# BIOGRAPHICAL DIRECTORY
## OF THE
## AMERICAN CONGRESS
## 1774-1996

John Plumbe, Jr.'s daguerreotype, taken about 1846, is the earliest known surviving photograph of the United States Capitol, and shows Charles Bulfinch's 140-foot high dome of copper-covered wood and highlights the east portico and stairs. (*Library of Congress*)

# BIOGRAPHICAL DIRECTORY
# OF THE
# AMERICAN CONGRESS
# 1774-1996

**THE CONTINENTAL CONGRESS**

SEPTEMBER 5, 1774, TO OCTOBER 21, 1788

and

**THE CONGRESS OF THE UNITED STATES**

FROM THE FIRST THROUGH THE 104TH CONGRESSES

MARCH 4, 1789, TO JANUARY 3, 1997

CLOSING DATE OF COMPILATION, SEPTEMBER 30, 1996

CQ Staff Directories, Inc.

A Congressional Quarterly Company

Alexandria, Virginia

## Biographical Directory of the American Congress, 1774-1996

| | |
|---|---|
| *Editor:* | Joel D. Treese |
| *Associate Editor:* | Dorothy J. Countryman |
| *Editorial Assistant:* | Elizabeth A. Olson |
| *Production Director:* | Robert B. McNeil, Jr. |
| *Typesetter:* | Meltem Akbasli |

---

## CQ Staff Directories, Inc.

| | |
|---|---|
| Neil Skene | *Chairman* |
| Patrick Bernuth | *President* |
| Bruce B. Brownson | *Vice President, Marketing* |
| Robert E. Cuthriell | *Vice President, Editorial* |
| P. Wayne Walker | *Editorial Director* |

---

*Charles B. Brownson and Anna L. Brownson*
*Co-Founders of Staff Directories, Ltd.*

---

ISBN  0-87289-124-0
ISSN  1091-0859

Photo credits: Frederick A. C. Muhlenberg—reproduced from the collection of the Architect of the Capitol. John Gailliard—reproduced from the original in the South Caroliniana Library. John W. McCormack—Senate Historical Office. Carl Albert—Anton. Thomas P. O'Neill, Jr.—Bachrach. James C. Wright—Art Stein. Thomas S. Foley—R. Michael Jenkins—Congressional Quarterly. Newt Gingrich—Kathleen R. Beall. All other photographs were reproduced from the collection of the Library of Congress.

This *Biographical Directory of the American Congress, 1774-1996* is printed and bound in the United States of America for

## CQ Staff Directories, Inc.

815 Slaters Lane, Alexandria, Virginia 22314

Telephone 703-739-0900

e-mail: staffdir@staffdirectories.com

FAX 703-739-0234

# TABLE OF CONTENTS

———

# TABLE OF CONTENTS

# Foreword

Meeting for the first time in the spring of 1789, Congress was charged with an important and specific list of responsibilities. First on the list was overseeing the election of our President and Vice President. At the time, the President of the Senate was required to supervise the ballot counting. Congress also needed to find a way to fund the government, organize the executive branch and judicial branch, and (at James Madison's urging) draft a bill of rights. If there were ever a daunting task, our first Members of Congress had found it.

These fundamental decisions were made for a very impressive reason: We had agreed to strive to achieve the goals laid out in the preamble of our Constitution: "We the People of the United States, in Order to form a more perfect Union, establish Justice, insure domestic Tranquility, provide for the common defence, promote the general Welfare, and secure the Blessings of Liberty to ourselves and our Posterity, do ordain and establish this Constitution for the United States of America."

Members of Congress, from 1789 until today, have committed themselves to support and defend these goals. And so, Congress is a commonality, an integrated union of districts, states and individuals. Regardless of difference and division, be it geographical or ideological, Senators and Representatives serve together; the Constitution forever defending their presence in the Halls of Congress. And these Halls have grown. In 1790, we were a nation of 3.9 million. In 1996, our population had grown to 266 million. In 1790, Congress held 92 members. In 1996, 535 call Washington, D.C. their second home.

This growth has actually enriched the United States Congress. Each member, from the newest district to the oldest state, plays a role in changing the face of Congress. Congress and its members are inextricably linked. The character, insight, legacy, successes and failures of a Member of Congress can never be erased from the history of the Legislative Branch, and it never should be. Each bill introduced, each statement made, and each amendment defeated serves as both a record of our past and a reflection of our legislative future.

This edition of the *Biographical Directory of the American Congress* is a useful window into the lives of our Congressional Members, past and present. The names of each member may not be familiar, but their contributions are nonetheless profound. I commend this directory to scholars, educators, librarians and interested citizens as a portrait of 207 years of challenging, yet rewarding progress for the United States of America.

> Mark O. Hatfield (R Oregon)
> Chairman, Senate Appropriations Committee
> and Joint Committee on the Library of Congress

August 1, 1996

# Introduction

When the fifty-five delegates to the Constitutional Convention met in Philadelphia during the summer of 1787 to lay foundation stones for a Senate and House of Representatives, they did so with a profound awareness of parliamentary tradition, their own colonial experience with representative assemblies, and the recent revolutionary struggle for self-government. They knew that the success of the national legislature would provide the world with an affirmation of the ability of Americans to govern themselves.

Congress has never been completely free of discord, or sharp words and fierce strife between individuals and political factions. Yet it also has never failed to serve as a most conspicuous public arena for debates and decisions about the most significant issues in our history. Some of those issues—such as temperance, slavery, railroad and canal construction, territorial expansion and bimetallism—are now part of our nation's collective historical memory. Others—taxation and government spending, immigration, national defense, and agricultural and environmental policy—continue to compel the attention of our public officials and citizens.

This ever-evolving institution's attempts to keep pace with complexity and change while performing its necessary and constitutionally sanctioned tasks have included the introduction of committee and seniority systems, the rise of party caucuses, the emergence of powerful party leaders, the simplification of processes by which bills are introduced and floor action taken, and the enhancement of rules governing ethics and accountability.

Congress has always possessed a remarkable pool of talent, which has provided the nation with Presidents and Vice Presidents, Supreme Court justices, federal judges, cabinet members, diplomats, and governors for every state in the Union.

The story of each of the more than 11,400 men and women who have served as a Member of Congress is illumined by the rich personal and career details in the *Biographical Directory of the American Congress 1774-1996*, the sixteenth in a series that has been published on an intermittent basis by both private publishers and the federal government since 1859. This edition endeavors to carry forward the high scholarly standards set by the 1989 *Biographical Directory of the United States Congress 1774-1988*, compiled under the direction of the Joint Committee on Printing and edited by Kathryn Allamong Jacob and Bruce A. Ragsdale. It was the first edition to be revised and updated by professional historians in the Senate Historical Office and the House of Representatives' Office for the Bicentennial (later Office of the Historian).

Published to commemorate the two-hundredth anniversary of the Congress, the 1989 *Biographical Directory* greatly enhanced the work's standing as a comprehensive record by enlisting the aid of many archivists, genealogists, historians, librarians and political scientists, particularly Dr. Kenneth C. Martis, author and editor of *The Historical Atlas of Political Parties in the United States Congress, 1789-1989* (Macmillan, 1989), and Dr. Garrison Nelson, co-author of *Committees in the U.S. Congress, 1947-1992* (Congressional Quarterly, 1993-94). The 1989 edition provided readers for the first time with a Member's standing committee chairmanships, service in a formal leadership position, more accurate and updated political labels and party affiliations, and bibliographic citations.

# Organization and Contents

The *Biographical Directory* is organized in five sections:

*Executive Officers 1789-1996* (pages 1 to 26). The name of every cabinet officer since the administration of George Washington is noted, including the dates each cabinet member assumed office. These listings now reflect the service of Presidents, Vice Presidents and cabinet members for the second administration of Ronald Reagan, and for the administrations of George Bush and William J. Clinton.

*The Continental Congress 1774-1788* (pages 27 to 34). The dates of each session of the Continental Congress and the locations of its meetings are shown. The names and dates of service of the presidents of the Congress and its delegates are also listed.

*Apportionment of Representatives* (page 37). A table shows how congressional seats have been apportioned among the various states following each census enumeration since 1790.

*The Congresses of the United States 1789-1997* (pages 39 to 548). The roster of each of the one hundred four Congresses lists the beginning and ending dates of each session, the names of officers elected by all Members of the House of Representatives and Senate at the commencement of each Congress, and all Senators and Representatives by state who served during that Congress. Beginning with the 79th Congress (1945-1947), the present edition adds to the rosters the political division of the Congresses, congressional district numbers for Representatives and party affiliations for all Members. Included are congressional leaders and assistants appointed by their respective parties. Photographs and engravings of the appropriate officers—Speakers of the House, Vice Presidents of the United States, and Presidents *pro tempore* of the Senate—have also been included for each Congress.

*Biographies* (pages 549 to 2108). Each biography follows a standardized format. Beginning with the complete name of the Member and family relationships to other Members of Congress, the biographies include the place and date of birth where available. Information about the Member's education, military service, occupation and career prior to service in Congress expand the personal data offered. Previous political office, as well as party affiliation and dates of service in Congress, standing committee chairmanships, service in elected leadership posts, and disciplinary actions such as censure or expulsion or other formal action against the Member are included. Biographies also present the subsequent career and current place of residence, or, in the case of those who have died, date of death and place of interment. Bibliographic citations provide guidance for those wishing further information.

This 1997 edition contains biographical entries on the additional 334 Representatives and Senators who have served since publication of the previous edition, and has taken note of 236 Members and former Members of Congress who have died since June 30, 1988, the closing date of that edition.

Where applicable, we have enhanced biographical entries with the following features:

- year of election and dates of terms of service for those Members who were elected and served as governors;

- dates of service for Members who served as appointed territorial governors;

- dates of nomination, confirmation and resignation for those Members who served on the United States Supreme Court;

- dates of appointment and termination of mission for Members appointed to diplomatic posts;

- dates of service for Members who were appointed to Cabinet offices;

- more detailed accounts of Members' Civil War military service, and the names, locations and dates of battles Members participated in during the war;

- when Members changed their party affiliation while serving (or, in some cases, after serving) in Congress, the date of the party change announcement is given. These changes have also been noted by appropriate footnotes in the Membership rosters;

- where Members sponsored or co-sponsored legislation generally known by their name (such as the Ludlow Resolution or the Volstead Act), brief descriptions of such legislation have been included.

## Acknowledgments

The extensive research for this edition of the *Biographical Directory* would not have been possible without the resources of both CQ Staff Directories, Inc., and its parent company, Congressional Quarterly Inc. Volumes of the *Congressional Staff Directory* dating back to 1959 have been invaluable tools in enhancing existing biographical entries by providing detailed information on the education, business and professional backgrounds, and military service, committee chairmanships and leadership positions of Members. Congressional Quarterly's *Guide to U.S. Elections* (3rd edition) and editions of its *Weekly Report* have enabled us to follow the careers of those Members who had been defeated for renomination or reelection, resigned from Congress, or attained other elective offices.

We are especially grateful to Kathleen Walton, Mike Williams, and Myra Engers Weinberg of Congressional Quarterly's library, who cheerfully and steadfastly answered a profusion of questions and guided us toward dependable research paths.

Nancy Lammers and William Gardner of Congressional Quarterly's Editorial Design and Production Department researched and acquired the portraits of Speakers of the House, Vice Presidents of the United States, and Presidents *pro tempore* of the Senate that augment our rosters, as well as John Plumbe, Jr.'s 1840s daguerreotype of the Capitol with Charles Bulfinch's wooden, copper-covered dome.

We are greatly in the debt of the 428 former Representatives and Senators, and their staffs and family members, who took time to review biographical sketches and contribute updates and corrections. We especially want to mention Sally C. Allen, Shirley A. Curtin, Peter J. De Muth, Susan J. Egloff, Bernice Holbrock, Priscilla S. Hunt, Nancy S. Love, Joan M. Plocharczyk, Burnette Staebler, and Virginia Van Gorp.

Librarians and library staff throughout the country were also kind enough to answer questions and assist us in our research. To the following, a special thanks: Shanla Brookshire, Lovett Memorial Library, Pampa, Texas; Julian Bruening, Warren County (Illinois) Public Library District; Julie Crump, assistant head of reference, Ouachita Parish Public Library, Monroe, Louisiana; Jean Gillmer, Tacoma, Washington Public Library's Northwest Room; Nina Johnson, librarian at the Columbia, Missouri *Daily Tribune*; Alline Merchant, Glendale, California Central Library; Linda G. Oaklander, Flint, Michigan Public Library; Donna Shermeyer, research coordinator of the York County, Pennsylvania Historical Society; D.A. Thomas, Kansas City, Kansas Public Library; Sharon Van Dorn, Texas-Dallas History Division, Dallas Public Library; and Sylvia A. Waters, Athens (Texas) *Daily Review*.

The resources of the Library of Congress were an indispensable help in our research, particularly the newspaper archives in the library's Newspaper and Current Periodical Reading Room.

We also relied extensively on the collections of the Joseph Mark Lauinger Memorial Library (Georgetown University), and the Jack and Dorothy G. Bender Library and Learning Resources Center (The American University).

For bibliographic citations, in addition to our own research, we were greatly aided by two reference works: Robert U. Goehlert, Fenton S. Martin and John R. Sayre's *Members of Congress: A Bibliography* (Congressional Quarterly, 1996); and *Senators of the United States: A Historical Bibliography 1789-1995*, compiled by Jo Anne McCormick Quatann-ens, Assistant Historian of the United States Senate Historical Office.

The particulars of contested Senate election cases were based on the research of Anne M. Butler and Wendy Wolff in the United States Senate Historical Office's *United States Senate Election, Expulsion and Censure Cases 1793-1990* (1995).

The Department of State's *Principal Officers of the Department of State and United States Chiefs of Mission 1778-1990*, the *Weekly Compilation of Presidential Documents*, and Congressional Quarterly's Washington Alert online congressional tracking service enabled us to provide dates of service for Members appointed to diplomatic posts.

The following reference works were of significant assistance to us: Congressional Quarterly's *Guide to the Supreme Court* (1979); Thomas A. McMullin and David Walker's *Biographical Directory of American Territorial Governors* (Meckler, 1984); Robert Sobel's *Biographical Directory of the United States Executive Branch, 1771-1989* (Greenwood Press, 1990); and Mary Mayo Boatner's *The Civil War Dictionary* (Vintage, 1991).

We relied heavily on the National Archives and Records Administration Office of the Federal Register's *Weekly Compilation of Presidential Documents* to update the listing of officers of the executive branch of the government.

The 1995-96 *Directory of the United States Association of Former Members of Congress* was used to mail entries to former Members, so they would have an opportunity to ensure the completeness and accuracy of their biographies.

Edward F. Murphy, founder and president of the Medal of Honor Historical Society, provided a list of Members of Congress who held the Medal of Honor.

This volume would not have been possible without the superb typesetting, composing and production work of Robert B. McNeil, Jr. and Meltem Akbasli, or without Dorothy J. Countryman's remarkable commitment to high standards of editorial accuracy and excellence. Elizabeth A. Olson did a splendid job of fact-checking and correcting member-ship rosters. Wayne Walker provided editorial guidance at every stage of this project.

It is our hope at CQ Staff Directories, Inc. that the 1997 edition of the *Biographical Directory of the American Congress* will enrich its readers' knowledge and comprehension of the old yet youthful institution that is the Congress of the United States.

We will continue to update and enhance the *Biographical Directory of the American Congress* between quadrennial editions. If our readers know of biographical changes or updates, new bibliographic citations, or errors or omissions, we would very much appreciate hearing from them. A detachable, postage-paid card has been provided elsewhere in this volume.

Although this edition of the *Biographical Directory* extends the admirable effort of the editors of the 1989 edition, any errors or omissions are the responsibility of CQ Staff Directories, Inc.

Joel D. Treese
Editor

# OFFICERS OF THE EXECUTIVE BRANCH
## OF THE GOVERNMENT

# EXPLANATORY NOTE

A Cabinet officer is not appointed for a fixed term and does not necessarily go out of office with the President who made the appointment. While it is customary to tender one's resignation at the time a change of administration takes place, each officer remains formally at the head of his department until a successor is appointed. Subordinates acting temporarily as heads of departments are not considered Cabinet officers, and in the earlier period of the Nation's history not all Cabinet officers were heads of executive departments. The names of all those exercising the duties and bearing the responsibilities of the executive departments, together with the period of service, are incorporated in the lists that follow.

The dates immediately following the names of executive officers are those upon which commissions were issued, unless otherwise specifically noted. Where periods of time are indicated by dates as, for instance, March 4, 1793-March 3, 1797, both such dates are included as portions of the time period.

The Twentieth Amendment to the Constitution (effective Oct. 15, 1933) changed the terms of the President and Vice President to end at noon on the 20th day of January and the terms of Senators and Representatives to end at noon on the 3d day of January when the terms of their successors shall begin.

# EXECUTIVE OFFICERS, 1789—1996

---

## First Administration of GEORGE WASHINGTON

### APRIL 30, 1789, TO MARCH 3, 1793

PRESIDENT OF THE UNITED STATES—GEORGE WASHINGTON, of Virginia.

VICE PRESIDENT OF THE UNITED STATES—JOHN ADAMS, of Massachusetts.

SECRETARY OF STATE—JOHN JAY, of New York, was Secretary for Foreign Affairs under the Confederation, and continued to act, at the request of Washington, until Jefferson took office. THOMAS JEFFERSON, of Virginia, September 26, 1789; entered upon duties March 22, 1790.

SECRETARY OF THE TREASURY—ALEXANDER HAMILTON, of New York, September 11, 1789.

SECRETARY OF WAR—HENRY KNOX, of Massachusetts, September 12, 1789.

ATTORNEY GENERAL—EDMUND RANDOLPH, of Virginia, September 26, 1789; entered upon duties February 2, 1790.

POSTMASTER GENERAL—SAMUEL OSGOOD, of Massachusetts, September 26, 1789. TIMOTHY PICKERING, of Pennsylvania, August 12, 1791; entered upon duties August 19, 1791.

---

## Second Administration of GEORGE WASHINGTON

### MARCH 4, 1793, TO MARCH 3, 1797

PRESIDENT OF THE UNITED STATES—GEORGE WASHINGTON, of Virginia.

VICE PRESIDENT OF THE UNITED STATES—JOHN ADAMS, of Massachusetts.

SECRETARY OF STATE—THOMAS JEFFERSON, of Virginia, continued from preceding administration. EDMUND RANDOLPH, of Virginia, January 2, 1794. TIMOTHY PICKERING, of Pennsylvania (Secretary of War), ad interim, August 20, 1795. TIMOTHY PICKERING, of Pennsylvania, December 10, 1795.

SECRETARY OF THE TREASURY—ALEXANDER HAMILTON, of New York, continued from preceding administration. OLIVER WOLCOTT, JR., of Connecticut, February 2, 1795.

SECRETARY OF WAR—HENRY KNOX, of Massachusetts, continued from preceding administration. TIMOTHY PICKERING, of Pennsylvania, January 2, 1795. TIMOTHY PICKERING, of Pennsylvania (Secretary of State), ad interim, December 10, 1795, to February 5, 1796. JAMES McHENRY, of Maryland, January 27, 1796; entered upon duties February 6, 1796.

ATTORNEY GENERAL—EDMUND RANDOLPH, of Virginia, continued from preceding administration. WILLIAM BRADFORD, of Pennsylvania, January 27, 1794; entered upon duties January 29, 1794. CHARLES LEE, of Virginia, December 10, 1795.

POSTMASTER GENERAL—TIMOTHY PICKERING, of Pennsylvania, continued from preceding administration. TIMOTHY PICKERING, of Pennsylvania, recommissioned June 1, 1794. JOSEPH HABERSHAM, of Georgia, February 25, 1795.

---

## Administration of JOHN ADAMS

### MARCH 4, 1797, TO MARCH 3, 1801

PRESIDENT OF THE UNITED STATES—JOHN ADAMS, of Massachusetts.

VICE PRESIDENT OF THE UNITED STATES—THOMAS JEFFERSON, of Virginia.

SECRETARY OF STATE—TIMOTHY PICKERING, of Pennsylvania, continued from preceding administration; resignation requested May 10, 1800, but declining to resign, he was dismissed May 12, 1800. CHARLES LEE, of Virginia, (Attorney General), ad interim, May 13, 1800. JOHN MARSHALL, of Virginia, May 13, 1800; entered upon duties June 6, 1800. JOHN MARSHALL, of Virginia (Chief Justice of the United States), ad interim, February 4, 1801, to March 3, 1801.

SECRETARY OF THE TREASURY—OLIVER WOLCOTT, JR., of Connecticut, continued from preceding administration. SAMUEL DEXTER of Massachusetts, January 1, 1801.

SECRETARY OF WAR—JAMES McHENRY, of Maryland, continued from preceding administration. BENJAMIN STODDERT, of Maryland (Secretary of the Navy), ad interim, June 1, 1800, to June 12, 1800. SAMUEL DEXTER, of Massachusetts, May 13, 1800; entered upon duties June 12, 1800. SAMUEL DEXTER, of Massachusetts (Secretary of the Treasury), ad interim, January 1, 1801.

ATTORNEY GENERAL—CHARLES LEE, of Virginia, continued from preceding administration.

POSTMASTER GENERAL—JOSEPH HABERSHAM, of Georgia, continued from preceding administration.

SECRETARY OF THE NAVY—BENJAMIN STODDERT, of Maryland, May 21, 1798; entered upon duties June 18, 1798.

## First Administration of THOMAS JEFFERSON

### MARCH 4, 1801, TO MARCH 3, 1805

PRESIDENT OF THE UNITED STATES—THOMAS JEFFERSON, of Virginia.

VICE PRESIDENT OF THE UNITED STATES—AARON BURR, of New York.

SECRETARY OF STATE—JOHN MARSHALL, of Virginia (Chief Justice of the United States), for one day (March 4, 1801), and for a special purpose. LEVI LINCOLN, of Massachusetts (Attorney General), ad interim, March 5, 1801. JAMES MADISON, of Virginia, March 5, 1801; entered upon duties May 2, 1801.

SECRETARY OF THE TREASURY—SAMUEL DEXTER, of Massachusetts, continued from preceding administration to May 6, 1801. ALBERT GALLATIN, of Pennsylvania, May 14, 1801.

SECRETARY OF WAR—HENRY DEARBORN, of Massachusetts, March 5, 1801.

ATTORNEY GENERAL—LEVI LINCOLN, of Massachusetts, March 5, 1801, to December 31, 1804.

POSTMASTER GENERAL—JOSEPH HABERSHAM, of Georgia, continued from preceding administration. GIDEON GRANGER, of Connecticut, November 28, 1801.

SECRETARY OF THE NAVY—BENJAMIN STODDERT, of Maryland, continued from preceding administration. HENRY DEARBORN, of Massachusetts (Secretary of War), ad interim, April 1, 1801. ROBERT SMITH, of Maryland, July 15, 1801; entered upon duties July 27, 1801.

## Second Administration of THOMAS JEFFERSON

### MARCH 4, 1805, TO MARCH 3, 1809

PRESIDENT OF THE UNITED STATES—THOMAS JEFFERSON, of Virginia.

VICE PRESIDENT OF THE UNITED STATES—GEORGE CLINTON, of New York.

SECRETARY OF STATE—JAMES MADISON, of Virginia, continued from preceding administration.

SECRETARY OF THE TREASURY—ALBERT GALLATIN, of Pennsylvania, continued from preceding administration.

SECRETARY OF WAR—HENRY DEARBORN, of Massachusetts, continued from preceding administration. JOHN SMITH (chief clerk), ad interim, February 17, 1809.

ATTORNEY GENERAL—JOHN BRECKENRIDGE, of Kentucky, August 7, 1805 (died December 14, 1806). CAESAR A. RODNEY, of Delaware, January 20, 1807.

POSTMASTER GENERAL—GIDEON GRANGER, of Connecticut, continued from preceding administration.

SECRETARY OF THE NAVY—ROBERT SMITH, of Maryland, continued from preceding administration.

## First Administration of JAMES MADISON

### MARCH 4, 1809, TO MARCH 3, 1813

PRESIDENT OF THE UNITED STATES—JAMES MADISON, of Virginia.

VICE PRESIDENT OF THE UNITED STATES—GEORGE CLINTON, of New York. (Died April 20, 1812.)

PRESIDENT PRO TEMPORE OF THE SENATE—WILLIAM H. CRAWFORD, of Georgia.

SECRETARY OF STATE—ROBERT SMITH, of Maryland, March 6, 1809. JAMES MONROE, of Virginia, April 2, 1811; entered upon duties April 6, 1811.

SECRETARY OF THE TREASURY—ALBERT GALLATIN, of Pennsylvania, continued from preceding administration.

SECRETARY OF WAR—JOHN SMITH (chief clerk), ad interim, continued from preceding administration. WILLIAM EUSTIS, of Massachusetts, March 7, 1809; entered upon duties April 8, 1809; served to December 31, 1812. JAMES MONROE, of Virginia (Secretary of State), ad interim, January 1, 1813. JOHN ARMSTRONG, of New York, January 13, 1813; entered upon duties February 5, 1813.

ATTORNEY GENERAL—CAESAR A. RODNEY, of Delaware, continued from preceding administration; resigned December 5, 1811. WILLIAM PINKNEY, of Maryland, December 11, 1811; entered upon duties January 6, 1812.

POSTMASTER GENERAL—GIDEON GRANGER, of Connecticut, continued from preceding administration.

SECRETARY OF THE NAVY—ROBERT SMITH, of Maryland, continued from preceding administration. CHARLES W. GOLDSBOROUGH (chief clerk), ad interim, March 8, 1809. PAUL HAMILTON, of South Carolina, March 7, 1809; entered upon duties May 15, 1809; served to December 31, 1812. CHARLES W. GOLDSBOROUGH (chief clerk), ad interim, January 7, 1813, to January 18, 1813. WILLIAM JONES, of Pennsylvania, January 12, 1813; entered upon duties January 19, 1813.

## Second Administration of JAMES MADISON

### MARCH 4, 1813, TO MARCH 3, 1817

PRESIDENT OF THE UNITED STATES—JAMES MADISON, of Virginia.

VICE PRESIDENT OF THE UNITED STATES—ELBRIDGE GERRY, of Massachusetts. (Died November 23, 1814.)

PRESIDENT PRO TEMPORE OF THE SENATE—JOHN GAILLARD, of South Carolina.

SECRETARY OF STATE—JAMES MONROE, of Virginia, continued from preceding administration. JAMES MONROE, of Virginia (Secretary of War), ad interim, October 1, 1814. JAMES MONROE, of Virginia, February 28, 1815.

SECRETARY OF THE TREASURY—ALBERT GALLATIN, of Pennsylvania, continued from preceding administration. WILLIAM JONES, of Pennsylvania (Secretary of the Navy), performed the duties of the Secretary of the Treasury during the absence of Mr. Gallatin in Europe (April 21, 1813, to February 9, 1814). GEORGE W. CAMPBELL, of Tennessee, February 9, 1814. ALEXANDER J. DALLAS, of Pennsylvania, October 6, 1814; entered upon duties October 14, 1814. WILLIAM H. CRAWFORD, of Georgia, October 22, 1816.

SECRETARY OF WAR—JOHN ARMSTRONG, of New York, continued from preceding administration. JAMES MONROE, of Virginia (Secretary of State), ad interim, August 30, 1814. JAMES MONROE, of Virginia, September 27, 1814; entered upon duties October 1, 1814. JAMES MONROE, of Virginia (Secretary of State), ad interim, March 1, 1815. ALEXANDER J. DALLAS, of Pennsylvania (Secretary of the Treasury), ad interim, March 14, 1815, to August 8, 1815. WILLIAM H. CRAWFORD, of Georgia, August 1, 1815; entered upon duties August 8, 1815. GEORGE GRAHAM (chief clerk), ad interim, October 22, 1816, to close of administration.

ATTORNEY GENERAL—WILLIAM PINKNEY, of Maryland, continued from preceding administration. RICHARD RUSH, of Pennsylvania, February 10, 1814; entered upon duties the day following.

POSTMASTER GENERAL—GIDEON GRANGER, of Connecticut, continued from preceding administration. RETURN J. MEIGS, JR., of Ohio, March 17, 1814; entered upon duties April 11, 1814.

SECRETARY OF THE NAVY—WILLIAM JONES, of Pennsylvania, continued from preceding administration. BENJAMIN HOMANS (chief clerk), ad interim, December 2, 1814. BENJAMIN W. CROWNINSHIELD, of Massachusetts, December 19, 1814; entered upon duties January 16, 1815.

---

## First Administration of JAMES MONROE

### MARCH 4, 1817, TO MARCH 3, 1821

PRESIDENT OF THE UNITED STATES—JAMES MONROE, of Virginia.

VICE PRESIDENT OF THE UNITED STATES—DANIEL D. TOMPKINS, of New York.

SECRETARY OF STATE—JOHN GRAHAM (chief clerk), ad interim, March 4, 1817. RICHARD RUSH, of Pennsylvania (Attorney General), ad interim, March 10, 1817. JOHN QUINCY ADAMS, of Massachusetts, March 5, 1817; entered upon duties September 22, 1817.

SECRETARY OF THE TREASURY—WILLIAM H. CRAWFORD, of Georgia, continued from preceding administration. WILLIAM H. CRAWFORD, of Georgia, recommissioned March 5, 1817.

SECRETARY OF WAR—GEORGE GRAHAM (chief clerk), ad interim, March 4, 1817. JOHN C. CALHOUN, of South Carolina, October 8, 1817; entered upon duties December 10, 1817.

ATTORNEY GENERAL—RICHARD RUSH, of Pennsylvania, continued from preceding administration to October 30, 1817. WILLIAM WIRT, of Virginia, November 13, 1817; entered upon duties November 15, 1817.

POSTMASTER GENERAL—RETURN J. MEIGS, JR., of Ohio, continued from preceding administration.

SECRETARY OF THE NAVY—BENJAMIN W. CROWNINSHIELD, of Massachusetts, continued from preceding administration. JOHN C. CALHOUN, of South Carolina (Secretary of War), ad interim, October 1, 1818. SMITH THOMPSON, of New York, November 9, 1818; entered upon duties January 1, 1819.

---

## Second Administration of JAMES MONROE

### MARCH 4, 1821, TO MARCH 3, 1825

PRESIDENT OF THE UNITED STATES—JAMES MONROE, of Virgina.

VICE PRESIDENT OF THE UNITED STATES—DANIEL D. TOMPKINS, of New York.

SECRETARY OF STATE—JOHN QUINCY ADAMS, of Massachusetts, continued from preceding administration.

SECRETARY OF THE TREASURY—WILLIAM H. CRAWFORD, of Georgia, continued from preceding administration.

SECRETARY OF WAR—JOHN C. CALHOUN, of South Carolina, continued from preceding administration.

ATTORNEY GENERAL—WILLIAM WIRT, of Virginia, continued from preceding administration.

POSTMASTER GENERAL—RETURN J. MEIGS, JR., of Ohio, continued from preceding administration. JOHN MCLEAN, of Ohio, commissioned June 26, 1823, to take effect July 1, 1823.

SECRETARY OF THE NAVY—SMITH THOMPSON, of New York, continued from preceding administration. JOHN RODGERS (Commodore, United States Navy, and President of the Board of Navy Commissioners), ad interim, September 1, 1823. SAMUEL L. SOUTHARD, of New Jersey, September 16, 1823.

## Administration of JOHN QUINCY ADAMS

### MARCH 4, 1825, TO MARCH 3, 1829

PRESIDENT OF THE UNITED STATES—JOHN QUINCY ADAMS, of Massachusetts.

VICE PRESIDENT OF THE UNITED STATES—JOHN C. CALHOUN, of South Carolina.

SECRETARY OF STATE—DANIEL BRENT (chief clerk), ad interim, March 4, 1825. HENRY CLAY, of Kentucky, March 7, 1825.

SECRETARY OF THE TREASURY—SAMUEL L. SOUTHARD, of New Jersey (Secretary of the Navy), ad interim, March 7, 1825. RICHARD RUSH, of Pennsylvania, March 7, 1825; entered upon duties August 1, 1825.

SECRETARY OF WAR—JAMES BARBOUR, of Virginia, March 7, 1825. SAMUEL L. SOUTHARD, of New Jersey (Secretary of the Navy), ad interim, May 26, 1828. PETER B. PORTER, of New York, May 26, 1828; entered upon duties June 21, 1828.

ATTORNEY GENERAL—WILLIAM WIRT, of Virginia, continued from preceding administration.

POSTMASTER GENERAL—JOHN MCLEAN, of Ohio, continued from preceding administration.

SECRETARY OF THE NAVY—SAMUEL L. SOUTHARD, of New Jersey, continued from preceding administration.

---

## First Administration of ANDREW JACKSON

### MARCH 4, 1829, TO MARCH 3, 1833

PRESIDENT OF THE UNITED STATES—ANDREW JACKSON, of Tennessee.

VICE PRESIDENT OF THE UNITED STATES—JOHN C. CALHOUN, of South Carolina. (Resigned December 28, 1832.)

PRESIDENT PRO TEMPORE OF THE SENATE—HUGH LAWSON WHITE, of Tennessee.

SECRETARY OF STATE—JAMES A. HAMILTON, of New York, ad interim, March 4, 1829. MARTIN VAN BUREN, of New York, March 6, 1829; entered upon duties March 28, 1829. EDWARD LIVINGSTON, of Louisiana, May 24, 1831.

SECRETARY OF THE TREASURY—SAMUEL D. INGHAM, of Pennsylvania, March 6, 1829. ASBURY DICKINS (chief clerk), ad interim, June 21, 1831. LOUIS MCLANE, of Delaware, August 8, 1831.

SECRETARY OF WAR—JOHN H. EATON, of Tennessee, March 9, 1829. PHILIP G. RANDOLPH (chief clerk), ad interim, June 20, 1831. ROGER B. TANEY, of Maryland (Attorney General), ad interim, July 21, 1831. LEWIS CASS, of Ohio, August 1, 1831; entered upon duties August 8, 1831.

ATTORNEY GENERAL—JOHN M. BERRIEN, of Georgia, March 9, 1829. ROGER B. TANEY, of Maryland, July 20, 1831.

POSTMASTER GENERAL—JOHN MCLEAN, of Ohio, continued from preceding administration. WILLIAM T. BARRY, of Kentucky, March 9, 1829; entered upon duties April 6, 1829.

SECRETARY OF THE NAVY—CHARLES HAY (chief clerk), ad interim, March 4, 1829. JOHN BRANCH, of North Carolina, March 9, 1829. JOHN BOYLE (chief clerk), ad interim, May 12, 1831. LEVI WOODBURY, of New Hampshire, May 23, 1831.

---

## Second Administration of ANDREW JACKSON

### MARCH 4, 1833, TO MARCH 3, 1837

PRESIDENT OF THE UNITED STATES—ANDREW JACKSON, of Tennessee.

VICE PRESIDENT OF THE UNITED STATES—MARTIN VAN BUREN, of New York.

SECRETARY OF STATE—EDWARD LIVINGSTON, of Louisiana, continued from preceding administration. LOUIS MCLANE, of Delaware, May 29, 1833. JOHN FORSYTH, of Georgia, June 27, 1834; entered upon duties July 1, 1834.

SECRETARY OF THE TREASURY—LOUIS MCLANE, of Delaware, continued from preceding administration. WILLIAM J. DUANE, of Pennsylvania, May 29, 1833; entered upon duties June 1, 1833. ROGER B. TANEY, of Maryland, September 23, 1833. MCCLINTOCK YOUNG (chief clerk), ad interim, June 25, 1834. LEVI WOODBURY, of New Hampshire, June 27, 1834; entered upon duties July 1, 1834.

SECRETARY OF WAR—LEWIS CASS, of Ohio, continued from preceding administration. CAREY A. HARRIS, of Tennessee (Commissioner of Indian Affairs), ad interim, October 5, 1836. BENJAMIN F. BUTLER, of New York (Attorney General), ad interim, October 26, 1836. BENJAMIN F. BUTLER, of New York, commissioned March 3, 1837, ad interim, "during the pleasure of the President, until a successor, duly appointed, shall accept such office and enter upon the duties thereof."

ATTORNEY GENERAL—ROGER B. TANEY, of Maryland, continued from preceding administration to September 23, 1833. BENJAMIN F. BUTLER, of New York, November 15, 1833; entered upon duties November 18, 1833.

POSTMASTER GENERAL—WILLIAM T. BARRY, of Kentucky, continued from preceding administration. AMOS KENDALL, of Kentucky, May 1, 1835.

SECRETARY OF THE NAVY—LEVI WOODBURY, of New Hampshire, continued from preceding administration. MAHLON DICKERSON, of New Jersey, June 30, 1834.

## Administration of MARTIN VAN BUREN

### MARCH 4, 1837, TO MARCH 3, 1841

PRESIDENT OF THE UNITED STATES—Martin Van Buren, of New York.

VICE PRESIDENT OF THE UNITED STATES—Richard M. Johnson, of Kentucky.

SECRETARY OF STATE—John Forsyth, of Georgia, continued from preceding administration.

SECRETARY OF THE TREASURY—Levi Woodbury, of New Hampshire, continued from preceding administration.

SECRETARY OF WAR—Benjamin F. Butler, of New York, ad interim, continued from preceding administration. Joel R. Poinsett, of South Carolina, March 7, 1837; entered upon duties March 14, 1837.

ATTORNEY GENERAL—Benjamin F. Butler, of New York, continued from preceding administration. Felix Grundy, of Tennessee, July 5, 1838, to take effect September 1, 1838. Henry D. Gilpin, of Pennsylvania, January 11, 1840.

POSTMASTER GENERAL—Amos Kendall, of Kentucky, continued from preceding administration. John M. Niles, of Connecticut, May 19, 1840, to take effect May 25, 1840; entered upon duties May 26, 1840.

SECRETARY OF THE NAVY—Mahlon Dickerson, of New Jersey, continued from preceding administration. James K. Paulding, of New York, June 25, 1838, to take effect "after the 30th instant"; entered upon duties July 1, 1838.

---

## Administration of WILLIAM HENRY HARRISON

### MARCH 4, 1841, TO APRIL 4, 1841

PRESIDENT OF THE UNITED STATES—William Henry Harrison, of Ohio. (Died April 4, 1841.)

VICE PRESIDENT OF THE UNITED STATES—John Tyler, of Virginia.

SECRETARY OF STATE—J. L. Martin (chief clerk), ad interim, March 4, 1841. Daniel Webster, of Massachusetts, March 5, 1841.

SECRETARY OF THE TREASURY—McClintock Young (chief clerk), ad interim, March 4, 1841. Thomas Ewing, of Ohio, March 5, 1841.

SECRETARY OF WAR—John Bell, of Tennessee, March 5, 1841.

ATTORNEY GENERAL—John J. Crittenden, of Kentucky, March 5, 1841.

POSTMASTER GENERAL—Selah R. Hobbie, of New York (First Assistant Postmaster General), ad interim, March 4, 1841. Francis Granger, of New York, March 6, 1841; entered upon duties March 8, 1841.

SECRETARY OF THE NAVY—John D. Simms (chief clerk), ad interim, March 4, 1841. George E. Badger, of North Carolina, March 5, 1841.

---

## Administration of JOHN TYLER

### APRIL 4, 1841, TO MARCH 3, 1845

PRESIDENT OF THE UNITED STATES—John Tyler, of Virginia.

PRESIDENT PRO TEMPORE OF THE SENATE—Samuel L. Southard, of New Jersey; Willie P. Mangum, of North Carolina.

SECRETARY OF STATE—Daniel Webster, of Massachusetts, continued from preceding administration. Hugh S. Legare, of South Carolina (Attorney General), ad interim, May 9, 1843. William S. Derrick (chief clerk), ad interim, June 21, 1843. Abel P. Upshur, of Virginia (Secretary of the Navy), ad interim, June 24, 1843. Abel P. Upshur, of Virginia, July 24, 1843 (killed by the explosion of a gun on the U.S.S. *Princeton* February 28, 1844). John Nelson, of Maryland (Attorney General), ad interim, February 29, 1844. John C. Calhoun, of South Carolina, March 6, 1844; entered upon duties April 1, 1844.

SECRETARY OF THE TREASURY—Thomas Ewing, of Ohio, continued from preceding administration. McClintock Young (chief clerk), ad interim, September 13, 1841. Walter Forward, of Pennsylvania, September 13, 1841. McClintock Young (chief clerk), ad interim, March 1, 1843. John C. Spencer, of New York, March 3, 1843; entered upon duties March 8, 1843. McClintock Young (chief clerk), ad interim, May 2, 1844. George M. Bibb, of Kentucky, June 15, 1844; entered upon duties July 4, 1844.

SECRETARY OF WAR—John Bell, of Tennessee, continued from preceding administration. Albert M. Lea, of Maryland (chief clerk), ad interim, September 12, 1841. John C. Spencer, of New York, October 12, 1841. James M. Porter of Pennsylvania, March 8, 1843. William Wilkins, of Pennsylvania, February 15, 1844; entered upon duties February 20, 1844.

ATTORNEY GENERAL—John J. Crittenden, of Kentucky, continued from preceding administration. Hugh S. Legare, of South Carolina, September 13, 1841; entered upon duties September 20, 1841 (died June 20, 1843). John Nelson, of Maryland, July 1, 1843.

POSTMASTER GENERAL—Francis Granger, of New York, continued from preceding administration. Selah R. Hobbie, of New York (First Assistant Postmaster General), ad interim, September 14, 1841. Charles A. Wickliffe, of Kentucky, September 13, 1841; entered upon duties October 13, 1841.

SECRETARY OF THE NAVY—George E. Badger, of North Carolina, continued from preceding administration. John D. Simms (chief clerk), ad interim, September 11, 1841. Abel P. Upshur, of Virginia, September 13, 1841; entered upon duties October 11, 1841. David Henshaw, of Massachusetts, July 24, 1843. Thomas W. Gilmer, of Virginia, February 15, 1844; entered upon duties February 19, 1844 (killed by the explosion of a gun on the U.S.S. *Princeton* February 28, 1844). Lewis Warrington (captain, United States Navy), ad interim, February 29, 1844. John Y. Mason, of Virginia, March 14, 1844; entered upon duties March 26, 1844.

### Administration of JAMES K. POLK

### MARCH 4, 1845, TO MARCH 3, 1849

PRESIDENT OF THE UNITED STATES—James K. Polk, of Tennessee.

VICE PRESIDENT OF THE UNITED STATES—George M. Dallas, of Pennsylvania.

SECRETARY OF STATE—John C. Calhoun, of South Carolina, continued from preceding administration. James Buchanan, of Pennsylvania, March 6, 1845; entered upon duties March 10, 1845.

SECRETARY OF THE TREASURY—George M. Bibb, of Kentucky, continued from preceding administration. Robert J. Walker, of Mississippi, March 6, 1845; entered upon duties March 8, 1845.

SECRETARY OF WAR—William Wilkins, of Pennsylvania, continued from preceding administration. William L. Marcy, of New York, March 6, 1845; entered upon duties March 8, 1845.

ATTORNEY GENERAL—John Nelson, of Maryland, continued from preceding administration. John Y. Mason, of Virginia, March 6, 1845; entered upon duties March 11, 1845. Nathan Clifford, of Maine, October 17, 1846. Isaac Toucey, of Connecticut, June 21, 1848; entered upon duties June 29, 1848.

POSTMASTER GENERAL—Charles A. Wickliffe, of Kentucky, continued from preceding administration. Cave Johnson, of Tennessee, March 6, 1845.

SECRETARY OF THE NAVY—John Y. Mason, of Virginia, continued from preceding administration. George Bancroft, of Massachusetts, March 10, 1845. John Y. Mason, of Virginia, September 9, 1846.

---

### Administration of ZACHARY TAYLOR

### MARCH 4, 1849, TO JULY 9, 1850

PRESIDENT OF THE UNITED STATES—Zachary Taylor, of Louisiana. (Oath administered March 5, 1849. Died July 9, 1850.)

VICE PRESIDENT OF THE UNITED STATES—Millard Fillmore, of New York.

SECRETARY OF STATE—James Buchanan, of Pennsylvania, continued from preceding administration. John M. Clayton, of Delaware, March 7, 1849.

SECRETARY OF THE TREASURY—Robert J. Walker, of Mississippi, continued from preceding administration. McClintock Young (chief clerk), ad interim, March 6, 1849. William M. Meredith, of Pennsylvania, March 8, 1849.

SECRETARY OF WAR—William L. Marcy, of New York, continued from preceding administration. Reverdy Johnson, of Maryland (Attorney General), ad interim, March 8, 1849. George W. Crawford, of Georgia, March 8, 1849; entered upon duties March 14, 1849.

ATTORNEY GENERAL—Isaac Toucey, of Connecticut, continued from preceding administration. Reverdy Johnson, of Maryland, March 8, 1849.

POSTMASTER GENERAL—Cave Johnson, of Tennessee, continued from preceding administration. Selah R. Hobbie, of New York (First Assistant Postmaster General), ad interim, March 6, 1849. Jacob Collamer, of Vermont, March 8, 1849.

SECRETARY OF THE NAVY—John Y. Mason, of Virginia, continued from preceding administration. William B. Preston, of Virginia, March 8, 1849.

SECRETARY OF THE INTERIOR—Thomas Ewing, of Ohio, March 8, 1849.

---

### Administration of MILLARD FILLMORE

### JULY 10, 1850, TO MARCH 3, 1853

PRESIDENT OF THE UNITED STATES—Millard Fillmore, of New York.

PRESIDENT PRO TEMPORE OF THE SENATE—William R. King, of Alabama; David R. Atchison, of Missouri.

SECRETARY OF STATE—John M. Clayton, of Delaware, continued from preceding administration. Daniel Webster, of Massachusetts, July 22, 1850 (died October 24, 1852). Charles M. Conrad, of Louisiana (Secretary of War), ad interim, October 25, 1852. Edward Everett, of Massachusetts, November 6, 1852.

SECRETARY OF THE TREASURY—William M. Meredith, of Pennsylvania, continued from preceding administration. Thomas Corwin, of Ohio July 23, 1850.

SECRETARY OF WAR—George W. Crawford, of Georgia, continued from preceding administration. Samuel J. Anderson (chief clerk), ad interim, July 23, 1850. Winfield Scott (major general, U.S. Army), ad interim, July 24, 1850. Charles M. Conrad, of Louisiana, August 15, 1850.

ATTORNEY GENERAL—Reverdy Johnson, of Maryland, continued from preceding administration, served to July 22, 1850. John J. Crittenden, of Kentucky, July 22, 1850; entered upon duties August 14, 1850.

POSTMASTER GENERAL—Jacob Collamer, of Vermont, continued from preceding administration. Nathan K. Hall, of New York, July 23, 1850. Samuel D. Hubbard, of Connecticut, August 31, 1852; entered upon duties September 14, 1852.

SECRETARY OF THE NAVY—William B. Preston, of Virginia, continued from preceding administration. Lewis Warrington (captain, U.S. Navy), ad interim, July 23, 1850. William A. Graham, of North Carolina, July 22, 1850; entered upon duties August 2, 1850. John P. Kennedy, of Maryland, July 22, 1852; entered upon duties July 26, 1852.

SECRETARY OF THE INTERIOR—Thomas Ewing, of Ohio, continued from preceding administration. Daniel C. Goddard (chief clerk), ad interim, July 23, 1850. Thomas M. T. McKennan, of Pennsylvania, August 15, 1850. Daniel C. Goddard (chief clerk), ad interim, August 27, 1850. Alexander H. H. Stuart, of Virginia, September 12, 1850; entered upon duties September 16, 1850.

## Administration of FRANKLIN PIERCE

### MARCH 4, 1853, TO MARCH 3, 1857

PRESIDENT OF THE UNITED STATES—FRANKLIN PIERCE, of New Hampshire.

VICE PRESIDENT OF THE UNITED STATES—WILLIAM R. KING, of Alabama. (Died April 18, 1853.)

PRESIDENT PRO TEMPORE OF THE SENATE—DAVID R. ATCHISON, of Missouri; LEWIS CASS, of Michigan; JESSE D. BRIGHT, of Indiana; CHARLES E. STUART, of Michigan; JAMES M. MASON, of Virginia.

SECRETARY OF STATE—WILLIAM HUNTER (chief clerk), ad interim, March 4, 1853. WILLIAM L. MARCY, of New York, March 7, 1853.

SECRETARY OF THE TREASURY—THOMAS CORWIN, of Ohio, continued from preceding administration. JAMES GUTHRIE, of Kentucky, March 7, 1853.

SECRETARY OF WAR—CHARLES M. CONRAD, of Louisiana, continued from preceding administration. JEFFERSON DAVIS, of Mississippi, March 7, 1853. SAMUEL COOPER (Adjutant General, U.S. Army), ad interim, March 3, 1857.

ATTORNEY GENERAL—JOHN J. CRITTENDEN, of Kentucky, continued from preceding administration. CALEB CUSHING, of Massachusetts, March 7, 1853.

POSTMASTER GENERAL—SAMUEL D. HUBBARD, of Connecticut, continued from preceding administration. JAMES CAMPBELL, of Pennsylvania, March 7, 1853.

SECRETARY OF THE NAVY—JOHN P. KENNEDY, of Maryland, continued from preceding administration. JAMES C. DOBBIN, of North Carolina, March 7, 1853.

SECRETARY OF THE INTERIOR—ALEXANDER H. H. STUART, of Virginia, continued from preceding administration. ROBERT MCCLELLAND, of Michigan, March 7, 1853.

---

## Administration of JAMES BUCHANAN

### MARCH 4, 1857, TO MARCH 3, 1861

PRESIDENT OF THE UNITED STATES—JAMES BUCHANAN, of Pennsylvania.

VICE PRESIDENT OF THE UNITED STATES—JOHN C. BRECKINRIDGE, of Kentucky.

SECRETARY OF STATE—WILLIAM L. MARCY, of New York, continued from preceding administration. LEWIS CASS, of Michigan, March 6, 1857. WILLIAM HUNTER (chief clerk), ad interim, December 15, 1860. JEREMIAH S. BLACK, of Pennsylvania, December 17, 1860.

SECRETARY OF THE TREASURY—JAMES GUTHRIE, of Kentucky, continued from preceding administration. HOWELL COBB, of Georgia, March 6, 1857. ISAAC TOUCEY, of Connecticut (Secretary of the Navy), ad interim, December 10, 1860. PHILIP F. THOMAS, of Maryland, December 12, 1860. JOHN A. DIX, of New York, January 11, 1861; entered upon duties January 15, 1861.

SECRETARY OF WAR—SAMUEL COOPER (Adjutant General, U.S. Army), ad interim, March 4, 1857. JOHN B. FLOYD, of Virginia, March 6, 1857. JOSEPH HOLT, of Kentucky (Postmaster General), ad interim, January 1, 1861. JOSEPH HOLT, of Kentucky, January 18, 1861.

ATTORNEY GENERAL—CALEB CUSHING, of Massachusetts, continued from preceding administration. JEREMIAH S. BLACK, of Pennsylvania, March 6, 1857; entered upon duties March 11, 1857. EDWIN M. STANTON, of Pennsylvania, December 20, 1860; entered upon duties December 22, 1860.

POSTMASTER GENERAL—JAMES CAMPBELL, of Pennsylvania, continued from preceding administration. AARON V. BROWN, of Tennessee, March 6, 1857 (died March 8, 1859). HORATIO KING, of Maine (First Assistant Postmaster General), ad interim, March 9, 1859. JOSEPH HOLT, of Kentucky, March 14, 1859. HORATIO KING, of Maine (First Assistant Postmaster General), ad interim, January 1, 1861. HORATIO KING, of Maine, February 12, 1861.

SECRETARY OF THE NAVY—JAMES C. DORBIN, of North Carolina, continued from preceding administration. ISAAC TOUCEY, of Connecticut, March 6, 1857.

SECRETARY OF THE INTERIOR—ROBERT MCCLELLAND, of Michigan, continued from preceding administration. JACOB THOMPSON, of Mississippi, March 6, 1857; entered upon duties March 10, 1857. MOSES KELLY (chief clerk), ad interim, January 10, 1861.

---

## First Administration of ABRAHAM LINCOLN

### MARCH 4, 1861, TO MARCH 3, 1865

PRESIDENT OF THE UNITED STATES—ABRAHAM LINCOLN, of Illinois.

VICE PRESIDENT OF THE UNITED STATES—HANNIBAL HAMLIN, of Maine.

SECRETARY OF STATE—JEREMIAH S. BLACK, of Pennsylvania, continued from preceding administration. WILLIAM H. SEWARD, of New York, March 5, 1861.

SECRETARY OF THE TREASURY—JOHN A. DIX, of New York, continued from preceding administration. SALMON P. CHASE, of Ohio, March 5, 1861; entered upon duties March 7, 1861. GEORGE HARRINGTON, of the District of Columbia (Assistant Secretary), ad interim, July 1, 1864. WILLIAM P. FESSENDEN, of Maine, July 1, 1864; entered upon duties July 5, 1864.

SECRETARY OF WAR—JOSEPH HOLT, of Kentucky, continued from preceding administration. SIMON CAMERON, of Pennsylvania, March 5, 1861; entered upon duties March 11, 1861. EDWIN M. STANTON, of Pennsylvania, January 15, 1862; entered upon duties January 20, 1862.

ATTORNEY GENERAL—EDWIN M. STANTON, of Pennsylvania, continued from preceding administration. EDWARD BATES, of Missouri, March 5, 1861. JAMES SPEED, of Kentucky, December 2, 1864; entered upon duties December 5, 1864.

POSTMASTER GENERAL—Horatio King, of Maine, continued from preceding administration. Montgomery Blair, of the District of Columbia, March 5, 1861; entered upon duties March 9, 1861. William Dennison, of Ohio, September 24, 1864; entered upon duties October 1, 1864.

SECRETARY OF THE NAVY—Isaac Toucey, of Connecticut, continued from preceding administration. Gideon Welles, of Connecticut, March 5, 1861; entered upon duties March 7, 1861.

SECRETARY OF THE INTERIOR—Moses Kelly (chief clerk), ad interim, March 4, 1861. Caleb B. Smith, of Indiana, March 5, 1861. John P. Usher, of Indiana (Assistant Secretary), ad interim, January 1, 1863. John P. Usher, of Indiana, January 8, 1863.

---

## Second Administration of ABRAHAM LINCOLN

### MARCH 4, 1865, TO APRIL 15, 1865

PRESIDENT OF THE UNITED STATES—Abraham Lincoln, of Illinois. (Died April 15, 1865.)

VICE PRESIDENT OF THE UNITED STATES—Andrew Johnson, of Tennessee.

SECRETARY OF STATE—William H. Seward, of New York, continued from preceding administration.

SECRETARY OF THE TREASURY—George Harrington, of the District of Columbia (Assistant Secretary), ad interim, March 4, 1865. Hugh McCulloch, of Indiana, March 7, 1865; entered upon duties March 9, 1865.

SECRETARY OF WAR—Edwin M. Stanton, of Pennsylvania, continued from preceding administration.

ATTORNEY GENERAL—James Speed, of Kentucky, continued from preceding administration.

POSTMASTER GENERAL—William Dennison, of Ohio, continued from preceding administration.

SECRETARY OF THE NAVY—Gideon Welles, of Connecticut, continued from preceding administration.

SECRETARY OF THE INTERIOR—John P. Usher, of Indiana, continued from preceding administration.

---

## Administration of ANDREW JOHNSON

### APRIL 15, 1865, TO MARCH 3, 1869

PRESIDENT OF THE UNITED STATES—Andrew Johnson, of Tennessee.

PRESIDENT PRO TEMPORE OF THE SENATE—Lafayette S. Foster, of Connecticut; Benjamin F. Wade, of Ohio.

SECRETARY OF STATE—William H. Seward, of New York, continued from preceding administration.

SECRETARY OF THE TREASURY—Hugh McCulloch, of Indiana, continued from preceding administration.

SECRETARY OF WAR—Edwin M. Stanton, of Pennsylvania, continued from preceding administration; suspended August 12, 1867. Ulysses S. Grant (General of the Army), ad interim, August 12, 1867. Edwin M. Stanton, of Pennsylvania, reinstated January 13, 1868, to May 26, 1868. John M. Schofield, of Illinois, May 28, 1868; entered upon duties June 1, 1868.

ATTORNEY GENERAL—James Speed, of Kentucky, continued from preceding administration. J. Hubley Ashton, of Pennsylvania (Assistant Attorney General), acting, July 17, 1866. Henry Stanberry, of Ohio, July 23, 1866. Orville H. Browning, of Illinois (Secretary of the Interior), ad interim, March 13, 1868. William M. Evarts, of New York, July 15, 1868; entered upon duties July 20, 1868.

POSTMASTER GENERAL—William Dennison, of Ohio, continued from preceding administration. Alexander W. Randall, of Wisconsin (First Assistant Postmaster General), ad interim, July 17, 1866. Alexander W. Randall, of Wisconsin, July 25, 1866.

SECRETARY OF THE NAVY—Gideon Welles, of Connecticut, continued from preceding administration.

SECRETARY OF THE INTERIOR—John P. Usher, of Indiana, continued from preceding administration. James Harlan, of Iowa, May 15, 1865. Orville H. Browning, of Illinois, July 27, 1866, to take effect September 1, 1866.

---

## First Administration of ULYSSES S. GRANT

### MARCH 4, 1869, TO MARCH 3, 1873

PRESIDENT OF THE UNITED STATES—Ulyssess S. Grant, of Illinois.

VICE PRESIDENT OF THE UNITED STATES—Schuyler Colfax, of Indiana.

SECRETARY OF STATE—William H. Seward, of New York, continued from preceding administration. Elihu B. Washburne, of Illinois, March 5, 1869. Hamilton Fish, of New York, March 11, 1869; entered upon duties March 17, 1869.

SECRETARY OF THE TREASURY—Hugh McCulloch, of Indiana, continued from preceding administration. John F. Hartley, of Maine (Assistant Secretary), ad interim, March 5, 1869. George S. Boutwell, of Massachusetts, March 11, 1869.

SECRETARY OF WAR—John M. Schofield, of Illinois, continued from preceding administration. John A. Rawlins, of Illinois, March 11, 1869. William T. Sherman, of Ohio, September 9, 1869; entered upon duties September 11, 1869. William W. Belknap, of Iowa, October 25, 1869; entered upon duties November 1, 1869.

ATTORNEY GENERAL—WILLIAM M. EVARTS, of New York, continued from preceding administration. J. HUBLEY ASHTON, of Pennsylvania (Assistant Attorney General), acting, March 5, 1869. EBENEZER R. HOAR, of Massachusetts, March 5, 1869; entered upon duties March 11, 1869. AMOS T. AKERMAN, of Georgia, June 23, 1870; entered upon duties July 8, 1870. GEORGE H. WILLIAMS, of Oregon, December 14, 1871, to take effect January 10, 1872.

POSTMASTER GENERAL—ST. JOHN B. L. SKINNER, of New York (First Assistant Postmaster General), ad interim, March 4, 1869. JOHN A. J. CRESWELL, of Maryland, March 5, 1869.

SECRETARY OF THE NAVY—WILLIAM FAXON, of Connecticut (Assistant Secretary), ad interim, March 4, 1869. ADOLPH E. BORIE, of Pennsylvania, March 5, 1869; entered upon duties March 9, 1869. GEORGE M. ROBESON, of New Jersey, June 25, 1869.

SECRETARY OF THE INTERIOR—WILLIAM T. OTTO, of Indiana (Assistant Secretary), ad interim, March 4, 1869. JACOB D. COX, of Ohio, March 5, 1869; entered upon duties March 9, 1869. COLUMBUS DELANO, of Ohio, November 1, 1870.

---

## Second Administration of ULYSSES S. GRANT

### MARCH 4, 1873, TO MARCH 3, 1877

PRESIDENT OF THE UNITED STATES—ULYSSESS S. GRANT, of Illinois.

VICE PRESIDENT OF THE UNITED STATES—HENRY WILSON, of Massachusetts. (Died November 22, 1875.)

PRESIDENT PRO TEMPORE OF THE SENATE—THOMAS W. FERRY, of Michigan.

SECRETARY OF STATE—HAMILTON FISH, of New York, continued from preceding administration. HAMILTON FISH, of New York, recommissioned March 17, 1873.

SECRETARY OF THE TREASURY—GEORGE S. BOUTWELL, of Massachusetts, continued from preceding administration. WILLIAM A. RICHARDSON, of Massachusetts, March 17, 1873. BENJAMIN H. BRISTOW, of Kentucky, June 2, 1874; entered upon duties June 4, 1874. CHARLES F. CONANT, of New Hampshire (Assistant Secretary), ad interim, June 21, 1876, to June 30, 1876. LOT M. MORRILL, of Maine, June 21, 1876; entered upon duties July 7, 1876.

SECRETARY OF WAR—WILLIAM W. BELKNAP, of Iowa, continued from preceding administration. WILLIAM W. BELKNAP, of Iowa, recommissioned March 17, 1873. GEORGE M. ROBESON, of New Jersey (Secretary of the Navy), ad interim, March 2, 1876. ALPHONSO TAFT, of Ohio, March 8, 1876; entered upon duties March 11, 1876. JAMES D. CAMERON, of Pennsylvania, May 22, 1876; entered upon duties June 1, 1876.

ATTORNEY GENERAL—GEORGE H. WILLIAMS, of Oregon, continued from preceding administration. GEORGE H. WILLIAMS, of Oregon, recommissioned March 17, 1873. EDWARDS PIERREPONT, of New York, April 26, 1875, to take effect May 15, 1875. ALPHONSO TAFT, of Ohio, May 22, 1876; entered upon duties June 1, 1876.

POSTMASTER GENERAL—JOHN A. J. CRESWELL, of Maryland, continued from preceding administration. JOHN A. J. CRESWELL, of Maryland, recommissioned March 17, 1873. JAMES W. MARSHALL, of Virginia, July 3, 1874; entered upon duties July 7, 1874. MARSHALL JEWELL, of Connecticut, August 24, 1874; entered upon duties September 1, 1874. JAMES N. TYNER, of Indiana, July 12, 1876.

SECRETARY OF THE NAVY—GEORGE M. ROBESON, of New Jersey, continued from preceding administration. GEORGE M. ROBESON, of New Jersey, recommissioned March 17, 1873.

SECRETARY OF THE INTERIOR—COLUMBUS DELANO, of Ohio, continued from preceding administration. COLUMBUS DELANO, of Ohio, recommissioned March 17, 1873. BENJAMIN R. COWEN, of Ohio (Assistant Secretary), ad interim, October 1, 1875. ZACHARIAH CHANDLER, of Michigan, October 19, 1875.

---

## Administration of RUTHERFORD B. HAYES

### MARCH 4, 1877, TO MARCH 3, 1881

PRESIDENT OF THE UNITED STATES—RUTHERFORD B. HAYES, of Ohio. (Oath administered March 5, 1877.)

VICE PRESIDENT OF THE UNITED STATES—WILLIAM A. WHEELER, of New York.

SECRETARY OF STATE—HAMILTON FISH, of New York, continued from preceding administration. WILLIAM M. EVARTS, of New York, March 12, 1877.

SECRETARY OF THE TREASURY—LOT M. MORRILL, of Maine, continued from preceding administration. JOHN SHERMAN, of Ohio, March 8, 1877; entered upon duties March 10, 1877.

SECRETARY OF WAR—JAMES D. CAMERON, of Pennsylvania, continued from preceding administration. GEORGE W. McCRARY, of Iowa, March 12, 1877. ALEXANDER RAMSEY, of Minnesota, December 10, 1879; entered upon duties December 12, 1879.

ATTORNEY GENERAL—ALPHONSO TAFT, of Ohio, continued from preceding administration. CHARLES DEVENS, of Massachusetts, March 12, 1877.

POSTMASTER GENERAL—JAMES N. TYNER, of Indiana, continued from preceding administration. DAVID M. KEY, of Tennessee, March 12, 1877; resigned June 1, 1880; served to August 24, 1880. HORACE MAYNARD, of Tennessee, June 2, 1880; entered upon duties August 25, 1880.

SECRETARY OF THE NAVY—GEORGE M. ROBESON, of New Jersey, continued from preceding administration. RICHARD W. THOMPSON, of Indiana, March 12, 1877. ALEXANDER RAMSEY, of Minnesota (Secretary of War), ad interim, December 20, 1880. NATHAN GOFF, JR., of West Virginia, January 6, 1881.

SECRETARY OF THE INTERIOR—ZACHARIAH CHANDLER, of Michigan, continued from preceding administration. CARL SCHURZ, of Missouri, March 12, 1877.

## Administration of JAMES A. GARFIELD
### MARCH 4, 1881, TO SEPTEMBER 19, 1881

PRESIDENT OF THE UNITED STATES—James A. Garfield, of Ohio (Died September 19, 1881.)

VICE PRESIDENT OF THE UNITED STATES—Chester A. Arthur, of New York.

SECRETARY OF STATE—William M. Evarts, of New York, continued from preceding administration. James G. Blaine, of Maine, March 5, 1881; entered upon duties March 7, 1881.

SECRETARY OF THE TREASURY—Henry F. French, of Massachusetts (Assistant Secretary), ad interim, March 4, 1881. William Windom, of Minnesota, March 5, 1881; entered upon duties March 8, 1881.

SECRETARY OF WAR—Alexander Ramsey, of Minnesota, continued from preceding administration. Robert T. Lincoln, of Illinois, March 5, 1881. entered upon duties March 11, 1881.

ATTORNEY GENERAL—Charles Devens, of Massachusetts, continued from preceding administration. Wayne MacVeagh, of Pennsylvania, March 5, 1881; entered upon duties March 7, 1881.

POSTMASTER GENERAL—Horace Maynard, of Tennessee, continued from preceding administration. Thomas L. James, of New York, March 5, 1881; entered upon duties March 8, 1881.

SECRETARY OF THE NAVY—Nathan Goff, Jr., of West Virginia, continued from preceding administration. William H. Hunt, of Louisiana, March 5, 1881; March 5, 1881; entered upon duties March 7, 1881.

SECRETARY OF THE INTERIOR—Carl Schurz, of Missouri, continued from preceding administration. Samuel J. Kirkwood, of Iowa, March 5, 1881; entered upon duties March 8, 1881.

---

## Administration of CHESTER A. ARTHUR
### SEPTEMBER 20, 1881, TO MARCH 3, 1885

PRESIDENT OF THE UNITED STATES—Chester A. Arthur, of New York.

VICE PRESIDENT OF THE UNITED STATES—Thomas F. Bayard, of Delaware; David Davis, of Illinois; George F. Edmunds, of Vermont.

SECRETARY OF STATE—James G. Blaine, of Maine, continued from preceding administration. Frederick T. Frelinghuysen, of New Jersey, December 12, 1881; entered upon duties December 19, 1881.

SECRETARY OF THE TREASURY—William Windom, of Minnesota, continued from preceding administration. Charles J. Folger, of New York, October 27, 1881; entered upon duties November 14, 1881 (died September 4, 1884). Charles E. Coon, of New York (Assistant Secretary), ad interim, September 4, 1884. Henry F. French, of Massachusetts (Assistant Secretary), ad interim, September 8, 1884. Charles E. Coon, of New York (Assistant Secretary), ad interim, September 15, 1884. Walter Q. Gresham, of Indiana, September 24, 1884. Henry F. French, of Massachusetts (Assistant Secretary), ad interim, October 29, 1884. Hugh McCulloch, of Indiana, October 28, 1884; entered upon duties October 31, 1884.

SECRETARY OF WAR—Robert T. Lincoln, of Illinois, continued from preceding administration.

ATTORNEY GENERAL—Wayne MacVeagh, of Pennsylvania, continued from preceding administration. Samuel F. Phillips, of North Carolina (Solicitor General), ad interim, November 14, 1881. Benjamin H. Brewster, of Pennsylvania, December 19, 1881; entered upon duties January 3, 1882.

POSTMASTER GENERAL—Thomas L. James, of New York, continued from preceding administration. Thomas L. James, of New York, recommissioned October 27, 1881; Timothy O. Howe, of Wisconsin, December 20, 1881; entered upon duties January 5, 1982 (died March 25, 1883). Frank Hatton of Iowa (First Assistant Postmaster General), ad interim, March 26, 1883. Walter Q. Gresham, of Indiana, April 3, 1883; entered upon duties April 11, 1883. Frank Hatton, of Iowa (First Assistant Postmaster General), ad interim, September 25, 1884. Frank Hatton, of Iowa, October 14, 1884.

SECRETARY OF THE NAVY—William H. Hunt, of Louisiana, continued from preceding administration. William E. Chandler, of New Hampshire, April 12, 1882; entered upon duties April 17, 1882.

SECRETARY OF THE INTERIOR—Samuel J. Kirkwood, of Iowa, continued from preceding administration. Henry M. Teller, of Colorado, April 6, 1882; entered upon duties April 17, 1882.

---

## First Administration of GROVER CLEVELAND
### MARCH 4, 1885, TO MARCH 3, 1889

PRESIDENT OF THE UNITED STATES—Grover Cleveland, of New York.

VICE PRESIDENT OF THE UNITED STATES—Thomas A. Hendricks, of Indiana. (Died November 25, 1885.)

PRESIDENT PRO TEMPORE OF THE SENATE—John Sherman, of Ohio; John J. Ingalls, of Kansas.

SECRETARY OF STATE—Frederick T. Frelinghuysen, of New Jersey, continued from preceding administration. Thomas F. Bayard, of Delaware, March 6, 1885.

SECRETARY OF THE TREASURY—Hugh McCulloch, of Indiana, continued from preceding administration. Daniel Manning, of New York, March 6, 1885; entered upon duties March 8, 1885. Charles S. Fairchild, of New York, April 1, 1887.

SECRETARY OF WAR—Robert T. Lincoln, of Illinois, continued from preceding administration. William C. Endicott, of Massachusetts, March 6, 1885.

ATTORNEY GENERAL—Benjamin H. Brewster, of Pennsylvania, continued from preceding administration. Augustus H. Garland, of Arkansas, March 6, 1885; entered upon duties March 9, 1885.

POSTMASTER GENERAL—Frank Hatton, of Iowa, continued from preceding administration. William F. Vilas, of Wisconsin, March 6, 1885. Don M. Dickinson, of Michigan, January 16, 1888.

SECRETARY OF THE NAVY—William E. Chandler, of New Hampshire, continued from preceding administration. William C. Whitney, of New York, March 6, 1885.

SECRETARY OF THE INTERIOR—Merritt L. Joslyn, of Illinois, (Assistant Secretary), ad interim, March 4, 1885. Lucius Q. C. Lamar, of Mississippi, March 6, 1885. Henry L. Muldrow, of Mississippi (First Assistant Secretary), ad interim, January 11, 1888. William F. Vilas, of Wisconsin, January 16, 1888.

SECRETARY OF AGRICULTURE—Norman J. Colman, of Missouri, February 13, 1889.

---

## Administration of BENJAMIN HARRISON

### MARCH 4, 1889, TO MARCH 3, 1893

PRESIDENT OF THE UNITED STATES—Benjamin Harrison, of Indiana.

VICE PRESIDENT OF THE UNITED STATES—Levi P. Morton, of New York.

SECRETARY OF STATE—Thomas F. Bayard, of Delaware, continued from preceding administration. James G. Blaine, of Maine, March 5, 1889; entered upon duties March 7, 1889. William F. Wharton, of Massachusetts (Assistant Secretary), ad interim, June 4, 1892. John W. Foster, of Indiana, June 29, 1892. William F. Wharton, of Massachusetts (Assistant Secretary), ad interim, February 23, 1893.

SECRETARY OF THE TREASURY—Charles S. Fairchild, of New York, continued from preceding administration. William Windom, of Minnesota, March 5, 1889; entered upon duties March 7, 1889 (died January 29, 1891). Allured B. Nettleton, of Minnesota (Assistant Secretary), ad interim, January 30, 1891. Charles Foster, of Ohio, February 24, 1891.

SECRETARY OF WAR—William C. Endicott, of Massachusetts, continued from preceding administration. Redfield Proctor, of Vermont, March 5, 1889; Lewis A. Grant, of Minnesota (Assistant Secretary), ad interim, December 6, 1891. Stephen B. Elkins, of West Virginia, December 22, 1891; entered upon duties December 24, 1891.

ATTORNEY GENERAL—Augustus H. Garland, of Arkansas, continued from preceding administration. William H. H. Miller, of Indiana, March 5, 1889.

POSTMASTER GENERAL—Don M. Dickinson, of Michigan, continued from preceding administration. John Wanamaker, of Pennsylvania, March 5, 1889.

SECRETARY OF THE NAVY—William C. Whitney, of New York, continued from preceding administration. Benjamin F. Tracy, of New York, March 5, 1889.

SECRETARY OF THE INTERIOR—William F. Vilas, of Wisconsin, continued from preceding administration. John W. Noble, of Missouri, March 5, 1889; entered upon duties March 7, 1889.

SECRETARY OF AGRICULTURE—Norman J. Colman, of Missouri, continued from preceding administration. Jeremiah M. Rusk, of Wisconsin, March 5, 1889; entered upon duties March 7, 1889.

---

## Second Administration of GROVER CLEVELAND

### MARCH 4, 1893, TO MARCH 3, 1897

PRESIDENT OF THE UNITED STATES—Grover Cleveland, of New York.

VICE PRESIDENT OF THE UNITED STATES—Adlai E. Stevenson, of Illinois.

SECRETARY OF STATE—William F. Wharton, of Massachusetts (Assistant Secretary), ad interim, continued from preceding administration. Walter Q. Gresham, of Illinois, March 6, 1893 (died May 28, 1895). Edwin F. Uhl, of Michigan (Assistant Secretary), ad interim, May 28, 1895. Alvey A. Adee, of the District of Columbia (Second Assistant Secretary), ad interim, May 31, 1895. Edwin F. Uhl, of Michigan (Assistant Secretary), ad interim, June 1, 1895. Richard Olney, of Massachusetts, June 8, 1895; entered upon duties June 10, 1895.

SECRETARY OF THE TREASURY—Charles Foster, of Ohio, continued from preceding administration. John G. Carlisle, of Kentucky, March 6, 1893.

SECRETARY OF WAR—Stephen B. Elkins, of West Virginia, continued from preceding administration. Daniel S. Lamont, of New York, March 6, 1893.

ATTORNEY GENERAL—William H. H. Miller, of Indiana, continued from preceding administration. Richard Olney, of Massachusetts, March 6, 1893. Judson Harmon, of Ohio, June 8, 1895; entered upon duties June 11, 1895.

POSTMASTER GENERAL—John Wanamaker, of Pennsylvania, continued from preceding administration. Wilson S. Bissell, of New York, March 6, 1893. William L. Wilson, of West Virginia, March 1, 1895; entered upon duties April 4, 1895.

SECRETARY OF THE NAVY—Benjamin F. Tracy, of New York, continued from preceding administration. Hilary A. Herbert, of Alabama, March 6, 1893.

SECRETARY OF THE INTERIOR—John W. Noble, of Missouri, continued from preceding administration. Hoke Smith, of Georgia, March 6, 1893. John M. Reynolds, of Pennsylvania (Assistant Secretary), ad interim, September 1, 1896. David R. Francis, of Missouri, September 1, 1896; entered upon duties September 4, 1896.

SECRETARY OF AGRICULTURE—Jeremiah M. Rusk, of Wisconsin, continued from preceding administration. Julius Sterling Morton, of Nebraska, March 6, 1893.

## First Administration of WILLIAM McKINLEY

### MARCH 4, 1897, TO MARCH 3, 1901

PRESIDENT OF THE UNITED STATES—WILLIAM McKINLEY, of Ohio.

VICE PRESIDENT OF THE UNITED STATES—GARRET A. HOBART, of New Jersey. (Died November 21, 1899.)

PRESIDENT PRO TEMPORE OF THE SENATE—WILLIAM P. FRYE, of Maine.

SECRETARY OF STATE—RICHARD OLNEY, of Massachusetts, continued from preceding administration. JOHN SHERMAN, of Ohio, March 5, 1897. WILLIAM R. DAY, of Ohio, April 26, 1898; entered upon duties April 28, 1898. ALVEY A. ADEE (Second Assistant Secretary), ad interim, September 17, 1898. JOHN HAY, of the District of Columbia, September 20, 1898; entered upon duties September 30, 1898.

SECRETARY OF THE TREASURY—JOHN G. CARLISLE, of Kentucky, continued from preceding administration. LYMAN J. GAGE, of Illinois, March 5, 1897.

SECRETARY OF WAR—DANIEL S. LAMONT, of New York, continued from preceding administration. RUSSELL A. ALGER, of Michigan, March 5, 1897. ELIHU ROOT, of New York, August 1, 1899.

ATTORNEY GENERAL—JUDSON HARMON, of Ohio, continued from preceding administration. JOSEPH McKENNA, of California, March 5, 1897; entered upon duties March 7, 1897. JOHN K, RICHARDS, of Ohio, (Solicitor General), ad interim, January 26, 1898. JOHN W. GRIGGS, of New Jersey, January 25, 1898; entered upon duties February 1, 1898.

POSTMASTER GENERAL—WILLIAM L. WILSON, of West Virginia, continued from preceding administration. JAMES A. GARY, of Maryland, March 5, 1897. CHARLES EMORY SMITH, of Pennsylvania, April 21, 1898.

SECRETARY OF THE NAVY—HILARY A. HERBERT, of Alabama, continued from preceding administration. JOHN D. LONG, of Massachusetts, March 5, 1897.

SECRETARY OF THE INTERIOR—DAVID R. FRANCIS, of Missouri, continued from preceding administration. CORNELIUS N. BLISS, of New York, March 5, 1897. ETHAN A. HITCHCOCK, of Missouri, December 21, 1898; entered upon duties February 20, 1899.

SECRETARY OF AGRICULTURE—JULIUS STERLING MORTON, of Nebraska, continued from preceding administration. JAMES WILSON, of Iowa, March 5, 1897.

---

## Second Administration of WILLIAM McKINLEY

### MARCH 4, 1901, TO SEPTEMBER 14, 1901

PRESIDENT OF THE UNITED STATES—WILLIAM McKINLEY, of Ohio. (Died September 14, 1901.)

VICE PRESIDENT OF THE UNITED STATES—THEODORE ROOSEVELT, of New York.

SECRETARY OF STATE—JOHN HAY, of the District of Columbia, continued from preceding administration. JOHN HAY, of the District of Columbia, recommissioned March 5, 1901.

SECRETARY OF THE TREASURY—LYMAN J. GAGE, of Illinois, continued from preceding administration. LYMAN J. GAGE, of Illinois, recommissioned March 5, 1901.

SECRETARY OF WAR—ELIHU ROOT, of New York, continued from preceding administration. ELIHU ROOT, of New York, recommissioned March 5, 1901.

ATTORNEY GENERAL—JOHN W. GRIGGS, of New Jersey, continued from preceding administration. JOHN W. GRIGGS, of New Jersey, recommissioned March 5, 1901. JOHN K. RICHARDS, of Ohio (Solicitor General), ad interim, April 1, 1901. PHILANDER C. KNOX, of Pennsylvania, April 5, 1901; entered upon duties April 10, 1901.

POSTMASTER GENERAL—CHARLES EMORY SMITH, of Pennsylvania, continued from preceding administration. CHARLES EMORY SMITH, of Pennsylvania, recommissioned March 5, 1901.

SECRETARY OF THE NAVY—JOHN D. LONG, of Massachusetts, continued from preceding administration. JOHN D. LONG, of Massachusetts, recommissioned March 5, 1901.

SECRETARY OF THE INTERIOR—ETHAN A. HITCHCOCK, of Missouri, continued from preceding administration. ETHAN A. HITCHCOCK, of Missouri, recommissioned March 5, 1901.

SECRETARY OF AGRICULTURE—JAMES WILSON, of Iowa, continued from preceding administration. JAMES WILSON, of Iowa, recommissioned March 5, 1901.

---

## First Administration of THEODORE ROOSEVELT

### SEPTEMBER 14, 1901, TO MARCH 3, 1905

PRESIDENT OF THE UNITED STATES—THEODORE ROOSEVELT, of New York.

PRESIDENT PRO TEMPORE OF THE SENATE—WILLIAM P. FRYE, of Maine.

SECRETARY OF STATE—JOHN HAY, of the District of Columbia, continued from preceding administration.

SECRETARY OF THE TREASURY—LYMAN J. GAGE, of Illinois, continued from preceding administration. LESLIE M. SHAW, of Iowa, January 9, 1902; entered upon duties February 1, 1902.

SECRETARY OF WAR—Elihu Root, of New York, continued from preceding administration. William H. Taft, of Ohio, January 11, 1904, to take effect February 1, 1904.

ATTORNEY GENERAL—Philander C. Knox, of Pennsylvania, continued from preceding administration. Philander C. Knox, of Pennsylvania, recommissioned December 16, 1901. William H. Moody, of Massachusetts, July 1, 1904.

POSTMASTER GENERAL—Charles Emory Smith, of Pennsylvania, continued from preceding administration. Henry C. Payne, of Wisconsin, January 9, 1902. Robert J. Wynne, of Pennsylvania, October 10, 1904.

SECRETARY OF THE NAVY—John D. Long, of Massachusetts, continued from preceding administration. William H. Moody, of Massachusetts, April 29, 1902; entered upon duties May 1, 1902. Paul Morton, of Illinois, July 1, 1904.

SECRETARY OF THE INTERIOR—Ethan A. Hitchcock, of Missouri, continued from preceding administration.

SECRETARY OF AGRICULTURE—James Wilson, of Iowa, continued from preceding administration.

SECRETARY OF COMMERCE AND LABOR—George B. Cortelyou, of New York, February 16, 1903. Victor H. Metcalf, of California, July 1, 1904.

---

## Second Administration of THEODORE ROOSEVELT

### MARCH 4, 1905, TO MARCH 3, 1909

PRESIDENT OF THE UNITED STATES—Theodore Roosevelt, of New York.

PRESIDENT PRO TEMPORE OF THE SENATE—Charles Warren Fairbanks, of Indiana.

SECRETARY OF STATE—John Hay, of the District of Columbia, continued from preceding administration. John Hay, of the District of Columbia, recommissioned March 6, 1905 (died July 1, 1905). Francis B. Loomis, of Ohio (Assistant Secretary), ad interim, July 1, 1905, to July 18, 1905. Elihu Root, of New York, July 7, 1905; entered upon duties July 19, 1905. Robert Bacon, of New York, January 27, 1909.

SECRETARY OF THE TREASURY—Leslie M. Shaw, of Iowa, continued from preceding administration. Leslie M. Shaw, of Iowa, recommissioned March 6, 1905. George B. Cortelyou, of New York, January 15, 1907; to take effect March 4, 1907.

SECRETARY OF WAR—William H. Taft, of Ohio, continued from preceding administration. William H. Taft, of Ohio, recommissioned March 6, 1905. Luke E. Wright, of Tennessee, June 29, 1908; entered upon duties July 1, 1908.

ATTORNEY GENERAL—William H. Moody, of Massachusets, continued from preceding administration. William H. Moody, of Massachusetts, recommissioned March 6, 1905. Charles J. Bonaparte, of Maryland, December 12, 1906; entered upon duties December 17, 1906.

POSTMASTER GENERAL—Robert J. Wynne, of Pennsylvania, continued from preceding administration. George B. Cortelyou, of New York, March 6, 1905. George von L. Meyer, of Massachusetts, January 15, 1907, to take effect March 4, 1907.

SECRETARY OF THE NAVY—Paul Morton, of Illinois, continued from preceding administration. Paul Morton, of Illinois, recommissioned March 6, 1905. Charles J. Bonaparte, of Maryland, July 1, 1905. Victor H. Metcalf, of California, December 12, 1906; entered upon duties December 17, 1906. Truman H. Newberry, of Michigan, December 1, 1908.

SECRETARY OF THE INTERIOR—Ethan A. Hitchcock, of Missouri, continued from preceding administration. Ethan A. Hitchcock, of Missouri, recommissioned March 6, 1905. James R. Garfield, of Ohio, January 15, 1907, to take effect March 4, 1907.

SECRETARY OF AGRICULTURE—James Wilson, of Iowa, continued from preceding administration. James Wilson, of Iowa, recommissioned March 6, 1905.

SECRETARY OF COMMERCE AND LABOR—Victor H. Metcalf, of California, continued from preceding administration. Victor H. Metcalf, of California, recommissioned March 6, 1905. Oscar S. Straus, of New York, December 12, 1906; entered upon duties December 17, 1906.

---

## Administration of WILLIAM H. TAFT

### MARCH 4, 1909, TO MARCH 3, 1913

PRESIDENT OF THE UNITED STATES—William H. Taft, of Ohio.

VICE PRESIDENT OF THE UNITED STATES—James S. Sherman, of New York. (Died October 30, 1912.)

PRESIDENT PRO TEMPORE OF THE SENATE—William P. Frye, of Maine (resigned April 27, 1911). Jacob H. Gallinger, of New Hampshire, and Augustus O. Bacon, of Georgia, alternating.

SECRETARY OF STATE—Robert Bacon, of New York, continued from preceding administration. Philander C. Knox, of Pennsylvania, March 5, 1909.

SECRETARY OF THE TREASURY—George B. Cortelyou, of New York, continued from preceding administration. Franklin MacVeagh, of Illinois, March 5, 1909; entered upon duties March 8, 1909.

SECRETARY OF WAR—Luke E. Wright, of Tennessee, continued from preceding administration. Jacob M. Dickinson, of Tennessee, March 5, 1909; entered upon duties March 12, 1909. Henry L. Stimson, of New York, May 16, 1911; entered upon duties May 22, 1911.

ATTORNEY GENERAL—Charles J. Bonaparte, of Maryland, continued from preceding administration. George W. Wickersham, of New York, March 5, 1909.

POSTMASTER GENERAL—George von L. Meyer, of Massachusetts, continued from preceding administration. Frank H. Hitchcock, of Massachusetts, March 5, 1909.

SECRETARY OF THE NAVY—Truman H. Newberry, of Michigan, continued from preceding administration. George von L. Meyer, of Massachusetts, March 5, 1909.

SECRETARY OF THE INTERIOR—James R. Garfield, of Ohio, continued from preceding administration. Richard A. Ballinger, of Washington, March 5, 1909. Walter Lowrie Fisher, of Illinois, March 7, 1911.

SECRETARY OF AGRICULTURE—James Wilson, of Iowa, continued from preceding administration. James Wilson, of Iowa, recommissioned March 5, 1909.

SECRETARY OF COMMERCE AND LABOR—Oscar S. Straus, of New York, continued from preceding administration. Charles Nagel, of Missouri, March 5, 1909.

## First Administration of WOODROW WILSON
### MARCH 4, 1913, TO MARCH 3, 1917

PRESIDENT OF THE UNITED STATES—Woodrow Wilson, of New Jersey

VICE PRESIDENT OF THE UNITED STATES—Thomas R. Marshall, of Indiana.

SECRETARY OF STATE—Philander C. Knox, of Pennsylvania, continued from preceding administration. William Jennings Bryan, of Nebraska, March 5, 1913. Robert Lansing, of New York (counselor), ad interim, June 9, 1915. Robert Lansing, of New York, June 23, 1915.

SECRETARY OF THE TREASURY—Franklin MacVeagh, of Illinois, continued from preceding administration. William Gibbs McAdoo, of New York, March 5, 1913; entered upon duties March 6, 1913.

SECRETARY OF WAR—Henry L. Stimson, of New York, continued from preceding administration. Lindley M. Garrison, of New Jersey, March 5, 1913. Hugh L. Scott (United States Army), ad interim, February 12, 1916; served from February 11 to March 8, 1916. Newton D. Baker, of Ohio, March 7, 1916; entered upon duties March 9, 1916.

ATTORNEY GENERAL—George W. Wickersham, of New York, continued from preceding administration. James Clark McReynolds, of Tennessee, March 5, 1913; entered upon duties March 6, 1913. Thomas Watt Gregory, of Texas, August 29, 1914; entered upon duties September 3, 1914.

POSTMASTER GENERAL—Frank H. Hitchcock, of Massachusetts, continued from preceding administration. Albert Sidney Burleson, of Texas, March 5, 1913.

SECRETARY OF THE NAVY—George von L. Meyer, of Massachusetts, continued from preceding administration. Josephus Daniels, of North Carolina, March 5, 1913.

SECRETARY OF THE INTERIOR—Walter Lowrie Fisher, of Illinois, continued from preceding administration. Franklin Knight Lane, of California, March 5, 1913.

SECRETARY OF AGRICULTURE—James Wilson, of Iowa, continued from preceding administration. David Franklin Houston, of Missouri, March 5, 1913; entered upon duties March 6, 1913.

SECRETARY OF COMMERCE—Charles Nagel, of Missouri (Secretary of Commerce and Labor), continued from preceding administration. William C. Redfield, of New York, March 5, 1913.

SECRETARY OF LABOR—Charles Nagel, of Missouri (Secretary of Commerce and Labor), continued from preceding administration. William Bauchop Wilson, of Pennsylvania, March 5, 1913.

## Second Administration of WOODROW WILSON
### MARCH 4, 1917, TO MARCH 3, 1921

PRESIDENT OF THE UNITED STATES—Woodrow Wilson, of New Jersey, (Oath administered March 5, 1917.)

VICE PRESIDENT OF THE UNITED STATES—Thomas R. Marshall, of Indiana.

SECRETARY OF STATE—Robert Lansing, of New York, continued from preceding administration. Frank L. Pole, of New York (Under Secretary), ad interim, February 14, 1920, to March 13, 1920. Bainbridge Colby, of New York, March 22, 1920; entered upon duties March 23, 1920.

SECRETARY OF THE TREASURY—William Gibbs McAdoo, of New York, continued from preceding administration. Carter Glass, of Virginia, December 6, 1918; entered upon duties December 16, 1918. David F. Houston, of Missouri, January 31, 1920; entered upon duties February 2, 1920.

SECRETARY OF WAR—Newton D. Baker, of Ohio, continued from preceding administration.

ATTORNEY GENERAL—Thomas Watt Gregory, of Texas, continued from preceding administration. A. Mitchell Palmer, of Pennsylvania, March 5, 1919.

POSTMASTER GENERAL—Albert Sidney Burleson, of Texas, continued from preceding administration. Albert Sidney Burleson, of Texas, recommissioned January 24, 1918.

SECRETARY OF THE NAVY—Josephus Daniels of North Carolina, continued from preceding administration.

SECRETARY OF THE INTERIOR—Franklin Knight Lane, of California, continued from preceding administration. John Barton Payne, of Illinois, February 28, 1920; entered upon duties March 13, 1920.

SECRETARY OF AGRICULTURE—David Franklin Houston, of Missouri, continued from preceding administration. Edwin T. Meredith, of Iowa, January 31, 1920; entered upon duties February 2, 1920.

SECRETARY OF COMMERCE—William C. Redfield, of New York, continued from preceding administration. Joshua Willis Alexander, of Missouri, December 11, 1919; entered upon duties December 16, 1919.

SECRETARY OF LABOR—William Bauchop Wilson, of Pennsylvania, continued from preceding administration.

## Administration of WARREN G. HARDING

### MARCH 4, 1921, TO AUGUST 2, 1923

PRESIDENT OF THE UNITED STATES—Warren G. Harding, of Ohio. (Died August 2, 1923.)

VICE PRESIDENT OF THE UNITED STATES—Calvin Coolidge, of Massachusetts.

SECRETARY OF STATE—Bainbridge Colby, of New York, continued from preceding administration. Charles Evans Hughes, of New York, March 4, 1921; entered upon duties March 5, 1921.

SECRETARY OF THE TREASURY—David F. Houston, of Missouri, continued from preceding administration. Andrew W. Mellon, of Pennsylvania, March 4, 1921; entered upon duties March 5, 1921.

SECRETARY OF WAR—Newton D. Baker, of Ohio, continued from preceding administration. John W. Weeks, of Massachusetts, March 5, 1921.

ATTORNEY GENERAL—A. Mitchell Palmer, of Pennsylvania, continued from preceding administration. Harry M. Daugherty, of Ohio, March 5, 1921.

POSTMASTER GENERAL—Albert Sidney Burleson, of Texas, continued from preceding administration. Will H. Hays, of Indiana, March 5, 1921. Hubert Work, of Colorado, March 4, 1922. Harry S. New, of Indiana, February 27, 1923; entered upon duties March 5, 1923.

SECRETARY OF THE NAVY—Josephus Daniels, of North Carolina, continued from preceding administration. Edwin Denby, of Michigan, March 5, 1921.

SECRETARY OF THE INTERIOR—John Barton Payne, of Illinois, continued from preceding administration. Albert B. Fall, of New Mexico, March 5, 1921. Hubert Work, of Colorado, Feburary 27, 1923; entered upon duties March 5, 1923.

SECRETARY OF AGRICULTURE—Edwin T. Meredith, of Iowa, continued from preceding administration. Henry C. Wallace, of Iowa, March 5, 1921.

SECRETARY OF COMMERCE—Joshua Willis Alexander, of Missouri, continued from preceding administration. Herbert C. Hoover, of California, March 5, 1921.

SECRETARY OF LABOR—William Bauchop Wilson, of Pennsylvania, continued from preceding administration. James J. Davis, of Pennsylvania, March 5, 1921.

---

## First Administration of CALVIN COOLIDGE

### AUGUST 3, 1923, TO MARCH 3, 1925

PRESIDENT OF THE UNITED STATES—Calvin Coolidge, of Massachusetts.

PRESIDENT PRO TEMPORE OF THE SENATE—Albert B. Cummins, of Iowa.

SECRETARY OF STATE—Charles Evans Hughes, of New York, continued from preceding administration.

SECRETARY OF THE TREASURY—Andrew W. Mellon, of Pennsylvania, continued from preceding administration.

SECRETARY OF WAR—John W. Weeks, of Massachusetts, continued from preceding administration.

ATTORNEY GENERAL—Harry M. Daugherty, of Ohio, continued from preceding administration. Harlan F. Stone, of New York, April 7, 1924; entered upon duties April 9, 1924.

POSTMASTER GENERAL—Harry S. New, of Indiana, continued from preceding administration.

SECRETARY OF THE NAVY—Edwin Denby, of Michigan, continued from preceding administration. Curtis D. Wilbur, of California, March 18, 1924.

SECRETARY OF THE INTERIOR—Hubert Work, of Colorado, continued from preceding administration.

SECRETARY OF AGRICULTURE—Henry C. Wallace, of Iowa, continued from preceding administration (died October 25, 1924). Howard M. Gore, of West Virginia (Assistant Secretary), ad interim, October 26, 1924, to November 22, 1924. Howard M. Gore, of West Virginia, November 21, 1924; entered upon duties November 22, 1924.

SECRETARY OF COMMERCE—Hebert C. Hoover, of California, continued from preceding administration.

SECRETARY OF LABOR—James J. Davis, of Pennsylvania, continued from preceding administration.

---

## Second Administration of CALVIN COOLIDGE

### MARCH 4, 1925, TO MARCH 3, 1929

PRESIDENT OF THE UNITED STATES—Calvin Coolidge, of Massachusetts.

VICE PRESIDENT OF THE UNITED STATES—Charles G. Dawes, of Illinois.

SECRETARY OF STATE—Charles Evans Hughes, of New York, continued from preceding administration. Frank B. Kellogg, of Minnesota, February 16, 1925; entered upon duties March 5, 1925.

SECRETARY OF THE TREASURY—Andrew W. Mellon, of Pennsylvania, continued from preceding administration.

SECRETARY OF WAR—John W. Weeks, of Massachusetts, continued from preceding administration. Dwight F. Davis, of Missouri, October 13, 1925; entered upon duties October 14, 1925.

ATTORNEY GENERAL—James M. Beck, of Pennsylvania (Solicitor General), ad interim, March 4, 1925, to March 16, 1925. John G. Sargent, of Vermont, March 17, 1925; entered upon duties March 18, 1925.

POSTMASTER GENERAL—HARRY S. NEW, of Indiana, continued from preceding administration. HARRY S. NEW, of Indiana, recommissioned March 5, 1925.

SECRETARY OF THE NAVY—CURTIS D. WILBUR, of California, continued from preceding administration.

SECRETARY OF THE INTERIOR—HUBERT WORK, of Colorado, continued from preceding administration. ROY O. WEST, of Illinois, ad interim, July 25, 1928, to January 21, 1929. ROY O. WEST, January 21, 1929.

SECRETARY OF AGRICULTURE—HOWARD M. GORE, of West Virginia, continued from preceding administration. WILLIAM M. JARDINE, of Kansas, February 18, 1925; entered upon duties March 5, 1925.

SECRETARY OF COMMERCE—HERBERT C. HOOVER, of California, continued from preceding administration. WILLIAM F. WHITING, of Massachusetts, ad interim, August 21, 1928, to December 1, 1928. WILLIAM F. WHITING, December 11, 1928.

SECRETARY OF LABOR—JAMES J. DAVIS, of Pennsylvania, continued from preceding administration.

## Administration of HERBERT C. HOOVER

### MARCH 4, 1929 TO MARCH 3, 1933

PRESIDENT OF THE UNITED STATES—HERBERT C. HOOVER, of California.

VICE PRESIDENT OF THE UNITED STATES—CHARLES CURTIS, of Kansas.

SECRETARY OF STATE—FRANK B. KELLOGG, of Minnesota, continued from preceding administration. HENRY L. STIMSON, of New York, March 4, 1929; entered upon duties March 29, 1929.

SECRETARY OF THE TREASURY—ANDREW W. MELLON, of Pennsylvania, continued from preceding administration. OGDEN L. MILLS, of New York, Feburary 10, 1932; entered upon duties February 13, 1932.

SECRETARY OF WAR—DWIGHT F. DAVIS, of Missouri, continued from preceding administration. JAMES W. GOOD, of Illinois, March 5, 1929; entered upon duties March 6, 1929. PATRICK J. HURLEY, of Oklahoma, December 9, 1929.

ATTORNEY GENERAL—JAMES. G. SARGENT, of Vermont, continued from preceding administration. JAMES DEWITT MITCHELL, of Minnesota, March 5, 1929; entered upon duties March 6, 1929.

POSTMASTER GENERAL—HARRY S. NEW, of Indiana, continued from preceding administration. WALTER F. BROWN, of Ohio, March 5, 1929; entered upon duties March 6, 1929.

SECRETARY OF THE NAVY—CURTIS D. WILBUR, of California, continued from preceding administration. CHARLES F. ADAMS, of Massachusetts, March 5, 1929.

SECRETARY OF THE INTERIOR—ROY O. WEST, of Illinois, continued from preceding administration. RAY L. WILBUR, of California, March 5, 1929.

SECRETARY OF AGRICULTURE—WILLIAM M. JARDINE, of Kansas, continued from preceding administration. ARTHUR M. HYDE, of Missouri, March 5, 1929; entered upon duties March 6, 1929.

SECRETARY OF COMMERCE—WILLIAM F. WHITING, of Massachusetts, continued from preceding administration. ROBERT P. LAMONT, of Illinois, March 5, 1929. ROY D. CHAPIN, of Michigan, ad interim, August 8, 1932, to December 14, 1932. ROY D. CHAPIN, of Michigan, December 14, 1932.

SECRETARY OF LABOR—JAMES J. DAVIS, of Pennsylvania, continued from preceding administration. WILLIAM N. DOAK, of Virginia, December 8, 1930; entered upon duties December 9, 1930.

## First Administration of FRANKLIN DELANO ROOSEVELT

### MARCH 4, 1933 TO JANUARY 20, 1937

PRESIDENT OF THE UNITED STATES—FRANKLIN DELANO ROOSEVELT, of New York.

VICE PRESIDENT OF THE UNITED STATES—JOHN N. GARNER, of Texas.

SECRETARY OF STATE—CORDELL HULL, of Tennessee, March 4, 1933.

SECRETARY OF THE TREASURY—WILLIAM H. WOODIN, of New York, March 4, 1933. HENRY MORGENTHAU, JR., of New York (Under Secretary), ad interim, January 1, 1934, to January 8, 1934. HENRY MORGENTHAU, JR., of New York, January 8, 1934.

SECRETARY OF WAR—GEORGE H. DERN, of Utah, March 4, 1933.

ATTORNEY GENERAL—HOMER S. CUMMINGS, of Connecticut, March 4, 1933.

POSTMASTER GENERAL—JAMES A. FARLEY, of New York, March 4, 1933.

SECRETARY OF THE NAVY—CLAUDE A. SWANSON, of Virginia, March 4, 1933.

SECRETARY OF THE INTERIOR—HAROLD L. ICKES, of Illinois, March 4, 1933.

SECRETARY OF AGRICULTURE—HENRY A. WALLACE, of Iowa, March 4, 1933.

SECRETARY OF COMMERCE—DANIEL C. ROPER, of South Carolina, March 4, 1933.

SECRETARY OF LABOR—FRANCES PERKINS, of New York, March 4, 1933.

## Second Administration of FRANKLIN DELANO ROOSEVELT

### JANUARY 20, 1937, TO JANUARY 20, 1941

PRESIDENT OF THE UNITED STATES—FRANKLIN DELANO ROOSEVELT, of New York.

VICE PRESIDENT OF THE UNITED STATES—JOHN H. GARNER, of Texas.

SECRETARY OF STATE—CORDELL HULL, of Tennessee, continued from preceding administration.

SECRETARY OF THE TREASURY—HENRY MORGENTHAU, JR., of New York, continued from preceding administration.

SECRETARY OF WAR—GEORGE H. DERN, of Utah, continued from preceding administration (died August 27, 1936). HARRY H. WOODRING, of Kansas (Assistant Secretary), ad interim, September 25, 1936, to May 6, 1937. HARRY H. WOODRING, of Kansas, May 6, 1937. HENRY L. STIMSON, of New York, July 10, 1940.

ATTORNEY GENERAL—HOMER S. CUMMINGS, of Connecticut, continued from preceding administration. FRANK MURPHY, of Michigan, ad interim, January 2, 1939, to January 17, 1939. FRANK MURPHY, of Michigan, January 17, 1939. ROBERT H. JACKSON, of New York, January 18 1940.

POSTMASTER GENERAL—JAMES A. FARLEY, of New York, continued from preceding administration. JAMES A. FARLEY, of New York, recommissioned January 22, 1937. FRANK C. WALKER, of Pennsylvania, September 10, 1940.

SECRETARY OF THE NAVY—CLAUDE A. SWANSON, of Virginia, continued from preceding administration (died July 7, 1939). CHARLES EDISON, of New Jersey, Acting Secretary from August 5, 1939, to December 30, 1939. CHARLES EDISON, of New Jersey (Assistant Secretary), ad interim, December 30, 1939, to January 11, 1940. CHARLES EDISON, of New Jersey, January 11, 1940. FRANK KNOX, of Illinois, July 10, 1940.

SECRETARY OF THE INTERIOR—HAROLD L. ICKES, of Illinois, continued from preceding administration.

SECRETARY OF AGRICULTURE—HENRY A. WALLACE, of Iowa, continued from preceding administration. CLAUDE R. WICKARD, of Indiana, August 27, 1940; entered upon duties September 5, 1940.

SECRETARY OF COMMERCE—DANIEL C. ROPER, of South Carolina, continued from preceding administration. HARRY L. HOPKINS, of New York ad interim, December 24, 1938, to January 23, 1939. HARRY L. HOPKINS, of New York, January 23, 1939. JESSE H. JONES, of Texas, September 16, 1940; entered upon duties September 19, 1940.

SECRETARY OF LABOR—FRANCES PERKINS, of New York, continued from preceding administration.

---

## Third Administration of FRANKLIN DELANO ROOSEVELT

### JANUARY 20, 1941, TO JANUARY 20, 1945

PRESIDENT OF THE UNITED STATES—FRANKLIN DELANO ROOSEVELT, of New York.

VICE PRESIDENT OF THE UNITED STATES—HENRY A. WALLACE, of Iowa.

SECRETARY OF STATE—CORDELL HULL, of Tennessee, continued from preceding administration. EDWARD R. STETTINIUS, of Virginia, November 30, 1944; entered upon duties December 1, 1944.

SECRETARY OF THE TREASURY—HENRY MORGENTHAU, JR., of New York, continued from preceding administration.

SECRETARY OF WAR—HENRY L. STIMSON, of New York, continued from preceding administration.

ATTORNEY GENERAL—ROBERT H. JACKSON, of New York, continued from preceding administration. FRANCIS BIDDLE, of Pennsylvania, September 5, 1941.

POSTMASTER GENERAL—FRANK C. WALKER, of Pennsylvania, continued from preceding administration. FRANK C. WALKER, of Pennsylvania, recommissioned January 27, 1941.

SECRETARY OF THE NAVY—FRANK KNOX, of Illinois, continued from preceding administration (died April 28, 1944). JAMES V. FORRESTAL, of New York, May 18, 1944.

SECRETARY OF THE INTERIOR—HAROLD L. ICKES, of Illinois, continued from preceding administration.

SECRETARY OF AGRICULTURE—CLAUDE R. WICKARD of Indiana, continued from preceding administration.

SECRETARY OF COMMERCE—JESSE H. JONES, of Texas, continued from preceding administration.

SECRETARY OF LABOR—FRANCES PERKINS, of New York, continued from preceding administration.

---

## Fourth Administration of FRANKLIN DELANO ROOSEVELT

### JANUARY 20, 1945, TO APRIL 12, 1945

PRESIDENT OF THE UNITED STATES—FRANKLIN DELANO ROOSEVELT, of New York. (Died April 12, 1945.)

VICE PRESIDENT OF THE UNITED STATES—HARRY S TRUMAN, of Missouri.

SECRETARY OF STATE—EDWARD R. STETTINIUS, of Virginia, continued from preceding administration.

SECRETARY OF THE TREASURY—HENRY MORGENTHAU, JR., of New York, continued from preceding administration.

SECRETARY OF WAR—HENRY L. STIMSON, of New York, continued from preceding administration.

ATTORNEY GENERAL—FRANCIS BIDDLE, of Pennsylvania, continued from preceding administration.

POSTMASTER GENERAL—FRANK C. WALKER, of Pennsylvania, continued from preceding administration. FRANK C. WALKER, of Pennsylvania, recommissioned February 6, 1945.

SECRETARY OF THE NAVY—James V. Forrestal, of New York, continued from preceding administration.

SECRETARY OF THE INTERIOR—Harold L. Ickes, of Illinois, continued from preceding administration.

SECRETARY OF AGRICULTURE—Claude R. Wickard, of Indiana, continued from preceding administration.

SECRETARY OF COMMERCE—Jesse H. Jones, of Texas, continued from preceding administration. Henry A. Wallace, of Iowa, March 1, 1945; entered upon duties March 2, 1945.

SECRETARY OF LABOR—Frances Perkins, of New York, continued from preceding administration.

---

## First Administration of HARRY S TRUMAN
### APRIL 12, 1945, TO JANUARY 20, 1949

PRESIDENT OF THE UNITED STATES—Harry S Truman, of Missouri.

PRESIDENT PRO TEMPORE OF THE SENATE—Kenneth McKellar, of Tennessee. Arthur S. Vandenberg, of Michigan, January 4, 1947.

SECRETARY OF STATE—Edward R. Stettinius, of Virginia, continued from preceding administration. James F. Byrnes, of South Carolina, July 2, 1945; entered upon duties July 3, 1945. Geroge C. Marshall, of Pennsylvania, January 8, 1947; entered upon duties January 21, 1947.

SECRETARY OF THE TREASURY—Henry Morgenthau, Jr., of New York, continued from preceding administration. Fred M. Vinson, of Kentucky, July 18, 1945; entered upon duties July 23, 1945. John W. Snyder, of Missouri, June 12, 1946; entered upon duties June 25, 1946.

SECRETARY OF DEFENSE—James Forrestal, of New York, July 26, 1947; entered upon duties September 17, 1947.

SECRETARY OF WAR—Henry L. Stimson, of New York, continued from preceding administration. Robert Porter Patterson, of New York, September 26, 1945; entered upon duties September 27, 1945. Kenneth C. Royall, of North Carolina, July 21, 1947; entered upon duties July 25, 1947, and served until September 17, 1947.

ATTORNEY GENERAL—Francis Biddle, of Pennsylvania, continued from preceding administration. Tom C. Clark, of Texas, June 15, 1945; entered upon duties July 1, 1945.

POSTMASTER GENERAL—Frank C. Walker, of Pennsylvania, continued from preceding administration. Robert E. Hannegan, of Missouri, May 8, 1945; entered upon duties July 1, 1945. Jesse M. Donaldson, of Missouri, December 16, 1947.

SECRETARY OF THE NAVY—James V. Forrestal, of New York, continued from preceding administration; served until September 17, 1947.

SECRETARY OF THE INTERIOR—Harold L. Ickes, of Illinois, continued from preceding administration. Julius A. Krug, of Wisconsin, March 6, 1946; entered upon duties March 18, 1946.

SECRETARY OF AGRICULTURE—Claude R. Wickard, of Indiana, continued from preceding administration. Clinton P. Anderson, of New Mexico, June 2, 1945; entered upon duties June 30, 1945. Charles F. Brannan, of Colorado, May 29, 1948; entered upon duties June 2, 1948.

SECRETARY OF COMMERCE—Henry A. Wallace, of Iowa, continued from preceding administration. William Averell Harriman, of New York, ad interim, September 28, 1946, to January 28, 1947. William Averell Harriman, of New York, January 28, 1947. Charles Sawyer, of Ohio, May 6, 1948.

SECRETARY OF LABOR—Frances Perkins, of New York, continued from preceding administration. Lewis B. Schwellenbach, of Washington, June 1, 1945; entered upon duties July 1, 1945 (died June 10, 1948). Maurice J. Tobin, of Massachusetts, ad interim, August 13, 1948.

---

## Second Administration of HARRY S TRUMAN
### JANUARY 20, 1949, TO JANUARY 20, 1953

PRESIDENT OF THE UNITED STATES—Harry S Truman, of Missouri.

VICE PRESIDENT OF THE UNITED STATES—Alben W. Barkley, of Kentucky.

SECRETARY OF STATE—Dean G. Acheson, of Connecticut, January 19, 1949; entered upon duties January 2, 1949.

SECRETARY OF THE TREASURY—John W. Snyder, of Missouri, continued from preceding administration.

SECRETARY OF DEFENSE—James Forrestal, of New York, continued from preceding administration. Louis A. Johnson, of West Virginia, March 23, 1949; entered upon duties March 28, 1949. George C. Marshall, of Pennsylvania, September 20, 1950; entered upon duties September 21, 1950. Robert A. Lovett, of New York, September 14, 1951; entered upon duties September 17, 1951.

ATTORNEY GENERAL—Tom C. Clark, of Texas, continued from preceding administration. J. Howard McGrath, of Rhode Island, August 19, 1949; entered upon duties August 14, 1949. James. P. McGranery, of Pennsylvania, May 21, 1952; entered upon duties May 27, 1952.

POSTMASTER GENERAL—Jesse M. Donaldson, of Missouri, continued from preceding administration. Jesse M. Donaldson, of Missouri, recommissioned February 8, 1949.

SECRETARY OF THE INTERIOR—Julius A. Krug, of Wisconsin, continued from preceding administration. Oscar L. Chapman, of Colorado (Under Secretary), ad interim, December 1, 1949, to January 19, 1950. Oscar L. Chapman, of Colorado, January 19, 1950.

SECRETARY OF AGRICULTURE—Charles F. Brannan, of Colorado, continued from preceding administration.

SECRETARY OF COMMERCE—Charles Sawyer, of Ohio, continued from preceding administration.

SECRETARY OF LABOR—Maurice J. Tobin, of Massachusetts, ad interim, continued from preceding administration. Maurice J. Tobin, of Massachusetts, February 1, 1949.

## First Administration of DWIGHT D. EISENHOWER

### JANUARY 20, 1953, TO JANUARY 20, 1957

PRESIDENT OF THE UNITED STATES—Dwight D. Eisenhower, of New York.

VICE PRESIDENT OF THE UNITED STATES—Richard M. Nixon, of California.

SECRETARY OF STATE—John Foster Dulles, of New York, January 21, 1953.

SECRETARY OF THE TREASURY—George M. Humphrey, of Ohio, January 21, 1953.

SECRETARY OF DEFENSE—Charles E. Wilson, of Michigan, January 26, 1953; entered upon duties January 28, 1953.

ATTORNEY GENERAL—Herbert Brownell, Jr., of New York, January 21, 1953.

POSTMASTER GENERAL—Arthur E. Summerfield, of Michigan, January 21, 1953.

SECRETARY OF THE INTERIOR—Douglas McKay, of Oregon, January 21, 1953. Frederick A. Seaton, of Nebraska, June 6, 1956; entered upon duties June 8, 1956.

SECRETARY OF AGRICULTURE—Ezra Taft Benson, of Utah, January 21, 1953.

SECRETARY OF COMMERCE—Sinclair Weeks, of Massachusetts, January 21, 1953.

SECRETARY OF LABOR—Martin P. Durkin, of Maryland, January 21, 1953. James P. Mitchell, of New Jersey, ad interim, October 9, 1953, to Janaury 19, 1954. James P. Mitchell, of New Jersey, January 19, 1954.

SECRETARY OF HEALTH, EDUCATION, AND WELFARE—Oveta Culp Hobby, of Texas, April 10, 1953; entered upon duties April 11, 1953. Marion B. Folsom, of New York, July 20, 1955; entered upon duties August 1, 1955.

---

## Second Administration of DWIGHT D. EISENHOWER

### JANUARY 20, 1957, TO JANUARY 20, 1961

PRESIDENT OF THE UNITED STATES—Dwight D. Eisenhower, of Pennsylvania.

VICE PRESIDENT OF THE UNITED STATES—Richard M. Nixon, of California.

SECRETARY OF STATE—John Foster Dulles, of New York, continued from preceding administration. Christian A. Herter, of Massachusetts, April 21, 1959; entered upon duties April 22, 1959.

SECRETARY OF THE TREASURY—George M. Humphrey, of Ohio, continued from preceding administration. Robert Bernerd Anderson, of Connecticut, July 2, 1957; entered upon duties July 29, 1957.

SECRETARY OF DEFENSE—Charles E. Wilson, of Michigan, continued from preceding administration. Neil H. McElroy, of Ohio, August 19, 1957; entered upon duties October 9, 1957. Thomas S. Gates, Jr., of Pennsylvania, ad interim, December 1, 1959, to January 26, 1960. Thomas S. Gates, Jr., of Pennsylvania, January 26, 1960.

ATTORNEY GENERAL—Herbert Brownell, Jr., of New York, continued from preceding administration. William P. Rogers, of Maryland, ad interim, November 8, 1957, to January 27, 1958. William P. Rogers, of Maryland, January 27, 1958.

POSTMASTER GENERAL—Arthur E. Summerfield, of Michigan, continued from preceding administration. Arthur E. Summerfield of Michigan, February 4, 1957.

SECRETARY OF THE INTERIOR—Frederick A. Seaton, of Nebraska, continued from preceding administration.

SECRETARY OF AGRICULTURE—Ezra Taft Benson, of Utah, continued from preceding administration.

SECRETARY OF COMMERCE—Sinclair Weeks, of Massachusetts, continued from preceding administration. Lewis L. Strauss, of New York, ad interim, November 13, 1958, to June 27, 1959. Frederick H. Mueller of Michigan (Under Secretary), ad interim, July 21, 1959, to August 6, 1959. Frederick H. Mueller, of Michigan, August 6, 1959.

SECRETARY OF LABOR—James P. Mitchell, of New Jersey, continued from preceding administration.

SECRETARY OF HEALTH, EDUCATION, AND WELFARE—Marion B. Folsom, of New York, continued from preceding administration. Authur S. Flemming, of Ohio, July 9, 1958; entered upon duties August 1, 1958.

---

## Administration of JOHN F. KENNEDY

### JANUARY 20, 1961, TO NOVEMBER 22, 1963

PRESIDENT OF THE UNITED STATES—John F. Kennedy, of Massachusetts. (Died November 22, 1963.)

VICE PRESIDENT OF THE UNITED STATES—Lyndon B. Johnson, of Texas.

SECRETARY OF STATE—Dean Rusk, of New York, January 21, 1961.

SECRETARY OF THE TREASURY—Douglas Dillon, of New Jersey, January 21, 1961.

SECRETARY OF DEFENSE—Robert S. McNamara, of Michigan, January 21, 1961.

ATTORNEY GENERAL—Robert F. Kennedy, of Massachusetts, January 21, 1961.

POSTMASTER GENERAL—J. Edward Day, of California, January 21, 1961. John A. Gronouski, of Wisconsin, September 24, 1963; entered upon duties September 30, 1963.

SECRETARY OF THE INTERIOR—STEWART L. UDALL, of Arizona, January 21, 1961.

SECRETARY OF AGRICULTURE—ORVILLE L. FREEMAN, of Minnesota, January 21, 1961.

SECRETARY OF COMMERCE—LUTHER H. HODGES, of North Carolina, January 21, 1961.

SECRETARY OF LABOR—ARTHUR J. GOLDBERG, of Illinois, January 21, 1961. W. WILLARD WIRTZ, of Illinois, September 20, 1962; entered upon duties September 25, 1962.

SECRETARY OF HEALTH, EDUCATION, AND WELFARE—ABRAHAM A. RIBICOFF, of Connecticut, January 21, 1961. ANTHONY J. CELEBREZZE, of Ohio, July 20, 1962; entered upon duties July 31, 1962.

---

## First Administration of LYNDON B. JOHNSON
### NOVEMBER 22, 1963, TO JANUARY 20, 1965

PRESIDENT OF THE UNITED STATES—LYNDON B. JOHNSON, of Texas.

VICE PRESIDENT OF THE UNITED STATES—JOHN W. MCCORMACK, of Massachusetts.

SECRETARY OF STATE—DEAN RUSK, of New York, continued from preceding administration.

SECRETARY OF THE TREASURY—DOUGLAS DILLON, of New Jersey, continued from preceding administration.

SECRETARY OF DEFENSE—ROBERT S. MCNAMARA, of Michigan, continued from preceding administration.

ATTORNEY GENERAL—ROBERT F. KENNEDY, of Massachusetts, continued from preceding administration. NICHOLAS DEB. KATZENBACH, of Illinois (Deputy Attorney General), ad interim, September 4, 1964.

POSTMASTER GENERAL—JOHN A. GRONOUSKI, of Wisconsin, continued from preceding administration.

SECRETARY OF THE INTERIOR—STEWART L. UDALL, of Arizona, continued from preceding administration.

SECRETARY OF AGRICULTURE—ORVILLE L. FREEMAN, of Minnesota, continued from preceding administration.

SECRETARY OF COMMERCE—LUTHER H. HODGES, of North Carolina, continued from preceding administration. JOHN T. O'CONNOR, of New Jersey, January 15, 1965; entered upon duties January 18, 1965.

SECRETARY OF LABOR—W. WILLARD WIRTZ, of Illinois, continued from preceding administration.

SECRETARY OF HEALTH, EDUCATION, AND WELFARE—ANTHONY J. CELEBREZZE, of Ohio, continued from preceding administration.

---

## Second Administration of LYNDON B. JOHNSON
### JANUARY 20, 1965, TO JANUARY 20, 1969

PRESIDENT OF THE UNITED STATES—LYNDON B. JOHNSON, of Texas.

VICE PRESIDENT OF THE UNITED STATES—HUBERT H. HUMPHREY, of Minnesota.

SECRETARY OF STATE—DEAN RUSK, of New York, continued from preceding administration.

SECRETARY OF THE TREASURY—DOUGLAS DILLON, of New Jersey, continued from preceding administration. HARRY H. FOWLER, of Virginia, March 25, 1965; entered upon duties April 1, 1965. JOSEPH W. BARR, of Indiana, entered upon duties December 21, 1968 (recess appointment); confirmed January 9, 1969.

SECRETARY OF DEFENSE—ROBERT S. MCNAMARA, of Michigan, continued from preceding administration. CLARK M. CLIFFORD, of Maryland, January 30, 1968; entered upon duties March 1, 1968.

ATTORNEY GENERAL—NICHOLAS DEB. KATZENBACH, of Illinois (Deputy Attorney General), ad interim, continued from preceding administration. NICHOLAS DEB. KATZENBACH, of Illinois, confirmed February 10, 1965; entered upon duties February 11, 1965. RAMSEY CLARK, of Texas, March 2, 1967.

POSTMASTER GENERAL—JOHN A. GRONOUSKI, of Wisconsin, continued from preceding administration. JOHN A. GRONOUSKI, of Wisconsin, recommissioned February 17, 1965. LAWRENCE F. O'BRIEN, of Massachusetts, September 1, 1965; entered upon duties November 3, 1965. W. MARVIN WATSON, of Texas, April 23, 1968; entered upon duties April 26, 1968.

SECRETARY OF THE INTERIOR—STEWART L. UDALL, of Arizona, continued from preceding administration.

SECRETARY OF AGRICULTURE—ORVILLE L. FREEMAN, of Minnesota, continued from preceding administration.

SECRETARY OF COMMERCE—JOHN T. O'CONNOR, of New Jersey, continued from preceding administration. ALEXANDER B. TROWBRIDGE, of New York, ad interim, February 1, 1967. ALEXANDER B. TROWBRIDGE, of New York, June 8, 1967; entered upon duties June 14, 1967. CYRUS R. SMITH, of New York, March 1, 1968; entered upon duties March 6, 1968.

SECRETARY OF LABOR—W. WILLARD WIRTZ, of Illinois, continued from preceding administration.

SECRETARY OF HEALTH, EDUCATION, AND WELFARE—ANTHONY J. CELEBREZZE, of Ohio, continued from preceding administration. JOHN W. GARDNER, of New York, August 11, 1965; entered upon duties August 18, 1965. WILBUR J. COHEN, of Michigan, ad interim, March 2, 1968. WILBUR J. COHEN, of Michigan, May 16, 1968.

SECRETARY OF HOUSING AND URBAN DEVELOPMENT—ROBERT C. WEAVER, of New York, January 17, 1966; entered upon duties January 18, 1966. ROBERT C. WOOD, of Florida, ad interim, January 2, 1969.

SECRETARY OF TRANSPORTATION—ALAN S. BOYD, of Florida, January 12, 1967; entered upon duties January 16, 1967.

## First Administration of RICHARD M. NIXON

### JANUARY 20, 1969, TO JANUARY 20, 1973

PRESIDENT OF THE UNITED STATES—RICHARD M. NIXON, of California.

VICE PRESIDENT OF THE UNITED STATES—SPIRO T. AGNEW, of Maryland.

SECRETARY OF STATE—WILLIAM P. ROGERS, of Maryland, January 20, 1969; entered upon duties January 22, 1969.

SECRETARY OF THE TREASURY—DAVID M. KENNEDY, of Illinois, January 20, 1969; entered upon duties January 21, 1969. JOHN B. CONNALLY, of Texas; entered upon duties February 11, 1971. GEORGE P. SHULTZ, of Illinois, June 8, 1972; entered upon duties June 12, 1972.

SECRETARY OF DEFENSE—MELVIN R. LAIRD, of Wisconsin, January 20, 1969; entered upon duties January 21, 1969.

ATTORNEY GENERAL—JOHN N. MITCHELL, of New York, January 20, 1969; entered upon duties January 21, 1969. RICHARD G. KLEINDIENST, of Arizona (Deputy Attorney General), ad interim, March 1, 1979. RICHARD G. KLEINDIENST, of Arizona, June 8, 1972; entered upon duties June 12, 1972.

POSTMASTER GENERAL—WINTON M. BLOUNT, of Alabama, January 20, 1969; entered upon duties January 21, 1969.

SECRETARY OF THE INTERIOR—WALTER J. HICKEL, of Alaska, January 23, 1969; entered upon duties January 24, 1969. FRED J. RUSSELL, of California, ad interim, November 26, 1970. ROGERS C.B. MORTON, of Maryland; entered upon duties January 29, 1971.

SECRETARY OF AGRICULTURE—CLIFFORD M. HARDIN, of Nebraska, January 20, 1969; entered upon duties January 21, 1969. EARL L. BUTZ, of Indiana, December 2, 1971; entered upon duties December 2, 1971.

SECRETARY OF COMMERCE—MAURICE H. STANS, of New York, January 20, 1969; entered upon duties January 21, 1969. PETER G. PETERSON, of Illinois, February 21, 1972; entered upon duties February 29, 1972.

SECRETARY OF LABOR—GEORGE P. SCHULTZ, of Illinois, January 20, 1969; entered upon duties January 21, 1969. JAMES D. HODGSON, of California, June 17, 1970; entered upon duties July 2, 1970.

SECRETARY OF HEALTH, EDUCATION, AND WELFARE—ROBERT H. FINCH, of California, January 21, 1969. ELLIOT L. RICHARDSON, of Massachusetts, June 15, 1970; entered upon duties June 24, 1970.

SECRETARY OF HOUSING AND URBAN DEVELOPMENT—GEORGE ROMNEY, of Michigan, January 20, 1969; entered upon duties January 21, 1969.

SECRETARY OF TRANSPORTATION—JOHN A. VOLPE, of Massachusetts, January 20, 1969; entered upon duties January 21, 1969.

---

## Second Administration of RICHARD M. NIXON

### JANUARY 20, 1973, TO AUGUST 9, 1974

PRESIDENT OF THE UNITED STATES—RICHARD M. NIXON, of California. (Resigned August 9, 1974.)

VICE PRESIDENT OF THE UNITED STATES—SPIRO T. AGNEW, of Maryland. (Resigned October 10, 1973.) GERALD R. FORD, JR., of Michigan, December 6, 1973. (First Vice President to be nominated by the President and confirmed by the Congress, pursuant to the Twenty-fifth Amendment to the Constitution of the United States.)

SECRETARY OF STATE—WILLIAM P. ROGERS, of Maryland, continued from preceding administration. KENNETH RUSH, of New York (Deputy Secretary), ad interim, September 4, 1973. HENRY A. KISSINGER, of the District of Columbia, September 21, 1973; entered upon duties September 21, 1973.

SECRETARY OF THE TREASURY—GEORGE P. SHULTZ, of Illinois, continued from preceding administration. WILLIAM E. SIMON, of New Jersey; entered upon duties May 7, 1974.

SECRETARY OF DEFENSE—MELVIN R. LAIRD, of Wisconsin, continued from preceding administration. ELLIOT L. RICHARDSON, of Massachusetts, January 29, 1973; entered upon duties February 2, 1973. WILLIAM P. CLEMENTS, JR., of Texas, ad interim, May 26, 1973. JAMES R. SCHLESINGER, of Virginia, June 28, 1973; entered upon duties June 29, 1973.

ATTORNEY GENERAL—RICHARD G. KLEINDIENST, of Arizona, continued from preceding administration. ELLIOT L. RICHARDSON, of Massachusetts, May 23, 1973; entered upon duties May 24, 1973. ROBERT H. BORK, of Pennsylvania (Solicitor General), ad interim, October 20, 1973. WILLIAM B. SAXBE, of Ohio, December 17, 1973; entered upon duties January 4, 1974.

SECRETARY OF THE INTERIOR—ROGERS C.B. MORTON, of Maryland, continued from preceding administration.

SECRETARY OF AGRICULTURE—EARL L. BUTZ, of Indiana, continued from preceding administration.

SECRETARY OF COMMERCE—PETER G. PETERSON, of Illinois, continued from preceding administration. FREDERICK B. DENT, of South Carolina, January 18, 1973; entered upon duties February 2, 1973.

SECRETARY OF LABOR—JAMES D. HODGSON, of California, continued from preceding administration. PETER J. BRENNAN, of New York, January 31, 1973; entered upon duties February 2, 1973.

SECRETARY OF HEALTH, EDUCATION, AND WELFARE—ELLIOT L. RICHARDSON, of Massachusetts, continued from preceding administration. CASPAR W. WEINBERGER, of California, February 8, 1973; entered upon duties February 8, 1973.

SECRETARY OF HOUSING AND URBAN DEVELOPMENT—GEORGE ROMNEY, of Michigan, continued from preceding administration. JAMES T. LYNN, of Ohio, January 21, 1973; entered upon duties February 2, 1973.

SECRETARY OF TRANSPORTATION—JOHN A. VOLPE, of Massachusetts, continued from preceding administration. CLAUDE S. BRINEGAR, of California, January 18, 1973; entered upon duties February 2, 1973.

## Administration of GERALD R. FORD, JR.

### AUGUST 9, 1974, TO JANUARY 20, 1977

PRESIDENT OF THE UNITED STATES—Gerald R. Ford, Jr., of Michigan, December 6, 1973.

VICE PRESIDENT OF THE UNITED STATES—Nelson A. Rockefeller, of New York, December 19, 1974. (Nominated by the President and confirmed by the Congress, pursuant to the Twenty-fifth Amendment of the Constitution.)

SECRETARY OF STATE—Henry A. Kissinger, of the District of Columbia, continued from preceding administration.

SECRETARY OF THE TREASURY—William E. Simon, of New Jersey, continued from preceding administration.

SECRETARY OF DEFENSE—James R. Schlesinger, of Virginia, continued from preceding administration. Donald H. Rumsfeld, of Illinois, November 18, 1975; entered upon duties November 18, 1975.

ATTORNEY GENERAL—William B. Saxbe, of Ohio, continued from preceding administration. Edward Hirsch Levi, of Illinois, February 5, 1975; entered upon duties February 6, 1975.

SECRETARY OF THE INTERIOR—Rogers C.B. Morton, of Maryland, continued from preceding administration. D. Kent Frizzell, of Kansas (Solicitor), ad interim, May 1, 1975. Stanley K. Hathaway, of Wyoming, June 11, 1975; entered upon duties June 12, 1975. D. Kent Frizzell, of Kansas (Solicitor), ad interim, July 25, 1975. Thomas Savig Kleppe, of North Dakota, October 9, 1975; entered upon duties October 13, 1975.

SECRETARY OF AGRICULTURE—Earl L. Butz, of Indiana, continued from preceding administration. John A. Knebel, of Oklahoma (Under Secretary), ad interim, October 5, 1976. John A. Knebel, of Oklahoma (recess appointment); entered upon duties November 3, 1976.

SECRETARY OF COMMERCE—Frederick B. Dent, of South Carolina, continued from preceding administration. John K. Tabor, of Pennsylvania (Under Secretary), ad interim, March 12, 1975. Rogers C.B. Morton, of Maryland, April 25, 1975; entered upon duties May 1, 1975. Elliot L. Richardson, of Massachusetts, December 11, 1975; entered upon duties February 1, 1976.

SECRETARY OF LABOR—Peter J. Brennan, of New York, continued from preceding administration. John T. Dunlop, of Massachusetts, March 6, 1975; entered upon duties March 18, 1975. Willie J. Usery, Jr., of Georgia, February 4, 1976; entered upon duties February 10, 1976.

SECRETARY OF HEALTH, EDUCATION, AND WELFARE—Casper W. Weinberger, of California, continued from preceding administration. Forrest David Mathews, of Alabama, June 26, 1975; entered upon duties August 8, 1975.

SECRETARY OF HOUSING AND URBAN DEVELOPMENT—James T. Lynn, of Ohio, continued from preceding administration. Carla A. Hills, of California, March 5, 1975; entered upon duties March 10, 1975.

SECRETARY OF TRANSPORTATION—Claude S. Brinegar, of California, continued from preceding administration. William T. Coleman, Jr., of Pennsylvania, March 3, 1975; entered upon duties March 4, 1975.

---

## Administration of JAMES EARL (JIMMY) CARTER, JR.

### JANUARY 20, 1977, TO JANUARY 20, 1981

PRESIDENT OF THE UNITED STATES—James Earl (Jimmy) Carter, Jr., of Georgia.

VICE PRESIDENT OF THE UNITED STATES—Walter F. Mondale, of Minnesota.

SECRETARY OF STATE—Cyrus R. Vance, of New York, January 20, 1977; entered upon duties January 21, 1977. Warren M. Christopher, of California (Deputy Secretary), ad interim, April 28, 1980. Edmund S. Muskie, of Maine, May 7, 1980; entered upon duties May 8, 1980.

SECRETARY OF THE TREASURY—W. Michael Blumenthal, of Michigan, January 20, 1977; entered upon duties January 21, 1977. G. William Miller, of California, August 2, 1979; entered upon duties August 6, 1979.

SECRETARY OF DEFENSE—Harold Brown, of California, January 20, 1977; entered upon duties January 21, 1977.

ATTORNEY GENERAL—Griffin B. Bell, of Georgia, January 25, 1977; entered upon duties January 26, 1977. Benjamin R. Civiletti, of Maryland, August 1, 1979; entered upon duties August 16, 1979.

SECRETARY OF THE INTERIOR—Cecil D. Andrus, of Idaho, January 20, 1977; entered upon duties January 23, 1977.

SECRETARY OF AGRICULTURE—Robert Selmer Bergland, of Minnesota, January 20, 1977; entered upon duties January 21, 1977.

SECRETARY OF COMMERCE—Juanita M. Kreps, of North Carolina, January 20, 1977; entered upon duties January 21, 1977. Luther H. Hodges, Jr., of North Carolina (Under Secretary), ad interim, November 5, 1979. Philip M. Klutznick, of Illinois, December 20, 1979; entered upon duties December 21, 1979.

SECRETARY OF LABOR—F. Ray Marshall, of Texas, January 26, 1977; entered upon duties January 26, 1977.

SECRETARY OF HEALTH, EDUCATION, AND WELFARE (Renamed Health and Human Services, under the Department of Education Organization Act (Public Law 96-88), approved October 17, 1979; effective May 4, 1980.)—Joseph A. Califano, Jr., of the District of Columbia, January 24, 1977; entered upon duties January 25, 1977. Patricia Roberts Harris, of the District of Columbia, July 27, 1979; entered upon duties August 3, 1979.

SECRETARY OF HOUSING AND URBAN DEVELOPMENT.—Patricia Roberts Harris, of the District of Columbia, January 20, 1977; entered upon duties January 21, 1977. Jay Janis, of Florida (Under Secretary), ad interim, August 3, 1979. Moon Landrieu, of Louisiana, September 12, 1979; entered upon duties September 14, 1979.

SECRETARY OF TRANSPORTATION—Brockman Adams, of Washington, January 20, 1977; entered upon duties January 20, 1977. W. Graham Claytor, Jr., of the District of Columbia, ad interim, July 24, 1979. Neil E. Goldschmidt, of Oregon; entered upon duties August 10, 1979 (recess appointment); confirmed September 21, 1979.

SECRETARY OF ENERGY—James R. Schlesinger, of Virginia, August 4, 1977; entered upon duties August 5, 1977. Charles W. Duncan, Jr., of Texas, July 31, 1979; entered upon duties August 24, 1979.

SECRETARY OF EDUCATION—Shirley M. Hufstedler, of California, November 30, 1979; entered upon duties December 6, 1979.

## First Administration of RONALD W. REAGAN

### JANUARY 20, 1981, TO JANUARY 20, 1985

PRESIDENT OF THE UNITED STATES—Ronald W. Reagan, of California.

VICE PRESIDENT OF THE UNITED STATES—George Bush, of Texas.

SECRETARY OF STATE—Alexander Meigs Haig, Jr., of Connecticut, January 21, 1981; entered upon duties January 22, 1981. Walter J. Stoessel, Jr., of the District of Columbia (Deputy Secretary), ad interim, July 5, 1982. George P. Shultz, of California, July 15, 1982; entered upon duties July 16, 1982.

SECRETARY OF THE TREASURY—Donald T. Regan, of New Jersey, January 21, 1981; entered upon duties January 22, 1981.

SECRETARY OF DEFENSE—Caspar Willard Weinberger, of California, January 20, 1981; entered upon duties January 20, 1981.

ATTORNEY GENERAL—William French Smith, of California, January 22, 1981; entered upon duties January 23, 1981.

SECRETARY OF THE INTERIOR—James Gaius Watt, of Colorado, January 22, 1981; entered upon duties January 23, 1981. J.J. Simpson III, of New Jersey (Under Secretary), ad interim, November 8, 1983. William P. Clark, of California, November 18, 1983; entered upon duties November 18, 1983.

SECRETARY OF AGRICULTURE—John R. Block, of Illinois, January 22, 1981; entered upon duties January 23, 1981.

SECRETARY OF COMMERCE—Malcolm Baldrige, of Connecticut, January 23, 1981; entered upon duties January 23, 1981.

SECRETARY OF LABOR—Raymond J. Donovan, of New Jersey, February 3, 1981; entered upon duties February 4, 1981. (October 1, 1984, Secretary Donovan took a leave of absence, which continued into the second administration of Ronald Reagan.)

SECRETARY OF HEALTH AND HUMAN SERVICES—Richard S. Schweiker, of Pennsylvania, January 21, 1981; entered upon duties January 22, 1981. Thomas R. Donnelly, of Virginia (Assistant Secretary for Legislation), ad interim, February 4, 1983. Margaret M. Heckler, of Massachusetts, March 3, 1983; entered upon duties March 9, 1983.

SECRETARY OF HOUSING AND URBAN DEVELOPMENT—Samuel R. Pierce, Jr., of New York, January 22, 1981; entered upon duties January 23, 1981.

SECRETARY OF TRANSPORTATION—Andrew L. Lewis, Jr., of Pennsylvania, January 22, 1981; entered upon duties January 23, 1981. Darrell M. Trent, of Kansas (Deputy Secretary), ad interim, February 1, 1983. Elizabeth Hanford Dole, of Kansas, February 1, 1983; entered upon duties, February 7, 1983.

SECRETARY OF ENERGY—James B. Edwards, of South Carolina, January 22, 1981; entered upon duties January 23, 1981. Donald P. Hodel, of Oregon; entered upon duties November 5, 1982 (recess appointment); confirmed December 8, 1982.

SECRETARY OF EDUCATION—Terrell H. Bell, of Utah, January 22, 1981; entered upon duties January 23, 1981. Gary L. Jones, of Michigan (Under Secretary), ad interim, December 31, 1984.

---

## Second Administration of RONALD W. REAGAN

### JANUARY 20, 1985, TO JANUARY 20, 1989

PRESIDENT OF THE UNITED STATES—Ronald W. Reagan, of California.

VICE PRESIDENT OF THE UNITED STATES—George Bush, of Texas.

SECRETARY OF STATE—George P. Shultz, of California, continued from preceding administration.

SECRETARY OF THE TREASURY—James A. Baker III, of Texas, January 29, 1985; entered upon duties February 3, 1985. Nicholas F. Brady, of New Jersey, September 14, 1988; entered upon duties September 15, 1988.

SECRETARY OF DEFENSE—Caspar Willard Weinberger, of California, continued from preceding administration. Frank C. Carlucci III, of Virginia, November 20, 1987; entered upon duties November 23, 1987.

ATTORNEY GENERAL—Edwin Meese III, of California, February 23, 1985; entered upon duties February 23, 1985. Richard L. Thronburgh, of Pennsylvania, August 12, 1988; entered upon duties August 12, 1988.

SECRETARY OF THE INTERIOR—Donald P. Hodel, of Virginia, February 6, 1985; entered upon duties February 7, 1985.

SECRETARY OF AGRICULTURE—John R. Block, of Illinois, continued from preceding administration. Richard E. Lyng, of California, March 6, 1986; entered upon duties March 7, 1986.

SECRETARY OF COMMERCE—Malcolm Baldrige, of Connecticut, continued from preceding administration. Clarence J. Brown, of Ohio (Deputy Secretary), ad interim, July 25, 1987. C. William Verity, Jr., of Ohio, October 13, 1987; entered upon duties October 15, 1987.

SECRETARY OF LABOR—Raymond J. Donovan, of New Jersey, continued from preceding administration. (Secretary Donovan remained on leave of absence until his resignation March 15, 1985.) William Emerson Brock III, of Tennessee, April 26, 1985; entered upon duties April 29, 1985. Dennis E. Whitfield, of Georgia (Deputy Secretary), ad interim, October 31, 1987. Ann Dore McLaughlin, of the District of Columbia, December 11, 1987; entered upon duties December 14, 1987.

SECRETARY OF HEALTH AND HUMAN SERVICES—Margaret M. Heckler, of Massachusetts, continued from preceding administration. Otis R. Bowen, of Indiana, December 12, 1985; entered upon duties December 13, 1985.

SECRETARY OF HOUSING AND URBAN DEVELOPMENT—Samuel R. Pierce, Jr., of New York, continued from preceding administration.

SECRETARY OF TRANSPORTATION—Elizabeth Hanford Dole, of Kansas, continued from preceding administration. James H. Burnley IV, of North Carolina (Deputy Secretary), ad interim, October 1, 1987. James H. Burnley IV, November 30, 1987; entered upon duties December 2, 1987.

SECRETARY OF ENERGY—John S. Herrington, of California, February 6, 1985; entered upon duties February 7, 1985.

SECRETARY OF EDUCATION—William J. Bennett, of North Carolina, February 6, 1985; entered upon duties February 6, 1985. Lauro F. Cavazos, of Texas, September 20, 1988; entered upon duties September 21, 1988.

## Administration of GEORGE BUSH
### JANUARY 20, 1989, TO JANUARY 20, 1993

PRESIDENT OF THE UNITED STATES—George Bush, of Texas.

VICE PRESIDENT OF THE UNITED STATES—J. Danforth Quayle, of Indiana.

SECRETARY OF STATE—James A. Baker III, of Texas, January 25, 1989; entered upon duties January 27, 1989. Lawrence S. Eagleburger, of Wisconsin, December 8, 1992; entered upon duties December 8, 1992.

SECRETARY OF THE TREASURY—Nicholas F. Brady, of New Jersey, continued from preceding administration.

SECRETARY OF DEFENSE—Richard B. Cheney, of Wyoming, entered upon duties March 21, 1989

ATTORNEY GENERAL—Richard L. Thornburgh, of Pennsylvania, continued from preceding administration. William P. Barr, of the District of Columbia, November 20, 1991; entered upon duties November 26, 1991.

SECRETARY OF THE INTERIOR—Manuel Lujan, Jr., of New Mexico, February 2, 1989; entered upon duties February 8, 1989.

SECRETARY OF AGRICULTURE—Clayton K. Yeutter, of Nebraska, entered upon duties February 16, 1989. Edward R. Madigan, of Illinois, March 7, 1991; entered upon duties March 12, 1991.

SECRETARY OF COMMERCE—Robert A. Mosbacher, of Texas, January 31, 1989; entered upon duties February 3, 1989. Barbara Hackman Franklin, of Pennsylvania, February 27, 1992; entered upon duties March 23, 1992.

SECRETARY OF LABOR—Elizabeth Hanford Dole, of North Carolina, January 25, 1989; entered upon duties January 30, 1989. Lynn M. Martin, of Illinois, December 17, 1990; entered upon duties February 22, 1991.

SECRETARY OF HEALTH AND HUMAN SERVICES—Louis W. Sullivan, of Georgia, March 10, 1989; entered upon duties March 11, 1989.

SECRETARY OF HOUSING AND URBAN DEVELOPMENT—Jack F. Kemp, of New York, February 2, 1989; entered upon duties February 13, 1989.

SECRETARY OF TRANSPORTATION—Samuel K. Skinner, of Illinois, January 31, 1989; entered upon duties February 6, 1989. Andrew H. Card, Jr., of Massachusetts, February 21, 1992; entered upon duties February 24, 1992.

SECRETARY OF ENERGY—James D. Watkins, of California, March 1, 1989; entered upon duties March 9, 1989.

SECRETARY OF EDUCATION—Lauro F. Cavazos, of Texas, continued from preceding administration. Lamar Alexander, of Tennessee, March 14, 1991; entered upon duties March 22, 1991.

SECRETARY OF VETERANS AFFAIRS—Edward J. Derwinski, of Illinois, March 2, 1989; entered upon duties March 15, 1989.

---

## Administration of WILLIAM J. CLINTON
### JANUARY 20, 1993, TO JANUARY 20, 1997

PRESIDENT OF THE UNITED STATES—William J. Clinton, of Arkansas.

VICE PRESIDENT OF THE UNITED STATES—Albert A. Gore, Jr., of Tennessee.

SECRETARY OF STATE—Warren M. Christopher, of California, January 20, 1993; entered upon duties January 22, 1993.

SECRETARY OF THE TREASURY—Lloyd M. Bentsen, of Texas, January 20, 1993; entered upon duties January 22, 1993. Robert E. Rubin, of New York, January 10, 1995; entered upon duties January 11, 1995.

SECRETARY OF DEFENSE—Leslie Aspin, of Wisconsin, January 20, 1993; entered upon duties January 22, 1993. William J. Perry, of California, February 3, 1994; entered upon duties February 3, 1994.

ATTORNEY GENERAL—Janet Reno, of Florida, March 3, 1993; entered upon duties March 12, 1993.

SECRETARY OF THE INTERIOR—Bruce E. Babbitt, of Arizona, January 21, 1993; entered upon duties January 22, 1993.

SECRETARY OF AGRICULTURE—Albert Michael (Mike) Espy, of Mississippi, January 20, 1993; entered upon duties January 22, 1993. Daniel R. Glickman, of Kansas, March 30, 1995; entered upon duties March 30, 1995.

SECRETARY OF COMMERCE—Ronald H. Brown, of the District of Columbia, January 21, 1993; entered upon duties January 22, 1993. Michael (Mickey) Kantor, of California, April 12, 1996; entered upon duties April 12, 1996.

SECRETARY OF LABOR—Robert B. Reich, of Massachusetts, January 21, 1993; entered upon duties January 22, 1993.

SECRETARY OF HEALTH AND HUMAN SERVICES—Donna E. Shalala, of Wisconsin, January 21, 1993; entered upon duties January 22, 1993.

SECRETARY OF HOUSING AND URBAN DEVELOPMENT—Henry G. Cisneros, of Texas, January 21, 1993; entered upon duties January 22, 1993.

SECRETARY OF TRANSPORTATION—Federico F. Peña, of Colorado, January 21, 1993; entered upon duties January 22, 1993.

SECRETARY OF ENERGY—Hazel Rollins O'Leary, of Minnesota, January 21, 1993; entered upon duties January 22, 1993.

SECRETARY OF EDUCATION—Richard W. Riley, of South Carolina, January 21, 1993; entered upon duties January 22, 1993.

SECRETARY OF VETERANS AFFAIRS—Jesse Brown, of Illinois, January 21, 1993; entered upon duties January 22, 1993.

# THE CONTINENTAL CONGRESS

## 1774 — 1779

# THE CONTINENTAL CONGRESS

## PLACE AND TIME OF MEETING

| | |
|---|---|
| Philadelphia, Pa. | From September 5, 1774 to October 26, 1774 |
| Philadelphia, Pa. | From May 10, 1775 to December 12, 1776 |
| Baltimore, Md. | From December 20, 1776, to March 4, 1777 |
| Philadelphia, Pa. | From March 5, 1777, to September 18, 1777 |
| Lancaster, Pa. | From September 27, 1777 (one day only) |
| York, Pa. | From September 30, 1777, to June 27, 1778 |
| Philadelphia, Pa. | From July 2, 1778, to June 21, 1783 |
| Princeton, NJ | From June 30, 1783, to November 4, 1783 |
| Annapolis, Md. | From November 26, 1783, to June 3, 1784 |
| Trenton, NJ. | From November 1, 1784, to December 24, 1784 |
| New York City | From January 11, 1785, to November 4, 1785 |
| New York City | From November 7, 1785, to November 3, 1786 |
| New York City | From November 6, 1786, to October 30, 1787 |
| New York City | From November 5, 1787, to October 21, 1788 |
| New York City | From November 3, 1788, to March 2, 1789 |

## PRESIDENTS OF THE CONGRESS

| | |
|---|---|
| PEYTON RANDOLPH,[1] of Virginia | Elected September 5, 1774 |
| HENRY MIDDLETON, of South Carolina | Elected October 22, 1774 |
| PEYTON RANDOLPH,[2] of Virginia | Elected May 10, 1775 |
| JOHN HANCOCK, of Massachusetts | Elected May 24, 1775 |
| HENRY LAURENS, of South Carolina | Elected November 1, 1777 |
| JOHN JAY, of New York | Elected December 10, 1778 |
| SAMUEL HUNTINGTON, of Connecticut | Elected September 28, 1779 |
| THOMAS McKEAN, of Delaware | Elected July 10, 1781 |
| JOHN HANSON, of Maryland | Elected November 5, 1781 |
| ELIAS BOUDINOT, of New Jersey | Elected November 4, 1782 |
| THOMAS MIFFLIN, of Pennsylvania | Elected November 3, 1783 |
| RICHARD HENRY LEE, of Virginia | Elected November 30, 1784 |
| JOHN HANCOCK,[3] of Massachusetts | Elected November 23, 1785 |
| NATHANIEL GORHAM, of Massachusetts | Elected June 6, 1786 |
| ARTHUR ST. CLAIR, of Pennsylvania | Elected February 2, 1787 |
| CYRUS GRIFFIN, of Virginia | Elected January 22, 1788 |

## SECRETARY OF THE CONGRESS

| | |
|---|---|
| CHARLES THOMSON, of Pennsylvania | Elected September 5, 1774 |

---

[1] Resigned October 22, 1774.
[2] Departed Congress May 23, 1775, to resume duties as Speaker of the Virginia House of Burgesses.
[3] Resigned May 29, 1786, never having served, owing to continued illness.

# DELEGATES IN THE CONTINENTAL CONGRESS

## CONNECTICUT

### Dates of Attendance

| | | |
|---|---|---|
| Andrew Adams . . . . . . . . . . . 1778 | Benjamin Huntington . . . . . . . . 1780, | Joseph Spencer . . . . . . . . . . . 1779 |
| Joseph P. Cooke . . . . . . . 1784-1785, | 1782-1783, 1788 | Jonathan Sturges . . . . . . . . . . 1786 |
| 1787-1788 | Samuel Huntington . . . 1776, 1778-1781, | James Wadsworth . . . . . . . . . . 1788 |
| Silas Deane . . . . . . . . . . . 1774-1776 | 1783 | Jeremiah Wadsworth . . . . . . . . 1788 |
| Eliphalet Dyer . . . . . . . . . 1774-1779, | William S. Johnson . . . . . . . 1785-1787 | William Williams . . . . . . . . 1776-1777 |
| 1782-1783 | Richard Law . . . . . . 1777, 1781-1782 | Oliver Wolcott . . . . . . . . . 1776-1778, |
| Pierpont Edwards . . . . . . . . . . 1788 | Stephen Mitchell . . . . . . . . 1785-1788 | 1780-1783 |
| Oliver Ellsworth . . . . . . . . 1778-1783 | Jesse Root . . . . . . . . . . . 1778-1782 | |
| Titus Hosmer . . . . . . . . . . . . 1778 | Roger Sherman . . . . . . 1774-1781, 1784 | |

### Delegates Who Did Not Attend and Dates of Election

| | | |
|---|---|---|
| John Canfield . . . . . . . . . . . . 1786 | William Hillhouse . . . . . . . 1783, 1785 | Joseph Trumbull . . . . . . . . . . 1774 |
| Charles C. Chandler . . . . . . . . . 1784 | William Pitkin . . . . . . . . . . . 1784 | Erastus Wolcott . . . . . . 1774, 1787, 1788 |
| John Chester . . . . . . . . . 1787, 1788 | Jedediah Strong . . . . . 1782, 1783, 1784 | |
| James Hillhouse . . . . . . . 1786, 1788 | John Treadwell . . . . . 1784, 1785, 1787 | |

## DELAWARE

### Dates of Attendance

| | | |
|---|---|---|
| Gunning Bedford, Jr. . . . . . . 1783-1785 | Nathaniel Mitchell . . . . . . . . 1787-1788 | James Tilton . . . . . . . . . . 1783-1784 |
| John Dickinson . . . . . . . . . . . 1779 | John Patten . . . . . . . . . . . . 1786 | Nicholas Van Dyke . . . . . . 1777-1781 |
| Philemon Dickinson . . . . . . . 1782-1783 | William Perry . . . . . . . . . . . 1786 | John Vining . . . . . . . . . 1784-1785 |
| Dyre Kearney . . . . . . . . . . 1787-1788 | George Read . . . . . . . . . . 1774-1777 | Samuel Wharton . . . . . . . . 1782-1783 |
| Eleazar McComb . . . . . . . . 1783-1784 | Caesar Rodney . . . . . . . . . 1774-1776 | |
| Thomas McKean . . . . . . . . 1774-1776, | Thomas Rodney . . . . . . 1781-82, 1786 | |
| 1778-1782 | James Sykes . . . . . . . . . . . . 1777 | |

### Delegates Who Did Not Attend and Dates of Election

| | | |
|---|---|---|
| Gunning Bedford, Sr. . . . . . . . . 1786 | Isaac Grantham . . . . . . . . . . 1787 | John McKinly . . . . . . . . . . . 1784 |
| John Evans . . . . . . . . . . . . 1776 | Henry Latimer . . . . . . . . . . 1784 | Samuel Patterson . . . . . . . . . . 1784 |

## GEORGIA

### Dates of Attendance

| | | |
|---|---|---|
| Abraham Baldwin . . . . . . . . . 1785, | John Habersham . . . . . . . . . . 1785 | Edward Telfair . . . . . . 1778, 1780-1782 |
| 1787-1788 | Lyman Hall . . . . . . . . . . . 1775-1777 | George Walton . . . . . . . . . 1776-1777, |
| Nathan Brownson . . . . . . . . . . 1777 | John Houstoun . . . . . . . . . . . 1775 | 1780-1781 |
| Archibald Bulloch . . . . . . . . . 1775 | William Houstoun . . . . . . . 1784-1786 | John Walton . . . . . . . . . . . . 1778 |
| William Few . . . . . . . . . 1780-1782, | Richard Howly . . . . . . . . . 1780-1781 | Joseph Wood . . . . . . . . . . 1777-1778 |
| 1786-1788 | Noble Wimberly Jones . . . . . 1781-1782 | John Zubly . . . . . . . . . . . . 1775 |
| William Gibbons . . . . . . . . . . 1784 | Edward Langworthy . . . . . . . 1777-1779 | |
| Button Gwinnett . . . . . . . . . . 1776 | William Pierce . . . . . . . . . . . 1787 | |

### Delegates Who Did Not Attend and Dates of Election

| | | |
|---|---|---|
| Benjamin Andrew . . . . . . . . . . 1780 | Joseph Habersham . . . . . . . . . 1784 | Nathaniel Pendleton . . . . . . . . 1789 |
| Joseph Clay . . . . . . . . . . . . 1778 | Lachlan McIntosh . . . . . . . . . 1784 | Samuel Stirk . . . . . . . . . . . 1781 |
| Samuel Elbert . . . . . . . . . . 1784 | William O'Bryen . . . . . . . . . . 1789 | |
| James Gunn . . . . . . . . . . . . 1787 | Henry Osborne . . . . . . . . . . 1786 | |

## MARYLAND
### Dates of Attendance

Robert Alexander . . . . . . . . . . 1776
William Carmichael . . . . . . . 1778-1778
Charles Carroll ("Barrister") . 1776-1777
Charles Carroll of Carrollton . 1776-1777
Daniel Carroll . . . . . . . . . . 1781-1783
Jeremiah T. Chase . . . . . . . . 1783-1784
Samuel Chase . . . . . . . . . . 1774-1778
Benjamin Contee . . . . . . . . . . 1788
James Forbes . . . . . . . . . . 1778-1780
Uriah Forrest . . . . . . . . . . . 1787
Robert Goldsborough . . . . . . 1774-1776
John Hall . . . . . . . . . . . . . 1775
John Hanson . . . . . . . . . . 1780-1782

William Harrison . . . . . . . . . . 1786
William Hemsley . . . . . . . 1782-1783
John Henry . . . . . . . . . . . 1778-1780,
1785-1786
William Hindman . . . . . . . . . . 1788
John E. Howard . . . . . . . . . . 1788
Daniel of St. Thomas Jenifer . 1779-1781
Thomas Johnson . . . . . . . . 1774-1776
Thomas Sim Lee . . . . . . . . . . 1783
Edward Lloyd . . . . . . . . . . 1783-1784
James McHenry . . . . . . . . 1783-1785
William Paca . . . . . . . . . . 1774-1779

George Plater . . . . . . . . . . 1778-1780
Richard Potts . . . . . . . . . . . 1781
Nathaniel Ramsey . . . . . . . 1786-1787
John Rogers . . . . . . . . . . 1775-1776
David Ross . . . . . . . . . . 1787-1789
Benjamin Rumsey . . . . . . . 1776-1777
Joshua Seney . . . . . . . . . . . 1788
William Smith . . . . . . . . . . . 1777
Thomas Stone . . . . . . . . . 1775-1776,
1778, 1784
Matthew Tilghman . . . . . . . 1774-1776
Turbutt Wright . . . . . . . . . . 1782

### Delegates Who Did Not Attend and Dates of Election

Edward Giles . . . . . . . . . . . . 1782
Luther Martin . . . . . . . . . . . 1784
Joseph Nicholson . . . . . . . . . 1777

Richard Ridgely . . . . . . . 1784, 1785
Gustavus Scott . . . . . . . . . . 1784

William Smallwood . . . . . . . . 1784
Stephen West . . . . . . . . . . . 1780

## MASSACHUSETTS
### Dates of Attendance

John Adams . . . . . . . . . . 1774-1777
Samuel Adams . . . . . . . . . 1774-1781
Thomas Cushing . . . . . . . . 1774-1776
Francis Dana . . . . . . 1777-1778, 1784
Nathan Dane . . . . . . . . . 1785-1788
Elbridge Gerry . . . . . . . . 1776-1780,
1783-1785
Nathaniel Gorham . . . . . . . 1782-1783,
1786-1787, 1789

John Hancock . . . . . . . . . 1775-1778
Stephen Higginson . . . . . . . . . 1783
Samuel Holten . . . . . . . . 1778-1780,
1783-1785, 1787
Jonathan Jackson . . . . . . . . . 1782
Rufus King . . . . . . . . . . 1784-1787
James Lovell . . . . . . . . . 1777-1782
John Lowell . . . . . . . . . . . . 1782
Samuel Osgood . . . . . . . 1781-1784

Samuel A. Otis . . . . . . . . 1787-1788
Robert Treat Paine . . . . . . 1774-1776
George Partridge . . . . . . . 1779-1785
Theodore Sedgwick . . . . . 1785-86, 1788
George Thatcher . . . . . . . 1787-1789
Artemas Ward . . . . . . . . 1780-1781

### Delegates Who Did Not Attend and Dates of Election

James Bowdoin . . . . . . . . . . . 1774
Tristram Dalton . . . . . . . . 1783, 1784
Timothy Danielson . . . 1780, 1782, 1783

Timothy Edwards . . . . . . . . . 1778
Levi Lincoln . . . . . . . . . . . 1781
Caleb Strong . . . . . . . . . . . 1780

James Sullivan . . . . . . . . 1782, 1783
James Warren . . . . . . . . . . . 1782

## NEW HAMPSHIRE
### Dates of Attendance

Josiah Bartlett . . . . . 1775-1776, 1778
Jonathan Blanchard . . . . . . . . 1784
Nathaniel Folsom . . . . 1774, 1777-1780
Abiel Foster . . . . . . . . . . 1783-1785
George Frost . . . . . . . . . . 1777-1779
John Taylor Gilman . . . . . . 1782-1783
Nicholas Gilman . . . . . . . . 1787-1789

John Langdon . . . . . . 1775-1776, 1787
Woodbury Langdon . . . . . . . . . 1779
Samuel Livermore . . . . . . . 1780-1782,
1785-1786
Pierse Long . . . . . . . . . . 1785-1786
Nathaniel Peabody . . . . . . . 1779-1780
John Sullivan . . . . . . . . . 1774-1775,
1780-1781
Matthew Thornton . . . . . . . 1776-1777
John Wentworth, Jr. . . . . . . . . 1778
William Whipple . . . . . . . . 1776-1779
Phillips White . . . . . . . . . 1782-1783
Paine Wingate . . . . . . . . . . . 1788

### Delegates Who Did Not Attend and Dates of Election

Samuel Ashley . . . . . . . . . . . 1779
George Atkinson . . . . . . . . 1780, 1785
Benjamin Bellows . . . . . . . . . 1781
Moses Dow . . . . . . . . . . . . . 1784

Elisha Payne . . . . . . . . . . . 1784
John Pickering . . . . . . . . . . 1787
John Sparhawk . . . . . . . . . . 1786
Ebenezer Thompson . . . . . 1778, 1783

Timothy Walker, Jr. . . . . . . 1777, 1778,
1782, 1785
Joshua Wentworth . . . . . . . . . 1779
Benjamin West . . . . . . . . . . 1787

## NEW JERSEY
### Dates of Attendance

| | | |
|---|---|---|
| John Beatty . . . . . . . . . . 1784-1785 | Jonathan Elmer . . . . . . . . 1777-1778, | James Schureman . . . . . . . 1786-1787 |
| Elias Boudinot . . . . . 1778, 1781-1783 | 1781-1783, 1787-1788 | Nathaniel Scudder . . . . . . 1778-1779 |
| William Burnet . . . . . . . . 1780-1781 | John Fell . . . . . . . . . . . 1778-1780 | Jonathan D. Sergeant . . . . . 1776-1777 |
| Lambert Cadwalader . . . . . 1785-1787 | Frederick Frelinghuysen . . . . . 1779 | Richard Smith . . . . . . . . 1774-1776 |
| Abraham Clark . . . . . . . . .1776-1778, | John Hart . . . . . . . . . . . . . 1776 | John Stevens . . . . . . . . . . . 1784 |
| 1780-1783, 1786-1788 | Francis Hopkinson . . . . . . . . . 1776 | Charles Stewart . . . . . . . . 1784-1785 |
| Silas Condict . . . . . . . . . 1781-1783 | Josiah Hornblower . . . . . . . 1785-1786 | Richard Stockton . . . . . . . . . 1776 |
| Stephen Crane . . . . . . . . . 1774-1776 | William C. Houston . . . . . . 1779-1781, | John C. Symmes . . . . . . . . 1785-1786 |
| Jonathan Dayton . . . . . . . . 1787-1788 | 1784-1785 | John Witherspoon . . . . . . . 1776-1782 |
| John De Hart . . . . . . . . . 1774-1776 | James Kinsey . . . . . . . . 1774-1775 | |
| Samuel Dick . . . . . . . . . 1784-1785 | William Livingston . . . . . . 1774-1776 | |

### Delegates Who Did Not Attend and Dates of Election

| | | |
|---|---|---|
| John Cooper . . . . . . . . . . . . 1776 | Thomas Henderson . . . . . . . . 1779 | William Paterson . . . . . . . 1780, 1787 |
| Elias Dayton . . . . . . . . . . . 1778 | John Neilson . . . . . . . . . . . 1778 | |

## NEW YORK
### Dates of Attendance

| | | |
|---|---|---|
| John Alsop . . . . . . . . . . 1774-1776 | John Jay . . . . . . . . . 1774-1776, | Lewis Morris . . . . . . . . . 1775-1777 |
| Egbert Benson . . . . . 1784, 1787-1788 | 1778-1779 | Ephraim Paine . . . . . . . . . . . 1784 |
| Simon Boerum . . . . . . . . . 1774-1775 | John Lansing, Jr. . . . . . . . . . 1785 | Philip Pell . . . . . . . . . . . . . 1789 |
| George Clinton . . . . . . . . 1775-1776 | John Laurance . . . . . . . . 1785-1787 | Zephanian Platt . . . . . . . . 1785-1786 |
| Charles DeWitt . . . . . . . . . . 1784 | Francis Lewis . . . . . . . . 1775-1779 | Philip Schuyler . . . . . . . . 1775, 1777, |
| James Duane . . . . . . . . . 1774-1783 | Ezra L'Hommedieu . . . . . . 1779-1783, | 1779-1780 |
| William Duer . . . . . . . . . 1777-1778 | 1788 | John Morin Scott . . . . . . 1780, 1782 |
| William Floyd . . . . . . 1774-1776, | Philip LIvingston . . . . . . . 1775-1778 | Melancton Smith . . . . . . . 1785-1787 |
| 1779-1783 | Robert R. Livingston . . . . . 1775-1776, | Henry Wisner . . . . . . . . . 1775-1776 |
| Leonard Gansevoort . . . . . . . . 1788 | 1779-1780, 1784 | Abraham Yates . . . . . . . . 1787-1788 |
| David Gelston . . . . . . . . . . . 1789 | Walter Livingston . . . . . . . 1784-1785 | Peter W. Yates . . . . . . . . . . 1786 |
| Alexander Hamilton . . . . . . 1782-1783, | Isaac Low . . . . . . . . . . . . . 1774 | |
| 1788 | Alexander McDougall . . . . . . . 1781 | |
| John Haring . . . . . . . 1774, 1785-1787 | Gouverneur Morris . . . . . . 1778-1779 | |

### Delegates Who Did Not Attend and Dates of Election

| | |
|---|---|
| John Hathorn . . . . . . . . . . . 1788 | Samuel Jones . . . . . . . . . . . 1788 |

## NORTH CAROLINA
### Dates of Attendance

| | | |
|---|---|---|
| John R. Ashe . . . . . . . . . . . 1787 | Benjamin Hawkins . . . 1781-1783, 1787 | John Penn . . . . . . . . . . . 1775-1780 |
| Timothy Bloodworth . . . . . . . . 1786 | Joseph Hewes . . . . . 1774-1776, 1779 | William Sharpe . . . . . . . . 1779-1781 |
| William Blount . . . . . . . . . 1782-1783, | Whitmell Hill . . . . . . . . . 1778-1780 | John Sitgreaves . . . . . . . . . . 1785 |
| 1786-1787 | William Hooper . . . . . . . . 1774-1777 | Richard D. Spaight . . . . . . 1783-1785 |
| Thomas Burke . . . . . . . . . 1777-1781 | Samuel Johnston . . . . . . . 1780-1781 | John Swann . . . . . . . . . . . . 1788 |
| Robert Burton . . . . . . . . . . . 1787 | Allen Jones . . . . . . . . . . 1779-1780 | James White . . . . . . . . . 1786-1788 |
| Richard Caswell . . . . . . . . 1774-1775 | Willie Jones . . . . . . . . . . . 1780 | John Williams . . . . . . . . . 1778-1779 |
| William Cumming . . . . . . . . . 1785 | Abner Nash . . . . . . . . . . 1782-1783 | Hugh Williamson . . . . 1782-1785, 1788 |
| Cornelius Harnett . . . . . . . 1777-1779 | | |

### Delegates Who Did Not Attend and Dates of Election

| | | |
|---|---|---|
| Ephraim Brevard . . . . . . . . . 1781 | Alexander Martin . . . . . . . . . 1786 | Benjamin Smith . . . . . . . . . . 1784 |
| Charles Johnson . . . . 1781, 1784, 1785 | Adlai Osborn . . . . . . . . . . . 1784 | John Stokes . . . . . . . . . . . . 1787 |
| Joseph McDowell . . . . . . . . . 1787 | Thomas Person . . . . . . . . . . 1784 | |
| Nathaniel Macon . . . . . . . . . 1785 | Thomas Polk . . . . . . . . . . . 1786 | |

## PENNSYLVANIA
### Dates of Attendance

| | | |
|---|---|---|
| Andrew Allen . . . . . . . . . 1775-1776 | Charles Humphreys . . . . . . 1774-1776 | James R. Reid . . . . . . . . . . 1787-1789 |
| John Armstrong, Sr. . . . . . . 1779-1780 | Jared Ingersoll . . . . . . . . . . . . 1780 | Samuel Rhoads . . . . . . . . . . . . 1774 |
| John Armstrong, Jr. . . . . . . . 1787-1788 | William Irvine . . . . . . . . . 1787-1788 | Daniel Roberdeau . . . . . . . 1777-1779 |
| Samuel J. Atlee . . . . . . . . . 1778-1782 | David Jackson . . . . . . . . . . . . 1785 | George Ross . . . . . . . . . . . 1774-1777 |
| John B. Bayard . . . . . . . . . 1785-1786 | James McLene . . . . . . . . . 1779-1780 | Benjamin Rush . . . . . . . . . 1776-1777 |
| Edward Biddle . . . . . . . . . 1774-1775 | Timothy Matlack . . . . . . . . . . 1780 | Arthur St. Clair . . . . . . . . . 1786-1787 |
| William Bingham . . . . . . . 1786-1788 | Samuel Meredith . . . . . . . . 1786-1788 | James Searle . . . . . . . . . . . 1778-1780 |
| William Clingan . . . . . . . . 1777-1779 | Thomas Mifflin . . . . . . . . . .1774-1775, | William Shippen, Sr. . . . . . . 1779-1780 |
| George Clymer . . . . . . . . . .1776-1777, | 1782-1784 | James Smith . . . . . . . . . . . 1776-1778 |
| 1780-1782 | John Montgomery . . . . . . . . 1782-1784 | Jonathan B. Smith . . . . . . . 1777-1778 |
| Tench Coxe . . . . . . . . . . . . 1789 | Joseph Montgomery . . . . . . 1780-1782 | Thomas Smith . . . . . . . . . . 1781-1782 |
| John Dickinson . . . . . . . . . 1774-1776 | Cadwalader Morris . . . . . . . 1783-1784 | George Taylor . . . . . . . . . . . . . 1776 |
| Thomas Fitzsimmons . . . . . . 1782-1783 | Robert Morris . . . . . . . . . . 1775-1778 | Thomas Willing . . . . . . . . . 1775-1777 |
| Benjamin Franklin . . . . . . . 1775-1776 | John Morton . . . . . . . . . . . 1774-1776 | James Wilson . . . . . . 1775-1777, 1783, |
| Joseph Galloway . . . . . . . . . . . 1774 | Frederick A. C. Muhlenberg . . 1779-1780 | 1785-1786 |
| Joseph Gardner . . . . . . . . . 1784-1785 | Richard Peters, Jr. . . . . . . . . 1782-1783 | Henry Wynkoop . . . . . . . . . 1779-1782 |
| Edward Hand . . . . . . . . . . 1783-1784 | Charles Pettit . . . . . . . . . . 1785-1787 | |
| William Henry . . . . . . . . . 1784-1785 | Joseph Reed . . . . . . . . . . . . 1778 | |

### Delegates Who Did Not Attend and Dates of Election

| | | |
|---|---|---|
| Matthew Clarkson . . . . . . . . . . 1785 | William Montgomery . . . . . . . . 1784 | William Moore . . . . . . . . . . . . 1777 |
| Samuel Duffield . . . . . . . . . . 1777 | | |

## RHODE ISLAND
### Dates of Attendance

| | | |
|---|---|---|
| Jonathan Arnold . . . . . . . . 1782-1783 | John Gerdner . . . . . . . . . . . . 1789 | Nathan Miller . . . . . . . . . . . . 1786 |
| Peleg Arnold . . . . . . . . . . 1787-1788 | Jonathan J. Hazard . . . . . . . . 1788 | Daniel Mowry, Jr. . . . . . . . . . 1781 |
| John Collins . . . . . . . . . . .1778-1780, | Stephen Hopkins . . . . . . . . 1774-1776 | James M. Varnum . . . . . . . 1780-1781, |
| 1782-1783 | David Howell . . . . . . . . . . 1782-1785 | 1787 |
| Ezekiel Cornell . . . . . . . . . 1780-1782 | James Manning . . . . . . . . . . . 1786 | Samuel Ward . . . . . . . . . . 1774-1776 |
| William Ellery . . . . . . . . . 1776-1785 | Henry Marchant . . . . . . . . 1777-1779 | |

### Delegates Who Did Not Attend and Dates of Election

| | | |
|---|---|---|
| William Bradford . . . . . . . . . . 1776 | Sylvester Gardner . . . . . . . . . 1787 | Paul Mumford . . . . . . . . . . . 1785 |
| John Brown . . . . . . . . . . 1784, 1785 | Thomas Holden . . . . . . . . 1788, 1789 | Peter Philips . . . . . . . . . . . . 1785 |
| George Champlin . . . . . . . 1785, 1786 | Daniel Manton . . . . . . . . . . . 1787 | |

## SOUTH CAROLINA
### Dates of Attendance

| | | |
|---|---|---|
| Robert Barnwell . . . . . . . . . . 1789 | Richard Hutson . . . . . . . . . 1778-1779 | Isaac Motte . . . . . . . . . . . 1780-1782 |
| Thomas Bee . . . . . . . . . . 1780-1782 | Ralph Izard . . . . . . . . . . . 1782-1783 | John Parker . . . . . . . . . . . 1786-1788 |
| Richard Beresford . . . . . . . 1783-1784 | John Kean . . . . . . . . . . . . 1785-1787 | Charles Pinckney . . . . . . . 1785-1787 |
| John Bull . . . . . . . . . . . 1784-1787 | Francis Kinloch . . . . . . . . . . . 1780 | David Ramsay . . . . . . . . . .1782-1783, |
| Pierce Butler . . . . . . . . . . . 1787 | Henry Laurens . . . . . . . . . 1777-1780 | 1785-1786 |
| William H. Drayton . . . . . . 1778-1779 | Thomas Lynch, Sr. . . . . . . . 1774-1776 | Jacob Read . . . . . . . . . . . 1783-1785 |
| Nicholas Eveleigh . . . . . . . 1781-1782 | Thomas Lynch, Jr. . . . . . . . . . 1776 | Edward Rutledge . . . . . . . . 1774-1776 |
| Christopher Gadsden . . . . . 1774-1776 | John Mathews . . . . . . . . . 1778-1781 | John Rutledge . . . . . . . . . .1774-1775, |
| John L. Gervais . . . . . . . . 1782-1783 | Arthur Middleton . . . . . . . 1776-1777, | 1782-1783 |
| Thomas Heyward, Jr. . . . . . 1776-1778 | 1781-1782 | Thomas T. Tucker . . . . . . . 1787-1788 |
| Daniel Huger . . . . . . . . . . 1786-1788 | Henry Middleton . . . . . . . . 1774-1775 | |

### Delegates Who Did Not Attend and Dates of Election

| | | |
|---|---|---|
| John Barnwell . . . . . . . . . . . 1784 | Rawlins Lowndes . . . . . . . . . . 1779 | Thomas Sumter . . . . . . . . . . 1783 |
| Alexander Gillon . . . . . . . . . . 1784 | William Moultrie . . . . . . . . . . 1784 | Paul Trapier . . . . . . . . . . . . 1777 |

# VIRGINIA

## Dates of Attendance

Thomas Adams . . . . . . . . . . 1778-1779
John Banister . . . . . . . . . . . . . 1778
Richard Bland . . . . . . . . . . 1774-1775
Theodorick Bland . . . . . . . 1780-1783
Carter Braxton . . . . . . . . . . . 1776
John Brown . . . . . . . . . . 1787-1788
Edward Carrington . . . . . . 1786-1788
John Dawson . . . . . . . . . . . . 1788
William Fitzhugh . . . . . . . . . 1779
William Fleming . . . . . . . . . 1779
William Grayson . . . . . . . . 1785-1787
Cryus Griffin . . . . . . . . . 1778-1780,
1787-1788
Samuel Hardy . . . . . . . . . 1783-1785
Benjamin Harrison . . . . . . . 1774-1777

John Harvie . . . . . . . . . . . 1777-1778
James Henry . . . . . . . . . . . . 1780
Patrick Henry . . . . . . . . . . 1774-1775
Thomas Jefferson . . . . . . . . 1775-1776,
1783-1784
Joseph Jones . . . . . . . 1777, 1780-1783
Arthur Lee . . . . . . . . . . . 1782-1784
Francis Lightfoot Lee . . . . . . 1775-1779
Henry Lee . . . . . . . . . . . . 1786-1788
Richard Henry Lee . . . . . . . 1774-1779,
1784-1785, 1787
James Madison . . . . . . . . . 1780-1783,
1787-1788
James Mercer . . . . . . . . . . . 1779
John F. Mercer . . . . . . . . . 1783-1784

James Monroe . . . . . . . . . 1783-1786
Thomas Nelson, Jr. . . . . . 1775-1777,
1779
Mann Page . . . . . . . . . . . . . 1777
Edmund Pendleton . . . . . . . 1774-1775
Edmund J. Randolph . . . . . . . . 1779,
1781-1782
Peyton Randolph . . . . . . . . . 1774-1775
Meriwether Smith . . . . . . . . 1778-1779,
1781
John Walker . . . . . . . . . . . . . 1780
George Washington . . . . . . . 1774-1775
George Wythe . . . . . . . . . . 1775-1776

## Delegates Who Did Not Attend and Dates of Election

John Blair . . . . . . . . . . . . . . 1781

Gabriel Jones . . . . . . . . . . . . 1779

George Mason . . . . . . . . . . . . 1777

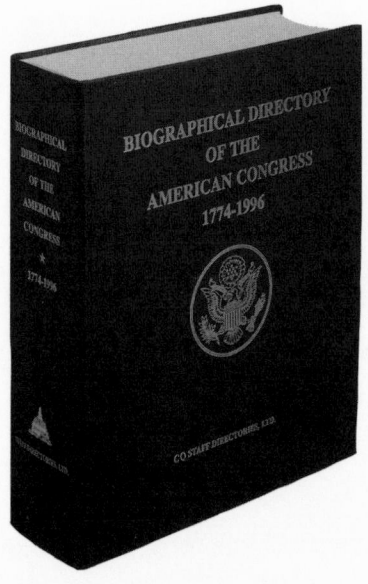

**H**ere at CQ Staff Directories we are constantly striving to enhance and update the *Biographical Directory of the American Congress*. If you know of any information regarding biographical changes or updates, or of new bibliographic citations, we would very much appreciate hearing from you. Please take a moment to fill out the postage-paid card below, detach and mail it to us.

Thank you for helping us to serve you better by further ensuring the accuracy and timeliness of the *Biographical Directory of the American Congress.*

---

## UPDATE/CORRECTION CARD

Name_____ Daytime phone (so that we may verify) _____

Page # _____

Addition, Correction or Update _____
_____
_____
_____
_____
_____

Source of information _____

---

## BIOGRAPHICAL DIRECTORY ORDER CARD

❏ **YES!** Send me _____ copies of the *Biographical Directory of the American Congress, 1774 - 1996* for only $295 each. ISBN 0-87289-124-0. PUBLICATION: NOVEMBER 1996, APPROX. 2,200 PAGES. CLOTH

❏ Check enclosed for $ _____ , payable to CQ Staff Directories.

❏ Please charge my:
   ❏ VISA    ❏ MasterCard    ❏ AmExpress

ACCT. #_____ EXP. DATE _____

SIGNATURE _____

❏ Please bill me (organizations only)

*Virginia residents add 4.5% sales tax. D.C. 5.75% sales tax. Shipping charges are paid by CQ Staff Directories.*

NAME _____
TITLE _____
COMPANY_____
ADDRESS _____
CITY/STATE/ZIP_____
PHONE _____ FAX _____

**Mail to: CQ Staff Directories, Inc.**
815 Slaters Lane
Alexandria, VA 22314

(703) 739-0900 (phone)
(703) 739-0234 (fax)
(800) 252-1722 (toll-free)

**or Visit our Web Site at: http:// www.staffdirectories.com**

**H**ere at CQ Staff Directories we are constantly striving to enhance and update the *Biographical Directory of the American Congress*. If you know of any information regarding biographical changes or updates, or of new bibliographic citations, we would very much appreciate hearing from you. Please take a moment to fill out the postage-paid card below, detach and mail it to us.

Thank you for helping us to serve you better by further ensuring the accuracy and timeliness of the *Biographical Directory of the American Congress*.

Name_____

Address _____

_____

City _____

State _____ Zip _____

## BUSINESS REPLY MAIL
**FIRST-CLASS MAIL**    **PERMIT NO. 754**    **ALEXANDRIA, VA**

### CQ Staff Directories, Inc.
Post Office Box 1411
Alexandria, VA 22313-9972

Name_____

Address _____

_____

City _____

State _____ Zip _____

## BUSINESS REPLY MAIL
**FIRST-CLASS MAIL**    **PERMIT NO. 754**    **ALEXANDRIA, VA**

### CQ Staff Directories, Inc.
Post Office Box 1411
Alexandria, VA 22313-9972

# CENSUS APPORTIONMENT OF
# REPRESENTATIVES

# REPRESENTATIVES UNDER EACH APPORTIONMENT

| States | Constitutional apportionment | 1st Census 1790 | 2nd Census 1800 | 3rd Census 1810 | 4th Census 1820 | 5th Census 1830 | 6th Census 1840 | 7th Census 1850 | 8th Census 1860 | 9th Census 1870 | 10th Census 1880 | 11th Census 1890 | 12th Census 1900 | 13th Census 1910 [1] | 15th Census 1930 | 16th Census 1940 | 17th Census 1950 | 18th Census 1960 | 19th Census 1970 | 20th Census 1980 | 21st Census 1990 |
|---|---|---|---|---|---|---|---|---|---|---|---|---|---|---|---|---|---|---|---|---|---|
| Alabama | | | | [2]1 | 3 | 5 | 7 | 7 | 6 | 8 | 8 | 9 | 9 | 10 | 9 | 9 | 9 | 8 | 7 | 7 | 7 |
| Alaska | | | | | | | | | | | | | | | | | [2]1 | 1 | 1 | 1 | 1 |
| Arizona | | | | | | | | | | | | | | [2]1 | 1 | 2 | 2 | 3 | 4 | 5 | 6 |
| Arkansas | | | | | | [2]1 | 1 | 2 | 3 | 4 | 5 | 6 | 7 | 7 | 7 | 7 | 6 | 4 | 4 | 4 | 4 |
| California | | | | | | | [2]2 | 2 | 3 | 4 | 6 | 7 | 8 | 11 | 20 | 23 | 30 | 38 | 43 | 45 | 52 |
| Colorado | | | | | | | | | | [2]1 | 1 | 2 | 3 | 4 | 4 | 4 | 4 | 4 | 5 | 6 | 6 |
| Connecticut | 5 | 7 | 7 | 7 | 6 | 6 | 4 | 4 | 4 | 4 | 4 | 4 | 5 | 5 | 6 | 6 | 6 | 6 | 6 | 6 | 6 |
| Delaware | 1 | 1 | 1 | 2 | 1 | 1 | 1 | 1 | 1 | 1 | 1 | 1 | 1 | 1 | 1 | 1 | 1 | 1 | 1 | 1 | 1 |
| Florida | | | | | | | [2]1 | 1 | 1 | 2 | 2 | 2 | 3 | 4 | 5 | 6 | 8 | 12 | 15 | 19 | 23 |
| Georgia | 3 | 2 | 4 | 6 | 7 | 9 | 8 | 8 | 7 | 9 | 10 | 11 | 11 | 12 | 10 | 10 | 10 | 10 | 10 | 10 | 11 |
| Hawaii | | | | | | | | | | | | | | | | | [2]1 | 2 | 2 | 2 | 2 |
| Idaho | | | | | | | | | | | [2]1 | 1 | 1 | 2 | 2 | 2 | 2 | 2 | 2 | 2 | 2 |
| Illinois | | | | [2]1 | 1 | 3 | 7 | 9 | 14 | 19 | 20 | 22 | 25 | 27 | 27 | 26 | 25 | 24 | 24 | 22 | 20 |
| Indiana | | | | [2]1 | 3 | 7 | 10 | 11 | 11 | 13 | 13 | 13 | 13 | 13 | 12 | 11 | 11 | 11 | 11 | 10 | 10 |
| Iowa | | | | | | | [2]2 | 2 | 6 | 9 | 11 | 11 | 11 | 11 | 9 | 8 | 8 | 7 | 6 | 6 | 5 |
| Kansas | | | | | | | | | 1 | 3 | 7 | 8 | 8 | 8 | 7 | 6 | 6 | 5 | 5 | 5 | 4 |
| Kentucky | | 2 | 6 | 10 | 12 | 13 | 10 | 10 | 9 | 10 | 11 | 11 | 11 | 11 | 9 | 9 | 8 | 7 | 7 | 7 | 6 |
| Louisiana | | | | [2]1 | 3 | 3 | 4 | 4 | 5 | 6 | 6 | 6 | 7 | 8 | 8 | 8 | 8 | 8 | 8 | 8 | 7 |
| Maine | | | | [3]7 | 7 | 8 | 7 | 6 | 5 | 5 | 4 | 4 | 4 | 4 | 3 | 3 | 3 | 2 | 2 | 2 | 2 |
| Maryland | 6 | 8 | 9 | 9 | 9 | 8 | 6 | 6 | 5 | 6 | 6 | 6 | 6 | 6 | 6 | 6 | 7 | 8 | 8 | 8 | 8 |
| Massachusetts | 8 | 14 | 17 | [3]13 | 13 | 12 | 10 | 11 | 10 | 11 | 12 | 13 | 14 | 16 | 15 | 14 | 14 | 12 | 12 | 11 | 10 |
| Michigan | | | | | | [2]1 | 3 | 4 | 6 | 9 | 11 | 12 | 12 | 13 | 17 | 17 | 18 | 19 | 19 | 18 | 16 |
| Minnesota | | | | | | | | [2]2 | 2 | 3 | 5 | 7 | 9 | 10 | 9 | 9 | 9 | 8 | 8 | 8 | 8 |
| Mississippi | | | | [2]1 | 1 | 2 | 4 | 5 | 5 | 6 | 7 | 7 | 8 | 8 | 7 | 7 | 6 | 5 | 5 | 5 | 5 |
| Missouri | | | | | 1 | 2 | 5 | 7 | 9 | 13 | 14 | 15 | 16 | 16 | 13 | 13 | 11 | 10 | 10 | 9 | 9 |
| Montana | | | | | | | | | | | [2]1 | 1 | 1 | 2 | 2 | 2 | 2 | 2 | 2 | 2 | 1 |
| Nebraska | | | | | | | | | [2]1 | 1 | 3 | 6 | 6 | 6 | 5 | 4 | 4 | 3 | 3 | 3 | 3 |
| Nevada | | | | | | | | | [2]1 | 1 | 1 | 1 | 1 | 1 | 1 | 1 | 1 | 1 | 1 | 2 | 2 |
| New Hampshire | 3 | 4 | 5 | 6 | 6 | 5 | 4 | 3 | 3 | 3 | 2 | 2 | 2 | 2 | 2 | 2 | 2 | 2 | 2 | 2 | 2 |
| New Jersey | 4 | 5 | 6 | 6 | 6 | 6 | 5 | 5 | 5 | 7 | 7 | 8 | 10 | 12 | 14 | 14 | 14 | 15 | 15 | 14 | 13 |
| New Mexico | | | | | | | | | | | | | | 1 | 1 | 2 | 2 | 2 | 2 | 3 | 3 |
| New York | 6 | 10 | 17 | 27 | 34 | 40 | 34 | 33 | 31 | 33 | 34 | 34 | 37 | 43 | 45 | 45 | 43 | 41 | 39 | 34 | 31 |
| North Carolina | 5 | 10 | 12 | 13 | 13 | 13 | 9 | 8 | 7 | 8 | 9 | 9 | 10 | 10 | 11 | 12 | 12 | 11 | 11 | 11 | 12 |
| North Dakota | | | | | | | | | | | [2]1 | 1 | 2 | 3 | 2 | 2 | 2 | 2 | 1 | 1 | 1 |
| Ohio | | | [2]1 | 6 | 14 | 19 | 21 | 21 | 19 | 20 | 21 | 21 | 21 | 22 | 24 | 23 | 23 | 24 | 23 | 21 | 19 |
| Oklahoma | | | | | | | | | | | | | [2]5 | 8 | 9 | 8 | 6 | 6 | 6 | 6 | 6 |
| Oregon | | | | | | | | [2]1 | 1 | 1 | 1 | 2 | 2 | 3 | 3 | 4 | 4 | 4 | 4 | 5 | 5 |
| Pennsylvania | 8 | 13 | 18 | 23 | 26 | 28 | 24 | 25 | 24 | 27 | 28 | 30 | 32 | 36 | 34 | 33 | 30 | 27 | 25 | 23 | 21 |
| Rhode Island | 1 | 2 | 2 | 2 | 2 | 2 | 2 | 2 | 2 | 2 | 2 | 2 | 2 | 3 | 2 | 2 | 2 | 2 | 2 | 2 | 2 |
| South Carolina | 5 | 6 | 8 | 9 | 9 | 9 | 7 | 6 | 4 | 5 | 7 | 7 | 7 | 7 | 6 | 6 | 6 | 6 | 6 | 6 | 6 |
| South Dakota | | | | | | | | | | | [2]2 | 2 | 2 | 3 | 2 | 2 | 2 | 2 | 2 | 1 | 1 |
| Tennessee | | [2]1 | 3 | 6 | 9 | 13 | 11 | 10 | 8 | 10 | 10 | 10 | 10 | 10 | 9 | 10 | 9 | 9 | 8 | 9 | 9 |
| Texas | | | | | | | [2]2 | 2 | 4 | 6 | 11 | 13 | 16 | 18 | 21 | 21 | 22 | 23 | 24 | 27 | 30 |
| Utah | | | | | | | | | | | | [2]1 | 1 | 2 | 2 | 2 | 2 | 2 | 2 | 3 | 3 |
| Vermont | | 2 | 4 | 6 | 5 | 5 | 4 | 3 | 3 | 3 | 2 | 2 | 2 | 2 | 1 | 1 | 1 | 1 | 1 | 1 | 1 |
| Virginia | 10 | 19 | 22 | 23 | 22 | 21 | 15 | 13 | 11 | 9 | 10 | 10 | 10 | 10 | 9 | 9 | 10 | 10 | 10 | 10 | 11 |
| Washington | | | | | | | | | | | [2]1 | 2 | 3 | 5 | 6 | 6 | 7 | 7 | 7 | 8 | 9 |
| West Virginia | | | | | | | | | | 3 | 4 | 4 | 5 | 6 | 6 | 6 | 6 | 5 | 4 | 4 | 3 |
| Wisconsin | | | | | | | [2]2 | 3 | 6 | 8 | 9 | 10 | 11 | 11 | 10 | 10 | 10 | 10 | 9 | 9 | 9 |
| Wyoming | | | | | | | | | | | [2]1 | 1 | 1 | 1 | 1 | 1 | 1 | 1 | 1 | 1 | 1 |
| Total | 65 | 106 | 142 | 186 | 213 | 242 | 232 | 237 | 243 | 293 | 332 | 357 | 391 | 435 | 435 | 435 | [4]437 | 435 | 435 | 435 | 435 |

[1] No apportionment was made in 1920.

[2] Indicates the state's original apportionment after admission, which occurs after the census indicated, but before the next census.

[3] Twenty Members were assigned to Massachusetts, but seven of these were credited to Maine when that area became a State.

[4] Apportionment temporarily increased by Public Laws 85-508 and 86-3 due to the admission of Alaska and Hawaii as States.

# THE CONGRESS OF THE UNITED STATES

## 1789-1996

# TIME AND PLACE OF MEETING

The Constitution (Art. I, sec.4) provided that "The Congress shall assemble at least once in every year * * * on the first Monday in December, unless they shall by law appoint a different day." Pursuant to a resolution of the Continental Congress the first session of the First Congress convened March 4, 1789. Up to and including May 20, 1820, eighteen acts were passed providing for the meeting of Congress on other days in the year. Since that year Congress met regularly on the first Monday in December until January 1934. The date for convening of Congress was changed by the Twentieth Amendment to the Constitution in 1933 to the 3d day of January unless a different day shall be appointed by law. The first and second sessions of the First Congress were held in New York City; subsequently, including the first session of the Sixth Congress, Philadelphia was the meeting place; since then Congress has convened in Washington, D.C.

# PARTY DESIGNATIONS

We have added political party designations to the membership rosters for the Seventy-ninth through the One Hundred Fourth Congresses. The designations we have used follow: American Labor — AL; Conservative — C; Democrat — D; Independent — I; Liberal — L; New Progressive — NP; Popular Democrat — PD; Progressive — P; Republican — R.

# FIRST CONGRESS

## MARCH 4, 1789, TO MARCH 3, 1791

FIRST SESSION— *March 4, 1789,*[1] *to September 29, 1789*
SECOND SESSION— *January 4, 1790, to August 12, 1790*
THIRD SESSION— *December 6, 1790, to March 3, 1791*

---

VICE PRESIDENT OF THE UNITED STATES— John Adams, of Massachusetts
PRESIDENT PRO TEMPORE OF THE SENATE— John Langdon,[2] of New Hampshire
SECRETARY OF THE SENATE— Samuel A. Otis,[3] of Massachusetts
DOORKEEPER OF THE SENATE— James Mathers,[4] of New York

---

SPEAKER OF THE HOUSE OF REPRESENTATIVES— Frederick A. C. Muhlenberg,[5] of Pennsylvania
CLERK OF THE HOUSE— John Beckley,[6] of Virginia
SERGEANT AT ARMS OF THE HOUSE— Joseph Wheaton,[7] of Rhode Island
DOORKEEPER OF THE HOUSE— Gifford Dalley

John Adams
Vice President

Frederick A. C. Muhlenberg
Speaker

## CONNECTICUT

### SENATORS

Oliver Ellsworth
William S. Johnson

### REPRESENTATIVES AT LARGE

Benjamin Huntington
Roger Sherman
Jonathan Sturges
Jonathan Trumbull
Jeremiah Wadsworth

## DELAWARE

### SENATORS

Richard Bassett
George Read

### REPRESENTATIVE AT LARGE

John Vining

## GEORGIA

### SENATORS

William Few
James Gunn

### REPRESENTATIVES

Abraham Baldwin
James Jackson
George Matthews

## MARYLAND

### SENATORS

John Henry
Charles Carroll

### REPRESENTATIVES

Daniel Carroll
Benjamin Contee
George Gale
Joshua Seney
William Smith
Michael Jenifer Stone

## MASSACHUSETTS

### SENATORS

Tristram Dalton
Caleb Strong

### REPRESENTATIVES

Fisher Ames
Elbridge Gerry
Benjamin Goodhue
Jonathan Grout
George Leonard
George Partridge[8]

Theodore Sedgwick
George Thacher

## NEW HAMPSHIRE

### SENATORS

John Langdon
Paine Wingate

### REPRESENTATIVES AT LARGE

Abiel Foster
Nicholas Gilman
Samuel Livermore

## NEW JERSEY

### SENATORS

Jonathan Elmer
William Paterson[9]
Philemon Dickinson[10]

### REPRESENTATIVES AT LARGE[11]

Elias Boudinot
Lambert Cadwalader
Thomas Sinnickson
James Schureman

---

[1] Neither a quorum of the Senate nor of the House of Representatives appeared in their respective chambers on Wednesday, March 4, 1789. But eight Senators appeared and the minority adjourned from day to day until Monday, April 6, when a quorum of the Senate was first present. Thirteen Members of the House of Representatives appeared on March 4 and a quorum was not present until April 1, when the body proceeded to the transaction of business. When both Houses were organized, on April 6, they met in joint convention, in the hall of the Senate, and proceeded to open and count the electoral vote for President and Vice-President. John Adams, the Vice President elect, appeared in the Senate Chamber and assumed the duties of the chair on Tuesday, April 21, 1789. On May 15, 1789, the

Senate determined by lot the classes into which the membership should be divided according to paragraph 2, section 3, of Article I of the Constitution, as follows: Class 1, term expires March 3, 1791—Messrs. Carroll, Dalton, Ellsworth, Elmer, Maclay, Read, and Grayson. Class 2, term expires March 3, 1793—Messrs. Bassett, Butler, Few, Lee, Strong, Paterson, and Wingate. Class 3, term expires March 3, 1795—Messrs. Gunn, Henry, Johnson, Izard, Langdon, and Morris.

[2] Elected April 6, 1789.
[3] Elected April 8, 1789.
[4] Elected April 7, 1789.
[5] Elected April 1, 1789.
[6] Elected April 1, 1789.
[7] Elected May 12, 1789.

[8] Resigned August 14, 1790.
[9] Resigned November 13, 1790, having been elected governor.
[10] Elected to fill vacancy caused by resignation of William Paterson, and took his seat December 6, 1790.
[11] The election of all four Representatives was contested, but owing to the burning of the papers and documents from the First to the Sixth Congress, by the British in 1814, it is not possible to ascertain the grounds upon which the contest was based. It is known that it related to questions of regularity and procedure, and that the decision was favorable to the sitting Members.

## NEW YORK

### SENATORS

Rufus King[12]
Philip John Schuyler[13]

### REPRESENTATIVES

Egbert Benson
William Floyd
John Hathorn[14]
John Laurance
Peter Silvester[15]
Jeremiah Van Rensselaer[16]

## NORTH CAROLINA

### SENATORS

Benjamin Hawkins[17]
Samuel Johnston[18]

### REPRESENTATIVES

John Baptista Ashe[19]
Timothy Bloodworth[20]
John Sevier[21]
John Steele[22]
Hugh Williamson[23]

## PENNSYLVANIA

### SENATORS

William Maclay
Robert Morris

### REPRESENTATIVES AT LARGE

George Clymer
Thomas Fitzsimons
Thomas Hartley
Daniel Hiester
Frederick A. C. Muhlenberg
John Peter G. Muhlenberg
Thomas Scott
Henry Wynkoop

## RHODE ISLAND

### SENATORS

Theodore Foster[24]
Joseph Stanton, Jr.[25]

### REPRESENTATIVE AT LARGE

Benjamin Bourne[26]

## SOUTH CAROLINA

### SENATORS

Pierce Butler
Ralph Izard

### REPRESENTATIVES

Aedanus Burke
Daniel Huger
William L. Smith[27]

Thomas Sumter
Thomas Tudor Tucker

## VIRGINIA

### SENATORS

William Grayson[28]
John Walker[29]
James Monroe[30]
Richard Henry Lee

### REPRESENTATIVES

Theodorick Bland[31]
William B. Giles[32]
John Brown
Isaac Coles
Richard Bland Lee
James Madison
Andrew Moore
John Page
Josiah Parker
Alexander White
Samuel Griffin

---

[12] Took his seat July 25, 1789; term to expire, as determined by lot, March 3, 1795.
[13] Took his seat July 27, 1789; term to expire, as determined by lot, March 3, 1791.
[14] Took his seat April 23, 1789.
[15] Took his seat April 22, 1789.
[16] Took his seat May 9, 1789.
[17] Took his seat January 13, 1790; term to expire, as determined by lot, March 3, 1795.
[18] Took his seat January 29, 1790; term to expire, as determined by lot, March 3, 1793.
[19] Took his seat March 24, 1790.
[20] Took his seat April 6, 1790.

[21] Took his seat June 16, 1790.
[22] Took his seat April 19, 1790.
[23] Took his seat March 19, 1790.
[24] Took his seat June 25, 1790; term to expire, as determined by lot, March 3, 1791.
[25] Took his seat June 25, 1790; term to expire, as determined by lot, March 3, 1793.
[26] Took his seat December 17, 1790.
[27] Took his seat April 15, 1789; on April 15, 1789, David Ramsay presented a petition claiming that Smith was ineligible because at the time of his election he had not been a citizen of the United States the term of years required by the Constitution, which was referred to the Committee on Elections; the committee reported on April 18, 1789, and on May 22, 1789, the House adopted a resolution that Mr. Smith was eligible at the time he was elected.
[28] Died March 12, 1790.
[29] Appointed to fill vacancy caused by death of William Grayson, and took his seat April 26, 1790.
[30] Elected to fill vacancy caused by death of William Grayson, and took his seat December 6, 1790.
[31] Died June 1, 1790.
[32] Elected to fill vacancy caused by death of Theodorick Bland, and took his seat December 7, 1790.

# SECOND CONGRESS

## MARCH 4, 1791, TO MARCH 3, 1793

FIRST SESSION— *October 24, 1791, to May 8, 1792*
SECOND SESSION— *November 5, 1792, to March 2, 1793*
SPECIAL SESSION OF THE SENATE— *March 4, 1791, for one day only*

———————

VICE PRESIDENT OF THE UNITED STATES— JOHN ADAMS, of Massachusetts
PRESIDENT PRO TEMPORE OF THE SENATE— RICHARD HENRY LEE,[1] of Virginia; JOHN LANGDON,[2] of New Hampshire
SECRETARY OF THE SENATE— SAMUEL A. OTIS, of Massachusetts
DOORKEEPER OF THE SENATE— JAMES MATHERS, of New York

———————

SPEAKER OF THE HOUSE OF REPRESENTATIVES— JONATHAN TRUMBULL,[3] of Connecticut
CLERK OF THE HOUSE— JOHN BECKLEY,[4] of Virginia
SERGEANT AT ARMS OF THE HOUSE— JOSEPH WHEATON, of Rhode Island
DOORKEEPER OF THE HOUSE— GIFFORD DALLEY

John Adams
Vice President

Jonathan Trumbull
Speaker

## CONNECTICUT

### SENATORS

Oliver Ellsworth
William S. Johnson[5]
Roger Sherman[6]

### REPRESENTATIVES AT LARGE

James Hillhouse
Amasa Learned
Jonathan Sturges
Jonathan Trumbull
Jeremiah Wadsworth

## DELAWARE

### SENATORS

Richard Bassett
George Read

### REPRESENTATIVE AT LARGE

John Vining

## GEORGIA

### SENATORS

William Few
James Gunn

### REPRESENTATIVES

Abraham Baldwin
Francis Willis
Anthony Wayne[7]
John Milledge[8]

## KENTUCKY[9]

### SENATORS

John Edwards[10]
John Brown[11]

### REPRESENTATIVES

Alexander D. Orr[12]
Christopher Greenup[13]

## MARYLAND

### SENATORS

John Henry
Charles Carroll[14]
Richard Potts[15]

### REPRESENTATIVES

Philip Key
William Pinkney[16]
John Francis Mercer[17]
William Vans Murray
Joshua Seney[18]
William Hindman[19]
Upton Sheridine
Samuel Sterett

## MASSACHUSETTS

### SENATORS

Caleb Strong
George Cabot

### REPRESENTATIVES

Fisher Ames
Shearjashub Bourne
Elbridge Gerry
Benjamin Goodhue
George Leonard
Theodore Sedgwick
George Thacher
Artemas Ward

## NEW HAMPSHIRE

### SENATORS

John Langdon
Paine Wingate

### REPRESENTATIVES AT LARGE

Nicholas Gilman
Samuel Livermore
Jeremiah Smith

## NEW JERSEY

### SENATORS

Philemon Dickinson
John Rutherfurd

### REPRESENTATIVES AT LARGE

Elias Boudinot
Abraham Clark
Jonathan Dayton
Aaron Kitchell

---

[1] Elected April 18, 1792.
[2] Elected November 5, 1792, and March 1, 1793.
[3] Elected October 24, 1791.
[4] Reelected October 24, 1791.
[5] Resigned March 4, 1791.
[6] Elected to fill vacancy caused by resignation of William S. Johnson, and took his seat October 24, 1791. Vacancy in this class from March 4 to June 13, 1791.
[7] Served until March 21, 1792; election contested by James Jackson, and, by separate resolutions, it was determined that neither was entitled to the seat.

[8] Elected to fill vacancy caused by declaring the seat of Anthony Wayne vacant, and took his seat November 22, 1792.
[9] Formed from a portion of the territory of the State of Virginia; admitted as a State into the Union June 1, 1792.
[10] Took his seat November 5, 1792; term to expire, as determined by lot, March 3, 1795.
[11] Took his seat November 5, 1792; term to expire, as determined by lot, March 3, 1793.
[12] Took his seat November 8, 1792.
[13] Took his seat November 9, 1792.

[14] Resigned November 30, 1792.
[15] Elected to fill vacancy caused by resignation of Charles Carroll, and took his seat February 4, 1793.
[16] Resigned in November 1791, due to questions of ineligibility.
[17] Elected to fill vacancy caused by resignation of William Pinkney, and took his seat February 6, 1792.
[18] Resigned May 1, 1792.
[19] Elected to fill vacancy caused by resignation of Joshua Seney, and took his seat January 30, 1793.

## NEW YORK

### SENATORS

Rufus King
Aaron Burr

### REPRESENTATIVES

Egbert Benson
James Gordon
John Laurance
Cornelius C. Schoonmaker
Peter Silvester
Thomas Tredwell[20]

## NORTH CAROLINA

### SENATORS

Benjamin Hawkins
Samuel Johnston

### REPRESENTATIVES

John Baptista Ashe
William Barry Grove
Nathaniel Macon
John Steele
Hugh Williamson

## PENNSYLVANIA

### SENATORS

Robert Morris
Vacant[21]

### REPRESENTATIVES

William Findley
Thomas Fitzsimons
Andrew Gregg
Thomas Hartley
Daniel Hiester
Israel Jacobs
John W. Kittera
Frederick A. C. Muhlenberg

## RHODE ISLAND

### SENATORS

Theodore Foster
Joseph Stanton, Jr.

### REPRESENTATIVE AT LARGE

Benjamin Bourne

## SOUTH CAROLINA

### SENATORS

Pierce Butler
Ralph Izard

### REPRESENTATIVES

Robert Barnwell
Daniel Huger
William L. Smith
Thomas Sumter
Thomas Tudor Tucker

## VERMONT[22]

### SENATORS

Moses Robinson[23]
Stephen R. Bradley[24]

### REPRESENTATIVES

Nathaniel Niles[25]
Israel Smith[26]

## VIRGINIA

### SENATORS

Richard Henry Lee[27]
John Taylor[28]
James Monroe

### REPRESENTATIVES

John Brown[29]
William B. Giles
Samuel Griffin
Richard Bland Lee
James Madison
Andrew Moore
John Page
Josiah Parker
Abraham B. Venable
Alexander White

---

[20] Elected to fill vacancy caused by death of Representative-elect James Townsend (May 24, 1790, before the commencement of the congressional term), and took his seat October 24, 1791.

[21] Credentials of Albert Gallatin were presented February 28, 1793, and ordered placed in the files; no further action taken during the Congress. (See U.S. Senate Election, Expulsion and Censure Cases, 1793-1990, Senate Document 103-33, pp. 3-5.)

[22] Formed from a portion of the territory of the State of New York; admitted as a State into the Union March 4, 1791.

[23] Took his seat October 31, 1791; term to expire, as determined by lot, March 3, 1797.

[24] Took his seat November 4, 1791; term to expire, as determined by lot, March 3, 1795.

[25] Took his seat October 31, 1791.

[26] Took his seat October 31, 1791.

[27] Resigned October 8, 1792.

[28] Elected to fill vacancy caused by resignation of Richard Henry Lee, and took his seat December 12, 1792.

[29] Served until June 1, 1792, when the district in which he resided was admitted into the Union as the State of Kentucky; subsequently elected a Senator from the new State.

# THIRD CONGRESS

## MARCH 4, 1793, TO MARCH 3, 1795

FIRST SESSION— *December 2, 1793, to June 9, 1794*
SECOND SESSION— *November 3, 1794, to March 3, 1795*
SPECIAL SESSION OF THE SENATE— *March 4, 1793, for one day only*

---

VICE PRESIDENT OF THE UNITED STATES— JOHN ADAMS, of Massachusetts
PRESIDENT PRO TEMPORE OF THE SENATE— RALPH IZARD,[1] of South Carolina;
HENRY TAZEWELL,[2] of Virginia
SECRETARY OF THE SENATE— SAMUEL A. OTIS, of Massachusetts
DOORKEEPER OF THE SENATE— JAMES MATHERS, of New York

John Adams
Vice President

Frederick A. C. Muhlenberg
Speaker

SPEAKER OF THE HOUSE OF REPRESENTATIVES— FREDERICK A. C. MUHLENBERG,[3] of Pennsylvania
CLERK OF THE HOUSE— JOHN BECKLEY,[4] of Virginia
SERGEANT AT ARMS OF THE HOUSE— JOSEPH WHEATON, of Rhode Island
DOORKEEPER OF THE HOUSE— GIFFORD DALLEY

## CONNECTICUT

### SENATORS

Oliver Ellsworth
Roger Sherman[5]
Stephen M. Mitchell[6]

### REPRESENTATIVES AT LARGE

Joshua Coit
James Hillhouse
Amasa Learned
Zephaniah Swift
Uriah Tracy
Jonathan Trumbull
Jeremiah Wadsworth

## DELAWARE

### SENATORS

George Read[7]
Henry Latimer[8]
John Vining

### REPRESENTATIVES

John Patten[9]
Henry Latimer[10]

## GEORGIA

### SENATORS

James Gunn
James Jackson

### REPRESENTATIVES AT LARGE

Abraham Baldwin
Thomas P. Carnes

## KENTUCKY

### SENATORS

John Edwards
John Brown

### REPRESENTATIVES

Christopher Greenup
Alexander D. Orr

## MARYLAND

### SENATORS

John Henry
Richard Potts

### REPRESENTATIVES

Gabriel Christie
George Dent
John F. Mercer[11]
Gabriel Duvall[12]
William Vans Murray
Uriah Forrest[13]
Benjamin Edwards[14]
William Hindman
Samuel Smith
Thomas Sprigg

## MASSACHUSETTS

### SENATORS

Caleb Strong
George Cabot

### REPRESENTATIVES

Fisher Ames
Shearjashub Bourne
David Cobb
Peleg Coffin, Jr.
Henry Dearborn
Samuel Dexter
Dwight Foster
Benjamin Goodhue
Samuel Holten
William Lyman
Theodore Sedgwick
George Thacher
Peleg Wadsworth
Artemas Ward

## NEW HAMPSHIRE

### SENATORS

John Langdon
Samuel Livermore

### REPRESENTATIVES AT LARGE

Nicholas Gilman
John S. Sherburne
Jeremiah Smith
Paine Wingate

---

[1] Elected May 31, 1794. Samuel Livermore was elected February 20, 1795, but declined.

[2] Elected February 20, 1795.

[3] Elected December 2, 1793.

[4] Reelected December 2, 1793.

[5] Died July 23, 1793.

[6] Elected to fill vacancy caused by death of Roger Sherman, and took his seat December 2, 1793.

[7] Resigned September 18, 1793.

[8] Elected to fill vacancy caused by resignation of

George Read, and took his seat February 28, 1795. Kensey Johns was appointed on March 19, 1794, to fill the vacancy and his credentials were presented March 24, 1794, but he was not permitted to qualify; March 28, 1794, the Senate declared he was not entitled to the seat; vacancy in this class from September 18, 1793, to February 7, 1795. (See U.S. Senate Election, Expulsion and Censure Cases, 1793-1990, Senate Document 103-33, pp. 6-7.)

[9] Served until February 14, 1794; succeeded by Henry Latimer, who contested his election.

[10] Successfully contested the election of John Patten, and took his seat February 14, 1794; resigned February 7, 1795, having been elected Senator.

[11] Resigned April 13, 1794.

[12] Elected to fill vacancy caused by resignation of John F. Mercer, and took his seat November 11, 1794.

[13] Resigned November 8, 1794.

[14] Elected to fill vacancy caused by resignation of Uriah Forrest, and took his seat January 2, 1795.

## NEW JERSEY

SENATORS

John Rutherfurd
Frederick Frelinghuysen

REPRESENTATIVES AT LARGE

John Beatty
Elias Boudinot
Lambert Cadwallader
Abraham Clark[15]
Aaron Kitchell[16]
Jonathan Dayton

## NEW YORK

SENATORS

Rufus King
Aaron Burr

REPRESENTATIVES

Theodorus Bailey
Peter Van Gaasbeck
Ezekiel Gilbert
James Gordon
Henry Glen
Silas Talbot
Thomas Tredwell
John E. Van Alen[17]
Philip Van Cortlandt
John Watts

## NORTH CAROLINA

SENATORS

Benjamin Hawkins
Alexander Martin

REPRESENTATIVES

Thomas Blount
William Johnston Dawson
James Gillespie
William Barry Grove
Matthew Locke
Nathaniel Macon
Joseph McDowell
Alexander Mebane
Benjamin Williams
Joseph Winston

## PENNSYLVANIA

SENATORS

Robert Morris
Albert Gallatin[18]
James Ross[19]

REPRESENTATIVES AT LARGE

James Armstrong
William Findley
Thomas Fitzsimons
Andrew Gregg
Thomas Hartley
Daniel Hiester
William Irvine
John Wilkes Kittera
William Montgomery
Frederick A. C. Muhlenberg
John Peter G. Muhlenberg
Thomas Scott
John Smilie

## RHODE ISLAND

SENATORS

Theodore Foster
William Bradford

REPRESENTATIVES AT LARGE

Benjamin Bourne
Francis Malbone

## SOUTH CAROLINA

SENATORS

Pierce Butler
Ralph Izard

REPRESENTATIVES

Lemuel Benton
Alexander Gillon[20]
Robert Goodloe Harper[21]
John Hunter
Andrew Pickens
William L. Smith
Richard Winn

## VERMONT

SENATORS

Moses Robinson
Stephen R. Bradley

REPRESENTATIVES

Nathaniel Niles
Israel Smith

## VIRGINIA

SENATORS

James Monroe[22]
Stevens T. Mason[23]
John Taylor[24]
Henry Tazewell[25]

REPRESENTATIVES

Isaac Coles
Thomas Claiborne
William B. Giles
Samuel Griffin
George Hancock
Carter B. Harrison
John Heath
Richard Bland Lee
James Madison
Andrew Moore
Joseph Neville
Anthony New
John Nicholas
John Page
Josiah Parker
Francis Preston[26]
Robert Rutherford
Abraham B. Venable
Francis Walker

## TERRITORY SOUTH OF THE RIVER OHIO[27]

DELEGATE

James White[28]

---

[15] Died September 15, 1794.

[16] Elected to fill vacancy caused by death of Abraham Clark, and took his seat January 29, 1795.

[17] Election unsuccessfully contested by Henry K. Van Rensselaer.

[18] Credentials presented in preceding Congress; took his seat December 2, 1793 and served until February 28, 1794, when the election was declared void, "he not having been a citizen of the United States the term of years required by the Constitution." (See U.S. Senate Election, Expulsion and Censure Cases, 1793-1990, Senate Document 103-33, pp. 3-5.)

[19] Elected to fill vacancy caused by the Senate declaring the election of Albert Gallatin void, and took his seat April 24, 1794.

[20] Died October 6, 1794.

[21] Elected to fill vacancy caused by death of Alexander Gillon, and took his seat February 9, 1795.

[22] Resigned, effective May 27, 1794, having been appointed minister plenipotentiary to France.

[23] Elected to fill vacancy caused by the resignation of James Monroe, but did not take his seat until June 8, 1795, in the succeeding Congress.

[24] Resigned May 11, 1794.

[25] Elected to fill vacancy caused by resignation of John Taylor, and took his seat December 29, 1794.

[26] Election unsuccessfully contested by Abraham Trigg.

[27] Created a district for the purposes of temporary government by act approved May 26, 1790, from territory ceded to the United States by the State of North Carolina and granted a Delegate in Congress.

[28] Took his seat November 18, 1794.

# FOURTH CONGRESS

MARCH 4, 1795, TO MARCH 3, 1797

FIRST SESSION— *December 7, 1795, to June 1, 1796*
SECOND SESSION— *December 5, 1796, to March 3, 1797*
SPECIAL SESSION OF THE SENATE— *June 8, 1795, to June 26, 1795*

———————

VICE PRESIDENT OF THE UNITED STATES— JOHN ADAMS, of Massachusetts
PRESIDENT PRO TEMPORE OF THE SENATE— HENRY TAZEWELL,[1] of Virginia; SAMUEL LIVERMORE,[2] of New Hampshire; WILLIAM BINGHAM,[3] of Pennsylvania
SECRETARY OF THE SENATE— SAMUEL A. OTIS, of Massachusetts
DOORKEEPER OF THE SENATE— JAMES MATHERS, of New York

———————

SPEAKER OF THE HOUSE OF REPRESENTATIVES— JONATHAN DAYTON,[4] of New Jersey
CLERK OF THE HOUSE— JOHN BECKLEY,[5] of Virginia
SERGEANT AT ARMS OF THE HOUSE— JOSEPH WHEATON, of Rhode Island
DOORKEEPER OF THE HOUSE— THOMAS CLAXTON

John Adams
Vice President

Jonathan Dayton
Speaker

## CONNECTICUT

### SENATORS

Oliver Ellsworth[6]
James Hillhouse[7]
Jonathan Trumbull[8]
Uriah Tracy[9]

### REPRESENTATIVES AT LARGE

Joshua Coit
Chauncey Goodrich
Roger Griswold
James Hillhouse[10]
James Davenport[11]
Nathaniel Smith
Zephaniah Swift
Uriah Tracy[12]
Samuel Whittlesey Dana[13]

## DELAWARE

### SENATORS

John Vining
Henry Latimer

### REPRESENTATIVE AT LARGE

John Patten

## GEORGIA

### SENATORS

James Gunn
James Jackson[14]

George Walton[15]
Josiah Tattnall[16]

### REPRESENTATIVES AT LARGE

Abraham Baldwin
John Milledge

## KENTUCKY

### SENATORS

John Brown
Humphrey Marshall

### REPRESENTATIVES

Christopher Greenup
Alexander D. Orr

## MARYLAND

### SENATORS

John Henry
Richard Potts[17]
John Eager Howard[18]

### REPRESENTATIVES

Gabriel Christie
Jeremiah Crabb[19]
William Craik[20]
Gabriel Duvall[21]
Richard Sprigg, Jr.[22]
George Dent
William Hindman
Samuel Smith
Thomas Sprigg
William Vans Murray

## MASSACHUSETTS

### SENATORS

Caleb Strong[23]
Theodore Sedgwick[24]
George Cabot[25]
Benjamin Goodhue[26]

### REPRESENTATIVES

Fisher Ames
Theophilus Bradbury
Henry Dearborn
Dwight Foster
Nathaniel Freeman, Jr.

---

[1] Elected December 7, 1795.
[2] Elected May 6, 1796.
[3] Elected February 16, 1797.
[4] Elected December 7, 1795.
[5] Reelected December 7, 1795.
[6] Resigned March 8, 1796.
[7] Elected to fill vacancy caused by resignation of Oliver Ellsworth, and took his seat December 6, 1796.
[8] Resigned June 10, 1796.
[9] Elected to fill vacancy caused by resignation of Jonathan Trumbull, and took his seat December 6, 1796.
[10] Resigned in the fall of 1796, having been elected Senator.

[11] Elected to fill vacancy caused by resignation of James Hillhouse, and took his seat December 5, 1796.
[12] Resigned, effective October 13, 1796, having been elected Senator.
[13] Elected to fill vacancy caused by resignation of Uriah Tracy, and took his seat January 3, 1797.
[14] Resigned in 1795.
[15] Appointed to fill vacancy caused by resignation of James Jackson, and took his seat December 18, 1795.
[16] Elected to fill vacancy caused by resignation of James Jackson, and took his seat April 12, 1796.
[17] Resigned October 24, 1796.
[18] Elected to fill vacancy caused by resignation of

Richard Potts, and took his seat December 27, 1796.
[19] Resigned in 1796.
[20] Elected to fill vacancy caused by resignation of Jeremiah Crabb, and took his seat December 5, 1796.
[21] Resigned March 28, 1796, having been elected judge of the Supreme Court of Maryland.
[22] Elected to fill vacancy caused by resignation of Gabriel Duvall, and took his seat May 5, 1796.
[23] Resigned June 1, 1796.
[24] Elected to fill vacancy caused by resignation of Caleb Strong, and took his seat December 21, 1796.
[25] Resigned June 9, 1796.
[26] Elected to fill vacancy caused by resignation of George Cabot, and took his seat December 6, 1796.

## MASSACHUSETTS—
### Continued

#### REPRESENTATIVES—CONTINUED
Benjamin Goodhue[27]
Samuel Sewall[28]
George Leonard
Samuel Lyman
William Lyman
John Reed
Theodore Sedgwick[29]
Thomson J. Skinner[30]
George Thacher
Joseph B. Varnum[31]
Peleg Wadsworth

## NEW HAMPSHIRE

#### SENATORS
John Langdon
Samuel Livermore

#### REPRESENTATIVES AT LARGE
Abiel Foster
Nicholas Gilman
John S. Sherburne
Jeremiah Smith

## NEW JERSEY

#### SENATORS
John Rutherfurd
Frederick Frelinghuysen[32]
Richard Stockton[33]

#### REPRESENTATIVES AT LARGE
Jonathan Dayton
Thomas Henderson
Aaron Kitchell
Isaac Smith
Mark Thomson

## NEW YORK

#### SENATORS
Rufus King[34]
John Laurance[35]
Aaron Burr

#### REPRESENTATIVES
Theodorus Bailey
William Cooper
Ezekiel Gilbert
Henry Glen
John Hathorn
Jonathan N. Havens
Edward Livingston
John E. Van Alen
Philip Van Cortlandt
John Williams

## NORTH CAROLINA

#### SENATORS
Alexander Martin
Timothy Bloodworth

#### REPRESENTATIVES
Thomas Blount
Nathan Bryan
Dempsey Burges
Jesse Franklin
James Gillespie
William Barry Grove
James Holland
Matthew Locke
Nathaniel Macon
Absalom Tatom[36]
William F. Strudwick[37]

## PENNSYLVANIA

#### SENATORS
James Ross
William Bingham

#### REPRESENTATIVES
David Bard[38]
William Findley
Albert Gallatin
Andrew Gregg
Thomas Hartley
Daniel Hiester[39]
George Ege[40]
John Wilkes Kittera
Samuel Maclay
John Richards[41]
Frederick A. C. Muhlenberg
Samuel Sitgreaves
John Swanwick
Richard Thomas

## RHODE ISLAND

#### SENATORS
Theodore Foster
William Bradford

#### REPRESENTATIVES AT LARGE
Francis Malbone
Benjamin Bourne[42]
Elisha R. Potter[43]

## SOUTH CAROLINA

#### SENATORS
Pierce Butler[44]
John Hunter[45]
Jacob Read

#### REPRESENTATIVES
Lemuel Benton
Samuel Earle
Wade Hampton
Robert Goodloe Harper
William L. Smith
Richard Winn

## TENNESSEE[46]

#### SENATORS
William Blount[47]
William Cocke[48]

#### REPRESENTATIVE AT LARGE
Andrew Jackson[49]

## VERMONT

#### SENATORS
Moses Robinson[50]
Isaac Tichenor[51]
Elijah Paine

#### REPRESENTATIVES
Daniel Buck
Israel Smith[52]

## VIRGINIA

#### SENATORS
Henry Tazewell
Stevens T. Mason

---

[27] Resigned in June 1796, having been elected Senator.

[28] Elected to fill vacancy caused by resignation of Benjamin Goodhue, and took his seat December 7, 1796.

[29] Resigned in June 1796, having been elected Senator.

[30] Elected to fill vacancy caused by resignation of Theodore Sedgwick, and took his seat January 27, 1797.

[31] Election contested by petition from sundry citizens of Massachusetts; Committee on Elections reported favorably for him, and added "that the attempt to deprive him of his seat was rather the act of malevolence than a desire to promote the public good." On January 25, 1797, these words were stricken and expressions of compliment to the sitting Member were substituted, and the report was agreed to.

[32] Resigned November 12, 1796.

[33] Elected to fill vacancy caused by resignation of Frederick Frelinghuysen, and took his seat December 6, 1796.

[34] Resigned May 23, 1796, having been appointed minister to England.

[35] Elected to fill vacancy caused by resignation of Rufus King, and took his seat December 8, 1796.

[36] Resigned June 1, 1796.

[37] Elected to fill vacancy caused by resignation of Absalom Tatom, and took his seat December 13, 1796.

[38] Election of David Bard investigated on account of informality in time of making return; committee reported that Mr. Bard was entitled to the seat and the House agreed to the report.

[39] Resigned July 1, 1796.

[40] Elected to fill vacancy caused by resignation of Daniel Hiester, and took his seat December 8, 1796.

[41] Presented a memorial on December 10, 1795, claiming election, the governor having declined to issue a certificate to either candidate; the committee of election reported that James Morris had been duly elected, but having died subsequent to the election the seat had become vacant; this report was recommitted and subsequently a resolution was reported that John Richards was entitled to the seat, which was adopted

by the House on January 18, 1796, and Mr. Richards took his seat the same day.

[42] Resigned in 1796, before the commencement of the Fifth Congress, to which he had been reelected.

[43] Elected to fill vacancy caused by resignation of Benjamin Bourn, and took his seat December 19, 1796.

[44] Resigned October 25, 1796.

[45] Elected to fill vacancy caused by resignation of Pierce Butler, and took his seat January 27, 1797.

[46] Admitted as a State into the Union June 1, 1796, formerly known as "Territory South of the River Ohio."

[47] Took his seat December 5, 1796; term to expire, as determined by lot, March 3, 1799.

[48] Took his seat December 5, 1796; term to expire, as determined by lot, March 3, 1797.

[49] Took his seat December 5, 1796.

[50] Resigned October 15, 1796.

[51] Elected to fill vacancy caused by resignation of Moses Robinson, and took his seat December 6, 1796.

[52] Election unsuccessfully contested by Matthew Lyon.

REPRESENTATIVES
Richard Brent
Samuel J. Cabell
Thomas Claiborne
John Clopton[53]
Isaac Coles
William B. Giles
George Hancock
Carter B. Harrison

John Heath
George Jackson
James Madison
Andrew Moore
Anthony New
John Nicholas
John Page
Josiah Parker

Francis Preston
Robert Rutherford
Abraham B. Venable

## TERRITORY SOUTH OF THE RIVER OHIO

DELEGATE
James White[54]

---

[53] Election unsuccessfully contested by Burwell Bassett.

[54] Served until June 1, 1796, when the Territory South of the River Ohio was granted statehood as the State of Tennessee.

# FIFTH CONGRESS

MARCH 4, 1797, TO MARCH 3, 1799

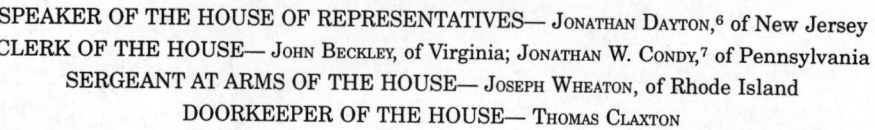

FIRST SESSION— *May 15, 1797, to July 10, 1797*
SECOND SESSION— *November 13, 1797, to July 16, 1798*
THIRD SESSION— *December 3, 1798, to March 3, 1799*
SPECIAL SESSIONS OF THE SENATE— *March 4, 1797, for one day only;
July 17, 1798, to July 19, 1798*

———————

VICE PRESIDENT OF THE UNITED STATES— THOMAS JEFFERSON, of Virginia
PRESIDENT PRO TEMPORE OF THE SENATE— WILLIAM BRADFORD,[1] of Rhode Island;
JACOB READ,[2] of South Carolina; THEODORE SEDGWICK,[3] of Massachusetts; JOHN LAURANCE,[4] of
New York; JAMES ROSS,[5] of Pennsylvania
SECRETARY OF THE SENATE— SAMUEL A. OTIS, of Massachusetts
DOORKEEPER OF THE SENATE— JAMES MATHERS, of New York

———————

SPEAKER OF THE HOUSE OF REPRESENTATIVES— JONATHAN DAYTON,[6] of New Jersey
CLERK OF THE HOUSE— JOHN BECKLEY, of Virginia; JONATHAN W. CONDY,[7] of Pennsylvania
SERGEANT AT ARMS OF THE HOUSE— JOSEPH WHEATON, of Rhode Island
DOORKEEPER OF THE HOUSE— THOMAS CLAXTON

Thomas Jefferson
Vice President

Jonathan Dayton
Speaker

## CONNECTICUT

### SENATORS

James Hillhouse
Uriah Tracy

### REPRESENTATIVES AT LARGE

John Allen
Joshua Coit[8]
Jonathan Brace[9]
Samuel W. Dana
Nathaniel Smith
James Davenport[10]
William Edmond[11]
Chauncey Goodrich
Roger Griswold[12]

## DELAWARE

### SENATORS

John Vining[13]
Joshua Clayton[14]
William H. Wells[15]
Henry Latimer

### REPRESENTATIVE AT LARGE

James A. Bayard

## GEORGIA

### SENATORS

James Gunn
Josiah Tattnall

### REPRESENTATIVES AT LARGE

Abraham Baldwin
John Milledge

## KENTUCKY

### SENATORS

John Brown
Humphrey Marshall

### REPRESENTATIVES

Thomas T. Davis
John Fowler

## MARYLAND

### SENATORS

John Henry[16]
James Lloyd[17]
John E. Howard

### REPRESENTATIVES

George Baer, Jr.
William Craik
John Dennis

George Dent
William Hindman
William Matthews
Samuel Smith
Richard Sprigg, Jr.

## MASSACHUSETTS

### SENATORS

Benjamin Goodhue
Theodore Sedgwick

### REPRESENTATIVES

Theophilus Bradbury[18]
Bailey Bartlett[19]
Stephen Bullock
Dwight Foster
Nathaniel Freeman, Jr.
Samuel Lyman
Harrison Gray Otis
Isaac Parker
John Reed
Samuel Sewall
William Shepard
Thomson J. Skinner
George Thacher
Joseph Bradley Varnum
Peleg Wadsworth

---

[1] Elected July 6, 1797.
[2] Elected November 22, 1797.
[3] Elected June 27, 1798.
[4] Elected December 6, 1798.
[5] Elected March 1, 1799.
[6] Reelected May 15, 1797; George Dent, of Maryland, was elected Speaker pro tempore for April 20, 1798, and again for May 28, 1798.
[7] Elected May 15, 1797.
[8] Died September 5, 1798.
[9] Elected to fill vacancy caused by death of Joshua Coit, and took his seat December 3, 1798.

[10] Died August 3, 1797.
[11] Elected to fill vacancy caused by death of James Davenport, and took his seat November 13, 1797.
[12] Unsuccessful motion made to expel after his personal encounter with Matthew Lyon, of Vermont, February 15, 1798.
[13] Resigned January 19, 1798.
[14] Elected to fill vacancy caused by resignation of John Vining, and took his seat February 19, 1798; died August 11, 1798.
[15] Elected to fill vacancy caused by death of

Joshua Clayton, and took his seat February 4, 1799.
[16] Resigned December 10, 1797, having been elected governor.
[17] Elected to fill vacancy caused by resignation of John Henry, and took his seat January 11, 1798.
[18] Resigned July 24, 1797.
[19] Elected to fill vacancy caused by resignation of Theophilus Bradbury, and took his seat November 27, 1797.

## NEW HAMPSHIRE

SENATORS

John Langdon
Samuel Livermore

REPRESENTATIVES AT LARGE

Abiel Foster
Jonathan Freeman
William Gordon
Jeremiah Smith[20]
Peleg Sprague[21]

## NEW JERSEY

SENATORS

John Rutherfurd[22]
Franklin Davenport[23]
Richard Stockton

REPRESENTATIVES AT LARGE

Jonathan Dayton
James H. Imlay
James Schureman[24]
Thomas Sinnickson
Mark Thomson

## NEW YORK

SENATORS

John Laurance
Philip John Schuyler[25]
John Sloss Hobart[26]
William North[27]
James Watson[28]

REPRESENTATIVES

David Brooks
James Cochran
Lucas C. Elmendorf
Henry Glen
Jonathan N. Havens
Hezekiah L. Hosmer
Edward Livingston
John E. Van Alen
Philip Van Cortlandt
John Williams

## NORTH CAROLINA

SENATORS

Alexander Martin
Timothy Bloodworth

REPRESENTATIVES

Thomas Blount
Nathan Bryan[29]
Richard Dobbs Spaight[30]
Dempsey Burges
James Gillespie
William Barry Grove
Matthew Locke
Nathaniel Macon
Joseph McDowell
Richard Stanford
Robert Williams

## PENNSYLVANIA

SENATORS

James Ross
William Bingham

REPRESENTATIVES

David Bard
Samuel Sitgreaves[31]
Robert Brown[32]
John Chapman
William Findley
Albert Gallatin
Andrew Gregg
John A. Hanna
Thomas Hartley
George Ege[33]
Joseph Hiester[34]
John Wilkes Kittera
Blair McClenachan
John Swanwick[35]
Robert Waln[36]
Richard Thomas

## RHODE ISLAND

SENATORS

Theodore Foster
William Bradford[37]
Ray Greene[38]

REPRESENTATIVES AT LARGE

Christopher G. Champlin
Elisha R. Potter[39]
Thomas Tillinghast[40]

## SOUTH CAROLINA

SENATORS

Jacob Read
John Hunter[41]
Charles Pinckney[42]

REPRESENTATIVES

Lemuel Benton
Robert Goodloe Harper
John Rutledge, Jr.
William L. Smith,[43] *Charleston district*[44]
Thomas Pinckney[45]
William Smith, *Spartan district*[44]
Thomas Sumter

## TENNESSEE

SENATORS

William Blount[46]
Joseph Anderson[47]
William Cocke[48]
Andrew Jackson[49]
Daniel Smith[50]

---

[20] Resigned July 26, 1797.

[21] Elected to fill vacancy caused by resignation of Jeremiah Smith, and took his seat December 15, 1797.

[22] Resigned November 26, 1798.

[23] Appointed to fill vacancy caused by resignation of John Rutherfurd, and took his seat December 19, 1798.

[24] Elected on February 14, 1799, to fill vacancy in Senate caused by resignation of John Rutherfurd, but did not take his seat until the following Congress, finishing out his term in the House.

[25] Resigned January 3, 1798.

[26] Elected to fill vacancy caused by resignation of Philip Schuyler, and took his seat February 2, 1798; resigned April 16, 1798, having been appointed judge of the United States district court of New York.

[27] Appointed to fill vacancy caused by resignation of John Sloss Hobart, and took his seat May 21, 1798.

[28] Elected to fill vacancy caused by resignation of John Sloss Hobart, and took his seat December 11, 1798.

[29] Died June 4, 1798.

[30] Elected to fill vacancy caused by death of Nathan Bryan, and took his seat December 10, 1798.

[31] Resigned in 1798, having been appointed commissioner to Great Britain.

[32] Elected to fill vacancy caused by resignation of Samuel Sitgreaves, and took his seat December 4, 1798.

[33] Resigned in October 1797.

[34] Elected to fill vacancy caused by resignation of George Ege, and took his seat December 1, 1797.

[35] Died August 1, 1798.

[36] Elected to fill vacancy caused by death of John Swanwick, and took his seat December 3, 1798.

[37] Resigned in October 1797.

[38] Elected to fill vacancy caused by resignation of William Bradford, and took his seat November 22, 1797.

[39] Elected to fill vacancy caused by resignation of Representative-elect Benjamin Bourn, in the preceding Congress; resigned in 1797.

[40] Elected to fill vacancy caused by resignation of Elisha R. Potter, and took his seat November 13, 1797.

[41] Resigned November 26, 1798.

[42] Elected to fill vacancy caused by resignation of John Hunter, and took his seat February 16, 1799.

[43] Resigned July 10, 1797, having been appointed minister plenipotentiary to Portugal.

[44] Many biographical errors have resulted from the fact that Smith of Charleston district and Smith of Spartan district both formerly were known as "William Smith." It was about this time that Smith of Charleston district changed his name to "William Loughton Smith."

[45] Elected to fill vacancy caused by resignation of William L. Smith, and took his seat November 23, 1797.

[46] Expelled for "high misdemeanor" July 8, 1797. (See U.S. Senate Election, Expulsion and Censure Cases, 1793-1990, Senate Document 103-33, pp. 13-15.)

[47] Elected to fill vacancy caused by expulsion of William Blount, and took his seat November 22, 1797, for the term ending March 3, 1799. (See footnote 50.)

[48] Appointed to fill vacancy in the term beginning March 4, 1797 (the legislature having failed to elect his successor), and took his seat May 15, 1797.

[49] Elected to fill vacancy in the term beginning March 4, 1797, and took his seat November 22, 1797; resigned in April 1798.

[50] Appointed to fill vacancy in the term beginning March 4, 1797, caused by the resignation of Andrew Jackson, and took his seat December 6, 1797; vacancy in this class from April 1798, to October 5, 1798. Joseph Anderson was elected December 12, 1798, to fill vacancy in the term beginning March 4, 1797, caused by resignation of Andrew Jackson, but did not present his credentials under this election until the Sixth Congress, continuing to serve in the other class, and on December 31, 1798, obtained leave of absence for Daniel Smith for the remainder of the session; technically, the term of Smith expired on the election of Anderson.

## TENNESSEE—Continued
### REPRESENTATIVE AT LARGE
William C. C. Claiborne[51]

## VERMONT
### SENATORS
Elijah Paine
Isaac Tichenor[52]
Nathaniel Chipman[53]
### REPRESENTATIVES
Matthew Lyon
Lewis R. Morris

## VIRGINIA
### SENATORS
Henry Tazewell[54]
Stevens T. Mason
### REPRESENTATIVES
Richard Brent
Samuel J. Cabell
Thomas Claiborne
Matthew Clay
John Clopton
John Dawson
William B. Giles[55]

Joseph Eggleston[56]
Thomas Evans
Carter B. Harrison
David Holmes
Walter Jones
James Machir
Daniel Morgan[57]
Anthony New
John Nicholas
Josiah Parker
Abram Trigg
John Trigg
Abraham B. Venable

---

[51] Took his seat November 23, 1797.

[52] Resigned October 17, 1797, having been elected governor.

[53] Elected to fill vacancy caused by resignation of Isaac Tichenor, and took his seat November 22, 1797.

[54] Died January 24, 1799. Letter from governor of Virginia (Senate Journal, p. 584) stating appointment would be deferred until legislature meets.

[55] Resigned October 2, 1798.

[56] Elected to fill vacancy caused by resignation of William B. Giles, and took his seat December 3, 1798.

[57] Election unsuccessfully contested by Robert Rutherford.

# SIXTH CONGRESS

## MARCH 4, 1799, TO MARCH 3, 1801

FIRST SESSION— *December 2, 1799, to May 14, 1800*
SECOND SESSION— *November 17, 1800, to March 3, 1801*

VICE PRESIDENT OF THE UNITED STATES— THOMAS JEFFERSON, of Virginia
PRESIDENT PRO TEMPORE OF THE SENATE— SAMUEL LIVERMORE,[1] of New Hampshire; URIAH TRACY,[2] of Connecticut; JOHN E. HOWARD,[3] of Maryland; JAMES HILLHOUSE,[4] of Connecticut
SECRETARY OF THE SENATE— SAMUEL A. OTIS, of Massachusetts
DOORKEEPER OF THE SENATE— JAMES MATHERS, of New York

SPEAKER OF THE HOUSE OF REPRESENTATIVES— THEODORE SEDGWICK,[5] of Massachusetts
CLERK OF THE HOUSE— JONATHAN W. CONDY,[6] of Pennsylvania; JOHN H. OSWALD,[7] of Pennsylvania
SERGEANT AT ARMS OF THE HOUSE— JOSEPH WHEATON, of Rhode Island
DOORKEEPER OF THE HOUSE— THOMAS CLAXTON

Thomas Jefferson
Vice President

Theodore Sedgwick
Speaker

## CONNECTICUT

### SENATORS

James Hillhouse
Uriah Tracy

### REPRESENTATIVES AT LARGE

Jonathan Brace[8]
John C. Smith[9]
Samuel W. Dana
John Davenport
William Edmond
Chauncey Goodrich
Elizur Goodrich
Roger Griswold

## DELAWARE

### SENATORS

Henry Latimer[10]
Samuel White[11]
William H. Wells

### REPRESENTATIVE AT LARGE

James A. Bayard

## GEORGIA

### SENATORS

James Gunn
Abraham Baldwin

## REPRESENTATIVES AT LARGE

James Jones[12]
Benjamin Taliaferro

## KENTUCKY

### SENATORS

John Brown
Humphrey Marshall

### REPRESENTATIVES

Thomas T. Davis
John Fowler

## MARYLAND

### SENATORS

John E. Howard
James Lloyd[13]
William Hindman[14]

### REPRESENTATIVES

George Baer
Gabriel Christie
William Craik
George Dent
John Dennis
Joseph H. Nicholson
Samuel Smith
John C. Thomas

## MASSACHUSETTS

### SENATORS

Benjamin Goodhue[15]
Jonathan Mason[16]
Samuel Dexter[17]
Dwight Foster[18]

### REPRESENTATIVES

Bailey Bartlett
Phanuel Bishop
Dwight Foster[19]
Levi Lincoln[20]
Silas Lee
Samuel Lyman[21]
Ebenezer Mattoon[22]
Harrison Gray Otis
John Reed
Theodore Sedgwick
Samuel Sewall[23]
Nathan Read[24]
William Shepard
George Thacher
Joseph B. Varnum
Peleg Wadsworth
Lemuel Williams

## NEW HAMPSHIRE

### SENATORS

John Langdon
Samuel Livermore

---

[1] Elected December 2, 1799.
[2] Elected May 14, 1800.
[3] Elected November 21, 1800.
[4] Elected February 28, 1801.
[5] Elected December 2, 1799.
[6] Reelected December 2, 1799; resigned December 4, 1799.
[7] Elected December 9, 1799.
[8] Resigned in 1800.
[9] Elected to fill vacancy caused by resignation of Jonathan Brace, and took his seat November 17, 1800.
[10] Resigned February 28, 1801.
[11] Appointed and subsequently elected to fill

vacancy caused by resignation of Henry Latimer, service to date from February 28, 1801; did not take his seat until March 4, 1801, in the special session of the Senate of the Seventh Congress.
[12] Died January 13, 1801.
[13] Resigned December 1, 1800.
[14] Elected to fill vacancy caused by resignation of James Lloyd, and took his seat December 15, 1800.
[15] Resigned November 8, 1800.
[16] Elected to fill vacancy caused by resignation of Benjamin Goodhue, and took his seat December 19, 1800.
[17] Resigned May 30, 1800.

[18] Elected to fill vacancy caused by resignation of Samuel Dexter, and took his seat November 21, 1800.
[19] Resigned June 6, 1800, having been elected Senator.
[20] Elected to fill vacancy caused by resignation of Dwight Foster, and took his seat February 6, 1801.
[21] Resigned November 6, 1800.
[22] Elected to fill vacancy caused by resignation of Samuel Lyman, and took his seat February 2, 1801.
[23] Resigned January 10, 1800.
[24] Elected to fill vacancy caused by resignation of Samuel Sewall, and took his seat November 25, 1800.

## NEW HAMPSHIRE— Continued

### REPRESENTATIVES AT LARGE
Jonathan Freeman
William Gordon[25]
Samuel Tenney[26]
Abiel Foster
James Sheafe

## NEW JERSEY

### SENATORS
James Schureman[27]
Aaron Ogden[28]
Jonathan Dayton

### REPRESENTATIVES
John Condit
Franklin Davenport
James H. Imlay
Aaron Kitchell
James Linn

## NEW YORK

### SENATORS
John Laurance[29]
John Armstrong[30]
James Watson[31]
Gouverneur Morris[32]

### REPRESENTATIVES
Theodorus Bailey
John Bird
William Cooper
Lucas C. Elmendorf
Henry Glen
Jonathan N. Havens[33]
John Smith[34]
Edward Livingston
Jonas Platt
John Thompson
Philip Van Cortlandt

## NORTH CAROLINA

### SENATORS
Timothy Bloodworth
Jesse Franklin

### REPRESENTATIVES
Willis Alston
Joseph Dickson
William Barry Grove

Archibald Henderson
William H. Hill
Nathaniel Macon
Richard Dobbs Spaight
Richard Stanford
David Stone
Robert Williams

## PENNSYLVANIA

### SENATORS
James Ross
William Bingham

### REPRESENTATIVES
Robert Brown
Albert Gallatin
Andrew Gregg
John A. Hanna
Thomas Hartley[35]
John Stewart[36]
Joseph Hiester
John Wilkes Kittera
Michael Leib
John Peter G. Muhlenberg
John Smilie
Richard Thomas
Robert Waln
Henry Woods

## RHODE ISLAND

### SENATORS
Theodore Foster
Ray Greene

### REPRESENTATIVES AT LARGE
John Brown
Christopher G. Champlin

## SOUTH CAROLINA

### SENATORS
Jacob Read
Charles Pinckney

### REPRESENTATIVES
Robert Goodloe Harper
Benjamin Huger
Abraham Nott
Thomas Pinckney
John Rutledge, Jr.
Thomas Sumter

## TENNESSEE

### SENATORS
Joseph Anderson[37]
William Cocke

### REPRESENTATIVE AT LARGE
William C. C. Claiborne

## VERMONT

### SENATORS
Elijah Paine
Nathaniel Chipman

### REPRESENTATIVES
Matthew Lyon
Lewis R. Morris

## VIRGINIA

### SENATORS
Stevens T. Mason
Wilson C. Nicholas[38]

### REPRESENTATIVES
Samuel J. Cabell
Matthew Clay
John Dawson
Joseph Eggleston
Thomas Evans
Samuel Goode
Edwin Gray
David Holmes
George Jackson
Henry Lee
John Marshall[39]
Littleton W. Tazewell[40]
Anthony New
John Nicholas
Robert Page
Josiah Parker
Levin Powell
John Randolph
Abram Trigg
John Trigg

## TERRITORY NORTHWEST OF THE RIVER OHIO[41]

### DELEGATE
William Henry Harrison[42]
William McMillan[43]

---

[25] Resigned June 12, 1800.

[26] Elected to fill vacancy caused by resignation of William Gordon, and took his seat December 8, 1800.

[27] Elected to fill vacancy caused by resignation of John Rutherfurd, in preceding Congress, and took his seat December 3, 1799; resigned February 16, 1801.

[28] Elected to fill vacancy caused by resignation of James Schureman, and took his seat March 3, 1801.

[29] Resigned in August 1800.

[30] Elected to fill vacancy caused by resignation of John Laurance, and took his seat January 8, 1801.

[31] Resigned March 19, 1800.

[32] Elected to fill vacancy caused by resignation of James Watson, and took his seat May 3, 1800.

[33] Died October 25, 1799, before Congress assembled.

[34] Elected to fill vacancy caused by death of Jonathan N. Havens, and took his seat February 27, 1800.

[35] Died December 21, 1800.

[36] Elected to fill vacancy caused by death of Thomas Hartley, and took his seat February 3, 1801.

[37] Elected December 12, 1798, to fill vacancy in the term beginning March 4, 1797, caused by resignation of Andrew Jackson, in preceding Congress, and took his seat December 2, 1799.

[38] Elected to fill vacancy caused by death of Henry Tazewell, in preceding Congress, and took his seat January 3, 1800.

[39] Resigned June 7, 1800.

[40] Elected to fill vacancy caused by resignation of John Marshall, and took his seat November 26, 1800.

[41] Created a district for the purposes of temporary government by act approved July 13, 1787, from territory ceded to the United States by the State of Virginia and granted a Delegate in Congress.

[42] Resigned in March 1800.

[43] Elected to fill vacancy caused by resignation of William Henry Harrison, and took his seat November 24, 1800.

# SEVENTH CONGRESS

## MARCH 4, 1801, TO MARCH 3, 1803

FIRST SESSION— *December 7, 1801, to May 3, 1802*
SECOND SESSION— *December 6, 1802, to March 3, 1803*
SPECIAL SESSION OF THE SENATE— *March 4, 1801, to March 5, 1801*

———————

VICE PRESIDENT OF THE UNITED STATES— Aaron Burr, of New York
PRESIDENT PRO TEMPORE OF THE SENATE— Abraham Baldwin,[1] of Georgia;
Stephen R. Bradley,[2] of Vermont
SECRETARY OF THE SENATE— Samuel A. Otis, of Massachusetts
DOORKEEPER OF THE SENATE— James Mathers, of New York

———————

SPEAKER OF THE HOUSE OF REPRESENTATIVES— Nathaniel Macon,[3] of North Carolina
CLERK OF THE HOUSE— John H. Oswald, of Pennsylvania; John Beckley,[4] of Virginia
SERGEANT AT ARMS OF THE HOUSE— Joseph Wheaton, of Rhode Island
DOORKEEPER OF THE HOUSE— Thomas Claxton

Aaron Burr
Vice President

Nathaniel Macon
Speaker

## CONNECTICUT

### SENATORS

James Hillhouse
Uriah Tracy

### REPRESENTATIVES AT LARGE

Samuel W. Dana
John Davenport
Roger Griswold
Calvin Goddard[5]
Elias Perkins
John C. Smith
Benjamin Tallmadge

## DELAWARE

### SENATORS

William H. Wells
Samuel White

### REPRESENTATIVE AT LARGE

James A. Bayard

## GEORGIA

### SENATORS

Abraham Baldwin
James Jackson

### REPRESENTATIVES AT LARGE

John Milledge[6]
Peter Early[7]
Benjamin Taliaferro[8]
David Meriwether[9]

## KENTUCKY

### SENATORS

John Brown
John Breckinridge

### REPRESENTATIVES

Thomas T. Davis
John Fowler

## MARYLAND

### SENATORS

John E. Howard
William Hindman[10]
Robert Wright[11]

### REPRESENTATIVES

John Archer
John Campbell
John Dennis
Daniel Hiester
Joseph H. Nicholson

Thomas Plater
Samuel Smith
Richard Sprigg, Jr.[12]
Walter Bowie[13]

## MASSACHUSETTS

### SENATORS

Dwight Foster[14]
Jonathan Mason

### REPRESENTATIVES

John Bacon
Phanuel Bishop
Manasseh Cutler
Richard Cutts
William Eustis
Silas Lee[15]
Samuel Thatcher[16]
Levi Lincoln[17]
Seth Hastings[18]
Ebenezer Mattoon
Nathan Read
William Shepard
Josiah Smith
Joseph B. Varnum
Peleg Wadsworth
Lemuel Williams

———————

[1] Elected December 7, 1801; April 17, 1802.
[2] Elected December 14, 1802; February 25, 1803; March 2, 1803.
[3] Elected December 7, 1801.
[4] Elected December 7, 1801.
[5] Elected to fill vacancy caused by resignation of Representative-elect Elizur Goodrich (March 3, 1801, before the beginning of the congressional term), and took his seat December 7, 1801.
[6] Resigned in May 1802.
[7] Elected to fill vacancy caused by resignation of

John Milledge, and took his seat January 10, 1803.
[8] Resigned in 1802.
[9] Elected to fill vacancy caused by resignation of Benjamin Taliaferro, and took his seat December 6, 1802.
[10] Reappointed to fill vacancy in term beginning March 4, 1801, caused by failure of legislature to elect his successor, and took his seat March 5, 1801.
[11] Elected to fill vacancy in term beginning March 4, 1801, and took his seat December 7, 1801.
[12] Resigned February 11, 1802.

[13] Elected to fill vacancy caused by resignation of Richard Sprigg, Jr., and took his seat March 24, 1802.
[14] Resigned March 2, 1803.
[15] Resigned August 20, 1801.
[16] Elected to fill vacancy caused by resignation of Silas Lee, and took his seat December 6, 1802.
[17] Resigned March 5, 1801, before Congress assembled having been appointed Attorney General of the United States.
[18] Elected to fill vacancy caused by resignation of Levi Lincoln, and took his seat January 11, 1802.

## NEW HAMPSHIRE

### SENATORS

Samuel Livermore[19]
Simeon Olcott[20]
James Sheafe[21]
William Plumer[22]

### REPRESENTATIVES AT LARGE

Abiel Foster
Joseph Peirce[23]
Samuel Hunt[24]
Samuel Tenney
George B. Upham

## NEW JERSEY

### SENATORS

Jonathan Dayton
Aaron Ogden

### REPRESENTATIVES AT LARGE

John Condit
Ebenezer Elmer
William Helms
James Mott
Henry Southard

## NEW YORK

### SENATORS

Gouverneur Morris
John Armstrong[25]
De Witt Clinton[26]

### REPRESENTATIVES

John Bird[27]
John P. Van Ness[28]
Lucas C. Elmendorf
Samuel L. Mitchill
Thomas Morris
John Smith
Thomas Tillotson[29]
Theodorus Bailey[30]
David Thomas
Philip Van Cortlandt
Killian K. Van Rensselaer
Benjamin Walker

## NORTH CAROLINA

### SENATORS

Jesse Franklin
David Stone

### REPRESENTATIVES

Willis Alston
William Barry Grove
Archibald Henderson
William H. Hill
Charles Johnson[31]
Thomas Wynns[32]
James Holland
Nathaniel Macon
Richard Stanford
John Stanly
Robert Williams

## OHIO[33]

### SENATORS

Vacant

### REPRESENTATIVE AT LARGE

Vacant

## PENNSYLVANIA

### SENATORS

James Ross
John Peter G. Muhlenberg[34]
George Logan[35]

### REPRESENTATIVES

Robert Brown
Thomas Boude
Andrew Gregg
John A. Hanna
Joseph Hiester
Joseph Hemphill
William Hoge
William Jones
Michael Leib
John Smilie
John Stewart
Isaac Van Horne
Henry Woods

## RHODE ISLAND

### SENATORS

Theodore Foster
Ray Greene[36]
Christopher Ellery[37]

### REPRESENTATIVES AT LARGE

Joseph Stanton, Jr.
Thomas Tillinghast

## SOUTH CAROLINA

### SENATORS

Charles Pinckney[38]
Thomas Sumter[39]
John Ewing Colhoun[40]
Pierce Butler[41]

### REPRESENTATIVES

William Butler
Benjamin Huger
Thomas Lowndes
Thomas Moore
John Rutledge
Thomas Sumter[42]
Richard Winn[43]

## TENNESSEE

### SENATORS

Joseph Anderson
William Cocke

### REPRESENTATIVE AT LARGE

William Dickson

## VERMONT

### SENATORS

Elijah Paine[44]
Stephen R. Bradley[45]
Nathaniel Chipman

### REPRESENTATIVES

Lewis R. Morris
Israel Smith

---

[19] Resigned June 12, 1801.
[20] Elected to fill vacancy caused by resignation of Samuel Livermore, and took his seat December 7, 1801.
[21] Resigned June 14, 1802.
[22] Elected to fill vacancy caused by resignation of James Sheafe, and took his seat December 14, 1802.
[23] Resigned in 1802.
[24] Elected to fill vacancy caused by resignation of Joseph Peirce, and took his seat December 6, 1802.
[25] Resigned February 5, 1802.
[26] Elected to fill vacancy caused by resignation of John Armstrong, and took his seat February 23, 1802.
[27] Resigned July 25, 1801, before Congress assembled.
[28] Elected to fill vacancy caused by resignation of John Bird, and took his seat December 7, 1801; seat declared forfeited January 17, 1803, because he had accepted and exercised the office of major of militia,

under authority of the United States, within the Territory of Columbia.
[29] Resigned August 10, 1801, before Congress assembled, having been appointed Secretary of State of New York.
[30] Elected to fill vacancy caused by resignation of Thomas Tillotson, and took his seat December 7, 1801.
[31] Died in 1802.
[32] Elected to fill vacancy caused by death of Charles Johnson, and took his seat December 7, 1802.
[33] Admitted as a State into the Union, November 29, 1802, from territory known as the "Territory Northwest of the River Ohio," which was originally ceded to the United States by the State of Virginia.
[34] Resigned June 30, 1801; attended special session of the Senate only, March 4 5, 1801.
[35] Appointed to fill vacancy caused by resignation of John Peter G. Muhlenberg, and took his seat December 7, 1801; subsequently elected.

[36] Resigned March 5, 1801.
[37] Elected to fill vacancy caused by resignation of Ray Greene, and took his seat December 7, 1801.
[38] Resigned in 1801.
[39] Elected to fill vacancy caused by resignation of Charles Pinckney, and took his seat December 19, 1801.
[40] Died October 26, 1802.
[41] Elected November 4, 1802, to fill vacancy caused by death of John E. Colhoun.
[42] Resigned December 15, 1801, having been elected Senator.
[43] Elected to fill vacancy caused by resignation of Thomas Sumter, and took his seat January 24, 1803.
[44] Resigned September 1, 1801.
[45] Elected to fill vacancy caused by resignation of Elijah Paine, and took his seat December 7, 1801.

## VIRGINIA

SENATORS

Stevens T. Mason
Wilson C. Nicholas

REPRESENTATIVES

Richard Brent
Samuel J. Cabell
Thomas Claiborne
Matthew Clay
John Clopton
John Dawson
William B. Giles

Edwin Gray
David Holmes
George Jackson
Anthony New
Thomas Newton, Jr.
John Randolph
John Smith
John Stratton
John Taliaferro
Philip R. Thompson
Abram Trigg
John Trigg

## MISSISSIPPI TERRITORY[46]

DELEGATE

Narsworthy Hunter[47]
Thomas M. Greene[48]

## TERRITORY NORTHWEST OF THE RIVER OHIO

DELEGATE

Paul Fearing[49]

---

[46] Formed by act of April 7, 1798, from territory ceded to the United States by the States of Georgia and South Carolina.

[47] Died March 11, 1802.

[48] Elected to fill vacancy caused by death of Narsworthy Hunter, and took his seat December 6, 1802.

[49] Question raised as to his right to retain his seat after November 29, 1802, when the Territory was granted statehood as the State of Ohio; no other representative appearing, was permitted to retain the seat.

# EIGHTH CONGRESS

## MARCH 4, 1803, TO MARCH 3, 1805

Aaron Burr
Vice President

FIRST SESSION— *October 17, 1803, to March 27, 1804*
SECOND SESSION— *November 5, 1804, to March 3, 1805*

———

VICE PRESIDENT OF THE UNITED STATES— Aaron Burr, of New York
PRESIDENT PRO TEMPORE OF THE SENATE— John Brown,[1] of Kentucky; Jesse Franklin,[2] of North Carolina; Joseph Anderson,[3] of Tennessee
SECRETARY OF THE SENATE— Samuel A. Otis, of Massachusetts
SERGEANT AT ARMS OF THE SENATE[4] — James Mathers, of New York

———

SPEAKER OF THE HOUSE OF REPRESENTATIVES— Nathaniel Macon,[5] of North Carolina
CLERK OF THE HOUSE— John Beckley,[6] of Virginia
SERGEANT AT ARMS OF THE HOUSE— Joseph Wheaton, of Rhode Island
DOORKEEPER OF THE HOUSE— Thomas Claxton

Nathaniel Macon
Speaker

## CONNECTICUT

### SENATORS

James Hillhouse
Uriah Tracy

### REPRESENTATIVES AT LARGE

Simeon Baldwin
Samuel W. Dana
John Davenport
Calvin Goddard
Roger Griswold
John C. Smith
Benjamin Tallmadge

## DELAWARE

### SENATORS

William H. Wells[7]
James A. Bayard[8]
Samuel White

### REPRESENTATIVE AT LARGE

Caesar A. Rodney

## GEORGIA

### SENATORS

Abraham Baldwin
James Jackson

### REPRESENTATIVES AT LARGE

Joseph Bryan
Peter Early
Samuel Hammond[9]
David Meriwether

## KENTUCKY

### SENATORS

John Brown
John Breckinridge

### REPRESENTATIVES

George M. Bedinger
John Boyle
John Fowler
Matthew Lyon
Thomas Sandford
Matthew Walton

## MARYLAND

### SENATORS

Robert Wright
Samuel Smith

### REPRESENTATIVES

John Archer
Walter Bowie
John Campbell
John Dennis
Nicholas R. Moore
William McCreery
Daniel Hiester[10]
Roger Nelson[11]
Joseph H. Nicholson
Thomas Plater

## MASSACHUSETTS

### SENATORS

Timothy Pickering[12]
John Quincy Adams

### REPRESENTATIVES

Phanuel Bishop
Phineas Bruce[13]
Jacob Crowninshield
Manasseh Cutler
Richard Cutts
Thomas Dwight
William Eustis
Seth Hastings
Nahum Mitchell
Ebenezer Seaver
Thomson J. Skinner[14]
Simon Larned[15]
William Stedman
Samuel Taggart
Samuel Thatcher
Joseph B. Varnum
Peleg Wadsworth
Lemuel Williams

## NEW HAMPSHIRE

### SENATORS

Simeon Olcott
William Plumer

### REPRESENTATIVES AT LARGE

Silas Betton
Clifton Clagett
David Hough
Samuel Hunt
Samuel Tenney

---

[1] Elected October 17, 1803; January 23, 1804.
[2] Elected March 10, 1804.
[3] Elected January 15, 1805; February 28, 1805; March 2, 1805.
[4] Official designation of "Sergeant at Arms" was fixed March 3, 1805.
[5] Reelected October 17, 1803.
[6] Reelected October 17, 1803.
[7] Resigned November 6, 1804.

[8] Elected to fill vacancy caused by resignation of William H. Wells, and took his seat January 15, 1805.
[9] Seat declared vacant February 2, 1805, because he had accepted appointment to be civil and military governor of upper Louisiana Territory.
[10] Died March 7, 1804.
[11] Elected to fill vacancy caused by death of Daniel Hiester, and took his seat November 6, 1804.

[12] Elected to fill vacancy caused by resignation of Dwight Foster in preceding Congress, and took his seat October 17, 1803.
[13] Never qualified, owing to illness.
[14] Resigned August 10, 1804.
[15] Elected to fill vacancy caused by resignation of Thomson J. Skinner, and took his seat November 5, 1804.

## NEW JERSEY

### SENATORS

Jonathan Dayton
John Condit[16]

### REPRESENTATIVES AT LARGE

Adam Boyd
Ebenezer Elmer
William Helms
James Mott
James Sloan
Henry Southard

## NEW YORK

### SENATORS

De Witt Clinton[17]
John Armstrong[18]
John Smith[19]
Theodorus Bailey[20]
John Armstrong[21]
Samuel L. Mitchill[22]

### REPRESENTATIVES

Isaac Bloom[23]
Daniel C. Verplanck[24]
Gaylord Griswold
Josiah Hasbrouck[25]
Henry W. Livingston
Andrew McCord
Samuel L. Mitchill[26]
George Clinton, Jr.[27]
Beriah Palmer
John Patterson
Oliver Phelps
Erastus Root
Joshua Sands
Thomas Sammons
John Smith[28]
Samuel Riker[29]
David Thomas
George Tibbitts
Philip Van Cortlandt
Killian K. Van Rensselaer

## NORTH CAROLINA

### SENATORS

Jesse Franklin
David Stone

### REPRESENTATIVES

Nathaniel Alexander
Willis Alston
William Blackledge
James Gillespie[30]
James Holland
William Kennedy
Nathaniel Macon
Samuel D. Purviance[31]
Richard Stanford
Marmaduke Williams
Joseph Winston
Thomas Wynns

## OHIO

### SENATORS

John Smith[32]
Thomas Worthington[33]

### REPRESENTATIVE AT LARGE

Jeremiah Morrow[34]

## PENNSYLVANIA

### SENATORS

George Logan
Samuel Maclay

### REPRESENTATIVES

Isaac Anderson
David Bard
Robert Brown
Joseph Clay
Frederick Conrad
William Findley
Andrew Gregg
John A. Hanna
Joseph Hiester
William Hoge[35]
John Hoge[36]
Michael Leib
John B. C. Lucas
John Rea
Jacob Richards
John Smilie
John Stewart
Isaac Van Horne
John Whitehill

## RHODE ISLAND

### SENATORS

Christopher Ellery
Samuel J. Potter[37]
Benjamin Howland[38]

### REPRESENTATIVES AT LARGE

Nehemiah Knight
Joseph Stanton, Jr.

## SOUTH CAROLINA

### SENATORS

Thomas Sumter
Pierce Butler[39]
John Gaillard[40]

### REPRESENTATIVES

William Butler
Levi Casey
John B. Earle
Wade Hampton
Benjamin Huger
Thomas Lowndes
Thomas Moore
Richard Winn

## TENNESSEE

### SENATORS

Joseph Anderson
William Cocke

### REPRESENTATIVES AT LARGE

George W. Campbell
William Dickson
John Rhea

## VERMONT

### SENATORS

Stephen R. Bradley
Israel Smith

### REPRESENTATIVES

William Chamberlain
Martin Chittenden
James Elliott
Gideon Olin

---

[16] Appointed to fill vacancy in term beginning March 4, 1803, to serve until the next meeting of the legislature, subsequently elected and took his seat October 17, 1803; vacancy in this class from March 4, 1803, to August 31, 1803.

[17] Resigned November 4, 1803.

[18] Appointed to fill vacancy caused by resignation of De Witt Clinton, and took his seat December 8, 1803. (See footnote 21.)

[19] Elected to fill vacancy caused by resignation of De Witt Clinton, and took his seat February 23, 1804.

[20] Resigned January 16, 1804.

[21] Elected to fill vacancy caused by resignation of Theodorus Bailey, and took his seat under the new credentials February 25, 1804; served in this class until June 30, 1804, when he resigned, having been appointed minister to France.

[22] Elected to fill vacancy caused by resignation of John Armstrong, and took his seat November 23, 1804.

[23] Died April 26, 1803, before Congress assembled.

[24] Elected to fill vacancy caused by death of Isaac Bloom, and took his seat October 17, 1803.

[25] Elected to fill vacancy caused by resignation of Representative-elect John Cantine, before the beginning of the congressional term, and took his seat October 17, 1803.

[26] Resigned November 22, 1804, before the commencement of the Ninth Congress, to which he had been reelected, having been elected Senator.

[27] Elected to fill vacancy caused by resignation of Samuel L. Mitchill, and took his seat February 14, 1805.

[28] Resigned effective February 23, 1804, having been elected Senator.

[29] Elected to fill vacancy caused by resignation of John Smith, and took his seat November 5, 1804.

[30] Died January 10, 1805.

[31] Election unsuccessfully contested by Duncan McFarland.

[32] Took his seat October 25, 1803; term to expire, as determined by lot, March 3, 1809.

[33] Took his seat October 17, 1803; term to expire as determined by lot, March 3, 1807.

[34] Took his seat October 17, 1803.

[35] Resigned October 15, 1804.

[36] Elected to fill vacancy caused by resignation of William Hoge, and took his seat November 27, 1804.

[37] Died October 14, 1804.

[38] Elected to fill vacancy caused by death of Samuel J. Potter, and took his seat December 3, 1804.

[39] Resigned November 21, 1804.

[40] Elected to fill vacancy caused by resignation of Pierce Butler, and took his seat January 31, 1805.

## VIRGINIA

### SENATORS

Stevens T. Mason[41]
John Taylor[42]
Abraham B. Venable[43]
William B. Giles[44]
Andrew Moore[45]
Wilson C. Nicholas[46]
Andrew Moore[47]
William B. Giles[48]

### REPRESENTATIVES

Thomas Claiborne
John Trigg[49]

Christopher Clark[50]
Matthew Clay
John Clopton
John Dawson
John W. Eppes
Peterson Goodwyn
Edwin Gray
Thomas Griffin
David Holmes
John G. Jackson
Walter Jones
Thomas Lewis[51]
Andrew Moore[52]
Alexander Wilson[53]

Anthony New
Thomas Newton, Jr.
John Randolph
Thomas M. Randolph
John Smith
James Stephenson
Philip R. Thompson
Abram Trigg
Joseph Lewis, Jr.

## MISSISSIPPI TERRITORY

### DELEGATE

William Lattimore

---

[41] Died May 10, 1803.

[42] Appointed to fill vacancy caused by death of Stevens T. Mason, and took his seat October 17, 1803.

[43] Elected to fill vacancy caused by death of Stevens T. Mason, and took his seat December 13, 1803; resigned June 7, 1804.

[44] Appointed to fill vacancy caused by resignation of Abraham B. Venable, and took his seat November 5, 1804; subsequently elected to fill vacancy caused by resignation of Wilson C. Nicholas. (See footnote 48.)

[45] Elected to fill vacancy caused by resignation of Abraham B. Venable, and qualified under these cre-

dentials December 17, 1804; antecedently appointed to fill vacancy caused by resignation of Wilson C. Nicholas. (See footnote 47.)

[46] Resigned May 22, 1804.

[47] Appointed to fill vacancy caused by resignation of Wilson C. Nicholas, and took his seat November 6, 1804; subsequently elected to fill vacancy caused by resignation of Abraham B. Venable. (See footnote 45.)

[48] Elected to fill vacancy caused by resignation of Wilson C. Nicholas, and took his seat December 17, 1804; antecedently appointed to fill vacancy caused by resignation of Abraham B. Venable. (See footnote 44.)

[49] Died June 28, 1804.

[50] Elected to fill vacancy caused by death of John Trigg, and took his seat November 5, 1804.

[51] Served until March 5, 1804 when he was succeeded by Andrew Moore, who contested his election. By formal action of the House of Representatives, counsel for the claimants in this case were heard at the bar of the House.

[52] Successfully contested the election of Thomas Lewis, and took his seat March 5, 1804; resigned November 6, 1804, having been appointed Senator.

[53] Elected to fill vacancy caused by resignation of Andrew Moore, and took his seat December 4, 1804.

# NINTH CONGRESS

MARCH 4, 1805, TO MARCH 3, 1807

George Clinton
Vice President

Nathaniel Macon
Speaker

FIRST SESSION— *December 2, 1805, to April 21, 1806*
SECOND SESSION— *December 1, 1806, to March 3, 1807*
SPECIAL SESSION OF THE SENATE— *March 4, 1805, for one day only*

———

VICE PRESIDENT OF THE UNITED STATES— George Clinton, of New York
PRESIDENT PRO TEMPORE OF THE SENATE— Samuel Smith,[1] of Maryland
SECRETARY OF THE SENATE— Samuel A. Otis, of Massachusetts
SERGEANT AT ARMS OF THE SENATE— James Mathers, of New York

———

SPEAKER OF THE HOUSE OF REPRESENTATIVES— Nathaniel Macon,[2] of North Carolina
CLERK OF THE HOUSE— John Beckley,[3] of Virginia
SERGEANT AT ARMS OF THE HOUSE— Joseph Wheaton, of Rhode Island
DOORKEEPER OF THE HOUSE— Thomas Claxton

## CONNECTICUT

### SENATORS

James Hillhouse
Uriah Tracy

### REPRESENTATIVES AT LARGE

Samuel W. Dana
John Davenport
Calvin Goddard[4]
Timothy Pitkin[5]
Roger Griswold[6]
Lewis B. Sturges[7]
Jonathan O. Moseley
John Cotton Smith[8]
Theodore Dwight[9]
Benjamin Tallmadge

## DELAWARE

### SENATORS

Samuel White
James A. Bayard

### REPRESENTATIVE AT LARGE

James M. Broom

## GEORGIA

### SENATORS

Abraham Baldwin
James Jackson[10]
John Milledge[11]

### REPRESENTATIVES AT LARGE

Joseph Bryan[12]
Dennis Smelt[13]
Peter Early
David Meriwether
Cowles Mead[14]
Thomas Spalding[15]
William W. Bibb[16]

## KENTUCKY

### SENATORS

John Breckinridge[17]
John Adair[18]
Henry Clay[19]
Buckner Thruston

### REPRESENTATIVES

George M. Bedinger
John Boyle
John Fowler

Matthew Lyon
Thomas Sandford
Matthew Walton

## MARYLAND

### SENATORS

Robert Wright[20]
Philip Reed[21]
Samuel Smith

### REPRESENTATIVES

John Archer
John Campbell
Leonard Covington
Joseph H. Nicholson[22]
Edward Lloyd[23]
Patrick Magruder
William McCreery
Nicholas R. Moore
Roger Nelson
Charles Goldsborough

## MASSACHUSETTS

### SENATORS

Timothy Pickering
John Quincy Adams

---

[1] Elected December 2, 1805; March 18, 1806; and March 2, 1807.
[2] Reelected December 2, 1805.
[3] Reelected December 2, 1805.
[4] Resigned in 1805, before Congress assembled.
[5] Elected to fill in part the vacancies caused by resignations of Calvin Goddard and Roger Griswold, and took his seat December 10, 1805.
[6] Resigned in 1805, before Congress assembled.
[7] Elected to fill in part the vacancies caused by resignations of Calvin Goddard and Roger Griswold, and took his seat December 2, 1805.
[8] Resigned in August 1806.
[9] Elected to fill vacancy caused by resignation of John Cotton Smith, and took his seat December 1, 1806.

[10] Died March 19, 1806.
[11] Elected to fill vacancy caused by death of James Jackson, and took his seat December 11, 1806.
[12] Resigned in 1806.
[13] Elected to fill vacancy caused by resignation of Joseph Bryan, and took his seat December 26, 1806.
[14] Served until December 24, 1805; succeeded by Thomas Spalding, who contested his election.
[15] Successfully contested the election of Cowles Mead, and took his seat December 24, 1805; resigned in 1806.
[16] Elected to fill vacancy caused by resignation of Thomas Spalding, and took his seat January 26, 1807.
[17] Resigned August 7, 1805, to become Attorney General.

[18] Elected to fill vacancy caused by resignation of John Breckinridge, and took his seat December 9, 1805; resigned November 18, 1806.
[19] Elected to fill vacancy caused by resignation of John Adair, and took his seat December 29, 1806.
[20] Resigned in 1806.
[21] Elected to fill vacancy caused by resignation of Robert Wright, and took his seat December 29, 1806.
[22] Resigned March 1, 1806.
[23] Elected to fill vacancy caused by resignation of Joseph H. Nicholson, and took his seat December 3, 1806.

## MASSACHUSETTS— Continued

### REPRESENTATIVES

Joseph Barker
Barnabas Bidwell
Phanuel Bishop
John Chandler
Orchard Cook
Jacob Crowninshield
Richard Cutts
William Ely
Isaiah L. Green
Seth Hastings
Jeremiah Nelson
Josiah Quincy
Ebenezer Seaver
William Stedman
Samuel Taggart
Joseph B. Varnum
Peleg Wadsworth

## NEW HAMPSHIRE

### SENATORS

William Plumer
Nicholas Gilman

### REPRESENTATIVES AT LARGE

Silas Betton
Caleb Ellis
David Hough
Samuel Tenney
Thomas W. Thompson

## NEW JERSEY

### SENATORS

John Condit
Aaron Kitchell

### REPRESENTATIVES AT LARGE

Ezra Darby
Ebenezer Elmer
William Helms
John Lambert
James Sloan
Henry Southard

## NEW YORK

### SENATORS

John Smith
Samuel L. Mitchill

### REPRESENTATIVES

John Blake, Jr.
George Clinton, Jr.[24]
Silas Halsey
Henry W. Livingston
Josiah Masters
Gurdon S. Mumford[25]
John Russell
Peter Sailly
Thomas Sammons
Martin G. Schuneman
David Thomas
Uri Tracy
Philip Van Cortlandt
Killian K. Van Rensselaer
Daniel C. Verplanck
Eliphalet Wickes
Nathan Williams

## NORTH CAROLINA

### SENATORS

David Stone[26]
James Turner

### REPRESENTATIVES

Nathaniel Alexander[27]
Evan S. Alexander[28]
Willis Alston
William Blackledge
Thomas Blount
James Holland
Thomas Kenan
Nathaniel Macon
Duncan McFarlan
Richard Stanford
Marmaduke Williams
Joseph Winston
Thomas Wynns

## OHIO

### SENATORS

John Smith
Thomas Worthington

### REPRESENTATIVE AT LARGE

Jeremiah Morrow

## PENNSYLVANIA

### SENATORS

George Logan
Samuel Maclay

### REPRESENTATIVES

Issac Anderson
David Bard
Robert Brown
Joseph Clay
Frederick Conrad
William Findley
Andrew Gregg
John Hamilton
John A. Hanna[29]
Robert Whitehill[30]
James Kelly
Michael Leib[31]
John Porter[32]
Christian Lower[33]
John B. C. Lucas[34]
Samuel Smith[35]
John Pugh
John Rea
Jacob Richards
John Smilie
John Whitehill

## RHODE ISLAND

### SENATORS

Benjamin Howland
James Fenner

### REPRESENTATIVES AT LARGE

Nehemiah Knight
Joseph Stanton, Jr.

## SOUTH CAROLINA

### SENATORS

Thomas Sumter
John Gaillard

### REPRESENTATIVES

William Butler
Levi Casey[36]
Elias Earle
Robert Marion
Thomas Moore
O'Brien Smith
David R. Williams
Richard Winn

## TENNESSEE

### SENATORS

Joseph Anderson
Daniel Smith

### REPRESENTATIVES

George W. Campbell
William Dickson
John Rhea

## VERMONT

### SENATORS

Stephen R. Bradley
Israel Smith

### REPRESENTATIVES

Martin Chittenden
James Elliott
James Fisk
Gideon Olin

---

[24] Elected to fill vacancy caused by resignation of Representative-elect Samuel L. Mitchill in preceding Congress.

[25] Elected to fill vacancy caused by resignation of Representative-elect Daniel D. Tompkins, before the beginning of the congressional term, and took his seat December 2, 1805.

[26] Resigned about February 17, 1807.

[27] Resigned in November 1805, having been elected governor.

[28] Elected to fill vacancy caused by resignation of Nathaniel Alexander and took his seat February 24, 1806.

[29] Died July 23, 1805, before Congress assembled.

[30] Elected to fill vacancy caused by death of John A. Hanna, and took his seat December 2, 1805.

[31] Election unsuccessfully contested by John Douglas; resigned February 14, 1806.

[32] Elected to fill vacancy caused by resignation of Michael Leib, and took his seat December 8, 1806.

[33] Died December 19, 1806, never having qualified.

[34] Resigned before Congress assembled.

[35] Elected to fill vacancy caused by resignation of John B. C. Lucas, and took his seat December 2, 1805.

[36] Died February 3, 1807, before the commencement of the Tenth Congress, to which he had been reelected.

## VIRGINIA

### SENATORS

William B. Giles
Andrew Moore

### REPRESENTATIVES

Burwell Bassett
John Claiborne
Christopher Clark[37]
William A. Burwell[38]
Matthew Clay
John Clopton
John Dawson
John W. Eppes
James M. Garnett

Peterson Goodwyn
Edwin Gray
David Holmes
John G. Jackson
Walter Jones
Joseph Lewis, Jr.
John Morrow
Thomas Newton, Jr.
John Randolph
Thomas M. Randolph
John Smith
Philip R. Thompson
Abram Trigg
Alexander Wilson

## INDIANA TERRITORY[39]

### DELEGATE

Benjamin Parke[40]

## MISSISSIPPI TERRITORY

### DELEGATE

William Lattimore

## TERRITORY OF ORLEANS[41]

### DELEGATE

Daniel Clark[42]

---

[37] Resigned July 1, 1806.

[38] Elected to fill vacancy caused by resignation of Christopher Clark, and took his seat December 1, 1806.

[39] Formed by act approved May 7, 1800, from a portion of lands of the Territory Northwest of the River Ohio originally ceded to the United States by the State of Virginia, with seat of government at Vincennes.

[40] Took his seat December 12, 1805.

[41] Formed by act approved March 26, 1804, from a portion of lands ceded by France to the United States under the name of Louisiana by the treaty of Paris of April 30, 1803.

[42] Took his seat December 1, 1806.

# TENTH CONGRESS

## MARCH 4, 1807, TO MARCH 3, 1809

FIRST SESSION— *October 26, 1807, to April 25, 1808*
SECOND SESSION— *November 7, 1808, to March 3, 1809*

---

VICE PRESIDENT OF THE UNITED STATES— GEORGE CLINTON, of New York
PRESIDENT PRO TEMPORE OF THE SENATE— SAMUEL SMITH,[1] of Maryland; STEPHEN
R. BRADLEY,[2] of Vermont; JOHN MILLEDGE,[3] of Georgia
SECRETARY OF THE SENATE— SAMUEL A. OTIS, of Massachusetts
SERGEANT AT ARMS OF THE SENATE— JAMES MATHERS, of New York

---

SPEAKER OF THE HOUSE OF REPRESENTATIVES— JOSEPH B. VARNUM,[4] of
Massachusetts
CLERK OF THE HOUSE— JOHN BECKLEY, of Virginia; PATRICK MAGRUDER,[5] of Maryland
SERGEANT AT ARMS OF THE HOUSE— JOSEPH WHEATON, of Rhode Island; THOMAS DUNN,[6] of Maryland
DOORKEEPER OF THE HOUSE— THOMAS CLAXTON

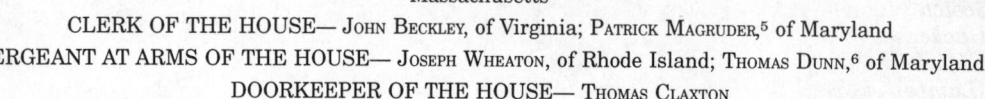

George Clinton
Vice President

Joseph B. Varnum
Speaker

---

## CONNECTICUT

### SENATORS
James Hillhouse, *New Haven*
Uriah Tracy,[7] *Litchfield*
Chauncey Goodrich,[8] *Hartford*

### REPRESENTATIVES AT LARGE
Epaphroditus Champion, *East Haddam*
Samuel W. Dana, *Middlesex*
John Davenport, *Stamford*
Jonathan O. Moseley, *East Haddam*
Timothy Pitkin, *Farmington*
Lewis B. Sturges, *Fairfield*
Benjamin Tallmadge, *Litchfield*

## DELAWARE

### SENATORS
Samuel White, *Wilmington*
James A. Bayard, *Wilmington*

### REPRESENTATIVE AT LARGE
James M. Broom,[9] *Wilmington*
Nicholas Van Dyke,[10] *New Castle*

## GEORGIA

### SENATORS
Abraham Baldwin,[11] *Augusta*
George Jones,[12] *Savannah*
William H. Crawford,[13] *Lexington*
John Milledge, *Augusta*

### REPRESENTATIVES AT LARGE
William W. Bibb, *Petersburg*
Howell Cobb, *Louisville*
Dennis Smelt, *Savannah*
George M. Troup, *Dublin*

## KENTUCKY

### SENATORS
Buckner Thruston, *Lexington*
John Pope, *Springfield*

### REPRESENTATIVES
John Boyle, *Lancaster*
Joseph Desha, *Mays Lick*
Benjamin Howard, *Lexington*
Richard M. Johnson, *Great Crossings*
Matthew Lyon, *Eddyville*
John Rowan, *Louisville*

## MARYLAND

### SENATORS
Samuel Smith, *Baltimore*
Philip Reed, *Chestertown*

### REPRESENTATIVES
John Campbell, *Port Tobacco*
Charles Goldsborough, *Cambridge*
Philip B. Key,[14] *Rockville*
Edward Lloyd, *Wye Mills*
William McCreery,[15] *Reisterstown*
John Montgomery, *Bel Air*
Nicholas R. Moore, *Ruxton*

Roger Nelson, *Frederick*
Archibald Van Horne, *Prince Goerges County*

## MASSACHUSETTS

### SENATORS
Timothy Pickering, *Wendham*
John Quincy Adams,[16] *Boston*
James Lloyd,[17] *Boston*

### REPRESENTATIVES
Barnabas Bidwell,[18] *Stockbridge*
Ezekiel Bacon,[19] *Pittsfield*
Joseph Barker, *Middleboro*
John Chandler, *Monmouth*
Orchard Cook, *Wiscasset*
Jacob Crowninshield,[20] *Salem*
Joseph Story,[21] *Salem*
Richard Cutts, *Pepperelboro*
Josiah Dean, *Raynham*
William Ely, *Springfield*
Isaiah L. Green, *Barnstable*
Daniel Ilsley, *Falmouth*
Edward St. Loe Livermore, *Newburyport*
Josiah Quincy, *Boston*
Ebenezer Seaver, *Roxbury*
William Stedman, *Worcester*
Samuel Taggart, *Colerain*
Jabez Upham, *Brookfield*
Joseph B. Varnum, *Dracut*

---

[1] Elected April 16, 1808.
[2] Elected December 28, 1808.
[3] Elected January 30, 1809.
[4] Elected October 26, 1807.
[5] Elected October 26, 1807.
[6] Elected October 27, 1807.
[7] Died July 19, 1807.
[8] Elected to fill vacancy caused by death of Uriah Tracy, and took his seat November 27, 1807.
[9] Resigned before Congress assembled.
[10] Elected to fill vacancy caused by resignation of James M. Broom, and took his seat December 2, 1807.
[11] Died March 4, 1807.

[12] Appointed to fill vacancy caused by death of Abraham Baldwin, and took his seat October 26, 1807.
[13] Elected to fill vacancy caused by death of Abraham Baldwin, and took his seat December 9, 1807.
[14] Election was questioned upon the grounds that he was not a resident of the district from which elected and that he was a British pensioner; a resolution declaring him entitled to his seat was passed by a vote of 57 to 52, March 18, 1808.
[15] Election unsuccessfully contested by Joshua Barney.
[16] Resigned June 8, 1808.

[17] Elected to fill vacancy caused by resignation of John Quincy Adams, and took his seat November 7, 1808.
[18] Resigned July 13, 1807, before Congress assembled.
[19] Elected to fill vacancy caused by resignation of Barnabas Bidwell, and took his seat November 2, 1807.
[20] Died April 15, 1808.
[21] Elected to fill vacancy caused by death of Jacob Crowninshield, and took his seat December 20, 1808.

## NEW HAMPSHIRE

SENATORS

Nicholas Gilman, *Exeter*
Nahum Parker, *Fitzwilliam*

REPRESENTATIVES AT LARGE

Peter Carleton, *Landaff*
Daniel M. Durell, *Dover*
Francis Gardner, *Keene*
Jedediah K. Smith, *Amherst*
Clement Storer, *Portsmouth*

## NEW JERSEY

SENATORS

John Condit, *Orange*
Aaron Kitchell, *Hanover*

REPRESENTATIVES AT LARGE

Ezra Darby,[22] *Scotch Plains*
Adam Boyd,[23] *Hackensack*
William Helms, *Hackettstown*
John Lambert, *Lambertville*
Thomas Newbold, *Springfield
Township*
James Sloan, *Newton Township*
Henry Southard, *Baskingridge*

## NEW YORK

SENATORS

John Smith, *Mastic*
Samuel L. Mitchill, *New York City*

REPRESENTATIVES

John Blake, Jr., *Montgomery*
George Clinton, Jr., *New York City*
Barent Gardenier, *Kingston*
John Harris, *Aurelias*
Reuben Humphrey, *Marcellus*
William Kirkpatrick, *Salina*
Josiah Masters, *Schaghticoke*
Gurdon S. Mumford, *New York City*
Samuel Riker, *Newtown*
John Russell, *Cooperstown*
Peter Swart, *Schoharie*
David Thomas,[24] *Salem*
Nathan Wilson,[25] *Salem*
John Thompson, *Stillwater*
James I. Van Alen, *Kinderhook*
Philip Van Cortlandt, *Croton*
Killian K. Van Rensselaer, *Albany*
Daniel C. Verplanck, *Fishkill*

## NORTH CAROLINA

SENATORS

James Turner, *Warrenton*
Jesse Franklin, *Surry County*

REPRESENTATIVES

Evan S. Alexander, *Salisbury*
Willis Alston, *Greenville*
William Blackledge, *Spring Hill*
Thomas Blount, *Tarboro*
John Culpepper,[26] *Allenton*
Meshack Franklin, *Surry County*
James Holland, *Rutherford County*
Thomas Kenan, *Kenansville*
Nathaniel Macon, *Warrenton*
Lemuel Sawyer, *Elizabeth City*
Richard Stanford, *Hawfields*
Marmaduke Williams, *Caswell
County*

## OHIO

SENATORS

John Smith,[27] *Columbia*
Return J. Meigs, Jr.,[28] *Marietta*
Edward Tiffin,[29] *Chillicothe*

REPRESENTATIVE AT LARGE

Jeremiah Morrow, *Montgomery*

## PENNSYLVANIA

SENATORS

Samuel Maclay,[30] *Lewisburg*
Michael Leib,[31] *Philadelphia*
Andrew Gregg, *Pennvalley*

REPRESENTATIVES

David Bard, *Frankstown*
Robert Brown, *Weaversville*
Joseph Clay,[32] *Philadelphia*
Benjamin Say,[33] *Philadelphia*
William Findley, *Youngstown*
John Hiester, *Parker Ford*
William Hoge, *Washington*
Robert Jenkins, *Churchtown*
James Kelly, *Philadelphia*
William Milnor, *Philadelphia*
John Porter, *Philadelphia*
John Pugh, *Doylestown*
John Rea, *Chambersburg*
Jacob Richards, *Chester*
Matthias Richards, *Pottstown*

John Smilie, *Fayette*
Samuel Smith, *Erie*
Robert Whitehill, *Camp Hill*
Daniel Montgomery, Jr., *Danville*

## RHODE ISLAND

SENATORS

Benjamin Howland, *Tiverton*
James Fenner,[34] *Providence*
Elisha Mathewson,[35] *Scituate*

REPRESENTATIVES AT LARGE

Nehemiah Knight,[36] *Cranston*
Richard Jackson, Jr.,[37] *Providence*
Isaac Wilbour, *Little Compton*

## SOUTH CAROLINA

SENATORS

Thomas Sumter, *Stateburg*
John Gaillard, *Charleston*

REPRESENTATIVES

Lemuel J. Alston, *Greenville*
William Butler, *Saluda*
Joseph Calhoun,[38] *Calhoun Mills*
Robert Marion, *Charleston*
Thomas Moore, *Prices Store*
John Taylor, *Columbia*
David R. Williams, *Society Hill*
Richard Winn, *Winnsboro*

## TENNESSEE

SENATORS

Joseph Anderson
Daniel Smith, *Hendersonville*

REPRESENTATIVES

George W. Campbell, *Nashville*
John Rhea, *Sullivan*
Jesse Wharton, *Nashville*

## VERMONT

SENATORS

Stephen R. Bradley, *Westminster*
Israel Smith,[39] *Rutland*
Jonathan Robinson,[40] *Bennington*

REPRESENTATIVES

Martin Chittenden, *Williston*
James Elliott, *Brattleboro*
James Fisk, *Barre*

---

[22] Died January 28, 1808.
[23] Elected to fill vacancy caused by death of Ezra Darby, and took his seat April 1, 1808.
[24] Resigned May 1, 1808.
[25] Elected to fill vacancy caused by resignation of David Thomas, and took his seat November 7, 1808.
[26] Election contested by Duncan McFarland; the House on January 2, 1808, declared the seat vacant on account of irregularities; subsequently elected, and took his seat February 23, 1808.
[27] Tried by Senate for complicity with Aaron Burr; but resolution of expulsion was rejected April 9, 1808; resigned April 25, 1808. (See U.S. Senate Election,

Expulsion and Censure Cases, 1793-1990, Senate Document 103-33, pp. 18-21.)
[28] Elected to fill vacancy caused by resignation of John Smith, and took his seat January 6, 1809.
[29] Resigned March 3, 1809.
[30] Resigned January 4, 1809.
[31] Elected to fill vacancy caused by resignation of Samuel Maclay, and took his seat January 19, 1809.
[32] Resigned in 1808.
[33] Elected to fill vacancy caused by resignation of Joseph Clay, and took his seat November 16, 1808.
[34] Resigned in September 1807, having been elected governor.

[35] Elected to fill vacancy caused by resignation of James Fenner, and took his seat November 20, 1807.
[36] Died June 13, 1808.
[37] Elected to fill vacancy caused by death of Nehemiah Knight, and took his seat November 11, 1808.
[38] Elected to fill vacancy caused by death of Representative-elect Levi Casey, in preceding Congress, and took his seat October 26, 1807.
[39] Resigned October 1, 1807, having been elected governor.
[40] Elected to fill vacancy caused by resignation of Israel Smith, and took his seat October 26, 1807.

## VERMONT—Continued

REPRESENTATIVES—CONTINUED

James Witherell,[41] *Fair Haven*
Samuel Shaw,[42] *Castleton*

## VIRGINIA

SENATORS

William B. Giles, *Ladore*
Andrew Moore, *Lexington*

REPRESENTATIVES

Burwell Bassett, *Williamsburg*
William A. Burwell, *Rocky Mount*
John Claiborne,[43] *Brunswick*
Thomas Gholson, Jr.,[44] *Brunswick*
Matthew Clay, *Halifax*
John Clopton, *Tunstall*

John Dawson
John W. Eppes, *Charles City*
James M. Garnett, *Loretto*
Peterson Goodwyn, *Petersburg*
Edwin Gray
David Holmes, *Winchester*
John G. Jackson, *Clarksburg*
Walter Jones, *Northumberland County*
Joseph Lewis, Jr., *Upperville*
John Love, *Alexandria*
John Morrow
Thomas Newton, Jr., *Norfolk*
Wilson C. Nicholas, *Charlottesville*
John Randolph, *Charlotte*
John Smith, *Frederick County*
Abram Trigg, *Christiansburg*

Alexander Wilson

## INDIANA TERRITORY

DELEGATE

Benjamin Parke,[45] *Vincennes*
Jesse B. Thomas,[46] *Lawrenceburg*

## MISSISSIPPI TERRITORY

DELEGATE

George Poindexter, *Woodville*

## TERRITORY OF ORLEANS

DELEGATE

Daniel Clark, *New Orleans*

---

[41] Resigned May 1, 1808.
[42] Elected to fill vacancy caused by resignation of James Witherell, and took his seat November 8, 1808.

[43] Died October 9, 1808.
[44] Elected to fill vacancy caused by death of John Claiborne, and took his seat November 7, 1808.

[45] Resigned March 1, 1808.
[46] Elected to fill vacancy caused by resignation of Benjamin Parke, and took his seat December 1, 1808.

# 11TH CONGRESS

## MARCH 4, 1809, TO MARCH 3, 1811

George Clinton
Vice President

Joseph B. Varnum
Speaker

FIRST SESSION— *May 22, 1809, to June 28, 1809*
SECOND SESSION— *November 27, 1809, to May 1, 1810*
THIRD SESSION— *December 3, 1810, to March 3, 1811*
SPECIAL SESSION OF THE SENATE— *March 4, 1809, to March 7, 1809*

---

VICE PRESIDENT OF THE UNITED STATES— GEORGE CLINTON, of New York
PRESIDENT PRO TEMPORE OF THE SENATE— ANDREW GREGG,[1] of Pennsylvania;
JOHN GAILLARD,[2] of South Carolina; JOHN POPE,[3] of Kentucky
SECRETARY OF THE SENATE— SAMUEL A. OTIS, of Massachusetts
SERGEANT AT ARMS OF THE SENATE— JAMES MATHERS, of New York

---

SPEAKER OF THE HOUSE OF REPRESENTATIVES— JOSEPH B. VARNUM,[4] of Massachusetts
CLERK OF THE HOUSE— PATRICK MAGRUDER,[5] of Maryland
SERGEANT AT ARMS OF THE HOUSE— THOMAS DUNN, of Maryland
DOORKEEPER OF THE HOUSE— THOMAS CLAXTON

## CONNECTICUT

### SENATORS

James Hillhouse,[6] *New Haven*
Samuel W. Dana,[7] *Middlesex*
Chauncey Goodrich, *Hartford*

### REPRESENTATIVES AT LARGE

Epaphroditus Champion, *East Haddam*
Samuel W. Dana,[8] *Middlesex*
Ebenezer Huntington,[9] *Norwich*
John Davenport, *Stamford*
Jonathan O. Moseley, *East Haddam*
Timothy Pitkin, *Farmington*
Lewis B. Sturges, *Fairfield*
Benjamin Tallmadge, *Litchfield*

## DELAWARE

### SENATORS

Samuel White,[10] *Wilmington*
Outerbridge Horsey,[11] *Wilmington*
James A. Bayard, *Wilmington*

### REPRESENTATIVE AT LARGE

Nicholas Van Dyke, *New Castle*

## GEORGIA

### SENATORS

John Milledge,[12] *Augusta*
Charles Tait,[13] *Elbert*

William H. Crawford, *Lexington*

### REPRESENTATIVES AT LARGE

William W. Bibb, *Petersburg*
Howell Cobb, *Louisville*
Dennis Smelt, *Savannah*
George M. Troup, *Dublin*

## KENTUCKY

### SENATORS

Buckner Thruston,[14] *Lexington*
Henry Clay,[15] *Lexington*
John Pope, *Springfield*

### REPRESENTATIVES

Benjamin Howard,[16] *Lexington*
William T. Barry,[17] *Lexington*
Henry Crist, *Shepherdsville*
Joseph Desha, *Mays Lick*
Richard M. Johnson, *Great Crossings*
Matthew Lyon, *Eddyville*
Samuel McKee, *Lancaster*

## MARYLAND

### SENATORS

Samuel Smith,[18] *Baltimore*
Philip Reed, *Chestertown*

### REPRESENTATIVES

John Brown,[19] *Centerville*
Robert Wright,[20] *Queenstown*
John Campbell, *Port Tobacco*
Charles Goldsborough, *Cambridge*
Philip B. Key, *Rockville*
Alexander McKim, *Baltimore*
John Montgomery, *Bel Air*
Nicholas R. Moore, *Ruxton*
Roger Nelson,[21] *Frederick*
Samuel Ringgold,[22] *Hagerstown*
Archibald Van Horne, *Prince Georges County*

## MASSACHUSETTS

### SENATORS

Timothy Pickering, *Wendham*
James Lloyd, *Boston*

### REPRESENTATIVES

Ezekiel Bacon, *Pittsfield*
William Baylies,[23] *Bridgewater*
Charles Turner, Jr.,[24] *Scituate*
Orchard Cook, *Wiscasset*
Richard Cutts, *Pepperelboro*
William Ely, *Springfield*
Gideon Gardner, *Nantucket*
Barzillai Gannett, *Gardiner*
Edward St. Loe Livermore, *Newburyport*

---

[1] Elected June 26, 1809.
[2] Elected February 28, 1810; reelected April 17, 1810.
[3] Elected February 23, 1811.
[4] Reelected May 22, 1809.
[5] Reelected May 22, 1809.
[6] Resigned June 10, 1810.
[7] Elected to fill vacancy caused by resignation of James Hillhouse, and took his seat December 4, 1810.
[8] Resigned in May, 1810, having been elected Senator.
[9] Elected to fill vacancy caused by resignation of Samuel W. Dana, and took his seat December 3, 1810.
[10] Died November 4, 1809.

[11] Elected to fill vacancy caused by death of Samuel White, and took his seat January 29, 1810.
[12] Resigned November 14, 1809.
[13] Elected to fill vacancy caused by resignation of John Milledge, and took his seat December 28, 1809.
[14] Resigned December 18, 1809.
[15] Elected to fill vacancy caused by resignation of Buckner Thruston, and took his seat February 5, 1810.
[16] Resigned April 10, 1810, to become governor of Upper Louisiana.
[17] Elected to fill vacancy caused by resignation of Benjamin Howard, and took his seat December 13, 1810.

[18] Appointed and subsequently reelected for the term beginning March 4, 1809.
[19] Resigned in 1810, before the commencement of the Twelfth Congress, to which he had been reelected.
[20] Elected to fill vacancy caused by resignation of John Brown, and took his seat December 3, 1810.
[21] Resigned May 14, 1810.
[22] Elected to fill vacancy caused by resignation of Roger Nelson, and took his seat December 7, 1810.
[23] Served until June 28, 1809; succeeded by Charles Turner, Jr., who contested his election.
[24] Successfully contested the election of William Baylies, and took his seat June 28, 1809.

## MASSACHUSETTS— Continued

### REPRESENTATIVES—CONTINUED

Benjamin Pickman, Jr., *Salem*
Josiah Quincy, *Boston*
Ebenezer Seaver, *Roxbury*
William Stedman,[25] *Worcester*
Abijah Bigelow,[26] *Leominster*
Samuel Taggart, *Colerain*
Jabez Upham,[27] *Brookfield*
Joseph Allen,[28] *Worcester*
Joseph B. Varnum, *Dracut*
Laban Wheaton, *Easton*
Ezekiel Whitman, *Portland*

## NEW HAMPSHIRE

### SENATORS

Nicholas Gilman, *Exeter*
Nahum Parker,[29] *Fitzwilliam*
Charles Cutts,[30] *Portsmouth*

### REPRESENTATIVES AT LARGE

Daniel Blaisdell, *Canaan*
John C. Chamberlain, *Charlestown*
William Hale, *Dover*
Nathaniel A. Haven, *Portsmouth*
James Wilson, *Peterboro*

## NEW JERSEY

### SENATORS

Aaron Kitchell,[31] *Hanover*
John Condit,[32] *Orange*
John Lambert, *Lambertville*

### REPRESENTATIVES AT LARGE

Adam Boyd, *Hackensack*
James Cox,[33] *Monmouth*
John A. Scudder,[34] *Monmouth*
William Helms, *Hackettstown*
Thomas Newbold, *Springfield Township*
Henry Southard, *Baskingridge*
Jacob Hufty, *Salem*

## NEW YORK

### SENATORS

John Smith, *Mastic*
Obadiah German, *Norwich*

### REPRESENTATIVES

William Denning,[35] *New York City*
Samuel L. Mitchill,[36] *New York City*

James Emott, *Albany*
Jonathan Fisk, *Newburgh*
Barent Gardenier, *Kingston*
Thomas R. Gold, *Whitestown*
Herman Knickerbocker, *Schaghticoke*
Robert Le Roy Livingston, *Hudson*
Vincent Mathews, *Elmira*
Gurdon S. Mumford, *New York City*
John Nicholson, *Herkimer*
Peter B. Porter, *Buffalo*
Erastus Root, *Delhi*
Ebenezer Sage, *Sag Harbor*
Thomas Sammons, *Johnstown*
John Thompson, *Stillwater*
Uri Tracy, *Oxford*
Killian K. Van Rensselaer, *Albany*

## NORTH CAROLINA

### SENATORS

James Turner, *Warrenton*
Jesse Franklin, *Surry County*

### REPRESENTATIVES

Willis Alston, *Greenville*
James Cochran, *Roxboro*
Meshack Franklin, *Surry County*
James Holland, *Rutherford County*
Thomas Kenan, *Kenansville*
William Kennedy, *Washington*
Nathaniel Macon, *Warrenton*
Archibald McBryde, *Carthage*
Joseph Pearson, *Salisbury*
Lemuel Sawyer, *Elizabeth City*
Richard Stanford, *Hawfields*
John Stanly, *New Bern*

## OHIO

### SENATORS

Return J. Meigs, Jr.,[37] *Marietta*
Thomas Worthington,[38] *Chillicothe*
Stanley Griswold,[39] *Doan's Corners*
Alexander Campbell,[40] *Ripley*

### REPRESENTATIVE AT LARGE

Jeremiah Morrow, *Montgomery*

## PENNSYLVANIA

### SENATORS

Andrew Gregg, *Pennvalley*
Michael Leib, *Philadelphia*

### REPRESENTATIVES

William Anderson, *Chester*
David Bard, *Frankstown*
Robert Brown, *Weaversville*
William Crawford, *Gettysburg*
William Findley, *Youngstown*
Daniel Hiester, *West Chester*
Robert Jenkins, *Churchtown*
Aaron Lyle, *West Middletown*
William Milnor, *Philadelphia*
John Porter, *Philadelphia*
John Rea, *Chambersburg*
Matthias Richards, *Pottstown*
John Ross, *Easton*
Benjamin Say,[41] *Philadelphia*
Adam Seybert,[42] *Philadelphia*
John Smilie, *Fayette*
George Smith
Samuel Smith, *Erie*
Robert Whitehill, *Camp Hill*

## RHODE ISLAND

### SENATORS

Elisha Mathewson, *Scituate*
Francis Malbone,[43] *Newport*
Christopher G. Champlin,[44] *Newport*

### REPRESENTATIVES AT LARGE

Richard Jackson, Jr., *Providence*
Elisha R. Potter, *Kingston*

## SOUTH CAROLINA

### SENATORS

Thomas Sumter,[45] *Stateburg*
John Taylor,[46] *Columbia*
John Gaillard, *Charleston*

### REPRESENTATIVES

Lemuel J. Alston, *Greenville*
William Butler, *Saluda*
Joseph Calhoun, *Calhoun Mills*
Robert Marion,[47] *Charleston*
Langdon Cheves,[48] *Charleston*
Thomas Moore, *Prices Store*
John Taylor,[49] *Columbia*
Richard Winn, *Winnsboro*
Robert Witherspoon, *Mayesville*

## TENNESSEE

### SENATORS

Joseph Anderson[50]
Daniel Smith,[51] *Hendersonville*

---

[25] Resigned July 16, 1810.
[26] Elected to fill vacancy caused by resignation of William Stedman, and took his seat December 14, 1810.
[27] Resigned in 1810.
[28] Elected to fill vacancy caused by resignation of Jabez Upham, and took his seat December 13, 1810.
[29] Resigned June 1, 1810.
[30] Elected to fill vacancy caused by resignation of Nahum Parker, and took his seat December 4, 1810.
[31] Resigned March 12, 1809.
[32] Appointed to fill vacancy caused by resignation of Aaron Kitchill, and took his seat May 24, 1809; subsequently elected.
[33] Died September 12, 1810.
[34] Elected to fill vacancy caused by death of James Cox, and took his seat December 3, 1810.

[35] Resigned before qualifying.
[36] Elected to fill vacancy caused by resignation of William Denning, and took his seat December 4, 1810.
[37] Resigned May 1, 1810.
[38] Elected to fill vacancy caused by resignation of Return J. Meigs, Jr., and took his seat January 8, 1811.
[39] Appointed to fill vacancy caused by resignation of Edward Tiffin, in preceding Congress, and took his seat June 2, 1809.
[40] Elected to fill vacancy caused by resignation of Edward Tiffin, and took his seat January 12, 1810.
[41] Resigned June, 1809.
[42] Elected to fill vacancy caused by resignation of Benjamin Say, and took his seat November 27, 1809.
[43] Died June 4, 1809.

[44] Elected to fill vacancy caused by death of Francis Malbone, and took his seat January 12, 1810.
[45] Resigned December 16, 1810.
[46] Elected December 19, 1810, to fill vacancy caused by resignation of Thomas Sumter, and took his seat December 31, 1810.
[47] Resigned December 4, 1810.
[48] Elected to fill vacancy caused by resignation of Robert Marion, and took his seat January 24, 1811.
[49] Resigned December 30, 1810, having been elected Senator.
[50] Appointed to fill vacancy in term commencing March 4, 1809, caused by failure of legislature to elect; subsequently elected, and took his seat May 22, 1809.
[51] Resigned March 31, 1809.

Jenkin Whiteside,[52] *Knoxville*

### REPRESENTATIVES
Pleasant M. Miller, *Knoxville*
John Rhea, *Sullivan*
Robert Weakley, *Nashville*

## VERMONT

### SENATORS
Stephen R. Bradley, *Westminster*
Jonathan Robinson, *Bennington*

### REPRESENTATIVES
William Chamberlain, *Peacham*
Martin Chittenden, *Williston*
Jonathan H. Hubbard, *Windsor*
Samuel Shaw, *Castleton*

## VIRGINIA

### SENATORS
William B. Giles, *Ladore*
Richard Brent, *Aquia*

### REPRESENTATIVES
Burwell Bassett, *Williamsburg*
James Breckinridge, *Fincastle*
William A. Burwell, *Rocky Mount*
Matthew Clay, *Halifax*
John Clopton, *Tunstall*
John G. Jackson,[53] *Clarksburg*
William McKinley[54]
John Dawson
John W. Eppes, *Charles City*
Thomas Gholson, Jr., *Brunswick*
Peterson Goodwyn, *Petersburg*
Edwin Gray
Walter Jones, *Northumberland County*
Joseph Lewis, Jr., *Upperville*
John Love, *Alexandria*
Thomas Newton, Jr., *Norfolk*
Wilson C. Nicholas,[55] *Charlottesville*
David S. Garland,[56] *Clifford*
John Randolph, *Charlotte*

John Roane, *Uppowac*
Daniel Sheffey, *Wythe*
John Smith, *Frederick County*
James Stephenson, *Martinsburg*
Jacob Swoope, *Staunton*

## INDIANA TERRITORY

### DELEGATE
Jonathan Jennings,[57] *Charlestown*

## MISSISSIPPI TERRITORY

### DELEGATE
George Poindexter, *Woodville*

## TERRITORY OF ORLEANS

### DELEGATE
Julien de L. Poydras, *New Orleans*

---

[52] Elected to fill vacancy caused by resignation of Daniel Smith, and took his seat May 26, 1809.

[53] Resigned September 28, 1810.

[54] Elected to fill vacancy caused by resignation of John G. Jackson, and took his seat December 21, 1810.

[55] Resigned November 27, 1809.

[56] Elected to fill vacancy caused by resignation of Wilson C. Nicholas, and took his seat January 17, 1810.

[57] Took his seat November 27, 1809; election unsuccessfully contested by Thomas Randolph.

# 12TH CONGRESS

## MARCH 4, 1811, TO MARCH 3, 1813

FIRST SESSION— *November 4, 1811, to July 6, 1812*
SECOND SESSION— *November 2, 1812, to March 3, 1813*

George Clinton
Vice President

Henry Clay
Speaker

VICE PRESIDENT OF THE UNITED STATES— GEORGE CLINTON,[1] of New York
PRESIDENT PRO TEMPORE OF THE SENATE— WILLIAM H. CRAWFORD,[2] of Georgia
SECRETARY OF THE SENATE— SAMUEL A. OTIS, of Massachusetts
SERGEANT AT ARMS OF THE SENATE— JAMES MATHERS,[3] of New York; MOUNTJOY BAYLY,[4] of Maryland

SPEAKER OF THE HOUSE OF REPRESENTATIVES— HENRY CLAY,[5] of Kentucky
CLERK OF THE HOUSE— PATRICK MAGRUDER,[6] of Maryland
SERGEANT AT ARMS OF THE HOUSE— THOMAS DUNN, of Maryland
DOORKEEPER OF THE HOUSE— THOMAS CLAXTON

## CONNECTICUT

### SENATORS
Chauncey Goodrich, *Hartford*
Samuel W. Dana, *Middlesex*

### REPRESENTATIVES AT LARGE
Epaphroditus Champion, *East Haddam*
John Davenport, *Stamford*
Lyman Law, *New London*
Jonathan O. Moseley, *East Haddam*
Timothy Pitkin, *Farmington*
Lewis B. Sturges, *Fairfield*
Benjamin Tallmadge, *Litchfield*

## DELAWARE

### SENATORS
James A. Bayard,[7] *Wilmington*
Outerbridge Horsey, *Wilmington*

### REPRESENTATIVE AT LARGE
Henry M. Ridgely, *Dover*

## GEORGIA

### SENATORS
William H. Crawford, *Lexington*
Charles Tait, *Elbert*

### REPRESENTATIVES AT LARGE
William W. Bibb, *Petersburg*
Howell Cobb,[8] *Louisville*
William Barnett,[9] *Washington*
Bolling Hall, *Milledgeville*

George M. Troup, *Dublin*

## KENTUCKY

### SENATORS
John Pope, *Springfield*
George M. Bibb, *Lexington*

### REPRESENTATIVES
Henry Clay, *Lexington*
Joseph Desha, *Mays Lick*
Richard M. Johnson, *Great Crossings*
Samuel McKee, *Lancaster*
Anthony New, *Elkton*
Stephen Ormsby, *Louisville*

## LOUISIANA[10]

### SENATORS
Allan B. Magruder,[11] *Opelousas*
John N. Destréhan,[12] *Destrehan*
Thomas Posey,[13] *Attakapas*
James Brown,[14] *New Orleans*

### REPRESENTATIVE AT LARGE
Thomas B. Robertson,[15] *New Orleans*

## MARYLAND

### SENATORS
Samuel Smith, *Baltimore*
Philip Reed, *Chestertown*

### REPRESENTATIVES
Charles Goldsborough, *Cambridge*
Joseph Kent, *Bladensburg*

Philip B. Key, *Rockville*
Peter Little, *Baltimore*
Alexander McKim, *Baltimore*
John Montgomery,[16] *Bel Air*
Stevenson Archer,[17] *Bel Air*
Samuel Ringgold, *Hagerstown*
Philip Stuart, *Port Tobacco*
Robert Wright,[18] *Queenstown*

## MASSACHUSETTS

### SENATORS
James Lloyd, *Boston*
Joseph B. Varnum,[19] *Dracut*

### REPRESENTATIVES
Ezekiel Bacon, *Pittsfield*
Abijah Bigelow, *Leominster*
Elijah Brigham, *Westboro*
Richard Cutts, *Pepperelboro*
William Ely, *Springfield*
Barzillai Gannett,[20] *Gardiner*
Francis Carr,[21] *Orrington*
Isaiah L. Green, *Barnstable*
Josiah Quincy, *Boston*
William Reed, *Marblehead*
Ebenezer Seaver, *Roxbury*
Samuel Taggart, *Colerain*
Peleg Tallman, *Bath*
Charles Turner, Jr., *Scituate*

---

[1] Died April 20, 1812.
[2] Elected March 24, 1812.
[3] Died September 2, 1811.
[4] Elected November 6, 1811.
[5] Elected November 4, 1811.
[6] Reelected November 4, 1811.
[7] Resigned March 3, 1813.
[8] Resigned in 1812.
[9] Elected to fill vacancy caused by resignation of Howell Cobb, and took his seat November 27, 1812.
[10] Admitted as a State into the Union April 30, 1812; formerly known as "Territory of Orleans."
[11] Took his seat November 18, 1812; term to expire, as determined by lot, March 3, 1813.

[12] Resigned October 1, 1812, never having qualified.
[13] Appointed to fill vacancy caused by resignation of John N. Destréhan, and took his seat December 7, 1812; term to expire, as determined by lot, March 3, 1817.
[14] Elected to fill vacancy caused by resignation of John N. Destréhan, and took his seat February 5, 1813.
[15] Took his seat December 23, 1812.
[16] Resigned April 29, 1811, before Congress assembled.
[17] Elected to fill vacancy caused by resignation of

John Montgomery, and took his seat November 4, 1811.
[18] Elected to fill vacancy caused by resignation of Representative-elect John Brown, in preceding Congress.
[19] Elected to fill vacancy in the term beginning March 4, 1811, caused by failure of legislature to elect, and took his seat November 4, 1811; vacancy in this class from March 4, 1811, to June 7, 1811.
[20] Resigned in 1812, never having qualified.
[21] Elected to fill vacancy caused by failure of Barzillai Gannett to qualify; took his seat June 3, 1812.

Joseph B. Varnum,[22] *Dracut*
William M. Richardson,[23] *Groton*
Laban Wheaton, *Easton*
Leonard White, *Haverhill*
William Widgery, *Portland*

## NEW HAMPSHIRE

SENATORS

Nicholas Gilman, *Exeter*
Charles Cutts, *Portsmouth*

REPRESENTATIVES AT LARGE

Josiah Bartlett, Jr., *Stratham*
Samuel Dinsmoor, *Keene*
Obed Hall, *Bartlett*
John A. Harper, *Meredith Bridge*
George Sullivan, *Exeter*

## NEW JERSEY

SENATORS

John Lambert, *Lambertville*
John Condit, *Orange*

REPRESENTATIVES AT LARGE

Adam Boyd, *Hackensack*
Lewis Condict, *Morristown*
Jacob Hufty, *Salem*
George C. Maxwell, *Raritan*
James Morgan, *South Amboy*
Thomas Newbold, *Springfield Township*

## NEW YORK

SENATORS

John Smith, *Mastic*
Obadiah German, *Norwich*

REPRESENTATIVES

Daniel Avery, *Aurora*
Harmanus Bleecker, *Albany*
Thomas B. Cooke, *Catskill*
James Emott, *Albany*
Asa Fitch, *Salem*
Thomas R. Gold, *Whitestown*
Robert Le Roy Livingston,[24] *Hudson*
Thomas P. Grosvenor,[25] *Hudson*
Arunah Metcalf, *Otsego*
Samuel L. Mitchill, *New York City*
William Paulding, Jr., *New York City*
Benjamin Pond, *Schroon*
Peter B. Porter, *Buffalo*
Ebenezer Sage, *Sag Harbor*
Thomas Sammons, *Johnstown*
Silas Stow, *Lowville*
Uri Tracy, *Oxford*
Pierre Van Cortlandt, Jr., *Peekskill*

## NORTH CAROLINA

SENATORS

James Turner, *Warrenton*
Jesse Franklin, *Surry County*

REPRESENTATIVES

Willis Alston, *Greenville*
William Blackledge, *Spring Hill*
Thomas Blount,[26] *Tarboro*
William Kennedy,[27] *Washington*
James Cochran, *Roxboro*
Meshack Franklin, *Surry County*
William R. King, *Wilmington*
Nathaniel Macon, *Warrenton*
Archibald McBryde, *Carthage*
Joseph Pearson, *Salisbury*
Israel Pickens, *Morgantown*
Lemuel Sawyer, *Elizabeth City*
Richard Stanford, *Hawfields*

## OHIO

SENATORS

Alexander Campbell, *Ripley*
Thomas Worthington, *Chillicothe*

REPRESENTATIVE AT LARGE

Jeremiah Morrow, *Montgomery*

## PENNSYLVANIA

SENATORS

Andrew Gregg, *Pennvalley*
Michael Leib, *Philadelphia*

REPRESENTATIVES

William Anderson, *Chester*
David Bard, *Frankstown*
Robert Brown, *Weaversville*
William Crawford, *Gettysburg*
Roger Davis, *Charlestown*
William Findley, *Youngstown*
John M. Hyneman, *Reading*
Abner Lacock,[28] *Beavertown*
Joseph Lefever, *Paradise*
Aaron Lyle, *West Middletown*
James Milnor, *Philadelphia*
William Piper, *Bloodyrun*
Jonathan Roberts, *Norristown*
William Rodman, *Bristol*
Adam Seybert, *Philadelphia*
John Smilie,[29] *Fayette*
George Smith
Robert Whitehill, *Camp Hill*

## RHODE ISLAND

SENATORS

Christopher G. Champlin,[30] *Newport*
William Hunter,[31] *Newport*
Jeremiah B. Howell, *Providence*

REPRESENTATIVES AT LARGE

Richard Jackson, Jr., *Providence*
Elisha R. Potter, *Kingston*

## SOUTH CAROLINA

SENATORS

John Gaillard, *Charleston*
John Taylor, *Columbia*

REPRESENTATIVES

William Butler, *Saluda*
John C. Calhoun, *Willington*
Langdon Cheves, *Charleston*
Elias Earle, *Centerville*
William Lowndes, *Jacksonboro*
Thomas Moore, *Prices Store*
David R. Williams, *Society Hill*
Richard Winn, *Winnsboro*

## TENNESSEE

SENATORS

Joseph Anderson
Jenkin Whiteside,[32] *Knoxville*
George W. Campbell,[33] *Nashville*

REPRESENTATIVES

Felix Grundy, *Nashville*
John Sevier, *Knoxville*
John Rhea, *Sullivan*

## VERMONT

SENATORS

Stephen R. Bradley, *Westminster*
Jonathan Robinson, *Bennington*

REPRESENTATIVES

Martin Chittenden, *Williston*
James Fisk, *Barre*
Samuel Shaw, *Castleton*
William Strong, *Hartford*

## VIRGINIA

SENATORS

William B. Giles, *Lodore*
Richard Brent, *Aquia*

REPRESENTATIVES

Burwell Bassett, *Williamsburg*
James Breckinridge, *Fincastle*
William A. Burwell, *Rocky Mount*
Matthew Clay, *Halifax*
John Clopton, *Tunstall*
John Dawson
Thomas Gholson, Jr., *Brunswick*
Peterson Goodwyn, *Petersburg*
Edwin Gray
Aylett Hawes, *Woodville*

---

[22] Resigned June 29, 1811, before Congress assembled, having been elected Senator.
[23] Elected to fill vacancy caused by resignation of Joseph B. Varnum, and took his seat January 22, 1812.
[24] Resigned May 6, 1812.
[25] Elected to fill vacancy caused by resignation of Robert Le Roy Livingston, and took his seat January 29, 1813.

[26] Died February 7, 1812.
[27] Elected to fill vacancy caused by death of Thomas Blount, and took his seat January 30, 1813.
[28] Reelected to the Thirteenth Congress, but resigned, having been elected Senator.
[29] Died December 30, 1812, before the commencement of the Thirteenth Congress, to which he had been reelected.

[30] Resigned October 2, 1811.
[31] Elected to fill vacancy caused by resignation of Christopher G. Champlin, and took his seat November 25, 1811.
[32] Resigned October 8, 1811.
[33] Elected to fill vacancy caused by resignation of Jenkin Whiteside, and took his seat November 4, 1811.

## VIRGINIA—Continued

REPRESENTATIVES—CONTINUED

John P. Hungerford,[34] *Leedstown*
John Taliaferro,[35] *Fredericksburg*
John Baker, *Shepherdstown*
Joseph Lewis, Jr., *Upperville*
William McCoy, *Franklin*
Hugh Nelson, *Milton*
Thomas Newton, Jr., *Norfolk*
James Pleasants, *Goochland*
John Randolph, *Charlotte*
John Roane, *Uppowac*

Daniel Sheffey, *Wythe*
John Smith, *Frederick County*
Thomas Wilson, *Morgantown*

## ILLINOIS TERRITORY[36]

DELEGATE

Shadrack Bond,[37] *Kaskaskia*

## INDIANA TERRITORY

DELEGATE

Jonathan Jennings, *Charlestown*

## MISSISSIPPI TERRITORY

DELEGATE

George Poindexter, *Woodville*

## TERRITORY OF MISSOURI[38]

DELEGATE

Edward Hempstead,[39] *St. Louis*

## TERRITORY OF ORLEANS[40]

DELEGATE

Vacant[41]

---

[34] Served until November 29, 1811; succeeded by John Taliaferro, who contested his election.

[35] Successfully contested the election of John P. Hungerford, and took his seat December 2, 1811.

[36] Formed by act approved February 3, 1809, from a portion of Indiana Territory and from lands originally ceded to the United States by the State of Virginia, and granted a Delegate in Congress.

[37] Took his seat December 3, 1812.

[38] Formed by the act approved June 4, 1812, from lands ceded by France to the United States by the treaty of Paris of April 30, 1803, theretofore known as the "District of Louisiana," and granted a Delegate in Congress.

[39] Took his seat January 4, 1813.

[40] Granted statehood April 30, 1812, as the State of Louisiana.

[41] Allen B. Magruder and Elegius Fromentin, agents were accorded the privilege of the floor March 6, 1812.

# 13TH CONGRESS

## MARCH 4, 1813, TO MARCH 3, 1815

FIRST SESSION— *May 24, 1813, to August 2, 1813*
SECOND SESSION— *December 6, 1813, to April 18, 1814*
THIRD SESSION— *September 19, 1814, to March 3, 1815*

Elbridge Gerry
Vice President

VICE PRESIDENT OF THE UNITED STATES— Elbridge Gerry,[1] of Massachusetts
PRESIDENT PRO TEMPORE OF THE SENATE— Joseph B. Varnum,[2] of Massachusetts; John Gaillard,[3] of South Carolina
SECRETARY OF THE SENATE— Samuel A. Otis,[4] of Massachusetts; Charles Cutts,[5] of New Hampshire
SERGEANT AT ARMS OF THE SENATE— Mountjoy Bayly, of Maryland

Henry Clay
Speaker

SPEAKER OF THE HOUSE OF REPRESENTATIVES— Henry Clay,[6] of Kentucky; Langdon Cheves,[7] of South Carolina
CLERK OF THE HOUSE— Patrick Magruder,[8] of Maryland; Thomas Dougherty,[9] of Kentucky
SERGEANT AT ARMS OF THE HOUSE— Thomas Dunn, of Maryland
DOORKEEPER OF THE HOUSE— Thomas Claxton

## CONNECTICUT

### SENATORS

Chauncey Goodrich,[10] *Hartford*
David Daggett,[11] *New Haven*
Samuel W. Dana, *Middlesex*

### REPRESENTATIVES AT LARGE

Epaphroditus Champion, *East Haddam*
John Davenport, *Stamford*
Lyman Law, *New London*
Jonathan O. Moseley, *East Haddam*
Timothy Pitkin, *Farmington*
Lewis B. Sturges, *Fairfield*
Benjamin Tallmadge, *Litchfield*

## DELAWARE

### SENATORS

Outerbridge Horsey, *Wilmington*
William H. Wells,[12] *Dagsborough*

### REPRESENTATIVES AT LARGE

Thomas Cooper, *Georgetown*
Henry M. Ridgely, *Dover*

## GEORGIA

### SENATORS

William H. Crawford,[13] *Lexington*
William B. Bulloch,[14] *Savannah*
William W. Bibb,[15] *Petersburg*
Charles Tait, *Elbert*

### REPRESENTATIVES AT LARGE

William Barnett, *Washington*
William W. Bibb,[16] *Petersburg*
Alfred Cuthbert,[17] *Eaton*
John Forsyth, *Augusta*
Bolling Hall, *Milledgeville*
Thomas Telfair, *Savannah*
George M. Troup, *Dublin*

## KENTUCKY

### SENATORS

George M. Bibb,[18] *Lexington*
George Walker,[19] *Nicholasville*
William T. Barry,[20] *Lexington*
Jesse Bledsoe,[21] *Lexington*
Isham Talbot,[22] *Frankfort*

### REPRESENTATIVES

James Clark, *Winchester*
Henry Clay,[23] *Lexington*

Joseph H. Hawkins,[24] *Lexington*
Joseph Desha, *Mays Lick*
William P. Duval, *Bardstown*
Samuel Hopkins, *Henderson*
Richard M. Johnson, *Great Crossings*
Samuel McKee, *Lancaster*
Thomas Montgomery, *Stanford*
Stephen Ormsby,[25] *Louisville*
Solomon P. Sharp, *Russellville*

## LOUISIANA

### SENATORS

James Brown, *New Orleans*
Eligius Fromentin, *New Orleans*

### REPRESENTATIVE AT LARGE

Thomas B. Robertson, *New Orleans*

## MARYLAND

### SENATORS

Samuel Smith, *Baltimore*
Robert H. Goldsborough,[26] *Easton*

### REPRESENTATIVES

Stevenson Archer, *Bel Air*
Charles Goldsborough, *Cambridge*

---

[1] Died November 23, 1814.
[2] Elected December 6, 1813.
[3] Elected April 18, 1814; November 25, 1814, upon the death of Vice President Elbridge Gerry.
[4] Died April 22, 1814.
[5] Elected October 11, 1814; Samuel Turner, Jr., the chief clerk, was appointed on September 19, 1814, to act in the interim.
[6] Reelected May 24, 1813; resigned from Congress January 19, 1814.
[7] Elected January 19, 1814, to fill vacancy caused by resignation of Henry Clay.
[8] Reelected May 24, 1813; resigned January 28, 1815, while resolution was pending to remove him from office and to elect a successor.
[9] Elected January 30, 1815.
[10] Resigned in May 1813.
[11] Elected to fill vacancy caused by resignation of Chauncey Goodrich, and took his seat May 24, 1813.

[12] Elected to fill vacancy caused by resignation of James A. Bayard, in preceding Congress, and took his seat June 10, 1813.
[13] Resigned March 23, 1813.
[14] Appointed to fill vacancy caused by resignation of William H. Crawford, and took his seat May 24, 1813.
[15] Elected to fill vacancy caused by resignation of William H. Crawford, and took his seat December 6, 1813.
[16] Resigned November 6, 1813, having been elected Senator.
[17] Elected to fill vacancy caused by resignation of William W. Bibb, and took his seat February 7, 1814.
[18] Resigned August 23, 1814.
[19] Appointed to fill vacancy caused by resignation of George M. Bibb, and took his seat October 10, 1814.
[20] Elected to fill vacancy caused by resignation of George M. Bibb, and took his seat February 2, 1815.

[21] Resigned December 24, 1814. In response to personal inquiry, Senate passed resolution January 20, 1815, declaring seat vacant. (See U.S. Senate Election, Expulsion and Censure Cases, 1793-1990, Senate Document 103-33, pp. 29-30.)
[22] Elected to fill vacancy caused by resignation of Jesse Bledsoe, and took his seat February 2, 1815.
[23] Resigned January 19, 1814, to accept "special and important diplomatic mission."
[24] Elected to fill vacancy caused by resignation of Henry Clay, and took his seat March 29, 1814.
[25] Elected to fill vacancy caused by death of Representative-elect John Simpson (January 22, 1813) before the beginning of the congressional term, and took his seat May 28, 1813.
[26] Elected for term beginning March 4, 1813, and took his seat May 27, 1813; vacancy in this class from March 4, 1813, to May 12, 1813.

## MARYLAND—Continued

REPRESENTATIVES—CONTINUED

Alexander C. Hanson, *Rockville*
Joseph Kent, *Bladensburg*
Alexander McKim, *Baltimore*
Nicholas R. Moore, *Ruxton*
Samuel Ringgold, *Hagerstown*
Philip Stuart, *Port Tobacco*
Robert Wright, *Queenstown*

## MASSACHUSETTS

SENATORS

James Lloyd,[27] *Boston*
Christopher Gore,[28] *Boston*
Joseph B. Varnum, *Dracut*

REPRESENTATIVES

William Baylies, *Bridgewater*
Abijah Bigelow, *Leominster*
George Bradbury, *Portland*
Elijah Brigham, *Westboro*
William M. Richardson,[29] *Groton*
Samuel Dana,[30] *Groton*
Samuel Davis, *Bath*
Daniel Dewey,[31] *Williamstown*
John W. Hulbert,[32] *Pittsfield*
William Ely, *Springfield*
Levi Hubbard, *Paris*
Cyrus King, *Saco*
James Parker, *Gardiner*
Timothy Pickering, *Wendham*
John Reed, *Yarmouth*
William Reed, *Marblehead*
Nathaniel Ruggles, *Boston*
Samuel Taggart, *Colerain*
Artemas Ward, Jr., *Boston*
Laban Wheaton, *Easton*
John Wilson, *Belfast*
Abiel Wood, *Wiscasset*

## NEW HAMPSHIRE

SENATORS

Nicholas Gilman,[33] *Exeter*
Thomas W. Thompson,[34] *Concord*
Charles Cutts,[35] *Portsmouth*
Jeremiah Mason,[36] *Portsmouth*

REPRESENTATIVES AT LARGE

Bradbury Cilley, *Nottingham*
William Hale, *Dover*
Samuel Smith, *Peterboro*
Roger Vose, *Walpole*
Daniel Webster, *Portsmouth*
Jeduthun Wilcox, *Orford*

## NEW JERSEY

SENATORS

John Lambert, *Lambertville*
John Condit, *Orange*

REPRESENTATIVES

Lewis Condict, *Morristown*
William Coxe, *Burlington*
Jacob Hufty,[37] *Salem*
Thomas Bines,[38] *Pennsville*
James Schureman, *New Brunswick*
Richard Stockton, *Princeton*
Thomas Ward, *Newark*

## NEW YORK

SENATORS

Obadiah German, *Norwich*
Rufus King, *New York City*

REPRESENTATIVES

Daniel Avery, *Aurora*
Egbert Benson,[39] *New York City*
William Irving,[40] *New York City*
John M. Bowers,[41] *Cooperstown*
Isaac Williams, Jr.,[42] *Cooperstown*
Alexander Boyd, *Middleburg*
Oliver C. Comstock, *Trumansburg*
Peter Denoyelles, *Haverstraw*
Jonathan Fisk, *Newburgh*
James Geddes, *Onondaga*
Thomas P. Grosvenor, *Hudson*
Abraham J. Hasbrouck, *Kingston*
Samuel M. Hopkins, *New York City*
Nathaniel W. Howell, *Canadaigua*
Moss Kent, *Leraysville*
John Lefferts, *Brooklyn*
John Lovett, *Albany*
Jacob Markell, *Manheim*
Morris S. Miller, *Utica*
Hosea Moffitt, *Nassau*
Thomas J. Oakley, *Poughkeepsie*
Jotham Post, Jr., *New York City*

Ebenezer Sage, *Sag Harbor*
Samuel Sherwood, *Delhi*
Zebulon R. Shipherd, *Granville*
William S. Smith, *Lebanon*
John W. Taylor, *Ballston Spa*
Joel Thompson, *Smyrna*
Elisha J. Winter, *Peru*

## NORTH CAROLINA

SENATORS

James Turner, *Warrenton*
David Stone,[43] *Raleigh*
Francis Locke,[44] *Salisbury*

REPRESENTATIVES

Willis Alston, *Greenville*
John Culpepper, *Allenton*
Peter Forney, *Lincolnton*
Meshack Franklin, *Surry County*
William Gaston, *New Bern*
William Kennedy, *Washington*
William R. King, *Wilmington*
Nathaniel Macon, *Warrenton*
William H. Murfree, *Murfreesburg*
Joseph Pearson, *Salisbury*
Israel Pickens, *Morgantown*
Richard Stanford, *Hawfields*
Bartlett Yancy, *Caswell*

## OHIO

SENATORS

Thomas Worthington,[45] *Chillicothe*
Joseph Kerr,[46] *Chillicothe*
Jeremiah Morrow, *Montgomery*

REPRESENTATIVES

John Alexander, *Xenia*
Reasin Beall,[47] *Wooster*
David Clendenin,[48] *Youngstown*
James Caldwell, *St. Clairsville*
Duncan MacArthur,[49] *Chillicothe*
William Creighton, Jr.,[50] *Chillicothe*
James Kilbourne, *Worthington*
John McLean, *Lebanon*

## PENNSYLVANIA

SENATORS

Michael Leib,[51] *Philadelphia*
Jonathan Roberts,[52] *Norristown*

---

[27] Resigned May 1, 1813.
[28] Appointed to fill vacancy caused by resignation of James Lloyd, and took his seat May 28, 1813; subsequently elected.
[29] Resigned April 18, 1814.
[30] Elected to fill vacancy caused by resignation of William M. Richardson, and took his seat September 22, 1814.
[31] Resigned February 24, 1814, having been appointed justice of supreme judicial court of Massachusetts.
[32] Elected to fill vacancy caused by resignation of Daniel Dewey, and took his seat September 26, 1814.
[33] Died May 2, 1814.
[34] Elected to fill vacancy caused by death of Nicholas Gilman, and took his seat September 19, 1814.
[35] Appointed to fill vacancy in term commencing March 4, 1813, there having been no election, and took his seat May 24, 1813.

[36] Elected to fill vacancy in term commencing March 4, 1813, and took his seat June 21, 1813.
[37] Died May 20, 1814.
[38] Elected to fill vacancy caused by death of Jacob Hufty, and took his seat November 2, 1814.
[39] Resigned August 2, 1813.
[40] Elected to fill vacancy caused by resignation of Egbert Benson, and took his seat January 22, 1814.
[41] Presented credentials as a Member-elect to fill vacancy caused by death of Representative-elect William Dowse (February 18, 1813, before the beginning of the congressional term), and took his seat June 21, 1813; served until December 20, 1813; succeeded by Isaac Williams, Jr., who contested his election.
[42] Successfully contested the election of John M. Bowers, and took his seat January 24, 1814.
[43] Resigned December 24, 1814.
[44] Chosen to fill vacancy caused by resignation of David Stone, but did not qualify.

[45] Resigned December 1, 1814.
[46] Elected to fill vacancy caused by resignation of Thomas Worthington, and took his seat December 30, 1814.
[47] Elected to fill vacancy caused by death of Representative-elect John S. Edwards (February 22, 1813, before the beginning of the congressional term), and took his seat June 8, 1813; resigned June 7, 1814.
[48] Elected to fill vacancy caused by resignation of Reasin Beall, and took his seat December 22, 1814.
[49] Resigned April 5, 1813, before Congress assembled.
[50] Elected to fill vacancy caused by resignation of Duncan MacArthur, and took his seat June 15, 1813.
[51] Resigned February 14, 1814, to become postmaster of Philadelphia.
[52] Elected to fill vacancy caused by resignation of Michael Leib, and took his seat February 28, 1814.

Abner Lacock, *Beavertown*

REPRESENTATIVES

William Anderson, *Chester*
David Bard, *Frankstown*
Robert Brown, *Weaversville*
John Conard, *Germantown*
William Crawford, *Gettysburg*
Roger Davis, *Charlestown*
William Findley, *Youngstown*
Hugh Glasgow, *York*
John Gloninger,[53] *Lebanon*
Edward Crouch,[54] *Paxtang*
Isaac Griffin,[55] *New Geneva*
Jonathan Roberts,[56] *Norristown*
Samuel Henderson,[57] *Norristown*
Charles J. Ingersoll, *Philadelphia*
Samuel D. Ingham, *New Hope*
Jared Irwin, *Sunbury*
Aaron Lyle, *West Middletown*
William Piper, *Bloodyrun*
Adam Seybert, *Philadelphia*
Isaac Smith, *Jersey Shore*
Adamson Tannehill, *Pittsburgh*
John M. Hyneman,[58] *Reading*
Daniel Udree,[59] *Reading*
James Whitehill,[60] *Strasburg*
Amos Slaymaker,[61] *Lancaster*
Robert Whitehill,[62] *Camp Hill*
John Rea,[63] *Chambersburg*
Thomas Wilson,[64] *Erie*

## RHODE ISLAND

SENATORS

Jeremiah B. Howell, *Providence*
William Hunter, *Newport*

REPRESENTATIVES AT LARGE

Richard Jackson, Jr., *Providence*
Elisha R. Potter, *Kingston*

## SOUTH CAROLINA

SENATORS

John Gaillard, *Charleston*
John Taylor, *Columbia*

REPRESENTATIVES

John C. Calhoun, *Willington*
John J. Chappell, *Columbia*

Langdon Cheves, *Charleston*
Elias Earle, *Centerville*
David R. Evans, *Winnsboro*
Samuel Farrow, *Spartanburg*
Theodore Gourdin, *Pineville*
John Kershaw, *Camden*
William Lowndes, *Jacksonboro*

## TENNESSEE

SENATORS

Joseph Anderson
George W. Campbell,[65] *Nashville*
Jesse Wharton,[66] *Nashville*

REPRESENTATIVES

John H. Bowen, *Gallatin*
Felix Grundy,[67] *Nashville*
Newton Cannon,[68] *Harpeth*
Thomas K. Harris,[69] *Sparta*
Parry W. Humphreys, *Nashville*
John Rhea, *Sullivan*
John Sevier, *Knoxville*

## VERMONT

SENATORS

Jonathan Robinson, *Bennington*
Dudley Chase, *Randolph*

REPRESENTATIVES AT LARGE

William C. Bradley, *Westminster*
Ezra Butler, *Waterbury*
James Fisk, *Barre*
Charles Rich, *Shoreham*
Richard Skinner, *Manchester*
William Strong, *Hartford*

## VIRGINIA

SENATORS

William B. Giles,[70] *Lodore*
Richard Brent,[71] *Aquia*
James Barbour,[72] *Barboursville*

REPRESENTATIVES

Thomas M. Bayly,[73] *Drummondtown*
James Breckinridge, *Fincastle*
William A. Burwell, *Rocky Mount*

Hugh Caperton, *Union*
John Clopton, *Tunstall*
John Dawson[74]
Philip P. Barbour,[75] *Orange*
John W. Eppes, *Charles City*
Thomas Gholson, Jr., *Brunswick*
Peterson Goodwyn, *Petersburg*
Aylett Hawes, *Woodville*
John P. Hungerford,[76] *Leedstown*
John G. Jackson, *Clarksburg*
James Johnson, *Suffolk*
John Kerr, *Mountpleasant*
Joseph Lewis, Jr., *Upperville*
William McCoy, *Franklin*
Hugh Nelson, *Milton*
Thomas Newton, Jr., *Norfolk*
James Pleasants, *Goochland*
John Roane, *Uppowoc*
Daniel Sheffey, *Wythe*
John Smith, *Frederick County*
Francis White, *Romney*

## ILLINOIS TERRITORY

DELEGATE

Shadrack Bond,[77] *Kaskaskia*
Benjamin Stephenson,[78] *Edwardsville*

## INDIANA TERRITORY

DELEGATE

Jonathan Jennings, *Charlestown*

## MISSISSIPPI TERRITORY

DELEGATE

William Lattimore, *Liberty*

## TERRITORY OF MISSOURI

DELEGATE

Edward Hempstead,[79] *St. Louis*
Rufus Easton,[80] *St. Louis*

---

[53] Resigned August 2, 1813.
[54] Elected to fill vacancy caused by resignation of John Gloninger, and took his seat December 6, 1813.
[55] Elected to fill vacancy caused by death of Representative-elect John Smilie, in preceding Congress, and took his seat May 24, 1813.
[56] Resigned February 24, 1814, having been elected Senator.
[57] Elected to fill vacancy caused by resignation of Jonathan Roberts, and took his seat November 29, 1814.
[58] Resigned August 2, 1813.
[59] Elected to fill vacancy caused by resignation of John M. Hyneman; took his seat December 6, 1813.
[60] Resigned September 1, 1814.
[61] Elected to fill vacancy caused by resignation of

James Whitehill, and took his seat December 12, 1814.
[62] Died April 8, 1813.
[63] Elected to fill vacancy caused by death of Robert Whitehill, and took his seat May 28, 1813.
[64] Elected to fill vacancy caused by resignation of Representative-elect Abner Lacock, in preceding Congress, and took his seat May 28, 1813.
[65] Resigned February 11, 1814.
[66] Appointed to fill vacancy caused by resignation of George W. Campbell, and took his seat April 9, 1814.
[67] Resigned in 1814.
[68] Elected to fill vacancy caused by resignation of Felix Grundy, and took his seat October 15, 1814.
[69] Election unsuccessfully contested by William Kelly.
[70] Resigned March 3, 1815.

[71] Died December 30, 1814.
[72] Elected to fill vacancy caused by death of Richard Brent, and took his seat January 11, 1815.
[73] Election unsuccessfully contested by Burwell Bassett.
[74] Died March 31, 1814.
[75] Elected to fill vacancy caused by death of John Dawson, and took his seat September 19, 1814.
[76] Election unsuccessfully contested by John Taliaferro.
[77] Served during the first session.
[78] Presented credentials, and took his seat November 14, 1814.
[79] Served during the first and second sessions.
[80] Presented credentials and took his seat November 16, 1814.

# 14TH CONGRESS

MARCH 4, 1815, TO MARCH 3, 1817

FIRST SESSION— *December 4, 1815, to April 30, 1816*
SECOND SESSION— *December 2, 1816, to March 3, 1817*

———

VICE PRESIDENT OF THE UNITED STATES[1]
PRESIDENT PRO TEMPORE OF THE SENATE— JOHN GAILLARD, of South Carolina
SECRETARY OF THE SENATE— CHARLES CUTTS, of New Hampshire
SERGEANT AT ARMS OF THE SENATE— MOUNTJOY BAYLY, of Maryland

———

SPEAKER OF THE HOUSE OF REPRESENTATIVES— HENRY CLAY,[2] of Kentucky
CLERK OF THE HOUSE— THOMAS DOUGHERTY,[3] of Kentucky
SERGEANT AT ARMS OF THE HOUSE— THOMAS DUNN, of Maryland
DOORKEEPER OF THE HOUSE— THOMAS CLAXTON

John Gaillard
President Pro Tempore

Henry Clay
Speaker

## CONNECTICUT

### SENATORS

Samuel W. Dana, *Middlesex*
David Daggett, *New Haven*

### REPRESENTATIVES AT LARGE

Epaphroditus Champion, *East Haddam*
John Davenport, *Stamford*
Lyman Law, *New London*
Jonathan O. Moseley, *East Haddam*
Timothy Pitkin, *Farmington*
Lewis B. Sturges, *Fairfield*
Benjamin Tallmadge, *Litchfield*

## DELAWARE

### SENATORS

Outerbridge Horsey, *Wilmington*
William H. Wells, *Dagsborough*

### REPRESENTATIVES AT LARGE

Thomas Clayton, *Dover*
Thomas Cooper, *Georgetown*

## GEORGIA

### SENATORS

Charles Tait, *Elbert*
William W. Bibb,[4] *Petersburg*
George M. Troup,[5] *Dublin*

### REPRESENTATIVES AT LARGE

Alfred Cuthbert,[6] *Eatonton*

Zadock Cook,[7] *Watkinsville*
John Forsyth, *Augusta*
Bolling Hall, *Milledgeville*
Wilson Lumpkin, *Lexington*
Thomas Telfair, *Savannah*
Richard Henry Wilde, *Augusta*

## INDIANA[8]

### SENATORS

James Noble,[9] *Brookville*
Waller Taylor,[10] *Vincennes*

### REPRESENTATIVE AT LARGE

William Hendricks,[11] *Madison*

## KENTUCKY

### SENATORS

William T. Barry,[12] *Lexington*
Martin D. Hardin,[13] *Frankfort*
Isham Talbot, *Frankfort*

### REPRESENTATIVES

James Clark,[14] *Winchester*
Thomas Fletcher,[15] *Owingsville*
Henry Clay, *Lexington*
Joseph Desha, *Mays Lick*
Benjamin Hardin, *Bardstown*
Richard M. Johnson, *Great Crossings*
Alney McLean, *Greenville*
Samuel McKee, *Lancaster*
Stephen Ormsby, *Louisville*

Solomon P. Sharp, *Bowling Green*
Micah Taul, *Monticello*

## LOUISIANA

### SENATORS

James Brown, *New Orleans*
Eligius Fromentin, *New Orleans*

### REPRESENTATIVE AT LARGE

Thomas B. Robertson, *New Orleans*

## MARYLAND

### SENATORS

Robert H. Goldsborough, *Easton*
Robert G. Harper,[16] *Baltimore*
Alexander C. Hanson,[17] *Rockville*

### REPRESENTATIVES

Stevenson Archer, *Bel Air*
George Baer, *Frederick*
Charles Goldsborough, *Cambridge*
John C. Herbert, *Vannsville*
William Pinkney,[18] *Baltimore*
Peter Little,[19] *Baltimore*
Alexander C. Hanson,[20] *Rockville*
George Peter,[21] *Darnestown*
Nicholas R. Moore,[22] *Ruxton*
Samuel Smith,[23] *Baltimore*
Philip Stuart, *Port Tobacco*
Robert Wright, *Queenstown*

———

[1] Vice President Elbridge Gerry died in preceding Congress.
[2] Elected December 4, 1815.
[3] Reelected December 4, 1815.
[4] Resigned November 9, 1816.
[5] Elected to fill vacancy caused by resignation of William W. Bibb, and took his seat December 12, 1816.
[6] Resigned November 9, 1816.
[7] Elected to fill vacancy caused by resignation of Alfred Cuthbert, and took his seat January 23, 1817.
[8] Admitted as a State into the Union December 11, 1816.
[9] Took his seat December 12, 1816; term to expire, as determined by lot, March 3, 1821.

[10] Took his seat December 12, 1816; term to expire, as determined by lot, March 3, 1819.
[11] Took his seat December 11, 1816.
[12] Resigned May 1, 1816.
[13] Appointed to fill vacancy caused by resignation of William T. Barry, and took his seat December 5, 1816; subsequently elected.
[14] Resigned in 1816.
[15] Elected to fill vacancy caused by resignation of James Clark, and took his seat December 2, 1816.
[16] Elected to serve "from January 29, 1816, to March 3, 1821," and took his seat February 5, 1816; resigned December 6, 1816; vacancy in this class from March 4, 1815, to January 28, 1816, caused by failure

of legislature to elect.
[17] Elected to fill vacancy caused by resignation of Robert G. Harper, and took his seat January 2, 1817.
[18] Resigned April 18, 1816, having been appointed minister to Russia.
[19] Elected to fill vacancy caused by resignation of William Pinkney, and took his seat December 2, 1816.
[20] Resigned in 1816.
[21] Elected to fill vacancy caused by resignation of Alexander C. Hanson, and took his seat December 2, 1816.
[22] Resigned in 1815, before Congress assembled.
[23] Elected to fill vacancy caused by resignation of Nicholas R. Moore, and took his seat February 4, 1816.

## MASSACHUSETTS

### SENATORS

Joseph B. Varnum, *Dracut*
Christopher Gore,[24] *Boston*
Eli P. Ashmun,[25] *Northampton*

### REPRESENTATIVES

William Baylies, *Bridgewater*
George Bradbury, *Portland*
Elijah Brigham,[26] *Westboro*
Benjamin Adams,[27] *Uxbridge*
Benjamin Brown, *Waldoborough*
James Carr, *Bangor*
Samuel S. Connor, *Waterville*
John W. Hulbert, *Pittsfield*
Cyrus King, *Saco*
Elijah H. Mills, *Northampton*
Jeremiah Nelson, *Newburyport*
Albion K. Parris, *Paris*
Timothy Pickering, *Wendham*
John Reed, *Yarmouth*
Thomas Rice, *Augusta*
Nathaniel Ruggles, *Boston*
Asahel Stearns, *Charlestown*
Solomon Strong, *Westminster*
Samuel Taggart, *Colerain*
Artemas Ward, Jr., *Boston*
Laban Wheaton, *Easton*

## NEW HAMPSHIRE

### SENATORS

Jeremiah Mason, *Portsmouth*
Thomas W. Thompson, *Concord*

### REPRESENTATIVES AT LARGE

Charles H. Atherton, *Amhurst*
Bradbury Cilley, *Nottingham*
William Hale, *Dover*
Roger Vose, *Walpole*
Daniel Webster, *Portsmouth*
Jeduthun Wilcox, *Orford*

## NEW JERSEY

### SENATORS

John Condit, *Orange*
James J. Wilson, *Trenton*

### REPRESENTATIVES AT LARGE

Ezra Baker, *Tuckerton*
Ephraim Bateman, *Cedarsville*
Benjamin Bennet, *Middletown*
Lewis Condict, *Morristown*

Henry Southard, *Baskingridge*
Thomas Ward, *Newark*

## NEW YORK

### SENATORS

Rufus King, *New York City*
Nathan Sanford, *New York City*

### REPRESENTATIVES

Asa Adgate,[28] *Chesterfield*
Enos T. Throop,[29] *Auburn*
Daniel Avery,[30] *Aurora*
Samuel R. Betts, *Newburgh*
James Birdsall, *Norwich*
Victory Birdseye, *Pompey*
Micah Brooks, *East Bloomfield*
Jonathan Fisk,[31] *Newburgh*
James W. Wilkin,[32] *Goshen*
Daniel Cady, *Johnston*
Oliver C. Comstock, *Trumansburg*
Henry Crocheron, *Castletown*
Thomas R. Gold, *Whitestown*
Thomas P. Grosvenor, *Hudson*
Jabez D. Hammond, *Cherry Valley*
William Irving, *New York City*
Moss Kent, *Leraysville*
John Lovett, *Albany*
Hosea Moffitt, *Nassau*
Peter B. Porter,[33] *Buffalo*
Archibald S. Clarke,[34] *Clarence*
John Adams,[35] *Catskill*
Erastus Root,[36] *Delhi*
John Savage, *Salem*
Abraham H. Schenck, *Fishkill Landing*
John W. Taylor, *Ballston Spa*
George Townsend, *Oyster Bay*
Jonathan Ward, *New Rochelle*
Peter H. Wendover, *New York City*
Westel Willoughby, Jr.,[37] *Herkimer*
John B. Yates, *Utica*

## NORTH CAROLINA

### SENATORS

James Turner,[38] *Warrenton*
Montfort Stokes,[39] *Wilkesboro*
Francis Locke,[40] *Salisbury*
Nathaniel Macon,[41] *Warrenton*

### REPRESENTATIVES

Joseph H. Bryan, *Windsor*
James W. Clark, *Tarboro*

John Culpepper, *Allenton*
Daniel M. Forney, *Lincolnton*
William Gaston, *New Bern*
William R. King,[42] *Wilmington*
Charles Hooks,[43] *Dublin*
William C. Love, *Salisbury*
Nathaniel Macon,[44] *Warrenton*
Weldon N. Edwards,[45] *Warrenton*
William H. Murfree, *Murfreesburg*
Israel Pickens, *Morgantown*
Richard Stanford,[46] *Hawfields*
Samuel Dickens,[47] *Mount Tirzah*
Lewis Williams, *Panther Creek*
Bartlett Yancy, *Caswell*

## OHIO

### SENATORS

Jeremiah Morrow, *Montgomery*
Benjamin Ruggles, *St. Clairsville*

### REPRESENTATIVES

John Alexander, *Xenia*
James Caldwell, *St. Clairsville*
David Clendenin, *Youngtown*
William Creighton, Jr., *Chillicothe*
James Kilbourne, *Worthington*
John McLean,[48] *Lebanon*
William Henry Harrison,[49] *Cincinnati*

## PENNSYLVANIA

### SENATORS

Abner Lacock, *Beavertown*
Jonathan Roberts, *Norristown*

### REPRESENTATIVES

David Bard,[50] *Frankstown*
Thomas Burnside,[51] *Bellefonte*
William P. Maclay,[52] *Lewistown*
William Crawford, *Gettysburg*
William Darlington, *West Chester*
William Findley, *Youngstown*
Hugh Glasgow, *York*
Isaac Griffin, *New Geneva*
John Hahn, *Pottsgrove*
Joseph Hiester, *Reading*
Joseph Hopkinson, *Philadelphia*
Samuel D. Ingham, *New Hope*
Jared Irwin, *Sunbury*
William Maclay, *Fannetsburg*
William Milnor, *Philadelphia*
William Piper, *Bloodyrun*
John Ross, *Easton*

---

[24] Resigned May 30, 1816.
[25] Elected to fill vacancy caused by resignation of Christopher Gore, and took his seat December 2, 1816.
[26] Died February 22, 1816.
[27] Elected to fill vacancy caused by death of Elijah Brigham, and took his seat December 2, 1816.
[28] Elected to fill vacancy caused by death of Representative-elect Benjamin Pond (October 6, 1814, before the beginning of the congressional term), and took his seat December 7, 1815.
[29] Resigned June 4, 1816.
[30] Elected to fill vacancy caused by resignation of Enos T. Throop, and took his seat December 3, 1816.
[31] Resigned in March, 1815, before Congress assembled.
[32] Elected to fill vacancy caused by resignation of Jonathan Fisk, and took his seat December 4, 1815.
[33] Resigned January 23, 1816.

[34] Elected to fill vacancy caused by resignation of Peter B. Porter, and took his seat December 2, 1816.
[35] Served until December 26, 1815; succeeded by Erastus Root, who contested his election.
[36] Successfully contested the election of John Adams, and took his seat December 26, 1815.
[37] Successfully contested the election of William S. Smith, and took his seat December 13, 1815. (Mr. Smith did not appear or claim the seat, although credentials had been presented.)
[38] Resigned November 21, 1816.
[39] Elected to fill vacancy caused by resignation of James Turner, and took his seat December 16, 1816.
[40] Resigned December 5, 1815, never having qualified.
[41] Elected to fill vacancy caused by resignation of Francis Locke, and took his seat December 13, 1815.
[42] Resigned November 4, 1816.

[43] Elected to fill vacancy caused by resignation of William R. King, and took his seat December 2, 1816.
[44] Resigned December 13, 1815, having been elected Senator.
[45] Elected to fill vacancy caused by resignation of Nathaniel Macon, and took his seat February 7, 1816.
[46] Died April 9, 1816.
[47] Elected to fill vacancy caused by death of Richard Stanford, and took his seat December 2, 1816.
[48] Resigned in 1816.
[49] Elected to fill vacancy caused by resignation of John McLean, and took his seat December 2, 1816.
[50] Died March 12, 1815.
[51] Elected to fill vacancy caused by death of David Bard, and took his seat December 11, 1815; resigned in April, 1816.
[52] Elected to fill vacancy caused by resignation of Thomas Burnside, and took his seat December 3, 1816.

## PENNSYLVANIA—Continued

REPRESENTATIVES—CONTINUED

Thomas Smith, *Darby*
Amos Ellmaker,[53] *Harrisburg*
James M. Wallace,[54] *Hummelstown*
John Whiteside, *Lancaster*
Jonathan Williams,[55] *Philadelphia*
John Sergeant,[56] *Philadelphia*
Thomas Wilson, *Erie*
William Wilson, *Williamsport*
Aaron Lyle, *West Middletown*
John Woods,[57] *Pittsburgh*

## RHODE ISLAND

SENATORS

Jeremiah B. Howell, *Providence*
William Hunter, *Newport*

REPRESENTATIVES AT LARGE

John L. Boss, Jr., *Newport*
James B. Mason, *Providence*

## SOUTH CAROLINA

SENATORS

John Gaillard, *Charleston*
John Taylor,[58] *Columbia*
William Smith,[59] *Yorkville*

REPRESENTATIVES

John J. Chappell, *Columbia*
Benjamin Huger, *Georgetown*
William Lowndes, *Jacksonboro*
William Mayrant,[60] *Stateburg*
Stephen D. Miller,[61] *Stateburg*
John C. Calhoun, *Willington*
Henry Middleton, *Charleston*
Thomas Moore, *Prices Store*
John Taylor, *Pendleton*
William Woodward, *Monticello*

## TENNESSEE

SENATORS

Jesse Wharton, *Nashville*
John Williams,[62] *Knoxville*

George W. Campbell,[63] *Nashville*

REPRESENTATIVES

Newton Cannon, *Harpeth*
Bennett H. Henderson, *Hendersonville*
Samuel Powell, *Rogersville*
James B. Reynolds, *Clarksville*
John Sevier,[64] *Knoxville*
William G. Blount,[65] *Knoxville*
Isaac Thomas, *Sparta*

## VERMONT

SENATORS

Dudley Chase, *Randolph*
Isaac Tichenor, *Bennington*

REPRESENTATIVES AT LARGE

Daniel Chipman,[66] *Middleburg*
Luther Jewett, *St. Johnsbury*
Chauncey Langdon, *Castleton*
Asa Lyon, *Grand Isle*
Charles Marsh, *Woodstock*
John Noyes, *Brattleboro*

## VIRGINIA

SENATORS

James Barbour, *Barboursville*
Armistead T. Mason,[67] *Rasburg Plain*

REPRESENTATIVES

Philip P. Barbour, *Orange*
Burwell Bassett, *Williamsburg*
James Breckinridge, *Fincastle*
William A. Burwell, *Rocky Mount*
Matthew Clay,[68] *Halifax*
John Kerr,[69] *Mountpleasant*
John Clopton,[70] *Tunstall*

John Tyler,[71] *Charles City*
Peterson Goodwyn, *Petersburg*
Aylett Hawes, *Woodville*
John P. Hungerford, *Leedstown*
John G. Jackson, *Clarksburg*
James Johnson, *Suffolk*
Joseph Lewis, Jr., *Upperville*
William McCoy,[72] *Franklin*
Hugh Nelson, *Milton*
Thomas Gholson, Jr.,[73] *Brunswick*
Thomas M. Nelson,[74] *Mecklenburg*
Thomas Newton, Jr., *Norfolk*
James Pleasants, *Goochland*
John Randolph, *Charlotte*
William H. Roane, *Dunkirk*
Daniel Sheffey, *Wythe*
Ballard Smith, *Lewisburg*
Magnus Tate, *Martinsburg*
Henry St. George Tucker, *Winchester*

## ILLINOIS TERRITORY

DELEGATE

Benjamin Stephenson,[75] *Edwardsville*
Nathaniel Pope,[76] *Kaskaskia*

## INDIANA TERRITORY

DELEGATE

Jonathan Jennings,[77] *Charlestown*

## MISSISSIPPI TERRITORY

DELEGATE

William Lattimore, *Liberty*

## TERRITORY OF MISSOURI

DELEGATE

Rufus Easton,[78] *St. Louis*
John Scott,[79] *Ste. Genevieve*

---

[53] Resigned July 3, 1815, without qualifying, having been appointed judge.

[54] Elected to fill vacancy caused by resignation of Amos Ellmaker, and took his seat December 4, 1815.

[55] Died May 16, 1815, before Congress assembled.

[56] Elected to fill vacancy caused by death of Jonathan Williams, and took his seat December 6, 1815.

[57] Never qualified owing to illness.

[58] Resigned in November, 1816.

[59] Elected to fill vacancy caused by resignation of John Taylor, and took his seat January 10, 1817.

[60] Resigned October 21, 1816.

[61] Elected to fill vacancy caused by resignation of William Mayrant, and took his seat January 2, 1817.

[62] Elected to fill vacancy in term ending March 3, 1817, caused by resignation of George W. Campbell from this class in the preceding Congress (Jesse Wharton having served by appointment from March

17, 1814, to October 10, 1815), and took his seat December 4, 1815.

[63] Elected for the term commencing March 4, 1815, and took his seat December 4, 1815; vacancy from March 4, 1815, to October 10, 1815.

[64] Died September 24, 1815, before Congress assembled.

[65] Elected to fill vacancy caused by death of John Sevier, and took his seat January 8, 1816.

[66] Resigned May 5, 1816; seat remained vacant.

[67] Elected to fill vacancy caused by resignation of William B. Giles, in preceding Congress, and took his seat January 22, 1816.

[68] Died May 27, 1815, before Congress assembled.

[69] Elected to fill vacancy caused by death of Matthew Clay, and took his seat December 5, 1815.

[70] Died September 11, 1816.

[71] Elected to fill vacancy caused by death of John Clopton, and took his seat December 17, 1816.

[72] Election unsuccessfully contested by Robert Porterfield.

[73] Died July 4, 1816.

[74] Elected to fill vacancy caused by death of Thomas Gholson, Jr., and took his seat December 4, 1816.

[75] Served during the first session.

[76] Presented credentials and took his seat December 2, 1816.

[77] Served until December 11, 1816, when Indiana Territory was granted statehood.

[78] Served during first session; unsuccessfully contested the election of John Scott in the second session.

[79] Presented credentials and took his seat December 2, 1816; Rufus Easton contested, and on January 13, 1817, the election was declared illegal and the seat vacant.

# 15TH CONGRESS

## MARCH 4, 1817, TO MARCH 3, 1819

Daniel D. Tompkins
Vice President

FIRST SESSION— *December 1, 1817, to April 20, 1818*
SECOND SESSION— *November 16, 1818, to March 3, 1819*
SPECIAL SESSION OF THE SENATE— *March 4, 1817, to March 6, 1817*

———————

VICE PRESIDENT OF THE UNITED STATES— Daniel D. Tompkins, of New York
PRESIDENT PRO TEMPORE OF THE SENATE— John Gaillard,[1] of South Carolina;
James Barbour,[2] of Virginia
SECRETARY OF THE SENATE— Charles Cutts, of New Hampshire
SERGEANT AT ARMS OF THE SENATE— Mountjoy Bayly, of Maryland

———————

SPEAKER OF THE HOUSE OF REPRESENTATIVES— Henry Clay,[3] of Kentucky
CLERK OF THE HOUSE— Thomas Dougherty,[4] of Kentucky
SERGEANT AT ARMS OF THE HOUSE— Thomas Dunn, of Maryland
DOORKEEPER OF THE HOUSE— Thomas Claxton

Henry Clay
Speaker

## CONNECTICUT

### SENATORS
Samuel W. Dana,[5] *Middlesex*
David Daggett, *New Haven*

### REPRESENTATIVES AT LARGE
Uriel Holmes,[6] *Litchfield*
Sylvester Gilbert,[7] *Hebron*
Ebenezer Huntington, *Norwich*
Jonathan O. Moseley, *East Haddam*
Timothy Pitkin, *Farmington*
Samuel B. Sherwood, *Saugatuck*
Nathaniel Terry, *Hartford*
Thomas S. Williams, *Hartford*

## DELAWARE

### SENATORS
Outerbridge Horsey, *Wilmington*
Nicholas Van Dyke, *New Castle*

### REPRESENTATIVES AT LARGE
Willard Hall, *Dover*
Louis McLane, *Wilmington*

## GEORGIA

### SENATORS
Charles Tait, *Elbert*
George M. Troup,[8] *Dublin*
John Forsyth,[9] *Augusta*

### REPRESENTATIVES AT LARGE
Joel Abbot, *Washington*
Thomas W. Cobb, *Lexington*
Zadock Cook, *Watkinsville*
Joel Crawford, *Milledgeville*
John Forsyth,[10] *Augusta*
Robert R. Reid,[11] *Augusta*
William Terrell, *Sparta*

## ILLINOIS[12]

### SENATORS
Jesse B. Thomas,[13] *Edwardsville*
Ninian Edwards,[14] *Edwardsville*

### REPRESENTATIVE AT LARGE
John McLean,[15] *Shawneetown*

## INDIANA

### SENATORS
James Noble, *Brookville*
Waller Taylor, *Vincennes*

### REPRESENTATIVE AT LARGE
William Hendricks, *Madison*

## KENTUCKY

### SENATORS
Isham Talbot, *Frankfort*
John J. Crittenden,[16] *Russellville*

## REPRESENTATIVES
Richard C. Anderson, Jr., *Louisville*
Henry Clay, *Lexington*
Joseph Desha, *Mays Lick*
Richard M. Johnson, *Great Crossings*
Anthony New, *Elkton*
Tunstall Quarles, *Somerset*
George Robertson, *Lancaster*
Thomas Speed, *Bardstown*
David Trimble, *Mount Sterling*
David Walker, *Russellville*

## LOUISIANA

### SENATORS
Eligius Fromentin, *New Orleans*
William C. C. Claiborne,[17] *New Orleans*
Henry Johnson,[18] *Donaldsonville*

### REPRESENTATIVE AT LARGE
Thomas B. Robertson,[19] *New Orleans*
Thomas Butler,[20] *St. Francisville*

## MARYLAND

### SENATORS
Robert H. Goldsborough, *Easton*
Alexander C. Hanson, *Elkridge*

### REPRESENTATIVES
Thomas Bayly, *Princess Anne*
Thomas Culbreth, *Denton*

---

[1] Continuing from preceding session; elected March 6, 1817 (special session of the Senate); March 31, 1818.
[2] Elected February 15, 1819.
[3] Reelected December 1, 1817.
[4] Reelected December 1, 1817.
[5] The rule requiring Senators to stand when addressing the Chair was suspended in his favor April 9, 1818.
[6] Resigned in 1818.
[7] Elected to fill vacancy caused by resignation of Uriel Holmes, and took his seat November 16, 1818.
[8] Resigned September 23, 1818.

[9] Elected to fill vacancy caused by resignation of George M. Troup, and took his seat November 23, 1818; resigned February 17, 1819, having been appointed minister to Spain.
[10] Resigned, effective November 23, 1818, having been elected Senator.
[11] Elected to fill vacancy caused by resignation of John Forsyth, and took his seat February 18, 1819.
[12] Admitted as a State into the Union December 3, 1818.
[13] Took his seat December 4, 1818; term to expire, as determined by lot, March 3, 1823.
[14] Took his seat December 4, 1818; term to expire, as determined by lot, March 3, 1819.

[15] Took his seat December 4, 1818.
[16] Resigned March 3, 1819.
[17] Died November 23, 1817, never having qualified.
[18] Elected to fill vacancy caused by death of William C. C. Claiborne, and took his seat February 26, 1818.
[19] Resigned April 20, 1818.
[20] Elected to fill vacancy caused by resignation of Thomas B. Robertson, and took his seat November 16, 1818.

## MARYLAND—Continued

REPRESENTATIVES—CONTINUED

John C. Herbert, *Vannsville*
Peter Little, *Freedom*
George Peter, *Darnestown*
Philip Reed, *Chestertown*
Samuel Ringgold, *Hagerstown*
Samuel Smith, *Baltimore*
Philip Stuart, *Port Tobacco*

## MASSACHUSETTS

SENATORS

Eli P. Ashmun,[21] *Northampton*
Prentiss Mellen,[22] *Portland*
Harrison Gray Otis, *Boston*

REPRESENTATIVES

Benjamin Adams, *Uxbridge*
Samuel C. Allen, *Greenfield*
Walter Folger, Jr., *Nantucket*
Timothy Fuller, *Boston*
Joshua Gage, *Augusta*
John Holmes, *Alfred*
Jonathan Mason, *Boston*
Elijah H. Mills, *Northampton*
Marcus Morton, *Taunton*
Jeremiah Nelson, *Newburyport*
Benjamin Orr, *Brunswick*
Albion K. Parris,[23] *Paris*
Enoch Lincoln,[24] *Paris*
Thomas Rice, *Augusta*
Nathaniel Ruggles, *Boston*
Zabdiel Sampson, *Plymouth*
Henry Shaw, *Lanesboro*
Nathaniel Silsbee, *Salem*
Solomon Strong, *Westminster*
Ezekiel Whitman, *Portland*
John Wilson, *Belfast*

## MISSISSIPPI[25]

SENATORS

Walter Leake,[26] *Red Bluff*
Thomas H. Williams,[27] *Washington*

REPRESENTATIVE AT LARGE

George Poindexter,[28] *Woodville*

## NEW HAMPSHIRE

SENATORS

Jeremiah Mason,[29] *Portsmouth*
Clement Storer,[30] *Portsmouth*
David L. Morril, *Goffstown*

REPRESENTATIVES AT LARGE

Josiah Butler, *South Deerfield*
Clifton Clagett, *Amherst*
Salma Hale, *Keene*
Arthur Livermore, *Plymouth*
John F. Parrott, *Portsmouth*
Nathaniel Upham, *Rochester*

## NEW JERSEY

SENATORS

James J. Wilson, *Trenton*
Mahlon Dickerson, *Suckasunny*

REPRESENTATIVES AT LARGE

Ephraim Bateman, *Cedarsville*
Benjamin Bennet, *Middletown*
Joseph Bloomfield, *Burlington*
Charles Kinsey, *Paterson*
John Linn, *Monroe*
Henry Southard, *Baskingridge*

## NEW YORK

SENATORS

Rufus King, *New York City*
Nathan Sanford, *New York City*

REPRESENTATIVES

Oliver C. Comstock, *Trumansburg*
Daniel Cruger, *Bath*
John P. Cushman, *Troy*
John R. Drake, *Owego*
Benjamin Ellicott, *Batavia*
Josiah Hasbrouck, *New Paltz*
John Herkimer, *Danube*
Thomas H. Hubbard, *Hamilton*
William Irving, *New York City*
Dorrance Kirtland, *Coxsackie*
Thomas Lawyer, *Cobleskill*
David A. Ogden, *Madrid*
John Palmer, *Plattsburg*
James Porter, *Skaneateles*
John Savage, *Salem*
Philip J. Schuyler, *Rhinebeck*
Tredwell Scudder, *Islip*
John C. Spencer, *Canandaigua*
Henry R. Storrs, *Whitestown*
James Tallmadge, Jr.,[31] *Poughkeepsie*
John W. Taylor, *Ballston Spa*
Caleb Tompkins, *White Plains*
George Townsend, *Oyster Bay*
Peter H. Wendover, *New York City*
Rensselaer Westerlo, *Albany*
James W. Wilkin, *Goshen*
Isaac Williams, Jr., *Cooperstown*

## NORTH CAROLINA

SENATORS

Nathaniel Macon, *Warrenton*
Montfort Stokes, *Wilkesboro*

REPRESENTATIVES

Joseph H. Bryan, *Windsor*
Weldon N. Edwards, *Warrenton*
Daniel M. Forney,[32] *Lincolnton*
William Davidson,[33] *Charlotte*
Thomas H. Hall, *Tarboro*
Alexander McMillan[34]
James Stewart,[35] *Laurinburg*
George Mumford,[36] *Salisbury*
Charles Fisher,[37] *Salisbury*
James Owen, *Elizabethtown*
Lemuel Sawyer, *Elizabeth City*
Thomas Settle, *Lenox Castle*
Jesse Slocumb, *Waynesborough*
James S. Smith, *Hillsboro*
Felix Walker, *Waynesville*
Lewis Williams, *Panther Creek*

## OHIO

SENATORS

Jeremiah Morrow, *Montgomery*
Benjamin Ruggles, *St. Clairsville*

REPRESENTATIVES

Levi Barber, *Point Harmer*
Philemon Beecher, *Lancaster*
John W. Campbell, *West Union*
William Henry Harrison, *Cincinnati*
Samuel Herrick,[38] *Zanesville*
Peter Hitchcock, *Burton*

## PENNSYLVANIA

SENATORS

Abner Lacock, *Beavertown*
Jonathan Roberts, *Norristown*

REPRESENTATIVES

William Anderson, *Chester*
Henry Baldwin, *Pittsburgh*
Andrew Boden, *Carlisle*
Isaac Darlington, *West Chester*
Joseph Hiester, *Reading*
Joseph Hopkinson, *Philadelphia*
Samuel D. Ingham,[39] *New Hope*
Samuel Moore,[40] *Doylestown*
William Maclay, *Fannetsburg*
William P. Maclay, *Lewistown*
David Marchand, *Greensburg*
Robert Moore, *Beavertown*

---

[21] Resigned May 10, 1818.
[22] Elected to fill vacancy caused by resignation of Eli P. Ashmun, and took his seat November 16, 1818.
[23] Resigned February 3, 1818.
[24] Elected to fill vacancy caused by resignation of Albion K. Parris, and took his seat November 16, 1818.
[25] Admitted as a State into the Union December 10, 1817.
[26] Took his seat December 11, 1817; term to expire, as determined by lot, March 3, 1821.
[27] Took his seat December 11, 1817; term to expire, as determined by lot, March 3, 1823.
[28] Took his seat December 15, 1817.
[29] Resigned June 16, 1817.
[30] Elected to fill vacancy caused by resignation of

Jeremiah Mason, and took his seat December 1, 1817.
[31] Elected to fill vacancy caused by death of Representative-elect Henry B. Lee (February 18, 1817, before the beginning of the congressional term), and took his seat December 1, 1817.
[32] Resigned in 1818.
[33] Elected to fill vacancy caused by resignation of Daniel M. Forney, and took his seat December 2, 1818.
[34] Died before Congress assembled.
[35] Elected to fill vacancy caused by death of Alexander McMillan, and took his seat January 26, 1818.
[36] Died December 31, 1818.
[37] Elected to fill vacancy caused by death of

George Mumford, and took his seat February 11, 1819.
[38] Election unsuccessfully contested by Charles Hammond. This case was one of a number in the same Congress that have been frequently referred to as determining the rights of a Representative-elect to hold a Federal office after the 4th of March—the day of the beginning of the congressional term to which they were elected. They are reported at length in Clark & Hall's publication, and also in the Digest of House Election Cases, edition of 1901, pp. 70-74.
[39] Resigned July 6, 1818.
[40] Elected to fill vacancy caused by resignation of Samuel D. Ingham, and took his seat November 16, 1818.

Alexander Ogle, *Somerset*
Thomas Patterson, *West Middleton*
Levi Pawling, *Norristown*
John Ross,[41] *Easton*
Thomas J. Rogers,[42] *Easton*
David Scott[43]
John Murray,[44] *Milton*
John Sergeant, *Philadelphia*
Adam Seybert, *Philadelphia*
Jacob Spangler,[45] *York*
Jacob Hostetter,[46] *Hanover*
Christian Tarr, *Brownsville*
James M. Wallace, *Hummelstown*
John Whiteside, *Lancaster*
William Wilson, *Williamsport*

## RHODE ISLAND

### SENATORS

William Hunter, *Newport*
James Burrill, Jr., *Providence*

### REPRESENTATIVES AT LARGE

John L. Boss, Jr., *Newport*
James B. Mason, *Providence*

## SOUTH CAROLINA

### SENATORS

John Gaillard, *Charleston*
William Smith, *Yorkville*

### REPRESENTATIVES

Joseph Bellinger, *Duncansville*
Elias Earle, *Centerville*
James Ervin, *Darlington*
William Lowndes, *Jacksonboro*
Henry Middleton, *Charleston*
Stephen D. Miller, *Stateburg*
Wilson Nesbitt, *New Hope*
John C. Calhoun,[47] *Willington*
Eldred Simkins,[48] *Edgefield*
Starling Tucker, *Mountain Shoals*

## TENNESSEE

### SENATORS

George W. Campbell,[49] *Nashville*
John H. Eaton,[50] *Nashville*
John Williams, *Knoxville*

### REPRESENTATIVES

William G. Blount, *Knoxville*
Thomas Claiborne, *Nashville*
Samuel Hogg, *Lebanon*
Francis Jones, *Winchester*
George W. L. Marr, *Clarksville*
John Rhea, *Sullivan*

## VERMONT

### SENATORS

Dudley Chase,[51] *Randolph*
James Fisk,[52] *Barre*
William A. Palmer,[53] *Danville*
Isaac Tichenor, *Bennington*

### REPRESENTATIVES AT LARGE

Heman Allen,[54] *Burlington*
Samuel C. Crafts, *Craftsbury*
William Hunter, *Windsor*
Orsamus C. Merrill, *Bennington*
Charles Rich, *Shoreham*
Mark Richards, *Westminster*

## VIRGINIA

### SENATORS

James Barbour, *Barboursville*
John W. Eppes, *Charles City*

### REPRESENTATIVES

Archibald Austin, *Buckingham*
William Lee Ball, *Lancaster*
Philip P. Barbour, *Orange*
Burwell Bassett, *Williamsburg*

William A. Burwell, *Rocky Mount*
Edward Colston, *Martinsburg*
John Floyd, *Newbern*
Robert S. Garnett, *Loyds*
Peterson Goodwyn,[55] *Petersburg*
John Pegram,[56] *Dinwiddie*
James Johnson, *Bowersville*
William J. Lewis, *Lynchburg*
William McCoy, *Franklin*
Charles F. Mercer, *Aldie*
Hugh Nelson, *Milton*
Thomas M. Nelson, *Mecklenburg*
Thomas Newton, Jr., *Norfolk*
James Pindall, *Clarksburg*
James Pleasants, *Goochland*
Ballard Smith, *Lewisburg*
Alexander Smyth, *Wythe*
George F. Strother, *Culpeper*
Henry St. George Tucker, *Winchester*
John Tyler, *Charles City*

## ALABAMA TERRITORY[57]

### DELEGATE

John Crowell,[58] *St. Stephens*

## ILLINOIS TERRITORY

### DELEGATE

Nathaniel Pope,[59] *Kaskaskia*

## MISSISSIPPI TERRITORY[60]

### DELEGATE

Vacant

## TERRITORY OF MISSOURI

### DELEGATE

John Scott,[61] *Ste. Genevieve*

---

[41] Resigned February 24, 1818.
[42] Elected to fill vacancy caused by resignation of John Ross, and took his seat March 24, 1818.
[43] Resigned before Congress assembled, having been appointed judge of the court of common pleas.
[44] Elected to fill vacancy caused by resignation of David Scott, and took his seat December 1, 1817.
[45] Resigned April 20, 1818.
[46] Elected to fill vacancy caused by resignation of Jacob Spangler, and took his seat November 16, 1818.
[47] Resigned November 3, 1817, having been appointed Secretary of War.
[48] Elected to fill vacancy caused by resignation of John C. Calhoun, and took his seat February 9, 1818.
[49] Resigned, to take effect at the close of the

ensuing session (April 20, 1818), to become minister to Russia.
[50] Appointed to fill vacancy caused by resignation of George W. Campbell, and took his seat November 16, 1818; subsequently elected.
[51] Resigned November 3, 1817, having been appointed chief judge of the supreme court of Vermont.
[52] Elected to fill vacancy caused by resignation of Dudley Chase, and took his seat December 1, 1817; resigned January 8, 1818.
[53] Elected to fill vacancy caused by resignations of Dudley Chase and James Fisk, and took his seat November 16, 1818.
[54] Resigned, to take effect April 20, 1818.

[55] Died February 21, 1818.
[56] Elected to fill vacancy caused by death of Peterson Goodwyn, and took his seat November 16, 1818.
[57] Formed from a portion of Mississippi Territory of lands originally ceded to the United States by the States of Georgia and South Carolina, by act of March 3, 1817; granted a Delegate in Congress by the same act.
[58] Took his seat March 9, 1818.
[59] Served during the first session; the Territory was granted statehood December 3, 1818.
[60] Granted statehood December 10, 1817.
[61] Elected August 4, 1817, and took his seat December 8, 1817.

# 16TH CONGRESS

MARCH 4, 1819, TO MARCH 3, 1821

FIRST SESSION— *December 6, 1819, to May 15, 1820*
SECOND SESSION— *November 13, 1820, to March 3, 1821*

---

VICE PRESIDENT OF THE UNITED STATES— DANIEL D. TOMPKINS, of New York
PRESIDENT PRO TEMPORE OF THE SENATE— JAMES BARBOUR, of Virginia; JOHN
GAILLARD,[1] of South Carolina
SECRETARY OF THE SENATE— CHARLES CUTTS, of New Hampshire
SERGEANT AT ARMS OF THE SENATE— MOUNTJOY BAYLY, of Maryland

---

SPEAKER OF THE HOUSE OF REPRESENTATIVES— HENRY CLAY,[2] of Kentucky; JOHN
W. TAYLOR,[3] of New York
CLERK OF THE HOUSE— THOMAS DOUGHERTY,[4] of Kentucky
SERGEANT AT ARMS OF THE HOUSE— THOMAS DUNN, of Maryland
DOORKEEPER OF THE HOUSE— THOMAS CLAXTON

*Daniel D. Tompkins*
*Vice President*

*Henry Clay*
*Speaker*

## ALABAMA[5]

SENATORS

John W. Walker,[6] *Huntsville*
William R. King,[7] *Cahaba*

REPRESENTATIVE AT LARGE

John Crowell,[8] *St. Stephens*

## CONNECTICUT

SENATORS

Samuel W. Dana, *Middlesex*
James Lanman, *Norwich*

REPRESENTATIVES AT LARGE

Henry W. Edwards, *New Haven*
Samuel A. Foote, *Cheshire*
Jonathan O. Moseley, *East Haddam*
Elisha Phelps, *Simsbury*
John Russ, *Hartford*
James Stevens, *Stamford*
Gideon Tomlinson, *Fairfield*

## DELAWARE

SENATORS

Outerbridge Horsey, *Wilmington*
Nicholas Van Dyke, *New Castle*

REPRESENTATIVES AT LARGE

Willard Hall,[9] *Dover*
Louis McLane, *Wilmington*

## GEORGIA

SENATORS

John Elliott, *Sunbury*
Freeman Walker,[10] *Augusta*

REPRESENTATIVES AT LARGE

Joel Abbot, *Washington*
Thomas W. Cobb, *Lexington*
Joel Crawford, *Milledgeville*
John A. Cuthbert, *Eatonton*
Robert R. Reid, *Augusta*
William Terrell, *Sparta*

## ILLINOIS

SENATORS

Jesse B. Thomas, *Edwardsville*
Ninian Edwards, *Edwardsville*

REPRESENTATIVE AT LARGE

Daniel P. Cook, *Edwardsville*

## INDIANA

SENATORS

James Noble, *Brookville*
Waller Taylor, *Vincennes*

REPRESENTATIVE AT LARGE

William Hendricks, *Madison*

## KENTUCKY

SENATORS

William Logan,[11] *Shelbyville*
Isham Talbot,[12] *Frankfort*
Richard M. Johnson,[13] *Great
Crossings*

REPRESENTATIVES

Richard C. Anderson, Jr., *Louisville*
William Brown, *Cynthiana*
Henry Clay, *Lexington*
Benjamin Hardin, *Bardstown*
David Walker,[14] *Russellville*
Francis Johnson,[15] *Bowling Green*
Thomas Metcalfe, *Carlisle*
Tunstall Quarles,[16] *Somerset*
Thomas Montgomery,[17] *Stanford*
George Robertson, *Lancaster*
David Trimble, *Mount Sterling*
Alney McLean, *Greenville*

## LOUISIANA

SENATORS

Henry Johnson, *Donaldsonville*
James Brown, *New Orleans*

REPRESENTATIVE AT LARGE

Thomas Butler, *St. Francisville*

---

[1] Elected January 25, 1820.
[2] Reelected December 6, 1819; resigned as Speaker October 28, 1820.
[3] Elected November 15, 1820.
[4] Reelected December 6, 1819.
[5] Admitted as a State into the Union December 14, 1819.
[6] Took his seat December 14, 1819; term to expire, as determined by lot, March 3, 1825.
[7] Took his seat December 22, 1819; term to expire, as determined by lot, March 3, 1823.

[8] Took his seat December 14, 1819.
[9] Resigned January 22, 1821.
[10] Elected to fill vacancy caused by resignation of John Forsyth, in preceding Congress, and took his seat December 15, 1819; vacancy in this class from February 18, 1819, to November 5, 1819.
[11] Resigned May 28, 1820.
[12] Elected to fill vacancy caused by resignation of William Logan, and took his seat November 27, 1820.
[13] Elected to fill vacancy caused by resignation of

John J. Crittenden, in preceding Congress, and took his seat January 3, 1820.
[14] Died March 1, 1820.
[15] Elected to fill vacancy caused by death of David Walker, and took his seat November 13, 1820.
[16] Resigned, effective June 15, 1820.
[17] Elected to fill vacancy caused by resignation of Tunstall Quarles, and took his seat November 13, 1820.

## MAINE[18]

### SENATORS

John Chandler,[19] *Monmouth*
John Homes,[20] *Alfred*

### REPRESENTATIVE AT LARGE[21]

Joseph Dane,[22] *Kennebunk*

## MARYLAND

### SENATORS

Alexander C. Hanson,[23] *Elkridge*
William Pinkney,[24] *Baltimore*
Edward Lloyd,[25] *Easton*

### REPRESENTATIVES

Stevenson Archer, *Bel Air*
Thomas Bayly, *Princess Anne*
Thomas Culbreth, *Denton*
Joseph Kent, *Bladensburg*
Peter Little, *Freedom*
Raphael Neale, *Leonardtown*
Samuel Ringgold, *Hagerstown*
Samuel Smith, *Baltimore*
Henry R. Warfield, *Middleburg*

## MASSACHUSETTS

### SENATORS

Harrison Gray Otis, *Boston*
Prentiss Mellen,[26] *Portland*
Elijah H. Mills,[27] *Northampton*

### REPRESENTATIVES[28]

Benjamin Adams, *Uxbridge*
Samuel C. Allen, *Northfield*
Joshua Cushman, *Winslow*
Edward Dowse,[29] *Dedham*
William Eustis,[30] *Boston*
Walter Folger, Jr., *Nantucket*
Timothy Fuller, *Boston*
Mark L. Hill, *Phippsburg*
John Holmes,[31] *Alfred*
Jonas Kendall, *Leominster*
Martin Kinsley, *Hampden*
Samuel Lathrop, *West Springfield*

Enoch Lincoln, *Paris*
Jonathan Mason,[32] *Boston*
Benjamin Gorham,[33] *Boston*
Marcus Morton, *Taunton*
Jeremiah Nelson, *Newburyport*
James Parker, *Gardner*
Zabdiel Sampson,[34] *Plymouth*
Aaron Hobart,[35] *Hanover*
Henry Shaw, *Lanesboro*
Nathaniel Silsbee, *Salem*
Ezekiel Whitman, *Portland*

## MISSISSIPPI

### SENATORS

Walter Leake,[36] *Bay St. Louis*
David Holmes,[37] *Washington*
Thomas H. Williams, *Washington*

### REPRESENTATIVE AT LARGE

Christopher Rankin, *Natchez*

## NEW HAMPSHIRE

### SENATORS

David L. Morril, *Goffstown*
John F. Parrott, *Portsmouth*

### REPRESENTATIVES AT LARGE

Joseph Buffum, Jr., *Westmoreland*
Josiah Butler, *South Deerfield*
Clifton Clagett, *Amherst*
Arthur Livermore, *Plymouth*
William Plumer, Jr., *Epping*
Nathaniel Upham, *Rochester*

## NEW JERSEY

### SENATORS

James J. Wilson,[38] *Trenton*
Samuel L. Southard,[39] *Trenton*
Mahlon Dickerson, *Succasunna*

### REPRESENTATIVES AT LARGE

Ephraim Bateman, *Cedarville*
Joseph Bloomfield, *Burlington*
John Condit,[40] *Orange*

Charles Kinsey,[41] *Paterson*
John Linn,[42] *Monroe*
Bernard Smith, *New Brunswick*
Henry Southard, *Baskingridge*

## NEW YORK

### SENATORS

Rufus King, *New York City*
Nathan Sanford, *New York City*

### REPRESENTATIVES

Nathaniel Allen, *Richmond*
Caleb Baker, *Elmira*
Walter Case, *Newbury*
Robert Clark, *Roseville*
Jacob H. De Witt, *Kingston*
John D. Dickinson, *Troy*
John Fay, *Northampton*
William D. Ford, *Watertown*
Ezra C. Gross, *Elizabeth*
Aaron Hackley, Jr., *Herkimer*
George Hall, *Onondaga*
Joseph S. Lyman, *Cooperstown*
Henry Meigs, *New York City*
Robert Monell, *Greene*
Hermanus Peek, *Schenectady*
Nathaniel Pitcher, *Sandy Hill*
Jonathan Richmond, *Aurora*
Ebenezer Sage,[43] *Sag Harbor*
James Guyon, Jr.,[44] *Richmond*
Henry R. Storrs, *Whitestown*
Randall S. Street, *Poughkeepsie*
James Strong, *Hudson*
John W. Taylor, *Ballston Spa*
Caleb Tompkins, *White Plains*
Albert H. Tracy, *Buffalo*
Solomon Van Rensselaer, *Albany*
Peter H. Wendover, *New York City*
Silas Wood, *Huntington*

---

[18] Admitted as a State into the Union March 15, 1820. Previous to March 3, 1820, Maine was a part of Massachusetts, and was called the "District of Maine" and its Representatives were numbered with those of Massachusetts; by compact between the two States, Maine became a separate and independent State, and by act of Congress of March 3, 1820, was admitted into the Union as such—the admission to date from the 15th of the same month.

[19] Took his seat November 13, 1820; term to expire, as determined by lot, March 3, 1823.

[20] Took his seat November 13, 1820; term to expire, as determined by lot, March 3, 1821.

[21] The act of Congress approved April 7, 1820, provided "That in the election of Representatives in the Seventeenth Congress, the State of Massachusetts shall be entitled to choose 13 Representatives only; and the State of Maine shall be entitled to choose 7 Representatives, ... That if the seat of any of the Representatives in the present Congress, who were elected in and under the authority of the State of Massachusetts, and who are now inhabitants of the State of Maine, shall be vacated by death, resignation, or otherwise, such vacancy shall be supplied by a successor, who shall, at the time of his election, be an inhabitant of the State of Maine."

[22] Elected to fill vacancy caused by resignation of John Holmes, a Representative from Massachusetts,

but residing in the new State of Maine, and took his seat December 11, 1820. (See footnote 21.)

[23] Died April 23, 1819.

[24] Elected to fill vacancy caused by death of Alexander C. Hanson, and took his seat January 4, 1820.

[25] Elected for the term beginning March 4, 1819, and took his seat December 27, 1819; vacancy in this class from March 4, 1819, to December 20, 1819.

[26] Resigned May 15, 1820.

[27] Elected to fill vacancy caused by resignation of Prentiss Mellen, and took his seat December 1, 1820.

[28] The act of Congress approved April 7, 1820, provided "That in the election of Representatives in the Seventeenth Congress, the State of Massachusetts shall be entitled to choose 13 Representatives only; and the State of Maine shall be entitled to choose 7 Representatives, ... That if the seat of any of the Representatives in the present Congress, who were elected in and under the authority of the State of Massachusetts, and who are now inhabitants of the State of Maine, shall be vacated by death, resignation, or otherwise, such vacancy shall be supplied by a successor, who shall, at the time of his election, be an inhabitant of the State of Maine."

[29] Resigned May 26, 1820.

[30] Elected to fill vacancy caused by resignation of Edward Dowse, and took his seat November 13, 1820.

[31] Resigned March 15, 1820; subsequently elected Senator from Maine. (See footnote 28.)

[32] Resigned May 15, 1820.

[33] Elected to fill vacancy caused by resignation of Jonathan Mason, and took his seat November 27, 1820.

[34] Resigned July 26, 1820.

[35] Elected to fill vacancy caused by resignation of Zabdiel Sampson, and took his seat December 18, 1820.

[36] Resigned May 15, 1820.

[37] Appointed to fill vacancy caused by resignation of Walter Leake, and took his seat November 13, 1820; subsequently elected.

[38] Resigned January 8, 1821.

[39] Appointed to fill vacancy caused by resignation of James J. Wilson, and took his seat February 16, 1821; subsequently elected.

[40] Resigned November 4, 1819, having been appointed assistant collector of customs.

[41] Elected to fill vacancy caused by resignation of John Condit, and took his seat February 16, 1820.

[42] Died January 5, 1821.

[43] Never appeared to claim seat; succeeded by James Guyon, Jr., who contested his election.

[44] Successfully contested the election of Ebenezer Sage, and took his seat January 14, 1820.

## NORTH CAROLINA

SENATORS

Nathaniel Macon, *Monroe*
Montfort Stokes, *Wilkesboro*

REPRESENTATIVES

Hutchins G. Burton, *Halifax*
John Culpepper, *Wadesboro*
William Davidson, *Charlotte*
Weldon N. Edwards, *Warrenton*
Charles Fisher, *Salisbury*
Thomas H. Hall, *Tarboro*
Charles Hooks, *Dublin*
Lemuel Sawyer, *Elizabeth City*
Thomas Settle, *Lenox Castle*
Jesse Slocumb,[45] *Waynesborough*
William S. Blackledge,[46] *New Bern*
James S. Smith, *Hillsboro*
Felix Walker, *Waynesville*
Lewis Williams, *Panther Creek*

## OHIO

SENATORS

Benjamin Ruggles, *St. Clairsville*
William A. Trimble, *Hillsboro*

REPRESENTATIVES

Philemon Beecher, *Lancaster*
Henry Brush, *Chillicothe*
John W. Campbell, *West Union*
Samuel Herrick, *Zanesville*
Thomas R. Ross, *Lebanon*
John Sloane, *Wooster*

## PENNSYLVANIA

SENATORS

Jonathan Roberts, *Norristown*
Walter Lowrie, *Butler*

REPRESENTATIVES

Henry Baldwin, *Pittsburgh*
Andrew Boden, *Carlisle*
William Darlington, *West Chester*
George Denison, *Wilkes-Barre*
Samuel Edwards, *Chester*
Thomas Forrest, *Germantown*
David Fullerton,[47] *Greencastle*
Thomas G. McCullough,[48] *Chambersburg*
Samuel Gross, *Trappe*
Joseph Hemphill, *Philadelphia*
Jacob Hibshman, *Ephrata*
Jacob Hostetter, *Hanover*
William P. Maclay, *Lewistown*
David Marchand, *Greensburg*

Robert Moore, *Beavertown*
Samuel Moore, *Doylestown*
John Murray, *Milton*
Thomas Patterson, *West Middletown*
Robert Philson, *Somerset*
Thomas J. Rogers, *Easton*
John Sergeant, *Philadelphia*
Christian Tarr, *Brownsville*
Joseph Hiester,[49] *Reading*
Daniel Udree,[50] *Reading*
James M. Wallace, *Hummelstown*

## RHODE ISLAND

SENATORS

William Hunter, *Newport*
James Burrill, Jr.,[51] *Providence*
Nehemiah R. Knight,[52] *Providence*

REPRESENTATIVES AT LARGE

Samuel Eddy, *Providence*
Nathaniel Hazard,[53] *Newport*

## SOUTH CAROLINA

SENATORS

John Gaillard, *Pendleton*
William Smith, *Pinckneyville*

REPRESENTATIVES

Joseph Brevard, *Camden*
Elias Earle, *Centerville*
James Ervin, *Darlington*
William Lowndes, *Jacksonboro*
John McCreary, *Cedar Shoals*
James Overstreet, *King Creek*
Charles Pinckney, *Charleston*
Eldred Simkins, *Edgefield*
Starling Tucker, *Mountain Shoals*

## TENNESSEE

SENATORS

John Williams, *Knoxville*
John H. Eaton, *Nashville*

REPRESENTATIVES

Robert Allen, *Carthage*
Henry H. Bryan, *Palmyra*
Newton Cannon, *Harpeth*
John Cocke, *Rutledge*
Francis Jones, *Winchester*
John Rhea, *Sullivan*

## VERMONT

SENATORS

Isaac Tichenor, *Bennington*
William A. Palmer, *Danville*

REPRESENTATIVES AT LARGE

Samuel C. Crafts, *Craftsbury*
Ezra Meech, *Charlotte*
Orsamus C. Merrill,[54] *Bennington*
Rollin C. Mallary,[55] *Poultney*
Charles Rich, *Shoreham*
Mark Richards, *Westminster*
William Strong, *Hartford*

## VIRGINIA

SENATORS

James Barbour, *Barboursville*
John W. Eppes,[56] *Charles City*
James Pleasants,[57] *Goochland*

REPRESENTATIVES

Mark Alexander, *Lombardy Grove*
William Lee Ball, *Nuttsville*
Philip P. Barbour, *Lucketsville*
William A. Burwell,[58] *Rocky Mount*
John Floyd, *Newbern*
Robert S. Garnett, *Lloyds*
James Johnson,[59] *Lawrenceville*
John C. Gray,[60] *Courtland*
James Jones, *Hendersonville*
William McCoy, *Franklin*
Charles F. Mercer, *Aldie*
Hugh Nelson, *Milton*
Thomas Newton, Jr., *Norfolk*
Severn E. Parker, *Eastville*
James Pindall,[61] *Clarksburg*
Edward B. Jackson,[62] *Clarksburg*
James Pleasants,[63] *Goochland*
William S. Archer,[64] *Amelia*
John Randolph, *Charlotte*
Ballard Smith, *Lewisburg*
Alexander Smyth, *Wythe*
George F. Strother,[65] *Culpeper*
Thomas L. Moore,[66] *Warrenton*
George Tucker, *Lynchburg*
John Tyler, *Charles City*
Thomas Van Swearingen, *Shepherdstown*
Jared Williams, *Newton*

## ALABAMA TERRITORY [67]

DELEGATE

Vacant

---

[45] Died December 20, 1820.
[46] Elected to fill vacancy caused by death of Jesse Slocumb, and took his seat February 7, 1821.
[47] Resigned May 15, 1820.
[48] Elected to fill vacancy caused by resignation of David Fullerton, and took his seat November 13, 1820.
[49] Resigned in December 1820, having been elected governor.
[50] Elected to fill vacancy caused by resignation of Joseph Hiester, and took his seat January 8, 1821.
[51] Died December 25, 1820.
[52] Elected to fill vacancy caused by death of James Burrill, Jr., and took his seat January 20, 1821.
[53] Died December 17, 1820.

[54] Served until January 12, 1820; succeeded by Rollin C. Mallary, who contested his election.
[55] Successfully contested the election of Orsamus C. Merrill, and took his seat January 13, 1820.
[56] Resigned December 4, 1819.
[57] Elected to fill vacancy caused by resignation of John W. Eppes, and took his seat December 14, 1819.
[58] Died February 16, 1821.
[59] Resigned February 1, 1820.
[60] Elected to fill vacancy caused by resignation of James Johnson, and took his seat November 13, 1820.
[61] Resigned July 26, 1820.
[62] Elected to fill vacancy caused by resignation of

James Pindall, and took his seat November 13, 1820.
[63] Resigned December 14, 1819, having been elected Senator.
[64] Elected to fill vacancy caused by resignation of James Pleasants, and took his seat January 18, 1820.
[65] Resigned February 10, 1820.
[66] Elected to fill vacancy caused by resignation of George F. Strother, and took his seat November 13, 1820.
[67] Granted statehood December 14, 1819.

## ARKANSAS TERRITORY[68]

DELEGATE
James W. Bates,[69] *Arkansas*

## MICHIGAN TERRITORY [70]

DELEGATE
William W. Woodbridge,[71] *Detroit*
Solomon Sibley,[72] *Detroit*

## TERRITORY OF MISSOURI

DELEGATE
John Scott, *Ste. Genevieve*

---

[68] Formed from a portion of the lands of the Territory of Missouri and granted a Delegate in Congress by Act of March 2, 1819.

[69] Took his seat March 2, 1820.

[70] Formed by act approved January 11, 1805, from a portion of lands of Indiana Territory with Detroit as the seat of government.

[71] Took his seat March 2, 1820; resigned August 9, 1820.

[72] Elected to fill vacancy caused by resignation of William W. Woodbridge, and took his seat November 20, 1820.

# 17TH CONGRESS

MARCH 4, 1821, TO MARCH 3, 1823

FIRST SESSION— *December 3, 1821, to May 8, 1822*
SECOND SESSION— *December 2, 1822, to March 3, 1823*

VICE PRESIDENT OF THE UNITED STATES— Daniel D. Tompkins, of New York
PRESIDENT PRO TEMPORE OF THE SENATE— John Gaillard,[1] of South Carolina
SECRETARY OF THE SENATE— Charles Cutts, of New Hampshire
SERGEANT AT ARMS OF THE SENATE— Mountjoy Bayly, of Maryland

SPEAKER OF THE HOUSE OF REPRESENTATIVES— Philip P. Barbour,[2] of Virginia
CLERK OF THE HOUSE— Thomas Dougherty,[3] of Kentucky; Matthew St. Clair Clarke,[4] of Pennsylvania
SERGEANT AT ARMS OF THE HOUSE— Thomas Dunn, of Maryland
DOORKEEPER OF THE HOUSE— Benjamin Birch, of Maryland

Daniel D. Tompkins
Vice President

Philip P. Barbour
Speaker

## ALABAMA

### SENATORS
John W. Walker,[5] *Huntsville*
William Kelly,[6] *Huntsville*
William R. King, *Cahaba*

### REPRESENTATIVE AT LARGE
Gabriel Moore, *Huntsville*

## CONNECTICUT

### SENATORS
James Lanman, *Norwich*
Elijah Boardman, *Litchfield*

### REPRESENTATIVES AT LARGE
Noyes Barber, *Groton*
Daniel Burrows, *Hebron*
Henry W. Edwards, *New Haven*
Gideon Tomlinson, *Fairfield*
John Russ, *Hartford*
Ansel Sterling, *Sharon*
Ebenezer Stoddard, *Woodstock*

## DELAWARE

### SENATORS
Nicholas Van Dyke, *New Castle*
Caesar A. Rodney,[7] *Wilmington*

### REPRESENTATIVES AT LARGE
Louis McLane, *Wilmington*
Caesar A. Rodney,[8] *Wilmington*
Daniel Rodney,[9] *Lewes*

## GEORGIA

### SENATORS
John Elliott, *Sunbury*
Freeman Walker,[10] *Augusta*
Nicholas Ware,[11] *Richmond*

### REPRESENTATIVES AT LARGE
Joel Abbot, *Washington*
Alfred Cuthbert, *Eatonton*
George R. Gilmer, *Lexington*
Robert R. Reid, *Augusta*
Edward F. Tattnall, *Savannah*
Wiley Thompson, *Elberton*

## ILLINOIS

### SENATORS
Jesse B. Thomas, *Edwardsville*
Ninian Edwards, *Edwardsville*

### REPRESENTATIVE AT LARGE
Daniel P. Cook, *Edwardsville*

## INDIANA

### SENATORS
James Noble, *Brookville*
Waller Taylor, *Vincennes*

### REPRESENTATIVE AT LARGE
William Hendricks,[12] *Madison*
Jonathan Jennings,[13] *Charlestown*

## KENTUCKY

### SENATORS
Richard M. Johnson, *Great Crossings*
Isham Talbot, *Frankfort*

### REPRESENTATIVES
Wingfield Bullock,[14] *Shelbyville*
James D. Breckinridge,[15] *Louisville*
Benjamin Hardin, *Bardstown*
Francis Johnson, *Bowling Green*
John T. Johnson, *Georgetown*
Thomas Metcalfe, *Carlisle*
Thomas Montgomery, *Stanford*
Anthony New, *Elkton*
George Robertson,[16] *Lancaster*
John S. Smith,[17] *Richmond*
David Trimble, *Mount Sterling*
Samuel H. Woodson, *Lexington*

## LOUISIANA

### SENATORS
Henry Johnson, *Donaldsonville*
James Brown, *New Orleans*

### REPRESENTATIVE AT LARGE
Josiah S. Johnston, *Alexandria*

## MAINE

### SENATORS
John Chandler, *Monmouth*
John Holmes, *Alfred*

### REPRESENTATIVES
Joshua Cushman, *Winslow*
Joseph Dane, *Kennebunk*

---

[1] Elected February 1, 1822; February 19, 1823.
[2] Elected December 4, 1821.
[3] Reelected December 4, 1821; died in 1822.
[4] Elected December 3, 1822; Samuel Burch, the principal clerk, acted as clerk in the interim.
[5] Resigned December 12, 1822.
[6] Elected to fill vacancy caused by resignation of John W. Walker, and took his seat January 21, 1823.
[7] Elected to fill vacancy in term commencing March 4, 1821, and took his seat January 24, 1822; resigned January 29, 1823, having been appointed minister to Buenos Aires; vacancy in this class from March 4, 1821, to January 23, 1822.
[8] Resigned January 24, 1822, having been elected Senator.
[9] Elected to fill vacancy caused by resignation of Caesar A. Rodney, and took his seat December 2, 1822.
[10] Resigned August 8, 1821.
[11] Elected to fill vacancy caused by resignation of Freeman Walker, and took his seat December 11, 1821.
[12] Resigned July 25, 1822.
[13] Elected to fill vacancy caused by resignation of William Hendricks, and took his seat December 2, 1822.
[14] Died October 13, 1821, before Congress assembled.
[15] Elected to fill vacancy caused by death of Wingfield Bullock, and took his seat January 2, 1822.
[16] Resigned before Congress assembled.
[17] Elected to fill vacancy caused by resignation of George Robertson, and took his seat December 3, 1821.

Ebenezer Herrick, *Bowdoinham*
Mark L. Hill, *Phippsburg*
Enoch Lincoln, *Paris*
Ezekiel Whitman,[18] *Portland*
Mark Harris,[19] *Portland*
William D. Williamson, *Bangor*

## MARYLAND

### SENATORS

Edward Lloyd, *Easton*
William Pinkney,[20] *Baltimore*
Samuel Smith,[21] *Baltimore*

### REPRESENTATIVES

Thomas Bayly, *Princess Anne*
Jeremiah Cosden,[22] *Elkton*
Philip Reed,[23] *Chestertown*
Joseph Kent, *Bladensburg*
Peter Little, *Freedom*
Raphael Neale, *Leonardtown*
John Nelson, *Frederick*
Samuel Smith,[24] *Baltimore*
Isaac McKim,[25] *Baltimore*
Henry R. Warfield, *Middleburg*
Robert Wright, *Queenstown*

## MASSACHUSETTS

### SENATORS

Harrison Gray Otis,[26] *Boston*
James Lloyd,[27] *Boston*
Elijah H. Mills, *Northampton*

### REPRESENTATIVES

Samuel C. Allen, *Greenfield*
Gideon Barstow, *Salem*
Francis Baylies, *Taunton*
Lewis Bigelow, *Petersham*
Henry W. Dwight, *Stockbridge*
William Eustis, *Boston*
Timothy Fuller, *Boston*
Benjamin Gorham, *Boston*
Aaron Hobart, *Hanover*
Samuel Lathrop, *West Springfield*
Jeremiah Nelson, *Newburyport*
John Reed, *Yarmouth*
Jonathan Russell, *Mendon*

## MISSISSIPPI

### SENATORS

Thomas H. Williams, *Washington*
David Holmes, *Washington*

### REPRESENTATIVE AT LARGE

Christopher Rankin, *Natchez*

## MISSOURI[28]

### SENATORS

David Barton,[29] *St. Louis*
Thomas Hart Benton,[30] *St. Louis*

### REPRESENTATIVE AT LARGE

John Scott,[31] *Ste. Genevieve*

## NEW HAMPSHIRE

### SENATORS

David L. Morril, *Goffstown*
John F. Parrott, *Portsmouth*

### REPRESENTATIVES AT LARGE

Josiah Butler, *South Deerfield*
Matthew Harvey, *Hopkinton*
Aaron Matson, *Stoddard*
William Plumer, Jr., *Epping*
Nathaniel Upham, *Rochester*
Thomas Whipple, Jr., *Wentworth*

## NEW JERSEY

### SENATORS

Mahlon Dickerson, *Succasunna*
Samuel L. Southard,[32] *Trenton*

### REPRESENTATIVES AT LARGE

Ephraim Bateman, *Cedarville*
George Cassedy, *Hackensack*
Lewis Condict, *Morristown*
George Holcombe, *Allentown*
James Matlack, *Woodbury*
Samuel Swan, *Somerville*

## NEW YORK

### SENATORS

Rufus King, *New York City*
Martin Van Buren, *Albany*

### REPRESENTATIVES

Selah Tuthill,[33] *Goshen*
Charles Borland, Jr.,[34] *Wardsbridge*
Churchill C. Cambreleng, *New York City*
Samuel Campbell, *Columbus*
Peter Sharpe,[35] *New York City*
Cadwallader D. Colden,[36] *New York City*
Alfred Conkling, *Canajoharie*

John D. Dickinson, *Troy*
John Gebhard, *Schoharie*
James Hawkes, *Richfield*
Thomas H. Hubbard, *Hamilton*
Joseph Kirkland, *Utica*
Elisha Litchfield, *Delphi*
Richard McCarty, *Coxsackie*
John J. Morgan, *New York City*
Walter Patterson, *Livingston*
Jeremiah H. Pierson, *Ramapo*
Nathaniel Pitcher, *Sandy Hill*
William B. Rochester, *Bath*
Charles H. Ruggles, *Kingston*
Elijah Spencer, *Benton*
Micah Sterling, *Watertown*
John W. Taylor, *Ballston Spa*
Albert H. Tracy, *Buffalo*
Solomon Van Rensselaer,[37] *Albany*
Stephen Van Rensselaer,[38] *Albany*
William W. Van Wyck, *Fishkill*
Reuben H. Walworth, *Plattsburg*
Silas Wood, *Huntington*
David Woodcock, *Ithaca*

## NORTH CAROLINA

### SENATORS

Nathaniel Macon, *Monroe*
Montfort Stokes, *Wilkesboro*

### REPRESENTATIVES

William S. Blackledge, *New Bern*
Hutchins G. Burton, *Halifax*
Henry W. Connor, *Sherrills Ford*
Josiah Crudup, *Raleigh*
Weldon N. Edwards, *Warrenton*
Thomas H. Hall, *Tarboro*
Charles Hooks, *Dublin*
John Long, *Longs Mills*
Archibald McNeill, *McNeills Store*
Romulus M. Saunders, *Milton*
Lemuel Sawyer, *Elizabeth City*
Felix Walker, *Waynesville*
Lewis Williams, *Panther Creek*

## OHIO

### SENATORS

Benjamin Ruggles, *St. Clairsville*
William A. Trimble,[39] *Hillsboro*
Ethan Allen Brown,[40] *Cincinnati*

---

[18] Resigned June 1, 1822.
[19] Elected to fill vacancy caused by resignation of Ezekiel Whitman, and took his seat December 2, 1822.
[20] Died February 25, 1822.
[21] Elected to fill vacancy caused by death of William Pinkney, and took his seat December 17, 1822.
[22] Served until March 19, 1822; succeeded by Philip Reed, who contested his election.
[23] Successfully contested the election of Jeremiah Cosden, and took his seat March 19, 1822.
[24] Resigned December 17, 1822, before the commencement of the Eighteenth Congress, to which he had been reelected, having been elected Senator.
[25] Elected to fill vacancy caused by resignation of Samuel Smith, and took his seat January 8, 1823.
[26] Resigned May 30, 1822.

[27] Elected to fill vacancy caused by resignation of Harrison Gray Otis, and took his seat December 2, 1822.
[28] Admitted as a State into the Union August 10, 1821.
[29] Took his seat December 3, 1821; term to expire, as determined by lot, March 3, 1825.
[30] Took his seat December 6, 1821; term to expire, as determined by lot, March 3, 1827.
[31] Took his seat December 3, 1821.
[32] Resigned March 3, 1823.
[33] Died September 7, 1821, before Congress assembled.
[34] Elected to fill vacancy caused by death of Selah Tuthill, and took his seat December 3, 1821.
[35] Never qualified; succeeded by Caldwallader D. Colden, who contested his election.

[36] Successfully contested the election of Peter Sharpe, and took his seat December 12, 1821.
[37] Resigned January 14, 1822.
[38] Elected to fill vacancy caused by resignation of Solomon Van Rensselaer, and took his seat March 12, 1822.
[39] Died December 13, 1821.
[40] Elected to fill vacancy caused by death of William A. Trimble, and took his seat January 15, 1822.

## OHIO—Continued

### REPRESENTATIVES

Levi Barber, *Point Harmer*
John W. Campbell, *West Union*
David Chambers,[41] *Zanesville*
Thomas R. Ross, *Lebanon*
John Sloane, *Wooster*
Joseph Vance,[42] *Urbana*

## PENNSYLVANIA

### SENATORS

Walter Lowrie, *Butler*
William Findlay,[43] *Franklinton*

### REPRESENTATIVES

Henry Baldwin,[44] *Pittsburgh*
Walter Forward,[45] *Pittsburgh*
John Brown, *Lewistown*
James Buchanan, *Lancaster*
William Darlington, *West Chester*
George Denison, *Wilkes-Barre*
James Duncan,[46] *Carlisle*
John Findlay,[47] *Chambersburg*
Samuel Edwards, *Chester*
William Cox Ellis,[48] *Muncy*
Thomas Murray, Jr.,[49] *Milton*
Patrick Farrelly, *Meadville*
Samuel Gross, *Trappe*
Joseph Hemphill, *Philadelphia*
James McSherry, *Petersburg*
William Milnor,[50] *Philadelphia*
Thomas Forrest,[51] *Philadelphia*
James S. Mitchell, *Rossville*
Samuel Moore,[52] *Doylestown*
Samuel D. Ingham,[53] *New Hope*
Thomas Patterson, *West Middletown*
John Phillips, *Hummelstown*
George Plumer, *Robbstown*
Thomas J. Rogers, *Easton*
John Sergeant, *Philadelphia*
Andrew Stewart, *Uniontown*
John Tod, *Bedford*
Ludwig Worman,[54] *Pottstown*
Daniel Udree,[55] *Reading*

## RHODE ISLAND

### SENATORS

Nehemiah R. Knight, *Providence*
James De Wolf, *Bristol*

### REPRESENTATIVES AT LARGE

Job Durfee, *Tiverton*
Samuel Eddy, *Providence*

## SOUTH CAROLINA

### SENATORS

John Gaillard, *Pendleton*
William Smith, *Pinckneyville*

### REPRESENTATIVES

James Blair,[56] *Camden*
John Carter,[57] *Camden*
Joseph Gist, *Pinckneyville*
James Overstreet,[58] *King Creek*
Andrew R. Govan,[59] *Orangeburg*
William Lowndes,[60] *Jacksonboro*
James Hamilton, Jr.,[61] *Charleston*
George McDuffie, *Edgefield*
Thomas R. Mitchell, *Georgetown*
Joel R. Poinsett, *Charleston*
Starling Tucker, *Mountain Shoals*
John Wilson, *Golden Grove*

## TENNESSEE

### SENATORS

John Williams, *Knoxville*
John H. Eaton,[62] *Nashville*

### REPRESENTATIVES

Robert Allen, *Carthage*
Henry H. Bryan,[63] *Palmyra*
Newton Cannon, *Harpeth*
John Cocke, *Rutledge*
Francis Jones, *Winchester*
John Rhea, *Sullivan*

## VERMONT

### SENATORS

William A. Palmer, *Danville*
Horatio Seymour, *Middlebury*

### REPRESENTATIVES

Samuel C. Crafts, *Craftsbury*
Elias Keyes, *Stockbridge*
Rollin C. Mallary, *Poultney*
John Mattocks, *Peacham*
Charles Rich, *Shoreham*
Phineas White, *Putney*

## VIRGINIA

### SENATORS

James Barbour, *Barboursville*
James Pleasants,[64] *Goochland*
John Taylor,[65] *Port Royal*

### REPRESENTATIVES

Mark Alexander, *Lombardy Grove*
William S. Archer, *Amelia*
William L. Ball, *Nuttsville*
Philip P. Barbour, *Lucketsville*
Burwell Bassett, *Williamsburg*
John Floyd, *Newbern*
Robert S. Garnett, *Lloyds*
Edward B. Jackson, *Clarksburg*
James Jones, *Hendersonville*
Jabez Leftwich, *Liberty*
William McCoy, *Franklin*
Charles F. Mercer, *Aldie*
Thomas L. Moore, *Warrenton*
Hugh Nelson,[66] *Milton*
Thomas Newton, Jr., *Norfolk*
John Randolph, *Charlotte*
Arthur Smith, *Smithfield*
William Smith, *Lewisburg*
Alexander Smyth, *Wythe*
Andrew Stevenson, *Richmond*
George Tucker, *Lynchburg*
Thomas Van Sweringen,[67]
   *Shepherdstown*
James Stephenson,[68] *Martinsburg*
Jared Williams, *Newton*

## ARKANSAS TERRITORY

### DELEGATE

James W. Bates,[69] *Arkansas*

---

[41] Elected to fill vacancy caused by resignation of Representative-elect John C. Wright (March 3, 1821, before the beginning of the congressional term), and took his seat December 3, 1821.

[42] In previous issues of this publication this name appears as "John Vance." It is believed that this is an error arising through a printer's blunder in the first issue of the Congressional Directory for the Seventeenth Congress, caused by the typesetter carrying the name of "John" of Sloane's down to that of "Vance." The House Journal does not show that a "John Vance" was ever a Representative from Ohio, but in the same directory, under "Alphabetical List of Boarding Houses with the Members in each," the list of boarders at Miss Polk's home included "Joseph" Vance, but no "John."

[43] Elected for term beginning March 4, 1821, and took his seat December 17, 1821; vacancy in this class from March 4, 1821, to December 9, 1821.

[44] Resigned May 8, 1822.

[45] Elected to fill vacancy caused by resignation of Henry Baldwin, and took his seat December 2, 1822.

[46] Resigned before Congress assembled.

[47] Elected to fill vacancy caused by resignation of James Duncan, and took his seat December 12, 1821.

[48] Resigned before Congress assembled.

[49] Elected to fill vacancy caused by resignation of William Cox Ellis, and took his seat December 12, 1821.

[50] Resigned May 8, 1822.

[51] Elected to fill vacancy caused by resignation of William Milnor, and took his seat December 2, 1822.

[52] Resigned May 20, 1822.

[53] Elected to fill vacancy caused by resignation of Samuel Moore, and took his seat December 2, 1822.

[54] Died October 17, 1822.

[55] Elected to fill vacancy caused by death of Ludwig Worman, and took his seat December 23, 1822.

[56] Resigned May 8, 1822.

[57] Elected to fill vacancy caused by resignation of James Blair, and took his seat December 11, 1822.

[58] Died May 24, 1822.

[59] Elected to fill vacancy caused by death of James Overstreet, and took his seat December 4, 1822.

[60] Resigned May 8, 1822.

[61] Elected to fill vacancy caused by resignation of William Lowndes, and took his seat January 6, 1823.

[62] Reelected for the term commencing March 4, 1821, and took his seat December 3, 1821; vacancy in this class from March 4, 1821, to September 26, 1821, caused by recess of legislature.

[63] Committee on Elections reported on February 17, 1823, that he had been duly elected, but appears never to have taken his seat.

[64] Resigned December 15, 1822.

[65] Elected to fill vacancy caused by resignation of James Pleasants, and took his seat December 30, 1822.

[66] Resigned January 14, 1823.

[67] Died August 19, 1822.

[68] Elected to fill vacancy caused by death of Thomas Van Sweringen, and took his seat December 2, 1822.

[69] Election unsuccessfully contested by Matthew Lyon.

## TERRITORY OF FLORIDA[70]

DELEGATE
Joseph M. Hernandez,[71] *St. Augustine*

## MICHIGAN TERRITORY

DELEGATE
Solomon Sibley, *Detroit*

## TERRITORY OF MISSOURI[72]

DELEGATE
Vacant

---

[70] Formed March 30, 1822, from lands ceded by Spain to the United States by treaty of Washington of February 22, 1819, and theretofore known as "East and West Florida," and granted a Delegate in Congress.

[71] Took his seat January 3, 1823.

[72] Granted statehood August 10, 1821.

# 18TH CONGRESS

MARCH 4, 1823, TO MARCH 3, 1825

FIRST SESSION— *December 1, 1823, to May 27, 1824*
SECOND SESSION— *December 6, 1824, to March 3, 1825*

VICE PRESIDENT OF THE UNITED STATES— DANIEL D. TOMPKINS, of New York
PRESIDENT PRO TEMPORE OF THE SENATE— JOHN GAILLARD,[1] of South Carolina
SECRETARY OF THE SENATE— CHARLES CUTTS, of New Hampshire
SERGEANT AT ARMS OF THE SENATE— MOUNTJOY BAYLY, of Maryland

SPEAKER OF THE HOUSE OF REPRESENTATIVES— HENRY CLAY,[2] of Kentucky
CLERK OF THE HOUSE— MATTHEW ST. CLAIR CLARKE,[3] of Pennsylvania
SERGEANT AT ARMS OF THE HOUSE— THOMAS DUNN, of Maryland; JOHN O. DUNN,[4] of
District of Columbia
DOORKEEPER OF THE HOUSE— BENJAMIN BIRCH, of Maryland

Daniel D. Tompkins
Vice President

Henry Clay
Speaker

## ALABAMA

### SENATORS
William R. King, *Cahaba*
William Kelly, *Huntsville*

### REPRESENTATIVES
John McKee, *Tuscaloosa*
Gabriel Moore, *Huntsville*
George W. Owen, *Claiborne*

## CONNECTICUT

### SENATORS
James Lanman, *Norwich*
Elijah Boardman,[5] *Litchfield*
Henry W. Edwards,[6] *New Haven*

### REPRESENTATIVES AT LARGE
Noyes Barber, *Groton*
Samuel A. Foote, *Cheshire*
Ansel Sterling, *Sharon*
Ebenezer Stoddard, *Woodstock*
Gideon Tomlinson, *Fairfield*
Lemuel Whitman, *Farmington*

## DELAWARE

### SENATORS
Nicholas Van Dyke, *New Castle*
Thomas Clayton,[7] *Dover*

### REPRESENTATIVE AT LARGE
Louis McLane, *Wilmington*

## GEORGIA

### SENATORS
John Elliott, *Sunbury*
Nicholas Ware,[8] *Richmond*
Thomas W. Cobb,[9] *Greensboro*

### REPRESENTATIVES AT LARGE
Joel Abbot, *Washington*
George Cary, *Appling*
Thomas W. Cobb,[10] *Greensboro*
Richard H. Wilde,[11] *Augusta*
Alfred Cuthbert, *Eatonton*
John Forsyth, *Augusta*
Edward F. Tattnall, *Savannah*
Wiley Thompson, *Elberton*

## ILLINOIS

### SENATORS
Jesse B. Thomas, *Edwardsville*
Ninian Edwards,[12] *Edwardsville*
John McLean,[13] *Shawneetown*

### REPRESENTATIVE AT LARGE
Daniel P. Cook, *Edwardsville*

## INDIANA

### SENATORS
James Noble, *Brookville*
Waller Taylor, *Vincennes*

### REPRESENTATIVES
Jonathan Jennings, *Charlestown*
John Test, *Brookville*
William Prince,[14] *Princeton*
Jacob Call,[15] *Princeton*

## KENTUCKY

### SENATORS
Richard M. Johnson, *Great Crossings*
Isham Talbot, *Frankfort*

### REPRESENTATIVES
Richard A. Buckner, *Greensburg*
Henry Clay, *Lexington*
Robert P. Henry, *Hopkinsville*
Francis Johnson, *Bowling Green*
John T. Johnson, *Georgetown*
Robert P. Letcher, *Lancaster*
Thomas Metcalfe, *Carlisle*
Thomas P. Moore, *Harrodsburg*
Philip Thompson, *Yellow Banks*
David Trimble, *Mount Sterling*
David White, *New Castle*
Charles A. Wickliffe, *Bardstown*

## LOUISIANA

### SENATORS
Henry Johnson,[16] *Donaldsonville*
Dominique Bouligny,[17] *New Orleans*
James Brown,[18] *New Orleans*
Josiah S. Johnston,[19] *Alexandria*

### REPRESENTATIVES
William L. Brent, *St. Martinsville*
Henry H. Gurley, *Baton Rouge*
Edward Livingston, *New Orleans*

---

[1] Elected May 21, 1824.
[2] Elected December 1, 1823.
[3] Reelected December 1, 1823.
[4] Elected December 6, 1824.
[5] Died October 8, 1823.
[6] Appointed to fill vacancy caused by death of Elijah Boardman, and took his seat December 1, 1823; subsequently elected.
[7] Elected to fill vacancy caused by resignation of Caesar A. Rodney, in preceding Congress, and took his seat January 15, 1824. Vacancy in this class from

January 29, 1823, to January 8, 1824.
[8] Died September 7, 1824.
[9] Elected to fill vacancy caused by death of Nicholas Ware, and took his seat December 6, 1824.
[10] Resigned December 6, 1824, having been elected Senator.
[11] Elected to fill vacancy caused by resignation of Thomas W. Cobb, and took his seat February 7, 1825.
[12] Resigned March 4, 1824, having been appointed minister to Mexico.
[13] Elected to fill vacancy caused by resignation of

Ninian Edwards, and took his seat December 20, 1824.
[14] Died September 4, 1824.
[15] Elected to fill vacancy caused by death of William Prince, and took his seat December 23, 1824.
[16] Resigned May 27, 1824.
[17] Elected to fill vacancy caused by resignation of Henry Johnson, and took his seat December 21, 1824.
[18] Resigned December 10, 1823, having been appointed minister to France.
[19] Elected to fill vacancy caused by resignation of James Brown, and took his seat March 12, 1824.

## MAINE

### SENATORS
John Chandler, *Monmouth*
John Holmes, *Alfred*

### REPRESENTATIVES
William Burleigh, *South Berwick*
Joshua Cushman, *Winslow*
Ebenezer Herrick, *Bowdoinham*
David Kidder, *Norridgewock*
Enoch Lincoln, *Paris*
Stephen Longfellow, *Portland*
Jeremiah O'Brien, *Machias*

## MARYLAND

### SENATORS
Edward Lloyd, *Easton*
Samuel Smith, *Baltimore*

### REPRESENTATIVES
William Heyward, Jr., *Easton*
Joseph Kent, *Bladensburg*
John Lee, *Petersville*
Peter Little, *Freedom*
Isaac McKim,[20] *Baltimore*
George E. Mitchell, *Elkton*
Raphael Neale, *Leonardtown*
John S. Spence, *Poplartown*
Henry R. Warfield, *Middleburg*

## MASSACHUSETTS

### SENATORS
Elijah H. Mills, *Northampton*
James Lloyd, *Boston*

### REPRESENTATIVES
Samuel C. Allen, *Greenfield*
John Bailey,[21] *Canton*
Francis Baylies, *Taunton*
Benjamin W. Crowninshield, *Salem*
Henry W. Dwight, *Stockbridge*
Timothy Fuller, *Boston*
Aaron Hobart, *Hanover*
Samuel Lathrop, *West Springfield*
John Locke, *Ashby*
Jeremiah Nelson, *Newburyport*
John Reed, *Yarmouth*
Jonas Sibley, *Worcester*
Daniel Webster, *Boston*

## MISSISSIPPI

### SENATORS
Thomas H. Williams, *Washington*
David Holmes, *Washington*

### REPRESENTATIVE AT LARGE
Christopher Rankin, *Natchez*

## MISSOURI

### SENATORS
David Barton, *St. Louis*
Thomas Hart Benton, *St. Louis*

### REPRESENTATIVE AT LARGE
John Scott, *Ste. Genevieve*

## NEW HAMPSHIRE

### SENATORS
John F. Parrott, *Portsmouth*
Samuel Bell, *Chester*

### REPRESENTATIVES AT LARGE
Ichabod Bartlett, *Portsmouth*
Matthew Harvey, *Hopkinton*
Arthur Livermore, *Plymouth*
Aaron Matson, *Stoddard*
William Plumer, Jr., *Epping*
Thomas Whipple, Jr., *Wentworth*

## NEW JERSEY

### SENATORS
Mahlon Dickerson, *Succasunna*
Joseph McIlvaine,[22] *Burlington*

### REPRESENTATIVES AT LARGE
George Cassedy, *Hackensack*
Lewis Condict, *Morristown*
Daniel Garrison, *Salem*
George Holcombe, *Allentown*
James Matlack, *Woodbury*
Samuel Swan, *Somerville*

## NEW YORK

### SENATORS
Rufus King, *New York City*
Martin Van Buren, *Albany*

### REPRESENTATIVES
John W. Cady, *Johnstown*
Churchill C. Cambreleng, *New York City*
Lot Clark, *Norwich*
Ela Collins, *Lowville*
Hector Craig, *Chester*
Rowland Day, *Simpronius*
Justin Dwinell, *Cazenovia*
Lewis Eaton, *Schoharie Bridge*
Charles A. Foote, *Delhi*
Joel Frost, *Carmel*
Moses Hayden, *York*
John Herkimer, *Danube*
James L. Hogeboom, *Castleton*
Lemuel Jenkins, *Bloomingburg*
Samuel Lawrence, *Johnsons Settlement*
Elisha Litchfield, *Delphi*
Henry C. Martindale, *Sandy Hill*

Dudley Marvin, *Canandaigua*
John J. Morgan, *New York City*
John Richards, *Johnsburg*
William B. Rochester,[23] *Bath*
William Woods,[24] *Bath*
Robert S. Rose, *Geneva*
Peter Sharpe, *New York City*
Henry R. Storrs, *Whitestown*
James Strong, *Hudson*
John W. Taylor, *Ballston Spa*
Egbert Ten Eyck, *Watertown*
Albert H. Tracy, *Buffalo*
Jacob Tyson, *Castletown*
Stephen Van Rensselaer, *Albany*
William W. Van Wyck, *Fishkill*
Isaac Williams, Jr., *Cooperstown*
Isaac Wilson,[25] *Middlebury*
Parmenio Adams,[26] *Batavia*
Silas Wood, *Huntington*

## NORTH CAROLINA

### SENATORS
Nathan Macon, *Monroe*
John Branch, *Enfield*

### REPRESENTATIVES
Hutchins G. Burton,[27] *Halifax*
George Outlaw,[28] *Windsor*
Henry W. Connor, *Sherrills Ford*
John Culpepper, *Lawrenceville*
Weldon N. Edwards, *Warrenton*
Alfred M. Gatlin, *Edenton*
Thomas H. Hall, *Tarboro*
Charles Hooks, *Dublin*
John Long, *Longs Mills*
Willie P. Mangum, *Red Mountain*
Romulus M. Saunders, *Milton*
Richard D. Spaight, Jr., *New Bern*
Robert B. Vance, *Nashville*
Lewis Williams, *Panther Creek*

## OHIO

### SENATORS
Benjamin Ruggles, *St. Clairsville*
Ethan Allen Brown, *Cincinnati*

### REPRESENTATIVES
Mordecai Bartley, *Mansfield*
Philemon Beecher, *Lancaster*
John W. Campbell, *West Union*
John W. Gazlay, *Cincinnati*
Duncan McArthur, *Chillicothe*
William McLean, *Piqua*
John Patterson, *St. Clairsville*
Thomas R. Ross, *Lebanon*
John Sloane, *Wooster*
Joseph Vance, *Urbana*
Samuel F. Vinton, *Gallipolis*

---

[20] Elected to fill vacancy caused by resignation of Representative-elect Samuel Smith, in preceding Congress.
[21] By resolution of March 18, 1824, was declared not entitled to seat; subsequently elected, and took his seat December 13, 1824.
[22] Elected to fill vacancy caused by resignation of

Samuel L. Southard, in preceding Congress, and took his seat December 1, 1823.
[23] Resigned before Congress assembled.
[24] Elected to fill vacancy caused by resignation of William B. Rochester, and took his seat December 1, 1823.
[25] Served until January 7, 1824; succeeded by

Parmenio Adams, who contested his election.
[26] Successfully contested the election of Isaac Wilson, and took his seat January 7, 1824.
[27] Resigned March 23, 1824.
[28] Elected to fill vacancy caused by resignation of Hutchins G. Burton, and took his seat January 19, 1825.

## OHIO—Continued

REPRESENTATIVES—CONTINUED
Elisha Whittlesey, *Canfield*
William Wilson, *Newark*
John C. Wright, *Steubenville*

## PENNSYLVANIA

SENATORS
Walter Lowrie, *Butler*
William Findlay, *Franklinton*

REPRESENTATIVES
James Allison, Jr., *Beaver*
Samuel Breck, *Philadelphia*
John Brown, *Lewistown*
James Buchanan, *Lancaster*
Samuel Edwards, *Chester*
William Cox Ellis, *Muncy*
Patrick Farrelly, *Meadville*
John Findlay, *Chambersburg*
Walter Forward, *Pittsburgh*
Robert Harris, *Harrisburg*
Joseph Hemphill, *Philadelphia*
Samuel D. Ingham, *New Hope*
George Kremer, *Lewisburg*
Samuel McKean, *Burlington*
Philip S. Markley, *Norristown*
Daniel H. Miller, *Philadelphia*
James S. Mitchell, *Rossville*
Thomas Patterson, *West Middletown*
George Plumer, *Robbstown*
Andrew Stewart, *Uniontown*
John Tod,[29] *Bedford*
Alexander Thomson,[30] *Bedford*
Daniel Udree, *Reading*
Isaac Wayne, *Warren*
Henry Wilson, *Allentown*
James Wilson, *Fairfield*
Thomas J. Rogers,[31] *Easton*
George Wolf,[32] *Easton*

## RHODE ISLAND

SENATORS
Nehemiah R. Knight, *Providence*
James De Wolf, *Bristol*

REPRESENTATIVES AT LARGE
Job Durfee, *Tiverton*
Samuel Eddy, *Providence*

## SOUTH CAROLINA

SENATORS
John Gaillard, *Pendleton*
Robert Y. Hayne, *Charleston*

REPRESENTATIVES
Robert B. Campbell, *Brownsville*
John Carter, *Camden*
Joseph Gist, *Pinckneyville*
Andrew R. Govan, *Orangeburg*
James Hamilton, Jr., *Charleston*
George McDuffie, *Edgefield*
Joel R. Poinsett, *Charleston*
Starling Tucker, *Mountain Shoals*
John Wilson, *Golden Grove*

## TENNESSEE

SENATORS
John H. Eaton, *Nashville*
Andrew Jackson, *Nashville*

REPRESENTATIVES
Adam R. Alexander, *Jackson*
Robert Allen, *Carthage*
John Blair, *Jonesboro*
John Cocke, *Rutledge*
Sam Houston, *Nashville*
Jacob C. Isacks, *Winchester*
James B. Reynolds, *Clarksville*
James T. Sandford, *Columbia*
James Standifer, *Pikeville*

## VERMONT

SENATORS
William A. Palmer, *Danville*
Horatio Seymour, *Middlebury*

REPRESENTATIVES AT LARGE
William C. Bradley, *Westminster*
Daniel A. A. Buck, *Chelsea*
Samuel C. Crafts, *Craftsbury*
Rollin C. Mallary, *Poultney*
Charles Rich,[33] *Shoreham*

Henry Olin,[34] *Salisbury*

## VIRGINIA

SENATORS
James Barbour, *Barboursville*
John Taylor,[35] *Port Royal*
Littleton W. Tazewell,[36] *Norfolk*

REPRESENTATIVES
Mark Alexander, *Lombardy Grove*
William S. Archer, *Amelia*
John S. Barbour, *Culpeper*
Philip P. Barbour, *Lucketsville*
Burwell Bassett, *Williamsburg*
John Floyd, *Newbern*
Robert S. Garnett, *Lloyds*
Joseph Johnson, *Bridgeport*
Jabez Leftwich, *Liberty*
William McCoy, *Franklin*
Charles F. Mercer, *Aldie*
Thomas Newton, Jr., *Norfolk*
John Randolph, *Charlotte*
William C. Rives, *Milton*
Arthur Smith, *Smithfield*
William Smith, *Lewisburg*
Alexander Smyth, *Wythe*
James Stephenson, *Martinsburg*
Andrew Stevenson, *Richmond*
William L. Ball,[37] *Nuttsville*
John Taliaferro,[38] *Fredericksburg*
George Tucker, *Lynchburg*
Jared Williams,[39] *Newton*

## ARKANSAS TERRITORY

DELEGATE
Henry W. Conway, *Little Rock*

## TERRITORY OF FLORIDA

DELEGATE
Richard K. Call, *Pensacola*

## MICHIGAN TERRITORY

DELEGATE
Gabriel Richard,[40] *Detroit*

---

[29] Resigned in 1824.
[30] Elected to fill vacancy caused by resignation of John Tod, and took his seat December 6, 1824.
[31] Resigned April 20, 1824.
[32] Elected to fill vacancy caused by resignation of Thomas J. Rogers, and took his seat December 9, 1824.

[33] Died October 15, 1824.
[34] Elected to fill vacancy caused by death of Charles Rich, and took his seat December 13, 1824.
[35] Died August 20, 1824.
[36] Elected to fill vacancy caused by death of John Taylor, and took his seat December 29, 1824.
[37] Died February 28, 1824.

[38] Elected to fill vacancy caused by death of William L. Ball, and took his seat April 8, 1824.
[39] Election unsuccessfully contested by Alfred H. Powell.
[40] Election unsuccessfully contested by John Biddle.

# 19TH CONGRESS

## MARCH 4, 1825, TO MARCH 3, 1827

John C. Calhoun
Vice President

FIRST SESSION— *December 5, 1825, to May 22, 1826*

SECOND SESSION— *December 4, 1826, to March 3, 1827*

SPECIAL SESSION OF THE SENATE— *March 4, 1825, to March 9, 1825*

---

VICE PRESIDENT OF THE UNITED STATES— JOHN C. CALHOUN, of South Carolina

PRESIDENT PRO TEMPORE OF THE SENATE— JOHN GAILLARD,[1] of South Carolina; NATHANIEL MACON,[2] of North Carolina

SECRETARY OF THE SENATE— CHARLES CUTTS, of New Hampshire; WALTER LOWRIE,[3] of Pennsylvania

SERGEANT AT ARMS OF THE SENATE— MOUNTJOY BAYLY, of Maryland

---

SPEAKER OF THE HOUSE OF REPRESENTATIVES— JOHN W. TAYLOR,[4] of New York

CLERK OF THE HOUSE— MATTHEW ST. CLAIR CLARKE,[5] of Pennsylvania

SERGEANT AT ARMS OF THE HOUSE— JOHN O. DUNN, of District of Columbia

DOORKEEPER OF THE HOUSE— BENJAMIN BIRCH, of Maryland

John W. Taylor
Speaker

## ALABAMA

### SENATORS
William R. King, *Cahaba*
Henry H. Chambers,[6] *Madison*
Israel Pickens,[7] *Cahaba*
John McKinley,[8] *Huntsville*

### REPRESENTATIVES
John McKee, *Tuscaloosa*
Gabriel Moore, *Huntsville*
George W. Owen, *Claiborne*

## CONNECTICUT

### SENATORS
Henry W. Edwards, *New Haven*
Calvin Willey,[9] *Tolland*

### REPRESENTATIVES AT LARGE
John Baldwin, *Windham*
Noyes Barber, *Groton*
Ralph I. Ingersoll, *New Haven*
Orange Merwin, *New Milford*
Elisha Phelps, *Simsbury*
Gideon Tomlinson, *Fairfield*

## DELAWARE

### SENATORS
Nicholas Van Dyke,[10] *New Castle*
Daniel Rodney,[11] *Wilmington*
Henry M. Ridgely,[12] *Dover*

Thomas Clayton, *Dover*

### REPRESENTATIVE AT LARGE
Louis McLane,[13] *Wilmington*

## GEORGIA

### SENATORS
Thomas W. Cobb, *Greensboro*
John Macpherson Berrien, *Savannah*

### REPRESENTATIVES AT LARGE
George Cary, *Appling*
Alfred Cuthbert, *Eatonton*
John Forsyth, *Augusta*
Charles E. Haynes, *Sparta*
James Meriwether, *Athens*
Edward F. Tattnall, *Savannah*
Wiley Thompson, *Elberton*

## ILLINOIS

### SENATORS
Jesse B. Thomas, *Edwardsville*
Elias K. Kane, *Kaskaskia*

### REPRESENTATIVE AT LARGE
Daniel P. Cook, *Edwardsville*

## INDIANA

### SENATORS
James Noble, *Brookville*
William Hendricks, *Madison*

### REPRESENTATIVES
Ratliff Boon, *Boonville*
Jonathan Jennings, *Charlestown*
John Test, *Brookville*

## KENTUCKY

### SENATORS
Richard M. Johnson, *Great Crossings*
John Rowan, *Louisville*

### REPRESENTATIVES
Richard A. Buckner, *Greensburg*
Henry Clay,[14] *Lexington*
James Clark,[15] *Winchester*
Robert P. Henry,[16] *Hopkinsville*
John F. Henry,[17] *Hopkinsville*
Francis Johnson, *Bowling Green*
James Johnson,[18] *Great Crossings*
Robert McHatton,[19] *Georgetown*
Robert P. Letcher, *Lancaster*
Thomas Metcalfe, *Carlisle*
Thomas P. Moore, *Harrodsburg*
David Trimble, *Mount Sterling*
Charles A. Wickliffe, *Bardstown*
William S. Young, *Elizabethtown*

[1] Elected March 9, 1825 (special session of the Senate).

[2] Elected May 20, 1826; January 2, 1827; and March 2, 1827.

[3] Elected December 12, 1825.

[4] Elected December 5, 1825.

[5] Reelected December 5, 1825.

[6] Died January 24, 1826.

[7] Appointed to fill vacancy caused by death of Henry Chambers, and took his seat April 10, 1826.

[8] Elected to fill vacancy caused by death of Henry Chambers, and took his seat December 21, 1826.

[9] Elected for term commencing March 4, 1825; took his seat December 5, 1825. James Lanman was appointed, but the Senate, on March 5, 1825, would not permit him to qualify; vacancy in this class from March 4, 1825, to May 4, 1825, because of recess of legislature. (See U.S. Senate Election, Expulsion and Censure Cases, 1793-1990, Senate Document 103-33, pp. 31-32.)

[10] Died May 21, 1826.

[11] Appointed to fill vacancy caused by death of Nicholas Van Dyke, and took his seat December 4, 1826.

[12] Elected to fill vacancy caused by death of Nicholas Van Dyke, and took his seat January 23, 1827.

[13] Reelected to the Twentieth Congress, but resigned, having been elected Senator.

[14] Resigned March 6, 1825, before Congress assembled.

[15] Elected to fill vacancy caused by resignation of Henry Clay, and took his seat December 5, 1825.

[16] Died August 25, 1826.

[17] Elected to fill vacancy caused by death of Robert P. Henry, and took his seat December 11, 1826.

[18] Died August 14, 1826.

[19] Elected to fill vacancy caused by death of James Johnson, and took his seat December 7, 1826.

## KENTUCKY—Continued

### REPRESENTATIVES—CONTINUED

Joseph Lecompte, *New Castle*

## LOUISIANA

### SENATORS

Josiah S. Johnston, *Alexandria*
Dominique Bouligny, *New Orleans*

### REPRESENTATIVES

William L. Brent, *St. Martinsville*
Henry H. Gurley, *Baton Rouge*
Edward Livingston, *New Orleans*

## MAINE

### SENATORS

John Chandler, *Monmouth*
John Holmes, *Alfred*

### REPRESENTATIVES

John Anderson, *Portland*
William Burleigh, *South Berwick*
Ebenezer Herrick, *Bowdoinham*
David Kiddler, *Norridgewock*
Enoch Lincoln,[20] *Paris*
James W. Ripley,[21] *Fryeburg*
Jeremiah O'Brien, *Machias*
Peleg Sprague, *Hallowell*

## MARYLAND

### SENATORS

Edward Lloyd,[22] *Easton*
Ezekiel F. Chambers,[23] *Chestertown*
Samuel Smith, *Baltimore*

### REPRESENTATIVES

John Barney, *Baltimore*
Clement Dorsey, *Chaptico*
Joseph Kent,[24] *Bladensburg*
John C. Weems,[25] *Waterloo*
John L. Kerr, *Easton*
Peter Little, *Freedom*
Robert N. Martin, *Princess Anne*
George E. Mitchell, *Elkton*
George Peter, *Darnestown*
Thomas C. Worthington, *Frederick*

## MASSACHUSETTS

### SENATORS

Elijah H. Mills, *Northampton*
James Lloyd,[26] *Boston*
Nathaniel Silsbee,[27] *Salem*

### REPRESENTATIVES

Samuel C. Allen, *Greenfield*
John Bailey, *Milton*
Francis Baylies, *Taunton*
Benjamin W. Crowninshield, *Salem*
John Davis, *Worcester*
Henry W. Dwight, *Stockbridge*
Edward Everett, *Cambridge*
Aaron Hobart, *East Bridgewater*
Samuel Lathrop, *West Springfield*
John Locke, *Ashby*
John Reed, *Yarmouth*
John Varnum, *Haverhill*
Daniel Webster, *Boston*

## MISSISSIPPI

### SENATORS

Thomas H. Williams, *Washington*
David Holmes,[28] *Washington*
Powhatan Ellis,[29] *Winchester*
Thomas B. Reed,[30] *Natchez*

### REPRESENTATIVE AT LARGE

Christopher Rankin,[31] *Natchez*
William Haile,[32] *Woodville*

## MISSOURI

### SENATORS

David Barton, *St. Louis*
Thomas Hart Benton, *St. Louis*

### REPRESENTATIVE AT LARGE

John Scott, *Ste. Genevieve*

## NEW HAMPSHIRE

### SENATORS

Samuel Bell, *Chester*
Levi Woodbury,[33] *Portsmouth*

### REPRESENTATIVES AT LARGE

Ichabod Bartlett, *Portsmouth*
Titus Brown, *Francestown*
Nehemiah Eastman, *Farmington*
Jonathan Harvey, *Sutton*
Joseph Healy, *Washington*
Thomas Whipple, Jr., *Wentworth*

## NEW JERSEY

### SENATORS

Mahlon Dickerson, *Succasunna*
Joseph McIlvaine,[34] *Burlington*
Ephraim Bateman,[35] *Cedarville*

### REPRESENTATIVES AT LARGE

George Cassedy, *Hackensack*
Lewis Condict, *Morristown*
Daniel Garrison, *Salem*
George Holcombe, *Allentown*
Samuel Swan, *Somerville*
Ebenezer Tucker, *Tuckerton*

## NEW YORK

### SENATORS

Martin Van Buren, *Albany*
Nathan Sanford,[36] *Albany*

### REPRESENTATIVES

Parmenio Adams, *Batavia*
William G. Angel, *Burlington*
Henry Ashley, *Catskill*
Luther Badger, *Janesville*
Churchill C. Cambreleng, *New York City*
William Dietz, *Schoharie*
Nicoll Fosdick, *Morristown*
Daniel G. Garnsey, *Fredonia*
John Hallock, Jr., *Ridgebury*
Abraham B. Hasbrouck, *Kingston*
Moses Hayden, *York*
Michael Hoffman, *Herkimer*
Charles Humphrey, *Ithaca*
Jeromus Johnson, *New York City*
Charles Kellogg, *Kelloggsville*
William McManus, *Troy*
Henry Markell, *Palatine*
Henry C. Martindale, *Sandy Hill*
Dudley Marvin, *Canandaigua*
John Miller, *Truxton*
Timothy H. Porter, *Olean*
Robert S. Rose, *Geneva*
Henry H. Ross, *Essex*
Joshua Sands, *Brooklyn*
Henry R. Storrs, *Whitestown*
James Strong, *Hudson*
John W. Taylor, *Ballston Spa*
Egbert Ten Eyck,[37] *Watertown*
Daniel Hugunin, Jr.,[38] *Oswego*
Stephen Van Rensselaer, *Albany*
Gulian C. Verplanck, *New York City*
Aaron Ward, *Mount Pleasant*
Bartow White, *Fishkill*
Elias Whitmore, *Windsor*
Silas Wood, *Huntington*

---

[20] Resigned in January, 1826, having been elected governor.

[21] Elected to fill vacancy caused by resignation of Enoch Lincoln, and took his seat December 4, 1826.

[22] Resigned in January 1826.

[23] Elected to fill vacancy caused by resignation of Edward Lloyd, and took his seat February 22, 1826.

[24] Resigned January 6, 1826, having been elected governor.

[25] Elected to fill vacancy caused by resignation of Joseph Kent, and took his seat February 7, 1826.

[26] Resigned May 23, 1826.

[27] Elected to fill vacancy caused by resignation of James Lloyd, and took his seat December 4, 1826.

[28] Resigned September 25, 1825.

[29] Appointed to fill vacancy caused by resignation of David Holmes, and took his seat December 12, 1825.

[30] Elected to fill vacancy caused by resignation of David Holmes, and took his seat March 11, 1826.

[31] Died March 14, 1826.

[32] Elected to fill vacancy caused by death of Christopher Rankin, and took his seat December 4, 1826.

[33] Elected to fill vacancy in term commencing March 4, 1825, and took his seat December 5, 1825; vacancy in this class from March 4, 1825, to June 15, 1825.

[34] Died August 19, 1826.

[35] Elected to fill vacancy caused by death of Joseph McIlvaine, and took his seat December 7, 1826.

[36] Elected to fill vacancy in term commencing March 4, 1825, and took his seat January 31, 1826; vacancy in this class from March 4, 1825, to January 14, 1826.

[37] Served until December 15, 1825; succeeded by Daniel Hugunin, Jr., who contested his election.

[38] Successfully contested the election of Egbert Ten Eyck, and took his seat December 15, 1825.

## NORTH CAROLINA

### SENATORS

Nathaniel Macon, *Monroe*
John Branch, *Enfield*

### REPRESENTATIVES

Willis Alston, *Hyde Park*
John H. Bryan, *New Bern*
Samuel P. Carson, *Pleasant Garden*
Henry W. Connor, *Sherrills Ford*
Weldon N. Edwards, *Warrenton*
Richard Hines, *Edgecombe*
Gabriel Holmes, *Clinton*
John Long, *Longs Mills*
Archibald McNeill, *McNeills Store*
Willie P. Mangum,[39] *Red Mountain*
Daniel L. Barringer,[40] *Raleigh*
Romulus M. Saunders, *Milton*
Lemuel Sawyer, *Elizabeth City*
Lewis Williams, *Panther Creek*

## OHIO

### SENATORS

Benjamin Ruggles, *St. Clairsville*
William Henry Harrison, *Cincinnati*

### REPRESENTATIVES

Mordecai Bartley, *Mansfield*
Philemon Beecher, *Lancaster*
John W. Campbell, *West Union*
James Findlay, *Cincinnati*
David Jennings,[41] *St. Clairsville*
Thomas Shannon,[42] *Barnesville*
William McLean, *Piqua*
John Sloane, *Wooster*
John Thomson, *Chillicothe*
Joseph Vance, *Urbana*
Samuel F. Vinton, *Gallipolis*
Elisha Whittlesey, *Canfield*
William Wilson, *Newark*
John Woods, *Hamilton*
John C. Wright, *Steubenville*

## PENNSYLVANIA

### SENATORS

William Findlay, *Franklinton*
William Marks, *Pittsburgh*

### REPRESENTATIVES

William Addams, *Reading*
James Allison, Jr.,[43] *Beaver*
Robert Orr, Jr.,[44] *Kittanning*
James Buchanan, *Lancaster*
Samuel Edwards, *Chester*
Patrick Farrelly,[45] *Meadville*
Thomas H. Sill,[46] *Erie*
John Findlay, *Chambersburg*
Robert Harris, *Harrisburg*
Joseph Hemphill,[47] *Philadelphia*
Thomas Kittera,[48] *Philadelphia*
Samuel D. Ingham, *New Hope*
George Kremer, *Lewisburg*
Joseph Lawrence, *Washington*
Samuel McKean, *Burlington*
Philip S. Markley, *Norristown*
Daniel H. Miller, *Philadelphia*
Charles Miner, *West Chester*
James S. Mitchell, *Rossville*
John Mitchell, *Bellefonte*
George Plumer, *Robbstown*
James S. Stevenson, *Pittsburgh*
Andrew Stewart, *Uniontown*
Alexander Thomson,[49] *Bedford*
Chauncey Forward,[50] *Somerset*
Espy Van Horne, *Williamsport*
Henry Wilson,[51] *Allentown*
Jacob Krebs,[52] *Orwigsburg*
James Wilson, *Fairfield*
George Wolf, *Easton*
John Wurts, *Philadelphia*

## RHODE ISLAND

### SENATORS

Nehemiah R. Knight, *Providence*
James De Wolf,[53] *Bristol*
Asher Robbins,[54] *Newport*

### REPRESENTATIVES AT LARGE

Tristam Burges, *Providence*
Dutee J. Pearce, *Newport*

## SOUTH CAROLINA

### SENATORS

John Gaillard,[55] *Pendleton*
William Harper,[56] *Charleston*
William Smith,[57] *Charleston*
Robert Y. Hayne, *Charleston*

### REPRESENTATIVES

John Carter, *Camden*
Joel R. Poinsett,[58] *Charleston*
William Drayton,[59] *Charleston*
Joseph Gist, *Pinckneyville*
Andrew R. Govan, *Orangeburg*
James Hamilton, Jr., *Charleston*
George McDuffie, *Edgefield*
Thomas R. Mitchell, *Georgetown*
Starling Tucker, *Mountain Shoals*

John Wilson, *Golden Grove*

## TENNESSEE

### SENATORS

John H. Eaton, *Nashville*
Andrew Jackson,[60] *Nashville*
Hugh Lawson White,[61] *Knoxville*

### REPRESENTATIVES

Adam R. Alexander, *Jackson*
Robert Allen, *Carthage*
John Blair, *Jonesboro*
John Cocke, *Rutledge*
Samuel Houston, *Nashville*
Jacob C. Isacks, *Winchester*
John H. Marable, *Yellow Creek*
James C. Mitchell, *Athens*
James K. Polk, *Columbia*

## VERMONT

### SENATORS

Horatio Seymour, *Middlebury*
Dudley Chase, *Randolph*

### REPRESENTATIVES

William C. Bradley, *Westminster*
Rollin C. Mallary, *Poultney*
John Mattocks, *Peacham*
Ezra Meech, *Shelburn*
George E. Wales, *Hartford*

## VIRGINIA

### SENATORS

James Barbour,[62] *Barboursville*
John Randolph,[63] *Charlotte*
Littleton W. Tazewell, *Norfolk*

### REPRESENTATIVES

Mark Alexander, *Lombardy Grove*
William S. Archer, *Amelia*
William Armstrong, *Romney*
John S. Barbour, *Culpeper*
Burwell Bassett, *Williamsburg*
Nathaniel H. Claiborne, *Rocky Mount*
Thomas Davenport, *Meadville*
Benjamin Estil, *Abingdon*
John Floyd, *Newbern*
Robert S. Garnett, *Lloyds*
Joseph Johnson, *Bridgeport*
William McCoy, *Franklin*
Charles F. Mercer, *Aldie*
Thomas Newton, Jr., *Norfolk*
Alfred H. Powell, *Winchester*
John Randolph,[64] *Charlotte*

---

[39] Resigned March 18, 1826.
[40] Elected to fill vacancy caused by resignation of Willie P. Mangum, and took his seat December 4, 1826.
[41] Resigned May 25, 1826.
[42] Elected to fill vacancy caused by resignation of David Jennings, and took his seat December 4, 1826.
[43] Resigned before Congress assembled.
[44] Elected to fill vacancy caused by resignation of James Allison, Jr., and took his seat December 5, 1825.
[45] Died January 12, 1826.
[46] Elected to fill vacancy caused by death of Patrick Farrelly, and took his seat April 3, 1826.
[47] Resigned in 1826.
[48] Elected to fill vacancy caused by resignation of Joseph Hemphill, and took his seat December 4, 1826.

[49] Resigned May 1, 1826.
[50] Elected to fill vacancy caused by resignation of Alexander Thomson, and took his seat December 4, 1826.
[51] Died August 14, 1826.
[52] Elected to fill vacancy caused by death of Henry Wilson, and took his seat December 4, 1826.
[53] Resigned October 31, 1825.
[54] Elected to fill vacancy caused by resignation of James De Wolf, and took his seat December 5, 1825.
[55] Died February 26, 1826.
[56] Appointed to fill vacancy caused by death of John Gaillard, and took his seat March 28, 1826.
[57] Elected to fill vacancy caused by death of John Gaillard, and took his seat December 7, 1826.

[58] Resigned March 7, 1825, to become minister to Mexico.
[59] Elected to fill vacancy caused by resignation of Joel R. Poinsett, and took his seat December 5, 1825.
[60] Resigned October 14, 1825.
[61] Elected to fill vacancy caused by resignation of Andrew Jackson, and took his seat December 12, 1825.
[62] Resigned March 7, 1825.
[63] Elected to fill vacancy caused by resignation of James Barbour, and took his seat December 26, 1825; vacancy in this class from March 28, 1825, to December 8, 1825.
[64] Resigned; effective December 26, 1825, without qualifying, having been elected Senator.

## VIRGINIA—Continued

REPRESENTATIVES—CONTINUED

George W. Crump,[65] *Cumberland*
William C. Rives, *Milton*
William Smith, *Lewisburg*
Andrew Stevenson, *Richmond*
John Taliaferro, *Fredericksburg*

Robert Taylor, *Orange*
James Trezvant, *Jerusalem*

## ARKANSAS TERRITORY

DELEGATE

Henry W. Conway, *Little Rock*

## TERRITORY OF FLORIDA

DELEGATE

Joseph M. White, *Pensacola*

## MICHIGAN TERRITORY

DELEGATE

Austin E. Wing,[66] *Detroit*

---

[65] Elected to fill vacancy caused by resignation of John Randolph, and took his seat February 6, 1826.

[66] Election unsuccessfully contested by John Biddle and Gabriel Richard.

# 20TH CONGRESS

MARCH 4, 1827, TO MARCH 3, 1829

FIRST SESSION— *December 3, 1827, to May 26, 1828*
SECOND SESSION— *December 1, 1828, to March 3, 1829*

---

VICE PRESIDENT OF THE UNITED STATES— John C. Calhoun, of South Carolina
PRESIDENT PRO TEMPORE OF THE SENATE— Samuel Smith,[1] of Maryland
SECRETARY OF THE SENATE— Walter Lowrie,[2] of Pennsylvania
SERGEANT AT ARMS OF THE SENATE— Mountjoy Bayly, of Maryland

---

SPEAKER OF THE HOUSE OF REPRESENTATIVES— Andrew Stevenson,[3] of Virginia
CLERK OF THE HOUSE— Matthew St. Clair Clarke,[4] of Pennsylvania
SERGEANT AT ARMS OF THE HOUSE— John O. Dunn, of District of Columbia
DOORKEEPER OF THE HOUSE— Benjamin Birch, of Maryland

John C. Calhoun
Vice President

Andrew Stevenson
Speaker

## ALABAMA

### SENATORS
William R. King, *Selma*
John McKinley, *Huntsville*

### REPRESENTATIVES
John McKee, *Tuscaloosa*
Gabriel Moore, *Huntsville*
George W. Owen, *Claiborne*

## CONNECTICUT

### SENATORS
Calvin Willey, *Tolland*
Samuel A. Foote, *Cheshire*

### REPRESENTATIVES AT LARGE
John Baldwin, *Windham*
Noyes Barber, *Groton*
Ralph I. Ingersoll, *New Haven*
Orange Merwin, *New Milford*
Elisha Phelps, *Simsbury*
David Plant, *Stratford*

## DELAWARE

### SENATORS
Henry M. Ridgely, *Dover*
Louis McLane, *Wilmington*

### REPRESENTATIVE AT LARGE
Kensey Johns, Jr.,[5] *New Castle*

## GEORGIA

### SENATORS
Thomas W. Cobb,[6] *Greensboro*

Oliver H. Prince,[7] *Macon*
John Macpherson Berrien, *Savannah*

### REPRESENTATIVES
John Floyd, *Jefferson*
John Forsyth,[8] *Augusta*
Richard H. Wilde,[9] *Augusta*
Tomlinson Fort, *Milledgeville*
Charles E. Haynes, *Sparta*
Wilson Lumpkin, *Madison*
Edward F. Tattnall,[10] *Savannah*
George R. Gilmer,[11] *Lexington*
Wiley Thompson, *Elberton*

## ILLINOIS

### SENATORS
Jesse B. Thomas, *Edwardsville*
Elias K. Kane, *Kaskaskia*

### REPRESENTATIVE AT LARGE
Joseph Duncan, *Brownsville*

## INDIANA

### SENATORS
James Noble, *Brookville*
William Hendricks, *Madison*

### REPRESENTATIVES
Thomas H. Blake, *Terre Haute*
Jonathan Jennings, *Charlestown*
Oliver H. Smith, *Connersville*

## KENTUCKY

### SENATORS
Richard M. Johnson, *Great Crossings*
John Rowan, *Louisville*

### REPRESENTATIVES
Richard A. Buckner, *Greensburg*
William S. Young,[12] *Elizabethtown*
John Calhoon,[13] *Hardinsburg*
Thomas Chilton,[14] *Elizabethtown*
James Clark, *Winchester*
Henry Daniel, *Mount Sterling*
Joseph Lecompte, *New Castle*
Robert P. Letcher, *Lancaster*
Chittenden Lyon, *Eddyville*
Robert McHatton, *Georgetown*
Thomas Metcalfe,[15] *Carlisle*
John Chambers,[16] *Washington*
Thomas P. Moore, *Harrodsburg*
Charles A. Wickliffe, *Bardstown*
Joel Yancey, *Glasgow*

## LOUISIANA

### SENATORS
Josiah S. Johnston, *Alexandria*
Dominique Bouligny, *New Orleans*

### REPRESENTATIVES
William L. Brent, *St. Martinsville*
Henry H. Gurley, *Baton Rouge*
Edward Livingston, *New Orleans*

---

[1] Elected May 15, 1828. Nathaniel Macon, of North Carolina, was first elected on the same day, but declined to serve.
[2] Reelected December 10, 1827.
[3] Elected December 3, 1827.
[4] Reelected December 3, 1827.
[5] Elected to fill vacancy caused by resignation of Representative-elect Louis McLane, in preceding Congress, and took his seat December 3, 1827.
[6] Resigned in 1828.
[7] Elected to fill vacancy caused by resignation of Thomas W. Cobb, and took his seat December 1, 1828.

[8] Resigned; effective November 7, 1827, before Congress assembled, having been elected governor.
[9] Elected to fill vacancy caused by resignation of John Forsyth, and took his seat January 14, 1828.
[10] Resigned before Congress assembled.
[11] Elected to fill vacancy caused by resignation of Edward Tattnall, and took his seat December 3, 1827; reelected to the Twenty-first Congress but failed to signify his acceptance.
[12] Died September 20, 1827, before Congress assembled.
[13] John Calhoon and Thomas Chilton were can-

didates to fill vacancy caused by death of William S. Young and the vote of one county being thrown out the certificate of election was given to Mr. Calhoon; by mutual agreement Calhoon resigned and both contestants then petitioned the governor for a new election.
[14] Elected to fill vacancy caused by resignation of John Calhoon, and took his seat January 11, 1828.
[15] Resigned June 1, 1828.
[16] Elected to fill vacancy caused by resignation of Thomas Metcalfe, and took his seat December 1, 1828.

## MAINE

### SENATORS

John Chandler, *Monmouth*
Albion K. Parris,[17] *Portland*
John Holmes,[18] *Alfred*

### REPRESENTATIVES

John Anderson, *Portland*
Samuel Butman, *Dixmont*
William Burleigh,[19] *South Berwick*
Rufus McIntire,[20] *Parsonsfield*
Jeremiah O'Brien, *Machias*
James W. Ripley, *Fryeburg*
Peleg Sprague,[21] *Hallowell*
Joseph F. Wingate, *Bath*

## MARYLAND

### SENATORS

Samuel Smith, *Baltimore*
Ezekiel F. Chambers, *Chestertown*

### REPRESENTATIVES

John Barney, *Baltimore*
Clement Dorsey, *Chaptico*
Levin Gale, *Elkton*
John L. Kerr, *Easton*
Peter Little, *Freedom*
Michael C. Sprigg, *Frostburg*
George C. Washington, *Rockville*
John C. Weems, *Waterloo*
Ephraim K. Wilson, *Snow Hill*

## MASSACHUSETTS

### SENATORS

Nathaniel Silsbee, *Salem*
Daniel Webster,[22] *Boston*

### REPRESENTATIVES

Samuel C. Allen, *Greenfield*
John Baily, *Milton*
Isaac C. Bates, *Northampton*
Benjamin W. Crowninshield, *Salem*
John Davis, *Worcester*
Henry W. Dwight, *Stockbridge*
Edward Everett, *Cambridge*
James L. Hodges, *Taunton*
John Locke, *Ashby*
John Reed, *Yarmouth*
Joseph Richardson, *Hingham*
John Varnum, *Haverhill*
Daniel Webster,[23] *Boston*

Benjamin Gorham,[24] *Boston*

## MISSISSIPPI

### SENATORS

Thomas H. Williams, *Washington*
Powhatan Ellis, *Winchester*

### REPRESENTATIVE AT LARGE

William Haile,[25] *Woodville*
Thomas Hinds,[26] *Greenville*

## MISSOURI

### SENATORS

David Barton, *St. Louis*
Thomas Hart Benton, *St. Louis*

### REPRESENTATIVE AT LARGE

Edward Bates, *St. Louis*

## NEW HAMPSHIRE

### SENATORS

Samuel Bell, *Chester*
Levi Woodbury, *Portsmouth*

### REPRESENTATIVES AT LARGE

David Barker, Jr., *Rochester*
Ichabod Bartlett, *Portsmouth*
Titus Brown, *Francestown*
Jonathan Harvey, *Sutton*
Joseph Healy, *Washington*
Thomas Whipple, Jr., *Wentworth*

## NEW JERSEY

### SENATORS

Ephraim Bateman,[27] *Cedarville*
Mahlon Dickerson,[28] *Succasunna*

### REPRESENTATIVES AT LARGE

Lewis Condict, *Morristown*
George Holcombe,[29] *Allentown*
James F. Randolph,[30] *New Brunswick*
Isaac Pierson, *Orange*
Hedge Thompson,[31] *Salem*
Thomas Sinnickson,[32] *Salem*
Samuel Swan, *Somerville*
Ebenezer Tucker, *Tuckerton*

## NEW YORK

### SENATORS

Martin Van Buren,[33] *Albany*

Charles E. Dudley,[34] *Albany*
Nathan Sanford, *Albany*

### REPRESENTATIVES

Daniel D. Barnard, *Rochester*
George O. Belden, *Monticello*
Rudolph Bunner, *Oswego*
Churchill C. Cambreleng, *New York City*
Samuel Chase, *Cooperstown*
John C. Clark, *Bainbridge*
David E. Evans,[35] *Batavia*
Phineas L. Tracy,[36] *Batavia*
John I. De Graff, *Schenectady*
John D. Dickinson, *Troy*
Jonas Earll, Jr., *Onondaga*
Daniel G. Garnsey, *Fredonia*
Nathaniel Garrow, *Auburn*
John Hallock, Jr., *Ridgebury*
Selah R. Hobbie, *Delhi*
Michael Hoffman, *Herkimer*
Jeromus Johnson, *New York City*
Richard Keese, *Keeseville*
John Magee, *Bath*
Henry Markell, *Palatine*
Henry C. Martindale, *Sandy Hill*
Dudley Marvin, *Canandaigua*
John Maynard, *Ovid Village*
Thomas J. Oakley,[37] *Poughkeepsie*
Thomas Taber, 2d,[38] *Dover*
Henry R. Storrs, *Whitestown*
John G. Stower, *Hamilton*
James Strong, *Hudson*
John W. Taylor, *Ballston Spa*
Stephen Van Rensselaer, *Albany*
Gulian C. Verplanck, *New York City*
Aaron Ward, *Mount Pleasant*
John J. Wood, *Clarkstown*
Silas Wood, *Huntington*
David Woodcock, *Ithaca*
Silas Wright, Jr.,[39] *Canton*

## NORTH CAROLINA

### SENATORS

Nathaniel Macon,[40] *Warrenton*
James Iredell,[41] *Edenton*
John Branch, *Enfield*

### REPRESENTATIVES

Willis Alston, *Hyde Park*
Daniel L. Barringer, *Raleigh*
John H. Bryan, *New Bern*

---

[17] Resigned August 26, 1828.
[18] Elected to fill vacancy caused by resignation of Albion K. Parris, and took his seat January 26, 1829.
[19] Died July 2, 1827, before Congress assembled.
[20] Elected to fill vacancy caused by death of William Burleigh, and took his seat December 3, 1827.
[21] Reelected to the Twenty-first Congress, but resigned, having been elected Senator.
[22] Elected to fill vacancy in the term beginning March 4, 1827, caused by failure of legislature to elect, and took his seat December 17, 1827.
[23] Resigned May 30, 1827, before Congress assembled, having been elected Senator.
[24] Elected to fill vacancy caused by resignation of Daniel Webster, and took his seat December 3, 1827.
[25] Resigned September 12, 1828.
[26] Elected to fill vacancy caused by resignation of William Haile, and took his seat December 8, 1828.
[27] A remonstrance against the legality of his

election was considered by a select committee of five Senators; it revealed that, as chairman of the joint convention of the general assembly of New Jersey, Mr. Bateman had voted for himself for Senator, had broken a tie vote thereby, and upon such state of facts the certificate had been issued to him; May 22, 1828, the committee reported, that, in its opinion, he had only exercised a legal right by thus voting, and, upon its request, was discharged; resigned January 12, 1829. (See U.S. Senate Election, Expulsion and Censure Cases, 1793-1990, Senate Document 103-33, pp. 33-34.)
[28] Elected to fill vacancy caused by resignation of Ephraim Bateman, and took his seat February 9, 1829; Resigned January 30, 1829 (see footnote 27); vacancy in this class from January 30, 1829, to March 3, 1829.
[29] Died January 14, 1828.
[30] Elected to fill vacancy caused by death of George Holcombe, and took his seat December 1, 1828.

[31] Died July 23, 1828.
[32] Elected to fill vacancy caused by death of Hedge Thompson, and took his seat December 1, 1828.
[33] Resigned December 20, 1828.
[34] Elected to fill vacancy caused by resignation of Martin Van Buren, and took his seat January 29, 1829.
[35] Resigned May 2, 1827, before Congress assembled.
[36] Elected to fill vacancy caused by resignation of David E. Evans, and took his seat December 3, 1827.
[37] Resigned May 9, 1828.
[38] Elected to fill vacancy caused by resignation of Thomas J. Oakley, and took his seat December 1, 1828.
[39] Resigned February 16, 1829.
[40] Resigned November 14, 1828.
[41] Elected to fill vacancy caused by resignation of Nathaniel Macon, and took his seat December 23, 1828.

Samuel P. Carson, *Pleasant Garden*
Henry W. Connor, *Sherrills Ford*
John Culpepper, *Beards Store*
Thomas H. Hall, *Tarboro*
Gabriel Holmes, *Clinton*
John Long, *Longs Mills*
Lemuel Sawyer, *Elizabeth City*
Augustine H. Shepperd, *Germantown*
Daniel Turner, *Warrenton*
Lewis Williams, *Panther Creek*

## OHIO

SENATORS

Benjamin Ruggles, *St. Clairsville*
William Henry Harrison,[42] *Cincinnati*
Jacob Burnet,[43] *Cincinnati*

REPRESENTATIVES

Mordecai Bartley, *Mansfield*
Philemon Beecher, *Lancaster*
William Creighton, Jr.,[44] *Chillicothe*
Francis S. Muhlenberg,[45] *Circleville*
John Davenport, *Barnesville*
James Findlay, *Cincinnati*
William McLean, *Piqua*
William Russell, *West Union*
John Sloane, *Wooster*
Joseph Vance, *Urbana*
Samuel F. Vinton, *Gallipolis*
Elisha Whittlesey, *Canfield*
William Wilson,[46] *Newark*
William Stanbery,[47] *Newark*
John Woods, *Hamilton*
John C. Wright, *Steubenville*

## PENNSYLVANIA

SENATORS

Williams Marks, *Pittsburgh*
Isaac D. Barnard, *West Chester*

REPRESENTATIVES

William Addams, *Reading*
Samuel Anderson, *Providence*
Stephen Barlow, *Meadville*
James Buchanan, *Lancaster*
Richard Coulter, *Greensburg*
Chauncey Forward, *Somerset*
Joseph Fry, Jr., *Fryburg*
Innis Green, *Dauphin*
Samuel D. Ingham, *New Hope*
Adam King, *York*
George Kremer, *Lewisburg*
Joseph Lawrence, *Washington*
Samuel McKean, *Burlington*
Daniel H. Miller, *Philadelphia*

Charles Miner, *West Chester*
John Mitchell, *Bellefonte*
Robert Orr, Jr., *Kittanning*
William Ramsey, *Carlisle*
John Sergeant,[48] *Philadelphia*
John B. Sterigere, *Upper Dublin*
James S. Stevenson, *Pittsburgh*
Andrew Stewart, *Uniontown*
Joel B. Sutherland, *Philadelphia*
Espy Van Horne, *Williamsport*
James Wilson, *Fairfield*
George Wolf, *Easton*

## RHODE ISLAND

SENATORS

Nehemiah R. Knight, *Providence*
Asher Robbins, *Newport*

REPRESENTATIVES AT LARGE

Tristam Burges, *Providence*
Dutee J. Pearce, *Newport*

## SOUTH CAROLINA

SENATORS

Robert Y. Hayne, *Charleston*
William Smith, *Charleston*

REPRESENTATIVES

John Carter, *Camden*
Warren R. Davis, *Pendleton*
William Drayton, *Charleston*
James Hamilton, Jr., *Charleston*
George McDuffie, *Edgefield*
William D. Martin, *Barnwell*
Thomas R. Mitchell, *Georgetown*
William T. Nuckolls, *Spartanburg*
Starling Tucker, *Mountain Shoals*

## TENNESSEE

SENATORS

John H. Eaton, *Nashville*
Hugh Lawson White, *Knoxville*

REPRESENTATIVES

John Bell, *Nashville*
John Blair, *Jonesboro*
David Crockett, *Trenton*
Robert Desha, *Gallatin*
Jacob C. Isacks, *Winchester*
Pryor Lea, *Knoxville*
John H. Marable, *Yellow Creek*
James C. Mitchell, *Athens*
James K. Polk, *Columbia*

## VERMONT

SENATORS

Horatio Seymour, *Middlebury*
Dudley Chase, *Randolph*

REPRESENTATIVES

Daniel A. A. Buck, *Chelsea*
Jonathan Hunt, *Brattleboro*
Rollin C. Mallary, *Poultney*
Benjamin Swift, *St. Albans*
George E. Wales, *Hartford*

## VIRGINIA

SENATORS

Littleton W. Tazewell, *Norfolk*
John Tyler, *Charles City*

REPRESENTATIVES

Mark Alexander, *Lombardy Grove*
Robert Allen, *Mount Jackson*
William S. Archer, *Elk Hill*
William Armstrong, *Romney*
John S. Barbour, *Culpeper*
Philip P. Barbour, *Gordonsville*
Burwell Bassett, *Williamsburg*
Nathaniel H. Claiborne, *Rocky Mount*
Thomas Davenport, *Meadville*
John Floyd, *Newbern*
Isaac Leffler, *Wheeling*
Lewis Maxwell, *Weston*
Charles F. Mercer, *Aldie*
William McCoy, *Franklin*
Thomas Newton, Jr., *Norfolk*
John Randolph, *Charlotte*
William C. Rives, *Milton*
John Roane, *Rumford Academy*
Alexander Smyth, *Wythe*
Andrew Stevenson, *Richmond*
John Taliaferro, *Fredericksburg*
James Trezvant, *Jerusalem*

## ARKANSAS TERRITORY

DELEGATE

Henry W. Conway,[49] *Little Rock*
Ambrose H. Sevier,[50] *Little Rock*

## TERRITORY OF FLORIDA

DELEGATE

Joseph M. White, *Pensacola*

## MICHIGAN TERRITORY

DELEGATE

Austin E. Wing, *Detroit*

---

[42] Resigned May 20, 1828.
[43] Elected to fill vacancy caused by resignation of William Henry Harrison, and took his seat December 29, 1828.
[44] Resigned in 1828.
[45] Elected to fill vacancy caused by resignation of

William Creighton, Jr., and took his seat December 19, 1828.
[46] Died June 6, 1827, before Congress assembled.
[47] Elected to fill vacancy caused by death of William Wilson, and took his seat December 3, 1827.
[48] Election questioned by sundry citizens of Penn-

sylvania. On January 14, 1828, resolution was adopted declaring him entitled to his seat.
[49] Died November 9, 1827, before Congress assembled.
[50] Elected to fill vacancy caused by death of Henry W. Conway, and took his seat February 13, 1828.

# 21ST CONGRESS

## MARCH 4, 1829, TO MARCH 3, 1831

John C. Calhoun
Vice President

FIRST SESSION— *December 7, 1829, to May 31, 1830*
SECOND SESSION— *December 6, 1830, to March 3, 1831*
SPECIAL SESSION OF THE SENATE— *March 4, 1829, to March 17, 1829*

—————

VICE PRESIDENT OF THE UNITED STATES— JOHN C. CALHOUN, of South Carolina
PRESIDENT PRO TEMPORE OF THE SENATE— SAMUEL SMITH,[1] of Maryland
SECRETARY OF THE SENATE— WALTER LOWRIE,[2] of Pennsylvania
SERGEANT AT ARMS OF THE SENATE— MOUNTJOY BAYLY, of Maryland

—————

SPEAKER OF THE HOUSE OF REPRESENTATIVES— ANDREW STEVENSON,[3] of Virginia
CLERK OF THE HOUSE— MATTHEW ST. CLAIR CLARKE,[4] of Pennsylvania
SERGEANT AT ARMS OF THE HOUSE— JOHN O. DUNN, of District of Columbia
DOORKEEPER OF THE HOUSE— BENJAMIN BIRCH, of Maryland

Andrew Stevenson
Speaker

## ALABAMA

### SENATORS

William R. King, *Selma*
John McKinley, *Florence*

### REPRESENTATIVES

Robert E. B. Baylor, *Tuscaloosa*
Clement C. Clay, *Huntsville*
Dixon H. Lewis, *Montgomery*

## CONNECTICUT

### SENATORS

Calvin Willey, *Tolland*
Samuel A. Foote, *Cheshire*

### REPRESENTATIVES AT LARGE

Noyes Barber, *Groton*
William W. Ellsworth, *Hartford*
Jabez W. Huntington, *Litchfield*
Ralph I. Ingersoll, *New Haven*
William L. Storrs, *Middletown*
Ebenezer Young, *Killingly Center*

## DELAWARE

### SENATORS

Louis McLane,[5] *Wilmington*
Arnold Naudain,[6] *Wilmington*
John M. Clayton, *Dover*

### REPRESENTATIVE AT LARGE

Kensey Johns, Jr., *New Castle*

## GEORGIA

### SENATORS

John Macpherson Berrien,[7] *Savannah*
John Forsyth,[8] *Augusta*
George M. Troup, *Dublin*

### REPRESENTATIVES AT LARGE

Thomas F. Foster, *Greensboro*
Charles E. Haynes, *Sparta*
Henry G. Lamar,[9] *Macon*
Wilson Lumpkin, *Monroe*
Wiley Thompson, *Elberton*
James M. Wayne, *Savannah*
Richard H. Wilde, *Augusta*

## ILLINOIS

### SENATORS

Elias K. Kane, *Kaskaskia*
John McLean,[10] *Shawneetown*
David J. Baker,[11] *Shawneetown*
John M. Robinson,[12] *Carmi*

### REPRESENTATIVE AT LARGE

Joseph Duncan, *Brownsville*

## INDIANA

### SENATORS

James Noble,[13] *Brookville*
William Hendricks, *Madison*

### REPRESENTATIVES

Ratliff Boon, *Boonville*
Jonathan Jennings, *Charlestown*
John Test, *Lawrenceburg*

## KENTUCKY

### SENATORS

John Rowan, *Louisville*
George M. Bibb, *Yellow Banks*

### REPRESENTATIVES

Thomas Chilton, *Elizabethtown*
James Clark, *Winchester*
Nicholas D. Coleman, *Washington*
Henry Daniel, *Mount Sterling*
Nathan Gaither, *Columbia*
Richard M. Johnson, *Great Crossings*
John Kincaid, *Stanford*
Joseph Lecompte, *New Castle*
Robert P. Letcher, *Lancaster*
Chittenden Lyon, *Eddyville*
Charles A. Wickliffe, *Bardstown*
Joel Yancey, *Glasgow*

## LOUISIANA

### SENATORS

Josiah S. Johnston, *Alexandria*
Edward Livingston, *New Orleans*

### REPRESENTATIVES

Henry H. Gurley, *Baton Rouge*
Walter H. Overton, *Alexandria*
Edward D. White, *Donaldsonville*

## MAINE

### SENATORS

John Holmes, *Alfred*
Peleg Sprague, *Hallowell*

---

[1] Elected March 13, 1829 (special session of the Senate); May 29, 1830; March 1, 1831; Littleton W. Tazewell, of Virginia, was first elected on the last-named date, but declined to serve.
[2] Reelected December 14, 1829.
[3] Reelected December 7, 1829.
[4] Reelected December 7, 1829.
[5] Resigned April 16, 1829.

[6] Elected to fill vacancy caused by resignation of Louis McLane, and took his seat January 13, 1830.
[7] Resigned March 9, 1829.
[8] Elected to fill vacancy caused by resignation of John Macpherson Berrien, and took his seat December 8, 1829.
[9] Elected to fill vacancy caused by failure of Representative-elect George R. Gilmer to signify his

acceptance, and took his seat December 7, 1829.
[10] Died October 14, 1830.
[11] Appointed to fill vacancy caused by death of John McLean, and took his seat December 6, 1830.
[12] Elected to fill vacancy caused by death of John McLean, and took his seat January 4, 1831.
[13] Died February 26, 1831.

## REPRESENTATIVES

John Anderson, *Portland*
Samuel Butman, *Dixmont*
George Evans,[14] *Gardiner*
Leonard Jarvis, *Ellsworth*
Rufus McIntire, *Parsonsfield*
James W. Ripley,[15] *Fryeburg*
Cornelius Holland,[16] *Canton*
Joseph F. Wingate, *Bath*

## MARYLAND

### SENATORS

Samuel Smith, *Baltimore*
Ezekiel F. Chambers, *Chestertown*

### REPRESENTATIVES

Elias Brown, *Freedom*
Clement Dorsey, *Chaptico*
Benjamin C. Howard, *Baltimore*
George E. Mitchell, *Elkton*
Benedict J. Semmes, *Piscataway*
Richard Spencer, *Easton*
Michael C. Sprigg, *Frostburg*
George C. Washington, *Rockville*
Ephraim K. Wilson, *Snow Hill*

## MASSACHUSETTS

### SENATORS

Nathaniel Silsbee, *Salem*
Daniel Webster, *Boston*

### REPRESENTATIVES

John Bailey, *Milton*
Isaac C. Bates, *Northampton*
Benjamin W. Crowninshield, *Salem*
John Davis, *Worcester*
Henry W. Dwight, *Stockbridge*
Edward Everett, *Charlestown*
Benjamin Gorham, *Boston*
George Grennell, Jr., *Greenfield*
James L. Hodges, *Taunton*
Joseph G. Kendall, *Leominster*
John Reed, *Yarmouth*
Joseph Richardson, *Hingham*
John Varnum, *Haverhill*

## MISSISSIPPI

### SENATORS

Powhatan Ellis, *Winchester*
Thomas B. Reed,[17] *Natchez*
Robert H. Adams,[18] *Natchez*
George Poindexter,[19] *Natchez*

### REPRESENTATIVE AT LARGE

Thomas Hinds, *Greenville*

## MISSOURI

### SENATORS

David Barton, *St. Louis*
Thomas Hart Benton, *St. Louis*

### REPRESENTATIVE AT LARGE

Spencer D. Pettis, *Fayette*

## NEW HAMPSHIRE

### SENATORS

Samuel Bell, *Chester*
Levi Woodbury, *Portsmouth*

### REPRESENTATIVES AT LARGE

John Brodhead, *Newmarket*
Thomas Chandler, *Hillsboro*
Joseph Hammons, *Farmington*
Jonathan Harvey, *Sutton*
Henry Hubbard, *Charlestown*
John W. Weeks, *Lancaster*

## NEW JERSEY

### SENATORS

Mahlon Dickerson, *Succasunna*
Theodore Frelinghuysen, *Newark*

### REPRESENTATIVES AT LARGE

Lewis Condict, *Morristown*
Richard M. Cooper, *Camden*
Thomas H. Hughes, *Cold Spring*
Isaac Pierson, *Orange*
James F. Randolph, *New Brunswick*
Samuel Swan, *Somerville*

## NEW YORK

### SENATORS

Nathan Sanford, *Albany*
Charles E. Dudley, *Albany*

### REPRESENTATIVES

William G. Angel, *Burlington*
Benedict Arnold, *Amsterdam*
Thomas Beekman, *Peterboro*
Abraham Bockee, *Federal Store*
Peter I. Borst, *Middleburg*

Churchill C. Cambreleng, *New York City*
Timothy Childs, *Rochester*
Jonas Earll, Jr., *Onondaga*
Isaac Finch, *Jay*
George Fisher,[20] *Oswego*
Silas Wright, Jr.,[21] *Canton*
Jonah Sanford,[22] *Oswego*
Jehiel H. Halsey, *Lodi*
Joseph Hawkins, *Henderson*
Michael Hoffman, *Herkimer*
Perkins King, *Freehold*
James Lent, *Newtown*
John Magee, *Bath*
Henry C. Martindale, *Sandy Hill*
Henry B. Cowles, *Carmel*
Hector Craig,[23] *Craigville*
Samuel W. Eager,[24] *Montgomery*
Jacob Crocheron, *Smithfield*
Charles G. De Witt, *Kingston*
John D. Dickinson, *Troy*
Thomas Maxwell, *Elmira*
Robert Monell,[25] *Greene*
Ebenezer F. Norton, *Buffalo*
Gershom Powers, *Auburn*
Robert S. Rose, *Geneva*
Ambrose Spencer, *Albany*
James Strong, *Hudson*
Henry R. Storrs, *Whitestown*
John W. Taylor, *Ballston Spa*
Phineas L. Tracy, *Batavia*
Gulian C. Verplanck, *New York City*
Campbell P. White, *New York City*

## NORTH CAROLINA

### SENATORS

John Branch,[26] *Enfield*
Bedford Brown,[27] *Browns Store*
James Iredell, *Edenton*

### REPRESENTATIVES

Willis Alston, *Hyde Park*
Daniel L. Barringer, *Raleigh*
Samuel P. Carson, *Pleasant Garden*
Henry W. Connor, *Sherrills Ford*
Edmund Deberry, *Lawrenceville*
Thomas H. Hall, *Tarboro*
Gabriel Holmes,[28] *Clinton*
Edward B. Dudley,[29] *Wilmington*
Robert Potter, *Oxford*
Abraham Rencher, *Pittsboro*
William B. Shepard, *Elizabeth City*
Augustine H. Shepperd, *Germantown*
Jesse Speight, *Stantonsburg*
Lewis Williams, *Panther Creek*

---

[14] Elected to fill vacancy caused by resignation of Representative-elect Peleg Sprague, in preceding Congress, and took his seat December 7, 1829.
[15] Election unsuccessfully contested by Reuel Washburn; resigned March 12, 1830.
[16] Elected to fill vacancy caused by resignation of James W. Ripley, and took his seat December 6, 1830.
[17] Died November 26, 1829.
[18] Elected to fill vacancy caused by death of Thomas B. Reed, and took his seat February 8, 1830; died July 2, 1830.
[19] Appointed to fill vacancy caused by deaths of

Thomas B. Reed and Robert H. Adams, and took his seat December 6, 1830; subsequently elected.
[20] Served until February 5, 1830; election successfully contested by Silas Wright, Jr.
[21] Successfully contested the election of George Fisher, but resigned March 9, 1830, never having qualified, preferring to continue as comptroller of the State.
[22] Elected to fill vacancy caused by resignation of Silas Wright, Jr., and took his seat December 6, 1830.
[23] Resigned July 12, 1830.
[24] Elected to fill vacancy caused by resignation of

Hector Craig, and took his seat December 6, 1830.
[25] Resigned February 21, 1831.
[26] Resigned March 9, 1829, having been appointed Secretary of the Navy.
[27] Elected to fill vacancy caused by resignation of John Branch, and took his seat December 28, 1829.
[28] Died September 26, 1829, before Congress assembled.
[29] Elected to fill vacancy caused by death of Gabriel Holmes, and took his seat December 14, 1829.

## OHIO

SENATORS

Benjamin Ruggles, *St. Clairsville*
Jacob Burnet, *Cincinnati*

REPRESENTATIVES

Mordecai Bartley, *Mansfield*
Joseph H. Crane, *Dayton*
William Creighton, Jr., *Chillicothe*
James Findlay, *Cincinnati*
John M. Goodenow,[30] *Steubenville*
Humphrey H. Leavitt,[31] *Steubenville*
William W. Irvin, *Lancaster*
William Kennon, Sr., *St. Clairsville*
William Russell, *West Union*
James Shields, *Dicks Mills*
William Stanbery, *Newark*
John Thomson, *New Lisbon*
Joseph Vance, *Urbana*
Samuel F. Vinton, *Gallipolis*
Elisha Whittlesey, *Canfield*

## PENNSYLVANIA

SENATORS

William Marks, *Pittsburgh*
Isaac D. Barnard, *West Chester*

REPRESENTATIVES

James Buchanan, *Lancaster*
Richard Coulter, *Greensburg*
Thomas H. Crawford, *Chambersburg*
Joshua Evans, Jr., *Paoli*
James Ford, *Lawrenceville*
Chauncey Forward, *Somerset*
Joseph Fry, Jr., *Fryburg*
John Gilmore, *Butler*
Innis Green, *Dauphin*
Joseph Hemphill, *Philadelphia*
Samuel D. Ingham,[32] *New Hope*
Peter Ihrie, Jr.,[33] *Easton*
George Wolf,[34] *Easton*
Samuel A. Smith,[35] *Doylestown*
Thomas Irwin, *Uniontown*
Adam King, *York*
George C. Leiper, *Leiperville*
Alem Marr, *Danville*
William McCreery, *Florence*
Daniel H. Miller, *Philadelphia*
Henry A. P. Muhlenberg, *Reading*
William Ramsey, *Carlisle*
John Scott, *Alexandria*

Thomas H. Sill, *Erie*
Philander Stephens, *Montrose*
John B. Sterigere, *Norristown*
Joel B. Sutherland, *Philadelphia*
William Wilkins,[36] *Pittsburgh*
Harmar Denny,[37] *Pittsburgh*

## RHODE ISLAND

SENATORS

Nehemiah R. Knight, *Providence*
Asher Robbins, *Newport*

REPRESENTATIVES AT LARGE

Tristam Burges, *Providence*
Dutee J. Pearce, *Newport*

## SOUTH CAROLINA

SENATORS

Robert Y. Hayne, *Charleston*
William Smith, *Charleston*

REPRESENTATIVES

Robert W. Barnwell, *Beaufort*
James Blair, *Camden*
John Campbell, *Brownsville*
Warren R. Davis, *Pendleton*
William Drayton, *Charleston*
William D. Martin, *Barnwell*
George McDuffie, *Edgefield*
William T. Nuckolls, *Hancockville*
Starling Tucker, *Mountain Shoals*

## TENNESSEE

SENATORS

John H. Eaton,[38] *Nashville*
Felix Grundy,[39] *Nashville*
Hugh Lawson White, *Knoxville*

REPRESENTATIVES

John Bell, *Nashville*
John Blair, *Jonesboro*
David Crockett, *Crockett*
Robert Desha, *Gallatin*
Jacob C. Isacks, *Winchester*
Cave Johnson, *Clarksville*

Pryor Lea,[40] *Knoxville*
James K. Polk, *Columbia*
James Standifer, *Mountairy*

## VERMONT

SENATORS

Horatio Seymour, *Middlebury*
Dudley Chase, *Randolph*

REPRESENTATIVES

William Cahoon, *Lyndon*
Horace Everett, *Windsor*
Jonathan Hunt, *Brattleboro*
Rollin C. Mallary, *Poultney*
Benjamin Swift, *St. Albans*

## VIRGINIA

SENATORS

Littleton W. Tazewell, *Norfolk*
John Tyler, *Charles City*

REPRESENTATIVES

Mark Alexander, *Lombardy Grove*
Robert Allen, *Mount Jackson*
William S. Archer, *Elk Hill*
William Armstrong, *Romney*
John S. Barbour, *Culpeper*
Philip P. Barbour,[41] *Gordonsville*
John M. Patton,[42] *Fredericksburg*
Thomas T. Bouldin, *Charlotte*
Nathaniel H. Claiborne, *Rocky Mount*
Richard Coke, Jr., *Williamsburg*
Robert Craig, *Montgomery*
Thomas Davenport, *Meadville*
Philip Doddridge, *Wellsburg*
Alexander Smyth,[43] *Wythe*
Joseph Draper,[44] *Wythe*
Thomas Newton, Jr.,[45] *Norfolk*
George Loyall,[46] *Norfolk*
William C. Rives,[47] *Milton*
William F. Gordon,[48] *Lindseys Store*
Lewis Maxwell, *Weston*
William McCoy, *Franklin*
Charles F. Mercer, *Leesburg*
John Roane, *Rumford Academy*
Andrew Stevenson, *Richmond*
John Taliaferro, *Fredericksburg*
James Trezvant, *Jerusalem*

---

[30] Resigned April 9, 1830, before Congress assembled.
[31] Elected to fill vacancy caused by resignation of John M. Goodenow, and took his seat December 6, 1830.
[32] Resigned before Congress assembled.
[33] Elected to fill in part vacancies caused by resignations of George Wolf and Samuel D. Ingham, and took his seat December 7, 1829.
[34] Resigned before Congress assembled, having been elected governor.
[35] Elected to fill in part vacancies caused by

resignations of George Wolf and Samuel D. Ingham, and took his seat December 7, 1829.
[36] Resigned before Congress assembled.
[37] Elected to fill vacancy caused by resignation of William Wilkins, and took his seat December 30, 1829.
[38] Resigned March 9, 1829.
[39] Elected to fill vacancy caused by resignation of John H. Eaton, and took his seat December 7, 1829.
[40] Election unsuccessfully contested by Thomas D. Arnold.
[41] Resigned October 15, 1830.
[42] Elected to fill vacancy caused by resignation of

Philip P. Barbour, and took his seat December 6, 1830.
[43] Died April 17, 1830.
[44] Elected to fill vacancy caused by death of Alexander Smyth, and took his seat December 6, 1830.
[45] Served until March 9, 1830; succeeded by George Loyall, who contested his election.
[46] Successfully contested the election of Thomas Newton, Jr., and took his seat March 9, 1830.
[47] Resigned in 1829, having been appointed minister to France.
[48] Elected to fill vacancy caused by resignation of William C. Rives, and took his seat January 25, 1830.

## ARKANSAS TERRITORY

DELEGATE

Ambrose H. Sevier, *Little Rock*

## TERRITORY OF FLORIDA

DELEGATE

Joseph M. White, *Monticello*

## MICHIGAN TERRITORY

DELEGATE

John Biddle,[49] *Detroit*

[49] Resigned February 21, 1831.

# 22ND CONGRESS

MARCH 4, 1831, TO MARCH 3, 1833

FIRST SESSION— *December 5, 1831, to July 16, 1832*
SECOND SESSION— *December 3, 1832, to March 2, 1833*

---

VICE PRESIDENT OF THE UNITED STATES— John C. Calhoun,[1] of South Carolina
PRESIDENT PRO TEMPORE OF THE SENATE— Littleton W. Tazewell,[2] of Virginia;
Hugh L. White,[3] of Tennessee
SECRETARY OF THE SENATE— Walter Lowrie,[4] of Pennsylvania
SERGEANT AT ARMS OF THE SENATE— Mountjoy Bayly, of Maryland

---

SPEAKER OF THE HOUSE OF REPRESENTATIVES— Andrew Stevenson,[5] of Virginia
CLERK OF THE HOUSE— Matthew St. Clair Clarke,[6] of Pennsylvania
SERGEANT AT ARMS OF THE HOUSE— John O. Dunn, of District of Columbia
DOORKEEPER OF THE HOUSE— Overton Carr, of Maryland

John C. Calhoun
Vice President

Andrew Stevenson
Speaker

## ALABAMA

SENATORS
William R. King, *Selma*
Gabriel Moore, *Huntsville*

REPRESENTATIVES
Clement C. Clay, *Huntsville*
Dixon H. Lewis, *Montgomery*
Samuel W. Mardis, *Montevallo*

## CONNECTICUT

SENATORS
Samuel A. Foote, *Cheshire*
Gideon Tomlinson, *Fairfield*

REPRESENTATIVES AT LARGE
Noyes Barber, *Groton*
William W. Ellsworth, *Hartford*
Jabez W. Huntington, *Litchfield*
Ralph I. Ingersoll, *New Haven*
William L. Storrs, *Middletown*
Ebenezer Young, *Killingly Center*

## DELAWARE

SENATORS
John M. Clayton, *Dover*
Arnold Naudain, *Wilmington*

REPRESENTATIVE AT LARGE
John J. Milligan, *Wilmington*

## GEORGIA

SENATORS
George M. Troup, *Dublin*
John Forsyth, *Augusta*

REPRESENTATIVES AT LARGE
Thomas F. Foster, *Greensboro*
Henry G. Lamar, *Macon*
Wilson Lumpkin,[7] *Monroe*
Augustin S. Clayton,[8] *Athens*
Daniel Newnan, *McDonough*
Wiley Thompson, *Elberton*
James M. Wayne, *Savannah*
Richard H. Wilde, *Augusta*

## ILLINOIS

SENATORS
Elias K. Kane, *Kaskaskia*
John M. Robinson, *Carmi*

REPRESENTATIVE AT LARGE
Joseph Duncan, *Jacksonville*

## INDIANA

SENATORS
William Hendricks, *Madison*
Robert Hanna,[9] *Brookville*
John Tipton,[10] *Logansport*

REPRESENTATIVES
Ratliff Boon, *Boonville*
John Carr, *Charlestown*
Johnathan McCarty, *Connersville*

## KENTUCKY

SENATORS
George M. Bibb, *Yellow Banks*
Henry Clay,[11] *Lexington*

REPRESENTATIVES
John Adair, *Harrodsburg*
Chilton Allan, *Winchester*
Henry Daniel, *Mount Sterling*
Nathan Gaither, *Columbia*
Albert G. Hawes, *Hawesville*
Richard M. Johnson, *Great Crossings*
Joseph Lecompte, *New Castle*
Robert P. Letcher, *Lancaster*
Chittenden Lyon, *Eddyville*
Thomas A. Marshall, *Paris*
Christopher Tompkins, *Glasgow*
Charles A. Wickliffe, *Bardstown*

## LOUISIANA

SENATORS
Josiah S. Johnston, *Alexandria*
Edward Livingston,[12] *New Orleans*
George A. Waggaman,[13] *New Orleans*

REPRESENTATIVES
Henry A. Bullard, *Alexandria*
Philemon Thomas, *Baton Rouge*
Edward D. White, *Donaldsonville*

## MAINE

SENATORS
John Holmes, *Alfred*
Peleg Sprague, *Hallowell*

REPRESENTATIVES
John Anderson, *Portland*
James Bates, *Norridgewock*
George Evans, *Gardiner*
Cornelius Holland, *Canton*

---

[1] Resigned December 28, 1832, having been elected United States Senator.
[2] Elected July 9, 1832.
[3] Elected December 3, 1832.
[4] Reelected December 19, 1831.
[5] Reelected December 5, 1831.
[6] Reelected December 5, 1831.
[7] Resigned in 1831, before Congress assembled, having been elected governor.

[8] Elected to fill vacancy caused by resignation of Wilson Lumpkin, and took his seat January 21, 1832.
[9] Appointed to fill vacancy caused by death of James Noble, in preceding Congress, and took his seat December 5, 1831.
[10] Elected to fill vacancy caused by death of James Noble, in preceding Congress, and took his seat January 3, 1832.

[11] Elected for term beginning March 4, 1831, and took his seat December 5, 1831: vacancy in this class from March 4, 1831, to November 9, 1831.
[12] Resigned May 24, 1831, having been appointed Secretary of State.
[13] Elected to fill vacancy caused by resignation of Edward Livingston, and took his seat January 3, 1832.

Leonard Jarvis, *Ellsworth*
Edward Kavanagh, *Damariscotta Mills*
Rufus McIntire, *Parsonsfield*

## MARYLAND

### SENATORS
Samuel Smith, *Baltimore*
Ezekiel F. Chambers, *Chestertown*

### REPRESENTATIVES
Benjamin C. Howard, *Baltimore*
Daniel Jenifer, *Allens Fresh*
John L. Kerr, *Easton*
George E. Mitchell,[14] *Elkton*
Charles S. Sewall,[15] *Elkton*
Benedict J. Semmes, *Piscataway*
John S. Spence, *Berlin*
Francis Thomas, *Frederick*
George C. Washington, *Rockville*
John T. H. Worthington, *Golden*

## MASSACHUSETTS

### SENATORS
Nathaniel Silsbee, *Salem*
Daniel Webster, *Boston*

### REPRESENTATIVES
John Quincy Adams, *Quincy*
Nathan Appleton, *Boston*
Isaac C. Bates, *Northampton*
George N. Briggs, *Lanesboro*
Rufus Choate, *Salem*
John David, *Worcester*
Henry A. S. Dearborn, *Brookline*
Edward Everett, *Charlestown*
George Grennell, Jr., *Greenfield*
James L. Hodges, *Bristol*
Joseph G. Kendall, *Leominster*
Jeremiah Nelson, *Essex*
John Reed, *Yarmouth*

## MISSISSIPPI

### SENATORS
Powhatan Ellis,[16] *Winchester*
John Black,[17] *Monroe*
George Poindexter, *Wilkinson*

### REPRESENTATIVE AT LARGE
Franklin E. Plummer, *Westville*

## MISSOURI

### SENATORS
Thomas Hart Benton, *St. Louis*
Alexander Buckner, *Jackson*

### REPRESENTATIVE AT LARGE
Spencer D. Pettis,[18] *Fayette*
William H. Ashley,[19] *St. Louis*

## NEW HAMPSHIRE

### SENATORS
Samuel Bell, *Chester*
Isaac Hill, *Concord*

### REPRESENTATIVES AT LARGE
John Brodhead, *Newmarket*
Thomas Chandler, *Hillsboro*
Joseph Hammons, *Farmington*
Joseph M. Harper, *Canterbury*
Henry Hubbard, *Charlestown*
John W. Weeks, *Lancaster*

## NEW JERSEY

### SENATORS
Mahlon Dickerson, *Succasunna*
Theodore Frelinghuysen, *Newark*

### REPRESENTATIVES AT LARGE
Lewis Condict, *Morristown*
Silas Condit, *Newark*
Richard M. Cooper, *Camden*
Thomas H. Hughes, *Cold Spring*
James F. Randolph, *New Brunswick*
Isaac Southard, *Somerville*

## NEW YORK

### SENATORS
Charles E. Dudley, *Albany*
William L. Marcy,[20] *Albany*
Silas Wright, Jr.,[21] *Canton*

### REPRESENTATIVES
William G. Angel, *Burlington*
William Babcock, *Pen Yan*
Gamaliel H. Barstow, *Nichols*
Samuel Beardsley, *Utica*
John T. Bergen, *Brooklyn*
Joseph Bouck, *Middleburg*
John C. Brodhead, *Modena*
Churchill C. Cambreleng, *New York City*
John A. Collier, *Binghamton*
Bates Cooke, *Lewiston*
Charles Dayan, *Lowville*
John Dickson, *West Bloomfield*
Ulysses F. Doubleday, *Auburn*
Michael Hoffman, *Herkimer*
William Hogan, *Hogansburg*
Freeborn G. Jewett, *Skaneateles*
John King, *North Lebanon*
Gerrit Y. Lansing, *Albany*
James Lent,[22] *Newtown*
Edmund H. Pendleton, *Hyde Park*
Job Pierson, *Schaghticoke*
Nathaniel Pitcher, *Sandyhill*
Edward C. Reed, *Homer*
Erastus Root, *Delhi*
Nathan Soule, *Fort Plain*

John W. Taylor, *Ballston Spa*
Phineas L. Tracy, *Batavia*
Gulian C. Verplanck, *New York City*
Aaron Ward, *Mount Pleasant*
Daniel Wardwell, *Mannsville*
Grattan H. Wheeler, *Wheeler*
Campbell P. White, *New York City*
Frederick Whittlesey, *Rochester*
Samuel J. Wilkin, *Goshen*

## NORTH CAROLINA

### SENATORS
Bedford Brown, *Browns Store*
Willie P. Mangum, *Red Mountain*

### REPRESENTATIVES
Daniel L. Barringer, *Raleigh*
Lauchlin Bethune, *Fayetteville*
John Branch,[23] *Enfield*
Samuel P. Carson, *Pleasant Garden*
Henry W. Connor, *Sherrills Ford*
Thomas H. Hall, *Tarboro*
Robert Potter,[24] *Oxford*
Micajah T. Hawkins,[25] *Warrenton*
James I. McKay, *Elizabethtown*
Abraham Rencher, *Pittsboro*
William B. Shepard, *Elizabeth City*
Augustine H. Shepperd, *Germantown*
Jesse Speight, *Stantonsburg*
Lewis Williams, *Panther Creek*

## OHIO

### SENATORS
Benjamin Ruggles, *St. Clairsville*
Thomas Ewing, *Lancaster*

### REPRESENTATIVES
Eleutheros Cooke, *Sandusky*
Thomas Corwin, *Lebanon*
Joseph H. Crane, *Dayton*
William Creighton, Jr., *Chillicothe*
James Findlay, *Cincinnati*
William W. Irvin, *Lancaster*
William Kennon, Sr., *St. Clairsville*
Humphrey H. Leavitt, *Steubenville*
William Russell, *West Union*
William Stanbery, *Newark*
John Thomson, *New Lisbon*
Joseph Vance, *Urbana*
Samuel F. Vinton, *Gallipolis*
Elisha Whittlesey, *Canfield*

---

[14] Died June 28, 1832.
[15] Elected to fill vacancy caused by death of George E. Mitchell, and took his seat December 3, 1832.
[16] Resigned July 16, 1832, having been appointed judge of United States court.
[17] Appointed to fill vacancy caused by resignation of Powhatan Ellis, and took his seat December 12, 1832; subsequently elected.

[18] Died August 28, 1831, before Congress assembled.
[19] Elected to fill vacancy caused by death of Spencer D. Pettis, and took his seat December 5, 1831.
[20] Resigned January 1, 1833, having been elected governor.
[21] Elected to fill vacancy caused by resignation of William L. Marcy, and took his seat January 14, 1833.

[22] Died February 22, 1833.
[23] Served as Secretary of the Navy until he resigned May 12, 1831 to take his seat in Congress.
[24] Resigned in November, 1831, before Congress assembled.
[25] Elected to fill vacancy caused by resignation of Robert Potter, and took his seat January 6, 1832.

## PENNSYLVANIA

### SENATORS

Isaac D. Barnard,[26] *West Chester*
George M. Dallas,[27] *Philadelphia*
William Wilkins, *Pittsburgh*

### REPRESENTATIVES

Robert Allison, *Huntingdon Center*
John Banks, *Mercer*
John C. Bucher, *Harrisburg*
George Burd, *Bedford*
Richard Coulter, *Greensburg*
Thomas H. Crawford, *Chambersburg*
Harmar Denny, *Pittsburgh*
Lewis Dewart, *Sunbury*
Joshua Evans, Jr., *Paoli*
James Ford, *Lawrenceville*
John Gilmore, *Butler*
William Hiester, *New Holland*
Henry Horn, *Philadelphia*
Peter Ihrie, Jr., *Easton*
Adam King, *York*
Henry King, *Allentown*
Thomas M. T. McKennan,
    *Washington*
Joel K. Mann, *Jenkintown*
Henry A. P. Muhlenberg, *Reading*
David Potts, Jr., *Pottstown*
William Ramsey,[28] *Carlisle*
Robert McCoy,[29] *Carlisle*
Samuel A. Smith, *Rockhill*
Philander Stephens, *Montrose*
Andrew Stewart, *Uniontown*
Joel B. Sutherland, *Philadelphia*
John G. Watmough, *Philadelphia*

## RHODE ISLAND

### SENATORS

Nehemiah R. Knight, *Providence*
Asher Robbins, *Newport*

### REPRESENTATIVES AT LARGE

Tristam Burges, *Providence*
Dutee J. Pearce, *Newport*

## SOUTH CAROLINA

### SENATORS

Robert Y. Hayne,[30] *Charleston*
John C. Calhoun,[31] *Fort Hill*

Stephen D. Miller,[32] *Camden*

### REPRESENTATIVES

Robert W. Barnwell, *Beaufort*
James Blair, *Lynchwood*
Warren R. Davis, *Pendleton*
William Drayton, *Charleston*
John M. Felder, *Orangeburg*
John K. Griffin, *Milton*
George McDuffie, *Edgefield*
Thomas R. Mitchell, *Georgetown*
William T. Nuckolls, *Hancockville*

## TENNESSEE

### SENATORS

Hugh Lawson White, *Knoxville*
Felix Grundy, *Nashville*

### REPRESENTATIVES

Thomas D. Arnold, *Campbell Station*
John Bell, *Nashville*
John Blair, *Jonesboro*
William Fitzgerald,[33] *Dresden*
William Hall, *Green Garden*
Jacob C. Isacks, *Winchester*
Cave Johnson, *Clarksville*
James K. Polk, *Columbia*
James Standifer, *Mountairy*

## VERMONT

### SENATORS

Horatio Seymour, *Middlebury*
Samuel Prentiss, *Montpelier*

### REPRESENTATIVES

Heman Allen, *Burlington*
William Cahoon, *Lyndon*
Horace Everett, *Windsor*
Jonathan Hunt,[34] *Brattleboro*
Hiland Hall,[35] *Bennington*
Rollin C. Mallary,[36] *Poultney*
William Slade,[37] *Middlebury*

## VIRGINIA

### SENATORS

Littleton W. Tazewell,[38] *Norfolk*
William C. Rives,[39] *Milton*
John Tyler, *Gloucester*

### REPRESENTATIVES

Mark Alexander, *Lombardy Grove*
Robert Allen, *Mount Jackson*
William S. Archer, *Elk Hill*
William Armstrong, *Romney*
John S. Barbour, *Culpeper*
Thomas T. Bouldin, *Charlotte*
Joseph W. Chinn, *Nuttsville*
Nathaniel H. Claiborne, *Rocky Mount*
Richard Coke, Jr., *Williamsburg*
Robert Craig, *Montgomery*
Thomas Davenport, *Meadville*
Philip Doddridge,[40] *Wellsburg*
Joseph Johnson,[41] *Bridgeport*
William F. Gordon, *Lindseys Store*
Charles C. Johnston,[42] *Abingdon*
Joseph Draper,[43] *Wythe*
John Y. Mason, *Hicksford*
Lewis Maxwell, *Weston*
Charles F. Mercer, *Leesburg*
William McCoy, *Franklin*
Thomas Newton, Jr., *Norfolk*
John M. Patton, *Fredericksburg*
John J. Roane, *Rumford Academy*
Andrew Stevenson, *Richmond*

## ARKANSAS TERRITORY

### DELEGATE

Ambrose H. Sevier, *Little Rock*

## TERRITORY OF FLORIDA

### DELEGATE

Joseph M. White, *Monticello*

## MICHIGAN TERRITORY

### DELEGATE

Austin E. Wing, *Monroe*

---

[26] Resigned December 6, 1831.
[27] Elected to fill vacancy caused by resignation of Isaac D. Barnard, and took his seat December 21, 1831.
[28] Died September 29, 1831, before Congress assembled.
[29] Elected to fill vacancy caused by death of William Ramsey, and took his seat December 5, 1831.
[30] Resigned December 13, 1832, having been elected governor.
[31] Elected to fill vacancy caused by resignation of Robert Y. Hayne, and took his seat January 4, 1833.

[32] Resigned March 2, 1833.
[33] Election unsuccessfully contested by David Crockett.
[34] Died May 14, 1832.
[35] Elected to fill vacancy caused by death of Jonathan Hunt, and took his seat January 21, 1833.
[36] Died April 16, 1831, before Congress assembled.
[37] Elected to fill vacancy caused by death of Rollin C. Mallary, and took his seat December 5, 1831.
[38] Resigned July 16, 1832.

[39] Elected to fill vacancy caused by resignation of Littleton W. Tazewell; took his seat January 4, 1833.
[40] Died November 19, 1832.
[41] Elected to fill vacancy caused by death of Philip Doddridge, and took his seat January 21, 1833.
[42] Election unsuccessfully contested by Joseph Draper; died June 17, 1832.
[43] Unsuccessfully contested the election of Charles C. Johnston; subsequently elected to fill vacancy caused by death of Mr. Johnston, and took his seat December 12, 1832.

# 23RD CONGRESS

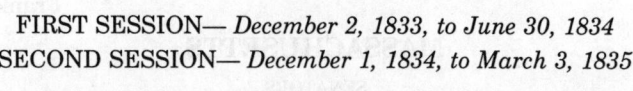

MARCH 4, 1833, TO MARCH 3, 1835

FIRST SESSION— *December 2, 1833, to June 30, 1834*
SECOND SESSION— *December 1, 1834, to March 3, 1835*

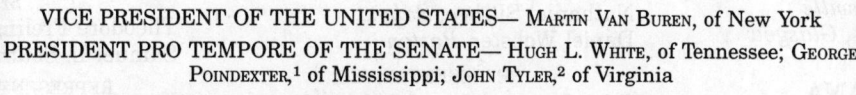

VICE PRESIDENT OF THE UNITED STATES— MARTIN VAN BUREN, of New York
PRESIDENT PRO TEMPORE OF THE SENATE— HUGH L. WHITE, of Tennessee; GEORGE
POINDEXTER,[1] of Mississippi; JOHN TYLER,[2] of Virginia
SECRETARY OF THE SENATE— WALTER LOWRIE,[3] of Pennsylvania
SERGEANT AT ARMS OF THE SENATE— MOUNTJOY BAYLY, of Maryland; JOHN
SHACKFORD,[4] of New Hampshire

SPEAKER OF THE HOUSE OF REPRESENTATIVES— ANDREW STEVENSON,[5] of Virginia;
JOHN BELL,[6] of Tennessee
CLERK OF THE HOUSE— MATTHEW ST. CLAIR CLARKE, of Pennsylvania; WALTER S. FRANKLIN,[7] of Pennsylvania
SERGEANT AT ARMS OF THE HOUSE— JOHN O. DUNN, of District of Columbia; THOMAS B. RANDOLPH,[8] of Virginia
DOORKEEPER OF THE HOUSE— OVERTON CARR, of Maryland

Martin Van Buren
Vice President

Andrew Stevenson
Speaker

## ALABAMA

### SENATORS

William R. King, *Selma*
Gabriel Moore, *Huntsville*

### REPRESENTATIVES

Clement C. Clay, *Huntsville*
Dixon H. Lewis, *Lowndesboro*
John McKinley, *Florence*
Samuel W. Mardis, *Montevallo*
John Murphy, *Claiborne*

## CONNECTICUT

### SENATORS

Gideon Tomlinson, *Fairfield*
Nathan Smith, *New Haven*

### REPRESENTATIVES AT LARGE

Noyes Barber, *Groton*
William W. Ellsworth,[9] *Hartford*
Joseph Trumbull,[10] *Hartford*
Samuel A. Foote,[11] *Cheshire*
Ebenezer Jackson, Jr.,[12] *Middletown*
Jabez W. Huntington,[13] *Litchfield*
Phineas Miner,[14] *Litchfield*
Samuel Tweedy, *Danbury*
Ebenezer Young, *Killingly Center*

## DELAWARE

### SENATORS

John M. Clayton, *Dover*
Arnold Naudain, *Wilmington*

### REPRESENTATIVE AT LARGE

John J. Milligan, *Wilmington*

## GEORGIA

### SENATORS

George M. Troup,[15] *Dublin*
John P. King,[16] *Augusta*
John Forsyth,[17] *Columbus*
Alfred Cuthbert,[18] *Monticello*

### REPRESENTATIVES AT LARGE

Augustin S. Clayton, *Athens*
John Coffee, *Jacksonville*
Thomas F. Foster, *Greensboro*
Roger L. Gamble, *Louisville*
George R. Gilmer, *Lexington*
Seaborn Jones, *Columbus*
William Schley, *Augusta*
James M. Wayne,[19] *Savannah*
Richard H. Wilde, *Augusta*

## ILLINOIS

### SENATORS

Elias K. Kane, *Kaskaskia*
John M. Robinson, *Carmi*

## REPRESENTATIVES

Zadoc Casey, *Mount Vernon*
Joseph Duncan,[20] *Jacksonville*
William L. May,[21] *Springfield*
Charles Slade,[22] *Carlyle*
John Reynolds,[23] *Belleville*

## INDIANA

### SENATORS

William Hendricks, *Madison*
John Tipton, *Logansport*

### REPRESENTATIVES

Ratliff Boon, *Boonville*
John Carr, *Charlestown*
John Ewing, *Vincennes*
Edward A. Hannegan, *Covington*
George L. Kinnard, *Indianapolis*
Amos Lane, *Lawrenceburg*
Johnathan McCarty, *Fort Wayne*

## KENTUCKY

### SENATORS

George M. Bibb, *Yellow Banks*
Henry Clay, *Lexington*

### REPRESENTATIVES

Chilton Allan, *Winchester*
Martin Beaty, *South Fork*
Thomas Chilton, *Elizabethtown*
Amos Davis, *Mount Sterling*
Benjamin Hardin, *Bardstown*

---

[1] Elected June 28, 1834.
[2] Elected March 3, 1835.
[3] Reelected December 9, 1833.
[4] Elected December 9, 1833.
[5] Reelected December 2, 1833; resigned from the House June 2, 1834; Henry Hubbard, of New Hampshire, was elected Speaker pro tempore for May 16, 1834.
[6] Elected June 2, 1834.
[7] Elected December 2, 1833.
[8] Elected December 3, 1833.
[9] Resigned July 8, 1834.
[10] Elected to fill vacancy caused by resignation of

William W. Ellsworth, took his seat December 1, 1834.
[11] Resigned May 9, 1834, having been elected governor.
[12] Elected to fill vacancy caused by resignation of Samuel A. Foote, and took his seat December 1, 1834.
[13] Resigned August 16, 1834, having been appointed judge of the supreme court of errors.
[14] Elected to fill vacancy caused by resignation of Jabez W. Huntington, and took his seat December 1, 1834.
[15] Resigned November 8, 1833.
[16] Elected to fill vacancy caused by resignation of George M. Troup, and took his seat December 31, 1833.

[17] Resigned June 27, 1834, having been appointed Secretary of State.
[18] Elected to fill vacancy caused by resignation of John Forsyth, and took his seat January 12, 1835.
[19] Resigned January 13, 1835.
[20] Elected September 21, 1834, having been elected governor.
[21] Elected to fill vacancy caused by resignation of Joseph Duncan, and took his seat December 1, 1834.
[22] Died July 26, 1834.
[23] Elected to fill vacancy caused by death of Charles Slade, and took his seat December 1, 1834.

## KENTUCKY—Continued

### REPRESENTATIVES—CONTINUED

Albert G. Hawes, *Hawesville*
Richard M. Johnson, *Great Crossings*
Robert P. Letcher,[24] *Lancaster*
James Love, *Barbourville*
Chittenden Lyon, *Eddyville*
Thomas A. Marshall, *Paris*
Patrick H. Pope, *Louisville*
Christopher Tompkins, *Glasgow*

## LOUISIANA

### SENATORS

Josiah S. Johnston,[25] *Alexandria*
Alexander Porter,[26] *Attakapas*
George A. Waggaman, *New Orleans*

### REPRESENTATIVES

Henry A. Bullard,[27] *Alexandria*
Rice Garland,[28] *Opelousas*
Philemon Thomas, *Baton Rouge*
Edward D. White,[29] *Donaldsonville*
Henry Johnson,[30] *Donaldsonville*

## MAINE

### SENATORS

Peleg Sprague,[31] *Hallowell*
John Ruggles,[32] *Thomaston*
Ether Shepley, *Saco*

### REPRESENTATIVES

George Evans, *Gardiner*
Joseph Hall, *Camden*
Leonard Jarvis, *Ellsworth*
Edward Kavanagh, *Damariscotta Mills*
Moses Mason, Jr., *Bethel*
Rufus McIntire, *Parsonsfield*
Gorham Parks, *Bangor*
Francis O. J. Smith, *Portland*

## MARYLAND

### SENATORS

Ezekiel F. Chambers,[33] *Chestertown*
Robert H. Goldsborough,[34] *Easton*
Joseph Kent, *Bladensburg*

### REPRESENTATIVES

Richard B. Carmichael, *Centerville*
Littleton P. Dennis,[35] *Princess Anne*
John N. Steele,[36] *Vienna*
James P. Heath, *Baltimore*

William Cost Johnson, *Jefferson*
Isaac McKim, *Baltimore*
John T. Stoddert, *Harris Lot*
Francis Thomas, *Frederick*
James Turner, *Wiseburg*

## MASSACHUSETTS

### SENATORS

Nathaniel Silsbee, *Salem*
Daniel Webster, *Boston*

### REPRESENTATIVES

John Quincy Adams, *Quincy*
Isaac C. Bates, *Northampton*
William Baylies, *West Bridgewater*
George N. Briggs, *Lanesboro*
Rufus Choate,[37] *Salem*
Stephen C. Phillips,[38] *Salem*
John Davis,[39] *Worcester*
Levi Lincoln,[40] *Worcester*
Edward Everett, *Charlestown*
Benjamin Gorham, *Boston*
George Grennell, Jr., *Greenfield*
William Jackson, *Newton*
Gayton P. Osgood, *North Andover*
John Reed, *Yarmouth*

## MISSISSIPPI

### SENATORS

George Poindexter, *Wilkinson*
John Black,[41] *Monroe*

### REPRESENTATIVES AT LARGE

Harry Cage, *Woodville*
Franklin E. Plummer, *Westville*

## MISSOURI

### SENATORS

Thomas Hart Benton, *St. Louis*
Alexander Buckner,[42] *Jackson*
Lewis F. Linn,[43] *Ste. Genevieve*

### REPRESENTATIVES AT LARGE

William H. Ashley, *St. Louis*
John Bull, *Chariton*

## NEW HAMPSHIRE

### SENATORS

Samuel Bell, *Chester*
Isaac Hill, *Concord*

### REPRESENTATIVES AT LARGE

Benning M. Bean, *Moultonboro*
Robert Burns, *Hebron*
Joseph M. Harper, *Canterbury*
Henry Hubbard, *Charlestown*
Franklin Pierce, *Hillsboro*

## NEW JERSEY

### SENATORS

Theodore Frelinghuysen, *Newark*
Samuel L. Southard, *Trenton*

### REPRESENTATIVES AT LARGE

Philemon Dickerson, *Paterson*
Samuel Fowler, *Hamburg*
Thomas Lee, *Port Elizabeth*
James Parker, *Perth Amboy*
Ferdinand S. Schenck, *Six Mile Run*
William N. Shinn, *Mount Holly*

## NEW YORK

### SENATORS

Silas Wright, Jr., *Canton*
Nathaniel P. Tallmadge, *Poughkeepsie*

### REPRESENTATIVES

John Adams, *Catskill*
Samuel Beardsley, *Utica*
Abraham Bockee, *Federal Store*
Charles Bodle, *Bloomingburg*
John W. Brown, *Newburgh*
Churchill C. Cambreleng, *New York City*
Samuel Clark, *Waterloo*
John Cramer, *Waterford*
Rowland Day, *Sempronius*
John Dickson, *West Bloomfield*
Millard Fillmore, *Buffalo*
Philo C. Fuller, *Genesco*
William K. Fuller, *Chittenango*
Ransom H. Gillet, *Ogdensburg*
Nicoll Halsey, *Trumansburg*
Gideon Hard, *Albion*
Samuel G. Hathaway, *Solon*
Abner Hazeltine, *Jamestown*
Edward Howell, *Bath*
Abel Huntington, *East Hampton*
Noadiah Johnson, *Delhi*
Gerrit Y. Lansing, *Albany*
Cornelius W. Lawrence,[44] *New York City*
John J. Morgan,[45] *New York City*
George W. Lay, *Batavia*

---

[24] Thomas P. Moore presented credentials on December 2, 1833, but was not sworn pending a contest by Robert P. Letcher, and on June 2, 1834, the House ordered a new election, "it being impracticable for this House to determine with any certainty who is the rightful Representative of this district." Mr. Letcher was subsequently elected and took his seat December 1, 1834.

[25] Died May 19, 1833.

[26] Elected to fill vacancy caused by death of Josiah S. Johnston, and took his seat January 6, 1834.

[27] Resigned January 4, 1834, having been appointed judge of the supreme court of Louisiana.

[28] Elected to fill vacancy caused by resignation of Henry A. Bullard, and took his seat April 28, 1834.

[29] Resigned November 15, 1834, having been elected Governor.

[30] Elected to fill vacancy caused by resignation of Edward D. White, and took his seat December 1, 1834.

[31] Resigned January 1, 1835.

[32] Elected to fill vacancy caused by resignation of Peleg Sprague, and took his seat February 6, 1835.

[33] Resigned in 1834.

[34] Elected to fill vacancy caused by resignation of Ezekiel F. Chambers, and took his seat January 23, 1835.

[35] Died April 14, 1834.

[36] Elected to fill vacancy caused by death of Littleton P. Dennis, and took his seat June 9, 1834.

[37] Resigned June 30, 1834.

[38] Elected to fill vacancy caused by resignation of Rufus Choate, and took his seat December 1, 1834.

[39] Resigned January 14, 1834, having been elected governor.

[40] Elected to fill vacancy caused by resignation of John Davis, and took his seat March 5, 1834.

[41] Elected to fill vacancy in term commencing March 4, 1833, and took his seat December 23, 1833; vacancy in this class from March 4, 1833, to November 21, 1833, because of recess of legislature.

[42] Died June 6, 1833.

[43] Appointed to fill vacancy caused by death of Alexander Buckner, and took his seat December 16, 1833; subsequently elected.

[44] Resigned May 14, 1834, having been elected mayor of New York City.

[45] Elected to fill vacancy caused by resignation of Cornelius W. Lawrence, and took his seat December 1, 1834.

Charles McVean, *Canajoharie*
Abijah Mann, Jr., *Fairfield*
Henry C. Martindale, *Sandy Hill*
Henry Mitchell, *Norwich*
Sherman Page, *Unadilla*
Job Pierson, *Schaghticoke*
Dudley Selden,[46] *New York City*
Charles G. Ferris,[47] *New York City*
William Taylor, *Manlius*
Joel Turrill, *Oswego*
Aaron Vanderpoel, *Kinderhook*
Isaac B. Van Houten, *Clarkstown*
Aaron Ward, *Mount Pleasant*
Daniel Wardwell, *Mannsville*
Reuben Whallon, *Split Rock*
Campbell P. White, *New York City*
Frederick Whittlesey, *Rochester*

## NORTH CAROLINA

### SENATORS

Bedford Brown, *Browns Store*
Willie P. Mangum, *Red Mountain*

### REPRESENTATIVES

Daniel L. Barringer, *Raleigh*
Jesse A. Bynum, *Halifax*
Henry W. Connor, *Sherrills Ford*
Edmund Deberry, *Lawrenceville*
James Graham, *Rutherfordton*
Thomas H. Hall, *Tarboro*
Micajah T. Hawkins, *Warrenton*
James I. McKay, *Elizabethtown*
Abraham Rencher, *Pittsboro*
William B. Shepard, *Elizabeth City*
Augustine H. Shepperd, *Germantown*
Jesse Speight, *Stantonsburg*
Lewis Williams, *Panther Creek*

## OHIO

### SENATORS

Thomas Ewing, *Lancaster*
Thomas Morris, *Bethel*

### REPRESENTATIVES

William Allen,[48] *Chillicothe*
James M. Bell, *Cambridge*
John Chaney, *Courtwright*
Thomas Corwin, *Lebanon*
Joseph H. Crane, *Dayton*
Thomas L. Hamer, *Georgetown*
Benjamin Jones, *Wooster*
Humphrey H. Leavitt,[49] *Steubenville*
Daniel Kilgore,[50] *Cadiz*
Robert T. Lytle,[51] *Cincinnati*

Jeremiah McLene, *Columbus*
Robert Mitchell, *Zanesville*
William Patterson, *Mansfield*
Jonathan Sloane, *Ravenna*
David Spangler, *Coshocton*
John Thomson, *New Lisbon*
Joseph Vance, *Urbana*
Samuel F. Vinton, *Gallipolis*
Taylor Webster, *Hamilton*
Elisha Whittlesey, *Canfield*

## PENNSYLVANIA

### SENATORS

William Wilkins,[52] *Pittsburgh*
James Buchanan,[53] *Lancaster*
Samuel McKean, *Burlington*

### REPRESENTATIVES

Joseph B. Anthony, *Williamsport*
John Banks, *Mercer*
Charles A. Barnitz, *York*
Andrew Beaumont, *Wilkes-Barre*
Horace Binney, *Philadelphia*
George Burd, *Bedford*
George Chambers, *Chambersburg*
William Clark, *Dauphin*
Richard Coulter, *Greensburg*
Edward Darlington, *Chester*
Harmar Denny, *Pittsburgh*
John Galbraith, *Franklin*
James Harper, *Philadelphia*
Samuel S. Harrison, *Kittanning*
Joseph Henderson, *Browns Mills*
William Hiester, *New Holland*
Henry King, *Allentown*
John Laporte, *Asylum*
Thomas M. T. McKennan,
 *Washington*
Joel K. Mann, *Jenkintown*
Jesse Miller, *Landisburg*
Henry A. P. Muhlenberg, *Reading*
David Potts, Jr., *Pottstown*
Robert Ramsey, *Hartsville*
Andrew Stewart, *Uniontown*
Joel B. Sutherland, *Philadelphia*
David D. Wagener, *Easton*
John G. Watmough, *Philadelphia*

## RHODE ISLAND

### SENATORS

Nehemiah R. Knight, *Providence*
Asher Robbins,[54] *Newport*

REPRESENTATIVES AT LARGE
Tristam Burges, *Providence*
Dutee J. Pearce, *Newport*

## SOUTH CAROLINA

### SENATORS

John C. Calhoun, *Fort Hill*
William C. Preston,[55] *Columbia*

### REPRESENTATIVES

James Blair,[56] *Lynchwood*
Richard I. Manning,[57] *Fulton*
William K. Clowney, *Union*
Warren R. Davis,[58] *Pendleton*
John M. Felder, *Orangeburg*
William J. Grayson, *Beaufort*
John K. Griffin, *Milton*
George McDuffie,[59] *Willington*
Francis W. Pickens,[60] *Edgefield*
Henry L. Pinckney, *Charleston*
Thomas D. Singleton,[61] *Kingtree*
Robert B. Campbell,[62] *Brownsville*

## TENNESSEE

### SENATORS

Hugh Lawson White, *Knoxville*
Felix Grundy, *Nashville*

### REPRESENTATIVES

John Bell, *Nashville*
John Blair, *Jonesboro*
Samuel Bunch, *Rutledge*
David Crockett, *Crockett*
David W. Dickinson, *Murfreesboro*
William C. Dunlap, *Bolivar*
John B. Forester, *McMinnville*
William M. Inge, *Fayetteville*
Cave Johnson, *Clarksville*
Luke Lea, *Campbells Station*
Balie Peyton, *Gallatin*
James K. Polk, *Columbia*
James Standifer, *Mountairy*

## VERMONT

### SENATORS

Samuel Prentiss, *Montpelier*
Benjamin Swift, *St. Albans*

### REPRESENTATIVES

Heman Allen, *Burlington*
Benjamin F. Deming,[63] *Danville*
Henry F. Janes,[64] *Waterbury*
Horace Everett, *Windsor*
Hiland Hall, *Bennington*
William Slade, *Middlebury*

---

[46] Resigned July 1, 1834.
[47] Elected to fill vacancy caused by resignation of Dudley Selden, and took his seat December 1, 1834.
[48] Election unsuccessfully contested by Duncan McArthur.
[49] Resigned July 10, 1834, having been appointed judge of the United States district court.
[50] Elected to fill vacancy caused by resignation of Humphrey H. Leavitt, and took his seat December 1, 1834.
[51] Resigned March 10, 1834; elected to fill vacancy caused by his own resignation, and took his seat December 27, 1834.
[52] Resigned June 30, 1834, having been appointed minister to Russia.

[53] Elected to fill vacancy caused by resignation of William Wilkins, and took his seat December 15, 1834.
[54] Election unsuccessfully contested by Elisha R. Potter. (See U.S. Senate Election, Expulsion and Censure Cases, 1793-1990, Senate Document 103-33, pp. 35-37.)
[55] Elected to fill vacancy caused by resignation of Stephen D. Miller, in preceding Congress, and took his seat December 9, 1833.
[56] Died April 1, 1834.
[57] Elected to fill vacancy caused by death of James Blair, and took his seat December 8, 1834.
[58] Died January 29, 1835, before the commencement of the Twenty-fourth Congress, to which he had been reelected.

[59] Resigned in 1834.
[60] Elected to fill vacancy caused by resignation of George McDuffie, and took his seat December 8, 1834.
[61] Died November 25, 1833, before Congress assembled.
[62] Elected to fill vacancy caused by death of Thomas D. Singleton, and took his seat February 27, 1834.
[63] Died July 11, 1834.
[64] Elected to fill vacancy caused by death of Benjamin F. Deming, and took his seat December 2, 1834.

## VIRGINIA

### SENATORS

John Tyler, *Gloucester*
William C. Rives,[65] *Lindseys Store*
Benjamin W. Leigh,[66] *Richmond*

### REPRESENTATIVES

John J. Allen, *Clarksburg*
William S. Archer, *Elk Hill*
James M. H. Beale, *New Market*
John Randolph,[67] *Charlotte*
Thomas T. Bouldin,[68] *Charlotte*
James W. Bouldin,[69] *Charlotte*
Joseph W. Chinn, *Nuttsville*
Nathaniel H. Claiborne, *Rocky Mount*
Thomas Davenport, *Meadville*

John H. Fulton, *Abingdon*
James H. Gholson, *Percivals*
William F. Gordon, *Lindseys Store*
George Loyall, *Norfolk*
Edward Lucas, *Charlestown*
John Y. Mason, *Hicksford*
William McComas, *Greenbrier*
Samuel McDowell Moore, *Lexington*
Charles F. Mercer, *Aldie*
John M. Patton, *Fredericksburg*
Andrew Stevenson,[70] *Richmond*
John Robertson,[71] *Richmond*
William P. Taylor, *Fredericksburg*
Edgar C. Wilson, *Morgantown*
Henry A. Wise, *Onancock*

## ARKANSAS TERRITORY

### DELEGATE

Ambrose H. Sevier, *Little Rock*

## TERRITORY OF FLORIDA

### DELEGATE

Joseph M. White, *Monticello*

## MICHIGAN TERRITORY

### DELEGATE

Lucius Lyon, *Bronson*

---

[65] Resigned February 22, 1834.
[66] Elected to fill vacancy caused by resignation of William C. Rives, and took his seat March 5, 1834.
[67] Died May 24, 1833.
[68] Elected to fill vacancy caused by death of John

Randolph, and took his seat December 2, 1833; died February 11, 1834, while addressing the House.
[69] Elected to fill vacancy caused by death of Thomas T. Bouldin, and took his seat March 28, 1834.
[70] Resigned June 2, 1834.

[71] Elected to fill vacancy caused by resignation of Andrew Stevenson, and took his seat December 8, 1834.

# 24TH CONGRESS

## MARCH 4, 1835, TO MARCH 3, 1837

FIRST SESSION— *December 7, 1835, to July 4, 1836*
SECOND SESSION— *December 5, 1836, to March 3, 1837*

---

VICE PRESIDENT OF THE UNITED STATES— MARTIN VAN BUREN, of New York
PRESIDENT PRO TEMPORE OF THE SENATE— WILLIAM R. KING,[1] of Alabama
SECRETARY OF THE SENATE— WALTER LOWRIE,[2] of Pennsylvania; ASBURY DICKENS,[3] of North Carolina
SERGEANT AT ARMS OF THE SENATE— JOHN SHACKFORD, of New Hampshire

---

SPEAKER OF THE HOUSE OF REPRESENTATIVES— JAMES K. POLK,[4] of Tennessee
CLERK OF THE HOUSE— WALTER S. FRANKLIN,[5] of Pennsylvania
SERGEANT AT ARMS OF THE HOUSE— THOMAS B. RANDOLPH, of Virginia; RODERICK DORSEY,[6] of Maryland
DOORKEEPER OF THE HOUSE— OVERTON CARR, of Maryland

Martin Van Buren
Vice President

James K. Polk
Speaker

## ALABAMA

SENATORS
William R. King, *Selma*
Gabriel Moore, *Huntsville*

REPRESENTATIVES
Reuben Chapman, *Somerville*
Joshua L. Martin, *Athens*
Joab Lawler, *Mardisville*
Dixon H. Lewis, *Lowndesboro*
Francis S. Lyon, *Demopolis*

## ARKANSAS[7]

SENATORS
William S. Fulton,[8] *Little Rock*
Ambrose H. Sevier,[9] *Lake Port*

REPRESENTATIVE AT LARGE
Archibald Yell,[10] *Fayetteville*

## CONNECTICUT

SENATORS
Gideon Tomlinson, *Fairfield*
Nathan Smith,[11] *New Haven*
John M. Niles,[12] *Hartford*

REPRESENTATIVES AT LARGE
Elisha Haley, *Mystic*
Andrew T. Judson,[13] *Canterbury*
Orrin Holt,[14] *Willington*

Samuel Ingham, *Saybrook*
Lancelot Phelps, *Hitchcockville*
Isaac Toucey, *Hartford*
Zalmon Wildman,[15] *Danbury*
Thomas T. Whittlesey,[16] *Danbury*

## DELAWARE

SENATORS
John M. Clayton,[17] *Dover*
Thomas Clayton,[18] *New Castle*
Arnold Naudain,[19] *Wilmington*
Richard H. Bayard,[20] *Wilmington*

REPRESENTATIVE AT LARGE
John J. Milligan, *Wilmington*

## GEORGIA

SENATORS
John P. King, *Augusta*
Alfred Cuthbert, *Monticello*

REPRESENTATIVES AT LARGE
George W. B. Towns,[21] *Talbotton*
Julius C. Alford,[22] *Lagrange*
William Schley,[23] *Augusta*
Jesse F. Cleveland,[24] *Decatur*
John Coffee,[25] *Jacksonville*
William C. Dawson,[26] *Greensboro*
John W. A. Sanford,[27] *Milledgeville*
Thomas Glascock,[28] *Augusta*

Seaton Grantland, *Milledgeville*
Charles E. Haynes, *Sparta*
James C. Terrell,[29] *Carnesville*
Hopkins Holsey,[30] *Hamilton*
Jabez Y. Jackson,[31] *Clarkesville*
George W. Owens, *Savannah*

## ILLINOIS

SENATORS
Elias K. Kane,[32] *Kaskaskia*
William L. D. Ewing,[33] *Vandalia*
John M. Robinson, *Carmi*

REPRESENTATIVES
John Reynolds, *Belleville*
Zadoc Casey, *Mount Vernon*
William L. May, *Springfield*

## INDIANA

SENATORS
William Hendricks, *Madison*
John Tipton, *Logansport*

REPRESENTATIVES
Ratliff Boon, *Boonville*
John Carr, *Charlestown*
John W. Davis, *Carlisle*
Amos Lane, *Lawrenceburg*
Johnathan McCarty, *Fort Wayne*

---

[1] Elected July 1, 1836; January 28, 1837.
[2] Reelected December 15, 1835; resigned December 5, 1836.
[3] Elected December 12, 1836; Lewis H. Machen, the principal clerk, was appointed on December 5, 1836, to act in the interim.
[4] Elected December 7, 1835.
[5] Reelected December 7, 1835.
[6] Elected December 15, 1835.
[7] Admitted as a State into the Union June 15, 1836.
[8] Took his seat December 5, 1836; term to expire, as determined by lot, March 3, 1841.
[9] Took his seat December 5, 1836; term to expire, as determined by lot, March 3, 1837.
[10] Took his seat December 5, 1836.
[11] Died December 6, 1835.
[12] Appointed to fill vacancy caused by death of

Nathan Smith, and took his seat December 21, 1835; subsequently elected.
[13] Resigned July 4, 1836.
[14] Elected to fill vacancy caused by resignation of Andrew T. Judson, and took his seat December 5, 1836.
[15] Died December 10, 1835.
[16] Elected to fill vacancy caused by death of Zalmon Wildman, and took his seat April 29, 1836.
[17] Resigned December 29, 1836.
[18] Elected to fill vacancy caused by resignation of John M. Clayton, and took his seat January 19, 1837.
[19] Resigned June 16, 1836.
[20] Elected to fill vacancy caused by resignation of Arnold Naudain, and took his seat June 20, 1836.
[21] Resigned September 1, 1836.
[22] Elected to fill vacancy caused by resignation of George W. B. Towns: took his seat January 31, 1837.
[23] Resigned July 1, 1835.

[24] Elected to fill vacancy caused by resignation of William Schley, and took his seat December 7, 1835.
[25] Died September 25, 1836.
[26] Elected to fill vacancy caused by death of John Coffee, and took his seat December 26, 1836.
[27] Resigned July 25, 1835.
[28] Elected to fill vacancy caused by resignation of John W. A. Sanford, and took his seat December 7, 1835.
[29] Resigned July 8, 1835.
[30] Elected to fill vacancy caused by resignation of James C. Terrell, and took his seat December 7, 1835.
[31] Elected to fill vacancy caused by resignation of James M. Wayne in preceding Congress, and took his seat December 7, 1835.
[32] Died December 12, 1835.
[33] Elected to fill vacancy caused by death of Elias K. Kane, and took his seat January 25, 1836.

## INDIANA—Continued

REPRESENTATIVES—CONTINUED

George L. Kinnard,[34] *Indianapolis*
William Herod,[35] *Columbus*
Edward A. Hannegan, *Covington*

## KENTUCKY

SENATORS

Henry Clay, *Lexington*
John J. Crittenden, *Frankfort*

REPRESENTATIVES

Linn Boyd, *New Design*
Albert G. Hawes, *Hawesville*
Joseph R. Underwood, *Bowling Green*
Sherrod Williams, *Monticello*
James Harlan, *Harrodsburg*
John Calhoon, *Hardinsburg*
Benjamin Hardin, *Bardstown*
William J. Graves, *New Castle*
John White, *Richmond*
Chilton Allan, *Winchester*
Richard French, *Mount Sterling*
John Chambers, *Washington*
Richard M. Johnson, *Great Crossings*

## LOUISIANA

SENATORS

Alexander Porter,[36] *Attakapas*
Alexander Mouton,[37] *Vermilionville*
Robert C. Nicholas,[38] *Donaldsonville*

REPRESENTATIVES

Henry Johnson, *Donaldsonville*
Eleazer W. Ripley, *Jackson*
Rice Garland, *Opelousas*

## MAINE

SENATORS

Ether Shepley,[39] *Saco*
Judah Dana,[40] *Fryeburg*
John Ruggles, *Thomaston*

REPRESENTATIVES

Jeremiah Bailey, *Wiscasset*
George Evans, *Gardiner*
John Fairfield, *Saco*
Joseph Hall, *Camden*
Leonard Jarvis, *Ellsworth*
Moses Mason, Jr., *Bethel*
Gorham Parks, *Bangor*
Francis O. J. Smith, *Portland*

## MARYLAND

SENATORS

Robert H. Goldsborough,[41] *Easton*
John S. Spence,[42] *Berlin*
Joseph Kent, *Bladensburg*

REPRESENTATIVES

John N. Steele, *Vienna*
James A. Pearce, *Chestertown*
James Turner, *Wiseburg*
Benjamin C. Howard, *Baltimore*
Isaac McKim, *Baltimore*
George C. Washington, *Rockville*
Francis Thomas, *Frederick*
Daniel Jenifer, *Harris Lot*

## MASSACHUSETTS

SENATORS

Daniel Webster, *Boston*
John Davis, *Worcester*

REPRESENTATIVES

Abbott Lawrence, *Boston*
Stephen C. Phillips, *Salem*
Caleb Cushing, *Newburyport*
Samuel Hoar, *Concord*
Levi Lincoln, *Worcester*
George Grennell, Jr., *Greenfield*
George N. Briggs, *Lanesboro*
William B. Calhoun, *Springfield*
William Jackson, *Newton*
Nathaniel B. Borden, *Fall River*
John Reed, *Yarmouth*
John Quincy Adams, *Quincy*

## MICHIGAN[43]

SENATORS

Lucius Lyon,[44] *Bronson*
John Norvell,[45] *Detroit*

REPRESENTATIVE AT LARGE

Isaac E. Crary,[46] *Marshall*

## MISSISSIPPI

SENATORS

John Black, *Monroe*
Robert J. Walker, *Madisonville*

REPRESENTATIVES AT LARGE

John F. H. Claiborne, *Madisonville*
David Dickson,[47] *Jackson*
Samuel J. Gholson,[48] *Athens*

## MISSOURI

SENATORS

Thomas Hart Benton, *St. Louis*
Lewis F. Linn, *Ste. Genevieve*

REPRESENTATIVES AT LARGE

William H. Ashley, *St. Louis*
Albert G. Harrison, *Fulton*

## NEW HAMPSHIRE

SENATORS

Isaac Hill,[49] *Concord*
John Page,[50] *Haverhill*
Henry Hubbard, *Charlestown*

REPRESENTATIVES AT LARGE

Benning M. Bean, *Moultonboro*
Robert Burns, *Plymouth*
Samuel Cushman, *Portsmouth*
Franklin Pierce, *Hillsboro*
Joseph Weeks, *Richmond*

## NEW JERSEY

SENATORS

Samuel L. Southard, *Trenton*
Garret D. Wall, *Burlington*

REPRESENTATIVES AT LARGE

Philemon Dickerson,[51] *Paterson*
William Chetwood,[52] *Elizabethtown*
Samuel Fowler, *Hamburg*
Thomas Lee, *Port Elizabeth*
James Parker, *Perth Amboy*
Ferdinand S. Schenck, *Six Mile Run*
William N. Shinn, *Mount Holly*

## NEW YORK

SENATORS

Silas Wright, Jr., *Canton*
Nathaniel P. Tallmadge, *Poughkeepsie*

REPRESENTATIVES

Abel Huntington, *East Hampton*
Samuel Barton, *Richmond*
Churchill C. Cambreleng, *New York City*
Campbell P. White,[53] *New York City*
Gideon Lee,[54] *New York City*
John McKeon, *New York City*
Ely Moore, *New York City*
Aaron Ward, *Mount Pleasant*

---

[34] Died November 26, 1836.
[35] Elected to fill vacancy caused by death of George L. Kinnard, and took his seat January 25, 1837.
[36] Resigned January 5, 1837.
[37] Elected to fill vacancy caused by resignation of Alexander Porter, and took his seat February 2, 1837.
[38] Elected for the term beginning March 4, 1835, and took his seat March 4, 1836. Charles E. A. Gayarre was elected, but resigned on account of ill health without qualifying; vacancy in this class from March 4, 1835, to January 13, 1836.
[39] Resigned March 3, 1836.
[40] Appointed to fill vacancy caused by resignation

of Ether Shepley, and took his seat December 21, 1836.
[41] Died October 5, 1836.
[42] Elected to fill vacancy caused by death of Robert H. Goldborough, and took his seat January 11, 1837.
[43] Admitted as a State into the Union January 26, 1837.
[44] Took his seat January 26, 1837; term to expire, as determined by lot, March 3, 1839.
[45] Took his seat January 26, 1837; term to expire, as determined by lot, March 3, 1841.
[46] Took his seat January 27, 1837.
[47] Died in 1836.
[48] Elected to fill vacancy caused by death of David Dickson, and took his seat January 7, 1837.

[49] Resigned May 30, 1836, having been elected governor.
[50] Elected to fill vacancy caused by resignation of Isaac Hill, and took his seat June 13, 1836.
[51] Resigned November 3, 1836.
[52] Elected to fill vacancy caused by resignation of Philemon Dickerson and took his seat December 5, 1836.
[53] Resigned before Congress assembled.
[54] Elected to fill vacancy caused by resignation of Campbell P. White, and took his seat December 7, 1835.

Abraham Bockee, *Federal Store*
John W. Brown, *Newburgh*
Nicholas Sickles, *Kingston*
Valentine Efner, *Jefferson*
Aaron Vanderpoel, *Kinderhook*
Hiram P. Hunt, *Troy*
Gerrit Y. Lansing, *Albany*
John Cramer, *Waterford*
David A. Russell, *Salem*
Dudley Farlin, *Warrensburg*
Ranson H. Gillet, *Ogdensburg*
Matthias J. Bovee, *Amsterdam*
Abijah Mann, Jr., *Fairfield*
Samuel Beardsley,[55] *Utica*
Rutger B. Miller,[56] *Utica*
Joel Turrill, *Oswego*
Daniel Wardwell, *Mannsville*
Sherman Page, *Unadilla*
William Seymour, *Binghamton*
William Mason, *Preston*
Stephen B. Leonard, *Owego*
Joseph Reynolds, *Virgil*
William K. Fuller, *Chittenango*
William Taylor, *Manlius*
Ulysses F. Doubleday, *Auburn*
Graham H. Chapin, *Lyons*
Francis Granger, *Canandaigua*
Joshua Lee, *Penn Yan*
Timothy Childs, *Rochester*
George W. Lay, *Batavia*
Philo C. Fuller,[57] *Geneseo*
John Young,[58] *Geneseo*
Abner Hazeltine, *Jamestown*
Thomas C. Love, *Buffalo*
Gideon Hard, *Albion*

## NORTH CAROLINA

SENATORS

Bedford Brown, *Browns Store*
Willie P. Mangum,[59] *Red Mountain*
Robert Strange,[60] *Fayetteville*

REPRESENTATIVES

William B. Shepard, *Elizabeth City*
Jesse A. Bynum, *Halifax*
Ebenezer Pettigrew, *Cool Spring*
Jesse Speight, *Stantonsburg*
James I. McKay, *Elizabethtown*
Micajah T. Hawkins, *Warrenton*
Edmund Deberry, *Lawrenceville*
William Montgomery, *Albrights*
Augustine H. Shepperd, *Germantown*
Abraham Rencher, *Pittsboro*
Henry W. Connor, *Sherrills Ford*
James Graham,[61] *Rutherfordton*
Lewis Williams, *Panther Creek*

## OHIO

SENATORS

Thomas Ewing, *Lancaster*
Thomas Morris, *Bethel*

REPRESENTATIVES

Bellamy Storer, *Cincinnati*
Taylor Webster, *Hamilton*
Joseph H. Crane, *Dayton*
Thomas Corwin, *Lebanon*
Thomas L. Hamer, *Georgetown*
Samuel F. Vinton, *Gallipolis*
William K. Bond, *Chillicothe*
Jeremiah McLene, *Columbus*
John Chaney, *Courtwright*
Samson Mason, *Springfield*
William Kennon, Sr., *St. Clairsville*
Elias Howell, *Newark*
David Spangler, *Coshocton*
William Patterson, *Mansfield*
Jonathan Sloane, *Ravenna*
Elisha Whittlesey, *Canfield*
John Thomson, *New Lisbon*
Benjamin Jones, *Wooster*
Daniel Kilgore, *Cadiz*

## PENNSYLVANIA

SENATORS

Samuel McKean, *Burlington*
James Buchanan, *Lancaster*

REPRESENTATIVES

Joel B. Sutherland, *Philadelphia*
Joseph R. Ingersoll, *Philadelphia*
James Harper, *Philadelphia*
Michael W. Ash, *Philadelphia*
Edward Darlington, *Chester*
William Hiester, *New Holland*
David Potts, Jr., *Pottstown*
Jacob Fry, Jr., *Trappe*
Mathias Morris, *Doylestown*
David D. Wagener, *Easton*
Edward B. Hubley, *Orwigsburg*
Henry A. P. Muhlenberg, *Reading*
William Clark, *Dauphin*
Henry Logan, *Dillsburg*
George Chambers, *Chambersburg*
Jesse Miller,[62] *Landisburg*
James Black,[63] *Newport*
Joseph Henderson, *Browns Mills*
Andrew Beaumont, *Wilkes-Barre*
Joseph B. Anthony, *Williamsport*
John Laporte, *Asylum*
Job Mann, *Bedford*
John Klingensmith, Jr., *Stewartsville*
Andrew Buchanan, *Waynesburg*

Thomas M. T. McKennan, *Washington*
Harmar Denny, *Pittsburgh*
Samuel S. Harrison, *Kittanning*
John Banks,[64] *Mercer*
John J. Pearson,[65] *Mercer*
John Galbraith, *Franklin*

## RHODE ISLAND

SENATORS

Nehemiah R. Knight, *Providence*
Asher Robbins, *Newport*

REPRESENTATIVES AT LARGE

Dutee J. Pearce, *Newport*
William Sprague, *Natick*

## SOUTH CAROLINA

SENATORS

John C. Calhoun, *Fort Hill*
William C. Preston, *Columbia*

REPRESENTATIVES

Robert B. Campbell, *Brownsville*
William J. Grayson, *Beaufort*
John K. Griffin, *Milton*
James H. Hammond,[66] *Silverton*
Franklin H. Elmore,[67] *Columbia*
Francis W. Pickens, *Edgefield*
Henry L. Pinckney, *Charleston*
Richard I. Manning,[68] *Fulton*
John P. Richardson,[69] *Fulton*
James Rogers, *Yorkville*
Waddy Thompson, Jr.,[70] *Greenville*

## TENNESSEE

SENATORS

Hugh Lawson White, *Knoxville*
Felix Grundy, *Nashville*

REPRESENTATIVES

William B. Carter, *Elizabethton*
Samuel Bunch, *Rutledge*
Luke Lea, *Campbells Station*
James Standifer, *Mountairy*
John B. Forester, *McMinnville*
Balie Peyton, *Gallatin*
John Bell, *Nashville*
Abram P. Maury, *Franklin*
James K. Polk, *Columbia*
Ebenezer J. Shields, *Pulaski*
Cave Johnson, *Clarksville*
Adam Huntsman, *Jackson*
William C. Dunlap, *Bolivar*

---

[55] Resigned March 29, 1836.
[56] Elected to fill vacancy caused by resignation of Samuel Beardsley, and took his seat December 5, 1836.
[57] Resigned September 2, 1836.
[58] Elected to fill vacancy caused by resignation of Philo C. Fuller, and took his seat December 6, 1836.
[59] Resigned November 26, 1836.
[60] Elected to fill vacancy caused by resignation of Willie P. Mangum, and took his seat December 15, 1836.
[61] Presented credentials as a Member-elect and

took his seat December 7, 1835; David Newlands contested the election, and on March 29, 1836, the seat was declared vacant; subsequently elected and took his seat December 5, 1836.
[62] Resigned October 30, 1836.
[63] Elected to fill vacancy caused by resignation of Jesse Miller, and took his seat December 5, 1836.
[64] Resigned in 1836.
[65] Elected to fill vacancy caused by resignation of John Banks, and took his seat December 5, 1836.
[66] Resigned February 26, 1836.

[67] Elected to fill vacancy caused by resignation of James H. Hammond, and took his seat December 19, 1836.
[68] Died May 1, 1836.
[69] Elected to fill vacancy caused by death of Richard I. Manning, and took his seat December 19, 1836.
[70] Elected to fill vacancy caused by death of Representative-elect Warren R. Davis in preceding Congress, and took his seat December 16, 1835.

## VERMONT

SENATORS

Samuel Prentiss, *Montpelier*
Benjamin Swift, *St. Albans*

REPRESENTATIVES

Hiland Hall, *Bennington*
William Slade, *Middlebury*
Horace Everett, *Windsor*
Heman Allen, *Burlington*
Henry F. Janes, *Waterbury*

## VIRGINIA

SENATORS

John Tyler,[71] *Gloucester*
William C. Rives,[72] *Lindseys Store*
Benjamin W. Leigh,[73] *Richmond*
Richard E. Parker,[74] *Snickersville*

REPRESENTATIVES

James M. H. Beale, *Mount Jackson*
James W. Bouldin, *Charlotte*
Nathaniel H. Claiborne, *Rocky Mount*
Walter Coles, *Robertsons Store*
Robert Craig, *Christiansburg*
George C. Dromgoole, *Gholsonville*
James Garland, *Lovingston*
George W. Hopkins, *Lebanon*
Joseph Johnson, *Bridgeport*
John W. Jones, *Petersburg*
George Loyall, *Norfolk*
Edward Lucas, *Charlestown*
William McComas, *Cabell*
John Y. Mason,[75] *Hicksford*
Charles F. Mercer, *Aldie*
William S. Morgan, *White Day*
John M. Patton, *Fredericksburg*
John Roane, *Rumford Academy*
John Robertson, *Richmond*
John Taliaferro, *Fredericksburg*
Henry A. Wise, *Accomac*

## ARKANSAS TERRITORY

DELEGATE

Ambrose H. Sevier,[76] *Lake Port*

## TERRITORY OF FLORIDA

DELEGATE

Joseph M. White, *Monticello*

## MICHIGAN TERRITORY[77]

DELEGATE

George W. Jones,[78] *Sinsinawa Mound*

## TERRITORY OF WISCONSIN [79]

DELEGATE

George W. Jones,[78] *Sinsinawa Mound*

---

[71] Resigned February 29, 1836.
[72] Elected to fill vacancy caused by resignation of John Tyler, and took his seat March 14, 1836.
[73] Resigned July 4, 1836.
[74] Elected to fill vacancy caused by resignation of Benjamin W. Leigh; took his seat December 15, 1836.

[75] Resigned January 11, 1837.
[76] Served as a Delegate until June 15, 1836, when Arkansas Territory was granted statehood; subsequently elected Senator.
[77] A portion of this Territory was granted statehood as the State of Michigan on January 26, 1837.

[78] Served as a Delegate from Michigan Territory until December 5, 1836, when he became the Delegate from the new Territory of Wisconsin.
[79] Formed from a portion of Michigan Territory and granted a Delegate in Congress by an Act of April 20, 1836.

# 25TH CONGRESS

## MARCH 4, 1837, TO MARCH 3, 1839

Richard M. Johnson
Vice President

James K. Polk
Speaker

FIRST SESSION— *September 4, 1837, to October 16, 1837*
SECOND SESSION— *December 4, 1837, to July 9, 1838*
THIRD SESSION— *December 3, 1838, to March 3, 1839*
SPECIAL SESSION OF THE SENATE— *March 4, 1837, to March 10, 1837*

———————

VICE PRESIDENT OF THE UNITED STATES— RICHARD M. JOHNSON,[1] of Kentucky
PRESIDENT PRO TEMPORE OF THE SENATE— WILLIAM R. KING,[2] of Alabama
SECRETARY OF THE SENATE— ASBURY DICKENS,[3] of North Carolina
SERGEANT AT ARMS OF THE SENATE— JOHN SHACKFORD, of New Hampshire; STEPHEN
HAIGHT,[4] of New York

———————

SPEAKER OF THE HOUSE OF REPRESENTATIVES— JAMES K. POLK,[5] of Tennessee
CLERK OF THE HOUSE— WALTER S. FRANKLIN,[6] of Pennsylvania; HUGH A. GARLAND,[7] of Virginia
SERGEANT AT ARMS OF THE HOUSE— RODERICK DORSEY, of Maryland
DOORKEEPER OF THE HOUSE— OVERTON CARR, of Maryland

## ALABAMA

### SENATORS

William R. King, *Selma*
John McKinley,[8] *Florence*
Clement C. Clay,[9] *Huntsville*

### REPRESENTATIVES

Reuben Chapman, *Somerville*
Joshua L. Martin, *Athens*
Joab Lawler,[10] *Mardisville*
George W. Crabb,[11] *Tuscaloosa*
Dixon H. Lewis, *Lowndesboro*
Francis S. Lyon, *Demopolis*

## ARKANSAS

### SENATORS

William S. Fulton, *Little Rock*
Ambrose H. Sevier, *Lake Port*

### REPRESENTATIVE AT LARGE

Archibald Yell, *Fayetteville*

## CONNECTICUT

### SENATORS

John M. Niles, *Hartford*
Perry Smith, *New Milford*

### REPRESENTATIVES

Isaac Toucey, *Hartford*
Samuel Ingham, *Saybrook*
Thomas T. Whittlesey, *Danbury*
Elisha Haley, *Mystic*
Lancelot Phelps, *Hitchcockville*
Orrin Holt, *Willington*

## DELAWARE

### SENATORS

Richard H. Bayard, *Wilmington*
Thomas Clayton, *New Castle*

### REPRESENTATIVE AT LARGE

John J. Milligan, *Wilmington*

## GEORGIA

### SENATORS

Alfred Cuthbert, *Monticello*
John P. King,[12] *Augusta*
Wilson Lumpkin,[13] *Athens*

### REPRESENTATIVES AT LARGE

Jesse F. Cleveland, *Decatur*
William C. Dawson, *Greensboro*
Thomas Glascock, *Augusta*
Seaton Grantland, *Milledgeville*
Charles E. Haynes, *Sparta*
Hopkins Holsey, *Hamilton*
Jabez Jackson, *Clarkesville*
George W. Owens, *Savannah*
George W. B. Towns, *Talbotton*

## ILLINOIS

### SENATORS

John M. Robinson, *Carmi*
Richard M. Young, *Quincy*

### REPRESENTATIVES

Adam W. Snyder, *Belleville*
Zadoc Casey, *Mount Vernon*
William L. May, *Springfield*

## INDIANA

### SENATORS

John Tipton, *Logansport*
Oliver H. Smith, *Connersville*

### REPRESENTATIVES

Ratliff Boon, *Boonville*
John Ewing, *Vincennes*
William Graham, *Vallonia*
George H. Dunn, *Lawrenceburg*
James Rariden, *Centerville*
William Herod, *Columbus*
Albert S. White, *Lafayette*

## KENTUCKY

### SENATORS

Henry Clay, *Lexington*
John J. Crittenden, *Frankfort*

### REPRESENTATIVES

John L. Murray, *Wadesboro*
Edward Rumsey, *Greenville*
Joseph R. Underwood, *Bowling Green*
Sherrod Williams, *Monticello*
James Harlan, *Harrodsburg*
John Calhoon, *Hardinsburg*
John Pope, *Springfield*
William J. Graves, *New Castle*
John White, *Richmond*
Richard Hawes, *Winchester*
Richard H. Menifee, *Mount Sterling*
John Chambers, *Washington*
William W. Southgate, *Covington*

---

[1] Elected by the Senate February 8, 1837.
[2] Elected March 7, 1837 (special session of the Senate); October 13, 1837; July 2, 1838; February 25, 1839.
[3] Reelected September 11, 1837.
[4] Elected September 4, 1837.
[5] Reelected September 4, 1837.

[6] Reelected September 4, 1837; died September 20, 1838.
[7] Elected December 3, 1838; Samuel Burch, the chief clerk, acted as clerk in the interim.
[8] Resigned April 22, 1837, never having qualified.
[9] Elected to fill vacancy caused by resignation of John McKinley, and took his seat September 4, 1837.

[10] Died May 8, 1838.
[11] Elected to fill vacancy caused by death of Joab Lawler, and took his seat December 3, 1838.
[12] Resigned November 1, 1837.
[13] Elected to fill vacancy caused by resignation of John P. King, and took his seat December 13, 1837.

## LOUISIANA

SENATORS

Robert C. Nicholas, *Donaldsonville*
Alexander Mouton, *Vermilionville*

REPRESENTATIVES

Henry Johnson, *Donaldsonville*
Eleazer W. Ripley,[14] *Jackson*
Rice Garland, *Opelousas*

## MAINE

SENATORS

John Ruggles, *Thomaston*
Reuel Williams,[15] *Augusta*

REPRESENTATIVES

Hugh J. Anderson, *Belfast*
Timothy J. Carter,[16] *Paris*
Virgil D. Parris,[17] *Buckfield*
Jonathan Cilley,[18] *Thomaston*
Edward Robinson,[19] *Thomaston*
John Fairfield,[20] *Saco*
Joseph C. Noyes, *Eastport*
Francis O. J. Smith, *Portland*
Thomas Davee, *Blanchard*
George Evans, *Gardiner*

## MARYLAND

SENATORS

Joseph Kent,[21] *Bladensburg*
William D. Merrick,[22] *Allens Fresh*
John S. Spence, *Berlin*

REPRESENTATIVES

John Dennis, *Princess Anne*
James A. Pearce, *Chestertown*
John T. H. Worthington, *Golden*
Benjamin C. Howard, *Baltimore*
Isaac McKim,[23] *Baltimore*
John P. Kennedy,[24] *Baltimore*
William Cost Johnson, *Jefferson*
Francis Thomas, *Frederick*
Daniel Jenifer, *Harris Lot*

## MASSACHUSETTS

SENATORS

Daniel Webster, *Boston*
John Davis, *Worcester*

REPRESENTATIVES

Richard Fletcher, *Boston*
Stephen C. Phillips,[25] *Salem*
Leverett Saltonstall,[26] *Salem*
Caleb Cushing, *Newburyport*

William Parmenter, *East Cambridge*
Levi Lincoln, *Worcester*
George Grennell, Jr., *Greenfield*
George N. Briggs, *Lanesboro*
William B. Calhoun, *Springfield*
William S. Hastings, *Mendon*
Nathaniel B. Borden, *Fall River*
John Reed, *Yarmouth*
John Quincy Adams, *Quincy*

## MICHIGAN

SENATORS

Lucius Lyon, *Bronson*
John Norvell, *Detroit*

REPRESENTATIVE AT LARGE

Isaac E. Crary, *Marshall*

## MISSISSIPPI

SENATORS

John Black,[27] *Monroe*
James F. Trotter,[28] *Holly Springs*
Thomas H. Williams,[29] *Pontotoc*
Robert J. Walker, *Madisonville*

REPRESENTATIVES AT LARGE

John F. H. Claiborne,[30] *Madisonville*
Samuel J. Gholson,[30] *Athens*
Sergeant S. Prentiss,[30] *Vicksburg*
Thomas J. Word,[30] *Pontotoc*

## MISSOURI

SENATORS

Thomas Hart Benton, *St. Louis*
Lewis F. Linn, *Ste. Genevieve*

REPRESENTATIVES AT LARGE

Albert G. Harrison, *Fulton*
John Miller, *Boonville*

## NEW HAMPSHIRE

SENATORS

Henry Hubbard, *Charlestown*
Franklin Pierce, *Hillsboro*

REPRESENTATIVES AT LARGE

Charles G. Atherton, *Nashua*
Samuel Cushman, *Portsmouth*
James Farrington, *Rochester*
Joseph Weeks, *Richmond*
Jared W. Williams, *Lancaster*

## NEW JERSEY

SENATORS

Samuel L. Southard, *Trenton*
Garret D. Wall, *Burlington*

REPRESENTATIVES AT LARGE

John B. Aycrigg, *Hackensack*
William Halstead, *Trenton*
John P. B. Maxwell, *Belvidere*
Joseph F. Randolph, *Freehold*
Charles C. Stratton, *Swedesboro*
Thomas Jones Yorke, *Salem*

## NEW YORK

SENATORS

Silas Wright, Jr., *Canton*
Nathaniel P. Tallmadge, *Poughkeepsie*

REPRESENTATIVES

Thomas B. Jackson, *Newtown*
Abraham Vanderveer, *Brooklyn*
J. Ogden Hoffman, *New York City*
Edward Curtis, *New York City*
Churchill C. Cambreleng, *New York City*
Ely Moore, *New York City*
Gouverneur Kemble, *Cold Spring*
Obadiah Titus, *Washington*
Nathaniel Jones, *Warwick*
John C. Brodhead, *Modena*
Zadock Pratt, *Prattsville*
Robert McClellan, *Middleburg*
Henry Vail, *Troy*
Albert Gallup, *East Berne*
John I. De Graff, *Schenectady*
David A. Russell, *Salem*
John Palmer, *Plattsburg*
James B. Spencer, *Fort Covington*
John Edwards, *Ephrath*
Arphaxed Loomis, *Little Falls*
Henry A. Foster, *Rome*
Abraham P. Grant, *Oswego*
Isaac H. Bronson, *Watertown*
John H. Prentiss, *Cooperstown*
Amasa J. Parker, *Delhi*
John C. Clark, *Bainbridge*
Andrew D. W. Bruyn,[31] *Ithaca*

---

[14] Never qualified owing to prolonged illness.
[15] Elected to fill vacancy caused by resignation of Ether Shepley, in preceding Congress, and took his seat March 4, 1837.
[16] Died March 14, 1838.
[17] Elected to fill vacancy caused by death of Timothy J. Carter, and took his seat May 29, 1838.
[18] Killed in a duel with Rep. William J. Graves of Kentucky, February 24, 1838.
[19] Elected to fill vacancy caused by death of Jonathan Cilley, and took his seat April 28, 1838.
[20] Resigned December 24, 1838, having been elected governor.
[21] Died November 24, 1837.
[22] Elected to fill vacancy caused by death of Joseph Kent, and took his seat January 5, 1838.

[23] Died April 1, 1838.
[24] Elected to fill vacancy caused by death of Isaac McKim, and took his seat April 30, 1838.
[25] Resigned September 28, 1838.
[26] Elected to fill vacancy caused by resignation of Stephen C. Phillips, and took his seat December 5, 1838.
[27] Resigned January 22, 1838.
[28] Elected to fill vacancy caused by resignation of John Black, and took his seat February 19, 1838; resigned July 10, 1838.
[29] Appointed to fill vacancy caused by resignation of James F. Trotter, and took his seat December 13, 1838; subsequently elected.
[30] Mississippi elected its Representatives in November of odd numbered years (after the beginning

of the congressional term); as Congress had been called to meet in September, Governor Charles Lynch issued writs for a special election to fill vacancies until the regular election; John F. H. Claiborne and Samuel J. Gholson presented credentials and were seated September 4, 1837, when, at their request the question of the validity of their election was referred to the Committee on Elections; on October 3, 1837, the House decided they had been elected for the full term; Sergeant S. Prentiss and Thomas J. Word presented credentials on December 27, 1837, and on February 5, 1838, the House rescinded its former decision and declared the seats vacant; Prentiss and Word were subsequently elected, and took their seats May 30, 1838.
[31] Died July 27, 1838.

Cyrus Beers,[32] *Ithaca*
Hiram Gray, *Elmira*
William Taylor, *Manlius*
Bennet Bicknell, *Morrisville*
William H. Noble, *Cato*
Samuel Birdsall, *Waterloo*
Mark H. Sibley, *Canandaigua*
John T. Andrews, *North Reading*
Timothy Childs, *Rochester*
William Patterson,[33] *Warsaw*
Harvey Putnam,[34] *Attica*
Luther C. Peck, *Pike*
Richard P. Marvin, *Jamestown*
Millard Fillmore, *Buffalo*
Charles F. Mitchell, *Lockport*

## NORTH CAROLINA

### SENATORS

Bedford Brown, *Browns Store*
Robert Strange, *Fayetteville*

### REPRESENTATIVES

Samuel T. Sawyer, *Edenton*
Jesse A. Bynum, *Halifax*
Edward Stanly, *Washington*
Charles B. Shepard, *New Bern*
James I. McKay, *Elizabethtown*
Micajah T. Hawkins, *Warrenton*
Edmund Deberry, *Lawrenceville*
William Montgomery, *Albrights*
Augustine H. Shepperd, *Bethania*
Abraham Rencher, *Pittsboro*
Henry W. Connor, *Sherrills Ford*
James Graham, *Rutherfordton*
Lewis Williams, *Panther Creek*

## OHIO

### SENATORS

Thomas Morris, *Bethel*
William Allen, *Chillicothe*

### REPRESENTATIVES

Alexander Duncan, *Cincinnati*
Taylor Webster, *Hamilton*
Patrick G. Goode, *Sidney*
Thomas Corwin, *Lebanon*
Thomas L. Hamer, *Georgetown*
Calvary Morris, *Athens*
William K. Bond, *Chillicothe*
Joseph Ridgway, *Columbus*
John Chaney, *Courtwright*
Samson Mason, *Springfield*
James Alexander, Jr., *St. Clairsville*
Alexander Harper, *Zanesville*
Daniel P. Leadbetter, *Millersburg*
William H. Hunter, *Sandusky*
John W. Allen, *Cleveland*

Elisha Whittlesey,[35] *Canfield*
Joshua R. Giddings,[36] *Jefferson*
Andrew W. Loomis,[37] *New Lisbon*
Charles D. Coffin,[38] *New Lisbon*
Matthias Shepler, *Bethlehem*
Daniel Kilgore,[39] *Cadiz*
Henry Swearingen,[40] *Smithfield*

## PENNSYLVANIA

### SENATORS

Samuel McKean, *Burlington*
James Buchanan, *Lancaster*

### REPRESENTATIVES

Lemuel Paynter, *Philadelphia*
John Sergeant, *Philadelphia*
George W. Toland, *Philadelphia*
Francis J. Harper,[41] *Frankford*
Charles Naylor,[42] *Philadelphia*
Edward Davies, *Churchtown*
David Potts, Jr., *Pottstown*
Edward Darlington, *Chester*
Jacob Fry, Jr., *Trappe*
Mathias Morris, *Doylestown*
David D. Wagener, *Easton*
Edward B. Hubley, *Orwigsburg*
Henry A. P. Muhlenberg,[43] *Reading*
George M. Keim,[44] *Reading*
Luther Reily, *Harrisburg*
Henry Logan, *Dillsburg*
Daniel Sheffer, *York*
Charles McClure, *Carlisle*
William W. Potter, *Bellefonte*
David Petrikin, *Danville*
Robert H. Hammond, *Milton*
Samuel W. Morris, *Wellsboro*
Charles Ogle, *Somerset*
John Klingensmith, Jr., *Stewartsville*
Andrew Buchanan, *Waynesburg*
Thomas M. T. McKennan,
    *Washington*
Richard Biddle, *Pittsburgh*
William Beatty, *Butler*
Thomas Henry, *Beaver*
Arnold Plumer, *Franklin*

## RHODE ISLAND

### SENATORS

Nehemiah R. Knight, *Providence*
Asher Robbins, *Newport*

### REPRESENTATIVES AT LARGE

Robert B. Cranston, *Newport*
Joseph L. Tillinghast, *Providence*

## SOUTH CAROLINA

### SENATORS

John C. Calhoun, *Fort Hill*
William C. Preston, *Columbia*

### REPRESENTATIVES

John Campbell, *Parnassus*
William K. Clowney, *Union*
Franklin H. Elmore, *Columbia*
John K. Griffin, *Milton*
Hugh S. Legare, *Charleston*
Francis W. Pickens, *Edgefield*
R. Barnwell Rhett, *Beaufort*
John P. Richardson, *Fulton*
Waddy Thompson, Jr., *Greenville*

## TENNESSEE

### SENATORS

Hugh Lawson White, *Knoxville*
Felix Grundy,[45] *Nashville*
Ephraim H. Foster,[46] *Nashville*

### REPRESENTATIVES

William B. Carter, *Elizabethton*
Abraham McClellan, *Blountville*
Joseph L. Williams, *Knoxville*
James Standifer,[47] *Mountairy*
William Stone,[48] *Delphi*
Hopkins L. Turney, *Winchester*
William B. Campbell, *Carthage*
John Bell, *Nashville*
Abram P. Maury, *Franklin*
James K. Polk, *Columbia*
Ebenezer J. Shields, *Pulaski*
Richard Cheatham, *Springfield*
John W. Crockett, *Paris*
Christopher H. Williams, *Lexington*

## VERMONT

### SENATORS

Samuel Prentiss, *Montpelier*
Benjamin Swift, *St. Albans*

### REPRESENTATIVES

Hiland Hall, *Bennington*
William Slade, *Middlebury*
Horace Everett, *Windsor*
Heman Allen, *Burlington*
Isaac Fletcher, *Lyndon*

---

[32] Elected to fill vacancy caused by death of Andrew D. W. Bruyn, and took his seat December 3, 1838.
[33] Died August 14, 1838.
[34] Elected to fill vacancy caused by death of William Patterson, and took his seat December 3, 1828.
[35] Resigned July 9, 1838.
[36] Elected to fill vacancy caused by resignation of Elisha Whittlesey, and took his seat December 3, 1838.
[37] Resigned October 20, 1837.
[38] Elected to fill vacancy caused by resignation of

Andrew W. Loomis, and took his seat December 20, 1837.
[39] Resigned July 4, 1838.
[40] Elected to fill vacancy caused by resignation of Daniel Kilgore, and took his seat December 3, 1838.
[41] Died March 18, 1837, before Congress assembled.
[42] Elected to fill vacancy caused by death of Francis J. Harper, and took his seat September 4, 1837.
[43] Resigned February 9, 1838.
[44] Elected to fill vacancy caused by resignation of

Henry A. P. Muhlenberg, and took his seat March 17, 1838.
[45] Resigned July 4, 1838.
[46] Appointed to fill vacancy caused by resignation of Felix Grundy, and took his seat December 3, 1838; subsequently elected for full term commencing March 4, 1839, but resigned March 3, 1839.
[47] Died August 20, 1837, before Congress assembled.
[48] Elected to fill vacancy caused by death of James Standifer, and took his seat October 6, 1837.

## VIRGINIA

### SENATORS
William C. Rives, *Lindseys Store*
Richard E. Parker,[49] *Snickersville*
William H. Roane,[50] *Richmond*

### REPRESENTATIVES
Andrew Beirne, *Union*
James W. Bouldin, *Charlotte*
Walter Coles, *Robertsons Store*
Robert Craig, *Christiansburg*
George C. Dromgoole, *Gholsonville*
James Garland, *Lovingston*
George W. Hopkins, *Lebanon*
Robert M. T. Hunter, *Lloyds*

Joseph Johnson, *Bridgeport*
John W. Jones, *Petersburg*
Francis Mallory, *Hampton*
James M. Mason, *Winchester*
Charles F. Mercer, *Aldie*
William S. Morgan, *White Day*
John M. Patton,[51] *Fredericksburg*
Linn Banks,[52] *Madison*
Isaac S. Pennybacker, *Harrisonburg*
Francis E. Rives, *Littleton*
John Robertson, *Richmond*
Archibald Stuart, *Mount Airy*
John Talliaferro, *Fredericksburg*
Henry A. Wise, *Accomac*

## TERRITORY OF FLORIDA

### DELEGATE
Charles Downing, *St. Augustine*

## TERRITORY OF IOWA[53]

### DELEGATE
William W. Chapman,[54] *Burlington*

## TERRITORY OF WISCONSIN

### DELEGATE
George W. Jones,[55] *Sinsinawa Mound*
James D. Doty,[56] *Astor*

---

[49] Resigned March 13, 1837.
[50] Elected to fill vacancy caused by resignation of Richard E. Parker, and took his seat September 4, 1837.
[51] Resigned in 1838.

[52] Elected to fill vacancy caused by resignation of John M. Patton, and took his seat May 19, 1838.
[53] Formed from a portion of the Territory of Wisconsin and granted a Delegate in Congress by an Act of June 12, 1838.

[54] Took his seat December 3, 1838.
[55] Served until January 14, 1839; succeeded by James D. Doty, who contested his election.
[56] Successfully contested the election of George W. Jones, and took his seat January 14, 1839.

# 26TH CONGRESS

MARCH 4, 1839, TO MARCH 3, 1841

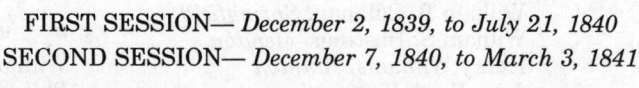

FIRST SESSION— *December 2, 1839, to July 21, 1840*
SECOND SESSION— *December 7, 1840, to March 3, 1841*

---

VICE PRESIDENT OF THE UNITED STATES— RICHARD M. JOHNSON, of Kentucky
PRESIDENT PRO TEMPORE OF THE SENATE— WILLIAM R. KING,[1] of Alabama
SECRETARY OF THE SENATE— ASBURY DICKENS,[2] of North Carolina
SERGEANT AT ARMS OF THE SENATE— STEPHEN HAIGHT, of New York

---

SPEAKER OF THE HOUSE OF REPRESENTATIVES— ROBERT M. T. HUNTER,[3] of Virginia
CLERK OF THE HOUSE— HUGH A. GARLAND,[4] of Virginia
SERGEANT AT ARMS OF THE HOUSE— RODERICK DORSEY, of Maryland
DOORKEEPER OF THE HOUSE— JOSEPH FOLLANSBEE, of Massachusetts

Richard M. Johnson
Vice President

Robert M. T. Hunter
Speaker

## ALABAMA

### SENATORS
William R. King, *Selma*
Clement C. Clay, *Huntsville*

### REPRESENTATIVES
Reuben Chapman, *Somerville*
David Hubbard, *Courtland*
George W. Crabb, *Tuscaloosa*
Dixon H. Lewis, *Lowndesboro*
James Dellet, *Claiborne*

## ARKANSAS

### SENATORS
William S. Fulton, *Little Rock*
Ambrose H. Sevier, *Lake Port*

### REPRESENTATIVE AT LARGE
Edward Cross, *Washington*

## CONNECTICUT

### SENATORS
Perry Smith, *New Milford*
Thaddeus Betts,[5] *Norwalk*
Jabez W. Huntington,[6] *Norwich*

### REPRESENTATIVES
Joseph Trumbull, *Hartford*
William L. Storrs,[7] *Middletown*
William W. Boardman,[8] *New Haven*
Thomas W. Williams, *New London*
Thomas B. Osborne, *Fairfield*
Truman Smith, *Litchfield*
John H. Brockway, *Ellington*

## DELAWARE

### SENATORS
Richard H. Bayard,[9] *Wilmington*
Thomas Clayton, *New Castle*

### REPRESENTATIVE AT LARGE
Thomas Robinson, Jr., *Georgetown*

## GEORGIA

### SENATORS
Alfred Cuthbert, *Monticello*
Wilson Lumpkin, *Athens*

### REPRESENTATIVES AT LARGE
Julius C. Alford, *Lagrange*
Edward J. Black, *Jacksonboro*
Walter T. Colquitt,[10] *Columbus*
Hines Holt,[11] *Columbus*
Mark A. Cooper, *Columbus*
William C. Dawson, *Greensboro*
Richard W. Habersham, *Clarkesville*
Thomas Butler King, *Waynesville*
Eugenius A. Nisbet, *Macon*
Lott Warren, *Palmyra*

## ILLINOIS

### SENATORS
John M. Robinson, *Carmi*
Richard M. Young, *Quincy*

### REPRESENTATIVES
John Reynolds, *Cadiz*
Zadoc Casey, *Mount Vernon*
John T. Stuart, *Springfield*

## INDIANA

### SENATORS
Oliver H. Smith, *Indianapolis*
Albert S. White, *Lafayette*

### REPRESENTATIVES
George H. Proffit, *Petersburg*
John W. Davis, *Carlisle*
John Carr, *Charlestown*
Thomas Smith, *Versailles*
James Rariden, *Centerville*
William W. Wick, *Indianapolis*
Tilghman A. Howard,[12] *Rockville*
Henry S. Lane,[13] *Crawfordsville*

## KENTUCKY

### SENATORS
Henry Clay, *Lexington*
John J. Crittenden, *Frankfort*

### REPRESENTATIVES
Linn Boyd, *Cadiz*
Philip Triplett, *Owensboro*
Joseph R. Underwood, *Bowling Green*
Sherrod Williams, *Monticello*
Simeon H. Anderson,[14] *Lancaster*
John B. Thompson,[15] *Harrodsburg*
Willis Green, *Green*
John Pope, *Springfield*
William J. Graves, *New Castle*
John White, *Richmond*
Richard Hawes, *Winchester*
Landaff W. Andrews, *Flemingsburg*
Garrett Davis, *Paris*
William O. Butler, *Carrollton*

---

[1] Continuing from preceding session; reelected July 3, 1840; March 3, 1841.
[2] Reelected December 9, 1839.
[3] Elected December 16, 1839.
[4] Reelected December 21, 1839.
[5] Died April 7, 1840.
[6] Elected to fill vacancy caused by death of Thaddeus Betts, and took his seat June 2, 1840.
[7] Resigned in June, 1840, to become associate judge of the court of errors.

[8] Elected to fill vacancy caused by resignation of William L. Storrs, and took his seat December 7, 1840.
[9] Resigned September 19, 1839, to become chief justice of Delaware; reelected to fill vacancy caused by his own resignation, and took his seat January 19, 1841; vacancy in this class from September 19, 1839, to January 11, 1841.
[10] Resigned July 21, 1840.
[11] Elected to fill vacancy caused by resignation

of Walter T. Colquitt, and took his seat February 1, 1841.
[12] Resigned August 1, 1840.
[13] Elected to fill vacancy caused by resignation of Tilghman A. Howard, and took his seat December 7, 1840.
[14] Died August 11, 1840.
[15] Elected to fill vacancy caused by death of Simeon H. Anderson, and took his seat December 7, 1840.

[119]

## LOUISIANA

SENATORS

Robert C. Nicholas, *Donaldsonville*
Alexander Mouton, *Vermilionville*

REPRESENTATIVES

Edward D. White, *Thibodaux*
Thomas W. Chinn, *Baton Rouge*
Rice Garland,[16] *Opelousas*
John Moore,[17] *Franklin*

## MAINE

SENATORS

John Ruggles, *Thomaston*
Reuel Williams, *Augusta*

REPRESENTATIVES

Hugh J. Anderson, *Belfast*
Nathan Clifford, *Newfield*
Thomas Davee, *Blanchard*
George Evans,[18] *Gardiner*
Joshua A. Lowell, *East Machias*
Virgil D. Parris, *Buckfield*
Benjamin Randall, *Bath*
Albert Smith, *Portland*

## MARYLAND

SENATORS

John S. Spence,[19] *Berlin*
John L. Kerr,[20] *Easton*
William D. Merrick, *Allens Fresh*

REPRESENTATIVES

John Dennis, *Princess Anne*
Philip F. Thomas, *Easton*
John T. H. Worthington, *Shawan*
Solomon Hillen, Jr., *Baltimore*
James Carroll, *Baltimore*
William Cost Johnson, *Jefferson*
Francis Thomas, *Frederick*
Daniel Jenifer, *Milton Hill*

## MASSACHUSETTS

SENATORS

Daniel Webster,[21] *Boston*
Rufus Choate,[22] *Boston*
John Davis,[23] *Worcester*
Isaac C. Bates,[24] *Northampton*

REPRESENTATIVES

Abbott Lawrence,[25] *Boston*
Robert C. Winthrop,[26] *Boston*
Leverett Saltonstall, *Salem*
Caleb Cushing, *Newburyport*

William Parmenter, *East Cambridge*
Levi Lincoln, *Worcester*
James C. Alvord,[27] *Greenfield*
Osmyn Baker,[28] *Amherst*
George N. Briggs, *Lanesboro*
William B. Calhoun, *Springfield*
William S. Hastings, *Mendon*
Henry Williams, *Taunton*
John Reed, *Yarmouth*
John Quincy Adams, *Quincy*

## MICHIGAN

SENATORS

John Norvell, *Detroit*
Augustus S. Porter,[29] *Detroit*

REPRESENTATIVE AT LARGE

Isaac E. Crary, *Marshall*

## MISSISSIPPI

SENATORS

Robert J. Walker, *Madisonville*
John Henderson, *Pass Christian*

REPRESENTATIVES AT LARGE

Albert G. Brown, *Gallatin*
Jacob Thompson, *Pontotoc*

## MISSOURI

SENATORS

Thomas Hart Benton, *St. Louis*
Lewis F. Linn, *Ste. Genevieve*

REPRESENTATIVES AT LARGE

Albert G. Harrison,[30] *Fulton*
John Jameson,[31] *Fulton*
John Miller, *Conners Mills*

## NEW HAMPSHIRE

SENATORS

Henry Hubbard, *Charlestown*
Franklin Pierce, *Concord*

REPRESENTATIVES AT LARGE

Charles G. Atherton, *Nashua*
Edmund Burke, *Newport*
Ira A. Eastman, *Gilmanton*
Tristram Shaw, *Exeter*
Jared W. Williams, *Lancaster*

## NEW JERSEY

SENATORS

Samuel L. Southard, *Trenton*
Garret D. Wall, *Burlington*

REPRESENTATIVES AT LARGE[32]

William R. Cooper, *Swedesboro*
Philemon Dickerson, *Paterson*
Joseph Kille, *Salem*
Joseph F. Randolph, *New Brunswick*
Daniel B. Ryall, *Freehold*
Peter D. Vroom, *Somerville*

## NEW YORK

SENATORS

Silas Wright, Jr., *Canton*
Nathaniel P. Tallmadge, *Poughkeepsie*

REPRESENTATIVES

Thomas B. Jackson, *Newtown*
James De la Montanya, *Haverstraw*
Ogden Hoffman, *New York City*
Edward Curtis, *New York City*
Moses H. Grinnell, *New York City*
James Monroe, *New York City*
Gouverneur Kemble, *Cold Spring*
Charles Johnston, *Poughkeepsie*
Nathaniel Jones, *Warwick*
Rufus Palen, *Fallsburg*
Aaron Vanderpoel, *Kinderhook*
John Ely, *Coxsackie*
Hiram P. Hunt, *Troy*
Daniel D. Barnard, *Albany*
Anson Brown,[33] *Ballston*
Nicholas B. Doe,[34] *Waterford*
David A. Russell, *Salem*
Augustus C. Hand, *Elizabethtown*
John Fine, *Ogdensburg*
Peter J. Wagner, *Fort Plain*
Andrew W. Doig, *Lowville*
John G. Floyd, *Utica*
David P. Brewster, *Oswego*
Thomas C. Chittenden, *Adams*
John H. Prentiss, *Cooperstown*
Judson Allen, *Harpersville*
John C. Clark, *Bainbridge*
Stephen B. Leonard, *Owego*
Amasa Dana, *Ithaca*
Edward Rogers, *Madison*
Nehemiah H. Earll, *Syracuse*
Christopher Morgan, *Aurora*
Theron R. Strong, *Palmyra*

---

[16] Resigned July 21, 1840.
[17] Elected to fill vacancy caused by resignation of Rice Garland, and took his seat December 17, 1840.
[18] Reelected to the Twenty-seventh Congress but resigned, having been elected Senator.
[19] Died October 24, 1840.
[20] Elected to fill vacancy caused by death of John S. Spence, and took his seat January 13, 1841.
[21] Resigned, effective February 22, 1841.
[22] Elected to fill vacancy caused by resignation of Daniel Webster, and took his seat March 1, 1841.
[23] Resigned January 5, 1841.
[24] Elected to fill vacancy caused by resignation of

John Davis, and took his seat January 21, 1841.
[25] Resigned September 18, 1840.
[26] Elected to fill vacancy caused by resignation of Abbott Lawrence, and took his seat December 7, 1840.
[27] Died September 27, 1839, before Congress assembled.
[28] Elected to fill vacancy caused by death of James C. Alvord, and took his seat January 14, 1840.
[29] Elected to fill vacancy in term commencing March 4, 1839, caused by failure of legislature to elect, and took his seat February 7, 1840; vacancy in this class from March 4, 1839, to January 19, 1840.
[30] Died September 7, 1839.

[31] Elected to fill vacancy caused by death of Albert G. Harrison, and took his seat December 12, 1839.
[32] Messrs. Aycrigg, Maxwell, Halsted, Stratton, and Yorke contested the election of Messrs. Vroom, Dickerson, Kille, Cooper, and Ryall; the House at first declined to seat either set of candidates, but by resolution of March 10, 1840, the five last named were admitted "without prejudice to the final rights of the claimants," and, on July 17, 1840, were adjudged entitled to their seats.
[33] Died June 14, 1840.
[34] Elected to fill vacancy caused by death of Anson Brown, and took his seat December 7, 1840.

Francis Granger, *Canandaigua*
Meredith Mallory, *Hammondsport*
Thomas Kempshall, *Rochester*
Seth M. Gates, *Leroy*
Luther C. Peck, *Pike*
Richard P. Marvin, *Jamestown*
Millard Fillmore, *Buffalo*
Charles F. Mitchell, *Lockport*

## NORTH CAROLINA

SENATORS

Bedford Brown,[35] *Browns Store*
Willie P. Mangum,[36] *Red Mountain*
Robert Strange,[37] *Fayetteville*
William A. Graham,[38] *Hillsboro*

REPRESENTATIVES

Kenneth Rayner, *Winton*
Jesse A. Bynum, *Halifax*
Edward Stanly, *Washington*
Charles B. Shepard, *New Bern*
James I. McKay, *Elizabethtown*
Micajah T. Hawkins, *Warrenton*
Edmund Deberry, *Lawrenceville*
William Montgomery, *Albrights*
John Hill, *Germantown*
Charles Fisher, *Salisbury*
Henry W. Connor, *Sherrills Ford*
James Graham, *Rutherfordton*
Lewis Williams, *Panther Creek*

## OHIO

SENATORS

William Allen, *Chillicothe*
Benjamin Tappan, *Steubenville*

REPRESENTATIVES

Alexander Duncan, *Cincinnati*
John B. Weller, *Hamilton*
Patrick G. Goode, *Sidney*
Thomas Corwin,[39] *Lebanon*
Jeremiah Morrow,[40] *Twentymile Stand*
William Doan, *Withamsville*
Calvary Morris, *Athens*
William K. Bond, *Chillicothe*
Joseph Ridgway, *Columbus*
William Medill, *Lancaster*
Samson Mason, *Springfield*
Isaac Parrish, *Cambridge*
Jonathan Taylor, *Newark*
Daniel P. Leadbetter, *Millersburg*
George Sweeny, *Bucyrus*
John W. Allen, *Cleveland*

Joshua R. Giddings, *Jefferson*
John Hastings, *Salem*
David A. Starkweather, *Canton*
Henry Swearingen, *Smithfield*

## PENNSYLVANIA

SENATORS

James Buchanan, *Lancaster*
Daniel Sturgeon,[41] *Uniontown*

REPRESENTATIVES

Lemuel Paynter, *Philadelphia*
John Sergeant, *Philadelphia*
George W. Toland, *Philadelphia*
Charles Naylor,[42] *Philadelphia*
Edward Davies, *Churchtown*
John Edwards, *Ivy Mills*
Francis James, *West Chester*
Joseph Fornance, *Norristown*
John Davis, *Davisville*
David D. Wagener, *Easton*
Peter Newhard, *Allentown*
George M. Keim, *Reading*
William Simonton, *Hummelstown*
James Gerry, *Shrewsbury*
James Cooper, *Gettysburg*
William S. Ramsey,[43] *Carlisle*
Charles McClure,[44] *Carlisle*
William W. Potter,[45] *Philadelphia*
George McCulloch,[46] *Center Line*
David Petrikin, *Danville*
Robert H. Hammond, *Milton*
Samuel W. Morris, *Wellsboro*
Charles Ogle, *Somerset*
Albert G. Marchand, *Greensburg*
Enos Hook, *Waynesburg*
Isaac Leet, *Washington*
Richard Biddle,[47] *Pittsburgh*
Henry M. Brackenridge,[48] *Tarentum*
William Beatty, *Butler*
Thomas Henry, *Beaver*
John Galbraith, *Erie*

## RHODE ISLAND

SENATORS

Nehemiah R. Knight, *Providence*
Nathan F. Dixon, *Westerly*

REPRESENTATIVES AT LARGE

Robert B. Cranston, *Newport*
Joseph L. Tillinghast, *Providence*

## SOUTH CAROLINA

SENATORS

John C. Calhoun, *Fort Hill*
William C. Preston, *Columbia*

REPRESENTATIVES

Sampson H. Butler, *Barnwell*
John Campbell, *Parnassus*
John K. Griffin, *Newberry*
Isaac E. Holmes, *Charleston*
Francis W. Pickens, *Edgefield*
R. Barnwell Rhett, *Blue House*
James Rogers, *Maybinton*
Thomas D. Sumter, *Stateburg*
Waddy Thompson, Jr., *Greenville*

## TENNESSEE

SENATORS

Hugh Lawson White,[49] *Knoxville*
Alexander Anderson,[50] *Knoxville*
Felix Grundy,[51] *Nashville*
Alfred O. P. Nicholson,[52] *Columbia*

REPRESENTATIVES

William B. Carter, *Elizabethton*
Abraham McClellan, *Blountville*
Joseph L. Williams, *Knoxville*
Julius W. Blackwell, *Athens*
Hopkins L. Turney, *Winchester*
William B. Campbell, *Carthage*
John Bell, *Nashville*
Meredith P. Gentry, *Harpeth*
Harvey M. Watterson, *Shelbyville*
Aaron V. Brown, *Pulaski*
Cave Johnson, *Clarksville*
John W. Crockett, *Trenton*
Christopher H. Williams, *Lexington*

## VERMONT

SENATORS

Samuel Prentiss, *Montpelier*
Samuel S. Phelps, *Middlebury*

REPRESENTATIVES

Hiland Hall, *Bennington*
William Slade, *Middlebury*
Horace Everett, *Windsor*
John Smith, *St. Albans*
Isaac Fletcher, *Lyndon*

---

[35] Resigned November 16, 1840.
[36] Elected to fill vacancy caused by resignation of Bedford Brown, and took his seat December 9, 1840.
[37] Resigned November 16, 1840.
[38] Elected to fill vacancy caused by resignation of Robert Strange, and took his seat December 10, 1840.
[39] Resigned May 30, 1840.
[40] Elected to fill vacancy caused by resignation of Thomas Corwin, and took his seat December 7, 1840.
[41] Elected January 14, 1840, to fill vacancy in the term commencing March 4, 1839, caused by failure of the legislature to elect, and took his seat January 24, 1840.

[42] Election unsuccessfully contested by Charles J. Ingersoll.
[43] Died October 17, 1840, before the commencement of the Twenty-seventh Congress, to which he had been reelected.
[44] Elected to fill vacancy caused by death of William S. Ramsey, and took his seat December 7, 1840.
[45] Died October 28, 1839, before Congress assembled.
[46] Elected to fill vacancy caused by death of William W. Potter and took his seat December 2, 1839.
[47] Resigned in 1840.

[48] Elected to fill vacancy caused by resignation of Richard Biddle, and took his seat December 10, 1840.
[49] Resigned January 13, 1840.
[50] Elected to fill vacancy caused by resignation of Hugh Lawson White, and took his seat February 26, 1840.
[51] Elected to fill vacancy in the term commencing March 4, 1839, caused by resignation of Ephraim H. Foster, in preceding Congress, and took his seat January 3, 1840; vacancy in this class from March 4 to December 14, 1839; died December 19, 1840.
[52] Appointed to fill vacancy caused by death of Felix Grundy, and took his seat January 11, 1841.

## VIRGINIA

### SENATORS

William H. Roane, *Richmond*
William C. Rives,[53] *Lindseys Store*

### REPRESENTATIVES

Linn Banks, *Madison*
Andrew Beirne, *Union*
John M. Botts, *Richmond*
Walter Coles, *Robertsons Store*
Robert Craig, *Christiansburg*
George C. Dromgoole, *Cholsonville*
James Garland, *Lovingston*
William L. Goggin, *Liberty*
John Hill, *Buckingham*

Joel Holleman,[54] *Burwell Bay*
Francis Mallory,[55] *Hampton*
George W. Hopkins, *Lebanon*
Robert M. T. Hunter, *Lloyds*
Joseph Johnson, *Bridgeport*
John W. Jones, *Petersburg*
William Lucas, *Charlestown*
Charles F. Mercer,[56] *Aldie*
William M. McCarty,[57] *Alexandria*
Francis E. Rives, *Littleton*
Green B. Samuels, *Woodstock*
Lewis Steenrod, *Wheeling*
John Taliaferro, *Fredericksburg*
Henry A. Wise, *Accomac*

## TERRITORY OF FLORIDA

### DELEGATE

Charles Downing, *St. Augustine*

## TERRITORY OF IOWA

### DELEGATE

William W. Chapman,[58] *Burlington*
Augustus C. Dodge,[59] *Burlington*

## TERRITORY OF WISCONSIN

### DELEGATE

James D. Doty, *Ashton*

---

[53] Elected to fill vacancy in term commencing March 4, 1839, caused by failure of legislature to elect, and took his seat January 30, 1841; vacancy in this class from March 4, 1839, to January 18, 1841.

[54] Resigned in 1840.

[55] Elected to fill vacancy caused by resignation of Joel Holleman, and took his seat January 7, 1841.

[56] Resigned December 26, 1839.

[57] Elected to fill vacancy caused by resignation of Charles F. Mercer, and took his seat January 25, 1840.

[58] Served until October 27, 1840, when his term expired under the provisions of the act of March 3, 1839.

[59] Elected in compliance with the act of March 3, 1839, and took his seat December 8, 1840.

# 27TH CONGRESS

## MARCH 4, 1841, TO MARCH 3, 1843

John Tyler
Vice President

John White
Speaker

FIRST SESSION— *May 31, 1841, to September 13, 1841*
SECOND SESSION— *December 6, 1841, to August 31, 1842*
THIRD SESSION— *December 5, 1842, to March 3, 1843*
SPECIAL SESSION OF THE SENATE— *March 4, 1841, to March 15, 1841*

---

VICE PRESIDENT OF THE UNITED STATES— JOHN TYLER,[1] of Virginia
PRESIDENT PRO TEMPORE OF THE SENATE— WILLIAM R. KING,[2] of Alabama; SAMUEL L. SOUTHARD,[3] of New Jersey; WILLIE P. MANGUM,[4] of North Carolina
SECRETARY OF THE SENATE— ASBURY DICKENS,[5] of North Carolina
SERGEANT AT ARMS OF THE SENATE— STEPHEN HAIGHT, of New York; EDWARD DYER,[6] of Maryland

---

SPEAKER OF THE HOUSE OF REPRESENTATIVES— JOHN WHITE,[7] of Kentucky
CLERK OF THE HOUSE— HUGH A. GARLAND, of Virginia; MATTHEW ST. CLAIR CLARKE,[8] of Pennsylvania
SERGEANT AT ARMS OF THE HOUSE— RODERICK DORSEY, of Maryland; ELEAZOR M. TOWNSEND,[9] of Connecticut
DOORKEEPER OF THE HOUSE— JOSEPH FOLLANSBEE, of Massachusetts

---

## ALABAMA

SENATORS

William R. King, *Selma*
Clement C. Clay,[10] *Huntsville*
Arthur P. Bagby,[11] *Tuscaloosa*

REPRESENTATIVES AT LARGE

Reuben Chapman, *Somerville*
George S. Houston, *Athens*
Dixon H. Lewis, *Lowndesboro*
William W. Payne, *Gainesville*
Benjamin G. Shields, *Demopolis*

## ARKANSAS

SENATORS

William S. Fulton, *Little Rock*
Ambrose H. Sevier, *Lake Port*

REPRESENTATIVE AT LARGE

Edward Cross, *Washington*

## CONNECTICUT

SENATORS

Perry Smith, *New Milford*
Jabez W. Huntington, *Norwich*

REPRESENTATIVES

Joseph Trumbull, *Hartford*
William W. Boardman, *New Haven*

Thomas W. Williams, *New London*
Thomas B. Osborne, *Fairfield*
Truman Smith, *Litchfield*
John H. Brockway, *Ellington*

## DELAWARE

SENATORS

Richard H. Bayard, *Wilmington*
Thomas Clayton, *New Castle*

REPRESENTATIVE AT LARGE

George B. Rodney, *New Castle*

## GEORGIA

SENATORS

Alfred Cuthbert, *Monticello*
John Macpherson Berrien, *Savannah*

REPRESENTATIVES AT LARGE

Julius C. Alford,[12] *Lagrange*
Edward J. Black,[13] *Jacksonboro*
William C. Dawson,[14] *Greensboro*
Walter T. Colquitt,[15] *Columbus*
Eugenius A. Nisbet,[16] *Macon*
Mark A. Cooper,[17] *Columbus*
Thomas F. Foster, *Columbus*
Roger L. Gamble, *Louisville*
Richard W. Habersham,[18] *Clarkesville*
George W. Crawford,[19] *Augusta*

Thomas Butler King, *Waynesville*
James A. Meriwether, *Edenton*
Lott Warren, *Palmyra*

## ILLINOIS

SENATORS

Richard M. Young, *Quincy*
Samuel McRoberts, *Danville*

REPRESENTATIVES

Zadoc Casey, *Mount Vernon*
John Reynolds, *Belleville*
John T. Stuart, *Springfield*

## INDIANA

SENATORS

Oliver H. Smith, *Indianapolis*
Albert S. White, *Lafayette*

REPRESENTATIVES

George H. Proffit, *Petersburg*
Richard W. Thompson, *Bedford*
Joseph L. White, *Madison*
James H. Cravens, *Marion*
Andrew Kennedy, *Muncietown*
David Wallace, *Indianapolis*
Henry S. Lane, *Crawfordsville*

---

[1] Became President upon the death of William Henry Harrison, April 4, 1841.
[2] Elected March 4, 1841 (special session of the Senate).
[3] Elected March 11, 1841 (special session of the Senate); resigned as President pro tempore May 31, 1842.
[4] Elected May 31, 1842.
[5] Reelected June 7, 1841.
[6] Elected March 8, 1841; reelected June 7, 1841.
[7] Elected May 31, 1841.
[8] Elected May 31, 1841.

[9] Elected June 8, 1841.
[10] Resigned November 15, 1841.
[11] Elected to fill vacancy caused by resignation of Clement C. Clay, and took his seat December 27, 1841.
[12] Resigned in 1841.
[13] Elected at large to fill, in part, vacancies caused by resignations of Julius C. Alford, William C. Dawson, and Eugenius A. Nisbet, and took his seat March 2, 1842.
[14] Resigned November 13, 1841.
[15] Elected at large to fill, in part, vacancies caused by resignations of Julius C. Alford, William C. Dawson,

and Eugenius A. Nisbet, and took his seat February 1, 1842.
[16] Resigned in 1841.
[17] Elected at large to fill, in part, vacancies caused by resignations of Julius C. Alford, William C. Dawson, and Eugenius A. Nisbet, and took his seat February 1, 1842.
[18] Died December 2, 1842.
[19] Elected to fill vacancy caused by death of Richard W. Habersham, and took his seat February 1, 1843.

## KENTUCKY

### SENATORS

Henry Clay,[20] *Lexington*
John J. Crittenden,[21] *Frankfort*
James T. Morehead, *Covington*

### REPRESENTATIVES

Linn Boyd, *Cadiz*
Philip Triplett, *Owensboro*
Joseph R. Underwood, *Bowling Green*
Bryan Y. Owsley, *Jamestown*
John B. Thompson, *Harrodsburg*
Willis Green, *Green*
John Pope, *Springfield*
James C. Sprigg, *Shelbyville*
John White, *Richmond*
Thomas F. Marshall, *Versailles*
Landaff W. Andrews, *Flemingsburg*
Garrett Davis, *Paris*
William O. Butler, *Carrollton*

## LOUISIANA

### SENATORS

Alexander Mouton,[22] *Vermilionville*
Charles M. Conrad,[23] *New Orleans*
Alexander Barrow, *Baton Rouge*

### REPRESENTATIVES

Edward D. White, *Thibodaux*
John B. Dawson, *St. Francisville*
John Moore, *Franklin*

## MAINE

### SENATORS

Reuel Williams,[24] *Augusta*
John Fairfield,[25] *Saco*
George Evans, *Gardiner*

### REPRESENTATIVES

Elisha H. Allen, *Bangor*
David Bronson,[26] *Anson*
Nathan Clifford, *Newfield*
William P. Fessenden, *Portland*
Nathaniel S. Littlefield, *Bridgeton*
Joshua A. Lowell,[27] *East Machias*
Alfred Marshall, *China*
Benjamin Randall, *Bath*

## MARYLAND

### SENATORS

William D. Merrick, *Allens Fresh*
John L. Kerr, *Easton*

### REPRESENTATIVES

Isaac D. Jones, *Princess Anne*
James A. Pearce, *Chestertown*
James W. Williams,[28] *Churchville*
Charles S. Sewall,[29] *Elkton*
John P. Kennedy, *Baltimore*
Alexander Randall, *Annapolis*
William Cost Johnson, *Jefferson*
John T. Mason, *Hagerstown*
Augustus R. Sollers, *Prince Frederick*

## MASSACHUSETTS

### SENATORS

Isaac C. Bates, *Northampton*
Rufus Choate, *Boston*

### REPRESENTATIVES

Robert C. Winthrop,[30] *Boston*
Nathan Appleton,[31] *Boston*
Leverett Saltonstall, *Salem*
Caleb Cushing, *Newburyport*
William Parmenter, *East Cambridge*
Levi Lincoln,[32] *Worcester*
Charles Hudson,[33] *Westminster*
Osmyn Baker, *Amherst*
George N. Briggs, *Lanesboro*
William B. Calhoun, *Springfield*
William S. Hastings,[34] *Mendon*
Nathaniel B. Borden, *Fall River*
Barker Burnell, *Nantucket*
John Quincy Adams, *Quincy*

## MICHIGAN

### SENATORS

Augustus S. Porter, *Detroit*
William Woodbridge, *Detroit*

### REPRESENTATIVE AT LARGE

Jacob M. Howard, *Detroit*

## MISSISSIPPI

### SENATORS

Robert J. Walker, *Madisonville*
John Henderson, *Pass Christian*

### REPRESENTATIVES AT LARGE

William M. Gwin, *Vicksburg*
Jacob Thompson, *Oxford*

## MISSOURI

### SENATORS

Thomas Hart Benton, *St. Louis*
Lewis F. Linn, *Ste. Genevieve*

### REPRESENTATIVES AT LARGE

John C. Edwards, *Jefferson City*
John Miller, *Conners Mills*

## NEW HAMPSHIRE

### SENATORS

Franklin Pierce,[35] *Concord*
Leonard Wilcox,[36] *Orford*
Levi Woodbury, *Portsmouth*

### REPRESENTATIVES AT LARGE

Charles G. Atherton, *Nashua*
Edmund Burke, *Newport*
Ira A. Eastman, *Gilmanton*
John R. Reding, *Haverhill*
Tristram Shaw, *Exeter*

## NEW JERSEY

### SENATORS

Samuel L. Southard,[37] *Trenton*
William L. Dayton,[38] *Trenton*
Jacob W. Miller, *Morristown*

### REPRESENTATIVES AT LARGE

John B. Aycrigg, *Pyramus*
William Halstead, *Trenton*
John P. B. Maxwell, *Belvidere*
Joseph F. Randolph, *New Brunswick*
Charles C. Stratton, *Swedesboro*
Thomas Jones Yorke, *Salem*

## NEW YORK

### SENATORS

Silas Wright, Jr., *Canton*
Nathaniel P. Tallmadge, *Poughkeepsie*

### REPRESENTATIVES

Charles A. Floyd, *Commack*
Joseph Egbert, *Tompkinsville*
John McKeon, *New York City*
James I. Roosevelt, *New York City*
Fernando Wood, *New York City*
Charles G. Ferris, *New York City*
Aaron Ward, *Mount Pleasant*
Richard D. Davis, *Poughkeepsie*
James G. Clinton, *Newburgh*
John Van Buren, *Kingston*
Robert McClellan, *Hudson*
Jacob Houck, Jr., *Schoharie*
Hiram P. Hunt, *Troy*
Daniel D. Barnard, *Albany*
Archibald L. Linn, *Schenectady*

---

[20] Resigned March 31, 1842.
[21] Elected to fill vacancy caused by resignation of Henry Clay, and took his seat March 31, 1842.
[22] Resigned March 1, 1842.
[23] Elected to fill vacancy caused by resignation of Alexander Mouton, and took his seat April 14, 1842.
[24] Resigned February 15, 1843.
[25] Elected to fill vacancy caused by resignation of Reuel Williams, but did not take his seat until December 4, 1843, in the next Congress.
[26] Elected to fill vacancy caused by resignation of Representative-elect George Evans, in preceding Congress, and took his seat May 31, 1841.

[27] Election unsuccessfully protested by sundry citizens of Maine.
[28] Died December 2, 1842.
[29] Elected to fill vacancy caused by death of James W. Williams, and took his seat January 7, 1843.
[30] Resigned May 25, 1842; subsequently elected to fill vacancy caused by resignation of his own successor, Nathan Appleton, and took his seat the second time December 5, 1842.
[31] Elected to fill vacancy caused by resignation of Robert C. Winthrop, and took his seat June 9, 1842; resigned September 28, 1842.
[32] Resigned March 16, 1841, before Congress

assembled, having been appointed collector of the port of Boston.
[33] Elected to fill vacancy caused by resignation of Levi Lincoln, and took his seat May 3, 1841.
[34] Died June 17, 1842.
[35] Resigned February 28, 1842.
[36] Appointed to fill vacancy caused by resignation of Franklin Pierce, and took his seat March 7, 1842; subsequently elected.
[37] Died June 26, 1842.
[38] Appointed to fill vacancy caused by death of Samuel L. Southard, and took his seat July 6, 1842; subsequently elected.

Barnard Blair, *Salem*
Thomas A. Tomlinson, *Keeseville*
Henry Van B. Rensselaer,
  *Ogdensburg*
John Sanford, *Amsterdam*
Andrew W. Doig, *Lowville*
John G. Floyd, *Utica*
David P. Brewster, *Oswego*
Thomas C. Chittenden, *Adams*
Samuel S. Bowne, *Cooperstown*
Samuel Gordon, *Delhi*
John C. Clark, *Bainbridge*
Lewis Riggs, *Homer*
Samuel Partridge, *Elmira*
Victory Birdseye, *Pompey*
A. Lawrence Foster, *Morrisville*
Christopher Morgan, *Aurora*
John Maynard, *Seneca Falls*
Francis Granger,[39] *Canandaigua*
John Greig,[40] *Canandaigua*
William M. Oliver, *Penn Yan*
Timothy Childs, *Rochester*
Seth M. Gates, *Leroy*
John Young, *Geneseo*
Staley N. Clarke, *Ellicottsville*
Millard Fillmore, *Buffalo*
Alfred Babcock, *Gaines*

## NORTH CAROLINA

### SENATORS

Willie P. Mangum, *Red Mountain*
William A. Graham, *Hillsboro*

### REPRESENTATIVES

Kenneth Rayner, *Winton*
John R. J. Daniel, *Halifax*
Edward Stanly, *Washington*
William H. Washington, *New Bern*
James I. McKay, *Elizabethtown*
Archibald H. Arrington, *Hilliardston*
Edmund Deberry, *Lawrenceville*
Romulus M. Saunders, *Raleigh*
Augustine H. Shepperd, *Salem*
Abraham Rencher, *Pittsboro*
Greene W. Caldwell, *Charlotte*
James Graham, *Rutherfordton*
Lewis Williams,[41] *Panther Creek*
Anderson Mitchell,[42] *Wilkesboro*

## OHIO

### SENATORS

William Allen, *Chillicothe*
Benjamin Tappan, *Steubenville*

### REPRESENTATIVES

Nathanael G. Pendleton, *Cincinnati*
John B. Weller, *Hamilton*
Patrick G. Goode, *Sidney*
Jeremiah Morrow, *Twentymile Stand*
William Doan, *Withamsville*
Calvary Morris, *Athens*
William Russell, *Portsmouth*
Joseph Ridgway, *Columbus*
William Medill, *Lancaster*
Samson Mason, *Springfield*
Benjamin S. Cowen, *St. Clairsville*
Joshua Mathiot, *Newark*
James Mathews, *Coshocton*
George Sweeny, *Bucyrus*
Sherlock J. Andrews, *Cleveland*
Joshua R. Giddings,[43] *Jefferson*
John Hastings, *Salem*
Ezra Dean, *Wooster*
Samuel Stokely, *Steubenville*

## PENNSYLVANIA

### SENATORS

James Buchanan, *Lancaster*
Daniel Sturgeon, *Uniontown*

### REPRESENTATIVES

Charles Brown, *Philadelphia*
John Sergeant,[44] *Philadelphia*
Joseph R. Ingersoll,[45] *Philadelphia*
George W. Toland, *Philadelphia*
Charles J. Ingersoll, *Philadelphia*
Jeremiah Brown, *Goshen*
Francis James, *West Chester*
John Edwards, *Ivy Mills*
Joseph Fornance, *Norristown*
Robert Ramsey, *Hartsville*
John Westbrook, *Dingmans Ferry*
Peter Newhard, *Allentown*
George M. Keim, *Reading*
William Simonton, *Hummelstown*
James Gerry, *Shrewsbury*
James Cooper, *Gettysburg*
Amos Gustine,[46] *Mifflintown*
James Irvin, *Milesburg*
Benjamin A. Bidlack, *Wilkes-Barre*
John Snyder, *Selinsgrove*

Davis Dimock, Jr.,[47] *Montrose*
Almon H. Read,[48] *Montrose*
Albert G. Marchand, *Greensburg*
Enos Hook,[49] *Waynesburg*
Henry W. Beeson,[50] *Uniontown*
Joseph Lawrence,[51] *Washington*
Thomas M. T. McKennan,[52]
  *Washington*
William W. Irwin, *Pittsburgh*
William Jack, *Brookville*
Thomas Henry, *Beaver*
Arnold Plumer, *Franklin*
Charles Ogle,[53] *Somerset*
Henry Black,[54] *Somerset*
James M. Russell,[55] *Bedford*

## RHODE ISLAND

### SENATORS

Nathan F. Dixon,[56] *Westerly*
William Sprague,[57] *Natick*
James F. Simmons, *Providence*

### REPRESENTATIVES AT LARGE

Robert B. Cranston, *Newport*
Joseph L. Tillinghast, *Providence*

## SOUTH CAROLINA

### SENATORS

John C. Calhoun,[58] *Fort Hill*
William C. Preston,[59] *Columbia*
George McDuffie,[60] *Edgefield*

### REPRESENTATIVES

Sampson H. Butler,[61] *Barnwell*
Samuel W. Trotti,[62] *Barnwell*
William Butler, *Greenville*
Patrick C. Caldwell, *Newberry*
John Campbell, *Parnassus*
Isaac E. Holmes, *Charleston*
Francis W. Pickens, *Edgefield*
R. Barnwell Rhett, *Blue House*
James Rogers, *Maybinton*
Thomas D. Sumter, *Stateburg*

## TENNESSEE

### SENATORS

Alfred O. P. Nicholson,[63] *Columbia*

---

[39] Resigned March 5, 1841, having been appointed Postmaster General; subsequently elected to fill vacancy caused by resignation of his own successor, John Greig, and took his seat the second time December 7, 1841.

[40] Elected to fill vacancy caused by resignation of Francis Granger, and took his seat May 31, 1841; resigned September 25, 1841.

[41] Died February 23, 1842.

[42] Elected to fill vacancy caused by death of Lewis Williams, and took his seat April 27, 1842.

[43] Resigned March 22, 1842; subsequently elected to fill vacancy caused by his own resignation, and took his seat December 5, 1842.

[44] Resigned September 15, 1841.

[45] Elected to fill vacancy caused by resignation of John Sergeant, and took his seat December 9, 1841.

[46] Elected to fill vacancy caused by death of Representative-elect William S. Ramsey, in preceding Congress, and took his seat May 31, 1841.

[47] Died January 13, 1842.

[48] Elected to fill vacancy caused by death of Davis Dimock, Jr., and took his seat March 18, 1842.

[49] Resigned April 18, 1841.

[50] Elected to fill vacancy caused by the resignation of Enos Hook, and took his seat May 31, 1841.

[51] Died April 17, 1842.

[52] Elected to fill vacancy caused by death of Joseph Lawrence, and took his seat May 30, 1842.

[53] Died May 10, 1841, before Congress assembled.

[54] Elected to fill vacancy caused by death of Charles Ogle, and took his seat June 28, 1841; died November 28, 1841.

[55] Elected to fill vacancy caused by death of Henry Black, and took his seat January 3, 1842.

[56] Died January 29, 1842.

[57] Elected to fill vacancy caused by death of Nathan F. Dixon, and took his seat February 18, 1842.

[58] Resigned March 3, 1843.

[59] Resigned November 29, 1842.

[60] Elected to fill vacancy caused by resignation of William C. Preston, and took his seat January 3, 1843.

[61] Resigned September 27, 1842.

[62] Elected to fill vacancy caused by resignation of Sampson H. Butler, and took his seat December 17, 1842.

[63] Served until February 7, 1842; State unrepresented for the remainder of the Congress, because of failure of legislature to elect.

## TENNESSEE—Continued

### SENATORS—CONTINUED

Vacant[64]

### REPRESENTATIVES

Thomas D. Arnold, *Greeneville*
Abraham McClellan, *Blountville*
Joseph L. Williams, *Knoxville*
Thomas J. Campbell, *Athens*
Hopkins L. Turney, *Winchester*
William B. Campbell, *Carthage*
Robert L. Caruthers, *Lebanon*
Meredith P. Gentry, *Harpeth*
Harvey M. Watterson, *Shelbyville*
Aaron V. Brown, *Pulaski*
Cave Johnson, *Clarksville*
Milton Brown, *Jackson*
Christopher H. Williams, *Lexington*

## VERMONT

### SENATORS

Samuel Prentiss,[65] *Montpelier*
Samuel C. Crafts,[66] *Craftsbury*
Samuel S. Phelps, *Middlebury*

### REPRESENTATIVES

Hiland Hall, *Bennington*
William Slade, *Middlebury*
Horace Everett, *Windsor*
Augustus Young, *Johnson*
John Mattocks, *Peacham*

## VIRGINIA

### SENATORS

William C. Rives, *Lindseys Store*
William S. Archer, *Elk Hill*

### REPRESENTATIVES

Francis Mallory, *Hampton*
George B. Cary, *Bethlehem*
John W. Jones, *Petersburg*
William O. Goode, *Boydton*
Edmund W. Hubard, *Curdsville*
Walter Coles, *Robertsons Store*
William L. Goggin, *Otter Bridge*
Henry A. Wise, *Accomac*
Robert M. T. Hunter, *Lloyds*
John Taliaferro, *Fredericksburg*
John M. Botts, *Richmond*

Thomas W. Gilmer, *Charlottesville*
Linn Banks,[67] *Madison*
William Smith,[68] *Culpeper*
Cuthbert Powell, *Upperville*
Richard W. Barton, *Winchester*
William A. Harris, *Luray*
Alexander H. H. Stuart, *Staunton*
George W. Hopkins, *Lebanon*
George W. Summers, *Kanawha*
Samuel L. Hayes, *Stewarts Creek*
Lewis Steenrod, *Wheeling*

## TERRITORY OF FLORIDA

### DELEGATE

David Levy (Yulee), *St. Augustine*

## TERRITORY OF IOWA

### DELEGATE

Augustus C. Dodge, *Burlington*

## TERRITORY OF WISCONSIN

### DELEGATE

Henry Dodge, *Dodgeville*

---

[64] Vacancy in this class throughout the Congress.
[65] Resigned April 11, 1842.
[66] Appointed to fill vacancy caused by resignation of Samuel Prentiss, and took his seat April 30, 1842; subsequently elected.
[67] Served until December 6, 1841; succeeded by William Smith, who contested his election.
[68] Successfully contested the election of Linn Banks, and took his seat December 6, 1841.

# 28TH CONGRESS

## MARCH 4, 1843, TO MARCH 3, 1845

FIRST SESSION— *December 4, 1843, to June 17, 1844*
SECOND SESSION— *December 2, 1844, to March 3, 1845*

---

VICE PRESIDENT OF THE UNITED STATES[1]
PRESIDENT PRO TEMPORE OF THE SENATE— WILLIE P. MANGUM, of North Carolina
SECRETARY OF THE SENATE— ASBURY DICKENS,[2] of North Carolina
SERGEANT AT ARMS OF THE SENATE— EDWARD DYER, of Maryland

---

Willie P. Mangum
President Pro Tempore

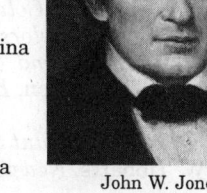

John W. Jones
Speaker

SPEAKER OF THE HOUSE OF REPRESENTATIVES— JOHN W. JONES,[3] of Virginia
CLERK OF THE HOUSE— MATTHEW ST. CLAIR CLARKE, of Pennsylvania; CALEB J. McNULTY,[4] of Ohio; BENJAMIN B. FRENCH,[5] of New Hampshire
SERGEANT AT ARMS OF THE HOUSE— ELEAZOR M. TOWNSEND, of Connecticut; NEWTON LANE,[6] of Kentucky
DOORKEEPER OF THE HOUSE— JESSE E. DOW, of Connecticut

## ALABAMA

### SENATORS
William R. King,[7] *Selma*
Dixon H. Lewis,[8] *Lowndesboro*
Arthur P. Bagby, *Tuscaloosa*

### REPRESENTATIVES
James Dellet, *Clairborne*
James E. Belser, *Montgomery*
Dixon H. Lewis,[9] *Lowndesboro*
William L. Yancey,[10] *Wetumpka*
William W. Payne, *Cainesville*
George S. Houston, *Athens*
Reuben Chapman, *Somerville*
Felix G. McConnell, *Talladega*

## ARKANSAS

### SENATORS
William S. Fulton,[11] *Little Rock*
Chester Ashley,[12] *Little Rock*
Ambrose H. Sevier, *Lake Port*

### REPRESENTATIVE AT LARGE
Edward Cross, *Washington*

## CONNECTICUT

### SENATORS
Jabez W. Huntington, *Norwich*
John M. Niles, *Hartford*

### REPRESENTATIVES
Thomas H. Seymour, *Hartford*
John Stewart, *Middle Haddam*
George S. Catlin, *Windham*

Samuel Simons, *Bridgeport*

## DELAWARE

### SENATORS
Richard H. Bayard, *Wilmington*
Thomas Clayton, *New Castle*

### REPRESENTATIVE AT LARGE
George B. Rodney, *New Castle*

## GEORGIA

### SENATORS
John Macpherson Berrien, *Savannah*
Walter T. Colquitt, *Columbus*

### REPRESENTATIVES AT LARGE
Edward J. Black, *Jacksonboro*
John B. Lamar,[13] *Macon*
Absalom H. Chappell,[14] *Macon*
Howell Cobb, *Athens*
Hugh A. Haralson, *Lagrange*
William H. Stiles, *Cassville*
John H. Lumpkin, *Rome*
John Millen,[15] *Savannah*
Duncan L. Clinch,[16] *St. Marys*
Mark A. Cooper,[17] *Columbus*
Alexander H. Stephens,[18]
    *Crawfordville*

## ILLINOIS

### SENATORS
Samuel McRoberts,[19] *Danville*
James Semple,[20] *Alton*

Sidney Breese, *Carlyle*

### REPRESENTATIVES
Robert Smith, *Alton*
John A. McClernand, *Shawneetown*
Orlando B. Ficklin, *Charleston*
John Wentworth, *Chicago*
Stephen A. Douglas, *Quincy*
Joseph P. Hoge, *Galena*
John J. Hardin, *Jacksonville*

## INDIANA

### SENATORS
Albert S. White, *Lafayette*
Edward A. Hannegan, *Covington*

### REPRESENTATIVES
Robert D. Owen, *New Harmony*
Thomas J. Henley, *New Washington*
Thomas Smith, *Versailles*
Caleb B. Smith, *Connersville*
William J. Brown, *Indianapolis*
John W. Davis, *Carlisle*
Joseph A. Wright, *Rockville*
John Pettit, *Lafayette*
Samuel C. Sample, *South Bend*
Andrew Kennedy, *Muncietown*

---

[1] John Tyler became President on the death of William Henry Harrison in preceding Congress.
[2] Reelected December 11, 1843.
[3] Elected December 4, 1843; the Speaker having withdrawn, George W. Hopkins, of Virginia, was substituted to act as Speaker on February 28, 1845, and officiated as such for the remainder of the day.
[4] Elected December 6, 1843; dismissed from office January 18, 1845.
[5] Elected January 18, 1845.
[6] Elected December 7, 1843.
[7] Resigned April 15, 1844, having been appointed minister to France.

[8] Appointed to fill vacancy caused by resignation of William R. King, and took his seat May 7, 1844; subsequently elected.
[9] Resigned April 22, 1844, having been appointed Senator.
[10] Elected to fill vacancy caused by resignation of Dixon H. Lewis, and took his seat December 2, 1844.
[11] Died August 15, 1844.
[12] Elected to fill vacancy caused by death of William S. Fulton, and took his seat December 4, 1844.
[13] Resigned July 29, 1843, before Congress assembled.
[14] Elected to fill vacancy caused by resignation of

John B. Lamar, and took his seat December 4, 1843.
[15] Died October 15, 1843, before Congress assembled.
[16] Elected to fill vacancy caused by death of John Millen, and took his seat February 15, 1844.
[17] Resigned June 26, 1843, before Congress assembled.
[18] Elected to fill vacancy caused by resignation of Mark A. Cooper, and took his seat December 4, 1843.
[19] Died March 27, 1843.
[20] Appointed to fill vacancy caused by death of Samuel McRoberts, and took his seat December 4, 1843; subsequently elected.

## KENTUCKY

SENATORS

James T. Morehead, *Covington*
John J. Crittenden, *Frankfort*

REPRESENTATIVES

Linn Boyd, *Cadiz*
Willis Green, *Green*
Henry Grider, *Bowling Green*
George A. Caldwell, *Columbia*
James W. Stone, *Taylorsville*
John White, *Richmond*
William P. Thomasson, *Louisville*
Garrett Davis, *Paris*
Richard French, *Mount Sterling*
John W. Tibbatts, *Newport*

## LOUISIANA

SENATORS

Alexander Barrow, *Baton Rouge*
Henry Johnson,[21] *New River*

REPRESENTATIVES

John Slidell, *New Orleans*
Alcée L. La Branche, *New Orleans*
John B. Dawson, *St. Francisville*
Pierre E. J. B. Bossier,[22] *Natchitoches*
Isaac E. Morse,[23] *St. Martinville*

## MAINE

SENATORS

George Evans, *Gardiner*
John Fairfield, *Saco*

REPRESENTATIVES

Joshua Herrick, *Kennebunkport*
Robert P. Dunlap, *Brunswick*
Luther Severance, *Augusta*
Freeman H. Morse, *Bath*
Benjamin White,[24] *Montville*
Hannibal Hamlin, *Hampden*
Shepard Cary,[25] *Houlton*

## MARYLAND

SENATORS

William D. Merrick, *Allens Fresh*
James A. Pearce, *Chestertown*

REPRESENTATIVES

John M. S. Causin, *Leonardtown*
Francis Brengle, *Frederick*
John Wethered, *Franklin*
John P. Kennedy, *Baltimore*
Jacob A. Preston, *Perryman*
Thomas A. Spence, *Snow Hill*

## MASSACHUSETTS

SENATORS

Isaac C. Bates, *Northampton*
Rufus Choate, *Boston*

REPRESENTATIVES

Robert C. Winthrop, *Boston*
Daniel P. King, *South Danvers*
Amos Abbott, *Andover*
William Parmenter, *East Cambridge*
Charles Hudson, *Westminster*
Osmyn Baker, *Amherst*
Julius Rockwell, *Pittsfield*
John Quincy Adams, *Quincy*
Henry Williams, *Taunton*
Barker Burnell,[26] *Nantucket*
Joseph Grinnell,[27] *New Bedford*

## MICHIGAN

SENATORS

Augustus S. Porter, *Detroit*
William Woodbridge, *Detroit*

REPRESENTATIVES

Robert McClelland, *Monroe*
James B. Hunt, *Pontiac*
Lucius Lyon, *Grand Rapids*

## MISSISSIPPI

SENATORS

Robert J. Walker, *Madisonville*
John Henderson, *Pass Christian*

REPRESENTATIVES AT LARGE

William H. Hammett, *Princeton*
Robert W. Roberts, *Hillsboro*
Jacob Thompson, *Oxford*
Tilghman M. Tucker, *Columbus*

## MISSOURI

SENATORS

Thomas Hart Benton, *St. Louis*
Lewis F. Linn,[28] *Ste. Genevieve*
David R. Atchison,[29] *Platte City*

REPRESENTATIVES AT LARGE

Gustavus M. Bower, *Paris*
James B. Bowlin, *St. Louis*
James M. Hughes, *Liberty*
John Jameson, *Fulton*
James H. Relfe, *Caledonia*

## NEW HAMPSHIRE

SENATORS

Levi Woodbury, *Portsmouth*
Charles G. Atherton, *Nashua*

REPRESENTATIVES AT LARGE

Edmund Burke, *Newport*
John P. Hale, *Dover*
Moses Norris, Jr., *Pittsfield*
John R. Reding, *Haverhill*

## NEW JERSEY

SENATORS

Jacob W. Miller, *Morristown*
William L. Dayton, *Trenton*

REPRESENTATIVES

Lucius Q. C. Elmer, *Bridgeton*
George Sykes, *Mount Holly*
Isaac G. Farlee, *Flemington*
Littleton Kirkpatrick, *New Brunswick*
William Wright, *Newark*

## NEW YORK

SENATORS

Silas Wright, Jr.,[30] *Canton*
Henry A. Foster,[31] *Rome*
John A. Dix,[32] *Albany*
Nathaniel P. Tallmadge,[33] *Poughkeepsie*
Daniel S. Dickinson,[34] *Binghamton*

REPRESENTATIVES

Selah B. Strong, *Setauket*
Henry C. Murphy, *Brooklyn*
J. Phillips Phoenix, *New York City*
William B. Maclay, *New York City*
Moses G. Leonard, *New York City*
Hamilton Fish, *New York City*
Joseph H. Anderson, *White Plains*
Richard D. Davis, *Poughkeepsie*
James G. Clinton, *Newburgh*
Jeremiah Russell, *Saugerties*
Zadock Pratt, *Prattsville*
David L. Seymour, *Troy*
Daniel D. Barnard, *Albany*
Charles Rogers, *Sandy Hill*
Lemuel Stetson, *Keeseville*
Chesselden Ellis, *Waterford*
Charles S. Benton, *Mohawk*
Preston King, *Ogdensburg*
Orville Hungerford, *Watertown*
Samuel Beardsley,[35] *Utica*

---

[21] Elected for term beginning March 4, 1843, and took his seat March 4, 1844. Alexander Porter was elected for this term but his credentials were not presented, and he died January 23, 1844. Out of consideration of his prior service, 1833 1837, the Senate adopted resolutions and adjourned in respect to his memory February 2, 1844; vacancy in this class from March 4, 1843, to February 12, 1844.

[22] Died April 24, 1844.

[23] Elected to fill vacancy caused by death of Pierre E. J. B. Bossier, and took his seat December 2, 1844.

[24] Took his seat December 2, 1844.

[25] Took his seat May 10, 1844.

[26] Died June 15, 1843, before Congress assembled.

[27] Elected to fill vacancy caused by death of Barker Burnell, and took his seat December 7, 1843.

[28] Died October 3, 1843.

[29] Appointed to fill vacancy caused by death of Lewis F. Linn, and took his seat December 4, 1843; subsequently elected.

[30] Resigned November 26, 1844, having been elected governor.

[31] Appointed to fill vacancy caused by resignation of Silas Wright, Jr., and took his seat December 9, 1844.

[32] Elected to fill vacancy caused by resignation of Silas Wright, Jr., and took his seat January 27, 1845.

[33] Resigned June 17, 1844, having been appointed Governor of Wisconsin Territory.

[34] Appointed to fill vacancy caused by resignation of Nathaniel P. Tallmadge, and took his seat December 9, 1844; subsequently elected.

[35] Resigned March 6, 1844.

Levi D. Carpenter,[36] *Waterville*
Jeremiah E. Cary, *Cherry Valley*
Smith M. Purdy, *Norwich*
Orville Robinson, *Mexico*
Horace Wheaton, *Pompey*
George Rathbun, *Auburn*
Amasa Dana, *Ithaca*
Byram Green, *Sodus*
Thomas J. Patterson, *Rochester*
Charles H. Carroll, *Groveland Center*
William S. Hubbell, *Bath*
Asher Tyler, *Ellicottsville*
William A. Moseley, *Buffalo*
Albert Smith, *Batavia*
Washington Hunt, *Lockport*

## NORTH CAROLINA

SENATORS

Willie P. Mangum, *Red Mountain*
William H. Haywood, Jr., *Raleigh*

REPRESENTATIVES

Thomas L. Clingman, *Asheville*
Daniel M. Barringer, *Concord*
David S. Reid, *Reidsville*
Edmund Deberry, *Lawrenceville*
Romulus M. Saunders, *Raleigh*
James I. McKay, *Elizabethtown*
John R. J. Daniel, *Halifax*
Archibald H. Arrington, *Hilliardston*
Kenneth Rayner, *Winton*

## OHIO

SENATORS

William Allen, *Chillicothe*
Benjamin Tappan, *Steubenville*

REPRESENTATIVES

Alexander Duncan, *Cincinnati*
John B. Weller, *Hamilton*
Robert C. Schenck, *Dayton*
Joseph Vance, *Urbana*
Emery D. Potter, *Toledo*
Henry St. John, *Tiffin*
Joseph J. McDowell, *Hillsboro*
John I. Vanmeter, *Piketon*
Elias Florence, *Circleville*
Heman Allen Moore,[37] *Columbus*
Alfred P. Stone,[38] *Columbus*
Jacob Brinkerhoff, *Mansfield*
Samuel F. Vinton, *Gallipolis*
Perley B. Johnson, *McConnellsville*
Alexander Harper, *Zanesville*
Joseph Morris, *Woodsfield*
James Mathews, *Coshocton*

William C. McCauslen, *Steubenville*
Ezra Dean, *Wooster*
Daniel R. Tilden, *Ravenna*
Joshua R. Giddings, *Jefferson*
Henry R. Brinkerhoff,[39] *Plymouth*
Edward S. Hamlin,[40] *Elyria*

## PENNSYLVANIA

SENATORS

James Buchanan, *Lancaster*
Daniel Sturgeon, *Uniontown*

REPRESENTATIVES

Edward Joy Morris, *Philadelphia*
Joseph R. Ingersoll, *Philadelphia*
John T. Smith, *Philadelphia*
Charles J. Ingersoll, *Philadelphia*
Jacob S. Yost, *Pottstown*
Michael H. Jenks, *Newtown*
Abraham R. McIlvaine, *Brandywine*
Jeremiah Brown, *Goshen*
John Ritter, *Reading*
Richard Brodhead, *Easton*
Benjamin A. Bidlack, *Wilkes-Barre*
Almon H. Read,[41] *Montrose*
George Fuller,[42] *Montrose*
Henry Frick,[43] *Milton*
James Pollock,[44] *Milton*
Alexander Ramsey, *Harrisburg*
Henry Nes, *York*
James Black, *Newport*
James Irvin, *Milesburg*
Andrew Stewart, *Uniontown*
Henry D. Foster, *Greensburg*
John Dickey, *Beaver*
William Wilkins,[45] *Pittsburgh*
Cornelius Darragh,[46] *Pittsburgh*
Samuel Hays, *Franklin*
Charles M. Reed, *Erie*
Joseph Buffington, *Kittanning*

## RHODE ISLAND

SENATORS

James F. Simmons, *Providence*
William Sprague,[47] *Natick*
John B. Francis,[48] *Providence*

REPRESENTATIVES

Henry Y. Cranston, *Newport*
Elisha R. Potter, *Kingston*

## SOUTH CAROLINA

SENATORS

George McDuffie, *Edgefield*
Daniel E. Huger,[49] *Charleston*

REPRESENTATIVES

James A. Black, *Cherokee Iron Works*
Richard F. Simpson, *Pendletonville*
Joseph A. Woodward, *Winnsboro*
John Campbell, *Parnassus*
Armistead Burt, *Abbeville*
Isaac E. Holmes, *Charleston*
R. Barnwell Rhett, *Blue House*

## TENNESSEE

SENATORS

Ephraim H. Foster,[50] *Nashville*
Spencer Jarnagin,[51] *Athens*

REPRESENTATIVES

Andrew Johnson, *Greeneville*
William T. Senter, *Panther Springs*
Julius W. Blackwell, *Athens*
Alvan Cullom, *Livingston*
George W. Jones, *Fayetteville*
Aaron V. Brown, *Pulaski*
David W. Dickinson, *Murfreesboro*
Joseph H. Peyton, *Gallatin*
Cave Johnson, *Clarksville*
John B. Ashe, *Brownsville*
Milton Brown, *Jackson*

## VERMONT

SENATORS

Samuel S. Phelps, *Middlebury*
William Upham, *Montpelier*

REPRESENTATIVES

Solomon Foot, *Rutland*
Jacob Collamer, *Woodstock*
George P. Marsh, *Burlington*
Paul Dillingham, Jr., *Waterbury*

## VIRGINIA

SENATORS

William C. Rives, *Lindseys Store*
William S. Archer, *Elk Hill*

REPRESENTATIVES

Archibald Atkinson, *Smithfield*
George C. Dromgoole, *Summit*
Walter Coles, *Robertsons Store*
Edmund W. Hubard, *Curdsville*
Thomas W. Gilmer,[52] *Charlottesville*

[36] Elected to fill vacancy caused by resignation of Samuel Beardsley, and took his seat December 2, 1844.

[37] Died April 3, 1844.

[38] Elected to fill vacancy caused by death of Heman Allen Moore, and took his seat December 2, 1844.

[39] Died April 30, 1844; never qualified owing to illness.

[40] Elected to fill vacancy caused by death of Henry R. Brinkerhoff, and took his seat December 2, 1844.

[41] Died June 3, 1844.

[42] Elected to fill vacancy caused by death of Almon

H. Read, and took his seat December 2, 1844.

[43] Died March 1, 1844.

[44] Elected to fill vacancy caused by death of Henry Frick, and took his seat April 23, 1844.

[45] Resigned February 14, 1844, having been appointed Secretary of War.

[46] Elected to fill vacancy caused by resignation of William Wilkins, and took his seat March 26, 1844.

[47] Resigned January 17, 1844.

[48] Elected to fill vacancy caused by resignation of William Sprague, and took his seat February 7, 1844.

[49] Elected to fill vacancy caused by resignation of

John C. Calhoun, in preceding Congress, and took his seat December 7, 1843; resigned March 3, 1845, in order that Mr. Calhoun might return to the Senate.

[50] Elected to fill vacancy caused by death of Felix Grundy in the Twenty-sixth Congress, and took his seat December 4, 1843; vacancy in this class from October 17, 1841, to October 16, 1843, because of failure of legislature to elect.

[51] Elected October 17, 1843, to fill vacancy in term beginning March 4, 1841, caused by failure of legislature to elect, and took his seat December 4, 1843.

[52] Election unsuccessfully contested by William L. Goggin; resigned February 16, 1844.

## VIRGINIA—Continued

REPRESENTATIVES—CONTINUED

William L. Goggin,[53] *Otter Bridge*
John W. Jones,[54] *Petersburg*
Henry A. Wise,[55] *Accomac*
Thomas H. Bayly,[56] *Accomac*
Willoughby Newton, *Hague*
Samuel Chilton, *Warrenton*
William Lucas, *Charlestown*
William Taylor, *Lexington*

Augustus A. Chapman, *Union*
George W. Hopkins, *Abingdon*
George W. Summers, *Kanawha*
Lewis Steenrod, *Wheeling*

## TERRITORY OF FLORIDA[57]

DELEGATE

David Levy (Yulee), *St. Augustine*

## TERRITORY OF IOWA

DELEGATE

Augustus C. Dodge, *Burlington*

## TERRITORY OF WISCONSIN

DELEGATE

Henry Dodge, *Dodgeville*

---

[53] Elected to fill vacancy caused by resignation of Thomas W. Gilmer, and took his seat May 10, 1844.
[54] Election unsuccessfully contested by John M. Botts.

[55] Resigned February 12, 1844.
[56] Elected to fill vacancy caused by resignation of Henry A. Wise, and took his seat May 6, 1844.

[57] Granted statehood by act of March 3, 1845.

# 29TH CONGRESS

## MARCH 4, 1845, TO MARCH 3, 1847

George M. Dallas
Vice President

FIRST SESSION— *December 1, 1845, to August 10, 1846*
SECOND SESSION— *December 7, 1846, to March 3, 1847*
SPECIAL SESSION OF THE SENATE— *March 4, 1845, to March 20, 1845*

---

VICE PRESIDENT OF THE UNITED STATES— George M. Dallas, of Pennsylvania
PRESIDENT PRO TEMPORE OF THE SENATE— Ambrose H. Sevier,[1] of Arkansas;
David R. Atchison,[2] of Missouri
SECRETARY OF THE SENATE— Asbury Dickens,[3] of North Carolina
SERGEANT AT ARMS OF THE SENATE— Edward Dyer,[4] of Maryland; Robert Beale,[5] of
Virginia

---

SPEAKER OF THE HOUSE OF REPRESENTATIVES— John W. Davis,[6] of Indiana
CLERK OF THE HOUSE— Benjamin B. French,[7] of New Hampshire
SERGEANT AT ARMS OF THE HOUSE— Newton Lane, of Kentucky
DOORKEEPER OF THE HOUSE— Cornelius S. Whitney, of District of Columbia

John W. Davis
Speaker

---

## ALABAMA

### SENATORS

Arthur P. Bagby, *Tuscaloosa*
Dixon H. Lewis, *Lowndesboro*

### REPRESENTATIVES

Reuben Chapman, *Somerville*
Edmund S. Dargan, *Mobile*
Henry W. Hilliard, *Montgomery*
George S. Houston, *Athens*
Felix G. McConnell,[8] *Talladega*
Franklin W. Bowdon,[9] *Talladega*
William W. Payne, *Gainesville*
William L. Yancey,[10] *Wetumpka*
James L. F. Cottrell,[11] *Hayneville*

## ARKANSAS

### SENATORS

Ambrose H. Sevier, *Lake Port*
Chester Ashley, *Little Rock*

### REPRESENTATIVE AT LARGE

Archibald Yell,[12] *Fayetteville*
Thomas W. Newton,[13] *Little Rock*

## CONNECTICUT

### SENATORS

Jabez W. Huntington, *Norwich*
John M. Niles, *Hartford*

### REPRESENTATIVES

James Dixon, *Hartford*
Samuel D. Hubbard, *Middletown*
John A. Rockwell, *Norwich*
Truman Smith, *Litchfield*

## DELAWARE

### SENATORS

Thomas Clayton, *New Castle*
John M. Clayton, *New Castle*

### REPRESENTATIVE AT LARGE

John W. Houston, *Georgetown*

## FLORIDA[14]

### SENATORS

David Levy Yulee,[15] *St. Augustine*
James D. Westcott, Jr.,[16] *Tallahassee*

### REPRESENTATIVE AT LARGE

Edward C. Cabell,[17] *Tallahassee*
William H. Brockenbrough,[18]
*Tallahassee*

## GEORGIA

### SENATORS

John Macpherson Berrien,[19]
*Savannah*
Walter T. Colquitt, *Columbus*

### REPRESENTATIVES

Howell Cobb, *Athens*
Hugh A. Haralson, *Lagrange*
Seaborn Jones, *Columbus*
Thomas Butler King, *Frederica*
John H. Lumpkin, *Rome*
George W. B. Towns,[20] *Talbotton*
Alexander H. Stephens,
*Crawfordville*
Robert Toombs, *Washington*

## ILLINOIS

### SENATORS

Sidney Breese, *Carlyle*
James Semple, *Alton*

### REPRESENTATIVES

Edward D. Baker,[21] *Springfield*
John Henry,[22] *Springfield*

---

[1] Served as President pro tempore one day, December 27, 1845, under designation by the Vice President.

[2] Elected August 8, 1846; January 11, 1847; March 3, 1847.

[3] Reelected December 9, 1845.

[4] Died September 8, 1845.

[5] Elected December 9, 1845.

[6] Elected December 1, 1845.

[7] Reelected December 2, 1845.

[8] Died September 10, 1846.

[9] Elected to fill vacancy caused by death of Felix G. McConnell, and took his seat December 7, 1846.

[10] Resigned September 1, 1846.

[11] Elected to fill vacancy caused by resignation of William L. Yancey, and took his seat December 7, 1846.

[12] Resigned July 1, 1846, having been appointed colonel in the Army in Mexico.

[13] Elected to fill vacancy caused by resignation of Archibald Yell, and took his seat February 6, 1847.

[14] Admitted as a State into the Union March 3, 1845, the last day of the preceding Congress.

[15] Took his seat December 1, 1845; term to expire, as determined by lot, March 3, 1851. Presented credentials as "David Levy," but on January 12, 1846, in conformity with an act of the Florida Legislature, the Senate ordered the surname "Yulee" added to his name on the official records.

[16] Took his seat December 1, 1845; term to expire, as determined by lot, March 3, 1849.

[17] Served until January 24, 1846; succeeded by William H. Brockenbrough, who contested his election.

[18] Successfully contested the election of Edward C. Cabell, and took his seat January 24, 1846.

[19] Resigned in May, 1845, to accept a judicial appointment in Georgia; was reelected to fill vacancy caused by his own resignation, and took his seat December 8, 1845.

[20] Elected to fill vacancy caused by resignation of Representative-elect Washington Poe on March 4, 1845, before the beginning of the congressional term, and took his seat January 27, 1846.

[21] Resigned December 24, 1846, "to take effect January 15, 1847, or sooner if successor is elected"; again resigned December 30, 1846.

[22] Elected to fill vacancy caused by resignation of Edward D. Baker, and took his seat February 5, 1847.

## ILLINOIS—Continued

REPRESENTATIVES—CONTINUED

Stephen A. Douglas,[23] *Quincy*
Orlando B. Ficklin, *Charleston*
Joseph P. Hoge, *Galena*
John A. McClernand, *Shawneetown*
Robert Smith, *Alton*
John Wentworth, *Chicago*

## INDIANA

SENATORS

Edward A. Hannegan, *Covington*
Jesse D. Bright, *Madison*

REPRESENTATIVES

Charles W. Cathcart, *Laporte*
John W. Davis, *Carlisle*
Thomas J. Henley, *New Washington*
Andrew Kennedy, *Muncietown*
Edward W. McGaughey, *Greencastle*
Robert D. Owen, *New Harmony*
John Pettit, *Lafayette*
Caleb B. Smith, *Connersville*
Thomas Smith, *Versailles*
William W. Wick, *Indianapolis*

## IOWA[24]

SENATORS

Vacant[25]

REPRESENTATIVES AT LARGE

S. Clinton Hastings,[26] *Bloomington*
Shepherd Leffler,[26] *Burlington*

## KENTUCKY

SENATORS

James T. Morehead, *Covington*
John J. Crittenden, *Frankfort*

REPRESENTATIVES

Joshua F. Bell, *Danville*
Linn Boyd, *Cadiz*
Garrett Davis, *Paris*
Henry Grider, *Bowling Green*
John P. Martin, *Prestonburg*
John H. McHenry, *Hartford*
William P. Thomasson, *Louisville*
John W. Tibbatts, *Newport*
Andrew Trumbo, *Owingsville*
Bryan R. Young, *Elizabethtown*

## LOUISIANA

SENATORS

Alexander Barrow,[27] *Baton Rouge*

Pierre Soulé,[28] *New Orleans*
Henry Johnson, *New River*

REPRESENTATIVES

John H. Harmanson, *Simmsport*
Isaac E. Morse, *St. Martinville*
John Slidell,[29] *New Orleans*
Emile La Sére,[30] *New Orleans*
Bannon G. Thibodeaux, *Thibodaux*

## MAINE

SENATORS

George Evans, *Gardiner*
John Fairfield, *Saco*

REPRESENTATIVES

Robert P. Dunlap, *Brunswick*
Hannibal Hamlin, *Hampden*
John D. McCrate, *Wiscasset*
Cullen Sawtelle, *Norridgewock*
John F. Scammon, *Saco*
Luther Severance, *Augusta*
Hezekiah Williams, *Castine*

## MARYLAND

SENATORS

James A. Pearce, *Chestertown*
Reverdy Johnson, *Baltimore*

REPRESENTATIVES

John G. Chapman, *Port Tobacco*
Albert Constable, *Perryville*
William F. Giles, *Baltimore*
Thomas W. Ligon, *Ellicotts Mills*
Edward H. C. Long, *Princess Anne*
Thomas J. Perry, *Cumberland*

## MASSACHUSETTS

SENATORS

Isaac C. Bates,[31] *Northampton*
John Davis,[32] *Worcester*
Daniel Webster, *Boston*

REPRESENTATIVES

Amos Abbott, *Andover*
John Quincy Adams, *Quincy*
George Ashmun, *Springfield*
Joseph Grinnell, *New Bedford*
Artemas Hale, *Bridgewater*
Charles Hudson, *Westminster*
Daniel P. King, *South Danvers*
Julius Rockwell, *Pittsfield*
Benjamin Thompson, *Charlestown*
Robert C. Winthrop, *Boston*

## MICHIGAN

SENATORS

William Woodbridge, *Detroit*
Lewis Cass, *Detroit*

REPRESENTATIVES

John S. Chipman, *Centerville*
James B. Hunt, *Pontiac*
Robert McClelland, *Monroe*

## MISSISSIPPI

SENATORS

Robert J. Walker,[33] *Madisonville*
Joseph W. Chalmers,[34] *Holly Springs*
Jesse Speight, *Plymouth*

REPRESENTATIVES AT LARGE

Stephen Adams, *Aberdeen*
Jefferson Davis,[35] *Warrenton*
Henry T. Ellett,[36] *Port Gibson*
Robert W. Roberts, *Hillsboro*
Jacob Thompson, *Oxford*

## MISSOURI

SENATORS

Thomas Hart Benton, *St. Louis*
David R. Atchison, *Platte City*

REPRESENTATIVES AT LARGE

James B. Bowlin, *St. Louis*
Sterling Price,[37] *Keytesville*
William McDaniel,[38] *Palmyra*
James H. Relfe, *Caledonia*
John S. Phelps, *Springfield*
Leonard H. Sims, *Springfield*

## NEW HAMPSHIRE

SENATORS

Levi Woodbury,[39] *Portsmouth*
Benning W. Jenness,[40] *Strafford*
Joseph Cilley,[41] *Nottingham*
Charles G. Atherton, *Nashua*

REPRESENTATIVES AT LARGE

James H. Johnson, *Bath*
Mace Moulton, *Manchester*
Moses Norris, Jr., *Pittsfield*

---

[23] Reelected to the Thirtieth Congress, but resigned, having been elected Senator.
[24] Admitted as a State into the Union December 28, 1846.
[25] Senators were not elected to this Congress.
[26] Took his seat December 29, 1846.
[27] Died December 29, 1846.
[28] Elected to fill vacancy caused by death of Alexander Barrow, and took his seat February 3, 1847.
[29] Resigned November 10, 1845, before Congress assembled.
[30] Elected to fill vacancy caused by resignation of

John Slidell, and took his seat January 29, 1846.
[31] Died March 16, 1845.
[32] Elected to fill vacancy caused by death of Isaac C. Bates, and took his seat December 1, 1845.
[33] Resigned March 5, 1845, having been appointed Secretary of the Treasury.
[34] Appointed to fill vacancy caused by resignation of Robert J. Walker, and took his seat December 1, 1845; subsequently elected.
[35] Resigned in June, 1846, to participate in the war with Mexico.
[36] Elected to fill vacancy caused by resignation of

Jefferson Davis, and took his seat January 26, 1847.
[37] Resigned August 12, 1846, to command a cavalry regiment in the war with Mexico.
[38] Elected to fill vacancy caused by resignation of Sterling Price, and took his seat December 7, 1846.
[39] Resigned November 20, 1845, having been appointed to the Supreme Court of the United States.
[40] Appointed to fill vacancy caused by resignation of Levi Woodbury, and took his seat December 1, 1845.
[41] Elected to fill vacancy caused by resignation of Levi Woodbury, and took his seat June 22, 1846.

## NEW JERSEY

SENATORS

Jacob W. Miller, *Morristown*
William L. Dayton, *Trenton*

REPRESENTATIVES

Joseph E. Edsall, *Hamburg*
James G. Hampton, *Bridgeton*
John Runk,[42] *Kingwood*
Samuel G. Wright,[43] *Imlaystown*
George Sykes,[44] *Mount Holly*
William Wright, *Newark*

## NEW YORK

SENATORS

Daniel S. Dickinson, *Binghamton*
John A. Dix, *Albany*

REPRESENTATIVES

Joseph H. Anderson, *White Plains*
Charles S. Benton, *Mohawk*
William W. Campbell, *New York City*
Charles H. Carroll, *Groveland Center*
John F. Collin, *Hillsdale*
Erastus D. Culver, *Greenwich*
John De Mott, *Lodi*
Samuel S. Ellsworth, *Penn Yan*
Charles Goodyear, *Schoharie*
Samuel Gordon, *Delhi*
Martin Grover, *Angelica*
Richard P. Herrick,[45] *Greenbush*
Thomas C. Ripley,[46] *Schaghticoke*
Elias B. Holmes, *Brockport*
William J. Hough, *Cazenovia*
Orville Hungerford, *Watertown*
Washington Hunt, *Lockport*
Timothy Jenkins, *Oneida Castle*
Preston King, *Ogdensburg*
John W. Lawrence, *Flushing*
Abner Lewis, *Panama*
William B. Maclay, *New York City*
William S. Miller, *New York City*
William A. Moseley, *Buffalo*
Archibald C. Niven, *Monticello*
George Rathbun, *Auburn*
Joseph Russell, *Warrensburg*
Henry I. Seaman, *Richmond*
Albert Smith, *Batavia*
Stephen Strong, *Owego*
Horace Wheaton, *Pompey*
Hugh White, *Cohoes*
Bradford R. Wood, *Albany*
Thomas M. Woodruff, *New York City*
William W. Woodworth, *Hyde Park*

## NORTH CAROLINA

SENATORS

Willie P. Mangum, *Red Mountain*
William H. Haywood, Jr.,[47] *Raleigh*
George E. Badger,[48] *Raleigh*

REPRESENTATIVES

Daniel M. Barringer, *Concord*
Asa Biggs, *Williamston*
Henry S. Clark, *Washington*
John R. J. Daniel, *Halifax*
James C. Dobbin, *Fayetteville*
Alfred Dockery, *Dockerys Store*
James Graham, *Rutherfordton*
James I. McKay, *Elizabethtown*
David S. Reid, *Reidsville*

## OHIO

SENATORS

William Allen, *Chillicothe*
Thomas Corwin, *Lebanon*

REPRESENTATIVES

Jacob Brinkerhoff, *Mansfield*
John D. Cummins, *New Philadelphia*
Francis A. Cunningham, *Eaton*
Columbus Delano, *Mount Vernon*
James J. Faran, *Cincinnati*
George Fries, *Hanoverton*
Joshua R. Giddings, *Jefferson*
Alexander Harper, *Zanesville*
Joseph J. McDowell, *Hillsboro*
Joseph Morris, *Woodsfield*
Isaac Parrish, *Parrishs Mills*
Augustus L. Perrill, *Lithopolis*
Joseph M. Root, *Norwalk*
William Sawyer, *St. Marys*
Robert C. Schenck, *Dayton*
Henry St. John, *McCutchenville*
David A. Starkweather, *Canton*
Allen G. Thurman, *Chillicothe*
Daniel R. Tilden, *Ravenna*
Joseph Vance, *Urbana*
Samuel F. Vinton, *Gallipolis*

## PENNSYLVANIA

SENATORS

James Buchanan,[49] *Lancaster*
Simon Cameron,[50] *Middletown*
Daniel Sturgeon, *Uniontown*

REPRESENTATIVES

James Black, *Newport*
John Blanchard, *Bellefonte*
Richard Brodhead, *Easton*
Joseph Buffington, *Kittanning*
John H. Campbell, *Philadelphia*
Cornelius Darragh, *Pittsburgh*

Jacob Erdman, *Coopersburg*
John H. Ewing, *Washington*
Henry D. Foster, *Greensburg*
William S. Garvin, *Mercer*
Charles J. Ingersoll, *Philadelphia*
Joseph R. Ingersoll, *Philadelphia*
Owen D. Leib, *Catawissa*
Lewis C. Levin, *Philadelphia*
Moses McClean, *Gettysburg*
Abraham R. McIlvaine, *Brandywine*
James Pollock, *Milton*
Alexander Ramsey, *Harrisburg*
John Ritter, *Reading*
Andrew Stewart, *Uniontown*
John Strohm, *New Providence*
James Thompson, *Erie*
David Wilmot, *Towanda*
Jacob S. Yost, *Pottstown*

## RHODE ISLAND

SENATORS

James F. Simmons, *Providence*
Albert C. Greene, *Providence*

REPRESENTATIVES

Lemuel H. Arnold, *Wakefield*
Henry Y. Cranston, *Newport*

## SOUTH CAROLINA

SENATORS

George McDuffie,[51] *Cherry Hill*
Andrew P. Butler,[52] *Edgefield*
John C. Calhoun,[53] *Pendleton*

REPRESENTATIVES

James A. Black, *Cherokee Iron Works*
Armistead Burt, *Willington*
Isaac E. Holmes, *Charleston*
R. Barnwell Rhett, *Ashepoo*
Richard F. Simpson, *Pendleton*
Alexander D. Sims, *Darlington*
Joseph A. Woodward, *Winnsboro*

## TENNESSEE

SENATORS

Spencer Jarnagin, *Athens*
Hopkins L. Turney, *Winchester*

REPRESENTATIVES

Lucien B. Chase, *Clarksville*
William M. Cocke, *Rutledge*
John H. Crozier, *Knoxville*
Alvan Cullom, *Livingston*
Joseph H. Peyton,[54] *Gallatin*
Edwin H. Ewing,[55] *Nashville*

---

[42] Election unsuccessfully contested by Isaac G. Farlee.

[43] Died July 30, 1845, before Congress assembled.

[44] Elected to fill vacancy caused by death of Samuel G. Wright, and took his seat December 1, 1845.

[45] Died June 20, 1846.

[46] Elected to fill vacancy caused by death of Richard P. Herrick, and took his seat December 7, 1846.

[47] Resigned July 25, 1846.

[48] Elected to fill vacancy caused by resignation of William H. Haywood, Jr., and took his seat December 14, 1846.

[49] Resigned March 5, 1845.

[50] Elected to fill vacancy caused by resignation of James Buchanan, and took his seat March 17, 1845.

[51] Resigned August 17, 1846.

[52] Elected to fill vacancy caused by resignation of George McDuffie, and took his seat December 21, 1846; vacancy in this class from January 17, 1846, to

December 3, 1846.

[53] Elected to fill vacancy caused by resignation of Daniel E. Huger, in preceding Congress, and took his seat December 22, 1845; vacancy in this class from March 4, 1845, to November 25, 1845.

[54] Died November 12, 1845, before Congress assembled.

[55] Elected to fill vacancy caused by death of Joseph H. Peyton, and took his seat January 2, 1846.

## TENNESSEE—Continued

### REPRESENTATIVES—CONTINUED

Milton Brown, *Jackson*
Meredith P. Gentry, *Franklin*
Andrew Johnson, *Greeneville*
George W. Jones, *Fayetteville*
Barclay Martin, *Columbia*
Frederick P. Stanton, *Memphis*

## TEXAS[56]

### SENATORS

Sam Houston,[57] *Raven Hill*
Thomas J. Rusk,[58] *Nacogdoches*

### REPRESENTATIVES

David S. Kaufman,[59] *Lowes Ferry*
Timothy Pilsbury,[60] *Brazoria*

## VERMONT

### SENATORS

Samuel S. Phelps, *Middlebury*
William Upham, *Montpelier*

### REPRESENTATIVES

Jacob Collamer, *Woodstock*
Paul Dillingham, Jr., *Waterbury*
Solomon Foot, *Rutland*
George P. Marsh, *Burlington*

## VIRGINIA

### SENATORS

William S. Archer, *Elk Hill*
Isaac S. Pennybacker,[61] *New Market*
James M. Mason,[62] *Winchester*

### REPRESENTATIVES

Archibald Atkinson, *Smithfield*
Thomas H. Bayly, *Accomac*
Henry Bedinger, *Charlestown*
William G. Brown, *Kingwood*
Augustus A. Chapman, *Union*
George C. Dromgoole, *Summit*
George W. Hopkins, *Abingdon*
Edmund W. Hubard, *Curdsville*

Robert M. T. Hunter, *Lloyds*
Joseph Johnson, *Bridgeport*
Shelton F. Leake, *Charlottesville*
John S. Pendleton, *Culpeper*
James A. Seddon, *Richmond*
William Taylor,[63] *Lexington*
James McDowell,[64] *Lexington*
William M. Tredway, *Danville*

## TERRITORY OF IOWA

### DELEGATE

Augustus C. Dodge,[65] *Burlington*

## TERRITORY OF WISCONSIN

### DELEGATE

Morgan L. Martin, *Green Bay*

---

[56] Admitted as a State into the Union December 29, 1845, after compliance with certain conditions stipulated in the joint resolution approved March 1, 1845, providing for the annexation of the Republic of Texas.

[57] Took his seat March 30, 1846; term to expire, as determined by lot, March 3, 1847.

[58] Took his seat March 26, 1846; term to expire, as determined by lot, March 3, 1851.

[59] Took his seat June 1, 1846.

[60] Took his seat June 10, 1846.

[61] Died January 12, 1847.

[62] Elected to fill vacancy caused by death of Isaac S. Pennybacker, and took his seat January 25, 1847.

[63] Died January 17, 1846.

[64] Elected to fill vacancy caused by death of William Taylor, and took his seat March 6, 1846.

[65] Served until December 28, 1846, when the Territory of Iowa was granted statehood.

# 30TH CONGRESS

MARCH 4, 1847, TO MARCH 3, 1849

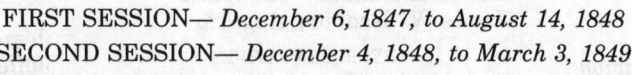

FIRST SESSION— *December 6, 1847, to August 14, 1848*
SECOND SESSION— *December 4, 1848, to March 3, 1849*

———————

VICE PRESIDENT OF THE UNITED STATES— GEORGE M. DALLAS, of Pennsylvania
PRESIDENT PRO TEMPORE OF THE SENATE— DAVID R. ATCHISON,[1] of Missouri
SECRETARY OF THE SENATE— ASBURY DICKENS,[2] of North Carolina
SERGEANT AT ARMS OF THE SENATE— ROBERT BEALE, of Virginia

———————

SPEAKER OF THE HOUSE OF REPRESENTATIVES— ROBERT C. WINTHROP,[3] of Massachusetts
CLERK OF THE HOUSE— BENJAMIN B. FRENCH, of New Hampshire; THOMAS J. CAMPBELL,[4] of Tennessee
SERGEANT AT ARMS OF THE HOUSE— NEWTON LANE, of Kentucky; NATHAN SARGENT,[5] of Vermont
DOORKEEPER OF THE HOUSE— ROBERT E. HORNER, of New Jersey

George M. Dallas
Vice President

Robert C. Winthrop
Speaker

## ALABAMA

### SENATORS

Arthur P. Bagby,[6] *Tuscaloosa*
William R. King,[7] *Selma*
Dixon H. Lewis,[8] *Lowndesboro*
Benjamin Fitzpatrick,[9] *Wetumpka*

### REPRESENTATIVES

John Gayle, *Mobile*
Henry W. Hilliard, *Montgomery*
Sampson W. Harris, *Wetumpka*
Samuel W. Inge, *Livingston*
George S. Houston, *Athens*
Williamson R. W. Cobb, *Bellefonte*
Franklin W. Bowdon, *Talladega*

## ARKANSAS

### SENATORS

Ambrose H. Sevier,[10] *Pine Bluff*
Solon Borland,[11] *Hot Springs*
Chester Ashley,[12] *Little Rock*
William K. Sebastian,[13] *Helena*

### REPRESENTATIVE AT LARGE

Robert W. Johnson, *Little Rock*

## CONNECTICUT

### SENATORS

Jabez W. Huntington,[14] *Norwich*

Roger S. Baldwin,[15] *New Haven*
John M. Niles, *Hartford*

### REPRESENTATIVES

James Dixon, *Hartford*
Samuel D. Hubbard, *Middletown*
John A. Rockwell, *Norwich*
Truman Smith, *Litchfield*

## DELAWARE

### SENATORS

John M. Clayton,[16] *New Castle*
John Wales,[17] *Wilmington*
Presley Spruance, *Smyrna*

### REPRESENTATIVE AT LARGE

John W. Houston, *Georgetown*

## FLORIDA

### SENATORS

David Levy Yulee, *St. Augustine*
James D. Westcott, Jr., *Tallahassee*

### REPRESENTATIVE AT LARGE

Edward C. Cabell, *Tallahassee*

## GEORGIA

### SENATORS

Walter T. Colquitt,[18] *Columbus*

Herschel V. Johnson,[19] *Milledgeville*
John Macpherson Berrien,[20] *Savannah*

### REPRESENTATIVES

Thomas Butler King, *Frederica*
Alfred Iverson, *Columbus*
John W. Jones, *Griffin*
Hugh A. Haralson, *Lagrange*
John H. Lumpkin, *Rome*
Howell Cobb, *Athens*
Alexander H. Stephens, *Crawfordville*
Robert Toombs, *Washington*

## ILLINOIS

### SENATORS

Sidney Breese, *Carlyle*
Stephen A. Douglas, *Quincy*

### REPRESENTATIVES

Robert Smith, *Alton*
John A. McClernand, *Shawneetown*
Orlando B. Ficklin, *Charleston*
John Wentworth, *Chicago*
William A. Richardson,[21] *Rushville*
Thomas J. Turner, *Freeport*
Abraham Lincoln, *Springfield*

---

[1] Elected February 2, 1848; June 1, 1848; June 26, 1848; July 29, 1848; December 26, 1848; and March 2, 1849.

[2] Reelected December 13, 1847.

[3] Elected December 6, 1847; Armistead Burt, of South Carolina, was elected Speaker pro tempore, and served from June 19 to 22, 1848.

[4] Elected December 7, 1847.

[5] Elected December 8, 1847.

[6] Resigned June 16, 1848.

[7] Appointed to fill vacancy caused by resignation of Arthur P. Bagby, and took his seat July 13, 1848.

[8] Died October 25, 1848.

[9] Appointed to fill vacancy caused by death of Dixon H. Lewis, and took his seat December 11, 1848.

[10] Resigned March 15, 1848.

[11] Appointed to fill vacancy caused by resignation of Ambrose H. Sevier, and took his seat April 24, 1848; subsequently elected.

[12] Died April 29, 1848.

[13] Appointed to fill vacancy caused by death of Chester Ashley, and took his seat May 31, 1848; subsequently elected.

[14] Died November 1, 1847.

[15] Appointed to fill vacancy caused by death of Jabez W. Huntington, and took his seat December 7, 1847; subsequently elected.

[16] Resigned February 23, 1849, having been appointed Secretary of State.

[17] Elected to fill vacancy caused by resignation of John M. Clayton, and took his seat February 26, 1849.

[18] Resigned in February, 1848.

[19] Appointed to fill vacancy caused by resignation of Walter T. Colquitt, and took his seat February 14, 1848.

[20] Reelected for the term beginning March 4, 1847, and took his seat December 16, 1847; vacancy in this class from March 4, 1847, to November 12, 1847.

[21] Elected to fill vacancy caused by resignation of Representative-elect Stephen A. Douglas, in preceding Congress, and took his seat December 6, 1847.

## INDIANA

### SENATORS

Edward A. Hannegan, *Covington*
Jesse D. Bright, *Madison*

### REPRESENTATIVES

Elisha Embree, *Princeton*
Thomas J. Henley, *New Washington*
John L. Robinson, *Rushville*
Caleb B. Smith, *Connersville*
William W. Wick, *Indianapolis*
George G. Dunn, *Bedford*
Richard W. Thompson, *Terre Haute*
John Pettit, *Lafayette*
Charles W. Cathcart, *Laporte*
William Rockhill, *Fort Wayne*

## IOWA

### SENATORS

Augustus C. Dodge,[22] *Burlington*
George W. Jones,[23] *Dubuque*

### REPRESENTATIVES

William Thompson, *Mount Pleasant*
Shepherd Leffler, *Burlington*

## KENTUCKY

### SENATORS

John J. Crittenden,[24] *Frankfort*
Thomas Metcalfe,[25] *Forest Retreat*
Joseph R. Underwood, *Bowling Green*

### REPRESENTATIVES

Linn Boyd, *Cadiz*
Beverly L. Clarke, *Franklin*
Samuel O. Peyton, *Hartford*
Aylett Buckner, *Greensburg*
John B. Thompson, *Harrodsburg*
Green Adams, *Barbourville*
W. Garnett Duncan, *Louisville*
Charles S. Morehead, *Frankfort*
Richard French, *Mount Sterling*
John P. Gaines, *Walton*

## LOUISIANA

### SENATORS

Henry Johnson, *New River*
Solomon W. Downs, *Monroe*

### REPRESENTATIVES

Emile La Sére, *New Orleans*
Bannon G. Thibodeaux, *Thibodaux*
John H. Harmanson, *Simmsport*
Isaac E. Morse, *St. Martinville*

## MAINE

### SENATORS

John Fairfield,[26] *Saco*
Wyman B. S. Moor,[27] *Bangor*
Hannibal Hamlin,[28] *Hampden*
James W. Bradbury, *Augusta*

### REPRESENTATIVES

David Hammons, *Lovell*
Asa W. H. Clapp, *Portland*
Hiram Belcher, *Farmington*
Franklin Clark, *Wiscasset*
Ephraim K. Smart, *Camden*
James S. Wiley, *Dover*
Hezekiah Williams, *Castine*

## MARYLAND

### SENATORS

James A. Pearce, *Chestertown*
Reverdy Johnson, *Baltimore*

### REPRESENTATIVES

John G. Chapman, *Port Tobacco*
J. Dixon Roman, *Hagerstown*
Thomas W. Ligon, *Ellicotts Mills*
Robert M. McLane, *Baltimore*
Alexander Evans, *Elkton*
John W. Crisfield, *Princess Anne*

## MASSACHUSETTS

### SENATORS

Daniel Webster, *Boston*
John Davis, *Worcester*

### REPRESENTATIVES

Robert C. Winthrop, *Boston*
Daniel P. King, *South Danvers*
Amos Abbott, *Andover*
John G. Palfrey, *Cambridge*
Charles Hudson, *Westminster*
George Ashmun, *Springfield*
Julius Rockwell, *Pittsfield*
John Quincy Adams,[29] *Quincy*
Horace Mann,[30] *West Newton*
Artemas Hale, *Bridgewater*
Joseph Grinnell, *New Bedford*

## MICHIGAN

### SENATORS

Lewis Cass,[31] *Detroit*
Thomas Fitzgerald,[32] *St. Joseph*
Alpheus Felch, *Ann Arbor*

### REPRESENTATIVES

Robert McClelland, *Monroe*
Edward Bradley,[33] *Marshall*

Charles E. Stuart,[34] *Kalamazoo*
Kinsley S. Bingham, *Kensington*

## MISSISSIPPI

### SENATORS

Jesse Speight,[35] *Plymouth*
Jefferson Davis,[36] *Warrenton*
Henry S. Foote, *Jackson*

### REPRESENTATIVES

Jacob Thompson, *Oxford*
Winfield S. Featherston, *Houston*
Patrick W. Tompkins, *Vicksburg*
Albert G. Brown, *Gallatin*

## MISSOURI

### SENATORS

Thomas Hart Benton, *St. Louis*
David R. Atchison, *Platte City*

### REPRESENTATIVES

James B. Bowlin, *St. Louis*
John Jameson, *Fulton*
James S. Green, *Canton*
Willard P. Hall, *St. Joseph*
John S. Phelps, *Springfield*

## NEW HAMPSHIRE

### SENATORS

Charles G. Atherton, *Nashua*
John P. Hale, *Dover*

### REPRESENTATIVES

Amos Tuck, *Exeter*
Charles H. Peaslee, *Concord*
James Wilson, *Keene*
James H. Johnson, *Bath*

## NEW JERSEY

### SENATORS

Jacob W. Miller, *Morristown*
William L. Dayton, *Trenton*

### REPRESENTATIVES

James G. Hampton, *Bridgeton*
William A. Newell, *Allentown*
Joseph E. Edsall, *Hamburg*
John Van Dyke, *New Brunswick*
Dudley S. Gregory, *Jersey City*

## NEW YORK

### SENATORS

Daniel S. Dickinson, *Binghamton*
John A. Dix, *Albany*

---

[22] Took his seat December 26, 1848; term to expire, as determined by lot, March 3, 1849.
[23] Took his seat December 26, 1848; term to expire, as determined by lot, March 3, 1853.
[24] Resigned June 12, 1848.
[25] Appointed to fill vacancy caused by resignation of John J. Crittenden, and took his seat July 3, 1848; subsequently elected.
[26] Died December 24, 1847.
[27] Appointed to fill vacancy caused by death of

John Fairfield, and took his seat January 17, 1848.
[28] Elected to fill vacancy caused by death of John Fairfield, and took his seat June 12, 1848.
[29] Died in the Speaker's room at the Capitol, February 23, 1848.
[30] Elected to fill vacancy caused by death of John Quincy Adams, and took his seat April 13, 1848.
[31] Resigned May 29, 1848; subsequently elected to fill vacancy caused by his own resignation, and took his seat March 4, 1849.

[32] Appointed to fill vacancy caused by resignation of Lewis Cass, and took his seat June 20, 1848.
[33] Died August 5, 1847, before Congress assembled.
[34] Elected to fill vacancy caused by death of Edward Bradley, and took his seat December 6, 1847.
[35] Died May 1, 1847.
[36] Appointed to fill vacancy caused by death of Jesse Speight, and took his seat December 6, 1847; subsequently elected.

## REPRESENTATIVES

Frederick W. Lord, *Greenport*
Henry C. Murphy, *Brooklyn*
Henry Nicoll, *New York City*
William B. Maclay, *New York City*
Frederick A. Tallmadge, *New York City*
David S. Jackson,[37] *New York City*
Horace Greeley,[38] *New York City*
William Nelson, *Peekskill*
Cornelius Warren, *Cold Spring*
Daniel B. St. John, *Monticello*
Eliakim Sherrill, *Shandaken*
Peter H. Silvester, *Coxsackie*
Gideon Reynolds, *Hoosick*
John I. Slingerland, *Bethlehem*
Orlando Kellogg, *Elizabethtown*
Sidney Lawrence, *Moira*
Hugh White, *Cohoes*
George Petrie, *Little Falls*
William Collins, *Lowville*
Joseph Mullin, *Watertown*
Timothy Jenkins, *Oneida Castle*
George A. Starkweather, *Cooperstown*
Ausburn Birdsall, *Binghamton*
William Duer, *Oswego*
Daniel Gott, *Pompey*
Harmon S. Conger, *Cortland*
William T. Lawrence, *Cayutaville*
John M. Holley,[39] *Lyons*
Esbon Blackmar,[40] *Newark*
Elias B. Holmes, *Brockport*
Robert L. Rose, *Allens Hill*
David Rumsey, Jr., *Bath*
Dudley Marvin, *Ripley*
Nathan K. Hall, *Buffalo*
Harvey Putnam, *Attica*
Washington Hunt, *Lockport*

## NORTH CAROLINA

### SENATORS

Willie P. Mangum, *Red Mountain*
George E. Badger, *Raleigh*

### REPRESENTATIVES

Thomas L. Clingman, *Asheville*
Nathaniel Boyden, *Salisbury*
Daniel M. Barringer, *Concord*
Augustine H. Shepperd, *Salem*
Abraham W. Venable, *Brownsville*
John R. J. Daniel, *Halifax*
James I. McKay, *Elizabethtown*
Richard S. Donnell, *New Bern*
David Outlaw, *Windsor*

## OHIO

### SENATORS

William Allen, *Chillicothe*
Thomas Corwin, *Lebanon*

### REPRESENTATIVES

James J. Faran, *Cincinnati*
David Fisher, *Wilmington*
Robert C. Schenck, *Dayton*
Richard S. Canby, *Bellefontaine*
William Sawyer, *St. Marys*
Rodolphus Dickinson, *Lower Sandusky*
Jonathan D. Morris,[41] *Batavia*
John L. Taylor, *Chillicothe*
Thomas O. Edwards, *Lancaster*
Daniel Duncan, *Newark*
John K. Miller, *Mount Vernon*
Samuel F. Vinton, *Gallipolis*
Thomas Ritchey, *Somerset*
Nathan Evans, *Cambridge*
William Kennon, Jr., *St. Clairsville*
John D. Cummins, *New Philadelphia*
George Fries, *Hanoverton*
Samuel Lahm, *Canton*
John Crowell, *Warren*
Joshua R. Giddings, *Jefferson*
Joseph M. Root, *Norwalk*

## PENNSYLVANIA

### SENATORS

Daniel Sturgeon, *Uniontown*
Simon Cameron, *Middletown*

### REPRESENTATIVES

Lewis C. Levin, *Philadelphia*
Joseph R. Ingersoll, *Philadelphia*
Charles Brown, *Philadelphia*
Charles J. Ingersoll, *Philadelphia*
John Freedley, *Norristown*
John W. Hornbeck,[42] *Allentown*
Samuel A. Bridges,[43] *Allentown*
Abraham R. McIlvaine, *Brandywine*
John Strohm, *New Providence*
William Strong, *Reading*
Richard Brodhead, *Easton*
Chester P. Butler, *Wilkes-Barre*
David Wilmot, *Towanda*
James Pollock, *Milton*
George N. Eckert, *Pottsville*
Henry Nes, *York*
Jasper E. Brady, *Chambersburg*
John Blanchard, *Bellefonte*
Andrew Stewart, *Uniontown*
Job Mann, *Bedford*
John Dickey, *Beaver*
Moses Hampton, *Pittsburgh*
John W. Farrelly, *Meadville*
James Thompson, *Erie*

Alexander Irvin, *Clearfield*

## RHODE ISLAND

### SENATORS

Albert C. Greene, *Providence*
John H. Clarke, *Providence*

### REPRESENTATIVES

Robert B. Cranston, *Newport*
Benjamin B. Thurston, *Hopkinton*

## SOUTH CAROLINA

### SENATORS

John C. Calhoun, *Pendleton*
Andrew P. Butler, *Edgefield*

### REPRESENTATIVES

James A. Black,[44] *Cherokee Iron Works*
Daniel Wallace,[45] *Union*
Richard F. Simpson, *Pendleton*
Joseph A. Woodward, *Winnsboro*
Alexander D. Sims,[46] *Darlington*
John McQueen,[47] *Bennettsville*
Armistead Burt, *Willington*
Isaac E. Holmes, *Charleston*
R. Barnwell Rhett, *Ashepoo*

## TENNESSEE

### SENATORS

Hopkins L. Turney, *Winchester*
John Bell, *Nashville*

### REPRESENTATIVES

Andrew Johnson, *Greeneville*
William M. Cocke, *Rutledge*
John H. Crozier, *Knoxville*
Hugh L. W. Hill, *Irving College*
George W. Jones, *Fayetteville*
James H. Thomas, *Columbia*
Meredith P. Gentry, *Franklin*
Washington Barrow, *Nashville*
Lucien B. Chase, *Clarksville*
Frederick P. Stanton, *Memphis*
William T. Haskell, *Jackson*

## TEXAS

### SENATORS

Sam Houston, *Raven Hill*
Thomas J. Rusk, *Nacogdoches*

### REPRESENTATIVES

David S. Kaufman, *Sabine*
Timothy Pilsbury, *Brazoria*

---

[37] Election contested by James Monroe, but the House declared, on April 19, 1848, that neither was entitled to the seat.

[38] Elected to fill vacancy declared to exist by resolutions of April 19, 1848, and took his seat December 4, 1848.

[39] Died March 8, 1848.

[40] Elected to fill vacancy caused by death of John M. Holley, and took his seat December 4, 1848.

---

[41] Elected to fill vacancy caused by death of Representative-elect Thomas L. Hamer (December 2, 1846, before the beginning of the congressional term, while serving in the war with Mexico), and took his seat December 6, 1847.

[42] Died January 16, 1848.

[43] Elected to fill vacancy caused by death of John W. Hornbeck, and took his seat March 6, 1848.

[44] Died April 3, 1848.

---

[45] Elected to fill vacancy caused by death of James A. Black, and took his seat on June 12, 1848.

[46] Died November 16, 1848, before the commencement of the Thirty-first Congress, to which he had been reelected.

[47] Elected to fill vacancy caused by death of Alexander D. Sims, and took his seat February 12, 1849.

## VERMONT

### SENATORS

Samuel S. Phelps, *Middlebury*
William Upham, *Montpelier*

### REPRESENTATIVES

William Henry, *Bellows Falls*
Jacob Collamer, *Woodstock*
George P. Marsh, *Burlington*
Lucius B. Peck, *Montpelier*

## VIRGINIA

### SENATORS

James M. Mason, *Winchester*
Robert M. T. Hunter, *Lloyds*

### REPRESENTATIVES

Archibald Atkinson, *Smithfield*
George C. Dromgoole,[48] *Summit*
Richard K. Meade,[49] *Petersburg*
Thomas S. Flournoy, *Halifax*
Thomas S. Bocock, *Appomattox*
William L. Goggin, *Otter Bridge*
John M. Botts, *Richmond*
Thomas H. Bayly, *Accomac*
Richard L. T. Beale, *Hague*
John S. Pendleton, *Culpeper*
Henry Bedinger, *Charlestown*
James McDowell, *Lexington*
William B. Preston, *Blacksburg*
Andrew S. Fulton, *Wytheville*
Robert A. Thompson, *Kanawha*

William G. Brown, *Kingwood*

## WISCONSIN[50]

### SENATORS

Henry Dodge,[51] *Dodgeville*
Isaac P. Walker,[52] *Milwaukee*

### REPRESENTATIVES AT LARGE

Mason C. Darling,[53] *Fond du Lac*
William P. Lynde,[54] *Milwaukee*

## TERRITORY OF WISCONSIN[55]

### DELEGATE

John H. Tweedy,[56] *Milwaukee*
Henry H. Sibley,[57] *Mendota*

---

[48] Died April 27, 1847, before Congress assembled.

[49] Elected to fill vacancy caused by death of George C. Dromgoole, and took his seat December 6, 1847.

[50] Formed from the eastern portion of the Territory of Wisconsin by authority of act approved August 6, 1846, and admitted as a State into the Union May 29, 1848.

[51] Took his seat June 23, 1848; term to expire, as determined by lot, March 3, 1851.

[52] Took his seat June 26, 1848; term to expire as determined by lot, March 3, 1849.

[53] Took his seat June 9, 1848.

[54] Took his seat June 5, 1848.

[55] The western portion of the Territory of Wisconsin retained its territorial organization under the same name until reorganized into the Territory of Minnesota by act of March 3, 1849, the eastern portion having been granted statehood as the State of Wisconsin.

[56] Served until May 29, 1848, when that portion of the Territory of Wisconsin in which he resided was admitted to statehood.

[57] Elected to fill vacancy caused by disqualification of John H. Tweedy, and took his seat January 15, 1849.

# 31st CONGRESS

## MARCH 4, 1849, TO MARCH 3, 1851

FIRST SESSION— *December 3, 1849, to September 30, 1850*
SECOND SESSION— *December 2, 1850, to March 3, 1851*
SPECIAL SESSION OF THE SENATE— *March 5, 1849, to March 23, 1849*

Millard Fillmore
Vice President

VICE PRESIDENT OF THE UNITED STATES— MILLARD FILLMORE,[1] of New York
PRESIDENT PRO TEMPORE OF THE SENATE— DAVID R. ATCHISON,[2] of Missouri;
WILLIAM R. KING,[3] of Alabama
SECRETARY OF THE SENATE— ASBURY DICKINS, of North Carolina
SERGEANT AT ARMS OF THE SENATE— ROBERT BEALE, of Virginia

Howell Cobb
Speaker

SPEAKER OF THE HOUSE OF REPRESENTATIVES— HOWELL COBB,[4] of Georgia
CLERK OF THE HOUSE— THOMAS J. CAMPBELL,[5] of Tennessee; RICHARD M. YOUNG,[6] of Illinois
SERGEANT AT ARMS OF THE HOUSE— NATHAN SARGENT, of Vermont; ADAM J. GLOSSBRENNER,[7] of Pennsylvania
DOORKEEPER OF THE HOUSE— ROBERT E. HORNER, of New Jersey

## ALABAMA

### SENATORS
William R. King, *Selma*
Benjamin Fitzpatrick, *Wetumpka*
Jeremiah Clemens,[8] *Huntsville*

### REPRESENTATIVES
William J. Alston, *Linden*
Henry W. Hilliard, *Montgomery*
Sampson W. Harris, *Wetumpka*
Samuel W. Inge, *Livingston*
David Hubbard, *Kinlock*
Williamson R. W. Cobb, *Bellefonte*
Franklin W. Bowdon, *Talladega*

## ARKANSAS

### SENATORS
Solon Borland, *Hot Springs*
William K. Sebastian, *Helena*

### REPRESENTATIVE AT LARGE
Robert W. Johnson, *Little Rock*

## CALIFORNIA[9]

### SENATORS
William M. Gwin,[10] *San Francisco*
John C. Fremont,[11] *San Francisco*

### REPRESENTATIVES AT LARGE
Edward Gilbert,[12] *San Francisco*
George W. Wright,[13] *San Francisco*

## CONNECTICUT

### SENATORS
Roger S. Baldwin, *New Haven*
Truman Smith, *Litchfield*

### REPRESENTATIVES
Loren P. Waldo, *Tolland*
Walter Booth, *Meriden*
Chauncey F. Cleveland, *Hampton*
Thomas B. Butler, *Norwalk*

## DELAWARE

### SENATORS
Presley Spruance, *Smyrna*
John Wales, *Wilmington*

### REPRESENTATIVE AT LARGE
John W. Houston, *Georgetown*

## FLORIDA

### SENATORS
David Levy Yulee, *St. Augustine*
Jackson Morton, *Pensacola*

### REPRESENTATIVE AT LARGE
Edward C. Cabell, *Tallahassee*

## GEORGIA

### SENATORS
J. Macpherson Berrien, *Savannah*
William C. Dawson, *Greensboro*

### REPRESENTATIVES
Thomas Butler King,[14] *Waynesville*
Joseph W. Jackson,[15] *Savannah*
Marshall J. Wellborn, *Columbus*
Allen F. Owen, *Talbotton*
Hugh A. Haralson, *Lagrange*
Thomas C. Hackett, *Rome*
Howell Cobb, *Athens*
Alexander H. Stephens,
 *Crawfordville*
Robert Toombs, *Washington*

## ILLINOIS

### SENATORS
Stephen A. Douglas, *Chicago*
James Shields,[16] *Belleville*

### REPRESENTATIVES
William H. Bissell, *Belleville*
John A. McClernand, *Shawneetown*
Timothy R. Young, *Marshall*
John Wentworth, *Chicago*
William A. Richardson, *Quincy*
Edward D. Baker, *Galena*
Thomas L. Harris, *Petersburg*

---

[1] Became President upon the death of Zachary Taylor, July 10, 1850.
[2] Elected March 5, 1849, and again March 16, 1849 (special session of the Senate).
[3] Elected May 6, 1850; July 11, 1850.
[4] Elected December 22, 1849, upon the sixty-third viva voce vote and the first vote under a plurality resolution adopted that day; Robert C. Winthrop, of Massachusetts, served as Speaker pro tempore on April 19, 1850.
[5] Reelected January 11, 1850; died April 13, 1850.
[6] Elected April 17, 1850.

[7] Elected January 15, 1850.
[8] Elected to fill vacancy caused by death of Dixon H. Lewis, in preceding Congress, and took his seat December 6, 1849.
[9] Formed from a portion of the territory ceded to the United States by Mexico by the treaty of Guadalupe Hidalgo of February 2, 1848, and admitted as a State into the Union September 9, 1850.
[10] Took his seat September 10, 1850; term to expire, as determined by lot, March 3, 1855.
[11] Took his seat September 10, 1850; term to expire, as determined by lot, March 3, 1851.
[12] Took his seat September 11, 1850.

[13] Took his seat September 11, 1850.
[14] Resigned in 1850.
[15] Elected to fill vacancy caused by resignation of Thomas Butler King, and took his seat March 4, 1850.
[16] Although seated on March 6, 1849, his election was declared void on March 15, 1849, "He not having been a citizen of the United States the term of years required as a qualification to be a Senator of the United States at the commencement of the term for which he was elected"; subsequently elected for the term beginning March 4, 1849, and took his seat December 3, 1849; vacancy in this class from March

## INDIANA

SENATORS

Jesse D. Bright, *Madison*
James Whitcomb, *Indianapolis*

REPRESENTATIVES

Nathaniel Albertson, *Greenville*
Cyrus L. Dunham, *Salem*
John L. Robinson, *Rushville*
George W. Julian, *Centerville*
William J. Brown, *Indianapolis*
Willis A. Gorman, *Bloomington*
Edward W. McGaughey, *Rockville*
Joseph E. McDonald, *Crawfordsville*
Graham N. Fitch, *Logansport*
Andrew J. Harlan, *Marion*

## IOWA

SENATORS

Augustus C. Dodge, *Burlington*
George W. Jones, *Dubuque*

REPRESENTATIVES

William Thompson,[17] *Mount Pleasant*
Daniel F. Miller,[18] *Fort Madison*
Shepherd Leffler, *Burlington*

## KENTUCKY

SENATORS

Joseph R. Underwood, *Bowling Green*
Henry Clay, *Lexington*

REPRESENTATIVES

Linn Boyd, *Cadiz*
James L. Johnson, *Owensboro*
Finis E. McLean, *Elkton*
George A. Caldwell, *Columbia*
John B. Thompson, *Harrodsburg*
Daniel Breck, *Richmond*
Humphrey Marshall, *Drennons Lick*
Charles S. Morehead, *Frankfort*
John C. Mason, *Owingsville*
Richard H. Stanton, *Maysville*

## LOUISIANA

SENATORS

Solomon W. Downs, *Monroe*
Pierre Soulé, *New Orleans*

REPRESENTATIVES

Emile La Sére, *New Orleans*
Charles M. Conrad,[19] *New Orleans*
Henry A. Bullard,[20] *New Orleans*

John H. Harmanson,[21] *Simmsport*
Alexander G. Penn,[22] *Covington*
Isaac E. Morse, *St. Martinville*

## MAINE

SENATORS

James W. Bradbury, *Augusta*
Hannibal Hamlin, *Hampden*

REPRESENTATIVES

Elbridge Gerry, *Waterford*
Nathaniel S. Littlefield, *Bridgeton*
John Otis, *Hallowell*
Rufus K. Goodenow, *Paris*
Cullen Sawtelle, *Norridgewock*
Charles Stetson, *Bangor*
Thomas J. D. Fuller, *Calais*

## MARYLAND

SENATORS

James A. Pearce, *Chestertown*
Reverdy Johnson,[23] *Baltimore*
David Stewart,[24] *Baltimore*
Thomas G. Pratt,[25] *Annapolis*

REPRESENTATIVES

Richard J. Bowie, *Rockville*
William T. Hamilton, *Hagerstown*
Edward Hammond, *Ellicotts Mills*
Robert M. McLane, *Baltimore*
Alexander Evans, *Elkton*
John B. Kerr, *Easton*

## MASSACHUSETTS

SENATORS

Daniel Webster,[26] *Boston*
Robert C. Winthrop,[27] *Boston*
Robert Rantoul, Jr.,[28] *Boston*
John Davis, *Worcester*

REPRESENTATIVES

Robert C. Winthrop,[29] *Boston*
Samuel A. Eliot,[30] *Boston*
James H. Duncan, *Haverhill*
Charles Allen, *Worcester*
George Ashmun, *Springfield*

Julius Rockwell, *Pittsfield*
Horace Mann, *West Newton*
Orin Fowler, *Fall River*
Joseph Grinnell, *New Bedford*
Daniel P. King,[31] *South Danvers*

## MICHIGAN

SENATORS

Lewis Cass, *Detroit*
Alpheus Felch, *Ann Arbor*

REPRESENTATIVES

Alexander W. Buel, *Detroit*
William Sprague, *Kalamazoo*
Kinsley S. Bingham, *Kensington*

## MISSISSIPPI

SENATORS

Henry S. Foote, *Jackson*
Jefferson Davis, *Palmyra*

REPRESENTATIVES

Jacob Thompson, *Oxford*
Winfield S. Featherston, *Houston*
William McWillie, *Camden*
Albert G. Brown, *Gallatin*

## MISSOURI

SENATORS

Thomas Hart Benton, *St. Louis*
David R. Atchison, *Platte City*

REPRESENTATIVES

James B. Bowlin, *St. Louis*
William V. N. Bay, *Union*
James S. Green, *Canton*
Willard P. Hall, *St. Joseph*
John S. Phelps, *Springfield*

## NEW HAMPSHIRE

SENATORS

John P. Hale, *Dover*
Moses Norris, Jr., *Manchester*

REPRESENTATIVES

Amos Tuck, *Exeter*
Charles H. Peaslee, *Concord*
James Wilson,[32] *Keene*
George W. Morrison,[33] *Manchester*
Harry Hibbard, *Bath*

---

[16] 1849, to December 2, 1849. (See U.S. Senate Election, Expulsion and Censure Cases, 1793-1990, Senate Document 103-33, 1954-56.)

[17] Election contested by Daniel F. Miller; served until June 29, 1850, when the House declared that neither was entitled to the seat.

[18] Unsuccessfully contested the election of William Thompson; subsequently elected at special election, and took his seat December 20, 1850.

[19] Resigned August 17, 1850.

[20] Elected to fill vacancy caused by resignation of Charles M. Conrad, and took his seat December 5, 1850.

[21] Died October 25, 1850.

[22] Elected to fill vacancy caused by death of John H. Harmanson, and took his seat December 30, 1850.

[23] Resigned March 7, 1849.

[24] Appointed to fill vacancy caused by resignation of Reverdy Johnson, and took his seat December 8, 1849.

[25] Elected to fill vacancy caused by resignation of Reverdy Johnson, and took his seat January 14, 1850.

[26] Resigned July 22, 1850, having been appointed Secretary of State.

[27] Appointed to fill vacancy caused by resignation

of Daniel Webster, and took his seat July 30, 1850.

[28] Elected to fill vacancy caused by resignation of Daniel Webster, and took his seat February 22, 1851.

[29] Resigned July 30, 1850, having been appointed Senator.

[30] Elected to fill vacancy caused by resignation of Robert C. Winthrop, and took his seat August 22, 1850.

[31] Died July 25, 1850.

[32] Resigned September 9, 1850.

[33] Elected to fill vacancy caused by resignation of James Wilson, and took his seat December 2, 1850; election unsuccessfully contested by Jared Perkins.

## NEW JERSEY

### SENATORS

Jacob W. Miller, *Morristown*
William L. Dayton, *Trenton*

### REPRESENTATIVES

Andrew K. Hay, *Winslow*
William A. Newell, *Allentown*
Isaac Wildrick, *Blairstown*
John Van Dyke, *New Brunswick*
James G. King, *Hoboken*

## NEW YORK

### SENATORS

Daniel S. Dickinson, *Binghamton*
William H. Seward, *Auburn*

### REPRESENTATIVES

John A. King, *Jamaica*
David A. Bokee, *Brooklyn*
J. Phillips Phoenix, *New York City*
Walter Underhill, *New York City*
George Briggs, *New York City*
James Brooks, *New York City*
William Nelson, *Peekskill*
Ransom Halloway, *Beekman*
Thomas McKissock, *Newburgh*
Herman D. Gould, *Delhi*
Peter H. Silvester, *Coxsackie*
Gideon Reynolds, *Hoosick*
John L. Schoolcraft, *Albany*
George R. Andrews, *Ticonderoga*
John R. Thurman, *Chestertown*
Hugh White, *Cohoes*
Henry P. Alexander, *Little Falls*
Preston King, *Ogdensburg*
Charles E. Clarke, *Great Bend*
Orsamus B. Matteson, *Utica*
Hiram Walden, *Waldensville*
Henry Bennett, *New Berlin*
William Duer, *Oswego*
Daniel Gott, *Pompey*
Harmon S. Conger, *Cortland*
William T. Jackson, *Havana*
William A. Sackett, *Seneca Falls*
Abraham M. Schermerhorn,
    *Rochester*
Robert L. Rose, *Allens Hill*
David Rumsey, Jr., *Bath*
Elijah Risley, *Fredonia*

Elbridge G. Spaulding, *Buffalo*
Harvey Putnam, *Attica*
Lorenzo Burrows, *Albion*

## NORTH CAROLINA

### SENATORS

Willie P. Mangum, *Red Mountain*
George E. Badger, *Raleigh*

### REPRESENTATIVES

Thomas L. Clingman, *Asheville*
Joseph P. Caldwell, *Statesville*
Edmund Deberry, *Mount Gilead*
Augustine H. Shepperd, *Salem*
Abraham W. Venable, *Brownsville*
John R. J. Daniel, *Halifax*
William S. Ashe, *Wilmington*
Edward Stanly, *Washington*
David Outlaw, *Windsor*

## OHIO

### SENATORS

Thomas Corwin,[34] *Lebanon*
Thomas Ewing,[35] *Lancaster*
Salmon P. Chase, *Cincinnati*

### REPRESENTATIVES

David T. Disney, *Cincinnati*
Lewis D. Campbell, *Hamilton*
Robert C. Schenck, *Dayton*
Moses B. Corwin, *Urbana*
Emery D. Potter, *Toledo*
Rodolphus Dickinson,[36] *Lower
    Sandusky*
Amos E. Wood,[37] *Woodville*
John Bell,[38] *Fremont*
Jonathan D. Morris, *Batavia*
John L. Taylor, *Chillicothe*
Edson B. Olds, *Circleville*
Charles Sweetser, *Delaware*
John K. Miller, *Mount Vernon*
Samuel F. Vinton, *Gallipolis*
William A. Whittlesey, *Marietta*
Nathan Evans, *Cambridge*
William F. Hunter, *Woodsfield*
Moses Hoagland, *Millersburg*
Joseph Cable, *Carrollton*
David K. Cartter, *Massillon*
John Crowell, *Warren*
Joshua R. Giddings, *Jefferson*
Joseph M. Root, *Sandusky*

## PENNSYLVANIA

### SENATORS

Daniel Sturgeon, *Uniontown*
James Cooper, *Pottsville*

### REPRESENTATIVES

Lewis C. Levin, *Philadelphia*
Joseph R. Chandler, *Philadelphia*
Henry D. Moore, *Philadelphia*
John Robbins, Jr.,[39] *Philadelphia*
John Freedley, *Norristown*
Thomas Ross, *Doylestown*
Jesse C. Dickey, *New London*
Thaddeus Stevens, *Lancaster*
William Strong, *Reading*
Milo M. Dimmick, *Stroudsburg*
David Wilmot, *Towanda*
Joseph Casey, *New Berlin*
Charles W. Pitman, *Pottsville*
Henry Nes,[40] *York*
Joel B. Danner,[41] *Gettysburg*
James X. McLanahan, *Chambersburg*
Samuel Calvin, *Hollidaysburg*
Andrew J. Ogle, *Somerset*
Job Mann, *Bedford*
Robert R. Reed, *Washington*
Moses Hampton, *Pittsburgh*
John W. Howe, *Franklin*
James Thompson, *Erie*
Alfred Gilmore, *Butler*
Chester P. Butler,[42] *Wilkes-Barre*
John Brisbin,[43] *Wilkes-Barre*

## RHODE ISLAND

### SENATORS

Albert C. Greene, *Providence*
John H. Clarke, *Providence*

### REPRESENTATIVES

George G. King, *Newport*
Nathan F. Dixon, *Westerly*

## SOUTH CAROLINA

### SENATORS

John C. Calhoun,[44] *Pendleton*
Franklin H. Elmore,[45] *Columbia*
Robert W. Barnwell,[46] *Beaufort*
R. Barnwell Rhett,[47] *Charleston*
Andrew P. Butler, *Edgefield*

---

[34] Resigned July 20, 1850, having been appointed Secretary of the Treasury.
[35] Appointed to fill vacancy caused by resignation of Thomas Corwin, and took his seat July 27, 1850.
[36] Died March 20, 1849.
[37] Elected to fill vacancy caused by death of Rodolphus Dickinson, and took his seat December 3, 1849; died November 19, 1850.
[38] Elected to fill vacancy caused by death of Amos

E. Wood, and took his seat January 7, 1851.
[39] Election unsuccessfully contested by John S. Littell.
[40] Died September 10, 1850.
[41] Elected to fill vacancy caused by death of Henry Nes, and took his seat December 2, 1850.
[42] Died October 5, 1850.
[43] Elected to fill vacancy caused by death of Chester P. Butler, and took his seat January 13, 1851.

[44] Died March 31, 1850.
[45] Appointed to fill vacancy caused by death of John C. Calhoun, and took his seat May 6, 1850; died May 29, 1850.
[46] Appointed to fill vacancy caused by deaths of John C. Calhoun and Franklin H. Elmore, and took his seat June 24, 1850.
[47] Elected to fill vacancy caused by death of John C. Calhoun, and took his seat January 6, 1851.

## SOUTH CAROLINA—
### Continued
#### REPRESENTATIVES
Daniel Wallace, *Union*
James L. Orr, *Anderson*
Joseph A. Woodward, *Winnsboro*
John McQueen,[48] *Bennettsville*
Armistead Burt, *Willington*
Isaac E. Holmes, *Charleston*
William F. Colcock, *Grahamville*

## TENNESSEE
#### SENATORS
Hopkins L. Turney, *Winchester*
John Bell, *Nashville*
#### REPRESENTATIVES
Andrew Johnson, *Greeneville*
Albert G. Watkins, *Panther Springs*
Josiah M. Anderson, *Fairview*
John H. Savage, *Smithville*
George W. Jones, *Fayetteville*
James H. Thomas, *Columbia*
Meredith P. Gentry, *Franklin*
Andrew Ewing, *Nashville*
Isham G. Harris, *Paris*
Frederick P. Stanton, *Memphis*
Christopher H. Williams, *Lexington*

## TEXAS
#### SENATORS
Sam Houston, *Huntsville*
Thomas J. Rusk, *Nacogdoches*

#### REPRESENTATIVES
David S. Kaufman,[49] *Sabine*
Volney E. Howard, *San Antonio*

## VERMONT
#### SENATORS
Samuel S. Phelps, *Middlebury*
William Upham, *Montpelier*

#### REPRESENTATIVES
William Henry, *Bellows Falls*
William Hebard, *Chelsea*
George P. Marsh,[50] *Burlington*
James Meacham,[51] *Middlebury*
Lucius B. Peck, *Montpelier*

## VIRGINIA
#### SENATORS
James M. Mason, *Winchester*
Robert M. T. Hunter, *Lloyds*

#### REPRESENTATIVES
John S. Millson, *Norfolk*
Richard K. Meade, *Petersburg*
Thomas H. Averett, *Halifax*
Thomas S. Bocock, *Appomattox*
Paulus Powell, *Amherst*
James A. Seddon, *Richmond*
Thomas H. Bayly, *Accomac*

Alexander R. Holladay, *Mansfield*
Jeremiah Morton, *Raccoon Ford*
Richard Parker, *Berryville*
James McDowell, *Lexington*
Henry A. Edmundson, *Salem*
Fayette McMullen, *Rye Cove*
James M. H. Beale, *Point Pleasant*
Alexander Newman,[52] *Wheeling*
Thomas S. Haymond,[53] *Fairmont*

## WISCONSIN
#### SENATORS
Henry Dodge, *Dodgeville*
Isaac P. Walker, *Milwaukee*

#### REPRESENTATIVES
Charles Durkee, *Kenosha*
Orsamus Cole, *Potosi*
James Duane Doty, *Menasha*

## TERRITORY OF
## MINNESOTA [54]

#### DELEGATE
Henry H. Sibley,[55] *Mendota*

## TERRITORY OF OREGON[56]

#### DELEGATE
Samuel R. Thurston,[57] *Linn City*

---

[48] Elected to fill vacancy caused by death of Representative-elect Alexander D. Sims in preceding Congress.

[49] Died January 31, 1851.

[50] Resigned in 1849, having been appointed minister to Turkey.

[51] Elected to fill vacancy caused by resignation of George P. Marsh, and took his seat December 3, 1849.

[52] Died September 8, 1849, before Congress Assembled.

[53] Elected to fill vacancy caused by death of Alexander Newman and took his seat December 3, 1849.

[54] Formed March 3, 1849, from the portion of Wisconsin Territory remaining after the State of Wisconsin had been admitted to statehood (May 29, 1848),

and granted a Delegate in Congress.

[55] Took his seat December 3, 1849.

[56] Formed August 14, 1848, from territory ceded to the United States by the treaty with France of April 30, 1803; the treaty with Spain of February 22, 1819, and the treaty with Great Britain of June 15, 1846, and granted a Delegate in Congress.

[57] Took his seat December 3, 1849.

# 32ND CONGRESS

MARCH 4, 1851, TO MARCH 3, 1853

William R. King
President Pro Tempore

Linn Boyd
Speaker

FIRST SESSION— *December 1, 1851, to August 31, 1852*
SECOND SESSION— *December 6, 1852, to March 3, 1853*
SPECIAL SESSION OF THE SENATE— *March 4, 1851, to March 13, 1851*

---

VICE PRESIDENT OF THE UNITED STATES[1]
PRESIDENT PRO TEMPORE OF THE SENATE— William R. King,[2] of Alabama; David R. Atchison,[3] of Missouri
SECRETARY OF THE SENATE— Asbury Dickens, of North Carolina
SERGEANT AT ARMS OF THE SENATE— Robert Beale, of Virginia

---

SPEAKER OF THE HOUSE OF REPRESENTATIVES— Linn Boyd,[4] of Kentucky
CLERK OF THE HOUSE— Richard M. Young, of Illinois; John W. Forney,[5] of Pennsylvania
SERGEANT AT ARMS OF THE HOUSE— Adam J. Glossbrenner, of Pennsylvania
DOORKEEPER OF THE HOUSE— Z. W. McKnew, of Maryland

## ALABAMA

### SENATORS

William R. King,[6] *Selma*
Benjamin Fitzpatrick,[7] *Wetumpka*
Jeremiah Clemens, *Huntsville*

### REPRESENTATIVES

John Bragg, *Mobile*
James Abercrombie, *Girard*
Sampson W. Harris, *Wetumpka*
William R. Smith, *Fayette*
George S. Houston, *Athens*
Williamson R. W. Cobb, *Bellefonte*
Alexander White, *Talladega*

## ARKANSAS

### SENATORS

William K. Sebastian, *Helena*
Solon Borland, *Hot Springs*

### REPRESENTATIVE AT LARGE

Robert W. Johnson, *Little Rock*

## CALIFORNIA

### SENATORS

William M. Gwin, *San Francisco*
John B. Weller,[8] *San Francisco*

### REPRESENTATIVES AT LARGE

Edward C. Marshall, *Sonora*
Joseph W. McCorkle, *Marysville*

## CONNECTICUT

### SENATORS

Truman Smith, *Litchfield*
Isaac Toucey,[9] *Hartford*

### REPRESENTATIVES

Charles Chapman, *Hartford*
Colin M. Ingersoll, *New Haven*
Chauncey F. Cleveland, *Hampton*
Origen S. Seymour, *Litchfield*

## DELAWARE

### SENATORS

Presley Spruance, *Smyrna*
James A. Bayard, *Wilmington*

### REPRESENTATIVE AT LARGE

George Read Riddle, *Wilmington*

## FLORIDA

### SENATORS

Jackson Morton, *Pensacola*
Stephen R. Mallory,[10] *Jacksonville*

### REPRESENTATIVE AT LARGE

Edward C. Cabell, *Tallahassee*

## GEORGIA

### SENATORS

John Macpherson Berrien,[11]
  *Savannah*
Robert M. Charlton,[12] *Savannah*

William C. Dawson, *Greensboro*

### REPRESENTATIVES

Joseph W. Jackson, *Savannah*
James Johnson, *Columbus*
David J. Bailey, *Jackson*
Charles Murphey, *Decatur*
Elijah W. Chastain, *Tacoah*
Junius Hillyer, *Monroe*
Alexander H. Stephens,
  *Crawfordville*
Robert Toombs, *Washington*

## ILLINOIS

### SENATORS

Stephen A. Douglas, *Chicago*
James Shields, *Belleville*

### REPRESENTATIVES

William H. Bissell, *Belleville*
Willis Allen, *Marion*
Orlando B. Ficklin, *Charleston*
Richard S. Molony, *Belvidere*
William A. Richardson, *Quincy*
Thompson Campbell, *Galena*
Richard Yates, *Jacksonville*

---

[1] Vice President Millard Fillmore became President on the death of Zachary Taylor in preceding Congress.
[2] Resigned as President pro tempore December 20, 1852.
[3] Elected December 20, 1852.
[4] Elected December 1, 1851.
[5] Elected December 1, 1851.
[6] Resigned December 20, 1852.

[7] Appointed to fill vacancy caused by resignation of William R. King, and took his seat January 20, 1853; subsequently elected.
[8] Elected for the term beginning March 4, 1851, and took his seat March 17, 1852; vacancy in this class from March 4, 1851, to January 30, 1852.
[9] Elected for the term beginning March 4, 1851, and took his seat May 14, 1852; vacancy in this class from March 4, 1851, to May 11, 1852, because of failure

of Governor to appoint.
[10] Election unsuccessfully contested by David Levy Yulee. (See U.S. Senate Election, Expulsion and Censure Cases, 1793-1990, Senate Document 103-33, pp. 62-64.)
[11] Resigned May 28, 1852.
[12] Appointed to fill vacancy caused by resignation of John Macpherson Berrien, and took his seat June 11, 1852.

## INDIANA

### SENATORS

Jesse D. Bright, *Madison*
James Whitcomb,[13] *Indianapolis*
Charles W. Cathcart,[14] *Laporte*
John Pettit,[15] *Lafayette*

### REPRESENTATIVES

James Lockhart, *Evansville*
Cyrus L. Dunham, *Salem*
John L. Robinson, *Rushville*
Samuel W. Parker, *Connersville*
Thomas A. Hendricks, *Shelbyville*
Willis A. Gorman, *Bloomington*
John G. Davis, *Rockville*
Daniel Mace, *Lafayette*
Graham N. Fitch, *Logansport*
Samuel Brenton, *Fort Wayne*

## IOWA

### SENATORS

Augustus C. Dodge, *Burlington*
George W. Jones, *Dubuque*

### REPRESENTATIVES

Bernhart Henn, *Fairfield*
Lincoln Clark, *Dubuque*

## KENTUCKY

### SENATORS

Joseph R. Underwood, *Bowling Green*
Henry Clay,[16] *Lexington*
David Meriwether,[17] *Louisville*
Archibald Dixon,[18] *Henderson*

### REPRESENTATIVES

Linn Boyd, *Paducah*
Benjamin E. Grey, *Hopkinsville*
Presley U. Ewing, *Russellville*
William T. Ward, *Greensburg*
James W. Stone, *Elizabethtown*
Addison White, *Richmond*
Humphrey Marshall,[19] *New Castle*
William Preston,[20] *Louisville*
John C. Breckinridge, *Lexington*
John C. Mason, *Owingsville*
Richard H. Stanton, *Maysville*

## LOUISIANA

### SENATORS

Solomon W. Downs, *Monroe*
Pierre Soulé, *New Orleans*

### REPRESENTATIVES

Louis St. Martin, *New Orleans*
J. Aristide Landry, *Donaldsonville*
Alexander G. Penn, *Covington*
John Moore, *New Iberia*

## MAINE

### SENATORS

James W. Bradbury, *Augusta*
Hannibal Hamlin, *Hampden*

### REPRESENTATIVES

Moses Macdonald, *Biddeford*
John Appleton, *Portland*
Robert Goodenow, *Farmington*
Charles Andrews,[21] *Paris*
Isaac Reed,[22] *Waldoboro*
Ephraim K. Smart, *Camden*
Israel Washburn, Jr., *Orono*
Thomas J. D. Fuller, *Calais*

## MARYLAND

### SENATORS

James A. Pearce, *Chestertown*
Thomas G. Pratt, *Annapolis*

### REPRESENTATIVES

Richard J. Bowie, *Rockville*
William T. Hamilton, *Hagerstown*
Edward Hammond, *Ellicotts Mills*
Thomas Yates Walsh, *Baltimore*
Alexander Evans, *Elkton*
Joseph S. Cottman, *Upper Trappe*

## MASSACHUSETTS

### SENATORS

John Davis, *Worcester*
Charles Sumner,[23] *Boston*

### REPRESENTATIVES

William Appleton, *Boston*
Orin Fowler,[24] *Fall River*
Edward P. Little,[25] *Marshfield*
James H. Duncan, *Haverhill*
Robert Rantoul, Jr.,[26] *Beverly*
Francis B. Fay,[27] *Chelsea*

Charles Allen, *Worcester*
George T. Davis, *Greenfield*
John Z. Goodrich, *Glendale*
Horace Mann, *West Newton*
Benjamin Thompson,[28] *Charlestown*
Lorenzo Sabine,[29] *Framingham*
Zeno Scudder, *Barnstable*

## MICHIGAN

### SENATORS

Lewis Cass, *Detroit*
Alpheus Felch, *Ann Arbor*

### REPRESENTATIVES

Ebenezer J. Penniman, *Plymouth*
Charles E. Stuart, *Kalamazoo*
James L. Conger, *Mount Clemens*

## MISSISSIPPI

### SENATORS

Henry S. Foote,[30] *Jackson*
Walker Brooke,[31] *Lexington*
Jefferson Davis,[32] *Palmyra*
John J. McRae,[33] *Enterprise*
Stephen Adams,[34] *Aberdeen*

### REPRESENTATIVES

Benjamin D. Nabers, *Hickory Flat*
John A. Wilcox, *Aberdeen*
John D. Freeman, *Jackson*
Albert G. Brown, *Gallatin*

## MISSOURI

### SENATORS

David R. Atchison, *Platte City*
Henry S. Geyer, *St. Louis*

### REPRESENTATIVES

John F. Darby, *St. Louis*
Gilchrist Porter, *Bowling Green*
John G. Miller, *Boonville*
Willard P. Hall, *St. Joseph*
John S. Phelps, *Springfield*

## NEW HAMPSHIRE

### SENATORS

John P. Hale, *Dover*
Moses Norris, Jr., *Manchester*

---

[13] Died October 4, 1852.

[14] Appointed to fill vacancy caused by death of James Whitcomb, and took his seat December 6, 1852.

[15] Elected to fill vacancy caused by death of James Whitcomb, and took his seat January 18, 1853.

[16] Tendered his resignation December 15, 1851, "to take effect on the first Monday of September, 1852"; died June 29, 1852.

[17] Appointed July 6, 1852, to fill vacancy caused by death of Henry Clay, and to serve "until the time the resignation of Henry Clay takes effect"; took his seat July 15, 1852, and served until the adjournment of the session, August 31, 1852.

[18] Elected December 30, 1851, to fill vacancy anticipated by the resignation of Henry Clay; credentials presented on December 6, 1852, but was not permitted to qualify until December 20, 1852, when a resolution was adopted declaring him duly elected "to

fill the vacancy occasioned by the resignation of Mr. Clay." (See U.S. Senate Election, Expulsion and Censure Cases, 1793-1990, Senate Document 103-33, pp. 65-66.)

[19] Resigned August 4, 1852.

[20] Elected to fill vacancy caused by resignation of Humphrey Marshall, and took his seat December 6, 1852.

[21] Died April 30, 1852.

[22] Elected to fill vacancy caused by death of Charles Andrews, and took his seat June 25, 1852.

[23] Elected for term beginning March 4, 1851, and took his seat December 1, 1851; vacancy in this class from March 4, 1851, to April 23, 1851.

[24] Died September 3, 1852.

[25] Elected to fill vacancy caused by death of Orin Fowler, and took his seat December 30, 1852.

[26] Died August 7, 1852.

[27] Elected to fill vacancy caused by death of Robert Rantoul, Jr., and took his seat December 29, 1852.

[28] Died September 24, 1852.

[29] Elected to fill vacancy caused by death of Benjamin Thompson, and took his seat December 28, 1852.

[30] Resigned January 8, 1852, having been elected Governor.

[31] Elected to fill vacancy caused by resignation of Henry S. Foote, and took his seat March 11, 1852.

[32] Resigned September 23, 1851.

[33] Appointed to fill vacancy caused by resignation of Jefferson Davis, and took his seat December 19, 1851.

[34] Elected to fill vacancy caused by resignation of Jefferson Davis, and took his seat March 17, 1852.

## REPRESENTATIVES

Amos Tuck, *Exeter*
Charles H. Peaslee, *Concord*
Jared Perkins, *Winchester*
Harry Hibbard, *Bath*

## NEW JERSEY

SENATORS

Jacob W. Miller, *Morristown*
Robert F. Stockton,[35] *Princeton*

REPRESENTATIVES

Nathan T. Stratton, *Mullica Hill*
Charles Skelton, *Trenton*
Isaac Wildrick, *Blairstown*
George H. Brown, *Somerville*
Rodman M. Price, *Hoboken*

## NEW YORK

SENATORS

William H. Seward, *Auburn*
Hamilton Fish, *New York City*

REPRESENTATIVES

John G. Floyd, *Moriches*
Obadiah Bowne, *Richmond*
Emanuel B. Hart, *New York City*
J. H. Hobart Haws, *New York City*
George Briggs, *New York City*
James Brooks, *New York City*
Abraham P. Stephens, *Nyack*
Gilbert Dean, *Poughkeepsie*
William Murray, *Goshen*
Marius Schoonmaker, *Kingston*
Josiah Sutherland, *Hudson*
David L. Seymour, *Troy*
John L. Schoolcraft, *Albany*
John H. Boyd, *Whitehall*
Joseph Russell, *Warrensburg*
John Wells, *Johnstown*
Alexander H. Buell,[36] *Fairfield*
Preston King, *Ogdensburg*
Willard Ives, *Watertown*
Timothy Jenkins, *Oneida Castle*
William W. Snow, *Oneonta*
Henry Bennett, *New Berlin*
Leander Babcock, *Oswego*
Daniel T. Jones, *Baldwinsville*
Thomas Y. Howe, Jr., *Auburn*
Henry S. Walbridge, *Ithaca*
William A. Sackett, *Seneca Falls*
Abraham M. Schermerhorn, *Rochester*
Jerediah Horsford, *Moscow*
Reuben Robie, *Bath*
Frederick S. Martin, *Olean*
Solomon G. Haven, *Buffalo*
Augustus P. Hascall, *Le Roy*
Lorenzo Burrows, *Albion*

## NORTH CAROLINA

SENATORS

Willie P. Mangum, *Red Mountain*
George E. Badger, *Raleigh*

REPRESENTATIVES

Thomas L. Clingman, *Asheville*
Joseph P. Caldwell, *Statesville*
Alfred Dockery, *Dockerys Store*
James T. Morehead, *Greensboro*
Abraham W. Venable, *Brownsville*
John R. J. Daniel, *Halifax*
William S. Ashe, *Wilmington*
Edward Stanly, *Washington*
David Outlaw, *Windsor*

## OHIO

SENATORS

Salmon P. Chase, *Cincinnati*
Benjamin F. Wade,[37] *Jefferson*

REPRESENTATIVES

David T. Disney, *Cincinnati*
Lewis D. Campbell, *Hamilton*
Hiram Bell, *Greenville*
Benjamin Stanton, *Bellefontaine*
Alfred P. Edgerton, *Hicksville*
Frederick W. Green, *Tiffin*
Nelson Barrere, *Hillsboro*
John L. Taylor, *Chillicothe*
Edson B. Olds, *Circleville*
Charles Sweetser, *Delaware*
George H. Busby, *Marion*
John Welch, *Athens*
James M. Gaylord, *McConnellsville*
Alexander Harper, *Zanesville*
William F. Hunter, *Woodsfield*
John Johnson, *Coshocton*
Joseph Cable, *Carrollton*
David K. Cartter, *Massillon*
Eben Newton, *Canfield*
Joshua R. Giddings, *Jefferson*
Norton S. Townshend, *Avon*

## PENNSYLVANIA

SENATORS

James Cooper, *Pottsville*
Richard Brodhead, *Easton*

REPRESENTATIVES

Thomas B. Florence, *Philadelphia*
Joseph R. Chandler, *Philadelphia*
Henry D. Moore, *Philadelphia*
John Robbins, Jr., *Kensington*
John McNair, *Norristown*
Thomas Ross, *Doylestown*
John A. Morrison, *Cochransville*
Thaddeus Stevens, *Lancaster*
J. Glancy Jones, *Reading*
Milo M. Dimmick, *Stroudsburg*
Henry M. Fuller,[38] *Wilkes-Barre*
Galusha A. Grow, *Glenwood*

James Gamble, *Jersey Shore*
Thomas M. Bibighaus, *Lebanon*
William H. Kurtz, *York*
James X. McLanahan, *Chambersburg*
Andrew Parker, *Mifflintown*
John L. Dawson, *Brownsville*
Joseph H. Kuhns, *Greensburg*
John Allison, *Beaver*
Thomas M. Howe, *Allegheny City*
John W. Howe, *Franklin*
Carlton B. Curtis, *Warren*
Alfred Gilmore, *Butler*

## RHODE ISLAND

SENATORS

John H. Clarke, *Providence*
Charles T. James, *Providence*

REPRESENTATIVES

George G. King, *Newport*
Benjamin B. Thurston, *Hopkinton*

## SOUTH CAROLINA

SENATORS

Andrew P. Butler, *Edgefield*
R. Barnwell Rhett,[39] *Charleston*
William F. De Saussure,[40] *Columbia*

REPRESENTATIVES

Daniel Wallace, *Jonesville*
James L. Orr, *Anderson*
Joseph A. Woodward, *Winnsboro*
John McQueen, *Bennettsville*
Armistead Burt, *Willington*
William Aiken, *Charleston*
William F. Colcock, *Grahamville*

## TENNESSEE

SENATORS

John Bell, *Nashville*
James C. Jones, *Memphis*

REPRESENTATIVES

Andrew Johnson, *Greeneville*
Albert G. Watkins, *Panther Springs*
William M. Churchwell, *Knoxville*
John H. Savage, *Smithville*
George W. Jones, *Fayetteville*
William H. Polk, *Columbia*
Meredith P. Gentry, *Franklin*
William Cullom, *Carthage*
Isham G. Harris, *Paris*
Frederick P. Stanton, *Memphis*
Christopher H. Williams, *Lexington*

---

[35] Resigned January 10, 1853; vacancy in this class during remainder of the Congress.
[36] Died January 29, 1853.
[37] Elected for term beginning March 4, 1851, and

took his seat December 1, 1851; vacancy in this class from March 4 to 14, 1851.
[38] Election unsuccessfully contested by Hendrick B. Wright.

[39] Resigned May 7, 1852.
[40] Appointed to fill vacancy caused by resignation of R. Barnwell Rhett, and took his seat May 24, 1852; subsequently elected.

## TEXAS

### SENATORS

Sam Houston, *Huntsville*
Thomas J. Rusk, *Nacogdoches*

### REPRESENTATIVES

Richardson Scurry, *Clarksville*
Volney E. Howard, *San Antonio*

## VERMONT

### SENATORS

William Upham,[41] *Montpelier*
Samuel S. Phelps,[42] *Middlebury*
Solomon Foot, *Rutland*

### REPRESENTATIVES

Ahiman L. Miner, *Manchester*
William Hebard, *Chelsea*
James Meacham, *Middlebury*
Thomas Bartlett, Jr., *Lyndon*

## VIRGINIA

### SENATORS

James M. Mason, *Winchester*
Robert M. T. Hunter, *Lloyds*

### REPRESENTATIVES

John S. Millson, *Norfolk*
Richard K. Meade, *Petersburg*
Thomas H. Averett, *Halifax*
Thomas S. Bocock, *Appomattox*
Paulus Powell, *Amherst*
John S. Caskie, *Richmond*
Thomas H. Bayly, *Accomac*
Alexander R. Holladay, *Mansfield*
James F. Strother, *Rappahannock*
Charles J. Faulkner, *Martinsburg*
John Letcher, *Lexington*
Henry A. Edmundson, *Salem*
Fayette McMullen, *Rye Cove*
James M. H. Beale, *Point Pleasant*
George W. Thompson,[43] *Wheeling*
Sherrard Clemens,[44] *Wheeling*

## WISCONSIN

### SENATORS

Henry Dodge, *Dodgeville*
Isaac P. Walker, *Milwaukee*

### REPRESENTATIVES

Charles Durkee, *Kenosha*
Ben C. Eastman, *Platteville*
James Duane Doty, *Menasha*

## TERRITORY OF MINNESOTA

### DELEGATE

Henry H. Sibley, *Mendota*

## TERRITORY OF NEW MEXICO[45]

### DELEGATE

Richard H. Weightman,[46] *Santa Fe*

## TERRITORY OF OREGON

### DELEGATE

Joseph Lane, *Oregon City*

## TERRITORY OF UTAH[47]

### DELEGATE

John M. Bernhisel,[48] *Salt Lake City*

---

[41] Died January 14, 1853.
[42] Appointed to fill vacancy caused by death of William Upham, and took his seat January 19, 1853.
[43] Resigned July 30, 1852.
[44] Elected to fill vacancy caused by resignation of George W. Thompson, and took his seat December 6, 1852.
[45] Formed from a portion of the territory ceded to the United States by Mexico by the treaty of Guadalupe Hidalgo of February 2, 1848, and granted a Delegate in Congress by act of September 9, 1850. Hugh N. Smith presented credentials February 4, 1850, in the preceding Congress, but was not admitted to a seat; the committee on elections held that no territorial government existed and the matter was laid on the table.

[46] Took his seat December 1, 1851.
[47] Formed from a portion of the territory ceded to the United States by Mexico by the treaty of Guadalupe Hidalgo of February 2, 1848, and granted a Delegate in Congress by act of September 9, 1850.
[48] Took his seat December 1, 1851.

# 33RD CONGRESS

## MARCH 4, 1853, TO MARCH 3, 1855

William R. King
Vice President

FIRST SESSION— *December 5, 1853, to August 7, 1854*
SECOND SESSION— *December 4, 1854, to March 3, 1855*
SPECIAL SESSION OF THE SENATE— *March 4, 1853, to April 11, 1853*

VICE PRESIDENT OF THE UNITED STATES— WILLIAM R. KING,[1] of Alabama
PRESIDENT PRO TEMPORE OF THE SENATE— DAVID R. ATCHISON,[2] of Missouri; LEWIS CASS,[3] of Michigan; JESSE D. BRIGHT,[4] of Indiana
SECRETARY OF THE SENATE— ASBURY DICKENS, of North Carolina
SERGEANT AT ARMS OF THE SENATE— ROBERT BEALE, of Virginia; DUNNING R. McNAIR,[5] of Pennsylvania

SPEAKER OF THE HOUSE OF REPRESENTATIVES— LINN BOYD,[6] of Kentucky
CLERK OF THE HOUSE— JOHN W. FORNEY,[7] of Pennsylvania
SERGEANT AT ARMS OF THE HOUSE— ADAM J. GLOSSBRENNER, of Pennsylvania
DOORKEEPER OF THE HOUSE— Z. W. McKNEW, of Maryland

Linn Boyd
Speaker

## ALABAMA

### SENATORS

Benjamin Fitzpatrick, *Wetumpka*
Clement C. Clay, Jr.,[8] *Huntsville*

### REPRESENTATIVES

Philip Phillips, *Mobile*
James Abercrombie, *Girard*
Sampson W. Harris, *Wetumpka*
William R. Smith, *Fayette*
George S. Houston, *Athens*
Williamson R. W. Cobb, *Bellefonte*
James F. Dowdell, *Chambers*

## ARKANSAS

### SENATORS

William K. Sebastian, *Helena*
Solon Borland,[9] *Hot Springs*
Robert W. Johnson,[10] *Little Rock*

### REPRESENTATIVES

Alfred B. Greenwood, *Bentonville*
Edward A. Warren, *Camden*

## CALIFORNIA

### SENATORS

William M. Gwin, *San Francisco*
John B. Weller, *San Francisco*

### REPRESENTATIVES AT LARGE

Milton S. Latham, *Sacramento*
James A. McDougall, *San Francisco*

## CONNECTICUT

### SENATORS

Truman Smith,[11] *Litchfield*
Francis Gillette,[12] *Hartford*
Isaac Toucey, *Hartford*

### REPRESENTATIVES

James T. Pratt, *Rockyhill*
Colin M. Ingersoll, *New Haven*
Nathan Belcher, *New London*
Origen S. Seymour, *Litchfield*

## DELAWARE

### SENATORS

James A. Bayard, *Wilmington*
John M. Clayton, *Chippewa*

### REPRESENTATIVE AT LARGE

George Read Riddle, *Wilmington*

## FLORIDA

### SENATORS

Jackson Morton, *Pensacola*
Stephen R. Mallory, *Jacksonville*

### REPRESENTATIVE AT LARGE

Augustus E. Maxwell, *Tallahassee*

## GEORGIA

### SENATORS

William C. Dawson, *Greensboro*
Robert Toombs, *Washington*

### REPRESENTATIVES

James L. Seward, *Thomasville*
Alfred H. Colquitt, *Newton*
David J. Bailey, *Jackson*
William B. W. Dent, *Newnan*
Elijah W. Chastain, *Tacoah*
Junius Hillyer, *Monroe*
David A. Reese, *Monticello*
Alexander H. Stephens,
 *Crawfordville*

## ILLINOIS

### SENATORS

Stephen A. Douglas, *Chicago*
James Shields, *Belleville*

### REPRESENTATIVES

Elihu B. Washburne, *Galena*
John Wentworth, *Chicago*
Jesse O. Norton, *Joliet*
James Knox, *Knoxville*
William A. Richardson, *Quincy*
Richard Yates, *Jacksonville*
James C. Allen, *Palestine*
William H. Bissell, *Belleville*
Willis Allen, *Marion*

## INDIANA

### SENATORS

Jesse D. Bright, *Madison*
John Pettit, *Lafayette*

### REPRESENTATIVES

Smith Miller, *Patoka*
William H. English, *Lexington*

---

[1] Died April 18, 1853, after taking the oath of office in Havana, Cuba, a privilege accorded by special act of Congress.
[2] Elected March 4, 1853.
[3] Elected December 4, 1854, for one day only.
[4] Elected December 5, 1854.
[5] Elected March 17, 1853.

[6] Reelected December 5, 1853.
[7] Reelected December 5, 1853.
[8] Elected for term beginning March 4, 1853, and took his seat December 14, 1853; vacancy in this class from March 4, 1853, to November 28, 1853.
[9] Resigned April 3, 1853, to become minister to Nicaragua and the other Central American Republics.

[10] Appointed to fill vacancy caused by resignation of Solon Borland, and took his seat December 5, 1853; subsequently elected.
[11] Resigned, effective May 24, 1854.
[12] Elected to fill vacancy caused by resignation of Truman Smith, and took his seat May 25, 1854.

## INDIANA—Continued

### REPRESENTATIVES—CONTINUED

Cyrus L. Dunham, *Salem*
James H. Lane, *Lawrenceburg*
Samuel W. Parker, *Connersville*
Thomas A. Hendricks, *Shelbyville*
John G. Davis, *Rockville*
Daniel Mace, *Lafayette*
Norman Eddy, *South Bend*
Ebenezer M. Chamberlain, *Goshen*
Andrew J. Harlan, *Marion*

## IOWA

### SENATORS

Augustus C. Dodge, *Burlington*
George W. Jones, *Dubuque*

### REPRESENTATIVES

Bernhart Henn, *Fairfield*
John P. Cook, *Davenport*

## KENTUCKY

### SENATORS

Archibald Dixon, *Henderson*
John B. Thompson, *Harrodsburg*

### REPRESENTATIVES

Linn Boyd, *Paducah*
Benjamin E. Grey, *Hopkinsville*
Presley U. Ewing,[13] *Russellville*
Francis M. Bristow,[14] *Elkton*
James S. Chrisman, *Monticello*
Clement S. Hill, *Lebanon*
John M. Elliott, *Prestonburg*
William Preston, *Louisville*
John C. Breckinridge, *Lexington*
Leander M. Cox, *Flemingsburg*
Richard H. Stanton, *Maysville*

## LOUISIANA

### SENATORS

Pierre Soulé,[15] *New Orleans*
John Slidell,[16] *New Orleans*
Judah P. Benjamin, *New Orleans*

### REPRESENTATIVES

William Dunbar, *New Orleans*
Theodore G. Hunt, *New Orleans*
John Perkins, Jr., *Ashwood*
Roland Jones, *Shreveport*

## MAINE

### SENATORS

Hannibal Hamlin, *Hampden*
William Pitt Fessenden,[17] *Portland*

### REPRESENTATIVES

Moses Macdonald, *Portland*
Samuel Mayall, *Gray*
E. Wilder Farley, *Newcastle*
Samuel P. Benson, *Winthrop*
Israel Washburn, Jr., *Orono*
Thomas J. D. Fuller, *Calais*

## MARYLAND

### SENATORS

James A. Pearce, *Chestertown*
Thomas G. Pratt, *Annapolis*

### REPRESENTATIVES

John R. Franklin, *Snow Hill*
Jacob Shower, *Manchester*
Joshua Vansant, *Baltimore*
Henry May, *Baltimore*
William T. Hamilton, *Hagerstown*
Augustus R. Sollers, *Prince Frederick*

## MASSACHUSETTS

### SENATORS

Charles Sumner, *Boston*
Edward Everett,[18] *Boston*
Julius Rockwell,[19] *Pittsfield*
Henry Wilson,[20] *Natick*

### REPRESENTATIVES

Zeno Scudder,[21] *Barnstable*
Thomas D. Eliot,[22] *New Bedford*
Samuel L. Crocker, *Taunton*
J. Wiley Edmands, *Lawrence*
Samuel H. Walley, *Roxbury*
William Appleton, *Boston*
Charles W. Upham, *Salem*
Nathaniel P. Banks, *Waltham*
Tappan Wentworth, *Lowell*
Alexander De Witt, *Oxford*
Edward Dickinson, *Amherst*
John Z. Goodrich, *Glendale*

## MICHIGAN

### SENATORS

Lewis Cass, *Detroit*
Charles E. Stuart, *Kalamazoo*

### REPRESENTATIVES

David Stuart, *Detroit*
David A. Noble, *Monroe*
Samuel Clarke, *Kalamazoo*

Hestor L. Stevens, *Pontiac*

## MISSISSIPPI

### SENATORS

Stephen Adams, *Aberdeen*
Albert G. Brown,[23] *Newton*

### REPRESENTATIVE AT LARGE

William Barksdale, *Columbus*

### REPRESENTATIVES

Daniel B. Wright, *Salem*
William T. S. Barry, *Greenwood*
Otho R. Singleton, *Canton*
Wiley P. Harris, *Monticello*

## MISSOURI

### SENATORS

David R. Atchison, *Platte City*
Henry S. Geyer, *St. Louis*

### REPRESENTATIVES

Thomas Hart Benton, *St. Louis*
Alfred W. Lamb, *Hannibal*
James J. Lindley, *Monticello*
Mordecai Oliver, *Richmond*
John G. Miller, *Boonville*
John S. Phelps, *Springfield*
Samuel Caruthers, *Cape Girardeau*

## NEW HAMPSHIRE

### SENATORS

Moses Norris, Jr.,[24] *Manchester*
John S. Wells,[25] *Exeter*
Charles G. Atherton,[26] *Nashua*
Jared W. Williams,[27] *Lancaster*

### REPRESENTATIVES

George W. Kittredge, *Newmarket*
George W. Morrison, *Manchester*
Harry Hibbard, *Bath*

## NEW JERSEY

### SENATORS

John R. Thomson,[28] *Princeton*
William Wright, *Newark*

### REPRESENTATIVES

Nathan T. Stratton, *Mullica Hill*
Charles Skelton, *Trenton*
Samuel Lilly, *Lambertville*
George Vail, *Morristown*
Alexander C. M. Pennington, *Newark*

---

[13] Died September 27, 1854.

[14] Elected to fill vacancy caused by death of Presley U. Ewing, and took his seat December 4, 1854.

[15] Resigned April 11, 1853.

[16] Elected to fill vacancy caused by resignation of Pierre Soulé, and took his seat December 5, 1853.

[17] Elected for the term beginning March 4, 1853, and took his seat February 23, 1854; vacancy in this class from March 4, 1853, to February 10, 1854.

[18] Resigned, effective June 1, 1854.

[19] Appointed to fill vacancy caused by resignation

of Edward Everett, and took his seat June 15, 1854.

[20] Elected to fill vacancy caused by resignation of Edward Everett, and took his seat February 10, 1855.

[21] Resigned March 4, 1854.

[22] Elected to fill vacancy caused by resignation of Zeno Scudder, and took his seat April 17, 1854.

[23] Elected for the term beginning March 4, 1853; took his seat January 26, 1854; vacancy in this class from March 4, 1853, to January 7, 1854.

[24] Died January 11, 1855.

[25] Appointed to fill vacancy caused by death of

Moses Norris, Jr., and took his seat January 22, 1855.

[26] Died November 15, 1853.

[27] Appointed to fill vacancy caused by death of Charles G. Atherton, and took his seat December 12, 1853; by resolution, August 3, 1854, Senate declared representation under the appointment had expired. (See U.S. Senate Election, Expulsion and Censure Cases, 1793-1990, Senate Document 103-33, pp. 69-70.)

[28] Elected to fill vacancy caused by resignation of Robert F. Stockton, in preceding Congress, and took his seat March 4, 1853.

## NEW YORK

### SENATORS

William H. Seward, *Auburn*
Hamilton Fish, *New York City*

### REPRESENTATIVES

James Maurice, *Maspeth*
Thomas W. Cumming, *Brooklyn*
Hiram Walbridge, *New York City*
Mike Walsh, *New York City*
William M. Tweed, *New York City*
John Wheeler, *New York City*
William A. Walker, *New York City*
Francis B. Cutting, *New York City*
Jared V. Peck, *Port Chester*
William Murray, *Goshen*
Theodore R. Westbrook, *Kingston*
Gilbert Dean,[29] *Poughkeepsie*
Isaac Teller,[30] *Mattawan*
Russell Sage, *Troy*
Rufus W. Peckham, *Albany*
Charles Hughes, *Sandy Hill*
George A. Simmons, *Keeseville*
Bishop Perkins, *Ogdensburg*
Peter Rowe, *Schenectady*
George W. Chase, *Schenevus*
Orsamus B. Matteson, *Utica*
Henry Bennett, *New Berlin*
Gerrit Smith,[31] *Petersboro*
Henry C. Goodwin,[32] *Hamilton*
Caleb Lyon, *Lyonsdale*
Daniel T. Jones, *Baldwinsville*
Edwin B. Morgan, *Aurora*
Andrew Oliver, *Penn Yan*
John J. Taylor, *Owego*
George Hastings, *Mount Morris*
Azariah Boody,[33] *Rochester*
Davis Carpenter,[34] *Brockport*
Benjamin Pringle, *Batavia*
Thomas T. Flagler, *Lockport*
Solomon G. Haven, *Buffalo*
Reuben E. Fenton, *Frewsburg*

## NORTH CAROLINA

### SENATORS

George E. Badger, *Raleigh*
David S. Reid,[35] *Wentworth*

### REPRESENTATIVES

Henry M. Shaw, *Indian Town*
Thomas Ruffin, *Goldsboro*
William S. Ashe, *Wilmington*
Sion H. Rogers, *Raleigh*
John Kerr, Jr., *Yanceyville*
Richard C. Puryear, *Huntsville*
F. Burton Craige, *Salisbury*
Thomas L. Clingman, *Asheville*

## OHIO

### SENATORS

Salmon P. Chase, *Cincinnati*
Benjamin F. Wade, *Jefferson*

### REPRESENTATIVES

David T. Disney, *Cincinnati*
John Scott Harrison, *Cleves*
Lewis D. Campbell, *Hamilton*
Matthias H. Nichols, *Lima*
Alfred P. Edgerton, *Hicksville*
Andrew Ellison, *Georgetown*
Aaron Harlan, *Yellow Springs*
Moses B. Corwin, *Urbana*
Frederick W. Green, *Tiffin*
John L. Taylor, *Chillicothe*
Thomas Ritchey, *Somerset*
Edson B. Olds, *Circleville*
William D. Lindsley, *Sandusky*
Harvey H. Johnson, *Ashland*
William R. Sapp, *Mount Vernon*
Edward Ball, *Zanesville*
Wilson Shannon, *St. Clairsville*
George Bliss, *Akron*
Edward Wade, *Cleveland*
Joshua R. Giddings, *Jefferson*
Andrew Stuart, *Steubenville*

## PENNSYLVANIA

### SENATORS

James Cooper, *Pottsville*
Richard Brodhead, *Easton*

### REPRESENTATIVES

Thomas B. Florence, *Philadelphia*
Joseph R. Chandler, *Philadelphia*
John Robbins, Jr., *Kensington*
William H. Witte, *Richmond*
John McNair, *Norristown*
William Everhart, *West Chester*
Samuel A. Bridges, *Allentown*
Henry A. Muhlenberg,[36] *Berks*
J. Glancy Jones,[37] *Reading*
Isaac E. Hiester, *Lancaster*
Ner Middleswarth, *Beavertown*
Christian M. Straub, *Pottsville*
Hendrick B. Wright, *Wilkes-Barre*
Asa Packer, *Mauch Chunk*
Galusha A. Grow, *Glenwood*
James Gamble, *Jersey Shore*
Carlton B. Curtis, *Warren*
Samuel L. Russell, *Bedford*
John McCulloch, *Shavers Creek*
Augustus Drum, *Indiana*
John L. Dawson, *Brownsville*
David Ritchie, *Pittsburgh*

Thomas M. Howe, *Allegheny City*
Michael C. Trout, *Sharon*
John Dick, *Meadville*
William H. Kurtz, *York*

## RHODE ISLAND

### SENATORS

Charles T. James, *Providence*
Philip Allen,[38] *Providence*

### REPRESENTATIVES

Thomas Davis, *Providence*
Benjamin B. Thurston, *Hopkinton*

## SOUTH CAROLINA

### SENATORS

Andrew P. Butler, *Edgefield*
Josiah J. Evans, *Society Hill*

### REPRESENTATIVES

John McQueen, *Marlboro*
William Aiken, *Charleston*
Laurence M. Keitt, *Orangeburg*
Preston S. Brooks, *Ninety Six*
James L. Orr, *Anderson*
William W. Boyce, *Winnsboro*

## TENNESSEE

### SENATORS

John Bell, *Nashville*
James C. Jones, *Memphis*

### REPRESENTATIVES

Brookins Campbell,[39] *Washington College*
Nathaniel G. Taylor,[40] *Happy Valley*
William M. Churchwell, *Knoxville*
Samuel A. Smith, *Charleston*
William Cullom, *Carthage*
Charles Ready, *Murfreesboro*
George W. Jones, *Fayetteville*
Robert M. Bugg, *Lynnville*
Felix K. Zollicoffer, *Nashville*
Emerson Etheridge, *Dresden*
Frederick P. Stanton, *Memphis*

## TEXAS

### SENATORS

Sam Houston, *Huntsville*
Thomas J. Rusk, *Nacogdoches*

### REPRESENTATIVES

George W. Smyth, *Jasper*
Peter H. Bell, *Austin*

---

[29] Resigned July 3, 1854.
[30] Elected to fill vacancy caused by resignation of Gilbert Dean, and took his seat December 4, 1854.
[31] Resigned August 7, 1854.
[32] Elected to fill vacancy caused by resignation of Gerrit Smith, and took his seat December 4, 1854.
[33] Resigned in October, 1853, before Congress assembled.
[34] Elected to fill vacancy caused by resignation of

Azariah Boody, and took his seat December 5, 1853.
[35] Elected for the term beginning March 4, 1853, and took his seat December 11, 1854; vacancy in this class from March 4, 1853, to December 6, 1854.
[36] Died January 9, 1854.
[37] Elected to fill vacancy caused by death of Henry A. Muhlenberg, and took his seat February 13, 1854.
[38] Elected on May 4, 1853, for the term beginning March 4, 1853, and took his seat December 5, 1853;

vacancy in this class from March 4, 1853, to July 20, 1853.
[39] Died December 25, 1853, never having qualified owing to illness.
[40] Elected to fill vacancy caused by death of Brookins Campbell, December 25, 1853, who did not qualify and took his seat March 30, 1854.

## VERMONT

### SENATORS

Solomon Foot, *Rutland*
Samuel S. Phelps,[41] *Middlebury*
Lawrence Brainerd,[42] *St. Albans*

### REPRESENTATIVES

James Meacham, *Middlebury*
Andrew Tracy, *Woodstock*
Alvah Sabin, *Georgia*

## VIRGINIA

### SENATORS

James M. Mason, *Winchester*
Robert M. T. Hunter, *Lloyds*

### REPRESENTATIVES

Thomas H. Bayly, *Accomac*
John S. Millson, *Norfolk*
John S. Caskie, *Richmond*
William O. Goode, *Boydton*
Thomas S. Bocock, *Appomattox*
Paulus Powell, *Amherst*
William Smith, *Warrenton*
Charles J. Faulkner, *Martinsburg*
John Letcher, *Lexington*
Zedekiah Kidwell, *Fairmont*
John F. Snodgrass,[43] *Parkersburg*

Charles S. Lewis,[44] *Clarksburg*
Henry A. Edmundson, *Salem*
Fayette McMullen, *Rye Cove*

## WISCONSIN

### SENATORS

Henry Dodge, *Dodgeville*
Isaac P. Walker, *Milwaukee*

### REPRESENTATIVES

Daniel Wells, Jr., *Milwaukee*
Ben C. Eastman, *Platteville*
John B. Macy, *Fond du Lac*

## TERRITORY OF KANSAS[45]

### DELEGATE

John W. Whitfield,[46] *Tecumseh*

## TERRITORY OF MINNESOTA

### DELEGATE

Henry M. Rice, *St. Paul*

## TERRITORY OF NEBRASKA[47]

### DELEGATE

Napoleon B. Giddings,[48] *Nebraska City*

## TERRITORY OF NEW MEXICO

### DELEGATE

José Manuel Gallegos,[49] *Albuquerque*

## TERRITORY OF OREGON[50]

### DELEGATE

Joseph Lane, *Winchester*

## TERRITORY OF UTAH

### DELEGATE

John M. Bernhisel, *Salt Lake City*

## TERRITORY OF WASHINGTON[51]

### DELEGATE

Columbia Lancaster,[52] *St. Helena*

---

[41] Appointed, in preceding Congress, to fill vacancy, caused by death of William Upham; by resolution of Senate of March 16, 1854, declared not entitled to retain his seat. (See U.S. Senate Election, Expulsion and Censure Cases, 1793-1990, Senate Document 103-33, pp. 67-68.)

[42] Elected to fill vacancy caused by death of William Upham, in preceding Congress, and took his seat December 4, 1854; vacancy in this class from March 17, 1854, to October 13, 1854.

[43] Died June 5, 1854.

[44] Elected to fill vacancy caused by death of John

F. Snodgrass, and took his seat December 4, 1854.

[45] Formed from territory ceded to the United States by France by the treaty of Paris of April 30, 1803, and by the State of Texas, in the settlement of her boundaries in 1850; erected into a Territorial government and granted a Delegate in Congress by act of May 30, 1854.

[46] Took his seat December 20, 1854.

[47] Formed from a portion of the territory ceded to the United States by France by the treaty of April 30, 1803, and granted a Delegate in Congress by act of May 30, 1854.

[48] Took his seat January 5, 1855.

[49] Election unsuccessfully contested by William Carr Lane.

[50] The Territory of Washington was formed from a portion of the Territory of Oregon by act of March 2, 1853.

[51] Formed March 2, 1853, from a portion of the Territory of Oregon, and granted a Delegate in Congress.

[52] Took his seat April 12, 1854.

# 34TH CONGRESS

## MARCH 4, 1855, TO MARCH 3, 1857

Jesse D. Bright
President Pro Tempore

Nathaniel P. Banks
Speaker

FIRST SESSION— *December 3, 1855, to August 18, 1856*
SECOND SESSION— *August 21, 1856, to August 30, 1856*
THIRD SESSION— *December 1, 1856, to March 3, 1857*

---

VICE PRESIDENT OF THE UNITED STATES[1]
PRESIDENT PRO TEMPORE OF THE SENATE— JESSE D. BRIGHT,[2] of Indiana; CHARLES E. STUART,[3] of Michigan; JAMES M. MASON,[4] of Virginia
SECRETARY OF THE SENATE— ASBURY DICKENS, of North Carolina
SERGEANT AT ARMS OF THE SENATE— DUNNING R. McNAIR, of Pennsylvania

---

SPEAKER OF THE HOUSE OF REPRESENTATIVES— NATHANIEL P. BANKS,[5] of Massachusetts
CLERK OF THE HOUSE— JOHN W. FORNEY, of Pennsylvania; WILLIAM CULLOM,[6] of Tennessee
SERGEANT AT ARMS OF THE HOUSE— ADAM J. GLOSSBRENNER, of Pennsylvania
DOORKEEPER OF THE HOUSE— NATHAN DARLING, of New York

## ALABAMA

### SENATORS

Clement C. Clay, Jr., *Huntsville*
Benjamin Fitzpatrick,[7] *Wetumpka*

### REPRESENTATIVES

Percy Walker, *Mobile*
Eli S. Shorter, *Eufaula*
James F. Dowdell, *Chambers*
William R. Smith, *Fayette*
George S. Houston, *Athens*
Williamson R. W. Cobb, *Bellefonte*
Sampson W. Harris, *Wetumpka*

## ARKANSAS

### SENATORS

William K. Sebastian, *Helena*
Robert W. Johnson, *Pine Bluff*

### REPRESENTATIVES

Alfred B. Greenwood, *Bentonville*
Albert Rust, *El Dorado*

## CALIFORNIA

### SENATORS

John B. Weller, *San Francisco*
William M. Gwin,[8] *San Francisco*

### REPRESENTATIVES AT LARGE

James W. Denver, *Weaverville*
Philemon T. Herbert, *Mariposa City*

## CONNECTICUT

### SENATORS

Isaac Toucey, *Hartford*
Lafayette S. Foster, *Norwich*

### REPRESENTATIVES

Ezra Clark, Jr., *Hartford*
John Woodruff, *New Haven*
Sidney Dean, *Putnam*
William W. Welch, *Norfolk*

## DELAWARE

### SENATORS

James A. Bayard, *Wilmington*
John M. Clayton,[9] *Chippewa*
Joseph P. Comegys,[10] *Dover*
Martin W. Bates,[11] *Dover*

### REPRESENTATIVE AT LARGE

Elisha D. Cullen, *Georgetown*

## FLORIDA

### SENATORS

Stephen R. Mallory, *Key West*
David Levy Yulee, *Homasassa*

### REPRESENTATIVE AT LARGE

Augustus E. Maxwell, *Tallahassee*

## GEORGIA

### SENATORS

Robert Toombs, *Washington*
Alfred Iverson, *Columbus*

### REPRESENTATIVES

James L. Seward, *Thomasville*
Martin J. Crawford, *Columbus*
Robert P. Trippe, *Forsyth*
Hiram Warner, *Greenville*
John H. Lumpkin, *Rome*
Howell Cobb, *Athens*
Nathaniel G. Foster, *Madison*
Alexander H. Stephens, *Crawfordville*

## ILLINOIS

### SENATORS

Stephen A. Douglas, *Chicago*
Lyman Trumbull, *Alton*

### REPRESENTATIVES

Elihu B. Washburne, *Galena*
James H. Woodworth, *Chicago*
Jesse O. Norton, *Joliet*
James Knox, *Knoxville*
William A. Richardson,[12] *Quincy*
Jacob C. Davis,[13] *Warsaw*
Thomas L. Harris, *Petersburg*
James C. Allen,[14] *Palestine*

---

[1] Vice President William R. King died in preceding Congress.

[2] Continued from preceding Congress; again elected June 11, 1856.

[3] Served June 5, 1856; elected June 9, 1856; resigned June 11, 1856.

[4] Served January 5, 1856; elected January 6, 1857.

[5] Elected February 2, 1856, upon the one hundred and thirty-third viva voce vote and the fourth vote under a plurality resolution adopted that day.

[6] Elected February 4, 1856.

[7] Elected for term beginning March 4, 1855, and took his seat December 3, 1855; vacancy in this class from March 4, 1855, to December 2, 1855.

[8] Elected for the term beginning March 4, 1855, and took his seat February 16, 1857; vacancy in this class from March 4, 1855, to January 12, 1857.

[9] Died November 9, 1856.

[10] Appointed to fill vacancy caused by death of John M. Clayton, and took his seat December 4, 1856.

[11] Elected January 14, 1857, to fill vacancy caused by death of John M. Clayton, but did not take his seat until March 4, 1857.

[12] Resigned August 25, 1856.

[13] Elected to fill vacancy caused by resignation of William A. Richardson, and took his seat December 4, 1856.

[14] Election contested by William B. Archer, and seat declared vacant July 18, 1856; subsequently elected, and took his seat December 1, 1856.

## ILLINOIS—Continued

REPRESENTATIVES—CONTINUED

James L. D. Morrison,[15] *Belleville*
Samuel S. Marshall,[16] *McLeansboro*

## INDIANA

SENATORS

Jesse D. Bright, *Madison*
Graham N. Fitch,[17] *Logansport*

REPRESENTATIVES

Smith Miller, *Patoka*
William H. English, *Lexington*
George G. Dunn, *Bedford*
William Cumback, *Greensburg*
David P. Holloway, *Richmond*
Lucien Barbour, *Indianapolis*
Harvey D. Scott, *Terre Haute*
Daniel Mace, *Lafayette*
Schuyler Colfax, *South Bend*
Samuel Brenton, *Fort Wayne*
John U. Pettit, *Wabash*

## IOWA

SENATORS

George W. Jones, *Dubuque*
James Harlan,[18] *Mount Pleasant*

REPRESENTATIVES

Augustus Hall,[19] *Keosauqua*
James Thorington, *Davenport*

## KENTUCKY

SENATORS

John B. Thompson, *Harrodsburg*
John J. Crittenden, *Frankfort*

REPRESENTATIVES

Henry C. Burnett, *Cadiz*
John P. Campbell, *Belleview*
Warner L. Underwood, *Bowling Green*
Albert G. Talbott, *Danville*
Joshua H. Jewett, *Elizabethtown*
John M. Elliott, *Prestonburg*
Humphrey Marshall, *Springport*
Alexander K. Marshall, *Nicholasville*
Leander M. Cox, *Flemingsburg*
Samuel F. Swope, *Falmouth*

## LOUISIANA

SENATORS

Judah P. Benjamin, *New Orleans*
John Slidell, *New Orleans*

REPRESENTATIVES

George Eustis, Jr.,[20] *New Orleans*
Miles Taylor, *Donaldsonville*
Thomas G. Davidson, *East Feliciana*
John M. Sandidge, *Pineville*

## MAINE

SENATORS

Hannibal Hamlin,[21] *Hampden*
Amos Nourse,[22] *Bath*
William Pitt Fessenden, *Portland*

REPRESENTATIVES

John M. Wood, *Portland*
John J. Perry, *Oxford*
Ebenezer Knowlton, *South Montville*
Samuel P. Benson, *Winthrop*
Israel Washburn, Jr., *Orono*
Thomas J. D. Fuller,[23] *Calais*

## MARYLAND

SENATORS

James A. Pearce, *Chestertown*
Thomas G. Pratt, *Annapolis*

REPRESENTATIVES

James A. Stewart, *Cambridge*
James B. Ricaud, *Chestertown*
J. Morrison Harris, *Baltimore*
H. Winter Davis, *Baltimore*
Henry W. Hoffman, *Cumberland*
Thomas F. Bowie, *Upper Marlboro*

## MASSACHUSETTS

SENATORS

Charles Sumner, *Boston*
Henry Wilson, *Natick*

REPRESENTATIVES

Robert B. Hall, *Plymouth*
James Buffington, *Fall River*
William S. Damrell, *Dedham*
Linus B. Comins, *Roxbury*
Anson Burlingame, *Cambridge*
Timothy Davis, *Gloucester*
Nathaniel P. Banks, *Waltham*
Chauncey L. Knapp, *Lowell*

Alexander De Witt, *Oxford*
Calvin C. Chaffee, *Springfield*
Mark Trafton, *Westfield*

## MICHIGAN

SENATORS

Lewis Cass, *Detroit*
Charles E. Stuart, *Kalamazoo*

REPRESENTATIVES

William A. Howard, *Detroit*
Henry Waldron, *Hillsdale*
David S. Walbridge, *Kalamazoo*
George W. Peck, *Lansing*

## MISSISSIPPI

SENATORS

Stephen Adams, *Aberdeen*
Albert G. Brown, *Newton*

REPRESENTATIVES

Daniel B. Wright, *Salem*
Hendley S. Bennett, *Grenada*
William Barksdale, *Columbus*
William A. Lake, *Vicksburg*
John A. Quitman, *Natchez*

## MISSOURI

SENATORS

Henry S. Geyer, *St. Louis*
James S. Green,[24] *Canton*

REPRESENTATIVES

Luther M. Kennett, *St. Louis*
Gilchrist Porter, *Hannibal*
James J. Lindley, *Monticello*
Mordecai Oliver, *Richmond*
John G. Miller,[25] *Boonville*
Thomas P. Akers,[26] *Lexington*
John S. Phelps, *Springfield*
Samuel Caruthers, *Cape Girardeau*

## NEW HAMPSHIRE

SENATORS

John P. Hale,[27] *Dover*
James Bell,[28] *Laconia*

REPRESENTATIVES

James Pike, *South Newmarket*
Mason W. Tappan, *Bradford*
Aaron H. Cragin, *Lebanon*

---

[15] Elected to fill vacancy caused by resignation of Representative-elect Lyman Trumbull, who was elected Senator before the beginning of the Congress, and took his seat December 1, 1856. Philip B. Fouke claimed the seat, contesting the election of Lyman Trumbull, but the House, on April 10, 1856, decided Fouke was not entitled to it, and, since Trumbull had been elected to the Senate, the seat remained vacant until the election of Morrison.

[16] Election unsuccessfully contested by L. Jay S. Turney.

[17] Elected for the term beginning March 4, 1855, and took his seat February 9, 1857; vacancy in this class from March 4, 1855, to February 3, 1857.

[18] Seat declared vacant by resolution, January 12,

1857; subsequently elected, and took his seat January 29, 1857. (See U.S. Senate Election, Expulsion and Censure Cases, 1793-1990, Senate Document 103-33, pp. 74-76.)

[19] Election unsuccessfully contested by R. L. B. Clarke.

[20] Election unsuccessfully contested by Albert Fabre.

[21] Resigned January 7, 1857, having been elected Governor.

[22] Elected to fill vacancy caused by resignation of Hannibal Hamlin, and took his seat January 24, 1857.

[23] Election unsuccessfully contested by James A. Milliken.

[24] Elected for the term beginning March 4, 1855, and took his seat January 21, 1857; vacancy in this class from March 4, 1855, to January 11, 1857.

[25] Died May 11, 1856; never qualified owing to illness.

[26] Elected to fill vacancy caused by death of John G. Miller, and took his seat August 18, 1856.

[27] Elected to fill vacancy caused by death of Charles G. Atherton, in preceding Congress, and took his seat December 4, 1855; vacancy in this class from July 16, 1854, to July 29, 1855.

[28] Elected for the term beginning March 4, 1855, and took his seat December 3, 1855; vacancy in this class from March 4, 1855, to July 29, 1855.

## NEW JERSEY

SENATORS

John R. Thompson, *Princeton*
William Wright, *Newark*

REPRESENTATIVES

Isaiah D. Clawson, *Woodstown*
George R. Robbins, *Hamilton Square*
James Bishop, *New Brunswick*
George Vail, *Morristown*
Alexander C. M. Pennington, *Newark*

## NEW YORK

SENATORS

William H. Seward, *Auburn*
Hamilton Fish, *New York*

REPRESENTATIVES

William W. Valk, *Flushing*
James S. T. Stranahan, *Brooklyn*
Guy R. Pelton, *New York City*
John Kelly, *New York City*
Thomas R. Whitney, *New York City*
John Wheeler, *New York City*
Thomas Child, Jr.,[29] *New York City*
Abram Wakeman, *New York City*
Bayard Clarke, *New York City*
Ambrose S. Murray, *Goshen*
Rufus H. King, *Catskill*
Killian Miller, *Hudson*
Russell Sage, *Troy*
Samuel Dickson, *New Scotland*
Edward Dodd, *Argyle*
George A. Simmons, *Keeseville*
Francis E. Spinner, *Mohawk*
Thomas R. Horton, *Fultonville*
Jonas A. Hughston, *Delhi*
Orsamus B. Matteson,[30] *Utica*
Henry Bennett, *New Berlin*
Andrew Z. McCarty, *Pulaski*
William A. Gilbert,[31] *Adams*
Amos P. Granger, *Syracuse*
Edwin B. Morgan, *Aurora*
Andrew Oliver, *Penn Yan*
John M. Parker, *Owego*
William H. Kelsey, *Geneseo*
John Williams, *Rochester*
Benjamin Pringle, *Batavia*
Thomas T. Flagler, *Lockport*
Solomon G. Haven, *Buffalo*
Francis S. Edwards,[32] *Fredonia*

## NORTH CAROLINA

SENATORS

David S. Reid, *Pleasantville*
Asa Biggs, *Williamston*

REPRESENTATIVES

Robert T. Paine, *Edenton*
Thomas Ruffin, *Goldsboro*
Warren Winslow, *Fayetteville*
Lawrence O'B. Branch, *Raleigh*

Edwin G. Reade, *Roxboro*
Richard C. Puryear, *Huntsville*
F. Burton Craige, *Salisbury*
Thomas L. Clingman, *Asheville*

## OHIO

SENATORS

Benjamin F. Wade, *Jefferson*
George E. Pugh, *Cincinnati*

REPRESENTATIVES

Timothy C. Day, *Cincinnati*
John Scott Harrison, *Cleves*
Lewis D. Campbell, *Hamilton*
Matthias H. Nichols, *Lima*
Richard Mott, *Toledo*
Jonas R. Emrie, *Hillsboro*
Aaron Harlan, *Yellow Springs*
Benjamin Stanton, *Bellefontaine*
Cooper K. Watson, *Tiffin*
Oscar F. Moore, *Portsmouth*
Valentine B. Horton, *Pomeroy*
Samuel Galloway, *Columbus*
John Sherman, *Mansfield*
Philemon Bliss, *Elyria*
William R. Sapp, *Mount Vernon*
Edward Ball, *Zanesville*
Charles J. Albright, *Cambridge*
Benjamin F. Leiter, *Canton*
Edward Wade, *Cleveland*
Joshua R. Giddings, *Jefferson*
John A. Bingham, *Cadiz*

## PENNSYLVANIA

SENATORS

Richard Brodhead, *Easton*
William Bigler,[33] *Philadelphia*

REPRESENTATIVES

Thomas B. Florence, *Philadelphia*
Job R. Tyson, *Philadelphia*
William Millward, *Philadelphia*
Jacob Broom, *Philadelphia*
John Cadwalader, *Philadelphia*
John Hickman, *West Chester*
Samuel C. Bradshaw, *Quakertown*
J. Glancy Jones, *Reading*
Anthony E. Roberts, *Lancaster*
John C. Kunkel, *Harrisburg*
James H. Campbell, *Pottsville*
Henry M. Fuller, *Wilkes-Barre*
Asa Packer, *Mauch Chunk*
Galusha A. Grow, *Glenwood*
John J. Pearce, *Williamsport*
Lemuel Todd, *Carlisle*
David F. Robison, *Chambersburg*
John R. Edie, *Somerset*
John Covode, *Lockport*
Jonathan Knight, *East Bethlehem*

David Ritchie, *Pittsburgh*
Samuel A. Purviance, *Butler*
John Allison, *New Brighton*
David Barclay, *Punxsutawney*
John Dick, *Meadville*

## RHODE ISLAND

SENATORS

Charles T. James, *Providence*
Philip Allen, *Providence*

REPRESENTATIVES

Nathaniel B. Durfee, *Tiverton*
Benjamin B. Thurston, *Hopkinton*

## SOUTH CAROLINA

SENATORS

Andrew P. Butler, *Edgefield*
Josiah J. Evans, *Society Hill*

REPRESENTATIVES

John McQueen, *Marlboro*
William Aiken, *Charleston*
Laurence M. Keitt,[34] *Orangeburg*
Preston S. Brooks,[35] *Ninety Six*
James L. Orr, *Anderson*
William W. Boyce, *Winnsboro*

## TENNESSEE

SENATORS

John Bell, *Nashville*
James C. Jones, *Memphis*

REPRESENTATIVES

Albert G. Watkins, *Panther Springs*
William H. Sneed, *Knoxville*
Samuel A. Smith, *Charleston*
John H. Savage, *Smithville*
Charles Ready, *Murfreesboro*
George W. Jones, *Fayetteville*
John V. Wright, *Purdy*
Felix K. Zollicoffer, *Nashville*
Emerson Etheridge, *Dresden*
Thomas Rivers, *Somerville*

## TEXAS

SENATORS

Sam Houston, *Huntsville*
Thomas J. Rusk, *Nacogdoches*

REPRESENTATIVES

Lemuel D. Evans, *Marshall*
Peter H. Bell, *Austin*

## VERMONT

SENATORS

Solomon Foot, *Rutland*
Jacob Collamer, *Woodstock*

---

[29] Never took his seat owing to prolonged illness.
[30] Resigned February 27, 1857.
[31] Resigned February 28, 1857.
[32] Resigned February 28, 1857.

[33] Elected for term beginning March 4, 1855, and took his seat January 28, 1856; vacancy in this class from March 4, 1855, to January 13, 1856.
[34] Resigned July 16, 1856; subsequently reelected,

and took his seat August 6, 1856.
[35] Resigned July 14, 1856; subsequently reelected and took his seat August 1, 1856; died January 27, 1857.

## VERMONT—Continued
REPRESENTATIVES
James Meacham,[36] *Middlebury*
George T. Hodges,[37] *Rutland*
Justin S. Morrill, *Strafford*
Alvah Sabin, *Georgia*

## VIRGINIA
SENATORS
James M. Mason, *Winchester*
Robert M. T. Hunter, *Lloyds*

REPRESENTATIVES
Thomas H. Bayly,[38] *Accomac*
Muscoe R. H. Garnett,[39] *Lloyds*
John S. Millson, *Norfolk*
John S. Caskie, *Richmond*
William O. Goode, *Boydton*
Thomas S. Bocock, *Appomattox*
Paulus Powell, *Amherst*
William Smith, *Warrenton*
Charles J. Faulkner, *Martinsburg*
John Letcher, *Lexington*
Zedekiah Kidwell, *Fairmont*
John S. Carlile, *Clarksburg*
Henry A. Edmundson, *Salem*
Fayette McMullen, *Rye Cove*

## WISCONSIN
SENATORS
Henry Dodge, *Dodgeville*
Charles Durkee, *Kenosha*

REPRESENTATIVES
Daniel Wells, Jr., *Milwaukee*
Cadwallader C. Washburn, *Mineral Point*
Charles Billingshurst, *Juneau*

## TERRITORY OF KANSAS
DELEGATE
John W. Whitfield,[40] *Tecumseh*

## TERRITORY OF MINNESOTA
DELEGATE
Henry M. Rice, *St. Paul*

## TERRITORY OF NEBRASKA
DELEGATE
Bird B. Chapman,[41] *Omaha City*

## TERRITORY OF NEW MEXICO
DELEGATE
José Manuel Gallegos,[42] *Albuquerque*
Miguel A. Otero,[43] *Albuquerque*

## TERRITORY OF OREGON
DELEGATE
Joseph Lane, *Winchester*

## TERRITORY OF UTAH
DELEGATE
John M. Bernhisel, *Salt Lake City*

## TERRITORY OF WASHINGTON
DELEGATE
J. Patton Anderson, *Olympia*

---

[36] Died August 23, 1856.
[37] Elected to fill vacancy caused by death of James Meacham, and took his seat December 1, 1856.
[38] Died June 23, 1856.
[39] Elected to fill vacancy caused by death of Thomas H. Bayly, and took his seat December 1, 1856.
[40] Presented credentials as a Delegate-elect to the Thirty-fourth Congress and served from March 4,

1855, until August 1, 1856, when the seat was declared vacant, the election having been unsuccessfully contested by Andrew H. Reeder; again elected to the Thirty-fourth Congress to fill vacancy caused by action of the House in declaring the seat vacant, and served from December 9, 1856, until March 3, 1857; this election also was unsuccessfully contested by Andrew H. Reeder.

[41] Election unsuccessfully contested by Hiram P. Bennett.
[42] Served until July 23, 1856; succeeded by Miguel A. Otero, who contested his election.
[43] Successfully contested the election of José Manuel Gallegos, and took his seat July 23, 1856.

# 35TH CONGRESS

MARCH 4, 1857, TO MARCH 3, 1859

John C. Breckinridge
Vice President

FIRST SESSION— *December 7, 1857, to June 14, 1858*
SECOND SESSION— *December 6, 1858, to March 3, 1859*
SPECIAL SESSIONS OF THE SENATE— *March 4, 1857, to March 14, 1857;*
*June 15, 1858, to June 16, 1858*

———————

VICE PRESIDENT OF THE UNITED STATES— JOHN C. BRECKINRIDGE, of Kentucky
PRESIDENT PRO TEMPORE OF THE SENATE— JAMES M. MASON,[1] of Virginia; THOMAS
J. RUSK,[2] of Texas; BENJAMIN FITZPATRICK,[3] of Alabama
SECRETARY OF THE SENATE— ASBURY DICKENS, of North Carolina
SERGEANT AT ARMS OF THE SENATE— DUNNING R. MCNAIR, of Pennsylvania

James L. Orr
Speaker

———————

SPEAKER OF THE HOUSE OF REPRESENTATIVES— JAMES L. ORR,[4] of South Carolina
CLERK OF THE HOUSE— WILLIAM CULLOM, of Tennessee; JAMES C. ALLEN,[5] of Illinois
SERGEANT AT ARMS OF THE HOUSE— ADAM J. GLOSSBRENNER, of Pennsylvania
DOORKEEPER OF THE HOUSE— ROBERT B. HACKNEY, of Virginia

## ALABAMA

### SENATORS

Benjamin Fitzpatrick, *Wetumpka*
Clement C. Clay, Jr., *Huntsville*

### REPRESENTATIVES

James A. Stallworth, *Evergreen*
Eli S. Shorter, *Eufaula*
James F. Dowdell, *Chambers*
Sydenham Moore, *Greensboro*
George S. Houston, *Athens*
Williamson R. W. Cobb, *Bellefonte*
Jabez L. M. Curry, *Talladega*

## ARKANSAS

### SENATORS

William K. Sebastian, *Helena*
Robert W. Johnson, *Pine Bluff*

### REPRESENTATIVES

Alfred B. Greenwood, *Bentonville*
Edward A. Warren, *Camden*

## CALIFORNIA

### SENATORS

William M. Gwin, *San Francisco*
David C. Broderick, *San Francisco*

### REPRESENTATIVES AT LARGE

Joseph C. McKibbin, *Downieville*
Charles L. Scott, *Sonora*

## CONNECTICUT

### SENATORS

Lafayette S. Foster, *Norwich*
James Dixon, *Hartford*

### REPRESENTATIVES

Ezra Clark, Jr., *Hartford*
Samuel Arnold, *Haddam*
Sidney Dean, *Putnam*
William D. Bishop, *Bridgeport*

## DELAWARE

### SENATORS

James A. Bayard, *Wilmington*
Martin W. Bates, *Dover*

### REPRESENTATIVE AT LARGE

William G. Whiteley, *New Castle*

## FLORIDA

### SENATORS

Stephen R. Mallory, *Key West*
David Levy Yulee, *Homasassa*

### REPRESENTATIVE AT LARGE

George S. Hawkins, *Pensacola*

## GEORGIA

### SENATORS

Robert Toombs, *Washington*
Alfred Iverson, *Columbus*

## REPRESENTATIVES

James L. Seward, *Thomasville*
Martin J. Crawford, *Columbus*
Robert P. Trippe, *Forsyth*
Lucius J. Gartrell, *Atlanta*
Augustus R. Wright, *Rome*
James Jackson, *Athens*
Joshua Hill, *Madison*
Alexander H. Stephens,
    *Crawfordville*

## ILLINOIS

### SENATORS

Stephen A. Douglas, *Chicago*
Lyman Trumbull, *Alton*

### REPRESENTATIVES

Elihu B. Washburne, *Galena*
John F. Farnsworth, *Chicago*
Owen Lovejoy, *Princeton*
William Kellogg, *Canton*
Isaac N. Morris, *Quincy*
Thomas L. Harris,[6] *Petersburg*
Charles D. Hodges,[7] *Carrollton*
Aaron Shaw, *Lawrenceville*
Robert Smith, *Alton*
Samuel S. Marshall, *McLeansboro*

## INDIANA

### SENATORS[8]

Jesse D. Bright, *Jeffersonville*
Graham N. Fitch, *Logansport*

---

[1] Elected March 4, 1857 (special session of the Senate).
[2] Elected March 14, 1857 (special session of the Senate).
[3] Elected December 7, 1857; March 29, 1858; June 14, 1858; January 25, 1859.

[4] Elected December 7, 1857.
[5] Elected December 7, 1857.
[6] Died November 24, 1858, before the commencement of the Thirty-sixth Congress, to which he had been reelected.
[7] Elected to fill vacancy caused by death of

Thomas L. Harris, and took his seat January 20, 1859.
[8] A protest of certain members of the legislature was presented, in the preceding Congress, against the legality of the election of both Mr. Fitch and Mr. Bright, setting out "they were not elected by the legislature, but by a convocation of a portion of the members

[155]

## INDIANA—Continued

### REPRESENTATIVES

James Lockhart,[9] *Evansville*
William E. Niblack,[10] *Vincennes*
William H. English, *Lexington*
James Hughes, *Bloomington*
James B. Foley, *Greensburg*
David Kilgore, *Yorktown*
James M. Gregg, *Danville*
John G. Davis, *Rockville*
James Wilson, *Crawfordsville*
Schuyler Colfax, *South Bend*
Samuel Brenton,[11] *Fort Wayne*
Charles Case,[12] *Fort Wayne*
John U. Pettit, *Wabash*

## IOWA

### SENATORS

George W. Jones, *Dubuque*
James Harlan, *Mount Pleasant*

### REPRESENTATIVES

Samuel R. Curtis, *Keokuk*
Timothy Davis, *Dubuque*

## KENTUCKY

### SENATORS

John B. Thompson, *Harrodsburg*
John J. Crittenden, *Frankfort*

### REPRESENTATIVES

Henry C. Burnett, *Cadiz*
Samuel O. Peyton, *Hartford*
Warner L. Underwood, *Bowling Green*
Albert G. Talbott, *Danville*
Joshua H. Jewett, *Elizabethtown*
John M. Elliott, *Prestonburg*
Humphrey Marshall, *Springport*
James B. Clay, *Lexington*
John C. Mason, *Owingsville*
John W. Stevenson, *Covington*

## LOUISIANA

### SENATORS

Judah P. Benjamin, *New Orleans*
John Slidell, *New Orleans*

### REPRESENTATIVES

George Eustis, Jr., *New Orleans*
Miles Taylor, *Donaldsonville*
Thomas G. Davidson, *East Feliciana*
John M. Sandidge, *Pineville*

## MAINE

### SENATORS

William Pitt Fessenden, *Portland*
Hannibal Hamlin, *Hampden*

### REPRESENTATIVES

John M. Wood, *Portland*
Charles J. Gilman, *Brunswick*
Nehemiah Abbott, *Belfast*
Freeman H. Morse, *Bath*
Israel Washburn, Jr., *Orono*
Stephen C. Foster, *Pembroke*

## MARYLAND

### SENATORS

James A. Pearce, *Chestertown*
Anthony Kennedy, *Baltimore*

### REPRESENTATIVES

James A. Stewart, *Cambridge*
James B. Ricaud, *Chestertown*
J. Morrison Harris,[13] *Baltimore*
H. Winter Davis,[14] *Baltimore*
Jacob M. Kunkel, *Frederick*
Thomas F. Bowie, *Upper Marlboro*

## MASSACHUSETTS

### SENATORS

Charles Sumner,[15] *Boston*
Henry Wilson, *Natick*

### REPRESENTATIVES

Robert B. Hall, *Plymouth*
James Buffington, *Fall River*
William S. Damrell, *Dedham*
Linus B. Comins, *Boston*
Anson Burlingame, *Cambridge*
Timothy Davis, *Gloucester*
Nathaniel P. Banks,[16] *Waltham*
Daniel W. Gooch,[17] *Melrose*
Chauncey L. Knapp, *Lowell*
Eli Thayer, *Worcester*
Calvin C. Chaffee, *Springfield*
Henry L. Dawes, *North Adams*

## MICHIGAN

### SENATORS

Charles E. Stuart, *Kalamazoo*
Zachariah Chandler, *Detroit*

### REPRESENTATIVES

William A. Howard, *Detroit*
Henry Waldron, *Hillsdale*
David S. Walbridge, *Kalamazoo*
De Witt C. Leach, *Lansing*

## MINNESOTA[18]

### SENATORS

Henry M. Rice,[19] *St. Paul*
James Shields,[20] *St. Paul*

### REPRESENTATIVES AT LARGE[21]

James M. Cavanaugh, *Chatfield*
William W. Phelps, *Red Wing*

## MISSISSIPPI

### SENATORS

Albert G. Brown, *Newton*
Jefferson Davis, *Hurricane*

### REPRESENTATIVES

Lucius Q. C. Lamar, *Abbeville*
Reuben Davis, *Aberdeen*
William Barksdale, *Columbus*
Otho R. Singleton, *Canton*
John A. Quitman,[22] *Natchez*
John J. McRae,[23] *State Line*

## MISSOURI

### SENATORS

James S. Green, *Canton*
Trusten Polk, *St. Louis*

### REPRESENTATIVES

Francis P. Blair, Jr., *St. Louis*
Thomas L. Anderson, *Palmyra*
John B. Clark,[24] *Fayette*
James Craig, *St. Joseph*
Samuel H. Woodson, *Independence*
John S. Phelps, *Springfield*
Samuel Caruthers, *Cape Girardeau*

---

thereof, not authorized by State law, legislative resolution, or constitutional provision"; both the Senators were seated upon their credentials, and the credentials and protest were referred to the Committee on the Judiciary; the committee reported May 24, 1858, that the sitting Senators were entitled to their seats, and this report was agreed to June 12, 1858. On January 24, 1859, a memorial of the State of Indiana was presented representing that it was the wish of the State that Henry S. Lane and William M. McCarty be admitted to seats as the only legally chosen Senators; February 3, 1859, the Senate Committee on the Judiciary, to which was referred the memorial, reported there was no vacancy in the Senate from the State of Indiana, and that the election of Messrs. Lane and McCarty was void; the Senate agreed to this report February 14, 1859. (See U.S. Senate Election, Expulsion and Censure Cases, 1793-1990, Senate Document 103-33, pp. 77-79.)

[9] Died September 7, 1857, before Congress assembled.

[10] Elected to fill vacancy caused by death of James Lockhart, and took his seat December 7, 1857.

[11] Died March 29, 1857.

[12] Elected to fill vacancy caused by the death of Samuel Brenton, and took his seat December 7, 1857.

[13] Election unsuccessfully contested by William Pinkney Whyte.

[14] Election unsuccessfully contested by Henry P. Brooks.

[15] Owing to ill health was present in this Congress but one day (December 7, 1857).

[16] Resigned December 24, 1857, having been elected Governor.

[17] Elected to fill vacancy caused by resignation of Nathaniel P. Banks, and took his seat January 21, 1858.

[18] Admitted as a State into the Union May 11, 1858.

[19] Took his seat May 12, 1858; term to expire, as determined by lot, March 3, 1863.

[20] Took his seat May 12, 1858; term to expire, as determined by lot, March 3, 1859.

[21] Credentials of James M. Cavanaugh and William W. Phelps were presented on May 13, 1858, and referred to the Committee on Elections "to inquire into and report upon the right of these gentlemen to be admitted and sworn as Members of this House," and on May 22, 1858, the committee resolution "that they be admitted and sworn" was adopted; took their seats the same day.

[22] Died July 17, 1858.

[23] Elected to fill vacancy caused by death of John A. Quitman, and took his seat December 7, 1858.

[24] Elected to fill vacancy caused by resignation of Representative-elect James S. Green (before the beginning of the congressional term), who had later been elected Senator, and took his seat December 7, 1857.

## NEW HAMPSHIRE

SENATORS

James Bell,[25] *Laconia*
Daniel Clark,[26] *Manchester*
John P. Hale, *Dover*

REPRESENTATIVES

James Pike, *Sanbornton Bridge*
Mason W. Tappan, *Bradford*
Aaron H. Cragin, *Lebanon*

## NEW JERSEY

SENATORS

John R. Thomson, *Princeton*
William Wright, *Newark*

REPRESENTATIVES

Isaiah D. Clawson, *Woodstown*
George R. Robbins, *Hamilton Square*
Garnett B. Adrain, *New Brunswick*
John Huyler, *Hackensack*
Jacob R. Wortendyke, *Jersey City*

## NEW YORK

SENATORS

William H. Seward, *Auburn*
Preston King, *Ogdensburg*

REPRESENTATIVES

John A. Searing, *Hempstead Branch*
George Taylor, *Brooklyn*
Daniel E. Sickles, *New York City*
John Kelly,[27] *New York City*
Thomas J. Barr,[28] *New York City*
William B. Maclay, *New York City*
John Cochrane, *New York City*
Elijah Ward, *New York City*
Horace F. Clark, *New York City*
John B. Haskin, *Fordham*
Ambrose S. Murray, *Goshen*
William F. Russell, *Saugerties*
John Thompson, *Poughkeepsie*
Abram B. Olin, *Troy*
Erastus Corning, *Albany*
Edward Dodd, *Argyle*
George W. Palmer, *Plattsburg*
Francis E. Spinner, *Mohawk*
Clark B. Cochrane, *Schenectady*
Oliver A. Morse, *Cherry Valley*
Orsamus B. Matteson, *Utica*
Henry Bennett, *New Berlin*
Henry C. Goodwin, *Hamilton*
Charles B. Hoard, *Watertown*
Amos P. Granger, *Syracuse*
Edwin B. Morgan, *Aurora*
Emory B. Pottle, *Naples*

John M. Parker, *Owego*
William H. Kelsey, *Geneseo*
Samuel G. Andrews, *Rochester*
Judson W. Sherman, *Angelica*
Silas M. Burroughs, *Medina*
Israel T. Hatch, *Buffalo*
Reuben E. Fenton, *Frewsburg*

## NORTH CAROLINA

SENATORS

David S. Reid, *Pleasantville*
Asa Biggs,[29] *Williamston*
Thomas L. Clingman,[30] *Asheville*

REPRESENTATIVES

Henry M. Shaw, *Indian Town*
Thomas Ruffin, *Goldsboro*
Warren Winslow, *Fayetteville*
Lawrence O'B. Branch, *Raleigh*
John A. Gilmer, *Greensboro*
Alfred M. Scales, *Madison*
F. Burton Craige, *Salisbury*
Thomas L. Clingman,[31] *Ashville*
Zebulon B. Vance,[32] *Asheville*

## OHIO

SENATORS

Benjamin F. Wade, *Jefferson*
George E. Pugh, *Cincinnati*

REPRESENTATIVES

George H. Pendleton, *Cincinnati*
William S. Groesbeck, *Cincinnati*
Lewis D. Campbell,[33] *Hamilton*
Clement L. Vallandigham,[34] *Dayton*
Matthias H. Nichols, *Lima*
Richard Mott, *Toledo*
Joseph R. Cockerill, *West Union*
Aaron Harlan, *Yellow Springs*
Benjamin Stanton, *Bellefontaine*
Lawrence W. Hall, *Bucyrus*
Joseph Miller, *Chillicothe*
Valentine B. Horton, *Pomeroy*
Samuel S. Cox, *Columbus*
John Sherman, *Mansfield*
Philemon Bliss, *Elyria*
Joseph Burns, *Coshocton*
Cydnor B. Tompkins, *McConnellsville*
William Lawrence, *Washington*
Benjamin F. Leiter, *Canton*
Edward Wade, *Cleveland*
Joshua R. Giddings, *Jefferson*
John A. Bingham, *Cadiz*

## OREGON[35]

SENATORS

Joseph Lane,[36] *Winchester*
Delazon Smith,[37] *Portland*

REPRESENTATIVE AT LARGE

La Fayette Grover,[38] *Salem*

## PENNSYLVANIA

SENATORS

William Bigler, *Clearfield*
Simon Cameron, *Harrisburg*

REPRESENTATIVES

Thomas B. Florence, *Philadelphia*
Edward Joy Morris, *Philadelphia*
James Landy, *Philadelphia*
Henry M. Phillips, *Philadelphia*
Owen Jones, *Cabinet*
John Hickman, *West Chester*
Henry Chapman, *Coylestown*
J. Glancy Jones,[39] *Reading*
William H. Keim,[40] *Reading*
Anthony E. Roberts, *Lancaster*
John C. Kunkel, *Harrisburg*
William L. Dewart, *Sunbury*
John G. Montgomery,[41] *Danville*
Paul Leidy,[42] *Danville*
William H. Dimmick, *Honesdale*
Galusha A. Grow, *Glenwood*
Allison White, *Lock Haven*
John A. Ahl, *Newville*
Wilson Reilly, *Chambersburg*
John R. Edie, *Somerset*
John Covode, *Lockport*
William Montgomery, *Washington*
David Ritchie, *Pittsburgh*
Samuel A. Purviance, *Butler*
William Stewart, *Mercer*
James L. Gillis, *Ridgway*
John Dick, *Meadville*

## RHODE ISLAND

SENATORS

Philip Allen, *Providence*
James F. Simmons, *Providence*

REPRESENTATIVES

Nathaniel B. Durfee, *Tiverton*
William D. Brayton, *Warwick*

---

[25] Died May 26, 1857.
[26] Elected to fill vacancy caused by death of James Bell, and took his seat December 7, 1857.
[27] Resigned December 25, 1858.
[28] Elected to fill vacancy caused by resignation of John Kelly, and took his seat January 17, 1859.
[29] Resigned May 5, 1858.
[30] Appointed to fill vacancy caused by resignation of Asa Biggs, and took his seat December 6, 1858; subsequently elected.
[31] Resigned May 7, 1858, having been elected Senator.

[32] Elected to fill vacancy caused by resignation of Thomas L. Clingman, and took his seat December 7, 1858.
[33] Served until May 25, 1858; succeeded by Clement L. Vallandigham, who contested his election.
[34] Successfully contested the election of Lewis D. Campbell, and took his seat May 25, 1858.
[35] Admitted as a State into the Union February 14, 1859.
[36] Took his seat February 14, 1859; term to expire, as determined by lot, March 3, 1861.

[37] Took his seat February 14, 1859; term to expire, as determined by lot, March 3, 1859.
[38] Took his seat February 15, 1859.
[39] Resigned October 30, 1858.
[40] Elected to fill vacancy caused by resignation of J. Glancy Jones, and took his seat December 7, 1858.
[41] Died April 24, 1857, before Congress assembled
[42] Elected to fill vacancy caused by death of John G. Montgomery, and took his seat December 7, 1857.

## SOUTH CAROLINA

SENATORS

Andrew P. Butler,[43] *Edgefield*
James H. Hammond,[44] *Beech Island*
Josiah J. Evans,[45] *Society Hill*
Arthur P. Hayne,[46] *Charleston*
James Chesnut, Jr.,[47] *Kershaw*

REPRESENTATIVES

John McQueen, *Marlboro*
William P. Miles, *Charleston*
Laurence M. Keitt, *Orangeburg*
Milledge L. Bonham, *Edgefield*
James L. Orr, *Anderson*
William W. Boyce, *Winnsboro*

## TENNESSEE

SENATORS

John Bell, *Nashville*
Andrew Johnson, *Greenville*

REPRESENTATIVES

Albert G. Watkins, *Panther Springs*
Horace Maynard, *Knoxville*
Samuel A. Smith, *Charleston*
John H. Savage, *Smithville*
Charles Ready, *Murfreesboro*
George W. Jones, *Fayetteville*
John V. Wright, *Purdy*
Felix K. Zollicoffer, *Nashville*
John D. C. Atkins, *Paris*
William T. Avery, *Memphis*

## TEXAS

SENATORS

Sam Houston, *Huntsville*
Thomas J. Rusk,[48] *Nacogdoches*
J. Pinckney Henderson,[49] *Marshville*
Matthias Ward,[50] *Jefferson*

REPRESENTATIVES

John H. Reagan, *Palestine*
Guy M. Bryan, *Brazoria*

## VERMONT

SENATORS

Solomon Foot, *Rutland*
Jacob Collamer, *Woodstock*

REPRESENTATIVES

Eliakim P. Walton, *Montpelier*
Justin S. Morrill, *Strafford*
Homer E. Royce, *Berkshire*

## VIRGINIA

SENATORS

James M. Mason, *Winchester*
Robert M. T. Hunter, *Lloyds*

REPRESENTATIVES

Muscoe R. H. Garnett, *Lovettsville*
John S. Millson, *Norfolk*
John S. Caskie, *Richmond*
William O. Goode, *Boydton*
Thomas S. Bocock, *Appomattox*
Paulus Powell, *Amherst*
William Smith, *Warrenton*
Charles J. Faulkner, *Martinsburg*
John Letcher, *Lexington*
Sherrard Clemens, *Wheeling*
Albert G. Jenkins, *Green Bottom*
Henry A. Edmundson, *Salem*
George W. Hopkins, *Abingdon*

## WISCONSIN

SENATORS

Charles Durkee, *Kenosha*
James R. Doolittle, *Racine*

REPRESENTATIVES

John F. Potter, *East Troy*
Cadwallader C. Washburn, *Mineral Point*
Charles Billinghurst, *Juneau*

## TERRITORY OF KANSAS

DELEGATE

Marcus J. Parrott, *Leavenworth*

## TERRITORY OF MINNESOTA

DELEGATE

William W. Kingsbury,[51] *Endion*

## TERRITORY OF NEBRASKA

DELEGATE

Fenner Ferguson,[52] *Belleview*

## TERRITORY OF NEW MEXICO

DELEGATE

Miguel A. Otero, *Albuquerque*

## TERRITORY OF OREGON

DELEGATE

Joseph Lane,[53] *Winchester*

## TERRITORY OF UTAH

DELEGATE

John M. Bernhisel, *Salt Lake City*

## TERRITORY OF WASHINGTON

DELEGATE

Isaac I. Stevens, *Olympia*

---

[43] Died May 25, 1857.
[44] Elected to fill vacancy caused by death of Andrew P. Butler, and took his seat January 7, 1858.
[45] Died May 6, 1858.
[46] Appointed to fill vacancy caused by death of Josiah J. Evans, and took his seat May 20, 1858.
[47] Elected to fill vacancy caused by death of Josiah J. Evans, and took his seat January 5, 1859.
[48] Died July 29, 1857.

[49] Elected to fill vacancy caused by death of Thomas J. Rusk, and took his seat March 1, 1858; died June 4, 1858.
[50] Appointed to fill vacancy caused by death of J. Pinckney Henderson, and took his seat December 6, 1858.
[51] Served until May 11, 1858, when a portion of the Territory was granted statehood; the House decided that the remainder was "without any legally organized

government and not entitled to a Delegate in Congress," although William W. Kingsbury and Alpheus G. Fuller both claimed to have been elected.
[52] Election unsuccessfully contested by Bird B. Chapman.
[53] Served until February 14, 1859, when the Territory of Oregon was granted statehood; then became one of the Senators from the new State.

# 36TH CONGRESS

MARCH 4, 1859, TO MARCH 3, 1861

John C. Breckinridge
Vice President

FIRST SESSION— *December 5, 1859, to June 25, 1860*
SECOND SESSION— *December 3, 1860, to March 3, 1861*
SPECIAL SESSIONS OF THE SENATE— *March 4, 1859, to March 10, 1859;
June 26, 1860, to June 28, 1860*

———

VICE PRESIDENT OF THE UNITED STATES— JOHN C. BRECKINRIDGE, of Kentucky
PRESIDENT PRO TEMPORE OF THE SENATE— BENJAMIN FITZPATRICK,[1] of Alabama;
JESSE D. BRIGHT,[2] of Indiana; SOLOMON FOOT,[3] of Vermont
SECRETARY OF THE SENATE— ASBURY DICKENS, of North Carolina
SERGEANT AT ARMS OF THE SENATE— DUNNING R. MCNAIR, of Pennsylvania

William Pennington
Speaker

———

SPEAKER OF THE HOUSE OF REPRESENTATIVES— WILLIAM PENNINGTON,[4] of New Jersey
CLERK OF THE HOUSE— JAMES C. ALLEN, of Illinois; JOHN W. FORNEY,[5] of Pennsylvania
SERGEANT AT ARMS OF THE HOUSE— ADAM J. GLOSSBRENNER, of Pennsylvania; HENRY W. HOFFMAN,[6] of Maryland
DOORKEEPER OF THE HOUSE— GEORGE MARSTON, of New Hampshire

## ALABAMA[7]

### SENATORS

Benjamin Fitzpatrick,[8] *Wetumpka*
Clement C. Clay, Jr.,[8] *Huntsville*

### REPRESENTATIVES

James A. Stallworth,[8] *Evergreen*
James L. Pugh,[8] *Eufaula*
David Clopton,[8] *Tuskegee*
Sydenham Moore,[8] *Greensboro*
George S. Houston,[8] *Athens*
Williamson R. W. Cobb,[9] *Bellefonte*
Jabez L. M. Curry,[8] *Talladega*

## ARKANSAS

### SENATORS

William K. Sebastian, *Helena*
Robert W. Johnson, *Pine Bluff*

### REPRESENTATIVES

Thomas C. Hindman, *Helena*
Albert Rust, *Little Rock*

## CALIFORNIA

### SENATORS

William M. Gwin, *San Francisco*
David C. Broderick,[10] *San Francisco*
Henry P. Haun,[11] *Marysville*
Milton S. Latham,[12] *San Francisco*

### REPRESENTATIVES AT LARGE

Charles L. Scott, *Sonora*
John C. Burch, *Weaverville*

## CONNECTICUT

### SENATORS

Lafayette S. Foster, *Norwich*
James Dixon, *Hartford*

### REPRESENTATIVES

Dwight Loomis, *Rockville*
John Woodruff, *New Haven*
Alfred A. Burnham, *Windham*
Orris S. Ferry, *Norwalk*

## DELAWARE

### SENATORS

James A. Bayard, *Wilmington*
Willard Saulsbury, *Georgetown*

### REPRESENTATIVE AT LARGE

William G. Whiteley, *New Castle*

## FLORIDA[13]

### SENATORS

Stephen R. Mallory,[14] *Pensacola*
David Levy Yulee,[14] *Homasassa*

### REPRESENTATIVE AT LARGE

George S. Hawkins,[14] *Pensacola*

## GEORGIA[15]

### SENATORS

Robert Toombs,[16] *Washington*
Alfred Iverson,[17] *Columbus*

### REPRESENTATIVES

Peter E. Love,[18] *Thomasville*
Martin J. Crawford,[18] *Columbus*
Thomas Hardeman, Jr.,[18] *Macon*
Lucius J. Gartrell,[18] *Atlanta*
John W. H. Underwood,[18] *Rome*
James Jackson,[18] *Athens*
Joshua Hill,[19] *Madison*
John J. Jones,[18] *Waynesboro*

## ILLINOIS

### SENATORS

Stephen A. Douglas, *Chicago*
Lyman Trumbull, *Alton*

### REPRESENTATIVES

Elihu B. Washburne, *Galena*
John F. Farnsworth, *Chicago*
Owen Lovejoy, *Princeton*
William Kellogg, *Canton*
Isaac N. Morris, *Quincy*
John A. McClernand,[20] *Springfield*
James C. Robinson, *Marshall*
Philip B. Fouke, *Belleville*
John A. Logan, *Benton*

---

[1] Elected March 9, 1859 (special session); December 19, 1859; February 20, 1860; June 26, 1860, in special session.
[2] Elected June 12, 1860.
[3] Elected February 16, 1861.
[4] Elected February 1, 1860, upon the forty-fourth viva voce vote.
[5] Elected February 3, 1860.
[6] Elected February 3, 1860.
[7] Seceded from the Union January 11, 1861.
[8] Withdrew January 21, 1861.

[9] Withdrew January 30, 1861.
[10] Died September 16, 1859.
[11] Appointed to fill vacancy caused by death of David C. Broderick, and took his seat December 5, 1859.
[12] Elected to fill vacancy caused by death of David C. Broderick and took his seat March 5, 1860.
[13] Seceded from the Union January 11, 1861.
[14] Withdrew January 21, 1861.
[15] Seceded from the Union January 28, 1861.

[16] Did not occupy his seat after February 4, 1861.
[17] Withdrew January 28, 1861.
[18] Withdrew January 23, 1861.
[19] Resigned January 23, 1861 (in written communication addressed to the Speaker).
[20] Elected to fill vacancy caused by death of Representative-elect Thomas L. Harris, in preceding Congress, and took his seat December 5, 1859.

## INDIANA

### SENATORS

Jesse D. Bright, *Jeffersonville*
Graham N. Fitch, *Logansport*

### REPRESENTATIVES

William E. Niblack, *Vincennes*
William H. English, *Lexington*
William McKee Dunn, *Madison*
William S. Holman, *Lawrenceburg*
David Kilgore, *Muncietown*
Albert G. Porter, *Indianapolis*
John G. Davis, *Rockville*
James Wilson, *Crawfordsville*
Schuyler Colfax, *South Bend*
Charles Case, *Fort Wayne*
John U. Pettit, *Wabash*

## IOWA

### SENATORS

James Harlan, *Mount Pleasant*
James W. Grimes, *Burlington*

### REPRESENTATIVES

Samuel R. Curtis, *Keokuk*
William Vandever, *Dubuque*

## KANSAS[21]

### SENATORS

Vacant[22]

### REPRESENTATIVE AT LARGE

Martin F. Conway,[23] *Lawrence*

## KENTUCKY

### SENATORS

John J. Crittenden, *Frankfort*
Lazarus W. Powell, *Henderson*

### REPRESENTATIVES

Henry C. Burnett, *Cadiz*
Samuel O. Peyton, *Hartford*
Francis N. Bristow, *Elkton*
William C. Anderson,[24] *Danville*
John Young Brown, *Elizabethtown*
Green Adams, *Barboursville*
Robert Mallory, *La Grange*
William E. Simms, *Paris*
Laban T. Moore, *Louisa*
John W. Stevenson, *Covington*

## LOUISIANA[25]

### SENATORS

Judah P. Benjamin,[26] *New Orleans*
John Slidell,[26] *New Orleans*

### REPRESENTATIVES

John E. Bouligny, *New Orleans*
Miles Taylor,[27] *Donaldsonville*
Thomas G. Davidson,[28] *Baton Rouge*
John M. Landrum, *Shreveport*

## MAINE

### SENATORS

William Pitt Fessenden, *Portland*
Hannibal Hamlin,[29] *Hampden*
Lot M. Morrill,[30] *Augusta*

### REPRESENTATIVES

Daniel E. Somes, *Biddeford*
John J. Perry, *Oxford*
Ezra B. French, *Damariscotta*
Freeman H. Morse, *Bath*
Israel Washburn, Jr.,[31] *Orono*
Stephen Coburn,[32] *Skowhegan*
Stephen C. Foster, *Pembroke*

## MARYLAND

### SENATORS

James A. Pearce, *Chestertown*
Anthony Kennedy, *Baltimore*

### REPRESENTATIVES

James A. Stewart, *Cambridge*
Edwin H. Webster, *Bel Air*
J. Morrison Harris,[33] *Baltimore*
H. Winter Davis,[34] *Baltimore*
Jacob M. Kunkel, *Frederick*
George W. Hughes, *West River*

## MASSACHUSETTS

### SENATORS

Charles Sumner, *Boston*
Henry Wilson, *Natick*

### REPRESENTATIVES

Thomas D. Eliot, *New Bedford*
James Buffington, *Fall River*
Charles Francis Adams, *Quincy*
Alexander H. Rice, *Boston*
Anson Burlingame, *Cambridge*
John B. Alley, *Lynn*
Daniel W. Gooch, *Melrose*
Charles R. Train, *Framingham*
Eli Thayer, *Worcester*
Charles Delano, *Northampton*
Henry L. Dawes, *North Adams*

## MICHIGAN

### SENATORS

Zachariah Chandler, *Detroit*
Kinsley S. Bingham, *Kensington*

### REPRESENTATIVES

George B. Cooper,[35] *Jackson*
William A. Howard,[36] *Detroit*
Henry Waldron, *Hillsdale*
Francis W. Kellogg, *Grand Rapids*
De Witt C. Leach, *Lansing*

## MINNESOTA

### SENATORS

Henry M. Rice, *St. Paul*
Morton S. Wilkinson, *Mankato*

### REPRESENTATIVES AT LARGE

Cyrus Aldrich, *Minneapolis*
William Windom, *Winona*

## MISSISSIPPI[37]

### SENATORS

Albert G. Brown,[38] *Terry*
Jefferson Davis,[39] *Hurricane*

### REPRESENTATIVES

Lucius Q. C. Lamar,[40] *Abbeville*
Reuben Davis, *Aberdeen*
William Barksdale, *Columbus*
Otho R. Singleton, *Canton*
John J. McRae, *State Line*

## MISSOURI

### SENATORS

James S. Green, *Canton*
Trusten Polk, *St. Louis*

### REPRESENTATIVES

John R. Barret,[41] *St. Louis*
Francis P. Blair, Jr.,[42] *St. Louis*
Thomas L. Anderson, *Palmyra*
John B. Clark, *Fayette*
James Craig, *St. Joseph*
Samuel H. Woodson, *Independence*
John S. Phelps, *Springfield*
John W. Noell, *Perryville*

---

[21] Admitted as a State into the Union January 29, 1861.

[22] Senators not elected to this Congress.

[23] Took his seat January 30, 1861.

[24] Election unsuccessfully contested by James S. Chrisman.

[25] Seceded from the Union January 26, 1861.

[26] Withdrew February 4, 1861.

[27] Withdrew February 5, 1861.

[28] Did not occupy his seat after February 5, 1861.

[29] Resigned effective January 17, 1861.

[30] Elected to fill vacancy caused by resignation of

Hannibal Hamlin, and took his seat January 17, 1861.

[31] Resigned effective January 1, 1861.

[32] Elected to fill vacancy caused by resignation of Israel Washburn, Jr., and took his seat January 2, 1861.

[33] Election Unsuccessfully contested by William P. Preston.

[34] Election unsuccessfully contested by William G. Harrison

[35] Served until May 15, 1860; succeeded by William A. Howard, who contested his election.

[36] Successfully contested the election of George B.

Cooper, and took his seat May 15, 1860.

[37] Seceded from the Union, January 9, 1861.

[38] Withdrew January 12, 1861.

[39] Withdrew January 21, 1861.

[40] Retired in December, 1860.

[41] Served until June 8, 1860; succeeded by Francis P. Blair, Jr., who contested his election; subsequently elected to fill vacancy caused by resignation of Francis P. Blair, Jr., and took his seat December 3, 1860.

[42] Successfully contested the election of John R. Barret, and took his seat June 8, 1860; resigned June 25, 1860.

## NEW HAMPSHIRE

### SENATORS

John P. Hale, *Dover*
Daniel Clark, *Manchester*

### REPRESENTATIVES

Gilman Marston, *Exeter*
Mason W. Tappan, *Bradford*
Thomas M. Edwards, *Keene*

## NEW JERSEY

### SENATORS

John R. Thomson, *Princeton*
John C. Ten Eyck, *Mount Holly*

### REPRESENTATIVES

John T. Nixon, *Bridgeton*
John L. N. Stratton, *Mount Holly*
Garnett B. Adrain, *New Brunswick*
Jetur R. Riggs, *Paterson*
William Pennington, *Newark*

## NEW YORK

### SENATORS

William H. Seward, *Auburn*
Preston King, *Ogdensburg*

### REPRESENTATIVES

Luther C. Carter, *Flushing*
James Humphrey, *Brooklyn*
Daniel E. Sickles,[43] *New York City*
Thomas J. Barr, *New York City*
William B. Maclay, *New York City*
John Cochrane, *New York City*
George Briggs, *New York City*
Horace F. Clark, *New York City*
John B. Haskin, *Fordham*
Charles H. Van Wyck, *Bloomingburg*
William S. Kenyon, *Kingston*
Charles L. Beale, *Kinderhook*
Abram B. Olin, *Troy*
John H. Reynolds, *Albany*
James B. McKean, *Saratoga Springs*
George W. Palmer, *Plattsburg*
Francis E. Spinner, *Mohawk*
Clark B. Cochrane, *Schenectady*
James H. Graham, *Delhi*
Roscoe Conkling, *Utica*
R. Holland Duell, *Cortland*
M. Lindley Lee, *Fulton*
Charles B. Hoard, *Watertown*
Charles B. Sedgwick, *Syracuse*
Martin Butterfield, *Palmyra*
Emory B. Pottle, *Naples*
Alfred Wells, *Ithaca*
William Irvine, *Corning*
Alfred Ely, *Rochester*
Augustus Frank, *Warsaw*
Silas M. Burroughs,[44] *Medina*

Edwin R. Reynolds,[45] *Albion*
Elbridge G. Spaulding, *Buffalo*
Reuben E. Fenton, *Frewsburg*

## NORTH CAROLINA

### SENATORS

Thomas L. Clingman, *Asheville*
Thomas Bragg, *Raleigh*

### REPRESENTATIVES

William N. H. Smith, *Murfreesboro*
Thomas Ruffin, *Goldsboro*
Warren Winslow, *Fayetteville*
Lawrence O'B. Branch, *Raleigh*
John A. Gilmer, *Greensboro*
James M. Leach, *Lexington*
F. Burton Craige, *Salisbury*
Zebulon B. Vance, *Asheville*

## OHIO

### SENATORS

Benjamin F. Wade, *Jefferson*
George E. Pugh, *Cincinnati*

### REPRESENTATIVES

George H. Pendleton, *Cincinnati*
John A. Gurley, *Cincinnati*
Clement L. Vallandigham, *Dayton*
William Allen, *Greenville*
James M. Ashley, *Toledo*
William Howard, *Batavia*
Thomas Corwin, *Lebanon*
Benjamin Stanton, *Bellefontaine*
John Carey, *Carey*
Carey A. Trimble, *Chillicothe*
Charles D. Martin, *Lancaster*
Samuel S. Cox, *Columbus*
John Sherman, *Mansfield*
Cyrus Spink,[46] *Wooster*
Harrison G. O. Blake,[47] *Medina*
William Helmick, *New Philadelphia*
Cydnor B. Tompkins, *McConnellsville*
Thomas C. Theaker, *Bridgeport*
Sidney Edgerton, *Tallmadge*
Edward Wade, *Cleveland*
John Hutchins, *Warren*
John A. Bingham, *Cadiz*

## OREGON

### SENATORS

Joseph Lane, *Winchester*
Edward D. Baker,[48] *Oregon City*

### REPRESENTATIVE AT LARGE

Lansing Stout, *Portland*

## PENNSYLVANIA

### SENATORS

William Bigler, *Clearfield*
Simon Cameron, *Harrisburg*

### REPRESENTATIVES

Thomas B. Florence, *Philadelphia*
Edward Joy Morris, *Philadelphia*
John P. Verree, *Philadelphia*
William Millward, *Philadelphia*
John Wood, *Conshohocken*
John Hickman, *West Chester*
Henry C. Longnecker, *Allentown*
John Schwartz,[49] *Reading*
Jacob K. McKenty,[50] *Reading*
Thaddeus Stevens, *Lancaster*
John W. Killinger, *Lebanon*
James H. Campbell, *Pottsville*
George W. Scranton, *Scranton*
William H. Dimmick, *Honesdale*
Galusha A. Grow, *Glenwood*
James T. Hale, *Bellefonte*
Benjamin F. Junkin, *New Bloomfield*
Edward McPherson, *Gettysburg*
Samuel S. Blair, *Hollidaysburg*
John Covode, *Lockport*
William Montgomery, *Washington*
James K. Moorhead, *Pittsburgh*
Robert McKnight, *Pittsburgh*
William Stewart, *Mercer*
Chapin Hall, *Warren*
Elijah Babbitt, *Erie*

## RHODE ISLAND

### SENATORS

James F. Simmons, *Providence*
Henry B. Anthony, *Providence*

### REPRESENTATIVES

Christopher Robinson, *Woonsocket*
William D. Brayton, *Warwick*

## SOUTH CAROLINA[51]

### SENATORS

James H. Hammond,[52] *Beech Island*
James Chesnut, Jr.,[53] *Camden*

### REPRESENTATIVES

John McQueen,[54] *Marlboro*
W. Porcher Miles,[55] *Charleston*
Laurence M. Keitt,[56] *Orangeburg*
Milledge L. Bonham,[54] *Edgefield*
John D. Ashmore,[54] *Anderson*
William W. Boyce,[54] *Winnsboro*

---

[43] Election unsuccessfully contested by Amor J. Williamson.
[44] Died June 3, 1860.
[45] Elected to fill vacancy caused by the death of Silar M. Burroughs, and took his seat December 5, 1860.
[46] Died May 31, 1859, before Congress assembled.
[47] Elected to fill vacancy caused by the death of

Cyrus Spink, and took his seat December 5, 1859.
[48] Elected for the term beginning March 4, 1859, and took his seat December 5, 1860; vacancy in this class from March 4, 1859 to October 1, 1860.
[49] Died June 20, 1860.
[50] Elected to fill vacancy caused by death of John Schwartz, and took his seat December 3, 1860.
[51] Seceded fromt he Union December 20, 1860.

[52] Withdrew November 11, 1860.
[53] Withdrew November 10, 1860.
[54] Withdrew December 21, 1860.
[55] Did not occupy his seat after December 13, 1860.
[56] Did not occupy his seat after December 10, 1860.

## TENNESSEE

### SENATORS

Andrew Johnson, *Greeneville*
Alfred O. P. Nicholson,[57] *Columbia*

### REPRESENTATIVES

Thomas A. R. Nelson, *Jonesboro*
Horace Maynard, *Knoxville*
Reese B. Brabson, *Chattanooga*
William B. Stokes, *Alexandria*
Robert H. Hatton, *Lebanon*
James H. Thomas, *Columbia*
John V. Wright, *Purdy*
James M. Quarles, *Clarksville*
Emerson Etheridge, *Dresden*
William T. Avery, *Memphis*

## TEXAS[58]

### SENATORS

Matthias Ward, *Jefferson*
Louis T. Wigfall,[59] *Marshall*
John Hemphill, *Austin*

### REPRESENTATIVES

John H. Reagan, *Palestine*
Andrew J. Hamilton, *Austin*

## VERMONT

### SENATORS

Solomon Foot, *Rutland*
Jacob Collamer, *Woodstock*

### REPRESENTATIVES

Justin S. Morrill, *Strafford*
Eliakim P. Walton, *Montpelier*
Homer E. Royce, *East Berkshire*

## VIRGINIA

### SENATORS

James M. Mason, *Winchester*
Robert M. T. Hunter, *Lloyds*

### REPRESENTATIVES

Muscoe R. H. Garnett, *Loretto*
John S. Millson, *Norfolk*
Daniel C. DeJarnette, *Bowling Green*
William O. Goode,[60] *Boydton*
Roger A. Pryor,[61] *Petersburg*
Thomas S. Bocock, *Appomattox*
Shelton F. Leake, *Charlottesville*
William Smith, *Warrenton*
Alexander R. Boteler, *Shepherdstown*
John T. Harris, *Harrisonburg*
Sherrard Clemens, *Wheeling*
Albert G. Jenkins, *Green Bottom*
Henry A. Edmundson, *Salem*
Elbert S. Martin, *Lee*

## WISCONSIN

### SENATORS

Charles Durkee, *Kenosha*
James R. Doolittle, *Racine*

### REPRESENTATIVES

John F. Potter, *East Troy*
Cadwallader C. Washburn, *La Crosse*
Charles H. Larrabee, *Horicon*

## TERRITORY OF KANSAS

### DELEGATE

Marcus J. Parrott,[62] *Leavenworth*

## TERRITORY OF NEBRASKA

### DELEGATE

Experience Estabrook,[63] *Omaha*
Samuel G. Daily,[64] *Peru*

## TERRITORY OF NEW MEXICO

### DELEGATE

Miguel A. Otero, *Albuquerque*

## TERRITORY OF UTAH

### DELEGATE

William H. Hooper, *Salt Lake City*

## TERRITORY OF WASHINGTON

### DELEGATE

Isaac I. Stevens, *Olympia*

---

[57] Withdrew March 3, 1861.
[58] Seceded from the Union February 1, 1861.
[59] Elected to fill vacancy cause dby death of J. Pinckney Henderson, in preceding Congress, and took his seat January 4, 1860.

[60] Died July 3, 1859.
[61] Elected to fill vacancy caused by death of William O. Goode, and took his seat December 7, 1859.
[62] Served until January 29, 1861, when the Territory of Kansas was granted statehood.

[63] Served until May 18, 1860; succeeded by Samuel G. Daily, who contested his election.
[64] Successfully contested the election of Experience Estabrook, and took his seat May 18, 1860.

# 37TH CONGRESS

## MARCH 4, 1861, TO MARCH 3, 1863

FIRST SESSION— *July 4, 1861, to August 6, 1861*
SECOND SESSION— *December 2, 1861, to July 17, 1862*
THIRD SESSION— *December 1, 1862, to March 3, 1863*
SPECIAL SESSION OF THE SENATE— *March 4, 1861, to March 28, 1861*

———

VICE PRESIDENT OF THE UNITED STATES— HANNIBAL HAMLIN, of Maine
PRESIDENT PRO TEMPORE OF THE SENATE— SOLOMON FOOT,[1] of Vermont
SECRETARY OF THE SENATE— ASBURY DICKENS, of North Carolina; JOHN W. FORNEY,[2] of Pennsylvania
SERGEANT AT ARMS OF THE SENATE— DUNNING R. McNAIR, of Pennsylvania; GEORGE T. BROWN,[3] of Illinois

———

SPEAKER OF THE HOUSE OF REPRESENTATIVES— GALUSHA A. GROW,[4] of Pennsylvania
CLERK OF THE HOUSE— JOHN W. FORNEY, of Pennsylvania; EMERSON ETHERIDGE,[5] of Tennessee
SERGEANT AT ARMS OF THE HOUSE— HENRY W. HOFFMAN, of Maryland; EDWARD BALL,[6] of Ohio
DOORKEEPER OF THE HOUSE— IRA GOODNOW, of Vermont

Hannibal Hamlin
Vice President

Galusha A. Grow
Speaker

## ALABAMA

### SENATORS
Clement C. Clay, Jr.,[7] *Huntsville*
Vacant

### REPRESENTATIVES
Vacant

## ARKANSAS[8]

### SENATORS
William K. Sebastian,[9] *Helena*
Charles B. Mitchel,[9] *Little Rock*

### REPRESENTATIVES
Vacant

## CALIFORNIA

### SENATORS
Milton S. Latham, *Sacramento*
James A. McDougall, *San Francisco*

### REPRESENTATIVES AT LARGE[10]
Frederick F. Low,[11] *San Francisco*
Timothy G. Phelps,[12] *San Mateo*
Aaron A. Sargent,[12] *Nevada City*

## CONNECTICUT

### SENATORS
Lafayette S. Foster, *Norwich*
James Dixon, *Hartford*

### REPRESENTATIVES
Alfred A. Burnham, *Windham*
James E. English, *New Haven*
Dwight Loomis, *Rockville*
George C. Woodruff, *Litchfield*

## DELAWARE

### SENATORS
James A. Bayard, *Wilmington*
Willard Saulsbury, *Georgetown*

### REPRESENTATIVE AT LARGE
George P. Fisher, *Dover*

## FLORIDA

### SENATORS
Stephen R. Mallory,[13] *Pensacola*
Vacant

## REPRESENTATIVE AT LARGE
Vacant

## GEORGIA

### SENATORS
Robert Toombs,[14] *Washington*
Vacant

### REPRESENTATIVES
Vacant

## ILLINOIS

### SENATORS
Stephen A. Douglas,[15] *Chicago*
Orville H. Browning,[16] *Quincy*
William A. Richardson,[17] *Quincy*
Lyman Trumbull, *Alton*

### REPRESENTATIVES
Isaac N. Arnold, *Chicago*
Philip B. Fouke, *Belleville*
William Kellogg, *Canton*
John A. Logan,[18] *Benton*
William J. Allen,[19] *Marion*
Owen Lovejoy, *Princeton*

---

[1] Elected March 23, 1861; July 18, 1861; January 15, 1862; March 31, 1862; June 19, 1862; and February 18, 1863.

[2] Elected July 15, 1861; William Hickey (chief clerk) was appointed acting secretary March 22, 1861, "to serve during the present infirmity of the secretary."

[3] Elected July 6, 1861.

[4] Elected July 4, 1861.

[5] Elected July 4, 1861.

[6] Elected July 5, 1861.

[7] Seat declared vacant by resolution of March 14, 1861. (See U.S. Senate Election, Expulsion and Censure Cases, 1793-1990, Senate Document 103-33, pp. 89-91.)

[8] Seceded from the Union May 8, 1861.

[9] Expelled by resolution of July 11, 1861. The resolution with its preamble was revoked and annulled, so far as Mr. Sebastian was concerned, by resolution of the Senate of March 3, 1877. (See U.S. Senate Election, Expulsion and Censure Cases, 1793-1990, Senate Document 103-33, pp. 95-98.)

[10] Elected September 4, 1861.

[11] Presented credentials and claimed a seat as a third representative from the State December 2, 1861; declared not entitled to a seat by resolution of May 6, 1862; upon approval of the act of June 2, 1862, allowing the State of California an additional representative, appeared and took his seat June 3, 1862.

[12] Took his seat December 2, 1861.

[13] Seat declared vacant by resolution of March 14, 1861. (See U.S. Senate Election, Expulsion and Censure Cases, 1793-1990, Senate Document 103-33, pp. 89-91.)

[14] Seat declared vacant by resolution of March 14, 1861. (See U.S. Senate Election, Expulsion and Censure Cases, 1793-1990, Senate Document 103-33, pp. 89-91.)

[15] Died June 3, 1861.

[16] Appointed to fill vacancy caused by death of Stephen A. Douglas, and took his seat July 4, 1861.

[17] Elected to fill vacancy caused by death of Stephen A. Douglas, and took his seat January 30, 1863.

[18] Resigned April 2, 1862.

[19] Elected to fill vacancy caused by resignation of John A. Logan, and took his seat June 2, 1862.

## ILLINOIS—Continued

REPRESENTATIVES—CONTINUED

John A. McClernand,[20] *Springfield*
Anthony L. Knapp,[21] *Jerseyville*
William A. Richardson,[22] *Quincy*
James C. Robinson, *Marshall*
Elihu B. Washburne, *Galena*

## INDIANA

SENATORS

Jesse D. Bright,[23] *Jeffersonville*
Joseph A. Wright,[24] *Indianapolis*
David Turpie,[25] *Indianapolis*
Henry S. Lane, *Crawfordsville*

REPRESENTATIVES

Schuyler Colfax, *South Bend*
James A. Cravens, *Hardinsburg*
William McKee Dunn, *Madison*
William S. Holman, *Aurora*
George W. Julian, *Centerville*
John Law, *Evansville*
William Mitchell, *Kendallville*
Albert G. Porter, *Indianapolis*
John P. C. Shanks, *Jay Court House*
Daniel W. Voorhees, *Terre Haute*
Albert S. White, *Stockwell*

## IOWA

SENATORS

James Harlan, *Mount Pleasant*
James W. Grimes, *Burlington*

REPRESENTATIVES

Samuel R. Curtis,[26] *Keokuk*
James F. Wilson,[27] *Fairfield*
William Vandever,[28] *Dubuque*

## KANSAS

SENATORS

Samuel C. Pomeroy,[29] *Atchison*
James H. Lane,[30] *Lawrence*

---

REPRESENTATIVE AT LARGE

Martin F. Conway, *Lawrence*

## KENTUCKY

SENATORS

Lazarus W. Powell, *Henderson*
John C. Breckinridge,[31] *Lexington*
Garrett Davis,[32] *Paris*

REPRESENTATIVES

Henry C. Burnett,[33] *Cadiz*
Samuel L. Casey,[34] *Caseyville*
John J. Crittenden, *Frankfort*
George W. Dunlap, *Lancaster*
Henry Grider, *Bowling Green*
Aaron Harding, *Greensburg*
James S. Jackson,[35] *Hopkinsville*
George H. Yeaman,[36] *Owensboro*
Robert Mallory, *La Grange*
John W. Menzies, *Covington*
William H. Wadsworth, *Maysville*
Charles A. Wickliffe, *Bardstown*

## LOUISIANA

SENATORS

Judah P. Benjamin,[37] *New Orleans*
Vacant

REPRESENTATIVES

Benjamin F. Flanders,[38] *New Orleans*
Michael Hahn,[39] *New Orleans*

## MAINE

SENATORS

William Pitt Fessenden, *Portland*
Lot M. Morrill, *Augusta*

REPRESENTATIVES

Samuel C. Fessenden, *Rockland*
John N. Goodwin, *South Berwick*
Anson P. Morrill, *Readfield*
Frederick A. Pike, *Calais*
John H. Rice, *Foxcroft*
Charles W. Walton,[40] *Auburn*
Thomas A. D. Fessenden,[41] *Auburn*

---

## MARYLAND

SENATORS

James A. Pearce,[42] *Chestertown*
Thomas H. Hicks,[43] *Cambridge*
Anthony Kennedy, *Ellicotts Mills*

REPRESENTATIVES

Charles B. Calvert, *Bladensburg*
John W. Crisfield, *Princess Anne*
Cornelius L. L. Leary, *Baltimore*
Henry May, *Baltimore*
Francis Thomas, *Frankville*
Edwin H. Webster, *Bel Air*

## MASSACHUSETTS

SENATORS

Charles Sumner, *Boston*
Henry Wilson, *Natick*

REPRESENTATIVES

Charles Francis Adams,[44] *Quincy*
Benjamin F. Thomas,[45] *Boston*
John B. Alley, *Lynn*
William Appleton,[46] *Boston*
Samuel Hooper,[47] *Boston*
Goldsmith F. Bailey,[48] *Fitchburg*
Amasa Walker,[49] *North Brookfield*
James Buffington, *Fall River*
Henry L. Dawes, *North Adams*
Charles Delano, *Northampton*
Thomas D. Eliot, *New Bedford*
Daniel W. Gooch, *Melrose*
Alexander H. Rice, *Boston*
Charles R. Train, *Framingham*

## MICHIGAN

SENATORS

Zachariah Chandler, *Detroit*
Kinsley S. Bingham,[50] *Oak Grove*
Jacob M. Howard,[51] *Detroit*

---

[20] Resigned October 28, 1861.
[21] Elected to fill vacancy caused by resignation of John A. McClernand, and took his seat December 12, 1861.
[22] Resigned January 29, 1863, having been elected Senator.
[23] Expelled February 5, 1862. (See U.S. Senate Election, Expulsion and Censure Cases, 1793-1990, Senate Document 103-33, pp. 106-108.)
[24] Appointed to fill vacancy caused by expulsion of Jesse D. Bright, and took his seat March 3, 1862.
[25] Elected to fill vacancy caused by expulsion of Jesse D. Bright, and took his seat January 22, 1863.
[26] Resigned August 4, 1861.
[27] Elected to fill vacancy caused by resignation of Samuel R. Curtis, and took his seat December 2, 1861.
[28] Took his seat July 4, 1861; election contested by Le Grand Byington. By resolution of January 20, 1863, House declared that Vandever had not been entitled to a seat since September 24, 1861, the day he was mustered into the military service of the United States as a colonel of volunteers without having resigned from Congress. Byington's case against Vandever remained undisposed of at close of the Congress.
[29] Took his seat July 4, 1861; term to expire, as determined by lot, March 3, 1867.

---

[30] Took his seat July 4, 1861; term to expire, as determined by lot, March 3, 1865. Election unsuccessfully contested by Frederick P. Stanton. (See U.S. Senate Election, Expulsion and Censure Cases, 1793-1990, Senate Document 103-33, pp. 92-94.)
[31] Expelled by resolution of December 4, 1861. (See U.S. Senate Election, Expulsion and Censure Cases, 1793-1990, Senate Document 103-33, pp. 102-103.)
[32] Elected to fill vacancy caused by expulsion of John C. Breckinridge and took his seat December 23, 1861.
[33] Expelled by resolution of December 3, 1861..
[34] Elected to fill vacancy caused by expulsion of Henry C. Burnett, and took his seat March 10, 1862.
[35] Resigned December 13, 1861, to enter the Union Army (killed at the battle of Perryville, Ky., October 8, 1862).
[36] Elected to fill vacancy caused by death of James S. Jackson, and took his seat December 1, 1862.
[37] Seat declared vacant by resolution of March 14, 1861. (See U.S. Senate Election, Expulsion and Censure Cases, 1793-1990, Senate Document 103-33, pp. 89-91.)
[38] Credentials presented December 19, 1862; declared entitled to his seat by resolution of February

---

17, 1863, and took his seat February 23, 1863.
[39] Credentials presented December 22, 1862; declared entitled to his seat by resolution of February 17, 1863, and took his seat the same day.
[40] Resigned May 26, 1862.
[41] Elected to fill vacancy caused by resignation of Charles W. Walton, and took his seat December 1, 1862.
[42] Died December 20, 1862.
[43] Appointed to fill vacancy caused by death of James A. Pearce, and took his seat January 14, 1863.
[44] Resigned May 1, 1861, having been appointed minister to England.
[45] Elected to fill vacancy caused by resignation of Charles Francis Adams, and took his seat July 4, 1861.
[46] Resigned September 27, 1861.
[47] Elected to fill vacancy caused by resignation of William Appleton, and took his seat December 2, 1861.
[48] Died May 8, 1862.
[49] Elected to fill vacancy caused by death of Goldsmith F. Bailey, and took his seat December 1, 1862.
[50] Died October 5, 1861.
[51] Elected to fill vacancy caused by death of Kinsley S. Bingham, and took his seat January 17, 1862.

REPRESENTATIVES

Fernando C. Beaman, *Adrian*
Bradley F. Granger, *Ann Arbor*
Francis W. Kellogg, *Grand Rapids*
Rowland E. Trowbridge, *Birmingham*

## MINNESOTA

SENATORS

Henry M. Rice, *St. Paul*
Morton S. Wilkinson, *Mankato*

REPRESENTATIVES AT LARGE

Cyrus Aldrich, *Minneapolis*
William Windom, *Winona*

## MISSISSIPPI

SENATORS

Albert G. Brown,[52] *Terry*
Jefferson Davis,[52] *Hurricane*

REPRESENTATIVES

Vacant

## MISSOURI

SENATORS

Trusten Polk,[53] *St. Louis*
John B. Henderson,[54] *Louisiana*
Waldo Porter Johnson,[55] *Osceola*
Robert Wilson,[56] *St. Joseph*

REPRESENTATIVES

Francis P. Blair, Jr.,[57] *St. Louis*
John W. Noell, *Perryville*
Elijah H. Norton, *Platte City*
John S. Phelps, *Springfield*
John W. Reid,[58] *Jefferson City*
Thomas L. Price,[59] *Jefferson City*
James S. Rollins, *Columbia*
John B. Clark,[60] *Fayette*
William A. Hall,[61] *Huntsville*

## NEW HAMPSHIRE

SENATORS

John P. Hale, *Dover*
Daniel Clark, *Manchester*

REPRESENTATIVES

Thomas M. Edwards, *Keene*
Gilman Marston, *Exeter*
Edward H. Rollins, *Concord*

## NEW JERSEY

SENATORS

John R. Thomson,[62] *Princeton*
Richard S. Field,[63] *Princeton*
James W. Wall,[64] *Burlington*
John C. Ten Eyck, *Mount Holly*

REPRESENTATIVES

George T. Cobb, *Morristown*
John T. Nixon, *Bridgeton*
Nehemiah Perry, *Newark*
William G. Steele, *Somerville*
J. L. N. Stratton, *Mount Holly*

## NEW YORK

SENATORS

Preston King, *Ogdensburg*
Ira Harris, *Albany*

REPRESENTATIVES

Stephen Baker, *Poughkeepsie*
Jacob P. Chamberlain, *Seneca Falls*
Ambrose W. Clark, *Watertown*
Frederick A. Conkling, *New York City*
Roscoe Conkling, *Utica*
Erastus Corning, *Albany*
Isaac C. Delaplaine, *New York City*
Alexander S. Diven, *Elmira*
R. Holland Duell, *Cortland*
Alfred Ely, *Rochester*
Reuben E. Fenton, *Frewsburg*
Richard Franchot, *Schenectady*
Augustus Frank, *Warsaw*
Edward Haight, *West Chester*
James E. Kerrigan, *New York City*
William E. Lansing, *Chittenango*
James B. McKean, *Saratoga Springs*
Moses F. Odell, *Brooklyn*
Abram B. Olin, *Troy*
Theodore M. Pomeroy, *Auburn*
Charles B. Sedgwick, *Syracuse*
Socrates N. Sherman, *Ogdensburg*
Edward H. Smith, *Smithtown*
Elbridge G. Spaulding, *Buffalo*

John B. Steele, *Kingston*
Burt Van Horn, *Newfane*
Robert B. Van Valkenburg, *Bath*
Charles H. Van Wyck, *Bloomingburg*
Chauncey Vibbard, *Schenectady*
William Wall, *Brooklyn*
Elijah Ward, *New York City*
William A. Wheeler, *Malone*
Benjamin Wood, *New York City*

## NORTH CAROLINA[65]

SENATORS

Thomas L. Clingman,[66] *Asheville*
Thomas Bragg,[67] *Raleigh*

REPRESENTATIVES

Vacant

## OHIO

SENATORS

Benjamin F. Wade, *Jefferson*
Salmon P. Chase,[68] *Cincinnati*
John Sherman,[69] *Mansfield*

REPRESENTATIVES

William Allen, *Greenville*
James M. Ashley, *Toledo*
John A. Bingham, *Cadiz*
Harrison G. O. Blake, *Medina*
Samuel S. Cox, *Columbus*
William P. Cutler, *Constitution*
Sidney Edgerton, *Tallmadge*
John A. Gurley, *Cincinnati*
Thomas Corwin,[70] *Lebanon*
Richard A. Harrison,[71] *London*
Valentine B. Horton, *Pomeroy*
John Hutchins, *Warren*
James R. Morris, *Woodsfield*
Warren P. Noble, *Tiffin*
Robert H. Nugen, *Newcomerstown*
George H. Pendleton, *Cincinnati*
Albert G. Riddle, *Cleveland*
Samuel Shellabarger, *Springfield*
Carey A. Trimble, *Chillicothe*
Clement L. Vallandigham, *Dayton*
Chilton A. White, *Georgetown*
John Sherman,[72] *Mansfield*
Samuel T. Worcester,[73] *Norwalk*

---

[52] Did not attend during this Congress; seat declared vacant by resolution of March 14, 1861. (See U.S. Senate Election, Expulsion and Censure Cases, 1793-1990, Senate Document 103-33, pp. 89-91.)

[53] Expelled by resolution of January 10, 1862. (See U.S. Senate Election, Expulsion and Censure Cases, 1793-1990, Senate Document 103-33, pp. 104-105.)

[54] Appointed to fill vacancy caused by expulsion of Trusten Polk, and took his seat January 29, 1862; subsequently elected.

[55] Expelled by resolution of January 10, 1862. (See U.S. Senate Election, Expulsion and Censure Cases, 1793-1990, Senate Document 103-33, pp. 104-105.)

[56] Appointed to fill vacancy caused by expulsion of Waldo P. Johnson, and took his seat January 24, 1862.

[57] Resigned in July, 1862.

[58] Did not occupy his seat after August 3, 1861; expelled by resolution of December 2, 1861.

[59] Elected to fill vacancy caused by expulsion of John W. Reid, and took his seat January 21, 1862.

[60] Expelled by resolution of July 13, 1861, never having qualified.

[61] Elected to fill vacancy caused by expulsion of John B. Clark, and took his seat January 20, 1862.

[62] Died September 12, 1862.

[63] Appointed to fill vacancy caused by death of John R. Thomson, and took his seat December 1, 1862.

[64] Elected to fill vacancy caused by death of John R. Thomson, and took his seat January 21, 1863.

[65] Seceded from the Union May 21, 1861. Charles Henry Foster claimed the right to represent the first congressional district.

[66] Withdrew March 28, 1861; expelled by resolution of July 11, 1861. (See U.S. Senate Election, Expulsion and Censure Cases, 1793-1990, Senate

Document 103-33, pp. 95-98.)

[67] Withdrew March 8, 1861; expelled by resolution of July 11, 1861. (See U.S. Senate Election, Expulsion and Censure Cases, 1793-1990, Senate Document 103-33, pp. 95-98.)

[68] Resigned March 6, 1861, having been appointed Secretary of the Treasury.

[69] Elected to fill vacancy caused by resignation of Salmon P. Chase, and took his seat March 23, 1861.

[70] Resigned March 12, 1861, having been appointed minister to Mexico.

[71] Elected to fill vacancy caused by the resignation of Thomas Corwin, and took his seat July 4, 1861.

[72] Resigned March 21, 1861, having been elected Senator.

[73] Elected to fill vacancy caused by the resignation of John Sherman, and took his seat July 4, 1861.

## OREGON

### SENATORS

Edward D. Baker,[74] *Oregon City*
Benjamin Stark,[75] *Portland*
Benjamin F. Harding,[76] *Salem*
James W. Nesmith, *Salem*

### REPRESENTATIVE AT LARGE

Andrew J. Thayer,[77] *Corvallis*
George K. Shiel,[78] *Salem*

## PENNSYLVANIA

### SENATORS

Simon Cameron,[79] *Harrisburg*
David Wilmot,[80] *Towanda*
Edgar Cowan, *Greensburg*

### REPRESENTATIVES

Sydenham E. Ancona, *Reading*
Elijah Babbitt, *Erie*
Joseph Bailey, *Newport*
E. Joy Morris,[81] *Philadelphia*
Charles J. Biddle,[82] *Philadelphia*
Samuel S. Blair, *Hollidaysburg*
James H. Campbell, *Pottsville*
Thomas B. Cooper,[83] *Coopersburg*
John D. Stiles,[84] *Allentown*
John Covode, *Lockport Station*
William Morris Davis, *Milestown*
Galusha A. Grow, *Glenwood*
James T. Hale, *Bellefonte*
John Hickman, *West Chester*
Philip Johnson, *Easton*
William D. Kelley, *Philadelphia*
John W. Killinger, *Lebanon*
Jesse Lazear, *Waynesburg*
William E. Lehman,[85] *Philadelphia*
Robert McKnight, *Pittsburgh*

Edward McPherson, *Gettysburg*
James K. Moorhead, *Pittsburgh*
John Patton, *Curwinsville*
Thaddeus Stevens, *Lancaster*
John P. Verree,[86] *Philadelphia*
John W. Wallace, *New Castle*
George W. Scranton,[87] *Scranton*
Hendrick B. Wright,[88] *Wilkes-Barre*

## RHODE ISLAND

### SENATORS

James F. Simmons,[89] *Providence*
Samuel G. Arnold,[90] *Providence*
Henry B. Anthony, *Providence*

### REPRESENTATIVES

George H. Browne, *Providence*
William P. Sheffield, *Newport*

## SOUTH CAROLINA

### SENATORS

James Chesnut, Jr.,[91] *Camden*
Vacant

### REPRESENTATIVES

Vacant

## TENNESSEE[92]

### SENATORS

Andrew Johnson,[93] *Greeneville*
Alfred O. P. Nicholson,[94] *Columbia*

### REPRESENTATIVES

George W. Bridges,[95] *Athens*
Andrew J. Clements,[96] *Lafayette*
Horace Maynard,[97] *Knoxville*

## TEXAS

### SENATORS

John Hemphill,[98] *Austin*
Louis T. Wigfall,[99] *Marshall*

### REPRESENTATIVES

Vacant

## VERMONT

### SENATORS

Solomon Foot, *Rutland*
Jacob Collamer, *Woodstock*

### REPRESENTATIVES

Portus Baxter, *Derby Line*
Justin S. Morrill, *Strafford*
Eliakim P. Walton, *Montpelier*

## VIRGINIA[100]

### SENATORS

James M. Mason,[101] *Winchester*
Waitman T. Willey,[102] *Morgantown*
Robert M. T. Hunter,[103] *Lloyds*
John S. Carlile,[104] *Wheeling*

### REPRESENTATIVES[105]

William G. Brown, *Kingwood*
John S. Carlile,[106] *Wheeling*
Jacob B. Blair,[107] *Parkersburg*
Joseph E. Segar,[108] *Elizabeth City*
Charles H. Upton,[109] *Falls Church*
Lewis McKenzie,[110] *Alexandria*
Kellian V. Whaley, *Ceredo*

## WISCONSIN

### SENATORS

James R. Doolittle, *Racine*
Timothy O. Howe, *Green Bay*

---

[74] Died October 21, 1861.

[75] Appointed to fill vacancy caused by death of Edward D. Baker; took his seat February 27, 1862.

[76] Elected to fill vacancy caused by death of Edward D. Baker, and took his seat December 1, 1862.

[77] Served until July 30, 1861; succeeded by George K. Shiel, who contested his election.

[78] Successfully contested the election of Andrew J. Thayer, and took his seat July 30, 1861.

[79] Resigned March 4, 1861, having been appointed Secretary of War.

[80] Elected to fill vacancy caused by resignation of Simon Cameron, and took his seat March 18, 1861.

[81] Resigned June 8, 1861, having been appointed minister resident to Turkey.

[82] Elected to fill vacancy caused by resignation of E. Joy Morris, and took his seat December 2, 1861.

[83] Died April 4, 1862.

[84] Elected to fill vacancy caused by death of Thomas B. Cooper, and took his seat June 3, 1862.

[85] Election unsuccessfully contested by John M. Butler.

[86] Election unsuccessfully contested by John Kline.

[87] Died March 24, 1861.

[88] Elected to fill vacancy caused by the death of George W. Scranton, and took his seat July 4, 1861.

[89] Resigned August 15, 1862.

[90] Elected to fill vacancy caused by resignation of James F. Simmons, and took his seat December 1, 1862.

[91] Did not attend during this Congress; expelled

by resolution of July 11, 1861. (See U.S. Senate Election, Expulsion and Censure Cases, 1793-1990, Senate Document 103-33, pp. 95-98.)

[92] Seceded from the Union June 24, 1861.

[93] Resigned March 4, 1862, to become military governor of Tennessee.

[94] Did not attend during this Congress; expelled by resolution of July 11, 1861. (See U.S. Senate Election, Expulsion and Censure Cases, 1793-1990, Senate Document 103-33, pp. 95-98.)

[95] Elected August 1, 1861; took his seat February 25, 1863.

[96] Elected August 1, 1861; presented memorial on December 3, 1861, claiming seat, and by resolution of January 13, 1862, was declared entitled to the same; took his seat same day.

[97] Elected August 1, 1861; took his seat December 2, 1861.

[98] Did not occupy his seat after March 4, 1861; expelled by resolution of July 11, 1861. (See U.S. Senate Election, Expulsion and Censure Cases, 1793-1990, Senate Document 103-33, pp. 95-98.)

[99] Did not occupy his seat after March 23, 1861; expelled by resolution of July 11, 1861. (See U.S. Senate Election, Expulsion and Censure Cases, 1793-1990, Senate Document 103-33, pp. 95-98.)

[100] Seceded from the Union April 17, 1861.

[101] Withdrew March 28, 1861; expelled by resolution of July 11, 1861. (See U.S. Senate Election, Expulsion and Censure Cases, 1793-1990, Senate Document 103-33, pp. 95-98.)

[102] Elected to fill vacancy caused by withdrawal of

James M. Mason, and took his seat July 13, 1861.

[103] Withdrew March 28, 1861; expelled by resolution of July 11, 1861. (See U.S. Senate Election, Expulsion and Censure Cases, 1793-1990, Senate Document 103-33, pp. 95-98.)

[104] Elected to fill vacancy caused by withdrawal of Robert M. T. Hunter, and took his seat July 13, 1861.

[105] J. B. McCloud and W. W. Wing both claimed election from the second district, but on February 14, 1863, the House decided that neither was entitled to the seat; Christopher L. Graffin presented credentials from the eighth district, but on March 3, 1863, was declared not entitled to seat.

[106] Resigned July 9, 1861, having been elected Senator.

[107] Elected to fill vacancy caused by resignation of John S. Carlile, and took his seat December 2, 1861.

[108] Declared not entitled to his seat under first credentials by resolution of February 11, 1862; subsequently elected and declared entitled to seat under second credentials by resolution of May 6, 1862; qualified and took his seat the same day.

[109] Presented credentials of an election held May 23, 1861, and took his seat July 4, 1861; declared not entitled to the seat February 27, 1862. S. Ferguson Beach presented memorial denying right of Upton, and claiming seat under an election held October 24, 1861, but on March 31, 1862, was declared not entitled to same.

[110] Elected to fill vacancy caused by the unseating of Charles H. Upton, and took his seat February 16, 1863.

REPRESENTATIVES

Luther Hanchett,[111] *Plover*
Walter D. McIndoe,[112] *Wausau*
John F. Potter, *East Troy*
A. Scott Sloan, *Beaver Dam*

## TERRITORY OF COLORADO[113]

DELEGATE

Hiram P. Bennett,[114] *Denver*

## TERRITORY OF DAKOTA[115]

DELEGATE

John B. S. Todd,[116] *Fort Randall*

## TERRITORY OF NEBRASKA

DELEGATE

Samuel G. Daily,[117] *Peru*

## TERRITORY OF NEVADA[118]

DELEGATE

John Cradlebaugh,[119] *Carson City*

## TERRITORY OF NEW MEXICO

DELEGATE

John S. Watts, *Santa Fe*

## TERRITORY OF UTAH

DELEGATE

John M. Bernhisel, *Salt Lake City*

## TERRITORY OF WASHINGTON

DELEGATE

William H. Wallace, *Steilacoom*

---

[111] Died November 24, 1862.

[112] Elected to fill vacancy caused by death of Luther Hanchett, and took his seat January 26, 1863.

[113] Formed from portions of the territory ceded to the United States by France by the treaty of Paris of April 30, 1803, and of that ceded by Mexico by the treaty of Guadalupe Hidalgo of February 2, 1848, and granted a Delegate in Congress by act of February 28, 1861.

[114] Took his seat December 2, 1861.

[115] Formed from a portion of the territory ceded to the United States by France by treaty of April 30, 1803, and granted a Delegate in Congress by act of March 2, 1861.

[116] Took his seat December 9, 1861.

[117] Election unsuccessfully contested by J. Sterling Morton.

[118] Formed from a portion of the territory ceded to the United States by Mexico by the treaty of Guadalupe Hidalgo of February 2, 1848, and granted a Delegate in Congress by act of March 2, 1861.

[119] Took his seat December 2, 1861.

# 38TH CONGRESS

## MARCH 4, 1863, TO MARCH 3, 1865

Hannibal Hamlin
Vice President

FIRST SESSION— *December 7, 1863, to July 4, 1864*
SECOND SESSION— *December 5, 1864, to March 3, 1865*
SPECIAL SESSION OF THE SENATE— *March 4, 1863, to March 14, 1863*

VICE PRESIDENT OF THE UNITED STATES— HANNIBAL HAMLIN, of Maine
PRESIDENT PRO TEMPORE OF THE SENATE— SOLOMON FOOT,[1] of Vermont; DANIEL CLARK,[2] of New Hampshire
SECRETARY OF THE SENATE— JOHN W. FORNEY, of Pennsylvania
SERGEANT AT ARMS OF THE SENATE— GEORGE T. BROWN, of Illinois

Schuyler Colfax
Speaker

SPEAKER OF THE HOUSE OF REPRESENTATIVES— SCHUYLER COLFAX,[3] of Indiana
CLERK OF THE HOUSE— EMERSON ETHERIDGE, of Tennessee; EDWARD McPHERSON,[4] of Pennsylvania
SERGEANT AT ARMS OF THE HOUSE— EDWARD BALL, of Ohio; NATHANIEL G. ORDWAY,[5] of New Hampshire
DOORKEEPER OF THE HOUSE— IRA GOODNOW, of Vermont
POSTMASTER OF THE HOUSE— WILLIAM S. KING

## ALABAMA

### SENATORS
Vacant

### REPRESENTATIVES
Vacant

## ARKANSAS

### SENATORS
Vacant

### REPRESENTATIVES
Vacant[6]

## CALIFORNIA

### SENATORS
James A. McDougall, *San Francisco*
John Conness, *Sacramento*

### REPRESENTATIVES AT LARGE
Cornelius Cole, *Santa Cruz*
William Higby, *Mokelumne Hill*
Thomas B. Shannon, *Quincy*

## CONNECTICUT

### SENATORS
Lafayette S. Foster, *Norwich*
James Dixon, *Hartford*

### REPRESENTATIVES
Augustus Brandegee, *New London*
Henry C. Deming, *Hartford*
James E. English, *New Haven*
John H. Hubbard, *Litchfield*

## DELAWARE

### SENATORS
James A. Bayard,[7] *Wilmington*
George R. Riddle,[8] *Wilmington*
Willard Saulsbury, *Georgetown*

### REPRESENTATIVE AT LARGE
William Temple,[9] *Smyrna*
Nathaniel B. Smithers,[10] *Dover*

## FLORIDA

### SENATORS
Vacant

### REPRESENTATIVE AT LARGE
Vacant

## GEORGIA

### SENATORS
Vacant

### REPRESENTATIVES
Vacant

## ILLINOIS

### SENATORS
Lyman Trumbull, *Alton*
William A. Richardson, *Quincy*

### REPRESENTATIVE AT LARGE
James C. Allen, *Palestine*

### REPRESENTATIVES
Isaac N. Arnold, *Chicago*
John F. Farnsworth, *St. Charles*
Elihu B. Washburne, *Galena*
Charles M. Harris, *Oquawka*
Owen Lovejoy,[11] *Princeton*
Ebon C. Ingersoll,[12] *Peoria*
Jesse O. Norton, *Joliet*
John R. Eden, *Sullivan*
John T. Stuart, *Springfield*
Lewis W. Ross, *Lewistown*
Anthony L. Knapp, *Jerseyville*
James C. Robinson, *Marshall*
William R. Morrison, *Waterloo*
William J. Allen, *Marion*

## INDIANA

### SENATORS
Henry S. Lane, *Crawfordsville*
Thomas A. Hendricks, *Indianapolis*

### REPRESENTATIVES
Schuyler Colfax, *South Bend*
James A. Cravens, *Hardinsburg*
Ebenezer Dumont, *Indianapolis*
Joseph K. Edgerton, *Fort Wayne*
Henry W. Harrington, *Madison*
William S. Holman, *Aurora*
George W. Julian, *Centerville*
John Law, *Evansville*
James F. McDowell, *Marion*
Godlove S. Orth, *Lafayette*

---

[1] Elected March 4, 1863 (special session of the Senate); December 18, 1863; February 23, 1864; March 11, 1864; and April 11, 1864.
[2] Elected April 26, 1864; February 9, 1865.
[3] Elected December 7, 1863.
[4] Elected December 8, 1863.
[5] Elected December 8, 1863.

[6] James M. Johnson, T. M. Jacks, and Anthony A. C. Rogers presented credentials as Members-elect, but their claims were not finally disposed of. By resolution of March 3, 1865, each was allowed the sum of $2,000 for "compensation, expenses, and mileage."
[7] Resigned January 29, 1864.
[8] Elected to fill vacancy caused by resignation of

James A. Bayard, and took his seat February 2, 1864.
[9] Died May 28, 1863, before Congress assembled.
[10] Elected to fill vacancy caused by death of William Temple, and took his seat December 7, 1863.
[11] Died March 25, 1864.
[12] Elected to fill vacancy caused by the death of Owen Lovejoy, and took his seat May 20, 1864.

Daniel W. Voorhees, *Terre Haute*

## IOWA

### SENATORS

James Harlan, *Mount Pleasant*
James W. Grimes, *Burlington*

### REPRESENTATIVES

William B. Allison, *Dubuque*
Josiah B. Grinnell,[13] *Grinnell*
Asahel W. Hubbard, *Sioux City*
John A. Kasson, *Des Moines*
Hiram Price, *Davenport*
James F. Wilson, *Fairfield*

## KANSAS

### SENATORS

Samuel C. Pomeroy, *Atchison*
James H. Lane, *Lawrence*

### REPRESENTATIVE AT LARGE

A. Carter Wilder, *Lawrence*

## KENTUCKY

### SENATORS

Lazarus W. Powell, *Henderson*
Garrett Davis, *Paris*

### REPRESENTATIVES

Lucien Anderson, *Mayfield*
Brutus J. Clay, *Paris*
Henry Grider, *Bristol*
Aaron Harding, *Greensburg*
Robert Mallory, *La Grange*
William H. Randall, *London*
Green C. Smith, *Covington*
William H. Wadsworth, *Maysville*
George H. Yeaman,[14] *Owensboro*

## LOUISIANA

### SENATORS

Vacant

### REPRESENTATIVES

Vacant[15]

## MAINE

### SENATORS

William Pitt Fessenden,[16] *Portland*
Nathan A. Farwell,[17] *Rockland*
Lot M. Morrill, *Augusta*

### REPRESENTATIVES

James G. Blaine, *Augusta*
Sidney Perham, *Paris*
Frederick A. Pike, *Calais*
John H. Rice, *Foxcroft*
Lorenzo D. M. Sweat, *Portland*

## MARYLAND

### SENATORS

Thomas H. Hicks,[18] *Cambridge*
Reverdy Johnson, *Baltimore*

### REPRESENTATIVES

John A. J. Creswell, *Elkton*
Henry Winter Davis, *Baltimore*
Benjamin G. Harris, *Leonardtown*
Francis Thomas, *Frankville*
Edwin H. Webster, *Bel Air*

## MASSACHUSETTS

### SENATORS

Charles Sumner, *Boston*
Henry Wilson, *Natick*

### REPRESENTATIVES

John B. Alley, *Lynn*
Oakes Ames, *North Easton*
John D. Baldwin, *Worcester*
George S. Boutwell, *Groton*
Henry L. Dawes, *Pittsfield*
Thomas D. Eliot, *New Bedford*
Daniel W. Gooch, *Melrose*
Samuel Hooper, *Boston*
Alexander H. Rice,[19] *Boston*
William B. Washburn, *Greenfield*

## MICHIGAN

### SENATORS

Zachariah Chandler, *Detroit*
Jacob M. Howard, *Detroit*

### REPRESENTATIVES

Augustus C. Baldwin, *Pontiac*
Fernando C. Beaman, *Adrian*
John F. Driggs, *East Saginaw*
Francis W. Kellogg, *Grand Rapids*
John W. Longyear, *Lansing*
Charles Upson, *Coldwater*

## MINNESOTA

### SENATORS

Morton S. Wilkinson, *Mankato*
Alexander Ramsey, *St. Paul*

### REPRESENTATIVES

Ignatius Donnelly, *Nininger*
William Windom, *Winona*

## MISSISSIPPI

### SENATORS

Vacant

### REPRESENTATIVES

Vacant

## MISSOURI

### SENATORS

John B. Henderson, *Louisiana*
Robert Wilson, *St. Joseph*
B. Gratz Brown,[20] *St. Louis*

### REPRESENTATIVES

Francis P. Blair, Jr.,[21] *St. Louis*
Samuel Knox,[22] *St. Louis*
Henry T. Blow, *St. Louis*
Sempronius H. Boyd, *Springfield*
William A. Hall, *Huntsville*
Austin A. King, *Richmond*
Benjamin F. Loan,[23] *St. Joseph*
Joseph W. McClurg,[24] *Linn Creek*
James S. Rollins, *Columbia*
John W. Noell,[25] *Perryville*
John G. Scott,[26] *Irondale*

## NEVADA[27]

### SENATORS

William M. Stewart,[28] *Virginia City*
James W. Nye,[29] *Carson City*

### REPRESENTATIVE AT LARGE

Henry G. Worthington,[30] *Austin*

## NEW HAMPSHIRE

### SENATORS

John P. Hale, *Dover*
Daniel Clark, *Manchester*

### REPRESENTATIVES

Daniel Marcy, *Portsmouth*
James W. Patterson, *Hanover*
Edward H. Rollins, *Concord*

## NEW JERSEY

### SENATORS

John C. Ten Eyck, *Mount Holly*
William Wright, *Newark*

---

[13] Election unsuccessfully contested by Hugh M. Martin.
[14] Election unsuccessfully contested by John H. McHenry, Jr.
[15] M. F. Bonzano, A. P. Field, W. D. Mann, T. M. Welles, and Robert W. Taliaferro presented credentials as Members-elect, but their claims were not finally disposed of.
[16] Resigned July 1, 1864, to become Secretary of the Treasury.
[17] Appointed to fill vacancy caused by resignation of William Pitt Fessenden, and took his seat December 5, 1864; subsequently elected.
[18] Died February 14, 1865.

[19] Election unsuccessfully contested by John S. Sleeper.
[20] Elected, on November 13, 1863, to fill vacancy caused by expulsion of Waldo Porter Johnson, in preceding Congress, and took his seat December 14, 1863; Robert Wilson, Senator-designate in previous Congress, attended on December 7, 1863, but the following day was declared not entitled to a seat.
[21] Served until June 10, 1864; succeeded by Samuel Knox, who contested his election.
[22] Successfully contested the election of Francis P. Blair, Jr., and took his seat June 15, 1864.
[23] Election unsuccessfully contested by John P. Bruce.

[24] Election unsuccessfully contested by Thomas L. Price.
[25] Died March 14, 1863.
[26] Elected to fill vacancy caused by the death of John W. Noell, and took his seat December 7, 1863; election unsuccessfully contested by James Lindsay.
[27] Admitted as a State into the Union October 31, 1864.
[28] Took his seat February 1, 1865; term to expire, as determined by lot, March 3, 1869.
[29] Took his seat February 1, 1865; term to expire, as determined by lot, March 3, 1867.
[30] Took his seat December 21, 1864.

## NEW JERSEY— Continued
### REPRESENTATIVES
George Middleton, *Allentown*
Nehemiah Perry, *Newark*
Andrew J. Rogers, *Newton*
John F. Starr, *Camden*
William G. Steele, *Somerville*

## NEW YORK
### SENATORS
Ira Harris, *Albany*
Edwin D. Morgan, *New York City*

### REPRESENTATIVES
James Brooks, *New York City*
John W. Chanler, *New York City*
Ambrose W. Clark, *Watertown*
Freeman Clarke, *Rochester*
Erastus Corning,[31] *Albany*
John V. L. Pruyn,[32] *Albany*
Thomas T. Davis, *Syracuse*
Reuben E. Fenton,[33] *Frewsburg*
Augustus Frank, *Warsaw*
John Ganson, *Buffalo*
John A. Griswold, *Troy*
Anson Herrick, *New York City*
Giles W. Hotchkiss, *Binghamton*
Calvin T. Hulburd, *Brasher Falls*
Martin Kalbfleisch, *Brooklyn*
Orlando Kellogg, *Elizabethtown*
Francis Kernan, *Utica*
De Witt C. Littlejohn, *Oswego*
James M. Marvin, *Saratoga Springs*
Samuel F. Miller, *Franklin*
Daniel Morris, *Penn Yan*
Homer A. Nelson, *Poughkeepsie*
Moses F. Odell, *Brooklyn*
Theodore M. Pomeroy, *Auburn*
William Radford, *Yonkers*
Henry G. Stebbins,[34] *New Brighton*
Dwight Townsend,[35] *Clifton*
John B. Steele, *Kingston*
Robert B. Van Valkenburg, *Bath*
Elijah Ward, *New York City*
Charles H. Winfield, *Goshen*
Benjamin Wood, *New York City*
Fernando Wood, *New York City*

## NORTH CAROLINA
### SENATORS
Vacant
### REPRESENTATIVES
Vacant

## OHIO
### SENATORS
Benjamin F. Wade, *Jefferson*
John Sherman, *Mansfield*

### REPRESENTATIVES
James M. Ashley, *Toledo*
George Bliss, *Wooster*
Samuel S. Cox, *Columbus*
Ephraim R. Eckley, *Carrollton*
William E. Finck, *Somerset*
James A. Garfield, *Hiram*
Wells A. Hutchins, *Portsmouth*
William Johnston, *Mansfield*
Francis C. Le Blond, *Celina*
Alexander Long, *Cincinnati*
John F. McKinney, *Piqua*
James R. Morris, *Woodsfield*
Warren P. Noble, *Tiffin*
John O'Neill, *Zanesville*
George H. Pendleton, *Cincinnati*
Robert C. Schenck, *Dayton*
Rufus P. Spalding, *Cleveland*
Chilton A. White, *Georgetown*
Joseph W. White, *Cambridge*

## OREGON
### SENATORS
James W. Nesmith, *Salem*
Benjamin F. Harding, *Salem*

### REPRESENTATIVE AT LARGE
John R. McBride, *Lafayette*

## PENNSYLVANIA
### SENATORS
Edgar Cowan, *Greensburg*
Charles R. Buckalew, *Bloomsburg*

### REPRESENTATIVES
Sydenham E. Ancona, *Reading*
Joseph Bailey, *Newport*
John M. Broomall, *Media*
Alexander H. Coffroth, *Somerset*
John L. Dawson, *Brownsville*
Charles Denison, *Wilkes-Barre*
James T. Hale, *Bellefonte*
Philip Johnson, *Easton*
William D. Kelley, *Philadelphia*
Jesse Lazear, *Waynesburg*
Archibald McAllister, *Springfield Furnace*
William H. Miller, *Harrisburg*
James K. Moorhead, *Pittsburgh*
Amos Myers, *Clarion*
Leonard Myers,[36] *Philadelphia*
Charles O'Neill, *Philadelphia*
Samuel J. Randall, *Philadelphia*
Glenni W. Schofield, *Warren*
Thaddeus Stevens, *Lancaster*

John D. Stiles, *Allentown*
Myer Strouse, *Pottsville*
M. Russell Thayer,[37] *Chestnut Hill*
Henry W. Tracy, *Standing Stone*
Thomas Williams, *Pittsburgh*

## RHODE ISLAND
### SENATORS
Henry B. Anthony, *Providence*
William Sprague, *Providence*

### REPRESENTATIVES
Nathan F. Dixon, *Westerly*
Thomas A. Jenckes, *Providence*

## SOUTH CAROLINA
### SENATORS
Vacant

### REPRESENTATIVES
Vacant

## TENNESSEE
### SENATORS
Vacant

### REPRESENTATIVES
Vacant

## TEXAS
### SENATORS
Vacant

### REPRESENTATIVES
Vacant

## VERMONT
### SENATORS
Solomon Foot, *Rutland*
Jacob Collamer, *Woodstock*

### REPRESENTATIVES
Portus Baxter, *Derby Line*
Justin S. Morrill, *Strafford*
Frederick E. Woodbridge, *Vergennes*

---

[31] Resigned October 5, 1863, before Congress assembled.
[32] Elected to fill vacancy caused by the resignation of Erastus Corning, and took his seat December 7, 1863.
[33] Resigned effective December 20, 1864.

[34] Resigned October 24, 1864.
[35] Elected to fill vacancy caused by resignation of Henry G. Stebbins, and took his seat December 5, 1864.
[36] Election unsuccessfully contested by John Kline.

[37] Election unsuccessfully contested by Charles W. Carrigan.

## VIRGINIA

SENATORS

John S. Carlile, *Clarksburg*

Lemuel J. Bowden,[38] *Williamsburg*

REPRESENTATIVES

Vacant[39]

## WEST VIRGINIA[40]

SENATORS

Peter G. Van Winkle,[41] *Parkersburg*

Waitman T. Willey,[42] *Morgantown*

REPRESENTATIVES

Jacob B. Blair,[43] *Parkersburg*

William G. Brown,[43] *Kingwood*

Kellian V. Whaley,[43] *Point Pleasant*

## WISCONSIN

SENATORS

James R. Doolittle, *Racine*

Timothy O. Howe, *Green Bay*

REPRESENTATIVES

James S. Brown, *Milwaukee*

Amasa Cobb, *Mineral Point*

Charles A. Eldridge, *Fond du Lac*

Walter D. McIndoe, *Wausau*

Ithamar C. Sloan, *Janesville*

Ezra Wheeler, *Berlin*

## TERRITORY OF ARIZONA[44]

DELEGATE

Charles D. Poston,[45] *Tubac*

## TERRITORY OF COLORADO

DELEGATE

Hiram P. Bennet, *Denver*

## TERRITORY OF DAKOTA

DELEGATE

William Jayne,[46] *Yankton*

John B. S. Todd,[47] *Yankton*

## TERRITORY OF IDAHO[48]

DELEGATE

William H. Wallace,[49] *Lewiston*

## TERRITORY OF MONTANA[50]

DELEGATE

Samuel McLean,[51] *Bannack*

## TERRITORY OF NEBRASKA

DELEGATE

Samuel G. Daily, *Peru*

## TERRITORY OF NEVADA

DELEGATE

Gordon N. Mott,[52] *Carson City*

## TERRITORY OF NEW MEXICO

DELEGATE

Francisco Perea,[53] *Bernalillo*

## TERRITORY OF UTAH

DELEGATE

John F. Kinney, *Salt Lake City*

## TERRITORY OF WASHINGTON

DELEGATE

George E. Cole, *Walla Walla*

---

[38] Died January 2, 1864. On February 17, 1865, the credentials of Joseph E. Segar, to fill vacancy caused by the death of Lemuel J. Bowden, were presented but were ordered to lie on the table; no further action taken. State unrepresented in this class from this date to October 20, 1869. (See U.S. Senate Election, Expulsion and Censure Cases, 1793-1990, Senate Document 103-33, pp. 124-126.)

[39] Joseph E. Segar, from the first district, Lucius H. Chandler, from the second district, and Bethuel M. Kitchen, from the seventh district, presented credentials. They were declared not entitled to seats, the first two by resolution of May 17, 1864; the last named by resolution of April 16, 1864. Lewis McKenzie also claimed to have been elected from the seventh district, and was declared not entitled to the seat by resolution of February 26, 1864. The first three claimants were

subsequently allowed mileage and pay to the dates of the adoption of the resolutions.

[40] Formed from a portion of the State of Virginia and admitted into the Union June 19, 1863.

[41] Took his seat December 7, 1863; term to expire, as determined by lot, March 3, 1869.

[42] Took his seat December 7, 1863; term to expire, as determined by lot, March 3, 1865.

[43] Took his seat December 7, 1863.

[44] Formed from a portion of the Territory of New Mexico and granted a Delegate in Congress by act of February 24, 1863.

[45] Took his seat December 5, 1864.

[46] Served until June 17, 1864; succeeded by John B. S. Todd, who contested his election.

[47] Successfully contested the election of William

Jayne, and took his seat June 17, 1864.

[48] Formed from a portion of the territory ceded to the United States by France by treaty of April 30, 1803, and granted a Delegate in Congress by act of March 3, 1863.

[49] Took his seat February 1, 1864.

[50] Formed from a portion of the territory ceded to the United States by France by treaty of April 30, 1803, and granted a Delegate in Congress by act of May 26, 1864.

[51] Took his seat January 6, 1865.

[52] Served until October 31, 1864, when the Territory of Nevada was granted statehood.

[53] Election unsuccessfully contested by José Manuel Gallegos.

# 39TH CONGRESS

## MARCH 4, 1865, TO MARCH 3, 1867

Andrew Johnson
Vice President

FIRST SESSION— *December 4, 1865, to July 28, 1866*
SECOND SESSION— *December 3, 1866, to March 3, 1867*
SPECIAL SESSION OF THE SENATE— *March 4, 1865, to March 11, 1865*

———

VICE PRESIDENT OF THE UNITED STATES— ANDREW JOHNSON,[1] of Tennessee
PRESIDENT PRO TEMPORE OF THE SENATE— LAFAYETTE S. FOSTER,[2] of Connecticut;
BENJAMIN F. WADE,[3] of Ohio
SECRETARY OF THE SENATE— JOHN W. FORNEY, of Pennsylvania
SERGEANT AT ARMS OF THE SENATE— GEORGE T. BROWN, of Illinois

———

SPEAKER OF THE HOUSE OF REPRESENTATIVES— SCHUYLER COLFAX,[4] of Indiana
CLERK OF THE HOUSE— EDWARD MCPHERSON,[5] of Pennsylvania
SERGEANT AT ARMS OF THE HOUSE— NATHANIEL G. ORDWAY, of New Hampshire
DOORKEEPER OF THE HOUSE— IRA GOODNOW, of Vermont
POSTMASTER OF THE HOUSE— JOSIAH GIVEN

Schuyler Colfax
Speaker

## ALABAMA

SENATORS

Vacant

REPRESENTATIVES[6]

Vacant

## ARKANSAS

SENATORS

Vacant

REPRESENTATIVES

Vacant

## CALIFORNIA

SENATORS

James A. McDougall, *San Francisco*
John Conness, *Sacramento*

REPRESENTATIVES

Donald C. McRuer, *San Francisco*
John Bidwell, *Chico*
William Higby, *Calaveras*

## CONNECTICUT

SENATORS

Lafayette S. Foster, *Norwich*
James Dixon, *Hartford*

REPRESENTATIVES

Henry C. Deming, *Hartford*
Samuel L. Warner, *Middletown*

Augustus Brandegee, *New London*
John H. Hubbard, *Litchfield*

## DELAWARE

SENATORS

Willard Saulsbury, *Georgetown*
George R. Riddle, *Wilmington*

REPRESENTATIVE AT LARGE

John A. Nicholson, *Dover*

## FLORIDA

SENATORS

Vacant[7]
Vacant[8]

REPRESENTATIVE AT LARGE

Vacant

## GEORGIA

SENATORS

Vacant

REPRESENTATIVES

Vacant

## ILLINOIS

SENATORS

Lyman Trumbull, *Chicago*
Richard Yates, *Jacksonville*

REPRESENTATIVE AT LARGE

Samuel W. Moulton, *Shelbyville*

REPRESENTATIVES

John Wentworth, *Chicago*
John F. Farnsworth, *St. Charles*
Elihu B. Washburne, *Galena*
Abner C. Harding, *Monmouth*
Ebon C. Ingersoll, *Peoria*
Burton C. Cook, *Ottawa*
Henry P. H. Bromwell, *Charleston*
Shelby M. Cullom, *Springfield*
Lewis W. Ross, *Lewistown*
Anthony Thornton, *Shelbyville*
Samuel S. Marshall, *McLeansboro*
Jehu Baker, *Belleville*
Andrew J. Kuykendall, *Vienna*

## INDIANA

SENATORS

Henry S. Lane, *Crawfordsville*
Thomas A. Hendricks, *Indianapolis*

REPRESENTATIVES

William E. Niblack, *Vincennes*
Michael C. Kerr, *New Albany*
Ralph Hill, *Columbus*
John H. Farquhar, *Brookville*
George W. Julian, *Centerville*
Ebenezer Dumont, *Indianapolis*
Daniel W. Voorhees,[9] *Terre Haute*
Henry D. Washburn,[10] *Clinton*
Godlove S. Orth, *Lafayette*

[1] Became President upon the death of Abraham Lincoln, April 15, 1865.
[2] Elected March 7, 1865 (special session of the Senate), "to serve in the absence of the Vice President," and did serve until March 2, 1867.
[3] Elected March 2, 1867.
[4] Reelected December 4, 1865.
[5] Reelected December 4, 1865.

[6] Credentials of Thomas J. Foster as Member-elect were presented to the House January 10, 1867, but were not acted upon.
[7] On January 19, 1866, William Marvin presented credentials as a Senator-elect for the term ending March 3, 1867, which were ordered to lie on the table and no further action taken thereon.
[8] On June 6, 1866, Wilkinson Call presented

credentials as a Senator-elect for the term ending March 3, 1869, which were ordered to lie on the table and no further action taken thereon.
[9] Served until February 23, 1866; succeeded by Henry D. Washburn, who contested his election.
[10] Successfully contested the election of Daniel W. Voorhees, and took his seat February 23, 1866.

Schuyler Colfax, *South Bend*
Joseph H. Defrees, *Goshen*
Thomas N. Stillwell, *Anderson*

## IOWA

### SENATORS

James Harlan,[11] *Mount Pleasant*
Samuel J. Kirkwood,[12] *Iowa City*
James W. Grimes, *Burlington*

### REPRESENTATIVES

James F. Wilson, *Fairfield*
Hiram Price, *Davenport*
William B. Allison, *Dubuque*
Josiah B. Grinnell, *Grinnell*
John A. Kasson, *Des Moines*
Asahel W. Hubbard, *Sioux City*

## KANSAS

### SENATORS

Samuel C. Pomeroy, *Atchison*
James H. Lane,[13] *Lawrence*
Edmund G. Ross,[14] *Lawrence*

### REPRESENTATIVE AT LARGE

Sidney Clarke, *Lawrence*

## KENTUCKY

### SENATORS

Garrett Davis, *Paris*
James Guthrie, *Louisville*

### REPRESENTATIVES

Lawrence S. Trimble, *Paducah*
Burwell C. Ritter, *Hopkinsville*
Henry Grider,[15] *Bowling Green*
Elijah Hise,[16] *Russellville*
Aaron Harding, *Greensburg*
Lovell H. Rousseau,[17] *Louisville*
Green C. Smith,[18] *Covington*
Andrew H. Ward,[19] *Cynthiana*
George S. Shanklin, *Nicholasville*
Samuel McKee, *Mount Sterling*
William H. Randall, *London*

## LOUISIANA

### SENATORS

Vacant

### REPRESENTATIVES

Vacant[20]

## MAINE

### SENATORS

Lot M. Morrill, *Augusta*
William Pitt Fessenden, *Portland*

### REPRESENTATIVES

John Lynch, *Portland*
Sidney Perham, *Paris*
James G. Blaine, *Augusta*
John H. Rice, *Foxcroft*
Frederick A. Pike, *Calais*

## MARYLAND

### SENATORS

Reverdy Johnson, *Baltimore*
John A. J. Creswell,[21] *Elkton*

### REPRESENTATIVES

Hiram McCullough, *Elkton*
Edwin H. Webster,[22] *Bel Air*
John L. Thomas, Jr.,[23] *Baltimore*
Charles E. Phelps, *Baltimore*
Francis Thomas, *Frankville*
Benjamin G. Harris, *Leonardtown*

## MASSACHUSETTS

### SENATORS

Charles Sumner, *Boston*
Henry Wilson, *Natick*

### REPRESENTATIVES

Thomas D. Eliot, *New Bedford*
Oakes Ames, *North Easton*
Alexander H. Rice, *Boston*
Samuel Hooper, *Boston*
John B. Alley, *Lynn*
Daniel W. Gooch,[24] *Melrose*
Nathaniel P. Banks,[25] *Waltham*
George S. Boutwell, *Groton*
John D. Baldwin, *Worcester*
William B. Washburn, *Greenfield*
Henry L. Dawes, *Pittsfield*

## MICHIGAN

### SENATORS

Zachariah Chandler, *Detroit*
Jacob M. Howard, *Detroit*

### REPRESENTATIVES

Fernando C. Beaman, *Adrian*
Charles Upson, *Coldwater*
John W. Longyear, *Lansing*
Thomas W. Ferry, *Grand Haven*

Rowland E. Trowbridge,[26]
*Birmingham*
John F. Driggs, *East Saginaw*

## MINNESOTA

### SENATORS

Alexander Ramsey, *St. Paul*
Daniel S. Norton, *Winona*

### REPRESENTATIVES

William Windom, *Winona*
Ignatius Donnelly, *Hastings*

## MISSISSIPPI

### SENATORS

Vacant

### REPRESENTATIVES

Vacant

## MISSOURI

### SENATORS

John B. Henderson, *Louisiana*
B. Gratz Brown, *St. Louis*

### REPRESENTATIVES

John Hogan, *St. Louis*
Henry T. Blow, *St. Louis*
Thomas E. Noell, *Perryville*
John R. Kelso,[27] *Springfield*
Joseph W. McClurg, *Linn Creek*
Robert T. Van Horn, *Kansas City*
Benjamin F. Loan, *St. Joseph*
John F. Benjamin, *Shelbyville*
George W. Anderson, *Louisiana*

## NEBRASKA[28]

### SENATORS

John M. Thayer,[29] *Omaha*
Thomas W. Tipton,[29] *Brownville*

### REPRESENTATIVE AT LARGE

Turner M. Marquette,[30] *Plattsmouth*

## NEVADA

### SENATORS

William M. Stewart, *Virginia City*
James W. Nye, *Carson City*

### REPRESENTATIVE AT LARGE

Delos R. Ashley, *Virginia City*

---

[11] Resigned May 15, 1865, having been appointed Secretary of the Interior.
[12] Elected to fill vacancy caused by resignation of James Harlan, and took his seat January 24, 1866.
[13] Died July 11, 1866.
[14] Appointed to fill vacancy caused by death of James H. Lane, and took his seat July 25, 1866; subsequently elected.
[15] Died September 14, 1866.
[16] Elected to fill vacancy caused by death of Henry Grider, and took his seat December 3, 1866.
[17] Resigned July 21, 1866; subsequently reelected, and took his seat December 3, 1866.
[18] Resigned in 1866.

[19] Elected to fill vacancy caused by resignation of Green C. Smith, and took his seat December 3, 1866.
[20] Credentials of Jacob Barker, Robert C. Wickliffe, Louis St. Martin, John E. King, and John Ray as Members-elect were presented and referred to the Select Committee on Reconstruction; no further action was taken.
[21] Elected to fill vacancy caused by death of Thomas H. Hicks, in preceding Congress, and took his seat December 4, 1865.
[22] Resigned in July, 1865, before Congress assembled, to become collector of the port of Baltimore.
[23] Elected to fill vacancy caused by resignation of Edwin H. Webster, and took his seat December 4, 1865.

[24] Resigned September 1, 1865, before Congress assembled.
[25] Elected to fill vacancy occasioned by resignation of Daniel W. Gooch, and took his seat December 4, 1865.
[26] Election unsuccessfully contested by Augustus C. Baldwin.
[27] Election unsuccessfully contested by S. H. Boyd.
[28] Admitted as a State into the Union, March 1, 1867.
[29] Elected, but did not take his seat until March 4, 1867.
[30] Took his seat March 2, 1867.

## NEW HAMPSHIRE

SENATORS

Daniel Clark,[31] *Manchester*
George G. Fogg,[32] *Concord*
Aaron H. Cragin, *Lebanon*

REPRESENTATIVES

Gilman Marston, *Exeter*
Edward H. Rollins, *Concord*
James W. Patterson, *Hanover*

## NEW JERSEY

SENATORS

William Wright,[33] *Newark*
Frederick T. Frelinghuysen,[34] *Newark*
John P. Stockton,[35] *Trenton*
Alexander G. Cattell,[36] *Camden*

REPRESENTATIVES

John F. Starr, *Camden*
William A. Newell, *Allentown*
Charles Sitgreaves, *Phillipsburg*
Andrew J. Rogers, *Newton*
Edwin R. V. Wright, *Hudson City*

## NEW YORK

SENATORS

Ira Harris, *Albany*
Edwin D. Morgan, *New York City*

REPRESENTATIVES

Stephen Taber, *Roslyn*
Teunis G. Bergen, *New Utrecht*
James Humphrey,[37] *Brooklyn*
John W. Hunter,[38] *Brooklyn*
Morgan Jones, *New York City*
Nelson Taylor, *New York City*
Henry J. Raymond, *New York City*
John W. Chanler, *New York City*
James Brooks,[39] *New York City*
William E. Dodge,[40] *New York City*
William A. Darling, *New York City*
William Radford, *Yonkers*
Charles H. Winfield, *Goshen*
John H. Ketcham, *Dover*
Edwin N. Hubbell, *Coxsackie*
Charles Goodyear, *Schoharie*
John A. Griswold, *Troy*
Orlando Kellogg,[41] *Elizabethtown*
Robert S. Hale,[42] *Elizabethtown*
Calvin T. Hulburd, *Brasher Falls*
James M. Marvin, *Saratoga Springs*

Demas Hubbard, Jr., *Smyrna*
Addison H. Laflin, *Herkimer*
Roscoe Conkling,[43] *Utica*
Sidney T. Holmes, *Morrisville*
Thomas T. Davis, *Syracuse*
Theodore M. Pomeroy, *Auburn*
Daniel Morris, *Penn Yan*
Giles W. Hotchkiss, *Binghamton*
Hamilton Ward, *Belmont*
Roswell Hart, *Rochester*
Burt Van Horn, *Newfane*
James M. Humphrey, *Buffalo*
Henry Van Aernam, *Franklinville*

## NORTH CAROLINA

SENATORS

Vacant

REPRESENTATIVES[44]

Vacant

## OHIO

SENATORS

Benjamin F. Wade, *Jefferson*
John Sherman, *Mansfield*

REPRESENTATIVES

Benjamin Eggleston, *Cincinnati*
Rutherford B. Hayes, *Cincinnati*
Robert C. Schenck, *Dayton*
William Lawrence, *Bellefontaine*
Francis C. Le Blond, *Celina*
Reader W. Clarke, *Batavia*
Samuel Shellabarger, *Springfield*
James R. Hubbell, *Delaware*
Ralph P. Buckland, *Fremont*
James M. Ashley, *Toledo*
Hezekiah S. Bundy, *Reeds Mill*
William E. Finck, *Somerset*
Columbus Delano,[45] *Mount Vernon*
Martin Welker, *Wooster*
Tobias A. Plants, *Pomeroy*
John A. Bingham, *Cadiz*
Ephraim R. Eckley, *Carrolton*
Rufus P. Spalding, *Cleveland*
James A. Garfield, *Hiram*

## OREGON

SENATORS

James W. Nesmith, *Salem*
George H. Williams, *Portland*

REPRESENTATIVE AT LARGE

James H. D. Henderson, *Eugene City*

## PENNSYLVANIA

SENATORS

Edgar Cowan, *Greensburg*
Charles R. Buckalew, *Bloomsburg*

REPRESENTATIVES

Samuel J. Randall, *Philadelphia*
Charles O'Neill, *Philadelphia*
Leonard Myers, *Philadelphia*
William D. Kelley, *Philadelphia*
M. Russell Thayer, *Chestnut Hill*
Benjamin M. Boyer, *Norristown*
John M. Broomall, *Media*
Sydenham E. Ancona, *Reading*
Thaddeus Stevens, *Lancaster*
Myer Strouse, *Pottsville*
Philip Johnson,[46] *Easton*
Charles Denison, *Wilkes-Barre*
Ulysses Mercur, *Towanda*
George F. Miller, *Lewisburg*
Adam J. Glossbrenner, *York*
Alexander H. Coffroth,[47] *Somerset*
William H. Koontz,[48] *Somerset*
Abraham A. Barker, *Edenburg*
Stephen F. Wilson, *Wellsboro*
Glenni W. Scofield, *Warren*
Charles V. Culver, *Franklin*
John L. Dawson,[49] *Brownsville*
James K. Moorhead, *Pittsburgh*
Thomas Williams, *Pittsburgh*
George V. Lawrence, *Monongahela City*

## RHODE ISLAND

SENATORS

Henry B. Anthony, *Providence*
William Sprague, *Providence*

REPRESENTATIVES

Thomas A. Jenckes, *Providence*
Nathan F. Dixon, *Westerly*

## SOUTH CAROLINA

SENATORS

Vacant

REPRESENTATIVES

Vacant

---

[31] Resigned July 27, 1866.
[32] Appointed to fill vacancy caused by resignation of Daniel Clark, and took his seat December 3, 1866.
[33] Died November 1, 1866.
[34] Appointed to fill vacancy caused by death of William Wright, and took his seat December 3, 1866; subsequently elected.
[35] Presented credentials and qualified December 4, 1865; protest of members of New Jersey Legislature against his admission filed the same day; served until March 27, 1866, when the seat was declared vacant. (See U.S. Senate Election, Expulsion and Censure Cases, 1793-1990, Senate Document 103-33, pp. 127-129.)
[36] Elected to fill vacancy caused by the Senate declaring the seat of John P. Stockton vacant, and took his seat December 3, 1866.

[37] Died June 16, 1866.
[38] Elected to fill vacancy caused by death of James Humphrey, and took his seat December 4, 1866.
[39] Served until April 7, 1866; succeeded by William E. Dodge, who contested his election.
[40] Successfully contested the election of James Brooks, and took his seat April 7, 1866.
[41] Died August 24, 1865.
[42] Elected to fill vacancy caused by death of Orlando Kellogg, and took his seat December 3, 1866.
[43] Reelected to the Fortieth Congress but resigned, effective March 4, 1867, having been elected Senator.
[44] Credentials of Alexander H. Jones and Lewis Hawes were presented and referred to the Select Committee on Reconstruction, but no further action

was taken.
[45] Election unsuccessfully contested by Charles Follett.
[46] Died January 29, 1867.
[47] Alexander H. Coffroth and William H. Koontz both claimed the election, the governor having declined to issue a certificate to either; the House, on February 19, 1866, adopted a resolution that Mr. Coffroth had the prima facie right to and should be permitted to occupy the seat without prejudice to the right to contest; took his seat the same day and served until July 18, 1866, when he was succeeded by William H. Koontz, who contested the election.
[48] Successfully contested the election of Alexander H. Coffroth, and took his seat July 18, 1866.
[49] Election unsuccessfully contested by Smith Fuller.

## TENNESSEE[50]

### SENATORS

Joseph S. Fowler,[51] *Nashville*
David T. Patterson,[52] *Greeneville*

### REPRESENTATIVES

Nathaniel G. Taylor,[53] *Happy Valley*
Horace Maynard,[53] *Knoxville*
William B. Stokes,[53] *Liberty*
Edmund Cooper,[54] *Shelbyville*
William B. Campbell,[55] *Lebanon*
Samuel M. Arnell,[56] *Columbia*
Isaac R. Hawkins,[55] *Huntingdon*
John W. Leftwich,[54] *Memphis*

## TEXAS

### SENATORS

Vacant

### REPRESENTATIVES

Vacant

## VERMONT

### SENATORS

Solomon Foot,[57] *Rutland*
George F. Edmunds,[58] *Burlington*
Jacob Collamer,[59] *Woodstock*
Luke P. Poland,[60] *St. Johnsbury*

### REPRESENTATIVES

Frederick E. Woodbridge, *Vergennes*
Justin S. Morrill, *Strafford*
Portus Baxter, *Derby Line*

## VIRGINIA

### SENATORS

Vacant

### REPRESENTATIVES

Vacant

## WEST VIRGINIA

### SENATORS

Peter G. Van Winkle, *Parkersburg*
Waitman T. Willey, *Morgantown*

### REPRESENTATIVES

Chester D. Hubbard, *Wheeling*
George R. Latham, *Grafton*
Kellian V. Whaley, *Point Pleasant*

## WISCONSIN

### SENATORS

James R. Doolittle, *Racine*
Timothy O. Howe, *Green Bay*

### REPRESENTATIVES

Halbert E. Paine, *Milwaukee*
Ithamar C. Sloan, *Janesville*
Amasa Cobb, *Mineral Point*
Charles A. Eldridge, *Fond du Lac*
Philetus Sawyer, *Oshkosh*
Walter D. McIndoe, *Wausau*

## TERRITORY OF ARIZONA

### DELEGATE

John N. Goodwin, *Prescott*

## TERRITORY OF COLORADO

### DELEGATE

Allen A. Bradford, *Denver*

## TERRITORY OF DAKOTA

### DELEGATE

Walter A. Burleigh, *Yankton*

## TERRITORY OF IDAHO

### DELEGATE

Edward D. Holbrook, *Idaho City*

## TERRITORY OF MONTANA

### DELEGATE

Samuel McLean, *Bannack*

## TERRITORY OF NEBRASKA

### DELEGATE

Phineas W. Hitchcock,[61] *Omaha*

## TERRITORY OF NEW MEXICO

### DELEGATE

J. Francisco Chaves, *Santa Fe*

## TERRITORY OF UTAH

### DELEGATE

William H. Hooper, *Salt Lake City*

## TERRITORY OF WASHINGTON

### DELEGATE

Arthur A. Denny, *Seattle*

---

[50] Readmitted to representation by joint resolution of July 24, 1866.
[51] Took his seat July 25, 1866; term to expire March 3, 1871.
[52] Took his seat July 28, 1866; term to expire March 3, 1869.
[53] Took his seat July 24, 1866.

[54] Took his seat July 25, 1866.
[55] Took his seat December 3, 1866.
[56] Took his seat December 3, 1866; election unsuccessfully contested by Dorsey B. Thomas.
[57] Died March 28, 1866.
[58] Appointed to fill vacancy caused by death of Solomon Foot, and took his seat April 5, 1866; subse-

quently elected.
[59] Died November 9, 1865.
[60] Appointed to fill vacancy caused by death of Jacob Collamer, and took his seat December 4, 1865; subsequently elected.
[61] Served until March 1, 1867, when the Territory of Nebraska was granted statehood.

# 40TH CONGRESS

## MARCH 4, 1867, TO MARCH 3, 1869

Benjamin F. Wade
President Pro Tempore

Schuyler Colfax
Speaker

FIRST SESSION— *March 4, 1867, to March 30, 1867; July 3, 1867,
to July 20, 1867; November 21, 1867, to December 1, 1867*
SECOND SESSION— *December 2, 1867, to July 27, 1868; September 21, 1868,
for one day only; October 16, 1868, for one day only; November 10, 1868,
for one day only*
THIRD SESSION— *December 7, 1868, to March 3, 1869*
SPECIAL SESSION OF THE SENATE— *April 1, 1867, to April 20, 1867*

———

VICE PRESIDENT OF THE UNITED STATES[1]
PRESIDENT PRO TEMPORE OF THE SENATE— BENJAMIN F. WADE, of Ohio
SECRETARY OF THE SENATE— JOHN W. FORNEY,[2] of Pennsylvania; GEORGE C. GORHAM,[3]
of California
SERGEANT AT ARMS OF THE SENATE— GEORGE T. BROWN, of Illinois

———

SPEAKER OF THE HOUSE OF REPRESENTATIVES— SCHUYLER COLFAX,[4] of Indiana; THEODORE M. POMEROY,[5] of New York
CLERK OF THE HOUSE— EDWARD McPHERSON,[6] of Pennsylvania
SERGEANT AT ARMS OF THE HOUSE— NATHANIEL G. ORDWAY, of New Hampshire
DOORKEEPER OF THE HOUSE— CHARLES E. LIPPINCOTT, of Illinois
POSTMASTER OF THE HOUSE— WILLIAM S. KING

## ALABAMA [7]

### SENATORS

George E. Spencer,[8] *Decatur*
Willard Warner,[9] *Montgomery*

### REPRESENTATIVES

Francis W. Kellogg,[10] *Mobile*
Charles W. Buckley,[11] *Montgomery*
Benjamin W. Norris,[11] *Elmore*
Charles W. Pierce,[11] *Demopolis*
John B. Callis,[11] *Huntsville*
Thomas Haughey,[11] *Decatur*

## ARKANSAS[12]

### SENATORS

Alexander McDonald,[13] *Little Rock*
Benjamin F. Rice,[14] *Little Rock*

### REPRESENTATIVES

Logan H. Roots,[15] *Devall Bluff*
James Hinds,[16] *Little Rock*
James T. Elliott,[17] *Camden*
Thomas Boles,[18] *Dardanelle*

## CALIFORNIA

### SENATORS

John Conness, *Georgetown*
Cornelius Cole, *San Francisco*

### REPRESENTATIVES[19]

Samuel B. Axtell,[20] *San Francisco*
William Higby,[20] *Calaveras*
James A. Johnson,[20] *Downieville*

## CONNECTICUT

### SENATORS

James Dixon, *Hartford*
Orris S. Ferry, *Norwalk*

### REPRESENTATIVES

Richard D. Hubbard, *Hartford*
Julius Hotchkiss, *Middletown*
Henry H. Starkweather, *Norwich*
William H. Barnum, *Lime Rock*

## DELAWARE

### SENATORS

George R. Riddle,[21] *Wilmington*
James A. Bayard,[22] *Wilmington*
Willard Saulsbury, *Georgetown*

### REPRESENTATIVE AT LARGE

John A. Nicholson, *Dover*

## FLORIDA[23]

### SENATORS

Thomas W. Osborn,[24] *Pensacola*
Adonijah S. Welch,[25] *Jacksonville*

### REPRESENTATIVE AT LARGE

Charles M. Hamilton,[26] *Marianna*

---

[1] Vice President Andrew Johnson became President in preceding Congress on the death of Abraham Lincoln.
[2] Resigned, effective June 4, 1868.
[3] Elected June 4, 1868.
[4] Reelected March 4, 1867; resigned as Speaker March 3, 1869, having been elected Vice President.
[5] Elected March 3, 1869.
[6] Reelected March 4, 1867.
[7] Readmitted to representation July 13, 1868.
[8] Took his seat July 25, 1868; term to expire March 3, 1873.
[9] Took his seat July 25, 1868; term to expire March 3, 1871.
[10] Took his seat July 22, 1868.

[11] Took his seat July 21, 1868.
[12] Readmitted to representation, by passage of bill in both Houses over the veto of President Johnson, June 22, 1868.
[13] Took his seat June 23, 1868; term to expire March 3, 1871.
[14] Took his seat June 23, 1868; term to expire March 3, 1873.
[15] Took his seat June 24, 1868.
[16] Took his seat June 24, 1868; died October 22, 1868.
[17] Elected to fill vacancy caused by death of James Hinds, and took his seat January 13, 1869.
[18] Took his seat June 24, 1868.
[19] Elected September 4, 1867.

[20] Took his seat November 21, 1867.
[21] Died March 29, 1867.
[22] Appointed to fill vacancy caused by death of George R. Riddle, and took his seat April 11, 1867; subsequently elected.
[23] Readmitted to representation June 25, 1868.
[24] Took his seat June 30, 1868; term to expire March 3, 1873; on the same day William Marvin presented credentials dated November 28, 1868, which were read and no further action taken thereon because Mr. Osborn was seated. (See U.S. Senate Election, Expulsion and Censure Cases, 1793-1990, Senate Document 103-33, pp. 143-144.)
[25] Took his seat July 2, 1868; term to expire March 3, 1869.
[26] Took his seat July 1, 1868.

## GEORGIA[27]

### SENATORS[28]

Vacant

### REPRESENTATIVES[29]

Joseph W. Clift,[30] *Savannah*
Nelson Tift,[30] *Albany*
William P. Edwards,[30] *Butler*
Samuel F. Gove,[30] *Griswoldville*
Charles H. Prince,[30] *Augusta*
Pierce M. B. Young,[30] *Cartersville*

## ILLINOIS

### SENATORS

Lyman Trumbull, *Chicago*
Richard Yates, *Jacksonville*

### REPRESENTATIVE AT LARGE

John A. Logan, *Carbondale*

### REPRESENTATIVES

Norman B. Judd, *Chicago*
John F. Farnsworth, *St. Charles*
Elihu B. Washburne, *Galena*
Abner C. Harding, *Monmouth*
Ebon C. Ingersoll, *Peoria*
Burton C. Cook, *Ottawa*
Henry P. H. Bromwell, *Charleston*
Shelby M. Cullom, *Springfield*
Lewis W. Ross, *Lewiston*
Albert G. Burr, *Winchester*
Samuel S. Marshall, *McLeansboro*
Jehu Baker, *Belleville*
Green B. Raum, *Harrisburg*

## INDIANA

### SENATORS

Thomas A. Hendricks, *Indianapolis*
Oliver H. P. T. Morton, *Indianapolis*

### REPRESENTATIVES

William E. Niblack, *Vincennes*
Michael C. Kerr, *New Albany*

Morton C. Hunter, *Bloomington*
William S. Holman, *Aurora*
George W. Julian, *Centerville*
John Coburn, *Indianapolis*
Henry D. Washburn, *Clinton*
Godlove S. Orth, *Lafayette*
Schuyler Colfax, *South Bend*
William Williams, *Warsaw*
John P. C. Shanks, *Jay Court House*

## IOWA

### SENATORS

James W. Grimes, *Burlington*
James Harlan, *Mount Pleasant*

### REPRESENTATIVES

James F. Wilson, *Fairfield*
Hiram Price, *Davenport*
William B. Allison, *Dubuque*
William Loughridge, *Oskaloosa*
Grenville M. Dodge, *Council Bluffs*
Asahel W. Hubbard, *Sioux City*

## KANSAS

### SENATORS

Samuel C. Pomeroy, *Atchison*
Edmund G. Ross, *Lawrence*

### REPRESENTATIVE AT LARGE

Sidney Clarke, *Lawrence*

## KENTUCKY

### SENATORS

Garrett Davis, *Paris*
James Guthrie,[31] *Louisville*
Thomas C. McCreery,[32] *Owensboro*

### REPRESENTATIVES[33]

Lawrence S. Trimble,[34] *Paducah*
Elijah Hise,[35] *Russellville*
Jacob S. Golladay,[36] *Allensville*
J. Proctor Knott,[37] *Lebanon*

Asa P. Grover,[37] *Louisville*
Thomas L. Jones,[38] *Newport*
James B. Beck,[37] *Lexington*
George M. Adams,[39] *Barbourville*
Samuel McKee,[40] *Mount Sterling*

## LOUISIANA[41]

### SENATORS

John S. Harris,[42] *Vidalia*
William Pitt Kellogg,[43] *New Orleans*

### REPRESENTATIVES

J. Hale Sypher,[44] *New Orleans*
James Mann,[45] *New Orleans*
Joseph P. Newsham,[44] *St. Francisville*
Michel Vidal,[44] *Opelousas*
W. Jasper Blackburn,[44] *Homer*

## MAINE

### SENATORS

Lot M. Morrill, *Augusta*
William Pitt Fessenden, *Portland*

### REPRESENTATIVES

John Lynch, *Portland*
Sidney Perham, *Paris*
James G. Blaine, *Augusta*
John A. Peters, *Bangor*
Frederick A. Pike, *Calais*

## MARYLAND

### SENATORS

Reverdy Johnson,[46] *Baltimore*
William Pinkney Whyte,[47] *Baltimore*
George Vickers,[48] *Chestertown*

### REPRESENTATIVES

Hiram McCullough, *Elkton*
Stevenson Archer, *Bel Air*
Charles E. Phelps, *Baltimore*
Francis Thomas, *Frankville*

---

[27] Although Georgia was not formally readmitted to representation until July 15, 1870 (in the succeeding Congress), the Representatives elected to this Congress qualified as indicated.

[28] On December 7, 1868, the credentials of Joshua Hill, elected by the legislature to fill vacancy in the term beginning March 4, 1867, were presented and referred to the Committee on the Judiciary; on January 11, 1869, the credentials of Homer V. M. Miller, elected in the same manner, for the term beginning March 4, 1865, were presented and were similarly referred; on January 25, 1869, the committee reported that the State of Georgia had not complied with the conditions of an act providing for her admission to representation, and that Mr. Hill "ought not now to be admitted"; February 17, 1869, the committee reported against admitting Mr. Miller to his seat, and the cases remained undisposed of. (See U.S. Senate Election, Expulsion and Censure Cases, 1793-1990, Senate Document 103-33, pp. 145-149.)

[29] John A. Wimpy and John H. Cristy both claimed election from the sixth district, but neither was seated.

[30] Took his seat July 25, 1868.

[31] Resigned February 7, 1868.

[32] Elected to fill vacancy caused by resignation of James Guthrie, and took his seat February 28, 1868.

[33] On July 3, 1867, it was proposed to seat all the Members-elect from Kentucky, but protests against

the manner of holding the election and charges of disloyal acts by certain individual members of the delegation were presented and a resolution was adopted directing an investigation and referring to the Committee on Elections the credentials of Messrs Lawrence S. Trimble, John Y. Brown, J. Proctor Knott, Asa P. Grover, Thomas L. Jones, James B. Beck, and John D. Young, who were not permitted to qualify pending this investigation; Samuel E. Smith contested the election of John Y. Brown, but the House, on February 15, 1868, decided that neither was entitled to the seat, which remained vacant throughout the Congress.

[34] Election unsuccessfully contested by G. G. Symes; took his seat January 10, 1868.

[35] Died May 8, 1867, never having qualified; the election of Mr. Hise was subsequently unsuccessfully contested by George D. Blakey.

[36] Elected to fill vacancy caused by death of Elijah Hise, and took his seat December 5, 1867; George D. Blakey, claiming to have been elected from this district instead of Mr. Hise, filed a protest against the seating of Mr. Golladay, but this protest was not allowed.

[37] Charges of disloyalty were unsustained, and took his seat December 3, 1867.

[38] Charges of disloyalty were unsustained, and took his seat December 4, 1867.

[39] Took his seat July 8, 1867.

[40] Successfully contested the election of John D. Young, and took his seat June 22, 1868.

[41] Readmitted to representation July 9, 1868.

[42] Took his seat July 17, 1868; term to expire March 3, 1871.

[43] Took his seat July 17, 1868; term to expire March 3, 1873.

[44] Took his seat July 18, 1868.

[45] Took his seat July 18, 1868; died August 26, 1868; Caleb S. Hunt and J. Willis Menard claimed to have been elected to fill the vacancy, and Simon Jones claimed he was elected, instead of Mann, in the first instance. The House decided against all claimants, and the seat remained vacant for the remainder of the session.

[46] Resigned July 10, 1868.

[47] Appointed to fill vacancy caused by resignation of Reverdy Johnson, and took his seat July 14, 1868.

[48] Elected for term beginning March 4, 1867, and took his seat March 9, 1868. The credentials of Philip F. Thomas, Senator-elect, were presented March 18, 1867, but he was not permitted to qualify; on February 19, 1868, the Senate adopted a resolution that he was not entitled to qualify as he had "voluntarily given aid, countenance, and encouragement to persons engaged in armed hostility to the United States." (See U.S. Senate Election, Expulsion and Censure Cases, 1793-1990, Senate Document 103-33, pp. 136-139.)

## MARYLAND—Continued

REPRESENTATIVES—CONTINUED

Frederick Stone, *Port Tobacco*

## MASSACHUSETTS

SENATORS

Charles Sumner, *Boston*
Henry Wilson, *Natick*

REPRESENTATIVES

Thomas D. Eliot, *New Bedford*
Oakes Ames, *North Easton*
Ginery Twichell, *Brookline*
Samuel Hooper, *Boston*
Benjamin F. Butler, *Lowell*
Nathaniel P. Banks, *Waltham*
George S. Boutwell, *Groton*
John D. Baldwin, *Worcester*
William B. Washburn, *Greenfield*
Henry L. Dawes, *Pittsfield*

## MICHIGAN

SENATORS

Zachariah Chandler, *Detroit*
Jacob M. Howard, *Detroit*

REPRESENTATIVES

Fernando C. Beaman, *Adrian*
Charles Upson, *Coldwater*
Austin Blair, *Jackson*
Thomas W. Ferry, *Grand Haven*
Rowland E. Trowbridge, *Birmingham*
John F. Driggs, *East Saginaw*

## MINNESOTA

SENATORS

Alexander Ramsey, *St. Paul*
Daniel S. Norton, *Winona*

REPRESENTATIVES

William Windom, *Winona*
Ignatius Donnelly, *Hastings*

## MISSISSIPPI

SENATORS

Vacant

REPRESENTATIVES

Vacant

## MISSOURI

SENATORS

John B. Henderson, *Louisiana*
Charles D. Drake, *St. Louis*

REPRESENTATIVES

William A. Pile,[49] *St. Louis*
Carman A. Newcomb, *Vineland*
Thomas E. Noell,[50] *Perryville*
James R. McCormick,[51] *Ironton*
Joseph J. Gravely, *Stockton*
Joseph W. McClurg,[52] *Linn Creek*
John H. Stover,[53] *Versailles*
Robert T. Van Horn,[54] *Kansas City*
Benjamin F. Loan, *St. Joseph*
John F. Benjamin, *Shelbyville*
George W. Anderson,[55] *Louisiana*

## NEBRASKA

SENATORS

John M. Thayer,[56] *Omaha*
Thomas W. Tipton,[57] *Brownville*

REPRESENTATIVE AT LARGE

John Taffe, *Omaha*

## NEVADA

SENATORS

William M. Stewart, *Virginia City*
James W. Nye, *Carson City*

REPRESENTATIVE AT LARGE

Delos R. Ashley, *Austin*

## NEW HAMPSHIRE

SENATORS

Aaron H. Cragin, *Lebanon*
James W. Patterson, *Hanover*

REPRESENTATIVES

Jacob H. Ela, *Rochester*
Aaron F. Stevens, *Nashua*
Jacob Benton, *Lancaster*

## NEW JERSEY

SENATORS

Alexander G. Cattell, *Camden*
Frederick T. Frelinghuysen, *Newark*

REPRESENTATIVES

William Moore, *Mays Landing*
Charles Haight, *Freehold*
Charles Sitgreaves, *Phillipsburg*
John Hill, *Boonton*
George A. Halsey, *Newark*

## NEW YORK

SENATORS

Edwin D. Morgan, *New York City*
Roscoe Conkling, *Utica*

REPRESENTATIVES

Stephen Taber, *Roslyn*
Demas Barnes, *Brooklyn*
William E. Robinson, *Brooklyn*
John Fox, *New York City*
John Morrissey, *New York City*
Thomas E. Stewart, *New York City*
John W. Chanler, *New York City*
James Brooks, *New York City*
Fernando Wood, *New York City*
William H. Robertson, *Katonah*
Charles H. Van Wyck, *Middletown*
John H. Ketsham, *Dover*
Thomas Cornell, *Rondout*
John V. L. Pruyn, *Albany*
John A. Griswold, *Troy*
Orange Ferriss, *Glens Falls*
Calvin T. Hulburd, *Brasher Falls*
James M. Marvin, *Saratoga Springs*
William C. Fields, *Laurens*
Addison H. Laflin, *Herkimer*
Alexander H. Bailey,[58] *Rome*
John C. Churchill, *Oswego*
Dennis McCarthy, *Syracuse*
Theodore M. Pomeroy, *Auburn*
William H. Kelsey, *Geneseo*
William S. Lincoln, *Owego*
Hamilton Ward, *Belmont*
Lewis Selye, *Rochester*
Burt Van Horn, *Lockport*
James M. Humphrey, *Buffalo*
Henry Van Aernam, *Franklinville*

## NORTH CAROLINA[59]

SENATORS

Joseph C. Abbott,[60] *Wilmington*
John Pool,[61] *Elizabeth City*

REPRESENTATIVES

John R. French,[62] *Edenton*
David Heaton,[63] *New Bern*
Oliver H. Dockery,[64] *Richmond*
John T. Deweese,[62] *Raleigh*
Israel G. Lash,[65] *Salem*
Nathaniel Boyden,[64] *Salisbury*
Alexander H. Jones,[62] *Asheville*

## OHIO

SENATORS

Benjamin F. Wade, *Jefferson*
John Sherman, *Mansfield*

REPRESENTATIVES

Benjamin Eggleston, *Cincinnati*
Rutherford B. Hayes,[66] *Cincinnati*

---

[49] Election unsuccessfully contested by John Hogan.
[50] Died October 3, 1867.
[51] Elected to fill vacancy caused by death of Thomas E. Noell, and took his seat December 17, 1867.
[52] Resigned in 1868.
[53] Elected to fill vacancy caused by resignation of Joseph W. McClurg, and took his seat December 7, 1868.
[54] Election unsuccessfully contested by James H. Birch.

[55] Election unsuccessfully contested by William F. Switzler.
[56] Took his seat March 4, 1867; term to expire, as determined by lot, March 3, 1871.
[57] Took his seat March 4, 1867; term to expire, as determined by lot, March 3, 1869.
[58] Elected to fill vacancy caused by resignation of Roscoe Conkling, in preceding Congress, and took his seat November 30, 1867.

[59] Readmitted to representation July 4, 1868.
[60] Took his seat July 17, 1868; term to expire March 3, 1871.
[61] Took his seat July 17, 1868; term to expire March 3, 1873.
[62] Took his seat July 6, 1868.
[63] Took his seat July 15, 1868.
[64] Took his seat July 13, 1868.
[65] Took his seat July 20, 1868.
[66] Resigned July 20, 1867.

Samuel F. Cary,[67] *Cincinnati*
Robert C. Schenck, *Dayton*
William Lawrence, *Bellefontaine*
William Mungen, *Findlay*
Reader W. Clarke, *Batavia*
Samuel Shellabarger, *Springfield*
Cornelius S. Hamilton,[68] *Marysville*
John Beatty,[69] *Cardington*
Ralph P. Buckland, *Fremont*
James M. Ashley, *Toledo*
John T. Wilson, *Tranquility*
Philadelph Van Trump, *Lancaster*
George W. Morgan,[70] *Mount Vernon*
Columbus Delano,[71] *Mount Vernon*
Martin Welker, *Wooster*
Tobias A. Plants, *Pomeroy*
John A. Bingham, *Cadiz*
Ephraim R. Eckley, *Carrollton*
Rufus P. Spalding, *Cleveland*
James A. Garfield, *Hiram*

## OREGON

### SENATORS

George H. Williams, *Portland*
Henry W. Corbett, *Portland*

### REPRESENTATIVE AT LARGE

Rufus Mallory, *Salem*

## PENNSYLVANIA

### SENATORS

Charles R. Buckalew, *Bloomsburg*
Simon Cameron, *Harrisburg*

### REPRESENTATIVES

Samuel J. Randall, *Philadelphia*
Charles O'Neill, *Philadelphia*
Leonard Myers, *Philadelphia*
William D. Kelley, *Philadelphia*
Caleb N. Taylor, *Bristol*
Benjamin M. Boyer, *Norristown*
John M. Broomall, *Media*
J. Lawrence Getz, *Reading*
Thaddeus Stevens,[72] *Lancaster*
Oliver J. Dickey,[73] *Lancaster*
Henry L. Cake, *Tamaqua*
Daniel M. Van Auken, *Milford*
Charles Denison,[74] *Wilkes-Barre*
George W. Woodward,[75] *Wilkes-Barre*
Ulysses Mercur, *Towanda*
George F. Miller, *Lewisburg*
Adam J. Glossbrenner, *York*
William H. Koontz, *Somerset*

Daniel J. Morrell, *Johnstown*
Stephen F. Wilson, *Wellsboro*
Glenni W. Scofield, *Warren*
Darwin A. Finney,[76] *Meadville*
S. Newton Pettis,[77] *Meadville*
John Covode, *Lockport*
James K. Moorhead, *Pittsburgh*
Thomas Williams, *Allegheny*
George V. Lawrence, *Monongahela City*

## RHODE ISLAND

### SENATORS

Henry B. Anthony, *Providence*
William Sprague, *Providence*

### REPRESENTATIVES

Thomas A. Jenckes, *Cumberland*
Nathan F. Dixon, *Westerly*

## SOUTH CAROLINA[78]

### SENATORS

Thomas J. Robertson,[79] *Columbia*
Frederick A. Sawyer,[80] *Charleston*

### REPRESENTATIVES

B. Frank Whittemore,[81] *Darlington*
Christopher C. Bowen,[82] *Charleston*
M. Simeon Corley,[83] *Lexington*
James H. Goss,[81] *Union Court House*

## TENNESSEE

### SENATORS

Joseph S. Fowler, *Nashville*
David T. Patterson, *Greeneville*

### REPRESENTATIVES[84]

Roderick R. Butler,[85] *Mountain City*
Horace Maynard,[86] *Knoxville*
William B. Stokes,[86] *Alexandria*
James Mullins,[86] *Shelbyville*
John Trimble,[86] *Nashville*
Samuel M. Arnell,[87] *Columbia*
Isaac R. Hawkins,[86] *Huntingdon*
David A. Nunn,[86] *Brownsville*

## TEXAS

### SENATORS

Vacant

### REPRESENTATIVES

Vacant

## VERMONT

### SENATORS

George F. Edmunds, *Burlington*
Justin S. Morrill, *Strafford*

### REPRESENTATIVES

Frederick E. Woodbridge, *Vergennes*
Luke P. Poland, *St. Johnsbury*
Worthington C. Smith, *St. Albans*

## VIRGINIA

### SENATORS

Vacant

### REPRESENTATIVES

Vacant

## WEST VIRGINIA

### SENATORS

Peter G. Van Winkle, *Parkersburg*
Waitman T. Willey, *Morgantown*
Chester D. Hubbard, *Wheeling*
Bethuel M. Kitchen, *Martinsburg*
Daniel Polsley, *Point Pleasant*

## WISCONSIN

### SENATORS

James R. Doolittle, *Racine*
Timothy O. Howe, *Green Bay*

### REPRESENTATIVES

Halbert E. Paine, *Milwaukee*
Benjamin F. Hopkins, *Madison*
Amasa Cobb, *Mineral Point*
Charles A. Eldridge, *Fond du Lac*
Philetus Sawyer, *Oshkosh*
Cadwallader C. Washburn, *La Crosse*

## TERRITORY OF ARIZONA

### DELEGATE

Coles Bashford, *Tucson*

---

[67] Elected to fill vacancy caused by resignation of Rutherford B. Hayes; took his seat November 21, 1867.
[68] Died December 22, 1867.
[69] Elected to fill vacancy caused by death of Cornelius S. Hamilton, and took his seat February 5, 1868.
[70] Served until June 3, 1868; succeeded by Columbus Delano, who contested his election.
[71] Successfully contested the election of George W. Morgan, and took his seat June 3, 1868.
[72] Died August 11, 1868.
[73] Elected to fill vacancy caused by death of Thaddeus Stevens, and took his seat December 7, 1868.
[74] Died June 27, 1867.

---

[75] Elected to fill vacancy caused by death of Charles Denison, and took his seat November 21, 1867.
[76] Died August 25, 1868.
[77] Elected to fill vacancy caused by death of Darwin A. Finney, and took his seat December 7, 1868.
[78] Readmitted to representation July 9, 1868.
[79] Took his seat July 20, 1868; term to expire March 3, 1871.
[80] Took his seat July 22, 1868; term to expire March 3, 1873.
[81] Took his seat July 18, 1868.
[82] Took his seat July 20, 1868.
[83] Took his seat July 25, 1868.

---

[84] The credentials of Thomas A. Hamilton, claiming to be a Member-elect from the State at large, were presented; claimant held that, inasmuch as Tennessee had voluntarily emancipated and enfranchised her slaves, she had added to her representative population a sufficient number to give her nine, instead of eight, Representatives, and he had been elected as such ninth Member. It was the first of many similar claims made by other readmitted States; the majority report was adverse to the claimant and, although the House took no formal action, he was not seated.
[85] Qualified under act of June 19, 1868, and took his seat June 26, 1868.
[86] Took his seat November 21, 1867.
[87] Took his seat November 25, 1867.

## TERRITORY OF COLORADO

DELEGATE

George M. Chilcott,[88] *Excelsior*

## TERRITORY OF DAKOTA

DELEGATE

Walter A. Burleigh, *Yankton*

## TERRITORY OF IDAHO

DELEGATE

Edward D. Holbrook, *Idaho City*

## TERRITORY OF MONTANA

DELEGATE

James M. Cavanaugh, *Helena*

## TERRITORY OF NEW MEXICO

DELEGATE

Charles P. Clever,[89] *Santa Fe*
J. Francisco Chaves,[90] *Santa Fe*

## TERRITORY OF UTAH

DELEGATE

William H. Hooper,[91] *Salt Lake City*

## TERRITORY OF WASHINGTON

DELEGATE

Alvan Flanders, *Walla Walla*

---

[88] George M. Chilcott and A. C. Hunt each presented credentials on March 5, 1867, which were referred to the Committee on Elections; the committee reported that neither was entitled to the seat; Chilcott was seated March 20, 1867, and Hunt subsequently abandoned the contest.

[89] Credentials certifying his election on September 2, 1867, were presented November 21, 1867, and referred to the Committee on Elections, together with letter of secretary of New Mexico claiming fraud in election; was seated on December 19, 1867, and served until February 20, 1869; succeeded by J. Francisco

Chaves, who contested his election.

[90] Successfully contested the election of Charles P. Clever, and took his seat February 20, 1869.

[91] Election unsuccessfully contested by William McGrorty.

# 41ST CONGRESS

## MARCH 4, 1869, TO MARCH 3, 1871

FIRST SESSION— *March 4, 1869, to April 10, 1869*
SECOND SESSION— *December 6, 1869, to July 15, 1870*
THIRD SESSION— *December 5, 1870, to March 3, 1871*
SPECIAL SESSION OF THE SENATE— *April 12, 1869, to April 22, 1869*

———

VICE PRESIDENT OF THE UNITED STATES— SCHUYLER COLFAX, of Indiana
PRESIDENT PRO TEMPORE OF THE SENATE— HENRY B. ANTHONY,[1] of Rhode Island
SECRETARY OF THE SENATE— GEORGE C. GORHAM, of California
SERGEANT AT ARMS OF THE SENATE— GEORGE T. BROWN, of Illinois; JOHN R. FRENCH,
[2] of New Hampshire

———

SPEAKER OF THE HOUSE OF REPRESENTATIVES— JAMES G. BLAINE,[3] of Maine
CLERK OF THE HOUSE— EDWARD MCPHERSON,[4] of Pennsylvania
SERGEANT AT ARMS OF THE HOUSE— NATHANIEL G. ORDWAY, of New Hampshire
DOORKEEPER OF THE HOUSE— OTIS S. BUXTON, of New York
POSTMASTER OF THE HOUSE— WILLIAM S. KING

Schuyler Colfax
Vice President

James G. Blaine
Speaker

## ALABAMA

### SENATORS

George E. Spencer, *Decatur*
Willard Warner, *Montgomery*

### REPRESENTATIVES[5]

Alfred E. Buck, *Mobile*
Charles W. Buckley, *Montgomery*
Robert S. Heflin, *Opelika*
Charles Hays, *Eutaw*
Peter M. Dox, *Huntsville*
William C. Sherrod, *Courtland*

## ARKANSAS

### SENATORS

Alexander McDonald, *Little Rock*
Benjamin F. Rice, *Little Rock*

### REPRESENTATIVES

Logan H. Roots, *Duvalls Bluff*
Anthony A. C. Rogers, *Pine Bluff*
Thomas Boles, *Dardanelle*

## CALIFORNIA

### SENATORS

Cornelius Cole, *San Francisco*
Eugene Casserly, *San Francisco*

### REPRESENTATIVES

Samuel B. Axtell, *San Francisco*
Aaron A. Sargent, *Nevada City*
James A. Johnson, *Downiesville*

## CONNECTICUT

### SENATORS

Orris S. Ferry, *Norwalk*
William A. Buckingham, *Norwich*

### REPRESENTATIVES[6]

Julius L. Strong, *Hartford*
Stephen W. Kellogg, *Waterbury*
Henry H. Starkweather, *Norwich*
William H. Barnum, *Lime Rock*

## DELAWARE

### SENATORS

Willard Saulsbury, *Georgetown*
Thomas F. Bayard, *Wilmington*

### REPRESENTATIVE AT LARGE

Benjamin T. Biggs, *Summit Bridge*

## FLORIDA

### SENATORS

Thomas W. Osborn, *Pensacola*
Abijah Gilbert, *St. Augustine*

### REPRESENTATIVE AT LARGE

Charles M. Hamilton, *Jacksonville*

## GEORGIA [7]

### SENATORS[8]

Joshua Hill,[9] *Madison*
Homer V. M. Miller,[10] *Rome*

### REPRESENTATIVES[11]

William W. Paine,[12] *Savannah*
Richard H. Whiteley,[13] *Bainbridge*

---

[1] Elected March 23, 1869; April 9, 1869; May 28, 1870; July 1, 1870; July 14, 1870.
[2] Elected March 22, 1869.
[3] Elected March 4, 1869.
[4] Reelected March 5, 1869.
[5] Elected August 3, 1869.
[6] Elected April 5, 1869.
[7] Formally readmitted to representation by act of July 15, 1870.
[8] The credentials of Mr. Hill and Mr. Miller, presented in the Fortieth Congress and undisposed of on the files of the Senate, were referred again to the Committee on the Judiciary March 9, 1869; they were reported back without recommendation and ordered to lie on the table March 17, 1869; they were again referred to the committee February 14, 1870. A new election was held in Georgia, and on July 15, 1870, the credentials of Richard H. Whiteley and Henry P. Farrow were presented and ordered to lie on the table, but were subsequently referred; on the same day of their presentation the act was approved readmitting Georgia to representation in Congress. The committee reported upon all the credentials January 23, 1871, resolving that Messrs. Hill and Miller were duly elected; that Mr. Hill should be permitted to take his seat, but that Mr. Miller was disqualified by reason of his service in the Confederate Army; this report was adopted February 1, 1871. A joint resolution prescribing a qualification oath for Mr. Miller was approved February 24, 1871; took his seat the same day. (See U.S. Senate Election, Expulsion and Censure Cases, 1793-1990, Senate Document 103-33, pp. 145-149.)

[9] Took his seat under the resolution of February 1, 1871, on that day; term to expire March 3, 1873.

[10] Qualified under the terms of the joint resolution approved February 24, 1871, and took his seat on that date; term to expire March 3, 1871.
[11] Pierce M. B. Young, Nelson Tift, W. P. Edwards, J. W. Clift, Samuel F. Gove, and C. H. Prince presented credentials alleging their election as Representatives, April 20, 1868, the same election in which they were elected to the Fortieth Congress; by resolution of January 28, 1870, the House declared they were not entitled to seats. Pierce M. B. Young subsequently presented credentials under a later election and was seated.
[12] Qualified under act of July 11, 1868, and took his seat January 23, 1871.
[13] Qualified under act of July 11, 1868, and took his seat February 9, 1871; election unsuccessful contested by Nelson Tift.

## GEORGIA—Continued

### REPRESENTATIVES—CONTINUED

Marion Bethune,[14] *Talbotton*
Jefferson F. Long,[15] *Macon*
Stephen A. Corker,[16] *Waynesboro*
William P. Price,[14] *Dahlonega*
Pierce M. B. Young,[14] *Cartersville*

## ILLINOIS

### SENATORS

Lyman Trumbull, *Chicago*
Richard Yates, *Jacksonville*

### REPRESENTATIVE AT LARGE

John A. Logan,[17] *Carbondale*

### REPRESENTATIVES

Norman B. Judd, *Chicago*
John F. Farnsworth, *St. Charles*
Elihu B. Washburne,[18] *Galena*
Horatio C. Burchard,[19] *Freeport*
John B. Hawley, *Rock Island*
Ebon C. Ingersoll, *Peoria*
Burton C. Cook, *Ottawa*
Jesse H. Moore, *Decatur*
Shelby M. Cullom, *Springfield*
Thompson W. McNeely, *Petersburg*
Albert G. Burr, *Carrollton*
Samuel S. Marshall, *McLeansboro*
John B. Hays, *Belleville*
John M. Crebs, *Carmi*

## INDIANA

### SENATORS

Oliver H. P. T. Morton, *Indianapolis*
Daniel D. Pratt, *Logansport*

### REPRESENTATIVES

William E. Niblack, *Vincennes*
Michael C. Kerr, *New Albany*
William S. Holman, *Aurora*
George W. Julian,[20] *Centerville*
John Coburn, *Indianapolis*
Daniel W. Voorhees, *Terre Haute*
Godlove S. Orth, *Lafayette*
James N. Tyner,[21] *Peru*

John P. C. Shanks, *Jay Court House*
William Williams, *Warsaw*
Jasper Packard, *Laporte*

## IOWA

### SENATORS

James W. Grimes,[22] *Burlington*
James B. Howell,[23] *Keokuk*
James Harlan, *Mount Pleasant*

### REPRESENTATIVES

George W. McCrary, *Keokuk*
William Smyth,[24] *Marion*
William P. Wolf,[25] *Tipton*
William B. Allison, *Dubuque*
William Loughridge, *Oskaloosa*
Frank W. Palmer, *Des Moines*
Charles Pomeroy, *Fort Dodge*

## KANSAS

### SENATORS

Samuel C. Pomeroy, *Atchison*
Edmund G. Ross, *Lawrence*

### REPRESENTATIVE AT LARGE

Sidney Clarke, *Lawrence*

## KENTUCKY

### SENATORS

Garrett Davis, *Paris*
Thomas C. McCreery, *Owensboro*

### REPRESENTATIVES

Lawrence S. Trimble, *Paducah*
William N. Sweeney, *Owensboro*
Jacob S. Golladay,[26] *Allensville*
Joseph H. Lewis,[27] *Glasgow*
J. Proctor Knott, *Lebanon*
Boyd Winchester, *Louisville*
Thomas L. Jones, *Newport*
James B. Beck, *Lexington*

George M. Adams,[28] *Barbourville*
John M. Rice,[29] *Louisa*

## LOUISIANA

### SENATORS

John S. Harris, *Vidalia*
William Pitt Kellogg, *New Orleans*

### REPRESENTATIVES[30]

J. Hale Sypher,[31] *New Orleans*
Lionel A. Sheldon,[32] *New Orleans*
Chester B. Darrall,[33] *Brashear*
Joseph P. Newsham,[34] *St. Francisville*
Frank Morey,[35] *Monroe*

## MAINE

### SENATORS

William Pitt Fessenden,[36] *Portland*
Lot M. Morrill,[37] *Augusta*
Hannibal Hamlin, *Bangor*

### REPRESENTATIVES

John Lynch, *Portland*
Samuel P. Morrill, *Farmington*
James G. Blaine, *Augusta*
John A. Peters, *Bangor*
Eugene Hale, *Ellsworth*

## MARYLAND

### SENATORS

George Vickers, *Chestertown*
William T. Hamilton, *Hagerstown*

### REPRESENTATIVES

Samuel Hambleton, *Easton*
Stevenson Archer, *Bel Air*
Thomas Swann, *Baltimore*
Patrick Hamill, *Oakland*
Frederick Stone, *Port Tobacco*

---

[14] Qualified under act of July 11, 1868, and took his seat January 16, 1871.

[15] Qualified under act of July 2, 1862, and took his seat January 16, 1871.

[16] Qualified under act of July 11, 1868, and took his seat January 24, 1871; election unsuccessfully contested by Thomas P. Beard.

[17] Reelected to the Forty-second Congress but resigned, having been elected Senator.

[18] Resigned March 6, 1869.

[19] Elected to fill vacancy caused by resignation of Elihu B. Washburne, and took his seat December 6, 1869.

[20] Election unsuccessfully contested by John S. Reid.

[21] Elected to fill vacancy caused by resignation of Representative-elect Daniel D. Pratt (January 27, 1869), before the beginning of the congressional term, who had been elected Senator, and took his seat March 4, 1869.

[22] Resigned December 6, 1869.

[23] Elected to fill vacancy caused by resignation of James W. Grimes, and took his seat January 26, 1870.

[24] Died September 30, 1870.

[25] Elected to fill vacancy caused by death of William Smyth, and took his seat December 6, 1870.

[26] Resigned February 28, 1870; the Governor of Kentucky peremptorily refused to accept the resignation and requested its withdrawl; the request was complied with; on March 7, 1870, a resolution was presented in the House as a question of privilege, citing these facts and granting him the right to resume his seat; the House refused to entertain it.

[27] Elected to fill vacancy caused by resignation of Jacob S. Golladay, and took his seat May 10, 1870.

[28] Election unsuccessfully contested by Sidney M. Barnes.

[29] Seated by resolution of March 5, 1869; election unsuccessfully contested by John T. Zeigler.

[30] The Governor of Louisiana having officially declared that the election held in the State of Louisiana on November 3, 1868, "Did not elicit an honest will of the people, * * *," a resolution was adopted on March 9, 1869, directing the Committee on Elections to inquire into the validity of the elections of those presenting credentials; all seats were contested, and the Members-elect were not sworn pending the contests.

[31] Contested the election of Louis St. Martin; committee reported in favor of seating Mr. Sypher, and House adopted the report by a vote of 78 to 73, moved to reconsider by a vote of 86 to 79, then adopted a substitute resolution declaring the seat vacant by a vote of 96 to 68 (April 20, 1870); subsequently elected, and took his seat December 5, 1870.

[32] Election unsuccessfully contested by Caleb S. Hunt; took his seat April 8, 1869.

[33] Election unsuccessfully contested by Adolphe Bailey; took his seat July 6, 1870.

[34] Successfully contested the election of Michael Ryan (who had not been permitted to qualify), and took his seat May 23, 1870.

[35] Frank Morey, G. W. McCranie, and P. J. Kennedy each presented credentials claiming to be the Member-elect from the fifth congressional district; by resolution of April 28, 1870, it was declared there was no lawful election in the district. Morey presented credentials under a subsequent election, and took his seat December 6, 1870.

[36] Died September 9, 1869.

[37] Appointed to fill vacancy caused by death of William Pitt Fessenden, and took his seat December 6, 1869; subsequently elected.

## MASSACHUSETTS

### SENATORS

Charles Sumner, *Boston*
Henry Wilson, *Natick*

### REPRESENTATIVES

James Buffington, *Fall River*
Oakes Ames, *North Easton*
Ginery Twichell, *Brookline*
Samuel Hooper, *Boston*
Benjamin F. Butler, *Lowell*
Nathaniel P. Banks, *Waltham*
George S. Boutwell,[38] *Groton*
George M. Brooks,[39] *Concord*
George F. Hoar, *Worcester*
William B. Washburn, *Greenfield*
Henry L. Dawes, *Pittsfield*

## MICHIGAN

### SENATORS

Zachariah Chandler, *Detroit*
Jacob M. Howard, *Detroit*

### REPRESENTATIVES

Fernando C. Beaman, *Adrain*
William L. Stoughton, *Sturgis*
Austin Blair, *Jackson*
Thomas W. Ferry,[40] *Grand Haven*
Omar D. Conger, *Port Huron*
Randolph Strickland, *St. Johns*

## MINNESOTA

### SENATORS

Alexander Ramsey, *St. Paul*
Daniel S. Norton,[41] *Winona*
William Windom,[42] *Winona*
Ozora P. Stearns,[43] *Rochester*

### REPRESENTATIVES

Morton S. Wilkinson, *Mankato*
Eugene M. Wilson, *Minneapolis*

## MISSISSIPPI[44]

### SENATORS

Hiram R. Revels,[45] *Natchez*
Adelbert Ames,[46] *Natchez*

### REPRESENTATIVES

George E. Harris,[47] *Hernando*
Joseph L. Morphis,[47] *Pontotoc*
Henry W. Barry,[48] *Columbus*
George C. McKee,[49] *Vicksburg*
Legrand W. Perce,[49] *Natchez*

## MISSOURI

### SENATORS

Charles D. Drake,[50] *St. Louis*
Daniel T. Jewett,[51] *St. Louis*
Francis P. Blair, Jr.,[52] *St. Louis*
Carl Schurz, *St. Louis*

### REPRESENTATIVES

Erastus Wells, *St. Louis*
Gustavus A. Finkelnburg, *St. Louis*
James R. McCormick, *Ironton*
Sempronius H. Boyd, *Springfield*
Samuel S. Burdett, *Osceola*
Robert T. Van Horn,[53] *Kansas City*
Joel F. Asper, *Chillicothe*
John F. Benjamin, *Shelbyville*
David P. Dyer,[54] *Louisiana*

## NEBRASKA

### SENATORS

John M. Thayer, *Omaha*
Thomas W. Tipton, *Brownville*

### REPRESENTATIVE AT LARGE

John Taffe, *Omaha*

## NEVADA

### SENATORS

William M. Stewart, *Virginia City*
James W. Nye, *Carson City*

### REPRESENTATIVE AT LARGE

Thomas Fitch, *Belmont*

## NEW HAMPSHIRE

### SENATORS

Aaron H. Cragin, *Lebanon*
James W. Patterson, *Hanover*

### REPRESENTATIVES

Jacob H. Ela, *Rochester*
Aaron F. Stevens, *Nashua*
Jacob Benton, *Lancaster*

## NEW JERSEY

### SENATORS

Alexander G. Cattell, *Camden*
John P. Stockton, *Trenton*

### REPRESENTATIVES

William Moore, *Mays Landing*
Charles Haight, *Freehold*

John T. Bird, *Flemington*
John Hill, *Boonton*
Orestes Cleveland, *Jersey City*

## NEW YORK

### SENATORS

Roscoe Conkling, *Utica*
Reuben E. Fenton, *Jamestown*

### REPRESENTATIVES

Henry A. Reeves, *Greenport*
John G. Schumaker, *Brooklyn*
Henry W. Slocum, *Brooklyn*
John Fox, *New York City*
John Morrissey, *New York City*
Samuel S. Cox, *New York City*
Hervey C. Calkin, *New York City*
James Brooks, *New York City*
Fernando Wood, *New York City*
Clarkson N. Potter, *New Rochelle*
George W. Greene,[55] *Goshen*
Charles H. Van Wyck,[56] *Middletown*
John H. Ketcham, *Dover*
John A. Griswold, *Catskill*
Stephen L. Mayham, *Schoharie*
Adolphus H. Tanner, *Whitehall*
Orange Ferriss, *Glens Falls*
William A. Wheeler, *Malone*
Stephen Sanford, *Amsterdam*
Charles Knapp, *Deposit*
Addison H. Laflin, *Herkimer*
Alexander H. Bailey, *Rome*
John C. Churchill, *Oswego*
Dennis McCarthy, *Syracuse*
George W. Cowles, *Clyde*
William H. Kelsey, *Geneseo*
Giles W. Hotchkiss, *Binghamton*
Hamilton Ward, *Belmont*
Noah Davis,[57] *Albion*
Charles H. Holmes,[58] *Albion*
John Fisher, *Batavia*
David S. Bennett, *Buffalo*
Porter Sheldon, *Jamestown*

## NORTH CAROLINA

### SENATORS

Joseph C. Abbott, *Wilmington*
John Pool, *Elizabeth City*

---

[38] Resigned March 12, 1869, having been appointed Secretary of the Treasury.

[39] Elected to fill vacancy caused by resignation of George S. Boutwell, and took his seat December 6, 1869.

[40] Reelected to the Forty-second Congress but resigned, having been elected Senator.

[41] Died July 13, 1870.

[42] Appointed to fill vacancy caused by death of Daniel S. Norton, and took his seat December 1, 1870.

[43] Elected to fill vacancy caused by death of Daniel S. Norton, and took his seat January 23, 1871.

[44] Readmitted to representation by act of February 23, 1870.

[45] Took his seat February 25, 1870; term to expire March 3, 1871.

[46] Took his seat April 1, 1870; term to expire March 3, 1875.

[47] Qualified under act of July 11, 1868, and took his seat February 23, 1870.

[48] Took his seat April 8, 1870.

[49] Qualified under act of July 2, 1862, and took his seat February 23, 1870.

[50] Resigned December 19, 1870.

[51] Appointed to fill vacancy caused by resignation of Charles D. Drake, and took his seat December 22, 1870.

[52] Elected to fill vacancy caused by resignation of Charles D. Drake, and took his seat January 25, 1871.

[53] Election unsuccessfully contested by James Shields.

[54] Election unsuccessfully contested by William F. Switzler.

[55] Served until February 17, 1870; succeeded by Charles H. Van Wyck, who contested his election.

[56] Successfully contested the election of George W. Greene, and took his seat February 17, 1870.

[57] Resigned July 15, 1870.

[58] Elected to fill vacancy caused by resignation of Noah Davis, and took his seat December 6, 1870.

## NORTH CAROLINA—
### Continued
#### REPRESENTATIVES

Clinton L. Cobb, *Elizabeth City*
David Heaton,[59] *New Bern*
Joseph Dixon,[60] *Hookerton*
Oliver H. Dockery, *Mangum*
John T. Deweese,[61] *Raleigh*
John Manning, Jr.,[62] *Pittsboro*
Israel G. Lash, *Salem*
Francis E. Shober,[63] *Salisbury*
Alexander H. Jones,[64] *Asheville*

## OHIO

#### SENATORS

John Sherman, *Mansfield*
Allen G. Thurman, *Columbus*

#### REPRESENTATIVES

Peter W. Strader,[65] *Cincinnati*
Job E. Stevenson, *Cincinnati*
Robert C. Schenck,[66] *Dayton*
William Lawrence, *Bellefontaine*
William Mungen, *Findlay*
John A. Smith, *Hillsboro*
James J. Winans, *Xenia*
John Beatty, *Cardington*
Edward F. Dickinson, *Fremont*
Truman H. Hoag,[67] *Toledo*
Erasmus D. Peck,[68] *Perrysburg*
John T. Wilson, *Tranquility*
Philadelph Van Trump, *Lancaster*
George W. Morgan, *Mount Vernon*
Martin Welker, *Wooster*
Eliakim H. Moore, *Athens*
John A. Bingham, *Cadiz*
Jacob A. Ambler, *Salem*
William H. Upson, *Akron*
James A. Garfield, *Hiram*

## OREGON

#### SENATORS

George H. Williams, *Portland*
Henry W. Corbett, *Portland*

#### REPRESENTATIVE AT LARGE

Joseph S. Smith, *Portland*

## PENNSYLVANIA

#### SENATORS

Simon Cameron, *Harrisburg*
John Scott, *Huntingdon*

#### REPRESENTATIVES

Samuel J. Randall, *Philadelphia*
Charles O'Neill, *Philadelphia*
John Moffet,[69] *Philadelphia*
Leonard Myers,[70] *Philadelphia*
William D. Kelley, *Philadelphia*
John R. Reading,[71] *Somerton*
Caleb N. Taylor,[72] *Bristol*
John D. Stiles, *Allentown*
Washington Townsend, *West Chester*
J. Lawrence Getz, *Reading*
Oliver J. Dickey, *Lancaster*
Henry L. Cake, *Tamaqua*
Daniel M. Van Auken, *Milford*
George W. Woodward, *Wilkes-Barre*
Ulysses Mercur, *Towanda*
John B. Packer, *Sunbury*
Richard J. Haldeman, *Harrisburg*
John Cessna, *Bedford*
Daniel J. Morrell, *Johnstown*
William H. Armstrong, *Williamsport*
Glenni W. Scofield, *Warren*
Calvin W. Gilfillan, *Franklin*
John Covode,[73] *Lockport*
James S. Negley, *Pittsburgh*
Darwin Phelps, *Kittanning*
Joseph B. Donley, *Waynesburg*

## RHODE ISLAND

#### SENATORS

Henry B. Anthony, *Providence*
William Sprague, *Providence*

#### REPRESENTATIVES

Thomas A. Jenckes, *Providence*
Nathan F. Dixon, *Westerly*

## SOUTH CAROLINA

#### SENATORS

Thomas J. Robertson, *Columbia*
Frederick A. Sawyer, *Charleston*

#### REPRESENTATIVES

B. Frank Whittemore,[74] *Darlington*
Joseph H. Rainey,[75] *Georgetown*
Christopher C. Bowen, *Charleston*
Solomon L. Hoge,[76] *Columbia*
Alexander S. Wallace,[77] *Yorkville*

## TENNESSEE

#### SENATORS

Joseph S. Fowler, *Nashville*
William G. Brownlow, *Knoxville*

#### REPRESENTATIVES[78]

Roderick R. Butler, *Taylorsville*
Horace Maynard, *Knoxville*
William B. Stokes, *Alexandria*
Lewis Tillman,[79] *Shelbyville*
William F. Prosser, *Nashville*
Samuel M. Arnell, *Columbia*
Isaac R. Hawkins, *Huntingdon*
William J. Smith, *Memphis*

## TEXAS [80]

#### SENATORS

Morgan C. Hamilton,[81] *Austin*
James W. Flanagan,[82] *Wallings Ferry*

---

[59] Died June 25, 1870.

[60] Elected to fill vacancy caused by death of David Heaton, and took his seat December 5, 1870.

[61] Resigned February 28, 1870; on March 1, 1870, the Committee on Military Affairs reported a resolution declaring that he had made "an appointment to the United States Naval Academy in violation of law, and that such appointment was influenced by pecuniary considerations," and condemning the action; upon a roll call the resolution was agreed to by a vote of 170 to 0.

[62] Elected to fill vacancy caused by the resignation of John T. Deweese, and took his seat December 7, 1870.

[63] Election unsuccessfully contested by Nathaniel Boyden.

[64] Election unsuccessfully contested by Plato Durham.

[65] Election unsuccessfully contested by Benjamin Eggleston.

[66] Resigned January 5, 1871.

[67] Died February 5, 1870.

[68] Elected to fill vacancy caused by death of Truman H. Hoag, and took his seat April 23, 1870.

[69] Served until April 9, 1869; succeeded by Leonard Myers, who contested his election.

[70] Successfully contested the election of John Moffet, and took his seat April 9, 1869.

[71] Served until April 13, 1870; succeeded by Caleb N. Taylor, who contested his election.

[72] Successfully contested the election of John R. Reading, and took his seat April 13, 1870.

[73] Both John Covode and Henry D. Foster claimed to have been elected, while the governor refused to sign a certificate or declare either elected; the House at first refused admission to either; case was recommitted for investigation and on February 9, 1870, the House declared Mr. Covode entitled to the seat; took his seat the same day; died January 11, 1871.

[74] February 21, 1870, the Committee on Military Affairs presented a report showing he had been "influenced by improper pecuniary considerations in making appointments to the Military and Naval Academies," and a resolution for his expulsion; pending action he resigned February 24, 1870; following the announcement, the House adopted a resolution, without a dissenting vote, declaring he had made such appointments in violation of law, that they were influenced by pecuniary considerations, that he was unworthy of a seat in the body, and condemning his

conduct. June 18, 1870, credentials of his reelection were presented; on June 21, 1870, the House passed a resolution citing its previous action, declining to allow him to be sworn, and directing the return of his credentials.

[75] Elected to fill vacancy caused by B. Frank Whittemore being refused his seat; took his seat December 12, 1870.

[76] Successfully contested the election of J. P. Reed, and took his seat April 8, 1869; the House had refused to permit Mr. Reed to qualify upon the ground of disloyalty.

[77] Successfully contested the election of William D. Simpson, who was not permitted to qualify on his credentials, and took his seat May 27, 1870.

[78] John B. Rogers claimed a seat as Representative at large, but claim was not seriously considered.

[79] Election unsuccessfully contested by C. A. Sheafe.

[80] Readmitted to representation by act of March 30, 1870.

[81] Took his seat March 31, 1870; term to expire March 3, 1871.

[82] Took his seat March 31, 1870; term to expire March 3, 1875.

REPRESENTATIVES
George W. Whitmore,[83] *Tyler*
John C. Conner,[84] *Sherman*
William T. Clark,[83] *Galveston*
Edward Degener,[83] *San Antonio*

## VERMONT

SENATORS
George F. Edmunds, *Burlington*
Justin S. Morrill, *Strafford*

REPRESENTATIVES
Charles W. Willard, *Montpelier*
Luke P. Poland, *St. Johnsbury*
Worthington C. Smith, *St. Albans*

## VIRGINIA[85]

SENATORS
John W. Johnston,[86] *Abingdon*
John F. Lewis,[87] *Port Republic*

REPRESENTATIVES[88]
Richard S. Ayer,[89] *Warsaw*
James H. Platt, Jr.,[90] *Petersburg*
Charles H. Porter,[90] *Richmond*
George W. Booker,[91] *Martinsville*
Robert Ridgway,[92] *Cool Well*
Richard T. W. Duke,[93] *Charlottesville*
William Milnes, Jr.,[90] *Shenandoah Iron Works*
Lewis McKenzie,[94] *Alexandria*
James King Gibson,[95] *Abingdon*

## WEST VIRGINIA

SENATORS
Waitman T. Willey, *Morgantown*
Arthur I. Boreman, *Parkersburg*

REPRESENTATIVES
Isaac H. Duval, *Wellsburg*
James C. McGrew, *Kingwood*
John S. Witcher, *Guyandotte*

## WISCONSIN

SENATORS
Timothy O. Howe, *Green Bay*
Matthew H. Carpenter, *Milwaukee*

REPRESENTATIVES
Halbert E. Paine, *Milwaukee*
Benjamin F. Hopkins,[96] *Madison*
David Atwood,[97] *Madison*
Amasa Cobb, *Mineral Point*
Charles A. Eldridge, *Fond du Lac*
Philetus Sawyer, *Oshkosh*
Cadwallader C. Washburn, *La Crosse*

## TERRITORY OF ARIZONA

DELEGATE
Richard C. McCormick, *Tucson*

## TERRITORY OF COLORADO

DELEGATE
Allen A. Bradford, *Pueblo*

## TERRITORY OF DAKOTA

DELEGATE
Solomon L. Spink, *Yankton*

## TERRITORY OF IDAHO

DELEGATE
Jacob K. Shafer, *Idaho City*

## TERRITORY OF MONTANA

DELEGATE
James M. Cavanaugh, *Helena*

## TERRITORY OF NEW MEXICO

DELEGATE
J. Francisco Chaves, *Santa Fe*

## TERRITORY OF UTAH

DELEGATE
William H. Hooper, *Salt Lake City*

## TERRITORY OF WASHINGTON

DELEGATE
Selucius Garfielde, *Olympia*

## TERRITORY OF WYOMING [98]

DELEGATE
Stephen F. Nuckolls,[99] *Cheyenne*

---

[83] Qualified under act of July 2, 1862, and took his seat March 31, 1870.

[84] Qualified under act of July 2, 1862, and took his seat March 31, 1870; election unsuccessfully contested by Benjamin F. Grafton.

[85] Readmitted to representation by act of January 26, 1870.

[86] Took his seat January 28, 1870; term to expire March 3, 1871.

[87] Took his seat January 27, 1870; term to expire March 3, 1875.

[88] The Virginia constitutional convention called under reconstruction laws passed an ordinance providing for a ninth Representative at large; credentials of Joseph Segar as such Representative were presented January 25, 1870; on July 11, 1870, the House adopted a resolution, without division, declaring him not entitled to a seat.

[89] Qualified under act of July 2, 1862, and took his seat January 31, 1870.

[90] Qualified under act of July 2, 1862, and took his seat January 27, 1870.

[91] Qualified under act of July 2, 1862, and took his seat February 1, 1870; election unsuccessfully contested by George Tucker.

[92] Qualified under act of July 2, 1862, and took his seat January 27, 1870; died October 16, 1870.

[93] Elected to fill vacancy caused by death of Robert Ridgway, qualified under act of July 11, 1868, and took his seat December 5, 1870.

[94] Qualified under act of July 2, 1862, and took his seat January 31, 1870; election unsuccessfully contested by Charles Whittlesey.

[95] Qualified under act of July 11, 1868, and took his seat January 28, 1870.

[96] Died January 1, 1870.

[97] Elected to fill vacancy caused by death of Benjamin F. Hopkins, and took his seat February 23, 1870.

[98] Formed from a portion of the territory ceded to the United States by France by treaty of Paris of April 30, 1803, and granted a Delegate in Congress by act of July 25, 1868.

[99] Took his seat December 6, 1869.

# 42ND CONGRESS

## MARCH 4, 1871, TO MARCH 3, 1873

FIRST SESSION— *March 4, 1871, to April 20, 1871*
SECOND SESSION— *December 4, 1871, to June 10, 1872*
THIRD SESSION— *December 2, 1872, to March 3, 1873*
SPECIAL SESSION OF THE SENATE— *May 10, 1871, to May 27, 1871*

———

VICE PRESIDENT OF THE UNITED STATES— Schuyler Colfax, of Indiana
PRESIDENT PRO TEMPORE OF THE SENATE— Henry B. Anthony,[1] of Rhode Island
SECRETARY OF THE SENATE— George C. Gorham, of California
SERGEANT AT ARMS OF THE SENATE— John R. French, of New Hampshire

———

SPEAKER OF THE HOUSE OF REPRESENTATIVES— James G. Blaine,[2] of Maine
CLERK OF THE HOUSE— Edward McPherson,[3] of Pennsylvania
SERGEANT AT ARMS OF THE HOUSE— Nathaniel G. Ordway, of New Hampshire
DOORKEEPER OF THE HOUSE— Otis S. Buxton, of New York
POSTMASTER OF THE HOUSE— William S. King

Schuyler Colfax
Vice President

James G. Blaine
Speaker

## ALABAMA

### SENATORS

George E. Spencer, *Decatur*
George T. Goldthwaite,[4] *Montgomery*

### REPRESENTATIVES

Benjamin S. Turner, *Selma*
Charles W. Buckley, *Montgomery*
William A. Handley,[5] *Roanoke*
Charles Hays, *Eutaw*
Peter M. Dox, *Huntsville*
Joseph H. Sloss, *Tuscumbia*

## ARKANSAS

### SENATORS

Benjamin F. Rice, *Little Rock*
Powell Clayton, *Little Rock*

### REPRESENTATIVES

James M. Hanks, *Helena*
Oliver P. Snyder, *Pine Bluff*
John Edwards,[6] *Fort Smith*
Thomas Boles,[7] *Dardanelle*

## CALIFORNIA

### SENATORS

Cornelius Cole, *San Francisco*
Eugene Casserly, *San Francisco*

### REPRESENTATIVES[8]

Sherman O. Houghton, *San Jose*
Aaron A. Sargent, *Nevada City*
John M. Coghlan, *Suisun City*

## CONNECTICUT

### SENATORS

Orris S. Ferry, *Norwalk*
William A. Buckingham, *Norwich*

### REPRESENTATIVES[9]

Julius L. Strong,[10] *Hartford*
Joseph R. Hawley,[11] *Hartford*
Stephen W. Kellogg, *Waterbury*
Henry H. Starkweather, *Norwich*
William H. Barnum, *Lime Rock*

## DELAWARE

### SENATORS

Thomas F. Bayard, *Wilmington*
Eli Saulsbury, *Dover*

### REPRESENTATIVE AT LARGE

Benjamin T. Biggs, *Summit Bridge*

## FLORIDA

### SENATORS

Thomas W. Osborn, *Pensacola*
Abijah Gilbert, *St. Augustine*

### REPRESENTATIVE AT LARGE

Josiah T. Walls,[12] *Gainesville*
Silas L. Niblack,[13] *Gainesville*

## GEORGIA

### SENATORS

Joshua Hill, *Madison*
Thomas M. Norwood,[14] *Savannah*

### REPRESENTATIVES

Archibald T. MacIntyre,[15] *Thomasville*
Richard H. Whiteley,[16] *Bainbridge*
John S. Bigby, *Newman*
Thomas J. Speer,[17] *Barnesville*
Erasmus W. Beck,[18] *Griffin*
Dudley M. DuBose,[19] *Washington*
William P. Price, *Dahlonega*
Pierce M. B. Young, *Cartersville*

---

[1] Elected March 10, 1871; April 17, 1871; May 23, 1871 (special session of the Senate); December 21, 1871; February 23, 1872; June 8, 1872; December 4, 1872; December 13, 1872; December 20, 1872; and January 24, 1873.

[2] Reelected March 4, 1871.

[3] Reelected March 4, 1871.

[4] Credentials presented February 6, 1871, in the preceding Congress; appeared to take the oath of office March 4, 1871; protest against his being seated presented the same day, and he was not permitted to qualify; on January 9, 1872, the Senate, by resolution, gave him permission to take his seat, pending further investigations; took his seat January 15, 1872; no further action. (See U.S. Senate Election, Expulsion and Censure Cases, 1793-1990, Senate Document 103-33, pp. 157-159.)

[5] Election unsuccessfully contested by B. W. Norris.

[6] Served until February 9, 1872; succeeded by Thomas Boles, who contested his election.

[7] Successfully contested the election of John Edwards, and took his seat February 9, 1872.

[8] Elected September 5, 1871.

[9] Elected April 4, 1871.

[10] Died September 7, 1872.

[11] Elected to fill vacancy caused by death of Julius L. Strong, and took his seat December 2, 1872.

[12] Served until January 29, 1873; succeeded by Silas L. Niblack, who contested his election.

[13] Successfully contested the election of Josiah T. Walls, and took his seat January 29, 1873.

[14] Took his seat December 19, 1871; Foster

Blodgett presented credentials as a Senator-elect, but the Senate declared him not elected in accordance with the Constitution; vacancy in this class from March 4, 1871, to November 13, 1871. (See U.S. Senate Election, Expulsion and Censure Cases, 1793-1990, Senate Document 103-33, pp. 160-163.)

[15] Election unsuccessfully contested by Virgil Hilyer.

[16] Election unsuccessfully contested by Nelson Tift.

[17] Died August 18, 1872.

[18] Elected to fill vacancy caused by death of Thomas J. Speer, and took his seat December 2, 1872.

[19] Election unsuccessfully contested by Isham S. Fannin.

## ILLINOIS

SENATORS

Lyman Trumbull, *Chicago*
John A. Logan, *Carbondale*

REPRESENTATIVE AT LARGE

John L. Beveridge,[20] *Evanston*

REPRESENTATIVES

Charles B. Farwell, *Chicago*
John F. Farnsworth, *St. Charles*
Horatio C. Burchard, *Freeport*
John B. Hawley, *Rock Island*
Bradford N. Stevens, *Tiskilwa*
Burton C. Cook,[21] *Ottawa*
Henry Snapp,[22] *Joliet*
Jesse H. Moore, *Decatur*
James C. Robinson, *Springfield*
Thompson W. McNeely, *Petersburg*
Edward Y. Rice, *Hillsboro*
Samuel S. Marshall, *McLeansboro*
John B. Hay, *Belleville*
John M. Crebs, *Carmi*

## INDIANA

SENATORS

Oliver H. P. T. Morton, *Indianapolis*
Daniel D. Pratt, *Logansport*

REPRESENTATIVES

William E. Niblack, *Vincennes*
Michael C. Kerr, *New Albany*
William S. Holman, *Aurora*
Jeremiah M. Wilson,[23] *Connersville*
John Coburn, *Indianapolis*
Daniel W. Voorhees, *Terre Haute*
Mahlon D. Manson, *Crawfordsville*
James N. Tyner, *Peru*
John P. C. Shanks, *Jay Court House*
William Williams, *Warsaw*
Jasper Packard, *Laporte*

## IOWA

SENATORS

James Harlan, *Mount Pleasant*
George G. Wright, *Des Moines*

REPRESENTATIVES

George W. McCrary, *Keokuk*
Aylett R. Cotton, *Lyons*
William G. Donnan, *Independence*
Madison M. Walden, *Centerville*

Frank W. Palmer, *Des Moines*
Jackson Orr, *Montana*

## KANSAS

SENATORS[24]

Samuel C. Pomeroy, *Atchison*
Alexander Caldwell, *Leavenworth*

REPRESENTATIVE AT LARGE

David P. Lowe, *Fort Scott*

## KENTUCKY

SENATORS

Garrett Davis,[25] *Paris*
Willis B. Machen,[26] *Eddyville*
John W. Stevenson, *Covington*

REPRESENTATIVES

Edward Crossland, *Mayfield*
Henry D. McHenry, *Hartford*
Joseph H. Lewis, *Glasgow*
William B. Read, *Hodgensville*
Boyd Winchester, *Louisville*
William E. Arthur, *Covington*
James B. Beck, *Lexington*
George M. Adams, *Barbourville*
John M. Rice, *Louisa*

## LOUISIANA

SENATORS

William Pitt Kellogg,[27] *New Orleans*
J. Rodman West, *New Orleans*

REPRESENTATIVES

J. Hale Sypher, *New Orleans*
Lionel A. Sheldon, *New Orleans*
Chester B. Darrall, *Brashear*
James McCleery,[28] *Shreveport*
Aleck Boarman,[29] *Shreveport*
Frank Morey, *Monroe*

## MAINE

SENATORS

Hannibal Hamlin, *Bangor*
Lot M. Morrill, *Augusta*

REPRESENTATIVES

John Lynch, *Portland*
William P. Frye, *Lewiston*

James G. Blaine, *Augusta*
John A. Peters, *Bangor*
Eugene Hale, *Ellsworth*

## MARYLAND

SENATORS

George Vickers, *Chestertown*
William T. Hamilton, *Hagerstown*

REPRESENTATIVES

Samuel Hambleton, *Easton*
Stevenson Archer, *Bel Air*
Thomas Swann, *Baltimore*
John Ritchie, *Frederick*
William M. Merrick, *Ilchester*

## MASSACHUSETTS

SENATORS

Charles Sumner, *Boston*
Henry Wilson,[30] *Natick*

REPRESENTATIVES

James Buffington, *Fall River*
Oakes Ames, *North Easton*
Ginery Twichell, *Brookline*
Samuel Hooper, *Boston*
Benjamin F. Butler, *Lowell*
Nathaniel P. Banks, *Waltham*
George M. Brooks,[31] *Concord*
Constantine C. Esty,[32] *Framingham*
George F. Hoar, *Worcester*
William B. Washburn,[33] *Greenfield*
Alvah Crocker,[34] *Fitchburg*
Henry L. Dawes, *Pittsfield*

## MICHIGAN

SENATORS

Zachariah Chandler, *Detroit*
Thomas W. Ferry, *Grand Haven*

REPRESENTATIVES

Henry Waldron, *Hillsdale*
William L. Stoughton, *Sturgis*
Austin Blair, *Jackson*
Wilder D. Foster,[35] *Grand Rapids*
Omar D. Conger, *Port Huron*
Jabez G. Sutherland, *Saginaw*

---

[20] Elected to fill vacancy caused by resignation of Representative-elect John A. Logan, in preceding Congress, and took his seat December 4, 1871; resigned January 4, 1873.
[21] Resigned August 26, 1871.
[22] Elected to fill vacancy caused by resignation of Burton C. Cook, and took his seat December 4, 1871.
[23] Election unsuccessfully contested by David S. Gooding.
[24] May 11, 1872, the Committee on Privileges and Elections was authorized to investigate charges of bribery and corruption in connection with the election of both the sitting Senators; June 3, 1872, it reported that in the case of Mr. Pomeroy such charges were totally unsustained; in the case of Mr. Caldwell the report was directly to the contrary, and on February 17, 1873, it reported a resolution declaring him "not duly and legally elected"; this report was not acted upon during the Congress, but early in the succeeding

Congress, during the special session of the Senate, while the report was pending and under discussion, Mr. Caldwell resigned (March 24, 1873). (See U.S. Senate Election, Expulsion and Censure Cases, 1793-1990, Senate Document 103-33, pp. 174-177.)
[25] Died September 22, 1872.
[26] Appointed to fill vacancy caused by death of Garrett Davis, and took his seat December 2, 1872.
[27] Resigned November 1, 1872; on January 22, 1873, credentials of John Ray and William L. McMillen, each claiming to have been elected to fill the vacancy, were presented and referred; February 20, 1873, the committee reported that neither of the claimants was entitled to a seat, as no State government existed at the time in Louisiana, and recommended the passage of a bill ordering a new election; such a bill was rejected February 27, 1873; no further action was taken on the credentials and the seat remained vacant to the close of the Congress. (See U.S.

Senate Election, Expulsion and Censure Cases, 1793-1990, Senate Document 103-33, pp. 182-188.)
[28] Died November 5, 1871, never having qualified.
[29] Elected to fill vacancy caused by death of James McCleery, and took his seat December 3, 1872.
[30] Resigned March 3, 1873, having been elected Vice President.
[31] Resigned May 13, 1872, to become judge of probate court.
[32] Elected to fill vacancy caused by resignation of George M. Brooks, and took his seat December 2, 1872.
[33] Resigned December 5, 1871, having been elected Governor.
[34] Elected to fill vacancy caused by resignation of William B. Washburn, and took his seat February 14, 1872.
[35] Elected to fill vacancy caused by resignation of Representative-elect Thomas W. Ferry, in preceding Congress, and took his seat December 4, 1871.

## MINNESOTA

### SENATORS

Alexander Ramsey, *St. Paul*
William Windom, *Winona*

### REPRESENTATIVES

Mark H. Dunnell, *Owatonna*
John T. Averill, *St. Paul*

## MISSISSIPPI

### SENATORS

Adelbert Ames, *Natchez*
James L. Alcorn,[36] *Friars Point*

### REPRESENTATIVES

George E. Harris, *Hernando*
Joseph L. Morphis, *Pontotoc*
Henry W. Barry, *Columbus*
George C. McKee, *Vicksburg*
Legrand W. Perce, *Natchez*

## MISSOURI

### SENATORS

Carl Schurz, *St. Louis*
Francis P. Blair, Jr., *St. Louis*

### REPRESENTATIVES

Erastus Wells, *St. Louis*
Gustavus A. Finkelnburg, *St. Louis*
James R. McCormick, *Arcadia*
Harrison E. Havens, *Springfield*
Samuel S. Burdett, *Osceola*
Abram Comingo, *Independence*
Isaac C. Parker, *St. Joseph*
James G. Blair, *Canton*
Andrew King, *St. Charles*

## NEBRASKA

### SENATORS

Thomas W. Tipton, *Brownville*
Phineas W. Hitchcock, *Omaha*

### REPRESENTATIVE AT LARGE

John Taffe, *Omaha*

## NEVADA

### SENATORS

William M. Stewart, *Virginia City*
James W. Nye, *Carson City*

### REPRESENTATIVE AT LARGE

Charles W. Kendall, *Hamilton*

## NEW HAMPSHIRE

### SENATORS

Aaron H. Cragin, *Lebanon*
James W. Patterson,[37] *Hanover*

### REPRESENTATIVES

Ellery A. Hibbard, *Laconia*
Samuel N. Bell, *Manchester*
Hosea W. Parker, *Claremont*

## NEW JERSEY

### SENATORS

John P. Stockton, *Trenton*
Frederick T. Frelinghuysen, *Newark*

### REPRESENTATIVES

John W. Hazelton, *Mullica Hill*
Samuel C. Forker, *Bordentown*
John T. Bird, *Flemington*
John Hill, *Boonton*
George A. Halsey, *Newark*

## NEW YORK

### SENATORS

Roscoe Conkling, *Utica*
Reuben E. Fenton, *Jamestown*

### REPRESENTATIVES

Dwight Townsend, *Stapleton*
Thomas Kinsella, *Brooklyn*
Henry W. Slocum, *Brooklyn*
Robert B. Roosevelt, *New York City*
William R. Roberts, *New York City*
Samuel S. Cox, *New York City*
Smith Ely, Jr., *New York City*
James Brooks, *New York City*
Fernando Wood, *New York City*
Clarkson N. Potter, *New Rochelle*
Charles St. John, *Port Jervis*
John H. Ketcham, *Dover Plains*
Joseph H. Tuthill, *Ellenville*
Eli Perry, *Albany*
Joseph M. Warren, *Troy*
John Rogers, *Black Brook*
William A. Wheeler, *Malone*
John M. Carroll, *Johnstown*
Elizur H. Prindle, *Norwich*
Clinton L. Merriam, *Locust Grove*
Ellis H. Roberts, *Utica*
William E. Lansing, *Chittenango*

R. Holland Duell, *Cortland*
John E. Seeley, *Ovid*
William H. Lamport, *Canandaigua*
Milo Goodrich, *Dryden*
H. Boardman Smith, *Elmira*
Freeman Clarke, *Rochester*
Seth Wakeman, *Batavia*
William Williams, *Buffalo*
Walter L. Sessions, *Panama*

## NORTH CAROLINA

### SENATORS

John Pool, *Elizabeth City*
Matt W. Ransom,[38] *Weldon*

### REPRESENTATIVES

Clinton L. Cobb, *Elizabeth City*
Charles R. Thomas, *New Bern*
Alfred M. Waddell, *Wilmington*
Sion H. Rogers,[39] *Raleigh*
James M. Leach, *Lexington*
Francis E. Shober, *Salisbury*
James C. Harper, *Patterson*

## OHIO

### SENATORS

John Sherman, *Mansfield*
Allen G. Thurman, *Columbus*

### REPRESENTATIVES

Aaron F. Perry,[40] *Cincinnati*
Ozro J. Dodds,[41] *Cincinnati*
Job E. Stevenson, *Cincinnati*
Lewis D. Campbell,[42] *Hamilton*
John F. McKinney, *Piqua*
Charles N. Lamison, *Lima*
John A. Smith, *Hillsboro*
Samuel Schellabarger, *Springfield*
John Beatty, *Cardington*
Charles Foster, *Fostoria*
Erasmus D. Peck, *Perrysburg*
John T. Wilson, *Tranquility*
Philadelph Van Trump, *Lancaster*
George W. Morgan, *Mount Vernon*
James Monroe, *Oberlin*
William P. Sprague, *McConnellsville*
John A. Bingham, *Cadiz*
Jacob A. Ambler, *Salem*
William H. Upson, *Akron*
James A. Garfield, *Hiram*

---

[36] Elected January 18, 1870, for the term beginning March 4, 1871, but did not accept or qualify until December 4, 1871, preferring to retain the governorship.

[37] February 5, 1873, a select committee was appointed to consider matters presented in a communication from the House of Representatives and accompanying testimony, reflecting upon the conduct of certain Senators in connection with the "Credit Mobilier of America"; February 27, 1873, the committee reported, exonerating other Senators mentioned in the report, and a resolution favoring the expulsion of Mr. Patterson; as the Congress and Mr. Patterson's term expired simultaneously on March 3, 1873, no final action was reached. (See U.S. Senate Election, Expulsion and Censure Cases, 1793-1990, Senate Document 103-33, pp. 189-195.)

[38] Joseph C. Abbott was a claimant for this seat; the Committee on Privileges and Elections reported February 28, 1872, that Zebulon B. Vance had received "a majority of the whole number of votes cast in each house," and Mr. Abbott received the next highest number of votes; the next day Mr. Vance was declared duly elected. Mr. Abbott rested his claim on what he assumed to be the legal result of the conceded ineligibility of Mr. Vance, who was barred by the provisions of the fourteenth amendment; Mr. Vance made no claim to the seat; on February 5, 1872, credentials of Mr. Ransom were presented, certifying he had been elected January 30, 1872, "to fill a vacancy existing by reason of the resignation of Zebulon B. Vance"; April 23, 1872, Senate declared, by resolution, that Mr. Abbott had not been elected, and the day following that Mr. Ransom was declared entitled to the seat; took his

seat April 24, 1872; resolutions were subsequently adopted allowing mileage and salary to Mr. Abbott from March 4, 1871, to April 23, 1872, and fixing Mr. Ransom's term and pay as beginning March 4, 1871. (See U.S. Senate Election, Expulsion and Censure Cases, 1793-1990, Senate Document 103-33, pp. 166-169.)

[39] Took his seat May 23, 1872; election unsuccessfully contested by James H. Harris.

[40] Resigned in 1872.

[41] Elected to fill vacancy caused by resignation of Aaron F. Perry, and took his seat December 2, 1872.

[42] Election unsuccessfully contested by R. C. Schenck.

## OREGON

### SENATORS

Henry W. Corbett, *Portland*
James K. Kelly, *Portland*

### REPRESENTATIVE AT LARGE

James H. Slater, *La Grande*

## PENNSYLVANIA

### SENATORS

Simon Cameron, *Harrisburg*
John Scott, *Huntingdon*

### REPRESENTATIVES

Samuel J. Randall, *Philadelphia*
John V. Creely, *Philadelphia*
Leonard Myers, *Philadelphia*
William D. Kelley, *Philadelphia*
Alfred C. Harmer, *Germantown*
Ephraim L. Acker, *Norristown*
Washington Townsend, *West Chester*
J. Lawrence Getz, *Reading*
Oliver J. Dickey, *Lancaster*
John W. Killinger, *Lebanon*
John B. Storm, *Stroudsburg*
Lazarus D. Shoemaker, *Wilkes-Barre*
Ulysses Mercur,[43] *Towanda*
Frank C. Bunnell,[44] *Tunkhannock*
John B. Packer, *Sunbury*
Richard J. Haldeman, *Harrisburg*
Benjamin F. Meyers,[45] *Bedford*
R. Milton Speer, *Huntingdon*
Henry Sherwood, *Wellsboro*
Glenni W. Scofield, *Warren*
Samuel Griffith, *Mercer*
Henry D. Foster, *Greensburg*
James S. Negley, *Pittsburgh*
Ebenezer McJunkin, *Butler*
William McClelland, *Mount Jackson*

## RHODE ISLAND

### SENATORS

Henry B. Anthony, *Providence*
William Sprague, *Providence*

### REPRESENTATIVES

Benjamin T. Eames, *Providence*
James M. Pendleton, *Westerly*

## SOUTH CAROLINA

### SENATORS

Thomas J. Robertson, *Columbia*
Frederick A. Sawyer, *Charleston*

### REPRESENTATIVES

Joseph H. Rainey, *Georgetown*
Robert C. De Large,[46] *Charleston*
Robert B. Elliott, *Columbia*
Alexander S. Wallace,[47] *Yorkville*

## TENNESSEE

### SENATORS

William G. Brownlow, *Knoxville*
Henry Cooper, *Nashville*

### REPRESENTATIVES[48]

Roderick R. Butler, *Taylorsville*
Horace Maynard, *Knoxville*
Abraham E. Garrett, *Carthage*
John M. Bright, *Fayetteville*
Edward I. Golladay, *Lebanon*
Washington C. Whitthorne, *Columbia*
Robert P. Caldwell, *Trenton*
William W. Vaughan, *Brownsville*

## TEXAS

### SENATORS

Morgan C. Hamilton,[49] *Austin*
James W. Flanagan, *Flanagans Mills*

### REPRESENTATIVES[50]

William S. Herndon, *Tyler*
John C. Conner, *Sherman*
William T. Clark,[51] *Galveston*
De Witt C. Giddings,[52] *Brenham*
John Hancock, *Austin*

## VERMONT

### SENATORS

George F. Edmunds, *Burlington*
Justin S. Morrill, *Strafford*

### REPRESENTATIVES

Charles W. Willard, *Montpelier*
Luke P. Poland, *St. Johnsbury*
Worthington C. Smith, *St. Albans*

## VIRGINIA

### SENATORS

John W. Johnston, *Abingdon*
John F. Lewis, *Port Republic*

### REPRESENTATIVES

John Critcher, *Oak Grove*
James H. Platt, Jr., *Petersburg*
Charles H. Porter, *Richmond*
William H. H. Stowell, *Burkeville*
Richard T. W. Duke, *Charlottesville*
John T. Harris, *Harrisonburg*
Elliott M. Braxton,[53] *Fredericksburg*
William Terry, *Wytheville*

## WEST VIRGINIA

### SENATORS

Arthur I. Boreman, *Parkersburg*
Henry Gassaway Davis, *Piedmont*

### REPRESENTATIVES

John J. Davis, *Clarksburg*
James C. McGrew, *Kingwood*
Frank Hereford, *Union*

## WISCONSIN

### SENATORS

Timothy O. Howe, *Green Bay*
Matthew H. Carpenter, *Milwaukee*

### REPRESENTATIVES

Alexander Mitchell, *Milwaukee*
Gerry W. Hazelton, *Columbus*
J. Allen Barber, *Lancaster*
Charles A. Eldredge, *Fond du Lac*
Philetus Sawyer, *Oshkosh*
Jeremiah M. Rusk, *Viroqua*

## TERRITORY OF ARIZONA

### DELEGATE

Richard C. McCormick, *Tucson*

## TERRITORY OF COLORADO

### DELEGATE

Jerome B. Chaffee, *Denver*

## TERRITORY OF DAKOTA

### DELEGATE

Moses K. Armstrong,[54] *Yankton*

---

[43] Resigned December 2, 1872.
[44] Elected to fill vacancy caused by resignation of Ulysses Mercur, and took his seat January 7, 1873.
[45] Election unsuccessfully contested by John Cessna.
[46] Election contested by Christopher C. Bowen; seat declared vacant January 24, 1873.
[47] Election unsuccessfully contested by Isaac G. McKissick.
[48] Thomas H. Reeves claimed a seat as Representative at large, but claim was not considered.

[49] Presented himself to take the oath of office March 4, 1871; a certified copy of a joint resolution of the Texas Legislature declaring his election by the preceding legislature illegal was offered and he was not permitted to qualify; March 15, 1871, credentials of Joseph J. Reynolds, claiming to be the Senator-elect, were presented; March 18, 1871, the Senate agreed to a reported resolution declaring Mr. Hamilton duly elected; took his seat March 20, 1871. (See U.S. Senate Election, Expulsion and Censure Cases, 1793-1990, Senate Document 103-33, pp. 164-165.)

[50] Elected October 3 to 6, 1871.
[51] Given a seat by resolution of January 10, 1872; served until May 13, 1872; succeeded by De Witt C. Giddings, who contested his election.
[52] Successfully contested the election of William T. Clark, and took his seat May 13, 1872.
[53] Election unsuccessfully contested by Lewis McKenzie.
[54] Election unsuccessfully contested by Walter A. Burleigh and Solomon L. Spink.

## DISTRICT OF COLUMBIA[55]

DELEGATE
Norton P. Chipman,[56] *Washington*

## TERRITORY OF IDAHO

DELEGATE
Samuel A. Merritt, *Idaho City*

## TERRITORY OF MONTANA

DELEGATE
William H. Clagett,[57] *Deer Lodge*

## TERRITORY OF NEW MEXICO

DELEGATE
José Manuel Gallegos,[58] *Santa Fe*

## TERRITORY OF UTAH

DELEGATE
William H. Hooper,[59] *Salt Lake City*

## TERRITORY OF WASHINGTON

DELEGATE
Selucius Garfielde, *Olympia*

## TERRITORY OF WYOMING

DELEGATE
William T. Jones, *Cheyenne*

---

[55] Established under the seventeenth clause of the eighth section of Article I of the Constitution of the United States; formed from territory ceded to the United States by the State of Maryland, legislative act of December 23, 1788; and by the State of Virginia, legislative act of December 3, 1789; cessions accepted by Congress by act of July 16, 1790, and lines and bounds were established by proclamation of the President, George Washington, March 30, 1791. By act of July 9, 1846, Congress retroceded the county of Alexandria, incorporated in the District, to the State of Virginia; by act of February 21, 1871, a territorial form of government was provided, with the right to Delegate representation in Congress.

[56] Took his seat December 4, 1871.
[57] Elected August 7, 1871.
[58] Elected September 4, 1871.
[59] Election unsuccessfully contested by G. R. Maxwell.

# 43RD CONGRESS

## MARCH 4, 1873, TO MARCH 3, 1875

Henry Wilson
Vice President

FIRST SESSION— *December 1, 1873, to June 23, 1874*
SECOND SESSION— *December 7, 1874, to March 3, 1875*
SPECIAL SESSION OF THE SENATE— *March 4, 1873, to March 26, 1873*

---

VICE PRESIDENT OF THE UNITED STATES— HENRY WILSON, of Massachusetts
PRESIDENT PRO TEMPORE OF THE SENATE— MATTHEW H. CARPENTER,[1] of Wisconsin;
HENRY B. ANTHONY,[2] of Rhode Island
SECRETARY OF THE SENATE— GEORGE C. GORHAM, of California
SERGEANT AT ARMS OF THE SENATE— JOHN R. FRENCH, of New Hampshire

---

SPEAKER OF THE HOUSE OF REPRESENTATIVES— JAMES G. BLAINE,[3] of Maine
CLERK OF THE HOUSE— EDWARD MCPHERSON,[4] of Pennsylvania
SERGEANT AT ARMS OF THE HOUSE— NATHANIEL G. ORDWAY, of New Hampshire
DOORKEEPER OF THE HOUSE— OTIS S. BUXTON, of New York
POSTMASTER OF THE HOUSE— HENRY SHERWOOD

James G. Blaine
Speaker

## ALABAMA

### SENATORS
George E. Spencer,[5] *Decatur*
George T. Goldthwaite, *Montgomery*

### REPRESENTATIVES AT LARGE
Alexander White, *Selma*
Charles C. Sheats, *Decatur*

### REPRESENTATIVES
Frederick G. Bromberg, *Mobile*
James T. Rapier, *Montgomery*
Charles Pelham, *Talladega*
Charles Hays, *Eutaw*
John H. Caldwell, *Jacksonville*
Joseph H. Sloss, *Tuscumbia*

## ARKANSAS

### SENATORS
Powell Clayton, *Little Rock*
Stephen W. Dorsey, *Helena*

### REPRESENTATIVE AT LARGE
William J. Hynes, *Little Rock*

### REPRESENTATIVES
Asa Hodges,[6] *Marion*
Oliver P. Snyder,[7] *Pine Bluff*
William W. Wilshire,[8] *Little Rock*
Thomas M. Gunter,[9] *Fayetteville*

## CALIFORNIA

### SENATORS
Eugene Casserly,[10] *San Francisco*
John S. Hager,[11] *San Francisco*
Aaron A. Sargent, *Nevada City*

### REPRESENTATIVES
Charles Clayton, *San Francisco*
Horace F. Page, *Placerville*
John K. Luttrell, *Santa Rosa*
Sherman O. Houghton, *San Jose*

## CONNECTICUT

### SENATORS
Orris S. Ferry, *Norwalk*
William A. Buckingham,[12] *Norwich*
William W. Eaton,[13] *Hartford*

### REPRESENTATIVES
Joseph R. Hawley, *Hartford*
Stephen W. Kellogg, *Waterbury*
Henry H. Starkweather, *Norwich*
William H. Barnum, *Lime Rock*

## DELAWARE

### SENATORS
Thomas F. Bayard, *Wilmington*
Eli Saulsbury, *Dover*

### REPRESENTATIVE AT LARGE
James R. Lofland, *Milford*

## FLORIDA

### SENATORS
Abijah Gilbert, *St. Augustine*
Simon B. Conover, *Tallahassee*

### REPRESENTATIVES AT LARGE
Josiah T. Walls, *Gainesville*
William J. Purman,[14] *Tallahassee*

## GEORGIA

### SENATORS
Thomas M. Norwood, *Savannah*
John B. Gordon, *Atlanta*

### REPRESENTATIVES
Morgan Rawls,[15] *Guyton*
Andrew Sloan,[16] *Savannah*
Richard H. Whiteley, *Bainbridge*
Philip Cook, *Americus*

---

[1] Elected March 12, 1873, and March 26, 1873 (special session of the Senate); December 11, 1873; December 23, 1874.

[2] Elected January 25, 1875, and February 15, 1875.

[3] Reelected December 1, 1873.

[4] Reelected December 1, 1873.

[5] Appeared on March 6, 1873, to take oath of office, having presented credentials in the preceding congress; objection was made, as a memorial was on file from Francis W. Sykes, claiming the seat; on March 7, 1873, a motion to refer the credentials and memorial to the Committee on Privileges and Elections was not agreed to, and Mr. Spencer was permitted to qualify; December 8, 1873, the memorial of Mr. Sykes was referred, and April 20, 1874, the committee, upon its motion, was discharged from further consideration

thereof. (See U.S. Senate Election, Expulsion and Censure Cases, 1793-1990, Senate Document 103-33, pp. 178-181.)

[6] Credentials as Member-elect, together with notice of contest by Lucien C. Gause, were presented and referred to Committee on Elections on December 2, 1873; the House adopted resolution reported by committee that Mr. Hodges was entitled prima facie to the seat without prejudice to the right of Mr. Gause to contest; took his seat February 4, 1874; the Committee reported unfavorably on the contest.

[7] Election unsuccessfully contested by Marcus L. Bell.

[8] Credentials as Member-elect, together with notice of contest by Thomas M. Gunter, were presented and referred to Committee on Elections on December 2, 1873; on recommendation of the committee he was

seated on February 18, 1874; served until June 16, 1874, when the House decided that Mr. Gunter was entitled to the seat.

[9] Successfully contested the election of William W. Wilshire, and took his seat June 16, 1874.

[10] Resigned November 29, 1873.

[11] Elected to fill vacancy caused by resignation of Eugene Casserly, and took his seat February 9, 1874.

[12] Died February 5, 1875.

[13] Appointed to fill vacancy caused by death of William A. Buckingham.

[14] Resigned January 25, 1875.

[15] Served until March 24, 1874; succeeded by Andrew Sloan, who contested his election.

[16] Successfully contested the election of Morgan Rawls, and took his seat March 24, 1874.

## GEORGIA—Continued

### REPRESENTATIVES—CONTINUED

Henry R. Harris,[17] *Greenville*
James C. Freeman, *Griffin*
James H. Blount, *Macon*
Pierce M. B. Young, *Cartersville*
Alexander H. Stephens,[18]
    *Crawfordville*
Hiram P. Bell, *Cumming*

## ILLINOIS

### SENATORS

John A. Logan, *Chicago*
Richard J. Oglesby, *Decatur*

### REPRESENTATIVES

John B. Rice,[19] *Chicago*
Bernard G. Caulfield,[20] *Chicago*
Jasper D. Ward, *Chicago*
Charles B. Farwell, *Chicago*
Stephen A. Hurlbut, *Belvidere*
Horatio C. Burchard, *Freeport*
John B. Hawley, *Rock Island*
Franklin Corwin, *Peru*
Greenbury L. Fort, *Lacon*
Granville Barrere, *Canton*
William H. Ray, *Rushville*
Robert M. Knapp, *Jerseyville*
James C. Robinson, *Springfield*
John McNulta, *Bloomington*
Joseph G. Cannon, *Tuscola*
John R. Eden, *Sullivan*
James S. Martin, *Salem*
William R. Morrison, *Waterloo*
Isaac Clements, *Carbondale*
Samuel S. Marshall, *McLeansboro*

## INDIANA

### SENATORS

Oliver H. P. T. Morton, *Indianapolis*
Daniel D. Pratt, *Logansport*

### REPRESENTATIVES AT LARGE

William Williams, *Warsaw*
Godlove S. Orth, *Lafayette*

### REPRESENTATIVES

William E. Niblack, *Vincennes*
Simeon K. Wolfe, *New Albany*
William S. Holman, *Aurora*

Jeremiah M. Wilson, *Connersville*
John Coburn, *Indianapolis*
Morton C. Hunter, *Bloomington*
Thomas J. Cason, *Lebanon*
James N. Tyner, *Peru*
John P. C. Shanks,[21] *Portland*
Henry B. Sayler, *Huntington*
Jasper Packard, *Laporte*

## IOWA

### SENATORS

George G. Wright, *Des Moines*
William B. Allison, *Dubuque*

### REPRESENTATIVES

George W. McCrary, *Keokuk*
Aylett R. Cotton, *Lyons*
William G. Donnan, *Independence*
Henry O. Pratt, *Charles City*
James Wilson, *Traer*
William Loughridge, *Oskaloosa*
John A. Kasson, *Des Moines*
James W. McDill, *Afton*
Jackson Orr, *Boone*

## KANSAS

### SENATORS

Alexander Caldwell,[22] *Leavenworth*
Robert Crozier,[23] *Leavenworth*
James M. Harvey,[24] *Vinton*
John J. Ingalls, *Atchison*

### REPRESENTATIVES AT LARGE

Stephen A. Cobb, *Wyandotte*
David P. Lowe, *Fort Scott*
William A. Phillips, *Salina*

## KENTUCKY

### SENATORS

John W. Stevenson, *Covington*
Thomas C. McCreery, *Owensboro*

### REPRESENTATIVES

Edward Crossland, *Mayfield*
John Y. Brown, *Henderson*
Charles W. Milliken, *Franklin*
William B. Read, *Hodgensville*
Elisha D. Standiford, *Louisville*
William E. Arthur, *Covington*
James B. Beck, *Lexington*

Milton J. Durham, *Danville*
George M. Adams, *Barbourville*
John D. Young,[25] *Owingsville*

## LOUISIANA

### SENATORS

J. Rodman West, *New Orleans*
Vacant[26]

### REPRESENTATIVE AT LARGE

George A. Sheridan,[27] *Lake
Providence*

### REPRESENTATIVES[28]

J. Hale Sypher,[29] *New Orleans*
Effingham Lawrence,[30] *New Orleans*
Lionel A. Sheldon,[31] *New Orleans*
Chester B. Darrall, *Brashear*
George L. Smith,[32] *Shreveport*
Frank Morey, *Monroe*

## MAINE

### SENATORS

Hannibal Hamlin, *Bangor*
Lot M. Morrill, *Augusta*

### REPRESENTATIVES

John H. Burleigh, *South Berwick*
William P. Frye, *Lewiston*
James G. Blaine, *Augusta*
Samuel Hersey,[33] *Bangor*
Eugene Hale, *Ellsworth*

## MARYLAND

### SENATORS

William T. Hamilton, *Hagerstown*
George R. Dennis, *Kingston*

### REPRESENTATIVES

Ephraim K. Wilson, *Snow Hill*
Stevenson Archer, *Bel Air*
William J. O'Brien, *Baltimore*
Thomas Swann, *Baltimore*
William J. Albert, *Baltimore*
Lloyd Lowndes, Jr., *Cumberland*

---

[17] Election unsuccessfully contested by M. Bethune.

[18] Elected to fill vacancy caused by death of Representative-elect Ambrose R. Wright (December 21, 1872, before the beginning of the congressional term), and took his seat December 1, 1873.

[19] Died December 17, 1874.

[20] Elected to fill vacancy caused by death of John B. Rice, and took his seat February 1, 1875.

[21] Election unsuccessfully contested by John E. Neff.

[22] Resigned March 24, 1873, while a resolution was pending and under discussion declaring he "was not duly and legally elected." (See U.S. Senate Election, Expulsion and Censure Cases, 1793-1990, Senate Document 103-33, pp. 174-177.)

[23] Appointed to fill vacancy caused by resignation of Alexander Caldwell, and took his seat December 1, 1873.

[24] Elected to fill vacancy caused by resignation of Alexander Caldwell, and took his seat February 12, 1874.

[25] Election unsuccessfully contested by John M. Burns.

[26] Pinckney B. S. Pinchback and William L. McMillen, were claimants for the seat and the contest continued throughout the Congress without settlement. (See U.S. Senate Election, Expulsion and Censure Cases, 1793-1990, Senate Document 103-33, pp. 182-188.)

[27] Took his seat March 3, 1875, after an unsuccessful contest by Pinckney B. S. Pinchback.

[28] A dual government existed in Louisiana at this time, and certificates of election for Representative at large and for the first, second, and fourth districts, signed by acting Governor Pinchback, were presented by Messrs. Pinchback, Lawrence, Gibson, and Davidson, respectively; credentials, signed by Governor

Warmoth, were also presented by Messrs. Sheridan, Sypher, Sheldon, and Smith, and the three last named were seated pending contests.

[29] Served until March 3, 1875; succeeded by Effingham Lawrence, who contested his election.

[30] Successfully contested the election of J. Hale Sypher, and took his seat March 3, 1875.

[31] Randall L. Gibson filed a contest, but no further action was taken.

[32] Elected to fill vacancy caused by death of Representative-elect Samuel Peters, before the beginning of the congressional term, and took his seat December 3, 1873; E. C. Davidson filed a contest under the original election, but no further action was taken.

[33] Died February 3, 1875, before the commencement of the Forty-fourth Congress, to which he had been reelected.

## MASSACHUSETTS

### SENATORS

Charles Sumner,[34] *Boston*
William B. Washburn,[35] *Greenfield*
George S. Boutwell,[36] *Groton*

### REPRESENTATIVES

James Buffington, *Fall River*
Benjamin W. Harris, *East Bridgewater*
William Whiting,[37] *Boston*
Henry L. Pierce,[38] *Boston*
Samuel Hooper,[39] *Boston*
Daniel W. Gooch, *Melrose*
Benjamin F. Butler, *Lowell*
Ebenezer R. Hoar, *Concord*
John M. S. Williams, *Cambridge*
George F. Hoar, *Worcester*
Alvah Crocker,[40] *Fitchburg*
Charles A. Stevens,[41] *Ware*
Henry L. Dawes, *Pittsfield*

## MICHIGAN

### SENATORS

Zachariah Chandler, *Detroit*
Thomas W. Ferry, *Grand Haven*

### REPRESENTATIVES

Moses W. Field, *Detroit*
Henry Waldron, *Hillsdale*
George Willard, *Battle Creek*
Julius C. Burrows, *Kalamazoo*
Wilder D. Foster,[42] *Grand Rapids*
William B. Williams,[43] *Allegan*
Josiah W. Begole, *Flint*
Omar D. Conger, *Port Huron*
Nathan B. Bradley, *Bay City*
Jay A. Hubbell, *Houghton*

## MINNESOTA

### SENATORS

Alexander Ramsey, *St. Paul*
William Windom, *Winoma*

### REPRESENTATIVES

Mark H. Dunnell, *Owatonna*
Horace B. Strait, *Shakopee*
John T. Averill, *St. Paul*

## MISSISSIPPI

### SENATORS

Adelbert Ames,[44] *Natchez*
Henry R. Pease,[45] *Jackson*
James L. Alcorn, *Friars Point*

### REPRESENTATIVES

Lucius Q. C. Lamar, *Oxford*
Albert R. Howe, *Sardis*
Henry W. Barry, *Columbus*
Jason Niles, *Kosciusko*
George C. McKee, *Vicksburg*
John R. Lynch, *Natchez*

## MISSOURI

### SENATORS

Carl Schurz, *St. Louis*
Lewis V. Bogy, *St. Louis*

### REPRESENTATIVES

Edwin O. Stanard, *St. Louis*
Erastus Wells, *St. Louis*
William H. Stone, *St. Louis*
Robert A. Hatcher, *New Madrid*
Richard P. Bland, *Lebanon*
Harrison E. Havens, *Springfield*
Thomas T. Crittenden, *Warrensburg*
Abram Comingo, *Independence*
Isaac C. Parker, *St. Joseph*
Ira B. Hyde, *Princeton*
John B. Clark, Jr., *Fayette*
John M. Glover, *La Grange*
Aylett H. Buckner, *Mexico*

## NEBRASKA

### SENATORS

Thomas W. Tipton, *Brownville*
Phineas W. Hitchcock, *Omaha*

### REPRESENTATIVE AT LARGE

Lorenzo Crounse, *Fort Calhoun*

## NEVADA

### SENATORS

William M. Stewart, *Virginia City*
John P. Jones, *Gold Hill*

### REPRESENTATIVE AT LARGE

Charles W. Kendall, *Hamilton*

## NEW HAMPSHIRE

### SENATORS

Aaron H. Cragin, *Lebanon*
Bainbridge Wadleigh, *Milford*

### REPRESENTATIVES

William B. Small, *New Market*
Austin F. Pike, *Franklin*
Hosea W. Parker, *Claremont*

## NEW JERSEY

### SENATORS

John P. Stockton, *Trenton*
Frederick T. Frelinghuysen, *Newark*

### REPRESENTATIVES

John W. Hazelton, *Mullica Hill*
Samuel A. Dobbins, *Mount Holly*
Amos Clark, Jr., *Elizabeth*
Robert Hamilton, *Newton*
William W. Phelps, *Englewood*
Marcus L. Ward, *Newark*
Isaac W. Scudder, *Jersey City*

## NEW YORK

### SENATORS

Roscoe Conkling, *Utica*
Reuben E. Fenton, *Jamestown*

### REPRESENTATIVE AT LARGE

Lyman Tremain, *Albany*

### REPRESENTATIVES

Henry J. Scudder, *New York City*
John G. Schumaker, *Brooklyn*
Stewart L. Woodford,[46] *Brooklyn*
Simeon B. Chittenden,[47] *Brooklyn*
Philip S. Crooke, *Flatbush*
William R. Roberts, *New York City*
James Brooks,[48] *New York City*
Samuel S. Cox,[49] *New York City*
Thomas J. Creamer, *New York City*
John D. Lawson, *New York City*
David B. Mellish,[50] *New York City*
Richard Schell,[51] *New York City*
Fernando Wood, *New York City*
Clarkson N. Potter, *New Rochelle*
Charles St. John, *Port Jervis*
John O. Whitehouse, *Poughkeepsie*
David M. De Witt, *Kingston*
Eli Perry, *Albany*
James S. Smart, *Cambridge*
Robert S. Hale, *Elizabethtown*
William A. Wheeler, *Malone*
Henry H. Hathorn, *Saratoga Springs*
David Wilber, *Milford*
Clinton L. Merriam, *Locust Grove*
Ellis H. Roberts, *Utica*
William E. Lansing, *Chittenango*
R. Holland Duell, *Cortland*
Clinton D. MacDougall, *Auburn*
William H. Lamport, *Canandaigua*
Thomas C. Platt, *Owego*
H. Boardman Smith, *Elmira*
Freeman Clarke, *Rochester*

---

[34] Died March 11, 1874.
[35] Elected to fill vacancy caused by death of Charles Sumner, and took his seat May 1, 1874.
[36] Elected to fill vacancy caused by resignation of Henry Wilson, in preceding Congress, and took his seat March 17, 1873.
[37] Died June 29, 1873, before Congress assembled.
[38] Elected to fill vacancy caused by the death of William Whiting, and took his seat December 1, 1873.
[39] Died February 13, 1875.
[40] Died December 26, 1874.

[41] Elected to fill vacancy caused by death of Alvah Crocker, and took his seat January 27, 1875.
[42] Died September 20, 1873, before Congress assembled.
[43] Elected to fill vacancy caused by death of Wilder D. Foster, and took his seat December 1, 1873.
[44] Resigned January 10, 1874, having been elected Governor.
[45] Elected to fill vacancy caused by resignation of Adelbert Ames, and took his seat February 12, 1874.
[46] Resigned July 1, 1874.

[47] Elected to fill vacancy caused by resignation of Stewart L. Woodford, and took his seat December 7, 1874.
[48] Died April 30, 1873.
[49] Elected to fill vacancy caused by the death of James Brooks, and took his seat December 1, 1873.
[50] Died May 23, 1874.
[51] Elected to fill vacancy caused by death of David B. Mellish, and took his seat December 7, 1874.

## NEW YORK— Continued

REPRESENTATIVES—CONTINUED

George G. Hoskins, *Attica*
Lyman K. Bass, *Buffalo*
Walter L. Sessions, *Panama*

## NORTH CAROLINA

SENATORS

Matt W. Ransom, *Weldon*
Augustus S. Merrimon, *Raleigh*

REPRESENTATIVES

Clinton L. Cobb, *Elizabeth City*
Charles R. Thomas, *New Bern*
Alfred M. Waddell, *Wilmington*
William A. Smith, *Princeton*
James M. Leach, *Lexington*
Thomas S. Ashe, *Wadesboro*
William M. Robbins, *Statesville*
Robert B. Vance, *Asheville*

## OHIO

SENATORS

John Sherman, *Mansfield*
Allen G. Thurman, *Columbus*

REPRESENTATIVES

Milton Sayler, *Cincinnati*
Henry B. Banning, *Cincinnati*
John Q. Smith, *Oakland*
Lewis B. Gunckel, *Dayton*
Charles N. Lamison, *Lima*
Isaac R. Sherwood, *Bryan*
Lawrence T. Neal, *Chillicothe*
William Lawrence, *Bellefontaine*
James W. Robinson, *Marysville*
Charles Foster, *Fostoria*
Hezekiah S. Bundy, *Wellston*
Hugh J. Jewett,[52] *Columbus*
William E. Finck,[53] *Somerset*
Milton I. Southard, *Zanesville*
John Berry, *Upper Sandusky*
William P. Sprague, *McConnellsville*
Lorenzo Danford, *St. Clairsville*
Laurin D. Woodworth, *Youngstown*
James Monroe, *Oberlin*
James A. Garfield, *Hiram*
Richard C. Parsons, *Cleveland*

## OREGON

SENATORS

James K. Kelly, *Portland*
John H. Mitchell, *Portland*

REPRESENTATIVE AT LARGE

Joseph G. Wilson,[54] *The Dalles*
James W. Nesmith,[55] *Rickreall*

## PENNSYLVANIA

SENATORS

Simon Cameron, *Harrisburg*
John Scott, *Huntingdon*

REPRESENTATIVES AT LARGE

Lemuel Todd, *Carlisle*
Glenni W. Scofield, *Warren*
Charles Albright, *Mauch Chunk*

REPRESENTATIVES

Samuel J. Randall, *Philadelphia*
Charles O'Neill, *Philadelphia*
Leonard Myers, *Philadelphia*
William D. Kelley, *Philadelphia*
Alfred C. Harmer, *Germantown*
James S. Biery, *Allentown*
Washington Townsend, *West Chester*
Hiester Clymer, *Reading*
A. Herr Smith, *Lancaster*
John W. Killinger, *Lebanon*
John B. Storm, *Stroudsburg*
Lazarus D. Shoemaker, *Wilkes-Barre*
James D. Strawbridge, *Danville*
John B. Packer, *Sunbury*
John A. Magee, *New Bloomfield*
John Cessna, *Bedford*
R. Milton Speer, *Huntingdon*
Sobieski Ross, *Coudersport*
Carlton B. Curtis, *Erie*
Hiram L. Richmond, *Meadville*
Alexander W. Taylor, *Indiana*
James S. Negley, *Pittsburgh*
Ebenezer McJunkin,[56] *Butler*
John M. Thompson,[57] *Butler*
William S. Moore, *Washington*

## RHODE ISLAND

SENATORS

Henry B. Anthony, *Providence*
William Sprague, *Providence*

REPRESENTATIVES

Benjamin T. Eames, *Providence*
James M. Pendleton, *Westerly*

## SOUTH CAROLINA

SENATORS

Thomas J. Robertson, *Columbia*
John J. Patterson, *Columbia*

REPRESENTATIVE AT LARGE

Richard H. Cain, *Columbia*

REPRESENTATIVES

Joseph H. Rainey, *Georgetown*
Alonzo J. Ransier, *Charleston*
Robert B. Elliott,[58] *Columbia*
Lewis C. Carpenter,[59] *Columbia*
Alexander S. Wallace, *Yorkville*

## TENNESSEE

SENATORS

William G. Brownlow, *Knoxville*
Henry Cooper, *Nashville*

REPRESENTATIVE AT LARGE

Horace Maynard, *Knoxville*

REPRESENTATIVES

Roderick R. Butler, *Taylorsville*
Jacob M. Thornburgh, *Knoxville*
William Crutchfield, *Chattanooga*
John M. Bright, *Fayetteville*
Horace H. Harrison, *Nashville*
Washington C. Whitthorne, *Columbia*
John D. C. Atkins, *Paris*
David A. Nunn, *Brownsville*
Barbour Lewis, *Memphis*

## TEXAS

SENATORS

Morgan C. Hamilton, *Austin*
James W. Flanagan, *Flanagans Mills*

REPRESENTATIVES AT LARGE

Roger Q. Mills, *Corsicana*
Asa H. Willie, *Galveston*

REPRESENTATIVES

William S. Herndon, *Tyler*
William P. McLean, *Mount Pleasant*
De Witt C. Giddings, *Brenham*
John Hancock, *Austin*

## VERMONT

SENATORS

George F. Edmunds, *Burlington*
Justin S. Morrill, *Strafford*

REPRESENTATIVES

Charles W. Willard, *Montpelier*
Luke P. Poland, *St. Johnsbury*
George W. Hendee, *Morrisville*

## VIRGINIA

SENATORS

John W. Johnston, *Abingdon*
John F. Lewis, *Port Republic*

REPRESENTATIVES

James B. Sener, *Fredericksburg*
James H. Platt, Jr., *Norfolk*
J. Ambler Smith, *Richmond*
William H. H. Stowell, *Burkeville*
Alexander M. Davis,[60] *Independence*
Christopher Y. Thomas,[61]
    *Martinsville*
Thomas Whitehead, *Amherst*
John T. Harris, *Harrisonburg*
Eppa Hunton, *Warrenton*
Rees T. Bowen, *Maiden Spring*

---

[52] Resigned June 23, 1874.
[53] Elected to fill vacancy caused by resignation of Hugh J. Jewett, and took his seat December 7, 1874.
[54] Died July 2, 1873, before Congress assembled.
[55] Elected to fill vacancy caused by death of Joseph G. Wilson, and took his seat December 1, 1873.

[56] Resigned January 1, 1875.
[57] Elected to fill vacancy caused by resignation of Ebenezer McJunkin, and took his seat January 5, 1875.
[58] Resigned, effective November 1, 1874.
[59] Elected to fill vacancy caused by resignation of

Robert B. Elliott, and took his seat December 7, 1874.
[60] Served until March 5, 1874; succeeded by Christopher Y. Thomas, who contested his election.
[61] Successfully contested the election of Alexander M. Davis, and took his seat March 5, 1874.

## WEST VIRGINIA

### SENATORS

Arthur I. Boreman, *Parkersburg*
Henry Gassaway Davis, *Piedmont*

### REPRESENTATIVES

John J. Davis,[62] *Clarksburg*
John M. Hagans,[63] *Morgantown*
Frank Hereford, *Union*

## WISCONSIN

### SENATORS

Timothy O. Howe, *Green Bay*
Matthew H. Carpenter, *Milwaukee*

### REPRESENTATIVES

Charles G. Williams, *Janesville*
Gerry W. Hazelton, *Columbus*
J. Allen Barber, *Lancaster*
Alexander Mitchell, *Milwaukee*
Charles A. Eldridge, *Fond du Lac*
Philetus Sawyer, *Oshkosh*
Jeremiah M. Rusk, *Viroqua*
Alexander S. McDill, *Plover*

## TERRITORY OF ARIZONA

### DELEGATE

Richard C. McCormick, *Tucson*

## TERRITORY OF COLORADO

### DELEGATE

Jerome B. Chaffee, *Denver*

## TERRITORY OF DAKOTA

### DELEGATE

Moses K. Armstrong, *Yankton*

## DISTRICT OF COLUMBIA[64]

### DELEGATE

Norton P. Chipman,[65] *Washington*

## TERRITORY OF IDAHO

### DELEGATE

John Hailey, *Boise City*

## TERRITORY OF MONTANA

### DELEGATE

Martin Maginnis, *Helena*

## TERRITORY OF NEW MEXICO

### DELEGATE

Stephen B. Elkins, *Santa Fe*

## TERRITORY OF UTAH

### DELEGATE

George Q. Cannon,[66] *Salt Lake City*

## TERRITORY OF WASHINGTON

### DELEGATE

Obadiah B. McFadden, *Olympia*

## TERRITORY OF WYOMING

### DELEGATE

William R. Steele, *Cheyenne*

---

[62] Election unsuccessfully contested by Benjamin Wilson; took his seat January 27, 1874.

[63] Election unsuccessfully contested by Benjamin F. Martin; took his seat January 27, 1874.

[64] Territorial form of government withdrawn and a government administered by a board of three commissioners, appointed by the President, by and with the advice and consent of the Senate, established by act of June 20, 1874.

[65] Served until March 3, 1875, under the provisions of the act of June 20, 1874.

[66] Election unsuccessfully contested by George R. Maxwell.

# 44TH CONGRESS

## MARCH 4, 1875, TO MARCH 3, 1877

Henry Wilson
Vice President

FIRST SESSION— *December 6, 1875, to August 15, 1876*
SECOND SESSION— *December 4, 1876, to March 3, 1877*
SPECIAL SESSION OF THE SENATE— *March 5, 1875, to March 24, 1875*

———

VICE PRESIDENT OF THE UNITED STATES— HENRY WILSON,[1] of Massachusetts
PRESIDENT PRO TEMPORE OF THE SENATE— THOMAS W. FERRY,[2] of Michigan
SECRETARY OF THE SENATE— GEORGE C. GORHAM, of California
SERGEANT AT ARMS OF THE SENATE— JOHN R. FRENCH, of New Hampshire

———

Michael C. Kerr
Speaker

SPEAKER OF THE HOUSE OF REPRESENTATIVES— MICHAEL C. KERR,[3] of Indiana;
SAMUEL J. RANDALL,[4] of Pennsylvania
CLERK OF THE HOUSE— EDWARD McPHERSON, of Pennsylvania; GEORGE M. ADAMS,[5] of Kentucky
SERGEANT AT ARMS OF THE HOUSE— NATHANIEL G. ORDWAY, of New Hampshire; JOHN G. THOMPSON,[6] of Ohio
DOORKEEPER OF THE HOUSE— JOHN H. PATTERSON, of New Jersey
POSTMASTER OF THE HOUSE— JAMES M. STEUART

## ALABAMA

### SENATORS

George E. Spencer, *Decatur*
George T. Goldthwaite, *Montgomery*

### REPRESENTATIVES AT LARGE

William H. Forney, *Jacksonville*
Burwell B. Lewis, *Tuscaloosa*

### REPRESENTATIVES

Jeremiah Haralson,[7] *Selma*
Jeremiah N. Williams, *Clayton*
Taul Bradford, *Talladega*
Charles Hays, *Haysville*
John H. Caldwell, *Jacksonville*
Goldsmith W. Hewitt, *Birmingham*

## ARKANSAS

### SENATORS

Powell Clayton, *Little Rock*
Stephen W. Dorsey, *Helena*

### REPRESENTATIVES

Lucien C. Gause, *Jacksonport*
William F. Slemons, *Monticello*
William W. Wilshire, *Little Rock*
Thomas M. Gunter, *Fayetteville*

## CALIFORNIA

### SENATORS

Aaron A. Sargent, *Nevada City*
Newton Booth, *Sacramento*

### REPRESENTATIVES

William A. Piper, *San Francisco*
Horace F. Page, *Placerville*
John K. Luttrell, *Santa Rosa*
Peter D. Wigginton, *Merced*

## COLORADO[8]

### SENATORS

Jerome B. Chaffee,[9] *Denver*
Henry M. Teller,[10] *Central City* 1

### REPRESENTATIVE AT LARGE

James B. Belford,[11] *Central City*

## CONNECTICUT

### SENATORS

Orris S. Ferry,[12] *Norwalk*
James E. English,[13] *New Haven*
William H. Barnum,[14] *Lime Rock*
William W. Eaton, *Hartford*

### REPRESENTATIVES

George M. Landers, *New Britain*
James Phelps, *Essex*

Henry H. Starkweather,[15] *Norwich*
John Turner Wait,[16] *Norwich*
William H. Barnum,[17] *Lime Rock*
Levi Warner,[18] *Norwalk*

## DELAWARE

### SENATORS

Thomas F. Bayard, *Wilmington*
Eli Saulsbury, *Dover*

### REPRESENTATIVE AT LARGE

James Williams, *Kenton*

## FLORIDA

### SENATORS

Simon B. Conover, *Tallahassee*
Charles W. Jones, *Pensacola*

### REPRESENTATIVES

William J. Purman, *Tallahassee*
Josiah T. Walls,[19] *Gainesville*
Jesse J. Finley,[20] *Jacksonville*

## GEORGIA

### SENATORS

Thomas M. Norwood, *Savannah*
John B. Gordon, *Atlanta*

---

[1] Died November 22, 1875.
[2] Elected March 9, 1875, and March 19, 1875 (special session of the Senate); December 20, 1875.
[3] Elected December 6, 1875; died August 19, 1876.
[4] Elected December 4, 1876.
[5] Elected December 6, 1875.
[6] Elected December 6, 1875.
[7] Election unsuccessfully contested by Frederick G. Bromberg.
[8] Admitted as a State into the Union August 1, 1876.
[9] Took his seat December 4, 1876; term to expire, as determined by lot, March 3, 1879.

[10] Took his seat December 4, 1876; term to expire, as determined by lot, March 3, 1877.
[11] Presented credentials as a Member-elect on December 4, 1876, which were referred to the Committee on the Judiciary, who reported favorably thereon, and the House, on January 31, 1877, decided that Colorado was a State, and that the Representative-elect should be admitted; took his seat the same day.
[12] Died November 21, 1875.
[13] Appointed to fill vacancy caused by death of Orris S. Ferry, and took his seat December 7, 1875.
[14] Elected to fill vacancy caused by death of Orris

S. Ferry, and took his seat May 22, 1876.
[15] Died January 28, 1876.
[16] Elected to fill vacancy caused by death of Henry H. Starkweather, and took his seat April 12, 1876.
[17] Resigned May 18, 1876, having been elected Senator.
[18] Elected to fill vacancy caused by resignation of William H. Barnum, and took his seat December 4, 1876.
[19] Served until April 19, 1876; succeeded by Jesse J. Finley, who contested his election.
[20] Successfully contested the election of Josiah T. Walls, and took his seat April 19, 1876.

### REPRESENTATIVES

Julian Hartridge, *Savannah*
William E. Smith, *Albany*
Philip Cook, *Americus*
Henry R. Harris, *Greenville*
Milton A. Candler, *Atlanta*
James H. Blount, *Macon*
William H. Felton, *Cartersville*
Alexander H. Stephens, *Crawfordville*
Benjamin H. Hill,[21] *Atlanta*

## ILLINOIS

### SENATORS

John A. Logan, *Chicago*
Richard J. Oglesby, *Decatur*

### REPRESENTATIVES

Bernard G. Caulfield, *Chicago*
Carter H. Harrison, *Chicago*
Charles B. Farwell,[22] *Chicago*
John V. Le Moyne,[23] *Chicago*
Stephen A. Hurlbut, *Belvidere*
Horatio C. Burchard, *Freeport*
Thomas J. Henderson, *Princeton*
Alexander Campbell, *La Salle*
Greenbury L. Fort, *Lacon*
Richard H. Whiting, *Peoria*
John C. Bagby, *Rushville*
Scott Wike, *Pittsville*
William M. Springer, *Springfield*
Adlai E. Stevenson, *Bloomington*
Joseph G. Cannon, *Tuscola*
John R. Eden, *Sullivan*
William A. J. Sparks, *Carlyle*
William R. Morrison, *Waterloo*
William Hartzell, *Chester*
William B. Anderson, *Elk Prairie*

## INDIANA

### SENATORS

Oliver H. P. T. Morton, *Indianapolis*
Joseph E. McDonald, *Indianapolis*

### REPRESENTATIVES

Benoni S. Fuller, *Boonville*
James D. Williams,[24] *Wheatland*
Andrew Humphreys,[25] *Linton*
Michael C. Kerr,[26] *New Albany*
Nathan T. Carr,[27] *Columbus*

Jeptha D. New, *Vernon*
William S. Holman, *Aurora*
Milton S. Robinson, *Anderson*
Franklin Landers, *Indianapolis*
Morton C. Hunter, *Bloomington*
Thomas J. Cason, *Lebanon*
William S. Haymond, *Monticello*
James L. Evans, *Noblesville*
Andrew H. Hamilton, *Fort Wayne*
John H. Baker, *Goshen*

## IOWA

### SENATORS

George G. Wright, *Des Moines*
William B. Allison, *Dubuque*

### REPRESENTATIVES

George W. McCrary, *Keokuk*
John Q. Tufts, *Wilton Junction*
Lucien L. Ainsworth, *West Union*
Henry O. Pratt, *Charles City*
James Wilson, *Traer*
Ezekiel S. Sampson, *Sigourney*
John A. Kasson, *Des Moines*
James W. McDill, *Afton*
S. Addison Oliver, *Onawa*

## KANSAS

### SENATORS

John J. Ingalls, *Atchison*
James M. Harvey, *Vinton*

### REPRESENTATIVES

William A. Phillips, *Salina*
John R. Goodin, *Humboldt*
William R. Brown, *Hutchinson*

## KENTUCKY

### SENATORS

John W. Stevenson, *Covington*
Thomas C. McCreery, *Owensboro*

### REPRESENTATIVES

Andrew R. Boone, *Mayfield*
John Y. Brown, *Henderson*
Charles W. Milliken, *Franklin*
J. Proctor Knott, *Lebanon*
Edward Y. Parsons,[28] *Louisville*
Henry Watterson,[29] *Louisville*
Thomas L. Jones, *Newport*

Joseph C. S. Blackburn, *Versailles*
Milton J. Durham, *Danville*
John D. White, *Manchester*
John B. Clarke, *Brooksville*

## LOUISIANA

### SENATORS

J. Rodman West, *New Orleans*
James B. Eustis,[30] *New Orleans*

### REPRESENTATIVES

Randall L. Gibson, *New Orleans*
E. John Ellis, *New Orleans*
Chester B. Darrall,[31] *Brashear*
William M. Levy, *Natchitoches*
Frank Morey,[32] *Monroe*
William B. Spencer,[33] *Vidalia*
Charles E. Nash, *Washington*

## MAINE

### SENATORS

Hannibal Hamlin, *Bangor*
Lot M. Morrill,[34] *Augusta*
James G. Blaine,[35] *Augusta*

### REPRESENTATIVES

John H. Burleigh, *South Berwick*
William P. Frye, *Lewiston*
James G. Blaine,[36] *Augusta*
Edwin Flye,[37] *New Castle*
Harris M. Plaisted,[38] *Bangor*
Eugene Hale, *Ellsworth*

## MARYLAND

### SENATORS

George R. Dennis, *Kingston*
William Pinkney Whyte, *Baltimore*

### REPRESENTATIVES

Philip F. Thomas, *Easton*
Charles B. Roberts, *Westminster*
William J. O'Brien, *Baltimore*
Thomas Swann, *Baltimore*
Eli J. Henkle, *Brooklyn*
William Walsh, *Cumberland*

---

[21] Elected to fill vacancy caused by death of Representative-elect Garnett McMillan (January 14, 1875, before the beginning of the congressional term), and took his seat December 6, 1875; resigned, effective March 3, 1877, before the commencement of the Forty-fifth Congress, to which he had been reelected, having been elected Senator.

[22] Served until May 6, 1876; succeeded by John V. Le Moyne, who contested his election.

[23] Successfully contested the election of Charles B. Farwell, and took his seat May 6, 1876.

[24] Resigned December 1, 1876, having been elected Governor.

[25] Elected to fill vacancy caused by resignation of James D. Williams, and took his seat December 5, 1876.

[26] Died August 19, 1876.

[27] Elected to fill vacancy caused by death of

Michael C. Kerr, and took his seat December 5, 1876.

[28] Died July 8, 1876.

[29] Elected to fill vacancy caused by death of Edward Y. Parsons, and took his seat August 12, 1876.

[30] Elected on January 12, 1876, for the term beginning March 4, 1873, but as his rights were not finally determined until December 10, 1877, the seat remained vacant throughout the Congress. The contest of Pinckney B. S. Pinchback and William L. McMillen were continued from the preceding Congress, but on December 14, 1875, McMillen was permitted to withdraw his credentials, and on March 8, 1876, the Senate adopted a resolution that Pinchback "be not admitted to a seat." (See U.S. Senate Election, Expulsion and Censure Cases, 1793-1990, Senate Document 103-33, pp. 182-188.)

[31] Election unsuccessfully contested by J. A. Preux.

[32] Served until June 8, 1876; succeeded by William B. Spencer, who contested his election.

[33] Successfully contested the election of Frank Morey, and took his seat June 8, 1876; resigned January 8, 1877.

[34] Resigned July 7, 1876, having been appointed Secretary of the Treasury.

[35] Appointed to fill vacancy caused by the resignation of Lot M. Morrill, and took his seat December 4, 1876; subsequently elected.

[36] Resigned July 10, 1876.

[37] Elected to fill vacancy caused by resignation of James G. Blaine, and took his seat December 4, 1876.

[38] Elected to fill vacancy caused by death of Representative-elect Samuel F. Hersey, in preceding Congress, and took his seat December 6, 1875.

## MASSACHUSETTS

SENATORS
George S. Boutwell, *Groton*
Henry L. Dawes, *Pittsfield*

REPRESENTATIVES
James Buffington,[39] *Fall River*
William W. Crapo,[40] *New Bedford*
Benjamin W. Harris, *East Bridgewater*
Henry L. Pierce, *Boston*
Rufus S. Frost,[41] *Chelsea*
Josiah G. Abbott,[42] *Boston*
Nathaniel P. Banks, *Waltham*
Charles P. Thompson, *Gloucester*
John K. Tarbox, *Lawrence*
William W. Warren, *Boston*
George F. Hoar, *Worcester*
Julius H. Seelye, *Amherst*
Chester W. Chapin, *Springfield*

## MICHIGAN

SENATORS
Thomas W. Ferry, *Grand Haven*
Isaac P. Christiancy, *Lansing*

REPRESENTATIVES
Alpheus S. Williams, *Detroit*
Henry Waldron, *Hillsdale*
George Willard, *Battle Creek*
Allen Potter, *Kalamazoo*
William B. Williams, *Allegan*
George H. Durand, *Flint*
Omar D. Conger, *Port Huron*
Nathan B. Bradley, *Bay City*
Jay A. Hubbell, *Houghton*

## MINNESOTA

SENATORS
William Windom, *Winona*
Samuel J. R. McMillan, *St. Paul*

REPRESENTATIVES
Mark H. Dunnell, *Owatonna*
Horace B. Strait,[43] *Shakopee*
William S. King, *Minneapolis*

## MISSISSIPPI

SENATORS
James L. Alcorn, *Friars Point*
Blanche K. Bruce, *Floreyville*

REPRESENTATIVES
Lucius Q. C. Lamar, *Oxford*
G. Wiley Wells, *Holly Springs*
Hernando D. Money, *Winona*
Otho R. Singleton, *Canton*
Charles E. Hooker, *Jackson*
John R. Lynch, *Natchez*

## MISSOURI

SENATORS
Lewis V. Bogy, *St. Louis*
Francis M. Cockrell, *Warrensburg*

REPRESENTATIVES
Edward C. Kehr, *St. Louis*
Erastus Wells, *St. Louis*
William H. Stone, *St. Louis*
Robert A. Hatcher, *New Madrid*
Richard P. Bland, *Lebanon*
Charles H. Morgan, *Lamar*
John F. Philips, *Sedalia*
Benjamin J. Franklin, *Kansas City*
David Rea, *Savannah*
Rezin A. De Bolt, *Trenton*
John B. Clark, Jr., *Fayette*
John M. Glover, *La Grange*
Aylett H. Buckner, *Mexico*

## NEBRASKA

SENATORS
Phineas W. Hitchcock, *Omaha*
Algernon S. Paddock, *Beatrice*

REPRESENTATIVE AT LARGE
Lorenzo Crounse, *Fort Calhoun*

## NEVADA

SENATORS
John P. Jones, *Gold Hill*
William Sharon, *Virginia City*

REPRESENTATIVE AT LARGE
William Woodburn, *Virginia City*

## NEW HAMPSHIRE

SENATORS
Aaron H. Cragin, *Lebanon*
Bainbridge Wadleigh, *Milford*

REPRESENTATIVES
Frank Jones, *Portsmouth*
Samuel N. Bell, *Manchester*
Henry W. Blair, *Plymouth*

## NEW JERSEY

SENATORS
Frederick T. Frelinghuysen, *Newark*
Theodore F. Randolph, *Morristown*

REPRESENTATIVES
Clement H. Sinnickson, *Salem*
Samuel A. Dobbins, *Mount Holly*
Miles Ross, *New Brunswick*
Robert Hamilton, *Newton*
Augustus W. Cutler, *Morristown*
Frederick H. Teese, *Newark*
Augustus A. Hardenbergh, *Jersey City*

## NEW YORK

SENATORS
Roscoe Conkling, *Utica*
Francis Kernan, *Utica*

REPRESENTATIVES
Henry B. Metcalfe, *Westfield*
John G. Schumaker, *Brooklyn*
Simeon B. Chittenden, *Brooklyn*
Archibald M. Bliss, *Brooklyn*
Edwin R. Meade, *New York City*
Samuel S. Cox, *New York City*
Smith Ely, Jr.,[44] *New York City*
David Dudley Field,[45] *New York City*
Elijah Ward, *New York City*
Fernando Wood, *New York City*
Abram S. Hewitt, *New York City*
Benjamin A. Willis, *New York City*
N. Holmes Odell, *White Plains*
John O. Whitehouse, *Poughkeepsie*
George M. Beebe, *Monticello*
John H. Bagley, Jr., *Catskill*
Charles H. Adams, *Cohoes*
Martin I. Townsend, *Troy*
Andrew Williams, *Plattsburg*
William A. Wheeler, *Malone*
Henry H. Hathorn, *Saratoga Springs*
Samuel F. Miller, *Franklin*
George A. Bagley, *Watertown*
Scott Lord, *Utica*
William H. Baker, *Constantia*
Elias W. Leavenworth, *Syracuse*
Clinton D. MacDougall, *Auburn*
Elbridge G. Lapham, *Canandaigua*
Thomas C. Platt, *Owego*
Charles C. B. Walker, *Corning*
John M. Davy, *Rochester*
George G. Hoskins, *Attica*
Lyman K. Bass, *Buffalo*
Nelson I. Norton,[46] *Hinsdale*

## NORTH CAROLINA

SENATORS
Matt W. Ransom, *Weldon*
Augustus S. Merrimon, *Raleigh*

REPRESENTATIVES
Jesse J. Yeates, *Murfreesboro*
John A. Hyman, *Warrenton*
Alfred M. Waddell, *Wilmington*
Joseph J. Davis, *Louisburg*
Alfred M. Scales, *Greensboro*
Thomas S. Ashe, *Wadesboro*
William M. Robbins, *Statesville*
Robert B. Vance, *Asheville*

## OHIO

SENATORS
John Sherman, *Mansfield*
Allen G. Thurman, *Columbus*

---

[39] Died March 7, 1875, before Congress assembled.

[40] Elected to fill vacancy caused by death of James Buffinton, and took his seat December 6, 1875.

[41] Served until July 28, 1876; succeeded by Josiah G. Abbott, who contested his election.

[42] Successfully contested the election of Rufus S. Frost, and took his seat July 28, 1876.

[43] Election unsuccessfully contested by E. St. Julien Cox.

[44] Resigned December 11, 1876, having been elected mayor of New York City.

[45] Elected to fill vacancy caused by resignation of Smith Ely, Jr., and took his seat January 11, 1877.

[46] Elected to fill vacancy caused by death of Representative-elect Augustus F. Allen (January 22, 1875, before the beginning of the congressional term), and took his seat December 6, 1875.

## REPRESENTATIVES

Milton Sayler, *Cincinnati*
Henry B. Banning, *Cincinnati*
John S. Savage, *Wilmington*
John A. McMahon, *Dayton*
Americus V. Rice, *Ottawa*
Frank H. Hurd, *Toledo*
Lawrence T. Neal, *Chillicothe*
William Lawrence, *Bellefontaine*
Earley F. Poppleton, *Delaware*
Charles Foster, *Fostoria*
John L. Vance, *Gallipolis*
Ansel T. Walling, *Circleville*
Milton I. Southard, *Zanesville*
Jacob P. Cowan, *Ashland*
Nelson H. Van Vorhes, *Athens*
Lorenzo Danford, *St. Clairsville*
Laurin D. Woodworth, *Youngstown*
James Monroe, *Oberlin*
James A. Garfield, *Hiram*
Henry B. Payne, *Cleveland*

## OREGON

### SENATORS

James K. Kelly, *Portland*
John H. Mitchell, *Portland*

### REPRESENTATIVE AT LARGE

George A. La Dow,[47] *Pendleton*
La Fayette Lane,[48] *Roseburg*

## PENNSYLVANIA

### SENATORS

Simon Cameron, *Harrisburg*
William A. Wallace, *Clearfield*

### REPRESENTATIVES

Chapman Freeman, *Philadelphia*
Charles O'Neill, *Philadelphia*
Samuel J. Randall, *Philadelphia*
William D. Kelley, *Philadelphia*
John Robbins, *Philadelphia*
Washington Townsend, *West Chester*
Alan Wood, Jr., *Conshohocken*
Hiester Clymer, *Reading*
A. Herr Smith, *Lancaster*
William Mutchler, *Easton*
Francis D. Collins, *Scranton*
Winthrop W. Ketchum,[49] *Wilkes-Barre*
William H. Stanton,[50] *Scranton*
James B. Reilly, *Pottsville*
John B. Packer, *Sunbury*
Joseph Powell, *Towanda*
Sobieski Ross, *Coudersport*

John Reilly, *Altoona*
William S. Stenger, *Chambersburg*
Levi Maish, *York*
Levi A. Mackey, *Lockhaven*
Jacob Turney, *Greensburg*
James H. Hopkins, *Pittsburgh*
Alexander G. Cochran, *Allegheny City*
John W. Wallace, *New Castle*
George A. Jenks, *Brookville*
James Sheakley, *Greenville*
Albert G. Egbert, *Franklin*

## RHODE ISLAND

### SENATORS

Henry B. Anthony, *Providence*
Ambrose E. Burnside, *Providence*

### REPRESENTATIVES

Benjamin T. Eames, *Providence*
Latimer W. Ballou, *Woonsocket*

## SOUTH CAROLINA

### SENATORS

Thomas J. Robertson, *Columbia*
John J. Patterson, *Columbia*

### REPRESENTATIVES

Joseph H. Rainey,[51] *Georgetown*
Edmund W. M. Mackey,[52] *Charleston*
Charles W. Buttz,[53] *Charleston*
Solomon L. Hoge, *Columbia*
Alexander S. Wallace, *Yorkville*
Robert Smalls, *Beaufort*

## TENNESSEE

### SENATORS

Henry Cooper, *Nashville*
Andrew Johnson,[54] *Greeneville*
David M. Key,[55] *Chattanooga*
James E. Bailey,[56] *Clarksville*

### REPRESENTATIVES

William McFarland, *Morristown*
Jacob M. Thornburgh, *Knoxville*
George G. Dibrell, *Sparta*
Samuel M. Fite,[57] *Carthage*
Haywood Y. Riddle,[58] *Lebanon*
John M. Bright, *Fayetteville*
John F. House, *Clarksville*
Washington C. Whitthorne, *Columbia*
John D. C. Atkins, *Paris*
William P. Caldwell, *Gardner*
H. Casey Young, *Memphis*

## TEXAS

### SENATORS

Morgan C. Hamilton, *Austin*
Samuel B. Maxey, *Paris*

### REPRESENTATIVES

John H. Reagan, *Palestine*
David B. Culberson, *Jefferson*
James W. Throckmorton, *McKinney*
Roger Q. Mills, *Corsicana*
John Hancock, *Austin*
Gustave Schleicher, *Cuero*

## VERMONT

### SENATORS

George F. Edmunds, *Burlington*
Justin S. Morrill, *Strafford*

### REPRESENTATIVES

Charles H. Joyce, *Rutland*
Dudley C. Denison, *Royalton*
George W. Hendee, *Morrisville*

## VIRGINIA

### SENATORS

John W. Johnston, *Abingdon*
Robert E. Withers, *Wytheville*

### REPRESENTATIVES

Beverly B. Douglas, *Ayletts*
John Goode, Jr.,[59] *Norfolk*
Gilbert C. Walker, *Richmond*
William H. H. Stowell, *Burkeville*
George C. Cabell, *Danville*
John R. Tucker, *Lexington*
John T. Harris, *Harrisonburg*
Eppa Hunton, *Warrenton*
William Terry, *Wytheville*

## WEST VIRGINIA

### SENATORS

Henry Gassaway Davis, *Piedmont*
Allen T. Caperton,[60] *Union*
Samuel Price,[61] *Lewisburg*
Frank Hereford,[62] *Union*

### REPRESENTATIVES

Benjamin Wilson, *Wilsonburg*
Charles J. Faulkner, *Martinsburg*
Frank Hereford,[63] *Union*

---

[47] Died May 1, 1875, before Congress assembled.
[48] Elected to fill vacancy caused by death of George A. La Dow, and took his seat December 6, 1875.
[49] Resigned July 19, 1876.
[50] Elected to fill vacancy caused by resignation of Winthrop W. Ketchum, and took his seat December 4, 1876.
[51] Election unsuccessfully contested by Samuel Lee.
[52] Election contested by Charles W. Buttz; seat declared vacant by resolution of July 19, 1876.
[53] Contested the election of Edmund W. M.

Mackey; by resolution, July 19, 1876, House declared neither contestant nor contestee duly elected and the seat to be vacant; subsequently elected, and took his seat January 23, 1877.
[54] Died July 31, 1875.
[55] Appointed to fill vacancy caused by death of Andrew Johnson, and took his seat December 6, 1875.
[56] Elected to fill vacancy caused by death of Andrew Johnson, and took his seat January 29, 1877.
[57] Elected to fill vacancy caused by death of Representative-elect John W. Head on November 9, 1874, before the beginning of the congress term;

died October 23, 1875, before Congress assembled.
[58] Elected to fill vacancy caused by death of Samuel M. Fite, and took his seat January 5, 1876.
[59] Election unsuccessfully contested by James H. Platt, Jr.
[60] Died July 26, 1876.
[61] Appointed to fill vacancy caused by death of Allen T. Caperton, and took his seat December 4, 1876.
[62] Elected to fill vacancy caused by death of Allen T. Caperton, and took his seat January 31, 1877.
[63] Resigned January 31, 1877, having been elected Senator.

## WISCONSIN

SENATORS

Timothy O. Howe, *Green Bay*
Angus Cameron, *La Crosse*

REPRESENTATIVES

Charles G. Williams, *Janesville*
Lucien B. Caswell, *Fort Atkinson*
Henry S. Magoon, *Darlington*
William P. Lynde, *Milwaukee*
Samuel D. Burchard, *Beaver Dam*
Alanson M. Kimball, *Pine River*
Jeremiah M. Rusk, *Viroqua*
George W. Cate, *Stevens Point*

## TERRITORY OF ARIZONA

DELEGATE

Hiram S. Stevens, *Tucson*

## TERRITORY OF COLORADO

DELEGATE

Thomas M. Patterson,[64] *Denver*

## TERRITORY OF DAKOTA

DELEGATE

Jefferson P. Kidder, *Vermilion*

## TERRITORY OF IDAHO

DELEGATE

Thomas W. Bennett,[65] *Boise City*
Stephen S. Fenn,[66] *Mount Idaho*

## TERRITORY OF MONTANA

DELEGATE

Martin Maginnis, *Helena*

## TERRITORY OF NEW MEXICO

DELEGATE

Stephen B. Elkins, *Santa Fe*

## TERRITORY OF UTAH

DELEGATE

George Q. Cannon, *Salt Lake City*

## TERRITORY OF WASHINGTON

DELEGATE

Orange Jacobs, *Seattle*

## TERRITORY OF WYOMING

DELEGATE

William R. Steele, *Cheyenne*

[64] Served until August 1, 1876, when the Territory of Colorado was granted statehood by act of Congress approved March 3, 1876.

[65] Served until June 23, 1876; succeeded by Stephen S. Fenn, who contested his election.

[66] Successfully contested the election of Thomas W. Bennett, and took his seat June 23, 1876.

# 45TH CONGRESS

## MARCH 4, 1877, TO MARCH 3, 1879

FIRST SESSION— *October 15, 1877, to December 3, 1877*
SECOND SESSION— *December 3, 1877, to June 20, 1878*
THIRD SESSION— *December 2, 1878, to March 3, 1879*
SPECIAL SESSION OF THE SENATE— *March 5, 1877, to March 17, 1877*

———

VICE PRESIDENT OF THE UNITED STATES— WILLIAM A. WHEELER, of New York
PRESIDENT PRO TEMPORE OF THE SENATE— THOMAS W. FERRY,[1] of Michigan
SECRETARY OF THE SENATE— GEORGE C. GORHAM, of California
SERGEANT AT ARMS OF THE SENATE— JOHN R. FRENCH, of New Hampshire

———

SPEAKER OF THE HOUSE OF REPRESENTATIVES— SAMUEL J. RANDALL,[2] of Pennsylvania
CLERK OF THE HOUSE— GEORGE M. ADAMS,[3] of Kentucky
SERGEANT AT ARMS OF THE HOUSE— JOHN G. THOMPSON, of Ohio
DOORKEEPER OF THE HOUSE— CHARLES W. FIELD, of Georgia
POSTMASTER OF THE HOUSE— JAMES M. STEUART

William A. Wheeler
Vice President

Samuel J. Randall
Speaker

## ALABAMA

### SENATORS

George E. Spencer, *Decatur*
John T. Morgan, *Selma*

### REPRESENTATIVES

James T. Jones, *Demopolis*
Hilary A. Herbert, *Montgomery*
Jeremiah N. Williams, *Clayton*
Charles M. Shelley,[4] *Selma*
Robert F. Ligon, *Tuskegee*
Goldsmith W. Hewitt, *Birmingham*
William H. Forney, *Jacksonville*
William W. Garth, *Huntsville*

## ARKANSAS

### SENATORS

Stephen W. Dorsey, *Helena*
Augustus H. Garland, *Little Rock*

### REPRESENTATIVES

Lucien C. Gause, *Jacksonport*
William F. Slemons, *Monticello*
Jordan E. Cravens, *Clarksville*
Thomas M. Gunter, *Fayetteville*

## CALIFORNIA

### SENATORS

Aaron A. Sargent, *Nevada City*
Newton Booth, *Sacramento*

### REPRESENTATIVES

Horace Davis, *San Francisco*
Horace F. Page, *Placerville*
John K. Luttrell, *Santa Rosa*
Romualdo Pacheco,[5] *San Luis Obispo*
Peter D. Wigginton,[6] *Merced*

## COLORADO

### SENATORS

Jerome B. Chaffee, *Denver*
Henry M. Teller, *Central City*

### REPRESENTATIVE AT LARGE

James B. Belford,[7] *Central City*
Thomas M. Patterson,[8] *Denver*

## CONNECTICUT

### SENATORS

William W. Eaton, *Hartford*
William H. Barnum, *Lime Rock*

### REPRESENTATIVES

George M. Landers, *New Britain*
James Phelps, *Essex*
John T. Wait, *Norwich*
Levi Warner, *Norwalk*

## DELAWARE

### SENATORS

Thomas F. Bayard, *Wilmington*
Eli Saulsbury, *Dover*

## REPRESENTATIVE AT LARGE

James Williams, *Kenton*

## FLORIDA

### SENATORS

Simon B. Conover, *Tallahassee*
Charles W. Jones, *Pensacola*

### REPRESENTATIVES

Horatio Bisbee, Jr.,[9] *Jacksonville*
Jesse J. Finley,[10] *Jacksonville*
Robert H. M. Davidson, *Quincy*

## GEORGIA

### SENATORS

John B. Gordon, *Atlanta*
Benjamin H. Hill, *Atlanta*

### REPRESENTATIVES

Julian Hartridge,[11] *Savannah*
William B. Fleming,[12] *Savannah*
William E. Smith, *Albany*
Philip Cook, *Americus*
Henry R. Harris, *Greenville*
Milton A. Candler, *Atlanta*
James H. Blount, *Macon*
William H. Felton, *Cartersville*
Alexander H. Stephens,
  *Crawfordville*
Hiram P. Bell,[13] *Cumming*

———

[1] Elected March 5, 1877 (special session of the Senate); February 26, 1878; April 17, 1878; and March 3, 1879.
[2] Reelected October 15, 1877.
[3] Reelected October 15, 1877.
[4] Election unsuccessfully contested by Jeremiah Haralson.
[5] Served until February 7, 1878; succeeded by Peter D. Wigginton, who contested his election.

[6] Successfully contested the election of Romualdo Pacheco, and took his seat February 7, 1878.
[7] Served until December 13, 1877; succeeded by Thomas M. Patterson, who contested his election.
[8] Successfully contested the election of James B. Belford, and took his seat December 13, 1877.
[9] Served until February 20, 1879; succeeded by Jesse J. Finley, who contested his election.
[10] Successfully contested the election of Horatio

Bisbee, Jr., and took his seat February 20, 1879.
[11] Died January 8, 1879.
[12] Elected to fill vacancy caused by death of Julian Hartridge, and took his seat February 17, 1879.
[13] Elected to fill vacancy caused by resignation of Representative-elect Benjamin H. Hill, in preceding Congress, and took his seat October 15, 1877.

## ILLINOIS

### SENATORS

Richard J. Oglesby, *Decatur*
David Davis, *Bloomington*

### REPRESENTATIVES

William Aldrich, *Chicago*
Carter H. Harrison, *Chicago*
Lorenzo Brentano, *Chicago*
William Lathrop, *Rockford*
Horatio C. Burchard, *Freeport*
Thomas J. Henderson, *Princeton*
Philip C. Hayes, *Morris*
Greenbury L. Fort, *Lacon*
Thomas A. Boyd, *Lewiston*
Benjamin F. Marsh, *Warsaw*
Robert M. Knapp, *Jerseyville*
William M. Springer, *Springfield*
Thomas F. Tipton, *Bloomington*
Joseph G. Cannon, *Danville*
John R. Eden, *Sullivan*
William A. J. Sparks, *Carlyle*
William R. Morrison, *Waterloo*
William Hartzell, *Chester*
Richard W. Townshend, *Shawneetown*

## INDIANA

### SENATORS

Oliver H. P. T. Morton,[14] *Indianapolis*
Daniel W. Voorhees,[15] *Terre Haute*
Joseph E. McDonald, *Indianapolis*

### REPRESENTATIVES

Benoni S. Fuller, *Boonville*
Thomas R. Cobb, *Vincennes*
George A. Bicknell, *New Albany*
Leonidas Sexton, *Rushville*
Thomas M. Browne, *Winchester*
Milton S. Robinson, *Anderson*
John Hanna, *Indianapolis*
Morton C. Hunter, *Bloomington*
Michael D. White, *Crawfordsville*
William H. Calkins, *Laporte*
James L. Evans, *Noblesville*
Andrew H. Hamilton, *Fort Wayne*
John H. Baker, *Goshen*

## IOWA

### SENATORS

William B. Allison, *Dubuque*
Samuel J. Kirkwood, *Iowa City*

### REPRESENTATIVES

Joseph C. Stone, *Burlington*
Hiram Price, *Davenport*
Theodore W. Burdick, *Decorah*
Nathaniel C. Deering, *Osage*
Rush Clark, *Iowa City*
Ezekiel S. Sampson, *Sigourney*
Henry J. B. Cummings, *Winterset*
William F. Sapp, *Council Bluffs*
S. Addison Oliver, *Onawa*

## KANSAS

### SENATORS

John J. Ingalls, *Atchison*
Preston B. Plumb, *Emporia*

### REPRESENTATIVES

William A. Phillips, *Salina*
Dudley C. Haskell, *Lawrence*
Thomas Ryan, *Topeka*

## KENTUCKY

### SENATORS

Thomas McCreery, *Owensboro*
James B. Beck, *Lexington*

### REPRESENTATIVES

Andrew R. Boone, *Mayfield*
James A. McKenzie, *Long View*
John W. Caldwell, *Russellville*
J. Proctor Knott, *Lebanon*
Albert S. Willis, *Louisville*
John G. Carlisle, *Covington*
Joseph C. S. Blackburn, *Versailles*
Milton J. Durham, *Danville*
Thomas Turner, *Mount Sterling*
John B. Clarke, *Brooksville*

## LOUISIANA

### SENATORS

William Pitt Kellogg,[16] *New Orleans*
James B. Eustis,[17] *New Orleans*

### REPRESENTATIVES

Randall L. Gibson, *New Orleans*
E. John Ellis, *New Orleans*
Chester B. Darrall,[18] *Brashear*
Joseph H. Acklen,[19] *Pattersonville*
Joseph B. Elam,[20] *Mansfield*
John E. Leonard,[21] *Lake Providence*
John S. Young,[22] *Homer*
Edward W. Robertson,[23] *Baton Rouge*

## MAINE

### SENATORS

Hannibal Hamlin, *Bangor*
James G. Blaine, *Augusta*

### REPRESENTATIVES

Thomas B. Reed, *Portland*
William P. Frye, *Lewiston*
Stephen D. Lindsey, *Norridgewock*
Llewellyn Powers, *Houlton*
Eugene Hale, *Ellsworth*

## MARYLAND

### SENATORS

George R. Dennis, *Kingston*
William Pinkney Whyte, *Baltimore*

### REPRESENTATIVES

Daniel M. Henry, *Cambridge*
Charles B. Roberts, *Westminster*
William Kimmel, *Baltimore*
Thomas Swann, *Baltimore*
Eli J. Henkle, *Brooklyn*
William Walsh, *Cumberland*

## MASSACHUSETTS

### SENATORS

Henry L. Dawes, *Pittsfield*
George F. Hoar, *Worcester*

### REPRESENTATIVES

William W. Crapo, *New Bedford*
Benjamin W. Harris, *East Bridgewater*
Walbridge A. Field,[24] *Boston*
Benjamin Dean,[25] *Boston*
Leopold Morse, *Boston*
Nathaniel P. Banks, *Waltham*
George B. Loring, *Salem*
Benjamin F. Butler, *Lowell*

---

[14] Died November 1, 1877.
[15] Appointed to fill vacancy caused by death of Oliver H. P. T. Morton, and took his seat November 12, 1877; subsequently elected.
[16] This seat was claimed by Henry M. Spofford; March 5, 1877 (in the special session of the Senate), Mr. Kellogg presented himself to be sworn, but objection was made and his credentials were ordered to lie on the table; October 17, 1877, the credentials of Mr. Spofford were presented, and they, with the credentials of Mr. Kellogg, were referred to the Committee on Privileges and Elections; November 26, 1877, the committee reported in favor of Mr. Kellogg; the report was adopted November 30, 1877; he took his seat the same day. In the succeeding Congress the case was reopened upon petition of Mr. Spofford and a report was made in his favor, but he died August 20, 1880, before action was taken. (See U.S. Senate Election,

Expulsion and Censure Cases, 1793-1990, Senate Document 103-33, pp. 182-188.)
[17] James B. Eustis' papers claiming the seat were presented to the Senate on January 18, 1876, and his case was referred to the Committee on Privileges and Elections. The committee reported that inasmuch as Pinckney B. S. Pinchback had been elected to the seat and had a clear title, there was no vacancy, and it recommended that Mr. Eustis' papers be laid on the table. However the Senate, on March 8, 1876, voted not to seat Mr. Pinchback. On March 9, 1877 the Senate agreed to reconsider the claim of Mr. Eustis, and his case was again referred to the Committee on Privileges and Elections. The committee reported on December 1, 1877 that the March 1876 refusal of the Senate to seat Mr. Pinchback be taken as the final adjudication of the case. The Senate voted December 10, 1877 to seat Mr. Eustis, and he took the oath of office the same day. (See

U.S. Senate Election, Expulsion and Censure Cases, 1793-1990, Senate Document 103-33, pp. 182-188.)
[18] Served until February 20, 1878; succeeded by Joseph H. Acklen, who contested his election.
[19] Successfully contested the election of Chester B. Darrall, and took his seat February 20, 1878.
[20] Election unsuccessfully contested by George L. Smith.
[21] Died March 15, 1878.
[22] Elected to fill vacancy caused by death of John E. Leonard, and took his seat December 2, 1878.
[23] Election unsuccessfully contested by Charles E. Nash.
[24] Served until March 28, 1878; succeeded by Benjamin Dean, who contested his election.
[25] Successfully contested the election of Walbridge A. Field, and took his seat March 28, 1878.

William Claflin, *Newton*
William W. Rice, *Worcester*
Amasa Norcross, *Fitchburg*
George D. Robinson, *Chicopee*

## MICHIGAN

### SENATORS

Thomas W. Ferry, *Grand Haven*
Isaac P. Christiancy,[26] *Lansing*
Zachariah Chandler,[27] *Detroit*

### REPRESENTATIVES

Alpheus S. Williams,[28] *Detroit*
Edwin Willits, *Monroe*
Jonas H. McGowan, *Coldwater*
Edwin W. Keightley, *Constantine*
John W. Stone, *Grand Rapids*
Mark S. Brewer, *Pontiac*
Omar D. Conger, *Port Huron*
Charles C. Ellsworth, *Greenville*
Jay A. Hubbell, *Houghton*

## MINNESOTA

### SENATORS

William Windom, *Winona*
Samuel J. R. McMillan, *St. Paul*

### REPRESENTATIVES

Mark H. Dunnell, *Owatonna*
Horace B. Strait, *Shakopee*
Jacob H. Stewart, *St. Paul*

## MISSISSIPPI

### SENATORS

Blanche K. Bruce, *Floreyville*
Lucius Q. C. Lamar, *Oxford*

### REPRESENTATIVES

Henry L. Muldrow, *Starkville*
Vannoy H. Manning, *Holly Springs*
Hernando D. Money, *Winona*
Otho R. Singleton, *Canton*
Charles E. Hooker, *Jackson*
James R. Chalmers,[29] *Vicksburg*

## MISSOURI

### SENATORS

Lewis V. Bogy,[30] *St. Louis*
David H. Armstrong,[31] *St. Louis*
James Shields,[32] *Carrollton*
Francis M. Cockrell, *Warrensburg*

### REPRESENTATIVES

Anthony Ittner, *St. Louis*
Nathan Cole, *St. Louis*
Lyne S. Metcalfe,[33] *St. Louis*

Robert A. Hatcher, *Charleston*
Richard P. Bland, *Lebanon*
Charles H. Morgan, *Lamar*
Thomas T. Crittenden, *Warrensburg*
Benjamin J. Franklin, *Kansas City*
David Rea, *Savannah*
Henry M. Pollard, *Chillicothe*
John B. Clark, Jr., *Fayette*
John M. Glover, *La Grange*
Aylett H. Buckner, *Mexico*

## NEBRASKA

### SENATORS

Algernon S. Paddock, *Beatrice*
Alvin Saunders, *Omaha*

### REPRESENTATIVE AT LARGE

Frank Welch,[34] *Norfolk*
Thomas J. Majors,[35] *Peru*

## NEVADA

### SENATORS

John P. Jones, *Gold Hill*
William Sharon, *Virginia City*

### REPRESENTATIVE AT LARGE

Thomas Wren, *Eureka*

## NEW HAMPSHIRE

### SENATORS

Bainbridge Wadleigh, *Milford*
Edward H. Rollins, *Concord*

### REPRESENTATIVES

Frank Jones, *Portsmouth*
James F. Briggs, *Manchester*
Henry W. Blair, *Plymouth*

## NEW JERSEY

### SENATORS

Theodore F. Randolph, *Morristown*
John R. McPherson, *Jersey City*

### REPRESENTATIVES

Clement H. Sinnickson, *Salem*
John H. Pugh, *Burlington*
Miles Ross, *New Brunswick*
Alvah A. Clark, *Somerville*
Augustus W. Cutler, *Morristown*
Thomas B. Peddie, *Newark*
Augustus A. Hardenbergh, *Jersey City*

## NEW YORK

### SENATORS

Roscoe Conkling, *Utica*
Francis Kernan, *Utica*

### REPRESENTATIVES

James W. Covert, *Flushing*
William D. Veeder, *Brooklyn*
Simeon B. Chittenden, *Brooklyn*
Archibald M. Bliss, *Brooklyn*
Nicholas Muller, *New York City*
Samuel S. Cox, *New York City*
Anthony Eickhoff, *New York City*
Anson G. McCook, *New York City*
Fernando Wood, *New York City*
Abram S. Hewitt, *New York City*
Benjamin A. Willis, *New York City*
Clarkson N. Potter, *New Rochelle*
John H. Ketcham, *Dover Plains*
George M. Beebe, *Monticello*
Stephen L. Mayham, *Schoharie*
Terence J. Quinn,[36] *Albany*
John M. Bailey,[37] *Albany*
Martin I. Townsend, *Troy*
Andrew Williams, *Plattsburg*
Amaziah B. James, *Ogdensburg*
John H. Starin, *Fultonville*
Solomon Bundy, *Oxford*
George A. Bagley, *Watertown*
William J. Bacon, *Utica*
William H. Baker, *Constantia*
Frank Hiscock, *Syracuse*
John H. Camp, *Lyons*
Elbridge G. Lapham, *Canandaigua*
Jeremiah W. Dwight, *Dryden*
John N. Hungerford, *Corning*
E. Kirke Hart, *Albion*
Charles B. Benedict, *Attica*
Daniel N. Lockwood, *Buffalo*
George W. Patterson, *Westerfield*

## NORTH CAROLINA

### SENATORS

Matt W. Ransom, *Weldon*
Augustus S. Merrimon, *Raleigh*

### REPRESENTATIVES

Jesse J. Yeates, *Murfreesboro*
Curtis H. Brogden, *Goldsboro*
Alfred M. Waddell, *Wilmington*
Joseph J. Davis, *Louisburg*
Alfred M. Scales, *Greensboro*
Walter L. Steele, *Rockingham*
William M. Robbins, *Statesville*
Robert B. Vance, *Asheville*

---

[26] Resigned February 10, 1879.
[27] Elected to fill vacancy caused by the resignation of Isaac P. Christiancy, and took his seat February 22, 1879.
[28] Died December 20, 1878.
[29] Election unsuccessfully contested by John R. Lynch.

[30] Died September 20, 1877.
[31] Appointed to fill vacancy caused by death of Lewis V. Bogy, and took his seat October 15, 1877.
[32] Elected to fill vacancy caused by death of Lewis V. Bogy, and took his seat January 27, 1879.
[33] Richard G. Frost filed a contest, which was referred to the Committee on Elections; the committee

reported in favor of Metcalfe; no further action taken.
[34] Died September 4, 1878.
[35] Elected to fill vacancy caused by death of Frank Welch, and took his seat December 2, 1878.
[36] Died June 18, 1878.
[37] Elected to fill vacancy caused by death of Terence J. Quinn, and took his seat December 2, 1878.

## OHIO

SENATORS

John Sherman,[38] *Mansfield*
Stanley Matthews,[39] *Glendale*
Allen G. Thurman, *Columbus*

REPRESENTATIVES

Milton Sayler, *Cincinnati*
Henry B. Banning, *Cincinnati*
Mills Gardner, *Washington Court House*
John A. McMahon, *Dayton*
Americus V. Rice, *Ottawa*
Jacob D. Cox, *Toledo*
Henry L. Dickey, *Greenfield*
J. Warren Keifer, *Springfield*
John S. Jones, *Delaware*
Charles Foster, *Fostoria*
Henry S. Neal, *Ironton*
Thomas Ewing, *Lancaster*
Milton I. Southard, *Zanesville*
Ebenezer B. Finley, *Bucyrus*
Nelson H. Van Vorhes, *Athens*
Lorenzo Danford, *St. Clairsville*
William McKinley, Jr., *Canton*
James Monroe, *Oberlin*
James A. Garfield, *Mentor*
Amos Townsend, *Cleveland*

## OREGON

SENATORS

John H. Mitchell, *Portland*
La Fayette Grover, *Salem*

REPRESENTATIVE AT LARGE

Richard Williams,[40] *Portland*

## PENNSYLVANIA

SENATORS

Simon Cameron,[41] *Harrisburg*
J. Donald Cameron,[42] *Harrisburg*
William A. Wallace, *Clearfield*

REPRESENTATIVES

Chapman Freeman, *Philadelphia*
Charles O'Neill, *Philadelphia*
Samuel J. Randall, *Philadelphia*
William D. Kelley, *Philadelphia*
Alfred C. Harmer, *Germantown*
William Ward, *Chester*
I. Newton Evans, *Hatboro*
Hiester Clymer, *Reading*
A. Herr Smith, *Lancaster*
Samuel A. Bridges, *Allentown*
Francis D. Collins, *Scranton*
Hendrick B. Wright, *Wilkes-Barre*
James B. Reilly, *Pottsville*

John W. Killinger, *Lebanon*
Edward Overton, Jr., *Towanda*
John I. Mitchell, *Wellsboro*
Jacob M. Campbell, *Johnstown*
William S. Stenger, *Chambersburg*
Levi Maish, *York*
Levi A. Mackey, *Lock Haven*
Jacob Turney, *Greensburg*
Russell Errett, *Pittsburgh*
Thomas M. Bayne, *Allegheny*
William S. Shallenberger, *Rochester*
Harry White, *Indiana*
John M. Thompson, *Butler*
Lewis F. Watson, *Warren*

## RHODE ISLAND

SENATORS

Henry B. Anthony, *Providence*
Ambrose E. Burnside, *Providence*

REPRESENTATIVES

Benjamin T. Eames, *Providence*
Latimer W. Ballou, *Woonsocket*

## SOUTH CAROLINA

SENATORS

John J. Patterson, *Charleston*
Matthew C. Butler,[43] *Edgefield*

REPRESENTATIVES

Joseph H. Rainey,[44] *Georgetown*
Richard H. Cain, *Charleston*
D. Wyatt Aiken, *Cokesbury*
John H. Evins, *Spartanburg*
Robert Smalls, *Beaufort*

## TENNESSEE

SENATORS

James E. Bailey, *Clarksville*
Isham G. Harris, *Memphis*

REPRESENTATIVES

James H. Randolph, *Newport*
Jacob M. Thornburgh, *Knoxville*
George G. Dibrell, *Sparta*
Haywood Y. Riddle, *Lebanon*
John M. Bright, *Fayetteville*
John F. House, *Clarksville*
Washington C. Whitthorne, *Columbia*
John D. C. Atkins, *Paris*
William P. Caldwell, *Gardner*
H. Casey Young, *Memphis*

## TEXAS

SENATORS

Samuel B. Maxey, *Paris*
Richard Coke, *Waco*

REPRESENTATIVES

John H. Reagan, *Palestine*
David B. Culberson, *Jefferson*
James W. Throckmorton, *McKinney*
Roger Q. Mills, *Corsicana*
De Witt C. Giddings, *Brenham*
Gustave Schleicher,[45] *Cuero*

## VERMONT

SENATORS

George F. Edmunds, *Burlington*
Justin S. Morrill, *Strafford*

REPRESENTATIVES

Charles H. Joyce, *Rutland*
Dudley C. Denison, *Royalton*
George W. Hendee, *Morrisville*

## VIRGINIA

SENATORS

John W. Johnston, *Abingdon*
Robert E. Withers, *Wytheville*

REPRESENTATIVES

Beverly B. Douglas,[46] *Ayletts*
Richard Lee T. Beale,[47] *Hague*
John Goode, Jr., *Norfolk*
Gilbert C. Walker, *Richmond*
Joseph Jorgensen, *Petersburg*
George C. Cabell, *Danville*
John R. Tucker, *Lexington*
John T. Harris, *Harrisonburg*
Eppa Hunton, *Warrenton*
Auburn L. Pridemore, *Jonesville*

## WEST VIRGINIA

SENATORS

Henry G. Davis, *Piedmont*
Frank Hereford, *Union*

REPRESENTATIVES

Benjamin Wilson, *Wilsonburg*
Benjamin F. Martin, *Pruntytown*
John E. Kenna, *Kanawha*

## WISCONSIN

SENATORS

Timothy O. Howe, *Green Bay*
Angus Cameron, *La Crosse*

---

[38] Resigned March 8, 1877, having been appointed Secretary of the Treasury.

[39] Elected to fill vacancy caused by resignation of John Sherman, and took his seat October 16, 1877.

[40] Election unsuccessfully contested by Samuel W. McDowell.

[41] Resigned effective March 12, 1877.

[42] Elected to fill vacancy caused by resignation of Simon Cameron, and took his seat October 15, 1877.

[43] David T. Corbin claimed this seat; his credentials, with those of Mr. Butler, were referred to the Committee on Privileges and Elections; November 26,

1877, the committee, upon its request, was discharged from further consideration of Mr. Butler's credentials; November 30, 1877, a resolution that Mr. Butler be sworn in was agreed to by a vote of 29 to 28, the Vice President voting to break a tie; appeared and qualified the same day. On February 4, 1879, the committee reported that Mr. Corbin was entitled to the seat, and a resolution that he be sworn; the Senate refused to consider this report February 25, 1879, and on February 28 following the Vice President laid before the Senate a letter from Mr. Corbin withdrawing his claim, and no further action was taken. (See U.S. Senate

Election, Expulsion and Censure Cases, 1793-1990, Senate Document 103-33, pp. 198-202.)

[44] Election unsuccessfully contested by John S. Richardson.

[45] Died January 10, 1879, before the commencement of the Forty-sixth Congress, to which he was reelected.

[46] Died December 22, 1878.

[47] Elected to fill vacancy caused by death of Beverly B. Douglas, and took his seat February 8, 1879.

REPRESENTATIVES

Charles G. Williams, *Janesville*
Lucien B. Caswell, *Fort Atkinson*
George C. Hazelton, *Boscobel*
William P. Lynde, *Milwaukee*
Edward S. Bragg, *Fond du Lac*
Gabriel Bouck, *Oshkosh*
Herman L. Humphrey, *Hudson*
Thaddeus C. Pound, *Chippewa Falls*

## TERRITORY OF ARIZONA

DELEGATE

Hiram S. Stevens, *Tucson*

## TERRITORY OF DAKOTA

DELEGATE

Jefferson P. Kidder, *Vermilion*

## TERRITORY OF IDAHO

DELEGATE

Stephen S. Fenn, *Mount Idaho*

## TERRITORY OF MONTANA

DELEGATE

Martin Maginnis, *Helena*

## TERRITORY OF NEW MEXICO

DELEGATE

Trinidad Romero, *Las Vegas*

## TERRITORY OF UTAH

DELEGATE

George Q. Cannon, *Salt Lake City*

## TERRITORY OF WASHINGTON

DELEGATE

Orange Jacobs, *Seattle*

## TERRITORY OF WYOMING

DELEGATE

William W. Corlett, *Cheyenne*

# 46TH CONGRESS

## MARCH 4, 1879, TO MARCH 3, 1881

FIRST SESSION— *March 18, 1879, to July 1, 1879*
SECOND SESSION— *December 1, 1879, to June 16, 1880*
THIRD SESSION— *December 6, 1880, to March 3, 1881*

William A. Wheeler
Vice President

Samuel J. Randall
Speaker

VICE PRESIDENT OF THE UNITED STATES— William A. Wheeler, of New York
PRESIDENT PRO TEMPORE OF THE SENATE— Allen G. Thurman,[1] of Ohio
SECRETARY OF THE SENATE— George C. Gorham, of Massachusetts; John C. Burch,[2] of Tennessee
SERGEANT AT ARMS OF THE SENATE— John R. French, of New Hampshire; Richard J. Bright,[3] of Indiana

SPEAKER OF THE HOUSE OF REPRESENTATIVES— Samuel J. Randall,[4] of Pennsylvania
CLERK OF THE HOUSE— George M. Adams,[5] of Kentucky
SERGEANT AT ARMS OF THE HOUSE— John G. Thompson, of Ohio
DOORKEEPER OF THE HOUSE— Charles W. Field, of Georgia
POSTMASTER OF THE HOUSE— A. W. C. Nowlin

## ALABAMA

### SENATORS

John T. Morgan, *Selma*
George S. Houston,[6] *Athens*
Luke Pryor,[7] *Athens*
James L. Pugh,[8] *Eufaula*

### REPRESENTATIVES

Thomas H. Herndon, *Mobile*
Hilary A. Herbert, *Montgomery*
William J. Samford, *Opelika*
Charles M. Shelley, *Selma*
Thomas Williams, *Wetumpka*
Burwell B. Lewis,[9] *Tuscaloosa*
Newton N. Clements,[10] *Tuscaloosa*
William H. Forney, *Jacksonville*
William M. Lowe, *Huntsville*

## ARKANSAS

### SENATORS

Augustus H. Garland, *Little Rock*
James D. Walker, *Fayetteville*

### REPRESENTATIVES

Poindexter Dunn, *Forest City*
William F. Slemons,[11] *Monticello*
Jordan E. Cravens, *Clarksville*
Thomas M. Gunter, *Fayetteville*

## CALIFORNIA

### SENATORS

Newton Booth, *San Francisco*
James T. Farley, *Jackson*

### REPRESENTATIVES[12]

Horace Davis, *San Francisco*
Horace F. Page, *Placerville*
Campbell P. Berry, *Wheatland*
Romualdo Pacheco, *San Luis Obispo*

## COLORADO

### SENATORS

Henry M. Teller, *Central City*
Nathaniel P. Hill, *Denver*

### REPRESENTATIVE AT LARGE

James B. Belford, *Central City*

## CONNECTICUT

### SENATORS

William W. Eaton, *Hartford*
Orville H. Platt, *West Meriden*

### REPRESENTATIVES

Joseph R. Hawley, *Hartford*
James Phelps, *Essex*
John T. Wait, *Norwich*
Frederick Miles, *Chapinville*

## DELAWARE

### SENATORS

Thomas F. Bayard, *Wilmington*
Eli Saulsbury, *Dover*

### REPRESENTATIVE AT LARGE

Edward L. Martin, *Seaford*

## FLORIDA

### SENATORS

Charles W. Jones, *Pensacola*
Wilkinson Call, *Jacksonville*

### REPRESENTATIVES

Robert H. M. Davidson, *Quincy*
Noble A. Hull,[13] *Sanford*
Horatio Bisbee, Jr.,[14] *Jacksonville*

## GEORGIA

### SENATORS

Benjamin H. Hill, *Atlanta*
John B. Gordon,[15] *Atlanta*
Joseph E. Brown,[16] *Atlanta*

### REPRESENTATIVES

John C. Nicholls, *Blackshear*
William E. Smith, *Albany*
Philip Cook, *Americus*
Henry Persons, *Geneva*
Nathaniel J. Hammond, *Atlanta*
James H. Blount, *Macon*

---

[1] Elected April 15, 1879; April 7, 1880; and May 6, 1880.
[2] Elected March 24, 1879.
[3] Elected March 23, 1879.
[4] Reelected March 18, 1879.
[5] Reelected March 18, 1879.
[6] Died December 31, 1879.
[7] Appointed to fill vacancy caused by death of George S. Houston and took his seat January 15, 1880.

[8] Elected to fill vacancy caused by death of George S. Houston, and took his seat December 6, 1880.
[9] Resigned October 1, 1880.
[10] Elected to fill vacancy caused by resignation of Burwell B. Lewis, and took his seat December 8, 1880.
[11] Election unsuccessfully contested by John M. Bradley.
[12] Elected September 3, 1879; took their seats December 1, 1879.

[13] Served until January 22, 1881; succeeded by Horatio Bisbee, Jr., who contested his election.
[14] Successfully contested the election of Noble A. Hull, and took his seat January 22, 1881.
[15] Resigned in May 1880.
[16] Appointed to fill vacancy caused by resignation of John B. Gordon, and took his seat May 26, 1880; subsequently elected.

William H. Felton, *Cartersville*
Alexander H. Stephens, *Crawfordville*
Emory Speer, *Athens*

## ILLINOIS

SENATORS

David Davis, *Bloomington*
John A. Logan, *Chicago*

REPRESENTATIVES

William Aldrich, *Chicago*
George R. Davis, *Chicago*
Hiram Barber, Jr., *Chicago*
John C. Sherwin, *Aurora*
Robert M. A. Hawk, *Mount Carroll*
Thomas J. Henderson, *Princeton*
Philip C. Hayes, *Morris*
Greenbury L. Fort, *Lacon*
Thomas A. Boyd, *Lewiston*
Benjamin F. Marsh, *Warsaw*
James W. Singleton, *Quincy*
William M. Springer, *Springfield*
Adlai E. Stevenson, *Bloomington*
Joseph G. Cannon, *Danville*
Albert P. Forsythe, *Isabel*
William A. J. Sparks, *Carlyle*
William R. Morrison, *Waterloo*
John R. Thomas, *Metropolis*
Richard W. Townshend, *Shawneetown*

## INDIANA

SENATORS

Joseph E. McDonald, *Indianapolis*
Daniel W. Voorhees, *Terre Haute*

REPRESENTATIVES

William Heilman, *Evansville*
Thomas R. Cobb, *Vincennes*
George A. Bicknell, *New Albany*
Jeptha D. New, *Vernon*
Thomas M. Browne, *Winchester*
William R. Myers, *Anderson*
Gilbert De La Matyr, *Indianapolis*
Abraham J. Hostetler, *Bedford*
Godlove S. Orth,[17] *Lafayette*
William H. Calkins, *Laporte*
Calvin Cowgill, *Wabash*
Walpole G. Colerick, *Fort Wayne*
John H. Baker, *Goshen*

## IOWA

SENATORS

William B. Allison, *Dubuque*
Samuel J. Kirkwood, *Iowa City*

REPRESENTATIVES

Moses A. McCoid, *Fairfield*
Hiram Price, *Davenport*
Thomas Updegraff, *McGregor*
Nathaniel C. Deering, *Osage*
Rush Clark,[18] *Iowa City*
William G. Thompson,[19] *Marion*
James B. Weaver, *Bloomfield*
Edward H. Gillette, *Des Moines*
William F. Sapp, *Council Bluffs*
Cyrus C. Carpenter, *Fort Dodge*

## KANSAS

SENATORS

John J. Ingalls, *Atchison*
Preston B. Plumb, *Emporia*

REPRESENTATIVES

John A. Anderson, *Manhattan*
Dudley C. Haskell, *Lawrence*
Thomas Ryan, *Topeka*

## KENTUCKY

SENATORS

James B. Beck, *Lexington*
John S. Williams, *Mount Sterling*

REPRESENTATIVES

Oscar Turner, *Oscar*
James A. McKenzie, *Long View*
John William Caldwell, *Russellville*
J. Proctor Knott, *Lebanon*
Albert S. Willis, *Louisville*
John G. Carlisle, *Covington*
Joseph C. S. Blackburn, *Versailles*
Philip B. Thompson, Jr., *Harrodsburg*
Thomas Turner, *Mount Sterling*
Elijah C. Phister, *Maysville*

## LOUISIANA

SENATORS

William Pitt Kellogg,[20] *New Orleans*
Benjamin F. Jonas, *New Orleans*

REPRESENTATIVES

Randall L. Gibson, *New Orleans*
E. John Ellis, *New Orleans*
Joseph H. Acklen, *Franklin*
Joseph B. Elam, *Mansfield*
J. Floyd King, *Vidalia*
Edward W. Robertson, *Baton Rouge*

## MAINE

SENATORS

Hannibal Hamlin, *Bangor*
James G. Blaine, *Augusta*

REPRESENTATIVES

Thomas B. Reed, *Portland*
William P. Frye, *Lewiston*
Stephen D. Lindsey, *Norridgewock*
George W. Ladd, *Bangor*
Thompson H. Murch, *Rockland*

## MARYLAND

SENATORS

William Pinkney Whyte, *Baltimore*
James B. Groome, *Elkton*

REPRESENTATIVES

Daniel M. Henry, *Cambridge*
J. Fred C. Talbott, *Towsontown*
William Kimmel, *Baltimore*
Robert M. McLane, *Baltimore*
Eli J. Henkle, *Brooklyn*
Milton G. Urner, *Frederick*

## MASSACHUSETTS

SENATORS

Henry L. Dawes, *Pittsfield*
George F. Hoar, *Worcester*

REPRESENTATIVES

William W. Crapo, *New Bedford*
Benjamin W. Harris, *East Bridgewater*
Walbridge A. Field, *Boston*
Leopold Morse, *Boston*
Selwyn Z. Bowman, *Somerville*
George B. Loring,[21] *Salem*
William A. Russell, *Lawrence*
William Claflin, *Newton*
William W. Rice, *Worcester*
Amasa Norcross, *Fitchburg*
George D. Robinson, *Chicopee*

## MICHIGAN

SENATORS

Thomas W. Ferry, *Grand Haven*
Zachariah Chandler,[22] *Detroit*
Henry P. Baldwin,[23] *Detroit*

REPRESENTATIVES

John S. Newberry, *Detroit*
Edwin Willits, *Monroe*
Jonas H. McGowan, *Coldwater*
Julius C. Burrows, *Kalamazoo*
John W. Stone, *Grand Rapids*
Mark S. Brewer, *Pontiac*
Omar D. Conger,[24] *Port Huron*
Roswell G. Horr, *East Saginaw*
Jay A. Hubbell, *Houghton*

---

[17] Election unsuccessfully contested by James McCabe.

[18] Died April 29, 1879.

[19] Elected to fill vacancy caused by the death of Rush Clark, and took his seat December 1, 1879.

[20] The credentials of Thomas C. Manning, appointed to fill vacancy caused by the death of Henry M. Spofford (August 20, 1880), contestant for this seat in the preceding Congress, were presented December 7, 1880; inasmuch as the Senate had taken no action upon the report that was favorable to Mr. Spofford, no action was taken upon Mr. Manning's credentials beyond referring them to the committee. (See U.S. Senate Election, Expulsion and Censure Cases, 1793-1990, Senate Document 103-33, pp. 182-188.)

[21] Election unsuccessfully contested by E. Moody Boynton.

[22] Died November 1, 1879.

[23] Appointed to fill vacancy caused by death of Zachariah Chandler, and took his seat December 3, 1879; subsequently elected.

[24] Resigned March 3, 1881, before the commencement of the Forty-seventh Congress to which he had been reelected, having been elected Senator.

## MINNESOTA

### SENATORS

William Windom, *Winona*
Samuel J. R. McMillan, *St. Paul*

### REPRESENTATIVES

Mark H. Dunnell, *Owatonna*
Henry Poehler, *Henderson*
William D. Washburn, *Minneapolis*

## MISSISSIPPI

### SENATORS

Blanche K. Bruce, *Floreyville*
Lucius Q. C. Lamar, *Oxford*

### REPRESENTATIVES

Henry L. Muldrow, *Starkville*
Vannoy H. Manning, *Holly Springs*
Hernando D. Money, *Winona*
Otho R. Singleton, *Canton*
Charles E. Hooker, *Jackson*
James R. Chalmers, *Vicksburg*

## MISSOURI

### SENATORS

Francis M. Cockrell, *Warrensburg*
George G. Vest, *Kansas City*

### REPRESENTATIVES

Martin L. Clardy, *Farmington*
Erastus Wells, *St. Louis*
Richard G. Frost, *St. Louis*
Lowndes H. Davis, *Jackson*
Richard P. Bland, *Lebanon*
James R. Waddill, *Springfield*
Alfred M. Lay,[25] *Jefferson City*
John F. Phillips,[26] *Sedalia*
Samuel L. Sawyer, *Independence*
Nicholas Ford, *Rochester*
Gideon F. Rothwell, *Moberly*
John B. Clark, Jr., *Fayette*
William H. Hatch, *Hannibal*
Aylett H. Buckner, *Mexico*

## NEBRASKA

### SENATORS

Algernon S. Paddock, *Beatrice*
Alvin Saunders, *Omaha*

### REPRESENTATIVE AT LARGE

Edward K. Valentine, *West Point*

## NEVADA

### SENATORS

John P. Jones, *Gold Hill*
William Sharon, *Virginia City*

### REPRESENTATIVE AT LARGE

Rollin M. Daggett, *Virginia City*

## NEW HAMPSHIRE

### SENATORS

Edward H. Rollins, *Concord*
Charles H. Bell,[27] *Exeter*
Henry W. Blair,[28] *Plymouth*

### REPRESENTATIVES

Joshua G. Hall, *Dover*
James F. Briggs, *Manchester*
Evarts W. Farr,[29] *Littleton*
Ossian Ray,[30] *Lancaster*

## NEW JERSEY

### SENATORS

Theodore F. Randolph, *Morristown*
John R. McPherson, *Jersey City*

### REPRESENTATIVES

George M. Robeson, *Camden*
Hezekiah B. Smith, *Smithville*
Miles Ross, *New Brunswick*
Alvah A. Clark, *Somerville*
Charles H. Voorhis, *Hackensack*
John L. Blake, *Orange*
Lewis A. Brigham, *Jersey City*

## NEW YORK

### SENATORS

Roscoe Conkling, *Utica*
Francis Kernan, *Utica*

### REPRESENTATIVES

James W. Covert, *Flushing*
Daniel O'Reilly, *Brooklyn*
Simeon B. Chittenden, *Brooklyn*
Archibald M. Bliss, *Brooklyn*
Nicholas Muller, *New York City*
Samuel S. Cox, *New York City*
Edwin Einstein, *New York City*
Anson G. McCook, *New York City*
Fernando Wood,[31] *New York City*
James O'Brien, *New York City*
Levi P. Morton, *New York City*
Waldo Hutchins,[32] *Kingsbridge*
John H. Ketcham, *Dover Plains*
John W. Ferdon, *Piermont*
William Lounsbery, *Kingston*
John M. Bailey, *Albany*

Walter A. Wood, *Hoosick Falls*
John Hammond, *Crown Point*
Amaziah B. James, *Ogdensburg*
John H. Starin, *Fultonville*
David Wilber, *Milford*
Warner Miller, *Herkimer*
Cyrus D. Prescott, *Rome*
Joseph Mason,[33] *Hamilton*
Frank Hiscock, *Syracuse*
John H. Camp, *Lyons*
Elbridge G. Lapham, *Canandaigua*
Jeremiah W. Dwight, *Dryden*
David P. Richardson, *Angelica*
John Van Voorhis, *Rochester*
Richard Crowley, *Lockport*
Ray V. Pierce,[34] *Buffalo*
Jonathan Scoville,[35] *Salisbury*
Henry Van Aernam, *Franklinville*

## NORTH CAROLINA

### SENATORS

Matt W. Ransom, *Weldon*
Zebulon B. Vance, *Charlotte*

### REPRESENTATIVES

Joseph J. Martin,[36] *Williamston*
Jesse J. Yeates,[37] *Murfreesboro*
William H. Kitchin, *Scotland Neck*
Daniel L. Russell, *Wilmington*
Joseph J. Davis, *Louisburg*
Alfred M. Scales, *Greensborough*
Walter L. Steele, *Rockingham*
Robert F. Armfield, *Statesville*
Robert B. Vance, *Asheville*

## OHIO

### SENATORS

Allen G. Thurman, *Columbus*
George H. Pendleton, *Cincinnati*

### REPRESENTATIVES

Benjamin Butterworth, *Cincinnati*
Thomas L. Young, *Cincinnati*
John A. McMahon, *Dayton*
J. Warren Keifer, *Springfield*
Benjamin Le Fevre, *Sidney*
William D. Hill, *Defiance*
Frank H. Hurd, *Toledo*
Ebenezer B. Finley, *Bucyrus*
George L. Converse, *Columbus*
Thomas Ewing, *Lancaster*
Henry L. Dickey, *Greenfield*
Henry S. Neal, *Ironton*
Adoniram J. Warner, *Marietta*
Gibson Atherton, *Newark*
George W. Geddes, *Mansfield*

---

[25] Died December 8, 1879.

[26] Elected to fill vacancy caused by the death of Alfred M. Lay, and took his seat January 26, 1880.

[27] Appointed to fill vacancy in term beginning March 4, 1879; credentials presented and referred March 18, 1879; majority of Committee on Privileges and Elections reported resolution, April 2, 1879, declaring him not entitled to seat; by resolution, April 10, 1879, was declared entitled to seat; appeared and qualified same day. (See U.S. Senate Election, Expulsion and Censure Cases, 1793-1990, Senate Document 103-33, pp. 216-218.)

[28] Elected to fill vacancy in term beginning March 4, 1879, and took his seat June 20, 1879.

[29] Died November 30, 1880.

[30] Elected to fill vacancy caused by death of Evarts W. Farr, and took his seat January 8, 1881.

[31] Died February 13, 1881, before the commencement of the Forty-seventh Congress, to which he had been reelected.

[32] Elected to fill vacancy caused by death of Representative-elect Alexander Smith (November 5, 1878, before the beginning of the congressional term),

and took his seat December 1, 1879.

[33] Election unsuccessfully contested by Sebastian Duffy.

[34] Resigned September 18, 1880.

[35] Elected to fill vacancy caused by resignation of Ray V. Pierce, and took his seat December 6, 1880.

[36] Served until January 29, 1881; succeeded by Jesse J. Yeates, who contested his election.

[37] Successfully contested the election of Joseph J. Martin, and took his seat January 29, 1881.

William McKinley, Jr., *Canton*
James Monroe, *Oberlin*
Jonathan T. Updegraff, *Mount Pleasant*
James A. Garfield,[38] *Mentor*
Ezra B. Taylor,[39] *Warren*
Amos Townsend, *Cleveland*

## OREGON

### SENATORS

La Fayette Grover, *Salem*
James H. Slater, *La Grande*

### REPRESENTATIVE AT LARGE

John Whiteaker, *Pleasant Hill*

## PENNSYLVANIA

### SENATORS

William A. Wallace, *Clearfield*
J. Donald Cameron, *Harrisburg*

### REPRESENTATIVES

Henry H. Bingham, *Philadelphia*
Charles O'Neill, *Philadelphia*
Samuel J. Randall, *Philadelphia*
William D. Kelley, *Philadelphia*
Alfred C. Harmer, *Germantown*
William Ward, *Chester*
William Godshalk, *New Britain*
Hiester Clymer, *Reading*
A. Herr Smith, *Lancaster*
Reuben K. Bachman, *Durham*
Robert Klotz, *Mauch Chunk*
Hendrick B. Wright, *Wilkes-Barre*
John W. Ryon, *Pottsville*
John W. Killinger, *Lebanon*
Edward Overton, Jr., *Towanda*
John I. Mitchell, *Wellsboro*
Alexander H. Coffroth, *Somerset*
Horatio G. Fisher, *Huntingdon*
Frank E. Beltzhoover, *Carlisle*
Seth H. Yocum,[40] *Bellefonte*
Morgan R. Wise, *Waynesburg*
Russell Errett, *Pittsburgh*
Thomas M. Bayne, *Allegheny*
William S. Shallenberger, *Rochester*
Harry White, *Indiana*
Samuel B. Dick, *Meadville*
James H. Osmer, *Franklin*

## RHODE ISLAND

### SENATORS

Henry B. Anthony, *Providence*
Ambrose E. Burnside, *Providence*

### REPRESENTATIVES

Nelson W. Aldrich, *Providence*
Latimer W. Ballou, *Woonsocket*

## SOUTH CAROLINA

### SENATORS

Matthew C. Butler, *Edgefield*
Wade Hampton, *Columbia*

### REPRESENTATIVES

John S. Richardson, *Sumter*
Michael P. O'Connor, *Charleston*
D. Wyatt Aiken, *Cokesbury*
John H. Evins, *Spartanburg*
George D. Tillman, *Edgefield*

## TENNESSEE

### SENATORS

James E. Bailey, *Clarksville*
Isham G. Harris, *Memphis*

### REPRESENTATIVES

Robert L. Taylor, *Jonesboro*
Leonidas C. Houk, *Knoxville*
George G. Dibrell, *Sparta*
Benton McMillin, *Carthage*
John M. Bright, *Fayetteville*
John F. House, *Clarksville*
Washington C. Whitthorne, *Columbia*
John D. C. Atkins, *Paris*
Charles B. Simonton, *Covington*
H. Casey Young, *Memphis*

## TEXAS

### SENATORS

Samuel B. Maxey, *Paris*
Richard Coke, *Waco*

### REPRESENTATIVES

John H. Reagan, *Palestine*
David B. Culberson, *Jefferson*
Olin Wellborn, *Dallas*
Roger Q. Mills, *Corsicana*
George W. Jones, *Bastrop*
Christopher C. Upson,[41] *San Antonio*

## VERMONT

### SENATORS

George F. Edmunds, *Burlington*
Justin S. Morrill, *Strafford*

### REPRESENTATIVES

Charles H. Joyce, *Rutland*
James M. Tyler, *Brattleboro*
Bradley Barlow, *St. Albans*

## VIRGINIA

### SENATORS

John W. Johnston, *Abingdon*
Robert E. Withers, *Wytheville*

### REPRESENTATIVES

Richard Lee T. Beale, *Hague*
John Goode, Jr., *Norfolk*
Joseph E. Johnston, *Longwood*

Joseph Jorgensen, *Petersburg*
George C. Cabell, *Danville*
John R. Tucker, *Lexington*
John T. Harris, *Harrisonburg*
Eppa Hunton, *Warrenton*
James B. Richmond, *Estillville*

## WEST VIRGINIA

### SENATORS

Henry Gassaway Davis, *Piedmont*
Frank Hereford, *Union*

### REPRESENTATIVES

Benjamin Wilson, *Wilsonburg*
Benjamin F. Martin, *Pruntytown*
John E. Kenna, *Kanawha*

## WISCONSIN

### SENATORS

Angus Cameron, *La Crosse*
Matthew H. Carpenter,[42] *Milwaukee*

### REPRESENTATIVES

Charles G. Williams, *Janesville*
Lucien B. Caswell, *Fort Atkinson*
George C. Hazelton, *Boscobel*
Peter V. Deuster, *Milwaukee*
Edward S. Bragg, *Fond du Lac*
Gabriel Bouck, *Oshkosh*
Herman L. Humphrey, *Hudson*
Thaddeus C. Pound, *Chippewa Falls*

## TERRITORY OF ARIZONA

### DELEGATE

John G. Campbell, *Prescott*

## TERRITORY OF DAKOTA

### DELEGATE

Granville G. Bennett, *Yankton*

## TERRITORY OF IDAHO

### DELEGATE

George Ainslie, *Idaho City*

## TERRITORY OF MONTANA

### DELEGATE

Martin Maginnis, *Helena*

## TERRITORY OF NEW MEXICO

### DELEGATE

Mariano S. Otero, *Peralta*

---

[38] Resigned November 8, 1880, having been elected President of the United States.
[39] Elected to fill vacancy caused by resignation of James A. Garfield, and took his seat December 13, 1880.

[40] Election unsuccessfully contested by Andrew G. Curtin.
[41] Elected to fill vacancy caused by death of Representative-elect Gustave Schleicher, in preceding

Congress, and took his seat June 2, 1879.
[42] Died February 24, 1881.

## TERRITORY OF UTAH

DELEGATE

George Q. Cannon, *Salt Lake City*

## TERRITORY OF WASHINGTON

DELEGATE

Thomas H. Brents, *Walla Walla*

## TERRITORY OF WYOMING

DELEGATE

Stephen W. Downey, *Laramie City*

# 47TH CONGRESS

## MARCH 4, 1881, TO MARCH 3, 1883

Chester A. Arthur
Vice President

J. Warren Keifer
Speaker

FIRST SESSION— *December 5, 1881, to August 8, 1882*
SECOND SESSION— *December 4, 1882, to March 3, 1883*
SPECIAL SESSIONS OF THE SENATE— *March 4, 1881, to May 20, 1881;*
*October 10, 1881, to October 29, 1881*

———

VICE PRESIDENT OF THE UNITED STATES— CHESTER A. ARTHUR,[1] of New York
PRESIDENT PRO TEMPORE OF THE SENATE— THOMAS F. BAYARD,[2] of Delaware; DAVID
DAVIS,[3] of Illinois; GEORGE F. EDMUNDS,[4] of Vermont
SECRETARY OF THE SENATE— JOHN C. BURCH,[5] of Tennessee; FRANCIS E. SHOBER[6]
(Chief Clerk), of North Carolina
SERGEANT AT ARMS OF THE SENATE— RICHARD J. BRIGHT, of Indiana

———

SPEAKER OF THE HOUSE OF REPRESENTATIVES— J. WARREN KEIFER,[7] of Ohio
CLERK OF THE HOUSE— GEORGE M. ADAMS, of Kentucky; EDWARD McPHERSON,[8] of Pennsylvania
SERGEANT AT ARMS OF THE HOUSE— JOHN G. THOMPSON, of Ohio; GEORGE W. HOOKER,[9] of Vermont
DOORKEEPER OF THE HOUSE— WALTER P. BROWNLOW, of Tennessee
POSTMASTER OF THE HOUSE— HENRY SHERWOOD

## ALABAMA

### SENATORS

John T. Morgan, *Selma*
James L. Pugh, *Eufaula*

### REPRESENTATIVES

Thomas H. Herndon, *Mobile*
Hilary A. Herbert, *Montgomery*
William C. Oates, *Abbeville*
Charles M. Shelley,[10] *Selma*
Thomas Williams, *Wetumpka*
Goldsmith W. Hewitt, *Birmingham*
William H. Forney, *Jacksonville*
Joseph Wheeler,[11] *Wheeler*
William M. Lowe,[12] *Huntsville*

## ARKANSAS

### SENATORS

Augustus H. Garland, *Little Rock*
James D. Walker, *Fayetteville*

### REPRESENTATIVES

Poindexter Dunn, *Forest City*
James K. Jones, *Washington*
Jordan E. Cravens, *Clarksville*
Thomas M. Gunter, *Fayetteville*

## CALIFORNIA

### SENATORS

James T. Farley, *Jackson*
John F. Miller, *San Francisco*

### REPRESENTATIVES

William S. Rosecrans, *San Francisco*
Horace F. Page, *Placerville*
Campbell P. Berry, *Wheatland*
Romualdo Pacheco, *San Luis Obispo*

## COLORADO

### SENATORS

Henry M. Teller,[13] *Denver*
George M. Chilcott,[14] *Denver*
Horace A. W. Tabor,[15] *Denver*
Nathaniel P. Hill, *Denver*

### REPRESENTATIVE AT LARGE

James B. Belford, *Central City*

## CONNECTICUT

### SENATORS

Orville H. Platt, *West Meriden*
Joseph R. Hawley, *Hartford*

### REPRESENTATIVES

John R. Buck, *Hartford*
James Phelps, *Essex*

John T. Wait, *Norwich*
Frederick Miles, *Chapinville*

## DELAWARE

### SENATORS

Thomas F. Bayard, *Wilmington*
Eli Saulsbury, *Dover*

### REPRESENTATIVE AT LARGE

Edward L. Martin, *Seaford*

## FLORIDA

### SENATORS

Charles W. Jones, *Pensacola*
Wilkinson Call, *Jacksonville*

### REPRESENTATIVES

Robert H. M. Davidson, *Quincy*
Jesse J. Finley,[16] *Jacksonville*
Horatio Bisbee, Jr.,[17] *Jacksonville*

---

[1] Became President on the death of James A. Garfield, September 19, 1881.
[2] Elected October 10, 1881 (special session of the Senate).
[3] Elected October 13, 1881 (special session of the Senate); resigned March 3, 1883.
[4] Elected March 3, 1883.
[5] Died July 28, 1881.
[6] Appointed Acting Secretary by resolution of October 24, 1881, to fill vacancy caused by death of John C. Burch; served throughout the Congress.
[7] Elected December 5, 1881.
[8] Elected December 5, 1881.

[9] Elected December 5, 1881.
[10] Election contested by James Q. Smith; report of the committee favorable to contestant, but contestant died and seat was declared vacant July 20, 1882; subsequently elected to fill vacancy thus caused, and took his seat December 4, 1882; this election was contested by John W. Jones, but was undisposed of at close of the Congress.
[11] Served until June 3, 1882; succeeded by William M. Lowe, who contested his election; subsequently elected to fill vacancy caused by the death of Mr. Lowe, and took his seat January 15, 1883.
[12] Successfully contested the election of Joseph

Wheeler, and took his seat June 3, 1882; died August 12, 1882.
[13] Resigned April 17, 1882, having been appointed Secretary of the Interior.
[14] Appointed to fill vacancy caused by resignation of Henry M. Teller, and took his seat April 17, 1882.
[15] Elected to fill vacancy caused by resignation of Henry m. Teller, and took his seat February 2, 1883.
[16] Served until June 1, 1882; succeeded by Horatio Bisbee, Jr., who contested his election.
[17] Successfully contested the election of Jesse J. Finley, and took his seat June 1, 1882.

## GEORGIA

### SENATORS

Benjamin H. Hill,[18] *Atlanta*
M. Pope Barrow,[19] *Athens*
Joseph E. Brown, *Atlanta*

### REPRESENTATIVES

George R. Black, *Sylvania*
Henry G. Turner, *Quitman*
Philip Cook, *Americus*
Hugh Buchanan, *Newnan*
Nathaniel J. Hammond, *Atlanta*
James H. Blount, *Macon*
Judson C. Clements, *La Fayette*
Alexander H. Stephens,[20]
    *Crawfordville*
Seaborn Reese,[21] *Sparta*
Emory Speer, *Athens*

## ILLINOIS

### SENATORS

David Davis, *Bloomington*
John A. Logan, *Chicago*

### REPRESENTATIVES

William Aldrich, *Chicago*
George R. Davis, *Chicago*
Charles B. Farwell, *Chicago*
John C. Sherwin, *Aurora*
Robert M. A. Hawk,[22] *Mount Carroll*
Robert R. Hitt,[23] *Mount Morris*
Thomas J. Henderson, *Princeton*
William Cullen, *Ottawa*
Lewis E. Payson, *Pontiac*
John H. Lewis, *Knoxville*
Benjamin F. Marsh, *Warsaw*
James W. Singleton, *Quincy*
William M. Springer, *Springfield*
Dietrich C. Smith, *Pekin*
Joseph G. Cannon, *Danville*
Samuel W. Moulton, *Shelbyville*
William A. J. Sparks, *Carlyle*
William R. Morrison, *Waterloo*
John R. Thomas, *Metropolis*
Richard W. Townshend, *Shawneetown*

## INDIANA

### SENATORS

Daniel W. Voorhees, *Terre Haute*
Benjamin Harrison, *Indianapolis*

### REPRESENTATIVES

William Heilman, *Evansville*
Thomas R. Cobb, *Vincennes*
Strother M. Stockslager, *Corydon*
William S. Holman, *Aurora*

Courtland C. Matson, *Greencastle*
Thomas M. Browne, *Winchester*
Stanton J. Peelle, *Indianapolis*
Robert B. F. Peirce, *Crawfordsville*
Godlove S. Orth,[24] *Lafayette*
Charles T. Doxey,[25] *Anderson*
Mark L. DeMotte, *Valparaiso*
George W. Steele, *Marion*
Walpole G. Colerick, *Fort Wayne*
William H. Calkins, *Laporte*

## IOWA

### SENATORS

William B. Allison, *Dubuque*
Samuel J. Kirkwood,[26] *Iowa City*
James W. McDill,[27] *Afton*

### REPRESENTATIVES

Moses A. McCoid, *Fairfield*
Sewall S. Farwell, *Monticello*
Thomas Updegraff, *McGregor*
Nathaniel C. Deering, *Osage*
William G. Thompson, *Marion*
Marsena E. Cutts,[28] *Oskaloosa*
John C. Cook,[29] *Newton*
John A. Kasson, *Des Moines*
William P. Hepburn, *Clarinda*
Cyrus C. Carpenter, *Fort Dodge*

## KANSAS

### SENATORS

John J. Ingalls, *Atchison*
Preston B. Plumb, *Emporia*

### REPRESENTATIVES

John A. Anderson, *Manhattan*
Dudley C. Haskell, *Lawrence*
Thomas Ryan, *Topeka*

## KENTUCKY

### SENATORS

James B. Beck, *Lexington*
John S. Williams, *Mount Sterling*

### REPRESENTATIVES

Oscar Turner, *Oscar*
James A. McKenzie, *Long View*
John W. Caldwell, *Russellville*
J. Proctor Knott, *Lebanon*
Albert S. Willis, *Louisville*
John G. Carlisle, *Covington*
Joseph C. S. Blackburn, *Versailles*
Philip B. Thompson, Jr., *Harrodsburg*
John D. White, *Manchester*
Elijah C. Phister, *Maysville*

## LOUISIANA

### SENATORS

William Pitt Kellogg, *New Orleans*
Benjamin F. Jonas, *New Orleans*

### REPRESENTATIVES

Randall L. Gibson, *New Orleans*
E. John Ellis, *New Orleans*
Chester B. Darrall, *Morgan City*
Newton C. Blanchard, *Shreveport*
J. Floyd King, *Vidalia*
Edward W. Robertson, *Baton Rouge*

## MAINE

### SENATORS

James G. Blaine,[30] *Augusta*
William P. Frye,[31] *Lewiston*
Eugene Hale, *Ellsworth*

### REPRESENTATIVES

Thomas B. Reed,[32] *Portland*
William P. Frye,[33] *Lewiston*
Nelson Dingley, Jr.,[34] *Lewiston*
Stephen D. Lindsey, *Norridgewock*
George W. Ladd, *Bangor*
Thompson H. Murch, *Rockland*

## MARYLAND

### SENATORS

James B. Groome, *Elkton*
Arthur Pue Gorman, *Laurel*

### REPRESENTATIVES

George W. Covington, *Snow Hill*
J. Fred. C. Talbott, *Towsontown*
Fetter S. Hoblitzell, *Baltimore*
Robert M. McLane, *Baltimore*
Andrew G. Chapman, *La Plata*
Milton G. Urner, *Frederick*

## MASSACHUSETTS

### SENATORS

Henry L. Dawes, *Pittsfield*
George F. Hoar, *Worcester*

### REPRESENTATIVES

William W. Crapo, *New Bedford*
Benjamin W. Harris, *East
    Bridgewater*
Ambrose A. Ranney, *Boston*
Leopold Morse, *Boston*
Selwyn Z. Bowman, *Somerville*

---

[18] Died August 16, 1882.
[19] Elected to fill vacancy caused by death of Benjamin H. Hill, and took his seat December 5, 1882.
[20] Resigned November 4, 1882, having been elected Governor.
[21] Elected to fill vacancy caused by resignation of Alexander H. Stephens, and took his seat December 4, 1882.
[22] Died June 29, 1882.
[23] Elected to fill vacancy caused by death of Robert M. A. Hawk, and took his seat December 4, 1882.
[24] Died December 16, 1882.

[25] Elected to fill vacancy caused by death of Godlove S. Orth, and took his seat January 17, 1883.
[26] Resigned March 7, 1881, to become Secretary of the Interior.
[27] Appointed to fill vacancy caused by resignation of Samuel J. Kirkwood, and took his seat March 14, 1881 (special session of the Senate); subsequently elected.
[28] Served until March 3, 1883; succeeded by John C. Cook, who contested his election.
[29] Successfully contested election of Marsena E. Cutts, and took his seat March 3, 1883—closing day of

the Congress.
[30] Resigned March 5, 1881, having been appointed Secretary of State.
[31] Elected to fill vacancy caused by resignation of James G. Blaine, and took his seat March 18, 1881.
[32] Election unsuccessfully contested by Samuel J. Anderson.
[33] Resigned March 17, 1881, having been elected Senator.
[34] Elected to fill vacancy caused by resignation of William P. Frye, and took his seat December 5, 1881.

Eben F. Stone, *Newburyport*
William A. Russell, *Lawrence*
John W. Candler, *Brookline*
William W. Rice, *Worcester*
Amasa Norcross, *Fitchburg*
George D. Robinson, *Chicopee*

## MICHIGAN

SENATORS

Thomas W. Ferry, *Grand Haven*
Omar D. Conger, *Port Huron*

REPRESENTATIVES

Henry W. Lord, *Detroit*
Edwin Willits, *Monroe*
Edward S. Lacey, *Charlotte*
Julius C. Burrows, *Kalamazoo*
George W. Webber, *Ionia*
Oliver L. Spaulding, *St. Johns*
John T. Rich,[35] *Elba*
Roswell G. Horr, *East Saginaw*
Jay A. Hubbell, *Houghton*

## MINNESOTA

SENATORS

Samuel J. R. McMillan, *St. Paul*
William Windom,[36] *Winona*
Alonzo J. Edgerton,[37] *Kasson*
William Windom,[38] *Winona*

REPRESENTATIVES

Mark H. Dunnell, *Owatonna*
Horace B. Strait, *Shakopee*
William D. Washburn, *Minneapolis*

## MISSISSIPPI

SENATORS

Lucius Q. C. Lamar, *Oxford*
James Z. George, *Jackson*

REPRESENTATIVES

Henry L. Muldrow, *Starkville*
Vannoy H. Manning,[39] *Holly Springs*
Hernando D. Money, *Winona*
Otho R. Singleton, *Canton*
Charles E. Hooker, *Jackson*
James R. Chalmers,[40] *Vicksburg*
John R. Lynch,[41] *Natchez*

## MISSOURI

SENATORS

Francis M. Cockrell, *Warrensburg*
George G. Vest, *Kansas City*

REPRESENTATIVES

Martin L. Clardy, *Farmington*
Thomas Allen,[42] *St. Louis*
James H. McLean,[43] *St. Louis*
Richard G. Frost,[44] *St. Louis*
Gustavus Sessinghaus,[45] *St. Louis*
Lowndes H. Davis, *Jackson*
Richard P. Bland, *Lebanon*
Ira S. Hazeltine, *Springfield*
Theron M. Rice, *Booneville*
Robert T. Van Horn, *Kansas City*
Nicholas Ford, *Rochester*
Joseph H. Burrows, *Cainsville*
John B. Clark, Jr., *Fayette*
William H. Hatch, *Hannibal*
Aylett H. Buckner, *Mexico*

## NEBRASKA

SENATORS

Alvin Saunders, *Omaha*
Charles H. Van Wyck, *Nebraska City*

REPRESENTATIVE AT LARGE[46]

Edward K. Valentine, *West Point*

## NEVADA

SENATORS

John P. Jones, *Gold Hill*
James G. Fair, *Virginia City*

REPRESENTATIVE AT LARGE

George W. Cassidy, *Eureka*

## NEW HAMPSHIRE

SENATORS

Edward H. Rollins, *Concord*
Henry W. Blair, *Plymouth*

REPRESENTATIVES

Joshua G. Hall, *Dover*
James F. Briggs, *Manchester*
Ossian Ray,[47] *Lancaster*

## NEW JERSEY

SENATORS

John R. McPherson, *Jersey City*
William J. Sewell, *Camden*

REPRESENTATIVES

George M. Robeson, *Camden*
J. Hart Brewer, *Trenton*
Miles Ross, *New Brunswick*
Henry S. Harris, *Belvidere*
John Hill, *Boonton*
Phineas Jones, *Newark*
Augustus A. Hardenbergh, *Jersey City*

## NEW YORK

SENATORS

Roscoe Conkling,[48] *Utica*
Elbridge G. Lapham,[49] *Canandaigua*
Thomas C. Platt,[50] *Owego*
Warner Miller,[51] *Herkimer*

REPRESENTATIVES

Perry Belmont, *Babylon*
William E. Robinson, *Brooklyn*
J. Hyatt Smith, *Brooklyn*
Archibald M. Bliss, *Brooklyn*
Benjamin Wood, *New York City*
Samuel S. Cox, *New York City*
P. Henry Dugro, *New York City*
Anson G. McCook, *New York City*
John Hardy,[52] *New York City*
Abram S. Hewitt, *New York City*
Levi P. Morton,[53] *New York City*
Roswell P. Flower,[54] *New York City*
Waldo Hutchins, *Kingsbridge*
John H. Ketcham, *Dover Plains*
Lewis Beach, *Cornwall*
Thomas Cornell, *Rondout*
Michael N. Nolan, *Albany*
Walter A. Wood, *Hoosick Falls*
John Hammond, *Crown Point*
Abraham X. Parker, *Potsdam*
George West, *Ballston Spa*
Ferris Jacobs, Jr., *Delhi*
Warner Miller,[55] *Herkimer*
Charles R. Skinner,[56] *Watertown*
Cyrus D. Prescott, *Rome*
Joseph Mason, *Hamilton*
Frank Hiscock, *Syracuse*
John H. Camp, *Lyons*
Elbridge G. Lapham,[57] *Canandaigua*
James W. Wadsworth,[58] *Livingstone*
Jeremiah W. Dwight, *Dryden*
David P. Richardson, *Angelica*
John Van Voorhis, *Rochester*
Richard Crowley, *Lockport*
Jonathan Scoville, *Buffalo*
Henry Van Aernam, *Franklinville*

---

[35] Elected to fill vacancy caused by resignation of Representative-elect Omar D. Conger, in preceding Congress, and took his seat December 5, 1881.

[36] Resigned March 4, 1881, to become Secretary of the Treasury.

[37] Appointed to fill vacancy caused by resignation of William Windom, and took his seat March 17, 1881.

[38] Elected to fill vacancy caused by his own resignation, and took his seat December 5, 1881.

[39] Election unsuccessfully contested by George M. Buchanan.

[40] Served until April 29, 1882; succeeded by John R. Lynch, who contested his election.

[41] Successfully contested the election of James R. Chalmers, and took his seat April 29, 1882.

[42] Died April 8, 1882.

[43] Elected to fill vacancy caused by death of Thomas Allen, and took his seat December 15, 1882.

[44] Served until March 2, 1883; succeeded by Gustavus Sessinghaus, who contested his election.

[45] Successfully contested the election of Richard G. Frost, and took his seat March 2, 1883.

[46] Thomas J. Majors presented credentials as a contingent (or additional) Representative, but was not permitted to take a seat.

[47] Elected to fill vacancy caused by death of Representative-elect Evarts W. Farr, in preceding Congress.

[48] Resigned May 16, 1881.

[49] Elected to fill vacancy caused by resignation of Roscoe Conkling, and took his seat October 11, 1881.

[50] Resigned May 16, 1881.

[51] Elected to fill vacancy caused by resignation of Thomas C. Platt, and took his seat October 11, 1881.

[52] Elected to fill vacancy caused by death of Representative-elect Fernando Wood, in the preceding Congress, and took his seat December 5, 1881.

[53] Resigned, effective March 21, 1881, before Congress assembled, having been appointed minister to France.

[54] Elected to fill vacancy caused by the resignation of Levi P. Morton, and took his seat December 5, 1881.

[55] Resigned July 26, 1881, having been elected Senator.

[56] Elected to fill vacancy caused by resignation of Warner Miller, and took his seat December 5, 1881.

[57] Resigned July 29, 1881, having been elected Senator.

[58] Elected to fill vacancy caused by resignation of Elbridge G. Lapham, and took his seat December 5, 1881.

## NORTH CAROLINA

### SENATORS

Matt W. Ransom, *Weldon*
Zebulon B. Vance, *Charlotte*

### REPRESENTATIVES

Louis C. Latham, *Greenville*
Orlando Hubbs, *New Bern*
John W. Shackelford,[59] *Jacksonville*
William R. Cox, *Raleigh*
Alfred M. Scales, *Greensboro*
Clement Dowd, *Charlotte*
Robert F. Armfield, *Statesville*
Robert B. Vance, *Asheville*

## OHIO

### SENATORS

George H. Pendleton, *Cincinnati*
John Sherman,[60] *Mansfield*

### REPRESENTATIVES

Benjamin Butterworth, *Cincinnati*
Thomas L. Young, *Cincinnati*
Henry L. Morey, *Hamilton*
Emanuel Shultz, *Dayton*
Benjamin Le Fevre, *Sidney*
James M. Ritchie, *Toledo*
John P. Leedom, *West Union*
J. Warren Keifer, *Springfield*
James S. Robinson, *Kenton*
John B. Rice, *Fremont*
Henry S. Neal, *Ironton*
George L. Converse, *Columbus*
Gibson Atherton, *Newark*
George W. Geddes, *Mansfield*
Rufus R. Dawes, *Marietta*
Jonathan T. Updegraff,[61] *Mount Pleasant*
Joseph D. Taylor,[62] *Cambridge*
William McKinley, Jr., *Canton*
Addison S. McClure, *Wooster*
Ezra B. Taylor, *Warren*
Amos Townsend, *Cleveland*

## OREGON

### SENATORS

La Fayette Grover, *Salem*
James H. Slater, *La Grande*

### REPRESENTATIVE AT LARGE

Melvin C. George, *Portland*

## PENNSYLVANIA

### SENATORS

J. Donald Cameron, *Harrisburg*
John I. Mitchell, *Wellsboro*

### REPRESENTATIVES

Henry H. Bingham, *Philadelphia*
Charles O'Neill, *Philadelphia*
Samuel J. Randall, *Philadelphia*
William D. Kelley, *Philadelphia*
Alfred C. Harmer, *Philadelphia*
William Ward, *Chester*
William Godshalk, *New Britain*
Daniel Ermentrout, *Reading*
A. Herr Smith, *Lancaster*
William Mutchler, *Easton*
Robert Klotz, *Mauch Chunk*
Joseph A. Scranton, *Scranton*
Charles N. Brumm, *Minersville*
Samuel F. Barr, *Harrisburg*
Cornelius C. Jadwin, *Honesdale*
Robert J. C. Walker, *Williamsport*
Jacob M. Campbell, *Johnstown*
Horatio G. Fisher, *Huntingdon*
Frank E. Beltzhoover, *Carlisle*
Andrew G. Curtin, *Bellefonte*
Morgan R. Wise, *Waynesburg*
Russell Errett, *Pittsburgh*
Thomas M. Bayne, *Allegheny*
William S. Shallenberger, *Rochester*
James Mosgrove, *Kittanning*
Samuel H. Miller, *Mercer*
Lewis F. Watson, *Warren*

## RHODE ISLAND

### SENATORS

Henry B. Anthony, *Providence*
Ambrose E. Burnside,[63] *Providence*
Nelson W. Aldrich,[64] *Providence*

### REPRESENTATIVES

Nelson W. Aldrich,[65] *Providence*
Henry J. Spooner,[66] *Providence*
Jonathan Chace, *Providence*

## SOUTH CAROLINA

### SENATORS

Matthew C. Butler, *Edgefield*
Wade Hampton, *Columbia*

### REPRESENTATIVES

John S. Richardson, *Sumter*
Michael P. O'Connor,[67] *Charleston*
Samuel Dibble,[68] *Orangeburg*
Edmund W. M. Mackey,[69] *Charleston*
D. Wyatt Aiken, *Cokesbury*
John H. Evins, *Spartanburg*
George D. Tillman,[70] *Edgefield*
Robert Smalls,[71] *Beaufort*

## TENNESSEE

### SENATORS

Isham G. Harris, *Memphis*
Howell E. Jackson, *Jackson*

### REPRESENTATIVES

Augustus H. Pettibone, *Greeneville*
Leonidas C. Houk, *Knoxville*
George G. Dibrell, *Sparta*
Benton McMillin, *Carthage*
Richard Warner, *Lewisburg*
John F. House, *Clarksville*
Washington C. Whitthorne, *Columbia*
John D. C. Atkins, *Paris*
Charles B. Simonton, *Covington*
William R. Moore, *Memphis*

## TEXAS

### SENATORS

Samuel B. Maxey, *Paris*
Richard Coke, *Waco*

### REPRESENTATIVES

John H. Reagan, *Palestine*
David B. Culberson, *Jefferson*
Olin Wellborn, *Dallas*
Roger Q. Mills, *Corsicana*
George W. Jones, *Bastrop*
Christopher C. Upson, *San Antonio*

## VERMONT

### SENATORS

George F. Edmunds, *Burlington*
Justin S. Morrill, *Strafford*

### REPRESENTATIVES

Charles H. Joyce, *Rutland*
James M. Tyler, *Brattleboro*
William W. Grout, *Barton*

## VIRGINIA

### SENATORS

John W. Johnston, *Abingdon*
William Mahone, *Petersburg*

### REPRESENTATIVES

George T. Garrison, *Accomac*
John F. Dezendorf, *Norfolk*
George D. Wise, *Richmond*
Joseph Jorgensen, *Petersburg*

---

[59] Died January 18, 1883.
[60] Elected for the term beginning March 4, 1881. James A. Garfield was elected but declined December 23, 1880, having been elected President of the United States.
[61] Died November 30, 1882, before the commencement of the Forty-eighth Congress, to which he had been reelected.
[62] Elected to fill vacancy caused by the death of Jonathan T. Updegraff, and took his seat January 16, 1883.
[63] Died September 13, 1881.

[64] Elected to fill vacancy caused by death of Ambrose E. Burnside, and took his seat October 11, 1881.
[65] Resigned October 4, 1881, having been elected Senator.
[66] Elected to fill vacancy caused by resignation of Nelson W. Aldrich, and took his seat December 5, 1881.
[67] Died April 26, 1881, while a contest of his election was pending, instituted by Edmund W. M. Mackey.
[68] Elected to fill vacancy caused by death of

Michael P. O'Connor; took his seat December 5, 1881, and served until May 31, 1882; succeeded by Edmund W. M. Mackey, who had previously contested the election of Mr. O'Connor and continued the contest against Mr. Dibble.
[69] Successfully contested the election of Samuel Dibble, as the successor of the original contestee, Mr. O'Connor, and took his seat May 31, 1882.
[70] Served until July 19, 1882; succeeded by Robert Smalls, who contested his election.
[71] Successfully contested the election of George D. Tillman, and took his seat July 19, 1882.

George C. Cabell,[72] *Danville*
John R. Tucker, *Lexington*
John Paul, *Harrisonburg*
John S. Barbour,[73] *Alexandria*
Abram Fulkerson, *Bristol*

## WEST VIRGINIA

### SENATORS
Henry Gassaway Davis, *Piedmont*
Johnson N. Camden, *Parkersburg*
### REPRESENTATIVES
Benjamin Wilson, *Clarksburg*
John B. Hoge, *Martinsburg*
John E. Kenna,[74] *Kanawha*

## WISCONSIN

### SENATORS
Angus Cameron,[75] *La Crosse*
Philetus Sawyer, *Oshkosh*
### REPRESENTATIVES
Charles G. Williams, *Janesville*
Lucien B. Caswell, *Fort Atkinson*

George C. Hazelton, *Boscobel*
Peter V. Deuster, *Milwaukee*
Edward S. Bragg, *Fond du Lac*
Richard W. Guenther, *Oshkosh*
Herman L. Humphrey, *Hudson*
Thaddeus C. Pound, *Chippewa Falls*

## TERRITORY OF ARIZONA

### DELEGATE
Granville H. Oury, *Florence*

## TERRITORY OF DAKOTA

### DELEGATE
Richard F. Pettigrew, *Sioux Falls*

## TERRITORY OF IDAHO

### DELEGATE
George Ainslie, *Idaho City*

## TERRITORY OF MONTANA

### DELEGATE
Martin Maginnis, *Helena*

## TERRITORY OF NEW MEXICO

### DELEGATE
Tranquilino Luna, *Los Lunas*

## TERRITORY OF UTAH

### DELEGATE
John T. Caine,[76] *Salt Lake City*

## TERRITORY OF WASHINGTON

### DELEGATE
Thomas H. Brents, *Walla Walla*

## TERRITORY OF WYOMING

### DELEGATE
Morton E. Post, *Cheyenne*

---

[72] Election unsuccessfully contested by John T. Stovell.

[73] Election unsuccessfully contested by S. P. Bayley.

[74] Reelected to the Forty-eighth Congress, but resigned effective March 4, 1883, having been elected Senator.

[75] Elected to fill vacancy caused by death of

Matthew H. Carpenter, in preceding Congress, and took his seat March 14, 1881.

[76] Allen G. Campbell and George Q. Cannon were contestants for this seat; by resolution of April 20, 1882, it was declared that neither was entitled to qualify and seat was declared vacant; on December 4, 1882, Mr. Caine submitted a petition stating that on November 7, 1882, at the election for Delegate to the

Forty-eighth Congress, he received 15,490 votes to fill the vacancy in the Forty-seventh Congress, no nomination having been made; the petition was referred to the Committee on Elections, and on January 17, 1883, a resolution was reported and adopted to the effect that he was entitled to the seat; took his seat the same day.

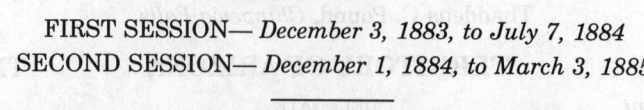

# 48TH CONGRESS

## MARCH 4, 1883, TO MARCH 3, 1885

FIRST SESSION— *December 3, 1883, to July 7, 1884*
SECOND SESSION— *December 1, 1884, to March 3, 1885*

---

VICE PRESIDENT OF THE UNITED STATES[1]
PRESIDENT PRO TEMPORE OF THE SENATE— GEORGE F. EDMUNDS,[2] of Vermont
SECRETARY OF THE SENATE— FRANCIS E. SHOBER (Chief Clerk), of North Carolina;
ANSON G. McCOOK,[3] of New York
SERGEANT AT ARMS OF THE SENATE— RICHARD J. BRIGHT, of Indiana; WILLIAM P.
CANADAY,[4] of North Carolina

SPEAKER OF THE HOUSE OF REPRESENTATIVES— JOHN G. CARLISLE,[5] of Kentucky
CLERK OF THE HOUSE— EDWARD McPHERSON, of Pennsylvania; JOHN B. CLARK, JR.,[6] of Missouri
SERGEANT AT ARMS OF THE HOUSE— GEORGE W. HOOKER, of Vermont; JOHN P. LEEDOM,[7] of Ohio
DOORKEEPER OF THE HOUSE— JAMES W. WINTERSMITH, of Texas
POSTMASTER OF THE HOUSE— LYCURGUS DALTON

George F. Edmunds
President Pro Tempore

John G. Carlisle
Speaker

## ALABAMA

### SENATORS

John T. Morgan, *Selma*
James L. Pugh, *Eufaula*

### REPRESENTATIVES

Thomas H. Herndon,[8] *Mobile*
James T. Jones,[9] *Demopolis*
Hilary A. Herbert, *Montgomery*
William C. Oates, *Abbeville*
Charles M. Shelley,[10] *Selma*
George H. Craig,[11] *Selma*
Thomas Williams, *Wetumpka*
Goldsmith W. Hewitt, *Birmingham*
William H. Forney, *Jacksonville*
Luke Pryor, *Athens*

## ARKANSAS

### SENATORS

Augustus H. Garland, *Little Rock*
James D. Walker, *Fayetteville*

### REPRESENTATIVE AT LARGE

Clifton R. Breckinridge, *Pine Bluff*

### REPRESENTATIVES

Poindexter Dunn, *Forest City*
James K. Jones,[12] *Washington*
John H. Rogers, *Fort Smith*
Samuel W. Peel, *Bentonville*

## CALIFORNIA

### SENATORS

James T. Farley, *Jackson*
John F. Miller, *San Francisco*

### REPRESENTATIVES AT LARGE

Charles A. Sumner, *San Francisco*
John R. Glascock, *Oakland*

### REPRESENTATIVES

William S. Rosecrans, *San Francisco*
James H. Budd, *Stocken*
Barclay Henley, *Santa Rosa*
Pleasant B. Tulley, *Gilroy*

## COLORADO

### SENATORS

Nathaniel P. Hill, *Denver*
Thomas M. Bowen, *Del Norte*

### REPRESENTATIVE AT LARGE

James B. Belford, *Central City*

## CONNECTICUT

### SENATORS

Orville H. Platt, *West Meriden*
Joseph R. Hawley, *Hartford*

### REPRESENTATIVES

William W. Eaton, *Hartford*
Charles L. Mitchell, *New Haven*
John T. Wait, *Norwich*
Edward W. Seymour, *Litchfield*

## DELAWARE

### SENATORS

Thomas F. Bayard, *Wilmington*
Eli Saulsbury, *Dover*

### REPRESENTATIVE AT LARGE

Charles B. Lore, *Wilmington*

## FLORIDA

### SENATORS

Charles W. Jones, *Pensacola*
Wilkinson Call, *Jacksonville*

### REPRESENTATIVES

Robert H. M. Davidson, *Quincy*
Horatio Bisbee, Jr., *Jacksonville*

## GEORGIA

### SENATORS

Joseph E. Brown, *Atlanta*
Alfred H. Colquitt, *Atlanta*

### REPRESENTATIVE AT LARGE

Thomas Hardeman, *Macon*

### REPRESENTATIVES

John C. Nicholls, *Blackshear*
Henry G. Turner, *Quitman*
Charles F. Crisp, *Americus*
Hugh Buchanan, *Newnan*
Nathaniel J. Hammond, *Atlanta*
James H. Blount, *Macon*
Judson C. Clements, *La Fayette*
Seaborn Reese, *Sparta*
Allen D. Candler, *Gainesville*

---

[1] Chester A. Arthur became President on the death of James A. Garfield in preceding Congress.
[2] Reelected January 14, 1884.
[3] Elected December 18, 1883.
[4] Elected December 18, 1883.
[5] Elected December 3, 1883.
[6] Elected December 4, 1883.

[7] Elected December 4, 1883.
[8] Died March 28, 1883, before Congress assembled.
[9] Elected to fill vacancy caused by death of Thomas H. Herndon, and took his seat December 3, 1883.
[10] Served until January 9, 1885; succeeded by

George H. Craig, who contested his election.
[11] Successfully contested the election of Charles M. Shelley, and took his seat January 9, 1885.
[12] Reelected to the Forty-ninth Congress, but tendered his resignation February 19, 1885, having been elected Senator.

## ILLINOIS

### SENATORS

John A. Logan, *Chicago*
Shelby M. Cullom, *Springfield*

### REPRESENTATIVES

Ransom W. Dunham, *Chicago*
John F. Finerty, *Chicago*
George R. Davis, *Chicago*
George E. Adams, *Chicago*
Reuben Ellwood, *Sycamore*
Robert R. Hitt, *Mount Morris*
Thomas J. Henderson, *Princeton*
William Cullen, *Ottawa*
Lewis E. Payson, *Pontiac*
Nicholas E. Worthington, *Peoria*
William H. Neece, *Macomb*
James M. Riggs, *Winchester*
William M. Springer, *Springfield*
Jonthan H. Rowell, *Bloomington*
Joseph G. Cannon, *Danville*
Aaron Shaw, *Olney*
Samuel W. Moulton, *Shelbyville*
William R. Morrison, *Waterloo*
Richard W. Townshend, *Shawneetown*
John R. Thomas, *Metropolis*

## INDIANA

### SENATORS

Daniel W. Voorhees, *Terre Haute*
Benjamin Harrison, *Indianapolis*

### REPRESENTATIVES

John J. Kleiner, *Evansville*
Thomas R. Cobb, *Vincennes*
Strother M. Stockslager, *Corydon*
William S. Holman, *Aurora*
Courtland C. Matson, *Greencastle*
Thomas M. Browne, *Winchester*
Stanton J. Peelle,[13] *Indianapolis*
William E. English,[14] *Indianapolis*
John E. Lamb, *Terre Haute*
Thomas B. Ward, *Lafayette*
Thomas J. Wood, *Crown Point*
George W. Steele, *Marion*
Robert Lowry, *Fort Wayne*
William H. Calkins,[15] *Laporte*
Benjamin F. Shively,[16] *South Bend*

## IOWA

### SENATORS

William B. Allison, *Dubuque*
James F. Wilson, *Fairfield*

### REPRESENTATIVES

Moses A. McCoid, *Fairfield*
Jeremiah H. Murphy, *Davenport*
David B. Henderson, *Dubuque*
Luman H. Weller, *Nashua*
James Wilson,[17] *Traer*
Benjamin T. Frederick,[18]
    *Marshalltown*
Marsena E. Cutts,[19] *Oskaloosa*
John C. Cook,[20] *Newton*
John A. Kasson,[21] *Des Moines*
Hiram Y. Smith,[22] *Des Moines*
William P. Hepburn, *Clarinda*
William H. M. Pusey, *Council Bluffs*
Adoniram J. Holmes, *Boone*
Isaac S. Struble, *Le Mars*

## KANSAS

### SENATORS

John J. Ingalls, *Atchison*
Preston B. Plumb, *Emporia*

### REPRESENTATIVES AT LARGE

Edmund N. Morrill, *Hiawatha*
Lewis Hanback, *Osborne*
Samuel R. Peters,[23] *Newton*
Bishop W. Perkins, *Oswego*

### REPRESENTATIVES

John A. Anderson, *Manhattan*
Dudley C. Haskell,[24] *Lawrence*
Edward H. Funston,[25] *Iola*
Thomas Ryan, *Topeka*

## KENTUCKY

### SENATORS

James B. Beck, *Lexington*
John S. Williams, *Mount Sterling*

### REPRESENTATIVES

Oscar Turner, *Oscar*
James F. Clay, *Henderson*
John E. Halsell, *Bowling Green*
Thomas A. Robertson, *Elizabethtown*
Albert S. Willis, *Louisville*
John G. Carlisle, *Covington*
Joseph C. S. Blackburn, *Versailles*
Philip B. Thompson, Jr., *Harrodsburg*
William W. Culbertson, *Ashland*
John D. White, *Manchester*
Frank L. Wolford, *Columbia*

## LOUISIANA

### SENATORS

Benjamin F. Jonas, *New Orleans*
Randall L. Gibson, *New Orleans*

### REPRESENTATIVES

Carleton Hunt, *New Orleans*
E. John Ellis, *New Orleans*
William Pitt Kellogg, *New Orleans*
Newton C. Blanchard, *Shreveport*
J. Floyd King, *Vidalia*
Edward T. Lewis,[26] *Opelousas*

## MAINE

### SENATORS

Eugene Hale, *Ellsworth*
William P. Frye, *Lewiston*

### REPRESENTATIVES AT LARGE

Thomas B. Reed, *Portland*
Nelson Dingley, Jr., *Lewiston*
Charles A. Boutelle, *Bangor*
Seth L. Milliken, *Belfast*

## MARYLAND

### SENATORS

James B. Groome, *Elkton*
Arthur Pue Gorman, *Laurel*

### REPRESENTATIVES

George W. Covington, *Snow Hill*
J. Fred. C. Talbott, *Towsontown*
Fetter S. Hoblitzell, *Baltimore*
John V. L. Findlay, *Baltimore*
Hart B. Holton, *Powhatan*
Louis E. McComas, *Hagerstown*

## MASSACHUSETTS

### SENATORS

Henry L. Dawes, *Pittsfield*
George F. Hoar, *Worcester*

### REPRESENTATIVES

Robert T. Davis, *Fall River*
John D. Long, *Hingham*
Ambrose A. Ranney, *Boston*
Patrick A. Collins, *Boston*
Leopold Morse, *Boston*
Henry B. Lovering, *Lynn*
Eben F. Stone, *Newburyport*
William A. Russell, *Lawrence*
Theodore Lyman, *Brookline*
William W. Rice, *Worcester*
William Whiting, *Holyoke*
George D. Robinson,[27] *Chicopee*
Francis W. Rockwell,[28] *Pittsfield*

---

[13] Served until May 22, 1884; succeeded by William E. English, who contested his election.

[14] Successfully contested the election of Stanton J. Peelle, and took his seat May 22, 1884.

[15] Resigned October 20, 1884.

[16] Elected to fill vacancy caused by resignation of William H. Calkins, and took his seat December 1, 1884.

[17] Served until March 3, 1885 (closing day of the Congress); succeeded by Benjamin T. Frederick, who contested his election.

[18] Successfully contested the election of James

Wilson, and took his seat March 3, 1885.

[19] Died August 31, 1883, before Congress assembled.

[20] Elected to fill vacancy caused by death of Marsena E. Cutts, and took his seat December 3, 1883.

[21] Resigned July 13, 1884.

[22] Elected to fill vacancy caused by resignation of John A. Kasson, and took his seat December 2, 1884.

[23] Election unsuccessfully contested by Samuel N. Wood.

[24] Died December 16, 1883.

[25] Elected to fill vacancy caused by death of Dudley C. Haskell, and took his seat March 21, 1884.

[26] Elected to fill vacancy caused by death of Representative-elect Andrew S. Herron (November 27, 1882, before the beginning of the congressional term), and took his seat December 3, 1883.

[27] Resigned January 7, 1884.

[28] Elected to fill vacancy caused by resignation of George D. Robinson, and took his seat January 26, 1884.

## MICHIGAN

SENATORS

Omar D. Conger, *Port Huron*
Thomas W. Palmer, *Detroit*

REPRESENTATIVES

William C. Maybury, *Detroit*
Nathaniel B. Eldredge, *Adrian*
Edward S. Lacey, *Charlotte*
George L. Yaple, *Mendon*
Julius Houseman, *Grand Rapids*
Edwin B. Winans, *Hamburg*
Ezra C. Carleton, *Port Huron*
Roswell G. Horr, *East Saginaw*
Byron M. Cutcheon, *Manistee*
Herschel H. Hatch, *Bay City*
Edward Breitung, *Negaunee*

## MINNESOTA

SENATORS

Samuel J. R. McMillan, *St. Paul*
Dwight M. Sabin, *Stillwater*

REPRESENTATIVES

Milo White, *Chatfield*
James B. Wakefield, *Blue Earth City*
Horace B. Strait, *Shakopee*
William D. Washburn, *Minneapolis*
Knute Nelson, *Alexandria*

## MISSISSIPPI

SENATORS

Lucius Q. C. Lamar, *Oxford*
James Z. George, *Jackson*

REPRESENTATIVES

Henry L. Muldrow, *Starkville*
James R. Chalmers,[29] *Sardis*
Elza Jeffords, *Mayersville*
Hernando D. Money, *Winona*
Otho R. Singleton, *Forest*
Henry S. Van Eaton, *Woodville*
Ethelbert Barksdale, *Jackson*

## MISSOURI

SENATORS

Francis M. Cockrell, *Warrensburg*
George G. Vest, *Kansas City*

REPRESENTATIVES

William H. Hatch, *Hannibal*
Armstead M. Alexander, *Paris*

Alexander M. Dockery, *Gallatin*
James N. Burnes, *St. Joseph*
Alexander Graves, *Lexington*
John Cosgrove, *Boonville*
Aylett H. Buckner, *Mexico*
John J. O'Neill, *St. Louis*
James O. Broadhead, *St. Louis*
Martin L. Clardy, *Farmington*
Richard P. Bland, *Lebanon*
Charles H. Morgan, *Lamar*
Robert W. Fyan, *Marshfield*
Lowndes H. Davis, *Jackson*

## NEBRASKA

SENATORS

Charles H. Van Wyck, *Nebraska City*
Charles F. Manderson, *Omaha*

REPRESENTATIVES

Archibald J. Weaver, *Falls City*
James Laird, *Hastings*
Edward K. Valentine, *West Point*

## NEVADA

SENATORS

John P. Jones, *Gold Hill*
James G. Fair, *Virginia City*

REPRESENTATIVE AT LARGE

George W. Cassidy, *Eureka*

## NEW HAMPSHIRE

SENATORS

Henry W. Blair, *Manchester*
Austin F. Pike, *Franklin*

REPRESENTATIVES

Martin A. Haynes, *Lake Village*
Ossian Ray, *Lancaster*

## NEW JERSEY

SENATORS

John R. McPherson, *Jersey City*
William J. Sewell, *Camden*

REPRESENTATIVES

Thomas M. Ferrell, *Glassboro*
J. Hart Brewer, *Trenton*
John Kean, *Elizabeth*
Benjamin F. Howey, *Columbia*
William W. Phelps, *Englewood*
William H. F. Fiedler, *Newark*
William McAdoo, *Jersey City*

## NEW YORK

SENATORS

Warner Miller, *Herkimer*
Elbridge G. Lapham, *Canandaigua*

REPRESENTATIVE AT LARGE

Henry W. Slocum, *Brooklyn*

REPRESENTATIVES

Perry Belmont, *Babylon*
William E. Robinson, *Brooklyn*
Darwin R. James, *Brooklyn*
Felix Campbell, *Brooklyn*
Nicholas Muller, *New York City*
Samuel S. Cox, *New York City*
William Dorsheimer, *New York City*
John J. Adams, *New York City*
John Hardy, *New York City*
Abram S. Hewitt, *New York City*
Orlando B. Potter, *New York City*
Waldo Hutchins, *Kingsbridge*
John H. Ketcham, *Dover Plains*
Lewis Beach, *Cornwall*
John H. Bagley, Jr., *Catskill*
Thomas J. Van Alstyne, *Albany*
Henry G. Burleigh, *Whitehall*
Frederick A. Johnson, *Glens Falls*
Abraham X. Parker, *Potsdam*
Edward Wemple, *Fultonville*
George W. Ray, *Chenango*
Charles R. Skinner, *Watertown*
John T. Spriggs, *Utica*
Newton W. Nutting, *Oswego*
Frank Hiscock, *Syracuse*
Sereno E. Payne, *Auburn*
James W. Wadsworth, *Geneseo*
Stephen C. Millard, *Binghamton*
John Arnot, Jr., *Elmira*
Halbert S. Greenleaf, *Rochester*
Robert S. Stevens, *Attica*
William F. Rogers, *Buffalo*
Francis B. Brewer, *Westfield*

## NORTH CAROLINA

SENATORS

Matt W. Ransom, *Weldon*
Zebulon B. Vance, *Charlotte*

REPRESENTATIVE AT LARGE

Risden T. Bennett, *Wadesboro*

REPRESENTATIVES

Walter F. Pool,[30] *Elizabeth*
Thomas G. Skinner,[31] *Hertford*
James E. O'Hara, *Enfield*
Wharton J. Green, *Fayetteville*
William R. Cox, *Raleigh*
Alfred M. Scales,[32] *Greensboro*
James W. Reid,[33] *Wentworth*
Clement Dowd, *Charlotte*
Tyre York, *Trap Hill*
Robert B. Vance, *Asheville*

---

[29] Credentials of election regularly issued to Vannoy H. Manning were not filed with Clerk of the House, but were presented on December 3, 1883, and referred, with papers of contest by James R. Chalmers, to the Committee on Elections for report as to the prima facie right of one of the contestants; the committee was discharged from further consideration of

the question of prima facie right on February 15, 1884, and on June 20, 1884, reported a resolution declaring Chalmers duly elected, which was adopted by the House June 25, 1884; took his seat the same day.

[30] Died August 25, 1883, before Congress assembled.

[31] Elected to fill vacancy caused by death of Walter

F. Pool, and took his seat December 19, 1883.

[32] Resigned December 30, 1884, to become Governor.

[33] Elected to fill vacancy caused by resignation of Alfred M. Scales, and took his seat January 28, 1885.

## OHIO

### SENATORS

George H. Pendleton, *Cincinnati*
John Sherman, *Mansfield*

### REPRESENTATIVES

John F. Follett, *Cincinnati*
Isaac M. Jordan, *Cincinnati*
Robert M. Murray, *Piqua*
Benjamin Le Fevre, *Maplewood*
George E. Seney, *Tiffin*
William D. Hill, *Defiance*
Henry L. Morey,[34] *Hamilton*
James E. Campbell,[35] *Hamilton*
J. Warren Keifer, *Springfield*
James S. Robinson,[36] *Kenton*
Frank H. Hurd, *Toledo*
John W. McCormick, *Gallipolis*
Alphonso Hart, *Hillsboro*
George L. Converse, *Columbus*
George W. Geddes, *Mansfield*
Adoniram J. Warner, *Marietta*
Beriah Wilkins, *Urichsville*
Joseph D. Taylor,[37] *Cambridge*
William McKinley, Jr.,[38] *Canton*
Jonathan H. Wallace,[39] *New Lisbon*
Ezra B. Taylor, *Warren*
David R. Paige, *Akron*
Martin A. Foran, *Cleveland*

## OREGON

### SENATORS

James H. Slater, *La Grande*
Joseph N. Dolph, *Portland*

### REPRESENTATIVE AT LARGE

Melvin C. George, *Portland*

## PENNSYLVANIA

### SENATORS

J. Donald Cameron, *Harrisburg*
John I. Mitchell, *Wellsboro*

### REPRESENTATIVE AT LARGE

Mortimer F. Elliott, *Wellsboro*

### REPRESENTATIVES

Henry H. Bingham, *Philadelphia*
Charles O'Neill, *Philadelphia*
Samuel J. Randall, *Philadelphia*
William D. Kelley, *Philadelphia*
Alfred C. Harmer, *Philadelphia*
James B. Everhart, *West Chester*
I. Newton Evans, *Hatboro*
Daniel Ermentrout, *Reading*
A. Herr Smith, *Lancaster*

William Mutchler, *Easton*
John B. Storm, *Stroudsburg*
Daniel W. Connolly, *Scranton*
Charles N. Brumm, *Minersville*
Samuel F. Barr, *Harrisburg*
George A. Post, *Susquehanna*
William W. Brown, *Bradford*
Jacob M. Campbell, *Johnstown*
Louis E. Atkinson, *Mifflintown*
William A. Duncan,[40] *Gettysburg*
John A. Swope,[41] *Gettysburg*
Andrew G. Curtin, *Bellefonte*
Charles E. Boyle, *Uniontown*
James H. Hopkins, *Pittsburgh*
Thomas M. Bayne, *Allegheny*
George V. Lawrence, *Monongahela*
John D. Patton, *Indiana*
Samuel H. Miller, *Mercer*
Samuel M. Brainerd, *Erie*

## RHODE ISLAND

### SENATORS

Henry B. Anthony,[42] *Providence*
William P. Sheffield,[43] *Newport*
Jonathan Chace,[44] *Providence*
Nelson W. Aldrich, *Providence*

### REPRESENTATIVES

Henry J. Spooner, *Providence*
Jonathan Chace,[45] *Providence*
Nathan F. Dixon,[46] *Westerly*

## SOUTH CAROLINA

### SENATORS

Matthew C. Butler, *Edgefield*
Wade Hampton, *Columbia*

### REPRESENTATIVES

Samuel Dibble, *Orangeburg*
George D. Tillman, *Clarks Hill*
D. Wyatt Aiken, *Cokesbury*
John H. Evins,[47] *Spartanburg*
John Bratton,[48] *White Oak*
John J. Hemphill, *Chester*
George W. Dargan, *Darlington*
Edmund W. M. Mackey,[49] *Berkeley*
Robert Smalls,[50] *Beaufort*

## TENNESSEE

### SENATORS

Isham G. Harris, *Memphis*
Howell E. Jackson, *Nashville*

### REPRESENTATIVES

Augustus H. Pettibone, *Greeneville*
Leonidas C. Houk, *Knoxville*

George G. Dibrell, *Sparta*
Benton McMillin, *Carthage*
Richard Warner, *Lewisburg*
Andrew J. Caldwell, *Nashville*
John G. Ballentine, *Pulaski*
John M. Taylor, *Lexington*
Rice A. Pierce, *Union City*
H. Casey Young, *Memphis*

## TEXAS

### SENATORS

Samuel B. Maxey, *Paris*
Richard Coke, *Waco*

### REPRESENTATIVES

Charles Stewart, *Houston*
John H. Reagan, *Palestine*
James H. Jones, *Henderson*
David B. Culberson, *Jefferson*
James W. Throckmorton, *McKinney*
Olin Wellborn, *Dallas*
Thomas P. Ochiltree, *Galveston*
James F. Miller, *Gonzales*
Roger Q. Mills, *Corsicana*
John Hancock, *Austin*
Samuel W. T. Lanham, *Weatherford*

## VERMONT

### SENATORS

George F. Edmunds, *Burlington*
Justin S. Morrill, *Strafford*

### REPRESENTATIVES

John W. Stewart, *Middlebury*
Luke P. Poland, *St. Johnsbury*

## VIRGINIA

### SENATORS

William Mahone, *Petersburg*
Harrison H. Riddleberger, *Woodstock*

### REPRESENTATIVE AT LARGE

John S. Wise, *Richmond*

### REPRESENTATIVES

Robert M. Mayo,[51] *Hague*
George T. Garrison,[52] *Accomac*
Harry Libbey, *Old Point Comfort*
George D. Wise, *Richmond*
Benjamin S. Hooper, *Farmville*
George C. Cabell, *Danville*
John R. Tucker, *Lexington*
John Paul,[53] *Harrisonburg*
Charles T. O'Ferrall,[54] *Harrisonburg*
John S. Barbour, *Alexandria*
Henry Bowen, *Tazewell*

---

[34] Served until June 20, 1884; succeeded by James E. Campbell, who contested his election.
[35] Successfully contested the election of Henry L. Morey, and took his seat June 20, 1884.
[36] Resigned January 12, 1885.
[37] Elected to fill vacancy caused by death of Representative-elect Jonathan T. Updegraff, in preceding Congress.
[38] Served until May 27, 1884; succeeded by Jonathan H. Wallace, who contested his election.
[39] Successfully contested the election of William McKinley, Jr., and took his seat May 27, 1884.
[40] Died November 14, 1884, before the commencement of the Forty-ninth Congress, to which he had

been reelected.
[41] Elected to fill vacancy caused by death of William A. Duncan, and took his seat January 5, 1885.
[42] Died September 2, 1884.
[43] Appointed to fill vacancy caused by death of Henry B. Anthony; took his seat December 2, 1884.
[44] Elected to fill vacancy caused by death of Henry B. Anthony, and took his seat January 26, 1885.
[45] Resigned January 26, 1885, having been elected Senator.
[46] Elected to fill vacancy caused by resignation of Jonathan Chace, and took his seat February 12, 1885.
[47] Died October 20, 1884.
[48] Elected to fill vacancy caused by death of John

H. Evins, and took his seat December 8, 1884.
[49] Died January 27, 1884.
[50] Elected to fill vacancy caused by death of Edmund W. M. Mackey, and took his seat March 31, 1884.
[51] Served until March 20, 1884; succeeded by George T. Garrison, who contested his election.
[52] Successfully contested the election of Robert M. Mayo, and took his seat March 20, 1884.
[53] Resigned September 5, 1883, before Congress assembled; succeeded by Charles T. O'Ferrall, who contested his election.
[54] Successfully contested the election of John Paul, and took his seat May 5, 1884.

## WEST VIRGINIA

### SENATORS

Johnson N. Camden, *Parkersburg*
John E. Kenna, *Kanawha*

### REPRESENTATIVES

Nathan Goff, Jr., *Clarksburg*
William L. Wilson, *Charles Town*
Charles P. Snyder,[55] *Charleston*
Eustace Gibson, *Huntington*

## WISCONSIN

### SENATORS

Angus Cameron, *La Crosse*
Philetus Sawyer, *Oshkosh*

### REPRESENTATIVES

John Winans, *Janesville*
Daniel H. Sumner, *Waukesha*
Burr W. Jones, *Madison*
Peter V. Deuster, *Milwaukee*
Joseph Rankin, *Manitowoc*
Richard W. Guenther, *Oshkosh*

Gilbert M. Woodward, *La Crosse*
William T. Price, *Black River Falls*
Isaac Stephenson, *Marinette*

## TERRITORY OF ARIZONA

### DELEGATE

Granville H. Oury, *Florence*

## TERRITORY OF DAKOTA

### DELEGATE

John B. Raymond, *Fargo*

## TERRITORY OF IDAHO

### DELEGATE

Theodore F. Singiser, *Boise City*

## TERRITORY OF MONTANA

### DELEGATE

Martin Maginnis,[56] *Helena*

## TERRITORY OF NEW MEXICO

### DELEGATE

Tranquilino Luna,[57] *Los Lunas*
Francisco A. Manzanares,[58] *Las Vegas*

## TERRITORY OF UTAH

### DELEGATE

John T. Caine, *Salt Lake City*

## TERRITORY OF WASHINGTON

### DELEGATE

Thomas H. Brents, *Walla Walla*

## TERRITORY OF WYOMING

### DELEGATE

Morton E. Post, *Cheyenne*

---

[55] Elected to fill vacancy caused by resignation of Representative-elect John E. Kenna, in preceding Congress, and took his seat December 3, 1883.

[56] Election unsuccessfully contested by A. C. Botkin.

[57] Served until March 5, 1884; succeeded by Francisco A. Manzanares, who contested his election.

[58] Successfully contested the election of Tranquilino Luna, and took his seat March 5, 1884.

# 49TH CONGRESS

## MARCH 4, 1885, TO MARCH 3, 1887

FIRST SESSION— *December 7, 1885, to August 5, 1886*
SECOND SESSION— *December 6, 1886, to March 3, 1887*
SPECIAL SESSION OF THE SENATE— *March 4, 1885, to April 2, 1885*

Thomas A. Hendricks
Vice President

VICE PRESIDENT OF THE UNITED STATES— THOMAS A. HENDRICKS,[1] of Indiana
PRESIDENT PRO TEMPORE OF THE SENATE— JOHN SHERMAN,[2] of Ohio; JOHN J. INGALLS,[3] of Kansas
SECRETARY OF THE SENATE— ANSON G. MCCOOK, of New York
SERGEANT AT ARMS OF THE SENATE— WILLIAM P. CANADAY, of North Carolina

John G. Carlisle
Speaker

SPEAKER OF THE HOUSE OF REPRESENTATIVES— JOHN G. CARLISLE,[4] of Kentucky
CLERK OF THE HOUSE— JOHN B. CLARK, JR.,[5] of Missouri
SERGEANT AT ARMS OF THE HOUSE— JOHN P. LEEDOM, of Ohio
DOORKEEPER OF THE HOUSE— SAMUEL DONALDSON, of Tennessee
POSTMASTER OF THE HOUSE— LYCURGUS DALTON

## ALABAMA

SENATORS

John T. Morgan, *Selma*
James L. Pugh, *Eufaula*

REPRESENTATIVES

James T. Jones, *Demopolis*
Hilary A. Herbert, *Montgomery*
William C. Oates, *Abbeville*
Alexander C. Davidson, *Uniontown*
Thomas W. Sadler, *Prattville*
John M. Martin, *Tuscaloosa*
William H. Forney, *Jacksonville*
Joseph Wheeler, *Wheeler*

## ARKANSAS

SENATORS

Augustus H. Garland,[6] *Little Rock*
James H. Berry,[7] *Bentonville*
James K. Jones, *Washington*

REPRESENTATIVES

Poindexter Dunn, *Forest City*
Clifton R. Breckinridge, *Pine Bluff*
Thomas C. McRae,[8] *Prescott*
John H. Rogers, *Fort Smith*
Samuel W. Peel, *Bentonville*

## CALIFORNIA

SENATORS

John F. Miller,[9] *San Francisco*
George Hearst,[10] *San Francisco*

Abram P. Williams,[11] *San Francisco*
Leland Stanford, *San Francisco*

REPRESENTATIVES

Barclay Henley, *Santa Rosa*
James A. Louttit, *Stockton*
Joseph McKenna, *Suisun*
William W. Morrow, *San Francisco*
Charles N. Felton, *San Francisco*
Henry H. Markham, *Pasadena*

## COLORADO

SENATORS

Thomas M. Bowen, *Del Norte*
Henry M. Teller, *Central City*

REPRESENTATIVE AT LARGE

George G. Symes, *Denver*

## CONNECTICUT

SENATORS

Orville H. Platt, *Meriden*
Joseph R. Hawley, *Hartford*

REPRESENTATIVES

John R. Buck, *Hartford*
Charles L. Mitchell, *New Haven*
John T. Wait, *Norwich*
Edward W. Seymour, *Litchfield*

## DELAWARE

SENATORS

Thomas F. Bayard,[12] *Wilmington*
George Gray,[13] *New Castle*
Eli Saulsbury, *Dover*

REPRESENTATIVE AT LARGE

Charles B. Lore, *Wilmington*

## FLORIDA

SENATORS

Charles W. Jones, *Pensacola*
Wilkinson Call, *Jacksonville*

REPRESENTATIVES

Robert H. M. Davidson, *Quincy*
Charles Dougherty, *Port Orange*

## GEORGIA

SENATORS

Joseph E. Brown, *Atlanta*
Alfred H. Colquitt, *Atlanta*

REPRESENTATIVES

Thomas M. Norwood, *Savannah*
Henry G. Turner, *Quitman*
Charles F. Crisp, *Americus*
Henry R. Harris, *Greenville*
Nathaniel J. Hammond, *Atlanta*
James H. Blount, *Macon*
Judson C. Clements, *La Fayette*
Seaborn Reese, *Sparta*
Allen D. Candler, *Gainesville*
George T. Barnes, *Augusta*

---

[1] Died November 25, 1885.
[2] Elected December 7, 1885; resigned, effective February 26, 1887.
[3] Elected February 25, 1887.
[4] Reelected December 7, 1885.
[5] Reelected December 7, 1885.
[6] Resigned March 6, 1885, having been appointed Attorney General.

[7] Elected to fill vacancy caused by resignation of Augustus H. Garland, and took his seat March 25, 1885.
[8] Elected to fill vacancy caused by resignation of Representative-elect James K. Jones, in preceding Congress, and took his seat December 7, 1885.
[9] Died March 8, 1886.
[10] Appointed to fill vacancy caused by death of

John F. Miller, and took his seat April 9, 1886.
[11] Elected to fill vacancy caused by death of John F. Miller, and took his seat December 6, 1886.
[12] Resigned March 6, 1885, having been appointed Secretary of State.
[13] Elected to fill vacancy caused by resignation of Thomas F. Bayard, and took his seat March 19, 1885.

## ILLINOIS

### SENATORS

John A. Logan,[14] *Chicago*
Charles B. Farwell,[15] *Chicago*
Shelby M. Cullom, *Springfield*

### REPRESENTATIVES

Ransom W. Dunham, *Chicago*
Frank Lawler, *Chicago*
James H. Ward, *Chicago*
George E. Adams, *Chicago*
Reuben Ellwood,[16] *Sycamore*
Albert J. Hopkins,[17] *Aurora*
Robert R. Hitt, *Mount Morris*
Thomas J. Henderson, *Princeton*
Ralph Plumb, *Streator*
Lewis E. Payson, *Pontiac*
Nicholas E. Worthington, *Peoria*
William H. Neece, *Macomb*
James M. Riggs, *Winchester*
William M. Springer, *Springfield*
Jonathan H. Rowell, *Bloomington*
Joseph G. Cannon, *Danville*
Silas Z. Landes, *Mount Carmel*
John R. Eden, *Sullivan*
William R. Morrison, *Waterloo*
Richard W. Townshend, *Shawneetown*
John R. Thomas, *Metropolis*

## INDIANA

### SENATORS

Daniel W. Voorhees, *Terre Haute*
Benjamin Harrison, *Indianapolis*

### REPRESENTATIVES

John J. Kleiner, *Evansville*
Thomas R. Cobb, *Vincennes*
Jonas G. Howard, *Jeffersonville*
William S. Holman, *Aurora*
Courtland C. Matson, *Greencastle*
Thomas M. Browne, *Winchester*
William D. Bynum, *Indianapolis*
James T. Johnston, *Rockville*
Thomas B. Ward, *Lafayette*
William D. Owen, *Logansport*
George W. Steele,[18] *Marion*
Robert Lowry, *Fort Wayne*
George Ford, *South Bend*

## IOWA

### SENATORS

William B. Allison, *Dubuque*
James F. Wilson, *Fairfield*

### REPRESENTATIVES

Benton J. Hall, *Burlington*
Jeremiah H. Murphy, *Davenport*
David B. Henderson, *Dubuque*
William E. Fuller, *West Union*
Benjamin T. Frederick, *Marshalltown*

James B. Weaver,[19] *Bloomfield*
Edwin H. Conger, *Des Moines*
William P. Hepburn, *Clarinda*
Joseph Lyman, *Council Bluffs*
Adoniram J. Holmes, *Boone*
Isaac S. Struble, *Le Mars*

## KANSAS

### SENATORS

John J. Ingalls, *Atchison*
Preston B. Plumb, *Emporia*

### REPRESENTATIVES

Edmund N. Morrill, *Hiawatha*
Edward H. Funston, *Iola*
Bishop W. Perkins, *Oswego*
Thomas Ryan, *Topeka*
John A. Anderson, *Manhattan*
Lewis Hanback, *Osborne*
Samuel R. Peters, *Newton*

## KENTUCKY

### SENATORS

James B. Beck, *Lexington*
Joseph C. S. Blackburn, *Versailles*

### REPRESENTATIVES

William J. Stone, *Kuttawa*
Polk Laffoon, *Madisonville*
John E. Halsell, *Bowling Green*
Thomas A. Robertson, *Elizabethtown*
Albert S. Willis, *Louisville*
John G. Carlisle, *Covington*
William C. P. Breckinridge, *Lexington*
James B. McCreary, *Richmond*
William H. Wadsworth, *Maysville*
William P. Taulbee, *Saylersville*
Frank L. Wolford, *Columbia*

## LOUISIANA

### SENATORS

Randall L. Gibson, *New Orleans*
James B. Eustis, *New Orleans*

### REPRESENTATIVES

Louis St. Martin, *New Orleans*
Michael Hahn,[20] *New Orleans*
Nathaniel D. Wallace,[21] *New Orleans*
Edward J. Gay, *Plaquemine*
Newton C. Blanchard, *Shreveport*
J. Floyd King, *Vidalia*
Alfred B. Irion, *Marksville*

## MAINE

### SENATORS

Eugene Hale, *Ellsworth*
William P. Frye, *Lewiston*

### REPRESENTATIVES

Thomas B. Reed, *Portland*
Nelson Dingley, Jr., *Lewiston*
Seth L. Milliken, *Belfast*
Charles A. Boutelle, *Bangor*

## MARYLAND

### SENATORS

Arthur Pue Gorman, *Laurel*
Ephraim K. Wilson, *Snow Hill*

### REPRESENTATIVES

Charles H. Gibson, *Easton*
Frank T. Shaw, *Westminster*
William H. Cole,[22] *Baltimore*
Harry W. Rusk,[23] *Baltimore*
John V. L. Findlay, *Baltimore*
Barnes Compton, *Laurel*
Louis E. McComas, *Hagerstown*

## MASSACHUSETTS

### SENATORS

Henry L. Dawes, *Pittsfield*
George F. Hoar, *Worcester*

### REPRESENTATIVES

Robert T. Davis, *Fall River*
John D. Long, *Hingham*
Ambrose A. Ranney, *Boston*
Patrick A. Collins, *Boston*
Edward D. Hayden, *Woburn*
Henry B. Lovering, *Lynn*
Eben F. Stone, *Newburyport*
Charles H. Allen, *Lowell*
Frederick D. Ely, *Dedham*
William W. Rice, *Worcester*
William Whiting, *Holyoke*
Francis W. Rockwell, *Pittsfield*

## MICHIGAN

### SENATORS

Omar D. Conger, *Port Huron*
Thomas W. Palmer, *Detroit*

### REPRESENTATIVES

William C. Maybury, *Detroit*
Nathaniel B. Eldredge, *Adrian*
James O'Donnell, *Jackson*
Julius C. Burrows, *Kalamazoo*
Charles C. Comstock, *Grand Rapids*
Edwin B. Winans, *Hamburg*
Ezra C. Carleton, *Port Huron*
Timothy E. Tarsney, *East Saginaw*
Byron M. Cutcheon, *Manistee*
Spencer O. Fisher, *West Bay City*
Seth C. Moffatt, *Traverse City*

---

[14] Died December 26, 1886.
[15] Elected to fill vacancy caused by death of John A. Logan, and took his seat January 25, 1887.
[16] Died July 1, 1885, before Congress assembled.
[17] Elected to fill vacancy caused by death of Reuben Ellwood, and took his seat December 7, 1885.

[18] Election unsuccessfully contested by Meredith H. Kidd.
[19] Election unsuccessfully contested by Frank G. Campbell.
[20] Died March 15, 1886.
[21] Elected to fill vacancy caused by death of

Michael Hahn, and took his seat December 9, 1886.
[22] Died July 8, 1886.
[23] Elected to fill vacancy caused by death of William H. Cole, and took his seat December 6, 1886.

## MINNESOTA

### SENATORS

Samuel J. R. McMillan, *St. Paul*
Dwight M. Sabin, *Stillwater*

### REPRESENTATIVES

Milo White, *Chatfield*
James B. Wakefield, *Blue Earth City*
Horace B. Strait, *Shakopee*
John B. Gilfillan, *Minneapolis*
Knute Nelson, *Alexandria*

## MISSISSIPPI

### SENATORS

Lucius Q. C. Lamar,[24] *Oxford*
Edward C. Walthall,[25] *Grenada*
James Z. George, *Jackson*

### REPRESENTATIVES

John M. Allen, *Tupelo*
James B. Morgan, *Hernando*
Thomas C. Catchings, *Vicksburg*
Frederick G. Barry, *West Point*
Otho R. Singleton, *Forest*
Henry S. Van Eaton, *Woodville*
Ethelbert Barksdale, *Jackson*

## MISSOURI

### SENATORS

Francis M. Cockrell, *Warrenburg*
George G. Vest, *Kansas City*

### REPRESENTATIVES

William H. Hatch, *Hannibal*
John B. Hale, *Carrollton*
Alexander M. Dockery, *Gallatin*
James N. Burnes, *St. Joseph*
William Warner, *Kansas City*
John T. Heard, *Sedalia*
John E. Hutton, *Mexico*
John J. O'Neill, *St. Louis*
John M. Glover, *St. Louis*
Martin L. Clardy, *Farmington*
Richard P. Bland, *Lebanon*
William J. Stone, *Nevada*
William H. Wade, *Springfield*
William Dawson, *New Madrid*

## NEBRASKA

### SENATORS

Charles H. Van Wyck, *Nebraska City*
Charles F. Manderson, *Omaha*

### REPRESENTATIVES

Archibald J. Weaver, *Falls City*
James Laird, *Hastings*
George W. E. Dorsey, *Fremont*

## NEVADA

### SENATORS

John P. Jones, *Gold Hill*
James G. Fair, *Virginia City*

### REPRESENTATIVE AT LARGE

William Woodburn, *Virginia City*

## NEW HAMPSHIRE

### SENATORS

Austin F. Pike,[26] *Franklin*
Person C. Cheney,[27] *Manchester*
Henry W. Blair,[28] *Manchester*

### REPRESENTATIVES

Martin A. Haynes, *Lake Village*
Jacob H. Gallinger, *Concord*

## NEW JERSEY

### SENATORS

John R. McPherson, *Jersey City*
William J. Sewell, *Camden*

### REPRESENTATIVES

George Hires, *Salem*
James Buchanan, *Trenton*
Robert S. Green,[29] *Elizabeth*
James N. Pidcock, *Whitehouse Station*
William W. Phelps, *Englewood*
Herman Lehlbach, *Newark*
William McAdoo, *Jersey City*

## NEW YORK

### SENATORS

Warner Miller, *Herkimer*
William M. Evarts, *New York City*

### REPRESENTATIVES

Perry Belmont, *Babylon*
Felix Campbell, *Brooklyn*
Darwin R. James, *Brooklyn*
Peter P. Mahoney, *Brooklyn*
Archibald M. Bliss, *Brooklyn*
Nicholas Muller, *New York City*
John J. Adams, *New York City*
Samuel S. Cox,[30] *New York City*
Timothy J. Campbell[31] *New York City*
Joseph Pulitzer,[32] *New York City*

Samuel S. Cox,[33] *New York City*
Abram S. Hewitt,[34] *New York City*
Truman A. Merriman, *New York City*
Abraham Dowdney,[35] *New York City*
Egbert L. Viele, *New York City*
William G. Stahlnecker, *Yonkers*
Lewis Beach,[36] *Cornwall*
Henry Bacon,[37] *Goshen*
John H. Ketcham, *Dover Plains*
James G. Lindsley, *Rondout*
Henry G. Burleigh, *Whitehall*
John Swinburne, *Albany*
George West, *Ballston Spa*
Frederick A. Johnson, *Glens Falls*
Abraham X. Parker, *Potsdam*
John T. Spriggs, *Utica*
John S. Pindar, *Cobleskill*
Frank Hiscock,[38] *Syracuse*
Stephen C. Millard, *Binghamton*
Sereno E. Payne, *Auburn*
John Arnot, Jr.,[39] *Elmira*
Ira Davenport, *Bath*
Charles S. Baker, *Rochester*
John G. Sawyer, *Albion*
John M. Farquhar, *Buffalo*
John B. Weber, *Buffalo*
Walter L. Sessions, *Jamestown*

## NORTH CAROLINA

### SENATORS

Matt W. Ransom, *Weldon*
Zebulon B. Vance, *Charlotte*

### REPRESENTATIVES

Thomas G. Skinner, *Hertford*
James E. O'Hara, *Enfield*
Wharton J. Green, *Fayetteville*
William R. Cox, *Raleigh*
James W. Reid,[40] *Wentworth*
Risden T. Bennett, *Wadesboro*
John S. Henderson, *Salisbury*
William H. H. Cowles, *Wilkesboro*
Thomas D. Johnston, *Asheville*

## OHIO

### SENATORS

John Sherman, *Mansfield*
Henry B. Payne, *Cleveland*

### REPRESENTATIVES

Benjamin Butterworth, *Cincinnati*
Charles E. Brown, *Cincinnati*
James E. Campbell, *Hamilton*
Charles M. Anderson, *Greenville*
Benjamin Le Fevre, *Maplewood*

---

[24] Resigned March 6, 1885, having been appointed Secretary of the Interior.
[25] Appointed to fill vacancy caused by resignation of Lucius Q. C. Lamar, and took his seat March 12, 1885 (special session of the Senate); subsequently elected.
[26] Died October 8, 1886.
[27] Appointed to fill vacancy caused by death of Austin F. Pike, and took his seat December 7, 1886.
[28] Appointed March 5, 1885, to fill vacancy in the term beginning March 4, 1885, to serve until the next

meeting of the legislature; subsequently elected, and took his seat December 7, 1885.
[29] Resigned January 17, 1887, having been elected Governor.
[30] Resigned May 20, 1885, before Congress assembled, having been appointed minister to Turkey.
[31] Elected to fill vacancy caused by resignation of Samuel S. Cox, and took his seat December 7, 1885.
[32] Resigned April 10, 1886.
[33] Elected to fill vacancy caused by resignation of Joseph Pulitzer, and took his seat December 6, 1886.

[34] Resigned December 30, 1886.
[35] Died December 10, 1886; seat vacant for remainder of the Congress.
[36] Died August 10, 1886.
[37] Elected to fill vacancy caused by death of Lewis Beach, and took his seat December 6, 1886.
[38] Reelected to the Fiftieth Congress, but resigned, having been elected Senator.
[39] Died November 20, 1886; seat vacant for remainder of the Congress.
[40] Resigned December 31, 1886.

## OHIO—Continued

### REPRESENTATIVES—CONTINUED

William D. Hill, *Defiance*
George E. Seney, *Tiffin*
John Little, *Xenia*
William C. Cooper, *Mount Vernon*
Jacob Romeis,[41] *Toledo*
William W. Ellsberry, *Georgetown*
Albert C. Thompson, *Portsmouth*
Joseph H. Outhwaite, *Columbus*
Charles H. Grosvenor, *Athens*
Beriah Wilkins, *Uhrichsville*
George W. Geddes, *Mansfield*
Adoniram J. Warner, *Marietta*
Isaac H. Taylor, *Carrollton*
Ezra B. Taylor, *Warren*
William McKinley, Jr. *Canton*
Martin A. Foran, *Cleveland*

## OREGON

### SENATORS

Joseph N. Dolph, *Portland*
John H. Mitchell,[42] *Portland*

### REPRESENTATIVE AT LARGE

Binger Hermann, *Roseburg*

## PENNSYLVANIA

### SENATORS

J. Donald Cameron, *Harrisburg*
John I. Mitchell, *Wellsboro*

### REPRESENTATIVE AT LARGE

Edwin S. Osborne, *Wilkes-Barre*

### REPRESENTATIVES

Henry H. Bingham, *Philadelphia*
Charles O'Neill, *Philadelphia*
Samuel J. Randall, *Philadelphia*
William D. Kelley, *Philadelphia*
Alfred C. Harmer, *Philadelphia*
James B. Everhart, *West Chester*
I. Newton Evans, *Hatboro*
Daniel Ermentrout, *Reading*
John A. Hiestand, *Lancaster*
William H. Sowden, *Allentown*
John B. Storm, *Stroudsburg*
Joseph A. Scranton, *Scranton*
Charles N. Brumm, *Minersville*
Franklin Bound, *Milton*
Frank C. Bunnell, *Tunkhannock*
William W. Brown, *Bradford*
Jacob M. Campbell, *Johnstown*
Louis E. Atkinson, *Mifflintown*
John A. Swope,[43] *Gettysburg*
Andrew G. Curtin, *Bellefonte*
Charles E. Boyle, *Uniontown*
James S. Negley, *Pittsburgh*
Thomas M. Bayne, *Allegheny*

Oscar L. Jackson, *New Castle*
Alexander C. White, *Brookville*
George W. Fleeger, *Butler*
William L. Scott, *Erie*

## RHODE ISLAND

### SENATORS

Nelson W. Aldrich, *Providence*
Jonathan Chace, *Providence*

### REPRESENTATIVES

Henry J. Spooner, *Providence*
William A. Pirce,[44] *Olneyville*
Charles H. Page,[45] *Scituate*

## SOUTH CAROLINA

### SENATORS

Matthew C. Butler, *Edgefield*
Wade Hampton, *Columbia*

### REPRESENTATIVES

Samuel Dibble, *Orangeburg*
George D. Tillman, *Edgefield*
D. Wyatt Aiken, *Cokesbury*
William H. Perry, *Greenville*
John J. Hemphill, *Chester*
George W. Dargan, *Darlington*
Robert Smalls, *Beaufort*

## TENNESSEE

### SENATORS

Isham G. Harris, *Memphis*
Howell E. Jackson,[46] *Nashville*
Washington C. Whitthorne,[47]
　*Columbia*

### REPRESENTATIVES

Augustus H. Pettibone, *Greeneville*
Leonidas C. Houk, *Knoxville*
John R. Neal, *Rhea Springs*
Benton McMillin, *Carthage*
James D. Richardson, *Murfreesboro*
Andrew J. Caldwell, *Nashville*
John G. Ballentine, *Pulaski*
John M. Taylor, *Lexington*
Presley T. Glass, *Ripley*
Zachary Taylor, *Covington*

## TEXAS

### SENATORS

Samuel B. Maxey, *Paris*
Richard Coke, *Waco*

### REPRESENTATIVES

Charles Stewart, *Houston*
John H. Reagan,[48] *Palestine*
James H. Jones, *Henderson*
David B. Culberson, *Jefferson*
James W. Throckmorton, *McKinney*

Olin Wellborn, *Dallas*
William H. Crain, *Cuero*
James F. Miller, *Gonzales*
Roger Q. Mills, *Corsicana*
Joseph D. Sayers, *Bastrop*
Samuel W. T. Lanham, *Weatherford*

## VERMONT

### SENATORS

George F. Edmunds, *Burlington*
Justin S. Morrill, *Strafford*

### REPRESENTATIVES

John W. Stewart, *Middlebury*
William W. Grout, *Barton*

## VIRGINIA

### SENATORS

William Mahone, *Petersburg*
Harrison H. Riddleberger, *Woodstock*

### REPRESENTATIVES

Thomas Croxton, *Tappahannock*
Harry Libbey, *Old Point Comfort*
George D. Wise, *Richmond*
James D. Brady, *Petersburg*
George C. Cabell, *Danville*
John W. Daniel, *Lynchburg*
Charles T. O'Ferrall, *Harrisonburg*
John S. Barbour, *Alexandria*
Connally F. Trigg, *Abingdon*
John R. Tucker, *Lexington*

## WEST VIRGINIA

### SENATORS

Johnson N. Camden, *Parkersburg*
John E. Kenna, *Charleston*

### REPRESENTATIVES

Nathan Goff, Jr., *Clarksburg*
William L. Wilson, *Charles Town*
Charles P. Snyder, *Charleston*
Eustace Gibson, *Huntington*

## WISCONSIN

### SENATORS

Philetus Sawyer, *Oshkosh*
John C. Spooner, *Hudson*

### REPRESENTATIVES

Lucien B. Caswell, *Fort Atkinson*
Edward S. Bragg, *Fond du Lac*
Robert M. La Follette, *Madison*
Isaac W. Van Schaick, *Milwaukee*
Joseph Rankin,[49] *Manitowoc*

---

[41] Election unsuccessfully contested by Frank H. Hurd.

[42] Elected to fill vacancy in term beginning March 4, 1885, caused by failure of legislature to elect, and took his seat December 17, 1885; vacancy in this class from March 4, 1885, to November 17, 1885.

[43] Elected to fill vacancy caused by death of Representative-elect William A. Duncan, in preceding Congress, and took his seat December 7, 1885.

[44] Served until January 25, 1887, when seat was declared vacant.

[45] Elected to fill vacancy caused by declaring the seat of William A. Pirce vacant, and took his seat February 25, 1887.

[46] Resigned April 14, 1886, to become United States circuit judge, sixth circuit.

[47] Appointed to fill vacancy caused by resignation of Howell E. Jackson, and took his seat April 26, 1886; subsequently elected.

[48] Reelected to the Fiftieth Congress, but resigned, having been elected Senator.

[49] Died January 24, 1886.

Thomas R. Hudd,[50] *Green Bay*
Richard W. Guenther, *Oshkosh*
Ormsby B. Thomas, *Prairie du Chien*
William T. Price,[51] *Black River Falls*
Hugh H. Price,[52] *Black River Falls*
Isaac Stephenson, *Marinette*

## TERRITORY OF ARIZONA

DELEGATE
Curtis C. Bean, *Prescott*

## TERRITORY OF DAKOTA

DELEGATE
Oscar S. Gifford, *Canton*

## TERRITORY OF IDAHO

DELEGATE
John Hailey, *Boise City*

## TERRITORY OF MONTANA

DELEGATE
Joseph K. Toole, *Helena*

## TERRITORY OF NEW MEXICO

DELEGATE
Antonio Joseph, *Ojo Caliente*

## TERRITORY OF UTAH

DELEGATE
John T. Caine, *Salt Lake City*

## TERRITORY OF WASHINGTON

DELEGATE
Charles S. Voorhees, *Colfax*

## TERRITORY OF WYOMING

DELEGATE
Joseph M. Carey, *Cheyenne*

---

[50] Elected to fill vacancy caused by death of Joseph Rankin, and took his seat March 8, 1886.
[51] Died December 6, 1886, before the commencement of the Fiftieth Congress, to which he had been reelected.
[52] Elected to fill vacancy caused by death of his father, William T. Price, and took his seat February 2, 1887.

# 50TH CONGRESS

MARCH 4, 1887, TO MARCH 3, 1889

FIRST SESSION— *December 5, 1887, to October 20, 1888*
SECOND SESSION— *December 3, 1888, to March 3, 1889*

---

VICE PRESIDENT OF THE UNITED STATES— [1]
PRESIDENT PRO TEMPORE OF THE SENATE— John J. Ingalls, of Kansas
SECRETARY OF THE SENATE— Anson G. McCook of New York
SERGEANT AT ARMS OF THE SENATE— William P. Canaday, of North Carolina

---

SPEAKER OF THE HOUSE OF REPRESENTATIVES— John G. Carlisle,[2] of Kentucky
CLERK OF THE HOUSE— John B. Clark, Jr.,[3] of Missouri
SERGEANT AT ARMS OF THE HOUSE— John P. Leedom, of Ohio
DOORKEEPER OF THE HOUSE— A. B. Hurd, of Mississippi
POSTMASTER OF THE HOUSE— Lycurgus Dalton

John J. Ingalls
President Pro Tempore

John G. Carlisle
Speaker

## ALABAMA

### SENATORS

John T. Morgan, *Selma*
James L. Pugh, *Eufaula*

### REPRESENTATIVES

James T. Jones, *Demopolis*
Hilary A. Herbert, *Montgomery*
William C. Oates, *Abbeville*
Alexander C. Davidson,[4] *Uniontown*
James E. Cobb, *Tuskegee*
John H. Bankhead, *Fayette*
William H. Forney, *Jacksonville*
Joseph Wheeler, *Wheeler*

## ARKANSAS

### SENATORS

James K. Jones, *Washington*
James H. Berry, *Bentonville*

### REPRESENTATIVES

Poindexter Dunn, *Forest City*
Clifton R. Breckinridge, *Pine Bluff*
Thomas C. McRae, *Prescott*
John H. Rogers, *Fort Smith*
Samuel W. Peel, *Bentonville*

## CALIFORNIA

### SENATORS

Leland Stanford, *San Francisco*
George Hearst, *San Francisco*

### REPRESENTATIVES

Thomas L. Thompson, *Santa Rosa*
Marion Biggs, *Gridley*
Joseph McKenna, *Suisun*
William W. Morrow, *San Francisco*
Charles N. Felton, *San Francisco*
William Vandever,[5] *Pasadena*

## COLORADO

### SENATORS

Thomas M. Bowen, *Del Norte*
Henry M. Teller, *Central City*

### REPRESENTATIVE AT LARGE

George G. Symes, *Denver*

## CONNECTICUT

### SENATORS

Orville H. Platt, *Meriden*
Joseph R. Hawley, *Hartford*

### REPRESENTATIVES

Robert J. Vance, *New Britain*
Carlos French, *Seymour*
Charles A. Russell, *Killingly*
Miles T. Granger, *Canaan*

## DELAWARE

### SENATORS

Eli Saulsbury, *Dover*
George Gray, *New Castle*

### REPRESENTATIVE AT LARGE

John B. Penington, *Dover*

## FLORIDA

### SENATORS

Wilkinson Call, *Jacksonville*
Samuel Pasco,[6] *Monticello*

### REPRESENTATIVES

Robert H. M. Davidson, *Quincy*
Charles Dougherty, *Port Orange*

## GEORGIA

### SENATORS

Joseph E. Brown, *Atlanta*
Alfred H. Colquitt, *Atlanta*

### REPRESENTATIVES

Thomas M. Norwood, *Savannah*
Henry G. Turner, *Quitman*
Charles F. Crisp, *Americus*
Thomas W. Grimes, *Columbus*
John D. Stewart, *Griffin*
James H. Blount, *Macon*
Judson C. Clements, *Rome*
Henry H. Carlton, *Athens*
Allen D. Candler, *Gainesville*
George T. Barnes, *Augusta*

## ILLINOIS

### SENATORS

Shelby M. Cullom, *Springfield*
Charles B. Farwell, *Chicago*

---

REPRESENTATIVES

Ransom W. Dunham, *Chicago*
Frank Lawler, *Chicago*
William E. Mason, *Chicago*
George E. Adams, *Chicago*
Albert J. Hopkins, *Aurora*
Robert R. Hitt, *Mount Morris*
Thomas J. Henderson, *Princeton*
Ralph Plumb, *Streator*
Lewis E. Payson, *Pontiac*
Philip S. Post,[7] *Galesburg*
William H. Gest, *Rock Island*
George A. Anderson, *Qunicy*
William M. Springer, *Springfield*
Jonathan H. Rowell, *Bloomington*
Joseph G. Cannon, *Danville*
Silas Z. Landes, *Mount Carmel*
Edward Lane, *Hillsboro*
Jehu Baker, *Belleville*
Richard W. Townshend, *Shawneetown*
John R. Thomas, *Metropolis*

## INDIANA

SENATORS

Daniel W. Voorhees, *Terre Haute*
David Turpie, *Indianapolis*

REPRESENTATIVES

Alvin P. Hovey,[8] *Mount Vernon*
Francis B. Posey,[9] *Poseyville*
John H. O'Neall, *Washington*
Jonas G. Howard, *Jeffersonville*
William S. Holman, *Aurora*
Courtland C. Matson, *Greencastle*
Thomas M. Browne, *Winchester*
William D. Bynum, *Indianapolis*
James T. Johnston, *Rockville*
Joseph B. Cheadle, *Frankfort*
William D. Owen, *Logansport*
George W. Steele, *Marion*
James B. White,[10] *Fort Wayne*
Benjamin F. Shively, *South Bend*

## IOWA

SENATORS

William B. Allison, *Dubuque*
James F. Wilson, *Fairfield*

REPRESENTATIVES

John H. Gear, *Burlington*
Walter I. Hayes, *Clinton*
David B. Henderson, *Dubuque*
William E. Fuller, *West Union*
Daniel Kerr, *Grundy Center*
James B. Weaver, *Bloomfield*
Edwin H. Conger, *Des Moines*
Albert R. Anderson, *Sidney*
Joseph Lyman, *Council Bluffs*

Adoniram J. Holmes, *Boone*
Isaac S. Struble, *Le Mars*

## KANSAS

SENATORS

John J. Ingalls, *Atchison*
Preston B. Plumb, *Emporia*

REPRESENTATIVES

Edmund N. Morrill, *Hiawatha*
Edward H. Funston, *Iola*
Bishop W. Perkins, *Oswego*
Thomas Ryan, *Topeka*
John A. Anderson, *Manhattan*
Erastus J. Turner, *Hoxie*
Samuel R. Peters, *Newton*

## KENTUCKY

SENATORS

James B. Beck, *Lexington*
Joseph C. S. Blackburn, *Versailles*

REPRESENTATIVES

William J. Stone, *Kuttawa*
Polk Laffoon, *Madisonville*
W. Godfrey Hunder, *Burksville*
Alexander B. Montgomery,
 *Elizabethtown*
Asher G. Caruth, *Louisville*
John G. Carlisle,[11] *Covington*
William C. P. Breckinridge, *Lexington*
James B. McCreary, *Richmond*
George M. Thomas, *Vanceburg*
William P. Taulbee, *Saylersville*
Hugh F. Finley, *Williamsburg*

## LOUISIANA

SENATORS

Randall L. Gibson, *New Orleans*
James B. Eustis, *New Orleans*

REPRESENTATIVES

Theodore S. Wilkinson, *Plaquemines
 Parish*
Matthew D. Lagan, *New Orleans*
Edward J. Gay, *Plaquemine*
Newton C. Blanchard, *Shreveport*
Cherubusco Newton, *Bastrop*
Edward W. Robertson,[12] *Baton Rouge*
Samuel M. Robertson,[13] *Baton Rouge*

## MAINE

SENATORS

Eugene Hale, *Ellsworth*
William P. Frye, *Lewiston*

REPRESENTATIVES

Thomas B. Reed, *Portland*
Nelson Dingley, Jr., *Lewiston*
Seth L. Milliken, *Belfast*
Charles A. Boutelle, *Bangor*

## MARYLAND

SENATORS

Arthur Pue Gorman, *Laurel*
Ephraim K. Wilson, *Snow Hill*

REPRESENTATIVES

Charles H. Gibson, *Easton*
Frank T. Shaw, *Westminster*
Harry W. Rusk, *Baltimore*
Isidor Rayner, *Baltimore*
Barnes Compton, *Laurel*
Louis E. McComas, *Hagerstown*

## MASSACHUSETTS

SENATORS

Henry L. Dawes, *Pittsfield*
George F. Hoar, *Worcester*

REPRESENTATIVES

Robert T. Davis, *Fall River*
John D. Long, *Hingham*
Leopold Morse, *Boston*
Patrick A. Collins, *Boston*
Edward D. Hayden, *Woburn*
Henry Cabot Lodge, *Nahant*
William Cogswell, *Salem*
Charles H. Allen, *Lowell*
Edward Burnett, *Southboro*
John E. Russell, *Leicester*
William Whiting, *Holyoke*
Francis W. Rockwell, *Pittsfield*

## MICHIGAN

SENATORS

Thomas W. Palmer, *Detroit*
Francis B. Stockbridge, *Kalamazoo*

REPRESENTATIVES

J. Logan Chipman, *Detroit*
Edward P. Allen, *Ypsilanti*
James O'Donnell, *Jackson*
Julius C. Burrows, *Kalamazoo*
Melbourne H. Ford, *Grand Rapids*
Mark S. Brewer, *Pontiac*
Justin R. Whiting, *St. Clair*
Timothy E. Tarsney, *East Saginaw*
Byron M. Cutcheon, *Manistee*
Spencer O. Fisher, *West Bay City*

---

[7] Election unsuccessfully contested by Nicholas E. Worthington.

[8] Resigned January 17, 1889.

[9] Elected to fill vacancy caused by resignation of Alvin P. Hovey, and took his seat February 6, 1889.

[10] Election unsuccessfully contested by Robert Lowry.

[11] Election unsuccessfully contested by George H. Thobe.

[12] Died August 2, 1887, before Congress assembled.

[13] Elected to fill vacancy caused by death of Edward W. Robertson, and took his seat December 5, 1887.

## MICHIGAN—Continued

REPRESENTATIVES—CONTINUED

Seth C. Moffatt,[14] *Traverse City*
Henry W. Seymour,[15] *Sault Ste. Marie*

## MINNESOTA

SENATORS

Dwight M. Sabin, *Stillwater*
Cushman K. Davis, *St. Paul*

REPRESENTATIVES

Thomas Wilson, *Winona*
John Lind, *New Ulm*
John L. MacDonald, *Shakopee*
Edmund Rise, *St. Paul*
Knute Nelson, *Alexandria*

## MISSISSIPPI

SENATORS

James Z. George, *Jackson*
Edward C. Walthall, *Grenada*

REPRESENTATIVES

John M. Allen, *Tupelo*
James B. Morgan, *Hernando*
Thomas C. Catchings, *Vicksburg*
Frederick G. Barry, *West Point*
Chapman L. Anderson, *Kosciusko*
Thomas R. Stockdale, *Summit*
Charles E. Hooker, *Jackson*

## MISSOURI

SENATORS

Francis M. Cockrell, *Warrenburg*
George G. Vest, *Kansas City*

REPRESENTATIVES

William H. Hatch, *Hannibal*
Charles H. Mansur, *Chillicothe*
Alexander M. Dockery, *Gallatin*
James N. Burnes,[16] *St. Joseph*
Charles F. Booher,[17] *St. Joseph*
William Warner, *Kansas City*
John T. Heard, *Sedalia*
John E. Hutton, *Mexico*
John J. O'Neill, *St. Louis*
John M. Glover,[18] *St. Louis*
Martin L. Clardy, *Farmington*
Richard P. Bland, *Lebanon*
William J. Stone, *Nevada*
William H. Wade, *Springfield*
James P. Walker, *Dexter*

## NEBRASKA

SENATORS

Charles F. Manderson, *Omaha*
Algernon S. Paddock, *Beatrice*

REPRESENTATIVES

John A. McShane, *Omaha*
James Laird, *Hastings*
George W. E. Dorsey, *Fremont*

## NEVADA

SENATORS

John P. Jones, *Gold Hill*
William M. Stewart, *Carson City*

REPRESENTATIVE AT LARGE

William Woodburn, *Virginia City*

## NEW HAMPSHIRE

SENATORS

Henry W. Blair, *Manchester*
Person C. Cheney, *Manchester*
William E. Chandler,[19] *Concord*

REPRESENTATIVES

Luther F. McKinney, *Manchester*
Jacob H. Gallinger, *Concord*

## NEW JERSEY

SENATORS

John R. McPherson, *Jersey City*
Rufus Blodgett, *Long Branch*

REPRESENTATIVES

George Hires, *Salem*
James Buchanan, *Trenton*
John Kean, *Elizabeth*
James N. Pidcock, *Whitehouse Station*
William W. Phelps, *Englewood*
Herman Lehlbach, *Newark*
William McAdoo, *Jersey City*

## NEW YORK

SENATORS

William M. Evarts, *New York City*
Frank Hiscock, *Syracuse*

REPRESENTATIVES

Perry Belmont,[20] *Babylon*
Felix Campbell, *Brooklyn*
Stephen V. White, *Brooklyn*
Peter P. Mahoney, *Brooklyn*
Archibald M. Bliss, *Brooklyn*
Amos J. Cummings, *New York City*

Lloyd S. Bryce, *New York City*
Timothy J. Campbell *New York City*
Samuel S. Cox, *New York City*
Francis B. Spinola, *New York City*
Truman A. Merriman, *New York City*
W. Bourke Cockran, *New York City*
Ashbel P. Fitch, *New York City*
William G. Stahlnecker, *Yonkers*
Henry Bacon, *Goshen*
John H. Ketcham, *Dover Plains*
Stephen T. Hopkins, *Catskill*
Edward W. Greenman, *Troy*
Nicholas T. Kane,[21] *Albany*
Charles Tracey,[22] *Albany*
George West, *Ballston Spa*
John H. Moffitt, *Chateaugay Lake*
Abraham X. Parker, *Potsdam*
James S. Sherman, *Utica*
David Wilber, *Oneonta*
James J. Belden,[23] *Syracuse*
Milton De Lano, *Canastota*
Newton W. Nutting, *Oswego*
Thomas S. Flood, *Elmira*
Ira Davenport, *Bath*
Charles S. Baker, *Rochester*
John G. Sawyer, *Albion*
John M. Farquhar, *Buffalo*
John B. Weber, *Buffalo*
William G. Laidlaw, *Ellicottville*

## NORTH CAROLINA

SENATORS

Matt W. Ransom, *Weldon*
Zebulon B. Vance, *Charlotte*

REPRESENTATIVES

Louis C. Latham, *Greenville*
Furnifold McL. Simmons, *New Bern*
Charles W. McClammy, *Scotts Hill*
John Nichols, *Raleigh*
James M. Brower, *Mount Airy*
Alfred Rowland, *Lumberton*
John S. Henderson, *Salisbury*
William H. H. Cowles, *Wilkesboro*
Thomas D. Johnston, *Asheville*

## OHIO

SENATORS

John Sherman, *Mansfield*
Henry B. Payne, *Cleveland*

REPRESENTATIVES

Benjamin Butterworth, *Cincinnati*
Charles E. Brown, *Cincinnati*
Elihu S. Williams, *Troy*
Samuel S. Yoder, *Lima*
George E. Seney, *Tiffin*

---

[14] Died December 22, 1887.
[15] Elected to fill vacancy caused by death of Seth C. Moffatt, and took his seat March 3, 1888.
[16] Died January 23, 1889, before the commencement of the Fifty-first Congress, to which he had been reelected.
[17] Elected to fill vacancy caused by death of James N. Burnes, and took his seat February 25, 1889.

[18] Election unsuccessfully contested by Nathan Frank.
[19] Elected to fill vacancy caused by death of Austin F. Pike, in preceding Congress, and took his seat December 5, 1887.
[20] Resigned December 1, 1888, having been appointed minister to Spain; seat vacant for remainder of the Congress.

[21] Died September 14, 1887, before Congress assembled.
[22] Elected to fill vacancy caused by death of Nicholas T. Kane, and took his seat December 5, 1887.
[23] Elected to fill vacancy caused by resignation of Representative-elect Frank Hiscock, in preceding Congress, and took his seat December 5, 1887.

Melvin M. Boothman, *Bryan*
James E. Campbell, *Hamilton*
Robert P. Kennedy, *Bellefontaine*
William C. Cooper, *Mount Vernon*
Jacob Romeis, *Toledo*
Albert C. Thompson, *Portsmouth*
Jacob J. Pugsley, *Hillsboro*
Joseph H. Outhwaite, *Columbus*
Charles P. Wickham, *Norwalk*
Charles H. Grosvenor, *Athens*
Beriah Wilkins, *Uhrichsville*
Joseph D. Taylor, *Cambridge*
William McKinley, Jr. *Canton*
Ezra B. Taylor, *Warren*
George W. Crouse, *Akron*
Martin A. Foran, *Cleveland*

## OREGON

SENATORS

Joseph N. Dolph, *Portland*
John H. Mitchell, *Portland*

REPRESENTATIVE AT LARGE

Binger Hermann, *Roseburg*

## PENNSYLVANIA

SENATORS

J. Donald Cameron, *Harrisburg*
Matthew S. Quay, *Beaver*

REPRESENTATIVE AT LARGE

Edwin S. Osborne, *Wilkes-Barre*

REPRESENTATIVES

Henry H. Bingham, *Philadelphia*
Charles O'Neill, *Philadelphia*
Samuel J. Randall, *Philadelphia*
William D. Kelley, *Philadelphia*
Alfred C. Harmer, *Philadelphia*
Smedley Darlington, *West Chester*
Robert M. Yardley, *Doylestown*
Daniel Ermentrout, *Reading*
John A. Hiestand, *Lancaster*
William H. Sowden, *Allentown*
Charles R. Buckalew, *Bloomsburg*
John Lynch, *Wilkes-Barre*
Charles N. Brumm, *Minersville*
Franklin Bound, *Milton*
Frank C. Bunnell, *Tunkhannock*
Henry C. McCormick, *Williamsport*
Edward Scull, *Somerset*
Louis E. Atkinson, *Mifflintown*
Levi Maish, *York*
John Patton, *Curwensville*
Welty McCullogh, *Greensburg*
John Dalzell, *Pittsburgh*
Thomas M. Bayne, *Allegheny*

Oscar L. Jackson, *New Castle*
James T. Maffett, *Clairon*
Norman Hall, *Sharon*
William L. Scott, *Erie*

## RHODE ISLAND

SENATORS

Nelson W. Aldrich, *Providence*
Jonathan Chace, *Providence*

REPRESENTATIVES

Henry J. Spooner, *Providence*
Warren O. Arnold, *Gloucester*

## SOUTH CAROLINA

SENATORS

Matthew C. Butler, *Edgefield*
Wade Hampton, *Columbia*

REPRESENTATIVES

Samuel Dibble, *Orangeburg*
George D. Tillman, *Edgefield*
James S. Cothran, *Abbeville*
William H. Perry, *Greenville*
John J. Hemphill, *Chester*
George W. Dargan, *Darlington*
William Elliott,[24] *Beaufort*

## TENNESSEE

SENATORS

Isham G. Harris, *Memphis*
William B. Bate, *Nashville*

REPRESENTATIVES

Roderick R. Butler, *Mountain City*
Leonidas C. Houk, *Knoxville*
John R. Neal, *Rhea Springs*
Benton McMillin, *Carthage*
James D. Richardson, *Murfreesboro*
Joseph E. Washington, *Cedar Hill*
Washington C. Whitthorne, *Columbia*
Benjamin A. Enloe, *Jackson*
Presley T. Glass, *Ripley*
James Phelan, *Memphis*

## TEXAS

SENATORS

Richard Coke, *Waco*
John H. Reagan, *Palestine*

REPRESENTATIVES

Charles Stewart, *Houston*
William H. Martin,[25] *Athens*
Constantine B. Kilgore, *Wills Point*

David B. Culberson, *Jefferson*
Silas Hare, *Sherman*
Jo Abbott, *Hillsboro*
William H. Crain, *Cuero*
Littleton W. Moore, *Legrange*
Roger Q. Mills, *Corsicana*
Joseph D. Sayers, *Bastrop*
Samuel W. T. Lanham, *Weatherford*

## VERMONT

SENATORS

George F. Edmunds, *Burlington*
Justin S. Morrill, *Strafford*

REPRESENTATIVES

John W. Stewart, *Middlebury*
William W. Grout, *Barton*

## VIRGINIA

SENATORS

Harrison H. Riddleberger, *Woodstock*
John W. Daniel, *Lynchburg*

REPRESENTATIVES

Thomas H. B. Browne, *Accomac*
George E. Bowden, *Norfolk*
George D. Wise, *Richmond*
William E. Gaines, *Burkeville*
John R. Brown, *Martinsville*
Samuel I. Hopkins, *Lynchburg*
Charles T. O'Ferrall, *Harrisonburg*
William H. F. Lee, *Burkes Station*
Henry Bowen, *Tazewell*
Jacob Yost, *Staunton*

## WEST VIRGINIA

SENATORS

John E. Kenna, *Charleston*
Charles J. Faulkner,[26] *Martinsburg*

REPRESENTATIVES

Nathan Goff, Jr., *Clarksburg*
William L. Wilson, *Charles Town*
Charles P. Snyder, *Charleston*
Charles E. Hogg, *Point Pleasant*

## WISCONSIN

SENATORS

Philetus Sawyer, *Oshkosh*
John C. Spooner, *Hudson*

REPRESENTATIVES

Lucien B. Caswell, *Fort Atkinson*
Richard W. Guenther, *Oshkosh*

---

[24] Election unsuccessfully contested by Robert Smalls.

[25] Elected to fill vacancy caused by resignation of Representative-elect John H. Reagan, in preceding Congress, and took his seat December 5, 1887.

[26] The Legislature of West Virginia had met and adjourned without electing a Senator for the term beginning March 4, 1887; on March 5, 1887, the governor appointed Daniel B. Lucas to fill such

vacancy; on the same day he issued a proclamation calling the legislature in extraordinary session for eight specific purposes, the election of Senator not being named as one of them; the legislature proceeded to choose a Senator, and Charles J. Faulkner was elected; credentials of both Mr. Lucas and Mr. Faulkner were presented on December 5, 1887, and Mr. Faulkner appeared to be sworn, but objection was made and he was not permitted to qualify; December

14, 1887, the Senate adopted a report from the Committee on Privileges and Elections, to whom all papers were referred on the 12th, declaring Mr. Faulkner duly elected and entitled to the seat; appeared, qualified, and took his seat the same day. (See U.S. Senate Election, Expulsion and Censure Cases, 1793-1990, Senate Document 103-32, pp. 230-31.)

## WISCONSIN—Continued

REPRESENTATIVES—CONTINUED

Robert M. La Follette, *Madison*
Henry Smith, *Milwaukee*
Thomas R. Hudd, *Green Bay*
Charles B. Clark, *Neenah*
Ormsby B. Thomas, *Prairie du Chien*
Nils P. Haugen,[27] *River Falls*
Isaac Stephenson, *Marinette*

## TERRITORY OF ARIZONA

DELEGATE

Marcus A. Smith, *Tombstone*

## TERRITORY OF DAKOTA

DELEGATE

Oscar S. Gifford, *Canton*

## TERRITORY OF IDAHO

DELEGATE

Fred T. Dubois, *Blackfoot*

## TERRITORY OF MONTANA

DELEGATE

Joseph K. Toole, *Helena*

## TERRITORY OF NEW MEXICO

DELEGATE

Antonio Joseph, *Ojo Caliente*

## TERRITORY OF UTAH

DELEGATE

John T. Caine, *Salt Lake City*

## TERRITORY OF WASHINGTON

DELEGATE

Charles S. Voorhees, *Colfax*

## TERRITORY OF WYOMING

DELEGATE

Joseph M. Carey, *Cheyenne*

---

[27] Elected on January 18, 1887, to fill vacancy caused by death of Representative-elect William T. Price, in preceding Congress, but on account of illness did not take his seat until January 4, 1888.

# 51ST CONGRESS

## MARCH 4, 1889, TO MARCH 3, 1891

Levi P. Morton
Vice President

Thomas B. Reed
Speaker

FIRST SESSION— *December 2, 1889, to October 1, 1890*
SECOND SESSION— *December 1, 1890, to March 2, 1891*
SPECIAL SESSION OF THE SENATE— *March 4, 1889, to April 2, 1889*

---

VICE PRESIDENT OF THE UNITED STATES— LEVI P. MORTON, of New York
PRESIDENT PRO TEMPORE OF THE SENATE— JOHN J. INGALLS,[1] of Kansas; CHARLES F. MANDERSON,[2] of Nebraska
SECRETARY OF THE SENATE— ANSON G. McCOOK, of New York
SERGEANT AT ARMS OF THE SENATE— WILLIAM P. CANADAY, of North Carolina; EDWARD K. VALENTINE,[3] of Nebraska

---

SPEAKER OF THE HOUSE OF REPRESENTATIVES— THOMAS B. REED,[4] of Maine
CLERK OF THE HOUSE— JOHN B. CLARK, JR., of Missouri; EDWARD McPHERSON,[5] of Pennsylvania
SERGEANT AT ARMS OF THE HOUSE— JOHN P. LEEDOM, of Ohio; ADONIRAM J. HOLMES,[6] of Iowa
DOORKEEPER OF THE HOUSE— CHARLES E. ADAMS, of Maryland
POSTMASTER OF THE HOUSE— JAMES L. WHEAT

## ALABAMA

### SENATORS

John T. Morgan, *Selma*
James L. Pugh, *Eufaula*

### REPRESENTATIVES

Richard H. Clarke,[7] *Mobile*
Hilary A. Herbert, *Montgomery*
William C. Oates, *Abbeville*
Louis W. Turpin,[8] *Newbern*
John V. McDuffie,[9] *Hayneville*
James E. Cobb, *Tuskegee*
John H. Bankhead, *Fayette*
William H. Forney, *Jacksonville*
Joseph Wheeler, *Wheeler*

## ARKANSAS

### SENATORS

James K. Jones, *Washington*
James H. Berry, *Bentonville*

### REPRESENTATIVES

William H. Cate,[10] *Jonesboro*
Lewis P. Featherston,[11] *Forest City*
Clifton R. Breckinridge,[12] *Pine Bluff*
Thomas C. McRae, *Prescott*
John H. Rogers, *Fort Smith*
Samuel W. Peel, *Bentonville*

## CALIFORNIA

### SENATORS

Leland Stanford, *San Francisco*
George Hearst,[13] *San Francisco*

### REPRESENTATIVES

John J. De Haven,[14] *Eureka*
Thomas J. Geary,[15] *Santa Rosa*
Marion Biggs, *Gridley*
Joseph McKenna, *Suisun*
William W. Morrow, *San Francisco*
Thomas J. Clunie, *San Francisco*
William Vandever, *San Buenaventura*

## COLORADO

### SENATORS

Henry M. Teller, *Central City*
Edward O. Wolcott, *Denver*

### REPRESENTATIVE AT LARGE

Hosea Townsend, *Silver Cliff*

## CONNECTICUT

### SENATORS

Orville H. Platt, *Meriden*
Joseph R. Hawley, *Hartford*

### REPRESENTATIVES

William E. Simonds, *Canton*
Washington F. Willcox, *Chester*
Charles A. Russell, *Killingly*
Frederick Miles, *Chapinville*

## DELAWARE

### SENATORS

George Gray, *New Castle*
Anthony Higgins, *Wilmington*

### REPRESENTATIVE AT LARGE

John B. Penington, *Dover*

## FLORIDA

### SENATORS

Wilkinson Call, *Jacksonville*
Samuel Pasco, *Monticello*

### REPRESENTATIVES

Robert H. M. Davidson, *Quincy*
Robert Bullock, *Ocala*

## GEORGIA

### SENATORS

Joseph E. Brown, *Atlanta*
Alfred H. Colquitt, *Atlanta*

### REPRESENTATIVES

Rufus E. Lester, *Savannah*
Henry G. Turner, *Quitman*
Charles F. Crisp, *Americus*
Thomas W. Grimes, *Columbus*
John D. Stewart, *Griffin*

---

[1] Elected March 7, 1889, and April 2, 1889 (special session of the Senate); February 28, 1890, and April 3, 1890; resigned as President pro tempore, effective March 2, 1891.
[2] Elected March 2, 1891.
[3] Elected June 30, 1890.
[4] Elected December 2, 1889.
[5] Elected December 2, 1889.
[6] Elected December 2, 1889.
[7] Election unsuccessfully contested by Frank H. Threet.

[8] Served until June 4, 1890; succeeded by John V. McDuffie, who contested his election.
[9] Successfully contested the election of Louis W. Turpin, and took his seat June 4, 1890.
[10] Served until March 5, 1890; succeeded by Lewis P. Featherston, who contested his election.
[11] Successfully contested the election of William H. Cate, and took his seat March 5, 1890.
[12] Election contested by John M. Clayton, who died January 29, 1889 (before the beginning of the

congressional term), while case was pending; served until September 5, 1890, when Clayton was declared to have been elected and the seat vacant; subsequently elected to fill vacancy caused by death of John M. Clayton, and took his seat December 1, 1890.
[13] Died February 28, 1891.
[14] Resigned October 1, 1890.
[15] Elected to fill vacancy caused by resignation of John J. De Haven, and took his seat December 9, 1890.

## GEORGIA—Continued

REPRESENTATIVES—CONTINUED

James H. Blount, *Macon*
Judson C. Clements, *Rome*
Henry H. Carlton, *Athens*
Allen D. Candler, *Gainesville*
George T. Barnes, *Augusta*

## IDAHO[16]

SENATORS[17]

George L. Shoup,[18] *Salmon City*
William J. McConnell,[19] *Moscow*

REPRESENTATIVE AT LARGE

Willis Sweet,[20] *Moscow*

## ILLINOIS

SENATORS

Shelby M. Cullom, *Springfield*
Charles B. Farwell, *Chicago*

REPRESENTATIVES

Abner Taylor, *Chicago*
Frank Lawler, *Chicago*
William E. Mason, *Chicago*
George E. Adams, *Chicago*
Albert J. Hopkins, *Aurora*
Robert R. Hitt, *Mount Morris*
Thomas J. Henderson, *Princeton*
Charles A. Hill, *Joliet*
Lewis E. Payson, *Pontiac*
Philip S. Post, *Galesburg*
William H. Gest, *Rock Island*
Scott Wike, *Pittsfield*
William M. Springer, *Springfield*
Jonathan H. Rowell, *Bloomington*
Joseph G. Cannon, *Danville*
George W. Fithian, *Newton*
Edward Lane, *Hillsboro*
William S. Forman, *Nashville*
Richard W. Townshend,[21]
　*Shawneetown*
James R. Williams,[22] *Carmi*
George W. Smith, *Murphysboro*

## INDIANA

SENATORS

Daniel W. Voorhees, *Terre Haute*
David Turpie, *Indianapolis*

REPRESENTATIVES

William F. Parrett,[23] *Evansville*
John H. O'Neall, *Washington*

Jason B. Brown, *Seymour*
William S. Holman, *Aurora*
George W. Cooper, *Columbus*
Thomas M. Browne, *Winchester*
William D. Bynum, *Indianapolis*
Elijah V. Brookshire, *Crawfordsville*
Joseph B. Cheadle, *Frankfort*
William D. Owen, *Logansport*
Augustus N. Martin, *Bluffton*
Charles A. O. McClellan, *Auburn*
Benjamin F. Shively, *South Bend*

## IOWA

SENATORS

William B. Allison, *Dubuque*
James F. Wilson, *Fairfield*

REPRESENTATIVES

John H. Gear, *Burlington*
Walter I. Hayes, *Clinton*
David B. Henderson, *Dubuque*
Joseph H. Sweney, *Osage*
Daniel Kerr, *Grundy Center*
John F. Lacey, *Oskaloosa*
Edwin H. Conger,[24] *Des Moines*
Edward R. Hays,[25] *Knoxville*
James P. Flick, *Bedford*
Joseph R. Reed, *Council Bluffs*
Jonathan P. Dolliver, *Fort Dodge*
Isaac S. Struble, *Le Mars*

## KANSAS

SENATORS

John J. Ingalls, *Atchison*
Preston B. Plumb, *Emporia*

REPRESENTATIVES

Edmund N. Morrill, *Hiawatha*
Edward H. Funston, *Iola*
Bishop W. Perkins, *Oswego*
Thomas Ryan,[26] *Topeka*
Harrison Kelley,[27] *Burlington*
John A. Anderson, *Manhattan*
Erastus J. Turner, *Hoxie*
Samuel R. Peters, *Newton*

## KENTUCKY

SENATORS

James B. Beck,[28] *Lexington*
John G. Carlisle,[29] *Covington*
Joseph C. S. Blackburn, *Versailles*

REPRESENTATIVES

William J. Stone, *Kuttawa*
William T. Ellis, *Owensboro*
Isaac H. Goodnight, *Franklin*
Alexander B. Montgomery,
　*Elizabethtown*
Asher G. Caruth, *Louisville*
John G. Carlisle,[30] *Covington*
William W. Dickerson,[31]
　*Williamstown*
William C. P. Breckinridge, *Lexington*
James B. McCreary, *Richmond*
Thomas H. Paynter, *Greenup*
John H. Wilson, *Barboursville*
Hugh F. Finley, *Williamsburg*

## LOUISIANA

SENATORS

Randall L. Gibson, *New Orleans*
James B. Eustis, *New Orleans*

REPRESENTATIVES

Theodore S. Wilkinson, *Plaquemines
　Parish*
Hamilton D. Coleman, *New Orleans*
Edward J. Gay,[32] *Plaquemine*
Andrew Price,[33] *Thibodaux*
Newton C. Blanchard, *Shreveport*
Charles J. Boatner, *Monroe*
Samuel M. Robertson, *Baton Rouge*

## MAINE

SENATORS

Eugene Hale, *Ellsworth*
William P. Frye, *Lewiston*

REPRESENTATIVES

Thomas B. Reed, *Portland*
Nelson Dingley, Jr., *Lewiston*
Seth L. Milliken, *Belfast*
Charles A. Boutelle, *Bangor*

## MARYLAND

SENATORS

Arthur Pue Gorman, *Laurel*
Ephraim K. Wilson,[34] *Snow Hill*

REPRESENTATIVES

Charles H. Gibson, *Easton*
Herman Stump, *Bel Air*
Harry W. Rusk, *Baltimore*
Henry Stockbridge, Jr., *Baltimore*

---

[16] Admitted as a State into the Union July 3, 1890.
[17] In addition to the Senators named, the credentials of Fred T. Dubois, who had been elected "for the term of six years from March 4, 1891," were presented December 30, 1890, but the Senate refused to consider them prior to the beginning of the Fifty-second Congress, when they were to become effective. (See U.S. Senate Election, Expulsion and Censure Cases, 1793-1990, Senate Document 103-33, pp. 235-38.)
[18] Took his seat December 29, 1890; term to expire, as determined by lot, March 3, 1895.
[19] Took his seat January 5, 1891; term to expire, as determined by lot, March 3, 1891.
[20] Took his seat December 1, 1890.

[21] Died March 9, 1889, before Congress assembled.
[22] Elected to fill vacancy caused by death of Richard W. Townshend, and took his seat December 2, 1889.
[23] Election unsuccessfully contested by Francis B. Posey.
[24] Resigned October 3, 1890.
[25] Elected to fill vacancy caused by resignation of Edwin H. Conger, and took his seat December 1, 1890.
[26] Resigned April 4, 1889, before Congress assembled.
[27] Elected to fill vacancy caused by resignation of

Thomas Ryan, and took his seat December 2, 1889.
[28] Died May 3, 1890.
[29] Elected to fill vacancy caused by death of James B. Beck, and took his seat May 26, 1890.
[30] Resigned May 26, 1890, having been elected Senator.
[31] Elected to fill vacancy caused by resignation of John G. Carlisle, and took his seat June 30, 1890.
[32] Died May 30, 1889, before Congress assembled.
[33] Elected to fill vacancy caused by death of Edward J. Gay, and took his seat December 2, 1889.
[34] Died February 24, 1891; had been reelected for the term beginning March 4, 1891.

Barnes Compton,[35] *Laurel*
Sydney E. Mudd,[36] *Bryantown*
Louis E. McComas, *Hagerstown*

## MASSACHUSETTS

### SENATORS

Henry L. Dawes, *Pittsfield*
George F. Hoar, *Worcester*

### REPRESENTATIVES

Charles S. Randall, *New Bedford*
Elijah A. Morse, *Canton*
John F. Andrew, *Boston*
Joseph H. O'Neil, *Boston*
Nathaniel P. Banks, *Waltham*
Henry Cabot Lodge, *Nahant*
William Cogswell, *Salem*
Frederic T. Greenhalge, *Lowell*
John W. Candler, *Brookline*
Joseph H. Walker, *Worcester*
Rodney Wallace, *Fitchburg*
Francis W. Rockwell, *Pittsfield*

## MICHIGAN

### SENATORS

Francis B. Stockbridge, *Kalamazoo*
James McMillan, *Detroit*

### REPRESENTATIVES

J. Logan Chipman, *Detroit*
Edward P. Allen, *Ypsilanti*
James O'Donnell, *Jackson*
Julius C. Burrows, *Kalamazoo*
Charles E. Belknap, *Grand Rapids*
Mark S. Brewer, *Pontiac*
Justin R. Whiting, *St. Clair*
Aaron T. Bliss, *Saginaw*
Byron M. Cutcheon, *Manistee*
Frank W. Wheeler, *West Bay City*
Samuel M. Stephenson, *Menominee*

## MINNESOTA

### SENATORS

Cushman K. Davis, *St. Paul*
William D. Washburn, *Minneapolis*

### REPRESENTATIVES

Mark H. Dunnell, *Owatonna*
John Lind, *New Ulm*
Darwin S. Hall, *Stewart*
Samuel P. Snider, *Minneapolis*
Solomon G. Comstock, *Moorhead*

## MISSISSIPPI

### SENATORS

James Z. George, *Carrollton*
Edward C. Walthall, *Grenada*

### REPRESENTATIVES

John M. Allen, *Tupelo*
James B. Morgan,[37] *Hernando*
Thomas C. Catchings, *Vicksburg*
Clarke Lewis, *Cliftonville*
Chapman L. Anderson, *Kosciusko*
Thomas R. Stockdale, *Summit*
Charles E. Hooker, *Jackson*

## MISSOURI

### SENATORS

Francis M. Cockrell, *Warrensburg*
George G. Vest, *Kansas City*

### REPRESENTATIVES

William H. Hatch, *Hannibal*
Charles H. Mansur, *Chillicothe*
Alexander M. Dockery, *Gallatin*
Robert P. C. Wilson,[38] *Platte City*
John C. Tarsney, *Kansas City*
John T. Heard, *Sedalia*
Richard H. Norton, *Troy*
Frederick G. Niedringhaus, *St. Louis*
Nathan Frank, *St. Louis*
William M. Kinsey, *St. Louis*
Richard P. Bland, *Lebanon*
William J. Stone, *Nevada*
William H. Wade, *Springfield*
James P. Walker,[39] *Dexter*
Robert H. Whitelaw,[40] *Cape Girardeau*

## MONTANA[41]

### SENATORS[42]

Thomas C. Power,[43] *Helena*
Wilbur F. Sanders,[44] *Helena*

### REPRESENTATIVE AT LARGE

Thomas H. Carter,[45] *Helena*

## NEBRASKA

### SENATORS

Charles F. Manderson, *Omaha*
Algernon S. Paddock, *Beatrice*

### REPRESENTATIVES

William J. Connell, *Omaha*
James Laird,[46] *Hastings*
Gilbert L. Laws,[47] *McCook*
George W. E. Dorsey, *Fremont*

## NEVADA

### SENATORS

John P. Jones, *Gold Hill*
William M. Stewart, *Carson City*

### REPRESENTATIVE AT LARGE

Horace F. Bartine, *Carson City*

## NEW HAMPSHIRE

### SENATORS

Henry W. Blair, *Manchester*
Gilman Marston,[48] *Exeter*
William E. Chandler,[49] *Concord*

### REPRESENTATIVES

Alonzo Nute, *Farmington*
Orren C. Moore, *Nashua*

## NEW JERSEY

### SENATORS

John R. McPherson, *Jersey City*
Rufus Blodgett, *Long Branch*

### REPRESENTATIVES

Christopher A. Bergen, *Camden*
James Buchanan, *Trenton*
Jacob A. Geissenhainer, *Freehold*
Samuel Fowler, *Newton*
Charles D. Beckwith, *Paterson*
Herman Lehlbach, *Newark*
William McAdoo, *Jersey City*

## NEW YORK

### SENATORS

William M. Evarts, *New York City*
Frank Hiscock, *Syracuse*

### REPRESENTATIVES

James W. Covert, *Long Island City*
Felix Campbell, *Brooklyn*
William C. Wallace, *Brooklyn*
John M. Clancy, *Brooklyn*
Thomas F. Magner, *Brooklyn*
Frank T. Fitzgerald,[50] *New York City*
Charles H. Turner,[51] *New York City*
Edward J. Dunphy, *New York City*
John H. McCarthy,[52] *New York City*
Samuel S. Cox,[53] *New York City*

---

[35] Served until March 20, 1890; succeeded by Sydney E. Mudd, who contested his election.

[36] Successfully contested the election of Barnes Compton, and took his seat March 20, 1890.

[37] Election unsuccessfully contested by James R. Chalmers.

[38] Elected to fill vacancy caused by death of Representative-elect James N. Burnes, in the preceding Congress, and took his seat December 2, 1889.

[39] Died July 20, 1890.

[40] Elected to fill vacancy caused by death of James P. Walker, and took his seat December 1, 1890.

[41] Admitted as a State into the Union November 8, 1889.

[42] William A. Clark and Martin Maginnis pre-

sented papers purporting to be credentials of their election January 23, 1890; the four claimants were given privileges of the floor pending the contest; by resolutions of April 16, 1890, Clark and Maginnis were declared not entitled to seats and Power and Sanders entitled thereto. (See U.S. Senate Election, Expulsion and Censure Cases, 1793-1990, Senate Document 103-33, pp. 232-34.)

[43] Took his seat April 16, 1890; term to expire, as determined by lot, March 3, 1895.

[44] Took his seat April 16, 1890; term to expire, as determined by lot, March 3, 1893.

[45] Took his seat December 2, 1889.

[46] Died August 17, 1889, before Congress assembled.

[47] Elected to fill vacancy caused by death of James Laird, and took his seat December 2, 1889.

[48] Appointed to fill vacancy in term beginning March 4, 1889, during the recess of the legislature.

[49] Elected to fill vacancy in the term beginning March 4, 1889, and took his seat December 2, 1889.

[50] Resigned November 4, 1889, before Congress assembled.

[51] Elected to fill vacancy caused by resignation of Frank T. Fitzgerald, and took his seat December 9, 1889.

[52] Resigned January 14, 1891.

[53] Died September 10, 1889, before Congress assembled.

## NEW YORK—Continued

### REPRESENTATIVES—CONTINUED

Amos J. Cummings,[54] *New York City*
Francis B. Spinola, *New York City*
John Quinn, *New York City*
Roswell P. Flower, *New York City*
Ashbel P. Fitch, *New York City*
William G. Stahlnecker, *Yonkers*
Moses D. Stivers, *Middletown*
John H. Ketcham, *Dover Plains*
Charles J. Knapp, *Deposit*
John A. Quackenbush, *Stillwater*
Charles Tracey, *Albany*
John Sanford, *Amsterdam*
John H. Moffitt, *Chateaugay Lake*
Frederick Lansing, *Watertown*
James S. Sherman, *Utica*
David Wilber,[55] *Oneonta*
John S. Pindar,[56] *Cobleskill*
James J. Belden, *Syracuse*
Milton De Lano, *Canastota*
Newton W. Nutting,[57] *Oswego*
Sereno E. Payne,[58] *Auburn*
Thomas S. Flood, *Elmira*
John Raines, *Canandaigua*
Charles S. Baker, *Rochester*
John G. Sawyer, *Albion*
John M. Farquhar, *Buffalo*
John McC. Wiley, *East Aurora*
William G. Laidlaw, *Ellicottville*

## NORTH CAROLINA

### SENATORS

Matt W. Ransom, *Weldon*
Zebulon B. Vance, *Charlotte*

### REPRESENTATIVES

Thomas G. Skinner, *Hertford*
Henry P. Cheatham, *Henderson*
Charles W. McClammy, *Scotts Hill*
Benjamin H. Bunn, *Rocky Mount*
John M. Brower, *Mount Airy*
Alfred Rowland, *Lumberton*
John S. Henderson, *Salisbury*
William H. H. Cowles, *Wilkesboro*
Hamilton G. Ewart, *Hendersonville*

## NORTH DAKOTA[59]

### SENATORS

Lyman R. Casey,[60] *Jamestown*
Gilbert A. Pierce,[61] *Fargo*

### REPRESENTATIVE AT LARGE

Henry C. Hansbrough,[62] *Devils Lake*

## OHIO

### SENATORS

John Sherman, *Mansfield*
Henry B. Payne, *Cleveland*

### REPRESENTATIVES

Benjamin Butterworth, *Cincinnati*
John A. Caldwell, *Cincinnati*
Elihu S. Williams, *Troy*
Samuel S. Yoder, *Lima*
George E. Seney, *Tiffin*
Melvin M. Boothman, *Bryan*
Henry L. Morey, *Hamilton*
Robert P. Kennedy, *Bellefontaine*
William C. Cooper, *Mount Vernon*
William E. Haynes, *Fremont*
Albert C. Thompson, *Portsmouth*
Jacob J. Pugsley, *Hillsboro*
Joseph H. Outhwaite, *Columbus*
Charles P. Wickham, *Norwalk*
Charles H. Grosvenor, *Athens*
James W. Owens, *Newark*
Joseph D. Taylor, *Cambridge*
William McKinley, Jr., *Canton*
Ezra B. Taylor, *Warren*
Martin L. Smyser, *Wooster*
Theodore E. Burton, *Cleveland*

## OREGON

### SENATORS

Joseph N. Dolph, *Portland*
John H. Mitchell, *Portland*

### REPRESENTATIVE AT LARGE

Binger Hermann, *Roseburg*

## PENNSYLVANIA

### SENATORS

J. Donald Cameron, *Harrisburg*
Matthew S. Quay, *Beaver*

### REPRESENTATIVES

Henry H. Bingham, *Philadelphia*
Charles O'Neill, *Philadelphia*
Samuel J. Randall,[63] *Philadelphia*
Richard Vaux,[64] *Philadelphia*
William D. Kelley,[65] *Philadelphia*
John E. Reyburn,[66] *Philadelphia*
Alfred C. Harmer, *Philadelphia*
Smedley Darlington, *West Chester*
Robert M. Yardley, *Doylestown*
William Mutchler, *Easton*

David B. Brunner, *Reading*
Marriott Brosius, *Lancaster*
Joseph A. Scranton, *Scranton*
Edwin S. Osborne, *Wilkes-Barre*
James B. Reilly, *Pottsville*
John W. Rife, *Middletown*
Myron B. Wright, *Susquehanna*
Henry C. McCormick, *Williamsport*
Charles R. Buckalew, *Bloomsburg*
Louis E. Atkinson, *Miffintown*
Levi Maish, *York*
Edward Scull, *Somerset*
Samuel A. Craig, *Brookville*
John Dalzell, *Pittsburgh*
Thomas M. Bayne, *Allegheny*
Joseph W. Ray, *Waynesburg*
Charles C. Townsend, *New Brighton*
William C. Culbertson, *Girard*
Lewis F. Watson,[67] *Warren*
Charles W. Stone,[68] *Warren*
James Kerr, *Clearfield*

## RHODE ISLAND

### SENATORS

Nelson W. Aldrich, *Providence*
Jonathan Chace,[69] *Providence*
Nathan F. Dixon,[70] *Westerly*

### REPRESENTATIVES

Henry J. Spooner, *Providence*
Warren O. Arnold, *Gloucester*

## SOUTH CAROLINA

### SENATORS

Matthew C. Butler, *Edgefield*
Wade Hampton, *Charleston*

### REPRESENTATIVES

Samuel Dibble, *Orangeburg*
George D. Tillman, *Clarks Hill*
James S. Cothran, *Abbeville*
William H. Perry, *Greenville*
John J. Hemphill, *Chester*
George W. Dargan, *Darlington*
William Elliott,[71] *Beaufort*
Thomas E. Miller,[72] *Beaufort*

## SOUTH DAKOTA[73]

### SENATORS

Richard F. Pettigrew,[74] *Sioux Falls*
Gideon C. Moody,[75] *Deadwood*

---

[54] Elected to fill vacancy caused by death of Samuel S. Cox, and took his seat December 2, 1889.

[55] Died April 1, 1890.

[56] Elected to fill vacancy caused by death of David Wilber, and took his seat December 1, 1890.

[57] Died October 15, 1889, before Congress assembled.

[58] Elected to fill vacancy caused by death of Newton W. Nutting, and took his seat December 2, 1889.

[59] Formed from a portion of the Territory of Dakota, and admitted as a State into the Union November 2, 1889.

[60] Took his seat December 4, 1889; term to expire, as determined by lot, March 3, 1893.

[61] Took his seat December 4, 1889; term to expire, as determined by lot, March 3, 1891.

[62] Took his seat December 2, 1889.

[63] Died April 13, 1890.

[64] Elected to fill vacancy caused by death of Samuel J. Randall, and took his seat May 28, 1890.

[65] Died January 9, 1890.

[66] Elected to fill vacancy caused by death of William D. Kelley, and took his seat February 24, 1890.

[67] Died August 25, 1890.

[68] Elected to fill vacancy caused by death of Lewis F. Watson, and took his seat December 1, 1890.

[69] Resigned April 9, 1889.

[70] Elected to fill vacancy caused by resignation

of Jonathan Chace, and took his seat December 2, 1889.

[71] Served until September 23, 1890; succeeded by Thomas E. Miller, who contested his election.

[72] Successfully contested the election of William Elliott, and took his seat September 24, 1890.

[73] Formed from a portion of the Territory of Dakota, and admitted as a State into the Union November 2, 1889.

[74] Took his seat December 2, 1889; term to expire, as determined by lot, March 3, 1895.

[75] Took his seat December 2, 1889; term to expire, as determined by lot, March 3, 1891.

REPRESENTATIVES AT LARGE

Oscar S. Gifford,[76] *Canton*
John A. Pickler,[76] *Faulkton*

## TENNESSEE

SENATORS

Isham G. Harris, *Memphis*
William B. Bate, *Nashville*

REPRESENTATIVES

Alfred A. Taylor, *Johnson City*
Leonidas C. Houk, *Knoxville*
H. Clay Evans, *Chattanooga*
Benton McMillin, *Carthage*
James D. Richardson, *Murfreesboro*
Joseph E. Washington, *Cedar Hill*
Washington C. Whitthorne, *Columbia*
Benjamin A. Enloe, *Jackson*
Rice A. Pierce, *Union City*
James Phelan,[77] *Memphis*

## TEXAS

SENATORS

Richard Coke, *Waco*
John H. Reagan, *Palestine*

REPRESENTATIVES

Charles Stewart, *Houston*
William H. Martin, *Athens*
Constantine B. Kilgore, *Wills Point*
David B. Culberson, *Jefferson*
Silas Hare, *Sherman*
Jo Abbott, *Hillsboro*
William H. Crain, *Cuero*
Littleton W. Moore, *Lagrange*
Roger Q. Mills, *Corsicana*
Joseph D. Sayers, *Bastrop*
Samuel W. T. Lanham, *Weatherford*

## VERMONT

SENATORS

George F. Edmunds, *Burlington*
Justin S. Morrill, *Strafford*

REPRESENTATIVES

John W. Stewart, *Middlebury*
William W. Grout, *Barton*

## VIRGINIA

SENATORS

John W. Daniel, *Lynchburg*
John S. Barbour, *Alexandria*

REPRESENTATIVES

Thomas H. B. Browne, *Accomac*
George E. Bowden, *Norfolk*
George D. Wise,[78] *Richmond*
Edmund Waddill, Jr.,[79] *Richmond*
Edward C. Venable,[80] *Petersburg*
John M. Langston,[81] *Petersburg*
Posey G. Lester, *Floyd*
Paul C. Edmunds, *Halifax*
Charles T. O'Ferrall, *Harrisonburg*
William H. F. Lee, *Burkes Station*
John A. Buchanan,[82] *Abingdon*
Henry St. George Tucker, *Staunton*

## WASHINGTON[83]

SENATORS

John B. Allen,[84] *Walla Walla*
Watson C. Squire,[85] *Seattle*

REPRESENTATIVE AT LARGE

John L. Wilson,[86] *Spokane Falls*

## WEST VIRGINIA

SENATORS

John E. Kenna, *Charleston*
Charles J. Faulkner, *Martinsburg*

REPRESENTATIVES

John O. Pendleton,[87] *Wheeling*
George W. Atkinson,[88] *Wheeling*
William L. Wilson, *Charles Town*
John D. Alderson, *Nicholas*
J. Monroe Jackson,[89] *Parkersburg*
Charles B. Smith,[90] *Parkersburg*

## WISCONSIN

SENATORS

Philetus Sawyer, *Oshkosh*
John C. Spooner, *Hudson*

REPRESENTATIVES

Lucien B. Caswell, *Fort Atkinson*
Charles Barwig, *Mayville*
Robert M. La Follette, *Madison*
Isaac W. Van Schaick, *Milwaukee*
George H. Brickner, *Sheboygan Falls*

Charles B. Clark, *Neenah*
Ormsby B. Thomas, *Prairie du Chien*
Nils P. Haugen, *River Falls*
Myron H. McCord, *Merrill*

## WYOMING[91]

SENATORS

Joseph M. Carey,[92] *Cheyenne*
Francis E. Warren,[93] *Cheyenne*

REPRESENTATIVE AT LARGE

Clarence D. Clark,[94] *Evanston*

## TERRITORY OF ARIZONA

DELEGATE

Marcus A. Smith, *Tombstone*

## TERRITORY OF DAKOTA

DELEGATE

George A. Mathews,[95] *Brookings*

## TERRITORY OF IDAHO

DELEGATE

Fred T. Dubois,[96] *Blackfoot*

## TERRITORY OF MONTANA

DELEGATE

Thomas H. Carter,[97] *Helena*

## TERRITORY OF NEW MEXICO

DELEGATE

Antonio Joseph, *Ojo Caliente*

## TERRITORY OF OKLAHOMA [98]

DELEGATE

David A. Harvey,[99] *Oklahoma City*

---

[76] Took his seat December 2, 1889.

[77] Died January 30, 1891.

[78] Served until April 10, 1890; succeeded by Edmond Waddill, Jr., who contested his election.

[79] Successfully contested the election of George D. Wise, and took his seat April 12, 1890.

[80] Served until September 23, 1890; succeeded by John M. Langston, who contested his election.

[81] Successfully contested the election of Edward C. Venable, and took his seat September 23, 1890. It was in connection with this case that the minority party adopted for the first time the plan of withdrawing in a body from the Hall of the House, to avoid being counted as part of a quorum.

[82] Election unsuccessfully contested by Henry Bowen.

[83] Admitted as a State into the Union November 11, 1889.

[84] Took his seat December 2, 1889; term to expire, as determined by lot, March 3, 1893.

[85] Took his seat December 2, 1889; term to expire, as determined by lot, March 3, 1891.

[86] Took his seat December 2, 1889.

[87] Served until February 26, 1890; succeeded by George W. Atkinson, who contested his election.

[88] Successfully contested the election of John O. Pendleton, and took his seat February 26, 1890.

[89] Served until February 3, 1890; succeeded by Charles B. Smith, who contested his election. It was in connection with this case that Speaker Reed, for the first time, made his parliamentary ruling regarding the "counting of a quorum."

[90] Successfully contested the election of J. Monroe Jackson and took his seat February 3, 1890.

[91] Admitted as a State into the Union July 10, 1890.

[92] Took his seat December 1, 1890; term to expire, as determined by lot, March 3, 1895.

[93] Took his seat December 1, 1890; term to expire,

as determined by lot, March 3, 1893.

[94] Took his seat December 1, 1890.

[95] Served until November 2, 1889, when the Territory of Dakota was divided and granted statehood as the States of North and South Dakota by act of Congress approved February 22, 1889.

[96] Served until July 3, 1890, when the Territory of Idaho was granted statehood by act of Congress approved that date.

[97] Served until November 8, 1889, when the Territory of Montana was granted statehood by act of Congress approved February 22, 1889; subsequently elected the first Representative from the new State.

[98] Formed from a portion of Indian Territory and from that portion of the United States known as the "Public Land Strip," and granted a Delegate in Congress by act of May 2, 1890.

[99] Took his seat December 1, 1890.

## TERRITORY OF UTAH

DELEGATE
John T. Caine, *Salt Lake City*

## TERRITORY OF WASHINGTON

DELEGATE
John B. Allen,[100] *Seattle*

## TERRITORY OF WYOMING

DELEGATE
Joseph M. Carey,[101] *Cheyenne*

---

[100] Served until November 11, 1889, when the Territory of Washington was granted statehood by act of Congress approved February 22, 1889; subsequently elected Senator from the new State.

[101] Served until July 10, 1890, when the Territory of Wyoming was granted statehood by act of Congress approved July 10, 1890; subsequently elected Senator from the new State.

# 52ND CONGRESS

## MARCH 4, 1891, TO MARCH 3, 1893

Levi P. Morton
Vice President

FIRST SESSION— *December 7, 1891, to August 5, 1892*
SECOND SESSION— *December 5, 1892, to March 3, 1893*

VICE PRESIDENT OF THE UNITED STATES— Levi P. Morton, of New York
PRESIDENT PRO TEMPORE OF THE SENATE— Charles F. Manderson, of Nebraska
SECRETARY OF THE SENATE— Anson G. McCook, of New York
SERGEANT AT ARMS OF THE SENATE— Edward K. Valentine, of Nebraska

SPEAKER OF THE HOUSE OF REPRESENTATIVES— Charles F. Crisp,[1] of Georgia
CLERK OF THE HOUSE— Edward McPherson, of Pennsylvania; James Kerr,[2] of Pennsylvania
SERGEANT AT ARMS OF THE HOUSE— Adoniram J. Holmes, of Iowa; Samuel S. Yoder,[3] of Ohio
DOORKEEPER OF THE HOUSE— Charles H. Turner, of New York
POSTMASTER OF THE HOUSE— J. W. Hathaway

Charles F. Crisp
Speaker

## ALABAMA

### SENATORS
John T. Morgan, *Selma*
James L. Pugh, *Eufaula*

### REPRESENTATIVES
Richard H. Clarke, *Mobile*
Hilary A. Herbert, *Montgomery*
William C. Oates, *Abbeville*
Louis W. Turpin,[4] *Newbern*
James E. Cobb, *Tuskegee*
John H. Bankhead, *Fayette*
William H. Forney, *Jacksonville*
Joseph Wheeler, *Wheeler*

## ARKANSAS

### SENATORS
James K. Jones, *Washington*
James H. Berry, *Bentonville*

### REPRESENTATIVES
William H. Cate, *Jonesboro*
Clifton R. Breckinridge, *Pine Bluff*
Thomas C. McRae, *Prescott*
William L. Terry, *Little Rock*
Samuel W. Peel, *Bentonville*

## CALIFORNIA

### SENATORS
Leland Stanford, *San Francisco*
Charles N. Felton,[5] *San Francisco*

### REPRESENTATIVES
Thomas J. Geary, *Santa Rosa*
Anthony Caminetti, *Jackson*
Joseph McKenna,[6] *Suisun*

Samuel G. Hilborn,[7] *Oakland*
John T. Cutting, *San Francisco*
Eugene F. Loud, *San Francisco*
William W. Bowers, *San Diego*

## COLORADO

### SENATORS
Henry M. Teller, *Central City*
Edward O. Wolcott, *Denver*

### REPRESENTATIVE AT LARGE
Hosea Townsend, *Silver Cliff*

## CONNECTICUT

### SENATORS
Orville H. Platt, *Meriden*
Joseph R. Hawley, *Hartford*

### REPRESENTATIVES
Lewis Sperry, *Hartford*
Washington F. Willcox, *Chester*
Charles A. Russell, *Killingly*
Robert E. De Forest, *Bridgeport*

## DELAWARE

### SENATORS
George Gray, *New Castle*
Anthony Higgins, *Wilmington*

### REPRESENTATIVE AT LARGE
John W. Causey, *Milford*

## FLORIDA

### SENATORS
Wilkinson Call,[8] *Jacksonville*
Samuel Pasco, *Monticello*

### REPRESENTATIVES
Stephen R. Mallory, *Pensacola*
Robert Bullock, *Ocala*

## GEORGIA

### SENATORS
Alfred H. Colquitt, *Atlanta*
John B. Gordon, *Atlanta*

### REPRESENTATIVES
Rufus E. Lester, *Savannah*
Henry G. Turner, *Quitman*
Charles F. Crisp, *Americus*
Charles L. Moses, *Turin*
Leonidas F. Livingston, *Atlanta*
James H. Blount, *Macon*
Robert W. Everett, *Fish*
Thomas G. Lawson, *Eatonton*
Thomas E. Winn, *Lawrenceville*
Thomas E. Watson, *Thomson*

## IDAHO

### SENATORS
George L. Shoup, *Salmon City*
Fred T. Dubois,[9] *Blackfoot*

### REPRESENTATIVE AT LARGE
Willis Sweet, *Moscow*

---

[1] Elected December 8, 1891.
[2] Elected December 8, 1891.
[3] Elected December 8, 1891.
[4] Election unsuccessfully contested by John V. McDuffie.
[5] Elected to fill vacancy caused by death of George Hearst, in preceding Congress, and took his seat

December 7, 1891.
[6] Resigned March 28, 1892.
[7] Elected to fill vacancy caused by resignation of Joseph McKenna, and took his seat December 5, 1892.
[8] Election unsuccessfully contested by Robert H. M. Davidson. (See U.S. Senate Election, Expulsion and Censure Cases, 1793-1990, Senate Document 103-33,

pp. 239-40.)

[9] Election unsuccessfully contested by William H. Clagett. (See U.S. Senate Election, Expulsion and Censure Cases, 1793-1990, Senate Document 103-33, pp. 235-38.)

## ILLINOIS

SENATORS

Shelby M. Cullom, *Springfield*
John McAuley Palmer, *Springfield*

REPRESENTATIVES

Abner Taylor, *Chicago*
Lawrence E. McGann, *Chicago*
Allan C. Durborow, Jr., *Chicago*
Walter C. Newberry, *Chicago*
Albert J. Hopkins, *Aurora*
Robert R. Hitt, *Mount Morris*
Thomas J. Henderson, *Princeton*
Lewis Steward, *Plano*
Herman W. Snow, *Sheldon*
Philip S. Post, *Galesburg*
Benjamin T. Cable, *Rock Island*
Scott Wike, *Pittsfield*
William M. Springer, *Springfield*
Owen Scott, *Bloomington*
Samuel T. Busey, *Urbana*
George W. Fithian, *Newton*
Edward Lane, *Hillsboro*
William S. Forman, *Nashville*
James R. Williams, *Carmi*
George W. Smith, *Murphysboro*

## INDIANA

SENATORS

Daniel W. Voorhees, *Terre Haute*
David Turpie, *Indianapolis*

REPRESENTATIVES

William F. Parrett, *Evansville*
John L. Bretz, *Jasper*
Jason B. Brown, *Seymour*
William S. Holman, *Aurora*
George W. Cooper, *Columbus*
Henry U. Johnson, *Richmond*
William D. Bynum, *Indianapolis*
Elijah V. Brookshire, *Crawfordsville*
Daniel W. Waugh, *Tipton*
David H. Patton, *Remington*
Augustus N. Martin, *Bluffton*
Charles A. O. McClellan, *Auburn*
Benjamin F. Shively, *South Bend*

## IOWA

SENATORS

William B. Allison, *Dubuque*
James F. Wilson, *Fairfield*

REPRESENTATIVES

John J. Seerley, *Burlington*
Walter I. Hayes, *Clinton*
David B. Henderson, *Dubuque*
Walter H. Butler, *West Union*
John T. Hamilton, *Cedar Rapids*

Frederick E. White, *Webster*
John A. T. Hull, *Des Moines*
James P. Flick, *Bedford*
Thomas Bowman, *Council Bluffs*
Jonathan P. Dolliver, *Fort Dodge*
George D. Perkins, *Sioux City*

## KANSAS

SENATORS

Preston B. Plumb,[10] *Emporia*
Bishop W. Perkins,[11] *Oswego*
William A. Peffer, *Topeka*

REPRESENTATIVES

Case Broderick, *Holton*
Edward H. Funston, *Iola*
Benjamin H. Clover, *Cambridge*
John G. Otis, *Topeka*
John Davis, *Junction City*
William Baker, *Lincoln*
Jeremiah Simpson, *Medicine Lodge*

## KENTUCKY

SENATORS

Joseph C. S. Blackburn, *Versailles*
John G. Carlisle,[12] *Covington*
William Lindsay,[13] *Frankfort*

REPRESENTATIVES

William J. Stone, *Kuttawa*
William T. Ellis, *Owensboro*
Isaac H. Goodnight, *Franklin*
Alexander B. Montgomery,
  *Elizabethtown*
Asher G. Caruth, *Louisville*
William W. Dickerson, *Williamstown*
William C. P. Breckinridge, *Lexington*
James B. McCreary, *Richmond*
Thomas H. Paynter, *Greenup*
John W. Kendall,[14] *West Liberty*
Joseph M. Kendall,[15] *Prestonsburg*
John H. Wilson, *Barboursville*

## LOUISIANA

SENATORS

Randall L. Gibson,[16] *New Orleans*
Donelson Caffery,[17] *Franklin*
Edward D. White, *New Orleans*

REPRESENTATIVES

Adolph Meyer, *New Orleans*
Matthew D. Lagan, *New Orleans*
Andrew Price, *Thibodaux*
Newton C. Blanchard, *Shreveport*
Charles J. Boatner, *Monroe*
Samuel M. Robertson, *Baton Rouge*

## MAINE

SENATORS

Eugene Hale, *Ellsworth*
William P. Frye, *Lewiston*

REPRESENTATIVES

Thomas B. Reed, *Portland*
Nelson Dingley, Jr., *Lewiston*
Seth L. Milliken, *Belfast*
Charles A. Boutelle, *Bangor*

## MARYLAND

SENATORS

Arthur Pue Gorman, *Laurel*
Charles H. Gibson,[18] *Easton*

REPRESENTATIVES

Henry Page,[19] *Princess Anne*
John B. Brown,[20] *Centerville*
Herman Stump, *Bel Air*
Harry W. Rusk, *Baltimore*
Isidor Rayner, *Baltimore*
Barnes Compton, *Laurel*
William M. McKaig, *Cumberland*

## MASSACHUSETTS

SENATORS

Henry L. Dawes, *Pittsfield*
George F. Hoar, *Worcester*

REPRESENTATIVES

Charles S. Randall, *New Bedford*
Elijah A. Morse, *Canton*
John F. Andrew, *Boston*
Joseph H. O'Neil, *Boston*
Sherman Hoar, *Waltham*
Henry Cabot Lodge,[21] *Nahant*
William Cogswell, *Salem*
Moses T. Stevens, *North Andover*
George F. Williams, *Dedham*
Joseph H. Walker, *Worcester*
Frederick S. Coolidge, *Ashburnham*
John C. Crosby, *Pittsfield*

## MICHIGAN

SENATORS

Francis B. Stockbridge, *Kalamazoo*
James McMillan, *Detroit*

REPRESENTATIVES

J. Logan Chipman, *Detroit*
James S. Gorman, *Chelsea*
James O'Donnell, *Jackson*
Julius C. Burrows, *Kalamazoo*
Melbourne H. Ford,[22] *Grand Rapids*

---

[10] Died December 20, 1891.
[11] Appointed to fill vacancy caused by death of Preston B. Plumb, and took his seat January 5, 1892.
[12] Resigned February 4, 1893.
[13] Elected to fill vacancy caused by resignation of John G. Carlisle, and took his seat February 21, 1893.
[14] Died March 7, 1892.
[15] Elected to fill vacancy caused by death of John W. Kendall, and took his seat May 5, 1892.

[16] Died December 15, 1892.
[17] Appointed to fill vacancy caused by death of Randall L. Gibson, and took his seat January 14, 1893; subsequently elected.
[18] Appointed to fill vacancy caused by death of Ephraim K. Wilson, in preceding Congress, and took his seat December 7, 1891; subsequently elected; vacancy in this class from February 25 to November 18, 1891.

[19] Resigned September 3, 1892, having been appointed judge of first judicial district of Maryland.
[20] Elected to fill vacancy caused by resignation of Henry Page, and took his seat December 5, 1892.
[21] Resigned March 3, 1893, before the commencement of the Fifty-third Congress, to which he had been reelected, having been elected Senator.
[22] Died April 20, 1891, before Congress assembled.

Charles E. Belknap,[23] *Grand Rapids*
Byron G. Stout, *Pontiac*
Justin R. Whiting, *St. Clair*
Henry M. Youmans, *Saginaw*
Harrison H. Wheeler, *Ludington*
Thomas A. E. Weadock, *Bay City*
Samuel M. Stephenson, *Menominee*

## MINNESOTA

### SENATORS

Cushman K. Davis, *St. Paul*
William D. Washburn, *Minneapolis*

### REPRESENTATIVES

William H. Harries, *Caledonia*
John Lind, *New Ulm*
Osee M. Hall, *Red Wing*
James N. Castle, *Stillwater*
Kittel Halvorson, *North Fork*

## MISSISSIPPI

### SENATORS

James Z. George, *Carrollton*
Edward C. Walthall, *Grenada*

### REPRESENTATIVES

John M. Allen, *Tupelo*
John C. Kyle, *Sardis*
Thomas C. Catchings, *Vicksburg*
Clarke Lewis, *Macon*
Joseph H. Beeman, *Eley*
Thomas R. Stockdale, *Summit*
Charles E. Hooker, *Jackson*

## MISSOURI

### SENATORS

Francis M. Cockrell, *Warrensburg*
George G. Vest, *Kansas City*

### REPRESENTATIVES

William H. Hatch, *Hannibal*
Charles H. Mansur, *Chillicothe*
Alexander M. Dockery, *Gallatin*
Robert P. C. Wilson, *Platte City*
John C. Tarsney, *Kansas City*
John T. Heard, *Sedalia*
Richard H. Norton, *Troy*
John J. O'Neill, *St. Louis*
Seth W. Cobb, *St. Louis*
Samuel Byrns, *Potosi*
Richard P. Bland, *Lebanon*
David A. De Armond, *Butler*
Robert W. Fyan, *Marshfield*
Marshall Arnold, *Benton*

## MONTANA

### SENATORS

Thomas C. Power, *Helena*
Wilber F. Sanders, *Helena*

### REPRESENTATIVE AT LARGE

William W. Dixon, *Butte*

## NEBRASKA

### SENATORS

Charles F. Manderson, *Omaha*
Algernon S. Paddock, *Beatrice*

### REPRESENTATIVES

William J. Bryan, *Lincoln*
William A. McKeighan, *Red Cloud*
Omer M. Kem, *Broken Bow*

## NEVADA

### SENATORS

John P. Jones, *Gold Hill*
William M. Stewart, *Carson City*

### REPRESENTATIVE AT LARGE

Horace F. Bartine, *Carson City*

## NEW HAMPSHIRE

### SENATORS

William E. Chandler, *Concord*
Jacob H. Gallinger, *Concord*

### REPRESENTATIVES

Luther F. McKinney, *Manchester*
Warren F. Daniell, *Franklin*

## NEW JERSEY

### SENATORS

John R. McPherson, *Jersey City*
Rufus Blodgett, *Long Branch*

### REPRESENTATIVES

Christopher A. Bergen, *Camden*
James Buchanan, *Trenton*
Jacob A. Geissenhainer, *Freehold*
Samuel Fowler, *Newton*
Cornelius A. Cadmus, *Paterson*
Thomas D. English, *Newark*
Edward F. McDonald,[24] *Harrison*

## NEW YORK

### SENATORS

Frank Hiscock, *Syracuse*
David B. Hill,[25] *Elmira*

### REPRESENTATIVES

James W. Covert, *Long Island City*
David A. Boody,[26] *Brooklyn*
Alfred C. Chapin,[27] *Brooklyn*

William J. Coombs, *Brooklyn*
John M. Clancy, *Brooklyn*
Thomas F. Magner, *Brooklyn*
John R. Fellows, *New York City*
Edward J. Dunphy, *New York City*
Timothy J. Campbell, *New York City*
Amos J. Cummings, *New York City*
Francis B. Spinola,[28] *New York City*
W. Bourke Cockran,[29] *New York City*
J. De Witt Warner, *New York City*
Roswell P. Flower,[30] *New York City*
Joseph J. Little,[31] *New York City*
Ashbel P. Fitch, *New York City*
William G. Stahlnecker, *Yonkers*
Henry Bacon, *Goshen*
John H. Ketcham, *Dover Plains*
Isaac N. Cox, *Ellenville*
John A. Quackenbush, *Stillwater*
Charles Tracey, *Albany*
John Sanford, *Amsterdam*
John M. Wever, *Plattsburg*
Leslie W. Russell,[32] *Ogdensburg*
Newton M. Curtis,[33] *Ogdensburg*
Henry W. Bentley, *Boonville*
George Van Horn, *Cooperstown*
James J. Belden, *Syracuse*
George W. Ray, *Norwich*
Sereno E. Payne, *Auburn*
Hosea H. Rockwell,[34] *Elmira*
John Raines, *Canandaigua*
Halbert S. Greenleaf, *Rochester*
James W. Wadsworth, *Geneseo*
Daniel N. Lockwood, *Buffalo*
Thomas L. Bunting, *Hamburg*
Warren B. Hooker, *Fredonia*

## NORTH CAROLINA

### SENATORS

Matt W. Ransom, *Weldon*
Zebulon B. Vance, *Charlotte*

### REPRESENTATIVES

William A. B. Branch, *Washington*
Henry P. Cheatham, *Littleton*
Benjamin F. Grady, *Wallace*
Benjamin H. Bunn, *Rocky Mount*
Archibald H. A. Williams, *Oxford*
Sydenham B. Alexander, *Charlotte*
John S. Henderson, *Salisbury*
William H. H. Cowles, *Wilkesboro*
William T. Crawford, *Waynesville*

## NORTH DAKOTA

### SENATORS

Lyman R. Casey, *Jamestown*
Henry C. Hansbrough, *Devils Lake*

### REPRESENTATIVE AT LARGE

Martin N. Johnson, *Petersburg*

---

[23] Elected to fill vacancy caused by death of Melbourne H. Ford, and took his seat December 7, 1891.

[24] Died November 5, 1892; seat remained vacant.

[25] Elected January 21, 1891, for the term beginning March 4, 1891, and took his seat January 7, 1892; governor during interim.

[26] Resigned October 13, 1891, before Congress assembled.

[27] Elected to fill vacancy caused by resignation of David A. Boody, and took his seat December 7, 1891; resigned November 16, 1892.

[28] Died April 14, 1891, before Congress assembled.

[29] Elected to fill vacancy caused by death of Francis B. Spinola, and took his seat December 7, 1891.

[30] Resigned September 16, 1891, before Congress assembled.

[31] Elected to fill vacancy caused by resignation of Roswell P. Flower, and took his seat December 7, 1891.

[32] Resigned September 11, 1891, before Congress assembled.

[33] Elected to fill vacancy caused by resignation of Leslie W. Russell, and took his seat December 7, 1891.

[34] Election unsuccessfully contested by Henry T. Noyes.

## OHIO

SENATORS

John Sherman, *Mansfield*
Calvin S. Brice, *Lima*

REPRESENTATIVES

Bellamy Storer, *Cincinnati*
John A. Caldwell, *Cincinnati*
George W. Houk, *Dayton*
Martin K. Gantz, *Troy*
Fernando C. Layton, *Wapakoneta*
Dennis D. Donovan, *Deshler*
William E. Haynes, *Fremont*
Darius D. Hare, *Upper Sandusky*
Joseph H. Outhwaite, *Columbus*
Robert E. Doan, *Wilmington*
John M. Pattison, *Milford*
William H. Enochs, *Ironton*
Irvine Dungan, *Jackson*
James W. Owens, *Newark*
Michael D. Harter, *Mansfield*
John G. Warwick,[35] *Massillon*
Lewis P. Ohliger,[36] *Wooster*
Albert J. Pearson, *Woodsfield*
Joseph D. Taylor, *Cambridge*
Ezra B. Taylor, *Warren*
Vincent A. Taylor, *Bedford*
Tom L. Johnson, *Cleveland*

## OREGON

SENATORS

Joseph N. Dolph, *Portland*
John H. Mitchell, *Portland*

REPRESENTATIVE AT LARGE

Binger Hermann, *Roseburg*

## PENNSYLVANIA

SENATORS

J. Donald Cameron, *Harrisburg*
Matthew S. Quay, *Beaver*

REPRESENTATIVES

Henry H. Bingham, *Philadelphia*
Charles O'Neill, *Philadelphia*
William McAleer, *Philadelphia*
John E. Reyburn, *Philadelphia*
Alfred C. Harmer, *Philadelphia*
John B. Robinson, *Media*
Edwin Hallowell, *Willow Grove*
William Mutchler, *Easton*
David B. Brunner, *Reading*
Marriott Brosius, *Lancaster*
Lemuel Amerman, *Scranton*
George W. Shonk,[37] *Plymouth*
James B. Reilly, *Pottsville*

John W. Rife, *Middletown*
Myron B. Wright, *Susquehanna*
Albert C. Hopkins, *Lock Haven*
Simon P. Wolverton, *Sunbury*
Louis E. Atkinson, *Miffintown*
Frank E. Beltzhoover, *Carlisle*
Edward Scull, *Somerset*
George F. Huff, *Greensburg*
John Dalzell, *Pittsburgh*
William A. Stone, *Allegheny*
Andrew Stewart,[38] *Uniontown*
Alexander K. Craig,[39] *Pittsburgh*
William A. Sipe,[40] *Pittsburgh*
Eugene P. Gillespie, *Greenville*
Matthew Griswold, *Erie*
Charles W. Stone, *Warren*
George F. Kribbs, *Clarion*

## RHODE ISLAND

SENATORS

Nelson W. Aldrich, *Providence*
Nathan F. Dixon, *Westerly*

REPRESENTATIVES

Oscar Lapham, *Providence*
Charles H. Page, *Scituate*

## SOUTH CAROLINA

SENATORS

Matthew C. Butler, *Edgefield*
John L. M. Irby, *Laurens*

REPRESENTATIVES

William H. Brawley, *Charleston*
George D. Tillman, *Clarks Hill*
George Johnstone, *Newberry*
George W. Shell, *Laurens*
John J. Hemphill, *Chester*
Eli T. Stackhouse,[41] *Little Rock*
John L. McLaurin,[42] *Bennettsville*
William Elliott, *Beaufort*

## SOUTH DAKOTA

SENATORS

Richard F. Pettigrew, *Sioux Falls*
James H. Kyle, *Aberdeen*

REPRESENTATIVES AT LARGE

John R. Gamble,[43] *Yankton*
John L. Jolley,[44] *Vermilion*
John A. Pickler, *Faulkton*

## TENNESSEE

SENATORS

Isham G. Harris, *Memphis*
William B. Bate, *Nashville*

REPRESENTATIVES

Alfred A. Taylor, *Johnson City*
Leonidas C. Houk,[45] *Knoxville*
John C. Houk,[46] *Knoxville*
Henry C. Snodgrass, *Sparta*
Benton McMillin, *Carthage*
James D. Richardson, *Murfreesboro*
Joseph E. Washington, *Cedar Hill*
Nicholas N. Cox, *Franklin*
Benjamin A. Enloe, *Jackson*
Rice A. Pierce, *Union City*
Josiah Patterson, *Memphis*

## TEXAS

SENATORS

Richard Coke, *Waco*
John H. Reagan,[47] *Palestine*
Horace Chilton,[48] *Tyler*
Roger Q. Mills,[49] *Corsicana*

REPRESENTATIVES

Charles Stewart, *Houston*
John B. Long, *Rusk*
Constantine B. Kilgore, *Wills Point*
David B. Culberson, *Jefferson*
Joseph W. Bailey, *Gainesville*
Jo Abbott, *Hillsboro*
William H. Crain, *Cuero*
Littleton W. Moore, *La Grange*
Roger Q. Mills,[50] *Corsicana*
Edwin Le Roy Antony,[51] *Cameron*
Joseph D. Sayers, *Bastrop*
Samuel W. T. Lanham, *Weatherford*

## VERMONT

SENATORS

George F. Edmunds,[52] *Burlington*
Redfield Proctor,[53] *Proctor*
Justin S. Morrill, *Strafford*

REPRESENTATIVES

H. Henry Powers, *Morrisville*
William W. Grout, *Barton*

## VIRGINIA

SENATORS

John W. Daniel, *Lynchburg*
John S. Barbour,[54] *Alexandria*
Eppa Hunton,[55] *Warrenton*

---

[35] Died August 14, 1892.

[36] Elected to fill vacancy caused by death of John G. Warwick, and took his seat December 5, 1892.

[37] Election unsuccessfully contested by John B. Reynolds.

[38] Served until February 26, 1892; succeeded by Alexander K. Craig, who contested his election.

[39] Successfully contested the election of Andrew Stewart, and took his seat February 26, 1892; died July 29, 1892.

[40] Elected to fill vacancy caused by death of Alexander K. Craig, and took his seat December 5, 1892.

[41] Died June 14, 1892.

[42] Elected to fill vacancy caused by death of Eli T. Stackhouse, and took his seat December 5, 1892.

[43] Died August 14, 1891, before Congress assembled.

[44] Elected to fill vacancy caused by death of John R. Gamble, and took his seat December 7, 1891.

[45] Died May 25, 1891, before Congress assembled.

[46] Elected to fill vacancy caused by death of Leonidas C. Houk, and took his seat December 7, 1891.

[47] Resigned June 10, 1891.

[48] Appointed to fill vacancy caused by resignation of John H. Reagan, and took his seat December 7, 1891.

[49] Elected to fill vacancy caused by resignation of

John H. Reagan, and took his seat March 30, 1892.

[50] Resigned March 28, 1892, having been elected Senator.

[51] Elected to fill vacancy caused by resignation of Roger Q. Mills, and took his seat July 28, 1892.

[52] Resigned, effective November 1, 1891.

[53] Appointed to fill vacancy caused by resignation of George F. Edmunds, and took his seat December 7, 1891; subsequently elected.

[54] Died May 14, 1892.

[55] Appointed to fill vacancy caused by death of John S. Barbour, and took his seat June 1, 1892; subsequently elected.

REPRESENTATIVES

William A. Jones, *Warsaw*
John W. Lawson, *Isle of Wight*
George D. Wise, *Richmond*
James F. Epes, *Blackstone*
Posey G. Lester, *Floyd*
Paul C. Edmunds, *Halifax*
Charles T. O'Ferrall, *Harrisonburg*
William H. F. Lee,[56] *Burkes Station*
Elisha E. Meredith,[57] *Brentsville*
John A. Buchanan, *Abingdon*
Henry St. George Tucker, *Staunton*

## WASHINGTON

SENATORS

John B. Allen, *Walla Walla*
Watson C. Squire, *Seattle*

REPRESENTATIVE AT LARGE

John L. Wilson, *Spokane*

## WEST VIRGINIA

SENATORS

John E. Kenna,[58] *Charleston*
Johnson N. Camden,[59] *Parkersburg*

Charles J. Faulkner, *Martinsburg*

REPRESENTATIVES

John O. Pendleton, *Wheeling*
William L. Wilson, *Charles Town*
John D. Alderson, *Nicholas*
James Capehart, *Point Pleasant*

## WISCONSIN

SENATORS

Philetus Sawyer, *Oshkosh*
William F. Vilas, *Madison*

REPRESENTATIVES

Clinton Babbitt, *Beloit*
Charles Barwig, *Mayville*
Allen R. Bushnell, *Madison*
John L. Mitchell,[60] *Milwaukee*
George H. Brickner, *Sheboygan Falls*
Lucas M. Miller, *Oshkosh*
Frank P. Coburn, *West Salem*
Nils P. Haugen, *River Falls*
Thomas Lynch, *Antigo*

## WYOMING

SENATORS

Joseph M. Carey, *Cheyenne*
Francis E. Warren, *Cheyenne*

REPRESENTATIVE AT LARGE

Clarence D. Clark, *Evanston*

## TERRITORY OF ARIZONA

DELEGATE

Marcus A. Smith, *Tombstone*

## TERRITORY OF NEW MEXICO

DELEGATE

Antonio Joseph, *Ojo Caliente*

## TERRITORY OF OKLAHOMA

DELEGATE

David A. Harvey, *Oklahoma City*

## TERRITORY OF UTAH

DELEGATE

John T. Caine, *Salt Lake City*

---

[56] Died October 15, 1891, before Congress assembled.
[57] Elected to fill vacancy caused by death of William H. F. Lee, and took his seat December 23, 1891.

[58] Died January 11, 1893.
[59] Elected to fill vacancy caused by death of John E. Kenna, and took his seat January 28, 1893.
[60] Resigned March 3, 1893, before the commence-

ment of the Fifty-third Congress, to which he had been reelected, having been elected Senator.

# 53RD CONGRESS

## MARCH 4, 1893, TO MARCH 3, 1895

FIRST SESSION— *August 7, 1893, to November 3, 1893*
SECOND SESSION— *December 4, 1893, to August 28, 1894*
THIRD SESSION— *December 3, 1894, to March 3, 1895*
SPECIAL SESSION OF THE SENATE— *March 4, 1893, to April 15, 1893*

———

VICE PRESIDENT OF THE UNITED STATES— Adlai E. Stevenson, of Illinois
PRESIDENT PRO TEMPORE OF THE SENATE— Charles F. Manderson,[1] of Nebraska;
Isham G. Harris,[2] of Tennessee; Matt W. Ransom,[3] of North Carolina
SECRETARY OF THE SENATE— Anson G. McCook, of New York; William R. Cox,[4] of
North Carolina
SERGEANT AT ARMS OF THE SENATE— Edward K. Valentine, of Nebraska; Richard J.
Bright,[5] of Indiana

———

SPEAKER OF THE HOUSE OF REPRESENTATIVES— Charles F. Crisp,[6] of Georgia
CLERK OF THE HOUSE— James Kerr,[7] of Pennsylvania
SERGEANT AT ARMS OF THE HOUSE— Samuel S. Yoder, of Ohio; Herman W. Snow,[8] of Illinois
DOORKEEPER OF THE HOUSE— A. B. Hurd, of Mississippi
POSTMASTER OF THE HOUSE— Lycurgus Dalton

Adlai E. Stevenson
Vice President

Charles F. Crisp
Speaker

## ALABAMA

### SENATORS
John T. Morgan, *Selma*
James L. Pugh, *Eufaula*

### REPRESENTATIVES
Richard H. Clarke, *Mobile*
Jesse F. Stallings, *Greenville*
William C. Oates,[9] *Abbeville*
George P. Harrison,[10] *Opelika*
Gaston A. Robbins, *Selma*
James E. Cobb,[11] *Tuskegee*
John H. Bankhead, *Fayette*
William H. Denson, *Gadsden*
Joseph Wheeler, *Wheeler*
Louis W. Turpin, *Newbern*

## ARKANSAS

### SENATORS
James K. Jones, *Washington*
James H. Berry, *Bentonville*

### REPRESENTATIVES
Philip D. McCulloch, Jr., *Marianna*
Clifton R. Breckinridge,[12] *Pine Bluff*
John S. Little,[13] *Greenwood*
Thomas C. McRae, *Prescott*
William L. Terry, *Little Rock*

Hugh A. Dinsmore, *Fayetteville*
Robert Neill, *Batesville*

## CALIFORNIA

### SENATORS
Leland Stanford,[14] *San Francisco*
George C. Perkins,[15] *Oakland*
Stephen M. White, *Los Angeles*

### REPRESENTATIVES
Thomas J. Geary, *Santa Rosa*
Anthony Caminetti, *Jackson*
Samuel G. Hilborn,[16] *Oakland*
Warren B. English,[17] *Oakland*
James G. Maguire, *San Francisco*
Eugene F. Loud, *San Francisco*
Marion Cannon, *Ventura*
William W. Bowers, *San Diego*

## COLORADO

### SENATORS
Henry M. Teller, *Central City*
Edward O. Wolcott, *Denver*

### REPRESENTATIVES
Lafayette Pence, *Denver*
John C. Bell, *Montrose*

## CONNECTICUT

### SENATORS
Orville H. Platt, *Meriden*
Joseph R. Hawley, *Hartford*

### REPRESENTATIVES
Lewis Sperry, *Hartford*
James P. Pigott, *New Haven*
Charles A. Russell, *Killingly*
Robert E. DeForest, *Bridgeport*

## DELAWARE

### SENATORS
George Gray, *New Castle*
Anthony Higgins, *Wilmington*

### REPRESENTATIVE AT LARGE
John W. Causey, *Milford*

## FLORIDA

### SENATORS
Wilkinson Call, *Jacksonville*
Samuel Pasco,[18] *Monticello*

### REPRESENTATIVES
Stephen R. Mallory, *Pensacola*
Charles M. Cooper, *Jacksonville*

---

[1] Resigned as President pro tempore March 22, 1893.
[2] Elected March 22, 1893 (special session of the Senate), and January 10, 1895.
[3] Elected January 7, 1895; resigned as President pro tempore January 10, 1895.
[4] Elected April 6, 1893.
[5] Reelected August 8, 1893.
[6] Reelected August 7, 1893.
[7] Reelected August 7, 1893.

[8] Elected August 7, 1893.
[9] Resigned, effective November 5, 1894.
[10] Elected to fill vacancy caused by resignation of William C. Oates, and took his seat December 3, 1894.
[11] Election unsuccessfully contested by W. W. Whatley.
[12] Resigned August 14, 1894.
[13] Elected to fill vacancy caused by resignation of Clifton R. Breckinridge, and took his seat December 3, 1894.

[14] Died June 21, 1893.
[15] Appointed to fill vacancy caused by death of Leland Stanford, and took his seat August 8, 1893; subsequently elected.
[16] Served until April 4, 1894; succeeded by Warren B. English, who contested his election.
[17] Successfully contested the election of Samuel G. Hilborn, and took his seat April 4, 1894.
[18] Reappointed to fill vacancy in the term beginning March 4, 1893, and subsequently reelected.

## GEORGIA

### SENATORS
Alfred H. Colquitt,[19] *Atlanta*
Patrick Walsh,[20] *Augusta*
John B. Gordon, *Atlanta*

### REPRESENTATIVES
Rufus E. Lester, *Savannah*
Benjamin E. Russell, *Bainbridge*
Charles F. Crisp, *Americus*
Charles L. Moses, *Turin*
Leonidas F. Livingston, *Kings*
Thomas B. Cabaniss, *Forsyth*
John W. Maddox, *Rome*
Thomas G. Lawson, *Eatonton*
Farish C. Tate, *Jasper*
James C. C. Black,[21] *Augusta*
Henry G. Turner, *Quitman*

## IDAHO

### SENATORS
George L. Shoup, *Salmon City*
Fred T. Dubois, *Blackfoot*

### REPRESENTATIVE AT LARGE
Willis Sweet, *Moscow*

## ILLINOIS

### SENATORS
Shelby M. Cullom, *Springfield*
John McAuley Palmer, *Springfield*

### REPRESENTATIVES AT LARGE
John C. Black,[22] *Chicago*
Andrew J. Hunter, *Paris*

### REPRESENTATIVES
J. Frank Aldrich, *Chicago*
Lawrence E. McGann, *Chicago*
Allan C. Durborow, Jr., *Chicago*
Julius Goldzier, *Chicago*
Albert J. Hopkins, *Aurora*
Robert R. Hitt, *Mount Morris*
Thomas J. Henderson, *Princeton*
Robert A. Childs, *Hinsdale*
Hamilton K. Wheeler, *Kankakee*
Philip S. Post,[23] *Galesburg*
Benjamin F. Marsh, *Warsaw*
John J. McDannold, *Mount Sterling*
William M. Springer, *Springfield*
Benjamin F. Funk, *Bloomington*
Joseph G. Cannon, *Danville*
George W. Fithian, *Newton*
Edward Lane, *Hillsboro*
William S. Forman, *Nashville*
James R. Williams, *Carmi*
George W. Smith, *Murphysboro*

## INDIANA

### SENATORS
Daniel W. Voorhees, *Terre Haute*
David Turpie, *Indianapolis*

### REPRESENTATIVES
Arthur H. Taylor, *Petersburg*
John L. Bretz, *Jasper*
Jason B. Brown, *Seymour*
William S. Holman, *Aurora*
George W. Cooper, *Columbus*
Henry U. Johnson, *Richmond*
William D. Bynum, *Indianapolis*
Elijah V. Brookshire, *Crawfordsville*
Daniel W. Waugh, *Tipton*
Thomas Hammond, *Hammond*
Augustus N. Martin, *Bluffton*
William F. McNagny, *Columbia City*
Charles G. Conn, *Elkhart*

## IOWA

### SENATORS
William B. Allison, *Dubuque*
James F. Wilson, *Fairfield*

### REPRESENTATIVES
John H. Gear, *Burlington*
Walter I. Hayes, *Clinton*
David B. Henderson, *Dubuque*
Thomas Updegraff, *McGregor*
Robert G. Cousins, *Tipton*
John F. Lacey, *Oskaloosa*
John A. T. Hull, *Des Moines*
William P. Hepburn, *Clarinda*
Alva L. Hager, *Greenfield*
Jonathan P. Dolliver, *Fort Dodge*
George D. Perkins, *Sioux City*

## KANSAS

### SENATORS
William A. Peffer, *Topeka*
John Martin,[24] *Topeka*

### REPRESENTATIVE AT LARGE
William A. Harris, *Linwood*

### REPRESENTATIVES
Case Broderick, *Holton*
Edward H. Funston,[25] *Iola*
Horace L. Moore,[26] *Lawrence*
Thomas J. Hudson, *Fredonia*
Charles Curtis, *Topeka*
John Davis, *Junction City*
William Baker, *Lincoln*
Jeremiah Simpson, *Medicine Lodge*

## KENTUCKY

### SENATORS
Joseph C. S. Blackburn, *Versailles*
William Lindsay, *Frankfort*

### REPRESENTATIVES
William J. Stone, *Kuttawa*
William T. Ellis, *Owensboro*
Isaac H. Goodnight, *Franklin*
Alexander B. Montgomery,
　*Elizabethtown*
Asher G. Caruth, *Louisville*
Albert S. Berry, *Newport*
William C. P. Breckinridge, *Lexington*
James B. McCreary, *Richmond*
Thomas H. Paynter,[27] *Greenup*
Marcus C. Lisle,[28] *Winchester*
William M. Beckner,[29] *Winchester*
Silas Adams, *Liberty*

## LOUISIANA

### SENATORS
Edward D. White,[30] *New Orleans*
Newton C. Blanchard,[31] *Shreveport*
Donelson Caffery, *Franklin*

### REPRESENTATIVES
Adolph Meyer, *New Orleans*
Robert C. Davey, *New Orleans*
Andrew Price, *Thibodaux*
Newton C. Blanchard,[32] *Shreveport*
Henry W. Ogden,[33] *Benton*
Charles J. Boatner, *Monroe*
Samuel M. Robertson, *Baton Rouge*

## MAINE

### SENATORS
Eugene Hale, *Ellsworth*
William P. Frye, *Lewiston*

### REPRESENTATIVES
Thomas B. Reed, *Portland*
Nelson Dingley, Jr., *Lewiston*
Seth L. Milliken, *Belfast*
Charles A. Boutelle, *Bangor*

## MARYLAND

### SENATORS
Arthur Pue Gorman, *Laurel*
Charles H. Gibson, *Easton*

### REPRESENTATIVES
Robert F. Bratton,[34] *Princess Anne*
W. Laird Henry,[35] *Cambridge*

---

[19] Died March 26, 1894.
[20] Appointed to fill vacancy caused by death of Alfred H. Colquitt, and took his seat April 9, 1894; subsequently elected.
[21] Election unsuccessfully contested by Thomas E. Watson.
[22] Resigned January 12, 1895.
[23] Died January 6, 1895, before the commencement of the Fifty-fourth Congress, to which he had been reelected.
[24] Elected to fill vacancy caused by death of Preston B. Plumb in preceding Congress, and took his seat March 4, 1893; election unsuccessfully contested

by Joseph W. Ady. (See U.S. Senate Election, Expulsion and Censure Cases, 1793-1990, Senate Document 103-33, pp. 243-45.)
[25] Served until August 2, 1894; succeeded by Horace L. Moore, who contested his election.
[26] Successfully contested the election of Edward H. Funston, and took his seat August 2, 1894.
[27] Resigned effective January 5, 1895.
[28] Died July 7, 1894.
[29] Elected to fill vacancy caused by death of Marcus C. Lisle, and took his seat December 3, 1894.
[30] Resigned, effective March 12, 1894, having

been appointed Associate Justice of the United States Supreme Court.
[31] Appointed to fill vacancy caused by resignation of Edward D. White, and took his seat March 12, 1894; subsequently elected.
[32] Resigned, effective March 12, 1894, having been elected Senator.
[33] Elected to fill vacancy caused by resignation of Newton C. Blanchard, and took his seat May 12, 1894.
[34] Died May 10, 1894.
[35] Elected to fill vacancy caused by death of Robert F. Bratton, and took his seat December 3, 1894.

## MARYLAND—Continued

REPRESENTATIVES—CONTINUED

J. Fred. C. Talbott, *Towson*
Harry W. Rusk, *Baltimore*
Isidor Rayner, *Baltimore*
Barnes Compton,[36] *Laurel*
Charles E. Coffin,[37] *Muirkirk*
William M. McKaig, *Cumberland*

## MASSACHUSETTS

SENATORS

George F. Hoar, *Worcester*
Henry Cabot Lodge, *Nahant*

REPRESENTATIVES

Ashley B. Wright, *North Adams*
Frederick H. Gillett, *Springfield*
Joseph H. Walker, *Worcester*
Lewis D. Apsley, *Hudson*
Moses T. Stevens, *North Andover*
William Cogswell, *Salem*
William Everett,[38] *Quincy*
Samuel W. McCall, *Winchester*
Joseph H. O'Neil, *Boston*
Michael J. McEttrick, *Boston*
William F. Draper, *Hopedale*
Elijah A. Morse, *Canton*
Charles S. Randall, *New Bedford*

## MICHIGAN

SENATORS

Francis B. Stockbridge,[39] *Kalamazoo*
John Patton, Jr.,[40] *Grand Rapids*
Julius C. Burrows,[41] *Kalamazoo*
James McMillan, *Detroit*

REPRESENTATIVES

J. Logan Chipman,[42] *Detroit*
Levi T. Griffin,[43] *Detroit*
James S. Gorman, *Chelsea*
Julius C. Burrows,[44] *Kalamazoo*
Henry F. Thomas, *Allegan*
George F. Richardson,[45] *Grand Rapids*
David D. Aitken, *Flint*
Justin R. Whiting, *St. Clair*
William S. Linton, *Saginaw*
John W. Moon, *Muskegon*
Thomas A. E. Weadock, *Bay City*
John Avery, *Greenville*
Samuel M. Stephenson, *Menominee*

## MINNESOTA

SENATORS

Cushman K. Davis, *St. Paul*
William D. Washburn, *Minneapolis*

REPRESENTATIVES

James A. Tawney, *Winona*
James T. McCleary, *Mankato*
Osee M. Hall, *Red Wing*
Andrew R. Kiefer, *St. Paul*
Loren Fletcher, *Minneapolis*
Melvin R. Baldwin, *Duluth*
Haldor E. Boen, *Fergus Falls*

## MISSISSIPPI

SENATORS

James Z. George, *Carrollton*
Edward C. Walthall,[46] *Grenada*
Anselm J. McLaurin,[47] *Brandon*

REPRESENTATIVES

John M. Allen, *Tupelo*
John C. Kyle, *Sardis*
Thomas C. Catchings, *Vicksburg*
Hernando D. Money, *Carrollton*
John Sharp Williams, *Yazoo City*
Thomas R. Stockdale, *Summit*
Charles E. Hooker, *Jackson*

## MISSOURI

SENATORS

Francis M. Cockrell, *Warrensburg*
George G. Vest, *Kansas City*

REPRESENTATIVES

William H. Hatch, *Hannibal*
Uriel S. Hall, *Hubbard*
Alexander M. Dockery, *Gallatin*
Daniel D. Burnes, *St. Joseph*
John C. Tarsney, *Kansas City*
David A. De Armond, *Butler*
John T. Heard, *Sedalia*
Richard P. Bland, *Lebanon*
James Beauchamp Clark, *Bowling Green*
Richard Bartholdt, *St. Louis*
Charles F. Joy,[48] *St. Louis*
John J. O'Neill,[49] *St. Louis*
Seth W. Cobb, *St. Louis*
Robert W. Fyan, *Marshfield*
Marshall Arnold, *Benton*
Charles H. Morgan, *Lamar*

## MONTANA

SENATORS

Thomas C. Power, *Helena*
Lee Mantle,[50] *Butte*

REPRESENTATIVE AT LARGE

Charles S. Hartman, *Bozeman*

## NEBRASKA

SENATORS

Charles F. Manderson, *Omaha*
William V. Allen, *Madison*

REPRESENTATIVES

William J. Bryan, *Lincoln*
David H. Mercer, *Omaha*
George D. Meiklejohn, *Fullerton*
Eugene J. Hainer, *Aurora*
William A. McKeighan, *Red Cloud*
Omer M. Kem, *Broken Bow*

## NEVADA

SENATORS

John P. Jones, *Gold Hill*
William M. Stewart, *Carson City*

REPRESENTATIVE AT LARGE

Francis G. Newlands, *Reno*

## NEW HAMPSHIRE

SENATORS

William E. Chandler, *Concord*
Jacob H. Gallinger, *Concord*

REPRESENTATIVES

Henry W. Blair, *Manchester*
Henry M. Baker, *Bow*

## NEW JERSEY

SENATORS

John R. McPherson, *Jersey City*
James Smith, Jr., *Newark*

REPRESENTATIVES

Henry C. Loudenslager, *Paulsboro*
John J. Gardner, *Atlantic City*
Jacob A. Geissenhainer, *Freehold*
Johnston Cornish, *Washington*
Cornelius A. Cadmus, *Paterson*
Thomas D. English, *Newark*
George B. Fielder, *Jersey City*
John T. Dunn, *Elizabeth*

---

[36] Resigned, effective May 15, 1894.

[37] Elected to fill vacancy caused by resignation of Barnes Compton, and took his seat December 3, 1894.

[38] Elected to fill vacancy caused by resignation of Representative-elect Henry Cabot Lodge, in preceding Congress, and took his seat August 7, 1893.

[39] Died April 30, 1894.

[40] Appointed to fill vacancy caused by death of Francis B. Stockbridge, and took his seat May 10, 1894.

[41] Elected to fill vacancy caused by death of Francis B. Stockbridge, and took his seat January 23, 1895.

[42] Died August 17, 1893.

[43] Elected to fill vacancy caused by death of J.

Logan Chipman, and took his seat December 4, 1893.

[44] Resigned January 23, 1895, before the commencement of the Fifty-fourth Congress, to which he had been reelected, having been elected Senator.

[45] Credentials presented December 22, 1892; credentials of Charles E. Belknap, issued by new officials, filed February 20, 1893; resolutions that Mr. Richardson be sworn adopted August 8, 1893, and he took his seat; September 9, 1893, Belknap was granted right to contest; Committee on Elections reported in favor of Richardson February 27, 1895; minority report filed for Belknap; no action by House.

[46] Resigned January 24, 1894.

[47] Elected to fill vacancy caused by resignation of Edward C. Walthall, and took his seat February 15, 1894.

[48] Served until April 3, 1894; succeeded by John J. O'Neill, who contested his election.

[49] Successfully contested the election of Charles F. Joy, and took his seat April 3, 1894.

[50] Appointed to fill vacancy in the term beginning March 4, 1893, caused by failure of legislature to elect; credentials presented March 9, 1893; on August 28, 1893, the Senate decided he was not entitled to a seat; subsequently elected and took his seat February 2, 1895; State unrepresented in this class from March 4, 1893, to January 15, 1895. (See U.S. Senate Election, Expulsion and Censure Cases, 1793-1990, Senate Document 103-33, pp. 243-45.)

## NEW YORK

SENATORS

David B. Hill, *Albany*
Edward Murphy, Jr., *Troy*

REPRESENTATIVES

James W. Covert, *Long Island City*
John M. Clancy, *Brooklyn*
Joseph C. Hendrix, *Brooklyn*
William J. Coombs, *Brooklyn*
John H. Graham, *Brooklyn*
Thomas F. Magner, *Brooklyn*
Franklin Bartlett, *New York City*
Edward J. Dunphy, *New York City*
Timothy J. Campbell, *New York City*
Daniel E. Sickles, *New York City*
Amos J. Cummings,[51] *New York City*
W. Bourke Cockran, *New York City*
J. De Witt Warner, *New York City*
John R. Fellows,[52] *New York City*
Lemuel E. Quigg,[53] *New York City*
Ashbel P. Fitch,[54] *New York City*
Isidor Straus,[55] *New York City*
William Ryan, *Port Chester*
Francis Marvin, *Port Jervis*
Jacob Le Fever, *New Paltz*
Charles D. Haines, *Kinderhook*
Charles Tracey, *Albany*
Simon J. Schermerhorn, *Schenectady*
Newton M. Curtis, *Ogdensburg*
John M. Wever, *Plattsburg*
Charles A. Chickering, *Copenhagen*
James S. Sherman, *Utica*
George W. Ray, *Norwich*
James J. Belden, *Syracuse*
Sereno E. Payne, *Auburn*
Charles W. Gillet, *Addison*
James W. Wadsworth, *Geneseo*
John Van Voorhis, *Rochester*
Daniel N. Lockwood, *Buffalo*
Charles Daniels, *Buffalo*
Warren B. Hooker, *Fredonia*

## NORTH CAROLINA

SENATORS

Matt W. Ransom, *Weldon*
Zebulon B. Vance,[56] *Charlotte*
Thomas J. Jarvis,[57] *Greenville*
Jeter C. Pritchard,[58] *Marshall*

REPRESENTATIVES

William A. B. Branch, *Washington*
Frederick A. Woodard, *Wilson*
Benjamin F. Grady, *Wallace*
Benjamin H. Bunn, *Rocky Mount*
Thomas Settle, *Reidsville*

Sydenham B. Alexander, *Charlotte*
John S. Henderson, *Salisbury*
William H. Bower, *Lenoir*
William T. Crawford, *Waynesville*

## NORTH DAKOTA

SENATORS

Henry C. Hansbrough, *Devils Lake*
William N. Roach, *Larimore*

REPRESENTATIVE AT LARGE

Martin N. Johnson, *Petersburg*

## OHIO

SENATORS

John Sherman, *Mansfield*
Calvin S. Brice, *Lima*

REPRESENTATIVES

Bellamy Storer, *Cincinnati*
Jacob A. Caldwell,[59] *Cincinnati*
Jacob H. Bromwell,[60] *Cincinnati*
George W. Houk,[61] *Dayton*
Paul J. Sorg,[62] *Middletown*
Fernando C. Layton, *Wapakoneta*
Dennis D. Donovan, *Deshler*
George W. Hulick, *Batavia*
George W. Wilson, *London*
Luther M. Strong, *Kenton*
Byron F. Ritchie, *Toledo*
William H. Enochs,[63] *Ironton*
Hezekiah S. Bundy,[64] *Wellston*
Charles H. Grosvenor, *Athens*
Joseph H. Outhwaite, *Columbus*
Darius D. Hare, *Upper Sandusky*
Michael D. Harter, *Mansfield*
Henry C. Van Voorhis, *Zanesville*
Albert J. Pearson, *Woodsfield*
James A. D. Richards, *New Philadelphia*
George P. Ikirt, *East Liverpool*
Stephen A. Northway, *Jefferson*
William J. White, *Cleveland*
Tom L. Johnson, *Cleveland*

## OREGON

SENATORS

Joseph N. Dolph, *Portland*
John H. Mitchell, *Portland*

REPRESENTATIVES

Binger Hermann, *Roseburg*
William R. Ellis, *Heppner*

## PENNSYLVANIA

SENATORS

J. Donald Cameron, *Harrisburg*
Matthew S. Quay, *Beaver*

REPRESENTATIVES AT LARGE

Alexander McDowell, *Sharon*
William Lilly,[65] *Mauch Chunk*
Galusha A. Grow,[66] *Glenwood*

REPRESENTATIVES

Henry H. Bingham, *Philadelphia*
Charles O'Neill,[67] *Philadelphia*
Robert Adams, Jr.,[68] *Philadelphia*
William McAleer, *Philadelphia*
John E. Reyburn, *Philadelphia*
Alfred C. Harmer, *Philadelphia*
John B. Robinson, *Media*
Irving P. Wanger, *Norristown*
William Mutchler,[69] *Easton*
Howard Mutchler,[70] *Easton*
Constantine J. Erdman, *Allentown*
Marriott Brosius, *Lancaster*
Joseph A. Scranton, *Scranton*
William H. Hines, *Wilkes-Barre*
James B. Reilly, *Pottsville*
Ephraim M. Woomer, *Lebanon*
Myron B. Wright,[71] *Susquehanna*
Edwin J. Jorden,[72] *Coudersport*
Albert C. Hopkins, *Lock Haven*
Simon P. Wolverton, *Sunbury*
Thaddeus M. Mahon, *Chambersburg*
Frank E. Beltzhoover, *Carlisle*
Josiah D. Hicks, *Altoona*
Daniel B. Heiner, *Kittanning*
John Dalzell, *Pittsburgh*
William A. Stone, *Allegheny*
William A. Sipe, *Pittsburgh*
Thomas W. Phillips, *New Castle*
Joseph C. Sibley, *Franklin*
Charles W. Stone, *Warren*
George F. Dribbs, *Clarion*

## RHODE ISLAND

SENATORS

Nelson W. Aldrich, *Providence*
Nathan F. Dixon, *Westerly*

REPRESENTATIVES

Oscar Lapham, *Providence*
Charles H. Page,[73] *Providence*

---

[51] Resigned November 21, 1894.
[52] Resigned effective December 31, 1893.
[53] Elected to fill vacancy caused by resignation of John R. Fellows, and took his seat February 14, 1894.
[54] Resigned December 26, 1893.
[55] Elected to fill vacancy caused by resignation of Ashbel P. Fitch, and took his seat February 14, 1894.
[56] Died April 14, 1894.
[57] Appointed to fill vacancy caused by death of Zebulon B. Vance, and took his seat April 26, 1894.
[58] Elected to fill vacancy caused by death of Zebulon B. Vance, and took his seat January 24, 1895.
[59] Resigned effective May 4, 1894.

[60] Elected to fill vacancy caused by resignation of John A. Caldwell, and took his seat December 3, 1894.
[61] Died February 9, 1894.
[62] Elected to fill vacancy caused by death of George W. Houk, and took his seat May 21, 1894.
[63] Died July 13, 1893, before Congress assembled.
[64] Elected to fill vacancy caused by death of William H. Enochs, and took his seat December 4, 1893.
[65] Died December 1, 1893.
[66] Elected to fill vacancy caused by death of William Lilly, and took his seat March 2, 1894.
[67] Died November 25, 1893.

[68] Elected to fill vacancy caused by death of Charles O'Neill, and took his seat January 3, 1894.
[69] Died June 23, 1893, before Congress assembled.
[70] Elected to fill vacancy caused by death of William Mutchler, and took his seat August 7, 1893.
[71] Died November 13, 1894, before the commencement of the Fifty-fourth Congress, to which he had been reelected.
[72] Elected to fill vacancy caused by death of Myron B. Wright, and took his seat February 23, 1895.
[73] Elected April 5, 1893, and took his seat August 7, 1893.

## SOUTH CAROLINA

SENATORS
Matthew C. Butler, *Edgefield*
John L. M. Irby, *Laurens*

REPRESENTATIVES
William H. Brawley,[74] *Charleston*
James F. Izlar,[75] *Orangeburg*
W. Jasper Talbert, *Parksville*
Asbury C. Latimer, *Belton*
George W. Shell, *Laurens*
Thomas J. Strait, *Lancaster*
John L. McLaurin, *Bennettsville*
George W. Murray, *Sumter*

## SOUTH DAKOTA

SENATORS
Richard F. Pettigrew, *Sioux Falls*
James H. Kyle, *Aberdeen*

REPRESENTATIVES AT LARGE
John A. Pickler, *Faulton*
William V. Lucas, *Hot Springs*

## TENNESSEE

SENATORS
Isham G. Harris, *Memphis*
William B. Bate, *Nashville*

REPRESENTATIVES
Alfred A. Taylor, *Johnson City*
John C. Houk, *Knoxville*
Henry C. Snodgrass, *Sparta*
Benton McMillin, *Carthage*
James D. Richardson, *Murfreesboro*
Joseph E. Washington, *Cedar Hill*
Nicholas N. Cox, *Franklin*
Benjamin A. Enloe,[76] *Jackson*
James C. McDearmon, *Trenton*
Josiah Patterson, *Memphis*

## TEXAS

SENATORS
Richard Coke, *Waco*
Roger Q. Mills, *Corsicana*

REPRESENTATIVES
Joseph C. Hutcheson, *Houston*
Samuel B. Cooper, *Woodville*
Constantine B. Kilgore, *Wills Point*
David B. Culberson, *Jefferson*

Joseph W. Bailey, *Gainesville*
Jo Abbott, *Hillsboro*
George C. Pendleton, *Belton*
Charles K. Bell, *Fort Worth*
Joseph D. Sayers, *Bastrop*
Walter Gresham, *Galveston*
William H. Crain, *Cuero*
Thomas M. Paschal, *Castroville*
Jeremiah V. Cockrell, *Anson*

## VERMONT

SENATORS
Justin S. Morrill, *Strafford*
Redfield Proctor, *Proctor*

REPRESENTATIVES
H. Henry Powers, *Morrisville*
William W. Grout, *Barton*

## VIRGINIA

SENATORS
John W. Daniel, *Lynchburg*
Eppa Hunton, *Warrenton*

REPRESENTATIVES
William A. Jones, *Warsaw*
D. Gardiner Tyler, *Sturgeon Point*
George D. Wise, *Richmond*
James F. Epes, *Blackstone*
Claude A. Swanson, *Chatham*
Paul C. Edmunds, *Halifax*
Charles T. O'Ferrall,[77] *Harrisonburg*
Smith S. Turner,[78] *Front Royal*
Elisha E. Meredith, *Brentsville*
James W. Marshall, *New Castle*
Henry St. George Tucker, *Staunton*

## WASHINGTON

SENATORS
Watson C. Squire, *Seattle*
John L. Wilson,[79] *Spokane*

REPRESENTATIVES AT LARGE
John L. Wilson,[80] *Spokane*
William H. Doolittle, *Tacoma*

## WEST VIRGINIA

SENATORS
Charles J. Faulkner, *Martinsburg*
Johnson N. Camden, *Parkersburg*

REPRESENTATIVES
John O. Pendleton, *Wheeling*
William L. Wilson, *Charles Town*
John D. Alderson, *Nicholas*
James Capehart, *Point Pleasant*

## WISCONSIN

SENATORS
William F. Vilas, *Madison*
John L. Mitchell, *Milwaukee*

REPRESENTATIVES
Henry Allen Cooper, *Racine*
Charles Barwig, *Mayville*
Joseph W. Babcock, *Necedah*
Peter J. Somers,[81] *Milwaukee*
George H. Brickner, *Sheboygan Falls*
Owen A. Wells, *Fond du Lac*
George B. Shaw,[82] *Eau Claire*
Michael Griffin,[83] *Eau Claire*
Lyman E. Barnes, *Appleton*
Thomas Lynch, *Antigo*
Nils P. Haugen, *River Falls*

## WYOMING

SENATORS
Joseph M. Carey, *Cheyenne*
Clarence D. Clark,[84] *Evanston*

REPRESENTATIVE AT LARGE
Henry A. Coffeen, *Big Horn*

## TERRITORY OF ARIZONA

DELEGATE
Marcus A. Smith, *Tombstone*

## TERRITORY OF NEW MEXICO

DELEGATE
Antonio Joseph, *Ojo Caliente*

## TERRITORY OF OKLAHOMA

DELEGATE
Dennis T. Flynn, *Guthrie*

## TERRITORY OF UTAH

DELEGATE
Joseph L. Rawlins, *Salt Lake City*

---

[74] Resigned February 12, 1894.

[75] Elected to fill vacancy caused by resignation of William H. Brawley, and took his seat April 15, 1894.

[76] Election unsuccessfully contested by P. H. Thrasher.

[77] Resigned December 28, 1893, having been elected governor.

[78] Elected to fill vacancy caused by resignation of Charles T. O'Ferrall, and took his seat February 12, 1894.

[79] Elected to fill vacancy in the term commencing March 4, 1893, and took his seat February 19, 1895. John B. Allen was appointed to fill such vacancy, the

legislature having adjourned without electing his successor; credentials presented March 20, 1893 (special session of the Senate), but he was not permitted to qualify; on August 28, 1893, the Senate decided he was not entitled to the seat. Vacancy in this class from March 4, 1893, to January 31, 1895. (See U.S. Senate Election, Expulsion and Censure Cases, 1793-1990, Senate Document 103-33, pp. 243-45.)

[80] Resigned, effective February 18, 1895, having been elected Senator.

[81] Elected to fill vacancy caused by resignation of Representative-elect John L. Mitchell, in preceding Congress, and took his seat August 27, 1893.

[82] Died August 27, 1894.

[83] Elected to fill vacancy caused by death of George B. Shaw, and took his seat December 3, 1894.

[84] Elected to fill vacancy in the term beginning March 4, 1893, caused by failure of legislature to elect, and took his seat February 6, 1895. Asahel C. Beckwith presented credentials as a Senator-designate March 15, 1893 (special session of the Senate), but was not sworn pending investigation of his right to the seat; resigned July 11, 1893, before final action by Senate; vacancy in this class from March 4, 1893, to January 22, 1895. (See U.S. Senate Election, Expulsion and Censure Cases, 1793-1990, Senate Document 103-33, pp. 243-45.)

# 54TH CONGRESS

## MARCH 4, 1895, TO MARCH 3, 1897

FIRST SESSION— *December 2, 1895, to June 11, 1896*
SECOND SESSION— *December 7, 1896, to March 3, 1897*

---

VICE PRESIDENT OF THE UNITED STATES— ADLAI E. STEVENSON, of Illinois
PRESIDENT PRO TEMPORE OF THE SENATE— WILLIAM P. FRYE,[1] of Maine
SECRETARY OF THE SENATE— WILLIAM R. COX, of North Carolina
SERGEANT AT ARMS OF THE SENATE— RICHARD J. BRIGHT, of Indiana

---

SPEAKER OF THE HOUSE OF REPRESENTATIVES— THOMAS B. REED,[2] of Maine
CLERK OF THE HOUSE— JAMES KERR, of Pennsylvania; ALEXANDER McDOWELL,[3] of Pennsylvania
SERGEANT AT ARMS OF THE HOUSE— HERMAN W. SNOW, of Illinois; BENJAMIN F. RUSSELL,[4] of Missouri
DOORKEEPER OF THE HOUSE— WILLIAM J. GLENN, of New York
POSTMASTER OF THE HOUSE— J. C. McELROY

Adlai E. Stevenson
Vice President

Thomas B. Reed
Speaker

## ALABAMA

### SENATORS
John T. Morgan, *Selma*
James L. Pugh, *Eufaula*

### REPRESENTATIVES
Richard H. Clarke, *Mobile*
Jesse F. Stallings, *Greenville*
George P. Harrison,[5] *Opelika*
Gaston A. Robbins,[6] *Selma*
William F. Aldrich,[7] *Aldrich*
James E. Cobb,[8] *Tuskegee*
Albert T. Goodwyn,[9] *Robinson Springs*
John H. Bankhead, *Fayette*
Milford W. Howard, *Fort Payne*
Joseph Wheeler, *Wheeler*
Oscar W. Underwood,[10] *Birmingham*
Truman H. Aldrich,[11] *Birmingham*

## ARKANSAS

### SENATORS
James K. Jones, *Washington*
James H. Berry, *Bentonville*

### REPRESENTATIVES
Philip D. McCulloch, Jr., *Marianna*
John S. Little, *Greenwood*
Thomas C. McRae, *Prescott*
William L. Terry, *Little Rock*
Hugh A. Dinsmore, *Fayetteville*
Robert Neill, *Batesville*

## CALIFORNIA

### SENATORS
Stephen M. White, *Los Angeles*
George C. Perkins, *Oakland*

### REPRESENTATIVES
John A. Barham, *Santa Rosa*
Grove L. Johnson, *Sacramento*
Samuel G. Hilborn, *Oakland*
James G. Maguire, *San Francisco*
Eugene F. Loud, *San Francisco*
James McLachlan, *Pasadena*
William W. Bowers, *San Diego*

## COLORADO

### SENATORS
Henry M. Teller, *Central City*
Edward O. Wolcott, *Denver*

### REPRESENTATIVES
John F. Shafroth, *Denver*
John C. Bell, *Montrose*

## CONNECTICUT

### SENATORS
Orville H. Platt, *Meriden*
Joseph R. Hawley, *Hartford*

### REPRESENTATIVES
E. Stevens Henry, *Rockville*

Nehemiah D. Sperry, *New Haven*
Charles A. Russell, *Killingly*
Ebenezer J. Hill, *Norwalk*

## DELAWARE

### SENATORS
George Gray, *New Castle*
Richard R. Kenney,[12] *Dover*

### REPRESENTATIVE AT LARGE
Jonathan S. Willis, *Milford*

## FLORIDA

### SENATORS
Wilkinson Call, *Jacksonville*
Samuel Pasco, *Monticello*

### REPRESENTATIVES
Stephen M. Sparkman, *Tampa*
Charles M. Cooper, *Jacksonville*

## GEORGIA

### SENATORS
John B. Gordon, *Atlanta*
Augustus O. Bacon, *Macon*

### REPRESENTATIVES
Rufus E. Lester, *Savannah*
Benjamin E. Russell, *Bainbridge*

---

[1] Elected February 7, 1896.
[2] Elected December 2, 1895.
[3] Elected December 2, 1895.
[4] Elected December 2, 1895.
[5] Election unsuccessfully contested by W. C. Robinson.
[6] Served until March 13, 1896; succeeded by William F. Aldrich, who contested his election.
[7] Successfully contested the election of Gaston A. Robbins, and took his seat March 13, 1896.
[8] Served until April 21, 1896; succeeded by Albert T. Goodwyn, who contested his election.
[9] Successfully contested the election of James E.

Cobb, and took his seat April 22, 1896.
[10] Served until June 9, 1896; succeeded by Truman H. Aldrich, who contested his election.
[11] Successfully contested the election of Oscar W. Underwood, and took his seat June 9, 1896.
[12] A petition and papers, certifying to the election of Henry A. du Pont for the term beginning March 4, 1895, were presented December 4, 1895; numerous affidavits and papers challenging the regularity of the election were also presented; the Committee on Privileges and Elections reported favorably to Mr. du Pont, February 17, 1896, but on May 15, 1896, the Senate, by a vote of 31 to 30, decided he was not entitled to a

seat; papers and legislative records were presented January 21, 1897, attesting the election of John Edwards Addicks on the day preceding, for the term beginning March 4, 1895; credentials of Richard R. Kenney, duly signed by the governor, and certifying to his election on January 19, 1897, were presented on February 5, 1897; appeared, qualified, and took his seat on the same day. The contest was continued in the succeeding Congress. Vacancy in this class from March 4, 1895, to January 18, 1897. (See U.S. Senate Election, Expulsion and Censure Cases, 1793-1990, Senate Document 103-33, pp. 249-52.)

## GEORGIA—Continued

### REPRESENTATIVES—CONTINUED

Charles F. Crisp,[13] *Americus*
Charles R. Crisp,[14] *Americus*
Charles L. Moses, *Turin*
Leonidas F. Livingston, *Kings*
Charles L. Bartlett, *Macon*
John W. Maddox,[15] *Rome*
Thomas G. Lawson, *Eatonton*
Farish C. Tate, *Jasper*
James C. C. Black,[16] *Augusta*
Henry G. Turner, *Quitman*

## IDAHO

### SENATORS

George L. Shoup, *Salmon City*
Fred T. Dubois, *Blackfoot*

### REPRESENTATIVE AT LARGE

Edgar Wilson, *Boise City*

## ILLINOIS

### SENATORS

Shelby M. Cullom, *Springfield*
John McAuley Palmer, *Springfield*

### REPRESENTATIVES

J. Frank Aldrich, *Chicago*
William Lorimer, *Chicago*
Lawrence E. McGann,[17] *Chicago*
Hugh R. Belknap,[18] *Chicago*
Charles W. Woodman, *Chicago*
George E. White, *Chicago*
Edward D. Cooke, *Chicago*
George E. Foss, *Chicago*
Albert J. Hopkins, *Aurora*
Robert R. Hitt, *Mount Morris*
George W. Prince,[19] *Galesburg*
Walter Reeves, *Streator*
Joseph G. Cannon, *Danville*
Vespasian Warner, *Clinton*
Joseph V. Graff, *Pekin*
Benjamin F. Marsh, *Warsaw*
Finis E. Downing,[20] *Virginia*
John I. Rinaker,[21] *Carlinville*
James A. Connolly, *Springfield*
Frederick Remann,[22] *Vandalia*
William F. L. Hadley,[23] *Edwardsville*
Benson Wood, *Effingham*
Orlando Burrell, *Carmi*
Everett J. Murphy, *East St. Louis*
George W. Smith, *Murphysboro*

## INDIANA

### SENATORS

Daniel W. Voorhees, *Terre Haute*
David Turpie, *Indianapolis*

### REPRESENTATIVES

James A. Hemenway, *Boonville*
Alexander M. Hardy, *Washington*
Robert J. Tracewell, *Corydon*
James E. Watson, *Rushville*
Jesse Overstreet, *Franklin*
Henry U. Johnson, *Richmond*
Charles L. Henry, *Anderson*
George W. Faris, *Terre Haute*
J. Frank Hanly, *Williamsport*
Jethro A. Hatch, *Kentland*
George W. Steele, *Marion*
Jacob D. Leighty, *St. Joe*
Lemuel W. Royse, *Warsaw*

## IOWA

### SENATORS

William B. Allison, *Dubuque*
John H. Gear, *Burlington*

### REPRESENTATIVES

Samuel M. Clark, *Keokuk*
George M. Curtis, *Clinton*
David B. Henderson, *Dubuque*
Thomas Updegraff, *McGregor*
Robert G. Cousins, *Tipton*
John F. Lacy, *Oskaloosa*
John A. T. Hull, *Des Moines*
William P. Hepburn, *Clarinda*
Alva L. Hager, *Greenfield*
Jonathan P. Dolliver, *Fort Dodge*
George D. Perkins, *Sioux City*

## KANSAS

### SENATORS

William A. Peffer, *Topeka*
Lucien Baker, *Leavenworth*

### REPRESENTATIVE AT LARGE

Richard W. Blue, *Pleasanton*

### REPRESENTATIVES

Case Broderick, *Holton*
Orrin L. Miller, *Kansas City*
Snyder S. Kirkpatrick, *Fredonia*
Charles Curtis, *Topeka*
William A. Calderhead, *Marysville*
William Baker, *Lincoln*
Chester I. Long, *Medicine Lodge*

## KENTUCKY

### SENATORS

Joseph C. S. Blackburn, *Versailles*
William Lindsay, *Frankfort*

### REPRESENTATIVES

John K. Hendrick, *Smithland*
John D. Clardy, *Newstead*
W. Godfrey Hunter, *Burkesville*
John W. Lewis, *Springfield*
Walter Evans, *Louisville*
Albert S. Berry, *Newport*
William C. Owens,[24] *Georgetown*
James B. McCreary, *Richmond*
Samuel J. Pugh, *Vanceburg*
Joseph M. Kendall,[25] *Prestonsburg*
Nathan T. Hopkins,[26] *Marshall*
David G. Colson, *Middlesboro*

## LOUISIANA

### SENATORS

Donelson Caffery, *Franklin*
Newton C. Blanchard, *Shreveport*

### REPRESENTATIVES

Adolph Meyer, *New Orleans*
Charles F. Buck,[27] *New Orleans*
Andrew Price,[28] *Thibodaux*
Henry W. Ogden, *Benton*
Charles J. Boatner,[29] *Monroe*
Samuel M. Robertson, *Baton Rouge*

## MAINE

### SENATORS

Eugene Hale, *Ellsworth*
William P. Frye, *Lewiston*

### REPRESENTATIVES

Thomas B. Reed, *Portland*
Nelson Dingley, Jr., *Lewiston*
Seth L. Milliken, *Belfast*
Charles A. Boutelle, *Bangor*

## MARYLAND

### SENATORS

Arthur Pue Gorman, *Laurel*
Charles H. Gibson, *Easton*

### REPRESENTATIVES

Joshua W. Miles, *Princess Anne*
William B. Baker, *Aberdeen*
Harry W. Rusk,[30] *Baltimore*
John K. Cowen, *Baltimore*
Charles E. Coffin, *Muirkirk*
George L. Wellington, *Cumberland*

---

[13] Died October 23, 1896.

[14] Elected to fill vacancy caused by death of his father, Charles F. Crisp, and took his seat December 19, 1896.

[15] Election unsuccessfully contested by William H. Felton.

[16] Resigned March 4, 1895, subsequently elected to fill vacancy caused by his own resignation, and took his seat December 2, 1895; election unsuccessfully contested by Thomas E. Watson.

[17] Resigned December 2, 1895; succeeded by Hugh R. Belknap, who contested his election.

[18] Successfully contested the election of Lawrence E. McGann, and took his seat December 27, 1895.

[19] Elected to fill vacancy caused by death of Representative-elect Philip S. Post, in preceding Congress, and took his seat December 2, 1895.

[20] Served until June 5, 1896; succeeded by John I. Rinaker, who contested his election.

[21] Successfully contested the election of Finis E. Downing, and took his seat June 5, 1896.

[22] Died July 14, 1895, before Congress assembled.

[23] Elected to fill vacancy caused by death of Frederick Remann, and took his seat December 2, 1895.

[24] Election unsuccessfully contested by George Denny, Jr.

[25] Served until February 18, 1897; succeeded by

N. T. Hopkins, who contested his election.

[26] Successfully contested the election of Joseph M. Kendall, and took his seat February 18, 1897.

[27] Election unsuccessfully contested by H. Dudley Coleman.

[28] Election unsuccessfully contested by Taylor Beattie.

[29] Election contested by Alexis Benoit; seat declared vacant March 20, 1896; subsequently elected and took his seat December 10, 1896; this election also unsuccessfully contested by Alexis Benoit.

[30] Election unsuccessfully contested by William S. Booze.

## MASSACHUSETTS

SENATORS

George F. Hoar, *Worcester*
Henry Cabot Lodge, *Nahant*

REPRESENTATIVES

Ashley B. Wright, *North Adams*
Frederick H. Gillett, *Springfield*
Joseph H. Walker, *Worcester*
Lewis D. Apsley, *Hudson*
William S. Knox, *Lawrence*
William Cogswell,[31] *Salem*
William H. Moody,[32] *Haverhill*
William E. Barrett, *Melrose*
Samuel W. McCall, *Winchester*
John F. Fitzgerald, *Boston*
Harrison H. Atwood, *Boston*
William F. Draper, *Hopedale*
Elijah A. Morse, *Canton*
John Simpkins, *Yarmouth*

## MICHIGAN

SENATORS

James McMillan, *Detroit*
Julius C. Burrows, *Kalamazoo*

REPRESENTATIVES

John B. Corliss, *Detroit*
George Spalding, *Monroe*
Alfred Milnes,[33] *Coldwater*
Henry F. Thomas, *Allegan*
William Alden Smith, *Grand Rapids*
David D. Aitken, *Flint*
Horace G. Snover, *Port Austin*
William S. Linton, *Saginaw*
Roswell P. Bishop, *Ludington*
Rousseau O. Crump, *West Bay City*
John Avery, *Greenville*
Samuel M. Stephenson, *Menominee*

## MINNESOTA

SENATORS

Cushman K. Davis, *St. Paul*
Knute Nelson, *Alexandria*

REPRESENTATIVES

James A. Tawney, *Winona*
James T. McCleary, *Mankato*
Joel P. Heatwole, *Northfield*
Andrew R. Keifer, *St. Paul*
Loren Fletcher, *Minneapolis*
Charles A. Towne, *Duluth*
Frank M. Eddy, *Glenwood*

## MISSISSIPPI

SENATORS

James Z. George, *Carrollton*
Edward C. Walthall, *Grenada*

REPRESENTATIVES

John M. Allen, *Tupelo*
John C. Kyle, *Sardis*
Thomas C. Catchings, *Vicksburg*
Hernando D. Money, *Carrollton*
John Sharp Williams, *Yazoo City*
Walter McK. Denny, *Scranton*
James G. Spencer, *Port Gibson*

## MISSOURI

SENATORS

Francis M. Cockrell, *Warrensburg*
George G. Vest, *Kansas City*

REPRESENTATIVES

Charles N. Clark, *Hannibal*
Uriel S. Hall, *Hubbard*
Alexander M. Dockery, *Gallatin*
George C. Crowther, *St. Joseph*
John C. Tarsney,[34] *Kansas City*
Robert T. Van Horn,[35] *Kansas City*
David A. De Armond, *Butler*
John P. Tracey, *Springfield*
Joel D. Hubbard, *Versailles*
William M. Treloar, *Mexico*
Richard Bartholdt, *St. Louis*
Charles F. Joy, *St. Louis*
Seth W. Cobb, *St. Louis*
John H. Raney, *Piedmont*
Norman A. Mozley, *Dexter*
Charles G. Burton, *Nevada*

## MONTANA

SENATORS

Lee Mantle, *Butte*
Thomas H. Carter, *Helena*

REPRESENTATIVE AT LARGE

Charles S. Hartman, *Bozeman*

## NEBRASKA

SENATORS

William V. Allen, *Madison*
John M. Thurston, *Omaha*

REPRESENTATIVES

Jesse B. Strode, *Lincoln*
David H. Mercer, *Omaha*
George D. Meiklejohn, *Fullerton*
Eugene J. Hainer, *Aurora*
William E. Andrews, *Hastings*
Omer M. Kem, *Broken Bow*

## NEVADA

SENATORS

John P. Jones, *Gold Hill*
William M. Stewart, *Carson City*

REPRESENTATIVE AT LARGE

Francis G. Newlands, *Reno*

## NEW HAMPSHIRE

SENATORS

William E. Chandler, *Concord*
Jacob H. Gallinger, *Concord*

REPRESENTATIVES

Cyrus A. Sulloway, *Manchester*
Henry M. Baker, *Bow*

## NEW JERSEY

SENATORS

James Smith, Jr., *Newark*
William J. Sewell, *Camden*

REPRESENTATIVES

Henry C. Loudenslager, *Paulsboro*
John J. Gardner, *Atlantic City*
Benjamin F. Howell, *New Brunswick*
Mahlon Pitney, *Morristown*
James F. Stewart, *Paterson*
Richard Wayne Parker, *Newark*
Thomas McEwan, Jr., *Jersey City*
Charles N. Fowler, *Elizabeth*

## NEW YORK

SENATORS

David B. Hill, *Albany*
Edward Murphy, Jr., *Troy*

REPRESENTATIVES

Richard C. McCormick, *Jamaica*
Denis M. Hurley, *Brooklyn*
Francis H. Wilson, *Brooklyn*
Israel F. Fischer, *Brooklyn*
Charles G. Bennett, *Brooklyn*
James R. Howe, *Brooklyn*
Franklin Bartlett, *New York City*
James J. Walsh,[36] *New York City*
John M. Mitchell,[37] *New York City*
Henry Clay Miner,[38] *New York City*
Amos J. Cummings,[39] *New York City*
William Sulzer, *New York City*
George B. McClellan,[40] *New York City*
Richard C. Shannon, *New York City*
Lemuel E. Quigg, *New York City*
Philip B. Low, *New York City*
Benjamin L. Fairchild, *Pelham
 Heights*
Benjamin B. Odell, Jr., *Newburgh*
Jacob Le Fever, *New Paltz*
Frank S. Black,[41] *Troy*
George N. Southwick, *Albany*
David F. Wilber, *Oneonta*
Newton M. Curtis, *Ogdensburg*
Wallace T. Foote, Jr., *Port Henry*
Charles A. Chickering, *Copenhagen*
James S. Sherman, *Utica*
George W. Ray, *Norwich*
Theodore L. Poole, *Syracuse*

---

[31] Died May 22, 1895, before Congress assembled.
[32] Elected to fill vacancy caused by death of William Cogswell, and took his seat December 2, 1895.
[33] Elected to fill vacancy caused by resignation of Representative-elect Julius C. Burrows, in preceding Congress, and took his seat December 2, 1895.
[34] Served until February 27, 1896; succeeded by Robert T. Van Horn, who contested his election.

[35] Successfully contested the election of John C. Tarsney, and took his seat February 27, 1896.
[36] Served until June 2, 1896; succeeded by John M. Mitchell, who contested his election.
[37] Successfully contested the election of James J. Walsh, and took his seat June 2, 1896.
[38] Election unsuccessfully contested by Timothy J. Campbell.

[39] Elected to fill vacancy caused by death of Representative-elect Andrew J. Campbell (December 6, 1894, before the beginning of the congressional term), and took his seat December 2, 1895.
[40] Election unsuccessfully contested by Robert A. Chesebrough.
[41] Resigned January 7, 1897, having been elected Governor.

## NEW YORK— Continued

REPRESENTATIVES—CONTINUED

Sereno E. Payne, *Auburn*
Charles W. Gillet, *Addison*
James W. Wadsworth, *Geneseo*
Henry C. Brewster, *Rochester*
Rowland B. Mahany, *Buffalo*
Charles Daniels, *Buffalo*
Warren B. Hooker, *Fredonia*

## NORTH CAROLINA

SENATORS

Jeter C. Pritchard, *Marshall*
Marion Butler, *Elliott*

REPRESENTATIVES

Harry Skinner, *Greenville*
Frederick A. Woodard,[42] *Wilson*
John G. Shaw,[43] *Fayetteville*
William F. Strowd, *Pittsboro*
Thomas Settle, *Reidsville*
James A. Lockhart,[44] *Wadesboro*
Charles H. Martin,[45] *Polkton*
Alonzo C. Shuford, *Newton*
Romulus Z. Linney, *Taylorsville*
Richmond Pearson, *Asheville*

## NORTH DAKOTA

SENATORS

Henry C. Hansbrough, *Devils Lake*
William N. Roach, *Larimore*

REPRESENTATIVE AT LARGE

Martin N. Johnson, *Petersburg*

## OHIO

SENATORS

John Sherman, *Mansfield*
Calvin S. Brice, *Lima*

REPRESENTATIVES

Charles P. Taft, *Cincinnati*
Jacob H. Bromwell, *Cincinnati*
Paul J. Sorg, *Middletown*
Fernando C. Layton, *Wapakoneta*
Francis B. De Witt, *Paulding*
George W. Hulick, *Batavia*
George W. Wilson, *London*
Luther M. Strong, *Kenton*
James H. Southard, *Toledo*
Lucien J. Fenton, *Winchester*
Charles H. Grosvenor, *Athens*
David K. Watson, *Columbus*
Stephen R. Harris, *Bucyrus*
Winfield S. Kerr, *Mansfield*
Henry C. Van Voorhis, *Zanesville*
Lorenzo Danford, *St. Clairsville*
Addison S. McClure, *Wooster*

Robert W. Tayler, *New Lisbon*
Stephen A. Northway, *Jefferson*
Clifton B. Beach, *Cleveland*
Theodore E. Burton, *Cleveland*

## OREGON

SENATORS

John H. Mitchell, *Portland*
George W. McBride, *St. Helens*

REPRESENTATIVES

Binger Hermann, *Roseburg*
William R. Ellis, *Heppner*

## PENNSYLVANIA

SENATORS

J. Donald Cameron, *Harrisburg*
Matthew S. Quay, *Beaver*

REPRESENTATIVES AT LARGE

Galusha A. Grow, *Glenwood*
George F. Huff, *Greensburg*

REPRESENTATIVES

Henry H. Bingham, *Philadelphia*
Robert Adams, Jr., *Philadelphia*
Frederick Halterman, *Philadelphia*
John E. Reyburn, *Philadelphia*
Alfred C. Harmer, *Philadelphia*
John B. Robinson, *Media*
Irving P. Wanger, *Norristown*
Joseph J. Hart, *Milford*
Constantine J. Erdman, *Allentown*
Marriott Brosius, *Lancaster*
Joseph A. Scranton, *Scranton*
John Leisenring, *Upper Lehigh*
Charles N. Brumm, *Minersville*
Ephraim M. Woomer, *Lebanon*
James H. Codding,[46] *Towanda*
Fred C. Leonard, *Coudersport*
Monroe H. Kulp, *Shamokin*
Thaddeus M. Mahon, *Chambersburg*
James A. Stahle, *Emigsville*
Josiah D. Hicks, *Altoona*
Daniel B. Heiner, *Kittanning*
John Dalzell, *Pittsburgh*
William A. Stone, *Allegheny*
Ernest F. Acheson, *Washington*
Thomas W. Phillips, *New Castle*
Matthew Griswold, *Erie*
Charles W. Stone, *Warren*
William C. Arnold, *Dubois*

## RHODE ISLAND

SENATORS

Nelson W. Aldrich, *Providence*
George P. Wetmore, *Newport*

REPRESENTATIVES

Melville Bull, *Middletown*
Warren O. Arnold, *Chepatchet*

## SOUTH CAROLINA

SENATORS

John L. M. Irby, *Laurens*
Benjamin R. Tillman, *Trenton*

REPRESENTATIVES

William Elliott,[47] *Beaufort*
George W. Murray,[48] *Rembert*
W. Jasper Talbert, *Parksville*
Asbury C. Latimer,[49] *Belton*
Stanyarne Wilson, *Spartanburg*
Thomas J. Strait, *Lancaster*
John L. McLaurin,[50] *Bennettsville*
J. William Stokes,[51] *Orangeburg*

## SOUTH DAKOTA

SENATORS

Richard F. Pettigrew, *Sioux Falls*
James H. Kyle, *Aberdeen*

REPRESENTATIVES AT LARGE

John A. Pickler, *Faulkton*
Robert J. Gamble, *Yankton*

## TENNESSEE

SENATORS

Isham G. Harris, *Memphis*
William B. Bate, *Nashville*

REPRESENTATIVES

William C. Anderson, *Newport*
Henry R. Gibson, *Knoxville*
Foster V. Brown, *Chattanooga*
Benton McMillin, *Carthage*
James D. Richardson, *Murfreesboro*
Joseph E. Washington, *Cedar Hill*
Nicholas N. Cox, *Franklin*
John E. McCall, *Lexington*
James C. McDearmon, *Trenton*
Josiah Patterson, *Memphis*

## TEXAS

SENATORS

Roger Q. Mills, *Corsicana*
Horace Chilton, *Tyler*

REPRESENTATIVES

Joseph C. Hutcheson, *Houston*
Samuel B. Cooper, *Woodville*
Charles H. Yoakum, *Greenville*
David B. Culberson,[52] *Jefferson*
Joseph W. Bailey, *Gainesville*

---

[42] Election unsuccessfully contested by Henry P. Cheatham.

[43] Election unsuccessfully contested by Cyrus Thompson.

[44] Served until June 5, 1896; succeeded by Charles H. Martin, who contested his election.

[45] Successfully contested election of James A. Lockhart, and took his seat June 5, 1896.

[46] Elected to fill vacancy caused by death of

Representative-elect Myron B. Wright, in preceding Congress, and took his seat December 2, 1895.

[47] Served until June 4, 1896; succeeded by George W. Murray, who contested his election.

[48] Successfully contested the election of William Elliott, and took his seat June 4, 1896.

[49] Election unsuccessfully contested by Robert Moorman.

[50] Election unsuccessfully contested by Joshua E. Wilson.

[51] Election contested by James B. Johnston, but the House on June 1, 1896, declared the election invalid and seat vacant; subsequently elected and took his seat December 7, 1896.

[52] Election unsuccessfully contested by John H. Davis.

Jo Abbott,[53] *Hillsboro*
George C. Pendleton, *Belton*
Charles K. Bell, *Fort Worth*
Joseph D. Sayers, *Bastrop*
Miles Crowley,[54] *Galveston*
William H. Crain,[55] *Cuero*
Rudolph Kleberg,[56] *Cuero*
George H. Noonan, *San Antonio*
Jeremiah V. Cockrell, *Anson*

## UTAH[57]

SENATORS

Frank J. Cannon,[58] *Ogden*
Arthur Brown,[59] *Salt Lake City*

REPRESENTATIVE AT LARGE

Clarence E. Allen,[60] *Salt Lake City*

## VERMONT

SENATORS

Justin S. Morrill, *Strafford*
Redfield Proctor, *Proctor*

REPRESENTATIVES

H. Henry Powers, *Morrisville*
William W. Grout, *Barton*

## VIRGINIA

SENATORS

John W. Daniel, *Lynchburg*
Thomas S. Martin, *Scottsville*

REPRESENTATIVES

William A. Jones,[61] *Warsaw*
D. Gardiner Tyler, *Sturgeon Point*
Tazewell Ellett, *Richmond*
William R. McKenney,[62] *Petersburg*

Robert T. Thorp,[63] *Mecklenburg*
Claude A. Swanson,[64] *Chatham*
Peter J. Otey,[65] *Lynchburg*
Smith S. Turner, *Front Royal*
Elisha E. Meredith, *Brentsville*
James A. Walker, *Wytheville*
Henry St. George Tucker,[66] *Staunton*

## WASHINGTON

SENATORS

Watson C. Squire, *Seattle*
John L. Wilson, *Spokane*

REPRESENTATIVES AT LARGE

William H. Doolittle, *Tacoma*
Samuel C. Hyde, *Spokane*

## WEST VIRGINIA

SENATORS

Charles J. Faulkner, *Martinsburg*
Stephen B. Elkins, *Elkins*

REPRESENTATIVES

Blackburn B. Dovener, *Wheeling*
Alston G. Dayton, *Philippi*
James H. Huling, *Charleston*
Warren Miller, *Jackson*

## WISCONSIN

SENATORS

William F. Vilas, *Madison*
John L. Mitchell, *Milwaukee*

REPRESENTATIVES

Henry Allen Cooper, *Racine*
Edward Sauerhering, *Mayville*
Joseph W. Babcock, *Necedah*

Theobald Otjen, *Milwaukee*
Samuel S. Barney, *West Bend*
Samuel A. Cook, *Neenah*
Michael Griffin, *Eau Claire*
Edward S. Minor, *Sturgeon Bay*
Alexander Stewart, *Wausau*
John J. Jenkins, *Chippewa Falls*

## WYOMING

SENATORS

Clarence D. Clark, *Evanston*
Francis E. Warren, *Cheyenne*

REPRESENTATIVE AT LARGE

Frank W. Mondell, *Newcastle*

## TERRITORY OF ARIZONA

DELEGATE

Nathan O. Murphy, *Phoenix*

## TERRITORY OF NEW MEXICO

DELEGATE

Thomas B. Catron, *Santa Fe*

## TERRITORY OF OKLAHOMA

DELEGATE

Dennis T. Flynn, *Guthrie*

## TERRITORY OF UTAH

DELEGATE

Frank J. Cannon,[67] *Ogden*

---

[53] Election unsuccessfully contested by J. C. Kearby.

[54] Election unsuccessfully contested by A. J. Rosenthal.

[55] Died February 10, 1896.

[56] Elected to fill vacancy caused by death of William H. Crain, and took his seat May 5, 1896.

[57] Admitted as a State into the Union January 4, 1896.

[58] Took his seat January 27, 1896; term to expire, as determined by lot, March 3, 1899.

[59] Took his seat January 27, 1896; term to expire, as determined by lot, March 3, 1897.

[60] Took his seat January 7, 1896.

[61] Election unsuccessfully contested by James J. McDonald.

[62] Served until May 2, 1896; succeeded by Robert T. Thorp, who contested his election.

[63] Successfully contested the election of William R. McKenney, and took his seat May 2, 1896.

[64] Election unsuccessfully contested by George W. Cornell.

[65] Election unsuccessfully contested by J. Hampton Hoge.

[66] Election unsuccessfully contested by Jacob Yost.

[67] Served until January 4, 1896, when the Territory of Utah was granted statehood; subsequently elected Senator from the new State.

# 55TH CONGRESS

MARCH 4, 1897, TO MARCH 3, 1899

Garret A. Hobart
Vice President

Thomas B. Reed
Speaker

FIRST SESSION— *March 15, 1897, to July 24, 1897*
SECOND SESSION— *December 6, 1897, to July 8, 1898*
THIRD SESSION— *December 5, 1898, to March 3, 1899*
SPECIAL SESSION OF THE SENATE— *March 4, 1897, to March 10, 1897*

---

VICE PRESIDENT OF THE UNITED STATES— Garret A. Hobart, of New Jersey
PRESIDENT PRO TEMPORE OF THE SENATE— William P. Frye, of Maine
SECRETARY OF THE SENATE— William R. Cox, of North Carolina
SERGEANT AT ARMS OF THE SENATE— Richard J. Bright, of Indiana

---

SPEAKER OF THE HOUSE OF REPRESENTATIVES— Thomas B. Reed,[1] of Maine
CLERK OF THE HOUSE— Alexander McDowell,[2] of Pennsylvania
SERGEANT AT ARMS OF THE HOUSE— Benjamin F. Russell, of Missouri
DOORKEEPER OF THE HOUSE— William J. Glenn, of New York
POSTMASTER OF THE HOUSE— J. C. McElroy

## ALABAMA

SENATORS

John T. Morgan, *Selma*
Edmund W. Pettus, *Selma*

REPRESENTATIVES

George W. Taylor, *Demopolis*
Jesse F. Stallings,[3] *Greenville*
Henry D. Clayton,[4] *Eufaula*
Thomas S. Plowman,[5] *Talladega*
William F. Aldrich,[6] *Aldrich*
Willis Brewer, *Hayneville*
John H. Bankhead, *Fayette*
Milford W. Howard, *Fort Payne*
Joseph Wheeler, *Wheeler*
Oscar W. Underwood,[7] *Birmingham*

## ARKANSAS

SENATORS

James K. Jones, *Washington*
James H. Berry, *Bentonville*

REPRESENTATIVES

Philip D. McCulloch, Jr., *Marianna*
John S. Little, *Greenwood*
Thomas C. McRae, *Prescott*
William L. Terry, *Little Rock*
Hugh A. Dinsmore, *Fayetteville*
Stephen Brundidge, Jr., *Searcy*

## CALIFORNIA

SENATORS

Stephen M. White, *Los Angeles*
George C. Perkins, *Oakland*

REPRESENTATIVES

John A. Barham, *Santa Rosa*
Marion De Vries, *Stockton*
Samuel G. Hilborn, *Oakland*
James G. Maguire, *San Francisco*
Eugene F. Loud, *San Francisco*
Charles A. Barlow, *San Luis Obispo*
Curtis H. Castle, *Merced*

## COLORADO

SENATORS

Henry M. Teller, *Central City*
Edward O. Wolcott, *Denver*

REPRESENTATIVES

John F. Shafroth, *Denver*
John C. Bell, *Montrose*

## CONNECTICUT

SENATORS

Orville H. Platt, *Meriden*
Joseph R. Hawley, *Hartford*

REPRESENTATIVES

E. Stevens Henry, *Rockville*
Nehemiah D. Sperry, *New Haven*
Charles A. Russell, *Killingly*
Ebenezer J. Hill, *Norwalk*

## DELAWARE

SENATORS

George Gray, *Wilmington*
Richard R. Kenney, *Dover*

## REPRESENTATIVE AT LARGE

Levin I. Handy,[8] *Newark*

## FLORIDA

SENATORS

Samuel Pasco, *Monticello*
Stephen R. Mallory,[9] *Pensacola*

REPRESENTATIVES

Stephen M. Sparkman, *Tampa*
Robert W. Davis, *Palatka*

## GEORGIA

SENATORS

Augustus O. Bacon, *Macon*
Alexander S. Clay, *Marietta*

REPRESENTATIVES

Rufus E. Lester, *Savannah*
James M. Griggs, *Dawson*
Elijah B. Lewis, *Montezuma*
William C. Adamson, *Carrollton*
Leonidas F. Livingston, *Kings*
Charles L. Bartlett, *Macon*
John W. Maddox, *Rome*
William M. Howard, *Lexington*
Farish C. Tate, *Jasper*
William H. Fleming, *Augusta*
William G. Brantley, *Brunswick*

## IDAHO

SENATORS

George L. Shoup, *Boise*
Henry Heitfeld, *Lewiston*

---

[1] Reelected March 15, 1897.
[2] Reelected March 15, 1897.
[3] Election unsuccessfully contested by Thomas H. Clark.
[4] Election unsuccessfully contested by George L. Comer.
[5] Served until February 9, 1898; succeeded by

William F. Aldrich, who contested his election.
[6] Successfully contested the election of Thomas S. Plowman, and took his seat February 9, 1898.
[7] Election unsuccessfully contested by Grattan B. Crowe.
[8] Election unsuccessfully contested by Jonathan S. Willis.

[9] Elected to fill vacancy in the term beginning March 4, 1897, and took his seat May 25, 1897; John A. Henderson presented credentials as a Senator-designate on March 16, 1897, which were referred to the Committee on Privileges and Elections; no further action was taken.

REPRESENTATIVE AT LARGE
James Gunn, *Boise*

## ILLINOIS

SENATORS
Shelby M. Cullom, *Springfield*
William E. Mason, *Chicago*

REPRESENTATIVES
James R. Mann, *Chicago*
William Lorimer, *Chicago*
Hugh R. Belknap, *Chicago*
Daniel W. Mills, *Chicago*
George E. White, *Chicago*
Edward D. Cooke,[10] *Chicago*
Henry S. Boutell,[11] *Chicago*
George E. Foss, *Chicago*
Albert J. Hopkins, *Aurora*
Robert R. Hitt, *Mount Morris*
George W. Prince, *Galesburg*
Walter Reeves, *Streator*
Joseph G. Cannon, *Danville*
Vespasian Warner, *Clinton*
Joseph V. Graff, *Pekin*
Benjamin F. Marsh, *Warsaw*
William H. Hinrichsen, *Jacksonville*
James A. Connolly, *Springfield*
Thomas M. Jett, *Hillsboro*
Andrew J. Hunter, *Paris*
James R. Campbell, *McLeansboro*
Jehu Baker, *Belleville*
George W. Smith, *Murphysboro*

## INDIANA

SENATORS
David Turpie, *Indianapolis*
Charles W. Fairbanks, *Indianapolis*

REPRESENTATIVES
James A. Hemenway, *Boonville*
Robert W. Miers, *Bloomington*
William T. Zenor, *Corydon*
William S. Holman,[12] *Aurora*
Francis M. Griffith,[13] *Vevay*
George W. Faris, *Terre Haute*
Henry U. Johnson, *Richmond*
Jesse Overstreet, *Indianapolis*
Charles L. Henry, *Anderson*
Charles B. Landis, *Delphi*
Edgar D. Crumpacker, *Valparaiso*
George W. Steele, *Marion*
James M. Robinson, *Fort Wayne*
Lemuel W. Royse, *Warsaw*

## IOWA

SENATORS
William B. Allison, *Dubuque*
John H. Gear, *Burlington*

REPRESENTATIVES
Samuel M. Clark, *Keokuk*
George M. Curtis, *Clinton*
David B. Henderson, *Dubuque*
Thomas Updegraff, *McGregor*
Robert G. Cousins, *Tipton*
John F. Lacey, *Oskaloosa*
John A. T. Hull, *Des Moines*
William P. Hepburn, *Clarinda*
Alva L. Hager, *Greenfield*
Jonathan P. Dolliver, *Fort Dodge*
George D. Perkins, *Sioux City*

## KANSAS

SENATORS
Lucien Baker, *Leavenworth*
William A. Harris, *Linwood*

REPRESENTATIVE AT LARGE
Jeremiah D. Botkin, *Winfield*

REPRESENTATIVES
Case Broderick, *Holton*
Mason S. Peters, *Kansas City*
Edwin R. Ridgely, *Pittsburg*
Charles Curtis, *Topeka*
William D. Vincent, *Clay Center*
Nelson B. McCormick, *Phillipsburg*
Jeremiah Simpson, *Medicine Lodge*

## KENTUCKY

SENATORS
William Lindsay, *Frankfort*
William J. Deboe, *Marion*

REPRESENTATIVES
Charles K. Wheeler, *Paducah*
John D. Clardy, *Newstead*
John S. Rhea,[14] *Russellville*
David H. Smith, *Hodgensville*
Walter Evans, *Louisville*
Albert S. Berry, *Newport*
Evan E. Settle, *Owenton*
George M. Davison, *Stanford*
Samuel J. Pugh, *Vanceburg*
Thomas Y. Fitzpatrick, *Prestonburg*
David G. Colson, *Middlesboro*

## LOUISIANA

SENATORS
Donelson Caffery, *Franklin*
Samuel D. McEnery, *New Orleans*

REPRESENTATIVES
Adolph Meyer,[15] *New Orleans*
Robert C. Davey, *New Orleans*
Robert F. Broussard, *New Iberia*
Henry W. Ogden, *Benton*
Samuel T. Baird, *Bastrop*
Samuel M. Robertson, *Baton Rouge*

## MAINE

SENATORS
Eugene Hale, *Ellsworth*
William P. Frye, *Lewiston*

REPRESENTATIVES
Thomas B. Reed, *Portland*
Nelson Dingley, Jr.,[16] *Lewiston*
Seth L. Milliken,[17] *Belfast*
Edwin C. Burleigh,[18] *Augusta*
Charles A. Boutelle, *Bangor*

## MARYLAND

SENATORS
Arthur Pue Gorman, *Laurel*
George L. Wellington, *Cumberland*

REPRESENTATIVES
Isaac A. Barber, *Easton*
William B. Baker, *Aberdeen*
William S. Booze, *Baltimore*
William W. McIntire, *Baltimore*
Sydney E. Mudd, *La Plata*
John McDonald, *Rockville*

## MASSACHUSETTS

SENATORS
George F. Hoar, *Worcester*
Henry Cabot Lodge, *Nahant*

REPRESENTATIVES
Ashley B. Wright,[19] *North Adams*
George P. Lawrence,[20] *North Adams*
Frederick H. Gillett, *Springfield*
Joseph H. Walker, *Worcester*
George W. Weymouth, *Fitchburg*
William S. Knox, *Lawrence*
William H. Moody, *Haverhill*
William E. Barrett, *Melrose*
Samuel W. McCall, *Winchester*
John F. Fitzgerald, *Boston*
Samuel J. Barrows, *Boston*
Charles F. Sprague, *Brookline*
William C. Lovering, *Taunton*
John Simpkins,[21] *Yarmouth*
William S. Greene,[22] *Fall River*

## MICHIGAN

SENATORS
James McMillan, *Detroit*
Julius C. Burrows, *Kalamazoo*

REPRESENTATIVES
John B. Corliss, *Detroit*
George Spalding, *Monroe*
Albert M. Todd, *Kalamazoo*
Edward L. Hamilton, *Niles*
William Alden Smith, *Grand Rapids*
Samuel W. Smith, *Pontiac*
Horace G. Snover, *Port Austin*

---

[10] Died June 24, 1897.
[11] Elected to fill vacancy caused by death of Edward D. Cooke, and took his seat December 6, 1897.
[12] Died April 22, 1897.
[13] Elected to fill vacancy caused by death of William S. Holman, and took his seat December 6, 1897.
[14] Election unsuccessfully contested by W. God-
frey Hunter.
[15] Election unsuccessfully contested by Joseph Gazin and Armand Romain.
[16] Died January 13, 1899, before the commencement of the Fifty-sixth Congress, to which he had been reelected.
[17] Died April 18, 1897.
[18] Elected to fill vacancy caused by death of Seth
L. Milliken, and took his seat July 1, 1897.
[19] Died August 14, 1897.
[20] Elected to fill vacancy caused by death of Ashley B. Wright, and took his seat December 6, 1897.
[21] Died March 27, 1898.
[22] Elected to fill vacancy caused by death of John Simpkins, and took his seat June 15, 1898.

## MICHIGAN—Continued

### REPRESENTATIVES—CONTINUED

Ferdinand Brucker, *Saginaw*
Roswell P. Bishop, *Ludington*
Rousseau O. Crump, *West Bay City*
William S. Mesick, *Mancelona*
Carlos D. Shelden, *Houghton*

## MINNESOTA

### SENATORS

Cushman K. Davis, *St. Paul*
Knute Nelson, *Alexandria*

### REPRESENTATIVES

James A. Tawney, *Winona*
James T. McCleary, *Mankato*
Joel P. Heatwole, *Northfield*
Frederick C. Stevens, *St. Paul*
Loren Fletcher, *Minneapolis*
R. Page W. Morris, *Duluth*
Frank M. Eddy, *Glenwood*

## MISSISSIPPI

### SENATORS

James Z. George,[23] *Carrollton*
Hernando D. Money,[24] *Carrollton*
Edward C. Walthall,[25] *Grenada*
William V. Sullivan,[26] *Oxford*

### REPRESENTATIVES

John M. Allen, *Tupelo*
William V. Sullivan,[27] *Oxford*
Thomas Spight,[28] *Ripley*
Thomas C. Catchings, *Vicksburg*
Andrew F. Fox, *West Point*
John Sharp Williams, *Yazoo City*
William F. Love,[29] *Gloster*
Frank A. McLain,[30] *Gloster*
Patrick Henry, *Brandon*

## MISSOURI

### SENATORS

Francis M. Cockrell, *Warrensburg*
George G. Vest, *Kansas City*

### REPRESENTATIVES

James T. Lloyd,[31] *Shelbyville*
Robert N. Bodine, *Paris*
Alexander M. Dockery, *Gallatin*
Charles F. Cochran, *St. Joseph*
William S. Cowherd, *Kansas City*
David A. De Armond, *Butler*
James Cooney, *Marshall*
Richard P. Bland, *Lebanon*
James Beauchamp Clark, *Bowling Green*
Richard Bartholdt, *St. Louis*
Charles F. Joy, *St. Louis*

Charles E. Pearce, *St. Louis*
Edward Robb, *Perryville*
Willard D. Vandiver, *Cape Girardeau*
Maecenas E. Benton, *Neosho*

## MONTANA

### SENATORS

Lee Mantle, *Butte*
Thomas H. Carter, *Helena*

### REPRESENTATIVE AT LARGE

Charles S. Hartman, *Bozeman*

## NEBRASKA

### SENATORS

William V. Allen, *Madison*
John M. Thurston, *Omaha*

### REPRESENTATIVES

Jesse B. Strode, *Lincoln*
David H. Mercer, *Omaha*
Samuel Maxwell, *Fremont*
William L. Stark, *Aurora*
Roderick D. Sutherland, *Nelson*
William L. Greene, *Kearney*

## NEVADA

### SENATORS

John P. Jones, *Gold Hill*
William M. Stewart, *Carson City*

### REPRESENTATIVE AT LARGE

Francis G. Newlands, *Reno*

## NEW HAMPSHIRE

### SENATORS

William E. Chandler, *Concord*
Jacob H. Gallinger, *Concord*

### REPRESENTATIVES

Cyrus A. Sulloway, *Manchester*
Frank G. Clarke, *Peterboro*

## NEW JERSEY

### SENATORS

James Smith, Jr., *Newark*
William J. Sewell, *Camden*

### REPRESENTATIVES

Henry C. Loudenslager, *Paulsboro*
John J. Gardner, *Atlantic City*
Benjamin F. Howell, *New Brunswick*
Mahlon Pitney,[32] *Morristown*
James F. Stewart, *Paterson*
Richard Wayne Parker, *Newark*
Thomas McEwan, Jr., *Jersey City*
Charles N. Fowler, *Elizabeth*

## NEW YORK

### SENATORS

Edward Murphy, Jr., *Troy*
Thomas C. Platt, *Owego*

### REPRESENTATIVES

Joseph M. Belford, *Riverhead*
Denis M. Hurley,[33] *Brooklyn*
Francis H. Wilson,[34] *Brooklyn*
Edmund H. Driggs,[35] *Brooklyn*
Israel F. Fischer, *Brooklyn*
Charles G. Bennett, *Brooklyn*
James R. Howe, *Brooklyn*
John H. G. Vehslage, *New York City*
John M. Mitchell, *New York City*
Thomas J. Bradley, *New York City*
Amos J. Cummings, *New York City*
William Sulzer, *New York City*
George B. McClellan, *New York City*
Richard C. Shannon, *New York City*
Lemuel E. Quigg, *New York City*
Philip B. Low, *New York City*
William L. Ward,[36] *Port Chester*
Benjamin B. Odell, Jr., *Newburgh*
John H. Ketcham, *Dover Plains*
Aaron V. S. Cochrane, *Hudson*
George N. Southwick, *Albany*
David F. Wilber, *Oneonta*
Lucius N. Littauer, *Gloversville*
Wallace T. Foote, Jr., *Port Henry*
Charles A. Chickering, *Copenhagen*
James S. Sherman, *Utica*
George W. Ray, *Norwich*
James J. Belden, *Syracuse*
Sereno E. Payne, *Auburn*
Charles W. Gillet, *Addison*
James W. Wadsworth, *Geneseo*
Henry C. Brewster, *Rochester*
Rowland B. Mahany, *Buffalo*
De Alva S. Alexander, *Buffalo*
Warren B. Hooker,[37] *Fredonia*

## NORTH CAROLINA

### SENATORS

Jeter C. Pritchard, *Marshall*
Marion Butler, *Elliot*

### REPRESENTATIVES

Harry Skinner, *Greenville*
George H. White, *Tarboro*
John E. Fowler, *Clinton*
William F. Strowd, *Pittsboro*
William W. Kitchin, *Roxboro*
Charles H. Martin, *Polkton*
Alonzo C. Shuford, *Newton*
Romulus Z. Linney, *Taylorsville*
Richmond Pearson, *Asheville*

---

[23] Died August 14, 1897.
[24] Appointed to fill vacancy caused by death of James Z. George, and took his seat December 7, 1897; subsequently elected.
[25] Died April 21, 1898.
[26] Appointed to fill vacancy caused by death of Edward C. Walthall, and took his seat May 31, 1898; subsequently elected.
[27] Resigned May 31, 1898, having been appointed Senator.

[28] Elected to fill vacancy caused by resignation of William V. Sullivan, and took his seat December 5, 1898.
[29] Died October 16, 1898.
[30] Elected to fill vacancy caused by death of William F. Love, and took his seat December 12, 1898.
[31] Elected to fill vacancy caused by death of Representative-elect Richard P. Giles (November 17, 1896, before the beginning of the congressional term), and took his seat June 10, 1897.

[32] Resigned January 10, 1899.
[33] Died February 26, 1899.
[34] Resigned September 30, 1897.
[35] Elected to fill vacancy caused by resignation of Francis H. Wilson, and took his seat December 6, 1897.
[36] Election unsuccessfully contested by Benjamin L. Fairchild.
[37] Resigned November 10, 1898, before the commencement of the Fifty-Sixth Congress, to which he had been reelected.

## NORTH DAKOTA

SENATORS

Henry C. Hansbrough, *Devils Lake*
William N. Roach, *Larimore*

REPRESENTATIVE AT LARGE

Martin N. Johnson, *Petersburg*

## OHIO

SENATORS

John Sherman,[38] *Mansfield*
Marcus A. Hanna,[39] *Cleveland*
Joseph B. Foraker, *Cincinnati*

REPRESENTATIVES

William B. Shattuc, *Madisonville*
Jacob H. Bromwell, *Cincinnati*
John L. Brenner, *Dayton*
George A. Marshall, *Sidney*
David Meekison, *Napoleon*
Seth W. Brown, *Lebanon*
Walter L. Weaver, *Springfield*
Archibald Lybrand, *Delaware*
James H. Southard, *Toledo*
Lucien J. Fenton, *Winchester*
Charles H. Grosvenor, *Athens*
John J. Lentz, *Columbus*
James A. Norton, *Tiffin*
Winfield S. Kerr, *Mansfield*
Henry C. Van Voorhis, *Zanesville*
Lorenzo Danford, *St. Clairsville*
John A. McDowell, *Millersburg*
Robert W. Tayler, *Lisbon*
Stephen A. Northway,[40] *Jefferson*
Charles W. F. Dick,[41] *Akron*
Clifton B. Beach, *Cleveland*
Theodore E. Burton, *Cleveland*

## OREGON

SENATORS

George W. McBride, *St. Helens*
Joseph Simon,[42] *Portland*

REPRESENTATIVES

Thomas H. Tongue,[43] *Hillsboro*
William R. Ellis, *Heppner*

## PENNSYLVANIA

SENATORS

Matthew S. Quay, *Beaver*
Boies Penrose, *Philadelphia*

REPRESENTATIVES AT LARGE

Galusha A. Grow, *Glenwood*
Samuel A. Davenport, *Erie*

REPRESENTATIVES

Henry H. Bingham, *Philadelphia*
Robert Adams, Jr., *Philadelphia*
William McAleer,[44] *Philadelphia*
James R. Young, *Philadelphia*
Alfred C. Harmer, *Philadelphia*
Thomas S. Butler, *Westchester*
Irving P. Wanger, *Norristown*
William S. Kirkpatrick, *Easton*
Daniel Ermentrout, *Reading*
Marriott Brosius, *Lancaster*
William Connell, *Scranton*
Morgan B. Williams, *Wilkes-Barre*
Charles N. Brumm, *Minersville*
Marlin E. Olmsted, *Harrisburg*
James H. Codding, *Towanda*
Horace B. Packer, *Wellsboro*
Monroe H. Kulp, *Shamokin*
Thaddeus M. Mahon, *Chambersburg*
George J. Benner, *Gettysburg*
Josiah D. Hicks, *Altoona*
Edward E. Robbins, *Greensburg*
John Dalzell, *Pittsburgh*
William A. Stone,[45] *Allegheny*
William H. Graham,[46] *Allegheny*
Ernest F. Acheson, *Washington*
Joseph B. Showalter,[47] *Chicora*
John C. Sturtevant, *Conneautville*
Charles W. Stone, *Warren*
William C. Arnold, *Dubois*

## RHODE ISLAND

SENATORS

Nelson W. Aldrich, *Providence*
George P. Wetmore, *Newport*

REPRESENTATIVES

Melville Bull, *Middletown*
Adin B. Capron, *Stillwater*

## SOUTH CAROLINA

SENATORS

Benjamin R. Tillman, *Trenton*
Joseph H. Earle,[48] *Greenville*
John L. McLaurin,[49] *Bennettsville*

REPRESENTATIVES

William Elliott, *Beaufort*
W. Jasper Talbert, *Parksville*

Asbury C. Latimer, *Belton*
Stanyarne Wilson, *Spartanburg*
Thomas J. Strait, *Lancaster*
John L. McLaurin,[50] *Bennettsville*
James Norton,[51] *Mullins*
J. William Stokes, *Orangeburg*

## SOUTH DAKOTA

SENATORS

Richard F. Pettigrew, *Sioux Falls*
James H. Kyle, *Aberdeen*

REPRESENTATIVES AT LARGE

Freeman Knowles, *Deadwood*
John E. Kelley, *Flandreau*

## TENNESSEE

SENATORS

Isham G. Harris,[52] *Memphis*
Thomas B. Turley,[53] *Memphis*
William B. Bate, *Nashville*

REPRESENTATIVES

Walter P. Brownlow, *Jonesboro*
Henry R. Gibson, *Knoxville*
John A. Moon, *Chattanooga*
Benton McMillin,[54] *Carthage*
James D. Richardson, *Murfreesboro*
John W. Gaines, *Nashville*
Nicholas N. Cox, *Franklin*
Thetus W. Sims, *Linden*
Rice A. Pierce, *Union City*
Edward W. Carmack,[55] *Memphis*

## TEXAS

SENATORS

Roger Q. Mills, *Corsicana*
Horace Chilton, *Tyler*

REPRESENTATIVES

Thomas H. Ball, *Huntsville*
Samuel B. Cooper, *Woodville*
Reese C. De Graffenreid, *Longview*
John W. Cranford,[56] *Sulphur Springs*
Joseph W. Bailey, *Gainesville*
Robert E. Burke, *Dallas*
Robert L. Henry, *Waco*
Samuel W. T. Lanham, *Weatherford*
Joseph D. Sayers,[57] *Bastrop*
Robert B. Hawley, *Galveston*
Rudolph Kleberg, *Cuero*
James L. Slayden, *San Antonio*
John H. Stephens, *Vernon*

---

[38] Resigned March 4, 1897, to become Secretary of State.

[39] Appointed to fill vacancy caused by resignation of John Sherman, and took his seat March 5, 1897; subsequently elected.

[40] Died September 18, 1898.

[41] Elected to fill vacancy caused by death of Stephen A. Northway, and took his seat December 5, 1898.

[42] Elected to fill vacancy in the term beginning March 4, 1897, caused by failure of legislature to elect, and took his seat December 5, 1898. Henry W. Corbett presented credentials as a Senator-designate March 15, 1897, but was not sworn; the Senate, on February 28, 1898, decided he was not entitled to the seat; vacancy in this class from March 4, 1897, to October 7, 1898. (See U.S. Senate Election, Expulsion and Censure Cases, 1793-1990, Senate Document 103-33, pp. 253-55.)

[43] Election unsuccessfully contested by W. S. Vanderburg.

[44] Election unsuccessfully contested by Samuel E. Hudson.

[45] Resigned November 9, 1898, having been elected Governor.

[46] Elected to fill vacancy caused by resignation of William A. Stone, and took his seat December 5, 1898.

[47] Elected to fill vacancy caused by death of Representative-elect James J. Davidson (January 2, 1897, before the beginning of the congressional term), and took his seat May 3, 1897.

[48] Died May 20, 1897.

[49] Appointed to fill vacancy caused by death of Joseph H. Earle, and took his seat June 1, 1897; subsequently elected.

[50] Resigned May 31, 1897, having been appointed Senator.

[51] Elected to fill vacancy caused by resignation of John L. McLaurin, and took his seat December 6, 1897.

[52] Died July 8, 1897.

[53] Appointed to fill vacancy caused by death of Isham G. Harris, and took his seat December 6, 1897; subsequently elected.

[54] Resigned January 16, 1899, having been elected Governor.

[55] Election unsuccessfully contested by Josiah Patterson.

[56] Died March 2, 1899.

[57] Resigned January 16, 1899, having been elected Governor.

## UTAH

SENATORS
Frank J. Cannon, *Ogden*
Joseph L. Rawlins, *Salt Lake City*

REPRESENTATIVE AT LARGE
William H. King, *Salt Lake City*

## VERMONT

SENATORS
Justin S. Morrill,[58] *Strafford*
Jonathan Ross,[59] *St. Johnsbury*
Redfield Proctor, *Proctor*

REPRESENTATIVES
H. Henry Powers, *Morrisville*
William W. Grout, *Barton*

## VIRGINIA

SENATORS
John W. Daniel, *Lynchburg*
Thomas S. Martin, *Scottsville*

REPRESENTATIVES
William A. Jones, *Warsaw*
William A. Young,[60] *Norfolk*
Richard A. Wise,[61] *Williamsburg*
John Lamb, *Richmond*
Sydney P. Epes,[62] *Blackstone*
Robert T. Thorp,[63] *Mecklenberg*
Claude A. Swanson, *Chatham*
Peter J. Otey, *Lynchburg*
James Hay, *Madison*

John F. Rixey, *Brandy*
James A. Walker, *Wytheville*
Jacob Yost, *Staunton*

## WASHINGTON

SENATORS
John L. Wilson, *Spokane*
George Turner, *Spokane*

REPRESENTATIVES AT LARGE
James Hamilton Lewis, *Seattle*
William C. Jones, *Spokane*

## WEST VIRGINIA

SENATORS
Charles J. Faulkner, *Martinsburg*
Stephen B. Elkins, *Elkins*

REPRESENTATIVES
Blackburn B. Dovener, *Wheeling*
Alston G. Dayton, *Philippi*
Charles P. Dorr, *Addison*
Warren Miller, *Jackson*

## WISCONSIN

SENATORS
John L. Mitchell, *Milwaukee*
John C. Spooner, *Madison*

REPRESENTATIVES
Henry Allen Cooper, *Racine*
Edward Sauerhering, *Mayville*
Joseph W. Babcock, *Necedah*

Theobald Otjen, *Milwaukee*
Samuel S. Barney, *West Bend*
James H. Davidson, *Oshkosh*
Michael Griffin, *Eau Claire*
Edward S. Minor, *Sturgeon Bay*
Alexander Stewart, *Wausau*
John J. Jenkins, *Chippewa Falls*

## WYOMING

SENATORS
Clarence D. Clark, *Evanston*
Francis E. Warren, *Cheyenne*

REPRESENTATIVE AT LARGE
John E. Osborne, *Rawlins*

## TERRITORY OF ARIZONA

DELEGATE
Marcus A. Smith, *Tucson*

## TERRITORY OF NEW MEXICO

DELEGATE
Harvey B. Fergusson, *Albuquerque*

## TERRITORY OF OKLAHOMA

DELEGATE
James Y. Callahan, *Kingfisher*

---

[58] Died December 28, 1898.
[59] Appointed to fill vacancy caused by death of Justin S. Morrill, and took his seat January 16, 1899.
[60] Served until April 26, 1898; succeeded by

Richard A. Wise, who contested his election.
[61] Successfully contested the election of William A. Young, and took his seat April 26, 1898.
[62] Served until March 23, 1898; succeeded by

Robert T. Thorp, who contested his election.
[63] Successfully contested the election of Sydney P. Epes, and took his seat March 23, 1898.

# 56TH CONGRESS

MARCH 4, 1899, TO MARCH 3, 1901

FIRST SESSION *December 4, 1899, to June 7, 1900*
SECOND SESSION *December 3, 1900, to March 3, 1901*

---

VICE PRESIDENT OF THE UNITED STATES— Garret A. Hobart,[1] of New Jersey
PRESIDENT PRO TEMPORE OF THE SENATE— William P. Frye, of Maine
SECRETARY OF THE SENATE— William R. Cox, of North Carolina; Charles G. Bennett,[2] of New York
SERGEANT AT ARMS OF THE SENATE— Richard J. Bright, of Indiana; Daniel M. Ransdell,[3] of Indiana

---

SPEAKER OF THE HOUSE OF REPRESENTATIVES— David B. Henderson,[4] of Iowa
CLERK OF THE HOUSE— Alexander McDowell,[5] of Pennsylvania
SERGEANT AT ARMS OF THE HOUSE— Benjamin F. Russell, of Missouri; Henry Casson,[6] of Wisconsin
DOORKEEPER OF THE HOUSE— William J. Glenn, of New York
POSTMASTER OF THE HOUSE— J. C. McElroy

Garret A. Hobart
Vice President

David B. Henderson
Speaker

## ALABAMA

### SENATORS

John T. Morgan, *Selma*
Edmund W. Pettus, *Selma*

### REPRESENTATIVES

George W. Taylor, *Demopolis*
Jesse F. Stallings, *Greenville*
Henry D. Clayton, *Eufaula*
Gaston A. Robbins,[7] *Selma*
William F. Aldrich,[8] *Aldrich*
Willis Brewer, *Hayneville*
John H. Bankhead, *Fayette*
John L. Burnett, *Gadsden*
Joseph Wheeler,[9] *Wheeler*
William Richardson,[10] *Huntsville*
Oscar W. Underwood, *Birmingham*

## ARKANSAS

### SENATORS

James K. Jones, *Washington*
James H. Berry, *Bentonville*

### REPRESENTATIVES

Philip D. McCulloch, *Marianna*
John S. Little, *Greenwood*
Thomas C. McRae, *Prescott*
William L. Terry, *Little Rock*
Hugh A. Dinsmore, *Fayetteville*
Stephen Brundidge, Jr., *Searcy*

## CALIFORNIA

### SENATORS

George C. Perkins, *Oakland*
Thomas R. Bard,[11] *Hueneme*

### REPRESENTATIVES

John A. Barham, *Santa Rosa*
Marion De Vries,[12] *Stockton*
Samuel D. Woods,[13] *Stockton*
Victor H. Metcalf, *Oakland*
Julius Kahn, *San Francisco*
Eugene F. Loud, *San Francisco*
Russell J. Waters, *Los Angeles*
James C. Needham, *Modesto*

## COLORADO

### SENATORS

Henry M. Teller, *Central City*
Edward O. Wolcott, *Denver*

### REPRESENTATIVES

John F. Shafroth, *Denver*
John C. Bell, *Montrose*

## CONNECTICUT

### SENATORS

Orville H. Platt, *Meriden*
Joseph R. Hawley, *Hartford*

### REPRESENTATIVES

E. Stevens Henry, *Rockville*
Nehemiah D. Sperry, *New Haven*
Charles A. Russell, *Killingly*
Ebenezer J. Hill, *Norwalk*

## DELAWARE

### SENATORS

Richard R. Kenney, *Dover*
Vacant[14]

### REPRESENTATIVE AT LARGE

John H. Hoffecker,[15] *Smyrna*
Walter O. Hoffecker,[16] *Smyrna*

## FLORIDA

### SENATORS

Samuel Pasco,[17] *Monticello*
James P. Taliaferro,[18] *Jacksonville*
Stephen R. Mallory, *Pensacola*

### REPRESENTATIVES

Stephen M. Sparkman, *Tampa*
Robert W. Davis, *Palatka*

## GEORGIA

### SENATORS

Augustus O. Bacon, *Macon*
Alexander S. Clay, *Marietta*

### REPRESENTATIVES

Rufus E. Lester, *Savannah*
James M. Griggs, *Dawson*
Elijah B. Lewis, *Montezuma*
William C. Adamson, *Carrollton*
Leonidas F. Livingston, *Kings*
Charles L. Bartlett, *Macon*

---

[1] Died November 21, 1899.
[2] Elected January 29, 1900.
[3] Elected January 29, 1900.
[4] Elected December 4, 1899.
[5] Reelected December 4, 1899.
[6] Elected December 4, 1899.
[7] Served until March 8, 1900; succeeded by William F. Aldrich, who contested his election.
[8] Successfully contested the election of Gaston A. Robbins, and took his seat March 8, 1900.

[9] Resigned April 20, 1900.
[10] Elected to fill vacancy caused by resignation of Joseph Wheeler, and took his seat December 3, 1900.
[11] Elected to fill vacancy in the term beginning March 4, 1899, caused by failure of legislature to elect, and took his seat March 5, 1900; vacancy in this class from March 4, 1899, to February 6, 1900.
[12] Resigned August 20, 1900.
[13] Elected to fill vacancy caused by resignation of Marion De Vries, and took his seat December 3, 1900.

[14] Vacancy in this class from March 4, 1899, to March 2, 1903, because of failure of legislature to elect.
[15] Died June 16, 1900.
[16] Elected to fill vacancy caused by death of John H. Hoffecker, and took his seat December 3, 1900.
[17] Reappointed to fill vacancy in the term beginning March 4, 1899, to serve until the next meeting of the legislature.
[18] Elected to fill vacancy in the term beginning March 4, 1899, and took his seat December 4, 1899.

## GEORGIA—Continued

REPRESENTATIVES—CONTINUED

John W. Maddox, *Rome*
William M. Howard, *Lexington*
Farish C. Tate, *Jasper*
William H. Fleming, *Augusta*
William G. Brantley, *Brunswick*

## IDAHO

SENATORS

George L. Shoup, *Boise*
Henry Heitfeld, *Lewiston*

REPRESENTATIVE AT LARGE

Edgar Wilson, *Boise*

## ILLINOIS

SENATORS

Shelby M. Cullom, *Springfield*
William E. Mason, *Chicago*

REPRESENTATIVES

James R. Mann, *Chicago*
William Lorimer, *Chicago*
George P. Foster, *Chicago*
Thomas Cusack, *Chicago*
Edward T. Noonan, *Chicago*
Henry S. Boutell, *Chicago*
George E. Foss, *Chicago*
Albert J. Hopkins, *Aurora*
Robert R. Hitt, *Mount Morris*
George W. Prince, *Galesburg*
Walter Reeves, *Streator*
Joseph G. Cannon, *Danville*
Vespasian Warner, *Clinton*
Joseph V. Graff, *Peoria*
Benjamin F. Marsh, *Warsaw*
William E. Williams, *Pittsfield*
Ben F. Caldwell, *Chatham*
Thomas M. Jett, *Hillsboro*
Joseph B. Crowley, *Robinson*
James R. Williams, *Carmi*
William A. Rodenberg, *East St. Louis*
George W. Smith, *Murphysboro*

## INDIANA

SENATORS

Charles W. Fairbanks, *Indianapolis*
Albert J. Beveridge, *Indianapolis*

REPRESENTATIVES

James A. Hemenway, *Boonville*
Robert W. Miers, *Bloomington*

William T. Zenor, *Corydon*
Francis M. Griffith, *Vevay*
George W. Faris, *Terre Haute*
James E. Watson, *Rushville*
Jesse Overstreet, *Indianapolis*
George W. Cromer, *Muncie*
Charles B. Landis, *Delphi*
Edgar D. Crumpacker, *Valparaiso*
George W. Steele, *Marion*
James M. Robinson, *Fort Wayne*
Abraham L. Brick, *South Bend*

## IOWA

SENATORS

William B. Allison, *Dubuque*
John H. Gear,[19] *Burlington*
Jonathan P. Dolliver,[20] *Fort Dodge*

REPRESENTATIVES

Thomas Hedge, *Burlington*
Joseph R. Lane, *Davenport*
David B. Henderson, *Dubuque*
Gilbert N. Haugen, *Northwood*
Robert G. Cousins, *Tipton*
John F. Lacey, *Oskaloosa*
John A. T. Hull, *Des Moines*
William P. Hepburn, *Clarinda*
Smith McPherson,[21] *Red Oak*
Walter I. Smith,[22] *Council Bluffs*
Jonathan P. Dolliver,[23] *Fort Dodge*
James P. Conner,[24] *Denison*
Lot Thomas, *Storm Lake*

## KANSAS

SENATORS

Lucien Baker, *Leavenworth*
William A. Harris, *Linwood*

REPRESENTATIVE AT LARGE

Willis J. Bailey, *Baileyville*

REPRESENTATIVES

Charles Curtis, *Topeka*
Justin D. Bowersock, *Lawrence*
Edwin R. Ridgely, *Pittsburg*
James M. Miller, *Council Grove*
William A. Calderhead, *Marysville*
William A. Reeder, *Logan*
Chester I. Long, *Medicine Lodge*

## KENTUCKY

SENATORS

William Lindsay, *Frankfort*
William J. Deboe, *Marion*

REPRESENTATIVES

Charles K. Wheeler, *Paducah*
Henry D. Allen, *Morganfield*
John S. Rhea, *Russellville*
David H. Smith, *Hodgensville*
Oscar Turner,[25] *Louisville*
Albert S. Berry, *Newport*
Evan E. Settle,[26] *Owenton*
June W. Gayle,[27] *Owenton*
George G. Gilbert, *Shelbyville*
Samuel J. Pugh, *Vanceburg*
Thomas Y. Fitzpatrick, *Prestonburg*
Vincent S. Boreing,[28] *London*

## LOUISIANA

SENATORS

Donelson Caffery, *Franklin*
Samuel D. McEnery, *New Orleans*

REPRESENTATIVES

Adolph Meyer, *New Orleans*
Robert C. Davey, *New Orleans*
Robert F. Broussard, *New Iberia*
Phanor Breazeale, *Natchitoches*
Samuel T. Baird,[29] *Bastrop*
Joseph E. Ransdell,[30] *Lake Providence*
Samuel M. Robertson, *Baton Rouge*

## MAINE

SENATORS

Eugene Hale, *Ellsworth*
William P. Frye, *Lewiston*

REPRESENTATIVES

Thomas B. Reed,[31] *Portland*
Amos L. Allen,[32] *Alfred*
Charles E. Littlefield,[33] *Rockland*
Edwin C. Burleigh, *Augusta*
Charles A. Boutelle,[34] *Bangor*

## MARYLAND

SENATORS

George L. Wellington, *Cumberland*
Louis E. McComas, *Williamsport*

REPRESENTATIVES

John W. Smith,[35] *Snow Hill*
Josiah L. Kerr,[36] *Cambridge*
William B. Baker, *Aberdeen*
Frank C. Wachter, *Baltimore*
James W. Denny, *Baltimore*
Sydney E. Mudd, *La Plata*
George A. Pearre, *Cumberland*

---

[19] Died July 14, 1900; had been reelected for the term beginning March 4, 1901.

[20] Appointed to fill vacancy caused by death of John H. Gear, and took his seat December 4, 1900.

[21] Resigned June 6, 1900.

[22] Elected to fill vacancy caused by resignation of Smith McPherson; took his seat December 3, 1900.

[23] Resigned August 22, 1900, having been appointed Senator.

[24] Elected to fill vacancy caused by resignation of Jonathan P. Dolliver, took his seat December 4, 1900.

[25] Election unsuccessfully contested by Walter Evans.

[26] Died November 16, 1899, before Congress assembled.

[27] Elected to fill vacancy caused by death of Evan E. Settle, and took his seat January 15, 1900.

[28] Election unsuccessfully contested by John D. White.

[29] Died April 22, 1899, before Congress assembled.

[30] Elected to fill vacancy caused by death of Samuel T. Baird, and took his seat December 4, 1899.

[31] Resigned September 4, 1899, before Congress assembled.

[32] Elected to fill vacancy caused by resignation of Thomas B. Reed, and took his seat December 4, 1899.

[33] Elected to fill vacancy caused by death of Representative-elect Nelson Dingley, Jr., in preceding Congress, and took his seat December 4, 1899.

[34] Resigned March 3, 1901, before the commencement of the Fifty-seventh Congress, to which he had been reelected.

[35] Resigned January 12, 1900.

[36] Elected to fill vacancy caused by resignation of John W. Smith, and took his seat December 3, 1900.

## MASSACHUSETTS

### SENATORS

George F. Hoar, *Worcester*
Henry Cabot Lodge, *Nahant*

### REPRESENTATIVES

George P. Lawrence, *North Adams*
Frederick H. Gillett, *Springfield*
John R. Thayer, *Worcester*
George W. Weymouth, *Fitchburg*
William S. Knox, *Lawrence*
William H. Moody, *Haverhill*
Ernest W. Roberts, *Chelsea*
Samuel W. McCall, *Winchester*
John F. Fitzgerald, *Boston*
Henry F. Naphen, *Boston*
Charles F. Sprague, *Brookline*
William C. Lovering, *Taunton*
William S. Greene, *Fall River*

## MICHIGAN

### SENATORS

James McMillan, *Detroit*
Julius C. Burrows, *Kalamazoo*

### REPRESENTATIVES

John B. Corliss, *Detroit*
Henry C. Smith, *Adrian*
Washington Gardner, *Albion*
Edward L. Hamilton, *Niles*
William Alden Smith, *Grand Rapids*
Samuel W. Smith, *Pontiac*
Edgar Weeks, *Mount Clemens*
Joseph W. Fordney, *Saginaw*
Roswell P. Bishop, *Ludington*
Rousseau O. Crump, *West Bay City*
William S. Mesick, *Mancelona*
Carlos D. Shelden, *Houghton*

## MINNESOTA

### SENATORS

Cushman K. Davis,[37] *St. Paul*
Charles A. Towne,[38] *Duluth*
Moses E. Clapp,[39] *St. Paul*
Knute Nelson, *Alexandria*

### REPRESENTATIVES

James A. Tawney, *Winona*
James T. McCleary, *Mankato*
Joel P. Heatwole, *Northfield*
Frederick C. Stevens, *St. Paul*
Loren Fletcher, *Minneapolis*
R. Page W. Morris, *Duluth*
Frank M. Eddy, *Glenwood*

## MISSISSIPPI

### SENATORS

Hernando D. Money, *Carrollton*
William V. Sullivan, *Oxford*

### REPRESENTATIVES

John M. Allen, *Tupelo*
Thomas Spight, *Ripley*
Thomas C. Catchings, *Vicksburg*
Andrew F. Fox, *West Point*
John Sharp Williams, *Yazoo City*
Frank McLain, *Gloster*
Patrick Henry, *Brandon*

## MISSOURI

### SENATORS

Francis M. Cockrell, *Warrensburg*
George G. Vest, *Sweet Springs*

### REPRESENTATIVES

James T. Lloyd, *Shelbyville*
William W. Rucker, *Keytesville*
John Dougherty, *Liberty*
Charles F. Cochran, *St. Joseph*
William S. Cowherd, *Kansas City*
David A. De Armond, *Butler*
James Cooney, *Marshall*
Richard P. Bland,[40] *Lebanon*
Dorsey W. Shackleford,[41] *Jefferson City*
James Beauchamp Clark, *Bowling Green*
Richard Bartholdt, *St. Louis*
Charles F. Joy, *St. Louis*
Charles E. Pearce, *St. Louis*
Edward Robb, *Perryville*
Willard D. Vandiver, *Cape Girardeau*
Maecenas E. Benton, *Neosho*

## MONTANA

### SENATORS

Thomas H. Carter, *Helena*
William A. Clark,[42] *Butte*

### REPRESENTATIVE AT LARGE

Albert J. Campbell, *Butte*

## NEBRASKA

### SENATORS

John M. Thurston, *Omaha*
Monroe L. Hayward,[43] *Nebraska City*
William V. Allen,[44] *Madison*

### REPRESENTATIVES

Elmer J. Burkett, *Lincoln*
David H. Mercer, *Omaha*

John S. Robinson, *Madison*
William L. Stark, *Aurora*
Roderick D. Sutherland, *Nelson*
William L. Greene,[45] *Kearney*
William Neville,[46] *North Platte*

## NEVADA

### SENATORS

John P. Jones, *Gold Hill*
William M. Stewart, *Carson City*

### REPRESENTATIVE AT LARGE

Francis G. Newlands, *Reno*

## NEW HAMPSHIRE

### SENATORS

William E. Chandler, *Concord*
Jacob H. Gallinger, *Concord*

### REPRESENTATIVES

Cyrus A. Sulloway, *Manchester*
Frank G. Clarke,[47] *Peterboro*

## NEW JERSEY

### SENATORS

William J. Sewell, *Camden*
John Kean, *Ursino*

### REPRESENTATIVES

Henry C. Loudenslager, *Paulsboro*
John J. Gardner, *Atlantic City*
Benjamin F. Howell, *New Brunswick*
Joshua S. Salmon, *Boonton*
James F. Stewart, *Paterson*
Richard Wayne Parker, *Newark*
William D. Daly,[48] *Hoboken*
Allan L. McDermott,[49] *Jersey City*
Charles N. Fowler, *Elizabeth*

## NEW YORK

### SENATORS

Thomas C. Platt, *Owego*
Chauncey M. Depew, *Peekskill*

### REPRESENTATIVES

Townsend Scudder, *Oyster Bay*
John J. Fitzgerald, *Brooklyn*
Edmund H. Driggs, *Brooklyn*
Bertram T. Clayton, *Brooklyn*
Frank E. Wilson, *Brooklyn*
Mitchell May, *Brooklyn*
Nicholas Muller, *New Brighton*

---

[37] Died November 27, 1900.
[38] Appointed to fill vacancy caused by death of Cushman K. Davis, and took his seat December 10, 1900.
[39] Elected to fill vacancy caused by death of Cushman K. Davis, and took his seat January 28, 1901.
[40] Died June 15, 1899, before Congress assembled.
[41] Elected to fill vacancy caused by death of Richard P. Bland, and took his seat December 4, 1899.
[42] Protests and a memorial of certain citizens of Montana against the validity of the election were presented and referred December 4, 1899; while reso-

lution declaring his election void was pending, tendered his resignation effective May 15, 1900; appointed by the lieutenant governor, as acting governor, to fill the vacancy caused by his own resignation, but did not qualify. Martin Maginnis also presented credentials of appointment, signed by the governor, but was not permitted to qualify. Seat remained vacant throughout the remainder of the Congress. (See U.S. Senate Election, Expulsion and Censure Cases, 1793-1990, Senate Document 103-33, pp. 263-65.)
[43] Elected March 8, 1899, to fill vacancy caused by failure of legislature to act in the term beginning March 4, 1899, but died December 5, 1899, before

qualifying.
[44] Appointed to fill vacancy caused by death of Monroe L. Hayward, and took his seat December 19, 1899.
[45] Died March 11, 1899, before Congress assembled.
[46] Elected to fill vacancy caused by death of William L. Greene, and took his seat December 4, 1899.
[47] Died January 9, 1901.
[48] Died July 31, 1900.
[49] Elected to fill vacancy caused by death of William D. Daly, and took his seat December 3, 1900.

## NEW YORK— Continued

### REPRESENTATIVES—CONTINUED

Daniel J. Riordan, *New York City*
Thomas J. Bradley, *New York City*
Amos J. Cummings, *New York City*
William Sulzer, *New York City*
George B. McClellan, *New York City*
Jefferson M. Levy, *New York City*
William A. Chanler, *New York City*
Jacob Ruppert, Jr., *New York City*
John Q. Underhill, *New Rochelle*
Arthur S. Tompkins, *Nyack*
John H. Ketcham, *Dover Plains*
Aaron V. S. Cochrane, *Hudson*
Martin H. Glynn, *Albany*
John K. Stewart, *Amsterdam*
Lucius N. Littauer, *Gloversville*
Louis W. Emerson, *Warrensburg*
Charles A. Chickering,[50] *Copenhagen*
Albert D. Shaw,[51] *Watertown*
James S. Sherman, *Utica*
George W. Ray, *Norwich*
Michael E. Driscoll, *Syracuse*
Sereno E. Payne, *Auburn*
Charles W. Gillet, *Addison*
James W. Wadsworth, *Geneseo*
James M. E. O'Grady, *Rochester*
William H. Ryan, *Buffalo*
De Alva S. Alexander, *Buffalo*
Edward B. Vreeland,[52] *Salamanca*

## NORTH CAROLINA

### SENATORS

Marion Butler, *Elliot*
Jeter C. Pritchard, *Marshall*

### REPRESENTATIVES

John H. Small, *Washington*
George H. White, *Tarboro*
Charles R. Thomas, *New Bern*
John W. Atwater, *Rialto*
William W. Kitchin, *Roxboro*
John D. Bellamy, *Wilmington*
Theodore F. Kluttz, *Salisbury*
Romulus Z. Linney, *Taylorsville*
William T. Crawford,[53] *Waynesville*
Richmond Pearson,[54] *Asheville*

## NORTH DAKOTA

### SENATORS

Henry C. Hansbrough, *Devils Lake*
Porter J. McCumber, *Wahpeton*

### REPRESENTATIVE AT LARGE

Burleigh F. Spalding, *Fargo*

## OHIO

### SENATORS

Joseph B. Foraker, *Cincinnati*
Marcus A. Hanna, *Cleveland*

### REPRESENTATIVES

William B. Shattuc, *Madisonville*
Jacob H. Bromwell, *Cincinnati*
John L. Brenner, *Dayton*
Robert B. Gordon, *St. Marys*
David Meekison, *Napoleon*
Seth W. Brown, *Lebanon*
Walter L. Weaver, *Springfield*
Archibald Lybrand, *Delaware*
James H. Southard, *Toledo*
Stephen Morgan, *Oak Hill*
Charles H. Grosvenor, *Athens*
John J. Lentz, *Columbus*
James A. Norton, *Tiffin*
Winfield S. Kerr, *Mansfield*
Henry C. Van Voorhis, *Zanesville*
Lorenzo Danford,[55] *St. Clairsville*
Joseph J. Gill,[56] *Steubenville*
John A. McDowell, *Millersburg*
Robert W. Tayler, *Lisbon*
Charles W. F. Dick, *Akron*
Fremont O. Phillips, *Medina*
Theodore E. Burton, *Cleveland*

## OREGON

### SENATORS

George W. McBride, *St. Helens*
Joseph Simon, *Portland*

### REPRESENTATIVES

Thomas H. Tongue, *Hillsboro*
Malcolm A. Moody, *The Dalles*

## PENNSYLVANIA

### SENATORS

Boies Penrose, *Philadelphia*
Matthew S. Quay,[57] *Beaver*

### REPRESENTATIVES AT LARGE

Galusha A. Grow, *Glenwood*
Samuel A. Davenport, *Erie*

### REPRESENTATIVES

Henry H. Bingham, *Philadelphia*
Robert Adams, Jr., *Philadelphia*
William McAleer, *Philadelphia*
James R. Young, *Philadelphia*
Alfred C. Harmer,[58] *Philadelphia*
Edward de V. Morrell,[59] *Torresdale*
Thomas S. Butler, *West Chester*
Irving P. Wanger, *Norristown*
Laird H. Barber, *Mauch Chunk*

Daniel Ermentrout,[60] *Reading*
Henry D. Green,[61] *Reading*
Marriott Brosius, *Lancaster*
William Connell, *Scranton*
Stanley W. Davenport, *Plymouth*
James W. Ryan, *Pottsville*
Marlin E. Olmsted, *Harrisburg*
Charles F. Wright, *Susquehanna*
Horace B. Packer, *Wellsboro*
Rufus K. Polk, *Danville*
Thaddeus M. Mahon, *Chambersburg*
Edward D. Ziegler, *York*
Joseph E. Thropp, *Everett*
Summers M. Jack, *Indiana*
John Dalzell, *Pittsburgh*
William H. Graham, *Allegheny*
Ernest F. Acheson, *Washington*
Joseph B. Showalter, *Butler*
Athelston Gaston, *Meadville*
Joseph C. Sibley, *Franklin*
James K. P. Hall, *Ridgway*

## RHODE ISLAND

### SENATORS

Nelson W. Aldrich, *Providence*
George P. Wetmore, *Newport*

### REPRESENTATIVES

Melville Bull, *Middletown*
Adin B. Capron, *Stillwater*

## SOUTH CAROLINA

### SENATORS

Benjamin R. Tillman, *Trenton*
John L. McLaurin, *Bennettsville*

### REPRESENTATIVES

William Elliott, *Beaufort*
W. Jasper Talbert, *Parksville*
Asbury C. Latimer, *Belton*
Stanyarne Wilson, *Spartanburg*
David E. Finley, *Yorkville*
James Norton, *Mullins*
J. William Stokes, *Orangeburg*

## SOUTH DAKOTA

### SENATORS

Richard F. Pettigrew, *Sioux Falls*
James H. Kyle, *Aberdeen*

### REPRESENTATIVES AT LARGE

Robert J. Gamble, *Yorkton*
Charles H. Burke, *Pierre*

---

[50] Died February 13, 1900.
[51] Elected to fill vacancy caused by death of Charles A. Chickering, and took his seat December 3, 1900; died February 10, 1901, before the commencement of the Fifty-seventh Congress, to which he had been reelected.
[52] Elected to fill vacancy caused by resignation of Representative-elect Warren B. Hooker, in preceding Congress, and took his seat December 4, 1899.
[53] Served until May 10, 1900; succeeded by Richmond Pearson, who contested his election.

[54] Successfully contested the election of William T. Crawford, and took his seat May 10, 1900.
[55] Died June 19, 1899, before Congress assembled.
[56] Elected to fill vacancy caused by death of Lorenzo Danford, and took his seat December 4, 1899.
[57] Appointed to fill vacancy in the term beginning March 4, 1899, the legislature having met and adjourned without electing; credentials presented December 25, 1899, but not permitted to qualify; on April 24, 1900, a resolution declaring him not entitled to a seat was agreed to; subsequently elected and took

his seat January 17, 1901; vacancy in this class from March 4, 1899, to January 15, 1901. (See U.S. Senate Election, Expulsion and Censure Cases, 1793-1990, Senate Document 103-33, pp. 261-62.)
[58] Died March 6, 1900.
[59] Elected to fill vacancy caused by the death of Alfred C. Harmer, and took his seat December 3, 1900.
[60] Died September 17, 1899, before Congress assembled.
[61] Elected to fill vacancy caused by death of Daniel Ermentrout, and took his seat December 4, 1899.

## TENNESSEE

### SENATORS

William B. Bate, *Nashville*
Thomas B. Turley, *Memphis*

### REPRESENTATIVES

Walter P. Brownlow, *Jonesboro*
Henry R. Gibson, *Knoxville*
John A. Moon, *Chattanooga*
Charles E. Snodgrass, *Crossville*
James D. Richardson, *Murfreesboro*
John W. Gaines, *Nashville*
Nicholas N. Cox, *Franklin*
Thetus W. Sims, *Linden*
Rice A. Pierce, *Union City*
Edward W. Carmack, *Memphis*

## TEXAS

### SENATORS

Horace Chilton, *Tyler*
Charles A. Culberson, *Dallas*

### REPRESENTATIVES

Thomas H. Ball, *Huntsville*
Samuel B. Cooper, *Beaumont*
Reese C. De Graffenreid, *Longview*
John L. Sheppard, *Texarkana*
Joseph W. Bailey, *Gainsville*
Robert E. Burke, *Dallas*
Robert L. Henry, *Waco*
Samuel W. T. Lanham, *Weatherford*
Albert S. Burleson, *Austin*
Robert B. Hawley, *Galveston*
Rudolph Kleberg, *Cuero*
James L. Slayden, *San Antonio*
John H. Stephens, *Vernon*

## UTAH

### SENATORS

Joseph L. Rawlins, *Salt Lake City*
Thomas Kearns,[62] *Salt Lake City*

### REPRESENTATIVE AT LARGE

William H. King,[63] *Salt Lake City*

## VERMONT

### SENATORS

Redfield Proctor, *Proctor*
Jonathan Ross, *St. Johnsbury*

William P. Dillingham,[64] *Waterbury*

### REPRESENTATIVES

H. Henry Powers, *Morrisville*
William W. Grout, *Barton*

## VIRGINIA

### SENATORS

John W. Daniel, *Lynchburg*
Thomas S. Martin, *Scottsville*

### REPRESENTATIVES

William A. Jones, *Warsaw*
William A. Young,[65] *Norfolk*
Richard A. Wise,[66] *Williamsburg*
John Lamb, *Richmond*
Sydney P. Epes,[67] *Blackstone*
Francis R. Lassiter,[68] *Petersburg*
Claude A. Swanson, *Chatham*
Peter J. Otey, *Lynchburg*
James Hay, *Madison*
John F. Rixey, *Brandy*
William F. Rhea, *Bristol*
Julian M. Quarles, *Staunton*

## WASHINGTON

### SENATORS

George Turner, *Spokane*
Addison G. Foster, *Tacoma*

### REPRESENTATIVES AT LARGE

Wesley L. Jones, *North Yakima*
Francis W. Cushman, *Tacoma*

## WEST VIRGINIA

### SENATORS

Stephen B. Elkins, *Elkins*
Nathan B. Scott,[69] *Wheeling*

### REPRESENTATIVES

Blackburn B. Dovener, *Wheeling*
Alston G. Dayton, *Philippi*
David E. Johnston, *Bluefield*
Romeo H. Freer, *Harrisville*

## WISCONSIN

### SENATORS

John C. Spooner, *Madison*
Joseph V. Quarles, *Milwaukee*

### REPRESENTATIVES

Henry Allen Cooper, *Racine*
Herman B. Dahle, *Mount Horeb*
Joseph W. Babcock, *Necedah*
Theobald Otjen, *Milwaukee*
Samuel S. Barney, *West Bend*
James H. Davidson, *Oshkosh*
John J. Esch, *La Crosse*
Edward S. Minor, *Sturgeon Bay*
Alexander Stewart, *Wausau*
John J. Jenkins, *Chippewa Falls*

## WYOMING

### SENATORS

Clarence D. Clark, *Evanston*
Francis E. Warren, *Cheyenne*

### REPRESENTATIVE AT LARGE

Frank W. Mondell, *Newcastle*

## TERRITORY OF ARIZONA

### DELEGATE

John F. Wilson, *Prescott*

## TERRITORY OF HAWAII[70]

### DELEGATE

Robert W. Wilcox,[71] *Honolulu*

## TERRITORY OF NEW MEXICO

### DELEGATE

Pedro Perea, *Bernalillo*

## TERRITORY OF OKLAHOMA

### DELEGATE

Dennis T. Flynn, *Guthrie*

---

[62] Elected to fill vacancy in the term beginning March 1, 1899, caused by failure of legislature to elect, and took his seat February 4, 1901; vacancy in this class from March 4, 1899, to January 22, 1901.

[63] Brigham H. Roberts presented credentials as a Member-elect December 5, 1899, but was not sworn owing to protests against his eligibility; the House, on January 5, 1900, adopted a resolution declaring he "ought not to have or hold a seat, and the seat to which he was elected is hereby declared vacant." Mr. King was elected to fill vacancy caused by action of the House, and took his seat April 25, 1900.

[64] Elected to fill vacancy caused by death of Justin S. Morrill, in preceding Congress, and took his seat December 3, 1900.

[65] Served until March 12, 1900; succeeded by Richard A. Wise, who contested his election.

[66] Successfully contested the election of William A. Young, and took his seat March 12, 1900; died December 21, 1900.

[67] Died March 3, 1900.

[68] Elected to fill vacancy caused by death of Sydney P. Epes, and took his seat April 28, 1900.

[69] In the preceding Congress memorials were filed remonstrating against the seating of Mr. Scott; December 5, 1899, appeared, qualified, and took his seat, without objection; subsequently other memorials were filed and a resolution was introduced declaring him not entitled to a seat; the Committee on Privileges and Elections was directed to investigate the election, and reported, March 20, 1900, with a resolution declaring Mr. Scott duly elected and entitled to retain the seat; this resolution was agreed to April 27, 1900, by a vote of 52 to 3. (See U.S. Senate Election, Expulsion and Censure Cases, 1793-1990, Senate Document 103-33, pp. 258-60.)

[70] Formed from the territory of the Republic of Hawaii, annexed to the United States by act of July 7, 1898, and granted a Delegate in Congress by act of April 30, 1900.

[71] Took his seat December 15, 1900, after the investigation of charges preferred against him as to eligibility.

# 57TH CONGRESS

## MARCH 4, 1901, TO MARCH 3, 1903

FIRST SESSION— *December 2, 1901, to July 1, 1902*
SECOND SESSION— *December 1, 1902, to March 3, 1903*
SPECIAL SESSION OF THE SENATE— *March 4, 1901, to March 9, 1901*

———

VICE PRESIDENT OF THE UNITED STATES— THEODORE ROOSEVELT,[1] of New York
PRESIDENT PRO TEMPORE OF THE SENATE— WILLIAM P. FRYE,[2] of Maine
SECRETARY OF THE SENATE— CHARLES G. BENNETT, of New York
SERGEANT AT ARMS OF THE SENATE— DANIEL M. RANSDELL, of Indiana

———

SPEAKER OF THE HOUSE OF REPRESENTATIVES— DAVID B. HENDERSON,[3] of Iowa
CLERK OF THE HOUSE— ALEXANDER MCDOWELL,[4] of Pennsylvania
SERGEANT AT ARMS OF THE HOUSE— HENRY CASSON, of Wisconsin
DOORKEEPER OF THE HOUSE— FRANK B. LYON, of New York
POSTMASTER OF THE HOUSE— J. C. MCELROY

Theodore Roosevelt
Vice President

David B. Henderson
Speaker

## ALABAMA

### SENATORS

John T. Morgan, *Selma*
Edmund W. Pettus, *Selma*

### REPRESENTATIVES

George W. Taylor, *Demopolis*
Ariosto A. Wiley, *Montgomery*
Henry D. Clayton, *Eufaula*
Sydney J. Bowie, *Anniston*
Charles W. Thompson, *Tuskegee*
John H. Bankhead, *Fayette*
John L. Burnett,[5] *Gadsden*
William Richardson, *Huntsville*
Oscar W. Underwood, *Birmingham*

## ARKANSAS

### SENATORS

James K. Jones, *Washington*
James H. Berry, *Bentonville*

### REPRESENTATIVES

Philip D. McCulloch, *Marianna*
John S. Little, *Greenwood*
Thomas C. McRae, *Prescott*
Charles C. Reid, *Morrillton*
Hugh A. Dinsmore, *Fayetteville*
Stephen Brundidge, Jr., *Searcy*

## CALIFORNIA

### SENATORS

George C. Perkins, *Oakland*
Thomas R. Bard, *Hueneme*

### REPRESENTATIVES

Frank L. Coombs, *Napa*
Samuel D. Woods, *Stockton*
Victor H. Metcalf, *Oakland*
Julius Kahn, *San Francisco*
Eugene F. Loud, *San Francisco*
James McLachlan, *Pasadena*
James C. Needham, *Modesto*

## COLORADO

### SENATORS

Henry M. Teller, *Central City*
Thomas M. Patterson, *Denver*

### REPRESENTATIVES

John F. Shafroth, *Denver*
John C. Bell, *Montrose*

## CONNECTICUT

### SENATORS

Orville H. Platt, *Meriden*
Joseph R. Hawley, *Hartford*

### REPRESENTATIVES

E. Stevens Henry, *Rockville*
Nehemiah D. Sperry, *New Haven*
Charles A. Russell,[6] *Killingly*
Frank B. Brandegee,[7] *New London*
Ebenezer J. Hill, *Norwalk*

## DELAWARE

### SENATORS

L. Heisler Ball,[8] *Faulkland*
J. Frank Allee,[9] *Dover*

## REPRESENTATIVE AT LARGE

L. Heisler Ball,[10] *Faulkland*

## FLORIDA

### SENATORS

Stephen R. Mallory, *Pensacola*
James P. Taliaferro, *Jacksonville*

### REPRESENTATIVES

Stephen M. Sparkman, *Tampa*
Robert W. Davis, *Palatka*

## GEORGIA

### SENATORS

Augustus O. Bacon, *Macon*
Alexander S. Clay, *Marietta*

### REPRESENTATIVES

Rufus E. Lester, *Savannah*
James M. Griggs, *Dawson*
Elijah B. Lewis, *Montezuma*
William C. Adamson, *Carrollton*
Leonidas F. Livingston, *Kings*
Charles L. Bartlett, *Macon*
John W. Maddox, *Rome*
William M. Howard, *Lexington*
Farish C. Tate, *Jasper*
William H. Fleming, *Augusta*
William G. Brantley, *Brunswick*

## IDAHO

### SENATORS

Henry Heitfeld, *Lewiston*
Fred T. Dubois, *Blackfoot*

———

[1] Became President upon the death of William McKinley September 14, 1901.
[2] Reelected March 7, 1901 (special session of the Senate).
[3] Elected December 2, 1901.
[4] Elected December 2, 1901.
[5] Election unsuccessfully contested by N. B. Spears.

———

[6] Died October 23, 1902.
[7] Elected to fill vacancy caused by death of Charles A. Russell, and took his seat December 1, 1902.
[8] Elected to fill vacancy in the term beginning March 4, 1899, caused by failure of legislature to elect, and took his seat March 3, 1903; vacancy in this class from March 4, 1899, to March 1, 1903.

———

[9] Elected to fill vacancy in the term beginning March 4, 1901, caused by failure of legislature to elect, and took his seat March 3, 1903; vacancy in this class from March 4, 1901, to March 1, 1903.
[10] Resigned March 3, 1903, having been elected Senator.

REPRESENTATIVE AT LARGE
Thomas L. Glenn, *Montpelier*

## ILLINOIS

SENATORS
Shelby M. Cullom, *Springfield*
William E. Mason, *Chicago*

REPRESENTATIVES
James R. Mann, *Chicago*
John J. Feely, *Chicago*
George P. Foster, *Chicago*
James McAndrews, *Chicago*
William F. Mahoney, *Chicago*
Henry S. Boutell, *Chicago*
George E. Foss, *Chicago*
Albert J. Hopkins, *Aurora*
Robert R. Hitt, *Mount Morris*
George W. Prince, *Galesburg*
Walter Reeves, *Streator*
Joseph G. Cannon, *Danville*
Vespasian Warner, *Clinton*
Joseph V. Graff, *Peoria*
J. Ross Mickey, *Macomb*
Thomas J. Selby, *Hardin*
Ben F. Caldwell, *Chatham*
Thomas M. Jett, *Hillsboro*
Joseph B. Crowley, *Robinson*
James R. Williams, *Carmi*
Frederick J. Kern, *Belleville*
George W. Smith, *Murphysboro*

## INDIANA

SENATORS
Charles W. Fairbanks, *Indianapolis*
Albert J. Beveridge, *Indianapolis*

REPRESENTATIVES
James A. Hemenway, *Boonville*
Robert W. Miers, *Bloomington*
William T. Zenor, *Corydon*
Francis M. Griffith, *Vevay*
Elias S. Holliday, *Brazil*
James E. Watson, *Rushville*
Jesse Overstreet, *Indianapolis*
George W. Cromer, *Muncie*
Charles B. Landis, *Delphi*
Edgar D. Crumpacker, *Valparaiso*
George W. Steele, *Marion*
James M. Robinson, *Fort Wayne*
Abraham L. Brick, *South Bend*

## IOWA

SENATORS
William B. Allison, *Dubuque*
Jonathan P. Dolliver,[11] *Fort Dodge*

REPRESENTATIVES
Thomas Hedge, *Burlington*
John N. W. Rumple,[12] *Marengo*

David B. Henderson, *Dubuque*
Gilbert N. Haugen, *Northwood*
Robert G. Cousins, *Tipton*
John F. Lacey, *Oskaloosa*
John A. T. Hull, *Des Moines*
William P. Hepburn, *Clarinda*
Walter I. Smith, *Council Bluffs*
James P. Conner, *Denison*
Lot Thomas, *Storm Lake*

## KANSAS

SENATORS
William A. Harris, *Linwood*
Joseph R. Burton, *Abilene*

REPRESENTATIVE AT LARGE
Charles F. Scott, *Iola*

REPRESENTATIVES
Charles Curtis, *Topeka*
Justin D. Bowersock, *Lawrence*
Alfred M. Jackson, *Winfield*
James M. Miller, *Council Grove*
William A. Calderhead, *Marysville*
William A. Reeder, *Logan*
Chester I. Long,[13] *Medicine Lodge*

## KENTUCKY

SENATORS
William J. Deboe, *Marion*
Joseph C. S. Blackburn, *Versailles*

REPRESENTATIVES
Charles K. Wheeler, *Paducah*
Henry D. Allen, *Morganfield*
John S. Rhea,[14] *Russellville*
J. McKenzie Moss,[15] *Bowling Green*
David H. Smith, *Hodgensville*
Harvey S. Irwin, *Louisville*
Daniel L. Gooch, *Covington*
South Trimble, *Frankfort*
George G. Gilbert, *Shelbyville*
James N. Kehoe, *Maysville*
James B. White, *Irvine*
Vincent Boreing, *London*

## LOUISIANA

SENATORS
Samuel D. McEnery, *New Orleans*
Murphy J. Foster, *Franklin*

REPRESENTATIVES
Adolph Meyer, *New Orleans*
Robert C. Davey, *New Orleans*
Robert F. Broussard, *New Iberia*
Phanor Breazeale, *Natchitoches*
Joseph E. Ransdell, *Lake Providence*
Samuel M. Robertson, *Baton Rouge*

## MAINE

SENATORS
Eugene Hale, *Ellsworth*
William P. Frye, *Lewiston*

REPRESENTATIVES
Amos L. Allen, *Alfred*
Charles E. Littlefield, *Rockland*
Edwin C. Burleigh, *Augusta*
Llewellyn Powers,[16] *Houlton*

## MARYLAND

SENATORS
George L. Wellington, *Cumberland*
Louis E. McComas, *Williamsport*

REPRESENTATIVES
William H. Jackson, *Salisbury*
Albert A. Blakeney, *Franklinville*
Frank C. Wachter, *Baltimore*
Charles R. Schirm, *Baltimore*
Sydney E. Mudd, *La Plata*
George A. Pearre, *Cumberland*

## MASSACHUSETTS

SENATORS
George F. Hoar, *Worcester*
Henry Cabot Lodge, *Nahant*

REPRESENTATIVES
George P. Lawrence, *North Adams*
Frederick H. Gillett, *Springfield*
John R. Thayer, *Worcester*
Charles Q. Tirrell, *Natick*
William S. Knox, *Lawrence*
William H. Moody,[17] *Haverhill*
Augustus P. Gardner,[18] *Hamilton*
Ernest W. Roberts, *Chelsea*
Samuel W. McCall, *Winchester*
Joseph A. Conry, *Boston*
Henry F. Naphen, *Boston*
Samuel L. Powers, *Newton*
William C. Lovering, *Taunton*
William S. Greene, *Fall River*

## MICHIGAN

SENATORS
James McMillan,[19] *Detroit*
Russell A. Alger,[20] *Detroit*
Julius C. Burrows, *Kalamazoo*

REPRESENTATIVES
John B. Corliss, *Detroit*
Henry C. Smith, *Adrian*
Washington Gardner, *Albion*
Edward L. Hamilton, *Niles*

---

[11] Appointed to fill vacancy in the term beginning March 4, 1901, caused by death of Senator-elect John H. Gear, in preceding Congress, and took his seat March 4, 1901; subsequently elected.

[12] Died January 31, 1903.

[13] Resigned, effective March 4, 1903, before the commencement of the Fifty-eighth Congress, to which he had been reelected, having been elected Senator.

[14] Served until March 25, 1902; succeeded by J.

McKenzie Moss, who contested his election.

[15] Successfully contested the election of John S. Rhea, and took his seat March 25, 1902.

[16] Elected to fill vacancy caused by resignation of Representative-elect Charles A. Boutelle, in preceding Congress, and took his seat December 2, 1901.

[17] Resigned May 1, 1902, to become Secretary of the Navy.

[18] Elected to fill vacancy caused by resignation of William H. Moody, and took his seat December 1, 1902.

[19] Died August 10, 1902.

[20] Appointed to fill vacancy caused by death of James McMillan, and took his seat December 2, 1902; subsequently elected.

## MICHIGAN—Continued

REPRESENTATIVES—CONTINUED

William Alden Smith, *Grand Rapids*
Samuel W. Smith, *Pontiac*
Edgar Weeks, *Mount Clemens*
Joseph W. Fordney, *Saginaw*
Roswell P. Bishop, *Ludington*
Rosseau O. Crump,[21] *West Bay City*
Henry H. Aplin,[22] *West Bay City*
Archibald B. Darragh, *St. Louis*
Carlos D. Shelden, *Houghton*

## MINNESOTA

SENATORS

Knute Nelson, *Alexandria*
Moses E. Clapp, *St. Paul*

REPRESENTATIVES

James A. Tawney, *Winona*
James T. McCleary, *Mankato*
Joel P. Heatwole, *Northfield*
Frederick C. Stevens, *St. Paul*
Loren Fletcher, *Minneapolis*
R. Page W. Morris, *Duluth*
Frank M. Eddy, *Glenwood*

## MISSISSIPPI

SENATORS

Hernando D. Money, *Carrollton*
Anselm J. McLaurin, *Brandon*

REPRESENTATIVES

Ezekiel S. Candler, Jr., *Corinth*
Thomas Spight, *Ripley*
Patrick Henry, *Vicksburg*
Andrew F. Fox, *West Point*
John Sharp Williams, *Yazoo City*
Frank A. McLain, *Gloster*
Charles E. Hooker, *Jackson*

## MISSOURI

SENATORS

Francis M. Cockrell, *Warrensburg*
George G. Vest, *Sweet Springs*

REPRESENTATIVES

James T. Lloyd, *Shelbyville*
William W. Rucker, *Keytesville*
John Dougherty, *Liberty*
Charles F. Cochran, *St. Joseph*
William S. Cowherd, *Kansas City*
David A. De Armond, *Butler*
James Cooney, *Marshall*
Dorsey W. Shackleford, *Jefferson City*

James Beauchamp Clark, *Bowling Green*
Richard Bartholdt, *St. Louis*
Charles F. Joy, *St. Louis*
James J. Butler,[23] *St. Louis*
George C. R. Wagoner,[24] *St. Louis*
Edward Robb, *Perryville*
Willard D. Vandiver, *Cape Girardeau*
Maecenas E. Benton, *Neosho*

## MONTANA

SENATORS

William A. Clark, *Butte*
Paris Gibson,[25] *Great Falls*

REPRESENTATIVE AT LARGE

Caldwell Edwards, *Bozeman*

## NEBRASKA

SENATORS

William V. Allen, *Madison*
Charles H. Dietrich,[26] *Hastings*
Joseph H. Millard, *Omaha*

REPRESENTATIVES

Elmer J. Burkett, *Lincoln*
David H. Mercer, *Omaha*
John S. Robinson, *Madison*
William L. Stark, *Aurora*
Ashton C. Shallenberger, *Alma*
William Neville, *North Platte*

## NEVADA

SENATORS

John P. Jones, *Gold Hill*
William M. Stewart, *Carson City*

REPRESENTATIVE AT LARGE

Francis G. Newlands, *Reno*

## NEW HAMPSHIRE

SENATORS

Jacob H. Gallinger, *Concord*
Henry E. Burnham, *Manchester*

REPRESENTATIVES

Cyrus A. Sulloway, *Manchester*
Frank D. Currier, *Canaan*

## NEW JERSEY

SENATORS

William J. Sewell,[27] *Camden*
John F. Dryden,[28] *Newark*
John Kean, *Ursino*

REPRESENTATIVES

Henry C. Loudenslager, *Paulsboro*
John J. Gardner, *Atlantic City*
Benjamin F. Howell, *New Brunswick*
Joshua S. Salmon,[29] *Boonton*
De Witt C. Flanagan,[30] *Morristown*
James F. Stewart, *Paterson*
Richard Wayne Parker, *Newark*
Allan L. McDermott, *Jersey City*
Charles N. Fowler, *Elizabeth*

## NEW YORK

SENATORS

Thomas C. Platt, *Owego*
Chauncey M. Depew, *Peekskill*

REPRESENTATIVES

Frederic Storm, *Bayside*
John J. Fitzgerald, *Brooklyn*
Henry Bristow, *Brooklyn*
Harry A. Hanbury, *Brooklyn*
Frank E. Wilson, *Brooklyn*
George H. Lindsay, *Brooklyn*
Nicholas Muller,[31] *New York City*
Montague Lessler,[32] *New York City*
Thomas J. Creamer, *New York City*
Henry M. Goldfogle, *New York City*
Amos J. Cummings,[33] *New York City*
Edward Swann,[34] *New York City*
William Sulzer, *New York City*
George B. McClellan, *New York City*
Oliver H. P. Belmont, *New York City*
William H. Douglas, *New York City*
Jacob Ruppert, Jr., *New York City*
Cornelius A. Pugsley, *Peekskill*
Arthur S. Tompkins, *Nyack*
John H. Ketcham, *Dover Plains*
William H. Draper, *Troy*
George N. Southwick, *Albany*
John K. Stewart, *Amsterdam*
Lucius N. Littauer, *Gloversville*
Louis W. Emerson, *Warrensburg*
Charles L. Knapp,[35] *Lowville*
James S. Sherman, *Utica*
George W. Ray,[36] *Norwich*
John W. Dwight,[37] *Dryden*
Michael E. Driscoll, *Syracuse*
Sereno E. Payne, *Auburn*
Charles W. Gillet, *Addison*
James W. Wadsworth, *Geneseo*
James B. Perkins, *Rochester*
William H. Ryan, *Buffalo*
De Alva S. Alexander, *Buffalo*
Edward B. Vreeland, *Salamanca*

---

[21] Died May 1, 1901, before Congress assembled.
[22] Elected to fill vacancy caused by death of Rosseau O. Crump, and took his seat December 2, 1901.
[23] Election contested by William M. Horton; on June 28, 1902, resolution adopted declaring no valid election and seat vacant; credentials presented of a subsequent election, and took his seat December 1, 1902; served until February 26, 1903; succeeded by George C. R. Wagoner, who contested this election.
[24] Successfully contested the election of James J. Butler, and took his seat February 26, 1903.
[25] Elected to fill vacancy caused by resignation of William A. Clark, in preceding Congress, and took his

seat December 2, 1901; vacancy in this class from May 16, 1900, to March 6, 1901.
[26] Elected to fill vacancy caused by death of Monroe L. Hayward, in preceding Congress, and took his seat December 2, 1901.
[27] Died December 27, 1901.
[28] Elected to fill vacancy caused by death of William J. Sewell, and took his seat February 4, 1902.
[29] Died May 6, 1902.
[30] Elected to fill vacancy caused by death of Joshua S. Salmon, and took his seat January 5, 1903.
[31] Resigned November 22, 1901, before Congress assembled.

[32] Elected January 7, 1902, to fill vacancy caused by resignation of Nicholas Muller, and took his seat January 15, 1902.
[33] Died May 2, 1902.
[34] Elected to fill vacancy caused by death of Amos J. Cummings, and took his seat December 2, 1902.
[35] Elected to fill vacancy caused by death of Representative-elect Albert D. Shaw, in preceding Congress, and took his seat December 2, 1901.
[36] Resigned September 11, 1902.
[37] Elected to fill vacancy caused by resignation of George W. Ray, and took his seat December 1, 1902.

## NORTH CAROLINA

### SENATORS

Jeter C. Pritchard, *Marshall*
Furnifold McL. Simmons, *Raleigh*

### REPRESENTATIVES

John H. Small, *Washington*
Claude Kitchin, *Scotland Neck*
Charles R. Thomas,[38] *New Bern*
Edward W. Pou, *Smithfield*
William W. Kitchin, *Roxboro*
John D. Bellamy, *Wilmington*
Theodore F. Kluttz, *Salisbury*
Edmond Spencer Blackburn,
   *Wilkesboro*
James M. Moody,[39] *Waynesville*

## NORTH DAKOTA

### SENATORS

Henry C. Hansbrough, *Devils Lake*
Porter J. McCumber, *Wahpeton*

### REPRESENTATIVE AT LARGE

Thomas F. Marshall, *Oakes*

## OHIO

### SENATORS

Joseph B. Foraker, *Cincinnati*
Marcus A. Hanna, *Cleveland*

### REPRESENTATIVES

William B. Shattuc, *Madisonville*
Jacob H. Bromwell, *Cincinnati*
Robert M. Nevin, *Dayton*
Robert B. Gordon, *St. Marys*
John S. Snook, *Paulding*
Charles Q. Hildebrant, *Wilmington*
Thomas B. Kyle, *Troy*
William R. Warnock, *Urbana*
James H. Southard, *Toledo*
Stephen Morgan, *Oak Hill*
Charles H. Grosvenor, *Athens*
Emmett Tompkins,[40] *Columbus*
James A. Norton, *Tiffin*
William W. Skiles, *Shelby*
Henry C. Van Voorhis, *Zanesville*
Joseph J. Gill, *Steubenville*
John W. Cassingham, *Coshocton*
Robert W. Tayler, *Lisbon*
Charles W. F. Dick, *Akron*
Jacob A. Beidler, *Willoughby*
Theodore E. Burton, *Cleveland*

## OREGON

### SENATORS

Joseph Simon, *Portland*
John H. Mitchell, *Portland*

### REPRESENTATIVES

Thomas H. Tongue,[41] *Hillsboro*
Malcolm A. Moody, *The Dalles*

## PENNSYLVANIA

### SENATORS

Boies Penrose, *Philadelphia*
Matthew S. Quay, *Beaver*

### REPRESENTATIVES AT LARGE

Galusha A. Grow, *Glenwood*
Robert H. Foerderer, *Philadelphia*

### REPRESENTATIVES

Henry H. Bingham, *Philadelphia*
Robert Adams, Jr., *Philadelphia*
Henry Burk, *Philadelphia*
James R. Young, *Philadelphia*
Edward de V. Morrell, *Torresdale*
Thomas S. Butler, *West Chester*
Irving P. Wanger, *Norristown*
Howard Mutchler, *Easton*
Henry D. Green, *Reading*
Marriott Brosius,[42] *Lancaster*
Henry B. Cassel,[43] *Marietta*
William Connell, *Scranton*
Henry W. Palmer, *Wilkes-Barre*
George R. Patterson, *Ashland*
Marlin E. Olmsted, *Harrisburg*
Charles F. Wright, *Susquehanna*
Elias Deemer, *Williamsport*
Rufus K. Polk,[44] *Danville*
Alexander Billmeyer,[45]
   *Washingtonville*
Thaddeus M. Mahon, *Chambersburg*
Robert J. Lewis, *York*
Alvin Evans, *Ebensburg*
Summers M. Jack, *Indiana*
John Dalzell, *Pittsburgh*
William H. Graham, *Allegheny*
Ernest F. Acheson, *Washington*
Joseph B. Showalter, *Butler*
Arthur L. Bates, *Meadville*
Joseph C. Sibley, *Franklin*
James K. P. Hall,[46] *Ridgway*

## RHODE ISLAND

### SENATORS

Nelson W. Aldrich, *Providence*
George P. Wetmore, *Newport*

### REPRESENTATIVES

Melville Bull, *Middletown*
Adin B. Capron, *Stillwater*

## SOUTH CAROLINA

### SENATORS

Benjamin R. Tillman, *Trenton*
John L. McLaurin, *Bennettsville*

### REPRESENTATIVES

William Elliott, *Beaufort*
William J. Talbert, *Parksville*
Asbury C. Latimer, *Belton*
Joseph T. Johnson, *Spartanburg*
David E. Finley, *Yorkville*
Robert B. Scarborough, *Conway*
J. William Stokes,[47] *Orangeburg*
Asbury F. Lever,[48] *Lexington*

## SOUTH DAKOTA

### SENATORS

James H. Kyle,[49] *Aberdeen*
Alfred B. Kittredge,[50] *Sioux Falls*
Robert J. Gamble, *Yankton*

### REPRESENTATIVES AT LARGE

Charles H. Burke, *Pierre*
Eben W. Martin, *Deadwood*

## TENNESSEE

### SENATORS

William B. Bate, *Nashville*
Edward W. Carmack, *Memphis*

### REPRESENTATIVES

Walter P. Brownlow, *Jonesboro*
Henry R. Gibson, *Knoxville*
John A. Moon, *Chattanooga*
Charles E. Snodgrass, *Crossville*
James D. Richardson, *Murfreesboro*
John W. Gaines, *Nashville*
Lemuel P. Padgett, *Columbia*
Thetus W. Sims, *Linden*
Rice A. Pierce, *Union City*
Malcolm R. Patterson, *Memphis*

## TEXAS

### SENATORS

Charles A. Culberson, *Dallas*
Joseph W. Bailey, *Gainsville*

### REPRESENTATIVES

Thomas H. Ball, *Huntsville*
Samuel B. Cooper, *Beaumont*
Reese C. De Graffenreid,[51] *Longview*
Gordon J. Russell,[52] *Tyler*
John L. Sheppard,[53] *Texarkana*

---

[38] Election unsuccessfully contested by John E. Fowler.

[39] Died February 5, 1903.

[40] Election unsuccessfully contested by John J. Lentz.

[41] Died January 11, 1903, before the commencement of the Fifty-eighth Congress, to which he had been reelected.

[42] Died March 16, 1901, before Congress assembled.

---

[43] Elected to fill vacancy caused by death of Marriott Brosius, and took his seat December 2, 1901.

[44] Died March 5, 1902.

[45] Elected to fill vacancy caused by death of Rufus K. Polk, and took his seat December 1, 1902.

[46] Resigned November 29, 1902.

[47] Died July 6, 1901, before Congress assembled.

[48] Elected to fill vacancy caused by death of J. William Stokes, and took his seat December 2, 1901.

---

[49] Died July 1, 1901.

[50] Appointed to fill vacancy caused by death of James H. Kyle, and took his seat December 2, 1901; subsequently elected.

[51] Died August 29, 1902.

[52] Elected to fill vacancy caused by death of Reese C. De Graffenreid, and took his seat December 2, 1902.

[53] Died October 11, 1902.

## TEXAS—Continued

REPRESENTATIVES—CONTINUED

Morris Sheppard,[54] *Texarkana*
Choice B. Randell, *Sherman*
Robert E. Burke,[55] *Dallas*
Dudley G. Wooten,[56] *Dallas*
Robert L. Henry, *Waco*
Samuel W. T. Lanham,[57] *Weatherford*
Albert S. Burleson, *Austin*
George F. Burgess, *Gonzales*
Rudolph Kleberg, *Cuero*
James L. Slayden, *San Antonio*
John H. Stephens, *Vernon*

## UTAH

SENATORS

Joseph L. Rawlins, *Salt Lake City*
Thomas Kearns, *Salt Lake City*

REPRESENTATIVE AT LARGE

George Sutherland, *Salt Lake City*

## VERMONT

SENATORS

Redfield Proctor, *Proctor*
William P. Dillingham, *Montpelier*

REPRESENTATIVES

David J. Foster, *Burlington*
Kittredge Haskins, *Brattleboro*

## VIRGINIA

SENATORS

John W. Daniel, *Lynchburg*
Thomas S. Martin, *Scottsville*

REPRESENTATIVES

William A. Jones, *Warsaw*
Harry L. Maynard, *Portsmouth*

John Lamb, *Richmond*
Francis R. Lassiter, *Petersburg*
Claude A. Swanson, *Chatham*
Peter J. Otey,[58] *Lynchburg*
Carter Glass,[59] *Lynchburg*
James Hay, *Madison*
John F. Rixey, *Brandy*
William F. Rhea,[60] *Bristol*
Henry D. Flood, *Appomattox*

## WASHINGTON

SENATORS

George Turner, *Spokane*
Addison G. Foster, *Tacoma*

REPRESENTATIVES AT LARGE

Wesley L. Jones, *North Yakima*
Francis W. Cushman, *Tacoma*

## WEST VIRGINIA

SENATORS

Stephen B. Elkins, *Elkins*
Nathan B. Scott, *Wheeling*

REPRESENTATIVES

Blackburn B. Dovener, *Wheeling*
Alston G. Dayton, *Philippi*
Joseph Holt Gaines, *Charleston*
James A. Hughes, *Huntington*

## WISCONSIN

SENATORS

John C. Spooner, *Madison*
Joseph V. Quarles, *Milwaukee*

REPRESENTATIVES

Henry Allen Cooper, *Racine*
Herman B. Dahle, *Mount Horeb*
Joseph W. Babcock, *Necedah*

Theobald Otjen, *Milwaukee*
Samuel S. Barney, *West Bend*
James H. Davidson, *Oshkosh*
John J. Esch, *La Crosse*
Edward S. Minor, *Sturgeon Bay*
Webster E. Brown, *Rhinelander*
John J. Jenkins, *Chippewa Falls*

## WYOMING

SENATORS

Clarence D. Clark, *Evanston*
Francis E. Warren, *Cheyenne*

REPRESENTATIVE AT LARGE

Frank W. Mondell, *Newcastle*

## TERRITORY OF ARIZONA

DELEGATE

Marcus A. Smith, *Tucson*

## TERRITORY OF HAWAII

DELEGATE

Robert W. Wilcox, *Honolulu*

## TERRITORY OF NEW MEXICO

DELEGATE

Bernard S. Rodey, *Albuquerque*

## TERRITORY OF OKLAHOMA

DELEGATE

Dennis T. Flynn, *Guthrie*

## PORTO RICO[61]

RESIDENT COMMISSIONER

Federico Degetau,[62] *San Juan*

---

[54] Elected to fill vacancy caused by death of his father, John L. Sheppard, and took his seat December 1, 1902.
[55] Died June 5, 1901, before Congress assembled.
[56] Elected to fill vacancy caused by death of Robert E. Burke, and took his seat December 2, 1901.
[57] Resigned January 15, 1903, having been elected Governor.

[58] Died May 4, 1902.
[59] Elected to fill vacancy caused by death of Peter J. Otey, and took his seat December 1, 1902.
[60] Election unsuccessfully contested by James A. Walker.
[61] Part of the territory ceded to the United States by Spain by the treaty of Paris of December 10, 1898; granted a civil government and the right to elect a

Resident Commissioner to the United States by act of April 12, 1900.
[62] Elected for a term of two years beginning March 4, 1901; granted the privilege of the floor of the House of Representatives June 28, 1902.

# 58TH CONGRESS

## MARCH 4, 1903, to MARCH 3, 1905

FIRST SESSION— *November 9, 1903, to December 7, 1903*
SECOND SESSION— *December 7, 1903, to April 28, 1904*
THIRD SESSION— *December 5, 1904, to March 3, 1905*
SPECIAL SESSION OF THE SENATE— *March 5, 1903, to March 19, 1903*

William P. Frye
President Pro Tempore

Joseph G. Cannon
Speaker

VICE PRESIDENT OF THE UNITED STATES[1]
PRESIDENT PRO TEMPORE OF THE SENATE— WILLIAM P. FRYE, of Maine
SECRETARY OF THE SENATE— CHARLES G. BENNETT, of New York
SERGEANT AT ARMS OF THE SENATE— DANIEL M. RANSDELL, of Indiana

SPEAKER OF THE HOUSE OF REPRESENTATIVES— JOSEPH G. CANNON,[2] of Illinois
CLERK OF THE HOUSE— ALEXANDER McDOWELL,[3] of Pennsylvania
SERGEANT AT ARMS OF THE HOUSE— HENRY CASSON, of Wisconsin
DOORKEEPER OF THE HOUSE— FRANK B. LYON, of New York
POSTMASTER OF THE HOUSE— J. C. McELROY

## ALABAMA

### SENATORS
John T. Morgan, *Selma*
Edmund W. Pettus, *Selma*

### REPRESENTATIVES
George W. Taylor, *Demopolis*
Ariosto A. Wiley, *Montgomery*
Henry D. Clayton, *Eufaula*
Sydney J. Bowie, *Anniston*
Charles W. Thompson,[4] *Tuskegee*
J. Thomas Heflin,[5] *Lafayette*
John H. Bankhead, *Fayette*
John L. Burnett, *Gadsden*
William Richardson, *Huntsville*
Oscar W. Underwood, *Birmingham*

## ARKANSAS

### SENATORS
James H. Berry, *Bentonville*
James P. Clarke, *Little Rock*

### REPRESENTATIVES
Robert B. Macon, *Helena*
Stephen Brundidge, Jr., *Searcy*
Hugh A. Dinsmore, *Fayetteville*
John S. Little, *Greenwood*
Charles C. Reid, *Morrillton*
Joseph T. Robinson, *Lonoke*
Robert M. Wallace, *Magnolia*

## CALIFORNIA

### SENATORS
George C. Perkins, *Oakland*
Thomas R. Bard, *Hueneme*

### REPRESENTATIVES
James N. Gillett, *Eureka*
Theodore A. Bell, *Napa*
Victor H. Metcalf,[6] *Oakland*
Joseph R. Knowland,[7] *Alameda*
Edward J. Livernash,[8] *San Francisco*
William J. Wynn, *San Francisco*
James C. Needham, *Modesto*
James McLachlan, *Pasadena*
Milton J. Daniels, *Riverside*

## COLORADO

### SENATORS
Henry M. Teller, *Central City*
Thomas M. Patterson, *Denver*

### REPRESENTATIVE AT LARGE
Franklin E. Brooks, *Colorado Springs*

### REPRESENTATIVES
John F. Shafroth,[9] *Denver*
Robert W. Bonynge,[10] *Denver*
Herschel M. Hogg, *Telluride*

## CONNECTICUT

### SENATORS
Orville H. Platt, *Meriden*
Joseph R. Hawley, *Hartford*

### REPRESENTATIVE AT LARGE
George L. Lilley, *Waterbury*

### REPRESENTATIVES
E. Stevens Henry, *Rockville*
Nehemiah D. Sperry, *New Haven*
Frank B. Brandegee, *New London*
Ebenezer J. Hill, *Norwalk*

## DELAWARE

### SENATORS
L. Heisler Ball, *Faulkland*
J. Frank Allee, *Dover*

### REPRESENTATIVE AT LARGE
Henry A. Houston, *Millsboro*

## FLORIDA

### SENATORS
Stephen R. Mallory,[11] *Pensacola*
James P. Taliaferro, *Jacksonville*

### REPRESENTATIVES
Stephen M. Sparkman, *Tampa*
Robert W. Davis, *Palatka*
William B. Lamar, *Monticello*

## GEORGIA

### SENATORS
Augustus O. Bacon, *Macon*
Alexander S. Clay, *Marietta*

---

[1] Vice President Theodore Roosevelt became President on the death of William McKinley in preceding Congress.
[2] Elected November 9, 1903.
[3] Reelected November 9, 1903.
[4] Died March 20, 1904.
[5] Elected to fill vacancy caused by death of Charles W. Thompson, and took his seat December 5, 1904.

[6] Resigned July 1, 1904, having been appointed Secretary of Commerce and Labor.
[7] Elected to fill vacancy caused by resignation of Victor H. Metcalf, and took his seat December 5, 1904.
[8] Election unsuccessfully contested by Julius Kahn.
[9] Election contested by Robert W. Bonynge; served until February 15, 1904, when he declared the conviction that contestant was duly elected and entitled

to seat held by him; contestant then seated by unanimous vote.
[10] Successfully contested the election of John F. Shafroth, and took his seat February 16, 1904.
[11] Reappointed to fill vacancy in the term beginning March 4, 1903, to serve until the next meeting of the legislature; subsequently reelected.

## GEORGIA—Continued

### REPRESENTATIVES

Rufus E. Lester, *Savannah*
James M. Griggs, *Dawson*
Elijah B. Lewis, *Montezuma*
William C. Adamson, *Carrollton*
Leonidas F. Livingston, *Covington*
Charles L. Bartlett, *Macon*
John W. Maddox, *Rome*
William M. Howard, *Lexington*
Farish C. Tate, *Jasper*
Thomas W. Hardwick, *Sandersville*
William G. Brantley, *Brunswick*

## IDAHO

### SENATORS

Fred T. Dubois, *Blackfoot*
Weldon B. Heyburn, *Wallace*

### REPRESENTATIVE AT LARGE

Burton L. French, *Moscow*

## ILLINOIS

### SENATORS

Shelby M. Cullom, *Springfield*
Albert J. Hopkins, *Aurora*

### REPRESENTATIVES

Martin Emerich, *Chicago*
James R. Mann, *Chicago*
William W. Wilson, *Chicago*
George P. Foster, *Chicago*
James McAndrews, *Chicago*
William Lorimer,[12] *Chicago*
Philip Knopf, *Chicago*
William F. Mahoney,[13] *Chicago*
Henry S. Boutell, *Chicago*
George E. Foss, *Chicago*
Howard M. Snapp, *Joliet*
Charles E. Fuller, *Belvidere*
Robert R. Hitt, *Mount Morris*
Benjamin F. Marsh, *Warsaw*
George W. Prince, *Galesburg*
Joseph V. Graff, *Peoria*
John A. Sterling, *Bloomington*
Joseph G. Cannon, *Danville*
Vespasian Warner, *Clinton*
Henry T. Rainey, *Carrollton*
Ben F. Caldwell, *Chatham*
William A. Rodenberg, *East St. Louis*
Joseph B. Crowley, *Robinson*
James R. Williams, *Carmi*
George W. Smith, *Murphysboro*

## INDIANA

### SENATORS

Charles W. Fairbanks,[14] *Indianapolis*
Albert J. Beveridge, *Indianapolis*

### REPRESENTATIVES

James A. Hemenway,[15] *Boonville*
Robert W. Miers, *Bloomington*
William T. Zenor, *Corydon*
Francis M. Griffith, *Vevay*
Elias S. Holliday, *Brazil*
James E. Watson, *Rushville*
Jesse Overstreet, *Indianapolis*
George W. Cromer, *Muncie*
Charles B. Landis, *Delphi*
Edgar D. Crumpacker, *Valparaiso*
Frederick Landis, *Logansport*
James M. Robinson, *Fort Wayne*
Abraham L. Brick, *South Bend*

## IOWA

### SENATORS

William B. Allison, *Dubuque*
Jonathan P. Dolliver, *Fort Dodge*

### REPRESENTATIVES

Thomas Hedge, *Burlington*
Martin J. Wade, *Iowa City*
Benjamin P. Birdsall, *Clarion*
Gilbert N. Haugen, *Northwood*
Robert G. Cousins, *Tipton*
John F. Lacey, *Oskaloosa*
John A. T. Hull, *Des Moines*
William P. Hepburn, *Clarinda*
Walter I. Smith, *Council Bluffs*
James P. Conner, *Denison*
Lot Thomas, *Storm Lake*

## KANSAS

### SENATORS

Joseph R. Burton, *Abilene*
Chester I. Long, *Medicine Lodge*

### REPRESENTATIVE AT LARGE

Charles F. Scott, *Iola*

### REPRESENTATIVES

Charles Curtis, *Topeka*
Justin D. Bowersock, *Lawrence*
Philip P. Campbell, *Pittsburg*
James M. Miller, *Council Grove*
William A. Calderhead, *Marysville*
William A. Reeder, *Logan*
Victor Murdock,[16] *Wichita*

## KENTUCKY

### SENATORS

Joseph C. S. Blackburn, *Versailles*
James B. McCreary, *Richmond*

### REPRESENTATIVES

Ollie M. James, *Marion*
Augustus O. Stanley, *Henderson*
John S. Rhea, *Russellville*
David H. Smith, *Hodgensville*
J. Swagar Sherley, *Louisville*

D. Linn Gooch, *Covington*
South Trimble, *Frankfort*
George G. Gilbert, *Shelbyville*
James N. Kehoe, *Maysville*
Frank A. Hopkins, *Prestonsburg*
Vincent Boreing,[17] *London*
W. Godfrey Hunter,[18] *Burkesville*

## LOUISIANA

### SENATORS

Samuel D. McEnery, *New Orleans*
Murphy J. Foster, *Franklin*

### REPRESENTATIVES

Adolph Meyer, *New Orleans*
Robert C. Davey, *New Orleans*
Robert F. Broussard, *New Iberia*
Phanor Breazeale, *Natchitoches*
Joseph E. Ransdell, *Lake Providence*
Samuel M. Robertson, *Baton Rouge*
Arsène P. Pujo, *Lake Charles*

## MAINE

### SENATORS

Eugene Hale, *Ellsworth*
William P. Frye, *Lewiston*

### REPRESENTATIVES

Amos L. Allen, *Alfred*
Charles E. Littlefield, *Rockland*
Edwin C. Burleigh, *Augusta*
Llewellyn Powers, *Houlton*

## MARYLAND

### SENATORS

Louis E. McComas, *Williamsport*
Arthur Pue Gorman, *Laurel*

### REPRESENTATIVES

William H. Jackson, *Salisbury*
J. Fred. C. Talbott, *Towson*
Frank C. Wachter, *Baltimore*
James W. Denny, *Baltimore*
Sydney E. Mudd, *La Plata*
George A. Pearre, *Cumberland*

## MASSACHUSETTS

### SENATORS

George F. Hoar,[19] *Worcester*
Winthrop Murray Crane,[20] *Dalton*
Henry Cabot Lodge, *Nahant*

### REPRESENTATIVES

George P. Lawrence, *North Adams*
Frederick H. Gillett, *Springfield*
John R. Thayer, *Worcester*
Charles Q. Tirrell, *Natick*
Butler Ames, *Lowell*
Augustus P. Gardner, *Hamilton*
Ernest W. Roberts, *Chelsea*

---

[12] Election unsuccessfully contested by Allan C. Durborow.

[13] Died December 27, 1904.

[14] Resigned, effective March 3, 1905, having been elected Vice President of the United States.

[15] Resigned, effective March 3, 1905, before the commencement of the Fifty-ninth Congress, to which he had been reelected, having been elected Senator.

[16] Elected to fill vacancy caused by resignation of Representative-elect Chester I. Long, in preceding Congress, and took his seat November 9, 1903.

[17] Died September 16, 1903, before Congress assembled.

[18] Elected to fill vacancy caused by death of Vincent Boreing, and took his seat December 4, 1903.

[19] Died September 30, 1904.

[20] Appointed to fill vacancy caused by death of George F. Hoar, and took his seat December 6, 1904; subsequently elected.

Samuel W. McCall, *Winchester*
John A. Keliher,[21] *Boston*
William S. McNary, *Boston*
John A. Sullivan, *Boston*
Samuel L. Powers, *Newton*
William S. Greene, *Fall River*
William C. Lovering, *Taunton*

## MICHIGAN

SENATORS

Julius C. Burrows, *Kalamazoo*
Russell A. Alger, *Detroit*

REPRESENTATIVES

Alfred Lucking, *Detroit*
Charles E. Townsend, *Jackson*
Washington Gardner, *Albion*
Edward L. Hamilton, *Niles*
William Alden Smith, *Grand Rapids*
Samuel W. Smith, *Pontiac*
Henry McMorran, *Port Huron*
Joseph W. Fordney, *Saginaw*
Roswell P. Bishop, *Ludington*
George A. Loud, *Au Sable*
Archibald B. Darragh, *St. Louis*
H. Olin Young, *Ishpeming*

## MINNESOTA

SENATORS

Knute Nelson, *Alexandria*
Moses E. Clapp, *St. Paul*

REPRESENTATIVES

James A. Tawney, *Winona*
James T. McCleary, *Mankato*
Charles R. Davis, *St. Peter*
Frederick C. Stevens, *St. Paul*
John Lind, *Minneapolis*
Clarence B. Buckman, *Little Falls*
Andrew J. Volstead, *Granite Falls*
J. Adam Bede, *Pine City*
Halvor Steenerson, *Crookston*

## MISSISSIPPI

SENATORS

Hernando D. Money, *Carrollton*
Anselm J. McLaurin, *Brandon*

REPRESENTATIVES

Ezekiel S. Candler, Jr., *Corinth*
Thomas Spight, *Ripley*
Benjamin G. Humphreys, *Greenville*
Wilson S. Hill, *Winona*
Adam M. Byrd, *Philadelphia*
Eaton J. Bowers, *Bay St. Louis*
Frank A. McLain, *Gloster*
John Sharp Williams, *Yazoo City*

## MISSOURI

SENATORS

Francis M. Cockrell, *Warrensburg*
William J. Stone, *Jefferson City*

REPRESENTATIVES

James T. Lloyd, *Shelbyville*
William W. Rucker, *Keytesville*
John Dougherty, *Liberty*
Charles F. Cochran, *St. Joseph*
William S. Cowherd, *Kansas City*
David A. De Armond, *Butler*
Courtney W. Hamlin, *Springfield*
Dorsey W. Shackleford, *Jefferson City*
James Beauchamp Clark, *Bowling Green*
Richard Bartholdt, *St. Louis*
John T. Hunt, *St. Louis*
James J. Butler, *St. Louis*
Edward Robb, *Perryville*
Willard D. Vandiver, *Cape Girardeau*
Maecenas E. Benton, *Neosho*
J. Robert Lamar, *Houston*

## MONTANA

SENATORS

William A. Clark, *Butte*
Paris Gibson, *Great Falls*

REPRESENTATIVE AT LARGE

Joseph M. Dixon, *Missoula*

## NEBRASKA

SENATORS

Charles H. Dietrich, *Hastings*
Joseph H. Millard, *Omaha*

REPRESENTATIVES

Elmer J. Burkett,[22] *Lincoln*
Gilbert M. Hitchcock, *Omaha*
John J. McCarthy, *Ponca*
Edmund H. Hinshaw, *Fairbury*
George W. Norris, *McCook*
Moses P. Kinkaid, *O'Neill*

## NEVADA

SENATORS

William M. Stewart, *Carson City*
Francis G. Newlands, *Reno*

REPRESENTATIVE AT LARGE

Clarence D. Van Duzer, *Tonopah*

## NEW HAMPSHIRE

SENATORS

Jacob H. Gallinger, *Concord*
Henry E. Burnham, *Manchester*

REPRESENTATIVES

Cyrus A. Sulloway, *Manchester*
Frank D. Currier, *Canaan*

## NEW JERSEY

SENATORS

John Kean, *Elizabeth*
John F. Dryden, *Newark*

REPRESENTATIVES

Henry C. Loudenslager, *Paulsboro*
John J. Gardner, *Atlantic City*
Benjamin F. Howell, *New Brunswick*
William M. Lanning,[23] *Trenton*
Ira W. Wood,[24] *Trenton*
Charles N. Fowler, *Elizabeth*
William Hughes, *Paterson*
Richard Wayne Parker, *Newark*
William H. Wiley, *East Orange*
Allan Benny, *Bayonne*
Allan L. McDermott, *Jersey City*

## NEW YORK

SENATORS

Thomas C. Platt, *Owego*
Chauncey M. Depew, *Peekskill*

REPRESENTATIVES

Townsend Scudder, *Glen Head*
George H. Lindsay, *Brooklyn*
Charles T. Dunwell, *Brooklyn*
Frank E. Wilson, *Brooklyn*
Edward M. Bassett, *Brooklyn*
Robert Baker, *Brooklyn*
John J. Fitzgerald, *Brooklyn*
Timothy D. Sullivan, *New York City*
Henry M. Goldfogle, *New York City*
William Sulzer, *New York City*
William R. Hearst, *New York City*
George B. McClellan,[25] *New York City*
W. Bourke Cockran,[26] *New York City*
Francis B. Harrison, *New York City*
Ira E. Rider, *New York City*
William H. Douglas, *New York City*
Jacob Ruppert, Jr., *New York City*
Francis E. Shober, *New York City*
Joseph A. Goulden, *Fordham*
Norton P. Otis,[27] *Yonkers*
Thomas W. Bradley, *Walden*
John H. Ketcham, *Dover Plains*
William H. Draper, *Troy*
George N. Southwick, *Albany*
George J. Smith, *Kingston*
Lucius N. Littauer, *Gloversville*
William H. Flack, *Malone*
James S. Sherman, *Utica*
Charles L. Knapp, *Lowville*
Michael E. Driscoll, *Syracuse*
John W. Dwight, *Dryden*
Sereno E. Payne, *Auburn*
James B. Perkins, *Rochester*
Charles W. Gillet, *Addison*
James W. Wadsworth, *Geneseo*
William H. Ryan, *Buffalo*
De Alva S. Alexander, *Buffalo*
Edward B. Vreeland, *Salamanca*

---

[21] Election unsuccessfully contested by Joseph A. Conry.

[22] Resigned, effective March 4, 1905, before the commencement of the Fifty-ninth Congress, to which he had been reelected, having been elected Senator.

[23] Resigned June 6, 1904, having been appointed United States district judge for New Jersey.

[24] Elected to fill vacancy caused by resignation of William M. Lanning, and took his seat December 5, 1904.

[25] Resigned December 21, 1903, having been elected mayor of New York City.

[26] Elected to fill vacancy caused by resignation of George B. McClellan, and took his seat March 9, 1904.

[27] Died February 20, 1905.

## NORTH CAROLINA

SENATORS

Furnifold McL. Simmons, *Raleigh*
Lee S. Overman, *Salisbury*

REPRESENTATIVES

John H. Small, *Washington*
Claude Kitchin, *Scotland Neck*
Charles R. Thomas, *New Bern*
Edward W. Pou, *Smithfield*
William W. Kitchin, *Roxboro*
Gilbert B. Patterson, *Maxton*
Robert N. Page, *Biscoe*
Theodore F. Kluttz, *Salisbury*
Edwin Y. Webb, *Shelby*
James N. Gudger, Jr.,[28] *Asheville*

## NORTH DAKOTA

SENATORS

Henry C. Hansbrough, *Devils Lake*
Porter J. McCumber, *Wahpeton*

REPRESENTATIVES AT LARGE

Thomas F. Marshall, *Oakes*
Burleigh F. Spalding, *Fargo*

## OHIO

SENATORS

Joseph B. Foraker, *Cincinnati*
Marcus A. Hanna,[29] *Cleveland*
Charles W. F. Dick,[30] *Akron*

REPRESENTATIVES

Nicholas Longworth, *Cincinnati*
Herman P. Goebel, *Cincinnati*
Robert M. Nevin, *Dayton*
Harvey C. Garber, *Greenville*
John S. Snook, *Paulding*
Charles Q. Hildebrant, *Wilmington*
Thomas B. Kyle, *Troy*
William R. Warnock, *Urbana*
James H. Southard, *Toledo*
Stephen Morgan, *Oak Hill*
Charles H. Grosvenor, *Athens*
De Witt C. Badger, *Columbus*
Amos H. Jackson, *Fremont*
William W. Skiles,[31] *Shelby*
Amos R. Webber,[32] *Elyria*
Henry C. Van Voorhis, *Zanesville*
Joseph J. Gill,[33] *Steubenville*
Capell L. Weems,[34] *St. Clairsville*
John W. Cassingham, *Coshocton*
James Kennedy, *Youngstown*
Charles W. F. Dick,[35] *Akron*
William Aubrey Thomas,[36] *Niles*

Jacob A. Beidler, *Willoughby*
Theodore E. Burton, *Cleveland*

## OREGON

SENATORS

John H. Mitchell, *Portland*
Charles W. Fulton, *Astoria*

REPRESENTATIVES

Binger Hermann,[37] *Roseburg*
John N. Williamson, *Prineville*

## PENNSYLVANIA

SENATORS

Boies Penrose, *Philadelphia*
Matthew S. Quay,[38] *Beaver*
Philander C. Knox,[39] *Pittsburgh*

REPRESENTATIVES

Henry H. Bingham, *Philadelphia*
Robert Adams, Jr., *Philadelphia*
Henry Burk,[40] *Philadelphia*
George A. Castor,[41] *Philadelphia*
Robert H. Foerderer,[42] *Philadelphia*
Reuben O. Moon,[43] *Philadelphia*
Edward de V. Morrell, *Torresdale*
George D. McCreary, *Philadelphia*
Thomas S. Butler, *West Chester*
Irving P. Wanger, *Norristown*
Henry B. Cassel, *Marietta*
George Howell,[44] *Scranton*
William Connell,[45] *Scranton*
Henry W. Palmer, *Wilkes-Barre*
George R. Patterson, *Ashland*
Marcus C. L. Kline, *Allentown*
Charles F. Wright, *Susquehanna*
Elias Deemer, *Williamsport*
Charles H. Dickerman, *Milton*
Thaddeus M. Mahon, *Chambersburg*
Marlin E. Olmsted, *Harrisburg*
Alvin Evans, *Ebensburg*
Daniel F. Lafean, *York*
Solomon R. Dresser, *Bradford*
George F. Huff, *Greensburg*
Allen F. Cooper, *Uniontown*
Ernest F. Acheson, *Washington*
Arthur L. Bates, *Meadville*
Joseph H. Shull, *Shroudsburg*
William O. Smith, *Punxsutawney*
Joseph C. Sibley, *Franklin*
George Shiras III, *Allegheny*
John Dalzell, *Pittsburgh*
Henry Kirk Porter, *Pittsburgh*
James W. Brown, *Pittsburgh*

## RHODE ISLAND

SENATORS

Nelson W. Aldrich, *Providence*
George P. Wetmore, *Newport*

REPRESENTATIVES

Daniel L. D. Granger, *Providence*
Adin B. Capron, *Stillwater*

## SOUTH CAROLINA

SENATORS

Benjamin R. Tillman, *Trenton*
Asbury C. Latimer, *Belton*

REPRESENTATIVES

George S. Legare, *Charleston*
George W. Croft,[46] *Aiken*
Theodore G. Croft,[47] *Aiken*
Wyatt Aiken, *Abbeville*
Joseph T. Johnson, *Spartanburg*
David E. Finley, *Yorkville*
Robert B. Scarborough, *Conway*
Asbury F. Lever,[48] *Lexington*

## SOUTH DAKOTA

SENATORS

Robert J. Gamble, *Yankton*
Alfred B. Kittredge, *Sioux Falls*

REPRESENTATIVES AT LARGE

Charles H. Burke, *Pierre*
Eben W. Martin, *Deadwood*

## TENNESSEE

SENATORS

William B. Bate, *Nashville*
Edward W. Carmack, *Memphis*

REPRESENTATIVES

Walter P. Brownlow, *Jonesboro*
Henry R. Gibson, *Knoxville*
John A. Moon, *Chattanooga*
Morgan C. Fitzpatrick, *Hartsville*
James D. Richardson, *Murfreesboro*
John W. Gaines, *Nashville*
Lemuel P. Padgett, *Columbia*
Thetus W. Sims,[49] *Linden*
Rice A. Pierce, *Union City*
Malcolm R. Patterson, *Memphis*

## TEXAS

SENATORS

Charles A. Culberson, *Dallas*
Joseph W. Bailey, *Gainesville*

---

[28] Election unsuccessfully contested by James M. Moody.

[29] Died February 15, 1904.

[30] Elected to fill vacancy caused by death of Marcus A. Hanna, and took his seat March 23, 1904.

[31] Died January 9, 1904.

[32] Elected to fill vacancy caused by death of William W. Skiles, and took his seat December 5, 1904.

[33] Resigned October 31, 1903, before Congress assembled.

[34] Elected to fill vacancy caused by resignation of Joseph J. Gill, and took his seat November 9, 1903.

[35] Resigned March 23, 1904, having been elected Senator.

[36] Elected to fill vacancy caused by resignation of Charles W. F. Dick, and took his seat December 5, 1904.

[37] Elected to fill vacancy caused by death of Representative-elect Thomas H. Tongue, in preceding Congress, and took his seat November 9, 1903.

[38] Died May 28, 1904.

[39] Appointed to fill vacancy caused by death of Matthew S. Quay, and took his seat January 25, 1905; subsequently elected.

[40] Died December 5, 1903.

[41] Elected to fill vacancy caused by death of Henry Burk, and took his seat February 29, 1904.

[42] Died July 26, 1903, before Congress assembled.

[43] Elected to fill vacancy caused by death of Robert H. Foerderer, and took his seat November 9, 1903.

[44] Served until February 10, 1904; succeeded by William Connell, who contested his election.

[45] Successfully contested the election of George Howell, and took his seat February 10, 1904.

[46] Died March 10, 1904.

[47] Elected to fill vacancy caused by death of his father, George W. Croft, and took his seat December 5, 1904.

[48] Election unsuccessfully contested by Alexander D. Dantzler.

[49] Election unsuccessfully contested by F. M. Davis.

## REPRESENTATIVES

Morris Sheppard, *Texarkana*
Samuel B. Cooper, *Beaumont*
Gordon J. Russell, *Tyler*
Choice B. Randell, *Sherman*
Jack Beall, *Waxahachie*
Scott Field, *Calvert*
Alexander W. Gregg, *Palestine*
Thomas H. Ball,[50] *Huntsville*
John M. Pinckney,[51] *Hempstead*
George F. Burgess, *Gonzales*
Albert S. Burleson, *Austin*
Robert L. Henry, *Waco*
Oscar W. Gillespie, *Fort Worth*
John H. Stephens, *Vernon*
James L. Slayden, *San Antonio*
John N. Garner, *Uvalde*
William R. Smith, *Colorado*

## UTAH

### SENATORS

Thomas Kearns, *Salt Lake City*
Reed Smoot, *Provo*

### REPRESENTATIVE AT LARGE

Joseph Howell, *Logan*

## VERMONT

### SENATORS

Redfield Proctor, *Proctor*
William P. Dillingham, *Montpelier*

### REPRESENTATIVES

David J. Foster, *Burlington*
Kittredge Haskins, *Brattleboro*

## VIRGINIA

### SENATORS

John W. Daniel, *Lynchburg*
Thomas S. Martin, *Scottsville*

### REPRESENTATIVES

William A. Jones, *Warsaw*
Harry L. Maynard, *Portsmouth*

John Lamb, *Richmond*
Robert G. Southall, *Amelia*
Claude A. Swanson, *Chatham*
Carter Glass, *Lynchburg*
James Hay, *Madison*
John F. Rixey, *Brandy*
Campbell Slemp, *Big Stone Gap*
Henry D. Flood, *Appomattox*

## WASHINGTON

### SENATORS

Addison G. Foster, *Tacoma*
Levi Ankeny, *Walla Walla*

### REPRESENTATIVES AT LARGE

Wesley L. Jones, *North Yakima*
Francis W. Cushman, *Tacoma*
William E. Humphrey, *Seattle*

## WEST VIRGINIA

### SENATORS

Stephen B. Elkins, *Elkins*
Nathan B. Scott, *Wheeling*

### REPRESENTATIVES

Blackburn B. Dovener, *Wheeling*
Alston G. Dayton, *Philippi*
Joseph Holt Gaines, *Charleston*
Harry C. Woodyard, *Spencer*
James A. Hughes, *Huntington*

## WISCONSIN

### SENATORS

John C. Spooner, *Madison*
Joseph V. Quarles, *Milwaukee*

### REPRESENTATIVES

Henry Allen Cooper, *Racine*
Henry C. Adams, *Madison*
Joseph W. Babcock, *Necedah*

Theobald Otjen, *Milwaukee*
William H. Stafford, *Milwaukee*
Charles H. Weisse, *Sheyboygan Falls*
John J. Esch, *La Crosse*
James H. Davidson, *Oshkosh*
Edward S. Minor, *Sturgeon Bay*
Webster E. Brown, *Rhinelander*
John J. Jenkins, *Chippewa Falls*

## WYOMING

### SENATORS

Clarence D. Clark, *Evanston*
Francis E. Warren, *Cheyenne*

### REPRESENTATIVE AT LARGE

Frank W. Mondell, *Newcastle*

## TERRITORY OF ARIZONA

### DELEGATE

John F. Wilson, *Prescott*

## TERRITORY OF HAWAII

### DELEGATE

Jonah K. Kalanianaole, *Waikiki*

## TERRITORY OF NEW MEXICO

### DELEGATE

Bernard S. Rodey, *Albuquerque*

## TERRITORY OF OKLAHOMA

### DELEGATE

Bird S. McGuire,[52] *Pawnee*

## PORTO RICO

### RESIDENT COMMISSIONER[53]

Federico Degetau, *San Juan*

---

[50] Resigned effective November 16, 1903.
[51] Elected to fill vacancy caused by resignation of Thomas H. Ball, and took his seat December 7, 1903.

[52] Election unsuccessfully contested by William M. Cross.
[53] Granted same powers and privileges possessed

by Delegates and made competent to serve as additional member of Committee on Insular Affairs February 2, 1904.

# 59TH CONGRESS

## MARCH 4, 1905, TO MARCH 3, 1907

FIRST SESSION— *December 4, 1905, to June 30, 1906*
SECOND SESSION— *December 3, 1906, to March 3, 1907*
SPECIAL SESSION OF THE SENATE— *March 4, 1905, to March 18, 1905*

———

VICE PRESIDENT OF THE UNITED STATES— CHARLES W. FAIRBANKS, of Indiana
PRESIDENT PRO TEMPORE OF THE SENATE— WILLIAM P. FRYE, of Maine
SECRETARY OF THE SENATE— CHARLES G. BENNETT, of New York
SERGEANT AT ARMS OF THE SENATE— DANIEL M. RANSDELL, of Indiana
SPEAKER OF THE HOUSE OF REPRESENTATIVES— JOSEPH G. CANNON,[1] of Illinois
CLERK OF THE HOUSE— ALEXANDER McDOWELL,[2] of Pennsylvania
SERGEANT AT ARMS OF THE HOUSE— HENRY CASSON, of Wisconsin
DOORKEEPER OF THE HOUSE— FRANK B. LYON, of New York
POSTMASTER OF THE HOUSE— J. C. McELROY

Charles W. Fairbanks
Vice President

Joseph G. Cannon
Speaker

## ALABAMA

### SENATORS
John T. Morgan, *Selma*
Edmund W. Pettus, *Selma*

### REPRESENTATIVES
George W. Taylor, *Demopolis*
Ariosto A. Wiley, *Montgomery*
Henry D. Clayton, *Eufaula*
Sydney J. Bowie, *Anniston*
J. Thomas Heflin, *Lafayette*
John H. Bankhead, *Fayette*
John L. Burnett, *Gadsden*
William Richardson, *Huntsville*
Oscar W. Underwood, *Birmingham*

## ARKANSAS

### SENATORS
James H. Berry, *Bentonville*
James P. Clarke, *Little Rock*

### REPRESENTATIVES
Robert B. Macon, *Helena*
Stephen Brundidge, Jr., *Searcy*
John C. Floyd, *Yellville*
John S. Little,[3] *Greenwood*
Charles C. Reid, *Morrillton*
Joseph T. Robinson, *Lonoke*
Robert M. Wallace, *Magnolia*

## CALIFORNIA

### SENATORS
George C. Perkins, *Oakland*
Frank P. Flint, *Los Angeles*

### REPRESENTATIVES
James N. Gillett,[4] *Eureka*
William F. Englebright,[5] *Nevada City*
Duncan E. McKinlay, *Santa Rosa*
Joseph R. Knowland, *Alameda*
Julius Kahn, *San Francisco*
Everis A. Hayes, *San Jose*
James C. Needham, *Modesto*
James McLachlan, *Pasadena*
Sylvester C. Smith, *Bakersfield*

## COLORADO

### SENATORS
Henry M. Teller, *Central City*
Thomas M. Patterson, *Denver*

### REPRESENTATIVE AT LARGE
Franklin E. Brooks, *Colorado Springs*

### REPRESENTATIVES
Robert W. Bonynge, *Denver*
Herschel M. Hogg, *Telluride*

## CONNECTICUT

### SENATORS
Orville H. Platt,[6] *Meriden*
Frank B. Brandegee,[7] *New London*
Morgan G. Bulkeley, *Hartford*

### REPRESENTATIVE AT LARGE
George L. Lilley, *Waterbury*

### REPRESENTATIVES
E. Stevens Henry, *Rockville*
Nehemiah D. Sperry, *New Haven*
Frank B. Brandegee,[8] *New London*

Edwin W. Higgins,[9] *Norwich*
Ebenezer J. Hill, *Norwalk*

## DELAWARE

### SENATORS
J. Frank Allee, *Dover*
Henry A. du Pont,[10] *Winterthur*

### REPRESENTATIVE AT LARGE
Hiram R. Burton, *Lewes*

## FLORIDA

### SENATORS
Stephen R. Mallory, *Pensacola*
James P. Taliaferro,[11] *Jacksonville*

### REPRESENTATIVES
Stephen M. Sparkman, *Tampa*
Frank Clark, *Lake City*
William B. Lamar, *Monticello*

## GEORGIA

### SENATORS
Augustus O. Bacon, *Macon*
Alexander S. Clay, *Marietta*

### REPRESENTATIVES
Rufus E. Lester,[12] *Savannah*
James W. Overstreet,[13] *Sylvania*
James M. Griggs, *Dawson*
Elijah B. Lewis, *Montezuma*
William C. Adamson, *Carrollton*
Leonidas F. Livingston, *Covington*
Charles L. Bartlett, *Macon*

---

[1] Reelected December 4, 1905.
[2] Reelected December 4, 1905.
[3] Resigned, to take effect January 14, 1907, having been elected Governor.
[4] Resigned November 4, 1906, having been elected Governor.
[5] Elected to fill vacancy caused by resignation of James N. Gillett, and took his seat January 3, 1907.
[6] Died April 21, 1905.

[7] Elected to fill vacancy caused by death of Orville H. Platt, and took his seat December 5, 1905.
[8] Resigned May 10, 1905, before Congress assembled, having been elected Senator.
[9] Elected to fill vacancy caused by resignation of Frank B. Brandegee, and took his seat December 4, 1905.
[10] Elected to fill vacancy in the term beginning March 4, 1905, caused by failure of legislature to elect,

and took his seat December 3, 1906; vacancy in this class from March 4, 1905, to June 12, 1906.
[11] Reappointed to fill vacancy in the term beginning March 4, 1905, to serve until the next meeting of the legislature; subsequently reelected.
[12] Died June 16, 1906.
[13] Elected to fill vacancy caused by death of Rufus E. Lester, and took his seat December 3, 1906.

Gordon Lee, *Chickamauga*
William M. Howard, *Lexington*
Thomas M. Bell, *Gainesville*
Thomas W. Hardwick, *Sandersville*
William G. Brantley, *Brunswick*

## IDAHO

### SENATORS

Fred T. Dubois, *Blackfoot*
Weldon B. Heyburn, *Wallace*

### REPRESENTATIVE AT LARGE

Burton L. French, *Moscow*

## ILLINOIS

### SENATORS

Shelby M. Cullom, *Springfield*
Albert J. Hopkins, *Aurora*

### REPRESENTATIVES

Martin B. Madden, *Chicago*
James R. Mann, *Chicago*
William W. Wilson, *Chicago*
Charles S. Wharton, *Chicago*
Anthony Michalek,[14] *Chicago*
William Lorimer, *Chicago*
Philip Knopf, *Chicago*
Charles McGavin, *Chicago*
Henry S. Boutell, *Chicago*
George E. Foss, *Chicago*
Howard M. Snapp, *Joliet*
Charles E. Fuller, *Belvidere*
Robert R. Hitt,[15] *Mount Morris*
Frank O. Lowden,[16] *Oregon*
Benjamin F. Marsh,[17] *Warsaw*
James McKinney,[18] *Aledo*
George W. Prince, *Galesburg*
Joseph V. Graff, *Peoria*
John A. Sterling, *Bloomington*
Joseph G. Cannon, *Danville*
William B. McKinley, *Champaign*
Henry T. Rainey, *Carrollton*
Zeno J. Rives, *Litchfield*
William A. Rodenberg, *East St. Louis*
Frank S. Dickson, *Ramsey*
Pleasant T. Chapman, *Vienna*
George W. Smith, *Murphysboro*

## INDIANA

### SENATORS

Albert J. Beveridge, *Indianapolis*
James A. Hemenway,[19] *Boonville*

### REPRESENTATIVES

John H. Foster,[20] *Evansville*
John C. Chaney, *Sullivan*
William T. Zenor, *Corydon*
Lincoln Dixon, *North Vernon*
Elias S. Holliday, *Brazil*
James E. Watson, *Rushville*
Jesse Overstreet, *Indianapolis*
George W. Cromer, *Muncie*
Charles B. Landis, *Delphi*
Edgar D. Crumpacker, *Valparaiso*
Frederick Landis, *Logansport*
Newton W. Gilbert,[21] *Fort Wayne*
Clarence C. Gilhams,[22] *La Grange*
Abraham L. Brick, *South Bend*

## IOWA

### SENATORS

William B. Allison, *Dubuque*
Jonathan P. Dolliver, *Fort Dodge*

### REPRESENTATIVES

Thomas Hedge, *Burlington*
Albert F. Dawson, *Preston*
Benjamin P. Birdsall, *Clarion*
Gilbert N. Haugen, *Northwood*
Robert G. Cousins, *Tipton*
John F. Lacey, *Oskaloosa*
John A. T. Hull, *Des Moines*
William P. Hepburn, *Clarinda*
Walter I. Smith, *Council Bluffs*
James P. Conner, *Denison*
Elbert H. Hubbard, *Sioux City*

## KANSAS

### SENATORS

Joseph R. Burton,[23] *Abilene*
Alfred W. Benson,[24] *Ottawa*
Charles Curtis,[25] *Topeka*
Chester I. Long, *Medicine Lodge*

### REPRESENTATIVE AT LARGE

Charles F. Scott, *Iola*

### REPRESENTATIVES

Charles Curtis,[26] *Topeka*
Justin D. Bowersock, *Lawrence*
Philip P. Campbell, *Pittsburg*
James M. Miller, *Council Grove*
William A. Calderhead, *Marysville*
William A. Reeder, *Logan*
Victor Murdock, *Wichita*

## KENTUCKY

### SENATORS

Joseph C. S. Blackburn, *Versailles*
James B. McCreary, *Richmond*

### REPRESENTATIVES

Ollie M. James, *Marion*
Augustus O. Stanley, *Henderson*
James M. Richardson, *Glasgow*
David H. Smith, *Hodgensville*
J. Swagar Sherley, *Louisville*
Joseph L. Rhinock, *Covington*
South Trimble, *Frankfort*
George G. Gilbert, *Shelbyville*
Joseph B. Bennett, *Greenup*
Frank A. Hopkins, *Prestonsburg*
Don C. Edwards, *London*

## LOUISIANA

### SENATORS

Samuel D. McEnery, *New Orleans*
Murphy J. Foster, *Franklin*

### REPRESENTATIVES

Adolph Meyer, *New Orleans*
Robert C. Davey, *New Orleans*
Robert F. Broussard, *New Iberia*
John T. Watkins, *Minden*
Joseph E. Ransdell, *Lake Providence*
Samuel M. Robertson, *Baton Rouge*
Arsène P. Pujo, *Lake Charles*

## MAINE

### SENATORS

Eugene Hale, *Ellsworth*
William P. Frye, *Lewiston*

### REPRESENTATIVES

Amos L. Allen, *Alfred*
Charles E. Littlefield, *Rockland*
Edwin C. Burleigh, *Augusta*
Llewellyn Powers, *Houlton*

## MARYLAND

### SENATORS

Arthur Pue Gorman,[27] *Laurel*
William Pinkney Whyte,[28] *Baltimore*
Isidor Rayner, *Baltimore*

### REPRESENTATIVES

Thomas A. Smith, *Ridgely*
J. Fred. C. Talbott, *Towson*
Frank C. Wachter, *Baltimore*
John Gill, Jr., *Baltimore*
Sydney E. Mudd, *La Plata*
George A. Pearre, *Cumberland*

---

[14] Protests of certain citizens of Fifth District were filed against his being seated upon grounds he was not of legal age and an alien; committee reported resolution declaring him qualified and entitled to the seat, which was agreed to March 6, 1906.

[15] Died September 19, 1906.

[16] Elected to fill vacancy caused by death of Robert R. Hitt, and took his seat December 3, 1906.

[17] Died June 2, 1905, before Congress assembled.

[18] Elected to fill vacancy caused by death of Benjamin F. Marsh, and took his seat December 4, 1905.

[19] Elected to fill vacancy caused by resignation of

Charles W. Fairbanks, in preceding Congress, and took his seat March 4, 1905.

[20] Elected to fill vacancy caused by resignation of Representative-elect James A. Hemenway, in preceding Congress, and took his seat December 4, 1905.

[21] Resigned November 6, 1906, having been appointed judge in the Philippine Islands.

[22] Elected to fill vacancy caused by resignation of Newton W. Gilbert, and took his seat December 3, 1906.

[23] Resigned June 4, 1906. (See U.S. Senate Election, Expulsion and Censure Cases, 1793-1990, Senate Document 103-33, pp. 275-76.)

[24] Appointed to fill vacancy caused by resignation of Joseph R. Burton, and took his seat June 14, 1906.

[25] Elected to fill vacancy caused by resignation of Joseph R. Burton, and took his seat January 29, 1907.

[26] Resigned January 28, 1907, before the commencement of the Sixtieth Congress, to which he had been reelected, having been elected Senator.

[27] Died June 4, 1906.

[28] Appointed to fill vacancy caused by death of Arthur Pue Gorman, and took his seat June 11, 1906; subsequently elected.

## MASSACHUSETTS

### SENATORS

Henry Cabot Lodge, *Nahant*
W. Murray Crane, *Dalton*

### REPRESENTATIVES

George P. Lawrence, *North Adams*
Frederick H. Gillett, *Springfield*
Rockwood Hoar,[29] *Worcester*
Charles G. Washburn,[30] *Worcester*
Charles Q. Tirrell, *Natick*
Butler Ames, *Lowell*
Augustus P. Gardner, *Hamilton*
Ernest W. Roberts, *Chelsea*
Samuel W. McCall, *Winchester*
John A. Keliher, *Boston*
William S. McNary, *Boston*
John A. Sullivan, *Boston*
John W. Weeks, *Newton*
William S. Greene, *Fall River*
William C. Lovering, *Taunton*

## MICHIGAN

### SENATORS

Julius C. Burrows, *Kalamazoo*
Russell A. Alger,[31] *Detroit*
William Alden Smith,[32] *Grand Rapids*

### REPRESENTATIVES

Edwin Denby, *Detroit*
Charles E. Townsend, *Jackson*
Washington Gardner, *Albion*
Edward L. Hamilton, *Niles*
William Alden Smith,[33] *Grand Rapids*
Samuel W. Smith, *Pontiac*
Henry McMorran, *Port Huron*
Joseph W. Fordney, *Saginaw*
Roswell P. Bishop, *Ludington*
George A. Loud, *Au Sable*
Archibald B. Darragh, *St. Louis*
H. Olin Young, *Ishpeming*

## MINNESOTA

### SENATORS

Knute Nelson, *Alexandria*
Moses E. Clapp, *St. Paul*

### REPRESENTATIVES

James A. Tawney, *Winona*
James T. McCleary, *Mankato*
Charles R. David, *St. Peter*
Frederick C. Stevens, *St. Paul*
Loren Fletcher, *Minneapolis*
Clarence B. Buckman, *Little Falls*
Andrew J. Volstead, *Granite Falls*
J. Adam Bede, *Pine City*
Halvor Steenerson, *Crookston*

## MISSISSIPPI

### SENATORS

Hernando D. Money, *Carrollton*
Anselm J. McLaurin, *Brandon*

### REPRESENTATIVES

Ezekiel S. Candler, Jr., *Corinth*
Thomas Spight, *Ripley*
Benjamin G. Humphreys, *Greenville*
Wilson S. Hill, *Winona*
Adam M. Byrd, *Philadelphia*
Eaton J. Bowers, *Bay St. Louis*
Frank A. McLain, *Gloster*
John Sharp Williams, *Yazoo City*

## MISSOURI

### SENATORS

William J. Stone, *Jefferson City*
William Warner, *Kansas City*

### REPRESENTATIVES

James T. Lloyd, *Shelbyville*
William W. Rucker, *Keytesville*
Frank B. Klepper, *Kingston*
Frank B. Fulkerson, *St. Joseph*
Edgar C. Ellis, *Kansas City*
David A. De Armond, *Butler*
John Welborn, *Lexington*
Dorsey W. Shackleford, *Jefferson City*
James Beauchamp Clark, *Bowling Green*
Richard Bartholdt, *St. Louis*
John T. Hunt, *St. Louis*
Ernest E. Wood,[34] *St. Louis*
Harry M. Coudrey,[35] *St. Louis*
Marion E. Rhodes, *Potosi*
William T. Tyndall, *Sparta*
Cassius M. Shartel, *Neosho*
Arthur P. Murphy, *Rolla*

## MONTANA

### SENATORS

William A. Clark, *Butte*
Thomas H. Carter, *Helena*

### REPRESENTATIVE AT LARGE

Joseph M. Dixon, *Missoula*

## NEBRASKA

### SENATORS

Joseph H. Millard, *Omaha*
Elmer J. Burkett, *Lincoln*

### REPRESENTATIVES

Ernest M. Pollard,[36] *Nehawka*
John L. Kennedy, *Omaha*
John J. McCarthy, *Ponca*
Edmund H. Hinshaw, *Fairbury*
George W. Norris, *McCook*
Moses P. Kinkaid, *O'Neill*

## NEVADA

### SENATORS

Francis G. Newlands, *Reno*
George S. Nixon, *Winnemucca*

### REPRESENTATIVE AT LARGE

Clarence D. Van Duzer, *Tonopah*

## NEW HAMPSHIRE

### SENATORS

Jacob H. Gallinger, *Concord*
Henry E. Burnham, *Manchester*

### REPRESENTATIVES

Cyrus A. Sulloway, *Manchester*
Frank D. Currier, *Canaan*

## NEW JERSEY

### SENATORS

John Kean, *Elizabeth*
John F. Dryden, *Newark*

### REPRESENTATIVES

Henry C. Loudenslager, *Paulsboro*
John J. Gardner, *Atlantic City*
Benjamin F. Howell, *New Brunswick*
Ira W. Wood, *Trenton*
Charles N. Fowler, *Elizabeth*
Henry C. Allen, *Little Falls*
Richard Wayne Parker, *Newark*
William H. Wiley, *East Orange*
Marshall Van Winkle, *Jersey City*
Allan L. McDermott, *Jersey City*

## NEW YORK

### SENATORS

Thomas C. Platt, *Owego*
Chauncey M. Depew, *Peekskill*

### REPRESENTATIVES

William W. Cocks, *Westbury*
George H. Lindsay, *Brooklyn*
Charles T. Dunwell, *Brooklyn*
Charles B. Law, *Brooklyn*
George E. Waldo, *Brooklyn*
William M. Calder, *Brooklyn*
John J. Fitzgerald, *Brooklyn*
Timothy D. Sullivan,[37] *New York City*
Daniel J. Riordan,[38] *New York City*
Henry M. Goldfogle, *New York City*
William Sulzer, *New York City*
William R. Hearst, *New York City*
W. Bourke Cockran, *New York City*
Herbert Parsons, *New York City*
Charles A. Towne, *New York City*
J. Van Vechten Olcott, *New York City*
Jacob Ruppert, Jr., *New York City*
William S. Bennet, *New York City*
Joseph A. Goulden, *Fordham*
John E. Andrus, *Yonkers*
Thomas W. Bradley, *Walden*

---

[29] Died November 1, 1906.
[30] Elected to fill vacancy caused by death of Rockwood Hoar, and took his seat January 3, 1907.
[31] Died January 24, 1907.
[32] Elected to fill vacancy caused by death of Russell A. Alger, and took his seat February 11, 1907.
[33] Resigned effective February 9, 1907, before the

commencement of the Sixtieth Congress, to which he had been reelected, having been elected Senator.
[34] Served until June 23, 1906; succeeded by Harry M. Coudrey, who contested his election.
[35] Successfully contested the election of Ernest E. Wood, and took his seat June 23, 1906.
[36] Elected to fill vacancy caused by resignation of

Representative-elect Elmer J. Burkett, in preceding Congress, and took his seat December 4, 1905.
[37] Resigned July 27, 1906.
[38] Elected to fill vacancy caused by resignation of Timothy D. Sullivan, and took his seat December 3, 1906.

John H. Ketcham,[39] *Dover Plains*
William H. Draper, *Troy*
George N. Southwick, *Albany*
Frank J. Le Fevre, *New Paltz*
Lucius N. Littauer, *Gloversville*
William H. Flack,[40] *Malone*
James S. Sherman, *Utica*
Charles L. Knapp, *Lowville*
Michael E. Driscoll, *Syracuse*
John W. Dwight, *Dryden*
Sereno E. Payne, *Auburn*
James B. Perkins, *Rochester*
J. Sloat Fassett, *Elmira*
James W. Wadsworth, *Geneseo*
William H. Ryan, *Buffalo*
De Alva S. Alexander, *Buffalo*
Edward B. Vreeland, *Salamanca*

## NORTH CAROLINA

### SENATORS

Furnifold McL. Simmons, *Raleigh*
Lee S. Overman, *Salisbury*

### REPRESENTATIVES

John H. Small, *Washington*
Claude Kitchin, *Scotland Neck*
Charles R. Thomas, *New Bern*
Edward W. Pou, *Smithfield*
William W. Kitchin, *Roxboro*
Gilbert B. Patterson, *Maxton*
Robert N. Page, *Biscoe*
E. Spencer Blackburn, *Wilkesboro*
Edwin Y. Webb, *Shelby*
James M. Gudger, Jr., *Asheville*

## NORTH DAKOTA

### SENATORS

Henry C. Hansbrough, *Devils Lake*
Porter J. McCumber, *Wahpeton*

### REPRESENTATIVES AT LARGE

Thomas F. Marshall, *Oakes*
Asle J. Gronna, *Lakota*

## OHIO

### SENATORS

Joseph B. Foraker, *Cincinnati*
Charles W. F. Dick, *Akron*

### REPRESENTATIVES

Nicholas Longworth, *Cincinnati*
Herman P. Goebel, *Cincinnati*
Robert M. Nevin, *Dayton*
Harvey C. Garber, *Greenville*
William W. Campbell, *Napoleon*
Thomas E. Scroggy, *Xenia*
J. Warren Keifer, *Springfield*
Ralph D. Cole, *Findlay*

James H. Southard, *Toledo*
Henry T. Bannon, *Portsmouth*
Charles H. Grosvenor, *Athens*
Edward L. Taylor, Jr., *Columbus*
Grant E. Mouser, *Marion*
Amos R. Webber, *Elyria*
Beman G. Dawes, *Marietta*
Capell L. Weems, *St. Clairsville*
Martin L. Smyser, *Wooster*
James Kennedy, *Youngstown*
W. Aubrey Thomas, *Niles*
Jacob A. Beidler, *Willoughby*
Theodore E. Burton, *Cleveland*

## OREGON

### SENATORS

John H. Mitchell,[41] *Portland*
John M. Gearin,[42] *Portland*
Frederick W. Mulkey,[43] *Portland*
Charles W. Fulton, *Astoria*

### REPRESENTATIVES

Binger Hermann, *Roseburg*
John N. Williamson,[44] *Prineville*

## PENNSYLVANIA

### SENATORS

Boies Penrose, *Philadelphia*
Philander C. Knox, *Pittsburgh*

### REPRESENTATIVES

Henry H. Bingham, *Philadelphia*
Robert Adams, Jr.,[45] *Philadelphia*
John E. Reyburn,[46] *Philadelphia*
George A. Castor,[47] *Philadelphia*
J. Hampton Moore,[48] *Philadelphia*
Reuben O. Moon, *Philadelphia*
Edward de V. Morrell, *Torresdale*
George D. McCreary, *Philadelphia*
Thomas S. Butler, *West Chester*
Irving P. Wanger, *Norristown*
Henry B. Cassel, *Marietta*
Thomas H. Dale, *Scranton*
Henry W. Palmer, *Wilkes-Barre*
George R. Patterson,[49] *Ashland*
Charles N. Brumm,[50] *Minersville*
Marcus C. L. Kline, *Allentown*
Mial E. Lilley, *Towanda*
Elias Deemer, *Williamsport*
Edmund W. Samuel, *Mount Carmel*
Thaddeus M. Mahon, *Chambersburg*
Marlin E. Olmsted, *Harrisburg*
John M. Reynolds, *Bedford*
Daniel F. Lafean, *York*
Solomon R. Dresser, *Bradford*
George F. Huff, *Greensburg*
Allen F. Cooper, *Uniontown*
Ernest F. Acheson, *Washington*

Arthur L. Bates, *Meadville*
Gustav A. Schneebeli, *Nazareth*
William O. Smith, *Punxsutawney*
Joseph C. Sibley, *Franklin*
William H. Graham, *Allegheny*
John Dalzell, *Pittsburgh*
James F. Burke, *Pittsburgh*
Andrew J. Barchfeld, *Pittsburgh*

## RHODE ISLAND

### SENATORS

Nelson W. Aldrich, *Providence*
George P. Wetmore, *Newport*

### REPRESENTATIVES

Daniel L. D. Granger, *Providence*
Adin B. Capron, *Stillwater*

## SOUTH CAROLINA

### SENATORS

Benjamin R. Tillman, *Trenton*
Asbury C. Latimer, *Belton*

### REPRESENTATIVES

George S. Legare,[51] *Charleston*
James O'H. Patterson,[52] *Barnwell*
Wyatt Aiken, *Abbeville*
Joseph T. Johnson, *Spartanburg*
David E. Finley, *Yorkville*
J. Edwin Ellerbe, *Marion*
Asbury F. Lever,[53] *Lexington*

## SOUTH DAKOTA

### SENATORS

Robert J. Gamble, *Yankton*
Alfred B. Kittredge, *Sioux Falls*

### REPRESENTATIVES AT LARGE

Charles H. Burke, *Pierre*
Eben W. Martin, *Deadwood*

## TENNESSEE

### SENATORS

William B. Bate,[54] *Nashville*
James B. Frazier,[55] *Chattanooga*
Edward W. Carmack, *Memphis*

### REPRESENTATIVES

Walter P. Brownlow, *Jonesboro*
Nathan W. Hale, *Knoxville*
John A. Moon, *Chattanooga*
Mounce G. Butler, *Gainesboro*
William C. Houston, *Woodbury*
John W. Gaines, *Nashville*
Lemuel P. Padgett, *Columbia*
Thetus W. Sims, *Linden*
Finis J. Garrett, *Dresden*
Malcolm R. Patterson,[56] *Memphis*

---

[39] Died November 4, 1906.
[40] Died February 2, 1907.
[41] Died December 8, 1905.
[42] Appointed to fill vacancy caused by death of John H. Mitchell, and took his seat December 21, 1905.
[43] Elected to fill vacancy caused by death of John H. Mitchell, and took his seat January 30, 1907.
[44] Never qualified.
[45] Died June 1, 1906.
[46] Elected to fill vacancy caused by death of Robert

Adams, Jr., and took his seat December 3, 1906.
[47] Died February 19, 1906.
[48] Elected to fill vacancy caused by death of George A. Castor, and took his seat December 3, 1906.
[49] Died March 21, 1906.
[50] Elected to fill vacancy caused by death of George R. Patterson, and took his seat December 3, 1906.
[51] Election unsuccessfully contested by Aaron P. Prioleau and John A. Noland.

[52] Election unsuccessfully contested by Isaac Myers.
[53] Election unsuccessfully contested by Charles C. Jacobs.
[54] Died March 9, 1905.
[55] Elected to fill vacancy caused by death of William B. Bate, and took his seat December 4, 1905.
[56] Resigned November 5, 1906, having been elected Governor.

## TEXAS

### SENATORS

Charles A. Culberson, *Dallas*
Joseph W. Bailey, *Gainesville*

### REPRESENTATIVES

Morris Sheppard, *Texarkana*
Moses L. Broocks,[57] *San Augustine*
Gordon J. Russell, *Tyler*
Choice B. Randell, *Sherman*
Jack Beall, *Waxahachie*
Scott Field, *Calvert*
Alexander W. Gregg, *Palestine*
John M. Pinckney,[58] *Hempstead*
John M. Moore,[59] *Richmond*
George F. Burgess, *Gonzales*
Albert S. Burleson, *Austin*
Robert L. Henry, *Waco*
Oscar W. Gillespie, *Fort Worth*
John H. Stephens, *Vernon*
James L. Slayden, *San Antonio*
John N. Garner, *Uvalde*
William R. Smith, *Colorado*

## UTAH

### SENATORS

Reed Smoot, *Provo*
George Sutherland, *Salt Lake City*

### REPRESENTATIVE AT LARGE

Joseph Howell, *Logan*

## VERMONT

### SENATORS

Redfield Proctor, *Proctor*
William P. Dillingham, *Waterbury*

### REPRESENTATIVES

David J. Foster, *Burlington*
Kittredge Haskins, *Brattleboro*

## VIRGINIA

### SENATORS

John W. Daniel, *Lynchburg*
Thomas S. Martin, *Charlottesville*

### REPRESENTATIVES

William A. Jones, *Warsaw*
Harry L. Maynard, *Portsmouth*
John Lamb, *Richmond*
Robert G. Southall, *Amelia*
Claude A. Swanson,[60] *Chatham*
Edward W. Saunders,[61] *Rockymount*
Carter Glass, *Lynchburg*
James Hay, *Madison*
John F. Rixey,[62] *Brandy*
Campbell Slemp, *Big Stone Gap*
Henry D. Flood, *Appomattox*

## WASHINGTON

### SENATORS

Levi Ankeny, *Walla Walla*
Samuel H. Piles, *Seattle*

### REPRESENTATIVES AT LARGE

Wesley L. Jones, *North Yakima*
Francis W. Cushman, *Tacoma*
William E. Humphrey, *Seattle*

## WEST VIRGINIA

### SENATORS

Stephen B. Elkins, *Elkins*
Nathan B. Scott, *Wheeling*

### REPRESENTATIVES

Blackburn B. Dovener, *Wheeling*
Alston G. Dayton,[63] *Philippi*
Thomas B. Davis,[64] *Keyser*
Joseph Holt Gaines, *Charleston*
Harry C. Woodyard, *Spencer*
James A. Hughes, *Huntington*

## WISCONSIN

### SENATORS

John C. Spooner, *Madison*
Robert M. La Follette,[65] *Madison*

### REPRESENTATIVES

Henry Allen Cooper, *Racine*
Henry C. Adams,[66] *Madison*
John M. Nelson,[67] *Madison*

Joseph W. Babcock, *Necedah*
Theobald Otjen, *Milwaukee*
William H. Stafford, *Milwaukee*
Charles H. Weisse, *Sheboygan Falls*
John J. Esch, *La Crosse*
James H. Davidson, *Oshkosh*
Edward S. Minor, *Sturgeon Bay*
Webster E. Brown, *Rhinelander*
John J. Jenkins, *Chippewa Falls*

## WYOMING

### SENATORS

Clarence D. Clark, *Evanston*
Francis E. Warren, *Cheyenne*

### REPRESENTATIVE AT LARGE

Frank W. Mondell, *Newcastle*

## TERRITORY OF ALASKA[68]

### DELEGATE

Frank N. H. Waskey,[69] *Nome*

## TERRITORY OF ARIZONA

### DELEGATE

Marcus A. Smith, *Tucson*

## TERRITORY OF HAWAII

### DELEGATE

Jonah K. Kalanianaole,[70] *Waikiki*

## TERRITORY OF NEW MEXICO

### DELEGATE

William H. Andrews, *Albuquerque*

## TERRITORY OF OKLAHOMA

### DELEGATE

Bird S. McGuire, *Pawnee*

## PORTO RICO

### RESIDENT COMMISSIONER

Tulio Larrinaga, *San Juan*

---

[57] Election unsuccessfully contested by A. J. Houston.

[58] Died April 24, 1905, before Congress assembled.

[59] Elected to fill vacancy caused by death of John M. Pinckney, and took his seat December 4, 1905.

[60] Resigned January 30, 1906, having been elected Governor.

[61] Elected to fill vacancy caused by resignation of Claude A. Swanson, and took his seat December 3, 1906.

[62] Died February 8, 1907, before the commencement of the Sixtieth Congress, to which he had been reelected.

[63] Resigned March 16, 1905, having been appointed United States district judge.

[64] Elected to fill vacancy caused by resignation of Alston G. Dayton, and took his seat December 4, 1905.

[65] Elected January 25, 1905, for the term beginning March 4, 1905, but did not qualify until January 4, 1906, preferring to retain the governorship.

[66] Died July 9, 1906.

[67] Elected to fill vacancy caused by death of Henry C. Adams, and took his seat December 3, 1906.

[68] Formed from territory ceded to the United States by Russia by treaty of March 30, 1867; granted a civil government without representation in Congress, by act of May 17, 1884; granted a Delegate in Congress by act of May 8, 1906.

[69] Took his seat December 3, 1906.

[70] Election unsuccessfully contested by Curtis P. Iaokea.

# 60TH CONGRESS

MARCH 4, 1907, TO MARCH 3, 1909

FIRST SESSION— *December 2, 1907, to May 30, 1908*
SECOND SESSION— *December 7, 1908, to March 3, 1909*

---

VICE PRESIDENT OF THE UNITED STATES— CHARLES W. FAIRBANKS, of Indiana
PRESIDENT PRO TEMPORE OF THE SENATE— WILLIAM P. FRYE,[1] of Maine
SECRETARY OF THE SENATE— CHARLES G. BENNETT, of New York
SERGEANT AT ARMS OF THE SENATE— DANIEL M. RANSDELL, of Indiana

---

SPEAKER OF THE HOUSE OF REPRESENTATIVES— JOSEPH G. CANNON,[2] of Illinois
CLERK OF THE HOUSE— ALEXANDER McDOWELL,[3] of Pennsylvania
SERGEANT AT ARMS OF THE HOUSE— HENRY CASSON, of Wisconsin
DOORKEEPER OF THE HOUSE— FRANK B. LYON, of New York
POSTMASTER OF THE HOUSE— SAMUEL LANGUM

Charles W. Fairbanks
Vice President

Joseph G. Cannon
Speaker

## ALABAMA

### SENATORS

John T. Morgan,[4] *Selma*
John H. Bankhead,[5] *Fayette*
Edmund W. Pettus,[6] *Selma*
Joseph F. Johnston,[7] *Birmingham*

### REPRESENTATIVES

George W. Taylor, *Demopolis*
Ariosto A. Wiley,[8] *Montgomery*
Oliver C. Wiley,[9] *Troy*
Henry D. Clayton, *Eufaula*
William B. Craig, *Selma*
J. Thomas Heflin, *Lafayette*
Richmond P. Hobson, *Greensboro*
John L. Burnett, *Gadsden*
William Richardson, *Huntsville*
Oscar W. Underwood, *Birmingham*

## ARKANSAS

### SENATORS

James P. Clarke, *Little Rock*
Jeff Davis, *Little Rock*

### REPRESENTATIVES

Robert B. Macon, *Helena*
Stephen Brundidge, Jr., *Searcy*
John C. Floyd, *Yellville*
William B. Cravens, *Fort Smith*
Charles C. Reid, *Morrillton*
Joseph T. Robinson, *Lonoke*
Robert M. Wallace, *Magnolia*

## CALIFORNIA

### SENATORS

George C. Perkins, *Oakland*
Frank P. Flint, *Los Angeles*

### REPRESENTATIVES

William F. Englebright, *Nevada City*
Duncan E. McKinlay, *Santa Rosa*
Joseph R. Knowland, *Alameda*
Julius Kahn, *San Francisco*
Everis A. Hayes, *San Jose*
James C. Needham, *Modesto*
James McLachlan, *Pasadena*
Sylvester C. Smith, *Bakersfield*

## COLORADO

### SENATORS

Henry M. Teller, *Central City*
Simon Guggenheim, *Denver*

### REPRESENTATIVE AT LARGE

George W. Cook, *Denver*

### REPRESENTATIVES

Robert W. Bonynge, *Denver*
Warren A. Haggott, *Idaho Springs*

## CONNECTICUT

### SENATORS

Morgan G. Bulkeley, *Hartford*
Frank B. Brandegee, *New London*

### REPRESENTATIVE AT LARGE

George L. Lilley,[10] *Waterbury*

### REPRESENTATIVES

E. Stevens Henry, *Rockville*
Nehemiah D. Sperry, *New Haven*
Edwin W. Higgins, *Norwich*
Ebenezer J. Hill, *Norwalk*

## DELAWARE

### SENATORS

Henry A. du Pont, *Winterthur*
Harry A. Richardson, *Dover*

### REPRESENTATIVE AT LARGE

Hiram R. Burton, *Lewes*

## FLORIDA

### SENATORS

Stephen R. Mallory,[11] *Pensacola*
William J. Bryan,[12] *Jacksonville*
William H. Milton,[13] *Marianna*
James P. Taliaferro, *Jacksonville*

### REPRESENTATIVES

Stephen M. Sparkman, *Tampa*
Frank Clark, *Gainesville*
William B. Lamar, *Monticello*

## GEORGIA

### SENATORS

Augustus O. Bacon, *Macon*
Alexander S. Clay, *Marietta*

### REPRESENTATIVES

Charles G. Edwards, *Savannah*
James M. Griggs, *Dawson*
Elijah B. Lewis, *Montezuma*
William C. Adamson, *Carrollton*

---

## GEORGIA—Continued

### REPRESENTATIVES—CONTINUED

Leonidas F. Livingston, *Covington*
Charles L. Bartlett, *Macon*
Gordon Lee, *Chickamauga*
William M. Howard, *Lexington*
Thomas M. Bell, *Gainesville*
Thomas W. Hardwick, *Sandersville*
William G. Brantley, *Brunswick*

## IDAHO

### SENATORS

Weldon B. Heyburn, *Wallace*
William E. Borah, *Boise*

### REPRESENTATIVE AT LARGE

Burton L. French, *Moscow*

## ILLINOIS

### SENATORS

Shelby M. Cullom, *Springfield*
Albert J. Hopkins, *Aurora*

### REPRESENTATIVES

Martin B. Madden, *Chicago*
James R. Mann, *Chicago*
William W. Wilson, *Chicago*
James T. McDermott, *Chicago*
Adolph J. Sabath,[14] *Chicago*
William Lorimer, *Chicago*
Philip Knopf, *Chicago*
Charles McGavin,[15] *Chicago*
Henry S. Boutell, *Chicago*
George E. Foss, *Chicago*
Howard M. Snapp, *Joliet*
Charles E. Fuller, *Belvidere*
Frank O. Lowden, *Oregon*
James McKinney, *Aledo*
George W. Prince, *Galesburg*
Joseph V. Graff, *Peoria*
John A. Sterling, *Bloomington*
Joseph G. Cannon, *Danville*
William B. McKinley, *Champaign*
Henry T. Rainey, *Carrollton*
Benjamin F. Caldwell, *Chatham*
William A. Rodenberg, *East St. Louis*
Martin D. Foster, *Olney*
Pleasant T. Chapman, *Vienna*
George W. Smith,[16] *Murphysboro*
Napoleon B. Thistlewood,[17] *Cairo*

## INDIANA

### SENATORS

Albert J. Beveridge, *Indianapolis*
James A. Hemenway, *Boonville*

### REPRESENTATIVES

John H. Foster, *Evansville*
John C. Chaney, *Sullivan*
William E. Cox, *Jasper*
Lincoln Dixon, *North Vernon*
Elias S. Holliday, *Brazil*
James E. Watson, *Rushville*
Jesse Overstreet, *Indianapolis*
John A. M. Adair, *Portland*
Charles B. Landis, *Delphi*
Edgar D. Crumpacker, *Valparaiso*
George W. Rauch, *Marion*
Clarence C. Gilhams, *La Grange*
Abraham L. Brick,[18] *South Bend*
Henry A. Barnhart,[19] *Rochester*

## IOWA

### SENATORS

William B. Allison,[20] *Dubuque*
Albert B. Cummins,[21] *Des Moines*
Jonathan P. Dolliver, *Fort Dodge*

### REPRESENTATIVES

Charles A. Kennedy, *Montrose*
Albert F. Dawson, *Preston*
Benjamin P. Birdsall, *Clarion*
Gilbert N. Haugen, *Northwood*
Robert G. Cousins, *Tipton*
Daniel W. Hamilton, *Sigourney*
John A. T. Hull, *Des Moines*
William P. Hepburn, *Clarinda*
Walter I. Smith, *Council Bluffs*
James P. Conner, *Denison*
Elbert H. Hubbard, *Sioux City*

## KANSAS

### SENATORS

Chester I. Long, *Medicine Lodge*
Charles Curtis, *Topeka*

### REPRESENTATIVES

Daniel R. Anthony, Jr.,[22] *Leavenworth*
Charles F. Scott, *Iola*
Philip P. Campbell, *Pittsburg*
James M. Miller, *Council Grove*
William A. Calderhead, *Marysville*
William A. Reeder, *Logan*
Edmond H. Madison, *Dodge City*
Victor Murdock, *Wichita*

## KENTUCKY

### SENATORS

James B. McCreary, *Richmond*
Thomas H. Paynter, *Greenup*

### REPRESENTATIVES

Ollie M. James, *Marion*
Augustus O. Stanley, *Henderson*
Addison D. James, *Penrod*
Ben Johnson, *Bardstown*
J. Swagar Sherley, *Louisville*
Joseph L. Rhinock, *Covington*
William P. Kimball, *Lexington*
Harvey Helm, *Stanford*
Joseph B. Bennett, *Greenup*
John W. Langley, *Pikeville*
Don C. Edwards, *London*

## LOUISIANA

### SENATORS

Samuel D. McEnery, *New Orleans*
Murphy J. Foster, *Franklin*

### REPRESENTATIVES

Adolph Meyer,[23] *New Orleans*
Albert Estopinal,[24] *Estopinal*
Robert C. Davey,[25] *New Orleans*
Robert F. Broussard, *New Iberia*
John T. Watkins, *Minden*
Joseph E. Ransdell, *Lake Providence*
George K. Favrot, *Baton Rouge*
Arsène P. Pujo, *Lake Charles*

## MAINE

### SENATORS

Eugene Hale, *Ellsworth*
William P. Frye, *Lewiston*

### REPRESENTATIVES

Amos L. Allen, *Alfred*
Charles E. Littlefield,[26] *Rockland*
John P. Swasey,[27] *Canton*
Edwin C. Burleigh, *Augusta*
Llewellyn Powers,[28] *Houlton*
Frank E. Guernsey,[29] *Dover*

## MARYLAND

### SENATORS

Isidor Rayner, *Baltimore*
William Pinkney Whyte,[30] *Baltimore*
John Walter Smith,[31] *Snow Hill*

### REPRESENTATIVES

William H. Jackson, *Salisbury*
J. Fred. C. Talbott, *Towson*
Harry B. Wolf, *Baltimore*

---

[14] Election unsuccessfully contested by Anthony Michalek.
[15] Election unsuccessfully contested by Stanley H. Kunz.
[16] Died November 30, 1907, before Congress assembled.
[17] Elected to fill vacancy caused by death of George W. Smith, and took his seat February 26, 1908.
[18] Died April 7, 1908.
[19] Elected to fill vacancy caused by death of Abraham L. Brick, and took his seat December 7, 1908.
[20] Died August 4, 1908.

[21] Elected to fill vacancy caused by death of William B. Allison, and took his seat December 8, 1908.
[22] Elected to fill vacancy caused by resignation of Representative-elect Charles Curtis, in preceding Congress, and took his seat December 2, 1907.
[23] Died March 8, 1908.
[24] Elected to fill vacancy caused by death of Adolph Meyer, and took his seat December 7, 1908.
[25] Died Dec. 26, 1908, before the commencement of the Sixty-first Congress, to which he had been reelected.
[26] Resigned effective September 30, 1908.

[27] Elected to fill vacancy caused by resignation of Charles E. Littlefield, and took his seat December 7, 1908.
[28] Died July 28, 1908.
[29] Elected to fill vacancy caused by death of Llewellyn Powers, and took his seat December 7, 1908.
[30] Died March 17, 1908.
[31] Elected to fill vacancy caused by death of William Pinkney Whyte, and took his seat March 26, 1908. (See U.S. Senate Election, Expulsion and Censure Cases, 1793-1990, Senate Document 103-33, pp. 279-80.)

John Gill, Jr., *Baltimore*
Sydney E. Mudd, *La Plata*
George A. Pearre, *Cumberland*

## MASSACHUSETTS

### SENATORS

Henry Cabot Lodge, *Nahant*
W. Murray Crane, *Dalton*

### REPRESENTATIVES

George P. Lawrence, *North Adams*
Frederick H. Gillett, *Springfield*
Charles G. Washburn, *Worcester*
Charles Q. Tirrell, *Natick*
Butler Ames, *Lowell*
Agustus P. Gardner, *Hamilton*
Ernest W. Roberts, *Chelsea*
Samuel W. McCall, *Winchester*
John A. Keliher, *Boston*
Joseph F. O'Connell, *Boston*
Andrew J. Peters, *Boston*
John W. Weeks, *Newton*
William S. Greene, *Fall River*
William C. Lovering, *Taunton*

## MICHIGAN

### SENATORS

Julius C. Burrows, *Kalamazoo*
William Alden Smith, *Grand Rapids*

### REPRESENTATIVES

Edwin Denby, *Detroit*
Charles E. Townsend, *Jackson*
Washington Gardner, *Albion*
Edward L. Hamilton, *Niles*
Gerrit J. Dickema,[32] *Holland*
Samuel W. Smith, *Pontiac*
Henry McMorran, *Port Huron*
Joseph W. Fordney, *Saginaw*
James C. McLaughlin, *Muskegon*
George A. Loud, *Au Sable*
Archibald B. Darragh, *St. Louis*
H. Olin Young, *Ishpeming*

## MINNESOTA

### SENATORS

Knute Nelson, *Alexandria*
Moses E. Clapp, *St. Paul*

### REPRESENTATIVES

James A. Tawney, *Winona*
Winfield S. Hammond, *St. James*
Charles R. Davis, *St. Peter*
Frederick C. Stevens, *St. Paul*
Frank M. Nye, *Minneapolis*
Charles A. Lindbergh, *Little Falls*
Andrew G. Volstead, *Granite Falls*
J. Adam Bede, *Pine City*
Halvor Steenerson, *Crookston*

## MISSISSIPPI

### SENATORS

Hernando D. Money, *Mississippi City*
Anselm J. McLaurin, *Brandon*

### REPRESENTATIVES

Ezekiel S. Candler, Jr., *Corinth*
Thomas Spight, *Ripley*
Benjamin G. Humphreys, *Greenville*
Wilson S. Hill, *Winona*
Adam M. Byrd, *Philadelphia*
Eaton J. Bowers, *Bay St. Louis*
Frank A. McLain, *Gloster*
John Sharp Williams, *Yazoo City*

## MISSOURI

### SENATORS

William J. Stone, *Jefferson City*
William Warner, *Kansas City*

### REPRESENTATIVES

James T. Lloyd, *Shelbyville*
William W. Rucker, *Keytesville*
Joshua W. Alexander, *Gallatin*
Charles F. Booher, *Savannah*
Edgar C. Ellis, *Kansas City*
David A. De Armond, *Butler*
Courtney W. Hamlin, *Springfield*
Dorsey W. Shackleford, *Jefferson City*
James Beauchamp Clark, *Bowling Green*
Richard Bartholdt, *St. Louis*
Henry S. Caulfield, *St. Louis*
Harry M. Coudrey, *St. Louis*
Madison R. Smith, *Farmington*
Joseph J. Russell, *Charleston*
Thomas Hackney, *Carthage*
J. Robert Lamar, *Houston*

## MONTANA

### SENATORS

Thomas H. Carter, *Helena*
Joseph M. Dixon, *Missoula*

### REPRESENTATIVE AT LARGE

Charles N. Pray, *Fort Benton*

## NEBRASKA

### SENATORS

Elmer J. Burkett, *Lincoln*
Norris Brown, *Kearney*

### REPRESENTATIVES

Ernest M. Pollard, *Nehawka*
Gilbert M. Hitchcock, *Omaha*
John F. Boyd, *Neligh*
Edmund H. Hinshaw, *Fairbury*
George W. Norris, *McCook*
Moses P. Kinkaid, *O'Neill*

## NEVADA

### SENATORS

Francis G. Newlands, *Reno*
George S. Nixon, *Reno*

### REPRESENTATIVE AT LARGE

George A. Bartlett, *Tonopah*

## NEW HAMPSHIRE

### SENATORS

Jacob H. Gallinger, *Concord*
Henry E. Burnham, *Manchester*

### REPRESENTATIVES

Cyrus A. Sulloway, *Manchester*
Frank D. Currier, *Canaan*

## NEW JERSEY

### SENATORS

John Kean, *Elizabeth*
Frank O. Briggs, *Trenton*

### REPRESENTATIVES

Henry C. Loudenslager, *Paulsboro*
John J. Gardner, *Atlantic City*
Benjamin F. Howell, *New Brunswick*
Ira W. Wood, *Trenton*
Charles N. Fowler, *Elizabeth*
William Hughes, *Paterson*
Richard Wayne Parker, *Newark*
Le Gage Pratt, *East Orange*
Eugene W. Leake, *Jersey City*
James A. Hamill, *Jersey City*

## NEW YORK

### SENATORS

Thomas C. Platt, *Owego*
Chauncey M. Depew, *Peekskill*

### REPRESENTATIVES

William W. Cocks, *Westbury*
George H. Lindsay, *Brooklyn*
Charles T. Dunwell,[33] *Brooklyn*
Otto G. Foelker,[34] *Brooklyn*
Charles B. Law, *Brooklyn*
George E. Waldo, *Brooklyn*
William M. Calder, *Brooklyn*
John J. Fitzgerald, *Brooklyn*
Daniel J. Riordan, *New York City*
Henry M. Goldfogle, *New York City*
William Sulzer, *New York City*
Charles V. Fornes, *New York City*
W. Bourke Cockran, *New York City*
Herbert Parsons, *New York City*
William Willett, Jr., *Far Rockaway*
J. Van Vechten Olcott, *New York City*
Francis B. Harrison, *New York City*
William S. Bennet, *New York City*
Joseph A. Goulden, *Fordham*
John E. Andrus, *Yonkers*
Thomas W. Bradley, *Walden*
Samuel McMillan, *Lake Mahopac*
William H. Draper, *Troy*
George N. Southwick, *Albany*

---

[32] Elected to fill vacancy caused by resignation of Representative-elect William Alden Smith, in preceding Congress, and took his seat December 2, 1907.

[33] Died June 12, 1908.
[34] Elected to fill vacancy caused by death of

Charles T. Dunwell, and took his seat December 7, 1908.

## NEW YORK—Continued

REPRESENTATIVES—CONTINUED

George W. Fairchild, *Oneonta*
Cyrus Durey, *Johnstown*
George R. Malby, *Ogdensburg*
James S. Sherman, *Utica*
Charles L. Knapp, *Lowville*
Michael E. Driscoll, *Syracuse*
John W. Dwight, *Dryden*
Sereno E. Payne, *Auburn*
James B. Perkins, *Rochester*
J. Sloat Fassett, *Elmira*
Peter A. Porter, *Niagara Falls*
William H. Ryan, *Buffalo*
De Alva S. Alexander, *Buffalo*
Edward B. Vreeland, *Salamanca*

## NORTH CAROLINA

SENATORS

Furnifold McL. Simmons, *Trenton*
Lee S. Overman, *Salisbury*

REPRESENTATIVES

John H. Small, *Washington*
Claude Kitchin, *Scotland Neck*
Charles R. Thomas, *New Bern*
Edward W. Pou, *Smithfield*
William W. Kitchin,[35] *Roxboro*
Hannibal L. Godwin, *Dunn*
Robert N. Page, *Biscoe*
Richard N. Hackett, *Wilkesboro*
Edwin Y. Webb, *Shelby*
William T. Crawford, *Waynesville*

## NORTH DAKOTA

SENATORS

Henry C. Hansbrough, *Devils Lake*
Porter J. McCumber, *Wahpeton*

REPRESENTATIVES AT LARGE

Thomas F. Marshall, *Oakes*
Asle J. Gronna, *Lakota*

## OHIO

SENATORS

Joseph B. Foraker, *Cincinnati*
Charles W. F. Dick, *Akron*

REPRESENTATIVES

Nicholas Longworth, *Cincinnati*
Herman P. Goebel, *Cincinnati*
J. Eugene Harding, *Excello*
William E. Tou Velle, *Celina*
Timothy T. Ansberry, *Defiance*
Matthew R. Denver, *Wilmington*

J. Warren Keifer, *Springfield*
Ralph D. Cole, *Findlay*
Isaac R. Sherwood, *Toledo*
Henry T. Bannon, *Portsmouth*
Albert Douglas, *Chillicothe*
Edward L. Taylor, Jr., *Columbus*
Grant E. Mouser, *Marion*
J. Ford Laning, *Norwalk*
Beman G. Dawes, *Marietta*
Capell L. Weems, *St. Clairsville*
William A. Ashbrook, *Johnstown*
James Kennedy, *Youngstown*
W. Aubrey Thomas, *Niles*
L. Paul Howland, *Cleveland*
Theodore E. Burton,[36] *Cleveland*

## OKLAHOMA[37]

SENATORS

Thomas P. Gore,[38] *Lawton*
Robert L. Owen,[39] *Muskogee*

REPRESENTATIVES[40]

Bird S. McGuire, *Pawnee*
Elmer L. Fulton, *Oklahoma City*
James S. Davenport, *Vinita*
Charles D. Carter, *Ardmore*
Scott Ferris, *Lawton*

## OREGON

SENATORS

Charles W. Fulton, *Astoria*
Jonathan Bourne, Jr., *Portland*

REPRESENTATIVES

Willis C. Hawley, *Salem*
William R. Ellis, *Pendleton*

## PENNSYLVANIA

SENATORS

Boies Penrose, *Philadelphia*
Philander C. Knox,[41] *Pittsburgh*

REPRESENTATIVES

Henry H. Bingham, *Philadelphia*
John E. Reyburn,[42] *Philadelphia*
Joel Cook,[43] *Philadelphia*
J. Hampton Moore, *Philadelphia*
Reuben O. Moon, *Philadelphia*
William W. Foulkrod, *Philadelphia*
George D. McCreary, *Philadelphia*
Thomas S. Butler, *West Chester*
Irving P. Wanger, *Norristown*
Henry B. Cassel, *Marietta*
Thomas D. Nicholls, *Scranton*
John T. Lenahan, *Wilkes-Barre*
Charles N. Brumm,[44] *Minersville*

John H. Rothermel, *Reading*
George W. Kipp, *Towanda*
William B. Wilson, *Blossburg*
John G. McHenry, *Benton*
Benjamin K. Focht, *Lewisburg*
Marlin E. Olmsted, *Harrisburg*
John M. Reynolds, *Bedford*
Daniel F. Lafean, *York*
Charles F. Barclay, *Sinnemahoning*
George F. Huff, *Greensburg*
Allen F. Cooper, *Uniontown*
Ernest F. Acheson, *Washington*
Arthur L. Bates, *Meadville*
J. Davis Brodhead, *South Bethlehem*
Joseph G. Beale, *Leechburg*
Nelson P. Wheeler, *Endeavor*
William H. Graham, *Allegheny*
John Dalzell, *Pittsburgh*
James F. Burke, *Pittsburgh*
Andrew J. Barchfeld, *Pittsburgh*

## RHODE ISLAND

SENATORS

Nelson W. Aldrich, *Providence*
George P. Wetmore,[45] *Newport*

REPRESENTATIVES

Daniel L. D. Granger,[46] *Providence*
Adin B. Capron, *Stillwater*

## SOUTH CAROLINA

SENATORS

Benjamin R. Tillman, *Trenton*
Asbury C. Latimer,[47] *Belton*
Frank B. Gary,[48] *Abbeville*

REPRESENTATIVES

George S. Legare,[49] *Charleston*
James O'H. Patterson,[50] *Barnwell*
Wyatt Aiken, *Abbeville*
Joseph T. Johnson, *Spartanburg*
David E. Finley, *Yorkville*
J. Edwin Ellerbe, *Marion*
Asbury F. Lever,[51] *Lexington*

## SOUTH DAKOTA

SENATORS

Robert J. Gamble, *Yankton*
Alfred B. Kittredge, *Sioux Falls*

REPRESENTATIVES AT LARGE

Philo Hall, *Brookings*
William H. Parker,[52] *Deadwood*
Eben W. Martin,[53] *Deadwood*

---

[35] Resigned effective January 11, 1909, having been elected Governor.
[36] Reelected to the Sixty-first Congress, but resigned effective March 4, 1909, having been elected Senator.
[37] Admitted as a State into the Union November 16, 1907.
[38] Took his seat December 16, 1907; term to expire, as determined by lot, March 3, 1909.
[39] Took his seat December 16, 1907; term to expire, as determined by lot, March 3, 1913.
[40] All Representatives took their seats December 2, 1907.

[41] Resigned effective March 4, 1909, having been appointed Secretary of State.
[42] Resigned March 31, 1907, before Congress assembled, having been elected mayor of Philadelphia.
[43] Elected to fill vacancy caused by resignation of John E. Reyburn, and took his seat December 2, 1907.
[44] Resigned January 4, 1909.
[45] Elected to fill vacancy in term beginning March 4, 1907, caused by failure of legislature to elect, and took his seat January 27, 1908; vacancy in this class from March 4, 1907, to January 21, 1908.
[46] Died February 14, 1909.
[47] Died February 20, 1908.

[48] Elected to fill vacancy caused by death of Asbury C. Latimer, and took his seat March 16, 1908.
[49] Election unsuccessfully contested by Aaron P. Prioleau.
[50] Election unsuccessfully contested by Isaac Myers.
[51] Election unsuccessfully contested by Alexander D. Dantzer.
[52] Died June 26, 1908.
[53] Elected to fill vacancy caused by death of William H. Parker, and took his seat December 7, 1908.

## TENNESSEE

### SENATORS

James B. Frazier, *Chattanooga*
Robert L. Taylor, *Nashville*

### REPRESENTATIVES

Walter P. Brownlow, *Jonesboro*
Nathan W. Hale, *Knoxville*
John A. Moon, *Chattanooga*
Cordell Hull, *Carthage*
William C. Houston, *Woodbury*
John W. Gaines, *Nashville*
Lemuel P. Padgett, *Columbia*
Thetus W. Sims, *Linden*
Finis J. Garrett, *Dresden*
George W. Gordon, *Memphis*

## TEXAS

### SENATORS

Charles A. Culberson, *Dallas*
Joseph W. Bailey, *Gainesville*

### REPRESENTATIVES

Morris Sheppard, *Texarkana*
Samuel B. Cooper, *Beaumont*
Gordon J. Russell, *Tyler*
Choice B. Randell, *Sherman*
Jack Beall, *Waxahachie*
Rufus Hardy, *Corsicana*
Alexander W. Gregg, *Palestine*
John M. Moore, *Richmond*
George F. Burgess, *Gonzales*
Albert S. Burleson, *Austin*
Robert L. Henry, *Waco*
Oscar W. Gillespie, *Fort Worth*
John H. Stephens, *Vernon*
James L. Slayden, *San Antonio*
John N. Garner, *Uvalde*
William R. Smith, *Colorado*

## UTAH

### SENATORS

Reed Smoot, *Provo*
George Sutherland, *Salt Lake City*

### REPRESENTATIVE AT LARGE

Joseph Howell, *Logan*

## VERMONT

### SENATORS

Redfield Proctor,[54] *Proctor*
John W. Stewart,[55] *Middlebury*
Carroll S. Page,[56] *Hyde Park*
William P. Dillingham, *Waterbury*

### REPRESENTATIVES

David J. Foster, *Burlington*
Kittredge Haskins, *Brattleboro*

## VIRGINIA

### SENATORS

John W. Daniel, *Lynchburg*
Thomas S. Martin, *Charlottesville*

### REPRESENTATIVES

William A. Jones, *Warsaw*
Harry L. Maynard, *Portsmouth*
John Lamb, *Richmond*
Francis R. Lassiter, *Petersburg*
Edward W. Saunders, *Rockymount*
Carter Glass, *Lynchburg*
James Hay, *Madison*
Charles C. Carlin,[57] *Alexandria*
Campbell Slemp,[58] *Big Stone Gap*
C. Bascom Slemp,[59] *Big Stone Gap*
Henry D. Flood, *Appomattox*

## WASHINGTON

### SENATORS

Levi Ankeny, *Walla Walla*
Samuel H. Piles, *Seattle*

### REPRESENTATIVES AT LARGE

Wesley L. Jones, *North Yakima*
Francis W. Cushman, *Tacoma*
William E. Humphrey, *Seattle*

## WEST VIRGINIA

### SENATORS

Stephen B. Elkins, *Elkins*
Nathan B. Scott, *Wheeling*

### REPRESENTATIVES

William P. Hubbard, *Wheeling*
George C. Sturgiss, *Morgantown*
Joseph Holt Gaines, *Charleston*
Harry C. Woodyard, *Spencer*
James A. Hughes, *Huntington*

## WISCONSIN

### SENATORS

John C. Spooner,[60] *Madison*
Isaac Stephenson,[61] *Marinette*
Robert M. La Follette, *Madison*

### REPRESENTATIVES

Henry Allen Cooper, *Racine*
John M. Nelson, *Madison*
James W. Murphy, *Platteville*

William J. Cary, *Milwaukee*
William H. Stafford, *Milwaukee*
Charles H. Weisse, *Sheboygan Falls*
John J. Esch, *La Crosse*
James H. Davidson, *Oshkosh*
Gustav Küstermann, *Green Bay*
Elmer A. Morse, *Antigo*
John J. Jenkins, *Chippewa Falls*

## WYOMING

### SENATORS

Clarence D. Clark, *Evanston*
Francis E. Warren, *Cheyenne*

### REPRESENTATIVE AT LARGE

Frank W. Mondell, *Newcastle*

## TERRITORY OF ALASKA

### DELEGATE

Thomas Cale, *Fairbanks*

## TERRITORY OF ARIZONA

### DELEGATE

Marcus A. Smith, *Tucson*

## TERRITORY OF HAWAII

### DELEGATE

Jonah K. Kalanianaole, *Honolulu*

## TERRITORY OF NEW MEXICO

### DELEGATE

William H. Andrews,[62] *Albuquerque*

## TERRITORY OF OKLAHOMA[63]

Vacant

## PHILIPPINE ISLANDS[64]

### RESIDENT COMMISSIONERS

Benito Legarda,[65] *Manila*
Pablo Ocampo,[65] *Manila*

## PORTO RICO

### RESIDENT COMMISSIONER

Tulio Larrinaga, *San Juan*

---

[54] Died March 4, 1908.
[55] Appointed to fill vacancy caused by death of Redfield Proctor, and took his seat March 30, 1908.
[56] Elected to fill vacancy caused by death of Redfeild Proctor, and took his seat December 7, 1908.
[57] Elected to fill vacancy caused by death of Representative-elect John F. Rixey, in preceding Congress, and took his seat December 2, 1907.
[58] Died October 13, 1907, before Congress assembled.
[59] Elected to fill vacancy caused by death of Campbell Slemp, and took his seat January 6, 1908.
[60] Resigned April 30, 1907.
[61] Elected to fill vacancy caused by resignation of John C. Spooner, and took his seat December 2, 1907.
[62] Election unsuccessfully contested by Octavius A. Larrazola.
[63] Granted statehood November 16, 1907.
[64] Part of the territory ceded to the United States by Spain by the treaty of Paris of December 10, 1898; granted the right to elect two Resident Commissioners to the United States by act of July 1, 1902.
[65] Elected November 22, 1907, for a term of two years; granted the privileges of the floor of the House of Representatives, with the right of debate, February 4, 1908.

# 61ST CONGRESS

## MARCH 4, 1909, TO MARCH 3, 1911

FIRST SESSION— *March 15, 1909, to August 5, 1909*
SECOND SESSION— *December 6, 1909, to June 25, 1910*
THIRD SESSION— *December 5, 1910, to March 3, 1911*
SPECIAL SESSION OF THE SENATE— *March 4, 1909, to March 6, 1909*

VICE PRESIDENT OF THE UNITED STATES— JAMES S. SHERMAN, of New York
PRESIDENT PRO TEMPORE OF THE SENATE— WILLIAM P. FRYE, of Maine
SECRETARY OF THE SENATE— CHARLES G. BENNETT, of New York
SERGEANT AT ARMS OF THE SENATE— DANIEL M. RANSDELL, of Indiana

SPEAKER OF THE HOUSE OF REPRESENTATIVES— JOSEPH G. CANNON,[1] of Illinois
CLERK OF THE HOUSE— ALEXANDER MCDOWELL,[2] of Pennsylvania
SERGEANT AT ARMS OF THE HOUSE— HENRY CASSON, of Wisconsin
DOORKEEPER OF THE HOUSE— FRANK B. LYON, of New York
POSTMASTER OF THE HOUSE— SAMUEL LANGUM

James S. Sherman
Vice President

Joseph G. Cannon
Speaker

## ALABAMA

### SENATORS
John H. Bankhead, *Fayette*
Joseph F. Johnston, *Birmingham*

### REPRESENTATIVES
George W. Taylor, *Demopolis*
S. Hubert Dent, Jr., *Montgomery*
Henry D. Clayton, *Eufaula*
William B. Craig, *Selma*
J. Thomas Heflin, *Lafayette*
Richmond P. Hobson, *Greensboro*
John L. Burnett, *Gadsden*
William Richardson, *Huntsville*
Oscar W. Underwood, *Birmingham*

## ARKANSAS

### SENATORS
James P. Clarke, *Little Rock*
Jeff Davis, *Little Rock*

### REPRESENTATIVES
Robert B. Macon, *Helena*
William A. Oldfield, *Batesville*
John C. Floyd, *Yellville*
William B. Cravens, *Fort Smith*
Charles C. Reid, *Morrillton*
Joseph T. Robinson, *Lonoke*
Robert M. Wallace, *Magnolia*

## CALIFORNIA

### SENATORS
George C. Perkins, *Oakland*
Frank P. Flint, *Los Angeles*

### REPRESENTATIVES
William F. Englebright, *Nevada City*
Duncan E. McKinlay, *Santa Rosa*
Joseph R. Knowland, *Alameda*
Julius Kahn, *San Francisco*
Everis A. Hayes, *San Jose*
James C. Needham, *Modesto*
James McLachlan, *Pasadena*
Sylvester C. Smith, *Bakersfield*

## COLORADO

### SENATORS
Simon Guggenheim, *Denver*
Charles J. Hughes, Jr.,[3] *Denver*

### REPRESENTATIVE AT LARGE
Edward T. Taylor, *Glenwood Springs*

### REPRESENTATIVES
Atterson W. Rucker, *Fort Logan*
John A. Martin, *Pueblo*

## CONNECTICUT

### SENATORS
Morgan G. Bulkeley, *Hartford*
Frank B. Brandegee, *New London*

### REPRESENTATIVE AT LARGE
John Q. Tilson, *New Haven*

### REPRESENTATIVES
E. Stevens Henry, *Rockville*
Nehemiah D. Sperry, *New Haven*
Edwin W. Higgins, *Norwich*
Ebenezer J. Hill, *Norwalk*

## DELAWARE

### SENATORS
Henry A. du Pont, *Winterthur*
Harry A. Richardson, *Dover*

### REPRESENTATIVE AT LARGE
William H. Heald, *Wilmington*

## FLORIDA

### SENATORS
James P. Taliaferro, *Jacksonville*
Duncan U. Fletcher,[4] *Jacksonville*

### REPRESENTATIVES
Stephen M. Sparkman, *Tampa*
Frank Clark, *Gainesville*
Dannitte H. Mays, *Monticello*

## GEORGIA

### SENATORS
Augustus O. Bacon, *Macon*
Alexander S. Clay,[5] *Marietta*
Joseph M. Terrell,[6] *Greenville*

### REPRESENTATIVES
Charles G. Edwards, *Savannah*
James M. Griggs,[7] *Dawson*
Seaborn A. Roddenberry,[8]
    *Thomasville*
Dudley M. Hughes, *Danville*
William C. Adamson, *Carrollton*
Leonidas F. Livingston, *Covington*
Charles L. Bartlett, *Macon*
Gordon Lee, *Chickamauga*
William M. Howard, *Lexington*
Thomas M. Bell, *Gainesville*
Thomas W. Hardwick, *Sandersville*
William G. Brantley, *Brunswick*

---

[1] Reelected March 15, 1909.
[2] Reelected March 15, 1909.
[3] Died January 11, 1911.
[4] Appointed to fill vacancy in the term beginning

March 4, 1909, and took his seat March 4, 1909; subsequently elected.
[5] Died November 13, 1910.
[6] Appointed to fill vacancy caused by death of

Alexander S. Clay, and took his seat December 6, 1910.
[7] Died January 5, 1910.
[8] Elected to fill vacancy caused by death of James M. Griggs, and took his seat February 28, 1910.

[282]

## IDAHO

### SENATORS

Weldon B. Heyburn, *Wallace*
William E. Borah, *Boise*

### REPRESENTATIVE AT LARGE

Thomas R. Hamer, *St. Anthony*

## ILLINOIS

### SENATORS

Shelby M. Cullom, *Springfield*
William Lorimer,[9] *Chicago*

### REPRESENTATIVES

Martin B. Madden, *Chicago*
James R. Mann, *Chicago*
William W. Wilson, *Chicago*
James T. McDermott, *Chicago*
Adolph J. Sabath, *Chicago*
William Lorimer,[10] *Chicago*
William J. Moxley,[11] *Chicago*
Frederick Lundin, *Chicago*
Thomas Gallagher, *Chicago*
Henry S. Boutell, *Chicago*
George E. Foss, *Chicago*
Howard M. Snapp, *Joliet*
Charles E. Fuller, *Belvidere*
Frank O. Lowden, *Oregon*
James McKinney, *Aledo*
George W. Prince, *Galesburg*
Joseph V. Graff, *Peoria*
John A. Sterling, *Bloomington*
Joseph G. Cannon, *Danville*
William B. McKinley, *Champaign*
Henry T. Rainey, *Carrollton*
James M. Graham, *Springfield*
William A. Rodenberg, *East St. Louis*
Martin D. Foster, *Olney*
Pleasant T. Chapman, *Vienna*
Napoleon B. Thistlewood, *Cairo*

## INDIANA

### SENATORS

Albert J. Beveridge, *Indianapolis*
Benjamin F. Shively, *South Bend*

### REPRESENTATIVES

John W. Boehne, *Evansville*
William A. Cullop, *Vincennes*
William E. Cox, *Jasper*
Lincoln Dixon, *North Vernon*
Ralph W. Moss, *Center Point*
William O. Barnard, *Newcastle*
Charles A. Korbly, *Indianapolis*
John A. M. Adair, *Portland*
Martin A. Morrison, *Frankfort*
Edgar D. Crumpacker, *Valparaiso*

George W. Rauch, *Marion*
Cyrus Cline, *Angola*
Henry A. Barnhart, *Rochester*

## IOWA

### SENATORS

Jonathan P. Dolliver,[12] *Fort Dodge*
Lafayette Young,[13] *Des Moines*
Albert B. Cummins, *Des Moines*

### REPRESENTATIVES

Charles A. Kennedy, *Montrose*
Albert F. Dawson, *Preston*
Charles E. Pickett, *Waterloo*
Gilbert N. Haugen, *Northwood*
James W. Good, *Cedar Rapids*
Nathan E. Kendall, *Albia*
John A. T. Hull, *Des Moines*
William D. Jamieson,[14] *Shenandoah*
Walter I. Smith, *Council Bluffs*
Frank P. Woods, *Estherville*
Elbert H. Hubbard, *Sioux City*

## KANSAS

### SENATORS

Charles Curtis, *Topeka*
Joseph L. Bristow, *Salina*

### REPRESENTATIVES

Daniel R. Anthony, Jr., *Leavenworth*
Charles F. Scott, *Iola*
Philip P. Campbell, *Pittsburg*
James M. Miller, *Council Grove*
William A. Calderhead, *Marysville*
William A. Reeder, *Logan*
Edmond H. Madison, *Dodge City*
Victor Murdock, *Wichita*

## KENTUCKY

### SENATORS

Thomas H. Paynter, *Frankfort*
William O. Bradley, *Louisville*

### REPRESENTATIVES

Ollie M. James, *Marion*
Augustus O. Stanley, *Henderson*
Robert Y. Thomas, Jr., *Central City*
Ben Johnson, *Bardstown*
J. Swagar Sherley, *Louisville*
Joseph L. Rhinock, *Covington*
James C. Cantrill, *Georgetown*
Harvey Helm, *Stanford*
Joseph B. Bennett, *Greenup*
John W. Langley, *Pikeville*
Don C. Edwards, *London*

## LOUISIANA

### SENATORS

Samuel D. McEnery,[15] *New Orleans*
John R. Thornton,[16] *Alexandria*
Murphy J. Foster, *Franklin*

### REPRESENTATIVES

Albert Estopinal,[17] *Estopinal*
Samuel L. Gilmore,[18] *New Orleans*
H.Garland Dupré,[19] *New Orleans*
Robert F. Broussard, *New Iberea*
John T. Watkins, *Minden*
Joseph E. Ransdell, *Lake Providence*
Robert C. Wickliffe, *St. Francisville*
Arsène P. Pujo, *Lake Charles*

## MAINE

### SENATORS

Eugene Hale, *Ellsworth*
William P. Frye, *Lewiston*

### REPRESENTATIVES

Amos L. Allen,[20] *Alfred*
John P. Swasey, *Canton*
Edwin C. Burleigh, *Augusta*
Frank E. Guernsey, *Dover*

## MARYLAND

### SENATORS

Isidor Rayner, *Baltimore*
John Walter Smith, *Snow Hill*

### REPRESENTATIVES

J. Harry Covington, *Easton*
J. Fred. C. Talbott, *Towson*
John Kronmiller, *Baltimore*
John Gill, Jr., *Baltimore*
Sydney E. Mudd, *La Plata*
George A. Pearre, *Cumberland*

## MASSACHUSETTS

### SENATORS

Henry Cabot Lodge, *Nahant*
W. Murray Crane, *Dalton*

### REPRESENTATIVES

George P. Lawrence, *North Adams*
Frederick H. Gillett, *Springfield*
Charles G. Washburn, *Worcester*
Charles Q. Tirrell,[21] *Natick*
John J. Mitchell,[22] *Marlboro*
Butler Ames, *Lowell*
Augustus P. Gardner, *Hamilton*

---

[9] Elected to fill vacancy in the term beginning March 4, 1909, and took his seat June 18, 1909; vacancy in this class from March 4, 1909, to May 27, 1909, because of failure of legislature to elect; and then until June 17, 1909, because Mr. Lorimer did not resign his seat in the House until the last-named date.

[10] Resigned, effective June 17, 1909, having been elected Senator.

[11] Elected to fill vacancy caused by resignation of William Lorimer, and took his seat December 10, 1909.

[12] Died October 15, 1910.

[13] Appointed to fill vacancy caused by death of Jonathan P. Dolliver; took his seat December 6, 1910.

[14] Election unsuccessfully contested by William P. Hepburn.

[15] Died June 28, 1910.

[16] Elected to fill vacancy caused by death of Samuel D. McEnery, and took his seat December 12, 1910; vacancy from June 29, 1910, to December 6, 1910.

[17] Election unsuccessfully contested by Henry C. Warmoth.

[18] Elected to fill vacancy caused by death of Representative-elect Robert C. Davey, in preceding Congress, and took his seat April 22, 1909; died July 18, 1910.

[19] Elected to fill vacancy caused by death of Samuel L. Gilmore, and took his seat December 12, 1910.

[20] Died February 20, 1911.

[21] Died July 31, 1910.

[22] Elected to fill vacancy caused by death of Charles Q. Tirrell, and took his seat December 5, 1910.

## MASSACHUSETTS—Continued

### REPRESENTATIVES—CONTINUED

Ernest W. Roberts, *Chelsea*
Samuel W. McCall, *Winchester*
John A. Keliher, *Boston*
Joseph F. O'Connell,[23] *Boston*
Andrew J. Peters, *Boston*
John W. Weeks, *Newton*
William S. Greene, *Fall River*
William C. Lovering,[24] *Taunton*
Eugene N. Foss,[25] *Jamaica Plains*

## MICHIGAN

### SENATORS

Julius C. Burrows, *Kalamazoo*
William Alden Smith, *Grand Rapids*

### REPRESENTATIVES

Edwin Denby, *Detroit*
Charles E. Townsend, *Jackson*
Washington Gardner, *Albion*
Edward L. Hamilton, *Niles*
Gerrit J. Diekema, *Holland*
Samuel W. Smith, *Pontiac*
Henry McMorran, *Port Huron*
Joseph W. Fordney, *Saginaw*
James C. McLaughlin, *Muskegon*
George A. Loud, *Au Sable*
Francis H. Dodds, *Mount Pleasant*
H. Olin Young, *Ishpeming*

## MINNESOTA

### SENATORS

Knute Nelson, *Alexandria*
Moses E. Clapp, *St. Paul*

### REPRESENTATIVES

James A. Tawney, *Winona*
Winfield S. Hammond, *St. James*
Charles R. Davis, *St. Peter*
Frederick C. Stevens, *St. Paul*
Frank M. Nye, *Minneapolis*
Charles A. Lindbergh, *Little Falls*
Andrew J. Volstead, *Granite Falls*
Clarence B. Miller, *Duluth*
Halvor Steenerson, *Crookston*

## MISSISSIPPI

### SENATORS

Hernando D. Money, *Mississippi City*
Anselm J. McLaurin,[26] *Brandon*
James Gordon,[27] *Okolona*
Le Roy Percy,[28] *Greenville*

### REPRESENTATIVES

Ezekiel S. Candler, Jr., *Corinth*
Thomas Spight, *Ripley*
Benjamin G. Humphreys, *Greenville*
Thomas U. Sisson, *Winona*

Adam M. Byrd, *Philadelphia*
Eaton J. Bowers, *Bay St. Louis*
William A. Dickson, *Centerville*
James W. Collier, *Vicksburg*

## MISSOURI

### SENATORS

William J. Stone, *Jefferson City*
William Warner, *Kansas City*

### REPRESENTATIVES

James T. Lloyd, *Shelbyville*
William W. Rucker, *Keytesville*
Joshua W. Alexander, *Gallatin*
Charles F. Booher, *Savannah*
William P. Borland, *Kansas City*
David A. De Armond,[29] *Butler*
Clement C. Dickinson,[30] *Clinton*
Courtney W. Hamlin, *Springfield*
Dorsey W. Shackleford, *Jefferson City*
James Beauchamp Clark, *Bowling Green*
Richard Bartholdt, *St. Louis*
Patrick F. Gill, *St. Louis*
Harry M. Coudrey, *St. Louis*
Politte Elvins, *Elvins*
Charles A. Crow, *Caruthersville*
Charles H. Morgan, *Joplin*
Arthur P. Murphy, *Rolla*

## MONTANA

### SENATORS

Thomas H. Carter, *Helena*
Joseph M. Dixon, *Missoula*

### REPRESENTATIVE AT LARGE

Charles N. Pray, *Fort Benton*

## NEBRASKA

### SENATORS

Elmer J. Burkett, *Lincoln*
Norris Brown, *Kearney*

### REPRESENTATIVES

John A. Maguire, *Lincoln*
Gilbert M. Hitchcock, *Omaha*
James P. Latta, *Tekamah*
Edmund H. Hinshaw, *Fairbury*
George W. Norris, *McCook*
Moses P. Kinkaid, *O'Neill*

## NEVADA

### SENATORS

Francis G. Newlands, *Reno*
George S. Nixon, *Reno*

### REPRESENTATIVE AT LARGE

George A. Bartlett, *Tonopah*

## NEW HAMPSHIRE

### SENATORS

Jacob H. Gallinger, *Concord*
Henry E. Burnham, *Manchester*

### REPRESENTATIVES

Cyrus A. Sulloway, *Manchester*
Frank D. Currier, *Canaan*

## NEW JERSEY

### SENATORS

John Kean, *Elizabeth*
Frank O. Briggs, *Trenton*

### REPRESENTATIVES

Henry C. Loudenslager, *Paulsboro*
John J. Gardner, *Atlantic City*
Benjamin F. Howell, *New Brunswick*
Ira W. Wood, *Trenton*
Charles N. Fowler, *Elizabeth*
William Hughes, *Paterson*
Richard Wayne Parker, *Newark*
William H. Wiley, *East Orange*
Eugene F. Kinkead, *Jersey City*
James A. Hamill, *Jersey City*

## NEW YORK

### SENATORS

Chauncey M. Depew, *Peekskill*
Elihu Root, *New York City*

### REPRESENTATIVES

William W. Cocks, *Westbury*
George H. Lindsay, *Brooklyn*
Otto G. Foelker, *Brooklyn*
Charles B. Law, *Brooklyn*
Richard Young, *Flatbush*
William M. Calder, *Brooklyn*
John J. Fitzgerald, *Brooklyn*
Daniel J. Riordan, *New York City*
Henry M. Goldfogle, *New York City*
William Sulzer, *New York City*
Charles V. Fornes, *New York City*
Michael F. Conry, *New York City*
Herbert Parsons, *New York City*
William Willett, Jr., *Long Island City*
J. Van Vechten Olcott, *New York City*
Francis B. Harrison, *New York City*
William S. Bennet, *New York City*
Joseph A. Goulden, *Fordham*
John E. Andrus, *Yonkers*
Thomas W. Bradley, *Walden*
Hamilton Fish, *Garrison*
William H. Draper, *Troy*
George N. Southwick, *Albany*
George W. Fairchild, *Oneonta*
Cyrus Durey, *Johnstown*
George R. Malby, *Ogdensburg*
Charles S. Millington, *Herkimer*
Charles L. Knapp, *Lowville*
Michael E. Driscoll, *Syracuse*

---

[23] Election unsuccessfully contested by J. Mitchell Galvin.
[24] Died February 4, 1910.
[25] Elected to fill vacancy caused by death of William C. Lovering, and took his seat April 7, 1910; resigned, effective January 4, 1911, having been

elected Governor.
[26] Died December 22, 1909.
[27] Appointed to fill vacancy caused by death of Anselm J. McLaurin, and took his seat January 5, 1910.
[28] Elected to fill vacancy caused by death of

Anselm J. McLaurin, and took his seat March 15, 1910.
[29] Died November 23, 1909.
[30] Elected to fill vacancy caused by death of David A. De Armond, and took his seat February 7, 1910.

John W. Dwight, *Dryden*
Sereno E. Payne, *Auburn*
James B. Perkins,[31] *Rochester*
James S. Havens,[32] *Rochester*
J. Sloat Fassett, *Elmira*
James S. Simmons, *Niagara Falls*
Daniel A. Driscoll, *Buffalo*
De Alva S. Alexander, *Buffalo*
Edward B. Vreeland, *Salamanca*

## NORTH CAROLINA

### SENATORS

Furnifold McL. Simmons, *New Bern*
Lee S. Overman, *Salisbury*

### REPRESENTATIVES

John H. Small, *Washington*
Claude Kitchin, *Scotland Neck*
Charles R. Thomas, *New Bern*
Edward W. Pou, *Smithfield*
John M. Morehead, *Spray*
Hannibal L. Godwin, *Dunn*
Robert N. Page, *Biscoe*
Charles H. Cowles, *Wilkesboro*
Edwin Y. Webb,[33] *Shelby*
John G. Grant, *Hendersonville*

## NORTH DAKOTA

### SENATORS

Porter J. McCumber, *Wahpeton*
Martin N. Johnson,[34] *Petersburg*
Fountain L. Thompson,[35] *Cando*
William E. Purcell,[36] *Wahpeton*
Asle J. Gronna,[37] *Lakota*

### REPRESENTATIVES AT LARGE

Louis B. Hanna, *Fargo*
Asle J. Gronna,[38] *Lakota*

## OHIO

### SENATORS

Charles W. F. Dick, *Akron*
Theodore E. Burton, *Cleveland*

### REPRESENTATIVES

Nicholas Longworth, *Cincinnati*
Herman P. Goebel, *Cincinnati*
James M. Cox, *Dayton*
William E. Tou Velle, *Celina*
Timothy T. Ansberry, *Defiance*
Matthew R. Denver, *Wilmington*
J. Warren Keifer, *Springfield*
Ralph D. Cole, *Findlay*
Isaac R. Sherwood, *Toledo*
Adna R. Johnson, *Ironton*

Albert Douglas, *Chillicothe*
Edward L. Taylor, Jr., *Columbus*
Carl C. Anderson, *Fostoria*
William G. Sharp, *Elyria*
James Joyce, *Cambridge*
David A. Hollingsworth, *Cadiz*
William A. Ashbrook, *Johnstown*
James Kennedy, *Youngstown*
William A. Thomas, *Niles*
L. Paul Howland, *Cleveland*
James H. Cassidy,[39] *Cleveland*

## OKLAHOMA

### SENATORS

Thomas P. Gore, *Lawton*
Robert L. Owen, *Muskogee*

### REPRESENTATIVES

Bird S. McGuire, *Pawnee*
Dick T. Morgan, *Woodward*
Charles E. Creager, *Muskogee*
Charles D. Carter, *Ardmore*
Scott Ferris, *Lawton*

## OREGON

### SENATORS

Jonathan Bourne, Jr., *Portland*
George E. Chamberlain, *Portland*

### REPRESENTATIVES

Willis C. Hawley, *Salem*
William R. Ellis, *Pendleton*

## PENNSYLVANIA

### SENATORS

Boies Penrose, *Philadelphia*
George T. Oliver,[40] *Pittsburgh*

### REPRESENTATIVES

Henry H. Bingham, *Philadelphia*
Joel Cook,[41] *Philadelphia*
J. Hampton Moore, *Philadelphia*
Reuben O. Moon, *Philadelphia*
William W. Foulkrod,[42] *Philadelphia*
George D. McCreary, *Philadelphia*
Thomas S. Butler, *West Chester*
Irving P. Wanger, *Norristown*
William W. Griest, *Lancaster*
Thomas D. Nicholls, *Scranton*
Henry W. Palmer, *Wilkes-Barre*
Alfred B. Garner, *Ashland*
John H. Rothermel, *Reading*
Charles C. Pratt, *New Milford*
William B. Wilson, *Blossburg*
John G. McHenry, *Benton*

Benjamin K. Focht, *Lewisburg*
Marlin E. Olmsted, *Harrisburg*
John M. Reynolds,[43] *Bedford*
Daniel F. Lafean, *York*
Charles F. Barclay, *Sinnemahoning*
George F. Huff, *Greensburg*
Allen F. Cooper, *Uniontown*
John K. Tener,[44] *Charleroi*
Arthur L. Bates, *Meadville*
A. Mitchell Palmer, *Stroudsburg*
Jonathan N. Langham, *Indiana*
Nelson P. Wheeler, *Endeavor*
William H. Graham, *Allegheny*
John Dalzell, *Pittsburgh*
James F. Burke, *Pittsburgh*
Andrew J. Barchfeld, *Pittsburgh*

## RHODE ISLAND

### SENATORS

Nelson W. Aldrich, *Providence*
George P. Wetmore, *Newport*

### REPRESENTATIVES

William P. Sheffield, *Newport*
Adin B. Capron, *Stillwater*

## SOUTH CAROLINA

### SENATORS

Benjamin R. Tillman, *Trenton*
Ellison D. Smith, *Florence*

### REPRESENTATIVES

George S. Legare,[45] *Charleston*
James O'H. Patterson,[46] *Barnwell*
Wyatt Aiken, *Abbeville*
Joseph T. Johnson, *Spartanburg*
David E. Finley, *Yorkville*
J. Edwin Ellerbe, *Marion*
Asbury F. Lever,[47] *Lexington*

## SOUTH DAKOTA

### SENATORS

Robert J. Gamble, *Yankton*
Coe I. Crawford, *Huron*

### REPRESENTATIVES AT LARGE

Eben W. Martin, *Deadwood*
Charles H. Burke, *Pierre*

## TENNESSEE

### SENATORS

James B. Frazier, *Chattanooga*
Robert L. Taylor, *Nashville*

---

[31] Died March 11, 1910.
[32] Elected to fill vacancy caused by death of James B. Perkins, and took his seat April 29, 1910.
[33] Election unsuccessfully contested by John A. Smith.
[34] Died October 21, 1909.
[35] Appointed to fill vacancy caused by death of Martin N. Johnson, and took his seat December 7, 1909; resigned effective January 31, 1910.
[36] Appointed to fill vacancy caused by death of Martin N. Johnson and resignation of Fountain L. Thompson, and took his seat February 1, 1910.
[37] Elected to fill vacancy caused by death of

Martin N. Johnson, and took his seat February 2, 1911.
[38] Resigned effective February 2, 1911, having been elected Senator.
[39] Elected to fill vacancy caused by resignation of Representative-elect Theodore E. Burton, in preceding Congress, and took his seat April 26, 1909.
[40] Elected to fill vacancy caused by resignation of Philander C. Knox, in preceding Congress, and took his seat March 19, 1909.
[41] Died December 15, 1910, before the commencement of the Sixty-second Congress, to which he had been reelected.
[42] Died November 13, 1910; vacancy throughout

the remainder of the Congress.
[43] Resigned January 17, 1911, having been elected Lieutenant Governor.
[44] Resigned January 16, 1911, having been elected Governor.
[45] Election unsuccessfully contested by Aaron P. Prioleau.
[46] Election unsuccessfully contested by Isaac Myers.
[47] Election unsuccessfully contested by R. H. Richardson.

## TENNESSEE—Continued
### REPRESENTATIVES
Walter P. Brownlow,[48] *Jonesboro*
Zachary D. Massey,[49] *Sevierville*
Richard W. Austin, *Knoxville*
John A. Moon, *Chattanooga*
Cordell Hull, *Carthage*
William C. Houston, *Woodbury*
Joseph W. Byrns, *Nashville*
Lemuel P. Padgett, *Columbia*
Thetus W. Sims, *Linden*
Finis J. Garrett, *Dresden*
George W. Gordon, *Memphis*

## TEXAS
### SENATORS
Charles A. Culberson, *Dallas*
Joseph W. Bailey, *Gainesville*
### REPRESENTATIVES
Morris Sheppard, *Texarkana*
Martin Dies, *Beaumont*
Gordon J. Russell,[50] *Tyler*
Robert M. Lively,[51] *Canton*
Choice B. Randell, *Sherman*
Jack Beall, *Waxahachie*
Rufus Hardy, *Corsicana*
Alexander W. Gregg, *Palestine*
John M. Moore, *Richmond*
George F. Burgess, *Gonzales*
Albert S. Burleson, *Austin*
Robert L. Henry, *Waco*
Oscar W. Gillespie, *Fort Worth*
John H. Stephens, *Vernon*
James L. Slayden, *San Antonio*
John N. Garner, *Uvalde*
William R. Smith, *Colorado*

## UTAH
### SENATORS
Reed Smoot, *Provo*
George Sutherland, *Salt Lake City*
### REPRESENTATIVE AT LARGE
Joseph Howell, *Logan*

## VERMONT
### SENATORS
William P. Dillingham, *Montpelier*
Carroll S. Page, *Hyde Park*
### REPRESENTATIVES
David J. Foster, *Burlington*
Frank Plumley, *Northfield*

## VIRGINIA
### SENATORS
John W. Daniel,[52] *Lynchburg*
Claude A. Swanson,[53] *Chatham*
Thomas S. Martin, *Charlottesville*
### REPRESENTATIVES
William A. Jones, *Warsaw*
Harry L. Maynard, *Portsmouth*
John Lamb, *Richmond*
Francis R. Lassiter,[54] *Petersburg*
Robert Turnbull,[55] *Lawrenceville*
Edward W. Saunders, *Rockymount*
Carter Glass, *Lynchburg*
James Hay, *Madison*
Charles C. Carlin, *Alexandria*
C. Bascom Slemp, *Big Stone Gap*
Henry D. Flood, *Appomattox*

## WASHINGTON
### SENATORS
Samuel H. Piles, *Seattle*
Wesley L. Jones, *North Yakima*
### REPRESENTATIVES[56]
William E. Humphrey, *Seattle*
Francis W. Cushman,[57] *Tacoma*
William W. McCredie,[58] *Vancouver*
Miles Poindexter, *Spokane*

## WEST VIRGINIA
### SENATORS
Stephen B. Elkins,[59] *Elkins*
Davis Elkins,[60] *Morgantown*
Clarence W. Watson,[61] *Fairmont*
Nathan B. Scott, *Wheeling*
### REPRESENTATIVES
William P. Hubbard, *Wheeling*
George C. Sturgiss, *Morgantown*
Joseph Holt Gaines, *Charleston*
Harry C. Woodyard, *Spencer*
James A. Hughes, *Huntington*

## WISCONSIN
### SENATORS
Robert M. La Follette, *Madison*
Isaac Stephenson, *Marinette*
### REPRESENTATIVES
Henry Allen Cooper, *Racine*
John M. Nelson, *Madison*
Arthur W. Kopp, *Platteville*
William J. Cary, *Milwaukee*
William H. Stafford, *Milwaukee*
Charles H. Weisse, *Sheboygan Falls*

John J. Esch, *La Crosse*
James H. Davidson, *Oshkosh*
Gustav Küstermann, *Green Bay*
Elmer A. Morse, *Antigo*
Irvine L. Lenroot, *Superior*

## WYOMING
### SENATORS
Clarence D. Clark, *Evanston*
Francis E. Warren, *Cheyenne*
### REPRESENTATIVE AT LARGE
Frank W. Mondell, *Newcastle*

## TERRITORY OF ALASKA
### DELEGATE
James Wickersham, *Fairbanks*

## TERRITORY OF ARIZONA
### DELEGATE
Ralph H. Cameron, *Flagstaff*

## TERRITORY OF HAWAII
### DELEGATE
Jonah K. Kalanianaole, *Waikiki*

## TERRITORY OF NEW MEXICO
### DELEGATE
William H. Andrews, *Albuquerque*

## PHILIPPINE ISLANDS
### RESIDENT COMMISSIONERS
Benito Legarda,[62] *Manila*
Pablo Ocampo,[63] *Manila*
Manuel L. Quezon,[64] *Lucena*

## PORTO RICO
### RESIDENT COMMISSIONER
Tulio Larrinaga, *San Juan*

---

[48] Died July 8, 1910.
[49] Elected to fill vacancy caused by death of Walter P. Brownlow, and took his seat December 5, 1910.
[50] Resigned June 14, 1910, having been appointed a Federal judge.
[51] Elected to fill vacancy caused by resignation of Gordon J. Russell, and took his seat December 5, 1910.
[52] Died June 29, 1910; had been reelected for the term beginning March 4, 1911.
[53] Appointed to fill vacancy caused by death of

John W. Daniel, and took his seat December 6, 1910.
[54] Died October 31, 1909.
[55] Elected to fill vacancy caused by death of Francis R. Lassiter, and took his seat March 16, 1910.
[56] Heretofore elected from State at large; congressional districts first established in 1909.
[57] Died July 6, 1909.
[58] Elected to fill vacancy caused by death of Francis W. Cushman, and took his seat December 6, 1909.
[59] Died January 4, 1911.

[60] Appointed to fill vacancy caused by death of his father, Stephen B. Elkins, and took his seat January 9, 1911.
[61] Elected to fill vacancy caused by death of Stephen B. Elkins, and took his seat February 2, 1911.
[62] Reelected for a term of two years beginning November 23, 1909.
[63] Term expired November 22, 1909.
[64] Elected for a term of two years beginning November 23, 1909.

# 62ND CONGRESS

## MARCH 4, 1911, TO MARCH 3, 1913

James S. Sherman
Vice President

James Beauchamp Clark
Speaker

FIRST SESSION— *April 4, 1911, to August 22, 1911*
SECOND SESSION— *December 4, 1911, to August 26, 1912*
THIRD SESSION— *December 2, 1912, to March 3, 1913*

---

VICE PRESIDENT OF THE UNITED STATES— James S. Sherman,[1] of New York
PRESIDENT PRO TEMPORE OF THE SENATE— William P. Frye,[2] of Maine; Charles
Curtis,[3] of Kansas; Augustus O. Bacon,[4] of Georgia; Jacob H. Gallinger,[5] of New
Hampshire; Henry Cabot Lodge,[6] of Massachusetts; Frank B. Brandegee,[7] of Connecticut
SECRETARY OF THE SENATE— Charles G. Bennett, of New York
SERGEANT AT ARMS OF THE SENATE— Daniel M. Ransdell, of Indiana; Edgar
Livingstone Cornelius,[8] of Maryland

---

SPEAKER OF THE HOUSE OF REPRESENTATIVES— James Beauchamp Clark,[9] of Missouri
CLERK OF THE HOUSE— Alexander McDowell, of Pennsylvania; South Trimble,[10] of Kentucky
SERGEANT AT ARMS OF THE HOUSE— Henry Casson, of Wisconsin; Ulysses S. Jackson,[11] of Indiana; Charles F. Riddell,[12] of Indiana
DOORKEEPER OF THE HOUSE— Joseph J. Sinnott, of Virginia
POSTMASTER OF THE HOUSE— William M. Dunbar

---

## ALABAMA

### SENATORS

John H. Bankhead, *Fayette*
Joseph F. Johnston, *Birmingham*

### REPRESENTATIVES

George W. Taylor, *Demopolis*
S. Hubert Dent, Jr., *Montgomery*
Henry D. Clayton, *Eufaula*
Fred L. Blackmon, *Anniston*
J. Thomas Heflin, *Lafayette*
Richmond P. Hobson, *Greensboro*
John L. Burnett, *Gadsden*
William Richardson, *Huntsville*
Oscar W. Underwood, *Birmingham*

## ARIZONA[13]

### SENATORS

Henry F. Ashurst,[14] *Prescott*
Marcus A. Smith,[15] *Tucson*

### REPRESENTATIVE AT LARGE

Carl Hayden,[16] *Phoenix*

## ARKANSAS

### SENATORS

James P. Clarke, *Little Rock*
Jeff Davis,[17] *Little Rock*
John N. Heiskell,[18] *Little Rock*
William M. Kavanaugh,[19] *Little Rock*

### REPRESENTATIVES

Robert B. Macon, *Helena*
William A. Oldfield, *Batesville*
John C. Floyd, *Yellville*
William B. Cravens, *Fort Smith*
Henderson M. Jacoway, *Dardanelle*
Joseph T. Robinson,[20] *Lonoke*
Samuel M. Taylor,[21] *Pine Bluff*
William S. Goodwin, *Warren*

## CALIFORNIA

### SENATORS

George C. Perkins, *Oakland*
John D. Works, *Los Angeles*

### REPRESENTATIVES

John E. Raker, *Alturas*
William Kent, *Kentfield*
Joseph R. Knowland, *Alameda*
Julius Kahn, *San Francisco*
Everis A. Hayes, *San Jose*

James C. Needham, *Modesto*
William D. Stephens, *Los Angeles*
Sylvester C. Smith,[22] *Bakersfield*

## COLORADO

### SENATORS

Simon Guggenheim, *Denver*
Charles S. Thomas,[23] *Denver*

### REPRESENTATIVE AT LARGE

Edward T. Taylor, *Glenwood Springs*

### REPRESENTATIVES

Atterson W. Rucker, *Fort Logan*
John A. Martin, *Pueblo*

## CONNECTICUT

### SENATORS

Frank B. Brandegee, *New London*
George P. McLean, *Simsbury*

### REPRESENTATIVE AT LARGE

John Q. Tilson, *New Haven*

### REPRESENTATIVES

E. Stevens Henry, *Rockville*
Thomas L. Reilly, *Meriden*
Edwin W. Higgins,[24] *Norwich*
Ebenezer J. Hill, *Norwalk*

---

[1] Died October 30, 1912.
[2] Resigned as President pro tempore April 27, 1911.
[3] Elected to serve December 4 to 12, 1911.
[4] Elected to serve January 15 to 17, March 11 and 12, April 8, May 10, May 30 to June 3, June 13 to July 5, August 1 to 10, August 27 to December 15, 1912; January 5 to 18 and February 2 to 15, 1913.
[5] Elected to serve February 12 to 14, April 26 and 27, May 7, July 6 to 31, August 12 to 26, 1912; December 16, 1912, to January 4, 1913; January 19 to February 1 and February 16 to March 3, 1913.
[6] Elected to serve March 25 and 26, 1912.
[7] Elected to serve May 25, 1912.
[8] Elected December 10, 1912.

[9] Elected April 4, 1911.
[10] Elected April 4, 1911.
[11] Elected April 4, 1911.
[12] Elected July 18, 1912.
[13] Admitted as a State into the Union February 14, 1912.
[14] Took his seat April 2, 1912; term to expire, as determined by lot, March 3, 1917.
[15] Took his seat April 2, 1912; term to expire, as determined by lot, March 3, 1915.
[16] Took his seat February 19, 1912.
[17] Died January 3, 1913.
[18] Appointed to fill vacancy caused by death of Jeff Davis, and took his seat January 9, 1913.
[19] Elected to fill vacancy caused by death of Jeff

Davis, and took his seat January 31, 1913.
[20] Resigned effective January 14, 1913, having been elected Governor.
[21] Elected to fill vacancy caused by resignation of Joseph T. Robinson, and took his seat January 27, 1913.
[22] Died January 26, 1913.
[23] Elected to fill vacancy caused by death of Charles J. Hughes, Jr., in preceding Congress, and took his seat January 20, 1913; vacancy in this class from January 12, 1911, to January 14, 1913, because of failure of legislature to elect.

[24] Election unsuccessfully contested by Raymond J. Jodoin.

## DELAWARE

### SENATORS

Henry A. du Pont, *Winterthur*
Harry A. Richardson, *Dover*

### REPRESENTATIVE AT LARGE

William H. Heald, *Wilmington*

## FLORIDA

### SENATORS

Duncan U. Fletcher, *Jacksonville*
Nathan P. Bryan,[25] *Jacksonville*

### REPRESENTATIVES

Stephen M. Sparkman, *Tampa*
Frank Clark, *Gainesville*
Dannitte H. Mays, *Monticello*

## GEORGIA

### SENATORS

Augustus O. Bacon, *Macon*
Joseph M. Terrell,[26] *Greenville*
Hoke Smith,[27] *Atlanta*

### REPRESENTATIVES

Charles G. Edwards, *Savannah*
Seaborn A. Roddenbery, *Thomasville*
Dudley M. Hughes, *Danville*
William C. Adamson, *Carrollton*
William S. Howard, *Decatur*
Charles L. Bartlett, *Macon*
Gordon Lee, *Chickamauga*
Samuel J. Tribble, *Athens*
Thomas M. Bell, *Gainesville*
Thomas W. Hardwick, *Sandersville*
William G. Brantley, *Brunswick*

## IDAHO

### SENATORS

Weldon B. Heyburn,[28] *Wallace*
Kirtland I. Perky,[29] *Boise*
James H. Brady,[30] *Pocatello*
William E. Borah, *Boise*

### REPRESENTATIVE AT LARGE

Burton L. French, *Moscow*

## ILLINOIS

### SENATORS

Shelby M. Cullom, *Springfield*
William Lorimer,[31] *Chicago*

### REPRESENTATIVES

Martin B. Madden, *Chicago*
James R. Mann, *Chicago*
William W. Wilson,[32] *Chicago*
James T. McDermott, *Chicago*
Adolph J. Sabath, *Chicago*
Edmund J. Stack, *Chicago*
Frank Buchanan, *Chicago*
Thomas Gallagher, *Chicago*
Lynden Evans, *Chicago*
George E. Foss, *Chicago*
Ira C. Copley, *Aurora*
Charles E. Fuller, *Belvidere*
John C. McKenzie, *Elizabeth*
James McKinney, *Aledo*
George W. Prince, *Galesburg*
Claudius U. Stone, *Peoria*
John A. Sterling, *Bloomington*
Joseph G. Cannon, *Danville*
William B. McKinely, *Champaign*
Henry T. Rainey, *Carrollton*
James M. Graham, *Springfield*
William A. Rodenberg, *East St. Louis*
Martin D. Foster, *Olney*
H. Robert Fowler, *Elizabethtown*
Napoleon B. Thistlewood, *Cairo*

## INDIANA

### SENATORS

Benjamin F. Shively, *South Bend*
John W. Kern, *Indianapolis*

### REPRESENTATIVES

John W. Boehne, *Evansville*
William A. Cullop, *Vincennes*
William E. Cox, *Jasper*
Lincoln Dixon, *North Vernon*
Ralph W. Moss, *Center Point*
Finly H. Gray, *Connersville*
Charles A. Korbly, *Indianapolis*
John A. M. Adair, *Portland*
Martin A. Morrison, *Frankfort*
Edgar D. Crumpacker, *Valparaiso*
George W. Rauch, *Marion*
Cyrus Cline, *Angola*
Henry A. Barnhardt, *Rochester*

## IOWA

### SENATORS

Albert B. Cummins, *Des Moines*
Lafayette Young, *Des Moines*
William S. Kenyon,[33] *Fort Dodge*

### REPRESENTATIVES

Charles A. Kennedy, *Montrose*
Irvin S. Pepper, *Muscatine*
Charles E. Pickett, *Waterloo*
Gilbert N. Haugen,[34] *Northwood*
James W. Good, *Cedar Rapids*
Nathan E. Kendall, *Albia*
Solomon F. Prouty, *Des Moines*
Horace M. Towner, *Corning*
Walter I. Smith,[35] *Council Bluffs*
William R. Green,[36] *Audubon*
Frank P. Woods, *Estherville*
Elbert H. Hubbard,[37] *Sioux City*
George C. Scott,[38] *Sioux City*

## KANSAS

### SENATORS

Charles Curtis, *Topeka*
Joseph L. Bristow, *Salina*

### REPRESENTATIVES

Daniel R. Anthony, Jr., *Leavenworth*
Alexander C. Mitchell,[39] *Lawrence*
Joseph Taggart,[40] *Kansas City*
Philip P. Campbell, *Pittsburg*
Fred S. Jackson, *Eureka*
Rollin R. Rees, *Minneapolis*
Isaac D. Young, *Beloit*
Edmond H. Madison,[41] *Dodge City*
George A. Neeley,[42] *Hutchinson*
Victor Murdock, *Wichita*

## KENTUCKY

### SENATORS

Thomas H. Paynter, *Frankfort*
William O. Bradley, *Louisville*

### REPRESENTATIVES

Ollie M. James, *Marion*
Augustus O. Stanley, *Henderson*
Robert Y. Thomas, Jr., *Central City*
Ben Johnson, *Bardstown*
J. Swagar Sherley, *Louisville*
Arthur B. Rouse, *Burlington*
James C. Cantrill, *Georgetown*
Harvey Helm, *Stanford*
William J. Fields, *Olive Hill*
John W. Langley, *Pikeville*
Caleb Powers, *Barbourville*

---

[25] Appointed to fill vacancy in the term beginning March 4, 1911, to serve until the next meeting of the legislature, and took his seat April 4, 1911; subsequently elected.

[26] Resigned July 14, 1911.

[27] Elected July 12, 1911, to fill vacancy caused by death of Alexander S. Clay, in preceding Congress, but did not qualify until December 4, 1911, preferring to retain the governorship.

[28] Died October 17, 1912.

[29] Appointed to fill vacancy caused by death of Weldon B. Heyburn, and took his seat December 3, 1912.

[30] Elected to fill vacancy caused by death of

Weldon B. Heyburn, and took his seat February 6, 1913.

[31] Election declared invalid July 13, 1912. (See U.S. Senate Election, Expulsion and Censure Cases, 1793-1990, Senate Document 103-33, pp. 281-84.)

[32] Election unsuccessfully contested by Fred J. Crowley.

[33] Elected to fill vacancy caused by death of Jonathan P. Dolliver, in preceding Congress, and took his seat April 24, 1911.

[34] Election unsuccessfully contested by Daniel D. Murphy.

[35] Resigned March 15, 1911.

[36] Elected to fill vacancy caused by resignation of

Walter I. Smith, and took his seat June 21, 1911.

[37] Died June 4, 1912.

[38] Elected to fill vacancy caused by death of Elbert H. Hubbard, and took his seat December 2, 1912.

[39] Died July 7, 1911.

[40] Elected to fill vacancy caused by death of Alexander C. Mitchell, and took his seat December 4, 1911.

[41] Died September 18, 1911.

[42] Elected to fill vacancy caused by death of Edmond H. Madison, and took his seat January 29, 1912.

## LOUISIANA

SENATORS

Murphy J. Foster, *Franklin*
John R. Thornton, *Alexandria*

REPRESENTATIVES

Albert Estopinal, *Estopinal*
H. Garland Dupré, *New Orleans*
Robert F. Broussard, *New Iberia*
John T. Watkins, *Minden*
Joseph E. Ransdell, *Lake Providence*
Robert C. Wickliffe,[43] *St. Francisville*
Lewis L. Morgan,[44] *Covington*
Arsène P. Pujo, *Lake Charles*

## MAINE

SENATORS

William P. Frye,[45] *Lewiston*
Obadiah Gardner,[46] *Rockland*
Charles F. Johnson, *Waterville*

REPRESENTATIVES

Asher C. Hinds, *Portland*
Daniel J. McGillicuddy, *Lewiston*
Samuel W. Gould, *Skowhegan*
Frank E. Guernsey, *Dover*

## MARYLAND

SENATORS

Isidor Rayner,[47] *Baltimore*
William P. Jackson,[48] *Salisbury*
John Walter Smith, *Snow Hill*

REPRESENTATIVES

J. Harry Covington, *Easton*
J. Fred. C. Talbott, *Towson*
George Konig, *Baltimore*
J. Charles Linthicum, *Baltimore*
Thomas Parran, *St. Leonard*
David J. Lewis, *Cumberland*

## MASSACHUSETTS

SENATORS

Henry Cabot Lodge, *Nahant*
W. Murray Crane, *Dalton*

REPRESENTATIVES

George P. Lawrence, *North Adams*
Frederick H. Gillett, *Springfield*
John A. Thayer, *Worcester*
William H. Wilder, *Gardner*
Butler Ames, *Lowell*
Augustus P. Gardner, *Hamilton*
Ernest W. Roberts, *Chelsea*
Samuel W. McCall, *Winchester*
William F. Murray, *Boston*

James M. Curley, *Boston*
Andrew J. Peters, *Boston*
John W. Weeks,[49] *West Newton*
William S. Greene, *Fall River*
Robert O. Harris, *East Bridgewater*

## MICHIGAN

SENATORS

William Alden Smith, *Grand Rapids*
Charles E. Townsend, *Jackson*

REPRESENTATIVES

Frank E. Doremus, *Detroit*
William W. Wedemeyer,[50] *Ann Arbor*
John M. C. Smith, *Charlotte*
Edward L. Hamilton, *Niles*
Edwin F. Sweet, *Grand Rapids*
Samuel W. Smith, *Pontiac*
Henry McMorran, *Port Huron*
Joseph W. Fordney, *Saginaw*
James C. McLaughlin, *Muskegon*
George A. Loud, *Au Sable*
Francis H. Dodds, *Mount Pleasant*
H. Olin Young, *Ishpeming*

## MINNESOTA

SENATORS

Knute Nelson, *Alexandria*
Moses E. Clapp, *St. Paul*

REPRESENTATIVES

Sydney Anderson, *Lanesboro*
Winfield S. Hammond, *St. James*
Charles R. Davis, *St. Peter*
Frederick C. Stevens, *St. Paul*
Frank M. Nye, *Minneapolis*
Charles A. Lindbergh, *Little Falls*
Andrew J. Volstead, *Granite Falls*
Clarence B. Miller, *Duluth*
Halvor Steenerson, *Crookston*

## MISSISSIPPI

SENATORS

Le Roy Percy, *Greenville*
John Sharp Williams, *Yazoo City*

REPRESENTATIVES

Ezekiel S. Candler, Jr., *Corinth*
Hubert D. Stephens, *New Albany*
Benjamin G. Humphreys, *Greenville*
Thomas U. Sisson, *Winona*
Samuel A. Witherspoon, *Meridian*
Pat Harrison, *Gulfport*
William A. Dickson, *Centerville*
James W. Collier, *Vicksburg*

## MISSOURI

SENATORS

William J. Stone, *Jefferson City*
James A. Reed, *Kansas City*

REPRESENTATIVES

James T. Lloyd, *Shelbyville*
William W. Rucker, *Keytesville*
Joshua W. Alexander, *Gallatin*
Charles F. Booher, *Savannah*
William P. Borland, *Kansas City*
Clement C. Dickinson, *Clinton*
Courtney W. Hamlin, *Springfield*
Dorsey W. Shackleford, *Jefferson City*
James Beauchamp Clark, *Bowling Green*
Richard Bartholdt,[51] *St. Louis*
Theron E. Catlin,[52] *St. Louis*
Patrick F. Gill,[53] *St. Louis*
Leonidas C. Dyer,[54] *St. Louis*
Walter L. Hensley, *Farmington*
Joseph J. Russell, *Charleston*
James A. Daugherty, *Webb City*
Thomas L. Rubey, *Lebanon*

## MONTANA

SENATORS

Joseph M. Dixon, *Missoula*
Henry L. Myers, *Hamilton*

REPRESENTATIVE AT LARGE

Charles N. Pray, *Fort Benton*

## NEBRASKA

SENATORS

Norris Brown, *Kearney*
Gilbert M. Hitchcock, *Omaha*

REPRESENTATIVES

John A. Maguire, *Lincoln*
Charles O. Lobeck, *Omaha*
James P. Latta,[55] *Tekamah*
Daniel V. Stephens,[56] *Fremont*
Charles H. Sloan, *Geneva*
George W. Norris, *McCook*
Moses P. Kinkaid, *O'Neill*

## NEVADA

SENATORS

Francis G. Newlands, *Reno*
George S. Nixon,[57] *Reno*
William A. Massey,[58] *Reno*
Key Pittman,[59] *Tonopah*

REPRESENTATIVE AT LARGE

Edwin E. Roberts, *Carson City*

---

[43] Died June 11, 1912.
[44] Elected to fill vacancy caused by death of Robert C. Wickliffe, and took his seat December 2, 1912.
[45] Died August 8, 1911.
[46] Appointed to fill vacancy caused by death of William P. Frye, and took his seat December 4, 1911; subsequently elected.
[47] Died November 25, 1912.
[48] Appointed to fill vacancy caused by death of Isidor Rayner, and took his seat December 3, 1912.

[49] Reelected to the Sixty-third Congress but resigned, effective March 4, 1913, having been elected Senator.
[50] Died January 2, 1913.
[51] Election unsuccessfully contested by Charles J. Maurer.
[52] Served until August 12, 1912; succeeded by Patrick F. Gill, who contested his election.
[53] Successfully contested the election of Theron E. Catlin, and took his seat August 12, 1912.

[54] Election unsuccessfully contested by Thomas E. Kinney.
[55] Died September 11, 1911.
[56] Elected to fill vacancy caused by death of James P. Latta, and took his seat December 4, 1911.
[57] Died June 5, 1912.
[58] Appointed to fill vacancy caused by death of George S. Nixon, and took his seat July 13, 1912.
[59] Elected to fill vacancy caused by death of George S. Nixon, and took his seat February 18, 1913.

## NEW HAMPSHIRE

SENATORS

Jacob H. Gallinger, *Concord*
Henry E. Burnham, *Manchester*

REPRESENTATIVES

Cyrus A. Sulloway, *Manchester*
Frank D. Currier, *Canaan*

## NEW JERSEY

SENATORS

Frank O. Briggs, *Trenton*
James E. Martine, *Plainfield*

REPRESENTATIVES

Henry C. Loudenslager,[60] *Paulsboro*
William J. Browning,[61] *Camden*
John J. Gardner, *Atlantic City*
Thomas J. Scully, *South Amboy*
Ira W. Wood, *Trenton*
William E. Tuttle, Jr., *Westfield*
William Hughes,[62] *Paterson*
Archibald C. Hart,[63] *Hackensack*
Edward W. Townsend, *Montclair*
Walter I. McCoy, *South Orange*
Eugene F. Kinkead, *Jersey City*
James A. Hamill, *Jersey City*

## NEW MEXICO[64]

SENATORS

Thomas B. Catron,[65] *Santa Fe*
Albert B. Fall,[66] *Three Rivers*

REPRESENTATIVES AT LARGE

George Curry,[67] *Tularosa*
Harvey B. Fergusson,[68] *Albuquerque*

## NEW YORK

SENATORS

Elihu Root, *New York City*
James A. O'Gorman, *New York City*

REPRESENTATIVES

Martin W. Littleton, *Port Washington*
George H. Lindsay, *Brooklyn*
James P. Maher, *Brooklyn*
Frank E. Wilson, *Brooklyn*
William C. Redfield, *Brooklyn*
William M. Calder, *Brooklyn*
John J. Fitzgerald, *Brooklyn*
Daniel J. Riordan, *New York City*
Henry M. Goldfogle, *New York City*
William Sulzer,[69] *New York City*
Charles V. Fornes, *New York City*
Michael F. Conry, *New York City*
Jefferson M. Levy, *New York City*
John J. Kindred, *Long Island City*
Thomas G. Patten, *New York City*

Francis B. Harrison, *New York City*
Henry George, Jr., *New York City*
Steven B. Ayres, *New York City*
John E. Andrus, *Yonkers*
Thomas W. Bradley, *Walden*
Richard E. Connell,[70] *Poughkeepsie*
William H. Draper, *Troy*
Henry S. De Forest, *Schenectady*
George W. Fairchild, *Oneonta*
Theron Akin, *Akin*
George R. Malby,[71] *Ogdensburg*
Edwin A. Merritt, Jr.,[72] *Potsdam*
Charles A. Talcott, *Utica*
Luther W. Mott, *Oswego*
Michael E. Driscoll, *Syracuse*
John W. Dwight, *Dryden*
Sereno E. Payne, *Auburn*
Henry G. Danforth, *Rochester*
Edwin S. Underhill, *Bath*
James S. Simmons, *Niagara Falls*
Daniel A. Driscoll, *Buffalo*
Charles B. Smith, *Buffalo*
Edward B. Vreeland, *Salamanca*

## NORTH CAROLINA

SENATORS

Furnifold McL. Simmons, *New Bern*
Lee S. Overman, *Salisbury*

REPRESENTATIVES

John H. Small, *Washington*
Claude Kitchin, *Scotland Neck*
John M. Faison, *Faison*
Edward W. Pou, *Smithfield*
Charles M. Stedman, *Greensboro*
Hannibal L. Godwin, *Dunn*
Robert N. Page, *Biscoe*
Robert L. Doughton, *Laurel Springs*
Edwin Y. Webb, *Shelby*
James M. Gudger, Jr., *Asheville*

## NORTH DAKOTA

SENATORS

Porter J. McCumber, *Wahpeton*
Asle J. Gronna, *Lakota*

REPRESENTATIVES AT LARGE

Louis B. Hanna,[73] *Fargo*
Henry T. Helgesen, *Milton*

## OHIO

SENATORS

Theodore E. Burton, *Cleveland*
Atlee Pomerene, *Canton*

REPRESENTATIVES

Nicholas Longworth, *Cincinnati*
Alfred G. Allen, *Cincinnati*

James M. Cox,[74] *Dayton*
J. Henry Goeke, *Wapakoneta*
Timothy T. Ansberry, *Defiance*
Matthew R. Denver, *Wilmington*
James D. Post, *Washington Courthouse*
Frank B. Willis, *Ada*
Isaac R. Sherwood, *Toledo*
Robert M. Switzer, *Gallipolis*
Horatio C. Claypool, *Chillicothe*
Edward L. Taylor, Jr., *Columbus*
Carl C. Anderson,[75] *Fostoria*
William G. Sharp, *Elyria*
George White, *Marietta*
William B. Francis, *Martins Ferry*
William A. Ashbrook, *Johnstown*
John J. Whitacre, *Canton*
Ellsworth R. Bathrick, *Akron*
L. Paul Howland, *Cleveland*
Robert J. Bulkley, *Cleveland*

## OKLAHOMA

SENATORS

Thomas P. Gore, *Lawton*
Robert L. Owen, *Muskogee*

REPRESENTATIVES

Bird S. McGuire, *Pawnee*
Dick T. Morgan, *Woodward*
James S. Davenport, *Vinita*
Charles D. Carter, *Ardmore*
Scott Ferris, *Lawton*

## OREGON

SENATORS

Jonathan Bourne, Jr., *Portland*
George E. Chamberlain, *Portland*

REPRESENTATIVES

Willis C. Hawley, *Salem*
Abraham W. Lafferty, *Portland*

## PENNSYLVANIA

SENATORS

Boies Penrose, *Philadelphia*
George T. Oliver, *Pittsburgh*

REPRESENTATIVES

Henry H. Bingham,[76] *Philadelphia*
William S. Vare,[77] *Philadelphia*
William S. Reyburn,[78] *Philadelphia*
J. Hampton Moore, *Philadelphia*
Reuben O. Moon, *Philadelphia*
Michael Donohoe, *Philadelphia*
George D. McCreary,[79] *Philadelphia*

---

[60] Died August 12, 1911.
[61] Elected to fill vacancy caused by death of Henry C. Loudenslager, and took his seat December 4, 1911.
[62] Resigned September 27, 1912.
[63] Elected to fill vacancy caused by resignation of William Hughes, and took his seat December 2, 1912.
[64] Admitted as a State into the Union January 6, 1912.
[65] Took his seat April 2, 1912; term to expire, as determined by lot, March 3, 1917.
[66] Took his seat April 2, 1912; term to expire, as determined by lot, March 3, 1913.

[67] Took his seat January 8, 1912.
[68] Took his seat January 8, 1912.
[69] Resigned December 31, 1912, having been elected Governor.
[70] Died October 30, 1912; vacancy throughout remainder of the Congress.
[71] Died July 5, 1912.
[72] Elected to fill vacancy caused by death of George R. Malby, and took his seat December 2, 1912.
[73] Resigned January 7, 1913, having been elected Governor.

[74] Resigned January 12, 1913, having been elected Governor.
[75] Died October 1, 1912.
[76] Died March 22, 1912.
[77] Elected to fill vacancy caused by death of Henry H. Bingham, and took his seat May 6, 1912.
[78] Elected to fill vacancy caused by death of Representative-elect Joel Cook, in preceding Congress, and took his seat June 2, 1911.
[79] Election unsuccessfully contested by Frank H. Hawkins.

Thomas S. Butler,[80] *West Chester*
Robert E. Difenderfer, *Jenkintown*
William W. Griest, *Lancaster*
John R. Farr, *Scranton*
Charles C. Bowman,[81] *Pittston*
Robert E. Lee, *Pottsville*
John H. Rothermel, *Reading*
George W. Kipp,[82] *Towanda*
William D. B. Ainey,[83] *Montrose*
William B. Wilson, *Blossburg*
John G. McHenry,[84] *Benton*
Benjamin K. Focht, *Lewisburg*
Marlin E. Olmsted, *Harrisburg*
Jesse L. Hartman, *Hollidaysburg*
Daniel F. Lafean, *York*
Charles E. Patton, *Curwensville*
Curtis H. Gregg, *Greensburg*
Thomas S. Crago,[85] *Waynesburg*
Charles Matthews, *New Castle*
Arthur L. Bates, *Meadville*
A. Mitchell Palmer, *Stroudsburg*
Jonathan N. Langham, *Indiana*
Peter M. Speer, *Oil City*
Stephen G. Porter, *Pittsburgh*
John Dalzell, *Pittsburgh*
James F. Burke, *Pittsburgh*
Andrew J. Barchfeld, *Pittsburgh*

## RHODE ISLAND

SENATORS

George P. Wetmore, *Newport*
Henry F. Lippitt, *Providence*

REPRESENTATIVES

George F. O'Shaunessy, *Providence*
George H. Utter,[86] *Westerly*

## SOUTH CAROLINA

SENATORS

Benjamin R. Tillman, *Trenton*
Ellison D. Smith, *Florence*

REPRESENTATIVES

George S. Legare,[87] *Charleston*
James F. Byrnes, *Aiken*
Wyatt Aiken, *Abbeville*
Joseph T. Johnson, *Spartanburg*
David E. Finley, *Yorkville*
J. Edwin Ellerbe, *Marion*
Asbury F. Lever, *Lexington*

## SOUTH DAKOTA

SENATORS

Robert J. Gamble, *Yankton*
Coe I. Crawford, *Huron*

REPRESENTATIVES AT LARGE

Charles H. Burke, *Pierre*
Eben W. Martin, *Deadwood*

## TENNESSEE

SENATORS

Robert L. Taylor,[88] *Nashville*
Newell Sanders,[89] *Chattanooga*
William R. Webb,[90] *Bellbuckle*
Luke Lea, *Nashville*

REPRESENTATIVES

Sam R. Sells, *Johnson City*
Richard W. Austin, *Knoxville*
John A. Moon, *Chattanooga*
Cordell Hull, *Carthage*
William C. Houston, *Woodbury*
Joseph W. Byrns, *Nashville*
Lemuel P. Padgett, *Columbia*
Thetus W. Sims, *Linden*
Finis J. Garrett, *Dresden*
George W. Gordon,[91] *Memphis*
Kenneth D. McKellar,[92] *Memphis*

## TEXAS

SENATORS

Charles A. Culberson, *Dallas*
Joseph W. Bailey,[93] *Gainesville*
Rienzi M. Jonston,[94] *Houston*
Morris Sheppard,[95] *Texarkana*

REPRESENTATIVES

Morris Sheppard,[96] *Texarkana*
Martin Dies, *Beaumont*
James Young, *Kaufman*
Choice B. Randell, *Sherman*
Jack Beall, *Waxahachie*
Rufus Hardy, *Corsicana*
Alexander W. Gregg, *Palestine*
John M. Moore, *Richmond*
George F. Burgess, *Gonzales*
Albert S. Burleson, *Austin*
Robert L. Henry, *Waco*
Oscar Callaway, *Comanche*
John H. Stephens, *Vernon*
James L. Slayden, *San Antonio*
John N. Garner, *Uvalde*
William R. Smith, *Colorado*

## UTAH

SENATORS

Reed Smoot, *Provo*
George Sutherland, *Salt Lake City*

REPRESENTATIVE AT LARGE

Joseph Howell, *Logan*

## VERMONT

SENATORS

William P. Dillingham, *Montpelier*
Carroll S. Page, *Hyde Park*

REPRESENTATIVES

David J. Foster,[97] *Burlington*
Frank L. Greene,[98] *St. Albans*
Frank Plumley, *Northfield*

## VIRGINIA

SENATORS

Thomas S. Martin, *Charlottesville*
Claude A. Swanson,[99] *Chatham*

REPRESENTATIVES

William A. Jones, *Warsaw*
Edward E. Holland, *Suffolk*
John Lamb, *Richmond*
Robert Turnbull, *Lawrenceville*
Edward W. Saunders, *Rockymount*
Carter Glass, *Lynchburg*
James Hay, *Madison*
Charles C. Carlin, *Alexandria*
C. Bascom Slemp, *Big Stone Gap*
Henry D. Flood, *Appomattox*

## WASHINGTON

SENATORS

Wesley L. Jones, *North Yakima*
Miles Poindexter, *Spokane*

REPRESENTATIVES

William E. Humphrey, *Seattle*
Stanton Warburton, *Tacoma*
William L. La Follette, *Pullman*

## WEST VIRGINIA

SENATORS

Clarence W. Watson, *Fairmont*
William E. Chilton, *Charleston*

REPRESENTATIVES

John W. Davis, *Clarksburg*
William G. Brown, Jr., *Kingwood*
Adam B. Littlepage, *Charleston*
John M. Hamilton, *Grantsville*
James A. Hughes,[100] *Huntington*

---

[80] Election unsuccessfully contested by Eugene C. Bonniwell.

[81] Election unsuccessfully contested by George R. McLean; seat declared vacant December 12, 1912.

[82] Died July 24, 1911.

[83] Elected to fill vacancy caused by death of George W. Kipp, and took his seat December 4, 1911.

[84] Died December 27, 1912.

[85] Election unsuccessfully contested by Jesse H. Wise.

[86] Died November 3, 1912; vacancy throughout remainder of the Congress.

[87] Election unsuccessfully contested by Aaron P. Prioleau; died January 31, 1913, before the commence-

ment of the Sixty-third Congress, to which he had been reelected.

[88] Died March 31, 1912.

[89] Appointed to fill vacancy caused by death of Robert L. Taylor, and took his seat April 11, 1912.

[90] Elected to fill vacancy caused by death of Robert L. Taylor, and took his seat February 3, 1913.

[91] Died August 9, 1911.

[92] Elected to fill vacancy caused by death of George W. Gordon, and took his seat December 4, 1911.

[93] Resigned January 3, 1913.

[94] Appointed to fill vacancy caused by resignation of Joseph W. Bailey, and took his seat January 7, 1913.

[95] Elected to fill vacancy caused by resignation of

Joseph W. Bailey, and took his seat February 3, 1913.

[96] Resigned February 3, 1913, having been elected Senator.

[97] Died March 21, 1912.

[98] Elected to fill vacancy caused by death of David J. Foster, and took his seat August 14, 1912.

[99] Reappointed to fill vacancy in the term beginning March 4, 1911, caused by death of Senator-elect John W. Daniel in preceding Congress, to serve until the next meeting of the legislature; subsequently reelected.

[100] Election unsuccessfully contested by Rankin Wiley.

## WISCONSIN

SENATORS

Robert M. La Follette, *Madison*
Isaac Stephenson, *Marinette*

REPRESENTATIVES

Henry Allen Cooper, *Racine*
John M. Nelson, *Madison*
Arthur W. Kopp, *Platteville*
William J. Cary, *Milwaukee*
Victor L. Berger, *Milwaukee*
Michael E. Burke, *Beaver Dam*
John J. Esch, *La Crosse*
James H. Davidson, *Oshkosh*
Thomas F. Konop, *Kewaunee*
Elmer A. Morse, *Antigo*
Irvine L. Lenroot, *Superior*

## WYOMING

SENATORS

Clarence D. Clark, *Evanston*
Francis E. Warren, *Cheyenne*

REPRESENTATIVE AT LARGE

Frank W. Mondell, *Newcastle*

## TERRITORY OF ALASKA

DELEGATE

James Wickersham, *Fairbanks*

## TERRITORY OF ARIZONA

DELEGATE

Ralph H. Cameron,[101] *Flagstaff*

## TERRITORY OF HAWAII

DELEGATE

J. Kuhio Kalanianaole, *Waikiki*

## TERRITORY OF NEW MEXICO

DELEGATE

William H. Andrews,[102] *Albuquerque*

## PHILIPPINE ISLANDS

RESIDENT COMMISSIONERS[103]

Benito Legarda, *Manila*
Manuel L. Quezon, *Tayabas*

## PORTO RICO

RESIDENT COMMISSIONER

Luis Muñoz Rivera, *San Juan*

---

[101] Served until February 18, 1912, the Territory of Arizona having been granted statehood by act of Congress approved June 20, 1910.

[102] Served until January 7, 1912, the Territory of New Mexico having been granted statehood by act of Congress approved June 20, 1910.

[103] By act of Congress approved February 15, 1911, term of office increased to four years, beginning March 4, 1913, present Commissioners to hold office until successors are elected and qualified.

# 63RD CONGRESS

## MARCH 4, 1913, TO MARCH 3, 1915

Thomas R. Marshall
Vice President

FIRST SESSION— *April 7, 1913, to December 1, 1913*
SECOND SESSION— *December 1, 1913, to October 24, 1914*
THIRD SESSION— *December 7, 1914, to March 3, 1915*
SPECIAL SESSION OF THE SENATE— *March 4, 1913, to March 17, 1913*

———————

VICE PRESIDENT OF THE UNITED STATES— THOMAS R. MARSHALL, of Indiana
PRESIDENT PRO TEMPORE OF THE SENATE— JAMES P. CLARKE,[1] of Arkansas
SECRETARY OF THE SENATE— CHARLES G. BENNETT, of New York; JAMES M. BAKER,[2] of
South Carolina
SERGEANT AT ARMS OF THE SENATE— EDGAR LIVINGSTONE CORNELIUS, of Maryland;
CHARLES P. HIGGINS,[3] of Missouri

———————

SPEAKER OF THE HOUSE OF REPRESENTATIVES— JAMES BEAUCHAMP CLARK,[4] of Missouri
CLERK OF THE HOUSE— SOUTH TRIMBLE,[5] of Kentucky
SERGEANT AT ARMS OF THE HOUSE— CHARLES F. RIDDELL, of Indiana; ROBERT B. GORDON,[6] of Ohio
DOORKEEPER OF THE HOUSE— JOSEPH J. SINNOTT, of Virginia
POSTMASTER OF THE HOUSE— WILLIAM M. DUNBAR

James Beauchamp Clark
Speaker

## ALABAMA

### SENATORS

John H. Bankhead, *Jasper*
Joseph F. Johnston,[7] *Birmingham*
Frank S. White,[8] *Birmingham*

### REPRESENTATIVE AT LARGE

John W. Abercrombie, *Tuscaloosa*

### REPRESENTATIVES

George W. Taylor, *Demopolis*
S. Hubert Dent, Jr., *Montgomery*
Henry D. Clayton,[9] *Eufaula*
William O. Mulkey,[10] *Geneva*
Fred L. Blackmon, *Anniston*
J. Thomas Heflin, *Lafayette*
Richmond P. Hobson, *Greensboro*
John L. Burnett, *Gadsden*
William Richardson,[11] *Huntsville*
Christopher C. Harris,[12] *Decatur*
Oscar W. Underwood, *Birmingham*

## ARIZONA

### SENATORS

Henry F. Ashurst, *Prescott*
Marcus A. Smith, *Tucson*

### REPRESENTATIVE AT LARGE

Carl Hayden, *Phoenix*

## ARKANSAS

### SENATORS

James P. Clarke, *Little Rock*
Joseph T. Robinson, *Little Rock*

### REPRESENTATIVES

Thaddeus H. Caraway, *Jonesboro*
William A. Oldfield, *Batesville*
John C. Floyd, *Yellville*
Otis Wingo, *De Queen*
Henderson M. Jacoway, *Dardanelle*
Samuel M. Taylor, *Pine Bluff*
William S. Goodwin, *Warren*

## CALIFORNIA

### SENATORS

George C. Perkins, *Oakland*
John D. Works, *Los Angeles*

### REPRESENTATIVES

William Kent, *Kentfield*
John E. Raker, *Alturas*
Charles F. Curry, *Sacramento*
Julius Kahn, *San Francisco*
John I. Nolan, *San Francisco*
Joseph R. Knowland, *Alameda*
Denver S. Church, *Fresno*
Everis A. Hayes, *San Jose*
Charles W. Bell, *Pasadena*
William D. Stephens, *Los Angeles*
William Kettner, *San Diego*

## COLORADO

### SENATORS

Charles S. Thomas, *Denver*
John F. Shafroth, *Denver*

### REPRESENTATIVES AT LARGE

Edward T. Taylor, *Glenwood Springs*
Edward Keating, *Pueblo*

### REPRESENTATIVES

George J. Kindel, *Denver*
Harry H. Seldomridge, *Colorado
Springs*

## CONNECTICUT

### SENATORS

Frank B. Brandegee, *New London*
George P. McLean, *Simsbury*

### REPRESENTATIVES

Augustine Lonergan, *Hartford*
Bryan F. Mahan, *New London*
Thomas L. Reilly, *Meriden*
Jeremiah Donovan, *South Norwalk*
William Kennedy, *Naugatuck*

## DELAWARE

### SENATORS

Henry A. du Pont, *Winterthur*
Willard Saulsbury, *Wilmington*

### REPRESENTATIVE AT LARGE

Franklin Brockson, *Clayton*

———————

[1] Elected March 13, 1913.
[2] Elected March 13, 1913.
[3] Elected March 13, 1913.
[4] Reelected April 7, 1913.
[5] Reelected April 7, 1913.
[6] Elected April 7, 1913.
[7] Died August 8, 1913.
[8] Elected to fill vacancy caused by death of Joseph
F. Johnston, and took his seat May 22, 1914. Vacancy

in this class from August 8, 1913, to May 11, 1914;
Henry D. Clayton was appointed by governor August
12, 1913, to fill vacancy; credentials withdrawn October 21, 1913; Frank P. Glass was appointed by governor November 17, 1913, but by Senate resolution of
February 4, 1914, was declared not entitled to a seat.
(See U.S. Senate Election, Expulsion and Censure
Cases, 1793-1990, Senate Document 103-33, pp. 290-
92.)

[9] Resigned May 25, 1914, having been appointed
a Federal district judge.
[10] Elected to fill vacancy caused by resignation of
Henry D. Clayton, and took his seat July 16, 1914.
[11] Died March 31, 1914.
[12] Elected to fill vacancy caused by death of
William Richardson, and took his seat May 19, 1914.

## FLORIDA

### SENATORS

Duncan U. Fletcher, *Jacksonville*
Nathan P. Bryan, *Jacksonville*

### REPRESENTATIVE AT LARGE

Claude L'Engle, *Jacksonville*

### REPRESENTATIVES

Stephen M. Sparkman, *Tampa*
Frank Clark, *Gainesville*
Emmett Wilson, *Pensacola*

## GEORGIA

### SENATORS

Augustus O. Bacon,[13] *Macon*
William S. West,[14] *Valdosta*
Thomas W. Hardwick,[15] *Sandersville*
Hoke Smith, *Atlanta*

### REPRESENTATIVES

Charles G. Edwards, *Savannah*
Seaborn A. Roddenbery,[16]
  *Thomasville*
Frank Park,[17] *Sylvester*
Charles S. Crisp, *Americus*
William C. Adamson, *Carrollton*
William S. Howard, *Decatur*
Charles L. Bartlett, *Macon*
Gordon Lee, *Chickamauga*
Samuel J. Tribble, *Athens*
Thomas M. Bell, *Gainesville*
Thomas W. Hardwick,[18] *Sandersville*
Carl Vinson,[19] *Milledgeville*
John R. Walker, *Valdosta*
Dudley M. Hughes, *Danville*

## IDAHO

### SENATORS

William E. Borah, *Boise*
James H. Brady, *Pocatello*

### REPRESENTATIVES AT LARGE

Burton L. French, *Moscow*
Addison T. Smith, *Twin Falls*

## ILLINOIS

### SENATORS

James Hamilton Lewis,[20] *Chicago*
Lawrence Y. Sherman,[21] *Springfield*

### REPRESENTATIVES AT LARGE

Lawrence B. Stringer, *Lincoln*
William E. Williams, *Pittsfield*

### REPRESENTATIVES

Martin B. Madden, *Chicago*
James R. Mann, *Chicago*
George E. Gorman, *Chicago*
James T. McDermott,[22] *Chicago*
Adolph J. Sabath, *Chicago*
James McAndrews, *Chicago*
Frank Buchanan, *Chicago*
Thomas Gallagher, *Chicago*
Fred A. Britten, *Chicago*
Charles M. Thomson, *Chicago*
Ira C. Copley, *Aurora*
William H. Hinebaugh, *Ottawa*
John C. McKenzie, *Elizabeth*
Clyde H. Tavenner, *Cordova*
Stephen A. Hoxworth, *Rapatee*
Claudius U. Stone, *Peoria*
Louis FitzHenry, *Bloomington*
Frank T. O'Hair, *Paris*
Charles M. Borchers, *Decatur*
Henry T. Rainey, *Carrollton*
James M. Graham, *Springfield*
William N. Baltz, *Millstadt*
Martin D. Foster, *Olney*
H. Robert Fowler, *Elizabethtown*
Robert P. Hill, *Marion*

## INDIANA

### SENATORS

Benjamin F. Shively, *South Bend*
John W. Kern, *Indianapolis*

### REPRESENTATIVES

Charles Lieb, *Rockport*
William A. Cullop, *Vincennes*
William E. Cox, *Jasper*
Lincoln Dixon, *North Vernon*
Ralph W. Moss, *Center Point*
Finly H. Gray, *Connersville*
Charles A. Korbly, *Indianapolis*
John A. M. Adair, *Portland*
Martin A. Morrison, *Frankfort*
John B. Peterson, *Crown Point*
George W. Rauch, *Marion*
Cyrus Cline, *Angola*
Henry A. Barnhart, *Rochester*

## IOWA

### SENATORS

Albert B. Cummins, *Des Moines*
William S. Kenyon, *Fort Dodge*

### REPRESENTATIVES

Charles A. Kennedy, *Montrose*
Irvin S. Pepper,[23] *Muscatine*
Henry Vollmer,[24] *Davenport*
Maurice Connolly, *Dubuque*
Gilbert N. Haugen, *Northwood*
James W. Good, *Cedar Rapids*
Sanford Kirkpatrick, *Ottumwa*
Solomon F. Prouty, *Des Moines*
Horace M. Towner, *Corning*
William R. Green, *Audubon*
Frank P. Woods, *Estherville*
George C. Scott, *Sioux City*

## KANSAS

### SENATORS

Joseph L. Bristow, *Salina*
William H. Thompson, *Garden City*

### REPRESENTATIVES

Daniel R. Anthony, Jr., *Leavenworth*
Joseph Taggart, *Kansas City*
Philip P. Campbell, *Pittsburg*
Dudley Doolittle, *Strong City*
Guy T. Helvering, *Marysville*
John R. Connelly, *Colby*
George A. Neeley, *Hutchinson*
Victor Murdock, *Wichita*

## KENTUCKY

### SENATORS

William O. Bradley,[25] *Beechmont*
Johnson N. Camden,[26] *Versailles*
Ollie M. James, *Marion*

### REPRESENTATIVES

Alben W. Barkley, *Paducah*
Augustus O. Stanley, *Henderson*
Robert Y. Thomas, Jr., *Central City*
Ben Johnson, *Bardstown*
J. Swagar Sherley, *Louisville*
Arthur B. Rouse, *Burlington*
James C. Cantrill, *Georgetown*
Harvey Helm, *Stanford*
William J. Fields, *Olive Hill*
John W. Langley, *Pikeville*
Caleb Powers, *Barbourville*

## LOUISIANA

### SENATORS

John R. Thornton, *Alexandria*
Joseph E. Ransdell, *Lake Providence*

### REPRESENTATIVES

Albert Estopinal, *Estopinal*
H. Garland Dupré, *New Orleans*

---

[13] Reappointed to fill vacancy in the term beginning March 4, 1913, to serve until the next meeting of the legislature; subsequently reelected; died February 14, 1914.
[14] Appointed to fill vacancy caused by death of Augustus O. Bacon, and took his seat March 6, 1914.
[15] Elected to fill vacancy caused by death of Augustus O. Bacon, and took his seat December 7, 1914.
[16] Died September 25, 1913.
[17] Elected to fill vacancy caused by death of Seaborn A. Roddenbery, and took his seat November 20, 1913.

[18] Resigned effective November 2, 1914; subsequently elected Senator.
[19] Elected to fill vacancy caused by resignation of Thomas W. Hardwick; took his seat December 7, 1914.
[20] Elected to fill vacancy in the term beginning March 4, 1913, and took his seat April 17, 1913; vacancy in this class from March 4 to 25, 1913, because of recess of legislature.
[21] Elected to fill vacancy in the term ending March 3, 1915, caused by action of Senate, in preceding Congress, in declaring invalid the election of William

Lorimer, and took his seat April 7, 1913; vacancy in this class from July 14, 1912, to March 25, 1913.
[22] Resigned July 21, 1914; vacancy throughout remainder of the Congress.
[23] Died December 22, 1913.
[24] Elected to fill vacancy caused by death of Irvin S. Pepper, and took his seat February 25, 1914.
[25] Died May 23, 1914.
[26] Appointed to fill vacancy caused by death of William O. Bradley, and took his seat June 18, 1914; subsequently elected.

Robert F. Broussard, *New Iberia*
John T. Watkins, *Minden*
J. Walter Elder, *Monroe*
Lewis L. Morgan, *Covington*
Ladislas Lazaro, *Washington*
James B. Aswell, *Natchitoches*

## MAINE

### SENATORS

Charles F. Johnson, *Waterville*
Edwin C. Burleigh, *Augusta*

### REPRESENTATIVES

Asher C. Hinds, *Portland*
Daniel J. McGillicuddy, *Lewiston*
Forrest Goodwin,[27] *Skowhegan*
John A. Peters,[28] *Ellsworth*
Frank E. Guernsey, *Dover*

## MARYLAND

### SENATORS

John Walter Smith, *Snow Hill*
William P. Jackson, *Salisbury*
Blair Lee,[29] *Silver Spring*

### REPRESENTATIVES

J. Harry Covington,[30] *Easton*
Jesse D. Price,[31] *Salisbury*
J. Fred. C. Talbott, *Lutherville*
George Konig,[32] *Baltimore*
Charles P. Coady,[33] *Baltimore*
J. Charles Linthicum, *Baltimore*
Frank O. Smith, *Dunkirk*
David J. Lewis, *Cumberland*

## MASSACHUSETTS

### SENATORS

Henry Cabot Lodge, *Nahant*
John W. Weeks, *West Newton*

### REPRESENTATIVES

Allen T. Treadway, *Stockbridge*
Frederick H. Gillett, *Springfield*
William H. Wilder,[34] *Gardner*
Calvin D. Paige,[35] *Southbridge*
Samuel E. Winslow, *Worcester*
John Jacob Rogers, *Lowell*
Augustus P. Gardner, *Hamilton*
Michael F. Phelan, *Lynn*
Frederick S. Deitrick, *Cambridge*
Ernest W. Roberts, *Chelsea*

William F. Murray,[36] *Boston*
Andrew J. Peters,[37] *Boston*
James M. Curley,[38] *Boston*
James A. Gallivan,[39] *Boston*
John J. Mitchell,[40] *Marlboro*
Edward Gilmore, *Brockton*
William S. Greene, *Fall River*
Thomas C. Thacher, *Yarmouth*

## MICHIGAN

### SENATORS

William Alden Smith, *Grand Rapids*
Charles E. Townsend, *Jackson*

### REPRESENTATIVE AT LARGE

Patrick H. Kelly, *Lansing*

### REPRESENTATIVES

Frank E. Doremus, *Detroit*
Samuel W. Beakes, *Ann Arbor*
John M. C. Smith,[41] *Charlotte*
Edward L. Hamilton, *Niles*
Carl E. Mapes, *Grand Rapids*
Samuel W. Smith, *Pontiac*
Louis C. Cramton, *Lapeer*
Joseph W. Fordney, *Saginaw*
James C. McLaughlin, *Muskegon*
Roy O. Woodruff, *Bay City*
Francis O. Lindquist, *Greenville*
H. Olin Young,[42] *Ishpeming*
William J. MacDonald,[43] *Calumet*

## MINNESOTA

### SENATORS

Knute Nelson, *Alexandria*
Moses E. Clapp, *St. Paul*

### REPRESENTATIVE AT LARGE

James Manahan, *Minneapolis*

### REPRESENTATIVES

Sydney Anderson, *Lanesboro*
Winfield S. Hammond,[44] *St. James*
Charles R. Davis, *St. Peter*
Frederick C. Stevens, *St. Paul*
George R. Smith, *Minneapolis*
Charles A. Lindbergh, *Little Falls*
Andrew J. Volstead, *Granite Falls*
Clarence B. Miller, *Duluth*
Halvor Steenerson, *Crookston*

## MISSISSIPPI

### SENATORS

John Sharp Williams, *Yazoo City*
James K. Vardaman, *Jackson*

### REPRESENTATIVES

Ezekiel S. Candler, Jr., *Corinth*
Hubert D. Stephens, *New Albany*
Benjamin G. Humphreys, *Greenville*
Thomas U. Sisson, *Winona*
Samuel A. Witherspoon, *Meridian*
Pat Harrison, *Gulfport*
Percy E. Quin, *McComb City*
James W. Collier, *Vicksburg*

## MISSOURI

### SENATORS

William J. Stone, *Jefferson City*
James A. Reed, *Kansas City*

### REPRESENTATIVES

James T. Lloyd, *Shelbyville*
William W. Rucker, *Keytesville*
Joshua W. Alexander, *Gallatin*
Charles F. Booher, *Savannah*
William P. Borland, *Kansas City*
Clement C. Dickinson, *Clinton*
Courtney W. Hamlin, *Springfield*
Dorsey W. Shackleford, *Jefferson City*
James Beauchamp Clark, *Bowling Green*
Richard Bartholdt, *St. Louis*
William L. Igoe, *St. Louis*
Leonidas C. Dyer,[45] *St. Louis*
Michael J. Gill,[46] *St. Louis*
Walter L. Hensley, *Farmington*
Joseph J. Russell, *Charleston*
Perl D. Decker, *Joplin*
Thomas L. Rubey, *Lebanon*

## MONTANA

### SENATORS

Henry L. Myers, *Hamilton*
Thomas J. Walsh, *Helena*

### REPRESENTATIVES AT LARGE

John M. Evans, *Missoula*
Tom Stout, *Lewistown*

---

[27] Died May 28, 1913.
[28] Elected to fill vacancy caused by death of Forrest Goodwin, and took his seat September 22, 1913.
[29] Elected on November 4, 1913, to fill vacancy caused by death of Isidor Rayner (in preceding Congress); credentials were presented on December 5, 1913, and referred to the Committee on Privileges and Elections, and pending report he did not attempt to qualify; on January 19, 1914, a resolution was reported to the effect that he had been legally elected and was entitled to the seat; on January 28, 1914, the Senate adopted the resolution and he took his seat the same day. This was the first election by popular vote held pursuant to the seventeenth amendment to the Constitution. (See U.S. Senate Election, Expulsion and Censure Cases, 1793-1990, Senate Document 103-33, pp. 295-96.)
[30] Resigned September 30, 1914.

[31] Elected to fill vacancy caused by resignation of J. Harry Covington, and took his seat December 7, 1914.
[32] Died May 31, 1913.
[33] Elected to fill vacancy caused by death of George Konig, and took his seat November 26, 1913.
[34] Died September 11, 1913.
[35] Elected to fill vacancy caused by death of William H. Wilder, and took his seat November 29, 1913.
[36] Resigned September 28, 1914; vacancy throughout remainder of the Congress.
[37] Resigned, effective August 15, 1914, having been appointed Assistant Secretary of the Treasury; vacancy throughout remainder of the Congress.
[38] Resigned effective February 4, 1914.
[39] Elected to fill vacancy caused by resignation of James M. Curley, and took his seat April 18, 1914.

[40] Elected to fill vacancy caused by resignation of Representative-elect John W. Weeks, in preceding Congress, and took his seat April 26, 1913.
[41] Election unsuccessfully contested by Claud S. Carney.
[42] Resigned effective May 16, 1913; subsequently succeeded by William J. MacDonald, who contested his election.
[43] Successfully contested the election of H. Olin Young (who had resigned effective May 16, 1913), and took his seat August 26, 1913.
[44] Resigned January 6, 1915, having been elected Governor.
[45] Served until June 19, 1914; succeeded by Michael J. Gill, who contested his election.
[46] Successfully contested the election of Leonidas C. Dyer, and took his seat June 19, 1914.

## NEBRASKA

### SENATORS

Gilbert M. Hitchcock, *Omaha*
George W. Norris, *McCook*

### REPRESENTATIVES

John A. Maguire, *Lincoln*
Charles O. Lobeck, *Omaha*
Daniel V. Stephens, *Fremont*
Charles H. Sloan, *Geneva*
Silas R. Barton, *Grand Island*
Moses P. Kinkaid, *O'Neill*

## NEVADA

### SENATORS

Francis G. Newlands, *Reno*
Key Pittman, *Tonopah*

### REPRESENTATIVE AT LARGE

Edwin E. Roberts, *Carson City*

## NEW HAMPSHIRE

### SENATORS

Jacob H. Gallinger, *Concord*
Henry F. Hollis,[47] *Concord*

### REPRESENTATIVES

Eugene E. Reed, *Manchester*
Raymond B. Stevens, *Landaff*

## NEW JERSEY

### SENATORS

James E. Marinte, *Plainfield*
William Hughes, *Paterson*

### REPRESENTATIVES

William J. Browning, *Camden*
J. Thompson Baker, *Wildwood*
Thomas J. Scully, *South Amboy*
Allan B. Walsh, *Trenton*
William E. Tuttle, Jr. *Westfield*
Lewis J. Martin,[48] *Newton*
Archibald C. Hart,[49] *Hackensack*
Robert G. Bremner,[50] *Passaic*
Dow H. Drukker,[51] *Passaic*
Eugene F. Kinkead,[52] *Jersey City*
Walter I. McCoy,[53] *East Orange*
Richard Wayne Parker,[54] *Newark*
Edward W. Townsend, *Montclair*
John J. Eagan, *Weehawken*
James A. Hamill, *Jersey City*

## NEW MEXICO

### SENATORS

Thomas B. Catron, *Santa Fe*
Albert B. Fall, *Three Rivers*

### REPRESENTATIVE AT LARGE

Harvey B. Fergusson, *Albuquerque*

## NEW YORK

### SENATORS

Elihu Root, *New York City*
James A. O'Gorman, *New York City*

### REPRESENTATIVES

Lathrop Brown, *St. James*
Denis O'Leary,[55] *Douglaston*
Frank E. Wilson, *Brooklyn*
Harry H. Dale, *Brooklyn*
James P. Maher, *Brooklyn*
William M. Calder, *Brooklyn*
John J. Fitzgerald, *Brooklyn*
Daniel J. Griffin, *Brooklyn*
James H. O'Brien, *Brooklyn*
Herman A. Metz, *Brooklyn*
Daniel J. Riordan, *New York City*
Henry M. Goldfogle, *New York City*
Timothy D. Sullivan,[56] *New York City*
George W. Loft,[57] *New York City*
Jefferson M. Levy, *New York City*
Michael F. Conry, *New York City*
Peter J. Dooling, *New York City*
John F. Carew, *New York City*
Thomas G. Patten, *New York City*
Walter M. Chandler, *New York City*
Francis B. Harrison,[58] *New York City*
Jacob A. Cantor,[59] *New York City*
Henry George, Jr., *New York City*
Henry Bruckner, *New York City*
Joseph A. Goulden, *Fordham*
Woodson R. Oglesby, *Yonkers*
Benjamin I. Taylor, *Harrison*
Edmund Platt, *Poughkeepsie*
George McClellan, *Chatham*
Peter G. Ten Eyck, *Albany*
James S. Parker, *Salem*
Samuel Wallin, *Amsterdam*
Edwin A. Merritt, Jr.,[60] *Potsdam*
Luther W. Mott, *Oswego*
Charles A. Talcott, *Utica*
George W. Fairchild, *Oneonta*
John R. Clancy, *Syracuse*
Sereno E. Payne,[61] *Auburn*
Edwin S. Underhill, *Bath*
Thomas B. Dunn, *Rochester*
Henry G. Danforth, *Rochester*
Robert H. Gittins, *Niagara Falls*
Charles B. Smith, *Buffalo*
Daniel A. Driscoll, *Buffalo*
Charles M. Hamilton, *Ripley*

## NORTH CAROLINA

### SENATORS

Furnifold McL. Simmons, *New Bern*
Lee S. Overman, *Salisbury*

### REPRESENTATIVES

John H. Small, *Washington*
Claude Kitchin, *Scotland Neck*
John M. Faison, *Faison*
Edward W. Pou, *Smithfield*
Charles M. Stedman, *Greensboro*
Hannibal L. Godwin, *Dunn*
Robert N. Page, *Biscoe*
Robert L. Doughton, *Laurel Springs*
Edwin Y. Webb, *Shelby*
James M. Gudger, Jr., *Asheville*

## NORTH DAKOTA

### SENATORS

Porter J. McCumber, *Wahpeton*
Asle J. Gronna, *Lakota*

### REPRESENTATIVES

Henry T. Helgesen, *Milton*
George M. Young, *Valley City*
Patrick D. Norton, *Hettinger*

## OHIO

### SENATORS

Theodore E. Burton, *Cleveland*
Atlee Pomerene, *Canton*

### REPRESENTATIVE AT LARGE

Robert Crosser, *Cleveland*

### REPRESENTATIVES

Stanley E. Bowdle, *Cincinnati*
Alfred G. Allen, *Cincinnati*
Warren Gard, *Hamilton*
J. Henry Goeke, *Wapakoneta*
Timothy T. Ansberry,[62] *Defiance*
Simeon D. Fess, *Yellow Springs*
James D. Post, *Washington Courthouse*
Frank B. Willis,[63] *Ada*
Isaac R. Sherwood, *Toledo*
Robert M. Switzer, *Gallipolis*
Horatio C. Claypool, *Chillicothe*
Clement L. Brumbaugh, *Columbus*
John A. Key, *Marion*
William G. Sharp,[64] *Elyria*
George White, *Marietta*
William B. Francis, *Martins Ferry*
William A. Ashbrook, *Johnstown*
John J. Whitacre, *Canton*
Ellsworth R. Bathrick, *Akron*
William Gordon, *Cleveland*
Robert J. Bulkley, *Cleveland*

---

[47] Elected March 13, 1913, for the term beginning March 4, 1913, and took his seat March 15, 1913.
[48] Died May 5, 1913.
[49] Elected to fill vacancy caused by death of Lewis J. Martin, and took his seat August 12, 1913.
[50] Died February 5, 1914.
[51] Elected to fill vacancy caused by death of Robert G. Bremner, and took his seat April 22, 1914.
[52] Resigned February 4, 1915.
[53] Resigned October 3, 1914.
[54] Elected to fill vacancy caused by resignation of Walter I. McCoy, and took his seat December 7, 1914.
[55] Resigned December 31, 1914.
[56] Died August 31, 1913.
[57] Elected to fill vacancy caused by death of Timothy D. Sullivan, and took his seat November 29, 1913.
[58] Resigned, effective September 1, 1913, having been appointed Governor General of the Philippine Islands.
[59] Elected to fill vacancy caused by resignation of Francis B. Harrison, and took his seat November 29, 1913.
[60] Died December 4, 1914, before the commencement of the Sixty-fourth Congress, to which he had been reelected.
[61] Died December 10, 1914, before the commencement of the Sixty-fourth Congress, to which he had been reelected.
[62] Resigned January 9, 1915.
[63] Resigned, effective January 9, 1915, having been elected Governor.
[64] Resigned, effective July 23, 1914.

## OKLAHOMA

### SENATORS

Thomas P. Gore, *Lawton*
Robert L. Owen, *Muskogee*

### REPRESENTATIVES AT LARGE

William H. Murray, *Tishomingo*
Joseph B. Thompson, *Pauls Valley*
Claude Weaver, *Oklahoma City*

### REPRESENTATIVES

Bird S. McGuire, *Pawnee*
Dick T. Morgan, *Woodward*
James S. Davenport, *Vinita*
Charles D. Carter, *Ardmore*
Scott Ferris, *Lawton*

## OREGON

### SENATORS

George E. Chamberlain, *Portland*
Harry Lane, *Portland*

### REPRESENTATIVES

Willis C. Hawley, *Salem*
Nicholas J. Sinnott, *The Dalles*
Abraham W. Lafferty, *Portland*

## PENNSYLVANIA

### SENATORS

Boies Penrose, *Philadelphia*
George T. Oliver, *Pittsburgh*

### REPRESENTATIVES AT LARGE

Fred E. Lewis, *Allentown*
John M. Morin, *Pittsburgh*
Arthur R. Rupley, *Carlisle*
Anderson H. Walters, *Johnstown*

### REPRESENTATIVES

William S. Vare, *Philadelphia*
George S. Graham, *Philadelphia*
J. Hampton Moore, *Philadelphia*
George W. Edmonds, *Philadelphia*
Michael Donohoe, *Philadelphia*
J. Washington Logue, *Philadelphia*
Thomas S. Butler, *West Chester*
Robert E. Difenderfer, *Jenkintown*
William W. Griest, *Lancaster*
John R. Farr, *Scranton*
John J. Casey, *Wilkes-Barre*
Robert E. Lee, *Pottsville*
John H. Rothermel, *Reading*
William D. B. Ainey, *Montrose*
Edgar R. Kiess, *Williamsport*
John V. Lesher, *Sunbury*
Frank L. Dershem, *Lewisburg*
Aaron S. Kreider, *Annville*
Warren W. Bailey, *Johnstown*
Andrew R. Brodbeck, *Hanover*
Charles E. Patton, *Curwensville*
Abraham L. Keister, *Scottdale*
Wooda N. Carr, *Uniontown*
Henry W. Temple, *Washington*
Milton W. Shreve, *Erie*
A. Mitchell Palmer, *Stroudsburg*

Jonathan N. Langham, *Indiana*
Willis J. Hulings, *Oil City*
Stephen G. Porter, *Pittsburgh*
M. Clyde Kelly, *Braddock*
James F. Burke, *Pittsburgh*
Andrew J. Barchfeld, *Pittsburgh*

## RHODE ISLAND

### SENATORS

Henry F. Lippitt, *Providence*
LeBaron B. Colt, *Bristol*

### REPRESENTATIVES

George F. O'Shaunessy, *Providence*
Peter G. Gerry, *Providence*
Ambrose Kennedy, *Woonsocket*

## SOUTH CAROLINA

### SENATORS

Benjamin R. Tillman, *Trenton*
Ellison D. Smith, *Florence*

### REPRESENTATIVES

Richard S. Whaley,[65] *Charleston*
James F. Byrnes, *Aiken*
Wyatt Aiken, *Abbeville*
Joseph T. Johnson, *Spartanburg*
David E. Finley, *Yorkville*
J. Willard Ragsdale, *Florence*
Asbury F. Lever, *Lexington*

## SOUTH DAKOTA

### SENATORS

Coe I. Crawford, *Huron*
Thomas Sterling, *Vermilion*

### REPRESENTATIVES

Charles H. Dillon, *Yankton*
Charles H. Burke, *Pierre*
Eben W. Martin, *Deadwood*

## TENNESSEE

### SENATORS

Luke Lea, *Nashville*
John K. Shields, *Knoxville*

### REPRESENTATIVES

Sam R. Sells, *Johnson City*
Richard W. Austin, *Knoxville*
John A. Moon, *Chattanooga*
Cordell Hull, *Carthage*
William C. Houston, *Woodbury*
Joseph W. Byrns, *Nashville*
Lemuel P. Padgett, *Columbia*
Thetus W. Sims, *Linden*
Finis J. Garrett, *Dresden*
Kenneth D. McKellar, *Memphis*

## TEXAS

### SENATORS

Charles A. Culberson, *Dallas*
Morris Sheppard, *Texarkana*

### REPRESENTATIVES AT LARGE

Daniel E. Garrett, *Houston*
Hatton W. Sumners, *Dallas*

### REPRESENTATIVES

Horace W. Vaughan, *Texarkana*
Martin Dies, *Beaumont*
James Young, *Kaufman*
Sam Rayburn, *Bonham*
Jack Beall, *Waxahachie*
Rufus Hardy, *Corsicana*
Alexander W. Gregg, *Palestine*
Joe H. Eagle, *Houston*
George F. Burgess, *Gonzales*
Albert S. Burleson,[66] *Austin*
James P. Buchanan,[67] *Brenham*
Robert L. Henry, *Waco*
Oscar Callaway, *Comanche*
John H. Stephens, *Vernon*
James L. Slayden, *San Antonio*
John N. Garner, *Uvalde*
William R. Smith, *Colorado*

## UTAH

### SENATORS

Reed Smoot, *Provo*
George Sutherland, *Salt Lake City*

### REPRESENTATIVES AT LARGE

Joseph Howell, *Logan*
Jacob Johnson, *Spring City*

## VERMONT

### SENATORS

William P. Dillingham, *Montpelier*
Carroll S. Page, *Hyde Park*

### REPRESENTATIVES

Frank L. Greene, *St. Albans*
Frank Plumley, *Northfield*

## VIRGINIA

### SENATORS

Thomas S. Martin, *Charlottesville*
Claude A. Swanson, *Chatham*

### REPRESENTATIVES

William A. Jones, *Warsaw*
Edward E. Holland, *Suffolk*
Andrew J. Montague, *Richmond*
Walter A. Watson, *Jennings Ordinary*
Edward W. Saunders, *Rockymount*
Carter Glass, *Lynchburg*
James Hay, *Madison*
Charles C. Carlin, *Alexandria*
C. Bascom Slemp, *Big Stone Gap*
Henry D. Flood, *Appomattox*

## WASHINGTON

### SENATORS

Wesley L. Jones, *North Yakima*
Miles Poindexter, *Spokane*

---

[65] Elected to fill vacancy caused by death of Representative-elect George S. Legare, in preceding Congress, and took his seat May 9, 1913; election unsuccessfully contested by John P. Grace.

[66] Resigned March 6, 1913, having been appointed Postmaster General.

[67] Elected to fill vacancy caused by resignation of Albert S. Burleson, and took his seat April 17, 1913.

## WASHINGTON—Continued

### REPRESENTATIVES AT LARGE

James W. Bryan, *Seattle*
Jacob A. Falconer, *Everett*

### REPRESENTATIVES

William E. Humphrey, *Seattle*
Albert Johnson, *Hoquiam*
William L. La Follette, *Pullman*

## WEST VIRGINIA

### SENATORS

William E. Chilton, *Charleston*
Nathan Goff,[68] *Clarksburg*

### REPRESENTATIVE AT LARGE

Howard Sutherland, *Elkins*

### REPRESENTATIVES

John W. Davis,[69] *Clarksburg*
Matthew M. Neely,[70] *Fairmont*
William G. Brown, Jr., *Kingwood*
Samuel B. Avis, *Charleston*
Hunter H. Moss, Jr., *Parkersburg*
James A. Hughes, *Huntington*

## WISCONSIN

### SENATORS

Robert M. La Follette, *Madison*
Isaac Stephenson, *Marinette*

### REPRESENTATIVES

Henry Allen Cooper, *Racine*
Michael E. Burke, *Beaver Dam*
John M. Nelson, *Madison*
William J. Cary, *Milwaukee*
William H. Stafford, *Milwaukee*
Michael K. Reilly, *Fond du Lac*
John J. Esch, *La Crosse*
Edward E. Browne, *Waupaca*
Thomas F. Konop, *Kewaunee*
James A. Frear, *Hudson*
Irvine L. Lenroot, *Superior*

## WYOMING

### SENATORS

Clarence D. Clark, *Evanston*
Francis E. Warren, *Cheyenne*

### REPRESENTATIVE AT LARGE

Frank W. Mondell, *Newcastle*

## TERRITORY OF ALASKA

### DELEGATE

James Wickersham, *Fairbanks*

## TERRITORY OF HAWAII

### DELEGATE

J. Kuhio Kalanianaole, *Waikiki*

## PHILIPPINE ISLANDS

### RESIDENT COMMISSIONERS

Manuel L. Quezon, *Tayabas*
Manuel Earnshaw, *Manila*

## PORTO RICO

### RESIDENT COMMISSIONER

Luis Muñoz Rivera, *San Juan*

---

[68] Elected February 21, 1913, for the term beginning March 4, 1913, but did not qualify until April 7, 1913, preferring to retain the judgeship.

[69] Resigned August 29, 1913, having been appointed Solicitor General of the United States.

[70] Elected to fill vacancy caused by resignation of John W. Davis, and took his seat November 1, 1913.

# 64TH CONGRESS

## MARCH 4, 1915, TO MARCH 3, 1917

FIRST SESSION— *December 6, 1915, to September 8, 1916*
SECOND SESSION— *December 4, 1916, to March 3, 1917*

---

VICE PRESIDENT OF THE UNITED STATES— Thomas R. Marshall, of Indiana
PRESIDENT PRO TEMPORE OF THE SENATE— James P. Clarke,[1] of Arkansas;
Willard Saulsbury,[2] of Delaware
SECRETARY OF THE SENATE— James M. Baker, of South Carolina
SERGEANT AT ARMS OF THE SENATE— Charles P. Higgins, of Missouri

---

SPEAKER OF THE HOUSE OF REPRESENTATIVES— James Beauchamp Clark,[3] of
Missouri
CLERK OF THE HOUSE— South Trimble,[4] of Kentucky
SERGEANT AT ARMS OF THE HOUSE— Robert B. Gordon,[5] of Ohio
DOORKEEPER OF THE HOUSE— Joseph J. Sinnott, of Virginia
POSTMASTER OF THE HOUSE— William M. Dunbar

**Thomas R. Marshall**
Vice President

**James Beauchamp Clark**
Speaker

---

## ALABAMA

### SENATORS
John H. Bankhead, *Jasper*
Oscar W. Underwood, *Birmingham*

### REPRESENTATIVE AT LARGE
John W. Abercrombie, *Tuscaloosa*

### REPRESENTATIVES
Oscar L. Gray, *Butler*
S. Hubert Dent, Jr., *Montgomery*
Henry B. Steagall, *Ozark*
Fred L. Blackmon, *Anniston*
J. Thomas Heflin, *Lafayette*
William B. Oliver, *Tuscaloosa*
John L. Burnett, *Gadsden*
Edward B. Almon, *Tuscumbia*
George Huddleston, *Birmingham*

## ARIZONA

### SENATORS
Henry F. Ashurst, *Prescott*
Marcus A. Smith, *Tucson*

### REPRESENTATIVE AT LARGE
Carl Hayden, *Phoenix*

## ARKANSAS

### SENATORS
James P. Clarke,[6] *Little Rock*
William F. Kirby,[7] *Little Rock*
Joseph T. Robinson, *Little Rock*

### REPRESENTATIVES
Thaddeus H. Caraway, *Jonesboro*
William A. Oldfield, *Batesville*

John N. Tillman, *Fayetteville*
Otis Wingo, *De Queen*
Henderson M. Jacoway, *Dardanelle*
Samuel M. Taylor, *Pine Bluff*
William S. Goodwin, *Warren*

## CALIFORNIA

### SENATORS
John D. Works, *Los Angeles*
James D. Phelan, *San Francisco*

### REPRESENTATIVES
William Kent, *Kentfield*
John E. Raker, *Alturas*
Charles F. Curry, *Sacramento*
Julius Kahn, *San Francisco*
John I. Nolan, *San Francisco*
John A. Elston, *Berkeley*
Denver S. Church, *Fresno*
Everis A. Hayes, *San Jose*
Charles H. Randall, *Los Angeles*
William D. Stephens,[8] *Los Angeles*
H. Stanley Benedict,[9] *Los Angeles*
William Kettner, *San Diego*

## COLORADO

### SENATORS
Charles S. Thomas, *Denver*
John F. Shafroth, *Denver*

### REPRESENTATIVES
Benjamin C. Hilliard, *Denver*
Charles B. Timberlake, *Sterling*
Edward Keating, *Pueblo*
Edward T. Taylor, *Glenwood Springs*

## CONNECTICUT

### SENATORS
Frank B. Brandegee, *New London*
George P. McLean, *Simsbury*

### REPRESENTATIVES
P. Davis Oakey, *Hartford*
Richard P. Freeman, *New London*
John Q. Tilson, *New Haven*
Ebenezer J. Hill,[10] *Norwalk*
James P. Glynn, *Winsted*

## DELAWARE

### SENATORS
Henry A. du Pont, *Winterthur*
Willard Saulsbury, *Wilmington*

### REPRESENTATIVE AT LARGE
Thomas W. Miller, *Wilmington*

## FLORIDA

### SENATORS
Duncan U. Fletcher, *Jacksonville*
Nathan P. Bryan, *Jacksonville*

### REPRESENTATIVES
Stephen M. Sparkman, *Tampa*
Frank Clark, *Gainesville*
Emmett Wilson, *Pensacola*
William J. Sears, *Kissimmee*

---

[1] Reelected December 6, 1915; died October 1, 1916.
[2] Elected December 14, 1916.
[3] Reelected December 6, 1915.
[4] Reelected December 6, 1915.

[5] Reelected December 6, 1915.
[6] Died October 1, 1916.
[7] Elected to fill vacancy caused by death of James P. Clarke, and took his seat December 5, 1916.
[8] Resigned July 22, 1916.

[9] Elected to fill vacancy caused by resignation of William D. Stephens, and took his seat December 4, 1916.
[10] Election unsuccessfully contested by Jeremiah Donovan.

## GEORGIA

### SENATORS

Hoke Smith, *Atlanta*
Thomas W. Hardwick, *Sandersville*

### REPRESENTATIVES

Charles G. Edwards, *Savannah*
Frank Park, *Sylvester*
Charles R. Crisp, *Americus*
William C. Adamson, *Carrollton*
William S. Howard, *Kirkwood*
James W. Wise, *Fayetteville*
Gordon Lee, *Chickamauga*
Samuel J. Tribble,[11] *Athens*
Tinsley W. Rucker,[12] *Athens*
Thomas M. Bell, *Gainesville*
Carl Vinson, *Milledgeville*
John R. Walker, *Valdosta*
Dudley M. Hughes, *Danville*

## IDAHO

### SENATORS

William E. Borah, *Boise*
James H. Brady, *Pocatello*

### REPRESENTATIVES AT LARGE

Robert M. McCracken, *Boise*
Addison T. Smith, *Twin Falls*

## ILLINOIS

### SENATORS

James Hamilton Lewis, *Chicago*
Lawrence Y. Sherman, *Springfield*

### REPRESENTATIVE AT LARGE

William E. Williams,[13] *Pittsfield*

### REPRESENTATIVES

Martin B. Madden, *Chicago*
James R. Mann, *Chicago*
William W. Wilson, *Chicago*
James T. McDermott, *Chicago*
Adolph J. Sabath, *Chicago*
James McAndrews, *Chicago*
Frank Buchanan, *Chicago*
Thomas Gallagher, *Chicago*
Fred A. Britten, *Chicago*
George E. Foss, *Chicago*
Ira C. Copley, *Aurora*
Charles E. Fuller, *Belvidere*
John C. McKenzie, *Elizabeth*
Clyde H. Tavenner, *Cordova*
Edward J. King, *Galesburg*
Claudius U. Stone, *Peoria*
John A. Sterling, *Bloomington*
Joseph G. Cannon, *Danville*
William B. McKinley, *Champaign*
Henry T. Rainey, *Carrollton*
Loren E. Wheeler, *Springfield*
William A. Rodenberg, *East St. Louis*
Martin D. Foster, *Olney*

Thomas S. Williams, *Louisville*
Edward E. Denison, *Marion*
Burnett M. Chiperfield, *Canton*

## INDIANA

### SENATORS

Benjamin F. Shively,[14] *South Bend*
Thomas Taggart,[15] *French Lick*
James E. Watson,[16] *Rushville*
John W. Kern, *Indianapolis*

### REPRESENTATIVES

Charles Lieb, *Rockport*
William A. Cullop, *Vincennes*
William E. Cox, *Jasper*
Lincoln Dixon, *North Vernon*
Ralph W. Moss, *Center Point*
Finly H. Gray, *Connersville*
Merrill Moores, *Indianapolis*
John A. M. Adair, *Portland*
Martin A. Morrison, *Frankfort*
William R. Wood, *La Fayette*
George W. Rauch, *Marion*
Cyrus Cline, *Angola*
Henry A. Barnhart, *Rochester*

## IOWA

### SENATORS

Albert B. Cummins, *Des Moines*
William S. Kenyon, *Fort Dodge*

### REPRESENTATIVES

Charles A. Kennedy, *Montrose*
Harry E. Hull, *Williamsburg*
Burton E. Sweet, *Waverly*
Gilbert N. Haugen, *Northwood*
James W. Good, *Cedar Rapids*
C. William Ramseyer, *Bloomfield*
Cassius C. Dowell, *Des Moines*
Horace M. Towner, *Corning*
William R. Green, *Council Bluffs*
Frank P. Woods, *Estherville*
Thomas J. Steele, *Sioux City*

## KANSAS

### SENATORS

William H. Thompson, *Garden City*
Charles Curtis, *Topeka*

### REPRESENTATIVES

Daniel R. Anthony, Jr., *Leavenworth*
Joseph Taggart, *Kansas City*
Philip P. Campbell, *Pittsburg*
Dudley Doolittle, *Strong City*
Guy T. Helvering, *Marysville*
John R. Connelly, *Colby*
Jouett Shouse, *Kinsley*
William A. Ayres, *Wichita*

## KENTUCKY

### SENATORS

Ollie M. James, *Marion*
Joseph C. W. Beckham, *Frankfort*

### REPRESENTATIVES

Alben W. Barkley, *Paducah*
David H. Kincheloe, *Madisonville*
Robert Y. Thomas, Jr., *Central City*
Ben Johnson, *Bardstown*
J. Swagar Sherley, *Louisville*
Arthur B. Rouse, *Burlington*
James C. Cantrill, *Georgetown*
Harvey Helm, *Stanford*
William J. Fields, *Olive Hill*
John W. Langley, *Pikeville*
Caleb Powers, *Barbourville*

## LOUISIANA

### SENATORS

Joseph E. Ransdell, *Lake Providence*
Robert F. Broussard, *New Iberia*

### REPRESENTATIVES

Albert Estopinal, *Estopinal*
H. Garland Dupré, *New Orleans*
Whitmell P. Martin, *Thibodaux*
John T. Watkins, *Minden*
Riley J. Wilson, *Harrisonburg*
Lewis L. Morgan, *Covington*
Ladislas Lazaro, *Washington*
James B. Aswell, *Natchitoches*

## MAINE

### SENATORS

Charles F. Johnson, *Waterville*
Edwin C. Burleigh,[17] *Augusta*
Bert M. Fernald,[18] *West Poland*

### REPRESENTATIVES

Asher C. Hinds, *Portland*
Daniel J. McGillicuddy, *Lewiston*
John A. Peters, *Ellsworth*
Frank E. Guernsey, *Dover*

## MARYLAND

### SENATORS

John Walter Smith, *Snow Hill*
Blair Lee, *Silver Spring*

### REPRESENTATIVES

Jesse D. Price, *Salisbury*
J. Fred. C. Talbott, *Lutherville*
Charles P. Coady, *Baltimore*
J. Charles Linthicum, *Baltimore*
Sydney E. Mudd, *La Plata*
David J. Lewis, *Cumberland*

---

[11] Died December 8, 1916, before the commencement of the Sixty-fifth Congress, to which he had been reelected.
[12] Elected to fill vacancy caused by death of Samuel J. Tribble, and took his seat January 15, 1917.
[13] Election unsuccessfully contested by J. McCan Davis.

[14] Died March 14, 1916.
[15] Appointed to fill vacancy caused by death of Benjamin F. Shively, and took his seat March 27, 1916.
[16] Elected to fill vacancy caused by death of Benjamin F. Shively, and took his seat December 5, 1916.

[17] Died June 16, 1916.
[18] Elected to fill vacancy caused by death of Edwin C. Burleigh, and took his seat December 5, 1916.

## MASSACHUSETTS

### SENATORS

Henry Cabot Lodge, *Nahant*
John W. Weeks, *West Newton*

### REPRESENTATIVES

Allen T. Treadway, *Stockbridge*
Frederick H. Gillett, *Springfield*
Calvin D. Paige, *Southbridge*
Samuel E. Winslow, *Worcester*
John Jacob Rogers, *Lowell*
Augustus P. Gardner, *Hamilton*
Michael F. Phelan, *Lynn*
Frederick W. Dallinger, *Cambridge*
Ernest W. Roberts, *Chelsea*
Peter F. Tague, *Boston*
George H. Tinkham,[19] *Boston*
James A. Gallivan, *Boston*
William H. Carter, *Needham Heights*
Richard Olney, *Dedham*
William S. Greene, *Fall River*
Joseph Walsh, *New Bedford*

## MICHIGAN

### SENATORS

William Alden Smith, *Grand Rapids*
Charles E. Townsend, *Jackson*

### REPRESENTATIVES

Frank E. Doremus, *Detroit*
Samuel W. Beakes, *Ann Arbor*
John M. C. Smith, *Charlotte*
Edward L. Hamilton, *Niles*
Carl E. Mapes, *Grand Rapids*
Patrick H. Kelley, *Lansing*
Louis C. Cramton, *Lapeer*
Joseph W. Fordney, *Saginaw*
James C. McLaughlin, *Muskegon*
George A. Loud, *Bay City*
Frank D. Scott, *Alpena*
W. Frank James, *Hancock*
Charles A. Nichols, *Detroit*

## MINNESOTA

### SENATORS

Knute Nelson, *Alexandria*
Moses E. Clapp, *St. Paul*

### REPRESENTATIVES

Sydney Anderson, *Lanesboro*
Franklin F. Ellsworth, *Mankato*
Charles R. Davis, *St. Peter*
Carl C. Van Dyke, *St. Paul*
George R. Smith, *Minneapolis*
Charles A. Lindbergh, *Little Falls*
Andrew J. Volstead, *Granite Falls*
Clarence B. Miller, *Duluth*
Halvor Steenerson, *Crookston*
Thomas D. Schall, *Excelsior*

## MISSISSIPPI

### SENATORS

John Sharp Williams, *Yazoo City*
James K. Vardaman, *Jackson*

### REPRESENTATIVES

Ezekiel S. Candler, Jr., *Corinth*
Hubert D. Stephens, *New Albany*
Benjamin G. Humphreys, *Greenville*
Thomas U. Sisson, *Winona*
Samuel A. Witherspoon,[20] *Meridian*
William W. Venable,[21] *Meridian*
Pat Harrison, *Gulfport*
Percy E. Quin, *McComb City*
James W. Collier, *Vicksburg*

## MISSOURI

### SENATORS

William J. Stone, *Jefferson City*
James A. Reed, *Kansas City*

### REPRESENTATIVES

James T. Lloyd, *Shelbyville*
William W. Rucker, *Keytesville*
Joshua W. Alexander, *Gallatin*
Charles F. Booher, *Savannah*
William P. Borland, *Kansas City*
Clement C. Dickinson, *Clinton*
Courtney W. Hamlin, *Springfield*
Dorsey W. Shackleford, *Jefferson City*
James Beauchamp Clark, *Bowling Green*
Jacob E. Meeker, *St. Louis*
William L. Igoe, *St. Louis*
Leonidas C. Dyer, *St. Louis*
Walter L. Hensley, *Farmington*
Joseph J. Russell, *Charleston*
Perl D. Decker, *Joplin*
Thomas L. Rubey, *Lebanon*

## MONTANA

### SENATORS

Henry L. Myers, *Hamilton*
Thomas J. Walsh, *Helena*

### REPRESENTATIVES AT LARGE

John M. Evans, *Missoula*
Tom Stout, *Lewistown*

## NEBRASKA

### SENATORS

Gilbert M. Hitchcock, *Omaha*
George W. Norris, *McCook*

### REPRESENTATIVES

C. Frank Reavis, *Falls City*
Charles O. Lobeck, *Omaha*
Daniel V. Stephens, *Fremont*
Charles H. Sloan, *Geneva*
Ashton C. Shallenberger, *Alma*
Moses P. Kinkaid, *O'Neill*

## NEVADA

### SENATORS

Francis G. Newlands, *Reno*
Key Pittman, *Tonopah*

### REPRESENTATIVE AT LARGE

Edwin E. Roberts, *Carson City*

## NEW HAMPSHIRE

### SENATORS

Jacob H. Gallinger, *Concord*
Henry F. Hollis, *Concord*

### REPRESENTATIVES

Cyrus A. Sulloway, *Manchester*
Edward H. Wason, *Nashua*

## NEW JERSEY

### SENATORS

James E. Martine, *Plainfield*
William Hughes, *Paterson*

### REPRESENTATIVES

William J. Browning, *Camden*
Isaac Bacharach, *Atlantic City*
Thomas J. Scully, *South Amboy*
Elijah C. Hutchinson, *Trenton*
John H. Capstick, *Montville*
Archibald C. Hart, *Hackensack*
Dow H. Drukker, *Passaic*
Edward W. Gray, *Newark*
Richard Wayne Parker, *Newark*
Frederick R. Lehlbach, *Newark*
John J. Eagan, *Weehawken*
James A. Hamill, *Jersey City*

## NEW MEXICO

### SENATORS

Thomas B. Catron, *Santa Fe*
Albert B. Fall, *Three Rivers*

### REPRESENTATIVE AT LARGE

Benigno C. Hernandez, *Tierra Amarilla*

## NEW YORK

### SENATORS

James A. O'Gorman, *New York City*
James W. Wadsworth, Jr., *Groveland*

### REPRESENTATIVES

Frederick C. Hicks,[22] *Port Washington*
Charles P. Caldwell, *Forest Hills*
Joseph V. Flynn, *Brooklyn*
Harry H. Dale, *Brooklyn*
James P. Maher, *Brooklyn*
Frederick W. Rowe, *Brooklyn*
John J. Fitzgerald, *Brooklyn*
Daniel J. Griffin, *Brooklyn*

---

[19] Election unsuccessfully contested by Francis J. Horgan.
[20] Died November 24, 1915.

[21] Elected to fill vacancy caused by death of Samuel A. Witherspoon, and took his seat January 17, 1916.

[22] Election unsuccessfully contested by Lathrop Brown.

## NEW YORK—Continued

### REPRESENTATIVES—CONTINUED

Oscar W. Swift, *Brooklyn*
Reuben L. Haskell, *Brooklyn*
Daniel J. Riordan, *New York City*
Meyer London, *New York City*
George W. Loft, *New York City*
Michael F. Farley, *New York City*
Michael F. Conry,[23] *New York City*
Peter J. Dooling, *New York City*
John F. Carew, *New York City*
Thomas G. Patten, *New York City*
Walter M. Chandler, *New York City*
Isaac Siegel,[24] *New York City*
G. Murray Hulbert, *New York City*
Henry Bruckner, *New York City*
Joseph A. Goulden,[25] *Fordham*
William S. Bennet,[26] *New York City*
Woodson R. Oglesby, *Yonkers*
James W. Husted, *Peekskill*
Edmund Platt, *Poughkeepsie*
Charles B. Ward, *Debruce*
Rollin B. Sanford, *Albany*
James S. Parker, *Salem*
William B. Charles, *Amsterdam*
Bertrand H. Snell,[27] *Potsdam*
Luther W. Mott, *Oswego*
Homer P. Snyder, *Little Falls*
George W. Fairchild, *Oneonta*
Walter W. Magee, *Syracuse*
Norman J. Gould,[28] *Seneca Falls*
Harry H. Pratt, *Corning*
Thomas B. Dunn, *Rochester*
Henry G. Danforth, *Rochester*
S. Wallace Dempsey, *Lockport*
Charles B. Smith, *Buffalo*
Daniel A. Driscoll, *Buffalo*
Charles M. Hamilton, *Ripley*

## NORTH CAROLINA

### SENATORS

Furnifold McL. Simmons, *New Bern*
Lee S. Overman, *Salisbury*

### REPRESENTATIVES

John H. Small, *Washington*
Claude Kitchin, *Scotland Neck*
George E. Hood, *Goldsboro*
Edward W. Pou, *Smithfield*
Charles M. Stedman, *Greensboro*
Hannibal L. Godwin, *Dunn*
Robert N. Page, *Biscoe*
Robert L. Doughton, *Laurel Springs*
Edwin Y. Webb, *Shelby*
James J. Britt, *Asheville*

## NORTH DAKOTA

### SENATORS

Porter J. McCumber, *Wahpeton*
Asle J. Gronna, *Lakota*

### REPRESENTATIVES

Henry T. Helgesen, *Milton*
George M. Young, *Valley City*
Patrick D. Norton, *Hettinger*

## OHIO

### SENATORS

Atlee Pomerene, *Canton*
Warren G. Harding, *Marion*

### REPRESENTATIVES

Nicholas Longworth, *Cincinnati*
Alfred G. Allen, *Cincinnati*
Warren Gard, *Hamilton*
J. Edward Russell, *Sidney*
Nelson E. Matthews, *Ottawa*
Charles C. Kearns, *Batavia*
Simeon D. Fess, *Yellow Springs*
John A. Key, *Marion*
Isaac R. Sherwood, *Toledo*
Robert M. Switzer, *Gallipolis*
Edwin D. Ricketts, *Logan*
Clement L. Brumbaugh, *Columbus*
Arthur W. Overmyer, *Fremont*
Seward H. Williams, *Lorain*
William C. Mooney, *Woodsfield*
Roscoe C. McCulloch, *Canton*
William A. Ashbrook, *Johnstown*
David A. Hollingsworth, *Cadiz*
John G. Cooper, *Youngstown*
William Gordon, *Cleveland*
Robert Crosser, *Cleveland*
Henry I. Emerson, *Cleveland*

## OKLAHOMA

### SENATORS

Thomas P. Gore, *Lawton*
Robert L. Owen, *Muskogee*

### REPRESENTATIVES

James S. Davenport, *Vinita*
William W. Hastings, *Tahlequah*
Charles D. Carter, *Ardmore*
William H. Murray, *Tishomingo*
Joseph B. Thompson, *Pauls Valley*
Scott Ferris, *Lawton*
James V. McClintic, *Snyder*
Dick T. Morgan, *Woodward*

## OREGON

### SENATORS

George E. Chamberlain, *Portland*
Harry Lane, *Portland*

### REPRESENTATIVES

Willis C. Hawley, *Salem*
Nicholas J. Sinnott, *The Dalles*
Clifton N. McArthur, *Portland*

## PENNSYLVANIA

### SENATORS

Boies Penrose, *Philadelphia*
George T. Oliver, *Pittsburgh*

### REPRESENTATIVES AT LARGE

Thomas S. Crago, *Waynesburg*
Mahlon M. Garland, *Pittsburgh*
Daniel F. Lafean, *York*
John R. K. Scott, *Philadelphia*

### REPRESENTATIVES

William S. Vare, *Philadelphia*
George S. Graham, *Philadelphia*
J. Hampton Moore, *Philadelphia*
George W. Edmonds, *Philadelphia*
Peter E. Costello, *Philadelphia*
George P. Darrow, *Philadelphia*
Thomas S. Butler, *West Chester*
Henry W. Watson, *Langhorne*
William W. Griest, *Lancaster*
John R. Farr, *Scranton*
John J. Casey, *Wilkes-Barre*
Robert D. Heaton, *Ashland*
Arthur G. Dewalt, *Allentown*
Louis T. McFadden, *Canton*
Edgar R. Kiess, *Williamsport*
John V. Lesher, *Sunbury*
Benjamin K. Focht, *Lewisburg*
Aaron S. Kreider, *Annville*
Warren W. Bailey, *Johnstown*
C. William Beales, *Gettysburg*
Charles H. Rowland, *Philipsburg*
Abraham L. Keister, *Scottdale*
Robert F. Hopwood, *Uniontown*
Henry W. Temple,[29] *Washington*
Michael Liebel, Jr., *Erie*
Henry J. Steele, *Easton*
S. Taylor North, *Punxsutawney*
Samuel H. Miller, *Mercer*
Stephen G. Porter, *Pittsburgh*
William H. Coleman, *McKeesport*
John M. Morin, *Pittsburgh*
Andrew J. Barchfeld, *Pittsburgh*

## RHODE ISLAND

### SENATORS

Henry F. Lippitt, *Providence*
LeBaron B. Colt, *Bristol*

### REPRESENTATIVES

George F. O'Shaunessy, *Providence*
Walter R. Stiness, *Warwick*
Ambrose Kennedy, *Woonsocket*

---

[23] Died March 2, 1917, before the commencement of the Sixty-fifth Congress, to which he had been reelected.

[24] Election unsuccessfully contested by Jacob A. Cantor.

[25] Died May 3, 1915.

[26] Elected to fill vacancy caused by death of Joseph A. Goulden, and took his seat December 6, 1915.

[27] Elected to fill vacancy caused by death of Representative-elect Edwin A. Merritt, Jr., in preceding Congress, and took his seat December 6, 1915.

[28] Elected to fill vacancy caused by death of

Representative-elect Sereno E. Payne, in preceding Congress, and took his seat December 6, 1915.

[29] Elected to fill vacancy caused by death of Representative-elect William M. Brown (January 31, 1915, before the beginning of the congressional term), and took his seat December 6, 1915.

## SOUTH CAROLINA

### SENATORS

Benjamin R. Tillman, *Trenton*
Ellison D. Smith, *Florence*

### REPRESENTATIVES

Richard S. Whaley,[30] *Charleston*
James F. Byrnes, *Aiken*
Wyatt Aiken, *Abbeville*
Joseph T. Johnson,[31] *Spartanburg*
Samuel J. Nicholls,[32] *Spartanburg*
David E. Finley,[33] *Yorkville*
Paul G. McCorkle,[34] *York*
J. Willard Ragsdale, *Florence*
Asbury F. Lever, *Lexington*

## SOUTH DAKOTA

### SENATORS

Thomas Sterling, *Vermilion*
Edwin S. Johnson, *Yankton*

### REPRESENTATIVES

Charles H. Dillon, *Yankton*
Royal C. Johnson, *Aberdeen*
Harry L. Gandy, *Rapid City*

## TENNESSEE

### SENATORS

Luke Lea, *Nashville*
John K. Shields, *Knoxville*

### REPRESENTATIVES

Sam R. Sells, *Johnson City*
Richard W. Austin, *Knoxville*
John A. Moon, *Chattanooga*
Cordell Hull, *Carthage*
William C. Houston, *Woodbury*
Joseph W. Byrns, *Nashville*
Lemuel P. Padgett, *Columbia*
Thetus W. Sims, *Linden*
Finis J. Garrett, *Dresden*
Kenneth D. McKellar, *Memphis*

## TEXAS

### SENATORS

Charles A. Culberson, *Dallas*
Morris Sheppard, *Texarkana*

### REPRESENTATIVES AT LARGE

A. Jeff. McLemore, *Houston*
James H. Davis, *Sulphur Springs*

### REPRESENTATIVES

Eugene Black, *Clarksville*
Martin Dies, *Beaumont*
James Young, *Kaufman*

Sam Rayburn, *Bonham*
Hatton W. Sumners, *Dallas*
Rufus Hardy, *Corsicana*
Alexander W. Gregg, *Palestine*
Joe H. Eagle, *Houston*
George F. Burgess, *Gonzales*
James P. Buchanan, *Brenham*
Robert L. Henry, *Waco*
Oscar Callaway, *Comanche*
John H. Stephens, *Vernon*
James L. Slayden, *San Antonio*
John N. Garner, *Uvalde*
William R. Smith, *Colorado*

## UTAH

### SENATORS

Reed Smoot, *Provo*
George Sutherland, *Salt Lake City*

### REPRESENTATIVES

Joseph Howell, *Logan*
James H. Mays, *Salt Lake City*

## VERMONT

### SENATORS

William P. Dillingham, *Montpelier*
Carroll S. Page, *Hyde Park*

### REPRESENTATIVES

Frank L. Greene, *St. Albans*
Porter H. Dale, *Island Pond*

## VIRGINIA

### SENATORS

Thomas S. Martin, *Charlottesville*
Claude A. Swanson, *Chatham*

### REPRESENTATIVES

William A. Jones, *Warsaw*
Edward E. Holland, *Suffolk*
Andrew J. Montague, *Richmond*
Walter A. Watson, *Jennings Ordinary*
Edward W. Saunders, *Rockymount*
Carter Glass, *Lynchburg*
James Hay,[35] *Madison*
Thomas W. Harrison,[36] *Winchester*
Charles C. Carlin, *Alexandria*
C. Bascom Slemp, *Big Stone Gap*
Henry D. Flood, *Appomattox*

## WASHINGTON

### SENATORS

Wesley L. Jones, *North Yakima*
Miles Poindexter, *Spokane*

### REPRESENTATIVES

William E. Humphrey, *Seattle*
Lindley H. Hadley, *Bellingham*
Albert Johnson, *Hoquiam*
William L. La Follette, *Pullman*
Clarence C. Dill, *Spokane*

## WEST VIRGINIA

### SENATORS

William E. Chilton, *Charleston*
Nathan Goff, *Clarksburg*

### REPRESENTATIVE AT LARGE

Howard Sutherland, *Elkins*

### REPRESENTATIVES

Matthew M. Neely, *Fairmont*
William G. Brown, Jr.,[37] *Kingwood*
George M. Bowers,[38] *Martinsburg*
Adam B. Littlepage, *Charleston*
Hunter H. Moss, Jr.,[39] *Parkersburg*
Harry C. Woodyard,[40] *Spencer*
Edward Cooper, *Bramwell*

## WISCONSIN

### SENATORS

Robert M. La Follette, *Madison*
Paul O. Husting, *Mayville*

### REPRESENTATIVES

Henry Allen Cooper, *Racine*
Michael E. Burke, *Beaver Dam*
John M. Nelson, *Madison*
William J. Cary,[41] *Milwaukee*
William H. Stafford, *Milwaukee*
Michael K. Reilly, *Fond du Lac*
John J. Esch, *La Crosse*
Edward E. Browne, *Waupaca*
Thomas F. Konop, *Green Bay*
James A. Frear, *Hudson*
Irvine L. Lenroot, *Superior*

## WYOMING

### SENATORS

Clarence D. Clark, *Evanston*
Francis E. Warren, *Cheyenne*

### REPRESENTATIVE AT LARGE

Frank W. Mondell, *Newcastle*

## TERRITORY OF ALASKA

### DELEGATE

James Wickersham, *Fairbanks*

---

[30] Election unsuccessfully contested by Aaron P. Prioleau.
[31] Resigned April 19, 1915.
[32] Elected to fill vacancy caused by resignation of Joseph T. Johnson, and took his seat December 6, 1915.
[33] Died January 26, 1917, before the commencement of the Sixty-fifth Congress, to which he had been reelected.

[34] Elected to fill vacancy caused by death of David E. Finley, and took his seat February 24, 1917.
[35] Resigned October 1, 1916.
[36] Elected to fill vacancy caused by resignation of James Hay, and took his seat December 4, 1916.
[37] Died March 9, 1916.
[38] Elected to fill vacancy caused by death of William G. Brown, Jr., and took his seat May 18, 1916.

[39] Died July 15, 1916.
[40] Elected to fill vacancy caused by death of Hunter H. Moss, Jr., and took his seat December 4, 1916.
[41] Election unsuccessfully contested by Winfield R. Gaylord.

## TERRITORY OF HAWAII

DELEGATE
J. Kuhio Kalanianaole, *Waikiki*

## PHILIPPINE ISLANDS

RESIDENT COMMISSIONERS
Manuel L. Quezon,[42] *Tayabas*
Manuel Earnshaw, *Manila*

## PORTO RICO

RESIDENT COMMISSIONER
Luis Muñoz Rivera,[43] *San Juan*

---

[42] Resigned October 15, 1916; vacancy throughout remainder of the Congress.

[43] Died November 15, 1916; vacancy until August 6, 1917.

# 65TH CONGRESS

## MARCH 4, 1917, TO MARCH 3, 1919

Thomas R. Marshall
Vice President

FIRST SESSION— *April 2, 1917, to October 6, 1917*
SECOND SESSION— *December 3, 1917, to November 21, 1918*
THIRD SESSION— *December 2, 1918, to March 3, 1919*
SPECIAL SESSION OF THE SENATE— *March 5, 1917, to March 16, 1917*

VICE PRESIDENT OF THE UNITED STATES— Thomas R. Marshall, of Indiana
PRESIDENT PRO TEMPORE OF THE SENATE— Willard Saulsbury, of Delaware
SECRETARY OF THE SENATE— James M. Baker, of South Carolina
SERGEANT AT ARMS OF THE SENATE— Charles P. Higgins, of Missouri

James Beauchamp Clark
Speaker

SPEAKER OF THE HOUSE OF REPRESENTATIVES— James Beauchamp Clark,[1] of Missouri
CLERK OF THE HOUSE— South Trimble,[2] of Kentucky
SERGEANT AT ARMS OF THE HOUSE— Robert B. Gordon, of Ohio
DOORKEEPER OF THE HOUSE— Joseph J. Sinnott, of Virginia
POSTMASTER OF THE HOUSE— William M. Dunbar

## ALABAMA

### SENATORS
John H. Bankhead, *Jasper*
Oscar W. Underwood, *Birmingham*

### REPRESENTATIVES
Oscar L. Gray, *Butler*
S. Hubert Dent, Jr., *Montgomery*
Henry B. Steagall, *Ozark*
Fred L. Blackmon, *Anniston*
J. Thomas Heflin, *Lafayette*
William B. Oliver, *Tuscaloosa*
John L. Burnett, *Gadsden*
Edward B. Almon, *Tuscumbia*
George Huddleston, *Birmingham*
William B. Bankhead, *Jasper*

## ARIZONA

### SENATORS
Henry F. Ashurst, *Prescott*
Marcus A. Smith, *Tucson*

### REPRESENTATIVE AT LARGE
Carl Hayden, *Phoenix*

## ARKANSAS

### SENATORS
Joseph T. Robinson, *Little Rock*
William F. Kirby, *Little Rock*

### REPRESENTATIVES
Thaddeus H. Caraway, *Jonesboro*
William A. Oldfield, *Batesville*
John N. Tillman, *Fayetteville*
Otis Wingo, *De Queen*
Henderson M. Jacoway, *Dardanelle*
Samuel M. Taylor, *Pine Bluff*
William S. Goodwin, *Warren*

## CALIFORNIA

### SENATORS
James D. Phelan, *San Francisco*
Hiram W. Johnson,[3] *San Francisco*

### REPRESENTATIVES
Clarence F. Lea, *Santa Rosa*
John E. Raker, *Alturas*
Charles F. Curry, *Sacramento*
Julius Kahn, *San Francisco*
John I. Nolan, *San Francisco*
John A. Elston, *Berkeley*
Denver S. Church, *Fresno*
Everis A. Hayes, *San Jose*
Charles H. Randall, *Los Angeles*
Henry Z. Osborne, *Los Angeles*
William Kettner, *San Diego*

## COLORADO

### SENATORS
Charles S. Thomas, *Denver*
John F. Shafroth, *Denver*

### REPRESENTATIVES
Benjamin C. Hilliard, *Denver*
Charles B. Timberlake, *Sterling*
Edward Keating, *Pueblo*
Edward T. Taylor, *Glenwood Springs*

## CONNECTICUT

### SENATORS
Frank B. Brandegee, *New London*
George P. McLean, *Simsbury*

### REPRESENTATIVES
Augustine Lonergan, *Hartford*
Richard P. Freeman, *New London*
John Q. Tilson, *New Haven*

Ebenezer J. Hill,[4] *Norwalk*
Schuyler Merritt,[5] *Stamford*
James P. Glynn, *Winsted*

## DELAWARE

### SENATORS
Willard Saulsbury, *Wilmington*
Josiah O. Wolcott, *Dover*

### REPRESENTATIVE AT LARGE
Albert F. Polk, *Georgetown*

## FLORIDA

### SENATORS
Duncan U. Fletcher, *Jacksonville*
Park Trammell, *Lakeland*

### REPRESENTATIVES
Herbert J. Drane, *Lakeland*
Frank Clark, *Gainesville*
J. Walter Kehoe, *Pensacola*
William J. Sears, *Kissimmee*

## GEORGIA

### SENATORS
Hoke Smith, *Atlanta*
Thomas W. Hardwick, *Sandersville*

### REPRESENTATIVES
James W. Overstreet, *Sylvania*
Frank Park, *Sylvester*
Charles R. Crisp, *Americus*
William C. Adamson,[6] *Carrollton*

---

[1] Reelected April 2, 1917.
[2] Reelected April 2, 1917.
[3] Elected November 7, 1916, for the term begin-

ning March 4, 1917, but did not qualify until April 2, 1917, preferring to retain the governorship.
[4] Died September 27, 1917.

[5] Elected to fill vacancy caused by death of Ebenezer J. Hill, and took his seat December 3, 1917.
[6] Resigned December 18, 1917.

## GEORGIA—Continued

### REPRESENTATIVES—CONTINUED

William C. Wright,[7] *Newnan*
William S. Howard, *Kirkwood*
James W. Wise, *Fayetteville*
Gordon Lee, *Chickamauga*
Charles H. Brand,[8] *Athens*
Thomas M. Bell, *Gainesville*
Carl Vinson, *Milledgeville*
John R. Walker, *Valdosta*
William W. Larsen, *Dublin*

## IDAHO

### SENATORS

William E. Borah, *Boise*
James H. Brady,[9] *Pocatello*
John F. Nugent,[10] *Boise*

### REPRESENTATIVES AT LARGE

Burton L. French, *Moscow*
Addison T. Smith, *Twin Falls*

## ILLINOIS

### SENATORS

James Hamilton Lewis, *Chicago*
Lawrence Y. Sherman, *Springfield*

### REPRESENTATIVES AT LARGE

Medill McCormick, *Chicago*
William E. Mason, *Chicago*

### REPRESENTATIVES

Martin B. Madden, *Chicago*
James R. Mann, *Chicago*
William W. Wilson, *Chicago*
Charles Martin,[11] *Chicago*
John W. Rainey,[12] *Chicago*
Adolph J. Sabath, *Chicago*
James McAndrews, *Chicago*
Niels Juul, *Chicago*
Thomas Gallagher, *Chicago*
Fred A. Britten, *Chicago*
George E. Foss, *Chicago*
Ira C. Copley, *Aurora*
Charles E. Fuller, *Belvidere*
John C. McKenzie, *Elizabeth*
William J. Graham, *Aledo*
Edward J. King, *Galesburg*
Clifford Ireland, *Peoria*
John A. Sterling,[13] *Bloomington*
Joseph G. Cannon, *Danville*
William B. McKinley, *Champaign*
Henry T. Rainey, *Carrollton*
Loren E. Wheeler, *Springfield*
William A. Rodenberg, *East St. Louis*
Martin D. Foster, *Olney*

Thomas S. Williams, *Louisville*
Edward E. Denison, *Marion*

## INDIANA

### SENATORS

James E. Watson, *Rushville*
Harry S. New, *Indianapolis*

### REPRESENTATIVES

George K. Denton, *Evansville*
Oscar E. Bland, *Linton*
William E. Cox, *Jasper*
Lincoln Dixon, *North Vernon*
Everett Sanders, *Terre Haute*
Daniel W. Comstock,[14] *Richmond*
Richard N. Elliot,[15] *Connersville*
Merrill Moores, *Indianapolis*
Albert H. Vestal, *Anderson*
Fred S. Purnell, *Attica*
William R. Wood, *La Fayette*
Milton Kraus, *Peru*
Louis W. Fairfield, *Angola*
Henry A. Barnhart, *Rochester*

## IOWA

### SENATORS

Albert B. Cummins, *Des Moines*
William S. Kenyon, *Fort Dodge*

### REPRESENTATIVES

Charles A. Kennedy, *Montrose*
Harry E. Hull, *Williamsburg*
Burton E. Sweet, *Waverly*
Gilbert N. Haugen, *Northwood*
James W. Good, *Cedar Rapids*
C. William Ramseyer, *Bloomfield*
Cassius C. Dowell, *Des Moines*
Horace M. Towner, *Corning*
William R. Green, *Council Bluffs*
Frank P. Woods, *Estherville*
George C. Scott,[16] *Sioux City*

## KANSAS

### SENATORS

William H. Thompson, *Kansas City*
Charles Curtis, *Topeka*

### REPRESENTATIVES

Daniel R. Anthony, Jr., *Leavenworth*
Edward C. Little, *Kansas City*
Philip P. Campbell, *Pittsburg*
Dudley Doolittle, *Strong City*
Guy T. Helvering, *Marysville*
John R. Connelly, *Colby*
Jouett Shouse, *Kinsley*
William A. Ayres, *Wichita*

## KENTUCKY

### SENATORS

Ollie M. James,[17] *Marion*
George B. Martin,[18] *Catlettsburg*
Joseph C. W. Beckham, *Frankfort*

### REPRESENTATIVES

Alben W. Barkley, *Paducah*
David H. Kincheloe, *Madisonville*
Robert Y. Thomas, Jr., *Central City*
Ben Johnson, *Bardstown*
J. Swagar Sherley, *Louisville*
Arthur B. Rouse, *Burlington*
James C. Cantrill, *Georgetown*
Harvey Helm,[19] *Stanford*
William J. Fields, *Olive Hill*
John W. Langley, *Pikeville*
Caleb Powers, *Barbourville*

## LOUISIANA

### SENATORS

Joseph E. Ransdell, *Lake Providence*
Robert F. Broussard,[20] *New Iberia*
Walter Guion,[21] *Napoleonville*
Edward J. Gay,[22] *Plaquemine*

### REPRESENTATIVES

Alber Estopinal, *Estopinal*
H. Garland Dupré, *New Orleans*
Whitmell P. Martin, *Thibodaux*
John T. Watkins, *Minden*
Riley J. Wilson, *Harrisonburg*
Jared Y. Sanders, *Bogalusa*
Ladislas Lazaro, *Washington*
James B. Aswell, *Natchitoches*

## MAINE

### SENATORS

Bert M. Fernald, *West Poland*
Frederick Hale, *Portland*

### REPRESENTATIVES

Louis B. Goodall, *Sanford*
Wallace H. White, Jr., *Lewiston*
John A. Peters, *Ellsworth*
Ira G. Hersey, *Houlton*

## MARYLAND

### SENATORS

John Walter Smith, *Snow Hill*
Joseph I. France, *Port Deposit*

### REPRESENTATIVES

Jesse D. Price, *Salisbury*
J. Fred. C. Talbott,[23] *Lutherville*
Carville D. Benson,[24] *Halethorpe*

---

[7] Elected to fill vacancy caused by resignation of William C. Adamson, and took his seat January 24, 1918.

[8] Elected to fill vacancy caused by death of Representative-elect Samuel J. Tribble, in preceding Congress, and took his seat April 2, 1917.

[9] Died January 13, 1918.

[10] Appointed to fill vacancy caused by death of James H. Brady, and took his seat January 30, 1918; subsequently elected.

[11] Died October 28, 1917.

[12] Elected to fill vacancy caused by death of

Charles Martin, and took his seat April 16, 1918.

[13] Died October 17, 1918; vacancy throughout remainder of the Congress.

[14] Died May 19, 1917.

[15] Elected to fill vacancy caused by death of Daniel W. Comstock, and took his seat July 3, 1917.

[16] Election unsuccessfully contested by Thomas J. Steele.

[17] Died August 28, 1918.

[18] Appointed to fill vacancy caused by death of Ollie M. James, and took his seat September 17, 1918.

[19] Died March 3, 1919, before the commencement

of the Sixty-sixth Congress, to which he had been reelected.

[20] Died April 12, 1918.

[21] Appointed to fill vacancy caused by death of Robert F. Broussard, and took his seat April 24, 1918.

[22] Elected to fill vacancy caused by death of Robert F. Broussard, and took his seat December 2, 1918.

[23] Died October 5, 1918.

[24] Elected to fill vacancy caused by death of J. Fred. C. Talbott, and took his seat November 18, 1918.

Charles P. Coady, *Baltimore*
J. Charles Linthicum, *Baltimore*
Sydney E. Mudd, *La Plata*
Frederick N. Zihlman, *Cumberland*

## MASSACHUSETTS

### SENATORS

Henry Cabot Lodge, *Nahant*
John W. Weeks, *West Newton*

### REPRESENTATIVES

Allen T. Treadway, *Stockbridge*
Frederick H. Gillett, *Springfield*
Calvin D. Paige, *Southbridge*
Samuel E. Winslow, *Worcester*
John Jacob Rogers, *Lowell*
Augustus P. Gardner,[25] *Hamilton*
Willfred W. Lufkin,[26] *Essex*
Michael F. Phelan, *Lynn*
Frederick W. Dallinger, *Cambridge*
Alvan T. Fuller, *Malden*
Peter F. Tague, *Boston*
George H. Tinkham, *Boston*
James A. Gallivan, *Boston*
William H. Carter, *Needham Heights*
Richard Olney, *Dedham*
William S. Greene, *Fall River*
Joseph Walsh, *New Bedford*

## MICHIGAN

### SENATORS

William Alden Smith, *Grand Rapids*
Charles E. Townsend, *Jackson*

### REPRESENTATIVES

Frank E. Doremus, *Detroit*
Mark R. Bacon,[27] *Wyandotte*
Samuel W. Beakes,[28] *Ann Arbor*
John M. C. Smith, *Charlotte*
Edward L. Hamilton, *Niles*
Carl E. Mapes, *Grand Rapids*
Patrick H. Kelley, *Lansing*
Louis C. Cramton, *Lapeer*
Joseph W. Fordney, *Saginaw*
James C. McLaughlin, *Muskegon*
Gilbert A. Currie, *Midland*
Frank D. Scott, *Alpena*
W. Frank James, *Hancock*
Charles A. Nichols, *Detroit*

## MINNESOTA

### SENATORS

Knute Nelson, *Alexandria*
Frank B. Kellogg, *St. Paul*

### REPRESENTATIVES

Sydney Anderson, *Lanesboro*
Franklin F. Ellsworth, *Mankato*
Charles R. Davis, *St. Peter*
Carl C. Van Dyke, *St. Paul*
Ernest Lundeen, *Minneapolis*
Harold Knutson, *St. Cloud*
Andrew J. Volstead, *Granite Falls*
Clarence B. Miller, *Duluth*
Halvor Steenerson, *Crookston*
Thomas D. Schall, *Excelsior*

## MISSISSIPPI

### SENATORS

John Sharp Williams, *Yazoo City*
James K. Vardaman, *Jackson*

### REPRESENTATIVES

Ezekiel S. Candler, Jr., *Corinth*
Hubert D. Stephens, *New Albany*
Benjamin G. Humphreys, *Greenville*
Thomas U. Sisson, *Winona*
William W. Venable, *Meridian*
Pat Harrison, *Gulfport*
Percy E. Quin, *McComb City*
James W. Collier, *Vicksburg*

## MISSOURI

### SENATORS

William J. Stone,[29] *Jefferson City*
Xenophon P. Wilfley,[30] *St. Louis*
Selden P. Spencer,[31] *St. Louis*
James A. Reed, *Kansas City*

### REPRESENTATIVES

Milton A. Romjue, *Macon*
William W. Rucker, *Keytesville*
Joshua W. Alexander, *Gallatin*
Charles F. Booher, *Savannah*
William P. Borland,[32] *Kansas City*
Clement C. Dickinson, *Clinton*
Courtney W. Hamlin, *Springfield*
Dorsey W. Shackleford, *Jefferson City*
James Beauchamp Clark, *Bowling Green*
Jacob E. Meeker,[33] *St. Louis*
Frederick Essen,[34] *Clayton*
William L. Igoe, *St. Louis*
Leonidas C. Dyer, *St. Louis*
Walter L. Hensley, *Farmington*
Joseph J. Russell, *Charleston*
Perl D. Decker, *Joplin*
Thomas L. Rubey, *Lebanon*

## MONTANA

### SENATORS

Henry L. Myers, *Hamilton*
Thomas J. Walsh, *Helena*

### REPRESENTATIVES AT LARGE

John M. Evans, *Missoula*
Jeannette Rankin, *Missoula*

## NEBRASKA

### SENATORS

Gilbert M. Hitchcock, *Omaha*
George W. Norris, *McCook*

### REPRESENTATIVES

C. Frank Reavis, *Falls City*
Charles O. Lobeck, *Omaha*
Daniel V. Stephens, *Fremont*
Charles H. Sloan, *Geneva*
Ashton C. Shallenberger, *Alma*
Moses P. Kinkaid, *O'Neill*

## NEVADA

### SENATORS

Francis G. Newlands,[35] *Reno*
Charles B. Henderson,[36] *Elko*
Key Pittman, *Tonopah*

### REPRESENTATIVE AT LARGE

Edwin E. Roberts, *Carson City*

## NEW HAMPSHIRE

### SENATORS

Jacob H. Gallinger,[37] *Concord*
Irving W. Drew,[38] *Lancaster*
George H. Moses,[39] *Concord*
Henry F. Hollis, *Concord*

### REPRESENTATIVES

Cyrus A. Sulloway,[40] *Manchester*
Sherman E. Burroughs,[41] *Manchester*
Edward H. Wason, *Nashua*

## NEW JERSEY

### SENATORS

William Hughes,[42] *Paterson*
David Baird,[43] *Camden*
Joseph S. Frelinghuysen, *Raritan*

### REPRESENTATIVES

William J. Browning, *Camden*
Isaac Bacharach, *Atlantic City*
Thomas J. Scully, *South Amboy*
Elijah C. Hutchinson, *Trenton*
John H. Capstick,[44] *Montville*

---

[25] Resigned May 15, 1917.
[26] Elected to fill vacancy caused by resignation of Augustus P. Gardner; took his seat December 3, 1917.
[27] Served until December 13, 1917; succeeded by Samuel W. Beakes, who contested his election.
[28] Successfully contested the election of Mark R. Bacon, and took his seat December 13, 1917.
[29] Died April 14, 1918.
[30] Appointed to fill vacancy caused by death of William J. Stone, and took his seat May 7, 1918.
[31] Elected to fill vacancy caused by death of William J. Stone, and took his seat November 21, 1918.

[32] Died February 20, 1919.
[33] Died October 16, 1918.
[34] Elected to fill vacancy caused by death of Jacob E. Meeker, and took his seat November 11, 1918.
[35] Died December 24, 1917.
[36] Appointed to fill vacancy caused by death of Francis G. Newlands, and took his seat January 24, 1918; subsequently elected.
[37] Died August 17, 1918.
[38] Appointed to fill vacancy caused by death of Jacob H. Gallinger; took his seat September 11, 1918.
[39] Elected to fill vacancy caused by death of Jacob

H. Gallinger, and took his seat November 18, 1918.
[40] Died March 11, 1917.
[41] Elected to fill vacancy caused by death of Cyrus A. Sulloway, and took his seat June 7, 1917.
[42] Died January 30, 1918.
[43] Appointed to fill vacancy caused by death of William Hughes, and took his seat March 7, 1918; subsequently elected.
[44] Died March 17, 1918.

## NEW JERSEY— Continued

REPRESENTATIVES—CONTINUED

William F. Birch,[45] *Dover*
John R. Ramsey, *Hackensack*
Dow H. Drukker, *Passaic*
Edward W. Gray, *Newark*
Richard Wayne Parker, *Newark*
Frederick R. Lehlbach, *Newark*
John J. Eagan, *Weehawken*
James A. Hamill, *Jersey City*

## NEW MEXICO

SENATORS

Albert B. Fall, *Three Rivers*
Andrieus A. Jones, *East Las Vegas*

REPRESENTATIVE AT LARGE

William B. Walton, *Silver City*

## NEW YORK

SENATORS

James W. Wadsworth, Jr., *Groveland*
William M. Calder, *Brooklyn*

REPRESENTATIVES

Frederick C. Hicks, *Port Washington*
Charles P. Caldwell, *Forest Hills*
Joseph V. Flynn, *Brooklyn*
Harry H. Dale,[46] *Brooklyn*
James P. Maher, *Brooklyn*
Frederick W. Rowe, *Brooklyn*
John J. Fitzgerald,[47] *Brooklyn*
John J. Delaney,[48] *Brooklyn*
Daniel J. Griffin,[49] *Brooklyn*
William E. Cleary,[50] *Brooklyn*
Oscar W. Swift, *Brooklyn*
Reuben L. Haskell, *Brooklyn*
Daniel J. Riordan, *New York City*
Meyer London, *New York City*
Christopher D. Sullivan, *New York City*
Fiorello H. LaGuardia, *New York City*
Thomas F. Smith,[51] *New York City*
Peter J. Dooling, *New York City*
John F. Carew, *New York City*
George B. Francis, *New York City*
Walter M. Chandler, *New York City*
Isaac Siegel, *New York City*
G. Murray Hulbert,[52] *New York City*
Jerome F. Donovan,[53] *New York City*
Henry Bruckner,[54] *New York City*
Anthony J. Griffin,[55] *New York City*
Daniel C. Oliver, *New York City*
Benjamin L. Fairchild, *Pelham*

James W. Husted, *Peekskill*
Edmund Platt, *Poughkeepsie*
Charles B. Ward, *Debruce*
Rollin B. Sanford, *Albany*
James S. Parker, *Salem*
George R. Lunn, *Schenectady*
Bertrand H. Snell, *Potsdam*
Luther W. Mott, *Oswego*
Homer P. Snyder, *Little Falls*
George W. Fairchild, *Oneonta*
Walter W. Magee, *Syracuse*
Norman J. Gould, *Seneca Falls*
Harry H. Pratt, *Corning*
Thomas B. Dunn,[56] *Rochester*
Archie D. Sanders, *Stafford*
S. Wallace Dempsey, *Lockport*
Charles B. Smith, *Buffalo*
William F. Waldow, *Buffalo*
Charles M. Hamilton, *Ripley*

## NORTH CAROLINA

SENATORS

Furnifold McL. Simmons, *New Bern*
Lee S. Overman, *Salisbury*

REPRESENTATIVES

John H. Small, *Washington*
Claude Kitchin, *Scotland Neck*
George E. Hood, *Goldsboro*
Edward W. Pou, *Smithfield*
Charles M. Stedman, *Greensboro*
Hannibal L. Godwin, *Dunn*
Leonidas D. Robinson, *Wadesboro*
Robert L. Doughton, *Laurel Springs*
Edwin Y. Webb, *Shelby*
Zebulon Weaver,[57] *Asheville*
James J. Britt,[58] *Asheville*

## NORTH DAKOTA

SENATORS

Porter J. McCumber, *Wahpeton*
Asle J. Gronna, *Lakota*

REPRESENTATIVES

Henry T. Helgesen,[59] *Milton*
John M. Baer,[60] *Fargo*
George M. Young, *Valley City*
Patrick D. Norton, *Hettinger*

## OHIO

SENATORS

Atlee Pomerene, *Canton*
Warren G. Harding, *Marion*

REPRESENTATIVES

Nicholas Longworth, *Cincinnati*
Victor Heintz, *Cincinnati*
Warren Gard, *Hamilton*
Benjamin F. Welty, *Lima*
John S. Snook, *Paulding*
Charles C. Kearns, *Batavia*
Simeon D. Fess, *Yellow Springs*
John A. Key, *Marion*
Isaac R. Sherwood, *Toledo*
Robert M. Switzer, *Gallipolis*
Horatio C. Claypool, *Chillicothe*
Clement L. Brumbaugh, *Columbus*
Arthur W. Overmyer, *Fremont*
Ellsworth R. Bathrick,[61] *Akron*
Martin L. Davey,[62] *Kent*
George White, *Marietta*
Roscoe C. McCulloch, *Canton*
William A. Ashbrook, *Johnstown*
David A. Hollinsworth, *Cadiz*
John G. Cooper, *Youngstown*
William Gordon, *Cleveland*
Robert Crosser, *Cleveland*
Henry I. Emerson, *Cleveland*

## OKLAHOMA

SENATORS

Thomas P. Gore, *Lawton*
Robert L. Owen, *Muskogee*

REPRESENTATIVES

Thomas A. Chandler, *Vinita*
William W. Hastings, *Tahlequah*
Charles D. Carter, *Ardmore*
Thomas D. McKeown, *Ada*
Joseph B. Thompson, *Pauls Valley*
Scott Ferris, *Lawton*
James V. McClintic, *Snyder*
Dick T. Morgan, *Woodward*

## OREGON

SENATORS

George E. Chamberlain, *Portland*
Harry Lane,[63] *Portland*
Charles L. McNary,[64] *Salem*
Frederick W. Mulkey,[65] *Portland*
Charles L. McNary,[66] *Salem*

REPRESENTATIVES

Willis C. Hawley, *Salem*
Nicholas J. Sinnott, *The Dalles*
Clifton N. McArthur, *Portland*

---

[45] Elected to fill vacancy caused by death of John H. Capstick, and took his seat November 21, 1918.
[46] Resigned January 6, 1919.
[47] Resigned December 31, 1917.
[48] Elected to fill vacancy caused by resignation of John J. Fitzgerald, and took his seat March 14, 1918.
[49] Resigned December 31, 1917.
[50] Elected to fill vacancy caused by resignation of Daniel J. Griffin, and took his seat March 14, 1918.
[51] Elected to fill vacancy caused by death of Representative-elect Michael F. Conry, in preceding Congress, and took his seat April 18, 1917.
[52] Resigned January 1, 1918.
[53] Elected to fill vacancy caused by resignation of

G. Murray Hulbert, and took his seat March 14, 1918.
[54] Resigned December 31, 1917.
[55] Elected to fill vacancy caused by resignation of Henry Bruckner, and took his seat March 14, 1918.
[56] Election unsuccessfully contested by Jacob Gerling.
[57] Served until March 1, 1919; succeeded by James J. Britt, who contested his election.
[58] Successfully contested the election of Zebulon Weaver, and took his seat March 1, 1919.
[59] Died April 10, 1917.
[60] Elected to fill vacancy caused by death of Henry T. Helgesen, and took his seat August 10, 1917.
[61] Died December 23, 1917.

[62] Elected to fill vacancy caused by death of Ellsworth R. Bathrick, and took his seat December 2, 1918.
[63] Died May 23, 1917.
[64] Appointed to fill vacancy caused by death of Harry Lane, to serve until the next general election, and took his seat June 8, 1917.
[65] Elected to fill vacancy caused by death of Harry Lane, and took his seat December 9, 1918; resigned, effective December 17, 1918.
[66] Appointed to fill vacancy caused by resignation of Frederick W. Mulkey, and took his seat December 17, 1918.

## PENNSYLVANIA

SENATORS

Boies Penrose, *Philadelphia*
Philander C. Knox, *Pittsburgh*

REPRESENTATIVES AT LARGE

Thomas S. Crago, *Waynesburg*
Mahlon M. Garland, *Pittsburgh*
Joseph McLaughlin, *Philadelphia*
John R. K. Scott,[67] *Philadelphia*

REPRESENTATIVES

William S. Vare, *Philadelphia*
George S. Graham, *Philadelphia*
J. Hampton Moore, *Philadelphia*
George W. Edmonds, *Philadelphia*
Peter E. Costello, *Philadelphia*
George P. Darrow, *Philadelphia*
Thomas S. Butler, *West Chester*
Henry W. Watson, *Langhorne*
William W. Griest, *Lancaster*
John R. Farr, *Scranton*
Thomas W. Templeton, *Plymouth*
Robert D. Heaton, *Ashland*
Arthur G. Dewalt, *Allentown*
Louis T. McFadden, *Canton*
Edgar R. Kiess, *Williamsport*
John V. Lesher, *Sunbury*
Benjamin K. Focht, *Lewisburg*
Aaron S. Kreider, *Annville*
John M. Rose, *Johnstown*
Andrew R. Brodbeck, *Hanover*
Charles H. Rowland, *Philipsburg*
Edward E. Robbins,[68] *Greensburg*
Bruce F. Sterling, *Uniontown*
Henry W. Temple, *Washington*
Henry A. Clark, *Erie*
Henry J. Steele, *Easton*
Nathan L. Strong, *Brookville*
Orrin D. Bleakley,[69] *Franklin*
Earl H. Beshlin,[70] *Warren*
Stephen G. Porter, *Pittsburgh*
M. Clyde Kelly, *Braddock*
John M. Morin, *Pittsburgh*
Guy E. Campbell, *Crafton*

## RHODE ISLAND

SENATORS

LeBaron B. Colt, *Bristol*
Peter G. Gerry, *Warwick*

REPRESENTATIVES

George F. O'Shaunessy, *Providence*
Walter R. Stiness, *Cowesett*
Ambrose Kennedy, *Woonsocket*

## SOUTH CAROLINA

SENATORS

Benjamin R. Tillman,[71] *Trenton*
Christie Benet,[72] *Columbia*
William P. Pollock,[73] *Cheraw*
Ellison D. Smith, *Florence*

REPRESENTATIVES

Richard S. Whaley, *Charleston*
James F. Byrnes, *Aiken*
Fred H. Dominick, *Newberry*
Samuel J. Nicholls, *Spartanburg*
William F. Stevenson,[74] *Cheraw*
J. Willard Ragsdale, *Florence*
Asbury F. Lever, *Lexington*

## SOUTH DAKOTA

SENATORS

Thomas Sterling, *Vermilion*
Edwin S. Johnson, *Yankton*

REPRESENTATIVES

Charles H. Dillon, *Yankton*
Royal C. Johnson, *Aberdeen*
Harry L. Gandy, *Rapid City*

## TENNESSEE

SENATORS

John K. Shields, *Knoxville*
Kenneth D. McKellar, *Memphis*

REPRESENTATIVES

Sam R. Sells, *Johnson City*
Richard W. Austin, *Knoxville*
John A. Moon, *Chattanooga*
Cordell Hull, *Carthage*
William C. Houston, *Woodbury*
Joseph W. Byrns, *Nashville*
Lemuel P. Padgett, *Columbia*
Thetus W. Sims, *Linden*
Finis J. Garrett, *Dresden*
Hubert F. Fisher, *Memphis*

## TEXAS

SENATORS

Charles A. Culberson, *Dallas*
Morris Sheppard, *Texarkana*

REPRESENTATIVES AT LARGE

A. Jeff. McLemore, *Houston*
Daniel E. Garrett, *Houston*

REPRESENTATIVES

Eugene Black, *Clarksville*
Martin Dies, *Beaumont*
James Young, *Kaufman*
Sam Rayburn, *Bonham*
Hatton W. Sumners, *Dallas*
Rufus Hardy, *Corsicana*

Alexander W. Gregg, *Palestine*
Joe H. Eagle, *Houston*
Joseph J. Mansfield, *Columbus*
James P. Buchanan, *Brenham*
Tom T. Connally, *Marlin*
James C. Wilson, *Fort Worth*
Marvin Jones, *Amarillo*
James L. Slayden, *San Antonio*
John N. Garner, *Uvalde*
Thomas L. Blanton, *Abilene*

## UTAH

SENATORS

Reed Smoot, *Provo*
William H. King, *Salt Lake City*

REPRESENTATIVES

Milton H. Welling, *Fielding*
James H. Mays, *Salt Lake City*

## VERMONT

SENATORS

William P. Dillingham, *Montpelier*
Carroll S. Page, *Hyde Park*

REPRESENTATIVES

Frank L. Greene, *St. Albans*
Porter H. Dale, *Island Pond*

## VIRGINIA

SENATORS

Thomas S. Martin, *Charlottesville*
Claude A. Swanson, *Chatham*

REPRESENTATIVES

William A. Jones,[75] *Warsaw*
Schuyler Otis Bland,[76] *Newport News*
Edward E. Holland, *Suffolk*
Andrew J. Montague, *Richmond*
Walter A. Watson, *Jennings Ordinary*
Edward W. Saunders, *Rockymount*
Carter Glass,[77] *Lynchburg*
James P. Woods,[78] *Roanoke*
Thomas W. Harrison, *Winchester*
Charles C. Carlin,[79] *Alexandria*
C. Bascom Slemp, *Big Stone Gap*
Henry D. Flood, *Appomattox*

## WASHINGTON

SENATORS

Wesley L. Jones, *Seattle*
Miles Poindexter, *Spokane*

REPRESENTATIVES

John F. Miller, *Seattle*
Lindley H. Hadley, *Bellingham*
Albert Johnson, *Hoquiam*
William L. La Follette, *Pullman*
Clarence C. Dill, *Spokane*

---

[67] Resigned effective January 5, 1919.

[68] Died January 25, 1919, before the commencement of the Sixty-sixth Congress, to which he had been reelected.

[69] Resigned April 3, 1917, never having qualified.

[70] Elected to fill vacancy caused by resignation of Orrin D. Bleakley, and took his seat December 3, 1917.

[71] Died July 3, 1918.

[72] Appointed to fill vacancy caused by death of Benjamin R. Tillman, and took his seat July 8, 1918.

[73] Elected to fill vacancy caused by death of Benjamin R. Tillman, and took his seat December 2, 1918.

[74] Elected to fill vacancy caused by death of Representative-elect David E. Finely, in preceding Congress, and took his seat April 2, 1917.

[75] Died April 17, 1918.

[76] Elected to fill vacancy caused by death of

William A. Jones, and took his seat July 3, 1918.

[77] Resigned December 16, 1918, before the commencement of the Sixty-sixth Congress, to which he had been reelected, having been appointed Secretary of the Treasury.

[78] Elected to fill vacancy caused by resignation of Carter Glass, and took his seat March 1, 1919.

[79] Resigned March 3, 1919, before the commencement of the Sixty-sixth Congress, to which he had been reelected.

## WEST VIRGINIA

SENATORS

Nathan Goff, *Clarksburg*
Howard Sutherland,[80] *Elkins*

REPRESENTATIVES

Matthew M. Neely, *Fairmont*
George M. Bowers, *Martinsburg*
Stuart F. Reed, *Clarksburg*
Harry C. Woodyard, *Spencer*
Edward Cooper, *Bramwell*
Adam B. Littlepage, *Charleston*

## WISCONSIN

SENATORS

Robert M. La Follette, *Madison*
Paul O. Husting,[81] *Mayville*
Irvine L. Lenroot,[82] *Superior*

REPRESENTATIVES

Henry Allen Cooper, *Racine*
Edward Voigt, *Sheboygan*

John M. Nelson, *Madison*
William J. Cary, *Milwaukee*
William H. Stafford, *Milwaukee*
James H. Davidson,[83] *Oshkosh*
Florian Lampert,[84] *Oshkosh*
John J. Esch, *La Crosse*
Edward E. Browne, *Waupaca*
David G. Classon, *Oconto*
James A. Frear, *Hudson*
Irvine L. Lenroot,[85] *Superior*
Adolphus P. Nelson,[86] *Grantsburg*

## WYOMING

SENATORS

Francis E. Warren, *Cheyenne*
John B. Kendrick, *Sheridan*

REPRESENTATIVE AT LARGE

Frank W. Mondell, *Newcastle*

## TERRITORY OF ALASKA

DELEGATE

Charles A. Sulzer,[87] *Sulzer*
James Wickersham,[88] *Fairbanks*

## TERRITORY OF HAWAII

DELEGATE

J. Kuhio Kalanianaole, *Waikiki*

## PHILIPPINE ISLANDS

RESIDENT COMMISSIONERS[89]

Jaime C. de Veyra, *Leyte*
Teodoro R. Yangco, *Zambales*

## PORTO RICO

RESIDENT COMMISSIONER[90]

Felix Cordova Davila,[91] *San Juan*

---

[80] Election unsuccessfully contested by William E. Chilton. (See U.S. Senate Election, Expulsion and Censure Cases, 1793-1990, Senate Document 103-33, pp. 297-98.)
[81] Died October 21, 1917.
[82] Elected to fill vacancy caused by death of Paul O. Husting, and took his seat April 18, 1918.
[83] Died August 6, 1918.
[84] Elected to fill vacancy caused by death of James

H. Davidson, and took his seat December 2, 1918.
[85] Resigned April 17, 1918, having been elected Senator.
[86] Elected to fill vacancy caused by resignation of Irvine L. Lenroot, and took his seat December 2, 1918.
[87] Served until January 7, 1919; succeeded by James Wickersham, who contested his election.
[88] Successfully contested the election of Charles A. Sulzer, and took his seat January 7, 1919.

[89] By act of Congress approved August 29, 1916, term of office decreased from four to three years beginning March 4, 1917.
[90] By act of Congress approved March 2, 1917, term of office increased to four years beginning March 4, 1921.
[91] Elected July 16, 1917, to serve from August 7, 1917, to March 3, 1921.

# 66TH CONGRESS

## MARCH 4, 1919, TO MARCH 3, 1921

FIRST SESSION— *May 19, 1919, to November 19, 1919*
SECOND SESSION— *December 1, 1919, to June 5, 1920*
THIRD SESSION— *December 6, 1920, to March 3, 1921*

———

VICE PRESIDENT OF THE UNITED STATES— Thomas R. Marshall, of Indiana
PRESIDENT PRO TEMPORE OF THE SENATE— Albert B. Cummins,[1] of Iowa
SECRETARY OF THE SENATE— James M. Baker, of South Carolina; George A. Sanderson,[2] of Illinois
SERGEANT AT ARMS OF THE SENATE— Charles P. Higgins, of Missouri; David S. Barry,[3] of Rhode Island

———

SPEAKER OF THE HOUSE OF REPRESENTATIVES— Frederick H. Gillett,[4] of Massachusetts
CLERK OF THE HOUSE— South Trimble, of Kentucky; William Tyler Page,[5] of Maryland
SERGEANT AT ARMS OF THE HOUSE— Robert B. Gordon, of Ohio; Joseph G. Rogers,[6] of Pennsylvania
DOORKEEPER OF THE HOUSE— Bert W. Kennedy, of Michigan
POSTMASTER OF THE HOUSE— Frank W. Collier

Thomas R. Marshall
Vice President

Frederick H. Gillett
Speaker

## ALABAMA

### SENATORS
John H. Bankhead,[7] *Jasper*
Braxton B. Comer,[8] *Birmingham*
J. Thomas Heflin,[9] *Lafayette*
Oscar W. Underwood, *Birmingham*

### REPRESENTATIVES
John McDuffie, *Monroeville*
S. Hubert Dent, Jr., *Montgomery*
Henry B. Steagall, *Ozark*
Fred L. Blackmon,[10] *Anniston*
J. Thomas Heflin,[11] *Lafayette*
William B. Bowling,[12] *Lafayette*
William B. Oliver, *Tuscaloosa*
John L. Burnett,[13] *Gadsden*
Lilius B. Rainey,[14] *Gadsden*
Edward B. Almon, *Tuscumbia*
George Huddleston, *Birmingham*
William B. Bankhead, *Jasper*

## ARIZONA

### SENATORS
Henry F. Ashurst, *Prescott*
Marcus A. Smith, *Tucson*

### REPRESENTATIVE AT LARGE
Carl Hayden, *Phoenix*

## ARKANSAS

### SENATORS
Joseph T. Robinson, *Little Rock*
William F. Kirby, *Little Rock*

### REPRESENTATIVES
Thaddeus H. Caraway, *Jonesboro*
William A. Oldfield, *Batesville*
John N. Tillman, *Fayetteville*
Otis Wingo, *De Queen*
Henderson M. Jacoway, *Dardanelle*
Samuel M. Taylor, *Pine Bluff*
William S. Goodwin, *Warren*

## CALIFORNIA

### SENATORS
James D. Phelan, *San Francisco*
Hiram W. Johnson, *San Francisco*

### REPRESENTATIVES
Clarence F. Lea, *Santa Rosa*
John E. Raker, *Alturas*
Charles F. Curry, *Sacramento*
Julius Kahn, *San Francisco*
John I. Nolan, *San Francisco*
John A. Elston, *Berkeley*
Henry E. Barbour, *Fresno*
Hugh S. Hersman, *Gilroy*
Charles H. Randall, *Los Angeles*
Henry Z. Osborne, *Los Angeles*
William Kettner, *San Diego*

## COLORADO

### SENATORS
Charles S. Thomas, *Denver*
Lawrence C. Phipps, *Denver*

### REPRESENTATIVES
William N. Vaile, *Denver*
Charles B. Timberlake, *Sterling*
Guy U. Hardy, *Canon City*
Edward T. Taylor, *Glenwood Springs*

## CONNECTICUT

### SENATORS
Frank B. Brandegee, *New London*
George P. McLean, *Simsbury*

### REPRESENTATIVES
Augustine Lonergan, *Hartford*
Richard P. Freeman, *New London*
John Q. Tilson, *New Haven*
Schuyler Merritt, *Stamford*
James P. Glynn, *Winsted*

## DELAWARE

### SENATORS
Josiah O. Wolcott, *Dover*
L. Heisler Ball, *Marshallton*

### REPRESENTATIVE AT LARGE
Caleb R. Layton, *Georgetown*

## FLORIDA

### SENATORS
Duncan U. Fletcher, *Jacksonville*
Park Trammell, *Lakeland*

———

[1] Elected May 19, 1919.
[2] Elected May 19, 1919.
[3] Elected May 19, 1919.
[4] Elected May 19, 1919.
[5] Elected May 19, 1919.
[6] Elected May 19, 1919.
[7] Died March 1, 1920.

[8] Appointed to fill vacancy caused by death of John H. Bankhead, and took his seat March 15, 1920.
[9] Elected to fill vacancy caused by death of John H. Bankhead, and took his seat December 6, 1920.
[10] Died February 8, 1921.
[11] Resigned November 1, 1920, subsequently elected Senator.

[12] Elected to fill vacancy caused by resignation of J. Thomas Heflin, and took his seat December 29, 1920.
[13] Died May 13, 1919, before Congress assembled.
[14] Elected to fill vacancy caused by death of John L. Burnett, and took his seat October 13, 1919.

## FLORIDA—Continued

### REPRESENTATIVES

Herbert J. Drane, *Lakeland*
Frank Clark, *Gainesville*
John H. Smithwick, *Pensacola*
William J. Sears, *Kissimmee*

## GEORGIA

### SENATORS

Hoke Smith, *Atlanta*
William J. Harris, *Cedartown*

### REPRESENTATIVES

James W. Overstreet, *Sylvania*
Frank Park, *Sylvester*
Charles R. Crisp, *Americus*
William C. Wright, *Newnan*
William D. Upshaw, *Atlanta*
James W. Wise, *Fayetteville*
Gordon Lee, *Chickamauga*
Charles H. Brand, *Athens*
Thomas M. Bell, *Gainesville*
Carl Vinson, *Milledgeville*
William C. Lankford, *Douglas*
William W. Larsen, *Dublin*

## IDAHO

### SENATORS

William E. Borah, *Boise*
John F. Nugent,[15] *Boise*
Frank R. Gooding,[16] *Gooding*

### REPRESENTATIVES

Burton L. French, *Moscow*
Addison T. Smith, *Twin Falls*

## ILLINOIS

### SENATORS

Lawrence Y. Sherman, *Springfield*
Medill McCormick, *Chicago*

### REPRESENTATIVES AT LARGE

Richard Yates, *Springfield*
William E. Mason, *Chicago*

### REPRESENTATIVES

Martin B. Madden, *Chicago*
James R. Mann, *Chicago*
William W. Wilson, *Chicago*
John W. Rainey, *Chicago*
Adolph J. Sabath, *Chicago*
James McAndrews, *Chicago*
Niels Juul, *Chicago*
Thomas Gallagher, *Chicago*
Fred A. Britten, *Chicago*
Carl R. Chindblom, *Chicago*
Ira C. Copley, *Aurora*
Charles E. Fuller, *Belvidere*
John C. McKenzie, *Elizabeth*
William J. Graham, *Aledo*
Edward J. King, *Galesburg*
Clifford Ireland, *Peoria*
Frank L. Smith, *Dwight*

Joseph G. Cannon, *Danville*
William B. McKinley, *Champaign*
Henry T. Rainey, *Carrollton*
Loren E. Wheeler, *Springfield*
William A. Rodenberg, *East St. Louis*
Edwin B. Brooks, *Newton*
Thomas S. Williams, *Louisville*
Edward E. Denison, *Marion*

## INDIANA

### SENATORS

James E. Watson, *Rushville*
Harry S. New, *Indianapolis*

### REPRESENTATIVES

Oscar R. Luhring, *Evansville*
Oscar E. Bland, *Linton*
James W. Dunbar, *New Albany*
John S. Benham, *Benham*
Everett Sanders, *Terre Haute*
Richard N. Elliott, *Connersville*
Merrill Moores, *Indianapolis*
Albert H. Vestal, *Anderson*
Fred S. Purnell, *Attica*
William R. Wood, *La Fayette*
Milton Kraus, *Peru*
Louis W. Fairfield, *Angola*
Andrew J. Hickey, *La Porte*

## IOWA

### SENATORS

Albert B. Cummins, *Des Moines*
William S. Kenyon, *Fort Dodge*

### REPRESENTATIVES

Charles A. Kennedy, *Montrose*
Harry E. Hull, *Williamsburg*
Burton E. Sweet, *Waverly*
Gilbert N. Haugen, *Northwood*
James W. Good, *Cedar Rapids*
C. William Ramseyer, *Bloomfield*
Cassius C. Dowell, *Des Moines*
Horace M. Towner, *Corning*
William R. Green, *Council Bluffs*
Lester J. Dickinson, *Algona*
William D. Boies, *Sheldon*

## KANSAS

### SENATORS

Charles Curtis, *Topeka*
Arthur Capper, *Topeka*

### REPRESENTATIVES

Daniel R. Anthony, Jr., *Leavenworth*
Edward C. Little, *Kansas City*
Philip P. Campbell, *Pittsburg*
Homer Hoch, *Marion*
James G. Strong, *Blue Rapids*
Hays B. White, *Mankato*
Jasper N. Tincher, *Medicine Lodge*
William A. Ayres, *Wichita*

## KENTUCKY

### SENATORS

Joseph C. W. Beckham, *Frankfort*
Augustus O. Stanley,[17] *Henderson*

### REPRESENTATIVES

Alben W. Barkley, *Paducah*
David H. Kincheloe, *Madisonville*
Robert Y. Thomas, Jr., *Central City*
Ben Johnson, *Bardstown*
Charles F. Ogden, *Louisville*
Arthur B. Rouse, *Burlington*
James C. Cantrill, *Georgetown*
King Swope,[18] *Danville*
William J. Fields, *Olive Hill*
John W. Langley, *Pikeville*
John M. Robsion, *Barbourville*

## LOUISIANA

### SENATORS

Joseph E. Ransdell, *Lake Providence*
Edward J. Gay, *Plaquemine*

### REPRESENTATIVES

Albert Estopinal,[19] *Estopinal*
James O'Connor,[20] *New Orleans*
H. Garland Dupré, *New Orleans*
Whitmell P. Martin, *Thibodaux*
John T. Watkins, *Minden*
Riley J. Wilson, *Harrisonburg*
Jared Y. Sanders, *Bogalusa*
Ladislas Lazaro, *Washington*
James B. Aswell, *Natchitoches*

## MAINE

### SENATORS

Bert M. Fernald, *West Poland*
Frederick Hale, *Portland*

### REPRESENTATIVES

Louis B. Goodall, *Sanford*
Wallace H. White, Jr., *Lewiston*
John A. Peters, *Ellsworth*
Ira G. Hersey, *Houlton*

## MARYLAND

### SENATORS

John Walter Smith, *Snow Hill*
Joseph I. France, *Port Deposit*

### REPRESENTATIVES

William N. Andrews, *Cambridge*
Carville D. Benson, *Halethorpe*
Charles P. Coady, *Baltimore*
J. Charles Linthicum, *Baltimore*
Sydney E. Mudd, *La Plata*
Frederick N. Zihlman, *Cumberland*

---

[15] Resigned, effective January 14, 1921.
[16] Appointed to fill vacancy caused by resignation of John F. Nugent, and took his seat January 15, 1921.
[17] Elected November 5, 1918, for term beginning March 4, 1919, but did not qualify until May 19, 1919,

preferring to retain the governorship.
[18] Elected to fill vacancy caused by death of Representative-elect Harvey Helm, in preceding Congress, and took his seat August 19, 1919.

[19] Died April 28, 1919, before Congress assembled.
[20] Elected to fill vacancy caused by death of Albert Estopinal, and took his seat June 10, 1919.

## MASSACHUSETTS

### SENATORS
Henry Cabot Lodge, *Nahant*
David I. Walsh, *Fitchburg*

### REPRESENTATIVES
Allen T. Treadway, *Stockbridge*
Frederick H. Gillett, *Springfield*
Calvin D. Paige, *Southbridge*
Samuel E. Winslow, *Worcester*
John Jacob Rogers, *Lowell*
Willfred W. Lufkin, *Essex*
Michael F. Phelan, *Lynn*
Frederick W. Dallinger, *Cambridge*
Alvan T. Fuller,[21] *Malden*
John F. Fitzgerald,[22] *Boston*
Peter F. Tague,[23] *Boston*
George H. Tinkham, *Boston*
James A. Gallivan, *Boston*
Robert Luce, *Waltham*
Richard Olney, *Dedham*
William S. Greene, *Fall River*
Joseph Walsh, *New Bedford*

## MICHIGAN

### SENATORS
Charles E. Townsend, *Jackson*
Truman H. Newberry, *Grosse Pointe Farms*

### REPRESENTATIVES
Frank E. Doremus, *Detroit*
Earl C. Michener, *Adrian*
John M. C. Smith, *Charlotte*
Edward L. Hamilton, *Niles*
Carl E. Mapes, *Grand Rapids*
Patrick H. Kelley, *Lansing*
Louis C. Cramton, *Lapeer*
Joseph W. Fordney, *Saginaw*
James C. McLaughlin, *Muskegon*
Gilbert A. Currie, *Midland*
Frank D. Scott, *Alpena*
W. Frank James, *Hancock*
Charles A. Nichols,[24] *Detroit*
Clarence J. McLeod,[25] *Detroit*

## MINNESOTA

### SENATORS
Knute Nelson, *Alexandria*
Frank B. Kellogg, *St. Paul*

### REPRESENTATIVES
Sydney Anderson, *Lanesboro*
Franklin F. Ellsworth, *Mankato*
Charles R. Davis, *St. Peter*
Carl C. Van Dyke,[26] *St. Paul*
Oscar E. Keller,[27] *St. Paul*
Walter H. Newton, *Minneapolis*

Harold Knutson, *St. Cloud*
Andrew J. Volstead, *Granite Falls*
William L. Carss, *Proctor*
Halvor Steenerson, *Crookston*
Thomas D. Schall, *Excelsior*

## MISSISSIPPI

### SENATORS
John Sharp Williams, *Yazoo City*
Pat Harrison, *Gulfport*

### REPRESENTATIVES
Ezekiel S. Candler, Jr., *Corinth*
Hubert D. Stephens, *New Albany*
Benjamin G. Humphreys, *Greenville*
Thomas U. Sisson, *Winona*
William W. Venable, *Meridian*
Paul B. Johnson, *Hattiesburg*
Percy E. Quin, *McComb City*
James W. Collier, *Vicksburg*

## MISSOURI

### SENATORS
James A. Reed, *Kansas City*
Selden P. Spencer, *St. Louis*

### REPRESENTATIVES
Milton A. Romjue, *Macon*
William W. Rucker, *Keytesville*
Joshua W. Alexander,[28] *Gallatin*
Jacob L. Milligan,[29] *Richmond*
Charles F. Booher,[30] *Savannah*
William T. Bland, *Kansas City*
Clement C. Dickinson, *Clinton*
Samuel C. Major, *Fayette*
William L. Nelson, *Columbia*
James Beauchamp Clark,[31] *Bowling Green*
Cleveland A. Newton, *St. Louis*
William L. Igoe, *St. Louis*
Leonidas C. Dyer, *St. Louis*
Marion E. Rhodes, *Potosi*
Edward D. Hays, *Cape Girardeau*
Isaac V. McPherson, *Aurora*
Thomas L. Rubey, *Lebanon*

## MONTANA

### SENATORS
Henry L. Myers, *Hamilton*
Thomas J. Walsh, *Helena*

### REPRESENTATIVES
John M. Evans, *Missoula*
Carl W. Riddick, *Lewistown*

## NEBRASKA

### SENATORS
Gilbert M. Hitchcock, *Omaha*
George W. Norris, *McCook*

### REPRESENTATIVES
C. Frank Reavis, *Falls City*
Albert W. Jefferis, *Omaha*
Robert E. Evans, *Dakota City*
Melvin O. McLaughlin, *York*
William E. Andrews, *Hastings*
Moses P. Kinkaid, *O'Neill*

## NEVADA

### SENATORS
Key Pittman, *Tonopah*
Charles B. Henderson, *Elko*

### REPRESENTATIVE AT LARGE
Charles R. Evans, *Goldfield*

## NEW HAMPSHIRE

### SENATORS
George H. Moses, *Concord*
Henry K. Keyes, *Haverhill*

### REPRESENTATIVES
Sherman E. Burroughs, *Manchester*
Edward H. Wason, *Nashua*

## NEW JERSEY

### SENATORS
Joseph S. Frelinghuysen, *Raritan*
Walter E. Edge, *Atlantic City*

### REPRESENTATIVES
William J. Browning,[32] *Camden*
Francis F. Patterson, Jr.,[33] *Camden*
Isaac Bacharach, *Atlantic City*
Thomas J. Scully, *South Amboy*
Elijah C. Hutchinson, *Trenton*
Ernest R. Ackerman, *Plainfield*
John R. Ramsey, *Hackensack*
Amos H. Radcliffe, *Paterson*
Cornelius A. McGlennon, *East Newark*
Daniel F. Minahan, *Orange*
Frederick R. Lehlbach, *Newark*
John J. Eagan, *Weehawken*
James A. Hamill, *Jersey City*

## NEW MEXICO

### SENATORS
Albert B. Fall, *Three Rivers*
Andrieus A. Jones, *East Las Vegas*

### REPRESENTATIVE AT LARGE
Bendigno C. Hernandez, *Tierra Amarilla*

---

[21] Resigned January 5, 1921, having been elected Lieutenant Governor.

[22] Served until October 23, 1919; succeeded by Peter F. Tague, who contested his election.

[23] Successfully contested the election of John F. Fitzgerald, and took his seat October 23, 1919.

[24] Died April 25, 1920.

[25] Elected to fill vacancy caused by death of Charles A. Nichols, and took his seat December 6, 1920.

[26] Died May 20, 1919.

[27] Elected to fill vacancy caused by death of Carl C. Van Dyke, and took his seat July 28, 1919.

[28] Resigned December 15, 1919, having been appointed Secretary of Commerce.

[29] Elected to fill vacancy caused by resignation of Joshua W. Alexander, and took his seat March 20, 1920.

[30] Died January 21, 1921. Election unsuccessfully contested by Albert L. Reeves.

[31] Died March 2, 1921. Election unsuccessfully contested by James D. Salts.

[32] Died March 24, 1920.

[33] Elected to fill vacancy caused by death of William J. Browning, and took his seat December 6, 1920.

## NEW YORK

### SENATORS

James W. Wadsworth, Jr., *Groveland*
William M. Calder, *Brooklyn*

### REPRESENTATIVES

Frederick C. Hicks, *Port Washington*
Charles P. Caldwell, *Forest Hills*
John MacCrate,[34] *Brooklyn*
Thomas H. Cullen, *Brooklyn*
John B. Johnston, *Brooklyn*
Frederick W. Rowe, *Brooklyn*
James P. Maher, *Brooklyn*
William E. Cleary, *Brooklyn*
David J. O'Connell, *Brooklyn*
Reuben L. Haskell,[35] *Brooklyn*
Lester D. Volk,[36] *Brooklyn*
Daniel J. Riordan, *New York City*
Henry M. Goldfogle, *New York City*
Christopher D. Sullivan, *New York City*
Fiorello H. LaGuardia,[37] *New York City*
Nathan D. Perlman,[38] *New York City*
Peter J. Dooling, *New York City*
Thomas F. Smith, *New York City*
Herbert C. Pell, Jr., *New York City*
John F. Carew, *New York City*
Joseph Rowan, *New York City*
Isaac Siegel, *New York City*
Jerome F. Donovan, *New York City*
Anthony J. Griffin, *New York City*
Richard F. McKiniry, *New York City*
James V. Ganly, *New York City*
James W. Husted, *Peekskill*
Edmund Platt,[39] *Poughkeepsie*
Hamilton Fish, Jr.,[40] *Garrison*
Charles B. Ward, *Debruce*
Rollin B. Sanford, *Albany*
James S. Parker, *Salem*
Frank Crowther, *Schenectady*
Bertrand H. Snell, *Potsdam*
Luther W. Mott, *Oswego*
Homer P. Snyder, *Little Falls*
William H. Hill, *Johnson City*
Walter W. Magee, *Syracuse*
Norman J. Gould, *Seneca Falls*
Alanson B. Houghton, *Corning*
Thomas B. Dunn, *Rochester*
Archie D. Sanders, *Stafford*
S. Wallace Dempsey, *Lockport*
Clarence MacGregor, *Buffalo*
James M. Mead, *Buffalo*
Daniel A. Reed, *Dunkirk*

## NORTH CAROLINA

### SENATORS

Furnifold McL. Simmons, *New Bern*
Lee S. Overman, *Salisbury*

### REPRESENTATIVES

John H. Small, *Washington*
Claude Kitchin, *Scotland Neck*
Samuel M. Brinson, *New Bern*
Edward W. Pou, *Smithfield*
Charles M. Stedman, *Greensboro*
Hannibal L. Godwin, *Dunn*
Leonidas D. Robinson, *Wadesboro*
Robert L. Doughton, *Laurel Springs*
Edwin Y. Webb,[41] *Shelby*
Clyde R. Hoey,[42] *Shelby*
Zebulon Weaver, *Asheville*

## NORTH DAKOTA

### SENATORS

Porter J. McCumber, *Wahpeton*
Asle J. Gronna, *Lakota*

### REPRESENTATIVES

John M. Baer, *Fargo*
George M. Young, *Valley City*
James H. Sinclair, *Kenmare*

## OHIO

### SENATORS

Atlee Pomerene, *Canton*
Warren G. Harding,[43] *Marion*
Frank B. Willis,[44] *Delaware*

### REPRESENTATIVES

Nicholas Longworth, *Cincinnati*
Ambrose E. B. Stephens, *North Bend*
Warren Gard, *Hamilton*
Benjamin F. Welty, *Lima*
Charles J. Thomson, *Defiance*
Charles C. Kearns, *Batavia*
Simeon D. Fess, *Yellow Springs*
R. Clint. Cole, *Findlay*
Isaac R. Sherwood, *Toledo*
Israel M. Foster, *Athens*
Edwin D. Ricketts, *Logan*
Clement L. Brumbaugh, *Columbus*
James T. Begg, *Sandusky*
Martin L. Davey, *Kent*
C. Ellis Moore, *Cambridge*
Roscoe C. McCulloch, *Canton*
William A. Ashbrook, *Johnstown*
B. Frank Murphy, *Steubenville*
John G. Cooper, *Youngstown*
Charles A. Mooney, *Cleveland*
John J. Babka, *Cleveland*

Henry I. Emerson, *Cleveland*

## OKLAHOMA

### SENATORS

Thomas P. Gore, *Lawton*
Robert L. Owen, *Muskogee*

### REPRESENTATIVES

Everette B. Howard, *Tulsa*
William W. Hastings, *Tahlequah*
Charles D. Carter, *Ardmore*
Thomas D. McKeown, *Ada*
Joseph B. Thompson,[45] *Pauls Valley*
John W. Harreld,[46] *Oklahoma City*
Scott Ferris, *Lawton*
James V. McClintic, *Snyder*
Dick T. Morgan,[47] *Woodward*
Charles Swindall,[48] *Woodward*

## OREGON

### SENATORS

George E. Chamberlain, *Portland*
Charles L. McNary, *Salem*

### REPRESENTATIVES

Willis C. Hawley, *Salem*
Nicholas J. Sinnott, *The Dalles*
Clifton N. McArthur, *Portland*

## PENNSYLVANIA

### SENATORS

Boies Penrose, *Philadelphia*
Philander C. Knox, *Pittsburgh*

### REPRESENTATIVES AT LARGE

William J. Burke, *Pittsburgh*
Thomas S. Crago, *Waynesburg*
Mahlon M. Garland,[49] *Pittsburgh*
Anderson H. Walters, *Johnstown*

### REPRESENTATIVES

William S. Vare, *Philadelphia*
George S. Graham, *Philadelphia*
J. Hampton Moore,[50] *Philadelphia*
Harry C. Ransley,[51] *Philadelphia*
George W. Edmonds, *Philadelphia*
Peter E. Costello, *Philadelphia*
George P. Darrow, *Philadelphia*
Thomas S. Butler, *West Chester*
Henry W. Watson, *Langhorne*
William W. Griest, *Lancaster*
Patrick McLane,[52] *Scranton*
John R. Farr,[53] *Scranton*
John J. Casey, *Wilkes-Barre*
John Reber, *Pottsville*
Authur G. Dewalt, *Allentown*
Louis T. McFadden, *Canton*

---

[34] Resigned December 30, 1920.
[35] Resigned December 31, 1919.
[36] Elected to fill vacancy caused by resignation of Reuben L. Haskell, and took his seat December 6, 1920.
[37] Resigned effective December 31, 1919.
[38] Elected to fill vacancy caused by resignation of Fiorello H. LaGuardia, and took his seat December 6, 1920.
[39] Resigned June 7, 1920.
[40] Elected to fill vacancy caused by resignation of Edmund Platt, and took his seat December 6, 1920.

[41] Resigned November 10, 1919.
[42] Elected to fill vacancy caused by resignation of Edwin Y. Webb, and took his seat January 5, 1920.
[43] Resigned, effective January 13, 1921, having been elected President of the United States.
[44] Appointed to fill vacancy caused by resignation of Warren G. Harding, and took his seat January 14, 1921.
[45] Died September 18, 1919.
[46] Elected to fill vacancy caused by death of Joseph B. Thompson, and took his seat November 17, 1919.
[47] Died July 4, 1920.

[48] Elected to fill vacancy caused by death of Dick T. Morgan, and took his seat December 6, 1920.
[49] Died November 19, 1920, before the commencement of the Sixty-seventh Congress, to which he had been reelected.
[50] Resigned January 4, 1920.
[51] Elected to fill vacancy caused by resignation of J. Hampton Moore, and took his seat December 6, 1920.
[52] Served until February 25, 1921; succeeded by John R. Farr, who contested his election.
[53] Successfully contested the election of Patrick McLane, and took his seat February 25, 1921.

Edgar R. Kiess, *Williamsport*
John V. Lesher, *Sunbury*
Benjamin K. Focht, *Lewisburg*
Aaron S. Kreider, *Annville*
John M. Rose, *Johnstown*
Edward S. Brooks, *York*
Evan J. Jones, *Bradford*
John H. Wilson,[54] *Butler*
Samuel A. Kendall, *Meyersdale*
Henry W. Temple, *Washington*
Milton W. Shreve, *Erie*
Henry J. Steele, *Easton*
Nathan L. Strong, *Brookville*
Willis J. Hulings, *Oil City*
Stephen G. Porter, *Pittsburgh*
M. Clyde Kelly, *Braddock*
John M. Morin, *Pittsburgh*
Guy E. Campbell, *Crafton*

## RHODE ISLAND

### SENATORS

LeBaron B. Colt, *Bristol*
Peter G. Gerry, *Warwick*

### REPRESENTATIVES

Clark Burdick, *Newport*
Walter R. Stiness, *Cowesett*
Ambrose Kennedy, *Woonsocket*

## SOUTH CAROLINA

### SENATORS

Ellison D. Smith, *Florence*
Nathaniel B. Dial, *Laurens*

### REPRESENTATIVES

Richard S. Whaley, *Charleston*
James F. Byrnes, *Aiken*
Fred H. Dominick, *Newberry*
Samuel J. Nicholls, *Spartanburg*
William F. Stevenson, *Cheraw*
J. Willard Ragsdale,[55] *Florence*
Philip H. Stoll,[56] *Kingstree*
Asbury F. Lever,[57] *Lexington*
Edward C. Mann,[58] *St. Matthews*

## SOUTH DAKOTA

### SENATORS

Thomas Sterling, *Vermilion*
Edwin S. Johnson, *Yankton*

### REPRESENTATIVES

Charles A. Christopherson, *Sioux Falls*
Royal C. Johnson, *Aberdeen*
Harry L. Gandy, *Rapid City*

## TENNESSEE

### SENATORS

John K. Shields, *Knoxville*
Kenneth D. McKellar, *Memphis*

### REPRESENTATIVES

Sam R. Sells, *Johnson City*
J. Will Taylor, *La Follette*
John A. Moon, *Chattanooga*
Cordell Hull, *Carthage*
Ewin L. Davis, *Tullahoma*
Joseph W. Byrns, *Nashville*
Lemuel P. Padgett, *Columbia*
Thetus W. Sims, *Linden*
Finis J. Garrett, *Dresden*
Hubert F. Fisher, *Memphis*

## TEXAS

### SENATORS

Charles A. Culberson, *Dallas*
Morris Sheppard, *Texarkana*

### REPRESENTATIVES

Eugene Black, *Clarksville*
John C. Box, *Jacksonville*
James Young, *Kaufman*
Sam Rayburn, *Bonham*
Hatton W. Sumners, *Dallas*
Rufus Hardy, *Corsicana*
Clay Stone Briggs, *Galveston*
Joe H. Eagle, *Houston*
Joseph J. Mansfield, *Columbus*
James P. Buchanan, *Brenham*
Tom T. Connally, *Marlin*
James C. Wilson,[59] *Fort Worth*
Fritz G. Lanham,[60] *Fort Worth*
Lucian W. Parrish, *Henrietta*
Carlos Bee, *San Antonio*
John N. Garner, *Uvalde*
Claude B. Hudspeth, *El Paso*
Thomas L. Blanton, *Abilene*
Marvin Jones, *Amarillo*

## UTAH

### SENATORS

Reed Smoot, *Provo*
William H. King, *Salt Lake City*

### REPRESENTATIVES

Milton H. Welling, *Fielding*
James H. Mays, *Salt Lake City*

## VERMONT

### SENATORS

William P. Dillingham, *Montpelier*
Carroll S. Page, *Hyde Park*

### REPRESENTATIVES

Frank L. Greene, *St. Albans*
Porter H. Dale, *Island Pond*

## VIRGINIA

### SENATORS

Thomas S. Martin,[61] *Charlottesville*
Carter Glass,[62] *Lynchburg*
Claude A. Swanson, *Chatham*

### REPRESENTATIVES

Schuyler Otis Bland, *Newport News*
Edward E. Holland, *Suffolk*
Andrew J. Montague, *Richmond*
Walter A. Watson,[63] *Jennings Ordinary*
Patrick Henry Drewry,[64] *Petersburg*
Edward W. Saunders,[65] *Rockymount*
Rorer A. James,[66] *Danville*
James P. Woods,[67] *Roanoke*
Thomas W. Harrison, *Winchester*
R. Walton Moore,[68] *Fairfax*
C. Bascom Slemp, *Big Stone Gap*
Henry D. Flood, *Appomattox*

## WASHINGTON

### SENATORS

Wesley L. Jones, *Seattle*
Miles Poindexter, *Spokane*

### REPRESENTATIVES

John F. Miller, *Seattle*
Lindley H. Hadley, *Bellingham*
Albert Johnson, *Hoquiam*
John W. Summers, *Walla Walla*
J. Stanley Webster, *Spokane*

## WEST VIRGINIA

### SENATORS

Howard Sutherland, *Elkins*
Davis Elkins, *Morgantown*

### REPRESENTATIVES

Matthew M. Neely, *Fairmont*
George M. Bowers, *Martinsburg*
Stuart F. Reed, *Clarksburg*
Harry C. Woodyard, *Spencer*
Wells Goodykoontz, *Williamson*
Leonard S. Echols, *Charleston*

---

[54] Elected to fill vacancy caused by death of Representative-elect Edward E. Robbins, in preceding Congress, and took his seat May 19, 1919.

[55] Died July 23, 1919.

[56] Elected to fill vacancy caused by death of J. Willard Ragsdale, and took his seat October 30, 1919.

[57] Resigned August 1, 1919.

[58] Elected to fill vacancy caused by resignation of Asbury F. Lever, and took his seat October 21, 1919.

[59] Resigned March 13, 1919, before Congress assembled.

[60] Elected to fill vacancy caused by resignation of James C. Wilson, and took his seat May 19, 1919.

[61] Died November 12, 1919.

[62] Appointed November 18, 1919, to fill vacancy caused by death of Thomas S. Martin, and took his seat February 2, 1920; Secretary of the Treasury during interim; subsequently elected.

[63] Died December 24, 1919.

[64] Elected to fill vacancy caused by death of Walter A. Watson, and took his seat May 10, 1920.

[65] Resigned February 29, 1920, having been elected judge of the circuit court of appeals.

[66] Elected to fill vacancy caused by resignation of Edward W. Saunders, and took his seat December 6, 1920.

[67] Elected to fill vacancy caused by resignation of Representative-elect Carter Glass, in preceding Congress.

[68] Elected to fill vacancy caused by resignation of Representative-elect Charles C. Carlin, in preceding Congress, and took his seat June 3, 1919.

## WISCONSIN

### SENATORS
Robert M. La Follette, *Madison*
Irvine L. Lenroot, *Superior*

### REPRESENTATIVES
Clifford E. Randall, *Kenosha*
Edward Voigt, *Sheboygan*
James G. Monahan, *Darlington*
John C. Kleczka, *Milwaukee*
Victor L. Berger,[69] *Milwaukee*
Florian Lampert, *Oshkosh*
John J. Esch, *La Crosse*
Edward E. Browne, *Waupaca*
David G. Classon, *Oconto*
James A. Frear, *Hudson*
Adolphus P. Nelson, *Grantsburg*

## WYOMING

### SENATORS
Francis E. Warren, *Cheyenne*
John B. Kendrick, *Sheridan*

### REPRESENTATIVE AT LARGE
Frank W. Mondell, *Newcastle*

## TERRITORY OF ALASKA

### DELEGATE
Charles A. Sulzer,[70] *Sulzer*
George B. Grigsby,[71] *Juneau*
James Wickersham,[72] *Fairbanks*

## TERRITORY OF HAWAII

### DELEGATE
J. Kuhio Kalanianaole, *Waikiki*

## PHILIPPINE ISLANDS

### RESIDENT COMMISSIONERS
Jaime C. de Veyra, *Manila*
Teodoro R. Yangco,[73] *Zambales*
Isauro Gabaldon,[74] *Nueva Ecija*

## PORTO RICO

### RESIDENT COMMISSIONER
Felix Cordova Davila, *San Juan*

---

[69] By resolution of the House adopted November 10, 1919, Victor L. Berger was declared "not entitled to take the oath of office as a Representative, or to hold a seat therein as such"; election unsuccessfully contested by Joseph P. Carney, and seat declared vacant; Victor L. Berger again presented credentials as Representative-elect to fill vacancy occasioned by resolution of November 10, 1919, declaring Mr. Berger not eligible to hold seat; on January 10, 1920, House again declared Victor L. Berger "not entitled to a seat in the Sixty-sixth Congress and declined to permit him to take the oath or qualify as a Representative"; Henry H. Bodenstab unsuccessfully contested the election of Victor L. Berger, who had been declared ineligible, and by resolution of House adopted February 25, 1921, seat was again declared vacant.

[70] Died April 15, 1919, before Congress assembled and pending a contest for the seat.

[71] Presented credentials as a Delegate-elect to fill vacancy caused by the death of Charles A. Sulzer, and took his seat July 1, 1919; served until March 1, 1921, succeeded by James Wickersham, who contested the election of Mr. Sulzer in the first instance, and continued the contest against Mr. Grigsby.

[72] Successfully contested the election of Charles A. Sulzer and George B. Grigsby, and took his seat March 1, 1921.

[73] Term expired March 3, 1920.

[74] Elected for a term of three years beginning March 4, 1920.

# 67TH CONGRESS

## MARCH 4, 1921, TO MARCH 3, 1923

FIRST SESSION— *April 11, 1921, to November 23, 1921*[1]
SECOND SESSION— *December 5, 1921, to September 22, 1922*[2]
THIRD SESSION— *November 20, 1922, to December 4, 1922*
FOURTH SESSION— *December 4, 1922, to March 3, 1923*
SPECIAL SESSION OF THE SENATE— *March 4, 1921, to March 15, 1921*

Calvin Coolidge
Vice President

Frederick H. Gillett
Speaker

VICE PRESIDENT OF THE UNITED STATES— CALVIN COOLIDGE, of Massachusetts
PRESIDENT PRO TEMPORE OF THE SENATE— ALBERT B. CUMMINS,[3] of Iowa
SECRETARY OF THE SENATE— GEORGE A. SANDERSON,[4] of Illinois
SERGEANT AT ARMS OF THE SENATE— DAVID S. BARRY, of Rhode Island

SPEAKER OF THE HOUSE OF REPRESENTATIVES— FREDERICK H. GILLETT,[5] of Massachusetts
CLERK OF THE HOUSE— WILLIAM TYLER PAGE,[6] of Maryland
SERGEANT AT ARMS OF THE HOUSE— JOSEPH G. ROGERS, of Pennsylvania
DOORKEEPER OF THE HOUSE— BERT W. KENNEDY, of Michigan
POSTMASTER OF THE HOUSE— FRANK W. COLLIER

## ALABAMA

### SENATORS

Oscar W. Underwood, *Birmingham*
J. Thomas Heflin, *Lafayette*

### REPRESENTATIVES

John McDuffie, *Monroeville*
John R. Tyson, *Montgomery*
Henry B. Steagall, *Ozark*
Lamar Jeffers,[7] *Anniston*
William B. Bowling, *Lafayette*
William B. Oliver, *Tuscaloosa*
Lilius B. Rainey,[8] *Gadsden*
Edward B. Almon, *Tuscumbia*
George Huddleston, *Birmingham*
William B. Bankhead, *Jasper*

## ARIZONA

### SENATORS

Henry F. Ashurst, *Prescott*
Ralph H. Cameron, *Phoenix*

### REPRESENTATIVE AT LARGE

Carl Hayden, *Phoenix*

## ARKANSAS

### SENATORS

Joseph T. Robinson, *Little Rock*
Thaddeus H. Caraway, *Jonesboro*

### REPRESENTATIVES

William J. Driver, *Osceola*
William A. Oldfield, *Batesville*
John N. Tillman, *Fayetteville*
Otis Wingo, *De Queen*
Henderson M. Jacoway, *Dardanelle*
Samuel M. Taylor,[9] *Pine Bluff*
Chester W. Taylor,[10] *Pine Bluff*
Tilman B. Parks, *Hope*

## CALIFORNIA

### SENATORS

Hiram W. Johnson, *San Francisco*
Samuel M. Shortridge, *Menlo Park*

### REPRESENTATIVES

Clarence F. Lea, *Santa Rosa*
John E. Raker, *Alturas*
Charles F. Curry, *Sacramento*
Julius Kahn, *San Francisco*
John I. Nolan,[11] *San Francisco*
Mae E. Nolan,[12] *San Francisco*
John A. Elston,[13] *Berkeley*
James H. MacLafferty,[14] *Oakland*
Henry E. Barbour, *Fresno*
Arthur M. Free, *San Jose*

Walter F. Lineberger,[15] *Long Beach*
Henry Z. Osborne,[16] *Los Angeles*
Philip D. Swing, *El Centro*

## COLORADO

### SENATORS

Lawrence C. Phipps, *Denver*
Samuel D. Nicholson, *Leadville*

### REPRESENTATIVES

William N. Vaile, *Denver*
Charles B. Timberlake, *Sterling*
Guy U. Hardy, *Canon City*
Edward T. Taylor, *Glenwood Springs*

## CONNECTICUT

### SENATORS

Frank B. Brandegee, *New London*
George P. McLean, *Simsbury*

### REPRESENTATIVES

E. Hart Fenn, *Wethersfield*
Richard P. Freeman, *New London*
John Q. Tilson, *New Haven*
Schuyler Merritt, *Stamford*
James P. Glynn, *Winsted*

---

[1] In recess from August 24, 1921, until September 21, 1921.

[2] The House of Representatives was in recess from June 30, 1922, until August 15, 1922.

[3] Reelected March 7, 1921.

[4] Reelected March 7, 1921.

[5] Reelected April 11, 1921.

[6] Reelected April 11, 1921.

[7] Elected to fill vacancy caused by death of Fred L. Blackmon, in preceding Congress, and took his seat June 27, 1921.

[8] Election unsuccessfully contested by Charles B. Kennamer.

[9] Died September 13, 1921.

[10] Elected to fill vacancy caused by death of his father, Samuel M. Taylor, and took his seat October 31, 1921.

[11] Died November 18, 1922, before the commencement of the Sixty-eighth Congress, to which he had been reelected.

[12] Elected to fill vacancy caused by death of her husband, John I. Nolan; took her seat February 12, 1923.

[13] Died December 15, 1921.

[14] Elected to fill vacancy caused by death of John A. Elston, and took his seat November 20, 1922.

[15] Elected to fill vacancy caused by death of Representative-elect Charles F. Van de Water (November 20, 1920, before the beginning of the congressional term), and took his seat April 11, 1921.

[16] Died February 8, 1923, before the commencement of the Sixty-eighth Congress, to which he had been reelected.

## DELAWARE

### SENATORS

Josiah O. Wolcott,[17] *Dover*
T. Coleman du Pont,[18] *Wilmington*
Thomas F. Bayard, Jr.,[19] *Wilmington*
L. Heisler Ball, *Marshallton*

### REPRESENTATIVE AT LARGE

Caleb R. Layton, *Georgetown*

## FLORIDA

### SENATORS

Duncan U. Fletcher, *Jacksonville*
Park Trammell, *Lakeland*

### REPRESENTATIVES

Herbert J. Drane, *Lakeland*
Frank Clark, *Gainesville*
John H. Smithwick, *Pensacola*
William J. Sears, *Kissimmee*

## GEORGIA

### SENATORS

William J. Harris, *Cedartown*
Thomas E. Watson,[20] *Thomson*
Rebecca L. Felton,[21] *Cartersville*
Walter F. George,[22] *Vienna*

### REPRESENTATIVES

James W. Overstreet, *Sylvania*
Frank Park, *Sylvester*
Charles R. Crisp, *Americus*
William C. Wright, *Newnan*
William D. Upshaw, *Atlanta*
James W. Wise, *Fayetteville*
Gordon Lee, *Chickamauga*
Charles H. Brand, *Athens*
Thomas M. Bell, *Gainesville*
Carl Vinson, *Milledgeville*
William C. Lankford, *Douglas*
William W. Larsen, *Dublin*

## IDAHO

### SENATORS

William E. Borah, *Boise*
Frank R. Gooding, *Gooding*

### REPRESENTATIVES

Burton L. French, *Moscow*
Addison T. Smith, *Twin Falls*

## ILLINOIS

### SENATORS

Medill McCormick, *Chicago*
William B. McKinley, *Champaign*

### REPRESENTATIVES AT LARGE

Richard Yates, *Springfield*
William E. Mason,[23] *Chicago*
Winnifred S. M. Huck,[24] *Chicago*

### REPRESENTATIVES

Martin B. Madden, *Chicago*
James R. Mann,[25] *Chicago*
Elliott W. Sproul, *Chicago*
John W. Rainey,[26] *Chicago*
Adolph J. Sabath,[27] *Chicago*
John J. Gorman, *Chicago*
M. Alfred Michaelson, *Chicago*
Stanley H. Kunz,[28] *Chicago*
Fred A. Britten, *Chicago*
Carl R. Chindblom, *Chicago*
Ira C. Copley, *Aurora*
Charles E. Fuller, *Belvidere*
John C. McKenzie, *Elizabeth*
William J. Graham, *Aledo*
Edward J. King, *Galesburg*
Clifford Ireland, *Peoria*
Frank H. Funk, *Bloomington*
Joseph G. Cannon, *Danville*
Allen F. Moore, *Monticello*
Guy L. Shaw,[29] *Beardstown*
Loren E. Wheeler, *Springfield*
William A. Rodenberg, *East St. Louis*
Edwin B. Brooks, *Newton*
Thomas S. Williams, *Louisville*
Edward E. Denison, *Marion*

## INDIANA

### SENATORS

James E. Watson, *Rushville*
Harry S. New, *Indianapolis*

### REPRESENTATIVES

Oscar R. Luhring, *Evansville*
Oscar E. Bland, *Linton*
James W. Dunbar, *New Albany*
John S. Benham, *Benham*
Everett Sanders, *Terre Haute*
Richard N. Elliott, *Connersville*
Merrill Moores, *Indianapolis*
Albert H. Vestal, *Anderson*
Fred S. Purnell, *Attica*
William R. Wood, *La Fayette*
Milton Kraus, *Peru*
Louis W. Fairfield, *Angola*
Andrew J. Hickey, *La Porte*

## IOWA

### SENATORS

Albert B. Cummins, *Des Moines*
William S. Kenyon,[30] *Fort Dodge*
Charles A. Rawson,[31] *Des Moines*
Smith W. Brookhart,[32] *Washington*

### REPRESENTATIVES

William F. Kopp, *Mount Pleasant*
Harry E. Hull, *Williamsburg*
Burton E. Sweet, *Waverly*
Gilbert N. Haugen, *Northwood*
James W. Good,[33] *Cedar Rapids*
Cyrenus Cole,[34] *Cedar Rapids*
C. William Ramseyer, *Bloomfield*
Cassius C. Dowell, *Des Moines*
Horace M. Towner, *Corning*
William R. Green, *Council Bluffs*
Lester J. Dickinson, *Algona*
William D. Boies, *Sheldon*

## KANSAS

### SENATORS

Charles Curtis, *Topeka*
Arthur Capper, *Topeka*

### REPRESENTATIVES

Daniel R. Anthony, Jr., *Leavenworth*
Edward C. Little, *Kansas City*
Philip P. Campbell, *Pittsburg*
Homer Hoch, *Marion*
James G. Strong, *Blue Rapids*
Hays B. White, *Mankato*
Jasper N. Tincher, *Medicine Lodge*
Richard E. Bird, *Wichita*

## KENTUCKY

### SENATORS

Augustus O. Stanley, *Henderson*
Richard P. Ernst, *Covington*

### REPRESENTATIVES

Alben W. Barkley, *Paducah*
David H. Kincheloe, *Madisonville*
Robert Y. Thomas, Jr., *Central City*
Ben Johnson, *Bardstown*
Charles F. Ogden, *Louisville*
Arthur B. Rouse, *Burlington*
James C. Cantrill, *Georgetown*
Ralph Gilbert, *Shelbyville*
William J. Fields, *Olive Hill*
John W. Langley, *Pikeville*
John M. Robsion, *Barbourville*

---

[17] Resigned July 2, 1921, having been appointed State chancellor.

[18] Appointed to fill vacancy caused by resignation of Josiah O. Wolcott, and took his seat July 26, 1921.

[19] Elected to fill vacancy caused by resignation of Josiah O. Wolcott, and took his seat November 21, 1922.

[20] Died September 26, 1922.

[21] Appointed to fill vacancy caused by death of Thomas E. Watson, and took her seat November 21, 1922.

[22] Elected November 7, 1922, to fill vacancy caused by death of Thomas E. Watson, but did not present his credentials until November 22, 1922

(Rebecca L. Felton having qualified on the day preceding), and took his seat the same day.

[23] Died June 16, 1921.

[24] Elected to fill vacancy caused by death of her father, William E. Mason, and took her seat November 20, 1922.

[25] Died November 30, 1922, before the commencement of the Sixty-eighth Congress, to which he had been reelected.

[26] Election unsuccessfully contested by John Golombiewski.

[27] Election unsuccessfully contested by Jacob Gartenstein.

[28] Election unsuccessfully contested by Dan Parillo.

[29] Election unsuccessfully contested by Henry T. Rainey.

[30] Resigned February 24, 1922.

[31] Appointed to fill vacancy caused by resignation of William S. Kenyon, and took his seat February 24, 1922.

[32] Elected to fill vacancy caused by resignation of William S. Kenyon, and took his seat December 2, 1922.

[33] Resigned June 15, 1921.

[34] Elected to fill vacancy caused by resignation of James W. Good, and took his seat July 28, 1921.

## LOUISIANA

### SENATORS

Joseph E. Ransdell, *Lake Providence*
Edwin S. Broussard, *New Iberia*

### REPRESENTATIVES

James O'Connor, *New Orleans*
H. Garland Dupré, *New Orleans*
Whitmell P. Martin, *Thibodaux*
John N. Sandlin, *Minden*
Riley J. Wilson, *Harrisonburg*
George K. Favrot, *Baton Rouge*
Ladislas Lazaro, *Washington*
James B. Aswell, *Natchitoches*

## MAINE

### SENATORS

Bert M. Fernald, *West Poland*
Frederick Hale, *Portland*

### REPRESENTATIVES

Carroll L. Beedy, *Portland*
Wallace H. White, Jr., *Lewiston*
John A. Peters,[35] *Ellsworth*
John E. Nelson,[36] *Augusta*
Ira G. Hersey, *Houlton*

## MARYLAND

### SENATORS

Joseph I. France, *Port Deposit*
Ovington E. Weller, *Baltimore*

### REPRESENTATIVES

T. Alan Goldsborough, *Denton*
Albert A. Blakeney, *Ten Hills*
John Philip Hill, *Baltimore*
J. Charles Linthicum, *Baltimore*
Sydney E. Mudd, *La Plata*
Frederick N. Zihlman, *Cumberland*

## MASSACHUSETTS

### SENATORS

Henry Cabot Lodge, *Nahant*
David I. Walsh, *Fitchburg*

### REPRESENTATIVES

Allen T. Treadway, *Stockbridge*
Frederick H. Gillett, *Springfield*
Calvin D. Paige, *Southbridge*
Samuel E. Winslow, *Worcester*
John Jacob Rogers, *Lowell*
Willfred W. Lufkin,[37] *Essex*
A. Piatt Andrew, Jr.,[38] *Gloucester*
Robert S. Maloney, *Lawrence*
Frederick W. Dallinger, *Cambridge*
Charles L. Underhill, *Somerville*
Peter F. Tague, *Boston*

George H. Tinkham, *Boston*
James A. Gallivan, *Boston*
Robert Luce, *Waltham*
Louis A. Frothingham, *Easton*
William S. Greene, *Fall River*
Joseph Walsh,[39] *New Bedford*
Charles L. Gifford,[40] *Cotuit*

## MICHIGAN

### SENATORS

Charles E. Townsend, *Jackson*
Truman H. Newberry,[41] *Grosse Pointe Farms*
James Couzens,[42] *Detroit*

### REPRESENTATIVES

George P. Codd, *Detroit*
Earl C. Michener, *Adrian*
William H. Frankhouser,[43] *Hillsdale*
John M. C. Smith,[44] *Charlotte*
John C. Ketcham, *Hastings*
Carl E. Mapes, *Grand Rapids*
Patrick H. Kelley, *Lansing*
Louis C. Cramton, *Lapeer*
Joseph W. Fordney, *Saginaw*
James C. McLaughlin, *Muskegon*
Roy O. Woodruff, *Bay City*
Frank D. Scott, *Alpena*
W. Frank James, *Hancock*
Vincent M. Brennan, *Detroit*

## MINNESOTA

### SENATORS

Knute Nelson, *Alexandria*
Frank B. Kellogg, *St. Paul*

### REPRESENTATIVES

Sydney Anderson, *Lanesboro*
Frank Clague, *Redwood Falls*
Charles R. Davis, *St. Peter*
Oscar E. Keller, *St. Paul*
Walter H. Newton, *Minneapolis*
Harold Knutson, *St. Cloud*
Andrew J. Volstead, *Granite Falls*
Oscar J. Larson, *Duluth*
Halvor Steenerson, *Crookston*
Thomas D. Schall, *Excelsior*

## MISSISSIPPI

### SENATORS

John Sharp Williams, *Yazoo City*
Pat Harrison, *Gulfport*

### REPRESENTATIVES

John E. Rankin, *Tupelo*
Bill G. Lowrey, *Blue Mountain*

Benjamin G. Humphreys, *Greenville*
Thomas U. Sisson, *Winona*
Ross A. Collins, *Meridian*
Paul B. Johnson, *Hattiesburg*
Percy E. Quin, *McComb City*
James W. Collier, *Vicksburg*

## MISSOURI

### SENATORS

James A. Reed, *Kansas City*
Selden P. Spencer, *St. Louis*

### REPRESENTATIVES

Frank C. Millspaugh,[45] *Canton*
William W. Rucker, *Keytesville*
Henry F. Lawrence, *Cameron*
Charles L. Faust, *St. Joseph*
Edgar C. Ellis, *Kansas City*
William O. Atkeson, *Butler*
Roscoe C. Patterson, *Springfield*
Sidney C. Roach, *Linn Creek*
Theodore W. Hukriede, *Warrenton*
Cleveland A. Newton, *St. Louis*
Harry B. Hawes,[46] *St. Louis*
Leonidas C. Dyer, *St. Louis*
Marion E. Rhodes, *Potosi*
Edward D. Hays, *Cape Girardeau*
Isaac V. McPherson, *Aurora*
Samuel A. Shelton, *Marshfield*

## MONTANA

### SENATORS

Henry L. Myers, *Hamilton*
Thomas J. Walsh, *Helena*

### REPRESENTATIVES

Washington J. McCormick, *Missoula*
Carl W. Riddick, *Lewistown*

## NEBRASKA

### SENATORS

Gilbert M. Hitchcock, *Omaha*
George W. Norris, *McCook*

### REPRESENTATIVES

C. Frank Reavis,[47] *Falls City*
Roy H. Thorpe,[48] *Lincoln*
Albert W. Jefferis, *Omaha*
Robert E. Evans, *Dakota City*
Melvin O. McLaughlin, *York*
William E. Andrews, *Hastings*
Moses P. Kinkaid,[49] *O'Neill*
Augustin R. Humphrey,[50] *Broken Bow*

---

[35] Resigned January 2, 1922.
[36] Elected to fill vacancy caused by resignation of John A. Peters, and took his seat March 27, 1922.
[37] Resigned June 30, 1921, to become collector of the port of Boston.
[38] Elected to fill vacancy caused by resignation of Willfred W. Lufkin, and took his seat October 10, 1921.
[39] Resigned August 2, 1922.
[40] Elected to fill vacancy caused by resignation of Joseph Walsh, and took his seat November 20, 1922.
[41] Election unsuccessfully contested by Henry

Ford; resigned November 18, 1922. (See U.S. Senate Election, Expulsion and Censure Cases, 1793-1990, Senate Document 103-33, pp. 302-05.)
[42] Appointed to fill vacancy caused by resignation of Truman H. Newberry, and took his seat December 7, 1922; subsequently elected.
[43] Died May 9, 1921; illness prevented his taking his seat.
[44] Elected to fill vacancy caused by death of William H. Frankhouser, and took his seat July 20, 1921.

[45] Resigned December 5, 1922; vacancy throughout remainder of the Congress.
[46] Election unsuccessfully contested by Bernard P. Bogg.
[47] Resigned June 3, 1922.
[48] Elected to fill vacancy caused by resignation of C. Frank Reavis, and took his seat November 27, 1922.
[49] Died July 6, 1922.
[50] Elected to fill vacancy caused by death of Moses P. Kinkaid, and took his seat November 20, 1922.

## NEVADA

### SENATORS
Key Pittman, *Tonopah*
Tasker L. Oddie, *Reno*

### REPRESENTATIVE AT LARGE
Samuel S. Arentz, *Simpson*

## NEW HAMPSHIRE

### SENATORS
George H. Moses, *Concord*
Henry W. Keyes, *Haverhill*

### REPRESENTATIVES
Sherman E. Burroughs,[51] *Manchester*
Edward H. Wason, *Nashua*

## NEW JERSEY

### SENATORS
Joseph S. Frelinghuysen, *Raritan*
Walter E. Edge, *Atlantic City*

### REPRESENTATIVES
Francis F. Patterson, Jr., *Camden*
Isaac Bacharach, *Atlantic City*
T. Frank Appleby, *Asbury Park*
Elijah C. Hutchinson, *Trenton*
Ernest R. Ackerman, *Plainfield*
Randolph Perkins, *Woodcliff Lake*
Amos H. Radcliffe, *Paterson*
Herbert W. Taylor, *Newark*
Richard Wayne Parker, *Newark*
Frederick R. Lehlbach, *Newark*
Archibald E. Olpp, *West Hoboken*
Charles F. X. O'Brien, *Jersey City*

## NEW MEXICO

### SENATORS
Albert B. Fall,[52] *Three Rivers*
Holm O. Bursum,[53] *Socorro*
Andrieus A. Jones, *East Las Vegas*

### REPRESENTATIVE AT LARGE
Nestor Montoya,[54] *Albuquerque*

## NEW YORK

### SENATORS
James W. Wadsworth, Jr., *Groveland*
William M. Calder, *Brooklyn*

### REPRESENTATIVES
Frederick C. Hicks, *Port Washington*
John J. Kindred, *Astoria*
John Kissel, *Brooklyn*
Thomas H. Cullen, *Brooklyn*
Ardolph L. Kline, *Brooklyn*
Warren I. Lee, *Brooklyn*
Michael J. Hogan, *Brooklyn*
Charles G. Bond, *Brooklyn*
Andrew N. Petersen, *Brooklyn*
Lester D. Volk, *Brooklyn*

Daniel J. Riordan, *New York City*
Meyer London, *New York City*
Christopher D. Sullivan, *New York City*
Nathan D. Perlman, *New York City*
Thomas J. Ryan, *New York City*
W. Bourke Cockran,[55] *New York City*
Ogden L. Mills, *New York City*
John F. Carew, *New York City*
Walter M. Chandler, *New York City*
Isaac Siegel, *New York City*
Martin C. Ansorge, *New York City*
Anthony J. Griffin, *New York City*
Albert B. Rossdale, *New York City*
Benjamin L. Fairchild, *Pelham*
James W. Husted, *Peekskill*
Hamilton Fish, Jr., *Garrison*
Charles B. Ward, *Debruce*
Peter G. Ten Eyck, *Albany*
James S. Parker, *Salem*
Frank Crowther, *Schenectady*
Bertrand H. Snell, *Potsdam*
Luther W. Mott, *Oswego*
Homer P. Snyder, *Little Falls*
John D. Clarke, *Fraser*
Walter W. Magee, *Syracuse*
Norman J. Gould, *Seneca Falls*
Alanson B. Houghton,[56] *Corning*
Lewis Henry,[57] *Elmira*
Thomas B. Dunn, *Rochester*
Archie D. Sanders, *Stafford*
S. Wallace Dempsey, *Lockport*
Clarence MacGregor, *Buffalo*
James M. Mead, *Buffalo*
Daniel A. Reed, *Dunkirk*

## NORTH CAROLINA

### SENATORS
Furnifold McL. Simmons, *New Bern*
Lee S. Overman, *Salisbury*

### REPRESENTATIVES
Hallett S. Ward, *Washington*
Claude Kitchin, *Scotland Neck*
Samuel M. Brinson,[58] *New Bern*
Charles L. Abernethy,[59] *New Bern*
Edward W. Pou, *Smithfield*
Charles M. Stedman, *Greensboro*
Homer L. Lyon, *Whiteville*
William C. Hammer, *Asheboro*
Robert L. Doughton,[60] *Laurel Springs*
Alfred L. Bulwinkle, *Gastonia*
Zebulon Weaver, *Asheville*

## NORTH DAKOTA

### SENATORS
Porter J. McCumber, *Wahpeton*
Edwin F. Ladd, *Fargo*

### REPRESENTATIVES
Olger B. Burtness, *Grand Forks*
George M. Young, *Valley City*
James H. Sinclair, *Kenmare*

## OHIO

### SENATORS
Atlee Pomerene, *Canton*
Frank B. Willis, *Delaware*

### REPRESENTATIVES
Nicholas Longworth, *Cincinnati*
Ambrose E. B. Stephens, *North Bend*
Roy G. Fitzgerald, *Dayton*
John L. Cable, *Lima*
Charles J. Thompson, *Defiance*
Charles C. Kearns, *Batavia*
Simeon D. Fess, *Yellow Springs*
R. Clint. Cole, *Findlay*
William W. Chalmers, *Toledo*
Israel M. Foster, *Athens*
Edwin D. Ricketts, *Logan*
John C. Speaks, *Columbus*
James T. Begg, *Sandusky*
Charles L. Knight, *Akron*
C. Ellis Moore, *Cambridge*
Joseph H. Himes, *Canton*
William M. Morgan, *Newark*
B. Frank Murphy, *Steubenville*
John G. Cooper, *Youngstown*
Miner G. Norton, *Cleveland*
Harry C. Gahn, *Cleveland*
Theodore E. Burton, *Cleveland*

## OKLAHOMA

### SENATORS
Robert L. Owen, *Muskogee*
John W. Harreld, *Oklahoma City*

### REPRESENTATIVES
Thomas A. Chandler, *Vinita*
Alice M. Robertson, *Muskogee*
Charles D. Carter, *Ardmore*
Joseph C. Pringey, *Chandler*
Fletcher B. Swank, *Norman*
Lorraine M. Gensman, *Lawton*
James V. McClintic, *Snyder*
Manuel Herrick, *Perry*

## OREGON

### SENATORS
Charles L. McNary, *Salem*
Robert N. Stanfield, *Portland*

### REPRESENTATIVES
Willis C. Hawley, *Salem*
Nicholas J. Sinnott, *The Dalles*
Clinton N. McArthur, *Portland*

[51] Died January 27, 1923.
[52] Resigned March 4, 1921, having been appointed Secretary of the Interior.
[53] Appointed to fill vacancy caused by resignation of Albert B. Fall, and took his seat April 11, 1921; subsequently elected.
[54] Died January 13, 1923.

[55] Died March 1, 1923, before the commencement of the Sixty-eighth Congress, to which he had been reelected.
[56] Resigned February 28, 1922.
[57] Elected to fill vacancy caused by resignation of Alanson B. Houghton, and took his seat April 21, 1922.
[58] Died April 13, 1922.

[59] Elected to fill vacancy caused by death of Samuel M. Brinson, and took his seat November 20, 1922.
[60] Election unsuccessfully contested by James I. Campbell.

## PENNSYLVANIA

### SENATORS

Boies Penrose,[61] *Philadelphia*
George Wharton Pepper,[62] *Philadelphia*
Philander C. Knox,[63] *Pittsburgh*
William E. Crow,[64] *Uniontown*
David A. Reed,[65] *Pittsburgh*

### REPRESENTATIVES AT LARGE

William J. Burke, *Pittsburgh*
Thomas S. Crago,[66] *Waynesburg*
Joseph McLaughlin, *Philadelphia*
Anderson H. Walters, *Johnstown*

### REPRESENTATIVES

William S. Vare,[67] *Philadelphia*
George S. Graham, *Philadelphia*
Harry C. Ransley, *Philadelphia*
George W. Edmonds, *Philadelphia*
James J. Connolly, *Philadelphia*
George P. Darrow, *Philadelphia*
Thomas S. Butler, *West Chester*
Henry W. Watson, *Langhorne*
William W. Griest, *Lancaster*
Charles R. Connell,[68] *Scranton*
Clarence D. Coughlin, *Wilkes-Barre*
John Reber, *Pottsville*
Fred B. Gernerd, *Allentown*
Louis T. McFadden, *Canton*
Edgar R. Kiess, *Williamsport*
I. Clinton Kline, *Sunbury*
Benjamin K. Focht, *Lewisburg*
Aaron S. Kreider, *Annville*
John M. Rose, *Johnstown*
Edward S. Brooks, *York*
Evan J. Jones, *Bradford*
Adam M. Wyant, *Greensburg*
Samuel A. Kendall, *Meyersdale*
Henry W. Temple, *Washington*
Milton W. Shreve, *Erie*
William H. Kirkpatrick, *Easton*
Nathan L. Strong, *Brookville*
Harris J. Bixler, *Johnsonburg*
Stephen G. Porter, *Pittsburgh*
M. Clyde Kelly, *Edgewood*
John M. Morin, *Pittsburgh*
Guy E. Campbell, *Crafton*

## RHODE ISLAND

### SENATORS

LeBaron B. Colt, *Bristol*
Peter G. Gerry, *Warwick*

### REPRESENTATIVES

Clark Burdick, *Newport*
Walter R. Stiness, *Cowesett*

Ambrose Kennedy, *Woonsocket*

## SOUTH CAROLINA

### SENATORS

Ellison D. Smith, *Lynchburg*
Nathaniel B. Dial, *Laurens*

### REPRESENTATIVES

W. Turner Logan, *Charleston*
James F. Byrnes, *Aiken*
Fred H. Dominick, *Newberry*
John J. McSwain, *Greenville*
William F. Stevenson, *Cheraw*
Philip H. Stoll, *Kingstree*
Hampton P. Fulmer, *Norway*

## SOUTH DAKOTA

### SENATORS

Thomas Sterling, *Vermilion*
Peter Norbeck, *Redfield*

### REPRESENTATIVES

Charles A. Christopherson, *Sioux Falls*
Royal C. Johnson, *Aberdeen*
William Williamson, *Oacoma*

## TENNESSEE

### SENATORS

John K. Shields, *Knoxville*
Kenneth D. McKellar, *Memphis*

### REPRESENTATIVES

B. Carroll Reece, *Butler*
J. Will Taylor, *La Follette*
Joseph Brown, *Chattanooga*
Wynne F. Clouse, *Cookeville*
Ewin L. Davis, *Tullahoma*
Joseph W. Byrns, *Nashville*
Lemuel P. Padgett,[69] *Columbia*
Clarence W. Turner,[70] *Waverly*
Lon A. Scott, *Savannah*
Finis J. Garrett, *Dresden*
Hubert F. Fisher, *Memphis*

## TEXAS

### SENATORS

Charles A. Culberson, *Dallas*
Morris Sheppard, *Texarkana*

### REPRESENTATIVES

Eugene Black, *Clarksville*
John C. Box, *Jacksonville*
Morgan G. Sanders, *Canton*
Sam Rayburn, *Bonham*

Hatton W. Sumners, *Dallas*
Rufus Hardy, *Corsicana*
Clay Stone Briggs, *Galveston*
Daniel E. Garrett, *Houston*
Joseph J. Mansfield, *Columbus*
James P. Buchanan, *Brenham*
Tom T. Connally, *Marlin*
Fritz G. Lanham, *Fort Worth*
Lucian W. Parrish,[71] *Henrietta*
Guinn Williams,[72] *Decatur*
Harry M. Wurzbach, *Seguin*
John N. Garner, *Uvalde*
Claude B. Hudspeth, *El Paso*
Thomas L. Blanton, *Abilene*
Marvin Jones, *Amarillo*

## UTAH

### SENATORS

Reed Smoot, *Provo*
William H. King, *Salt Lake City*

### REPRESENTATIVES

Don B. Colton, *Vernal*
Elmer O. Leatherwood, *Salt Lake City*

## VERMONT

### SENATORS

William P. Dillingham, *Montpelier*
Carroll S. Page, *Hyde Park*

### REPRESENTATIVES

Frank L. Greene, *St. Albans*
Porter H. Dale, *Island Pond*

## VIRGINIA

### SENATORS

Claude A. Swanson, *Chatham*
Carter Glass, *Lynchburg*

### REPRESENTATIVES

Schuyler Otis Bland, *Newport News*
Joseph T. Deal, *Norfolk*
Andrew J. Montague, *Richmond*
Patrick Henry Drewry, *Petersburg*
Rorer A. James,[73] *Danville*
James M. Hooker,[74] *Stuart*
James P. Woods, *Roanoke*
Thomas W. Harrison,[75] *Winchester*
John Paul,[76] *Harrisonburg*
R. Walton Moore, *Fairfax*
C. Bascom Slemp, *Big Stone Gap*
Henry D. Flood,[77] *Appomattox*
Henry St. George Tucker,[78] *Lexington*

---

[61] Died December 31, 1921.
[62] Appointed to fill vacancy caused by death of Boies Penrose, and took his seat January 10, 1922; subsequently elected.
[63] Died October 12, 1921.
[64] Appointed to fill vacancy caused by death of Philander C. Knox, and took his seat October 24, 1921; died August 2, 1922.
[65] Appointed to fill vacancy caused by deaths of Philander C. Knox and William E. Crow, and took his seat August 16, 1922; subsequently elected.
[66] Elected to fill vacancy caused by death of

Representative-elect Mahlon M. Garland, in preceding Congress, and took his seat October 10, 1921. John P. Bracken filed a memorial claiming a seat in the Sixty-seventh Congress.
[67] Resigned January 2, 1923.
[68] Died September 26, 1922; vacancy throughout remainder of the Congress.
[69] Died August 2, 1922.
[70] Elected to fill vacancy caused by death of Lemuel P. Padgett, and took his seat November 20, 1922.
[71] Died March 27, 1922.

[72] Elected to fill vacancy caused by death of Lucian W. Parrish, and took his seat May 22, 1922.
[73] Died August 6, 1921.
[74] Elected to fill vacancy caused by death of Rorer A. James, and took his seat November 21, 1921.
[75] Served until December 15, 1922; succeeded by John Paul, who contested his election.
[76] Successfully contested the election of Thomas W. Harrison, and took his seat December 15, 1922.
[77] Died December 8, 1921.

## WASHINGTON

SENATORS

Wesley L. Jones, *Seattle*
Miles Poindexter, *Spokane*

REPRESENTATIVES

John F. Miller, *Seattle*
Lindley H. Hadley, *Bellingham*
Albert Johnson, *Hoquiam*
John W. Summers, *Walla Walla*
J. Stanley Webster, *Spokane*

## WEST VIRGINIA

SENATORS

Howard Sutherland, *Elkins*
Davis Elkins, *Morgantown*

REPRESENTATIVES

Benjamin L. Rosenbloom, *Wheeling*
George M. Bowers, *Martinsburg*
Stuart F. Reed, *Clarksburg*
Harry C. Woodyard, *Spencer*
Wells Goodykoontz, *Williamson*
Leonard S. Echols, *Charleston*

## WISCONSIN

SENATORS

Robert M. La Follette, *Madison*
Irvine L. Lenroot, *Superior*

REPRESENTATIVES

Henry Allen Cooper, *Racine*
Edward Voigt, *Sheboygan*
John M. Nelson, *Madison*
John C. Kleczka, *Milwaukee*
William H. Stafford, *Milwaukee*
Florian Lampert, *Oshkosh*
Joseph D. Beck, *Viroqua*
Edward E. Browne, *Waupaca*
David G. Classon, *Oconto*
James A. Frear, *Hudson*
Adolphus P. Nelson, *Grantsburg*

## WYOMING

SENATORS

Francis E. Warren, *Cheyenne*
John B. Kendrick, *Sheridan*

REPRESENTATIVE AT LARGE
Frank W. Mondell, *Newcastle*

## TERRITORY OF ALASKA

DELEGATE

Dan A. Sutherland, *Juneau*

## TERRITORY OF HAWAII

DELEGATE

J. Kuhio Kalanianaole,[78] *Waikiki*
Henry A. Baldwin,[79] *Paia*

## PHILIPPINE ISLANDS

RESIDENT COMMISSIONERS

Jaime C. de Veyra, *Manila*
Isauro Gabaldon, *Nueva Ecija*

## PORTO RICO

RESIDENT COMMISSIONER

Felix Cordova Davila, *San Juan*

---

[78] Died January 7, 1922.  [79] Elected to fill vacancy caused by death of J. Kuhio Kalanianaole, and took his seat April 18, 1922.

# 68TH CONGRESS

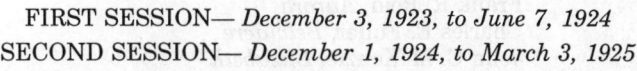

## MARCH 4, 1923, TO MARCH 3, 1925

FIRST SESSION— *December 3, 1923, to June 7, 1924*
SECOND SESSION— *December 1, 1924, to March 3, 1925*

---

VICE PRESIDENT OF THE UNITED STATES— CALVIN COOLIDGE,[1] of Massachusetts
PRESIDENT PRO TEMPORE OF THE SENATE— ALBERT B. CUMMINS, of Iowa
SECRETARY OF THE SENATE— GEORGE A. SANDERSON,[2] of Illinois
SERGEANT AT ARMS OF THE SENATE— DAVID S. BARRY, of Rhode Island

---

SPEAKER OF THE HOUSE OF REPRESENTATIVES— FREDERICK H. GILLETT,[3] of Massachusetts
CLERK OF THE HOUSE— WILLIAM TYLER PAGE,[4] of Maryland
SERGEANT AT ARMS OF THE HOUSE— JOSEPH G. ROGERS, of Pennsylvania
DOORKEEPER OF THE HOUSE— BERT W. KENNEDY, of Michigan
POSTMASTER OF THE HOUSE— FRANK W. COLLIER

Calvin Coolidge
Vice President

Frederick H. Gillett
Speaker

## ALABAMA

### SENATORS

Oscar W. Underwood, *Birmingham*
J. Thomas Heflin, *Lafayette*

### REPRESENTATIVES

John McDuffie, *Monroeville*
John R. Tyson,[5] *Montgomery*
Lister Hill,[6] *Montgomery*
Henry B. Steagall, *Ozark*
Lamar Jeffers, *Anniston*
William B. Bowling, *Lafayette*
William B. Oliver, *Tuscaloosa*
Miles C. Allgood, *Allgood*
Edward B. Almon, *Tuscumbia*
George Huddleston, *Birmingham*
William B. Bankhead, *Jasper*

## ARIZONA

### SENATORS

Henry F. Ashurst, *Prescott*
Ralph H. Cameron, *Phoenix*

### REPRESENTATIVE AT LARGE

Carl Hayden, *Phoenix*

## ARKANSAS

### SENATORS

Joseph T. Robinson, *Little Rock*
Thaddeus H. Caraway, *Jonesboro*

### REPRESENTATIVES

William J. Driver, *Osceola*
William A. Oldfield, *Batesville*
John N. Tillman, *Fayetteville*
Otis Wingo, *De Queen*
Heartsill Ragon, *Clarksville*
Lewis E. Sawyer,[7] *Hot Springs*
James B. Reed,[8] *Lonoke*
Tilman B. Parks, *Hope*

## CALIFORNIA

### SENATORS

Hiram W. Johnson, *San Francisco*
Samuel M. Shortridge, *Menlo Park*

### REPRESENTATIVES

Clarence F. Lea, *Santa Rosa*
John E. Raker, *Alturas*
Charles F. Curry, *Sacramento*
Julius Kahn,[9] *San Francisco*
Mae E. Nolan,[10] *San Francisco*
James H. MacLafferty, *Oakland*
Henry E. Barbour, *Fresno*
Arthur M. Free, *San Jose*
Walter F. Lineberger, *Long Beach*
John D. Fredericks,[11] *Los Angeles*
Philip D. Swing, *El Centro*

## COLORADO

### SENATORS

Lawrence C. Phipps, *Denver*
Samuel D. Nicholson,[12] *Leadville*

Alva B. Adams,[13] *Pueblo*
Rice W. Means,[14] *Denver*

### REPRESENTATIVES

William N. Vaile, *Denver*
Charles B. Timberlake, *Sterling*
Guy U. Hardy, *Canon City*
Edward T. Taylor, *Glenwood Springs*

## CONNECTICUT

### SENATORS

Frank B. Brandegee,[15] *New London*
Hiram Bingham,[16] *New Haven*
George P. McLean, *Simsbury*

### REPRESENTATIVES

E. Hart Fenn, *Wethersfield*
Richard P. Freeman, *New London*
John Q. Tilson, *New Haven*
Schuyler Merritt, *Stamford*
Patrick B. O'Sullivan, *Derby*

## DELAWARE

### SENATORS

L. Heisler Ball, *Marshallton*
Thomas F. Bayard, Jr., *Wilmington*

### REPRESENTATIVE AT LARGE

William H. Boyce, *Dover*

---

[1] Became President upon the death of Warren G. Harding, August 3, 1923.
[2] Reelected December 17, 1923.
[3] Reelected December 3, 1923.
[4] Reelected December 3, 1923.
[5] Died March 27, 1923, before Congress assembled.
[6] Elected to fill vacancy caused by death of John R. Tyson, and took his seat December 5, 1923.
[7] Died May 5, 1923, before Congress assembled.
[8] Elected to fill vacancy caused by death of Lewis

E. Sawyer, and took his seat December 5, 1923.
[9] Died December 18, 1924, before the commencement of the Sixty-ninth Congresss, to which he had been reelected.
[10] Elected to fill vacancy caused by death of her husband, Representative-elect John I. Nolan, in preceding Congress.
[11] Elected to fill vacancy caused by death of Representative-elect Henry Z. Osborne, in preceding Congress, and took his seat December 5, 1923.
[12] Died March 24, 1923.

[13] Appointed to fill vacancy caused by death of Samuel D. Nicholson, and took his seat December 3, 1923.
[14] Elected to fill vacancy caused by death of Samuel D. Nicholson, and took his seat December 1, 1924.
[15] Died October 14, 1924.
[16] Elected to fill vacancy caused by death of Frank B. Brandegee, and took his seat January 9, 1925. Vacancy from October 15, 1924, to December 17, 1924.

## FLORIDA

SENATORS

Duncan U. Fletcher, *Jacksonville*
Park Trammell, *Lakeland*

REPRESENTATIVES

Herbert J. Drane, *Lakeland*
Frank Clark, *Gainesville*
John H. Smithwick, *Pensacola*
William J. Sears, *Kissimmee*

## GEORGIA

SENATORS

William J. Harris, *Cedartown*
Walter F. George, *Vienna*

REPRESENTATIVES

R. Lee Moore,[17] *Statesboro*
Frank Park, *Sylvester*
Charles R. Crisp, *Americus*
William C. Wright, *Newnan*
William D. Upshaw, *Atlanta*
James W. Wise,[18] *Fayetteville*
Gordon Lee, *Chickamauga*
Charles H. Brand, *Athens*
Thomas M. Bell, *Gainesville*
Carl Vinson, *Milledgeville*
William C. Lankford, *Douglas*
William W. Larsen, *Dublin*

## IDAHO

SENATORS

William E. Borah, *Boise*
Frank R. Gooding, *Gooding*

REPRESENTATIVES

Burton L. French, *Moscow*
Addison T. Smith, *Twin Falls*

## ILLINOIS

SENATORS

Medill McCormick,[19] *Chicago*
Charles S. Deneen,[20] *Chicago*
William B. McKinley, *Champaign*

REPRESENTATIVES AT LARGE

Richard Yates, *Springfield*
Henry R. Rathbone, *Kenilworth*

REPRESENTATIVES

Martin B. Madden, *Chicago*
Morton D. Hull,[21] *Chicago*
Elliott W. Sproul, *Chicago*
John W. Rainey,[22] *Chicago*
Thomas A. Doyle,[23] *Chicago*
Adolph J. Sabath, *Chicago*

James R. Buckley,[24] *Chicago*
M. Alfred Michaelson, *Chicago*
Stanley H. Kunz, *Chicago*
Fred A. Britten, *Chicago*
Carl R. Chindblom, *Chicago*
Frank R. Reid, *Aurora*
Charles E. Fuller, *Belvidere*
John C. McKenzie, *Elizabeth*
William J. Graham,[25] *Aledo*
Edward J. King, *Galesburg*
William E. Hull, *Peoria*
Frank H. Funk, *Bloomington*
William P. Holaday, *Georgetown*
Allen F. Moore, *Monticello*
Henry T. Rainey, *Carrollton*
J. Earl Major, *Hillsboro*
Edward E. Miller, *East St. Louis*
William W. Arnold, *Robinson*
Thomas S. Williams, *Louisville*
Edward E. Denison, *Marion*

## INDIANA

SENATORS

James E. Watson, *Rushville*
Samuel M. Ralston, *Indianapolis*

REPRESENTATIVES

William E. Wilson, *Evansville*
Arthur H. Greenwood, *Washington*
Frank Gardner, *Scottsburg*
Harry C. Canfield, *Batesville*
Everett Sanders, *Terre Haute*
Richard N. Elliott, *Connersville*
Merrill Moores, *Indianapolis*
Albert H. Vestal, *Anderson*
Fred S. Purnell, *Attica*
William R. Wood, *La Fayette*
Samuel E. Cook, *Huntington*
Louis W. Fairfield, *Angola*
Andrew J. Hickey, *La Porte*

## IOWA

SENATORS

Albert B. Cummins, *Des Moines*
Smith W. Brookhart, *Washington*

REPRESENTATIVES

William F. Kopp, *Mount Pleasant*
Harry E. Hull, *Williamsburg*
Thomas J. B. Robinson, *Hampton*
Gilbert N. Haugen, *Northwood*
Cyrenus Cole, *Cedar Rapids*
C. William Ramseyer, *Bloomfield*
Cassius C. Dowell, *Des Moines*
Horace M. Towner,[26] *Corning*

Hiram K. Evans,[27] *Corydon*
William R. Green, *Council Bluffs*
Lester J. Dickinson, *Algona*
William D. Boies, *Sheldon*

## KANSAS

SENATORS

Charles Curtis, *Topeka*
Arthur Capper, *Topeka*

REPRESENTATIVES

Daniel R. Anthony, Jr., *Leavenworth*
Edward C. Little,[28] *Kansas City*
Ulysses S. Guyer,[29] *Kansas City*
William H. Sproul, *Sedan*
Homer Hoch, *Marion*
James G. Strong, *Blue Rapids*
Hays B. White, *Mankato*
Jasper N. Tincher, *Medicine Lodge*
William A. Ayres, *Wichita*

## KENTUCKY

SENATORS

Augustus O. Stanley, *Henderson*
Richard P. Ernst, *Covington*

REPRESENTATIVES

Alben W. Barkley, *Paducah*
David H. Kincheloe, *Madisonville*
Robert Y. Thomas, Jr., *Central City*
Ben Johnson, *Bardstown*
Maurice H. Thatcher, *Louisville*
Arthur B. Rouse, *Burlington*
James C. Cantrill,[30] *Georgetown*
Joseph W. Morris,[31] *New Castle*
Ralph Gilbert, *Shelbyville*
William J. Fields,[32] *Olive Hill*
Fred M. Vinson,[33] *Louisa*
John W. Langley, *Pikeville*
John M. Robsion, *Barbourville*

## LOUISIANA

SENATORS

Joseph E. Ransdell, *Lake Providence*
Edwin S. Broussard, *New Iberia*

REPRESENTATIVES

James O'Connor, *New Orleans*
H. Garland Dupré,[34] *New Orleans*
J. Zach Spearing,[35] *New Orleans*
Whitmell P. Martin, *Thibodaux*
John N. Sandlin, *Minden*
Riley J. Wilson, *Harrisonburg*
George K. Favrot, *Baton Rouge*
Ladislas Lazaro, *Washington*
James B. Aswell, *Natchitoches*

---

[17] Election unsuccessfully contested by Don H. Clark.
[18] Never qualified owing to prolonged illness.
[19] Died February 25, 1925.
[20] Appointed to fill vacancy caused by death of Medill McCormick, and took his seat February 28, 1925.
[21] Elected to fill vacancy caused by death of Representative-elect James R. Mann, in preceding Congress, and took his seat December 5, 1923.
[22] Died May 4, 1923.
[23] Elected to fill vacancy caused by death of John

W. Rainey, and took his seat December 5, 1923.
[24] Election unsuccessfully contested by John J. Gorman.
[25] Resigned June 7, 1924; vacancy throughout remainder of the Congress.
[26] Resigned April 1, 1923, before Congress assembled.
[27] Elected to fill vacancy caused by resignation of Horace M. Towner, and took his seat December 5, 1923.
[28] Died June 27, 1924.
[29] Elected to fill vacancy caused by death of Edward C. Little, and took his seat December 1, 1924.

[30] Died September 2, 1923, before Congress assembled.
[31] Elected to fill vacancy caused by death of James C. Cantrill, and took his seat December 5, 1923.
[32] Resigned December 11, 1923.
[33] Elected to fill vacancy caused by resignation of William J. Fields, and took his seat January 31, 1924.
[34] Died February 21, 1924.
[35] Elected to fill vacancy caused by death of H. Garland Dupré, and took his seat May 15, 1924.

## MAINE

SENATORS

Bert M. Fernald, *West Poland*
Frederick Hale, *Portland*

REPRESENTATIVES

Carroll L. Beedy, *Portland*
Wallace H. White, Jr., *Lewiston*
John E. Nelson, *Augusta*
Ira G. Hersey, *Houlton*

## MARYLAND

SENATORS

Ovington E. Weller, *Baltimore*
William Cabell Bruce, *Baltimore*

REPRESENTATIVES

T. Alan Goldsborough, *Denton*
Millard E. Tydings, *Havre de Grace*
John Philip Hill, *Baltimore*
J. Charles Linthicum, *Baltimore*
Sydney E. Mudd,[36] *La Plata*
Stephen W. Gambrill,[37] *Laurel*
Frederick N. Zihlman, *Cumberland*

## MASSACHUSETTS

SENATORS

Henry Cabot Lodge,[38] *Nahant*
William M. Butler,[39] *Boston*
David I. Walsh, *Fitchburg*

REPRESENTATIVES

Allen T. Treadway, *Stockbridge*
Frederick H. Gillett, *Springfield*
Calvin D. Paige, *Southbridge*
Samuel E. Winslow, *Worcester*
John Jacob Rogers, *Lowell*
A. Piatt Andrew, Jr., *Gloucester*
William P. Connery, Jr., *Lynn*
Frederick W. Dallinger, *Cambridge*
Charles L. Underhill, *Somerville*
Peter F. Tague, *Boston*
George H. Tinkham, *Boston*
James A. Gallivan, *Boston*
Robert Luce, *Waltham*
Louis A. Frothingham, *Easton*
William S. Greene,[40] *Fall River*
Robert M. Leach,[41] *Taunton*
Charles L. Gifford, *Cotuit*

## MICHIGAN

SENATORS

James Couzens, *Detroit*
Woodbridge N. Ferris, *Big Rapids*

REPRESENTATIVES

Robert H. Clancy, *Detroit*
Earl C. Michener, *Adrian*
John M. C. Smith,[42] *Charlotte*
Arthur B. Williams,[43] *Battle Creek*

John C. Ketcham, *Hastings*
Carl E. Mapes, *Grand Rapids*
Grant M. Hudson, *East Lansing*
Louis C. Cramton, *Lapeer*
Bird J. Vincent, *Saginaw*
James C. McLaughlin, *Muskegon*
Roy O. Woodruff, *Bay City*
Frank D. Scott, *Alpena*
W. Frank James, *Hancock*
Clarence J. McLeod, *Detroit*

## MINNESOTA

SENATORS

Knute Nelson,[44] *Alexandria*
Magnus Johnson,[45] *Kimball*
Henrik Shipstead, *Minneapolis*

REPRESENTATIVES

Sydney Anderson, *Lanesboro*
Frank Clague, *Redwood Falls*
Charles R. Davis, *St. Peter*
Oscar E. Keller, *St. Paul*
Walter H. Newton, *Minneapolis*
Harold Knutson, *St. Cloud*
O. J. Kvale, *Benson*
Oscar J. Larson, *Duluth*
Knud Wefald, *Hawley*
Thomas D. Schall, *Excelsior*

## MISSISSIPPI

SENATORS

Pat Harrison, *Gulfport*
Hubert D. Stephens, *New Albany*

REPRESENTATIVES

John E. Rankin, *Tupelo*
Bill G. Lowrey, *Blue Mountain*
Benjamin G. Humphreys,[46] *Greenville*
William Y. Humphreys,[47] *Greenville*
T. Jeff. Busby, *Houston*
Ross A. Collins, *Meridian*
T. Webber Wilson, *Laurel*
Percy E. Quin, *McComb City*
James W. Collier, *Vicksburg*

## MISSOURI

SENATORS

James A. Reed, *Kansas City*
Selden P. Spencer, *St. Louis*

REPRESENTATIVES

Milton A. Romjue, *Macon*
Ralph F. Lozier, *Carrollton*
Jacob L. Milligan, *Richmond*
Charles L. Faust, *St. Joseph*
Henry L. Jost, *Kansas City*
Clement C. Dickinson, *Clinton*
Samuel C. Major, *Fayette*
Sidney C. Roach, *Linn Creek*
Clarence Cannon, *Elsberry*

Cleveland A. Newton, *St. Louis*
Harry B. Hawes, *St. Louis*
Leonidas C. Dyer, *St. Louis*
J. Scott Wolff, *Festus*
James F. Fulbright, *Doniphan*
Joe J. Manlove, *Joplin*
Thomas L. Rubey, *Lebanon*

## MONTANA

SENATORS

Thomas J. Walsh, *Helena*
Burton K. Wheeler, *Butte*

REPRESENTATIVES

John M. Evans, *Missoula*
Scott Leavitt, *Great Falls*

## NEBRASKA

SENATORS

George W. Norris, *McCook*
Robert B. Howell, *Omaha*

REPRESENTATIVES

John H. Morehead, *Falls City*
Willis G. Sears, *Omaha*
Edgar Howard, *Columbus*
Melvin O. McLaughlin, *York*
Ashton C. Shallenberger, *Alma*
Robert G. Simmons, *Scottsbluff*

## NEVADA

SENATORS

Key Pittman, *Tonopah*
Tasker L. Oddie, *Reno*

REPRESENTATIVE AT LARGE

Charles L. Richards, *Reno*

## NEW HAMPSHIRE

SENATORS

George H. Moses, *Concord*
Henry W. Keyes, *Haverhill*

REPRESENTATIVES

William N. Rogers, *Sanbornville*
Edward H. Wason, *Nashua*

## NEW JERSEY

SENATORS

Walter E. Edge, *Atlantic City*
Edward I. Edwards, *Jersey City*

REPRESENTATIVES

Francis F. Patterson, Jr., *Camden*
Isaac Bacharach, *Atlantic City*
Elmer H. Geran, *Matawan*
Charles Browne, *Princeton*
Ernest R. Ackerman, *Plainfield*
Randolph Perkins, *Woodcliff Lake*
George N. Seger, *Passaic*

---

[36] Died October 11, 1924.
[37] Elected to fill vacancy caused by death of Sydney E. Mudd, and took his seat December 1, 1924.
[38] Died November 9, 1924.
[39] Appointed to fill vacancy caused by death of Henry Cabot Lodge, and took his seat December 1, 1924.
[40] Died September 22, 1924.

[41] Elected to fill vacancy caused by death of William S. Greene, and took his seat December 1, 1924.
[42] Died March 30, 1923, before Congress assembled.
[43] Elected to fill vacancy caused by death of John M. C. Smith, and took his seat December 5, 1923.
[44] Died April 28, 1923.

[45] Elected to fill vacancy caused by death of Knute Nelson, and took his seat December 3, 1923.
[46] Died October 16, 1923, before Congress assembled.
[47] Elected to fill vacancy caused by death of his father, Benjamin G. Humphreys, and took his seat December 5, 1923.

## NEW JERSEY— Continued

REPRESENTATIVES—CONTINUED

Frank J. McNulty, *Newark*
Daniel F. Minahan, *Orange*
Frederick R. Lehlbach, *Newark*
John J. Eagan, *Weehawken*
Charles F.X. O'Brien, *Jersey City*

## NEW MEXICO

SENATORS

Andrieus A. Jones, *East Las Vegas*
Holm O. Bursum, *Socorro*

REPRESENTATIVE AT LARGE

John Morrow, *Raton*

## NEW YORK

SENATORS

James W. Wadsworth, Jr., *Groveland*
Royal S. Copeland, *New York City*

REPRESENTATIVES

Robert L. Bacon, *Westbury*
John J. Kindred, *Astoria*
George W. Lindsay, *Brooklyn*
Thomas H. Cullen, *Brooklyn*
Loring M. Black, Jr., *Brooklyn*
Charles I. Stengle, *Brooklyn*
John F. Quayle, *Brooklyn*
William E. Cleary, *Brooklyn*
David J. O'Connell, *Brooklyn*
Emanuel Celler, *Brooklyn*
Daniel J. Riordan,[48] *New York City*
Anning S. Prall,[49] *West New Brighton*
Samuel Dickstein, *New York City*
Christopher D. Sullivan, *New York City*
Nathan D. Perlman, *New York City*
John J. Boylan, *New York City*
John J. O'Connor,[50] *New York City*
Ogden L. Mills, *New York City*
John F. Carew, *New York City*
Sol Bloom,[51] *New York City*
Fiorello H. LaGuardia,[52] *New York City*
Royal H. Weller,[53] *New York City*
Anthony J. Griffin, *New York City*
Frank Oliver, *Bronx*
James V. Ganly,[54] *Bronx*
Benjamin L. Fairchild,[55] *Pelham*
J. Mayhew Wainwright, *Rye*
Hamilton Fish, Jr., *Garrison*
Charles B. Ward, *Debruce*
Parker Cornig, *Albany*
James S. Parher, *Salem*
Frank Crowter, *Schenectady*
Bertrand H. Snell, *Potsdam*

Luther W. Mott,[56] *Oswego*
Thaddeus C. Sweet,[57] *Phoenix*
Homer P. Snyder, *Little Falls*
John D. Clarke, *Fraser*
Walter W. Magee, *Syracuse*
John Taber, *Auburn*
Gale H. Stalker, *Elmira*
Meyer Jacobstein, *Rochester*
Archie D. Sanders, *Stafford*
S. Wallace Dempsey, *Lockport*
Clarence MacGregor, *Buffalo*
James M. Mead, *Buffalo*
Daniel A. Reed, *Dunkirk*

## NORTH CAROLINA

SENATORS

Furnifold McL. Simmons, *New Bern*
Lee S. Overman, *Salisbury*

REPRESENTATIVES

Hallett S. Ward, *Washington*
Claude Kitchin,[58] *Scotland Neck*
John H. Kerr,[59] *Warrenton*
Charles L. Abernethy, *New Bern*
Edward W. Pou, *Smithfield*
Charles M. Stedman, *Greensboro*
Homer L. Lyon, *Whiteville*
William C. Hammer, *Asheboro*
Robert L. Doughton, *Laurel Springs*
Alfred L. Bulwinkle, *Gastonia*
Zebulon Weaver, *Asheville*

## NORTH DAKOTA

SENATORS

Edwin F. Ladd, *Fargo*
Lynn J. Frazier, *Hoople*

REPRESENTATIVES

Olger B. Burtness, *Grand Forks*
George M. Young,[60] *Valley City*
Thomas Hall,[61] *Bismarck*
James H. Sinclair, *Kenmare*

## OHIO

SENATORS

Frank B. Willis, *Delaware*
Simeon D. Fess, *Yellow Springs*

REPRESENTATIVES

Nicholas Longworth, *Cincinnati*
Ambrose E. B. Stephens, *North Bend*
Roy G. Fitzgerald, *Dayton*
John L. Cable, *Lima*
Charles J. Thompson, *Defiance*
Charles C. Kearns, *Batavia*
Charles Brand, *Urbana*
R. Clint. Cole, *Findlay*
Isaac R. Sherwood, *Toledo*

Israel M. Foster, *Athens*
Mell G. Underwood, *New Lexington*
John C. Speaks, *Columbus*
James T. Begg, *Sandusky*
Martin L. Davey, *Kent*
C. Ellis Moore, *Cambridge*
John McSweeney, *Wooster*
William M. Morgan, *Newark*
B. Frank Murphy, *Steubenville*
John G. Cooper, *Youngstown*
Charles A. Mooney, *Cleveland*
Robert Crosser, *Cleveland*
Theodore E. Burton, *Cleveland*

## OKLAHOMA

SENATORS

Robert L. Owen, *Muskogee*
John W. Harreld, *Oklahoma City*

REPRESENTATIVES

Everette B. Howard, *Tulsa*
William W. Hastings, *Tahlequah*
Charles D. Carter, *Ardmore*
Thomas D. McKeown, *Ada*
Fletcher B. Swank, *Norman*
J. W. Elmer Thomas, *Medicine Park*
James V. McClintic, *Snyder*
Milton C. Garber, *Enid*

## OREGON

SENATORS

Charles L. McNary, *Salem*
Robert N. Stanfield, *Portland*

REPRESENTATIVES

Willis C. Hawley, *Salem*
Nicholas J. Sinnott, *The Dalles*
Elton Watkins, *Portland*

## PENNSYLVANIA

SENATORS

George Wharton Pepper, *Philadelphia*
David A. Reed, *Pittsburgh*

REPRESENTATIVES

William S. Vare, *Philadelphia*
George S. Graham, *Philadelphia*
Harry C. Ransley, *Philadelphia*
George W. Edmonds, *Philadelphia*
James J. Connolly, *Philadelphia*
George A. Welsh, *Philadelphia*
George P. Darrow, *Philadelphia*
Thomas S. Butler, *West Chester*
Henry W. Watson, *Langhorne*
William W. Griest, *Lancaster*
Laurence H. Watres, *Scranton*
John J. Casey, *Wilkes-Barre*

---

[48] Died April 28, 1923, before Congress assembled.
[49] Elected to fill vacancy caused by death of Daniel J. Riordan, and took his seat December 5, 1923.
[50] Elected to fill vacancy caused by death of Representative-elect W. Bourke Cockran, in preceding Congress, and took his seat December 5, 1923.
[51] Elected to fill vacancy caused by death of Representative-elect Samuel Marx (November 29, 1922, before the beginning of the congressional term),

and took his seat December 5, 1923; election unsuccessfully contested by Walter M. Chandler.
[52] Election unsuccessfully contested by Henry Frank.
[53] Election unsuccessfully contested by Martin C. Ansorge.
[54] Died September 7, 1923, before Congress assembled.
[55] Elected to fill vacancy caused by death of James V. Ganly, and took his seat December 5, 1923.

[56] Died July 10, 1923, before Congress assembled.
[57] Elected to fill vacancy caused by death of Luther W. Mott, and took his seat December 5, 1923.
[58] Died May 31, 1923.
[59] Elected to fill vacancy caused by death of Claude Kitchin, and took his seat December 5, 1923.
[60] Resigned September 2, 1924.
[61] Elected to fill vacancy caused by resignation of George M. Young, and took his seat December 1, 1924.

George F. Brumm, *Minersville*
William M. Croll, *Reading*
Louis T. McFadden, *Canton*
Edgar R. Kiess, *Williamsport*
Herbert W. Cummings, *Sunbury*
Edward M. Beers, *Mount Union*
Frank C. Sites, *Harrisburg*
George M. Wertz, *Johnstown*
J. Banks Kurtz, *Altoona*
Samuel F. Glatfelter, *York*
William I. Swoope, *Clearfield*
Samuel A. Kendall, *Meyersdale*
Henry W. Temple, *Washington*
Thomas W. Phillips, Jr., *Butler*
Nathan L. Strong, *Brookville*
Harris J. Bixler, *Johnsonburg*
Milton W. Shreve, *Erie*
Everett Kent, *Bangor*
Adam M. Wyant, *Greensburg*
Stephen G. Porter, *Pittsburgh*
M. Clyde Kelly, *Edgewood*
John M. Morin, *Pittsburgh*
James M. Magee, *Pittsburgh*
Guy E. Campbell, *Crafton*

## RHODE ISLAND

### SENATORS

LeBaron B. Colt,[62] *Bristol*
Jesse H. Metcalf,[63] *Providence*
Peter G. Gerry, *Warwick*

### REPRESENTATIVES

Clark Burdick, *Newport*
Richard S. Aldrich, *Warwick*
Jeremiah E. O'Connell, *Providence*

## SOUTH CAROLINA

### SENATORS

Ellison D. Smith, *Lynchburg*
Nathaniel B. Dial, *Laurens*

### REPRESENTATIVES

W. Turner Logan, *Charleston*
James F. Byrnes, *Aiken*
Fred H. Dominick, *Newberry*
John J. McSwain, *Greenville*
William F. Stevenson, *Cheraw*
Allard H. Gasque, *Florence*
Hampton P. Fulmer, *Norway*

## SOUTH DAKOTA

### SENATORS

Thomas Sterling, *Vermilion*
Peter Norbeck, *Redfield*

### REPRESENTATIVES

Charles A. Christopherson, *Sioux Falls*
Royal C. Johnson, *Aberdeen*
William Williamson, *Oacoma*

## TENNESSEE

### SENATORS

John K. Shields, *Knoxville*
Kenneth D. McKellar, *Memphis*

### REPRESENTATIVES

B. Carroll Reece, *Butler*
J. Will Taylor, *La Follette*
Sam D. McReynolds, *Chattanooga*
Cordell Hull, *Carthage*
Ewin L. Davis, *Tullahoma*
Joseph W. Byrns, *Nashville*
William C. Salmon, *Columbia*
Gordon Browning, *Huntingdon*
Finis J. Garrett, *Dresden*
Hubert F. Fisher, *Memphis*

## TEXAS

### SENATORS

Morris Sheppard, *Texarkana*
Earle B. Mayfield,[64] *Austin*

### REPRESENTATIVES[65]

Eugene Black, *Clarksville*
John C. Box, *Jacksonville*
Morgan G. Sanders, *Canton*
Sam Rayburn, *Bonham*
Hatton W. Sumners, *Dallas*
Luther A. Johnson, *Corsicana*
Clay Stone Briggs, *Galveston*
Daniel E. Garrett, *Houston*
Joseph J. Mansfield, *Columbus*
James P. Buchanan, *Brenham*
Tom T. Connally, *Marlin*
Fritz G. Lanham, *Fort Worth*
Guinn Williams, *Decatur*
Harry M. Wurzbach, *Seguin*
John N. Garner, *Uvalde*
Claude B. Hudspeth, *El Paso*
Thomas L. Blanton, *Abilene*
Marvin Jones, *Amarillo*

## UTAH

### SENATORS

Reed Smoot, *Provo*
William H. King, *Salt Lake City*

### REPRESENTATIVES

Don B. Colton, *Vernal*
Elmer O. Leatherwood, *Salt Lake City*

## VERMONT

### SENATORS

William P. Dillingham,[66] *Montpelier*
Porter H. Dale,[67] *Island Pond*
Frank L. Greene, *St. Albans*

### REPRESENTATIVES

Frederick G. Fleetwood, *Morrisville*
Porter H. Dale,[68] *Island Pond*
Ernest Willard Gibson,[69] *Brattleboro*

## VIRGINIA

### SENATORS

Claude A. Swanson, *Chatham*
Carter Glass, *Lynchburg*

### REPRESENTATIVES

Schuyler Otis Bland, *Newport News*
Joseph T. Deal, *Norfolk*
Andrew J. Montague, *Richmond*
Patrick Henry Drewry, *Petersburg*
James M. Hooker, *Stuart*
Clifton A. Woodrum, *Roanoke*
Thomas W. Harrison, *Winchester*
R. Walton Moore, *Fairfax*
George C. Peery, *Tazewell*
Henry St. George Tucker, *Lexington*

## WASHINGTON

### SENATORS

Wesley L. Jones, *Seattle*
Clarence C. Dill, *Spokane*

### REPRESENTATIVES

John F. Miller, *Seattle*
Lindley H. Hadley, *Bellingham*
Albert Johnson, *Hoquiam*
John W. Summers, *Walla Walla*
J. Stanley Webster,[70] *Spokane*
Samuel B. Hill,[71] *Waterville*

## WEST VIRGINIA

### SENATORS

Davis Elkins, *Morgantown*
Matthew M. Neely, *Fairmont*

### REPRESENTATIVES

Benjamin L. Rosenbloom, *Wheeling*
Robert E. L. Allen, *Morgantown*
Stuart F. Reed, *Clarksburg*
George W. Johnson, *Parkersburg*
Thomas J. Lilly, *Hinton*
J. Alfred Taylor, *Fayetteville*

---

[62] Died August 18, 1924.
[63] Elected to fill vacancy caused by the death of LeBaron B. Colt, and took his seat December 1, 1924.
[64] Election unsuccessfully contested by George E. B. Peddy. (See U.S. Senate Election, Expulsion and Censure Cases, 1793-1990, Senate Document 103-33, pp. 306-08.)
[65] E. W. Cole presented credentials and claimed a seat as a Representative at large, based upon the official census of 1920, in accordance with which no reapportionment law had been enacted; House, by resolution adopted June 3, 1924, declared him not entitled to a seat.
[66] Died July 12, 1923.
[67] Elected to fill vacancy caused by death of William P. Dillingham, and took his seat December 3, 1923.
[68] Resigned August 11, 1923, before Congress assembled; subsequently elected Senator.
[69] Elected to fill vacancy caused by resignation of Porter H. Dale, and took his seat December 5, 1923.
[70] Resigned May 8, 1923, before Congress assembled.
[71] Elected to fill vacancy caused by resignation of J. Stanley Webster, and took his seat December 5, 1923.

## WISCONSIN

SENATORS

Robert M. La Follette, *Madison*
Irvine L. Lenroot, *Superior*

REPRESENTATIVES

Henry Allen Cooper, *Racine*
Edward Voigt, *Sheboygan*
John M. Nelson, *Madison*
John C. Schafer, *Milwaukee*
Victor L. Berger, *Milwaukee*
Florian Lampert, *Oshkosh*
Joseph D. Beck, *Viroqua*
Edward E. Browne, *Waupaca*
George J. Schneider, *Appleton*

James A. Frear, *Hudson*
Hubert H. Peavey, *Washburn*

## WYOMING

SENATORS

Francis E. Warren, *Cheyenne*
John B. Kendrick, *Sheridan*

REPRESENTATIVE AT LARGE

Charles E. Winter, *Casper*

## TERRITORY OF ALASKA

DELEGATE

Dan A. Sutherland, *Fairbanks*

## TERRITORY OF HAWAII

DELEGATE

William P. Jarrett, *Honolulu*

## PHILIPPINE ISLANDS

RESIDENT COMMISSIONERS

Isauro Gabaldon, *Nueva Ecija*
Pedro Guevara, *Santa Cruz*

## PORTO RICO

RESIDENT COMMISSIONER

Felix Cordova Davila, *San Juan*

# 69TH CONGRESS

## MARCH 4, 1925, TO MARCH 3, 1927

Charles G. Dawes
Vice President

Nicholas Longworth
Speaker

FIRST SESSION— *December 7, 1925, to July 3, 1926; November 10, 1926*[1]
SECOND SESSION— *December 6, 1926, to March 3, 1927*
SPECIAL SESSION OF THE SENATE— *March 4, 1925, to March 18, 1925*

---

VICE PRESIDENT OF THE UNITED STATES— CHARLES G. DAWES, of Illinois
PRESIDENT PRO TEMPORE OF THE SENATE— ALBERT B. CUMMINS, of Iowa; GEORGE H. MOSES,[2] of New Hampshire
SECRETARY OF THE SENATE— GEORGE A. SANDERSON,[3] of Illinois; EDWIN P. THAYER,[4] of Indiana
SERGEANT AT ARMS OF THE SENATE— DAVID S. BARRY, of Rhode Island

---

SPEAKER OF THE HOUSE OF REPRESENTATIVES— NICHOLAS LONGWORTH,[5] of Ohio
CLERK OF THE HOUSE— WILLIAM TYLER PAGE,[6] of Maryland
SERGEANT AT ARMS OF THE HOUSE— JOSEPH G. ROGERS, of Pennsylvania
DOORKEEPER OF THE HOUSE— BERT W. KENNEDY, of Michigan
POSTMASTER OF THE HOUSE— FRANK W. COLLIER

## ALABAMA

### SENATORS

Oscar W. Underwood, *Birmingham*
J. Thomas Heflin, *Lafayette*

### REPRESENTATIVES

John McDuffie, *Monroeville*
Lister Hill, *Montgomery*
Henry B. Steagall, *Ozark*
Lamar Jeffers, *Anniston*
William B. Bowling, *Lafayette*
William B. Oliver, *Tuscaloosa*
Miles C. Allgood, *Allgood*
Edward B. Almon, *Tuscumbia*
George Huddleston, *Birmingham*
William B. Bankhead, *Jasper*

## ARIZONA

### SENATORS

Henry F. Ashurst, *Prescott*
Ralph H. Cameron, *Phoenix*

### REPRESENTATIVE AT LARGE

Carl Hayden, *Phoenix*

## ARKANSAS

### SENATORS

Joseph T. Robinson, *Little Rock*
Thaddeus H. Caraway, *Jonesboro*

### REPRESENTATIVES

William J. Driver, *Osceola*
William A. Oldfield, *Batesville*

John N. Tillman, *Fayetteville*
Otis Wingo, *De Queen*
Heartsill Ragon, *Clarksville*
James B. Reed, *Lonoke*
Tilman B. Parks, *Hope*

## CALIFORNIA

### SENATORS

Hiram W. Johnson, *San Francisco*
Samuel M. Shortridge, *Menlo Park*

### REPRESENTATIVES

Clarence F. Lea, *Santa Rosa*
John E. Raker,[7] *Alturas*
Harry L. Englebright,[8] *Nevada City*
Charles F. Curry, *Sacramento*
Florence P. Kahn,[9] *San Francisco*
Lawrence J. Flaherty,[10] *San Francisco*
Richard J. Welch,[11] *San Francisco*
Albert E. Carter, *Oakland*
Henry E. Barbour, *Fresno*
Arthur M. Free, *San Jose*
Walter F. Lineberger, *Long Beach*
John D. Fredericks, *Los Angeles*
Philip D. Swing, *El Centro*

## COLORADO

### SENATORS

Lawrence C. Phipps, *Denver*
Rice W. Means, *Denver*

### REPRESENTATIVES

William N. Vaile, *Denver*
Charles B. Timberlake, *Sterling*
Guy U. Hardy, *Canon City*
Edward T. Taylor, *Glenwood Springs*

## CONNECTICUT

### SENATORS

George P. McLean, *Simsbury*
Hiram Bingham, *New Haven*

### REPRESENTATIVES

E. Hart Fenn, *Wethersfield*
Richard P. Freeman, *New London*
John Q. Tilson, *New Haven*
Schuyler Merritt, *Stamford*
James P. Glynn, *Winsted*

## DELAWARE

### SENATORS

Thomas F. Bayard, Jr., *Wilmington*
T. Coleman du Pont, *Wilmington*

### REPRESENTATIVE AT LARGE

Robert G. Houston, *Georgetown*

## FLORIDA

### SENATORS

Duncan U. Fletcher, *Jacksonville*
Park Trammell, *Lakeland*

---

[1] The Senate met pursuant to adjournment for the purpose of sitting as a court of impeachment in trial of Judge George W. English; adjourned sine die the same day.
[2] Elected March 6, 1925.
[3] Reelected March 6, 1925; died April 24, 1925.
[4] Elected December 7, 1925.

[5] Elected December 7, 1925.
[6] Reelected December 7, 1925.
[7] Owing to illness, oath of office administered at his residence on January 7, 1926; died January 22, 1926.
[8] Elected to fill vacancy caused by death of John E. Raker, and took his seat December 6, 1926.

[9] Elected to fill vacancy caused by death of her husband, Representative-elect Julius Kahn, in preceding Congress, and took her seat December 7, 1925.
[10] Died June 13, 1926.
[11] Elected to fill vacancy caused by death of Lawrence J. Flaherty, and took his seat December 6, 1926.

## FLORIDA—Continued

### REPRESENTATIVES

Herbert J. Drane, *Lakeland*
Robert A. Green,[12] *Starke*
John H. Smithwick, *Pensacola*
William J. Sears, *Kissimmee*

## GEORGIA

### SENATORS

William J. Harris, *Cedartown*
Walter F. George, *Vienna*

### REPRESENTATIVES

Charles G. Edwards,[13] *Savannah*
Edward E. Cox, *Camilla*
Charles R. Crisp, *Americus*
William C. Wright, *Newnan*
William D. Upshaw, *Atlanta*
Samuel Rutherford, *Forsyth*
Gordon Lee, *Chickamauga*
Charles H. Brand, *Athens*
Thomas M. Bell, *Gainesville*
Carl Vinson, *Milledgeville*
William C. Lankford, *Douglas*
William W. Larsen, *Dublin*

## IDAHO

### SENATORS

William E. Borah, *Boise*
Frank R. Gooding, *Gooding*

### REPRESENTATIVES

Burton L. French, *Moscow*
Addison T. Smith, *Twin Falls*

## ILLINOIS

### SENATORS

William B. McKinley,[14] *Champaign*
Frank L. Smith,[15] *Dwight*
Charles S. Deneen, *Chicago*

### REPRESENTATIVES AT LARGE

Richard Yates, *Springfield*
Henry R. Rathbone, *Kenilworth*

### REPRESENTATIVES

Martin B. Madden, *Chicago*
Morton D. Hull, *Chicago*
Elliott W. Sproul, *Chicago*
Thomas A. Doyle, *Chicago*
Adolph J. Sabath, *Chicago*
John J. Gorman, *Chicago*
M. Alfred Michaelson, *Chicago*
Stanley H. Kunz, *Chicago*
Fred A. Britten, *Chicago*
Carl R. Chindblom, *Chicago*
Frank R. Reid, *Aurora*

Charles E. Fuller,[16] *Belvidere*
William R. Johnson, *Freeport*
John C. Allen, *Monmouth*
Edward J. King, *Galesburg*
William E. Hull, *Peoria*
Frank H. Funk, *Bloomington*
William P. Holaday, *Georgetown*
Charles Adkins, *Decatur*
Henry T. Rainey, *Carrollton*
Loren E. Wheeler, *Springfield*
Edward M. Irwin, *Belleville*
William W. Arnold, *Robinson*
Thomas S. Williams, *Louisville*
Edward E. Denison, *Marion*

## INDIANA

### SENATORS

James E. Watson, *Rushville*
Samuel M. Ralston,[17] *Indianapolis*
Arthur R. Robinson,[18] *Indianapolis*

### REPRESENTATIVES

Harry E. Rowbottom, *Evansville*
Arthur H. Greenwood, *Washington*
Frank Gardner, *Scottsburg*
Harry C. Canfield, *Batesville*
Noble J. Johnson, *Terre Haute*
Richard N. Elliott, *Connersville*
Ralph E. Updike, *Indianapolis*
Albert H. Vestal, *Anderson*
Fred S. Purnell, *Attica*
William R. Wood, *La Fayette*
Albert R. Hall, *Marion*
David Hogg, *Fort Wayne*
Andrew J. Hickey, *La Porte*

## IOWA

### SENATORS

Albert B. Cummins,[19] *Des Moines*
David W. Stewart,[20] *Sioux City*
Smith W. Brookhart,[21] *Washington*
Daniel F. Steck,[22] *Ottumwa*

### REPRESENTATIVES

William F. Kopp, *Mount Pleasant*
F. Dickinson Letts, *Davenport*
Thomas J. B. Robinson, *Hampton*
Gilbert N. Haugen, *Northwood*
Cyrenus Cole, *Cedar Rapids*
C. William Ramseyer, *Bloomfield*
Cassius C. Dowell, *Des Moines*
Lloyd Thurston, *Osceola*
William R. Green, *Council Bluffs*
Lester J. Dickinson, *Algona*
William D. Boies, *Sheldon*

## KANSAS

### SENATORS

Charles Curtis, *Topeka*
Arthur Capper, *Topeka*

### REPRESENTATIVES

Daniel R. Anthony, Jr., *Leavenworth*
Chauncey B. Little, *Olathe*
William H. Sproul, *Sedan*
Homer Hoch, *Marion*
James G. Strong, *Blue Rapids*
Hays B. White, *Mankato*
Jasper N. Tincher, *Medicine Lodge*
William A. Ayres, *Wichita*

## KENTUCKY

### SENATORS

Richard P. Ernst, *Covington*
Frederic M. Sackett, *Louisville*

### REPRESENTATIVES

Alben W. Barkley, *Paducah*
David H. Kincheloe, *Madisonville*
Robert Y. Thomas, Jr.,[23] *Central City*
John W. Moore,[24] *Morgantown*
Ben Johnson, *Bardstown*
Maurice H. Thatcher, *Louisville*
Arthur B. Rouse, *Burlington*
Virgil M. Chapman, *Paris*
Ralph Gilbert, *Shelbyville*
Fred M. Vinson, *Louisa*
John W. Langley,[25] *Pikeville*
Andrew J. Kirk,[26] *Jenkins*
John M. Robsion, *Barbourville*

## LOUISIANA

### SENATORS

Joseph E. Ransdell, *Lake Providence*
Edwin S. Broussard, *New Iberia*

### REPRESENTATIVES

James O'Connor, *New Orleans*
J. Zach Spearing, *New Orleans*
Whitmell P. Martin, *Thibodaux*
John N. Sandlin, *Minden*
Riley J. Wilson, *Ruston*
Bolivar E. Kemp, *Amite*
Ladislas Lazaro, *Washington*
James B. Aswell, *Natchitoches*

---

[12] Election unsuccessfully contested by H. O. Brown.

[13] Election unsuccessfully contested by Don H. Clark.

[14] Died December 7, 1926.

[15] Credentials as Senator-designate to fill vacancy caused by death of William B. McKinley were presented on January 19, 1927, and were referred to the Committee on Privileges and Elections for report; meanwhile Mr. Smith was not permitted to qualify. No further action was taken. (See U.S. Senate Election, Expulsion and Censure Cases, 1793-1990, Senate Document 103-33, pp. 330-33.)

[16] Died June 25, 1926; vacancy throughout remainder of the Congress.

[17] Died October 14, 1925.

[18] Appointed to fill vacancy caused by death of Samuel M. Ralston, and took his seat December 7, 1925; subsequently elected.

[19] Died July 30, 1926.

[20] Appointed to fill vacancy caused by death of Albert B. Cummins, and took his seat November 10, 1926; subsequently elected.

[21] Served until April 12, 1926; succeeded by Daniel F. Steck, who contested his election.

[22] Successfully contested the election of Smith W. Brookhart, and took his seat April 12, 1926. (See U.S. Senate Election, Expulsion and Censure Cases, 1793-1990, Senate Document 103-33, pp. 312-15.)

[23] Died September 3, 1925, before Congress assembled.

[24] Elected to fill vacancy caused by death of Robert Y. Thomas, Jr., and took his seat December 7, 1925.

[25] Resigned January 11, 1926, never having qualified.

[26] Elected to fill vacancy caused by resignation of John W. Langley, and took his seat February 25, 1926.

## MAINE

### SENATORS

Bert M. Fernald,[27] *West Poland*
Arthur R. Gould,[28] *Presque Isle*
Frederick Hale, *Portland*

### REPRESENTATIVES

Carroll L. Beedy, *Portland*
Wallace H. White, Jr., *Lewiston*
John E. Nelson, *Augusta*
Ira G. Hersey, *Houlton*

## MARYLAND

### SENATORS

Ovington E. Weller, *Baltimore*
William Cabell Bruce, *Baltimore*

### REPRESENTATIVES

T. Alan Goldsborough, *Denton*
Millard E. Tydings, *Havre de Grace*
John Philip Hill, *Baltimore*
J. Charles Linthicum, *Baltimore*
Stephen W. Gambrill, *Laurel*
Frederick N. Zihlman, *Cumberland*

## MASSACHUSETTS

### SENATORS

William M. Butler, *Boston*
David I. Walsh,[29] *Fitchburg*
Frederick H. Gillett, *Springfield*

### REPRESENTATIVES

Allen T. Treadway, *Stockbridge*
George B. Churchill,[30] *Amherst*
Henry L. Bowles,[31] *Springfield*
Frank H. Foss, *Fitchburg*
George R. Stobbs, *Worcester*
John Jacob Rogers,[32] *Lowell*
Edith Nourse Rogers,[33] *Lowell*
A. Piatt Andrew, Jr., *Gloucester*
William P. Connery, Jr., *Lynn*
Harry I. Thayer,[34] *Wakefield*
Frederick W. Dallinger,[35] *Cambridge*
Charles L. Underhill, *Somerville*
John J. Douglass, *Boston*
George H. Tinkham, *Boston*
James A. Gallivan, *Boston*
Robert Luce, *Waltham*
Louis A. Frothingham, *Easton*
Joseph W. Martin, Jr., *North Attleboro*
Charles L. Gifford, *Cotuit*

## MICHIGAN

### SENATORS

James Couzens, *Detroit*
Woodbridge N. Ferris, *Big Rapids*

### REPRESENTATIVES

John B. Sosnowski, *Detroit*
Earl C. Michener, *Adrian*
Arthur B. Williams,[36] *Battle Creek*
Joseph L. Hooper,[37] *Battle Creek*
John C. Ketcham, *Hastings*
Carl E. Mapes, *Grand Rapids*
Grant M. Hudson, *East Lansing*
Louis C. Cramton, *Lapeer*
Bird J. Vincent, *Saginaw*
James C. McLaughlin, *Muskegon*
Roy O. Woodruff, *Bay City*
Frank D. Scott, *Alpena*
W. Frank James, *Hancock*
Clarence J. McLeod, *Detroit*

## MINNESOTA

### SENATORS

Henrik Shipstead, *Minneapolis*
Thomas D. Schall,[38] *Excelsior*

### REPRESENTATIVES

Allen J. Furlow, *Rochester*
Frank Clague, *Redwood Falls*
August H. Andresen, *Red Wing*
Oscar E. Keller, *St. Paul*
Walter H. Newton, *Minneapolis*
Harold Knutson, *St. Cloud*
O. J. Kvale, *Benson*
William L. Carss, *Proctor*
Knud Wefald, *Hawley*
Godfrey G. Goodwin, *Cambridge*

## MISSISSIPPI

### SENATORS

Pat Harrison, *Gulfport*
Hubert D. Stephens, *New Albany*

### REPRESENTATIVES

John E. Rankin, *Tupelo*
Bill G. Lowrey, *Blue Mountain*
William M. Whittington, *Greenwood*
T. Jeff. Busby, *Houston*
Ross A. Collins, *Meridian*
T. Webber Wilson, *Laurel*
Percy E. Quin, *McComb City*
James W. Collier, *Vicksburg*

## MISSOURI

### SENATORS

James A. Reed, *Kansas City*
Selden P. Spencer,[39] *St. Louis*
George H. Williams,[40] *St. Louis*
Harry B. Hawes,[41] *St. Louis*

### REPRESENTATIVES

Milton A. Romjue, *Macon*
Ralph F. Lozier, *Carrollton*
Jacob L. Milligan, *Richmond*
Charles L. Faust, *St. Joseph*
Edgar C. Ellis, *Kansas City*
Clement C. Dickinson, *Clinton*
Samuel C. Major, *Fayette*
William L. Nelson, *Columbia*
Clarence Cannon, *Elsberry*
Cleveland A. Newton, *St. Louis*
Harry B. Hawes,[42] *St. Louis*
John J. Cochran,[43] *St. Louis*
Leonidas C. Dyer, *St. Louis*
Charles E. Kiefner, *Perryville*
Ralph E. Bailey, *Sikeston*
Joe J. Manlove, *Joplin*
Thomas L. Rubey, *Lebanon*

## MONTANA

### SENATORS

Thomas J. Walsh, *Helena*
Burton K. Wheeler, *Butte*

### REPRESENTATIVES

John M. Evans, *Missoula*
Scott Leavitt, *Great Falls*

## NEBRASKA

### SENATORS

George W. Norris, *McCook*
Robert B. Howell, *Omaha*

### REPRESENTATIVES

John H. Morehead, *Falls City*
Willis G. Sears, *Omaha*
Edgar Howard, *Columbus*
Melvin O. McLaughlin, *York*
Ashton C. Shallenberger, *Alma*
Robert G. Simmons, *Scottsbluff*

## NEVADA

### SENATORS

Key Pittman, *Tonopah*
Tasker L. Oddie, *Reno*

### REPRESENTATIVE AT LARGE

Samuel S. Arentz, *Simpson*

---

[27] Died August 23, 1926.
[28] Elected to fill vacancy caused by death of Bert M. Fernald, and took his seat December 6, 1926.
[29] Elected to fill vacancy caused by death of Henry Cabot Lodge, in preceding Congress, and took his seat December 6, 1926.
[30] Died July 1, 1925, before Congress assembled.
[31] Elected to fill vacancy caused by death of George B. Churchill, and took his seat December 7, 1925.
[32] Died March 28, 1925, before Congress assembled.
[33] Elected to fill vacancy caused by death of her husband, John Jacob Rogers, and took her seat December 7, 1925.
[34] Died March 10, 1926.
[35] Elected to fill vacancy caused by death of Harry I. Thayer, and took his seat December 6, 1926.
[36] Died May 1, 1925, before Congress assembled.
[37] Elected to fill vacancy caused by death of Arthur B. Williams, and took his seat December 7, 1925.
[38] Election unsuccessfully contested by Mangus Johnson. (See U.S. Senate Election, Expulsion and Censure Cases, 1793-1990, Senate Document 103-33, pp. 316-17.)
[39] Died May 16, 1925.
[40] Appointed to fill vacancy caused by death of Selden P. Spencer, and took his seat December 7, 1925.
[41] Elected to fill vacancy caused by death of Selden P. Spencer, and took his seat December 6, 1926.
[42] Resigned October 15, 1926, having been nominated for the Senate.
[43] Elected to fill vacancy caused by resignation of Harry B. Hawes, and took his seat December 6, 1926.

## NEW HAMPSHIRE

SENATORS

George H. Moses, *Concord*
Henry W. Keyes, *Haverhill*

REPRESENTATIVES

Fletcher Hale, *Laconia*
Edward H. Wason, *Nashua*

## NEW JERSEY

SENATORS

Walter E. Edge, *Atlantic City*
Edward I. Edwards, *Jersey City*

REPRESENTATIVES

Francis F. Patterson, Jr., *Camden*
Isaac Bacharach, *Atlantic City*
Stewart H. Appleby,[44] *Asbury Park*
Charles A. Eaton, *North Plainfield*
Ernest R. Ackerman, *Plainfield*
Randolph Perkins, *Woodcliff Lake*
George N. Seger, *Passaic*
Herbert W. Taylor, *Newark*
Franklin W. Fort, *East Orange*
Frederick R. Lehlbach, *Newark*
Oscar L. Auf der Heide, *West New York*
Mary T. Norton, *Jersey City*

## NEW MEXICO

SENATORS

Andrieus A. Jones, *East Las Vegas*
Sam G. Bratton,[45] *Albuquerque*

REPRESENTATIVE AT LARGE

John Morrow, *Raton*

## NEW YORK

SENATORS

James W. Wadsworth, Jr., *Groveland*
Royal S. Copeland, *New York City*

REPRESENTATIVES

Robert L. Bacon, *Westbury*
John J. Kindred, *Astoria*
George W. Lindsay, *Brooklyn*
Thomas H. Cullen, *Brooklyn*
Loring M. Black, Jr., *Brooklyn*
Andrew L. Somers, *Brooklyn*
John F. Quayle, *Brooklyn*
William E. Cleary, *Brooklyn*
David J. O'Connell, *Brooklyn*
Emanuel Celler, *Brooklyn*
Anning S. Prall, *West New Brighton*
Samuel Dickstein, *New York City*
Christopher D. Sullivan, *New York City*
Nathan D. Perlman,[46] *New York City*

John J. Boylan, *New York City*
John J. O'Connor, *New York City*
Ogden L. Mills, *New York City*
John F. Carew, *New York City*
Sol Bloom, *New York City*
Fiorello H. LaGuardia, *New York City*
Royal H. Weller, *New York City*
Anthony J. Griffin, *New York City*
Frank Oliver, *Bronx*
Benjamin L. Fairchild, *Pelham*
J. Mayhew Wainwright, *Rye*
Hamilton Fish, Jr., *Garrison*
Harcourt J. Pratt, *Highland*
Parker Corning, *Albany*
James S. Parker, *Salem*
Frank Crowther, *Schenectady*
Bertrand H. Snell, *Potsdam*
Thaddeus C. Sweet, *Phoenix*
Frederick M. Davenport, *Clinton*
Harold S. Tolley, *Binghamton*
Walter W. Magee, *Syracuse*
John Taber, *Auburn*
Gale H. Stalker, *Elmira*
Meyer Jacobstein, *Rochester*
Archie D. Sanders, *Stafford*
S. Wallace Dempsey, *Lockport*
Clarence MacGregor, *Buffalo*
James M. Mead, *Buffalo*
Daniel A. Reed, *Dunkirk*

## NORTH CAROLINA

SENATORS

Furnifold McL. Simmons, *New Bern*
Lee S. Overman, *Salisbury*

REPRESENTATIVES

Lindsay C. Warren, *Washington*
John H. Kerr, *Warrenton*
Charles L. Abernethy, *New Bern*
Edward W. Pou, *Smithfield*
Charles M. Stedman, *Greensboro*
Homer L. Lyon, *Whiteville*
William C. Hammer, *Asheboro*
Robert L. Doughton, *Laurel Springs*
Alfred L. Bulwinkle, *Gastonia*
Zebulon Weaver, *Asheville*

## NORTH DAKOTA

SENATORS

Edwin F. Ladd,[47] *Fargo*
Gerald P. Nye,[48] *Cooperstown*
Lynn J. Frazier, *Hoople*

REPRESENTATIVES

Olger B. Burtness, *Grand Forks*
Thomas Hall, *Bismarck*
James H. Sinclair, *Kenmare*

## OHIO

SENATORS

Frank B. Willis, *Delaware*
Simeon D. Fess, *Yellow Springs*

REPRESENTATIVES

Nicholas Longworth, *Cincinnati*
Ambrose E. B. Stephens,[49] *North Bend*
Roy G. Fitzgerald, *Dayton*
William T. Fitzgerald, *Greenville*
Charles J. Thompson, *Defiance*
Charles C. Kearns, *Amelia*
Charles Brand, *Urbana*
Thomas Brooks Fletcher, *Marion*
William W. Chalmers, *Toledo*
Thomas A. Jenkins, *Ironton*
Mell G. Underwood, *New Lexington*
John C. Speaks, *Columbus*
James T. Begg, *Sandusky*
Martin L. Davey, *Kent*
C. Ellis Moore, *Cambridge*
John McSweeney, *Wooster*
William M. Morgan, *Newark*
B. Frank Murphy, *Steubenville*
John G. Cooper, *Youngstown*
Charles A. Mooney, *Cleveland*
Robert Crosser, *Cleveland*
Theodore E. Burton, *Cleveland*

## OKLAHOMA

SENATORS

John W. Harreld, *Oklahoma City*
William B. Pine, *Okmulgee*

REPRESENTATIVES

Samuel J. Montgomery, *Bartlesville*
William W. Hastings, *Tahlequah*
Charles D. Carter, *Ardmore*
Thomas D. McKeown, *Ada*
Fletcher B. Swank, *Norman*
J. W. Elmer Thomas, *Medicine Park*
James V. McClintic, *Snyder*
Milton C. Garber, *Enid*

## OREGON

SENATORS

Charles L. McNary, *Salem*
Robert N. Stanfield, *Portland*

REPRESENTATIVES

Willis C. Hawley, *Salem*
Nicholas J. Sinnott, *The Dalles*
Maurice E. Crumpacker, *Portland*

## PENNSYLVANIA

SENATORS

George Wharton Pepper, *Philadelphia*
David A. Reed, *Pittsburgh*

---

[44] Elected to fill vacancy caused by death of his father, Representative-elect T. Frank Appleby (December 14, 1924, before the beginning of the congressional term), and took his seat December 7, 1925.

[45] Election unsuccessfully contested by Holm O. Bursum. (See U.S. Senate Election, Expulsion and Censure Cases, 1793-1990, Senate Document 103-33, pp. 318-19.)

[46] Election unsuccessfully contested by William I. Sirovich.

[47] Died June 22, 1925.

[48] Appointed to fill vacancy caused by death of

Edwin F. Ladd, and took his seat January 12, 1926; subsequently elected.

[49] Died February 12, 1927, before the commencement of the Seventieth Congress, to which he had been reelected.

## REPRESENTATIVES

William S. Vare, *Philadelphia*
George S. Graham, *Philadelphia*
Harry C. Ransley, *Philadelphia*
Benjamin M. Golder, *Philadelphia*
James J. Connolly, *Philadelphia*
George A. Welsh, *Philadelphia*
George P. Darrow, *Philadelphia*
Thomas S. Butler, *West Chester*
Henry W. Watson, *Langhorne*
William W. Griest, *Lancaster*
Laurence H. Watres, *Scranton*
Edmund N. Carpenter, *Wilkes-Barre*
George F. Brumm, *Minersville*
Charles J. Esterly, *Reading*
Louis T. McFadden, *Canton*
Edgar R. Kiess, *Williamsport*
Frederick W. Magrady, *Mount Carmel*
Edward M. Beers, *Mount Union*
Joshua W. Swartz, *Harrisburg*
Anderson H. Walters,[50] *Johnstown*
J. Banks Kurtz, *Altoona*
Franklin Menges, *York*
William I. Swoope, *Clearfield*
Samuel A. Kendall, *Meyersdale*
Henry W. Temple, *Washington*
Thomas W. Phillips, Jr., *Butler*
Nathan L. Strong, *Brookville*
Harris J. Bixler, *Johnsonburg*
Milton W. Shreve, *Erie*
William R. Coyle, *Bethlehem*
Adam M. Wyant, *Greensburg*
Stephen G. Porter, *Pittsburgh*
M. Clyde Kelly, *Edgewood*
John M. Morin, *Pittsburgh*
James M. Magee, *Pittsburgh*
Guy E. Campbell, *Crafton*

## RHODE ISLAND

### SENATORS

Peter G. Gerry, *Warwick*
Jesse H. Metcalf, *Providence*

### REPRESENTATIVES

Clark Burdick, *Newport*
Richard S. Aldrich, *Warwick*
Jeremiah E. O'Connell, *Providence*

## SOUTH CAROLINA

### SENATORS

Ellison D. Smith, *Lynchburg*
Coleman L. Blease, *Columbia*

### REPRESENTATIVES

Thomas S. McMillan, *Charleston*
Butler B. Hare, *Saluda*
Fred H. Dominick, *Newberry*
John J. McSwain, *Greenville*
William F. Stevenson, *Cheraw*
Allard H. Gasque, *Florence*
Hampton P. Fulmer, *Orangeburg*

## SOUTH DAKOTA

### SENATORS

Peter Norbeck, *Redfield*
William H. McMaster, *Yankton*

### REPRESENTATIVES

Charles A. Christopherson, *Sioux Falls*
Royal C. Johnson, *Aberdeen*
William Williamson, *Custer*

## TENNESSEE

### SENATORS

Kenneth D. McKellar, *Memphis*
Lawrence D. Tyson, *Knoxville*

### REPRESENTATIVES

B. Carroll Reece, *Butler*
J. Will Taylor, *La Follette*
Sam D. McReynolds, *Chattanooga*
Cordell Hull, *Carthage*
Ewin L. Davis, *Tullahoma*
Joseph W. Byrns, *Nashville*
Edward E. Eslick, *Pulaski*
Gordon Browning, *Huntingdon*
Finis J. Garrett, *Dresden*
Hubert F. Fisher, *Memphis*

## TEXAS

### SENATORS

Morris Sheppard, *Texarkana*
Earle B. Mayfield, *Austin*

### REPRESENTATIVES

Eugene Black, *Clarksville*
John C. Box, *Jacksonville*
Morgan G. Sanders, *Canton*
Sam Rayburn, *Bonham*
Hatton W. Sumners, *Dallas*
Luther A. Johnson, *Corsicana*
Clay Stone Briggs, *Galveston*
Daniel E. Garrett, *Houston*
Joseph J. Mansfield, *Columbus*
James P. Buchanan, *Brenham*
Tom T. Connally, *Marlin*
Fritz G. Lanham, *Fort Worth*
Guinn Williams, *Decatur*
Harry M. Wurzbach, *Seguin*
John N. Garner, *Uvalde*
Claude B. Hudspeth, *El Paso*
Thomas L. Blanton, *Abilene*
Marvin Jones, *Amarillo*

## UTAH

### SENATORS

Reed Smoot, *Provo*
William H. King, *Salt Lake City*

### REPRESENTATIVES

Don B. Colton, *Vernal*
Elmer O. Leatherwood, *Salt Lake City*

## VERMONT

### SENATORS

Frank L. Greene, *St. Albans*
Porter H. Dale, *Island Pond*

### REPRESENTATIVES

Elbert S. Brigham, *St. Albans*
Ernest Willard Gibson, *Brattleboro*

## VIRGINIA

### SENATORS

Claude A. Swanson, *Chatham*
Carter Glass, *Lynchburg*

### REPRESENTATIVES

Schuyler Otis Bland, *Newport News*
Joseph T. Deal, *Norfolk*
Andrew J. Montague, *Richmond*
Patrick Henry Drewry, *Petersburg*
Joseph Whitehead, *Chatham*
Clifton A. Woodrum, *Roanoke*
Thomas W. Harrison, *Winchester*
R. Walton Moore, *Fairfax*
George C. Peery, *Tazewell*
Henry St. George Tucker, *Lexington*

## WASHINGTON

### SENATORS

Wesley L. Jones, *Seattle*
Clarence C. Dill, *Spokane*

### REPRESENTATIVES

John F. Miller, *Seattle*
Lindley H. Hadley, *Bellingham*
Albert Johnson, *Hoquiam*
John W. Summers, *Walla Walla*
Samuel B. Hill, *Waterville*

## WEST VIRGINIA

### SENATORS

Matthew M. Neely, *Fairmont*
Guy D. Goff, *Clarksburg*

### REPRESENTATIVES

Carl G. Bachmann, *Wheeling*
Frank L. Bowman, *Morgantown*
John M. Wolverton, *Richwood*
Harry C. Woodyard, *Spencer*
James French Strother, *Welch*
J. Alfred Taylor, *Fayetteville*

## WISCONSIN

### SENATORS

Robert M. La Follette,[51] *Madison*
Robert M. La Follette, Jr.,[52] *Madison*
Irvine L. Lenroot, *Superior*

### REPRESENTATIVES

Henry Allen Cooper, *Racine*
Edward Voigt, *Sheboygan*
John M. Nelson, *Madison*
John C. Schafer, *Milwaukee*

---

[50] Election unsuccessfully contested by Warren Worth Bailey.
[51] Died June 18, 1925.
[52] Elected to fill vacancy caused by death of his father, Robert M. La Follette, and took his seat December 7, 1925.

## WISCONSIN—Continued

### REPRESENTATIVES—CONTINUED

Victor L. Berger, *Milwaukee*
Florian Lampert, *Oshkosh*
Joseph D. Beck, *Viroqua*
Edward E. Browne, *Waupaca*
George J. Schneider, *Appleton*
James A. Frear, *Hudson*
Hubert H. Peavey, *Washburn*

## WYOMING

### SENATORS

Francis E. Warren, *Cheyenne*
John B. Kendrick, *Sheridan*

### REPRESENTATIVE AT LARGE

Charles E. Winter, *Casper*

## TERRITORY OF ALASKA

### DELEGATE

Dan A. Sutherland, *Juneau*

## TERRITORY OF HAWAII

### DELEGATE

William P. Jarrett, *Honolulu*

## PHILIPPINE ISLANDS

### RESIDENT COMMISSIONERS

Isauro Gabaldon, *Nueva Ecija*
Pedro Guevara, *Santa Cruz*

## PORTO RICO

### RESIDENT COMMISSIONER

Felix Cordova Davila, *San Juan*

# 70TH CONGRESS

## MARCH 4, 1927, TO MARCH 3, 1929

FIRST SESSION— *December 5, 1927, to May 29, 1928*
SECOND SESSION— *December 3, 1928, to March 3, 1929*

---

VICE PRESIDENT OF THE UNITED STATES— CHARLES G. DAWES, of Illinois
PRESIDENT PRO TEMPORE OF THE SENATE— GEORGE H. MOSES,[1] of New Hampshire
SECRETARY OF THE SENATE— EDWIN P. THAYER,[2] of Indiana
SERGEANT AT ARMS OF THE SENATE— DAVID S. BARRY, of Rhode Island

---

SPEAKER OF THE HOUSE OF REPRESENTATIVES— NICHOLAS LONGWORTH,[3] of Ohio
CLERK OF THE HOUSE— WILLIAM TYLER PAGE,[4] of Maryland
SERGEANT AT ARMS OF THE HOUSE— JOSEPH G. ROGERS, of Pennsylvania
DOORKEEPER OF THE HOUSE— BERT W. KENNEDY, of Michigan
POSTMASTER OF THE HOUSE— FRANK W. COLLIER

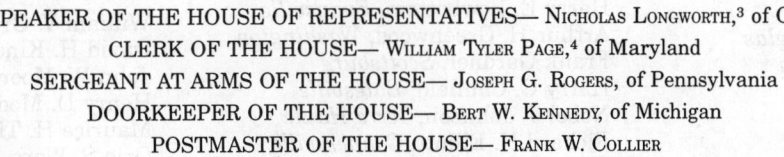

Charles G. Dawes
Vice President

Nicholas Longworth
Speaker

## ALABAMA

### SENATORS

J. Thomas Heflin, *Lafayette*
Hugo L. Black, *Birmingham*

### REPRESENTATIVES

John McDuffie, *Monroeville*
Lister Hill, *Montgomery*
Henry B. Steagall, *Ozark*
Lamar Jeffers, *Anniston*
William B. Bowling,[5] *Lafayette*
LaFayette L. Patterson,[6] *Alexander City*
William B. Oliver, *Tuscaloosa*
Miles C. Allgood, *Allgood*
Edward B. Almon, *Tuscumbia*
George Huddleston, *Birmingham*
William B. Bankhead, *Jasper*

## ARIZONA

### SENATORS

Henry F. Ashurst, *Prescott*
Carl Hayden, *Phoenix*

### REPRESENTATIVE AT LARGE

Lewis W. Douglas, *Phoenix*

## ARKANSAS

### SENATORS

Joseph T. Robinson, *Little Rock*
Thaddeus H. Caraway, *Jonesboro*

### REPRESENTATIVES

William J. Driver, *Osceola*
William A. Oldfield,[7] *Batesville*

Pearl Peden Oldfield,[8] *Batesville*
John N. Tillman, *Fayetteville*
Otis Wingo, *De Queen*
Heartsill Ragon, *Clarksville*
James B. Reed, *Lonoke*
Tilman B. Parks, *Camden*

## CALIFORNIA

### SENATORS

Hiram W. Johnson, *San Francisco*
Samuel M. Shortridge, *Menlo Park*

### REPRESENTATIVES

Clarence F. Lea, *Santa Rosa*
Harry L. Englebright, *Nevada City*
Charles F. Curry, *Sacramento*
Florence P. Kahn, *San Francisco*
Richard J. Welch, *San Francisco*
Albert E. Carter, *Oakland*
Henry E. Barbour, *Fresno*
Arthur M. Free, *San Jose*
William E. Evans, *Glendale*
Joe Crail, *Los Angeles*
Philip D. Swing, *El Centro*

## COLORADO

### SENATORS

Lawrence C. Phipps, *Denver*
Charles W. Waterman, *Denver*

### REPRESENTATIVES

William N. Vaile,[9] *Denver*
S. Harrison White,[10] *Denver*
Charles B. Timberlake, *Sterling*
Guy U. Hardy, *Canon City*
Edward T. Taylor, *Glenwood Springs*

## CONNECTICUT

### SENATORS

George P. McLean, *Simsbury*
Hiram Bingham, *New Haven*

### REPRESENTATIVES

E. Hart Fenn, *Wethersfield*
Richard P. Freeman, *New London*
John Q. Tilson, *New Haven*
Schuyler Merritt, *Stamford*
James P. Glynn, *Winsted*

## DELAWARE

### SENATORS

Thomas F. Bayard, Jr., *Wilmington*
T. Coleman du Pont,[11] *Wilmington*
Daniel O. Hastings,[12] *Wilmington*

### REPRESENTATIVE AT LARGE

Robert G. Houston, *Georgetown*

## FLORIDA

### SENATORS

Duncan U. Fletcher, *Jacksonville*
Park Trammell, *Lakeland*

### REPRESENTATIVES

Herbert J. Drane, *Lakeland*
Robert A. Green, *Starke*
Thomas A. Yon, *Tallahassee*
William J. Sears, *Kissimmee*

---

[1] Reelected December 15, 1927.
[2] Reelected December 15, 1927.
[3] Reelected December 5, 1927.
[4] Reelected December 5, 1927.
[5] Resigned August 16, 1928, having been appointed a justice of the circuit court of the State of Alabama.
[6] Elected to fill vacancy caused by resignation of

William B. Bowling, and took his seat December 3, 1928.
[7] Died November 19, 1928, before the commencement of the Seventy-first Congress, to which he had been reelected.
[8] Elected to fill vacancy caused by death of her husband, William A. Oldfield, and took her seat January 11, 1929.

[9] Died July 2, 1927, before Congress assembled.
[10] Elected to fill vacancy caused by death of William N. Vaile, and took his seat December 5, 1927.
[11] Resigned December 9, 1928.
[12] Appointed to fill vacancy caused by resignation of T. Coleman du Pont, and took his seat December 13, 1928.

## GEORGIA

SENATORS

William J. Harris, *Cedartown*
Walter F. George, *Vienna*

REPRESENTATIVES

Charles G. Edwards, *Savannah*
Edward E. Cox, *Camilla*
Charles R. Crisp, *Americus*
William C. Wright, *Newnan*
Leslie J. Steele, *Decatur*
Samuel Rutherford, *Forsyth*
Malcolm C. Tarver, *Dalton*
Charles H. Brand, *Athens*
Thomas M. Bell, *Gainesville*
Carl Vinson, *Milledgeville*
William C. Lankford, *Douglas*
William W. Larsen, *Dublin*

## IDAHO

SENATORS

William E. Borah, *Boise*
Frank R. Gooding,[13] *Gooding*
John Thomas,[14] *Gooding*

REPRESENTATIVES

Burton L. French, *Moscow*
Addison T. Smith, *Twin Falls*

## ILLINOIS

SENATORS

Charles S. Deneen, *Chicago*
Frank L. Smith,[15] *Dwight*
Otis F. Glenn,[16] *Murphysboro*

REPRESENTATIVES AT LARGE

Richard Yates, *Springfield*
Henry R. Rathbone,[17] *Kenilworth*

REPRESENTATIVES

Martin B. Madden,[18] *Chicago*
Morton D. Hull, *Chicago*
Elliott W. Sproul, *Chicago*
Thomas A. Doyle, *Chicago*
Adolph J. Sabath, *Chicago*
James T. Igoe, *Chicago*
M. Alfred Michaelson, *Chicago*
Stanley H. Kunz, *Chicago*
Fred A. Britten, *Chicago*
Carl R. Chindblom, *Chicago*
Frank R. Reid, *Aurora*
John T. Buckbee, *Rockford*
William R. Johnson, *Freeport*
John C. Allen, *Monmouth*
Edward J. King,[19] *Galesburg*
William E. Hull, *Peoria*
Homer W. Hall, *Bloomington*
William P. Holaday, *Georgetown*

Charles Adkins, *Decatur*
Henry T. Rainey, *Carrollton*
J. Earl Major, *Hillsboro*
Edward M. Irwin, *Belleville*
William W. Arnold, *Robinson*
Thomas S. Williams, *Louisville*
Edward E. Denison, *Marion*

## INDIANA

SENATORS

James E. Watson, *Rushville*
Arthur R. Robinson, *Indianapolis*

REPRESENTATIVES

Harry E. Rowbottom, *Evansville*
Arthur H. Greenwood, *Washington*
Frank Gardner, *Scottsburg*
Harry C. Canfield, *Batesville*
Nobel J. Johnson, *Terre Haute*
Richard N. Elliott, *Connersville*
Ralph E. Updike, *Indianapolis*
Albert H. Vestal, *Anderson*
Fred S. Purnell, *Attica*
William R. Wood, *La Fayette*
Albert R. Hall, *Marion*
David Hogg, *Fort Wayne*
Andrew J. Hickey, *La Porte*

## IOWA

SENATORS

Daniel F. Steck, *Ottumwa*
Smith W. Brookhart, *Washington*

REPRESENTATIVES

William F. Kopp, *Mount Pleasant*
F. Dickinson Letts, *Davenport*
Thomas J. B. Robinson, *Hampton*
Gilbert N. Haugen, *Northwood*
Cyrenus Cole, *Cedar Rapids*
C. William Ramseyer, *Bloomfield*
Cassius C. Dowell, *Des Moines*
Lloyd Thurston, *Osceola*
William R. Green,[20] *Council Bluffs*
Earl W. Vincent,[21] *Guthrie Center*
Lester J. Dickinson, *Algona*
William D. Boies, *Sheldon*

## KANSAS

SENATORS

Charles Curtis,[22] *Topeka*
Arthur Capper, *Topeka*

REPRESENTATIVES

Daniel R. Anthony, Jr., *Leavenworth*
Ulysses S. Guyer, *Kansas City*

William H. Sproul, *Sedan*
Homer Hoch, *Marion*
James G. Strong, *Blue Rapids*
Hays B. White,[23] *Mankato*
Clifford R. Hope, *Garden City*
William A. Ayres, *Wichita*

## KENTUCKY

SENATORS

Frederic M. Sackett, *Louisville*
Alben W. Barkley, *Paducah*

REPRESENTATIVES

William V. Gregory, *Mayfield*
David H. Kincheloe, *Madisonville*
John W. Moore, *Morgantown*
Henry D. Moorman, *Hardinsburg*
Maurice H. Thatcher, *Louisville*
Orie S. Ware, *Covington*
Virgil M. Chapman, *Paris*
Ralph Gilbert, *Shelbyville*
Fred M. Vinson, *Louisa*
Katherine Langley, *Pikeville*
John M. Robsion, *Barbourville*

## LOUISIANA

SENATORS

Joseph E. Ransdell, *Lake Providence*
Edwin S. Broussard, *New Iberia*

REPRESENTATIVES

James O'Connor, *New Orleans*
J. Zach Spearing, *New Orleans*
Whitmell P. Martin, *Thibodaux*
John N. Sandlin, *Minden*
Riley J. Wilson, *Ruston*
Bolivar E. Kemp, *Amite*
Ladislas Lazaro,[24] *Washington*
René L. DeRouen,[25] *Ville Platte*
James B. Aswell, *Natchitoches*

## MAINE

SENATORS

Frederick Hale, *Portland*
Arthur R. Gould, *Presque Isle*

REPRESENTATIVES

Carroll L. Beedy, *Portland*
Wallace H. White, Jr., *Lewiston*
John E. Nelson, *Augusta*
Ira G. Hersey, *Houlton*

---

[13] Died June 24, 1928.
[14] Appointed to fill vacancy caused by death of Frank R. Gooding, and took his seat December 3, 1928; subsequently elected.
[15] A Senator-elect whom the Senate refused to seat and who resigned February 9, 1928. (See U.S. Senate Election, Expulsion and Censure Cases, 1793-1990, Senate Document 103-33, pp. 330-33.)
[16] Elected to fill vacancy caused by resignation of Frank L. Smith, and took his seat December 3, 1928.
[17] Died July 15, 1928; vacancy throughout

remainder of the Congress.
[18] Died April 27, 1928; vacancy throughout remainder of the Congress.
[19] Died February 17, 1929, before the commencement of the Seventy-first Congress, to which he had been reelected. Vacancy in the Seventieth Congress not filled.
[20] Resigned March 31, 1928, having been appointed a judge of the Court of Claims of the United States.
[21] Elected to fill vacancy caused by resignation of

William R. Green, and took his seat December 3, 1928.
[22] Resigned effective March 3, 1929, having been elected Vice President of the United States.
[23] Election unsuccessfully contested by W. H. Clark.
[24] Died March 30, 1927, before Congress assembled.
[25] Elected to fill vacancy caused by death of Ladislas Lazaro, and took his seat December 5, 1927.

## MARYLAND

SENATORS

William Cabell Bruce, *Baltimore*
Millard E. Tydings, *Havre de Grace*

REPRESENTATIVES

T. Alan Goldsborough, *Denton*
William P. Cole, Jr., *Towson*
Vincent L. Palmisano, *Baltimore*
J. Charles Linthicum, *Baltimore*
Stephen W. Gambrill, *Laurel*
Frederick N. Zihlman, *Cumberland*

## MASSACHUSETTS

SENATORS

Frederick H. Gillett, *Springfield*
David I. Walsh, *Fitchburg*

REPRESENTATIVES

Allen T. Treadway, *Stockbridge*
Henry L. Bowles, *Springfield*
Frank H. Foss, *Fitchburg*
George R. Stobbs, *Worcester*
Edith Nourse Rogers, *Lowell*
A. Piatt Andrew, Jr., *Gloucester*
William P. Connery, Jr., *Lynn*
Frederick W. Dallinger, *Cambridge*
Charles L. Underhill, *Somerville*
John J. Douglass, *Boston*
George H. Tinkham, *Boston*
James A. Gallivan,[26] *Boston*
John W. McCormack,[27] *Dorchester*
Robert Luce, *Waltham*
Louis A. Frothingham,[28] *Easton*
Richard B. Wigglesworth,[29] *Milton*
Joseph W. Martin, Jr., *North Attleboro*
Charles L. Gifford, *Cotuit*

## MICHIGAN

SENATORS

James Couzens, *Detroit*
Woodbridge N. Ferris,[30] *Big Rapids*
Arthur H. Vandenberg,[31] *Grand Rapids*

REPRESENTATIVES

Robert H. Clancy, *Detroit*
Earl C. Michener, *Adrian*
Joseph L. Hooper, *Battle Creek*
John C. Ketcham, *Hastings*
Carl E. Mapes, *Grand Rapids*
Grant M. Hudson, *East Lansing*
Louis C. Cramton, *Lapeer*
Bird J. Vincent, *Saginaw*
James C. McLaughlin, *Muskegon*
Roy O. Woodruff, *Bay City*
Frank P. Bohn, *Newberry*
W. Frank James, *Hancock*
Clarence J. McLeod, *Detroit*

## MINNESOTA

SENATORS

Henrik Shipstead, *Minneapolis*
Thomas D. Schall, *Excelsior*

REPRESENTATIVES

Allen J. Furlow, *Rochester*
Frank Clague, *Redwood Falls*
August H. Andresen, *Red Wing*
Melvin J. Maas, *St. Paul*
Walter H. Newton, *Minneapolis*
Harold Knutson, *St. Cloud*
Ole J. Kvale, *Benson*
William L. Carss, *Proctor*
Conrad G. Selvig, *Crookston*
Godfrey G. Goodwin, *Cambridge*

## MISSISSIPPI

SENATORS

Pat Harrison, *Gulfport*
Hubert D. Stephens, *New Albany*

REPRESENTATIVES

John E. Rankin, *Tupelo*
Bill G. Lowrey, *Blue Mountain*
William M. Whittington, *Greenwood*
T. Jeff. Busby, *Houston*
Ross A. Collins, *Meridian*
T. Webber Wilson, *Laurel*
Percy E. Quin, *McComb*
James W. Collier, *Vicksburg*

## MISSOURI

SENATORS

James A. Reed, *Kansas City*
Harry B. Hawes, *St. Louis*

REPRESENTATIVES

Milton A. Romjue, *Macon*
Ralph F. Lozier, *Carrollton*
Jacob L. Milligan, *Richmond*
Charles L. Faust,[32] *St. Joseph*
David W. Hopkins,[33] *St. Joseph*
George H. Combs, Jr., *Kansas City*
Clement C. Dickinson, *Clinton*
Samuel C. Major, *Fayette*
William L. Nelson, *Columbia*
Clarence Cannon, *Elsberry*
Henry F. Niedringhaus, *St. Louis*
John J. Cochran, *St. Louis*
Leonidas C. Dyer, *St. Louis*
Clyde Williams, *Hillsboro*
James F. Fulbright, *Doniphan*
Joe J. Manlove, *Joplin*
Thomas L. Rubey,[34] *Lebanon*

## MONTANA

SENATORS

Thomas J. Walsh, *Helena*
Burton K. Wheeler, *Butte*

REPRESENTATIVES

John M. Evans, *Missoula*
Scott Leavitt, *Great Falls*

## NEBRASKA

SENATORS

George W. Norris, *McCook*
Robert B. Howell, *Omaha*

REPRESENTATIVES

John H. Morehead, *Falls City*
Willis G. Sears, *Omaha*
Edgar Howard, *Columbus*
John N. Norton, *Polk*
Ashton C. Shallenberger, *Alma*
Robert G. Simmons, *Scottsbluff*

## NEVADA

SENATORS

Key Pittman, *Tonopah*
Tasker L. Oddie, *Reno*

REPRESENTATIVE AT LARGE

Samuel S. Arentz, *Simpson*

## NEW HAMPSHIRE

SENATORS

George H. Moses, *Concord*
Henry W. Keyes, *Haverhill*

REPRESENTATIVES

Fletcher Hale, *Laconia*
Edward H. Wason, *Nashua*

## NEW JERSEY

SENATORS

Walter E. Edge, *Atlantic City*
Edward I. Edwards, *Jersey City*

REPRESENTATIVES

Charles A. Wolverton, *Camden*
Isaac Bacharach, *Atlantic City*
Harold G. Hoffman, *South Amboy*
Charles A. Eaton, *North Plainfield*
Ernest R. Ackerman, *Plainfield*
Randolph Perkins, *Woodcliff Lake*
George N. Seger, *Passaic*
Paul J. Moore, *Newark*
Franklin W. Fort, *East Orange*
Frederick R. Lehlbach, *Newark*
Oscar L. Auf der Heide, *West New York*
Mary T. Norton, *Jersey City*

---

[26] Died April 3, 1928.
[27] Elected to fill vacancy caused by death of James A. Gallivan, and took his seat December 3, 1928.
[28] Died August 23, 1928.
[29] Elected to fill vacancy caused by death of Louis A. Frothingham, and took his seat December 3, 1928.

[30] Died March 23, 1928.
[31] Appointed to fill vacancy caused by death of Woodbridge N. Ferris, and took his seat April 5, 1928; subsequently elected.
[32] Died December 17, 1928, before the commencement of the Seventy-first Congress, to which he had

been reelected.
[33] Elected to fill vacancy caused by death of Charles L. Faust, and took his seat February 20, 1929.
[34] Died November 2, 1928; vacancy throughout remainder of the Congress.

## NEW MEXICO

### SENATORS

Andrieus A. Jones,[35] *East Las Vegas*
Bronson M. Cutting,[36] *Santa Fe*
Octaviano A. Larrazolo,[37]
　*Albuquerque*
Sam G. Bratton, *Albuquerque*

### REPRESENTATIVE AT LARGE

John Morrow, *Raton*

## NEW YORK

### SENATORS

Royal S. Copeland, *New York City*
Robert F. Wagner, *New York City*

### REPRESENTATIVES

Robert L. Bacon, *Westbury*
John J. Kindred, *Astoria*
George W. Lindsay, *Brooklyn*
Thomas H. Cullen, *Brooklyn*
Loring M. Black, Jr., *Brooklyn*
Andrew L. Somers, *Brooklyn*
John F. Quayle, *Brooklyn*
Patrick J. Carley, *Brooklyn*
David J. O'Connell, *Brooklyn*
Emanuel Celler, *Brooklyn*
Anning S. Prall, *West New Brighton*
Samuel Dickstein, *New York City*
Christopher D. Sullivan, *New York City*
William I. Sirovich, *New York City*
John J. Boylan, *New York City*
John J. O'Connor, *New York City*
William W. Cohen, *New York City*
John F. Carew, *New York City*
Sol Bloom, *New York City*
Fiorello H. LaGuardia,[38] *New York City*
Royal H. Weller,[39] *New York City*
Anthony J. Griffin, *New York City*
Frank Oliver, *Bronx*
James M. Fitzpatrick, *New York City*
J. Mayhew Wainwright, *Rye*
Hamilton Fish, Jr., *Garrison*
Harcourt J. Pratt, *Highland*
Parker Corning, *Albany*
James S. Parker, *Salem*
Frank Crowther, *Schenectady*
Bertrand H. Snell, *Potsdam*

Thaddeus C. Sweet,[40] *Phoenix*
Francis D. Culkin,[41] *Oswego*
Frederick M. Davenport, *Clinton*
John D. Clarke, *Fraser*
Walter W. Magee,[42] *Syracuse*
Clarence E. Hancock,[43] *Syracuse*
John Taber, *Auburn*
Gale H. Stalker, *Elmira*
Meyer Jacobstein, *Rochester*
Archie D. Sanders, *Stafford*
S. Wallace Dempsey, *Lockport*
Clarence MacGregor,[44] *Buffalo*
James M. Mead, *Buffalo*
Daniel A. Reed, *Dunkirk*

## NORTH CAROLINA

### SENATORS

Furnifold McL. Simmons, *New Bern*
Lee S. Overman, *Salisbury*

### REPRESENTATIVES

Lindsay C. Warren, *Washington*
John H. Kerr, *Warrenton*
Charles L. Abernethy, *New Bern*
Edward W. Pou, *Smithfield*
Charles M. Stedman, *Greensboro*
Homer L. Lyon, *Whiteville*
William C. Hammer, *Asheboro*
Robert L. Doughton, *Laurel Springs*
Alfred L. Bulwinkle, *Gastonia*
Zebulon Weaver, *Asheville*

## NORTH DAKOTA

### SENATORS

Lynn J. Frazier, *Hoople*
Gerald P. Nye, *Cooperstown*

### REPRESENTATIVES

Olger B. Burtness, *Grand Forks*
Thomas Hall, *Bismarck*
James H. Sinclair, *Kenmare*

## OHIO

### SENATORS

Frank B. Willis,[45] *Delaware*
Cyrus Locher,[46] *Cleveland*
Theodore E. Burton,[47] *Cleveland*
Simeon D. Fess, *Yellow Springs*

### REPRESENTATIVES

Nicholas Longworth, *Cincinnati*
Charles Tatgenhorst, Jr.,[48] *Cleves*
Roy G. Fitzgerald, *Dayton*
William T. Fitzgerald, *Greenville*
Charles J. Thompson, *Defiance*
Charles C. Kearns, *Amelia*
Charles Brand, *Urbana*
Thomas Brooks Fletcher, *Marion*
William W. Chalmers, *Toledo*
Thomas A. Jenkins, *Ironton*
Mell G. Underwood, *New Lexington*
John C. Speaks, *Columbus*
James T. Begg, *Sandusky*
Martin L. Davey, *Kent*
C. Ellis Moore, *Cambridge*
John McSweeney, *Wooster*
William M. Morgan, *Newark*
B. Frank Murphy, *Steubenville*
John G. Cooper, *Youngstown*
Charles A. Mooney, *Cleveland*
Robert Crosser, *Cleveland*
Theodore E. Burton,[49] *Cleveland*

## OKLAHOMA

### SENATORS

William B. Pine, *Okmulgee*
J. W. Elmer Thomas, *Medicine Park*

### REPRESENTATIVES

Everette B. Howard, *Tulsa*
William W. Hastings, *Tahlequah*
Wilburn Cartwright, *McAlester*
Thomas D. McKeown, *Ada*
Fletcher B. Swank, *Norman*
Jed Johnson, *Anadarko*
James V. McClintic, *Snyder*
Milton C. Garber, *Enid*

## OREGON

### SENATORS

Charles L. McNary, *Salem*
Frederick Steiwer, *Portland*

### REPRESENTATIVES

Willis C. Hawley, *Salem*
Nicholas J. Sinnott,[50] *The Dalles*
Robert R. Butler,[51] *The Dalles*
Maurice E. Crumpacker,[52] *Portland*
Franklin F. Korell,[53] *Portland*

---

[35] Died December 20, 1927.
[36] Appointed to fill vacancy caused by death of Andrieus A. Jones, and took his seat January 4, 1928.
[37] Elected to fill vacancy caused by death of Andrieus A. Jones, and took his seat December 7, 1928.
[38] Election unsuccessfully contested by H. Warren Hubbard.
[39] Died March 1, 1929, before the commencement of the Seventy-first Congress, to which he had been reelected. Vacancy in the Seventieth Congress not filled.
[40] Died May 1, 1928.
[41] Elected to fill vacancy caused by death of Thaddeus C. Sweet, and took his seat December 3, 1928.

[42] Died May 25, 1927, before Congress assembled.
[43] Elected to fill vacancy caused by death of Walter W. Magee, and took his seat December 5, 1927.
[44] Resigned December 31, 1928, having been appointed a justice of the Supreme Court of the State of New York; vacancy throughout remainder of Congress.
[45] Died March 30, 1928.
[46] Appointed to fill vacancy caused by death of Frank B. Willis, and took his seat April 16, 1928.
[47] Elected to fill vacancy caused by death of Frank B. Willis, and took his seat December 15, 1928.
[48] Elected to fill vacancy caused by death of Representative-elect Ambrose E. B. Stephens in pre-

ceding Congress, and took his seat December 5, 1927.
[49] Resigned December 15, 1928, having been elected to the Senate; vacancy throughout remainder of the Congress.
[50] Resigned May 31, 1928, having been appointed a judge of the Court of Claims of the United States.
[51] Elected to fill vacancy caused by resignation of Nicholas J. Sinnott, and took his seat December 3, 1928.
[52] Died July 24, 1927, before Congress assembled.
[53] Elected to fill vacancy caused by death of Maurice E. Crumpacker, and took his seat December 5, 1927.

## PENNSYLVANIA

SENATORS

David A. Reed, *Pittsburgh*
William S. Vare,[54] *Philadelphia*

REPRESENTATIVES

James M. Hazlett,[55] *Philadelphia*
James M. Beck,[56] *Philadelphia*
George S. Graham, *Philadelphia*
Harry C. Ransley, *Philadelphia*
Benjamin M. Golder, *Philadelphia*
James J. Connolly, *Philadelphia*
George A. Welsh, *Philadelphia*
George P. Darrow, *Philadelphia*
Thomas S. Butler,[57] *West Chester*
James Wolfenden,[58] *Upper Darby*
Henry W. Watson, *Langhorne*
William W. Griest, *Lancaster*
Laurence H. Watres, *Scranton*
John J. Casey, *Wilkes-Barre*
Cyrus M. Palmer, *Pottsville*
Robert G. Bushong, *Sinking Spring*
Louis T. McFadden, *Canton*
Edgar R. Kiess, *Williamsport*
Frederick W. Magrady, *Mount Carmel*
Edward M. Beers, *Mount Union*
Isaac H. Doutrich, *Harrisburg*
J. Russell Leech, *Ebensburg*
J. Banks Kurtz, *Altoona*
Franklin Menges, *York*
J. Mitchell Chase, *Clearfield*
Samuel A. Kendall, *Meyersdale*
Henry W. Temple, *Washington*
J. Howard Swick, *Beaver Falls*
Nathan L. Strong, *Brookville*
Thomas C. Cochran, *Mercer*
Milton W. Shreve, *Erie*
Everett Kent, *Bangor*
Adam M. Wyant, *Greensburg*
Stephen G. Porter, *Pittsburgh*
M. Clyde Kelly, *Edgewood*
John M. Morin, *Pittsburgh*
Harry A. Estep, *Pittsburgh*
Guy E. Campbell, *Crafton*

## RHODE ISLAND

SENATORS

Peter G. Gerry, *Warwick*
Jesse H. Metcalf, *Providence*

REPRESENTATIVES

Clark Burdick, *Newport*
Richard S. Aldrich, *Warwick*
Louis Monast, *Pawtucket*

## SOUTH CAROLINA

SENATORS

Ellison D. Smith, *Lynchburg*
Coleman L. Blease, *Columbia*

REPRESENTATIVES

Thomas S. McMillan, *Charleston*
Butler B. Hare, *Saluda*
Fred H. Dominick, *Newberry*
John J. McSwain, *Greenville*
William F. Stevenson, *Cheraw*
Allard H. Gasque, *Florence*
Hampton P. Fulmer, *Orangeburg*

## SOUTH DAKOTA

SENATORS

Peter Norbeck, *Redfield*
William H. McMaster, *Yankton*

REPRESENTATIVES

Charles A. Christopherson, *Sioux Falls*
Royal C. Johnson, *Aberdeen*
William Williamson, *Rapid City*

## TENNESSEE

SENATORS

Kenneth D. McKellar, *Memphis*
Lawrence D. Tyson, *Knoxville*

REPRESENTATIVES

B. Carroll Reece, *Butler*
J. Will Taylor, *La Follette*
Sam D. McReynolds, *Chattanooga*
Cordell Hull, *Carthage*
Ewin L. Davis, *Tullahoma*
Joseph W. Byrns, *Nashville*
Edward E. Eslick, *Pulaski*
Gordon Browning, *Huntingdon*
Finis J. Garrett, *Dresden*
Hubert F. Fisher, *Memphis*

## TEXAS

SENATORS

Morris Sheppard, *Texarkana*
Earle B. Mayfield, *Austin*

REPRESENTATIVES

Eugene Black, *Clarksville*
John C. Box, *Jacksonville*
Morgan G. Sanders, *Canton*
Sam Rayburn, *Bonham*
Hatton W. Sumners, *Dallas*
Luther A. Johnson, *Corsicana*
Clay Stone Briggs, *Galveston*
Daniel E. Garrett, *Houston*
Joseph J. Mansfield, *Columbus*
James P. Buchanan, *Brenham*
Tom T. Connally, *Marlin*
Fritz G. Lanham, *Fort Worth*
Guinn Williams, *Decatur*
Harry M. Wurzbach, *Seguin*
John N. Garner, *Uvalde*
Claude B. Hudspeth, *El Paso*
Thomas L. Blanton, *Abilene*
Marvin Jones, *Amarillo*

## UTAH

SENATORS

Reed Smoot, *Provo*
William H. King, *Salt Lake City*

REPRESENTATIVES

Don B. Colton, *Vernal*
Elmer O. Leatherwood, *Salt Lake City*

## VERMONT

SENATORS

Frank L. Greene, *St. Albans*
Porter H. Dale, *Island Pond*

REPRESENTATIVES

Elbert S. Brigham, *St. Albans*
Ernest Willard Gibson, *Brattleboro*

## VIRGINIA

SENATORS

Claude A. Swanson, *Chatham*
Carter Glass, *Lynchburg*

REPRESENTATIVES

Schuyler Otis Bland, *Newport News*
Joseph T. Deal, *Norfolk*
Andrew J. Montague, *Richmond*
Patrick Henry Drewry, *Petersburg*
Joseph Whitehead, *Chatham*
Clifton A. Woodrum, *Roanoke*
Thomas W. Harrison, *Winchester*
R. Walton Moore, *Fairfax*
George C. Peery, *Tazewell*
Henry St. George Tucker, *Lexington*

## WASHINGTON

SENATORS

Wesley L. Jones, *Seattle*
Clarence C. Dill, *Spokane*

REPRESENTATIVES

John F. Miller, *Seattle*
Lindley H. Hadley, *Bellingham*
Albert Johnson, *Hoquiam*
John W. Summers, *Walla Walla*
Samuel B. Hill, *Waterville*

## WEST VIRGINIA

SENATORS

Matthew M. Neely, *Fairmont*
Guy D. Goff, *Clarksburg*

REPRESENTATIVES

Carl G. Bachmann, *Wheeling*
Frank L. Bowman, *Morgantown*
William S. O'Brien, *Buckhannon*
James A. Hughes, *Huntington*
James French Strother, *Welch*

---

[54] Credentials as Senator-elect were presented and referred to the Committee on Privileges and Elections for report; meanwhile Mr. Vare was not permitted to qualify. No action taken during the session. (See U.S. Senate Election, Expulsion and Censure Cases, 1793-1990, Senate Document 103-33, pp. 323-29.)

[55] Resigned October 20, 1927, before Congress assembled.

[56] Elected to fill vacancy caused by resignation of James M. Hazlett, and took his seat December 5, 1927. Election unsuccessfully contested by House Resolution No. 9.

[57] Died May 26, 1928.

[58] Elected to fill vacancy caused by death of Thomas S. Butler, and took his seat December 3, 1928.

## WEST VIRGINIA— Continued

REPRESENTATIVES—CONTINUED

Edward T. England,[59] *Charleston*

## WISCONSIN

SENATORS

Robert M. La Follette, Jr., *Madison*
John J. Blaine, *Boscobel*

REPRESENTATIVES

Henry Allen Cooper, *Racine*
Charles A. Kading, *Watertown*
John M. Nelson, *Madison*
John C. Schafer, *Milwaukee*
Victor L. Berger, *Milwaukee*
Florian Lampert, *Oshkosh*
Joseph D. Beck, *Viroqua*

Edward E. Browne, *Waupaca*
George J. Schneider, *Appleton*
James A. Frear, *Hudson*
Hubert H. Peavey, *Washburn*

## WYOMING

SENATORS

Francis E. Warren, *Cheyenne*
John B. Kendrick, *Sheridan*

REPRESENTATIVE AT LARGE

Charles E. Winter, *Casper*

## TERRITORY OF ALASKA

DELEGATE

Dan A. Sutherland, *Juneau*

## TERRITORY OF HAWAII

DELEGATE

Victor S. K. Houston, *Honolulu*

## PHILIPPINE ISLANDS

RESIDENT COMMISSIONERS

Isauro Gabaldon,[60] *Nueva Ecija*
Pedro Guevara, *Santa Cruz*

## PORTO RICO

RESIDENT COMMISSIONER

Felix Cordova Davila, *San Juan*

---

[59] Election unsuccessfully contested by J. Alfred Taylor.

[60] Resigned July 16, 1928, having been nominated for election to the Philippine House of Representatives; vacancy throughout the remainder of the Congress.

# 71st CONGRESS

## MARCH 4, 1929, TO MARCH 3, 1931

FIRST SESSION— *April 15, 1929, to November 22, 1929*
SECOND SESSION— *December 2, 1929, to July 3, 1930*
THIRD SESSION— *December 1, 1930, to March 3, 1931*
SPECIAL SESSIONS OF THE SENATE— *March 4, 1929, to March 5, 1929;*
*July 7, 1930, to July 21, 1930*

VICE PRESIDENT OF THE UNITED STATES— CHARLES CURTIS, of Kansas
PRESIDENT PRO TEMPORE OF THE SENATE— GEORGE H. MOSES, of New Hampshire
SECRETARY OF THE SENATE— EDWIN P. THAYER, of Indiana
SERGEANT AT ARMS OF THE SENATE— DAVID S. BARRY, of Rhode Island

Charles Curtis
Vice President

Nicholas Longworth
Speaker

SPEAKER OF THE HOUSE OF REPRESENTATIVES— NICHOLAS LONGWORTH,[1] of Ohio
CLERK OF THE HOUSE— WILLIAM TYLER PAGE,[2] of Maryland
SERGEANT AT ARMS OF THE HOUSE— JOSEPH G. ROGERS, of Pennsylvania
DOORKEEPER OF THE HOUSE— BERT W. KENNEDY, of Michigan
POSTMASTER OF THE HOUSE— FRANK W. COLLIER

## ALABAMA

### SENATORS
J. Thomas Heflin, *Lafayette*
Hugo L. Black, *Birmingham*

### REPRESENTATIVES
John McDuffie, *Monroeville*
Lister Hill, *Montgomery*
Henry B. Steagall, *Ozark*
Lamar Jeffers, *Anniston*
LaFayette L. Patterson, *Alexander City*
William B. Oliver, *Tuscaloosa*
Miles C. Allgood, *Allgood*
Edward B. Almon, *Tuscumbia*
George Huddleston, *Birmingham*
William B. Bankhead, *Jasper*

## ARIZONA

### SENATORS
Henry F. Ashurst, *Prescott*
Carl Hayden, *Phoenix*

### REPRESENTATIVE AT LARGE
Lewis W. Douglas, *Phoenix*

## ARKANSAS

### SENATORS
Joseph T. Robinson, *Little Rock*
Thaddeus H. Caraway, *Jonesboro*

### REPRESENTATIVES
William J. Driver, *Osceola*
Pearl Peden Oldfield,[3] *Batesville*
Claude A. Fuller, *Eureka Springs*

Otis Wingo,[4] *De Queen*
Effiegene (Locke) Wingo,[5] *De Queen*
Heartsill Ragon, *Clarksville*
David D. Glover, *Malvern*
Tilman B. Parks, *Camden*

## CALIFORNIA

### SENATORS
Hiram W. Johnson, *San Francisco*
Samuel M. Shortridge, *Menlo Park*

### REPRESENTATIVES
Clarence F. Lea, *Santa Rosa*
Harry L. Englebright, *Nevada City*
Charles F. Curry,[6] *Sacramento*
Florence P. Kahn, *San Francisco*
Richard J. Welch, *San Francisco*
Albert E. Carter, *Oakland*
Henry E. Barbour, *Fresno*
Arthur M. Free, *San Jose*
William E. Evans, *Glendale*
Joe Crail, *Los Angeles*
Philip D. Swing, *El Centro*

## COLORADO

### SENATORS
Lawrence C. Phipps, *Denver*
Charles W. Waterman, *Denver*

### REPRESENTATIVES
William R. Eaton, *Denver*
Charles B. Timberlake, *Sterling*
Guy U. Hardy, *Canon City*
Edward T. Taylor, *Glenwood Springs*

## CONNECTICUT

### SENATORS
Hiram Bingham, *New Haven*
Frederic C. Walcott, *Norfolk*

### REPRESENTATIVES
E. Hart Fenn, *Wethersfield*
Richard P. Freeman, *New London*
John Q. Tilson, *New Haven*
Schuyler Merritt, *Stamford*
James P. Glynn,[7] *Winsted*
Edward W. Goss,[8] *Waterbury*

## DELAWARE

### SENATORS
Daniel O. Hastings, *Wilmington*
John G. Townsend, Jr., *Selbyville*

### REPRESENTATIVE AT LARGE
Robert G. Houston, *Georgetown*

## FLORIDA

### SENATORS
Duncan U. Fletcher, *Jacksonville*
Park Trammell, *Lakeland*

### REPRESENTATIVES
Herbert J. Drane, *Lakeland*
Robert A. Green, *Starke*
Thomas A. Yon, *Tallahassee*
Ruth Bryan Owen,[9] *Miami*

---

[1] Reelected April 15, 1929.
[2] Reelected April 15, 1929.
[3] Elected to fill vacancy caused by death of her husband, Representative-elect William A. Oldfield, in preceding Congress.
[4] Died October 21, 1930.

[5] Elected to fill vacancy caused by death of her husband, Otis Wingo, and took her seat December 1, 1930.
[6] Died October 10, 1930; vacancy throughout remainder of the Congress.
[7] Died March 6, 1930.

[8] Elected to fill vacancy caused by death of James P. Glynn, and took his seat December 1, 1930.
[9] Election unsuccessfully contested by William C. Lawson.

## GEORGIA

### SENATORS

William J. Harris, *Cedartown*
Walter F. George, *Vienna*

### REPRESENTATIVES

Charles G. Edwards, *Savannah*
Edward E. Cox, *Camilla*
Charles R. Crisp, *Americus*
William C. Wright, *Newnan*
Leslie J. Steele,[10] *Decatur*
Robert Ramspeck,[11] *Decatur*
Samuel Rutherford, *Forsyth*
Malcolm C. Tarver, *Dalton*
Charles H. Brand, *Athens*
Thomas M. Bell, *Gainesville*
Carl Vinson, *Milledgeville*
William C. Lankford, *Douglas*
William W. Larsen, *Dublin*

## IDAHO

### SENATORS

William E. Borah, *Boise*
John Thomas, *Gooding*

### REPRESENTATIVES

Burton L. French, *Moscow*
Addison T. Smith, *Twin Falls*

## ILLINOIS

### SENATORS

Charles S. Deneen, *Chicago*
Otis F. Glenn, *Murphysboro*

### REPRESENTATIVES AT LARGE

Richard Yates, *Springfield*
Ruth Hanna McCormick, *Byron*

### REPRESENTATIVES

Oscar De Priest, *Chicago*
Morton D. Hull, *Chicago*
Elliott W. Sproul, *Chicago*
Thomas A. Doyle, *Chicago*
Adolph J. Sabath, *Chicago*
James T. Igoe, *Chicago*
M. Alfred Michaelson, *Chicago*
Stanley H. Kunz, *Chicago*
Fred A. Britten, *Chicago*
Carl R. Chindblom, *Chicago*
Frank R. Reid, *Aurora*
John T. Buckbee, *Rockford*
William R. Johnson, *Freeport*
John C. Allen, *Monmouth*

Burnett M. Chiperfield,[12] *Canton*
William E. Hull, *Peoria*
Homer W. Hall, *Bloomington*
William P. Holaday, *Georgetown*
Charles Adkins, *Decatur*
Henry T. Rainey, *Carrollton*
Frank M. Ramey, *Hillsboro*
Edward M. Irwin, *Belleville*
William W. Arnold, *Robinson*
Thomas S. Williams,[13] *Louisville*
Claude V. Parsons,[14] *Golconda*
Edward E. Denison, *Marion*

## INDIANA

### SENATORS

James E. Watson, *Rushville*
Arthur R. Robinson, *Indianapolis*

### REPRESENTATIVES

Harry E. Rowbottom, *Evansville*
Arthur H. Greenwood, *Washington*
James W. Dunbar, *New Albany*
Harry C. Canfield, *Batesville*
Noble J. Johnson, *Terre Haute*
Richard N. Elliott, *Connersville*
Louis Ludlow,[15] *Indianapolis*
Albert H. Vestal, *Anderson*
Fred S. Purnell, *Attica*
William R. Wood, *La Fayette*
Albert R. Hall, *Marion*
David Hogg, *Fort Wayne*
Andrew J. Hickey, *La Porte*

## IOWA

### SENATORS

Daniel F. Steck, *Ottumwa*
Smith W. Brookhart, *Washington*

### REPRESENTATIVES

William F. Kopp, *Mount Pleasant*
F. Dickinson Letts, *Davenport*
Thomas J. B. Robinson, *Hampton*
Gilbert N. Haugen, *Northwood*
Cyrenus Cole, *Cedar Rapids*
C. William Ramseyer, *Bloomfield*
Cassius C. Dowell, *Des Moines*
Lloyd Thurston, *Osceola*
Charles E. Swanson, *Council Bluffs*
Lester J. Dickinson, *Algona*
Ed H. Campbell, *Battle Creek*

## KANSAS

### SENATORS

Arthur Capper, *Topeka*
Henry J. Allen,[16] *Wichita*
George McGill,[17] *Wichita*

### REPRESENTATIVES

William P. Lambertson, *Fairview*
Ulysses S. Guyer, *Kansas City*
William H. Sproul, *Sedan*
Homer Hoch, *Marion*
James G. Strong, *Blue Rapids*
Charles I. Sparks, *Goodland*
Clifford R. Hope, *Garden City*
William A. Ayres, *Wichita*

## KENTUCKY

### SENATORS

Frederic M. Sackett,[18] *Louisville*
John M. Robsion,[19] *Barbourville*
Ben M. Williamson,[20] *Ashland*
Alben W. Barkley, *Paducah*

### REPRESENTATIVES

William V. Gregory, *Mayfield*
David H. Kincheloe,[21] *Madisonville*
John L. Dorsey, Jr.,[22] *Henderson*
Charles W. Roark,[23] *Greenville*
John W. Moore,[24] *Morgantown*
John D. Craddock, *Munfordville*
Maurice H. Thatcher, *Louisville*
J. Lincoln Newhall, *Covington*
Robert E. Lee Blackburn, *Lexington*
Lewis L. Walker, *Lancaster*
Elva R. Kendall, *Carlisle*
Katherine Langley, *Pikeville*
John M. Robsion,[25] *Barbourville*
Charles Finley,[26] *Williamsburg*

## LOUISIANA

### SENATORS

Joseph E. Ransdell, *Lake Providence*
Edwin S. Broussard, *New Iberia*

### REPRESENTATIVES

James O'Connor, *New Orleans*
J. Zach Spearing, *New Orleans*
Whitmell P. Martin,[27] *Thibodaux*
Numa F. Montet,[28] *Thibodaux*
John N. Sandlin, *Minden*
Riley J. Wilson, *Ruston*
Bolivar E. Kemp, *Amite*
René I. DeRouen, *Ville Platte*
James B. Aswell, *Natchitoches*

---

[10] Died July 24, 1929.
[11] Elected to fill vacancy caused by death of Leslie J. Steele, and took his seat November 11, 1929.
[12] Elected to to fill vacancy caused by death of Representative-elect Edward J. King, in preceding Congress, and took his seat December 1, 1930.
[13] Resigned November 11, 1929, having been appointed a judge of the Court of Claims of the United States.
[14] Elected to fill vacancy caused by the resignation of Thomas S. Williams, and took his seat December 1, 1930.
[15] Election unsuccessfully contested by Ralph E. Updike.
[16] Appointed to fill vacancy caused by resignation of Charles Curtis, in preceding Congress, and took his

seat April 15, 1929.
[17] Elected to fill vacancy caused by resignation of Charles Curtis, in preceding Congress, and took his seat December 1, 1930.
[18] Resigned January 9, 1930, having been appointed ambassador to Germany.
[19] Appointed to fill vacancy caused by resignation of Frederic M. Sackett, and took his seat January 11, 1930.
[20] Elected to fill vacancy caused by resignation of Frederic M. Sackett, and took his seat December 1, 1930.
[21] Resigned October 5, 1930, having been appointed a judge for the United States Customs Court.

[22] Elected to fill vacancy caused by resignation of David H. Kincheloe, and took his seat December 1, 1930.
[23] Died April 5, 1929, before Congress assembled.
[24] Elected to fill vacancy caused by death of Charles W. Roark, and took his seat June 19, 1929.
[25] Resigned January 10, 1930, having been appointed a Senator.
[26] Elected to fill vacancy caused by resignation of John M. Robsion, and took his seat March 1, 1930.
[27] Died April 6, 1929, before Congress assembled.
[28] Elected to fill vacancy caused by death of Whitmell P. Martin, and took his seat October 14, 1929.

## MAINE

### SENATORS

Frederick Hale, *Portland*
Arthur R. Gould, *Presque Isle*

### REPRESENTATIVES

Carroll L. Beedy, *Portland*
Wallace H. White, Jr., *Lewiston*
John E. Nelson, *Augusta*
Donald F. Snow, *Bangor*

## MARYLAND

### SENATORS

Millard E. Tydings, *Havre de Grace*
Phillips Lee Goldsborough, *Baltimore*

### REPRESENTATIVES

T. Alan Goldsborough, *Denton*
Linwood L. Clark, *Baltimore*
Vincent L. Palmisano,[29] *Baltimore*
J. Charles Linthicum, *Baltimore*
Stephen W. Gambrill, *Laurel*
Frederick N. Zihlman, *Cumberland*

## MASSACHUSETTS

### SENATORS

Frederick H. Gillett, *Springfield*
David I. Walsh, *Fitchburg*

### REPRESENTATIVES

Allen T. Tredway, *Stockbridge*
William Kirk Kaynor,[30] *Springfield*
William J. Granfield,[31] *Longmeadow*
Frank H. Foss, *Fitchburg*
George R. Stobbs, *Worcester*
Edith Nourse Rogers, *Lowell*
A. Piatt Andrew, Jr., *Gloucester*
William P. Connery, Jr., *Lynn*
Frederick W. Dallinger, *Cambridge*
Charles L. Underhill, *Somerville*
John J. Douglass, *Boston*
George H. Tinkham, *Boston*
John W. McCormack, *Dorchester*
Robert Luce, *Waltham*
Richard B. Wigglesworth, *Milton*
Joseph W. Martin, Jr., *North Attleboro*
Charles L. Gifford, *Cotuit*

## MICHIGAN

### SENATORS

James Couzens, *Detroit*
Arthur H. Vandenberg, *Grand Rapids*

### REPRESENTATIVES

Robert H. Clancy, *Detroit*
Earl C. Michener, *Adrian*
Joseph L. Hooper, *Battle Creek*
John C. Ketcham, *Hastings*
Carl E. Mapes, *Grand Rapids*
Grant M. Hudson, *East Lansing*
Louis C. Cramton, *Lapeer*
Bird J. Vincent, *Saginaw*
James C. McLaughlin, *Muskegon*
Roy O. Woodruff, *Bay City*
Frank P. Bohn, *Newberry*
W. Frank James, *Hancock*
Clarence J. McLeod, *Detroit*

## MINNESOTA

### SENATORS

Henrik Shipstead, *Minneapolis*
Thomas D. Schall, *Excelsior*

### REPRESENTATIVES

Victor Christgau, *Austin*
Frank Clague, *Redwood Falls*
August H. Andresen, *Red Wing*
Melvin J. Maas, *St. Paul*
Walter H. Newton,[32] *Minneapolis*
William I. Nolan,[33] *Minneapolis*
Harold Knutson, *St. Cloud*
Ole J. Kvale,[34] *Benson*
Paul J. Kvale,[35] *Benson*
William A. Pittenger, *Duluth*
Conrad G. Selvig, *Crookston*
Godfrey G. Goodwin, *Cambridge*

## MISSISSIPPI

### SENATORS

Pat Harrison, *Gulfport*
Hubert D. Stephens, *New Albany*

### REPRESENTATIVES

John E. Rankin, *Tupelo*
Wall Doxey, *Holly Springs*
William M. Whittington, *Greenwood*
T. Jeff. Busby, *Houston*
Ross A. Collins, *Meridian*
Robert S. Hall, *Hattiesburg*
Percy E. Quin, *McComb*
James W. Collier, *Vicksburg*

## MISSOURI

### SENATORS

Harry B. Hawes, *St. Louis*
Roscoe C. Patterson, *Kansas City*

### REPRESENTATIVES

Milton A. Romjue, *Macon*
Ralph F. Lozier, *Carrollton*
Jacob L. Milligan,[36] *Richmond*
David W. Hopkins,[37] *St. Joseph*
Edgar C. Ellis, *Kansas City*
Thomas J. Halsey, *Holden*
John W. Palmer, *Sedalia*
William L. Nelson, *Columbia*
Clarence Cannon, *Elsberry*
Henry F. Niedringhaus, *St. Louis*
John J. Cochran, *St. Louis*
Leonidas C. Dyer, *St. Louis*
Charles E. Kiefner, *Perryville*
Dewey Short, *Galena*
Joe J. Manlove, *Joplin*
Rowland L. Johnston, *Rolla*

## MONTANA

### SENATORS

Thomas J. Walsh, *Helena*
Burton K. Wheeler, *Butte*

### REPRESENTATIVES

John M. Evans, *Missoula*
Scott Leavitt, *Great Falls*

## NEBRASKA

### SENATORS

George W. Norris, *McCook*
Robert B. Howell, *Omaha*

### REPRESENTATIVES

John H. Morehead, *Falls City*
Willis G. Sears, *Omaha*
Edgar Howard, *Columbus*
Charles H. Sloan, *Geneva*
Fred G. Johnson, *Hastings*
Robert G. Simmons, *Scottsbluff*

## NEVADA

### SENATORS

Key Pittman, *Tonopah*
Tasker L. Oddie, *Reno*

### REPRESENTATIVE AT LARGE

Samuel S. Arentz, *Simpson*

## NEW HAMPSHIRE

### SENATORS

George H. Moses, *Concord*
Henry W. Keyes, *Haverhill*

### REPRESENTATIVES

Fletcher Hale, *Laconia*
Edward H. Wason, *Nashua*

---

[29] Election unsuccessfully contested by John P. Hill.

[30] Died December 20, 1929.

[31] Elected to fill vacancy caused by death of William Kirk Kaynor, and took his seat February 17, 1930.

[32] Resigned June 30, 1929, having been appointed Secretary to the President.

[33] Elected to fill vacancy caused by resignation of Walter H. Newton, and took his seat October 14, 1929.

[34] Died September 11, 1929.

[35] Elected to fill vacancy caused by death of his father, Ole J. Kvale, and took his seat November 11, 1929.

[36] Election unsuccessfully contested by Henry F. Lawrence.

[37] Elected to fill vacancy caused by death of Representative-elect Charles L. Faust, in preceding Congress.

## NEW JERSEY

SENATORS

Walter E. Edge,[38] *Atlantic City*
David Baird, Jr.,[39] *Camden*
Dwight W. Morrow,[40] *Englewood*
Hamilton F. Kean, *Elizabeth*

REPRESENTATIVES

Charles A. Wolverton, *Camden*
Isaac Bacharach, *Atlantic City*
Harold G. Hoffman, *South Amboy*
Charles A. Eaton, *North Plainfield*
Ernest R. Ackerman, *Plainfield*
Randolph Perkins, *Woodcliff Lake*
George N. Seger, *Passaic*
Fred A. Hartley, Jr., *Kearny*
Franklin W. Fort, *East Orange*
Frederick R. Lehlbach, *Newark*
Oscar L. Auf der Heide, *West New York*
Mary T. Norton, *Jersey City*

## NEW MEXICO

SENATORS

Sam G. Bratton, *Albuquerque*
Bronson M. Cutting, *Santa Fe*

REPRESENTATIVE AT LARGE

Albert Gallatin Simms, *Albuquerque*

## NEW YORK

SENATORS

Royal S. Copeland, *New York City*
Robert F. Wagner, *New York City*

REPRESENTATIVES

Robert L. Bacon, *Westbury*
William F. Brunner, *Rockaway Park*
George W. Lindsay, *Brooklyn*
Thomas H. Cullen, *Brooklyn*
Loring M. Black, Jr., *Brooklyn*
Andrew L. Somers, *Brooklyn*
John F. Quayle,[41] *Brooklyn*
Patrick J. Carley, *Brooklyn*
David J. O'Connell,[42] *Brooklyn*
Emanuel Celler, *Brooklyn*
Anning S. Prall, *West New Brighton*
Samuel Dickstein, *New York City*
Christopher D. Sullivan, *New York City*
William I. Sirovich, *New York City*
John J. Boylan, *New York City*
John J. O'Connor, *New York City*
Ruth S. B. Pratt, *New York City*
John F. Carew,[43] *New York City*
Martin J. Kennedy,[44] *New York City*

Sol Bloom, *New York City*
Fiorello H. LaGuardia, *New York City*
Joseph A. Gavagan,[45] *New York City*
Anthony J. Griffin, *New York City*
Frank Oliver, *Bronx*
James M. Fitzpatrick, *New York City*
J. Mayhew Wainwright, *Rye*
Hamilton Fish, Jr., *Garrison*
Harcourt J. Pratt, *Highland*
Parker Corning, *Albany*
James S. Parker, *Salem*
Frank Crowther, *Schenectady*
Bertrand H. Snell, *Potsdam*
Francis D. Culkin, *Oswego*
Frederick M. Davenport, *Clinton*
John D. Clarke, *Fraser*
Clarence E. Hancock, *Syracuse*
John Taber, *Auburn*
Gale H. Stalker, *Elmira*
James L. Whitley, *Rochester*
Archie D. Sanders, *Stafford*
S. Wallace Dempsey, *Lockport*
Edmund F. Cooke, *Alden*
James M. Mead, *Buffalo*
Daniel A. Reed, *Dunkirk*

## NORTH CAROLINA

SENATORS

Furnifold McL. Simmons, *New Bern*
Lee S. Overman,[46] *Salisbury*
Cameron Morrison,[47] *Charlotte*

REPRESENTATIVES

Lindsay C. Warren, *Washington*
John H. Kerr, *Warrenton*
Charles L. Abernethy, *New Bern*
Edward W. Pou, *Smithfield*
Charles M. Stedman,[48] *Greensboro*
Franklin W. Hancock, Jr.,[49] *Oxford*
J. Bayard Clark, *Fayetteville*
William C. Hammer,[50] *Asheboro*
Hinton James,[51] *Laurinburg*
Robert L. Doughton, *Laurel Springs*
Charles A. Jonas, *Lincolnton*
George M. Pritchard, *Asheville*

## NORTH DAKOTA

SENATORS

Lynn J. Frazier, *Hoople*
Gerald P. Nye, *Cooperstown*

REPRESENTATIVES

Olger B. Burtness, *Grand Forks*
Thomas Hall, *Bismarck*
James H. Sinclair, *Kenmare*

## OHIO

SENATORS

Simeon D. Fess, *Yellow Springs*
Theodore E. Burton,[52] *Cleveland*
Roscoe C. McCulloch,[53] *Canton*
Robert J. Bulkley,[54] *Cleveland*

REPRESENTATIVES

Nicholas Longworth, *Cincinnati*
William E. Hess, *Cincinnati*
Roy G. Fitzgerald, *Dayton*
John L. Cable, *Lima*
Charles J. Thompson, *Defiance*
Charles C. Kearns, *Amelia*
Charles Brand, *Urbana*
Grant E. Mouser, Jr., *Marion*
William W. Chalmers, *Toledo*
Thomas A. Jenkins, *Ironton*
Mell G. Underwood, *New Lexington*
John C. Speaks, *Columbus*
Joseph E. Baird, *Bowling Green*
Francis Seiberling, *Akron*
C. Ellis Moore, *Cambridge*
Charles B. McClintock, *Canton*
William M. Morgan, *Newark*
B. Frank Murphy, *Steubenville*
John G. Cooper, *Youngstown*
Charles A. Mooney, *Cleveland*
Robert Crosser, *Cleveland*
Chester C. Bolton, *Cleveland*

## OKLAHOMA

SENATORS

William B. Pine, *Okmulgee*
J. W. Elmer Thomas, *Medicine Park*

REPRESENTATIVES

Charles O'Connor, *Tulsa*
William W. Hastings, *Tahlequah*
Wilburn Cartwright, *McAlester*
Thomas D. McKeown, *Ada*
Ulysses S. Stone, *Norman*
Jed Johnson, *Anadarko*
James V. McClintic, *Snyder*
Milton C. Garber, *Enid*

## OREGON

SENATORS

Charles L. McNary, *Salem*
Frederick Steiwer, *Portland*

REPRESENTATIVES

Willis C. Hawley, *Salem*
Robert R. Butler, *The Dalles*
Franklin F. Korell, *Portland*

---

[38] Resigned November 21, 1929, having been appointed ambassador to France.

[39] Appointed to fill vacancy caused by resignation of Walter E. Edge, and took his seat December 9, 1929.

[40] Elected to fill vacancy caused by resignation of Walter E. Edge, and took his seat December 3, 1930.

[41] Died November 27, 1930, before the commencement of the Seventy-second Congress, to which he had been reelected. Vacancy in the Seventy-first Congress not filled.

[42] Died December 29, 1930, before the commencement of the Seventy-second Congress, to which he had been reelected. Vacancy in the Seventy-first Congress not filled.

[43] Resigned December 28, 1929, having been appointed a justice of the Supreme Court of the State of New York.

[44] Elected to fill vacancy caused by resignation of John F. Carew, and took his seat April 16, 1930.

[45] Elected to fill vacancy caused by death of Representative-elect Royal H. Weller, in preceding Congress, and took his seat November 21, 1929.

[46] Died December 12, 1930.

[47] Appointed to fill vacancy caused by death of Lee S. Overman, and took his seat December 17, 1930.

[48] Died September 23, 1930.

[49] Elected to fill vacancy caused by death of

Charles M. Stedman, and took his seat December 1, 1930.

[50] Died September 26, 1930.

[51] Elected to fill vacancy caused by death of William C. Hammer, and took his seat December 1, 1930.

[52] Died October 28, 1929.

[53] Appointed to fill vacancy caused by death of Theodore E. Burton, and took his seat November 12, 1929.

[54] Elected to fill vacancy caused by death of Theodore E. Burton, and took his seat December 1, 1930.

## PENNSYLVANIA

### SENATORS

David A. Reed, *Pittsburgh*
William S. Vare,[55] *Philadelphia*
Joseph R. Grundy,[56] *Bristol*
James J. Davis,[57] *Pittsburgh*

### REPRESENTATIVES

James M. Beck, *Philadelphia*
George S. Graham, *Philadelphia*
Harry C. Ransley, *Philadelphia*
Benjamin M. Golder, *Philadelphia*
James J. Connolly, *Philadelphia*
George A. Welsh, *Philadelphia*
George P. Darrow, *Philadelphia*
James Wolfenden, *Upper Darby*
Henry W. Watson, *Langhorne*
William W. Griest,[58] *Lancaster*
J. Roland Kinzer,[59] *Lancaster*
Laurence H. Watres, *Scranton*
John J. Casey,[60] *Wilkes-Barre*
C. Murray Turpin,[61] *Kingston*
George F. Brumm, *Minersville*
Charles J. Esterly, *Sally Ann Furnace*
Louis T. McFadden, *Canton*
Edgar R. Kiess,[62] *Williamsport*
Robert F. Rich,[63] *Woolrich*
Frederick W. Magrady, *Mount Carmel*
Edward M. Beers, *Mount Union*
Isaac H. Doutrich, *Harrisburg*
J. Russell Leech, *Ebensburg*
J. Banks Kurtz, *Altoona*
Franklin Menges, *York*
J. Mitchell Chase, *Clearfield*
Samuel A. Kendall, *Meyersdale*
Henry W. Temple, *Washington*
J. Howard Swick, *Beaver Falls*
Nathan L. Strong, *Brookville*
Thomas C. Cochran, *Mercer*
Milton W. Shreve, *Erie*
William R. Coyle, *Bethlehem*
Adam M. Wyant, *Greensburg*
Stephen G. Porter,[64] *Pittsburgh*
Edmund F. Erk,[65] *Pittsburgh*
M. Clyde Kelly, *Edgewood*
Patrick J. Sullivan, *Pittsburgh*
Harry A. Estep, *Pittsburgh*
Guy E. Campbell, *Crafton*

## RHODE ISLAND

### SENATORS

Jesse H. Metcalf, *Providence*
Felix Hébert, *West Warwick*

### REPRESENTATIVES

Clark Burdick, *Newport*
Richard S. Aldrich, *Warwick*
Jeremiah E. O'Connell,[66] *Providence*
Francis B. Condon,[67] *Central Falls*

## SOUTH CAROLINA

### SENATORS

Ellison D. Smith, *Lynchburg*
Coleman L. Blease, *Columbia*

### REPRESENTATIVES

Thomas S. McMillan, *Charleston*
Butler B. Hare, *Saluda*
Fred H. Dominick, *Newberry*
John J. McSwain, *Greenville*
William F. Stevenson, *Cheraw*
Allard H. Gasque, *Florence*
Hampton P. Fulmer, *Orangeburg*

## SOUTH DAKOTA

### SENATORS

Peter Norbeck, *Redfield*
William H. McMaster, *Yankton*

### REPRESENTATIVES

Charles A. Christopherson, *Sioux Falls*
Royal C. Johnson, *Aberdeen*
William Williamson, *Rapid City*

## TENNESSEE

### SENATORS

Kenneth D. McKellar, *Memphis*
Lawrence D. Tyson,[68] *Knoxville*
William E. Brock,[69] *Chattanooga*

### REPRESENTATIVES

B. Carroll Reece, *Butler*
J. Will Taylor, *La Follette*
Sam D. McReynolds, *Chattanooga*
Cordell Hull, *Carthage*
Ewin L. Davis, *Tullahoma*
Joseph W. Byrns, *Nashville*
Edward E. Eslick, *Pulaski*
Gordon Browning, *Huntingdon*
Jere Cooper, *Dyersburg*
Hubert F. Fisher, *Memphis*

## TEXAS

### SENATORS

Morris Sheppard, *Texarkana*
Tom T. Connally, *Marlin*

### REPRESENTATIVES

Wright Patman, *Texarkana*
John C. Box, *Jacksonville*
Morgan G. Sanders, *Canton*
Sam Rayburn, *Bonham*
Hatton W. Sumners, *Dallas*
Luther A. Johnson, *Corsicana*
Clay Stone Briggs, *Galveston*
Daniel E. Garrett, *Houston*
Joseph J. Mansfield, *Columbus*
James P. Buchanan, *Brenham*
Oliver H. Cross, *Waco*
Fritz G. Lanham, *Fort Worth*
Guinn Williams, *Decatur*
Augustus McCloskey,[70] *San Antonio*
Harry M. Wurzbach,[71] *Seguin*
John N. Garner, *Uvalde*
Claude B. Hudspeth, *El Paso*
Robert Q. Lee,[72] *Cisco*
Thomas L. Blanton,[73] *Abilene*
Marvin Jones, *Amarillo*

## UTAH

### SENATORS

Reed Smoot, *Provo*
William H. King, *Salt Lake City*

### REPRESENTATIVES

Don B. Colton, *Vernal*
Elmer O. Leatherwood,[74] *Salt Lake City*
Frederick C. Loofbourow,[75] *Salt Lake City*

## VERMONT

### SENATORS

Frank L. Greene,[76] *St. Albans*
Frank C. Partridge,[77] *Proctor*
Porter H. Dale, *Island Pond*

### REPRESENTATIVES

Elbert S. Brigham, *St. Albans*
Ernest Willard Gibson, *Brattleboro*

## VIRGINIA

### SENATORS

Claude A. Swanson, *Chatham*
Carter Glass, *Lynchburg*

---

[55] Credentials as Senator-elect were presented in preceding Congress, and referred to the Committee on Privileges and Elections for report; meanwhile Mr. Vare was not permitted to qualify, and by Senate Resolution No. 111, of December 6, 1929, was declared not entitled to a seat. (See U.S. Senate Election, Expulsion and Censure Cases, 1793-1990, Senate Document 103-33, pp. 323-29.)

[56] Appointed to fill vacancy caused by refusal of the Senate to seat William S. Vare, and took his seat December 12, 1929.

[57] Elected to fill vacancy caused by refusal of the Senate to seat William S. Vare, and took his seat December 2, 1930.

[58] Died December 5, 1929.

[59] Elected to fill vacancy caused by death of William W. Griest, and took his seat February 4, 1930.

[60] Died May 5, 1929.

[61] Elected to fill vacancy caused by death of John J. Casey, and took his seat June 11, 1929.

[62] Died July 20, 1930.

[63] Elected to fill vacancy caused by death of Edgar R. Kiess, and took his seat December 1, 1930.

[64] Died June 27, 1930.

[65] Elected to fill vacancy caused by death of Stephen G. Porter, and took his seat December 1, 1930.

[66] Resigned May 9, 1930, having been appointed an associate justice of the Superior Court of Rhode Island.

[67] Elected to fill vacancy caused by resignation of Jeremiah E. O'Connell, and took his seat December 1, 1930.

[68] Died August 24, 1929.

[69] Appointed to fill vacancy caused by death of Lawrence D. Tyson, and took his seat September 9, 1929; subsequently elected.

[70] Served until February 10, 1930; succeeded by Harry M. Wurzbach, who contested his election.

[71] Successfully contested the election of Augustus McCloskey, and took his seat February 10, 1930.

[72] Died April 18, 1930.

[73] Elected to fill vacancy caused by death of Robert Q. Lee, and took his seat June 2, 1930.

[74] Died December 24, 1929.

[75] Elected to fill vacancy caused by death of Elmer O. Leatherwood, and took his seat December 1, 1930.

[76] Died December 17, 1930.

[77] Appointed to fill vacancy caused by death of Frank L. Greene, and took his seat January 5, 1931.

## VIRGINIA—Continued
### REPRESENTATIVES
Schuyler Otis Bland, *Newport News*
Menalcus Lankford, *Norfolk*
Andrew J. Montague, *Richmond*
Patrick Henry Drewry, *Petersburg*
Joseph Whitehead, *Chatham*
Clifton A. Woodrum, *Roanoke*
Jacob A. Garber, *Harrisonburg*
R. Walton Moore, *Fairfax*
Joseph C. Shaffer, *Wytheville*
Henry St. George Tucker, *Lexington*

## WASHINGTON
### SENATORS
Wesley L. Jones, *Seattle*
Clarence C. Dill, *Spokane*
### REPRESENTATIVES
John F. Miller, *Seattle*
Lindley H. Hadley, *Bellingham*
Albert Johnson, *Hoquiam*
John W. Summers, *Walla Walla*
Samuel B. Hill, *Waterville*

## WEST VIRGINIA
### SENATORS
Guy D. Goff, *Clarksburg*
Henry D. Hatfield, *Huntington*

### REPRESENTATIVES
Carl G. Bachmann, *Wheeling*
Frank L. Bowman, *Morgantown*
John M. Wolverton, *Richwood*
James A. Hughes,[78] *Huntington*
Robert L. Hogg,[79] *Point Pleasant*
Hugh Ike Shott, *Bluefield*
Joe L. Smith, *Beckley*

## WISCONSIN
### SENATORS
Robert M. La Follette, Jr., *Madison*
John J. Blaine, *Boscobel*

### REPRESENTATIVES
Henry Allen Cooper,[80] *Racine*
Charles A. Kading, *Watertown*
John M. Nelson, *Madison*
John C. Schafer, *Milwaukee*
William H. Stafford, *Milwaukee*
Florian Lampert,[81] *Oshkosh*
Michael K. Reilly,[82] *Fond du Lac*
Merlin Hull, *Black River Falls*
Edward E. Browne, *Waupaca*
George J. Schneider, *Appleton*
James A. Frear, *Hudson*
Hubert H. Peavey, *Washburn*

## WYOMING
### SENATORS
Francis E. Warren,[83] *Cheyenne*
Patrick J. Sullivan,[84] *Casper*
Robert D. Carey,[85] *Careyhurst*
John B. Kendrick, *Sheridan*
### REPRESENTATIVE AT LARGE
Vincent M. Carter, *Kemmerer*

## TERRITORY OF ALASKA
### DELEGATE
Dan A. Sutherland, *Juneau*

## TERRITORY OF HAWAII
### DELEGATE
Victor S. K. Houston, *Honolulu*

## PHILIPPINE ISLANDS
### RESIDENT COMMISSIONERS
Pedro Guevara, *Santa Cruz*
Camilo Osias, *Balaoan*

## PORTO RICO
### RESIDENT COMMISSIONER
Felix Cordova Davila, *San Juan*

---

[78] Died March 2, 1930.
[79] Elected to fill vacancy caused by death of James A. Hughes, and took his seat December 1, 1930.
[80] Died March 1, 1931, before the commencement of the Seventy-second Congress, to which he had been reelected. Vacancy in the Seventy-first Congress not filled.

[81] Died July 18, 1930.
[82] Elected to fill vacancy caused by death of Florian Lampert, and took his seat December 1, 1930.
[83] Died November 24, 1929.
[84] Appointed to fill vacancy caused by death of Francis E. Warren, and took his seat December 9, 1929.

[85] Elected to fill vacancy caused by death of Francis E. Warren, and took his seat December 1, 1930.

# 72ND CONGRESS

## MARCH 4, 1931, TO MARCH 3, 1933

FIRST SESSION— *December 7, 1931, to July 16, 1932*
SECOND SESSION— *December 5, 1932, to March 3, 1933*

---

VICE PRESIDENT OF THE UNITED STATES— CHARLES CURTIS, of Kansas
PRESIDENT PRO TEMPORE OF THE SENATE— GEORGE H. MOSES, of New Hampshire
SECRETARY OF THE SENATE— EDWIN P. THAYER, of Indiana
SERGEANT AT ARMS OF THE SENATE— DAVID S. BARRY, of Rhode Island

---

SPEAKER OF THE HOUSE OF REPRESENTATIVES— JOHN N. GARNER,[1] of Texas
CLERK OF THE HOUSE— SOUTH TRIMBLE,[2] of Kentucky
SERGEANT AT ARMS OF THE HOUSE— JOSEPH G. ROGERS, of Pennsylvania; KENNETH ROMNEY,[3] of Montana
DOORKEEPER OF THE HOUSE— JOSEPH J. SINNOTT, of Virginia
POSTMASTER OF THE HOUSE— FINIS E. SCOTT

Charles Curtis
Vice President

John N. Garner
Speaker

## ALABAMA

### SENATORS
Hugo L. Black, *Birmingham*
John H. Bankhead II, *Jasper*

### REPRESENTATIVES
John McDuffie, *Monroeville*
Lister Hill, *Montgomery*
Henry B. Steagall, *Ozark*
Lamar Jeffers, *Anniston*
LaFayette L. Patterson, *Gadsden*
William B. Oliver, *Tuscaloosa*
Miles C. Allgood, *Gadsden*
Edward B. Almon, *Tuscumbia*
George Huddleston, *Birmingham*
William B. Bankhead, *Jasper*

## ARIZONA

### SENATORS
Henry F. Ashurst, *Prescott*
Carl Hayden, *Phoenix*

### REPRESENTATIVE AT LARGE
Lewis W. Douglas,[4] *Phoenix*

## ARKANSAS

### SENATORS
Joseph T. Robinson, *Little Rock*
Thaddeus H. Caraway,[5] *Jonesboro*
Hattie W. Caraway,[6] *Jonesboro*

### REPRESENTATIVES
William J. Driver, *Osceola*
John E. Miller, *Searcy*
Claude A. Fuller, *Eureka Springs*
Effiegene (Locke) Wingo, *De Queen*

Heartsill Ragon, *Clarksville*
David D. Glover, *Malvern*
Tilman B. Parks, *Camden*

## CALIFORNIA

### SENATORS
Hiram W. Johnson, *San Francisco*
Samuel M. Shortridge, *Menlo Park*

### REPRESENTATIVES
Clarence F. Lea, *Santa Rosa*
Harry L. Englebright, *Nevada City*
Charles F. Curry, Jr., *Sacramento*
Florence P. Kahn, *San Francisco*
Richard J. Welch, *San Francisco*
Albert E. Carter, *Oakland*
Henry E. Barbour, *Fresno*
Arthur M. Free, *San Jose*
William E. Evans, *Glendale*
Joe Crail, *Los Angeles*
Philip D. Swing, *El Centro*

## COLORADO

### SENATORS
Charles W. Waterman,[7] *Denver*
Walter Walker,[8] *Grand Junction*
Karl C. Schuyler,[9] *Denver*
Edward P. Costigan, *Denver*

### REPRESENTATIVES
William R. Eaton, *Denver*
Charles B. Timberlake, *Sterling*
Guy U. Hardy, *Canon City*
Edward T. Taylor, *Glenwood Springs*

## CONNECTICUT

### SENATORS
Hiram Bingham, *New Haven*
Frederic C. Walcott, *Norfolk*

### REPRESENTATIVES
Augustine Lonergan, *Hartford*
Richard P. Freeman, *New London*
John Q. Tilson,[10] *New Haven*
William L. Tierney, *Greenwich*
Edward W. Goss, *Waterbury*

## DELAWARE

### SENATORS
Daniel O. Hastings, *Wilmington*
John G. Townsend, Jr., *Selbyville*

### REPRESENTATIVE AT LARGE
Robert G. Houston, *Georgetown*

## FLORIDA

### SENATORS
Duncan U. Fletcher, *Jacksonville*
Park Trammell, *Lakeland*

### REPRESENTATIVES
Herbert J. Drane, *Lakeland*
Robert A. Green, *Starke*
Thomas A. Yon, *Tallahassee*
Ruth Bryan Owen, *Miami*

## GEORGIA

### SENATORS
William J. Harris,[11] *Cedartown*
John S. Cohen,[12] *Atlanta*

---

[1] Elected December 7, 1931.
[2] Elected December 7, 1931.
[3] Elected December 7, 1931.
[4] Resigned, effective March 4, 1933, before the commencement of the Seventy-third Congress, to which he had been reelected, having been appointed Director of the Bureau of the Budget.
[5] Died November 6, 1931.

[6] Appointed to fill vacancy caused by death of Thaddeus H. Caraway, and took her seat December 8, 1931; subsequently elected.
[7] Died August 27, 1932.
[8] Appointed to fill vacancy caused by death of Charles W. Waterman, and took his seat December 5, 1932.
[9] Elected to fill vacancy caused by death of

Charles W. Waterman, and took his seat December 7, 1932.
[10] Resigned December 3, 1932; vacancy throughout remainder of the Congress.
[11] Died April 18, 1932.
[12] Appointed to fill vacancy caused by death of William J. Harris, and took his seat April 27, 1932.

[347]

## GEORGIA—Continued

SENATORS—CONTINUED

Richard B. Russell,[13] *Winder*
Walter F. George, *Vienna*

REPRESENTATIVES

Charles G. Edwards,[14] *Savannah*
Homer C. Parker,[15] *Statesboro*
Edward E. Cox, *Camilla*
Charles R. Crisp,[16] *Americus*
Bryant T. Castellow,[17] *Cuthbert*
William C. Wright, *Newnan*
Robert Ramspeck, *Atlanta*
Samuel Rutherford,[18] *Forsyth*
W. Carlton Mobley,[19] *Forsyth*
Malcolm C. Tarver, *Dalton*
Charles H. Brand, *Athens*
John S. Wood, *Canton*
Carl Vinson, *Milledgeville*
William C. Lankford, *Douglas*
William W. Larsen, *Dublin*

## IDAHO

SENATORS

William E. Borah, *Boise*
John Thomas, *Gooding*

REPRESENTATIVES

Burton L. French, *Moscow*
Addison T. Smith, *Twin Falls*

## ILLINOIS

SENATORS

Otis F. Glenn, *Murphysboro*
J. Hamilton Lewis, *Chicago*

REPRESENTATIVES AT LARGE

Richard Yates, *Springfield*
William H. Dieterich, *Beardstown*

REPRESENTATIVES

Oscar De Priest, *Chicago*
Morton D. Hull, *Chicago*
Edward A. Kelly, *Chicago*
Harry P. Beam, *Chicago*
Adolph J. Sabath, *Chicago*
James T. Igoe, *Chicago*
Leonard W. Schuetz, *Chicago*
Peter C. Granata,[20] *Chicago*
Stanley H. Kunz,[21] *Chicago*
Fred A. Britten, *Chicago*
Carl R. Chindblom, *Evanston*
Frank R. Reid, *Aurora*
John T. Buckbee, *Rockford*
William R. Johnson, *Freeport*
John C. Allen, *Monmouth*
Burnett M. Chiperfield, *Canton*
William E. Hull, *Peoria*
Homer W. Hall, *Bloomington*

William P. Holaday, *Georgetown*
Charles Adkins, *Decatur*
Henry T. Rainey, *Carrollton*
J. Earl Major, *Hillsboro*
Charles A. Karch,[22] *East St. Louis*
William W. Arnold, *Robinson*
Claude V. Parsons, *Golconda*
Kent E. Keller, *Ava*

## INDIANA

SENATORS

James E. Watson, *Rushville*
Arthur R. Robinson, *Indianapolis*

REPRESENTATIVES

John W. Boehne, Jr., *Evansville*
Arthur H. Greenwood, *Washington*
Eugene B. Crowe, *Bedford*
Harry C. Canfield, *Batesville*
Courtland C. Gillen, *Greencastle*
William H. Larrabee, *New Palestine*
Louis Ludlow, *Indianapolis*
Albert H. Vestal,[23] *Anderson*
Fred S. Purnell, *Attica*
William R. Wood, *La Fayette*
Glenn Griswold, *Peru*
David Hogg, *Fort Wayne*
Samuel B. Pettengill, *South Bend*

## IOWA

SENATORS

Smith W. Brookhart, *Washington*
Lester J. Dickinson, *Algona*

REPRESENTATIVES

William F. Kopp, *Mount Pleasant*
Bernhard M. Jacobsen, *Clinton*
Thomas J. B. Robinson, *Hampton*
Gilbert N. Haugen, *Northwood*
Cyrenus Cole, *Cedar Rapids*
C. William Ramseyer, *Bloomfield*
Cassius C. Dowell, *Des Moines*
Lloyd Thurston, *Osceola*
Charles E. Swanson, *Council Bluffs*
Fred C. Gilchrist, *Laurens*
Ed H. Campbell, *Battle Creek*

## KANSAS

SENATORS

Arthur Capper, *Topeka*
George McGill, *Wichita*

REPRESENTATIVES

William P. Lambertson, *Fairview*
Ulysses S. Guyer, *Kansas City*
Harold McGugin, *Coffeyville*
Homer Hoch, *Marion*
James G. Strong, *Blue Rapids*

Charles I. Sparks, *Goodland*
Clifford R. Hope, *Garden City*
William A. Ayres, *Wichita*

## KENTUCKY

SENATORS

Alben W. Barkley, *Paducah*
Marvel M. Logan, *Bowling Green*

REPRESENTATIVES

William V. Gregory, *Mayfield*
Glover H. Cary, *Owensboro*
John W. Moore, *Morgantown*
Cap R. Carden, *Munfordville*
Maurice H. Thatcher, *Louisville*
Brent Spence, *Fort Thomas*
Virgil M. Chapman, *Paris*
Ralph Gilbert, *Shelbyville*
Fred M. Vinson, *Ashland*
Andrew J. May, *Prestonsburg*
Charles Finley, *Williamsburg*

## LOUISIANA

SENATORS

Edwin S. Broussard, *New Iberia*
Huey P. Long,[24] *New Orleans*

REPRESENTATIVES

Joachim O. Fernandez, *New Orleans*
Paul H. Maloney, *New Orleans*
Numa F. Montet, *Thibodaux*
John N. Sandlin, *Minden*
Riley J. Wilson, *Ruston*
Bolivar E. Kemp, *Amite*
René L. DeRouen, *Ville Platte*
James B. Aswell,[25] *Natchitoches*
John H. Overton,[26] *Alexandria*

## MAINE

SENATORS

Frederick Hale, *Portland*
Wallace H. White, Jr., *Auburn*

REPRESENTATIVES

Carroll L. Beedy, *Portland*
Donald B. Partridge, *Norway*
John E. Nelson, *Augusta*
Donald F. Snow, *Bangor*

## MARYLAND

SENATORS

Millard E. Tydings, *Havre de Grace*
Phillips Lee Goldsborough, *Baltimore*

REPRESENTATIVES

T. Alan Goldsborough, *Denton*
William P. Cole, Jr., *Towson*
Vincent L. Palmisano, *Baltimore*

---

[13] Elected to fill vacancy caused by death of William J. Harris, and took his seat January 12, 1933.
[14] Died July 13, 1931.
[15] Elected to fill vacancy caused by death of Charles G. Edwards, and took his seat December 7, 1931.
[16] Resigned October 7, 1932, having been appointed a member of the United States Tariff Commission.
[17] Elected to fill vacancy caused by resignation of

Charles R. Crisp, and took his seat December 5, 1932.
[18] Died February 4, 1932.
[19] Elected to fill vacancy caused by death of Samuel Rutherford, and took his seat March 7, 1932.
[20] Served until April 5, 1932; succeeded by Stanley H. Kunz, who contested his election.
[21] Successfully contested the election of Peter C. Granata, and took his seat April 5, 1932.
[22] Died November 6, 1932; vacancy throughout

remainder of the Congress.
[23] Died April 1, 1932; vacancy throughout remainder of the Congress.
[24] Elected November 4, 1930, for the term beginning March 4, 1931, but did not qualify until January 25, 1932, preferring to retain the governorship.
[25] Died March 16, 1931.
[26] Elected to fill vacancy caused by death of James B. Aswell, and took his seat December 7, 1931.

J. Charles Linthicum,[27] *Baltimore*
Ambrose J. Kennedy,[28] *Baltimore*
Stephen W. Gambrill, *Laurel*
David J. Lewis, *Cumberland*

## MASSACHUSETTS

SENATORS

David I. Walsh, *Fitchburg*
Marcus A. Coolidge, *Fitchburg*

REPRESENTATIVES

Allen T. Treadway, *Stockbridge*
William J. Granfield, *Springfield*
Frank H. Foss, *Fitchburg*
Pehr G. Holmes, *Worcester*
Edith Nourse Rogers, *Lowell*
A. Piatt Andrews, Jr., *Gloucester*
William P. Connery, Jr., *Lynn*
Frederick W. Dallinger,[29] *Cambridge*
Charles L. Underhill, *Somerville*
John J. Douglass, *Boston*
George H. Tinkham, *Boston*
John W. McCormack, *Dorchester*
Robert Luce, *Waltham*
Richard B. Wigglesworth, *Milton*
Joseph W. Martin, Jr., *North Attleboro*
Charles L. Gifford, *Cotuit*

## MICHIGAN

SENATORS

James Couzens, *Detroit*
Arthur H. Vandenberg, *Grand Rapids*

REPRESENTATIVES

Robert H. Clancy, *Detroit*
Earl C. Michener, *Adrian*
Joseph L. Hooper, *Battle Creek*
John C. Ketcham, *Hastings*
Carl E. Mapes, *Grand Rapids*
Seymour H. Person, *Lansing*
Jesse P. Wolcott, *Port Huron*
Bird J. Vincent,[30] *Saginaw*
Michael J. Hart,[31] *Saginaw*
James C. McLaughlin,[32] *Muskegon*
Roy O. Woodruff, *Bay City*
Frank P. Bohn, *Newberry*
W. Frank James, *Hancock*
Clarence J. McLeod, *Detroit*

## MINNESOTA

SENATORS

Henrik Shipstead, *Minneapolis*
Thomas D. Schall, *Excelsior*

REPRESENTATIVES

Victor Christgau, *Austin*
Frank Clague, *Redwood Falls*
August H. Andresen, *Red Wing*
Melvin J. Maas, *St. Paul*
William I. Nolan, *Minneapolis*
Harold Knutson, *St. Cloud*
Paul J. Kvale, *Benson*
William A. Pittenger, *Duluth*
Conrad G. Selvig, *Crookston*
Godfrey G. Goodwin,[33] *Cambridge*

## MISSISSIPPI

SENATORS

Pat Harrison, *Gulfport*
Hubert D. Stephens, *New Albany*

REPRESENTATIVES

John E. Rankin, *Tupelo*
Wall Doxey, *Holly Springs*
William M. Whittington, *Greenwood*
T. Jeff. Busby, *Houston*
Ross A. Collins, *Meridian*
Robert S. Hall, *Hattiesburg*
Percy E. Quin,[34] *McComb*
Lawrence Russell Ellzey,[35] *Wesson*
James W. Collier, *Vicksburg*

## MISSOURI

SENATORS

Harry B. Hawes,[36] *St. Louis*
Joel Bennett Clark,[37] *St. Louis*
Roscoe C. Patterson, *Kansas City*

REPRESENTATIVES

Milton A. Romjue, *Macon*
Ralph F. Lozier, *Carrollton*
Jacob L. Milligan, *Richmond*
David W. Hopkins, *St. Joseph*
Joseph B. Shannon, *Kansas City*
Clement C. Dickinson, *Clinton*
Samuel C. Major,[38] *Fayette*
Robert D. Johnson,[39] *Marshall*
William L. Nelson, *Columbia*
Clarence Cannon, *Elsberry*
Henry F. Niedringhaus, *St. Louis*
John J. Cochran, *St. Louis*
Leonidas C. Dyer, *St. Louis*
Clyde Williams, *Hillsboro*
James F. Fulbright, *Doniphan*
Joe J. Manlove, *Joplin*
William E. Barton, *Houston*

## MONTANA

SENATORS

Thomas J. Walsh,[40] *Helena*
Burton K. Wheeler, *Butte*

REPRESENTATIVES

John M. Evans, *Missoula*
Scott Leavitt, *Great Falls*

## NEBRASKA

SENATORS

George W. Norris, *McCook*
Robert B. Howell, *Omaha*

REPRESENTATIVES

John H. Morehead, *Falls City*
H. Malcolm Baldrige, *Omaha*
Edgar Howard, *Columbus*
John N. Norton, *Polk*
Ashton C. Shallenberger, *Alma*
Robert G. Simmons, *Scottsbluff*

## NEVADA

SENATORS

Key Pittman, *Tonopah*
Tasker L. Oddie, *Reno*

REPRESENTATIVE AT LARGE

Samuel S. Arentz, *Simpson*

## NEW HAMPSHIRE

SENATORS

George H. Moses, *Concord*
Henry W. Keyes, *Haverhill*

REPRESENTATIVES

Fletcher Hale,[41] *Laconia*
William N. Rogers,[42] *Sanbornville*
Edward H. Wason, *Nashua*

## NEW JERSEY

SENATORS

Hamilton F. Kean, *Elizabeth*
Dwight W. Morrow,[43] *Englewood*
W. Warren Barbour,[44] *Locust*

REPRESENTATIVES

Charles A. Wolverton, *Camden*
Isaac Bacharach, *Atlantic City*
William H. Sutphin, *Matawan*
Charles A. Eaton, *North Plainfield*
Ernest R. Ackerman,[45] *Plainfield*
Percy H. Stewart,[46] *Plainfield*
Randolph Perkins, *Woodcliff Lake*
George N. Seger, *Passaic*
Fred A. Hartley, Jr., *Kearny*
Peter A. Cavicchia, *Newark*

---

[27] Died October 5, 1932.
[28] Elected to fill vacancy caused by death of J. Charles Linthicum, and took his seat December 5, 1932.
[29] Resigned October 1, 1932, having been appointed a judge of the United States Customs Court; vacancy throughout remainder of the Congress.
[30] Died July 18, 1931.
[31] Elected to fill vacancy caused by death of Bird J. Vincent, and took his seat December 7, 1931.
[32] Died November 29, 1932; vacancy throughout remainder of the Congress.
[33] Died February 16, 1933; vacancy throughout

remainder of the Congress.
[34] Died February 4, 1932.
[35] Elected to fill vacancy caused by death of Percy E. Quin, and took his seat March 30, 1932.
[36] Resigned February 3, 1933.
[37] Appointed to fill vacancy caused by resignation of Harry B. Hawes, and took his seat February 3, 1933; was previously elected for the term commencing March 4, 1933.
[38] Died July 28, 1931.
[39] Elected to fill vacancy caused by death of Samuel C. Major, and took his seat December 7, 1931.
[40] Died March 2, 1933; vacancy throughout

remainder of the Congress.
[41] Died October 22, 1931.
[42] Elected to fill vacancy caused by death of Fletcher Hale, and took his seat January 20, 1932.
[43] Died October 5, 1931.
[44] Appointed to fill vacancy caused by death of Dwight W. Morrow, and took his seat December 8, 1931; subsequently elected.
[45] Died October 18, 1931.
[46] Elected to fill vacancy caused by death of Ernest R. Ackerman, and took his seat December 7, 1931.

## NEW JERSEY— Continued

REPRESENTATIVES—CONTINUED
Frederick R. Lehlbach, *Newark*
Oscar L. Auf der Heide, *West New York*
Mary T. Norton, *Jersey City*

## NEW MEXICO

SENATORS
Sam G. Bratton, *Albuquerque*
Bronson M. Cutting, *Santa Fe*

REPRESENTATIVE AT LARGE
Dennis Chavez, *Albuquerque*

## NEW YORK

SENATORS
Royal S. Copeland, *New York City*
Robert F. Wagner, *New York City*

REPRESENTATIVES
Robert L. Bacon, *Westbury*
William F. Brunner, *Rockaway Park*
George W. Lindsay, *Brooklyn*
Thomas H. Cullen, *Brooklyn*
Loring M. Black, Jr., *Brooklyn*
Andrew L. Somers, *Brooklyn*
Matthew V. O'Malley,[47] *Brooklyn*
John J. Delaney,[48] *Brooklyn*
Patrick J. Carley, *Brooklyn*
Stephen A. Rudd,[49] *Brooklyn*
Emanuel Celler, *Brooklyn*
Anning S. Prall, *West New Brighton*
Samuel Dickstein, *New York City*
Christopher D. Sullivan, *New York City*
William I. Sirovich, *New York City*
John J. Boylan, *New York City*
John J. O'Connor, *New York City*
Ruth S. B. Pratt, *New York City*
Martin J. Kennedy, *New York City*
Sol Bloom, *New York City*
Fiorello H. LaGuardia, *New York City*
Joseph A. Gavagan, *New York City*
Anthony J. Griffin, *New York City*
Frank Oliver, *Bronx*
James M. Fitzpatrick, *New York City*
Charles D. Millard, *Tarrytown*
Hamilton Fish, Jr., *Garrison*
Harcourt J. Pratt, *Highland*
Parker Corning, *Albany*
James S. Parker, *Salem*
Frank Crowther, *Schenectady*
Bertrand H. Snell, *Potsdam*
Francis D. Culkin, *Oswego*
Frederick M. Davenport, *Clinton*

John D. Clarke, *Fraser*
Clarence E. Hancock, *Syracuse*
John Taber, *Auburn*
Gale H. Stalker, *Elmira*
James L. Whitley, *Rochester*
Archie D. Sanders, *Stafford*
Walter G. Andrews, *Buffalo*
Edmund F. Cooke, *Alden*
James M. Mead, *Buffalo*
Daniel A. Reed, *Dunkirk*

## NORTH CAROLINA

SENATORS
Cameron Morrison,[50] *Charlotte*
Robert R. Reynolds,[51] *Asheville*
Josiah W. Bailey, *Raleigh*

REPRESENTATIVES
Lindsay C. Warren, *Washington*
John H. Kerr, *Warrenton*
Charles L. Abernethy, *New Bern*
Edward W. Pou, *Smithfield*
Franklin W. Hancock, Jr., *Oxford*
J. Bayard Clark, *Fayetteville*
J. Walter Lambeth, *Thomasville*
Robert L. Doughton, *Laurel Springs*
Alfred L. Bulwinkle, *Gastonia*
Zebulon Weaver, *Asheville*

## NORTH DAKOTA

SENATORS
Lynn J. Frazier, *Hoople*
Gerald P. Nye, *Cooperstown*

REPRESENTATIVES
Olger B. Burtness, *Grand Forks*
Thomas Hall, *Bismarck*
James H. Sinclair, *Kenmare*

## OHIO

SENATORS
Simeon D. Fess, *Yellow Springs*
Robert J. Bulkley, *Cleveland*

REPRESENTATIVES
Nicholas Longworth,[52] *Cincinnati*
John B. Hollister,[53] *Cincinnati*
William E. Hess, *Cincinnati*
Byron B. Harlan, *Dayton*
John L. Cable, *Lima*
Frank C. Kniffin, *Napoleon*
James G. Polk, *Highland*
Charles Brand, *Urbana*
Grant E. Mouser, Jr., *Marion*
Wilbur M. White, *Toledo*
Thomas A. Jenkins, *Ironton*
Mell G. Underwood, *New Lexington*

Authur P. Lamneck, *Columbus*
William L. Fiesinger, *Sandusky*
Francis Seiberling, *Akron*
C. Ellis Moore, *Cambridge*
Charles B. McClintock, *Canton*
Charles West, *Granville*
B. Frank Murphy, *Steubenville*
John G. Cooper, *Youngstown*
Charles A. Mooney,[54] *Cleveland*
Martin L. Sweeney,[55] *Cleveland*
Robert Crosser, *Cleveland*
Chester C. Bolton, *Cleveland*

## OKLAHOMA

SENATORS
J. W. Elmer Thomas, *Medicine Park*
Thomas P. Gore, *Oklahoma City*

REPRESENTATIVES
Wesley E. Disney, *Tulsa*
William W. Hastings, *Tahlequah*
Wilburn Cartwright, *McAlester*
Thomas D. McKeown, *Ada*
Fletcher B. Swank, *Norman*
Jed Johnson, *Anadarko*
James V. McClintic, *Snyder*
Milton C. Garber, *Enid*

## OREGON

SENATORS
Charles L. McNary, *Salem*
Frederick Steiwer, *Portland*

REPRESENTATIVES
Willis C. Hawley, *Salem*
Robert R. Butler,[56] *The Dalles*
Charles H. Martin, *Portland*

## PENNSYLVANIA

SENATORS
David A. Reed, *Pittsburgh*
James J. Davis, *Pittsburgh*

REPRESENTATIVES
James M. Beck, *Philadelphia*
George S. Graham,[57] *Philadelphia*
Edward L. Stokes,[58] *Philadelphia*
Harry C. Ransley, *Philadelphia*
Benjamin M. Golder, *Philadelphia*
James J. Connolly, *Philadelphia*
George A. Welsh,[59] *Philadelphia*
Robert L. Davis,[60] *Philadelphia*
George P. Darrow, *Philadelphia*
James Wolfenden, *Upper Darby*
Henry W. Watson, *Langhorne*
J. Roland Kinzer, *Lancaster*

---

[47] Elected February 17, 1931, to fill vacancy caused by death of Representative-elect John F. Quayle, in preceding Congress; died May 26, 1931, before Congress assembled, and was therefore not sworn in.

[48] Elected to fill vacancy caused by deaths of Representatives-elect John F. Quayle and Matthew V. O'Malley, and took his seat December 7, 1931.

[49] Elected to fill vacancy caused by death of Representative-elect David J. O'Connell, in preceding Congress, and took his seat December 7, 1931.

[50] Appointed to fill vacancy caused by death of Lee

S. Overman in preceding Congress.

[51] Elected to fill vacancy caused by death of Lee S. Overman, in preceding Congress, and took his seat December 5, 1932.

[52] Died April 9, 1931.

[53] Elected to fill vacancy caused by death of Nicholas Longworth, and took his seat December 7, 1931.

[54] Died May 29, 1931.

[55] Elected to fill vacancy caused by death of Charles A. Mooney, and took his seat December 7, 1931.

[56] Died January 7, 1933; vacancy throughout remainder of the Congress.

[57] Died July 4, 1931.

[58] Elected to fill vacancy caused by death of George S. Graham, and took his seat December 7, 1931.

[59] Resigned May 31, 1932, having been appointed judge of the United States district court, eastern district of Pennsylvania.

[60] Elected to fill vacancy caused by resignation of George A. Welsh, and took his seat December 5, 1932.

Patrick J. Boland, *Scranton*
C. Murray Turpin, *Kingston*
George F. Brumm, *Minersville*
Norton L. Lichtenwalner, *Allentown*
Louis T. McFadden, *Canton*
Robert F. Rich, *Woolrich*
Frederick W. Magrady, *Mount Carmel*
Edward M. Beers,[61] *Mount Union*
Joseph F. Biddle,[62] *Huntingdon*
Isaac H. Doutrich, *Harrisburg*
J. Russell Leech,[63] *Ebensburg*
Howard W. Stull,[64] *Johnstown*
J. Banks Kurtz, *Altoona*
Harry L. Haines, *Red Lion*
J. Mitchell Chase, *Clearfield*
Samuel A. Kendall,[65] *Meyersdale*
Henry W. Temple, *Washington*
J. Howard Swick, *Beaver Falls*
Nathan L. Strong, *Brookville*
Thomas C. Cochran, *Mercer*
Milton W. Shreve, *Erie*
William R. Coyle, *Bethlehem*
Adam M. Wyant, *Greensburg*
Edmund F. Erk, *Pittsburgh*
M. Clyde Kelly, *Edgewood*
Patrick J. Sullivan, *Pittsburgh*
Harry A. Estep, *Pittsburgh*
Guy E. Campbell, *Crafton*

## RHODE ISLAND

### SENATORS

Jesse H. Metcalf, *Providence*
Felix Hébert, *West Warwick*

### REPRESENTATIVES

Clark Burdick, *Newport*
Richard S. Aldrich, *Warwick*
Francis B. Condon, *Central Falls*

## SOUTH CAROLINA

### SENATORS

Ellison D. Smith, *Lynchburg*
James F. Byrnes, *Spartanburg*

### REPRESENTATIVES

Thomas S. McMillan, *Charleston*
Butler B. Hare, *Saluda*
Fred H. Dominick, *Newberry*
John J. McSwain, *Greenville*
William F. Stevenson, *Cheraw*
Allard H. Gasque, *Florence*
Hampton P. Fulmer, *Orangeburg*

## SOUTH DAKOTA

### SENATORS

Peter Norbeck, *Redfield*
William J. Bulow, *Beresford*

### REPRESENTATIVES

Charles A. Christopherson, *Sioux Falls*
Royal C. Johnson, *Aberdeen*
William Williamson, *Rapid City*

## TENNESSEE

### SENATORS

Kenneth D. McKellar, *Memphis*
Cordell Hull,[66] *Carthage*

### REPRESENTATIVES

Oscar B. Lovette, *Greeneville*
J. Will Taylor, *La Follette*
Sam D. McReynolds, *Chattanooga*
John R. Mitchell, *Cookeville*
Ewin L. Davis, *Tullahoma*
Joseph W. Byrns, *Nashville*
Edward E. Eslick,[67] *Pulaski*
Willa M. B. Eslick,[68] *Pulaski*
Gordon Browning, *Huntingdon*
Jere Cooper, *Dyersburg*
Edward H. Crump, *Memphis*

## TEXAS

### SENATORS

Morris Sheppard, *Texarkana*
Tom T. Connally, *Marlin*

### REPRESENTATIVES

Wright Patman, *Texarkana*
Martin Dies, Jr., *Orange*
Morgan G. Sanders, *Canton*
Sam Rayburn, *Bonham*
Hatton W. Sumners, *Dallas*
Luther A. Johnson, *Corsicana*
Clay Stone Briggs, *Galveston*
Daniel E. Garrett,[69] *Houston*
Joe H. Eagle,[70] *Houston*
Joseph J. Mansfield, *Columbus*
James P. Buchanan, *Brenham*
Oliver H. Cross, *Waco*
Fritz G. Lanham, *Fort Worth*
Guinn Williams, *Decatur*
Harry M. Wurzbach,[71] *Seguin*
Richard M. Kleberg,[72] *Corpus Christi*
John N. Garner,[73] *Uvalde*
R. Ewing Thomason, *El Paso*
Thomas L. Blanton, *Abilene*
Marvin Jones, *Amarillo*

## UTAH

### SENATORS

Reed Smoot, *Provo*
William H. King, *Salt Lake City*

### REPRESENTATIVES

Don B. Colton, *Vernal*
Frederick C. Loofbourow, *Salt Lake City*

## VERMONT

### SENATORS

Porter H. Dale, *Island Pond*
Frank C. Partridge,[74] *Proctor*
Warren R. Austin,[75] *Burlington*

### REPRESENTATIVES

John E. Weeks, *Middlebury*
Ernest Willard Gibson, *Brattleboro*

## VIRGINIA

### SENATORS

Claude A. Swanson,[76] *Chatham*
Carter Glass, *Lynchburg*

### REPRESENTATIVES

Schuyler Otis Bland, *Newport News*
Menalcus Lankford, *Norfolk*
Andrew J. Montague, *Richmond*
Patrick Henry Drewry, *Petersburg*
Thomas G. Burch, *Martinsville*
Clifton A. Woodrum, *Roanoke*
John W. Fishburne, *Charlottesville*
Howard W. Smith, *Alexandria*
John W. Flannagan, Jr., *Bristol*
Henry St. George Tucker,[77] *Lexington*
Joel W. Flood,[78] *Appomattox*

## WASHINGTON

### SENATORS

Wesley L. Jones,[79] *Seattle*
Elijah S. Grammer,[80] *Seattle*
Clarence C. Dill, *Spokane*

### REPRESENTATIVES

Ralph A. Horr, *Seattle*
Lindley H. Hadley, *Bellingham*
Albert Johnson, *Hoquiam*
John W. Summers, *Walla Walla*
Samuel B. Hill, *Waterville*

---

[61] Died April 21, 1932.
[62] Elected to fill vacancy caused by death of Edward M. Beers, and took his seat December 5, 1932.
[63] Resigned January 29, 1932, having been appointed a member of the United States Board of Tax Appeals.
[64] Elected to fill vacancy caused by resignation of J. Russell Leech, and took his seat May 6, 1932.
[65] Died January 8, 1933; vacancy throughout remainder of the Congress.
[66] Resigned, effective March 3, 1933, having been appointed Secretary of State.
[67] Died June 14, 1932.
[68] Elected to fill vacancy caused by death of her husband, Edward E. Eslick, and took her seat December 5, 1932.
[69] Died December 13, 1932, before the commencement of the Seventy-third Congress, to which he had been reelected.
[70] Elected to fill vacancy caused by death of Daniel E. Garrett, and took his seat February 7, 1933.
[71] Died November 6, 1931.
[72] Elected to fill vacancy caused by death of Harry M. Wurzbach, and took his seat December 7, 1931.
[73] Resigned, effective March 3, 1933, before the commencement of the Seventy-third Congress, to which he had been reelected, having been elected Vice President of the United States.
[74] Appointed to fill vacancy caused by death of Frank L. Greene in preceding Congress.
[75] Elected March 31, 1931, to fill vacancy caused by death of Frank L. Greene, in preceding Congress. His term commenced April 1, 1931.
[76] Resigned, effective March 3, 1933, having been appointed Secretary of the Navy.
[77] Died July 23, 1932.
[78] Elected to fill vacancy caused by death of Henry St. George Tucker, and took his seat December 5, 1932.
[79] Died November 19, 1932.
[80] Appointed to fill vacancy caused by death of Wesley L. Jones, and took his seat December 5, 1932.

## WEST VIRGINIA

### SENATORS
Henry D. Hatfield, *Huntington*
Matthew M. Neely, *Fairmont*

### REPRESENTATIVES
Carl G. Bachmann, *Wheeling*
Frank L. Bowman, *Morgantown*
Lynn S. Hornor, *Clarksburg*
Robert L. Hogg, *Point Pleasant*
Hugh Ike Shott, *Bluefield*
Joe L. Smith, *Beckley*

## WISCONSIN

### SENATORS
Robert M. La Follette, Jr., *Madison*
John J. Blaine, *Boscobel*

### REPRESENTATIVES
Thomas R. Amlie,[81] *Elkhorn*
Charles A. Kading, *Watertown*

John M. Nelson, *Madison*
John C. Schafer, *Milwaukee*
William H. Stafford, *Milwaukee*
Michael K. Reilly, *Fond du Lac*
Gardner R. Withrow, *La Crosse*
Gerald J. Boileau, *Wausau*
George J. Schneider, *Appleton*
James A. Frear, *Hudson*
Hubert H. Peavey, *Washburn*

## WYOMING

### SENATORS
John B. Kendrick, *Sheridan*
Robert D. Carey, *Careyhurst*

### REPRESENTATIVE AT LARGE
Vincent M. Carter, *Kemmerer*

## TERRITORY OF ALASKA

### DELEGATE
James Wickersham, *Juneau*

## TERRITORY OF HAWAII

### DELEGATE
Victor S. K. Houston, *Honolulu*

## PHILIPPINE ISLANDS

### RESIDENT COMMISSIONERS
Pedro Guevara, *Santa Cruz*
Camilo Osias, *Balaoan*

## PUERTO RICO[82]

### RESIDENT COMMISSIONERS
Felix Cordova Davila,[83] *San Juan*
José L. Pesquera,[84] *Bayamon*

---

[81] Elected to fill vacancy caused by death of Representative-elect Henry Allen Cooper, in preceding Congress, and took his seat December 7, 1931.

[82] The spelling of this name was changed from Porto Rico to Puerto Rico by an act of Congress (47 Stat 158), approved May 17, 1932.

[83] Resigned April 11, 1932.

[84] Appointed to fill vacancy caused by resignation of Felix Cordova Davila, and took his seat April 28, 1932.

# 73RD CONGRESS

## MARCH 4, 1933, TO JANUARY 3,[1] 1935

John N. Garner
Vice President

Henry T. Rainey
Speaker

FIRST SESSION— *March 9, 1933, to June 15, 1933*
SECOND SESSION— *January 3,[1] 1934, to June 18, 1934*
SPECIAL SESSION OF THE SENATE— *March 4, 1933, to March 6, 1933*

---

VICE PRESIDENT OF THE UNITED STATES— John N. Garner, of Texas
PRESIDENT PRO TEMPORE OF THE SENATE— Key Pittman,[2] of Nevada
SECRETARY OF THE SENATE— Edwin A. Halsey,[3] of Virginia
SERGEANT AT ARMS OF THE SENATE— Chesley W. Jurney,[4] of Texas

---

SPEAKER OF THE HOUSE OF REPRESENTATIVES— Henry T. Rainey,[5] of Illinois
CLERK OF THE HOUSE— South Trimble,[6] of Kentucky
SERGEANT AT ARMS OF THE HOUSE— Kenneth Romney, of Montana
DOORKEEPER OF THE HOUSE— Joseph J. Sinnott, of Virginia
POSTMASTER OF THE HOUSE— Finis E. Scott

## ALABAMA

### SENATORS
Hugo L. Black, *Birmingham*
John H. Bankhead II, *Jasper*

### REPRESENTATIVES
John McDuffie, *Monroeville*
Lister Hill, *Montgomery*
Henry B. Steagall, *Ozark*
Lamar Jeffers, *Anniston*
Miles C. Allgood, *Gadsden*
William B. Oliver, *Tuscaloosa*
William B. Bankhead, *Jasper*
Edward B. Almon,[7] *Tuscumbia*
Archibald H. Carmichael,[8] *Tuscumbia*
George Huddleston, *Birmingham*

## ARIZONA

### SENATORS
Henry F. Ashurst, *Prescott*
Carl Hayden, *Phoenix*

### REPRESENTATIVE AT LARGE
Isabella S. Greenway,[9] *Ajo*

## ARKANSAS

### SENATORS
Joseph T. Robinson, *Little Rock*
Hattie W. Caraway, *Jonesboro*

### REPRESENTATIVES
William J. Driver, *Osceola*
John E. Miller, *Searcy*

Claude A. Fuller, *Eureka Springs*
William B. Cravens, *Fort Smith*
Heartsill Ragon,[10] *Clarksville*
David D. Terry,[11] *Little Rock*
David D. Glover, *Malvern*
Tilman B. Parks, *Camden*

## CALIFORNIA

### SENATORS
Hiram W. Johnson, *San Francisco*
William Gibbs McAdoo, *Los Angeles*

### REPRESENTATIVES
Clarence F. Lea, *Santa Rosa*
Harry L. Englebright, *Nevada City*
Frank H. Buck, *Vacaville*
Florence P. Kahn, *San Francisco*
Richard J. Welch, *San Francisco*
Albert E. Carter, *Oakland*
Ralph R. Eltse, *Berkeley*
John J. McGrath, *San Mateo*
Denver S. Church, *Fresno*
Henry E. Stubbs, *Santa Maria*
William E. Evans, *Glendale*
John H. Hoeppel, *Arcadia*
Charles Kramer, *Los Angeles*
Thomas F. Ford, *Los Angeles*
William I. Traeger, *Los Angeles*
John F. Dockweiler, *Los Angeles*
Charles J. Colden, *San Pedro*
John H. Burke, *Long Beach*
Samuel L. Collins, *Fullerton*
George Burnham,[12] *San Diego*

## COLORADO

### SENATORS
Edward P. Costigan, *Denver*
Alva B. Adams, *Pueblo*

### REPRESENTATIVES
Lawrence Lewis, *Denver*
Fred Cummings, *Fort Collins*
John A. Martin, *Pueblo*
Edward T. Taylor, *Glenwood Springs*

## CONNECTICUT

### SENATORS
Frederic C. Walcott, *Norfolk*
Augustine Lonergan, *Hartford*

### REPRESENTATIVE AT LARGE
Charles M. Bakewell,
*New Haven*

### REPRESENTATIVES
Herman P. Kopplemann, *Hartford*
William L. Higgins,[13] *South Coventry*
Francis T. Maloney, *Meriden*
Schuyler Merritt, *Stamford*
Edward W. Goss,[14] *Waterbury*

## DELAWARE

### SENATORS
Daniel O. Hastings, *Wilmington*
John G. Townsend, Jr., *Selbyville*

### REPRESENTATIVE AT LARGE
Wilbur L. Adams, *Wilmington*

---

[1] Pursuant to the twentieth amendment to the Constitution, the regular sessions of Congress will hereafter begin on January 3 of each year.
[2] Elected March 9, 1933.
[3] Unanimously elected March 9, 1933.
[4] Elected March 9, 1933.
[5] Elected March 9, 1933; died August 19, 1934.
[6] Reelected March 9, 1933.

[7] Died June 22, 1933.
[8] Elected to fill vacancy caused by death of Edward B. Almon, and took his seat January 3, 1934.
[9] Elected to fill vacancy caused by resignation of Representative-elect Lewis W. Douglas, in preceding Congress, and took her seat January 3, 1934.
[10] Resigned June 16, 1933, having been appointed a judge of the United States district court, western district of Arkansas.

[11] Elected to fill vacancy caused by resignation of Heartsill Ragon, and took his seat January 3, 1934.
[12] Election unsuccessfully contested by Claude Chandler.
[13] Election unsuccessfully contested by William C. Fox.
[14] Election unsuccessfully contested by Martin E. Gormley.

## FLORIDA

### SENATORS

Duncan U. Fletcher, *Jacksonville*
Park Trammell, *Lakeland*

### REPRESENTATIVE AT LARGE

William J. Sears, *Jacksonville*

### REPRESENTATIVES

J. Hardin Peterson, *Lakeland*
Robert A. Green, *Starke*
Millard F. Caldwell, *Milton*
J. Mark Wilcox, *West Palm Beach*

## GEORGIA

### SENATORS

Walter F. George, *Vienna*
Richard B. Russell, *Winder*

### REPRESENTATIVES

Homer C. Parker, *Statesboro*
Edward E. Cox, *Camilla*
Bryant T. Castellow, *Cuthbert*
Emmett M. Owen, *Griffin*
Robert Ramspeck, *Decatur*
Carl Vinson, *Milledgeville*
Malcolm C. Tarver, *Dalton*
Braswell D. Deen, *Alma*
John S. Wood, *Canton*
Charles H. Brand,[15] *Athens*
Paul Brown,[16] *Elberton*

## IDAHO

### SENATORS

William E. Borah, *Boise*
James P. Pope, *Boise*

### REPRESENTATIVES

Compton I. White, *Clark Fork*
Thomas C. Coffin,[17] *Pocatello*

## ILLINOIS

### SENATORS

J. Hamilton Lewis, *Chicago*
William H. Dieterich, *Beardstown*

### REPRESENTATIVES AT LARGE

Martin A. Brennan, *Bloomington*
Walter Nesbit, *Belleville*

### REPRESENTATIVES

Oscar De Priest, *Chicago*
Patrick H. Moynihan, *Chicago*
Edward A. Kelly, *Chicago*
Harry P. Beam, *Chicago*
Adolph J. Sabath, *Chicago*
Thomas J. O'Brien, *Chicago*
Leonard W. Schuetz, *Chicago*
Leo Kocialkowski, *Chicago*

Fred A. Britten,[18] *Chicago*
James Simpson, Jr.,[19] *Wadsworth*
Frank R. Reid, *Aurora*
John T. Buckbee, *Rockford*
Leo E. Allen, *Galena*
Chester C. Thompson, *Rock Island*
J. Leroy Adair, *Quincy*
Everett M. Dirksen, *Pekin*
James Frank Gillespie, *Bloomington*
James A. Meeks, *Danville*
Donald C. Dobbins, *Champaign*
Henry T. Rainey,[20] *Carrollton*
J. Earl Major,[21] *Hillsboro*
Edwin M. Schaefer, *Belleville*
William W. Arnold, *Robinson*
Claude V. Parsons, *Golconda*
Kent E. Keller, *Ava*

## INDIANA

### SENATORS

Arthur R. Robinson, *Indianapolis*
Frederick Van Nuys, *Indianapolis*

### REPRESENTATIVES

William T. Schulte, *Hammond*
George R. Durgan, *La Fayette*
Samuel B. Pettengill, *South Bend*
James I. Farley, *Auburn*
Glenn Griswold, *Peru*
Virginia E. Jenckes, *Terre Haute*
Arthur H. Greenwood, *Washington*
John W. Boehne, Jr., *Evansville*
Eugene B. Crowe, *Bedford*
Finly H. Gray, *Connersville*
William H. Larrabee, *New Palestine*
Louis Ludlow, *Indianapolis*

## IOWA

### SENATORS

Lester J. Dickinson, *Algona*
Richard Louis Murphy, *Dubuque*

### REPRESENTATIVES

Edward C. Eicher, *Washington*
Bernhard M. Jacobsen, *Clinton*
Albert C. Willford, *Waterloo*
Fred Biermann, *Decorah*
Lloyd Thurston,[22] *Osceola*
Cassius C. Dowell, *Des Moines*
Otha D. Wearin, *Hastings*
Fred C. Gilchrist, *Laurens*
Guy M. Gillette, *Cherokee*

## KANSAS

### SENATORS

Arthur Capper, *Topeka*
George McGill, *Wichita*

### REPRESENTATIVES

William P. Lambertson, *Fairview*
Ulysses S. Guyer, *Kansas City*
Harold McGugin, *Coffeyville*
William Randolph Carpenter, *Marion*
William A. Ayres,[23] *Wichita*
Kathryn E. O'Loughlin,[24] *Hays*
Clifford R. Hope, *Garden City*

## KENTUCKY

### SENATORS

Alben W. Barkley, *Paducah*
Marvel M. Logan, *Bowling Green*

### REPRESENTATIVES AT LARGE

Fred M. Vinson, *Ashland*
John Y. Brown, *Lexington*
Andrew J. May, *Prestonsburg*
Brent Spence, *Fort Thomas*
Virgil M. Chapman, *Paris*
Glover H. Cary, *Owensboro*
William V. Gregory, *Mayfield*
Cap R. Carden, *Munfordville*
Finley Hamilton, *London*

## LOUISIANA

### SENATORS

Huey P. Long, *New Orleans*
John H. Overton, *Alexandria*

### REPRESENTATIVES

Joachim O. Fernandez, *New Orleans*
Paul H. Maloney, *New Orleans*
Numa F. Montet, *Thibodaux*
John N. Sandlin, *Minden*
Riley J. Wilson, *Ruston*
Bolivar E. Kemp,[25] *Amite*
Jared Y. Sanders, Jr.,[26] *Baton Rouge*
René L. DeRouen, *Ville Platte*
Cleveland Dear, *Alexandria*

## MAINE

### SENATORS

Frederick Hale, *Portland*
Wallace H. White, Jr., *Auburn*

### REPRESENTATIVES

Carroll L. Beedy, *Portland*
Edward C. Moran, Jr., *Rockland*
John G. Utterback,[27] *Bangor*

---

[15] Died May 17, 1933.
[16] Elected to fill vacancy caused by death of Charles H. Brand, and took his seat January 3, 1934.
[17] Died June 8, 1934; vacancy throughout remainder of the Congress.
[18] Election unsuccessfully contested by James McAndrews.
[19] Election unsuccessfully contested by Charles H. Weber.
[20] Died August 19, 1934; vacancy throughout remainder of the Congress.

[21] Resigned October 6, 1933, having been appointed a judge of the United States district court, southern district of Illinois; vacancy throughout remainder of the Congress.
[22] Election unsuccessfully contested by Lloyd Ellis.
[23] Resigned August 22, 1934, having been appointed a member of the Federal Trade Commission; vacancy throughout remainder of the Congress.
[24] After election was married and name changed to Kathryn O'Loughlin McCarthy.

[25] Died June 19, 1933.
[26] Contested the election of Esther C. Kemp, who had presented credentials as a Member-elect to fill the vacancy caused by the death of her husband, Bolivar E. Kemp, but who was not permitted to qualify, the seat being declared vacant; subsequently elected to fill this vacancy, and took his seat May 21, 1934.
[27] Election unsuccessfully contested by Ralph O. Brewster.

## MARYLAND

SENATORS

Millard E. Tydings, *Havre de Grace*
Phillips Lee Goldsborough, *Baltimore*

REPRESENTATIVES

T. Alan Goldsborough, *Denton*
William P. Cole, Jr., *Towson*
Vincent L. Palmisano, *Baltimore*
Ambrose J. Kennedy, *Baltimore*
Stephen W. Gambrill, *Laurel*
David J. Lewis, *Cumberland*

## MASSACHUSETTS

SENATORS

David I. Walsh, *Fitchburg*
Marcus A. Coolidge, *Fitchburg*

REPRESENTATIVES

Allen T. Treadway, *Stockbridge*
William J. Granfield, *Springfield*
Frank H. Foss, *Fitchburg*
Pehr G. Holmes, *Worcester*
Edith Nourse Rogers, *Lowell*
A. Piatt Andrew, Jr., *Gloucester*
William P. Connery, Jr., *Lynn*
Arthur D. Healey, *Somerville*
Robert Luce, *Waltham*
George H. Tinkham, *Boston*
John J. Douglass, *Boston*
John W. McCormack, *Dorchester*
Richard B. Wigglesworth, *Milton*
Joseph W. Martin, Jr., *North Attleboro*
Charles L. Gifford, *Cotuit*

## MICHIGAN

SENATORS

James Couzens, *Detroit*
Arthur H. Vandenberg, *Grand Rapids*

REPRESENTATIVES

George G. Sadowski, *Detroit*
John C. Lehr, *Monroe*
Joseph L. Hooper,[28] *Battle Creek*
George E. Foulkes, *Hartford*
Carl E. Mapes, *Grand Rapids*
Claude E. Cady, *Lansing*
Jesse P. Wolcott, *Port Huron*
Michael J. Hart, *Saginaw*
Harry W. Musselwhite, *Manistee*
Roy O. Woodruff, *Bay City*
Prentiss M. Brown, *St. Ignace*
W. Frank James, *Hancock*
Clarence J. McLeod, *Detroit*
Carl M. Weideman, *Detroit*
John D. Dingell,[29] *Detroit*
John Lesinski, *Dearborn*
George A. Dondero, *Royal Oak*

## MINNESOTA

SENATORS

Henrik Shipstead, *Miltona*
Thomas D. Schall, *Excelsior*

REPRESENTATIVES AT LARGE

Magnus John, *Kimball*
Paul J. Kvale, *Benson*
Henry Arens, *Jordan*
Ernest Lundeen, *Minneapolis*
Theodore Christianson, *Minneapolis*
Einar Hoidale, *Minneapolis*
Ray P. Chase, *Anoka*
Francis H. Shoemaker, *Red Wing*
Harold Knutson, *St. Cloud*

## MISSISSIPPI

SENATORS

Pat Harrison, *Gulfport*
Hubert D. Stephens, *New Albany*

REPRESENTATIVES

John E. Rankin, *Tupelo*
Wall Doxey, *Holly Springs*
William M. Whittington, *Greenwood*
T. Jeff. Busby, *Houston*
Ross A. Collins, *Meridian*
William M. Colmer, *Pascagoula*
Lawrence Russell Ellzey,[30] *Wesson*

## MISSOURI

SENATORS

Roscoe C. Patterson, *Kansas City*
Joel Bennett Clark, *St. Louis*

REPRESENTATIVES AT LARGE

John J. Cochran, *St. Louis*
James R. Claiborne, *St. Louis*
Joseph B. Shannon, *Kansas City*
Clyde Williams, *Hillsboro*
Clarence Cannon, *Elsberry*
Frank H. Lee, *Joplin*
James E. Ruffin, *Springfield*
Ralph F. Lozier, *Carrollton*
Jacob L. Milligan, *Richmond*
Reuben T. Wood, *Springfield*
Milton A. Romjue, *Macon*
Richard M. Duncan, *St. Joseph*
Clement C. Dickinson, *Clinton*

## MONTANA

SENATORS

Burton K. Wheeler, *Butte*
John E. Erickson,[31] *Kalispell*
James E. Murray,[32] *Butte*

REPRESENTATIVES

Joseph P. Monaghan, *Butte*
Roy E. Ayers, *Lewistown*

## NEBRASKA

SENATORS

George W. Norris, *McCook*
Robert B. Howell,[33] *Omaha*
William H. Thompson,[34] *Grand Island*
Richard C. Hunter,[35] *Omaha*

REPRESENTATIVES

John H. Morehead, *Falls City*
Edward R. Burke, *Omaha*
Edgar Howard, *Columbus*
Ashton C. Shallenberger, *Alma*
Terry M. Carpenter, *Scottsbluff*

## NEVADA

SENATORS

Key Pittman, *Tonopah*
Patrick A. McCarran, *Reno*

REPRESENTATIVE AT LARGE

James G. Scrugham, *Reno*

## NEW HAMPSHIRE

SENATORS

Henry W. Keyes, *Haverhill*
Fred H. Brown, *Somersworth*

REPRESENTATIVES

William N. Rogers, *Sanbornville*
Charles W. Tobey, *Temple*

## NEW JERSEY

SENATORS

Hamilton F. Kean, *Elizabeth*
W. Warren Barbour, *Locust*

REPRESENTATIVES

Charles A. Wolverton, *Camden*
Isaac Bacharach, *Atlantic City*
William H. Sutphin, *Matawan*
D. Lane Powers, *Trenton*
Charles A. Eaton, *North Plainfield*
Donald H. McLean, *Elizabeth*
Randolph Perkins, *Woodcliff Lake*
George N. Seger, *Passaic*
Edward A. Kenney, *Cliffside Park*
Fred A. Hartley, Jr., *Kearny*
Peter A. Cavicchia, *Newark*
Frederick R. Lehlbach, *Newark*
Mary T. Norton, *Jersey City*
Oscar L. Auf der Heide, *West New York*

---

[28] Died February 22, 1934; vacancy throughout remainder of the Congress.

[29] Election unsuccessfully contested by Charles Bowles.

[30] Election unsuccessfully contested by L. G. Reese.

[31] Appointed to fill vacancy caused by death of Thomas J. Walsh, in preceding Congress, and took his seat March 20, 1933.

[32] Elected November 6, 1934, to fill vacancy caused by death of Thomas J. Walsh, and took his seat January 3, 1935.

[33] Died March 11, 1933.

[34] Appointed to fill vacancy caused by death of Robert B. Howell, and took his seat May 26, 1933.

[35] Elected to fill vacancy caused by death of Robert B. Howell, and served from November 7, 1934, to January 3, 1935.

## NEW MEXICO

SENATORS

Sam G. Bratton,[36] *Albuquerque*
Carl A. Hatch,[37] *Clovis*
Bronson M. Cutting, *Santa Fe*

REPRESENTATIVE AT LARGE

Dennis Chavez, *Albuquerque*

## NEW YORK

SENATORS

Royal S. Copeland, *New York City*
Robert F. Wagner, *New York City*

REPRESENTATIVES AT LARGE

Elmer E. Studley, *Flushing*
John Fitzgibbons, *Oswego*

REPRESENTATIVES

Robert L. Bacon, *Old Westbury*
William F. Brunner, *Rockaway Park*
George W. Lindsay, *Brooklyn*
Thomas H. Cullen, *Brooklyn*
Loring M. Black, Jr., *Brooklyn*
Andrew L. Somers, *Brooklyn*
John J. Delaney, *Brooklyn*
Patrick J. Carley, *Brooklyn*
Stephen A. Rudd, *Brooklyn*
Emanuel Celler, *Brooklyn*
Anning S. Prall, *West New Brighton*
Samuel Dickstein, *New Yorl City*
Christopher D. Sullivan, *New York City*
William I. Sirovich, *New York City*
John J. Boylan, *New York City*
John J. O'Connor, *New York City*
Theodore A. Peyser, *New York City*
Martin J. Kennedy, *New York City*
Sol Bloom, *New York City*
James J. Lanzetta, *New York City*
Joseph A. Gavagan, *New York City*
Anthony J. Griffin, *New York City*
Frank Oliver,[38] *Bronx*
James M. Fitzpatrick, *New York City*
Charles D. Millard, *Tarrytown*
Hamilton Fish, Jr., *Garrison*
Philip A. Goodwin, *Coxsackie*
Parker Corning, *Albany*
James S. Parker,[39] *Salem*
William D. Thomas,[40] *Hoosick Falls*
Frank Crowther, *Schenectady*
Bertrand H. Snell, *Potsdam*
Francis D. Culkin, *Oswego*
Fred J. Sisson, *Whitesboro*
John D. Clarke,[41] *Fraser*
Marian W. Clarke,[42] *Fraser*

Clarence E. Hancock, *Syracuse*
John Taber, *Auburn*
Gale H. Stalker, *Elmira*
James L. Whitley, *Rochester*
James W. Wadsworth, Jr., *Geneseo*
Walter G. Andrews, *Buffalo*
Alfred F. Beiter, *Williamsville*
James M. Mead, *Buffalo*
Daniel A. Reed, *Dunkirk*

## NORTH CAROLINA

SENATORS

Josiah W. Bailey, *Raleigh*
Robert R. Reynolds, *Asheville*

REPRESENTATIVES

Lindsay C. Warren, *Washington*
John H. Kerr, *Warrenton*
Charles L. Abernethy, *New Bern*
Edward W. Pou,[43] *Smithfield*
Harold D. Cooley,[44] *Nashville*
Franklin W. Hancock, Jr., *Oxford*
William B. Umstead, *Durham*
J. Bayard Clark, *Fayetteville*
J. Walter Lambeth, *Thomasville*
Robert L. Doughton, *Laurel Springs*
Alfred L. Bulwinkle, *Gastonia*
Zebulon Weaver, *Asheville*

## NORTH DAKOTA

SENATORS

Lynn J. Frazier, *Hoople*
Gerald P. Nye, *Cooperstown*

REPRESENTATIVES AT LARGE

James H. Sinclair, *Kenmare*
William Lemke, *Fargo*

## OHIO

SENATORS

Simeon D. Fess, *Yellow Springs*
Robert J. Bulkley, *Cleveland*

REPRESENTATIVES AT LARGE

Charles V. Truax, *Bucyrus*
Stephen M. Young, *Cleveland*

REPRESENTATIVES

John B. Hollister, *Cincinnati*
William E. Hess, *Cincinnati*
Byron B. Harlan, *Dayton*
Frank L. Kloeb, *Celina*
Frank C. Kniffin, *Napoleon*
James G. Polk, *Highland*
Leroy T. Marshall, *Xenia*
Thomas Brooks Fletcher, *Marion*
Warren J. Duffey, *Toledo*
Thomas A. Jenkins, *Ironton*
Mell G. Underwood, *New Lexington*
Arthur P. Lamneck, *Columbus*

William L. Fiesinger, *Sandusky*
Dow W. Harter, *Akron*
Robert T. Secrest, *Senecaville*
William R. Thom, *Canton*
Charles West, *Granville*
Lawrence E. Imhoff, *St. Clairsville*
John G. Cooper, *Youngstown*
Martin L. Sweeney, *Cleveland*
Robert Crosser, *Cleveland*
Chester C. Bolton, *Cleveland*

## OKLAHOMA

SENATORS

J. W. Elmer Thomas, *Medicine Park*
Thomas P. Gore, *Oklahoma City*

REPRESENTATIVE AT LARGE

Will Rogers, *Oklahoma City*

REPRESENTATIVES

Wesley E. Disney, *Tulsa*
William W. Hastings, *Tahlequah*
Wilburn Cartwright, *McAlester*
Thomas D. McKeown, *Ada*
Fletcher B. Swank, *Norman*
Jed Johnson, *Anadarko*
James V. McClintic, *Snyder*
Ernest W. Marland, *Ponca City*

## OREGON

SENATORS

Charles L. McNary, *Salem*
Frederick Steiwer, *Portland*

REPRESENTATIVES

James W. Mott, *Salem*
Walter M. Pierce, *La Grande*
Charles H. Martin, *Portland*

## PENNSYLVANIA

SENATORS

David A. Reed, *Pittsburgh*
James J. Davis, *Pittsburgh*

REPRESENTATIVES

Harry C. Ransley, *Philadelphia*
James M. Beck,[45] *Philadelphia*
Alfred M. Waldron, *Philadelphia*
George W. Edmonds, *Philadelphia*
James J. Connolly, *Philadelphia*
Edward L. Stokes, *Philadelphia*
George P. Darrow, *Philadelphia*
James Wolfenden, *Upper Darby*
Henry W. Watson,[46] *Langhorne*
Oliver W. Frey,[47] *Allentown*
J. Roland Kinzer, *Lancaster*
Patrick J. Boland, *Scranton*

---

[36] Resigned June 24, 1933, having been appointed a judge of the Circuit Court of Appeals of the United States.

[37] Appointed to fill vacancy caused by resignation of Sam G. Bratton, and took his seat January 3, 1934; subsequently elected.

[38] Resigned June 18, 1934, having been appointed a magistrate in the city of New York; vacancy throughout remainder of the Congress.

[39] Died December 19, 1933.

[40] Elected to fill vacancy caused by death of James S. Parker, and took his seat February 5, 1934.

[41] Died November 5, 1933.

[42] Elected to fill vacancy caused by death of her husband, John D. Clarke, and took her seat January 3, 1934.

[43] Died April 1, 1934.

[44] Elected to fill vacancy caused by death of Edward W. Pou, and served from July 7, 1934, to January 3, 1935.

[45] Election unsuccessfully contested by John J. Shanahan; resigned September 30, 1934; vacancy throughout remainder of the Congress.

[46] Died August 27, 1933.

[47] Elected to fill vacancy caused by death of Henry W. Watson, and took his seat January 3, 1934.

C. Murray Turpin,[48] *Kingston*
George F. Brumm,[49] *Minersville*
William E. Richardson, *Reading*
Louis T. McFadden, *Canton*
Robert F. Rich, *Woolrich*
J. William Ditter, *Ambler*
Benjamin K. Focht, *Lewisburg*
Isaac H. Doutrich, *Harrisburg*
Thomas C. Cochran, *Mercer*
Francis E. Walter, *Easton*
Harry L. Haines, *Red Lion*
J. Banks Kurtz, *Altoona*
J. Buell Snyder, *Perryopolis*
Charles I. Faddis, *Waynesburg*
J. Howard Swick, *Beaver Falls*
Nathan L. Strong, *Brookville*
William M. Berlin, *Greensburg*
Charles N. Crosby, *Meadville*
J. Twing Brooks, *Sewickley*
M. Clyde Kelly, *Edgewood*
Michael J. Muldowney, *Pittsburgh*
Henry Ellenbogen,[50] *Pittsburgh*
Matthew A. Dunn, *Pittsburgh*

## RHODE ISLAND

SENATORS

Jesse H. Metcalf, *Providence*
Felix Hébert, *West Warwick*

REPRESENTATIVES

Francis B. Condon, *Central Falls*
John M. O'Connell, *Westerly*

## SOUTH CAROLINA

SENATORS

Ellison D. Smith, *Lynchburg*
James F. Byrnes, *Spartanburg*

REPRESENTATIVES

Thomas S. McMillan, *Charleston*
Hampton P. Fulmer, *Orangeburg*
John C. Taylor, *Anderson*
John J. McSwain, *Greenville*
James P. Richards, *Lancaster*
Allard H. Gasque, *Florence*

## SOUTH DAKOTA

SENATORS

Peter Norbeck, *Redfield*
William J. Bulow, *Beresford*

REPRESENTATIVES

Fred H. Hildebrandt, *Watertown*
Theodore B. Werner, *Rapid City*

## TENNESSEE

SENATORS

Kenneth D. McKellar, *Memphis*
Nathan L. Bachman,[51] *Chattanooga*

REPRESENTATIVES

B. Carroll Reece,[52] *Johnson City*
J. Will Taylor, *La Follette*
Sam D. McReynolds, *Chattanooga*
John R. Mitchell, *Cookeville*
Joseph W. Byrns, *Nashville*
Clarence W. Turner, *Waverly*
Gordon Browning, *Huntingdon*
Jere Cooper, *Dyersburg*
Edward H. Crump, *Memphis*

## TEXAS

SENATORS

Morris Sheppard, *Texarkana*
Tom T. Connally, *Marlin*

REPRESENTATIVES AT LARGE

George B. Terrell, *Alto*
Sterling P. Strong, *Dallas*
Joseph W. Bailey, Jr., *Dallas*

REPRESENTATIVES

Wright Patman, *Texarkana*
Martin Dies, Jr., *Orange*
Morgan G. Sanders, *Canton*
Sam Rayburn, *Bonham*
Hatton W. Sumners, *Dallas*
Luther A. Johnson, *Corsicana*
Clay Stone Briggs,[53] *Galveston*
Clark W. Thompson,[54] *Galveston*
Joe H. Eagle,[55] *Houston*
Joseph J. Mansfield, *Columbus*
James P. Buchanan, *Brenham*
Oliver H. Cross, *Waco*
Fritz G. Lanham, *Fort Worth*
William D. McFarlane, *Graham*
Richard M. Kleberg, *Corpus Christi*
Milton H. West,[56] *Brownsville*
R. Ewing Thomason, *El Paso*
Thomas L. Blanton, *Abilene*
Marvin Jones, *Amarillo*

## UTAH

SENATORS

William H. King, *Salt Lake City*
Elbert D. Thomas, *Salt Lake City*

REPRESENTATIVES

Abe Murdock, *Beaver*
J. W. Robinson, *Provo*

## VERMONT

SENATORS

Porter H. Dale,[57] *Island Pond*
Ernest Willard Gibson,[58] *Brattleboro*
Warren R. Austin, *Burlington*

REPRESENTATIVE AT LARGE

Ernest Willard Gibson,[59] *Brattleboro*
Charles A. Lumley,[60] *Northfield*

## VIRGINIA

SENATORS

Carter Glass, *Lynchburg*
Harry Flood Byrd,[61] *Berryville*

REPRESENTATIVES AT LARGE

Clifton A. Woodrum, *Roanoke*
Andrew J. Montague, *Richmond*
Schuyler Otis Bland, *Newport News*
Thomas G. Burch, *Martinsville*
A. Willis Robertson, *Lexington*
Howard W. Smith, *Alexandria*
Patrick Henry Drewry, *Petersburg*
Colgate W. Darden, Jr., *Norfolk*
John W. Flannagan, Jr., *Bristol*

## WASHINGTON

SENATORS

Clarence C. Dill, *Spokane*
Homer T. Bone, *Tacoma*

REPRESENTATIVES

Marion A. Zioncheck, *Seattle*
Monrad C. Wallgren, *Everett*
Martin F. Smith, *Hoquiam*
Knute Hill, *Prosser*
Samuel B. Hill, *Waterville*
Wesley Lloyd, *Tacoma*

## WEST VIRGINIA

SENATORS

Henry D. Hatfield, *Huntington*
Matthew M. Neely, *Fairmont*

REPRESENTATIVES

Robert L. Ramsay, *Follansbee*
Jennings Randolph, *Elkins*
Lynn S. Hornor,[62] *Clarksburg*
Andrew Edmiston,[63] *Weston*
George W. Johnson, *Parkersburg*
John Kee, *Bluefield*
Joe L. Smith, *Beckley*

---

[48] Election unsuccessfully contested by John J. Casey.
[49] Died May 29, 1934; vacancy throughout remainder of the Congress.
[50] Election unsuccessfully contested by Harry E. Estep.
[51] Appointed to fill vacancy caused by resignation of Cordell Hull, and took his seat March 4, 1933; subsequently elected.
[52] Election unsuccessfully contested by O. B. Lovette.
[53] Died April 29, 1933.

[54] Elected to fill vacancy caused by death of Clay Stone Briggs, and took his seat January 3, 1934.
[55] Elected to fill vacancy caused by death of Representative-elect Daniel E. Garrett, in preceding Congress.
[56] Elected to fill vacancy caused by resignation of Representative-elect John N. Garner, in preceding Congress, and took his seat May 2, 1933.
[57] Died October 6, 1933.
[58] Appointed to fill vacancy caused by death of Porter H. Dale, and took his seat February 1, 1934; subsequently elected.

[59] Resigned October 19, 1933, having been appointed Senator.
[60] Elected to fill vacancy caused by resignation of Ernest W. Gibson, and took his seat January 18, 1934.
[61] Appointed to fill vacancy caused by resignation of Claude A. Swanson, and took his seat March 4, 1933; subsequently elected.
[62] Died September 23, 1933.
[63] Elected to fill vacancy caused by death of Lynn S. Hornor, and took his seat January 3, 1934.

## WISCONSIN

### SENATORS
Robert M. La Follette, Jr., *Madison*
F. Ryan Duffy, *Fond du Lac*

### REPRESENTATIVES
George W. Blanchard, *Edgerton*
Charles W. Henney, *Portage*
Gardner R. Withrow, *La Crosse*
Raymond J. Cannon, *Milwaukee*
Thomas O'Malley, *Milwaukee*
Michael K. Reilly, *Fond du Lac*
Gerald J. Boileau, *Wausau*
James F. Hughes, *De Pere*
James A. Frear, *Hudson*

Hubert H. Peavey, *Washburn*

## WYOMING

### SENATORS
John B. Kendrick,[64] *Sheridan*
Joseph C. O'Mahoney,[65] *Cheyenne*
Robert D. Carey, *Careyhurst*

### REPRESENTATIVE AT LARGE
Vincent M. Carter, *Kemmerer*

## TERRITORY OF ALASKA

### DELEGATE
Anthony J. Dimond, *Valdez*

## TERRITORY OF HAWAII

### DELEGATE
Lincoln L. McCandless, *Honolulu*

## PHILIPPINE ISLANDS

### RESIDENT COMMISSIONERS
Pedro Guevara, *Santa Cruz*
Camilo Osias, *Balaoan*

## PUERTO RICO

### RESIDENT COMMISSIONER
Santiago Iglesias, *San Juan*

---

[64] Died November 3, 1933.
[65] Appointed to fill vacancy caused by death of John B. Kendrick, and took his seat January 3, 1934; subsequently elected.

# 74TH CONGRESS

JANUARY 3, 1935, TO JANUARY 3, 1937

FIRST SESSION— *January 3, 1935, to August 26, 1935*
SECOND SESSION— *January 3, 1936, to June 20, 1936*

———————

VICE PRESIDENT OF THE UNITED STATES— JOHN N. GARNER, of Texas
PRESIDENT PRO TEMPORE OF THE SENATE— KEY PITTMAN,[1] of Nevada
SECRETARY OF THE SENATE— EDWIN A. HALSEY, of Virginia
SERGEANT AT ARMS OF THE SENATE— CHESLEY W. JURNEY, of Texas

———————

SPEAKER OF THE HOUSE OF REPRESENTATIVES— JOSEPH W. BYRNS,[2] of Tennessee;
WILLIAM B. BANKHEAD,[3] of Alabama
CLERK OF THE HOUSE— SOUTH TRIMBLE,[4] of Kentucky
SERGEANT AT ARMS OF THE HOUSE— KENNETH ROMNEY, of Montana
DOORKEEPER OF THE HOUSE— JOSEPH J. SINNOTT, of Virginia
POSTMASTER OF THE HOUSE— FINIS E. SCOTT

John N. Garner
Vice President

Joseph W. Byrns
Speaker

## ALABAMA

### SENATORS
Hugo L. Black, *Birmingham*
John H. Bankhead II, *Jasper*

### REPRESENTATIVES
John McDuffie,[5] *Monroeville*
Frank W. Boykin,[6] *Mobile*
Lister Hill, *Montgomery*
Henry B. Steagall, *Ozark*
Sam Hobbs, *Selma*
Joe Starnes, *Guntersville*
William B. Oliver, *Tuscaloosa*
William B. Bankhead, *Jasper*
Archibald H. Carmichael, *Tuscumbia*
George Huddleston, *Birmingham*

## ARIZONA

### SENATORS
Henry F. Ashurst, *Prescott*
Carl Hayden, *Phoenix*

### REPRESENTATIVE AT LARGE
Isabella S. Greenway, *Ajo*

## ARKANSAS

### SENATORS
Joseph T. Robinson, *Little Rock*
Hattie W. Caraway, *Jonesboro*

### REPRESENTATIVES
William J. Driver, *Osceola*
John E. Miller, *Searcy*
Claude A. Fuller, *Eureka Springs*
William B. Cravens, *Fort Smith*
David D. Terry, *Little Rock*
John L. McClellan, *Malvern*
Tilman B. Parks, *Camden*

## CALIFORNIA

### SENATORS
Hiram W. Johnson, *San Francisco*
William Gibbs McAdoo, *Los Angeles*

### REPRESENTATIVES
Clarence F. Lea, *Santa Rosa*
Harry L. Englebright, *Nevada City*
Frank H. Buck, *Vacaville*
Florence P. Kahn, *San Francisco*
Richard J. Welch, *San Francisco*
Albert E. Carter, *Oakland*
John H. Tolan, *Oakland*
John J. McGrath, *San Mateo*
Bertrand W. Gearhart, *Fresno*
Henry E. Stubbs, *Santa Maria*
John S. McGroarty, *Tujunga*
John H. Hoeppel, *Arcadia*
Charles Kramer, *Los Angeles*
Thomas F. Ford, *Los Angeles*
John M. Costello, *Hollywood*
John F. Dockweiler, *Los Angeles*
Charles J. Colden, *San Pedro*
Byron N. Scott, *Long Beach*
Samuel L. Collins, *Fullerton*
George Burnham, *San Diego*

## COLORADO

### SENATORS
Edward P. Costigan, *Denver*
Alva B. Adams, *Pueblo*

### REPRESENTATIVES
Lawrence Lewis, *Denver*
Fred Cummings, *Fort Collins*
John A. Martin, *Pueblo*
Edward T. Taylor, *Glenwood Springs*

## CONNECTICUT

### SENATORS
Augustine Lonergan, *Hartford*
Francis T. Maloney, *Meriden*

### REPRESENTATIVE AT LARGE
William M. Citron, *Middletown*

### REPRESENTATIVES
Herman P. Kopplemann, *Hartford*
William L. Higgins, *South Coventry*
James A. Shanley, *New Haven*
Schuyler Merritt, *Stamford*
J. Joseph Smith, *Waterbury*

## DELAWARE

### SENATORS
Daniel O. Hastings, *Wilmington*
John G. Townsend, Jr., *Selbyville*

### REPRESENTATIVE AT LARGE
John G. Stewart, *Wilmington*

## FLORIDA

### SENATORS
Duncan U. Fletcher,[7] *Jacksonville*
William L. Hill,[8] *Gainesville*
Claude Pepper,[9] *Tallahassee*
Park Trammell,[10] *Lakeland*
Scott M. Loftin,[11] *Jacksonville*
Charles O. Andrews,[12] *Orlando*

### REPRESENTATIVE AT LARGE
William J. Sears, *Jacksonville*

---

[1] Reelected January 7, 1935.
[2] Elected January 3, 1935; died June 4, 1936.
[3] Elected June 4, 1936.
[4] Reelected January 3, 1935.
[5] Resigned March 2, 1935, having been appointed a judge in the United States District Court.
[6] Elected to fill vacancy caused by resignation of

John McDuffie, and took his seat August 12, 1935.
[7] Died June 17, 1936.
[8] Appointed to fill vacancy caused by death of Duncan U. Fletcher, and served from July 1, 1936, to November 3, 1936, but was unable to be sworn in as Congress was not in session.
[9] Elected to fill vacancy caused by death of

Duncan U. Fletcher, and took his seat January 5, 1937.
[10] Died May 8, 1936.
[11] Appointed to fill vacancy caused by death of Park Trammell, and took his seat May 27, 1936.
[12] Elected to fill vacancy caused by death of Park Trammell, and took his seat January 5, 1937.

## FLORIDA—Continued

### REPRESENTATIVES

J. Hardin Peterson, *Lakeland*
Robert A. Green, *Starke*
Millard F. Caldwell, *Milton*
J. Mark Wilcox, *West Palm Beach*

## GEORGIA

### SENATORS

Walter F. George, *Vienna*
Richard B. Russell, *Winder*

### REPRESENTATIVES

Hugh Peterson, *Ailey*
Edward E. Cox, *Camilla*
Bryant T. Castellow, *Cuthbert*
Emmett M. Owen, *Griffin*
Robert Ramspeck, *Atlanta*
Carl Vinson, *Milledgeville*
Malcolm C. Tarver, *Dalton*
Braswell D. Deen, *Alma*
B. Frank Whelchel, *Gainesville*
Paul Brown, *Elberton*

## IDAHO

### SENATORS

William E. Borah, *Boise*
James P. Pope, *Boise*

### REPRESENTATIVES

Compton I. White, *Clark Fork*
D. Worth Clark, *Pocatello*

## ILLINOIS

### SENATORS

J. Hamilton Lewis, *Chicago*
William H. Dieterich, *Beardstown*

### REPRESENTATIVES AT LARGE

Martin A. Brennan, *Bloomington*
Michael L. Igoe,[13] *Chicago*

### REPRESENTATIVES

Arthur W. Mitchell, *Chicago*
Raymond S. McKeough, *Chicago*
Edward A. Kelly, *Chicago*
Harry P. Beam, *Chicago*
Adolph J. Sabath, *Chicago*
Thomas J. O'Brien, *Chicago*
Leonard W. Schuetz, *Chicago*
Leo Kocialkowski, *Chicago*
James McAndrews, *Chicago*
Ralph E. Church, *Evanston*
Chauncey W. Reed, *West Chicago*
John T. Buckbee,[14] *Rockford*

Leo E. Allen, *Galena*
Chester C. Thompson, *Rock Island*
J. Leroy Adair, *Quincy*
Everett M. Dirksen, *Pekin*
Leslie C. Arends, *Melvin*
James A. Meeks, *Danville*
Donald C. Dobbins, *Champaign*
Scott W. Lucas, *Havana*
Harry H. Mason, *Pawnee*
Edwin M. Schaefer, *Belleville*
William W. Arnold,[15] *Robinson*
Claude V. Parsons, *Golconda*
Kent E. Keller, *Ava*

## INDIANA

### SENATORS

Frederick Van Nuys, *Indianapolis*
Sherman Minton, *New Albany*

### REPRESENTATIVES

William T. Schulte, *Hammond*
Charles A. Halleck,[16] *Rensselaer*
Samuel B. Pettengill, *South Bend*
James I. Farley, *Auburn*
Glenn Griswold, *Peru*
Virginia E. Jenckes, *Terre Haute*
Arthur H. Greenwood, *Washington*
John W. Boehne, Jr., *Evansville*
Eugene B. Crowe, *Bedford*
Finly H. Gray, *Connersville*
William H. Larrabee, *New Palestine*
Louis Ludlow, *Indianapolis*

## IOWA

### SENATORS

Lester J. Dickinson, *Algona*
Richard Louis Murphy,[17] *Dubuque*
Guy M. Gillette,[18] *Cherokee*

### REPRESENTATIVES

Edward C. Eicher, *Washington*
Bernhard M. Jacobsen,[19] *Clinton*
John W. Gwynne, *Waterloo*
Fred Biermann, *Decorah*
Lloyd Thurston, *Osceola*
Hubert Utterback, *Des Moines*
Otha D. Wearin, *Hastings*
Fred C. Gilchrist, *Laurens*
Guy M. Gillette,[20] *Cherokee*

## KANSAS

### SENATORS

Arthur Capper, *Topeka*
George McGill, *Wichita*

### REPRESENTATIVES

William P. Lambertson, *Fairview*
Ulysses S. Guyer, *Kansas City*
Edward W. Patterson, *Pittsburg*
William Randolph Carpenter, *Marion*
John M. Houston, *Newton*
Frank Carlson, *Concordia*
Clifford R. Hope, *Garden City*

## KENTUCKY

### SENATORS

Alben W. Barkley, *Paducah*
Marvel M. Logan, *Bowling Green*

### REPRESENTATIVES

William V. Gregory,[21] *Mayfield*
Glover H. Cary,[22] *Owensboro*
Emmet O'Neal, *Louisville*
Cap R. Carden,[23] *Munfordville*
Edward W. Creal,[24] *Hodgenville*
Brent Spence, *Fort Thomas*
Virgil M. Chapman, *Paris*
Andrew J. May, *Prestonsburg*
Fred M. Vinson, *Ashland*
John M. Robsion, *Barbourville*

## LOUISIANA

### SENATORS

Huey P. Long,[25] *New Orleans*
Rose McConnell Long,[26] *New Orleans*
John H. Overton, *Alexandria*

### REPRESENTATIVES

Joachim O. Fernandez, *New Orleans*
Paul H. Maloney, *New Orleans*
Numa F. Montet, *Thibodaux*
John N. Sandlin, *Minden*
Riley J. Wilson, *Ruston*
Jared Y. Sanders, Jr., *Baton Rouge*
René L. DeRouen, *Ville Platte*
Cleveland Dear, *Alexandria*

## MAINE

### SENATORS

Frederick Hale, *Portland*
Wallace H. White, Jr., *Auburn*

### REPRESENTATIVES

Simon M. Hamlin, *South Portland*
Edward C. Moran, Jr., *Rockland*
Ralph O. Brewster, *Dexter*

---

[13] Resigned June 2, 1935, having been appointed a United States attorney, northern district of Illinois; vacancy throughout remainder of the Congress.

[14] Died April 23, 1936; vacancy throughout remainder of the Congress.

[15] Resigned September 16, 1935, having been appointed a member of the United States Board of Tax Appeals; vacancy throughout remainder of the Congress.

[16] Elected to fill vacancy caused by death of Representative-elect Frederick Landis (November 15, 1934, before the beginning of the congressional term), and took his seat February 5, 1935.

[17] Died July 16, 1936; vacancy in this class from July 17, 1936, to November 3, 1936.

[18] Elected November 3, 1936, to fill vacancy caused by death of Richard Louis Murphy, and took his seat January 5, 1937.

[19] Died June 30, 1936; vacancy throughout remainder of the Congress.

[20] Resigned November 3, 1936; subsequently elected Senator; vacancy throughout the remainder of the Congress.

[21] Died October 10, 1936; vacancy throughout remainder of the Congress.

[22] Died December 5, 1936, before the commencement of the Seventy-fifth Congress, to which he had been reelected; vacancy throughout remainder of the Congress.

[23] Died June 13, 1935.

[24] Elected to fill vacancy caused by death of Cap R. Carden, and took his seat January 3, 1936.

[25] Died September 10, 1935; vacancy in this class from September 11, 1935, to January 30, 1936.

[26] Appointed to fill vacancy caused by death of her husband, Huey P. Long, and took her seat February 10, 1936; subsequently elected.

## MARYLAND

SENATORS

Millard E. Tydings, *Havre de Grace*
George L. Radcliffe, *Baltimore*

REPRESENTATIVES

T. Alan Goldsborough, *Denton*
William P. Cole, Jr., *Towson*
Vincent L. Palmisano, *Baltimore*
Ambrose J. Kennedy, *Baltimore*
Stephen W. Gambrill, *Laurel*
David J. Lewis, *Cumberland*

## MASSACHUSETTS

SENATORS

David I. Walsh, *Fitchburg*
Marcus A. Coolidge, *Fitchburg*

REPRESENTATIVES

Allen T. Treadway, *Stockbridge*
William J. Granfield, *Springfield*
Joseph E. Casey, *Clinton*
Pehr G. Holmes, *Worcester*
Edith Nourse Rogers, *Lowell*
A. Piatt Andrew, Jr.,[27] *Gloucester*
William P. Connery, Jr., *Lynn*
Arthur D. Healey, *Somerville*
Richard M. Russell, *Cambridge*
George H. Tinkham, *Boston*
John P. Higgins, *Boston*
John W. McCormack, *Dorchester*
Richard B. Wigglesworth, *Milton*
Joseph W. Martin, Jr., *North Attleboro*
Charles L. Gifford, *Cotuit*

## MICHIGAN

SENATORS

James Couzens,[28] *Detroit*
Prentiss M. Brown,[29] *St. Ignace*
Arthur H. Vandenberg, *Grand Rapids*

REPRESENTATIVES

George G. Sadowski, *Detroit*
Earl C. Michener, *Adrian*
Henry M. Kimball,[30] *Kalamazoo*
Verner W. Main,[31] *Battle Creek*
Clare E. Hoffman, *Allegan*
Carl E. Mapes, *Grand Rapids*
William W. Blackney, *Flint*
Jesse P. Wolcott, *Port Huron*
Fred L. Crawford, *Saginaw*
Albert J. Engel, *Lake City*
Roy O. Woodruff, *Bay City*
Prentiss M. Brown,[32] *St. Ignace*
Frank E. Hook, *Ironwood*
Clarence J. McLeod, *Detroit*
Louis C. Rabaut, *Detroit*

John D. Dingell, *Detroit*
John Lesinski, *Dearborn*
George A. Dondero, *Royal Oak*

## MINNESOTA

SENATORS

Henrik Shipstead, *Minneapolis*
Thomas D. Schall,[33] *Excelsior*
Elmer A. Benson,[34] *Appleton*
Guy V. Howard,[35] *Minneapolis*

REPRESENTATIVES

August H. Andresen, *Red Wing*
Elmer J. Ryan, *South St. Paul*
Ernest Lundeen, *Minneapolis*
Melvin J. Maas, *St. Paul*
Theodore Christianson, *Minneapolis*
Harold Knutson, *St. Cloud*
Paul J. Kvale, *Benson*
William A. Pittenger, *Duluth*
Richard T. Buckler, *Crookston*

## MISSISSIPPI

SENATORS

Pat Harrison, *Gulfport*
Theodore G. Bilbo, *Poplarville*

REPRESENTATIVES

John E. Rankin, *Tupelo*
Wall Doxey, *Holly Springs*
William M. Whittington, *Greenwood*
Aaron Lane Ford, *Ackerman*
Aubert C. Dunn, *Meridian*
William M. Colmer, *Pascagoula*
Dan R. McGehee, *Meadville*

## MISSOURI

SENATORS

Joel Bennett Clark, *St. Louis*
Harry S Truman, *Independence*

REPRESENTATIVES

Milton A. Romjue, *Macon*
William L. Nelson, *Columbia*
Richard M. Duncan, *St. Joseph*
C. Jasper Bell, *Kansas City*
Joseph B. Shannon, *Kansas City*
Reuben T. Wood, *Springfield*
Dewey Short, *Galena*
Clyde Williams, *Hillsboro*
Clarence Cannon, *Elsberry*
Orville Zimmerman, *Kennett*
Thomas C. Hennings, Jr., *St. Louis*
James R. Clairborne, *St. Louis*
John J. Cochran, *St. Louis*

## MONTANA

SENATORS

Burton K. Wheeler, *Butte*
James E. Murray, *Butte*

REPRESENTATIVES

Joseph P. Monaghan, *Butte*
Roy E. Ayers, *Lewistown*

## NEBRASKA

SENATORS

George W. Norris, *McCook*
Edward R. Burke, *Omaha*

REPRESENTATIVES

Henry C. Luckey, *Lincoln*
Charles F. McLaughlin, *Omaha*
Karl Stefan, *Norfolk*
Charles G. Binderup, *Minden*
Harry B. Coffee, *Chadron*

## NEVADA

SENATORS

Key Pittman, *Tonopah*
Patrick A. McCarran, *Reno*

REPRESENTATIVE AT LARGE

James G. Scrugham, *Reno*

## NEW HAMPSHIRE

SENATORS

Henry W. Keyes, *Haverhill*
Fred H. Brown, *Somersworth*

REPRESENTATIVES

William N. Rogers, *Sanbornville*
Charles W. Tobey, *Temple*

## NEW JERSEY

SENATORS

W. Warren Barbour, *Locust*
A. Harry Moore, *Jersey City*

REPRESENTATIVES

Charles A. Wolverton, *Camden*
Isaac Bacharach, *Atlantic City*
William H. Sutphin, *Matawan*
D. Lane Powers, *Trenton*
Charles A. Eaton, *North Plainfield*
Donald H. McLean, *Elizabeth*
Randolph Perkins,[36] *Woodcliff Lake*
George N. Seger, *Passaic*
Edward A. Kenney, *Cliffside Park*
Fred A. Hartley, Jr., *Kearny*
Peter A. Cavacchia, *Newark*
Frederick R. Lehlbach, *Newark*
Mary T. Norton, *Jersey City*
Edward J. Hart, *Jersery City*

---

[27] Died June 3, 1936; vacancy throughout remainder of the Congress.

[28] Died October 22, 1936; vacancy in this class from October 23, 1936, to November 18, 1936.

[29] Appointed to fill vacancy caused by death of James Couzens, and served from November 19, 1936; was previously elected for term commencing January 3, 1937.

[30] Died October 19, 1935.

[31] Elected to fill vacancy caused by death of Henry M. Kimball, and took his seat January 3, 1936.

[32] Resigned November 18, 1936, having been appointed a Senator; vacancy throughout remainder of the Congress.

[33] Died December 22, 1935.

[34] Appointed to fill vacancy caused by death of Thomas D. Schall, and took his seat January 3, 1936.

[35] Elected to fill vacancy caused by death of Thomas D. Schall, and served from November 4, 1936, to January 3, 1937, but was unable to be sworn in as Congress was not in session.

[36] Died May 25, 1936; vacancy throughout remainder of the Congress.

## NEW MEXICO

### SENATORS

Bronson M. Cutting,[37] *Santa Fe*
Dennis Chavez,[38] *Albuquerque*
Carl A. Hatch, *Clovis*

### REPRESENTATIVE AT LARGE

John J. Dempsey, *Santa Fe*

## NEW YORK

### SENATORS

Royal S. Copeland, *New York City*
Robert F. Wagner, *New York City*

### REPRESENTATIVES AT LARGE

Matthew J. Merritt, *Flushing*
Caroline O'Day, *Rye*

### REPRESENTATIVES

Robert L. Bacon, *Old Westbury*
William F. Brunner,[39] *Rockaway Park*
William B. Barry,[40] *Hollis*
Joseph L. Pfeifer, *Brooklyn*
Thomas H. Cullen, *Brooklyn*
Marcellus H. Evans, *Brooklyn*
Andrew L. Somers, *Brooklyn*
John J. Delaney, *Brooklyn*
Richard J. Tonry, *Brooklyn*
Stephen A. Rudd,[41] *Brooklyn*
Emanuel Celler, *Brooklyn*
James A. O'Leary, *West New Brighton*
Samuel Dickstein, *New York City*
Christopher D. Sullivan, *New York City*
William I. Sirovich, *New York City*
John J. Boylan, *New York City*
John J. O'Connor, *New York City*
Theodore A. Peyser, *New York City*
Martin J. Kennedy, *New York City*
Sol Bloom, *New York City*
Vito Marcantonio,[42] *New York City*
Joseph A. Gavagan, *New York City*
Anthony J. Griffin,[43] *New York City*
Edward W. Curley,[44] *New York City*
Charles A. Buckley, *New York City*
James M. Fitzpatrick, *New York City*
Charles D. Millard, *Tarrytown*
Hamilton Fish, Jr., *Garrison*
Philip A. Goodwin, *Coxsackie*
Parker Corning, *Albany*
William D. Thomas,[45] *Hoosick Falls*
Frank Crowther, *Schenectady*
Bertrand H. Snell, *Potsdam*
Francis D. Culkin, *Oswego*
Fred J. Sisson, *Whitesboro*
Bert Lord, *Afton*
Clarence E. Hancock, *Syracuse*
John Taber, *Auburn*

W. Sterling Cole, *Bath*
James P. B. Duffy, *Rochester*
James W. Wadsworth, Jr., *Geneseo*
Walter G. Andrews, *Buffalo*
Alfred F. Beiter, *Williamsville*
James M. Mead, *Buffalo*
Daniel A. Reed, *Dunkirk*

## NORTH CAROLINA

### SENATORS

Josiah W. Bailey, *Raleigh*
Robert R. Reynolds, *Asheville*

### REPRESENTATIVES

Lindsay C. Warren, *Washington*
John H. Kerr, *Warrenton*
Graham A. Barden, *New Bern*
Harold D. Cooley, *Nashville*
Franklin W. Hancock, Jr., *Oxford*
William B. Umstead, *Durham*
J. Bayard Clark, *Fayetteville*
J. Walter Lambeth, *Thomasville*
Robert L. Doughton, *Laurel Springs*
Alfred L. Bulwinkle, *Gastonia*
Zebulon Weaver, *Asheville*

## NORTH DAKOTA

### SENATORS

Lynn J. Frazier, *Hoople*
Gerald P. Nye, *Cooperstown*

### REPRESENTATIVES AT LARGE

Usher L. Burdick, *Bismarck*
William Lemke, *Fargo*

## OHIO

### SENATORS

Robert J. Bulkley, *Cleveland*
A. Victor Donahey, *Huntsville, R.F.D.*

### REPRESENTATIVES AT LARGE

Charles V. Truax,[46] *Bucyrus*
Daniel S. Earhart,[47] *Columbus*
Stephen M. Young, *Cleveland*

### REPRESENTATIVES

John B. Hollister, *Cincinnati*
William E. Hess, *Cincinnati*
Byron B. Harlan, *Dayton*
Frank L. Kloeb, *Celina*
Frank C. Kniffin, *Napoleon*
James G. Polk, *Highland*
Leroy T. Marshall, *Xenia*
Thomas Brooks Fletcher, *Marion*
Warren J. Duffey,[48] *Toledo*
Thomas A. Jenkins, *Ironton*
Mell G. Underwood,[49] *New Lexington*
Peter F. Hammond,[50] *Lancaster*

Arthur P. Lamneck, *Columbus*
William L. Fiesinger, *Sandusky*
Dow W. Harter, *Akron*
Robert T. Secrest, *Caldwell*
William R. Thom, *Canton*
William A. Ashbrook, *Johnstown*
Lawrence E. Imhoff, *St. Clairsville*
John G. Cooper,[51] *Youngstown*
Martin L. Sweeney, *Cleveland*
Robert Crosser, *Cleveland*
Chester C. Bolton, *Cleveland*

## OKLAHOMA

### SENATORS

J. W. Elmer Thomas, *Medicine Park*
Thomas P. Gore, *Oklahoma City*

### REPRESENTATIVE AT LARGE

Will Rogers, *Oklahoma City*

### REPRESENTATIVES

Wesley E. Disney, *Tulsa*
Jack Nichols, *Eufaula*
Wilburn Cartwright, *McAlester*
P. L. Gassaway, *Coalgate*
Josh Lee, *Norman*
Jed Johnson, *Anadarko*
Sam C. Massingale, *Cordell*
Phil Ferguson, *Woodward*

## OREGON

### SENATORS

Charles L. McNary, *Salem*
Frederick Steiwer, *Portland*

### REPRESENTATIVES

James W. Mott, *Salem*
Walter M. Pierce, *La Grande*
William A. Ekwall, *Portland*

## PENNSYLVANIA

### SENATORS

James J. Davis, *Pittsburgh*
Joseph F. Guffey, *Pittsburgh*

### REPRESENTATIVES

Harry C. Ransley, *Philadelphia*
William H. Wilson, *Philadelphia*
Clare G. Fenerty, *Philadelphia*
J. Burrwood Daly, *Philadelphia*
Frank J. G. Dorsey, *Philadelphia*
Michael J. Stack, *Philadelphia*
George P. Darrow, *Philadelphia*
James Wolfenden, *Upper Darby*
Oliver W. Frey, *Allentown*
J. Roland Kinzer, *Lancaster*
Patrick J. Boland, *Scranton*
C. Murray Turpin, *Kingston*

---

[37] Died May 6, 1935. (See U.S. Senate Election, Expulsion and Censure Cases, 1793-1990, Senate Document 103-33, pp. 355-58.)

[38] Appointed to fill vacancy caused by death of Bronson M. Cutting, and took his seat May 20, 1935; subsequently elected.

[39] Resigned September 27, 1935, having been nominated and elected sheriff of Queens County, N. Y.

[40] Elected to fill vacancy caused by resignation of William F. Brunner, and took his seat January 3, 1936.

[41] Died March 31, 1936; vacancy throughout remainder of the Congress.

[42] Election unsuccessfully contested by James J. Lanzetta.

[43] Died January 13, 1935.

[44] Elected to fill vacancy caused by death of Anthony J. Griffin, and took his seat January 3, 1936.

[45] Died May 17, 1936; vacancy throughout remainder of the Congress.

[46] Died August 9, 1935.

[47] Elected to fill vacancy caused by death of Charles V. Truax, and served from November 3, 1936, to January 3, 1937, but was unable to be sworn in as Congress was not in session.

[48] Died July 7, 1936; vacancy throughout remainder of the Congress.

[49] Resigned effective April 10, 1936, having been appointed a judge of the United States District Court for the Southern District of Ohio on February 12, 1936.

[50] Elected to fill vacancy caused by resignation of Mell G. Underwood, and served from November 3, 1936, to January 3, 1937, but was unable to be sworn in as Congress was not in session.

[51] Election unsuccessfully contested by Locke Miller.

James H. Gildea, *Coaldale*
William E. Richardson, *Reading*
C. Elmer Dietrich, *Tunkhannock*
Robert F. Rich, *Woolrich*
J. William Ditter, *Ambler*
Benjamin K. Focht, *Lewisburg*
Isaac H. Doutrich, *Harrisburg*
D. J. Driscoll, *St. Marys*
Francis E. Walter, *Easton*
Harry L. Haines, *Red Lion*
Don Gingery, *Clearfield*
J. Buell Snyder, *Perryopolis*
Charles I. Faddis, *Waynesburg*
Charles R. Eckert, *Beaver*
Joseph Gray, *Spangler*
William M. Berlin, *Greensburg*
Charles N. Crosby, *Meadville*
J. Twing Brooks, *Sewickley*
James L. Quinn, *Braddock*
Theodore L. Moritz, *Pittsburgh*
Henry Ellenbogen, *Pittsburgh*
Matthew A. Dunn, *Pittsburgh*

## RHODE ISLAND

### SENATORS

Jesse H. Metcalf, *Providence*
Peter G. Gerry, *Warwick*

### REPRESENTATIVES

Francis B. Condon,[52] *Central Falls*
Charles F. Risk,[53] *Saylesville*
John M. O'Connell, *Westerly*

## SOUTH CAROLINA

### SENATORS

Ellison D. Smith, *Lynchburg*
James F. Byrnes, *Spartanburg*

### REPRESENTATIVES

Thomas S. McMillan, *Charleston*
Hampton P. Fulmer, *Orangeburg*
John C. Taylor, *Anderson*
John J. McSwain,[54] *Greenville*
G. Heyward Mahon, Jr.,[55] *Greenville*
James P. Richards, *Lancaster*
Allard H. Gasque, *Florence*

## SOUTH DAKOTA

### SENATORS

Peter Norbeck,[56] *Redfield*
Herbert E. Hitchcock,[57] *Mitchell*
William J. Bulow, *Beresford*

### REPRESENTATIVES

Fred H. Hildebrandt, *Watertown*
Theodore B. Werner, *Rapid City*

## TENNESSEE

### SENATORS

Kenneth D. McKellar, *Memphis*
Nathan L. Bachman, *Chattanooga*

### REPRESENTATIVES

B. Carroll Reece, *Johnson City*
J. Will Taylor, *La Follette*
Sam D. McReynolds, *Chattanooga*
John R. Mitchell, *Cookeville*
Joseph W. Byrns,[58] *Nashville*
Clarence W. Turner, *Waverly*
Herron Pearson, *Jackson*
Jere Cooper, *Dyersburg*
Walter Chandler, *Memphis*

## TEXAS

### SENATORS

Morris Sheppard, *Texarkana*
Tom T. Connally, *Marlin*

### REPRESENTATIVES

Wright Patman, *Texarkana*
Martin Dies, Jr., *Orange*
Morgan G. Sanders, *Canton*
Sam Rayburn, *Bonham*
Hatton W. Sumners, *Dallas*
Luther A. Johnson, *Corsicana*
Nat Patton, *Crockett*
Joe H. Eagle, *Houston*
Joseph J. Mansfield, *Columbus*
James P. Buchanan, *Brenham*
Oliver H. Cross, *Waco*
Fritz G. Lanham, *Fort Worth*
William D. McFarlane, *Graham*
Richard M. Kleberg, *Corpus Christi*
Milton H. West, *Brownsville*
R. Ewing Thomason, *El Paso*
Thomas L. Blanton, *Abilene*
Marvin Jones, *Amarillo*
George H. Mahon, *Colorado*
Maury Maverick, *San Antonio*
Charles L. South, *Coleman*

## UTAH

### SENATORS

William H. King, *Salt Lake City*
Elbert D. Thomas, *Salt Lake City*

### REPRESENTATIVES

Abe Murdock, *Beaver*
J. W. Robinson, *Provo*

## VERMONT

### SENATORS

Warren R. Austin, *Burlington*
Ernest Willard Gibson, *Brattleboro*

REPRESENTATIVE AT LARGE
Charles A. Plumley, *Northfield*

## VIRGINIA

### SENATORS

Carter Glass, *Lynchburg*
Harry Flood Byrd, *Berryville*

### REPRESENTATIVES

Schuyler Otis Bland, *Newport News*
Colgate W. Darden, Jr., *Norfolk*
Andrew J. Montague, *Richmond*
Patrick Henry Drewry, *Petersburg*
Thomas C. Burch, *Martinsville*
Clifton A. Woodrum, *Roanoke*
A. Willis Robertson, *Lexington*
Howard W. Smith, *Alexandria*
John W. Flannagan, Jr., *Bristol*

## WASHINGTON

### SENATORS

Homer T. Bone, *Tacoma*
Lewis B. Schwellenbach, *Neppel*

### REPRESENTATIVES

Marion A. Zioncheck,[59] *Seattle*
Monrad C. Wallgren, *Everett*
Martin F. Smith, *Hoquiam*
Knute Hill, *Prosser*
Samuel B. Hill,[60] *Waterville*
Wesley Lloyd,[61] *Tacoma*

## WEST VIRGINIA

### SENATORS

Matthew M. Neely, *Fairmont*
Rush D. Holt,[62] *Weston*

### REPRESENTATIVES

Robert L. Ramsay, *Follansbee*
Jennings Randolph, *Elkins*
Andrew Edmiston, *Weston*
George W. Johnson, *Parkersburg*
John Kee, *Bluefield*
Joe L. Smith, *Beckley*

## WISCONSIN

### SENATORS

Robert M. La Follette, Jr., *Madison*
F. Ryan Duffy, *Fond du Lac*

### REPRESENTATIVES

Thomas R. Amlie, *Elkhorn*
Harry Sauthoff, *Madison*
Gardner R. Withrow, *La Crosse*
Raymond J. Cannon, *Milwaukee*
Thomas O'Malley, *Milwaukee*
Michael K. Reilly, *Fond du Lac*
Gerald J. Boileau, *Wausau*

---

[52] Resigned January 10, 1935, having been appointed an associate justice of the Supreme Court of the State of Rhode Island.

[53] Elected to fill vacancy caused by the resignation of Francis B. Condon, and took his seat August 19, 1935.

[54] Died August 6, 1936.

[55] Elected to fill vacancy caused by death of John J. McSwain, and served from November 3, 1936, to January 3, 1937, but was unable to be sworn in as Congress was not in session.

[56] Died December 20, 1936.

[57] Appointed to fill vacancy caused by death of Peter Norbeck, and took his seat January 5, 1937.

[58] Died June 4, 1936; vacancy throughout remainder of the Congress.

[59] Died August 7, 1936; vacancy throughout remainder of the Congress.

[60] Resigned effective June 25, 1936, having been appointed a member of the United States Board of Tax Appeals on May 21, 1936; vacancy throughout remain-

der of the Congress.

[61] Died January 10, 1936; vacancy throughout remainder of the Congress.

[62] Elected for the term commencing January 3, 1935, but not having attained the age required by the Constitution, did not take his seat until June 21, 1935. (See U.S. Senate Election, Expulsion and Censure Cases, 1793-1990, Senate Document 103-33, pp. 359-61.)

## WISCONSIN—Continued

### REPRESENTATIVES—CONTINUED

George J. Schneider, *Appleton*
Merlin Hull, *Black River Falls*
Bernard J. Gehrmann, *Mellon, R.F.D.*

## WYOMING

### SENATORS

Robert D. Carey, *Careyhurst*
Joseph C. O'Mahoney, *Cheyenne*

### REPRESENTATIVE AT LARGE

Paul R. Greever, *Cody*

## TERRITORY OF ALASKA

### DELEGATE

Anthony J. Dimond, *Valdez*

## TERRITORY OF HAWAII

### DELEGATE

Samuel W. King,[63] *Honolulu*

## PHILIPPINE ISLANDS[64]

### RESIDENT COMMISSIONERS

Pedro Guevara,[64] *Santa Cruz*
Francisco A. Delgado,[64] *Bulacan*
Quintin Paredes,[65] *Bangued, Abra*

## PUERTO RICO

### RESIDENT COMMISSIONER

Santiago Iglesias, *San Juan*

---

[63] Election unsuccessfully contested by Lincoln L. McCandless.

[64] The terms of office of the Resident Commissioners of the Philippine Islands expired when the new government of the Commonwealth of the Philippine Islands was inaugurated; both served until February 14, 1936, when a selected successor qualified. (See 48 Stat. 456.) This law also reduced from 2 to 1 the number of Resident Commissioners.

[65] Appointed December 21, 1935, to fill the vacancy caused by the expiration of the terms of Pedro Guevara and Francisco A. Delgado, due to the new form of government, and took his seat February 14, 1936.

# 75TH CONGRESS

### JANUARY 3,[1] 1937, TO JANUARY 3, 1939

John N. Garner
Vice President

FIRST SESSION— *January 5,[1] 1937, to August 21, 1937*
SECOND SESSION— *November 15, 1937, to December 21, 1937*
THIRD SESSION— *January 3, 1938, to June 16, 1938*

———

VICE PRESIDENT OF THE UNITED STATES— John N. Garner, of Texas
PRESIDENT PRO TEMPORE OF THE SENATE— Key Pittman, of Nevada
SECRETARY OF THE SENATE— Edwin A. Halsey, of Virginia
SERGEANT AT ARMS OF THE SENATE— Chesley W. Jurney, of Texas

———

SPEAKER OF THE HOUSE OF REPRESENTATIVES— William B. Bankhead,[2] of Alabama
CLERK OF THE HOUSE— South Trimble,[3] of Kentucky
SERGEANT AT ARMS OF THE HOUSE— Kenneth Romney, of Montana
DOORKEEPER OF THE HOUSE— Joseph J. Sinnott, of Virginia
POSTMASTER OF THE HOUSE— Finis E. Scott

William B. Bankhead
Speaker

## ALABAMA

### SENATORS

Hugo L. Black,[4] *Birmingham*
Dixie Bibb Graves,[5] *Montgomery*
Lister Hill,[6] *Montgomery*
John H. Bankhead II, *Jasper*

### REPRESENTATIVES

Frank W. Boykin, *Mobile*
Lister Hill,[7] *Montgomery*
George M. Grant,[8] *Troy*
Henry B. Steagall, *Ozark*
Sam Hobbs, *Selma*
Joe Starnes, *Guntersville*
Pete Jarman, *Livingston*
William B. Bankhead, *Jasper*
John J. Sparkman, *Huntsville*
Luther Patrick, *Birmingham*

## ARIZONA

### SENATORS

Henry F. Ashurst, *Prescott*
Carl Hayden, *Phoenix*

### REPRESENTATIVE AT LARGE

John R. Murdock, *Tempe*

## ARKANSAS

### SENATORS

Joseph T. Robinson,[9] *Little Rock*

John E. Miller,[10] *Searcy*
Hattie W. Caraway, *Jonesboro*

### REPRESENTATIVES

William J. Driver, *Osceola*
John E. Miller,[11] *Searcy*
Claude A. Fuller, *Eureka Springs*
William B. Cravens, *Fort Smith*
David D. Terry, *Little Rock*
John L. McClellan, *Malvern*
Wade H. Kitchens, *Magnolia*

## CALIFORNIA

### SENATORS

Hiram W. Johnson, *San Francisco*
William Gibbs McAdoo,[12] *Los Angeles*
Thomas M. Storke,[13] *Santa Barbara*

### REPRESENTATIVES

Clarence F. Lea, *Santa Rosa*
Harry L. Englebright, *Nevada City*
Frank H. Buck, *Vacaville*
Franck R. Havenner, *San Francisco*
Richard J. Welch, *San Francisco*
Albert E. Carter, *Oakland*
John H. Tolan, *Oakland*
John J. McGrath, *San Mateo*
Bertrand W. Gearhart, *Fresno*
Henry E. Stubbs,[14] *Santa Maria*
Alfred J. Elliott,[15] *Tulare*
John S. McGroarty, *Tujunga*

H. Jerry Voorhis, *San Dimas*
Charles Kramer, *Los Angeles*
Thomas F. Ford, *Los Angeles*
John M. Costello, *Hollywood*
John F. Dockweiler, *Los Angeles*
Charles J. Colden,[16] *San Pedro*
Byron N. Scott, *Long Beach*
Harry R. Sheppard, *Yucaipa*
Edouard V. M. Izac, *San Diego*

## COLORADO

### SENATORS

Alva B. Adams, *Pueblo*
Edwin C. Johnson, *Denver*

### REPRESENTATIVES

Lawrence Lewis, *Denver*
Fred Cummings, *Fort Collins*
John A. Martin, *Pueblo*
Edward T. Taylor, *Glenwood Springs*

## CONNECTICUT

### SENATORS

Augustine Lonergan, *Hartford*
Francis T. Maloney, *Meriden*

### REPRESENTATIVE AT LARGE

William M. Citron, *Middletown*

———

[1] By joint resolution (Pub. Law No. 120, 74th Cong.) the date of assembling the first session of the Seventy-fifth Congress was fixed for January 5, 1937.

[2] Reelected January 5, 1937.

[3] Reelected January 5, 1937.

[4] Resigned August 19, 1937, having been appointed an Associate Justice of the Supreme Court of the United States.

[5] Appointed to fill vacancy caused by resignation of Hugo L. Black, and took her seat August 20, 1937; resigned January 10, 1938.

[6] Appointed to fill vacancy caused by resignations of Hugo L. Black and Dixie Bibb Graves, and took his

seat January 11, 1938; subsequently elected.

[7] Resigned January 11, 1938, having been appointed Senator.

[8] Elected to fill vacancy caused by resignation of Lister Hill, and served from June 14, 1938, to January 3, 1939, but was not sworn in as Congress adjourned shortly after his election.

[9] Died July 14, 1937.

[10] Elected to fill vacancy caused by death of Joseph T. Robinson, and took his seat November 15, 1937; vacancy in this class from July 15, 1937, to November 14, 1937.

[11] Resigned November 14, 1937, having been

elected Senator; vacancy throughout remainder of the Congress.

[12] Resigned November 8, 1938.

[13] Appointed to fill vacancy caused by resignation of William Gibbs McAdoo, and served from November 9, 1938, to January 3, 1939, but was unable to be sworn in as Congress was not in session.

[14] Died February 28, 1937.

[15] Elected to fill vacancy caused by death of Henry E. Stubbs, and took his seat June 7, 1937.

[16] Died April 15, 1938; vacancy throughout remainder of the Congress.

[365]

## CONNECTICUT—Continued

### REPRESENTATIVES
Herman P. Kopplemann, *Hartford*
William J. Fitzgerald, *Norwich*
James A. Shanley, *New Haven*
Alfred N. Phillips, Jr., *Stamford*
J. Joseph Smith, *Waterbury*

## DELAWARE

### SENATORS
John G. Townsend, Jr., *Selbyville*
James H. Hughes, *Dover*

### REPRESENTATIVE AT LARGE
William F. Allen, *Seaford*

## FLORIDA

### SENATORS
Charles O. Andrews, *Orlando*
Claude Pepper, *Tallahasse*

### REPRESENTATIVES
J. Hardin Peterson, *Lakeland*
Robert A. Green, *Starke*
Millard F. Caldwell, *Milton*
J. Mark Wilcox, *West Palm Beach*
Joe Hendricks, *De Land*

## GEORGIA

### SENATORS
Walter F. George, *Vienna*
Richard B. Russell, *Winder*

### REPRESENTATIVES
Hugh Peterson, *Ailey*
Edward E. Cox, *Camilla*
Stephen Pace, *Americus*
Emmett M. Owen, *Griffin*
Robert Ramspeck, *Atlanta*
Carl Vinson, *Milledgeville*
Malcolm C. Tarver, *Dalton*
Braswell D. Deen, *Alma*
B. Frank Whelchel, *Gainesville*
Paul Brown, *Elberton*

## IDAHO

### SENATORS
William E. Borah, *Boise*
James P. Pope, *Boise*

### REPRESENTATIVES
Compton I. White, *Clark Fork*
D. Worth Clark, *Pocatello*

## ILLINOIS

### SENATORS
J. Hamilton Lewis, *Chicago*
William H. Dieterich, *Beardstown*

### REPRESENTATIVES AT LARGE
Edwin V. Champion, *Peoria*
Lewis M. Long, *Sandwich*

### REPRESENTATIVES
Arthur W. Mitchell, *Chicago*
Raymond S. McKeough, *Chicago*
Edward A. Kelly, *Chicago*
Harry P. Beam, *Chicago*
Adolph J. Sabath, *Chicago*
Thomas J. O'Brien, *Chicago*
Leonard W. Schuetz, *Chicago*
Leo Kocialkowski, *Chicago*
James McAndrews, *Chicago*
Ralph E. Church, *Evanston*
Chauncey W. Reed, *West Chicago*
Noah M. Mason, *Oglesby*
Leo E. Allen, *Galena*
Chester C. Thompson, *Rock Island*
Lewis L. Boyer, *Quincy*
Everett M. Dirksen, *Pekin*
Leslie C. Arends, *Melvin*
James A. Meeks, *Danville*
Hugh M. Rigney, *Arthur*
Scott W. Lucas, *Havana*
Frank W. Fries, *Carlinville*
Edwin M. Schaefer, *Belleville*
Laurence F. Arnold, *Newton*
Claude V. Parsons, *Golconda*
Kent E. Keller, *Ava*

## INDIANA

### SENATORS
Frederick Van Nuys, *Indianapolis*
Sherman Minton, *New Albany*

### REPRESENTATIVES
William T. Schulte, *Hammond*
Charles A. Halleck, *Rensselaer*
Samuel B. Pettengill, *South Bend*
James I. Farley, *Auburn*
Glenn Griswold, *Peru*
Virginia E. Jenckes, *Terre Haute*
Arthur H. Greenwood, *Washington*
John W. Boehne, Jr., *Evansville*
Eugene B. Crowe, *Bedford*
Finly H. Gray, *Connersville*
William H. Larrabee, *New Palestine*
Louis Ludlow, *Indianapolis*

## IOWA

### SENATORS
Guy M. Gillette, *Cherokee*
Clyde L. Herring, *Des Moines*

### REPRESENTATIVES
Edward C. Eicher,[17] *Washington*
William S. Jacobsen, *Clinton*
John W. Gwynne, *Waterloo*
Fred Biermann, *Decorah*
Lloyd Thurston, *Osceola*
Cassius C. Dowell, *Des Moines*
Otha D. Wearin, *Hastings*
Fred C. Gilchrist, *Laurens*
Vincent F. Harrington, *Sioux City*

## KANSAS

### SENATORS
Arthur Capper, *Topeka*
George McGill, *Wichita*

### REPRESENTATIVES
William P. Lambertson, *Fairview*
Ulysses S. Guyer, *Kansas City*
Edward W. Patterson, *Pittsburg*
Edward H. Rees, *Emporia*
John M. Houston, *Newton*
Frank Carlson, *Concordia*
Clifford R. Hope, *Garden City*

## KENTUCKY

### SENATORS
Alben W. Barkley, *Paducah*
Marvel M. Logan, *Bowling Green*

### REPRESENTATIVES
Noble J. Gregory, *Mayfield*
Beverly M. Vincent,[18] *Brownsville*
Emmet O'Neal, *Louisville*
Edward W. Creal, *Hodgenville*
Brent Spence, *Fort Thomas*
Virgil M. Chapman, *Paris*
Andrew J. May, *Prestonsburg*
Fred M. Vinson,[19] *Ashland*
Joe B. Bates,[20] *Greenup*
John M. Robsion, *Barbourville*

## LOUISIANA

### SENATORS
John H. Overton, *Alexandria*
Allen J. Ellender, *Houma*

### REPRESENTATIVES
Joachim O. Fernandez, *New Orleans*
Paul H. Maloney, *New Orleans*
Robert L. Mouton, *Lafayette*
Overton Brooks, *Shreveport*
Newt V. Mills, *Mer Rouge*
John K. Griffith, *Slidell*
René L. DeRouen, *Ville Platte*
A. Leonard Allen, *Winnfield*

## MAINE

### SENATORS
Frederick Hale, *Portland*
Wallace H. White, Jr., *Auburn*

### REPRESENTATIVES
James C. Oliver, *South Portland*
Clyde H. Smith, *Skowhegan*
Ralph O. Brewster, *Dexter*

---

[17] Resigned December 2, 1938, having been appointed a commissioner of the Securities and Exchange Commission; vacancy throughout remainder of the Congress.

[18] Elected to fill vacancy caused by death of Representative-elect Glover H. Cary, in preceding Congress, and took his seat March 11, 1937.

[19] Resigned May 12, 1938, having been appointed

an associate justice of the United States Court of Appeals for the District of Columbia.

[20] Elected to fill vacancy caused by resignation of Fred M. Vinson, and took his seat June 9, 1938.

## MARYLAND

### SENATORS

Millard E. Tydings, *Havre de Grace*
George L. Radcliffe, *Baltimore*

### REPRESENTATIVES

T. Alan Goldsborough, *Denton*
William P. Cole, Jr., *Towson*
Vincent L. Palmisano, *Baltimore*
Ambrose J. Kennedy, *Baltimore*
Stephen W. Gambrill,[21] *Laurel*
David J. Lewis, *Cumberland*

## MASSACHUSETTS

### SENATORS

David I. Walsh, *Fitchburg*
Henry Cabot Lodge, Jr., *Beverly*

### REPRESENTATIVES

Allen T. Treadway, *Stockbridge*
Charles R. Clason, *Springfield*
Joseph E. Casey, *Clinton*
Pehr G. Holmes, *Worcester*
Edith Nourse Rogers, *Lowell*
George J. Bates, *Salem*
William P. Connery, Jr.,[22] *Lynn*
Lawrence J. Connery,[23] *Lynn*
Arthur D. Healey, *Somerville*
Robert Luce, *Waltham*
George H. Tinkham, *Boston*
John P. Higgins,[24] *Boston*
Thomas A. Flaherty,[25] *Boston*
John W. McCormack, *Dorchester*
Richard B. Wigglesworth, *Milton*
Joseph W. Martin, Jr., *North Attleboro*
Charles L. Gifford, *Cotuit*

## MICHIGAN

### SENATORS

Arthur H. Vandenberg, *Grand Rapids*
Prentiss M. Brown, *St. Ignace*

### REPRESENTATIVES

George G. Sadowski, *Detroit*
Earl C. Michener, *Adrian*
Paul W. Shafer, *Battle Creek*
Clare E. Hoffman, *Allegan*
Carl E. Mapes, *Grand Rapids*
Andrew J. Transue, *Flint*
Jesse P. Wolcott, *Port Huron*
Fred L. Crawford, *Saginaw*
Albert J. Engel, *Lake City*
Roy O. Woodruff, *Bay City*
John Luecke, *Escanaba*
Frank E. Hook, *Ironwood*
George D. O'Brien, *Detroit*
Louis C. Rabaut, *Detroit*

John D. Dingell, *Detroit*
John Lesinski, *Dearborn*
George A. Dondero, *Royal Oak*

## MINNESOTA

### SENATORS

Henrik Shipstead, *Minneapolis*
Ernest Lundeen, *Minneapolis*

### REPRESENTATIVES

August H. Andresen, *Red Wing*
Elmer J. Ryan, *South St. Paul*
Henry G. Teigan, *Minneapolis*
Melvin J. Maas, *St. Paul*
Dewey W. Johnson, *Minneapolis*
Harold Knutson, *St. Cloud*
Paul J. Kvale, *Benson*
John T. Bernard, *Eveleth*
Richard T. Buckler, *Crookston*

## MISSISSIPPI

### SENATORS

Pat Harrison, *Gulfport*
Theodore G. Bilbo, *Poplarville*

### REPRESENTATIVES

John E. Rankin, *Tupelo*
Wall Doxey, *Holly Springs*
William M. Whittington, *Greenwood*
Aaron Lane Ford, *Ackerman*
Ross A. Collins, *Meridian*
William M. Colmer, *Pascagoula*
Dan R. McGehee, *Meadville*

## MISSOURI

### SENATORS

Joel Bennett Clark, *St. Louis*
Harry S Truman, *Independence*

### REPRESENTATIVES

Milton A. Romjue, *Macon*
William L. Nelson, *Columbia*
Richard M. Duncan, *St. Joseph*
C. Jasper Bell, *Kansas City*
Joseph B. Shannon, *Kansas City*
Reuben T. Wood, *Springfield*
Dewey Short, *Galena*
Clyde Williams, *Hillsboro*
Clarence Cannon, *Elsberry*
Orville Zimmerman, *Kennett*
Thomas C. Hennings, Jr., *St. Louis*
C. Arthur Anderson, *St. Louis*
John J. Cochran, *St. Louis*

## MONTANA

### SENATORS

Burton K. Wheeler, *Butte*
James E. Murray, *Butte*

### REPRESENTATIVES

Jerry J. O'Connell, *Butte*
James F. O'Connor, *Livingston*

## NEBRASKA

### SENATORS

George W. Norris, *McCook*
Edward R. Burke, *Omaha*

### REPRESENTATIVES

Henry C. Luckey, *Lincoln*
Charles F. McLaughlin, *Omaha*
Karl Stefan, *Norfolk*
Charles G. Binderup, *Minden*
Harry B. Coffee, *Chadron*

## NEVADA

### SENATORS

Key Pittman, *Tonopah*
Patrick A. McCarran, *Reno*

### REPRESENTATIVE AT LARGE

James G. Scrugham, *Reno*

## NEW HAMPSHIRE

### SENATORS

Fred H. Brown, *Somersworth*
H. Styles Bridges, *East Concord*

### REPRESENTATIVES

Arthur B. Jenks,[26] *Manchester*
Alphonse Roy,[27] *Manchester*
Charles W. Tobey, *Temple*

## NEW JERSEY

### SENATORS

A. Harry Moore,[28] *Jersey City*
John Milton,[29] *Jersey City*
W. Warren Barbour,[30] *Locust*
William H. Smathers,[31] *Atlantic City*

### REPRESENTATIVES

Charles A. Wolverton, *Camden*
Elmer H. Wene, *Vineland*
William H. Sutphin, *Matawan*
D. Lane Powers, *Trenton*
Charles A. Eaton, *North Plainfield*
Donald H. McLean, *Elizabeth*
J. Parnell Thomas, *Allendale*
George N. Seger, *Passaic*
Edward A. Kenney,[32] *Cliffside Park*
Fred A. Hartley, Jr., *Kearny*
Edward L. O'Neill, *Newark*

---

[21] Died December 19, 1938, before the commencement of the Seventy-sixth Congress, to which he had been reelected; vacancy throughout remainder of the Congress.

[22] Died June 15, 1937.

[23] Elected to fill vacancy caused by death of his brother, William P. Connery, Jr., and took his seat November 15, 1937.

[24] Resigned September 30, 1937, having been appointed chief justice of the Superior Court of Massachusetts.

[25] Elected to fill vacancy caused by resignation of John P. Higgins, and took his seat January 3, 1938.

[26] Served until June 9, 1938; succeeded by Alphonse Roy, who contested his election.

[27] Successfully contested the election of Arthur B. Jenks, and took his seat June 9, 1938.

[28] Resigned January 18, 1938, having been elected Governor of New Jersey.

[29] Appointed to fill vacancy caused by resignation

of A. Harry Moore, and took his seat January 24, 1938.

[30] Elected November 8, 1938, to fill vacancy caused by resignation of A. Harry Moore, and took his seat January 3, 1939.

[31] Elected November 3, 1936, for the term beginning January 3, 1937, but did not qualify until April 15, 1937, serving as a State senator until that time.

[32] Died January 27, 1938; vacancy throughout remainder of the Congress.

## NEW JERSEY— Continued

REPRESENTATIVES—CONTINUED

Frank W. Towey, Jr., *Caldwell*
Mary T. Norton, *Jersey City*
Edward J. Hart, *Jersey City*

## NEW MEXICO

SENATORS

Carl A. Hatch, *Clovis*
Dennis Chavez, *Albuquerque*

REPRESENTATIVE AT LARGE

John J. Dempsey, *Santa Fe*

## NEW YORK

SENATORS

Royal S. Copeland,[33] *New York City*
James M. Mead,[34] *Buffalo*
Robert F. Wagner, *New York City*

REPRESENTATIVES AT LARGE

Matthew J. Merritt, *Flushing*
Caroline O'Day, *Rye*

REPRESENTATIVES

Robert L. Bacon,[35] *Old Westbury*
William B. Barry, *Hollis*
Joseph L. Pfeifer, *Brooklyn*
Thomas H. Cullen, *Brooklyn*
Marcellus H. Evans, *Brooklyn*
Andrew L. Somers, *Brooklyn*
John J. Delaney, *Brooklyn*
Donald L. O'Toole, *Brooklyn*
Eugene J. Keogh, *Brooklyn*
Emanuel Celler, *Brooklyn*
James A. O'Leary, *West New Brighton*
Samuel Dickstein, *New York City*
Christopher D. Sullivan, *New York City*
William I. Sirovich, *New York City*
John J. Boylan,[36] *New York City*
John J. O'Connor, *New York City*
Theodore A. Peyser,[37] *New York City*
Bruce Barton,[38] *New York City*
Martin J. Kennedy, *New York City*
Sol Bloom, *New York City*
James J. Lanzetta, *New York City*
Joseph A. Gavagan, *New York City*
Edward W. Curley, *New York City*
Charles A. Buckley, *New York City*
James M. Fitzpatrick, *New York City*
Charles D. Millard,[39] *Tarrytown*
Ralph A. Gamble,[40] *Larchmont*
Hamilton Fish, Jr., *Garrison*
Philip A. Goodwin,[41] *Coxsackie*

Lewis K. Rockefeller,[42] *Chatham*
William T. Byrne, *Loudonville*
E. Harold Cluett, *Troy*
Frank Crowther, *Schenectady*
Bertrand H. Snell, *Potsdam*
Francis D. Culkin, *Oswego*
Fred J. Douglas, *Utica*
Bert Lord, *Afton*
Clarence E. Hancock, *Syracuse*
John Taber, *Auburn*
W. Sterling Cole, *Bath*
George B. Kelly, *Rochester*
James W. Wadsworth, Jr., *Geneseo*
Walter G. Andrews, *Buffalo*
Alfred F. Beiter, *Williamsville*
James M. Mead,[43] *Buffalo*
Daniel A. Reed, *Dunkirk*

## NORTH CAROLINA

SENATORS

Josiah W. Bailey, *Raleigh*
Robert R. Reynolds, *Asheville*

REPRESENTATIVES

Lindsay C. Warren, *Washington*
John H. Kerr, *Warrenton*
Graham A. Barden, *New Bern*
Harold D. Cooley, *Nashville*
Franklin W. Hancock, Jr., *Oxford*
William B. Umstead, *Durham*
J. Bayard Clark, *Fayetteville*
J. Walter Lambeth, *Thomasville*
Robert L. Doughton, *Laurel Springs*
Alfred L. Bulwinkle, *Gastonia*
Zebulon Weaver, *Asheville*

## NORTH DAKOTA

SENATORS

Lynn J. Frazier, *Hoople*
Gerald P. Nye, *Cooperstown*

REPRESENTATIVES AT LARGE

Usher L. Burdick, *Bismarck*
William Lemke, *Fargo*

## OHIO

SENATORS

Robert J. Bulkley, *Cleveland*
A. Victor Donahey, *Huntsville, R.F.D.*

REPRESENTATIVES AT LARGE

John McSweeney, *Wooster*
Harold G. Mosier, *Cleveland*

REPRESENTATIVES

Joseph A. Dixon, *Cincinnati*
Herbert S. Bigelow, *Cincinnati*
Byron B. Harlan, *Dayton*
Frank L. Kloeb,[44] *Celina*
Walter H. Albaugh,[45] *Troy*
Frank C. Kniffin, *Napoleon*
James G. Polk, *Highland*
Arthur W. Aleshire, *Springfield*
Thomas Brooks Fletcher, *Marion*
John F. Hunter, *Toledo*
Thomas A. Jenkins, *Ironton*
Harold K. Claypool, *Chillicothe*
Arthur P. Lamneck, *Columbus*
Dudley A. White, *Norwalk*
Dow W. Harter, *Akron*
Robert T. Secrest, *Caldwell*
William R. Thom, *Canton*
William A. Ashbrook, *Johnstown*
Lawrence E. Imhoff, *St. Clairsville*
Michael J. Kirwan, *Youngstown*
Martin L. Sweeney, *Cleveland*
Robert Crosser, *Cleveland*
Anthony A. Fleger, *Parma*

## OKLAHOMA

SENATORS

J. W. Elmer Thomas, *Medicine Park*
Josh Lee, *Norman*

REPRESENTATIVE AT LARGE

Will Rogers, *Oklahoma City*

REPRESENTATIVES

Wesley E. Disney, *Tulsa*
Jack Nichols, *Eufaula*
Wilburn Cartwright, *McAlester*
Lyle H. Boren, *Seminole*
Robert P. Hill,[46] *Oklahoma City*
Gomer Smith,[47] *Oklahoma City*
Jed Johnson, *Anadarko*
Sam C. Massingale, *Cordell*
Phil Ferguson, *Woodward*

## OREGON

SENATORS

Charles L. McNary, *Salem*
Frederick Steiwer,[48] *Portland*
Alfred Evan Reames,[49] *Medford*
Alexander G. Berry,[50] *Portland*

REPRESENTATIVES

James W. Mott, *Salem*
Walter M. Pierce, *La Grande*
Nan W. Honeyman, *Portland*

---

[33] Died June 17, 1938.
[34] Elected November 8, 1938, to fill vacancy caused by death of Royal S. Copeland, and took his seat January 3, 1939; vacancy in this class from June 18, 1938, to December 2, 1938.
[35] Died September 12, 1938; vacancy throughout remainder of the Congress.
[36] Died October 5, 1938; vacancy throughout remainder of the Congress.
[37] Died August 8, 1937.
[38] Elected to fill vacancy caused by death of Theodore A. Peyser, and took his seat November 15, 1937.
[39] Resigned September 29, 1937, having been

elected surrogate of Westchester County, N. Y.
[40] Elected to fill vacancy caused by resignation of Charles D. Millard, and took his seat November 15, 1937.
[41] Died June 6, 1937.
[42] Elected to fill vacancy caused by death of Philip A. Goodwin, and took his seat November 15, 1937.
[43] Resigned December 2, 1938, having been elected Senator; vacancy throughout remainder of the Congress.
[44] Resigned August 19, 1937, having been appointed a judge of the United States district court, northern district of Ohio.
[45] Elected to fill vacancy caused by resignation of

Frank L. Kloeb, and served from November 8, 1938, to January 3, 1939, but was unable to be sworn in as Congress was not in session.
[46] Died October 29, 1937.
[47] Elected to fill vacancy caused by death of Robert P. Hill, and took his seat January 3, 1938.
[48] Resigned January 31, 1938.
[49] Appointed to fill vacancy caused by resignation of Frederick Steiwer, and took his seat February 11, 1938.
[50] Elected to fill vacancy caused by resignation of Frederick Steiwer, and served from November 9, 1938, to January 3, 1939, but was unable to be sworn in as Congress was not in session.

## PENNSYLVANIA

### SENATORS

James J. Davis, *Pittsburgh*
Joseph F. Guffey, *Pittsburgh*
J. Burrwood Daly, *Philadelphia*

### REPRESENTATIVES

Leon Sacks, *Philadelphia*
James P. McGranery, *Philadelphia*
Michael J. Bradley, *Philadelphia*
Frank J. G. Dorsey, *Philadelphia*
Michael J. Stack, *Philadelphia*
Ira W. Drew, *Philadelphia*
James Wolfenden, *Upper Darby*
Oliver W. Frey, *Allentown*
J. Roland Kinzer, *Lancaster*
Patrick J. Boland, *Scranton*
J. Harold Flannery, *Pittston*
James H. Gildea, *Coaldale*
Guy L. Moser, *Douglassville*
Albert G. Rutherford, *Honesdale*
Robert F. Rich, *Woolrich*
J. William Ditter, *Ambler*
Benjamin K. Focht,[51] *Lewisburg*
Richard M. Simpson,[52] *Huntingdon*
Guy J. Swope, *Harrisburg*
Benjamin Jarrett, *Farrell*
Francis E. Walter, *Easton*
Harry L. Haines, *Red Lion*
Don Gingery, *Clearfield*
J. Buell Snyder, *Perryopolis*
Charles I. Faddis, *Waynesburg*
Charles R. Eckert, *Beaver*
Joseph Gray, *Spangler*
Robert G. Allen, *Greensburg*
Charles N. Crosby, *Meadville*
Peter J. DeMuth, *Pittsburgh*
James L. Quinn, *Braddock*
Herman P. Eberharter, *Pittsburgh*
Henry Ellenbogen,[53] *Pittsburgh*
Matthew A. Dunn, *Pittsburgh*

## RHODE ISLAND

### SENATORS

Peter G. Gerry, *Warwick*
Theodore F. Green, *Providence*

### REPRESENTATIVES

Aime J. Forand, *Central Falls*
John M. O'Connell, *Westerly*

## SOUTH CAROLINA

### SENATORS

Ellison D. Smith, *Lynchburg*
James F. Byrnes, *Spartanburg*

### REPRESENTATIVES

Thomas S. McMillan, *Charleston*
Hampton P. Fulmer, *Orangeburg*
John C. Taylor, *Anderson*
G. Heyward Mahon, Jr., *Greenville*
James P. Richards, *Lancaster*
Allard H. Gasque,[54] *Florence*
Elizabeth H. Gasque,[55] *Florence*

## SOUTH DAKOTA

### SENATORS

William J. Bulow, *Beresford*
Herbert E. Hitchcock,[56] *Mitchell*
Gladys Pyle,[57] *Huron*

### REPRESENTATIVES

Fred H. Hildebrandt, *Watertown*
Francis H. Case, *Custer*

## TENNESSEE

### SENATORS

Kenneth D. McKellar, *Memphis*
Nathan L. Bachman,[58] *Chattanooga*
George L. Berry,[59] *Pressmen's Home*
A. Tom Stewart,[60] *Winchester*

### REPRESENTATIVES

B. Carroll Reece, *Johnson City*
J. Will Taylor, *La Follette*
Sam D. McReynolds, *Chattanooga*
John R. Mitchell, *Cookeville*
Richard M. Atkinson, *Nashville*
Clarence W. Turner, *Waverly*
Herron C. Pearson, *Jackson*
Jere Cooper, *Dyersburg*
Walter Chandler, *Memphis*

## TEXAS

### SENATORS

Morris Sheppard, *Texarkana*
Tom T. Connally, *Marlin*

### REPRESENTATIVES

Wright Patman, *Texarkana*
Martin Dies, Jr., *Orange*
Morgan G. Sanders, *Canton*
Sam Rayburn, *Bonham*
Hatton W. Sumners, *Dallas*
Luther A. Johnson, *Corsicana*
Nat Patton, *Crockett*
Albert Thomas, *Houston*
Joseph J. Mansfield, *Columbus*
James P. Buchanan,[61] *Brenham*
Lyndon B. Johnson,[62] *Johnson City*
William R. Poage, *Waco*
Fritz G. Lanham, *Fort Worth*
William D. McFarlane, *Graham*

Richard M. Kleberg, *Corpus Christi*
Milton H. West, *Brownsville*
R. Ewing Thomason, *El Paso*
Clyde L. Garrett, *Eastland*
Marvin Jones, *Amarillo*
George H. Mahon, *Colorado*
Maury Maverick, *San Antonio*
Charles L. South, *Coleman*

## UTAH

### SENATORS

William H. King, *Salt Lake City*
Elbert D. Thomas, *Salt Lake City*

### REPRESENTATIVES

Abe Murdock, *Beaver*
J. W. Robinson, *Provo*

## VERMONT

### SENATORS

Warren R. Austin, *Burlington*
Ernest Willard Gibson, *Brattleboro*

### REPRESENTATIVE AT LARGE

Charles A. Plumley, *Northfield*

## VIRGINIA

### SENATORS

Carter Glass, *Lynchburg*
Harry Flood Byrd, *Berryville*

### REPRESENTATIVES

Schuyler Otis Bland, *Newport News*
Norman R. Hamilton, *Portsmouth*
Andrew J. Montague,[63] *Richmond*
Dave E. Satterfield, Jr.,[64] *Richmond*
Patrick Henry Drewry, *Petersburg*
Thomas G. Burch, *Martinsville*
Clifton A. Woodrum, *Roanoke*
A. Willis Robertson, *Lexington*
Howard W. Smith, *Alexandria*
John W. Flannagan, Jr., *Bristol*

## WASHINGTON

### SENATORS

Homer T. Bone, *Tacoma*
Lewis B. Schwellenbach, *Neppel*

### REPRESENTATIVES

Warren G. Magnuson, *Seattle*
Monrad C. Wallgren, *Everett*
Martin F. Smith, *Hoquiam*
Knute Hill, *Prosser*
Charles H. Leavy, *Spokane*
John M. Coffee, *Tacoma*

---

[51] Died March 27, 1937.
[52] Elected to fill vacancy caused by death of Benjamin K. Focht, and took his seat May 24, 1937.
[53] Resigned January 3, 1938, having been elected judge of the common pleas court of Allegheny County, Pa.; vacancy throughout remainder of the Congress.
[54] Died June 17, 1938.
[55] Elected to fill vacancy caused by death of her husband, Allard H. Gasque, and served from September 13, 1938, to January 3, 1939, but was unable to be sworn in as Congress was not in session.
[56] Appointed to fill vacancy caused by death of

Peter Norbeck in preceding Congress.
[57] Elected to fill vacancy caused by death of Peter Norbeck, in preceding Congress, and served from November 9, 1938, to January 3, 1939, but was unable to be sworn in as Congress was not in session.
[58] Died April 23, 1937.
[59] Appointed to fill vacancy caused by death of Nathan L. Bachman, and took his seat May 10, 1937. (See U.S. Senate Election, Expulsion and Censure Cases, 1793-1990, Senate Document 103-33, pp. 362-63.)

[60] Elected November 8, 1938, to fill vacancy caused by death of Nathan L. Bachman, and took his seat January 16, 1939.
[61] Died February 22, 1937.
[62] Elected to fill vacancy caused by death of James B. Buchanan, and took his seat May 13, 1937.
[63] Died January 24, 1937.
[64] Elected to fill vacancy caused by death of Andrew J. Montague, and took his seat November 15, 1937.

## WEST VIRGINIA

### SENATORS

Matthew M. Neely, *Fairmont*
Rush D. Holt, *Weston*

### REPRESENTATIVES

Robert L. Ramsay, *Follansbee*
Jennings Randolph, *Elkins*
Andrew Edmiston, *Weston*
George W. Johnson, *Parkersburg*
John Kee, *Bluefield*
Joe L. Smith, *Beckley*

## WISCONSIN

### SENATORS

Robert M. La Follette, Jr., *Madison*
F. Ryan Duffy, *Fond du Lac*

### REPRESENTATIVES

Thomas R. Amlie, *Elkhorn*
Harry Sauthoff, *Madison*

Gardner R. Withrow, *La Crosse*
Raymond J. Cannon, *Milwaukee*
Thomas O'Malley, *Milwaukee*
Michael K. Reilly, *Fond du Lac*
Gerald J. Boileau, *Wausau*
George J. Schneider, *Appleton*
Merlin Hull, *Black River Falls*
Bernard J. Gehrmann, *Mellon, R.F.D.*

## WYOMING

### SENATORS

Joseph C. O'Mahoney, *Cheyenne*
H. H. Schwartz, *Casper*

### REPRESENTATIVE AT LARGE

Paul R. Greever, *Cody*

## TERRITORY OF ALASKA

### DELEGATE

Anthony J. Dimond, *Valdez*

## TERRITORY OF HAWAII

### DELEGATE

Samuel W. King, *Honolulu*

## COMMONWEALTH OF THE PHILLIPPINES

### RESIDENT COMMISSIONER

Quintin Paredes,[65] *Bangued Abra*
Joaquin M. Elizalde,[66] *Manila*

## PUERTO RICO

### RESIDENT COMMISSIONER

Santiago Iglesias, *San Juan*

---

[65] Resigned September 29, 1938.
[66] Appointed September 29, 1938, to fill vacancy

caused by resignation of Quintin Paredes, and took his seat January 3, 1939, upon the convening of the

Seventy-sixth Congress.

# 76TH CONGRESS

### JANUARY 3, 1939, TO JANUARY 3, 1941

FIRST SESSION— *January 3, 1939, to August 5, 1939*
SECOND SESSION— *September 21, 1939, to November 3, 1939*
THIRD SESSION— *January 3, 1940, to January 3, 1941*

———

VICE PRESIDENT OF THE UNITED STATES— JOHN N. GARNER, of Texas
PRESIDENT PRO TEMPORE OF THE SENATE— KEY PITTMAN,[1] of Nevada; WILLIAM H. KING,[2] of Utah
SECRETARY OF THE SENATE— EDWIN A. HALSEY, of Virginia
SERGEANT AT ARMS OF THE SENATE— CHESLEY W. JURNEY, of Texas

———

SPEAKER OF THE HOUSE OF REPRESENTATIVES— WILLIAM B. BANKHEAD,[3] of Alabama; SAM RAYBURN,[4] of Texas
CLERK OF THE HOUSE— SOUTH TRIMBLE,[5] of Kentucky
SERGEANT AT ARMS OF THE HOUSE— KENNETH ROMNEY, of Montana
DOORKEEPER OF THE HOUSE— JOSEPH J. SINNOTT, of Virginia
POSTMASTER OF THE HOUSE— FINIS E. SCOTT

John N. Garner
Vice President

William B. Bankhead
Speaker

## ALABAMA

### SENATORS
John H. Bankhead II, *Jasper*
Lister Hill, *Montgomery*

### REPRESENTATIVES
Frank W. Boykin, *Mobile*
George M. Grant, *Troy*
Henry B. Steagall, *Ozark*
Sam Hobbs, *Selma*
Joe Starnes, *Guntersville*
Pete Jarman, *Livingston*
William B. Bankhead,[6] *Jasper*
Zadoc L. Weatherford,[7] *Red Bay*
John J. Sparkman, *Huntsville*
Luther Patrick, *Birmingham*

## ARIZONA

### SENATORS
Henry F. Ashurst, *Prescott*
Carl Hayden, *Phoenix*

### REPRESENTATIVE AT LARGE
John R. Murdock, *Tempe*

## ARKANSAS

### SENATORS
Hattie W. Caraway, *Jonesboro*
John E. Miller, *Searcy*

### REPRESENTATIVES
E. C. Gathings, *West Memphis*
Wilbur D. Mills, *Kensett*
Clyde T. Ellis, *Bentonville*
William B. Cravens,[8] *Fort Smith*

Fadjo Cravens,[9] *Fort Smith*
David D. Terry, *Little Rock*
William F. Norrell, *Monticello*
Wade H. Kitchens, *Magnolia*

## CALIFORNIA

### SENATORS
Hiram W. Johnson, *San Francisco*
Sheridan Downey, *Atherton*

### REPRESENTATIVES
Clarence F. Lea, *Santa Rosa*
Harry L. Englebright, *Nevada City*
Frank H. Buck, *Vacaville*
Franck R. Havenner, *San Francisco*
Richard J. Welch, *San Francisco*
Albert E. Carter, *Oakland*
John H. Tolan, *Oakland*
John Z. Anderson, *San Juan Bautista*
Bertrand W. Gearhart, *Fresno*
Alfred J. Elliott, *Tulare*
Carl Hinshaw, *Pasadena*
H. Jerry Voorhis, *San Dimas*
Charles Kramer, *Los Angeles*
Thomas F. Ford, *Los Angeles*
John M. Costello, *Hollywood*
Leland M. Ford, *Santa Monica*
Lee E. Geyer, *Gardena*
Thomas M. Eaton,[10] *Long Beach*
Harry R. Sheppard, *Yucaipa*
Edouard V. M. Izac, *San Diego*

## COLORADO

### SENATORS
Alva B. Adams, *Pueblo*
Edwin C. Johnson, *Denver*

### REPRESENTATIVES
Lawrence Lewis, *Denver*
Fred Cummings, *Fort Collins*
John A. Martin,[11] *Pueblo*
William E. Burney,[12] *Pueblo*
Edward T. Taylor, *Glenwood Springs*

## CONNECTICUT

### SENATORS
Francis T. Maloney, *Meriden*
John A. Danaher, *Hartford*

### REPRESENTATIVE AT LARGE
Boleslaus J. Monkiewicz, *New Britain*

### REPRESENTATIVES
William J. Miller, *Wethersfield*
Thomas R. Ball, *Old Lyme*
James A. Shanley, *New Haven*
Albert E. Austin, *Old Greenwich*
J. Joseph Smith, *Waterbury*

## DELAWARE

### SENATORS
John G. Townsend, Jr., *Selbyville*
James H. Hughes, *Dover*

### REPRESENTATIVE AT LARGE
George S. Williams, *Millsboro*

---

[1] Died November 10, 1940.
[2] Elected November 19, 1940.
[3] Reelected January 3, 1939; died September 15, 1940.
[4] Elected September 16, 1940.
[5] Reelected January 3, 1939.
[6] Died September 15, 1940.

[7] Elected to fill vacancy caused by death of William B. Bankhead, and took his seat November 11, 1940.
[8] Died January 13, 1939.
[9] Elected to fill vacancy caused by death of his father, William B. Cravens, and took his seat September 21, 1939.

[10] Died September 16, 1939; vacancy throughout remainder of the Congress; election unsuccessfully contested by Byron N. Scott.
[11] Died December 23, 1939.
[12] Elected to fill vacancy caused by death of John A. Martin, and took his seat November 28, 1940.

## FLORIDA

SENATORS

Charles O. Andrews, *Orlando*
Claude Pepper, *Tallahassee*

REPRESENTATIVES

J. Hardin Peterson, *Lakeland*
Robert A. Green, *Starke*
Millard F. Caldwell, *Milton*
Arthur P. Cannon, *Miami*
Joe Hendricks, *De Land*

## GEORGIA

SENATORS

Walter F. George, *Vienna*
Richard B. Russell, *Winder*

REPRESENTATIVES

Hugh Peterson, *Ailey*
Edward E. Cox, *Camilla*
Stephen Pace, *Americus*
Emmett M. Owen,[13] *Griffin*
A. Sidney Camp,[14] *Newnan*
Robert Ramspeck, *Atlanta*
Carl Vinson, *Milledgeville*
Malcolm C. Tarver, *Dalton*
W. Benjamin Gibbs,[15] *Jesup*
Florence R. Gibbs,[16] *Jesup*
B. Frank Whelchel, *Gainesville*
Paul Brown, *Elberton*

## IDAHO

SENATORS

William E. Borah,[17] *Boise*
John Thomas,[18] *Gooding*
D. Worth Clark, *Pocatello*

REPRESENTATIVES

Compton I. White, *Clark Fork*
Henry C. Dworshak, *Burley*

## ILLINOIS

SENATORS

J. Hamilton Lewis,[19] *Chicago*
James M. Slattery,[20] *Chicago*
C. Wayland Brooks,[21] *Chicago*
Scott W. Lucas, *Havana*

REPRESENTATIVES AT LARGE

John C. Martin, *Salem*
Thomas V. Smith, *Chicago*

REPRESENTATIVES

Arthur W. Mitchell, *Chicago*
Raymond S. McKeough, *Chicago*
Edward A. Kelly, *Chicago*
Harry P. Beam, *Chicago*
Adolph J. Sabath, *Chicago*
Anton F. Maciejewski, *Cicero*

Leonard W. Schuetz, *Chicago*
Leo Kocialkowski, *Chicago*
James McAndrews, *Chicago*
Ralph E. Church, *Evanston*
Chauncey W. Reed, *West Chicago*
Noah M. Mason, *Oglesby*
Leo E. Allen, *Galena*
Anton J. Johnson, *Macomb*
Robert B. Chiperfield, *Canton*
Everett M. Dirksen, *Pekin*
Leslie C. Arends, *Melvin*
Jessie Sumner, *Milford*
William H. Wheat, *Rantoul*
James M. Barnes, *Jacksonville*
Frank W. Fries, *Carlinville*
Edwin M. Schaefer, *Belleville*
Laurence F. Arnold, *Newton*
Claude V. Parsons, *Golconda*
Kent E. Keller, *Ava*

## INDIANA

SENATORS

Frederick Van Nuys, *Indianapolis*
Sherman Minton, *New Albany*

REPRESENTATIVES

William T. Schulte, *Hammond*
Charles A. Halleck, *Rensselaer*
Robert A. Grant, *South Bend*
George W. Gillie, *Fort Wayne*
Forest A. Harness, *Kokomo*
Noble J. Johnson, *Terre Haute*
Gerald W. Landis, *Linton*
John W. Boehne, Jr., *Evansville*
Eugene B. Crowe, *Bedford*
Raymond S. Springer, *Connersville*
William H. Larrabee, *New Palestine*
Louis Ludlow, *Indianapolis*

## IOWA

SENATORS

Guy M. Gillette, *Cherokee*
Clyde L. Herring, *Des Moines*

REPRESENTATIVES

Thomas E. Martin, *Iowa City*
William S. Jacobsen, *Clinton*
John W. Gwynne, *Waterloo*
Henry O. Talle, *Decorah*
Karl M. LeCompte, *Corydon*
Cassius C. Dowell,[22] *Des Moines*
Robert K. Goodwin,[23] *Redfield*
Ben F. Jensen, *Exira*
Fred C. Gilchrist, *Laurens*
Vincent F. Harrington,[24] *Sioux City*

## KANSAS

SENATORS

Arthur Capper, *Topeka*
Clyde M. Reed, *Parsons*

REPRESENTATIVES

William P. Lambertson, *Fairview*
Ulysses S. Guyer, *Kansas City*
Thomas D. Winter, *Girard*
Edward H. Rees, *Emporia*
John M. Houston, *Newton*
Frank Carlson, *Concordia*
Clifford R. Hope, *Garden City*

## KENTUCKY

SENATORS

Alben W. Barkley, *Paducah*
Marvel M. Logan,[25] *Bowling Green*
Albert B. Chandler,[26] *Versailles*

REPRESENTATIVES

Noble J. Gregory, *Mayfield*
Beverly M. Vincent, *Brownsville*
Emmet O'Neal, *Louisville*
Edward W. Creal, *Hodgenville*
Brent Spence, *Fort Thomas*
Virgil M. Chapman, *Paris*
Andrew J. May, *Prestonsburg*
Joe B. Bates, *Greenup*
John M. Robsion, *Barbourville*

## LOUISIANA

SENATORS

John H. Overton, *Alexandria*
Allen J. Ellender, *Houma*

REPRESENTATIVES

Joachim O. Fernandez, *New Orleans*
Paul H. Maloney,[27] *New Orleans*
Robert L. Mouton, *Lafayette*
Overton Brooks, *Shreveport*
Newt V. Mills, *Monroe*
John K. Griffith, *Slidell*
René L. DeRouen, *Ville Platte*
A. Leonard Allen, *Winnfield*

## MAINE

SENATORS

Frederick Hale, *Portland*
Wallace H. White, Jr., *Auburn*

REPRESENTATIVES

James C. Oliver, *South Portland*
Clyde H. Smith,[28] *Skowhegan*
Margaret Chase Smith,[29] *Skowhegan*
Ralph O. Brewster, *Dexter*

---

[13] Died June 21, 1939.
[14] Elected to fill vacancy caused by death of Emmett M. Owen, and took his seat August 5, 1939.
[15] Died August 7, 1940.
[16] Elected to fill vacancy caused by death of her husband, W. Benjamin Gibbs, and took her seat October 3, 1940.
[17] Died January 19, 1940.
[18] Appointed to fill vacancy caused by death of William E. Borah, and took his seat February 6, 1940; subsequently elected.

[19] Died April 9, 1939.
[20] Appointed to fill vacancy caused by death of J. Hamilton Lewis, and took his seat April 24, 1939.
[21] Elected November 5, 1940, to fill vacancy caused by death of J. Hamilton Lewis, and took his seat November 22, 1940.
[22] Died February 4, 1940.
[23] Elected to fill vacancy caused by death of Cassius C. Dowell, and took his seat March 12, 1940.
[24] Election unsuccessfully contested by Albert F. Swanson.

[25] Died October 3, 1939.
[26] Appointed to fill vacancy caused by death of Marvel M. Logan, and took his seat October 10, 1939; subsequently elected.
[27] Resigned December 15, 1940; vacancy throughout remainder of the Congress.
[28] Died April 8, 1940.
[29] Elected to fill vacancy caused by death of her husband, Clyde H. Smith, and took her seat June 10, 1940.

## MARYLAND

### SENATORS

Millard E. Tydings, *Havre de Grace*
George L. Radcliffe, *Baltimore*

### REPRESENTATIVES

T. Alan Goldsborough,[30] *Denton*
David J. Ward,[31] *Salisbury*
William P. Cole, Jr., *Towson*
Thomas D'Alesandro, Jr., *Baltimore*
Ambrose J. Kennedy, *Baltimore*
Lansdale G. Sasscer,[32] *Upper Marlboro*
William D. Byron, *Williamsport*

## MASSACHUSETTS

### SENATORS

David I. Walsh, *Fitchburg*
Henry Cabot Lodge, Jr., *Beverly*

### REPRESENTATIVES

Allen T. Treadway, *Stockbridge*
Charles R. Clason, *Springfield*
Joseph E. Casey, *Clinton*
Pehr G. Holmes, *Worcester*
Edith Nourse Rogers, *Lowell*
George J. Bates, *Salem*
Lawrence J. Connery, *Lynn*
Arthur D. Healey, *Somerville*
Robert Luce, *Waltham*
George H. Tinkham, *Boston*
Thomas A. Flaherty, *Boston*
John W. McCormack, *Dorchester*
Richard B. Wigglesworth, *Milton*
Joseph W. Martin, Jr., *North Attleboro*
Charles L. Gifford, *Cotuit*

## MICHIGAN

### SENATORS

Arthur H. Vandenberg, *Grand Rapids*
Prentiss M. Brown, *St. Ignace*

### REPRESENTATIVES

Rudolph G. Tenerowicz, *Detroit*
Earl C. Michener, *Adrian*
Paul W. Shafer, *Battle Creek*
Clare E. Hoffman, *Allegan*
Carl E. Mapes,[33] *Grand Rapids*
Bartel J. Jonkman,[34] *Grand Rapids*
William W. Blackney, *Flint*
Jesse P. Wolcott, *Port Huron*
Fred L. Crawford, *Saginaw*
Albert J. Engel, *Muskegon*
Roy O. Woodruff, *Bay City*
Frederick V. Bradley, *Rogers City*
Frank E. Hook, *Ironwood*
Clarence J. McLeod, *Detroit*
Louis C. Rabaut, *Detroit*

John D. Dingell, *Detroit*
John Lesinski, *Dearborn*
George A. Dondero, *Royal Oak*

## MINNESOTA

### SENATORS

Henrik Shipstead, *Minneapolis*
Ernest Lundeen,[35] *Wayzata, R.F.D.*
Joseph H. Ball,[36] *St. Paul*

### REPRESENTATIVES

August H. Andresen, *Red Wing*
Elmer J. Ryan, *South St. Paul*
John G. Alexander, *Minneapolis*
Melvin J. Maas, *St. Paul*
Oscar Youngdahl, *Minneapolis*
Harold Knutson, *St. Cloud*
H. Carl Andersen, *Tyler*
William A. Pittenger, *Duluth*
Richard T. Buckler, *Crookston*

## MISSISSIPPI

### SENATORS

Pat Harrison, *Gulfport*
Theodore G. Bilbo, *Poplarville*

### REPRESENTATIVES

John E. Rankin, *Tupelo*
Wall Doxey, *Holly Springs*
William M. Whittington, *Greenwood*
Aaron Lane Ford, *Ackerman*
Ross A. Collins, *Meridian*
William M. Colmer, *Pascagoula*
Dan R. McGehee, *Meadville*

## MISSOURI

### SENATORS

Joel Bennett Clark, *St. Louis*
Harry S Truman, *Independence*

### REPRESENTATIVES

Milton A. Romjue, *Macon*
William L. Nelson, *Columbia*
Richard M. Duncan, *St. Joseph*
C. Jasper Bell, *Kansas City*
Joseph B. Shannon, *Kansas City*
Reuben T. Wood, *Springfield*
Dewey Short, *Galena*
Clyde Williams, *Hillsboro*
Clarence Cannon, *Elsberry*
Orville Zimmerman, *Kennett*
Thomas C. Hennings, Jr.,[37] *St. Louis*
C. Arthur Anderson, *St. Louis*
John J. Cochran, *St. Louis*

## MONTANA

### SENATORS

Burton K. Wheeler, *Butte*
James E. Murray, *Butte*

### REPRESENTATIVES

Jacob Thorkelson, *Butte*
James F. O'Connor, *Livingston*

## NEBRASKA

### SENATORS

George W. Norris, *McCook*
Edward R. Burke, *Omaha*

### REPRESENTATIVES

George H. Heinke,[38] *Nebraska City*
John Hyde Sweet,[39] *Nebraska City*
Charles F. McLaughlin, *Omaha*
Karl Stefan, *Norfolk*
Carl T. Curtis, *Minden*
Harry B. Coffee, *Chadron*

## NEVADA

### SENATORS

Key Pittman,[40] *Tonopah*
Berkeley L. Bunker,[41] *Las Vegas*
Patrick A. McCarran, *Reno*

### REPRESENTATIVE AT LARGE

James G. Scrugham, *Reno*

## NEW HAMPSHIRE

### SENATORS

H. Styles Bridges, *East Concord*
Charles W. Tobey, *Temple*

### REPRESENTATIVES

Arthur B. Jenks, *Manchester*
Foster Stearns, *Hancock*

## NEW JERSEY

### SENATORS

William H. Smathers, *Atlantic City*
W. Warren Barbour, *Locust*

### REPRESENTATIVES

Charles A. Wolverton, *Camden*
Walter S. Jeffries, *Atlantic City*
William H. Sutphin, *Matawan*
D. Lane Powers, *Trenton*
Charles A. Eaton, *North Plainfield*
Donald H. McLean, *Elizabeth*
J. Parnell Thomas, *Allendale*
George N. Seger,[42] *Passaic*
Frank C. Osmers, Jr., *Haworth*
Fred A. Hartley, Jr., *Kearny*
Albert L. Vreeland, *East Orange*
Robert W. Kean, *Livingston*
Mary T. Norton, *Jersey City*
Edward J. Hart, *Jersey City*

---

[30] Resigned April 5, 1939, having been appointed an associate justice of the District Court of the United States for the District of Columbia.

[31] Elected to fill vacancy caused by resignation of T. Alan Goldsborough, and took his seat June 13, 1939.

[32] Elected to fill vacancy caused by death of Representative-elect Stephen W. Gambrill in preceding Congress, and took his seat February 16, 1939.

[33] Died December 12, 1939.

[34] Elected to fill vacancy caused by death of Carl E. Mapes, and took his seat February 29, 1940.

[35] Died August 31, 1940.

[36] Appointed to fill vacancy caused by death of Ernest Lundeen, and took his seat October 17, 1940.

[37] Resigned December 31, 1940, to become circuit attorney for the city of St. Louis; vacancy throughout remainder of the Congress.

[38] Died January 2, 1940.

[39] Elected to fill vacancy caused by death of George H. Heinke, and took his seat April 17, 1940.

[40] Died November 10, 1940.

[41] Appointed to fill vacancy caused by death of Key Pittman, and took his seat December 12, 1940.

[42] Died August 26, 1940; vacancy throughout remainder of the Congress.

## NEW MEXICO

### SENATORS

Carl A. Hatch, *Clovis*
Dennis Chavez, *Albuquerque*

### REPRESENTATIVE AT LARGE

John J. Dempsey, *Santa Fe*

## NEW YORK

### SENATORS

Robert F. Wagner, *New York City*
James M. Mead, *Buffalo*

### REPRESENTATIVES AT LARGE

Matthew J. Merritt, *Flushing*
Caroline O'Day, *Rye*

### REPRESENTATIVES

Leonard W. Hall, *Oyster Bay*
William B. Barry, *St. Albans*
Joseph L. Pfeifer, *Brooklyn*
Thomas H. Cullen, *Brooklyn*
Marcellus H. Evans, *Brooklyn*
Andrew L. Somers, *Brooklyn*
John J. Delaney, *Brooklyn*
Donald L. O'Toole, *Brooklyn*
Eugene J. Keogh, *Brooklyn*
Emanuel Celler, *Brooklyn*
James A. O'Leary, *West New Brighton*
Samuel Dickstein, *New York City*
Christopher D. Sullivan, *New York City*
William I. Sirovich,[43] *New York City*
M. Michael Edelstein,[44] *New York City*
Michael J. Kennedy, *New York City*
James H. Fay, *New York City*
Bruce Barton, *New York City*
Martin J. Kennedy, *New York City*
Sol Bloom, *New York City*
Vito Marcantonio, *New York City*
Joseph A. Gavagan, *New York City*
Edward W. Curley,[45] *New York City*
Walter A. Lynch,[46] *New York City*
Charles A. Buckley, *New York City*
James M. Fitzpatrick, *New York City*
Ralph A. Gamble, *Larchmont*
Hamilton Fish, Jr., *Garrison*
Lewis K. Rockefeller, *Chatham*
William T. Byrne, *Loudonville*
E. Harold Cluett, *Troy*
Frank Crowther, *Schenectady*
Wallace E. Pierce,[47] *Plattsburgh*
Clarence E. Kilburn,[48] *Malone*
Francis D. Culkin, *Oswego*
Fred J. Douglas, *Utica*
Bert Lord,[49] *Afton*
Edwin Arthur Hall,[50] *Binghamton*
Clarence E. Hancock, *Syracuse*

John Taber, *Auburn*
W. Sterling Cole, *Bath*
Joseph J. O'Brien, *East Rochester*
James W. Wadsworth, Jr., *Geneseo*
Walter G. Andrews, *Buffalo*
J. Francis Harter, *Eggertsville*
Pius L. Schwert, *Buffalo*
Daniel A. Reed, *Dunkirk*

## NORTH CAROLINA

### SENATORS

Josiah W. Bailey, *Raleigh*
Robert R. Reynolds, *Asheville*

### REPRESENTATIVES

Lindsay C. Warren,[51] *Washington*
Herbert C. Bonner,[52] *Washington*
John H. Kerr, *Warrenton*
Graham A. Barden, *New Bern*
Harold D. Cooley, *Nashville*
Alonzo D. Folger, *Mount Airy*
Carl T. Durham, *Chapel Hill*
J. Bayard Clark, *Fayetteville*
William O. Burgin, *Lexington*
Robert L. Doughton, *Laurel Springs*
Alfred L. Bulwinkle, *Gastonia*
Zebulon Weaver, *Asheville*

## NORTH DAKOTA

### SENATORS

Lynn J. Frazier, *Hoople*
Gerald P. Nye, *Cooperstown*

### REPRESENTATIVES AT LARGE

Usher L. Burdick, *Williston*
William Lemke, *Fargo*

## OHIO

### SENATORS

A. Victor Donahey, *Huntsville, R.F.D.*
Robert A. Taft, *Cincinnati*

### REPRESENTATIVES AT LARGE

George H. Bender, *Cleveland Heights*
Lycurgus L. Marshall, *Euclid*

### REPRESENTATIVES

Charles H. Elston, *Newtown, R.F.D.*
William E. Hess, *Cincinnati*
Harry N. Routzohn, *Dayton*
Robert F. Jones, *Lima*
Cliff Clevenger, *Bryan*
James G. Polk,[53] *Highland*
Clarence J. Brown, *Blanchester*
Frederick C. Smith, *Marion*
John F. Hunter, *Toledo*
Thomas A. Jenkins, *Ironton*
Harold K. Claypool, *Chillicothe*
John M. Vorys, *Columbus*

Dudley A. White, *Norwalk*
Dow W. Harter, *Akron*
Robert T. Secrest, *Caldwell*
James Seccombe, *Canton*
William A. Ashbrook,[54] *Johnstown*
J. Harry McGregor,[55] *West Lafayette*
Earl R. Lewis, *St. Clairsville*
Michael J. Kirwan, *Youngstown*
Martin L. Sweeney, *Cleveland*
Robert Crosser, *Cleveland*
Chester C. Bolton,[56] *Lyndhurst*
Frances P. Bolton,[57] *Lyndhurst*

## OKLAHOMA

### SENATORS

J. W. Elmer Thomas, *Medicine Park*
Josh Lee, *Norman*

### REPRESENTATIVE AT LARGE

Will Rogers, *Oklahoma City*

### REPRESENTATIVES

Wesley E. Disney, *Tulsa*
Jack Nichols, *Eufaula*
Wilburn Cartwright, *McAlester*
Lyle H. Boren, *Seminole*
A. S. Mike Monroney, *Oklahoma City*
Jed Johnson, *Anadarko*
Sam C. Massingale, *Cordell*
Phil Ferguson, *Woodward*

## OREGON

### SENATORS

Charles L. McNary, *Salem*
Rufus C. Holman, *Portland*

### REPRESENTATIVES

James W. Mott, *Salem*
Walter M. Pierce, *La Grande*
Homer D. Angell, *Portland*

## PENNSYLVANIA

### SENATORS

James J. Davis, *Pittsburgh*
Joseph F. Guffey, *Pittsburgh*

### REPRESENTATIVES

Leon Sacks, *Philadelphia*
James P. McGranery, *Philadelphia*
Michael J. Bradley, *Philadelphia*
J. Burrwood Daly,[58] *Philadelphia*
John Edward Sheridan,[59] *Philadelphia*
Fred C. Gartner, *Philadelphia*
Francis J. Myers, *Philadelphia*
George P. Darrow, *Philadelphia*

---

[43] Died December 17, 1939.
[44] Elected to fill vacancy caused by death of William I. Sirovich, and took his seat February 14, 1940.
[45] Died January 6, 1940.
[46] Elected to fill vacancy caused by death of Edward W. Curley, and took his seat March 4, 1940.
[47] Died January 3, 1940.
[48] Elected to fill vacancy caused by death of Wallace E. Pierce, and took his seat February 21, 1940.

[49] Died May 24, 1939.
[50] Elected to fill vacancy caused by death of Bert Lord, and took his seat January 3, 1940.
[51] Resigned October 31, 1940, having been appointed Comptroller General of the United States.
[52] Elected to fill vacancy caused by resignation of Lindsay C. Warren; took his seat November 11, 1940.
[53] Election unsuccessfully contested by Emory F. Smith.
[54] Died January 1, 1940.

[55] Elected to vacancy caused by death of William A. Ashbrook, and took his seat March 5, 1940.
[56] Died October 29, 1939.
[57] Elected to fill vacancy caused by death of her husband, Chester C. Bolton, and took her seat March 5, 1940.
[58] Died March 12, 1939.
[59] Elected to fill the vacancy caused by the death of J. Burrwood Daly, and took his seat January 3, 1940.

James Wolfenden, *Upper Darby*
Charles L. Gerlach, *Allentown*
J. Roland Kinzer, *Lancaster*
Patrick J. Boland, *Scranton*
J. Harold Flannery, *Pittston*
Ivor D. Fenton, *Mahanoy City*
Guy L. Moser, *Douglassville*
Albert G. Rutherford, *Honesdale*
Robert F. Rich, *Woolrich*
J. William Ditter, *Ambler*
Richard M. Simpson, *Huntingdon*
John C. Kunkel, *Harrisburg*
Benjamin Jarrett, *Farrell*
Francis E. Walter, *Easton*
Chester H. Gross, *Manchester*
James E. Van Zandt, *Altoona*
J. Buell Snyder, *Perryopolis*
Charles I. Faddis, *Waynesburg*
Louis E. Graham, *Beaver*
Harve Tibbott, *Ebensburg*
Robert G. Allen, *Greensburg*
Robert L. Rodgers, *Erie*
Robert J. Corbett, *Bellevue*
John McDowell, *Wilkinsburg*
Herman P. Eberharter, *Pittsburgh*
Joseph A. McArdle, *Pittsburgh*
Matthew A. Dunn, *Pittsburgh*

## RHODE ISLAND

### SENATORS

Peter G. Gerry, *Warwick*
Theodore F. Green, *Providence*

### REPRESENTATIVES

Charles F. Risk, *Saylesville*
Harry Sandager, *Cranston*

## SOUTH CAROLINA

### SENATORS

Ellison D. Smith, *Lynchburg*
James F. Byrnes, *Spartanburg*

### REPRESENTATIVES

Thomas S. McMillan,[60] *Charleston*
Clara G. McMillan,[61] *Charleston*
Hampton P. Fulmer, *Orangeburg*
Butler B. Hare, *Saluda*
Joseph R. Bryson, *Greenville*
James P. Richards, *Lancaster*
John L. McMillan, *Florence*

## SOUTH DAKOTA

### SENATORS

William J. Bulow, *Beresford*
J. Chandler Gurney, *Yankton*

### REPRESENTATIVES

Karl E. Mundt, *Madison*
Francis H. Case, *Custer*

## TENNESSEE

### SENATORS

Kenneth D. McKellar, *Memphis*
A. Tom Stewart,[62] *Winchester*

### REPRESENTATIVES

B. Carroll Reece, *Johnson City*
J. Will Taylor,[63] *La Follette*
John Jennings, Jr.,[64] *Knoxville*
Sam D. McReynolds,[65] *Chattanooga*
Estes Kefauver,[66] *Chattanooga*
Albert A. Gore, *Carthage*
Joseph W. Byrns, Jr., *Nashville*
Clarence W. Turner,[67] *Waverly*
Wirt Courtney,[68] *Franklin*
Herron Pearson, *Jackson*
Jere Cooper, *Dyersburg*
Walter Chandler,[69] *Memphis*
Clifford Davis,[70] *Memphis*

## TEXAS

### SENATORS

Morris Sheppard, *Texarkana*
Tom T. Connally, *Marlin*

### REPRESENTATIVES

Wright Patman, *Texarkana*
Martin Dies, Jr., *Orange*
Lindley Beckworth, *Gilmer*
Sam Rayburn, *Bonham*
Hatton W. Sumners, *Dallas*
Luther A. Johnson, *Corsicana*
Nat Patton, *Crockett*
Albert Thomas, *Houston*
Joseph J. Mansfield, *Columbus*
Lyndon B. Johnson, *Johnson City*
William R. Poage, *Waco*
Fritz G. Lanham, *Fort Worth*
Ed Gossett, *Wichita Falls*
Richard M. Kleberg, *Corpus Christi*
Milton H. West, *Brownsville*
R. Ewing Thomason, *El Paso*
Clyde L. Garrett, *Eastland*
Marvin Jones,[71] *Amarillo*
George H. Mahon, *Colorado City*
Paul J. Kilday, *San Antonio*

Charles L. South, *Coleman*

## UTAH

### SENATORS

William H. King, *Salt Lake City*
Elbert D. Thomas, *Salt Lake City*

### REPRESENTATIVES

Abe Murdock, *Beaver*
J. W. Robinson, *Provo*

## VERMONT

### SENATORS

Warren R. Austin, *Burlington*
Ernest Willard Gibson,[72] *Brattleboro*
Ernest William Gibson,[73] *Brattleboro*

### REPRESENTATIVE AT LARGE

Charles A. Plumley, *Northfield*

## VIRGINIA

### SENATORS

Carter Glass, *Lynchburg*
Harry Flood Byrd, *Berryville*

### REPRESENTATIVES

Schuyler Otis Bland, *Newport News*
Colgate W. Darden, Jr., *Norfolk*
Dave E. Satterfield, Jr., *Richmond*
Patrick Henry Drewry, *Petersburg*
Thomas G. Burch, *Martinsville*
Clifton A. Woodrum, *Roanoke*
A. Willis Robertson, *Lexington*
Howard W. Smith, *Alexandria*
John W. Flannagan, Jr., *Bristol*

## WASHINGTON

### SENATORS

Homer T. Bone, *Tacoma*
Lewis B. Schwellenbach,[74] *Neppel*
Monrad C. Wallgren,[75] *Everett*

### REPRESENTATIVES

Warren G. Magnuson, *Seattle*
Monrad C. Wallgren,[76] *Everett*
Martin F. Smith, *Hoquiam*
Knute Hill, *Prosser*
Charles H. Leavy, *Veradale*
John M. Coffee, *Tacoma*

## WEST VIRGINIA

### SENATORS

Matthew M. Neely, *Fairmont*
Rush D. Holt, *Weston*

---

[60] Died September 29, 1939.
[61] Elected to fill vacancy caused by death of her husband, Thomas S. McMillan, and took her seat January 3, 1940.
[62] Elected November 8, 1938, to fill vacancy caused by death of Nathan L. Bachman in preceding Congress, but did not qualify until January 16, 1939; vacancy from November 9, 1938, to January 15, 1939. Election unsuccessfully contested by John R. Neal. (See U.S. Senate Election, Expulsion and Censure Cases, 1793-1990, Senate Document 103-33, pp. 364-65.)
[63] Died November 14, 1939.
[64] Elected to fill vacancy caused by death of J. Will Taylor, and took his seat January 8, 1940.

[65] Died July 11, 1939.
[66] Elected to fill vacancy caused by death of Sam D. McReynolds, and took his seat September 21, 1939.
[67] Died March 23, 1939.
[68] Elected to fill vacancy caused by death of Clarence W. Turner, and took his seat May 24, 1939.
[69] Resigned January 2, 1940, to serve as mayor of Memphis, Tenn.
[70] Elected to fill vacancy caused by resignation of Walter Chandler, and took his seat February 21, 1940.
[71] Resigned November 20, 1940, having been appointed judge of the United States Court of Claims; vacancy throughout remainder of the Congress.
[72] Died June 20, 1940.

[73] Appointed to fill vacancy caused by death of his father, Ernest Willard Gibson, and took his seat July 3, 1940.
[74] Resigned December 16, 1940, having been appointed United States district judge for the Eastern District of Washington.
[75] Appointed to fill vacancy caused by resignation of Lewis B. Schwellenbach, and took his seat December 19, 1940.
[76] Resigned December 19, 1940, having been appointed United States Senator; vacancy throughout remainder of the Congress.

## WEST VIRGINIA— Continued
### REPRESENTATIVES
Andrew C. Schiffler, *Wheeling*
Jennings Randolph, *Elkins*
Andrew Edmiston, *Weston*
George W. Johnson, *Parkersburg*
John Kee, *Bluefield*
Joe L. Smith, *Beckley*

## WISCONSIN
### SENATORS
Robert M. La Follette, Jr., *Madison*
Alexander Wiley, *Chippewa Falls*
### REPRESENTATIVES
Stephen Bolles, *Janesville*
Charles Hawks, Jr., *Horicon*
Harry W. Griswold,[77] *West Salem*
John C. Schafer, *Milwaukee*

Lewis D. Thill, *Milwaukee*
Frank B. Keefe, *Oshkosh*
Reid F. Murray, *Waupaca*
Joshua L. Johns, *Appleton*
Merlin Hull, *Black River Falls*
Bernard J. Gehrmann, *Mellon, R.F.D.*

## WYOMING
### SENATORS
Joseph C. O'Mahoney, *Cheyenne*
H. H. Schwartz, *Casper*
### REPRESENTATIVE AT LARGE
Frank O. Horton, *Saddlestring*

## TERRITORY OF ALASKA
### DELEGATE
Anthony J. Dimond, *Valdez*

## TERRITORY OF HAWAII
### DELEGATE
Samuel W. King, *Honolulu*

## COMMONWEALTH OF THE PHILIPPINES
### RESIDENT COMMISSIONER
Joaquin M. Elizalde, *Manila*

## PUERTO RICO
### RESIDENT COMMISSIONER
Santiago Iglesias,[78] *San Juan*
Bolívar Pagán,[79] *San Juan*

---

[77] Died July 4, 1939; vacancy throughout remainder of the Congress.

[78] Died December 5, 1939.
[79] Appointed December 26, 1939, to fill vacancy

caused by death of Santiago Iglesias, and took his seat January 3, 1940.

# 77TH CONGRESS

## JANUARY 3, 1941, TO JANUARY 3, 1943

FIRST SESSION— *January 3, 1941, to January 2, 1942*
SECOND SESSION— *January 5,[1] 1942, to December 16, 1942*

VICE PRESIDENT[2] OF THE UNITED STATES— John N. Garner,[3] of Texas; Henry A. Wallace,[4] of Iowa
PRESIDENT PRO TEMPORE OF THE SENATE— Pat Harrison,[5] of Mississippi; Carter Glass,[6] of Virginia
SECRETARY OF THE SENATE— Edwin A. Halsey, of Virginia
SERGEANT AT ARMS OF THE SENATE— Chesley W. Jurney, of Texas

SPEAKER OF THE HOUSE OF REPRESENTATIVES— Sam Rayburn,[7] of Texas
CLERK OF THE HOUSE— South Trimble,[8] of Kentucky
SERGEANT AT ARMS OF THE HOUSE— Kenneth Romney, of Montana
DOORKEEPER OF THE HOUSE— Joseph J. Sinnott, of Virginia
POSTMASTER OF THE HOUSE— Finis E. Scott

Henry A. Wallace
Vice President

Sam Rayburn
Speaker

## ALABAMA

### SENATORS
John H. Bankhead II, *Jasper*
Lister Hill, *Montgomery*

### REPRESENTATIVES
Frank W. Boykin, *Mobile*
George M. Grant, *Troy*
Henry B. Steagall, *Ozark*
Sam Hobbs, *Selma*
Joe Starnes, *Guntersville*
Pete Jarman, *Livingston*
Walter W. Bankhead,[9] *Jasper*
Carter Manasco,[10] *Jasper*
John J. Sparkman, *Huntsville*
Luther Patrick, *Birmingham*

## ARIZONA

### SENATORS
Carl Hayden, *Phoenix*
Ernest W. McFarland, *Florence*

### REPRESENTATIVE AT LARGE
John R. Murdock, *Tempe*

## ARKANSAS

### SENATORS
Hattie W. Caraway, *Jonesboro*
John E. Miller,[11] *Searcy*
George Lloyd Spencer,[12] *Hope*

### REPRESENTATIVES
E. C. Gathings, *West Memphis*
Wilbur D. Mills, *Kensett*
Clyde T. Ellis, *Bentonville*
Fadjo Cravens, *Fort Smith*
David D. Terry, *Little Rock*
William F. Norrell, *Monticello*
Oren Harris, *El Dorado*

## CALIFORNIA

### SENATORS
Hiram W. Johnson, *San Francisco*
Sheridan Downey, *Atherton*

### REPRESENTATIVES
Clarence F. Lea, *Santa Rosa*
Harry L. Englebright, *Nevada City*
Frank H. Buck,[13] *Vacaville*
Thomas Rolph, *San Francisco*
Richard J. Welch, *San Francisco*
Albert E. Carter, *Oakland*
John H. Tolan, *Oakland*
John Z. Anderson, *San Juan Bautista*
Bertrand W. Gearhart, *Fresno*
Alfred J. Elliott, *Tulare*
Carl Hinshaw, *Pasadena*
H. Jerry Voorhis, *San Dimas*
Charles Kramer, *Los Angeles*
Thomas F. Ford, *Los Angeles*
John M. Costello, *Hollywood*
Leland M. Ford, *Santa Monica*
Lee E. Geyer,[14] *Gardena*

Cecil R. King,[15] *Los Angeles*
Ward Johnson, *Long Beach*
Harry R. Sheppard, *Yucaipa*
Edouard V. M. Izac, *San Diego*

## COLORADO

### SENATORS
Alva B. Adams,[16] *Pueblo*
Eugene D. Millikin,[17] *Denver*
Edwin C. Johnson, *Denver*

### REPRESENTATIVES
Lawrence Lewis, *Denver*
William S. Hill, *Fort Collins*
J. Edgar Chenoweth, *Trinidad*
Edward T. Taylor,[18] *Glenwood Springs*
Robert F. Rockwell,[19] *Paonia*

## CONNECTICUT

### SENATORS
Francis T. Maloney, *Meriden*
John A. Danaher, *Hartford*

### REPRESENTATIVE AT LARGE
Lucien J. Maciora, *New Britain*

### REPRESENTATIVES
Herman P. Kopplemann, *Hartford*
William J. Fitzgerald, *Norwich*
James A. Shanley, *New Haven*
Le Roy D. Downs, *South Norwalk*
J. Joseph Smith,[20] *Prospect*

---

[1] By joint resolution (Pub. Law 395, 77th Cong., 1st sess.) the date of assembling the second session of the Seventy-seventh Congress was fixed for January 5, 1942.
[2] Pursuant to the twentieth amendment to the Constitution, the term of the Vice President expires or begins, as the case may be, at noon on January 20, and does not run concurrently with the terms of Congress.
[3] Term expired at noon on January 20, 1941.
[4] Term began at noon on January 20, 1941.
[5] Elected January 6, 1941; died June 22, 1941.
[6] Elected July 10, 1941.

[7] Reelected January 3, 1941.
[8] Reelected January 3, 1941.
[9] Resigned February 1, 1941.
[10] Elected to fill vacancy caused by resignation of Walter W. Bankhead, and took his seat July 3, 1941.
[11] Resigned effective March 31, 1941, having been appointed United States district judge for the Western District of Arkansas.
[12] Appointed to fill vacancy caused by resignation of John E. Miller, and took his seat April 2, 1941.
[13] Died September 17, 1942; vacancy throughout remainder of the Congress.

[14] Died October 11, 1941.
[15] Elected to fill vacancy caused by death of Lee E. Geyer, and took his seat October 12, 1942.
[16] Died December 1, 1941.
[17] Appointed to fill vacancy caused by death of Alva B. Adams, and took his seat January 5, 1942; subsequently elected.
[18] Died September 3, 1941.
[19] Elected to fill vacancy caused by death of Edward T. Taylor, and took his seat January 5, 1941.
[20] Resigned November 4, 1942.

## CONNECTICUT—Continued

REPRESENTATIVES—CONTINUED

Joseph E. Talbot,[21] *Naugatuck*

## DELAWARE

SENATORS

James H. Hughes, *Dover*
James M. Tunnell, *Georgetown*

REPRESENTATIVE AT LARGE

Philip A. Traynor, *Wilmington*

## FLORIDA

SENATORS

Charles O. Andrews, *Orlando*
Claude Pepper, *Tallahassee*

REPRESENTATIVES

J. Hardin Peterson, *Lakeland*
Robert A. Green, *Starke*
Robert L. F. Sikes, *Crestview*
Arthur P. Cannon, *Miami*
Joe Hendricks, *De Land*

## GEORGIA

SENATORS

Walter F. George, *Vienna*
Richard B. Russell, *Winder*

REPRESENTATIVES

Hugh Peterson, *Ailey*
Edward E. Cox, *Camilla*
Stephen Pace, *Americus*
A. Sidney Camp, *Newnan*
Robert Ramspeck, *Atlanta*
Carl Vinson, *Milledgeville*
Malcolm C. Tarver, *Dalton*
John S. Gibson, *Douglas*
B. Frank Whelchel, *Gainesville*
Paul Brown, *Elberton*

## IDAHO

SENATORS

D. Worth Clark, *Pocatello*
John Thomas, *Gooding*

REPRESENTATIVES

Compton I. White, *Clark Fork*
Henry C. Dworshak, *Burley*

## ILLINOIS

SENATORS

Scott W. Lucas, *Havana*
C. Wayland Brooks, *Chicago*

REPRESENTATIVES AT LARGE

Stephen A. Day, *Evanston*
William G. Stratton, *Morris*

REPRESENTATIVES

Arthur W. Mitchell, *Chicago*
Raymond S. McKeough, *Chicago*
Edward A. Kelly, *Chicago*

---

Harry P. Beam,[22] *Chicago*
Adolph J. Sabath, *Chicago*
Anton F. Maciejewski,[23] *Cicero*
Leonard W. Schuetz, *Chicago*
Leo Kocialkowski, *Chicago*
Charles S. Dewey, *Chicago*
George A. Paddock, *Evanston*
Chauncey W. Reed, *West Chicago*
Noah M. Mason, *Oglesby*
Leo E. Allen, *Galena*
Anton J. Johnson, *Macomb*
Robert B. Chiperfield, *Canton*
Everett M. Dirksen, *Pekin*
Leslie C. Arends, *Melvin*
Jessie Sumner, *Milford*
William H. Wheat, *Rantoul*
James M. Barnes, *Jacksonville*
Evan Howell, *Springfield*
Edwin M. Schaefer, *Belleville*
Laurence F. Arnold, *Newton*
James V. Heidinger, *Fairfield*
Cecil W. (Runt) Bishop, *Carterville*

## INDIANA

SENATORS

Frederick Van Nuys, *Indianapolis*
Raymond E. Willis, *Angola*

REPRESENTATIVES

William T. Schulte, *Hammond*
Charles A. Halleck, *Rensselaer*
Robert A. Grant, *South Bend*
George W. Gillie, *Fort Wayne*
Forest A. Harness, *Kokomo*
Noble J. Johnson, *Terre Haute*
Gerald W. Landis, *Linton*
John W. Boehne, Jr., *Evansville*
Earl Wilson, *Huron*
Raymond S. Springer, *Connersville*
William H. Larrabee, *New Palestine*
Louis Ludlow, *Indianapolis*

## IOWA

SENATORS

Guy M. Gillette, *Cherokee*
Clyde L. Herring, *Des Moines*

REPRESENTATIVES

Thomas E. Martin, *Iowa City*
William S. Jacobsen, *Clinton*
John W. Gwynne, *Waterloo*
Henry O. Talle, *Decorah*
Karl M. LeCompte, *Corydon*
Paul Cunningham, *Des Moines*
Ben F. Jensen, *Exira*
Fred C. Gilchrist, *Laurens*
Vincent F. Harrington,[24] *Sioux City*
Harry E. Narey,[25] *Spirit Lake*

---

## KANSAS

SENATORS

Arthur Capper, *Topeka*
Clyde M. Reed, *Parsons*

REPRESENTATIVES

William P. Lambertson, *Fairview*
Ulysses S. Guyer, *Kansas City*
Thomas D. Winter, *Girard*
Edward H. Rees, *Emporia*
John M. Houston, *Wichita, R.F.D.*
Frank Carlson, *Concordia*
Clifford R. Hope, *Garden City*

## KENTUCKY

SENATORS

Alben W. Barkley, *Paducah*
Albert B. Chandler, *Versailles*

REPRESENTATIVES

Noble J. Gregory, *Mayfield*
Beverly M. Vincent, *Brownsville*
Emmet O'Neal, *Louisville*
Edward W. Creal, *Hodgenville*
Brent Spence, *Fort Thomas*
Virgil M. Chapman, *Paris*
Andrew J. May, *Prestonsburg*
Joe B. Bates, *Greenup*
John M. Robsion, *Barbourville*

## LOUISIANA

SENATORS

John H. Overton, *Alexandria*
Allen J. Ellender, *Houma*

REPRESENTATIVES

F. Edward Hébert, *New Orleans*
T. Hale Boggs, *New Orleans*
James Domengeaux, *Lafayette*
Overton Brooks, *Shreveport*
Newt V. Mills, *Monroe*
Jared Y. Sanders, Jr., *Baton Rouge*
Vance Plauché, *Lake Charles*
A. Leonard Allen, *Winnfield*

## MAINE

SENATORS

Wallace H. White, Jr., *Auburn*
Ralph O. Brewster, *Dexter*

REPRESENTATIVES

James C. Oliver, *South Portland*
Margaret Chase Smith, *Skowhegan*
Frank Fellows, *Bangor*

## MARYLAND

SENATORS

Millard E. Tydings, *Havre de Grace*
George L. Radcliffe, *Baltimore*

---

[21] Elected to fill vacancy caused by resignation of J. Joseph Smith, and took his seat February 5, 1942.

[22] Resigned December 6, 1942; vacancy throughout remainder of the Congress.

[23] Resigned December 8, 1942; vacancy throughout remainder of the Congress.

[24] Resigned September 5, 1942.

[25] Elected to fill vacancy caused by resignation of Vincent F. Harrington, and took his seat November 16, 1942.

REPRESENTATIVES
David J. Ward, *Salisbury*
William P. Cole, Jr.,[26] *Towson*
Thomas D'Alesandro, Jr., *Baltimore*
John A. Meyer, *Baltimore*
Lansdale G. Sasscer, *Upper Marlboro*
William D. Byron,[27] *Williamsport*
Katharine E. Byron,[28] *Williamsport*

## MASSACHUSETTS

SENATORS
David I. Walsh, *Fitchburg*
Henry Cabot Lodge, Jr., *Beverly*

REPRESENTATIVES
Allen T. Treadway, *Stockbridge*
Charles R. Clason, *Springfield*
Joseph E. Casey, *Clinton*
Pehr G. Holmes, *Worcester*
Edith Nourse Rogers, *Lowell*
George J. Bates, *Salem*
Lawrence J. Connery,[29] *Lynn*
Thomas J. Lane,[30] *Lawrence*
Arthur D. Healey,[31] *Somerville*
Thomas H. Eliot, *Cambridge*
George H. Tinkham, *Boston*
Thomas A. Flaherty, *Boston*
John W. McCormack, *Boston*
Richard B. Wigglesworth, *Milton*
Joseph W. Martin, Jr., *North Attleboro*
Charles L. Gifford, *Cotuit*

## MICHIGAN

SENATORS
Arthur H. Vandenberg, *Grand Rapids*
Prentiss M. Brown, *St. Ignace*

REPRESENTATIVES
Rudolph G. Tenerowicz, *Detroit*
Earl C. Michner, *Adrian*
Paul W. Shafer, *Battle Creek*
Clare E. Hoffman, *Allegan*
Bartel J. Jonkman, *Grand Rapids*
William W. Blackney, *Flint*
Jesse P. Wolcott, *Port Huron*
Fred L. Crawford, *Saginaw*
Albert J. Engel, *Muskegon*
Roy O. Woodruff, *Bay City*
Frederick V. Bradley, *Rogers City*
Frank E. Hook, *Ironwood*
George D. O'Brien, *Detroit*
Louis C. Rabaut, *Detroit*
John D. Dingell, *Detroit*
John Lensinki, *Dearborn*
George A. Dondero, *Royal Oak*

## MINNESOTA

SENATORS
Henrik Shipstead, *Minneapolis*
Joseph H. Ball,[32] *St. Paul*
Arthur E. Nelson,[33] *St. Paul*

REPRESENTATIVES
August H. Andresen, *Red Wing*
Joseph P. O'Hara, *Glencoe*
Richard P. Gale, *Mound*
Melvin J. Maas, *St. Paul*
Oscar Youngdahl, *Minneapolis*
Harold Knutson, *St. Cloud*
H. Carl Andersen, *Tyler*
William A. Pittenger, *Duluth*
Richard T. Buckler, *Crookston*

## MISSISSIPPI

SENATORS
Pat Harrison,[34] *Gulfport*
James O. Eastland,[35] *Ruleville*
Wall Doxey,[36] *Holly Springs*
Theodore G. Bilbo, *Poplarville*

REPRESENTATIVES
John E. Rankin, *Tupelo*
Wall Doxey,[37] *Holly Springs*
Jamie L. Whitten,[38] *Charleston*
William M. Whittington, *Greenwood*
Aaron Lane Ford, *Ackerman*
Ross A. Collins, *Meridian*
William M. Colmer, *Pascagoula*
Dan R. McGehee, *Meadville*

## MISSOURI

SENATORS
Joel Bennett Clark, *St. Louis*
Harry S Truman, *Independence*

REPRESENTATIVES
Milton A. Romjue, *Macon*
William L. Nelson, *Columbia*
Richard M. Duncan, *St. Joseph*
C. Jasper Bell, *Blue Springs*
Joseph B. Shannon, *Kansas City*
Philip A. Bennett,[39] *Springfield*
Dewey Short, *Galena*
Clyde Williams, *Hillsboro*
Clarence Cannon, *Elsberry*
Orville Zimmerman, *Kennett*
John B. Sullivan, *St. Louis*
Walter C. Ploeser, *St. Louis*
John J. Cochran, *St. Louis*

## MONTANA

SENATORS
Burton K. Wheeler, *Butte*
James E. Murray, *Butte*

REPRESENTATIVES
Jeannette Rankin, *Missoula*
James F. O'Connor, *Livingston*

## NEBRASKA

SENATORS
George W. Norris, *McCook*
Hugh A. Butler, *Omaha*

REPRESENTATIVES
Oren S. Copeland, *Lincoln*
Charles F. McLaughlin, *Omaha*
Karl Stefan, *Norfolk*
Carl T. Curtis, *Minden*
Harry B. Coffee, *Chadron*

## NEVADA

SENATORS
Patrick A. McCarran, *Reno*
Berkeley L. Bunker,[40] *Las Vegas*
James G. Scrugham,[41] *Reno*

REPRESENTATIVE AT LARGE
James G. Scrugham,[42] *Reno*

## NEW HAMPSHIRE

SENATORS
H. Styles Bridges, *Concord*
Charles W. Tobey, *Temple*

REPRESENTATIVES
Arthur B. Jenks, *Manchester*
Foster Stearns, *Hancock*

## NEW JERSEY

SENATORS
William H. Smathers, *Atlantic City*
W. Warren Barbour, *Locust*

REPRESENTATIVES
Charles A. Wolverton, *Camden*
Elmer H. Wene, *Vineland*
William H. Sutphin, *Matawan*
D. Lane Powers, *Trenton*
Charles A. Eaton, *North Plainfield*
Donald H. McLean, *Elizabeth*
J. Parnell Thomas, *Allendale*
Gordon Canfield, *Paterson*
Frank C. Osmers, Jr., *Haworth*
Fred A. Hartley, Jr., *Kearny*
Albert L. Vreeland, *East Orange*

[26] Resigned October 26, 1942; vacancy throughout remainder of the Congress.
[27] Died February 27, 1941.
[28] Elected to fill vacancy caused by death of her husband, William D. Byron, and took her seat June 11, 1941.
[29] Died October 19, 1941.
[30] Elected to fill vacancy caused by death of Lawrence J. Connery, and took his seat January 12, 1942.
[31] Resigned August 3, 1942; vacancy throughout remainder of the Congress.
[32] Appointed in preceding Congress to fill vacancy

caused by death of Ernest Lundeen.
[33] Elected to fill vacancy caused by death of Ernest Lundeen, in preceding Congress, and took his seat November 18, 1942.
[34] Died June 22, 1941.
[35] Appointed to fill vacancy caused by death of Pat Harrison, and took his seat June 30, 1941.
[36] Elected to fill vacancy caused by death of Pat Harrison, and took his seat September 29, 1941.
[37] Resigned September 29, 1941, having been elected Senator.
[38] Elected to fill vacancy caused by resignation of Wall Doxey, and took his seat November 14, 1941.

[39] Died December 7, 1942, before the commencement of the Seventy-eighth Congress, to which he had been reelected; vacancy throughout remainder of the Congress.
[40] Appointed in preceding Congress to fill vacancy caused by death of Key Pittman.
[41] Elected to fill vacancy caused by death of Key Pittman in preceding Congress, and took his seat December 7, 1942.
[42] Resigned December 7, 1942, having been elected Senator; vacancy throughout remainder of the Congress.

## NEW JERSEY—Continued

REPRESENTATIVES—CONTINUED

Robert W. Kean, *Livingston*
Mary T. Norton, *Jersey City*
Edward J. Hart, *Jersey City*

## NEW MEXICO

SENATORS

Carl A. Hatch, *Clovis*
Dennis Chavez, *Albuquerque*

REPRESENTATIVE AT LARGE

Clinton P. Anderson, *Albuquerque*

## NEW YORK

SENATORS

Robert F. Wagner, *New York City*
James M. Mead, *Buffalo*

REPRESENTATIVES AT LARGE

Matthew J. Merritt, *Flushing*
Caroline O'Day, *Rye*

REPRESENTATIVES

Leonard W. Hall, *Oyster Bay*
William B. Barry, *St. Albans*
Joseph L. Pfeifer, *Brooklyn*
Thomas H. Cullen, *Brooklyn*
James J. Heffernan, *Brooklyn*
Andrew L. Somers, *Brooklyn*
John J. Delaney, *Brooklyn*
Donald L. O'Toole, *Brooklyn*
Eugene J. Keogh, *Brooklyn*
Emanuel Celler, *Brooklyn*
James A. O'Leary, *West New Brighton*
Samuel Dickstein, *New York City*
Louis J. Capozzoli, *New York City*
M. Michael Edelstein,[43] *New York City*
Arthur G. Klein,[44] *New York City*
Michael J. Kennedy, *New York City*
William T. Pheiffer, *New York City*
Kenneth F. Simpson,[45] *New York City*
Joseph Clark Baldwin,[46] *New York City*
Martin J. Kennedy, *New York City*
Sol Bloom, *New York City*
Vito Marcantonio, *New York City*
Joseph A. Gavagan, *New York City*
Walter A. Lynch, *New York City*
Charles A. Buckley, *New York City*
James M. Fitzpatrick, *New York City*
Ralph A. Gamble, *Larchmont*
Hamilton Fish, Jr., *Garrison*
Lewis K. Rockefeller, *Chatham*
William T. Byrne, *Loudonville*
E. Harold Cluett, *Troy*
Frank Crowther, *Schenectady*
Clarence E. Kilburn, *Malone*
Francis D. Culkin, *Oswego*

Fred J. Douglas, *Utica*
Edwin Arthur Hall, *Binghamton*
Clarence E. Hancock, *Syracuse*
John Taber, *Auburn*
W. Sterling Cole, *Bath*
Joseph J. O'Brien, *East Rochester*
James W. Wadsworth, Jr., *Geneseo*
Walter G. Andrews, *Buffalo*
Alfred F. Beiter, *Williamsville*
Pius L. Schwert,[47] *Buffalo*
John C. Butler,[48] *Buffalo*
Daniel A. Reed, *Dunkirk*

## NORTH CAROLINA

SENATORS

Josiah W. Bailey, *Raleigh*
Robert R. Reynolds, *Asheville*

REPRESENTATIVES

Herbert C. Bonner, *Washington*
John H. Kerr, *Warrenton*
Graham A. Barden, *New Bern*
Harold D. Cooley, *Nashville*
Alonzo D. Folger,[49] *Mount Airy*
John H. Folger,[50] *Mount Airy*
Carl T. Durham, *Chapel Hill*
J. Bayard Clark, *Fayetteville*
William O. Burgin, *Lexington*
Robert L. Doughton, *Laurel Springs*
Alfred L. Bulwinkle, *Gastonia*
Zebulon Weaver, *Asheville*

## NORTH DAKOTA

SENATORS

Gerald P. Nye, *Cooperstown*
William Langer, *Bismarck*

REPRESENTATIVES AT LARGE

Usher L. Burdick, *Williston*
Charles R. Robertson, *Bismarck*

## OHIO

SENATORS

Robert A. Taft, *Cincinnati*
Harold H. Burton, *Cleveland*

REPRESENTATIVES AT LARGE

George H. Bender, *Cleveland Heights*
Stephen M. Young, *Cleveland*

REPRESENTATIVES

Charles H. Elston, *Newtown, R.F.D.*
William E. Hess, *Cincinnati*
Greg J. Holbrock, *Hamilton*
Robert F. Jones, *Lima*
Cliff Clevenger, *Bryan*
Jacob E. Davis, *Waverly*
Clarence J. Brown, *Blanchester*
Frederick C. Smith, *Marion*
John F. Hunter, *Toledo*
Thomas A. Jenkins, *Ironton*

Harold K. Claypool, *Chillicothe*
John M. Vorys, *Columbus*
Albert D. Baumhart, Jr.,[51] *Vermilion*
Dow W. Harter, *Akron*
Robert T. Secrest,[52] *Caldwell*
William R. Thom, *Canton*
J. Harry McGregor, *West Lafayette*
Lawrence E. Imhoff, *St. Clairsville*
Michael J. Kirwan, *Youngstown*
Martin L. Sweeney, *Cleveland*
Robert Crosser, *Cleveland*
Frances P. Bolton, *Lyndhurst*

## OKLAHOMA

SENATORS

J. W. Elmer Thomas, *Medicine Park*
Josh Lee, *Norman*

REPRESENTATIVE AT LARGE

Will Rogers, *Oklahoma City*

REPRESENTATIVES

Wesley E. Disney, *Tulsa*
Jack Nichols, *Eufaula*
Wilburn Cartwright, *McAlester*
Lyle H. Boren, *Seminole*
A. S. Mike Monroney, *Oklahoma City*
Jed Johnson, *Anadarko*
Sam C. Massingale,[53] *Cordell*
Victor Wickersham,[54] *Mangum*
Ross Rizley, *Guymon*

## OREGON

SENATORS

Charles L. McNary, *Salem*
Rufus C. Holman, *Portland*

REPRESENTATIVES

James W. Mott, *Salem*
Walter M. Pierce, *La Grande*
Homer D. Angell, *Portland*

## PENNSYLVANIA

SENATORS

James J. Davis, *Pittsburgh*
Joseph F. Guffey, *Pittsburgh*

REPRESENTATIVES

Leon Sacks, *Philadelphia*
James P. McGranery, *Philadelphia*
Michael J. Bradley, *Philadelphia*
John Edward Sheridan, *Philadelphia*
Francis R. Smith, *Philadelphia*
Francis J. Myers, *Philadelphia*
Hugh D. Scott, Jr., *Philadelphia*
James Wolfenden, *Upper Darby*
Charles L. Gerlach, *Allentown*
J. Roland Kinzer, *Lancaster*

---

[43] Died June 4, 1941.
[44] Elected to fill vacancy caused by death of M. Michael Edelstein, and took his seat August 7, 1941.
[45] Died January 25, 1941.
[46] Elected to fill vacancy caused by death of Kenneth F. Simpson, and took his seat March 19, 1941.
[47] Died March 11, 1941.

[48] Elected to fill vacancy caused by death of Pius L. Schwert, and took his seat May 5, 1941.
[49] Died April 30, 1941.
[50] Elected to fill vacancy caused by death of his brother, Alonzo D. Folger, and took his seat June 20, 1941.
[51] Resigned September 2, 1942; vacancy through-

out remainder of the Congress.
[52] Resigned August 3, 1942; vacancy throughout remainder of the Congress.
[53] Died January 17, 1941.
[54] Elected to fill vacancy caused by death of Sam C. Massingale, and took his seat April 14, 1941.

Patrick J. Boland,[55] *Scranton*
Veronica G. Boland,[56] *Scranton*
J. Harold Flannery,[57] *Pittston*
Thomas Byron Miller,[58] *Plymouth*
Ivor D. Fenton, *Mahanoy City*
Guy L. Moser, *Douglassville*
Albert G. Rutherford,[59] *Honesdale*
Wilson D. Gillette,[60] *Towanda*
Robert F. Rich, *Woolrich*
J. William Ditter, *Ambler*
Richard M. Simpson, *Huntingdon*
John C. Kunkel, *Harrisburg*
Benjamin Jarrett, *Farrell*
Francis E. Walter, *Easton*
Harry L. Haines, *Red Lion*
James E. Van Zandt, *Altoona*
J. Buell Snyder, *Perryopolis*
Charles I. Faddis,[61] *Waynesburg*
Louis E. Graham, *Beaver*
Harve Tibbott, *Ebensburg*
Augustine B. Kelley, *Greensburg*
Robert L. Rodgers, *Erie*
Thomas E. Scanlon, *Pittsburgh*
Samuel A. Weiss, *Glassport*
Herman P. Eberharter, *Pittsburgh*
Joseph A. McArdle,[62] *Pittsburgh*
Elmer J. Holland,[63] *Pittsburgh*
James A. Wright, *Carnegie*

## RHODE ISLAND

SENATORS

Peter G. Gerry, *Warwick*
Theodore F. Green, *Providence*

REPRESENTATIVES

Aime J. Forand, *Cumberland*
John E. Fogarty, *Harmony*

## SOUTH CAROLINA

SENATORS

Ellison D. Smith, *Lynchburg*
James F. Byrnes,[64] *Spartanburg*
Alva M. Lumpkin,[65] *Columbia*
Roger C. Peace,[66] *Greenville*
Burnet R. Maybank,[67] *Charleston*

REPRESENTATIVES

L. Mendel Rivers, *North Charleston*
Hampton P. Fulmer, *Orangeburg*
Butler B. Hare, *Saluda*
Joseph R. Bryson, *Greenville*
James P. Richards, *Lancaster*
John L. McMillan, *Florence*

## SOUTH DAKOTA

SENATORS

William J. Bulow, *Beresford*
J. Chandler Gurney, *Yankton*

REPRESENTATIVES

Karl E. Mundt, *Madison*
Francis H. Case, *Custer*

## TENNESSEE

SENATORS

Kenneth D. McKellar, *Memphis*
A. Tom Stewart, *Winchester*

REPRESENTATIVES

B. Carroll Reece, *Johnson City*
John Jennings, Jr., *Knoxville*
Estes Kefauver, *Chattanooga*
Albert A. Gore, *Carthage*
J. Percey Priest, *Nashville*
Wirt Courtney, *Franklin*
Herron Pearson, *Jackson*
Jere Cooper, *Dyersburg*
Clifford Davis, *Memphis*

## TEXAS

SENATORS

Morris Sheppard,[68] *Texarkana*
Andrew Jackson Houston,[69] *La Porte*
W. Lee O'Daniel,[70] *Fort Worth*
Tom T. Connally, *Marlin*

REPRESENTATIVES

Wright Patman, *Texarkana*
Martin Dies, Jr., *Orange*
Lindley Beckworth, *Gilmer*
Sam Rayburn, *Bonham*
Hatton W. Sumners, *Dallas*
Luther A. Johnson, *Corsicana*
Nat Patton, *Crockett*
Albert Thomas, *Houston*
Joseph J. Mansfield, *Columbus*
Lyndon B. Johnson, *Johnson City*
William R. Poage, *Waco*
Fritz G. Lanham, *Fort Worth*
Ed Gossett, *Wichita Falls*
Richard M. Kleberg, *Corpus Christi*
Milton H. West, *Brownsville*
R. Ewing Thomason, *El Paso*
Sam M. Russell, *Stephenville*
Eugene Worley, *Shamrock*
George H. Mahon, *Colorado City*
Paul J. Kilday, *San Antonio*
Charles L. South, *Coleman*

## UTAH

SENATORS

Elbert D. Thomas, *Salt Lake City*
Abe Murdock, *Beaver*

REPRESENTATIVES

Walter K. Granger, *Cedar City*
J. W. Robinson, *Provo*

## VERMONT

SENATORS

Warren R. Austin, *Burlington*
George D. Aiken,[71] *Putney*

REPRESENTATIVE AT LARGE

Charles A. Plumley, *Northfield*

## VIRGINIA

SENATORS

Carter Glass, *Lynchburg*
Harry Flood Byrd, *Berryville*

REPRESENTATIVES

Schuyler Otis Bland, *Newport News*
Colgate W. Darden, Jr.,[72] *Norfolk*
Winder R. Harris,[73] *Norfolk*
Dave E. Satterfield, Jr., *Richmond*
Patrick Henry Drewry, *Petersburg*
Thomas G. Burch, *Martinsville*
Clifton A. Woodrum, *Roanoke*
A. Willis Robertson, *Lexington*
Howard W. Smith, *Alexandria*
John W. Flannagan, Jr., *Bristol*

## WASHINGTON

SENATORS

Homer T. Bone, *Tacoma*
Monrad C. Wallgren, *Everett*

REPRESENTATIVES

Warren G. Magnuson, *Seattle*
Henry M. Jackson, *Everett*
Martin F. Smith, *Hoquiam*
Knute Hill, *Prosser*
Charles H. Leavy,[74] *Spokane*
John M. Coffee, *Tacoma*

---

[55] Died May 18, 1942.

[56] Elected to fill vacancy caused by death of her husband, Patrick J. Boland, and took her seat November 19, 1942.

[57] Resigned January 3, 1942.

[58] Elected to fill vacancy caused by resignation of J. Harold Flannery, and took his seat June 15, 1942.

[59] Died August 10, 1941.

[60] Elected to fill vacancy caused by death of Albert G. Rutherford, and took his seat December 4, 1941.

[61] Resigned December 4, 1942; vacancy throughout remainder of the Congress.

[62] Resigned January 5, 1942.

[63] Elected to fill vacancy caused by resignation of

Joseph A. McArdle, and took his seat June 15, 1942.

[64] Resigned July 8, 1941, having been appointed Associate Justice of the United States Supreme Court.

[65] Appointed to fill vacancy caused by resignation of James F. Byrnes, and took his seat July 22, 1941; died August 1, 1941, while serving as an appointee.

[66] Appointed to fill vacancy caused by resignation of James F. Byrnes and death of Alva M. Lumpkin, and took his seat August 6, 1941.

[67] Elected to fill vacancy caused by resignation of James F. Byrnes, and took his seat November 5, 1941.

[68] Died April 9, 1941.

[69] Appointed to fill vacancy caused by death of Morris Sheppard, and took his seat June 2, 1941; died

June 26, 1941, while serving as an appointee.

[70] Elected June 28, 1941, to fill vacancy caused by deaths of Morris Sheppard and Andrew Jackson Houston, but did not qualify until August 4, 1941; vacancy from June 27 to August 3, 1941.

[71] Elected November 5, 1940, to fill vacancy caused by death of Ernest Willard Gibson in preceding Congress, but did not qualify until January 10, 1941; vacancy from January 3 to 9, 1941.

[72] Resigned March 1, 1941.

[73] Elected to fill vacancy caused by resignation of Colgate W. Darden, Jr., and took his seat April 15, 1941.

[74] Resigned August 1, 1942; vacancy throughout remainder of the Congress.

## WEST VIRGINIA

### SENATORS

Matthew M. Neely,[75] *Fairmont*
Joseph Rosier,[76] *Fairmont*
Hugh Ike Shott,[77] *Bluefield*
Harley M. Kilgore, *Beckley*

### REPRESENTATIVES

Robert L. Ramsay, *Follansbee*
Jennings Randolph, *Elkins*
Andrew Edmiston, *Weston*
George W. Johnson, *Parkersburg*
John Kee, *Bluefield*
Joe L. Smith, *Beckley*

## WISCONSIN

### SENATORS

Robert M. La Follette, Jr., *Madison*
Alexander Wiley, *Chippewa Falls*

### REPRESENTATIVES

Stephen Bolles,[78] *Janesville*
Lawrence H. Smith,[79] *Racine*
Harry Sauthoff, *Madison*
William H. Stevenson, *La Crosse*
Thaddeus F. B. Wasielewski,
   *Milwaukee*
Lewis D. Thill, *Milwaukee*
Frank B. Keefe, *Oshkosh*
Reid F. Murray, *Ogdensburg*
Joshua L. Johns, *Appleton*
Merlin Hull, *Black River Falls*
Bernard J. Gehrmann, *Mellon, R.F.D.*

## WYOMING

### SENATORS

Joseph C. O'Mahoney, *Cheyenne*
H. H. Schwartz, *Casper*

### REPRESENTATIVE AT LARGE

John J. McIntyre, *Douglas*

## TERRITORY OF ALASKA

### DELEGATE

Anthony J. Dimond, *Valdez*

## TERRITORY OF HAWAII

### DELEGATE

Samuel W. King, *Honolulu*

## COMMONWEALTH OF THE PHILLIPPINES

### RESIDENT COMMISSIONER

Joaquin M. Elizalde, *Manila*

## PUERTO RICO

### RESIDENT COMMISSIONER

Bolívar Pagán, *San Juan*

---

[75] Resigned January 12, 1941.
[76] The outgoing Governor of West Virginia appointed Clarence E. Martin and the incoming Governor appointed Joseph Rosier to fill the vacancy caused by the resignation of Matthew M. Neely. The Senate decided on May 13, 1941 (S. Res. 106), that Joseph Rosier was entitled to a seat as a Senator from West Virginia, and he took his seat May 14, 1941. (See U.S. Senate Election, Expulsion and Censure Cases, 1793-1990, Senate Document 103-33, pp. 371-73.)

[77] Elected to fill vacancy caused by resignation of Matthew M. Neely and took his seat November 18, 1942.

[78] Died July 8, 1941.

[79] Elected to fill vacancy caused by death of Stephen Bolles, and took his seat September 16, 1941.

# 78TH CONGRESS

## JANUARY 3, 1943, TO JANUARY 3, 1945

FIRST SESSION— *January 6,[1] 1943, to December 21, 1943*
SECOND SESSION— *January 10,[2] 1944, to December 19, 1944*

---

VICE PRESIDENT OF THE UNITED STATES— HENRY A. WALLACE, of Iowa
PRESIDENT PRO TEMPORE OF THE SENATE— CARTER GLASS, of Virginia
SECRETARY OF THE SENATE— EDWIN A. HALSEY, of Virginia
SERGEANT AT ARMS OF THE SENATE— CHESLEY W. JURNEY, of Texas; WALL DOXY,[3] of Mississippi

---

SPEAKER OF THE HOUSE OF REPRESENTATIVES— SAM RAYBURN,[4] of Texas
CLERK OF THE HOUSE— SOUTH TRIMBLE,[5] of Kentucky
SERGEANT AT ARMS OF THE HOUSE— KENNETH ROMNEY, of Montana
DOORKEEPER OF THE HOUSE— JOSEPH J. SINNOTT, of Virginia
POSTMASTER OF THE HOUSE— FINIS E. SCOTT

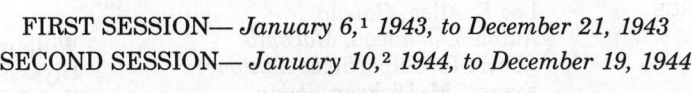

Henry A. Wallace
Vice President

Sam Rayburn
Speaker

## ALABAMA

### SENATORS
John H. Bankhead II, *Jasper*
Lister Hill, *Montgomery*

### REPRESENTATIVES
Frank W. Boykin, *Mobile*
George M. Grant, *Troy*
Henry B. Steagall,[6] *Ozark*
George W. Andrews,[7] *Union Springs*
Sam Hobbs, *Selma*
Joe Starnes, *Guntersville*
Pete Jarman, *Livingston*
Carter Manasco, *Jasper*
John J. Sparkman, *Huntsville*
John P. Newsome, *Birmingham*

## ARIZONA

### SENATORS
Carl Hayden, *Phoenix*
Ernest W. McFarland, *Florence*

### REPRESENTATIVES AT LARGE
Richard F. Harless, *Phoenix*
John R. Murdock, *Tempe*

## ARKANSAS

### SENATORS
Hattie W. Caraway, *Jonesboro*
John L. McClellan, *Camden*

### REPRESENTATIVES
E. C. Gathings, *West Memphis*
Wilbur D. Mills, *Kensett*
J. William Fulbright, *Fayetteville*

Fadjo Cravens, *Fort Smith*
Brooks Hays, *Little Rock*
William F. Norrell, *Monticello*
Oren Harris, *El Dorado*

## CALIFORNIA

### SENATORS
Hiram W. Johnson, *San Francisco*
Sheridan Downey, *Claremont*

### REPRESENTATIVES
Clarence F. Lea, *Santa Rosa*
Harry L. Englebright,[8] *Nevada City*
Clair Engle,[9] *Red Bluff*
Leroy Johnson, *Stockton*
Thomas Rolph, *San Francisco*
Richard J. Welch, *San Francisco*
Albert E. Carter, *Oakland*
John H. Tolan, *Oakland*
John Z. Anderson, *San Juan Bautista*
Bertrand W. Gearhart, *Fresno*
Alfred J. Elliott, *Tulare*
George E. Outland, *Santa Barbara*
H. Jerry Voorhis, *San Dimas*
Norris Poulson, *Los Angeles*
Thomas F. Ford, *Los Angeles*
John M. Costello, *Hollywood*
Will Rogers, Jr.,[10] *Culver City*
Cecil R. King, *Los Angeles*
Ward Johnson, *Long Beach*
Chet Holifield, *Montebello*
Carl Hinshaw, *Pasadena*
Harry R. Sheppard, *Yucaipa*
John Phillips, *Banning*
Edouard V. M. Izac, *San Diego*

## COLORADO

### SENATORS
Edwin C. Johnson, *Craig*
Eugene D. Millikin, *Denver*

### REPRESENTATIVES
Lawrence Lewis,[11] *Denver*
Dean M. Gillespie,[12] *Denver*
William S. Hill, *Fort Collins*
J. Edgar Chenoweth, *Trindad*
Robert F. Rockwell, *Paonia*

## CONNECTICUT

### SENATORS
Francis T. Maloney, *Meriden*
John A. Danaher, *Portland*

### REPRESENTATIVE AT LARGE
Boleslaus J. Monkiewicz, *New Britain*

### REPRESENTATIVES
William J. Miller, *Wethersfield*
John D. McWilliams, *Norwich*
Ranulf Compton, *Madison*
Clare Boothe Luce, *Greenwich*
Joseph E. Talbot, *Naugatuck*

## DELAWARE

### SENATORS
James M. Tunnell, *Georgetown*
C. Douglass Buck, *Wilmington*

### REPRESENTATIVE AT LARGE
Earle D. Willey, *Dover*

---

[1] By joint resolution (Pub. Law 819, 77th Cong., 2d sess.) the date of assembling the first session of the Seventy-eighth Congress was fixed for January 6, 1943.

[2] By joint resolution (Pub. Law 210, 78th Cong., 1st sess.) the date of assembling the second session of the Seventy-eighth Congress was fixed for January 10, 1944.

[3] Elected February 1, 1943.
[4] Reelected January 6, 1943.
[5] Reelected January 6, 1943.
[6] Died November 22, 1943.
[7] Elected to fill vacancy caused by death of Henry B. Steagall, and took his seat March 20, 1944.
[8] Died May 13, 1943.

[9] Elected to fill vacancy caused by death of Harry L. Englebright, and took his seat September 23, 1943.

[10] Resigned May 23, 1944; vacancy throughout remainder of the Congress.

[11] Died December 9, 1943.

[12] Elected to fill vacancy caused by death of Lawrence Lewis, and took his seat March 30, 1944.

## FLORIDA

SENATORS

Charles O. Andrews, *Orlando*
Claude Pepper, *Tallahassee*

REPRESENTATIVE AT LARGE

Robert A. Green,[13] *Starke*

REPRESENTATIVES

J. Hardin Peterson, *Lakeland*
Emory H. Price, *Jacksonville*
Robert L. F. Sikes,[14] *Crestview*
Arthur P. Cannon, *Miami*
Joe Hendricks, *De Land*

## GEORGIA

SENATORS

Walter F. George, *Vienna*
Richard B. Russell, *Winder*

REPRESENTATIVES

Hugh Peterson,[15] *Ailey*
Edward E. Cox, *Camilla*
Stephen Pace, *Americus*
A. Sidney Camp, *Newnan*
Robert Ramspeck, *Atlanta*
Carl Vinson, *Milledgeville*
Malcolm C. Tarver, *Dalton*
John S. Gibson, *Douglas*
B. Frank Whelchel, *Gainesville*
Paul Brown, *Elberton*

## IDAHO

SENATORS

D. Worth Clark, *Pocatello*
John Thomas, *Gooding*

REPRESENTATIVES

Compton I. White, *Clark Fork*
Henry C. Dworshak, *Burley*

## ILLINOIS

SENATORS

Scott W. Lucas, *Havana*
C. Wayland Brooks, *Chicago*

REPRESENTATIVE AT LARGE

Stephen A. Day, *Evanston*

REPRESENTATIVES

William L. Dawson, *Chicago*
William A. Rowan, *Chicago*
Fred E. Busbey, *Chicago*
Martin Gorski, *Chicago*
Adolph J. Sabath, *Chicago*
Thomas J. O'Brien, *Chicago*
Leonard W. Schuetz,[16] *Chicago*

Thomas S. Gordon, *Chicago*
Charles S. Dewey, *Chicago*
Ralph E. Church, *Evanston*
Chauncey W. Reed, *West Chicago*
Noah M. Mason, *Oglesby*
Leo E. Allen, *Galena*
Anton J. Johnson, *Macomb*
Robert B. Chiperfield, *Canton*
Everett M. Dirksen, *Pekin*
Leslie C. Arends, *Melvin*
Jessie Sumner, *Milford*
William H. Wheat,[17] *Rantoul*
Rolla C. McMillen,[18] *Decatur*
Sidney E. Simpson, *Carrollton*
Evan Howell, *Springfield*
Calvin D. Johnson, *Belleville*
Charles W. Vursell, *Salem*
James V. Heidinger, *Fairfield*
Cecil W. (Runt) Bishop, *Carterville*

## INDIANA

SENATORS

Frederick Van Nuys,[19] *Indianapolis*
Samuel D. Jackson,[20] *Fort Wayne*
William E. Jenner,[21] *Bedford*
Raymond E. Willis, *Angola*

REPRESENTATIVES

Ray J. Madden, *Gary*
Charles A. Halleck, *Rensselaer*
Robert A. Grant, *South Bend*
George W. Gillie, *Fort Wayne*
Forest A. Harness, *Kokomo*
Noble J. Johnson, *Terre Haute*
Gerald W. Landis, *Linton*
Charles M. La Follette, *Evansville*
Earl Wilson, *Bedford*
Raymond S. Springer, *Connersville*
Louis Ludlow, *Indianapolis*

## IOWA

SENATORS

Guy M. Gillette, *Cherokee*
George A. Wilson, *Des Moines*

REPRESENTATIVES

Thomas E. Martin, *Iowa City*
Henry O. Talle, *Decorah*
John W. Gwynne, *Waterloo*
Karl M. LeCompte, *Corydon*
Paul Cunningham, *Des Moines*
Fred C. Gilchrist, *Laurens*
Ben F. Jensen, *Exira*
Charles B. Hoeven, *Alton*

## KANSAS

SENATORS

Arthur Capper, *Topeka*
Clyde M. Reed, *Parsons*

REPRESENTATIVES

William P. Lambertson, *Fairview*
Ulysses S. Guyer,[22] *Kansas City*
Errett P. Scrivner,[23] *Kansas City*
Thomas D. Winter, *Girard*
Edward H. Rees, *Emporia*
Clifford R. Hope, *Garden City*
Frank Carlson, *Concordia*

## KENTUCKY

SENATORS

Alben W. Barkley, *Paducah*
Albert B. Chandler, *Versailles*

REPRESENTATIVES

Noble J. Gregory, *Mayfield*
Beverly M. Vincent, *Brownsville*
Emmet O'Neal, *Louisville*
Edward W. Creal,[24] *Hodgenville*
Chester O. Carrier,[25] *Leitchfield*
Brent Spence, *Fort Thomas*
Virgil M. Chapman, *Paris*
Andrew J. May, *Prestonsburg*
Joe B. Bates, *Greenup*
John M. Robsion, *Barbourville*

## LOUISIANA

SENATORS

John H. Overton, *Alexandria*
Allen J. Ellender, *Houma*

REPRESENTATIVES

F. Edward Hébert, *New Orleans*
Paul H. Maloney, *New Orleans*
James Domengeaux,[26] *Lafayette*
Overton Brooks, *Shreveport*
Charles E. McKenzie, *Monroe*
James H. Morrison, *Hammond*
Henry D. Larcade, Jr., *Opelousas*
A. Leonard Allen, *Winnfield*

## MAINE

SENATORS

Wallace H. White, Jr., *Auburn*
Ralph O. Brewster, *Dexter*

REPRESENTATIVES

Robert Hale, *Portland*
Margaret Chase Smith, *Skowhegan*
Frank Fellows, *Bangor*

---

[13] Resigned November 25, 1944; vacancy throughout remainder of the Congress.
[14] Resigned October 19, 1944; vacancy throughout remainder of the Congress.
[15] Election unsuccessfully contested by Edward T. McEvoy.
[16] Election unsuccessfully contested by James C. Moreland. Died February 13, 1944; vacancy throughout remainder of the Congress.
[17] Died January 16, 1944.

[18] Elected to fill vacancy caused by death of William H. Wheat, and took his seat August 1, 1944.
[19] Died January 25, 1944.
[20] Appointed to fill vacancy caused by death of Frederick Van Nuys; took his seat January 31, 1944.
[21] Elected to fill vacancy caused by death of Frederick Van Nuys, and took his seat November 14, 1944.
[22] Died June 5, 1943.

[23] Elected to fill vacancy caused by death of Ulysses S. Guyer, and took his seat September 28, 1943.
[24] Died October 13, 1943.
[25] Elected to fill vacancy caused by death of Edward W. Creal, and took his seat December 10, 1943.
[26] Resigned April 15, 1944; subsequently reelected, and took his seat November 20, 1944.

## MARYLAND

SENATORS

Millard E. Tydings, *Havre de Grace*
George L. Radcliffe, *Baltimore*

REPRESENTATIVES

David J. Ward, *Salisbury*
H. Streett Baldwin, *Towson*
Thomas D'Alesandro, Jr., *Baltimore*
Daniel Ellison, *Baltimore*
Lansdale G. Sasscer, *Upper Marlboro*
J. Glenn Beall, *Frostburg*

## MASSACHUSETTS

SENATORS

David I. Walsh, *Clinton*
Henry Cabot Lodge, Jr.,[27] *Beverly*
Sinclair Weeks,[28] *West Newton*

REPRESENTATIVES

Allen T. Treadway, *Stockbridge*
Charles R. Clason, *Springfield*
Philip J. Philbin, *Clinton*
Pehr G. Holmes, *Worcester*
Edith Nourse Rogers, *Lowell*
George J. Bates, *Salem*
Thomas J. Lane, *Lawrence*
Angier L. Goodwin, *Melrose*
Charles L. Gifford, *Cotuit*
Christian A. Herter, *Boston*
James M. Curley, *Boston*
John W. McCormack, *Boston*
Richard B. Wigglesworth, *Milton*
Joseph W. Martin, Jr., *North Attleboro*

## MICHIGAN

SENATORS

Arthur H. Vandenberg, *Grand Rapids*
Homer Ferguson, *Detroit*

REPRESENTATIVES

George G. Sadowski, *Detroit*
Earl C. Michener, *Adrian*
Paul W. Shafer, *Battle Creek*
Clare E. Hoffman, *Allegan*
Bartel J. Jonkman, *Grand Rapids*
William W. Blackney, *Flint*
Jesse P. Wolcott, *Port Huron*
Fred L. Crawford, *Saginaw*
Albert J. Engel, *Muskegon*
Roy O. Woodruff, *Bay City*
Frederick V. Bradley, *Rogers City*
John B. Bennett, *Ontonagon*
George D. O'Brien, *Detroit*
Louis C. Rabaut, *Detroit*
John D. Dingell, *Detroit*
John Lesinski, *Dearborn*
George A. Dondero, *Royal Oak*

## MINNESOTA

SENATORS

Henrik Shipstead, *Carlos, R.F.D.*
Joseph H. Ball, *St. Paul*

REPRESENTATIVES

August H. Andresen, *Red Wing*
Joseph P. O'Hara, *Glencoe*
Richard P. Gale, *Mound*
Melvin J. Maas, *St. Paul*
Walter H. Judd, *Minneapolis*
Harold Knutson, *St. Cloud*
H. Carl Andersen, *Tyler*
William A. Pittenger, *Duluth*
Harold C. Hagen, *Crookston*

## MISSISSIPPI

SENATORS

Theodore G. Bilbo, *Poplarville*
James O. Eastland, *Ruleville*

REPRESENTATIVES

John E. Rankin, *Tupelo*
Jamie L. Whitten, *Charleston*
William M. Whittington, *Greenwood*
Thomas G. Abernethy, *Okolona*
W. Arthur Winstead, *Philadelphia*
William M. Colmer, *Pascagoula*
Dan R. McGehee, *Meadville*

## MISSOURI

SENATORS

Joel Bennett Clark, *St. Louis*
Harry S Truman, *Independence*

REPRESENTATIVES

Samuel W. Arnold, *Kirksville*
Max Schwabe, *Columbia*
William C. Cole, *St. Joseph*
C. Jasper Bell, *Blue Springs*
Roger C. Slaughter, *Kansas City*
Marion T. Bennett,[29] *Springfield*
Dewey Short, *Galena*
William P. Elmer, *Salem*
Clarence Cannon, *Elsberry*
Orville Zimmerman, *Kennett*
Louis E. Miller,[30] *St. Louis*
Walter C. Ploeser, *St. Louis*
John J. Cochran, *St. Louis*

## MONTANA

SENATORS

Burton K. Wheeler, *Butte*
James E. Murray, *Butte*

REPRESENTATIVES

Mike Mansfield, *Missoula*
James F. O'Connor, *Livingston*

## NEBRASKA

SENATORS

Hugh A. Butler, *Omaha*
Kenneth S. Wherry, *Pawnee City*

REPRESENTATIVES

Carl T. Curtis, *Minden*
Howard H. Buffett, *Omaha*
Karl Stefan, *Norfolk*
Arthur L. Miller, *Kimball*

## NEVADA

SENATORS

Patrick A. McCarran, *Reno*
James G. Scrugham, *Reno*

REPRESENTATIVE AT LARGE

Maurice J. Sullivan, *Reno*

## NEW HAMPSHIRE

SENATORS

H. Styles Bridges, *Concord*
Charles W. Tobey, *Temple*

REPRESENTATIVES

Chester E. Merrow, *Center Ossipee*
Foster Stearns, *Hancock*

## NEW JERSEY

SENATORS

W. Warren Barbour,[31] *Locust*
Arthur Walsh,[32] *South Orange*
H. Alexander Smith,[33] *Princeton*
Albert W. Hawkes, *Montclair*

REPRESENTATIVES

Charles A. Wolverton, *Camden*
Elmer H. Wene, *Vineland*
James C. Auchincloss, *Rumson*
D. Lane Powers, *Trenton*
Charles A. Eaton, *North Plainfield*
Donald H. McLean, *Elizabeth*
J. Parnell Thomas, *Allendale*
Gordon Canfield, *Paterson*
Harry L. Towe, *Rutherford*
Fred A. Hartley, Jr., *Kearny*
Frank L. Sundstrom, *East Orange*
Robert W. Kean, *Livingston*
Mary T. Norton, *Jersey City*
Edward J. Hart, *Jersey City*

## NEW MEXICO

SENATORS

Carl A. Hatch, *Clovis*
Dennis Chavez, *Albuquerque*

REPRESENTATIVES AT LARGE

Clinton P. Anderson, *Albuquerque*
Antonio M. Fernandez, *Santa Fe*

---

[27] Resigned February 3, 1944.
[28] Appointed to fill vacancy caused by resignation of Henry Cabot Lodge, Jr., and took his seat February 15, 1944.
[29] Elected to fill vacancy caused by death of his father, Philip A. Bennett, in preceding Congress and took his seat January 21, 1943.
[30] Election unsuccessfully contested by John B. Sullivan.
[31] Died November 22, 1943.
[32] Appointed to fill vacancy caused by death of W. Warren Barbour, and took his seat December 2, 1943.
[33] Elected to fill vacancy caused by death of W. Warren Barbour, and took his seat December 7, 1944.

## NEW YORK

### SENATORS
Robert F. Wagner, *New York City*
James M. Mead, *Buffalo*

### REPRESENTATIVES AT LARGE
Matthew J. Merritt, *Flushing*
Winifred C. Stanley, *Buffalo*

### REPRESENTATIVES
Leonard W. Hall, *Oyster Bay*
William B. Barry, *St. Albans*
Joseph L. Pfeifer, *Brooklyn*
Thomas H. Cullen,[34] *Brooklyn*
John J. Rooney,[35] *Brooklyn*
James J. Heffernan, *Brooklyn*
Andrew L. Somers, *Brooklyn*
John J. Delaney, *Brooklyn*
Donald L. O'Toole, *Brooklyn*
Eugene J. Keogh, *Brooklyn*
Emanuel Celler, *Brooklyn*
James A. O'Leary,[36] *West New Brighton*
Ellsworth B. Buck,[37] *Staten Island*
Samuel Dickstein, *New York City*
Louis J. Capozzoli, *New York City*
Arthur G. Klein, *New York City*
Thomas F. Burchill, *New York City*
James H. Fay, *New York City*
Joseph Clark Baldwin, *New York City*
Martin J. Kennedy, *New York City*
Sol Bloom, *New York City*
Vito Marcantonio, *New York City*
Joseph A. Gavagan,[38] *New York City*
James H. Torrens,[39] *New York City*
Walter A. Lynch, *New York City*
Charles A. Buckley, *New York City*
James M. Fitzpatrick, *New York City*
Ralph A. Gamble, *Larchmont*
Hamilton Fish, Jr., *Garrison*
Jay LeFevre, *New Paltz*
William T. Byrne, *Loudonville*
Dean P. Taylor, *Troy*
Bernard W. Kearney, *Gloversville*
Clarence E. Kilburn, *Malone*
Francis D. Culkin,[40] *Oswego*
Hadwen C. Fuller,[41] *Parish*
Fred J. Douglas, *Utica*
Edwin Arthur Hall, *Binghamton*
Clarence E. Hancock, *Syracuse*
John Taber, *Auburn*
W. Sterling Cole, *Bath*
Joseph J. O'Brien, *East Rochester*
James W. Wadsworth, Jr., *Geneseo*
Walter G. Andrews, *Buffalo*
Joseph Mruk, *Buffalo*
John C. Butler, *Buffalo*
Daniel A. Reed, *Dunkirk*

## NORTH CAROLINA

### SENATORS
Josiah W. Bailey, *Raleigh*
Robert R. Reynolds, *Asheville*

### REPRESENTATIVES
Herbert C. Bonner, *Washington*
John H. Kerr, *Warrenton*
Graham A. Barden, *New Bern*
Harold D. Cooley, *Nashville*
John H. Folger, *Mount Airy*
Carl T. Durham, *Chapel Hill*
J. Bayard Clark, *Fayetteville*
William O. Burgin, *Lexington*
Robert L. Doughton, *Laurel Springs*
Cameron Morrison, *Charlotte*
Alfred L. Bulwinkle, *Gastonia*
Zebulon Weaver, *Asheville*

## NORTH DAKOTA

### SENATORS
Gerald P. Nye, *Cooperstown*
William Langer, *Bismarck*

### REPRESENTATIVES AT LARGE
Usher L. Burdick, *Williston*
William Lemke, *Fargo*

## OHIO

### SENATORS
Robert A. Taft, *Cincinnati*
Harold H. Burton, *Cleveland*

### REPRESENTATIVE AT LARGE
George H. Bender, *Cleveland Heights*

### REPRESENTATIVES
Charles H. Elston, *Cincinnati*
William E. Hess, *Cincinnati*
Harry P. Jeffrey, *Dayton*
Robert F. Jones, *Lima*
Cliff Clevenger, *Bryan*
Edward O. McCowen, *Wheelersburg*
Clarence J. Brown, *Blanchester*
Frederick C. Smith, *Marion*
Homer A. Ramey, *Toledo*
Thomas A. Jenkins, *Ironton*
Walter E. Brehm, *Logan*
John M. Vorys, *Columbus*
Alvin F. Weichel, *Sandusky*
Ed Rowe, *Akron*
Percy W. Griffiths, *Marietta*
Henderson H. Carson, *Canton*
J. Harry McGregor, *West Lafayette*
Earl R. Lewis, *St. Clairsville*
Michael J. Kirwan, *Youngstown*
Michael A. Feighan, *Cleveland*
Robert Crosser, *Cleveland*
Frances P. Bolton, *Lyndhurst*

## OKLAHOMA

### SENATORS
J. W. Elmer Thomas, *Medicine Park*
Edward H. Moore, *Tulsa*

### REPRESENTATIVES
Wesley E. Disney, *Tulsa*
Jack Nichols,[42] *Eufaula*
William C. Stigler,[43] *Stigler*
Paul Stewart, *Antlers*
Lyle H. Boren, *Seminole*
A. S. Mike Monroney, *Oklahoma City*
Jed Johnson, *Anadarko*
Victor Wickersham, *Mangum*
Ross Rizley, *Guymon*

## OREGON

### SENATORS
Charles L. McNary,[44] *Salem*
Guy Cordon,[45] *Roseburg*
Rufus C. Holman, *Portland*

### REPRESENTATIVES
James W. Mott, *Salem*
Lowell Stockman, *Pendleton*
Homer D. Angell, *Portland*
Harris Ellsworth, *Roseburg*

## PENNSYLVANIA

### SENATORS
James J. Davis, *Pittsburgh*
Joseph F. Guffey, *Pittsburgh*

### REPRESENTATIVE AT LARGE
William I. Troutman,[46] *Shamokin*

### REPRESENTATIVES
James Gallagher, *Philadelphia*
James P. McGranery,[47] *Philadelphia*
Joseph M. Pratt,[48] *Philadelphia*
Michael J. Bradley, *Philadelphia*
John Edward Sheridan, *Philadelphia*
C. Frederick Pracht, *Philadelphia*
Francis J. Myers, *Philadelphia*
Hugh D. Scott, Jr., *Philadelphia*
James Wolfenden, *Upper Darby*
Charles L. Gerlach, *Allentown*
J. Roland Kinzer, *Lancaster*
John W. Murphy, *Dunmore*
Thomas Byron Miller, *Plymouth*
Ivor D. Fenton, *Mahanoy City*
Daniel K. Hoch, *Reading*
Wilson D. Gillette, *Towanda*
Thomas E. Scanlon, *Pittsburgh*
J. William Ditter,[49] *Ambler*
Samuel K. McConnell, Jr.,[50] *Penn Wynne*

---

[34] Died March 1, 1944.
[35] Elected to fill vacancy caused by death of Thomas H. Cullen, and took his seat June 15, 1944.
[36] Died March 16, 1944.
[37] Elected to fill vacancy caused by death of James A. O'Leary, and took his seat June 14, 1944.
[38] Resigned December 30, 1943, having been elected a justice of the New York Supreme Court.
[39] Elected to fill vacancy caused by resignation of Joseph A. Gavagan, and took his seat March 9, 1944.

[40] Died August 4, 1943.
[41] Elected to fill vacancy caused by death of Francis D. Culkin, and took his seat November 10, 1943.
[42] Election unsuccessfully contested by E. O. Clark. Resigned July 3, 1943.
[43] Elected to fill vacancy caused by resignation of Jack Nichols, and took his seat April 12, 1944.
[44] Died February 25, 1944.
[45] Appointed to fill vacancy caused by death of

Charles L. McNary, and took his seat March 13, 1944; subsequently elected.
[46] Resigned January 2, 1945.
[47] Resigned November 17, 1943.
[48] Elected to fill vacancy caused by resignation of James P. McGranery, and took his seat February 8, 1944.
[49] Died November 21, 1943.
[50] Elected to fill vacancy caused by death of J. William Ditter, and took his seat February 8, 1944.

Richard M. Simpson, *Huntingdon*
John C. Kunkel, *Harrisburg*
Leon H. Gavin, *Oil City*
Francis E. Walter, *Easton*
Chester H. Gross, *Manchester*
James E. Van Zandt,[51] *Altoona*
D. Emmert Brumbaugh,[52] *Claysburg*
J. Buell Snyder, *Perryopolis*
Grant Furlong, *Donora*
Louis E. Graham, *Beaver*
Harve Tibbott, *Ebensburg*
Augustine B. Kelley, *Greensburg*
Robert L. Rodgers, *Erie*
Samuel A. Weiss, *Glassport*
Herman P. Eberharter, *Pittsburgh*
James A. Wright, *Carnegie*

## RHODE ISLAND

SENATORS

Peter G. Gerry, *Warwick*
Theodore F. Green, *Providence*

REPRESENTATIVES

Aime J. Forand, *Cumberland*
John E. Fogarty,[53] *Harmony*

## SOUTH CAROLINA

SENATORS

Ellison D. Smith,[54] *Lynchburg*
Wilton E. Hall,[55] *Anderson*
Burnet R. Maybank, *Charleston*

REPRESENTATIVES

L. Mendel Rivers, *North Charleston*
Hampton P. Fulmer,[56] *Orangeburg*
Willa E. Fulmer,[57] *Orangeburg*
Butler B. Hare, *Saluda*
Joseph R. Bryson, *Greenville*
James P. Richards, *Lancaster*
John L. McMillan, *Florence*

## SOUTH DAKOTA

SENATORS

J. Chandler Gurney, *Yankton*
Harlan J. Bushfield, *Miller*

REPRESENTATIVES

Karl E. Mundt, *Madison*
Francis H. Case, *Custer*

## TENNESSEE

SENATORS

Kenneth D. McKellar, *Memphis*
A. Tom Stewart, *Winchester*

REPRESENTATIVES

B. Carroll Reece, *Johnson City*
John Jennings, Jr., *Knoxville*
Estes Kefauver, *Chattanooga*
Albert A. Gore,[58] *Carthage*
Jim Nance McCord, *Lewisburg*
J. Percy Priest, *Nashville*
Wirt Courtney, *Franklin*
Thomas J. Murray, *Jackson*
Jere Cooper, *Dyersburg*
Clifford Davis, *Memphis*

## TEXAS

SENATORS

Tom T. Connally, *Marlin*
W. Lee O'Daniel, *Fort Worth*

REPRESENTATIVES

Wright Patman, *Texarkana*
Martin Dies, Jr., *Orange*
Lindley Beckworth, *Gilmer*
Sam Rayburn, *Bonham*
Hatton W. Sumners, *Dallas*
Luther A. Johnson, *Corsicana*
Nat Patton, *Crockett*
Albert Thomas, *Houston*
Joseph J. Mansfield, *Columbus*
Lyndon B. Johnson, *Johnson City*
William R. Poage, *Waco*
Fritz G. Lanham, *Fort Worth*
Ed Gossett, *Wichita Falls*
Richard M. Kleberg, *Corpus Christi*
Milton H. West, *Brownsville*
R. Ewing Thomason, *El Paso*
Sam M. Russell, *Stephenville*
Eugene Worley, *Shamrock*
George H. Mahon, *Colorado City*
Paul J. Kilday, *San Antonio*
O. Clark Fisher, *San Angelo*

## UTAH

SENATORS

Elbert D. Thomas, *Salt Lake City*
Abe Murdock, *Beaver*

REPRESENTATIVES

Walter K. Granger, *Cedar City*
J. W. Robinson, *Provo*

## VERMONT

SENATORS

Warren R. Austin, *Burlington*
George D. Aiken, *Putney*

REPRESENTATIVE AT LARGE

Charles A. Plumley, *Northfield*

## VIRGINIA

SENATORS

Carter Glass, *Lynchburg*
Harry Flood Byrd, *Berryville*

REPRESENTATIVES

Schuyler Otis Bland, *Newport News*
Winder R. Harris,[59] *Norfolk*
Ralph H. Daughton,[60] *Norfolk*
Dave E. Satterfield, Jr., *Richmond*
Patrick Henry Drewry, *Petersburg*
Thomas G. Burch, *Martinsville*
Clifton A. Woodrum, *Roanoke*
A. Willis Robertson, *Lexington*
Howard W. Smith, *Alexandria*
John W. Flannagan, Jr., *Bristol*

## WASHINGTON

SENATORS

Homer T. Bone,[61] *Tacoma*
Warren G. Magnuson,[62] *Seattle*
Monrad C. Wallgren, *Everett*

REPRESENTATIVES

Warren G. Magnuson,[63] *Seattle*
Henry M. Jackson, *Everett*
Fred Norman, *Raymond*
Hal Holmes, *Ellensburg*
Walter F. Horan, *Wenatchee*
John M. Coffee, *Tacoma*

## WEST VIRGINIA

SENATORS

Harley M. Kilgore, *Beckley*
Chapman Revercomb, *Charleston*

REPRESENTATIVES

Andrew C. Schiffler, *Wheeling*
Jennings Randolph, *Elkins*
Edward G. Rohrbough, *Glenville*
Hubert S. Ellis, *Huntington*
John Kee, *Bluefield*
Joe L. Smith, *Beckley*

## WISCONSIN

SENATORS

Robert M. La Follette, Jr., *Madison*
Alexander Wiley, *Chippewa Falls*

REPRESENTATIVES

Lawrence H. Smith, *Racine*
Harry Sauthoff, *Madison*
William H. Stevenson, *La Crosse*
Thaddeus F. B. Wasielewski,[64]
  *Milwaukee*
Howard J. McMurray,[65] *Milwaukee*
Frank B. Keefe, *Oshkosh*

---

[51] Resigned September 24, 1943.
[52] Elected to fill vacancy caused by resignation of James E. Van Zandt, took his seat November 23, 1943.
[53] Resigned December 7, 1944; vacancy throughout remainder of the Congress.
[54] Died November 17, 1944.
[55] Appointed to fill vacancy caused by death of Ellison D. Smith, and took his seat November 27, 1944.
[56] Died October 19, 1944.

[57] Elected to fill vacancy caused by death of Hampton P. Fulmer, and took her seat November 16, 1944.
[58] Resigned December 4, 1944; vacancy throughout remainder of the Congress.
[59] Resigned September 15, 1944.
[60] Elected to fill vacancy caused by resignation of Winder R. Harris, and took his seat November 14, 1944.
[61] Resigned November 13, 1944.

[62] Appointed to fill vacancy caused by resignation of Homer T. Bone, and took his seat December 14, 1944.
[63] Resigned December 13, 1944; vacancy throughout remainder of the Congress.
[64] Election unsuccessfully contested by John C. Schafer.
[65] Election unsuccessfully contested by Lewis D. Thill.

## WISCONSIN—Continued

REPRESENTATIVES—CONTINUED

Reid F. Murray, *Ogdensburg*
LaVern R. Dilweg, *Green Bay*
Merlin Hull, *Black River Falls*
Alvin E. O'Konski, *Mercer*

## WYOMING

SENATORS

Joseph C. O'Mahoney, *Cheyenne*
Edward V. Robertson, *Cody*

REPRESENTATIVE AT LARGE

Frank A. Barrett, *Lusk*

## TERRITORY OF ALASKA

DELEGATE

Anthony J. Dimond, *Valdez*

## TERRITORY OF HAWAII

DELEGATE

Joseph R. Farrington, *Honolulu*

## COMMONWEALTH OF THE PHILIPPINES

RESIDENT COMMISSIONER

Joaquin M. Elizalde,[66] *Manila*
Carlos P. Romulo,[67] *Manila*

## PUERTO RICO

RESIDENT COMMISSIONER

Bolívar Pagán, *San Juan*

[66] Resigned August 9, 1944.
[67] Appointed to fill vacancy caused by resignation of Joaquin M. Elizalde, and took his seat August 21, 1944.

# 79TH CONGRESS

## JANUARY 3, 1945, TO JANUARY 3, 1947

FIRST SESSION— *January 3, 1945, to December 21, 1945*
SECOND SESSION— *January 14,[1] 1946, to August 2, 1946*

Harry S Truman
Vice President

Sam Rayburn
Speaker

---

### Senate

Democrats 57 — Republicans 38 — Progressive 1

VICE PRESIDENT OF THE UNITED STATES— Henry A. Wallace,[2] of Iowa; Harry S Truman,[3] of Missouri

PRESIDENT PRO TEMPORE OF THE SENATE— Kenneth McKellar,[4] of Tennessee

SECRETARY OF THE SENATE— Edwin A. Halsey,[5] of Virginia; Leslie L. Biffle,[6] of Arkansas

SERGEANT AT ARMS OF THE SENATE— Wall Doxey, of Mississippi

MAJORITY FLOOR LEADER— Alben W. Barkley, of Kentucky

DEMOCRATIC WHIP— Lister Hill, of Alabama

REPUBLICAN FLOOR LEADER— Wallace H. White, Jr., of Maine

ASSISTANT REPUBLICAN LEADER— Kenneth S. Wherry, of Nebraska

---

### House of Representatives

Democrats 243 — Republicans 190 — American Labor 1 — Progressive 1

SPEAKER OF THE HOUSE OF REPRESENTATIVES— Sam Rayburn,[7] of Texas

CLERK OF THE HOUSE— South Trimble,[8] of Kentucky; Harry Newlin Megill[9]

SERGEANT AT ARMS OF THE HOUSE— Kenneth Romney, of Montana

DOORKEEPER OF THE HOUSE— Ralph R. Roberts, of Indiana

POSTMASTER OF THE HOUSE— Finis E. Scott

MAJORITY LEADER— John W. McCormack, of Massachusetts

MAJORITY WHIP— Robert C. Ramspeck,[10] of Georgia; John J. Sparkman,[11] of Alabama

REPUBLICAN LEADER— Joseph W. Martin, Jr., of Massachusetts

REPUBLICAN WHIP— Leslie C. Arends, of Illinois

---

## ALABAMA

### SENATORS

John H. Bankhead II (D),[12] *Jasper*
George R. Swift (D),[13] *Atmore*
John J. Sparkman (D),[14] *Huntsville*
Lister Hill (D), *Montgomery*

### REPRESENTATIVES

1 Frank W. Boykin (D), *Mobile*
2 George M. Grant (D), *Troy*
3 George W. Andrews (D), *Union Springs*
4 Sam Hobbs (D), *Selma*
5 Albert Rains (D), *Gadsden*
6 Pete Jarman (D), *Livingston*
7 Carter Manasco (D), *Jasper*
8 John J. Sparkman (D),[15] *Huntsville*
9 Luther Patrick (D), *Birmingham*

## ARIZONA

### SENATORS

Carl Hayden (D), *Phoenix*
Ernest W. McFarland (D), *Florence*

### REPRESENTATIVES AT LARGE

Richard F. Harless (D), *Phoenix*
John R. Murdock (D), *Tempe*

## ARKANSAS

### SENATORS

John L. McClellan (D), *Camden*
J. William Fulbright (D), *Fayetteville*

### REPRESENTATIVES

1 E. C. Gathings (D), *West Memphis*
2 Wilbur D. Mills (D), *Kensett*

3 James W. Trimble (D), *Berryville*
4 Fadjo Cravens (D), *Fort Smith*
5 Brooks Hays (D), *Little Rock*
6 William F. Norrell (D), *Monticello*
7 Oren Harris (D), *El Dorado*

## CALIFORNIA

### SENATORS

Hiram W. Johnson (R),[16] *San Francisco*
William F. Knowland (R),[17] *Piedmont*
Sheridan Downey (D), *Laguna Beach*

### REPRESENTATIVES

1 Clarence F. Lea (D), *Santa Rosa*
2 Clair Engle (D), *Red Bluff*
3 Leroy Johnson (R), *Stockton*

---

[1] By joint resolution (Pub. Law 289, 79th Cong., 1st sess.) the date of assembling the second session of the Seventy-ninth Congress was fixed for January 14, 1946.

[2] Term expired at noon on January 20, 1945.

[3] Term began at noon on January 20, 1945. Became President on the death of Franklin D. Roosevelt, April 12, 1945.

[4] Elected January 6, 1945.

[5] Died January 29, 1945.

[6] Elected acting secretary January 29, 1945;

elected secretary February 8, 1945.

[7] Reelected January 3, 1945.

[8] Reelected January 3, 1945; died November 23, 1946.

[9] Assistant to the Clerk, acted as Clerk following the death of South Trimble.

[10] Resigned from the House, December 31, 1945.

[11] Elected January 14, 1946.

[12] Died June 12, 1946.

[13] Appointed to fill vacancy caused by death of

John H. Bankhead II, and took his seat June 20, 1946.

[14] Elected November 5, 1946, to fill vacancy caused by death of John H. Bankhead II, but was unable to be sworn in as Congress was not in session.

[15] Resigned November 5, 1946, having been elected Senator; vacancy throughout remainder of the Congress.

[16] Died August 6, 1945.

[17] Appointed to fill vacancy caused by death of Hiram W. Johnson, and took his seat September 5, 1945.

## CALIFORNIA—Continued

REPRESENTATIVES—CONTINUED

4  Franck R. Havenner (D), *San Francisco*
5  Richard J. Welch (R), *San Francisco*
6  George P. Miller (D), *Alameda*
7  John H. Tolan (D), *Oakland*
8  John Z. Anderson (R), *San Juan Bautista*
9  Bertrand W. Gearhart (R), *Fresno*
10  Alfred J. Elliott (D), *Tulare*
11  George E. Outland (D), *Santa Barbara*
12  H. Jerry Voorhis (D), *San Dimas*
13  Ned R. Healy (D), *Los Angeles*
14  Helen Gahagan Douglas (D), *Los Angeles*
15  Gordon L. McDonough (R), *Los Angeles*
16  Ellis E. Patterson (D), *Los Angeles*
17  Cecil R. King (D), *Los Angeles*
18  Clyde G. Doyle (D), *Long Beach*
19  Chet Holifield (D), *Montebello*
20  Carl Hinshaw (R), *Pasadena*
21  Harry R. Sheppard (D), *Yucaipa*
22  John Phillips (R), *Banning*
23  Edouard V. M. Izac (D), *San Diego*

## COLORADO

SENATORS

Edwin C. Johnson (D), *Craig*
Eugene D. Millikin (R), *Denver*

REPRESENTATIVES

1  Dean M. Gillespie (R), *Denver*
2  William S. Hill (R), *Fort Collins*
3  J. Edgar Chenoweth (R), *Trinidad*
4  Robert F. Rockwell (R), *Paonia*

## CONNECTICUT

SENATORS

Francis T. Maloney (D),[18] *Meriden*
Thomas C. Hart (R),[19] *Sharon*
Raymond E. Baldwin (R),[20] *Stratford*
Brien McMahon (D), *Norwalk*

REPRESENTATIVE AT LARGE

Joseph F. Ryter (D), *Hartford*

REPRESENTATIVES

1  Herman P. Kopplemann (D), *Hartford*
2  Chase Going Woodhouse (D), *New London*

3  James P. Geelan (D), *New Haven*
4  Clare Boothe Luce (R), *Greenwich*
5  Joseph E. Talbot (R), *Naugatuck*

## DELAWARE

SENATORS

James M. Tunnell (D), *Georgetown*
C. Douglass Buck (R), *Wilmington*

REPRESENTATIVE AT LARGE

Philip A. Traynor (D), *Wilmington*

## FLORIDA

SENATORS

Charles O. Andrews (D),[21] *Orlando*
Spessard L. Holland (D),[22] *Bartow*
Claude D. Pepper (D), *Tallahassee*

REPRESENTATIVES

1  J. Hardin Peterson (D), *Lakeland*
2  Emory H. Price (D), *Jacksonville*
3  Robert L. F. Sikes (D), *Crestview*
4  Arthur P. Cannon (D), *Miami*
5  Joe Hendricks (D), *De Land*
6  Dwight L. Rogers (D), *Fort Lauderdale*

## GEORGIA

SENATORS

Walter F. George (D), *Vienna*
Richard B. Russell (D), *Winder*

REPRESENTATIVES

1  Hugh Peterson (D), *Ailey*
2  Edward E. Cox (D), *Camilla*
3  Stephen Pace (D), *Americus*
4  A. Sidney Camp (D), *Newnan*
5  Robert Ramspeck (D),[23] *Atlanta*
5  Helen Douglas Mankin (D),[24] *Atlanta*
6  Carl Vinson (D), *Milledgeville*
7  Malcolm C. Tarver (D), *Dalton*
8  John S. Gibson (D), *Douglas*
9  John S. Wood (D), *Canton*
10  Paul Brown (D), *Elberton*

## IDAHO

SENATORS

John Thomas (R),[25] *Gooding*
Charles C. Gossett (D),[26] *Nampa*
Henry C. Dworshak (R),[27] *Burley*
Glen H. Taylor (D), *Pocatello*

REPRESENTATIVES

1  Compton I. White (D), *Clark Fork*
2  Henry C. Dworshak (R),[28] *Burley*

## ILLINOIS

SENATORS

Scott W. Lucas (D), *Havana*
C. Wayland Brooks (R), *Chicago*

REPRESENTATIVE AT LARGE

Emily Taft Douglas (D), *Chicago*

REPRESENTATIVES

1  William L. Dawson (D), *Chicago*
2  William A. Rowan (D), *Chicago*
3  Edward A. Kelly (D), *Chicago*
4  Martin Gorski (D), *Chicago*
5  Adolph J. Sabath (D), *Chicago*
6  Thomas J. O'Brien (D), *Chicago*
7  William W. Link (D), *Chicago*
8  Thomas S. Gordon (D), *Chicago*
9  Alexander J. Resa (D), *Chicago*
10  Ralph E. Church (R), *Evanston*
11  Chauncey W. Reed (R), *West Chicago*
12  Noah M. Mason (R), *Oglesby*
13  Leo E. Allen (R), *Galena*
14  Anton J. Johnson (R), *Macomb*
15  Robert B. Chiperfield (R), *Canton*
16  Everett McKinley Dirksen (R), *Pekin*
17  Leslie C. Arends (R), *Melvin*
18  Jessie Sumner (R), *Milford*
19  Rolla C. McMillen (R), *Decatur*
20  Sidney E. Simpson (R), *Carrollton*
21  Evan Howell (R), *Springfield*
22  Melvin Price (D), *East St. Louis*
23  Charles W. Vursell (R), *Salem*
24  James V. Heidinger (R),[29] *Fairfield*
24  Roy Clippinger (R),[30] *Carmi*
25  Cecil W. (Runt) Bishop (R), *Carterville*

## INDIANA

SENATORS

Raymond E. Willis (R), *Angola*
Homer E. Capehart (R), *Washington*

REPRESENTATIVES

1  Ray J. Madden (D), *Gary*
2  Charles A. Halleck (R), *Rensselaer*
3  Robert A. Grant (R), *South Bend*
4  George W. Gillie (R), *Fort Wayne*
5  Forest A. Harness (R), *Kokomo*
6  Noble J. Johnson (R), *Terre Haute*
7  Gerald W. Landis (R), *Linton*
8  Charles M. La Follette (R), *Evansville*
9  Earl Wilson (R), *Huron*
10  Raymond S. Springer (R), *Connersville*
11  Louis Ludlow (D), *Indianapolis*

---

[18] Died January 16, 1945.
[19] Appointed to fill vacancy caused by death of Francis T. Maloney; took his seat February 15, 1945.
[20] Elected November 5, 1946, to fill vacancy caused by death of Francis T. Maloney, but was unable to be sworn in as Congress was not in session.
[21] Died September 18, 1946.
[22] Appointed September 25, 1946, to fill vacancy caused by death of Charles O. Andrews, but was

unable to be sworn in as Congress was not in session.
[23] Resigned December 31, 1945.
[24] Elected to fill vacancy caused by resignation of Robert Ramspeck, and took her seat February 25, 1946.
[25] Died November 10, 1945.
[26] Appointed to fill vacancy caused by death of John Thomas, and took his seat November 29, 1945.
[27] Elected November 5, 1946, to fill vacancy

caused by death of John Thomas, but was unable to be sworn in as Congress was not in session.
[28] Resigned November 5, 1946, having been elected Senator; vacancy throughout remainder of the Congress.
[29] Died March 22, 1945.
[30] Elected to fill vacancy caused by death of James V. Heidinger, and took his seat November 26, 1945.

## IOWA

### SENATORS

George A. Wilson (R), *Des Moines*
Bourke B. Hickenlooper (R), *Cedar Rapids*

### REPRESENTATIVES

1 Thomas E. Martin (R), *Iowa City*
2 Henry O. Talle (R), *Decorah*
3 John W. Gwynne (R), *Waterloo*
4 Karl M. LeCompte (R), *Corydon*
5 Paul Cunningham (R), *Des Moines*
6 James I. Dolliver (R), *Fort Dodge*
7 Ben F. Jensen (R), *Exira*
8 Charles B. Hoeven (R), *Alton*

## KANSAS

### SENATORS

Arthur Capper (R), *Topeka*
Clyde M. Reed (R), *Parsons*

### REPRESENTATIVES

1 Albert M. Cole (R), *Holton*
2 Errett P. Scrivner (R), *Kansas City*
3 Thomas D. Winter (R), *Girard*
4 Edward H. Rees (R), *Emporia*
5 Clifford R. Hope (R), *Garden City*
6 Frank Carlson (R), *Concordia*

## KENTUCKY

### SENATORS

Alben W. Barkley (D), *Paducah*
Albert B. Chandler (D),[31] *Versailles*
William A. Stanfill (R),[32] *Hazard*
John Sherman Cooper (R),[33] *Somerset*

### REPRESENTATIVES

1 Noble J. Gregory (D), *Mayfield*
2 Earle C. Clements (D), *Morganfield*
3 Emmet O'Neal (D), *Louisville*
4 Frank L. Chelf (D), *Lebanon*
5 Brent Spence (D), *Fort Thomas*
6 Virgil M. Chapman (D), *Paris*
7 Andrew J. May (D), *Prestonsburg*
8 Joe B. Bates (D), *Greenup*
9 John M. Robsion (R), *Barbourville*

## LOUISIANA

### SENATORS

John H. Overton (D), *Alexandria*
Allen J. Ellender (D), *Houma*

### REPRESENTATIVES

1 F. Edward Hébert (D), *New Orleans*
2 Paul H. Maloney (D), *New Orleans*
3 James Domengeaux (D), *Lafayette*
4 Overton Brooks (D), *Shreveport*
5 Charles E. McKenzie (D), *Monroe*
6 James H. Morrison (D), *Hammond*
7 Henry D. Larcade, Jr. (D), *Opelousas*
8 A. Leonard Allen (D), *Winnfield*

## MAINE

### SENATORS

Wallace H. White, Jr. (R), *Auburn*
Ralph O. Brewster (R), *Dexter*

### REPRESENTATIVES

1 Robert Hale (R), *Portland*
2 Margaret Chase Smith (R), *Skowhegan*
3 Frank Fellows (R), *Bangor*

## MARYLAND

### SENATORS

Millard E. Tydings (D), *Havre de Grace*
George L. Radcliffe (D), *Baltimore*

### REPRESENTATIVES

1 Dudley G. Roe (D), *Sudlersville*
2 H. Streett Baldwin (D), *Hydes*
3 Thomas D'Alesandro, Jr. (D), *Baltimore*
4 George H. Fallon (D), *Baltimore*
5 Lansdale G. Sasscer (D), *Upper Marlboro*
6 J. Glenn Beall (R), *Frostburg*

## MASSACHUSETTS

### SENATORS

David I. Walsh (D), *Clinton*
Leverett Saltonstall (R),[34] *Chestnut Hill*

### REPRESENTATIVES

1 John W. Heselton (R), *Deerfield*
2 Charles R. Clason (R), *Springfield*
3 Philip J. Philbin (D), *Clinton*
4 Pehr G. Holmes (R), *Worcester*
5 Edith Nourse Rogers (R), *Lowell*
6 George J. Bates (R), *Salem*
7 Thomas J. Lane (D), *Lawrence*
8 Angier L. Goodwin (R), *Melrose*
9 Charles L. Gifford (R), *Cotuit*
10 Christian A. Herter (R), *Boston*
11 James M. Curley (D), *Boston*
12 John W. McCormack (D), *Boston*
13 Richard B. Wigglesworth (R), *Milton*
14 Joseph W. Martin, Jr. (R), *North Attleboro*

## MICHIGAN

### SENATORS

Arthur H. Vandenberg (R), *Grand Rapids*
Homer Ferguson (R), *Detroit*

### REPRESENTATIVES

1 George G. Sadowski (D), *Detroit*
2 Earl C. Michener (R), *Adrian*
3 Paul W. Shafer (R), *Battle Creek*
4 Clare E. Hoffman (R), *Allegan*
5 Bartel J. Jonkman (R), *Grand Rapids*
6 William W. Blackney (R), *Flint*
7 Jesse P. Wolcott (R), *Port Huron*
8 Fred L. Crawford (R), *Saginaw*
9 Albert J. Engel (R), *Muskegon*
10 Roy O. Woodruff (R), *Bay City*
11 Frederick V. Bradley (R), *Rogers City*
12 Frank E. Hook (D), *Ironwood*
13 George D. O'Brien (D), *Detroit*
14 Louis C. Rabaut (D), *Detroit*
15 John D. Dingell (D), *Detroit*
16 John Lesinski (D), *Dearborn*
17 George A. Dondero (R),[35] *Royal Oak*

## MINNESOTA

### SENATORS

Henrik Shipstead (R), *Carlos*
Joseph H. Ball (R), *St. Paul*

### REPRESENTATIVES

1 August H. Andresen (R), *Red Wing*
2 Joseph P. O'Hara (R), *Glencoe*
3 William J. Gallagher (D),[36] *Minneapolis*
4 Frank T. Starkey (D), *St. Paul*
5 Walter H. Judd (R), *Minneapolis*
6 Harold Knutson (R), *St. Cloud*
7 H. Carl Andersen (R), *Tyler*
8 William A. Pittenger (R), *Duluth*
9 Harold C. Hagen (R), *Crookston*

## MISSISSIPPI

### SENATORS

Theodore G. Bilbo (D), *Poplarville*
James O. Eastland (D), *Ruleville*

### REPRESENTATIVES

1 John E. Rankin (D), *Tupelo*
2 Jamie L. Whitten (D), *Charleston*
3 William M. Whittington (D), *Greenwood*
4 Thomas G. Abernethy (D), *Okolona*
5 W. Arthur Winstead (D), *Philadelphia*

---

[31] Resigned November 1, 1945.
[32] Appointed to fill vacancy caused by resignation of Albert B. Chandler, and took his seat November 23, 1945.
[33] Elected November 5, 1946, to fill vacancy caused by resignation of Albert B. Chandler, but was unable to be sworn in as Congress was not in session.
[34] Elected November 7, 1944, to fill vacancy caused by resignation of Henry Cabot Lodge, Jr., in preceding Congress, and took his seat January 10, 1945.
[35] Election unsuccessfully contested by John W. L. Hicks.
[36] Died August 13, 1946; vacancy throughout remainder of the Congress.

## MISSISSIPPI—Continued

REPRESENTATIVES—CONTINUED

6 William M. Colmer (D), *Pascagoula*
7 Dan R. McGehee (D), *Meadville*

## MISSOURI

SENATORS

Harry S Truman (D),[37] *Independence*
Frank P. Briggs (D),[38] *Macon*
Forrest C. Donnell (R), *Webster Groves*

REPRESENTATIVES

1 Samuel W. Arnold (R), *Kirksville*
2 Max Schwabe (R), *Columbia*
3 William C. Cole (R), *St. Joseph*
4 C. Jasper Bell (D), *Blue Springs*
5 Roger C. Slaughter (D), *Kansas City*
6 Marion T. Bennett (R), *Springfield*
7 Dewey Short (R), *Galena*
8 Albert S. J. Carnahan (D), *Ellsinore*
9 Clarence Cannon (D), *Elsberry*
10 Orville Zimmerman (D), *Kennett*
11 John B. Sullivan (D), *St. Louis*
12 Walter C. Ploeser (R), *Clayton*
13 John J. Cochran (D), *St. Louis*

## MONTANA

SENATORS

Burton K. Wheeler (D), *Butte*
James E. Murray (D), *Butte*

REPRESENTATIVES

1 Mike Mansfield (D), *Missoula*
2 James F. O'Connor (D),[39] *Livingston*
2 Wesley A. D'Ewart (R),[40] *Wilsall*

## NEBRASKA

SENATORS

Hugh A. Butler (R), *Omaha*
Kenneth S. Wherry (R), *Pawnee City*

REPRESENTATIVES

1 Carl T. Curtis (R), *Minden*
2 Howard H. Buffett (R), *Omaha*
3 Karl Stefan (R), *Norfolk*
4 Arthur L. Miller (R), *Kimball*

## NEVADA

SENATORS

Patrick A. McCarran (D), *Reno*
James G. Scrugham (D),[41] *Reno*
Edward P. Carville (D),[42] *Reno*

REPRESENTATIVE AT LARGE

Berkeley L. Bunker (D), *Las Vegas*

## NEW HAMPSHIRE

SENATORS

H. Styles Bridges (R), *Concord*
Charles W. Tobey (R), *Temple*

REPRESENTATIVES

1 Chester E. Merrow (R), *Center Ossipee*
2 Sherman Adams (R), *Lincoln*

## NEW JERSEY

SENATORS

Albert W. Hawkes (R), *Montclair*
H. Alexander Smith (R), *Princeton*

REPRESENTATIVES

1 Charles A. Wolverton (R), *Camden*
2 T. Millet Hand (R), *Cape May City*
3 James C. Auchincloss (R), *Rumson*
4 D. Lane Powers (R),[43] *Trenton*
4 Frank A. Mathews, Jr. (R),[44] *Riverton*
5 Charles A. Eaton (R), *North Plainfield*
6 Clifford P. Case (R), *Rahway*
7 J. Parnell Thomas (R), *Allendale*
8 Gordon Canfield (R), *Paterson*
9 Harry L. Towe (R), *Rutherford*
10 Fred A. Hartley, Jr. (R), *Kearny*
11 Frank L. Sundstrom (R), *East Orange*
12 Robert W. Kean (R), *Livingston*
13 Mary T. Norton (D), *Jersey City*
14 Edward J. Hart (D), *Jersey City*

## NEW MEXICO

SENATORS

Carl A. Hatch (D), *Clovis*
Dennis Chavez (D), *Albuquerque*

REPRESENTATIVES AT LARGE

Clinton P. Anderson (D),[45] *Albuquerque*
Antonio M. Fernandez (D), *Santa Fe*

## NEW YORK

SENATORS

Robert F. Wagner (D), *New York City*
James M. Mead (D), *Buffalo*

REPRESENTATIVES

1 Edgar A. Sharp (R), *Patchogue*
2 Leonard W. Hall (R), *Oyster Bay*
3 Henry J. Latham (R), *Queens Village*
4 William B. Barry (D),[46] *St. Albans*
5 James A. Roe (D), *Flushing*
6 James J. Delaney (D), *Long Island City*
7 John J. Delaney (D), *Brooklyn*
8 Joseph L. Pfeifer (D), *Brooklyn*
9 Eugene J. Keogh (D), *Brooklyn*
10 Andrew L. Somers (D), *Brooklyn*
11 James J. Heffernan (D), *Brooklyn*
12 John J. Rooney (D), *Brooklyn*
13 Donald L. O'Toole (D), *Brooklyn*
14 Leo F. Rayfiel (D), *Brooklyn*
15 Emanuel Celler (D), *Brooklyn*
16 Ellsworth B. Buck (R), *Staten Island*
17 Joseph Clark Baldwin (R), *New York City*
18 Vito Marcantonio (AL), *New York City*
19 Samuel Dickstein (D),[47] *New York City*
19 Arthur G. Klein (D),[48] *New York City*
20 Sol Bloom (D), *New York City*
21 James H. Torrens (D), *New York City*
22 Adam C. Powell, Jr. (D), *New York City*
23 Walter A. Lynch (D), *New York City*
24 Benjamin J. Rabin (D), *New York City*
25 Charles A. Buckley (D), *New York City*
26 Peter A. Quinn (D), *New York City*
27 Ralph W. Gwinn (R), *Bronxville*
28 Ralph A. Gamble (R), *Larchmont*
29 Augustus W. Bennet (R), *Newburgh*
30 Jay LeFevre (R), *New Paltz*
31 Bernard W. Kearney (R), *Gloversville*
32 William T. Byrne (D), *Loudonville*
33 Dean P. Taylor (R), *Troy*
34 Clarence E. Kilburn (R), *Malone*
35 Hadwen C. Fuller (R), *Parish*
36 Clarence E. Hancock (R), *Syracuse*
37 Edwin Arthur Hall (R), *Binghamton*
38 John Taber (R), *Auburn*
39 W. Sterling Cole (R), *Bath*
40 George F. Rogers (D), *Rochester*
41 James W. Wadsworth, Jr. (R), *Geneseo*
42 Walter G. Andrews (R), *Buffalo*
43 Edward J. Elsaesser (R), *Buffalo*
44 John C. Butler (R), *Buffalo*
45 Daniel A. Reed (R), *Dunkirk*

---

[37] Resigned January 17, 1945, having been elected Vice President of the United States.

[38] Appointed to fill vacancy caused by resignation of Harry S Truman, and took his seat January 22, 1945.

[39] Died January 15, 1945.

[40] Elected to fill vacancy caused by death of James F. O'Connor, and took his seat June 25, 1945.

[41] Died June 23, 1945.

[42] Appointed to fill vacancy caused by death of James G. Scrugham, and took his seat July 26, 1945.

[43] Resigned August 30, 1945.

[44] Elected to fill vacancy caused by resignation of D. Lane Powers, and took his seat November 27, 1945.

[45] Resigned June 30, 1945; vacancy throughout remainder of the Congress.

[46] Died October 20, 1946; vacancy throughout remainder of the Congress.

[47] Resigned December 30, 1945.

[48] Elected to fill vacancy caused by resignation of Samuel Dickstein, and took his seat March 4, 1946.

## NORTH CAROLINA

SENATORS

Josiah W. Bailey (D),[49] *Raleigh*
William B. Umstead (D),[50] *Durham*
Clyde R. Hoey (D), *Shelby*

REPRESENTATIVES

1 Herbert C. Bonner (D),
 *Washington*
2 John H. Kerr (D), *Warrenton*
3 Graham A. Barden (D), *New Bern*
4 Harold D. Cooley (D), *Nashville*
5 John H. Folger (D), *Mount Airy*
6 Carl T. Durham (D), *Chapel Hill*
7 J. Bayard Clark (D), *Fayetteville*
8 William O. Burgin (D),[51]
 *Lexington*
8 Eliza Jane Pratt (D),[52] *Lexington*
9 Robert L. Doughton (D), *Laurel
 Springs*
10 Joe W. Ervin (D),[53] *Charlotte*
10 Sam J. Ervin, Jr. (D),[54]
 *Morganton*
11 Alfred L. Bulwinkle (D), *Gastonia*
12 Zebulon Weaver (D), *Asheville*

## NORTH DAKOTA

SENATORS

William Langer (R), *Bismarck*
John Moses (D),[55] *Hazen*
Milton R. Young (R),[56] *Berlin*

REPRESENTATIVES AT LARGE

William Lemke (R), *Fargo*
Charles R. Robertson (R), *Bismarck*

## OHIO

SENATORS

Robert A. Taft (R), *Cincinnati*
Harold H. Burton (R),[57] *Cleveland*
James W. Huffman (D),[58] *Columbus*
Kingsley A. Taft (R),[59] *Shaker
 Heights*

REPRESENTATIVE AT LARGE

George H. Bender (R), *Cleveland
 Heights*

REPRESENTATIVES

1 Charles H. Elston (R), *Cincinnati*
2 William E. Hess (R), *Cincinnati*
3 Edward J. Gardner (D), *Hamilton*
4 Robert F. Jones (R), *Lima*
5 Cliff Clevenger (R), *Bryan*
6 Edward O. McCowen (R),
 *Wheelersburg*

7 Clarence J. Brown (R),
 *Blanchester*
8 Frederick C. Smith (R), *Marion*
9 Homer A. Ramey (R), *Toledo*
10 Thomas A. Jenkins (R), *Ironton*
11 Walter E. Brehm (R), *Logan*
12 John M. Vorys (R), *Columbus*
13 Alvin F. Weichel (R), *Sandusky*
14 Walter B. Huber (D), *Akron*
15 Percy W. Griffiths (R), *Marietta*
16 William R. Thom (D), *Canton*
17 J. Harry McGregor (R), *West
 Lafayette*
18 Earl R. Lewis (R), *St. Clairsville*
19 Michael J. Kirwan (D),
 *Youngstown*
20 Michael A. Feighan (D), *Cleveland*
21 Robert Crosser (D), *Cleveland*
22 Frances P. Bolton (R), *Lyndhurst*

## OKLAHOMA

SENATORS

J. W. Elmer Thomas (D), *Medicine
 Park*
Edward H. Moore (R), *Tulsa*

REPRESENTATIVES

1 George B. Schwabe (R), *Tulsa*
2 William G. Stigler (D), *Stigler*
3 Paul Stewart (D), *Antlers*
4 Lyle H. Boren (D), *Seminole*
5 A. S. Mike Monroney (D),
 *Oklahoma City*
6 Jed Johnson (D), *Anadarko*
7 Victor Wickersham (D), *Mangum*
8 Ross Rizley (R), *Guymon*

## OREGON

SENATORS

Guy Cordon (R), *Roseburg*
Wayne L. Morse (R), *Eugene*

REPRESENTATIVES

1 James W. Mott (R),[60] *Salem*
1 A. Walter Norblad, Jr. (R),[61]
 *Astoria*
2 Lowell Stockman (R), *Pendleton*
3 Homer D. Angell (R), *Portland*
4 Harris Ellsworth (R), *Roseburg*

## PENNSYLVANIA

SENATORS

Joseph F. Guffey (D), *Pittsburgh*
Francis J. Myers (D), *Philadelphia*

REPRESENTATIVES

1 William A. Barrett (D),
 *Philadelphia*
2 William T. Granahan (D),
 *Philadelphia*
3 Michael J. Bradley (D),
 *Philadelphia*
4 John Edward Sheridan (D),
 *Philadelphia*
5 William J. Green, Jr. (D),
 *Philadelphia*
6 Herbert J. McGlinchey (D),
 *Philadelphia*
7 James Wolfenden (R), *Upper
 Darby*
8 Charles L. Gerlach (R), *Allentown*
9 J. Roland Kinzer (R), *Lancaster*
10 John W. Murphy (D),[62] *Dunmore*
10 James P. Scoblick (R),[63] *Archbald*
11 Daniel J. Flood (D), *Wilkes-Barre*
12 Ivor D. Fenton (R), *Mahanoy City*
13 Daniel K. Hoch (D), *Reading*
14 Wilson D. Gillette (R), *Towanda*
15 Robert F. Rich (R), *Woolrich*
16 Samuel K. McConnell, Jr. (R),
 *Penn Wynne*
17 Richard M. Simpson (R),
 *Huntingdon*
18 John C. Kunkel (R), *Harrisburg*
19 Leon H. Gavin (R), *Oil City*
20 Francis E. Walter (D), *Easton*
21 Chester H. Gross (R), *Manchester*
22 D. Emmett Brumbaugh (R),
 *Claysburg*
23 J. Buell Snyder (D),[64] *Perryopolis*
23 Carl H. Hoffman (R),[65] *Somerset*
24 Thomas E. Morgan (D),
 *Fredericktown*
25 Louis E. Graham (R), *Beaver*
26 Harve Tibbott (R), *Ebensburg*
27 Augustine B. Kelley (D),
 *Greensburg*
28 Robert L. Rodgers (R), *Erie*
29 Howard E. Campbell (R),
 *Pittsburgh*
30 Robert J. Corbett (R), *Bellevue*
31 James G. Fulton (R), *Dormont*
32 Herman P. Eberharter (D),
 *Pittsburgh*
33 Samuel A. Weiss (D),[66] *Glassport*
33 Frank Buchanan (D),[67]
 *McKeesport*

[49] Died December 15, 1946.
[50] Appointed December 18, 1946, to fill vacancy caused by death of Josiah W. Bailey, but was unable to be sworn in as Congress was not in session.
[51] Died April 11, 1946.
[52] Elected to fill vacancy caused by death of William O. Burgin, and took her seat June 3, 1946.
[53] Died December 25, 1945.
[54] Elected to fill vacancy caused by death of his brother, Joe W. Ervin, and took his seat February 4, 1946.
[55] Died March 3, 1945.
[56] Appointed to fill vacancy caused by death of

John Moses, and took his seat March 19, 1945; subsequently elected.
[57] Resigned September 30, 1945, having been appointed Associate Justice of the Supreme Court of the United States.
[58] Appointed to fill vacancy caused by resignation of Harold H. Burton, and took his seat October 9, 1945.
[59] Elected to fill vacancy caused by resignation of Harold H. Burton and served from November 6, 1946, to January 3, 1947, but was unable to be sworn in as Congress was not in session.
[60] Died November 12, 1945.
[61] Elected to fill vacancy caused by death of James

W. Mott, and took his seat January 29, 1946.
[62] Resigned July 17, 1946.
[63] Elected on November 5, 1946, to fill vacancy caused by resignation of John W. Murphy, but was unable to be sworn in as Congress was not in session.
[64] Died February 24, 1946.
[65] Elected to fill vacancy caused by death of J. Buell Snyder, and took his seat June 11, 1946.
[66] Resigned January 7, 1946.
[67] Elected to fill vacancy caused by resignation of Samuel A. Weiss, and took his seat June 19, 1946.

## RHODE ISLAND

### SENATORS

Peter G. Gerry (D), *Providence*
Theodore F. Green (D), *Providence*

### REPRESENTATIVES

1 Aime J. Forand (D), *Cumberland*
2 John E. Fogarty (D), *Harmony*

## SOUTH CAROLINA

### SENATORS

Burnet R. Maybank (D), *Charleston*
Olin D. Johnston (D), *Spartanburg*

### REPRESENTATIVES

1 L. Mendel Rivers (D), *North Charleston*
2 John J. Riley (D), *Sumter*
3 Butler B. Hare (D), *Saluda*
4 Joseph R. Bryson (D), *Greenville*
5 James P. Richards (D), *Lancaster*
6 John L. McMillan (D), *Florence*

## SOUTH DAKOTA

### SENATORS

J. Chandler Gurney (R), *Yankton*
Harlan J. Bushfield (R), *Miller*

### REPRESENTATIVES

1 Karl E. Mundt (R), *Madison*
2 Francis H. Case (R), *Custer*

## TENNESSEE

### SENATORS

Kenneth D. McKellar (D), *Memphis*
A. Tom Stewart (D), *Winchester*

### REPRESENTATIVES

1 B. Carroll Reece (R), *Johnson City*
2 John Jennings, Jr. (R), *Knoxville*
3 Estes Kefauver (D), *Chattanooga*
4 Albert A. Gore (D), *Carthage*
5 Harold H. Earthman (D), *Murfreesboro*
6 J. Percy Priest (D), *Nashville*
7 Wirt Courtney (D), *Franklin*
8 Thomas J. Murray (D), *Jackson*
9 Jere Cooper (D), *Dyersburg*
10 Clifford Davis (D), *Memphis*

## TEXAS

### SENATORS

Tom T. Connally (D), *Marlin*
W. Lee O'Daniel (D), *Fort Worth*

### REPRESENTATIVES

1 Wright Patman (D), *Texarkana*
2 Jesse M. Combs (D), *Beaumont*
3 Lindley Beckworth (D), *Gladewater*
4 Sam Rayburn (D), *Bonham*
5 Hattan W. Sumners (D), *Dallas*
6 Luther A. Johnson (D),[68] *Corsicana*
6 Olin E. Teague (D),[69] *College Station*
7 Tom Pickett (D), *Palestine*
8 Albert Thomas (D), *Houston*
9 Joseph J. Mansfield (D), *Columbus*
10 Lyndon B. Johnson (D), *Johnson City*
11 William R. Poage (D), *Waco*
12 Fritz G. Lanham (D), *Fort Worth*
13 Ed Gossett (D), *Wichita Falls*
14 John E. Lyle, Jr. (D), *Corpus Christi*
15 Milton H. West (D), *Brownsville*
16 R. Ewing Thomason (D), *El Paso*
17 Sam M. Russell (D), *Stephenville*
18 Eugene Worley (D), *Shamrock*
19 George H. Mahon (D), *Colorado City*
20 Paul J. Kilday (D), *San Antonio*
21 O. Clark Fisher (D), *San Angelo*

## UTAH

### SENATORS

Elbert D. Thomas (D), *Salt Lake City*
Abe Murdock (D), *Beaver*

### REPRESENTATIVES

1 Walter K. Granger (D), *Cedar City*
2 J. W. Robinson (D), *Provo*

## VERMONT

### SENATORS

Warren R. Austin (R),[70] *Burlington*
Ralph E. Flanders (R),[71] *Springfield*
George D. Aiken (R), *Putney*

### REPRESENTATIVE AT LARGE

Charles A. Plumley (R), *Northfield*

## VIRGINIA

### SENATORS

Carter Glass (D),[72] *Lynchburg*
Thomas G. Burch (D),[73] *Martinsville*

A. Willis Robertson (D),[74] *Lexington*
Harry Flood Byrd (D), *Berryville*

### REPRESENTATIVES

1 Schuyler Otis Bland (D), *Newport News*
2 Ralph H. Daughton (D), *Norfolk*
3 Dave E. Satterfield, Jr. (D),[75] *Richmond*
3 J. Vaughan Gary (D),[76] *Richmond*
4 Patrick Henry Drewry (D), *Petersburg*
5 Thomas G. Burch (D),[77] *Martinsville*
5 Thomas B. Stanley (D),[78] *Stanleytown*
6 Clifton A. Woodrum (D),[79] *Roanoke*
6 J. Lindsay Almond, Jr. (D),[80] *Roanoke*
7 A. Willis Robertson (D),[81] *Lexington*
7 Burr P. Harrison (D),[82] *Winchester*
8 Howard W. Smith (D), *Alexandria*
9 John W. Flannagan, Jr. (D), *Bristol*

## WASHINGTON

### SENATORS

Warren G. Magnuson (D), *Seattle*
Monrad C. Wallgren (D),[83] *Everett*
Hugh B. Mitchell (D),[84] *Everett*
Harry P. Cain (R),[85] *Tacoma*

### REPRESENTATIVES

1 Hugh De Lacy (D), *Seattle*
2 Henry M. Jackson (D), *Everett*
3 Charles R. Savage (D), *Shelton*
4 Hal Holmes (R), *Ellensburg*
5 Walter F. Horan (R), *Wenatchee*
6 John M. Coffee (D), *Tacoma*

## WEST VIRGINIA

### SENATORS

Harley M. Kilgore (D), *Beckley*
Chapman Revercomb (R), *Charleston*

### REPRESENTATIVES

1 Matthew M. Neely (D), *Fairmont*
2 Jennings Randolph (D), *Elkins*
3 Cleveland M. Bailey (D), *Clarksburg*
4 Hubert S. Ellis (R), *Huntington*
5 John Kee (D), *Bluefield*
6 Erland H. Hedrick (D), *Beckley*

---

[68] Resigned July 17, 1946.
[69] Elected August 24, 1946, to fill vacancy caused by resignation of Luther A. Johnson, but was unable to be sworn in as Congress was not in session.
[70] Resigned August 2, 1946.
[71] Appointed November 1, 1946, to fill vacancy caused by resignation of Warren R. Austin, but was unable to be sworn in as Congress was not in session.
[72] Died May 28, 1946.
[73] Appointed to fill vacancy caused by death of Carter Glass, and took his seat May 31, 1946.
[74] Elected November 5, 1946, to fill vacancy caused by death of Carter Glass, but was unable to be sworn in as Congress was not in session.

[75] Resigned February 15, 1945.
[76] Elected to fill vacancy caused by resignation of Dave E. Satterfield, Jr., and took his seat March 16, 1945.
[77] Resigned May 31, 1946, having been appointed Senator.
[78] Elected November 5, 1946, to fill vacancy caused by resignation of Thomas B. Burch, but was unable to be sworn in as Congress was not in session.
[79] Resigned December 31, 1945.
[80] Elected to fill vacancy caused by resignation of Clifton A. Woodrum, and took his seat February 4, 1946.

[81] Resigned November 5, 1946, having been elected Senator.
[82] Elected November 5, 1946, to fill vacancy caused by resignation of A. Willis Robertson, but was unable to be sworn in as Congress was not in session.
[83] Resigned January 9, 1945.
[84] Appointed to fill vacancy caused by resignation of Monrad C. Wallgren, and took his seat January 18, 1945; resigned December 25, 1946.
[85] Appointed December 26, 1946, to fill vacancy caused by resignations of Monrad C. Wallgren and Hugh B. Mitchell, but was unable to be sworn in as Congress was not in session.

## WISCONSIN

SENATORS

Robert M. La Follette, Jr. (P),[86]
*Madison*

Alexander Wiley (R), *Chippewa Falls*

REPRESENTATIVES

1 Lawrence H. Smith (R), *Racine*
2 Robert K. Henry (R),[87] *Jefferson*
3 William H. Stevenson (R), *La Crosse*
4 Thaddeus F. B. Wasielewski (D), *Milwaukee*
5 Andrew J. Biemiller (D), *Milwaukee*
6 Frank B. Keefe (R), *Oshkosh*
7 Reid F. Murray (R), *Ogdensburg*
8 John W. Byrnes (R), *Green Bay*
9 Merlin Hull (P),[88] *Black River Falls*
10 Alvin E. O'Konski (R), *Mercer*

## WYOMING

SENATORS

Joseph C. O'Mahoney (D), *Cheyenne*
Edward V. Robertson (R), *Cody*

REPRESENTATIVE AT LARGE

Frank A. Barrett (R), *Lusk*

## TERRITORY OF ALASKA

DELEGATE

E. L. (Bob) Bartlett (D), *Juneau*

## TERRITORY OF HAWAII

DELEGATE

Joseph R. Farrington (R), *Honolulu*

## COMMONWEALTH OF THE PHILIPPINES

RESIDENT COMMISSIONER

Carlos P. Romulo,[89] *Manila*

## PUERTO RICO

RESIDENT COMMISSIONER

Jesús T. Piñero (PD),[90] *Canovanas*
Antonio Fernós-Isern (PD),[91] *San Juan*

---

[86] Changed party affiliation to Republican, March 17, 1946.

[87] Died November 20, 1946; vacancy throughout remainder of the Congress.

[88] Changed party affiliation to Republican, March 17, 1946.

[89] Office of Resident Commissioner terminated on July 4, 1946 (Public Law 127, 73d Cong.)

[90] Resigned September 2, 1946.

[91] Appointed September 11, 1946, to fill vacancy caused by resignation of Jesús T. Piñero, but was unable to be sworn in as Congress was not in session.

# 80TH CONGRESS

## JANUARY 3, 1947, TO JANUARY 3, 1949

FIRST SESSION— *January 3, 1947, to December 19, 1947*
SECOND SESSION— *January 6, 1948,*[1] *to December 31, 1948*

**Arthur H. Vandenberg**
President Pro Tempore

---

### Senate
Democrats 45 — Republicans 51
VICE PRESIDENT OF THE UNITED STATES[2]
PRESIDENT PRO TEMPORE OF THE SENATE— Arthur H. Vandenberg,[3] of Michigan
SECRETARY OF THE SENATE— Carl A. Loeffler,[4] of Pennsylvania
SERGEANT AT ARMS OF THE SENATE— Edward F. McGinnis,[5] of Illinois
MAJORITY FLOOR LEADER— Wallace H. White, Jr., of Maine
REPUBLICAN WHIP— Kenneth S. Wherry, of Nebraska
DEMOCRATIC FLOOR LEADER— Alben W. Barkley, of Kentucky
ASSISTANT DEMOCRATIC LEADER— Scott W. Lucas, of Illinois

**Joseph W. Martin, Jr.**
Speaker

---

### House of Representatives
Democrats 188 — Republicans 246 — American Labor 1
SPEAKER OF THE HOUSE OF REPRESENTATIVES— Joseph W. Martin, Jr.,[6] of Massachusetts
CLERK OF THE HOUSE— John Andrews,[7] of Massachusetts
SERGEANT AT ARMS OF THE HOUSE— William F. Russell, of Pennsylvania
DOORKEEPER OF THE HOUSE— M. L. Meletio, of Missouri
POSTMASTER OF THE HOUSE— Frank Collier
MAJORITY LEADER— Charles A. Halleck, of Indiana
MAJORITY WHIP— Leslie C. Arends, of Illinois
DEMOCRATIC LEADER— Sam Rayburn, of Texas
DEMOCRATIC WHIP— John W. McCormack, of Massachusetts

---

## ALABAMA

### SENATORS
Lister Hill (D), *Montgomery*
John J. Sparkman (D), *Huntsville*

### REPRESENTATIVES
1 Frank W. Boykin (D), *Mobile*
2 George M. Grant (D), *Troy*
3 George W. Andrews (D), *Union Springs*
4 Sam Hobbs (D), *Selma*
5 Albert Rains (D), *Gadsden*
6 Pete Jarman (D), *Livingston*
7 Carter Manasco (D), *Jasper*
8 Robert E. Jones, Jr. (D),[8] *Scottsboro*
9 Laurie C. Battle (D), *Birmingham*

## ARIZONA

### SENATORS
Carl Hayden (D), *Phoenix*
Ernest W. McFarland (D), *Florence*

### REPRESENTATIVES AT LARGE
Richard F. Harless (D), *Phoenix*
John R. Murdock (D), *Tempe*

## ARKANSAS

### SENATORS
John L. McClellan (D), *Camden*
J. William Fulbright (D), *Fayetteville*

### REPRESENTATIVES
1 E. C. Gathings (D), *West Memphis*
2 Wilbur D. Mills (D), *Kensett*
3 James W. Trimble (D), *Berryville*
4 Fadjo Cravens (D), *Fort Smith*
5 Brooks Hays (D), *Little Rock*
6 William F. Norrell (D), *Monticello*
7 Oren Harris (D), *El Dorado*

## CALIFORNIA

### SENATORS
Sheridan Downey (D), *San Francisco*
William F. Knowland (R), *Piedmont*

### REPRESENTATIVES
1 Clarence F. Lea (D), *Santa Rosa*
2 Clair Engle (D), *Red Bluff*
3 Leroy Johnson (R), *Stockton*
4 Franck R. Havenner (D), *San Francisco*
5 Richard J. Welch (R), *San Francisco*
6 George P. Miller (D), *Alameda*
7 John J. Allen, Jr. (R), *Oakland*
8 John Z. Anderson (R), *San Juan Bautista*
9 Bertrand W. Gearhart (R), *Fresno*
10 Alfred J. Elliott (D), *Tulare*
11 Ernest K. Bramblett (R), *Pacific Grove*
12 Richard M. Nixon (R), *Whittier*
13 Norris Poulson (R), *Los Angeles*
14 Helen Gahagan Douglas (D), *Los Angeles*
15 Gordon L. McDonough (R), *Los Angeles*
16 Donald L. Jackson (R), *Santa Monica*
17 Cecil R. King (D), *Los Angeles*
18 Willis W. Bradley (R), *Long Beach*
19 Chet Holifield (D), *Montebello*
20 Carl Hinshaw (R), *Pasadena*

---

21 Harry R. Sheppard (D), *Yucaipa*
22 John Phillips (R), *Banning*
23 Charles K. Fletcher (R), *San Diego*

## COLORADO

### SENATORS

Edwin C. Johnson (D), *Craig*
Eugene D. Millikin (R), *Denver*

### REPRESENTATIVES

1 John A. Carroll (D), *Denver*
2 William S. Hill (R), *Fort Collins*
3 J. Edgar Chenoweth (R), *Trinidad*
4 Robert F. Rockwell (R), *Paonia*

## CONNECTICUT

### SENATORS

Brien McMahon (D), *Norwalk*
Raymond E. Baldwin (R), *Stratford*

### REPRESENTATIVE AT LARGE

Antoni N. Sadlak (R), *Rockville*

### REPRESENTATIVES

1 William J. Miller (R), *Wethersfield*
2 Horace Seely-Brown, Jr. (R), *Pomfret Center*
3 Ellsworth B. Foote (R), *North Branford*
4 John Davis Lodge (R), *Westport*
5 James T. Patterson (R), *Naugatuck*

## DELAWARE

### SENATORS

C. Douglass Buck (R), *Wilmington*
John J. Williams (R), *Millsboro*

### REPRESENTATIVE AT LARGE

J. Caleb Boggs (R), *Wilmington*

## FLORIDA

### SENATORS

Claude D. Pepper (D), *Tallahassee*
Spessard L. Holland (D), *Bartow*

### REPRESENTATIVES

1 J. Hardin Peterson (D), *Lakeland*
2 Emory H. Price (D), *Jacksonville*
3 Robert L. F. Sikes (D), *Crestview*
4 George A. Smathers (D), *Miami*
5 Joe Hendricks (D), *De Land*
6 Dwight L. Rogers (D), *Fort Lauderdale*

## GEORGIA

### SENATORS

Walter F. George (D), *Vienna*
Richard B. Russell (D), *Winder*

### REPRESENTATIVES

1 Prince H. Preston, Jr. (D), *Statesboro*
2 Edward E. Cox (D), *Camilla*
3 Stephen Pace (D), *Americus*
4 A. Sidney Camp (D), *Newnan*
5 James C. Davis (D),[9] *Stone Mountain*
6 Carl Vinson (D), *Milledgeville*
7 Henderson L. Lanham (D), *Rome*
8 William M. Wheeler (D), *Alma*
9 John S. Wood (D), *Canton*
10 Paul Brown (D), *Elberton*

## IDAHO

### SENATORS

Glen H. Taylor (D), *Pocatello*
Henry C. Dworshak (R), *Burley*

### REPRESENTATIVES

1 Abe McGregor Goff (R), *Moscow*
2 John C. Sanborn (R), *Hagerman*

## ILLINOIS

### SENATORS

Scott W. Lucas (D), *Havana*
C. Wayland Brooks (R), *Chicago*

### REPRESENTATIVE AT LARGE

William G. Stratton (R), *Morris*

### REPRESENTATIVES

1 William L. Dawson (D), *Chicago*
2 Richard B. Vail (R), *Chicago*
3 Fred E. Busbey (R), *Chicago*
4 Martin Gorski (D), *Chicago*
5 Adolph J. Sabath (D), *Chicago*
6 Thomas J. O'Brien (D), *Chicago*
7 Thomas L. Owens (R),[10] *Chicago*
8 Thomas S. Gordon (D), *Chicago*
9 Robert J. Twyman (R), *Chicago*
10 Ralph E. Church (R), *Evanston*
11 Chauncey W. Reed (R), *West Chicago*
12 Noah M. Mason (R), *Oglesby*
13 Leo E. Allen (R), *Galena*
14 Anton J. Johnson (R), *Macomb*
15 Robert B. Chiperfield (R), *Canton*
16 Everett M. Dirksen (R), *Pekin*
17 Leslie C. Arends (R), *Melvin*
18 Edward H. Jenison (R), *Paris*
19 Rolla C. McMillen (R), *Decatur*
20 Sidney E. Simpson (R), *Carrollton*
21 Evan Howell (R),[11] *Springfield*
22 Melvin Price (D), *East St. Louis*
23 Charles W. Vursell (R), *Salem*
24 Roy Clippinger (R), *Carmi*
25 Cecil W. (Runt) Bishop (R), *Carterville*

## INDIANA

### SENATORS

Homer E. Capehart (R), *Washington*
William E. Jenner (R), *Bedford*

### REPRESENTATIVES

1 Ray J. Madden (D), *Gary*
2 Charles A. Halleck (R), *Rensselaer*
3 Robert A. Grant (R), *South Bend*
4 George W. Gillie (R), *Fort Wayne*
5 Forest A. Harness (R), *Kokomo*
6 Noble J. Johnson (R),[12] *Terre Haute*
7 Gerald W. Landis (R), *Linton*
8 Edward A. Mitchell (R), *Evansville*
9 Earl Wilson (R), *Bedford*
10 Raymond S. Springer (R),[13] *Connersville*
10 Ralph Harvey (R),[14] *New Castle*
11 Louis Ludlow (D), *Indianapolis*

## IOWA

### SENATORS

George A. Wilson (R), *Des Moines*
Bourke B. Hickenlooper (R), *Cedar Rapids*

### REPRESENTATIVES

1 Thomas E. Martin (R), *Iowa City*
2 Henry O. Talle (R), *Decorah*
3 John W. Gwynne (R), *Waterloo*
4 Karl M. LeCompte (R), *Corydon*
5 Paul Cunningham (R), *Des Moines*
6 James I. Dolliver (R), *Fort Dodge*
7 Ben F. Jensen (R), *Exira*
8 Charles B. Hoeven (R), *Alton*

## KANSAS

### SENATORS

Arthur Capper (R), *Topeka*
Clyde M. Reed (R), *Parsons*

### REPRESENTATIVES

1 Albert M. Cole (R), *Holton*
2 Errett P. Scrivner (R), *Kansas City*
3 Herbert A. Meyer (R), *Independence*
4 Edward H. Rees (R), *Emporia*
5 Clifford R. Hope (R), *Garden City*
6 Wint Smith (R), *Mankato*

## KENTUCKY

### SENATORS

Alben W. Barkley (D), *Paducah*
John Sherman Cooper (R), *Somerset*

### REPRESENTATIVES

1 Noble J. Gregory (D), *Mayfield*
2 Earle C. Clements (D),[15] *Morganfield*
2 John A. Whitaker (D),[16] *Russellville*

---

[9] Election unsuccessfully contested by Helen Douglas Mankin and Wyman C. Lowe.
[10] Died June 7, 1948; vacancy throughout remainder of Congress.
[11] Resigned October 5, 1947; vacancy throughout remainder of Congress.

[12] Resigned July 1, 1948; vacancy throughout remainder of Congress.
[13] Died August 28, 1947.
[14] Elected to fill vacancy caused by death of Raymond S. Springer, and took his seat November 17, 1947.

[15] Resigned January 6, 1948.
[16] Elected to fill vacancy caused by resignation of Earle C. Clements, and took his seat April 26, 1948.

## KENTUCKY—Continued

REPRESENTATIVES—CONTINUED

3 Thruston B. Morton (R), *Glenview*
4 Frank L. Chelf (D), *Lebanon*
5 Brent Spence (D), *Fort Thomas*
6 Virgil M. Chapman (D), *Paris*
7 W. Howes Meade (R), *Paintsville*
8 Joe B. Bates (D), *Greenup*
9 John M. Robsion (R),[17] *Barbourville*
9 William Lewis (R),[18] *London*

## LOUISIANA

SENATORS

John H. Overton (D),[19] *Alexandria*
William C. Feazel (D),[20] *West Monroe*
Russell B. Long (D),[21] *Baton Rouge*
Allen J. Ellender (D), *Houma*

REPRESENTATIVES

1 F. Edward Hébert (D), *New Orleans*
2 Hale Boggs (D), *New Orleans*
3 James Domengeaux (D), *Lafayette*
4 Overton Brooks (D), *Shreveport*
5 Otto E. Passman (D), *Monroe*
6 James H. Morrison (D), *Hammond*
7 Henry D. Larcade, Jr. (D), *Opelousas*
8 A. Leonard Allen (D), *Winnfield*

## MAINE

SENATORS

Wallace H. White, Jr. (R), *Auburn*
Ralph O. Brewster (R), *Dexter*

REPRESENTATIVES

1 Robert Hale (R), *Portland*
2 Margaret Chase Smith (R), *Skowhegan*
3 Frank Fellows (R), *Bangor*

## MARYLAND

SENATORS

Millard E. Tydings (D), *Havre de Grace*
Herbert R. O'Conor (D),[22] *Baltimore*

REPRESENTATIVES

1 Edward T. Miller (R), *Easton*
2 Hugh A. Meade (D), *Baltimore*
3 Thomas D'Alesandro, Jr. (D),[23] *Baltimore*

3 Edward A. Garmatz (D),[24] *Baltimore*
4 George H. Fallon (D), *Baltimore*
5 Lansdale G. Sasscer (D), *Upper Marlboro*
6 J. Glenn Beall (R), *Frostburg*

## MASSACHUSETTS

SENATORS

Leverett Saltonstall (R), *Dover*
Henry Cabot Lodge, Jr. (R), *Beverly*

REPRESENTATIVES

1 John W. Heselton (R), *Deerfield*
2 Charles R. Clason (R), *Springfield*
3 Philip J. Philbin (D), *Clinton*
4 Harold D. Donohue (D), *Worcester*
5 Edith Nourse Rogers (R), *Lowell*
6 George J. Bates (R), *Salem*
7 Thomas J. Lane (D), *Lawrence*
8 Angier L. Goodwin (R), *Melrose*
9 Charles L. Gifford (R),[25] *Cotuit*
9 Donald W. Nicholson (R),[26] *Wareham*
10 Christian A. Herter (R), *Boston*
11 John F. Kennedy (D), *Boston*
12 John W. McCormack (D), *Dorchester*
13 Richard B. Wigglesworth (R), *Milton*
14 Joseph W. Martin, Jr. (R), *North Attleboro*

## MICHIGAN

SENATORS

Arthur H. Vandenberg (R), *Grand Rapids*
Homer Ferguson (R), *Detroit*

REPRESENTATIVES

1 George G. Sadowski (D), *Detroit*
2 Earl C. Michener (R), *Adrian*
3 Paul W. Shafer (R), *Battle Creek*
4 Clare E. Hoffman (R), *Allegan*
5 Bartel J. Jonkman (R), *Grand Rapids*
6 William W. Blackney (R), *Flint*
7 Jesse P. Wolcott (R), *Port Huron*
8 Fred L. Crawford (R), *Saginaw*
9 Albert J. Engle (R), *Muskegon*
10 Roy O. Woodruff (R), *Bay City*
11 Frederick V. Bradley (R),[27] *Rogers City*

11 Charles E. Potter (R),[28] *Cheboygan*
12 John B. Bennett (R), *Ontonagon*
13 Howard A. Coffin (R), *Detroit*
14 Harold F. Youngblood (R), *Detroit*
15 John D. Dingell (D), *Detroit*
16 John Lesinski (D), *Dearborn*
17 George A. Dondero (R), *Royal Oak*

## MINNESOTA

SENATORS

Joseph H. Ball (R), *Stillwater*
Edward J. Thye (R), *Northfield*

REPRESENTATIVES

1 August H. Andresen (R), *Red Wing*
2 Joseph P. O'Hara (R), *Glencoe*
3 George E. MacKinnon (R), *Minneapolis*
4 Edward J. Devitt (R), *St. Paul*
5 Walter H. Judd (R), *Minneapolis*
6 Harold Knutson (R), *Manhattan Beach*
7 H. Carl Andersen (R), *Tyler*
8 John A. Blatnik (D), *Chisholm*
9 Harold C. Hagen (R), *Crookston*

## MISSISSIPPI

SENATORS

Theodore G. Bilbo (D),[29] *Poplarville*
John C. Stennis (D),[30] *De Kalb*,
James O. Eastland (D), *Doddsville*

REPRESENTATIVES

1 John E. Rankin (D), *Tupelo*
2 Jamie L. Whitten (D), *Charleston*
3 William M. Whittington (D), *Greenwood*
4 Thomas G. Abernethy (D), *Okolona*
5 W. Arthur Winstead (D), *Philadelphia*
6 William M. Colmer (D), *Pascagoula*
7 John Bell Williams (D), *Raymond*

## MISSOURI

SENATORS

Forrest C. Donnell (R), *Webster Groves*
James P. Kem (R), *Kansas City*

---

[17] Died February 17, 1948.
[18] Elected to fill vacancy caused by death of John M. Robsion, and took his seat May 3, 1948.
[19] Died May 14, 1948.
[20] Appointed to fill vacancy caused by death of John H. Overton, and took his seat May 24, 1948.
[21] Elected to fill vacancy caused by death of John H. Overton, and took his seat December 31, 1948.
[22] Election unsuccessfully contested by David John Markey. (See U.S. Senate Election, Expulsion and Censure Cases, 1793-1990, Senate Document 103-33, pp. 380-82.)
[23] Resigned May 16, 1947.
[24] Elected to fill vacancy caused by resignation of Thomas D'Alesandro, Jr., and took his seat July 24, 1947.

[25] Died August 23, 1947.
[26] Elected to fill vacancy caused by death of Charles L. Gifford, and took his seat November 28, 1947.
[27] Died May 24, 1947.
[28] Elected to fill vacancy caused by death of Frederick V. Bradley, and took his seat November 17, 1947.
[29] Controversy surrounding allegations that Bilbo had accepted gifts, services and contributions from wartime contractors and had made efforts to prevent African-Americans from voting in Mississippi's July 1946 primary election caused two Senate committees to investigate his activities. Faced with a filibuster by Bilbo's Senate partisans following the opening of the

80th Congress, Democratic and Republican leaders reached a compromise prohibiting Bilbo from taking his seat but permitting him to receive his salary, and agreeing to delay action on his seating until after he had returned to the Senate from receiving medical treatment. Bilbo's death on August 21, 1947 removed any reason for the Senate to act regarding his case. (See U.S. Senate Election, Expulsion and Censure Cases, 1793-1990, Senate Document 103-33, pp. 376-79.)
[30] Elected to fill vacancy caused by death of Theodore G. Bilbo, and took his seat November 17, 1947.

REPRESENTATIVES

1 Samuel W. Arnold (R), *Kirksville*
2 Max Schwabe (R), *Columbia*
3 William C. Cole (R), *St. Joseph*
4 C. Jasper Bell (D), *Blue Springs*
5 Albert L. Reeves, Jr. (R), *Kansas City*
6 Marion T. Bennett (R), *Springfield*
7 Dewey Short (R), *Galena*
8 Parke M. Banta (R), *Arcadia*
9 Clarence Cannon (D), *Elsberry*
10 Orville Zimmerman (D),[31] *Kennett*
10 Paul C. Jones (D),[32] *Kennett*
11 Claude I. Bakewell (R), *St. Louis*
12 Walter C. Ploeser (R), *Chesterfield*
13 Frank M. Karsten (D), *St. Louis*

## MONTANA

SENATORS

James E. Murray (D), *Butte*
Zales N. Ecton (R), *Manhattan*

REPRESENTATIVES

1 Mike Mansfield (D), *Missoula*
2 Wesley A. D'Ewart (R), *Wilsall*

## NEBRASKA

SENATORS

Hugh A. Butler (R), *Omaha*
Kenneth S. Wherry (R), *Pawnee City*

REPRESENTATIVES

1 Carl T. Curtis (R), *Minden*
2 Howard H. Buffett (R), *Omaha*
3 Karl Stefan (R), *Norfolk*
4 Arthur L. Miller (R), *Kimball*

## NEVADA

SENATORS

Patrick A. McCarran (D), *Reno*
George W. Malone (R), *Reno*

REPRESENTATIVE AT LARGE

Charles H. Russell (R), *Ely*

## NEW HAMPSHIRE

SENATORS

H. Styles Bridges (R), *Concord*
Charles W. Tobey (R), *Temple*

REPRESENTATIVES

1 Chester E. Merrow (R), *Center Ossipee*
2 Norris Cotton (R), *Lebanon*

## NEW JERSEY

SENATORS

Albert W. Hawkes (R), *Montclair*
H. Alexander Smith (R), *Princeton*

REPRESENTATIVES

1 Charles A. Wolverton (R), *Merchantville*
2 T. Millet Hand (R), *Cape May City*
3 James C. Auchincloss (R), *Rumson*
4 Frank A. Mathews, Jr. (R), *Riverton*
5 Charles A. Eaton (R), *Plainfield*
6 Clifford P. Case (R), *Rahway*
7 J. Parnell Thomas (R), *Allendale*
8 Gordon Canfield (R), *Paterson*
9 Harry L. Towe (R), *Rutherford*
10 Fred A. Hartley, Jr. (R), *Pittstown*
11 Frank L. Sundstrom (R), *East Orange*
12 Robert W. Kean (R), *Livingston*
13 Mary T. Norton (D), *Jersey City*
14 Edward J. Hart (D), *Jersey City*

## NEW MEXICO

SENATORS

Carl A. Hatch (D), *Clovis*
Dennis Chavez (D), *Albuquerque*

REPRESENTATIVES AT LARGE

Antonio M. Fernandez (D), *Santa Fe*
Georgia L. Lusk (D), *Santa Fe*

## NEW YORK

SENATORS

Robert F. Wagner (D), *New York City*
Irving M. Ives (R), *Norwich*

REPRESENTATIVES

1 W. Kingsland Macy (R), *Islip*
2 Leonard W. Hall (R), *Oyster Bay*
3 Henry J. Latham (R), *Queens Village*
4 Gregory McMahon (R), *Ozone Park*
5 Robert Tripp Ross (R), *Jackson Heights*
6 Robert J. Nodar, Jr. (R), *Maspeth*
7 John J. Delaney (D),[33] *Brooklyn*
8 Joseph L. Pfeifer (D), *Brooklyn*
9 Eugene J. Keogh (D), *Brooklyn*
10 Andrew L. Somers (D), *Brooklyn*
11 James J. Heffernan (D), *Brooklyn*
12 John J. Rooney (D), *Brooklyn*
13 Donald L. O'Toole (D), *Brooklyn*
14 Leo F. Rayfiel (D),[34] *Brooklyn*
14 Abraham J. Multer (D),[35] *Brooklyn*
15 Emanuel Celler (D), *Brooklyn*
16 Ellsworth B. Buck (R), *Staten Island*
17 Frederic R. Coudert, Jr. (R), *New York City*
18 Vito Marcantonio (AL), *New York City*

19 Arthur G. Klein (D), *New York City*
20 Sol Bloom (D), *New York City*
21 Jacob K. Javits (R), *New York City*
22 Adam Clayton Powell, Jr. (D), *New York City*
23 Walter A. Lynch (D), *New York City*
24 Benjamin J. Rabin (D),[36] *New York City*
24 Leo Isacson (AL),[37] *New York City*
25 Charles A. Buckley (D), *New York City*
26 David M. Potts (R), *New York City*
27 Ralph W. Gwinn (R), *Bronxville*
28 Ralph A. Gamble (R), *Larchmont*
29 Katharine St. George (R), *Tuxedo Park*
30 Jay LeFevre (R), *New Paltz*
31 Bernard W. Kearney (R), *Gloversville*
32 William T. Byrne (D), *Loudonville*
33 Dean P. Taylor (R), *Troy*
34 Clarence E. Kilburn (R), *Malone*
35 Hadwen C. Fuller (R), *Parish*
36 R. Walter Riehlman (R), *Tully*
37 Edwin Arthur Hall (R), *Binghamton*
38 John Taber (R), *Auburn*
39 W. Sterling Cole (R), *Bath*
40 Kenneth B. Keating (R), *Rochester*
41 James W. Wadsworth, Jr. (R), *Geneseo*
42 Walter G. Andrews (R), *Buffalo*
43 Edward J. Elsaesser (R), *Buffalo*
44 John C. Butler (R), *Buffalo*
45 Daniel A. Reed (R), *Dunkirk*

## NORTH CAROLINA

SENATORS

Clyde R. Hoey (D), *Shelby*
William B. Umstead (D),[38] *Durham*
J. Melville Broughton (D),[39] *Raleigh*

REPRESENTATIVES

1 Herbert C. Bonner (D), *Washington*
2 John H. Kerr (D), *Warrenton*
3 Graham A. Barden (D), *New Bern*
4 Harold D. Cooley (D), *Nashville*
5 John H. Folger (D), *Mount Airy*
6 Carl T. Durham (D), *Chapel Hill*
7 J. Bayard Clark (D), *Fayetteville*
8 Charles B. Deane (D), *Rockingham*
9 Robert L. Doughton (D), *Sparta*
10 Hamilton C. Jones (D), *Charlotte*
11 Alfred L. Bulwinkle (D), *Gastonia*
12 Monroe M. Redden (D), *Hendersonville*

---

[31] Died April 7, 1948.
[32] Elected to fill vacancy caused by death of Orville Zimmerman, and took his seat December 31, 1948.
[33] Died November 18, 1948; vacancy throughout remainder of Congress.
[34] Resigned September 13, 1947.

[35] Elected to fill vacancy caused by resignation of Leo F. Rayfiel, and took his seat November 17, 1947.
[36] Resigned December 31, 1947.
[37] Elected to fill vacancy caused by resignation of Benjamin J. Rabin, and took his seat March 1, 1948.
[38] Appointed to fill vacancy caused by death of

Josiah W. Bailey in preceding Congress; appointment expired Deecember 30, 1948.
[39] Elected to fill vacancy caused by death of Josiah W. Bailey, in preceding Congress, and took his seat December 31, 1948.

## NORTH DAKOTA

### SENATORS
William Langer (R), *Wheatland*
Milton R. Young (R), *Berlin*

### REPRESENTATIVES AT LARGE
William Lemke (R), *Fargo*
Charles R. Robertson (R), *Bismarck*

## OHIO

### SENATORS
Robert A. Taft (R), *Cincinnati*
John W. Bricker (R), *Columbus*

### REPRESENTATIVE AT LARGE
George H. Bender (R), *Cleveland Heights*

### REPRESENTATIVES
1 Charles H. Elston (R), *Cincinnati*
2 William E. Hess (R), *Cincinnati*
3 Raymond H. Burke (R), *Hamilton*
4 Robert F. Jones (R),[40] *Lima*
4 William M. McCulloch (R),[41] *Piqua*
5 Cliff Clevenger (R), *Bryan*
6 Edward O. McCowen (R), *Wheelersburg*
7 Clarence J. Brown (R), *Blanchester*
8 Frederick C. Smith (R), *Marion*
9 Homer A. Ramey (R), *Toledo*
10 Thomas A. Jenkins (R), *Ironton*
11 Walter E. Brehm (R), *Logan*
12 John M. Vorys (R), *Columbus*
13 Alvin F. Weichel (R), *Sandusky*
14 Walter B. Huber (D), *Akron*
15 Percy W. Griffiths (R), *Marietta*
16 Henderson H. Carson (R), *Canton*
17 J. Harry McGregor (R), *West Lafayette*
18 Earl R. Lewis (R), *St. Clairsville*
19 Michael J. Kirwan (D), *Youngstown*
20 Michael A. Feighan (D), *Cleveland*
21 Robert Crosser (D), *Cleveland*
22 Frances P. Bolton (R), *Lyndhurst*

## OKLAHOMA

### SENATORS
J. W. Elmer Thomas (D), *Medicine Park*
Edward H. Moore (R), *Tulsa*

### REPRESENTATIVES
1 George B. Schwabe (R), *Tulsa*
2 William G. Stigler (D), *Stigler*
3 Carl Albert (D), *McAlester*
4 Glen D. Johnson (D), *Okemah*
5 A. S. Mike Monroney (D), *Oklahoma City*
6 Toby Morris (D), *Lawton*

7 Preston E. Peden (D), *Altus*
8 Ross Rizley (R), *Guymon*

## OREGON

### SENATORS
Guy Cordon (R), *Roseburg*
Wayne L. Morse (R), *Eugene*

### REPRESENTATIVES
1 A. Walter Norblad, Jr. (R), *Astoria*
2 Lowell Stockman (R), *Pendleton*
3 Homer D. Angell (R), *Portland*
4 Harris Ellsworth (R), *Roseburg*

## PENNSYLVANIA

### SENATORS
Francis J. Myers (D), *Philadelphia*
Edward Martin (R), *Washington*

### REPRESENTATIVES
1 James Gallagher (R), *Philadelphia*
2 Robert N. McGarvey (R), *Philadelphia*
3 Hardie Scott (R), *Philadelphia*
4 Franklin J. Maloney (R), *Philadelphia*
5 George W. Sarbacher, Jr. (R), *Philadelphia*
6 Hugh D. Scott, Jr. (R), *Philadelphia*
7 E. Wallace Chadwick (R), *Rose Valley*
8 Charles L. Gerlach (R),[42] *Allentown*
8 Franklin H. Lichtenwalter (R),[43] *Center Valley,*
9 Paul B. Dague (R), *Downingtown*
10 James P. Scoblick (R), *Archbald*
11 Mitchell Jenkins (R), *Trucksville*
12 Ivor D. Fenton (R), *Mahonoy City*
13 Frederick A. Muhlenberg (R), *Wernersville*
14 Wilson D. Gillette (R), *Towanda*
15 Robert F. Rich (R), *Woolrich*
16 Samuel K. McConnell, Jr. (R), *Wynnewood*
17 Richard M. Simpson (R), *Huntingdon*
18 John C. Kunkel (R), *Harrisburg*
19 Leon H. Gavin (R), *Oil City*
20 Francis E. Walter (D), *Easton*
21 Chester H. Gross (R), *York*
22 James E. Van Zandt (R), *Altoona*
23 William J. Crow (R), *Uniontown*
24 Thomas E. Morgan (D), *Fredericktown*
25 Louis E. Graham (R), *Beaver*
26 Harve Tibbott (R), *Ebensburg*
27 Augustine B. Kelley (D), *Greensburg*

28 Carroll D. Kearns (R), *Farrell*
29 John R. McDowell (R), *Wilkinsburg*
30 Robert J. Corbett (R), *Bellevue*
31 James G. Fulton (R), *Dormont*
32 Herman P. Eberharter (D), *Pittsburgh*
33 Frank Buchanan (D), *McKeesport*

## RHODE ISLAND

### SENATORS
Theodore F. Green (D), *Providence*
J. Howard McGrath (D), *Providence*

### REPRESENTATIVES
1 Aime J. Forand (D), *Valley Falls*
2 John E. Fogarty (D), *Harmony*

## SOUTH CAROLINA

### SENATORS
Burnet R. Maybank (D), *Charleston*
Olin D. Johnston (D), *Spartanburg*

### REPRESENTATIVES
1 L. Mendel Rivers (D), *North Charleston*
2 John J. Riley (D), *Sumter*
3 W. J. Bryan Dorn (D), *Greenwood*
4 Joseph R. Bryson (D), *Greenville*
5 James P. Richards (D), *Lancaster*
6 John L. McMillan (D), *Florence*

## SOUTH DAKOTA

### SENATORS
J. Chandler Gurney (R), *Yankton*
Harlan J. Bushfield (R),[44] *Miller*
Vera C. Bushfield (R),[45] *Miller*
Karl E. Mundt (R),[46] *Madison*

### REPRESENTATIVES
1 Karl E. Mundt (R),[47] *Madison*
2 Francis H. Case (R), *Custer*

## TENNESSEE

### SENATORS
Kenneth D. McKellar (D), *Memphis*
A. Tom Stewart (D), *Winchester*

### REPRESENTATIVES
1 Dayton E. Phillips (R), *Elizabethton*
2 John Jennings, Jr. (R), *Knoxville*
3 Estes Kefauver (D), *Chattanooga*
4 Albert A. Gore (D), *Carthage*
5 Joseph L. Evins (D), *Smithville*
6 J. Percy Priest (D), *Nashville*
7 Wirt Courtney (D), *Franklin*
8 Thomas J. Murray (D), *Jackson*
9 Jere Cooper (D), *Dyersburg*
10 Clifford Davis (D), *Memphis*

---

[40] Resigned September 2, 1947.
[41] Elected to fill vacancy caused by resignation of Robert F. Jones, and took his seat November 17, 1947.
[42] Died May 5, 1947.
[43] Elected to fill vacancy caused by death of Charles L. Gerlach, and took his seat November 17, 1947.

---

[44] Died September 27, 1948.
[45] Appointed to fill vacancy caused by death of her husband, Harlan J. Bushfield, and took the oath of office in Pierre, S. Dak., October 6, 1948; resigned December 27, 1948.
[46] Elected to fill vacancy caused by death of

---

Harlan J. Bushfield, and took his seat December 31, 1948.
[47] Resigned December 30, 1948, having been elected to the Senate.

## TEXAS

### SENATORS

Tom T. Connally (D), *Marlin*
W. Lee O'Daniel (D), *Fort Worth*

### REPRESENTATIVES

1 Wright Patman (D), *Texarkana*
2 Jesse M. Combs (D), *Beaumont*
3 Lindley Beckworth (D), *Gladewater*
4 Sam Rayburn (D), *Bonham*
5 J. Frank Wilson (D), *Dallas*
6 Olin E. Teague (D), *College Station*
7 Tom Pickett (D), *Palestine*
8 Albert Thomas (D), *Houston*
9 Joseph J. Mansfield (D),[48] *Columbus*
9 Clark W. Thompson (D),[49] *Galveston*
10 Lyndon B. Johnson (D), *Johnson City*
11 William R. Poage (D), *Waco*
12 Wingate H. Lucas (D), *Grapevine*
13 Ed Gossett (D), *Wichita Falls*
14 John E. Lyle, Jr. (D), *Corpus Christi*
15 Milton H. West (D),[50] *Brownsville*
15 Lloyd M. Bentsen, Jr. (D),[51] *McAllen*
16 R. Ewing Thomason (D),[52] *El Paso*
16 Kenneth M. Regan (D),[53] *Midland*
17 Omar T. Burleson (D), *Anson*
18 Eugene Worley (D), *Shamrock*
19 George H. Mahon (D), *Colorado City*
20 Paul J. Kilday (D), *San Antonio*
21 O. Clark Fisher (D), *San Angelo*

## UTAH

### SENATORS

Elbert D. Thomas (D), *Salt Lake City*
Arthur V. Watkins (R), *Orem*

### REPRESENTATIVES

1 Walter K. Granger (D),[54] *Cedar City*
2 William A. Dawson (R), *Layton*

## VERMONT

### SENATORS

George D. Aiken (R), *Putney*
Ralph E. Flanders (R), *Springfield*

### REPRESENTATIVE AT LARGE

Charles A. Plumley (R), *Northfield*

## VIRGINIA

### SENATORS

Harry Flood Byrd (D), *Berryville*
A. Willis Robertson (D), *Lexington*

### REPRESENTATIVES

1 Schuyler Otis Bland (D), *Newport News*
2 Porter Hardy, Jr. (D), *Churchland*
3 J. Vaughan Gary (D), *Richmond*
4 Patrick Henry Drewry (D),[55] *Petersburg*
4 Watkins M. Abbitt (D),[56] *Appomattox*
5 Thomas B. Stanley (D), *Stanleytown*
6 J. Lindsay Almond, Jr. (D),[57] *Roanoke*
6 Clarence G. Burton (D),[58] *Lynchburg*
7 Burr P. Harrison (D), *Winchester*
8 Howard W. Smith (D), *Alexandria*
9 John W. Flannagan, Jr. (D), *Bristol*

## WASHINGTON

### SENATORS

Warren G. Magnuson (D), *Seattle*
Harry P. Cain (R), *Tacoma*

### REPRESENTATIVES

1 Homer R. Jones (R), *Bremerton*
2 Henry M. Jackson (D), *Everett*
3 Fred B. Norman (R),[59] *Raymond*
3 Russell V. Mack (R),[60] *Hoquiam*
4 Hal Holmes (R), *Ellensburg*
5 Walter F. Horan (R), *Wenatchee*
6 Thor C. Tollefson (R), *Tacoma*

## WEST VIRGINIA

### SENATORS

Harley M. Kilgore (D), *Beckley*
Chapman Revercomb (R), *Charleston*

### REPRESENTATIVES

1 Francis J. Love (R), *Wheeling*

2 Melvin C. Snyder (R), *Kingwood*
3 Edward G. Rohrbough (R), *Glenville*
4 Hubert S. Ellis (R), *Huntington*
5 John Kee (D), *Bluefield*
6 Erland H. Hedrick (D), *Beckley*

## WISCONSIN

### SENATORS

Alexander Wiley (R), *Chippewa Falls*
Joseph R. McCarthy (R), *Appleton*

### REPRESENTATIVES

1 Lawrence H. Smith (R), *Racine*
2 Glenn R. Davis (R),[61] *Waukesha*
3 William H. Stevenson (R), *La Crosse*
4 John C. Brophy (R), *Milwaukee*
5 Charles J. Kersten (R), *Milwaukee*
6 Frank B. Keefe (R), *Oshkosh*
7 Reid F. Murray (R), *Ogdensburg*
8 John W. Byrnes (R), *Green Bay*
9 Merlin Hull (R), *Black River Falls*
10 Alvin E. O'Konski (R), *Mercer*

## WYOMING

### SENATORS

Joseph C. O'Mahoney (D), *Cheyenne*
Edward V. Robertson (R), *Cody*

### REPRESENTATIVE AT LARGE

Frank A. Barrett (R), *Lusk*

## TERRITORY OF ALASKA

### DELEGATE

E. L. (Bob) Bartlett (D), *Juneau*

## TERRITORY OF HAWAII

### DELEGATE

Joseph R. Farrington (R), *Honolulu*

## PUERTO RICO

### RESIDENT COMMISSIONER

Antonio Fernós-Isern (PD), *San Juan*

---

[48] Died July 12, 1947.
[49] Elected to fill vacancy caused by death of Joseph J. Mansfield, and took his seat November 17, 1947.
[50] Died October 28, 1948.
[51] Elected to fill vacancy caused by death of Milton H. West, and took his seat December 31, 1948.
[52] Resigned July 31, 1947.
[53] Elected to fill vacancy caused by resignation of R. Ewing Thomason, and took his seat November 17, 1947.

[54] Election unsuccessfully contested by David J. Wilson.
[55] Died December 21, 1947.
[56] Elected to fill vacancy caused by death of Patrick Henry Drewry, and took his seat February 26, 1948.
[57] Resigned April 17, 1948.
[58] Elected to fill vacancy caused by resignation of J. Lindsay Almond, Jr., and took his seat December 31, 1948.

[59] Died April 18, 1947.
[60] Elected to fill vacancy caused by death of Fred B. Norman, and took his seat June 25, 1947.
[61] Elected to fill vacancy caused by death of Representative-elect Robert K. Henry, in preceding Congress, and took his seat May 5, 1947.

# 81st CONGRESS

JANUARY 3, 1949, TO JANUARY 3, 1951

Alben W. Barkley
Vice President

Sam Rayburn
Speaker

FIRST SESSION— *January 3, 1949, to October 19, 1949*
SECOND SESSION— *January 3, 1950, to January 2, 1951*

---

Senate
Democrats 54 — Republicans 42

VICE PRESIDENT OF THE UNITED STATES— Alben W. Barkley,[1] of Kentucky
PRESIDENT PRO TEMPORE OF THE SENATE— Kenneth D. McKellar,[2] of Tennessee
SECRETARY OF THE SENATE— Leslie L. Biffle,[3] of Arkansas
SERGEANT AT ARMS OF THE SENATE— Joseph C. Duke,[4] of Arizona
MAJORITY FLOOR LEADER— Scott W. Lucas, of Illinois
DEMOCRATIC WHIP— Francis J. Myers, of Pennsylvania
REPUBLICAN FLOOR LEADER— Kenneth S. Wherry, of Nebraska
ASSISTANT REPUBLICAN LEADER— Leverett Saltonstall, of Massachusetts

---

House of Representatives
Democrats 263 — Republicans 171 — American Labor 1

SPEAKER OF THE HOUSE OF REPRESENTATIVES— Sam Rayburn,[5] of Texas
CLERK OF THE HOUSE— Ralph R. Roberts,[6] of Indiana
SERGEANT AT ARMS OF THE HOUSE— Joseph H. Callahan,[7] of Kentucky
DOORKEEPER OF THE HOUSE— William M. Miller,[8] of Mississippi
POSTMASTER OF THE HOUSE— Finis E. Scott,[9] of Tennessee
MAJORITY LEADER— John W. McCormack, of Massachusetts
MAJORITY WHIP— J. Percy Priest, of Tennessee
REPUBLICAN LEADER— Joseph W. Martin, Jr., of Massachusetts
REPUBLICAN WHIP— Leslie C. Arends, of Illinois

---

## ALABAMA

### SENATORS

Lister Hill (D), *Montgomery*
John J. Sparkman (D), *Huntsville*

### REPRESENTATIVES

1 Frank W. Boykin (D), *Mobile*
2 George M. Grant (D), *Troy*
3 George W. Andrews (D), *Union Springs*
4 Sam Hobbs (D), *Selma*
5 Albert Rains (D), *Gadsden*
6 Edward deGraffenried (D), *Tuscaloosa*
7 Carl A. Elliott (D), *Jasper*
8 Robert E. Jones, Jr. (D), *Scottsboro*
9 Laurie C. Battle (D), *Birmingham*

## ARIZONA

### SENATORS

Carl Hayden (D), *Phoenix*
Ernest W. McFarland (D), *Florence*

### REPRESENTATIVES

1 John R. Murdock (D), *Tempe*
2 Harold A. Patten (D), *Tucson*

## ARKANSAS

### SENATORS

John L. McClellan (D), *Camden*
J. William Fulbright (D), *Fayetteville*

### REPRESENTATIVES

1 E. C. Gathings (D), *West Memphis*
2 Wilbur D. Mills (D), *Kensett*
3 James W. Trimble (D), *Berryville*
4 Boyd Tackett (D), *Nashville*
5 Brooks Hays (D), *Little Rock*
6 William F. Norrell (D), *Monticello*
7 Oren Harris (D), *El Dorado*

## CALIFORNIA

### SENATORS

Sheridan Downey (D),[10] *San Francisco*
Richard M. Nixon (R),[11] *Whittier*

William F. Knowland (R), *Piedmont*

### REPRESENTATIVES

1 Hubert B. Scudder (R), *Sebastopol*
2 Clair Engle (D), *Red Bluff*
3 Leroy Johnson (R), *Stockton*
4 Franck R. Havenner (D), *San Francisco*
5 Richard J. Welch (R),[12] *San Francisco*
5 John F. Shelley (D),[13] *San Francisco*
6 George P. Miller (D), *Alameda*
7 John J. Allen, Jr. (R), *Oakland*
8 John Z. Anderson (R), *San Juan Bautista*
9 Cecil F. White (D), *Fresno*
10 Thomas H. Werdel (R), *Bakersfield*
11 Ernest K. Bramblett (R), *Pacific Grove*
12 Richard M. Nixon (R),[14] *Whittier*
13 Norris Poulson (R), *Los Angeles*

---

[1] Elected Vice President and took the oath of office January 20, 1949.
[2] Elected January 3, 1949.
[3] Elected January 3, 1949.
[4] Elected January 3, 1949.
[5] Elected January 3, 1949.
[6] Elected January 3, 1949.

[7] Elected January 3, 1949.
[8] Elected January 3, 1949.
[9] Elected January 3, 1949.
[10] Resigned November 30, 1950.
[11] Appointed to fill vacancy caused by resignation of Sheridan Downey, and took his seat December 4, 1950.

[12] Died September 10, 1949.
[13] Elected to fill vacancy caused by death of Richard J. Welch, and took his seat January 3, 1950.
[14] Resigned November 30, 1950, having been appointed to the Senate; vacancy throughout remainder of the Congress.

14 Helen Gahagan Douglas (D), *Los Angeles*
15 Gordon L. McDonough (R), *Los Angeles*
16 Donald L. Jackson (R), *Santa Monica*
17 Cecil R. King (D), *Los Angeles*
18 Clyde G. Doyle (D), *Long Beach*
19 Chet Holifield (D), *Montebello*
20 Carl Hinshaw (R), *Pasadena*
21 Harry R. Sheppard (D), *Yucaipa*
22 John Phillips (R), *Banning*
23 Clinton D. McKinnon (D), *San Diego*

## COLORADO

### SENATORS

Edwin C. Johnson (D), *Craig*
Eugene D. Millikin (R), *Denver*

### REPRESENTATIVES

1 John A. Carroll (D), *Denver*
2 William S. Hill (R), *Fort Collins*
3 John H. Marsalis (D), *Pueblo*
4 Wayne N. Aspinall (D), *Palisade*

## CONNECTICUT

### SENATORS

Brien McMahon (D), *Norwalk*
Raymond E. Baldwin (R),[15] *Stratford*
William Benton (D),[16] *Southport*

### REPRESENTATIVE AT LARGE

Antoni N. Sadlak (R), *Rockville*

### REPRESENTATIVES

1 Abraham A. Ribicoff (D), *Hartford*
2 Chase Going Woodhouse (D), *Sprague*
3 John A. McGuire (D), *Wallingford*
4 John Davis Lodge (R), *Westport*
5 James T. Patterson (R), *Naugatuck*

## DELAWARE

### SENATORS

John J. Williams (R), *Millsboro*
J. Allen Frear, Jr. (D), *Dover*

### REPRESENTATIVE AT LARGE

J. Caleb Boggs (R), *Wilmington*

## FLORIDA

### SENATORS

Claude D. Pepper (D), *Tallahassee*
Spessard L. Holland (D), *Bartow*

### REPRESENTATIVES

1 J. Hardin Peterson (D), *Lakeland*
2 Charles E. Bennett (D), *Jacksonville*
3 Robert L. F. Sikes (D), *Crestview*
4 George A. Smathers (D), *Miami*
5 A. Sydney Herlong, Jr. (D), *Leesburg*
6 Dwight L. Rogers (D), *Fort Lauderdale*

## GEORGIA

### SENATORS

Walter F. George (D), *Vienna*
Richard B. Russell (D), *Winder*

### REPRESENTATIVES

1 Prince H. Preston, Jr. (D), *Statesboro*
2 Edward E. Cox (D), *Camilla*
3 Stephen Pace (D), *Americus*
4 A. Sidney Camp (D), *Newnan*
5 James C. Davis (D), *Stone Mountain*
6 Carl Vinson (D), *Milledgeville*
7 Henderson L. Lanham (D), *Rome*
8 William M. Wheeler (D), *Alma*
9 John S. Wood (D), *Canton*
10 Paul Brown (D), *Elberton*

## IDAHO

### SENATORS

Glen H. Taylor (D), *Pocatello*
Bert H. Miller (D),[17] *Boise*
Henry C. Dworshak (R),[18] *Burley*

### REPRESENTATIVES

1 Compton I. White (D), *Clark Fork*
2 John C. Sanborn (R), *Hagerman*

## ILLINOIS

### SENATORS

Scott W. Lucas (D), *Havana*
Paul H. Douglas (D), *Chicago*

### REPRESENTATIVES

1 William L. Dawson (D), *Chicago*
2 Barratt O'Hara (D), *Chicago*
3 Neil J. Linehan (D), *Chicago*
4 James V. Buckley (D), *Lansing*
5 Martin Gorski (D),[19] *Chicago*
6 Thomas J. O'Brien (D), *Chicago*
7 Adolph J. Sabath (D), *Chicago*
8 Thomas S. Gordon (D), *Chicago*
9 Sidney R. Yates (D), *Chicago*
10 Richard W. Hoffman (R), *Berwyn*
11 Chester A. Chesney (D), *Chicago*
12 Edgar A. Jonas (R), *Chicago*

13 Ralph E. Church (R),[20] *Evanston*
14 Chauncey W. Reed (R), *West Chicago*
15 Noah M. Mason (R), *Oglesby*
16 Leo E. Allen (R), *Galena*
17 Leslie C. Arends (R), *Melvin*
18 Harold H. Velde (R), *Pekin*
19 Robert B. Chiperfield (R), *Canton*
20 Sidney E. Simpson (R), *Carrollton*
21 Peter F. Mack, Jr. (D), *Carlinville*
22 Rolla C. McMillen (R), *Decatur*
23 Edward H. Jenison (R), *Paris*
24 Charles W. Vursell (R), *Salem*
25 Melvin Price (D), *East St. Louis*
26 Cecil W. (Runt) Bishop (R), *Carterville*

## INDIANA

### SENATORS

Homer E. Capehart (R), *Washington*
William E. Jenner (R), *Bedford*

### REPRESENTATIVES

1 Ray J. Madden (D), *Gary*
2 Charles A. Halleck (R), *Rensselaer*
3 Thurman C. Crook (D), *South Bend*
4 Edward H. Kruse, Jr. (D), *Fort Wayne*
5 John R. Walsh (D), *Anderson*
6 Cecil M. Harden (R), *Covington*
7 James E. Noland (D), *Bloomington*
8 Winfield K. Denton (D), *Evansville*
9 Earl Wilson (R), *Bedford*
10 Ralph Harvey (R), *New Castle*
11 Andrew Jacobs, Sr. (D), *Indianapolis*

## IOWA

### SENATORS

Bourke B. Hickenlooper (R), *Cedar Rapids*
Guy M. Gillette (D), *Cherokee*

### REPRESENTATIVES

1 Thomas E. Martin (R), *Iowa City*
2 Henry O. Talle (R), *Decorah*
3 H. R. Gross (R), *Waterloo*
4 Karl M. LeCompte (R), *Corydon*
5 Paul Cunningham (R),[21] *Des Moines*
6 James I. Dolliver (R), *Fort Dodge*
7 Ben F. Jensen (R), *Exira*
8 Charles B. Hoeven (R), *Alton*

---

[15] Resigned December 16, 1949.
[16] Appointed to fill vacancy caused by resignation of Raymond E. Baldwin, and took his seat January 3, 1950; subsequently elected.
[17] Died October 8, 1949.

[18] Appointed to fill vacancy caused by death of Bert H. Miller, and took his seat October 15, 1949; subsequently elected.
[19] Died December 4, 1949; vacancy throughout remainder of the Congress.

[20] Died March 21, 1950; vacancy throughout remainder of the Congress.
[21] Election unsuccessfully contested by Vincent L. Browner.

## KANSAS

### SENATORS

Clyde M. Reed (R),[22] *Parsons*
Harry Darby (R),[23] *Kansas City*
Frank Carlson (R),[24] *Concordia*
Andrew F. Schoeppel (R), *Wichita*

### REPRESENTATIVES

1 Albert M. Cole (R), *Holton*
2 Errett P. Scrivner (R), *Kansas City*
3 Herbert A. Meyer (R),[25] *Independence*
3 Myron V. George (R),[26] *Altamont*
4 Edward H. Rees (R), *Emporia*
5 Clifford R. Hope (R), *Garden City*
6 Wint Smith (R), *Mankato*

## KENTUCKY

### SENATORS

Alben W. Barkley (D),[27] *Paducah*
Garrett L. Withers (D),[28] *Dixon*
Earle C. Clements (D),[29] *Morganfield*
Virgil M. Chapman (D), *Paris*

### REPRESENTATIVES

1 Noble J. Gregory (D), *Mayfield*
2 John A. Whitaker (D), *Russellville*
3 Thruston B. Morton (R), *Glenview*
4 Frank L. Chelf (D), *Lebanon*
5 Brent Spence (D), *Fort Thomas*
6 Thomas R. Underwood (D), *Lexington*
7 Carl D. Perkins (D), *Hindman*
8 Joe B. Bates (D), *Greenup*
9 James S. Golden (R), *Pineville*

## LOUISIANA

### SENATORS

Allen J. Ellender, Sr. (D), *Houma*
Russell B. Long (D), *Baton Rouge*

### REPRESENTATIVES

1 F. Edward Hébert (D), *New Orleans*
2 Hale Boggs (D), *New Orleans*
3 Edwin E. Willis (D), *St. Martinville*
4 Overton Brooks (D), *Shreveport*
5 Otto E. Passman (D), *Monroe*
6 James H. Morrison (D), *Hammond*
7 Henry D. Larcade, Jr. (D), *Opelousas*
8 A. Leonard Allen (D), *Winnfield*

## MAINE

### SENATORS

Ralph O. Brewster (R), *Dexter*
Margaret Chase Smith (R), *Skowhegan*

### REPRESENTATIVES

1 Robert Hale (R), *Portland*
2 Charles P. Nelson (R), *Augusta*
3 Frank Fellows (R), *Bangor*

## MARYLAND

### SENATORS

Millard E. Tydings (D), *Havre de Grace*
Herbert R. O'Conor (D), *Baltimore*

### REPRESENTATIVES

1 Edward T. Miller (R), *Easton*
2 William P. Bolton (D), *Towson*
3 Edward A. Garmatz (D), *Baltimore*
4 George H. Fallon (D), *Baltimore*
5 Lansdale G. Sasscer (D), *Upper Marlboro*
6 J. Glenn Beall (R), *Frostburg*

## MASSACHUSETTS

### SENATORS

Leverett Saltonstall (R), *Dover*
Henry Cabot Lodge, Jr. (R), *Beverly*

### REPRESENTATIVES

1 John W. Heselton (R), *Deerfield*
2 Foster Furcolo (D), *Longmeadow*
3 Philip J. Philbin (D), *Clinton*
4 Harold D. Donohue (D), *Worcester*
5 Edith Nourse Rogers (R), *Lowell*
6 George J. Bates (R),[30] *Salem*
6 William H. Bates (R),[31] *Salem*
7 Thomas J. Lane (D), *Lawrence*
8 Angier L. Goodwin (R), *Melrose*
9 Donald W. Nicholson (R), *Wareham*
10 Christian A. Herter (R), *Boston*
11 John F. Kennedy (D), *Boston*
12 John W. McCormack (D), *Dorchester*
13 Richard B. Wigglesworth (R), *Milton*
14 Joseph W. Martin, Jr. (R), *North Attleboro*

## MICHIGAN

### SENATORS

Arthur H. Vandenberg (R), *Grand Rapids*
Homer Ferguson (R), *Detroit*

### REPRESENTATIVES

1 George G. Sadowski (D), *Detroit*
2 Earl C. Michener (R), *Adrian*
3 Paul W. Shafer (R), *Battle Creek*
4 Clare E. Hoffman (R), *Allegan*
5 Gerald R. Ford, Jr. (R), *Grand Rapids*
6 William W. Blackney (R),[32] *Flint*
7 Jesse P. Wolcott (R), *Port Huron*
8 Fred L. Crawford (R), *Saginaw*
9 Albert J. Engel (R), *Muskegon*
10 Roy O. Woodruff (R), *Bay City*
11 Charles E. Potter (R), *Cheboygan*
12 John B. Bennett (R), *Ontonagon*
13 George D. O'Brien (D), *Detroit*
14 Louis C. Rabaut (D), *Grosse Pointe Park*
15 John D. Dingell (D), *Detroit*
16 John Lesinski (D),[33] *Dearborn*
17 George A. Dondero (R), *Royal Oak*

## MINNESOTA

### SENATORS

Edward J. Thye (R), *Northfield*
Hubert H. Humphrey (D), *Minneapolis*

### REPRESENTATIVES

1 August H. Andresen (R), *Red Wing*
2 Joseph P. O'Hara (R), *Glencoe*
3 Roy W. Wier (D), *Minneapolis*
4 Eugene J. McCarthy (D), *St. Paul*
5 Walter H. Judd (R), *Minneapolis*
6 Fred Marshall (D), *Grove City*
7 H. Carl Andersen (R), *Tyler*
8 John A. Blatnik (D), *Chisholm*
9 Harold C. Hagen (R), *Crookston*

## MISSISSIPPI

### SENATORS

James O. Eastland (D), *Doddsville*
John C. Stennis (D), *De Kalb*

### REPRESENTATIVES

1 John E. Rankin (D), *Tupelo*
2 Jamie L. Whitten (D), *Charleston*
3 William M. Whittington (D), *Greenwood*
4 Thomas G. Abernethy (D), *Okolona*
5 W. Arthur Winstead (D), *Philadelphia*
6 William M. Colmer (D), *Pascagoula*
7 John Bell Williams (D), *Raymond*

---

[22] Died November 8, 1949.

[23] Appointed to fill vacancy caused by death of Clyde M. Reed, and took his seat January 3, 1950.

[24] Elected to fill vacancy caused by death of Clyde M. Reed, and took his seat November 29, 1950.

[25] Died October 2, 1950.

[26] Elected to fill vacancy caused by death of Herbert A. Meyer, and took his seat November 27, 1950.

[27] Resigned January 19, 1949, having been elected Vice President of the United States.

[28] Appointed to fill vacancy caused by resignation of Alben W. Barkley, and took his seat January 20, 1949.

[29] Elected to fill vacancy caused by resignation of Alben W. Barkley, and took his seat November 27, 1950.

[30] Died November 1, 1949.

[31] Elected to fill vacancy caused by death of his father, George J. Bates; took his seat February 28, 1950.

[32] Election unsuccessfully contested by George D. Stevens.

[33] Died May 27, 1950; vacancy throughout remainder of the Congress.

## MISSOURI

### SENATORS

Forrest C. Donnell (R), *Webster Groves*

James P. Kem (R), *Kansas City*

### REPRESENTATIVES

1 Clare Magee (D), *Unionville*
2 Morgan M. Moulder (D), *Camdenton*
3 Philip J. Welch (D), *St. Joseph*
4 Theodore Leonard Irving (D), *Independence*
5 Richard W. Bolling (D), *Kansas City*
6 George H. Christopher (D), *Amoret*
7 Dewey Short (R), *Galena*
8 Albert S. J. Carnahan (D), *Ellsinore*
9 Clarence Cannon (D), *Elsberry*
10 Paul C. Jones (D), *Kennett*
11 John B. Sullivan (D), *St. Louis*
12 Raymond W. Karst (D), *St. Louis*
13 Frank M. Karsten (D), *St. Louis*

## MONTANA

### SENATORS

James E. Murray (D), *Butte*

Zales N. Ecton (R), *Manhattan*

### REPRESENTATIVES

1 Mike Mansfield (D), *Missoula*
2 Wesley A. D'Ewart (R), *Wilsall*

## NEBRASKA

### SENATORS

Hugh A. Butler (R), *Omaha*

Kenneth S. Wherry (R), *Pawnee City*

### REPRESENTATIVES

1 Carl T. Curtis (R), *Minden*
2 Eugene D. O'Sullivan (D), *Omaha*
3 Karl Stefan (R), *Norfolk*
4 Arthur L. Miller (R), *Kimball*

## NEVADA

### SENATORS

Patrick A. McCarran (D), *Reno*

George W. Malone (R), *Reno*

### REPRESENTATIVE AT LARGE

Walter S. Baring (D), *Reno*

## NEW HAMPSHIRE

### SENATORS

H. Styles Bridges (R), *Concord*

Charles W. Tobey (R), *Temple*

### REPRESENTATIVES

1 Chester E. Merrow (R), *Center Ossipee*
2 Norris Cotton (R), *Lebanon*

## NEW JERSEY

### SENATORS

H. Alexander Smith (R), *Princeton*

Robert C. Hendrickson (R), *Woodbury*

### REPRESENTATIVES

1 Charles A. Wolverton (R), *Merchantville*
2 T. Millet Hand (R), *Cape May City*
3 James C. Auchincloss (R), *Rumson*
4 Charles R. Howell (D), *Pennington*
5 Charles A. Eaton (R), *Plainfield*
6 Clifford P. Case (R), *Rahway*
7 J. Parnell Thomas (R),[34] *Allendale*
7 William B. Widnall (R),[35] *Saddle River*
8 Gordon Canfield (R), *Paterson*
9 Harry L. Towe (R), *Rutherford*
10 Peter W. Rodino, Jr. (D), *Newark*
11 Hugh J. Addonizio (D), *Newark*
12 Robert W. Kean (R), *Livingston*
13 Mary T. Norton (D), *Jersey City*
14 Edward J. Hart (D), *Jersey City*

## NEW MEXICO

### SENATORS

Dennis Chavez (D), *Albuquerque*

Clinton P. Anderson (D), *Albuquerque*

### REPRESENTATIVES AT LARGE

Antonio M. Fernandez (D), *Santa Fe*

John E. Miles (D), *Santa Fe*

## NEW YORK

### SENATORS

Robert F. Wagner (D),[36] *New York City*

John Foster Dulles (R),[37] *New York City*

Herbert H. Lehman (D),[38] *New York City*

Irving M. Ives (R), *Norwich*

### REPRESENTATIVES

1 W. Kingsland Macy (R), *Islip*
2 Leonard W. Hall (R), *Oyster Bay*
3 Henry J. Latham (R), *Queens Village*
4 L. Gary Clemente (D), *Ozone Park*
5 T. Vincent Quinn (D), *Jackson Heights*
6 James J. Delaney (D), *Long Island City*
7 Louis B. Heller (D),[39] *Brooklyn*
8 Joseph L. Pfeifer (D), *Brooklyn*
9 Eugene J. Keogh (D), *Brooklyn*
10 Andrew L. Somers (D),[40] *Brooklyn*
10 Edna F. Kelly (D),[41] *Brooklyn*
11 James J. Heffernan (D), *Brooklyn*
12 John J. Rooney (D), *Brooklyn*
13 Donald L. O'Toole (D), *Brooklyn*
14 Abraham J. Multer (D), *Brooklyn*
15 Emanuel Celler (D), *Brooklyn*
16 James J. Murphy (D), *Staten Island*
17 Frederic R. Coudert, Jr. (R), *New York City*
18 Vito Marcantonio (AL), *New York City*
19 Arthur G. Klein (D), *New York City*
20 Sol Bloom (D),[42] *New York City*
20 Franklin D. Roosevelt, Jr. (D),[43] *New York City*
21 Jacob K. Javits (R), *New York City*
22 Adam Clayton Powell, Jr. (D), *New York City*
23 Walter A. Lynch (D), *New York City*
24 Isidore Dollinger (D), *New York City*
25 Charles A. Buckley (D), *New York City*
26 Christopher C. McGrath (D), *New York City*
27 Ralph W. Gwinn (R), *Bronxville*
28 Ralph A. Gamble (R), *Larchmont*
29 Katharine St. George (R), *Tuxedo Park*
30 Jay LeFevre (R), *New Paltz*
31 Bernard W. Kearney (R), *Gloversville*
32 William T. Byrne (D), *Loudonville*
33 Dean P. Taylor (R), *Troy*
34 Clarence E. Kilburn (R), *Malone*
35 John C. Davies (D),[44] *Utica*
36 R. Walter Riehlman (R), *Tully*
37 Edwin Arthur Hall (R), *Binghamton*
38 John Taber (R), *Auburn*
39 W. Sterling Cole (R), *Bath*
40 Kenneth B. Keating (R), *Rochester*
41 James W. Wadsworth, Jr. (R), *Geneseo*
42 William L. Pfeiffer (R), *Kenmore*
43 Anthony F. Tauriello (D), *Buffalo*
44 Chester C. Gorski (D), *Buffalo*
45 Daniel A. Reed (R), *Dunkirk*

---

[34] Resigned January 2, 1950.

[35] Elected to fill vacancy caused by resignation of J. Parnell Thomas, and took his seat February 14, 1950.

[36] Resigned June 28, 1949.

[37] Appointed to fill vacancy caused by resignation of Robert F. Wagner, and took his seat July 8, 1949.

[38] Elected to fill vacancy caused by resignation of Robert F. Wagner, and took his seat January 3, 1950.

[39] Elected to fill vacancy caused by death of Representative-elect John J. Delaney in preceding Congress, and took his seat February 28, 1949.

[40] Died April 6, 1949.

[41] Elected to fill vacancy caused by death of

Andrew L. Somers, and took her seat January 3, 1950.

[42] Died March 7, 1949.

[43] Elected to fill vacancy caused by death of Sol Bloom, and took his seat June 14, 1949.

[44] Election unsuccessfully contested by Hadwen C. Fuller.

## NORTH CAROLINA

### SENATORS

Clyde R. Hoey (D), *Shelby*
J. Melville Broughton (D),[45] *Raleigh*
Frank P. Graham (D),[46] *Chapel Hill*
Willis Smith (D),[47] *Raleigh*

### REPRESENTATIVES

1 Herbert C. Bonner (D),
   *Washington*
2 John H. Kerr (D), *Warrenton*
3 Graham A. Barden (D), *New Bern*
4 Harold D. Cooley (D), *Nashville*
5 Richard Thurmond Chatham (D),
   *Winston-Salem*
6 Carl T. Durham (D), *Chapel Hill*
7 F. Ertel Carlyle (D), *Lumberton*
8 Charles B. Deane (D),
   *Rockingham*
9 Robert L. Doughton (D), *Sparta*
10 Hamilton C. Jones (D), *Charlotte*
11 Alfred L. Bulwinkle (D),[48]
   *Gastonia*
11 Woodrow W. Jones (D),[49]
   *Rutherfordton*
12 Monroe M. Redden (D),
   *Hendersonville*

## NORTH DAKOTA

### SENATORS

William Langer (R), *Wheatland*
Milton R. Young (R), *La Moure*

### REPRESENTATIVES AT LARGE

William Lemke (R),[50] *Fargo*
Usher L. Burdick (R), *Williston*

## OHIO

### SENATORS

Robert A. Taft (R), *Cincinnati*
John W. Bricker (R), *Columbus*

### REPRESENTATIVE AT LARGE

Stephen M. Young (D), *Cleveland*

### REPRESENTATIVES

1 Charles H. Elston (R), *Cincinnati*
2 Earl T. Wagner (D), *Cincinnati*
3 Edward F. Breen (D), *Dayton*
4 William M. McCulloch (R), *Piqua*
5 Cliff Clevenger (R), *Bryan*
6 James G. Polk (D), *Highland*
7 Clarence J. Brown (R),
   *Blanchester*
8 Frederick C. Smith (R), *Marion*
9 Thomas H. Burke (D), *Toledo*
10 Thomas A. Jenkins (R), *Ironton*
11 Walter E. Brehm (R), *Millersport*
12 John M. Vorys (D), *Columbus*
13 Alvin F. Weichel (R), *Sandusky*
14 Walter B. Huber (D), *Akron*

15 Robert T. Secrest (D), *Senecaville*
16 John McSweeney (D), *Wooster*
17 J. Harry McGregor (R), *West Lafayette*
18 Wayne L. Hays (D), *Flushing*
19 Michael J. Kirwan (D),
   *Youngstown*
20 Michael A. Feighan (D),[51]
   *Cleveland*
21 Robert Crosser (D), *Cleveland*
22 Frances P. Bolton (R), *Lyndhurst*

## OKLAHOMA

### SENATORS

J. W. Elmer Thomas (D), *Medicine Park*
Robert S. Kerr (D), *Oklahoma City*

### REPRESENTATIVES

1 William Franklin (Dixie) Gilmer
   (D), *Tulsa*
2 William G. Stigler (D), *Stigler*
3 Carl Albert (D), *McAlester*
4 Thomas J. Steed (D), *Shawnee*
5 A. S. Mike Monroney (D),
   *Oklahoma City*
6 Toby Morris (D), *Lawton*
7 Victor E. Wickersham (D),
   *Mangum*
8 George H. Wilson (D), *Enid*

## OREGON

### SENATORS

Guy Cordon (R), *Roseburg*
Wayne L. Morse (R), *Eugene*

### REPRESENTATIVES

1 A. Walter Norblad, Jr. (R), *Astoria*
2 Lowell Stockman (R), *Pendleton*
3 Homer D. Angell (R), *Portland*
4 Harris Ellsworth (R), *Roseburg*

## PENNSYLVANIA

### SENATORS

Francis J. Myers (D), *Philadelphia*
Edward Martin (R), *Washington*

### REPRESENTATIVES

1 William A. Barrett (D),
   *Philadelphia*
2 William T. Granahan (D),
   *Philadelphia*
3 Hardie Scott (R), *Philadelphia*
4 Earl Chudoff (D), *Philadelphia*
5 William J. Green, Jr. (D),
   *Philadelphia*
6 Hugh D. Scott, Jr. (R),
   *Philadelphia*
7 Benjamin F. James (R), *Rosemont*

8 Franklin H. Lichtenwalter (R),
   *Center Valley*
9 Paul B. Dague (R), *Downingtown*
10 Harry P. O'Neill (D), *Dunmore*
11 Daniel J. Flood (D), *Wilkes-Barre*
12 Ivor D. Fenton (R), *Mahanoy City*
13 George M. Rhodes (D), *Reading*
14 Wilson D. Gillette (R), *Towanda*
15 Robert F. Rich (R), *Woolrich*
16 Samuel K. McConnell, Jr. (R),
   *Wynnewood*
17 Richard M. Simpson (R),
   *Huntingdon*
18 John C. Kunkel (R), *Harrisburg*
19 Leon H. Gavin (R), *Oil City*
20 Francis E. Walter (D), *Easton*
21 James F. Lind (D), *York*
22 James E. Van Zandt (R), *Altoona*
23 Anthony Cavalcante (D),
   *Uniontown*
24 Thomas E. Morgan (D),
   *Fredericktown*
25 Louis E. Graham (R), *Beaver*
26 Robert L. Coffey, Jr. (D),[52]
   *Johnstown*
26 John P. Saylor (R),[53] *Johnstown*
27 Augustine B. Kelley (D),
   *Greensburg*
28 Carroll D. Kearns (R), *Farrell*
29 Harry J. Davenport (D),
   *Pittsburgh*
30 Robert J. Corbett (R), *Pittsburgh*
31 James G. Fulton (R), *Pittsburgh*
32 Herman P. Eberharter (D),
   *Pittsburgh*
33 Frank Buchanan (D), *McKeesport*

## RHODE ISLAND

### SENATORS

Theodore F. Green (D), *Providence*
J. Howard McGrath (D),[54] *Providence*
Edward L. Leahy (D),[55] *Bristol*
John O. Pastore (D),[56] *Providence*

### REPRESENTATIVES

1 Aime J. Forand (D), *Valley Falls*
2 John E. Fogarty (D), *Harmony*

## SOUTH CAROLINA

### SENATORS

Burnet R. Maybank (D), *Charleston*
Olin D. Johnston (D), *Spartanburg*

### REPRESENTATIVES

1 L. Mendel Rivers (D), *Charleston*
2 Hugo S. Sims, Jr. (D), *Orangeburg*
3 James B. Hare (D), *Saluda*
4 Joseph R. Bryson (D), *Greenville*

[45] Died March 6, 1949.
[46] Appointed to fill vacancy caused by death of J. Melville Broughton, and took his seat March 29, 1949.
[47] Elected to fill vacancy caused by death of J. Melville Broughton, and took his seat November 27, 1950.
[48] Died August 31, 1950.
[49] Elected to fill vacancy caused by death of Alfred

L. Bulwinkle, and took his seat November 30, 1950.
[50] Died May 30, 1950; vacancy throughout remainder of the Congress.
[51] Election unsuccessfully contested by James F. Thierry.
[52] Died April 20, 1949.
[53] Elected to fill vacancy caused by death of Robert

L. Coffey, Jr., and took his seat September 28, 1949.
[54] Resigned August 23, 1949.
[55] Appointed to fill vacancy caused by resignation of J. Howard McGrath; took his seat August 24, 1949.
[56] Elected to fill vacancy caused by resignation of J. Howard McGrath, and took his seat December 19, 1950.

5 James P. Richards (D), *Lancaster*
6 John L. McMillan (D), *Florence*

## SOUTH DAKOTA

SENATORS

J. Chandler Gurney (R), *Yankton*
Karl E. Mundt (R), *Madison*

REPRESENTATIVES

1 Harold O. Lovre (R), *Watertown*
2 Francis H. Case (R), *Custer*

## TENNESSEE

SENATORS

Kenneth D. McKellar (D), *Memphis*
Estes Kefauver (D), *Chattanooga*

REPRESENTATIVES

1 Dayton E. Phillips (R), *Elizabethton*
2 John Jennings, Jr. (R), *Knoxville*
3 James B. Frazier, Jr. (D), *Chattanooga*
4 Albert A. Gore (D), *Carthage*
5 Joseph L. Evins (D), *Smithville*
6 J. Percy Priest (D), *Nashville*
7 James P. Sutton (D), *Lawrenceburg*
8 Thomas J. Murray (D), *Jackson*
9 Jere Cooper (D), *Dyersburg*
10 Clifford Davis (D), *Memphis*

## TEXAS

SENATORS

Tom T. Connally (D), *Marlin*
Lyndon B. Johnson (D), *Johnson City*

REPRESENTATIVES

1 Wright Patman (D), *Texarkana*
2 Jesse M. Combs (D), *Beaumont*
3 Lindley Beckworth (D), *Gladewater*
4 Sam Rayburn (D), *Bonham*
5 J. Frank Wilson (D), *Dallas*
6 Olin E. Teague (D), *College Station*
7 Tom Pickett (D), *Palestine*
8 Albert Thomas (D), *Houston*
9 Clark W. Thompson (D), *Galveston*
10 W. Homer Thornberry (D), *Austin*
11 W. R. Poage (D), *Waco*
12 Wingate H. Lucas (D), *Grapevine*
13 Ed Gossett (D), *Wichita Falls*
14 John E. Lyle, Jr. (D), *Corpus Christi*
15 Lloyd M. Bentsen, Jr. (D), *McAllen*
16 Kenneth M. Regan (D), *Midland*
17 Omar T. Burleson (D), *Anson*
18 Eugene Worley (D),[57] *Shamrock*
18 Ben H. Guill (R),[58] *Pampa*
19 George H. Mahon (D), *Colorado City*
20 Paul J. Kilday (D), *San Antonio*
21 O. Clark Fisher (D), *San Angelo*

## UTAH

SENATORS

Elbert D. Thomas (D), *Salt Lake City*
Arthur V. Watkins (R), *Orem*

REPRESENTATIVES

1 Walter K. Granger (D), *Cedar City*
2 Reva Z. B. Bosone (D), *Salt Lake City*

## VERMONT

SENATORS

George D. Aiken (R), *Putney*
Ralph E. Flanders (R), *Springfield*

REPRESENTATIVE AT LARGE

Charles A. Plumley (R), *Northfield*

## VIRGINIA

SENATORS

Harry Flood Byrd (D), *Berryville*
A. Willis Robertson (D), *Lexington*

REPRESENTATIVES

1 Schuyler Otis Bland (D),[59] *Newport News*
1 Edward J. Robeson, Jr. (D),[60] *Newport News*
2 Porter Hardy, Jr. (D), *Churchland*
3 J. Vaughan Gary (D), *Richmond*
4 Watkins M. Abbitt (D), *Appomattox*
5 Thomas B. Stanley (D), *Stanleytown*
6 Clarence G. Burton (D), *Lynchburg*
7 Burr P. Harrison (D), *Winchester*
8 Howard W. Smith (D), *Alexandria*
9 Thomas B. Fugate (D), *Ewing*

## WASHINGTON

SENATORS

Warren G. Magnuson (D), *Seattle*
Harry P. Cain (R), *Tacoma*

REPRESENTATIVES

1 Hugh B. Mitchell (D), *Seattle*
2 Henry M. Jackson (D), *Everett*
3 Russell V. Mack (R), *Hoquiam*
4 Hal Holmes (R), *Ellensburg*
5 Walter F. Horan (R), *Wenatchee*
6 Thor C. Tollefson (R), *Tacoma*

## WEST VIRGINIA

SENATORS

Harley M. Kilgore (D), *Beckley*
Matthew M. Neely (D), *Fairmont*

REPRESENTATIVES

1 Robert L. Ramsay (D), *Follansbee*
2 Harley O. Staggers (D), *Keyser*
3 Cleveland M. Bailey (D), *Clarksburg*
4 Maurice G. Burnside (D), *Huntington*
5 John Kee (D), *Bluefield*
6 Erland H. Hedrick (D), *Beckley*

## WISCONSIN

SENATORS

Alexander Wiley (R), *Chippewa Falls*
Joseph R. McCarthy (R), *Appleton*

REPRESENTATIVES

1 Lawrence H. Smith (R), *Racine*
2 Glenn R. Davis (R), *Waukesha*
3 Gardner R. Withrow (R), *La Crosse*
4 Clement J. Zablocki (D), *Milwaukee*
5 Andrew J. Biemiller (D), *Milwaukee*
6 Frank B. Keefe (R), *Oshkosh*
7 Reid F. Murray (R), *Ogdensburg*
8 John W. Byrnes (R), *Green Bay*
9 Merlin Hull (R), *Black River Falls*
10 Alvin E. O'Konski (R), *Mercer*

## WYOMING

SENATORS

Joseph C. O'Mahoney (D), *Cheyenne*
Lester C. Hunt (D), *Lander*

REPRESENTATIVE AT LARGE

Frank A. Barrett (R),[61] *Lusk*

## TERRITORY OF ALASKA

DELEGATE

E. L. (Bob) Bartlett (D), *Juneau*

## TERRITORY OF HAWAII

DELEGATE

Joseph R. Farrington (R), *Honolulu*

## PUERTO RICO

RESIDENT COMMISSIONER

Antonio Fernós-Isern (PD), *Santurce*

---

[57] Resigned April 3, 1950.
[58] Elected to fill vacancy caused by resignation of Eugene Worley, and took his seat May 15, 1950.

[59] Died February 16, 1950.
[60] Elected to fill vacancy caused by death of Schuyler Otis Bland, and took his seat May 11, 1950.

[61] Resigned December 31, 1950; vacancy throughout remainder of the Congress.

# 82ND CONGRESS

### JANUARY 3, 1951, TO JANUARY 3, 1953

FIRST SESSION— *January 3, 1951, to October 20, 1951*
SECOND SESSION— *January 8, 1952,[1] to July 7, 1952*

Alben W. Barkley
Vice President

Sam Rayburn
Speaker

---

### Senate
Democrats 49 — Republicans 47
VICE PRESIDENT OF THE UNITED STATES— ALBEN W. BARKLEY, of Kentucky
PRESIDENT PRO TEMPORE OF THE SENATE— KENNETH D. McKELLAR, of Tennessee
SECRETARY OF THE SENATE— LESLIE L. BIFFLE, of Arkansas
SERGEANT AT ARMS OF THE SENATE— JOSEPH C. DUKE,[2] of Arizona
MAJORITY FLOOR LEADER— ERNEST W. McFARLAND, of Arizona
DEMOCRATIC WHIP— LYNDON B. JOHNSON, of Texas
REPUBLICAN FLOOR LEADER— KENNETH S. WHERRY,[3] of Nebraska; STYLES BRIDGES,[4] of New Hampshire
ASSISTANT REPUBLICAN LEADER— LEVERETT SALTONSTALL, of Massachusetts

---

### House of Representatives
Democrats 235 — Republicans 199 — Independent 1
SPEAKER OF THE HOUSE OF REPRESENTATIVES— SAM RAYBURN,[5] of Texas
CLERK OF THE HOUSE— RALPH R. ROBERTS,[6] of Indiana
SERGEANT AT ARMS OF THE HOUSE— JOSEPH H. CALLAHAN,[7] of Kentucky
DOORKEEPER OF THE HOUSE— WILLIAM M. MILLER,[8] of Mississippi
POSTMASTER OF THE HOUSE— FINIS E. SCOTT,[9] of Tennessee
MAJORITY LEADER— JOHN W. McCORMACK, of Massachusetts
MAJORITY WHIP— J. PERCY PRIEST, of Tennessee
REPUBLICAN LEADER— JOSEPH W. MARTIN, JR., of Massachusetts
REPUBLICAN WHIP— LESLIE C. ARENDS, of Illinois

## ALABAMA

### SENATORS
Lister Hill (D), *Montgomery*
John J. Sparkman (D), *Huntsville*

### REPRESENTATIVES
1 Frank W. Boykin (D), *Mobile*
2 George M. Grant (D), *Troy*
3 George W. Andrews (D), *Union Springs*
4 Kenneth A. Roberts (D), *Piedmont*
5 Albert Rains (D), *Gadsden*
6 Edward deGraffenried (D), *Tuscaloosa*
7 Carl A. Elliott (D), *Jasper*
8 Robert E. Jones, Jr. (D), *Scottsboro*
9 Laurie C. Battle (D), *Birmingham*

## ARIZONA

### SENATORS
Carl Hayden (D), *Phoenix*
Ernest W. McFarland (D), *Florence*

### REPRESENTATIVES
1 John R. Murdock (D), *Tempe*
2 Harold A. Patten (D), *Tucson*

## ARKANSAS

### SENATORS
John L. McClellan (D), *Camden*
J. William Fulbright (D), *Fayetteville*

### REPRESENTATIVES
1 E. C. Gathings (D), *West Memphis*
2 Wilbur D. Mills (D), *Kensett*
3 James W. Trimble (D), *Berryville*
4 Boyd Tackett (D), *Nashville*
5 Brooks Hays (D), *Little Rock*
6 William F. Norrell (D), *Monticello*
7 Oren Harris (D), *El Dorado*

## CALIFORNIA

### SENATORS
William F. Knowland (R), *Piedmont*
Richard M. Nixon (R),[10] *Whittier*
Thomas H. Kuchel (R),[11] *Anaheim*

### REPRESENTATIVES
1 Hubert B. Scudder (R), *Sebastopol*
2 Clair Engle (D), *Red Bluff*
3 Leroy Johnson (R), *Stockton*
4 Franck R. Havenner (D), *San Francisco*
5 John F. Shelley (D), *San Francisco*
6 George P. Miller (D), *Alameda*
7 John J. Allen, Jr. (R), *Oakland*
8 John Z. Anderson (R), *San Juan Bautista*
9 Allan O. Hunter (R), *Fresno*
10 Thomas H. Werdel (R), *Bakersfield*
11 Ernest K. Bramblett (R), *Pacific Grove*
12 Patrick J. Hillings (R), *Arcadia*
13 Norris Poulson (R), *Los Angeles*
14 Samuel W. Yorty (D), *Los Angeles*
15 Gordon L. McDonough (R), *Los Angeles*
16 Donald L. Jackson (R), *Pacific Palisades*

---

[1] By joint resolution (Pub. Law 244, 82d Cong., 1st sess.), the date of assembling the second session of the Eighty-second Congress was fixed for January 8, 1952.
[2] Reelected January 3, 1951.
[3] Died November 29, 1951.
[4] Elected January 8, 1952.

[5] Reelected January 3, 1951.
[6] Reelected January 3, 1951.
[7] Reelected January 3, 1951.
[8] Reelected January 3, 1951.
[9] Reelected January 3, 1951.

[10] Resigned January 1, 1953, having been elected Vice President.
[11] Appointed December 22, 1952, to fill vacancy caused by resignation of Richard M. Nixon, and took his seat January 2, 1953.

17 Cecil R. King (D), *Los Angeles*
18 Clyde G. Doyle (D), *Long Beach*
19 Chet Holifield (D), *Montebella*
20 Carl Hinshaw (R), *Pasadena*
21 Harry R. Sheppard (D), *Yucaipa*
22 John Phillips (R), *Banning*
23 Clinton D. McKinnon (D), *San Diego*

## COLORADO

### SENATORS

Edwin C. Johnson (D), *Craig*
Eugene D. Millikin (R), *Denver*

### REPRESENTATIVES

1 Byron G. Rogers (D), *Denver*
2 William S. Hill (R), *Fort Collins*
3 J. Edgar Chenoweth (R), *Trinidad*
4 Wayne N. Aspinall (D), *Palisade*

## CONNECTICUT

### SENATORS

Brien McMahon (D),[12] *Norwalk*
William A. Purtell (R),[13] *West Hartford*
Prescott S. Bush (R),[14] *Greenwich*
William Benton (D), *Southport*

### REPRESENTATIVE AT LARGE

Antoni N. Sadlak (R), *Rockville*

### REPRESENTATIVES

1 Abraham A. Ribicoff (D), *Hartford*
2 Horace Seely-Brown, Jr. (R), *Pomfret Center*
3 John A. McGuire (D), *Wallingford*
4 Albert P. Morano (R), *Greenwich*
5 James T. Patterson (R), *Naugatuck*

## DELAWARE

### SENATORS

John J. Williams (R), *Millsboro*
J. Allen Frear, Jr. (D), *Dover*

### REPRESENTATIVE AT LARGE

J. Caleb Boggs (R), *Wilmington*

## FLORIDA

### SENATORS

Spessard L. Holland (D), *Bartow*
George A. Smathers (D), *Miami*

### REPRESENTATIVES

1 Chester B. McMullen (D), *Clearwater*
2 Charles E. Bennett (D), *Jacksonville*
3 Robert L. F. Sikes (D), *Crestview*
4 William C. Lantaff (D), *Miami Springs*
5 A. Sydney Herlong, Jr. (D), *Leesburg*

6 Dwight L. Rogers (D), *Fort Lauderdale*

## GEORGIA

### SENATORS

Walter F. George (D), *Vienna*
Richard B. Russell (D), *Winder*

### REPRESENTATIVES

1 Prince H. Preston, Jr. (D), *Statesboro*
2 Edward E. Cox (D),[15] *Camilla*
3 E. L. Forrester (D), *Leesburg*
4 A. Sidney Camp (D), *Newnan*
5 James C. Davis (D), *Stone Mountain*
6 Carl Vinson (D), *Milledgeville*
7 Henderson L. Lanham (D), *Rome*
8 William M. Wheeler (D), *Alma*
9 John S. Wood (D), *Canton*
10 Paul Brown (D), *Elberton*

## IDAHO

### SENATORS

Henry C. Dworshak (R), *Burley*
Herman Welker (R), *Payette*

### REPRESENTATIVES

1 John T. Wood (R), *Coeur d' Alene*
2 Hamer H. Budge (R), *Boise*

## ILLINOIS

### SENATORS

Paul H. Douglas (D), *Chicago*
Everett McKinley Dirksen (R), *Pekin*

### REPRESENTATIVES

1 William L. Dawson (D), *Chicago*
2 Richard B. Vail (R), *Chicago*
3 Fred E. Busbey (R), *Chicago*
4 William E. McVey (R), *Harvey*
5 John C. Kluczynski (D), *Chicago*
6 Thomas J. O'Brien (D), *Chicago*
7 Adolph J. Sabath (D),[16] *Chicago*
8 Thomas S. Gordon (D), *Chicago*
9 Sidney R. Yates (D), *Chicago*
10 Richard W. Hoffman (R), *Berwyn*
11 Timothy P. Sheehan (R), *Chicago*
12 Edgar A. Jonas (R), *Chicago*
13 Marguerite Stitt Church (R), *Evanston*
14 Chauncey W. Reed (R), *West Chicago*
15 Noah M. Mason (R), *Oglesby*
16 Leo E. Allen (R), *Galena*
17 Leslie C. Arends (R), *Melvin*
18 Harold H. Velde (R), *Pekin*
19 Robert B. Chiperfield (R), *Canton*
20 Sidney E. Simpson (R), *Carrollton*
21 Peter F. Mack, Jr. (D), *Carlinville*
22 William L. Springer (R), *Champaign*

23 Edward H. Jenison (R), *Paris*
24 Charles W. Vursell (R), *Salem*
25 Melvin Price (D), *East St. Louis*
26 Cecil W. (Runt) Bishop (R), *Carterville*

## INDIANA

### SENATORS

Homer E. Capehart (R), *Washington*
William E. Jenner (R), *Bedford*

### REPRESENTATIVES

1 Ray J. Madden (D), *Gary*
2 Charles A. Halleck (R), *Rensselaer*
3 Shepard J. Crumpacker, Jr. (R), *South Bend*
4 E. Ross Adair (R), *Fort Wayne*
5 John V. Beamer (R), *Wabash*
6 Cecil M. Harden (R), *Covington*
7 William G. Bray (R), *Martinsville*
8 Winfield K. Denton (D), *Evansville*
9 Earl Wilson (R), *Bedford*
10 Ralph Harvey (R), *Mount Summit*
11 Charles B. Brownson (R), *Indianapolis*

## IOWA

### SENATORS

Bourke B. Hickenlooper (R), *Cedar Rapids*
Guy M. Gillette (D), *Cherokee*

### REPRESENTATIVES

1 Thomas E. Martin (R), *Iowa City*
2 Henry O. Talle (R), *Decorah*
3 H. R. Gross (R), *Waterloo*
4 Karl M. LeCompte (R), *Corydon*
5 Paul Cunningham (R), *Des Moines*
6 James I. Dolliver (R), *Fort Dodge*
7 Ben F. Jensen (R), *Exira*
8 Charles B. Hoeven (R), *Alton*

## KANSAS

### SENATORS

Andrew F. Schoeppel (R), *Wichita*
Frank Carlson (R), *Concordia*

### REPRESENTATIVES

1 Albert M. Cole (R), *Holton*
2 Errett P. Scrivner (R), *Kansas City*
3 Myron V. George (R), *Altamont*
4 Edward H. Rees (R), *Emporia*
5 Clifford R. Hope (R), *Garden City*
6 Wint Smith (R), *Mankato*

---

[12] Died July 28, 1952.
[13] Appointed August 29, 1952, to fill vacancy caused by death of Brien McMahon, but was unable to be sworn in as Congress was not in session.
[14] Elected to fill vacancy caused by death of Brien McMahon, and took his seat January 3, 1953.
[15] Died December 24, 1952, before the commencement of the Eighty-third Congress, to which he had been reelected. Vacancy in the Eighty-second Congress not filled.
[16] Died November 6, 1952, before the commencement of the Eighty-third Congress, to which he had been reelected. Vacancy in the Eighty-second Congress not filled.

## KENTUCKY

SENATORS

Virgil M. Chapman (D),[17] *Paris*
Thomas R. Underwood (D),[18]
*Lexington*
John Sherman Cooper (R),[19] *Somerset*
Earle C. Clements (D), *Morganfield*

REPRESENTATIVES

1 Noble J. Gregory (D), *Mayfield*
2 John A. Whitaker (D),[20]
*Russellville*
2 Garrett L. Withers (D),[21] *Dixon*
3 Thruston B. Morton (R), *Glenview*
4 Frank L. Chelf (D), *Lebanon*
5 Brent Spence (D), *Fort Thomas*
6 Thomas R. Underwood (D),[22]
*Lexington*
6 John C. Watts (D),[23] *Nicholasville*
7 Carl D. Perkins (D), *Hindman*
8 Joe B. Bates (D), *Greenup*
9 James S. Golden (R), *Pineville*

## LOUISIANA

SENATORS

Allen J. Ellender, Sr. (D), *Houma*
Russell B. Long (D), *Baton Rouge*

REPRESENTATIVES

1 F. Edward Hébert (D), *New
Orleans*
2 Hale Boggs (D), *New Orleans*
3 Edwin E. Willis (D), *St.
Martinsville*
4 Overton Brooks (D), *Shreveport*
5 Otto E. Passman (D), *Monroe*
6 James H. Morrison (D),
*Hammond*
7 Henry D. Larcade, Jr. (D),
*Opelousas*
8 A. Leonard Allen (D), *Winnfield*

## MAINE

SENATORS

Ralph O. Brewster (R),[24] *Dexter*
Margaret Chase Smith (R),
*Skowhegan*

REPRESENTATIVES

1 Robert Hale (R), *Portland*
2 Charles P. Nelson (R), *Augusta*
3 Frank Fellows (R),[25] *Bangor*
3 Clifford G. McIntire (R),[26] *Perham*

## MARYLAND

SENATORS

Herbert R. O'Conor (D), *Baltimore*
John Marshall Butler (R), *Baltimore*

REPRESENTATIVES

1 Edward T. Miller (R), *Easton*
2 James P. S. Devereux (R),
*Stevenson*
3 Edward A. Garmatz (D),
*Baltimore*
4 George H. Fallon (D), *Baltimore*
5 Lansdale G. Sasscer (D), *Upper
Marlboro*
6 J. Glenn Beall (R), *Frostburg*

## MASSACHUSETTS

SENATORS

Leverett Saltonstall (R), *Dover*
Henry Cabot Lodge, Jr. (R), *Beverly*

REPRESENTATIVES

1 John W. Heselton (R), *Deerfield*
2 Foster Furcolo (D),[27] *Longmeadow*
3 Philip J. Philbin (D), *Clinton*
4 Harold D. Donohue (D), *Worcester*
5 Edith Nourse Rogers (R), *Lowell*
6 William H. Bates (R), *Salem*
7 Thomas J. Lane (D), *Lawrence*
8 Angier L. Goodwin (R), *Melrose*
9 Donald W. Nicholson (R),
*Wareham*
10 Christian A. Herter (R), *Boston*
11 John F. Kennedy (D), *Boston*
12 John W. McCormack (D),
*Dorchester*
13 Richard B. Wigglesworth (R),
*Milton*
14 Joseph W. Martin, Jr. (R), *North
Attleboro*

## MICHIGAN

SENATORS

Arthur H. Vandenberg (R),[28] *Grand
Rapids*
Arthur Edson Blair Moody (D),[29]
*Detroit*
Charles E. Potter (R),[30] *Cheboygan*
Homer Ferguson (R), *Detroit*

REPRESENTATIVES

1 Thaddeus M. Machrowicz (D),
*Hantramck*
2 George Meader (R), *Ann Arbor*
3 Paul W. Shafer (R), *Battle Creek*
4 Clare E. Hoffman (R), *Allegan*

5 Gerald R. Ford, Jr. (R), *Grand
Rapids*
6 William W. Blackney (R), *Flint*
7 Jesse P. Wolcott (R), *Port Huron*
8 Fred L. Crawford (R), *Saginaw*
9 Ruth Thompson (R), *Whitehall*
10 Roy O. Woodruff (R), *Bay City*
11 Charles E. Potter (R),[31]
*Cheboygan*
12 John B. Bennett (R), *Ontonagon*
13 George D. O'Brien (D), *Detroit*
14 Louis C. Rabaut (D), *Grosse
Pointe Park*
15 John D. Dingell (D), *Detroit*
16 John Lesinski, Jr. (D), *Dearborn*
17 George A. Dondero (R), *Royal Oak*

## MINNESOTA

SENATORS

Edward J. Thye (R), *Northfield*
Hubert H. Humphrey (D),
*Minneapolis*

REPRESENTATIVES

1 August H. Andresen (R), *Red
Wing*
2 Joseph P. O'Hara (R), *Glencoe*
3 Roy W. Wier (D), *Minneapolis*
4 Eugene J. McCarthy (D), *St. Paul*
5 Walter H. Judd (R), *Minneapolis*
6 Fred Marshall (D), *Grove City*
7 H. Carl Andersen (R), *Tyler*
8 John A. Blatnik (D), *Chisholm*
9 Harold C. Hagen (R), *Crookston*

## MISSISSIPPI

SENATORS

James O. Eastland (D), *Doddsville*
John C. Stennis (D), *De Kalb*

REPRESENTATIVES

1 John E. Rankin (D), *Tupelo*
2 Jamie L. Whitten (D), *Charleston*
3 Frank E. Smith (D), *Greenwood*
4 Thomas G. Abernethy (D),
*Okolona*
5 W. Arthur Winstead (D),
*Philadelphia*
6 William M. Colmer (D),
*Pascagoula*
7 John Bell Williams (D), *Raymond*

## MISSOURI

SENATORS

James P. Kem (R), *Kansas City*
Thomas C. Hennings, Jr. (D), *St.
Louis*

---

[17] Died March 8, 1951.
[18] Appointed to fill vacancy caused by death of Virgil M. Chapman, and took his seat March 19, 1951.
[19] Elected November 4, 1952, to fill vacancy caused by death of Virgil M. Chapman, and took his seat January 3, 1953.
[20] Died December 15, 1951.
[21] Elected August 2, 1952, to fill vacancy caused by death of John A. Whitaker, but was unable to be sworn in as Congress was not in session.
[22] Resigned March 17, 1951, having been appointed to the Senate.

[23] Elected April 14, 1951, to fill vacancy caused by resignation of Thomas R. Underwood, and took his seat April 23, 1951.
[24] Resigned December 31, 1952; vacancy throughout remainder of the Congress.
[25] Died August 27, 1951.
[26] Elected October 22, 1951, to fill vacancy caused by death of Frank Fellows; took his seat January 8, 1952.
[27] Resigned September 30, 1952; vacancy throughout remainder of the Congress.

[28] Died April 18, 1951.
[29] Appointed to fill vacancy caused by death of Arthur H. Vandenberg, and took his seat April 25, 1951.
[30] Elected November 4, 1952, to fill vacancy caused by death of Arthur H. Vandenberg; also elected to full term, and took his seat January 3, 1953.
[31] Resigned November 4, 1952; vacancy throughout remainder of the Congress.

REPRESENTATIVES
1 Clare Magee (D), *Unionville*
2 Morgan M. Moulder (D), *Camdenton*
3 Philip J. Welch (D), *St. Joseph*
4 Theodore Leonard Irving (D), *Independence*
5 Richard W. Bolling (D), *Kansas City*
6 Orland K. Armstrong (R), *Springfield*
7 Dewey Short (R), *Galena*
8 Albert S. J. Carnahan (D), *Ellsinore*
9 Clarence Cannon (D), *Elsberry*
10 Paul C. Jones (D), *Kennett*
11 John B. Sullivan (D),[32] *St. Louis*
11 Claude I. Bakewell (R),[33] *St. Louis*
12 Thomas B. Curtis (R), *Webster Groves*
13 Frank M. Karsten (D), *St. Louis*

## MONTANA

SENATORS
James E. Murray (D), *Butte*
Zales N. Ecton (R), *Manhattan*

REPRESENTATIVES
1 Mike Mansfield (D), *Missoula*
2 Wesley A. D'Ewart (R), *Wilsall*

## NEBRASKA

SENATORS
Hugh A. Butler (R), *Omaha*
Kenneth S. Wherry (R),[34] *Pawnee City*
Frederick A. Seaton (R),[35] *Hastings*
Dwight P. Griswold (R),[36] *Scotts Bluff*

REPRESENTATIVES
1 Carl T. Curtis (R), *Minden*
2 Howard H. Buffett (R), *Omaha*
3 Karl Stefan (R),[37] *Norfolk*
3 Robert D. Harrison (R),[38] *Norfolk*
4 Arthur L. Miller (R), *Kimball*

## NEVADA

SENATORS
Patrick A. McCarran (D), *Reno*
George W. Malone (R), *Reno*

REPRESENTATIVE AT LARGE
Walter S. Baring (D), *Reno*

## NEW HAMPSHIRE

SENATORS
H. Styles Bridges (R), *Concord*
Charles W. Tobey (R), *Temple*

REPRESENTATIVES
1 Chester E. Merrow (R), *Center Ossipee*
2 Norris Cotton (R), *Lebanon*

## NEW JERSEY

SENATORS
H. Alexander Smith (R), *Princeton*
Robert C. Hendrickson (R), *Woodbury*

REPRESENTATIVES
1 Charles A. Wolverton (R), *Merchantville*
2 T. Millet Hand (R), *Cape May City*
3 James C. Auchincloss (R), *Rumson*
4 Charles R. Howell (D), *Pennington*
5 Charles A. Eaton (R), *Watchung*
6 Clifford P. Case (R), *Rahway*
7 William B. Widnall (R), *Saddle River*
8 Gordon Canfield (R), *Paterson*
9 Harry L. Towe (R),[39] *Tenafly*
9 Frank C. Osmers, Jr. (R),[40] *Haworth*
10 Peter W. Rodino, Jr. (D), *Newark*
11 Hugh J. Addonizio (D), *Newark*
12 Robert W. Kean (R), *Livingston*
13 Alfred D. Sieminski (D), *Jersey City*
14 Edward J. Hart (D), *Jersey City*

## NEW MEXICO

SENATORS
Dennis Chavez (D), *Albuquerque*
Clinton P. Anderson (D), *Albuquerque*

REPRESENTATIVES AT LARGE
Antonio M. Fernandez (D), *Santa Fe*
John J. Dempsey (D), *Santa Fe*

## NEW YORK

SENATORS
Irving M. Ives (R), *Norwich*
Herbert H. Lehman (D), *New York City*

REPRESENTATIVES
1 Ernest Greenwood (D), *Bay Shore*
2 Leonard W. Hall (R),[41] *Oyster Bay*
3 Henry J. Latham (R), *Queens Village*
4 L. Gary Clemente (D), *Ozone Park*
5 T. Vincent Quinn (D),[42] *Jackson Heights*
5 Robert Tripp Ross (R),[43] *Jackson Heights*
6 James J. Delaney (D), *Long Island City*
7 Louis B. Heller (D), *Brooklyn*
8 Victor L. Anfuso (D), *Brooklyn*
9 Eugene J. Keogh (D), *Brooklyn*
10 Edna F. Kelly (D), *Brooklyn*
11 James J. Heffernan (D), *Brooklyn*
12 John J. Rooney (D), *Brooklyn*
13 Donald L. O'Toole (D), *Brooklyn*
14 Abraham J. Multer (D), *New York City*
15 Emanuel Celler (D), *Brooklyn*
16 James J. Murphy (D), *Staten Island*
17 Frederic R. Coudert, Jr. (R), *New York City*
18 James G. Donovan (D), *New York City*
19 Arthur G. Klein (D), *New York City*
20 Franklin D. Roosevelt, Jr. (D), *New York City*
21 Jacob K. Javits (R), *New York City*
22 Adam Clayton Powell, Jr. (D), *New York City*
23 Sidney A. Fine (D), *New York City*
24 Isidore Dollinger (D), *New York City*
25 Charles A. Buckley (D), *New York City*
26 Christopher C. McGrath (D), *New York City*
27 Ralph W. Gwinn (R), *Bronxville*
28 Ralph A. Gamble (R), *Larchmont*
29 Katharine St. George (R), *Tuxedo Park*
30 J. Ernest Wharton (R), *Richmondville*
31 Bernard W. Kearney (R), *Gloversville*
32 William T. Byrne (D),[44] *Loudonville*
32 Leo W. O'Brien (D),[45] *Albany*
33 Dean P. Taylor (R), *Troy*
34 Clarence E. Kilburn (R), *Malone*
35 William R. Williams (R), *Cassville*
36 R. Walter Riehlman (R), *Tully*
37 Edwin Arthur Hall (R), *Binghamton*
38 John Taber (R), *Auburn*
39 W. Sterling Cole (R), *Bath*
40 Kenneth B. Keating (R), *Rochester*
41 Harold C. Ostertag (R), *Attica*
42 William E. Miller (R), *Lockport*
43 Edmund P. Radwan (R), *Buffalo*
44 John C. Butler (R), *Buffalo*
45 Daniel A. Reed (R), *Dunkirk*

---

[32] Died January 29, 1951.
[33] Elected March 9, 1951, to fill vacancy caused by death of John B. Sullivan, and took his seat March 19, 1951.
[34] Died November 29, 1951.
[35] Appointed to fill vacancy caused by death of Kenneth S. Wherry, and took his seat January 8, 1952.
[36] Elected November 4, 1952, to fill vacancy caused by death of Kenneth S. Wherry, and took his seat January 3, 1953.

[37] Died October 2, 1951.
[38] Elected December 4, 1951, to fill vacancy caused by death of Karl Stefan, and took his seat January 8, 1952.
[39] Resigned September 7, 1951.
[40] Elected November 6, 1951, to fill vacancy caused by resignation of Harry L. Towe, and took his seat January 8, 1952.
[41] Resigned December 31, 1952; vacancy through-

out remainder of the Congress.
[42] Resigned December 30, 1951.
[43] Elected February 19, 1952, to fill vacancy caused by resignation of T. Vincent Quinn, and took his seat February 26, 1952.
[44] Died January 27, 1952.
[45] Elected April 1, 1952, to fill vacancy caused by death of William T. Byrne, and took his seat April 9, 1952.

## NORTH CAROLINA

### SENATORS

Clyde R. Hoey (D), *Shelby*
Willis Smith (D), *Raleigh*

### REPRESENTATIVES

1 Herbert C. Bonner (D),
   *Washington*
2 John H. Kerr (D), *Warrenton*
3 Graham A. Barden (D), *New Bern*
4 Harold D. Cooley (D), *Nashville*
5 Richard Thurmond Chatham (D),
   *Winston-Salem*
6 Carl T. Durham (D), *Chapel Hill*
7 F. Ertel Carlyle (D), *Lumberton*
8 Charles B. Deane (D),
   *Rockingham*
9 Robert L. Doughton (D), *Laurel
   Springs*
10 Hamilton C. Jones (D), *Charlotte*
11 Woodrow W. Jones (D),
   *Rutherfordton*
12 Monroe M. Redden (D),
   *Hendersonville*

## NORTH DAKOTA

### SENATORS

William Langer (R), *Wheatland*
Milton R. Young (R), *La Moure*

### REPRESENTATIVES AT LARGE

Usher L. Burdick (R), *Williston*
Fred G. Aandahl (R), *Litchville*

## OHIO

### SENATORS

Robert A. Taft (R), *Cincinnati*
John W. Bricker (R), *Columbus*

### REPRESENTATIVE AT LARGE

George H. Bender (R), *Chagrin Falls*

### REPRESENTATIVES

1 Charles H. Elston (R), *Cincinnati*
2 William E. Hess (R), *Cincinnati*
3 Edward F. Breen (D),[46] *Dayton*
3 Paul F. Schenck (R),[47] *Dayton*
4 William M. McCulloch (R), *Piqua*
5 Cliff Clevenger (R), *Bryan*
6 James G. Polk (D), *Highland*
7 Clarence J. Brown (R),
   *Blanchester*
8 Jackson E. Betts (R), *Findlay*
9 H. Frazier Reams (I), *Toledo*
10 Thomas A. Jenkins (R), *Ironton*
11 Walter E. Brehm (R), *Millersport*
12 John M. Vorys (R), *Columbus*
13 Alvin F. Weichel (R), *Sandusky*
14 William H. Ayres (R), *Akron*
15 Robert T. Secrest (D), *Senacaville*
16 Frank T. Bow (R), *Canton*

17 J. Harry McGregor (R), *West
   Lafayette*
18 Wayne L. Hays (D), *Flushing*
19 Michael J. Kirwan (D),
   *Youngstown*
20 Michael A. Feighan (D), *Cleveland*
21 Robert Crosser (D), *Cleveland*
22 Frances P. Bolton (R), *Lyndhurst*

## OKLAHOMA

### SENATORS

Robert S. Kerr (D), *Oklahoma City*
A. S. Mike Monroney (D), *Oklahoma
City*

### REPRESENTATIVES

1 George B. Schwabe (R),[48] *Tulsa*
2 William G. Stigler (D),[49] *Stigler*
3 Carl Albert (D), *McAlester*
4 Thomas J. Steed (D), *Shawnee*
5 John Jarman (D), *Oklahoma City*
6 Toby Morris (D), *Lawton*
7 Victor E. Wickersham (D),
   *Mangum*
8 Page H. Belcher (R), *Enid*

## OREGON

### SENATORS

Guy Cordon (R), *Roseberg*
Wayne L. Morse (R),[50] *Eugene*

### REPRESENTATIVES

1 A. Walter Norblad, Jr. (R), *Astoria*
2 Lowell Stockman (R), *Pendleton*
3 Homer D. Angell (R), *Portland*
4 Harris Ellsworth (R), *Roseberg*

## PENNSYLVANIA

### SENATORS

Edward Martin (R), *Washington*
James H. Duff (R), *Carnegie*

### REPRESENTATIVES

1 William A. Barrett (D),
   *Philadelphia*
2 William T. Granahan (D),
   *Philadelphia*
3 Hardie Scott (R), *Philadelphia*
4 Earl Chudoff (D), *Philadelphia*
5 William J. Green, Jr. (D),
   *Philadelphia*
6 Hugh D. Scott, Jr. (R),
   *Philadelphia*
7 Benjamin F. James (R), *Rosemont*
8 Albert C. Vaughn (R),[51] *Fullerton*
8 Karl C. King (R),[52] *Morrisville*
9 Paul B. Dague (R), *Downingtown*
10 Harry P. O'Neill (D), *Dunmore*
11 Daniel J. Flood (D), *Wilkes-Barre*
12 Ivor D. Fenton (R), *Mahanoy City*

13 George M. Rhodes (R), *Reading*
14 Wilson D. Gillette (R),[53] *Towanda*
14 Joseph L. Carrigg (R),[54]
   *Susquehanna*
15 Alvin R. Bush (R), *Muncy*
16 Samuel K. McConnell, Jr. (R),
   *Wynnewood*
17 Richard M. Simpson (R),
   *Huntingdon*
18 Walter M. Mumma (R),
   *Harrisburg*
19 Leon H. Gavin (R), *Oil City*
20 Francis E. Walter (D), *Easton*
21 James F. Lind (D), *York*
22 James E. Van Zandt (R), *Altoona*
23 Edward L. Sittler, Jr. (R),
   *Uniontown*
24 Thomas E. Morgan (D),
   *Fredericktown*
25 Louis E. Graham (R), *Beaver*
26 John P. Saylor (R), *Johnstown*
27 Augustine B. Kelley (D),
   *Greensburg*
28 Carroll D. Kearns (R), *Farrell*
29 Harmar D. Denny, Jr. (R),
   *Pittsburgh*
30 Robert J. Corbett (R), *Pittsburgh*
31 James G. Fulton (R), *Pittsburgh*
32 Herman P. Eberharter (D),
   *Pittsburgh*
33 Frank Buchanan (D),[55]
   *McKeesport*
33 Vera D. Buchanan (D),[56]
   *McKeesport*

## RHODE ISLAND

### SENATORS

Theodore F. Green (D), *Providence*
John O. Pastore (D), *Providence*

### REPRESENTATIVES

1 Aime J. Forand (D), *Cumberland*
2 John E. Fogarty (D), *Harmony*

## SOUTH CAROLINA

### SENATORS

Burnet R. Maybank (D), *Charleston*
Olin D. Johnston (D), *Spartanburg*

### REPRESENTATIVES

1 L. Mendel Rivers (D), *Charleston*
2 John J. Riley (D), *Sumter*
3 W. J. Bryan Dorn (D), *Greenwood*
4 Joseph R. Bryson (D), *Greenville*
5 James P. Richards (D), *Lancaster*
6 John L. McMillan (D), *Florence*

---

[46] Resigned October 1, 1951.
[47] Elected November 6, 1951, to fill vacancy caused by resignation of Edward F. Breen, and took his seat January 8, 1952.
[48] Died April 2, 1952; vacancy throughout remainder of the Congress.
[49] Died August 21, 1952; vacancy throughout remainder of the Congress.

[50] Announced October 24, 1952 that he was resigning from the Republican Party and would serve in the Senate as an Independent.
[51] Died September 1, 1951.
[52] Elected November 6, 1951, to fill vacancy caused by death of Albert C. Vaughn, and took his seat January 8, 1952.
[53] Died August 7, 1951.

[54] Elected November 6, 1951, to fill vacancy caused by death of Wilson D. Gillette, and took his seat January 8, 1952.
[55] Died April 27, 1951.
[56] Elected July 24, 1951, to fill vacancy caused by death of Frank Buchanan, and took her seat August 1, 1951.

## SOUTH DAKOTA

SENATORS

Karl E. Mundt (R), *Madison*
Francis H. Case (R), *Custer*

REPRESENTATIVES

1 Harold O. Lovre (R), *Watertown*
2 E. Y. Berry (R), *McLaughlin*

## TENNESSEE

SENATORS

Kenneth D. McKellar (D), *Memphis*
Estes Kefauver (D), *Chattanooga*

REPRESENTATIVES

1 B. Carroll Reece (R), *Johnson City*
2 Howard H. Baker (R), *Huntsville*
3 James B. Frazier, Jr. (D), *Chattanooga*
4 Albert A. Gore (D), *Carthage*
5 Joseph L. Evins (D), *Smithville*
6 J. Percy Priest (D), *Nashville*
7 James P. Sutton (D), *Lawrenceburg*
8 Thomas J. Murray (D), *Jackson*
9 Jere Cooper (D), *Dyersburg*
10 Clifford Davis (D), *Memphis*

## TEXAS

SENATORS

Tom T. Connally (D), *Marlin*
Lyndon B. Johnson (D), *Johnson City*

REPRESENTATIVES

1 Wright Patman (D), *Texarkana*
2 Jesse M. Combs (D), *Beaumont*
3 Lindley Beckworth (D), *Gladewater*
4 Sam Rayburn (D), *Bonham*
5 J. Frank Wilson (D), *Dallas*
6 Olin E. Teague (D), *College Station*
7 Tom Pickett (D),[57] *Palestine*
7 John V. Dowdy (D),[58] *Athens*
8 Albert Thomas (D), *Houston*
9 Clark W. Thompson (D), *Galveston*
10 W. Homer Thornberry (D), *Austin*
11 W. R. Poage (D), *Waco*
12 Wingate H. Lucas (D), *Grapevine*
13 Ed Gossett (D),[59] *Wichita Falls*
13 Frank N. Ikard (D),[60] *Wichita Falls*
14 John E. Lyle, Jr. (D), *Corpus Christi*
15 Lloyd M. Bentsen, Jr. (D), *McAllen*
16 Kenneth M. Regan (D), *Midland*
17 Omar T. Burleson (D), *Anson*
18 Walter E. Rogers (D), *Pampa*
19 George H. Mahon (D), *Lubbock*
20 Paul J. Kilday (D), *San Antonio*
21 O. Clark Fisher (D), *San Angelo*

## UTAH

SENATORS

Arthur V. Watkins (R), *Orem*
Wallace F. Bennett (R), *Salt Lake City*

REPRESENTATIVES

1 Walter K. Granger (D), *Cedar City*
2 Reva Z. B. Bosone (D), *Salt Lake City*

## VERMONT

SENATORS

George D. Aiken (R), *Putney*
Ralph E. Flanders (R), *Springfield*

REPRESENTATIVE AT LARGE

Winston L. Prouty (R), *Newport*

## VIRGINIA

SENATORS

Harry Flood Byrd (D), *Berryville*
A. Willis Robertson (D), *Lexington*

REPRESENTATIVES

1 Edward J. Robeson, Jr. (D), *Newport News*
2 Porter Hardy, Jr. (D), *Churchland*
3 J. Vaughan Gary (D), *Richmond*
4 Watkins M. Abbitt (D), *Appomattox*
5 Thomas B. Stanley (D), *Stanleytown*
6 Clarence G. Burton (D), *Lynchburg*
7 Burr P. Harrison (D), *Winchester*
8 Howard W. Smith (D), *Alexandria*
9 Thomas B. Fugate (D), *Ewing*

## WASHINGTON

SENATORS

Warren G. Magnuson (D), *Seattle*
Harry P. Cain (R), *Tacoma*

REPRESENTATIVES

1 Hugh B. Mitchell (D), *Seattle*
2 Henry M. Jackson (D), *Everett*
3 Russell V. Mack (R), *Hoquiam*
4 Hal Holmes (R), *Ellensburg*
5 Walter F. Horan (R), *Wenatchee*
6 Thor C. Tollefson (R), *Tacoma*

## WEST VIRGINIA

SENATORS

Harley M. Kilgore (D), *Beckley*
Matthew M. Neely (D), *Fairmont*

REPRESENTATIVES

1 Robert L. Ramsay (D), *Follansbee*
2 Harley O. Staggers (D), *Keyser*
3 Cleveland M. Bailey (D), *Clarksburg*
4 Maurice G. Burnside (D), *Huntington*
5 John Kee (D),[61] *Bluefield*
5 M. Elizabeth Kee (D),[62] *Bluefield*
6 Erland H. Hedrick (D), *Beckley*

## WISCONSIN

SENATORS

Alexander Wiley (R), *Chippewa Falls*
Joseph R. McCarthy (R), *Appleton*

REPRESENTATIVES

1 Lawrence H. Smith (R), *Racine*
2 Glenn R. Davis (R), *Waukesha*
3 Gardner R. Withrow (R), *La Crosse*
4 Clement J. Zablocki (D), *Milwaukee*
5 Charles J. Kersten (R), *Milwaukee*
6 William K. Van Pelt (R), *Fond du Lac*
7 Reid F. Murray (R),[63] *Ogdensburg*
8 John W. Byrnes (R), *Green Bay*
9 Merlin Hull (R), *Black River Falls*
10 Alvin E. O'Konski (R), *Mercer*

## WYOMING

SENATORS

Joseph C. O'Mahoney (D), *Cheyenne*
Lester C. Hunt (D), *Lander*

REPRESENTATIVE AT LARGE

William H. Harrison (R), *Sheridan*

## TERRITORY OF ALASKA

DELEGATE

E. L. (Bob) Bartlett (D), *Juneau*

## TERRITORY OF HAWAII

DELEGATE

Joseph R. Farrington (R), *Honolulu*

## COMMONWEALTH OF PUERTO RICO[64]

RESIDENT COMMISSIONER

Antonio Fernós-Isern (PD), *Santurce*

---

[57] Resigned June 30, 1952.
[58] Elected September 23, 1952, to fill vacancy caused by resignation of Tom Pickett, but was unable to be sworn in as Congress was not in session.
[59] Resigned July 31, 1951.
[60] Elected September 8, 1951, to fill vacancy caused by resignation of Ed Gossett, and took his seat September 17, 1951.
[61] Died May 8, 1951.
[62] Elected July 17, 1951, to fill vacancy caused by death of her husband, John Kee, and took her seat July 6, 1951.
[63] Died April 29, 1952; vacancy throughout remainder of the Congress.
[64] Became a Commonwealth by enactment of Public Law 447, 82d Congress (66 Stat. 327), effective July 25, 1952.

# 83RD CONGRESS

## JANUARY 3, 1953, TO JANUARY 3, 1955

Richard M. Nixon
Vice President

FIRST SESSION— *January 3, 1953, to August 3, 1953*
SECOND SESSION— *January 6, 1954,[1] to December 2,[2] 1954*

Joseph W. Martin, Jr.
Speaker

Senate
Democrats 47 — Republicans 48 — Independent 1

VICE PRESIDENT OF THE UNITED STATES— Alben W. Barkley,[3] of Kentucky; Richard M. Nixon,[4] of California

PRESIDENT PRO TEMPORE OF THE SENATE— H. Styles Bridges,[5] of New Hampshire

SECRETARY OF THE SENATE— J. Mark Trice,[6] of Maryland

SERGEANT AT ARMS OF THE SENATE— Forest A. Harness,[7] of Indiana

MAJORITY FLOOR LEADER— Robert A. Taft,[8] of Ohio; William F. Knowland,[9] of California

REPUBLICAN WHIP— Leverett Saltonstall, of Massachusetts

DEMOCRATIC FLOOR LEADER— Lyndon B. Johnson, of Texas

ASSISTANT DEMOCRATIC LEADER— Earle C. Clements, of Kentucky

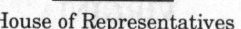

House of Representatives
Democrats 213 — Republicans 221 — Independent 1

SPEAKER OF THE HOUSE OF REPRESENTATIVES— Joseph W. Martin, Jr.,[10] of Massachusetts

CLERK OF THE HOUSE— Lyle O. Snader,[11] of Illinois

SERGEANT AT ARMS OF THE HOUSE— William F. Russell,[12] of Pennsylvania; Lyle O. Snader,[13] of Illinois; William R. Bonnell,[14] of Pennsylvania

DOORKEEPER OF THE HOUSE— Tom Kennamer,[15] of Missouri

POSTMASTER OF THE HOUSE— Beecher Hess,[16] of Ohio

MAJORITY LEADER— Charles A. Halleck, of Indiana

MAJORITY WHIP— Leslie C. Arends, of Illinois

DEMOCRATIC LEADER— Sam Rayburn, of Texas

DEMOCRATIC WHIP— John W. McCormack, of Massachusetts

---

## ALABAMA

### SENATORS

Lister Hill (D), *Montgomery*
John J. Sparkman (D), *Huntsville*

### REPRESENTATIVES

1 Frank W. Boykin (D), *Mobile*
2 George M. Grant (D), *Troy*
3 George W. Andrews (D), *Union Springs*
4 Kenneth A. Roberts (D), *Piedmont*
5 Albert Rains (D), *Gadsden*
6 Armistead I. Selden, Jr. (D), *Greensboro*
7 Carl A. Elliott (D), *Jasper*
8 Robert E. Jones, Jr. (D), *Scottsboro*
9 Laurie C. Battle (D), *Birmingham*

## ARIZONA

### SENATORS

Carl Hayden (D), *Phoenix*
Barry M. Goldwater (R), *Phoenix*

### REPRESENTATIVES

1 John J. Rhodes (R), *Mesa*
2 Harold A. Patten (D), *Tucson*

## ARKANSAS

### SENATORS

John L. McClellan (D), *Camden*
J. William Fulbright (D), *Fayetteville*

### REPRESENTATIVES

1 E. C. Gathings (D), *West Memphis*
2 Wilbur D. Mills (D), *Kensett*
3 James W. Trimble (D), *Berryville*

4 Oren Harris (D), *El Dorado*
5 Brooks Hays (D), *Little Rock*
6 William F. Norrell (D), *Monticello*

## CALIFORNIA

### SENATORS

William F. Knowland (R), *Piedmont*
Thomas H. Kuchel (R), *Anaheim*

### REPRESENTATIVES

1 Hubert B. Scudder (R), *Sebastopol*
2 Clair Engle (D), *Red Bluff*
3 John E. Moss, Jr. (D), *Sacramento*
4 William S. Mailliard (R), *San Francisco*
5 John F. Shelley (D), *San Francisco*
6 Robert L. Condon (D), *Walnut Creek*
7 John J. Allen, Jr. (R), *Oakland*

---

[1] By joint resolution (Pub. Law 199, 83d Cong., 1st sess.) the date of assembling the second session of the Eighty-third Congress was fixed for January 6, 1954
[2] The House adjourned sine die August 20, 1954, and the Senate adjourned sine die December 2, 1954.
[3] Term expired at noon January 20, 1953.
[4] Term began at noon January 20, 1953.
[5] Elected January 3, 1953.

[6] Elected January 3, 1953.
[7] Elected January 3, 1953.
[8] Died July 31, 1953.
[9] Elected August 4, 1953.
[10] Elected January 3, 1953.
[11] Elected January 3, 1953.
[12] Elected January 3, 1953; died July 7, 1953.

[13] Served from July 8, 1953, to September 15, 1953, to fill vacancy caused by death of William F. Russell.
[14] Appointed September 15, 1953.
[15] Elected January 3, 1953.
[16] Elected January 3, 1953.

[414]

8 George P. Miller (D), *Alameda*
9 J. Arthur Younger (R), *San Mateo*
10 Charles S. Gubser (R), *Gilroy*
11 Leroy Johnson (R), *Stockton*
12 Allan O. Hunter (R), *Fresno*
13 Ernest K. Bramblett (R), *Pacific Grove*
14 Harlan F. Hagen (D), *Hanford*
15 Gordon L. McDonough (R), *Los Angeles*
16 Donald L. Jackson (R), *Pacific Palisades*
17 Cecil R. King (D), *Los Angeles*
18 Craig Hosmer (R), *Long Beach*
19 Chet Holifield (D), *Montebello*
20 Carl Hinshaw (R), *Pasadena*
21 Edgar W. Hiestand (R), *Altadena*
22 Joseph F. Holt (R), *Van Nuys*
23 Clyde G. Doyle (D), *South Gate*
24 Norris Poulson (R),[17] *Los Angeles*
24 Glenard P. Lipscomb (R),[18] *Los Angeles*
25 Patrick J. Hillings (R), *Arcadia*
26 Samuel W. Yorty (D), *Los Angeles*
27 Harry R. Sheppard (D), *Yucaipa*
28 James B. Utt (R), *Santa Ana*
29 John Phillips (R), *Banning*
30 Robert C. Wilson (R), *Chula Vista*

## COLORADO

### SENATORS

Edwin C. Johnson (D), *Craig*
Eugene D. Millikin (R), *Denver*

### REPRESENTATIVES

1 Byron G. Rogers (D), *Denver*
2 William S. Hill (R), *Fort Collins*
3 J. Edgar Chenoweth (R), *Trinidad*
4 Wayne N. Aspinall (D), *Palisade*

## CONNECTICUT

### SENATORS

Prescott S. Bush (R), *Greenwich*
William A. Purtell (R), *West Hartford*

### REPRESENTATIVE AT LARGE

Antoni N. Sadlak (R), *Rockville*

### REPRESENTATIVES

1 Thomas J. Dodd (D), *West Hartford*
2 Horace Seely-Brown, Jr. (R), *Pomfret Center*
3 Albert W. Cretella (R), *North Haven*
4 Albert P. Morano (R), *Greenwich*
5 James T. Patterson (R), *Watertown*

## DELAWARE

### SENATORS

John J. Williams (R), *Millsboro*
J. Allen Frear, Jr. (D), *Dover*

### REPRESENTATIVE AT LARGE

Herbert B. Warburton (R), *Wilmington*

## FLORIDA

### SENATORS

Spessard L. Holland (D), *Bartow*
George A. Smathers (D), *Miami*

### REPRESENTATIVES

1 Courtney W. Campbell (D), *Clearwater*
2 Charles E. Bennett (D), *Jacksonville*
3 Robert L. F. Sikes (D), *Crestview*
4 William C. Lantaff (D), *Miami Springs*
5 A. Sydney Herlong, Jr. (D), *Leesburg*
6 Dwight L. Rogers (D),[19] *Fort Lauderdale*
7 James A. Haley (D), *Sarasota*
8 D. R. (Billy) Matthews (D), *Gainesville*

## GEORGIA

### SENATORS

Walter F. George (D), *Vienna*
Richard B. Russell (D), *Winder*

### REPRESENTATIVES

1 Prince H. Preston, Jr. (D), *Statesboro*
2 John L. Pilcher (D),[20] *Meigs*
3 E. L. Forrester (D), *Leesburg*
4 A. Sidney Camp (D),[21] *Newnan*
4 John J. Flynt, Jr. (D),[22] *Griffin*
5 James C. Davis (D), *Stone Mountain*
6 Carl Vinson (D), *Milledgeville*
7 Henderson L. Lanham (D), *Rome*
8 William M. Wheeler (D), *Alma*
9 Phillip M. Landrum (D), *Jasper*
10 Paul Brown (D), *Elberton*

## IDAHO

### SENATORS

Henry C. Dworshak (R), *Burley*
Herman Welker (R), *Payette*

### REPRESENTATIVES

1 Gracie B. Pfost (D), *Nampa*
2 Hamer H. Budge (R), *Boise*

## ILLINOIS

### SENATORS

Paul H. Douglas (D), *Chicago*
Everett McKinley Dirksen (R), *Pekin*

### REPRESENTATIVES

1 William L. Dawson (D), *Chicago*
2 Barratt O'Hara (D), *Chicago*
3 Fred E. Busbey (R), *Chicago*
4 William E. McVey (R), *Harvey*
5 John C. Kluczynski (D), *Chicago*
6 Thomas J. O'Brien (D), *Chicago*
7 James B. Bowler (D),[23] *Chicago*
8 Thomas S. Gordon (D), *Chicago*
9 Sidney R. Yates (D), *Chicago*
10 Richard W. Hoffman (R), *Riverside*
11 Timothy P. Sheehan (R), *Chicago*
12 Edgar A. Jonas (R), *Chicago*
13 Marguerite Stitt Church (R), *Evanston*
14 Chauncey W. Reed (R), *West Chicago*
15 Noah M. Mason (R), *Oglesby*
16 Leo E. Allen (R), *Galena*
17 Leslie C. Arends (R), *Melvin*
18 Harold H. Velde (R), *Pekin*
19 Robert B. Chiperfield (R), *Canton*
20 Sidney E. Simpson (R), *Carrollton*
21 Peter F. Mack, Jr. (D), *Carlinville*
22 William L. Springer (R), *Champaign*
23 Charles W. Vursell (R), *Salem*
24 Melvin Price (D), *East St. Louis*
25 Cecil W. (Runt) Bishop (R), *Carterville*

## INDIANA

### SENATORS

Homer E. Capehart (R), *Washington*
William E. Jenner (R), *Bedford*

### REPRESENTATIVES

1 Ray J. Madden (D), *Gary*
2 Charles A. Halleck (R), *Rensselaer*
3 Shepard J. Crumpacker, Jr. (R), *South Bend*
4 E. Ross Adair (R), *Fort Wayne*
5 John V. Beamer (R), *Wabash*
6 Cecil M. Harden (R), *Covington*
7 William G. Bray (R), *Martinsville*
8 D. Bailey Merrill (R), *Evansville*
9 Earl Wilson (R), *Bedford*
10 Ralph Harvey (R), *Mount Summit*
11 Charles B. Brownson (R), *Indianapolis*

---

[17] Resigned July 11, 1953.
[18] Elected to fill vacancy caused by resignation of Norris Poulson, and took his seat January 6, 1954.
[19] Died December 1, 1954, before the commencement of the Eighty-fourth Congress to which he had been reelected. Vacancy in the Eighty-third Congress not filled.

[20] Elected to fill vacancy caused by death of Representative-elect Edward E. Cox, in preceding Congress, and took his seat February 9, 1953.
[21] Died July 24, 1954.
[22] Elected November 2, 1954, to fill vacancy caused by death of A. Sidney Camp, but was unable to

be sworn in as Congress was not in session.
[23] Elected to fill vacancy caused by death of Representative-elect Adolph J. Sabath, in preceding Congress, and took his seat July 13, 1953.

## IOWA

SENATORS

Bourke B. Hickenlooper (R), *Cedar Rapids*
Guy M. Gillette (D), *Cherokee*

REPRESENTATIVES

1 Thomas E. Martin (R), *Iowa City*
2 Henry O. Talle (R), *Decorah*
3 H. R. Gross (R), *Waterloo*
4 Karl M. LeCompte (R), *Corydon*
5 Paul Cunningham (R), *Des Moines*
6 James I. Dolliver (R), *Fort Dodge*
7 Ben F. Jensen (R), *Exira*
8 Charles B. Hoeven (R), *Alton*

## KANSAS

SENATORS

Andrew F. Schoeppel (R), *Wichita*
Frank Carlson (R), *Concordia*

REPRESENTATIVES

1 Howard S. Miller (D), *Hiawatha*
2 Errett P. Scrivner (R), *Kansas City*
3 Myron V. George (R), *Altamont*
4 Edward H. Rees (R), *Emporia*
5 Clifford R. Hope (R), *Garden City*
6 Wint Smith (R), *Mankato*

## KENTUCKY

SENATORS

Earle C. Clements (D), *Morganfield*
John Sherman Cooper (R), *Somerset*

REPRESENTATIVES

1 Noble J. Gregory (D), *Mayfield*
2 Garrett L. Withers (D),[24] *Dixon*
2 William H. Natcher (D),[25] *Bowling Green*
3 John M. Robsion, Jr. (R), *Louisville*
4 Frank L. Chelf (D), *Lebanon*
5 Brent Spence (D), *Fort Thomas*
6 John C. Watts (D), *Nicholasville*
7 Carl D. Perkins (D), *Hindman*
8 James S. Golden (R), *Pineville*

## LOUISIANA

SENATORS

Allen J. Ellender, Sr. (D), *Houma*
Russell B. Long (D), *Baton Rouge*

REPRESENTATIVES

1 F. Edward Hébert (D), *New Orleans*
2 Hale Boggs (D), *New Orleans*
3 Edwin E. Willis (D), *St. Martinville*

4 Overton Brooks (D), *Shreveport*
5 Otto E. Passman (D), *Monroe*
6 James H. Morrison (D), *Hammond*
7 T. Ashton Thompson (D), *Ville Platte*
8 George S. Long (D), *Pineville*

## MAINE

SENATORS

Margaret Chase Smith (R), *Skowhegan*
Frederick G. Payne (R), *Waldoboro*

REPRESENTATIVES

1 Robert Hale (R), *Portland*
2 Charles P. Nelson (R), *Augusta*
3 Clifford G. McIntire (R), *Perham*

## MARYLAND

SENATORS

John Marshall Butler (R), *Baltimore*
J. Glenn Beall (R), *Frostburg*

REPRESENTATIVES

1 Edward T. Miller (R), *Easton*
2 James P. S. Devereux (R), *Stevenson*
3 Edward A. Garmatz (D), *Baltimore*
4 George H. Fallon (D), *Baltimore*
5 Frank Small, Jr. (R), *Clinton*
6 DeWitt S. Hyde (R), *Bethesda*
7 Samuel N. Friedel (D), *Baltimore*

## MASSACHUSETTS

SENATORS

Leverett Saltonstall (R), *Dover*
John F. Kennedy (D), *Boston*

REPRESENTATIVES

1 John W. Heselton (R), *Deerfield*
2 Edward P. Boland (D), *Springfield*
3 Philip J. Philbin (D), *Clinton*
4 Harold D. Donohue (D), *Worcester*
5 Edith Nourse Rogers (R), *Lowell*
6 William H. Bates (R), *Salem*
7 Thomas J. Lane (D), *Lawrence*
8 Angier L. Goodwin (R), *Melrose*
9 Donald W. Nicholson (R), *Wareham*
10 Laurence Curtis (R), *Boston*
11 Thomas P. O'Neill, Jr. (D), *Cambridge*
12 John W. McCormack (D), *Dorchester*

13 Richard B. Wigglesworth (R), *Milton*
14 Joseph W. Martin, Jr. (R), *North Attleboro*

## MICHIGAN

SENATORS

Homer Ferguson (R), *Detroit*
Charles E. Potter (R), *Cheboygan*

REPRESENTATIVES

1 Thaddeus M. Machrowicz (D), *Hamtramck*
2 George Meader (R), *Ann Arbor*
3 Paul W. Shafer (R),[26] *Battle Creek*
4 Clare E. Hoffman (R), *Allegan*
5 Gerald R. Ford, Jr. (R), *Grand Rapids*
6 Kit Clardy (R), *East Lansing*
7 Jesse P. Wolcott (R), *Port Huron*
8 Alvin M. Bentley (R), *Owosso*
9 Ruth Thompson (R), *Whitehall*
10 Elford A. Cederberg (R), *Bay City*
11 Victor A. Knox (R), *Sault Ste. Marie*
12 John B. Bennett (R), *Ontonagon*
13 George D. O'Brien (D), *Detroit*
14 Louis C. Rabaut (D), *Grosse Pointe Park*
15 John D. Dingell (D), *Detroit*
16 John Lesinski, Jr. (D), *Dearborn*
17 Charles G. Oakman (R), *Detroit*
18 George A. Dondero (R), *Royal Oak*

## MINNESOTA

SENATORS

Edward J. Thye (R), *Northfield*
Hubert H. Humphrey (D), *Minneapolis*

REPRESENTATIVES

1 August H. Andresen (R), *Red Wing*
2 Joseph P. O'Hara (R), *Glencoe*
3 Roy W. Wier (D), *Minneapolis*
4 Eugene J. McCarthy (D), *St. Paul*
5 Walter H. Judd (R), *Minneapolis*
6 Fred Marshall (D), *Grove City*
7 H. Carl Andersen (R), *Tyler*
8 John A. Blatnik (D), *Chisholm*
9 Harold C. Hagen (R), *Crookston*

## MISSISSIPPI

SENATORS

James O. Eastland (D), *Doddsville*
John C. Stennis (D), *De Kalb*

REPRESENTATIVES

1 Thomas G. Abernethy (D), *Okolona*
2 Jamie L. Whitten (D), *Charleston*
3 Frank E. Smith (D), *Greenwood*
4 John Bell Williams (D), *Raymond*

---

[24] Died April 30, 1953.
[25] Elected to fill vacancy caused by death of

Garrett L. Withers, and took his seat January 6, 1954.
[26] Died August 17, 1954; vacancy throughout

remainder of the Congress.

5 W. Arthur Winstead (D),
  *Philadelphia*
6 William M. Colmer (D),
  *Pascagoula*

## MISSOURI

SENATORS

Thomas C. Hennings, Jr. (D), *St. Louis*

Stuart Symington (D), *Creve Coeur*

REPRESENTATIVES

1 Frank M. Karsten (D), *St. Louis*
2 Thomas B. Curtis (R), *Webster Groves*
3 Leonor Kretzer Sullivan (D), *St. Louis*
4 Jeffrey P. Hillelson (R), *Independence*
5 Richard W. Bolling (D), *Kansas City*
6 William C. Cole (R), *St. Joseph*
7 Dewey Short (R), *Galena*
8 Albert S. J. Carnahan (D), *Ellsinore*
9 Clarence Cannon (D), *Elsberry*
10 Paul C. Jones (D), *Kennett*
11 Morgan M. Moulder (D), *Camdenton*

## MONTANA

SENATORS

James E. Murray (D), *Butte*

Mike Mansfield (D), *Missoula*

REPRESENTATIVES

1 Lee Metcalf (D), *Helena*
2 Wesley A. D'Ewart (D), *Wilsall*

## NEBRASKA

SENATORS

Hugh A. Butler (R),[27] *Omaha*

Sam W. Reynolds (R),[28] *Omaha*

Roman L. Hruska (R),[29] *Omaha*

Dwight P. Griswold (R),[30] *Scottsbluff*

Eva K. Bowring (R),[31] *Merriman*

Hazel H. Abel (R),[32] *Lincoln*

Carl T. Curtis (R),[33] *Minden*

REPRESENTATIVES

1 Carl T. Curtis (R),[34] *Minden*
2 Roman L. Hruska (R),[35] *Omaha*
3 Robert D. Harrison (R), *Norfolk*
4 Arthur L. Miller (R), *Kimball*

## NEVADA

SENATORS

Patrick A. McCarran (D),[36] *Reno*

Ernest S. Brown (R),[37] *Reno*

Alan H. Bible (D),[38] *Reno*

George W. Malone (R), *Reno*

REPRESENTATIVE AT LARGE

Clifton Young (R), *Reno*

## NEW HAMPSHIRE

SENATORS

H. Styles Bridges (R), *Concord*

Charles W. Tobey (R),[39] *Temple*

Robert W. Upton (R),[40] *Concord*

Norris Cotton (R),[41] *Lebanon*

REPRESENTATIVES

1 Chester E. Merrow (R), *Center Ossipee*
2 Norris Cotton (R),[42] *Lebanon*

## NEW JERSEY

SENATORS

H. Alexander Smith (R), *Princeton*

Robert C. Hendrickson (R), *Woodbury*

REPRESENTATIVES

1 Charles A. Wolverton (R), *Merchantville*
2 T. Millet Hand (R), *Cape May City*
3 James C. Auchincloss (R), *Rumson*
4 Charles R. Howell (D), *Pennington*
5 Peter H. B. Frelinghuysen, Jr. (R), *Morristown*
6 Clifford P. Case (R),[43] *Rahway*
6 Harrison A. Williams, Jr. (D),[44] *Plainfield*
7 William B. Widnall (R), *Saddle River*
8 Gordon Canfield (R), *Paterson*
9 Frank C. Osmers, Jr. (R), *Haworth*
10 Peter W. Rodino, Jr. (D), *Newark*
11 Hugh J. Addonizio (D), *Newark*
12 Robert W. Kean (R), *Livingston*
13 Alfred D. Sieminski (D), *Jersey City*
14 Edward J. Hart (D), *Jersey City*

## NEW MEXICO

SENATORS

Dennis Chavez (D), *Albuquerque*

Clinton P. Anderson (D), *Albuquerque*

REPRESENTATIVES AT LARGE

Antonio M. Fernandez (D), *Santa Fe*

John J. Dempsey (D), *Santa Fe*

## NEW YORK

SENATORS

Irving M. Ives (R), *Norwich*

Herbert H. Lehman (D), *New York City*

REPRESENTATIVES

1 Stuyvesant Wainwright II (R), *Wainscott*
2 Steven B. Derounian (R), *Roslyn*
3 Frank J. Becker (R), *Lynbrook*
4 Henry J. Latham (R), *Queens Village*
5 Albert H. Bosch (R), *Richmond Hill*
6 Lester Holtzman (D), *Rego Park*
7 James J. Delaney (D), *Long Island City*
8 Louis B. Heller (D),[45] *Brooklyn*
9 Eugene J. Keogh (D), *Brooklyn*
10 Edna F. Kelly (D), *Brooklyn*
11 Emanuel Celler (D), *Brooklyn*
12 Francis E. Dorn (R), *Brooklyn*
13 Abraham J. Multer (D), *Brooklyn*
14 John J. Rooney (D), *Brooklyn*
15 John H. Ray (R), *Staten Island*
16 Adam Clayton Powell, Jr. (D), *New York City*
17 Frederic R. Coudert, Jr. (R), *New York City*
18 James G. Donovan (D), *New York City*
19 Arthur G. Klein (D), *New York City*
20 Franklin D. Roosevelt, Jr. (D), *New York City*
21 Jacob K. Javits (R),[46] *New York City*
22 Sidney A. Fine (D), *New York City*
23 Isidore Dollinger (D), *New York City*
24 Charles A. Buckley (D), *New York City*
25 Paul A. Fino (R), *New York City*
26 Ralph A. Gamble (R), *Larchmont*

---

[27] Died July 1, 1954.

[28] Appointed to fill vacancy caused by death of Hugh A. Butler, and took his seat July 7, 1954.

[29] Elected November 2, 1954, to fill vacancy caused by death of Hugh A. Butler, and took his seat November 8, 1954.

[30] Died April 12, 1954.

[31] Appointed to fill vacancy caused by death of Dwight P. Griswold, and took her seat April 26, 1954.

[32] Elected November 2, 1954, to fill vacancy caused by death of Dwight P. Griswold, and took her seat November 8, 1954; resigned December 31, 1954.

[33] Appointed January 1, 1954, to fill vacancy caused by resignation of Hazel H. Abel, but was unable to be sworn in as Congress was not in session.

[34] Resigned December 31, 1954 having been appointed to the Senate; vacancy throughout remainder of the Congress.

[35] Resigned November 8, 1954 having been elected to the Senate; vacancy throughout remainder of the Congress.

[36] Died September 28, 1954.

[37] Appointed to fill vacancy caused by death of Patrick A. McCarran, and took his seat November 8, 1954.

[38] Elected November 2, 1954, to fill vacancy caused by death of Patrick A. McCarran, and took his seat December 2, 1954.

[39] Died July 24, 1953.

[40] Appointed to fill vacancy caused by death of Charles W. Tobey, and took his seat January 6, 1954.

[41] Elected November 2, 1954, to fill vacancy caused by death of Charles W. Tobey, and took his seat November 8, 1954.

[42] Resigned November 7, 1954 having been elected to the Senate; vacancy throughout remainder of the Congress.

[43] Resigned August 16, 1953.

[44] Elected to fill vacancy caused by resignation of Clifford P. Case, and took his seat January 6, 1954.

[45] Resigned July 21, 1954; vacancy throughout remainder of the Congress.

[46] Resigned December 31, 1954; vacancy throughout remainder of the Congress.

## NEW YORK— Continued

### REPRESENTATIVES—CONTINUED

27 Ralph W. Gwinn (R), *Bronxville*
28 Katharine St. George (R), *Tuxedo Park*
29 J. Ernest Wharton (R), *Richmondville*
30 Leo W. O'Brien (D), *Albany*
31 Dean P. Taylor (R), *Troy*
32 Bernard W. Kearney (R), *Gloversville*
33 Clarence E. Kilburn (R), *Malone*
34 William R. Williams (R), *Cassville*
35 R. Walter Riehlman (R), *Tully*
36 John Taber (R), *Auburn*
37 W. Sterling Cole (R), *Bath*
38 Kenneth B. Keating (R), *Rochester*
39 Harold C. Ostertag (R), *Attica*
40 William E. Miller (R), *Lockport*
41 Edmund P. Radwan (R), *Buffalo*
42 John R. Pillion (R), *Lackawanna*
43 Daniel A. Reed (R), *Dunkirk*

## NORTH CAROLINA

### SENATORS

Clyde R. Hoey (D),[47] *Shelby*
Sam J. Ervin, Jr. (D),[48] *Morganton*
Willis Smith (D),[49] *Raleigh*
Alton A. Lennon (D),[50] *Wilmington*
W. Kerr Scott (D),[51] *Haw River*

### REPRESENTATIVES

1 Herbert C. Bonner (D), *Washington*
2 L. H. Fountain (D), *Tarboro*
3 Graham A. Barden (D), *New Bern*
4 Harold D. Cooley (D), *Nashville*
5 Richard Thurmond Chatham (D), *Elkin*
6 Carl T. Durham (D), *Chapel Hill*
7 F. Ertel Carlyle (D), *Lumberton*
8 Charles B. Deane (D), *Rockingham*
9 Hugh Q. Alexander (D), *Kannapolis*
10 Charles Raper Jonas (R), *Lincolnton*
11 Woodrow W. Jones (D), *Rutherfordton*
12 George A. Shuford (D), *Asheville*

## NORTH DAKOTA

### SENATORS

William Langer (R), *Wheatland*
Milton R. Young (R), *La Moure*

### REPRESENTATIVES AT LARGE

Usher L. Burdick (R), *Williston*
Otto Krueger (R), *Fessenden*

## OHIO

### SENATORS

Robert A. Taft (R),[52] *Cincinnati*
Thomas A. Burke (D),[53] *Cleveland*
George H. Bender (R),[54] *Chagrin Falls*
John W. Bricker (R), *Columbus*

### REPRESENTATIVES

1 Gordon H. Scherer (R), *Cincinnati*
2 William E. Hess (R), *Cincinnati*
3 Paul F. Schenck (R), *Dayton*
4 William M. McCulloch (R), *Piqua*
5 Cliff Clevenger (R), *Bryan*
6 James G. Polk (D), *Highland*
7 Clarence J. Brown (R), *Blanchester*
8 Jackson E. Betts (R), *Findlay*
9 H. Frazier Reams (I), *Toledo*
10 Thomas A. Jenkins (R), *Ironton*
11 Oliver P. Bolton (R), *Mentor*
12 John M. Vorys (R), *Columbus*
13 Alvin F. Weichel (R), *Sandusky*
14 William H. Ayers (R), *Akron*
15 Robert T. Secrest (D),[55] *Senecaville*
16 Frank T. Bow (R), *Canton*
17 J. Harry McGregor (R), *West Lafayette*
18 Wayne L. Hays (D), *Flushing*
19 Michael J. Kirwan (D), *Youngstown*
20 Michael A. Feighan (D), *Cleveland*
21 Robert Crosser (D), *Cleveland*
22 Frances P. Bolton (R), *Lyndhurst*
23 George H. Bender (R),[56] *Chagrin Falls*

## OKLAHOMA

### SENATORS

Robert S. Kerr (D), *Oklahoma City*
A. S. Mike Monroney (D), *Oklahoma City*

### REPRESENTATIVES

1 Page H. Belcher (R), *Enid*
2 Edmond Edmondson (D), *Muskogee*
3 Carl Albert (D), *McAlester*
4 Thomas J. Steed (D), *Shawnee*
5 John Jarman (D), *Oklahoma City*
6 Victor E. Wickersham (D), *Mangum*

## OREGON

### SENATORS

Guy Cordon (R), *Roseburg*
Wayne L. Morse (I), *Eugene*

### REPRESENTATIVES

1 A. Walter Norblad (R), *Stayton*
2 Samuel H. Coon (R), *Baker*
3 Homer D. Angell (R), *Portland*
4 Harris Ellsworth (R), *Roseburg*

## PENNSYLVANIA

### SENATORS

Edward Martin (R), *Washington*
James H. Duff (R), *Carnegie*

### REPRESENTATIVES

1 William A. Barrett (D), *Philadelphia*
2 William T. Granahan (D), *Philadelphia*
3 James A. Byrne (D), *Philadelphia*
4 Earl Chudoff (D), *Philadelphia*
5 William J. Green, Jr. (D), *Philadelphia*
6 Hugh D. Scott, Jr. (R), *Philadelphia*
7 Benjamin F. James (R), *Rosemont*
8 Karl C. King (R), *Morrisville*
9 Paul B. Dague (R), *Downingtown*
10 Joseph L. Carrigg (R), *Susquehanna*
11 Edward J. Bonin (R), *Hazleton*
12 Ivor D. Fenton (R), *Mahanoy City*
13 Samuel K. McConnell, Jr. (R), *Wynnewood*
14 George M. Rhodes (D), *Reading*
15 Francis E. Walter (D), *Easton*
16 Walter M. Mumma (R), *Harrisburg*
17 Alvin R. Bush (R), *Muncy*
18 Richard M. Simpson (R), *Huntingdon*
19 S. Walter Stauffer (R), *York*
20 James E. Van Zandt (R), *Altoona*
21 Augustine B. Kelley (D), *Greensburg*
22 John P. Saylor (R), *Johnstown*
23 Leon H. Gavin (R), *Oil City*
24 Carroll D. Kearns (R), *Farrell*
25 Louis E. Graham (R), *Beaver*
26 Thomas E. Morgan (D), *Fredericktown*
27 James G. Fulton (R), *Pittsburgh*
28 Herman P. Eberharter (D), *Pittsburgh*
29 Robert J. Corbett (R), *Pittsburgh*
30 Vera D. Buchanan (D), *McKeesport*

---

[47] Died May 12, 1954.
[48] Appointed to fill vacancy caused by death of Clyde R. Hoey, and took his seat June 11, 1954; subsequently elected.
[49] Died June 26, 1953.
[50] Appointed to fill vacancy caused by death of Willis Smith, and took his seat July 15, 1953.

[51] Elected to fill vacancy caused by death of Willis Smith, and took his seat November 29, 1954.
[52] Died July 31, 1953.
[53] Appointed to fill vacancy caused by death of Robert A. Taft, and took his seat January 6, 1954.
[54] Elected November 2, 1954, to fill vacancy caused by death of Robert A. Taft, and took his seat

December 16, 1954.
[55] Resigned September 26, 1954; vacancy throughout remainder of the Congress.
[56] Resigned December 15, 1954 having been elected to the Senate; vacancy throughout remainder of the Congress.

## RHODE ISLAND

### SENATORS

Theodore F. Green (D), *Providence*
John O. Pastore (D), *Providence*

### REPRESENTATIVES

1 Aime J. Forand (D), *Cumberland*
2 John E. Fogarty (D), *Harmony*

## SOUTH CAROLINA

### SENATORS

Burnet R. Maybank (D),[57] *Charleston*
Charles E. Daniel (D),[58] *Greenville*
Strom Thurmond (D),[59] *Aiken*
Olin D. Johnston (D), *Spartanburg*

### REPRESENTATIVES

1 L. Mendel Rivers (D), *Charleston*
2 John J. Riley (D), *Sumter*
3 W. J. Bryan Dorn (D), *Greenwood*
4 Joseph R. Bryson (D),[60] *Greenville*
4 Robert T. Ashmore (D),[61] *Greenville*
5 James P. Richards (D), *Lancaster*
6 John L. McMillan (D), *Florence*

## SOUTH DAKOTA

### SENATORS

Karl E. Mundt (R), *Madison*
Francis H. Case (R), *Custer*

### REPRESENTATIVES

1 Harold O. Lovre (R), *Watertown*
2 E. Y. Berry (R), *McLaughlin*

## TENNESSEE

### SENATORS

Estes Kefauver (D), *Chattanooga*
Albert A. Gore (D), *Carthage*

### REPRESENTATIVES

1 B. Carroll Reece (R), *Johnson City*
2 Howard H. Baker (R), *Huntsville*
3 James B. Frazier, Jr. (D), *Chattanooga*
4 Joseph L. Evins (D), *Smithville*
5 J. Percy Priest (D), *Nashville*
6 James P. Sutton (D), *Lawrenceburg*
7 Thomas J. Murray (D), *Jackson*
8 Jere Cooper (D), *Dyersburg*
9 Clifford Davis (D), *Memphis*

## TEXAS

### SENATORS

Lyndon B. Johnson (D), *Johnson City*
M. Price Daniel (D), *Liberty*

### REPRESENTATIVE AT LARGE

Martin Dies, Jr. (D), *Lufkin*

### REPRESENTATIVES

1 Wright Patman (D), *Texarkana*
2 Jack B. Brooks (D), *Beaumont*
3 Brady P. Gentry (D), *Tyler*
4 Sam Rayburn (D), *Bonham*
5 J. Frank Wilson (D), *Dallas*
6 Olin E. Teague (D), *College Station*
7 John V. Dowdy (D), *Athens*
8 Albert Thomas (D), *Houston*
9 Clark W. Thompson (D), *Galveston*
10 W. Homer Thornberry (D), *Austin*
11 W. R. Poage (D), *Waco*
12 Wingate H. Lucas (D), *Grapevine*
13 Frank N. Ikard (D), *Wichita Falls*
14 John E. Lyle, Jr. (D), *Corpus Christi*
15 Lloyd M. Bentsen, Jr. (D), *McAllen*
16 Kenneth M. Regan (D), *Midland*
17 Omar T. Burleson (D), *Anson*
18 Walter E. Rogers (D), *Pampa*
19 George H. Mahon (D), *Lubbock*
20 Paul J. Kilday (D), *San Antonio*
21 O. Clark Fisher (D), *San Angelo*

## UTAH

### SENATORS

Arthur V. Watkins (R), *Orem*
Wallace F. Bennett (R), *Salt Lake City*

### REPRESENTATIVES

1 Douglas R. Stringfellow (R), *Ogden*
2 William A. Dawson (R), *Salt Lake City*

## VERMONT

### SENATORS

George D. Aiken (R), *Putney*
Ralph E. Flanders (R), *Springfield*

### REPRESENTATIVE AT LARGE

Winston L. Prouty (R), *Newport*

## VIRGINIA

### SENATORS

Harry Flood Byrd (D), *Berryville*
A. Willis Robertson (D), *Lexington*

### REPRESENTATIVES

1 Edward J. Robeson, Jr. (D), *Warwick*
2 Porter Hardy, Jr. (D), *Churchland*
3 J. Vaughan Gary (D), *Richmond*
4 Watkins M. Abbitt (D), *Appomattox*
5 Thomas B. Stanley (D),[62] *Stanleytown*
5 William M. Tuck (D),[63] *South Boston*
6 Richard H. Poff (R), *Radford*
7 Burr P. Harrison (D), *Winchester*
8 Howard W. Smith (D), *Broad Run*
9 William C. Wampler (R), *Bristol*
10 Joel T. Broyhill (R), *Arlington*

## WASHINGTON

### SENATORS

Warren G. Magnuson (D), *Seattle*
Henry M. Jackson (D), *Everett*

### REPRESENTATIVE AT LARGE

Don Magnuson (D), *Seattle*

### REPRESENTATIVES

1 Thomas M. Pelly (R), *Seattle*
2 Alfred John (Jack) Westland (R), *Everett*
3 Russell V. Mack (R), *Hoquiam*
4 Hal Holmes (R), *Ellensburg*
5 Walter F. Horan (R), *Wenatchee*
6 Thor C. Tollefson (R), *Tacoma*

## WEST VIRGINIA

### SENATORS

Harley M. Kilgore (D), *Beckley*
Matthew M. Neely (D), *Fairmont*

### REPRESENTATIVES

1 Robert H. Mollohan (D), *Fairmont*
2 Harley O. Staggers (D), *Keyser*
3 Cleveland M. Bailey (D), *Clarksburg*
4 William E. Neal (R), *Huntington*
5 M. Elizabeth Kee (D), *Bluefield*
6 Robert C. Byrd (D), *Beckley*

## WISCONSIN

### SENATORS

Alexander Wiley (R), *Chippewa Falls*
Joseph R. McCarthy (R), *Appleton*

### REPRESENTATIVES

1 Lawrence H. Smith (R), *Racine*
2 Glenn R. Davis (R), *Waukesha*
3 Gardner R. Withrow (R), *La Crosse*
4 Clement J. Zablocki (D), *Milwaukee*
5 Charles J. Kersten (R), *Milwaukee*
6 William K. Van Pelt (R), *Fond du Lac*
7 Melvin R. Laird (R), *Marshfield*
8 John W. Byrnes (R), *Green Bay*
9 Merlin Hull (R),[64] *Black River Falls*

---

[57] Died September 1, 1954.
[58] Appointed to fill vacancy caused by death of Burnet R. Maybank, and took his seat November 8, 1954; resigned December 23, 1954.
[59] Appointed December 24, 1954, to fill vacancy caused by the death of Burnet R. Maybank, but was unable to be sworn in as Congress was not in session.
[60] Died March 10, 1953.
[61] Elected to fill vacancy caused by death of Joseph R. Bryson, and took his seat June 15, 1953.

[62] Resigned February 3, 1953.
[63] Elected to fill vacancy caused by resignation of Thomas B. Stanley, and took his seat April 21, 1953.
[64] Died May 17, 1953.

## WISCONSIN—Continued

REPRESENTATIVES—CONTINUED

9 Lester R. Johnson (D),[65] *Black River Falls*

10 Alvin E. O'Konski (R), *Mercer*

## WYOMING

SENATORS

Lester C. Hunt (D),[66] *Lander*

Edward D. Crippa (R),[67] *Rock Springs*

Joseph C. O'Mahoney (D),[68] *Cheyenne*

Frank A. Barrett (R), *Lusk*

REPRESENTATIVE AT LARGE

William H. Harrison (R), *Sheridan*

## TERRITORY OF ALASKA

DELEGATE

E. L. (Bob) Bartlett (D), *Juneau*

## TERRITORY OF HAWAII

DELEGATE

Joseph R. Farrington (R),[69] *Honolulu*

Mary Elizabeth Pruett Farrington (R),[70] *Honolulu*

## COMMONWEALTH OF PUERTO RICO

RESIDENT COMMISSIONER

Antonio Fernós-Isern (PD), *Santurce*

---

[65] Elected to fill vacancy caused by death of Merlin Hull, and took his seat January 6, 1954.

[66] Died June 19, 1954.

[67] Appointed to fill vacancy caused by death of

Lester C. Hunt, and took his seat June 28, 1954.

[68] Elected to fill vacancy caused by death of Lester C. Hunt, and took his seat November 29, 1954.

[69] Died June 19, 1954.

[70] Elected to fill vacancy caused by death of her husband, Joseph R. Farrington, and took her seat August 4, 1954.

# 84TH CONGRESS

## JANUARY 3, 1955, TO JANUARY 3, 1957

FIRST SESSION— *January 5,[1] 1955, to August 2, 1955*
SECOND SESSION— *January 3, 1956, to July 27, 1956*

---

### Senate
#### Democrats 48 — Republicans 47 — Independent 1
VICE PRESIDENT OF THE UNITED STATES— Richard M. Nixon, of California
PRESIDENT PRO TEMPORE OF THE SENATE— Walter F. George,[2] of Georgia
SECRETARY OF THE SENATE— Felton McLellan Johnston,[3] of Mississippi
SERGEANT AT ARMS OF THE SENATE— Joseph C. Duke,[4] of Arizona
MAJORITY FLOOR LEADER— Lyndon B. Johnson, of Texas
DEMOCRATIC WHIP— Earle C. Clements, of Kentucky
REPUBLICAN FLOOR LEADER— William F. Knowland, of California
ASSISTANT REPUBLICAN LEADER— Leverett Saltonstall, of Massachusetts

---

### House of Representatives
#### Democrats 232 — Republicans 203
SPEAKER OF THE HOUSE OF REPRESENTATIVES— Sam Rayburn,[5] of Texas
CLERK OF THE HOUSE— Ralph R. Roberts,[6] of Indiana
SERGEANT AT ARMS OF THE HOUSE— Zeake W. Johnson, Jr.,[7] of Tennessee
DOORKEEPER OF THE HOUSE— William M. Miller,[8] of Mississippi
POSTMASTER OF THE HOUSE— H. H. Morris,[9] of Kentucky
MAJORITY LEADER— John W. McCormack, of Massachusetts
MAJORITY WHIP— Carl Albert, of Oklahoma
REPUBLICAN LEADER— Joseph W. Martin, Jr., of Massachusetts
REPUBLICAN WHIP— Leslie C. Arends, of Illinois

Richard M. Nixon
Vice President

Sam Rayburn
Speaker

---

## ALABAMA

### SENATORS
Lister Hill (D), *Montgomery*
John J. Sparkman (D), *Huntsville*

### REPRESENTATIVES
1 Frank W. Boykin (D), *Mobile*
2 George M. Grant (D), *Troy*
3 George W. Andrews (D), *Union Springs*
4 Kenneth A. Roberts (D), *Anniston*
5 Albert Rains (D), *Gadsden*
6 Armistead I. Selden, Jr. (D), *Greensboro*
7 Carl A. Elliott (D), *Jasper*
8 Robert E. Jones, Jr. (D), *Scottsboro*
9 George Huddleston, Jr. (D), *Birmingham*

## ARIZONA

### SENATORS
Carl Hayden (D), *Phoenix*
Barry M. Goldwater (R), *Phoenix*

### REPRESENTATIVES
1 John J. Rhodes (R), *Mesa*
2 Stewart L. Udall (D), *Tucson*

## ARKANSAS

### SENATORS
John L. McClellan (D), *Camden*
J. William Fulbright (D), *Fayetteville*

### REPRESENTATIVES
1 E. C. Gathings (D), *West Memphis*
2 Wilbur D. Mills (D), *Kensett*
3 James W. Trimble (D), *Berryville*
4 Oren Harris (D), *El Dorado*
5 Brooks Hays (D), *Little Rock*
6 William F. Norrell (D), *Monticello*

## CALIFORNIA

### SENATORS
William F. Knowland (R), *Piedmont*
Thomas H. Kuchel (R), *Anaheim*

### REPRESENTATIVES
1 Hubert B. Scudder (R), *Sebastopol*
2 Clair Engle (D), *Red Bluff*
3 John E. Moss, Jr. (D), *Sacramento*
4 William S. Mailliard (R), *San Francisco*
5 John F. Shelley (D), *San Francisco*
6 John F. Baldwin, Jr. (R), *Martinez*
7 John J. Allen, Jr. (R), *Oakland*
8 George P. Miller (D), *Alameda*
9 J. Arthur Younger (R), *San Mateo*
10 Charles S. Gubser (R), *Gilroy*
11 Leroy Johnson (R), *Stockton*
12 B. F. Sisk (D), *Fresno*
13 Charles M. Teague (R), *Ojai*
14 Harlan F. Hagen (D), *Hanford*
15 Gordon L. McDonough (R), *Los Angeles*
16 Donald L. Jackson (R), *Pacific Palisades*
17 Cecil R. King (D), *Los Angeles*
18 Craig Hosmer (R), *Long Beach*
19 Chet Holifield (D), *Montebello*
20 Carl Hinshaw (R),[10] *Pasadena*
21 Edgar W. Hiestand (R), *Altadena*
22 Joseph F. Holt (R), *Van Nuys*
23 Clyde G. Doyle (D), *South Gate*

---

[1] By joint resolution (Pub. Law 700, 83d Cong., 2d Sess.) the date of assembling the first session of the Eighty-fourth Congress was fixed for January 5, 1955.
[2] Elected January 5, 1955.
[3] Elected January 5, 1955.
[4] Elected January 5, 1955.
[5] Elected January 5, 1955.
[6] Elected January 5, 1955.
[7] Elected January 5, 1955.
[8] Elected January 5, 1955.
[9] Elected January 5, 1955.
[10] Died August 5, 1956; vacancy throughout remainder of the Congress.

## CALIFORNIA—Continued

REPRESENTATIVES—CONTINUED
24 Glenard P. Lipscomb (R), *Los Angeles*
25 Patrick J. Hillings (R), *Arcadia*
26 James Roosevelt (D), *Los Angeles*
27 Harry R. Sheppard (D), *Yucaipa*
28 James B. Utt (R), *Santa Ana*
29 John Phillips (R), *Banning*
30 Robert C. Wilson (R), *Chula Vista*

## COLORADO

SENATORS
Eugene D. Millikin (R), *Denver*
Gordon L. Allott (R), *Lamar*

REPRESENTATIVES
1 Byron G. Rogers (D), *Denver*
2 William S. Hill (R), *Fort Collins*
3 J. Edgar Chenoweth (R), *Trinidad*
4 Wayne N. Aspinall (D), *Palisade*

## CONNECTICUT

SENATORS
Prescott S. Bush (R), *Greenwich*
William A. Purtell (R), *West Hartford*

REPRESENTATIVE AT LARGE
Antoni N. Sadlak (R), *Rockville*

REPRESENTATIVES
1 Thomas J. Dodd (D), *West Hartford*
2 Horace Seely-Brown, Jr. (R), *Pomfret Center*
3 Albert W. Cretella (R), *North Haven*
4 Albert P. Morano (R), *Greenwich*
5 James T. Patterson (R), *Watertown*

## DELAWARE

SENATORS
John J. Williams (R), *Millsboro*
J. Allen Frear, Jr. (D), *Dover*

REPRESENTATIVE AT LARGE
Harris B. McDowell, Jr. (D), *Middletown*

## FLORIDA

SENATORS
Spessard L. Holland (D), *Bartow*
George A. Smathers (D), *Miami*

REPRESENTATIVES
1 William C. Cramer (R), *St. Petersburg*
2 Charles E. Bennett (D), *Jacksonville*
3 Robert L. F. Sikes (D), *Crestview*
4 Dante B. Fascell (D), *Miami*
5 A. Sydney Herlong, Jr. (D), *Leesburg*

6 Paul G. Rogers (D),[11] *West Palm Beach*
7 James A. Haley (D), *Sarasota*
8 D. R. (Billy) Matthews (D), *Gainesville*

## GEORGIA

SENATORS
Walter F. George (D), *Vienna*
Richard B. Russell (D), *Winder*

REPRESENTATIVES
1 Prince H. Preston, Jr. (D), *Statesboro*
2 John L. Pilcher (D), *Meigs*
3 E. L. Forrester (D), *Leesburg*
4 John J. Flynt, Jr. (D), *Griffin*
5 James C. Davis (D), *Stone Mountain*
6 Carl Vinson (D), *Milledgeville*
7 Henderson L. Lanham (D), *Rome*
8 Iris F. Blitch (D), *Homerville*
9 Phillip M. Landrum (D), *Jasper*
10 Paul Brown (D), *Elberton*

## IDAHO

SENATORS
Henry C. Dworshak (R), *Burley*
Herman Welker (R), *Payette*

REPRESENTATIVES
1 Gracie B. Pfost (D), *Nampa*
2 Hamer H. Budge (R), *Boise*

## ILLINOIS

SENATORS
Paul H. Douglas (D), *Chicago*
Everett McKinley Dirksen (R), *Pekin*

REPRESENTATIVES
1 William L. Dawson (D), *Chicago*
2 Barratt O'Hara (D), *Chicago*
3 James C. Murray (D), *Chicago*
4 William E. McVey (R), *Harvey*
5 John C. Kluczynski (D), *Chicago*
6 Thomas J. O'Brien (D), *Chicago*
7 James B. Bowler (D), *Chicago*
8 Thomas S. Gordon (D), *Chicago*
9 Sidney R. Yates (D), *Chicago*
10 Richard W. Hoffman (R), *Riverside*
11 Timothy P. Sheehan (R), *Chicago*
12 Charles A. Boyle (D), *Chicago*
13 Marguerite Stitt Church (R), *Evanston*
14 Chauncey W. Reed (R),[12] *West Chicago*
15 Noah M. Mason (R), *Oglesby*
16 Leo E. Allen (R), *Galena*
17 Leslie C. Arends (R), *Melvin*
18 Harold H. Velde (R), *Pekin*
19 Robert B. Chiperfield (R), *Canton*
20 Sidney E. Simpson (R), *Carrollton*
21 Peter F. Mack, Jr. (D), *Carlinville*

22 William L. Springer (R), *Champaign*
23 Charles W. Vursell (R), *Salem*
24 Melvin Price (D), *East St. Louis*
25 Kenneth J. Gray (D), *West Frankfort*

## INDIANA

SENATORS
Homer E. Capehart (R), *Washington*
William E. Jenner (R), *Bedford*

REPRESENTATIVES
1 Ray J. Madden (D), *Gary*
2 Charles A. Halleck (R), *Rensselaer*
3 Shepard J. Crumpacker, Jr. (R), *South Bend*
4 E. Ross Adair (R), *Fort Wayne*
5 John V. Beamer (R), *Wabash*
6 Cecil M. Harden (R), *Covington*
7 William G. Bray (R), *Martinsville*
8 Winfield K. Denton (D), *Evansville*
9 Earl Wilson (R), *Bedford*
10 Ralph Harvey (R), *Mount Summit*
11 Charles B. Brownson (R), *Indianapolis*

## IOWA

SENATORS
Bourke B. Hickenlooper (R), *Cedar Rapids*
Thomas E. Martin (R), *Iowa City*

REPRESENTATIVES
1 Frederic D. Schwengel (R), *Davenport*
2 Henry O. Talle (R), *Decorah*
3 H. R. Gross (R), *Waterloo*
4 Karl M. LeCompte (R), *Corydon*
5 Paul Cunningham (R), *Des Moines*
6 James I. Dolliver (R), *Fort Dodge*
7 Ben F. Jensen (R), *Exira*
8 Charles B. Hoeven (R), *Alton*

## KANSAS

SENATORS
Andrew F. Schoeppel (R), *Wichita*
Frank Carlson (R), *Concordia*

REPRESENTATIVES
1 William H. Avery (R), *Wakefield*
2 Errett P. Scrivner (R), *Kansas City*
3 Myron V. George (R), *Altamont*
4 Edward H. Rees (R), *Emporia*
5 Clifford R. Hope (R), *Garden City*
6 Wint Smith (R), *Mankato*

---

[11] Elected to fill vacancy caused by death of his father, Representative-elect Dwight L. Rogers, in the preceding Congress, and took his seat January 13, 1955.

[12] Died February 9, 1956; vacancy throughout remainder of the Congress.

## KENTUCKY

SENATORS

Earle C. Clements (D), *Morganfield*
Alben W. Barkley (D),[13] *Paducah*
Robert Humphreys (D),[14] *Frankfort*
John Sherman Cooper (R),[15] *Somerset*

REPRESENTATIVES

1 Noble J. Gregory (D), *Mayfield*
2 William H. Natcher (D), *Bowling Green*
3 John M. Robsion, Jr. (R), *Louisville*
4 Frank L. Chelf (D), *Lebanon*
5 Brent Spence (D), *Fort Thomas*
6 John C. Watts (D), *Nicholasville*
7 Carl D. Perkins (D), *Hindman*
8 Eugene Siler (R), *Williamsburg*

## LOUISIANA

SENATORS

Allen J. Ellender, Sr. (D), *Houma*
Russell B. Long (D), *Baton Rouge*

REPRESENTATIVES

1 F. Edward Hébert (D), *New Orleans*
2 Hale Boggs (D), *New Orleans*
3 Edwin E. Willis (D), *St. Martinville*
4 Overton Brooks (D), *Shreveport*
5 Otto E. Passman (D), *Monroe*
6 James H. Morrison (D), *Hammond*
7 T. Ashton Thompson (D), *Ville Platte*
8 George S. Long (D), *Pineville*

## MAINE

SENATORS

Margaret Chase Smith (R), *Skowhegan*
Frederick G. Payne (R), *Waldoboro*

REPRESENTATIVES

1 Robert Hale (R), *Portland*
2 Charles P. Nelson (R), *Waterville*
3 Clifford G. McIntire (R), *Perham*

## MARYLAND

SENATORS

John Marshall Butler (R), *Baltimore*
J. Glenn Beall (R), *Frostburg*

REPRESENTATIVES

1 Edward T. Miller (R), *Easton*
2 James P. S. Devereux (R), *Stevenson*
3 Edward A. Garmatz (D), *Baltimore*
4 George H. Fallon (D), *Baltimore*

5 Richard E. Lankford (D), *Annapolis*
6 DeWitt S. Hyde (R), *Bethesda*
7 Samuel N. Friedel (D), *Baltimore*

## MASSACHUSETTS

SENATORS

Leverett Saltonstall (R), *Dover*
John F. Kennedy (D), *Boston*

REPRESENTATIVES

1 John W. Heselton (R), *Deerfield*
2 Edward P. Boland (D), *Springfield*
3 Philip J. Philbin (D), *Clinton*
4 Harold D. Donohue (D), *Worcester*
5 Edith Nourse Rogers (R), *Lowell*
6 William H. Bates (R), *Salem*
7 Thomas J. Lane (D), *Lawrence*
8 Torbert H. Macdonald (D), *Malden*
9 Donald W. Nicholson (R), *Wareham*
10 Laurence Curtis (R), *Boston*
11 Thomas P. O'Neill, Jr. (D), *Cambridge*
12 John W. McCormack (D), *Dorchester*
13 Richard B. Wigglesworth (R), *Milton*
14 Joseph W. Martin, Jr. (R), *North Attleboro*

## MICHIGAN

SENATORS

Charles E. Potter (R), *Cheboygan*
Patrick V. McNamara (D), *Detroit*

REPRESENTATIVES

1 Thaddeus M. Machrowicz (D), *Hamtramck*
2 George Meader (R), *Ann Arbor*
3 August E. Johansen (R), *Battle Creek*
4 Clare E. Hoffman (R), *Allegan*
5 Gerald R. Ford, Jr. (R), *Grand Rapids*
6 Don Hayworth (D), *East Lansing*
7 Jesse P. Wolcott (R), *Port Huron*
8 Alvin M. Bentley (R), *Owosso*
9 Ruth Thompson (R), *Whitehall*
10 Elford A. Cederberg (R), *Bay City*
11 Victor A. Knox (R), *Sault Ste. Marie*
12 John B. Bennett (R), *Ontonagon*
13 Charles C. Diggs, Jr. (D), *Detroit*
14 Louis C. Rabaut (D), *Grosse Pointe Park*
15 John D. Dingell (D),[16] *Detroit*
15 John D. Dingell, Jr. (D),[17] *Detroit*
16 John Lesinski, Jr. (D), *Dearborn*
17 Martha W. Griffiths (D), *Detroit*
18 George A. Dondero (R), *Royal Oak*

## MINNESOTA

SENATORS

Edward J. Thye (R), *Northfield*
Hubert H. Humphrey (D), *Minneapolis*

REPRESENTATIVES

1 August H. Andresen (R), *Red Wing*
2 Joseph P. O'Hara (R), *Glencoe*
3 Roy W. Wier (D), *Minneapolis*
4 Eugene J. McCarthy (D), *St. Paul*
5 Walter H. Judd (R), *Minneapolis*
6 Fred Marshall (D), *Grove City*
7 H. Carl Andersen (R), *Tyler*
8 John A. Blatnik (D), *Chisholm*
9 Coya G. Knutson (D), *Oklee*

## MISSISSIPPI

SENATORS

James O. Eastland (D), *Doddsville*
John C. Stennis (D), *De Kalb*

REPRESENTATIVES

1 Thomas G. Abernethy (D), *Okolona*
2 Jamie L. Whitten (D), *Charleston*
3 Frank E. Smith (D), *Greenwood*
4 John Bell Williams (D), *Raymond*
5 W. Arthur Winstead (D), *Philadelphia*
6 William M. Colmer (D), *Pascagoula*

## MISSOURI

SENATORS

Thomas C. Hennings, Jr. (D), *St. Louis*
Stuart Symington (D), *Creve Coeur*

REPRESENTATIVES

1 Frank M. Karsten (D), *St. Louis*
2 Thomas B. Curtis (R), *Webster Groves*
3 Leonor Kretzer Sullivan (D), *St. Louis*
4 George H. Christopher (D), *Butler*
5 Richard W. Bolling (D), *Kansas City*
6 William R. Hull, Jr. (D), *Weston*
7 Dewey Short (R), *Galena*
8 Albert S. J. Carnahan (D), *Ellsinore*
9 Clarence Cannon (D), *Elsberry*
10 Paul C. Jones (D), *Kennett*
11 Morgan M. Moulder (D), *Camdenton*

## MONTANA

SENATORS

James E. Murray (D), *Butte*
Mike Mansfield (D), *Missoula*

---

[13] Died April 30, 1956.
[14] Appointed to fill vacancy caused by death of Alben W. Barkley, and took his seat June 25, 1956.
[15] Elected to fill vacancy caused by death of Alben W. Barkley, and took his seat January 3, 1957.
[16] Died September 19, 1955.
[17] Elected to fill vacancy caused by death of his father, John D. Dingell; took his seat January 3, 1956.

## MONTANA—Continued

### REPRESENTATIVES

1 Lee Metcalf (D), *Helena*
2 Orvin B. Fjare (R), *Big Timber*

## NEBRASKA

### SENATORS

Roman L. Hruska (R), *Omaha*
Carl T. Curtis (R), *Minden*

### REPRESENTATIVES

1 Phillip H. Weaver (R), *Falls City*
2 Jackson B. Chase (R), *Omaha*
3 Robert D. Harrison (R), *Norfolk*
4 Arthur L. Miller (R), *Kimball*

## NEVADA

### SENATORS

George W. Malone (R), *Reno*
Alan H. Bible (D), *Reno*

### REPRESENTATIVE AT LARGE

Clifton Young (R), *Reno*

## NEW HAMPSHIRE

### SENATORS

H. Styles Bridges (R), *Concord*
Norris Cotton (R), *Lebanon*

### REPRESENTATIVES

1 Chester E. Merrow (R), *Center Ossipee*
2 Perkins Bass (R), *Peterborough*

## NEW JERSEY

### SENATORS

H. Alexander Smith (R), *Princeton*
Clifford P. Case (R), *Rahway*

### REPRESENTATIVES

1 Charles A. Wolverton (R), *Merchantville*
2 T. Millet Hand (R),[18] *Cape May City*
3 James C. Auchincloss (R), *Rumson*
4 Frank Thompson, Jr. (D), *Trenton*
5 Peter H. B. Frelinghuysen, Jr. (R), *Morristown*
6 Harrison A. Williams, Jr. (D), *Westfield*
7 William B. Widnall (R), *Saddle River*
8 Gordon Canfield (R), *Paterson*
9 Frank C. Osmers, Jr. (R), *Tenafly*
10 Peter W. Rodino, Jr. (D), *Newark*
11 Hugh J. Addonizio (D), *Newark*
12 Robert W. Kean (R), *Livingston*
13 Alfred D. Sieminski (D), *Jersey City*
14 T. James Tumulty (D), *Jersey City*

## NEW MEXICO

### SENATORS

Dennis Chavez (D), *Albuquerque*
Clinton P. Anderson (D), *Albuquerque*

### REPRESENTATIVES AT LARGE

Antonio M. Fernandez (D),[19] *Santa Fe*
John J. Dempsey (D), *Santa Fe*

## NEW YORK

### SENATORS

Irving M. Ives (R), *Norwich*
Herbert H. Lehman (D), *New York City*

### REPRESENTATIVES

1 Stuyvesant Wainwright II (R), *Wainscott*
2 Steven B. Derounian (R), *Roslyn*
3 Frank J. Becker (R), *Lynbrook*
4 Henry J. Latham (R), *Queens Village*
5 Albert H. Bosch (R), *Richmond Hill*
6 Lester Holtzman (D), *Rego Park*
7 James J. Delaney (D), *Long Island City*
8 Victor L. Anfuso (D), *Brooklyn*
9 Eugene J. Keogh (D), *Brooklyn*
10 Edna F. Kelly (D), *Brooklyn*
11 Emanuel Celler (D), *Brooklyn*
12 Francis E. Dorn (R), *Brooklyn*
13 Abraham J. Multer (D), *Brooklyn*
14 John J. Rooney (D), *Brooklyn*
15 John H. Ray (R), *Staten Island*
16 Adam Clayton Powell, Jr. (D), *New York City*
17 Frederic R. Coudert, Jr. (R), *New York City*
18 James G. Donovan (D), *New York City*
19 Arthur G. Klein (D),[20] *New York City*
20 Irwin D. Davidson (D),[21] *New York City*
21 Herbert Zelenko (D), *New York City*
22 Sidney A. Fine (D),[22] *New York City*
22 James C. Healey (D),[23] *New York City*
23 Isidore Dollinger (D), *New York City*
24 Charles A. Buckley (D), *New York City*
25 Paul A. Fino (R), *New York City*
26 Ralph A. Gamble (R), *Larchmont*
27 Ralph W. Gwinn (R), *Bronxville*
28 Katharine St. George (R), *Tuxedo Park*

29 J. Ernest Wharton (R), *Richmondville*
30 Leo W. O'Brien (D), *Albany*
31 Dean P. Taylor (R), *Troy*
32 Bernard W. Kearney (R), *Gloversville*
33 Clarence E. Kilburn (R), *Malone*
34 William R. Williams (R), *Cassville*
35 R. Walter Riehlman (R), *Tully*
36 John Taber (R), *Auburn*
37 W. Sterling Cole (R), *Bath*
38 Kenneth B. Keating (R), *Rochester*
39 Harold C. Ostertag (R), *Attica*
40 William E. Miller (R), *Lockport*
41 Edmund P. Radwan (R), *Buffalo*
42 John R. Pillion (R), *Lackawanna*
43 Daniel A. Reed (R), *Dunkirk*

## NORTH CAROLINA

### SENATORS

Sam J. Ervin, Jr. (D), *Morganton*
W. Kerr Scott (D), *Haw River*

### REPRESENTATIVES

1 Herbert C. Bonner (D), *Washington*
2 L. H. Fountain (D), *Tarboro*
3 Graham A. Barden (D), *New Bern*
4 Harold D. Cooley (D), *Nashville*
5 Richard Thurmond Chatham (D), *Winston-Salem*
6 Carl T. Durham (D), *Chapel Hill*
7 F. Ertel Carlyle (D), *Lumberton*
8 Charles B. Deane (D), *Rockingham*
9 Hugh Q. Alexander (D), *Kannapolis*
10 Charles Raper Jonas (R), *Lincolnton*
11 Woodrow W. Jones (D), *Rutherfordton*
12 George A. Shuford (D), *Asheville*

## NORTH DAKOTA

### SENATORS

William Langer (R), *Wheatland*
Milton R. Young (R), *La Moure*

### REPRESENTATIVES AT LARGE

Usher L. Burdick (R), *Williston*
Otto Krueger (R), *Fessenden*

## OHIO

### SENATORS

John W. Bricker (R), *Columbus*
George H. Bender (R), *Chagrin Falls*

### REPRESENTATIVES

1 Gordon H. Scherer (R), *Cincinnati*

---

[18] Died December 26, 1956, before the commencement of the Eighty-fifth Congress to which he had been reelected. Vacancy in the Eighty-fourth Congress not filled.

[19] Died November 7, 1956, before the commencement of the Eighty-fifth Congress to which he had been reelected. Vacancy in the Eighty-fourth Congress not filled.

[20] Resigned December 31, 1956; vacancy throughout remainder of the Congress.

[21] Resigned December 31, 1956; vacancy throughout remainder of the Congress.

[22] Resigned January 2, 1956.

[23] Elected to fill vacancy caused by resignation of Sidney A. Fine, and took his seat February 20, 1956.

2 William E. Hess (R), *Cincinnati*
3 Paul F. Schenck (R), *Dayton*
4 William M. McCulloch (R), *Piqua*
5 Cliff Clevenger (R), *Bryan*
6 James G. Polk (D), *Highland*
7 Clarence J. Brown (R), *Blanchester*
8 Jackson E. Betts (R), *Findlay*
9 Thomas L. Ashley (D), *Toledo*
10 Thomas A. Jenkins (R), *Ironton*
11 Oliver P. Bolton (R), *Mentor*
12 John M. Vorys (R), *Columbus*
13 Albert D. Baumhart, Jr. (R), *Vermilion*
14 William H. Ayres (R), *Akron*
15 John E. Henderson (R), *Cambridge*
16 Frank T. Bow (R), *Canton*
17 J. Harry McGregor (R), *West Lafayette*
18 Wayne L. Hays (D), *Flushing*
19 Michael J. Kirwan (D), *Youngstown*
20 Michael A. Feighan (D), *Cleveland*
21 Charles A. Vanik (D), *Cleveland*
22 Frances P. Bolton (R), *Lyndhurst*
23 William E. Minshall (R), *Rocky River*

## OKLAHOMA

### SENATORS

Robert S. Kerr (D), *Oklahoma City*
A. S. Mike Monroney (D), *Oklahoma City*

### REPRESENTATIVES

1 Page H. Belcher (R), *Enid*
2 Edmond Edmondson (D), *Muskogee*
3 Carl Albert (D), *McAlester*
4 Thomas J. Steed (D), *Shawnee*
5 John Jarman (D), *Oklahoma City*
6 Victor E. Wickersham (D), *Mangum*

## OREGON

### SENATORS

Wayne L. Morse (I),[24] *Eugene*
Richard L. Neuberger (D), *Portland*

### REPRESENTATIVES

1 A. Walter Norblad (R), *Stayton*
2 Samuel H. Coon (R), *Baker*
3 Edith S. Green (D), *Portland*
4 Harris Ellsworth (R), *Roseburg*

## PENNSYLVANIA

### SENATORS

Edward Martin (R), *Washington*
James H. Duff (R), *Carnegie*

### REPRESENTATIVES

1 William A. Barrett (D), *Philadelphia*
2 William T. Granahan (D),[25] *Philadelphia*
2 Kathryn E. Granahan (D),[26] *Philadelphia*
3 James A. Byrne (D), *Philadelphia*
4 Earl Chudoff (D), *Philadelphia*
5 William J. Green, Jr. (D), *Philadelphia*
6 Hugh D. Scott, Jr. (R), *Philadelphia*
7 Benjamin F. James (R), *Rosemont*
8 Karl C. King (R), *Morrisville*
9 Paul B. Dague (R), *Downingtown*
10 Joseph L. Carrigg (R), *Susquehanna*
11 Daniel J. Flood (D), *Wilkes-Barre*
12 Ivor D. Fenton (R), *Mahanoy City*
13 Samuel K. McConnell, Jr. (R), *Wynnewood*
14 George M. Rhodes (D), *Reading*
15 Francis E. Walter (D), *Easton*
16 Walter M. Mumma (R), *Harrisburg*
17 Alvin R. Bush (R), *Muncy*
18 Richard M. Simpson (R), *Huntingdon*
19 James M. Quigley (D), *Highland Park*
20 James E. Van Zandt (R), *Altoona*
21 Augustine B. Kelley (D), *Greensburg*
22 John P. Saylor (R), *Johnstown*
23 Leon H. Gavin (R), *Oil City*
24 Carroll D. Kearns (R), *Farrell*
25 Frank M. Clark (D), *Bessemer*
26 Thomas E. Morgan (D), *Fredericktown*
27 James G. Fulton (R), *Pittsburgh*
28 Herman P. Eberharter (D), *Pittsburgh*
29 Robert J. Corbett (R), *Pittsburgh*
30 Vera D. Buchanan (D),[27] *McKeesport*
30 Elmer J. Holland (D),[28] *Pittsburgh*

## RHODE ISLAND

### SENATORS

Theodore F. Green (D), *Providence*
John O. Pastore (D), *Providence*

### REPRESENTATIVES

1 Aime J. Forand (D), *Cumberland*
2 John E. Fogarty (D), *Harmony*

## SOUTH CAROLINA

### SENATORS

Olin D. Johnston (D), *Spartanburg*
Strom Thurmond (D),[29] *Aiken*
Thomas A. Wofford (D),[30] *Greenville*
Strom Thurmond (D),[31] *Aiken*

### REPRESENTATIVES

1 L. Mendel Rivers (D), *Charleston*
2 John J. Riley (D), *Sumter*
3 W. J. Bryan Dorn (D), *Greenwood*
4 Robert T. Ashmore (D), *Greenville*
5 James P. Richards (D), *Lancaster*
6 John L. McMillan (D), *Florence*

## SOUTH DAKOTA

### SENATORS

Karl E. Mundt (R), *Madison*
Francis H. Case (R), *Custer*

### REPRESENTATIVES

1 Harold O. Lovre (R), *Watertown*
2 E. Y. Berry (R), *McLaughlin*

## TENNESSEE

### SENATORS

Estes Kefauver (D), *Chattanooga*
Albert A. Gore (D), *Carthage*

### REPRESENTATIVES

1 B. Carroll Reece (R), *Johnson City*
2 Howard H. Baker (R), *Huntsville*
3 James B. Frazier, Jr. (D), *Chattanooga*
4 Joseph L. Evins (D), *Smithville*
5 J. Percy Priest (D),[32] *Nashville*
6 Ross Bass (D), *Pulaski*
7 Thomas J. Murray (D), *Jackson*
8 Jere Cooper (D), *Dyersburg*
9 Clifford Davis (D), *Memphis*

## TEXAS

### SENATORS

Lyndon B. Johnson (D), *Johnson City*
M. Price Daniel (D), *Liberty*

### REPRESENTATIVE AT LARGE

Martin Dies, Jr. (D), *Lufkin*

### REPRESENTATIVES

1 Wright Patman (D), *Texarkana*
2 Jack B. Brooks (D), *Beaumont*
3 Brady P. Gentry (D), *Tyler*
4 Sam Rayburn (D), *Bonham*
5 Bruce R. Alger (R), *Dallas*
6 Olin E. Teague (D), *College Station*
7 John V. Dowdy (D), *Athens*
8 Albert Thomas (D), *Houston*
9 Clark W. Thompson (D), *Galveston*
10 W. Homer Thornberry (D), *Austin*

---

[24] Changed party affiliation to Democrat, February 17, 1955.
[25] Died May 25, 1956.
[26] Elected November 6, 1956, to fill vacancy caused by death of her husband, William T. Granahan, but was unable to be sworn in as Congress was not in session.

[27] Died November 26, 1955.
[28] Elected to fill vacancy caused by death of Vera D. Buchanan, and took his seat February 8, 1956.
[29] Resigned April 4, 1956.
[30] Appointed to fill vacancy caused by resignation

of Strom Thurmond, and took his seat April 9, 1956.
[31] Elected to fill vacancy caused by his own resignation, and took his seat January 3, 1957.
[32] Died October 12, 1956; vacancy throughout remainder of the Congress.

## TEXAS—Continued

### REPRESENTATIVES—CONTINUED
11 W. R. Poage (D), *Waco*
12 James C. Wright, Jr. (D),
    *Weatherford*
13 Frank N. Ikard (D), *Wichita Falls*
14 John J. Bell (D), *Cuero*
15 Joe M. Kilgore (D), *McAllen*
16 J. T. Rutherford (D), *Odessa*
17 Omar T. Burleson (D), *Anson*
18 Walter E. Rogers (D), *Pampa*
19 George H. Mahon (D), *Lubbock*
20 Paul J. Kilday (D), *San Antonio*
21 O. Clark Fisher (D), *San Angelo*

## UTAH

### SENATORS
Arthur V. Watkins (R), *Orem*
Wallace F. Bennett (R), *Salt Lake
City*

### REPRESENTATIVES
1 Henry A. Dixon (R), *Ogden*
2 William A. Dawson (R), *Salt Lake
City*

## VERMONT

### SENATORS
George D. Aiken (R), *Putney*
Ralph E. Flanders (R), *Springfield*

### REPRESENTATIVE AT LARGE
Winston L. Prouty (R), *Newport*

## VIRGINIA

### SENATORS
Harry Flood Byrd (D), *Berryville*
A. Willis Robertson (D), *Lexington*

### REPRESENTATIVES
1 Edward J. Robeson, Jr. (D),
    *Warwick*
2 Porter Hardy, Jr. (D), *Churchland*
3 J. Vaughan Gary (D), *Richmond*
4 Watkins M. Abbitt (D),
    *Appomattox*

5 William M. Tuck (D), *South
    Boston*
6 Richard H. Poff (R), *Radford*
7 Burr P. Harrison (D), *Winchester*
8 Howard W. Smith (D), *Broad Run*
9 W. Pat Jennings (D), *Marion*
10 Joel T. Broyhill (R), *Arlington*

## WASHINGTON

### SENATORS
Warren G. Magnuson (D), *Seattle*
Henry M. Jackson (D), *Everett*

### REPRESENTATIVE AT LARGE
Donald H. Magnuson (D), *Seattle*

### REPRESENTATIVES
1 Thomas M. Pelly (R), *Seattle*
2 Alfred John (Jack) Westland (R),
    *Everett*
3 Russell V. Mack (R), *Hoquiam*
4 Hal Holmes (R), *Ellensburg*
5 Walter F. Horan (R), *Wenatchee*
6 Thor C. Tollefson (R), *Tacoma*

## WEST VIRGINIA

### SENATORS
Harley M. Kilgore (D),[33] *Beckley*
William R. Laird III (D),[34]
    *Fayetteville*
Chapman Revercomb (R),[35]
    *Charleston*
Matthew M. Neely (D), *Fairmont*

### REPRESENTATIVES
1 Robert H. Mollohan (D), *Fairmont*
2 Harley O. Staggers (D), *Keyser*
3 Cleveland M. Bailey (D),
    *Clarksburg*
4 Maurice G. Burnside (D),
    *Huntington*
5 M. Elizabeth Kee (D), *Bluefield*
6 Robert C. Byrd (D), *Beckley*

## WISCONSIN

### SENATORS
Alexander Wiley (R), *Chippewa Falls*
Joseph R. McCarthy (R), *Appleton*

### REPRESENTATIVES
1 Lawrence H. Smith (R), *Racine*
2 Glenn R. Davis (R), *Waukesha*
3 Gardner R. Withrow (R), *La
    Crosse*
4 Clement J. Zablocki (D),
    *Milwaukee*
5 Henry S. Reuss (D), *Milwaukee*
6 William K. Van Pelt (R), *Fond du
    Lac*
7 Melvin R. Laird (R), *Marshfield*
8 John W. Byrnes (R), *Green Bay*
9 Lester R. Johnson (D), *Black
    River Falls*
10 Alvin E. O'Konski (R), *Mercer*

## WYOMING

### SENATORS
Frank A. Barrett (R), *Lusk*
Joseph C. O'Mahoney (D), *Cheyenne*

### REPRESENTATIVE AT LARGE
E. Keith Thomson (R), *Cheyenne*

## TERRITORY OF ALASKA

### DELEGATE
E. L. (Bob) Bartlett (D), *Juneau*

## TERRITORY OF HAWAII

### DELEGATE
Mary Elizabeth Pruett Farrington
(R), *Honolulu*

## COMMONWEALTH OF
PUERTO RICO

### RESIDENT COMMISSIONER
Antonio Fernós-Isern (PD), *Santurce*

---

[33] Died February 28, 1956.
[34] Appointed to fill vacancy caused by death of

Harley M. Kilgore, and took his seat March 15, 1956.
[35] Elected to fill vacancy caused by death of Harley

M. Kilgore, and took his seat January 3, 1957.

# 85TH CONGRESS

## JANUARY 3, 1957, TO JANUARY 3, 1959

FIRST SESSION— *January 3, 1957, to August 30, 1957*
SECOND SESSION— *January 7, 1958,[1] to August 24, 1958*

Richard M. Nixon
Vice President

Sam Rayburn
Speaker

---

### Senate
Democrats 49 — Republicans 47

VICE PRESIDENT OF THE UNITED STATES— RICHARD M. NIXON, of California
PRESIDENT PRO TEMPORE OF THE SENATE— CARL HAYDEN,[2] of Arizona
SECRETARY OF THE SENATE— FELTON MCLELLAN JOHNSTON,[3] of Mississippi
SERGEANT AT ARMS OF THE SENATE— JOSEPH C. DUKE,[4] of Arizona
MAJORITY FLOOR LEADER— LYNDON B. JOHNSON, of Texas
DEMOCRATIC WHIP— MIKE MANSFIELD, of Montana
REPUBLICAN FLOOR LEADER— WILLIAM F. KNOWLAND, of California
ASSISTANT REPUBLICAN LEADER— EVERETT MCKINLEY DIRKSEN, of Illinois

---

### House of Representatives
Democrats 234 — Republicans 201

SPEAKER OF THE HOUSE OF REPRESENTATIVES— SAM RAYBURN,[5] of Texas
CLERK OF THE HOUSE— RALPH R. ROBERTS,[6] of Indiana
SERGEANT AT ARMS OF THE HOUSE— ZEAKE W. JOHNSON, JR.,[7] of Tennessee
DOORKEEPER OF THE HOUSE— WILLIAM M. MILLER,[8] of Mississippi
POSTMASTER OF THE HOUSE— H. H. MORRIS,[9] of Kentucky
MAJORITY LEADER— JOHN W. McCORMACK, of Massachusetts
MAJORITY WHIP— CARL ALBERT, of Oklahoma
REPUBLICAN LEADER— JOSEPH W. MARTIN, JR., of Massachusetts
REPUBLICAN WHIP— LESLIE C. ARENDS, of Illinois

---

## ALABAMA

### SENATORS

Lister Hill (D), *Montgomery*
John J. Sparkman (D), *Huntsville*

### REPRESENTATIVES

1 Frank W. Boykin (D), *Mobile*
2 George M. Grant (D), *Troy*
3 George W. Andrews (D), *Union Springs*
4 Kenneth A. Roberts (D), *Anniston*
5 Albert Rains (D), *Gadsden*
6 Armistead I. Selden, Jr. (D), *Greensboro*
7 Carl A. Elliott (D), *Jasper*
8 Robert E. Jones, Jr. (D), *Scottsboro*
9 George Huddleston, Jr. (D), *Birmingham*

## ARIZONA

### SENATORS

Carl Hayden (D), *Phoenix*
Barry M. Goldwater (R), *Phoenix*

### REPRESENTATIVES

1 John J. Rhodes (R), *Mesa*
2 Stewart L. Udall (D), *Tucson*

## ARKANSAS

### SENATORS

John L. McClellan (D), *Camden*
J. William Fulbright (D), *Fayetteville*

### REPRESENTATIVES

1 E. C. Gathings (D), *West Memphis*
2 Wilbur D. Mills (D), *Kensett*
3 James W. Trimble (D), *Berryville*
4 Oren Harris (D), *El Dorado*
5 Brooks Hays (D), *Little Rock*
6 William F. Norrell (D), *Monticello*

## CALIFORNIA

### SENATORS

William F. Knowland (R), *Piedmont*
Thomas H. Kuchel (R), *Anaheim*

### REPRESENTATIVES

1 Hubert B. Scudder (R), *Sebastopol*
2 Clair Engle (D), *Red Bluff*
3 John E. Moss, Jr. (D), *Sacramento*
4 William S. Mailliard (R), *San Francisco*
5 John F. Shelley (D), *San Francisco*
6 John F. Baldwin, Jr. (R), *Martinez*
7 John J. Allen, Jr. (R), *Oakland*
8 George P. Miller (D), *Alameda*
9 J. Arthur Younger (R), *San Mateo*
10 Charles S. Gubser (R), *Gilroy*
11 John J. McFall (D), *Manteca*
12 B. F. Sisk (D), *Fresno*
13 Charles M. Teague (R), *Ojai*
14 Harlan F. Hagen (D), *Hanford*
15 Gordon L. McDonough (R), *Los Angeles*
16 Donald L. Jackson (R), *Pacific Palisades*
17 Cecil R. King (D), *Los Angeles*
18 Craig Hosmer (R), *Long Beach*
19 Chet Holifield (D), *Montebello*
20 H. Allen Smith (R), *Glendale*
21 Edgar W. Hiestand (R), *Altadena*
22 Joseph F. Holt (R), *Van Nuys*
23 Clyde G. Doyle (D), *South Gate*

---

[1] By joint resolution (Pub. Law 85-290, 85th Cong., 1st sess.) the date of assembling the second session of the Eighty-fifth Congress was fixed for January 7, 1958.
[2] Elected January 3, 1957.

[3] Reelected January 3, 1957.
[4] Reelected January 3, 1957.
[5] Reelected January 3, 1957.
[6] Reelected January 3, 1957.

[7] Reelected January 3, 1957.
[8] Reelected January 3, 1957.
[9] Reelected January 3, 1957.

[427]

## CALIFORNIA—Continued

REPRESENTATIVES—CONTINUED
24 Glenard P. Lipscomb (R), *Los Angeles*
25 Patrick J. Hillings (R), *Arcadia*
26 James Roosevelt (D), *Los Angeles*
27 Harry R. Sheppard (D), *Yucaipa*
28 James B. Utt (R), *Santa Ana*
29 Dalip S. Saund (D), *Westmorland*
30 Robert C. Wilson (R), *Chula Vista*

## COLORADO

SENATORS
Gordon L. Allott (R), *Lamar*
John A. Carroll (D), *Denver*

REPRESENTATIVES
1 Byron G. Rogers (D), *Denver*
2 William S. Hill (R), *Fort Collins*
3 J. Edgar Chenoweth (R), *Trinidad*
4 Wayne N. Aspinall (D), *Palisade*

## CONNECTICUT

SENATORS
Prescott S. Bush (R), *Greenwich*
William A. Purtell (R), *West Hartford*

REPRESENTATIVE AT LARGE
Antoni N. Sadlak (R), *Rockville*

REPRESENTATIVES
1 Edwin H. May, Jr. (R), *Wethersfield*
2 Horace Seely-Brown, Jr. (R), *Pomfret Center*
3 Albert W. Cretella (R), *North Haven*
4 Albert P. Morano (R), *Greenwich*
5 James T. Patterson (R), *Watertown*

## DELAWARE

SENATORS
John J. Williams (R), *Millsboro*
J. Allen Frear, Jr. (D), *Dover*

REPRESENTATIVE AT LARGE
Harry G. Haskell, Jr. (R), *Wilmington*

## FLORIDA

SENATORS
Spessard L. Holland (D), *Bartow*
George A. Smathers (D), *Miami*

REPRESENTATIVES
1 William C. Cramer (R), *St. Petersburg*
2 Charles E. Bennett (D), *Jacksonville*
3 Robert L. F. Sikes (D), *Crestview*
4 Dante B. Fascell (D), *Miami*

5 A. Sydney Herlong, Jr. (D), *Leesburg*
6 Paul G. Rogers (D), *West Palm Beach*
7 James A. Haley (D), *Sarasota*
8 D. R. (Billy) Matthews (D), *Gainesville*

## GEORGIA

SENATORS
Richard B. Russell (D), *Winder*
Herman E. Talmadge (D), *Lovejoy*

REPRESENTATIVES
1 Prince H. Preston, Jr. (D), *Statesboro*
2 John L. Pilcher (D), *Meigs*
3 E. L. Forrester (D), *Leesburg*
4 John J. Flynt, Jr. (D), *Griffin*
5 James C. Davis (D), *Stone Mountain*
6 Carl Vinson (D), *Milledgeville*
7 Henderson L. Lanham (D),[10] *Rome*
7 H. Erwin Mitchell (D),[11] *Dalton*
8 Iris F. Blitch (D), *Homerville*
9 Phillip M. Landrum (D), *Jasper*
10 Paul Brown (D), *Elberton*

## IDAHO

SENATORS
Henry C. Dworshak (R), *Burley*
Frank Church (D), *Boise*

REPRESENTATIVES
1 Gracie B. Pfost (D), *Nampa*
2 Hamer H. Budge (R), *Boise*

## ILLINOIS

SENATORS
Paul H. Douglas (D), *Chicago*
Everett McKinley Dirksen (R), *Pekin*

REPRESENTATIVES
1 William L. Dawson (D), *Chicago*
2 Barratt O'Hara (D), *Chicago*
3 Emmet F. Byrne (R), *Chicago*
4 William E. McVey (R),[12] *Harvey*
5 John C. Kluczynski (D), *Chicago*
6 Thomas J. O'Brien (D), *Chicago*
7 James B. Bowler (D),[13] *Chicago*
7 Roland V. Libonati (D),[14] *Chicago*
8 Thomas S. Gordon (D), *Chicago*
9 Sidney R. Yates (D), *Chicago*
10 Harold R. Collier (R), *Berwyn*
11 Timothy P. Sheehan (R), *Chicago*
12 Charles A. Boyle (D), *Chicago*
13 Marguerite Stitt Church (R), *Evanston*
14 Russell W. Keeney (R),[15] *Wheaton*
15 Noah M. Mason (R), *Oglesby*

16 Leo E. Allen (R), *Galena*
17 Leslie C. Arends (R), *Melvin*
18 Robert H. Michel (R), *Peoria*
19 Robert B. Chiperfield (R), *Canton*
20 Sidney E. Simpson (R),[16] *Carrollton*
21 Peter F. Mack, Jr. (D), *Carlinville*
22 William L. Springer (R), *Champaign*
23 Charles W. Vursell (R), *Salem*
24 Melvin Price (D), *East St. Louis*
25 Kenneth J. Gray (D), *West Frankfort*

## INDIANA

SENATORS
Homer E. Capehart (R), *Washington*
William E. Jenner (R), *Bedford*

REPRESENTATIVES
1 Ray J. Madden (D), *Gary*
2 Charles A. Halleck (R), *Rensselaer*
3 F. Jay Nimtz (R), *South Bend*
4 E. Ross Adair (R), *Fort Wayne*
5 John V. Beamer (R), *Wabash*
6 Cecil M. Harden (R), *Covington*
7 William G. Bray (R), *Martinsville*
8 Winfield K. Denton (D), *Evansville*
9 Earl Wilson (R), *Bedford*
10 Ralph Harvey (R), *New Castle*
11 Charles B. Brownson (R), *Indianapolis*

## IOWA

SENATORS
Bourke B. Hickenlooper (R), *Cedar Rapids*
Thomas E. Martin (R), *Iowa City*

REPRESENTATIVES
1 Frederic D. Schwengel (R), *Davenport*
2 Henry O. Talle (R), *Decorah*
3 H. R. Gross (R), *Waterloo*
4 Karl M. LeCompte (R),[17] *Corydon*
5 Paul Cunningham (R), *Des Moines*
6 Merwin Coad (D), *Boone*
7 Ben F. Jensen (R), *Exira*
8 Charles B. Hoeven (R), *Alton*

## KANSAS

SENATORS
Andrew F. Schoeppel (R), *Wichita*
Frank Carlson (R), *Concordia*

REPRESENTATIVES
1 William H. Avery (R), *Wakefield*
2 Errett P. Scrivner (R), *Kansas City*

---

[10] Died November 10, 1957.
[11] Elected to fill vacancy caused by death of Henderson L. Lanham, and took his seat January 13, 1958.
[12] Died August 10, 1958; vacancy throughout remainder of the Congress.

[13] Died July 18, 1957.
[14] Elected to fill vacancy caused by death of James B. Bowler, and took his seat January 7, 1958.
[15] Died January 11, 1958; vacancy throughout remainder of the Congress.

[16] Died October 26, 1958; vacancy throughout remainder of the Congress.
[17] Election unsuccessfully contested by Steven V. Carter.

3 Myron V. George (R), *Altamont*
4 Edward H. Rees (R), *Emporia*
5 J. Floyd Breeding (D), *Rolla*
6 Wint Smith (R), *Mankato*

## KENTUCKY

### SENATORS

John Sherman Cooper (R), *Somerset*
Thruston B. Morton (R), *Glenview*

### REPRESENTATIVES

1 Nobel J. Gregory (D), *Mayfield*
2 William H. Natcher (D), *Bowling Green*
3 John M. Robsion, Jr. (R), *Louisville*
4 Frank L. Chelf (D), *Lebanon*
5 Brent Spence (D), *Fort Thomas*
6 John C. Watts (D), *Nicholasville*
7 Carl D. Perkins (D), *Hindman*
8 Eugene Siler (R), *Williamsburg*

## LOUISIANA

### SENATORS

Allen J. Ellender (D), *Houma*
Russell B. Long (D), *Baton Rouge*

### REPRESENTATIVES

1 F. Edward Hébert (D), *New Orleans*
2 Hale Boggs (D), *New Orleans*
3 Edwin E. Willis (D), *St. Martinville*
4 Overton Brooks (D), *Shreveport*
5 Otto E. Passman (D), *Monroe*
6 James H. Morrison (D), *Hammond*
7 T. Ashton Thompson (D), *Ville Platte*
8 George S. Long (D),[18] *Pineville*

## MAINE

### SENATORS

Margaret Chase Smith (R), *Skowhegan*
Frederick G. Payne (R), *Waldoboro*

### REPRESENTATIVES

1 Robert Hale (R),[19] *Portland*
2 Frank M. Coffin (D), *Lewiston*
3 Clifford G. McIntire (R), *Perham*

## MARYLAND

### SENATORS

John Marshall Butler (R), *Baltimore*
J. Glenn Beall (R), *Frostburg*

### REPRESENTATIVES

1 Edward T. Miller (R), *Easton*
2 James P. S. Devereux (R), *Stevenson*
3 Edward A. Garmatz (D), *Baltimore*

4 George H. Fallon (D), *Baltimore*
5 Richard E. Lankford (D), *Annapolis*
6 DeWitt S. Hyde (R), *Bethesda*
7 Samuel N. Friedel (D), *Baltimore*

## MASSACHUSETTS

### SENATORS

Leverett Saltonstall (R), *Dover*
John F. Kennedy (D), *Boston*

### REPRESENTATIVES

1 John W. Heselton (R), *Deerfield*
2 Edward P. Boland (D), *Springfield*
3 Philip J. Philbin (D), *Clinton*
4 Harold D. Donohue (D), *Worcester*
5 Edith Nourse Rogers (R), *Lowell*
6 William H. Bates (R), *Salem*
7 Thomas J. Lane (D), *Lawrence*
8 Torbert H. Macdonald (D), *Malden*
9 Donald W. Nicholson (R), *Wareham*
10 Laurence Curtis (R), *Boston*
11 Thomas P. O'Neill, Jr. (D), *Cambridge*
12 John W. McCormack (D), *Dorchester*
13 Richard B. Wigglesworth (R),[20] *Milton*
14 Joseph W. Martin, Jr. (R), *North Attleboro*

## MICHIGAN

### SENATORS

Charles E. Potter (R), *Cheboygan*
Patrick V. McNamara (D), *Detroit*

### REPRESENTATIVES

1 Thaddeus M. Machrowicz (D), *Hamtramck*
2 George Meader (R), *Ann Arbor*
3 August E. Johansen (R), *Battle Creek*
4 Clare E. Hoffman (R), *Allegan*
5 Gerald R. Ford, Jr. (R), *Grand Rapids*
6 Charles E. Chamberlain (R), *East Lansing*
7 Robert J. McIntosh (R), *Port Huron*
8 Alvin M. Bentley (R), *Owosso*
9 Robert P. Griffin (R), *Traverse City*
10 Elford A. Cederberg (R), *Bay City*
11 Victor A. Knox (R), *Sault Ste. Marie*
12 John B. Bennett (R), *Ontonagon*
13 Charles C. Diggs, Jr. (D), *Detroit*
14 Louis C. Rabaut (D), *Grosse Pointe Park*
15 John D. Dingell, Jr. (D), *Detroit*
16 John Lesinski, Jr. (D), *Dearborn*

17 Martha W. Griffiths (D), *Detroit*
18 William S. Broomfield (R), *Royal Oak*

## MINNESOTA

### SENATORS

Edward J. Thye (R), *Northfield*
Hubert H. Humphrey (D), *Minneapolis*

### REPRESENTATIVES

1 August H. Andresen (R),[21] *Red Wing*
1 Albert H. Quie (R),[22] *Dennison*
2 Joseph P. O'Hara (R), *Glencoe*
3 Roy W. Wier (D), *Minneapolis*
4 Eugene J. McCarthy (D), *St. Paul*
5 Walter H. Judd (R), *Minneapolis*
6 Fred Marshall (D), *Grove City*
7 H. Carl Andersen (R), *Tyler*
8 John A. Blatnik (D), *Chisholm*
9 Coya G. Knutson (D), *Oklee*

## MISSISSIPPI

### SENATORS

James O. Eastland (D), *Doddsville*
John C. Stennis (D), *De Kalb*

### REPRESENTATIVES

1 Thomas G. Abernethy (D), *Okolona*
2 Jamie L. Whitten (D), *Charleston*
3 Frank E. Smith (D), *Greenwood*
4 John Bell Williams (D), *Raymond*
5 W. Arthur Winstead (D), *Philadelphia*
6 William M. Colmer (D), *Pascagoula*

## MISSOURI

### SENATORS

Thomas C. Hennings, Jr. (D), *St. Louis*
Stuart Symington (D), *Creve Coeur*

### REPRESENTATIVES

1 Frank M. Karsten (D), *St. Louis*
2 Thomas B. Curtis (R), *Webster Groves*
3 Leonor Kretzer Sullivan (D), *St. Louis*
4 George H. Christopher (D), *Butler*
5 Richard W. Bolling (D), *Kansas City*
6 William R. Hull, Jr. (D), *Weston*
7 Charles H. Brown (D), *Springfield*
8 Albert S. J. Carnahan (D), *Ellsinore*
9 Clarence Cannon (D), *Elsberry*
10 Paul C. Jones (D), *Kennett*
11 Morgan M. Moulder (D), *Camdenton*

---

[18] Died March 22, 1958; vacancy throughout remainder of the Congress.
[19] Election unsuccessfully contested by James C. Oliver.

[20] Resigned November 13, 1958; vacancy throughout remainder of the Congress.
[21] Died January 14, 1958.

[22] Elected to fill vacancy caused by death of August H. Andresen, and took his seat March 6, 1958.

## MONTANA

SENATORS

James E. Murray (D), *Butte*
Mike Mansfield (D), *Missoula*

REPRESENTATIVES

1 Lee Metcalf (D), *Helena*
2 LeRoy H. Anderson (D), *Conrad*

## NEBRASKA

SENATORS

Roman L. Hruska (R), *Omaha*
Carl T. Curtis (R), *Minden*

REPRESENTATIVES

1 Phillip H. Weaver (R), *Falls City*
2 Glenn C. Cunningham (R), *Omaha*
3 Robert D. Harrison (R), *Norfolk*
4 Arthur L. Miller (R), *Kimball*

## NEVADA

SENATORS

George W. Malone (R), *Reno*
Alan H. Bible (D), *Reno*

REPRESENTATIVE AT LARGE

Walter S. Baring (D), *Reno*

## NEW HAMPSHIRE

SENATORS

H. Styles Bridges (R), *Concord*
Norris Cotton (R), *Lebanon*

REPRESENTATIVES

1 Chester E. Merrow (R), *Center Ossipee*
2 Perkins Bass (R), *Peterborough*

## NEW JERSEY

SENATORS

H. Alexander Smith (R), *Princeton*
Clifford P. Case (R), *Rahway*

REPRESENTATIVES

1 Charles A. Wolverton (R), *Merchantville*
2 Milton W. Glenn (R),[23] *Margate City*
3 James C. Auchincloss (R), *Rumson*
4 Frank Thompson, Jr. (D), *Trenton*
5 Peter H. B. Frelinghuysen, Jr. (R), *Morristown*
6 Florence P. Dwyer (R), *Elizabeth*
7 William B. Widnall (R), *Saddle River*
8 Gordon Canfield (R), *Paterson*
9 Frank C. Osmers, Jr. (R), *Tenafly*
10 Peter W. Rodino, Jr. (D), *Newark*
11 Hugh J. Addonizio (D), *Newark*

12 Robert W. Kean (R), *Livingston*
13 Alfred D. Sieminski (D), *Jersey City*
14 Vincent J. Dellay (R),[24] *West New York*

## NEW MEXICO

SENATORS

Dennis Chavez (D), *Albuquerque*
Clinton P. Anderson (D), *Albuquerque*

REPRESENTATIVES AT LARGE

John J. Dempsey (D),[25] *Santa Fe*
Joseph M. Montoya (D),[26] *Santa Fe*

## NEW YORK

SENATORS

Irving M. Ives (R), *Norwich*
Jacob K. Javits (R), *New York City*

REPRESENTATIVES

1 Stuyvesant Wainwright II (R), *Wainscott*
2 Steven B. Derounian (R), *Roslyn*
3 Frank J. Becker (R), *Lynbrook*
4 Henry J. Latham (R),[27] *Queens Village*
5 Albert H. Bosch (R), *Woodhaven*
6 Lester Holtzman (D), *Rego Park*
7 James J. Delaney (D), *Long Island City*
8 Victor L. Anfuso (D), *Brooklyn*
9 Eugene J. Keogh (D), *Brooklyn*
10 Edna F. Kelly (D), *Brooklyn*
11 Emanuel Celler (D), *Brooklyn*
12 Francis E. Dorn (R), *Brooklyn*
13 Abraham J. Multer (D), *Brooklyn*
14 John J. Rooney (D), *Brooklyn*
15 John H. Ray (R), *Staten Island*
16 Adam Clayton Powell, Jr. (D), *New York City*
17 Frederic R. Coudert, Jr. (R), *New York City*
18 Alfred E. Santangelo (D), *New York City*
19 Leonard Farbstein (D), *New York City*
20 Ludwig Teller (D), *New York City*
21 Herbert Zelenko (D), *New York City*
22 James C. Healey (D), *New York City*
23 Isidore Dollinger (D), *New York City*
24 Charles A. Buckley (D), *New York City*
25 Paul A. Fino (R), *New York City*
26 Edwin B. Dooley (R), *Mamaroneck*
27 Ralph W. Gwinn (R), *Bronxville*

28 Katharine St. George (R), *Tuxedo Park*
29 J. Ernest Wharton (R), *Richmondville*
30 Leo W. O'Brien (D), *Albany*
31 Dean P. Taylor (R), *Troy*
32 Bernard W. Kearney (R), *Lake Pleasant*
33 Clarence E. Kilburn (R), *Malone*
34 William R. Williams (R), *Cassville*
35 R. Walter Riehlman (R), *Tully*
36 John Taber (R), *Auburn*
37 W. Sterling Cole (R),[28] *Bath*
37 Howard W. Robison (R),[29] *Owego*
38 Kenneth B. Keating (R), *Rochester*
39 Harold C. Ostertag (R), *Attica*
40 William E. Miller (R), *Lockport*
41 Edmund P. Radwan (R), *Buffalo*
42 John R. Pillion (R), *Hamburg*
43 Daniel A. Reed (R), *Dunkirk*

## NORTH CAROLINA

SENATORS

Sam J. Ervin, Jr. (D), *Morganton*
W. Kerr Scott (D),[30] *Haw River*
B. Everett Jordan (D),[31] *Saxapahaw*

REPRESENTATIVES

1 Herbert C. Bonner (D), *Washington*
2 L. H. Fountain (D), *Tarboro*
3 Graham A. Barden (D), *New Bern*
4 Harold D. Cooley (D), *Nashville*
5 Ralph J. Scott (D), *Danbury*
6 Carl T. Durham (D), *Chapel Hill*
7 Alton A. Lennon (D), *Wilmington*
8 A. Paul Kitchin (D), *Wadesboro*
9 Hugh Q. Alexander (D), *Kannapolis*
10 Charles Raper Jonas (R), *Lincolnton*
11 Basil L. Whitener (D), *Gastonia*
12 George A. Shuford (D), *Asheville*

## NORTH DAKOTA

SENATORS

William Langer (R), *Wheatland*
Milton R. Young (R), *La Moure*

REPRESENTATIVES AT LARGE

Usher L. Burdick (R), *Williston*
Otto Krueger (R), *Fessenden*

## OHIO

SENATORS

John W. Bricker (R), *Columbus*
Frank J. Lausche (D), *Cleveland*

REPRESENTATIVES

1 Gordon H. Scherer (R), *Cincinnati*
2 William E. Hess (R), *Cincinnati*

---

[23] Elected to fill vacancy caused by death of Representative-elect T. Millet Hand, in the preceding Congress, and took his seat January 7, 1958.
[24] Changed party affiliation to Democrat, October 29, 1957.
[25] Died March 11, 1958; vacancy throughout remainder of the Congress.

[26] Elected to fill vacancy caused by death of Representative-elect Antonio M. Fernandez, in the preceding Congress, and took his seat April 29, 1957.
[27] Resigned December 31, 1958; vacancy throughout remainder of the Congress.
[28] Resigned December 1, 1957.

[29] Elected to fill vacancy caused by resignation of Sterling Cole, and took his seat January 20, 1958.
[30] Died April 16, 1958.
[31] Appointed to fill vacancy caused by death of W. Kerr Scott, and took his seat May 5, 1958; subsequently elected.

3 Paul F. Schenck (R), *Dayton*
4 William M. McCulloch (R), *Piqua*
5 Cliff Clevenger (R), *Bryan*
6 James G. Polk (D), *Highland*
7 Clarence J. Brown (R), *Blanchester*
8 Jackson E. Betts (R), *Findlay*
9 Thomas L. Ashley (D), *Waterville*
10 Thomas A. Jenkins (R), *Ironton*
11 David S. Dennison (R), *Warren*
12 John M. Vorys (R), *Columbus*
13 Albert D. Baumhart, Jr. (R), *Vermilion*
14 William H. Ayres (R), *Akron*
15 John E. Henderson (R), *Cambridge*
16 Frank T. Bow (R), *Canton*
17 J. Harry McGregor (R),[32] *West Lafayette*
18 Wayne L. Hays (D), *Flushing*
19 Michael J. Kirwan (D), *Youngstown*
20 Michael A. Feighan (D), *Cleveland*
21 Charles A. Vanik (D), *Cleveland*
22 Frances P. Bolton (R), *Lyndhurst*
23 William E. Minshall (R), *Rocky River*

## OKLAHOMA

SENATORS

Robert S. Kerr (D), *Oklahoma City*
A. S. Mike Monroney (D), *Oklahoma City*

REPRESENTATIVES

1 Page H. Belcher (R), *Enid*
2 Edmond Edmondson (D), *Muskogee*
3 Carl Albert (D), *McAlester*
4 Thomas J. Steed (D), *Shawnee*
5 John Jarman (D), *Oklahoma City*
6 Toby Morris (D), *Lawton*

## OREGON

SENATORS

Wayne L. Morse (D), *Eugene*
Richard L. Neuberger (D), *Portland*

REPRESENTATIVES

1 A. Walter Norblad (R), *Stayton*
2 Albert C. Ullman (D), *Baker*
3 Edith S. Green (D), *Portland*
4 Charles O. Porter (D), *Eugene*

## PENNSYLVANIA

SENATORS

Edward Martin (R), *Washington*
Joseph S. Clark (D), *Philadelphia*

REPRESENTATIVES

1 William A. Barrett (D), *Philadelphia*
2 Kathryn E. Granahan (D), *Philadelphia*
3 James A. Byrne (D), *Philadelphia*
4 Earl Chudoff (D),[33] *Philadelphia*
4 Robert N. C. Nix (D),[34] *Philadelphia*
5 William J. Green, Jr. (D), *Philadelphia*
6 Hugh D. Scott, Jr. (R), *Philadelphia*
7 Benjamin F. James (R), *Rosemont*
8 Willard S. Curtin (R), *Morrisville*
9 Paul B. Dague (R), *Downingtown*
10 Joseph L. Carrigg (R), *Susquehanna*
11 Daniel J. Flood (D), *Wilkes-Barre*
12 Ivor D. Fenton (R), *Mahanoy City*
13 Samuel K. McConnell, Jr. (R),[35] *Wynnewood*
13 John A. Lafore, Jr. (R),[36] *Haverford*
14 George M. Rhodes (D), *Reading*
15 Francis E. Walter (D), *Easton*
16 Walter M. Mumma (R), *Harrisburg*
17 Alvin R. Bush (R), *Muncy*
18 Richard M. Simpson (R), *Huntingdon*
19 S. Walter Stauffer (R), *York*
20 James E. Van Zandt (R), *Altoona*
21 Augustine B. Kelley (D),[37] *Greensburg*
21 John H. Dent (D),[38] *Jeannette*
22 John P. Saylor (R), *Johnstown*
23 Leon H. Gavin (R), *Oil City*
24 Carroll D. Kearns (R), *Farrell*
25 Frank M. Clark (D), *Bessemer*
26 Thomas E. Morgan (D), *Fredericktown*
27 James G. Fulton (R), *Dormont*
28 Herman P. Eberharter (D),[39] *Pittsburgh*
29 Robert J. Corbett (R), *Ben Avon Heights*
30 Elmer J. Holland (D), *Pittsburgh*

## RHODE ISLAND

SENATORS

Theodore F. Green (D), *Providence*
John O. Pastore (D), *Providence*

REPRESENTATIVES

1 Aime J. Forand (D), *Cumberland*
2 John E. Fogarty (D), *Harmony*

## SOUTH CAROLINA

SENATORS

Olin D. Johnston (D), *Spartanburg*
Strom Thurmond (D), *Aiken*

REPRESENTATIVES

1 L. Mendel Rivers (D), *Charleston*
2 John J. Riley (D), *Sumter*
3 W. J. Bryan Dorn (D), *Greenwood*
4 Robert T. Ashmore (D), *Greenville*
5 Robert W. Hemphill (D), *Chester*
6 John L. McMillan (D), *Florence*

## SOUTH DAKOTA

SENATORS

Karl E. Mundt (R), *Madison*
Francis H. Case (R), *Custer*

REPRESENTATIVES

1 George S. McGovern (D), *Mitchell*
2 E. Y. Berry (R), *McLaughlin*

## TENNESSEE

SENATORS

Estes Kefauver (D), *Chattanooga*
Albert A. Gore (D), *Carthage*

REPRESENTATIVES

1 B. Carroll Reece (R), *Johnson City*
2 Howard H. Baker (R), *Huntsville*
3 James B. Frazier, Jr. (D), *Chattanooga*
4 Joseph L. Evins (D), *Smithville*
5 J. Carlton Loser (D), *Nashville*
6 Ross Bass (D), *Pulaski*
7 Thomas J. Murray (D), *Jackson*
8 Jere Cooper (D),[40] *Dyersburg*
8 Robert A. Everett (D),[41] *Union City*
9 Clifford Davis (D), *Memphis*

## TEXAS

SENATORS

Lyndon B. Johnson (D), *Johnson City*
M. Price Daniel (D),[42] *Liberty*
William A. Blakley (D),[43] *Dallas*
Ralph W. Yarborough (D),[44] *Austin*

REPRESENTATIVE AT LARGE

Martin Dies, Jr. (D), *Lufkin*

REPRESENTATIVES

1 Wright Patman (D), *Texarkana*
2 Jack B. Brooks (D), *Beaumont*
3 Lindley G. Beckworth (D), *Gladewater*
4 Sam Rayburn (D), *Bonham*
5 Bruce R. Alger (R), *Dallas*
6 Olin E. Teague (D), *College Station*

---

[32] Died October 7, 1958; vacancy throughout remainder of the Congress.
[33] Resigned January 5, 1958.
[34] Elected to fill vacancy caused by resignation of Earl Chudoff, and took his seat June 4, 1958.
[35] Resigned September 1, 1957.
[36] Elected to fill vacancy caused by resignation of Samuel K. McConnell, Jr., and took his seat January 7, 1958.

[37] Died November 20, 1957.
[38] Elected to fill vacancy caused by death of Augustine B. Kelley, and took his seat January 27, 1958.
[39] Died September 9, 1958; vacancy throughout remainder of the Congress.
[40] Died December 18, 1957.

[41] Elected to fill vacancy caused by death of Jere Cooper, and took his seat February 10, 1958.
[42] Resigned January 14, 1957.
[43] Appointed to fill vacancy caused by resignation of M. Price Daniel, and took his seat January 17, 1957.
[44] Elected to fill vacancy caused by resignation of M. Price Daniel, and took his seat April 29, 1957.

## TEXAS—Continued

### REPRESENTATIVES—CONTINUED

7  John V. Dowdy (D), *Athens*
8  Albert Thomas (D), *Houston*
9  Clark W. Thompson (D), *Galveston*
10  W. Homer Thornberry (D), *Austin*
11  W. R. Poage (D), *Waco*
12  James C. Wright, Jr. (D), *Fort Worth*
13  Frank N. Ikard (D), *Wichita Falls*
14  John A. Young (D), *Corpus Christi*
15  Joe M. Kilgore (D), *McAllen*
16  J. T. Rutherford (D), *Odessa*
17  Omar T. Burleson (D), *Anson*
18  Walter E. Rogers (D), *Pampa*
19  George H. Mahon (D), *Lubbock*
20  Paul J. Kilday (D), *San Antonio*
21  O. Clark Fisher (D), *San Angelo*

## UTAH

### SENATORS

Arthur V. Watkins (R), *Orem*
Wallace F. Bennett (R), *Salt Lake City*

### REPRESENTATIVES

1  Henry A. Dixon (R), *Ogden*
2  William A. Dawson (R), *Salt Lake City*

## VERMONT

### SENATORS

George D. Aiken (R), *Putney*
Ralph E. Flanders (R), *Springfield*

### REPRESENTATIVE AT LARGE

Winston L. Prouty (R), *Newport*

## VIRGINIA

### SENATORS

Harry Flood Byrd (D), *Berryville*
A. Willis Robertson (D), *Lexington*

### REPRESENTATIVES

1  Edward J. Robeson, Jr. (D), *Warwick*

2  Porter Hardy, Jr. (D), *Churchland*
3  J. Vaughan Gary (D), *Richmond*
4  Watkins M. Abbitt (D), *Appomattox*
5  William M. Tuck (D), *South Boston*
6  Richard H. Poff (R), *Radford*
7  Burr P. Harrison (D), *Winchester*
8  Howard W. Smith (D), *Broad Run*
9  W. Pat Jennings (D), *Marion*
10  Joel T. Broyhill (R), *Arlington*

## WASHINGTON

### SENATORS

Warren G. Magnuson (D), *Seattle*
Henry M. Jackson (D), *Everett*

### REPRESENTATIVE AT LARGE

Donald H. Magnuson (D), *Seattle*

### REPRESENTATIVES

1  Thomas M. Pelly (R), *Port Blakely*
2  Alfred John (Jack) Westland (R), *Everett*
3  Russell V. Mack (R), *Hoquiam*
4  Hal Holmes (R), *Ellensburg*
5  Walter F. Horan (R), *Wenatchee*
6  Thor C. Tollefson (R), *Tacoma*

## WEST VIRGINIA

### SENATORS

Matthew M. Neely (D),[45] *Fairmont*
John D. Hoblitzell, Jr. (R),[46] *Ravenswood*
Jennings Randolph (D),[47] *Elkins*
Chapman Revercomb (R), *Charleston*

### REPRESENTATIVES

1  Arch A. Moore, Jr. (R), *Glendale*
2  Harley O. Staggers (D), *Keyser*
3  Cleveland M. Bailey (D), *Clarksburg*
4  William E. Neal (R), *Huntington*
5  M. Elizabeth Kee (D), *Bluefield*
6  Robert C. Byrd (D), *Beckley*

## WISCONSIN

### SENATORS

Alexander Wiley (R), *Chippewa Falls*
Joseph R. McCarthy (R),[48] *Appleton*
William Proxmire (D),[49] *Madison*

### REPRESENTATIVES

1  Lawrence H. Smith (R),[50] *Racine*
2  Donald E. Tewes (R), *Waukesha*
3  Gardner R. Withrow (R), *La Crosse*
4  Clement J. Zablocki (D), *Milwaukee*
5  Henry S. Reuss (D), *Milwaukee*
6  William K. Van Pelt (R), *Fond du Lac*
7  Melvin R. Laird (R), *Marshfield*
8  John W. Byrnes (R), *Green Bay*
9  Lester R. Johnson (D), *Black River Falls*
10  Alvin E. O'Konski (R), *Mercer*

## WYOMING

### SENATORS

Frank A. Barrett (R), *Lusk*
Joseph C. O'Mahoney (D), *Cheyenne*

### REPRESENTATIVE AT LARGE

E. Keith Thomson (R), *Cheyenne*

## TERRITORY OF ALASKA

### DELEGATE

E. L. (Bob) Bartlett (D), *Juneau*

## TERRITORY OF HAWAII

### DELEGATE

John A. Burns (D), *Honolulu*

## COMMONWEALTH OF PUERTO RICO

### RESIDENT COMMISSIONER

Antonio Fernós-Isern (PD), *Santurce*

---

[45] Died January 18, 1958.
[46] Appointed to fill vacancy caused by death of Matthew M. Neely, and took his seat January 27, 1958.
[47] Elected November 5, 1958 to fill vacancy caused

by death of Matthew M. Neely, but was unable to be sworn in because Congress was not in session.
[48] Died May 2, 1957.
[49] Elected to fill vacancy caused by death of Joseph

R. McCarthy, and took his seat August 29, 1957.
[50] Died January 22, 1958; vacancy throughout remainder of the Congress.

# 86TH CONGRESS

### JANUARY 3, 1959, TO JANUARY 3, 1961

FIRST SESSION— *January 7, 1959,*[1] *to September 15, 1959*
SECOND SESSION— *January 6, 1960,*[2] *to September 1, 1960*

---

Senate
Democrats 64 — Republicans 34

VICE PRESIDENT OF THE UNITED STATES— RICHARD M. NIXON, of California
PRESIDENT PRO TEMPORE OF THE SENATE— CARL HAYDEN, of Arizona
SECRETARY OF THE SENATE— FELTON McLELLAN JOHNSTON, of Mississippi
SERGEANT AT ARMS OF THE SENATE— JOSEPH C. DUKE, of Arizona
MAJORITY FLOOR LEADER— LYNDON B. JOHNSON, of Texas
DEMOCRATIC WHIP— MIKE MANSFIELD, of Montana
REPUBLICAN FLOOR LEADER— EVERETT McKINLEY DIRKSEN, of Illinois
ASSISTANT REPUBLICAN LEADER— THOMAS H. KUCHEL, of California

---

House of Representatives
Democrats 283 — Republicans 153

SPEAKER OF THE HOUSE OF REPRESENTATIVES— SAM RAYBURN,[3] of Texas
CLERK OF THE HOUSE— RALPH R. ROBERTS,[4] of Indiana
SERGEANT AT ARMS OF THE HOUSE— ZEAKE W. JOHNSON, JR.,[5] of Tennessee
DOORKEEPER OF THE HOUSE— WILLIAM M. MILLER,[6] of Mississippi
POSTMASTER OF THE HOUSE— H. H. MORRIS,[7] of Kentucky
MAJORITY LEADER— JOHN W. McCORMACK, of Massachusetts
MAJORITY WHIP— CARL ALBERT, of Oklahoma
REPUBLICAN LEADER— CHARLES A. HALLECK, of Indiana
REPUBLICAN WHIP— LESLIE C. ARENDS, of Illinois

Richard M. Nixon
Vice President

Sam Rayburn
Speaker

## ALABAMA

SENATORS

Lister Hill (D), *Montgomery*
John J. Sparkman (D), *Huntsville*

REPRESENTATIVES

1  Frank W. Boykin (D), *Mobile*
2  George M. Grant (D), *Troy*
3  George W. Andrews (D), *Union Springs*
4  Kenneth A. Roberts (D), *Anniston*
5  Albert Rains (D), *Gadsden*
6  Armistead I. Selden, Jr. (D), *Greensboro*
7  Carl A. Elliott (D), *Jasper*
8  Robert E. Jones, Jr. (D), *Scottsboro*
9  George Huddleston, Jr. (D), *Birmingham*

## ALASKA [8]

SENATORS

E. L. (Bob) Bartlett (D),[9] *Juneau*

Ernest Gruening (D),[10] *Juneau*

REPRESENTATIVE AT LARGE

Ralph J. Rivers (D),[11] *Fairbanks*

## ARIZONA

SENATORS

Carl Hayden (D), *Phoenix*
Barry M. Goldwater (R), *Phoenix*

REPRESENTATIVES

1  John J. Rhodes (R), *Mesa*
2  Stewart L. Udall (D), *Tucson*

## ARKANSAS

SENATORS

John L. McClellan (D), *Camden*
J. William Fulbright (D), *Fayetteville*

REPRESENTATIVES

1  E. C. Gathings (D), *West Memphis*
2  Wilbur D. Mills (D), *Kensett*
3  James W. Trimble (D), *Berryville*

4  Oren Harris (D), *El Dorado*
5  T. Dale Alford (D),[12] *Little Rock*
6  William F. Norrell (D), *Monticello*

## CALIFORNIA

SENATORS

Thomas H. Kuchel (R), *Anaheim*
Clair Engle (D), *Red Bluff*

REPRESENTATIVES

1  Clement W. Miller (D), *Corte Madera*
2  Harold T. Johnson (D), *Roseville*
3  John E. Moss, Jr. (D), *Sacramento*
4  William S. Mailliard (R), *San Francisco*
5  John F. Shelley (D), *San Francisco*
6  John F. Baldwin (R), *Martinez*
7  Jeffery Cohelan (D), *Berkeley*
8  George P. Miller (D), *Alameda*
9  J. Arthur Younger (R), *San Mateo*
10  Charles S. Gubser (R), *Gilroy*

---

[1] By joint resolution (Pub. Law 85 819, 85th Cong., 2d sess.) the date of assembling the first session of the Eighty-sixth Congress was fixed for January 7, 1959.

[2] By joint resolution (Pub. Law 86 305, 86th Cong., 1st sess.) the date of assembling the second session of the Eighty-sixth Congress was fixed for January 6, 1960.

[3] Reelected January 7, 1959.

[4] Reelected January 7, 1959.
[5] Reelected January 7, 1959.
[6] Reelected January 7, 1959.
[7] Reelected January 7, 1959.
[8] Admitted as a State into the Union January 3, 1959.
[9] Took his seat January 7, 1959; term to expire, as

determined by lot, January 3, 1961.

[10] Took his seat January 7, 1959; term to expire, as determined by lot, January 3, 1963.

[11] Took his seat January 7, 1959.

[12] Election investigated by order of the House (H. Res. 1). H. Res. 380 declared T. Dale Alford was entitled to his seat.

[433]

## CALIFORNIA—Continued

### REPRESENTATIVES—CONTINUED

11 John J. McFall (D), *Manteca*
12 B. F. Sisk (D), *Fresno*
13 Charles M. Teague (R), *Ojai*
14 Harlan F. Hagen (D), *Hanford*
15 Gordon L. McDonough (R), *Los Angeles*
16 Donald L. Jackson (R), *Pacific Palisades*
17 Cecil R. King (D), *Los Angeles*
18 Craig Hosmer (R), *Long Beach*
19 Chet Holifield (D), *Montebello*
20 H. Allen Smith (R), *Glendale*
21 Edgar W. Hiestand (R), *Burbank*
22 Joseph F. Holt (R), *Van Nuys*
23 Clyde G. Doyle (D), *South Gate*
24 Glenard P. Lipscomb (R), *Los Angeles*
25 George A. Kasem (D), *West Covina*
26 James Roosevelt (D), *Los Angeles*
27 Harry R. Sheppard (D), *Yucaipa*
28 James B. Utt (R), *Santa Ana*
29 Dalip S. Saund (D), *Westmorland*
30 Robert C. Wilson (R), *Chula Vista*

## COLORADO

### SENATORS

Gordon L. Allott (R), *Lamar*
John A. Carroll (D), *Denver*

### REPRESENTATIVES

1 Byron G. Rogers (D), *Denver*
2 Byron L. Johnson (D), *Denver*
3 J. Edgar Chenoweth (R), *Trinidad*
4 Wayne N. Aspinall (D), *Palisade*

## CONNECTICUT

### SENATORS

Prescott S. Bush (R), *Greenwich*
Thomas J. Dodd (D), *West Hartford*

### REPRESENTATIVE AT LARGE

Frank Kowalski (D), *Meriden*

### REPRESENTATIVES

1 Emilio Q. Daddario (D), *Hartford*
2 Chester Bowles (D), *Essex*
3 Robert N. Giaimo (D), *North Haven*
4 Donald J. Irwin (D), *Norwalk*
5 John S. Monagan (D), *Waterbury*

## DELAWARE

### SENATORS

John J. Williams (R), *Millsboro*
J. Allen Frear, Jr. (D), *Dover*

### REPRESENTATIVE AT LARGE

Harris B. McDowell, Jr. (D), *Middletown*

## FLORIDA

### SENATORS

Spessard L. Holland (D), *Bartow*
George A. Smathers (D), *Miami*

### REPRESENTATIVES

1 William C. Cramer (R), *St. Petersburg*
2 Charles E. Bennett (D), *Jacksonville*
3 Robert L. F. Sikes (D), *Crestview*
4 Dante B. Fascell (D), *Miami*
5 A. Sydney Herlong, Jr. (D), *Leesburg*
6 Paul G. Rogers (D), *West Palm Beach*
7 James A. Haley (D), *Sarasota*
8 D. R. (Billy) Matthews (D), *Gainesville*

## GEORGIA

### SENATORS

Richard B. Russell (D), *Winder*
Herman E. Talmadge (D), *Lovejoy*

### REPRESENTATIVES

1 Prince H. Preston, Jr. (D), *Statesboro*
2 John L. Pilcher (D), *Meigs*
3 E. L. Forrester (D), *Leesburg*
4 John J. Flynt, Jr. (D), *Griffin*
5 James C. Davis (D), *Stone Mountain*
6 Carl Vinson (D), *Milledgeville*
7 H. Erwin Mitchell (D), *Dalton*
8 Iris F. Blitch (D), *Homerville*
9 Phillip M. Landrum (D), *Jasper*
10 Paul Brown (D), *Elberton*

## HAWAII[13]

### SENATORS

Hiram L. Fong (R),[14] *Honolulu*
Oren E. Long (D),[15] *Honolulu*

### REPRESENTATIVE AT LARGE

Daniel K. Inouye (D),[16] *Honolulu*

## IDAHO

### SENATORS

Henry C. Dworshak (R), *Burley*
Frank Church (D), *Boise*

### REPRESENTATIVES

1 Gracie B. Pfost (D), *Nampa*
2 Hamer H. Budge (R), *Boise*

## ILLINOIS

### SENATORS

Paul H. Douglas (D), *Chicago*
Everett McKinley Dirksen (R), *Pekin*

### REPRESENTATIVES

1 William L. Dawson (D), *Chicago*
2 Barratt O'Hara (D), *Chicago*
3 William T. Murphy (D), *Chicago*
4 Edward J. Derwinski (R), *Chicago*
5 John C. Kluczynski (D), *Chicago*
6 Thomas J. O'Brien (D), *Chicago*
7 Roland V. Libonati (D), *Chicago*
8 Dan Rostenkowski (D), *Chicago*
9 Sidney R. Yates (D), *Chicago*
10 Harold R. Collier (R), *Berwyn*
11 Roman C. Pucinski (D), *Chicago*
12 Charles A. Boyle (D),[17] *Chicago*
13 Marguerite Stitt Church (R), *Evanston*
14 Elmer J. Hoffman (R), *Wheaton*
15 Noah M. Mason (R), *Oglesby*
16 Leo E. Allen (R), *Galena*
17 Leslie C. Arends (R), *Melvin*
18 Robert H. Michel (R), *Peoria*
19 Robert B. Chiperfield (R), *Canton*
20 Edna Oakes Simpson (R), *Carrollton*
21 Peter F. Mack, Jr. (D), *Carlinville*
22 William L. Springer (R), *Champaign*
23 George E. Shipley (D), *Olney*
24 Melvin Price (D), *East St. Louis*
25 Kenneth J. Gray (D), *West Frankfort*

## INDIANA

### SENATORS

Homer E. Capehart (R), *Washington*
Vance Hartke (D), *Evansville*

### REPRESENTATIVES

1 Ray J. Madden (D), *Gary*
2 Charles A. Halleck (R), *Rensselaer*
3 John Brademas (D), *South Bend*
4 E. Ross Adair (R), *Fort Wayne*
5 J. Edward Roush (D), *Huntington*
6 Fred Wampler (D), *Terre Haute*
7 William G. Bray (R), *Martinsville*
8 Winfield K. Denton (D), *Evansville*
9 Earl Hogan (D), *Hope*
10 Randall S. Harmon (D), *Muncie*
11 Joseph W. Barr (D), *Indianapolis*

## IOWA

### SENATORS

Bourke B. Hickenlooper (R), *Cedar Rapids*
Thomas E. Martin (R), *Iowa City*

### REPRESENTATIVES

1 Frederic D. Schwengel (R), *Davenport*
2 Leonard G. Wolf (D), *Elkader*
3 H. R. Gross (R), *Waterloo*
4 Steven V. Carter (D),[18] *Leon*

---

[13] Admitted as a State into the Union August 21, 1959. See footnote 53.
[14] Took his seat August 24, 1959; term to expire, as determined by lot, January 3, 1965.

[15] Took his seat August 24, 1959; term to expire, as determined by lot, January 3, 1963.
[16] Took his seat August 24, 1959.

[17] Died November 4, 1959; vacancy throughout remainder of the Congress.
[18] Died November 4, 1959.

4 John H. Kyl (R),[19] *Bloomfield*
5 Neal Smith (D), *Altoona*
6 Merwin Coad (D), *Boone*
7 Ben F. Jensen (R), *Exira*
8 Charles B. Hoeven (R), *Alton*

## KANSAS

### SENATORS

Andrew F. Schoeppel (R), *Wichita*
Frank Carlson (R), *Concordia*

### REPRESENTATIVES

1 William H. Avery (R), *Wakefield*
2 Newell A. George (D), *Kansas City*
3 Denver D. Hargis (D), *Coffeyville*
4 Edward H. Rees (R), *Emporia*
5 J. Floyd Breeding (D), *Rolla*
6 Wint Smith (R),[20] *Mankato*

## KENTUCKY

### SENATORS

John Sherman Cooper (R), *Somerset*
Thruston B. Morton (R), *Glenview*

### REPRESENTATIVES

1 Frank A. Stubblefield (D), *Murray*
2 William H. Natcher (D), *Bowling Green*
3 Frank W. Burke (D), *Louisville*
4 Frank L. Chelf (D), *Lebanon*
5 Brent Spence (D), *Fort Thomas*
6 John C. Watts (D), *Nicholasville*
7 Carl D. Perkins (D), *Hindman*
8 Eugene Siler (R), *Williamsburg*

## LOUISIANA

### SENATORS

Allen J. Ellender (D), *Houma*
Russell B. Long (D), *Baton Rouge*

### REPRESENTATIVES

1 F. Edward Hébert (D), *New Orleans*
2 Hale Boggs (D), *New Orleans*
3 Edwin E. Willis (D), *St. Martinville*
4 Overton Brooks (D), *Shreveport*
5 Otto E. Passman (D), *Monroe*
6 James H. Morrison (D), *Hammond*
7 T. Ashton Thompson (D), *Ville Platte*
8 Harold B. McSween (D), *Alexandria*

## MAINE

### SENATORS

Margaret Chase Smith (R), *Skowhegan*
Edmund S. Muskie (D), *Waterville*

### REPRESENTATIVES

1 James C. Oliver (D), *South Portland*
2 Frank M. Coffin (D), *Lewiston*
3 Clifford G. McIntire (R), *Perham*

## MARYLAND

### SENATORS

John Marshall Butler (R), *Baltimore*
J. Glenn Beall (R), *Frostburg*

### REPRESENTATIVES

1 Thomas F. Johnson (D), *Berlin*
2 Daniel B. Brewster (D), *Glyndon*
3 Edward A. Garmatz (D), *Baltimore*
4 George H. Fallon (D), *Baltimore*
5 Richard E. Lankford (D), *Annapolis*
6 John R. Foley (D), *Kensington*
7 Samuel N. Friedel (D), *Baltimore*

## MASSACHUSETTS

### SENATORS

Leverett Saltonstall (R), *Dover*
John F. Kennedy (D),[21] *Boston*
Benjamin A. Smith II (D),[22] *Gloucester*

### REPRESENTATIVES

1 Silvio O. Conte (R), *Pittsfield*
2 Edward P. Boland (D), *Springfield*
3 Philip J. Philbin (D), *Clinton*
4 Harold D. Donohue (D), *Worcester*
5 Edith Nourse Rogers (R),[23] *Lowell*
6 William H. Bates (R), *Salem*
7 Thomas J. Lane (D), *Lawrence*
8 Torbert H. Macdonald (D), *Malden*
9 Hastings Keith (R), *West Bridgewater*
10 Laurence Curtis (R), *Boston*
11 Thomas P. O'Neill, Jr. (D), *Cambridge*
12 John W. McCormack (D), *Dorchester*
13 James A. Burke (D), *Milton*
14 Joseph W. Martin, Jr. (R), *North Attleboro*

## MICHIGAN

### SENATORS

Patrick V. McNamara (D), *Detroit*
Philip A. Hart (D), *Mackinac Island*

### REPRESENTATIVES

1 Thaddeus M. Machrowicz (D), *Hamtramck*
2 George Meader (R), *Ann Arbor*
3 August E. Johansen (R), *Battle Creek*
4 Clare E. Hoffman (R), *Allegan*
5 Gerald R. Ford, Jr. (R), *Grand Rapids*
6 Charles E. Chamberlain (R), *East Lansing*
7 James G. O'Hara (D), *Utica*
8 Alvin M. Bentley (R), *Owosso*
9 Robert P. Griffin (R), *Traverse City*
10 Elford A. Cederberg (R), *Bay City*
11 Victor A. Knox (R), *Sault Ste. Marie*
12 John B. Bennett (R), *Ontonagon*
13 Charles C. Diggs, Jr. (D), *Detroit*
14 Louis C. Rabaut (D), *Grosse Pointe Park*
15 John D. Dingell, Jr. (D), *Detroit*
16 John Lesinski, Jr. (D), *Dearborn*
17 Martha W. Griffiths (D), *Detroit*
18 William S. Broomfield (R), *Royal Oak*

## MINNESOTA

### SENATORS

Hubert H. Humphrey (D), *Waverly*
Eugene J. McCarthy (D), *St. Paul*

### REPRESENTATIVES

1 Albert H. Quie (R), *Dennison*
2 Ancher Nelsen (R), *Hutchinson*
3 Roy W. Wier (D), *Minneapolis*
4 Joseph E. Karth (D), *St. Paul*
5 Walter H. Judd (R), *Minneapolis*
6 Fred Marshall (D), *Grove City*
7 H. Carl Andersen (R), *Tyler*
8 John A. Blatnik (D), *Chisholm*
9 Odin Langen (R), *Kennedy*

## MISSISSIPPI

### SENATORS

James O. Eastland (D), *Doddsville*
John C. Stennis (D), *De Kalb*

### REPRESENTATIVES

1 Thomas G. Abernethy (D), *Okolona*
2 Jamie L. Whitten (D), *Charleston*
3 Frank E. Smith (D), *Greenwood*
4 John Bell Williams (D), *Raymond*
5 W. Arthur Winstead (D), *Philadelphia*
6 William M. Colmer (D), *Pascagoula*

## MISSOURI

### SENATORS

Thomas C. Hennings, Jr. (D),[24] *St. Louis*
Edward V. Long (D),[25] *Bowling Green*
Stuart Symington (D), *Richmond Heights*

---

[19] Elected to fill vacancy caused by death of Steven V. Carter, and took his seat January 6, 1960.
[20] Election unsuccessfully contested by Elmo J. Mahoney.
[21] Resigned December 22, 1960, having been elected President.
[22] Appointed December 27, 1960, to fill vacancy caused by resignation of John F. Kennedy but was unable to be sworn in as Congress was not in session.
[23] Died September 10, 1960; vacancy throughout remainder of the Congress.
[24] Died September 13, 1960.
[25] Appointed September 23, 1960, to fill vacancy caused by death of Thomas C. Hennings, Jr.; subsequently elected.

## MISSOURI—Continued

### REPRESENTATIVES

1 Frank M. Karsten (D), *St. Louis*
2 Thomas B. Curtis (R), *Webster Groves*
3 Leonor Kretzer Sullivan (D), *St. Louis*
4 George H. Christopher (D),[26] *Butler*
4 William J. Randall (D),[27] *Independence*
5 Richard W. Bolling (D), *Kansas City*
6 William R. Hull, Jr. (D), *Weston*
7 Charles H. Brown (D), *Springfield*
8 Albert S. J. Carnahan (D), *Ellsinore*
9 Clarence Cannon (D), *Elsberry*
10 Paul C. Jones (D), *Kennett*
11 Morgan M. Moulder (D), *Camdenton*

## MONTANA

### SENATORS

James E. Murray (D), *Butte*
Mike Mansfield (D), *Missoula*

### REPRESENTATIVES

1 Lee Metcalf (D), *Helena*
2 LeRoy H. Anderson (D), *Conrad*

## NEBRASKA

### SENATORS

Roman L. Hruska (R), *Omaha*
Carl T. Curtis (R), *Minden*

### REPRESENTATIVES

1 Phillip H. Weaver (R), *Falls City*
2 Glenn C. Cunningham (R), *Omaha*
3 Lawrence Brock (D), *Wakefield*
4 Donald F. McGinley (D), *Ogallala*

## NEVADA

### SENATORS

Alan H. Bible (D), *Reno*
Howard W. Cannon (D), *Las Vegas*

### REPRESENTATIVE AT LARGE

Walter S. Baring (D), *Reno*

## NEW HAMPSHIRE

### SENATORS

H. Styles Bridges (R), *Concord*
Norris Cotton (R), *Lebanon*

### REPRESENTATIVES

1 Chester E. Merrow (R), *Center Ossipee*
2 Perkins Bass (R), *Peterborough*

## NEW JERSEY

### SENATORS

Clifford P. Case (R), *Rahway*
Harrison A. Williams, Jr. (D), *Westfield*

### REPRESENTATIVES

1 William T. Cahill (R), *Collingswood*
2 Milton W. Glenn (R), *Margate City*
3 James C. Auchincloss (R), *Rumson*
4 Frank Thompson, Jr. (D), *Trenton*
5 Peter H. B. Frelinghuysen, Jr. (R), *Morristown*
6 Florence P. Dwyer (R), *Elizabeth*
7 William B. Widnall (R), *Saddle River*
8 Gordon Canfield (R), *Paterson*
9 Frank C. Osmers, Jr. (R), *Tenafly*
10 Peter W. Rodino, Jr. (D), *Newark*
11 Hugh J. Addonizio (D), *Newark*
12 George M. Wallhauser (R), *Maplewood*
13 Cornelius E. Gallagher (D), *Bayonne*
14 Dominick V. Daniels (D), *Jersey City*

## NEW MEXICO

### SENATORS

Dennis Chavez (D), *Albuquerque*
Clinton P. Anderson (D), *Albuquerque*

### REPRESENTATIVES AT LARGE

Joseph M. Montoya (D), *Santa Fe*
Thomas G. Morris (D), *Tucumcari*

## NEW YORK

### SENATORS

Jacob K. Javits (R), *New York City*
Kenneth B. Keating (R), *Rochester*

### REPRESENTATIVES

1 Stuyvesant Wainwright II (R), *Wainscott*
2 Steven B. Derounian (R), *Roslyn*
3 Frank J. Becker (R), *Lynbrook*
4 Seymour Halpern (R), *Forest Hills*
5 Albert H. Bosch (R),[28] *Woodhaven*
6 Lester Holtzman (D), *Rego Park*
7 James J. Delaney (D), *Long Island City*
8 Victor L. Anfuso (D), *Brooklyn*
9 Eugene J. Keogh (D), *Brooklyn*
10 Edna F. Kelly (D), *Brooklyn*
11 Emanuel Celler (D), *Brooklyn*
12 Francis E. Dorn (R), *Brooklyn*
13 Abraham J. Multer (D), *Brooklyn*
14 John J. Rooney (D), *Brooklyn*
15 John H. Ray (R), *Staten Island*
16 Adam Clayton Powell, Jr. (D), *New York City*
17 John V. Lindsay (R), *New York City*
18 Alfred E. Santangelo (D), *New York City*
19 Leonard Farbstein (D), *New York City*
20 Ludwig Teller (D), *New York City*
21 Herbert Zelenko (D), *New York City*
22 James C. Healey (D), *New York City*
23 Isidore Dollinger (D),[29] *New York City*
23 Jacob H. Gilbert (D),[30] *New York City*
24 Charles A. Buckley (D), *New York City*
25 Paul A. Fino (R), *New York City*
26 Edwin B. Dooley (R), *Mamaroneck*
27 Robert R. Barry (R), *Yonkers*
28 Katharine St. George (R), *Tuxedo Park*
29 J. Ernest Wharton (R), *Richmondville*
30 Leo W. O'Brien (D), *Albany*
31 Dean P. Taylor (R), *Troy*
32 Samuel S. Stratton (D), *Schenectady*
33 Clarence E. Kilburn (R), *Malone*
34 Alexander Pirnie (R), *Utica*
35 R. Walter Riehlman (R), *Tully*
36 John Taber (R), *Auburn*
37 Howard W. Robison (R), *Owego*
38 Jessica McC. Weis (R), *Rochester*
39 Harold C. Ostertag (R), *Attica*
40 William E. Miller (R), *Olcott*
41 Thaddeus J. Dulski (D), *Buffalo*
42 John R. Pillion (R), *Hamburg*
43 Daniel A. Reed (R),[31] *Dunkirk*
43 Charles E. Goodell (R),[32] *Jamestown*

## NORTH CAROLINA

### SENATORS

Sam J. Ervin, Jr. (D), *Morganton*
B. Everett Jordan (D), *Saxapahaw*

### REPRESENTATIVES

1 Herbert C. Bonner (D), *Washington*
2 L. H. Fountain (D), *Tarboro*
3 Graham A. Barden (D), *New Bern*
4 Harold D. Cooley (D), *Nashville*
5 Ralph J. Scott (D), *Danbury*
6 Carl T. Durham (D), *Chapel Hill*
7 Alton A. Lennon (D), *Wilmington*
8 A. Paul Kitchin (D), *Wadesboro*

---

[26] Died January 23, 1959.
[27] Elected to fill vacancy caused by death of George H. Christopher, and took his seat March 9, 1959.

[28] Resigned December 31, 1960; vacancy throughout remainder of the Congress.
[29] Resigned December 31, 1959.
[30] Elected to fill vacancy caused by resignation of Isidore Dollinger, and took his seat March 11, 1960.
[31] Died February 19, 1959.
[32] Elected to fill vacancy caused by death of Daniel A. Reed, and took his seat June 2, 1959.

9 Hugh Q. Alexander (D),
   *Kannapolis*
10 Charles Raper Jonas (R),
   *Lincolnton*
11 Basil L. Whitener (D), *Gastonia*
12 David M. Hall (D),[33] *Sylva*
12 Roy A. Taylor (D),[34] *Black
   Mountain*

## NORTH DAKOTA

### SENATORS

William Langer (R),[35] *Wheatland*
C. Norman Brunsdale (R),[36] *Mayville*
Quentin N. Burdick (D),[37] *Fargo*
Milton R. Young (R), *La Moure*

### REPRESENTATIVES AT LARGE

Quentin N. Burdick (D),[38] *Fargo*
Don L. Short (R), *Medora*

## OHIO

### SENATORS

Frank J. Lausche (D), *Cleveland*
Stephen M. Young (D), *Cleveland*

### REPRESENTATIVES

1 Gordon H. Scherer (R), *Cincinnati*
2 William E. Hess (R), *Cincinnati*
3 Paul F. Schenck (R), *Dayton*
4 William M. McCulloch (R), *Piqua*
5 Delbert L. Latta (R), *Bowling
   Green*
6 James G. Polk (D),[39] *Highland*
6 Ward M. Miller (R),[40] *Portsmouth*
7 Clarence J. Brown (R),
   *Blanchester*
8 Jackson E. Betts (R), *Findlay*
9 Thomas L. Ashley (D), *Waterville*
10 Walter H. Moeller (D), *Lancaster*
11 Robert E. Cook (D), *Ravenna*
12 Samuel L. Devine (R), *Columbus*
13 Albert D. Baumhart, Jr. (R),
   *Vermilion*
14 William H. Ayres (R), *Akron*
15 John E. Henderson (R),
   *Cambridge*
16 Frank T. Bow (R), *Canton*
17 Robert W. Levering (D),
   *Fredericktown*
18 Wayne L. Hays (D), *Flushing*
19 Michael J. Kirwan (D),
   *Youngstown*
20 Michael A. Feighan (D), *Cleveland*
21 Charles A. Vanik (D), *Cleveland*
22 Frances P. Bolton (R), *Lyndhurst*

23 William E. Minshall (R), *Rocky
   River*

## OKLAHOMA

### SENATORS

Robert S. Kerr (D), *Oklahoma City*
A. S. Mike Monroney (D), *Oklahoma
City*

### REPRESENTATIVES

1 Page H. Belcher (R), *Enid*
2 Edmond Edmondson (D),
   *Muskogee*
3 Carl Albert (D), *McAlester*
4 Thomas J. Steed (D), *Shawnee*
5 John Jarman (D), *Oklahoma City*
6 Toby Morris (D), *Lawton*

## OREGON

### SENATORS

Wayne L. Morse (D), *Eugene*
Richard L. Neuberger (D),[41] *Portland*
Hall S. Lusk (D),[42] *Portland*
Maurine B. Neuberger (D),[43]
   *Portland*

### REPRESENTATIVES

1 A. Walter Norblad (R), *Stayton*
2 Albert C. Ullman (D), *Baker*
3 Edith S. Green (D), *Portland*
4 Charles O. Porter (D), *Eugene*

## PENNSYLVANIA

### SENATORS

Joseph S. Clark (D), *Philadelphia*
Hugh D. Scott, Jr. (R), *Philadelphia*

### REPRESENTATIVES

1 William A. Barrett (D),
   *Philadelphia*
2 Kathryn E. Granahan (D),
   *Philadelphia*
3 James A. Byrne (D), *Philadelphia*
4 Robert N. C. Nix (D),
   *Philadelphia*
5 William J. Green, Jr. (D),
   *Philadelphia*
6 Herman Toll (D), *Philadelphia*
7 William H. Milliken, Jr. (R),
   *Sharon Hill*
8 Willard S. Curtin (R), *Morrisville*
9 Paul B. Dague (R), *Downingtown*
10 Stanley A. Prokop (D), *Lake Ariel*
11 Daniel J. Flood (D), *Wilkes-Barre*
12 Ivor D. Fenton (R), *Mahanoy City*
13 John A. Lafore, Jr. (R), *Haverford*
14 George M. Rhodes (D), *Reading*

15 Francis E. Walter (D), *Easton*
16 Walter M. Mumma (R),
   *Harrisburg*
17 Alvin R. Bush (R),[44] *Muncy*
17 Herman T. Schneebeli (R),[45]
   *Williamsport*
18 Richard M. Simpson (R),[46]
   *Huntingdon*
18 Douglas H. Elliott (R),[47]
   *Chambersburg*
18 J. Irving Whalley (R),[48] *Windber*
19 James M. Quigley (D), *Camp Hill*
20 James E. Van Zandt (R), *Altoona*
21 John H. Dent (D), *Jeannette*
22 John P. Saylor (R), *Johnstown*
23 Leon H. Gavin (R), *Oil City*
24 Carroll D. Kearns (R), *Farrell*
25 Frank M. Clark (D), *Bessemer*
26 Thomas E. Morgan (D),
   *Fredericktown*
27 James G. Fulton (R), *Dormont*
28 William S. Moorhead (D),
   *Pittsburgh*
29 Robert J. Corbett (R), *Pittsburgh*
30 Elmer J. Holland (D), *Pittsburgh*

## RHODE ISLAND

### SENATORS

Theodore F. Green (D), *Providence*
John O. Pastore (D), *Cranston*

### REPRESENTATIVES

1 Aime J. Forand (D), *Cumberland*
2 John E. Fogarty (D), *Harmony*

## SOUTH CAROLINA

### SENATORS

Olin D. Johnston (D), *Spartanburg*
Strom Thurmond (D), *Aiken*

### REPRESENTATIVES

1 L. Mendel Rivers (D), *Charleston*
2 John J. Riley (D), *Sumter*
3 W. J. Bryan Dorn (D), *Greenwood*
4 Robert T. Ashmore (D), *Greenville*
5 Robert W. Hemphill (D), *Chester*
6 John L. McMillan (D), *Florence*

## SOUTH DAKOTA

### SENATORS

Karl E. Mundt (R), *Madison*
Francis H. Case (R), *Custer*

### REPRESENTATIVES

1 George S. McGovern (D), *Mitchell*
2 E. Y. Berry (R), *McLaughlin*

---

[33] Died January 29, 1960.
[34] Elected to fill vacancy caused by death of David M. Hall, and took his seat July 2, 1960.
[35] Died November 8, 1959.
[36] Appointed to fill vacancy caused by death of William Langer, and took his seat January 6, 1960.
[37] Elected to fill vacancy caused by death of William Langer, and took his seat August 8, 1960.
[38] Resigned August 8, 1960, having been elected Senator; vacancy throughout remainder of the Congress.
[39] Died April 28, 1959.

[40] Elected November 8, 1960, to fill vacancy caused by death of James G. Polk but was unable to be sworn in as Congress was not in session.
[41] Died March 9, 1960.
[42] Appointed to fill vacancy caused by death of Richard L. Neuberger, and took his seat March 23, 1960.
[43] Elected November 8, 1960, to fill vacancy caused by death of her husband, Richard L. Neuberger, for the term ending January 3, 1961; elected at the same time for the term ending January 3, 1967, but was unable to be sworn in as Congress was not in session.

[44] Died November 5, 1959.
[45] Elected to fill vacancy caused by death of Alvin R. Bush, and took his seat May 5, 1960.
[46] Died January 7, 1960.
[47] Elected to fill vacancy caused by death of Richard M. Simpson, and took his seat May 5, 1960. Died June 19, 1960.
[48] Elected November 8, 1960, to fill vacancy caused by death of Douglas H. Elliott, but was unable to be sworn in as Congress was not in session.

## TENNESSEE

### SENATORS

Estes Kefauver (D), *Chattanooga*
Albert A. Gore (D), *Carthage*

### REPRESENTATIVES

1 B. Carroll Reece (R), *Johnson City*
2 Howard H. Baker (R), *Huntsville*
3 James B. Frazier, Jr. (D), *Chattanooga*
4 Joseph L. Evins (D), *Smithville*
5 J. Carlton Loser (D), *Nashville*
6 Ross Bass (D), *Pulaski*
7 Thomas J. Murray (D), *Jackson*
8 Robert A. Everett (D), *Union City*
9 Clifford Davis (D), *Memphis*

## TEXAS

### SENATORS

Lyndon B. Johnson (D), *Johnson City*
Ralph W. Yarborough (D), *Austin*

### REPRESENTATIVES

1 Wright Patman (D), *Texarkana*
2 Jack B. Brooks (D), *Beaumont*
3 Lindley G. Beckworth (D), *Gladewater*
4 Sam Rayburn (D), *Bonham*
5 Bruce R. Alger (R), *Dallas*
6 Olin E. Teague (D), *College Station*
7 John V. Dowdy (D), *Athens*
8 Albert Thomas (D), *Houston*
9 Clark W. Thompson (D), *Galveston*
10 W. Homer Thornberry (D), *Austin*
11 W. R. Poage (D), *Waco*
12 James C. Wright, Jr. (D), *Fort Worth*
13 Frank N. Ikard (D), *Wichita Falls*
14 John A. Young (D), *Corpus Christi*
15 Joe M. Kilgore (D), *McAllen*
16 J. T. Rutherford (D), *Odessa*
17 Omar T. Burleson (D), *Anson*
18 Walter E. Rogers (D), *Pampa*
19 George H. Mahon (D), *Lubbock*
20 Paul J. Kilday (D), *San Antonio*
21 O. Clark Fisher (D), *San Angelo*
22 Robert R. Casey (D), *Houston*

## UTAH

### SENATORS

Wallace F. Bennett (R), *Salt Lake City*

Frank E. Moss (D), *Salt Lake City*

### REPRESENTATIVES

1 Henry A. Dixon (R), *Ogden*
2 David S. King (D), *Salt Lake City*

## VERMONT

### SENATORS

George D. Aiken (R), *Putney*
Winston L. Prouty (R), *Newport*

### REPRESENTATIVE AT LARGE

William H. Meyer (D), *West Rupert*

## VIRGINIA

### SENATORS

Harry Flood Byrd (D), *Berryville*
A. Willis Robertson (D), *Lexington*

### REPRESENTATIVES

1 Thomas N. Downing (D), *Newport News*
2 Porter Hardy, Jr. (D), *Churchland*
3 J. Vaughan Gary (D), *Richmond*
4 Watkins M. Abbitt (D), *Appomattox*
5 William M. Tuck (D), *South Boston*
6 Richard H. Poff (R), *Radford*
7 Burr P. Harrison (D), *Winchester*
8 Howard W. Smith (D), *Broad Run*
9 W. Pat Jennings (D), *Marion*
10 Joel T. Broyhill (R), *Arlington*

## WASHINGTON

### SENATORS

Warren G. Magnuson (D), *Seattle*
Henry M. Jackson (D), *Everett*

### REPRESENTATIVES

1 Thomas M. Pelly (R), *Port Blakely*
2 Alfred John (Jack) Westland (R), *Everett*
3 Russell V. Mack (R),[49] *Hoquiam*
3 Julia Butler Hansen (D),[50] *Cathlamet*
4 Catherine D. May (R), *Yakima*
5 Walter F. Horan (R), *Wenatchee*
6 Thor C. Tollefson (R), *Tacoma*
7 Donald H. Magnuson (D), *Seattle*

## WEST VIRGINIA

### SENATORS

Jennings Randolph (D), *Elkins*
Robert C. Byrd (D), *Sophia*

### REPRESENTATIVES

1 Arch A. Moore, Jr. (R), *Glendale*
2 Harley O. Staggers (D), *Keyser*
3 Cleveland M. Bailey (D), *Clarksburg*
4 Ken Hechler (D), *Huntington*
5 M. Elizabeth Kee (D), *Bluefield*
6 John M. Slack, Jr. (D), *Charleston*

## WISCONSIN

### SENATORS

Alexander Wiley (R), *Chippewa Falls*
William Proxmire (D), *Madison*

### REPRESENTATIVES

1 Gerald T. Flynn (D), *Racine*
2 Robert W. Kastenmeier (D), *Watertown*
3 Gardner R. Withrow (R), *La Crosse*
4 Clement J. Zablocki (D), *Milwaukee*
5 Henry S. Reuss (D), *Milwaukee*
6 William K. Van Pelt (R), *Fond du Lac*
7 Melvin R. Laird (R), *Marshfield*
8 John W. Byrnes (R), *Green Bay*
9 Lester R. Johnson (D), *Black River Falls*
10 Alvin E. O'Konski (R), *Mercer*

## WYOMING

### SENATORS

Joseph C. O'Mahoney (D), *Cheyenne*
Gale W. McGee (D), *Laramie*

### REPRESENTATIVE AT LARGE

E. Keith Thomson (R),[51] *Cheyenne*

## TERRITORY OF HAWAII[52]

### DELEGATE

John A. Burns (D),[53] *Honolulu*

## COMMONWEALTH OF PUERTO RICO

### RESIDENT COMMISSIONER

Antonio Fernós-Isern (PD), *Santurce*

---

[49] Died March 28, 1960.
[50] Elected November 8, 1960, to fill vacancy caused by death of Russell V. Mack, but was unable to be sworn in as Congress was not in session.

[51] Died December 9, 1960; vacancy throughout remainder of the Congress.
[52] Admitted as a state into the Union August 21, 1959.

[53] Served during the first session; the Territory was granted statehood on August 21, 1959.

# 87TH CONGRESS

## JANUARY 3, 1961, TO JANUARY 3, 1963

FIRST SESSION— *January 3, 1961, to September 27, 1961*
SECOND SESSION— *January 10, 1962,[1] to October 13, 1962*

Lyndon B. Johnson
Vice President

Sam Rayburn
Speaker

---

### Senate
#### Democrats 65 — Republicans 35

VICE PRESIDENT OF THE UNITED STATES— Richard M. Nixon,[2] of California;
Lyndon B. Johnson,[3] of Texas
PRESIDENT PRO TEMPORE OF THE SENATE— Carl Hayden, of Arizona
SECRETARY OF THE SENATE— Felton McLellan Johnston, of Mississippi
SERGEANT AT ARMS OF THE SENATE— Joseph C. Duke, of Arizona
MAJORITY FLOOR LEADER— Mike Mansfield, of Montana
DEMOCRATIC WHIP— Hubert H. Humphrey, of Minnesota
REPUBLICAN FLOOR LEADER— Everett McKinley Dirksen, of Illinois
ASSISTANT REPUBLICAN LEADER— Thomas H. Kuchel, of California

---

### House of Representatives
#### Democrats 262 — Republicans 175

SPEAKER OF THE HOUSE OF REPRESENTATIVES— Sam Rayburn,[4] of Texas; John W. McCormack,[5] of Massachusetts
CLERK OF THE HOUSE— Ralph R. Roberts,[6] of Indiana
SERGEANT OF ARMS OF THE HOUSE— Zeake W. Johnson, Jr.,[7] of Tennessee
DOORKEEPER OF THE HOUSE— William M. Miller,[8] of Mississippi
POSTMASTER OF THE HOUSE— H. H. Morris,[9] of Kentucky
MAJORITY LEADER— John W. McCormack, of Massachusetts; Carl Albert,[10] of Oklahoma
MAJORITY WHIP— Carl Albert, of Oklahoma; Hale Boggs,[11] of Louisiana
REPUBLICAN LEADER— Charles A. Halleck, of Indiana
REPUBLICAN WHIP— Leslie C. Arends, of Illinois

---

## ALABAMA

### SENATORS

Lister Hill (D), *Montgomery*
John J. Sparkman (D), *Huntsville*

### REPRESENTATIVES

1 Frank W. Boykin (D), *Mobile*
2 George M. Grant (D), *Troy*
3 George W. Andrews (D), *Union Springs*
4 Kenneth A. Roberts (D), *Anniston*
5 Albert Rains (D), *Gadsden*
6 Armistead I. Selden, Jr. (D), *Greensboro*
7 Carl A. Elliott (D), *Jasper*
8 Robert E. Jones, Jr. (D), *Scottsboro*
9 George Huddleston, Jr. (D), *Birmingham*

## ALASKA

### SENATORS

E. L. (Bob) Bartlett (D), *Juneau*
Ernest Gruening (D), *Juneau*

### REPRESENTATIVE AT LARGE

Ralph J. Rivers (D), *Fairbanks*

## ARIZONA

### SENATORS

Carl Hayden (D), *Phoenix*
Barry M. Goldwater (R), *Phoenix*

### REPRESENTATIVES

1 John J. Rhodes (R), *Mesa*
2 Stewart L. Udall (D),[12] *Tucson*
2 Morris K. Udall (D),[13] *Tucson*

## ARKANSAS

### SENATORS

John L. McClellan (D), *Camden*
J. William Fulbright (D), *Fayetteville*

### REPRESENTATIVES

1 E. C. Gathings (D), *West Memphis*
2 Wilbur D. Mills (D), *Kensett*
3 James W. Trimble (D), *Berryville*
4 Oren Harris (D), *El Dorado*
5 T. Dale Alford (D), *Little Rock*
6 William F. Norrell (D),[14] *Monticello*
6 Catherine D. Norrell (D),[15] *Monticello*

## CALIFORNIA

### SENATORS

Thomas H. Kuchel (R), *Anaheim*
Clair Engle (D), *Red Bluff*

---

[1] By joint resolution (Pub. Law 348, 87th Cong., 1st sess.), the date of assembling the second session of the Eighty-seventh Congress was fixed for January 10, 1962.
[2] Term expired at noon on January 20, 1961.
[3] Term began at noon on January 20, 1961.
[4] Reelected January 3, 1961; died November 16, 1961.

[5] Elected January 10, 1962.
[6] Reelected January 3, 1961.
[7] Reelected January 3, 1961.
[8] Reelected January 3, 1961.
[9] Reelected January 3, 1961.
[10] Elected January 10, 1962.
[11] Elected January 10, 1962.

[12] Resigned January 18, 1961.
[13] Elected to fill vacancy caused by resignation of his brother, Stewart L. Udall, and took his seat May 17, 1961.
[14] Died February 15, 1961.
[15] Elected to fill vacancy caused by death of her husband, William F. Norrell, and took her seat April 25, 1961.

## CALIFORNIA—Continued
### REPRESENTATIVES
1 Clement W. Miller (D),[16] *Corte Madera*
2 Harold T. Johnson (D), *Roseville*
3 John E. Moss, Jr. (D), *Sacramento*
4 William S. Mailliard (R), *San Francisco*
5 John F. Shelley (D), *San Francisco*
6 John F. Baldwin (R), *Martinez*
7 Jeffery Cohelan (D), *Berkeley*
8 George P. Miller (D), *Alameda*
9 J. Arthur Younger (R), *San Mateo*
10 Charles S. Gubser (R), *Gilroy*
11 John J. McFall (D), *Manteca*
12 B. F. Sisk (D), *Fresno*
13 Charles M. Teague (R), *Ojai*
14 Harlan F. Hagen (D), *Hanford*
15 Gordon L. McDonough (R), *Los Angeles*
16 Alphonzo Bell (R), *Santa Monica*
17 Cecil R. King (D), *Los Angeles*
18 Craig Hosmer (R), *Long Beach*
19 Chet Holifield (D), *Montebello*
20 H. Allen Smith (R), *Glendale*
21 Edgar W. Hiestand (R), *Burbank*
22 James C. Corman (D), *Van Nuys*
23 Clyde G. Doyle (D), *South Gate*
24 Glenard P. Lipscomb (R), *Los Angeles*
25 John H. Rousselot (R), *San Gabriel*
26 James Roosevelt (D), *Los Angeles*
27 Harry R. Sheppard (D), *Yucaipa*
28 James B. Utt (R), *Santa Ana*
29 Dalip S. Saund (D), *Westmorland*
30 Robert C. Wilson (R), *Chula Vista*

## COLORADO
### SENATORS
Gordon L. Allott (R), *Lamar*
John A. Carroll (D), *Denver*

### REPRESENTATIVES
1 Byron G. Rogers (D), *Denver*
2 Peter H. Dominick (R), *Englewood*
3 J. Edgar Chenoweth (R), *Trinidad*
4 Wayne N. Aspinall (D), *Palisade*

## CONNECTICUT
### SENATORS
Prescott S. Bush (R), *Greenwich*
Thomas J. Dodd (D), *West Hartford*

### REPRESENTATIVE AT LARGE
Frank Kowalski (D), *Meriden*

### REPRESENTATIVES
1 Emilio Q. Daddario (D), *Hartford*
2 Horace Seely-Brown, Jr. (R), *Pomfret Center*
3 Robert N. Giaimo (D), *North Haven*

4 Abner W. Sibal (R), *Norwalk*
5 John S. Monagan (D), *Waterbury*

## DELAWARE
### SENATORS
John J. Williams (R), *Millsboro*
J. Caleb Boggs (R), *Wilmington*

### REPRESENTATIVE AT LARGE
Harris B. McDowell, Jr. (D), *Middletown*

## FLORIDA
### SENATORS
Spessard L. Holland (D), *Bartow*
George A. Smathers (D), *Miami*

### REPRESENTATIVES
1 William C. Cramer (R), *St. Petersburg*
2 Charles E. Bennett (D), *Jacksonville*
3 Robert L. F. Sikes (D), *Crestview*
4 Dante B. Fascell (D), *Miami*
5 A. Sydney Herlong, Jr. (D), *Leesburg*
6 Paul G. Rogers (D), *West Palm Beach*
7 James A. Haley (D), *Sarasota*
8 D. R. (Billy) Matthews (D), *Gainesville*

## GEORGIA
### SENATORS
Richard B. Russell (D), *Winder*
Herman E. Talmadge (D), *Lovejoy*

### REPRESENTATIVES
1 G. Elliott Hagan (D), *Sylvania*
2 John L. Pilcher (D), *Meigs*
3 E. L. Forrester (D), *Leesburg*
4 John J. Flynt, Jr. (D), *Griffin*
5 James C. Davis (D), *Stone Mountain*
6 Carl Vinson (D), *Milledgeville*
7 John W. Davis (D), *Summerville*
8 Iris F. Blitch (D), *Homerville*
9 Phillip M. Landrum (D), *Jasper*
10 Robert G. Stephens, Jr. (D), *Athens*

## HAWAII
### SENATORS
Hiram L. Fong (R), *Honolulu*
Oren E. Long (D), *Honolulu*

### REPRESENTATIVE AT LARGE
Daniel K. Inouye (D), *Honolulu*

## IDAHO
### SENATORS
Henry C. Dworshak (R),[17] *Burley*
Len B. Jordan (R),[18] *Boise*
Frank Church (D), *Boise*

### REPRESENTATIVES
1 Gracie B. Pfost (D), *Nampa*
2 Ralph R. Harding (D), *Blackfoot*

## ILLINOIS
### SENATORS
Paul H. Douglas (D), *Chicago*
Everett McKinley Dirksen (R), *Pekin*

### REPRESENTATIVES
1 William L. Dawson (D), *Chicago*
2 Barratt O'Hara (D), *Chicago*
3 William T. Murphy (D), *Chicago*
4 Edward J. Derwinski (R), *Chicago*
5 John C. Kluczynski (D), *Chicago*
6 Thomas J. O'Brien (D), *Chicago*
7 Roland V. Libonati (D), *Chicago*
8 Dan Rostenkowski (D), *Chicago*
9 Sidney R. Yates (D), *Chicago*
10 Harold R. Collier (R), *Berwyn*
11 Roman C. Pucinski (D), *Chicago*
12 Edward R. Finnegan (D), *Chicago*
13 Marguerite Stitt Church (R), *Evanston*
14 Elmer J. Hoffman (R), *Wheaton*
15 Noah M. Mason (R), *Oglesby*
16 John B. Anderson (R), *Rockford*
17 Leslie C. Arends (R), *Melvin*
18 Robert H. Michel (R), *Peoria*
19 Robert B. Chiperfield (R), *Canton*
20 Paul Findley (R), *Pittsfield*
21 Peter F. Mack, Jr. (D), *Carlinville*
22 William L. Springer (R), *Champaign*
23 George E. Shipley (D), *Olney*
24 Melvin Price (D), *East St. Louis*
25 Kenneth J. Gray (D), *West Frankfort*

## INDIANA
### SENATORS
Homer E. Capehart (R), *Washington*
Vance Hartke (D), *Evansville*

### REPRESENTATIVES
1 Ray J. Madden (D), *Gary*
2 Charles A. Halleck (R), *Rennselaer*
3 John Brademas (D), *South Bend*
4 E. Ross Adair (R), *Fort Wayne*
5 J. Edward Roush (D),[19] *Huntington*
6 Richard L. Roudebush (R), *Noblesville*
7 William G. Bray (R), *Martinsville*
8 Winfield K. Denton (D), *Evansville*
9 Earl Wilson (R), *Bedford*
10 Ralph Harvey (R), *New Castle*
11 Donald C. Bruce (R), *Indianapolis*

---

[16] Died October 7, 1962; vacancy throughout remainder of the Congress.
[17] Died July 23, 1962.

[18] Appointed to fill vacancy caused by death of Henry C. Dworshak, and took his seat August 7, 1962.
[19] Election investigated by order of the House (H.

Res. 1). H. Res. 339 declared that J. Edward Roush was entitled to this seat.

## IOWA

SENATORS

Bourke B. Hickenlooper (R), *Cedar Rapids*

Jack R. Miller (R), *Sioux City*

REPRESENTATIVES

1 Frederic D. Schwengel (R), *Davenport*
2 James E. Bromwell (R), *Cedar Rapids*
3 H. R. Gross (R), *Waterloo*
4 John H. Kyl (R), *Bloomfield*
5 Neal Smith (D), *Altoona*
6 Merwin Coad (D), *Boone*
7 Ben F. Jensen (R), *Exira*
8 Charles B. Hoeven (R), *Alton*

## KANSAS

SENATORS

Andrew F. Schoeppel (R),[20] *Wichita*

James B. Pearson (R),[21] *Prairie Village*

Frank Carlson (R), *Concordia*

REPRESENTATIVES

1 William H. Avery (R), *Wakefield*
2 Robert F. Ellsworth (R), *Lawrence*
3 Walter L. McVey (R), *Independence*
4 Garner E. Shriver (R), *Wichita*
5 J. Floyd Breeding (D), *Rolla*
6 Robert J. Dole (R), *Russell*

## KENTUCKY

SENATORS

John Sherman Cooper (R), *Somerset*

Thruston B. Morton (R), *Louisville*

REPRESENTATIVES

1 Frank A. Stubblefield (D), *Murray*
2 William H. Natcher (D), *Bowling Green*
3 Frank W. Burke (D), *Louisville*
4 Frank L. Chelf (D), *Lebanon*
5 Brent Spence (D), *Fort Thomas*
6 John C. Watts (D), *Nicholasville*
7 Carl D. Perkins (D), *Hindman*
8 Eugene Siler (R), *Williamsburg*

## LOUISIANA

SENATORS

Allen J. Ellender (D), *Houma*

Russell B. Long (D), *Baton Rouge*

REPRESENTATIVES

1 F. Edward Hébert (D), *New Orleans*
2 Hale Boggs (D), *New Orleans*
3 Edwin E. Willis (D), *Martinville*
4 Overton Brooks (D),[22] *Shreveport*
4 Joe D. Waggonner, Jr. (D),[23] *Plain Dealing*
5 Otto E. Passman (D), *Monroe*
6 James H. Morrison (D), *Hammond*
7 T. Ashton Thompson (D), *Ville Platte*
8 Harold B. McSween (D), *Alexandria*

## MAINE

SENATORS

Margaret Chase Smith (R), *Skowhegan*

Edmund S. Muskie (D), *Waterville*

REPRESENTATIVES

1 Peter A. Garland (R), *Saco*
2 Stanley R. Tupper (R), *Boothbay Harbor*
3 Clifford G. McIntire (R), *Perham*

## MARYLAND

SENATORS

John Marshall Butler (R), *Baltimore*

J. Glenn Beall (R), *Frostburg*

REPRESENTATIVES

1 Thomas F. Johnson (D), *Berlin*
2 Daniel B. Brewster (D), *Glyndon*
3 Edward A. Garmatz (D), *Baltimore*
4 George H. Fallon (D), *Baltimore*
5 Richard E. Lankford (D), *Annapolis*
6 Charles McC. Mathias, Jr. (R), *Frederick*
7 Samuel N. Friedel (D), *Baltimore*

## MASSACHUSETTS

SENATORS

Leverett Saltonstall (R), *Dover*

Benjamin A. Smith II (D),[24] *Gloucester*

Edward M. Kennedy (D),[25] *Boston*

REPRESENTATIVES

1 Silvio O. Conte (R), *Pittsfield*
2 Edward P. Boland (D), *Springfield*
3 Philip J. Philbin (D), *Clinton*
4 Harold D. Donohue (D), *Worcester*
5 F. Bradford Morse (R), *Lowell*
6 William H. Bates (R), *Salem*
7 Thomas J. Lane (D), *Lawrence*
8 Torbert H. Macdonald (D), *Malden*
9 Hastings Keith (R), *West Bridgewater*
10 Laurence Curtis (R), *Boston*
11 Thomas P. O'Neill, Jr. (D), *Cambridge*

12 John W. McCormack (D), *Dorchester*
13 James A. Burke (D), *Milton*
14 Joseph W. Martin, Jr. (R), *North Attleboro*

## MICHIGAN

SENATORS

Patrick V. McNamara (D), *Detroit*

Philip A. Hart (D), *Mackinac Island*

REPRESENTATIVES

1 Thaddeus M. Machrowicz (D),[26] *Hamtramck*
1 Lucien N. Nedzi (D),[27] *Detroit*
2 George Meader (R), *Ann Arbor*
3 August E. Johansen (R), *Battle Creek*
4 Clare E. Hoffman (R), *Allegan*
5 Gerald R. Ford, Jr. (R), *Grand Rapids*
6 Charles E. Chamberlain (R), *East Lansing*
7 James G. O'Hara (D), *Utica*
8 James Harvey (R), *Saginaw*
9 Robert P. Griffin (R), *Traverse City*
10 Elford A. Cederberg (R), *Bay City*
11 Victor A. Knox (R), *Sault Ste. Marie*
12 John B. Bennett (R), *Ontonagon*
13 Charles C. Diggs, Jr. (D), *Detroit*
14 Louis C. Rabaut (D),[28] *Grosse Pointe Park*
14 Harold M. Ryan (D),[29] *Detroit*
15 John D. Dingell, Jr. (D), *Detroit*
16 John Lesinski, Jr. (D), *Dearborn*
17 Martha W. Griffiths (D), *Detroit*
18 William S. Broomfield (R), *Royal Oak*

## MINNESOTA

SENATORS

Hubert H. Humphrey (D), *Waverly*

Eugene J. McCarthy (D), *St. Paul*

REPRESENTATIVES

1 Albert H. Quie (R), *Dennison*
2 Ancher Nelsen (R), *Hutchinson*
3 Clark MacGregor (R), *Plymouth*
4 Joseph E. Karth (D), *St. Paul*
5 Walter H. Judd (R), *Minneapolis*
6 Fred Marshall (D), *Grove City*
7 H. Carl Andersen (R), *Tyler*
8 John A. Blatnik (D), *Chisholm*
9 Odin Langen (R), *Kennedy*

## MISSISSIPPI

SENATORS

James O. Eastland (D), *Doddsville*

John C. Stennis (D), *De Kalb*

---

[20] Died January 21, 1962.
[21] Appointed to fill vacancy caused by death of Andrew F. Schoeppel, and took his seat February 5, 1962.
[22] Died September 16, 1961.
[23] Elected to fill vacancy caused by death of Overton Brooks, and took his seat January 10, 1962.

[24] Appointed December 27, 1960, to fill vacancy caused by resignation of John F. Kennedy in preceding Congress.
[25] Elected November 6, 1962, to fill vacancy caused by resignation of his brother, John F. Kennedy, but was unable to be sworn in as Congress was not in session.

[26] Resigned September 18, 1961.
[27] Elected to fill vacancy caused by resignation of Thaddeus M. Machrowicz, and took his seat January 10, 1962.
[28] Died November 12, 1961.
[29] Elected to fill vacancy caused by death of Louis C. Rabaut and took his seat February 21, 1962.

## MISSISSIPPI—Continued

### REPRESENTATIVES

1 Thomas G. Abernethy (D), *Okolona*
2 Jamie L. Whitten (D), *Charleston*
3 Frank E. Smith (D),[30] *Greenwood*
4 John Bell Williams (D), *Raymond*
5 W. Arthur Winstead (D), *Philadelphia*
6 William M. Colmer (D), *Pascagoula*

## MISSOURI

### SENATORS

Stuart Symington (D), *Richmond Heights*
Edward V. Long (D), *Clarksville*

### REPRESENTATIVES

1 Frank M. Karsten (D), *St. Louis*
2 Thomas B. Curtis (R), *Webster Groves*
3 Leonor Kretzer Sullivan (D), *St. Louis*
4 William J. Randall (D), *Independence*
5 Richard W. Bolling (D), *Kansas City*
6 William R. Hull, Jr. (D), *Weston*
7 Durward G. (Doc) Hall (R), *Springfield*
8 Richard H. Ichord (D), *Houston*
9 Clarence Cannon (D), *Elsberry*
10 Paul C. Jones (D), *Kennett*
11 Morgan M. Moulder (D), *Camdenton*

## MONTANA

### SENATORS

Mike Mansfield (D), *Missoula*
Lee Metcalf (D), *Helena*

### REPRESENTATIVES

1 Arnold Olsen (D), *Helena*
2 James F. Battin (R), *Billings*

## NEBRASKA

### SENATORS

Roman L. Hruska (R), *Omaha*
Carl T. Curtis (R), *Minden*

### REPRESENTATIVES

1 Phillip H. Weaver (R), *Falls City*
2 Glenn C. Cunningham (R), *Omaha*
3 Ralph F. Beermann (R), *Dakota City*
4 David T. Martin (R), *Kearney*

## NEVADA

### SENATORS

Alan H. Bible (D), *Reno*
Howard W. Cannon (D), *Las Vegas*

### REPRESENTATIVE AT LARGE

Walter S. Baring (D), *Reno*

## NEW HAMPSHIRE

### SENATORS

H. Styles Bridges (R),[31] *Concord*
Maurice J. Murphy, Jr. (R),[32] *Portsmouth*
Thomas J. McIntyre (D),[33] *Laconia*
Norris Cotton (R), *Lebanon*

### REPRESENTATIVES

1 Chester E. Merrow (R), *Center Ossipee*
2 Perkins Bass (R), *Peterborough*

## NEW JERSEY

### SENATORS

Clifford P. Case (R), *Rahway*
Harrison A. Williams, Jr. (D), *Westfield*

### REPRESENTATIVES

1 William T. Cahill (R), *Collingswood*
2 Milton W. Glenn (R), *Margate City*
3 James C. Auchincloss (R), *Rumson*
4 Frank Thompson, Jr. (D), *Trenton*
5 Peter H. B. Frelinghuysen, Jr. (R), *Morristown*
6 Florence P. Dwyer (R), *Elizabeth*
7 William B. Widnall (R), *Saddle River*
8 Charles S. Joelson (D), *Paterson*
9 Frank C. Osmers, Jr. (R), *Tenafly*
10 Peter W. Rodino, Jr. (D), *Newark*
11 Hugh J. Addonizio (D),[34] *Newark*
12 George M. Wallhauser (R), *Maplewood*
13 Cornelius E. Gallagher (D), *Bayonne*
14 Dominick V. Daniels (D), *Jersey City*

## NEW MEXICO

### SENATORS

Dennis Chavez (D),[35] *Albuquerque*
Edwin L. Mechem (R),[36] *Las Cruces*
Clinton P. Anderson (D), *Albuquerque*

### REPRESENTATIVES AT LARGE

Joseph M. Montoya (D), *Santa Fe*
Thomas G. Morris (D), *Tucumcari*

## NEW YORK

### SENATORS

Jacob K. Javits (R), *New York City*
Kenneth B. Keating (R), *Rochester*

### REPRESENTATIVES

1 Otis G. Pike (D), *Riverhead*
2 Steven B. Derounian (R), *Roslyn*
3 Frank J. Becker (R), *Lynbrook*
4 Seymour Halpern (R), *Forest Hills*
5 Joseph P. Addabbo (D), *Ozone Park*
6 Lester Holtzman (D),[37] *Rego Park*
6 Benjamin S. Rosenthal (D),[38] *Elmhurst*
7 James J. Delaney (D), *Long Island City*
8 Victor L. Anfuso (D), *Brooklyn*
9 Eugene J. Keogh (D), *Brooklyn*
10 Edna F. Kelly (D), *Brooklyn*
11 Emanuel Celler (D), *Brooklyn*
12 Hugh L. Carey (D), *Brooklyn*
13 Abraham J. Multer (D), *Brooklyn*
14 John J. Rooney (D), *Brooklyn*
15 John H. Ray (R), *Staten Island*
16 Adam Clayton Powell, Jr. (D), *New York City*
17 John V. Lindsay (R), *New York City*
18 Alfred E. Santangelo (D), *New York City*
19 Leonard Farbstein (D), *New York City*
20 William Fitts Ryan (D), *New York City*
21 Herbert Zelenko (D), *New York City*
22 James C. Healey (D), *New York City*
23 Jacob H. Gilbert (D), *New York City*
24 Charles A. Buckley (D), *New York City*
25 Paul A. Fino (R), *New York City*
26 Edwin B. Dooley (R), *Mamaroneck*
27 Robert R. Barry (R), *Yonkers*
28 Katharine St. George (R), *Tuxedo Park*
29 J. Ernest Wharton (R), *Richmondville*
30 Leo W. O'Brien (D), *Albany*
31 Carleton J. King (R), *Saratoga Springs*
32 Samuel S. Stratton (D), *Schenectady*
33 Clarence E. Kilburn (R), *Malone*
34 Alexander Pirnie (R), *Utica*
35 R. Walter Riehlman (R), *Tully*
36 John Taber (R), *Auburn*

---

[30] Resigned November 14, 1962; vacancy throughout remainder of the Congress.
[31] Died November 26, 1961.
[32] Appointed to fill vacancy caused by death of Styles Bridges, and took his seat January 10, 1962.
[33] Elected November 6, 1962, to fill vacancy caused by death of Styles Bridges, but was unable to be sworn in as Congress was not in session.
[34] Resigned June 30, 1962; vacancy throughout remainder of the Congress.
[35] Died November 18, 1962.
[36] Appointed November 30, 1962, to fill vacancy caused by death of Dennis Chavez, and took his seat January 9, 1963.
[37] Resigned December 31, 1961.
[38] Elected to fill vacancy caused by resignation of Lester Holtzman, and took his seat February 28, 1962.

37 Howard W. Robison (R), *Owego*
38 Jessica McC. Weis (R), *Rochester*
39 Harold C. Ostertag (R), *Attica*
40 William E. Miller (R), *Olcott*
41 Thaddeus J. Dulski (D), *Buffalo*
42 John R. Pillion (R), *Hamburg*
43 Charles E. Goodell (R),
   *Jamestown*

## NORTH CAROLINA

SENATORS

Sam J. Ervin, Jr. (D), *Morganton*
B. Everett Jordan (D), *Saxapahaw*

REPRESENTATIVES

1 Herbert C. Bonner (D),
   *Washington*
2 L. H. Fountain (D), *Tarboro*
3 David N. Henderson (D), *Wallace*
4 Harold D. Cooley (D), *Nashville*
5 Ralph J. Scott (D), *Danbury*
6 Horace R. Kornegay (D),
   *Greensboro*
7 Alton A. Lennon (D), *Wilmington*
8 A. Paul Kitchin (D), *Wadesboro*
9 Hugh Q. Alexander (D),
   *Kannapolis*
10 Charles Raper Jonas (R),
   *Lincolnton*
11 Basil L. Whitener (D), *Gastonia*
12 Roy A. Taylor (D), *Black
   Mountain*

## NORTH DAKOTA

SENATORS

Milton R. Young (R), *La Moure*
Quentin N. Burdick (D), *Fargo*

REPRESENTATIVES AT LARGE

Don L. Short (R), *Medora*
Hjalmar C. Nygaard (R), *Enderlin*

## OHIO

SENATORS

Frank J. Lausche (D), *Cleveland*
Stephen M. Young (D), *Cleveland*

REPRESENTATIVES

1 Gordon H. Scherer (R), *Cincinnati*
2 Donald D. Clancy (R), *Cincinnati*
3 Paul F. Schenck (R), *Dayton*
4 William M. McCulloch (R), *Piqua*
5 Delbert L. Latta (R), *Bowling
   Green*
6 William H. Harsha, Jr. (R),
   *Portsmouth*
7 Clarence J. Brown (R),
   *Blanchester*
8 Jackson E. Betts (R), *Findlay*
9 Thomas L. Ashley (D), *Waterville*
10 Walter H. Moeller (D), *Lancaster*
11 Robert E. Cook (D),[39] *Ravenna*

12 Samuel L. Devine (R), *Columbus*
13 Charles A. Mosher (R), *Oberlin*
14 William H. Ayres (R), *Akron*
15 Tom V. Moorehead (R), *Zanesville*
16 Frank T. Bow (R), *Canton*
17 John M. Ashbrook (R), *Johnstown*
18 Wayne L. Hays (D), *Flushing*
19 Michael J. Kirwan (D),
   *Youngstown*
20 Michael A. Feighan (D), *Cleveland*
21 Charles A. Vanik (D), *Cleveland*
22 Frances P. Bolton (R), *Lyndhurst*
23 William E. Minshall (R),
   *Lakewood*

## OKLAHOMA

SENATORS

Robert S. Kerr (D),[40] *Oklahoma City*
A. S. Mike Monroney (D), *Oklahoma
City*

REPRESENTATIVES

1 Page H. Belcher (R), *Enid*
2 Edmond Edmondson (D),
   *Muskogee*
3 Carl Albert (D), *McAlester*
4 Thomas J. Steed (D), *Shawnee*
5 John Jarman (D), *Oklahoma City*
6 Victor Wickersham (D), *Mangum*

## OREGON

SENATORS

Wayne L. Morse (D), *Eugene*
Maurine B. Neuberger (D), *Portland*

REPRESENTATIVES

1 A. Walter Norblad (R), *Stayton*
2 Albert C. Ullman (D), *Baker*
3 Edith S. Green (D), *Portland*
4 Edwin R. Durno (R), *Medford*

## PENNSYLVANIA

SENATORS

Joseph S. Clark (D), *Philadelphia*
Hugh D. Scott, Jr. (R), *Philadelphia*

REPRESENTATIVES

1 William A. Barrett (D),
   *Philadelphia*
2 Kathryn E. Granahan (D),
   *Philadelphia*
3 James A. Byrne (D), *Philadelphia*
4 Robert N. C. Nix (D),
   *Philadelphia*
5 William J. Greene, Jr. (D),
   *Philadelphia*
6 Herman Toll (D), *Philadelphia*
7 William H. Milliken, Jr. (R),
   *Sharon Hill*
8 Willard S. Curtin (R), *Morrisville*
9 Paul B. Dague (R), *Downingtown*
10 William W. Scranton (R), *Dalton*

11 Daniel J. Flood (D), *Wilkes-Barre*
12 Ivor D. Fenton (R), *Mahanoy City*
13 Richard S. Schweiker (R),
   *Lansdale*
14 George M. Rhodes (D), *Reading*
15 Francis E. Walter (D), *Easton*
16 Walter M. Mumma (R),[41]
   *Harrisburg*
16 John C. Kunkel (R),[42] *Harrisburg*
17 Herman T. Schneebeli (R),
   *Williamsport*
18 J. Irving Whalley (R), *Windber*
19 George A. Goodling (R),
   *Loganville*
20 James E. Van Zandt (R), *Altoona*
21 John H. Dent (D), *Jeannette*
22 John P. Saylor (R), *Johnstown*
23 Leon H. Gavin (R), *Oil City*
24 Carroll D. Kearns (R), *Farrell*
25 Frank M. Clark (D), *Bessemer*
26 Thomas E. Morgan (D),
   *Fredericktown*
27 James G. Fulton (R), *Pittsburgh*
28 William S. Moorhead (D),
   *Pittsburgh*
29 Robert J. Corbett (R), *Pittsburgh*
30 Elmer J. Holland (D), *Pittsburgh*

## RHODE ISLAND

SENATORS

John O. Pastore (D), *Cranston*
Claiborne Pell (D), *Newport*

REPRESENTATIVES

1 Fernand J. St Germain (D),
   *Woonsocket*
2 John E. Fogarty (D), *Harmony*

## SOUTH CAROLINA

SENATORS

Olin D. Johnston (D), *Spartanburg*
Strom Thurmond (D), *Aiken*

REPRESENTATIVES

1 L. Mendel Rivers (D), *Charleston*
2 John J. Riley (D),[43] *Sumter*
2 Corinne B. Riley (D),[44] *Sumter*
3 W. J. Bryan Dorn (D), *Greenwood*
4 Robert T. Ashmore (D), *Greenville*
5 Robert W. Hemphill (D), *Chester*
6 John L. McMillan (D), *Florence*

## SOUTH DAKOTA

SENATORS

Karl E. Mundt (R), *Madison*
Francis H. Case (R),[45] *Custer*
Joseph H. Bottum (R),[46] *Rapid City*

REPRESENTATIVES

1 Benjamin Reifel (R), *Aberdeen*
2 E. Y. Berry (R), *McLaughlin*

---

[39] Resigned December 13, 1962; vacancy through-out remainder of the Congress.
[40] Died January 1, 1963; vacancy throughout remainder of the Congress.
[41] Died February 25, 1961.

[42] Elected to fill vacancy caused by death of Walter M. Mumma, and took his seat May 22, 1961.
[43] Died January 1, 1962.
[44] Elected to fill vacancy caused by death of her husband, John J. Riley, and took her seat April 12, 1962.

[45] Died June 22, 1962.
[46] Appointed to fill vacancy caused by death of Francis H. Case, and took his seat July 11, 1962.

## TENNESSEE

### SENATORS

Estes Kefauver (D), *Lookout Mountain*
Albert A. Gore (D), *Carthage*

### REPRESENTATIVES

1 B. Carroll Reece (R),[47] *Johnson City*
1 Louise G. Reece (R),[48] *Johnson City*
2 Howard H. Baker (R), *Huntsville*
3 James B. Frazier, Jr. (D), *Chattanooga*
4 Joseph L. Evins (D), *Smithville*
5 J. Carlton Loser (D), *Nashville*
6 Ross Bass (D), *Pulaski*
7 Thomas J. Murray (D), *Jackson*
8 Robert A. Everett (D), *Union City*
9 Clifford Davis (D), *Memphis*

## TEXAS

### SENATORS

Lyndon B. Johnson (D),[49] *Johnson City*
William A. Blakley (D),[50] *Dallas*
John G. Tower (R),[51] *Wichita Falls*
Ralph W. Yarborough (D), *Austin*

### REPRESENTATIVES

1 Wright Patman (D), *Texarkana*
2 Jack B. Brooks (D), *Beaumont*
3 Lindley G. Beckworth (D), *Gladewater*
4 Sam Rayburn (D),[52] *Bonham*
4 H. Ray Roberts (D),[53] *McKinney*
5 Bruce R. Alger (R), *Dallas*
6 Olin E. Teague (D), *College Station*
7 John V. Dowdy (D), *Athens*
8 Albert Thomas (D), *Houston*
9 Clark W. Thompson (D), *Galveston*
10 W. Homer Thornberry (D), *Austin*
11 W. R. Poage (D), *Waco*
12 James C. Wright, Jr. (D), *Fort Worth*
13 Frank N. Ikard (D),[54] *Wichita Falls*
13 Graham B. Purcell, Jr. (D),[55] *Wichita Falls*
14 John A. Young (D), *Corpus Christi*
15 Joe M. Kilgore (D), *McAllen*
16 J. T. Rutherford (D), *Odessa*
17 Omar T. Burleson (D), *Anson*
18 Walter E. Rogers (D), *Pampa*
19 George H. Mahon (D), *Lubbock*
20 Paul J. Kilday (D),[56] *San Antonio*
20 Henry B. Gonzalez (D),[57] *San Antonio*
21 O. Clark Fisher (D), *San Angelo*
22 Robert R. Casey (D), *Houston*

## UTAH

### SENATORS

Wallace F. Bennett (R), *Salt Lake City*
Frank E. Moss (D), *Salt Lake City*

### REPRESENTATIVES

1 M. Blaine Peterson (D), *Ogden*
2 David S. King (D), *Salt Lake City*

## VERMONT

### SENATORS

George D. Aiken (R), *Putney*
Winston L. Prouty (R), *Newport*

### REPRESENTATIVE AT LARGE

Robert T. Stafford (R), *Rutland City*

## VIRGINIA

### SENATORS

Harry Flood Byrd (D), *Berryville*
A. Willis Robertson (D), *Lexington*

### REPRESENTATIVES

1 Thomas N. Downing (D), *Newport News*
2 Porter Hardy, Jr. (D), *Churchland*
3 J. Vaughan Gary (D), *Richmond*
4 Watkins M. Abbitt (D), *Appomattox*
5 William M. Tuck (D), *South Boston*
6 Richard H. Poff (R), *Radford*
7 Burr P. Harrison (D), *Winchester*
8 Howard W. Smith (D), *Broad Run*
9 W. Pat Jennings (D), *Marion*
10 Joel T. Broyhill (R), *Arlington*

## WASHINGTON

### SENATORS

Warren G. Magnuson (D), *Seattle*
Henry M. Jackson (D), *Everett*

### REPRESENTATIVES

1 Thomas M. Pelly (R), *Bainbridge Island*
2 Alfred John (Jack) Westland (R), *Everett*
3 Julia Butler Hansen (D), *Cathlamet*
4 Catherine D. May (R), *Yakima*
5 Walter F. Horan (R), *Wenatchee*
6 Thor C. Tollefson (R), *Tacoma*
7 Donald H. Magnuson (D), *Seattle*

## WEST VIRGINIA

### SENATORS

Jennings Randolph (D), *Elkins*
Robert C. Byrd (D), *Sophia*

### REPRESENTATIVES

1 Arch A. Moore, Jr. (R), *Glendale*
2 Harley O. Staggers (D), *Keyser*
3 Cleveland M. Bailey (D), *Clarksburg*
4 Ken Hechler (D), *Huntington*
5 M. Elizabeth Kee (D), *Bluefield*
6 John M. Slack, Jr. (D), *Charleston*

## WISCONSIN

### SENATORS

Alexander Wiley (R), *Chippewa Falls*
William Proxmire (D), *Madison*

### REPRESENTATIVES

1 Henry C. Schadeberg (R), *Burlington*
2 Robert W. Kastenmeier (D), *Watertown*
3 Vernon W. Thomson (R), *Richland Center*
4 Clement J. Zablocki (D), *Milwaukee*
5 Henry S. Reuss (D), *Milwaukee*
6 William K. Van Pelt (R), *Fond du Lac*
7 Melvin R. Laird (R), *Marshfield*
8 John W. Byrnes (R), *Green Bay*
9 Lester R. Johnson (D), *Black River Falls*
10 Alvin E. O'Konski (R), *Mercer*

## WYOMING

### SENATORS

Gale W. McGee (D), *Laramie*
J. J. Hickey (D),[58] *Cheyenne*
Milward L. Simpson (R),[59] *Cody*

### REPRESENTATIVE AT LARGE

William Henry Harrison (R), *Sheridan*

## COMMONWEALTH OF PUERTO RICO

### RESIDENT COMMISSIONER

Antonio Fernós-Isern (PD), *Santurce*

---

[47] Died March 19, 1961.
[48] Elected to fill vacancy caused by death of her husband, B. Carroll Reece, and took her seat May 23, 1961.
[49] Resigned January 3, 1961, having been elected Vice President.
[50] Appointed to fill vacancy caused by resignation of Lyndon B. Johnson, and took his seat January 3, 1961.
[51] Elected to fill vacancy caused by resignation of

Lyndon B. Johnson, and took his seat June 15, 1961.
[52] Died November 16, 1961.
[53] Elected to fill vacancy caused by death of Sam Rayburn, and took his seat February 5, 1962.
[54] Resigned December 15, 1961.
[55] Elected to fill vacancy caused by resignation of Frank N. Ikard, and took his seat January 29, 1962.
[56] Resigned September 24, 1961.
[57] Elected to fill vacancy caused by resignation of

Paul J. Kilday, and took his seat January 10, 1962.
[58] Appointed to fill vacancy caused by the death of Senator-elect E. Keith Thomson in the previous Congress, and took his seat January 3, 1961.
[59] Elected November 6, 1962, to fill vacancy caused by the death of Senator-elect E. Keith Thomson in the previous Congress, but was unable to be sworn in as Congress was not in session.

# 88TH CONGRESS

## JANUARY 3, 1963, TO JANUARY 3, 1965

FIRST SESSION— *January 9, 1963,*[1] to December 30, 1963
SECOND SESSION— *January 7, 1964,*[2] to October 3, 1964

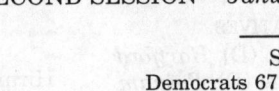

### Senate
Democrats 67 — Republicans 33

VICE PRESIDENT OF THE UNITED STATES— LYNDON B. JOHNSON,[3] of Texas
PRESIDENT PRO TEMPORE OF THE SENATE— CARL HAYDEN, of Arizona
SECRETARY OF THE SENATE— FELTON MCLELLAN JOHNSTON, of Mississippi
SERGEANT AT ARMS OF THE SENATE— JOSEPH C. DUKE, of Arizona
MAJORITY FLOOR LEADER— MIKE MANSFIELD, of Montana
DEMOCRATIC WHIP— HUBERT H. HUMPHREY, of Minnesota
REPUBLICAN FLOOR LEADER— EVERETT MCKINLEY DIRKSEN, of Illinois
ASSISTANT REPUBLICAN LEADER— THOMAS H. KUCHEL, of California

Lyndon B. Johnson
Vice President

John W. McCormack
Speaker

### House of Representatives
Democrats 258 — Republicans 177

SPEAKER OF THE HOUSE OF REPRESENTATIVES— JOHN W. MCCORMACK,[4] of Massachusetts
CLERK OF THE HOUSE— RALPH R. ROBERTS,[5] of Indiana
SERGEANT AT ARMS OF THE HOUSE— ZEAKE W. JOHNSON, JR.,[6] of Tennessee
DOORKEEPER OF THE HOUSE— WILLIAM M. MILLER,[7] of Mississippi
POSTMASTER OF THE HOUSE— H. H. MORRIS,[8] of Kentucky
MAJORITY LEADER— CARL ALBERT, of Oklahoma
MAJORITY WHIP— HALE BOGGS, of Louisiana
REPUBLICAN LEADER— CHARLES A. HALLECK, of Indiana
REPUBLICAN WHIP— LESLIE C. ARENDS, of Illinois

## ALABAMA

### SENATORS
Lister Hill (D), *Montgomery*
John J. Sparkman (D), *Huntsville*

### REPRESENTATIVES AT LARGE
George M. Grant (D), *Troy*
George W. Andrews (D), *Union
Springs*
Kenneth A. Roberts (D), *Anniston*
Albert Rains (D), *Gadsden*
Armistead I. Selden, Jr. (D),
*Greensboro*
Carl A. Elliott (D), *Jasper*
Robert E. Jones (D), *Scottsboro*
George Huddleston, Jr. (D),
*Birmingham*

## ALASKA

### SENATORS
E. L. (Bob) Bartlett (D), *Juneau*

Ernest Gruening (D), *Juneau*

### REPRESENTATIVE AT LARGE
Ralph J. Rivers (D), *Fairbanks*

## ARIZONA

### SENATORS
Carl Hayden (D), *Phoenix*
Barry M. Goldwater (R), *Phoenix*

### REPRESENTATIVES
1 John J. Rhodes (R), *Mesa*
2 Morris K. Udall (D), *Tucson*
3 George F. Senner, Jr. (D), *Miami*

## ARKANSAS

### SENATORS
John L. McClellan (D), *Camden*
J. William Fulbright (D), *Fayetteville*

### REPRESENTATIVES
1 E. C. Gathings (D), *West Memphis*
2 Wilbur D. Mills (D), *Kensett*
3 James W. Trimble (D), *Berryville*
4 Oren Harris (D), *El Dorado*

## CALIFORNIA

### SENATORS
Thomas H. Kuchel (R), *Anaheim*
Clair Engle (D),[9] *Red Bluff*
Pierre Salinger (D),[10] *San Francisco*
George L. Murphy (R),[11] *Beverly Hills*

### REPRESENTATIVES
1 Don H. Clausen (R),[12] *Crescent
City*
2 Harold T. Johnson (D), *Roseville*
3 John E. Moss, Jr. (D), *Sacramento*
4 Robert L. Leggett (D), *Vallejo*

[1] By joint resolution (Pub. Law 864, 87th Cong., 2d sess.), the date of assembling the first session of the Eighty-eighth Congress was fixed for January 9, 1963.

[2] By joint resolution (Pub. Law 247, 88th Cong., 1st sess.), the date of assembling the second session of the Eighty-eighth Congress was fixed for January 7, 1964.

[3] Lyndon B. Johnson became President on the death of John F. Kennedy November 22, 1963.

[4] Reelected January 9, 1963.
[5] Reelected January 9, 1963.
[6] Reelected January 9, 1963.
[7] Reelected January 9, 1963.
[8] Reelected January 9, 1963.
[9] Died July 30, 1964.
[10] Appointed to fill vacancy caused by death of Clair Engle, and took his seat August 5, 1964; resigned December 31, 1964. (See U.S. Senate Election, Expul-

sion and Censure Cases, 1793-1990, Senate Document 103-33, pp. 411-12.)

[11] Appointed January 1, 1965, to fill vacancy caused by resignation of Pierre Salinger.

[12] Elected to fill vacancy caused by death of Rep. Clement L. Miller. Rep. Miller had died a month before the election but had been posthumously elected to the Eighty-eighth Congress. Rep. Clausen was elected January 22, 1963, and took his seat January 28, 1963.

## CALIFORNIA—Continued

REPRESENTATIVES—CONTINUED

5 John F. Shelley (D),[13] *San Francisco*
5 Phillip Burton (D),[14] *San Francisco*
6 William S. Mailliard (R), *San Francisco*
7 Jeffery Cohelan (D), *Berkeley*
8 George P. Miller (D), *Alameda*
9 Don Edwards (D), *San Jose*
10 Charles S. Gubser (R), *Gilroy*
11 J. Arthur Younger (R), *San Mateo*
12 Burt L. Talcott (R), *Salinas*
13 Charles M. Teague (R), *Ojai*
14 John F. Baldwin (R), *Martinez*
15 John J. McFall (D), *Manteca*
16 B. F. Sisk (D), *Fresno*
17 Cecil R. King (D), *Los Angeles*
18 Harlan F. Hagen (D), *Hanford*
19 Chet Holifield (D), *Montebello*
20 H. Allen Smith (R), *Glendale*
21 Augustus F. Hawkins (D), *Los Angeles*
22 James C. Corman (D), *Van Nuys*
23 Clyde G. Doyle (D),[15] *South Gate*
23 Del M. Clawson (R),[16] *Compton*
24 Glenard P. Lipscomb (R), *Los Angeles*
25 Ronald Brooks Cameron (D), *Whittier*
26 James Roosevelt (D), *Los Angeles*
27 Everett G. Burkhalter (D), *North Hollywood*
28 Alphonzo Bell (R), *Beverly Hills*
29 George E. Brown, Jr. (D), *Monterey Park*
30 Edward R. Roybal (D), *Los Angeles*
31 Charles H. Wilson (D), *Los Angeles*
32 Craig Hosmer (R), *Long Beach*
33 Harry R. Sheppard (D), *Yucaipa*
34 Richard T. Hanna (D), *Fullerton*
35 James B. Utt (R), *Santa Ana*
36 Robert C. Wilson (R), *San Diego*
37 Lionel Van Deerlin (D), *San Diego*
38 Pat Minor Martin (R), *Riverside*

## COLORADO

SENATORS

Gordon L. Allott (R), *Lamar*
Peter H. Dominick (R), *Englewood*

REPRESENTATIVES

1 Byron G. Rogers (D), *Denver*
2 Donald G. Brotzman (R), *Boulder*
3 J. Edgar Chenoweth (R), *Trinidad*
4 Wayne N. Aspinall (D), *Palisade*

## CONNECTICUT

SENATORS

Thomas J. Dodd (D), *North Stonington*
Abraham A. Ribicoff (D), *Hartford*

REPRESENTATIVE AT LARGE

Bernard F. Grabowski (D), *Bristol*

REPRESENTATIVES

1 Emilio Q. Daddario (D), *Hartford*
2 William L. St. Onge (D), *Putnam*
3 Robert N. Giaimo (D), *North Haven*
4 Abner W. Sibal (R), *Norwalk*
5 John S. Monagan (D), *Waterbury*

## DELAWARE

SENATORS

John J. Williams (R), *Millsboro*
J. Caleb Boggs (R), *Wilmington*

REPRESENTATIVE AT LARGE

Harris B. McDowell, Jr. (D), *Middletown*

## FLORIDA

SENATORS

Spessard L. Holland (D), *Bartow*
George A. Smathers (D), *Miami*

REPRESENTATIVES

1 Robert L. F. Sikes (D), *Crestview*
2 Charles E. Bennett (D), *Jacksonville*
3 Claude D. Pepper (D), *Coral Gables*
4 Dante B. Fascell (D), *Miami*
5 A. Sydney Herlong, Jr. (D), *Leesburg*
6 Paul G. Rogers (D), *West Palm Beach*
7 James A. Haley (D), *Sarasota*
8 D. R. (Billy) Matthews (D), *Gainesville*
9 Don Fuqua (D), *Altha*
10 Sam M. Gibbons (D), *Tampa*
11 Edward J. Gurney (R), *Winter Park*
12 William C. Cramer (R), *St. Petersburg*

## GEORGIA

SENATORS

Richard B. Russell (D), *Winder*
Herman E. Talmadge (D), *Lovejoy*

REPRESENTATIVES

1 G. Elliott Hagan (D), *Sylvania*
2 John L. Pilcher (D), *Meigs*
3 E. L. Forrester (D), *Leesburg*
4 John J. Flynt, Jr. (D), *Griffin*
5 Charles L. Weltner (D), *Atlanta*
6 Carl Vinson (D), *Milledgeville*
7 John W. Davis (D), *Summerville*
8 J. Russell Tuten (D), *Brunswick*
9 Phillip M. Landrum (D), *Jasper*
10 Robert G. Stephens, Jr. (D), *Athens*

## HAWAII

SENATORS

Hiram L. Fong (R), *Honolulu*
Daniel K. Inouye (D), *Honolulu*

REPRESENTATIVES AT LARGE

Thomas P. Gill (D), *Honolulu*
Spark M. Matsunaga (D), *Honolulu*

## IDAHO

SENATORS

Frank Church (D), *Boise*
Len B. Jordan (R), *Boise*

REPRESENTATIVES

1 Compton I. White, Jr. (D), *Clark Fork*
2 Ralph R. Harding (D), *Blackfoot*

## ILLINOIS

SENATORS

Paul H. Douglas (D), *Chicago*
Everett McKinley Dirksen (R), *Pekin*

REPRESENTATIVES

1 William L. Dawson (D), *Chicago*
2 Barratt O'Hara (D), *Chicago*
3 William T. Murphy (D), *Chicago*
4 Edward J. Derwinski (R), *South Holland*
5 John C. Kluczynski (D), *Chicago*
6 Thomas J. O'Brien (D),[17] *Chicago*
7 Roland V. Libonati (R), *Chicago*
8 Dan Rostenkowski (D), *Chicago*
9 Edward R. Finnegan (D),[18] *Chicago*
10 Harold R. Collier (R), *Berwyn*
11 Roman C. Pucinski (D), *Chicago*
12 Robert McClory (R), *Lake Bluff*
13 Donald Rumsfeld (R), *Glenview*
14 Elmer J. Hoffman (R), *Wheaton*
15 Charlotte T. Reid (R), *Aurora*
16 John B. Anderson (R), *Rockford*
17 Leslie C. Arends (R), *Melvin*
18 Robert H. Michel (R), *Peoria*
19 Robert T. McLoskey (R), *Monmouth*
20 Paul Findley (R), *Pittsfield*
21 Kenneth J. Gray (D), *West Frankfort*
22 William L. Springer (R), *Champaign*
23 George E. Shipley (D), *Olney*
24 Melvin Price (D), *East St. Louis*

[13] Resigned January 7, 1964.
[14] Elected to fill vacancy caused by resignation of John F. Shelley, and took his seat February 25, 1964.
[15] Died March 14, 1963.

[16] Elected to fill vacancy caused by death of Clyde G. Doyle, and took his seat June 11, 1963.
[17] Died April 14, 1964; vacancy throughout remainder of the Congress.

[18] Resigned December 6, 1964; vacancy throughout remainder of the Congress.

## INDIANA

### SENATORS

Vance Hartke (D), *Evansville*
Birch E. Bayh (D), *Terre Haute*

### REPRESENTATIVES

1 Ray J. Madden (D), *Gary*
2 Charles A. Halleck (R), *Rensselaer*
3 John Brademas (D), *South Bend*
4 E. Ross Adair (R), *Fort Wayne*
5 J. Edward Roush (D), *Huntington*
6 Richard L. Roudebush (R), *Noblesville*
7 William G. Bray (R), *Martinsville*
8 Winfield K. Denton (D), *Evansville*
9 Earl Wilson (R), *Bedford*
10 Ralph Harvey (R), *New Castle*
11 Donald C. Bruce (R), *Indianapolis*

## IOWA

### SENATORS

Bourke B. Hickenlooper (R), *Cedar Rapids*
Jack R. Miller (R), *Sioux City*

### REPRESENTATIVES

1 Frederic D. Schwengel (R), *Davenport*
2 James E. Bromwell (R), *Cedar Rapids*
3 H. R. Gross (R), *Waterloo*
4 John H. Kyl (R), *Bloomfield*
5 Neal Smith (D), *Altoona*
6 Charles B. Hoeven (R), *Alton*
7 Ben F. Jensen (R), *Exira*

## KANSAS

### SENATORS

Frank Carlson (R), *Concordia*
James B. Pearson (R), *Prairie Village*

### REPRESENTATIVES

1 Robert J. Dole (R), *Russell*
2 William H. Avery (R), *Wakefield*
3 Robert F. Ellsworth (R), *Lawrence*
4 Garner E. Shriver (R), *Wichita*
5 Joe Skubitz (R), *Pittsburg*

## KENTUCKY

### SENATORS

John Sherman Cooper (R), *Somerset*
Thruston B. Morton (R), *Louisville*

### REPRESENTATIVES

1 Frank A. Stubblefield (D), *Murray*
2 William H. Natcher (D), *Bowling Green*
3 M. G. (Gene) Snyder (R), *Jeffersontown*
4 Frank L. Chelf (D), *Lebanon*
5 Eugene Siler (R), *Williamsburg*
6 John C. Watts (D), *Nicholasville*
7 Carl D. Perkins (D), *Hindman*

## LOUISIANA

### SENATORS

Allen J. Ellender (D), *Houma*
Russell B. Long (D), *Baton Rouge*

### REPRESENTATIVES

1 F. Edward Hébert (D), *New Orleans*
2 Hale Boggs (D), *New Orleans*
3 Edwin E. Willis (D), *St. Martinville*
4 Joe D. Waggonner, Jr. (D), *Plain Dealing*
5 Otto E. Passman (D), *Monroe*
6 James H. Morrison (D), *Hammond*
7 T. Ashton Thompson (D), *Ville Platte*
8 Gillis W. Long (D), *Winnfield*

## MAINE

### SENATORS

Margaret Chase Smith (R), *Skowhegan*
Edmund S. Muskie (D), *Waterville*

### REPRESENTATIVES

1 Stanley R. Tupper (R), *Boothbay Harbor*
2 Clifford G. McIntire (R), *Perham*

## MARYLAND

### SENATORS

J. Glenn Beall (R), *Frostburg*
Daniel B. Brewster (D), *Towson*

### REPRESENTATIVE AT LARGE

Carlton R. Sickles (D), *Lanham*

### REPRESENTATIVES

1 Rogers C. B. Morton (R), *Easton*
2 Clarence D. Long (D), *Ruxton*
3 Edward A. Garmatz (D), *Baltimore*
4 George H. Fallon (D), *Baltimore*
5 Richard E. Lankford (D), *Annapolis*
6 Charles McC. Mathias, Jr. (R), *Frederick*
7 Samuel N. Friedel (D), *Baltimore*

## MASSACHUSETTS

### SENATORS

Leverett Saltonstall (R), *Dover*
Edward M. Kennedy (D), *Boston*

### REPRESENTATIVES

1 Silvio O. Conte (R), *Pittsfield*
2 Edward P. Boland (D), *Springfield*
3 Philip J. Philbin (D), *Clinton*
4 Harold D. Donohue (D), *Worcester*
5 F. Bradford Morse (R), *Lowell*
6 William H. Bates (R), *Salem*
7 Torbert H. Macdonald (D), *Malden*
8 Thomas P. O'Neill, Jr. (D), *Cambridge*
9 John W. McCormack (D), *Dorchester*
10 Joseph W. Martin, Jr. (R), *North Attleboro*
11 James A. Burke (D), *Milton*
12 Hastings Keith (R), *West Bridgewater*

## MICHIGAN

### SENATORS

Patrick V. McNamara (D), *Detroit*
Philip A. Hart (D), *Mackinac Island*

### REPRESENTATIVE AT LARGE

Neil Staebler (D), *Ann Arbor*

### REPRESENTATIVES

1 Lucien N. Nedzi (D), *Detroit*
2 George Meader (R), *Ann Arbor*
3 August E. Johansen (R), *Battle Creek*
4 Edward Hutchinson (R), *Fennville*
5 Gerald R. Ford, Jr. (R), *Grand Rapids*
6 Charles E. Chamberlain (R), *East Lansing*
7 James G. O'Hara (D), *Utica*
8 James Harvey (R), *Saginaw*
9 Robert P. Griffin (R), *Traverse City*
10 Elford A. Cederberg (R), *Bay City*
11 Victor A. Knox (R), *Sault Ste. Marie*
12 John B. Bennett (R),[19] *Ontonagon*
13 Charles C. Diggs, Jr. (D), *Detroit*
14 Harold M. Ryan (D), *Detroit*
15 John D. Dingell, Jr. (D), *Detroit*
16 John Lesinski (D), *Dearborn*
17 Martha W. Griffiths (D), *Detroit*
18 William S. Broomfield (R), *Royal Oak*

## MINNESOTA

### SENATORS

Hubert H. Humphrey (D),[20] *Waverly*
Walter F. Mondale (D),[21] *Minneapolis*
Eugene J. McCarthy (D), *St. Paul*

### REPRESENTATIVES

1 Albert H. Quie (R), *Dennison*
2 Ancher Nelsen (R), *Hutchinson*
3 Clark MacGregor (R), *Plymouth Village*
4 Joseph E. Karth (D), *St. Paul*
5 Donald M. Fraser (D), *Minneapolis*
6 Alec G. Olson (D),[22] *Montevideo*
7 Odin Langen (R), *Kennedy*
8 John A. Blatnik (D), *Chisholm*

---

[19] Died August 9, 1964; vacancy throughout remainder of the Congress.
[20] Resigned December 29, 1964, having been elected Vice President.
[21] Appointed December 30, 1964, to fill vacancy caused by resignation of Hubert H. Humphrey.
[22] Election unsuccessfully contested by Robert J. Odegard.

## MISSISSIPPI

### SENATORS

James O. Eastland (D), *Doddsville*
John C. Stennis (D), *De Kalb*

### REPRESENTATIVES

1 Thomas G. Abernethy (D), *Okolona*
2 Jamie L. Whitten (D), *Charleston*
3 John Bell Williams (D), *Raymond*
4 W. Arthur Winstead (D), *Philadelphia*
5 William M. Colmer (D), *Pascagoula*

## MISSOURI

### SENATORS

Stuart Symington (D), *Richmond Heights*
Edward V. Long (D), *Clarksville*

### REPRESENTATIVES

1 Frank M. Karsten (D), *St. Louis*
2 Thomas B. Curtis (R), *Webster Groves*
3 Leonor Kretzer Sullivan (D), *St. Louis*
4 William J. Randall (D), *Independence*
5 Richard W. Bolling (D), *Kansas City*
6 William R. Hull, Jr. (D), *Weston*
7 Durward G. (Doc) Hall (R), *Springfield*
8 Richard H. Ichord (D), *Houston*
9 Clarence Cannon (D),[23] *Elsberry*
9 William L. Hungate (D),[24] *Troy*
10 Paul C. Jones (D), *Kennett*

## MONTANA

### SENATORS

Mike Mansfield (D), *Missoula*
Lee Metcalf (D), *Helena*

### REPRESENTATIVES

1 Arnold Olsen (D), *Helena*
2 James F. Battin (R), *Billings*

## NEBRASKA

### SENATORS

Roman L. Hruska (R), *Omaha*
Carl T. Curtis (R), *Minden*

### REPRESENTATIVES

1 Ralph F. Beermann (R), *Dakota City*
2 Glenn C. Cunningham (R), *Omaha*
3 David T. Martin (R), *Kearney*

## NEVADA

### SENATORS

Alan H. Bible (D), *Reno*
Howard W. Cannon (D), *Las Vegas*

### REPRESENTATIVE AT LARGE

Walter S. Baring (D), *Reno*

## NEW HAMPSHIRE

### SENATORS

Norris Cotton (R), *Lebanon*
Thomas J. McIntyre (D), *Laconia*

### REPRESENTATIVES

1 Louis C. Wyman (R), *Manchester*
2 James C. Cleveland (R), *New London*

## NEW JERSEY

### SENATORS

Clifford P. Case (R), *Rahway*
Harrison A. Williams, Jr. (D), *Westfield*

### REPRESENTATIVES

1 William T. Cahill (R), *Collingswood*
2 Milton W. Glenn (R), *Margate*
3 James C. Auchincloss (R), *Rumson*
4 Frank Thompson, Jr. (D), *Trenton*
5 Peter H. B. Frelinghuysen, Jr. (R), *Morristown*
6 Florence P. Dwyer (R), *Elizabeth*
7 William B. Widnall (R), *Saddle River*
8 Charles S. Joelson (D), *Paterson*
9 Frank C. Osmers, Jr. (R), *Tenafly*
10 Peter W. Rodino, Jr. (D), *Newark*
11 Joseph G. Minish (D), *West Orange*
12 George M. Wallhauser (R), *Maplewood*
13 Cornelius E. Gallagher (D), *Bayonne*
14 Dominick V. Daniels (D), *Jersey City*
15 Edward J. Patten (D), *Perth Amboy*

## NEW MEXICO

### SENATORS

Clinton P. Anderson (D), *Albuquerque*
Edwin L. Mechem (R),[25] *Las Cruces*
Joseph M. Montoya (D),[26] *Santa Fe*

### REPRESENTATIVES AT LARGE

Joseph M. Montoya (D),[27] *Santa Fe*
Thomas G. Morris (D), *Tucumcari*

## NEW YORK

### SENATORS

Jacob K. Javits (R), *New York City*
Kenneth B. Keating (R), *Rochester*

### REPRESENTATIVES

1 Otis G. Pike (D), *Riverhead*
2 James R. Grover, Jr. (R), *Babylon*
3 Steven B. Derounian (R), *Roslyn*
4 John W. Wydler (R), *Garden City*
5 Frank J. Becker (R), *Lynbrook*
6 Seymour Halpern (R), *Forest Hills*
7 Joseph P. Addabbo (D), *Ozone Park*
8 Benjamin S. Rosenthal (D), *Elmhurst*
9 James J. Delaney (D), *Long Island City*
10 Emanuel Celler (D), *Brooklyn*
11 Eugene J. Keogh (D), *Brooklyn*
12 Edna F. Kelly (D), *Brooklyn*
13 Abraham J. Multer (D), *Brooklyn*
14 John J. Rooney (D), *Brooklyn*
15 Hugh L. Carey (D), *Brooklyn*
16 John M. Murphy (D), *Staten Island*
17 John V. Lindsay (R), *New York City*
18 Adam Clayton Powell, Jr. (D), *New York City*
19 Leonard Farbstein (D), *New York City*
20 William Fitts Ryan (D), *New York City*
21 James C. Healey (D), *New York City*
22 Jacob H. Gilbert (D), *New York City*
23 Charles A. Buckley (D), *New York City*
24 Paul A. Fino (R), *New York City*
25 Robert R. Barry (R), *Yonkers*
26 Ogden R. Reid (R), *Purchase*
27 Katharine St. George (R), *Tuxedo Park*
28 J. Ernest Wharton (R), *Richmondville*
29 Leo W. O'Brien (D), *Albany*
30 Carleton J. King (R), *Saratoga Springs*
31 Clarence E. Kilburn (R), *Malone*
32 Alexander Pirnie (R), *Utica*
33 Howard W. Robison (R), *Owego*
34 R. Walter Riehlman (R), *Tully*
35 Samuel S. Stratton (D), *Amsterdam*
36 Frank J. Horton (R), *Rochester*
37 Harold C. Ostertag (R), *Attica*
38 Charles E. Goodell (R), *Jamestown*

---

[23] Died May 12, 1964.
[24] Elected to fill vacancy caused by death of Clarence Cannon, and took his seat November 3, 1964.
[25] Appointed November 30, 1962, to fill vacancy

caused by death of Dennis Chavez, and took his seat January 9, 1963.
[26] Elected to fill vacancy caused by death of Dennis Chavez, and took his seat November 4, 1964.

[27] Resigned November 3, 1964, having been elected to the Senate; vacancy throughout remainder of Congress.

39 John R. Pillion (R), *Lake View*
40 William E. Miller (R), *Olcott*
41 Thaddeus J. Dulski (D), *Buffalo*

## NORTH CAROLINA

SENATORS

Sam J. Ervin, Jr. (D), *Morganton*
B. Everett Jordan (D), *Saxapahaw*

REPRESENTATIVES

1 Herbert C. Bonner (D),
   *Washington*
2 L. H. Fountain (D), *Tarboro*
3 David N. Henderson (D), *Wallace*
4 Harold D. Cooley (D), *Nashville*
5 Ralph J. Scott (D), *Danbury*
6 Horace R. Kornegay (D),
   *Greensboro*
7 Alton A. Lennon (D), *Wilmington*
8 Charles Raper Jonas (R),
   *Lincolnton*
9 James T. Broyhill (R), *Lenoir*
10 Basil L. Whitener (D), *Gastonia*
11 Roy A. Taylor (D), *Black
   Mountain*

## NORTH DAKOTA

SENATORS

Milton R. Young (R), *La Moure*
Quentin N. Burdick (D), *Fargo*

REPRESENTATIVES

1 Hjalmar C. Nygaard (R),[28]
   *Enderlin*
1 Mark Andrews (R),[29] *Mapleton*
2 Don L. Short (R), *Medora*

## OHIO

SENATORS

Frank J. Lausche (D), *Cleveland*
Stephen M. Young (D), *Cleveland*

REPRESENTATIVE AT LARGE

Robert Taft, Jr. (R), *Indian Hill*

REPRESENTATIVES

1 Carl W. Rich (R), *Cincinnati*
2 Donald D. Clancy (R), *Cincinnati*
3 Paul F. Schenck (R), *Dayton*
4 William M. McCulloch (R), *Piqua*
5 Delbert L. Latta (R), *Bowling
   Green*
6 William H. Harsha, Jr. (R),
   *Portsmouth*
7 Clarence J. Brown (R),
   *Blanchester*
8 Jackson E. Betts (R), *Findlay*
9 Thomas L. Ashley (D), *Waterville*
10 Homer E. Abele (R), *McArthur*
11 Oliver P. Bolton (R), *Mentor*

12 Samuel L. Devine (R), *Columbus*
13 Charles A. Mosher (R), *Oberlin*
14 William H. Ayres (R), *Akron*
15 Robert T. Secrest (D), *Senecaville*
16 Frank T. Bow (R), *Canton*
17 John M. Ashbrook (R), *Johnstown*
18 Wayne L. Hays (D), *Flushing*
19 Michael J. Kirwan (D),
   *Youngstown*
20 Michael A. Feighan (D), *Cleveland*
21 Charles A. Vanik (D), *Cleveland*
22 Frances P. Bolton (R), *Lyndhurst*
23 William E. Minshall (R),
   *Cleveland*

## OKLAHOMA

SENATORS

A. S. Mike Monroney (D), *Oklahoma
City*
J. Howard Edmondson (D),[30]
*Oklahoma City*
Fred R. Harris (D),[31] *Lawton*

REPRESENTATIVES

1 Page H. Belcher (R), *Enid*
2 Edmond Edmondson (D),
   *Muskogee*
3 Carl Albert (D), *McAlester*
4 Thomas J. Steed (D), *Shawnee*
5 John Jarman (D), *Oklahoma City*
6 Victor Wickersham (D), *Mangum*

## OREGON

SENATORS

Wayne L. Morse (D), *Eugene*
Maurine B. Neuberger (D), *Portland*

REPRESENTATIVES

1 A. Walter Norblad (R),[32] *Stayton*
1 Wendell Wyatt (R),[33] *Astoria*
2 Albert C. Ullman (D), *Baker*
3 Edith S. Green (D), *Portland*
4 Robert B. Duncan (D), *Medford*

## PENNSYLVANIA

SENATORS

Joseph S. Clark (D), *Philadelphia*
Hugh D. Scott, Jr. (R), *Philadelphia*

REPRESENTATIVES

1 William A. Barrett (D),
   *Philadelphia*
2 Robert N. C. Nix (D),
   *Philadelphia*
3 James A. Byrne (D), *Philadelphia*
4 Herman Toll (D), *Philadelphia*
5 William J. Green, Jr. (D),[34]
   *Philadelphia*

5 William J. Green (D),[35]
   *Philadelphia*
6 George M. Rhodes (D), *Reading*
7 William H. Milliken (R), *Sharon
   Hill*
8 Willard S. Curtin (R), *Morrisville*
9 Paul B. Dague (R), *Downingtown*
10 Joseph M. McDade (R), *Scranton*
11 Daniel J. Flood (D), *Wilkes-Barre*
12 J. Irving Whalley (R), *Windber*
13 Richard S. Schweiker (R),
   *Lansdale*
14 William S. Moorhead (D),
   *Pittsburgh*
15 Francis E. Walter (D),[36] *Easton*
15 Fred B. Rooney (D),[37] *Bethlehem*
16 John C. Kunkel (R), *Harrisburg*
17 Herman T. Schneebeli (R),
   *Williamsport*
18 Robert J. Corbett (R), *Pittsburgh*
19 George A. Goodling (R),
   *Loganville*
20 Elmer J. Holland (D), *Pittsburgh*
21 John H. Dent (D), *Jeannette*
22 John P. Saylor (R), *Johnstown*
23 Leon H. Gavin (R),[38] *Oil City*
23 Albert W. Johnson (R),[39]
   *Smethport*
24 James D. Weaver (R), *Erie*
25 Frank M. Clark (D), *Bessemer*
26 Thomas E. Morgan (D),
   *Fredericktown*
27 James G. Fulton (R), *Pittsburgh*

## RHODE ISLAND

SENATORS

John O. Pastore (D), *Cranston*
Claiborne Pell (D), *Newport*

REPRESENTATIVES

1 Fernand J. St Germain (D),
   *Woonsocket*
2 John E. Fogarty (D), *Harmony*

## SOUTH CAROLINA

SENATORS

Olin D. Johnston (D), *Spartanburg*
Strom Thurmond (D),[40] *Aiken*

REPRESENTATIVES

1 L. Mendel Rivers (D), *Charleston*
2 Albert W. Watson (D), *Columbia*
3 W. J. Bryan Dorn (D), *Greenwood*
4 Robert T. Ashmore (D), *Greenville*
5 Robert W. Hemphill (D),[41] *Chester*
5 Thomas S. Gettys (D),[42] *Rock Hill*
6 John L. McMillan (D), *Florence*

---

[28] Died July 18, 1963.
[29] Elected to fill vacancy caused by death of Hjalmar C. Nygaard, and took his seat October 22, 1963.
[30] Appointed January 7, 1963, to fill vacancy caused by death of Robert S. Kerr.
[31] Elected to fill vacancy caused by death of Robert S. Kerr, and took his seat November 4, 1964.
[32] Died September 20, 1964.
[33] Elected to fill vacancy caused by death of

Walter Norblad, and took his seat November 3, 1964.
[34] Died December 21, 1963.
[35] Elected to fill vacancy caused by death of his father, William J. Green, Jr., and took his seat April 28, 1964.
[36] Died May 31, 1963.
[37] Elected to fill vacancy caused by death of Francis E. Walter, and took his seat July 30, 1963.
[38] Died September 15, 1963.

[39] Elected to fill vacancy caused by death of Leon H. Gavin, and took his seat November 5, 1963.
[40] Changed party affiliation to Republican, September 16, 1964.
[41] Resigned May 1, 1964.
[42] Elected to fill vacancy caused by resignation of Robert W. Hemphill, and took his seat November 3, 1964.

## SOUTH DAKOTA

### SENATORS

Karl E. Mundt (R), *Madison*
George S. McGovern (D), *Mitchell*

### REPRESENTATIVES

1 Benjamin Reifel (R), *Aberdeen*
2 E. Y. Berry (R), *McLaughlin*

## TENNESSEE

### SENATORS

Estes Kefauver (D),[43] *Lookout Mountain*
Herbert S. Walters (D),[44] *Morristown*
Ross Bass (D),[45] *Pulaski*
Albert A. Gore (D), *Carthage*

### REPRESENTATIVES

1 James H. Quillen (R), *Kingsport*
2 Howard H. Baker (R),[46] *Knoxville*
2 Irene Bailey Baker (R),[47] *Knoxville*
3 William E. Brock III (R), *Chattanooga*
4 Joseph L. Evins (D), *Smithville*
5 Richard H. Fulton (D), *Nashville*
6 Ross Bass (D),[48] *Pulaski*
7 Thomas J. Murray (D), *Jackson*
8 Robert A. Everett (D), *Union City*
9 Clifford Davis (D), *Memphis*

## TEXAS

### SENATORS

Ralph W. Yarborough (D), *Austin*
John G. Tower (R), *Wichita Falls*

### REPRESENTATIVE AT LARGE

Joe R. Pool (D), *Dallas*

### REPRESENTATIVES

1 Wright Patman (D), *Texarkana*
2 Jack B. Brooks (D), *Beaumont*
3 Lindley G. Beckworth (D), *Gladewater*
4 H. Ray Roberts (D), *McKinney*
5 Bruce R. Alger (R), *Dallas*
6 Olin E. Teague (D), *College Station*
7 John V. Dowdy (D), *Athens*
8 Albert Thomas (D), *Houston*
9 Clark W. Thompson (D), *Galveston*
10 W. Homer Thornberry (D),[49] *Austin*
10 J. J. (Jake) Pickle (D),[50] *Austin*
11 W. R. Poage (D), *Waco*
12 James C. Wright, Jr. (D), *Fort Worth*
13 Graham B. Purcell (D), *Wichita Falls*
14 John A. Young (D), *Corpus Christi*
15 Joe M. Kilgore (D), *McAllen*
16 Edgar F. Foreman (R), *Odessa*
17 Omar T. Burleson (D), *Anson*
18 Walter E. Rogers (D), *Pampa*
19 George H. Mahon (D), *Lubbock*
20 Henry B. Gonzalez (D), *San Antonio*
21 O. Clark Fisher (D), *San Angelo*
22 Robert R. Casey (D), *Houston*

## UTAH

### SENATORS

Wallace F. Bennett (R), *Salt Lake City*
Frank E. Moss (D), *Salt Lake City*

### REPRESENTATIVES

1 Laurence J. Burton (R), *Ogden*
2 Sherman P. Lloyd (R), *Salt Lake City*

## VERMONT

### SENATORS

George D. Aiken (R), *Putney*
Winston L. Prouty (R), *Newport*

### REPRESENTATIVE AT LARGE

Robert T. Stafford (R), *Rutland City*

## VIRGINIA

### SENATORS

Harry Flood Byrd (D), *Berryville*
A. Willis Robertson (D), *Lexington*

### REPRESENTATIVES

1 Thomas N. Downing (D), *Newport News*
2 Porter Hardy, Jr. (D), *Churchland*
3 J. Vaughan Gary (D), *Richmond*
4 Watkins M. Abbitt (D), *Appomattox*
5 William M. Tuck (D), *South Boston*
6 Richard H. Poff (R), *Radford*
7 John O. Marsh, Jr. (D), *Strasburg*
8 Howard W. Smith (D), *Broad Run*
9 W. Pat Jennings (D), *Marion*
10 Joel T. Broyhill (R), *Arlington*

## WASHINGTON

### SENATORS

Warren G. Magnuson (D), *Seattle*
Henry M. Jackson (D), *Everett*

### REPRESENTATIVES

1 Thomas M. Pelly (R), *Seattle*
2 Alfred John (Jack) Westland (R), *Everett*
3 Julia Butler Hansen (D), *Cathlamet*
4 Catherine May (R), *Yakima*
5 Walter F. Horan (R), *Wenatchee*
6 Thor C. Tollefson (R), *Tacoma*
7 K. William Stinson (R), *Bellevue*

## WEST VIRGINIA

### SENATORS

Jennings Randolph (D), *Elkins*
Robert C. Byrd (D), *Sophia*

### REPRESENTATIVES

1 Arch A. Moore, Jr. (R), *Glen Dale*
2 Harley O. Staggers (D), *Keyser*
3 John M. Slack, Jr. (D), *Charleston*
4 Ken Hechler (D), *Huntington*
5 M. Elizabeth Kee (D), *Bluefield*

## WISCONSIN

### SENATORS

William Proxmire (D), *Madison*
Gaylord A. Nelson (D), *Madison*

### REPRESENTATIVES

1 Henry C. Schadeberg (R), *Burlington*
2 Robert W. Kastenmeier (D), *Watertown*
3 Vernon W. Thomson (R), *Richland Center*
4 Clement J. Zablocki (D), *Milwaukee*
5 Henry S. Reuss (D), *Milwaukee*
6 William K. Van Pelt (R), *Fond du Lac*
7 Melvin R. Laird (R), *Marshfield*
8 John W. Byrnes (R), *Green Bay*
9 Lester R. Johnson (D), *Black River Falls*
10 Alvin E. O'Konski (R), *Mercer*

## WYOMING

### SENATORS

Gale W. McGee (D), *Laramie*
Milward L. Simpson (R), *Cody*

### REPRESENTATIVE AT LARGE

William Henry Harrison (R), *Sheridan*

## COMMONWEALTH OF PUERTO RICO

### RESIDENT COMMISSIONER

Antonio Fernós-Isern (PD), *Santurce*

---

[43] Died August 10, 1963.
[44] Appointed August 20, 1963, to fill vacancy caused by death of Estes Kefauver.
[45] Elected to fill vacancy caused by death of Estes Kefauver, and took his seat November 4, 1964.

[46] Died January 7, 1964.
[47] Elected to fill vacancy caused by death of her husband, Howard H. Baker, and took her seat March 10, 1964.
[48] Resigned November 3, 1964, having been

elected to the Senate.
[49] Resigned December 20, 1963.
[50] Elected to fill vacancy caused by resignation of Homer Thornberry, and took his seat December 21, 1963.

# 89TH CONGRESS

JANUARY 3, 1965, TO JANUARY 3, 1967

FIRST SESSION— *January 4, 1965, to October 23, 1965*
SECOND SESSION— *January 10, 1966,[1] to October 22, 1966*

---

Senate
Democrats 68 — Republicans 32

VICE PRESIDENT OF THE UNITED STATES— Hubert H. Humphrey,[2] of Minnesota

PRESIDENT PRO TEMPORE OF THE SENATE— Carl Hayden, of Arizona

SECRETARY OF THE SENATE— Felton McLellan Johnston,[3] of Mississippi; Emery L. Frazier,[4] of Kentucky; Francis R. Valeo,[5] of the District of Columbia

SERGEANT AT ARMS— Joseph C. Duke,[6] of Arizona, Robert G. Dunphy,[7] of Rhode Island

MAJORITY FLOOR LEADER— Mike Mansfield, of Montana

DEMOCRATIC WHIP— Russell B. Long, of Louisiana

REPUBLICAN FLOOR LEADER— Everett McKinley Dirksen, of Illinois

ASSISTANT REPUBLICAN LEADER— Thomas H. Kuchel, of California

Hubert H. Humphrey
Vice President

John W. McCormack
Speaker

House of Representatives
Democrats 295 — Republicans 140

SPEAKER OF THE HOUSE— John W. McCormack,[8] of Massachusetts

CLERK OF THE HOUSE— Ralph R. Roberts,[9] of Indiana

SERGEANT AT ARMS OF THE HOUSE— Zeake W. Johnson,[10] of Tennessee

DOORKEEPER OF THE HOUSE— William M. Miller,[11] of Mississippi

POSTMASTER OF THE HOUSE— H. H. Morris,[12] of Kentucky

MAJORITY LEADER— Carl Albert, of Oklahoma

MAJORITY WHIP— Hale Boggs, of Louisiana

REPUBLICAN LEADER— Gerald R. Ford, Jr., of Michigan

REPUBLICAN WHIP— Leslie C. Arends, of Illinois

---

## ALABAMA

SENATORS

Lister Hill (D), *Montgomery*
John J. Sparkman (D), *Huntsville*

REPRESENTATIVES

1 Jack Edwards (R), *Mobile*
2 William L. Dickinson (R), *Montgomery*
3 George W. Andrews (D), *Union Springs*
4 Glenn Andrews (R), *Anniston*
5 Armistead I. Selden, Jr. (D), *Greensboro*
6 John H. Buchanan, Jr. (R), *Birmingham*
7 James D. Martin (R), *Gadsden*
8 Robert E. Jones (D), *Scottsboro*

## ALASKA

SENATORS

E. L. (Bob) Bartlett (D), *Juneau*
Ernest Gruening (D), *Juneau*

REPRESENTATIVE AT LARGE
Ralph J. Rivers (D),[13] *Fairbanks*

## ARIZONA

SENATORS

Carl Hayden (D), *Phoenix*
Paul J. Fannin (R), *Phoenix*

REPRESENTATIVES

1 John J. Rhodes (R), *Mesa*
2 Morris K. Udall (D), *Tucson*
3 George F. Senner, Jr. (D), *Miami*

## ARKANSAS

SENATORS

John L. McClellan (D), *Camden*
J. William Fulbright (D), *Fayetteville*

REPRESENTATIVES

1 E. C. Gathings (D), *West Memphis*

2 Wilbur D. Mills (D), *Kensett*
3 James W. Trimble (D), *Berryville*
4 Oren Harris (D),[14] *El Dorado*
4 David H. Pryor (D),[15] *Camden*

## CALIFORNIA

SENATORS

Thomas H. Kuchel (R), *Anaheim*
George L. Murphy (R), *Beverly Hills*

REPRESENTATIVES

1 Don H. Clausen (R), *Crescent City*
2 Harold T. Johnson (D), *Roseville*
3 John E. Moss, Jr. (D), *Sacramento*
4 Robert L. Leggett (D), *Vallejo*
5 Phillip Burton (D), *San Francisco*
6 William S. Mailliard (R), *San Francisco*
7 Jeffery Cohelan (D), *Berkeley*
8 George P. Miller (D), *Alameda*

---

[1] By joint resolution (Pub. Law 89 340, 89th Cong., 1st sess.), the date of assembling the second session of the Eighty-ninth Congress was fixed for January 10, 1966.
[2] Term began at noon January 20, 1965.
[3] Resigned December 30, 1965.
[4] Elected to serve from January 1, 1966, through September 30, 1966.

[5] Term began October 1, 1966.
[6] Resigned December 30, 1965.
[7] Term began January 14, 1966.
[8] Reelected January 4, 1965.
[9] Reelected January 4, 1965.
[10] Reelected January 4, 1965.
[11] Reelected January 4, 1965.

[12] Reelected January 4, 1965.
[13] Resigned December 30, 1966; vacancy throughout remainder of the Congress.
[14] Resigned February 2, 1966.
[15] Elected November 8, 1966, to fill vacancy caused by resignation of Oren Harris, but was unable to be sworn in as Congress was not in session.

## CALIFORNIA—Continued

REPRESENTATIVES—CONTINUED

9 Don Edwards (D), *San Jose*
10 Charles S. Gubser (R), *Gilroy*
11 J. Arthur Younger (R), *San Mateo*
12 Burt L. Talcott (R), *Salinas*
13 Charles M. Teague (R), *Ojai*
14 John F. Baldwin (R),[16] *Martinez*
14 Jerome R. Waldie (D),[17] *Antioch*
15 John J. McFall (D), *Manteca*
16 B. F. Sisk (D), *Fresno*
17 Cecil R. King (D), *Los Angeles*
18 Harlan F. Hagen (D), *Hanford*
19 Chet Holifield (D), *Montebello*
20 H. Allen Smith (R), *Glendale*
21 Augustus F. Hawkins (D), *Los Angeles*
22 James C. Corman (D), *Van Nuys*
23 Del M. Clawson (R), *Compton*
24 Glenard P. Lipscomb (R), *Los Angeles*
25 Ronald Brooks Cameron (D), *Whittier*
26 James Roosevelt (D),[18] *Los Angeles*
26 Thomas M. Rees (D),[19] *Los Angeles*
27 Ed Reinecke (R), *Tujunga*
28 Alphonzo Bell (R), *Los Angeles*
29 George E. Brown, Jr. (D), *Monterey Park*
30 Edward R. Roybal (D), *Los Angeles*
31 Charles H. Wilson (D), *Los Angeles*
32 Craig Hosmer (R), *Long Beach*
33 Kenneth W. Dyal (D), *San Bernardino*
34 Richard T. Hanna (D), *Huntington Beach*
35 James B. Utt (R), *Santa Ana*
36 Robert C. Wilson (R), *San Diego*
37 Lionel Van Deerlin (D), *San Diego*
38 John V. Tunney (D), *Riverside*

## COLORADO

SENATORS

Gordon L. Allott (R), *Lamar*
Peter H. Dominick (R), *Englewood*

REPRESENTATIVES

1 Byron G. Rogers (D), *Denver*
2 Roy H. McVicker (D), *Wheat Ridge*
3 Frank E. Evans (D), *Pueblo*
4 Wayne N. Aspinall (D), *Palisade*

## CONNECTICUT

SENATORS

Thomas J. Dodd (D), *West Hartford*
Abraham A. Ribicoff (D), *Hartford*

REPRESENTATIVES

1 Emilio Q. Daddario (D), *Hartford*

2 William L. St. Onge (D), *Putnam*
3 Robert N. Giaimo (D), *North Haven*
4 Donald J. Irwin (D), *Norwalk*
5 John S. Monagan (D), *Waterbury*
6 Bernard F. Grabowski (D), *Bristol*

## DELAWARE

SENATORS

John J. Williams (R), *Millsboro*
J. Caleb Boggs (R), *Wilmington*

REPRESENTATIVE AT LARGE

Harris B. McDowell, Jr. (D), *Middletown*

## FLORIDA

SENATORS

Spessard L. Holland (D), *Bartow*
George A. Smathers (D), *Miami*

REPRESENTATIVES

1 Robert L. F. Sikes (D), *Crestview*
2 Charles E. Bennett (D), *Jacksonville*
3 Claude D. Pepper (D), *Miami*
4 Dante B. Fascell (D), *Miami*
5 A. Sydney Herlong, Jr. (D), *Leesburg*
6 Paul G. Rogers (D), *West Palm Beach*
7 James A. Haley (D), *Sarasota*
8 D. R. (Billy) Matthews (D), *Gainesville*
9 Don Fuqua (D), *Altha*
10 Sam M. Gibbons (D), *Tampa*
11 Edward J. Gurney (R), *Winter Park*
12 William C. Cramer (R), *St. Petersburg*

## GEORGIA

SENATORS

Richard B. Russell (D), *Winder*
Herman E. Talmadge (D), *Lovejoy*

REPRESENTATIVES

1 G. Elliott Hagan (D), *Sylvania*
2 Maston E. O'Neal, Jr. (D), *Bainbridge*
3 Howard H. Callaway (R), *Pine Mountain*
4 James A. Mackay (D), *Atlanta*
5 Charles L. Weltner (D), *Atlanta*
6 John J. Flynt, Jr. (D), *Griffin*
7 John W. Davis (D), *Summerville*
8 J. Russell Tuten (D), *Brunswick*
9 Phillip M. Landrum (D), *Jasper*
10 Robert G. Stephens, Jr. (D), *Athens*

## HAWAII

SENATORS

Hiram L. Fong (R), *Honolulu*
Daniel K. Inouye (D), *Honolulu*

REPRESENTATIVES AT LARGE

Spark M. Matsunaga (D), *Honolulu*
Patsy T. Mink (D), *Waipahu*

## IDAHO

SENATORS

Frank Church (D), *Boise*
Len B. Jordan (R), *Boise*

REPRESENTATIVES

1 Compton I. White, Jr. (D), *Clarkfork*
2 George V. Hansen (R), *Pocatello*

## ILLINOIS

SENATORS

Paul H. Douglas (D), *Chicago*
Everett McKinley Dirksen (R), *Pekin*

REPRESENTATIVES

1 William L. Dawson (D), *Chicago*
2 Barratt O'Hara (D), *Chicago*
3 William T. Murphy (D), *Chicago*
4 Edward J. Derwinski (R), *South Holland*
5 John C. Kluczynski (D), *Chicago*
6 Daniel J. Ronan (D), *Chicago*
7 Frank Annunzio (D), *Chicago*
8 Dan Rostenkowski (D), *Chicago*
9 Sidney R. Yates (D), *Chicago*
10 Harold R. Collier (R), *Berwyn*
11 Roman C. Pucinski (D), *Chicago*
12 Robert McClory (R), *Lake Bluff*
13 Donald Rumsfeld (R), *Glenview*
14 John N. Erlenborn (R), *Elmhurst*
15 Charlotte T. Reid (R), *Aurora*
16 John B. Anderson (R), *Rockford*
17 Leslie C. Arends (R), *Melvin*
18 Robert H. Michel (R), *Peoria*
19 Gale Schisler (D), *London Mills*
20 Paul Findley (R), *Pittsfield*
21 Kenneth J. Gray (D), *West Frankfort*
22 William L. Springer (R), *Champaign*
23 George E. Shipley (D), *Olney*
24 Melvin Price (D), *East St. Louis*

## INDIANA

SENATORS

Vance Hartke (D), *Evansville*
Birch E. Bayh (D), *Terre Haute*

REPRESENTATIVES

1 Ray J. Madden (D), *Gary*
2 Charles A. Halleck (R), *Rensselaer*
3 John Brademas (D), *South Bend*
4 E. Ross Adair (R), *Fort Wayne*
5 J. Edward Roush (D), *Huntington*

---

[16] Died March 9, 1966.
[17] Elected to fill vacancy caused by death of John F. Baldwin, and took his seat June 20, 1966.
[18] Resigned September 30, 1965.
[19] Elected to fill vacancy caused by resignation of James Roosevelt, and took his seat January 10, 1966.

6 Richard L. Roudebush (R), *Noblesville*
7 William G. Bray (R), *Martinsville*
8 Winfield K. Denton (D),[20] *Evansville*
9 Lee H. Hamilton (D), *Columbus*
10 Ralph Harvey (R),[21] *New Castle*
11 Andrew Jacobs, Jr. (D), *Indianapolis*

## IOWA

SENATORS

Bourke B. Hickenlooper (R), *Cedar Rapids*
Jack R. Miller (R), *Sioux City*

REPRESENTATIVES

1 John R. Schmidhauser (D), *Iowa City*
2 John C. Culver (D), *Marion*
3 H. R. Gross (R),[22] *Waterloo*
4 Bert A. Bandstra (D), *Pella*
5 Neal Smith (D), *Altoona*
6 Stanley L. Greigg (D), *Sioux City*
7 John R. Hansen (D), *Manning*

## KANSAS

SENATORS

Frank Carlson (R), *Concordia*
James B. Pearson (R), *Prairie Village*

REPRESENTATIVES

1 Robert J. Dole (R), *Russell*
2 Chester L. Mize (R), *Atchison*
3 Robert F. Ellsworth (R), *Lawrence*
4 Garner E. Shriver (R), *Wichita*
5 Joe Skubitz (R), *Pittsburg*

## KENTUCKY

SENATORS

John Sherman Cooper (R), *Somerset*
Thruston B. Morton (R), *Louisville*

REPRESENTATIVES

1 Frank A. Stubblefield (D), *Murray*
2 William H. Natcher (D), *Bowling Green*
3 Charles R. P. Farnsley (D), *Louisville*
4 Frank Chelf (D), *Lebanon*
5 Tim Lee Carter (R), *Tompkinsville*
6 John C. Watts (D), *Nicholasville*
7 Carl D. Perkins (D), *Hindman*

## LOUISIANA

SENATORS

Allen J. Ellender (D), *Houma*
Russell B. Long (D), *Baton Rouge*

REPRESENTATIVES

1 F. Edward Hébert (D), *New Orleans*

2 Hale Boggs (D), *New Orleans*
3 Edwin E. Willis (D), *St. Martinville*
4 Joe D. Waggonner, Jr. (D), *Plain Dealing*
5 Otto E. Passman (D), *Monroe*
6 James H. Morrison (D), *Hammond*
7 T. Ashton Thompson (D),[23] *Ville Platte*
7 Edwin W. Edwards (D),[24] *Crowley*
8 Speedy O. Long (D), *Jena*

## MAINE

SENATORS

Margaret Chase Smith (R), *Skowhegan*
Edmund S. Muskie (D), *Waterville*

REPRESENTATIVES

1 Stanley R. Tupper (R), *Boothbay Harbor*
2 William D. Hathaway (D), *Auburn*

## MARYLAND

SENATORS

Daniel B. Brewster (D), *Towson*
Joseph D. Tydings (D), *Harve de Grace*

REPRESENTATIVE AT LARGE

Carlton R. Sickles (D), *Lanham*

REPRESENTATIVES

1 Rogers C. B. Morton (R), *Easton*
2 Clarence D. Long (D), *Ruxton*
3 Edward A. Garmatz (D), *Baltimore*
4 George H. Fallon (D), *Baltimore*
5 Hervey G. Machen (D), *Hyattsville*
6 Charles McC. Mathias, Jr. (R), *Frederick*
7 Samuel N. Friedel (D), *Baltimore*

## MASSACHUSETTS

SENATORS

Leverett Saltonstall (R), *Dover*
Edward M. Kennedy (D), *Boston*

REPRESENTATIVES

1 Silvio O. Conte (R), *Pittsfield*
2 Edward P. Boland (D), *Springfield*
3 Philip J. Philbin (D), *Clinton*
4 Harold D. Donohue (D), *Worcester*
5 F. Bradford Morse (R), *Lowell*
6 William H. Bates (R), *Salem*
7 Torbert H. Macdonald (D), *Malden*
8 Thomas P. O'Neill, Jr. (D), *Cambridge*

9 John W. McCormack (D), *Dorchester*
10 Joseph W. Martin, Jr. (R), *North Attleboro*
11 James A. Burke (D), *Milton*
12 Hastings Keith (R), *West Bridgewater*

## MICHIGAN

SENATORS

Patrick V. McNamara (D),[25] *Detroit*
Robert P. Griffin (R),[26] *Traverse City*
Philip A. Hart (D), *Mackinac Island*

REPRESENTATIVES

1 John Conyers, Jr. (D), *Detroit*
2 Weston E. Vivian (D), *Ann Arbor*
3 Paul H. Todd, Jr. (D), *Kalamazoo*
4 Edward Hutchinson (R), *Fennville*
5 Gerald R. Ford, Jr. (R), *Grand Rapids*
6 Charles E. Chamberlain (R), *East Lansing*
7 John C. Mackie (D), *Flint*
8 James Harvey (R), *Saginaw*
9 Robert P. Griffin (R),[27] *Traverse City*
9 Guy A. Vander Jagt (R),[28] *Cadillac*
10 Elford A. Cederberg (R), *Bay City*
11 Raymond F. Clevenger (D), *Sault Ste. Marie*
12 James G. O'Hara (D), *Utica*
13 Charles C. Diggs, Jr. (D), *Detroit*
14 Lucien N. Nedzi (D), *Detroit*
15 William D. Ford (D), *Taylor*
16 John D. Dingell, Jr. (D), *Dearborn*
17 Martha W. Griffiths (D), *Detroit*
18 William S. Broomfield (R), *Royal Oak*
19 Billie S. Farnum (D), *Drayton Plains*

## MINNESOTA

SENATORS

Eugene J. McCarthy (D), *St. Paul*
Walter F. Mondale (D), *Minneapolis*

REPRESENTATIVES

1 Albert H. Quie (R), *Dennison*
2 Ancher Nelson (R), *Hutchinson*
3 Clark MacGregor (R), *Plymouth*
4 Joseph E. Karth (D), *St. Paul*
5 Donald M. Fraser (D), *Minneapolis*
6 Alec G. Olson (D), *Montevideo*
7 Odin Langen (R), *Kennedy*
8 John A. Blatnik (D), *Chisholm*

---

[20] Resigned December 30, 1966; vacancy throughout remainder of the Congress.
[21] Resigned December 30, 1966; vacancy throughout remainder of the Congress.
[22] Election unsuccessfully contested by Stephen M. Peterson.

[23] Died July 1, 1965.
[24] Elected to fill vacancy caused by death of T. Ashton Thompson, and took his seat October 18, 1965.
[25] Died April 30, 1966.
[26] Appointed May 11, 1966, to fill vacancy caused

by death of Patrick V. McNamara, subsequently elected.
[27] Resigned May 10, 1966.
[28] Elected November 8, 1966, to fill vacancy caused by resignation of Robert P. Griffin, but was unable to be sworn in as Congress was not in session.

## MISSISSIPPI

### SENATORS

James O. Eastland (D), *Doddsville*
John C. Stennis (D), *De Kalb*

### REPRESENTATIVES

1 Thomas G. Abernethy (D),[29] *Okolona*
2 Jamie L. Whitten (D),[30] *Charleston*
3 John Bell Williams (D),[31] *Raymond*
4 Prentiss L. Walker (R),[32] *Mize*
5 William M. Colmer (D),[33] *Pascagoula*

## MISSOURI

### SENATORS

Stuart Symington (D), *St. Louis*
Edward V. Long (D), *Clarksville*

### REPRESENTATIVES

1 Frank M. Karsten (D), *St. Louis*
2 Thomas B. Curtis (R), *Webster Groves*
3 Leonor Kretzer Sullivan (D), *St. Louis*
4 William J. Randall (D), *Independence*
5 Richard W. Bolling (D), *Kansas City*
6 William R. Hull, Jr. (D), *Weston*
7 Durward G. Hall (R), *Springfield*
8 Richard H. Ichord (D), *Houston*
9 William L. Hungate (D), *Troy*
10 Paul C. Jones (D), *Kennett*

## MONTANA

### SENATORS

Mike Mansfield (D), *Missoula*
Lee Metcalf (D), *Helena*

### REPRESENTATIVES

1 Arnold Olsen (D), *Helena*
2 James F. Battin (R), *Billings*

## NEBRASKA

### SENATORS

Roman L. Hruska (R), *Omaha*
Carl T. Curtis (R), *Minden*

### REPRESENTATIVES

1 Clair A. Callan (D), *Odell*
2 Glenn C. Cunningham (R), *Omaha*
3 David T. Martin (R), *Kearney*

## NEVADA

### SENATORS

Alan Bible (D), *Reno*
Howard W. Cannon (D), *Las Vegas*

### REPRESENTATIVE AT LARGE

Walter S. Baring (D), *Reno*

## NEW HAMPSHIRE

### SENATORS

Norris Cotton (R), *Lebanon*
Thomas J. McIntyre (D), *Laconia*

### REPRESENTATIVES

1 J. Oliva Huot (D), *Laconia*
2 James C. Cleveland (R), *New London*

## NEW JERSEY

### SENATORS

Clifford P. Case (R), *Rahway*
Harrison A. Williams, Jr. (D), *Westfield*

### REPRESENTATIVES

1 William T. Cahill (R), *Collingswood*
2 Thomas C. McGrath, Jr. (D), *Margate City*
3 James J. Howard (D), *Wall Township*
4 Frank Thompson, Jr. (D), *Trenton*
5 Peter H. B. Frelinghuysen (R), *Morristown*
6 Florence P. Dwyer (R), *Elizabeth*
7 William B. Widnall (R), *Saddle River*
8 Charles S. Joelson (D), *Paterson*
9 Henry Helstoski (D), *East Rutherford*
10 Peter W. Rodino, Jr. (D), *Newark*
11 Joseph G. Minish (D), *West Orange*
12 Paul J. Krebs (D), *Livingston*
13 Cornelius E. Gallagher (D), *Bayonne*
14 Dominick V. Daniels (D), *Jersey City*
15 Edward J. Patten (D), *Perth Amboy*

## NEW MEXICO

### SENATORS

Clinton P. Anderson (D), *Albuquerque*
Joseph M. Montoya (D), *Santa Fe*

### REPRESENTATIVES AT LARGE

Thomas G. Morris (D), *Tucumcari*
E. S. Johnny Walker (D), *Santa Fe*

## NEW YORK

### SENATORS

Jacob K. Javits (R), *New York City*
Robert F. Kennedy (D), *Glen Cove*

### REPRESENTATIVES

1 Otis G. Pike (D), *Riverhead*
2 James R. Grover, Jr. (R), *Babylon*
3 Lester L. Wolff (D), *Great Neck*
4 John W. Wydler (R), *Garden City*
5 Herbert Tenzer (D), *Lawrence*
6 Seymour Halpern (R), *Forest Hills*
7 Joseph P. Addabbo (D), *Ozone Park*
8 Benjamin S. Rosenthal (D), *Elmhurst*
9 James J. Delaney (D), *Long Island City*
10 Emanuel Celler (D), *Brooklyn*
11 Eugene J. Keogh (D), *Brooklyn*
12 Edna F. Kelly (D), *Brooklyn*
13 Abraham J. Multer (D), *Brooklyn*
14 John J. Rooney (D), *Brooklyn*
15 Hugh L. Carey (D), *Brooklyn*
16 John M. Murphy (D), *Staten Island*
17 John V. Lindsay (R),[34] *New York City*
17 Theodore R. Kupferman (R),[35] *New York City*
18 Adam Clayton Powell, Jr. (D), *New York City*
19 Leonard Farbstein (D), *New York City*
20 William Fitts Ryan (D), *New York City*
21 James H. Scheuer (D), *Bronx*
22 Jacob H. Gilbert (D), *Bronx*
23 Jonathan B. Bingham (D), *Bronx*
24 Paul A. Fino (R), *Bronx*
25 Richard L. Ottinger (D),[36] *Pleasantville*
26 Ogden R. Reid (R), *Purchase*
27 John G. Dow (D), *Grand View*
28 Joseph Y. Resnick (D), *Ellenville*
29 Leo W. O'Brien (D), *Albany*
30 Carleton J. King (R), *Saratoga Springs*
31 Robert C. McEwen (R), *Ogdensburg*
32 Alexander Pirnie (R), *Utica*
33 Howard W. Robison (R), *Owego*
34 James M. Hanley (D), *Syracuse*
35 Samuel S. Stratton (D), *Amsterdam*
36 Frank Horton (R), *Rochester*
37 Barber B. Conable, Jr. (R), *Alexander*
38 Charles E. Goodell (R), *Jamestown*
39 Richard D. McCarthy (D), *Buffalo*
40 Henry P. Smith III (R), *North Tonawanda*
41 Thaddeus J. Dulski (D), *Buffalo*

---

[29] Election unsuccessfully contested by Augusta Wheadon.
[30] Election unsuccessfully contested by Fannie Lou Hamer.
[31] Election unsuccessfully contested by Mildred Cosey, Evelyn Nelson, and Rev. Allen Johnson.
[32] Election unsuccessfully contested by Annie DeVine.
[33] Election unsuccessfully contested by Victoria Jackson Gray.

[34] Resigned December 31, 1965.
[35] Elected to fill vacancy caused by resignation of John V. Lindsay, and took his seat February 23, 1966.
[36] Election unsuccessfully contested by James R. Frankenberry.

## NORTH CAROLINA

### SENATORS

Sam J. Ervin, Jr. (D), *Morganton*
B. Everett Jordan (D), *Saxapahaw*

### REPRESENTATIVES

1 Herbert C. Bonner (D),[37] *Washington*
1 Walter B. Jones (D),[38] *Farmville*
2 L. H. Fountain (D), *Tarboro*
3 David N. Henderson (D), *Wallace*
4 Harold D. Cooley (D),[39] *Nashville*
5 Ralph J. Scott (D), *Danbury*
6 Horace R. Kornegay (D), *Greensboro*
7 Alton A. Lennon (D), *Wilmington*
8 Charles Raper Jonas (R), *Lincolnton*
9 James T. Broyhill (R), *Lenoir*
10 Basil L. Whitener (D), *Gastonia*
11 Roy A. Taylor (D), *Black Mountain*

## NORTH DAKOTA

### SENATORS

Milton R. Young (R), *LaMoure*
Quentin N. Burdick (D), *Fargo*

### REPRESENTATIVES

1 Mark Andrews (R), *Mapleton*
2 Rolland Redlin (D), *Crosby*

## OHIO

### SENATORS

Frank J. Lausche (D), *Cleveland*
Stephen M. Young (D), *Cleveland*

### REPRESENTATIVE AT LARGE

Robert E. Sweeney (D), *Bay Village*

### REPRESENTATIVES

1 John J. Gilligan (D), *Cincinnati*
2 Donald D. Clancy (R), *Cincinnati*
3 Rodney M. Love (D), *Dayton*
4 William M. McCulloch (R), *Piqua*
5 Delbert L. Latta (R), *Bowling Green*
6 William H. Harsha (R), *Portsmouth*
7 Clarence J. Brown (R),[40] *Blanchester*
7 Clarence J. Brown, Jr. (R),[41] *Urbana*
8 Jackson E. Betts (R), *Findlay*
9 Thomas L. Ashley (D), *Waterville*
10 Walter H. Moeller (D), *Lancaster*
11 J. William Stanton (R), *Painesville*
12 Samuel L. Devine (D), *Columbus*

13 Charles A. Mosher (R), *Oberlin*
14 William H. Ayres (R), *Akron*
15 Robert T. Secrest (D),[42] *Senecaville*
16 Frank T. Bow (R), *Canton*
17 John M. Ashbrook (R), *Johnstown*
18 Wayne L. Hays (D), *Flushing*
19 Michael J. Kirwan (D), *Youngstown*
20 Michael A. Feighan (D), *Cleveland*
21 Charles A. Vanik (D), *Cleveland*
22 Frances P. Bolton (R), *Cleveland*
23 William E. Minshall (R), *Lakewood*

## OKLAHOMA

### SENATORS

A. S. Mike Monroney (D), *Oklahoma City*
Fred R. Harris (D), *Lawton*

### REPRESENTATIVES

1 Page H. Belcher (R), *Enid*
2 Edmond Edmondson (D), *Muskogee*
3 Carl Albert (D), *McAlester*
4 Thomas J. Steed (D), *Shawnee*
5 John Jarman (D), *Oklahoma City*
6 Jed Johnson, Jr. (D), *Chickasha*

## OREGON

### SENATORS

Wayne L. Morse (D), *Eugene*
Maurine B. Neuberger (D), *Portland*

### REPRESENTATIVES

1 Wendell Wyatt (R), *Astoria*
2 Albert C. Ullman (D), *Baker*
3 Edith S. Green (D), *Portland*
4 Robert B. Duncan (D), *Medford*

## PENNSYLVANIA

### SENATORS

Joseph S. Clark (D), *Philadelphia*
Hugh D. Scott, Jr. (R), *Philadelphia*

### REPRESENTATIVES

1 William A. Barrett (D), *Philadelphia*
2 Robert N. C. Nix (D), *Philadelphia*
3 James A. Byrne (D), *Philadelphia*
4 Herman Toll (D), *Philadelphia*
5 William J. Green (D), *Philadelphia*
6 George M. Rhodes (D), *Reading*
7 G. Robert Watkins (R), *West Chester*
8 Willard S. Curtin (R), *Morrisville*

9 Paul B. Dague (R),[43] *Downingtown*
10 Joseph M. McDade (R), *Scranton*
11 Daniel J. Flood (D), *Wilkes-Barre*
12 J. Irving Whalley (R), *Windber*
13 Richard S. Schweiker (R), *Worcester*
14 William S. Moorhead (D), *Pittsburgh*
15 Fred B. Rooney (D), *Bethlehem*
16 John C. Kunkel (R),[44] *Harrisburg*
17 Herman T. Schneebeli (R), *Williamsport*
18 Robert J. Corbett (R), *Pittsburgh*
19 N. Neiman Craley, Jr. (D), *York*
20 Elmer J. Holland (D), *Pittsburgh*
21 John H. Dent (D), *Jeannette*
22 John P. Saylor (R), *Johnstown*
23 Albert W. Johnson (R), *Smethport*
24 Joseph P. Vigorito (D), *Erie*
25 Frank M. Clark (D), *Bessemer*
26 Thomas E. Morgan (D), *Fredericktown*
27 James G. Fulton (R), *Pittsburgh*

## RHODE ISLAND

### SENATORS

John O. Pastore (D), *Cranston*
Claiborne Pell (D), *Newport*

### REPRESENTATIVES

1 Fernand J. St Germain (D), *Woonsocket*
2 John E. Fogarty (D), *Harmony*

## SOUTH CAROLINA

### SENATORS

Olin D. Johnston (D),[45] *Spartanburg*
Donald S. Russell (D),[46] *Spartanburg*
Ernest F. Hollings (D),[47] *Charleston*
Strom Thurmond (R), *Aiken*

### REPRESENTATIVES

1 L. Mendel Rivers (D), *Charleston*
2 Albert W. Watson (D),[48] *Columbia*
3 W. J. Bryan Dorn (D), *Greenwood*
4 Robert T. Ashmore (D), *Greenville*
5 Thomas S. Gettys (D), *Rock Hill*
6 John L. McMillan (D), *Florence*

## SOUTH DAKOTA

### SENATORS

Karl E. Mundt (R), *Madison*
George S. McGovern (D), *Mitchell*

### REPRESENTATIVES

1 Benjamin Reifel (R), *Aberdeen*
2 E. Y. Berry (R), *McLaughlin*

---

[37] Died November 7, 1965.
[38] Elected to fill vacancy caused by death of Herbert C. Bonner, and took his seat February 10, 1966.
[39] Resigned December 30, 1966; vacancy throughout remainder of the Congress.
[40] Died August 23, 1965.
[41] Elected to fill vacancy caused by death of his father, Clarence J. Brown, and took his seat January 10, 1966.

[42] Resigned December 30, 1966; vacancy throughout remainder of the Congress.
[43] Resigned December 30, 1966; vacancy throughout remainder of the Congress.
[44] Resigned December 30, 1966; vacancy throughout remainder of the Congress.
[45] Died April 18, 1965.
[46] Appointed April 22, 1965, to fill vacancy caused by death of Olin D. Johnston.

[47] Elected November 8, 1966, to fill vacancy caused by death of Olin D. Johnston, for term ending January 3, 1969, but was unable to be sworn in as Congress was not in session.
[48] Changed party affiliation to Republican, January 12, 1965. Resigned February 1, 1965; elected as a Republican to fill vacancy caused by his own resignation and took his seat June 16, 1965.

## TENNESSEE

SENATORS

Albert A. Gore (D), *Carthage*
Ross Bass (D), *Pulaski*

REPRESENTATIVES

1 James H. Quillen (R), *Kingsport*
2 John J. Duncan (R), *Knoxville*
3 William E. Brock III (R), *Chattanooga*
4 Joseph L. Evins (D), *Smithville*
5 Richard H. Fulton (D), *Nashville*
6 William R. Anderson (D), *Waverly*
7 Thomas J. Murray (D),[49] *Jackson*
8 Robert A. Everett (D), *Union City*
9 George W. Grider (D), *Memphis*

## TEXAS

SENATORS

Ralph W. Yarborough (D), *Austin*
John G. Tower (R), *Wichita Falls*

REPRESENTATIVE AT LARGE

Joe R. Pool (D), *Dallas*

REPRESENTATIVES

1 Wright Patman (D), *Texarkana*
2 Jack B. Brooks (D), *Beaumont*
3 Lindley G. Beckworth (D), *Gladewater*
4 H. Ray Roberts (D), *McKinney*
5 Earle Cabell (D), *Dallas*
6 Olin E. Teague (D), *College Station*
7 John V. Dowdy (D), *Athens*
8 Albert Thomas (D),[50] *Houston*
8 Lera Thomas (D),[51] *Houston*
9 Clark W. Thompson (D),[52] *Galveston*
10 J. J. (Jake) Pickle (D), *Austin*
11 W. R. Poage (D), *Waco*
12 James C. Wright, Jr. (D), *Fort Worth*
13 Graham B. Purcell (D), *Wichita Falls*
14 John A. Young (D), *Corpus Christi*
15 Eligio (Kika) de la Garza (D), *Mission*
16 Richard C. White (D), *El Paso*
17 Omar T. Burleson (D), *Anson*
18 Walter E. Rogers (D), *Pampa*
19 George H. Mahon (D), *Lubbock*
20 Henry B. Gonzalez (D), *San Antonio*
21 O. Clark Fisher (D), *San Angelo*
22 Robert R. Casey (D), *Houston*

## UTAH

SENATORS

Wallace F. Bennett (R), *Salt Lake City*
Frank E. Moss (D), *Salt Lake City*

REPRESENTATIVES

1 Laurence J. Burton (R), *Ogden*
2 David S. King (D), *Salt Lake City*

## VERMONT

SENATORS

George D. Aiken (R), *Putney*
Winston L. Prouty (R), *Newport*

REPRESENTATIVE AT LARGE

Robert T. Stafford (R), *Rutland*

## VIRGINIA

SENATORS

Harry Flood Byrd (D),[53] *Berryville*
Harry Flood Byrd, Jr. (D),[54] *Winchester*
A. Willis Robertson (D),[55] *Lexington*
William B. Spong, Jr. (D),[56] *Portsmouth*

REPRESENTATIVES

1 Thomas N. Downing (D), *Newport News*
2 Porter Hardy, Jr. (D), *Churchland*
3 David E. Satterfield III (D), *Richmond*
4 Watkins M. Abbitt (D), *Appomattox*
5 William M. Tuck (D), *South Boston*
6 Richard H. Poff (R), *Radford*
7 John O. Marsh, Jr. (D), *Strasburg*
8 Howard W. Smith (D), *Broad Run*
9 W. Pat Jennings (D), *Marion*
10 Joel T. Broyhill (R), *Arlington*

## WASHINGTON

SENATORS

Warren G. Magnuson (D), *Seattle*
Henry M. Jackson (D), *Everett*

REPRESENTATIVES

1 Thomas M. Pelly (R), *Seattle*
2 Lloyd Meeds (D), *Everett*
3 Julia Butler Hansen (D), *Cathlamet*
4 Catherine May (R), *Yakima*
5 Thomas S. Foley (D), *Spokane*
6 Floyd V. Hicks (D), *Tacoma*
7 Brock Adams (D), *Seattle*

## WEST VIRGINIA

SENATORS

Jennings Randolph (D), *Elkins*
Robert C. Byrd (D), *Sophia*

REPRESENTATIVES

1 Arch A. Moore, Jr. (R), *Glendale*
2 Harley O. Staggers (D), *Keyser*
3 John M. Slack, Jr. (D), *Charleston*
4 Ken Hechler (D), *Huntington*
5 James Kee (D), *Bluefield*

## WISCONSIN

SENATORS

William Proxmire (D), *Madison*
Gaylord A. Nelson (D), *Madison*

REPRESENTATIVES

1 Lynn E. Stalbaum (D), *Racine*
2 Robert W. Kastenmeier (D), *Watertown*
3 Vernon W. Thomson (R), *Richland Center*
4 Clement J. Zablocki (D), *Milwaukee*
5 Henry S. Reuss (D), *Milwaukee*
6 John A. Race (D), *Fond du Lac*
7 Melvin R. Laird (R), *Marshfield*
8 John W. Byrnes (R), *Green Bay*
9 Glenn R. Davis (R), *New Berlin*
10 Alvin E. O'Konski (R), *Mercer*

## WYOMING

SENATORS

Gale W. McGee (D), *Laramie*
Milward L. Simpson (R), *Cody*

REPRESENTATIVE AT LARGE

Teno Roncalio (D), *Cheyenne*

## COMMONWEALTH OF PUERTO RICO

RESIDENT COMMISSIONER

Santiago Polanco-Abreu (PD), *Isabela*

---

[49] Resigned December 30, 1966; vacancy throughout remainder of the Congress.
[50] Died February 15, 1966.
[51] Elected to fill vacancy caused by death of her husband, Albert Thomas, and took her seat March 30, 1966.

[52] Resigned December 30, 1966; vacancy throughout remainder of the Congress.
[53] Resigned November 10, 1965.
[54] Appointed November 12, 1965, to fill vacancy caused by the resignation of his father, Harry Flood Byrd; subsequently elected.

[55] Resigned December 30, 1966.
[56] Appointed to fill vacancy caused by resignation of A. Willis Robertson, but was unable to be sworn in as Congress was not in session.

# 90TH CONGRESS

## JANUARY 3, 1967, TO JANUARY 3, 1969

FIRST SESSION— *January 10, 1967,*[1] *to December 15, 1967*
SECOND SESSION— *January 15, 1968,*[2] *to October 14, 1968*

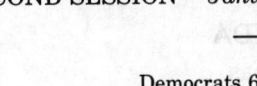

### Senate
#### Democrats 64 — Republicans 36

VICE PRESIDENT OF THE UNITED STATES— Hubert H. Humphrey, of Minnesota
PRESIDENT PRO TEMPORE OF THE SENATE— Carl Hayden, of Arizona
SECRETARY OF THE SENATE— Francis R. Valeo, of the District of Columbia
SERGEANT AT ARMS— Robert G. Dunphy, of Rhode Island
MAJORITY FLOOR LEADER— Mike Mansfield, of Montana
DEMOCRATIC WHIP— Russell B. Long, of Louisiana
REPUBLICAN FLOOR LEADER— Everett McKinley Dirksen, of Illinois
ASSISTANT REPUBLICAN LEADER— Thomas H. Kuchel, of California

### House of Representatives
#### Democrats 248 — Republicans 187

SPEAKER OF THE HOUSE— John W. McCormack,[3] of Massachusetts
CLERK OF THE HOUSE— W. Pat Jennings,[4] of Virginia
SERGEANT AT ARMS OF THE HOUSE— Zeake W. Johnson,[5] of Tennessee
DOORKEEPER OF THE HOUSE— William M. Miller,[6] of Mississippi
POSTMASTER OF THE HOUSE— H. H. Morris,[7] of Kentucky
MAJORITY LEADER— Carl Albert, of Oklahoma
MAJORITY WHIP— Hale Boggs, of Louisiana
REPUBLICAN LEADER— Gerald R. Ford, Jr., of Michigan
REPUBLICAN WHIP— Leslie C. Arends, of Illinois

Hubert H. Humphrey
Vice President

John W. McCormack
Speaker

## ALABAMA

### SENATORS
Lister Hill (D), *Montgomery*
John J. Sparkman (D), *Huntsville*

### REPRESENTATIVES
1  Jack Edwards (R), *Mobile*
2  William L. Dickinson (R), *Montgomery*
3  George W. Andrews (D), *Union Springs*
4  William Nichols (D), *Sylacauga*
5  Armistead I. Selden, Jr. (D), *Greensboro*
6  John H. Buchanan, Jr. (R), *Birmingham*
7  Tom Bevill (D), *Jasper*
8  Robert E. Jones (D), *Scottsboro*

## ALASKA

### SENATORS
E. L. (Bob) Bartlett (D),[8] *Juneau*
Theodore F. Stevens (R),[9] *Anchorage*
Ernest Gruening (D), *Juneau*

### REPRESENTATIVE AT LARGE
Howard W. Pollock (R), *Anchorage*

## ARIZONA

### SENATORS
Carl Hayden (D), *Phoenix*
Paul J. Fannin (R), *Phoenix*

### REPRESENTATIVES
1  John J. Rhodes (R), *Mesa*
2  Morris K. Udall (D), *Tucson*
3  Sam Steiger (R), *Prescott*

## ARKANSAS

### SENATORS
John L. McClellan (D), *Camden*
J. William Fulbright (D), *Fayetteville*

### REPRESENTATIVES
1  E. C. Gathings (D), *West Memphis*
2  Wilbur D. Mills (D), *Kensett*
3  John Paul Hammerschmidt (R), *Harrison*
4  David H. Pryor (D), *Camden*

## CALIFORNIA

### SENATORS
Thomas H. Kuchel (R), *Anaheim*
George L. Murphy (R), *Beverly Hills*

### REPRESENTATIVES
1  Don H. Clausen (R), *Crescent City*
2  Harold T. Johnson (D), *Roseville*
3  John E. Moss, Jr. (D), *Sacramento*
4  Robert L. Leggett (D), *Vallejo*
5  Phillip Burton (D), *San Francisco*
6  William S. Mailliard (R), *San Francisco*
7  Jeffery Cohelan (D), *Berkeley*
8  George P. Miller (D), *Alameda*
9  Don Edwards (D), *San Jose*
10  Charles S. Gubser (R), *Gilroy*
11  J. Arthur Younger (R),[10] *San Mateo*
11  Paul N. McCloskey, Jr. (R),[11] *Portola Valley*
12  Burt L. Talcott (R), *Salinas*
13  Charles M. Teague (R), *Ojai*
14  Jerome R. Waldie (D), *Antioch*

---

[1]  By joint resolution (Pub. Law 89 704, 89th Cong., 2d sess.), the date of assembling the first session of the Ninetieth Congress was fixed for January 10, 1967.
[2]  By joint resolution (Pub. Law 90 230, 90th Cong., 1st sess.), the date of assembling the second session of the Ninetieth Congress was fixed for January 15, 1968.
[3]  Reelected January 10, 1967.

[4]  Elected January 10, 1967.
[5]  Reelected January 10, 1967.
[6]  Reelected January 10, 1967.
[7]  Reelected January 10, 1967.
[8]  Died December 11, 1968.
[9]  Appointed December 23, 1968, to fill vacancy

caused by death of E. L. (Bob) Bartlett, but was unable to be sworn in as Congress was not in session.
[10]  Died June 20, 1967.
[11]  Elected to fill vacancy caused by death of J. Arthur Younger, and took his seat December 14, 1967.

## CALIFORNIA—Continued

REPRESENTATIVES—CONTINUED

15 John J. McFall (D), *Manteca*
16 B. F. Sisk (D), *Fresno*
17 Cecil R. King (D), *Los Angeles*
18 Robert B. Mathias (R), *Visalia*
19 Chet Holifield (D), *Montebello*
20 H. Allen Smith (R), *Glendale*
21 Augustus F. Hawkins (D), *Los Angeles*
22 James C. Corman (D), *Van Nuys*
23 Del M. Clawson (R), *Compton*
24 Glenard P. Lipscomb (R), *Los Angeles*
25 Charles E. Wiggins (R), *El Monte*
26 Thomas M. Rees (D), *Los Angeles*
27 Ed Reinecke (R), *Tujunga*
28 Alphonzo Bell (R), *Los Angeles*
29 George E. Brown, Jr. (D), *Monterey Park*
30 Edward R. Roybal (D), *Los Angeles*
31 Charles H. Wilson (D), *Los Angeles*
32 Craig Hosmer (R), *Long Beach*
33 Jerry L. Pettis (R), *Loma Linda*
34 Richard T. Hanna (D), *Huntington Beach*
35 James B. Utt (R), *Santa Ana*
36 Robert C. Wilson (R), *San Diego*
37 Lionel Van Deerlin (D), *San Diego*
38 John V. Tunney (D), *Riverside*

## COLORADO

SENATORS

Gordon L. Allott (R), *Lamar*
Peter H. Dominick (R), *Englewood*

REPRESENTATIVES

1 Byron G. Rogers (D), *Denver*
2 Donald G. Brotzman (R), *Boulder*
3 Frank E. Evans (D), *Pueblo*
4 Wayne N. Aspinall (D), *Palisade*

## CONNECTICUT

SENATORS

Thomas J. Dodd (D), *North Stonington*
Abraham A. Ribicoff (D), *Hartford*

REPRESENTATIVES

1 Emilio Q. Daddario (D), *Hartford*
2 William L. St. Onge (D), *Putnam*
3 Robert N. Giaimo (D), *North Haven*
4 Donald J. Irwin (D), *Norwalk*
5 John S. Monagan (D), *Waterbury*
6 Thomas J. Meskill (R), *New Britain*

## DELAWARE

SENATORS

John J. Williams (R), *Millsboro*
J. Caleb Boggs (R), *Wilmington*

REPRESENTATIVE AT LARGE

William V. Roth, Jr. (R), *Wilmington*

## FLORIDA

SENATORS

Spessard L. Holland (D), *Bartow*
George A. Smathers (D), *Miami*

REPRESENTATIVES

1 Robert L. F. Sikes (D), *Crestview*
2 Don Fuqua (D), *Altha*
3 Charles E. Bennett (D), *Jacksonville*
4 A. Sydney Herlong, Jr. (D), *Leesburg*
5 Edward J. Gurney (R), *Winter Park*
6 Sam M. Gibbons (D), *Tampa*
7 James A. Haley (D), *Sarasota*
8 William C. Cramer (R), *St. Petersburg*
9 Paul G. Rogers (D), *West Palm Beach*
10 J. Herbert Burke (R), *Hollywood*
11 Claude D. Pepper (D), *Miami*
12 Dante B. Fascell (D), *Miami*

## GEORGIA

SENATORS

Richard B. Russell (D), *Winder*
Herman E. Talmadge (D), *Lovejoy*

REPRESENTATIVES

1 G. Elliott Hagan (D), *Sylvania*
2 Maston E. O'Neal, Jr. (D), *Bainbridge*
3 Jack T. Brinkley (D), *Columbia*
4 Benjamin B. Blackburn (R),[12] *Atlanta*
5 Fletcher Thompson (R),[13] *East Point*
6 John J. Flynt, Jr. (D), *Griffin*
7 John W. Davis (D), *Summerfield*
8 Williamson S. Stuckey, Jr. (D), *Eastman*
9 Phillip M. Landrum (D), *Jasper*
10 Robert G. Stephens, Jr. (D), *Athens*

## HAWAII

SENATORS

Hiram L. Fong (R), *Honolulu*
Daniel K. Inouye (D), *Honolulu*

REPRESENTATIVES AT LARGE

Spark M. Matsunaga (D), *Honolulu*
Patsy T. Mink (D), *Waipahu*

## IDAHO

SENATORS

Frank Church (D), *Boise*
Len B. Jordan (R), *Boise*

REPRESENTATIVES

1 James A. McClure (R), *Payette*
2 George V. Hansen (R), *Pocatello*

## ILLINOIS

SENATORS

Everett McKinley Dirksen (R), *Pekin*
Charles H. Percy (R), *Kenilworth*

REPRESENTATIVES

1 William L. Dawson (D), *Chicago*
2 Barratt O'Hara (D), *Chicago*
3 William T. Murphy (D), *Chicago*
4 Edward J. Derwinski (R), *South Holland*
5 John C. Kluczynski (D), *Chicago*
6 Daniel J. Ronan (D), *Chicago*
7 Frank Annunzio (D), *Chicago*
8 Dan Rostenkowski (D), *Chicago*
9 Sidney R. Yates (D), *Chicago*
10 Harold R. Collier (R), *Western Springs*
11 Roman C. Pucinski (D), *Chicago*
12 Robert McClory (R), *Lake Bluff*
13 Donald Rumsfeld (R), *Wilmette*
14 John N. Erlenborn (R), *Elmhurst*
15 Charlotte T. Reid (R), *Aurora*
16 John B. Anderson (R), *Rockford*
17 Leslie C. Arends (R), *Melvin*
18 Robert H. Michel (R), *Peoria*
19 Thomas F. Railsback (R), *Moline*
20 Paul Findley (R), *Pittsfield*
21 Kenneth J. Gray (D), *West Frankfort*
22 William L. Springer (R), *Champaign*
23 George E. Shipley (D), *Olney*
24 Melvin Price (D), *East St. Louis*

## INDIANA

SENATORS

Vance Hartke (D), *Evansville*
Birch E. Bayh (D), *Terre Haute*

REPRESENTATIVES

1 Ray J. Madden (D), *Gary*
2 Charles A. Halleck (R), *Rensselaer*
3 John Brademas (D), *South Bend*
4 E. Ross Adair (R), *Fort Wayne*
5 J. Edward Roush (D), *Huntington*
6 William G. Bray (R), *Martinsville*
7 John T. Myers (R), *Covington*
8 Roger H. Zion (R), *Evansville*
9 Lee H. Hamilton (D), *Columbus*
10 Richard L. Roudebush (R), *Noblesville*
11 Andrew Jacobs, Jr. (D), *Indianapolis*

---

[12] Contested election by James A. Mackay withdrawn.

[13] Election unsuccessfully contested by Wyman C. Lowe.

## IOWA

SENATORS

Bourke B. Hickenlooper (R), *Cedar Rapids*
Jack R. Miller (R), *Sioux City*

REPRESENTATIVES

1 Frederic D. Schwengel (R), *Davenport*
2 John C. Culver (D), *Marion*
3 H. R. Gross (R), *Waterloo*
4 John H. Kyl (R), *Bloomfield*
5 Neal Smith (D), *Altoona*
6 Wiley Mayne (R), *Sioux City*
7 William J. Scherle (R), *Henderson*

## KANSAS

SENATORS

Frank Carlson (R), *Concordia*
James B. Pearson (R), *Prairie Village*

REPRESENTATIVES

1 Robert J. Dole (R), *Russell*
2 Chester L. Mize (R), *Atchison*
3 Larry Winn, Jr. (R), *Leawood*
4 Garner E. Shriver (R), *Wichita*
5 Joe Skubitz (R), *Pittsburg*

## KENTUCKY

SENATORS

John Sherman Cooper (R), *Somerset*
Thruston B. Morton (R),[14] *Louisville*
Marlow W. Cook (R),[15] *Louisville*

REPRESENTATIVES

1 Frank A. Stubblefield (D), *Murray*
2 William H. Natcher (D), *Bowling Green*
3 William O. Cowger (R), *Louisville*
4 M. G. (Gene) Snyder (R), *Jeffersontown*
5 Tim Lee Carter (R), *Tompkinsville*
6 John C. Watts (D), *Nicholasville*
7 Carl D. Perkins (D), *Hindman*

## LOUISIANA

SENATORS

Allen J. Ellender (D), *Houma*
Russell B. Long (D), *Baton Rouge*

REPRESENTATIVES

1 F. Edward Hébert (D), *New Orleans*
2 Hale Boggs (D), *New Orleans*
3 Edwin E. Willis (D), *St. Martinville*
4 Joe D. Waggonner, Jr. (D), *Plain Dealing*
5 Otto E. Passman (D), *Monroe*
6 John R. Rarick (D), *St. Francisville*
7 Edwin W. Edwards (D), *Crowley*
8 Speedy O. Long (D), *Jena*

## MAINE

SENATORS

Margaret Chase Smith (R), *Skowhegan*
Edmund S. Muskie (D), *Waterville*

REPRESENTATIVES

1 Peter N. Kyros (D), *Portland*
2 William D. Hathaway (D), *Auburn*

## MARYLAND

SENATORS

Daniel B. Brewster (D), *Towson*
Joseph D. Tydings (D), *Havre de Grace*

REPRESENTATIVES

1 Rogers C. B. Morton (R), *Easton*
2 Clarence D. Long (D), *Ruxton*
3 Edward A. Garmatz (D), *Baltimore*
4 George H. Fallon (D), *Baltimore*
5 Hervey G. Machen (D), *Hyattsville*
6 Charles McC. Mathias, Jr. (R), *Frederick*
7 Samuel N. Friedel (D), *Baltimore*
8 Gilbert Gude (R), *Bethesda*

## MASSACHUSETTS

SENATORS

Edward M. Kennedy (D), *Boston*
Edward W. Brooke (R), *Newton Centre*

REPRESENTATIVES

1 Silvio O. Conte (R), *Pittsfield*
2 Edward P. Boland (D), *Springfield*
3 Philip J. Philbin (D), *Clinton*
4 Harold D. Donohue (D), *Worcester*
5 F. Bradford Morse (R), *Lowell*
6 William H. Bates (R), *Salem*
7 Torbert H. Macdonald (D), *Malden*
8 Thomas P. O'Neill, Jr. (D), *Cambridge*
9 John W. McCormack (D), *Dorchester*
10 Margaret M. Heckler (R), *Wellesley*
11 James A. Burke (D), *Milton*
12 Hastings Keith (R), *West Bridgewater*

## MICHIGAN

SENATORS

Philip A. Hart (D), *Mackinac*
Robert P. Griffin (R), *Traverse City*

REPRESENTATIVES

1 John Conyers, Jr. (D), *Detroit*
2 Marvin L. Esch (R), *Ann Arbor*
3 Garry E. Brown (R), *Schoolcraft*
4 Edward Hutchinson (R), *Fennville*
5 Gerald R. Ford, Jr. (R), *Grand Rapids*
6 Charles E. Chamberlain (R), *East Lansing*
7 Donald W. Riegle, Jr. (R), *Flint*
8 James Harvey (R), *Saginaw*
9 Guy A. Vander Jagt (R), *Cadillac*
10 Elford A. Cederberg (R), *Bay City*
11 Philip E. Ruppe (R), *Houghton*
12 James G. O'Hara (D), *Utica*
13 Charles C. Diggs, Jr. (D), *Detroit*
14 Lucien N. Nedzi (D), *Detroit*
15 William D. Ford (D), *Taylor*
16 John D. Dingell, Jr. (D), *Dearborn*
17 Martha W. Griffiths (D), *Detroit*
18 William S. Broomfield (R), *Royal Oak*
19 Jack H. McDonald (R), *Detroit*

## MINNESOTA

SENATORS

Eugene J. McCarthy (D), *St. Paul*
Walter F. Mondale (D), *Minneapolis*

REPRESENTATIVES

1 Albert H. Quie (R), *Dennison*
2 Ancher Nelsen (R), *Hutchinson*
3 Clark MacGregor (R), *Plymouth*
4 Joseph E. Karth (D), *St. Paul*
5 Donald M. Fraser (D), *Minneapolis*
6 John M. Zwach (R), *Walnut Grove*
7 Odin Langen (R), *Kennedy*
8 John A. Blatnik (D), *Chisholm*

## MISSISSIPPI

SENATORS

James O. Eastland (D), *Doddsville*
John C. Stennis (D), *De Kalb*

REPRESENTATIVES

1 Thomas G. Abernethy (D), *Okolona*
2 Jamie L. Whitten (D), *Charleston*
3 John Bell Williams (D),[16] *Raymond*
3 Charles H. Griffin (D),[17] *Utica*
4 Gillespie V. (Sonny) Montgomery (D), *Meridian*
5 William M. Colmer (D), *Pascagoula*

## MISSOURI

SENATORS

Stuart Symington (D), *St. Louis*
Edward V. Long (D),[18] *Clarksville*
Thomas F. Eagleton (D),[19] *St. Louis*

REPRESENTATIVES

1 Frank M. Karsten (D), *St. Louis*
2 Thomas B. Curtis (R), *Webster Groves*

---

[14] Resigned December 16, 1968.
[15] Appointed to fill vacancy caused by resignation of Thruston B. Morton, but was unable to be sworn in as Congress was not in session.

[16] Resigned January 16, 1968.
[17] Elected to fill vacancy caused by resignation of John Bell Williams, and took his seat March 18, 1968.
[18] Resigned December 27, 1968.

[19] Appointed to fill vacancy caused by resignation of Edward V. Long, but was unable to be sworn in as Congress was not in session.

## MISSOURI—Continued

REPRESENTATIVES—CONTINUED
3 Leonor K. Sullivan (D), *St. Louis*
4 William J. Randall (D), *Independence*
5 Richard W. Bolling (D), *Kansas City*
6 William R. Hull, Jr. (D), *Weston*
7 Durward G. Hall (R), *Springfield*
8 Richard H. Ichord (D), *Houston*
9 William L. Hungate (D), *Troy*
10 Paul C. Jones (D), *Kennett*

## MONTANA

SENATORS
Mike Mansfield (D), *Missoula*
Lee Metcalf (D), *Helena*

REPRESENTATIVES
1 Arnold Olsen (D), *Helena*
2 James F. Battin (R), *Billinas*

## NEBRASKA

SENATORS
Roman L. Hruska (R), *Omaha*
Carl T. Curtis (R), *Minden*

REPRESENTATIVES
1 Robert V. Denney (R), *Fairbury*
2 Glenn C. Cunningham (R), *Omaha*
3 David T. Martin (R), *Kearneu*

## NEVADA

SENATORS
Alan Bible (D), *Reno*
Howard W. Cannon (D), *Las Vegas*

REPRESENTATIVE AT LARGE
Walter S. Baring (D), *Reno*

## NEW HAMPSHIRE

SENATORS
Norris Cotton (R), *Lebanon*
Thomas J. McIntyre (D), *Laconia*

REPRESENTATIVES
1 Louis C. Wyman (R), *Manchester*
2 James C. Cleveland (R), *New London*

## NEW JERSEY

SENATORS
Clifford P. Case (R), *Rahway*
Harrison A. Williams, Jr. (D), *Westfield*

REPRESENTATIVES
1 John E. Hunt (R), *Pitman*
2 Charles W. Sandman, Jr. (R), *Cape May*

3 James J. Howard (D), *Wall Township*
4 Frank Thompson, Jr. (D), *Trenton*
5 Peter H. B. Frelinghuysen (R), *Morristown*
6 William T. Cahill (R), *Collingswood*
7 William B. Widnall (R), *Saddle River*
8 Charles S. Joelson (D), *Paterson*
9 Henry Helstoski (D), *East Rutherford*
10 Peter W. Rodino, Jr. (D), *Newark*
11 Joseph G. Minish (D), *West Orange*
12 Florence P. Dwyer (R), *Elizabeth*
13 Cornelius E. Gallagher (D), *Bayonne*
14 Dominick V. Daniels (D), *Jersey City*
15 Edward J. Patten (D), *Perth Amboy*

## NEW MEXICO

SENATORS
Clinton P. Anderson (D), *Albuquerque*
Joseph M. Montoya (D), *Santa Fe*

REPRESENTATIVES AT LARGE
Thomas G. Morris (D), *Tucumcari*
E. S. Johnny Walker (D), *Santa Fe*

## NEW YORK

SENATORS
Jacob K. Javits (R), *New York City*
Robert F. Kennedy (D),[20] *New York City*
Charles E. Goodell (R),[21] *Jamestown*

REPRESENTATIVES
1 Otis G. Pike (D), *Riverhead*
2 James R. Grover, Jr. (R), *Babylon*
3 Lester L. Wolff (D), *Great Neck*
4 John W. Wydler (R), *Garden City*
5 Herbert Tenzer (D), *Cedarhurst*
6 Seymour Halpern (R), *Jamaica*
7 Joseph P. Addabbo (D), *Ozone Park*
8 Benjamin S. Rosenthal (D), *Elmhurst*
9 James J. Delaney (D), *Long Island City*
10 Emanuel Celler (D), *Brooklyn*
11 Frank J. Brasco (D), *Brooklyn*
12 Edna F. Kelly (D), *Brooklyn*
13 Abraham J. Multer (D),[22] *Brooklyn*
13 Bertram L. Podell (D),[23] *Brooklyn*
14 John J. Rooney (D), *Brooklyn*
15 Hugh L. Carey (D), *Brooklyn*

16 John M. Murphy (D), *Staten Island*
17 Theodore R. Kupferman (R), *New York City*
18 Adam Clayton Powell, Jr. (D),[24] *New York City*
19 Leonard Farbstein (D), *New York City*
20 William Fitts Ryan (D), *New York City*
21 James H. Scheuer (D), *Bronx*
22 Jacob H. Gilbert (D), *Bronx*
23 Jonathan B. Bingham (D), *Bronx*
24 Paul A. Fino (R),[25] *Bronx*
25 Richard L. Ottinger (D), *Pleasantville*
26 Ogden R. Reid (R), *Purchase*
27 John G. Dow (D), *Grand View*
28 Joseph Y. Resnick (D), *Ellenville*
29 Daniel E. Button (R), *Albany*
30 Carleton J. King (R), *Saratoga Springs*
31 Robert C. McEwen (R), *Ogdensburg*
32 Alexander Pirnie (R), *Utica*
33 Howard W. Robison (R), *Owego*
34 James M. Hanley (D), *Syracuse*
35 Samuel S. Stratton (D), *Amsterdam*
36 Frank Horton (R), *Rochester*
37 Barber B. Conable, Jr. (R), *Alexander*
38 Charles E. Goodell (R),[26] *Jamestown*
39 Richard D. McCarthy (D), *Buffalo*
40 Henry P. Smith III (R), *Tonawanda*
41 Thaddeus J. Dulski (D), *Buffalo*

## NORTH CAROLINA

SENATORS
Sam J. Ervin, Jr. (D), *Morganton*
B. Everett Jordan (D), *Saxapahaw*

REPRESENTATIVES
1 Walter B. Jones (D), *Farmville*
2 L. H. Fountain (D), *Tarboro*
3 David N. Henderson (D), *Wallace*
4 James C. Gardner (R), *Rocky Mount*
5 Nick Galifianakis (D), *Durham*
6 Horace R. Kornegay (D), *Greensboro*
7 Alton A. Lennon (D), *Wilmington*
8 Charles Raper Jonas (R), *Lincolnton*
9 James T. Broyhill (R), *Lenoir*
10 Basil L. Whitener (D), *Gastonia*
11 Roy A. Taylor (D), *Black Mountain*

---

[20] Died June 6, 1968.
[21] Appointed to fill vacancy caused by death of Robert F. Kennedy, and took his seat September 12, 1968.
[22] Resigned December 31, 1967.
[23] Elected to fill vacancy caused by resignation of Abraham Multer, and took his seat February 28, 1968.
[24] Served until February 28, 1967 when pursuant to H. Res. 278, he was excluded from membership in the 90th Congress. Elected as a Democrat in a special election held April 11, 1967 to fill vacancy caused by his exclusion but did not appear to be sworn in.
[25] Resigned December 31, 1968; vacancy throughout remainder of the Congress.
[26] Resigned September 9, 1968, having been appointed Senator; vacancy throughout remainder of the Congress.

## NORTH DAKOTA

### SENATORS

Milton R. Young (R), *LaMoure*
Quentin N. Burdick (D), *Fargo*

### REPRESENTATIVES

1 Mark Andrews (R), *Mapleton*
2 Thomas S. Kleppe (R), *Bismarck*

## OHIO

### SENATORS

Frank J. Lausche (D), *Cleveland*
Stephen M. Young (D), *Cleveland*

### REPRESENTATIVES

1 Robert Taft, Jr. (R), *Cincinnati*
2 Donald D. Clancy (R), *Cincinnati*
3 Charles W. Whalen, Jr. (R), *Dayton*
4 William M. McCulloch (R), *Piqua*
5 Delbert L. Latta (R), *Bowling Green*
6 William H. Harsha (R), *Portsmouth*
7 Clarence J. Brown, Jr. (R), *Urbana*
8 Jackson E. Betts (R), *Findlay*
9 Thomas L. Ashley (D), *Waterville*
10 Clarence E. Miller (R), *Lancaster*
11 J. William Stanton (R), *Painesville*
12 Samuel L. Devine (R), *Columbus*
13 Charles A. Mosher (R), *Oberlin*
14 William H. Ayres (R), *Akron*
15 Chalmers P. Wylie (R), *Columbus*
16 Frank T. Bow (R), *Canton*
17 John M. Ashbrook (R), *Johnstown*
18 Wayne L. Hays (D), *Flushing*
19 Michael J. Kirwan (D), *Youngstown*
20 Michael A. Feighan (D), *Cleveland*
21 Charles A. Vanik (D), *Cleveland*
22 Frances P. Bolton (R), *Cleveland*
23 William E. Minshall (R), *Lakewood*
24 Donald E. Lukens (R), *Middletown*

## OKLAHOMA

### SENATORS

A. S. Mike Monroney (D), *Oklahoma City*
Fred R. Harris (D), *Lawton*

### REPRESENTATIVES

1 Page H. Belcher (R), *Enid*
2 Edmond Edmondson (D), *Muskogee*
3 Carl Albert (D), *McAlester*
4 Thomas J. Steed (D), *Shawnee*
5 John Jarman (D), *Oklahoma City*
6 James V. Smith (R), *Chickasha*

## OREGON

### SENATORS

Wayne L. Morse (D), *Eugene*
Mark O. Hatfield (R), *Salem*

### REPRESENTATIVES

1 Wendell Wyatt (R), *Astoria*
2 Albert C. Ullman (D), *Baker*
3 Edith S. Green (D), *Portland*
4 John R. Dellenback (R), *Medford*

## PENNSYLVANIA

### SENATORS

Joseph S. Clark (D), *Philadelphia*
Hugh D. Scott, Jr. (R), *Philadelphia*

### REPRESENTATIVES

1 William A. Barrett (D), *Philadelphia*
2 Robert N. C. Nix (D), *Philadelphia*
3 James A. Byrne (D), *Philadelphia*
4 Joshua Eilberg (D), *Philadelphia*
5 William J. Green (D), *Philadelphia*
6 George M. Rhodes (D), *Reading*
7 Lawrence G. Williams (R), *Springfield*
8 Edward G. Biester, Jr. (R), *Furlong*
9 G. Robert Watkins (R), *West Chester*
10 Joseph M. McDade (R), *Scranton*
11 Daniel J. Flood (D), *Wilkes-Barre*
12 J. Irving Whalley (R), *Windber*
13 Richard S. Schweiker (R), *Worcester*
14 William S. Moorhead (D), *Pittsburgh*
15 Fred B. Rooney (D), *Bethlehem*
16 Edwin D. Eshleman (R), *Lancaster*
17 Herman T. Schneebeli (R), *Williamsport*
18 Robert J. Corbett (R), *Pittsburgh*
19 George A. Goodling (R), *Loganville*
20 Elmer J. Holland (D),[27] *Pittsburgh*
20 Joseph M. Gaydos (D),[28] *McKeesport*
21 John H. Dent (D), *Jeannette*
22 John P. Saylor (R), *Johnstown*
23 Albert W. Johnson (R), *Smethport*
24 Joseph P. Vigorito (D), *Erie*
25 Frank M. Clark (D), *Bessemer*
26 Thomas E. Morgan (D), *Fredericktown*
27 James G. Fulton (R), *Pittsburgh*

## RHODE ISLAND

### SENATORS

John O. Pastore (D), *Cranston*
Claiborne Pell (D), *Newport*

### REPRESENTATIVES

1 Fernand J. St Germain (D), *Woonsocket*
2 John E. Fogarty (D),[29] *Harmony*
2 Robert O. Tiernan (D),[30] *Warwick*

## SOUTH CAROLINA

### SENATORS

Strom Thurmond (R), *Aiken*
Ernest F. Hollings (D), *Charleston*

### REPRESENTATIVES

1 L. Mendel Rivers (D), *Charleston*
2 Albert W. Watson (R), *Columbia*
3 W. J. Bryan Dorn (D), *Greenwood*
4 Robert T. Ashmore (D), *Greenville*
5 Thomas S. Gettys (D), *Rock Hill*
6 John L. McMillan (D), *Florence*

## SOUTH DAKOTA

### SENATORS

Karl E. Mundt (R), *Madison*
George S. McGovern (D), *Mitchell*

### REPRESENTATIVES

1 Benjamin Reifel (R), *Aberdeen*
2 E. Y. Berry (R), *McLaughlin*

## TENNESSEE

### SENATORS

Albert A. Gore (D), *Carthage*
Howard H. Baker, Jr. (R), *Huntsville*

### REPRESENTATIVES

1 James H. Quillen (R), *Kingsport*
2 John J. Duncan (R), *Knoxville*
3 William E. Brock III (R), *Chattanooga*
4 Joseph L. Evins (D), *Smithfield*
5 Richard H. Fulton (D), *Nashville*
6 William R. Anderson (D), *Waverly*
7 L. Ray Blanton (D), *Adamsville*
8 Robert A. Everett (D), *Union City*
9 Dan H. Kuykendall (R), *Memphis*

## TEXAS

### SENATORS

Ralph W. Yarborough (D), *Austin*
John G. Tower (R), *Wichita Falls*

### REPRESENTATIVES

1 Wright Patman (D), *Texarkana*
2 John V. Dowdy (D), *Athens*
3 Joe R. Pool (D),[31] *Dallas*

---

[27] Died August 9, 1968.
[28] Elected to fill vacancy caused by death of Elmer J. Holland, but was unable to be sworn in as Congress was not in session.

[29] Died January 10, 1967, before the commencement of the Ninetieth Congress, to which he had been reelected.

[30] Elected to fill vacancy caused by death of John E. Fogarty, and took his seat April 13, 1967.
[31] Died July 14, 1968.

## TEXAS—Continued

### REPRESENTATIVES—CONTINUED

3 James M. Collins (R),[32] *Grand Prairie*
4 H. Ray Roberts (D), *McKinney*
5 Earle Cabell (D), *Dallas*
6 Olin E. Teague (D), *College Station*
7 George Bush (R), *Houston*
8 Robert C. Eckhardt (D), *Houston*
9 Jack B. Brooks (D), *Beaumont*
10 J. J. (Jake) Pickle (D), *Austin*
11 W. R. Poage (D), *Waco*
12 James C. Wright, Jr. (D), *Fort Worth*
13 Graham B. Purcell (D), *Wichita Falls*
14 John A. Young (D), *Corpus Christi*
15 Eligio (Kika) de la Garza (D), *Mission*
16 Richard C. White (D), *El Paso*
17 Omar T. Burleson (D), *Anson*
18 Robert D. Price (R), *Pampa*
19 George H. Mahon (D), *Lubbock*
20 Henry B. Gonzalez (D), *San Antonio*
21 O. Clark Fisher (D), *San Angelo*
22 Robert R. Casey (D), *Houston*
23 Abraham Kazen, Jr. (D), *Laredo*

## UTAH

### SENATORS

Wallace F. Bennett (R), *Salt Lake City*
Frank E. Moss (D), *Salt Lake City*

### REPRESENTATIVES

1 Laurence J. Burton (R), *Ogden*
2 Sherman P. Lloyd (R), *Salt Lake City*

## VERMONT

### SENATORS

George D. Aiken (R), *Putney*
Winston L. Prouty (R), *Newport*

### REPRESENTATIVE AT LARGE

Robert T. Stafford (R), *Rutland*

## VIRGINIA

### SENATORS

Harry Flood Byrd, Jr. (D), *Winchester*
William B. Spong, Jr. (D), *Portsmouth*

### REPRESENTATIVES

1 Thomas N. Downing (D), *Newport News*
2 Porter Hardy, Jr. (D), *Portsmouth*
3 David E. Satterfield III (D), *Richmond*
4 Watkins M. Abbitt (D), *Appomattox*
5 William M. Tuck (D), *South Boston*
6 Richard H. Poff (R), *Radford*
7 John O. Marsh, Jr. (D), *Strasburg*
8 William L. Scott (R), *Fairfax*
9 William C. Wampler (R), *Bristol*
10 Joel T. Broyhill (R), *Arlington*

## WASHINGTON

### SENATORS

Warren G. Magnuson (D), *Seattle*
Henry M. Jackson (D), *Everett*

### REPRESENTATIVES

1 Thomas M. Pelly (R), *Seattle*
2 Lloyd Meeds (D), *Everett*
3 Julia Butler Hansen (D), *Cathlamet*
4 Catherine May (R), *Yakima*
5 Thomas S. Foley (D), *Spokane*
6 Floyd V. Hicks (D), *Takoma*
7 Brock Adams (D), *Seattle*

## WEST VIRGINIA

### SENATORS

Jennings Randolph (D), *Elkins*
Robert C. Byrd (D), *Sophia*

### REPRESENTATIVES

1 Arch A. Moore, Jr. (R), *Glen Dale*
2 Harley O. Staggers (D), *Keyser*
3 John M. Slack, Jr. (D), *Charleston*
4 Ken Hechler (D), *Huntington*
5 James Kee (D), *Bluefield*

## WISCONSIN

### SENATORS

William Proxmire (D), *Madison*
Gaylord Nelson (D), *Madison*

### REPRESENTATIVES

1 Henry C. Schadeberg (R), *Burlington*
2 Robert W. Kastenmeier (D), *Watertown*
3 Vernon W. Thomson (R), *Richland Center*
4 Clement J. Zablocki (D), *Milwaukee*
5 Henry S. Reuss (D), *Milwaukee*
6 William A. Steiger (R), *Oshkosh*
7 Melvin R. Laird (R), *Marshfield*
8 John W. Byrnes (R), *Green Bay*
9 Glenn R. Davis (R), *New Berlin*
10 Alvin E. O'Konski (R), *Mercer*

## WYOMING

### SENATORS

Gale W. McGee (D), *Laramie*
Clifford P. Hansen (R), *Jackson Hole*

### REPRESENTATIVE AT LARGE

William Henry Harrison (R), *Sheridan*

## COMMONWEALTH OF PUERTO RICO

### RESIDENT COMMISSIONER

Santiago Polanco-Abreu (PD), *Isabela*

---

[32] Elected to fill vacancy caused by death of Joe R. Pool, and took his seat September 4, 1968.

# 91ST CONGRESS

### JANUARY 3, 1969, TO JANUARY 3, 1971

FIRST SESSION— *January 3, 1969, to December 23, 1969*
SECOND SESSION— *January 19, 1970,[1] to January 2, 1971*

Spiro T. Agnew
Vice President

John W. McCormack
Speaker

### Senate
### Democrats 57 — Republicans 43

VICE PRESIDENT OF THE UNITED STATES— Spiro T. Agnew,[2] of Maryland
PRESIDENT PRO TEMPORE OF THE SENATE— Richard B. Russell,[3] of Georgia
SECRETARY OF THE SENATE— Francis R. Valeo,[4] of the District of Columbia
SERGEANT OF ARMS OF THE SENATE— Robert G. Dunphy,[5] of Rhode Island
MAJORITY FLOOR LEADER— Mike Mansfield, of Montana
DEMOCRATIC WHIP— Edward M. Kennedy, of Massachusetts
REPUBLICAN FLOOR LEADER— Everett McKinley Dirksen,[6] of Illinois; Hugh D. Scott,[7] of Pennsylvania
ASSISTANT REPUBLICAN LEADER— Hugh D. Scott, of Pennsylvania; Robert P. Griffin,[8] of Michigan

### House of Representatives
### Democrats 243 — Republicans 192

SPEAKER OF THE HOUSE— John W. McCormack,[9] of Massachusetts
CLERK OF THE HOUSE— W. Pat Jennings,[10] of Virginia
SERGEANT AT ARMS OF THE HOUSE— Zeake W. Johnson,[11] of Tennessee
DOORKEEPER OF THE HOUSE— William M. Miller,[12] of Mississippi
POSTMASTER OF THE HOUSE— H. H. Morris,[13] of Kentucky
MAJORITY LEADER— Carl Albert, of Oklahoma
MAJORITY WHIP— Hale Boggs, of Louisiana
REPUBLICAN LEADER— Gerald R. Ford, Jr., of Michigan
REPUBLICAN WHIP— Leslie C. Arends, of Illinois

## ALABAMA

SENATORS

John J. Sparkman (D), *Huntsville*
James B. Allen (D), *Gadsden*

REPRESENTATIVES

1 Jack Edwards (R), *Mobile*
2 William L. Dickinson (R), *Montgomery*
3 George W. Andrews (D), *Union Springs*
4 William Nichols (D), *Sylacauga*
5 Walter Flowers (D), *Tuscaloosa*
6 John H. Buchanan, Jr. (R), *Birmingham*
7 Tom Bevill (D), *Jasper*
8 Robert E. Jones (D), *Scottsboro*

## ALASKA

SENATORS

Theodore F. Stevens (R), *Anchorage*
Maurice R. (Mike) Gravel (D), *Anchorage*

REPRESENTATIVE AT LARGE
Howard W. Pollock (R), *Anchorage*

## ARIZONA

SENATORS

Paul J. Fannin (R), *Phoenix*
Barry M. Goldwater (R), *Phoenix*

REPRESENTATIVES

1 John J. Rhodes (R), *Mesa*
2 Morris K. Udall (D), *Tucson*
3 Sam Steiger (R), *Prescott*

## ARKANSAS

SENATORS

John L. McClellan (D), *Camden*
J. William Fulbright (D), *Fayetteville*

REPRESENTATIVES

1 William V. Alexander, Jr. (D), *Osceola*
2 Wilbur D. Mills (D), *Kensett*
3 John Paul Hammerschmidt (R), *Harrison*

4 David H. Pryor (D), *Camden*

## CALIFORNIA

SENATORS

George L. Murphy (R),[14] *Beverly Hills*
John V. Tunney (D),[15] *Riverside*
Alan Cranston (D), *Los Angeles*

REPRESENTATIVES

1 Don H. Clausen (R), *Crescent City*
2 Harold T. Johnson (D), *Roseville*
3 John E. Moss, Jr. (D), *Sacramento*
4 Robert L. Leggett (D), *Vallejo*
5 Phillip Burton (D), *San Francisco*
6 William S. Mailliard (R), *San Francisco*
7 Jeffery Cohelan (D), *Berkeley*
8 George P. Miller (D), *Alameda*
9 Don Edwards (D), *San Jose*
10 Charles S. Gubser (R), *Gilroy*
11 Paul N. McCloskey, Jr. (R), *Portola Valley*
12 Burt L. Talcott (R), *Salinas*

[1] By joint resolution (Pub. Law 91 182, 91st Cong., 1st sess.), the date of assembling the second session of the Ninety-first Congress was fixed for January 19, 1970.
[2] Term began January 20, 1969.
[3] Elected January 3, 1969.
[4] Reelected January 3, 1969.
[5] Reelected January 3, 1969.

[6] Died September 7, 1969.
[7] Elected September 24, 1969.
[8] Elected September 24, 1969.
[9] Reelected January 3, 1969.
[10] Reelected January 3, 1969.
[11] Reelected January 3, 1969.

[12] Reelected January 3, 1969.
[13] Reelected January 3, 1969.
[14] Resigned January 2, 1971.
[15] Appointed to fill vacancy caused by resignation of George L. Murphy, and took his seat January 2, 1971.

## CALIFORNIA—Continued

### REPRESENTATIVES—CONTINUED

13 Charles M. Teague (R), *Ojai*
14 Jerome R. Waldie (D), *Antioch*
15 John J. McFall (D), *Manteca*
16 B. F. Sisk (D), *Fresno*
17 Glenn M. Anderson (D), *Torrance*
18 Robert B. Mathias (R), *Visalia*
19 Chet Holifield (D), *Montebello*
20 H. Allen Smith (R), *Glendale*
21 Augustus F. Hawkins (D), *Los Angeles*
22 James C. Corman (D), *Van Nuys*
23 Del M. Clawson (R), *Compton*
24 Glenard P. Lipscomb (R),[16] *Alhambra*
24 John H. Rousselot (R),[17] *San Marino*
25 Charles E. Wiggins (R), *El Monte*
26 Thomas M. Rees (D), *Los Angeles*
27 Ed Reinecke (R),[18] *Tujunga*
27 Barry M. Goldwater, Jr. (R),[19] *Burbank*
28 Alphonzo Bell (R), *Los Angeles*
29 George E. Brown, Jr. (D), *Monterey Park*
30 Edward R. Roybal (D), *Los Angeles*
31 Charles H. Wilson (D), *Los Angeles*
32 Craig Hosmer (R), *Long Beach*
33 Jerry L. Pettis (R), *Loma Linda*
34 Richard T. Hanna (D), *Huntington Beach*
35 James B. Utt (R),[20] *Santa Ana*
35 John G. Schmitz (R),[21] *Santa Ana*
36 Robert C. Wilson (R), *San Diego*
37 Lionel Van Deerlin (D), *San Diego*
38 John V. Tunney (D),[22] *Riverside*

## COLORADO

### SENATORS

Gordon L. Allott (R), *Lamar*
Peter H. Dominick (R), *Englewood*

### REPRESENTATIVES

1 Byron G. Rogers (D), *Denver*
2 Donald G. Brotzman (R), *Boulder*
3 Frank E. Evans (D), *Pueblo*
4 Wayne N. Aspinall (D), *Palisade*

## CONNECTICUT

### SENATORS

Thomas J. Dodd (D), *Old Lyme*
Abraham A. Ribicoff (D), *Hartford*

### REPRESENTATIVES

1 Emilio Q. Daddario (D), *Hartford*
2 William L. St. Onge (D),[23] *Putman*
2 Robert H. Steele (R),[24] *Vernon*
3 Robert N. Giaimo (D), *North Haven*
4 Lowell P. Weicker, Jr. (R), *Greenwich*
5 John S. Monagan (D), *Waterbury*
6 Thomas J. Meskill (R), *New Britain*

## DELAWARE

### SENATORS

John J. Williams (R),[25] *Millsboro*
William V. Roth, Jr. (R),[26] *Wilmington*
J. Caleb Boggs (R), *Wilmington*

### REPRESENTATIVE AT LARGE

William V. Roth, Jr. (R),[27] *Wilmington*

## FLORIDA

### SENATORS

Spessard L. Holland (D), *Bartow*
Edward J. Gurney (R), *Winter Haven*

### REPRESENTATIVES

1 Robert L. F. Sikes (D), *Crestview*
2 Don Fuqua (D), *Altha*
3 Charles E. Bennett (D), *Jacksonville*
4 William V. Chappell, Jr. (D), *Ocala*
5 Louis Frey, Jr. (R), *Winter Park*
6 Sam M. Gibbons (D), *Tampa*
7 James A. Haley (D), *Sarasota*
8 William C. Cramer (R), *St. Petersburg*
9 Paul G. Rogers (D), *West Palm Beach*
10 J. Herbert Burke (R), *Hollywood*
11 Claude D. Pepper (D), *Miami*
12 Dante B. Fascell (D), *Miami*

## GEORGIA

### SENATORS

Richard B. Russell (D), *Winder*
Herman E. Talmadge (D), *Lovejoy*

### REPRESENTATIVES

1 G. Elliott Hagan (D), *Sylvania*
2 Maston E. O'Neal, Jr. (D), *Bainbridge*
3 Jack T. Brinkley (D), *Columbus*
4 Benjamin B. Blackburn (R), *Atlanta*
5 Fletcher Thompson (R),[28] *East Point*
6 John J. Flynt, Jr. (D), *Griffin*
7 John W. Davis (D), *Summerville*
8 Williamson S. Stuckey, Jr. (D), *Eastman*
9 Phillip M. Landrum (D), *Jasper*
10 Robert G. Stephens, Jr. (D), *Athens*

## HAWAII

### SENATORS

Hiram L. Fong (R), *Honolulu*
Daniel K. Inouye (D), *Honolulu*

### REPRESENTATIVES AT LARGE

Spark M. Matsunaga (D), *Honolulu*
Patsy T. Mink (D), *Waipahu*

## IDAHO

### SENATORS

Frank Church (D), *Boise*
Len B. Jordan (R), *Boise*

### REPRESENTATIVES

1 James A. McClure (R), *Payette*
2 Orval Hansen (R), *Idaho Falls*

## ILLINOIS

### SENATORS

Everett McKinley Dirksen (R),[29] *Pekin*
Ralph T. Smith (R),[30] *Alton*
Adlai E. Stevenson III (D),[31] *Chicago*
Charles H. Percy (R), *Wilmette*

### REPRESENTATIVES

1 William L. Dawson (D),[32] *Chicago*
2 Abner J. Mikva (D), *Chicago*
3 William T. Murphy (D), *Chicago*
4 Edward J. Derwinski (R), *South Holland*
5 John C. Kluczynski (D), *Chicago*
6 Daniel J. Ronan (D),[33] *Chicago*
6 George W. Collins (D),[34] *Chicago*
7 Frank Annunzio (D), *Chicago*
8 Dan Rostenkowski (D), *Chicago*
9 Sidney R. Yates (D), *Chicago*
10 Harold R. Collier (R), *Western Springs*
11 Roman C. Pucinski (D), *Chicago*
12 Robert McClory (R), *Lake Bluff*
13 Donald Rumsfeld (R),[35] *Wilmette*

---

[16] Died February 1, 1970.
[17] Elected June 30, 1970, to fill vacancy caused by death of Glenard P. Lipscomb, and took his seat July 6, 1970.
[18] Resigned January 21, 1969.
[19] Elected April 29, 1969, to fill vacancy caused by resignation of Ed Reinecke, and took his seat May 5, 1969.
[20] Died March 1, 1970.
[21] Elected June 30, 1970, to fill vacancy caused by death of James B. Utt, and took his seat July 1, 1970.
[22] Resigned January 2, 1971, to become U.S. Senator by appointment of Governor to term ending

January 3, 1971.
[23] Died May 1, 1970.
[24] Elected November 3, 1970, to fill vacancy caused by death of William L. St. Onge, and took his seat November 16, 1970.
[25] Resigned December 31, 1970.
[26] Appointed to fill vacancy caused by resignation of John J. Williams, and took his seat January 2, 1971.
[27] Resigned December 31, 1970; vacancy throughout remainder of Congress.
[28] Election unsuccessfully contested by Wyman C. Lowe.
[29] Died September 7, 1969.

[30] Appointed to fill vacancy caused by death of Everett McKinley Dirksen, and took his seat September 18, 1969.
[31] Elected November 3, 1970, to fill vacancy caused by death of Everett McKinley Dirksen, and took his seat November 17, 1970.
[32] Died September 11, 1970; vacancy throughout remainder of Congress.
[33] Died August 13, 1969.
[34] Elected November 3, 1970, to fill vacancy caused by death of Daniel J. Ronan, and took his seat November 16, 1970.
[35] Resigned May 25, 1969.

13 Philip M. Crane (R),[36] *Winnetka*
14 John N. Erlenborn (R), *Elmhurst*
15 Charlotte T. Reid (R), *Aurora*
16 John B. Anderson (R), *Rockford*
17 Leslie C. Arends (R), *Melvin*
18 Robert H. Michel (R), *Peoria*
19 Thomas F. Railsback (R), *Moline*
20 Paul Findley (R), *Pittsfield*
21 Kenneth J. Gray (D), *West Frankfort*
22 William L. Springer (R), *Champaign*
23 George E. Shipley (D), *Olney*
24 Melvin Price (D), *East St. Louis*

## INDIANA

SENATORS

Vance Hartke (D), *Evansville*
Birch E. Bayh (D), *Terre Haute*

REPRESENTATIVES

1 Ray J. Madden (D), *Gary*
2 Earl F. Landgrebe (R), *Valparaiso*
3 John Brademas (D), *South Bend*
4 E. Ross Adair (R), *Fort Wayne*
5 Richard L. Roudebush (R), *Noblesville*
6 William G. Bray (R), *Martinsville*
7 John T. Myers (R), *Covington*
8 Roger H. Zion (R), *Evansville*
9 Lee H. Hamilton (D), *Columbus*
10 David W. Dennis (R), *Richmond*
11 Andrew Jacobs, Jr. (D), *Indianapolis*

## IOWA

SENATORS

Jack R. Miller (R), *Sioux City*
Harold E. Hughes (D), *Ida Grove*

REPRESENTATIVES

1 Frederic D. Schwengel (R), *Davenport*
2 John C. Culver (D), *Marion*
3 H. R. Gross (R), *Waterloo*
4 John H. Kyl (R), *Bloomfield*
5 Neal Smith (D), *Altoona*
6 Wiley Mayne (R), *Sioux City*
7 William J. Scherle (R), *Henderson*

## KANSAS

SENATORS

James B. Pearson (R), *Prairie Village*
Robert J. Dole (R), *Russell*

REPRESENTATIVES

1 Keith G. Sebelius (R), *Norton*
2 Chester L. Mize (R), *Atchison*
3 Larry Winn, Jr. (R), *Overland Park*
4 Garner E. Shriver (R), *Wichita*
5 Joe Skubitz (R), *Pittsburg*

## KENTUCKY

SENATORS

John Sherman Cooper (R), *Somerset*
Marlow W. Cook (R), *Louisville*

REPRESENTATIVES

1 Frank A. Stubblefield (D), *Murray*
2 William H. Natcher (D), *Bowling Green*
3 William O. Cowger (R), *Louisville*
4 M. G. (Gene) Snyder (R), *Jeffersontown*
5 Tim Lee Carter (R), *Tompkinsville*
6 John C. Watts (D), *Nicholasville*
7 Carl D. Perkins (D), *Hindman*

## LOUISIANA

SENATORS

Allen J. Ellender (D), *Houma*
Russell B. Long (D), *Baton Rouge*

REPRESENTATIVES

1 F. Edward Hébert (D), *New Orleans*
2 Hale Boggs (D), *New Orleans*
3 Patrick T. Caffery (D), *New Iberia*
4 Joe D. Waggonner, Jr. (D), *Plain Dealing*
5 Otto E. Passman (D), *Monroe*
6 John R. Rarick (D), *Baton Rouge*
7 Edwin W. Edwards (D), *Crowley*
8 Speedy O. Long (D), *Jena*

## MAINE

SENATORS

Margaret Chase Smith (R), *Skowhegan*
Edmund S. Muskie (D), *Waterville*

REPRESENTATIVES

1 Peter N. Kyros (D), *Portland*
2 William D. Hathaway (D), *Auburn*

## MARYLAND

SENATORS

Joseph D. Tyding (D), *Havre de Grace*
Charles McC. Mathias, Jr. (R), *Frederick*

REPRESENTATIVES

1 Rogers C. B. Morton (R), *Easton*
2 Clarence D. Long (D), *Ruxton*
3 Edward A. Garmatz (D), *Baltimore*
4 George H. Fallon (D), *Baltimore*
5 Lawrence J. Hogan (R), *Landover*
6 J. Glenn Beall, Jr. (R), *Frostburg*
7 Samuel N. Friedel (D), *Baltimore*
8 Gilbert Gude (R), *Bethesda*

## MASSACHUSETTS

SENATORS

Edward M. Kennedy (D), *Boston*
Edward W. Brooke (R), *Newton Centre*

REPRESENTATIVES

1 Silvio O. Conte (R), *Pittsfield*
2 Edward P. Boland (D), *Springfield*
3 Philip J. Philbin (D), *Clinton*
4 Harold D. Donohue (D), *Worcester*
5 F. Bradford Morse (R), *Lowell*
6 William H. Bates (R),[37] *Salem*
6 Michael J. Harrington (D),[38] *Beverly*
7 Torbert H. Macdonald (D), *Malden*
8 Thomas P. O'Neill, Jr. (D), *Cambridge*
9 John W. McCormack (D), *Dorchester*
10 Margaret M. Heckler (R), *Wellesley*
11 James A. Burke (D), *Milton*
12 Hastings Keith (R), *West Bridgewater*

## MICHIGAN

SENATORS

Philip A. Hart (D), *Mackinac Island*
Robert P. Griffin (R), *Traverse City*

REPRESENTATIVES

1 John Conyers, Jr. (D), *Detroit*
2 Marvin L. Esch (R), *Ann Arbor*
3 Garry E. Brown (R), *Schoolcraft*
4 Edward Hutchinson (R), *Fennville*
5 Gerald R. Ford, Jr. (R), *Grand Rapids*
6 Charles E. Chamberlain (R), *East Lansing*
7 Donald W. Riegle, Jr. (R), *Flint*
8 James Harvey (R), *Saginaw*
9 Guy A. Vander Jagt (R), *Cadillac*
10 Elford A. Cederberg (R), *Bay City*
11 Philip E. Ruppe (R), *Houghton*
12 James G. O'Hara (D), *Utica*
13 Charles C. Diggs, Jr. (D), *Detroit*
14 Lucien N. Nedzi (D), *Detroit*
15 William D. Ford (D), *Taylor*
16 John D. Dingell, Jr. (D), *Dearborn*
17 Martha W. Griffiths (D), *Detroit*
18 William S. Broomfield (R), *Royal Oak*
19 Jack H. McDonald (R), *Livonia*

## MINNESOTA

SENATORS

Eugene J. McCarthy (D), *St. Paul*
Walter F. Mondale (D), *Minneapolis*

REPRESENTATIVES

1 Albert H. Quie (R), *Dennison*
2 Ancher Nelsen (R), *Hutchinson*

---

[36] Elected November 25, 1969, to fill vacancy caused by resignation of Donald Rumsfeld, and took his seat December 1, 1969.

[37] Died June 22, 1969.
[38] Elected September 30, 1969, to fill vacancy caused by death of William H. Bates, and took his seat

October 3, 1969.

## MINNESOTA—Continued

### REPRESENTATIVES—CONTINUED

3 Clark MacGregor (R), *Plymouth*
4 Joseph E. Karth (D), *St. Paul*
5 Donald M. Fraser (D),
  *Minneapolis*
6 John M. Zwach (R), *Walnut Grove*
7 Odin Langen (R), *Kennedy*
8 John A. Blatnik (D), *Chisholm*

## MISSISSIPPI

### SENATORS

James O. Eastland (D), *Doddsville*
John C. Stennis (D), *De Kalb*

### REPRESENTATIVES

1 Thomas G. Abernethy (D),
  *Okolona*
2 Jamie L. Whitten (D), *Charleston*
3 Charles H. Griffin (D), *Utica*
4 Gillespie V. (Sonny) Montgomery
  (D), *Meridian*
5 William M. Colmer (D),
  *Pascagoula*

## MISSOURI

### SENATORS

Stuart Symington (D), *St. Louis*
Thomas F. Eagleton (D), *St. Louis*

### REPRESENTATIVES

1 William L. Clay (D), *St. Louis*
2 James W. Symington (D), *Clayton*
3 Leonor K. Sullivan (D), *St. Louis*
4 William J. Randall (D),
  *Independence*
5 Richard W. Bolling (D), *Kansas
  City*
6 William R. Hull, Jr. (D), *Weston*
7 Durward G. Hall (R), *Springfield*
8 Richard H. Ichord (D), *Houston*
9 William L. Hungate (D), *Troy*
10 Bill D. Burlison (D), *Cape
  Girardeau*

## MONTANA

### SENATORS

Mike Mansfield (D), *Missoula*
Lee Metcalf (D), *Helena*

### REPRESENTATIVES

1 Arnold Olsen (D), *Helena*
2 James F. Battin (R),[39] *Billings*
2 John Melcher (D),[40] *Forsyth*

## NEBRASKA

### SENATORS

Roman L. Hruska (R), *Omaha*
Carl T. Curtis (R), *Minden*

### REPRESENTATIVES

1 Robert V. Denney (R), *Fairbury*

2 Glenn C. Cunningham (R),
  *Omaha*
3 David T. Martin (R), *Kearney*

## NEVADA

### SENATORS

Alan Bible (D), *Reno*
Howard W. Cannon (D), *Las Vegas*

### REPRESENTATIVE AT LARGE

Walter S. Baring (D), *Reno*

## NEW HAMPSHIRE

### SENATORS

Norris Cotton (R), *Lebanon*
Thomas J. McIntyre (D), *Laconia*

### REPRESENTATIVES

1 Louis C. Wyman (R), *Manchester*
2 James C. Cleveland (R), *New
  London*

## NEW JERSEY

### SENATORS

Clifford P. Case (R), *Rahway*
Harrison A. Williams, Jr. (D),
  *Westfield*

### REPRESENTATIVES

1 John E. Hunt (R), *Pitman*
2 Charles W. Sandman, Jr. (R),
  *Cape May*
3 James J. Howard (D), *Wall
  Township*
4 Frank Thompson, Jr. (D), *Trenton*
5 Peter H. B. Frelinghuysen (R),
  *Morristown*
6 William T. Cahill (R),[41]
  *Collingswood*
6 Edwin B. Forsythe (R),[42]
  *Moorestown*
7 William B. Widnall (R), *Saddle
  River*
8 Charles S. Joelson (D),[43] *Paterson*
8 Robert A. Roe (D),[44] *Wayne*
9 Henry Helstoski (D), *East
  Rutherford*
10 Peter W. Rodino, Jr. (D), *Newark*
11 Joseph G. Minish (D), *West
  Orange*
12 Florence P. Dwyer (R), *Elizabeth*
13 Cornelius E. Gallagher (D),
  *Bayonne*
14 Dominick V. Daniels (D), *Jersey
  City*
15 Edward J. Patten (D), *Perth
  Amboy*

## NEW MEXICO

### SENATORS

Clinton P. Anderson (D), *Albuquerque*
Joseph M. Montoya (D), *Santa Fe*

### REPRESENTATIVES

1 Manuel Lujan, Jr. (R),
  *Albuquerque*
2 Edgar F. Foreman (R), *Las Cruces*

## NEW YORK

### SENATORS

Jacob K. Javits (R), *New York City*
Charles E. Goodell (R), *Jamestown*

### REPRESENTATIVES

1 Otis G. Pike (D), *Riverhead*
2 James R. Grover, Jr. (R), *Babylon*
3 Lester L. Wolff (D), *Great Neck*
4 John W. Wydler (R), *Garden City*
5 Allard K. Lowenstein (D), *Long
  Beach*
6 Seymour Halpern (R), *Jamaica*
7 Joseph P. Addabbo (D), *Ozone
  Park*
8 Benjamin S. Rosenthal (D),
  *Elmhurst*
9 James J. Delaney (D), *Long
  Island City*
10 Emanuel Celler (D), *Brooklyn*
11 Frank J. Brasco (D), *Brooklyn*
12 Shirley A. Chisholm (D), *Brooklyn*
13 Bertram L. Podell (D), *Brooklyn*
14 John J. Rooney (D), *Brooklyn*
15 Hugh L. Carey (D), *Brooklyn*
16 John M. Murphy (D), *Staten
  Island*
17 Edward I. Koch (D), *Manhattan*
18 Adam Clayton Powell, Jr. (D),
  *New York City*
19 Leonard Farbstein (D), *New York
  City*
20 William Fitts Ryan (D), *New York
  City*
21 James H. Scheuer (D), *Bronx*
22 Jacob H. Gilbert (D), *Bronx*
23 Jonathan B. Bingham (D), *Bronx*
24 Mario Biaggi (D), *Bronx*
25 Richard L. Ottinger (D),
  *Pleasantville*
26 Ogden R. Reid (R), *Purchase*
27 Martin B. McKneally (R),
  *Newburgh*
28 Hamilton Fish, Jr. (R), *Millbrook*
29 Daniel E. Button (R), *Albany*
30 Carleton J. King (R), *Saratoga
  Springs*
31 Robert C. McEwen (R),
  *Ogdensburg*
32 Alexander Pirnie (R), *Utica*
33 Howard W. Robison (R), *Owego*
34 James M. Hanley (D), *Syracuse*
35 Samuel S. Stratton (D),
  *Amsterdam*
36 Frank Horton (R), *Rochester*
37 Barber B. Conable, Jr. (R),
  *Alexander*

---

[39] Resigned February 27, 1969.
[40] Elected June 24, 1969, to fill vacancy caused by resignation of James F. Battin, and took his seat June 27, 1969.

[41] Resigned January 19, 1970.
[42] Elected November 3, 1970, to fill vacancy caused by resignation of William T. Cahill, and took his seat November 16, 1970.

[43] Resigned September 4, 1969.
[44] Elected November 4, 1969, to fill vacancy caused by resignation of Charles S. Joelson, and took his seat November 20, 1969.

38 James F. Hastings (R), *Allegany*
39 Richard D. McCarthy (D), *Buffalo*
40 Henry P. Smith III (R), *North Tonawanda*
41 Thaddeus J. Dulski (D), *Buffalo*

## NORTH CAROLINA

SENATORS

Sam J. Ervin, Jr. (D), *Morganton*
B. Everett Jordan (D), *Saxapahaw*

REPRESENTATIVES

1 Walter B. Jones (D), *Farmville*
2 L. H. Fountain (D), *Tarboro*
3 David N. Henderson (D), *Wallace*
4 Nick Galifianakis (D), *Durham*
5 Wilmer D. Mizell (R), *Winston-Salem*
6 L. Richardson Preyer (D), *Greensboro*
7 Alton A. Lennon (D), *Wilmington*
8 Earl B. Ruth (R), *Salisbury*
9 Charles Raper Jonas (R), *Lincolnton*
10 James T. Broyhill (R), *Lenoir*
11 Roy A. Taylor (D), *Black Mountain*

## NORTH DAKOTA

SENATORS

Milton R. Young (R), *LaMoure*
Quentin N. Burdick (D), *Fargo*

REPRESENTATIVES

1 Mark Andrews (R), *Mapleton*
2 Thomas S. Kleppe (R), *Bismarck*

## OHIO

SENATORS

Stephen M. Young (D), *Cleveland*
William B. Saxbe (R), *Mechanicsville*

REPRESENTATIVES

1 Robert Taft, Jr. (R), *Cincinnati*
2 Donald D. Clancy (R), *Cincinnati*
3 Charles W. Whalen, Jr. (R), *Dayton*
4 William M. McCulloch (R), *Piqua*
5 Delbert L. Latta (R), *Bowling Green*
6 William H. Harsha (R), *Portsmouth*
7 Clarence J. Brown (R), *Urbana*
8 Jackson E. Betts (R), *Findlay*
9 Thomas L. Ashley (D), *Waterville*
10 Clarence E. Miller (R), *Lancaster*
11 J. William Stanton (R), *Painesville*
12 Samuel L. Devine (R), *Columbus*
13 Charles A. Mosher (R), *Oberlin*
14 William H. Ayres (R), *Akron*
15 Chalmers P. Wylie (R), *Columbus*
16 Frank T. Bow (R), *Canton*

17 John M. Ashbrook (R), *Johnstown*
18 Wayne L. Hays (D), *Flushing*
19 Michael J. Kirwan (D),[45] *Youngstown*
19 Charles J. Carney (D),[46] *Youngstown*
20 Michael A. Feighan (D), *Cleveland*
21 Louis Stokes (D), *Cleveland*
22 Charles A. Vanik (D), *Cleveland*
23 William E. Minshall (R), *Lakewood*
24 Donald E. Lukens (R), *Middletown*

## OKLAHOMA

SENATORS

Fred R. Harris (D), *Lawton*
Henry L. Bellmon (R), *Billings*

REPRESENTATIVES

1 Page H. Belcher (R), *Tulsa*
2 Edmond Edmondson (D), *Muskogee*
3 Carl Albert (D), *McAlester*
4 Thomas J. Steed (D), *Shawnee*
5 John Jarman (D), *Oklahoma City*
6 John N. Happy Camp (R), *Waukomis*

## OREGON

SENATORS

Mark O. Hatfield (R), *Salem*
Robert W. Packwood (R), *Portland*

REPRESENTATIVES

1 Wendell Wyatt (R), *Astoria*
2 Albert C. Ullman (D), *Baker*
3 Edith S. Green (D), *Portland*
4 John R. Dellenback (R), *Medford*

## PENNSYLVANIA

SENATORS

Hugh D. Scott, Jr. (R), *Philadelphia*
Richard S. Schweiker (R), *Worcester*

REPRESENTATIVES

1 William A. Barrett (D), *Philadelphia*
2 Robert N. C. Nix (D), *Philadelphia*
3 James A. Byrne (D), *Philadelphia*
4 Joshua Eilberg (D), *Philadelphia*
5 William J. Green (D), *Philadelphia*
6 Gus Yatron (D), *Reading*
7 Lawrence G. Williams (R), *Springfield*
8 Edward G. Biester, Jr. (R), *Furlong*
9 G. Robert Watkins (R),[47] *West Chester*
9 John H. Ware (R),[48] *Oxford*
10 Joseph M. McDade (R), *Scranton*

11 Daniel J. Flood (D), *Wilkes-Barre*
12 J. Irving Whalley (R), *Windber*
13 R. Lawrence Coughlin (R), *Villanova*
14 William S. Moorhead (D), *Pittsburgh*
15 Fred B. Rooney (D), *Bethlehem*
16 Edwin D. Eshleman (R), *Lancaster*
17 Herman T. Schneebeli (R), *Williamsport*
18 Robert J. Corbett (R), *Pittsburgh*
19 George A. Goodling (R), *Loganville*
20 Joseph M. Gaydos (D), *McKeesport*
21 John H. Dent (D), *Jeannette*
22 John P. Saylor (R), *Johnstown*
23 Albert W. Johnson (R), *Smethport*
24 Joseph P. Vigorito (D), *Erie*
25 Frank M. Clark (D), *Bessemer*
26 Thomas E. Morgan (D), *Fredericktown*
27 James G. Fulton (R), *Pittsburgh*

## RHODE ISLAND

SENATORS

John O. Pastore (D), *Cranston*
Claiborne Pell (D), *Newport*

REPRESENTATIVES

1 Fernand J. St Germain (D), *Woonsocket*
2 Robert O. Tiernan (D), *Warwick*

## SOUTH CAROLINA

SENATORS

Strom Thurmond (R), *Aiken*
Ernest F. Hollings (D), *Charleston*

REPRESENTATIVES

1 L. Mendel Rivers (D),[49] *Charleston*
2 Albert W. Watson (R), *Columbia*
3 W. J. Bryan Dorn (D), *Greenwood*
4 James R. Mann (D), *Greenville*
5 Thomas S. Gettys (D), *Rock Hill*
6 John L. McMillan (D), *Florence*

## SOUTH DAKOTA

SENATORS

Karl E. Mundt (R), *Madison*
George S. McGovern (D), *Mitchell*

REPRESENTATIVES

1 Benjamin Reifel (R), *Aberdeen*
2 E. Y. Berry (R), *McLaughlin*

## TENNESSEE

SENATORS

Albert Gore (D), *Carthage*
Howard H. Baker, Jr. (R), *Huntsville*

---

[45] Died July 27, 1970.
[46] Elected November 3, 1970, to fill vacancy caused by death of Michael J. Kirwan, and took his seat November 16, 1970.

[47] Died August 7, 1970.
[48] Elected November 3, 1970, to fill vacancy caused by death of G. Robert Watkins, and took his

seat November 16, 1970.
[49] Died December 28, 1970; vacancy throughout remainder of Congress.

## TENNESSEE—Continued
### REPRESENTATIVES
1 James H. Quillen (R), *Kingsport*
2 John J. Duncan (R), *Knoxville*
3 William E. Brock III (R), *Chattanooga*
4 Joseph L. Evins (D), *Smithville*
5 Richard H. Fulton (D), *Nashville*
6 William R. Anderson (D), *Waverly*
7 L. Ray Blanton (D), *Adamsville*
8 Robert A. Everett (D),[50] *Union City*
8 Edward Jones (D),[51] *Yorkville*
9 Dan H. Kuykendall (R), *Memphis*

## TEXAS
### SENATORS
Ralph W. Yarborough (D), *Austin*
John G. Tower (R), *Wichita Falls*

### REPRESENTATIVES
1 Wright Patman (D), *Texarkana*
2 John Dowdy (D), *Athens*
3 James M. Collins (R), *Grand Prairie*
4 H. Ray Roberts (D), *McKinney*
5 Earle Cabell (D), *Dallas*
6 Olin E. Teague (D), *College Station*
7 George Bush (R), *Houston*
8 Robert C. Eckhardt (D), *Houston*
9 Jack B. Brooks (D), *Beaumont*
10 J. J. (Jake) Pickle (D), *Austin*
11 W. R. Poage (D), *Waco*
12 James C. Wright, Jr. (D), *Fort Worth*
13 Graham B. Purcell (D), *Wichita Falls*
14 John A. Young (D), *Corpus Christi*
15 Eligio (Kika) de la Garza (D), *Mission*
16 Richard C. White (D), *El Paso*
17 Omar T. Burleson (D), *Anson*
18 Robert D. Price (R), *Pampa*
19 George H. Mahon (D), *Lubbock*
20 Henry B. Gonzalez (D), *San Antonio*
21 O. Clark Fisher (D), *San Angelo*
22 Robert R. Casey (D), *Houston*
23 Abraham Kazen, Jr. (D), *Laredo*

## UTAH
### SENATORS
Wallace F. Bennett (R), *Salt Lake City*
Frank E. Moss (D), *Salt Lake City*

### REPRESENTATIVES
1 Laurence J. Burton (R), *Ogden*
2 Sherman P. Lloyd (R), *Salt Lake City*

## VERMONT
### SENATORS
George D. Aiken (R), *Putney*
Winston L. Prouty (R), *Newport*

### REPRESENTATIVE AT LARGE
Robert T. Stafford (R), *Rutland*

## VIRGINIA
### SENATORS
Harry Flood Byrd, Jr. (D),[52] *Winchester*
William B. Spong, Jr. (D), *Portsmouth*

### REPRESENTATIVES
1 Thomas N. Downing (D), *Newport News*
2 G. William Whitehurst (R), *Norfolk*
3 David E. Satterfield III (D), *Richmond*
4 Watkins M. Abbitt (D), *Appomattox*
5 W. C. (Dan) Daniel (D), *Danville*
6 Richard H. Poff (R), *Radford*
7 John O. Marsh, Jr. (D), *Strasburg*
8 William L. Scott (R), *Fairfax*
9 William C. Wampler (R), *Bristol*
10 Joel T. Broyhill (R), *Arlington*

## WASHINGTON
### SENATORS
Warren G. Magnuson (D), *Seattle*
Henry M. Jackson (D), *Everett*

### REPRESENTATIVES
1 Thomas M. Pelly (R), *Seattle*
2 Lloyd Meeds (D), *Everett*
3 Julia Butler Hansen (D), *Cathlamet*
4 Catherine May (R), *Yakima*
5 Thomas S. Foley (D), *Spokane*
6 Floyd V. Hicks (D), *Tacoma*
7 Brock Adams (D), *Seattle*

## WEST VIRGINIA
### SENATORS
Jennings Randolph (D), *Elkins*
Robert C. Byrd (D), *Sophia*

### REPRESENTATIVES
1 Robert H. Mollohan (D), *Fairmont*
2 Harley O. Staggers (D), *Keyser*
3 John M. Slack, Jr. (D), *Charleston*
4 Ken Hechler (D), *Huntington*
5 James Kee (D), *Bluefield*

## WISCONSIN
### SENATORS
William Proxmire (D), *Madison*
Gaylord Nelson (D), *Madison*

### REPRESENTATIVES
1 Henry C. Schadeberg (R), *Burlington*
2 Robert W. Kastenmeier (D), *Watertown*
3 Vernon W. Thomson (R), *Richland Center*
4 Clement J. Zablocki (D), *Milwaukee*
5 Henry S. Reuss (D), *Milwaukee*
6 William A. Steiger (R), *Oshkosh*
7 Melvin R. Laird (R),[53] *Marshfield*
7 David R. Obey (D),[54] *Wausau*
8 John W. Byrnes (R), *Green Bay*
9 Glenn R. Davis (R), *Waukesha*
10 Alvin E. O'Konski (D), *Rhinelander*

## WYOMING
### SENATORS
Gale W. McGee (D), *Laramie*
Clifford P. Hansen (R), *Jackson Hole*

### REPRESENTATIVE AT LARGE
John Wold (R), *Casper*

## COMMONWEALTH OF PUERTO RICO
### RESIDENT COMMISSIONER
Jorge L. Córdova (NP), *San Juan*

---

[50] Died January 26, 1969.
[51] Elected March 25, 1969, to fill vacancy caused by death of Robert A. Everett, and took his seat April 1, 1969.

[52] Changed party affiliation to Independent, March 17, 1970.
[53] Resigned January 21, 1969.

[54] Elected April 1, 1969, to fill vacancy caused by resignation of Melvin R. Laird, and took his seat April 3, 1969.

# 92ND CONGRESS

## JANUARY 3, 1971, TO JANUARY 3, 1973

Spiro T. Agnew
Vice President

Carl Albert
Speaker

FIRST SESSION— *January 21, 1971,*[1] *to December 17, 1971*
SECOND SESSION— *January 18, 1972,*[2] *to October 18, 1972*

---

Senate
Democrats 54 — Republicans 44 — Conservative 1 — Independent 1
VICE PRESIDENT OF THE UNITED STATES— SPIRO T. AGNEW, of Maryland
PRESIDENT PRO TEMPORE OF THE SENATE— RICHARD B. RUSSELL,[3] of Georgia; ALLEN J. ELLENDER,[4] of Louisiana; JAMES O. EASTLAND,[5] of Mississippi
SECRETARY OF THE SENATE— FRANCIS R. VALEO, of the District of Columbia
SERGEANT AT ARMS OF THE SENATE— ROBERT G. DUNPHY,[6] of Rhode Island; WILLIAM H. WANNALL,[7] of Maryland
MAJORITY FLOOR LEADER— MIKE MANSFIELD, of Montana
DEMOCRATIC WHIP— ROBERT C. BYRD, of West Virginia
REPUBLICAN FLOOR LEADER— HUGH D. SCOTT, of Pennsylvania
ASSISTANT REPUBLICAN LEADER— ROBERT P. GRIFFIN, of Michigan

---

House of Representatives
Democrats 255 — Republicans 180
SPEAKER OF THE HOUSE— CARL ALBERT,[8] of Oklahoma
CLERK OF THE HOUSE— W. PAT JENNINGS,[9] of Virginia
SERGEANT AT ARMS OF THE HOUSE— ZEAKE W. JOHNSON,[10] of Tennessee; KENNETH R. HARDING,[11] of New York
DOORKEEPER OF THE HOUSE— WILLIAM M. MILLER,[12] of Mississippi
POSTMASTER OF THE HOUSE— H.H. MORRIS,[13] of Kentucky; ROBERT V. ROTA,[14] of Pennsylvania
MAJORITY LEADER— HALE BOGGS, of Louisiana
MAJORITY WHIP— THOMAS P. O'NEILL, JR., of Massachusetts
REPUBLICAN LEADER— GERALD R. FORD, JR., of Michigan
REPUBLICAN WHIP— LESLIE C. ARENDS, of Illinois

---

## ALABAMA

### SENATORS

John J. Sparkman (D), *Huntsville*
James B. Allen (D), *Gadsden*

### REPRESENTATIVES

1 Jack Edwards (R), *Mobile*
2 William L. Dickinson (R), *Montgomery*
3 George W. Andrews (D),[15] *Union Springs*
3 Elizabeth B. Andrews (D),[16] *Union Springs*
4 William Nichols (D), *Sylacauga*
5 Walter Flowers (D), *Tuscaloosa*
6 John H. Buchanan, Jr. (R), *Birmingham*
7 Tom Bevill (D), *Jasper*

8 Robert E. Jones, Jr. (D), *Scottsboro*

## ALASKA

### SENATORS

Theodore F. Stevens (R), *Anchorage*
Maurice R. (Mike) Gravel (D), *Anchorage*

### REPRESENTATIVE AT LARGE

Nicholas J. Begich (D),[17] *Anchorage*

## ARIZONA

### SENATORS

Paul J. Fannin (R), *Phoenix*
Barry M. Goldwater (R), *Scottsdale*

### REPRESENTATIVES

1 John J. Rhodes (R), *Mesa*

2 Morris K. Udall (D), *Tucson*
3 Sam Steiger (R), *Prescott*

## ARKANSAS

### SENATORS

John L. McClellan (D), *Little Rock*
J. William Fulbright (D), *Fayetteville*

### REPRESENTATIVES

1 William V. Alexander, Jr. (D), *Osceola*
2 Wilbur D. Mills (D), *Kensett*
3 John Paul Hammerschmidt (R), *Harrison*
4 David H. Pryor (D), *Camden*

---

[1] By joint resolution (Pub. Law 91 463, 91st Cong., 2d sess.), the date of assembling the first session of the Ninety-second Congress was fixed for January 21, 1971.

[2] By joint resolution (Pub. Law 91 217, 92d Cong., 1st sess.), the date of assembling the second session of the Ninety-second Congress was fixed for January 18, 1972.

[3] Died January 21, 1971.

[4] Elected January 22, 1971; died July 27, 1972.

[5] Elected July 28, 1972.

[6] Resigned June 30, 1972.

[7] Elected July 1, 1972.

[8] Reelected January 21, 1971.

[9] Reelected January 21, 1971.

[10] Reelected January 21, 1971; resigned September 30, 1972.

[11] Elected October 1, 1972.

[12] Reelected January 21, 1971.

[13] Reelected January 21, 1971; resigned June 30, 1972.

[14] Elected July 1, 1972.

[15] Died December 25, 1971.

[16] Elected April 4, 1972, to fill vacancy caused by death of her husband, George W. Andrews, and took her seat April 10, 1972.

[17] Following an airplane crash on October 16, 1972, declared by the State of Alaska to be presumed dead December 29, 1972, before the commencement of the Ninety-third Congress, to which he had been reelected. Vacancy in the Ninety-second Congress was not filled.

## CALIFORNIA

SENATORS

Alan Cranston (D), *Los Angeles*
John V. Tunney (D), *Riverside*

REPRESENTATIVES

1 Don H. Clausen (R), *Crescent City*
2 Harold T. Johnson (D), *Roseville*
3 John E. Moss, Jr. (D), *Sacramento*
4 Robert L. Leggett (D), *Vallejo*
5 Phillip Burton (D), *San Francisco*
6 William S. Mailliard (R), *San Francisco*
7 Ronald V. Dellums (D), *Berkeley*
8 George P. Miller (D), *Alameda*
9 Don Edwards (D), *San Jose*
10 Charles S. Gubser (R), *Gilroy*
11 Paul N. McCloskey, Jr. (R), *Portola Valley*
12 Burt L. Talcott (R), *Salinas*
13 Charles M. Teague (R), *Ojai*
14 Jerome R. Waldie (D), *Antioch*
15 John J. McFall (D), *Manteca*
16 B. F. Sisk (D), *Fresno*
17 Glenn M. Anderson (D), *Harbor City*
18 Robert B. Mathias (R), *Visalia*
19 Chet Holifield (D), *Montebello*
20 H. Allen Smith (R), *Glendale*
21 Augustus F. Hawkins (D), *Los Angeles*
22 James C. Corman (D), *Van Nuys*
23 Del M. Clawson (R), *Compton*
24 John H. Rousselot (R), *San Marino*
25 Charles E. Wiggins (R), *El Monte*
26 Thomas M. Rees (D), *Los Angeles*
27 Barry M. Goldwater, Jr. (R), *Burbank*
28 Alphonzo Bell (R), *Los Angeles*
29 George E. Danielson (D), *Los Angeles*
30 Edward R. Roybal (D), *Los Angeles*
31 Charles H. Wilson (D), *Los Angeles*
32 Craig Hosmer (R), *Long Beach*
33 Jerry L. Pettis (R), *Loma Linda*
34 Richard T. Hanna (D), *Fullerton*
35 John G. Schmitz (R), *Santa Ana*
36 Robert C. Wilson (R), *San Diego*
37 Lionel Van Deerlin (D), *San Diego*
38 Victor V. Veysey (R),[18] *Brawley*

## COLORADO

SENATORS

Gordon L. Allott (R), *Lamar*
Peter H. Dominick (R), *Englewood*

REPRESENTATIVES

1 James D. McKevitt (R), *Denver*

2 Donald G. Brotzman (R), *Boulder*
3 Frank E. Evans (D), *Pueblo*
4 Wayne N. Aspinall (D), *Palisade*

## CONNECTICUT

SENATORS

Abraham A. Ribicoff (D), *Hartford*
Lowell P. Weicker, Jr. (R), *Greenwich*

REPRESENTATIVES

1 William R. Cotter (D), *Hartford*
2 Robert H. Steele (R), *Vernon*
3 Robert N. Giaimo (D), *North Haven*
4 Stewart B. McKinney (R), *Fairfield*
5 John S. Monagan (D), *Waterbury*
6 Ella T. Grasso (D), *Windsor Locks*

## DELAWARE

SENATORS

J. Caleb Boggs (R), *Wilmington*
William V. Roth, Jr. (R), *Wilmington*

REPRESENTATIVE AT LARGE

Pierre S. (Pete) du Pont IV (R), *Wilmington*

## FLORIDA

SENATORS

Edward J. Gurney (R), *Winter Park*
Lawton Chiles (D), *Lakeland*

REPRESENTATIVES

1 Robert L. F. Sikes (D), *Crestview*
2 Don Fuqua (D), *Altha*
3 Charles E. Bennett (D), *Jacksonville*
4 William V. Chappell, Jr. (D), *Ocala*
5 Louis Frey, Jr. (R), *Winter Park*
6 Sam M. Gibbons (D), *Tampa*
7 James A. Haley (D), *Sarasota*
8 C. W. Bill Young (R), *Seminole*
9 Paul G. Rogers (D), *West Palm Beach*
10 J. Herbert Burke (R), *Hollywood*
11 Claude D. Pepper (D), *Miami*
12 Dante B. Fascell (D), *Miami*

## GEORGIA

SENATORS

Richard B. Russell (D),[19] *Winder*
David H. Gambrell (D),[20] *Atlanta*
Sam Nunn (D),[21] *Perry*
Herman E. Talmadge (D), *Lovejoy*

REPRESENTATIVES

1 G. Elliott Hagan (D), *Sylvania*
2 Dawson Mathis (D), *Albany*
3 Jack T. Brinkley (D), *Columbus*

4 Benjamin B. Blackburn (R), *Atlanta*
5 Fletcher Thompson (R), *East Point*
6 John J. Flynt, Jr. (D), *Griffin*
7 John W. Davis (D), *Summerville*
8 Williamson S. Stuckey, Jr. (D), *Eastman*
9 Phillip M. Landrum (D), *Jasper*
10 Robert G. Stephens, Jr. (D), *Athens*

## HAWAII

SENATORS

Hiram L. Fong (R), *Honolulu*
Daniel K. Inouye (D), *Honolulu*

REPRESENTATIVES

1 Spark M. Matsunaga (D), *Honolulu*
2 Patsy T. Mink (D), *Waipahu*

## IDAHO

SENATORS

Frank Church (D), *Boise*
Len B. Jordan (R), *Boise*

REPRESENTATIVES

1 James A. McClure (R), *Payette*
2 Orval Hansen (R), *Idaho Falls*

## ILLINOIS

SENATORS

Charles H. Percy (R), *Wilmette*
Adlai E. Stevenson III (D), *Chicago*

REPRESENTATIVES

1 Ralph H. Metcalfe (D), *Chicago*
2 Abner J. Mikva (D), *Chicago*
3 Morgan F. Murphy (D), *Chicago*
4 Edward J. Derwinski (R), *South Holland*
5 John C. Kluczynski (D), *Chicago*
6 George W. Collins (D),[22] *Chicago*
7 Frank Annunzio (D), *Chicago*
8 Dan Rostenkowski (D), *Chicago*
9 Sidney R. Yates (D), *Chicago*
10 Harold R. Collier (R), *Western Springs*
11 Roman C. Pucinski (D), *Chicago*
12 Robert McClory (R), *Lake Bluff*
13 Philip M. Crane (R), *Winnetka*
14 John N. Erlenborn (R), *Elmhurst*
15 Charlotte T. Reid (R),[23] *Aurora*
15 Cliffard D. Carlson (R),[24] *Geneva*
16 John B. Anderson (R), *Rockford*
17 Leslie C. Arends (R), *Melvin*
18 Robert H. Michel (R), *Peoria*
19 Thomas F. Railsback (R), *Moline*
20 Paul Findley (R), *Pittsfield*

---

[18] Election unsuccessfully contested by David A. Tunno.
[19] Died January 21, 1971.
[20] Appointed February 2, 1971, to fill vacancy caused by death of Richard B. Russell, and took his seat the same day.

[21] Elected November 7, 1972, to fill vacancy caused by death of Richard B. Russell, but was unable to be sworn in as Congress was not in session.
[22] Died December 8, 1972, before the commencement of the Ninety-third Congress, to which he had been reelected; vacancy in the Ninety-second Congress

was not filled.
[23] Resigned October 7, 1971.
[24] Elected April 4, 1972, to fill vacancy caused by resignation of Charlotte T. Reid, and took his seat April 11, 1972.

21 Kenneth J. Gray (D), *West Frankfort*
22 William L. Springer (R), *Champaign*
23 George E. Shipley (D), *Olney*
24 Melvin Price (D), *East St. Louis*

## INDIANA

### SENATORS

Vance Hartke (D), *Evansville*
Birch E. Bayh (D), *Terre Haute*

### REPRESENTATIVES

1 Ray J. Madden (D), *Gary*
2 Earl F. Landgrebe (R), *Valparaiso*
3 John Brademas (D), *South Bend*
4 J. Edward Roush (D), *Huntington*
5 Elwood Hillis (R), *Kokomo*
6 William G. Bray (R), *Martinsville*
7 John T. Myers (R), *Covington*
8 Roger H. Zion (R), *Evansville*
9 Lee H. Hamilton (D), *Columbus*
10 David W. Dennis (R), *Richmond*
11 Andrew Jacobs, Jr. (D), *Indianapolis*

## IOWA

### SENATORS

Jack R. Miller (R), *Sioux City*
Harold E. Hughes (D), *Ida Grove*

### REPRESENTATIVES

1 Frederic D. Schwengel (R), *Davenport*
2 John C. Culver (D), *Marion*
3 H. R. Gross (R), *Waterloo*
4 John H. Kyl (R), *Bloomfield*
5 Neal Smith (D), *Altoona*
6 Wiley Mayne (R), *Sioux City*
7 William J. Scherle (R), *Henderson*

## KANSAS

### SENATORS

James B. Pearson (R), *Prairie Village*
Robert J. Dole (R), *Russell*

### REPRESENTATIVES

1 Keith G. Sebelius (R), *Norton*
2 William R. Roy (D), *Topeka*
3 Larry Winn, Jr. (R), *Leawood*
4 Garner E. Shriver (R), *Wichita*
5 Joe Skubitz (R), *Pittsburg*

## KENTUCKY

### SENATORS

John Sherman Cooper (R), *Somerset*
Marlow W. Cook (R), *Louisville*

### REPRESENTATIVES

1 Frank A. Stubblefield (D), *Murray*
2 William H. Natcher (D), *Bowling Green*
3 Romano L. Mazzoli (D), *Louisville*
4 M. G. (Gene) Snyder (R), *Jeffersontown*
5 Tim Lee Carter (R), *Tompkinsville*
6 John C. Watts (D),[25] *Nicholasville*
6 William P. Curlin, Jr. (D),[26] *Frankfort*
7 Carl D. Perkins (D), *Hindman*

## LOUISIANA

### SENATORS

Allen J. Ellender (D),[27] *Houma*
Elaine S. Edwards (D),[28] *Crowley*
J. Bennett Johnston (D),[29] *Shreveport*
Russell B. Long (D), *Baton Rouge*

### REPRESENTATIVES

1 F. Edward Hébert (D), *New Orleans*
2 Hale Boggs (D),[30] *New Orleans*
3 Patrick T. Caffery (D), *New Iberia*
4 Joe D. Waggonner, Jr. (D), *Plain Dealing*
5 Otto E. Passman (D), *Monroe*
6 John R. Rarick (D), *Baton Rouge*
7 Edwin W. Edwards (D),[31] *Crowley*
7 John B. Breaux (D),[32] *Crowley*
8 Speedy O. Long (D), *Jena*

## MAINE

### SENATORS

Margaret Chase Smith (R), *Skowhegan*
Edmund S. Muskie (D), *Waterville*

### REPRESENTATIVES

1 Peter N. Kyros (D), *Portland*
2 William D. Hathaway (D), *Auburn*

## MARYLAND

### SENATORS

Charles McC. Mathias, Jr. (R), *Frederick*
J. Glenn Beall, Jr. (R), *Frostburg*

### REPRESENTATIVES

1 Rogers C. B. Morton (R),[33] *Easton*
1 William O. Mills (R),[34] *Easton*
2 Clarence D. Long (D), *Ruxton*
3 Edward A. Garmatz (D), *Baltimore*
4 Paul S. Sarbanes (D), *Baltimore*
5 Lawrence J. Hogan (R), *Hyattsville*
6 Goodloe E. Byron (D), *Frederick*

7 Parren J. Mitchell (D), *Baltimore*
8 Gilbert Gude (R), *Bethesda*

## MASSACHUSETTS

### SENATORS

Edward M. Kennedy (D), *Boston*
Edward W. Brooke (R), *Newton Centre*

### REPRESENTATIVES

1 Silvio O. Conte (R), *Pittsfield*
2 Edward P. Boland (D), *Springfield*
3 Robert F. Drinan (D), *Newton*
4 Harold D. Donohue (D), *Worcester*
5 F. Bradford Morse (R),[35] *Lowell*
6 Michael J. Harrington (D), *Beverly*
7 Torbert H. Macdonald (D), *Malden*
8 Thomas P. O'Neill, Jr. (D), *Cambridge*
9 Louise Day Hicks (D), *Boston*
10 Margaret M. Heckler (R), *Wellesley*
11 James A. Burke (D), *Milton*
12 Hastings Keith (R), *West Bridgewater*

## MICHIGAN

### SENATORS

Philip A. Hart (D), *Mackinac Island*
Robert P. Griffin (R), *Traverse City*

### REPRESENTATIVES

1 John Conyers, Jr. (D), *Detroit*
2 Marvin L. Esch (R), *Ann Arbor*
3 Garry E. Brown (R), *Schoolcraft*
4 Edward Hutchinson (R), *Fennville*
5 Gerald R. Ford, Jr. (R), *Grand Rapids*
6 Charles E. Chamberlain (R), *East Lansing*
7 Donald W. Riegle, Jr. (R), *Flint*
8 James Harvey (R), *Saginaw*
9 Guy A. Vander Jagt (R), *Cadillac*
10 Elford A. Cederberg (R), *Bay City*
11 Philip E. Ruppe (R), *Houghton*
12 James G. O'Hara (D), *Utica*
13 Charles C. Diggs, Jr. (D), *Detroit*
14 Lucien N. Nedzi (D), *Detroit*
15 William D. Ford (D), *Taylor*
16 John D. Dingell, Jr. (D), *Detroit*
17 Martha W. Griffiths (D), *Detroit*
18 William S. Broomfield (R), *Royal Oak*
19 Jack H. McDonald (R), *Detroit*

---

[25] Died September 24, 1971.
[26] Elected December 4, 1971, to fill vacancy caused by death of John C. Watts, and took his seat December 6, 1971.
[27] Died July 27, 1972.
[28] Appointed August 1, 1972, to fill vacancy caused by death of Allen J. Ellender, and took her seat August 7, 1972; resigned November 13, 1972.
[29] Appointed November 14, 1972, to fill vacancy

caused by resignation of Elaine S. Edwards, but was unable to be sworn in as Congress was not in session.
[30] Missing in an airplane crash in Alaska on October 16, 1972. By House Resolution 1, Ninety-third Congress, January 3, 1973, the seat was declared vacant, and Mr. Boggs presumed dead.
[31] Resigned May 9, 1972.
[32] Elected September 30, 1972, to fill vacancy caused by resignation of Edwin W. Edwards, and took

his seat October 12, 1972.
[33] Resigned January 29, 1971.
[34] Elected May 25, 1971, to fill vacancy caused by resignation of Rogers C. B. Morton, and took his seat May 27, 1971.
[35] Resigned May 1, 1972; vacancy throughout remainder of Congress.

## MINNESOTA

### SENATORS

Walter F. Mondale (D), *Minneapolis*
Hubert H. Humphrey (D), *Waverly*

### REPRESENTATIVES

1　Albert H. Quie (R), *Dennison*
2　Ancher Nelsen (R), *Hutchinson*
3　Bill Frenzel (R), *Golden Valley*
4　Joseph E. Karth (D), *St. Paul*
5　Donald M. Fraser (D),
　　*Minneapolis*
6　John M. Zwach (R), *Walnut Grove*
7　Bob Bergland (D), *Roseau*
8　John A. Blatnik (D), *Chisholm*

## MISSISSIPPI

### SENATORS

James O. Eastland (D), *Doddsville*
John C. Stennis (D), *De Kalb*

### REPRESENTATIVES

1　Thomas G. Abernethy (D),
　　*Okolona*
2　Jamie L. Whitten (D), *Charleston*
3　Charles H. Griffin (D), *Utica*
4　Gillespie V. (Sonny) Montgomery
　　(D), *Meridian*
5　William M. Colmer (D),
　　*Pascagoula*

## MISSOURI

### SENATORS

Stuart Symington (D), *St. Louis*
Thomas F. Eagleton (D), *St. Louis*

### REPRESENTATIVES

1　William L. Clay (D), *St. Louis*
2　James W. Symington (D), *Clayton*
3　Leonor K. Sullivan (D), *St. Louis*
4　William J. Randall (D),
　　*Independence*
5　Richard W. Bolling (D), *Kansas City*
6　William R. Hull, Jr. (D), *Weston*
7　Durward G. Hall (R), *Springfield*
8　Richard H. Ichord (D), *Houston*
9　William L. Hungate (D), *Troy*
10　Bill D. Burlison (D), *Cape Girardeau*

## MONTANA

### SENATORS

Mike Mansfield (D), *Missoula*
Lee Metcalf (D), *Helena*

### REPRESENTATIVES

1　Richard G. Shoup (R), *Missoula*
2　John Melcher (D), *Forsyth*

## NEBRASKA

### SENATORS

Roman L. Hruska (R), *Omaha*
Carl T. Curtis (R), *Minden*

### REPRESENTATIVES

1　Charles Thone (R), *Lincoln*
2　John Y. McCollister (R), *Omaha*
3　David T. Martin (R), *Kearney*

## NEVADA

### SENATORS

Alan Bible (D), *Reno*
Howard W. Cannon (D), *Las Vegas*

### REPRESENTATIVE AT LARGE

Walter S. Baring (D), *Reno*

## NEW HAMPSHIRE

### SENATORS

Norris Cotton (R), *Lebanon*
Thomas J. McIntyre (D), *Laconia*

### REPRESENTATIVES

1　Louis C. Wyman (R), *Manchester*
2　James C. Cleveland (R), *New London*

## NEW JERSEY

### SENATORS

Clifford P. Case (R), *Rahway*
Harrison A. Williams, Jr. (D),
　　*Westfield*

### REPRESENTATIVES

1　John E. Hunt (R), *Pitman*
2　Charles W. Sandman, Jr. (R),
　　*Cape May*
3　James J. Howard (D), *Wall*
4　Frank Thompson, Jr. (D), *Trenton*
5　Peter H. B. Frelinghuysen (R),
　　*Morristown*
6　Edwin B. Forsythe (R),
　　*Moorestown*
7　William B. Widnall (R), *Saddle River*
8　Robert A. Roe (D), *Wayne*
9　Henry Helstoski (D), *East Rutherford*
10　Peter W. Rodino, Jr. (D), *Newark*
11　Joseph G. Minish (D), *West Orange*
12　Florence P. Dwyer (R), *Elizabeth*
13　Cornelius E. Gallagher (D),
　　*Bayonne*
14　Dominick V. Daniels (D), *Jersey City*
15　Edward J. Patten (D), *Perth Amboy*

## NEW MEXICO

### SENATORS

Clinton P. Anderson (D), *Albuquerque*
Joseph M. Montoya (D), *Santa Fe*

### REPRESENTATIVES

1　Manuel Lujan, Jr. (R),
　　*Albuquerque*
2　Harold Runnels (D), *Lovington*

## NEW YORK

### SENATORS

Jacob K. Javits (R), *New York City*
James L. Buckley (C),[36] *New York City*

### REPRESENTATIVES

1　Otis G. Pike (D), *Riverhead*
2　James R. Grover, Jr. (R), *Babylon*
3　Lester L. Wolff (D), *Great Neck*
4　John W. Wydler (R), *Garden City*
5　Norman F. Lent (R), *East Rockaway*
6　Seymour Halpern (R), *Forest Hills*
7　Joseph P. Addabbo (D), *Ozone Park*
8　Benjamin S. Rosenthal (D),
　　*Elmhurst*
9　James J. Delaney (D), *Long Island City*
10　Emanuel Celler (D), *Brooklyn*
11　Frank J. Brasco (D), *Brooklyn*
12　Shirley A. Chisholm (D), *Brooklyn*
13　Bertram L. Podell (D), *Brooklyn*
14　John J. Rooney (D), *Brooklyn*
15　Hugh L. Carey (D), *Brooklyn*
16　John M. Murphy (D), *Staten Island*
17　Edward I. Koch (D), *New York City*
18　Charles B. Rangel (D), *New York City*
19　Bella S. Abzug (D), *New York City*
20　William Fitts Ryan (D),[37] *New York*
21　Herman Badillo (D), *Bronx*
22　James H. Scheuer (D), *New York City*
23　Jonathan B. Bingham (D), *Bronx*
24　Mario Biaggi (D), *Bronx*
25　Peter A. Peyser (R), *Irvington*
26　Ogden R. Reid (R),[38] *Purchase*
27　John G. Dow (D), *Grand View*
28　Hamilton Fish, Jr. (R), *Millbrook*
29　Samuel S. Stratton (D),
　　*Amsterdam*
30　Carleton J. King (R), *Saratoga Springs*
31　Robert C. McEwen (R),
　　*Ogdensburg*
32　Alexander Pirnie (R), *Utica*
33　Howard W. Robison (R), *Owego*
34　John H. Terry (R), *Syracuse*
35　James M. Hanley (D), *Syracuse*
36　Frank Horton (R), *Rochester*
37　Barber B. Conable, Jr. (R),
　　*Alexander*
38　James F. Hastings (R), *Allegany*
39　Jack F. Kemp (R), *Hamburg*
40　Henry P. Smith III (R), *North Tonawanda*
41　Thaddeus J. Dulski (D), *Buffalo*

---

[36] Elected to the Senate as a Conservative.
[37] Died September 17, 1972; vacancy throughout remainder of Congress.
[38] Changed party affiliation to Democrat, March 22, 1972.

## NORTH CAROLINA

SENATORS

Sam J. Ervin, Jr. (D), *Morganton*
B. Everett Jordan (D), *Saxapahaw*

REPRESENTATIVES

1 Walter B. Jones (D), *Farmville*
2 L. H. Fountain (D), *Tarboro*
3 David N. Henderson (D), *Wallace*
4 Nick Galifianakis (D), *Durham*
5 Wilmer D. Mizell (R), *Winston-Salem*
6 L. Richardson Preyer (D), *Greensboro*
7 Alton A. Lennon (D), *Wilmington*
8 Earl B. Ruth (R), *Salisbury*
9 Charles Raper Jonas (R), *Lincolnton*
10 James T. Broyhill (R), *Lenoir*
11 Roy A. Taylor (D), *Black Mountain*

## NORTH DAKOTA

SENATORS

Milton R. Young (R), *La Moure*
Quentin N. Burdick (D), *Fargo*

REPRESENTATIVES

1 Mark Andrews (R), *Mapleton*
2 Arthur A. Link (D), *Alexander*

## OHIO

SENATORS

William B. Saxbe (R), *Mechanicsburg*
Robert Taft, Jr. (R), *Cincinnati*

REPRESENTATIVES

1 William J. Keating (R), *Cincinnati*
2 Donald D. Clancy (R), *Cincinnati*
3 Charles W. Whalen, Jr. (R), *Dayton*
4 William M. McCulloch (R), *Piqua*
5 Delbert L. Latta (R), *Bowling Green*
6 William H. Harsha (R), *Portsmouth*
7 Clarence J. Brown (R), *Urbana*
8 Jackson E. Betts (R), *Findlay*
9 Thomas L. Ashley (D), *Waterville*
10 Clarence E. Miller (R), *Lancaster*
11 J. William Stanton (R), *Painesville*
12 Samuel L. Devine (R), *Columbus*
13 Charles A. Mosher (R), *Oberlin*
14 John F. Seiberling (D), *Akron*
15 Chalmers P. Wylie (R), *Columbus*
16 Frank T. Bow (R),[39] *Canton*
17 John M. Ashbrook (R), *Johnstown*
18 Wayne L. Hays (D), *Flushing*
19 Charles J. Carney (D), *Youngstown*
20 James V. Stanton (D), *Cleveland*
21 Louis Stokes (D), *Cleveland*
22 Charles A. Vanik (D), *Euclid*
23 William E. Minshall (R), *Lakewood*
24 Walter E. Powell (R), *Fairfield*

## OKLAHOMA

SENATORS

Fred R. Harris (D), *Lawton*
Henry L. Bellmon (R), *Bedrock*

REPRESENTATIVES

1 Page H. Belcher (R), *Tulsa*
2 Edmond Edmondson (D), *Muskogee*
3 Carl Albert (D), *McAlester*
4 Thomas J. Steed (D), *Shawnee*
5 John Jarman (D), *Oklahoma City*
6 John N. Happy Camp (R), *Waukomis*

## OREGON

SENATORS

Mark O. Hatfield (R), *Salem*
Robert W. Packwood (R), *Portland*

REPRESENTATIVES

1 Wendell Wyatt (R), *Astoria*
2 Albert C. Ullman (D), *Baker*
3 Edith S. Green (D), *Portland*
4 John R. Dellenback (R), *Medford*

## PENNSYLVANIA

SENATORS

Hugh D. Scott, Jr. (R), *Philadelphia*
Richard S. Schweiker (R), *Worcester*

REPRESENTATIVES

1 William A. Barrett (D), *Philadelphia*
2 Robert N. C. Nix (D), *Philadelphia*
3 James A. Byrne (D), *Philadelphia*
4 Joshua Eilberg (D), *Philadelphia*
5 William J. Green (D), *Philadelphia*
6 Gus Yatron (D), *Reading*
7 Lawrence G. Williams (R), *Springfield*
8 Edward G. Biester, Jr. (R), *Furlong*
9 John H. Ware (R), *Oxford*
10 Joseph M. McDade (R), *Scranton*
11 Daniel J. Flood (D), *Wilkes-Barre*
12 J. Irving Whalley (R), *Windber*
13 R. Lawrence Coughlin (R), *Villanova*
14 William S. Moorhead (D), *Pittsburgh*
15 Fred B. Rooney (D), *Bethlehem*
16 Edwin D. Eshleman (R), *Lancaster*
17 Herman T. Schneebeli (R), *Williamsport*
18 Robert J. Corbett (R),[40] *Pittsburgh*
18 H. John Heinz III (R),[41] *Pittsburgh*
19 George A. Goodling (R), *Loganville*
20 Joseph M. Gaydos (D), *McKeesport*
21 John H. Dent (D), *Jeannette*
22 John P. Saylor (R), *Johnstown*
23 Albert W. Johnson (R), *Smethport*
24 Joseph P. Vigorito (D), *Erie*
25 Frank M. Clark (D), *Bessemer*
26 Thomas E. Morgan (D), *Fredericktown*
27 James G. Fulton (R),[42] *Pittsburgh*
27 William S. Conover (R),[43] *Pittsburgh*

## RHODE ISLAND

SENATORS

John O. Pastore (D), *Cranston*
Claiborne Pell (D), *Newport*

REPRESENTATIVES

1 Fernand J. St Germain (D), *Woonsocket*
2 Robert O. Tiernan (D), *Warwick*

## SOUTH CAROLINA

SENATORS

Strom Thurmond (R), *Aiken*
Ernest F. Hollings (D), *Charleston*

REPRESENTATIVES

1 Mendel J. Davis (D),[44] *North Charleston*
2 Floyd Spence (R), *Lexington*
3 W. J. Bryan Dorn (D), *Greenwood*
4 James R. Mann (D), *Greenville*
5 Thomas S. Gettys (D), *Rock Hill*
6 John L. McMillan (D), *Florence*

## SOUTH DAKOTA

SENATORS

Karl E. Mundt (R), *Madison*
George S. McGovern (D), *Mitchell*

REPRESENTATIVES

1 Frank E. Denholm (D), *Brookings*
2 James Abourezk (D), *Rapid City*

## TENNESSEE

SENATORS

Howard H. Baker, Jr. (R), *Huntsville*
William E. Brock III (R), *Lookout Mountain*

---

[39] Died November 13, 1972; vacancy throughout remainder of Congress.
[40] Died April 25, 1971.
[41] Elected November 2, 1971, to fill vacancy

caused by death of Robert J. Corbett, and took his seat November 4, 1971.
[42] Died October 6, 1971.
[43] Elected April 25, 1972, to fill vacancy caused by

death of James G. Fulton, and took his seat May 24, 1972.
[44] Elected April 27, 1971, to fill vacancy caused by death of Representative-elect L. Mendel Rivers, in the previous Congress, and took his seat April 29, 1971.

## TENNESSEE—Continued

### REPRESENTATIVES

1 James H. Quillen (R), *Kingsport*
2 John J. Duncan (R), *Knoxville*
3 E. LaMar Baker (R), *Chattanooga*
4 Joseph L. Evins (D), *Smithville*
5 Richard H. Fulton (D), *Nashville*
6 William R. Anderson (D), *Waverly*
7 L. Ray Blanton (D), *Adamsville*
8 Edward Jones (D), *Yorkville*
9 Dan H. Kuykendall (R), *Memphis*

## TEXAS

### SENATORS

John G. Tower (R), *Wichita Falls*
Lloyd M. Bentsen, Jr. (D), *Houston*

### REPRESENTATIVES

1 Wright Patman (D), *Texarkana*
2 John Dowdy (D), *Athens*
3 James M. Collins (R), *Grand Prairie*
4 H. Ray Roberts (D), *McKinney*
5 Earle Cabell (D), *Dallas*
6 Olin E. Teague (D), *College Station*
7 William R. Archer, Jr. (R), *Houston*
8 Robert C. Eckhardt (D), *Houston*
9 Jack B. Brooks (D), *Beaumont*
10 J. J. (Jake) Pickle (D), *Austin*
11 W. R. Poage (D), *Waco*
12 James C. Wright, Jr. (D), *Fort Worth*
13 Graham B. Purcell (D), *Wichita Falls*
14 John A. Young (D), *Corpus Christi*
15 Eligio (Kika) de la Garza (D), *Mission*
16 Richard C. White (D), *El Paso*
17 Omar T. Burleson (D), *Anson*
18 Robert D. Price (R), *Pampa*
19 George H. Mahon (D), *Lubbock*
20 Henry B. Gonzalez (D), *San Antonio*
21 O. Clark Fisher (D), *San Angelo*
22 Robert R. Casey (D), *Houston*
23 Abraham Kazen, Jr. (D), *Laredo*

## UTAH

### SENATORS

Wallace F. Bennett (R), *Salt Lake City*

Frank E. Moss (D), *Salt Lake City*

### REPRESENTATIVES

1 K. Gunn McKay (D), *Huntsville*
2 Sherman P. Lloyd (R), *Salt Lake City*

## VERMONT

### SENATORS

George D. Aiken (R), *Putney*
Winston L. Prouty (R),[45] *Newport*
Robert T. Stafford (R),[46] *Rutland City*

### REPRESENTATIVE AT LARGE

Robert T. Stafford (R),[47] *Rutland*
Richard W. Mallary (R),[48] *Bradford*

## VIRGINIA

### SENATORS

Harry Flood Byrd, Jr. (I), *Winchester*
William B. Spong, Jr. (D), *Portsmouth*

### REPRESENTATIVES

1 Thomas N. Downing (D), *Newport News*
2 G. William Whitehurst (R), *Norfolk*
3 David E. Satterfield III (D), *Richmond*
4 Watkins M. Abbitt (D), *Appomattox*
5 W. C. (Dan) Daniel (D), *Danville*
6 Richard H. Poff (R),[49] *Radford*
6 M. Caldwell Butler (R),[50] *Winchester*
7 J. Kenneth Robinson (R), *Winchester*
8 William L. Scott (R), *Fairfax*
9 William C. Wampler (R), *Bristol*
10 Joel T. Broyhill (R), *Arlington*

## WASHINGTON

### SENATORS

Warren G. Magnuson (D), *Seattle*
Henry M. Jackson (D), *Everett*

### REPRESENTATIVES

1 Thomas M. Pelly (R), *Seattle*
2 Lloyd Meeds (D), *Everett*
3 Julia Butler Hansen (D), *Cathlamet*
4 Mike McCormack (D), *Richland*
5 Thomas S. Foley (D), *Spokane*
6 Floyd V. Hicks (D), *Tacoma*
7 Brock Adams (D), *Seattle*

## WEST VIRGINIA

### SENATORS

Jennings Randolph (D), *Elkins*
Robert C. Byrd (D), *Sophia*

### REPRESENTATIVES

1 Robert H. Mollohan (D), *Fairmont*
2 Harley O. Staggers (D), *Keyser*
3 John M. Slack, Jr. (D), *Charleston*
4 Ken Hechler (D), *Huntington*
5 James Kee (D), *Bluefield*

## WISCONSIN

### SENATORS

William Proxmire (D), *Madison*
Gaylord Nelson (D), *Madison*

### REPRESENTATIVES

1 Les Aspin (D), *Racine*
2 Robert W. Kastenmeier (D), *Watertown*
3 Vernon W. Thomson (R), *Richland Center*
4 Clement J. Zablocki (D), *Milwaukee*
5 Henry S. Reuss (D), *Milwaukee*
6 William A. Steiger (R), *Oshkosh*
7 David R. Obey (D), *Wausau*
8 John W. Byrnes (R), *Green Bay*
9 Glenn R. Davis (R), *New Berlin*
10 Alvin E. O'Konski (R), *Mercer*

## WYOMING

### SENATORS

Gale W. McGee (D), *Laramie*
Clifford P. Hansen (R), *Jackson*

### REPRESENTATIVE AT LARGE

Teno Roncalio (D), *Cheyenne*

## COMMONWEALTH OF PUERTO RICO

### RESIDENT COMMISSIONER

Jorge L. Córdova (NP), *San Juan*

## DISTRICT OF COLUMBIA[51]

### DELEGATE

Walter E. Fauntroy (D),[52] *Washington, D.C.*

---

[45] Died September 10, 1971.

[46] Appointed September 16, 1971, to fill vacancy caused by death of Winston L. Prouty, and took his seat September 17, 1971; subsequently elected.

[47] Resigned September 16, 1971, having been appointed United States Senator.

[48] Elected January 7, 1972, to fill vacancy caused by resignation of Robert T. Stafford, and took his seat January 18, 1972.

[49] Resigned August 29, 1972.

[50] Elected November 7, 1972, to fill vacancy caused by resignation of Richard H. Poff, but was

unable to be sworn in as Congress was not in session.

[51] Granted a Delegate in Congress by Public Law 91 409, September 22, 1970.

[52] Elected March 23, 1971, and took his seat April 19, 1971.

# 93RD CONGRESS

## JANUARY 3, 1973, TO JANUARY 3, 1975

FIRST SESSION— *January 3, 1973, to December 22, 1973*
SECOND SESSION— *January 21, 1974,[1] to December 20, 1974*

### Senate

Democrats 56 — Republicans 42 — Conservative 1 — Independent 1

VICE PRESIDENT OF THE UNITED STATES— Spiro T. Agnew,[2] of Maryland; Gerald R. Ford, Jr.,[3] of Michigan; Nelson A. Rockefeller,[4] of New York

PRESIDENT PRO TEMPORE OF THE SENATE— James O. Eastland, of Mississippi

SECRETARY OF THE SENATE— Francis R. Valeo, of the District of Columbia

SERGEANT AT ARMS OF THE SENATE— William H. Wannall, of Maryland

MAJORITY FLOOR LEADER— Mike Mansfield, of Montana

DEMOCRATIC WHIP— Robert C. Byrd, of West Virginia

REPUBLICAN FLOOR LEADER— Hugh D. Scott, of Pennsylvania

ASSISTANT REPUBLICAN LEADER— Robert P. Griffin, of Michigan

Spiro T. Agnew
Vice President

Carl Albert
Speaker

### House of Representatives

Democrats 243 — Republicans 192

SPEAKER OF THE HOUSE— Carl Albert,[5] of Oklahoma

CLERK OF THE HOUSE— W. Pat Jennings,[6] of Virginia

SERGEANT AT ARMS OF THE HOUSE— Kenneth R. Harding,[7] of Virginia

DOORKEEPER OF THE HOUSE— William M. Miller,[8] of Mississippi; James T. Molloy,[9] of New York

POSTMASTER OF THE HOUSE— Robert V. Rota,[10] of Pennsylvania

MAJORITY LEADER— Thomas P. O'Neill, Jr., of Massachusetts

MAJORITY WHIP— John J. McFall, of California

REPUBLICAN LEADER— Gerald R. Ford, Jr.,[11] of Michigan; John J. Rhodes,[12] of Arizona

REPUBLICAN WHIP— Leslie C. Arends, of Illinois

---

## ALABAMA

### SENATORS

John J. Sparkman (D), *Huntsville*
James B. Allen (D), *Gadsden*

### REPRESENTATIVES

1 Jack Edwards (R), *Mobile*
2 William L. Dickinson (R), *Montgomery*
3 William Nichols (D), *Sylacauga*
4 Tom Bevill (D), *Jasper*
5 Robert E. Jones, Jr. (D), *Scottsboro*
6 John H. Buchanan, Jr. (R), *Birmingham*
7 Walter Flowers (D), *Tuscaloosa*

## ALASKA

### SENATORS

Theodore F. Stevens (R), *Anchorage*

Maurice R. (Mike) Gravel (D), *Anchorage*

### REPRESENTATIVE AT LARGE

Donald E. Young (R),[13] *Fort Yukon*

## ARIZONA

### SENATORS

Paul J. Fannin (R), *Phoenix*
Barry M. Goldwater (R), *Scottsdale*

### REPRESENTATIVES

1 John J. Rhodes (R), *Mesa*
2 Morris K. Udall (D), *Tucson*
3 Sam Steiger (R), *Prescott*
4 John B. Conlan (R), *Phoenix*

## ARKANSAS

### SENATORS

John L. McClellan (D), *Little Rock*

J. William Fulbright (D),[14] *Fayetteville*

### REPRESENTATIVES

1 William V. Alexander, Jr. (D), *Osceola*
2 Wilbur D. Mills (D), *Kensett*
3 John Paul Hammerschmidt (R), *Harrison*
4 Ray Thornton (D), *Sheridan*

## CALIFORNIA

### SENATORS

Alan Cranston (D), *Los Angeles*
John V. Tunney (D), *Riverside*

### REPRESENTATIVES

1 Don H. Clausen (R), *Crescent City*
2 Harold T. Johnson (D), *Roseville*
3 John E. Moss (D), *Sacramento*

---

[1] By joint resolution (Pub. Law 93 196, 93d Cong., 1st sess.), the date of assembling the second session of the Ninety-third Congress was fixed for January 21, 1974.

[2] Term began January 20, 1973; resigned October 10, 1973.

[3] Nominated by the President and confirmed by the Congress, December 6, 1973, to fill vacancy caused by the resignation of Spiro T. Agnew, and assumed office the same day; became President upon the resignation of Richard M. Nixon, August 9, 1974.

[4] Nominated by the President and confirmed by the Congress, December 19, 1974, to fill vacancy when Vice President Gerald R. Ford, Jr., assumed the office of the Presidency.

[5] Reelected January 3, 1973.

[6] Reelected January 3, 1973.

[7] Reelected January 3, 1973.

[8] Reelected January 3, 1973.

[9] Acted as Doorkeeper during the interim.

[10] Reelected January 3, 1973.

[11] Resigned from the House, December 6, 1973.

[12] Elected December 7, 1973.

[13] Elected March 6, 1973, to fill vacancy caused by the death of Representative-elect Nick Begich, in preceding Congress, and took his seat March 14, 1973.

[14] Resigned December 31, 1974; vacancy throughout remainder of Congress.

## CALIFORNIA—Continued
### REPRESENTATIVES—CONTINUED
4 Robert L. Leggett (D), _Vallejo_
5 Phillip Burton (D), _San Francisco_
6 William S. Mailliard (R),[15] _San Francisco_
6 John L. Burton (D),[16] _San Francisco_
7 Ronald V. Dellums (D), _Berkeley_
8 Fortney H. (Pete) Stark, Jr. (D), _Danville_
9 Don Edwards (D), _San Jose_
10 Charles S. Gubser (R),[17] _Gilroy_
11 Leo J. Ryan (D), _South San Francisco_
12 Burt L. Talcott (R), _Salinas_
13 Charles M. Teague (R),[18] _Santa Paula_
13 Robert J. Lagomarsino (R),[19] _Ojai_
14 Jerome R. Waldie (D), _Antioch_
15 John J. McFall (D), _Manteca_
16 B. F. Sisk (D), _Fresno_
17 Paul N. (Pete) McCloskey, Jr. (R), _Portola Valley_
18 Robert B. Mathias (R), _Tulare_
19 Chet Holifield (D),[20] _Montebello_
20 Carlos J. Moorhead (R), _Los Angeles_
21 Augustus F. Hawkins (D), _Los Angeles_
22 James C. Corman (D), _Van Nuys_
23 Del M. Clawson (R), _Downey_
24 John H. Rousselot (R), _San Marino_
25 Charles E. Wiggins (R), _West Covina_
26 Thomas M. Rees (D), _Los Angeles_
27 Barry M. Goldwater, Jr. (R), _Burbank_
28 Alphonzo Bell (R), _Los Angeles_
29 George E. Danielson (D), _Los Angeles_
30 Edward R. Roybal (D), _Los Angeles_
31 Charles H. Wilson (D), _Torrance_
32 Craig Hosmer (R),[21] _Long Beach_
33 Jerry L. Pettis (R), _Loma Linda_
34 Richard T. Hanna (D),[22] _Anaheim_
35 Glenn M. Anderson (D), _Harbor City_
36 William M. Ketchum (R), _Paso Robles_
37 Yvonne Brathwaite Burke (D), _Los Angeles_
38 George E. Brown, Jr. (D), _Colton_
39 Andrew J. Hinshaw (R), _Mission Viejo_
40 Robert C. Wilson (R), _San Diego_
41 Lionel Van Deerlin (D), _San Diego_
42 Clair W. Burgener (R), _Rancho Santa Fe_
43 Victor V. Veysey (R), _Brawley_

## COLORADO
### SENATORS
Peter H. Dominick (R), _Englewood_
Floyd K. Haskell (D), _Littleton_
### REPRESENTATIVES
1 Patricia Schroeder (D), _Denver_
2 Donald G. Brotzman (R), _Boulder_
3 Frank E. Evans (D), _Pueblo_
4 James P. Johnson (R), _Fort Collins_
5 William L. Armstrong (R), _Aurora_

## CONNECTICUT
### SENATORS
Abraham A. Ribicoff (D), _Hartford_
Lowell P. Weicker, Jr. (R), _Greenwich_
### REPRESENTATIVES
1 William R. Cotter (D), _Hartford_
2 Robert H. Steele (R), _Vernon_
3 Robert N. Giaimo (D), _North Haven_
4 Stewart B. McKinney (R), _Fairfield_
5 Ronald A. Sarasin (R), _Beacon Falls_
6 Ella T. Grasso (D), _Windsor Locks_

## DELAWARE
### SENATORS
William V. Roth, Jr. (R), _Wilmington_
Joseph R. Biden, Jr. (D), _Wilmington_
### REPRESENTATIVE AT LARGE
Pierre S. (Pete) du Pont IV (R), _Rockland_

## FLORIDA
### SENATORS
Edward J. Gurney (R),[23] _Winter Park_
Richard Stone (D),[24] _Tallahassee_
Lawton Chiles (D), _Lakeland_
### REPRESENTATIVES
1 Robert L. F. Sikes (D), _Crestview_
2 Don Fuqua (D), _Altha_
3 Charles E. Bennett (D), _Jacksonville_
4 William V. Chappell, Jr. (D), _Ocala_
5 Bill Gunter (D), _Orlando_
6 C. W. Bill Young (R), _St. Petersburg_
7 Sam M. Gibbons (D), _Tampa_
8 James A. Haley (D), _Sarasota_
9 Louis Frey, Jr. (R), _Winter Park_
10 L. A. (Skip) Bafalis (R), _Palm Beach Gardens_
11 Paul G. Rogers (D), _West Palm Beach_
12 J. Herbert Burke (R), _Hollywood_
13 William Lehman (D), _North Miami Beach_
14 Claude D. Pepper (D), _Miami_
15 Dante B. Fascell (D), _Miami_

## GEORGIA
### SENATORS
Herman E. Talmadge (D), _Lovejoy_
Sam Nunn (D), _Perry_
### REPRESENTATIVES
1 Ronald B. (Bo) Ginn (D), _Millen_
2 Dawson Mathis (D), _Albany_
3 Jack T. Brinkley (D), _Columbus_
4 Benjamin B. Blackburn (R), _Atlanta_
5 Andrew Young (D), _Atlanta_
6 John J. Flynt, Jr. (D), _Griffin_
7 John W. Davis (D), _Summerville_
8 Williamson S. Stuckey, Jr. (D), _Eastman_
9 Phillip M. Landrum (D), _Jasper_
10 Robert G. Stephens, Jr. (D), _Athens_

## HAWAII
### SENATORS
Hiram L. Fong (R), _Honolulu_
Daniel K. Inouye (D), _Honolulu_
### REPRESENTATIVES
1 Spark M. Matsunaga (D), _Honolulu_
2 Patsy T. Mink (D), _Waipahu_

## IDAHO
### SENATORS
Frank Church (D), _Boise_
James A. McClure (R), _Payette_
### REPRESENTATIVES
1 Steven D. Symms (R), _Caldwell_
2 Orval Hansen (R), _Idaho Falls_

## ILLINOIS
### SENATORS
Charles H. Percy (R), _Wilmette_
Adlai E. Stevenson III (D), _Chicago_
### REPRESENTATIVES
1 Ralph H. Metcalfe (D), _Chicago_
2 Morgan F. Murphy (D), _Chicago_
3 Robert P. Hanrahan (R), _Homewood_
4 Edward J. Derwinski (R), _Flossmoor_
5 John C. Kluczynski (D), _Chicago_

---

[15] Resigned March 5, 1974.
[16] Elected June 4, 1974, to fill vacancy caused by resignation of William S. Mailliard, and took his seat June 25, 1974.
[17] Resigned December 31, 1974.
[18] Died January 1, 1974.

[19] Elected March 5, 1974, to fill vacancy caused by death of Charles M. Teague, and took his seat March 13, 1974.
[20] Resigned December 31, 1974.
[21] Resigned December 31, 1974.
[22] Resigned December 31, 1974.

[23] Resigned December 31, 1974.
[24] Appointed January 1, 1975, to fill vacancy caused by resignation of Edward J. Gurney, but was unable to be sworn in as Congress was not in session.

6 Harold R. Collier (R), *Riverside*
7 Cardiss Collins (D),[25] *Chicago*
8 Dan Rostenkowski (D), *Chicago*
9 Sidney R. Yates (D), *Chicago*
10 Samuel H. Young (R), *Glenview*
11 Frank Annunzio (D), *Chicago*
12 Philip M. Crane (R), *Mount Prospect*
13 Robert McClory (R), *Lake Bluff*
14 John N. Erlenborn (R), *Elmhurst*
15 Leslie C. Arends (R),[26] *Melvin*
16 John B. Anderson (R), *Rockford*
17 George M. O'Brien (R), *Joliet*
18 Robert H. Michel (R), *Peoria*
19 Thomas F. Railsback (R), *Moline*
20 Paul Findley (R), *Pittsfield*
21 Edward R. Madigan (R), *Lincoln*
22 George E. Shipley (D), *Olney*
23 Melvin Price (D), *East St. Louis*
24 Kenneth J. Gray (D),[27] *West Frankfort*

## INDIANA

### SENATORS

Vance Hartke (D), *Evansville*
Birch E. Bayh (D), *Terre Haute*

### REPRESENTATIVES

1 Ray J. Madden (D), *Gary*
2 Earl F. Landgrebe (R), *Valparaiso*
3 John Brademas (D), *South Bend*
4 J. Edward Roush (D), *Huntington*
5 Elwood Hillis (R), *Kokomo*
6 William G. Bray (R), *Martinsville*
7 John T. Myers (R), *Covington*
8 Roger H. Zion (R), *Evansville*
9 Lee H. Hamilton (D), *Columbus*
10 David W. Dennis (R), *Richmond*
11 William H. Hudnut III (R), *Indianapolis*

## IOWA

### SENATORS

Harold E. Hughes (D), *Ida Grove*
Dick Clark (D), *Marion*

### REPRESENTATIVES

1 Edward Mezvinsky (D), *Iowa City*
2 John C. Culver (D), *Cedar Rapids*
3 H. R. Gross (R), *Waterloo*
4 Neal Smith (D), *Altoona*
5 William J. Scherle (R), *Henderson*
6 Wiley Mayne (R), *Sioux City*

## KANSAS

### SENATORS

James B. Pearson (R), *Prairie Village*
Robert J. Dole (R), *Russell*

### REPRESENTATIVES

1 Keith G. Sebelius (R), *Norton*
2 William R. Roy (D), *Topeka*
3 Larry Winn, Jr. (R), *Overland Park*
4 Garner E. Shriver (R), *Wichita*
5 Joe Skubitz (R), *Pittsburg*

## KENTUCKY

### SENATORS

Marlow W. Cook (R),[28] *Louisville*
Wendell H. Ford (D),[29] *Owensboro*
Walter (Dee) Huddleston (D), *Elizabethtown*

### REPRESENTATIVES

1 Frank A. Stubblefield (D),[30] *Murray*
2 William H. Natcher (D), *Bowling Green*
3 Romano L. Mazzoli (D), *Louisville*
4 M. G. (Gene) Snyder (R), *Jefferson County*
5 Tim Lee Carter (R), *Tompkinsville*
6 John Breckinridge (D), *Lexington*
7 Carl D. Perkins (D), *Hindman*

## LOUISIANA

### SENATORS

Russell B. Long (D), *Baton Rouge*
J. Bennett Johnston (D), *Shreveport*

### REPRESENTATIVES

1 F. Edward Hébert (D), *New Orleans*
2 Hale Boggs (D),[31] *New Orleans*
2 Corinne C. (Lindy) Boggs (D),[32] *New Orleans*
3 David C. Treen (R), *Metairie*
4 Joe D. Waggonner, Jr. (D), *Plain Dealing*
5 Otto E. Passman (D), *Monroe*
6 John R. Rarick (D), *Baton Rouge*
7 John B. Breaux (D), *Crowley*
8 Gillis W. Long (D), *Alexandria*

## MAINE

### SENATORS

Edmund S. Muskie (D), *Waterville*
William D. Hathaway (D), *Auburn*

### REPRESENTATIVES

1 Peter N. Kyros (D), *Portland*
2 William S. Cohen (R), *Bangor*

## MARYLAND

### SENATORS

Charles McC. Mathias, Jr. (R), *Frederick*

J. Glenn Beall, Jr. (R), *Frostburg*

### REPRESENTATIVES

1 William O. Mills (R),[33] *Easton*
1 Robert E. Bauman (R),[34] *Easton*
2 Clarence D. Long (D), *Ruxton*
3 Paul S. Sarbanes (D), *Baltimore*
4 Marjorie S. Holt (R), *Severna Park*
5 Lawrence J. Hogan (R), *Landover*
6 Goodloe E. Byron (D), *Frederick*
7 Parren J. Mitchell (D), *Baltimore*
8 Gilbert Gude (R), *Bethesda*

## MASSACHUSETTS

### SENATORS

Edward M. Kennedy (D), *Boston*
Edward W. Brooke (R), *Newton Centre*

### REPRESENTATIVES

1 Silvio O. Conte (R), *Pittsfield*
2 Edward P. Boland (D), *Springfield*
3 Harold D. Donohue (D),[35] *Worcester*
4 Robert F. Drinan (D), *Newton*
5 Paul W. Cronin (R), *Andover*
6 Michael J. Harrington (D), *Beverly*
7 Torbert H. Macdonald (D), *Malden*
8 Thomas P. O'Neill, Jr. (D), *Cambridge*
9 John Joseph Moakley (D), *Boston*
10 Margaret M. Heckler (R), *Wellesley*
11 James A. Burke (D), *Milton*
12 Gerry E. Studds (D), *Cohasset*

## MICHIGAN

### SENATORS

Philip A. Hart (D), *Mackinac Island*
Robert P. Griffin (R), *Traverse City*

### REPRESENTATIVES

1 John Conyers, Jr. (D), *Detroit*
2 Marvin L. Esch (R), *Ann Arbor*
3 Garry E. Brown (R), *Schoolcraft*
4 Edward Hutchinson (R), *St. Joseph*
5 Gerald R. Ford, Jr. (R),[36] *Grand Rapids*
5 Richard F. Vander Veen (D),[37] *Grand Rapids*

---

[25] Elected June 5, 1973, to fill vacancy caused by death of her husband, Representative-elect George W. Collins, in preceding Congress, and took her seat June 7, 1973.
[26] Resigned December 31, 1974.
[27] Resigned December 31, 1974.
[28] Resigned December 27, 1974.
[29] Appointed December 28, 1974, to fill vacancy caused by resignation of Marlow W. Cook, but was

unable to be sworn in as Congress was not in session.
[30] Resigned December 31, 1974.
[31] Pursuant to H. Res. 1, adopted on January 3, 1973, seat was declared vacant.
[32] Elected March 20, 1973, to fill vacancy caused by death of her husband, Hale Boggs, and took her seat March 27, 1973.
[33] Died May 24, 1973.
[34] Elected August 21, 1973, to fill vacancy caused

by death of William O. Mills, and took his seat September 5, 1973.
[35] Resigned December 31, 1974.
[36] Resigned December 6, 1973; having been nominated and confirmed as Vice President of the United States.
[37] Elected Febuary 18, 1974, to fill vacancy caused by resignation of Gerald R. Ford, Jr., and took his seat February 21, 1974.

## MICHIGAN—Continued

REPRESENTATIVES—CONTINUED

6 Charles E. Chamberlain (R),[38] *East Lansing*
7 Donald W. Riegle, Jr. (R),[39] *Flint*
8 James Harvey (R),[40] *Saginaw*
8 Bob Traxler (D),[41] *Saginaw*
9 Guy A. Vander Jagt (R), *Cadillac*
10 Elford A. Cederberg (R), *Midland*
11 Philip E. Ruppe (R), *Houghton*
12 James G. O'Hara (D), *Utica*
13 Charles C. Diggs, Jr. (D), *Detroit*
14 Lucien N. Nedzi (D), *Detroit*
15 William D. Ford (D), *Taylor*
16 John D. Dingell, Jr. (D), *Trenton*
17 Martha W. Griffiths (D),[42] *Detroit*
18 Robert J. Huber (R), *Troy*
19 William S. Broomfield (R), *Birmingham*

## MINNESOTA

SENATORS

Walter F. Mondale (D), *Minneapolis*
Hubert H. Humphrey (D), *Waverly*

REPRESENTATIVES

1 Albert H. Quie (R), *Dennison*
2 Ancher Nelsen (R),[43] *Hutchinson*
3 Bill Frenzel (R), *Golden Valley*
4 Joseph E. Karth (D), *St. Paul*
5 Donald M. Fraser (D), *Minneapolis*
6 John M. Zwach (R), *Walnut Grove*
7 Bob Bergland (D), *Roseau*
8 John A. Blatnik (D),[44] *Chisholm*

## MISSISSIPPI

SENATORS

James O. Eastland (D), *Doddsville*
John C. Stennis (D), *De Kalb*

REPRESENTATIVES

1 Jamie L. Whitten (D), *Charleston*
2 David R. Bowen (D), *Cleveland*
3 Gillespie V. (Sonny) Montgomery (D), *Meridian*
4 Thad Cochran (R), *Jackson*
5 Trent Lott (R), *Pascagoula*

## MISSOURI

SENATORS

Stuart Symington (D), *St. Louis*
Thomas F. Eagleton (D), *St. Louis*

REPRESENTATIVES

1 William L. Clay (D), *St. Louis*
2 James W. Symington (D), *Clayton*
3 Leonor K. Sullivan (D), *St. Louis*
4 William J. Randall (D), *Independence*
5 Richard W. Bolling (D), *Kansas City*
6 Jerry Litton (D), *Chillicothe*
7 Gene Taylor (R), *Sarcoxie*
8 Richard H. Ichord (D), *Houston*
9 William L. Hungate (D), *Troy*
10 Bill D. Burlison (D), *Cape Girardeau*

## MONTANA

SENATORS

Mike Mansfield (D), *Missoula*
Lee Metcalf (D), *Helena*

REPRESENTATIVES

1 Richard G. Shoup (R), *Missoula*
2 John Melcher (D), *Forsyth*

## NEBRASKA

SENATORS

Roman L. Hruska (R), *Omaha*
Carl T. Curtis (R), *Minden*

REPRESENTATIVES

1 Charles Thone (R), *Lincoln*
2 John Y. McCollister (R), *Omaha*
3 David T. Martin (R),[45] *Kearney*

## NEVADA

SENATORS

Alan Bible (D),[46] *Reno*
Paul Laxalt (R),[47] *Carson City*
Howard W. Cannon (D), *Las Vegas*

REPRESENTATIVE AT LARGE

David Towell (R), *Gardnerville*

## NEW HAMPSHIRE

SENATORS

Norris Cotton (R),[48] *Lebanon*
Louis C. Wyman (R),[49] *Manchester*
Thomas J. McIntyre (D), *Laconia*

REPRESENTATIVES

1 Louis C. Wyman (R),[50] *Manchester*
2 James C. Cleveland (R), *New London*

## NEW JERSEY

SENATORS

Clifford P. Case (R), *Rahway*
Harrison A. Williams, Jr. (D), *Westfield*

REPRESENTATIVES

1 John E. Hunt (R), *Pitman*
2 Charles W. Sandman, Jr. (R), *Cape May*
3 James J. Howard (D), *Wall*
4 Frank Thompson, Jr. (D), *Trenton*
5 Peter H. B. Frelinghuysen (R), *Morristown*
6 Edwin B. Forsythe (R), *Moorestown*
7 William B. Widnall (R),[51] *Saddle River*
8 Robert A. Roe (D), *Wayne*
9 Henry Helstoski (D), *East Rutherford*
10 Peter W. Rodino, Jr. (D), *Newark*
11 Joseph G. Minish (D), *West Orange*
12 Matthew J. Rinaldo (R), *Union*
13 Joseph J. Maraziti (R), *Boonton*
14 Dominick V. Daniels (D), *Jersey City*
15 Edward J. Patten (D), *Perth Amboy*

## NEW MEXICO

SENATORS

Joseph M. Montoya (D), *Santa Fe*
Pete V. Domenici (R), *Albuquerque*

REPRESENTATIVES

1 Manuel Lujan, Jr. (R), *Albuquerque*
2 Harold Runnels (D), *Lovington*

## NEW YORK

SENATORS

Jacob K. Javits (R), *New York*
James L. Buckley (C), *New York*

REPRESENTATIVES

1 Otis G. Pike (D), *Riverhead*
2 James R. Grover, Jr. (R), *Babylon*
3 Angelo D. Roncallo (R), *Massapequa*
4 Norman F. Lent (R), *East Rockaway*
5 John W. Wydler (R), *Garden City*
6 Lester L. Wolff (D), *Great Neck*
7 Joseph P. Addabbo (D), *Ozone Park*
8 Benjamin S. Rosenthal (D), *Elmhurst*
9 James J. Delaney (D), *Long Island City*
10 Mario Biaggi (D), *Brooklyn*
11 Frank J. Brasco (D), *Brooklyn*
12 Shirley A. Chisholm (D), *Brooklyn*
13 Bertram L. Podell (D), *Brooklyn*

---

[38] Resigned December 31, 1974.
[39] Changed party affiliation to Democrat, February 27, 1973.
[40] Resigned January 31, 1974.
[41] Elected April 16, 1974, to fill vacancy caused by resignation of James Harvey, and took his seat April 23, 1974.
[42] Resigned December 31, 1974.

[43] Resigned December 31, 1974.
[44] Resigned December 31, 1974.
[45] Resigned December 31, 1974.
[46] Resigned December 17, 1974.
[47] Appointed December 18, 1974, to fill vacancy caused by resignation of Alan Bible, and took his seat the same day.

[48] Resigned December 31, 1974.
[49] Appointed January 1, 1975, to fill vacancy caused by resignation of Norris Cotton, but was unable to be sworn in as Congress was not in session.
[50] Resigned December 31, 1974, having been appointed United States Senator; vacancy throughout remainder of Congress.
[51] Resigned December 31, 1974.

14 John J. Rooney (D),[52] *Brooklyn*
15 Hugh L. Carey (D),[53] *Brooklyn*
16 Elizabeth Holtzman (D), *Brooklyn*
17 John M. Murphy (D), *Staten Island*
18 Edward I. Koch (D), *New York*
19 Charles B. Rangel (D), *New York*
20 Bella S. Abzug (D), *New York*
21 Herman Badillo (D), *Bronx*
22 Jonathan B. Bingham (D), *Bronx*
23 Peter A. Peyser (R), *Irvington*
24 Ogden R. Reid (D), *Purchase*
25 Hamilton Fish, Jr. (R), *Millbrook*
26 Benjamin A. Gilman (R), *Middlebrook*
27 Howard W. Robison (R), *Candor*
28 Samuel S. Stratton (D), *Amsterdam*
29 Carleton J. King (R),[54] *Saratoga Springs*
30 Robert C. McEwen (R), *Ogdensburg*
31 Donald J. Mitchell (R), *Herkimer*
32 James M. Hanley (D), *Syracuse*
33 William F. Walsh (R), *Syracuse*
34 Frank Horton (R), *Rochester*
35 Barber B. Conable, Jr. (R), *Alexander*
36 Henry P. Smith III (R), *North Tonawanda*
37 Thaddeus J. Dulski (D),[55] *Buffalo*
38 Jack F. Kemp (R), *Hamburg*
39 James F. Hastings (R), *Rushford Lake, Caneadea*

## NORTH CAROLINA

### SENATORS

Sam J. Ervin, Jr. (D),[56] *Morganton*
Jesse Helms (R), *Raleigh*

### REPRESENTATIVES

1 Walter B. Jones (D), *Farmville*
2 L. H. Fountain (D), *Tarboro*
3 David N. Henderson (D), *Wallace*
4 Ike F. Andrews (D), *Siler City*
5 Wilmer D. Mizell (R), *Winston-Salem*
6 L. Richardson Preyer (D), *Greensboro*
7 Charles Rose (D), *Fayetteville*
8 Earl B. Ruth (R), *Salisbury*
9 James G. Martin (R), *Davidson*
10 James T. Broyhill (R), *Lenoir*
11 Roy A. Taylor (D), *Black Mountain*

## NORTH DAKOTA

### SENATORS

Milton R. Young (R), *La Moure*
Quentin N. Burdick (D), *Fargo*

### REPRESENTATIVE AT LARGE

Mark Andrews (R), *Mapleton*

## OHIO

### SENATORS

William B. Saxbe (R),[57] *Mechanicsburg*
Howard M. Metzenbaum (D),[58] *Cleveland*
John Glenn, Jr. (D),[59] *Columbus*
Robert Taft, Jr. (R), *Cincinnati*

### REPRESENTATIVES

1 William J. Keating (R),[60] *Cincinnati*
1 Thomas A. Luken (D),[61] *Cincinnati*
2 Donald D. Clancy (R), *Cincinnati*
3 Charles W. Whalen, Jr. (R), *Dayton*
4 Tennyson Guyer (R), *Findley*
5 Delbert L. Latta (R), *Bowling Green*
6 William H. Harsha (R), *Portsmouth*
7 Clarence J. Brown (R), *Urbana*
8 Walter E. Powell (R), *Fairfield*
9 Thomas L. Ashley (D), *Maumee*
10 Clarence E. Miller (R), *Lancaster*
11 J. William Stanton (R), *Painesville*
12 Samuel L. Devine (R), *Columbus*
13 Charles A. Mosher (R), *Oberlin*
14 John F. Seiberling (D), *Akron*
15 Chalmers P. Wylie (R), *Columbus*
16 Ralph S. Regula (R), *Navarre*
17 John M. Ashbrook (R), *Johnstown*
18 Wayne L. Hays (D), *Flushing*
19 Charles J. Carney (D), *Youngstown*
20 James V. Stanton (D), *Cleveland*
21 Louis Stokes (D), *Cleveland*
22 Charles A. Vanik (D), *Euclid*
23 William E. Minshall (R),[62] *Lakewood*

## OKLAHOMA

### SENATORS

Henry L. Bellmon (R), *Billings*
Dewey F. Bartlett (R), *Tulsa*

### REPRESENTATIVES

1 James R. Jones (D), *Tulsa*
2 Clem Rogers McSpadden (D), *Claremore*
3 Carl Albert (D), *McAlester*
4 Thomas J. Steed (D), *Shawnee*
5 John Jarman (D), *Oklahoma City*
6 John N. Happy Camp (R), *Waukomis*

## OREGON

### SENATORS

Mark O. Hatfield (R), *Salem*
Robert W. Packwood (R), *Portland*

### REPRESENTATIVES

1 Wendell Wyatt (R), *Gearhart*
2 Albert C. Ullman (D), *Baker*
3 Edith S. Green (D),[63] *Portland*
4 John R. Dellenback (R), *Medford*

## PENNSYLVANIA

### SENATORS

Hugh D. Scott, Jr. (R), *Philadelphia*
Richard S. Schweiker (R), *Worcester*

### REPRESENTATIVES

1 William A. Barrett (D), *Philadelphia*
2 Robert N. C. Nix (D), *Philadelphia*
3 William J. Green (D), *Philadelphia*
4 Joshua Eilberg (D), *Philadelphia*
5 John H. Ware (R), *Oxford*
6 Gus Yatron (D), *Reading*
7 Lawrence G. Williams (R), *Springfield*
8 Edward G. Biester, Jr. (R), *Furlong*
9 E. G. Shuster (R), *Everett*
10 Joseph M. McDade (R), *Scranton*
11 Daniel J. Flood (D), *Wilkes-Barre*
12 John P. Saylor (R),[64] *Johnstown*
12 John P. Murtha, Jr. (D),[65] *Johnstown*
13 R. Lawrence Coughlin (R), *Villanova*
14 William S. Moorhead (D), *Pittsburgh*
15 Fred B. Rooney (D), *Bethlehem*
16 Edwin D. Eshleman (R), *Lancaster*
17 Herman T. Schneebeli (R), *Williamsport*

---

[52] Resigned December 31, 1974.
[53] Resigned December 31, 1974.
[54] Resigned December 31, 1974.
[55] Resigned December 31, 1974.
[56] Resigned December 31, 1974.
[57] Resigned January 3, 1974.
[58] Appointed January 4, 1974, to fill vacancy caused by resignation of William B. Saxbe, but was unable to be sworn in as Congress was not in session; took his seat January 21, 1974; resigned December 23, 1974.
[59] Appointed December 24, 1974, to fill vacancy caused by resignation of Howard M. Metzenbaum, but was unable to be sworn in as Congress was not in session.
[60] Resigned January 3, 1974.
[61] Elected March 5, 1974, to fill vacancy caused by resignation of William J. Keating, and took his seat March 7, 1974.
[62] Resigned December 31, 1974.
[63] Resigned December 31, 1974.
[64] Died October 28, 1973.
[65] Elected February 5, 1974, to fill vacancy caused by death of John P. Saylor, and took his seat February 20, 1974.

## PENNSYLVANIA—Continued

### REPRESENTATIVES—CONTINUED
18 H. John Heinz III (R), *Pittsburgh*
19 George A. Goodling (R), *Loganville*
20 Joseph M. Gaydos (D), *McKeesport*
21 John H. Dent (D), *Ligonier*
22 Thomas E. Morgan (D), *Fredericktown*
23 Albert W. Johnson (R), *Smethport*
24 Joseph P. Vigorito (D), *Erie*
25 Frank M. Clark (D),[66] *Bessemer*

## RHODE ISLAND

### SENATORS
John O. Pastore (D), *Cranston*
Claiborne Pell (D), *Newport*

### REPRESENTATIVES
1 Fernand J. St Germain (D), *Woonsocket*
2 Robert O. Tiernan (D), *Warwick*

## SOUTH CAROLINA

### SENATORS
Strom Thurmond (R), *Aiken*
Ernest F. Hollings (D), *Charleston*

### REPRESENTATIVES
1 Mendel J. Davis (D), *North Charleston*
2 Floyd Spence (R), *Lexington*
3 W. J. Bryan Dorn (D),[67] *Greenwood*
4 James R. Mann (D), *Greenville*
5 Thomas S. Gettys (D),[68] *Rock Hill*
6 Edward L. Young (R), *Florence*

## SOUTH DAKOTA

### SENATORS
George S. McGovern (D), *Mitchell*
James Abourezk (D), *Rapid City*

### REPRESENTATIVES
1 Frank E. Denholm (D), *Brookings*
2 James Abdnor (R), *Kennebec*

## TENNESSEE

### SENATORS
Howard H. Baker, Jr. (R), *Huntsville*
William E. Brock III (R), *Lookout Mountain*

### REPRESENTATIVES
1 James H. Quillen (R), *Kingsport*
2 John J. Duncan (R), *Knoxville*
3 E. LaMar Baker (R), *Chattanooga*
4 Joseph L. Evins (D), *Smithville*
5 Richard H. Fulton (D), *Nashville*
6 Robin L. Beard (R), *Brentwood*
7 Edward Jones (D), *Yorkville*
8 Dan H. Kuykendall (R), *Memphis*

## TEXAS

### SENATORS
John G. Tower (R), *Wichita Falls*
Lloyd M. Bentsen, Jr. (D), *Houston*

### REPRESENTATIVES
1 Wright Patman (D), *Texarkana*
2 Charles Wilson (D), *Lufkin*
3 James M. Collins (R), *Irving*
4 H. Ray Roberts (D), *McKinney*
5 Alan Steelman (R), *Dallas*
6 Olin E. Teague (D), *College Station*
7 William R. Archer, Jr. (R), *Houston*
8 Robert C. Eckhardt (D), *Harris County*
9 Jack B. Brooks (D), *Beaumont*
10 J. J. (Jake) Pickle (D), *Austin*
11 W. R. Poage (D), *Waco*
12 James C. Wright, Jr. (D), *Fort Worth*
13 Robert D. Price (R), *Pampa*
14 John A. Young (D), *Corpus Christi*
15 Eligio (Kika) de la Garza (D), *Mission*
16 Richard C. White (D), *El Paso*
17 Omar T. Burleson (D), *Anson*
18 Barbara Jordan (D), *Houston*
19 George H. Mahon (D), *Lubbock*
20 Henry B. Gonzalez (D), *San Antonio*
21 O. Clark Fisher (D),[69] *San Angelo*
22 Robert R. Casey (D), *Houston*
23 Abraham Kazen, Jr. (D), *Laredo*
24 Dale Milford (D), *Grand Prairie*

## UTAH

### SENATORS
Wallace F. Bennett (R),[70] *Salt Lake City*
E. J. (Jake) Garn (R),[71] *Salt Lake City*
Frank E. Moss (D), *Salt Lake City*

### REPRESENTATIVES
1 K. Gunn McKay (D), *Huntsville*
2 Wayne Owens (D), *Salt Lake City*

## VERMONT

### SENATORS
George D. Aiken (R), *Putney*
Robert T. Stafford (R), *Rutland*

### REPRESENTATIVE AT LARGE
Richard W. Mallary (R), *Bradford*

## VIRGINIA

### SENATORS
Harry Flood Byrd, Jr. (I), *Winchester*
William L. Scott (R), *Fairfax*

### REPRESENTATIVES
1 Thomas N. Downing (D), *Newport News*
2 G. William Whitehurst (R), *Norfolk*
3 David E. Satterfield III (D), *Richmond*
4 Robert W. Daniel, Jr. (R), *Spring Cove*
5 W. C. (Dan) Daniel (D), *Danville*
6 M. Caldwell Butler (R), *Winchester*
7 J. Kenneth Robinson (R), *Winchester*
8 Stanford E. Parris (R), *Fairfax Station*
9 William C. Wampler (R), *Bristol*
10 Joel T. Broyhill (R),[72] *Arlington*

## WASHINGTON

### SENATORS
Warren G. Magnuson (D), *Seattle*
Henry M. Jackson (D), *Everett*

### REPRESENTATIVES
1 Joel Pritchard (R), *Seattle*
2 Lloyd Meeds (D), *Everett*
3 Julia Butler Hansen (D),[73] *Cathlamet*
4 Mike McCormack (D), *Richland*
5 Thomas S. Foley (D), *Spokane*
6 Floyd V. Hicks (D), *Tacoma*
7 Brock Adams (D), *Seattle*

## WEST VIRGINIA

### SENATORS
Jennings Randolph (D), *Elkins*
Robert C. Byrd (D), *Sophia*

### REPRESENTATIVES
1 Robert H. Mollohan (D), *Fairmont*
2 Harley O. Staggers (D), *Keyser*
3 John M. Slack, Jr. (D), *Charleston*
4 Ken Hechler (D), *Huntington*

## WISCONSIN

### SENATORS
William Proxmire (D), *Madison*
Gaylord Nelson (D), *Madison*

### REPRESENTATIVES
1 Les Aspin (D), *Racine*
2 Robert W. Kastenmeier (D), *Sun Prairie*
3 Vernon W. Thomson (R),[74] *Richland Center*
4 Clement J. Zablocki (D), *Milwaukee*

---

[66] Resigned December 31, 1974.
[67] Resigned December 31, 1974.
[68] Resigned December 31, 1974.
[69] Resigned December 31, 1974.
[70] Resigned December 20, 1974.
[71] Appointed December 21, 1974, to fill vacancy caused by resignation of Wallace F. Bennett, but was unable to be sworn in as Congress was not in session.
[72] Resigned December 31, 1974.
[73] Resigned December 31, 1974.
[74] Resigned December 31, 1974.

5 Henry S. Reuss (D), *Milwaukee*
6 William A. Steiger (R), *Oshkosh*
7 David R. Obey (D), *Wausau*
8 Harold V. Froehlich (R), *Appleton*
9 Glenn R. Davis (R),[75] *Waukesha*

## WYOMING

### SENATORS

Gale W. McGee (D), *Laramie*
Clifford P. Hansen (R), *Jackson*

#### REPRESENTATIVE AT LARGE

Teno Roncalio (D), *Cheyenne*

## COMMONWEALTH OF PUERTO RICO

### RESIDENT COMMISSIONER

Jaime Benitez (PD), *Carey*

## DISTRICT OF COLUMBIA

#### DELEGATE

Walter E. Fauntroy (D), *Washington, D.C.*

## GUAM[76]

### DELEGATE

Antonio Borja Won Pat (D),[77] *Sinajano*

## VIRGIN ISLANDS[78]

### DELEGATE

Ron de Lugo (D),[79] *St. Croix*

---

[75] Resigned December 31, 1974.
[76] Granted a Delegate in Congress by Public Law 92-271, dated April 10, 1972.

[77] Elected November 7, 1972, and took his seat January 3, 1973.
[78] Granted a Delegate in Congress by Pubic Law

92-271, dated April 10, 1972.
[79] Elected and took his seat January 3, 1973.

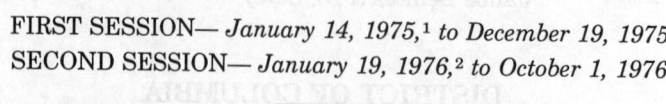

# 94TH CONGRESS

## JANUARY 3, 1975, TO JANUARY 3, 1977

FIRST SESSION— *January 14, 1975,*[1] *to December 19, 1975*
SECOND SESSION— *January 19, 1976,*[2] *to October 1, 1976*

Nelson A. Rockefeller
Vice President

Carl Albert
Speaker

### Senate

Democrats 60 — Republicans 37 — Conservative 1 — Independent 1 — Vacant 1

VICE PRESIDENT OF THE UNITED STATES— NELSON A. ROCKEFELLER, of New York
PRESIDENT PRO TEMPORE OF THE SENATE— JAMES O. EASTLAND, of Mississippi
SECRETARY OF THE SENATE— FRANCIS R. VALEO, of the District of Columbia
SERGEANT AT ARMS OF THE SENATE— WILLIAM H. WANNALL,[3] of Maryland; F. NORDY
HOFFMANN,[4] of Maryland
MAJORITY FLOOR LEADER— MIKE MANSFIELD, of Montana
DEMOCRATIC WHIP— ROBERT C. BYRD, of West Virginia
REPUBLICAN FLOOR LEADER— HUGH D. SCOTT, of Pennsylvania
ASSISTANT REPUBLICAN LEADER— ROBERT P. GRIFFIN, of Michigan

---

### House of Representatives

Democrats 290 — Republicans 144 — Vacant 1

SPEAKER OF THE HOUSE— CARL ALBERT,[5] of Oklahoma
CLERK OF THE HOUSE— W. PAT JENNINGS,[6] of Virginia; EDMUND L. HENSHAW, JR.,[7] of Virginia
SERGEANT AT ARMS OF THE HOUSE— KENNETH R. HARDING,[8] of Virginia
DOORKEEPER OF THE HOUSE— JAMES T. MOLLOY,[9] of New York
POSTMASTER OF THE HOUSE— ROBERT V. ROTA,[10] of Pennsylvania
MAJORITY LEADER— THOMAS P. O'NEILL, JR., of Massachusetts
MAJORITY WHIP— JOHN J. McFALL, of California
REPUBLICAN LEADER— JOHN J. RHODES, of Arizona
REPUBLICAN WHIP— ROBERT H. MICHEL, of Illinois

---

## ALABAMA

### SENATORS

John J. Sparkman (D), *Huntsville*
James B. Allen (D), *Gadsden*

### REPRESENTATIVES

1 Jack Edwards (R), *Mobile*
2 William L. Dickinson (R), *Montgomery*
3 William Nichols (D), *Sylacauga*
4 Tom Bevill (D), *Jasper*
5 Robert E. Jones, Jr. (D), *Scottsboro*
6 John H. Buchanan, Jr. (R), *Birmingham*
7 Walter Flowers (D), *Tuscaloosa*

## ALASKA

### SENATORS

Theodore F. Stevens (R), *Anchorage*
Maurice R. (Mike) Gravel (D), *Anchorage*

### REPRESENTATIVE AT LARGE

Donald E. Young (R), *Fort Yukon*

## ARIZONA

### SENATORS

Paul J. Fannin (D), *Phoenix*
Barry M. Goldwater (R), *Scottsdale*

### REPRESENTATIVES

1 John J. Rhodes (R), *Mesa*
2 Morris K. Udall (D), *Tucson*
3 Sam Steiger (R), *Prescott*
4 John B. Conlan (R), *Phoenix*

## ARKANSAS

### SENATORS

John L. McClellan (D), *Little Rock*
Dale Bumpers (D), *Charleston*

### REPRESENTATIVES

1 William V. Alexander, Jr. (D), *Osceola*
2 Wilbur D. Mills (D), *Kensett*
3 John Paul Hammerschmidt (R), *Harrison*
4 Ray Thornton (D), *Sheridan*

## CALIFORNIA

### SENATORS

Alan Cranston (D), *Los Angeles*
John V. Tunney (D),[11] *Riverside*
S. I. Hayakawa (R),[12] *Mill Valley*

### REPRESENTATIVES

1 Harold T. Johnson (D), *Roseville*
2 Don H. Clausen (R), *Crescent City*
3 John E. Moss (D), *Sacramento*
4 Robert L. Leggett (D), *Vallejo*
5 John Burton (D), *San Francisco*
6 Phillip Burton (D), *San Francisco*
7 George Miller (D), *Martinez*

---

[1] By joint resolution (Pub. Law 93 553, 93d Cong., 2d sess.), the date of assembling the first session of the Ninety-fourth Congress was fixed for January 14, 1975.

[2] By joint resolution (Pub. Law 94 186, 94th Cong., 1st sess.), the date of assembling the second session of the Ninety-fourth Congress was fixed for January 19, 1976.

[3] Resigned December 31, 1975.
[4] Elected effective January 1, 1976.
[5] Reelected January 14, 1975.
[6] Reelected January 14, 1975; resigned November 15, 1975.
[7] Appointed acting Clerk of the House of Representatives November 16, 1975; elected Clerk December 17, 1975.

[8] Reelected January 14, 1975.
[9] Elected January 14, 1975.
[10] Reelected January 14, 1975.
[11] Resigned January 1, 1977.
[12] Appointed January 2, 1977, to fill vacancy caused by resignation of John V. Tunney, but was unable to be sworn in as Congress was not in session.

8  Ronald V. Dellums (D), *Berkeley*
9  Fortney H. (Pete) Stark, Jr. (D), *Oakland*
10 Don Edwards (D), *San Jose*
11 Leo J. Ryan (D), *South San Francisco*
12 Paul N. (Pete) McCloskey, Jr. (R), *Menlo Park*
13 Norman Y. Mineta (D), *San Jose*
14 John J. McFall (D), *Manteca*
15 B. F. Sisk (D), *Fresno*
16 Burt L. Talcott (R), *Salinas*
17 John Krebs (D), *Fresno*
18 William M. Ketchum (R), *Bakersfield*
19 Robert J. Lagomarsino (R), *Ojai*
20 Barry M. Goldwater, Jr. (R), *Woodland Hills*
21 James C. Corman (D), *Van Nuys*
22 Carlos J. Moorhead (R), *Glendale*
23 Thomas M. Rees (D), *Los Angeles*
24 Henry A. Waxman (D), *Los Angeles*
25 Edward R. Roybal (D), *Los Angeles*
26 John H. Rousselot (R), *San Marino*
27 Alphonzo Bell (R), *Los Angeles*
28 Yvonne Brathwaite Burke (D), *Los Angeles*
29 Augustus F. Hawkins (D), *Los Angeles*
30 George E. Danielson (D), *Monterey Park*
31 Charles H. Wilson (D), *Hawthorne*
32 Glenn M. Anderson (D), *Harbor City*
33 Del M. Clawson (R), *Downey*
34 Mark W. Hannaford (D), *Lakewood*
35 Jim Lloyd (D), *West Covina*
36 George E. Brown, Jr. (D), *Colton*
37 Jerry L. Pettis (R),[13] *Loma Linda*
37 Shirley N. Pettis (R),[14] *Loma Linda*
38 Jerry M. Patterson (D), *Santa Ana*
39 Charles E. Wiggins (R), *Fullerton*
40 Andrew J. Hinshaw (R),[15] *Newport Beach*
41 Robert C. Wilson (R), *San Diego*
42 Lionel Van Deerlin (D), *Chula Vista*
43 Clair W. Burgener (R), *Rancho Santa Fe*

## COLORADO

SENATORS

Floyd K. Haskell (D), *Littleton*
Gary Hart (D), *Denver*

REPRESENTATIVES

1 Patricia Schroeder (D), *Denver*

---

2 Timothy E. Wirth (D), *Denver*
3 Frank E. Evans (D), *Beulah*
4 James P. Johnson (R), *Fort Collins*
5 William L. Armstrong (R), *Aurora*

## CONNECTICUT

SENATORS

Abraham A. Ribicoff (D), *Hartford*
Lowell P. Weicker, Jr. (R), *Greenwich*

REPRESENTATIVES

1 William R. Cotter (D), *Hartford*
2 Christopher J. Dodd (D), *North Stonington*
3 Robert N. Giaimo (D), *North Haven*
4 Stewart B. McKinney (R), *Fairfield*
5 Ronald A. Sarasin (R), *Beacon Falls*
6 Toby Moffett (D), *Unionville*

## DELAWARE

SENATORS

William V. Roth, Jr. (R), *Wilmington*
Joseph R. Biden, Jr. (D), *Wilmington*

REPRESENTATIVE AT LARGE

Pierre S. (Pete) du Pont IV (R), *Rockland*

## FLORIDA

SENATORS

Lawton Chiles (D), *Lakeland*
Richard Stone (D), *Tallahassee*

REPRESENTATIVES

1 Robert L. F. Sikes (D), *Crestview*
2 Don Fuqua (D), *Altha*
3 Charles E. Bennett (D), *Jacksonville*
4 William V. Chappell, Jr. (D), *Ocala*
5 Richard Kelly (R), *Holiday*
6 C. W. Bill Young (R), *Clearwater*
7 Sam M. Gibbons (D), *Tampa*
8 James A. Haley (D), *Sarasota*
9 Louis Frey, Jr. (R), *Winter Park*
10 L. A. (Skip) Bafalis (R), *Fort Myers Beach*
11 Paul G. Rogers (D), *West Palm Beach*
12 J. Herbert Burke (R), *Hollywood*
13 William Lehman (D), *North Miami Beach*
14 Claude D. Pepper (D), *Miami*
15 Dante B. Fascell (D), *Miami*

## GEORGIA

SENATORS

Herman E. Talmadge (D), *Lovejoy*
Sam Nunn (D), *Perry*

---

REPRESENTATIVES

1 Ronald B. (Bo) Ginn (D), *Millen*
2 Dawson Mathis (D), *Albany*
3 Jack T. Brinkley (D), *Columbus*
4 Elliott H. Levitas (D), *Atlanta*
5 Andrew Young (D), *Atlanta*
6 John J. Flynt, Jr. (D), *Griffin*
7 Larry McDonald (D), *Marietta*
8 Williamson S. Stuckey, Jr. (D), *Eastman*
9 Phillip M. Landrum (D), *Jasper*
10 Robert G. Stephens, Jr. (D), *Athens*

## HAWAII

SENATORS

Hiram L. Fong (R), *Honolulu*
Daniel K. Inouye (D), *Honolulu*

REPRESENTATIVES

1 Spark M. Matsunaga (D), *Honolulu*
2 Patsy T. Mink (D), *Waipahu*

## IDAHO

SENATORS

Frank Church (D), *Boise*
James A. McClure (R), *Payette*

REPRESENTATIVES

1 Steven D. Symms (R), *Caldwell*
2 George Hansen (R), *Pocatello*

## ILLINOIS

SENATORS

Charles H. Percy (R), *Wilmette*
Adlai E. Stevenson III (D), *Hanover*

REPRESENTATIVES

1 Ralph H. Metcalfe (D), *Chicago*
2 Morgan F. Murphy (D), *Chicago*
3 Martin A. Russo (D), *South Holland*
4 Edward J. Derwinski (R), *Flossmoor*
5 John C. Kluczynski (D),[16] *Chicago*
5 John G. Fary (D),[17] *Chicago*
6 Henry J. Hyde (R), *Park Ridge*
7 Cardiss Collins (D), *Chicago*
8 Dan Rostenkowski (D), *Chicago*
9 Sidney R. Yates (D), *Chicago*
10 Abner J. Mikva (D),[18] *Evanston*
11 Frank Annunzio (D), *Chicago*
12 Philip M. Crane (R), *Mount Prospect*
13 Robert McClory (R), *Lake Bluff*
14 John N. Erlenborn (R), *Glen Ellyn*
15 Tim L. Hall (D), *Dwight*
16 John B. Anderson (R), *Rockford*
17 George M. O'Brien (R), *Joliet*
18 Robert H. Michel (R), *Peoria*
19 Thomas F. Railsback (R), *Moline*
20 Paul Findley (R), *Pittsfield*
21 Edward R. Madigan (R), *Lincoln*

---

[13] Died February 14, 1975.
[14] Elected April 29, 1975, to fill vacancy caused by death of her husband, Jerry L. Pettis, and took her seat May 6, 1975.

[15] Election unsuccessfully contested by Roderick J. Wilson.
[16] Died January 26, 1975.
[17] Elected July 8, 1975, to fill vacancy caused by

death of John C. Kluczynski, and took his seat July 15, 1975.
[18] Election unsuccessfully contested by Samuel H. Young.

## ILLINOIS—Continued

### REPRESENTATIVES—CONTINUED

22 George E. Shipley (D), *Olney*
23 Melvin Price (D), *East St. Louis*
24 Paul Simon (D), *Carbondale*

## INDIANA

### SENATORS

Vance Hartke (D), *Evansville*
Birch E. Bayh (D), *Terre Haute*

### REPRESENTATIVES

1 Ray J. Madden (D), *Gary*
2 Floyd J. Fithian (D), *Lafayette*
3 John Brademas (D), *South Bend*
4 J. Edward Roush (D), *Huntington*
5 Elwood Hillis (R), *Kokomo*
6 David W. Evans (D), *Indianapolis*
7 John T. Myers (R), *Covington*
8 Philip H. Hayes (D), *Evansville*
9 Lee H. Hamilton (D), *Columbus*
10 Philip R. Sharp (D), *Muncie*
11 Andrew Jacobs, Jr. (D), *Indianapolis*

## IOWA

### SENATORS

Dick Clark (D), *Marion*
John C. Culver (D), *Cedar Rapids*

### REPRESENTATIVES

1 Edward Mezvinsky (D), *Iowa City*
2 Michael T. Blouin (D), *Dubuque*
3 Charles E. Grassley (R), *New Hartford*
4 Neal Smith (D), *Altoona*
5 Tom Harkin (D), *Ames*
6 Berkley Bedell (D), *Spirit Lake*

## KANSAS

### SENATORS

James B. Pearson (R), *Shawnee Mission*
Robert J. Dole (R), *Russell*

### REPRESENTATIVES

1 Keith G. Sebelius (R), *Norton*
2 Martha Keys (D), *Manhattan*
3 Larry Winn, Jr. (R), *Overland Park*
4 Garner E. Shriver (R), *Wichita*
5 Joe Skubitz (R), *Pittsburg*

## KENTUCKY

### SENATORS

Walter (Dee) Huddleston (D), *Elizabethtown*
Wendell H. Ford, *Owensboro*

### REPRESENTATIVES

1 Carroll Hubbard, Jr. (D), *Mayfield*

2 William H. Natcher (D), *Bowling Green*
3 Romano L. Mazzoli (D), *Louisville*
4 M. G. (Gene) Snyder (R), *Louisville*
5 Tim Lee Carter (R), *Tompkinsville*
6 John Breckinridge (D), *Lexington*
7 Carl D. Perkins (D), *Hindman*

## LOUISIANA

### SENATORS

Russell B. Long (D), *Baton Rouge*
J. Bennett Johnston, Jr. (D), *Shreveport*

### REPRESENTATIVES

1 F. Edward Hébert (D), *New Orleans*
2 Corinne C. (Lindy) Boggs (D), *New Orleans*
3 David C. Treen (R), *Metairie*
4 Joe D. Waggonner, Jr. (D), *Plain Dealing*
5 Otto E. Passman (D), *Monroe*
6 W. Henson Moore (R),[19] *Baton Rouge*
7 John B. Breaux (D), *Crowley*
8 Gillis W. Long (D), *Alexandria*

## MAINE

### SENATORS

Edmund S. Muskie (D), *Waterville*
William D. Hathaway (D), *Auburn*

### REPRESENTATIVES

1 David F. Emery (R),[20] *Portland*
2 William S. Cohen (R), *Bangor*

## MARYLAND

### SENATORS

Charles McC. Mathias, Jr. (R), *Frederick*
J. Glenn Beall, Jr. (R), *Frostburg*

### REPRESENTATIVES

1 Robert E. Bauman (R), *Easton*
2 Clarence D. Long (D), *Ruxton*
3 Paul S. Sarbanes (D), *Baltimore*
4 Marjorie S. Holt (R), *Severna Park*
5 Gladys Noon Spellman (D), *Laurel*
6 Goodloe E. Byron (D), *Frederick*
7 Parren J. Mitchell (D), *Baltimore*
8 Gilbert Gude (R), *Bethesda*

## MASSACHUSETTS

### SENATORS

Edward M. Kennedy (D), *Boston*
Edward W. Brooke (R), *Newton*

### REPRESENTATIVES

1 Silvio O. Conte (R), *Pittsfield*
2 Edward P. Boland (D), *Springfield*
3 Joseph D. Early (D), *Worcester*
4 Robert F. Drinan (D), *Newton*
5 Paul E. Tsongas (D), *Lowell*
6 Michael J. Harrington (D), *Beverly*
7 Torbert H. Macdonald (D),[21] *Malden*
7 Edward J. Markey (D),[22] *Malden*
8 Thomas P. O'Neill, Jr. (D), *Cambridge*
9 John Joseph Moakley (D), *Boston*
10 Margaret M. Heckler (R), *Wellesley*
11 James A. Burke (D), *Milton*
12 Gerry E. Studds (D), *Cohasset*

## MICHIGAN

### SENATORS

Philip A. Hart (D),[23] *Mackinac Island*
Donald W. Reigle, Jr. (D),[24] *Flint*
Robert P. Griffin (R), *Traverse City*

### REPRESENTATIVES

1 John Conyers, Jr. (D), *Detroit*
2 Marvin L. Esch (R), *Ann Arbor*
3 Garry E. Brown (R), *Schoolcraft*
4 Edward Hutchinson (R), *St. Joseph*
5 Richard F. Vander Veen (D), *Grand Rapids*
6 Bob Carr (D), *East Lansing*
7 Donald W. Riegle, Jr. (D),[25] *Flint*
8 Bob Traxler (D), *Bay City*
9 Guy A. Vander Jagt (R), *Luther*
10 Elford A. Cederberg (R), *Midland*
11 Philip E. Ruppe (R), *Houghton*
12 James G. O'Hara (D), *Utica*
13 Charles C. Diggs, Jr. (D), *Detroit*
14 Lucien N. Nedzi (D), *Detroit*
15 William D. Ford (D), *Taylor*
16 John D. Dingell, Jr. (D), *Trenton*
17 William M. Brodhead (D), *Detroit*
18 James J. Blanchard (D), *Pleasant Ridge*
19 William S. Broomfield (R), *Birmingham*

## MINNESOTA

### SENATORS

Walter F. Mondale (D),[26] *Minneapolis*
Wendell R. Anderson (D),[27] *Minneapolis*
Hubert H. Humphrey (D), *Waverly*

### REPRESENTATIVES

1 Albert H. Quie (R), *Dennison*
2 Tom Hagedorn (R), *Truman*

---

[19] Elected November 5, 1974, but election was contested by Jeff LaCaze and result was voided by the Louisiana Supreme Court on November 27, 1974; Rep. Moore was elected January 7, 1975.
[20] Election unsuccessfully contested by Peter N. Kyros.
[21] Died May 21, 1976.
[22] Elected November 2, 1976, to fill vacancy

caused by death of Torbert H. Macdonald, but was unable to be sworn in as Congress was not in session.
[23] Died December 26, 1976.
[24] Appointed December 30, 1976, to fill vacancy caused by death of Philip A. Hart, but was unable to be sworn in as Congress was not in session.
[25] Resigned December 30, 1976, having been

appointed United States Senator; vacancy throughout remainder of Congress.
[26] Resigned December 30, 1976, having been elected Vice President.
[27] Appointed December 30, 1976, to fill vacancy caused by resignation of Walter F. Mondale, but was unable to be sworn in as Congress was not in session.

3 Bill Frenzel (R), *Golden Valley*
4 Joseph E. Karth (D), *St. Paul*
5 Donald M. Fraser (D), *Minneapolis*
6 Richard Nolan (D), *Waite Park*
7 Bob Bergland (D), *Roseau*
8 James L. Oberstar (D), *Chisholm*

## MISSISSIPPI

### SENATORS

James O. Eastland (D), *Doddsville*
John C. Stennis (D), *De Kalb*

### REPRESENTATIVES

1 Jamie L. Whitten (D), *Charleston*
2 David R. Bowen (D), *Cleveland*
3 Gillespie V. (Sonny) Montgomery (D), *Meridian*
4 Thad Cochran (R), *Jackson*
5 Trent Lott (R), *Pascagoula*

## MISSOURI

### SENATORS

Stuart Symington (D),[28] *St. Louis*
John C. Danforth (R),[29] *Jefferson City*
Thomas F. Eagleton (D), *St. Louis*

### REPRESENTATIVES

1 William L. Clay (D), *St. Louis*
2 James W. Symington (D), *Ladue*
3 Leonor K. Sullivan (D), *St. Louis*
4 William J. Randall (D), *Independence*
5 Richard W. Bolling (D), *Kansas City*
6 Jerry Litton (D),[30] *Chillicothe*
6 E. Thomas Coleman (R),[31] *Kansas City*
7 Gene Taylor (R), *Sarcoxie*
8 Richard H. Ichord (D), *Houston*
9 William L. Hungate (D), *Troy*
10 Bill D. Burlison (D), *Cape Girardeau*

## MONTANA

### SENATORS

Mike Mansfield (D), *Missoula*
Lee Metcalf (D), *Helena*

### REPRESENTATIVES

1 Max Baucus (D), *Helena*
2 John Melcher (D), *Forsyth*

## NEBRASKA

### SENATORS

Roman L. Hruska (R),[32] *Omaha*
Edward Zorinsky (D),[33] *Omaha*
Carl T. Curtis (R), *Minden*

### REPRESENTATIVES

1 Charles Thone (R), *Lincoln*
2 John Y. McCollister (R), *Omaha*
3 Virginia Smith (R),[34] *Chappell*

## NEVADA

### SENATORS

Howard W. Cannon (D), *Las Vegas*
Paul Laxalt (R), *Carson City*

### REPRESENTATIVE AT LARGE

Jim Santini (D), *Las Vegas*

## NEW HAMPSHIRE

### SENATORS

Thomas J. McIntyre (D), *Laconia*
Norris Cotton (R),[35] *Lebanon*
John A. Durkin (D),[36] *Manchester*

### REPRESENTATIVES

1 Norman E. D'Amours (D), *Manchester*
2 James C. Cleveland (R), *New London*

## NEW JERSEY

### SENATORS

Clifford P. Case (R), *Rahway*
Harrison A. Williams, Jr. (D), *Bedminster*

### REPRESENTATIVES

1 James J. Florio (D), *Camden*
2 William J. Hughes (D), *Ocean City*
3 James J. Howard (D), *Spring Lake*
4 Frank Thompson, Jr. (D), *Trenton*
5 Millicent Fenwick (R), *Bernardsville*
6 Edwin B. Forsythe (R), *Moorestown*
7 Andrew Maguire (D), *Ridgewood*
8 Robert A. Roe (D), *Wayne*
9 Henry Helstoski (D), *East Rutherford*
10 Peter W. Rodino, Jr. (D), *Newark*
11 Joseph G. Minish (D), *West Orange*
12 Matthew J. Rinaldo (R), *Union*
13 Helen S. Meyner (D), *Phillipsburg*
14 Dominick V. Daniels (D), *Union City*
15 Edward J. Patten (D), *Perth Amboy*

## NEW MEXICO

### SENATORS

Joseph M. Montoya (D), *Santa Fe*
Pete V. Domenici (R), *Albuquerque*

### REPRESENTATIVES

1 Manuel Lujan, Jr. (R), *Albuquerque*
2 Harold Runnels (D), *Lovington*

## NEW YORK

### SENATORS

Jacob K. Javits (R), *New York*
James L. Buckley (C), *New York*

### REPRESENTATIVES

1 Otis G. Pike (D), *Riverhead*
2 Thomas J. Downey (D), *West Islip*
3 Jerome A. Ambro (D), *East Northport*
4 Norman F. Lent (R), *East Rockaway*
5 John W. Wydler (R), *Garden City*
6 Lester L. Wolff (D), *Great Neck*
7 Joseph P. Addabbo (D), *Ozone Park*
8 Benjamin S. Rosenthal (D), *Elmhurst*
9 James J. Delaney (D), *Long Island City*
10 Mario Biaggi (D), *Bronx*
11 James H. Scheuer (D), *Neponsit*
12 Shirley A. Chisholm (D), *Brooklyn*
13 Stephen J. Solarz (D), *Brooklyn*
14 Frederick W. Richmond (D), *Brooklyn*
15 Leo C. Zeferetti (D), *Brooklyn*
16 Elizabeth Holtzman (D), *Brooklyn*
17 John M. Murphy (D), *Staten Island*
18 Edward I. Koch (D), *New York*
19 Charles B. Rangel (D), *New York*
20 Bella S. Abzug (D), *New York*
21 Herman Badillo (D), *Bronx*
22 Jonathan B. Bingham (D), *Bronx*
23 Peter A. Peyser (R), *Irvington*
24 Richard L. Ottinger (D), *Pleasantville*
25 Hamilton Fish, Jr. (R), *Millbrook*
26 Benjamin A. Gilman (R), *Middletown*
27 Matthew F. McHugh (D), *Ithaca*
28 Samuel S. Stratton (D), *Amsterdam*
29 Edward W. Pattison (D), *West San Lake*
30 Robert C. McEwen (R), *Ogdensburg*

---

28 Resigned December 27, 1976.
29 Appointed December 27, 1976, to fill vacancy caused by resignation of Stuart Symington, but was unable to be sworn in as Congress was not in session.
30 Died August 3, 1976.
31 Elected November 2, 1976, to fill vacancy caused by death of Jerry Litton, but was unable to be sworn in as Congress was not in session.
32 Resigned December 27, 1976.

33 Appointed December 28, 1976, to fill vacancy caused by resignation of Roman L. Hruska, but was unable to be sworn in as Congress was not in session.
34 Election unsuccessfully contested by Wayne Ziebarth.
35 Appointed August 8, 1975, to fill vacancy created that day, when the Senate declared the seat vacant (S. Res. 54, 94th Congress) due to its inability to decide the winner of the November 5, 1974 general

election between John A. Durkin and Louis C. Wyman. Resigned September 18, 1975. (See U.S. Senate Election, Expulsion and Censure Cases, 1793-1990, Senate Document 103-33, pp. 421-25.)
36 Elected September 16, 1975, to fill vacancy created by the Senate's declaring the seat vacant (S. Res. 54, 94th Congress), and took his seat September 18, 1975. (See U.S. Senate Election, Expulsion and Censure Cases, 1793-1990, Senate Document 103-33, pp. 421-25.)

## NEW YORK— Continued

REPRESENTATIVES—CONTINUED

31 Donald J. Mitchell (R), *Herkimer*
32 James M. Hanley (D), *Syracuse*
33 William F. Walsh (R), *Syracuse*
34 Frank Horton (R), *Rochester*
35 Barber B. Conable, Jr. (R), *Alexander*
36 John J. LaFalce (D), *Tonawanda*
37 Henry J. Nowak (D), *Buffalo*
38 Jack F. Kemp (R), *Hamburg*
39 James F. Hastings (R),[37] *Caneadea*
39 Stanley N. Lundine (D),[38] *Jamestown*

## NORTH CAROLINA

SENATORS

Jesse Helms (R), *Raleigh*
Robert Morgan (D), *Lillington*

REPRESENTATIVES

1 Walter B. Jones (D), *Farmville*
2 L. H. Fountain (D), *Tarboro*
3 David N. Henderson (D), *Wallace*
4 Ike F. Andrews (D), *Siler City*
5 Stephen L. Neal (D), *Winston-Salem*
6 L. Richardson Preyer (D), *Greensboro*
7 Charles Rose (D), *Fayetteville*
8 W. G. (Bill) Hefner (D), *Concord*
9 James G. Martin (R), *Davidson*
10 James T. Broyhill (R), *Lenoir*
11 Roy A. Taylor (D), *Black Mountain*

## NORTH DAKOTA

SENATORS

Milton R. Young (R), *La Moure*
Quentin N. Burdick (D), *Fargo*

REPRESENTATIVE AT LARGE

Mark Andrews (R), *Mapleton*

## OHIO

SENATORS

Robert Taft, Jr. (R),[39] *Cincinnati*
Howard M. Metzenbaum (D),[40] *Cleveland*
John Glenn, Jr. (D), *Columbus*

REPRESENTATIVES

1 Willis D. Gradison, Jr. (R), *Cincinnati*
2 Donald D. Clancy (R), *Cincinnati*
3 Charles W. Whalen, Jr. (R), *Dayton*
4 Tennyson Guyer (R), *Findley*

5 Delbert L. Latta (R), *Bowling Green*
6 William H. Harsha (R), *Portsmouth*
7 Clarence J. Brown (R), *Urbana*
8 Thomas N. Kindness (R), *Hamilton*
9 Thomas L. Ashley (D), *Toledo*
10 Clarence E. Miller (R), *Lancaster*
11 J. William Stanton (R), *Painesville*
12 Samuel L. Devine (R), *Columbus*
13 Charles A. Mosher (R), *Oberlin*
14 John F. Seiberling (D), *Akron*
15 Chalmers P. Wylie (R), *Columbus*
16 Ralph S. Regula (R), *Navarre*
17 John M. Ashbrook (R), *Johnstown*
18 Wayne L. Hays (D),[41] *Flushing*
19 Charles J. Carney (D), *Youngstown*
20 James V. Stanton (D), *Cleveland*
21 Louis Stokes (D),[42] *Cleveland*
22 Charles A. Vanik (D), *Euclid*
23 Ronald M. Mottl (D), *Parma*

## OKLAHOMA

SENATORS

Henry L. Bellmon (R),[43] *Red Rock*
Dewey F. Bartlett (R), *Tulsa*

REPRESENTATIVES

1 James R. Jones (D), *Tulsa*
2 Theodore M. Risenhoover (D), *Tahlequah*
3 Carl Albert (D), *McAlester*
4 Thomas J. Steed (D), *Shawnee*
5 John Jarman (D),[44] *Oklahoma City*
6 Glenn English (D), *Cordell*

## OREGON

SENATORS

Mark O. Hatfield (R), *Newport*
Robert W. Packwood (R), *Portland*

REPRESENTATIVES

1 Les AuCoin (D), *Forest Grove*
2 Al Ullman (D), *Baker*
3 Robert Duncan (D), *Gresham*
4 James Weaver (D), *Eugene*

## PENNSYLVANIA

SENATORS

Hugh D. Scott, Jr. (R), *Philadelphia*
Richard S. Schweiker (R), *Worcester*

REPRESENTATIVES

1 William A. Barrett (D),[45] *Philadelphia*

1 Michael O. Myers (D),[46] *Philadelphia*
2 Robert N. C. Nix (D), *Philadelphia*
3 William J. Green (D), *Philadelphia*
4 Joshua Eilberg (D), *Philadelphia*
5 Richard T. Schulze (R), *Paoli*
6 Gus Yatron (D), *Reading*
7 Robert W. Edgar (D), *Broomall*
8 Edward G. Biester, Jr. (R), *Furlong*
9 E. G. Shuster (R), *Everett*
10 Joseph M. McDade (R), *Scranton*
11 Daniel J. Flood (D), *Wilkes-Barre*
12 John P. Murtha, Jr. (D), *Johnstown*
13 R. Lawrence Coughlin (R), *Villanova*
14 William S. Moorhead (D), *Pittsburgh*
15 Fred B. Rooney (D), *Bethlehem*
16 Edwin D. Eshleman (R), *Lancaster*
17 Herman T. Schneebeli (R), *Williamsport*
18 H. John Heinz III (R), *Pittsburgh*
19 William F. Goodling (R), *Jacobus*
20 Joseph M. Gaydos (D), *McKeesport*
21 John H. Dent (D), *Ligonier*
22 Thomas E. Morgan (D), *Fredericktown*
23 Albert W. Johnson (R), *Smethport*
24 Joseph P. Vigorito (D), *Erie*
25 Gary A. Myers (R), *Butler*

## RHODE ISLAND

SENATORS

John O. Pastore (D),[47] *Cranston*
John H. Chafee (R),[48] *Warwick*
Claiborne Pell (D), *Newport*

REPRESENTATIVES

1 Fernand J. St Germain (D), *Woonsocket*
2 Edward P. Beard (D), *Cranston*

## SOUTH CAROLINA

SENATORS

Strom Thurmond (R), *Aiken*
Ernest F. Hollings (D), *Charleston*

REPRESENTATIVES

1 Mendel J. Davis (D), *Charleston Heights*
2 Floyd Spence (R), *Lexington*
3 Butler Derrick (D), *Edgefield*
4 James R. Mann (D), *Greenville*

---

[37] Resigned January 20, 1976.
[38] Elected March 2, 1976, to fill vacancy caused by resignation of James F. Hastings, and took his seat March 8, 1976.
[39] Resigned December 28, 1976.
[40] Appointed December 29, 1976, to fill vacancy caused by resignation of Robert Taft, Jr., but was unable to be sworn in as Congress was not in session.
[41] Resigned September 1, 1976; vacancy through-out remainder of Congress.
[42] Election unsuccessfully contested by William Mack.
[43] Election unsuccessfully contested by Edmond Edmondson. (See U.S. Senate Election, Expulsion and Censure Cases, 1793-1990, Senate Document 103-33, pp. 426-28.)
[44] Changed party affiliation to Republican, January 24, 1975.

[45] Died April 12, 1976.
[46] Elected November 2, 1976, to fill vacancy caused by death of William A. Barrett, but was unable to be sworn in as Congress was not in session.
[47] Resigned December 28, 1976.
[48] Appointed December 29, 1976, to fill vacancy caused by resignation of John O. Pastore, but was unable to be sworn in as Congress was not in session.

5 Kenneth L. Holland (D), *Camden*
6 John W. Jenrette, Jr. (D), *North Myrtle Beach*

## SOUTH DAKOTA

### SENATORS

George S. McGovern (D), *Mitchell*
James Abourezk (D), *Rapid City*

### REPRESENTATIVES

1 Larry Pressler (R), *Humboldt*
2 James Abdnor (R), *Kennebec*

## TENNESSEE

### SENATORS

Howard H. Baker, Jr. (R), *Huntsville*
William E. Brock III (R), *Lookout Mountain*

### REPRESENTATIVES

1 James H. Quillen (R), *Kingsport*
2 John J. Duncan (R), *Knoxville*
3 Marilyn Lloyd (D), *Chattanooga*
4 Joseph L. Evins (D), *Smithville*
5 Richard H. Fulton (D),[49] *Goodlettsville*
5 Clifford R. Allen (D),[50] *Nashville*
6 Robin L. Beard (R), *Franklin*
7 Edward Jones (D), *Yorkville*
8 Harold E. Ford (D), *Memphis*

## TEXAS

### SENATORS

John G. Tower (R), *Wichita Falls*
Lloyd M. Bentsen, Jr. (D), *Houston*

### REPRESENTATIVES

1 Wright Patman (D),[51] *Texarkana*
1 Sam B. Hall, Jr. (D),[52] *Marshall*
2 Charles Wilson (D), *Lufkin*
3 James M. Collins (R), *Dallas*
4 H. Ray Roberts (D), *McKinney*
5 Alan Steelman (R), *Mesquite*
6 Olin E. Teague (D), *College Station*
7 William R. Archer, Jr. (R), *Houston*
8 Robert C. Eckhardt (D), *Houston*
9 Jack B. Brooks (D), *Beaumont*
10 J. J. (Jake) Pickle (D), *Austin*
11 W. R. Poage (D), *Waco*
12 James C. Wright, Jr. (D), *Fort Worth*
13 Jack Hightower (D), *Vernon*
14 John Young (D), *Corpus Christi*
15 Eligio (Kika) de la Garza (D), *Mission*
16 Richard C. White (D), *El Paso*
17 Omar T. Burleson (D), *Anson*
18 Barbara Jordan (D), *Houston*

19 George H. Mahon (D), *Lubbock*
20 Henry B. Gonzalez (D), *San Antonio*
21 Robert Krueger (D), *New Braunfels*
22 Robert R. Casey (D),[53] *Houston*
22 Ron Paul (R),[54] *Lake Jackson*
23 Abraham Kazen, Jr. (D), *Laredo*
24 Dale Milford (D), *Grand Prairie*

## UTAH

### SENATORS

Frank E. Moss (D), *Salt Lake City*
E. J. (Jake) Garn (R), *Salt Lake City*

### REPRESENTATIVES

1 K. Gunn McKay (D), *Huntsville*
2 Allan T. Howe (D), *Salt Lake City*

## VERMONT

### SENATORS

Robert T. Stafford (R), *Rutland*
Patrick J. Leahy (D), *Burlington*

### REPRESENTATIVE AT LARGE

James M. Jeffords (R), *Rutland*

## VIRGINIA

### SENATORS

Harry Flood Byrd, Jr. (I), *Winchester*
William L. Scott (R), *Fairfax*

### REPRESENTATIVES

1 Thomas N. Downing (D), *Newport News*
2 G. William Whitehurst (R), *Virginia Beach*
3 David E. Satterfield III (D), *Richmond*
4 Robert W. Daniel, Jr. (R), *Spring Cove*
5 W. C. (Dan) Daniel (D), *Danville*
6 M. Caldwell Butler (R), *Roanoke*
7 J. Kenneth Robinson (R), *Winchester*
8 Herbert E. Harris II (D), *Alexandria*
9 William C. Wampler (R), *Bristol*
10 Joseph L. Fisher (D), *Arlington*

## WASHINGTON

### SENATORS

Warren G. Magnuson (D), *Seattle*
Henry M. Jackson (D), *Everett*

### REPRESENTATIVES

1 Joel Pritchard (R), *Seattle*
2 Lloyd Meeds (D), *Lake Stevens*
3 Don Bonker (D), *Olympia*
4 Mike McCormack (D), *Richland*
5 Thomas S. Foley (D), *Spokane*

6 Floyd V. Hicks (D), *Tacoma*
7 Brock Adams (D), *Seattle*

## WEST VIRGINIA

### SENATORS

Jennings Randolph (D), *Elkins*
Robert C. Byrd (D), *Sophia*

### REPRESENTATIVES

1 Robert H. Mollohan (D), *Fairmont*
2 Harley O. Staggers (D), *Keyser*
3 John M. Slack, Jr. (D), *Charleston*
4 Ken Hechler (D), *Huntington*

## WISCONSIN

### SENATORS

William Proxmire (D), *Madison*
Gaylord Nelson (D), *Madison*

### REPRESENTATIVES

1 Les Aspin (D), *Racine*
2 Robert W. Kastenmeier (D), *Sun Prairie*
3 Alvin Baldus (D), *Menomonie*
4 Clement J. Zablocki (D), *Milwaukee*
5 Henry S. Reuss (D), *Milwaukee*
6 William A. Steiger (R), *Oshkosh*
7 David R. Obey (D), *Wausau*
8 Robert J. Cornell (D), *DePere*
9 Robert W. Kasten, Jr. (R), *Thiensville*

## WYOMING

### SENATORS

Gale W. McGee (D), *Laramie*
Clifford P. Hansen (R), *Jackson*

### REPRESENTATIVE AT LARGE

Teno Roncalio (D), *Cheyenne*

## COMMONWEALTH OF PUERTO RICO

### RESIDENT COMMISSIONER

Jaime Benitez (PD), *Cayey*

## DISTRICT OF COLUMBIA

### DELEGATE

Walter E. Fauntroy (D), *Washington, D.C.*

## GUAM

### DELEGATE

Antonio Borja Won Pat (D), *Agana*

## VIRGIN ISLANDS

### DELEGATE

Ron de Lugo (D), *St. Croix*

---

[49] Resigned August 14, 1975.
[50] Elected November 25, 1975, to fill vacancy caused by resignation of Richard H. Fulton, and took his seat December 2, 1975.

[51] Died March 7, 1976.
[52] Elected June 19, 1976, to fill vacancy caused by death of Wright Patman, and took his seat June 28, 1976.

[53] Resigned January 22, 1976.
[54] Elected April 3, 1976, to fill vacancy caused by resignation of Robert R. Casey, and took his seat April 7, 1976.

# 95TH CONGRESS

## JANUARY 3, 1977, TO JANUARY 3, 1979

FIRST SESSION— *January 4, 1977,[1] to December 15, 1977*
SECOND SESSION— *January 19, 1978,[2] to October 15, 1978*

Walter F. Mondale
Vice President

Thomas P. O'Neill, Jr.
Speaker

---

### Senate
Democrats 61 — Republicans 38 — Independent 1

VICE PRESIDENT OF THE UNITED STATES— NELSON A. ROCKEFELLER,[3] of New York;
WALTER F. MONDALE,[4] of Minnesota

PRESIDENT PRO TEMPORE OF THE SENATE— JAMES O. EASTLAND,[5] of Mississippi

DEPUTY PRESIDENT PRO TEMPORE OF THE SENATE— HUBERT H. HUMPHREY,[6] of
Minnesota

SECRETARY OF THE SENATE— FRANCIS R. VALEO,[7] of the District of Columbia;
J. STANLEY KIMMITT,[8] of Virginia

SERGEANT AT ARMS OF THE SENATE— F. NORDY HOFFMANN, of Maryland

MAJORITY FLOOR LEADER— ROBERT C. BYRD, of West Virginia

DEMOCRATIC WHIP— ALAN M. CRANSTON, of California

REPUBLICAN FLOOR LEADER— HOWARD H. BAKER, JR., of Tennessee

ASSISTANT REPUBLICAN LEADER— THEODORE F. STEVENS, of Alaska

---

### House of Representatives
Democrats 292 — Republicans 143

SPEAKER OF THE HOUSE— THOMAS P. O'NEILL, JR.,[9] of Massachusetts

CLERK OF THE HOUSE— EDMUND L. HENSHAW, JR.,[10] of Virginia

SERGEANT AT ARMS OF THE HOUSE— KENNETH R. HARDING,[11] of Virginia

DOORKEEPER OF THE HOUSE— JAMES T. MOLLOY,[12] of New York

POSTMASTER OF THE HOUSE— ROBERT V. ROTA,[13] of Pennsylvania

MAJORITY LEADER— JAMES C. WRIGHT, JR., of Texas

MAJORITY WHIP— JOHN BRADEMAS, of Indiana

REPUBLICAN LEADER— JOHN J. RHODES, of Arizona

REPUBLICAN WHIP— ROBERT H. MICHEL, of Illinois

---

## ALABAMA

### SENATORS
John J. Sparkman (D), *Huntsville*
James B. Allen (D),[14] *Gadsden*
Maryon Allen (D),[15] *Gadsden*
Donald Stewart (D),[16] *Anniston*

### REPRESENTATIVES
1 Jack Edwards (R), *Mobile*
2 William L. Dickinson (R),
   *Montgomery*
3 William Nichols (D), *Sylacauga*
4 Tom Bevill (D), *Jasper*
5 Ronnie G. Flippo (D), *Florence*
6 John H. Buchanan (R),
   *Birmingham*
7 Walter Flowers (D), *Tuscaloosa*

## ALASKA

### SENATORS
Theodore F. Stevens (R), *Anchorage*
Maurice R. (Mike) Gravel (D),
   *Anchorage*

### REPRESENTATIVE AT LARGE
Donald E. Young (R), *Fort Yukon*

## ARIZONA

### SENATORS
Barry M. Goldwater (R), *Scottsdale*
Dennis DeConcini (D), *Tucson*

### REPRESENTATIVES
1 John J. Rhodes (R), *Mesa*
2 Morris K. Udall (D), *Tucson*
3 Bob Stump (D), *Tolleson*
4 Eldon Rudd (R), *Scottsdale*

## ARKANSAS

### SENATORS
John L. McClellan (D),[17] *Little Rock*
Kaneaster Hodges, Jr. (D),[18] *Newport*
Dale Bumpers (D), *Charleston*

### REPRESENTATIVES
1 William V. Alexander (D), *Osceola*
2 Jim Guy Tucker, Jr. (D), *Little
   Rock*
3 John Paul Hammerschmidt (R),
   *Harrison*
4 Ray Thornton (D), *Sheridan*

---

[1] By joint resolution (Pub. Law 94 494, 94th Cong., 2d sess.), the date of assembling the first session of the Ninety-fifth Congress was fixed for January 4, 1977.

[2] By joint resolution (Pub. Law 95 221, 95th Cong., 1st sess.), the date of assembling the second session of the Ninety-fifth Congress was fixed for January 19, 1978.

[3] Term expired at noon on January 20, 1977.

[4] Term began at noon on January 20, 1977.

[5] Resigned December 27, 1978.

[6] Office of Deputy President Pro Tempore was established January 5, 1977, pursuant to Senate Resolution 17, Ninety-fifth Congress; Hubert H. Humphrey died January 13, 1978.

[7] Resigned March 31, 1977.

[8] Elected April 1, 1977.

[9] Elected January 4, 1977.

[10] Reelected January 4, 1977.

[11] Reelected January 4, 1977.

[12] Reelected January 4, 1977.

[13] Reelected January 4, 1977.

[14] Died June 1, 1978.

[15] Appointed June 8, 1978, to fill vacancy caused by death of her husband, James B. Allen, and took her seat June 12, 1978; resigned November 7, 1978.

[16] Elected November 7, 1978, to fill vacancy caused by death of James B. Allen, but was unable to be sworn in as Congress was not in session.

[17] Died November 28, 1977.

[18] Appointed December 10, 1977, to fill vacancy caused by death of John L. McClellan, and took his seat December 15, 1977.

## CALIFORNIA

### SENATORS

Alan Cranston (D), *Los Angeles*
S. I. Hayakawa (R), *Mill Valley*

### REPRESENTATIVES

1 Harold T. Johnson (D), *Roseville*
2 Don H. Clausen (R), *Crescent City*
3 John E. Moss (D),[19] *Sacramento*
4 Robert L. Leggett (D),[20] *Vallejo*
5 John L. Burton (D), *San Francisco*
6 Phillip Burton (D), *San Francisco*
7 George Miller (D), *Martinez*
8 Ronald V. Dellums (D), *Berkeley*
9 Fortney H. (Pete) Stark, Jr. (D), *Oakland*
10 Don Edwards (D), *San Jose*
11 Leo J. Ryan (D),[21] *Belmont*
12 Paul N. (Pete) McCloskey, Jr. (R), *Menlo Park*
13 Norman Y. Mineta (D), *San Jose*
14 John J. McFall (D),[22] *Manteca*
15 B. F. Sisk (D), *Fresno*
16 Leon E. Panetta (D), *Carmel Valley*
17 John Krebs (D), *Fresno*
18 William M. Ketchum (R),[23] *Bakersfield*
19 Robert J. Lagomarsino (R), *Ventura*
20 Barry M. Goldwater, Jr. (R), *Woodland Hills*
21 James C. Corman (D), *Van Nuys*
22 Carlos J. Moorhead (R), *Glendale*
23 Anthony C. Beilenson (D), *Los Angeles*
24 Henry A. Waxman (D), *Los Angeles*
25 Edward R. Roybal (D), *Los Angeles*
26 John H. Rousselot (R), *San Marino*
27 Robert K. Dornan (R), *Santa Monica*
28 Yvonne Brathwaite Burke (D), *Los Angeles*
29 Augustus F. Hawkins (D), *Los Angeles*
30 George E. Danielson (D), *Monterey Park*
31 Charles H. Wilson (D), *Hawthorne*
32 Glenn M. Anderson (D), *Harbor City*
33 Del M. Clawson (R),[24] *Downey*
34 Mark W. Hannaford (D), *Lakewood*
35 Jim Lloyd (D), *West Covina*
36 George E. Brown, Jr. (D), *Colton*
37 Shirley N. Pettis (R), *Loma Linda*
38 Jerry M. Patterson (D), *Buena Park*
39 Charles E. Wiggins (R), *Fullerton*
40 Robert E. Badham (R), *Newport Beach*
41 Robert C. Wilson (R), *San Diego*
42 Lionel Van Deerlin (D), *Chula Vista*
43 Clair W. Burgener (R), *Rancho Santa Fe*

## COLORADO

### SENATORS

Floyd K. Haskell (D), *Littleton*
Gary Hart (D), *Denver*

### REPRESENTATIVES

1 Patricia Schroeder (D), *Denver*
2 Timothy E. Wirth (D), *Denver*
3 Frank E. Evans (D), *Pueblo*
4 James P. Johnson (R), *Fort Collins*
5 William L. Armstrong (R), *Aurora*

## CONNECTICUT

### SENATORS

Abraham A. Ribicoff (D), *Hartford*
Lowell P. Weicker, Jr. (R), *Greenwich*

### REPRESENTATIVES

1 William R. Cotter (D), *Hartford*
2 Christopher J. Dodd (D), *Norwich*
3 Robert N. Giaimo (D), *North Haven*
4 Stewart B. McKinney (R), *Fairfield*
5 Ronald A. Sarasin (R), *Beacon Falls*
6 Toby Moffett (D), *Unionville*

## DELAWARE

### SENATORS

William V. Roth, Jr. (R), *Wilmington*
Joseph R. Biden, Jr. (D), *Wilmington*

### REPRESENTATIVE AT LARGE

Thomas B. Evans, Jr. (R), *Wilmington*

## FLORIDA

### SENATORS

Lawton Chiles (D), *Lakeland*
Richard Stone (D), *Tallahassee*

### REPRESENTATIVES

1 Robert L. F. Sikes (D), *Crestview*
2 Don Fuqua (D), *Altha*
3 Charles E. Bennett (D), *Jacksonville*
4 William V. Chappell, Jr. (D), *Ocala*
5 Richard Kelly (R),[25] *New Port Richey*
6 C. W. Bill Young (R), *St. Petersburg*
7 Sam M. Gibbons (D), *Tampa*
8 Andrew P. Ireland (D), *Winter Haven*
9 Louis Frey, Jr. (R), *Winter Park*
10 L. A. (Skip) Bafalis (R), *Fort Myers Beach*
11 Paul G. Rogers (D), *West Palm Beach*
12 J. Herbert Burke (R), *Hollywood*
13 William Lehman (D), *Miami*
14 Claude D. Pepper (D), *Miami*
15 Dante B. Fascell (D), *Miami*

## GEORGIA

### SENATORS

Herman E. Talmadge (D), *Lovejoy*
Sam Nunn (D), *Perry*

### REPRESENTATIVES

1 Ronald B. (Bo) Ginn (D), *Millen*
2 Dawson Mathis (D), *Albany*
3 Jack T. Brinkley (D), *Columbus*
4 Elliott H. Levitas (D), *Atlanta*
5 Andrew Young (D),[26] *Atlanta*
5 Wyche Fowler, Jr. (D),[27] *Atlanta*
6 John J. Flynt, Jr. (D), *Griffin*
7 Larry McDonald (D), *Marietta*
8 Billy Lee Evans (D), *Macon*
9 Edgar L. Jenkins (D), *Jasper*
10 D. Douglas Barnard, Jr. (D), *Augusta*

## HAWAII

### SENATORS

Daniel K. Inouye (D), *Honolulu*
Spark M. Matsunaga (D), *Honolulu*

### REPRESENTATIVES

1 Cecil Heftel (D), *Honolulu*
2 Daniel K. Akaka (D), *Honolulu*

## IDAHO

### SENATORS

Frank Church (D), *Boise*
James A. McClure (R), *Payette*

### REPRESENTATIVES

1 Steven D. Symms (R), *Caldwell*
2 George Hansen (R), *Pocatello*

---

[19] Resigned December 31, 1978; vacancy throughout remainder of Congress.
[20] Election unsuccessfully contested by Albert Dehr.
[21] Died November 18, 1978, before commencement of the Ninety-sixth Congress, to which he had been reelected; vacancy in the Ninety-fifth Congress not filled.

[22] Resigned December 31, 1978; vacancy throughout remainder of Congress.
[23] Died June 24, 1978; vacancy throughout remainder of Congress.
[24] Resigned December 31, 1978; vacancy throughout remainder of Congress.

[25] Election unsuccessfully contested by JoAnn Saunders.
[26] Resigned January 29, 1977.
[27] Elected April 5, 1977, to fill vacancy caused by resignation of Andrew Young, and took his seat April 6, 1977; election unsuccessfully contested by Wyman C. Lowe.

## ILLINOIS

### SENATORS

Charles H. Percy (R), *Wilmette*
Adlai E. Stevenson III (D), *Hanover*

### REPRESENTATIVES

1 Ralph H. Metcalfe (D),[28] *Chicago*
2 Morgan F. Murphy (D), *Chicago*
3 Martin A. Russo (D), *South Holland*
4 Edward J. Derwinski (R), *Flossmoor*
5 John G. Fary (D), *Chicago*
6 Henry J. Hyde (R), *Park Ridge*
7 Cardiss Collins (D), *Chicago*
8 Dan Rostenkowski (D), *Chicago*
9 Sidney R. Yates (D), *Chicago*
10 Abner J. Mikva (D), *Evanston*
11 Frank Annunzio (D), *Chicago*
12 Philip M. Crane (R), *Mount Prospect*
13 Robert McClory (R), *Lake Bluff*
14 John N. Erlenborn (R), *Glen Ellyn*
15 Thomas J. Corcoran (R), *Ottawa*
16 John B. Anderson (R), *Rockford*
17 George M. O'Brien (R), *Joliet*
18 Robert H. Michel (R), *Peoria*
19 Thomas F. Railsback (R), *Moline*
20 Paul Findley (R), *Pittsfield*
21 Edward R. Madigan (R), *Lincoln*
22 George E. Shipley (D), *Olney*
23 Melvin Price (D), *East St. Louis*
24 Paul Simon (D), *Carbondale*

## INDIANA

### SENATORS

Birch E. Bayh (D), *Terre Haute*
Richard G. Lugar (R), *Indianapolis*

### REPRESENTATIVES

1 Adam Benjamin, Jr. (D), *Hobart*
2 Floyd J. Fithian (D), *Lafayette*
3 John Brademas (D), *South Bend*
4 J. Danforth Quayle (R), *Huntington*
5 Elwood Hillis (R), *Kokomo*
6 David W. Evans (D), *Indianapolis*
7 John T. Myers (R), *Covington*
8 David L. Cornwell (D), *Paoli*
9 Lee H. Hamilton (D), *Columbus*
10 Philip R. Sharp (D), *Muncie*
11 Andrew Jacobs, Jr. (D), *Indianapolis*

## IOWA

### SENATORS

Dick Clark (D), *Marion*
John C. Culver (D), *Cedar Rapids*

### REPRESENTATIVES

1 James A. S. Leach (R), *Davenport*
2 Michael T. Blouin (D), *Dubuque*
3 Charles E. Grassley (R), *New Hartford*
4 Neal Smith (D), *Altoona*
5 Tom Harkin (D), *Ames*
6 Berkley Bedell (D), *Spirit Lake*

## KANSAS

### SENATORS

James B. Pearson (R),[29] *Prairie Village*
Nancy L. Kassebaum (R),[30] *Wichita*
Robert J. Dole (R), *Russell*

### REPRESENTATIVES

1 Keith G. Sebelius (R), *Norton*
2 Martha Keys (D), *Manhattan*
3 Larry Winn, Jr. (R), *Overland Park*
4 Daniel R. Glickman (D), *Wichita*
5 Joe Skubitz (R),[31] *Pittsburg*

## KENTUCKY

### SENATORS

Walter (Dee) Huddleston (D), *Elizabethtown*
Wendell H. Ford (D), *Owensboro*

### REPRESENTATIVES

1 Carroll Hubbard, Jr. (D), *Mayfield*
2 William H. Natcher (D), *Bowling Green*
3 Romano L. Mazzoli (D), *Louisville*
4 M. G. (Gene) Snyder (R), *Louisville*
5 Tim Lee Carter (R), *Tompkinsville*
6 John Breckinridge (D), *Lexington*
7 Carl D. Perkins (D), *Hindman*

## LOUISIANA

### SENATORS

Russell B. Long (D), *Baton Rouge*
J. Bennett Johnston, Jr. (D), *Shreveport*

### REPRESENTATIVES

1 Richard A. Tonry (D),[32] *Arabi*
1 Robert L. Livingston (R),[33] *New Orleans*
2 Corinne C. (Lindy) Boggs (D), *New Orleans*
3 David C. Treen (R), *Metairie*
4 Joe D. Waggonner, Jr. (D), *Plain Dealing*
5 Thomas J. Huckaby (D), *Ringgold*
6 W. Henson Moore (R), *Baton Rouge*
7 John B. Breaux (D), *Crowley*

8 Gillis W. Long (D), *Alexandria*

## MAINE

### SENATORS

Edmund S. Muskie (D), *Waterville*
William D. Hathaway (D), *Auburn*

### REPRESENTATIVES

1 David F. Emery (R), *Rockland*
2 William S. Cohen (R), *Bangor*

## MARYLAND

### SENATORS

Charles McC. Mathias, Jr. (R), *Frederick*
Paul S. Sarbanes (D), *Baltimore*

### REPRESENTATIVES

1 Robert E. Bauman (R), *Easton*
2 Clarence D. Long (D), *Ruxton*
3 Barbara A. Mikulski (D), *Baltimore*
4 Marjorie S. Holt (R), *Severna Park*
5 Gladys Noon Spellman (D), *Laurel*
6 Goodloe E. Byron (D),[34] *Frederick*
7 Parren J. Mitchell (D), *Baltimore*
8 Newton I. Steers, Jr. (R), *Bethesda*

## MASSACHUSETTS

### SENATORS

Edward M. Kennedy (D), *Hyannis Port*
Edward W. Brooke (R), *Newton*

### REPRESENTATIVES

1 Silvio O. Conte (R), *Pittsfield*
2 Edward P. Boland (D), *Springfield*
3 Joseph D. Early (D), *Worcester*
4 Robert F. Drinan (D), *Newton*
5 Paul E. Tsongas (D), *Lowell*
6 Michael J. Harrington (D), *Beverly*
7 Edward J. Markey (D), *Malden*
8 Thomas P. O'Neill, Jr. (D), *Cambridge*
9 John Joseph Moakley (D), *South Boston*
10 Margaret M. Heckler (R), *Wellesley*
11 James A. Burke (D), *Milton*
12 Gerry E. Studds (D), *Cohasset*

---

[28] Died October 10, 1978; vacancy throughout remainder of Congress.
[29] Resigned December 23, 1978.
[30] Appointed December 23, 1978, to fill vacancy caused by resignation of James B. Pearson, but was unable to be sworn in as Congress was not in session.
[31] Resigned December 31, 1978; vacancy throughout remainder of Congress.

[32] Primary runoff election contested by James A. Moreau. State District Judge Melvin Shortess ruled October 15, 1976 that insufficient evidence existed to prove that election fraud had taken place; he reversed this decision on April 21, 1977 but held that he lacked jurisdiction to overturn the result. Rep. Tonry resigned May 4, 1977.

[33] Elected August 27, 1977, to fill vacancy caused by resignation of Richard A. Tonry, and took his seat September 7, 1977.
[34] Died October 11, 1978; vacancy throughout remainder of Congress.

## MICHIGAN

### SENATORS

Robert P. Griffin (R), *Traverse City*
Donald W. Riegle, Jr. (D), *Flint*

### REPRESENTATIVES

1 John Conyers, Jr. (D), *Detroit*
2 Carl D. Pursell (R),[35] *Plymouth*
3 Garry E. Brown (R), *Schoolcraft*
4 David A. Stockman (R), *St. Joseph*
5 Harold S. Sawyer (R), *Rockford*
6 Bob Carr (D), *East Lansing*
7 Dale E. Kildee (D), *Flint*
8 Bob Traxler (D), *Bay City*
9 Guy A. Vander Jagt (R), *Luther*
10 Elford A. Cederberg (R),[36] *Midland*
11 Philip E. Ruppe (R), *Houghton*
12 David E. Bonior (D), *Mount Clemens*
13 Charles C. Diggs, Jr. (D), *Detroit*
14 Lucien N. Nedzi (D), *Detroit*
15 William D. Ford (D), *Taylor*
16 John D. Dingell, Jr. (D), *Trenton*
17 William M. Brodhead (D), *Detroit*
18 James J. Blanchard (D), *Pleasant Ridge*
19 William S. Broomfield (R), *Birmingham*

## MINNESOTA

### SENATORS

Hubert H. Humphrey (D),[37] *Waverly*
Muriel Humphrey (D),[38] *Waverly*
David F. Durenberger (R),[39] *Minneapolis*
Wendell R. Anderson (D),[40] *St. Paul*
Rudy Boschwitz (R),[41] *Plymouth*

### REPRESENTATIVES

1 Albert H. Quie (R), *Dennison*
2 Tom Hagedorn (R), *Truman*
3 Bill Frenzel (R), *Golden Valley*
4 Bruce F. Vento (D), *St. Paul*
5 Donald M. Fraser (D), *Minneapolis*
6 Richard Nolan (D), *Waite Park*
7 Bob Bergland (D),[42] *Roseau*
7 Arlan Stangeland (R),[43] *Barnesville*
8 James L. Oberstar (D), *Chisholm*

## MISSISSIPPI

### SENATORS

James O. Eastland (D),[44] *Doddsville*
Thad Cochran (R),[45] *Jackson*
John C. Stennis (D), *De Kalb*

### REPRESENTATIVES

1 Jamie L. Whitten (D), *Charleston*
2 David R. Bowen (D), *Cleveland*
3 Gillespie V. (Sonny) Montgomery (D), *Meridian*
4 Thad Cochran (R),[46] *Jackson*
5 Trent Lott (R), *Pascagoula*

## MISSOURI

### SENATORS

Thomas F. Eagleton (D), *St. Louis*
John C. Danforth (R), *Jefferson City*

### REPRESENTATIVES

1 William L. Clay (D),[47] *St. Louis*
2 Robert A. Young (D), *St. Ann*
3 Richard A. Gephardt (D), *St. Louis*
4 Ike Skelton (D), *Lexington*
5 Richard W. Bolling (D), *Kansas City*
6 E. Thomas Coleman (R), *Kansas City*
7 Gene Taylor (R), *Sarcoxie*
8 Richard H. Ichord (D), *Houston*
9 Harold A. Volkmer (D), *Hannibal*
10 Bill D. Burlison (D), *Cape Girardeau*

## MONTANA

### SENATORS

Lee Metcalf (D),[48] *Helena*
Paul Hatfield (D),[49] *Great Falls*
Max Baucus (D),[50] *Missoula*
John Melcher (D), *Forsyth*

### REPRESENTATIVES

1 Max Baucus (D),[51] *Missoula*
2 Ron Marlenee (R), *Scobey*

## NEBRASKA

### SENATORS

Carl T. Curtis (R), *Minden*
Edward Zorinsky (D), *Omaha*

### REPRESENTATIVES

1 Charles Thone (R), *Lincoln*
2 John J. Cavanaugh (D), *Omaha*
3 Virginia Smith (R), *Chappell*

## NEVADA

### SENATORS

Howard W. Cannon (D), *Las Vegas*
Paul Laxalt (R), *Carson City*

### REPRESENTATIVE AT LARGE

Jim Santini (D), *Las Vegas*

## NEW HAMPSHIRE

### SENATORS

Thomas J. McIntyre (D), *Laconia*
John A. Durkin (D), *Manchester*

### REPRESENTATIVES

1 Norman E. D'Amours (D), *Manchester*
2 James C. Cleveland (R), *New London*

## NEW JERSEY

### SENATORS

Clifford P. Case (R), *Rahway*
Harrison A. Williams, Jr. (D), *Bedminster*

### REPRESENTATIVES

1 James J. Florio (D), *Camden*
2 William J. Hughes (D), *Ocean City*
3 James J. Howard (D), *Spring Lake Heights*
4 Frank Thompson, Jr. (D), *Trenton*
5 Millicent Fenwick (R), *Bernardsville*
6 Edwin B. Forsythe (R), *Moorestown*
7 Andrew Maguire (D), *Ridgewood*
8 Robert A. Roe (D), *Wayne*
9 Harold C. Hollenbeck (R), *East Rutherford*
10 Peter W. Rodino, Jr. (D), *Newark*
11 Joseph G. Minish (D), *West Orange*
12 Matthew J. Rinaldo (R), *Union*
13 Helen S. Meyner (D), *Phillipsburg*
14 Joseph A. LeFante (D),[52] *Bayonne*
15 Edward J. Patten (D), *Perth Amboy*

---

[35] Election unsuccessfully contested by Edward C. Pierce.

[36] Resigned December 31, 1978; vacancy throughout remainder of Congress.

[37] Died January 13, 1978.

[38] Appointed January 25, 1978, to fill vacancy caused by death of her husband, Hubert H. Humphrey, and took her seat February 6, 1978; resigned November 7, 1978.

[39] Elected November 7, 1978, to fill vacancy caused by death of Hubert H. Humphrey, but was unable to be sworn in as Congress was not in session.

[40] Resigned December 29, 1978.

[41] Appointed December 30, 1978, to fill vacancy caused by resignation of Wendell R. Anderson, but was unable to be sworn in as Congress was not in session.

[42] Resigned January 22, 1977.

[43] Elected February 22, 1977, to fill vacancy caused by resignation of Bob Bergland, and took his seat March 1, 1977.

[44] Resigned December 27, 1978.

[45] Appointed December 27, 1978, to fill vacancy caused by resignation of James O. Eastland, but was unable to be sworn in as Congress was not in session.

[46] Resigned December 26, 1978, having been appointed United States Senator; vacancy throughout remainder of Congress.

[47] Election unsuccessfully contested by Elsa Debra Hill and Felix J. Panasigui.

[48] Died January 12, 1978.

[49] Appointed January 22, 1978, to fill vacancy caused by death of Lee Metcalf, and took his seat January 23, 1978; resigned December 14, 1978.

[50] Appointed December 15, 1978, to fill vacancy caused by resignation of Paul Hatfield, but was unable to be sworn in as Congress was not in session.

[51] Resigned December 14, 1978, having been appointed United States Senator; vacancy throughout remainder of Congress.

[52] Resigned December 14, 1978; vacancy throughout remainder of Congress.

## NEW MEXICO

SENATORS

Pete V. Domenici (R), *Albuquerque*
Harrison H. Schmitt (R), *Silver City*

REPRESENTATIVES

1 Manuel Lujan, Jr. (R),
  *Albuquerque*
2 Harold Runnels (D), *Lovington*

## NEW YORK

SENATORS

Jacob K. Javits (R), *New York*
Daniel P. Moynihan (D), *New York*

REPRESENTATIVES

1 Otis G. Pike (D), *Riverhead*
2 Thomas J. Downey (D), *West Islip*
3 Jerome A. Ambro (D), *East
  Northport*
4 Norman F. Lent (R), *East
  Rockaway*
5 John W. Wydler (R), *Garden City*
6 Lester L. Wolff (D), *Great Neck*
7 Joseph P. Addabbo (D), *Ozone
  Park*
8 Benjamin S. Rosenthal (D),
  *Elmhurst*
9 James J. Delaney (D),[53] *Long
  Island City*
10 Mario Biaggi (D), *Bronx*
11 James H. Scheuer (D), *Neponsit*
12 Shirley A. Chisholm (D), *Brooklyn*
13 Stephen J. Solarz (D), *Brooklyn*
14 Frederick W. Richmond (D),
  *Brooklyn*
15 Leo C. Zeferetti (D), *Brooklyn*
16 Elizabeth Holtzman (D), *Brooklyn*
17 John M. Murphy (D), *Staten
  Island*
18 Edward I. Koch (D),[54] *New York*
18 S. William Green (R),[55] *New York*
19 Charles B. Rangel (D), *New York*
20 Ted Weiss (D), *New York*
21 Herman Badillo (D),[56] *Bronx*
21 Robert Garcia (D),[57] *Bronx*
22 Jonathan B. Bingham (D), *Bronx*
23 Bruce F. Caputo (R), *Yonkers*
24 Richard L. Ottinger (D),
  *Pleasantville*
25 Hamilton Fish, Jr. (R), *Millbrook*
26 Benjamin A. Gilman (R),
  *Middletown*
27 Matthew F. McHugh (D), *Ithaca*
28 Samuel S. Stratton (D),
  *Amsterdam*
29 Edward W. Pattison (D), *West
  Sand Lake*
30 Robert C. McEwen (R),
  *Ogdensburg*
31 Donald J. Mitchell (R), *Herkimer*
32 James M. Hanley (D), *Syracuse*
33 William F. Walsh (R), *Syracuse*
34 Frank Horton (R), *Rochester*
35 Barber B. Conable, Jr. (R),
  *Alexander*
36 John J. LaFalce (D), *Buffalo*
37 Henry J. Nowak (D), *Buffalo*
38 Jack F. Kemp (R), *Hamburg*
39 Stanley N. Lundine (D),
  *Jamestown*

## NORTH CAROLINA

SENATORS

Jesse Helms (R), *Raleigh*
Robert Morgan (D), *Lillington*

REPRESENTATIVES

1 Walter B. Jones (D), *Farmville*
2 L. H. Fountain (D), *Tarboro*
3 Charles O. Whitley (D), *Mount
  Olive*
4 Ike F. Andrews (D), *Research
  Triangle Park*
5 Stephen L. Neal (D),
  *Winston-Salem*
6 L. Richardson Preyer (D),
  *Greensboro*
7 Charles Rose (D), *Fayetteville*
8 W. G. (Bill) Hefner (D), *Concord*
9 James G. Martin (R), *Davidson*
10 James T. Broyhill (R), *Lenoir*
11 V. Lamar Gudger (D), *Asheville*

## NORTH DAKOTA

SENATORS

Milton R. Young (R), *LaMoure*
Quentin N. Burdick (D), *Fargo*

REPRESENTATIVE AT LARGE

Mark Andrews (R), *Mapleton*

## OHIO

SENATORS

John Glenn, Jr. (D), *Columbus*
Howard M. Metzenbaum (D), *Shaker
Heights*

REPRESENTATIVES

1 Willis D. Gradison, Jr. (R),
  *Cincinnati*
2 Thomas A. Luken (D), *Cincinnati*
3 Charles W. Whalen, Jr. (R),
  *Dayton*
4 Tennyson Guyer (R), *Findley*
5 Delbert L. Latta (R), *Bowling
  Green*
6 William H. Harsha (R),
  *Portsmouth*
7 Clarence J. Brown (R), *Urbana*
8 Thomas N. Kindness (R),
  *Hamilton*
9 Thomas L. Ashley (D), *Toledo*
10 Clarence E. Miller (R), *Lancaster*
11 J. William Stanton (R),
  *Painesville*
12 Samuel L. Devine (R), *Columbus*
13 Donald J. Pease (D), *Oberlin*
14 John F. Seiberling (D), *Akron*
15 Chalmers P. Wylie (R), *Columbus*
16 Ralph S. Regula (R), *Navarre*
17 John M. Ashbrook (R), *Johnstown*
18 Douglas Applegate (D),
  *Steubenville*
19 Charles J. Carney (D),
  *Youngstown*
20 Mary Rose Oakar (D), *Cleveland*
21 Louis Stokes (D), *Cleveland*
22 Charles A. Vanik (D), *Euclid*
23 Ronald M. Mottl (D), *Parma*

## OKLAHOMA

SENATORS

Henry L. Bellmon (R), *Red Rock*
Dewey F. Bartlett (R), *Tulsa*

REPRESENTATIVES

1 James R. Jones (D), *Tulsa*
2 Theodore R. Risenhoover (D),
  *Tahlequah*
3 Wesley W. Watkins (D), *Ada*
4 Thomas J. Steed (D), *Shawnee*
5 Mickey Edwards (R), *Oklahoma
  City*
6 Glenn English (D), *Cordell*

## OREGON

SENATORS

Mark O. Hatfield (R), *Newport*
Robert W. Packwood (R), *Portland*

REPRESENTATIVES

1 Les AuCoin (D), *Forest Grove*
2 Albert C. Ullman (D), *Baker*
3 Robert Duncan (D), *Portland*
4 James Weaver (D), *Eugene*

## PENNSYLVANIA

SENATORS

Richard S. Schweiker (R), *Worcester*
H. John Heinz III (R), *Pittsburgh*

REPRESENTATIVES

1 Michael O. Myers (D),
  *Philadelphia*
2 Robert N. C. Nix (D),
  *Philadelphia*
3 Raymond F. Lederer (D),
  *Philadelphia*
4 Joshua Eilberg (D), *Philadelphia*
5 Richard T. Schulze (R), *Malvern*
6 Gus Yatron (D), *Reading*
7 Robert W. Edgar (D), *Broomall*
8 Peter H. Kostmayer (D), *Solebury*
9 E. G. Shuster (R), *Everett*

---

[53] Resigned December 31, 1978; vacancy throughout remainder of Congress.
[54] Resigned December 31, 1977, having been elected Mayor of New York City.
[55] Elected February 14, 1978, to fill vacancy caused by resignation of Edward I. Koch, and took his seat February 21, 1978.
[56] Resigned December 31, 1977.
[57] Elected February 14, 1978, as a Republican-Liberal to fill vacancy caused by resignation of Herman Badillo. Resumed his prior Democratic Party affiliation when he took his seat February 21, 1978.

10 Joseph M. McDade (R), *Clarks Summit*
11 Daniel J. Flood (D), *Wilkes-Barre*
12 John P. Murtha, Jr. (D), *Johnstown*
13 R. Lawrence Coughlin (R), *Villanova*
14 William S. Moorhead (D), *Pittsburgh*
15 Fred B. Rooney (D), *Bethlehem*
16 Robert S. Walker (R), *East Petersburg*
17 Allen E. Ertel (D), *Montoursville*
18 Doug Walgren (D), *Pittsburgh*
19 William F. Goodling (R), *York*
20 Joseph M. Gaydos (D), *McKeesport*
21 John H. Dent (D), *Ligonier*
22 Austin J. Murphy (D), *Charleroi*
23 Joseph S. Ammerman (D), *Curwensville*
24 Marc L. Marks (R), *Sharon*
25 Gary A. Myers (R), *Butler*

## RHODE ISLAND

### SENATORS

Claiborne Pell (D), *Newport*
John H. Chafee (R), *Warwick*

### REPRESENTATIVES

1 Fernand J. St Germain (D), *Woonsocket*
2 Edward P. Beard (D), *Cranston*

## SOUTH CAROLINA

### SENATORS

Strom Thurmond (R), *Aiken*
Ernest F. Hollings (D), *Charleston*

### REPRESENTATIVES

1 Mendel J. Davis (D), *Charleston*
2 Floyd Spence (R), *Lexington*
3 Butler Derrick (D), *Edgefield*
4 James R. Mann (D), *Greenville*
5 Kenneth L. Holland (D), *Lugoff*
6 John W. Jenrette, Jr. (D), *North Myrtle Beach*

## SOUTH DAKOTA

### SENATORS

George S. McGovern (D), *Mitchell*
James Abourezk (D), *Rapid City*

### REPRESENTATIVES

1 Larry Pressler (R), *Humboldt*
2 James Abdnor (R), *Kennebec*

## TENNESSEE

### SENATORS

Howard H. Baker, Jr. (R), *Huntsville*
James R. Sasser (D), *Nashville*

### REPRESENTATIVES

1 James H. Quillen (R), *Kingsport*
2 John J. Duncan (R), *Knoxville*
3 Marilyn Lloyd (D), *Chattanooga*
4 Albert A. Gore, Jr. (D), *Carthage*
5 Clifford R. Allen (D),[58] *Nashville*
6 Robin L. Beard (R), *Franklin*
7 Ed Jones (D), *Yorkville*
8 Harold E. Ford (D), *Memphis*

## TEXAS

### SENATORS

John G. Tower (R), *Wichita Falls*
Lloyd M. Bentsen, Jr. (D), *Houston*

### REPRESENTATIVES

1 Sam B. Hall, Jr. (D), *Marshall*
2 Charles Wilson (D), *Lufkin*
3 James M. Collins (R), *Dallas*
4 H. Ray Roberts (D), *McKinney*
5 James A. Mattox (D), *Dallas*
6 Olin E. Teague (D),[59] *College Station*
7 William R. Archer, Jr. (R), *Houston*
8 Robert C. Eckhardt (D), *Houston*
9 Jack B. Brooks (D), *Beaumont*
10 J. J. (Jake) Pickle (D), *Austin*
11 W. R. Poage (D),[60] *Waco*
12 James C. Wright, Jr. (D), *Fort Worth*
13 Jack Hightower (D), *Vernon*
14 John Young (D), *Corpus Christi*
15 Eligio (Kika) de la Garza (D), *Mission*
16 Richard C. White (D), *El Paso*
17 Omar T. Burleson (D),[61] *Anson*
18 Barbara Jordan (D), *Houston*
19 George H. Mahon (D), *Lubbock*
20 Henry B. Gonzalez (D), *San Antonio*
21 Robert Krueger (D), *New Braunfels*
22 Robert A. Gammage (D),[62] *Houston*
23 Abraham Kazen, Jr. (D), *Laredo*
24 Dale Milford (D), *Grand Prairie*

## UTAH

### SENATORS

E. J. (Jake) Garn (R), *Salt Lake City*
Orrin G. Hatch (R), *Salt Lake City*

### REPRESENTATIVES

1 K. Gunn McKay (D), *Huntsville*
2 David D. Marriott (R), *Salt Lake City*

## VERMONT

### SENATORS

Robert T. Stafford (R), *Rutland*
Patrick J. Leahy (D), *Burlington*

### REPRESENTATIVE AT LARGE

James M. Jeffords (R), *Rutland*

## VIRGINIA

### SENATORS

Harry Flood Byrd, Jr. (I), *Winchester*
William L. Scott (R),[63] *Fairfax*
John W. Warner (R),[64] *Middleburg*

### REPRESENTATIVES

1 Paul S. Trible, Jr. (R), *Tappahannock*
2 G. William Whitehurst (R), *Virginia Beach*
3 David E. Satterfield III (D), *Richmond*
4 Robert W. Daniel, Jr. (R), *Spring Cove*
5 W. C. (Dan) Daniel (D), *Danville*
6 M. Caldwell Butler (R), *Roanoke*
7 J. Kenneth Robinson (R), *Winchester*
8 Herbert E. Harris II (D), *Alexandria*
9 William C. Wampler (R), *Bristol*
10 Joseph L. Fisher (D), *Arlington*

## WASHINGTON

### SENATORS

Warren G. Magnuson (D), *Seattle*
Henry M. Jackson (D), *Everett*

### REPRESENTATIVES

1 Joel Pritchard (R), *Seattle*
2 Lloyd Meeds (D), *Lake Stevens*
3 Don Bonker (D), *Olympia*
4 Mike McCormack (D), *Richland*
5 Thomas S. Foley (D), *Spokane*
6 Norman D. Dicks (D), *Bremerton*
7 Brock Adams (D),[65] *Seattle*
7 John (Jack) Cunningham (R),[66] *Seattle*

## WEST VIRGINIA

### SENATORS

Jennings Randolph (D), *Elkins*
Robert C. Byrd (D), *Sophia*

### REPRESENTATIVES

1 Robert H. Mollohan (D), *Fairmont*
2 Harley O. Staggers (D), *Keyser*
3 John M. Slack, Jr. (D), *Charleston*
4 Nick J. Rahall II (D), *Beckley*

---

[58] Died June 18, 1978; vacancy throughout remainder of Congress.
[59] Resigned December 31, 1978; vacancy throughout remainder of Congress.
[60] Resigned December 31, 1978; vacancy throughout remainder of Congress.
[61] Resigned December 31, 1978; vacancy throughout remainder of Congress.
[62] Election unsuccessfully contested by Ronald E. Paul.
[63] Resigned January 1, 1979.
[64] Appointed January 2, 1979, to fill vacancy caused by resignation of William L. Scott, but was unable to be sworn in as Congress was not in session.
[65] Resigned January 22, 1977.
[66] Elected May 17, 1977, to fill vacancy caused by resignation of Brock Adams, and took his seat May 23, 1977.

## WISCONSIN

### SENATORS

William Proxmire (D), *Madison*
Gaylord Nelson (D), *Madison*

### REPRESENTATIVES

1 Les Aspin (D), *Racine*
2 Robert W. Kastenmeier (D), *Sun Prairie*
3 Alvin Baldus (D), *Menomonie*
4 Clement J. Zablocki (D), *Milwaukee*
5 Henry S. Reuss (D), *Milwaukee*
6 William A. Steiger (R),[67] *Oshkosh*
7 David R. Obey (D), *Wausau*
8 Robert J. Cornell (D), *DePere*
9 Robert W. Kasten, Jr. (R), *Brookfield*

## WYOMING

### SENATORS

Clifford P. Hansen (R),[68] *Jackson*
Alan K. Simpson (R),[69] *Cody*
Malcolm Wallop (R), *Big Horn*

### REPRESENTATIVE AT LARGE

Teno Roncalio (D),[70] *Cheyenne*

## COMMONWEALTH OF PUERTO RICO

### RESIDENT COMMISSIONER

Baltasar Corrada-del Rio (NP), *San Juan*

## DISTRICT OF COLUMBIA

### DELEGATE

Walter E. Fauntroy (D), *Washington, D.C.*

## GUAM

### DELEGATE

Antonio Borja Won Pat (D), *Agana*

## VIRGIN ISLANDS

### DELEGATE

Ron de Lugo (D), *St. Croix*

---

[67] Died December 4, 1978, before the commencement of the Ninety-sixth Congress, to which he had been reelected; vacancy in the Ninety-fifth Congress not filled.

[68] Resigned December 31, 1978.
[69] Appointed January 1, 1979, to fill vacancy caused by resignation of Clifford P. Hansen, but was unable to be sworn in as Congress was not in session.
[70] Resigned December 30, 1978; vacancy throughout remainder of Congress.

# 96TH CONGRESS

## JANUARY 3, 1979, TO JANUARY 3, 1981

FIRST SESSION— *January 15, 1979,*[1] to *January 3, 1980*[2]
SECOND SESSION— *January 3, 1980, to October 15, 1980*

Walter F. Mondale
Vice President

Thomas P. O'Neill, Jr.
Speaker

---

### Senate
Democrats 58 — Republicans 41 — Independent 1

VICE PRESIDENT OF THE UNITED STATES— Walter F. Mondale, of Minnesota
PRESIDENT PRO TEMPORE OF THE SENATE— Warren G. Magnuson,[3] of Washington
SECRETARY OF THE SENATE— J. S. Kimmitt, of Virginia
SERGEANT AT ARMS OF THE SENATE— F. Nordy Hoffmann, of Maryland
MAJORITY FLOOR LEADER— Robert C. Byrd, of West Virginia
DEMOCRATIC WHIP— Alan M. Cranston, of California
REPUBLICAN FLOOR LEADER— Howard H. Baker, Jr., of Tennessee
ASSISTANT REPUBLICAN LEADER— Theodore F. Stevens, of Alaska

---

### House of Representatives
Democrats 276 — Republicans 157 — Vacant 2

SPEAKER OF THE HOUSE— Thomas P. O'Neill, Jr.,[4] of Massachusetts
CLERK OF THE HOUSE— Edmund L. Henshaw, Jr.,[5] of Virginia
SERGEANT AT ARMS OF THE HOUSE— Kenneth R. Harding,[6] of Virginia; Benjamin J. Guthrie,[7] of Virginia
DOORKEEPER OF THE HOUSE— James T. Molloy,[8] of New York
POSTMASTER OF THE HOUSE— Robert V. Rota,[9] of Pennsylvania
MAJORITY LEADER— James C. Wright, Jr., of Texas
MAJORITY WHIP— John Brademas, of Indiana
REPUBLICAN LEADER— John J. Rhodes, of Arizona
REPUBLICAN WHIP— Robert H. Michel, of Illinois

---

## ALABAMA

### SENATORS
Donald W. Stewart (D),[10] *Anniston*
Jeremiah A. Denton, Jr. (R),[11] *Mobile*
Howell T. Heflin (D), *Tuscumbia*

### REPRESENTATIVES
1 Jack Edwards (R), *Mobile*
2 William L. Dickinson (R), *Montgomery*
3 William Nichols (D), *Sylacauga*
4 Tom Bevill (D), *Jasper*
5 Ronnie G. Flippo (D), *Florence*
6 John H. Buchanan, Jr. (R), *Birmingham*
7 Richard C. Shelby (D), *Tuscaloosa*

## ALASKA

### SENATORS
Theodore F. Stevens (R), *Anchorage*
Maurice R. (Mike) Gravel (D), *Anchorage*

### REPRESENTATIVE AT LARGE
Donald E. Young (R), *Fort Yukon*

## ARIZONA

### SENATORS
Barry M. Goldwater (R), *Scottsdale*
Dennis DeConcini (D), *Tucson*

### REPRESENTATIVES
1 John J. Rhodes (R), *Mesa*
2 Morris K. Udall (D), *Tucson*
3 Bob Stump (D), *Tolleson*
4 Eldon Rudd (R), *Scottsdale*

## ARKANSAS

### SENATORS
Dale Bumpers (D), *Charleston*
David H. Pryor (D), *Camden*

### REPRESENTATIVES
1 William V. Alexander (D), *Osceola*
2 Ed Bethune (R), *Searcy*
3 John Paul Hammerschmidt (R), *Harrison*
4 Beryl F. Anthony, Jr. (D), *El Dorado*

## CALIFORNIA

### SENATORS
Alan Cranston (D), *Los Angeles*
S. I. Hayakawa (R), *Mill Valley*

### REPRESENTATIVES
1 Harold T. Johnson (D), *Roseville*
2 Don H. Clausen (R), *Crescent City*
3 Robert T. Matsui (D), *Sacramento*
4 Vic Fazio (D), *Sacramento*
5 John L. Burton (D), *San Francisco*
6 Phillip Burton (D), *San Francisco*
7 George Miller (D), *Martinez*
8 Ronald V. Dellums (D), *Berkeley*
9 Fortney H. (Pete) Stark, Jr. (D), *Oakland*
10 Don Edwards (D), *San Jose*
11 William Royer (R),[12] *Redwood City*

---

[1] By joint resolution (Pub. Law 95 594, 95th Cong., 2d sess.), the date of assembling the first session of the Ninety-sixth Congress was fixed for January 15, 1979.
[2] The Senate adjourned sine die December 20, 1979.
[3] Elected January 15, 1979.
[4] Reelected January 15, 1979.

[5] Reelected January 15, 1979.
[6] Reelected January 15, 1979; resigned February 29, 1980.
[7] Acted as Sergeant at Arms during the interim.
[8] Reelected January 15, 1979.
[9] Reelected January 15, 1979.

[10] Resigned January 1, 1981.
[11] Appointed to fill vacancy caused by resignation of Donald W. Stewart, and took his seat January 2, 1981.
[12] Elected April 3, 1979, to fill vacancy caused by death of Representative-elect Leo J. Ryan, in preceding Congress, and took his seat April 9, 1979.

## CALIFORNIA—Continued

REPRESENTATIVES—CONTINUED

12 Paul N. (Pete) McCloskey, Jr. (R), *Menlo Park*
13 Norman Y. Mineta (D), *San Jose*
14 Norman D. Shumway (R), *Stockton*
15 Tony Coelho (D), *Merced*
16 Leon E. Panetta (D), *Carmel Valley*
17 Charles Pashayan, Jr. (R), *Fresno*
18 William M. Thomas (R), *Bakersfield*
19 Robert J. Lagomarsino (R), *Ventura*
20 Barry M. Goldwater, Jr. (R), *Woodland Hills*
21 James C. Corman (D), *Van Nuys*
22 Carlos J. Moorhead (R), *Glendale*
23 Anthony C. Beilenson (D), *Los Angeles*
24 Henry A. Waxman (D), *Los Angeles*
25 Edward R. Roybal (D), *Los Angeles*
26 John Rousselot (R), *San Marino*
27 Robert K. Dornan (R), *Santa Monica*
28 Julian C. Dixon (D), *Los Angeles*
29 Augustus F. Hawkins (D), *Los Angeles*
30 George E. Danielson (D), *Monterey Park*
31 Charles H. Wilson (D), *Hawthorne*
32 Glenn M. Anderson (D), *Harbor City*
33 Wayne R. Grisham (R), *La Mirada*
34 Dan Lungren (R), *Long Beach*
35 Jim Lloyd (D), *West Covina*
36 George E. Brown, Jr. (D), *Riverside*
37 Jerry Lewis (R), *San Bernardino*
38 Jerry M. Patterson (D), *Santa Ana*
39 William E. Dannemeyer (R), *Fullerton*
40 Robert E. Badham (R), *Newport Beach*
41 Robert C. Wilson (R), *San Diego*
42 Lionel Van Deerlin (D), *Chula Vista*
43 Clair W. Burgener (R), *Rancho Santa Fe*

## COLORADO

SENATORS

Gary Hart (D), *Denver*
William L. Armstrong (R), *Aurora*

REPRESENTATIVES

1 Patricia Schroeder (D), *Denver*
2 Timothy E. Wirth (D), *Denver*
3 Raymond P. Kogovsek (D), *Pueblo*
4 James P. Johnson (R), *Fort Collins*
5 Kenneth B. Kramer (R), *Colorado Springs*

## CONNECTICUT

SENATORS

Abraham A. Ribicoff (D), *Hartford*
Lowell P. Weicker, Jr. (R), *Stonington*

REPRESENTATIVES

1 William R. Cotter (D), *Hartford*
2 Christopher J. Dodd (D), *North Stonington*
3 Robert N. Giaimo (D), *North Haven*
4 Stewart B. McKinney (R), *Fairfield*
5 William R. Ratchford (D), *Danbury*
6 Toby Moffett (D), *Unionville*

## DELAWARE

SENATORS

William V. Roth, Jr. (R), *Wilmington*
Joseph R. Biden, Jr. (D), *Wilmington*

REPRESENTATIVE AT LARGE

Thomas B. Evans, Jr. (R), *Wilmington*

## FLORIDA

SENATORS

Lawton Chiles (D), *Lakeland*
Richard Stone (D),[13] *Tallahassee*
Paula Hawkins (R),[14] *Winter Park*

REPRESENTATIVES

1 Earl Hutto (D), *Panama City*
2 Don Fuqua (D), *Altha*
3 Charles E. Bennett (D), *Jacksonville*
4 William V. Chappell, Jr. (D), *Ocala*
5 Richard Kelly (R), *Holiday*
6 C. W. Bill Young (R), *St. Petersburg*
7 Sam M. Gibbons (D), *Tampa*
8 Andrew P. Ireland (D), *Winter Haven*
9 Bill Nelson (D), *Melbourne*
10 L. A. (Skip) Bafalis (R), *Fort Myers Beach*
11 Daniel A. Mica (D), *West Palm Beach*
12 Edward J. Stack (D), *Fort Lauderdale*
13 William Lehman (D), *North Miami Beach*
14 Claude D. Pepper (D), *Miami*
15 Dante B. Fascell (D), *Miami*

## GEORGIA

SENATORS

Herman E. Talmadge (D), *Lovejoy*
Sam Nunn (D), *Atlanta*

REPRESENTATIVES

1 Ronald B. (Bo) Ginn (D), *Millen*
2 Dawson Mathis (D), *Albany*
3 Jack T. Brinkley (D), *Columbus*
4 Elliott H. Levitas (D), *Atlanta*
5 Wyche Fowler, Jr. (D), *Atlanta*
6 Newt Gingrich (R), *Carrollton*
7 Larry McDonald (D), *Marietta*
8 Billy Lee Evans (D), *Macon*
9 Edgar L. Jenkins (D), *Jasper*
10 D. Douglas Barnard, Jr. (D), *Augusta*

## HAWAII

SENATORS

Daniel K. Inouye (D), *Honolulu*
Spark M. Matsunaga (D), *Honolulu*

REPRESENTATIVES

1 Cecil Heftel (D), *Honolulu*
2 Daniel K. Akaka (D), *Honolulu*

## IDAHO

SENATORS

Frank Church (D), *Boise*
James A. McClure (R), *Payette*

REPRESENTATIVES

1 Steven D. Symms (R), *Caldwell*
2 George Hansen (R), *Pocatello*

## ILLINOIS

SENATORS

Charles H. Percy (R), *Wilmette*
Adlai E. Stevenson III (D), *Chicago*

REPRESENTATIVES

1 Bennett Stewart (D),[15] *Chicago*
2 Morgan F. Murphy (D), *Chicago*
3 Martin A. Russo (D), *Chicago*
4 Edward J. Derwinski (R), *Flossmoor*
5 John G. Fary (D), *Chicago*
6 Henry J. Hyde (R), *Bensenville*
7 Cardiss Collins (D), *Chicago*
8 Dan Rostenkowski (D), *Chicago*
9 Sidney R. Yates (D), *Chicago*
10 Abner J. Mikva (D),[16] *Evanston*
10 John Edward Porter (R),[17] *Evanston*
11 Frank Annunzio (D), *Chicago*
12 Philip M. Crane (R), *Mount Prospect*
13 Robert McClory (R), *Lake Bluff*
14 John N. Erlenborn (R), *Glen Ellyn*
15 Thomas J. Corcoran (R), *Ottawa*
16 John B. Anderson (R), *Rockford*
17 George M. O'Brien (R), *Joliet*
18 Robert H. Michel (R), *Peoria*

---

[13] Resigned December 31, 1980.
[14] Appointed to fill vacancy caused by resignation of Richard Stone, and took her seat January 1, 1981.

[15] Election unsuccessfully contested by A. A. Sammy Rayner, Jr.
[16] Resigned September 26, 1979.

[17] Elected January 22, 1980, to fill vacancy caused by resignation of Abner J. Mikva, and took his seat January 24, 1980.

19 Thomas F. Railsback (R), *Moline*
20 Paul Findley (R), *Pittsfield*
21 Edward R. Madigan (R), *Lincoln*
22 Daniel B. Crane (R), *Danville*
23 Melvin Price (D), *East St. Louis*
24 Paul Simon (D), *Carbondale*

## INDIANA

### SENATORS

Birch E. Bayh (D), *Terre Haute*
Richard G. Lugar (R), *Indianapolis*

### REPRESENTATIVES

1 Adam Benjamin, Jr. (D), *Hobart*
2 Floyd J. Fithian (D), *Lafayette*
3 John Brademas (D), *South Bend*
4 J. Danforth Quayle (R), *Huntington*
5 Elwood Hillis (R), *Kokomo*
6 David W. Evans (D), *Indianapolis*
7 John T. Myers (R), *Covington*
8 H. Joel Deckard (R), *Evansville*
9 Lee H. Hamilton (D), *Columbus*
10 Philip R. Sharp (D), *Muncie*
11 Andrew Jacobs, Jr. (D), *Indianapolis*

## IOWA

### SENATORS

John C. Culver (D), *Cedar Rapids*
Roger W. Jepsen (R), *Davenport*

### REPRESENTATIVES

1 James A. S. Leach (R), *Davenport*
2 Thomas J. Tauke (R), *Dubuque*
3 Charles E. Grassley (R), *New Hartford*
4 Neal Smith (D), *Altoona*
5 Tom Harkin (D), *Ames*
6 Berkley Bedell (D), *Spirit Lake*

## KANSAS

### SENATORS

Robert J. Dole (R), *Russell*
Nancy L. Kassebaum (R), *Wichita*

### REPRESENTATIVES

1 Keith G. Sebelius (R), *Norton*
2 Jim Jeffries (R), *Atchison*
3 Larry Winn, Jr. (R), *Overland Park*
4 Daniel R. Glickman (D), *Wichita*
5 Bob Whittaker (R), *Augusta*

## KENTUCKY

### SENATORS

Walter (Dee) Huddleston (D), *Elizabethtown*
Wendell H. Ford (D), *Owensboro*

### REPRESENTATIVES

1 Carroll Hubbard, Jr. (D), *Mayfield*
2 William H. Natcher (D), *Bowling Green*
3 Romano L. Mazzoli (D), *Louisville*
4 M. G. (Gene) Snyder (R), *Brownsboro Farms*
5 Tim Lee Carter (R), *Tompkinsville*
6 Larry J. Hopkins (R), *Lexington*
7 Carl D. Perkins (D), *Hindman*

## LOUISIANA

### SENATORS

Russell B. Long (D), *Baton Rouge*
J. Bennett Johnston, Jr. (D), *Shreveport*

### REPRESENTATIVES

1 Robert L. Livingston (R), *New Orleans*
2 Corinne C. (Lindy) Boggs (D), *New Orleans*
3 David C. Treen (R),[18] *Metairie*
3 W. J. (Billy) Tauzin (D),[19] *Thibodaux*
4 Claude (Buddy) Leach, Jr. (D),[20] *Leesville*
5 Thomas J. (Jerry) Huckaby (D), *Ringgold*
6 W. Henson Moore (R), *Baton Rouge*
7 John B. Breaux (D), *Crowley*
8 Gillis W. Long (D), *Alexandria*

## MAINE

### SENATORS

Edmund S. Muskie (D),[21] *Waterville*
George J. Mitchell (D),[22] *Portland*
William S. Cohen (R), *Bangor*

### REPRESENTATIVES

1 David F. Emery (R), *Rockland*
2 Olympia J. Snowe (R), *Auburn*

## MARYLAND

### SENATORS

Charles McC. Mathias, Jr. (R), *Frederick*
Paul S. Sarbanes (D), *Baltimore*

### REPRESENTATIVES

1 Robert E. Bauman (R), *Easton*
2 Clarence D. Long (D), *Ruxton*
3 Barbara A. Mikulski (D), *Baltimore*
4 Marjorie S. Holt (R), *Severna Park*
5 Gladys Noon Spellman (D), *Laurel*
6 Beverly B. Byron (D),[23] *Frederick*

7 Parren J. Mitchell (D),[24] *Baltimore*
8 Michael D. Barnes (D), *Kensington*

## MASSACHUSETTS

### SENATORS

Edward M. Kennedy (D), *Boston*
Paul E. Tsongas (D), *Lowell*

### REPRESENTATIVES

1 Silvio O. Conte (R), *Pittsfield*
2 Edward P. Boland (D), *Springfield*
3 Joseph D. Early (D), *Worcester*
4 Robert F. Drinan (D), *Newton*
5 James M. Shannon (D), *Lawrence*
6 Nicholas Mavroules (D), *Peabody*
7 Edward J. Markey (D), *Malden*
8 Thomas P. O'Neill, Jr. (D), *Cambridge*
9 John Joseph Moakley (D), *Boston*
10 Margaret M. Heckler (R), *Wellesley*
11 Brian J. Donnelly (D), *Dorchester*
12 Gerry E. Studds (D), *Cohasset*

## MICHIGAN

### SENATORS

Donald W. Riegle, Jr. (D), *Flint*
Carl Levin (D), *Detroit*

### REPRESENTATIVES

1 John Conyers, Jr. (D), *Detroit*
2 Carl D. Pursell (R), *Plymouth*
3 Howard E. Wolpe (D), *Lansing*
4 David A. Stockman (R), *St. Joseph*
5 Harold S. Sawyer (R), *Rockford*
6 Bob Carr (D), *East Lansing*
7 Dale E. Kildee (D), *Flint*
8 Bob Traxler (D), *Bay City*
9 Guy A. Vander Jagt (R), *Luther*
10 Donald J. Albosta (D), *St. Charles*
11 Robert W. Davis (R), *Gaylord*
12 David E. Bonior (D), *Mount Clemens*
13 Charles C. Diggs, Jr. (D),[25] *Detroit*
13 George W. Crockett, Jr. (D),[26] *Detroit*
14 Lucien N. Nedzi (D), *Detroit*
15 William D. Ford (D), *Taylor*
16 John D. Dingell, Jr. (D), *Trenton*
17 William M. Brodhead (D), *Detroit*
18 James J. Blanchard (D), *Pleasant Ridge*
19 William S. Broomfield (R), *Birmingham*

---

[18] Resigned March 10, 1980.
[19] Elected May 17, 1980, to fill vacancy caused by resignation of David C. Treen, and took his seat May 22, 1980.
[20] Election unsuccessfully contested by Jimmy H. Wilson.

[21] Resigned May 7, 1980.
[22] Appointed May 17, 1980, to fill vacancy caused by resignation of Edmund S. Muskie, and took his seat May 19, 1980.
[23] Election unsuccessfully contested by Melvin Perkins.

[24] Election unsuccessfully contested by Debra Hannania Freeman.
[25] Resigned June 3, 1980.
[26] Elected November 4, 1980, to fill vacancy caused by resignation of Charles C. Diggs, Jr., and took his seat November 12, 1980.

## MINNESOTA

### SENATORS

David F. Durenberger (R),
*Minneapolis*
Rudy Boschwitz (R), *Plymouth*

### REPRESENTATIVES

1　Arlen I. Erdahl (R), *West St. Paul*
2　Tom Hagedorn (R), *Truman*
3　Bill Frenzel (R), *Golden Valley*
4　Bruce F. Vento (D), *St. Paul*
5　Martin Olav Sabo (D),
　　*Minneapolis*
6　Richard Nolan (D), *Waite Park*
7　Arlan Stangeland (R), *Barnesville*
8　James L. Oberstar (D), *Chisholm*

## MISSISSIPPI

### SENATORS

John C. Stennis (D), *De Kalb*
Thad Cochran (R), *Jackson*

### REPRESENTATIVES

1　Jamie L. Whitten (D), *Charleston*
2　David R. Bowen (D), *Cleveland*
3　Gillespie V. (Sonny) Montgomery
　　(D), *Meridian*
4　Jon C. Hinson (R), *Tylertown*
5　Trent Lott (R), *Pascagoula*

## MISSOURI

### SENATORS

Thomas F. Eagleton (D), *St. Louis*
John C. Danforth (R), *Jefferson City*

### REPRESENTATIVES

1　William L. Clay (D), *St. Louis*
2　Robert A. Young (D), *St. Ann*
3　Richard A. Gephardt (D), *St.
　　Louis*
4　Ike Skelton (D), *Lexington*
5　Richard W. Bolling (D), *Kansas
　　City*
6　E. Thomas Coleman (R), *Kansas
　　City*
7　Gene Taylor (R), *Sarcoxie*
8　Richard H. Ichord (D), *Houston*
9　Harold A. Volkmer (D), *Hannibal*
10　Bill D. Burlison (D), *Cape
　　Girardeau*

## MONTANA

### SENATORS

John Melcher (D), *Forsyth*
Max Baucus (D), *Missoula*

### REPRESENTATIVES

1　Pat Williams (D), *Helena*
2　Ron Marlenee (R), *Scobey*

## NEBRASKA

### SENATORS

Edward Zorinsky (D), *Omaha*
J. James Exon (D), *Lincoln*

### REPRESENTATIVES

1　Douglas K. Bereuter (R), *Utica*
2　John J. Cavanaugh (D), *Omaha*
3　Virginia Smith (R), *Chappell*

## NEVADA

### SENATORS

Howard W. Cannon (D), *Las Vegas*
Paul Laxalt (R), *Carson City*

### REPRESENTATIVE AT LARGE

Jim Santini (D), *Las Vegas*

## NEW HAMPSHIRE

### SENATORS

John A. Durkin (D),[27] *Manchester*
Warren B. Rudman (R),[28] *Nashua*
Gordon J. Humphrey (R), *Sunapee*

### REPRESENTATIVES

1　Norman E. D'Amours (D),
　　*Manchester*
2　James C. Cleveland (R), *New
　　London*

## NEW JERSEY

### SENATORS

Harrison A. Williams, Jr. (D),
　　*Bedminster*
Bill Bradley (D), *Denville*

### REPRESENTATIVES

1　James J. Florio (D), *Camden*
2　William J. Hughes (D), *Ocean
　　City*
3　James J. Howard (D), *Spring
　　Lake Heights*
4　Frank Thompson, Jr. (D),[29]
　　*Trenton*
5　Millicent Fenwick (R),
　　*Bernardsville*
6　Edwin B. Forsythe (R),
　　*Moorestown*
7　Andrew Maguire (D), *Ridgewood*
8　Robert A. Roe (D), *Wayne*
9　Harold C. Hollenbeck (R), *East
　　Rutherford*
10　Peter W. Rodino, Jr. (D), *Newark*
11　Joseph G. Minish (D), *West
　　Orange*
12　Matthew J. Rinaldo (R), *Union*
13　James A. Courter (R),
　　*Hackettstown*
14　Frank J. Guarini (D), *Jersey City*
15　Edward J. Patten (D), *Perth
　　Amboy*

## NEW MEXICO

### SENATORS

Pete V. Domenici (R), *Albuquerque*
Harrison H. Schmitt (R), *Silver City*

### REPRESENTATIVES

1　Manuel Lujan, Jr. (R),
　　*Albuquerque*
2　Harold Runnels (D),[30] *Lovington*

## NEW YORK

### SENATORS

Jacob K. Javits (R), *New York*
Daniel P. Moynihan (D), *New York*

### REPRESENTATIVES

1　William Carney (R), *Hauppauge*
2　Thomas J. Downey (D), *West Islip*
3　Jerome A. Ambro (D), *Huntington
　　Station*
4　Norman F. Lent (R), *East
　　Rockaway*
5　John W. Wydler (R), *Garden City*
6　Lester L. Wolff (D), *Great Neck*
7　Joseph P. Addabbo (D), *Ozone
　　Park*
8　Benjamin S. Rosenthal (D),
　　*Elmhurst*
9　Geraldine A. Ferraro (D), *Forest
　　Hills*
10　Mario Biaggi (D), *Bronx*
11　James H. Scheuer (D), *Neponsit*
12　Shirley A. Chisholm (D), *Brooklyn*
13　Stephen J. Solarz (D), *Brooklyn*
14　Frederick W. Richmond (D),
　　*Brooklyn*
15　Leo C. Zeferetti (D), *Brooklyn*
16　Elizabeth Holtzman (D), *Brooklyn*
17　John M. Murphy (D), *Staten
　　Island*
18　S. William Green (R), *New York*
19　Charles B. Rangel (D), *New York*
20　Ted Weiss (D), *New York*
21　Robert Garcia (D), *Bronx*
22　Jonathan B. Bingham (D), *Bronx*
23　Peter A. Peyser (D), *Irvington*
24　Richard L. Ottinger (D),
　　*Mamaroneck*
25　Hamilton Fish, Jr. (R), *Millbrook*
26　Benjamin A. Gilman (R),
　　*Middletown*
27　Matthew F. McHugh (D), *Ithaca*
28　Samuel S. Stratton (D),
　　*Amsterdam*
29　Gerald B. H. Solomon (R), *Glens
　　Falls*
30　Robert C. McEwen (R),
　　*Ogdensburg*
31　Donald J. Mitchell (R), *Herkimer*
32　James M. Hanley (D), *Syracuse*

---

[27] Resigned December 29, 1980.
[28] Appointed to fill vacancy caused by resignation of John A. Durkin, and took his seat December 29, 1980.

[29] Resigned December 29, 1980; vacancy throughout remainder of Congress.

[30] Died August 5, 1980; vacancy throughout remainder of Congress.

33 Gary A. Lee (R), *Dryden*
34 Frank Horton (R), *Rochester*
35 Barber B. Conable, Jr. (R), *Alexander*
36 John J. LaFalce (D), *Tonawanda*
37 Henry J. Nowak (D), *Buffalo*
38 Jack F. Kemp (R), *Hamburg*
39 Stanley N. Lundine (D), *Jamestown*

## NORTH CAROLINA

### SENATORS

Jesse Helms (R), *Raleigh*
Robert Morgan (D), *Lillington*

### REPRESENTATIVES

1 Walter B. Jones (D), *Farmville*
2 L. H. Fountain (D), *Tarboro*
3 Charles O. Whitley (D), *Mount Olive*
4 Ike F. Andrews (D), *Siler City*
5 Stephen L. Neal (D), *Winston-Salem*
6 L. Richardson Preyer (D), *Greensboro*
7 Charles Rose (D), *Fayetteville*
8 W. G. (Bill) Hefner (D), *Concord*
9 James G. Martin (R), *Davidson*
10 James T. Broyhill (R), *Lenoir*
11 V. Lamar Gudger (D), *Asheville*

## NORTH DAKOTA

### SENATORS

Milton R. Young (R), *LaMoure*
Quentin N. Burdick (D), *Fargo*

### REPRESENTATIVE AT LARGE

Mark Andrews (R), *Mapleton*

## OHIO

### SENATORS

John Glenn, Jr. (D), *Columbus*
Howard M. Metzenbaum (D), *Shaker Heights*

### REPRESENTATIVES

1 Willis D. Gradison, Jr. (R), *Cincinnati*
2 Thomas A. Luken (D), *Cincinnati*
3 Tony P. Hall (D), *Dayton*
4 Tennyson Guyer (R), *Findley*
5 Delbert L. Latta (R), *Bowling Green*
6 William H. Harsha (R), *Portsmouth*
7 Clarence J. Brown (R), *Urbana*
8 Thomas N. Kindness (R), *Hamilton*
9 Thomas L. Ashley (D), *Maumee*
10 Clarence E. Miller (R), *Lancaster*

11 J. William Stanton (R), *Painesville*
12 Samuel L. Devine (R), *Columbus*
13 Donald J. Pease (D), *Oberlin*
14 John F. Seiberling (D), *Akron*
15 Chalmers P. Wylie (R), *Worthington*
16 Ralph S. Regula (R), *Navarre*
17 John M. Ashbrook (R), *Johnstown*
18 Douglas Applegate (D), *Steubenville*
19 Lyle Williams (R), *Warren*
20 Mary Rose Oakar (D), *Cleveland*
21 Louis Stokes (D), *Cleveland*
22 Charles A. Vanik (D), *Euclid*
23 Ronald M. Mottl (D), *Parma*

## OKLAHOMA

### SENATORS

Henry L. Bellmon (R), *Billings*
David L. Boren (D), *Seminole*

### REPRESENTATIVES

1 James R. Jones (D), *Tulsa*
2 Mike Synar (D), *Muskogee*
3 Wesley W. Watkins (D), *Ada*
4 Thomas J. Steed (D), *Shawnee*
5 Mickey Edwards (R), *Oklahoma City*
6 Glenn English (D), *Cordell*

## OREGON

### SENATORS

Mark O. Hatfield (R), *Salem*
Robert W. Packwood (R), *Portland*

### REPRESENTATIVES

1 Les AuCoin (D), *Forest Grove*
2 Albert C. Ullman (D), *Baker*
3 Robert Duncan (D), *Gresham*
4 James Weaver (D), *Eugene*

## PENNSYLVANIA

### SENATORS

Richard S. Schweiker (R), *Worcester*
H. John Heinz III (R), *Pittsburgh*

### REPRESENTATIVES

1 Michael O. Myers (D),[31] *Philadelphia*
2 William H. Gray III (D), *Philadelphia*
3 Raymond F. Lederer (D), *Philadelphia*
4 Charles F. Dougherty (R), *Philadelphia*
5 Richard T. Schulze (R), *Malvern*
6 Gus Yatron (D), *Reading*
7 Robert W. Edgar (D), *Broomall*
8 Peter H. Kostmayer (D), *Solebury*
9 E. G. Shuster (R), *Everett*
10 Joseph M. McDade (R), *Scranton*

11 Daniel J. Flood (D),[32] *Wilkes-Barre*
11 Raphael Musto (D),[33] *Pittston*
12 John P. Murtha, Jr. (D), *Johnstown*
13 R. Lawrence Coughlin (R), *Villanova*
14 William S. Moorhead (D), *Pittsburgh*
15 Don Ritter (R), *Coopersburg*
16 Robert S. Walker (R), *East Petersburg*
17 Allen E. Ertel (D), *Montoursville*
18 Doug Walgren (D), *Pittsburgh*
19 William F. Goodling (R), *Jacobus*
20 Joseph M. Gaydos (D), *McKeesport*
21 Don Bailey (D), *Greensburg*
22 Austin J. Murphy (D), *Charleroi*
23 William F. Clinger, Jr. (R), *Warren*
24 Marc L. Marks (R), *Sharon*
25 Eugene V. Atkinson (D), *Aliquippa*

## RHODE ISLAND

### SENATORS

Claiborne Pell (D), *Newport*
John H. Chafee (R), *Warwick*

### REPRESENTATIVES

1 Fernand J. St Germain (D), *Woonsocket*
2 Edward P. Beard (D), *Cranston*

## SOUTH CAROLINA

### SENATORS

Strom Thurmond (R), *Aiken*
Ernest F. Hollings (D), *Charleston*

### REPRESENTATIVES

1 Mendel J. Davis (D), *Charleston*
2 Floyd Spence (R), *Lexington*
3 Butler Derrick (D), *Edgefield*
4 Carroll Campbell, Jr. (R), *Greenville*
5 Kenneth L. Holland (D), *Gaffney*
6 John W. Jenrette, Jr. (D),[34] *North Myrtle Beach*

## SOUTH DAKOTA

### SENATORS

George S. McGovern (D), *Mitchell*
Larry Pressler (R), *Humboldt*

### REPRESENTATIVES

1 Thomas A. Daschle (D),[35] *Aberdeen*
2 James Abdnor (R), *Kennebec*

---

[31] Expelled by H.Res. 794, October 2, 1980; vacancy throughout remainder of Congress.
[32] Resigned January 31, 1980.
[33] Elected April 9, 1980, to fill vacancy caused by resignation of Daniel J. Flood, and took his seat April 15, 1980.
[34] Resigned December 10, 1980; vacancy throughout remainder of Congress.
[35] Election unsuccessfully contested by Leo K. Thorsness.

## TENNESSEE

### SENATORS
Howard H. Baker, Jr. (R), *Huntsville*
James R. Sasser (D), *Nashville*

### REPRESENTATIVES
1 James H. Quillen (R), *Kingsport*
2 John J. Duncan (R), *Knoxville*
3 Marilyn Lloyd (D),[36] *Chattanooga*
4 Albert A. Gore, Jr. (D), *Carthage*
5 William H. Boner (D), *Nashville*
6 Robin L. Beard (R), *Franklin*
7 Edward Jones (D), *Yorkville*
8 Harold E. Ford (D), *Memphis*

## TEXAS

### SENATORS
John G. Tower (R), *Wichita Falls*
Lloyd M. Bentsen, Jr. (D), *Houston*

### REPRESENTATIVES
1 Sam B. Hall, Jr. (D), *Marshall*
2 Charles Wilson (D), *Lufkin*
3 James M. Collins (R), *Dallas*
4 H. Ray Roberts (D), *McKinney*
5 James A. Mattox (D), *Dallas*
6 Phil Gramm (D), *College Station*
7 William R. Archer, Jr. (R), *Houston*
8 Robert C. Eckhardt (D), *Houston*
9 Jack B. Brooks (D), *Beaumont*
10 J. J. (Jake) Pickle (D), *Austin*
11 J. Marvin Leath (D), *Marlin*
12 James C. Wright, Jr. (D), *Fort Worth*
13 Jack Hightower (D), *Vernon*
14 Joseph P. Wyatt, Jr. (D), *Bloomington*
15 Eligio (Kika) de la Garza (D), *Mission*
16 Richard C. White (D), *El Paso*
17 Charles W. Stenholm (D), *Stamford*
18 Mickey Leland (D), *Houston*
19 Kent R. Hance (D), *Lubbock*
20 Henry B. Gonzalez (D), *San Antonio*
21 Tom Loeffler (R), *Hunt*
22 Ronald E. Paul (R), *Lake Jackson*
23 Abraham Kazen, Jr. (D), *Laredo*
24 Martin Frost (D), *Dallas*

## UTAH

### SENATORS
E. J. (Jake) Garn (R), *Salt Lake City*
Orrin G. Hatch (R), *Salt Lake City*

### REPRESENTATIVES
1 K. Gunn McKay (D), *Huntsville*
2 David D. Marriott (R), *Salt Lake City*

## VERMONT

### SENATORS
Robert T. Stafford (R), *Rutland*
Patrick J. Leahy (D), *Burlington*

### REPRESENTATIVE AT LARGE
James M. Jeffords (R), *Montpelier*

## VIRGINIA

### SENATORS
Harry Flood Byrd, Jr. (I), *Winchester*
John W. Warner (R), *Middleburg*

### REPRESENTATIVES
1 Paul S. Trible, Jr. (R), *Newport News*
2 G. William Whitehurst (R), *Norfolk*
3 David E. Satterfield III (D), *Richmond*
4 Robert W. Daniel, Jr. (R), *Spring Cove*
5 W. C. (Dan) Daniel (D), *Danville*
6 M. Caldwell Butler (R), *Roanoke*
7 J. Kenneth Robinson (R), *Winchester*
8 Herbert E. Harris II (D), *Alexandria*
9 William C. Wampler (R), *Bristol*
10 Joseph L. Fisher (D), *Arlington*

## WASHINGTON

### SENATORS
Warren G. Magnuson (D), *Seattle*
Henry M. Jackson (D), *Everett*

### REPRESENTATIVES
1 Joel Pritchard (R), *Seattle*
2 Al Swift (D), *Bellingham*
3 Don Bonker (D), *Ridgefield*
4 Mike McCormack (D), *Richland*
5 Thomas S. Foley (D), *Spokane*
6 Norman D. Dicks (D), *Port Orchard*
7 Mike Lowry (D), *Mercer Island*

## WEST VIRGINIA

### SENATORS
Jennings Randolph (D), *Elkins*
Robert C. Byrd (D), *Sophia*

### REPRESENTATIVES
1 Robert H. Mollohan (D), *Fairmont*
2 Harley O. Staggers (D), *Keyser*
3 John M. Slack, Jr. (D),[37] *Charleston*
3 John G. Hutchinson (D),[38] *Charleston*
4 Nick J. Rahall II (D), *Beckley*

## WISCONSIN

### SENATORS
William Proxmire (D), *Madison*
Gaylord Nelson (D), *Madison*

### REPRESENTATIVES
1 Les Aspin (D), *Racine*
2 Robert W. Kastenmeier (D), *Sun Prairie*
3 Alvin Baldus (D), *Menomonie*
4 Clement J. Zablocki (D), *Milwaukee*
5 Henry S. Reuss (D), *Milwaukee*
6 Thomas E. Petri (R),[39] *Fond du Lac*
7 David R. Obey (D), *Wausau*
8 Toby A. Roth (R), *Appleton*
9 F. James Sensenbrenner, Jr. (R), *Shorewood*

## WYOMING

### SENATORS
Malcolm Wallop (R), *Big Horn*
Alan K. Simpson (R), *Cody*

### REPRESENTATIVE AT LARGE
Richard B. Cheney (R), *Casper*

## COMMONWEALTH OF PUERTO RICO

### RESIDENT COMMISSIONER
Baltasar Corrada-del Rio (NP), *Rio Piedras*

## DISTRICT OF COLUMBIA

### DELEGATE
Walter E. Fauntroy (D), *Washington, D.C.*

## GUAM

### DELEGATE
Antonio Borja Won Pat (D), *Agana*

## VIRGIN ISLANDS

### DELEGATE
Melvin H. Evans (R), *St. Croix*

---

[36] After election name changed to Marilyn Lloyd Bouquard.
[37] Died March 17, 1980.

[38] Elected June 3, 1980, to fill vacancy caused by death of John M. Slack, Jr., and took his seat June 10, 1980.

[39] Elected April 3, 1979, to fill vacancy caused by death of Representative-elect William A. Steiger, in preceding Congress, and took his seat April 9, 1979.

# 97TH CONGRESS

## JANUARY 3, 1981, TO JANUARY 3, 1983

George Bush
Vice President

Thomas P. O'Neill, Jr.
Speaker

FIRST SESSION— *January 5, 1981,*[1] *to December 16, 1981*
SECOND SESSION— *January 25, 1982,*[2] *to December 23, 1982*

Senate
Democrats 53 — Republicans 46 — Independent 1

VICE PRESIDENT OF THE UNITED STATES— Walter F. Mondale,[3] of Minnesota;
George Bush,[4] of Texas

PRESIDENT PRO TEMPORE OF THE SENATE— Strom Thurmond,[5] of South Carolina

SECRETARY OF THE SENATE— William F. Hildenbrand,[6] of Washington, D.C.

SERGEANT AT ARMS OF THE SENATE— Howard S. Liebengood,[7] of Virginia

MAJORITY FLOOR LEADER— Howard H. Baker, Jr., of Tennessee

REPUBLICAN WHIP— Theodore F. Stevens, of Alaska

DEMOCRATIC FLOOR LEADER— Robert C. Byrd, of West Virginia

ASSISTANT DEMOCRATIC LEADER— Alan M. Cranston, of California

House of Representatives
Democrats 242 — Republicans 193

SPEAKER OF THE HOUSE— Thomas P. O'Neill, Jr.,[8] of Massachusetts

CLERK OF THE HOUSE— Edmund L. Henshaw, Jr.,[9] of Virginia

SERGEANT AT ARMS OF THE HOUSE— Benjamin J. Guthrie,[10] of Virginia

DOORKEEPER OF THE HOUSE— James T. Molloy,[11] of New York

POSTMASTER OF THE HOUSE— Robert V. Rota,[12] of Pennsylvania

MAJORITY LEADER— James C. Wright, Jr., of Texas

MAJORITY WHIP— Thomas S. Foley, of Washington

REPUBLICAN LEADER— Robert H. Michel, of Illinois

REPUBLICAN WHIP— Trent Lott, of Mississippi

## ALABAMA

### SENATORS
Howell T. Heflin (D), *Tuscumbia*
Jeremiah A. Denton, Jr. (R), *Mobile*

### REPRESENTATIVES
1 Jack Edwards (R), *Mobile*
2 William L. Dickinson (R), *Montgomery*
3 William Nichols (D), *Sylacauga*
4 Tom Bevill (D), *Jasper*
5 Ronnie G. Flippo (D), *Florence*
6 Albert Lee Smith, Jr. (R), *Birmingham*
7 Richard C. Shelby (D), *Tuscaloosa*

## ALASKA

### SENATORS
Theodore F. Stevens (R), *Anchorage*
Frank H. Murkowski (R), *Fairbanks*

### REPRESENTATIVE AT LARGE
Donald E. Young (R), *Fort Yukon*

## ARIZONA

### SENATORS
Barry M. Goldwater (R), *Scottsdale*
Dennis DeConcini (D), *Tucson*

### REPRESENTATIVES
1 John J. Rhodes (R), *Mesa*
2 Morris K. Udall (D), *Tucson*
3 Bob Stump (D),[13] *Tolleson*
4 Eldon Rudd (R), *Scottsdale*

## ARKANSAS

### SENATORS
Dale Bumpers (D), *Charleston*
David H. Pryor (D), *Camden*

### REPRESENTATIVES
1 William V. Alexander (D), *Osceola*
2 Ed Bethune (R), *Searcy*

3 John Paul Hammerschmidt (R), *Harrison*
4 Beryl F. Anthony, Jr. (D), *El Dorado*

## CALIFORNIA

### SENATORS
Alan Cranston (D), *Los Angeles*
S. I. Hayakawa (R), *Mill Valley*

### REPRESENTATIVES
1 Eugene A. Chappie (R), *Roseville*
2 Don H. Clausen (R), *Crescent City*
3 Robert T. Matsui (D), *Sacramento*
4 Vic Fazio (D), *Sacramento*
5 John L. Burton (D), *San Francisco*
6 Phillip Burton (D), *San Francisco*
7 George Miller (D), *Martinez*
8 Ronald V. Dellums (D), *Berkeley*
9 Fortney H. (Pete) Stark, Jr. (D), *Oakland*

[1] By joint resolution (Pub. Law 96 566, 96th Cong., 2d sess.), the date of assembling the first session of the Ninety-seventh Congress was fixed for January 5, 1981.
[2] By joint resolution (Pub. Law 97 133, 97th Cong., 1st sess.), the date of assembling the second session of the Ninety-seventh Congress was fixed for January 25, 1982.

[3] Term expired at noon on January 20, 1981.
[4] Term began at noon on January 20, 1981.
[5] Elected January 5, 1981.
[6] Elected January 5, 1981.
[7] Elected January 5, 1981.
[8] Reelected January 5, 1981.

[9] Reelected January 5, 1981.
[10] Elected January 5, 1981.
[11] Reelected January 5, 1981.
[12] Reelected January 5, 1981.
[13] Changed party affiliation to Republican, September 24, 1981.

## CALIFORNIA—Continued
REPRESENTATIVES—CONTINUED
10 Don Edwards (D), *San Jose*
11 Tom Lantos (D), *San Mateo*
12 Paul N. (Pete) McCloskey, Jr. (R), *Menlo Park*
13 Norman Y. Mineta (D), *San Jose*
14 Norman D. Shumway (R), *Stockton*
15 Tony Coelho (D), *Merced*
16 Leon E. Panetta (D), *Carmel Valley*
17 Charles Pashayan, Jr., Jr. (R), *Fresno*
18 William M. Thomas (R), *Bakersfield*
19 Robert J. Lagomarsino (R), *Ojai*
20 Barry M. Goldwater, Jr. (R), *Woodland Hills*
21 Bobbi Fiedler (R), *Northridge*
22 Carlos J. Moorhead (R), *Glendale*
23 Anthony C. Beilenson (D), *Los Angeles*
24 Henry A. Waxman (D), *Los Angeles*
25 Edward R. Roybal (D), *Los Angeles*
26 John H. Rousselot (R), *San Marino*
27 Robert K. Dornan (R), *Los Angeles*
28 Julian C. Dixon (D), *Los Angeles*
29 Augustus F. Hawkins (D), *Los Angeles*
30 George E. Danielson (D),[14] *Monterey Park*
30 Matthew G. Martinez (D),[15] *Monterey Park*
31 Mervyn M. Dymally (D), *Compton*
32 Glenn M. Anderson (D), *Harbor City*
33 Wayne R. Grisham (R), *La Mirada*
34 Dan Lungren (R), *Long Beach*
35 David Dreier (R), *La Verne*
36 George E. Brown, Jr. (D), *Riverside*
37 Jerry Lewis (R), *San Bernardino*
38 Jerry M. Patterson (D), *Santa Ana*
39 William E. Dannemeyer (R), *Fullerton*
40 Robert E. Badham (R), *Newport Beach*
41 Bill Lowery (R), *San Diego*
42 Duncan L. Hunter (R), *Coronado*
43 Clair W. Burgener (R), *Rancho Santa Fe*

## COLORADO
SENATORS
Gary Hart (D), *Denver*
William L. Armstrong (R), *Aurora*

REPRESENTATIVES
1 Patricia Schroeder (D), *Denver*
2 Timothy E. Wirth (D), *Denver*
3 Raymond P. Kogovsek (D), *Pueblo*
4 Hank Brown (R), *Greeley*
5 Kenneth B. Kramer (R), *Colorado Springs*

## CONNECTICUT
SENATORS
Lowell P. Weicker, Jr. (R), *Stonington*
Christopher J. Dodd (D), *North Stonington*

REPRESENTATIVES
1 William R. Cotter (D),[16] *Hartford*
1 Barbara B. Kennelly (D),[17] *Hartford*
2 Samuel Gejdenson (D), *Bozrah*
3 Lawrence J. DeNardis (R), *Hamden*
4 Stewart B. McKinney (R), *Fairfield*
5 William R. Ratchford (D), *Danbury*
6 Toby Moffett (D), *Unionville*

## DELAWARE
SENATORS
William V. Roth, Jr. (R), *Wilmington*
Joseph R. Biden, Jr. (D), *Wilmington*

REPRESENTATIVE AT LARGE
Thomas B. Evans, Jr. (R), *Wilmington*

## FLORIDA
SENATORS
Lawton Chiles (D), *Lakeland*
Paula Hawkins (R), *Winter Park*

REPRESENTATIVES
1 Earl Hutto (D), *Panama City*
2 Don Fuqua (D), *Altha*
3 Charles E. Bennett (D), *Jacksonville*
4 William V. Chappell, Jr. (D), *Ocala*
5 Bill McCollum (R), *Altamonte Springs*
6 C. W. Bill Young (R), *St. Petersburg*
7 Sam M. Gibbons (D), *Tampa*
8 Andrew P. Ireland (D), *Winter Haven*
9 Bill Nelson (D), *Melbourne*
10 L. A. (Skip) Bafalis (R), *Fort Myers Beach*

11 Daniel A. Mica (D), *West Palm Beach*
12 Clay Shaw (R), *Fort Lauderdale*
13 William Lehman (D), *North Miami Beach*
14 Claude D. Pepper (D), *Miami*
15 Dante B. Fascell (D), *Miami*

## GEORGIA
SENATORS
Sam Nunn (D), *Perry*
Mack Mattingly (R), *St. Simons Island*

REPRESENTATIVES
1 Ronald B. (Bo) Ginn (D), *Millen*
2 Charles Hatcher (D), *Albany*
3 Jack T. Brinkley (D), *Columbus*
4 Elliott H. Levitas (D), *Atlanta*
5 Wyche Fowler, Jr. (D), *Atlanta*
6 Newt Gingrich (R), *Carrollton*
7 Larry McDonald (D), *Marietta*
8 Billy Lee Evans (D), *Macon*
9 Edgar L. Jenkins (D), *Jasper*
10 D. Douglas Barnard, Jr. (D), *Augusta*

## HAWAII
SENATORS
Daniel K. Inouye (D), *Honolulu*
Spark M. Matsunaga (D), *Honolulu*

REPRESENTATIVES
1 Cecil Heftel (D), *Honolulu*
2 Daniel K. Akaka (D), *Honolulu*

## IDAHO
SENATORS
James A. McClure (R), *Payette*
Steven D. Symms (R), *Boise*

REPRESENTATIVES
1 Larry Craig (R), *Midvale*
2 George Hansen (R), *Pocatello*

## ILLINOIS
SENATORS
Charles H. Percy (R), *Wilmette*
Alan J. Dixon (D), *Belleville*

REPRESENTATIVES
1 Harold Washington (D), *Chicago*
2 Gus Savage (D), *Chicago*
3 Martin A. Russo (D), *Chicago*
4 Edward J. Derwinski (R), *Flossmoor*
5 John G. Fary (D), *Chicago*
6 Henry J. Hyde (R), *Bensenville*
7 Cardiss Collins (D), *Chicago*
8 Dan Rostenkowski (D), *Chicago*
9 Sidney R. Yates (D), *Chicago*
10 John Edward Porter (R), *Evanston*

---

[14] Resigned March 9, 1982.
[15] Elected July 13, 1982, to fill vacancy caused by resignation of George E. Danielson, and took his seat July 15, 1982.

[16] Died September 8, 1981.
[17] Elected January 12, 1982, to fill vacancy caused by death of William R. Cotter, and took her seat

January 25, 1982.

11 Frank Annunzio (D), *Chicago*
12 Philip M. Crane (R), *Mount Prospect*
13 Robert McClory (R), *Lake Bluff*
14 John N. Erlenborn (R), *Glen Ellyn*
15 Thomas J. Corcoran (R), *Ottawa*
16 Lynn Martin (R), *Rockford*
17 George M. O'Brien (R), *Joliet*
18 Robert H. Michel (R), *Peoria*
19 Thomas F. Railsback (R), *Moline*
20 Paul Findley (R), *Pittsfield*
21 Edward R. Madigan (R), *Lincoln*
22 Daniel B. Crane (R), *Danville*
23 Melvin Price (D), *East St. Louis*
24 Paul Simon (D), *Carbondale*

## INDIANA

### SENATORS
Richard G. Lugar (R), *Indianapolis*
J. Danforth Quayle (R), *Huntington*

### REPRESENTATIVES
1 Adam Benjamin, Jr. (D),[18] *Hobart*
1 Katie Hall (D),[19] *Gary*
2 Floyd J. Fithian (D), *Lafayette*
3 John P. Hiler (R), *La Porte*
4 Dan R. Coats (R), *Fort Wayne*
5 Elwood Hillis (R), *Kokomo*
6 David W. Evans (D), *Indianapolis*
7 John T. Myers (R), *Covington*
8 H. Joel Deckard (R), *Evansville*
9 Lee H. Hamilton (D), *Columbus*
10 Philip R. Sharp (D), *Muncie*
11 Andrew Jacobs, Jr. (D), *Indianapolis*

## IOWA

### SENATORS
Roger W. Jepsen (R), *Davenport*
Charles E. Grassley (R), *New Hartford*

### REPRESENTATIVES
1 James A. S. Leach (R), *Davenport*
2 Thomas J. Tauke (R), *Dubuque*
3 Cooper Evans (R), *Grundy Center*
4 Neal Smith (D), *Altoona*
5 Tom Harkin (D), *Ames*
6 Berkley Bedell (D), *Spirit Lake*

## KANSAS

### SENATORS
Robert J. Dole (R), *Russell*
Nancy L. Kassebaum (R), *Wichita*

### REPRESENTATIVES
1 Pat Roberts (R), *Dodge City*
2 Jim Jeffries (R), *Atchison*
3 Larry Winn, Jr. (R), *Overland Park*
4 Daniel R. Glickman (D), *Wichita*
5 Bob Whittaker (R), *Augusta*

## KENTUCKY

### SENATORS
Walter (Dee) Huddleston (D), *Elizabethtown*
Wendell H. Ford (D), *Owensboro*

### REPRESENTATIVES
1 Carroll Hubbard, Jr. (D), *Mayfield*
2 William H. Natcher (D), *Bowling Green*
3 Romano L. Mazzoli (D), *Louisville*
4 M. G. (Gene) Snyder (R), *Brownsboro Farms*
5 Harold Rogers (R), *Somerset*
6 Larry J. Hopkins (R), *Lexington*
7 Carl D. Perkins (D), *Hindman*

## LOUISIANA

### SENATORS
Russell B. Long (D), *Baton Rouge*
J. Bennett Johnston, Jr. (D), *Shreveport*

### REPRESENTATIVES
1 Robert L. Livingston (R), *New Orleans*
2 Corinne C. (Lindy) Boggs (D), *New Orleans*
3 W. J. (Billy) Tauzin (D), *Thibodaux*
4 Charles (Buddy) Roemer (D), *Bossier City*
5 Thomas J. (Jerry) Huckaby (D), *Ringgold*
6 W. Henson Moore (R), *Baton Rouge*
7 John B. Breaux (D), *Crowley*
8 Gillis W. Long (D), *Alexandria*

## MAINE

### SENATORS
William S. Cohen (R), *Bangor*
George J. Mitchell (D), *Portland*

### REPRESENTATIVES
1 David F. Emery (R), *Rockland*
2 Olympia J. Snowe (R), *Auburn*

## MARYLAND

### SENATORS
Charles McC. Mathias, Jr. (R), *Frederick*
Paul S. Sarbanes (D), *Baltimore*

### REPRESENTATIVES
1 Roy Dyson (D), *Grest Mills*
2 Clarence D. Long (D), *Ruxton*
3 Barbara A. Mikulski (D), *Baltimore*
4 Marjorie S. Holt (R), *Severna Park*
5 Gladys Noon Spellman (D),[20] *Laurel*
5 Steny H. Hoyer (D),[21] *Berkshire*
6 Beverly B. Byron (D), *Frederick*
7 Parren J. Mitchell (D), *Baltimore*
8 Michael D. Barnes (D), *Kensington*

## MASSACHUSETTS

### SENATORS
Edward M. Kennedy (D), *Boston*
Paul E. Tsongas (D), *Lowell*

### REPRESENTATIVES
1 Silvio O. Conte (R), *Pittsfield*
2 Edward P. Boland (D), *Springfield*
3 Joseph D. Early (D), *Worcester*
4 Barney Frank (D), *Newton*
5 James M. Shannon (D), *Lawrence*
6 Nicholas Mavroules (D), *Peabody*
7 Edward J. Markey (D), *Malden*
8 Thomas P. O'Neill, Jr. (D), *Cambridge*
9 John Joseph Moakley (D), *Boston*
10 Margaret M. Heckler (R), *Wellesley*
11 Brian J. Donnelly (D), *Dorchester*
12 Gerry E. Studds (D), *Cohasset*

## MICHIGAN

### SENATORS
Donald W. Riegle, Jr. (D), *Flint*
Carl Levin (D), *Detroit*

### REPRESENTATIVES
1 John Conyers, Jr. (D), *Detroit*
2 Carl D. Pursell (R), *Plymouth*
3 Howard E. Wolpe (D), *Lansing*
4 David A. Stockman (R),[22] *St. Joseph*
4 Mark Siljander (R),[23] *Three Rivers*
5 Harold S. Sawyer (R), *Rockford*
6 Jim Dunn (R), *East Lansing*
7 Dale E. Kildee (D), *Flint*
8 Bob Traxler (D), *Bay City*
9 Guy A. Vander Jagt (R), *Luther*
10 Donald J. Albosta (D), *St. Charles*
11 Robert W. Davis (R), *Gaylord*
12 David E. Bonior (D), *Mount Clemens*
13 George W. Crockett, Jr. (D), *Detroit*
14 Dennis M. Hertel (D), *Detroit*
15 William D. Ford (D), *Taylor*
16 John D. Dingell, Jr. (D), *Trenton*
17 William M. Brodhead (D), *Detroit*
18 James J. Blanchard (D), *Pleasant Ridge*
19 William S. Broomfield (R), *Birmingham*

---

[18] Died September 7, 1982.
[19] Elected November 2, 1982, to fill vacancy caused by death of Adam Benjamin, Jr., and took her seat November 29, 1982.
[20] Pursuant to H. Res. 80, passed on February 24, 1981, seat was declared vacant.
[21] Elected May 19, 1981, to fill vacancy caused by incapacitating illness of Gladys Noon Spellman, and took his seat June 3, 1981.
[22] Resigned January 27, 1981.
[23] Elected April 21, 1981, to fill vacancy caused by resignation of David A. Stockman, and took his seat April 29, 1981.

## MINNESOTA

### SENATORS

David F. Durenberger (R), *Minneapolis*
Rudy Boschwitz (R), *Plymouth*

### REPRESENTATIVES

1 Arlen I. Erdahl (R), *West St. Paul*
2 Tom Hagedorn (R), *Truman*
3 Bill Frenzel (R), *Golden Valley*
4 Bruce F. Vento (D), *St. Paul*
5 Martin Olav Sabo (D), *Minneapolis*
6 Vin Weber (R), *St. Cloud*
7 Arlan Stangeland (R), *Barnesville*
8 James L. Oberstar (D), *Chisholm*

## MISSISSIPPI

### SENATORS

John C. Stennis (D), *De Kalb*
Thad Cochran (R), *Jackson*

### REPRESENTATIVES

1 Jamie L. Whitten (D), *Charleston*
2 David R. Bowen (D), *Cleveland*
3 Gillespie V. (Sonny) Montgomery (D), *Meridian*
4 Jon C. Hinson (R),[24] *Tylertown*
4 Wayne Dowdy (D),[25] *Summit*
5 Trent Lott (R), *Pascagoula*

## MISSOURI

### SENATORS

Thomas F. Eagleton (D), *St. Louis*
John C. Danforth (R), *Flat*

### REPRESENTATIVES

1 William L. Clay (D), *St. Louis*
2 Robert A. Young (D), *St. Ann*
3 Richard A. Gephardt (D), *St. Louis*
4 Ike Skelton (D), *Lexington*
5 Richard W. Bolling (D), *Kansas City*
6 E. Thomas Coleman (R), *Kansas City*
7 Gene Taylor (R), *Sarcoxie*
8 Wendell Bailey (R), *Willow Springs*
9 Harold L. Volkmer (D), *Hannibal*
10 Bill Emerson (R), *DeSoto*

## MONTANA

### SENATORS

John Melcher (D), *Forsyth*
Max Baucus (D), *Missoula*

### REPRESENTATIVES

1 Pat Williams (D), *Helena*
2 Ron Marlenee (R), *Scobey*

## NEBRASKA

### SENATORS

Edward Zorinsky (D), *Omaha*
J. James Exon (D), *Lincoln*

### REPRESENTATIVES

1 Douglas K. Bereuter (R), *Utica*
2 Hal Daub (R), *Omaha*
3 Virginia Smith (R), *Chappell*

## NEVADA

### SENATORS

Howard W. Cannon (D), *Las Vegas*
Paul Laxalt (R), *Carson City*

### REPRESENTATIVE AT LARGE

Jim Santini (D), *Las Vegas*

## NEW HAMPSHIRE

### SENATORS

Gordon J. Humphrey (R), *Sunapee*
Warren B. Rudman (R), *Nashua*

### REPRESENTATIVES

1 Norman E. D'Amours (D), *Manchester*
2 Judd Gregg (R), *Greenfield*

## NEW JERSEY

### SENATORS

Harrison A. Williams, Jr. (D),[26] *Bedminster*
Nicholas F. Brady (R),[27] *Farhills*
Frank R. Lautenberg (D),[28] *Montclair*
Bill Bradley (D), *Denville*

### REPRESENTATIVES

1 James J. Florio (D), *Camden*
2 William J. Hughes (D), *Ocean City*
3 James J. Howard (D), *Spring Lake Heights*
4 Christopher H. Smith (R), *Old Bridge*
5 Millicent Fenwick (R), *Bernardsville*
6 Edwin B. Forsythe (R), *Moorestown*
7 Marge Roukema (R), *Ridgewood*
8 Robert A. Roe (D), *Wayne*
9 Harold C. Hollenbeck (R), *East Rutherford*
10 Peter W. Rodino, Jr. (D), *Newark*
11 Joseph G. Minish (D), *West Orange*
12 Matthew J. Rinaldo (R), *Union*
13 James A. Courter (R), *Hackettstown*
14 Frank J. Guarini (D), *Jersey City*
15 Bernard J. Dwyer (D), *Edison*

## NEW MEXICO

### SENATORS

Pete V. Domenici (R), *Albuquerque*
Harrison H. Schmitt (R), *Silver City*

### REPRESENTATIVES

1 Manuel Lujan, Jr. (R), *Albuquerque*
2 Joe Skeen (R), *Picacho*

## NEW YORK

### SENATORS

Daniel P. Moynihan (D), *New York*
Alfonse M. D'Amato (R), *Island Park*

### REPRESENTATIVES

1 William Carney (R), *Hauppauge*
2 Thomas J. Downey (D), *West Islip*
3 Gregory W. Carman (R), *Farmingdale*
4 Norman F. Lent (R), *East Rockaway*
5 Raymond J. McGrath (R), *Valley Stream*
6 John LeBoutillier (R), *Westbury*
7 Joseph P. Addabbo (D), *Ozone Park*
8 Benjamin S. Rosenthal (D), *Elmhurst*
9 Geraldine A. Ferraro (D), *Forest Hills*
10 Mario Biaggi (D), *Bronx*
11 James H. Scheuer (D), *Neponsit*
12 Shirley A. Chisholm (D), *Brooklyn*
13 Stephen J. Solarz (D), *Brooklyn*
14 Frederick W. Richmond (D),[29] *Brooklyn*
15 Leo C. Zeferetti (D), *Brooklyn*
16 Charles E. Schumer (D), *Brooklyn*
17 Guy V. Molinari (R), *Staten Island*
18 S. William Green (R), *New York*
19 Charles B. Rangel (D), *New York*
20 Ted S. Weiss (D), *New York*
21 Robert Garcia (D), *Bronx*
22 Jonathan B. Bingham (D), *Bronx*
23 Peter A. Peyser (D), *Irvington*
24 Richard L. Ottinger (D), *Mamaroneck*
25 Hamilton Fish, Jr. (R), *Millbrook*
26 Benjamin A. Gilman (R), *Middletown*
27 Matthew F. McHugh (D), *Ithaca*
28 Samuel S. Stratton (D), *Amsterdam*
29 Gerald B. H. Solomon (R), *Glens Falls*
30 David O'B. Martin (R), *Canton*
31 Donald J. Mitchell (R), *Herkimer*
32 George C. Wortley (R), *Fayetteville*
33 Gary A. Lee (R), *Dryden*
34 Frank Horton (R), *Rochester*

---

[24] Resigned April 13, 1981.
[25] Elected July 7, 1981, to fill vacancy caused by resignation of Jon C. Hinson, and took his seat July 9, 1981.
[26] Resigned March 11, 1982.

[27] Appointed April 12, 1982, to fill vacancy caused by resignation of Harrison A. Williams, Jr., and took his seat April 12, 1982; resigned December 27, 1982.
[28] Appointed to fill vacancy caused by the resig-

nation of Nicholas F. Brady, and took his seat December 27, 1982.
[29] Resigned August 25, 1982; vacancy throughout remainder of Congress.

35 Barber B. Conable, Jr. (R), *Alexander*
36 John J. LaFalce (D), *Tonawanda*
37 Henry J. Nowak (D), *Buffalo*
38 Jack F. Kemp (R), *Hamburg*
39 Stanley N. Lundine (D), *Jamestown*

## NORTH CAROLINA

### SENATORS

Jesse Helms (R), *Raleigh*
John P. East (R), *Greenville*

### REPRESENTATIVES

1 Walter B. Jones (D), *Farmville*
2 L. H. Fountain (D), *Tarboro*
3 Charles O. Whitley (D), *Mount Olive*
4 Ike F. Andrews (D), *Siler City*
5 Stephen L. Neal (D), *Winston-Salem*
6 W. Eugene Johnston III (R), *Greensboro*
7 Charles Rose (D), *Fayetteville*
8 W. G. (Bill) Hefner (D), *Concord*
9 James G. Martin (R), *Davidson*
10 James T. Broyhill (R), *Lenoir*
11 Bill Hendon (R), *Asheville*

## NORTH DAKOTA

### SENATORS

Quentin N. Burdick (D), *Fargo*
Mark Andrews (R), *Mapleton*

### REPRESENTATIVE AT LARGE

Byron L. Dorgan (D), *Bismarck*

## OHIO

### SENATORS

John Glenn, Jr. (D), *Columbus*
Howard M. Metzenbaum (D), *Shaker Heights*

### REPRESENTATIVES

1 Willis D. Gradison, Jr. (R), *Cincinnati*
2 Thomas A. Luken (D), *Cincinnati*
3 Tony P. Hall (D), *Dayton*
4 Tennyson Guyer (R),[30] *Findley*
4 Michael G. Oxley (R),[31] *Findley*
5 Delbert L. Latta (R), *Bowling Green*
6 Robert McEwen (R), *Hillsboro*
7 Clarence J. Brown (R), *Urbana*
8 Thomas N. Kindness (R), *Hamilton*
9 Ed Weber (R), *Toledo*
10 Clarence E. Miller (R), *Lancaster*
11 J. William Stanton (R), *Painesville*
12 Bob Shamansky (D), *Columbus*
13 Donald J. Pease (D), *Oberlin*

14 John F. Seiberling (D), *Akron*
15 Chalmers P. Wylie (R), *Worthington*
16 Ralph S. Regula (R), *Navarre*
17 John M. Ashbrook (R),[32] *Johnstown*
17 Jean Ashbrook (R),[33] *Johnstown*
18 Douglas Applegate (D), *Steubenville*
19 Lyle Williams (R), *Warren*
20 Mary Rose Oakar (D), *Cleveland*
21 Louis Stokes (D), *Cleveland*
22 Dennis E. Eckart (D), *Euclid*
23 Ronald M. Mottl (D), *Parma*

## OKLAHOMA

### SENATORS

David L. Boren (D), *Seminole*
Don Nickles (R), *Ponca City*

### REPRESENTATIVES

1 James R. Jones (D), *Tulsa*
2 Mike Synar (D), *Muskogee*
3 Wesley W. Watkins (D), *Ada*
4 Dave McCurdy (D), *Norman*
5 Mickey Edwards (R), *Oklahoma City*
6 Glenn English (D), *Cordell*

## OREGON

### SENATORS

Mark O. Hatfield (R), *Salem*
Robert W. Packwood (R), *Portland*

### REPRESENTATIVES

1 Les AuCoin (D), *Forest Grove*
2 Denny Smith (R), *Salem*
3 Ron Wyden (D), *Portland*
4 James Weaver (D), *Eugene*

## PENNSYLVANIA

### SENATORS

H. John Heinz III (R), *Pittsburgh*
Arlen Specter (R), *Philadelphia*

### REPRESENTATIVES

1 Thomas M. Foglietta (D), *Philadelphia*
2 William H. Gray III (D), *Philadelphia*
3 Raymond F. Lederer (D),[34] *Philadelphia*
3 Joseph F. Smith (D),[35] *Philadelphia*
4 Charles F. Dougherty (R), *Philadelphia*
5 Richard T. Schulze (R), *Malvern*
6 Gus Yatron (D), *Reading*
7 Robert W. Edgar (D), *Broomall*
8 James K. Coyne (R), *Newtown*
9 E. G. Shuster (R), *Everett*
10 Joseph M. McDade (R), *Scranton*

11 James L. Nelligan (R), *Forty-Fort*
12 John P. Murtha, Jr. (D), *Johnstown*
13 R. Lawrence Coughlin (R), *Villanova*
14 William J. Coyne (D), *Pittsburgh*
15 Don Ritter (R), *Coopersburg*
16 Robert S. Walker (R), *East Petersburg*
17 Allen E. Ertel (D), *Montoursville*
18 Doug Walgren (D), *Pittsburgh*
19 William F. Goodling (R), *Jacobus*
20 Joseph M. Gaydos (D), *McKeesport*
21 Don Bailey (D), *Greensburg*
22 Austin J. Murphy (D), *Charleroi*
23 William F. Clinger, Jr. (R), *Warren*
24 Marc L. Marks (R), *Sharon*
25 Eugene V. Atkinson (D),[36] *Aliquippa*

## RHODE ISLAND

### SENATORS

Claiborne Pell (D), *Newport*
John H. Chafee (R), *Warwick*

### REPRESENTATIVES

1 Fernand J. St Germain (D), *Woonsocket*
2 Claudine Schneider (R), *Narragansett*

## SOUTH CAROLINA

### SENATORS

Strom Thurmond (R), *Aiken*
Ernest F. Hollings (D), *Charleston*

### REPRESENTATIVES

1 Thomas F. Hartnett (R), *Charleston*
2 Floyd Spence (R), *Lexington*
3 Butler Derrick (D), *Edgefield*
4 Carroll Campbell, Jr. (R), *Greenville*
5 Kenneth L. Holland (D), *Gaffney*
6 John L. Napier (R), *Bennettsville*

## SOUTH DAKOTA

### SENATORS

Larry Pressler (R), *Humboldt*
James Abdnor (R), *Kennebec*

### REPRESENTATIVES

1 Thomas A. Daschle (D), *Aberdeen*
2 Clint Roberts (R), *Presho*

## TENNESSEE

### SENATORS

Howard H. Baker, Jr. (R), *Huntsville*
James R. Sasser (D), *Nashville*

[30] Died April 12, 1981.
[31] Elected June 25, 1981, to fill vacancy caused by death of Tennyson Guyer, and took his seat July 21, 1981.
[32] Died April 24, 1982.

[33] Elected June 29, 1982, to fill vacancy caused by death of her husband, John M. Ashbrook, and took her seat July 12, 1982.
[34] Resigned April 29, 1981.
[35] Elected July 21, 1981, to fill vacancy caused by

resignation of Raymond F. Lederer, and took his seat July 28, 1981.
[36] Changed party affiliation to Republican, October 14, 1981.

## TENNESSEE—Continued
REPRESENTATIVES
1 James H. Quillen (R), *Kingsport*
2 John J. Duncan (R), *Knoxville*
3 Marilyn Lloyd Bouquard (D), *Chattanooga*
4 Albert A. Gore, Jr. (D), *Carthage*
5 William H. Boner (D), *Nashville*
6 Robin L. Beard (R), *Franklin*
7 Edward Jones (D), *Yorkville*
8 Harold E. Ford (D), *Memphis*

## TEXAS
SENATORS
John G. Tower (R), *Wichita Falls*
Lloyd M. Bentsen, Jr. (D), *Houston*
REPRESENTATIVES
1 Sam B. Hall, Jr. (D), *Marshall*
2 Charles Wilson (D), *Lufkin*
3 James M. Collins (R), *Dallas*
4 Ralph M. Hall (D), *Rockwall*
5 James A. Mattox (D), *Dallas*
6 Phil Gramm (D), *College Station*
7 William R. Archer, Jr. (R), *Houston*
8 Jack Fields (R), *Humble*
9 Jack B. Brooks (D), *Beaumont*
10 J. J. (Jake) Pickle (D), *Austin*
11 J. Marvin Leath (D), *Marlin*
12 James C. Wright, Jr. (D), *Fort Worth*
13 Jack Hightower (D), *Vernon*
14 William N. Patman (D), *Ganado*
15 Eligio (Kika) de la Garza (D), *Mission*
16 Richard C. White (D), *El Paso*
17 Charles W. Stenholm (D), *Stamford*
18 Mickey Leland (D), *Houston*
19 Kent R. Hance (D), *Lubbock*
20 Henry B. Gonzalez (D), *San Antonio*
21 Tom Loeffler (R), *Hunt*
22 Ronald E. Paul (R), *Lake Jackson*
23 Abraham Kazen, Jr. (D), *Laredo*
24 Martin Frost (D), *Dallas*

## UTAH
SENATORS
E. J. (Jake) Garn (R), *Salt Lake City*
Orrin G. Hatch (R), *Salt Lake City*
REPRESENTATIVES
1 James V. Hansen (R), *Farmington*
2 David D. Marriott (R), *Salt Lake City*

## VERMONT
SENATORS
Robert T. Stafford (R), *Rutland*
Patrick J. Leahy (D), *Burlington*
REPRESENTATIVE AT LARGE
James M. Jeffords (R), *Montpelier*

## VIRGINIA
SENATORS
Harry Flood Byrd, Jr. (I), *Winchester*
John W. Warner (R), *Middleburg*
REPRESENTATIVES
1 Paul S. Trible, Jr. (R), *Newport News*
2 G. William Whitehurst (R), *Norfolk*
3 Thomas J. Bliley, Jr. (R), *Richmond*
4 Robert W. Daniel, Jr. (R), *Spring Cove*
5 W. C. (Dan) Daniel (D), *Danville*
6 M. Caldwell Butler (R), *Roanoke*
7 J. Kenneth Robinson (R), *Winchester*
8 Stanford E. Parris (R), *Woodbridge*
9 William C. Wampler (R), *Bristol*
10 Frank R. Wolf (R), *Falls Church*

## WASHINGTON
SENATORS
Henry M. Jackson (D), *Everett*
Slade Gorton (R), *Olympia*
REPRESENTATIVES
1 Joel Pritchard (R), *Seattle*
2 Al Swift (D), *Bellingham*
3 Don Bonker (D), *Ridgefield*
4 Sid Morrison (R), *Zillah*
5 Thomas S. Foley (D), *Spokane*
6 Norman D. Dicks (D), *Port Orchard*
7 Mike Lowry (D), *Seattle*

## WEST VIRGINIA
SENATORS
Jennings Randolph (D), *Elkins*
Robert C. Byrd (D), *Sophia*
REPRESENTATIVES
1 Robert H. Mollohan (D), *Fairmont*
2 Cleve Benedict (R), *Lewisburg*

3 Mick Staton (R), *South Charleston*
4 Nick J. Rahall II (D), *Beckley*

## WISCONSIN
SENATORS
William Proxmire (D), *Madison*
Robert W. Kasten, Jr. (R), *Milwaukee*
REPRESENTATIVES
1 Les Aspin (D), *Racine*
2 Robert W. Kastenmeier (D), *Sun Prairie*
3 Steven Gunderson (R), *Osseo*
4 Clement J. Zablocki (D), *Milwaukee*
5 Henry S. Reuss (D), *Milwaukee*
6 Thomas E. Petri (R), *Fond du Lac*
7 David R. Obey (D), *Wausau*
8 Toby A. Roth (R), *Appleton*
9 F. James Sensenbrenner, Jr. (R), *Shorewood*

## WYOMING
SENATORS
Malcolm Wallop (R), *Big Horn*
Alan K. Simpson (R), *Cody*
REPRESENTATIVE AT LARGE
Richard B. Cheney (R), *Casper*

## AMERICAN SAMOA[37]
DELEGATE
Fofó I. F. Sunia (D),[38] *Pago Pago*

## COMMONWEALTH OF PUERTO RICO
RESIDENT COMMISSIONER
Baltasar Corrada-del Rio (NP), *Rio Piedras*

## DISTRICT OF COLUMBIA
DELEGATE
Walter E. Fauntroy (D), *Washington, D.C.*

## GUAM
DELEGATE
Antonio Borja Won Pat (D), *Sinajana*

## VIRGIN ISLANDS
DELEGATE
Ron de Lugo (D), *St. Thomas*

---

[37] Granted a delegate in Congress by Public Law 95-556, October 31, 1978.

[38] Elected November 4, 1980, and took his seat January 3, 1981.

# 98TH CONGRESS

## JANUARY 3, 1983, TO JANUARY 3, 1985

George Bush
Vice President

FIRST SESSION— *January 3, 1983, to November 18, 1983*
SECOND SESSION— *January 23, 1984,[1] to October 12, 1984*

Thomas P. O'Neill, Jr.
Speaker

### Senate
Democrats 46 — Republicans 54

VICE PRESIDENT OF THE UNITED STATES— George Bush, of Texas
PRESIDENT PRO TEMPORE OF THE SENATE— Strom Thurmond, of South Carolina
SECRETARY OF THE SENATE— William F. Hildenbrand, of Washington, D.C.
SERGEANT AT ARMS OF THE SENATE— Howard S. Liebengood, of Virginia; Larry E.
Smith,[2] of Virginia
MAJORITY FLOOR LEADER— Howard H. Baker, Jr., of Tennessee
REPUBLICAN WHIP— Theodore F. Stevens, of Alaska
DEMOCRATIC FLOOR LEADER— Robert C. Byrd, of West Virginia
ASSISTANT DEMOCRATIC LEADER— Alan M. Cranston, of California

### House of Representatives
Democrats 268 — Republicans 167

SPEAKER OF THE HOUSE— Thomas P. O'Neill, Jr.,[3] of Massachusetts
CLERK OF THE HOUSE— Benjamin J. Guthrie,[4] of Virginia
SERGEANT AT ARMS OF THE HOUSE— Jack Russ,[5] of Maryland
DOORKEEPER OF THE HOUSE— James T. Molloy,[6] of New York
POSTMASTER OF THE HOUSE— Robert V. Rota,[7] of Pennsylvania
MAJORITY LEADER— James C. Wright, Jr., of Texas
MAJORITY WHIP— Thomas S. Foley, of Washington
REPUBLICAN LEADER— Robert H. Michel, of Illinois
REPUBLICAN WHIP— Trent Lott, of Mississippi

## ALABAMA

### SENATORS
Howell T. Heflin (D), *Tuscumbia*
Jeremiah A. Denton, Jr. (R), *Mobile*

### REPRESENTATIVES
1 Jack Edwards (R), *Mobile*
2 William L. Dickinson (R), *Montgomery*
3 William Nichols (D), *Sylacauga*
4 Tom Bevill (D), *Jasper*
5 Ronnie G. Flippo (D), *Florence*
6 Ben Erdreich (D), *Birmingham*
7 Richard C. Shelby (D), *Tuscaloosa*

## ALASKA

### SENATORS
Theodore F. Stevens (R), *Anchorage*
Frank H. Murkowski (R), *Fairbanks*

### REPRESENTATIVE AT LARGE
Donald E. Young (R), *Fort Yukon*

## ARIZONA

### SENATORS
Barry M. Goldwater (R), *Scottsdale*
Dennis DeConcini (D), *Tucson*

### REPRESENTATIVES
1 John S. McCain III (R), *Tempe*
2 Morris K. Udall (D), *Tucson*
3 Bob Stump (R), *Tolleson*
4 Eldon Rudd (R), *Scottsdale*
5 James F. McNulty, Jr. (D), *Bisbee*

## ARKANSAS

### SENATORS
Dale Bumpers (D), *Charleston*
David H. Pryor (D), *Camden*

### REPRESENTATIVES
1 William V. Alexander (D), *Osceola*
2 Ed Bethune (R), *Searcy*
3 John Paul Hammerschmidt (R), *Harrison*
4 Beryl F. Anthony, Jr. (D), *El Dorado*

## CALIFORNIA

### SENATORS
Alan Cranston (D), *Los Angeles*
Pete Wilson (R), *San Diego*

### REPRESENTATIVES
1 Douglas H. Bosco (D), *Occidental*
2 Eugene A. Chappie (R), *Roseville*
3 Robert T. Matsui (D), *Sacramento*
4 Vic Fazio (D), *Sacramento*
5 Phillip Burton (D),[8] *San Francisco*
5 Sala Burton (D),[9] *San Francisco*
6 Barbara Boxer (D), *Greenbrae*
7 George Miller (D), *Martinez*
8 Ronald V. Dellums (D), *Berkeley*
9 Fortney H. (Pete) Stark, Jr. (D), *Oakland*
10 Don Edwards (D), *San Jose*
11 Tom Lantos (D), *San Mateo*
12 Edwin V. W. Zschau (R), *Los Altos*
13 Norman Y. Mineta (D), *San Jose*

---

## CALIFORNIA—Continued

### REPRESENTATIVES—CONTINUED

14 Norman D. Shumway (R), *Stockton*
15 Tony Coelho (D), *Merced*
16 Leon E. Panetta (D), *Carmel Valley*
17 Charles Pashayan, Jr. (R), *Fresno*
18 Richard H. Lehman (D), *Sanger*
19 Robert J. Lagomarsino (R), *Ventura*
20 William M. Thomas (R), *Bakersfield*
21 Bobbi Fiedler (R), *Northridge*
22 Carlos J. Moorhead (R), *Glendale*
23 Anthony C. Beilenson (D), *Los Angeles*
24 Henry A. Waxman (D), *Los Angeles*
25 Edward R. Roybal (D), *Los Angeles*
26 Howard L. Berman (D), *Studio City*
27 Mel Levine (D), *Santa Monica*
28 Julian C. Dixon (D), *Los Angeles*
29 Augustus F. Hawkins (D), *Los Angeles*
30 Matthew G. Martinez (D), *Monterey Park*
31 Mervyn M. Dymally (D), *Compton*
32 Glenn M. Anderson (D), *San Pedro*
33 David Dreier (R), *La Verna*
34 Esteban Edward Torres (D), *La Puente*
35 Jerry Lewis (R), *San Bernadino*
36 George E. Brown, Jr. (D), *Riverside*
37 Alfred A. McCandless (R), *Palm Desert*
38 Jerry M. Patterson (D), *Santa Ana*
39 William E. Dannemeyer (R), *Fullerton*
40 Robert E. Badham (R), *Newport Beach*
41 Bill Lowery (R), *San Diego*
42 Dan Lungren (R), *Long Beach*
43 Ron Packard (R), *Carlsbad*
44 Jim Bates (D), *San Diego*
45 Duncan L. Hunter (R), *Coronado*

## COLORADO

### SENATORS

Gary Hart (D), *Denver*
William L. Armstrong (R), *Aurora*

### REPRESENTATIVES

1 Patricia Schroeder (D), *Denver*
2 Timothy E. Wirth (D), *Denver*
3 Raymond P. Kogovsek (D), *Pueblo*

4 Hank Brown (R), *Greeley*
5 Kenneth B. Kramer (R), *Colorado Springs*
6 Dan Schaefer (R),[10] *Lakewood*

## CONNECTICUT

### SENATORS

Lowell P. Weicker, Jr. (R), *Stonington*
Christopher J. Dodd (D), *North Stonington*

### REPRESENTATIVES

1 Barbara B. Kennelly (D), *Hartford*
2 Samuel Gejdenson (D), *Bozrah*
3 Bruce A. Morrison (D), *Hamden*
4 Stewart B. McKinney (R), *Westport*
5 William R. Ratchford (D), *Danbury*
6 Nancy L. Johnson (R), *New Britain*

## DELAWARE

### SENATORS

William V. Roth, Jr. (R), *Wilmington*
Joseph R. Biden, Jr. (D), *Wilmington*

### REPRESENTATIVE AT LARGE

Thomas R. Carper (D), *New Castle*

## FLORIDA

### SENATORS

Lawton Chiles (D), *Lakeland*
Paula Hawkins (R), *Winter Park*

### REPRESENTATIVES

1 Earl Hutto (D), *Panama City*
2 Don Fuqua (D), *Altha*
3 Charles E. Bennett (D), *Jacksonville*
4 William V. Chappell, Jr. (D), *Ocala*
5 Bill McCollum (R), *Altamonte Springs*
6 Kenneth H. (Buddy) MacKay (D), *Ocala*
7 Sam M. Gibbons (D), *Tampa*
8 C. W. Bill Young (R), *St. Petersburg*
9 Michael Bilirakis (R), *Palm Harbor*
10 Andrew P. Ireland (D),[11] *Winter Haven*
11 Bill Nelson (D), *Melbourne*
12 Tom Lewis (R), *North Palm Beach*
13 Connie Mack (R), *Cape Coral*
14 Daniel A. Mica (D), *West Palm Beach*
15 Clay Shaw (R), *Fort Lauderdale*
16 Lawrence J. Smith (D), *Hollywood*

17 William Lehman (D), *North Miami Beach*
18 Claude D. Pepper (D), *Miami*
19 Dante B. Fascell (D), *Miami*

## GEORGIA

### SENATORS

Sam Nunn (D), *Perry*
Mack Mattingly (R), *St. Simons Island*

### REPRESENTATIVES

1 R. Lindsay Thomas (D), *Screven*
2 Charles Hatcher (D), *Albany*
3 Richard Ray (D), *Perry*
4 Elliott H. Levitas (D), *Atlanta*
5 Wyche Fowler, Jr. (D), *Atlanta*
6 Newt Gingrich (R), *Carrollton*
7 Larry McDonald (D),[12] *Marietta*
7 George (Buddy) Darden (D),[13] *Marietta*
8 J. Roy Rowland (D), *Dublin*
9 Edgar L. Jenkins (D), *Jasper*
10 D. Douglas Barnard, Jr. (D), *Augusta*

## HAWAII

### SENATORS

Daniel K. Inouye (D), *Honolulu*
Spark M. Matsunaga (D), *Honolulu*

### REPRESENTATIVES

1 Cecil Heftel (D), *Honolulu*
2 Daniel K. Akaka (D), *Honolulu*

## IDAHO

### SENATORS

James A. McClure (R), *Payette*
Steven D. Symms (R), *Boise*

### REPRESENTATIVES

1 Larry Craig (R), *Midvale*
2 George Hansen (R), *Pocatello*

## ILLINOIS

### SENATORS

Charles H. Percy (R), *Wilmette*
Alan J. Dixon (D), *Belleville*

### REPRESENTATIVES

1 Harold Washington (D),[14] *Chicago*
1 Charles A. Hayes (D),[15] *Chicago*
2 Gus Savage (D), *Chicago*
3 Martin A. Russo (D), *Chicago*
4 George M. O'Brien (R), *Joliet*
5 William O. Lipinski (D), *Chicago*
6 Henry J. Hyde (R), *Bensenville*
7 Cardiss Collins (D), *Chicago*
8 Dan Rostenkowski (D), *Chicago*
9 Sidney R. Yates (D), *Chicago*
10 John Edward Porter (R), *Winnetka*

---

[10] Elected March 29, 1983, to fill vacancy caused by death of Representative-elect John L. (Jack) Swigert, and took his seat April 7, 1983.
[11] Changed party affiliation to Republican, July 5, 1984.

[12] Died September 1, 1983.
[13] Elected November 8, 1983, to fill vacancy caused by death of Larry McDonald, and took his seat November 10, 1983.
[14] Resigned April 30, 1983.

[15] Elected August 23, 1983, to fill vacancy caused by resignation of Harold Washington, and took his seat September 12, 1983.

11 Frank Annunzio (D), *Chicago*
12 Philip M. Crane (R), *Mount Prospect*
13 John N. Erlenborn (R), *Glen Ellyn*
14 Thomas J. Corcoran (R),[16] *Ottawa*
15 Edward R. Madigan (R), *Lincoln*
16 Lynn Martin (R), *Rockford*
17 Lane A. Evans (D), *Rock Island*
18 Robert H. Michel (R), *Peoria*
19 Daniel B. Crane (R), *Danville*
20 Richard J. Durbin (D), *Springfield*
21 Melvin Price (D), *East St. Louis*
22 Paul Simon (D), *Carbondale*

## INDIANA

### SENATORS

Richard G. Lugar (R), *Indianapolis*
J. Danforth Quayle (R), *Huntington*

### REPRESENTATIVES

1 Katie Hall (D), *Gary*
2 Philip R. Sharp (D), *Muncie*
3 John P. Hiler (R), *La Porte*
4 Dan R. Coats (R), *Fort Wayne*
5 Elwood Hillis (R), *Kokomo*
6 Dan Burton (R), *Indianapolis*
7 John T. Myers (R), *Covington*
8 Frank McCloskey (D), *Bloomington*
9 Lee H. Hamilton (D), *Nashville*
10 Andrew Jacobs, Jr. (D), *Indianapolis*

## IOWA

### SENATORS

Roger W. Jepsen (R), *Davenport*
Charles E. Grassley (R), *New Hartford*

### REPRESENTATIVES

1 James A. S. Leach (R), *Davenport*
2 Thomas J. Tauke (R), *Dubuque*
3 Cooper Evans (R), *Grundy Center*
4 Neal Smith (D), *Altoona*
5 Tom Harkin (D), *Ames*
6 Berkley Bedell (D), *Spirit Lake*

## KANSAS

### SENATORS

Robert J. Dole (R), *Russell*
Nancy L. Kassebaum (R), *Wichita*

### REPRESENTATIVES

1 Pat Roberts (R), *Dodge City*
2 Jim Slattery (D), *Topeka*
3 Larry Winn, Jr. (R), *Overland Park*
4 Daniel R. Glickman (D), *Wichita*
5 Bob Whittaker (R), *Augusta*

## KENTUCKY

### SENATORS

Walter D. Huddleston (D), *Elizabethtown*
Wendell H. Ford (D), *Owensboro*

### REPRESENTATIVES

1 Carroll Hubbard, Jr. (D), *Mayfield*
2 William H. Natcher (D), *Bowling Green*
3 Romano L. Mazzoli (D), *Louisville*
4 M. G. (Gene) Snyder (R), *Brownsboro Farms*
5 Harold Rogers (R), *Somerset*
6 Larry J. Hopkins (R), *Lexington*
7 Carl D. Perkins (D),[17] *Hindman*
7 Carl C. Perkins (D),[18] *Leburn*

## LOUISIANA

### SENATORS

Russell B. Long (D), *Baton Rouge*
J. Bennett Johnston, Jr. (D), *Shreveport*

### REPRESENTATIVES

1 Robert L. Livingston (R), *New Orleans*
2 Corinne C. (Lindy) Boggs (D), *New Orleans*
3 W. J. (Billy) Tauzin (D), *Thibodaux*
4 Charles (Buddy) Roemer (D), *Bossier City*
5 Thomas J. (Jerry) Huckaby (D), *Ringgold*
6 W. Henson Moore (R), *Baton Rouge*
7 John B. Breaux (D), *Crowley*
8 Gillis W. Long (D), *Alexandria*

## MAINE

### SENATORS

William S. Cohen (R), *Bangor*
George J. Mitchell (D), *Portland*

### REPRESENTATIVES

1 John R. McKernan (R), *Cumberland*
2 Olympia J. Snowe (R), *Auburn*

## MARYLAND

### SENATORS

Charles McC. Mathias, Jr. (R), *Frederick*
Paul S. Sarbanes (D), *Baltimore*

### REPRESENTATIVES

1 Roy Dyson (D), *Great Mills*
2 Clarence D. Long (D), *Ruxton*
3 Barbara A. Mikulski (D), *Baltimore*
4 Marjorie S. Holt (R), *Severna Park*

5 Steny H. Hoyer (D), *Berkshire*
6 Beverly B. Byron (D), *Frederick*
7 Parren J. Mitchell (D), *Baltimore*
8 Michael D. Barnes (D), *Kensington*

## MASSACHUSETTS

### SENATORS

Edward M. Kennedy (D), *Boston*
Paul E. Tsongas (D),[19] *Lowell*
John F. Kerry (D),[20] *Boston*

### REPRESENTATIVES

1 Silvio O. Conte (R), *Pittsfield*
2 Edward P. Boland (D), *Springfield*
3 Joseph D. Early (D), *Worcester*
4 Barney Frank (D), *Newton*
5 James M. Shannon (D), *Lawrence*
6 Nicholas Mavroules (D), *Peabody*
7 Edward J. Markey (D), *Malden*
8 Thomas P. O'Neill, Jr. (D), *Cambridge*
9 John Joseph Moakley (D), *Boston*
10 Gerry E. Studds (D), *Cohasset*
11 Brian J. Donnelly (D), *Dorchester*

## MICHIGAN

### SENATORS

Donald W. Riegle, Jr. (D), *Flint*
Carl Levin (D), *Detroit*

### REPRESENTATIVES

1 John Conyers, Jr. (D), *Detroit*
2 Carl D. Pursell (R), *Plymouth*
3 Howard E. Wolpe (D), *Lansing*
4 Mark D. Siljander (R), *Three Rivers*
5 Harold S. Sawyer (R), *Rockford*
6 Bob Carr (D), *East Lansing*
7 Dale E. Kildee (D), *Flint*
8 Bob Traxler (D), *Bay City*
9 Guy A. Vander Jagt (R), *Luther*
10 Donald J. Albosta (D), *St. Charles*
11 Robert W. Davis (R), *Gaylord*
12 David E. Bonior (D), *Mount Clemens*
13 George W. Crockett, Jr. (D), *Detroit*
14 Dennis M. Hertel (D), *Detroit*
15 William D. Ford (D), *Taylor*
16 John D. Dingell, Jr. (D), *Trenton*
17 Sander M. Levin (D), *Southfield*
18 William S. Broomfield (R), *Birmingham*

## MINNESOTA

### SENATORS

David F. Durenberger (R), *Minneapolis*
Rudy Boschwitz (R), *Plymouth*

---

[16] Resigned November 28, 1984; vacancy throughout remainder of Congress.
[17] Died August 3, 1984.
[18] Elected November 6, 1984, to fill vacancy caused by death of his father, Carl D. Perkins, but was unable to be sworn in because Congress was not in session.
[19] Resigned January 2, 1985.

[20] Appointed and took his seat on January 2, 1985 to fill vacancy caused by resignation of Paul E. Tsongas.

## MINNESOTA—Continued
REPRESENTATIVES

1 Timothy J. Penny (D), *New Richland*
2 Vin Weber (R), *St. Cloud*
3 Bill Frenzel (R), *Golden Valley*
4 Bruce F. Vento (D), *St. Paul*
5 Martin Olav Sabo (D), *Minneapolis*
6 Gerry E. Sikorski (D), *Stillwater*
7 Arlan Stangeland (R), *Barnesville*
8 James L. Oberstar (D), *Chisholm*

## MISSISSIPPI
SENATORS

John C. Stennis (D), *De Kalb*
Thad Cochran (R), *Jackson*

REPRESENTATIVES

1 Jamie L. Whitten (D), *Charleston*
2 William W. Franklin (R), *Greenwood*
3 Gillespie V. (Sonny) Montgomery (D), *Meridian*
4 Wayne Dowdy (D), *Summit*
5 Trent Lott (R), *Pascagoula*

## MISSOURI
SENATORS

Thomas F. Eagleton (D), *St. Louis*
John C. Danforth (R), *Flat*

REPRESENTATIVES

1 William L. Clay (D), *St. Louis*
2 Robert A. Young (D), *St. Ann*
3 Richard A. Gephardt (D), *St. Louis*
4 Ike Skelton (D), *Lexington*
5 Alan D. Wheat (D), *Kansas City*
6 E. Thomas Coleman (R), *Kansas City*
7 Gene Taylor (R), *Sarcoxie*
8 Bill Emerson (R), *Cape Girardeau*
9 Harold L. Volkmer (D), *Hannibal*

## MONTANA
SENATORS

John Melcher (D), *Forsyth*
Max Baucus (D), *Missoula*

REPRESENTATIVES

1 Pat Williams (D), *Helena*
2 Ron Marlenee (R), *Scobey*

## NEBRASKA
SENATORS

Edward Zorinsky (D), *Omaha*
J. James Exon (D), *Lincoln*

REPRESENTATIVES

1 Douglas K. Bereuter (R), *Utica*
2 Hal Daub (R), *Omaha*
3 Virginia Smith (R), *Chappell*

## NEVADA
SENATORS

Paul Laxalt (R), *Carson City*
Chic Hecht (R), *Las Vegas*

REPRESENTATIVES

1 Harry M. Reid (D), *Las Vegas*
2 Barbara F. Vucanovich (R), *Reno*

## NEW HAMPSHIRE
SENATORS

Gordon J. Humphrey (R), *Sunapee*
Warren B. Rudman (R), *Nashua*

REPRESENTATIVES

1 Norman E. D'Amours (D), *Manchester*
2 Judd Gregg (R), *Greenfield*

## NEW JERSEY
SENATORS

Bill Bradley (D), *Denville*
Frank R. Lautenberg (D), *Montclair*

REPRESENTATIVES

1 James J. Florio (D), *Pine Hill*
2 William J. Hughes (D), *Ocean City*
3 James J. Howard (D), *Spring Lake Heights*
4 Christopher H. Smith (R), *Old Bridge*
5 Marge Roukema (R), *Ridgewood*
6 Bernard J. Dwyer (D), *Edison*
7 Matthew J. Rinaldo (R), *Union*
8 Robert A. Roe (D), *Wayne*
9 Robert G. Torricelli (D), *New Milford*
10 Peter W. Rodino, Jr. (D), *Newark*
11 Joseph G. Minish (D), *West Orange*
12 James A. Courter (R), *Hackettstown*
13 Edwin B. Forsythe (R),[21] *Moorestown*
13 H. James Saxton (R),[22] *Vincentown*
14 Frank J. Guarini (D), *Jersey City*

## NEW MEXICO
SENATORS

Pete V. Domenici (R), *Albuquerque*
Jeff Bingaman (D), *Santa Fe*

REPRESENTATIVES

1 Manuel Lujan, Jr. (R), *Albuquerque*
2 Joe Skeen (R), *Picacho*
3 William B. Richardson (D), *Santa Fe*

## NEW YORK
SENATORS

Daniel P. Moynihan (D), *Pindars Corners*
Alfonse M. D'Amato (R), *Island Park*

REPRESENTATIVES

1 William Carney (R), *Hauppauge*
2 Thomas J. Downey (D), *West Islip*
3 Robert J. Mrazek (D), *Huntington*
4 Norman F. Lent (R), *East Rockaway*
5 Raymond J. McGrath (R), *Valley Stream*
6 Joseph P. Addabbo (D), *Ozone Park*
7 Benjamin S. Rosenthal (D),[23] *Elmhurst*
7 Gary L. Ackerman (D),[24] *Flushing*
8 James H. Scheuer (D), *Neponsit*
9 Geraldine A. Ferraro (D), *Forest Hills Garden*
10 Charles E. Schumer (D), *Brooklyn*
11 Edolphus Towns (D), *Brooklyn*
12 Major R. Owens (D), *Brooklyn*
13 Stephen J. Solarz (D), *Brooklyn*
14 Guy V. Molinari (R), *Staten Island*
15 S. William Green (R), *New York*
16 Charles B. Rangel (D), *New York*
17 Ted Weiss (D), *New York*
18 Robert Garcia (D), *Bronx*
19 Mario Biaggi (D), *Bronx*
20 Richard L. Ottinger (D), *Mamaroneck*
21 Hamilton Fish, Jr. (R), *Millbrook*
22 Benjamin A. Gilman (R), *Middletown*
23 Samuel S. Stratton (D), *Amsterdam*
24 Gerald B. H. Solomon (R), *Glens Falls*
25 Sherwood L. Boehlert (R), *New Hartford*
26 David O'B. Martin (R), *Canton*
27 George C. Wortley (R), *Fayetteville*
28 Matthew F. McHugh (D), *Ithaca*
29 Frank Horton (R), *Rochester*
30 Barber B. Conable, Jr. (R), *Alexander*
31 Jack F. Kemp (R), *Hamburg*
32 John J. LaFalce (D), *Tonawanda*
33 Henry J. Nowak (D), *Buffalo*
34 Stanley N. Lundine (D), *Jamestown*

## NORTH CAROLINA
SENATORS

Jesse Helms (R), *Raleigh*
John P. East (R), *Greenville*

REPRESENTATIVES

1 Walter B. Jones (D), *Farmville*

---

[21] Died March 29, 1984.
[22] Elected November 6, 1984, to fill the vacancy caused by death of Edwin B. Forsythe, but was unable to be sworn in because Congress was not in session.
[23] Died January 4, 1983.
[24] Elected March 1, 1983, to fill vacancy caused by death of Benjamin S. Rosenthal, and took his seat March 2, 1983.

2 Tim Valentine (D), *Nashville*
3 Charles O. Whitley (D), *Mount Olive*
4 Ike F. Andrews (D), *Siler City*
5 Stephen L. Neal (D), *Winston-Salem*
6 Robin Britt (D), *Greensboro*
7 Charles Rose (D), *Fayetteville*
8 W. G. (Bill) Hefner (D), *Concord*
9 James G. Martin (R), *Davidson*
10 James T. Broyhill (R), *Lenoir*
11 James McClure Clarke (D), *Fairview*

## NORTH DAKOTA

### SENATORS

Quentin N. Burdick (D), *Fargo*
Mark Andrews (R), *Mapleton*

### REPRESENTATIVE AT LARGE

Byron L. Dorgan (D), *Bismarck*

## OHIO

### SENATORS

John Glenn, Jr. (D), *Columbus*
Howard M. Metzenbaum (D), *Shaker Heights*

### REPRESENTATIVES

1 Thomas A. Luken (D), *Cincinnati*
2 Willis D. Gradison, Jr. (R), *Cincinnati*
3 Tony P. Hall (D), *Dayton*
4 Michael G. Oxley (R), *Findley*
5 Delbert L. Latta (R), *Bowling Green*
6 Robert McEwen (R), *Hillsboro*
7 Michael DeWine (R), *Cedarville*
8 Thomas N. Kindness (R), *Hamilton*
9 Marcy Kaptur (D), *Toledo*
10 Clarence E. Miller (R), *Lancaster*
11 Dennis E. Eckart (D), *Concord Township*
12 John R. Kasich (R), *Westerville*
13 Donald J. Pease (D), *Oberlin*
14 John F. Seiberling (D), *Akron*
15 Chalmers P. Wylie (R), *Worthington*
16 Ralph Regula (R), *Navarre*
17 Lyle Williams (R), *Warren*
18 Douglas Applegate (D), *Steubenville*
19 Edward F. Feighan (D), *Cleveland*
20 Mary Rose Oakar (D), *Cleveland*
21 Louis Stokes (D), *Cleveland*

## OKLAHOMA

### SENATORS

David L. Boren (D), *Seminole*
Don Nickles (R), *Ponca City*

### REPRESENTATIVES

1 James R. Jones (D), *Tulsa*
2 Mike Synar (D), *Muskogee*

3 Wesley W. Watkins (D), *Ada*
4 Dave McCurdy (D), *Norman*
5 Mickey Edwards (R), *Oklahoma City*
6 Glenn English (D), *Cordell*

## OREGON

### SENATORS

Mark O. Hatfield (R), *Salem*
Robert W. Packwood (R), *Portland*

### REPRESENTATIVES

1 Les AuCoin (D), *Forest Grove*
2 Robert F. Smith (R), *Burns*
3 Ron Wyden (D), *Portland*
4 James Weaver (D), *Eugene*
5 Denny Smith (R), *Salem*

## PENNSYLVANIA

### SENATORS

H. John Heinz III (R), *Pittsburgh*
Arlen Specter (R), *Philadelphia*

### REPRESENTATIVES

1 Thomas M. Foglietta (D), *Philadelphia*
2 William H. Gray III (D), *Philadelphia*
3 Robert A. Borski, Jr. (D), *Philadelphia*
4 Joseph P. Kolter (D), *New Brighton*
5 Richard T. Schulze (R), *Malvern*
6 Gus Yatron (D), *Reading*
7 Robert W. Edgar (D), *Broomall*
8 Peter H. Kostmayer (D), *New Hope*
9 E. G. Shuster (R), *Everett*
10 Joseph M. McDade (R), *Scranton*
11 Frank Harrison (D), *Wilkes-Barre*
12 John P. Murtha, Jr. (D), *Johnstown*
13 R. Lawrence Coughlin (R), *Villanova*
14 William J. Coyne (D), *Pittsburgh*
15 Don Ritter (R), *Coopersburg*
16 Robert S. Walker (R), *East Petersburg*
17 George W. Gekas (R), *Harrisburg*
18 Doug Walgren (D), *Pittsburgh*
19 William F. Goodling (R), *Jacobus*
20 Joseph M. Gaydos (D), *McKeesport*
21 Thomas J. Ridge (R), *Erie*
22 Austin J. Murphy (D), *Charleroi*
23 William F. Clinger, Jr. (R), *Warren*

## RHODE ISLAND

### SENATORS

Claiborne Pell (D), *Newport*
John H. Chafee (R), *Warwick*

### REPRESENTATIVES

1 Fernand J. St Germain (D), *Woonsocket*

2 Claudine Schneider (R), *Narragansett*

## SOUTH CAROLINA

### SENATORS

Strom Thurmond (R), *Aiken*
Ernest F. Hollings (D), *Charleston*

### REPRESENTATIVES

1 Thomas F. Hartnett (R), *Charleston*
2 Floyd Spence (R), *Lexington*
3 Butler Derrick (D), *Edgefield*
4 Carroll Campbell, Jr. (R), *Fountain Inn*
5 John McK. Spratt, Jr. (D), *York*
6 Robert M. (Robin) Tallon (D), *Florence*

## SOUTH DAKOTA

### SENATORS

Larry Pressler (R), *Humboldt*
James Abdnor (R), *Kennebec*

### REPRESENTATIVE AT LARGE

Thomas A. Daschle (D), *Aberdeen*

## TENNESSEE

### SENATORS

Howard H. Baker, Jr. (R), *Huntsville*
James R. Sasser (D), *Nashville*

### REPRESENTATIVES

1 James H. Quillen (R), *Kingsport*
2 John J. Duncan (R), *Knoxville*
3 Marilyn Lloyd Bouquard (D), *Chattanooga*
4 James Cooper (D), *Shelbyville*
5 William H. Boner (D), *Nashville*
6 Albert A. Gore, Jr. (D), *Carthage*
7 Donald K. Sundquist (R), *Memphis*
8 Edward Jones (D), *Yorkville*
9 Harold E. Ford (D), *Memphis*

## TEXAS

### SENATORS

John G. Tower (R), *Wichita Falls*
Lloyd M. Bentsen, Jr. (D), *Houston*

### REPRESENTATIVES

1 Sam B. Hall, Jr. (D), *Marshall*
2 Charles Wilson (D), *Lufkin*
3 Steve Bartlett (R), *Dallas*
4 Ralph M. Hall (D), *Rockwall*
5 John W. Bryant (D), *Dallas*
6 Phil Gramm (D),[25] *College Station*
7 William R. Archer, Jr. (R), *Houston*
8 Jack Fields (R), *Humble*
9 Jack B. Brooks (D), *Beaumont*
10 J. J. (Jake) Pickle (D), *Austin*
11 J. Marvin Leath (D), *Marlin*
12 James C. Wright, Jr. (D), *Fort Worth*

[25] Resigned January 5, 1983; changed party affiliation to Republican; reelected February 12, 1983, and took his seat February 22, 1983.

## TEXAS—Continued

### REPRESENTATIVES—CONTINUED

13 Jack Hightower (D), *Vernon*
14 William N. Patman (D), *Ganado*
15 Eligio (Kika) de la Garza (D), *Mission*
16 Ronald Coleman (D), *El Paso*
17 Charles W. Stenholm (D), *Stamford*
18 Mickey Leland (D), *Houston*
19 Kent R. Hance (D), *Lubbock*
20 Henry B. Gonzalez (D), *San Antonio*
21 Tom Loeffler (R), *Hunt*
22 Ronald E. Paul (R), *Lake Jackson*
23 Abraham Kazen, Jr. (D), *Laredo*
24 Martin Frost (D), *Dallas*
25 Michael A. Andrews (D), *Houston*
26 Tommy J. Vandergriff (D), *Arlington*
27 Solomon P. Ortiz (D), *Corpus Christi*

## UTAH

### SENATORS

E. J. (Jake) Garn (R), *Salt Lake City*
Orrin G. Hatch (R), *Salt Lake City*

### REPRESENTATIVES

1 James V. Hansen (R), *Farmington*
2 David D. Marriott (R), *Salt Lake City*
3 Howard C. Nielson (R), *Provo*

## VERMONT

### SENATORS

Robert T. Stafford (R), *Rutland*
Patrick J. Leahy (D), *Burlington*

### REPRESENTATIVE AT LARGE

James M. Jeffords (R), *Montpelier*

## VIRGINIA

### SENATORS

John W. Warner (R), *Middleburg*
Paul S. Trible, Jr. (R), *Newport News*

### REPRESENTATIVES

1 Herbert H. Bateman (R), *Yorktown*

2 G. William Whitehurst (R), *Norfolk*
3 Thomas J. Bliley, Jr. (R), *Richmond*
4 Norman Sisisky (D), *Petersburg*
5 W. C. (Dan) Daniel (D), *Danville*
6 James R. Olin (D), *Roanoke*
7 J. Kenneth Robinson (R), *Winchester*
8 Stanford E. Parris (R), *Woodbridge*
9 Frederick C. Boucher (D), *Abington*
10 Frank R. Wolf (R), *Falls Church*

## WASHINGTON

### SENATORS

Henry M. Jackson (D),[26] *Everett*
Daniel J. Evans (R),[27] *Seattle*
Slade Gorton (R), *Olympia*

### REPRESENTATIVES

1 Joel Pritchard (R), *Seattle*
2 Al Swift (D), *Bellingham*
3 Don Bonker (D), *Ridgefield*
4 Sid Morrison (R), *Zillah*
5 Thomas S. Foley (D), *Spokane*
6 Norman D. Dicks (D), *Port Orchard*
7 Mike Lowry (D), *Seattle*
8 Rod D. Chandler (R), *Redmond*

## WEST VIRGINIA

### SENATORS

Jennings Randolph (D), *Elkins*
Robert C. Byrd (D), *Sophia*

### REPRESENTATIVES

1 Alan B. Mollohan (D), *Fairmont*
2 Harley O. Staggers, Jr. (D), *Keyser*
3 Robert E. Wise, Jr. (D), *Charleston*
4 Nick J. Rahall II (D), *Beckley*

## WISCONSIN

### SENATORS

William Proxmire (D), *Madison*
Robert W. Kasten, Jr. (R), *Milwaukee*

### REPRESENTATIVES

1 Les Aspin (D), *Racine*
2 Robert W. Kastenmeier (D), *Sun Prairie*
3 Steven Gunderson (R), *Osseo*
4 Clement J. Zablocki (D),[28] *Milwaukee*
4 Gerald D. Kleczka (D),[29] *Milwaukee*
5 Jim Moody (D), *Milwaukee*
6 Thomas E. Petri (R), *Fond du Lac*
7 David R. Obey (D), *Wausau*
8 Toby A. Roth (R), *Appleton*
9 F. James Sensenbrenner, Jr. (R), *Shorewood*

## WYOMING

### SENATORS

Malcolm Wallop (R), *Big Horn*
Alan K. Simpson (R), *Cody*

### REPRESENTATIVE AT LARGE

Richard B. Cheney (R), *Casper*

## AMERICAN SAMOA

### DELEGATE

Fofó I. F. Sunia (D), *Pago Pago*

## COMMONWEALTH OF PUERTO RICO

### RESIDENT COMMISSIONER

Baltasar Corrada-del Rio (NP), *Rio Piedras*

## DISTRICT OF COLUMBIA

### DELEGATE

Walter E. Fauntroy (D), *Washington, D.C.*

## GUAM

### DELEGATE

Antonio B. Won Pat (D), *Sinajana*

## VIRGIN ISLANDS

### DELEGATE

Ron de Lugo (D), *St. Thomas*

---

[26] Died September 1, 1983.
[27] Appointed September 8, 1983, to fill vacancy caused by death of Henry M. Jackson, and took his seat

September 12, 1983; elected November 8, 1983 for the remainder of the term ending January 3, 1989.
[28] Died December 3, 1983.

[29] Elected April 3, 1984, to fill vacancy caused by death of Clement J. Zablocki, and took his seat April 10, 1984.

# 99TH CONGRESS

## JANUARY 3, 1985, TO JANUARY 3, 1987

FIRST SESSION— *January 3, 1985, to December 20, 1985*
SECOND SESSION— *January 21, 1986,[1] to October 18, 1986*

George Bush
Vice President

Thomas P. O'Neill, Jr.
Speaker

---

### Senate
Democrats 53 — Republicans 47

VICE PRESIDENT OF THE UNITED STATES— George Bush, of Texas
PRESIDENT PRO TEMPORE OF THE SENATE— Strom Thurmond,[2] of South Carolina
SECRETARY OF THE SENATE— Jo-Anne L. Coe, of Virginia
SERGEANT AT ARMS OF THE SENATE— Larry E. Smith,[3] of Virginia; Ernest Garcia,[4] of Kansas
MAJORITY FLOOR LEADER— Robert J. Dole, of Kansas
REPUBLICAN WHIP— Alan K. Simpson, of Wyoming
DEMOCRATIC FLOOR LEADER— Robert C. Byrd, of West Virginia
ASSISTANT DEMOCRATIC LEADER— Alan M. Cranston, of California

---

### House of Representatives
Democrats 253 — Republicans 182

SPEAKER OF THE HOUSE— Thomas P. O'Neill, Jr.,[5] of Massachusetts
CLERK OF THE HOUSE— Benjamin J. Guthrie,[6] of Virginia
SERGEANT AT ARMS OF THE HOUSE— Jack Russ,[7] of Maryland
DOORKEEPER OF THE HOUSE— James T. Molloy,[8] of New York
POSTMASTER OF THE HOUSE— Robert V. Rota,[9] of Pennsylvania
MAJORITY LEADER— James C. Wright, Jr., of Texas
MAJORITY WHIP— Thomas S. Foley, of Washington
REPUBLICAN LEADER— Robert H. Michel, of Illinois
REPUBLICAN WHIP— Trent Lott, of Mississippi

---

## ALABAMA

### SENATORS
Howell T. Heflin (D), *Tuscumbia*
Jeremiah A. Denton, Jr. (R), *Mobile*

### REPRESENTATIVES
1  H. L. (Sonny) Callahan (R), *Mobile*
2  William L. Dickinson (R), *Montgomery*
3  William Nichols (D), *Sylacauga*
4  Tom Bevill (D), *Jasper*
5  Ronnie G. Flippo (D), *Florence*
6  Ben Erdreich (D), *Birmingham*
7  Richard C. Shelby (D), *Tuscaloosa*

## ALASKA

### SENATORS
Theodore F. Stevens (R), *Anchorage*
Frank H. Murkowski (R), *Fairbanks*

### REPRESENTATIVE AT LARGE
Donald E. Young (R), *Fort Yukon*

## ARIZONA

### SENATORS
Barry M. Goldwater (R), *Scottsdale*
Dennis DeConcini (D), *Tucson*

### REPRESENTATIVES
1  John S. McCain III (R), *Tempe*
2  Morris K. Udall (D), *Tucson*
3  Bob Stump (R), *Tolleson*
4  Eldon Rudd (R), *Scottsdale*
5  Jim Kolbe (R), *Bisbee*

## ARKANSAS

### SENATORS
Dale Bumpers (D), *Charleston*
David H. Pryor (D), *Little Rock*

### REPRESENTATIVES
1  William V. Alexander (D), *Osceola*
2  Tommy Robinson (D), *Jacksonville*
3  John Paul Hammerschmidt (R), *Harrison*
4  Beryl F. Anthony, Jr. (D), *El Dorado*

## CALIFORNIA

### SENATORS
Alan Cranston (D), *Los Angeles*
Pete Wilson (R), *San Diego*

### REPRESENTATIVES
1  Douglas H. Bosco (D), *Occidental*
2  Eugene A. Chappie (R), *Chico*
3  Robert T. Matsui (D), *Sacramento*
4  Vic Fazio (D), *Sacramento*
5  Sala Burton (D), *San Francisco*
6  Barbara Boxer (D), *Greenbrae*
7  George Miller (D), *Martinez*
8  Ronald V. Dellums (D), *Oakland*
9  Fortney H. (Pete) Stark, Jr. (D), *Oakland*
10  Don Edwards (D), *San Jose*
11  Tom Lantos (D), *San Mateo*
12  Edwin V. W. Zschau (R), *Los Altos*
13  Norman Y. Mineta (D), *San Jose*
14  Norman D. Shumway (R), *Stockton*
15  Tony Coelho (D), *Merced*

---

[1] By joint resolution (Pub. Law 99 233, 99th Cong., 1st sess.), the date of assembling the second session of the Ninety-ninth Congress was fixed for January 21, 1986.
[2] Reelected January 3, 1985.

[3] Resigned June 3, 1985.
[4] Elected May 16, 1985.
[5] Reelected January 3, 1985.
[6] Reelected January 3, 1985.

[7] Reelected January 3, 1985.
[8] Reelected January 3, 1985.
[9] Reelected January 3, 1985.

## CALIFORNIA—Continued

REPRESENTATIVES—CONTINUED

16 Leon E. Panetta (D), *Carmel Valley*
17 Charles Pashayan, Jr. (R), *Fresno*
18 Richard H. Lehman (D), *Sanger*
19 Robert J. Lagomarsino (R), *Ventura*
20 William M. Thomas (R), *Bakersfield*
21 Bobbi Fiedler (R), *Northridge*
22 Carlos J. Moorhead (R), *Glendale*
23 Anthony C. Beilenson (D), *Los Angeles*
24 Henry A. Waxman (D), *Los Angeles*
25 Edward R. Roybal (D), *Los Angeles*
26 Howard L. Berman (D), *Panorama City*
27 Mel Levine (D), *Los Angeles*
28 Julian C. Dixon (D), *Los Angeles*
29 Augustus F. Hawkins (D), *Los Angeles*
30 Matthew G. Martinez (D), *Montebello*
31 Mervyn M. Dymally (D), *Compton*
32 Glenn M. Anderson (D), *San Pedro*
33 David Dreier (R), *La Verna*
34 Esteban Edward Torres (D), *La Puente*
35 Jerry Lewis (R), *Redlands*
36 George E. Brown, Jr. (D), *Riverside*
37 Alfred A. McCandless (R), *Bermuda Dunes*
38 Robert K. Dornan (R), *Garden Grove*
39 William E. Dannemeyer (R), *Fullerton*
40 Robert E. Badham (R), *Newport Beach*
41 Bill Lowery (R), *San Diego*
42 Dan Lungren (R), *Long Beach*
43 Ron Packard (R), *Carlsbad*
44 Jim Bates (D), *San Diego*
45 Duncan L. Hunter (R), *Coronado*

## COLORADO

SENATORS

Gary Hart (D), *Denver*
William L. Armstrong (R), *Aurora*

REPRESENTATIVES

1 Patricia Schroeder (D), *Denver*
2 Timothy E. Wirth (D), *Boulder*
3 Michael L. Strang (R), *Carbondale*
4 Hank Brown (R), *Greeley*
5 Kenneth B. Kramer (R), *Colorado Springs*
6 Dan Schaefer (R), *Lakewood*

## CONNECTICUT

SENATORS

Lowell P. Weicker, Jr. (R), *Greenwich*
Christopher J. Dodd (D), *East Haddam*

REPRESENTATIVES

1 Barbara B. Kennelly (D), *Hartford*
2 Samuel Gejdenson (D), *Bozrah*
3 Bruce A. Morrison (D), *Hamden*
4 Stewart B. McKinney (R), *Green Farms*
5 John G. Rowland (R), *Waterbury*
6 Nancy L. Johnson (R), *New Britain*

## DELAWARE

SENATORS

William V. Roth, Jr. (R), *Wilmington*
Joseph R. Biden, Jr. (D), *Wilmington*

REPRESENTATIVE AT LARGE

Thomas R. Carper (D), *New Castle*

## FLORIDA

SENATORS

Lawton Chiles (D), *Lakeland*
Paula Hawkins (R), *Winter Park*

REPRESENTATIVES

1 Earl Hutto (D), *Panama City*
2 Don Fuqua (D), *Altha*
3 Charles E. Bennett (D), *Jacksonville*
4 William V. Chappell, Jr. (D), *Ocala*
5 Bill McCollum (R), *Altamonte Springs*
6 Kenneth H. (Buddy) MacKay (D), *Ocala*
7 Sam M. Gibbons (D), *Tampa*
8 C. W. Bill Young (R), *St. Petersburg*
9 Michael Bilirakis (R), *Palm Harbor*
10 Andrew P. Ireland (R), *Winter Haven*
11 Bill Nelson (D), *Melbourne*
12 Tom Lewis (R), *North Palm Beach*
13 Connie Mack (R), *Cape Coral*
14 Daniel A. Mica (D), *Lake Worth*
15 Clay Shaw (R), *Fort Lauderdale*
16 Lawrence J. Smith (D), *Hollywood*
17 William Lehman (D), *Biscayne Park*
18 Claude D. Pepper (D), *Miami*
19 Dante B. Fascell (D), *Miami*

## GEORGIA

SENATORS

Sam Nunn (D), *Perry*
Mack Mattingly (R), *St. Simons Island*

REPRESENTATIVES

1 R. Lindsay Thomas (D), *Statesboro*
2 Charles Hatcher (D), *Albany*
3 Richard Ray (D), *Perry*
4 Pat Swindall (R), *Dunwoody*
5 Wyche Fowler, Jr. (D), *Atlanta*
6 Newt Gingrich (R), *Jonesboro*
7 George (Buddy) Darden (D), *Marietta*
8 J. Roy Rowland (D), *Dublin*
9 Edgar L. Jenkins (D), *Jasper*
10 D. Douglas Barnard, Jr. (D), *Augusta*

## HAWAII

SENATORS

Daniel K. Inouye (D), *Honolulu*
Spark M. Matsunaga (D), *Honolulu*

REPRESENTATIVES

1 Cecil Heftel (D),[10] *Honolulu*
1 Neil Abercrombie (D),[11] *Honolulu*
2 Daniel K. Akaka (D), *Honolulu*

## IDAHO

SENATORS

James A. McClure (R), *McCall*
Steven D. Symms (R), *Caldwell*

REPRESENTATIVES

1 Larry Craig (R), *Midvale*
2 Richard Stallings (D), *Rexburg*

## ILLINOIS

SENATORS

Alan J. Dixon (D), *Belleville*
Paul Simon (D), *Makanda*

REPRESENTATIVES

1 Charles A. Hayes (D), *Chicago*
2 Gus Savage (D), *Chicago*
3 Martin A. Russo (D), *South Holland*
4 George M. O'Brien (R),[12] *Joliet*
5 William O. Lipinski (D), *Chicago*
6 Henry J. Hyde (R), *Bensenville*
7 Cardiss Collins (D), *Chicago*
8 Dan Rostenkowski (D), *Chicago*
9 Sidney R. Yates (D), *Chicago*
10 John Edward Porter (R), *Winnetka*
11 Frank Annunzio (D), *Chicago*
12 Philip M. Crane (R), *Mount Prospect*
13 Harris W. Fawell (R), *Naperville*
14 John E. Grotberg (R),[13] *St. Charles*

---

[10] Resigned July 11, 1986.
[11] Elected September 20, 1986, to fill vacancy caused by resignation of Cecil Heftel, and took his seat September 23, 1986.
[12] Died July 27, 1986; vacancy throughout remainder of Congress.
[13] Died November 15, 1986; vacancy throughout remainder of Congress.

15 Edward R. Madigan (R), *Lincoln*
16 Lynn Martin (R), *Rockford*
17 Lane A. Evans (D), *Rock Island*
18 Robert H. Michel (R), *Peoria*
19 Terry L. Bruce (D), *Olney*
20 Richard J. Durbin (D), *Springfield*
21 Melvin Price (D), *East St. Louis*
22 Kenneth J. Gray (D), *West Frankfort*

## INDIANA

### SENATORS

Richard G. Lugar (R), *Indianapolis*
J. Danforth Quayle (R), *Huntington*

### REPRESENTATIVES

1 Peter J. Visclosky (D), *Merrillville*
2 Philip R. Sharp (D), *Muncie*
3 John P. Hiler (R), *La Porte*
4 Dan R. Coats (R), *Fort Wayne*
5 Elwood Hillis (R), *Kokomo*
6 Dan Burton (R), *Indianapolis*
7 John T. Myers (R), *Covington*
8 Frank McCloskey (D),[14] *Bloomington*
9 Lee H. Hamilton (D), *Nashville*
10 Andrew Jacobs, Jr. (D), *Indianapolis*

## IOWA

### SENATORS

Charles E. Grassley (R), *New Hartford*
Tom Harkin (D), *Cumming*

### REPRESENTATIVES

1 James A. S. Leach (R), *Davenport*
2 Thomas J. Tauke (R), *Dubuque*
3 Cooper Evans (R), *Grundy Center*
4 Neal Smith (D), *Altoona*
5 Jim Ross Lightfoot (R), *Shenandoah*
6 Berkley Bedell (D), *Spirit Lake*

## KANSAS

### SENATORS

Robert J. Dole (R), *Russell*
Nancy L. Kassebaum (R), *Wichita*

### REPRESENTATIVES

1 Pat Roberts (R), *Dodge City*
2 Jim Slattery (D), *Topeka*
3 Jan Meyers (R), *Overland Park*
4 Daniel R. Glickman (D), *Wichita*
5 Bob Whittaker (R), *Augusta*

## KENTUCKY

### SENATORS

Wendell H. Ford (D), *Owensboro*
Mitch McConnell (R), *Louisville*

### REPRESENTATIVES

1 Carroll Hubbard, Jr. (D), *Mayfield*

2 William H. Natcher (D), *Bowling Green*
3 Romano L. Mazzoli (D), *Louisville*
4 M. G. (Gene) Snyder (R), *Brownsboro Farms*
5 Harold Rogers (R), *Somerset*
6 Larry J. Hopkins (R), *Lexington*
7 Carl C. Perkins (D), *Leburn*

## LOUISIANA

### SENATORS

Russell B. Long (D), *Baton Rouge*
J. Bennett Johnston, Jr. (D), *Shreveport*

### REPRESENTATIVES

1 Robert L. Livingston (R), *Metairie*
2 Corinne C. (Lindy) Boggs (D), *New Orleans*
3 W. J. (Billy) Tauzin (D), *Thibodaux*
4 Charles (Buddy) Roemer (D), *Bossier City*
5 Thomas J. (Jerry) Huckaby (D), *Ringgold*
6 W. Henson Moore (R), *Baton Rouge*
7 John B. Breaux (D), *Crowley*
8 Gillis W. Long (D),[15] *Alexandria*
8 Cathy Long (D),[16] *Alexandria*

## MAINE

### SENATORS

William S. Cohen (R), *Bangor*
George J. Mitchell (D), *Portland*

### REPRESENTATIVES

1 John R. McKernan (R), *Cumberland*
2 Olympia J. Snowe (R), *Auburn*

## MARYLAND

### SENATORS

Charles McC. Mathias, Jr. (R), *Frederick*
Paul S. Sarbanes (D), *Baltimore*

### REPRESENTATIVES

1 Roy Dyson (D), *Great Mills*
2 Helen Delich Bentley (R), *Lutherville*
3 Barbara A. Mikulski (D), *Baltimore*
4 Marjorie S. Holt (R), *Severna Park*
5 Steny H. Hoyer (D), *Berkshire*
6 Beverly B. Byron (D), *Frederick*
7 Parren J. Mitchell (D), *Baltimore*
8 Michael D. Barnes (D), *Kensington*

## MASSACHUSETTS

### SENATORS

Edward M. Kennedy (D), *Boston*
John F. Kerry (D), *Boston*

### REPRESENTATIVES

1 Silvio O. Conte (R), *Pittsfield*
2 Edward P. Boland (D), *Springfield*
3 Joseph D. Early (D), *Worcester*
4 Barney Frank (D), *Newton*
5 Chester G. Atkins (D), *Concord*
6 Nicholas Mavroules (D), *Peabody*
7 Edward J. Markey (D), *Malden*
8 Thomas P. O'Neill, Jr. (D), *Cambridge*
9 John Joseph Moakley (D), *Boston*
10 Gerry E. Studds (D), *Cohasset*
11 Brian J. Donnelly (D), *Dorchester*

## MICHIGAN

### SENATORS

Donald W. Riegle, Jr. (D), *Flint*
Carl Levin (D), *Detroit*

### REPRESENTATIVES

1 John Conyers, Jr. (D), *Detroit*
2 Carl D. Pursell (R), *Plymouth*
3 Howard E. Wolpe (D), *Lansing*
4 Mark D. Siljander (R), *Three Rivers*
5 Paul B. Henry (R), *Grand Rapids*
6 Bob Carr (D), *Okemos*
7 Dale E. Kildee (D), *Flint*
8 Bob Traxler (D), *Bay City*
9 Guy A. Vander Jagt (R), *Luther*
10 Bill Schuette (R), *Sanford*
11 Robert W. Davis (R), *Gaylord*
12 David E. Bonior (D), *Mount Clemens*
13 George W. Crockett, Jr. (D), *Detroit*
14 Dennis M. Hertel (D), *Harper Woods*
15 William D. Ford (D), *Taylor*
16 John D. Dingell, Jr. (D), *Trenton*
17 Sander M. Levin (D), *Southfield*
18 William S. Broomfield (R), *Birmingham*

## MINNESOTA

### SENATORS

David F. Durenberger (R), *Minneapolis*
Rudy Boschwitz (R), *Plymouth*

### REPRESENTATIVES

1 Timothy J. Penny (D), *New Richland*
2 Vin Weber (R), *North Mankato*
3 Bill Frenzel (R), *Golden Valley*
4 Bruce F. Vento (D), *St. Paul*
5 Martin Olav Sabo (D), *Minneapolis*
6 Gerry E. Sikorski (D), *Stillwater*

---

[14] Pursuant to House Resolution 146, the House seated the Democratic candidate of the November 6, 1984 election.

[15] Died January 20, 1985.
[16] Elected March 30, 1985, to fill vacancy caused by death of her husband, Gillis W. Long, and took her

seat April 4, 1985.

## MINNESOTA—Continued

### REPRESENTATIVES—CONTINUED

7 Arlan Stangeland (R), *Barnesville*
8 James L. Oberstar (D), *Chisholm*

## MISSISSIPPI

### SENATORS

John C. Stennis (D), *De Kalb*
Thad Cochran (R), *Jackson*

### REPRESENTATIVES

1 Jamie L. Whitten (D), *Charleston*
2 William W. Franklin (R), *Greenwood*
3 Gillespie V. (Sonny) Montgomery (D), *Meridian*
4 Wayne Dowdy (D), *Summit*
5 Trent Lott (R), *Pascagoula*

## MISSOURI

### SENATORS

Thomas F. Eagleton (D), *St. Louis*
John C. Danforth (R), *Newburg*

### REPRESENTATIVES

1 William L. Clay (D), *St. Louis*
2 Robert A. Young (D), *Maryland Heights*
3 Richard A. Gephardt (D), *St. Louis*
4 Ike Skelton (D), *Lexington*
5 Alan D. Wheat (D), *Kansas City*
6 E. Thomas Coleman (R), *Kansas City*
7 Gene Taylor (R), *Sarcoxie*
8 Bill Emerson (R), *Cape Girardeau*
9 Harold L. Volkmer (D), *Hannibal*

## MONTANA

### SENATORS

John Melcher (D), *Forsyth*
Max Baucus (D), *Missoula*

### REPRESENTATIVES

1 Pat Williams (D), *Helena*
2 Ron Marlenee (R), *Scobey*

## NEBRASKA

### SENATORS

Edward Zorinsky (D), *Omaha*
J. James Exon (D), *Lincoln*

### REPRESENTATIVES

1 Douglas K. Bereuter (R), *Utica*
2 Hal Daub (R), *Omaha*
3 Virginia Smith (R), *Chappell*

## NEVADA

### SENATORS

Paul Laxalt (R), *Carson City*
Chic Hecht (R), *Las Vegas*

### REPRESENTATIVES

1 Harry M. Reid (D), *Las Vegas*
2 Barbara F. Vucanovich (R), *Reno*

## NEW HAMPSHIRE

### SENATORS

Gordon J. Humphrey (R), *Chichester*
Warren B. Rudman (R), *Nashua*

### REPRESENTATIVES

1 Robert C. Smith (R), *Tuftonboro*
2 Judd Gregg (R), *Greenfield*

## NEW JERSEY

### SENATORS

Bill Bradley (D), *Denville*
Frank R. Lautenberg (D), *Montclair*

### REPRESENTATIVES

1 James J. Florio (D), *Pine Hill*
2 William J. Hughes (D), *Ocean City*
3 James J. Howard (D), *Spring Lake Heights*
4 Christopher H. Smith (R), *Hamilton*
5 Marge Roukema (R), *Ridgewood*
6 Bernard J. Dwyer (D), *Edison*
7 Matthew J. Rinaldo (R), *Union*
8 Robert A. Roe (D), *Wayne*
9 Robert G. Torricelli (D), *Hackensack*
10 Peter W. Rodino, Jr. (D), *Newark*
11 Dean A. Gallo (R), *Parsippany*
12 James A. Courter (R), *Hackettstown*
13 H. James Saxton (R), *Vincentown*
14 Frank J. Guarini (D), *Jersey City*

## NEW MEXICO

### SENATORS

Pete V. Domenici (R), *Albuquerque*
Jeff Bingaman (D), *Santa Fe*

### REPRESENTATIVES

1 Manuel Lujan, Jr. (R), *Albuquerque*
2 Joe Skeen (R), *Picacho*
3 William B. Richardson (D), *Santa Fe*

## NEW YORK

### SENATORS

Daniel P. Moynihan (D), *Pindars Corners*
Alfonse M. D'Amato (R), *Island Park*

### REPRESENTATIVES

1 William Carney (R), *Hauppauge*
2 Thomas J. Downey (D), *West Islip*
3 Robert J. Mrazek (D), *Huntington*
4 Norman F. Lent (R), *East Rockaway*
5 Raymond J. McGrath (R), *Valley Stream*
6 Joseph P. Addabbo (D),[17] *Ozone Park*
6 Alton R. Waldon, Jr. (D),[18] *Cambria Heights*
7 Gary L. Ackerman (D), *Queens*
8 James H. Scheuer (D), *Douglaston*
9 Thomas J. Manton (D), *Queens*
10 Charles E. Schumer (D), *Brooklyn*
11 Edolphus Towns (D), *Brooklyn*
12 Major R. Owens (D), *Brooklyn*
13 Stephen J. Solarz (D), *Brooklyn*
14 Guy V. Molinari (R), *Staten Island*
15 S. William Green (R), *New York*
16 Charles B. Rangel (D), *New York*
17 Ted Weiss (D), *New York*
18 Robert Garcia (D), *Bronx*
19 Mario Biaggi (D), *Bronx*
20 Joseph J. DioGuardi (R), *Scarsdale*
21 Hamilton Fish, Jr. (R), *Millbrook*
22 Benjamin A. Gilman (R), *Middletown*
23 Samuel S. Stratton (D), *Schenectady*
24 Gerald B. H. Solomon (R), *Glens Falls*
25 Sherwood L. Boehlert (R), *Utica*
26 David O'B. Martin (R), *Canton*
27 George C. Wortley (R), *Fayetteville*
28 Matthew F. McHugh (D), *Ithaca*
29 Frank Horton (R), *Rochester*
30 Fred J. Eckert (R), *Rochester*
31 Jack F. Kemp (R), *Hamburg*
32 John J. LaFalce (D), *Tonawanda*
33 Henry J. Nowak (D), *Buffalo*
34 Stanley N. Lundine (D), *Jamestown*

## NORTH CAROLINA

### SENATORS

Jesse Helms (R), *Raleigh*
John P. East (R),[19] *Greenville*
James T. Broyhill (R),[20] *Lenoir*
Terry Sanford (D),[21] *Durham*

### REPRESENTATIVES

1 Walter B. Jones (D), *Farmville*
2 Tim Valentine (D), *Nashville*
3 Charles O. Whitley (D),[22] *Mount Olive*
4 William W. Cobey, Jr. (R), *Chapel Hill*
5 Stephen L. Neal (D), *Winston-Salem*
6 Howard Coble (R), *Greensboro*
7 Charles Rose (D), *Fayetteville*
8 W. G. (Bill) Hefner (D), *Concord*
9 J. Alex McMillan (R), *Charlotte*

---

[17] Died April 10, 1986.
[18] Elected July 10, 1986, to fill vacancy caused by death of Joseph P. Addabbo, and took his seat July 29, 1986.

[19] Died June 29, 1986.
[20] Appointed to fill vacancy caused by death of John P. East, and took his seat July 14, 1986.
[21] Elected November 4, 1986, to fill the vacancy

caused by death of John P. East, and took his seat December 10, 1986.
[22] Resigned December 31, 1986; vacancy throughout remainder of Congress.

10  James T. Broyhill (R),[23] *Lenoir*
10  Cass Ballenger (R),[24] *Hickory*
11  William M. Hendon (R), *Asheville*

## NORTH DAKOTA

### SENATORS

Quentin N. Burdick (D), *Fargo*
Mark Andrews (R), *Mapleton*

### REPRESENTATIVE AT LARGE

Byron L. Dorgan (D), *Bismarck*

## OHIO

### SENATORS

John Glenn, Jr. (D), *Columbus*
Howard M. Metzenbaum (D),
   *Lyndhurst*

### REPRESENTATIVES

1  Thomas A. Luken (D), *Cincinnati*
2  Willis D. Gradison, Jr. (R),
   *Cincinnati*
3  Tony P. Hall (D), *Dayton*
4  Michael G. Oxley (R), *Findley*
5  Delbert L. Latta (R), *Bowling
   Green*
6  Robert McEwen (R), *Hillsboro*
7  Michael DeWine (R), *Cedarville*
8  Thomas N. Kindness (R),
   *Hamilton*
9  Marcy Kaptur (D), *Toledo*
10  Clarence E. Miller (R), *Lancaster*
11  Dennis E. Eckart (D), *Mentor*
12  John R. Kasich (R), *Westerville*
13  Donald J. Pease (D), *Oberlin*
14  John F. Seiberling (D), *Akron*
15  Chalmers P. Wylie (R),
   *Worthington*
16  Ralph Regula (R), *Navarre*
17  James A. Traficant, Jr. (D),
   *Poland*
18  Douglas Applegate (D),
   *Steubenville*
19  Edward F. Feighan (D), *Lakewood*
20  Mary Rose Oakar (D), *Cleveland*
21  Louis Stokes (D), *Warrensville
   Heights*

## OKLAHOMA

### SENATORS

David L. Boren (D), *Seminole*
Don Nickles (R), *Ponca City*

### REPRESENTATIVES

1  James R. Jones (D), *Tulsa*
2  Mike Synar (D), *Muskogee*
3  Wesley W. Watkins (D), *Ada*
4  Dave McCurdy (D), *Norman*
5  Mickey Edwards (R), *Oklahoma
   City*
6  Glenn English (D), *Cordell*

## OREGON

### SENATORS

Mark O. Hatfield (R), *Tigard*
Robert W. Packwood (R), *Portland*

### REPRESENTATIVES

1  Les AuCoin (D), *Portland*
2  Robert F. Smith (R), *Burns*
3  Ron Wyden (D), *Portland*
4  James Weaver (D), *Eugene*
5  Denny Smith (R), *Salem*

## PENNSYLVANIA

### SENATORS

H. John Heinz III (R), *Pittsburgh*
Arlen Specter (R), *Philadelphia*

### REPRESENTATIVES

1  Thomas M. Foglietta (D),
   *Philadelphia*
2  William H. Gray III (D),
   *Philadelphia*
3  Robert A. Borski, Jr. (D),
   *Philadelphia*
4  Joseph P. Kolter (D), *New
   Brighton*
5  Richard T. Schulze (R), *Berwyn*
6  Gus Yatron (D), *Reading*
7  Robert W. Edgar (D), *Middletown*
8  Peter H. Kostmayer (D), *Solebury*
9  E. G. Shuster (R), *Everett*
10  Joseph M. McDade (R), *Scranton*
11  Paul E. Kanjorski (D), *Nanticoke*
12  John P. Murtha, Jr. (D),
   *Johnstown*
13  R. Lawrence Coughlin (R),
   *Villanova*
14  William J. Coyne (D), *Pittsburgh*
15  Don Ritter (R), *Coopersburg*
16  Robert S. Walker (R), *East
   Petersburg*
17  George W. Gekas (R), *Harrisburg*
18  Doug Walgren (D), *Pittsburgh*
19  William F. Goodling (R), *Jacobus*
20  Joseph M. Gaydos (D),
   *McKeesport*
21  Thomas J. Ridge (R), *Erie*
22  Austin J. Murphy (D), *Charleroi*
23  William F. Clinger, Jr. (R), *Warren*

## RHODE ISLAND

### SENATORS

Claiborne Pell (D), *Newport*
John H. Chafee (R), *Warwick*

### REPRESENTATIVES

1  Fernand J. St Germain (D),
   *Woonsocket*
2  Claudine Schneider (R),
   *Narragansett*

## SOUTH CAROLINA

### SENATORS

Strom Thurmond (R), *Aiken*
Ernest F. Hollings (D), *Charleston*

### REPRESENTATIVES

1  Thomas F. Hartnett (R),
   *Charleston*
2  Floyd Spence (R), *Lexington*
3  Butler Derrick (D), *Edgefield*
4  Carroll Campbell, Jr. (R),
   *Greenville*
5  John McK. Spratt, Jr. (D), *York*
6  Robert M. (Robin) Tallon (D),
   *Florence*

## SOUTH DAKOTA

### SENATORS

Larry Pressler (R), *Humboldt*
James Abdnor (R), *Kennebec*

### REPRESENTATIVE AT LARGE

Thomas A. Daschle (D), *Aberdeen*

## TENNESSEE

### SENATORS

James R. Sasser (D), *Nashville*
Albert A. Gore, Jr. (D), *Carthage*

### REPRESENTATIVES

1  James H. Quillen (R), *Kingsport*
2  John J. Duncan (R), *Knoxville*
3  Marilyn Lloyd (D),[25] *Chattanooga*
4  James Cooper (D), *Shelbyville*
5  William H. Boner (D), *Nashville*
6  Bart Gordon (D), *Murfreesboro*
7  Donald K. Sundquist (R),
   *Memphis*
8  Edward Jones (D), *Yorkville*
9  Harold E. Ford (D), *Memphis*

## TEXAS

### SENATORS

Lloyd M. Bentsen, Jr. (D), *Houston*
Phil Gramm (R), *College Station*

### REPRESENTATIVES

1  Sam B. Hall, Jr. (D),[26] *Marshall*
1  Jim Chapman (D),[27] *Sulphur
   Springs*
2  Charles Wilson (D), *Lufkin*
3  Steve Bartlett (R), *Dallas*
4  Ralph M. Hall (D), *Rockwall*
5  John W. Bryant (D), *Dallas*
6  Joe Barton (R), *Ennis*
7  William R. Archer, Jr. (R),
   *Houston*
8  Jack Fields (R), *Humble*
9  Jack B. Brooks (D), *Beaumont*
10  J. J. (Jake) Pickle (D), *Austin*
11  J. Marvin Leath (D), *Waco*
12  James C. Wright, Jr. (D), *Fort
   Worth*

---

[23] Resigned July 13, 1986, having been appointed United States Senator.
[24] Elected November 4, 1986, to fill the vacancy caused by the resignation of James T. Broyhill, but was unable to be sworn in as Congress was not in session.
[25] Served under the name Marilyn Lloyd Bouquard in the 96th-98th Congresses.
[26] Resigned May 27, 1985.
[27] Elected August 3, 1985, to fill vacancy caused by resignation of Sam B. Hall, Jr., and took his seat September 4, 1985.

## TEXAS—Continued

REPRESENTATIVES—CONTINUED

13 Beau Boulter (R), *Amarillo*
14 Mac Sweeney (R), *Wharton*
15 Eligio (Kika) de la Garza (D), *Mission*
16 Ronald Coleman (D), *El Paso*
17 Charles W. Stenholm (D), *Avoca*
18 Mickey Leland (D), *Houston*
19 Larry Combest (R), *Lubbock*
20 Henry B. Gonzalez (D), *San Antonio*
21 Tom Loeffler (R), *Hunt*
22 Tom DeLay (R), *Sugar Land*
23 Albert G. Bustamante (D), *San Antonio*
24 Martin Frost (D), *Dallas*
25 Michael A. Andrews (D), *Houston*
26 Richard Armey (R), *Denton*
27 Solomon P. Ortiz (D), *Corpus Christi*

## UTAH

SENATORS

E. J. (Jake) Garn (R), *Salt Lake City*
Orrin G. Hatch (R), *Salt Lake City*

REPRESENTATIVES

1 James V. Hansen (R), *Farmington*
2 David S. Monson (R), *Salt Lake City*
3 Howard C. Nielson (R), *Provo*

## VERMONT

SENATORS

Robert T. Stafford (R), *Rutland*
Patrick J. Leahy (D), *Burlington*

REPRESENTATIVE AT LARGE

James M. Jeffords (R), *Rutland*

## VIRGINIA

SENATORS

John W. Warner (R), *Middleburg*
Paul S. Trible, Jr. (R), *Kilmarnock*

REPRESENTATIVES

1 Herbert H. Bateman (R), *Newport News*

2 G. William Whitehurst (R), *Norfolk*
3 Thomas J. Bliley, Jr. (R), *Richmond*
4 Norman Sisisky (D), *Petersburg*
5 W. C. (Dan) Daniel (D), *Danville*
6 James R. Olin (D), *Roanoke*
7 D. French Slaughter, Jr. (R), *Culpeper*
8 Stanford E. Parris (R), *Woodbridge*
9 Frederick C. Boucher (D), *Abington*
10 Frank R. Wolf (R), *Vienna*

## WASHINGTON

SENATORS

Slade Gorton (R), *Olympia*
Daniel J. Evans (R), *Seattle*

REPRESENTATIVES

1 John Miller (R), *Seattle*
2 Al Swift (D), *Bellingham*
3 Don Bonker (D), *Ridgefield*
4 Sid Morrison (R), *Zillah*
5 Thomas S. Foley (D), *Spokane*
6 Norman D. Dicks (D), *Bremerton*
7 Mike Lowry (D), *Seattle*
8 Rod D. Chandler (R), *Redmond*

## WEST VIRGINIA

SENATORS

Robert C. Byrd (D), *Sophia*
John D. Rockefeller IV (D), *Charleston*

REPRESENTATIVES

1 Alan B. Mollohan (D), *Fairmont*
2 Harley O. Staggers, Jr. (D), *Keyser*
3 Robert E. Wise, Jr. (D), *Clendenin*
4 Nick J. Rahall II (D), *Beckley*

## WISCONSIN

SENATORS

William Proxmire (D), *Madison*
Robert W. Kasten, Jr. (R), *Milwaukee*

REPRESENTATIVES

1 Les Aspin (D), *East Troy*
2 Robert W. Kastenmeier (D), *Sun Prairie*
3 Steven Gunderson (R), *Osseo*
4 Gerald D. Kleczka (D), *Milwaukee*
5 Jim Moody (D), *Milwaukee*
6 Thomas E. Petri (R), *Fond du Lac*
7 David R. Obey (D), *Wausau*
8 Toby A. Roth (R), *Appleton*
9 F. James Sensenbrenner, Jr. (R), *Menomonce Falls*

## WYOMING

SENATORS

Malcolm Wallop (R), *Big Horn*
Alan K. Simpson (R), *Cody*

REPRESENTATIVE AT LARGE

Richard B. Cheney (R), *Casper*

## AMERICAN SAMOA

DELEGATE

Fofó I. F. Sunia (D), *Pago Pago*

## COMMONWEALTH OF PUERTO RICO

RESIDENT COMMISSIONER

Jaime B. Fuster (D), *Santurce*

## DISTRICT OF COLUMBIA

DELEGATE

Walter E. Fauntroy (D), *Washington, D.C.*

## GUAM

DELEGATE

Ben Garrido Blaz (R), *Agana*

## VIRGIN ISLANDS

DELEGATE

Ron de Lugo (D), *St. Thomas*

# 100TH CONGRESS

## JANUARY 6, 1987, TO JANUARY 3, 1989

FIRST SESSION— *January 6, 1987,*[1] *to December 22, 1987*
SECOND SESSION— *January 25, 1988,*[2] *to October 22, 1988*

James C. Wright, Jr.,
Speaker

George Bush
Vice President

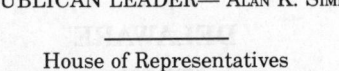

### Senate
Democrats 55 — Republicans 45

VICE PRESIDENT OF THE UNITED STATES— GEORGE BUSH, of Texas
PRESIDENT PRO TEMPORE OF THE SENATE— JOHN C. STENNIS,[3] of Mississippi
SECRETARY OF THE SENATE— WALTER J. STEWART,[4] of Washington, D.C.
SERGEANT AT ARMS OF THE SENATE— HENRY KUUALOHA GIUGNI,[5] of Hawaii
MAJORITY FLOOR LEADER— ROBERT C. BYRD, of West Virginia
DEMOCRATIC WHIP— ALAN M. CRANSTON, of California
REPUBLICAN FLOOR LEADER— ROBERT J. DOLE, of Kansas
ASSISTANT REPUBLICAN LEADER— ALAN K. SIMPSON, of Wyoming

### House of Representatives
Democrats 258 — Republicans 177

SPEAKER OF THE HOUSE— JAMES C. WRIGHT, JR.,[6] of Texas
CLERK OF THE HOUSE— DONNALD K. ANDERSON,[7] of California
SERGEANT AT ARMS OF THE HOUSE— JACK RUSS,[8] of Maryland
DOORKEEPER OF THE HOUSE— JAMES T. MOLLOY,[9] of New York
POSTMASTER OF THE HOUSE— ROBERT V. ROTA,[10] of Pennsylvania
MAJORITY LEADER— THOMAS S. FOLEY, of Washington
MAJORITY WHIP— ANTHONY L. COELHO, of California
REPUBLICAN LEADER— ROBERT H. MICHEL, of Illinois
REPUBLICAN WHIP— TRENT LOTT, of Mississippi

## ALABAMA

SENATORS
Howell T. Heflin (D), *Tuscumbia*
Richard C. Shelby (D), *Tuscaloosa*

REPRESENTATIVES
1 H. L. (Sonny) Callahan (R),
  *Mobile*
2 William L. Dickinson (R),
  *Montgomery*
3 William Nichols (D),* *Sylacauga*
4 Tom Bevill (D), *Jasper*
5 Ronnie G. Flippo (D), *Florence*
6 Ben Erdreich (D), *Birmingham*
7 Claude Harris (D), *Tuscaloosa*

## ALASKA

SENATORS
Theodore F. Stevens (R), *Anchorage*
Frank H. Murkowski (R), *Fairbanks*

REPRESENTATIVE AT LARGE
Donald E. Young (R), *Fort Yukon*

## ARIZONA

SENATORS
Dennis DeConcini (D), *Tucson*
John S. McCain III (R), *Tempe*

REPRESENTATIVES
1 John J. Rhodes III (R), *Mesa*
2 Morris K. Udall (D), *Tucson*
3 Bob Stump (R), *Tolleson*
4 Jon Kyl (R), *Scottsdale*
5 Jim Kolbe (R), *Bisbee*

## ARKANSAS

SENATORS
Dale Bumpers (D), *Charleston*
David H. Pryor (D), *Camden*

REPRESENTATIVES
1 William V. Alexander (D), *Osceola*
2 Tommy Robinson (D), *Jacksonville*
3 John Paul Hammerschmidt (R),
  *Harrison*

4 Beryl F. Anthony, Jr. (D), *El
  Dorado*

## CALIFORNIA

SENATORS
Alan Cranston (D), *Los Angeles*
Pete Wilson (R), *San Diego*

REPRESENTATIVES
1 Douglas H. Bosco (D), *Occidental*
2 Wally Herger (R), *Roseville*
3 Robert T. Matsui (D), *Sacramento*
4 Vic Fazio (D), *Sacramento*
5 Sala Burton (D),[11] *San Francisco*
5 Nancy Pelosi (D),[12] *San Francisco*
6 Barbara Boxer (D), *Greenbrae*
7 George Miller (D), *Martinez*
8 Ronald V. Dellums (D), *Berkeley*
9 Fortney H. (Pete) Stark, Jr. (D),
  *Oakland*
10 Don Edwards (D), *San Jose*
11 Tom Lantos (D), *Hillsborough*
12 Ernest L. Konnyu (R), *Saratoga*

[1] By joint resolution (Pub. Law 99-613, 99th Cong., 2d sess.), the date of assembling the first session of the One Hundredth Congress was fixed for January 6, 1987.

[2] By joint resolution (Pub. Law 100 229, 100th Cong., 1st sess.), the date of assembling the second session of the One Hundredth Congress was fixed for January 25, 1988.

[3] Elected January 6, 1987.
[4] Elected January 6, 1987.
[5] Elected January 6, 1987.
[6] Elected January 6, 1987.
[7] Elected January 6, 1987.
[8] Reelected January 6, 1987.

[9] Reelected January 6, 1987.
[10] Reelected January 6, 1987.
[11] Died February 1, 1987.
[12] Elected June 2, 1987, to fill vacancy caused by death of Sala Burton, and took her seat June 9, 1987.
* Died December 13, 1988.

## CALIFORNIA—Continued

REPRESENTATIVES—CONTINUED

13 Norman Y. Mineta (D), *San Jose*
14 Norman D. Shumway (R), *Stockton*
15 Tony Coelho (D), *Merced*
16 Leon E. Panetta (D), *Carmel Valley*
17 Charles Pashayan, Jr. (R), *Fresno*
18 Richard H. Lehman (D), *Sanger*
19 Robert J. Lagomarsino (R), *Ojai*
20 William M. Thomas (R), *Bakersfield*
21 Elton Gallegly (R), *Northridge*
22 Carlos J. Moorhead (R), *Glendale*
23 Anthony C. Beilenson (D), *Los Angeles*
24 Henry A. Waxman (D), *Los Angeles*
25 Edward R. Roybal (D), *Los Angeles*
26 Howard L. Berman (D), *Studio City*
27 Mel Levine (D), *Santa Monica*
28 Julian C. Dixon (D), *Los Angeles*
29 Augustus F. Hawkins (D), *Los Angeles*
30 Matthew G. Martinez (D), *Monterey Park*
31 Mervyn M. Dymally (D), *Compton*
32 Glenn M. Anderson (D), *Harbor City*
33 David Dreier (R), *La Verne*
34 Esteban Edward Torres (D), *La Puente*
35 Jerry Lewis (R), *Highland*
36 George E. Brown, Jr. (D), *Colton*
37 Alfred A. McCandless (R), *Bermuda Dunes*
38 Robert K. Dornan (R), *Garden Grove*
39 William E. Dannemeyer (R), *Fullerton*
40 Robert E. Badham (R), *Newport Beach*
41 Bill Lowery (R), *San Diego*
42 Dan Lungren (R), *Long Beach*
43 Ron Packard (R), *Carlsbad*
44 Jim Bates (D), *San Diego*
45 Duncan L. Hunter (R), *San Diego*

## COLORADO

SENATORS

William L. Armstrong (R), *Aurora*
Timothy E. Wirth (D), *Denver*

REPRESENTATIVES

1 Patricia Schroeder (D), *Denver*
2 David E. Skaggs (D), *Boulder*
3 Ben Nighthorse Campbell (D), *Ignacio*
4 Hank Brown (R), *Greeley*
5 Joel Hefley (R), *Colorado Springs*

6 Dan Schaefer (R), *Lakewood*

## CONNECTICUT

SENATORS

Lowell P. Weicker, Jr. (R), *Stonington*
Christopher J. Dodd (D), *North Stonington*

REPRESENTATIVES

1 Barbara B. Kennelly (D), *Hartford*
2 Samuel Gejdenson (D), *Bozrah*
3 Bruce A. Morrison (D), *Hamden*
4 Stewart B. McKinney (R),[13] *Westport*
4 Christopher Shays (R),[14] *Stamford*
5 John G. Rowland (R), *Danbury*
6 Nancy L. Johnson (R), *New Britain*

## DELAWARE

SENATORS

William V. Roth, Jr. (R), *Wilmington*
Joseph R. Biden, Jr. (D), *Wilmington*

REPRESENTATIVE AT LARGE

Thomas R. Carper (D), *New Castle*

## FLORIDA

SENATORS

Lawton Chiles (D), *Lakeland*
Bob Graham (D), *Tallahassee*

REPRESENTATIVES

1 Earl Hutto (D), *Panama City*
2 Bill Grant (D), *Madison*
3 Charles E. Bennett (D), *Jacksonville*
4 William V. Chappell, Jr. (D), *Ocala*
5 Bill McCollum (R), *Altamonte Springs*
6 Kenneth H. (Buddy) MacKay (D), *Ocala*
7 Sam M. Gibbons (D), *Tampa*
8 C. W. Bill Young (R), *St. Petersburg*
9 Michael Bilirakis (R), *Tarpon Springs*
10 Andrew P. Ireland (R), *Winter Haven*
11 Bill Nelson (D), *Melbourne*
12 Tom Lewis (R), *North Palm Beach*
13 Connie Mack (R), *Cape Coral*
14 Daniel A. Mica (D), *West Palm Beach*
15 Clay Shaw (R), *Fort Lauderdale*
16 Lawrence J. Smith (D), *Hollywood*
17 William Lehman (D), *North Miami Beach*
18 Claude D. Pepper (D), *Miami*
19 Dante B. Fascell (D), *Miami*

## GEORGIA

SENATORS

Sam Nunn (D), *Perry*
Wyche Fowler, Jr. (D), *Atlanta*

REPRESENTATIVES

1 R. Lindsay Thomas (D), *Screven*
2 Charles Hatcher (D), *Albany*
3 Richard Ray (D), *Perry*
4 Pat Swindall (R), *Atlanta*
5 John Lewis (D), *Atlanta*
6 Newt Gingrich (R), *Carrollton*
7 George (Buddy) Darden (D), *Marietta*
8 J. Roy Rowland (D), *Dublin*
9 Edgar L. Jenkins (D), *Jasper*
10 D. Douglas Barnard, Jr. (D), *Augusta*

## HAWAII

SENATORS

Daniel K. Inouye (D), *Honolulu*
Spark M. Matsunaga (D), *Honolulu*

REPRESENTATIVES

1 Patricia F. Saiki (R), *Honolulu*
2 Daniel K. Akaka (D), *Honolulu*

## IDAHO

SENATORS

James A. McClure (R), *Payette*
Steven D. Symms (R), *Boise*

REPRESENTATIVES

1 Larry Craig (R), *Midvale*
2 Richard Stallings (D), *Pocatello*

## ILLINOIS

SENATORS

Alan J. Dixon (D), *Belleville*
Paul Simon (D), *Makanda*

REPRESENTATIVES

1 Charles A. Hayes (D), *Chicago*
2 Gus Savage (D), *Chicago*
3 Martin A. Russo (D), *South Holland*
4 Jack Davis (R), *New Lenox*
5 William O. Lipinski (D), *Chicago*
6 Henry J. Hyde (R), *Bensenville*
7 Cardiss Collins (D), *Chicago*
8 Dan Rostenkowski (D), *Chicago*
9 Sidney R. Yates (D), *Chicago*
10 John Edward Porter (R), *Winnetka*
11 Frank Annunzio (D), *Chicago*
12 Philip M. Crane (R), *Mount Prospect*
13 Harris W. Fawell (R), *Glen Ellyn*
14 J. Dennis Hastert (R), *Oswego*
15 Edward R. Madigan (R), *Lincoln*
16 Lynn Martin (R), *Rockford*
17 Lane A. Evans (D), *Rock Island*
18 Robert H. Michel (R), *Peoria*
19 Terry L. Bruce (D), *Danville*

---

[13] Died May 7, 1987.
[14] Elected August 18, 1987, to fill vacancy caused by death of Stewart B. McKinney, and took his seat September 9, 1987.

20 Richard J. Durbin (D), *Springfield*
21 Melvin Price (D),[15] *East St. Louis*
21 Jerry F. Costello (D),[16] *Belleville*
22 Kenneth J. Gray (D), *Carbondale*

## INDIANA

### SENATORS

Richard G. Lugar (R), *Indianapolis*
J. Danforth Quayle (R), *Huntington*

### REPRESENTATIVES

1 Peter J. Visclosky (D), *Gary*
2 Philip R. Sharp (D), *Muncie*
3 John P. Hiler (R), *La Porte*
4 Dan R. Coats (R), *Fort Wayne*
5 Jim Jontz (D), *Brookston*
6 Dan Burton (R), *Indianapolis*
7 John T. Myers (R), *Covington*
8 Frank McCloskey (D),
   *Bloomington*
9 Lee H. Hamilton (D), *Columbus*
10 Andrew Jacobs, Jr. (D),
   *Indianapolis*

## IOWA

### SENATORS

Charles E. Grassley (R), *New Hartford*
Tom Harkin (D), *Ames*

### REPRESENTATIVES

1 James A. S. Leach (R), *Davenport*
2 Thomas J. Tauke (R), *Dubuque*
3 David R. Nagle (D), *Cedar Falls*
4 Neal Smith (D), *Altoona*
5 Jim Ross Lightfoot (R),
   *Shenandoah*
6 Fred Grandy (R), *Sioux City*

## KANSAS

### SENATORS

Robert J. Dole (R), *Russell*
Nancy L. Kassebaum (R), *Wichita*

### REPRESENTATIVES

1 Pat Roberts (R), *Dodge City*
2 Jim Slattery (D), *Topeka*
3 Jan Meyers (R), *Overland Park*
4 Daniel R. Glickman (D), *Wichita*
5 Bob Whittaker (R), *Augusta*

## KENTUCKY

### SENATORS

Wendell H. Ford (D), *Owensboro*
Mitch McConnell (R), *Louisville*

### REPRESENTATIVES

1 Carroll Hubbard, Jr. (D), *Mayfield*
2 William H. Natcher (D), *Bowling Green*
3 Romano L. Mazzoli (D), *Louisville*
4 Jim Bunning (R), *Fort Thomas*
5 Harold Rogers (R), *Somerset*
6 Larry J. Hopkins (R), *Lexington*

7 Carl C. Perkins (D), *Leburn*

## LOUISIANA

### SENATORS

J. Bennett Johnston, Jr. (D),
   *Shreveport*
John B. Breaux (D), *Crowley*

### REPRESENTATIVES

1 Robert L. Livingston (R), *New Orleans*
2 Corinne C. (Lindy) Boggs (D),
   *New Orleans*
3 W. J. (Billy) Tauzin (D),
   *Thibodaux*
4 Charles (Buddy) Roemer (D),[17]
   *Bossier City*
4 James O. McCrery III (R),[18]
   *Shreveport*
5 Thomas J. (Jerry) Huckaby (D),
   *Ringgold*
6 Richard H. Baker (R), *Baton Rouge*
7 James A. Hayes (D), *Lafayette*
8 Clyde C. Holloway (R), *Forest Hill*

## MAINE

### SENATORS

William S. Cohen (R), *Bangor*
George J. Mitchell (D), *South Portland*

### REPRESENTATIVES

1 Joseph E. Brennan (D), *Portland*
2 Olympia J. Snowe (R), *Auburn*

## MARYLAND

### SENATORS

Paul S. Sarbanes (D), *Baltimore*
Barbara A. Mikulski (D), *Baltimore*

### REPRESENTATIVES

1 Roy Dyson (D), *Great Mills*
2 Helen Delich Bentley (R), *Towson*
3 Benjamin L. Cardin (D),
   *Baltimore*
4 C. Thomas McMillen (D), *Crofton*
5 Steny H. Hoyer (D), *Berkshire*
6 Beverly B. Byron (D), *Frederick*
7 Kweisi Mfume (D), *Baltimore*
8 Constance A. Morella (R),
   *Bethesda*

## MASSACHUSETTS

### SENATORS

Edward M. Kennedy (D), *Boston*
John F. Kerry (D), *Boston*

### REPRESENTATIVES

1 Silvio O. Conte (R), *Pittsfield*
2 Edward P. Boland (D), *Springfield*
3 Joseph D. Early (D), *Worcester*
4 Barney Frank (D), *Newton*
5 Chester G. Atkins (D), *Lawrence*

6 Nicholas Mavroules (D), *Peabody*
7 Edward J. Markey (D), *Malden*
8 Joseph P. Kennedy II (D), *Boston*
9 John Joseph Moakley (D), *South Boston*
10 Gerry E. Studds (D), *Cohasset*
11 Brian J. Donnelly (D), *Dorchester*

## MICHIGAN

### SENATORS

Donald W. Riegle, Jr. (D), *Flint*
Carl Levin (D), *Detroit*

### REPRESENTATIVES

1 John Conyers, Jr. (D), *Detroit*
2 Carl D. Pursell (R), *Plymouth*
3 Howard E. Wolpe (D), *Lansing*
4 Fred Upton (R), *St. Joe*
5 Paul B. Henry (R), *Rockford*
6 Bob Carr (D), *East Lansing*
7 Dale E. Kildee (D), *Flint*
8 Bob Traxler (D), *Bay City*
9 Guy A. Vander Jagt (R), *Luther*
10 Bill Schuette (R), *St. Charles*
11 Robert W. Davis (R), *Gaylord*
12 David E. Bonior (D), *Mount Clemens*
13 George W. Crockett, Jr. (D),
   *Detroit*
14 Dennis M. Hertel (D), *Detroit*
15 William D. Ford (D), *Taylor*
16 John D. Dingell, Jr. (D), *Trenton*
17 Sander M. Levin (D), *Springfield*
18 William S. Broomfield (R),
   *Birmingham*

## MINNESOTA

### SENATORS

David F. Durenberger (R),
   *Minneapolis*
Rudy Boschwitz (R), *Wayzata*

### REPRESENTATIVES

1 Timothy J. Penny (D), *New Richland*
2 Vin Weber (R), *Slayton*
3 Bill Frenzel (R), *Bloomington*
4 Bruce F. Vento (D), *St. Paul*
5 Martin Olav Sabo (D),
   *Minneapolis*
6 Gerry E. Sikorski (D), *Stillwater*
7 Arlan Stangeland (R), *Barnesville*
8 James L. Oberstar (D), *Chisholm*

## MISSISSIPPI

### SENATORS

John C. Stennis (D), *De Kalb*
Thad Cochran (R), *Jackson*

### REPRESENTATIVES

1 Jamie L. Whitten (D), *Charleston*

---

[15] Died April 22, 1988.
[16] Elected August 9, 1988, to fill vacancy caused by the death of Melvin Price, and took his seat August 11, 1988.

[17] Resigned March 14, 1988.
[18] Elected April 16, 1988, to fill vacancy caused by

the resignation of Charles (Buddy) Roemer, and took his seat April 26, 1988.

## MISSISSIPPI—Continued

REPRESENTATIVES—CONTINUED
2 Mike Espy (D), *Yazoo City*
3 Gillespie V. (Sonny) Montgomery
   (D), *Meridian*
4 Wayne Dowdy (D), *McComb*
5 Trent Lott (R), *Pascagoula*

## MISSOURI

SENATORS
John C. Danforth (R), *Flat*
Christopher S. (Kit) Bond (R), *Kansas City*

REPRESENTATIVES
1 William L. Clay (D), *St. Louis*
2 Jack Buechner (R), *Kirkwood*
3 Richard A. Gephardt (D), *St. Louis*
4 Ike Skelton (D), *Jefferson City*
5 Alan D. Wheat (D), *Kansas City*
6 E. Thomas Coleman (R), *Kansas City*
7 Gene Taylor (R), *Sarcoxie*
8 Bill Emerson (R), *Cape Girardeau*
9 Harold L. Volkmer (D), *Hannibal*

## MONTANA

SENATORS
John Melcher (D), *Forsyth*
Max Baucus (D), *Missoula*

REPRESENTATIVES
1 Pat Williams (D), *Helena*
2 Ron Marlenee (R), *Scobey*

## NEBRASKA

SENATORS
Edward Zorinsky (D),[19] *Omaha*
David K. Karnes (R),[20] *Omaha*
J. James Exon (D), *Lincoln*

REPRESENTATIVES
1 Douglas K. Bereuter (R), *Utica*
2 Hal Daub (R), *Omaha*
3 Virginia Smith (R), *Chappell*

## NEVADA

SENATORS
Chic Hecht (R), *Las Vegas*
Harry M. Reid (D), *Las Vegas*

REPRESENTATIVES
1 James H. Bilbray (D), *Las Vegas*
2 Barbara F. Vucanovich (R), *Reno*

## NEW HAMPSHIRE

SENATORS
Gordon J. Humphrey (R), *Chichester*
Warren B. Rudman (R), *Nashua*

REPRESENTATIVES
1 Robert C. Smith (R), *Manchester*
2 Judd Gregg (R), *Greenfield*

## NEW JERSEY

SENATORS
Bill Bradley (D), *Denville*
Frank R. Lautenberg (D), *Montclair*

REPRESENTATIVES
1 James J. Florio (D), *Pine Hill*
2 William J. Hughes (D), *Ocean City*
3 James J. Howard (D),[21] *Spring Lake Heights*
3 Frank J. Pallone (D),[22] *Long Branch*
4 Christopher H. Smith (R), *Trenton*
5 Marge Roukema (R), *Ridgewood*
6 Bernard J. Dwyer (D), *Edison*
7 Matthew J. Rinaldo (R), *Union*
8 Robert A. Roe (D), *Wayne*
9 Robert G. Torricelli (D), *New Milford*
10 Peter W. Rodino, Jr. (D), *Newark*
11 Dean A. Gallo (R), *West Orange*
12 James A. Courter (R), *Hackettstown*
13 H. James Saxton (R), *Vincentown*
14 Frank J. Guarini (D), *Jersey City*

## NEW MEXICO

SENATORS
Pete V. Domenici (R), *Albuquerque*
Jeff Bingaman (D), *Santa Fe*

REPRESENTATIVES
1 Manuel Lujan, Jr. (R), *Albuquerque*
2 Joe Skeen (R), *Picacho*
3 William B. Richardson (D), *Santa Fe*

## NEW YORK

SENATORS
Daniel P. Moynihan (D), *Pindars Corners*
Alfonse M. D'Amato (R), *Island Park*

REPRESENTATIVES
1 George J. Hochbrueckner (D), *Coram*
2 Thomas J. Downey (D), *Amityville*
3 Robert J. Mrazek (D), *Centerport*
4 Norman F. Lent (R), *East Rockaway*
5 Raymond J. McGrath (R), *Valley Stream*
6 Floyd H. Flake (D), *Queens*
7 Gary L. Ackerman (D), *Flushing*
8 James H. Scheuer (D), *Flushing*
9 Thomas J. Manton (D), *Forest Hills*
10 Charles E. Schumer (D), *Brooklyn*
11 Edolphus Towns (D), *Brooklyn*
12 Major R. Owens (D), *Brooklyn*
13 Stephen J. Solarz (D), *Brooklyn*
14 Guy V. Molinari (R), *Staten Island*
15 S. William Green (R), *New York*
16 Charles B. Rangel (D), *New York*
17 Ted Weiss (D), *New York*
18 Robert Garcia (D), *Bronx*
19 Mario Biaggi (D),[23] *Bronx*
20 Joseph J. DioGuardi (R), *Mamaroneck*
21 Hamilton Fish, Jr. (R), *Millbrook*
22 Benjamin A. Gilman (R), *Middletown*
23 Samuel S. Stratton (D), *Amsterdam*
24 Gerald B. H. Solomon (R), *Glens Falls*
25 Sherwood L. Boehlert (R), *New Hartford*
26 David O'B. Martin (R), *Canton*
27 George C. Wortley (R), *Fayetteville*
28 Matthew F. McHugh (D), *Ithaca*
29 Frank Horton (R), *Rochester*
30 Louise McIntosh Slaughter (D), *Fairport*
31 Jack F. Kemp (R), *Buffalo*
32 John J. LaFalce (D), *Buffalo*
33 Henry J. Nowak (D), *Buffalo*
34 Amory Houghton, Jr. (R), *Corning*

## NORTH CAROLINA

SENATORS
Jesse Helms (R), *Raleigh*
Terry Sanford (D), *Durham*

REPRESENTATIVES
1 Walter B. Jones (D), *Farmville*
2 Tim Valentine (D), *Nashville*
3 Martin Lancaster (D), *Goldsboro*
4 David E. Price (D), *Chapel Hill*
5 Stephen L. Neal (D), *Winston-Salem*
6 Howard Coble (R), *Greensboro*
7 Charles Rose (D), *Fayetteville*
8 W. G. (Bill) Hefner (D), *Concord*
9 J. Alex McMillan (R), *Davidson*
10 Cass Ballenger (R), *Hickory*
11 James McClure Clarke (D), *Fairview*

## NORTH DAKOTA

SENATORS
Quentin N. Burdick (R), *Fargo*
Kent Conrad (D), *Bismarck*

REPRESENTATIVE AT LARGE
Byron L. Dorgan (D), *Bismarck*

---

[19] Died March 6, 1987.
[20] Appointed March 10, 1987, to fill vacancy caused by death of Edward Zorinsky, and took his seat March 13, 1987.

[21] Died March 25, 1988.
[22] Elected November 8, 1988 to fill vacancy caused by death of James J. Howard, but was unable to be sworn in because Congress was not in session.

[23] Resigned August 8, 1988.

## OHIO

SENATORS

John Glenn, Jr. (D), *Columbus*
Howard M. Metzenbaum (D), *Cleveland*

REPRESENTATIVES

1 Thomas A. Luken (D), *Cincinnati*
2 Willis D. Gradison, Jr. (R), *Cincinnati*
3 Tony P. Hall (D), *Dayton*
4 Michael G. Oxley (R), *Findley*
5 Delbert L. Latta (R), *Bowling Green*
6 Robert McEwen (R), *Hillsboro*
7 Michael DeWine (R), *Cedarville*
8 Donald E. Lukens (R), *Middletown*
9 Marcy Kaptur (D), *Toledo*
10 Clarence E. Miller (R), *Lancaster*
11 Dennis E. Eckart (D), *Mentor*
12 John R. Kasich (R), *Westerville*
13 Donald J. Pease (D), *Oberlin*
14 Thomas C. Sawyer (D), *Akron*
15 Chalmers P. Wylie (R), *Columbus*
16 Ralph Regula (R), *Navarre*
17 James A. Traficant, Jr. (D), *Warren*
18 Douglas Applegate (D), *Steubenville*
19 Edward F. Feighan (D), *Gates Mills*
20 Mary Rose Oakar (D), *Cleveland*
21 Louis Stokes (D), *Warrensville Heights*

## OKLAHOMA

SENATORS

David L. Boren (D), *Seminole*
Don Nickles (R), *Ponca City*

REPRESENTATIVES

1 James M. Inhofe (R), *Tulsa*
2 Mike Synar (D), *Muskogee*
3 Wesley W. Watkins (D), *Ada*
4 Dave McCurdy (D), *Norman*
5 Mickey Edwards (R), *Oklahoma City*
6 Glenn English (D), *Cordell*

## OREGON

SENATORS

Mark O. Hatfield (R), *Salem*
Robert W. Packwood (R), *Portland*

REPRESENTATIVES

1 Les AuCoin (D), *Forest Grove*
2 Robert F. Smith (R), *Burns*
3 Ron Wyden (D), *Portland*
4 Peter A. DeFazio (D), *Springfield*
5 Denny Smith (R), *Salem*

## PENNSYLVANIA

SENATORS

H. John Heinz III (R), *Pittsburgh*
Arlen Specter (R), *Philadelphia*

REPRESENTATIVES

1 Thomas M. Foglietta (D), *Philadelphia*
2 William H. Gray III (D), *Philadelphia*
3 Robert A. Borski, Jr. (D), *Philadelphia*
4 Joseph P. Kolter (D), *New Brighton*
5 Richard T. Schulze (R), *Wayne*
6 Gus Yatron (D), *Reading*
7 Curt Weldon (R), *Media*
8 Peter H. Kostmayer (D), *New Hope*
9 E. G. Shuster (R), *Everett*
10 Joseph M. McDade (R), *Clarks Summit*
11 Paul E. Kanjorski (D), *Wilkes-Barre*
12 John P. Murtha, Jr. (D), *Johnstown*
13 R. Lawrence Coughlin (D), *Villanova*
14 William J. Coyne (D), *Pittsburgh*
15 Don Ritter (R), *Coopersburg*
16 Robert S. Walker (R), *East Petersburg*
17 George W. Gekas (R), *Harrisburg*
18 Doug Walgren (D), *Pittsburgh*
19 William F. Goodling (R), *Jacobus*
20 Joseph M. Gaydos (D), *McKeesport*
21 Thomas J. Ridge (R), *Erie*
22 Austin J. Murphy (D), *Monongahela*
23 William F. Clinger, Jr. (R), *Warren*

## RHODE ISLAND

SENATORS

Claiborne Pell (D), *Newport*
John H. Chafee (R), *Warwick*

REPRESENTATIVES

1 Fernand J. St Germain (D), *Woonsocket*
2 Claudine Schneider (R), *Narragansett*

## SOUTH CAROLINA

SENATORS

Strom Thurmond (R), *Columbia*
Ernest F. Hollings (D), *Charleston*

REPRESENTATIVES

1 Arthur Ravenel, Jr. (R), *Charleston*
2 Floyd Spence (R), *Lexington*
3 Butler Derrick (D), *Edgefield*
4 Liz J. Patterson (D), *Spartanburg*
5 John M. Spratt, Jr. (D), *York*
6 Robert M. (Robin) Tallon (D), *Florence*

## SOUTH DAKOTA

SENATORS

Larry Pressler (R), *Humboldt*
Thomas A. Daschle (D), *Aberdeen*

REPRESENTATIVE AT LARGE

Tim Johnson (D), *Vermillion*

## TENNESSEE

SENATORS

James R. Sasser (D), *Nashville*
Albert A. Gore, Jr. (D), *Carthage*

REPRESENTATIVES

1 James H. Quillen (R), *Kingsport*
2 John J. Duncan (R),[24] *Knoxville*
2 John J. Duncan, Jr. (R),[25] *Knoxville*
3 Marilyn Lloyd (D), *Chattanooga*
4 James Cooper (D), *Shelbyville*
5 William H. Boner (D),[26] *Nashville*
5 Robert N. Clement (D),[27] *Nashville*
6 Bart Gordon (D), *Carthage*
7 Donald K. Sundquist (R), *Memphis*
8 Edward Jones (D), *Yorkville*
9 Harold E. Ford (D), *Memphis*

## TEXAS

SENATORS

Lloyd M. Bentsen, Jr. (D), *Austin*
Phil Gramm (R), *College Station*

REPRESENTATIVES

1 Jim Chapman (D), *Sulphur Springs*
2 Charles Wilson (D), *Lufkin*
3 Steve Bartlett (R), *Dallas*
4 Ralph M. Hall (D), *Rockwall*
5 John W. Bryant (D), *Dallas*
6 Joe Barton (R), *Ennis*
7 William R. Archer, Jr. (R), *Houston*
8 Jack Fields (R), *Humble*
9 Jack B. Brooks (D), *Beaumont*
10 J. J. (Jake) Pickle (D), *Austin*
11 J. Marvin Leath (D), *Marlin*
12 James C. Wright, Jr. (D), *Fort Worth*
13 Beau Boulter (R), *Vernon*
14 Mac Sweeney (R), *Ganado*
15 Eligio (Kika) de la Garza (D), *McAllen*
16 Ronald Coleman (D), *El Paso*
17 Charles W. Stenholm (D), *Avoca*
18 Mickey Leland (D), *Houston*
19 Larry Combest (R), *Lubbock*
20 Henry B. Gonzalez (D), *San Antonio*

---

[24] Died June 21, 1988.
[25] Elected November 8, 1988 to fill vacancy caused by death of his father, John J. Duncan, but was unable

to be sworn in because Congress was not in session.
[26] Resigned October 5, 1987.
[27] Elected January 19, 1988, to fill vacancy caused

by resignation of William H. Boner, and took his seat January 25, 1988.

## TEXAS—Continued

### REPRESENTATIVES—CONTINUED

21 Lamar S. Smith (R), *San Antonio*
22 Tom DeLay (R), *Lake Jackson*
23 Albert G. Bustamante (D), *Laredo*
24 Martin Frost (D), *Dallas*
25 Michael A. Andrews (D), *Houston*
26 Richard Armey (R), *Arlington*
27 Solomon P. Ortiz (D), *Corpus Christi*

## UTAH

### SENATORS

E. J. (Jake) Garn (R), *Salt Lake City*
Orrin G. Hatch (R), *Midvale*

### REPRESENTATIVES

1 James V. Hansen (R), *Farmington*
2 Wayne Owens (D), *Salt Lake City*
3 Howard C. Nielson (R), *Provo*

## VERMONT

### SENATORS

Robert T. Stafford (R), *Rutland*
Patrick J. Leahy (D), *Burlington*

### REPRESENTATIVE AT LARGE

James M. Jeffords (R), *Rutland*

## VIRGINIA

### SENATORS

John W. Warner (R), *Middleburg*
Paul S. Trible, Jr. (R), *Richmond*

### REPRESENTATIVES

1 Herbert H. Bateman (R), *Newport News*
2 Owen B. Pickett (D), *Virginia Beach*
3 Thomas J. Bliley, Jr. (R), *Richmond*
4 Norman Sisisky (D), *Petersburg*
5 W. C. (Dan) Daniel (D),[28] *Danville*
5 L. F. Payne, Jr. (D),[29] *Wintergreen*
6 James R. Olin (D), *Roanoke*

7 D. French Slaughter, Jr. (R), *Winchester*
8 Stanford E. Parris (R), *Alexandria*
9 Frederick C. Boucher (D), *Abingdon*
10 Frank R. Wolf (R), *Vienna*

## WASHINGTON

### SENATORS

Daniel J. Evans (R), *Seattle*
Brock Adams (D), *Seattle*

### REPRESENTATIVES

1 John Miller (R), *Bainbridge Island*
2 Al Swift (D), *Bellingham*
3 Don Bonker (D), *Vancouver*
4 Sid Morrison (R), *Zillah*
5 Thomas S. Foley (D), *Spokane*
6 Norman D. Dicks (D), *Port Orchard*
7 Mike Lowry (D), *Seattle*
8 Rod D. Chandler (R), *Belleview*

## WEST VIRGINIA

### SENATORS

Robert C. Byrd (D), *Sophia*
John D. Rockefeller IV (D), *Charleston*

### REPRESENTATIVES

1 Alan B. Mollohan (D), *Fairmont*
2 Harley O. Staggers, Jr. (D), *Keyser*
3 Robert E. Wise, Jr. (D), *Charleston*
4 Nick J. Rahall II (D), *Beckley*

## WISCONSIN

### SENATORS

William Proxmire (D), *Madison*
Robert W. Kasten, Jr. (R), *Milwaukee*

### REPRESENTATIVES

1 Les Aspin (D), *Racine*

2 Robert W. Kastenmeier (D), *Sun Prairie*
3 Steven Gunderson (R), *Osseo*
4 Gerald D. Kleczka (D), *Milwaukee*
5 Jim Moody (D), *Milwaukee*
6 Thomas E. Petri (R), *Fond du Lac*
7 David R. Obey (D), *Wausau*
8 Toby A. Roth (R), *Appleton*
9 F. James Sensenbrenner, Jr. (R), *Menomonee Falls*

## WYOMING

### SENATORS

Malcolm Wallop (R), *Big Horn*
Alan K. Simpson (R), *Cody*

### REPRESENTATIVE AT LARGE

Richard B. Cheney (R), *Casper*

## AMERICAN SAMOA

### DELEGATE

Fofó I. F. Sunia (D),[30] *Pago Pago*

## COMMONWEALTH OF PUERTO RICO

### RESIDENT COMMISSIONER

Jaime B. Fuster (D), *Rio Piedras*

## DISTRICT OF COLUMBIA

### DELEGATE

Walter E. Fauntroy (D), *Washington, D.C.*

## GUAM

### DELEGATE

Ben Garrido Blaz (R), *Agana*

## VIRGIN ISLANDS

### DELEGATE

Ron de Lugo (D), *St. Thomas*

---

[28] Died January 23, 1988.
[29] Elected June 14, 1988, to fill vacancy caused by death of W. C. (Dan) Daniel, and took his seat June 21, 1988.

[30] Resigned September 6, 1988; vacancy throughout remainder of the Congress.

# 101ST CONGRESS

## JANUARY 3, 1989, TO JANUARY 3, 1991

FIRST SESSION—JANUARY 3, 1989, TO NOVEMBER 22, 1989
SECOND SESSION—JANUARY 23, 1990, TO OCTOBER 28, 1990

J. Danforth Quayle
Vice President

James C. Wright, Jr.
Speaker

### Senate
Democrats 55 — Republicans 45

VICE PRESIDENT OF THE UNITED STATES—GEORGE BUSH,[1] of Texas; J. DANFORTH QUAYLE,[2] of Indiana

PRESIDENT PRO TEMPORE OF THE SENATE—ROBERT C. BYRD,[3] of West Virginia

SECRETARY OF THE SENATE—WALTER J. STEWART,[4] of Washington, D.C.

SERGEANT AT ARMS OF THE SENATE—HENRY KUUALOHA GIUGNI,[5] of Hawaii

CHAPLAIN OF THE SENATE—REV. RICHARD C. HALVERSON,[6] LL.D., D.D.

MAJORITY FLOOR LEADER—GEORGE J. MITCHELL,[7] of Maine

DEMOCRATIC WHIP—ALAN M. CRANSTON, of California

REPUBLICAN FLOOR LEADER—ROBERT J. DOLE, of Kansas

ASSISTANT REPUBLICAN LEADER—ALAN K. SIMPSON, of Wyoming

### House of Representatives
Democrats 260 — Republicans 175

SPEAKER OF THE HOUSE—JAMES C. WRIGHT, JR.,[8] of Texas; THOMAS S. FOLEY,[9] of Washington

CLERK OF THE HOUSE—DONNALD K. ANDERSON,[10] of California

SERGEANT AT ARMS OF THE HOUSE—JACK RUSS,[11] of Maryland

DOORKEEPER OF THE HOUSE—JAMES T. MOLLOY,[12] of New York

POSTMASTER OF THE HOUSE—ROBERT V. ROTA,[13] of Pennsylvania

CHAPLAIN OF THE HOUSE—REV. JAMES DAVID FORD,[14] D.D.

MAJORITY LEADER—THOMAS S. FOLEY,[15] of Washington; RICHARD A. GEPHARDT,[16] of Missouri

MAJORITY WHIP—ANTHONY L. COELHO,[17] of California; WILLIAM H. GRAY III,[18] of Pennsylvania

REPUBLICAN LEADER—ROBERT H. MICHEL, of Illinois

REPUBLICAN WHIP—RICHARD B. CHENEY,[19] of Wyoming; NEWT GINGRICH,[20] of Georgia

---

## ALABAMA

### SENATORS
Howell T. Heflin (D), *Tuscumbia*
Richard C. Shelby (D), *Tuscaloosa*

### REPRESENTATIVES
1 H. L. (Sonny) Callahan (R), *Mobile*
2 William L. Dickinson (R), *Montgomery*
3 J. Glen Browder (D),[21] *Jacksonville*
4 Tom Bevill (D), *Jasper*
5 Ronnie G. Flippo (D), *Florence*
6 Ben Erdreich (D), *Birmingham*
7 Claude Harris (D), *Tuscaloosa*

## ALASKA

### SENATORS
Theodore F. Stevens (R), *Girdwood*
Frank H. Murkowski (R), *Fairbanks*

### REPRESENTATIVE AT LARGE
Donald E. Young (R), *Fort Yukon*

## ARIZONA

### SENATORS
Dennis DeConcini (D), *Tucson*
John S. McCain III (R), *Phoenix*

### REPRESENTATIVES
1 John J. Rhodes III (R), *Mesa*
2 Morris K. Udall (D), *Tucson*
3 Bob Stump (R), *Tolleson*
4 Jon Kyl (R), *Phoenix*
5 Jim Kolbe (R), *Tucson*

## ARKANSAS

### SENATORS
Dale Bumpers (D), *Charleston*
David H. Pryor (D), *Little Rock*

### REPRESENTATIVES
1 William V. Alexander, Jr. (D), *Osceola*
2 Tommy F. Robinson (D),[22] *Jacksonville*
3 John Paul Hammerschmidt (R), *Harrison*

---

[1] Term expired at noon on January 20, 1989.
[2] Term began at noon on January 20, 1989.
[3] Elected January 3, 1989.
[4] Reelected January 3, 1989.
[5] Reelected January 3, 1989.
[6] Reelected January 3, 1989.
[7] Elected November 29, 1988.
[8] Reelected January 3, 1989; resigned as Speaker on June 6, 1989; resigned from the House on June 30, 1989.

[9] Elected June 6, 1989.
[10] Reelected January 3, 1989.
[11] Reelected January 3, 1989.
[12] Reelected January 3, 1989.
[13] Reelected January 3, 1989.
[14] Reelected January 3, 1989.
[15] Elected Speaker on June 6, 1989.
[16] Elected June 14, 1989.
[17] Resigned from the House on June 15, 1989.

[18] Elected June 14, 1989.
[19] Elected December 5, 1988; resigned from the House on March 17, 1989.
[20] Elected March 22, 1989.
[21] Elected April 4, 1989, to fill vacancy caused by death of Representative-elect William F. Nichols, and took his seat April 18, 1989.
[22] Changed party affiliation to Republican, July 28, 1989.

## ARKANSAS—Continued

REPRESENTATIVES—CONTINUED

4 Beryl F. Anthony, Jr. (D), *El Dorado*

## CALIFORNIA

SENATORS

Alan Cranston (D), *Los Angeles*
Pete Wilson (R), *San Diego*

REPRESENTATIVES

1 Douglas H. Bosco (D), *Occidental*
2 Wally Herger (R), *Rio Oso*
3 Robert T. Matsui (D), *Sacramento*
4 Vic Fazio (D), *West Sacramento*
5 Nancy Pelosi (D), *San Francisco*
6 Barbara Boxer (D), *Greenbrae*
7 George Miller (D), *Martinez*
8 Ronald V. Dellums (D), *Oakland*
9 Fortney H. (Pete) Stark, Jr. (D), *Oakland*
10 Don Edwards (D), *San Jose*
11 Tom Lantos (D), *San Mateo*
12 Thomas J. Campbell (R), *Stanford*
13 Norman Y. Mineta (D), *San Jose*
14 Norman D. Shumway (R), *Stockton*
15 Tony Coelho (D),[23] *Merced*
15 Gary A. Condit (D),[24] *Ceres*
16 Leon E. Panetta (D), *Carmel Valley*
17 Charles Pashayan, Jr. (R), *Fresno*
18 Richard H. Lehman (D), *Fresno*
19 Robert J. Lagomarsino (R), *Ventura*
20 William M. Thomas (R), *Bakersfield*
21 Elton W. Gallegly (R), *Simi Valley*
22 Carlos J. Moorhead (R), *Glendale*
23 Anthony C. Beilenson (D), *Los Angeles*
24 Henry A. Waxman (D), *Los Angeles*
25 Edward R. Roybal (D), *Pasadena*
26 Howard L. Berman (D), *Panorama City*
27 Mel Levine (D), *Los Angeles*
28 Julian C. Dixon (D), *Culver City*
29 Augustus F. Hawkins (D), *Los Angeles*
30 Matthew G. Martinez, Jr. (D), *Montebello*
31 Mervyn M. Dymally (D), *Compton*
32 Glenn M. Anderson (D), *San Pedro*
33 David Dreier (R), *La Verne*
34 Esteban Edward Torres (D), *La Puente*
35 Jerry Lewis (R), *Redlands*
36 George E. Brown, Jr. (D), *Riverside*
37 Alfred A. McCandless (R), *La Quinta*
38 Robert K. Dornan (R), *Garden Grove*
39 William E. Dannemeyer (R), *Fullerton*
40 C. Christopher Cox (R), *Newport Beach*
41 Bill Lowery (R), *San Diego*
42 Dana Rohrabacher (R), *Lomita*
43 Ron Packard (R), *Carlsbad*
44 Jim Bates (D), *San Diego*
45 Duncan L. Hunter (R), *Coronado*

## COLORADO

SENATORS

William L. Armstrong (R), *Aurora*
Timothy E. Wirth (D), *Boulder*

REPRESENTATIVES

1 Patricia Schroeder (D), *Denver*
2 David E. Skaggs (D), *Boulder*
3 Ben Nighthorse Campbell (D), *Ignacio*
4 Hank Brown (R), *Greeley*
5 Joel Hefley (R), *Colorado Springs*
6 Dan Schaefer (R), *Lakewood*

## CONNECTICUT

SENATORS

Christopher J. Dodd (D), *East Haddam*
Joseph I. Lieberman (D), *New Haven*

REPRESENTATIVES

1 Barbara B. Kennelly (D), *Hartford*
2 Samuel Gejdenson (D), *Bozrah*
3 Bruce A. Morrison (D), *Hamden*
4 Christopher Shays (R), *Stamford*
5 John G. Rowland (R), *Waterbury*
6 Nancy L. Johnson (R), *New Britain*

## DELAWARE

SENATORS

William V. Roth, Jr. (R), *Wilmington*
Joseph R. Biden, Jr. (D), *Wilmington*

REPRESENTATIVE AT LARGE

Thomas R. Carper (D), *Wilmington*

## FLORIDA

SENATORS

Bob Graham (D), *Miami Lakes*
Connie Mack (R), *Cape Coral*

REPRESENTATIVES

1 Earl Hutto (D), *Panama City*
2 Bill Grant (D),[25] *Madison*
3 Charles E. Bennett (D), *Jacksonville*
4 Craig T. James (R), *Deland*
5 Bill McCollum (R), *Longwood*
6 Clifford B. Stearns (R), *Ocala*
7 Sam M. Gibbons (D), *Tampa*
8 C. W. Bill Young (R), *St. Petersburg*
9 Michael Bilirakis (R), *Palm Harbor*
10 Andrew P. Ireland (R), *Winter Haven*
11 Bill Nelson (D), *Melbourne*
12 Tom Lewis (R), *North Palm Beach*
13 Porter J. Goss (R), *Sanibel*
14 Harry A. Johnston II (D), *West Palm Beach*
15 Clay Shaw (R), *Fort Lauderdale*
16 Lawrence J. Smith (D), *Hollywood*
17 William Lehman (D), *Biscayne Park*
18 Claude D. Pepper (D),[26] *Miami*
18 Ileana Ros-Lehtinen (R),[27] *Miami*
19 Dante B. Fascell (D), *Miami*

## GEORGIA

SENATORS

Sam Nunn (D), *Perry*
Wyche Fowler, Jr. (D), *Atlanta*

REPRESENTATIVES

1 R. Lindsay Thomas (D), *Statesboro*
2 Charles F. Hatcher (D), *Albany*
3 Richard B. Ray (D), *Perry*
4 Ben Jones (D), *Covington*
5 John R. Lewis (D), *Atlanta*
6 Newt Gingrich (R), *Jonesboro*
7 George (Buddy) Darden (D), *Marietta*
8 J. Roy Rowland (D), *Dublin*
9 Edgar L. Jenkins (D), *Jasper*
10 D. Douglas Barnard, Jr. (D), *Augusta*

## HAWAII

SENATORS

Daniel K. Inouye (D), *Honolulu*
Spark M. Matsunaga (D),[28] *Kailua*
Daniel K. Akaka (D),[29] *Honolulu*

REPRESENTATIVES

1 Patricia F. Saiki (R), *Honolulu*
2 Daniel K. Akaka (D),[30] *Honolulu*
2 Patsy T. Mink (D),[31] *Honolulu*

[23] Resigned June 15, 1989.
[24] Elected September 12, 1989, to fill vacancy caused by resignation of Tony Coelho, and took his seat September 20, 1989.
[25] Changed party affiliation to Republican, February 21, 1989.
[26] Died May 30, 1989.

[27] Elected August 29, 1989, to fill vacancy caused by death of Claude D. Pepper, and took her seat September 6, 1989.
[28] Died April 15, 1990.
[29] Appointed April 28, 1990, to fill vacancy caused by death of Spark M. Matsunaga, and took his seat May 16, 1990.

[30] Resigned May 16, 1990, having been appointed to the Senate.
[31] Elected September 22, 1990, to fill vacancy caused by resignation of Daniel K. Akaka, and took her seat September 27, 1990.

## IDAHO

SENATORS

James A. McClure (R), *McCall*
Steven D. Symms (R), *Caldwell*

REPRESENTATIVES

1 Larry Craig (R), *Boise*
2 Richard Stallings (D), *Rexburg*

## ILLINOIS

SENATORS

Alan J. Dixon (D), *Belleville*
Paul M. Simon (D), *Makanda*

REPRESENTATIVES

1 Charles A. Hayes (D), *Chicago*
2 Gus Savage (D), *Chicago*
3 Martin A. Russo (D), *South Holland*
4 George E. Sangmeister (D), *Mokena*
5 William O. Lipinski (D), *Chicago*
6 Henry J. Hyde (R), *Bensenville*
7 Cardiss Collins (D), *Chicago*
8 Dan Rostenkowski (D), *Chicago*
9 Sidney R. Yates (D), *Chicago*
10 John Edward Porter (R), *Wilmette*
11 Frank Annunzio (D), *Chicago*
12 Philip M. Crane (R), *Mount Prospect*
13 Harris W. Fawell (R), *Naperville*
14 J. Dennis Hastert (R), *Yorkville*
15 Edward R. Madigan (R), *Lincoln*
16 Lynn Martin (R), *Loves Park*
17 Lane A. Evans (D), *Rock Island*
18 Robert H. Michel (R), *Peoria*
19 Terry L. Bruce (D), *Olney*
20 Richard J. Durbin (D), *Springfield*
21 Jerry F. Costello (D), *Belleville*
22 Glenn Poshard (D), *Carterville*

## INDIANA

SENATORS

Richard G. Lugar (R), *Indianapolis*
J. Danforth Quayle (R),[32] *Huntington*
Dan R. Coats (R),[33] *Indianapolis*

REPRESENTATIVES

1 Peter J. Visclosky (D), *Merrillville*
2 Philip R. Sharp (D), *Muncie*
3 John P. Hiler (R), *La Porte*
4 Dan R. Coats (R),[34] *Indianapolis*
4 Jill L. Long (D),[35] *Larwill*
5 Jim Jontz (D), *Monticello*
6 Dan Burton (R), *Indianapolis*
7 John T. Myers (R), *Covington*
8 Frank McCloskey (D), *Bloomington*
9 Lee H. Hamilton (D), *Nashville*
10 Andrew Jacobs, Jr. (D), *Indianapolis*

## IOWA

SENATORS

Charles E. Grassley (R), *New Hartford*
Tom Harkin (D), *Cumming*

REPRESENTATIVES

1 James A. S. Leach (R), *Davenport*
2 Thomas J. Tauke (R), *Dubuque*
3 David R. Nagle (D), *Cedar Falls*
4 Neal Smith (D), *Altoona*
5 Jim Ross Lightfoot (R), *Shenandoah*
6 Fred Grandy (R), *Sioux City*

## KANSAS

SENATORS

Robert J. Dole (R), *Russell*
Nancy L. Kassebaum (R), *Burdick*

REPRESENTATIVES

1 Pat Roberts (R), *Dodge City*
2 Jim Slattery (D), *Topeka*
3 Jan Meyers (R), *Overland Park*
4 Daniel R. Glickman (D), *Wichita*
5 Bob Whittaker (R), *Augusta*

## KENTUCKY

SENATORS

Wendell H. Ford (D), *Owensboro*
Mitch McConnell (R), *Louisville*

REPRESENTATIVES

1 Carroll Hubbard, Jr. (D), *Mayfield*
2 William H. Natcher (D), *Bowling Green*
3 Romano L. Mazzoli (D), *Louisville*
4 Jim Bunning (R), *Southgate*
5 Harold Rogers (R), *Somerset*
6 Larry J. Hopkins (R), *Lexington*
7 Carl C. Perkins (D), *Leburn*

## LOUISIANA

SENATORS

J. Bennett Johnston, Jr. (D), *Shreveport*
John B. Breaux (D), *Crowley*

REPRESENTATIVES

1 Robert L. Livingston (R), *Metairie*
2 Corinne C. (Lindy) Boggs (D), *New Orleans*
3 W. J. (Billy) Tauzin (D), *Thibodaux*
4 James O. McCrery III (R), *Shreveport*
5 Thomas J. (Jerry) Huckaby (D), *Ringgold*
6 Richard H. Baker (R), *Baton Rouge*
7 James A. Hayes (D), *Lafayette*
8 Clyde C. Holloway (R), *Forest Hill*

## MAINE

SENATORS

William S. Cohen (R), *Bangor*
George J. Mitchell (D), *Portland*

REPRESENTATIVES

1 Joseph E. Brennan (D), *Portland*
2 Olympia J. Snowe (R), *Auburn*

## MARYLAND

SENATORS

Paul S. Sarbanes (D), *Baltimore*
Barbara A. Mikulski (D), *Baltimore*

REPRESENTATIVES

1 Roy Dyson (D), *Great Mills*
2 Helen Delich Bentley (R), *Lutherville*
3 Benjamin L. Cardin (D), *Baltimore*
4 C. Thomas McMillen (D), *Crofton*
5 Steny H. Hoyer (D), *Forestville*
6 Beverly B. Byron (D), *Frederick*
7 Kweisi Mfume (D), *Baltimore*
8 Constance A. Morella (R), *Bethesda*

## MASSACHUSETTS

SENATORS

Edward M. Kennedy (D), *Boston*
John F. Kerry (D), *Boston*

REPRESENTATIVES

1 Silvio O. Conte (R), *Pittsfield*
2 Richard E. Neal (D), *Springfield*
3 Joseph D. Early (D), *Worcester*
4 Barney Frank (D), *Newton*
5 Chester G. Atkins (D), *Concord*
6 Nicholas Mavroules (D), *Peabody*
7 Edward J. Markey (D), *Malden*
8 Joseph P. Kennedy II (D), *Brighton*
9 John Joseph Moakley (D), *South Boston*
10 Gerry E. Studds (D), *Cohasset*
11 Brian J. Donnelly (D), *Boston*

## MICHIGAN

SENATORS

Donald W. Riegle, Jr. (D), *Flint*
Carl Levin (D), *Detroit*

REPRESENTATIVES

1 John Conyers, Jr. (D), *Detroit*
2 Carl D. Pursell (R), *Plymouth*
3 Howard E. Wolpe (D), *Lansing*
4 Fred Upton (R), *St. Joseph*
5 Paul B. Henry (R), *Grand Rapids*
6 Bob Carr (D), *East Lansing*
7 Dale E. Kildee (D), *Flint*
8 Bob Traxler (D), *Bay City*
9 Guy A. Vander Jagt (R), *Luther*

---

[32] Resigned January 3, 1989, having been elected Vice President.
[33] Appointed December 27, 1988, to fill vacancy caused by resignation of J. Danforth Quayle, and took his seat January 3, 1989.

[34] Resigned January 3, 1989, having been appointed to the Senate.
[35] Elected March 28, 1989, to fill vacancy caused by resignation of Dan R. Coats, and took her seat April 10, 1989.

## MICHIGAN—Continued

### REPRESENTATIVES—CONTINUED

10 Bill Schuette (R), *Sanford*
11 Robert W. Davis (R), *Gaylord*
12 David E. Bonior (D), *Mount Clemens*
13 George W. Crockett, Jr. (D), *Detroit*
14 Dennis M. Hertel (D), *Harper Woods*
15 William D. Ford (D), *Taylor*
16 John D. Dingell, Jr. (D), *Trenton*
17 Sander M. Levin (D), *Southfield*
18 William S. Broomfield (R), *Birmingham*

## MINNESOTA

### SENATORS

David F. Durenberger (R), *Minneapolis*
Rudy Boschwitz (R), *Plymouth*

### REPRESENTATIVES

1 Timothy J. Penny (D), *New Richland*
2 Vin Weber (R), *North Mankato*
3 Bill Frenzel (R), *Golden Valley*
4 Bruce F. Vento (D), *St. Paul*
5 Martin Olav Sabo (D), *Minneapolis*
6 Gerry Sikorski (D), *Stillwater*
7 Arlan Stangeland (R), *Barnesville*
8 James L. Oberstar (D), *Chisholm*

## MISSISSIPPI

### SENATORS

Thad Cochran (R), *Jackson*
Trent Lott (R), *Pascagoula*

### REPRESENTATIVES

1 Jamie L. Whitten (D), *Charleston*
2 Mike Espy (D), *Yazoo City*
3 Gillespie V. (Sonny) Montgomery (D), *Meridian*
4 Michael Parker (D), *Brookhaven*
5 Larkin I. Smith (R),[36] *Gulfport*
5 Gary E. (Gene) Taylor (D),[37] *Bay St. Louis*

## MISSOURI

### SENATORS

John C. Danforth (R), *Newburg*
Christopher S. (Kit) Bond (R), *Mexico*

### REPRESENTATIVES

1 William L. Clay (D), *St. Louis*
2 Jack Buechner (R), *St. Louis*
3 Richard A. Gephardt (D), *St. Louis*
4 Ike Skelton (D), *Lexington*

5 Alan D. Wheat (D), *Kansas City*
6 E. Thomas Coleman (R), *Gladstone*
7 Melton D. Hancock (R), *Springfield*
8 Bill Emerson (R), *Cape Girardeau*
9 Harold L. Volkmer (D), *Hannibal*

## MONTANA

### SENATORS

Max Baucus (D), *Missoula*
Conrad Burns (R), *Billings*

### REPRESENTATIVES

1 Pat Williams (D), *Helena*
2 Ron Marlenee (R), *Scobey*

## NEBRASKA

### SENATORS

J. James Exon (D), *Lincoln*
J. Robert Kerrey (D), *Omaha*

### REPRESENTATIVES

1 Douglas K. Bereuter (R), *Utica*
2 Peter D. Hoagland (D), *Omaha*
3 Virginia Smith (R), *Chappell*

## NEVADA

### SENATORS

Harry M. Reid (D), *Searchlight*
Richard H. Bryan (D), *Las Vegas*

### REPRESENTATIVES

1 James H. Bilbray (D), *Las Vegas*
2 Barbara F. Vucanovich (R), *Reno*

## NEW HAMPSHIRE

### SENATORS

Gordon J. Humphrey (R),[38] *Chichester*
Robert C. Smith (R),[39] *Tuftonboro*
Warren B. Rudman (R), *Hollis*

### REPRESENTATIVES

1 Robert C. Smith (R),[40] *Tuftonboro*
2 Charles G. Douglas III (R), *Concord*

## NEW JERSEY

### SENATORS

Bill Bradley (D), *Denville*
Frank R. Lautenberg (D), *Secaucus*

### REPRESENTATIVES

1 James J. Florio (D),[41] *Gloucester Township*
1 Robert E. Andrews (D),[42] *Bellmawr*
2 William J. Hughes (D), *Ocean City*

3 Frank Pallone, Jr. (D), *Long Branch*
4 Christopher H. Smith (R), *Hamilton*
5 Marge Roukema (R), *Ridgewood*
6 Bernard J. Dwyer (D), *Edison*
7 Matthew J. Rinaldo (R), *Union*
8 Robert A. Roe (D), *Wayne*
9 Robert G. Torricelli (D), *Englewood*
10 Donald M. Payne (D), *Newark*
11 Dean A. Gallo (R), *Parsippany*
12 James A. Courter (R), *Hackettstown*
13 H. James Saxton (R), *Vincentown*
14 Frank J. Guarini (D), *Jersey City*

## NEW MEXICO

### SENATORS

Pete V. Domenici (R), *Albuquerque*
Jeff Bingaman (D), *Albuquerque*

### REPRESENTATIVES

1 Steven H. Schiff (R), *Albuquerque*
2 Joe Skeen (R), *Picacho*
3 William B. Richardson (D), *Tesuque*

## NEW YORK

### SENATORS

Daniel P. Moynihan (D), *Pindars Corners*
Alfonse M. D'Amato (R), *Island Park*

### REPRESENTATIVES

1 George J. Hochbrueckner (D), *Coram*
2 Thomas J. Downey (D), *Amityville*
3 Robert J. Mrazek (D), *Huntington*
4 Norman F. Lent (R), *East Rockaway*
5 Raymond J. McGrath (R), *Valley Stream*
6 Floyd H. Flake (D), *Rosedale*
7 Gary L. Ackerman (D), *Jamaica*
8 James H. Scheuer (D), *Douglaston*
9 Thomas J. Manton (D), *Sunnyside Queens*
10 Charles E. Schumer (D), *Brooklyn*
11 Edolphus Towns (D), *Brooklyn*
12 Major R. Owens (D), *Brooklyn*
13 Stephen J. Solarz (D), *Brooklyn*
14 Guy V. Molinari (R),[43] *Staten Island*
14 Susan Molinari (R),[44] *Staten Island*
15 S. William Green (R), *New York*
16 Charles B. Rangel (D), *New York*
17 Ted Weiss (D), *New York*

---

[36] Died August 13, 1989.
[37] Elected October 17, 1989, to fill vacancy caused by death of Larkin I. Smith, and took his seat October 24, 1989.
[38] Resigned December 4, 1990.
[39] Elected November 6, 1990; sworn in December 7, 1990, to fill vacancy caused by resignation of Gordon

J. Humphrey.
[40] Resigned December 7, 1990, having been elected to the Senate; vacancy throughout remainder of Congress.
[41] Resigned January 16, 1990.
[42] Elected by special election, November 6, 1990, to fill vacancy caused by resignation of James J. Florio;

elected at the same time to the One Hundred Second Congress.
[43] Resigned January 1, 1990.
[44] Elected March 20, 1990, to fill vacancy caused by the resignation of her father, Guy V. Molinari, and took her seat March 27, 1990.

18 Robert Garcia (D),[45] *Bronx*
18 José E. Serrano (D),[46] *Bronx*
19 Eliot L. Engel (D), *Bronx*
20 Nita M. Lowey (D), *Rye*
21 Hamilton Fish, Jr. (R), *Millbrook*
22 Benjamin A. Gilman (R), *Middletown*
23 Michael R. McNulty (D), *Green Island*
24 Gerald B. H. Solomon (R), *Glens Falls*
25 Sherwood L. Boehlert (R), *New Hartford*
26 David O'B. Martin (R), *Canton*
27 James T. Walsh (R), *Syracuse*
28 Matthew F. McHugh (D), *Ithaca*
29 Frank Horton (R), *Rochester*
30 Louise M. Slaughter (D), *Fairport*
31 L. William Paxon (R), *East Aurora*
32 John J. LaFalce (D), *Tonawanda*
33 Henry J. Nowak (D), *Buffalo*
34 Amory Houghton, Jr. (R), *Corning*

## NORTH CAROLINA

### SENATORS
Jesse Helms (R), *Raleigh*
Terry Sanford (D), *Durham*

### REPRESENTATIVES
1 Walter B. Jones (D), *Farmville*
2 Tim Valentine (D), *Nashville*
3 H. Martin Lancaster (D), *Goldsboro*
4 David E. Price (D), *Chapel Hill*
5 Stephen L. Neal (D), *Winston-Salem*
6 Howard Coble (R), *Greensboro*
7 Charles Rose (D), *Fayetteville*
8 W. G. (Bill) Hefner (D), *Concord*
9 J. Alex McMillan (R), *Charlotte*
10 Cass Ballenger (R), *Hickory*
11 James McClure Clarke (D), *Fairview*

## NORTH DAKOTA

### SENATORS
Quentin M. Burdick (D), *Fargo*
Kent Conrad (D), *Bismarck*

### REPRESENTATIVE AT LARGE
Byron L. Dorgan (D), *Bismarck*

## OHIO

### SENATORS
John Glenn, Jr. (D), *Columbus*
Howard M. Metzenbaum (D), *Lyndhurst*

### REPRESENTATIVES
1 Thomas A. Luken (D), *Cincinnati*
2 Willis D. Gradison, Jr. (R), *Cincinnati*
3 Tony P. Hall (D), *Dayton*
4 Michael G. Oxley (R), *Findlay*
5 Paul E. Gillmor (R), *Port Clinton*
6 Robert McEwen (R), *Hillsboro*
7 Michael DeWine (R), *Cedarville*
8 Donald E. Lukens (R),[47] *Middletown*
9 Marcy Kaptur (D), *Toledo*
10 Clarence E. Miller (R), *Lancaster*
11 Dennis E. Eckart (D), *Mentor*
12 John R. Kasich (R), *Westerville*
13 Donald J. Pease (D), *Oberlin*
14 Thomas C. Sawyer (D), *Akron*
15 Chalmers P. Wylie (R), *Columbus*
16 Ralph Regula (R), *Navarre*
17 James A. Traficant, Jr. (D), *Poland*
18 Douglas Applegate (D), *Steubenville*
19 Edward F. Feighan (D), *Lakewood*
20 Mary Rose Oakar (D), *Cleveland*
21 Louis Stokes (D), *Shaker Heights*

## OKLAHOMA

### SENATORS
David L. Boren (D), *Seminole*
Don Nickles (R), *Ponca City*

### REPRESENTATIVES
1 James M. Inhofe (R), *Tulsa*
2 Mike Synar (D), *Muskogee*
3 Wesley W. Watkins (D), *Ada*
4 Dave McCurdy (D), *Norman*
5 Mickey Edwards (R), *Oklahoma City*
6 Glenn English (D), *Cordell*

## OREGON

### SENATORS
Mark O. Hatfield (R), *Tigard*
Robert W. Packwood (R), *Portland*

### REPRESENTATIVES
1 Les AuCoin (D), *Portland*
2 Robert F. Smith (R), *Burns*
3 Ron Wyden (D), *Portland*
4 Peter A. DeFazio (D), *Springfield*
5 Denny Smith (R), *Salem*

## PENNSYLVANIA

### SENATORS
H. John Heinz III (R), *Pittsburgh*
Arlen Specter (R), *Philadelphia*

### REPRESENTATIVES
1 Thomas M. Foglietta (D), *Philadelphia*
2 William H. Gray III (D), *Philadelphia*
3 Robert A. Borski, Jr. (D), *Philadelphia*
4 Joseph P. Kolter (D), *New Brighton*
5 Richard T. Schulze (R), *Paoli*
6 Gus Yatron (D), *Reading*
7 Curt Weldon (R), *Aston*
8 Peter H. Kostmayer (D), *Solebury*
9 E. G. Shuster (R), *Everett*
10 Joseph M. McDade (R), *Clarks Summit*
11 Paul E. Kanjorski (D), *Nanticoke*
12 John P. Murtha, Jr. (D), *Johnstown*
13 R. Lawrence Coughlin (R), *Plymouth Meeting*
14 William J. Coyne (D), *Pittsburgh*
15 Don Ritter (R), *Coopersburg*
16 Robert S. Walker (R), *East Petersburg*
17 George W. Gekas (R), *Harrisburg*
18 Doug Walgren (D), *Mount Lebanon*
19 William F. Goodling (R), *Jacobus*
20 Joseph M. Gaydos (D), *McKeesport*
21 Thomas J. Ridge (R), *Erie*
22 Austin J. Murphy (D), *Monongahela*
23 William F. Clinger, Jr. (R), *Warren*

## RHODE ISLAND

### SENATORS
Claiborne Pell (D), *Newport*
John H. Chafee (R), *Warwick*

### REPRESENTATIVES
1 Ronald K. Machtley (R), *Portsmouth*
2 Claudine Schneider (R), *Narragansett*

## SOUTH CAROLINA

### SENATORS
Strom Thurmond (R), *Aiken*
Ernest F. Hollings (D), *Charleston*

### REPRESENTATIVES
1 Arthur Ravenel, Jr. (R), *Mount Pleasant*
2 Floyd Spence (R), *Lexington*
3 Butler Derrick (D), *Edgefield*
4 Liz J. Patterson (D), *Spartanburg*
5 John M. Spratt, Jr. (D), *York*
6 Robert M. (Robin) Tallon (D), *Florence*

## SOUTH DAKOTA

### SENATORS
Larry Pressler (R), *Humboldt*
Thomas A. Daschle (D), *Aberdeen*

### REPRESENTATIVE AT LARGE
Tim Johnson (R), *Vermillion*

## TENNESSEE

### SENATORS
James R. Sasser (D), *Nashville*
Albert A. Gore, Jr. (D), *Carthage*

---

[45] Resigned January 7, 1990.
[46] Elected March 20, 1990, to fill vacancy caused by the resignation of Robert Garcia, and took his seat March 28, 1990.
[47] Resigned October 24, 1990.

## TENNESSEE—Continued
### REPRESENTATIVES
1 James H. Quillen (R), *Kingsport*
2 John J. Duncan (R), *Knoxville*
3 Marilyn Lloyd (D), *Chattanooga*
4 James Cooper (D), *Shelbyville*
5 Robert N. Clement (D), *Nashville*
6 Bart Gordon (D), *Murfreesboro*
7 Donald K. Sundquist (R), *Memphis*
8 John S. Tanner (D), *Union City*
9 Harold E. Ford (D), *Memphis*

## TEXAS
### SENATORS
Lloyd M. Bentsen, Jr. (D), *Star County*
Phil Gramm (R), *College Station*
### REPRESENTATIVES
1 Jim Chapman (D), *Sulphur Springs*
2 Charles Wilson (D), *Lufkin*
3 Steve Bartlett (R), *Dallas*
4 Ralph M. Hall (D), *Rockwall*
5 John W. Bryant (D), *Dallas*
6 Joe Barton (R), *Ennis*
7 William R. Archer, Jr. (R), *Houston*
8 Jack Fields (R), *Humble*
9 Jack B. Brooks (D), *Beaumont*
10 J. J. (Jake) Pickle (D), *Austin*
11 J. Marvin Leath (D), *Waco*
12 James C. Wright, Jr. (D),[48] *Fort Worth*
12 Preston M. (Pete) Geren III (D),[49] *Fort Worth*
13 William Sarpalius (D), *Amarillo*
14 Gregory H. Laughlin (D), *West Columbia*
15 Eligio (Kika) de la Garza (D), *McAllen*
16 Ronald Coleman (D), *El Paso*
17 Charles W. Stenholm (D), *Avoca*
18 Mickey Leland (D),[50] *Houston*
18 Craig A. Washington (D),[51] *Houston*
19 Larry Combest (R), *Lubbock*
20 Henry B. Gonzalez (D), *San Antonio*
21 Lamar S. Smith (R), *San Antonio*
22 Tom DeLay (R), *Sugar Land*
23 Albert G. Bustamante (D), *San Antonio*
24 Martin Frost (D), *Dallas*
25 Michael A. Andrews (D), *Houston*
26 Richard K. Armey (R), *Copper Canyon*
27 Solomon P. Ortiz (D), *Corpus Christi*

## UTAH
### SENATORS
E. J. (Jake) Garn (R), *Salt Lake City*
Orrin G. Hatch (R), *Salt Lake City*
### REPRESENTATIVES
1 James V. Hansen (R), *Farmington*
2 Wayne Owens (D), *Salt Lake City*
3 Howard C. Nielson (R), *Provo*

## VERMONT
### SENATORS
Patrick J. Leahy (D), *Burlington*
James M. Jeffords (R), *Shrewsbury*
### REPRESENTATIVE AT LARGE
Peter P. Smith (R), *Middlesex*

## VIRGINIA
### SENATORS
John W. Warner (R), *Middleburg*
Charles S. Robb (D), *McLean*
### REPRESENTATIVES
1 Herbert H. Bateman (R), *Newport News*
2 Owen B. Pickett (D), *Virginia Beach*
3 Thomas J. Bliley, Jr. (R), *Richmond*
4 Norman Sisisky (D), *Petersburg*
5 L. F. Payne, Jr. (D), *Nellysford*
6 James R. Olin (D), *Roanoke*
7 D. French Slaughter, Jr. (R), *Culpeper*
8 Stanford E. Parris (R), *Alexandria*
9 Frederick C. Boucher (D), *Abingdon*
10 Frank R. Wolf (R), *Vienna*

## WASHINGTON
### SENATORS
Brock Adams (D), *Seattle*
Slade Gorton III (R), *Seattle*
### REPRESENTATIVES
1 John R. Miller (R), *Seattle*
2 Al Swift (D), *Bellingham*
3 Jolene Unsoeld (D), *Olympia*
4 Sid Morrison (R), *Zillah*
5 Thomas S. Foley (D), *Spokane*
6 Norman D. Dicks (D), *Bremerton*
7 James A. McDermott (D), *Seattle*
8 Rod D. Chandler (R), *Bellevue*

## WEST VIRGINIA
### SENATORS
Robert C. Byrd (D), *Sophia*
John D. Rockefeller IV (D), *Charleston*
### REPRESENTATIVES
1 Alan B. Mollohan (D), *Fairmont*
2 Harley O. Staggers, Jr. (D), *Keyser*
3 Robert E. Wise, Jr. (D), *Clendenin*
4 Nick J. Rahall II (D), *Beckley*

## WISCONSIN
### SENATORS
Robert W. Kasten, Jr. (R), *Milwaukee*
Herbert H. Kohl (D), *Milwaukee*
### REPRESENTATIVES
1 Les Aspin (D), *East Troy*
2 Robert W. Kastenmeier (D), *Sun Prairie*
3 Steven Gunderson (R), *Osseo*
4 Gerald D. Kleczka (D), *Milwaukee*
5 Jim Moody (D), *Milwaukee*
6 Thomas E. Petri (R), *Fond du Lac*
7 David R. Obey (D), *Wausau*
8 Toby A. Roth (R), *Appleton*
9 F. James Sensenbrenner, Jr. (R), *Menomonee Falls*

## WYOMING
### SENATORS
Malcolm Wallop (R), *Big Horn*
Alan K. Simpson (R), *Cody*
### REPRESENTATIVE AT LARGE
Richard B. Cheney (R),[52] *Casper*
Craig L. Thomas (R),[53] *Casper*

## AMERICAN SAMOA
### DELEGATE
Eni F. H. Faleomavaega, Jr. (D), *Pago Pago*

## COMMONWEALTH OF PUERTO RICO
### RESIDENT COMMISSIONER
Jaime B. Fuster (D), *Condado*

## DISTRICT OF COLUMBIA
### DELEGATE
Walter E. Fauntroy (D), *Washington, D.C.*

## GUAM
### DELEGATE
Ben Garrido Blaz (R), *Ordot*

## VIRGIN ISLANDS
### DELEGATE
Ron de Lugo (D), *St. Thomas*

---

[48] Resigned June 30, 1989.
[49] Elected September 12, 1989, to fill vacancy caused by the resignation of James C. Wright, Jr., and took his seat September 20, 1989.

[50] Died August 7, 1989.
[51] Elected December 9, 1989, to fill vacancy caused by death of Mickey Leland, and took his seat January 23, 1990.

[52] Resigned March 17, 1989.
[53] Elected April 26, 1989, to fill vacancy caused by resignation of Richard B. Cheney, and took his seat May 2, 1989.

# 102ND CONGRESS

## JANUARY 3, 1991, TO JANUARY 3, 1993

FIRST SESSION—JANUARY 3, 1991, TO JANUARY 3, 1992
SECOND SESSION—JANUARY 3, 1992, TO OCTOBER 9, 1992

J. Danforth Quayle
Vice President

Thomas S. Foley
Speaker

### Senate
Democrats 56 — Republicans 44

VICE PRESIDENT OF THE UNITED STATES—J. DANFORTH QUAYLE, of Indiana
PRESIDENT PRO TEMPORE OF THE SENATE—ROBERT C. BYRD, of West Virginia
SECRETARY OF THE SENATE—WALTER J. STEWART, of Washington, D.C.
SERGEANT AT ARMS OF THE SENATE—MARTHA S. POPE,[1] of Connecticut
CHAPLAIN OF THE SENATE—REV. RICHARD C. HALVERSON, LL.D., D.D.
MAJORITY FLOOR LEADER—GEORGE J. MITCHELL, of Maine
DEMOCRATIC WHIP—WENDELL H. FORD,[2] of Kentucky
REPUBLICAN FLOOR LEADER—ROBERT J. DOLE, of Kansas
ASSISTANT REPUBLICAN LEADER—ALAN K. SIMPSON, of Wyoming

### House of Representatives
Democrats 267 — Republicans 167 — Independent 1

SPEAKER OF THE HOUSE—THOMAS S. FOLEY, of Washington
CLERK OF THE HOUSE—DONNALD K. ANDERSON, of California
SERGEANT AT ARMS OF THE HOUSE—JACK RUSS,[3] of Maryland; WERNER W. BRANDT,[4] of Virginia
DOORKEEPER OF THE HOUSE—JAMES T. MOLLOY, of New York
POSTMASTER OF THE HOUSE[5]—ROBERT V. ROTA,[6] of Pennsylvania; MICHAEL J. SHINAY,[7] of Virginia
CHAPLAIN OF THE HOUSE—REV. JAMES DAVID FORD, D.D.
MAJORITY LEADER—RICHARD A. GEPHARDT, of Missouri
MAJORITY WHIP—WILLIAM H. GRAY III,[8] of Pennsylvania; DAVID E. BONIOR,[9] of Michigan
REPUBLICAN LEADER—ROBERT H. MICHEL, of Illinois
REPUBLICAN WHIP—NEWT GINGRICH, of Georgia

## ALABAMA

### SENATORS

Howell T. Heflin (D), *Tuscumbia*
Richard C. Shelby (D), *Tuscaloosa*

### REPRESENTATIVES

1 H. L. (Sonny) Callahan (R), *Mobile*
2 William L. Dickinson (R), *Montgomery*
3 J. Glen Browder (D), *Jacksonville*
4 Tom Bevill (D), *Jasper*
5 Robert E. (Bud) Cramer, Jr. (D), *Huntsville*
6 Ben Erdreich (D), *Birmingham*
7 Claude Harris (D), *Tuscaloosa*

## ALASKA

### SENATORS

Theodore F. Stevens (R), *Girdwood*
Frank H. Murkowski (R), *Fairbanks*

### REPRESENTATIVE AT LARGE

Donald E. Young (R), *Fort Yukon*

## ARIZONA

### SENATORS

Dennis DeConcini (D), *Tucson*
John S. McCain III (R), *Phoenix*

### REPRESENTATIVES

1 John J. Rhodes III (R), *Mesa*
2 Morris K. Udall (D),[10] *Tucson*
2 Edward L. Pastor (D),[11] *Phoenix*
3 Bob Stump (R), *Tolleson*

4 Jon L. Kyl (R), *Phoenix*
5 Jim Kolbe (R), *Tucson*

## ARKANSAS

### SENATORS

Dale Bumpers (D), *Charleston*
David H. Pryor (D), *Little Rock*

### REPRESENTATIVES

1 William V. Alexander, Jr. (D), *Osceola*
2 Raymond H. Thornton, Jr. (D), *Little Rock*
3 John Paul Hammerschmidt (R), *Harrison*
4 Beryl F. Anthony, Jr. (D), *El Dorado*

---

[1] Elected January 3, 1991.
[2] Elected November 13, 1990.
[3] Resigned March 12, 1992.
[4] Appointed March 12, 1992.
[5] The position of Postmaster was eliminated

pursuant to H. Res. 423, April 9, 1992.
[6] Resigned March 19, 1992.
[7] Appointed March 31, 1992.
[8] Resigned from the House September 11, 1991.
[9] Elected July 11, 1991.

[10] Resigned May 4, 1991.
[11] Elected September 24, 1991, to fill vacancy caused by resignation of Morris K. Udall, and took his seat October 3, 1991.

## CALIFORNIA

SENATORS

Alan Cranston (D), *Los Angeles*
Pete Wilson (R),[12] *San Diego*
John Seymour (R),[13] *Anaheim*
Dianne Feinstein (D),[14] *San Francisco*

REPRESENTATIVES

1 Frank D. Riggs (R), *Santa Rosa*
2 Wally Herger (R), *Rio Oso*
3 Robert T. Matsui (D), *Sacramento*
4 Vic Fazio (D), *Sacramento*
5 Nancy Pelosi (D), *San Francisco*
6 Barbara Boxer (D), *Greenbrae*
7 George Miller (D), *Martinez*
8 Ronald V. Dellums (D), *Oakland*
9 Fortney H. (Pete) Stark, Jr. (D), *Oakland*
10 Don Edwards (D), *San Jose*
11 Tom Lantos (D), *San Mateo*
12 Thomas J. Campbell (R), *Stanford*
13 Norman Y. Mineta (D), *San Jose*
14 John T. Doolittle (R), *Rocklin*
15 Gary A. Condit (D), *Ceres*
16 Leon E. Panetta (D), *Carmel Valley*
17 Calvin M. Dooley, Jr. (D), *Visalia*
18 Richard H. Lehman (D), *Fresno*
19 Robert J. Lagomarsino (R), *Ventura*
20 William M. Thomas (R), *Bakersfield*
21 Elton W. Gallegly (R), *Simi Valley*
22 Carlos J. Moorhead (R), *Glendale*
23 Anthony C. Beilenson (D), *Los Angeles*
24 Henry A. Waxman (D), *Los Angeles*
25 Edward R. Roybal (D), *Los Angeles*
26 Howard L. Berman (D), *Panorama City*
27 Mel Levine (D), *Los Angeles*
28 Julian C. Dixon (D), *Culver City*
29 Maxine Waters (D), *Los Angeles*
30 Matthew G. Martinez, Jr. (D), *Montebello*
31 Mervyn M. Dymally (D), *Compton*
32 Glenn M. Anderson (D), *San Pedro*
33 David Dreier (R), *Claremont*
34 Esteban Edward Torres (D), *West Covina*
35 Jerry Lewis (R), *Redlands*
36 George E. Brown, Jr. (D), *Riverside*
37 Alfred A. McCandless (R), *La Quinta*
38 Robert K. Dornan (R), *Garden Grove*
39 William E. Dannemeyer (R), *Fullerton*
40 C. Christopher Cox (R), *Newport Beach*
41 Bill Lowery (R), *San Diego*
42 Dana Rohrabacher (R), *Long Beach*
43 Ron Packard (R), *Carlsbad*
44 Randy (Duke) Cunningham (R), *Chula Vista*
45 Duncan L. Hunter (R), *Coronado*

## COLORADO

SENATORS

Timothy E. Wirth (D), *Boulder*
Hank Brown (R), *Greeley*

REPRESENTATIVES

1 Patricia Schroeder (D), *Denver*
2 David E. Skaggs (D), *Boulder*
3 Ben Nighthorse Campbell (D), *Ignacio*
4 A. Wayne Allard (R), *Loveland*
5 Joel Hefley (R), *Colorado Springs*
6 Dan Schaefer (R), *Lakewood*

## CONNECTICUT

SENATORS

Christopher J. Dodd (D), *East Haddam*
Joseph I. Lieberman (D), *New Haven*

REPRESENTATIVES

1 Barbara B. Kennelly (D), *Hartford*
2 Samuel Gejdenson (D), *Bozrah*
3 Rosa L. DeLauro (D), *New Haven*
4 Christopher Shays (R), *Stamford*
5 Gary A. Franks (R), *Waterbury*
6 Nancy L. Johnson (R), *New Britain*

## DELAWARE

SENATORS

William V. Roth, Jr. (R), *Wilmington*
Joseph R. Biden, Jr. (D), *Wilmington*

REPRESENTATIVE AT LARGE

Thomas R. Carper (D), *Wilmington*

## FLORIDA

SENATORS

Bob Graham (D), *Miami Lakes*
Connie Mack (R), *Cape Coral*

REPRESENTATIVES

1 Earl Hutto (D), *Panama City*
2 Douglas (Pete) Peterson (D), *Marianna*
3 Charles E. Bennett (D), *Jacksonville*
4 Craig T. James (R), *De Land*
5 Bill McCollum, Jr. (R), *Longwood*
6 Clifford B. Stearns (R), *Ocala*
7 Sam M. Gibbons (D), *Tampa*
8 C. W. Bill Young (R), *St. Petersburg*
9 Michael Bilirakis (R), *Palm Harbor*
10 Andrew P. Ireland (R), *Winter Haven*
11 James Bacchus (D), *Belle Isle*
12 Tom Lewis (R), *North Palm Beach*
13 Porter J. Goss (R), *Sanibel*
14 Harry A. Johnston II (D), *West Palm Beach*
15 Clay Shaw (R), *Fort Lauderdale*
16 Lawrence J. Smith (D), *Hollywood*
17 William Lehman (D), *Biscayne Park*
18 Ileana Ros-Lehtinen (R), *Miami*
19 Dante B. Fascell (D), *Miami*

## GEORGIA

SENATORS

Sam Nunn (D), *Perry*
Wyche Fowler, Jr. (D), *Atlanta*

REPRESENTATIVES

1 R. Lindsay Thomas (D), *Statesboro*
2 Charles F. Hatcher (D), *Albany*
3 Richard B. Ray (D), *Perry*
4 Ben Jones (D), *Covington*
5 John R. Lewis (D), *Atlanta*
6 Newt Gingrich (R), *Jonesboro*
7 George (Buddy) Darden (D), *Marietta*
8 J. Roy Rowland (D), *Dublin*
9 Edgar L. Jenkins (D), *Jasper*
10 D. Douglas Barnard, Jr. (D), *Augusta*

## HAWAII

SENATORS

Daniel K. Inouye (D), *Honolulu*
Daniel K. Akaka (D), *Honolulu*

REPRESENTATIVES

1 Neil Abercrombie (D), *Honolulu*
2 Patsy T. Mink (D), *Honolulu*

## IDAHO

SENATORS

Steven D. Symms (R), *Caldwell*
Larry Craig (R), *Payette*

REPRESENTATIVES

1 Larry LaRocco (D), *Boise*
2 Richard Stallings (D), *Rexburg*

## ILLINOIS

SENATORS

Alan J. Dixon (D), *Belleville*
Paul M. Simon (D), *Makanda*

REPRESENTATIVES

1 Charles A. Hayes (D), *Chicago*

---

[12] Resigned January 7, 1991.
[13] Appointed January 2, 1991, to fill vacancy caused by resignation of Pete Wilson, and took his seat January 10, 1991.

[14] Elected November 3, 1992, to fill vacancy caused by resignation of Pete Wilson, and took her seat November 4, 1992.

2 Gus Savage (D), *Chicago*
3 Martin A. Russo (D), *South Holland*
4 George E. Sangmeister (D), *Mokena*
5 William O. Lipinski (D), *Chicago*
6 Henry J. Hyde (R), *Bensenville*
7 Cardiss Collins (D), *Chicago*
8 Dan Rostenkowski (D), *Chicago*
9 Sidney R. Yates (D), *Chicago*
10 John Edward Porter (R), *Wilmette*
11 Frank Annunzio (D), *Chicago*
12 Philip M. Crane (R), *McHenry*
13 Harris W. Fawell (R), *Naperville*
14 J. Dennis Hastert (R), *Yorkville*
15 Edward R. Madigan (R),[15] *Lincoln*
15 Thomas W. Ewing (R),[16] *Pontiac*
16 John W. Cox, Jr. (D), *Galena*
17 Lane A. Evans (D), *Rock Island*
18 Robert H. Michel (R), *Peoria*
19 Terry L. Bruce (D), *Olney*
20 Richard J. Durbin (D), *Springfield*
21 Jerry F. Costello (D), *Belleville*
22 Glenn Poshard (D), *Carterville*

## INDIANA

### SENATORS

Richard G. Lugar (R), *Indianapolis*
Dan R. Coats (R), *Indianapolis*

### REPRESENTATIVES

1 Peter J. Visclosky (D), *Merrillville*
2 Philip R. Sharp (D), *Muncie*
3 Timothy J. Roemer (D), *South Bend*
4 Jill L. Long (D), *Larwill*
5 Jim Jontz (D), *Monticello*
6 Dan Burton (R), *Indianapolis*
7 John T. Myers (R), *Covington*
8 Frank McCloskey (D), *Bloomington*
9 Lee H. Hamilton (D), *Nashville*
10 Andrew Jacobs, Jr. (D), *Indianapolis*

## IOWA

### SENATORS

Charles E. Grassley (R), *New Hartford*
Tom Harkin (D), *Cumming*

### REPRESENTATIVES

1 James A. S. Leach (R), *Davenport*
2 James A. Nussle (R), *Manchester*
3 David R. Nagle (D), *Cedar Falls*
4 Neal Smith (D), *Altoona*
5 Jim Ross Lightfoot (R), *Shenandoah*
6 Fred Grandy (R), *Sioux City*

## KANSAS

### SENATORS

Robert J. Dole (R), *Russell*
Nancy L. Kassebaum (R), *Burdick*

### REPRESENTATIVES

1 Pat Roberts (R), *Dodge City*
2 Jim Slattery (D), *Topeka*
3 Jan Meyers (R), *Overland Park*
4 Daniel R. Glickman (D), *Wichita*
5 Richard Nichols (R), *McPherson*

## KENTUCKY

### SENATORS

Wendell H. Ford (D), *Owensboro*
Mitch McConnell (R), *Louisville*

### REPRESENTATIVES

1 Carroll Hubbard, Jr. (D), *Mayfield*
2 William H. Natcher (D), *Bowling Green*
3 Romano L. Mazzoli (D), *Louisville*
4 Jim Bunning (R), *Southgate*
5 Harold Rogers (R), *Somerset*
6 Larry J. Hopkins (R), *Lexington*
7 Carl C. Perkins (D), *Leburn*

## LOUISIANA

### SENATORS

J. Bennett Johnston, Jr. (D), *Shreveport*
John B. Breaux (D), *Crowley*

### REPRESENTATIVES

1 Robert L. Livingston (R), *Metairie*
2 William J. Jefferson (D), *New Orleans*
3 W. J. (Billy) Tauzin (D), *Thibodaux*
4 James O. McCrery III (R), *Shreveport*
5 Thomas J. (Jerry) Huckaby (D), *Ringgold*
6 Richard H. Baker (R), *Baton Rouge*
7 James A. Hayes (D), *Lafayette*
8 Clyde C. Holloway (R), *Forest Hill*

## MAINE

### SENATORS

William S. Cohen (R), *Bangor*
George J. Mitchell (D), *Portland*

### REPRESENTATIVES

1 Thomas H. Andrews (D), *Portland*
2 Olympia J. Snowe (R), *Auburn*

## MARYLAND

### SENATORS

Paul S. Sarbanes (D), *Baltimore*
Barbara A. Mikulski (D), *Baltimore*

### REPRESENTATIVES

1 Wayne T. Gilchrest (R), *Kennedyville*
2 Helen Delich Bentley (R), *Lutherville*
3 Benjamin L. Cardin (D), *Baltimore*
4 C. Thomas McMillen (D), *Crofton*
5 Steny H. Hoyer (D), *Forestville*
6 Beverly B. Byron (D), *Frederick*
7 Kweisi Mfume (D), *Baltimore*
8 Constance A. Morella (R), *Bethesda*

## MASSACHUSETTS

### SENATORS

Edward M. Kennedy (D), *Hyannis Port*
John F. Kerry (D), *Boston*

### REPRESENTATIVES

1 Silvio O. Conte (R),[17] *Pittsfield*
1 John W. Olver (D),[18] *Amherst*
2 Richard E. Neal (D), *Springfield*
3 Joseph D. Early (D), *Worcester*
4 Barney Frank (D), *Newton*
5 Chester G. Atkins (D), *Concord*
6 Nicholas Mavroules (D), *Peabody*
7 Edward J. Markey (D), *Malden*
8 Joseph P. Kennedy II (D), *Brighton*
9 John Joseph Moakley (D), *South Boston*
10 Gerry E. Studds (D), *Cohasset*
11 Brian J. Donnelly (D), *Dorchester*

## MICHIGAN

### SENATORS

Donald W. Riegle, Jr. (D), *Flint*
Carl Levin (D), *Detroit*

### REPRESENTATIVES

1 John Conyers, Jr. (D), *Detroit*
2 Carl D. Pursell (R), *Plymouth*
3 Howard E. Wolpe (D), *Lansing*
4 Fred Upton (R), *St. Joseph*
5 Paul B. Henry (R), *Grand Rapids*
6 Bob Carr (D), *East Lansing*
7 Dale E. Kildee (D), *Flint*
8 Bob Traxler (D), *Bay City*
9 Guy A. Vander Jagt (R), *Luther*
10 David L. Camp (R), *Midland*
11 Robert W. Davis (R), *Gaylord*
12 David E. Bonior (D), *Mount Clemens*
13 Barbara-Rose Collins (D), *Detroit*
14 Dennis M. Hertel (D), *Harper Woods*
15 William D. Ford (D), *Taylor*
16 John D. Dingell, Jr. (D), *Trenton*
17 Sander M. Levin (D), *Southfield*
18 William S. Broomfield (R), *Birmingham*

---

[15] Resigned March 8, 1991.
[16] Elected July 2, 1991, to fill vacancy caused by resignation of Edward R. Madigan, and took his seat July 10, 1991.

[17] Died February 8, 1991.
[18] Elected June 4, 1991, to fill vacancy caused by death of Silvio O. Conte, and took his seat June 18, 1991.

## MINNESOTA

SENATORS

David F. Durenberger (R), *Minneapolis*

Paul D. Wellstone (D), *Northfield*

REPRESENTATIVES

1 Timothy J. Penny (D), *New Richland*

2 Vin Weber (R), *North Mankato*

3 Jim Ramstad (R), *Minnetonka*

4 Bruce F. Vento (D), *St. Paul*

5 Martin Olav Sabo (D), *Minneapolis*

6 Gerry E. Sikorski (D), *Stillwater*

7 Collin C. Peterson (D), *Detroit Lakes*

8 James L. Oberstar (D), *Chisholm*

## MISSISSIPPI

SENATORS

Thad Cochran (R), *Jackson*

Trent Lott (R), *Pascagoula*

REPRESENTATIVES

1 Jamie L. Whitten (D), *Charleston*

2 Mike Espy (D), *Yazoo City*

3 Gillespie V. (Sonny) Montgomery (D), *Meridian*

4 Michael Parker (D), *Brookhaven*

5 Gary E. (Gene) Taylor (D), *Bay St. Louis*

## MISSOURI

SENATORS

John C. Danforth (R), *Newburg*

Christopher S. (Kit) Bond (R), *Mexico*

REPRESENTATIVES

1 William L. Clay (D), *St. Louis*

2 Joan Kelly Horn (D), *St. Louis*

3 Richard A. Gephardt (D), *St. Louis*

4 Ike Skelton (D), *Lexington*

5 Alan D. Wheat (D), *Kansas City*

6 E. Thomas Coleman (R), *Gladstone*

7 Melton D. Hancock (R), *Springfield*

8 Bill Emerson (R), *Cape Girardeau*

9 Harold L. Volkmer (D), *Hannibal*

## MONTANA

SENATORS

Max Baucus (D), *Missoula*

Conrad Burns (R), *Billings*

REPRESENTATIVES

1 Pat Williams (D), *Helena*

2 Ron Marlenee (R), *Scobey*

## NEBRASKA

SENATORS

J. James Exon (D), *Lincoln*

J. Robert Kerrey (D), *Omaha*

REPRESENTATIVES

1 Douglas K. Bereuter (R), *Utica*

2 Peter D. Hoagland (D), *Omaha*

3 William E. Barrett (R), *Lexington*

## NEVADA

SENATORS

Harry M. Reid (D), *Searchlight*

Richard H. Bryan (D), *Las Vegas*

REPRESENTATIVES

1 James H. Bilbray (D), *Las Vegas*

2 Barbara F. Vucanovich (R), *Reno*

## NEW HAMPSHIRE

SENATORS

Warren B. Rudman (R), *Hollis*

Robert C. Smith (R), *Tuftonboro*

REPRESENTATIVES

1 William H. Zeliff, Jr. (R), *Jackson*

2 Richard W. Swett (D), *Bow*

## NEW JERSEY

SENATORS

Bill Bradley (D), *Denville*

Frank R. Lautenberg (D), *Secaucus*

REPRESENTATIVES

1 Robert E. Andrews (D), *Bellmawr*

2 William J. Hughes (D), *Ocean City*

3 Frank Pallone, Jr. (D), *Long Branch*

4 Christopher H. Smith (R), *Robbinsville*

5 Marge Roukema (R), *Ridgewood*

6 Bernard J. Dwyer (D), *Edison*

7 Matthew J. Rinaldo (R), *Union*

8 Robert A. Roe (D), *Wayne*

9 Robert G. Torricelli (D), *Englewood*

10 Donald M. Payne (D), *Newark*

11 Dean A. Gallo (R), *Parsippany*

12 Richard Zimmer (R), *Flemington*

13 H. James Saxton (R), *Vincentown*

14 Frank J. Guarini (D), *Jersey City*

## NEW MEXICO

SENATORS

Pete V. Domenici (R), *Albuquerque*

Jeff Bingaman (D), *Santa Fe*

REPRESENTATIVES

1 Steven H. Schiff (R), *Albuquerque*

2 Joe Skeen (R), *Picacho*

3 William B. Richardson (D), *Santa Fe*

## NEW YORK

SENATORS

Daniel P. Moynihan (D), *Pindars Corners*

Alfonse M. D'Amato (R), *Island Park*

REPRESENTATIVES

1 George J. Hochbrueckner (D), *Coram*

2 Thomas J. Downey (D), *Amityville*

3 Robert J. Mrazek (D), *Huntington*

4 Norman F. Lent (R), *East Rockaway*

5 Raymond J. McGrath (R), *Valley Stream*

6 Floyd H. Flake (D), *Rosedale*

7 Gary L. Ackerman (D), *Jamaica*

8 James H. Scheuer (D), *Douglaston*

9 Thomas J. Manton (D), *Sunnyside Queens*

10 Charles E. Schumer (D), *Brooklyn*

11 Edolphus Towns (D), *Brooklyn*

12 Major R. Owens (D), *Brooklyn*

13 Stephen J. Solarz (D), *Brooklyn*

14 Susan Molinari (R), *Staten Island*

15 S. William Green (R), *New York*

16 Charles B. Rangel (D), *New York*

17 Ted Weiss (D),[19] *New York*

17 Jerrold L. Nadler (D),[20] *New York*

18 José E. Serrano (D), *Bronx*

19 Eliot L. Engel (D), *Bronx*

20 Nita M. Lowey (D), *Rye*

21 Hamilton Fish, Jr. (R), *Millbrook*

22 Benjamin A. Gilman (R), *Middletown*

23 Michael R. McNulty (D), *Green Island*

24 Gerald B. H. Solomon (R), *Glens Falls*

25 Sherwood L. Boehlert (R), *New Hartford*

26 David O'B. Martin (R), *Canton*

27 James T. Walsh (R), *Syracuse*

28 Matthew F. McHugh (D), *Ithaca*

29 Frank Horton (R), *Rochester*

30 Louise M. Slaughter (D), *Fairport*

31 L. William Paxon (R), *Williamsville*

32 John J. LaFalce (D), *Tonawanda*

33 Henry J. Nowak (D), *Buffalo*

34 Amory Houghton, Jr. (R), *Corning*

## NORTH CAROLINA

SENATORS

Jesse Helms (R), *Raleigh*

Terry Sanford (D), *Durham*

REPRESENTATIVES

1 Walter B. Jones (D),[21] *Farmville*

1 Eva M. Clayton (D),[22] *Littleton*

2 Tim Valentine, Jr. (D), *Nashville*

3 H. Martin Lancaster (D), *Goldsboro*

---

[19] Died September 14, 1992.

[20] Elected November 3, 1992, to fill vacancy caused by death of Ted Weiss, but was not sworn in because Congress was not in session.

[21] Died September 15, 1992.

[22] Elected November 3, 1992, to fill vacancy caused by death of Walter B. Jones, but was not sworn in because Congress was not in session.

4 David E. Price (D), *Chapel Hill*
5 Stephen L. Neal (D), *Winston-Salem*
6 Howard Coble (R), *Greensboro*
7 Charles Rose (D), *Fayetteville*
8 W. G. (Bill) Hefner (D), *Concord*
9 J. Alex McMillan (R), *Charlotte*
10 Cass Ballenger (R), *Hickory*
11 Charles H. Taylor (R), *Brevard*

## NORTH DAKOTA

### SENATORS

Quentin N. Burdick (D),[23] *Fargo*
Jocelyn B. Burdick (D),[24] *Fargo*
Kent Conrad (D),[25] *Bismarck*
Byron L. Dorgan (D),[26] *Bismarck*

### REPRESENTATIVE AT LARGE

Byron L. Dorgan (D),[27] *Bismarck*

## OHIO

### SENATORS

John Glenn, Jr. (D), *Columbus*
Howard M. Metzenbaum (D), *Lyndhurst*

### REPRESENTATIVES

1 Charles J. Luken (D), *Cincinnati*
2 Willis D. Gradison, Jr. (R), *Cincinnati*
3 Tony P. Hall (D), *Dayton*
4 Michael G. Oxley (R), *Findlay*
5 Paul E. Gillmor (R), *Port Clinton*
6 Robert McEwen (R), *Hillsboro*
7 David L. Hobson (R), *Springfield*
8 John A. Boehner (R), *Westchester*
9 Marcy Kaptur (D), *Toledo*
10 Clarence E. Miller (R), *Lancaster*
11 Dennis E. Eckart (D), *Mentor*
12 John R. Kasich (R), *Westerville*
13 Donald J. Pease (D), *Oberlin*
14 Thomas C. Sawyer (D), *Akron*
15 Chalmers P. Wylie (R), *Columbus*
16 Ralph Regula (R), *Navarre*
17 James A. Traficant, Jr. (D), *Poland*
18 Douglas Applegate (D), *Steubenville*
19 Edward F. Feighan (D), *Lakewood*
20 Mary Rose Oakar (D), *Cleveland*
21 Louis Stokes (D), *Shaker Heights*

## OKLAHOMA

### SENATORS

David L. Boren (D), *Seminole*
Don Nickles (R), *Ponca City*

### REPRESENTATIVES

1 James M. Inhofe (R), *Tulsa*
2 Mike Synar (D), *Muskogee*
3 William K. Brewster (D), *Marietta*

4 Dave McCurdy (D), *Norman*
5 Mickey Edwards (R), *Oklahoma City*
6 Glenn English (D), *Cordell*

## OREGON

### SENATORS

Mark O. Hatfield (R), *Portland*
Robert W. Packwood (R), *Portland*

### REPRESENTATIVES

1 Les AuCoin (D), *Portland*
2 Robert F. Smith (R), *Burns*
3 Ron Wyden (D), *Portland*
4 Peter A. DeFazio (D), *Springfield*
5 Michael J. Kopetski (D), *Keizer*

## PENNSYLVANIA

### SENATORS

H. John Heinz III (R),[28] *Pittsburgh*
Harris L. Wofford (D),[29] *Bryn Mawr*
Arlen Specter (R), *Philadelphia*

### REPRESENTATIVES

1 Thomas M. Foglietta (D), *Philadelphia*
2 William H. Gray III (D),[30] *Philadelphia*
2 Lucien E. Blackwell (D),[31] *Philadelphia*
3 Robert A. Borski, Jr. (D), *Philadelphia*
4 Joseph P. Kolter (D), *New Brighton*
5 Richard T. Schulze (R), *Berwyn*
6 Gus Yatron (D), *Reading*
7 Curt Weldon (R), *Aston*
8 Peter H. Kostmayer (D), *Solebury*
9 E. G. Shuster (R), *Everett*
10 Joseph M. McDade (R), *Clarks Summit*
11 Paul E. Kanjorski (D), *Nanticoke*
12 John P. Murtha, Jr. (D), *Johnstown*
13 R. Lawrence Coughlin (R), *Plymouth Meeting*
14 William J. Coyne (D), *Pittsburgh*
15 Don Ritter (R), *Coopersburg*
16 Robert S. Walker (R), *East Petersburg*
17 George W. Gekas (R), *Harrisburg*
18 Richard J. Santorum (R), *Mt. Lebanon*
19 William F. Goodling (R), *Jacobus*
20 Joseph M. Gaydos (D), *McKeesport*
21 Thomas J. Ridge (R), *Erie*
22 Austin J. Murphy (D), *Monongahela*
23 William F. Clinger, Jr. (R), *Warren*

## RHODE ISLAND

### SENATORS

Claiborne Pell (D), *Newport*
John H. Chafee (R), *Warwick*

### REPRESENTATIVES

1 Ronald K. Machtley (R), *Portsmouth*
2 John F. Reed (D), *Cranston*

## SOUTH CAROLINA

### SENATORS

Strom Thurmond (R), *Aiken*
Ernest F. Hollings (D), *Charleston*

### REPRESENTATIVES

1 Arthur Ravenel, Jr. (R), *Mount Pleasant*
2 Floyd Spence (R), *Lexington*
3 Butler Derrick (D), *Edgefield*
4 Liz J. Patterson (D), *Spartanburg*
5 John M. Spratt, Jr. (D), *York*
6 Robert M. (Robin) Tallon (D), *Florence*

## SOUTH DAKOTA

### SENATORS

Larry Pressler (R), *Humboldt*
Thomas A. Daschle (D), *Aberdeen*

### REPRESENTATIVE AT LARGE

Tim Johnson (D), *Vermillion*

## TENNESSEE

### SENATORS

James R. Sasser (D), *Nashville*
Albert A. Gore, Jr. (D),[32] *Carthage*
Harlan Mathews (D),[33] *Nashville*

### REPRESENTATIVES

1 James H. Quillen (R), *Kingsport*
2 John J. Duncan (R), *Knoxville*
3 Marilyn Lloyd (D), *Chattanooga*
4 James Cooper (D), *Shelbyville*
5 Robert N. Clement (D), *Nashville*
6 Bart Gordon (D), *Murfreesboro*
7 Donald K. Sundquist (R), *Memphis*
8 John S. Tanner (D), *Union City*
9 Harold E. Ford (D), *Memphis*

## TEXAS

### SENATORS

Lloyd M. Bentsen, Jr. (D), *Starr County*
Phil Gramm (R), *College Station*

### REPRESENTATIVES

1 Jim Chapman (D), *Sulphur Springs*
2 Charles Wilson (D), *Lufkin*

---

[23] Died September 8, 1992.
[24] Appointed to fill vacancy caused by death of Quentin N. Burdick, and took her seat September 16, 1992.
[25] Resigned December 14, 1992.
[26] Appointed to fill vacancy caused by resignation of Kent Conrad, and took his seat December 15, 1992.

[27] Resigned December 14, 1992, having been appointed to the Senate.
[28] Died April 4, 1991.
[29] Appointed to fill vacancy caused by death of H. John Heinz III, and took his seat May 9, 1991.
[30] Resigned September 11, 1991.
[31] Elected November 5, 1991, to fill vacancy

caused by resignation of William H. Gray III, and took his seat November 13, 1991.
[32] Resigned January 2, 1993, having been elected Vice President.
[33] Appointed to fill vacancy caused by resignation of Albert A. Gore, Jr., and took his seat January 2, 1993.

## TEXAS—Continued

### REPRESENTATIVES—CONTINUED

3 Steve Bartlett (R),[34] *Dallas*
3 Sam Johnson (R),[35] *Dallas*
4 Ralph M. Hall (D), *Rockwall*
5 John W. Bryant (D), *Dallas*
6 Joe Barton (R), *Ennis*
7 William R. Archer, Jr. (R), *Houston*
8 Jack Fields (R), *Humble*
9 Jack B. Brooks (D), *Beaumont*
10 J. J. (Jake) Pickle (D), *Austin*
11 Chet Edwards (D), *Waco*
12 Preston M. (Pete) Geren III (D), *Fort Worth*
13 William Sarpalius (D), *Amarillo*
14 Gregory H. Laughlin (D), *West Columbia*
15 Eligio (Kika) de la Garza (D), *McAllen*
16 Ronald Coleman (D), *El Paso*
17 Charles W. Stenholm (D), *Avoca*
18 Craig A. Washington (D), *Houston*
19 Larry Combest (R), *Lubbock*
20 Henry B. Gonzalez (D), *San Antonio*
21 Lamar S. Smith (R), *San Antonio*
22 Tom DeLay (R), *Sugar Land*
23 Albert G. Bustamante (D), *San Antonio*
24 Martin Frost (D), *Dallas*
25 Michael A. Andrews (D), *Houston*
26 Richard K. Armey (R), *Copper Canyon*
27 Solomon P. Ortiz (D), *Corpus Christi*

## UTAH

### SENATORS

E. J. (Jake) Garn (R), *Salt Lake City*
Orrin G. Hatch (R), *Salt Lake City*

### REPRESENTATIVES

1 James V. Hansen (R), *Farmington*
2 Wayne Owens (D), *Salt Lake City*
3 William Orton (D), *Provo*

## VERMONT

### SENATORS

Patrick J. Leahy (D), *Burlington*
James M. Jeffords (R), *Shrewsbury*

### REPRESENTATIVE AT LARGE

Bernard Sanders (I), *Burlington*

## VIRGINIA

### SENATORS

John W. Warner (R), *Middleburg*
Charles S. Robb (D), *McLean*

### REPRESENTATIVES

1 Herbert H. Bateman (R), *Newport News*
2 Owen B. Pickett (D), *Virginia Beach*
3 Thomas J. Bliley, Jr. (R), *Richmond*
4 Norman Sisisky (D), *Petersburg*
5 L. F. Payne, Jr. (D), *Nellysford*
6 James R. Olin (D), *Roanoke*
7 D. French Slaughter, Jr. (R),[36] *Culpeper*
7 George F. Allen, Jr. (R),[37] *Earlysville*
8 James P. Moran (D), *Alexandria*
9 Frederick C. Boucher (D), *Abingdon*
10 Frank R. Wolf (R), *Vienna*

## WASHINGTON

### SENATORS

Brock Adams (D), *Seattle*
Slade Gorton III (R), *Seattle*

### REPRESENTATIVES

1 John R. Miller (R), *Seattle*
2 Al Swift (D), *Bellingham*
3 Jolene Unsoeld (D), *Olympia*
4 Sid Morrison (R), *Zillah*
5 Thomas S. Foley (D), *Spokane*
6 Norman D. Dicks (D), *Bremerton*
7 James A. McDermott (D), *Seattle*
8 Rod D. Chandler (R), *Bellevue*

## WEST VIRGINIA

### SENATORS

Robert C. Byrd (D), *Sophia*
John D. Rockefeller IV (D), *Charleston*

### REPRESENTATIVES

1 Alan B. Mollohan (D), *Fairmont*
2 Harley O. Staggers, Jr. (D), *Keyser*
3 Robert E. Wise, Jr. (D), *Clendenin*
4 Nick J. Rahall II (D), *Beckley*

## WISCONSIN

### SENATORS

Robert W. Kasten, Jr. (R), *Milwaukee*
Herbert H. Kohl (D), *Milwaukee*

### REPRESENTATIVES

1 Les Aspin (D), *East Troy*
2 Scott L. Klug (R), *Madison*
3 Steven Gunderson (R), *Osseo*
4 Gerald D. Kleczka (D), *Milwaukee*
5 Jim Moody (D), *Milwaukee*
6 Thomas E. Petri (R), *Fond du Lac*
7 David R. Obey (D), *Wausau*
8 Toby A. Roth (R), *Appleton*
9 F. James Sensenbrenner, Jr. (R), *Menomomee Falls*

## WYOMING

### SENATORS

Malcolm Wallop (R), *Big Horn*
Alan K. Simpson (R), *Cody*

### REPRESENTATIVE AT LARGE

Craig L. Thomas (R), *Casper*

## AMERICAN SAMOA

### DELEGATE

Eni F. H. Faleomavaega, Jr. (D), *Pago Pago*

## COMMONWEALTH OF PUERTO RICO

### RESIDENT COMMISSIONER

Jaime B. Fuster (D),[38] *San Juan*
Antonio J. Colorado (D),[39] *San Juan*

## DISTRICT OF COLUMBIA

### DELEGATE

Eleanor Holmes Norton (D), *Washington, D.C.*

## GUAM

### DELEGATE

Ben Garrido Blaz (R), *Ordot*

## VIRGIN ISLANDS

### DELEGATE

Ron de Lugo (D), *St. Croix*

---

[34] Resigned March 11, 1991.
[35] Elected May 18, 1991, to fill vacancy caused by resignation of Steve Bartlett, and took his seat May 22, 1991.

[36] Resigned November 5, 1991.
[37] Elected November 5, 1991, to fill vacancy caused by resignation of D. French Slaughter, Jr., and took his seat November 12, 1991.

[38] Resigned March 4, 1992.
[39] Appointed February 21, 1992, to fill vacancy caused by resignation of Jaime B. Fuster, and took his seat March 4, 1992.

# 103RD CONGRESS

## JANUARY 3, 1993, TO JANUARY 3, 1995

FIRST SESSION—JANUARY 5, 1993, TO NOVEMBER 26, 1993
SECOND SESSION—JANUARY 25, 1994, TO DECEMBER 1, 1994

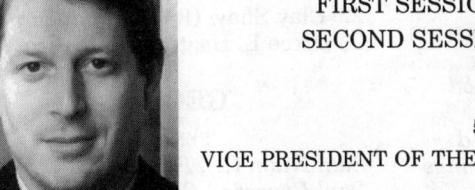

Albert A. Gore, Jr.
Vice President

Thomas S. Foley
Speaker

Senate
58 Democrats — 42 Republicans

VICE PRESIDENT OF THE UNITED STATES—J. DANFORTH QUAYLE,[1] of Indiana; ALBERT A. GORE, JR.,[2] of Tennessee
PRESIDENT PRO TEMPORE OF THE SENATE—ROBERT C. BYRD, of West Virginia
SECRETARY OF THE SENATE—WALTER J. STEWART, of Washington, D.C.
SERGEANT AT ARMS OF THE SENATE—MARTHA S. POPE, of Connecticut
CHAPLAIN OF THE SENATE—REV. RICHARD C. HALVERSON, LL.D., D.D.
MAJORITY FLOOR LEADER—GEORGE J. MITCHELL, of Maine
DEMOCRATIC WHIP—WENDELL H. FORD, of Kentucky
REPUBLICAN FLOOR LEADER—ROBERT J. DOLE, of Kansas
ASSISTANT REPUBLICAN LEADER—ALAN K. SIMPSON, of Wyoming

House of Representatives
258 Democrats — 176 Republicans — 1 Independent

SPEAKER OF THE HOUSE—THOMAS S. FOLEY, of Washington
CLERK OF THE HOUSE—DONNALD K. ANDERSON, of California
SERGEANT AT ARMS OF THE HOUSE—WERNER W. BRANDT, of Virginia
DOORKEEPER OF THE HOUSE—JAMES T. MOLLOY, of New York
CHAPLAIN OF THE HOUSE—REV. JAMES DAVID FORD, D.D.
MAJORITY LEADER—RICHARD A. GEPHARDT, of Missouri
MAJORITY WHIP—DAVID E. BONIOR, of Michigan
REPUBLICAN LEADER—ROBERT H. MICHEL, of Illinois
REPUBLICAN WHIP—NEWT GINGRICH, of Georgia

## ALABAMA

SENATORS
Howell T. Heflin (D), *Tuscumbia*
Richard C. Shelby (D),[3] *Tuscaloosa*

REPRESENTATIVES
1 H. L. (Sonny) Callahan (R), *Mobile*
2 Terry Everett (R), *Enterprise*
3 J. Glen Browder (D), *Jacksonville*
4 Tom Bevill (D), *Jasper*
5 Robert E. (Bud) Cramer, Jr. (D), *Huntsville*
6 Spencer T. Bachus III (R), *Birmingham*
7 Earl F. Hilliard (D), *Birmingham*

## ALASKA

SENATORS
Theodore F. Stevens (R), *Girdwood*
Frank H. Murkowski (R), *Fairbanks*

REPRESENTATIVE AT LARGE
Donald E. Young (R), *Fort Yukon*

## ARIZONA

SENATORS
Dennis DeConcini (D), *Tucson*
John S. McCain III (R), *Phoenix*

REPRESENTATIVES
1 Samuel G. Coppersmith (D), *Phoenix*
2 Edward L. Pastor (D), *Phoenix*
3 Bob Stump (R), *Tolleson*
4 Jon Kyl (R), *Phoenix*
5 Jim Kolbe (R), *Tucson*
6 Karan English (D), *Flagstaff*

## ARKANSAS

SENATORS
Dale Bumpers (D), *Charleston*
David H. Pryor (D), *Little Rock*

REPRESENTATIVES
1 Blanche M. Lambert (D), *Helena*
2 Raymond H. Thornton, Jr. (D), *Little Rock*

3 Y. Tim Hutchinson (R), *Bentonville*
4 Jay W. Dickey, Jr. (R), *Pine Bluff*

## CALIFORNIA

SENATORS
Dianne Feinstein (D), *San Francisco*
Barbara Boxer (D), *Greenbrae*

REPRESENTATIVES
1 Dan Hamburg (D), *Ukiah*
2 Wally Herger (R), *Marysville*
3 Vic Fazio (D), *Sacramento*
4 John T. Doolittle (R), *Rocklin*
5 Robert T. Matsui (D), *Sacramento*
6 Lynn C. Woolsey (D), *Petaluma*
7 George Miller (D), *Martinez*
8 Nancy Pelosi (D), *San Francsico*
9 Ronald V. Dellums (D), *Oakland*
10 William P. Baker (R), *Walnut Creek*
11 Richard W. Pombo (R), *Tracy*
12 Tom Lantos (D), *San Mateo*

[1] Term expired at noon on January 20, 1993.
[2] Term began at noon on January 20, 1993.
[3] Changed party affiliation to Republican, November 9, 1994.

## CALIFORNIA—Continued

### REPRESENTATIVES—CONTINUED

13 Fortney H. (Pete) Stark, Jr. (D), *Hayward*
14 Anna G. Eshoo (D), *Atherton*
15 Norman Y. Mineta (D), *San Jose*
16 Don Edwards (D), *San Jose*
17 Leon E. Panetta (D),[4] *Carmel Valley*
17 Sam Farr (D),[5] *Carmel*
18 Gary A. Condit (D), *Ceres*
19 Richard H. Lehman (D), *Fresno*
20 Calvin M. Dooley (D), *Visalia*
21 William M. Thomas (R), *Bakersfield*
22 Michael Huffington (R), *Santa Barbara*
23 Elton W. Gallegly (R), *Simi Valley*
24 Anthony C. Beilenson (D), *Woodland Hills*
25 Howard P. McKeon (R), *Santa Clarita*
26 Howard L. Berman (D), *Sherman Oaks*
27 Carlos J. Moorhead (R), *Glendale*
28 David Dreier (R), *La Verne*
29 Henry A. Waxman (D), *Los Angeles*
30 Xavier Becerra (D), *Montebello*
31 Matthew G. Martinez, Jr. (D), *Monterey Park*
32 Julian C. Dixon (D), *Los Angeles*
33 Lucille Roybal-Allard (D), *Bell Gardens*
34 Esteban Edward Torres (D), *West Covina*
35 Maxine Waters (D), *Los Angeles*
36 Jane Harman (D), *Marina Del Rey*
37 Walter R. Tucker III (D), *Compton*
38 Steve Horn (R), *Long Beach*
39 Edward R. Royce (R), *Fullerton*
40 Jerry Lewis (R), *Redlands*
41 Jay C. Kim (R), *Diamond Bar*
42 George E. Brown, Jr. (D), *San Bernardino*
43 Kenneth Calvert (R), *Riverside*
44 Alfred A. McCandless (R), *La Quinta*
45 Dana Rohrabacher (R), *Huntington Beach*
46 Robert K. Dornan (R), *Garden Grove*
47 C. Christopher Cox (R), *Newport Beach*
48 Ron Packard (R), *Oceanside*
49 Lynn Schenk (D), *San Diego*
50 Robert Filner (D), *San Diego*
51 Randy (Duke) Cunningham (R), *Del Mar*
52 Duncan L. Hunter (R), *Coronado*

## COLORADO

### SENATORS

Hank Brown (R), *Greeley*
Ben Nighthorse Campbell (D), *Ignacio*

### REPRESENTATIVES

1 Patricia Schroeder (D), *Denver*
2 David E. Skaggs (D), *Boulder*
3 Scott S. McInnis (R), *Glenwood Springs*
4 A. Wayne Allard (R), *Loveland*
5 Joel Hefley (R), *Colorado Springs*
6 Dan Schaefer (R), *Lakewood*

## CONNECTICUT

### SENATORS

Christopher J. Dodd (D), *East Haddam*
Joseph I. Lieberman (D), *New Haven*

### REPRESENTATIVES

1 Barbara B. Kennelly (D), *Hartford*
2 Samuel Gejdenson (D), *Bozrah*
3 Rosa L. DeLauro (D), *New Haven*
4 Christopher Shays (R), *Stamford*
5 Gary A. Franks (R), *Waterbury*
6 Nancy L. Johnson (R), *New Britain*

## DELAWARE

### SENATORS

William V. Roth, Jr. (R), *Wilmington*
Joseph R. Biden, Jr. (D), *Wilmington*

### REPRESENTATIVE AT LARGE

Michael N. Castle (R), *Dover*

## FLORIDA

### SENATORS

Bob Graham (D), *Miami Lakes*
Connie Mack (R), *Cape Coral*

### REPRESENTATIVES

1 Earl Hutto (D), *Panama City*
2 Douglas (Pete) Peterson (D), *Marianna*
3 Corrine Brown (D), *Jacksonville*
4 Tillie K. Fowler (R), *Jacksonville*
5 Karen L. Thurman (D), *Dunnellon*
6 Clifford B. Stearns (R), *Ocala*
7 John L. Mica (R), *Winter Park*
8 Bill McCollum, Jr. (R), *Longwood*
9 Michael Bilirakis (R), *Palm Harbor*
10 C. W. Bill Young (R), *Indian Rocks Beach*
11 Sam M. Gibbons (D), *Tampa*
12 Charles T. Canady (R), *Lakeland*
13 Dan Miller (R), *Bradenton*
14 Porter J. Goss (R), *Sanibel*
15 James Bacchus (D), *Belle Isle*
16 Tom Lewis (R), *Palm Beach Gardens*
17 Carrie P. Meek (D), *Miami*
18 Ileana Ros-Lehtinen (R), *Miami*
19 Harry A. Johnston II (D), *West Palm Beach*
20 Peter Deutsch (D), *Lauderhill*
21 Lincoln Diaz-Balart (R), *Miami*
22 Clay Shaw (R), *Fort Lauderdale*
23 Alcee L. Hastings (D), *Miramar*

## GEORGIA

### SENATORS

Sam Nunn (D), *Perry*
Paul Coverdell (R), *Atlanta*

### REPRESENTATIVES

1 Jack Kingston (R), *Savannah*
2 Sanford Bishop (D), *Columbus*
3 Michael A. (Mac) Collins (R), *Jackson*
4 John E. Linder (R), *Dunwoody*
5 John R. Lewis (D), *Atlanta*
6 Newt Gingrich (R), *Marietta*
7 George (Buddy) Darden (D), *Marietta*
8 J. Roy Rowland (D), *Dublin*
9 J. Nathan Deal (D), *Gainesville*
10 Donald Johnson, Jr. (D), *Royston*
11 Cynthia A. McKinney (D), *Lithonia*

## HAWAII

### SENATORS

Daniel K. Inouye (D), *Honolulu*
Daniel K. Akaka (D), *Honolulu*

### REPRESENTATIVES

1 Neil Abercrombie (D), *Honolulu*
2 Patsy T. Mink (D), *Honolulu*

## IDAHO

### SENATORS

Larry Craig (R), *Boise*
Dirk Kempthorne (R), *Boise*

### REPRESENTATIVES

1 Larry LaRocco (D), *Boise*
2 Michael D. Crapo (R), *Idaho Falls*

## ILLINOIS

### SENATORS

Paul M. Simon (D), *Makanda*
Carol Moseley–Braun (D), *Chicago*

### REPRESENTATIVES

1 Bobby L. Rush (D), *Chicago*
2 Mel Reynolds (D), *Chicago*
3 William O. Lipinski (D), *Chicago*
4 Luis V. Gutierrez (D), *Chicago*
5 Dan Rostenkowski (D), *Chicago*
6 Henry J. Hyde (R), *Bensenville*
7 Cardiss Collins (D), *Chicago*
8 Philip M. Crane (R), *Mount Prospect*
9 Sidney R. Yates (D), *Chicago*
10 John Edward Porter (R), *Wilmette*

---

[4] Resigned January 21, 1993.
[5] Elected June 8, 1993, to fill vacancy caused by resignation of Leon E. Panetta, and took his seat June 16, 1993.

11 George E. Sangmeister (D), *Mokena*
12 Jerry F. Costello (D), *Belleville*
13 Harris W. Fawell (R), *Naperville*
14 J. Dennis Hastert (R), *Yorkville*
15 Thomas W. Ewing (R), *Pontiac*
16 Donald A. Manzullo (R), *Egan*
17 Lane A. Evans (D), *Rock Island*
18 Robert H. Michel (R), *Peoria*
19 Glenn Poshard (D), *Carterville*
20 Richard J. Durbin (D), *Springfield*

## INDIANA

### SENATORS

Richard G. Lugar (R), *Indianapolis*
Dan R. Coats (R), *Indianapolis*

### REPRESENTATIVES

1 Peter J. Visclosky (D), *Merrillville*
2 Philip R. Sharp (D), *Muncie*
3 Timothy J. Roemer (D), *South Bend*
4 Jill L. Long (D), *Larwill*
5 Stephen E. Buyer (R), *Monticello*
6 Dan Burton (R), *Indianapolis*
7 John T. Myers (R), *Covington*
8 Frank McCloskey (D), *Smithville*
9 Lee H. Hamilton (D), *Nashville*
10 Andrew Jacobs, Jr. (D), *Indianapolis*

## IOWA

### SENATORS

Charles E. Grassley (R), *New Hartford*
Tom Harkin (D), *Cumming*

### REPRESENTATIVES

1 James A. S. Leach (R), *Davenport*
2 James A. Nussle (R), *Manchester*
3 Jim Ross Lightfoot (R), *Shenandoah*
4 Neal Smith (D), *Altoona*
5 Fred Grandy (R), *Sioux City*

## KANSAS

### SENATORS

Robert J. Dole (R), *Russell*
Nancy L. Kassebaum (R), *Burdick*

### REPRESENTATIVES

1 Pat Roberts (R), *Dodge City*
2 Jim Slattery (D), *Topeka*
3 Jan Meyers (R), *Overland Park*
4 Daniel R. Glickman (D), *Wichita*

## KENTUCKY

### SENATORS

Wendell H. Ford (D), *Owensboro*
Mitch McConnell (R), *Louisville*

### REPRESENTATIVES

1 Thomas J. Barlow III (D), *Paducah*
2 William H. Natcher (D),[6] *Bowling Green*
2 Ronald Lewis (R),[7] *Cecilia*
3 Romano L. Mazzoli (D), *Louisville*
4 Jim Bunning (R), *Southgate*
5 Harold Rogers (R), *Somerset*
6 Scotty Baesler (D), *Lexington*

## LOUISIANA

### SENATORS

J. Bennett Johnston, Jr. (D), *Shreveport*
John B. Breaux (D), *Crowley*

### REPRESENTATIVES

1 Robert L. Livingston (R), *Metairie*
2 William J. Jefferson (D), *New Orleans*
3 W. J. (Billy) Tauzin (D), *Thibodaux*
4 Cleo Fields (D), *Baton Rouge*
5 James O. McCrery III (R), *Shreveport*
6 Richard H. Baker (R), *Baton Rouge*
7 James A. Hayes (D), *Lafayette*

## MAINE

### SENATORS

William S. Cohen (R), *Bangor*
George J. Mitchell (D), *Portland*

### REPRESENTATIVES

1 Thomas H. Andrews (D), *Portland*
2 Olympia J. Snowe (R), *Auburn*

## MARYLAND

### SENATORS

Paul S. Sarbanes (D), *Baltimore*
Barbara A. Mikulski (D), *Baltimore*

### REPRESENTATIVES

1 Wayne T. Gilchrest (R), *Kennedyville*
2 Helen Delich Bentley (R), *Lutherville*
3 Benjamin L. Cardin (D), *Baltimore*
4 Albert R. Wynn (D), *Largo*
5 Steny H. Hoyer (D), *Mitchellville*
6 Roscoe G. Bartlett (R), *Frederick*
7 Kweisi Mfume (D), *Baltimore*
8 Constance A. Morella (R), *Bethesda*

## MASSACHUSETTS

### SENATORS

Edward M. Kennedy (D), *Boston*
John F. Kerry (D), *Boston*

### REPRESENTATIVES

1 John W. Olver (D), *Amherst*
2 Richard E. Neal (D), *Springfield*
3 Peter I. Blute (R), *Shrewsbury*
4 Barney Frank (D), *Newton*
5 Martin T. Meehan (D), *Lowell*
6 Peter G. Torkildsen (R), *Danvers*
7 Edward J. Markey (D), *Malden*
8 Joseph P. Kennedy II (D), *Boston*
9 John Joseph Moakley (D), *South Boston*
10 Gerry E. Studds (D), *Cohasset*

## MICHIGAN

### SENATORS

Donald W. Riegle, Jr. (D), *Flint*
Carl Levin (D), *Detroit*

### REPRESENTATIVES

1 Bart T. Stupak (D), *Menominee*
2 Peter Hoekstra (R), *Holland*
3 Paul B. Henry (R),[8] *Grand Rapids*
3 Vernon J. Ehlers (R),[9] *Grand Rapids*
4 David L. Camp (R), *Midland*
5 James A. Barcia (D), *Bay City*
6 Fred Upton (R), *St. Joseph*
7 Nick H. Smith (R), *Addison*
8 Bob Carr (D), *East Lansing*
9 Dale E. Kildee (D), *Flint*
10 David E. Bonior (D), *Mount Clemens*
11 Joseph K. Knollenberg (R), *Bloomfield Hills*
12 Sander M. Levin (D), *Southfield*
13 William D. Ford (D), *Ypsilanti*
14 John Conyers, Jr. (D), *Detroit*
15 Barbara-Rose Collins (D), *Detroit*
16 John D. Dingell, Jr. (D), *Trenton*

## MINNESOTA

### SENATORS

David F. Durenberger (R), *Minneapolis*
Paul D. Wellstone (D), *Northfield*

### REPRESENTATIVES

1 Timothy J. Penny (D), *New Richland*
2 David R. Minge (D), *Montevideo*
3 Jim Ramstad (R), *Minnetonka*
4 Bruce F. Vento (D), *St. Paul*
5 Martin Olav Sabo (D), *Minneapolis*
6 Rod Grams (R), *Anoka*
7 Collin C. Peterson (D), *Detroit Lakes*
8 James L. Oberstar (D), *Chisholm*

---

[6] Died March 29, 1994.
[7] Elected May 24, 1994, to fill vacancy caused by death of William H. Natcher, and took his seat May 26, 1994.

[8] Died July 31, 1993.
[9] Elected December 7, 1993, to fill vacancy caused by death of Paul B. Henry, and took his seat January 25, 1994.

## MISSISSIPPI

### SENATORS

Thad Cochran (R), *Jackson*
Trent Lott (R), *Pascagoula*

### REPRESENTATIVES

1 Jamie L. Whitten (D), *Charleston*
2 Mike Espy (D),[10] *Madison*
2 Bennie G. Thompson (D),[11] *Bolton*
3 Gillespie V. (Sonny) Montgomery (D), *Meridian*
4 Michael Parker (D), *Brookhaven*
5 Gary E. (Gene) Taylor (D), *Bay St. Louis*

## MISSOURI

### SENATORS

John C. Danforth (R), *Newburg*
Christopher S. (Kit) Bond (R), *Mexico*

### REPRESENTATIVES

1 William L. Clay (D), *St. Louis*
2 James M. Talent (R), *Chesterfield*
3 Richard A. Gephardt (D), *St. Louis*
4 Ike Skelton (D), *Lexington*
5 Alan D. Wheat (D), *Kansas City*
6 Pat Danner (D), *Smithville*
7 Melton D. Hancock (R), *Springfield*
8 Bill Emerson (R), *Cape Girardeau*
9 Harold L. Volkmer (D), *Hannibal*

## MONTANA

### SENATORS

Max Baucus (D), *Missoula*
Conrad Burns (R), *Billings*

### REPRESENTATIVE AT LARGE

Pat Williams (D), *Helena*

## NEBRASKA

### SENATORS

J. James Exon (D), *Lincoln*
J. Robert Kerrey (D), *Omaha*

### REPRESENTATIVES

1 Douglas K. Bereuter (R), *Utica*
2 Peter D. Hoagland (D), *Omaha*
3 William E. Barrett (R), *Lexington*

## NEVADA

### SENATORS

Harry M. Reid (D), *Searchlight*
Richard H. Bryan (D), *Las Vegas*

### REPRESENTATIVES

1 James H. Bilbray (D), *Las Vegas*
2 Barbara F. Vucanovich (R), *Reno*

## NEW HAMPSHIRE

### SENATORS

Robert C. Smith (R), *Tuftonboro*
Judd Gregg (R), *Greenfield*

### REPRESENTATIVES

1 William H. Zeliff, Jr. (R), *Jackson*
2 Richard W. Swett (D), *Bow*

## NEW JERSEY

### SENATORS

Bill Bradley (D), *Denville*
Frank R. Lautenberg (D), *Secaucus*

### REPRESENTATIVES

1 Robert E. Andrews (D), *Bellmawr*
2 William J. Hughes (D), *Ocean City*
3 H. James Saxton (R), *Mount Holly*
4 Christopher H. Smith (R), *Robbinsville*
5 Marge Roukema (R), *Ridgewood*
6 Frank Pallone, Jr. (D), *Long Branch*
7 Robert D. Franks (R), *New Providence*
8 Herbert C. Klein (D), *Clifton*
9 Robert G. Torricelli (D), *Englewood*
10 Donald M. Payne (D), *Newark*
11 Dean A. Gallo (R),[12] *Parsippany*
12 Richard Zimmer (R), *Flemington*
13 Robert Menendez (D), *Union City*

## NEW MEXICO

### SENATORS

Pete V. Domenici (R), *Albuquerque*
Jeff Bingaman (D), *Albuquerque*

### REPRESENTATIVES

1 Steven H. Schiff (R), *Albuquerque*
2 Joe Skeen (R), *Picacho*
3 William B. Richardson (D), *Santa Fe*

## NEW YORK

### SENATORS

Daniel P. Moynihan (D), *Pindars Corners*
Alfonse M. D'Amato (R), *Island Park*

### REPRESENTATIVES

1 George J. Hochbrueckner (D), *Coram*
2 Rick A. Lazio (R), *Brightwaters*
3 Peter T. King (R), *Seaford*
4 David A. Levy (R), *Baldwin*
5 Gary L. Ackerman (D), *Jamaica*
6 Floyd H. Flake (D), *Rosedale*
7 Thomas J. Manton (D), *Queens*
8 Jerrold L. Nadler (D), *New York*
9 Charles E. Schumer (D), *Brooklyn*
10 Edolphus Towns (D), *Brooklyn*
11 Major R. Owens (D), *Brooklyn*
12 Nydia M. Velázquez (D), *Brooklyn*
13 Susan Molinari (R), *Staten Island*
14 Carolyn B. Maloney (D), *New York*
15 Charles B. Rangel (D), *New York*
16 José E. Serrano (D), *Bronx*
17 Eliot L. Engel (D), *Bronx*
18 Nita M. Lowey (D), *Rye*
19 Hamilton Fish, Jr. (R), *Millbrook*
20 Benjamin A. Gilman (R), *Middletown*
21 Michael R. McNulty (D), *Green Island*
22 Gerald B. H. Solomon (R), *Queensbury*
23 Sherwood L. Boehlert (R), *New Hartford*
24 John M. McHugh (R), *Pierrepont Manor*
25 James T. Walsh (R), *Syracuse*
26 Maurice D. Hinchey (D), *Saugerties*
27 L. William Paxon (R), *Williamsville*
28 Louise M. Slaughter (D), *Fairport*
29 John J. LaFalce (D), *Kenmore*
30 Jack Quinn (R), *Hamburg*
31 Amory Houghton, Jr. (R), *Corning*

## NORTH CAROLINA

### SENATORS

Jesse Helms (R), *Raleigh*
Lauch Faircloth (R), *Clinton*

### REPRESENTATIVES

1 Eva M. Clayton (D), *Littleton*
2 Tim Valentine, Jr. (D), *Nashville*
3 H. Martin Lancaster (D), *Goldsboro*
4 David E. Price (D), *Chapel Hill*
5 Stephen L. Neal (D), *Winston-Salem*
6 Howard Coble (R), *Greensboro*
7 Charles Rose (D), *Fayetteville*
8 W. G. (Bill) Hefner (D), *Concord*
9 J. Alex McMillan (R), *Charlotte*
10 Cass Ballenger (R), *Hickory*
11 Charles H. Taylor (R), *Brevard*
12 Melvin Watt (D), *Charlotte*

## NORTH DAKOTA

### SENATORS

Kent Conrad (D), *Bismarck*
Byron L. Dorgan (D), *Bismarck*

### REPRESENTATIVE AT LARGE

Earl Pomeroy (D), *Bismarck*

## OHIO

### SENATORS

John Glenn, Jr. (D), *Columbus*
Howard M. Metzenbaum (D), *Lyndhurst*

### REPRESENTATIVES

1 David S. Mann (D), *Cincinnati*

[10] Resigned January 22, 1993.
[11] Elected April 13, 1993, to fill vacancy caused by resignation of Mike Espy, and took his seat April 20, 1993.
[12] Died November 6, 1994; vacancy throughout remainder of Congress.

2 Willis D. Gradison, Jr. (R),[13] *Cincinnati*
2 Robert J. Portman (R),[14] *Hyde Park*
3 Tony P. Hall (D), *Dayton*
4 Michael G. Oxley (R), *Findlay*
5 Paul E. Gillmor (R), *Port Clinton*
6 Ted Strickland (D), *Lucasville*
7 David L. Hobson (R), *Springfield*
8 John A. Boehner (R), *West Chester*
9 Marcy Kaptur (D), *Toledo*
10 Martin R. Hoke (R), *Shaker Heights*
11 Louis Stokes (D), *Shaker Heights*
12 John R. Kasich (R), *Westerville*
13 Sherrod C. Brown (D), *Chippewa Lake*
14 Thomas C. Sawyer (D), *Akron*
15 Deborah D. Pryce (R), *Dublin*
16 Ralph Regula (R), *Navarre*
17 James A. Traficant, Jr. (D), *Poland*
18 Douglas Applegate (D), *Steubenville*
19 Eric D. Fingerhut (D), *Cleveland*

## OKLAHOMA

### SENATORS

David L. Boren (D),[15] *Seminole*
James M. Inhofe (R),[16] *Tulsa*
Don Nickles (R), *Ponca City*

### REPRESENTATIVES

1 James M. Inhofe (R),[17] *Tulsa*
1 Steve Largent (R),[18] *Tulsa*
2 Mike Synar (D), *Muskogee*
3 William K. Brewster (D), *Marietta*
4 Dave McCurdy (D), *Norman*
5 Ernest J. Istook, Jr. (R), *Oklahoma City*
6 Glenn English (D),[19] *Cordell*
6 Frank D. Lucas (R),[20] *Cheyenne*

## OREGON

### SENATORS

Mark O. Hatfield (R), *Tigard*
Robert W. Packwood (R), *Portland*

### REPRESENTATIVES

1 Elizabeth Furse (D), *Hillsboro*
2 Bob Smith (R), *Burns*
3 Ron Wyden (D), *Portland*
4 Peter A. DeFazio (D), *Springfield*
5 Michael J. Kopetski (D), *Salem*

## PENNSYLVANIA

### SENATORS

Arlen Specter (R), *Philadelphia*
Harris L. Wofford (D), *Bryn Mawr*

### REPRESENTATIVES

1 Thomas M. Foglietta (D), *Philadelphia*
2 Lucien E. Blackwell (D), *Philadelphia*
3 Robert A. Borski, Jr. (D), *Philadelphia*
4 Ronald Klink (D), *Jeannette*
5 William F. Clinger, Jr. (R), *Warren*
6 Timothy Holden (D), *St. Clair*
7 Curt Weldon (R), *Aston*
8 James C. Greenwood (R), *Doylestown*
9 E. G. Shuster (R), *Everett*
10 Joseph M. McDade (R), *Clarks Summit*
11 Paul E. Kanjorski (D), *Nanticoke City*
12 John P. Murtha, Jr. (D), *Johnstown*
13 Marjorie Margolies–Mezvinsky (D), *Narberth*
14 William J. Coyne (D), *Pittsburgh*
15 Paul F. McHale, Jr. (D), *Bethlehem*
16 Robert S. Walker (R), *East Petersburg*
17 George W. Gekas (R), *Harrisburg*
18 Richard J. Santorum (R), *Mt. Lebanon*
19 William F. Goodling (R), *Jacobus*
20 Austin J. Murphy (D), *Monongahela*
21 Thomas J. Ridge (R), *Erie*

## RHODE ISLAND

### SENATORS

Claiborne Pell (D), *Newport*
John H. Chafee (R), *Warwick*

### REPRESENTATIVES

1 Ronald K. Machtley (R), *Portsmouth*
2 John F. Reed (D), *Cranston*

## SOUTH CAROLINA

### SENATORS

Strom Thurmond (R), *Aiken*
Ernest F. Hollings (D), *Charleston*

### REPRESENTATIVES

1 Arthur Ravenel, Jr. (R), *Mount Pleasant*

2 Floyd Spence (R), *Lexington*
3 Butler Derrick (D), *Edgefield*
4 Robert D. Inglis (R), *Greenville*
5 John M. Spratt, Jr. (D), *York*
6 James E. Clyburn (D), *Columbia*

## SOUTH DAKOTA

### SENATORS

Larry Pressler (R), *Humboldt*
Thomas A. Daschle (D), *Aberdeen*

### REPRESENTATIVE AT LARGE

Tim Johnson (D), *Vermillion*

## TENNESSEE

### SENATORS

James R. Sasser (D), *Nashville*
Harlan Mathews (D),[21] *Nashville*
Fred D. Thompson (R),[22] *Nashville*

### REPRESENTATIVES

1 James H. Quillen (R), *Kingsport*
2 John J. Duncan (R), *Knoxville*
3 Marilyn Lloyd (D), *Chattanooga*
4 James Cooper (D), *Shelbyville*
5 Robert N. Clement (D), *Nashville*
6 Bart Gordon (D), *Murfreesboro*
7 Donald K. Sundquist (R), *Memphis*
8 John S. Tanner (D), *Union City*
9 Harold E. Ford (D), *Memphis*

## TEXAS

### SENATORS

Lloyd M. Bentsen, Jr. (D),[23] *Star County*
Robert Krueger (D),[24] *New Braunfels*
Kay Bailey Hutchison (R),[25] *Dallas*
Phil Gramm (R), *College Station*

### REPRESENTATIVES

1 Jim Chapman (D), *Sulphur Springs*
2 Charles Wilson (D), *Lufkin*
3 Sam Johnson (R), *Dallas*
4 Ralph M. Hall (D), *Rockwall*
5 John W. Bryant (D), *Dallas*
6 Joe Barton (R), *Ennis*
7 William R. Archer, Jr. (R), *Houston*
8 Jack Fields (R), *Humble*
9 Jack B. Brooks (D), *Beaumont*
10 J. J. (Jake) Pickle (D), *Austin*
11 Chet Edwards (D), *Waco*
12 Preston M. (Pete) Geren III (D), *Fort Worth*
13 William Sarpalius (D), *Amarillo*

---

[13] Resigned January 31, 1993.
[14] Elected May 4, 1993, to fill vacancy caused by resignation of Willis D. Gradison, Jr., and took his seat May 5, 1993.
[15] Resigned November 15, 1994.
[16] Elected November 8, 1994, to fill vacancy caused by resignation of David L. Boren, and took his seat November 17, 1994.
[17] Resigned November 17, 1994, having been elected Senator.

[18] Elected to the One Hundred Fourth Congress, November 8, 1994; took oath of office as a member of the One Hundred Third Congress on November 29, 1994 pursuant to H. Res. 585, thereby filling vacancy caused by resignation of James M. Inhofe.
[19] Resigned January 7, 1994.
[20] Elected May 10, 1994, to fill vacancy caused by resignation of Glenn English, and took his seat May 17, 1994.
[21] Resigned December 1, 1994.

[22] Elected November 8, 1994, for remainder of term ending January 3, 1997; took his seat December 9, 1994 to fill vacancy caused by resignation of Harlan Mathews.
[23] Resigned January 20, 1993.
[24] Appointed to fill vacancy caused by resignation of Lloyd M. Bentsen, Jr., and took his seat January 21, 1992.
[25] Elected to fill vacancy caused by resignation of Lloyd M. Bentsen, Jr., and took her seat June 14, 1993.

## TEXAS—Continued

REPRESENTATIVES—CONTINUED

14 Gregory H. Laughlin (D), *West Columbia*
15 Eligio (Kika) de la Garza (D), *Mission*
16 Ronald Coleman (D), *El Paso*
17 Charles W. Stenholm (D), *Avoca*
18 Craig A. Washington (D), *Houston*
19 Larry Combest (R), *Lubbock*
20 Henry B. Gonzalez (D), *San Antonio*
21 Lamar S. Smith (R), *San Antonio*
22 Tom DeLay (R), *Sugar Land*
23 Henry Bonilla (R), *San Antonio*
24 Martin Frost (D), *Dallas*
25 Michael A. Andrews (D), *Houston*
26 Richard K. Armey (R), *Flower Mound*
27 Solomon P. Ortiz (D), *Corpus Christi*
28 Frank M. Tejeda (D), *San Antonio*
29 Gene Green (D), *Houston*
30 Eddie Bernice Johnson (D), *Dallas*

## UTAH

SENATORS

Orrin G. Hatch (R), *Salt Lake City*
Robert F. Bennett (R), *Salt Lake City*

REPRESENTATIVES

1 James V. Hansen (R), *Farmington*
2 Karen Shepherd (D), *Salt Lake City*
3 William Orton (D), *Sundance*

## VERMONT

SENATORS

Patrick J. Leahy (D), *Burlington*
James M. Jeffords (R), *Shrewsbury*

REPRESENTATIVE AT LARGE

Bernard Sanders (I), *Burlington*

## VIRGINIA

SENATORS

John W. Warner (R), *Middleburg*
Charles S. Robb (D), *McLean*

REPRESENTATIVES

1 Herbert H. Bateman (R), *Newport News*
2 Owen B. Pickett (D), *Virginia Beach*
3 Robert C. Scott (D), *Newport News*
4 Norman Sisisky (D), *Petersburg*
5 L. F. Payne, Jr. (D), *Nellysford*
6 Robert W. Goodlatte (R), *Roanoke*
7 Thomas J. Bliley, Jr. (R), *Richmond*
8 James P. Moran (D), *Alexandria*
9 Frederick C. Boucher (D), *Abingdon*
10 Frank R. Wolf (R), *Vienna*
11 Leslie L. Byrne (D), *Annandale*

## WASHINGTON

SENATORS

Slade Gorton III (R), *Seattle*
Patty Murray (D), *Seattle*

REPRESENTATIVES

1 Maria Cantwell (D), *Mountlake Terrace*
2 Al Swift (D), *Bellingham*
3 Jolene Unsoeld (D), *Olympia*
4 Jay R. Inslee (D), *Selah*
5 Thomas S. Foley (D), *Spokane*
6 Norman D. Dicks (D), *Bremerton*
7 James A. McDermott (D), *Seattle*
8 Jennifer B. Dunn (R), *Bellevue*
9 Myron B. Kreidler (D), *Federal Way*

## WEST VIRGINIA

SENATORS

Robert C. Byrd (D), *Sophia*
John D. Rockefeller IV (D), *Charleston*

REPRESENTATIVES

1 Alan B. Mollohan (D), *Fairmont*
2 Robert E. Wise, Jr. (D), *Clendenin*
3 Nick J. Rahall II (D), *Beckley*

## WISCONSIN

SENATORS

Herbert H. Kohl (D), *Milwaukee*
Russell D. Feingold (D), *Middleton*

REPRESENTATIVES

1 Les Aspin (D),[26] *East Troy*
1 Peter W. Barca (D),[27] *Kenosha*
2 Scott L. Klug (R), *Madison*
3 Steven Gunderson (R), *Osseo*
4 Gerald D. Kleczka (D), *Milwaukee*
5 Thomas M. Barrett (D), *Milwaukee*
6 Thomas E. Petri (R), *Fond du Lac*
7 David R. Obey (D), *Wausau*
8 Toby A. Roth (R), *Appleton*
9 F. James Sensenbrenner, Jr. (R), *Menomomee Falls*

## WYOMING

SENATORS

Malcolm Wallop (R), *Big Horn*
Alan K. Simpson (R), *Cody*

REPRESENTATIVE AT LARGE

Craig L. Thomas (R), *Casper*

## AMERICAN SAMOA

DELEGATE

Eni F. H. Faleomavaega, Jr. (D), *Pago Pago*

## COMMONWEALTH OF PUERTO RICO

RESIDENT COMMISSIONER

Carlos A. Romero-Barceló (D), *San Juan*

## DISTRICT OF COLUMBIA

DELEGATE

Eleanor Holmes Norton (D), *Washington, D.C.*

## GUAM

DELEGATE

Robert A. Underwood (D), *Agana*

## VIRGIN ISLANDS

DELEGATE

Ron de Lugo (D), *St. Croix*

[26] Resigned January 21, 1993.
[27] Elected May 4, 1993, to fill vacancy caused by resignation of Les Aspin, and took his seat June 8, 1993.

# 104TH CONGRESS

## JANUARY 3, 1995, TO JANUARY 3, 1997

FIRST SESSION—JANUARY 4, 1995, TO JANUARY 3, 1996
SECOND SESSION—JANUARY 3, 1996, TO OCTOBER 4, 1996

Albert A. Gore, Jr.
Vice President

Newt Gingrich
Speaker

### Senate
53 Republicans — 47 Democrats

VICE PRESIDENT OF THE UNITED STATES—ALBERT A. GORE, JR., of Tennessee
PRESIDENT PRO TEMPORE OF THE SENATE—STROM THURMOND,[1] of South Carolina
SECRETARY OF THE SENATE—SHEILA P. BURKE,[2] of Virginia; KELLY D. JOHNSTON,[3] of Oklahoma; GARY L. SISCO,[4] of Tennessee
SERGEANT AT ARMS OF THE SENATE—HOWARD O. GREENE, JR.,[5] of Delaware; GREGORY S. CASEY,[6] of Idaho
CHAPLAIN OF THE SENATE—DR. LLOYD JOHN OGILVIE, D.D.
MAJORITY FLOOR LEADER—ROBERT J. DOLE,[7] of Kansas; TRENT LOTT,[8] of Mississippi
REPUBLICAN WHIP—TRENT LOTT, of Mississippi; DONALD L. NICKLES,[9] of Oklahoma
DEMOCRATIC FLOOR LEADER—THOMAS A. DASCHLE, of South Dakota
ASSISTANT DEMOCRATIC LEADER—WENDELL H. FORD, of Kentucky

### House of Representatives
230 Republicans — 204 Democrats — 1 Independent

SPEAKER OF THE HOUSE—NEWT GINGRICH, of Georgia
CLERK OF THE HOUSE—ROBIN H. CARLE,[10] of Virginia
SERGEANT AT ARMS OF THE HOUSE—WILSON S. LIVINGOOD,[11] of Virginia
CHIEF ADMINISTRATIVE OFFICER OF THE HOUSE—SCOT M. FAULKNER,[12] of West Virginia
CHAPLAIN OF THE HOUSE—REV. JAMES DAVID FORD,[13] D.D.
MAJORITY LEADER—RICHARD K. ARMEY, of Texas
MAJORITY WHIP—TOM DELAY, of Texas
DEMOCRATIC LEADER—RICHARD A. GEPHARDT, of Missouri
DEMOCRATIC WHIP—DAVID E. BONIOR, of Michigan

## ALABAMA

### SENATORS

Howell T. Heflin (D), *Tuscumbia*
Richard C. Shelby (R), *Tuscaloosa*

### REPRESENTATIVES

1 H. L. (Sonny) Callahan (R), *Mobile*
2 Terry Everett (R), *Enterprise*
3 J. Glen Browder (D), *Jacksonville*
4 Tom Bevill (D), *Jasper*
5 Robert E. (Bud) Cramer, Jr. (D), *Huntsville*
6 Spencer T. Bachus III (R), *Birmingham*
7 Earl F. Hilliard (D), *Birmingham*

## ALASKA

### SENATORS

Theodore F. Stevens (R), *Girdwood*
Frank H. Murkowski (R), *Fairbanks*

### REPRESENTATIVE AT LARGE

Donald E. Young (R), *Fort Yukon*

## ARIZONA

### SENATORS

John S. McCain III (R), *Phoenix*
Jon L. Kyl (R), *Phoenix*

### REPRESENTATIVES

1 Matt Salmon (R), *Mesa*
2 Edward L. Pastor (D), *Phoenix*
3 Bob Stump (R), *Tolleson*
4 John Shadegg (R), *Phoenix*
5 Jim Kolbe (R), *Tucson*
6 John D. Hayworth, Jr. (R), *Scottsfield*

## ARKANSAS

### SENATORS

Dale Bumpers (D), *Charleston*
David H. Pryor (D), *Little Rock*

### REPRESENTATIVES

1 Blanche Lambert Lincoln (D), *Helena*
2 Raymond H. Thornton, Jr. (D), *Little Rock*
3 Y. Tim Hutchinson (R), *Bentonville*
4 Jay W. Dickey, Jr. (R), *Pine Bluff*

[1] Elected January 4, 1995.
[2] Elected January 4, 1995.
[3] Elected June 8, 1995.
[4] Elected pursuant to S.Res. 307, October 1, 1996.
[5] Elected January 4, 1995.
[6] Elected pursuant to S.Res. 289, September 6, 1996.
[7] Resigned as Majority Leader on June 11, 1996; resigned from the Senate on June 11, 1996.
[8] Elected June 12, 1996.
[9] Elected June 12, 1996.
[10] Elected January 4, 1995.
[11] Elected January 4, 1995.
[12] Elected January 4, 1995.
[13] Reelected January 4, 1995.

## CALIFORNIA

### SENATORS

Dianne Feinstein (D), *San Francisco*
Barbara Boxer (D), *Greenbrae*

### REPRESENTATIVES

1 Frank D. Riggs (R), *Windsor*
2 Wally Herger (R), *Marysville*
3 Vic Fazio (D), *West Sacramento*
4 John T. Doolittle (R), *Rocklin*
5 Robert T. Matsui (D), *Sacramento*
6 Lynn C. Woolsey (D), *Petaluma*
7 George Miller (D), *Martinez*
8 Nancy Pelosi (D), *San Franscisco*
9 Ronald V. Dellums (D), *Oakland*
10 William P. Baker (R), *Danville*
11 Richard W. Pombo (R), *Tracy*
12 Tom Lantos (D), *San Mateo*
13 Fortney H. (Pete) Stark, Jr. (D), *Hayward*
14 Anna G. Eshoo (D), *Atherton*
15 Norman Y. Mineta (D),[14] *San Jose*
15 Thomas J. Campbell (R),[15] *Campbell*
16 Zoe Lofgren (D), *San Jose*
17 Sam Farr (D), *Carmel*
18 Gary A. Condit (D), *Ceres*
19 George P. Radanovich (R), *Mariposa*
20 Calvin M. Dooley (D), *Visalia*
21 William M. Thomas (R), *Bakersfield*
22 Andrea Seastrand (R), *Shell Beach*
23 Elton W. Gallegly (R), *Simi Valley*
24 Anthony C. Beilenson (D), *Woodland Hills*
25 Howard P. McKeon (R), *Santa Clarita*
26 Howard L. Berman (D), *Mission Hills*
27 Carlos J. Moorhead (R), *Glendale*
28 David Dreier (R), *San Dimas*
29 Henry A. Waxman (D), *Los Angeles*
30 Xavier Becerra (D), *Los Angeles*
31 Matthew G. Martinez, Jr. (D), *Monterey Park*
32 Julian C. Dixon (D), *Los Angeles*
33 Lucille Roybal-Allard (D), *Los Angeles*
34 Esteban Edward Torres (D), *Pico Rivera*
35 Maxine Waters (D), *Los Angeles*
36 Jane Harman (D), *Rolling Hills*
37 Walter R. Tucker III (D),[16] *Compton*
37 Juanita Millender-McDonald (D),[17] *Carson*
38 Steve Horn (R), *Long Beach*
39 Edward R. Royce (R), *Fullerton*
40 Jerry Lewis (R), *Redlands*
41 Jay C. Kim (R), *Diamond Bar*
42 George E. Brown, Jr. (D), *Riverside*
43 Kenneth Calvert (R), *Corona*
44 Sonny Bono (R), *Palm Springs*
45 Dana Rohrabacher (R), *Huntington Beach*
46 Robert K. Dornan (R), *Garden Grove*
47 C. Christopher Cox (R), *Newport Beach*
48 Ron Packard (R), *Oceanside*
49 Brian P. Bilbray (R), *Imperial Beach*
50 Robert Filner (D), *San Diego*
51 Randy (Duke) Cunningham (R), *San Diego*
52 Duncan L. Hunter (R), *Alpine*

## COLORADO

### SENATORS

Hank Brown (R), *Greeley*
Ben Nighthorse Campbell (D),[18] *Ignacio*

### REPRESENTATIVES

1 Patricia Schroeder (D), *Denver*
2 David E. Skaggs (D), *Boulder*
3 Scott S. McInnis (R), *Grand Junction*
4 A. Wayne Allard (R), *Loveland*
5 Joel Hefley (R), *Colorado Springs*
6 Dan Schaefer (R), *Lakewood*

## CONNECTICUT

### SENATORS

Christopher J. Dodd (D), *East Haddam*
Joseph I. Lieberman (D), *New Haven*

### REPRESENTATIVES

1 Barbara B. Kennelly (D), *Hartford*
2 Samuel Gejdenson (D), *Bozrah*
3 Rosa L. DeLauro (D), *New Haven*
4 Christopher Shays (R), *Stamford*
5 Gary A. Franks (R), *Waterbury*
6 Nancy L. Johnson (R), *New Britain*

## DELAWARE

### SENATORS

William V. Roth, Jr. (R), *Wilmington*
Joseph R. Biden, Jr. (D), *Wilmington*

### REPRESENTATIVE AT LARGE

Michael N. Castle (R), *Wilmington*

## FLORIDA

### SENATORS

Bob Graham (D), *Miami Lakes*
Connie Mack (R), *Cape Coral*

### REPRESENTATIVES

1 C. Joseph Scarborough (R), *Pensacola*
2 Douglas (Pete) Peterson (D), *Marianna*
3 Corrine Brown (D), *Jacksonville*
4 Tillie K. Fowler (R), *Jacksonville*
5 Karen L. Thurman (D), *Dunnellon*
6 Clifford B. Stearns (R), *Ocala*
7 John L. Mica (R), *Winter Park*
8 Bill McCollum, Jr. (R), *Orlando*
9 Michael Bilirakis (R), *Palm Harbor*
10 C. W. Bill Young (R), *St. Petersburg*
11 Sam M. Gibbons (D), *Tampa*
12 Charles T. Canady (R), *Lakeland*
13 Dan Miller (R), *Bradenton*
14 Porter J. Goss (R), *Sanibel*
15 Dave Weldon (R), *Palm Bay*
16 Mark Foley (R), *West Palm Beach*
17 Carrie P. Meek (D), *Miami*
18 Ileana Ros-Lehtinen (R), *Miami*
19 Harry A. Johnston II (D), *Boynton Beach*
20 Peter Deutsch (D), *Tamarac*
21 Lincoln Diaz-Balart (R), *Miami*
22 Clay Shaw (R), *Fort Lauderdale*
23 Alcee L. Hastings (D), *Miramar*

## GEORGIA

### SENATORS

Sam Nunn (D), *Perry*
Paul D. Coverdell (R), *Atlanta*

### REPRESENTATIVES

1 Jack Kingston (R), *Savannah*
2 Sanford D. Bishop, Jr. (D), *Columbus*
3 Michael A. (Mac) Collins (R), *McDonough*
4 John E. Linder (R), *Atlanta*
5 John R. Lewis (D), *Atlanta*
6 Newt Gingrich (R), *Marietta*
7 Bob Barr (R), *Smyrna*
8 C. Saxby Chambliss (R), *Moultrie*
9 J. Nathan Deal (D),[19] *Lula*
10 Charles W. Norwood, Jr. (R), *Evans*
11 Cynthia A. McKinney (D), *Lithonia*

## HAWAII

### SENATORS

Daniel K. Inouye (D), *Honolulu*
Daniel K. Akaka (D), *Honolulu*

### REPRESENTATIVES

1 Neil Abercrombie (D), *Honolulu*
2 Patsy T. Mink (D), *Honolulu*

---

[14] Resigned October 10, 1995.
[15] Elected December 12, 1995 to fill vacancy caused by resignation of Norman Y. Mineta, and took his seat December 15, 1995.

[16] Resigned December 15, 1995.
[17] Elected March 26, 1996, to fill vacancy caused by resignation of Walter R. Tucker III, and took her seat April 16, 1996.

[18] Changed party affiliation to Republican, March 3, 1995.
[19] Changed party affiliation to Republican, April 10, 1995.

## IDAHO

SENATORS

Larry Craig (R), *Payette*
Dirk Kempthorne (R), *Boise*

REPRESENTATIVES

1 Helen P. Chenoweth (R), *Boise*
2 Michael D. Crapo (R), *Idaho Falls*

## ILLINOIS

SENATORS

Paul M. Simon (D), *Makanda*
Carol Moseley-Braun (D), *Chicago*

REPRESENTATIVES

1 Bobby L. Rush (D), *Chicago*
2 Mel Reynolds (D),[20] *Chicago*
2 Jesse L. Jackson, Jr. (D),[21] *Chicago*
3 William O. Lipinski (D), *Chicago*
4 Luis V. Gutierrez (D), *Chicago*
5 Michael P. Flanagan (R), *Chicago*
6 Henry J. Hyde (R), *Wood Dale*
7 Cardiss Collins (D), *Chicago*
8 Philip M. Crane (R), *Wauconda*
9 Sidney R. Yates (D), *Chicago*
10 John Edward Porter (R), *Wilmette*
11 Gerald C. Weller (R), *Morris*
12 Jerry F. Costello (D), *Belleville*
13 Harris W. Fawell (R), *Naperville*
14 J. Dennis Hastert (R), *Yorkville*
15 Thomas W. Ewing (R), *Pontiac*
16 Donald A. Manzullo (R), *Egan*
17 Lane A. Evans (D), *Rock Island*
18 Ray H. LaHood (R), *Peoria*
19 Glenn Poshard (D), *Marion*
20 Richard J. Durbin (D), *Springfield*

## INDIANA

SENATORS

Richard G. Lugar (R), *Indianapolis*
Dan R. Coats (R), *Fort Wayne*

REPRESENTATIVES

1 Peter J. Visclosky (D), *Merrillville*
2 David M. McIntosh (R), *Muncie*
3 Timothy J. Roemer (D), *South Bend*
4 Mark E. Souder (R), *Fort Wayne*
5 Stephen E. Buyer (R), *Monticello*
6 Dan Burton (R), *Indianapolis*
7 John T. Myers (R), *Covington*
8 John N. Hostettler (R), *Evansville*
9 Lee H. Hamilton (D), *Nashville*
10 Andrew Jacobs, Jr. (D), *Indianapolis*

## IOWA

SENATORS

Charles E. Grassley (R), *New Hartford*

Tom Harkin (D), *Cumming*

REPRESENTATIVES

1 James A. S. Leach (R), *Davenport*
2 James A. Nussle (R), *Manchester*
3 Jim Ross Lightfoot (R), *Shenandoah*
4 Greg Ganske (R), *Des Moines*
5 Tom Latham (R), *Alexander*

## KANSAS

SENATORS

Robert J. Dole (R), [22] *Russell*
Sheila Frahm (R), [23] *Colby*
Nancy L. Kassebaum (R), *Burdick*

REPRESENTATIVES

1 Pat Roberts (R), *Dodge City*
2 Samuel D. Brownback (R), *Topeka*
3 Jan Meyers (R), *Overland Park*
4 Todd Tiahrt (R), *Goddard*

## KENTUCKY

SENATORS

Wendell H. Ford (D), *Owensboro*
Mitch McConnell (R), *Louisville*

REPRESENTATIVES

1 Edward Whitfield (R), *Hopkinsville*
2 Ron Lewis (R), *South Shore*
3 Michael D. Ward (D), *Louisville*
4 Jim Bunning (R), *Southgate*
5 Harold Rogers (R), *Somerset*
6 Scotty Baesler (D), *Lexington*

## LOUISIANA

SENATORS

J. Bennett Johnston, Jr. (D), *Shreveport*
John B. Breaux (D), *Crowley*

REPRESENTATIVES

1 Robert L. Livingston (R), *Metairie*
2 William J. Jefferson (D), *New Orleans*
3 W. J. (Billy) Tauzin (D),[24] *Chackbay*
4 Cleo Fields (D), *Baton Rouge*
5 James O. McCrery III (R), *Shreveport*
6 Richard H. Baker (R), *Baton Rouge*
7 James A. Hayes (D),[25] *Lafayette*

## MAINE

SENATORS

William S. Cohen (R), *Bangor*
Olympia J. Snowe (R), *Auburn*

REPRESENTATIVES

1 James B. Longley, Jr. (R), *Falmouth*
2 John E. Baldacci (D), *Bangor*

## MARYLAND

SENATORS

Paul S. Sarbanes (D), *Baltimore*
Barbara A. Mikulski (D), *Baltimore*

REPRESENTATIVES

1 Wayne T. Gilchrest (R), *Kennedyville*
2 Robert L. Ehrlich, Jr. (R), *Timonium*
3 Benjamin L. Cardin (D), *Baltimore*
4 Albert R. Wynn (D), *Largo*
5 Steny H. Hoyer (D), *Forestville*
6 Roscoe G. Bartlett (R), *Frederick*
7 Kweisi Mfume (D),[26] *Baltimore*
7 Elijah E. Cummings (D),[27] *Baltimore*
8 Constance A. Morella (R), *Bethesda*

## MASSACHUSETTS

SENATORS

Edward M. Kennedy (D), *Barnstable*
John F. Kerry (D), *Boston*

REPRESENTATIVES

1 John W. Olver (D), *Amherst*
2 Richard E. Neal (D), *Springfield*
3 Peter I. Blute (R), *Shrewsbury*
4 Barney Frank (D), *Newton*
5 Martin T. Meehan (D), *Lowell*
6 Peter G. Torkildsen (R), *Danvers*
7 Edward J. Markey (D), *Malden*
8 Joseph P. Kennedy II (D), *Boston*
9 J. Joseph Moakley (D), *South Boston*
10 Gerry E. Studds (D), *Cohasset*

## MICHIGAN

SENATORS

Carl Levin (D), *Detroit*
Spencer Abraham (R), *Auburn Hills*

REPRESENTATIVES

1 Bart T. Stupak (D), *Menominee*
2 Peter Hoekstra (R), *Holland*
3 Vernon J. Ehlers (R), *Grand Rapids*
4 David L. Camp (R), *Midland*
5 James A. Barcia (D), *Bay City*
6 Fred Upton (R), *St. Joseph*
7 Nick H. Smith (R), *Addison*
8 Richard Chrysler (R), *Brighton*
9 Dale E. Kildee (D), *Flint*

---

[20] Resigned October 1, 1995.
[21] Elected December 12, 1995 to fill vacancy caused by resignation of Mel Reynolds, and took his seat December 14, 1995.
[22] Resigned June 11, 1996.
[23] Appointed May 24, 1996 to fill vacancy caused by resignation of Robert J. Dole, and took her seat June 11, 1996.
[24] Changed party affiliation to Republican, August 6, 1995.
[25] Changed party affiliation to Republican, December 1, 1995.
[26] Resigned February 18, 1996.
[27] Elected April 16, 1996 to fill vacancy caused by resignation of Kweisi Mfume, and took his seat April 25, 1996.

## MICHIGAN—Continued

REPRESENTATIVES—CONTINUED

10 David E. Bonior (D), *Mount Clemens*
11 Joseph K. Knollenberg (R), *Bloomfield Hills*
12 Sander M. Levin (D), *Royal Oak*
13 Lynn N. Rivers (D), *Ann Arbor*
14 John Conyers, Jr. (D), *Detroit*
15 Barbara-Rose Collins (D), *Detroit*
16 John D. Dingell, Jr. (D), *Dearborn*

## MINNESOTA

SENATORS

Paul D. Wellstone (D), *Northfield*
Rod Grams (R), *Ramsey*

REPRESENTATIVES

1 Gilbert W. Gutknecht (R), *Rochester*
2 David R. Minge (D), *Montevideo*
3 Jim Ramstad (R), *Minnetonka*
4 Bruce F. Vento (D), *St. Paul*
5 Martin Olav Sabo (D), *Minneapolis*
6 William P. Luther (D), *Stillwater*
7 Collin C. Peterson (D), *Detroit Lakes*
8 James L. Oberstar (D), *Chisholm*

## MISSISSIPPI

SENATORS

Thad Cochran (R), *Jackson*
C. Trent Lott (R), *Pascagoula*

REPRESENTATIVES

1 Roger F. Wicker (R), *Tupelo*
2 Bennie G. Thompson (D), *Bolton*
3 Gillespie V. (Sonny) Montgomery (D), *Meridian*
4 Michael Parker (D),[28] *Brookhaven*
5 Gary E. (Gene) Taylor (D), *Bay St. Louis*

## MISSOURI

SENATORS

Christopher S. (Kit) Bond (R), *Mexico*
John D. Ashcroft (R), *Ballwin*

REPRESENTATIVES

1 William L. Clay (D), *St. Louis*
2 James M. Talent (R), *Chesterfield*
3 Richard A. Gephardt (D), *St. Louis*
4 Ike Skelton (D), *Lexington*
5 Karen McCarthy (D), *Kansas City*
6 Pat Danner (D), *Kansas City North*
7 Melton D. Hancock (R), *Springfield*
8 Bill Emerson (R),[29] *Cape Girardeau*
9 Harold L. Volkmer (D), *Hannibal*

## MONTANA

SENATORS

Max Baucus (D), *Missoula*
Conrad Burns (R), *Billings*

REPRESENTATIVE AT LARGE

Pat Williams (D), *Helena*

## NEBRASKA

SENATORS

J. James Exon (D), *Lincoln*
J. Robert Kerrey (D), *Omaha*

REPRESENTATIVES

1 Douglas K. Bereuter (R), *Lincoln*
2 Jon Christensen (R), *Omaha*
3 William E. Barrett (R), *Lexington*

## NEVADA

SENATORS

Harry M. Reid (D), *Searchlight*
Richard H. Bryan (D), *Las Vegas*

REPRESENTATIVES

1 John Ensign (R), *Las Vegas*
2 Barbara F. Vucanovich (R), *Reno*

## NEW HAMPSHIRE

SENATORS

Robert C. Smith (R), *Tuftonboro*
Judd Gregg (R), *Greenfield*

REPRESENTATIVES

1 William H. Zeliff, Jr. (R), *Jackson*
2 Charles F. Bass (R), *Peterborough*

## NEW JERSEY

SENATORS

Bill Bradley (D), *Montclair*
Frank R. Lautenberg (D), *Cliffside Park*

REPRESENTATIVES

1 Robert E. Andrews (D), *Haddon Heights*
2 Frank A. LoBiondo (R), *Vineland*
3 H. James Saxton (R), *Mount Holly*
4 Christopher H. Smith (R), *Robbinsville*
5 Marge Roukema (R), *Ridgewood*
6 Frank Pallone, Jr. (D), *Long Branch*
7 Robert D. Franks (R), *New Providence*
8 Bill Martini (R), *Cedar Grove*
9 Robert G. Torricelli (D), *Englewood*
10 Donald M. Payne (D), *Newark*
11 Rodney P. Frelinghuysen (R), *Morristown*
12 Richard Zimmer (R), *Delaware*
13 Robert Menendez (D), *Union City*

## NEW MEXICO

SENATORS

Pete V. Domenici (R), *Albuquerque*
Jeff Bingaman (D), *Santa Fe*

REPRESENTATIVES

1 Steven H. Schiff (R), *Albuquerque*
2 Joe Skeen (R), *Picacho*
3 William B. Richardson (D), *Santa Fe*

## NEW YORK

SENATORS

Daniel P. Moynihan (D), *Oneonta*
Alfonse M. D'Amato (R), *Island Park*

REPRESENTATIVES

1 Michael P. Forbes (R), *Quogue*
2 Rick A. Lazio (R), *Brightwaters*
3 Peter T. King (R), *Seaford*
4 Daniel Frisa (R), *Westbury*
5 Gary L. Ackerman (D), *Queens*
6 Floyd H. Flake (D), *Rosedale*
7 Thomas J. Manton (D), *Queens*
8 Jerrold L. Nadler (D), *New York*
9 Charles E. Schumer (D), *Brooklyn*
10 Edolphus Towns (D), *Brooklyn*
11 Major R. Owens (D), *Brooklyn*
12 Nydia M. Velázquez (D), *New York*
13 Susan Molinari (R), *Staten Island*
14 Carolyn B. Maloney (D), *New York*
15 Charles B. Rangel (D), *New York*
16 José E. Serrano (D), *Bronx*
17 Eliot L. Engel (D), *Bronx*
18 Nita M. Lowey (D), *Rye*
19 Sue W. Kelly (R), *Katonah*
20 Benjamin A. Gilman (R), *Middletown*
21 Michael R. McNulty (D), *Green Island*
22 Gerald B. H. Solomon (R), *Glens Falls*
23 Sherwood L. Boehlert (R), *New Hartford*
24 John M. McHugh (R), *Pierrepont Manor*
25 James T. Walsh (R), *Syracuse*
26 Maurice D. Hinchey (D), *Saugerties*
27 L. William Paxon (R), *Williamsville*
28 Louise M. Slaughter (D), *Fairport*
29 John J. LaFalce (D), *Tonawanda*
30 Jack Quinn (R), *Hamburg*
31 Amory Houghton, Jr. (R), *Corning*

## NORTH CAROLINA

SENATORS

Jesse Helms (R), *Raleigh*
Lauch Faircloth (R), *Clinton*

---

[28] Changed party affiliation to Republican, November 10, 1995.

[29] Died June 22, 1996.

## REPRESENTATIVES

1 Eva M. Clayton (D), *Littleton*
2 David B. Funderburk (R), *Buies Creek*
3 Walter B. Jones, Jr. (R), *Farmville*
4 Frederick K. Heineman (R), *Raleigh*
5 Richard Burr (R), *Winston-Salem*
6 Howard Coble (R), *Greensboro*
7 Charles Rose (D), *Fayetteville*
8 W. G. (Bill) Hefner (D), *Concord*
9 Sue Myrick (R), *Charlotte*
10 Cass Ballenger (R), *Hickory*
11 Charles H. Taylor (R), *Brevard*
12 Melvin Watt (D), *Charlotte*

## NORTH DAKOTA

### SENATORS

Kent Conrad (D), *Bismarck*
Byron L. Dorgan (D), *Bismarck*

### REPRESENTATIVE AT LARGE

Earl R. Pomeroy (D), *Valley City*

## OHIO

### SENATORS

John Glenn, Jr. (D), *Columbus*
Michael DeWine (R), *Yellowsprings*

### REPRESENTATIVES

1 Steve Chabot (R), *Cincinnati*
2 Robert J. Portman (R), *Cincinnati*
3 Tony P. Hall (D), *Dayton*
4 Michael G. Oxley (R), *Findlay*
5 Paul E. Gillmor (R), *Old Fort*
6 Frank A. Cremeans (R), *Gallipolis*
7 David L. Hobson (R), *Springfield*
8 John A. Boehner (R), *West Chester*
9 Marcy Kaptur (D), *Toledo*
10 Martin R. Hoke (R), *Lakewood*
11 Louis Stokes (D), *Shaker Heights*
12 John R. Kasich (R), *Westerville*
13 Sherrod C. Brown (D), *Lorain*
14 Thomas C. Sawyer (D), *Akron*
15 Deborah D. Pryce (R), *Columbus*
16 Ralph Regula (R), *Navarre*
17 James A. Traficant, Jr. (D), *Poland*
18 Robert W. Ney (R), *Columbus*
19 Steven C. LaTourette (R), *Madison Village*

## OKLAHOMA

### SENATORS

Donald L. Nickles (R), *Ponca City*
James M. Inhofe (R), *Tulsa*

### REPRESENTATIVES

1 Steve Largent (R), *Tulsa*
2 Thomas A. Coburn (R), *Muskogee*
3 William K. Brewster (D), *Marietta*
4 J. C. Watts, Jr. (R), *Norman*

5 Ernest J. Istook, Jr. (R), *Oklahoma City*
6 Frank D. Lucas (R), *Cheyenne*

## OREGON

### SENATORS

Mark O. Hatfield (R), *Portland*
Robert W. Packwood (R),[30] *Portland*
Ron Wyden (D),[31] *Portland*

### REPRESENTATIVES

1 Elizabeth Furse (D), *Hillsboro*
2 Wester Cooley (R), *Alfalfa*
3 Ron Wyden (D),[32] *Portland*
3 Earl Blumenauer (D),[33] *Portland*
4 Peter A. DeFazio (D), *Springfield*
5 James L. Bunn (R), *Gleneden Beach*

## PENNSYLVANIA

### SENATORS

Arlen Specter (R), *Philadelphia*
Richard J. Santorum (R), *Mount Lebanon*

### REPRESENTATIVES

1 Thomas M. Foglietta (D), *Philadelphia*
2 Chaka Fattah (D), *Philadelphia*
3 Robert A. Borski, Jr. (D), *Philadelphia*
4 Ronald Klink (D), *Jeannette*
5 William F. Clinger, Jr. (R), *Warren*
6 Timothy Holden (D), *St. Clair*
7 Curt Weldon (R), *Aston*
8 James C. Greenwood (R), *Erwinna*
9 E. G. Shuster (R), *Everett*
10 Joseph M. McDade (R), *Clarks Summit*
11 Paul E. Kanjorski (D), *Nanticoke*
12 John P. Murtha, Jr. (D), *Johnstown*
13 Jon D. Fox (R), *Elkins Park*
14 William J. Coyne (D), *Pittsburgh*
15 Paul F. McHale, Jr. (D), *Bethlehem*
16 Robert S. Walker (R), *East Petersburg*
17 George W. Gekas (R), *Harrisburg*
18 Michael F. Doyle (D), *Pittsburgh*
19 William F. Goodling (R), *Jacobus*
20 Frank R. Mascara (D), *Charleroi*
21 Philip S. English (R), *Erie*

## RHODE ISLAND

### SENATORS

Claiborne Pell (D), *Newport*
John H. Chafee (R), *Warwick*

### REPRESENTATIVES

1 Patrick J. Kennedy (D), *Providence*

2 John F. Reed (D), *Cranston*

## SOUTH CAROLINA

### SENATORS

Strom Thurmond (R), *Aiken*
Ernest F. Hollings (D), *Charleston*

### REPRESENTATIVES

1 Marshall C. (Mark) Sanford, Jr. (R), *Charleston*
2 Floyd Spence (R), *Lexington*
3 Lindsey O. Graham (R), *Seneca*
4 Robert D. Inglis (R), *Greenville*
5 John M. Spratt, Jr. (D), *York*
6 James E. Clyburn (D), *Columbia*

## SOUTH DAKOTA

### SENATORS

Larry Pressler (R), *Humboldt*
Thomas A. Daschle (D), *Aberdeen*

### REPRESENTATIVE AT LARGE

Tim Johnson (D), *Vermillion*

## TENNESSEE

### SENATORS

Fred D. Thompson (R), *Nashville*
William H. Frist (R), *Nashville*

### REPRESENTATIVES

1 James H. Quillen (R), *Kingsport*
2 John J. Duncan (R), *Knoxville*
3 Zachary P. Wamp (R), *Chattanooga*
4 W. Van Hilleary (R), *Spring City*
5 Robert N. Clement (D), *Nashville*
6 Bart Gordon (D), *Murfreesboro*
7 Edward B. Bryant (R), *Henderson*
8 John S. Tanner (D), *Union City*
9 Harold E. Ford (D), *Memphis*

## TEXAS

### SENATORS

Phil Gramm (R), *College Station*
Kay Bailey Hutchison (R), *Dallas*

### REPRESENTATIVES

1 Jim Chapman (D), *Sulphur Springs*
2 Charles Wilson (D), *Lufkin*
3 Sam Johnson (R), *Dallas*
4 Ralph M. Hall (D), *Rockwall*
5 John W. Bryant (D), *Dallas*
6 Joe Barton (R), *Ennis*
7 William R. Archer, Jr. (R), *Houston*
8 Jack Fields (R), *Humble*
9 Steve Stockman (R), *Beaumont*
10 Lloyd A. Doggett (D), *Austin*
11 Chet Edwards (D), *Waco*
12 Preston M. (Pete) Geren III (D), *Fort Worth*

---

[30] Resigned October 1, 1995.
[31] Elected January 30, 1996 to fill vacancy caused by resignation of Robert W. Packwood, and took his seat February 6, 1996.

[32] Resigned February 5, 1996, having been elected Senator.
[33] Elected May 21, 1996 to fill vacancy caused by

resignation of Ron Wyden, and took his seat May 30, 1996.

## TEXAS—Continued

REPRESENTATIVES—CONTINUED

13 William M. (Mac) Thornberry (R), *Amarillo*
14 Gregory H. Laughlin (D),[34] *West Columbia*
15 Eligio (Kika) de la Garza (D), *McAllen*
16 Ronald Coleman (D), *El Paso*
17 Charles W. Stenholm (D), *Avoca*
18 Sheila Jackson Lee (D), *Houston*
19 Larry Combest (R), *Lubbock*
20 Henry B. Gonzalez (D), *San Antonio*
21 Lamar S. Smith (R), *San Antonio*
22 Tom DeLay (R), *Sugar Land*
23 Henry Bonilla (R), *San Antonio*
24 Martin Frost (D), *Dallas*
25 Kenneth E. Bentsen, Jr. (D), *Houston*
26 Richard K. Armey (R), *Lewisville*
27 Solomon P. Ortiz (D), *Corpus Christi*
28 Frank M. Tejeda (D), *San Antonio*
29 Gene Green (D), *Houston*
30 Eddie Bernice Johnson (D), *Dallas*

## UTAH

SENATORS

Orrin G. Hatch (R), *Salt Lake City*
Robert F. Bennett (R), *Salt Lake City*

REPRESENTATIVES

1 James V. Hansen (R), *Farmington*
2 Enid Greene Waldholtz (R), *Salt Lake City*
3 William Orton (D), *Provo*

## VERMONT

SENATORS

Patrick J. Leahy (D), *Burlington*
James M. Jeffords (R), *Shrewsbury*

REPRESENTATIVE AT LARGE

Bernard Sanders (I), *Burlington*

## VIRGINIA

SENATORS

John W. Warner (R), *Alexandria*
Charles S. Robb (D), *McLean*

REPRESENTATIVES

1 Herbert H. Bateman (R), *Newport News*
2 Owen B. Pickett (D), *Virginia Beach*
3 Robert C. Scott (D), *Newport News*
4 Norman Sisisky (D), *Petersburg*
5 L. F. Payne, Jr. (D), *Nellysford*
6 Robert W. Goodlatte (R), *Roanoke*
7 Thomas J. Bliley, Jr. (R), *Richmond*
8 James P. Moran (D), *Alexandria*
9 Frederick C. Boucher (D), *Abingdon*
10 Frank R. Wolf (R), *Vienna*
11 Thomas M. Davis III (R), *Falls Church*

## WASHINGTON

SENATORS

Slade Gorton III (R), *Seattle*
Patty Murray (D), *Seattle*

REPRESENTATIVES

1 Rick White (R), *Bainbridge Island*
2 Jack Metcalf (R), *Langley*
3 Linda A. Smith (R), *Vancouver*
4 Richard (Doc) Hastings (R), *Pasco*
5 George R. Nethercutt, Jr. (R), *Spokane*
6 Norman D. Dicks (D), *Bremerton*
7 James A. McDermott (D), *Seattle*
8 Jennifer B. Dunn (R), *Bellevue*
9 Randy Tate (R), *Puyallup*

## WEST VIRGINIA

SENATORS

Robert C. Byrd (D), *Sophia*
John D. Rockefeller IV (D), *Charleston*

REPRESENTATIVES

1 Alan B. Mollohan (D), *Fairmont*
2 Robert E. Wise, Jr. (D), *Clendenin*
3 Nick J. Rahall II (D), *Beckley*

## WISCONSIN

SENATORS

Herbert H. Kohl (D), *Milwaukee*
Russell D. Feingold (D), *Middleton*

REPRESENTATIVES

1 Mark W. Neumann (R), *Janesville*
2 Scott L. Klug (R), *Madison*
3 Steven Gunderson (R), *Osseo*
4 Gerald D. Kleczka (D), *Milwaukee*
5 Thomas M. Barrett (D), *Milwaukee*
6 Thomas E. Petri (R), *Fond du Lac*
7 David R. Obey (D), *Wausau*
8 Toby A. Roth (R), *Appleton*
9 F. James Sensenbrenner, Jr. (R), *Menomomee Falls*

## WYOMING

SENATORS

Alan K. Simpson (R), *Cody*
Craig L. Thomas (R), *Casper*

REPRESENTATIVE AT LARGE

Barbara Cubin (R), *Casper*

## AMERICAN SAMOA

DELEGATE

Eni F. H. Faleomavaega, Jr. (D), *Vailoatai Pago Pago*

## COMMONWEALTH OF PUERTO RICO

RESIDENT COMMISSIONER

Carlos A. Romero-Barceló (D), *San Juan*

## DISTRICT OF COLUMBIA

DELEGATE

Eleanor Holmes Norton (D), *Washington, D.C.*

## GUAM

DELEGATE

Robert A. Underwood (D), *Yona*

## VIRGIN ISLANDS

DELEGATE

Victor O. Frazer (I), *St. Thomas*

---

[34] Changed party affiliation to Republican, June 26, 1995.

# BIOGRAPHIES

# A

**AANDAHL, Fred George,** a Representative from North Dakota; born in Litchville, Barnes County, N.Dak., April 9, 1897; attended a one-room country school and Litchville High School; was graduated from the University of North Dakota at Grand Forks in 1921; engaged in agricultural pursuits; superintendent of schools in Litchville, N.Dak., 1922-1927; member of the North Dakota State senate in the 1931, 1939, and 1941 sessions; elected Governor of North Dakota in 1944, reelected in 1946 and 1948, and served from January 4, 1945 to January 3, 1951; elected as a Republican to the Eighty-second Congress (January 3, 1951-January 3, 1953); was not a candidate for renomination in 1952 to the House of Representatives, but was an unsuccessful candidate for nomination to the United States Senate; appointed Assistant Secretary of the Department of the Interior, Washington, D.C., and served from February 10, 1953, until January 20, 1961; resumed former agricultural pursuits; died in Fargo, N.Dak., April 7, 1966; interment in Hillside Cemetery, Valley City, N.Dak.

**ABBITT, Watkins Moorman,** a Representative from Virginia; born in Lynchburg, Va., May 21, 1908; attended the public schools; was graduated from Appomattox Agricultural High School in 1925; LL.B., University of Richmond School of Law, 1931; was admitted to the bar in December 1930 and commenced practice in Appomattox, Va.; Commonwealth attorney of Appomattox County, 1932-1948; member of the Virginia Constitutional Convention of 1945; delegate to the Democratic National Convention of 1964; director of Farmers National Bank; delegate to Virginia Democratic Conventions in 1932, 1936, 1940, 1944, 1948, and 1952; chairman, Virginia Democratic central committee, 1966-1972; elected as a Democrat to the Eightieth Congress, February 17, 1948, by special election to fill the vacancy caused by the death of Patrick H. Drewry; reelected to the twelve succeeding Congresses, and served from February 17, 1948 to January 3, 1973; was not a candidate for reelection in 1972 to the Ninety-third Congress; is a resident of Appomattox, Va.

**ABBOT, Joel,** a Representative from Georgia; born in Ridgefield, Conn., March 17, 1776; moved to Washington, Ga., in 1794 and practiced medicine; member of the city council, Washington, Ga.; member of the State house of representatives, 1799, 1802-1804, 1808, and 1811; elected as a Republican to the Fifteenth and reelected to the three succeeding Congresses (March 4, 1817-March 3, 1825); resumed the practice of medicine; delegate to the convention which met in Philadelphia, Pa., in 1820 to prepare the first National Pharmacopoeia; died in Lexington, Ga., November 19, 1826; interment in Rest Haven Cemetery.

**ABBOTT, Amos,** a Representative from Massachusetts; born in Andover, Mass., September 10, 1786; attended the district school and Bradford Academy; engaged in mercantile pursuits; highway surveyor in 1812, 1814, and 1816; clerk of the market in 1819, and 1820-1822; town clerk in 1822, 1826, and 1828; town treasurer, 1824-1829; member of the school committee, 1828-1829, and again in 1830; one of the founders of the Boston and Portland (later the Boston and Maine) Railroad in 1833, serving as director from 1833 to 1841; member of the Massachusetts house of representatives in 1835, 1836, 1837, and again in 1843; served in the Massachusetts senate, 1840-1842; elected as a Whig to the Twenty-eighth and to the two succeeding Congresses (March 4, 1843-March 3, 1849); was not a candidate for reelection in 1848 to the Thirty-first Congress; resumed his former mercantile pursuits; served as postmaster of Andover, Mass., from 1849 to 1853; died in Andover, Mass., November 2, 1868; interment in South Parish Cemetery.

**ABBOTT, Jo (Joseph),** a Representative from Texas; born near Decatur, Morgan County, Ala., January 15, 1840; attended the public schools; moved with his parents to Freestone County, Tex., in 1853; during the Civil War served in the Confederate Army as first lieutenant in the Twelfth Regiment, Texas Cavalry; studied law; was admitted to the bar in 1866 and commenced practice in Springfield, Limestone County, Tex.; subsequently moved to Hillsboro and continued the practice of law; member of the State house of representatives in 1870 and 1871; appointed district judge of the twenty-eighth judicial district by Governor Oran M. Roberts in February 1879; subsequently elected in November 1880 for a term of four years; elected as a Democrat to the Fiftieth and to the four succeeding Congresses (March 4, 1887-March 3, 1897); was not a candidate for renomination in 1896 to the Fifty-fifth Congress; resumed the practice of law in Hillsboro, Hill County, Tex., and died there February 11, 1908; interment in Old Cemetery.

**ABBOTT, Joseph Carter,** a Senator from North Carolina; born in Concord, N.H., July 15, 1825; was graduated from Phillips Academy, Andover, Mass., in 1846; studied law; was admitted to the bar in 1852; owner and editor of the Daily American, in Manchester, N.H., 1852-1857; adjutant general of New Hampshire 1855-1861; editor of the Boston Atlas in 1859; member of the commission to adjust the boundary between New Hampshire and Canada; entered the Union Army as lieutenant colonel of the Seventh New Hampshire on December 13, 1861; promoted to colonel November 17, 1863, and brevetted as brigadier general January 15, 1865; moved to Wilmington, N.C. and was for a time commandant of the city; delegate to the State constitutional convention in 1868; upon the readmission of the State of North Carolina was elected as a Republican to the United States Senate, and served from July 14, 1868 to March 3, 1871; collector of the port of Wilmington under President Ulysses S. Grant; inspector of posts along the eastern line of the southern coast under President Rutherford B. Hayes; established the town of Abbottsburg, in Bladen County, N.C.; engaged in the manufacture of lumber; employed as a special agent in the United States Treasury Department; editor of the Wilmington Post; died in Wilmington, New Hanover County, N.C., October 8, 1881; originally interred in the United States National Cemetery, Wilmington, N.C.; reinterred in Valley Cemetery, Manchester, N.H., in 1887.

**Bibliography:** *DAB.*

**ABBOTT, Josiah Gardner,** a Representative from Massachusetts; born in Chelmsford, Middlesex County, Mass., November 1, 1814; attended the common schools and Chelmsford Academy; was graduated from Harvard University in 1832; taught school; studied law; was admitted to the bar in 1835 and commenced practice in Lowell, Mass., in 1837; member of the Massachusetts house of representatives in 1836; served in the Massachusetts senate, 1841-1842; member of the staff of Governor Marcus Morton in 1843; master in chancery, 1850-1855; member of the Massachusetts constitutional convention in 1853; appointed justice of the superior court of Suffolk County in 1855 and served until 1858, when he resigned; resumed the practice of law; one of the overseers of Harvard College, 1859-1865; several times was the unsuccessful Democratic candidate for United States Senator; declined an appointment to the supreme court bench in 1860; moved to Boston in 1861 and continued the practice of law; declined the Democratic nomination for attorney general in 1861; successfully contested as a Democrat the election of Rufus S. Frost to the Forty-fourth Congress, and served from July 28, 1876 to March 3, 1877; was not a candidate for renomination in 1876 to the Forty-fifth Congress; appointed a member of the Electoral Commission created by the act of Congress approved January 29, 1877, to decide the contests in various States in the presidential election of 1876; resumed the practice of law; also interested in manufacturing and various other enterprises; died in Wellesley Hills, near Boston, Mass., June 2, 1891; interment in St. Mary's Cemetery, Newton Lower Falls, Mass.

**ABBOTT, Nehemiah,** a Representative from Maine; born in Sidney, Maine, March 29, 1804; studied law at the Litchfield (Conn.) Law School; was admitted to the bar in 1836 and commenced practice at Calais, Maine; moved to Columbus, Miss., in 1839 and continued the practice of law; returned to Maine in 1840 and settled in Belfast, Waldo County, where he resumed the practice of law; member of the State house of representatives in 1842, 1843, and 1845; elected as a Republican to the Thirty-fifth Congress (March 4, 1857-March 3, 1859); was not a candidate for reelection in 1858 to the Thirty-sixth Congress; engaged in the practice of his profession until his death; mayor of Belfast in 1865 and 1866; died in Belfast, Maine, July 26, 1877; interment in Grove Cemetery.

**ABDNOR, James,** a Representative and a Senator from South Dakota; born in Kennebec, Lyman County, S.Dak., February 13, 1923; attended the public schools; B.A., University of Nebraska, Lincoln, 1945; served in the United States Army, 1942-1943; worked as a farmer and rancher; school teacher and coach, 1946-1948; chairman, South Dakota Young Republicans, 1953-1955; served in the South Dakota State senate, 1956-1969; Lieutenant Governor of South Dakota, 1969-1970; elected as a Republican to the Ninety-third and to the three succeeding Congresses (January 3, 1973-January 3, 1981); was not a candidate for reelection in 1980 to the House of Representatives, but was elected as a Republican to the United States Senate, and served from January 3, 1981 to January 3, 1987; unsuccessful candidate for reelection; appointed Administrator of the Small Business Administration, 1987; is a resident of Kennebec, S.Dak.

**ABEL, Hazel Hempel,** a Senator from Nebraska; born in Plattsmouth, Cass County, Nebr., July 10, 1888; attended the public schools of Omaha, Nebr., graduated from the University of Nebraska at Lincoln in 1908; high school teacher of mathematics and principal of high schools in Papillion, Ashland, and Crete, Nebr., 1908-1916; president of Abel Construction Co., 1937-1952; chairwoman of the board of directors of Abel Investment Co., Lincoln, Nebr., in 1952 and 1953; vice chairwoman of State Republican Central Committee in 1954; elected as a Republican to the United States Senate to fill the vacancy in the term ending January 3, 1955, caused by the death of Dwight Griswold, and served from November 8, 1954, until her resignation December 31, 1954; delegate to White House Conference on Education in 1955; chairwoman of Nebraska delegation to the Republican National Convention of 1956; member of the Theodore Roosevelt Centennial Commission, 1955-1959; chairwoman, board of trustees, Doane College; member, board of trustees of Nebraska Wesleyan College; died in Lincoln, Nebr., on July 30, 1966; interment in Wyuka Cemetery.

**ABELE, Homer E.,** a Representative from Ohio; born in Wellston, Jackson County, Ohio, November 21, 1916; attended the public schools; graduated from Wellston High School in 1934; employed by Anchor Hocking Glass Corp., Lancaster, Ohio, and the Austin Powder Co., McArthur, Ohio, 1938-1941; member of the Ohio State Highway Patrol, 1941-1943, and for six months in 1946 after returning from military service; during the Second World War enlisted as a cadet in the Air Corps in May 1943, and served until discharged as a private first class, February 22, 1946; took prelaw studies at Ohio University at Athens, Ohio, 1946-1948; served in the Ohio State general assembly, 1949-1952; graduated from Ohio State University College of Law at Columbus in December 1953 and was admitted to the bar in 1954; legislative counsel for a special transportation committee, 1953-1957; solicitor for McArthur, Ohio; delegate to the Republican National Convention of 1956; chairman of the Vinton County Republican Executive Committee, 1954-1957; unsuccessful candidate for election in 1958 to the Eighty-sixth Congress; elected as a Republican to the Eighty-eighth Congress (January 3, 1963-January 3, 1965); unsuccessful candidate for reelection in 1964 to the Eighty-ninth Congress; elected judge,

Fourth District Court of Appeals of Ohio, for four terms commencing in 1966 and ending February 1991, and served as presiding judge, 1977-1978, 1983 and 1984; chief justice, Ohio Court of Appeals, 1978; is a resident of McArthur, Ohio.

**ABERCROMBIE, James,** a Representative from Alabama; born in Hancock County, Ga., in 1795; attended the common schools; moved to Alabama about 1812 and settled in Monroe (now Dallas) County, and later, in 1819, in Montgomery County; during the War of 1812 served as a corporal in Maj. F. Freeman's Squadron of Georgia Cavalry; studied law; member of the State house of representatives 1820-1822 and in 1824; captain in the Alabama Militia and in command of the cavalry at the reception for General Lafayette in 1825; served in the State senate 1825-1833; moved to Russell County in 1834; again a member of the State house of representatives in 1838 and 1839; again served in the State senate 1847-1850; elected as a Whig to the Thirty-second and Thirty-third Congresses (March 4, 1851-March 3, 1855); was not a candidate for renomination in 1854; moved to Florida in 1856 and became engaged as a Government brick contractor; died in Pensacola, Fla., July 2, 1861; interment in Linwood Cemetery, Columbus, Ga.

**ABERCROMBIE, John William,** a Representative from Alabama; born near Kellys Creek Post Office, St. Clair County, Ala., May 17, 1866; attended the rural schools; was graduated from Oxford (Ala.) College in 1886, and from the law department of the University of Alabama at Tuscaloosa in 1888; was admitted to the bar in 1888 and practiced in Cleburne County, Ala., in 1889 and 1890; high school principal, city school superintendent, and college president, 1888-1898; member of the Alabama State senate, 1896-1898; State superintendent of education, 1898-1902; president of the University of Alabama, 1902-1911; president of the Southern Educational Association in 1906 and 1907; organizer and president of the Alabama Association of Colleges, 1908-1912; elected as a Democrat to the Sixty-third and Sixty-fourth Congresses (March 4, 1913-March 3, 1917); was not a candidate for reelection in 1916 to the Sixty-fifth Congress; served as Solicitor and Acting Secretary of the United States Department of Labor, 1918-1920; appointed and subsequently elected State superintendent of education for the term 1920 to 1927; died in Montgomery, Ala., July 2, 1940; interment in Greenwood Cemetery.

**Bibliography:** Richardson, Jesse Monroe. *The Contributions of John William Abercrombie to Public Education.* Nashville, Tenn.: Bureau of Publications, John Peabody College for Teachers, 1949.

**ABERCROMBIE, Neil,** a Representative from Hawaii; born in Buffalo, N.Y., June 26, 1938; graduated from Williamsville (N.Y.) High School; B.A., Union College, Schenectady, N.Y., 1959; M.A., University of Hawaii, 1964; Ph.D., American studies, University of Hawaii, 1974; taught at the University of Hawaii, Hawaii Loa College and Leeward Community College; unsuccessful candidate in 1970 for nomination for the United States Senate; member, Hawaii State house of representatives, 1974-1978; Hawaii State senate, 1978-1986; elected as a Democrat to the Ninety-ninth Congress in a special election held September 20, 1986, to fill the vacancy caused by the resignation of Cecil Heftel and served until January 3, 1987; was an unsuccessful candidate for nomination in 1986 to the One Hundredth Congress; elected to the One Hundred Second and to the two succeeding Congresses (January 3, 1991-January 3, 1997); is a resident of Honolulu, Hawaii.

**ABERNETHY, Charles Laban,** a Representative from North Carolina; born in Rutherford College, Burke County, N.C., March 18, 1872; attended the public schools, Mount Olive (N.C.) High School, and Rutherford College; moved to Beaufort, Carteret County, N.C., in 1893; founded the Beaufort Herald in 1893; studied law at the University of North Carolina at Chapel Hill; was admitted to the bar in 1895 and commenced practice in Beaufort, N.C.; solicitor of the third (later the fifth) judicial circuit for twelve years; member of the State Democratic executive committee, 1898-1900; moved to New Bern, N.C., in 1913 and continued the practice of law; elected as a Democrat to the Sixty-seventh Congress to fill the vacancy caused by the death of Samuel M. Brinson; reelected to the Sixty-eighth and to the five succeeding Congresses, and served from November 7, 1922 to January 3, 1935; unsuccessful candidate for renomination in 1934 to the Seventy-fourth Congress; resumed the practice of law until his retirement in 1938; died in New Bern, N.C., February 23, 1955; interment in Cedar Grove Cemetery.

**ABERNETHY, Thomas Gerstle,** a Representative from Mississippi; born in Eupora, Webster County, Miss., May 16, 1903; attended the public schools, the University of Alabama at Tuscaloosa, and the University of Mississippi at Oxford; LL.B., Cumberland University School of Law, Lebanon, Tenn., 1924; was admitted to the bar in 1924 and commenced practice in Eupora, Miss., in 1925; mayor of Eupora, 1927-1929; moved to Okolona, Miss, in 1929 and continued the practice of law; district attorney of the third judicial district of Mississippi, 1936-1942; delegate to the Democratic National Conventions of 1956 and 1960; elected as a Democrat to the Seventy-eighth and to the fourteen succeeding Congresses (January 3, 1943-January 3, 1973); chairman, Committee on Elections No. 1 (Seventy-eighth Congress); was not a candidate for reelection in 1972 to the Ninety-third Congress; is a resident of Okolona and Jackson, Miss.

**ABOUREZK, James George,** a Representative and a Senator from South Dakota; born in Wood, Mellette County, S.Dak., February 24, 1931; attended the Wood and Mission public schools; B.S., South Dakota School of Mines, Rapid City, 1961; J.D., University of South Dakota Law School, Vermillion, 1966; admitted to the South Dakota bar in 1966 and commenced practice in Rapid City; served in the United States Navy from 1948 until 1952; elected as a Democrat to the Ninety-second Congress (January 3, 1971-January 3, 1973); was not a candidate in 1972 for reelection to the House of Representatives, but was elected to the United States Senate, and served from January 3, 1973 to January 3, 1979; was not a candidate for reelection in 1978; chairman, Select Committee on Indian Affairs (Ninety-fifth Congress); chairman, American Indian Policy Review Commission, 1976; resumed the practice of law and began a career in writing; is a resident of Sioux Falls, S.Dak.

**Bibliography:** Abourezk, James G. *Advise and Dissent: Memoirs of South Dakota and the U.S. Senate.* Chicago: Lawrence Hill Books, 1989; Abourezk, James G. "The Congressional Veto: A Contemporary Response to Executive Encroachment on Legislative Prerogative." *Indiana Law Journal* 52 (Winter 1977): 323-343.

**ABRAHAM, Spencer,** a Senator from Michigan; born in Lansing, Ingham County, Mich., June 12, 1952; attended East Lansing High School; B.A., Michigan State University, 1974, J.D., Harvard University School of Law, 1979; member of the faculty, Thomas M. Cooley School of Law, 1981-1983; chairman, Michigan State Republican Party, 1983-1991; deputy chief of staff to Vice President J. Danforth Quayle, 1990-1991; chair, National Republican Congressional Committee, 1991-1993; of counsel, Miller, Canfield, Paddock and Stone, 1994; elected as a Republican to the United States Senate in 1994 for the term ending January 3, 2001; is a resident of Auburn Hills, Mich.

**ABZUG, Bella Savitzky,** a Representative from New York; born in New York City, July 24, 1920; attended the local public schools; A.B., Hunter College, New York City, 1942; LL.B., Columbia University Law School, New York City, 1945; engaged in graduate work at the Jewish Theological Seminary of America; admitted to the New York Bar in 1947 and commenced practice in New York City; active in labor law; a founder and member, National and State New Democratic Coalition, 1968; an initiator and national legislative representative, Women Strike for Peace Movement, 1961-1971; delegate to Democratic National Convention, 1972 and 1980; elected as a Democrat to the Ninety-second and to the two succeeding Congresses (January 3, 1971-January 3, 1977); was not a candidate in 1976 for reelection to the House of Representatives, but was an unsuccessful candidate for nomination to the United States Senate; unsuccessful candidate for nomination in 1977 for mayor of New York City; unsuccessful candidate for election to the Ninety-fifth Congress in a special election, February 14, 1978; co-chair, National Advisory Committee for Women, 1978-1979; unsuccessful candidate for election in 1986 to the One Hundredth Congress; is a resident of New York City.

**Bibliography:** Abzug, Bella (Savitzky). *Bella! Ms. Abzug Goes to Washington.* Edited by Mel Ziegler. New York: Saturday Review Press, 1972; Faber, Doris. *Bella Abzug.* New York: Lothrop, 1976.

**ACHESON, Ernest Francis,** a Representative from Pennsylvania; born in Washington, Pa., September 19, 1855; attended the public schools; was graduated from Washington and Jefferson College, Washington, Pa., in 1875; studied law; was admitted to the bar in 1877 and practiced until 1879; purchased the Washington Weekly Observer, of which he was editor; delegate to the Republican National Conventions of 1884 and 1896; established a daily edition of the Observer in 1889; elected president of the Pennsylvania Editorial Association in January 1893, and in June of the same year was chosen recording secretary of the National Editorial Association; trustee of Washington and Jefferson College, Washington, Pa., 1894-1917; elected as a Republican to the Fifty-fourth and to the six succeeding Congresses (March 4, 1895-March 3, 1909); unsuccessful candidate for renomination in 1908 to the Sixty-first Congress; resumed editorial work until his retirement in 1912; died in Washington, Pa., May 16, 1917; interment in Washington Cemetery.

**ACKER, Ephraim Leister,** a Representative from Pennsylvania; born in Marlboro Township, Montgomery County, Pa., January 11, 1827; attended the common schools and the academy at Sumneytown; was graduated from Marshall College, Mercersburg, Pa., September 8, 1847; taught school for two years; was graduated in medicine from the University of Pennsylvania at Philadelphia in March 1852; editor and publisher of the Norristown Register 1853-1877; superintendent of the schools of Montgomery County from June 1854 to June 1860; appointed postmaster of Norristown, Pa., in March 1860 by President James Buchanan and after serving eleven months was removed by President Lincoln; served as inspector of Montgomery County Prison for three years; elected as a Democrat to the Forty-second Congress (March 4, 1871-March 3, 1873); unsuccessful candidate for reelection in 1872 to the Forty-third Congress; resumed the publication of his newspaper until 1877, when he began the study of law; was admitted to the bar and practiced until his death in Norristown, Pa., May 12, 1903; interment in Norris City Cemetery, Norriton Township, Montgomery County, Pa.

**ACKERMAN, Ernest Robinson,** a Representative from New Jersey; born in New York City, N.Y., June 17, 1863; moved with his parents to Plainfield, N.J., very shortly thereafter; educated at public and private schools and was graduated from the Plainfield High School in 1880; engaged in cement manufacturing; member of the common council of Plainfield, N.J., in 1891 and 1892; member of the State senate 1905-1911, serving as president in 1911; delegate to the Republican National Conventions of 1908 and 1916; member of the board of trustees of Rutgers College, New Brunswick, N.J., 1916-1920; Federal food administrator for Union County during the First World War; member of the State board of education 1918-1920; member of the New Jersey Geological Survey and associate of the American Society of Civil Engineers; elected as a Republican to the Sixty-sixth and to the six succeeding Congresses and served from

March 4, 1919, until his death in Plainfield, N.J., October 18, 1931; interment in the family plot, Hillside Cemetery.

**ACKERMAN, Gary Leonard,** a Representative from New York; born in Brooklyn, Kings County, N.Y., November 19, 1942; attended New York City public schools; graduated, Brooklyn Technical High School, 1960; B.A., Queens College, Flushing, N.Y., 1965; attended, St. John's University, Jamaica, N.Y., 1966; public school teacher, newspaper publisher, businessman; elected to the New York State senate, 1979-1983; elected as a Democrat to the Ninety-eighth Congress, by special election, March 1, 1983, to fill the vacancy caused by the death of Benjamin Rosenthal; reelected to the Ninety-ninth and to the five succeeding Congresses and served from March 1, 1983, to January 3, 1997; is a resident of Queens, N.Y.

**ACKLEN, Joseph Hayes,** a Representative from Louisiana; born in Nashville, Tenn., May 20, 1850; educated by private tutors; attended Burlington Military College, near Burlington, N.J., in 1864 and 1865, and was graduated from two foreign universities (École de Neuilly, Paris, and Swiss University, Vevay); returned to the United States and was graduated from the Lebanon Law School, Lebanon, Tenn., in 1871; commenced the practice of law in Nashville and later practiced in Memphis, Tenn.; abandoned the practice of law and moved to Louisiana to superintend his sugar plantations near Pattersonville (now Patterson), St. May Parish; colonel in the Louisiana Militia in 1876; successfully contested as a Democrat the election of Chester B. Darrall to the Forty-fifth Congress; reelected to the Forty-sixth Congress, and served from February 20, 1878 to March 3, 1881; was not a candidate for renomination in 1880 to the Forty-seventh Congress; resumed the practice of law at Franklin, La.; declined to accept the position of judge of the Federal district court of Louisiana tendered by President Rutherford B. Hayes in 1880; unsuccessful candidate for election in 1882 to the Forty-eighth Congress; returned to Nashville, Tenn., in 1885 and continued the practice of law; chairman of the Davidson County Democratic executive committee, 1886-1894; member of the Nashville City Council, 1900-1904; president of the State bar association in 1901 and 1902; general insurance counsel of Tennessee, 1903-1907; State warden of the department of game, fish, and forestry, 1903-1913; general counsel of the National Association of Game and Fish Commissioners of the United States, 1905-1912; middle Tennessee counsel of the St. Louis and San Francisco Railroad, 1907-1911; chief game warden of the United States in 1913 and 1914; author of numerous articles on ornithology, fish culture, forestry, and field sports; chairman of the State central committee on the constitutional convention, 1923-1927; died in Nashville, Tenn., September 28, 1938; interment in Mount Olivet Cemetery.

**ADAIR, Edwin Ross,** a Representative from Indiana; born in Albion, Noble County, Ind., December 14, 1907; attended grade and high schools in Albion, Ind.; A.B., Hillsdale (Mich.) College, 1928; LL.B., George Washington University Law School, Washington, D.C., 1933; was admitted to the Indiana bar in 1933 and commenced the practice of law in Fort Wayne, Ind.; probate commissioner of Allen County, Ind., 1940-1950; during the Second World War was called to active duty as a second lieutenant in the Quartermaster Corps Reserve in September 1941, and served until October 1945; elected as a Republican to the Eighty-second and to the nine succeeding Congresses (January 3, 1951-January 3, 1971); unsuccessful candidate for reelection in 1970 to the Ninety-second Congress; appointed Ambassador to Ethiopia on May 11, 1971 and served until February 1974; resumed the practice of law in Fort Wayne, Ind., where he resided until his death there on May 5, 1983; interment in Greenlawn Memorial Park and Mausoleum, Fort Wayne.

**ADAIR, Jackson Leroy,** a Representative from Illinois; born in Clayton, Adams County, Ill., February 23, 1887; attended public and high schools, and Illinois College at Jacksonville; was graduated from the law department of the University of Michigan at Ann Arbor in 1911; was admitted to the bar the same year and commenced practice in Muskogee, Okla.; moved to Quincy, Ill., in 1913 and continued the practice of law; also engaged in agricultural pursuits and in the manufacture of medicine for livestock; city attorney 1914-1916; prosecuting attorney of Adams County 1916-1920 and 1924-1928; member of the State senate 1928-1932; elected as a Democrat to the Seventy-third and Seventy-fourth Congresses (March 4, 1933-January 3, 1937); was not a candidate for renomination in 1936; appointed United States district judge for the southern district of Illinois in 1937 by President Franklin D. Roosevelt and served until his death in Quincy, Ill., January 19, 1956; interment in South Side Cemetery, Clayton, Ill.

**ADAIR, John,** a Senator and a Representative from Kentucky; born in Chester District, Chester County, S.C., January 9, 1757; attended the public schools in Charlotte, N.C.; served in the Revolutionary War; member of the South Carolina convention that ratified the Constitution of the United States; moved to Kentucky in 1788; major of volunteers in an expedition against the Indians under General James Wilkinson in 1791 and 1792; was a lieutenant colonel under General Charles Scott in 1793; member of the Kentucky constitutional convention in 1792; member of the Kentucky house of representatives, 1793-1795, 1798, and 1800-1803, serving as speaker in 1802 and 1803; register of the United States land office in 1805; elected to the United States Senate to fill the vacancy caused by the resignation of John Breckinridge and served from November 8, 1805, to November 18, 1806, when he resigned, having been an unsuccessful candidate for reelection; aide to Governor Isaac Shelby in the Battle of the Thames, October 5, 1813; commander of the Kentucky rifle brigade which served under General Andrew Jackson in 1814 and 1815; again a member of the Kentucky house of representatives in 1817; appointed adjutant general with the brevet rank of brigadier general; Governor of Kentucky from June 1, 1820 to June 1, 1824; elected as a Jacksonian to the Twenty-second Congress (March 4, 1831-March 3, 1833); was not a candidate for reelection in 1832 to the Twenty-third Congress; died in Harrodsburg, Ky., May 19, 1840; interment in State Cemetery, Frankfort, Ky., where a monument to his memory was erected by the Commonwealth of Kentucky.

**Bibliography:** *DAB*; Gillig, John S. "In the Pursuit of Truth and Honor: The Controversy Between Andrew Jackson and John Adair in 1817." *Filson Club History Quarterly* 58 (April 1984): 177-201; Leger, William G. "The Public Life Of John Adair." Ph.D. dissertation, University of Kentucky, 1960.

**ADAIR, John Alfred McDowell,** a Representative from Indiana; born near Portland, Jay County, Ind., December 22, 1864; attended the public schools and Portland High School; engaged in mercantile pursuits; clerk of the city of Portland 1888-1890; clerk of Jay County 1890-1895; studied law; was admitted to the bar in 1895 and commenced practice in Portland, Ind.; member of the State house of representatives in 1902 and 1903; engaged in banking, being elected president of the First National Bank of Portland in 1904; elected as a Democrat to the Sixtieth and to the four succeeding Congresses (March 4, 1907-March 3, 1917); chairman, Committee on Expenditures in the Department of War (Sixty-third and Sixty-fourth Congresses); did not seek renomination in 1916 to the Sixty-fifth Congress, but was an unsuccessful candidate for election for Governor of Indiana; resumed the banking business in Portland, Ind.; moved to Washington, D.C., in 1924 and served as vice president of Southern Dairies (Inc.) until 1931; chairman of the board of the Finance Service Co., in Baltimore, Md., 1933-1935; vice president of the Atlas Tack Corporation, Fairhaven, Mass., 1935-1937; director of the Artloom Corporation, Philadelphia, Pa., in 1937; died in Portland, Ind., October 5, 1938; interment in Green Park Cemetery.

**ADAMS, Alva Blanchard,** a Senator from Colorado; born in Del Norte, Rio Grande County, Colo., October 29, 1875; attended the common schools; graduated from Phillips Academy, Andover, Mass., in 1893; graduated from Yale University in 1896, and from Columbia Law School in 1899; was admitted to the bar in 1899 and commenced practice in Pueblo, Colo.; served as Pueblo County attorney, 1909-1911; member of the charter convention of Pueblo in 1911; regent of the State University of Colorado, 1911-1912; city attorney of Pueblo, 1911-1915; during the First World War served as a major in the Judge Advocate General's Department, 1918-1919; appointed as a Democrat to the United States Senate to fill the vacancy caused by the death of Samuel D. Nicholson, and served from May 17, 1923 to November 30, 1924, when a successor was elected and qualified; unsuccessful candidate for election to fill the vacancy in 1924; resumed the practice of law; elected as a Democrat to the United States Senate in 1932; reelected in 1938, and served from March 4, 1933 until his death in Washington, D.C., December 1, 1941; chairman, Committee on Irrigation and Reclamation (Seventy-third and Seventy-fourth Congresses), Committee on Public Lands and Surveys (Seventy-fifth through Seventy-seventh Congresses); interment in Roselawn Cemetery, Pueblo, Colorado.

**ADAMS, Andrew,** a Delegate from Connecticut; born in Stratford, Conn., January 7, 1736; pursued preparatory studies; was graduated from Yale College in 1760; studied law, and was admitted to the Fairfield County bar; prosecuting attorney of Litchfield County in 1772; moved in 1774 to Litchfield, which thereafter remained his home; member of the Connecticut Council of Safety for two years; served in the Revolutionary War with the rank of colonel; member of the State house of representatives 1776-1781, serving as speaker in 1779 and 1780; Member of the Continental Congress in 1778; signer of the Articles of Confederation in 1778; member of the executive council in 1789; appointed chief justice of the Connecticut Supreme Court in 1793 and served in this position until his death in Litchfield, Conn., November 26, 1797; interment in East Cemetery.

**Bibliography:** *DAB*.

**ADAMS, Benjamin,** a Representative from Massachusetts; born in Mendon, Mass., December 16, 1764; attended the public schools and was graduated from Brown University in 1788; studied law; was admitted to the bar and commenced practice in Uxbridge; member of the Massachusetts house of representatives 1809-1814; served in the Massachusetts senate in 1814, 1815, and 1822-1825; elected as a Federalist to the Fourteenth Congress to fill the vacancy caused by the death of Elijah Brigham; reelected to the Fifteenth and Sixteenth Congresses and served from December 2, 1816, to March 3, 1821; unsuccessful candidate for reelection in 1820 to the Seventeenth Congress and for election in 1822 to the Eighteenth Congress; resumed the practice of his profession; died in Uxbridge, Worcester County, Mass., March 28, 1837; interment in Prospect Hill Cemetery.

**ADAMS, Brockman (Brock),** a Representative and a Senator from Washington; born in Atlanta, Ga., January 13, 1927; attended the public schools in Portland, Oreg.; B.A., University of Washington, Seattle, 1949; J.D., Harvard University Law School, 1952; served in the United States Navy 1944-1946; admitted to the Washington State bar in 1952 and began practice in Seattle; taught law, American Institute of Banking 1954-1960; United States attorney for the Western District of Washington, 1961-1964; elected as a Democrat to the Eighty-ninth and to the six succeeding Congresses and served from January 3, 1965, until his resignation January 22, 1977; chairman, Committee on the Budget (Ninety-fourth Congress); appointed Secretary of Transportation in the Cabinet of President Jimmy Carter, and served from January 20, 1977 until July 20, 1979; resumed the practice of law in Washington State; elected as a Democrat to the United States Senate in 1986, and served from January 3, 1987 to January 3, 1993; was not a candidate for reelection in 1992; is a resident of Stevensville, Md.

**ADAMS, Charles Francis** (son of John Quincy Adams and grandson of John Adams), a Representative from Massachusetts; born in Boston, Mass., August 18, 1807; spent several years with his parents in St. Petersburg, Russia; attended the Boston Latin School, and was graduated from Harvard University in 1825; studied law; was admitted to the bar on January 6, 1829, and commenced practice in Boston; member of the Massachusetts house of representatives in 1831; served in the Massachusetts senate, 1835-1840; founded the Boston Whig in 1846; unsuccessful candidate of the Free Soil Party for Vice President of the United States in 1848 on the ticket headed by Martin Van Buren; elected as a Republican to the Thirty-sixth and Thirty-seventh Congresses, and served from March 4, 1859 to May 1, 1861, when he resigned to accept a diplomatic position; chairman, Committee on Manufactures (Thirty-sixth Congress); appointed by President Lincoln as Minister to Great Britain, and served from March 20, 1861 to May 13, 1868; declined the presidency of Harvard University but became one of its overseers in 1869; died in Boston, Mass., November 21, 1886; interment in Mount Wollaston Cemetery, Quincy, Mass.

**Bibliography:** *DAB*; Adams, Charles Francis. *Diary of Charles Francis Adams.* 6 vols. *The Adams Papers, Series I: Diaries.* Edited by William T. Doherty, Marc Friedlander, and L.H. Butterfield. Cambridge, Mass.: Belknap Press of Harvard University Press, 1975; Duberman, Martin B. *Charles Francis Adams, 1807-1886.* Boston: Houghton, 1961.

**ADAMS, Charles Henry,** a Representative from New York; born in Coxsackie, Greene County, N.Y., April 10, 1824; attended the public schools; studied law; was admitted to the bar about 1845 and commenced practice in New York City; moved to Cohoes, Albany County, N.Y., in 1850; appointed with rank of colonel to Governor Washington Hunt's staff in 1851; member of the State assembly in 1858; engaged in the manufacture of knit underwear, and in banking; retired from active business in 1870; served as first mayor of Cohoes 1870-1872; delegate to the Republican National Convention at Philadelphia in 1872; served in the State senate in 1872 and 1873; United States commissioner from New York to the Vienna Exposition in 1873; elected as a Republican to the Forty-fourth Congress (March 4, 1875-March 3, 1877); unsuccessful candidate for renomination in 1876; resumed banking in Cohoes, N.Y., until 1892, when he retired from active business pursuits and moved to New York City, where he died December 15, 1902; interment in Woodlawn Cemetery.

**ADAMS, George Everett,** a Representative from Illinois; born in Keene, Cheshire County, N.H., June 18, 1840; moved with his parents to Chicago, Ill., in 1853; attended Phillips Exeter Academy, Exeter, N.H.; was graduated from Harvard University in 1860; during the Civil War enlisted in the First Regiment, Illinois Volunteer Artillery; attended the Harvard Law School; was admitted to the bar in 1865 and commenced practice in Chicago, Ill.; member of the State senate from 1880 until March 3, 1883, when he resigned to enter Congress; elected as a Republican to the Forty-eighth and to the three succeeding Congresses (March 4, 1883-March 3, 1891); was an unsuccessful candidate for reelection in 1890 to the Fifty-second Congress; resumed the practice of his profession in Chicago, Ill., until his death at his summer home in Peterborough, Hillsborough County, N.H., October 5, 1917; interment in Pine Hill Cemetery.

**ADAMS, George Madison** (nephew of Green Adams), a Representative from Kentucky; born in Barbourville, Knox County, Ky., December 20, 1837; received private instruction from his father and attended Centre College, Danville, Ky.; studied law; clerk of the circuit court of Knox County, Ky., 1859-1861; during the Civil War raised a company of volunteers and was captain of Company H,

Seventh Regiment, Kentucky Volunteer Infantry, from 1861 to 1863; in 1864 was commissioned paymaster with the rank of major; elected as a Democrat to the Fortieth and to the three succeeding Congresses (March 4, 1867-March 3, 1875); unsuccessful candidate for reelection in 1874 to the Forty-fourth Congress; elected Clerk of the House of Representatives December 6, 1875, during the Forty-fourth Congress, and served until the commencement of the Forty-seventh Congress, December 5, 1881; appointed register of the Kentucky land office by Governor J. Proctor Knott and served from 1884 to 1887; appointed secretary of state for Kentucky by Governor Simon B. Buckner and served from 1887 to 1891; appointed State railroad commissioner in 1891; appointed United States pension agent at Louisville by President Grover Cleveland and served from 1894 to 1898; after retirement resided at Winchester, Clark County, Ky., until his death April 6, 1920; interment in Lexington Cemetery, Lexington, Ky.

**ADAMS, Green** (uncle of George Madison Adams), a Representative from Kentucky; born in Barbourville, Knox County, Ky., August 20, 1812; pursued preparatory studies; studied law; was admitted to the bar and practiced; member of the Kentucky house of representatives in 1839; presidential elector on the Whig ticket in 1844; elected as a Whig to the Thirtieth Congress (March 4, 1847-March 3, 1849); was not a candidate for renomination in 1848 to the Thirty-first Congress; judge of the circuit court of Kentucky 1851-1856; elected as the candidate of the Opposition Party to the Thirty-sixth Congress (March 4, 1859-March 3, 1861); was not a candidate for renomination in 1860 to the Thirty-seventh Congress; Sixth Auditor of the Treasury Department from April 17, 1861, to October 26, 1864; resumed the practice of law in Philadelphia; died in Philadelphia, Pa., January 18, 1884; interment in West Laurel Hill Cemetery.

**ADAMS, Henry Cullen**, a Representative from Wisconsin; born in Verona, Oneida County, N.Y., November 28, 1850; moved to Wisconsin in 1851 with his parents, who settled in Fort Atkinson, Jefferson County; attended the public schools, Albion Academy, and the University of Wisconsin at Madison; engaged in agricultural pursuits; member of the Wisconsin State assembly, 1883-1885; State superintendent of public property, 1884-1890; engaged in work with the Wisconsin farmers' institutes, 1887-1889; president of the Wisconsin Dairy Association and secretary of the State Horticultural Society; State dairy and food commissioner, 1895-1902; elected as a Republican to the Fifty-eighth and Fifty-ninth Congresses, and served from March 4, 1903 until his death in Chicago, Ill., July 9, 1906; sponsor of the Adams Act of 1906, which provided increased appropriations to the States for scientific investigations and research in agriculture; interment in Forest Hill Cemetery, Madison, Wis.

**Bibliography:** *DAB*; Rosenberg, Charles E. "The Adams Act: Politics and the Cause of Scientific Research." *Agricultural History* 38 (January 1964): 3-12.

**ADAMS, John** (father of John Quincy Adams and grandfather of Charles Francis Adams), a Delegate from Massachusetts and a Vice President and 2nd President of the United States; born in Braintree, Mass., October 19, 1735; was graduated from Harvard College in 1755; studied law; was admitted to the bar in 1758 and commenced practice in Suffolk County; joined the Sons of Liberty and argued against the Stamp Act; was elected to represent Boston in the general court in 1768; Member of the Continental Congress 1774-1777; signed the Declaration of Independence and proposed George Washington, of Virginia, for General of the American Army; became a member of the Board of War, but resigned to accept appointment as commissioner to the Court of France; appointed Minister Plenipotentiary to the Netherlands on January 1, 1781 and served until March 1788; appointed the first United States Minister to the court of Great Britain on February 24, 1785 and served until

his farewell audience February 20, 1788; elected in 1788 as the first Vice President of the United States with George Washington as President; reelected in 1792 and served from April 21, 1789, to March 3, 1797; elected President of the United States and served from March 4, 1797, to March 3, 1801; delegate to the constitutional convention of Massachusetts 1820; died in Quincy, Mass., July 4, 1826; interment under the old First Congregational Church, now called the United First Parish Church.

**Bibliography:** *DAB*; Adams, John. *The Adams Papers*. Edited by Richard Ryerson, L.H. Butterfield, Marc Friedlander, et al. 17 vols. relating to John Adams to date. Cambridge, Mass.: Harvard University Press, 1961-; Ferling, John E. *John Adams: A Life.* 1992. Reprint. New York: Henry Holt and Co., 1996. Guerrero, Linda. "John Adams' Vice Presidency, 1789-1797." Ph.D. dissertation, University of California, Santa Barbara, 1978.

**ADAMS, John,** a Representative from New York; born in Oak Hill, town of Durham, Greene County, N.Y., August 26, 1778; attended the common schools; taught school in Durham; studied law; was admitted to the bar in 1805 and commenced practice in Durham; appointed surrogate of Greene County by Governor Daniel D. Tompkins in 1810; member of the State assembly in 1812 and 1813; presented credentials as a Republican Member-elect to the Fourteenth Congress and served from March 4 to December 26, 1815, when he was succeeded by Erastus Root, who contested his election; elected as a Jacksonian to the Twenty-third Congress (March 4, 1833-March 3, 1835); was not a candidate for renomination in 1834; moved to Catskill, Greene County, N.Y., and continued the practice of law until his death; elected a director of the Catskill-Canajoharie Railroad in 1835; died in Catskill, N.Y., September 25, 1854; interment in Thomson Street Cemetery.

**ADAMS, John Joseph,** a Representative from New York; born in Douglas Town, Province of New Brunswick, Dominion of Canada, September 16, 1848; attended the local school; came to the United States and settled in New York City in 1864; engaged as a clerk with a dry-goods firm until 1874; was graduated from Columbia Law School in 1876; was admitted to the bar the same year and commenced practice in New York City; elected as a Democrat to the Forty-eighth and Forty-ninth Congresses (March 4, 1883-March 3, 1887); was not a candidate for renomination in 1886; resumed the practice of law in New York City and died there February 16, 1919; interment in Greenwood Cemetery, Brooklyn, N.Y.

**ADAMS, John Quincy** (son of John Adams and father of Charles Francis Adams), a Senator and a Representative from Massachusetts and 6th President of the United States; born in Braintree, Mass., July 11, 1767; acquired his early education in Europe at the University of Leyden; was graduated from Harvard University in 1787; studied law; was admitted to the bar and commenced practice in Boston, Mass.; appointed Minister to the Netherlands on May 30, 1794 and served until June 1797; appointed Minister to Portugal on May 30, 1796, but did not serve; appointed Minister to Prussia on June 1, 1797, and served until May 1801; commissioned to make a commercial treaty with Sweden in 1798; elected to the State senate in 1802; unsuccessful candidate for election in 1802 to the Eighth Congress; elected as a Federalist to the United States Senate and served from March 4, 1803, until June 8, 1808, when he resigned; appointed Minister to Russia on June 27, 1809 and served until April 1814; member of the commission which negotiated the Treaty of Ghent in 1814; appointed Minister to Great Britain on February 28, 1815, served until May 1817 and assisted in concluding the convention of commerce with Great Britain; appointed Secretary of State in the Cabinet of President James Monroe on March 5, 1817, and served until March 3, 1825; in 1825 the election of the President of the United States fell, according to the Constitution of the United States, upon the House of Representatives, as none of the candidates had secured a majority of the electors chosen by the States, and Adams, who stood second to Andrew Jackson in the electoral vote, was chosen on February 9, 1825, and served from March 4, 1825, to March 3, 1829; elected to the Twenty-second and to the eight succeeding Congresses and served from March 4, 1831, until his death; chairman, Committee on Manufactures (Twenty-second through Twenty-sixth, and Twenty-eighth and Twenty-ninth Congresses), Committee on Indian Affairs (Twenty-seventh Congress), Committee on Foreign Affairs (Twenty-seventh Congress); unsuccessful candidate for election in 1833 for Governor of Massachusetts; died in the Capitol Building, Washington, D.C., February 23, 1848; interment in the family burial ground at Quincy, Mass.; subsequently reinterred in United First Parish Church.

**Bibliography:** *DAB*; Adams, John Quincy. *The Diary of John Quincy Adams.* Edited by David Grayson Allen, Robert J. Taylor, et al. 2 vols. to date. Cambridge, Mass.: Harvard University Press, 1981-; Macoll, John Douglas. "Congressman John Quincy Adams." Ph.D. dissertation, Indiana University, 1973; Richards, Leonard. *The Life and Times of Congressman John Quincy Adams.* New York: Oxford University Press, 1986.

**ADAMS, Parmenio,** a Representative from New York; born in Hartford, Conn., September 9, 1776; attended the common schools; moved in 1806 to "Phelps Corners," then in the township of Batavia, Genesee County (now Attica, Wyoming County), N.Y.; held commissions in the New York State Militia from 1806 to 1816 as lieutenant of light Infantry, captain of Grenadiers, second and first major, and division inspector of Infantry; served in the War of 1812 as major and commandant of New York Volunteers for some months on the Niagara frontier and was recommended for a majority in the United States Army by Governor Daniel D. Tompkins, of New York; twice appointed sheriff of Genesee County, serving in 1815 and 1816, and again from 1818 to 1821; engaged in agricultural pursuits and also was a construction contractor on the Erie Canal; successfully contested the election of Isaac Wilson to the Eighteenth Congress; reelected to the Nineteenth Congress and served from January 7, 1824, to March 3, 1827; died in Alexander, Genesee County, N.Y., February 19, 1832.

**ADAMS, Robert, Jr.,** a Representative from Pennsylvania; born in Philadelphia, Pa., February 26, 1849; attended Doctor Fairies Physical Institute, Philadelphia, Pa., and was graduated from the University of Pennsylvania at Philadelphia in 1869; studied law; was admitted to the bar on April 27, 1872, and practiced; member of the United States Geological Survey during the explorations of Yellowstone Park, 1871-1875; member of the Pennsylvania militia, 1881-1895; served in the Pennsylvania senate from 1883 until 1886; was graduated from the Wharton School of Economy and Finance of the University of Pennsylvania in 1884; appointed United States Minister to Brazil on April 1, 1889, and served until June 1, 1890, when he resigned; elected as a Republican to the Fifty-third Congress to fill the vacancy caused by the death of Charles O'Neill; reelected to the Fifty-fourth and to the five succeeding Congresses and served from December 19, 1893, until his death in Washington, D.C., June 1, 1906; interment in Laurel Hill Cemetery, Philadelphia, Pa.

**Bibliography:** *DAB*.

**ADAMS, Robert Huntington,** a Senator from Mississippi; born in Rockbridge County, Va., in 1792; apprenticed to the cooper's trade; was graduated from Washington College (now Washington and Lee University) at Lexington, Va., in 1806; studied law; was admitted to the bar and commenced practice in Knoxville, Tenn.; moved to Natchez, Miss., in 1819; member of the Mississippi State house of representatives in 1828; elected as a Jacksonian to the United States Senate to fill the vacancy caused by the death of Thomas B. Reed and served from January 6, 1830, until his death in Natchez, Miss., July 2, 1830; interment in Natchez City Cemetery.

**ADAMS, Samuel** (uncle of Joseph Allen and granduncle of Charles Allen), a Delegate from Massachusetts; born in Boston, Mass., September 27, 1722; was graduated from Harvard College in 1740; received his M.A. degree in 1743; engaged in the brewing business; appointed tax collector of Boston, 1756-1764; drafted the instructions given by the town of Boston to its newly chosen representatives with reference to the proposed Stamp Act in May 1764; member of the general court of Massachusetts, 1765-1774; Member of the Continental Congress from 1774 to 1781; a signer of the Declaration of Independence; member of the Massachusetts constitutional convention in 1779; president of the Massachusetts senate in 1781; member of the Massachusetts constitutional convention in 1788; unsuccessful candidate for election in 1788 to the First Congress; lieutenant governor, 1789-1794; elected Governor of Massachusetts in 1794, 1795 and 1796, and served from October 8, 1793 to June 2, 1797; died in Boston, Mass., October 2, 1803; interment in Granary Burial Ground.

**Bibliography:** *DAB*; Adams, Samuel. *The Writings of Samuel Adams.* 4 vols. Edited by Harry Alonzo Cushing. New York: G.P. Putnam's Sons, 1904-1908; Hosmer, James K. *Samuel Adams.* 1898. Reprint. Introduction by Pauline Maier. New York: Chelsea House, 1980; Miller, John C. *Sam Adams: Pioneer in Propaganda.* 1936. Reprint. Stanford, Calif.: Stanford University Press, 1960.

**ADAMS, Sherman,** a Representative from New Hampshire; born in East Dover, Windham County, Vt., January 8, 1899; as an infant moved with his parents to Providence, R.I.; attended the public schools of Providence; served in the United States Marine Corps during the First World War; was graduated from Dartmouth College, Hanover, N.H., in 1920; engaged in the lumber business in Healdville, Vt., in 1921 and 1922 and in the paper and lumber business in Lincoln, N.H. from 1923 until 1944; also engaged in banking; member of the New Hampshire State house of representatives, 1941-1944, serving as speaker in 1943 and 1944; chairman of the Grafton County Republican Committee, 1942-1944; delegate to the Republican National Conventions of 1944 and 1952; elected as a Republican to the Seventy-ninth Congress (January 3, 1945-January 3, 1947); was not a candidate for renomination in 1946 to the Eightieth Congress, but was an unsuccessful candidate for the gubernatorial nomination; engaged as a representative of the American Pulpwood Industry in New York City, 1946-1948; elected Governor of New Hampshire in 1948, reelected in 1950, and served from January 6, 1949 until January 1, 1953; appointed The Assistant to President Dwight D. Eisenhower on January 21, 1953, and served until his resignation September 22, 1958; engaged in writing and lecturing; established a ski resort in 1966 and was president and chairman of the board of Loon Mountain Corporation; was a resident of Lincoln, N.H., until his death in Hanover, N.H., October 27, 1986.

**Bibliography:** Adams, Sherman. *Firsthand Report: The Story of the Eisenhower Administration.* 1961. Reprint. Westport, Conn.: Greenwood Press, 1974.

**ADAMS, Silas,** a Representative from Kentucky; born in Pulaski County, Ky., February 9, 1839; moved to Casey County with his parents in 1841; attended the public schools, Kentucky University at Harrodsburg, and Transylvania University at Lexington; entered the Union Army during the Civil War as a first lieutenant, First Regiment, Kentucky Volunteer Cavalry; promoted to captain, lieutenant colonel, and colonel of the regiment; was mustered out December 31, 1864; entered Lexington Law School in 1867; was admitted to the bar and practiced; served two terms as county attorney; member of the Kentucky house of representatives 1889-1892; unsuccessful Republican candidate for the United States Senate in 1892; elected as a Republican to the Fifty-third Congress (March 4, 1893-March 3, 1895); unsuccessful independent candidate for reelection in 1894 to the Fifty-fourth Congress; resumed the practice of law; died in Liberty, Casey County, Ky., May 5, 1896; interment in Brown Cemetery, Humphrey, Ky.

**ADAMS, Stephen,** a Representative and a Senator from Mississippi; born in the Pendleton District, S.C., October 17, 1807; moved with his parents to Franklin County, Tenn., in 1812; attended the public schools; studied law; was admitted to the bar in 1829; member of the State senate 1833-1834; moved to Aberdeen, Miss., in 1834 and commenced the practice of law; circuit court judge 1837-1845; elected as a Democrat to the Twenty-ninth Congress (March 4, 1845-March 3, 1847); again became judge of the circuit court in 1848; member of the State house of representatives in 1850; delegate to the State constitutional convention in 1851; elected as a Democrat to the United States Senate on February 19, 1852, to fill the vacancy caused by the resignation of Jefferson Davis and served from March 17, 1852, to March 3, 1857; chairman, Committee on Retrenchment (Thirty-third and the Thirty-fourth Congresses); moved to Memphis, Tenn. and resumed the practice of law; died in Memphis, Tenn., May 11, 1857; interment in Elmwood Cemetery.

**ADAMS, Thomas,** a Delegate from Virginia; born in New Kent County, Va., in 1730; attended the common schools; clerk of Henrico County; journeyed to Great Britain in 1762 and attended to his extensive business interests there until 1774; returned before the Revolutionary War; member of the Virginia House of Burgesses, and signed the Articles of Association on May 27, 1774; chairman of the New Kent County Committee of Safety in 1774; Member of the Continental Congress in 1778 and 1779; a signer of the Articles of Confederation; moved to Augusta County, Va., in 1780; member of the Virginia senate 1783-1786; died on his estate, "Cowpasture," in Augusta County, Va., in August 1788.

**ADAMS, Wilbur Louis,** a Representative from Delaware; born in Georgetown, Sussex County, Del., October 23, 1884; attended the public schools, Delaware College, Newark, Del., and Dickinson College, Carlisle, Pa.; was graduated from the law department of the University of Pennsylvania at Philadelphia in 1907; was admitted to the bar the same year and commenced practice in Wilmington, Del.; unsuccessful candidate for election as attorney general in 1924; elected as a Democrat to the Seventy-third Congress (March 4, 1933-January 3, 1935); was not a candidate for renomination in 1934, but was an unsuccessful candidate for election to the United States Senate; moved to Georgetown, Del., in 1934 and continued the practice of law; acting postmaster of Georgetown, Del., from May 6, 1937, until his death; died in Lewes, Del., on December 4, 1937; interment in Union Cemetery, Georgetown, Del.

**ADAMSON, William Charles,** a Representative from Georgia; born in Bowdon, Carroll County, Ga., August 13, 1854; attended the common schools; was graduated from Bowdon College in 1874; studied law; was admitted to the bar in 1876 and commenced practice in Carrollton, Carroll County, Ga.; judge of the city court of Carrollton, 1885-1889; attorney for the city of Carrollton for a number of years; delegate to the Democratic National Convention of 1892; elected as a Democrat to the Fifty-fifth and to the ten succeeding Congresses and served from March 4, 1897, until his resignation on December 18, 1917; chairman, Committee on Interstate and Foreign Commerce (Sixty-second through Sixty-fifth Congresses); appointed on December 17, 1917, a member of the Board of United States General Appraisers (now the United States Customs Court) and served until January 20, 1928, when he resigned; resumed the practice of law in Carrollton, Ga.; died while on a visit in New York City, January 3, 1929; interment in City Cemetery, Carrollton, Ga.

**ADDABBO, Joseph Patrick,** a Representative from New York; born in Ozone Park, Queens County, N.Y., March 17, 1925; attended Public School 59, Boys' High School, Brooklyn, and City College of New York; graduated from St. John's Law School in 1946 and commenced the practice of law in Ozone Park, N.Y., in 1947; president of Ozone Park Men's Association, 1948-1959 and Ferrini Welfare League of Catholic Charities, 1956-1958; elected as a Democrat to the Eighty-seventh and to the twelve succeeding Congresses, and served from January 3, 1961 until his death in Washington, D.C., April 10, 1986; interment in St. John's Cemetery, Queens, N.Y.

**ADDAMS, William,** a Representative from Pennsylvania; born in Lancaster County, Pa., April 11, 1777; moved to Berks County, near Reading, and served as auditor in 1813 and 1814; commissioner of Berks County from 1814 until 1817; member of the Pennsylvania house of representatives, 1822-1824; elected to the Nineteenth and Twentieth Congresses (March 4, 1825-March 3, 1829); unsuccessful candidate for renomination in 1828 to the Twenty-first Congress; member of the committee for the Deaf and Dumb Institution for the States of New York and Ohio; elected associate judge of Berks County and served from 1839 to 1842; captain of the Reading City Troop; largely interested in agricultural pursuits; died in Spring Township, Berks County, Pa., May 30, 1858; interment in St. John's Church Cemetery, Sinking Springs, Pa.

**ADDONIZIO, Hugh Joseph,** a Representative from New Jersey; born in Newark, Essex County, N.J., January 31, 1914; attended the public schools; graduated from West Side High School, Newark, N.J., in 1933, St. Benedict's Prep School, Newark, N.J., in 1935, and Fordham University, New York City, in 1939; employed with A and C Clothing Co., of Newark, N.J., in 1939 and became vice president in 1946; during the Second World War entered the United States Army as a private on January 13, 1941; attended Officers Candidate School, Fort Benning, Ga., and commissioned a second lieutenant of Infantry; served with the Sixtieth Infantry, Ninth Division, participating in eight major campaigns; discharged as a captain in February 1946; elected as a Democrat to the Eighty-first and to the six succeeding Congresses and served from January 3, 1949, until his resignation June 30, 1962; elected mayor of Newark, N.J., in 1962 and reelected in 1966, serving until July 1, 1970; unsuccessful candidate for reelection in 1970; resided in Tinton Falls, N.J., until his death in Red Bank, N.J., February 2, 1981; interment in Gate of Heaven Cemetery, Hanover, N.J.

**ADGATE, Asa,** a Representative from New York; born in Canaan, N.Y., November 17, 1767; in 1793 moved to what became known as Adgates Falls, on the Ausable River, then in the township of Peru, Clinton County, N.Y. (now Ausable Chasm, Chesterfield Township, Essex County, N.Y.), where he engaged in the manufacture of iron and agricultural pursuits; upon the organization of the town of Peru in 1793 was elected town clerk and reelected in 1794; supervisor in 1795; assessor in 1796 and 1797; commissioner of schools in 1798; member of the New York State general assembly from Clinton County in 1798; lieutenant of Infantry, Clinton County, New York Militia, in 1798 and 1799; named by Governor John Jay, of New York, March 9, 1799, in the first commission of the peace for Essex County, as one of the judges of the court of common pleas and served for several years; elected as a Republican to the Fourteenth Congress to fill the vacancy caused by the death of Benjamin Pond and served from June 7, 1815, to March 3, 1817; was not a candidate for renomination in 1816 to the Fifteenth Congress; resumed his former occupations; again a member of the State general assembly from Essex County, in 1823; died at Ausable Chasm, Chesterfield Township, Essex County, N.Y., February 15, 1832; interment in Ausable Chasm Cemetery, Ausable Township, Clinton County, N.Y.

**ADKINS, Charles,** a Representative from Illinois; born on a farm in Pickaway County, Ohio, near Mount Sterling, February 7, 1863; attended the common schools; taught school for several years; moved to Illinois in 1885 and settled on a farm in Piatt County near Bement; engaged in agricultural pursuits; president of the Piatt County (Ill.) Farmers' Institute; member of the board of education of

Bement, Ill., 1900-1920; member of the board of supervisors of Piatt County 1902-1906; member of the State house of representatives 1907-1913, serving as speaker 1911-1913; president of the Illinois Livestock Breeders' Association in 1914 and 1915; appointed State director of agriculture during the administration of Governor Frank M. Lowden and served from 1916 to 1920; moved to Decatur, Macon County, Ill., in 1918; elected as a Republican to the Sixty-ninth and to the three succeeding Congresses (March 4, 1925-March 3, 1933); unsuccessful candidate for reelection in 1932 to the Seventy-third Congress; resided in Decatur, Ill., until his death there on March 31, 1941; interment in Bement Cemetery, Bement, Ill.

**ADRAIN, Garnett Bowditch,** a Representative from New Jersey; born in New York City December 15, 1815; moved with his parents to New Brunswick, N.J.; attended the public schools; was graduated from Rutgers College, New Brunswick, in 1833; studied law in the office of his brother; was licensed as an attorney in 1836 and as a counselor in 1839; commenced the practice of law in New Brunswick, N.J.; elected as a Democrat to the Thirty-fifth Congress and as an Anti-Lecompton Democrat to the Thirty-sixth Congress (March 4, 1857-March 3, 1861); chairman, Committee on Engraving (Thirty-fifth and Thirty-sixth Congresses); was not a candidate for reelection in 1860; resumed the practice of his profession; died in New Brunswick, Middlesex County, N.J., August 17, 1878; interment in Van Liew Cemetery.

**AGNEW, Spiro Theodore,** Vice President of the United States; born in Baltimore, Md., November 9, 1918; educated in the public schools of Baltimore; attended the Johns Hopkins University, 1937-1939; graduated from the University of Baltimore Law School in 1947; served in the United States Army during the Second World War and the Korean conflict; insurance investigator and casualty claims adjuster; practiced law in Baltimore and in Towson, Md.; member, 1957-1958, and chair, 1958-1961, of the Baltimore County Board of Appeals; elected county executive of Baltimore County in 1962 and served from December 1, 1962 until 1966; elected Governor of Maryland in 1966 and served from January 25, 1967 until his resignation on January 7, 1969, having been elected Vice President of the United States on November 5, 1968, on the Republican ticket with Richard M. Nixon; reelected Vice President on November 7, 1972 and served from January 20, 1969 until his resignation; charged with accepting bribes and falsifying federal tax returns, pleaded nolo contendere to the latter charge in federal court, and resigned on October 10, 1973; international business consultant; was a resident of Ocean City, Md., and Rancho Mirage, Calif., until his death in Berlin, Md. on September 17, 1996; interment in Dulaney Valley Memorial Gardens, Timonium, Md.

**Bibliography:** Agnew, Spiro T. *Go Quietly...Or Else.* New York: Morrow, 1980; Lippman, Theo, Jr. *Spiro Agnew's America: The Vice President and the Politics of Suburbia.* New York: Norton, 1972; Whitcover, Jules. *White Knight: The Rise of Spiro Agnew.* New York: Random House, 1972.

**AHL, John Alexander,** a Representative from Pennsylvania; born in Strasburg, Franklin County, Pa., August 16, 1813; moved with his parents to Newville, Cumberland County, Pa., in 1825; attended the public schools; taught school for several terms; studied medicine and was graduated from the University of Maryland, Baltimore, Md., in 1832; practiced his profession at Centerville, Pa., until 1856; moved to Newville, Pa., in 1856 and engaged in the real estate business; also operated a paper mill; delegate to the Democratic National Convention at Cincinnati in 1856; elected as a Democrat to the Thirty-fifth Congress (March 4, 1857-March 3, 1859); declined to be a candidate for renomination in 1858 to the Thirty-sixth Congress; resumed the manufacture of paper, and operated an iron furnace at Antietam, Md.; served as surgeon in the Pennsylvania militia; projector and major builder of the Harrisburg

and Potomac Railroad; died in Newville, Pa., April 25, 1882; interment in Big Spring Presbyterian Cemetery.

**AIKEN, David Wyatt** (father of Wyatt Aiken and cousin of William Aiken), a Representative from South Carolina; born in Winnsboro, Fairfield County, S.C., March 17, 1828; received his early education under private tutors; attended Mount Zion Institute, Winnsboro, and was graduated from South Carolina University, at Columbia, in 1849; taught school two years; engaged in agricultural pursuits in 1852; during the Civil War served in the Confederate Army as a private; appointed adjutant and later elected colonel of the Seventh Regiment of Volunteers; relieved from service by reason of wounds received on September 17, 1862, at the Battle of Antietam, Md.; member of the South Carolina State house of representatives, 1864-1866; secretary and treasurer, Agricultural and Mechanical Society of South Carolina, 1869; member, executive committee, National Grange, 1873-1885, and served as chairman, 1875; delegate to the Democratic National Convention of 1876; elected as a Democrat to the Forty-fifth and to the four succeeding Congresses (March 4, 1877-March 3, 1887); chairman, Committee on Education (Forty-eighth and Forty-ninth Congresses); was not a candidate for renomination in 1886 to the Fiftieth Congress, being an invalid throughout his last term; died in Cokesbury, S.C., April 6, 1887; interment in Magnolia Cemetery, Greenwood, S.C.

**Bibliography:** *DAB*; Pritchard, Claudius Hornby, Jr. *Colonel D. Wyatt Aiken, 1828-1887, South Carolina's Militant Agrarian.* Privately printed in Hampden-Sydney, Va., 1970.

**AIKEN, George David,** a Senator from Vermont; born in Dummerston, Windham County, Vt., August 20, 1892; moved with his parents to Putney, Vt., in 1893; attended the public schools of Putney and Brattleboro, Vt.; engaged in fruit farming in 1912; also conducted an extensive nursery business, and in 1926 engaged in the commercial cultivation of wildflowers; served as school director of Putney from 1920 until 1937; member of the Vermont State house of representatives, 1931-1935, and served as speaker, 1933-1935; Lieutenant Governor of Vermont, 1935-1937; elected Governor of Vermont in 1936, reelected in 1938, and served from January 7, 1937 to January 9, 1941; elected as a Republican to the United States Senate, November 5, 1940, to fill the vacancy caused by the death of Ernest W. Gibson in the term ending January 3, 1945, but did not assume office until January 10, 1941; reelected in 1944, 1950, 1956, 1962, and 1968, and served from January 10, 1941, to January 3, 1975; was not a candidate for reelection in 1974; chairman, Committee on Expenditures in Executive Departments (Eightieth Congress), Committee on Agriculture and Forestry (Eighty-third Congress); died in Putney, Vt., November 19, 1984; interment in Putney, Vt.

**Bibliography:** Aiken, George D. *Aiken: Senate Diary, January 1972-January 1975.* Brattleboro, Vt.: The Stephen Greene Press, 1976; Sherman, Michael, ed. *The Political Legacy of George D. Aiken: Wise Old Owl of the U.S. Senate.* Foreword by Mike Mansfield. Woodstock, Vt.: Countryman Press, 1995.

**AIKEN, William** (cousin of David Wyatt Aiken), a Representative from South Carolina; born in Charleston, S.C., January 28, 1806; attended private schools; was graduated from the College of South Carolina (now the University of South Carolina) at Columbia in 1825; engaged in agricultural pursuits; member of the State house of representatives 1838-1842; served in the State senate 1842-1844; chosen Governor of South Carolina by the legislature of the State and served from December 1844 to December 1846; elected as a Democrat to the Thirty-second, Thirty-third, and Thirty-fourth Congresses (March 4, 1851-March 3, 1857); was an unsuccessful candidate for Speaker of the House of Representatives after 133 ballots in the Thirty-fourth Congress; was not a candidate for renomination in 1856 to the Thirty-fifth Congress; presented credentials as a Member-elect to the Thirty-ninth Congress on

February 12, 1867, but was not permitted to qualify; resumed his former pursuits near Charleston, S.C.; died at Flat Rock, Henderson County, N.C., September 6, 1887; interment in Magnolia Cemetery, Charleston, S.C.

**Bibliography:** *DAB.*

**AIKEN, Wyatt** (son of David Wyatt Aiken), a Representative from South Carolina; born near Macon, Ga., December 14, 1863; reared in Cokesbury, Abbeville (now Greenwood) County, S.C.; attended the public schools of Cokesbury and of Washington, D.C.; official court reporter for the second South Carolina judicial circuit and, later, for the eighth circuit; volunteered as a private in Company A, First South Carolina Regiment of Infantry, during the war with Spain; later appointed battalion adjutant by Governor William H. Ellerbe, and acted as regimental quartermaster during the greater portion of his service; was mustered out in Columbia, S.C., November 10, 1898; elected as a Democrat to the Fifty-eighth and to the six succeeding Congresses (March 4, 1903-March 3, 1917); unsuccessful candidate for renomination in 1916 and again in 1918; lived in retirement until his death in Abbeville, S.C., February 6, 1923; interment in Melrose Cemetery.

**AINEY, William David Blakeslee,** a Representative from Pennsylvania; born in New Milford, Pa., April 8, 1864; attended the public schools, the State Normal School at Mansfield, and Lehigh University, Bethlehem, Pa., in 1887; studied law; was admitted to the bar in 1887 and commenced practice in Montrose, Pa.; district attorney for Susquehanna County 1890-1896; organized Company G of the Pennsylvania National Guard and served as captain 1889-1894; elected as a Republican to the Sixty-second Congress to fill the vacancy caused by the death of George W. Kipp; reelected to the Sixty-third Congress and served from November 7, 1911, to March 3, 1915; was not a candidate for reelection in 1914 to the Sixty-fourth Congress; delegate to the International Parliamentary Union for International Peace held at Geneva, Switzerland, in 1912, and at The Hague in 1913; secretary and president of the Japanese-American group of interparliamentarians and delegate in 1914 to Tokyo, Japan, and to Stockholm, Sweden; resumed the practice of law in Montrose, Pa.; appointed a member of the Public Service Commission of Pennsylvania May 20, 1915, and on August 20, 1915, was elected chairman; reappointed for a ten-year term as member and chairman on July 1, 1917, and again on July 1, 1927; appointed chairman of the Pennsylvania Fuel Commission in August 1922; president of the National Association of Railroad and Utilities Commissioners in 1924; died in Harrisburg, Pa., September 4, 1932; interment in Montrose Cemetery, Montrose, Pa.

**AINSLIE, George,** a Delegate from the Territory of Idaho; born near Boonville, Cooper County, Mo., October 30, 1838; attended the common schools, and St. Louis (Mo.) University in 1856 and 1857; was graduated from the Jesuit College at St. Louis; studied law; was admitted to the bar in 1860 and commenced practice in Boonville, Mo.; moved to Colorado the same year, and in 1862 moved to that portion of the Territory of Washington that later became the Territory of Idaho; engaged in mining and also practiced law; member of the Idaho Territorial house of representatives in 1865 and 1866; edited the Idaho World from 1869 to 1873; district attorney of the second district in 1874 and 1876; elected as a Democrat to the Forty-sixth and Forty-seventh Congresses (March 4, 1879-March 3, 1883); unsuccessful candidate for reelection in 1882 to the Forty-eighth Congress; built the first electric street railway in Boise City, Idaho; settled in Oakland, Calif., and retired from active business pursuits; died in Oakland, Calif., May 19, 1913; the remains were cremated and the ashes deposited in the columbarium, Odd Fellows Cemetery, San Francisco, Calif.

**AINSWORTH, Lucien Lester,** a Representative from Iowa; born in New Woodstock, Madison County, N.Y., June 21, 1831; attended the public schools, and the Oneida Conference Seminary, Cazenovia, N.Y.; studied law; was admitted to the bar in Madison County, N.Y., in 1854; moved to Belvidere, Ill., and commenced practice the same year; moved to Iowa in 1855 and continued the practice of law in West Union; member of the State senate 1860-1862; during the Civil War entered the Union Army in 1862 as captain of Company C, Sixth Regiment, Iowa Volunteer Cavalry, and served three years against the Indians in the Northwest; after leaving the Army returned to West Union and resumed the practice of law; member of the State house of representatives 1871-1873; elected as a Democrat to the Forty-fourth Congress (March 4, 1875-March 3, 1877); declined to accept a renomination in 1876; resumed the practice of law in West Union, Fayette County, Iowa, and died there April 19, 1902; interment in West Union Cemetery.

**AITKEN, David Demerest,** a Representative from Michigan; born on a farm in Flint Township, Genesee County, Mich., September 5, 1853; attended the district schools and the local high school in Flint; taught in a district school of Genesee County in 1871 and 1872; moved to New Jersey in 1872 and was employed as a bookkeeper; studied law in New York City; was admitted to the bar in 1878 and commenced practice in Flint, Mich.; city clerk, 1883-1886; city attorney, 1886-1890; elected as a Republican to the Fifty-third and Fifty-fourth Congresses (March 4, 1893-March 3, 1897); chairman, Committee on Mining (Fifty-fourth Congress); was not a candidate for renomination in 1896 to the Fifty-fifth Congress, being an unsuccessful candidate for Governor of Michigan; resumed the practice of law; also engaged in banking; served as mayor of Flint in 1905 and 1906; died in Flint, Mich., May 26, 1930; interment in Glenwood Cemetery.

**AKAKA, Daniel Kahikina,** a Representative and a Senator from Hawaii; born in Honolulu, Hawaii, September 11, 1924; attended the public schools of Hawaii; graduated, Kamehameha School for Boys (high school), 1942; B.E., University of Hawaii, 1952; professional certificate in secondary education, 1953; professional school administrator's certificate, 1961; M.E., education, 1966; served in United States Army, 1945-1947; teacher, 1953-1960; vice principal, 1960; principal, 1963-1971, all in Hawaii; program specialist, Compensatory Education, 1968-1971; director, Hawaii Office of Economic Opportunity, 1971-1974; special assistant, Hawaii Office of the Governor, 1975-1976; elected as a Democrat to the Ninety-fifth and to the six succeeding Congresses and served from January 3, 1977, until May 15, 1990, when he resigned; appointed to the United States Senate, April 30, 1990, to fill the vacancy caused by the death of Spark M. Matsunaga and served from May 16, 1990, to January 3, 1991; elected November 6, 1990 to complete the term ending January 3, 1995; reelected in 1994 for the term ending January 3, 2001; is a resident of Honolulu, Hawaii.

**AKERS, Thomas Peter,** a Representative from Missouri; born in Knox County, Ohio, October 4, 1828; attended school in Cleveland, Ohio; was graduated from an Ohio college; studied law; was admitted to the bar; taught school for a time in Kentucky; moved to Lexington, Mo., in 1853; professor of mathematics and moral philosophy in Masonic College, Lexington, Mo., in 1855 and 1856; pastor of the local Methodist Church; elected as a candidate of the American Party to the Thirty-fourth Congress to fill the vacancy caused by the death of John G. Miller and served from August 18, 1856, to March 3, 1857; was not a candidate for reelection to the Thirty-fifth Congress; moved to New York City in 1861 and became vice president of the gold board; owing to ill health moved to Utah, and shortly thereafter returned to Lexington, Lafayette County, Mo., where he died on April 3, 1877; interment in Machpelah Cemetery.

**AKIN, Theron,** a Representative from New York; born in Johnstown, Fulton County, N.Y., May 23, 1855; attended the common schools of Amsterdam, N.Y., and also was privately tutored at home; engaged in agricultural pursuits; was graduated from the

New York Dental College and practiced for twelve years in Amsterdam, N.Y.; moved to Akin (later Fort Johnson), N.Y., and engaged in agricultural pursuits in Montgomery County; served as president of the village of Fort Johnson, N.Y.; elected as a Progressive Republican to the Sixty-second Congress (March 4, 1911-March 3, 1913); unsuccessful candidate for renomination on the Progressive ticket in 1912; resumed agricultural pursuits; unsuccessful candidate for election to the Sixty-fourth Congress on the Progressive ticket in 1914; mayor of Amsterdam, Montgomery County, N.Y., 1920-1923; resumed his former pursuits; unsuccessful candidate for the Republican and Democratic mayoralty nomination in 1927; died in Amsterdam, N.Y., March 26, 1933; interment in Pine Grove Cemetery, Tribes Hill, Montgomery County, N.Y.

**ALBAUGH, Walter Hugh,** a Representative from Ohio; born in Phoneton, Miami County, Ohio, January 2, 1890; attended the public and high schools of his native city; was graduated from the law department of Ohio State University at Columbus in 1914; was admitted to the bar the same year and commenced practice in Troy, Ohio; during the First World War served in the United States Infantry as a private unassigned, from May 28, 1918, to December 13, 1918; member of the State house of representatives 1921-1925; also engaged as a civil engineer, surveying fuel lands in Ohio and West Virginia 1910-1911; elected as a Republican to the Seventy-fifth Congress to fill the vacancy caused by the resignation of Frank L. Kloeb and served from November 8, 1938, until January 3, 1939; was not a candidate for nomination in 1938 to the full term; resumed the practice of law in Troy, Ohio, and died there January 21, 1942; interment in Memorial Park Cemetery, Dayton, Ohio.

**ALBERT, Carl Bert** (cousin of Charles Wesley Vursell), a Representative from Oklahoma; born in North McAlester, Pittsburg County, Okla., May 10, 1908; attended Flowery Mound Rural School; was graduated from McAlester High School in 1927; A.B., University of Oklahoma, Norman, 1931; having been awarded a Rhodes Scholarship, received a B.A. in 1933, and a B.C.L. in 1934 from Oxford University, England; studied law; was admitted to the bar in 1935 and commenced practice in McAlester, Okla.; legal clerk, Federal Housing Administration, 1934-1937; employed as an accountant, Sayre Oil Co., 1937-1938, and in the legal department of Ohio Oil Co., 1939-1940; during the Second World War enlisted in the United States Army on June 16, 1941, as a private; served in the Pacific Theater and was discharged as lieutenant colonel on February 17, 1946; awarded the Bronze Star; resumed the practice of law; delegate to the Democratic National Conventions of 1952, 1956, 1964 and 1968; elected as a Democrat to the Eightieth and to the fourteen succeeding Congresses (January 3, 1947-January 3, 1977); majority whip (Eighty-fourth through Eighty-seventh Congresses), majority leader (Eighty-seventh through Ninety-first Congresses), Speaker of the House of Representatives (Ninety-second through Ninety-fourth Congresses); was not a candidate for reelection in 1976 to the Ninety-fifth Congress; is a resident of McAlester, Okla.

Bibliography: Albert, Carl, with Danney Goble. *Little Giant: The Life and Times of Speaker Carl Albert.* Norman: University of Oklahoma Press, 1990.

**ALBERT, William Julian,** a Representative from Maryland; born in Baltimore, Md., August 4, 1816; was graduated from Mount St. Mary's College, near Emmittsburg, Md., in 1833; engaged in the hardware business until 1855 and, later, in banking; was a prominent Union leader in Maryland and worked to prevent the secession of the State; one of the founders and directors of the First National Bank of Maryland; director of several insurance companies, savings banks, and manufacturing companies; unsuccessful candidate for election in 1866 to the Fortieth Congress, and in 1868 to the Forty-first Congress; elected as a Republican to the Forty-third Congress (March 4, 1873-March 3, 1875); was not a

candidate for reelection in 1874 to the Forty-fourth Congress; resumed his former business pursuits; died in Baltimore, Md., March 29, 1879; interment in Greenmount Cemetery.

**ALBERTSON, Nathaniel,** a Representative from Indiana; born in Fairfax, Fairfax County, Va., June 10, 1800; moved to Salem, Washington County, Ind., and engaged in agricultural pursuits; member of the State house of representatives 1838-1840; moved to Floyd County in 1835 and settled in Greenville, near New Albany, and resumed agricultural pursuits; elected as a Democrat to the Thirty-first Congress (March 4, 1849-March 3, 1851); unsuccessful candidate for reelection in 1850 to the Thirty-second Congress; resumed agricultural pursuits; moved to Keokuk, Iowa, in 1853 and engaged in mercantile pursuits; moved to Boonville, Mo., in 1856 and continued mercantile pursuits; settled in Central City, Gilpin County, Colo., in 1860 and engaged in the hotel business; also became interested in mining; died in Central City, Colo., December 16, 1863; interment in Central City Graveyard.

**ALBOSTA, Donald Joseph,** a Representative from Michigan; born in Saginaw, Mich., December 5, 1925; attended the Saginaw and Chesaning public schools; graduated from Chesaning Agricultural School; attended Delta College, Saginaw, Mich.; served in the United States Navy; farmer; owner and developer of Misteguay Creek Farms; Albee Township Trustee; associate director, Saginaw County Soil Conservation District; Saginaw County Commissioner, 1970-1974; served in the Michigan house of representatives, 1974-1976; elected as a Democrat to the Ninety-sixth and to the two succeeding Congresses (January 3, 1979-January 3, 1985); unsuccessful candidate for reelection in 1984 to the Ninety-ninth Congress; farmer and businessman; is a resident of St. Charles, Mich.

**ALBRIGHT, Charles,** a Representative from Pennsylvania; born in Bucks County, Pa., December 13, 1830; attended Dickinson College, Carlisle, Pa.; studied law; was admitted to the bar in 1852 and commenced practice in Mauch Chunk, Pa.; moved to the Territory of Kansas in 1854 and participated in its early development; returned to Pennsylvania and resumed the practice of law in Mauch Chunk in 1856; delegate to the Republican National Convention in 1860 and 1872; during the Civil War served in the Union Army and was promoted through the ranks to colonel of the One Hundred and Thirty-second Regiment, Pennsylvania Volunteer Infantry; honorably mustered out May 24, 1865; recommissioned colonel of the Thirty-fourth Pennsylvania Militia July 3, 1863, and honorably mustered out August 10, 1863; recommissioned colonel of the Two Hundred and Second Regiment, Pennsylvania Volunteer Infantry, September 4, 1864; honorably mustered out August 3, 1865; resumed the practice of law in Mauch Chunk, Pa.; elected as a Republican to the Forty-third Congress (March 4, 1873-March 3, 1875); was not a candidate for reelection in 1874; resumed the practice of law and also engaged in manufacturing in Mauch Chunk, Pa., until his death there September 28, 1880; interment in Mauch Chunk Cemetery.

**ALBRIGHT, Charles Jefferson,** a Representative from Ohio; born in Carlisle, Cumberland County, Pa., May 9, 1816; moved with his parents in 1824 to Allegheny County, Pa.; received a limited schooling; was employed in a harness shop and as a clerk in a rural store; apprenticed as a printer; moved to Guernsey County, Ohio, in 1832 and settled on a farm near Cambridge; owner and publisher of the Guernsey Times, 1840-1845, and 1848-1855; served as secretary of the Guernsey County Board of School Examiners, 1841-1844; elected as a Republican to the Thirty-fourth Congress (March 4, 1855-March 3, 1857); unsuccessful candidate for reelection in 1856 to the Thirty-fifth Congress; served as vice president at the Republican State convention in 1855; delegate to the Republican National Conventions of 1856 and 1860; during the Civil War served as chairman of the Guernsey County Military Committee; internal revenue collector for the sixteenth Ohio district, by appointment of President Lincoln, 1862-1869; delegate to the third State constitutional convention in 1873; member of the State board of charities in 1875; president of the board of school examiners of the Cambridge Union School, 1881-1883; died in Cambridge, Ohio, October 21, 1883; interment in South Cemetery.

**ALCORN, James Lusk,** a Senator from Mississippi; born near Golconda, Ill., November 4, 1816; attended the public schools of Livingston County, Ky., and was graduated from Cumberland College, Ky.; deputy sheriff of Livingston County 1839-1844; member of the Kentucky house of representatives in 1843; studied law; was admitted to the bar in 1844 and commenced practice in Delta, Panola County, Miss.; member of the Mississippi house of representatives 1846, 1856, and 1857; served in the State senate 1848-1854; unsuccessful candidate for election to the Thirty-fifth Congress in 1856; declined the nomination for Governor in 1857; founder of the Mississippi levee system and was made president of the levee board of the Mississippi-Yazoo Delta in 1858; served in the Confederate Army during the Civil War as a brigadier general; presented credentials as a United States Senator-elect in 1865 but was not permitted to take his seat; elected Governor of Mississippi in 1869 and served from March 10, 1870, until his resignation on November 30, 1871, having previously been elected Senator; elected as a Republican to the United States Senate on January 18, 1870, for the term beginning March 4, 1871, but did not assume these duties until December 1, 1871, preferring to continue as Governor; served as Senator from December 1, 1871, to March 3, 1877; unsuccessful candidate for election in 1873 for Governor; resumed the practice of law in Friar Point; died at his plantation home, "Eagles Nest," in Coahoma County, Miss., December 19, 1894; interment in the family cemetery on his estate.

Bibliography: *DAB*; Pereyra, Lillian A. *James Lusk Alcorn: Persistent Whig.* Baton Rouge: Louisiana State University Press, 1966; Tubb, Jackson McWhirter. "Senatorial Career of James Lusk Alcorn." Ph.D. dissertation, University of Mississippi, 1927.

**ALDERSON, John Duffy,** a Representative from West Virginia; born at Nicholas Court House (now Summersville), W.Va., November 29, 1854; attended the common schools; sergeant at arms of the West Virginia State senate, 1871-1873; doorkeeper in 1872 and 1873; studied law; was admitted to the bar in 1876 and commenced practice at Nicholas Court House; appointed prosecuting attorney for the counties of Nicholas and Webster in 1876; elected prosecuting attorney for these counties, reelected in 1880 and 1884, and served until January 1, 1889; clerk of the State senate, 1883-1887; elected as a Democrat to the Fifty-first and to the two succeeding Congresses (March 4, 1889-March 3, 1895); unsuccessful candidate for reelection in 1894 to the Fifty-fourth Congress; resumed the practice of law in Nicholas, W.Va.; delegate to the Democratic National Conventions of 1900 and 1908; died in Richwood, Nicholas County, W.Va., December 5, 1910; interment in a private burial ground at Summersville, W.Va.

**ALDRICH, Cyrus,** a Representative from Minnesota; born in Smithfield, R.I., June 18, 1808; attended the common schools; followed the occupations of sailor, boatman, farmer, contractor on public works, and mail contractor; moved to Illinois and settled in Alton in 1837; member of the State house of representatives 1845-1847; register of deeds of Jo Daviess County 1847-1849; receiver of the United States land office at Dixon, Ill., 1849-1853; moved to Minneapolis, Minn., in 1855 and engaged in the lumber business; member of the State constitutional convention in 1857; elected as a Republican to the Thirty-sixth and Thirty-seventh Congresses (March 4, 1859-March 3, 1863); chairman, Committee on Indian Affairs (Thirty-seventh Congress); was not a candidate for renomination in 1862 to the Thirty-eighth Congress; unsuccessful candidate for election in 1863 to the United States Senate; member

of the State house of representatives in 1865; elected chairman of the board of supervisors of the town of Minneapolis in 1865; appointed by President Lincoln in 1863 one of the commissioners to examine claims for indemnity of those who had suffered during the Sioux War of 1862; postmaster of Minneapolis, Minn., from September 11, 1867, until April 15, 1871, when a successor was appointed; died in Minneapolis, Minn., October 5, 1871; interment in Lakewood Cemetery.

**ALDRICH, James Franklin** (son of William Aldrich), a Representative from Illinois; born at Two Rivers, Manitowoc County, Wis., April 6, 1853; moved with his parents to Chicago, Ill., in April 1861; attended the public schools and Chicago University; was graduated from Rensselaer Polytechnic Institute, Troy, N.Y., in 1877; engaged in the manufacture of linseed oil, and later engaged in the gas business; member of the Cook County Board of Commissioners, 1886-1888, serving as president in 1887; member of the Cook County board of education in 1887; commissioner of public works of Chicago from May 1, 1891 to January 1, 1893; elected as a Republican to the Fifty-third and Fifty-fourth Congresses (March 4, 1893-March 3, 1897); chairman, Committee on Accounts (Fifty-fourth Congress); was not a candidate for renomination in 1896 to the Fifty-fifth Congress; appointed consul general at Havana, Cuba, in 1897, but did not reach his post to serve, owing to the sinking of the battleship *Maine*, February 15, 1898, and to the war with Spain which followed in April; receiver of national banks and railroad appraiser from 1898 until 1923; died in Chicago, Ill., March 8, 1933; interment in Rosehill Cemetery.

**ALDRICH, Nelson Wilmarth** (father of Richard Steere Aldrich, cousin of William Aldrich, grandfather of Nelson Aldrich Rockefeller, and great-grandfather of John Davison Rockefeller), a Representative and a Senator from Rhode Island; born in Foster, R.I., November 6, 1841; attended the public schools of East Killingly, Conn., and the Academy of East Greenwich, R.I.; entered the wholesale grocery business in Providence; during the Civil War enlisted as a private in Company D, First Regiment, Rhode Island National Guard, in 1862; member of the city council, 1869-1874, serving as president in 1872 and 1873; member of the Rhode Island State house of representatives in 1875 and 1876, elected speaker in 1876; elected as a Republican to the Forty-sixth and Forty-seventh Congresses, and served from March 4, 1879 to October 4, 1881, when he resigned to become Senator; elected as a Republican to the United States Senate to fill the vacancy caused by the death of Ambrose E. Burnside; reelected 1886, 1892, 1898, and 1904, and served from October 5, 1881 to March 3, 1911; was not a candidate for reelection in 1911; Republican caucus chairman 1908-1909; chairman, Committee on Transportation Routes to the Seaboard (Forty-eighth and Forty-ninth Congresses), Committee on Rules (Fiftieth through Fifty-second and Fifty-fourth and Fifty-fifth Congresses), Select Committee on Corporations Organized in the District of Columbia (Fifty-third Congress), Committee on Finance (Fifty-fifth through Sixty-first Congresses), Republican Conference (Sixtieth Congress); chairman, National Monetary Commission, 1908-1912; retired to Providence, R.I.; died in New York City, April 16, 1915; interment in Swan Point Cemetery, Providence, R.I.

Bibliography: *DAB*; Stephenson, Nathaniel W. *Nelson W. Aldrich: A Leader In American Politics.* 1930. Reprint. New York: Kennikat Press, 1971; Sternstein, Jerome L. "Corruption in the Gilded Age Senate: Nelson W. Aldrich and the Sugar Trust." *Capitol Studies* 6 (Spring 1978): 13-37.

**ALDRICH, Richard Steere** (son of Nelson Wilmarth Aldrich), a Representative from Rhode Island; born in Washington, D.C., February 29, 1884; attended the public schools in Providence, R.I.; was graduated from Hope Street High School at Providence in 1902, from Yale University in 1906, and from the law department of Harvard University in 1909; was admitted to the bar in 1911 and commenced the practice of law in New York City; returned to Providence, R.I., in 1913 and continued the practice of his profession; member of the Rhode Island house of representatives 1914-1916; served in the State senate 1916-1918; elected as a Republican to the Sixty-eighth and to the four succeeding Congresses (March 4, 1923-March 3, 1933); was not a candidate for renomination in 1932; resumed legal pursuits in Providence, R.I., until his death there on December 25, 1941; interment in Swan Point Cemetery.

**ALDRICH, Truman Heminway** (brother of William Farrington Aldrich), a Representative from Alabama; born in Palmyra, Wayne County, N.Y., October 17, 1848; attended the public schools, the military academy at West Chester, Pa., and was graduated from the Rensselaer Polytechnic Institute, Troy, N.Y., in 1869; engaged in engineering in New York and New Jersey; moved to Selma, Ala., in 1871; engaged in banking and in the mining of coal, becoming vice president and general manager of the Tennessee Coal, Iron and Railroad Co., in 1892; founder of the Cahaba Coal Mining Co.; successfully contested as a Republican the election of Oscar W. Underwood to the Fifty-fourth Congress and served from June 9, 1896, to March 3, 1897; was not a candidate for renomination in 1896 to the Fifty-fifth Congress; served as postmaster at Birmingham, Ala., by appointment of President William Howard Taft, from September 1, 1911, to December 15, 1915; delegate to the Republican National Convention of 1904; served as a dollar-per-year man on the War Industries Board during the First World War; after the war was engaged as a mining engineer and geologist; died in Birmingham, Ala., April 28, 1932; interment in Elmwood Cemetery.

**ALDRICH, William** (father of James Franklin Aldrich and cousin of Nelson Wilmarth Aldrich), a Representative from Illinois; born in Greenfield Center, Saratoga County, N.Y., January 19, 1820; attended the common schools and the local academy; taught school until twenty-six years of age; moved to Jackson, Mich., in 1846 and engaged in mercantile pursuits; moved to Wisconsin and settled in Two Rivers, Manitowoc County, in 1851; continued mercantile pursuits and also engaged in the manufacture of lumber, woodenware, and furniture; superintendent of schools during 1855 and 1856; chairman of the county board of supervisors, 1857-1858; member of the Illinois State house of representatives in 1859; moved to Chicago, Ill., in 1861, and engaged in the wholesale grocery business; member of the Chicago City Council in 1876, serving as chairman; elected as a Republican to the Forty-fifth and to the two succeeding Congresses (March 4, 1877-March 3, 1883); unsuccessful candidate for renomination in 1882 to the Forty-eighth Congress; resumed his former business pursuits in Chicago and was also interested in the milling business at Fond du Lac, Wis., where he died while on a business trip, December 3, 1885; interment in Rosehill Cemetery, Chicago, Ill.

**ALDRICH, William Farrington** (brother of Truman Heminway Aldrich), a Representative from Alabama; born in Palmyra, Wayne County, N.Y., March 11, 1853; attended the public schools of his native city; moved with his father to New York City in 1865; attended several schools, and was graduated from Warren's Military Academy in Poughkeepsie, N.Y., in 1873; moved to Alabama in 1874; engaged in mining and manufacturing; built up the town that bears his name; successfully contested as a Republican the election of Gaston A. Robbins to the Fifty-fourth Congress and served from March 13, 1896, to March 3, 1897; successfully contested the election of Thomas S. Plowman to the Fifty-fifth Congress and served from February 9, 1898, to March 3, 1899; again successfully contested the election of Gaston A. Robbins to the Fifty-sixth Congress and served from March 8, 1900, to March 3, 1901; declined to be a candidate for renomination in 1900; editor, owner, and publisher of the Birmingham (Ala.) Times; delegate to the Republican National Convention at Chicago in 1904; engaged in the

development of mineral lands until his death in Birmingham, Ala., October 30, 1925; the remains were cremated and deposited in the family vault in Rock Creek Cemetery, Washington, D.C.

**ALESHIRE, Arthur William,** a Representative from Ohio; born near Luray, Page County, Va., February 15, 1900; attended the rural schools; moved to Clark County, Ohio, in 1912 with his parents, who settled on a farm near Springfield; employed by a railway express company in 1921 and 1922; engaged in dairy farming near Springfield, Ohio, in 1922 and 1923; due to an accident in 1923 lost the use of his legs and in a wheelchair operated a filling station and grocery store until elected to Congress; elected as a Democrat to the Seventy-fifth Congress (January 3, 1937-January 3, 1939); unsuccessful candidate for reelection in 1938 to the Seventy-sixth Congress; resumed his former business pursuits near Springfield, Ohio; died in Springfield, Ohio, March 11, 1940; interment in Ferncliff Cemetery.

**ALEXANDER, Adam Rankin,** a Representative from Tennessee; born in Rockbridge County, Va.; became a surveyor by profession; moved to Tennessee in 1801 and located in Blount County; moved to what is now Madison County, Tenn., about 1806 and established the town of Alexandria, named for him; member of the State senate in 1817; register of the land office for the tenth surveyors' district; member of the first county court of Madison County in 1821; elected to the Eighteenth and Nineteenth Congresses (March 4, 1823-March 3, 1827); unsuccessful candidate for reelection in 1828 to the Twentieth Congress; moved to Shelby County, Tenn., and represented that county at the State abolitionist convention in 1834; member of the State house of representatives in 1841 and 1843; died in Jackson, Madison County, Tenn.

**ALEXANDER, Armstead Milton,** a Representative from Missouri; born near Winchester, Clark County, Ky., May 26, 1834; moved to Monroe County, Mo., with his parents, who settled near Paris; attended the common schools; worked at the blacksmith trade in 1848; engaged in gold mining in California in 1849; was graduated from Bethany College, Bethany, Va. (now West Virginia), in 1853; moved to Paris, Mo., and became engaged in business; served in the Confederate Army during the Civil War; studied law; was admitted to the bar in 1870 and commenced practice at Paris, Mo., but did not sign the record there until 1881; prosecuting attorney of Monroe County, 1872-1876; delegate to the State constitutional convention in 1875; elected as a Democrat to the Forty-eighth Congress (March 4, 1883-March 3, 1885); unsuccessful candidate for renomination in 1884 to the Forty-ninth Congress; resumed the practice of law; died in Paris, Mo., November 7, 1892; interment in Walnut Grove Cemetery.

**ALEXANDER, De Alva Stanwood,** a Representative from New York; born in Richmond, Sagadahoc County, Maine, July 17, 1846; attended the common schools; moved with his mother to Ohio in 1859; at the age of fifteen enlisted in the Union Army as a private in the One Hundred and Twenty-eighth Regiment, Ohio Volunteer Infantry, and served from 1862 until the close of the Civil War, when he entered the Edward Little Institute, Auburn, Maine, to prepare for college; was graduated from Bowdoin College, Brunswick, Maine, in 1870 and served for many years as a member and president of its board of overseers; moved to Fort Wayne, Ind., in 1870; one of the editors and proprietors of the Daily Gazette, 1871-1874; delegate to the Republican National Convention of 1872; moved to Indianapolis, Ind., in 1874 and became a staff correspondent of the Cincinnati Gazette; secretary of the Indiana Republican State committee, 1874-1878; studied law; was admitted to the bar in 1877 and commenced practice in Indianapolis, Ind.; appointed Fifth Auditor of the Treasury Department in 1881 and served until 1885; commander of the Department of the Potomac, Grand Army of the Republic, for one term; moved to Buffalo, N.Y., in 1885; appointed United States attorney for the northern district of New York in May

1889 and served until his resignation in December 1893; elected as a Republican to the Fifty-fifth and to the six succeeding Congresses (March 4, 1897-March 3, 1911); chairman, Committee on Rivers and Harbors (Sixty-first Congress); unsuccessful candidate for reelection in 1910 to the Sixty-second Congress; author of "History and Procedure of the House of Representatives"; resumed the practice of law; died in Buffalo, N.Y., January 30, 1925; interment in Forest Lawn Cemetery.

Bibliography: *DAB*; Alexander, De Alva Stanwood. *History and Procedure of the House of Representatives*. 1916. Reprint. New York: Burt Franklin, 1970.

ALEXANDER, Evan Shelby (cousin of Nathaniel Alexander), a Representative from North Carolina; born in Mecklenburg County, N.C., about 1767; attended the common schools; was graduated from Princeton College in 1787; studied law; was admitted to the bar and commenced practice in Salisbury, Rowan County, N.C.; member of the State house of commons 1796-1803; trustee of the University of North Carolina at Chapel Hill 1799-1809; elected as a Republican to the Ninth Congress to fill the vacancy caused by the resignation of Nathaniel Alexander; reelected to the Tenth Congress and served from February 24, 1806, to March 3, 1809; died October 28, 1809.

ALEXANDER, Henry Porteous, a Representative from New York; born in Little Falls, Herkimer County, N.Y., September 13, 1801; attended the public schools; engaged in mercantile pursuits in Little Falls; also engaged in banking; president of the village of Little Falls in 1834 and 1835; became president of the Herkimer County Bank at Little Falls in 1839 and served until his death; unsuccessful candidate for election in 1846 to the Thirtieth Congress; elected as a Whig to the Thirty-first Congress (March 4, 1849-March 3, 1851); unsuccessful candidate for reelection in 1850 to the Thirty-second Congress; resumed his former business pursuits; died in Little Falls, N.Y., February 22, 1867; interment in Church Street Cemetery.

ALEXANDER, Hugh Quincy, a Representative from North Carolina; born on a farm near Glendon, Moore County, N.C., August 7, 1911; attended the public schools; graduated from Duke University, Durham, N.C., in 1932, and from the University of North Carolina, Chapel Hill, N.C., in 1937; studied law; was admitted to the bar in 1937 and began practice in Kannapolis, N.C.; during the Second World War served in the United States Navy 1942-1946 and had thirty-four months overseas duty; member of North Carolina house of representatives in 1947 and 1949; solicitor, Cabarrus County Recorders Court, 1950-1952; State commander, American Legion, 1951; elected as a Democrat to the Eighty-third and to the four succeeding Congresses (January 3, 1953-January 3, 1963); unsuccessful candidate for reelection to the Eighty-eighth Congress; chief counsel of the Senate Rules and Administration Committee 1963-1976; resumed the practice of law; was a resident of Kannapolis, N.C.; died September 17, 1989.

ALEXANDER, James, Jr., a Representative from Ohio; born near Delta, York County, Pa., October 17, 1789; moved to the Northwest Territory in 1799 with his father, who settled in what is now St. Clairsville, Belmont County, Ohio; engaged in agricultural pursuits, in river transportation on the Ohio and Mississippi Rivers, and, later, in mercantile pursuits in St. Clairsville; member of the State house of representatives in 1830 and again in 1833 and 1834; served as associate judge of the court of common pleas in 1831; elected as a Whig to the Twenty-fifth Congress (March 4, 1837-March 3, 1839); unsuccessful candidate for reelection in 1838 to the Twenty-sixth Congress; returned to St. Clairsville, Ohio, and resumed his former business pursuits; purchased a large tract of property in Wheeling, Va. (now West Virginia), in 1843 and moved to that city, living in retirement until his death; was an extensive owner of farming land in the State of Illinois; died, while visiting his

son, in McNabb, Putnam County, Ill., September 5, 1846; interment in Scotch Ridge Cemetery, eight miles north of St. Clairsville, Ohio.

ALEXANDER, John, a Representative from Ohio; born at Crowsville, in the Spartanburg District, S.C., April 16, 1777; attended the public schools; moved to Butler County, Ohio, and thence to Miamisburg, Montgomery County, in 1803; studied law; was admitted to the bar and commenced practice in 1804; moved to Xenia, Greene County, Ohio, in 1805 and continued his profession there, also practicing in Columbus, Chillicothe, and before the Supreme Court of the United States at Washington, D.C.; appointed prosecuting attorney in 1808 and held that office until 1833, except during the time he was a Member of Congress; elected as a Republican to the Thirteenth and Fourteenth Congresses (March 4, 1813-March 3, 1817); unsuccessful candidate for reelection in 1816 to the Fifteenth Congress; resumed the practice of law at Xenia; member of the State senate in 1822 and 1823; served in the State house of representatives two terms; retired from the practice of his profession in 1834; died at Xenia, Ohio, June 28, 1848; interment in Woodlawn Cemetery.

ALEXANDER, John Grant, a Representative from Minnesota; born in Texas Valley, Cortland County, N.Y., July 16, 1893; attended the public schools; was graduated from the law department of Cornell University, Ithaca, N.Y., in 1916; was admitted to the New York bar the same year; moved to Redwood Falls, Minn., in 1916; was admitted to the Minnesota bar in 1917 and commenced practice in Lynd, Minn.; engaged in the banking business 1917-1923; during the First World War served as a private in the Three Hundred and Eighty-sixth Ambulance Company in 1918; engaged in the insurance business and in real estate management in Minneapolis, Minn., in 1924; member of the Minnesota National Guard 1927-1937; elected as a Republican to the Seventy-sixth Congress (January 3, 1939-January 3, 1941); unsuccessful candidate for renomination in 1940 to the Seventy-seventh Congress; unsuccessful candidate for Governor in 1942; resumed the business of real estate management and insurance; resided in Minneapolis, Minn., where he died December 8, 1971; interment in Lakewood Cemetery.

ALEXANDER, Joshua Willis, a Representative from Missouri; born in Cincinnati, Ohio, January 22, 1852; moved to Missouri with his mother, who settled in Canton, Daviess County, in 1863; attended public, private, and high schools, and was graduated from Christian University (now Culver-Stockton College), Canton, Mo., in 1872; moved to Gallatin, Mo., in 1873; studied law; was admitted to the bar in 1875 and commenced practice in Gallatin; public administrator of Daviess County, 1877-1881; served as secretary and then as president of the board of education of Gallatin, Mo., 1882-1901; member of the Missouri State house of representatives, 1883-1887, serving as speaker in 1887; mayor of Gallatin, 1891-1892; member of the board of managers of State Hospital No. 2, 1893-1896; judge of the seventh judicial circuit of Missouri, 1901-1907; elected as a Democrat to the Sixtieth and to the six succeeding Congresses, and served from March 4, 1907 until December 15, 1919, when he resigned to accept a Cabinet portfolio; chairman, Committee on Merchant Marine and Fisheries (Sixty-second through Sixty-fifth Congresses); served as chairman of the commissioners of the United States to the International Conference on Safety of Life at Sea, which met in London on November 12, 1913, and continued until January 20, 1914; appointed Secretary of Commerce in the Cabinet of President Woodrow Wilson, and served from December 16, 1919 until March 4, 1921; returned to Gallatin, Mo., in 1921 and resumed the practice of law; delegate at large to the State constitutional convention in 1922; died in Gallatin, Mo., February 27, 1936; interment in Brown Cemetery.

ALEXANDER, Mark, a Representative from Virginia; born on a plantation near Boydton, Mecklenburg County, Va., February 7, 1792; attended the public schools; was graduated from the

University of North Carolina at Chapel Hill, in 1811; studied law; was admitted to the bar and commenced the practice of law in Boydton, Va.; member of the Virginia house of delegates 1815-1819; elected to the Sixteenth through Twentieth Congresses; elected as a Jacksonian to the Twenty-first and Twenty-second Congresses (March 4, 1819-March 3, 1833); chairman, Committee on District of Columbia (Nineteenth and Twentieth Congresses); declined to be a candidate for renomination in 1832; delegate to the Virginia constitutional convention of 1829-1830; again a member of the Virginia house of delegates, 1845-1846; retired from political life and engaged in the management of his large estate; died in Scotland Neck, Halifax County, N.C., October 7, 1883; interment in the cemetery of the old Episcopal Church.

**ALEXANDER, Nathaniel** (cousin of Evan Shelby Alexander), a Representative from North Carolina; born near Concord, Mecklenburg County, N.C., March 5, 1756; attended the common schools; was graduated from Princeton College in 1776; studied medicine and surgery; served in the Revolutionary War as a surgeon 1778-1782; after independence was established, practiced his profession at the High Hills of Santee in South Carolina; subsequently returned to Charlotte, N.C., and continued practice; member of the State house of commons in 1797; served in the State senate in 1801 and 1802; elected as a Republican to the Eighth and Ninth Congresses and served from March 4, 1803, until November 1805, when he resigned to become Governor; Governor of North Carolina from December 10, 1805 to December 1, 1807; died in Salisbury, Rowan County, N.C., March 7, 1808; interment in Old Cemetery, Charlotte, N.C.

**ALEXANDER, Robert,** a Delegate from Maryland; born on the family estate in Cecil County (now part of the city of Elkton), Md., around 1740; studied law; was admitted to the bar and practiced; member of the provincial convention of Maryland 1774, 1775, and 1776; secretary of the Baltimore committee of observation and member of the council of safety in 1775; commissioned a first lieutenant in the Baltimore militia June 6, 1776; Member of the Continental Congress in 1776; after the promulgation of the Declaration of Independence he fled from Maryland to the British Fleet, joined the Associated Loyalists of America, and in 1782 sailed for London, England, where he remained; in 1780 he was adjudged guilty of high treason and his property was confiscated; died in London, England, on November 20, 1805.

**ALEXANDER, Sydenham Benoni** (cousin of Adlai Ewing Stevenson and John Sharp Williams), a Representative from North Carolina; born at "Rosedale," near Charlotte, Mecklenburg County, N.C., December 8, 1840; attended preparatory schools at Rocky River and Wadesboro, N.C.; was graduated from the University of North Carolina at Chapel Hill in 1860; during the Civil War enlisted in the Confederate Army in 1861 as a private in the First Regiment, North Carolina Volunteer Infantry; elected captain of Company K, Forty-second North Carolina Regiment, in June 1862; detached from his company in 1864 and served as inspector general on the staff of Major General Robert F. Hoke; member of the State senate in 1879, 1883, 1885, 1887, and 1901; was instrumental in the establishment of the North Carolina Agricultural and Mechanical College (now North Carolina Agricultural and Technical State University) in 1891, and served as a member of its board of trustees; president of the North Carolina Railroad; elected as a Democrat to the Fifty-second and Fifty-third Congresses (March 4, 1891-March 3, 1895); was not a candidate for renomination in 1894 to the Fifty-fourth Congress; retired to his estate, "Enderly Plantation," in Mecklenburg County, N.C., and engaged in agricultural pursuits; moved to Charlotte, N.C., in 1906 and died there June 14, 1921; interment in Elmwood Cemetery.

**ALEXANDER, William Vollie, Jr.,** a Representative from Arkansas; born in Memphis, Shelby County, Tenn., January 16, 1934; attended the University of Arkansas; B.A., Southwestern at Memphis, 1957; LL.B., Vanderbilt University, 1960; served in the United States Army, Adjutant General Corps, 1951-1953; legal research assistant to Federal Judge Marion Boyd, Memphis, Tenn., 1960-1961; associate, firm of Montedonico, Boone, Gilliland, Heiskell & Loch, 1961-1963; partner, firm of Swift and Alexander, Osceola, Ark., 1963; admitted to practice before the United States Supreme Court; commissioner, Arkansas Waterways Commission; secretary, Osceola Port Authority; member, American Academy of Political and Social Science; elected as a Democrat to the Ninety-first and to the eleven succeeding Congresses (January 3, 1969-January 3, 1993); unsuccessful candidate for renomination in 1992 to the One Hundred Third Congress; is a resident of Osceola, Ark.

**ALFORD, Julius Caesar,** a Representative from Georgia; born in Greensboro, Ga., May 10, 1799; attended the common schools; studied law; was admitted to the bar and commenced practice in Lagrange, Ga.; also engaged in planting; member of the State house of representatives; commanded a company in the Creek War of 1836; elected as a State Rights candidate to the Twenty-fourth Congress to fill the vacancy caused by the resignation of George W. B. Towns and served from January 2 to March 3, 1837; unsuccessful candidate for reelection in 1836 to the Twenty-fifth Congress; elected as a Whig to the Twenty-sixth and Twenty-seventh Congresses and served from March 4, 1839, to October 1, 1841, when he resigned; moved to Tuskegee, Ala., and subsequently settled near Montgomery, Ala.; delegate to the Union convention at Montgomery in 1852; resumed the practice of law; unsuccessful candidate for election in 1855 to the Thirty-fourth Congress; member of the secession convention in 1861; died on his plantation near Montgomery, Ala., January 1, 1863; interment in the family cemetery on his estate near Montgomery.

**ALFORD, Thomas Dale,** a Representative from Arkansas; born in New Hope, Pike County, near Murfreesboro, Ark., January 28, 1916; attended the public schools of Rector, Ark., Arkansas State College at Jonesboro, State Teachers College at Conway, and graduated from the University of Arkansas School of Medicine at Little Rock; postgraduate training at the University of Illinois in Chicago; during the Second World War served in the United States Army Medical Corps with service at the Army and Navy General Hospital, Hot Springs, Ark., 1941-1943, and in the European Theater 1943-1945; private practice of medicine at Atlanta, Ga., 1946-1948, and taught at Emory University College of Medicine, 1947-1948; in 1948 returned to Little Rock, Ark., and continued the practice of medicine; member of active teaching faculty, University of Arkansas School of Medicine, 1948-1958; member of Little Rock Board of Education 1955-1958; delegate to the Democratic National Convention of 1960; elected as an Independent write-in candidate to the Eighty-sixth Congress, but served as a Democrat; reelected to the Eighty-seventh Congress (January 3, 1959-January 3, 1963); was not a candidate for reelection in 1962 to the Eighty-eighth Congress, but was an unsuccessful candidate for nomination for Governor of Arkansas; resumed practice of ophthalmic surgery; member of faculty, University of Arkansas School of Medicine; is a resident of Little Rock, Ark.

**ALGER, Bruce Reynolds,** a Representative from Texas; born in Dallas, Tex., June 12, 1918; moved to Webster Groves, Mo., with his parents in 1924, and attended the public schools; graduated from Princeton University in 1940; field representative with RCA Victor Manufacturing Co., 1940 and 1941; enlisted as an aviation cadet in the Army Air Corps in September 1941, served as a B-29 commander in the Pacific Area, and discharged in November 1945; returned to Dallas, Tex., and engaged in the real estate and construction business; elected as a Republican to the Eighty-fourth and to the four succeeding Congresses (January 3, 1955-January 3, 1965); unsuccessful candidate for reelection in 1964 to the Eighty-ninth Congress; resumed real estate pursuits; is a resident of Carrollton, Tex.

**ALGER, Russell Alexander,** a Senator from Michigan; born in Lafayette Township, Medina County, Ohio, February 27, 1836; worked on a farm; attended Richfield Academy, Summit County, Ohio; taught country school; studied law in Akron, Ohio; was admitted to the bar in March 1859; moved to Grand Rapids, Mich., and engaged in the lumber business; moved to Detroit; commissioned a captain, Second Michigan Cavalry, October 2, 1861, and was promoted to major April 2, 1862, lieutenant colonel October 30, 1862, and colonel June 11, 1863; resigned his commission on September 20, 1864; brevetted as a major general, United States Volunteers, June 11, 1865; resumed the lumber business; elected Governor of Michigan in 1884, and served from January 1, 1885 to January 1, 1887; declined renomination in 1886; presidential elector on the Republican ticket in 1888; was appointed Secretary of War in the Cabinet of President William McKinley on March 5, 1897, and resigned August 1, 1899; appointed and subsequently elected as a Republican to the United States Senate to fill the vacancy caused by the death of James McMillan, and served from September 27, 1902 until his death in Washington, D.C., January 24, 1907; chairman, Committee on Coast Defenses (Fifty-ninth Congress), Committee on the Pacific Railroads (Fifty-ninth Congress); interment in Elmwood Cemetery, Detroit, Mich.

**Bibliography:** *DAB*; Bell, Rodney E. "A Life of Russell Alexander Alger, 1836-1907." Ph.D. dissertation, University of Michigan, 1975.

**ALLAN, Chilton,** a Representative from Kentucky; born in Albemarle County, Va., April 6, 1786; moved with his mother to Winchester, Clark County, Ky., in 1797; attended the common schools, and also received private instructions; served an apprenticeship of three years as a wheelwright, studying law in his leisure time; was admitted to the bar in 1808 and commenced practice in Winchester; member of the Kentucky house of representatives in 1811, 1815, 1822, and 1830; member of the Kentucky senate, 1823-1827; elected as an Anti-Jacksonian to the Twenty-second and Twenty-third Congresses and reelected as a Whig to the Twenty-fourth Congress (March 4, 1831-March 3, 1837); chairman, Committee on Territories (Twenty-third Congress); was not a candidate for renomination in 1836; appointed president of the Kentucky board of internal improvements in 1837 and served until 1839, when he resigned; resumed the practice of law; again a member of the Kentucky house of representatives in 1842; died in Winchester, Ky., September 3, 1858; interment in Winchester Cemetery.

**ALLARD, Alan Wayne,** a Representative from Colorado; born in Fort Collins, Larimer County, Colo., December 2, 1943; graduated, Fort Collins High School; D.V.M., Colorado State University, 1968; veterinarian, director, Allard Animal Hospital; member, Colorado State senate, 1983-1990, Republican caucus chair, 1986-1990; elected as a Republican to the One Hundred Second and to the two succeeding Congresses (January 3, 1991-January 3, 1997); was not a candidate for reelection in 1996 to the House of Representatives, but was a candidate for election to the United States Senate; is a resident of Loveland, Colo.

**ALLEE, James Frank,** a Senator from Delaware; born in Dover, Del., December 2, 1857; attended the common schools; learned the trade of jeweler and watchmaker from his father, whom he succeeded in business; chairman of the Republican State committee 1886-1896; member of the State senate from January 3, 1899, to March 2, 1903, when he resigned to become a United States Senator; elected as a Republican to the United States Senate on March 2, 1903, to fill the vacancy in the term commencing March 4, 1901, caused by the failure of the legislature to elect, and served from March 2, 1903, to March 3, 1907; was not a candidate for reelection in 1907; chairman, Committee on the Organization, Conduct, and Expenditures of the Executive Departments (Fifty-eighth Congress), Committee on Indian Depredations (Fifty-ninth Congress), Committee on Railroads (Fifty-ninth Congress); resumed his former business pursuits, as well as engaging in the fruit and vegetable canning industry; died in Dover, Del., October 12, 1938; interment in Christ Church Cemetery.

**ALLEN, Alfred Gaither,** a Representative from Ohio; born on a farm near Wilmington, Clinton County, Ohio, July 23, 1867; attended the public schools; was graduated from Wilmington High School in 1886 and from the law school of the University of Cincinnati, Ohio, in 1890; was admitted to the bar in 1890 and commenced practice in Cincinnati, Ohio; United States commissioner 1896-1900; delegate to the Democratic State conventions at Columbus in 1901 and 1908; member of the city council 1906-1908; member of the board of the sinking-fund trustees of Cincinnati 1908-1910; elected as a Democrat to the Sixty-second, Sixty-third, and Sixty-fourth Congresses (March 4, 1911-March 3, 1917); declined to be a candidate for renomination in 1916; resumed the practice of his profession in Cincinnati; delegate to the Democratic National Convention at San Francisco in 1920; served as president of the Cincinnati Bar Association in 1925 and 1926; died in Cincinnati, Ohio, December 9, 1932; interment in Sugar Grove Cemetery, Wilmington, Ohio.

**ALLEN, Amos Lawrence,** a Representative from Maine; born in Waterboro, York County, Maine, March 17, 1837; attended the common schools, Whitestown Seminary, Whitestown, N.Y., and was graduated from Bowdoin College, Brunswick, Maine, in 1860; studied law at Columbian Law School, Washington, D.C.; was admitted to the bar of York County in 1866 but never practiced; served as a clerk in the United States Treasury Department, 1867-1870; elected clerk of the courts for York County, Maine, in 1870, reelected three times, and served until January 1, 1883; member of the Maine State house of representatives in 1886 and 1887; private secretary to the Speaker of the United States House of Representatives, Thomas B. Reed, 1889-1891 and 1895-1899; delegate at large to the Republican National Convention of 1896; elected as a Republican to the Fifty-sixth Congress to fill the vacancy caused by the resignation of Thomas B. Reed; reelected to the Fifty-seventh and to the four succeeding Congresses and served from November 6, 1899, until his death in Washington, D.C., February 20, 1911; interment in Evergreen Cemetery, Alfred, Maine.

**ALLEN, Andrew,** a Delegate from Pennsylvania; born in Philadelphia, Pa., in June 1740; was graduated from the University of Pennsylvania at Philadelphia in 1759; completed law studies at the Temple in London, England; was admitted to the bar in 1765 and commenced practice in Philadelphia; member of the provisional assembly and of the provisional council 1765-1775; appointed attorney general in 1766; member of the common council of Philadelphia in 1768; member of the committee of safety in 1775 and 1776; Member of the Continental Congress in 1775 and 1776, but disapproved of independence and withdrew in June 1776; when the Royalist Army entered New York he went within the British lines, took the oath of allegiance to the King, renouncing those he had taken as a Member of the Continental Congress, and went to London, England; was attainted of treason and his estates confiscated; compensated by the British Government with a pension of £400 per annum; died in London, England, on March 7, 1825.

**Bibliography:** *DAB*.

**ALLEN, Asa Leonard,** a Representative from Louisiana; born on a farm near Winnfield, Winn Parish, La., January 5, 1891; attended the rural schools; was graduated from Louisiana State

University at Baton Rouge in 1914; taught in the rural schools of Louisiana; principal of the Georgetown (La.) High School in 1914 and 1915 and of the Verda (La.) High School 1915-1917; superintendent of Winn Parish schools 1917-1922; studied law; was admitted to the bar in 1922 and commenced practice in Winnfield, La.; served as city attorney of Winnfield for several years; elected as a Democrat to the Seventy-fifth and to the seven succeeding Congresses (January 3, 1937-January 3, 1953); chairman, Committtee on the Census (Seventy-eighth and Seventy-ninth Congresses); was not a candidate for renomination in 1952; retired and resided in Winnfield, La., until his death January 5, 1969; interment in Winnfield Cemetery.

**ALLEN, Charles** (son of Joseph Allen and grandnephew of Samuel Adams), a Representative from Massachusetts; born in Worcester, Mass., August 9, 1797; attended the Leicester Academy 1809-1811 and Yale College in 1811 and 1812; studied law; was admitted to the bar in 1818 and commenced practice in New Braintree; moved to Worcester in 1824 and continued the practice of law; member of the Massachusetts house of representatives 1830, 1833, 1835, and 1840; served in the Massachusetts senate 1836 and 1837; member of the Northeastern Boundary Commission in 1842; judge of the court of common pleas 1842-1845; delegate to the Whig National Convention at Philadelphia in 1848; elected by the Free-soil Party to the Thirty-first and Thirty-second Congresses (March 4, 1849-March 3, 1853); was not a candidate for renomination in 1852; resumed the practice of law; member of the Massachusetts constitutional convention in 1853; chief justice of the Suffolk County Superior Court 1859-1867; delegate to the peace convention held at Washington, D.C., in 1861, in an effort to devise means to prevent the impending war; died in Worcester, Mass., August 6, 1869; interment in the Rural Cemetery.

**ALLEN, Charles Herbert,** a Representative from Massachusetts; born in Lowell, Mass., April 15, 1848; attended public and private schools; was graduated from Amherst College, Mass., in 1869; engaged in the manufacture of wooden boxes and in the lumber business with his father; held various local offices; member of the Massachusetts house of representatives in 1881 and 1882; served in the Massachusetts senate in 1883; colonel and aide-de-camp on the staff of Governor George D. Robinson in 1884; elected as a Republican to the Forty-ninth and Fiftieth Congresses (March 4, 1885-March 3, 1889); declined to be a candidate for renomination in 1888 to the Fifty-first Congress; unsuccessful candidate for election in 1891 for Governor of Massachusetts; served as Massachusetts Prison Commissioner in 1897 and 1898; Assistant Secretary of the Navy, 1898-1900; served as first civil Governor of Puerto Rico, 1900-1902; returned to Lowell, Mass., in 1902 and became financially interested in banking and other enterprises, serving as vice president of the Morton Trust Co. and of the Guaranty Trust Co. of New York and as president of the American Sugar Refining Co.; died in Lowell, Mass., April 20, 1934; interment in Lowell Cemetery.

**ALLEN, Clarence Emir,** a Representative from Utah; born in Girard Township, Erie County, Pa., September 8, 1852; attended the district school and Girard (Pa.) Academy; was graduated from Western Reserve College, then at Hudson, Ohio, in 1877; moved to Salt Lake City, Utah, in August 1881 and was an instructor in Salt Lake Academy until 1886, when he resigned to engage in mining pursuits; member of the Territorial house of representatives in 1888, 1890, and again in 1894; elected county clerk of Salt Lake County in August 1890 and served until January 1, 1893; studied law; was admitted to the bar in 1893 and commenced practice in Salt Lake City; unsuccessful Liberal candidate for election in 1892 as a Delegate to the Fifty-third Congress; delegate to the Republican National Convention in 1892 and 1896; upon the admission of Utah as a State into the Union was elected as a Republican to the

Fifty-fourth Congress and served from January 4, 1896, to March 3, 1897; declined to be a candidate for renomination in 1896; resumed his former mining pursuits until 1922, when he retired from active business and resided in Columbus, Ohio, until 1931; died in Escondido, Calif., July 9, 1932; the remains were cremated and the ashes interred in Mount Olivet Cemetery, Salt Lake City, Utah.

**ALLEN, Clifford Robertson,** a Representative from Tennessee; born in Jacksonville, Duval County, Fla., January 6, 1912; graduated, Friends Elementary and High School in Washington, D.C.; LL.B., Cumberland University School of Law, Lebanon, Tenn., 1931; admitted to the Tennessee Bar in 1931 and commenced practice in Nashville; member, Tennessee State senate 1949-1951, 1955-1959; unsuccessful candidate for nomination in 1950, 1952 and 1958 for Governor of Tennessee; tax assessor for Metropolitan Nashville and Davidson County, Tenn., 1960-1975; president, International Association of Assessing Officers, 1970; president, Tennessee Association of Assessing Officers, 1971; member, Tennessee Constitutional Convention, 1971; elected as a Democrat, by special election, November 25, 1975, to the Ninety-fourth Congress to fill the vacancy caused by the resignation of Richard H. Fulton; reelected to the Ninety-fifth Congress, and served from November 25, 1975, until his death in Nashville, Tenn., June 18, 1978; interment in Woodlawn Memorial Park.

**ALLEN, Edward Payson,** a Representative from Michigan; born in Sharon, Washtenaw County, Mich., October 28, 1839; attended the district and select schools; was graduated from the State normal school in 1864; enlisted and helped to raise a company for the Twenty-ninth Regiment, Michigan Volunteer Infantry; commissioned first lieutenant in September 1864 and later, captain; mustered out with his regiment in September 1865; was graduated from the law school of Michigan University at Ann Arbor in March 1867; was admitted to the bar; commenced practice in Ypsilanti, Washtenaw County; assistant assessor of internal revenue in 1869; prosecuting attorney of Washtenaw County in 1872; alderman of Ypsilanti 1872-1874; elected to the Michigan house of representatives in 1876 and again in 1878, at which time he was elected speaker pro tempore; mayor of Ypsilanti in 1880; appointed United States Indian agent for Michigan in August 1882 and served until December 1885; elected as a Republican to the Fiftieth and Fifty-first Congresses (March 4, 1887-March 3, 1891); unsuccessful candidate for reelection in 1890 to the Fifty-second Congress; resumed the practice of law; member of the State board of agriculture 1897-1903; again mayor of Ypsilanti in 1899 and 1900; member of the State soldiers' home board 1903-1909; died in Ypsilanti, Mich., November 25, 1909; interment in Highland Cemetery.

**ALLEN, Elisha Hunt** (son of Samuel Clesson Allen), a Representative from Maine; born in New Salem, Mass., January 28, 1804; attended New Salem Academy, and was graduated from Williams College, Williamstown, Mass., in 1823; studied law; was admitted to the bar in 1825 and commenced practice in Brattleboro, Vt.; moved to Bangor, Maine, and continued the practice of law; member of the Maine house of representatives 1835-1840, serving as speaker in 1838; elected as a Whig to the Twenty-seventh Congress (March 4, 1841-March 3, 1843); unsuccessful candidate for reelection in 1842 to the Twenty-eighth Congress; again elected to the Maine house of representatives in 1846; moved to Boston, Mass., in 1847 and resumed the practice of his profession; elected to the Massachusetts house of representatives in 1849; appointed consul to Honolulu in 1850; was prominently connected with the government of the Hawaiian Islands as chief justice and regent, and as envoy to the United States in 1856 and 1864; served as minister from the Kingdom of Hawaii to the United States from 1869 until his death on January 1, 1883, while attending a diplomatic reception given by

President Chester A. Arthur in the White House at Washington, D.C.; interment in Mount Auburn Cemetery, Cambridge, Mass.

**Bibliography:** *DAB.*

**ALLEN, George Felix, Jr.,** a Representative from Virginia; born in Whittier, Los Angeles County, Calif., March 8, 1952; B.A., University of Virginia, 1974; J.D., University of Virginia School of Law, 1977; admitted to Virginia bar and District of Columbia bar; practicing attorney for thirteen years in Charlottesville, Va.; member, Virginia house of delegates, 1982-1991; elected as a Republican to the One Hundred Second Congress, November 5, 1991, by special election to fill the vacancy caused by the resignation of D. French Slaughter, Jr., and served from November 5, 1991 to January 3, 1993; was not a candidate for reelection in 1992 to the One Hundred Third Congress; elected Governor of Virginia in 1993 for the term beginning January 15, 1994; is a resident of Earlysville, Va.

**ALLEN, Heman (of Colchester),** a Representative from Vermont; born in Poultney, Vt., February 23, 1779; attended the common schools; was graduated from Dartmouth College, Hanover, N.H., in 1795; studied law; was admitted to the bar in 1801 and commenced practice in Colchester, Vt.; sheriff of Chittenden County in 1808 and 1809; chief justice of the county court 1811-1814; member of the State house of representatives 1812-1817; elected as a Republican to the Fifteenth Congress and served from March 4, 1817, to April 20, 1818, when he resigned to become marshal; appointed United States marshal for the district of Vermont on December 14, 1818, and reappointed on December 24, 1822; United States Minister Plenipotentiary to Chile from January 27, 1823, to July 31, 1827; president of the Burlington branch of the United States Bank from 1830 until the expiration of its charter in 1836; resumed the practice of his profession in Highgate, Franklin County, Vt., where he died April 7, 1852; interment in Allen Cemetery, Burlington, Vt.

**ALLEN, Heman (of Milton),** a Representative from Vermont; born in Ashfield (now Deerfield), Mass., June 14, 1777; attended an academy in Chesterfield, N.H., for two years; moved to Grand Isle, Vt.; studied law; was admitted to the bar in 1803 and commenced practice in Milton, Vt.; member of the State house of representatives 1810-1814, 1816, 1817, 1822, and 1824-1826; moved to Burlington, Chittenden County, Vt., in 1828 and continued the practice of his profession; elected as an Anti-Jacksonian to the Twenty-second and Twenty-third Congresses and as a Whig to the Twenty-fourth and Twenty-fifth Congresses (March 4, 1831-March 3, 1839); chairman, Committee on Expenditures in the Department of the Treasury (Twenty-third through Twenty-fifth Congresses); unsuccessful candidate for reelection in 1838 to the Twenty-sixth Congress; resumed the practice of law; died in Burlington, Vt., on December 11, 1844; interment in Elmwood Avenue Cemetery.

**ALLEN, Henry Crosby,** a Representative from New Jersey; born in Paterson, N.J., May 13, 1872; attended private and public schools of his native city; was graduated from St. Paul's School, Garden City, Long Island, in 1889, from Yale University in 1893, and from the New York Law School in 1895; was admitted to the bar in 1895 and commenced practice in Paterson, N.J.; elected as a Republican to the Fifty-ninth Congress (March 4, 1905-March 3, 1907); was not a candidate for renomination in 1906; resumed the practice of law in Paterson, N.J.; postmaster of Paterson 1926-1935; died in Mystic, Conn., March 7, 1942, while visiting his daughter; interment in Cedar Lawn Cemetery, Paterson, N.J.

**ALLEN, Henry Dixon,** a Representative from Kentucky; born near Henderson, Henderson County, Ky., June 24, 1854; moved with his parents to Morganfield, Union County, in 1855; attended the common schools and Morganfield Collegiate Institute; taught school in Union County 1869-1875; studied medicine and was graduated

from the Missouri Medical College, St. Louis, Mo., in 1877; practiced medicine in Union County from 1877 to 1878; abandoned medicine and studied law; was admitted to the bar in 1878 and commenced practice in Morganfield, Ky.; county school commissioner 1879-1881; prosecuting attorney of Union County 1882-1891; elected as a Democrat to the Fifty-sixth and Fifty-seventh Congresses (March 4, 1899-March 3, 1903); was not a candidate for renomination in 1902; resumed the practice of law; also engaged in banking and agricultural pursuits; died in Morganfield, Ky., March 9, 1924; interment in Masonic Cemetery.

**ALLEN, Henry Justin,** a Senator from Kansas; born in Pittsfield, Warren County, Pa., September 11, 1868; moved with his parents to Kansas in 1870 and settled on a farm near Clifton, Clay County; attended the public schools, Washburn College, Topeka, Kans., and was graduated from Baker University, Baldwin, Kans., in 1890; became a newspaper reporter and editorial writer; during the Spanish-American War served as a war correspondent in Cuba; member of the press galleries of the United States Congress, 1914-1916; owner of several Kansas newspapers; served with the American Red Cross in France as head of the home communication service during the First World War; elected Governor of Kansas in 1918, reelected in 1920, and served from January 13, 1919 to January 8, 1923; special commissioner of the Near East Relief to Armenia, Turkey, Greece, and Southern Russia in 1923 and 1924; director of publicity for the Republican National Committee in the campaign of 1928; appointed as a Republican to the United States Senate to fill the vacancy caused by the resignation of Charles Curtis and served from April 1, 1929, to November 30, 1930, when a duly elected successor qualified; unsuccessful candidate for election to fill the vacancy; editor of the Topeka State Journal and chairman of the board of directors of the Wichita Beacon; died in Wichita, Kans., January 17, 1950; interment in Maple Grove Cemetery.

**Bibliography:** *DAB.*

**ALLEN, James Browning** (husband of Maryon Pittman Allen), a Senator from Alabama; born in Gadsden, Etowah County, Ala., December 28, 1912; attended public schools of Gadsden, the University of Alabama, and the University of Alabama Law School; practiced law in Gadsden, Ala., from 1935 to 1968; member of the Alabama State legislature, 1938-1942; resigned to enter active duty in the United States Naval Reserve, 1943-1946; member of the Alabama State senate, 1946-1950; lieutenant governor of Alabama 1951-1955, and 1963-1967; elected as a Democrat to the United States Senate, November 5, 1968; reelected in 1974, and served from January 3, 1969, until his death in Gulf Shores, Ala., June 1, 1978; interment in Forrest Cemetery, Gadsden, Ala.

**Bibliography:** *DAB.*

**ALLEN, James Cameron,** a Representative from Illinois; born in Shelby County, Ky., January 29, 1822; attended the public schools; moved to Indiana in 1830; studied law; was admitted to the bar in 1843 and commenced practice in Sullivan, Ind.; prosecuting attorney for the seventh judicial district of Indiana 1846-1848; moved to Palestine, Ill., in 1848 and continued the practice of law; member of the State house of representatives in 1850 and 1851; elected as a Democrat to the Thirty-third Congress (March 4, 1853-March 3, 1855); presented credentials as a Member-elect to the Thirty-fourth Congress and served from March 4, 1855, to July 18, 1856, when the House decided he was not entitled to the seat; subsequently elected to fill the vacancy thus caused and served from November 4, 1856, to March 3, 1857; was not a candidate for renomination in 1856 to the Thirty-fifth Congress; Clerk of the House of Representatives in the Thirty-fifth Congress; unsuccessful candidate for election in 1860 for Governor of Illinois; elected circuit court judge in April 1861 and served until he resigned in 1863; elected to the Thirty-eighth Congress (March 4, 1863-March 3, 1865); unsuccessful candidate for reelection in 1864 to the

Thirty-ninth Congress; resumed the practice of law; reelected circuit court judge in 1873 and upon the establishment of the appellate court was appointed its judge, occupying both positions and serving from 1873 to 1879; moved to Olney, Richland County, Ill., in 1876 and practiced law; retired from the practice of his profession in 1907; died in Olney, Ill., January 30, 1912; interment in Olney Cemetery.

**ALLEN, John** (father of John William Allen), a Representative from Connecticut; born in Great Barrington, Mass., June 12, 1763; attended the common schools; studied law at the Litchfield Law School; was admitted to the bar in 1786 and commenced practice in Litchfield, Conn.; member of the State house of representatives 1793-1796, serving as clerk in 1796; elected as a Federalist to the Fifth Congress (March 4, 1797-March 3, 1799); declined to be a candidate for renomination in 1798; member of the State council and of the supreme court of errors 1800-1806; continued the practice of law in Litchfield, Conn., until his death on July 31, 1812; interment in East Cemetery.

**ALLEN, John Beard,** a Delegate from the Territory of Washington and a Senator from Washington; born in Crawfordsville, Montgomery County, Ind., May 18, 1845; attended the public schools and Wabash College, Crawfordsville, Ind.; during the Civil War served as a private; moved to Rochester, Minn., in 1865 and engaged in business as a grain dealer; graduated from the law department of the University of Michigan at Ann Arbor, and was admitted to the bar in 1869; moved to Washington Territory in 1870 and commenced the practice of law in Olympia; appointed United States attorney for the Territory of Washington by President Ulysses S. Grant, and served from April 1875 to July 1885; reporter for the supreme court of the Territory, 1878-1885; moved to Walla Walla in 1881; elected as a Republican Delegate to the Fifty-first Congress (March 4, 1889-November 11, 1889); when the Territory was admitted as a State, elected as a Republican to the United States Senate, and served from November 20, 1889 to March 3, 1893; the legislature failing to elect a Senator, was appointed by the Governor to serve in the Senate until March 20, 1893; presented his credentials as a Senator-designate in 1893, but was not permitted to qualify; moved to Seattle and resumed the practice of law; died in Seattle, Wash., January 28, 1903; interment in Lakeview Cemetery.

**Bibliography:** Allen, John Beard. *Allen's Political Essays.* Walla Walla, Wash.: Allen-Chancey Agency, 1909.

**ALLEN, John Clayton,** a Representative from Illinois; born in Hinesburg, Chittenden County, Vt., February 14, 1860; attended the common schools and Beeman Academy, New Haven, Vt.; moved to Lincoln, Nebr., in 1881, and to McCook, Redwillow County, Nebr., in 1886 and engaged in mercantile pursuits at both places; member of the McCook City Council 1887-1889; mayor of McCook, Nebr., in 1890; secretary of state of Nebraska 1891-1895; moved to Monmouth, Warren County, Ill., in 1896 and became president of the John C. Allen Co. department store and of the People's National Bank of Monmouth; member of the State normal school board 1917-1927; elected as a Republican to the Sixty-ninth and to the three succeeding Congresses (March 4, 1925-March 3, 1933); unsuccessful candidate for reelection in 1932 to the Seventy-third Congress, and for election in 1934 to the Seventy-fourth Congress; resumed his former business pursuits in Monmouth, Ill., until his death there on January 12, 1939; interment in Vermont Cemetery, Vermont, Ill.

**ALLEN, John James** (brother of Robert Allen), a Representative from Virginia; born in Woodstock, Shenandoah County, Va., September 25, 1797; attended Dickinson College, Carlisle, Pa., in 1811 and 1812, and Washington College (now Washington and Lee University), Lexington, Va., in 1814 and 1815; studied law; was admitted to the bar in 1819 and commenced practice at Campbell Courthouse; moved to Clarksburg, Harrison County, Va., and continued practice; member of the Virginia senate 1828-1830;

Commonwealth attorney for Harrison, Lewis, and Preston Counties in 1834, serving while a Member of Congress; elected as an Anti-Jacksonian to the Twenty-third Congress (March 4, 1833-March 3, 1835); unsuccessful candidate for reelection in 1834 to the Twenty-fourth Congress; judge of the seventeenth circuit court of Virginia 1836-1840; judge of the Virginia supreme court of appeals 1840-1865, serving as presiding justice 1852-1865; president of the executive council in 1861; author of the "Botetourt resolutions" of 1861; retired to private life and engaged in the management of his large estate; died at Beaverdam, near Fincastle, Botetourt County, Va., September 18, 1871; interment in the family burying ground in Lauderdale Cemetery, near his estate in Botetourt County, Va.

**Bibliography:** *DAB.*

**ALLEN, John Joseph, Jr.,** a Representative from California; born in Oakland, Alameda County, Calif., November 27, 1899; attended the public schools; while a student in college enlisted during the First World War in the United States Navy and served as an apprentice seaman; was graduated from the University of California at Berkeley in 1920, and from its law department in 1922; was admitted to the bar in 1922 and commenced practice in Oakland, Calif.; member of the Oakland Board of Education from 1923 until 1943, serving several terms as president; president of the California State School Trustees Association, 1936-1938; member of the County Republican Central Committee, 1936-1944; during the Second World War served as a lieutenant commander in the United States Navy, 1942-1945, with twenty months service in the South Pacific area; vice chairman of the State commission on school districts in 1946 and 1947; elected as a Republican to the Eightieth and to the five succeeding Congresses (January 3, 1947-January 3, 1959); unsuccessful candidate for reelection in 1958 to the Eighty-sixth Congress; appointed Under Secretary of Commerce for Transportation, January 5, 1959, serving until January 20, 1961; resumed the practice of law until his retirement in 1969; member, McCall City Planning and Zoning Commission, 1973-1988; mayor of McCall, Idaho, 1988-1992; was a resident of McCall, Idaho, until his death on March 7, 1995.

**ALLEN, John Mills,** a Representative from Mississippi; born in Tishomingo County, Miss., July 8, 1846; attended the common schools; during the Civil War enlisted as a private in the Confederate Army and served throughout the war; attended the law school of Cumberland University, Lebanon, Tenn., and was graduated from the law department of the University of Mississippi in 1870; was admitted to the bar the same year and commenced practice in Tupelo, Lee County, Miss.; district attorney for the first judicial district of Mississippi 1875-1879; elected as a Democrat to the Forty-ninth and to the seven succeeding Congresses (March 4, 1885-March 3, 1901); chairman, Committee of Expenditures in the Department of Justice (Fifty-second Congress), Committee on Levees and Improvements of the Mississippi River (Fifty-third Congress); declined to be a candidate for reelection in 1900 to the Fifty-seventh Congress; appointed in March 1901 a United States commissioner to the St. Louis Exposition of 1904; resumed the practice of law in Tupelo, Miss., and died there October 30, 1917; interment in Glenwood Cemetery.

**Bibliography:** Faries, Clyde J. "The Rhetoric of Private John Allen." Ph.D. dissertation, University of Missouri, 1965; Gentry, Claude. *Private John Allen: Gentleman, Statesman, Sage, Prophet.* Baldwyn, Miss: The author, 1951.

**ALLEN, John William** (son of John Allen), a Representative from Ohio; born in Litchfield, Conn., in August 1802; attended preparatory schools; moved to Chenango County, N.Y., in 1818, where he received a classical education and studied law; moved to Cleveland, Ohio, in 1825 and continued the study of law; was admitted to the bar in 1826 and commenced practice in Cleveland; president of the village, 1831-1835; member of the board of directors of the Commercial Bank of Lake Erie upon its reorganization in 1832; one of the incorporators of the Cleveland and Newburg Railroad Co. in 1834, and an organizer of the Ohio Railroad Co. in 1836; served in the Ohio State senate, 1836-1837; elected as a Whig to the Twenty-fifth and Twenty-sixth Congresses (March 4, 1837-March 3, 1841); was not a candidate for reelection in 1840 to the Twenty-seventh Congress; elected mayor of Cleveland in 1841; elected president of the Cleveland, Columbus and Cincinnati Railroad in 1845; delegate to the first convention on river and harbor improvement, held in Chicago in 1847; appointed postmaster of Cleveland by President Ulysses S. Grant on April 4, 1870; reappointed April 4, 1874, and served until his resignation on January 11, 1875; one of the first bank commissioners of Ohio; died in Cleveland, Ohio, October 5, 1887; interment in Erie Street Cemetery.

**ALLEN, Joseph** (nephew of Samuel Adams), a Representative from Massachusetts; born in Boston, Mass., September 2, 1749; was graduated from Harvard College in 1774; engaged in business in Leicester, Mass.; moved to Worcester in 1776; member of the State constitutional convention of 1788; appointed clerk of the courts and held that office until 1810, when he resigned to serve in Congress; elected as a Federalist to the Eleventh Congress to fill the vacancy caused by the resignation of Jabez Upham and served from October 8, 1810, to March 3, 1811; declined to be a candidate for reelection in 1810; State councilor from 1815 to 1818; died in Worcester, Mass., September 2, 1827; interment in Mechanic Street Burying Ground.

**ALLEN, Judson,** a Representative from New York; born in Plymouth, Conn., April 3, 1797; attended the public schools; engaged in the lumber business; moved to Harpursville (formerly Harpersville), Broome County, N.Y.; appointed postmaster of Harpursville March 19, 1830, and served until November 20, 1839; judge of the Broome County Court for eight years; member of the State assembly in 1836 and 1837; elected as a Democrat to the Twenty-sixth Congress (March 4, 1839-March 3, 1841); was not a candidate for renomination in 1840; moved to St. Louis, Mo., and engaged in the produce, lumber, marble, and grocery business until his death in St. Louis, August 6, 1880; interment in Bellefontaine Cemetery.

**ALLEN, Leo Elwood,** a Representative from Illinois; born in Elizabeth, Jo Daviess County, Ill., October 5, 1898; attended the public schools; during the First World War served as a sergeant in the One Hundred and Twenty-third Field Artillery 1917-1919; was graduated from the University of Michigan at Ann Arbor in 1923; taught school at Galena, Ill., in 1922 and 1923; clerk of the circuit court of Jo Daviess County 1924-1932; studied law; was admitted to the bar in 1930 and commenced practice in Galena, Ill.; elected as a Republican to the Seventy-third Congress and to the thirteen succeeding Congresses (March 4, 1933-January 3, 1961); chairman, Committee on Rules (Eightieth and Eighty-third Congresses); was not a candidate for renomination in 1960; retired and resided in Galena, Ill., where he died January 19, 1973; interment in Greenwood Cemetery.

**ALLEN, Maryon Pittman** (wife of James Browning Allen), a Senator from Alabama; born in Meridian, Lauderdale County, Miss., November 30, 1925; moved to Birmingham, Ala., in 1926; educated in the public schools of Birmingham; attended the University of Alabama, 1944-1947, and the International Institute of Interior Design, 1970; medical office and business manager, Birmingham, 1959-1961; life underwriter, Protective Life Insurance Co., Birmingham, 1960-1961; women's editor, Sun Newspapers, Birmingham, 1962-1964; feature writer for the Birmingham News, 1964, and syndicated columnist, 1969-1978; contributing editor, Southern Accents Magazine, 1976-1978; vice president and partner in Pittman family companies; appointed chair of the Blair House Fine Arts Commission by President Gerald R. Ford in 1974; appointed as a Democrat to the United States Senate, June 8, 1978, to fill the

vacancy caused by the death of her husband, James B. Allen, and served from June 8, 1978 to November 7, 1978; unsuccessful candidate in 1978 for renomination to the unexpired term ending January 3, 1981; columnist for The Washington (D.C.) Post, 1978-1981, and for McCall's Needlework Magazine, 1993 to present; public relations and advertising director for a Washington, D.C. antique and auction firm, 1981; owner of The Maryon Allen Company, specializing in the restoration of antique textiles and in original clothing designs; is a resident of "Cliff House," Birmingham, Ala.

**ALLEN, Nathaniel** (father-in-law of Robert Lawson Rose), a Representative from New York; born in East Bloomfield, N.Y., in 1780; attended the common schools; worked as a blacksmith at Canandaigua, Ontario County, N.Y.; started a blacksmith shop at Richmond, near Allens Hill, in 1796; served as an officer in the militia; appointed postmaster of Honeoye Falls, N.Y., July 1, 1811; was commissioner and paymaster on the Niagara frontier in 1812; member of the New York State assembly in 1812; sheriff of Ontario County, N.Y., 1815-1819; elected to the Sixteenth Congress (March 4, 1819-March 3, 1821); was not a candidate for renomination in 1820 to the Seventeenth Congress; supervisor of the town of Richmond, 1824-1826; engaged in the prosecution of claims for money due in connection with the construction of the Louisville and Portland Canal; died in the Gault House at Louisville, Ky., while on a business trip to that city, December 22, 1832; interment in the churchyard of the Episcopal Church, Allens Hill, Ontario County, N.Y.

**Bibliography:** Baldwin, Aubrey H. "Commissioner Nathaniel Allen, Citizen of Two Worlds." *Pennsylvania Genealogical Magazine* 32 (1982): 189-218.

**ALLEN, Philip,** a Senator from Rhode Island; born in Providence, R.I., September 1, 1785; received his early education from private tutors; attended Taunton Academy and Robert Rogers School at Newport; was graduated from Rhode Island College (now Brown University) in 1803; engaged in mercantile pursuits and foreign commerce; when shipping was suspended during the War of 1812 he engaged in the manufacture of cotton goods in Smithfield, R.I.; member of the Rhode Island State house of representatives from 1819 until 1821; appointed pension agent and president of the Rhode Island branch of the United States Bank in 1827; continued the manufacture of cotton goods and began the printing of calicos at Providence, R.I., in 1831; elected Governor of Rhode Island in 1851, reelected in 1852 and 1853, and served from May 6, 1851 until July 20, 1853, when he resigned to become Senator; elected as a Democrat to the United States Senate on May 4, 1853 for the term beginning March 4, 1853, and served from July 20, 1853, to March 3, 1859; was not a candidate for reelection in 1859; chairman, Committee on Agriculture (Thirty-third and Thirty-fourth Congresses); retired from active political and business pursuits; died in Providence, R.I., December 16, 1865; interment in the North Burial Ground.

**Bibliography:** *DAB*.

**ALLEN, Robert,** a Representative from Tennessee; born in Augusta County, Va., June 19, 1778; attended the rural schools and William and Mary College, Williamsburg, Va.; studied law and practiced; moved to Carthage, Tenn., in 1804 and engaged in the mercantile business; clerk of Smith County for many years; during the War of 1812 served as colonel and commanded a regiment of Tennessee Volunteers under General Andrew Jackson; elected to the Sixteenth and to the three succeeding Congresses (March 4, 1819-March 3, 1827); chairman, Committee on Revolutionary Claims (Nineteenth Congress); declined to be a candidate for renomination in 1826 to the Twentieth Congress; engaged in agricultural and mercantile pursuits in Carthage, Tenn.; delegate to the State convention in 1834; died in Carthage, Tenn., August 19, 1844; interment in Greenwood Cemetery, Lebanon, Tenn.

**ALLEN, Robert** (brother of John James Allen), a Representative from Virginia; born in the village of Woodstock, Shenandoah County, Va., July 30, 1794; attended the rural schools, and Dickinson College at Carlisle 1811-1812; was graduated from Washington College (now Washington and Lee University), Lexington, Va., in 1815; engaged in agricultural pursuits in Shenandoah County; studied law; was admitted to the bar and commenced practice in Woodstock; prosecuting attorney of Shenandoah County; member of the Virginia senate in 1821-1826; elected as a Jacksonian to the Twentieth, Twenty-first and Twenty-second Congresses (March 4, 1827-March 3, 1833); chairman, Committee on Accounts (Twenty-second Congress); moved to Bedford County and continued agricultural pursuits; died in Mount Prospect, Va., December 30, 1859; interment in Longwood Cemetery, Liberty (now Bedford City), Va.

**ALLEN, Robert Edward Lee,** a Representative from West Virginia; born in Lima, Tyler County, W.Va., November 28, 1865; attended the country schools, Fairmont Normal School, and Peabody College, Nashville, Tenn.; was graduated from the literary department of the University of West Virginia at Morgantown in 1894 and from its law department in 1895; was admitted to the bar in 1895 and commenced practice at Morgantown, Monongalia County, W.Va.; member of the city council from 1895 to 1917; deputy collector of internal revenue for the district of West Virginia 1917-1921; judge of the city court 1921-1923; elected as a Democrat to the Sixty-eighth Congress (March 4, 1923-March 3, 1925); was an unsuccessful candidate for reelection in 1924 to the Sixty-ninth Congress and for election in 1926 to the Seventieth Congress; resumed the practice of law in Morgantown, W.Va., until his retirement in 1927; moved to Preston County, W.Va., and operated a summer resort at Brookside 1929-1939; resided in Aurora, W.Va., until his death in Mountain Lake Park, Md., January 28, 1951; interment in Kingwood Cemetery, Kingwood, W.Va.

**ALLEN, Robert Gray,** a Representative from Pennsylvania; born in Winchester, Middlesex County, Mass., August 24, 1902; moved to Minneapolis, Minn., in 1906 and attended public and private schools; was graduated from Phillips Academy at Andover, Mass., in 1922 and later attended Harvard University; moved to Greensburg, Pa., in 1929 and was a salesman and sales manager for a valve and fittings manufacturing business until 1937; district administrator of the Works Progress Administration in 1935 and 1936; elected as a Democrat to the Seventy-fifth and Seventy-sixth Congresses (January 3, 1937-January 3, 1941); was not a candidate for renomination in 1940 to the Seventy-seventh Congress; president of the Duff-Norton Manufacturing Co., Pittsburgh, Pa., 1940-1943; commissioned a major in the Ordnance Branch, United States Army, in July 1942, promoted to lieutenant colonel in February 1943, and served until his discharge in January 1945; sales manager for the Baldwin Locomotive Works, 1945-1946; vice president, Fisher Plastics Corp., Boston, Mass., 1946-1947; vice president, Great Lakes Carbon Corp., 1947-1954; president, Pesco Products, division of Borg-Warner Corp., 1954-1957; vice president of Bucyrus-Erie Co., in 1957 and 1958 and president in 1958; chairman of the board and president of Bucyrus-Erie Co. of Canada, Ltd., and chairman of the board of Ruston-Bucyrus, Ltd., Lincoln, England; director of the First Wisconsin National Bank of Milwaukee; retired from business activities in 1962 and moved from Milwaukee, Wis., to Keene, Va., where he died on August 9, 1963; interment in Christ Episcopal Church.

**ALLEN, Samuel Clesson** (father of Elisha Hunt Allen), a Representative from Massachusetts; born in Bernardston, Mass., January 5, 1772; attended the public schools of New Salem, and was graduated from Dartmouth College, Hanover, N.H., in 1794; studied theology; was ordained as a minister, became pastor of the Congregational Church in Northfield in 1795, and served until 1798; studied law; was admitted to the bar in 1800 and practiced in New Salem; member of the Massachusetts house of representatives 1806-1810; served in the Massachusetts senate 1812-1815; elected as a Federalist to the Fifteenth Congress and reelected to the five succeeding Congresses (March 4, 1817-March 3, 1829); chairman, Committee on Accounts (Seventeenth through Twentieth Congresses); was not a candidate for renomination in 1828; member of the Governor's executive council of Massachusetts 1829-1830; again elected to the State senate in 1831; retired from politics; engaged as a lecturer at Amherst College; member of the board of trustees of Amherst College and of the University of Vermont; died in Northfield, Mass., February 8, 1842; interment in the Village Cemetery, Bernardston, Franklin County, Mass.

**ALLEN, Thomas,** a Representative from Missouri; born in Pittsfield, Mass., August 29, 1813; attended Pittsfield Academy and Berkshire Gymnasium; was graduated from Union College in 1832; studied law in New York City; was admitted to the bar in 1835 and commenced practice in New York City in 1832; moved to Washington, D.C., and established the Madisonian in 1837; printer to the House of Representatives, 1837-1839; printer to the United States Senate, 1839-1842; moved to St. Louis, Mo., in 1842; member of the Missouri State senate, 1850-1854; was a contractor upon internal improvements and projected and built more than one thousand miles of railway; in 1852 took the first steam locomotive across the Mississippi River; president of the St. Louis, Iron Mountain and Southern Railway, but subsequently sold all his railway interests and retired from active pursuits; elected as a Democrat to the Forty-seventh Congress, and served from March 4, 1881 until his death in Washington, D.C., April 8, 1882; interment in Pittsfield Cemetery, Pittsfield, Mass.

**Bibliography:** *DAB.*

**ALLEN, William,** a Representative and a Senator from Ohio; born in Edenton, Chowan County, N.C., December 18 or December 27, 1803; moved to Lynchburg, Va., and attended private schools; moved to Chillicothe, Ohio, in 1819; attended Chillicothe Academy; studied law; was admitted to the bar in 1827 and commenced practice in Chillicothe; elected as a Jacksonian to the Twenty-third Congress (March 4, 1833-March 3, 1835); unsuccessful candidate for reelection in 1834 to the Twenty-fourth Congress; elected as a Democrat to the United States Senate in January 1837; reelected in 1843, and served from March 4, 1837, to March 3, 1849; was not a candidate for reelection; chairman, Committee on Foreign Relations (Twenty-ninth Congress); retired to his estate, "Fruit Hill," near Chillicothe, Ross County, Ohio, and engaged in farming and stock raising; elected Governor of Ohio in 1873 and served from January 12, 1874 to January 10, 1876; unsuccessful candidate for reelection in 1875; resumed agricultural pursuits; died at "Fruit Hill," July 11, 1879; interment in Grandview Cemetery, Chillicothe, Ohio.

**Bibliography:** *DAB*; McGrane, Reginald C. *William Allen: A Study in Western Democracy.* Columbus: Ohio State Archeological and Historical Society, 1925.

**ALLEN, William,** a Representative from Ohio; born near Hamilton, Butler County, Ohio, August 13, 1827; attended the public schools; taught school; studied law; was admitted to the bar in 1849 and commenced practice in Greenville, Ohio, in 1850; prosecuting attorney of Darke County 1850-1854; elected as a Democrat to the Thirty-sixth and Thirty-seventh Congresses (March 4, 1859-March 3, 1863); chairman, Committee on Expenditures in the Department of the Interior (Thirty-seventh Congress); declined to be a candidate for renomination in 1862; resumed the practice of law; affiliated with the Republican Party at the close of the Civil War; appointed judge of the court of common pleas of the second judicial district in 1865; declined the Republican nomination for election to the

Forty-sixth Congress in 1878 because of failing health; interested in banking until his death in Greenville, Darke County, Ohio, July 6, 1881; interment in Greenville Cemetery.

ALLEN, William Franklin, a Representative from Delaware; born in Bridgeville, Sussex County, Del., January 19, 1883; attended the public schools at Bridgeville, and Laurel, Del.; moved to Seaford, Del., and was employed as an agent and train dispatcher by a railroad company 1902-1922; served as school commissioner at Seaford, Del., 1920-1924; delegate to the Democratic National Convention at San Francisco, Calif., in 1920; member of the State senate 1925-1929, serving as president pro tempore in 1927; engaged in the manufacture of fruit packages and in the packing and shipping of farm products in 1926; also engaged in the brokerage of oil and petroleum in 1926; elected as a Democrat to the Seventy-fifth Congress (January 3, 1937-January 3, 1939); unsuccessful candidate for reelection in 1938 to the Seventy-sixth Congress; resumed the oil and gasoline distribution business; died in a hospital at Lewes, Del., June 14, 1946; interment in Odd Fellows Cemetery, Seaford, Del.

ALLEN, William Joshua (son of Willis Allen), a Representative from Illinois; born in Wilson County, Tenn., June 9, 1829; moved with his father to Franklin (now Williamson) County, Ill., about 1830, and in 1839 settled in Marion; attended the common schools; studied law; was admitted to the bar in 1849 and commenced practice in Metropolis; enrolling and engrossing clerk of the State house of representatives in 1849 and 1851; moved to Marion, Ill., in 1853 and continued the practice of his profession; appointed prosecuting attorney for the twenty-sixth judicial circuit of Illinois in 1854; member of the State senate in 1855; elected judge of the circuit court of the twenty-sixth judicial circuit on June 24, 1859, and served until 1861; elected as a Democrat to the Thirty-seventh Congress to fill the vacancy caused by the resignation of John A. Logan; reelected to the Thirty-eighth Congress and served from June 2, 1862, to March 3, 1865; was not a candidate for reelection in 1864; member of the State constitutional conventions in 1862 and 1870; delegate to all Democratic National Conventions from 1864 to 1888; moved to Springfield, Ill., in 1886; appointed United States district judge for the southern district of Illinois on April 18, 1887, and served until his death January 26, 1901, while visiting in Hot Springs, Ark.; interment in Oak Ridge Cemetery, Springfield, Ill.
Bibliography: *DAB.*

ALLEN, William Vincent, a Senator from Nebraska; born in Midway, Madison County, Ohio, January 28, 1847; moved with his parents to Iowa in 1857; attended the common schools and Upper Iowa University at Fayette; served as a private during the Civil War; studied law at West Union, Iowa; was admitted to the bar in 1869 and practiced in Iowa until 1884, when he moved to Madison, Nebr.; judge of the district court of the ninth judicial district of Nebraska 1891-1893; permanent chairman of the Populist State conventions in 1892, 1894, and 1896; elected as a Populist to the United States Senate and served from March 4, 1893, to March 3, 1899; unsuccessful candidate for reelection in 1899; appointed and subsequently elected judge of the district court of the ninth judicial district of Nebraska and served from March 9, 1899, until December 1899, when he resigned to return to the Senate; appointed to the United States Senate to fill the vacancy caused by the death of Monroe L. Hayward, and served from December 13, 1899, to March 28, 1901, when a successor was elected; was not a candidate for election to the vacancy; chairman, Committee on Forest Reservations and Game Protection (Fifty-fourth and Fifty-fifth Congresses); resumed the practice of law in Madison, Nebr.; again elected judge of the district court of the ninth judicial district of Nebraska in 1917 and served until his death; died in Los Angeles, Calif., January 12, 1924; interment in Crown Hill Cemetery, Madison, Nebr.
Bibliography: *DAB.*

ALLEN, Willis (father of William Joshua Allen), a Representative from Illinois; born near Roanoke, Va., December 15, 1806; attended the common schools; taught school; moved to Tennessee and settled in Wilson County; moved to Franklin (now Williamson) County, Ill., in 1830 and engaged in agricultural pursuits; studied law; was admitted to the bar and commenced practice in Marion; sheriff of Franklin County 1834-1838; member of the State house of representatives 1838-1840; prosecuting attorney of the first judicial circuit in 1841; member of the State senate 1844-1847; member of the State constitutional convention in 1847 and 1848; elected as a Democrat to the Thirty-second and Thirty-third Congresses (March 4, 1851-March 3, 1855); was not a candidate for reelection in 1854; resumed the practice of his profession; elected judge of the twenty-sixth circuit court of Illinois March 2, 1859, and served until his death while holding court in Harrisburg, Saline County, Ill., April 15, 1859; interment in Marion Cemetery, Marion, Ill.

ALLEY, John Bassett, a Representative from Massachusetts; born in Lynn, Essex County, Mass., January 7, 1817; attended the common schools; at the age of fourteen was apprenticed as a shoemaker, but was released at nineteen; moved to Cincinnati, Ohio, in 1836; freighted merchandise up and down the Mississippi River; moved to Lynn, Mass., in 1838 and entered the shoe manufacturing business; established a hide and leather house in Boston in 1847; member of the first board of aldermen of Lynn in 1850; member of the Governor's council 1847-1851; served in the Massachusetts senate in 1852; member of the constitutional convention of 1853; elected as a Republican to the Thirty-sixth and to the three succeeding Congresses (March 4, 1859-March 3, 1867); chairman, Committee on the Post Office and Post Roads (Thirty-eighth and Thirty-ninth Congresses); was not a candidate for renomination in 1866; became connected with the Union Pacific Railroad; abandoned active business pursuits in 1886 and lived in retirement until his death in West Newton, Mass., January 19, 1896; interment in Pine Grove Cemetery, Lynn, Mass.

ALLGOOD, Miles Clayton, a Representative from Alabama; born in Chepultepec (now Allgood), Blount County, Ala., February 22, 1878; attended the common schools of his native county and was graduated from the State Normal College at Florence, Ala., in 1898; taught school in Blount County; tax assessor of Blount County, Ala., 1900-1909; member of the State Democratic executive committee 1908-1910; Blount County agricultural demonstration agent 1910-1913; State auditor of Alabama 1914-1918; State commissioner of agriculture and industries 1918-1922; elected as a delegate at large from Alabama to the Democratic National Convention at San Francisco in 1920; elected as a Democrat to the Sixty-eighth Congress and to the five succeeding Congresses (March 4, 1923-January 3, 1935); chairman, Committee on War Claims (Seventy-second and Seventy-third Congresses); unsuccessful candidate for renomination in 1934 to the Seventy-fourth Congress; served as a member of the Farm Security Administration from September 4, 1935, until he retired on December 1, 1943; unsuccessful candidate for State treasurer in 1954; retired; died in Fort Payne, Ala., March 4, 1977; interment in Valley Head Cemetery, Valley Head, Ala.

ALLISON, James, Jr. (father of John Allison), a Representative from Pennsylvania; born near Elkton, Cecil County, Md., October 4, 1772; moved with his parents to Washington County, Pa., in 1774; at seventeen years of age he enrolled in the school of David Johnson, of Beaver, Pa.; saw service in the Indian warfare at Yellow Creek, Bedford County, Pa.; studied law; was admitted to the bar in 1796 and commenced practice in Washington, Pa.; returned to Beaver in 1803 and continued the practice of law until 1822, when he was elected to Congress; prosecuting attorney of Beaver County 1803-1809; elected to the Eighteenth and Nineteenth Congresses and served from March 4, 1823, until his resignation in 1825 before the assembling of the Nineteenth Congress; resumed the practice of law until 1848, after which he discontinued active pursuits and lived in retirement until his death in Beaver, Beaver County, Pa., June 17, 1854; interment in Old Cemetery.

**ALLISON, John** (son of James Allison, Jr.), a Representative from Pennsylvania; born in Beaver, Pa., August 5, 1812; attended the common schools; studied law; was admitted to the bar but did not practice extensively; engaged in the manufacture of hats; also operated a tannery; member of the Pennsylvania house of representatives in 1846, 1847, and 1849; elected as a Whig to the Thirty-second Congress (March 4, 1851-March 3, 1853); unsuccessful candidate for reelection in 1852 to the Thirty-third Congress; elected as a Whig to the Thirty-fourth Congress (March 4, 1855-March 3, 1857); declined to be a candidate for renomination in 1856; delegate to the Republican National Convention in 1856 and nominated Abraham Lincoln as a candidate for Vice President; also a delegate to the Republican National Convention at Chicago in 1860; appointed Register of the Treasury April 3, 1869, and served until his death in Washington, D.C., on March 23, 1878; interment in Beaver Cemetery, Beaver, Pa.

**ALLISON, Robert,** a Representative from Pennsylvania; born near Greencastle, Franklin County, Pa., March 10, 1777; attended local and private schools; moved to Huntingdon, Pa., in 1795; employed as a clerk in his brother's office; studied law; was admitted to the bar in April 1798 and commenced the practice of law in Huntingdon; served as a captain in the Huntingdon Volunteers during the War of 1812; at the close of the war returned to Huntingdon and resumed the practice of law; burgess of Huntingdon, Pa., in 1815, 1817, 1819, 1821-1824, and again in 1826; unsuccessful candidate for election in 1824 to the Nineteenth Congress, in 1826 to the Twentieth Congress, and in 1828 to the Twenty-first Congress; elected as an Anti-Masonic candidate to the Twenty-second Congress (March 4, 1831-March 3, 1833); was not a candidate for renomination in 1832 to the Twenty-third Congress; continued the practice of his profession in Huntingdon, Huntingdon County, Pa., until his death there on December 2, 1840; interment in River View Cemetery.

**ALLISON, William Boyd,** a Representative and a Senator from Iowa; born in Perry, Ohio, March 2, 1829; attended country schools, the academy in Wooster, Ohio, and Allegheny College, Meadville, Pa.; was graduated from Western Reserve College, Hudson, Ohio (now in Cleveland), in 1849; studied law; was admitted to the bar in 1852 and commenced practice in Ashland, Ohio; unsuccessful candidate for district attorney in 1856; settled in Dubuque, Iowa, in 1857 and resumed the practice of law; served as a lieutenant colonel in the Union Army during the Civil War; elected as a Republican to the Thirty-eighth and to the three succeeding Congresses (March 4, 1863-March 3, 1871); chairman, Expenditures in the Department of the Treasury (Forty-first Congress); declined to be a candidate in 1870 for renomination to the House of Representatives, but was an unsuccessful candidate for the United States Senate; resumed the practice of law in Dubuque; elected as a Republican to the United States Senate in 1872; reelected in 1878, 1884, 1890, 1896, and again in 1902, and served from March 4, 1873 until his death; Republican caucus chairman, 1897, 1904-1906, 1907-1908; chairman, Committee on Indian Affairs, (Forty-fourth and Forty-fifth Congresses), Committee on Appropriations (Forty-seventh through Sixtieth Congresses, except for the Fifty-third), Committee on Engrossed Bills (Fifty-third Congress), Republican Conference (Fifty-fifth, Fifty-sixth, Fifty-eighth and Fifty-ninth Congresses); co-sponsor of the Bland-Allison Silver Purchase Act of 1878, requiring the Federal government to encourage bimetallism and assist silver producers by making monthly purchases of silver bullion; died in Dubuque, Iowa, August 4, 1908; interment in Linwood Cemetery.

**Bibliography:** *DAB*; Cooper, Vernon. "The Public Career of William Boyd Allison." Ph.D. dissertation, State University of Iowa, 1927; Sage, Leland. *William Boyd Allison: A Study in Practical Politics.* Iowa City: State Historical Society, 1956.

**ALLOTT, Gordon Llewellyn,** a Senator from Colorado; born in Pueblo, Colo., January 2, 1907; attended the public schools of Pueblo, Colo.; B.A., University of Colorado, Boulder, 1927; LL.B., University of Colorado School of Law, 1929; was admitted to the bar in 1929 and commenced the practice of law in Pueblo, Colo.; moved to Lamar, Colo., in 1930 and continued practicing law; county attorney of Prowers County, Colo., in 1934 and 1941-1946; director, First Federal Savings and Loan Association of Lamar, Colo., 1934-1960; city attorney, Lamar, Colo., 1937-1941; during the Second World War served as a major in the United States Army Air Corps, 1942-1946; district attorney, fifteenth judicial district, 1946-1948; vice chairman State Board of Paroles, 1951-1955; lieutenant governor of Colorado, 1951-1955; elected as a Republican to the United States Senate in 1954; reelected in 1960 and again in 1966, and served from January 3, 1955 to January 3, 1973; unsuccessful candidate for reelection in 1972; chairman, Republican Policy Committee (Ninety-first and Ninety-second Congresses); was a resident of Englewood, Colo.; died January 17, 1989.

**ALMON, Edward Berton,** a Representative from Alabama; born near Moulton, Lawrence County, Ala., April 18, 1860; attended the rural schools; was graduated from the State Normal College, Florence, Ala., and from the law department of the University of Alabama, at Tuscaloosa, in 1883; was admitted to the bar in 1885 and commenced practice in Tuscumbia, Colbert County, Ala.; served in the State senate 1892-1894; judge of the circuit court of the eleventh judicial circuit of Alabama 1898-1906; member of the State house of representatives 1910-1915, serving as speaker in 1911; elected as a Democrat to the Sixty-fourth and to the nine succeeding Congresses and served from March 4, 1915, until his death in Washington, D.C., June 22, 1933; chairman, Committee on Roads (Seventy-second and Seventy-third Congresses); interment in Oakwood Cemetery, Tuscumbia, Ala.

**ALMOND, James Lindsay, Jr.,** a Representative from Virginia; born in Charlottesville, Albemarle County, Va., June 15, 1898; attended the graded schools in Locust Grove, Va.; law department of the University of Virginia at Charlottesville, LL.B., 1923; was admitted to the bar the same year and commenced practice in Roanoke, Va.; during the First World War served as a private in the Students Army Training Corps at the University of Virginia in 1917 and 1918; taught school at Locust Grove, Va., in 1919; principal of Zoar High School in 1921 and 1922; served as assistant Commonwealth's attorney of Virginia, 1930-1933; judge of the Hustings Court of Roanoke City, Va., 1933-1945; elected as a Democrat to the Seventy-ninth Congress to fill the vacancy caused by the resignation of Clifton A. Woodrum; reelected to the Eightieth Congress and served from January 22, 1946, until his resignation on April 17, 1948, having been elected attorney general of Virginia, in which capacity he served until August 28, 1957, when he resigned; elected Governor of Virginia in 1957, and served from January 11, 1958 to January 13, 1962; delegate to the Democratic National Convention of 1960; judge, United States Court of Customs and Patents Appeals; was a resident of Richmond, Va. until his death there on April 15, 1986.

**ALSOP, John,** a Delegate from New York; born in New Windsor, Orange County, N.Y., in 1724; completed preparatory studies; moved to New York City and engaged in mercantile pursuits and importing; represented New York City in the colonial legislature; one of the incorporators of the New York Hospital, serving as its governor from 1770 to 1784; Member of the Continental Congress, 1774-1776; member of a committee of one hundred appointed in 1775 by the citizens of the city to take charge of the government until a convention could be assembled; served as the eighth president of the New York Chamber of Commerce in 1784 and 1785; died in Newtown, Long Island, N.Y., November 22, 1794; interment in Trinity Church Cemetery, New York City.

**ALSTON, Lemuel James,** a Representative from South Carolina; born in the eastern part of Granville (now Warren) County, N.C., in 1760; moved to South Carolina after the Revolutionary War and settled near Greens Mill, which soon became the town of Greenville; studied law; was admitted to the bar and commenced practice in Greenville; member of the State house of representatives, 1789-1790; elected as a Republican to the Tenth and Eleventh Congresses (March 4, 1807-March 3, 1811); moved in 1816 to Clarke County, Ala., and settled near Grove Hill, where he presided over the orphans' court and the county court from November 1816 until May 1821; died at "Alston Place," Clarke County, Ala., in 1836.

**ALSTON, William Jeffreys,** a Representative from Alabama; born in Milledgeville, Ga., December 31, 1800; attended a private school in South Carolina; moved to Alabama and settled in Marengo County; taught school for several years; studied law; was admitted to the bar and commenced practice in Linden, Marengo County, in 1821; judge of the Marengo County Court for several years; member of the State house of representatives in 1837; served in the State senate 1839-1842; elected as a Whig to the Thirty-first Congress (March 4, 1849-March 3, 1851); was not a candidate for renomination in 1850; resumed the practice of his profession; again became a member of the State house of representatives, in 1855; engaged in agricultural pursuits; died in Magnolia, Marengo County, Ala., June 10, 1876; interment in Magnolia Cemetery.

**ALSTON, Willis** (nephew of Nathaniel Macon), a Representative from North Carolina; born near Littleton, Halifax County, N.C., in 1769; completed preparatory studies and attended Princeton College; engaged in agricultural pursuits; member of the State house of commons 1790-1792; served in the State senate 1794-1796; elected as a Republican to the Sixth and to the seven succeeding Congresses (March 4, 1799-March 3, 1815); chairman, Committee on Revisal and Unfinished Business (Thirteenth Congress); again a member of the State house of commons 1820-1824; elected to the Nineteenth and Twentieth Congresses and reelected as a Jacksonian to the Twenty-first Congress (March 4, 1825-March 3, 1831); chairman, Committee on Elections (Twenty-first Congress); was not a candidate for reelection to the Twenty-second Congress; resumed agricultural pursuits; died in Halifax, N.C., April 10, 1837; interment in a private burying ground on his plantation home, "Butterwood," near Littleton, Halifax County, N.C.

**ALVORD, James Church,** a Representative from Massachusetts; born in Greenwich, Mass., April 14, 1808; completed preparatory studies and was graduated from Dartmouth College, Hanover, N.H., in 1827; studied law; was admitted to the bar in 1830 and commenced the practice of his profession in Greenfield, Mass.; member of the Massachusetts house of representatives in 1837; served in the Massachusetts senate in 1838; elected as a Whig to the Twenty-sixth Congress and served from March 4, 1839, until his death in Greenfield, Franklin County, Mass., on September 27, 1839, before the Congress assembled; interment in Federal Street Cemetery.

**AMBLER, Jacob A.,** a Representative from Ohio; born in Pittsburgh, Pa., February 18, 1829; attended the local schools of Allegheny City and also received private instruction; moved to Salem, Ohio, and studied law in his brother's law office; was admitted to the bar on March 27, 1851, and commenced practice in Salem, Columbiana County, Ohio; elected to the State house of representatives in 1857 and served two terms; appointed judge of the ninth judicial district in 1859 and served until 1867; elected as a

Republican to the Forty-first and Forty-second Congresses (March 4, 1869-March 3, 1873); declined to be a candidate for renomination in 1872 to the Forty-third Congress; resumed the practice of law and also became interested in various business enterprises in Salem, Ohio; served as vice president of a bank and of a steel and wire nail mill corporation and also as president of a publishing company; delegate to every Republican National Convention between 1876 and 1896; appointed a member of the United States Tariff Commission by President Chester A. Arthur in 1882; retired from the general practice of law in 1898 but continued active business pursuits until his death in Canton, Stark County, Ohio, September 22, 1906; interment in Hope Cemetery, Salem, Ohio.

**AMBRO, Jerome Anthony, Jr.,** a Representative from New York; born in Brooklyn, Kings County, N.Y., June 27, 1928; attended the public schools of Brooklyn; graduated from Grover Cleveland High School, Queens, N.Y., 1946; B.A., New York University, 1955; served in the United States Army, Military Police, 1951-1953; budget officer, purchasing and personnel director, Town of Huntington, N.Y., 1960-1967; served on Suffolk County (N.Y.) Board of Supervisors, 1968-1969; elected to four terms as Supervisor, Town of Huntington, N.Y., 1968-1974; chairman, Huntington Urban Renewal Agency and president, Freeholders and Commonalty of the Town of Huntington, 1968-1974; elected as a Democrat to the Ninety-fourth and to the two succeeding Congresses (January 3, 1975-January 3, 1981); unsuccessful candidate for reelection in 1980 to the Ninety-seventh Congress; governmental and legislative consultant; was a resident of Huntington Station, N.Y.; died March 4, 1993.

**AMERMAN, Lemuel,** a Representative from Pennsylvania; born near Danville, Montour County, Pa., October 29, 1846; attended the common schools and Danville Academy; was graduated from Bucknell University, Lewisburg, Pa., in 1869; taught school three years; studied law; was admitted to the bar in 1873 and commenced practice in Philadelphia, Pa.; moved to Scranton, Pa., in 1876 and continued the practice of law; also engaged in banking; solicitor for Lackawanna County 1879 and 1880; member of the Pennsylvania house of representatives 1881-1884; elected city comptroller of Scranton in 1885 and 1886; reporter of the decisions of the supreme court of Pennsylvania in 1886 and 1887; elected as a Democrat to the Fifty-second Congress (March 4, 1891-March 3, 1893); unsuccessful candidate for reelection in 1892 to the Fifty-third Congress; continued the practice of his profession in Scranton, Pa., until his death in Blossburg, Tioga County, Pa., October 7, 1897; interment in Forest Hill Cemetery, Scranton, Pa.

**AMES, Adelbert** (father of Butler Ames and son-in-law of Benjamin Franklin Butler), a Senator from Mississippi; born in Rockland, Knox County, Maine, October 31, 1835; attended the common schools; was graduated from the United States Military Academy at West Point in 1861; during the Civil War served with the Union Army from 1861 to 1865 as lieutenant, colonel, and brigadier general; brevetted colonel; received the Congressional Medal of Honor for gallantry at the first Battle of Bull Run, July 21, 1861; captain in the Fifth Artillery of the Regular Army, 1864-1866; lieutenant colonel of the Twenty-fourth United States Infantry from July 28, 1866 until 1870, when he resigned; appointed Provisional Governor of Mississippi on March 15, 1868; appointed to the command of the fourth military district (Department of Mississippi) on March 17, 1869; upon the readmission of the State of Mississippi to representation was elected as a Republican to the United States Senate, and served from February 23, 1870 until January 10, 1874, when he resigned, having been elected Governor in 1873; chairman, Committee on Enrolled Bills (Fifty-third Congress); Governor of Mississippi from January 4, 1874 until March 29, 1876, when he resigned; moved to New York City and later to Lowell, Mass.; engaged in the flour business, with mills in Minnesota; also interested in various manufacturing industries in Lowell; was appointed brigadier general of Volunteers in the Spanish-American War, 1898-1899; discontinued active business pursuits and lived in retirement in Lowell, Mass.; died at his winter home in Ormond, Fla., April 12, 1933; interment in Hildreth Cemetery, Lowell, Mass.

**Bibliography:** *DAB*; Ames, Blanche. *Adelbert Ames, 1835-1933, General, Senator, Governor*. North Easton, Mass.: Argosy Antiquarian, 1964; Lord, Stuart B. "Adelbert Ames: Soldier and Politician: A Reevaluation." *Maine Historical Society Quarterly* 13 (Fall 1973): 81-97.

**AMES, Butler** (son of Adelbert Ames and grandson of Benjamin Franklin Butler), a Representative from Massachusetts; born in Lowell, Mass., August 22, 1871; attended the public schools and Phillips Exeter Academy, Exeter, N.H.; was graduated from the United States Military Academy at West Point in 1894; resigned from the United States Army after appointment as second lieutenant to the Eleventh Regiment, United States Infantry; took a postgraduate course at Massachusetts Institute of Technology and was graduated in 1896 as a mechanical and electrical engineer; engaged in manufacturing; served as a member of the common council of Lowell in 1896; enlisted during the Spanish-American War and was commissioned lieutenant and adjutant of the Sixth Regiment, Massachusetts Volunteer Infantry; appointed acting engineer officer of the Second Army Corps under General Graham, in addition to his duties as adjutant; was promoted to lieutenant colonel in August 1898; served as civil administrator of the Arecibo district of Puerto Rico until November 1898; member of the Massachusetts house of representatives 1897-1899; elected as a Republican to the Fifty-eighth and to the four succeeding Congresses (March 4, 1903-March 3, 1913); was not a candidate for renomination in 1912; resumed manufacturing pursuits; president of United States Cartridge Co., and treasurer of Heinze Electrical Co. of Lowell; at time of death was treasurer and a director of Wamesit Power Co. of Lowell, Mass.; director of Union Land and Grazing Co., Colorado Springs, Colo., and vice president and a director of Ames Textile Corp., Lowell, Mass.; died in Tewksbury, Mass., November 6, 1954; interment in Hildreth Family Cemetery, Lowell, Mass.

**AMES, Fisher,** a Representative from Massachusetts; born in Dedham, Mass., April 9, 1758; attended the town school of his native city and also received private instruction; was graduated from Harvard College in 1774; while teaching school, studied law; was admitted to the bar and commenced practice in Dedham in 1781; served in the Massachusetts house of representatives in 1788; member of the Massachusetts convention called for the ratification of the Federal Constitution in 1788; elected to the First through Third Congresses and as a Federalist to the Fourth Congress (March 4, 1789-March 3, 1797); chairman, Committtee on Elections (First Congress); was not a candidate for renomination in 1796; resumed the practice of law in Dedham; member of the Governor's council 1798-1800; chosen president of Harvard University in 1804, but declined to accept because of failing health; died in Dedham, Mass., July 4, 1808; interment in Old First Parish Cemetery.

**Bibliography:** *DAB*; Ames, Fisher. *Works of Fisher Ames: With a Selection from His Speeches and Correspondence*. Edited by Seth Ames. 2 vols. 1854. Reprint. New York: DaCapo Press, 1969; Bernhard, Winfred E.A. *Fisher Ames: Federalist and Statesman, 1758-1808*. Chapel Hill: University of North Carolina Press, 1965.

**AMES, Oakes,** a Representative from Massachusetts; born in Easton, Mass., January 10, 1804; attended the public schools and Dighton (Mass.) Academy; engaged in the manufacture of shovels in North Easton; member of the executive council of Massachusetts in 1860; elected as a Republican to the Thirty-eighth and to the four succeeding Congresses (March 4, 1863-March 3, 1873); was not a candidate for renomination in 1872 to the Forty-third Congress;

instrumental in accomplishing the construction of the first transcontinental railroad; on February 27, 1873, he received the censure of the House for "seeking to procure congressional attention to the affairs of a corporation in which he was interested," which was in connection with the construction by the Crédit Mobilier of America of a portion of the Union Pacific Railroad; in 1883 the legislature of Massachusetts passed resolutions of gratitude for his work and faith in his integrity and petitioned the United States Congress to extend him a like acknowledgment; died in North Easton, Mass., May 8, 1873; interment in Unity Cemetery.

**Bibliography:** *DAB*.

**AMLIE, Thomas Ryum,** a Representative from Wisconsin; born on a farm near Binford, Griggs County, N.Dak., April 17, 1897; attended the public schools, Cooperstown (N.Dak.) High School, the University of North Dakota at Grand Forks, and the University of Minnesota at Minneapolis; graduated from the law department of the University of Wisconsin at Madison in 1923; admitted to the Wisconsin bar the same year and commenced the practice of law in Beloit, Wis.; moved to Elkhorn, Wis., in 1927 and continued the practice of law; elected as a Republican to the Seventy-second Congress to fill the vacancy caused by the death of Henry Allen Cooper, and served from October 13, 1931, to March 3, 1933; was an unsuccessful candidate for renomination in 1932 to the Seventy-third Congress; elected as a Progressive to the Seventy-fourth and Seventy-fifth Congresses (January 3, 1935-January 3, 1939); was not a candidate for renomination to the House of Representatives, but was an unsuccessful Progressive candidate for nomination to the United States Senate; nominated by President Franklin D. Roosevelt, January 23, 1939, to be a member of the Interstate Commerce Commission, but his name was withdrawn on April 17, 1939; appointed a special assistant attorney general in the Lands Division of the Department of Justice, May 1939; resumed the practice of law; author; resided in Madison, Wis., until his death there on August 22, 1973; cremated; ashes interred at Sunset Memory Gardens.

**Bibliography:** Amlie, Thomas R. *Let's Look at the Record*. Madison, Wisconsin: Capital City Press, 1950; Long, Robert E. "Thomas Amlie: A Political Biography." Ph.D. dissertation, University of Wisconsin, 1969; Rosenof, Theodore. "The Political Education of an American Radical: Thomas R. Amlie in the 1930's." *Wisconsin Magazine of History* 58 (Autumn 1974): 19-30.

**AMMERMAN, Joseph Scofield,** a Representative from Pennsylvania; born in Curwensville, Clearfield County, Pa., July 14, 1924; attended the public schools and graduated from Curwensville High School in 1942; A.B., Dickinson College, Carlisle, Pa., 1948; J.D., Dickinson College School of Law, 1950; admitted to the Pennsylvania Bar in 1950 and commenced practice in Clearfield; served in the United States Army, 1943-1946; district attorney, Clearfield County, 1954-1961; United States attorney for the Western District of Pennsylvania, 1961-1963; served in the Pennsylvania senate, 1970-1977; elected to the Democratic State committee, 1968; delegate to the Democratic National Convention of 1952; elected as a Democrat to the Ninety-fifth Congress (January 3, 1977-January 3, 1979); unsuccessful candidate for reelection in 1978 to the Ninety-sixth Congress; judge, court of common pleas, Forty-sixth Judicial District of Pennsylvania, Clearfield County, Pa.; died in October 1993.

**ANCONA, Sydenham Elnathan,** a Representative from Pennsylvania; born near Lititz, Lancaster County, Pa., November 20, 1824; moved to Berks County, Pa., in 1826 with his parents, who settled near Sculls Hill; attended public and private schools; taught school; moved in 1856 to Reading, Pa., where he entered the employ of the Reading Railroad Co.; member of the board of education; elected as a Democrat to the Thirty-seventh, Thirty-eighth, and

Thirty-ninth Congresses (March 4, 1861-March 3, 1867); unsuccessful candidate for renomination in 1866; became engaged in the trust, fire-insurance, and relief-association businesses in Reading, Pa.; delegate to the Democratic National Convention at Cincinnati in 1880; during a visit to the Capitol at Washington, D.C., in 1912 was tendered a reception on the floor of the House of Representatives, it being stated at the time that he was the last surviving Member of the Thirty-seventh Congress which assembled at the extraordinary session called by Abraham Lincoln on July 4, 1861; engaged in banking and in the insurance business until his death in Reading, Pa., on June 20, 1913; interment in Charles Evans Cemetery.

**ANDERSEN, Herman Carl,** a Representative from Minnesota; born in Newcastle, Kings County, Wash., January 27, 1897; moved with his parents to a farm near Tyler, Lincoln County, Minn., in 1901; attended the rural schools; attended the University of Washington and later the Naval Academy; engaged in cattle raising and agricultural pursuits 1919-1925 and as a civil engineer 1925-1930; resumed agricultural pursuits near Tyler, Minn., 1930-1938; member of the State house of representatives in 1935; elected as a Republican to the Seventy-sixth and to the eleven succeeding Congresses (January 3, 1939-January 3, 1963); unsuccessful candidate for renomination as an Independent in 1962 to the Eighty-eighth Congress; resided in Falls Church, Va.; died in Arlington, Va., July 26, 1978; cremated; ashes interred in Danebod Lutheran Cemetery, Tyler, Minn.

**ANDERSON, Albert Raney,** a Representative from Iowa; born in Adams County, Ohio, November 8, 1837; moved with his parents to Galesburg, Ill.; attended the common schools and Knox College, Galesburg, Ill.; moved to Taylor County, Iowa, in 1857; studied law; was admitted to the bar in 1860 and commenced practice in Clarinda, Iowa; appointed postmaster of Clarinda by President Lincoln in 1861; resigned to enlist in the Union Army as a private in Company K, Fourth Regiment, Iowa Volunteer Infantry; promoted through the ranks to become major of his regiment; commissioned lieutenant colonel in 1865; mustered out in August 1865 and returned to Clarinda, Iowa; moved to Sidney, Iowa, in 1866; resumed the practice of law; assessor of internal revenue 1868-1871; delegate to the Republican National Convention at Philadelphia in 1872; district attorney 1876-1880; State railroad commissioner in 1881; unsuccessful candidate for election in 1882 to the Forty-eighth Congress; elected as an Independent Republican to the Fiftieth Congress (March 4, 1887-March 3, 1889); unsuccessful candidate for reelection in 1888 to the Fifty-first Congress; moved to Hot Springs, S.Dak., in 1892 and continued the practice of his profession; served as mayor of Hot Springs, Fall River County, S.Dak., in 1895 and 1896; elected State attorney of Fall River County November 8, 1898; died at Hot Springs, S.Dak., November 17, 1898; interment in Sidney Cemetery, Sidney, Iowa.

**ANDERSON, Alexander Outlaw** (son of Joseph Anderson), a Senator from Tennessee; born at "Soldiers' Rest," Jefferson County, Tenn., November 10, 1794; attended preparatory schools; was graduated from Washington College at Greeneville, Tenn.; enlisted in the War of 1812 and fought in the Battle of New Orleans, January 8, 1815; studied law in Washington, D.C., and in 1814 was admitted to the bar in Dandridge, Tenn., where he practiced law; later moved to Knoxville; superintendent of the United States land office in Alabama in 1836; government agent for removing the Indians from Alabama and Florida in 1838; elected as a Democrat to the United States Senate to fill the vacancy caused by the resignation of Hugh L. White, and served from February 26, 1840, to March 3, 1841; was not a candidate for reelection; leader of an overland company which went to California in 1849; member of the State senate in 1850 and 1851; supreme court judge of California 1851-1853; returned to Tennessee in 1853; later practiced law in Washington, D.C., before the Court of Claims and before the Supreme Court of the United

States; during the Civil War moved to Alabama and practiced law in Mobile and Camden; died in Knoxville, Tenn., May 23, 1869; interment in the Old Gray Cemetery.

**ANDERSON, Carl Carey,** a Representative from Ohio; born in Bluffton, Allen County, Ohio, December 2, 1877; moved to Sandusky County in 1881 with his parents, who settled in Fremont; attended the common schools; became employed as a traveling salesman; moved to Fostoria, Seneca County, and engaged in the manufacture of underwear; elected mayor of Fostoria, Ohio, in 1905 and again in 1907, on each occasion for a term of two years; president of the city hospital board and director in a number of manufacturing enterprises; elected as a Democrat to the Sixty-first and Sixty-second Congresses and served from March 4, 1909, until his death in an automobile accident near Fostoria, Ohio, October 1, 1912; interment in Oakwood Cemetery, Fremont, Ohio.

**ANDERSON, Chapman Levy,** a Representative from Mississippi; born near Macon, Noxubee County, Miss., March 15, 1845; attended the common schools in Jackson, Miss., and the University of Mississippi at Oxford; enlisted in the Confederate Army on March 5, 1862, as a private in the Thirty-ninth Regiment, Mississippi Volunteer Infantry; was promoted through the successive grades of noncommissioned officer until July 1864, when he was transferred to Bradford's cavalry corps of scouts with the rank of second lieutenant, in which capacity he served until the close of the war; studied law; was admitted to the bar in 1868 and commenced practice in Kosciusko, Miss.; mayor of Kosciusko, Miss., in 1875; member of the State house of representatives in 1879 and 1880; elected as a Democrat to the Fiftieth and Fifty-first Congresses (March 4, 1887-March 3, 1891); unsuccessful candidate for renomination in 1890; United States district attorney for the northern district of Mississippi in 1896 and 1897; engaged in the practice of law in Kosciusko, Miss., until his death, April 27, 1924; interment in Kosciusko Cemetery.

**ANDERSON, Charles Arthur,** a Representative from Missouri; born in St. Louis, Mo., September 26, 1899; attended the public schools; was graduated from St. Charles Military Academy in 1916 and from the law school of St. Louis University, LL.B., 1924; during the First World War served in the One Hundred and Twenty-eighth Field Artillery, Thirty-fifth Division, from April 1, 1917, to July 2, 1919, with nineteen months service overseas; was admitted to the bar in 1924 and commenced practice in St. Louis, Mo.; prosecuting attorney of St. Louis County 1933-1937; elected as a Democrat to the Seventy-fifth and to the Seventy-sixth Congresses (January 3, 1937-January 3, 1941); unsuccessful candidate for reelection in 1940 to the Seventy-seventh Congress; chairman of the Democratic State convention at St. Louis in 1940; resumed the practice of law in St. Louis, Mo., where he died April 26, 1977; interment in Sunset Burial Park.

**ANDERSON, Charles Marley,** a Representative from Ohio; born near Mifflintown, Juniata County, Pa., January 5, 1845; moved to Ohio in 1855 with his parents, who settled in Darke County; attended the common schools; was graduated from the Lebanon Normal School, Lebanon, Ohio, in 1868; enlisted in the Union Army and served from March 15, 1861, in Company B, Seventy-first Regiment, Ohio Volunteer Infantry, until discharged on November 30, 1865; studied law; was admitted to the bar in 1868 and commenced practice in Greenville, Ohio; manager of the Central Branch of the National Soldiers' Home, Dayton, Ohio, for twenty years; elected as a Democrat to the Forty-ninth Congress (March 4, 1885-March 3, 1887); was an unsuccessful candidate for renomination in 1886; resumed the practice of law; Ohio State commissioner to the World's Fair at Chicago in 1892 and 1893; died in Greenville, Ohio, December 28, 1908; interment in Greenville Cemetery.

**ANDERSON, Clinton Presba,** a Representative and a Senator from New Mexico; born in Centerville, Turner County, S.Dak., October 23, 1895; attended the public schools, Dakota Wesleyan University, Mitchell, S.Dak., and the University of Michigan at Ann Arbor; moved to Albuquerque, N.Mex., in 1917; newspaper reporter and editor at Albuquerque, 1918-1922; engaged in the general insurance business at Albuquerque from 1922 until 1946; served as treasurer of State of New Mexico, 1933-1934; administrator of the New Mexico Relief Administration in 1935; field representative of the Federal Emergency Relief Administration, 1935-1936; chairman and executive director of the Unemployment Compensation Commission of New Mexico, 1936-1938; managing director of the United States Coronado Exposition Commission, 1939-1940; elected as a Democrat to the Seventy-seventh and to the two succeeding Congresses, and served from January 3, 1941 until his resignation on June 30, 1945, having been appointed Secretary of Agriculture; served as Secretary of Agriculture in the Cabinet of President Harry S Truman from June 30, 1945 until his resignation on May 10, 1948; elected as a Democrat to the United States Senate in 1948; reelected in 1954, 1960, and again in 1966, and served from January 3, 1949 to January 3, 1973; was not a candidate for reelection in 1972; chairman, Joint Committee on Atomic Energy (Eighty-fourth and Eighty-sixth Congresses), Joint Committee on Construction of Building for Smithsonian (Eighty-fourth through Eighty-eighth Congresses), Joint Committee on Navaho-Hopi Indian (Eighty-fourth through the Ninety-second Congresses), Special Committee on Preservation of Senate Records (Eighty-fifth and Eighty-sixth Congresses), Committee on Interior and Insular Affairs (Eighty-seventh and Eighty-eighth Congresses), Special Committee on National Fuel Policy (Eighty-seventh Congress), Committee on Aeronautical and Space Sciences (Eighty-eighth through Ninety-second Congresses); retired from active pursuits and returned to Albuquerque, where he died on November 11, 1975; interment in Fairview Memorial Park.

**Bibliography:** Anderson, Clinton P. *Outsider in the Senate: Senator Clinton Anderson's Memoirs.* New York: World Publishing Co., 1970; Baker, Richard Allan. *Conservation Politics: The Senate Career of Clinton P. Anderson.* Albuquerque: University of New Mexico Press, 1985.

**ANDERSON, George Alburtus,** a Representative from Illinois; born in Botetourt County, Va., March 11, 1853; moved to Illinois in 1855 with his parents, who settled in Hancock County; attended the common schools; was graduated from Carthage (Ill.) College in 1876; studied law in Lincoln, Nebr., and Sedalia, Mo.; was admitted to the bar in 1878 and commenced practice in Quincy, Ill., in 1880; unsuccessful candidate for city attorney of Quincy in 1883; elected city attorney in 1884 and again in 1885; elected as a Democrat to the Fiftieth Congress (March 4, 1887-March 3, 1889); declined to be a candidate for renomination in 1888; engaged in the practice of law until his death in Quincy, Ill., January 31, 1896; interment in Woodlawn Cemetery.

**ANDERSON, George Washington,** a Representative from Missouri; born in Jefferson County, Tenn., May 22, 1832; attended the public schools; was graduated from Franklin College, Tennessee; moved to St. Louis, Mo., in 1853; studied law; was admitted to the bar in Louisiana, Pike County, Mo., in 1854 and began the practice of law; member of the State house of representatives in 1859 and 1860; served in the State senate in 1862; during the Civil War was captain of Company A, Pike County (Missouri), Home Guards from June 12 to July 17, 1861, when he was elected colonel of the regiment, and served until the organization was disbanded on September 3, 1861; colonel of the Forty-ninth Regiment, Enrolled Missouri Militia, from August 13, 1862, to January 25, 1863, and from September 29 to December 1, 1864; elected as a Republican to the Thirty-ninth and Fortieth Congresses (March 4, 1865-March 3, 1869); chairman, Committee on Mileage (Thirty-ninth and Fortieth

Congresses); declined to be a candidate for renomination in 1868; resumed the practice of law; died while on a visit to his brother at Rhea Springs, Tenn., February 26, 1902; interment in Leuty Cemetery, near Rhea Springs.

**ANDERSON, Glenn Malcolm,** a Representative from California; born in Hawthorne, Los Angeles County, Calif., February 21, 1913; B.A., University of California, 1936; served with the United States Army in the Second World War; elected mayor of Hawthorne in 1940; elected to the California State assembly, 1942-1948; lieutenant governor of California, 1959-1967; chairman and member, California State Lands Commission, 1959-1967; member of the Board of Trustees of California State Colleges, 1961-1967; elected as a Democrat to the Ninety-first and to the eleven succeeding Congresses (January 3, 1969-January 3, 1993); chairman, Committee on Public Works and Transportation (One Hundred First Congress); was not a candidate for reelection in 1992 to the One Hundred Third Congress; was a resident of San Pedro, Calif.; died December 13, 1994.

**ANDERSON, Hugh Johnston,** a Representative from Maine; born in Wiscasset, Maine, May 10, 1801; attended the local schools; moved to Belfast, Maine, in 1815 and was employed as a clerk in the mercantile establishment of his uncle; clerk of the Waldo County courts from 1824 until 1836; studied law; elected as a Democrat to the Twenty-fifth and Twenty-sixth Congresses (March 4, 1837-March 3, 1841); was not a candidate for reelection in 1840 to the Twenty-seventh Congress; elected Governor of Maine in 1843, reelected in 1844 and 1845, served from January 5, 1844 to May 12, 1847; was a candidate for United States Senator in 1847 but subsequently withdrew; moved to Washington, D.C., and served as commissioner of customs in the United States Treasury Department, 1853-1858; appointed head of the commission to reorganize and adjust the affairs of the United States Mint at San Francisco, Calif., in 1857; Sixth Auditor of the Treasury from 1866 to 1869; retired from public life in 1880 and settled in Portland, Oreg., where he died on May 31, 1881; interment in Grove Cemetery, Belfast, Maine.

**ANDERSON, Isaac,** a Representative from Pennsylvania; born at "Anderson Place," in Charlestown Township, near Valley Forge, Chester County, Pa., November 23, 1760; as a mere youth was the carrier of dispatches between the headquarters of the Revolutionary Army under General Washington at Valley Forge and the Congress then in session at York; served three terms of service in the Revolutionary War before attaining the age of eighteen and ultimately became an ensign in the Fifth Battalion of Chester County Militia; commissioned on May 24, 1779, as first lieutenant, Fifth Battalion, Sixth Company; justice of the peace in Charlestown Township for several years; member of the Pennsylvania house of representatives in 1801; elected as a Republican to the Eighth and Ninth Congresses (March 4, 1803-March 3, 1807); was not a candidate for renomination in 1806 to the Tenth Congress; engaged in agricultural pursuits and sawmilling; died at "Anderson Place," Charlestown Township, Pa., October 27, 1838; interment in the family burying ground near Valley Forge, Schuylkill Township, Chester County, Pa.

**ANDERSON, James Patton,** a Delegate from the Territory of Washington; born near Winchester, Franklin County, Tenn., February 16, 1822; was graduated from Jefferson College, Canonsburg, Pa., in 1842; moved to Kentucky; studied law at Montrose Law School, Frankfort, Ky.; was admitted to the bar and practiced in Hernando, Miss., from 1842 to 1846; raised a company of volunteers for the Mexican War; elected lieutenant colonel of the Second Battalion, Mississippi Rifles, and served in that capacity until the close of the war; member of the State house of representatives in 1850; appointed United States marshal for the Territory of Washington in 1853 and settled in Olympia; elected as a Democrat to the Thirty-fourth Congress (March 4, 1855-March 3, 1857); was not a candidate for renomination in 1856 to the Thirty-fifth Congress; appointed Governor of the Territory of Washington by President James Buchanan in 1857, but declined the office; moved to his plantation, "Casabianca," near Monticello, Fla., the same year; served in the Provisional Congress of the Confederate States; during the Civil War entered the Confederate Army as colonel of the First Regiment, Florida Infantry; appointed brigadier general February 10, 1862; promoted to major general February 17, 1864, and assigned to the command of the district of Florida; after the close of the war settled in Memphis, Tenn., and conducted a publication devoted to agriculture; collector of delinquent State taxes for Shelby County; died in Memphis, Tenn., September 20, 1872; interment in Elmwoo

**Bibliography:** *DAB*.

**ANDERSON, John,** a Representative from Maine; born in Windham, Maine, July 30, 1792; attended the common schools; was graduated from Bowdoin College, Brunswick, Maine, in 1813; studied law; was admitted to the bar in 1816 and commenced practice in Portland, Maine; member of the State senate in 1823; elected to the Nineteenth and Twentieth Congresses and elected as a Jacksonian to the Twenty-first and Twenty-second Congresses (March 4, 1825-March 3, 1833); chairman, Committee on Elections (Twentieth Congress), Committee on Naval Affairs (Twenty-second Congress); was not a candidate for renomination in 1832 to the Twenty-third Congress; mayor of Portland, 1833-1836 and again in 1842; United States attorney for the district of Maine, 1833-1836; collector of customs for the port of Portland, 1837-1841, and 1843-1848; resumed the practice of law; died in Portland, Maine, August 21, 1853; interment in Town Cemetery (then a part of the farm of his ancestors) on River Road, Windham, Maine.

**ANDERSON, John Alexander,** a Representative from Kansas; born near Pigeon Creek, Washington County, Pa., June 26, 1834; attended public and private schools; was graduated from Miami University, Oxford, Ohio, in 1853; ordained a Presbyterian minister in 1857 and began preaching in Stockton, Calif.; elected trustee of the California State insane asylum in 1860; appointed chaplain of the Third Regiment, California Volunteer Infantry, in 1862; accompanied General Patrick Connor's expedition to Salt Lake City in July 1862; mustered into the Federal service in March 1863; resigned in June 1863; California correspondent and agent of the United States Sanitary Commission, 1863-1865; moved to Junction City, Kans., in 1868, where he erected the First Presbyterian Church, of which he was pastor for five years; regent of the University of Kansas, 1872-1873; president of the Kansas State Agricultural College, 1873-1879; elected as a Republican to the Forty-sixth and to the three succeeding Congresses (March 4, 1879-March 3, 1887); unsuccessful candidate for renomination in 1886, but was elected as an Independent Republican to the Fiftieth Congress and reelected as a Republican to the Fifty-first Congress (March 4, 1887-March 3, 1891); unsuccessful candidate for renomination in 1890 to the Fifty-second Congress; appointed United States consul general to Cairo, Egypt, March 4, 1891, and remained there until shortly before his death in a hospital in Liverpool, England, May 18, 1892, en route to his home; interment in Highland Cemetery, Junction City, Kans.

**Bibliography:** *DAB*.

**ANDERSON, John Bayard,** a Representative from Illinois; born in Rockford, Winnebago County, Ill., February 15, 1922; attended Rockford public schools; A.B., University of Illinois, Urbana, 1942, J.D., 1946; LL.M., Harvard University Law School, 1949; served on the faculty of Northeastern University School of Law in Boston, Mass., while attending Harvard; during the Second World War enlisted in the United States Army and served from 1943 to 1945 in the Field Artillery, ten months of which was in France and Germany; admitted to the bar and commenced the practice of law in Rockford, Ill., in 1946; adviser on the staff of the United States High Commissioner for Germany, 1952-1955; elected State's attorney of Winnebago County in 1956 and served in that position until 1960; political author; elected as a Republican to the Eighty-seventh Congress and to the nine succeeding Congresses (January 3, 1961-January 3, 1981); chairman, Republican Conference, January 1969; was not a candidate for renomination in 1980 to the Ninety-seventh Congress, but was an unsuccessful independent candidate for President of the United States; visiting professor at Stanford University, 1981, University of Illinois College of Law, 1981, Brandeis University, 1985, Bryn Mawr College, 1985, Oregon State University, 1986, and the University of Massachusetts, 1986; distinguished visiting professor, Nova-Southeastern University Law School, 1987 to present; chair of the advisory board, Center for Voting and Democracy; is a resident of Fort Lauderdale, Fla.

**Bibliography:** Anderson, John B. *The American Economy We Need–and won't get from the Republicans or the Democrats.* New York: Atheneum, 1984.

**ANDERSON, John Zuinglius,** a Representative from California; born in Oakland, Alameda County, Calif., March 22, 1904; moved with his parents to Santa Cruz, Calif., the same year, and to San Jose, Calif., in 1913, attended the public schools; was graduated from San Jose High School in 1923; moved to San Juan Bautista, San Benito County, Calif., in 1925 and engaged in agricultural pursuits and fruit growing; elected as a Republican to the Seventy-sixth and to the six succeeding Congresses (January 3, 1939-January 3, 1953); was not a candidate for renomination in 1952 to the Eighty-third Congress; member of board of directors of Bank of America; president of California Canning Pear Association and Pacific States Canning Pear Association; with Department of Agriculture in 1954 and 1955; administrative assistant to President Dwight D. Eisenhower from December 15, 1956, to January 20, 1961; member of staff of Veterans' Affairs Committee, House of Representatives until June 30, 1962; retired; resided in Hollister, Calif., where he died February 9, 1981; cremated; ashes scattered at the top of Sonora Pass, Sierra Nevada Mountains.

**ANDERSON, Joseph** (father of Alexander Outlaw Anderson), a Senator from Tennessee; born in White Marsh, near Philadelphia, Pa., November 5, 1757; studied law; served throughout the Revolutionary War and attained the rank of brevet major; was admitted to the bar and practiced law in Delaware for several years; appointed on February 25, 1791, by President Washington as United States judge for the Territory South of the Ohio River; member of the first constitutional convention of Tennessee; elected in 1797 to the United States Senate to fill the vacancy in the term ending March 3, 1799, caused by the expulsion of William Blount; again elected December 12, 1798, to fill the vacancy in the term ending March 3, 1803, caused by the resignation of Andrew Jackson; reelected in 1803; appointed and subsequently reelected in 1809 for the ensuing term, and served continuously from September 26, 1797 to March 3, 1815; served as President pro tempore of the Senate during the Eighth Congress; First Comptroller of the Treasury, 1815-1836; lived in retirement until his death in Washington, D.C., on April 17, 1837; interment in the Congressional Cemetery.

**Bibliography:** *DAB*.

**ANDERSON, Joseph Halstead,** a Representative from New York; born in the town of Harrison, near White Plains, Westchester County, N.Y., August 25, 1800; attended the common schools; engaged in agricultural pursuits; member of the State assembly in 1833 and 1834; sheriff of Westchester County 1835-1838; elected as a Democrat to the Twenty-eighth and Twenty-ninth Congresses (March 4, 1843-March 3, 1847); chairman, Committee on Agriculture (Twenty-ninth Congress); was not a candidate for renomination in 1846 to the Thirtieth Congress; resumed farming pursuits; died in

White Plains, N.Y., June 23, 1870; interment in a private burying ground at "Anderson Hill," near White Plains, N.Y.

**ANDERSON, Josiah McNair,** a Representative from Tennessee; born near Pikeville, Bledsoe County, Tenn., November 29, 1807; attended the common schools; studied law; was admitted to the bar and commenced practice in Jasper, Tenn.; member of the State house of representatives 1833-1837, serving as speaker; member of the State senate 1843-1845, serving as presiding officer; elected as a Whig to the Thirty-first Congress (March 4, 1849-March 3, 1851); unsuccessful candidate for reelection in 1850 to the Thirty-second Congress; delegate from Tennessee to the peace convention of 1861, held in Washington, D.C., in an effort to devise means to prevent the impending war; colonel in the Tennessee State Militia 1861; was killed at Looneys Creek, near the present town of Whitwell, Marion County, Tenn., November 8, 1861, just after having made a secession speech; interment on a farm seven miles southeast of Dunlap, Sequatchie County, Tenn.

**ANDERSON, LeRoy Hagen,** a Representative from Montana; born in Ellendale, Dickey County, N.Dak., February 2, 1906; moved with his parents to Conrad, Mont., in 1909; B.S., Montana State College, Bozeman, 1927; engaged in postgraduate work in mathematics and physical chemistry in 1935-1938 at the California Institute of Technology in Pasadena; wheat and cattle rancher; during the Second World War served as commander of armored task force in the European Theater of Operations in combat from Normandy to the Elbe River; separated from the service as a lieutenant colonel in 1945; awarded Silver Star Medal and Croix de Guerre Medal with Palm; major general in Army Reserve, commanding the Ninety-sixth Infantry Division Reserve, 1948-1962; member of the Montana State house of representatives in 1947 and 1948, and the Montana State senate, 1949-1956, serving as Democratic floor leader, 1954-1956; unsuccessful candidate for election in 1954 to the Eighty-fourth Congress; elected as a Democrat to the Eighty-fifth and Eighty-sixth Congresses (January 3, 1957-January 3, 1961); was not a candidate for renomination in 1960 to the House of Representatives, but was an unsuccessful candidate for nomination to the United States Senate; resumed engineering pursuits; unsuccessful candidate for nomination in 1968 for Governor of Montana; member, Montana State senate, 1966-1970; was a resident of Conrad, Mont.; died September 25, 1991.

**ANDERSON, Lucian,** a Representative from Kentucky; born near Mayfield, Graves County, Ky., June 23, 1824; attended the public schools; studied law; was admitted to the bar in 1845 and commenced practice in Mayfield; presidential elector on the Whig ticket of Scott and Graham in 1852; member of the Kentucky house of representatives 1855-1857; elected as an Unconditional Unionist to the Thirty-eighth Congress (March 4, 1863-March 3, 1865); declined to be a candidate for renomination in 1864; delegate to the Republican National Convention in 1864; resumed the practice of his profession; died in Mayfield, Ky., October 18, 1898; interment in the Anderson family cemetery.

**Bibliography:** Hood, James Larry. "For the Union: Kentucky's Unconditional Unionist Congressmen and the Development of the Republican Party in Kentucky, 1863-1865." *Register of the Kentucky Historical Society* 76 (July 1978): 197-215.

**ANDERSON, Richard Clough, Jr.,** a Representative from Kentucky; born at "Soldiers' Retreat," near Louisville, Ky., August 4, 1788; attended private schools; was graduated from William and Mary College, Williamsburg, Va., in 1804; studied law; was admitted to the bar and commenced practice in Louisville; member of the Kentucky house of representatives in 1815; elected as a Republican to the Fifteenth and Sixteenth Congresses (March 4, 1817-March 3, 1821); chairman, Committee on Public Lands (Sixteenth Congress); declined to be a candidate for reelection in 1820 to the Seventeenth Congress; again a member of the Kentucky house of representatives,

in 1821 and 1822, serving as speaker the latter year; appointed the first United States Minister to the Republic of Colombia on January 27, 1823; took his leave on June 7, 1823, having been commissioned Envoy Extraordinary and Minister Plenipotentiary to the Panama Congress of Nations, but died, en route to his post, in Turbaco, near Cartagena, Colombia, July 24, 1826; interment at "Soldiers' Retreat," near Louisville, Ky.

**Bibliography:** *DAB*; Anderson, Richard Clough, Jr. *Diary and Journal, 1814-1826.* Edited by Alfred R. Tischendorf and E. Taylor Parks. Durham, N.C.: Duke University Press, 1964; Rubenstein, Asa L. "Richard Clough Anderson, Nathaniel Massie, and the Impact of Government on Western Land Speculation and Settlement, 1774-1830." Ph.D. dissertation, University of Illinois, Urbana-Champaign, 1986.

**ANDERSON, Samuel,** a Representative from Pennsylvania; born in Middletown, Dauphin County, Pa., in 1773; completed preparatory studies; studied medicine; was admitted to practice in 1796; entered the United States Navy as assistant surgeon in 1799; promoted to the rank of surgeon in 1800; resigned his commission and in 1801 settled in Chester, Pa., where he practiced his profession; during the War of 1812, raised a body of volunteers known as the Mifflin Guards; commissioned captain on September 10, 1814; served in the Pennsylvania Militia and was promoted to the rank of lieutenant colonel in the One Hundredth Regiment, Second Brigade, Third Division, on August 3, 1821; member of the State house of representatives 1815-1818 and 1823-1825; sheriff of Delaware County 1819-1823; again entered the naval service in 1823 as special physician but was soon forced to resign because of ill health; elected to the Twentieth Congress (March 4, 1827-March 3, 1829); again a member of the Pennsylvania house of representatives 1829-1835 and served as speaker in 1833; appointed inspector of customs in 1841; elected justice of the peace in 1846 and served until his death in Chester, Chester County, Pa., January 17, 1850; interment in Middletown Presbyterian Cemetery, near Media, Delaware County, Pa.

**ANDERSON, Simeon H.** (father of William Clayton Anderson), a Representative from Kentucky; born near Lancaster, Garrard County, Ky., March 2, 1802; pursued preparatory studies; studied law; was admitted to the bar in 1823 and commenced practice in Lancaster, Ky.; member of the Kentucky house of representatives 1828, 1829, 1832, and 1836-1838; elected as a Whig to the Twenty-sixth Congress and served from March 4, 1839, until his death near Lancaster, Garrard County, Ky., August 11, 1840; interment in the Anderson family cemetery.

**ANDERSON, Sydney,** a Representative from Minnesota; born in Zumbrota, Goodhue County, Minn., September 18, 1881; attended the common schools; was graduated from high school in 1899; attended Highland Park College, Des Moines, Iowa, and the University of Minnesota at Minneapolis; studied law; was admitted to the bar in 1903 and commenced practice in Minneapolis, Minn.; moved to Kansas City, Mo., and thence to Lanesboro, Minn., and continued the practice of law from 1904 to 1911; served as a private in Company D, Fourteenth Regiment, Minnesota Volunteer Infantry, during the Spanish-American War; elected as a Republican to the Sixty-second and to the six succeeding Congresses (March 4, 1911-March 3, 1925); chairman of the Congressional Joint Commission of Agricultural Inquiry in 1921 and 1922; declined to be a candidate for reelection in 1924 to the Sixty-ninth Congress; vice chairman of the research council of the National Transportation Institute at Washington, D.C., in 1923 and 1924; president of the Millers' National Federation, Chicago, Ill., and Washington, D.C., 1924-1929; vice president, secretary, and, later, member of the board of directors of General Mills, Inc., Minneapolis, Minn., 1930-1948; president of the Transportation Association of America, Chicago, Ill.,

1943-1948; died in Minneapolis, Minn., October 8, 1948; interment in Lakewood Cemetery.

**ANDERSON, Thomas Lilbourne,** a Representative from Missouri; born near Bowling Green, Green County, Ky., December 8, 1808; attended the rural schools; studied law; was admitted to the bar in 1828 and commenced practice in Franklin, Simpson County, Ky.; moved in 1830 to Palmyra, Marion County, Mo., where he continued the practice of law; member of the State house of representatives 1840-1844; presidential elector on the Whig ticket in 1844, 1848 and 1852; member of the State constitutional convention in 1845; elected as a candidate of the American Party to the Thirty-fifth Congress and as an Independent Democrat to the Thirty-sixth Congress (March 4, 1857-March 3, 1861); was not a candidate for renomination in 1860; resumed the practice of law in Marion County, Mo.; died in Palmyra, Mo., March 6, 1885; interment in the City Cemetery.

**ANDERSON, Wendell Richard,** a Senator from Minnesota; born in St. Paul, Ramsey County, Minn., February 1, 1933; educated in the public schools of St. Paul; B.A., University of Minnesota, 1954; LL.B., University of Minnesota Law School, 1960; admitted to the Minnesota bar in 1960 and commenced practice in St. Paul; represented the United States at the 1956 winter Olympic Games (hockey) at Cortina d'Ampezzo, Italy; served in the United States Army, 1956-1957; member, Minnesota State house of representatives, 1959-1963; Minnesota State senator, 1963-1971; elected Governor of Minnesota in 1970, reelected in 1974, and served from January 4, 1971 until his resignation on December 29, 1976; member of the Democratic National Committee's Executive Committee, 1974-1975; chairman of the Democratic National Convention Platform Committee in 1975; appointed as a Democrat to the United States Senate, December 30, 1976, to fill the vacancy caused by the resignation of Walter F. Mondale for the term ending January 3, 1979, and served from December 30, 1976, until his resignation December 29, 1978; unsuccessful candidate for election in 1978; is a resident of Wayzata, Minn.

**ANDERSON, William,** a Representative from Pennsylvania; born in Virginia in 1762; attended the common schools; during the Revolutionary War joined the Continental Army at the age of fifteen and served until the end of the war; was a major on the staff of General Lafayette and distinguished himself at Germantown and Yorktown; engaged in the hotel business as landlord of the Columbia House, Chester, Pa., in 1796; county auditor in 1804; county director of the poor in 1805; elected as a Republican to the Eleventh, Twelfth, and Thirteenth Congresses (March 4, 1809-March 3, 1815); elected to the Fifteenth Congress (March 4, 1817-March 3, 1819); appointed an associate judge of the county court on January 5, 1826; resigned in 1828 to become an inspector of customs in Philadelphia and served until his death in Chester, Pa., December 16, 1829; interment in Old St. Paul's Cemetery.

**ANDERSON, William Black,** a Representative from Illinois; born in Mount Vernon, Ill., April 2, 1830; attended the common schools; was graduated from McKendree College, Lebanon, Ill., in 1850; surveyor of Jefferson County in 1851; studied law; was admitted to the bar but never practiced; engaged in agricultural pursuits; member of the State house of representatives in 1856 and 1858; during the Civil War entered the Union Army as a private in the Sixtieth Regiment, Illinois Volunteer Infantry; commissioned lieutenant colonel of the regiment February 17, 1862, and colonel, April 4, 1863; brevetted brigadier general of Volunteers March 13, 1865; resigned December 26, 1864; member of the constitutional convention of Illinois in 1869; served in the State senate in 1871; elected as an Independent to the Forty-fourth Congress (March 4, 1875-March 3, 1877); was not a candidate for renomination in 1876; collector of internal revenue for the southern district of Illinois 1885-1889; United States pension agent in Chicago from November

9, 1893, to January 17, 1898; died in Chicago, Ill., August 28, 1901; interment in Oakwood Cemetery, Mount Vernon, Ill.

**ANDERSON, William Clayton** (son of Simeon H. Anderson and nephew of Albert Gallatin Talbott), a Representative from Kentucky; born in Lancaster, Garrard County, Ky., December 26, 1826; attended private schools and was graduated from Centre College, Danville, Ky., in 1845; studied law; was admitted to the bar and commenced practice in Lancaster; moved to Danville, Boyle County, in 1847 and continued the practice of law; member of the Kentucky house of representatives 1851-1853; presidential elector on the American Party ticket of Fillmore and Donaldson in 1856; unsuccessful candidate for election in 1856 to the Thirty-fifth Congress; elected as a candidate of the Opposition Party to the Thirty-sixth Congress (March 4, 1859-March 3, 1861); was not a candidate for renomination in 1860; elected as a Unionist to the Kentucky house of representatives in 1861; died, during the session of the legislature, at Frankfort, Ky., December 23, 1861; interment in Bell View Cemetery, Danville, Ky.

**ANDERSON, William Coleman,** a Representative from Tennessee; born at Tusculum, near Greeneville, Greene County, Tenn., July 10, 1853; attended a rural school; was graduated from Tusculum College, Greeneville, Tenn., in 1876; moved to Newport, Tenn., in 1876; while studying law was assistant clerk of Cocke County, 1877-1878; was admitted to the bar in 1878 and commenced practice in Newport; member of the Tennessee State house of representatives, 1881-1883; was a principal examiner in the General Land Office at Washington, D.C., 1889-1892; promoted to chief of the contest division on February 1, 1892, but resigned August 7, 1892; chief of the General Land Office from November 23, 1892, until April 11, 1893; returned to Newport, Cocke County, in 1893 and resumed the practice of law; elected as a Republican to the Fifty-fourth Congress (March 4, 1895-March 3, 1897); unsuccessful candidate for renomination in 1896 to the Fifty-fifth Congress; founder and editor of Plain Talk, a weekly newspaper published in Newport; member of the city council at the time of his death in Newport, Tenn., September 8, 1902; interment in Union Cemetery.

**ANDERSON, William Robert,** a Representative from Tennessee; born in Bakerville, Humphreys County, Tenn., June 17, 1921; attended the public schools in Waynesboro, Tenn., graduated from Columbia (Tenn.) Military Academy in 1939 and from the United States Naval Academy in 1942; participated in eleven submarine combat patrols in the Pacific; awarded the Bronze Star and other combat awards; commanding officer of the Nautilus, the first atomic submarine, 1957-1959; made the first transpolar voyage under ice in August 1958; served as assistant to Vice Admiral Hyman J. Rickover; retired from active Navy duty in July 1962; consultant to President John F. Kennedy for the National Service Corps in 1963; author; elected as a Democrat to the Eighty-ninth and to the three succeeding Congresses (January 3, 1965-January 3, 1973); unsuccessful candidate for reelection in 1972 to the Ninety-third Congress; chairman and chief executive officer, Public Office Corporation, Washington, D.C., 1978 to present; is a resident of Great Falls, Va.

**ANDRESEN, August Herman,** a Representative from Minnesota; born in Newark, Kendall County, Ill., October 11, 1890; attended the public schools; moved with his parents to Grand Forks, N.Dak., in 1900, to Eagle Grove, Iowa, in 1902, and to Red Wing, Goodhue County, Minn., in 1905, attending the local schools in each place; was graduated from Red Wing (Minn.) Seminary, and from St. Olaf College, Northfield, Minn., in 1912; special investigator for the Minnesota Department of Weights and Measures, 1912-1915; was graduated from the St. Paul (Minn.) College of Law; was admitted to the bar in 1914 and commenced practice in Red Wing in 1915; member of the Minnesota Home Guards in 1918 and 1919; interested in financial and business enterprises and also engaged in agricultural pursuits; elected as a Republican to the Sixty-ninth and to the three succeeding Congresses (March 4, 1925-March 3, 1933); unsuccessful candidate for reelection in 1932 to the Seventy-third Congress; elected to the Seventy-fourth and to the eleven succeeding Congresses, and served from January 3, 1935 until his death in Bethesda, Md., January 14, 1958; chairman, Select Committee on Commodity Exchanges (Eightieth Congress); interment in Oakwood Cemetery, Red Wing, Minn.

**ANDREW, Abram Piatt, Jr.,** a Representative from Massachusetts; born in La Porte, La Porte County, Ind., February 12, 1873; attended the public schools and the Lawrenceville (N.J.) School; was graduated from Princeton College in 1893; member of the Harvard Graduate School of Arts and Sciences, 1893-1898; pursued postgraduate studies in the Universities of Halle, Berlin, and Paris; moved to Gloucester, Mass., and was instructor and assistant professor of economics at Harvard University, 1900-1909; expert assistant and editor of publications of the National Monetary Commission, 1908-1911; director of the Mint in 1909 and 1910; Assistant Secretary of the Treasury, 1910-1912; served in France continuously for four and a half years during the First World War, first with the French Army and later with the United States Army; commissioned major, United States National Army, in September 1917 and promoted to lieutenant colonel in September 1918; delegate to the Republican National Conventions of 1924 and 1928; member of the board of trustees of Princeton University, 1932-1936; elected as a Republican to the Sixty-seventh Congress to fill the vacancy caused by the resignation of Willfred W. Lufkin; reelected to the Sixty-eighth and to the six succeeding Congresses, and served from September 27, 1921 until his death in Gloucester, Mass., on June 3, 1936; remains were cremated and the ashes scattered from an airplane flying over his estate at Eastern Point, Gloucester, Mass.

Bibliography: *DAB*.

**ANDREW, Benjamin,** a Delegate from Georgia; born in Dorchester, S.C., in 1730; moved to Georgia in 1754 and became a planter in St. John's Parish; president of State Executive Council in 1777; elected as a Delegate to the Continental Congress in 1780; associate justice for the County of Liberty for several terms; died in Liberty County, Georgia, about 1799.

**ANDREW, John Forrester,** a Representative from Massachusetts; born in Hingham, Plymouth County, Mass., November 26, 1850; attended private schools in Hingham and the Phillips School and Brooks School in Boston; was graduated from Harvard University in 1872 and from Harvard Law School in 1875; was admitted to the Suffolk bar in 1875 and commenced practice in Boston; member of the Massachusetts house of representatives 1880-1882; served in the Massachusetts senate in 1884 and 1885; commissioner of parks for Boston 1885-1890 and again in 1894; unsuccessful Democratic candidate for election in 1886 for Governor of Massachusetts; elected as a Democrat to the Fifty-first and Fifty-second Congresses (March 4, 1889-March 3, 1893); chairman, Committee on Reform in the Civil Service (Fifty-second Congress); unsuccessful candidate for reelection in 1892 to the Fifty-third Congress; resumed the practice of his profession; died in Boston, Mass., May 30, 1895; interment in Mount Auburn Cemetery, Cambridge, Mass.

**ANDREWS, Arthur Glenn,** a Representative from Alabama; born in Anniston, Calhoun County, Ala., January 15, 1909; attended the Birmingham public schools; graduated from Phillips High School and Mercersburg Academy; A.B., Princeton University, 1931; associated with the National City Bank of New York, 1931-1933; International Business Machines, 1933-1936; district manager of an Eastman Kodak subsidiary, 1936-1946, and in advertising, 1946-1970; candidate for the Alabama State house of representatives in 1956 and for Alabama secretary of state in 1958; delegate to the

Republican National Convention of 1964; elected as a Republican to the Eighty-ninth Congress (January 3, 1965-January 3, 1967); unsuccessful candidate for reelection in 1966 to the Ninetieth Congress; Republican Fourth District Chairman, Alabama; unsuccessful candidate for election in 1970 to the Ninety-second Congress; was a trustee in bankruptcy court, 1973-1985; engages in agricultural pursuits; is a resident of Anniston, Ala.

**ANDREWS, Charles,** a Representative from Maine; born in Paris, Oxford County, Maine, February 11, 1814; attended the district school; was graduated from Hebron (Maine) Academy; studied law; was admitted to the bar in 1837 and commenced practice in Turner, Androscoggin County, Maine; returned to Paris, Maine; member of the State house of representatives 1839-1843, serving as speaker in 1842; became clerk of the courts for Oxford County, Maine, on January 1, 1845, and served three years; delegate to the Democratic National Convention at Baltimore in 1848; elected as a Democrat to the Thirty-second Congress and served from March 4, 1851, until his death in Paris, Maine, April 30, 1852; interment in Hillside Cemetery.

**ANDREWS, Charles Oscar,** a Senator from Florida; born in Ponce de Leon, Holmes County, Fla., March 7, 1877; attended the public schools and the South Florida Military Institute at Bartow, Fla.; was graduated from the Florida State Normal School at Gainesville, Fla., in 1901 and the University of Florida at Gainesville in 1907; during the Spanish-American War served in the Florida National Guard; captain in the Florida National Guard 1903-1905; secretary of the Florida State senate 1905-1907 and 1909-1911; studied law; was admitted to the bar in 1907 and commenced practice in De Funiak Springs, Fla.; judge of the criminal court of record of Walton County, Fla., 1910-1911; assistant attorney general of Florida 1912-1919; circuit judge of the seventeenth judicial circuit 1919-1925; general counsel of the Florida Real Estate Commission 1925-1928; member of the State house of representatives in 1927; attorney for Orlando, Fla., 1926-1929; State supreme court commissioner 1929-1932; elected as a Democrat to the United States Senate to fill the vacancy caused by the death of Park Trammell; was reelected in 1940 and served from November 4, 1936, until his death in Washington, D.C., on September 18, 1946; chairman, Committee on Enrolled Bills (Seventy-ninth Congress), Committee on Public Buildings and Grounds (Seventy-ninth Congress), Special Committee on Reconstruction of the Senate Roof and Skylights (Seventy-ninth Congress); interment in Greenwood Cemetery, Orlando, Fla.

**ANDREWS, Elizabeth Bullock** (wife of George William Andrews), a Representative from Alabama; born in Geneva, Ala., February 12, 1911; attended the public schools of Geneva; B.S., Montevallo College, Montevallo, Ala., 1932; taught school in Livingston, Union Springs, and Coffee County, Ala.; elected as a Democrat, by special election, April 4, 1972, to the Ninety-second Congress to fill the vacancy caused by the death of her husband, George W. Andrews, and served from April 4, 1972, to January 3, 1973; was not a candidate for reelection in 1972 to the Ninety-third Congress; is a resident of Union Springs, Ala.

**ANDREWS, George Rex,** a Representative from New York; born in Ticonderoga, Essex County, N.Y., September 21, 1808; attended the common schools and was graduated from the Albany Law School; was admitted to the bar in 1836 and commenced the practice of law in Ticonderoga; elected as a Whig to the Thirty-first Congress (March 4, 1849-March 3, 1851); moved to Oshkosh, Wis., in 1852 and engaged in the timber and lumber business; died in Oshkosh, Wis., December 5, 1873; interment in Riverside Cemetery.

**ANDREWS, George William** (husband of Elizabeth Bullock Andrews), a Representative from Alabama; born in Clayton, Barbour County, Ala., December 12, 1906; attended the public schools; was graduated from the University of Alabama at Tuscaloosa in 1928; was admitted to the bar in 1928 and commenced practice in Union Springs, Ala.; district attorney for the third judicial circuit of Alabama 1931-1943; during the Second World War served as a lieutenant (jg) in the United States Naval Reserve from January 1943 until his election to Congress, at which time he was serving at Pearl Harbor, Hawaii; elected as a Democrat to the Seventy-eighth Congress to fill the vacancy caused by the death of Henry B. Steagall; reelected to the fourteen succeeding Congresses and served from March 14, 1944, until his death in Birmingham, Ala., December 25, 1971; interment in Oak Hill Cemetery, Union Springs, Ala.

**ANDREWS, Ike Franklin,** a Representative from North Carolina; born in Bonlee, Chatham County, N.C., September 2, 1925; attended the public schools; Fork Union Military Academy, Fork Union, Va., 1941-1942; B.S., University of North Carolina, Chapel Hill, 1950, and LL.B., 1952; served in the United States Army, field artillery forward observer, 1943-1945, attained the rank of master sergeant, received Bronze Star and Purple Heart; admitted to the North Carolina Bar in 1972 and commenced practice in Pittsboro; North Carolina State senator, 1959-1961; member, North Carolina State house of representatives, 1961-1963, 1967-1972; elected as a Democrat to the Ninety-third and to the five succeeding Congresses (January 3, 1973-January 3, 1985); unsuccessful candidate for reelection in 1984 to the Ninety-ninth Congress; is a resident of Fearrington Village, Pittsboro, N.C.

**ANDREWS, John Tuttle,** a Representative from New York; born near Schoharie Creek, Greene County, N.Y., May 29, 1803; moved with his parents in 1813 to Reading, near Dundee, Yates County; attended the district school and also was privately tutored; taught school for several years; engaged in mercantile pursuits in Irelandville and Watkins; justice of the peace and sheriff of Steuben County in 1836 and 1837; elected as a Democrat to the Twenty-fifth Congress (March 4, 1837-March 3, 1839); was not a candidate for renomination in 1838; after his term in Congress retired from active business and settled in Dundee, N.Y.; again engaged in mercantile pursuits, from 1866 until 1877, when he again retired from business pursuits to care for his personal estate; died in Dundee, N.Y., June 11, 1894; interment in Hillside Cemetery, Dundee, N.Y.

**ANDREWS, Landaff Watson,** a Representative from Kentucky; born in Flemingsburg, Fleming County, Ky., February 12, 1803; attended the public schools; was graduated from the law department of Transylvania University, Lexington, Ky., in 1826; was admitted to the bar the same year and commenced practice in Flemingsburg; prosecuting attorney of Fleming County 1829-1839; member of the Kentucky house of representatives 1834-1838; elected as a Whig to the Twenty-sixth and Twenty-seventh Congresses (March 4, 1839-March 3, 1843); unsuccessful candidate for reelection in 1842 to the Twenty-eighth Congress; served in the Kentucky senate as an independent candidate in 1857; again elected a member of the Kentucky house of representatives, in 1861, and served until 1862, when he resigned; judge of the circuit court 1862-1868; resumed the practice of law in Flemingsburg, Ky., where he died December 23, 1887; interment in Fleming County Cemetery.

**ANDREWS, Mark,** a Representative and a Senator from North Dakota; born in Cass County, N.Dak., May 19, 1926; attended the public schools; served in the United States Army from 1944 until 1946; cadet at United States Military Academy, West Point, N.Y., until receiving a disability discharge in 1946; B.S., North Dakota State University, Fargo, 1949; farmer and operator of a cattle feeding lot; director, Garrison Conservancy District, 1955-1964; member and past president of the North Dakota Crop Improvement Association; Republican national committeeman, 1958-1962; unsuccessful candidate in 1962 for election for Governor of North Dakota; elected as a Republican to the Eighty-eighth Congress, October 22, 1963, by special election to fill the vacancy caused by the death of Hjalmar Nygaard; reelected to the eight succeeding Congresses, and served from October 22, 1963 to January 3, 1981; was not a candidate for reelection in 1980 to the House of Representatives, but was elected to the United States Senate, and served from January 3, 1981 to January 3, 1987; unsuccessful candidate for reelection in 1986; chairman, Select Committee on Indian Affairs (Ninety-eighth and Ninety-ninth Congresses); a director of Tenneco, Inc. and the Case Corporation; established a government consulting firm in Washington, D.C.; is a resident of Mapleton, N.Dak.

**Bibliography:** Fenno, Richard F., Jr. *When Incumbency Fails: The Senate Career of Mark Andrews*. Washington: Congressional Quarterly Press, 1992.

**ANDREWS, Michael Allen,** a Representative from Texas; born in Houston, Harris County, Tex., February 7, 1944; attended the public schools of Forth Worth, Tex.; graduated from Arlington Heights High School, Fort Worth, Tex., 1962; B.A., University of Texas, Austin, 1967; J.D., Southern Methodist University, School of Law, Dallas, Tex., 1970; admitted to the Texas bar, 1971 and commenced practice in Houston; law clerk for United States District Court Judge Allen B. Hannay, Southern District of Texas, 1971-1972; assistant district attorney, Harris County, Tex., 1972-1976; private practice of law, 1976-1983; elected as a Democrat to the Ninety-eighth and to the five succeeding Congresses (January 3, 1983-January 3, 1995); was not a candidate in 1994 for renomination to the House of Representatives, but was an unsuccessful candidate for nomination to the United States Senate; resumed the practice of law in Houston, Tex., and Washington, D.C.; is a resident of Houston, Tex.

**ANDREWS, Robert Ernest,** a Representative from New Jersey; born in Camden, N.J., August 4, 1957; graduated from Triton High School, Runnemede, N.J., 1975; B.A., Bucknell University, Lewisburg, Pa., 1979; J.D., Cornell University Law School, 1982; professor, Rutgers University College of Law; elected as a Democrat to the One Hundred First Congress, November 6, 1990, by special election to fill the vacancy caused by the resignation of James J. Florio, and at the same time elected to the One Hundred Second Congress; reelected to the two succeeding Congresses, and served from November 6, 1990 to January 3, 1997; is a resident of Bellmawr, N.J.

**ANDREWS, Samuel George,** a Representative from New York; born in Derby, Conn., October 16, 1796; attended the public schools and a classical academy in Chester, Conn.; moved to New York in 1815 with his parents, who settled in Rochester; became engaged in the mercantile business; clerk of the New York State assembly in 1831 and 1832; clerk of Monroe County, 1834-1837; member of the board of aldermen in 1838; secretary of the State senate in 1840 and 1841; clerk of the court of errors for two years; appointed postmaster of Rochester on January 8, 1842 and served until July 18, 1845, when his successor was appointed; mayor of Rochester in 1846, and again in 1850; elected as a Republican to the Thirty-fifth Congress (March 4, 1857-March 3, 1859); engaged in the milling business; died in Rochester, N.Y., June 11, 1863; interment in Mount Hope Cemetery.

**ANDREWS, Sherlock James,** a Representative from Ohio; born in Wallingford, New Haven County, Conn., November 17, 1801; attended Cheshire Academy, Connecticut; was graduated from Union College, Schenectady, N.Y., in 1821; studied law at the New Haven (Conn.) Law School; was admitted to the bar and commenced practice in Cleveland, Cuyahoga County, Ohio, in 1825; prosecuting attorney of Cuyahoga County, Ohio, in 1830; elected as a Whig to the Twenty-seventh Congress (March 4, 1841-March 3, 1843); declined to be a candidate for renomination in 1842; resumed the practice of law in Cleveland; judge of the superior court of Cleveland 1848-1850; delegate to the second and third State constitutional conventions in 1849 and 1873; member of the village council of Cleveland, Ohio; died in Cleveland, Ohio, February 11, 1880; interment in Lakeview Cemetery.

**Bibliography:** *DAB.*

**ANDREWS, Thomas Hiram,** a Representative from Maine; born in North Easton, Barnstable County, Mass., March 27, 1953; graduated from North Easton High School; B.A., Bowdoin College, Brunswick, Maine, 1976; executive director, Maine Association of Handicapped Persons; member, Maine State house of representatives, 1983-1985; member, Maine State senate, 1985-1990; elected as a Democrat to the One Hundred Second and One Hundred Third Congresses (January 3, 1991-January 3, 1995); was not a candidate in 1994 for reelection to the House of Representatives, but was an unsuccessful candidate for election to the United States Senate; is a resident of Portland, Maine.

**ANDREWS, Walter Gresham,** a Representative from New York; born in Evanston, Cook County, Ill., July 16, 1889; moved with his parents to Buffalo, N.Y., in 1902; attended the public schools of Buffalo, N.Y.; was graduated from the Lawrenceville (N.J.) Academy in 1908 and from the law department of Princeton University, in 1913; coach of the Princeton University football team in 1913 and 1915; served on the Mexican border as a private, Troop I, First New York Cavalry, in 1916; commissioned second lieutenant, Machine Gun Group, First New York Cavalry, in 1917; served in France with the One Hundred and Seventh United States Infantry, Twenty-seventh Division; promoted to major; superintendent and central sales manager, Pratt and Lambert, Inc., Buffalo, N.Y., 1914-1925; supervisor of the fifteenth federal census for the seventh district of New York in 1929 and 1930; director of the Buffalo General Hospital; elected as a Republican to the Seventy-second and to the eight succeeding Congresses (March 4, 1931-January 3, 1949); chairman, Committee on Armed Services (Eightieth Congress); was not a candidate for renomination in 1948 to the Eighty-first Congress; died at Daytona Beach, Fla., March 5, 1949; interment in Old Fort Niagara Cemetery, Youngstown, N.Y.

**ANDREWS, William Ezekiel,** a Representative from Nebraska; born near Oskaloosa, Mahaska County, Iowa, December 17, 1854; became an orphan in early youth; worked as a farm hand, and attended the country schools in the winter; was graduated from Simpson College, Indianola, Iowa, in 1874, and from Parsons College, Fairfield, Iowa, in 1875; was elected superintendent of schools of Ringgold County in 1879; member of the faculty of Hastings (Nebr.) College from January 1, 1885, to January 1, 1893; elected vice president of Hastings College in 1889 and president of the Nebraska State Teachers' Association in 1890; served as private secretary to Governor Lorenzo Crounse of Nebraska in 1893 and 1894; was an unsuccessful candidate for election in 1892 to the Fifty-third Congress; elected as a Republican to the Fifty-fourth Congress (March 4, 1895-March 3, 1897); was an unsuccessful candidate for reelection in 1896 to the Fifty-fifth Congress; auditor for the Treasury Department, Washington, D.C., 1897-1915; elected to the Sixty-sixth and Sixty-seventh Congresses (March 4, 1919-March 3, 1923); chairman, Committee on the Election of President, Vice President, and Representatives (Sixty-seventh Congress); was an unsuccessful candidate for reelection in 1922 to the Sixty-eighth Congress; lived in Washington, D.C., until his death there on January 19, 1942; interment in Parkview Cemetery, Hastings, Nebr.

**ANDREWS, William Henry,** a Delegate from the Territory of New Mexico; born in Youngsville, Warren County, Pa., January 14, 1846; attended the public schools; engaged in mercantile pursuits at Cincinnati, Ohio, and at Meadville and Titusville, Pa., 1880-1890; was also a builder of railroads; president of the Santa Fe Central Railway Co.; chairman of the Republican State committee of Pennsylvania 1889-1891; member of the State house of representatives 1889-1893; served in the State senate in 1895; moved to the Territory of New Mexico in 1900 and engaged in the mining business in Sierra County; was a member of the Territorial council in 1903 and 1904; elected as a Republican to the Fifty-ninth, Sixtieth, Sixty-first, and Sixty-second Congresses and served from March 4, 1905, to January 7, 1912, when, pursuant to law, his term expired, the Territory of New Mexico having been admitted as a State into the Union and the Representative-elect having qualified; became engaged in the development of oil in the southern part of New Mexico in 1912; died in Carlsbad, Eddy County, N.Mex., January 16, 1919; interment in Woodlawn Cemetery, Titusville, Crawford County, Pa.

**ANDREWS, William Noble,** a Representative from Maryland; born in Hurlock, Dorchester County, Md., November 13, 1876; attended the public schools of the county and Dixon College; was graduated from Wesley Collegiate Institute, Dover, Del., in 1898 and from the law department of the University of Maryland at Baltimore in 1903; was admitted to the bar in 1903 and commenced the practice of law in Cambridge, Md.; served as State attorney for Dorchester County from 1904 to 1911; member of the State house of delegates in 1914; served in the State senate from 1918 until 1919, when he resigned to enter Congress; elected as a Republican to the Sixty-sixth Congress (March 4, 1919-March 3, 1921); unsuccessful candidate for reelection in 1920 to the Sixty-seventh Congress; resumed the practice of law in Cambridge, Md., until his death there on December 27, 1937; interment in Washington Cemetery, Hurlock, Md.

**ANDRUS, John Emory,** a Representative from New York; born in Pleasantville, Westchester County, N.Y., February 16, 1841; attended the local schools, and Charlotteville Seminary in Schoharie County, N.Y.; was graduated from Wesleyan University, Middletown, Conn., in 1862; taught school in New Jersey for four years; engaged in the manufacture of medicine in Yonkers, N.Y.; president of the New York Pharmaceutical Association, and of the Palisade Manufacturing Co. of Yonkers, Westchester County; trustee of Wesleyan University; mayor of Yonkers in 1903; elected as a Republican to the Fifty-ninth and to the three succeeding Congresses (March 4, 1905-March 3, 1913); was not a candidate for renomination in 1912; resumed his former business pursuits in Yonkers, N.Y., until his death there on December 26, 1934; interment in Kensico Cemetery, Valhalla, N.Y.

**Bibliography:** Morrill, George P. *Multimillionaire Straphanger: A Life of John Emory Andrus.* Middletown, Conn.: Wesleyan University Press, 1971.

**ANFUSO, Victor L'Episcopo,** a Representative from New York; born in Gagliano Castelferrato, Sicily, Italy, March 10, 1905; immigrated to the United States in 1914 and settled in Brooklyn, N.Y.; attended elementary and Commercial High School in Brooklyn, N.Y.; took preparatory courses at Columbia University in 1926 and 1927; LL.B., St. Lawrence University Law School (now Brooklyn Law School), 1927; was admitted to the bar in 1928 and commenced the practice of law in New York City; organized the Citizens Welfare Association of Brooklyn, and the Italian Board of Guardians, Brooklyn, N.Y.; during the Second World War served with the Office of Strategic Services in the Mediterranean Theater, 1943-1945; special assistant Commissioner of Immigration and Naturalization, United States Department of Justice, 1944-1946; elected as a Democrat to the Eighty-second Congress (January 3, 1951-January 3, 1953); was not a candidate for renomination in 1952 to the Eighty-third Congress; appointed city magistrate of Brooklyn, N.Y., in February 1954, and resigned in July 1954 to run for Congress; elected to the Eighty-fourth and to the three succeeding Congresses (January 3, 1955-January 3, 1963); was not a candidate for renomination in 1962 to the Eighty-eighth Congress; elected a judge in the State Supreme Court in New York in 1962; died in New York City, December 28, 1966; interment in St. Johns Cemetery, Middle Village, N.Y.

**ANGEL, William G.,** a Representative from New York; born in New Shoreham, Block Island, R.I., July 17, 1790; moved with his parents to Litchfield, Otsego County, N.Y., in 1792; attended the common schools; began the study of medicine in 1807; studied law; was admitted to the bar and commenced practice in Burlington, N.Y., in 1817; elected to the Nineteenth Congress (March 4, 1825-March 3, 1827); elected as a Jacksonian to the Twenty-first and Twenty-second Congresses (March 4, 1829-March 3, 1833); resumed the practice of law in Hammondsport, Steuben County, N.Y.; member of the State constitutional convention of 1846; was elected judge of Allegany County in 1847; died in Angelica, Allegany County, N.Y., on August 13, 1858; interment in Until the Day Dawn Cemetery.

**ANGELL, Homer Daniel,** a Representative from Oregon; born on a farm near The Dalles, Wasco County, Oreg., January 12, 1875; attended the public schools; was graduated from the University of Oregon at Eugene in 1900 and from the law school of Columbia University, New York City, in 1903; was admitted to the New York and Oregon bars the same year and commenced practice in Portland, Oreg.; member of the State house of representatives in 1929, 1931, and 1935; served in the State senate in 1937 and 1938, resigning to become a candidate for Congress; elected as a Republican to the Seventy-sixth and to the seven succeeding Congresses (January 3, 1939-January 3, 1955); unsuccessful candidate for renomination in 1954; retired but remained active in community activities for over a decade; died in Portland, Oreg., March 31, 1968; interment in Portland Memorial Indoor Cemetery.

**ANKENY, Levi,** a Senator from Washington; born near St. Joseph, Buchanan County, Mo., August 1, 1844; crossed the plains to Oregon in 1850 with his parents and settled in Portland; attended the rural schools and Kingsley Academy, Portland, Oreg.; engaged in business in Lewiston, Orofino, and Florence, Idaho; interested in the cattle business; first mayor of Lewiston; moved to Walla Walla, Wash., and engaged in banking; appointed a member of the Pan American Exposition Commission and became its chairman; elected as a Republican to the United States Senate, and served from March 4, 1903, to March 3, 1909; unsuccessful candidate for renomination in 1908; chairman, Committee on Coast and Insular Survey (Fifty-eighth and Fifty-ninth Congresses), Committee on Irrigation (Fifty-ninth Congress), Committee on Irrigation and Reclamation (Sixtieth Congress); engaged in banking in Walla Walla, Wash., until his death on March 29, 1921; interment in Masonic Cemetery.

**ANNUNZIO, Frank,** a Representative from Illinois; born in Chicago, Cook County, Ill., January 12, 1915; graduated from Crane Technical High School, Chicago, Ill., and from DePaul University, B.S., 1940, and M.A., 1942; teacher, Chicago public schools, 1936-1943; assistant supervisor of the National Defense Program at Austin High School 1942-1943; educational representative of the United Steelworkers of America, 1943-1948; chairman, War Ration Board 40-20, 1943-1945; Advisory Committee to Illinois Industrial Commission on Health and Safety, 1944-1949; Advisory Committee on Unemployment Compensation, 1944-1949; director of labor, State of Illinois, 1949-1952; engaged in private business 1954-1964; elected as a Democrat to the Eighty-ninth and to the thirteen succeeding Congresses (January 3, 1965-January 3, 1993); chairman, Committee on House Administration (Ninety-eighth through One Hundred First Congresses), Joint Committee on Printing (Ninety-eighth and One Hundredth Congresses), Joint Committee on the Library (Ninety-ninth and One Hundred First Congresses); was not a candidate for reelection in 1992 to the One Hundred Third Congress; is a resident of Chicago, Ill.

**ANSBERRY, Timothy Thomas,** a Representative from Ohio; born in Defiance, Defiance County, Ohio, December 24, 1871; attended the public schools; was graduated from the University of Notre Dame, South Bend, Ind., in June 1893; was admitted to the bar and commenced practice in Defiance, Ohio; justice of the peace 1893-1895; prosecuting attorney of Defiance County 1895-1903; was an unsuccessful candidate for election in 1904 to the Fifty-ninth Congress; elected as a Democrat to the Sixtieth and to the three succeeding Congresses and served from March 4, 1907, until January 9, 1915, when he resigned to accept a judicial position; chairman, Committee on Elections No. 1 (Sixty-second Congress); appointed associate judge of the Ohio Court of Appeals, in which capacity he served until his resignation in 1916; delegate to the Democratic National Conventions at San Francisco in 1920 and at New York in 1924; moved to Washington, D.C., in 1916 and engaged in the practice of law until his death; died in New York City, July 5, 1943; interment in Mount Olivet Cemetery, Washington, D.C.

**ANSORGE, Martin Charles,** a Representative from New York; born in Corning, Steuben County, N.Y., January 1, 1882; attended the public schools and the College of the City of New York; was graduated from Columbia College in 1903 and from the Columbia Law School in 1906; was admitted to the bar in 1906 and commenced practice in New York City; chairman of the Triborough Bridge Committee 1918-1921; unsuccessful Republican candidate for election to Congress in 1912, 1914, and 1916; declined the Republican nomination for Congress in 1918; during the First World War enlisted in the Motor Transport Corps; elected as a Republican to the Sixty-seventh Congress (March 4, 1921-March 3, 1923); unsuccessfully contested the election in 1922 of Royal H. Weller to the Sixty-eighth Congress; unsuccessful candidate for judge of the court of general sessions of New York City in 1924; unsuccessful candidate for justice of the supreme court of New York in 1927 and in 1928; resumed the practice of law in New York City; director of United Air Lines 1934-1961; engaged in general practice of law; died in New York City, February 4, 1967; interment in Temple Israel Cemetery, Hastings-on-Hudson, N.Y.

**ANTHONY, Beryl Franklin, Jr.,** a Representative from Arkansas; born in El Dorado, Union County, Ark., February 21, 1938; attended the Union County public schools; graduated, El Dorado High School, 1956; B.S., B.A., University of Arkansas, Fayetteville, 1961; J.D., same university, 1963; admitted to the Arkansas bar in 1963 and commenced practice in El Dorado; assistant attorney general, 1964-1965; deputy prosecuting attorney, Union County, Ark., 1966-1970; prosecuting attorney, Thirteenth Judicial District, 1971-1976; legal counsel, Anthony Forest Products Co., 1977; private practice of law, 1977; delegate to Arkansas State Democratic conventions, 1964-1978; elected as a Democrat to the Ninety-sixth and to the six succeeding Congresses (January 3, 1979-January 3, 1993); unsuccessful candidate for renomination in 1992 to the One Hundred Third Congress; is a resident of El Dorado, Ark.

**ANTHONY, Daniel Read, Jr.,** a Representative from Kansas; born in Leavenworth, Kans., August 22, 1870; attended the public schools, the Michigan Military Academy at Orchard Lake, and the University of Michigan at Ann Arbor; studied law; was admitted to the bar but did not practice extensively; engaged in newspaper work; appointed postmaster of Leavenworth, Kans., on June 22, 1898, and served until June 30, 1902, when a successor was appointed; mayor of Leavenworth 1903-1905; became manager and editor of the Leavenworth Daily Times in 1904; elected as a Republican to the Sixtieth Congress to fill the vacancy caused by the resignation of Charles Curtis; reelected to the Sixty-first and to the nine succeeding Congresses and served from May 23, 1907, to March 3, 1929; chairman, Committee on Appropriations (Seventieth Congress); was not a candidate for renomination in 1928; resumed his former business pursuits; died in Leavenworth, Kans., August 4, 1931; interment in Mount Muncie Cemetery.

**ANTHONY, Henry Bowen,** a Senator from Rhode Island; born in Coventry, R.I., April 1, 1815; attended a private school in Providence, R.I.; graduated from Brown University in 1833; editor of the Providence Journal in 1838, and afterwards became one of its owners; elected Governor of Rhode Island in 1849, reelected in 1850, and served from May 1, 1849 to May 6, 1851; declined to be a candidate for renomination; resumed editorial pursuits; elected as a Republican to the United States Senate in 1858, reelected in 1864, 1870, 1876, and again in 1882, and served from March 4, 1859, until his death in Providence, R.I., on September 2, 1884; served as President pro tempore of the Senate during the Forty-first, Forty-second and Forty-third Congresses; chairman, Committee on Printing (Thirty-seventh through Forty-eighth Congresses), Committee on Revolutionary Claims (Forty-sixth and Forty-seventh Congresses); interment in Swan Point Cemetery.

Bibliography: *DAB.*

**ANTHONY, Joseph Biles,** a Representative from Pennsylvania; born in Philadelphia, Pa., June 19, 1795; attended the public schools; studied law; was admitted to the bar and practiced; member of the Pennsylvania senate 1830-1833; elected as a Jacksonian to the Twenty-third and Twenty-fourth Congresses (March 4, 1833-March 3, 1837); appointed judge of the "Nichelson court"; engaged in the sale of titles to large tracts of lands in Pennsylvania; was elected president judge of the eighth district in 1844 and served until his death in Williamsport, Lycoming County, Pa., January 10, 1851; interment in Williamsport Cemetery.

**ANTONY, Edwin Le Roy,** a Representative from Texas; born in Waynesboro, Burke County, Ga., January 5, 1852; moved with his parents to Texas in 1859 and settled in Brazoria County; moved to Milam County in 1867; attended the common schools, and was graduated from the University of Georgia at Athens in 1873; studied law; was admitted to the bar in 1874 and commenced practice in Cameron, Tex.; prosecuting attorney of Milam County 1876, being also ex officio district attorney for his county; was appointed special judge during the illness of the regular district judge in 1886; member of the board of aldermen of Cameron 1890-1892; elected as a Democrat to the Fifty-second Congress to fill the vacancy caused by the resignation of Roger Q. Mills, and served from June 14, 1892, to March 3, 1893; unsuccessful candidate for renomination in 1892; resumed the practice of law in Cameron, Tex.; died in Dallas, Tex., January 16, 1913; interment in Oakland Cemetery.

**APLIN, Henry Harrison,** a Representative from Michigan; born in Thetford Township, Genesee County, Mich., April 15, 1841; moved with his parents to Flint, Mich., in 1848; attended the public schools; enlisted July 3, 1861, in Company C, Sixteenth Regiment, Michigan Volunteer Infantry; served until July 16, 1865, with the rank of second lieutenant; returned to Michigan and engaged in mercantile pursuits at Wenona (now West Bay City); postmaster of West Bay City from November 1869 to June 1886; served as township clerk and township treasurer, each for three years; delegate to the Republican National Convention at Chicago in 1884; elected auditor general of the State in 1886 and 1888; interested in the construction of the electric railways of West Bay City and served as general manager until 1891; member of the Michigan house of representatives in 1894 and 1895; was again appointed postmaster of West Bay City and served from October 1, 1898, to June 1902; elected as a Republican to the Fifty-seventh Congress to fill the vacancy caused by the death of Rousseau O. Crump and served from October 20, 1901, to March 3, 1903; unsuccessful candidate for renomination in 1902; engaged in agricultural pursuits and was also interested in the manufacture of ice; died in West Bay City, Mich., July 23, 1910; interment in Elm Lawn Cemetery, Bay City, Mich.

**APPLEBY, Stewart Hoffman** (son of Theodore Frank Appleby), a Representative from New Jersey; born in Asbury Park, Monmouth County, N.J., May 17, 1890; attended the public schools of Asbury Park, and Mercersburg Academy; was graduated from Rutgers University, New Brunswick, N.J., in 1913; engaged in the real estate and insurance business; organized and served as vice president of the First National Bank of Avon-by-the-Sea, N.J.; during the First World War enlisted in the United States Marine Corps on May 17, 1917, and served until May 17, 1921; commissioned a captain in the United States Marine Corps Reserve on November 24, 1925; elected as a Republican to the Sixty-ninth Congress to fill the vacancy caused by the death of his father, Representative-elect T. Frank Appleby, and served from November 3, 1925, to March 3, 1927; was not a candidate for renomination in 1926; during the Second World War served in the United States Coast Guard, being discharged in September 1945 as a coxswain; retired to Hallandale, Fla.; died in Miami, Fla., January 12, 1964; interment in Arlington National Cemetery, Va.

**APPLEBY, Theodore Frank** (father of Stewart Hoffman Appleby), a Representative from New Jersey; born in Old Bridge, Middlesex County, N.J., October 10, 1864; moved with his parents to Asbury Park, N.J., in 1875; attended the public schools and Pennington (N.J.) Seminary; was graduated from Fort Edwards Collegiate Institute, Glens Falls, N.Y., in 1885; engaged in the real estate and insurance business; member of the Asbury Park Board of Education 1887-1897; member of the State board of education 1894-1902; delegate to the Republican National Convention of 1896; member of the city council 1899-1906; mayor of Asbury Park 1908-1912; member of the Monmouth County Board of Taxation 1917-1920; elected as a Republican to the Sixty-seventh Congress (March 4, 1921-March 3, 1923); unsuccessful candidate for reelection in 1922 to the Sixty-eighth Congress; elected in 1924 to the Sixty-ninth Congress but died in Baltimore, Md., December 15, 1924, before the commencement of the congressional term; interment in Chestnut Hill Cemetery, Old Bridge, N.J.

**APPLEGATE, Douglas,** a Representative from Ohio; born in Steubenville, Jefferson County, Ohio, March 27, 1928; attended the public schools and graduated from Steubenville High School in 1947; engaged in real estate business; served in the Ohio State house of representatives, 1961-1969; Ohio State senator, 1969-1976; delegate to the Democratic National Conventions of 1964, 1980 and 1988; elected as a Democrat to the Ninety-fifth and to the eight succeeding Congresses (January 3, 1977-January 3, 1995); was not a candidate for reelection in 1994 to the One Hundred Fourth Congress; Democratic State Central Committeeman, 1994-1996; is a resident of Steubenville, Ohio.

**APPLETON, John,** a Representative from Maine; born in Beverly, Mass., February 11, 1815; was graduated from Bowdoin College, Brunswick, Maine, in 1834; studied law at the Cambridge Law School; was admitted to the Cumberland bar in 1837 and commenced practice in Portland, Maine; engaged in editorial work on the Eastern Argus and became editor in 1838; register of probate for Cumberland County, Maine, 1840, and 1842-1844; chief clerk of the Navy Department, 1845-1848, and of the Department of State from January 26 to April 25, 1848; appointed Minister to Bolivia on March 30, 1848, and served until May 1849; elected as a Democrat to the Thirty-second Congress (March 4, 1851-March 3, 1853); was not a candidate for reelection in 1852 to the Thirty-third Congress; resumed the practice of law; secretary of the United States legation in London from February 19 to November 16, 1855; Assistant Secretary of State from April 4, 1857 to June 10, 1860; appointed Minister to Russia on June 8, 1860, and served until June 1861, when he resigned; died in Portland, Maine, August 22, 1864; interment in Evergreen Cemetery.

Bibliography: *DAB.*

**APPLETON, Nathan** (cousin of William Appleton), a Representative from Massachusetts; born in New Ipswich, N.H., October 6, 1779; attended the common schools, the local academy in New Ipswich, N.H., and Dartmouth College, Hanover, N.H.; clerked in his brother's importing house in Boston; one of the founders of the cotton-mill industry of Waltham, Mass.; also one of the founders of the city of Lowell in 1821; served in the Massachusetts house of representatives in 1815, 1816, 1821, 1823, 1824, and 1827; elected as an Anti-Jacksonian to the Twenty-second Congress (March 4, 1831-March 3, 1833); was not a candidate for renomination in 1832 to the Twenty-third Congress; elected as a Whig to the Twenty-seventh Congress to fill the vacancy caused by the resignation of Robert C. Winthrop and served from June 9 to September 28, 1842, when he resigned; engaged in mercantile pursuits; died in Boston, Mass., July 14, 1861; interment in Mount Auburn Cemetery, Cambridge, Mass.

**Bibliography:** *DAB*; Gregory, Francis W. *Nathan Appleton, Merchant and Entrepreneur, 1779-1861.* Charlottesville: University Press of Virginia, 1975; Winthrop, Robert Charles. *Memoir of the Hon. Nathan Appleton, LL.D.* Westport, Conn.: Greenwood Press, 1969.

**APPLETON, William** (cousin of Nathan Appleton), a Representative from Massachusetts; born in Brookfield, Mass., November 16, 1786; attended schools in New Ipswich, N.H., Francestown, N.H., and Tyngsboro, Mass.; worked in a country store at Temple, Hillsboro County, N.H., when fifteen years of age; moved to Boston in 1807; engaged in mercantile pursuits; president of the Boston Branch of the United States Bank 1832-1836; elected as a Whig to the Thirty-second and Thirty-third Congresses (March 4, 1851-March 3, 1855); unsuccessful candidate for reelection in 1854 to the Thirty-fourth Congress and for election in 1856 to the Thirty-fifth Congress; elected as a Constitutional Unionist to the Thirty-seventh Congress and served from March 4, 1861, to September 27, 1861, when he resigned because of failing health; died at Longwood (Brookline), Mass., February 15, 1862; interment in Mount Auburn Cemetery, Cambridge, Mass.

**APSLEY, Lewis Dewart,** a Representative from Massachusetts; born in Northumberland, Pa., September 29, 1852; moved with his parents to Lock Haven, Clinton County, Pa., in 1861; attended public and private schools; moved to Philadelphia and engaged in business; early identified himself with the rubbergoods trade; moved to Massachusetts in 1877 and became a manufacturer of rubber clothing in Hudson in 1885; president of the Apsley Rubber Co., succeeded by the Firestone Apsley Rubber Co.; president of the Hudson Board of Trade and a director of the Hudson National Bank; elected as a Republican to the Fifty-third and Fifty-fourth Congresses (March 4, 1893-March 3, 1897); chairman, Committee on Manufactures (Fifty-fourth Congress); declined to be a candidate for renomination in 1896; resumed his former business pursuits in Hudson, Mass.; served two terms as vice chairman of the Republican National Congressional Committee; died in Colon, Panama, April 11, 1925; interment in Forestvale Cemetery, Hudson, Mass.

**ARCHER, John** (father of Stevenson Archer [1786-1848] and grandfather of Stevenson Archer [1827-1898]), a Representative from Maryland; born near Churchville, Harford (then Baltimore) County, Md., May 5, 1741; attended the West Nottingham Academy in Cecil County and was graduated from Princeton College in 1760; studied theology, but owing to a throat affection abandoned the same and began the study of medicine; was graduated as a physician from the College of Philadelphia in 1768, receiving the first medical diploma issued on the American continent; commenced the practice of his profession in Harford County, Md. in 1769; member of the Revolutionary committee 1774-1776; raised a military company during the Revolution; member of the first State constitutional convention of 1776; served in the State house of delegates 1777-1779; during the Revolutionary War was aide-de-camp to General Anthony Wayne at Stony Point; on June 1, 1779, was made a captain and subsequently a major in the Continental Army; elected as a Republican to the Seventh, Eighth, and Ninth Congresses (March 4, 1801-March 3, 1807); founded with his son, Dr. Thomas Archer, the medical and chirurgical faculty of Maryland in 1799; died at his country home, "Medical Hall," near Churchville, Harford County, Md., September 28, 1810; interment in the Presbyterian Cemetery, Churchville, Md.

**Bibliography:** *DAB.*

**ARCHER, Stevenson** (son of John Archer and father of Stevenson Archer [1827-1898]), a Representative from Maryland; born at "Medical Hall," near Churchville, Harford County, Md., October 11, 1786; attended Nottingham Academy, Maryland, and was graduated from Princeton College in 1805; studied law; was admitted to the bar of Harford County in 1808 and commenced practice the same year; member of the State house of delegates 1809-1810; elected as a Republican to the Twelfth Congress to fill the vacancy caused by the resignation of John Montgomery; reelected to the Thirteenth and Fourteenth Congresses and served from October 26, 1811, to March 3, 1817; chairman, Committee on Claims (Thirteenth Congress), Committee on Expenditures in the Department of the Navy (Fourteenth Congress); paymaster to the Fortieth Maryland Militia during the War of 1812; appointed on March 5, 1817, by President James Madison as United States judge for the Territory of Mississippi, with powers of Governor, holding court at St. Stephens; resigned within a year and returned to Maryland and practiced law; elected to the Sixteenth Congress (March 4, 1819-March 3, 1821); chairman, Committee on Expenditures in the Department of the Navy (Sixteenth Congress); appointed chief judge of the judicial circuit court of Baltimore and Harford Counties and Baltimore city in 1823; in 1844 was appointed by Governor Thomas G. Pratt as chief justice of the Maryland Court of Appeals and served until his death at "Medical Hall," near Churchville, Harford County, Md., June 26, 1848; interment in the Presbyterian Cemetery, Churchville, Md.

**Bibliography:** *DAB.*

**ARCHER, Stevenson** (son of Stevenson Archer [1786-1848] and grandson of John Archer), a Representative from Maryland; born at "Medical Hall," near Churchville, Harford County, Md., February 28, 1827; attended Bel Air Academy, and was graduated from Princeton College in 1848; studied law; was admitted to the bar in 1850 and commenced practice the same year; member of the State house of delegates in 1854; elected as a Democrat to the Fortieth and to the three succeeding Congresses (March 4, 1867-March 3, 1875); unsuccessful candidate for renomination in 1874; engaged in the practice of his chosen profession in Bel Air, Md., until his death on August 2, 1898; interment in the Presbyterian Cemetery, Churchville, Md.

**ARCHER, William Reynolds, Jr.,** a Representative from Texas; born in Houston, Harris County, Tex., March 22, 1928; attended private schools in Houston and Rice University, 1945-1946; B.B.A. and LL.B., University of Texas, Austin, 1946-1951; admitted to the Texas Bar in 1951 and commenced practice in Houston; served in the United States Air Force, captain, during Korean Conflict, 1951-1953; president, Uncle Johnny Mills, Inc., 1953-1961; councilman and mayor pro tem, City of Hunters Creek Village, Tex., 1955-1962; director, Heights State Bank, 1967-1970; member, Texas State house of representatives, 1967-1970; elected as a Republican to the Ninety-second and to the twelve succeeding Congresses (January 3, 1971-January 3, 1997); chairman, Committee on Ways and Means (One Hundred Fourth Congress), Joint Committee on Taxation (One Hundred Fourth Congress); is a resident of Houston, Tex.

**ARCHER, William Segar** (nephew of Joseph Eggleston), a Representative and a Senator from Virginia; born at "The Lodge," Amelia County, Va., March 5, 1789; received private instruction; was graduated from William and Mary College, Williamsburg, Va., in 1806; studied law; was admitted to the bar in 1810 and practiced in Amelia and Powhatan Counties; served four terms in the Virginia house of delegates between 1812 and 1819; elected to the Sixteenth Congress to fill the vacancy caused by the resignation of James Pleasants; reelected to the Seventeenth and to the six succeeding Congresses (January 3, 1820-March 3, 1835); unsuccessful candidate for reelection in 1834 to the Twenty-fourth Congress; chairman, Committee on Foreign Affairs (Twenty-first through Twenty-third Congresses); elected as a Whig to the United States Senate and served from March 4, 1841, to March 3, 1847; unsuccessful candidate for reelection in 1846; chairman, Committee on Foreign Affairs (Twenty-seventh and Twenty-eighth Congresses), Committee on Naval Affairs ( Twenty-seventh Congress); resumed the practice of law; died at "The Lodge," in Amelia County, Va., March 28, 1855; interment in a private cemetery at "The Lodge."

Bibliography: *DAB.*

**ARENDS, Leslie Cornelius,** a Representative from Illinois; born in Melvin, Ford County, Ill., September 27, 1895; attended public and high schools and Oberlin (Ohio) College; during the First World War served in the United States Navy in 1918 and 1919; engaged in agricultural pursuits and banking; in 1935 became member of the Ford County (Ill.) Farm Bureau and in 1938 a member of the board of trustees of the Illinois Wesleyan University at Bloomington; elected as a Republican to the Seventy-fourth Congress; reelected to the nineteen succeeding Congresses and served from January 3, 1935, until his resignation December 31, 1974; minority whip (Seventy-eighth and Seventy-ninth Congresses, Eighty-first and Eighty-second Congresses, and Eighty-fourth through Ninety-third Congresses), majority whip (Eightieth Congress and Eighty-third Congress); was not a candidate for reelection in 1974 to the Ninety-fourth Congress; was a resident of Naples, Fla. until his death there, July 17, 1985; interment in Melvin Cemetery, Melvin, Ill.

**ARENS, Henry Martin,** a Representative from Minnesota; born in Westphalia, Germany, November 21, 1873; attended the public schools and an agricultural school in Germany; immigrated to the United States in 1889 and settled near Jordan, Scott County, Minn.; engaged in agricultural pursuits in 1903; member of the board of aldermen of Jordan, Minn., 1905-1913; served on the board of education from 1913 to 1919; one of the organizers of Land O' Lakes Creamery in 1920 and a member of the board of directors for twelve years, and vice president, 1927-1933; member of the Minnesota State house of representatives, 1919-1923; served in the State senate, 1923-1929; lieutenant governor of Minnesota, 1929-1931; elected as a Farmer-Laborite to the Seventy-third Congress (March 4, 1933-January 3, 1935); unsuccessful candidate for reelection in 1934 to the Seventy-fourth Congress, and for election in 1936 to the Seventy-fifth Congress; resumed agricultural pursuits; unsuccessful candidate in 1942 for the Farmer-Labor nomination for United States Senator; retired from active business in 1944; died in Jordan Minn., October 6, 1963; interment in Calvary Cemetery.

**ARENTZ, Samuel Shaw (Ulysses),** a Representative from Nevada; born in Chicago, Ill., January 8, 1879; attended the public and high schools; was graduated from the Chicago Manual Training School in 1897 and from the South Dakota School of Mines at Rapid City in 1904; member of the South Dakota National Guard at Rapid City 1901-1904; moved to Ludering, Lyon County, Nev., in 1907, and to Salt Lake City, Utah, in 1912, and was engaged as surveyor, assessor, miner, and timberman in Bear Gulch and Butte, Mont., Bingham Canyon and Stockton, Utah, and the Lake Superior copper country; mining engineer and superintendent of mines in Idaho, Utah, Arizona, and Nevada; chief engineer of railway companies in Nevada; consulting engineer of the United States Bureau of Mines; captain of Engineers, United States Army, during the First World War; moved to a ranch in Lyon County, Nev., near Simpson, in 1917; also engaged in mining and irrigation projects; elected as a Republican to the Sixty-seventh Congress (March 4, 1921-March 3, 1923); was not a candidate for renomination but was an unsuccessful candidate in the 1922 primary election for the Republican nomination for United States Senator; elected to the Sixty-ninth and to the three succeeding Congresses (March 4, 1925-March 3, 1933); unsuccessful candidate for reelection in 1932 to the Seventy-third Congress; delegate to the Republican National Conventions in 1928 and 1932; again engaged as a rancher near Simpson; also resumed mining activities in Nevada and Utah; died in Reno, Nev., where he had gone to receive medical treatment, on June 17, 1934; interment in Mountain View Cemetery, Reno, Nev.

**ARMEY, Richard Keith,** a Representative from Texas; born in Cando, Towner County, N.Dak., July 7, 1940; attended the public schools; graduated, Cando High School, 1958; graduated from Jamestown College, Jamestown, N.Dak. in 1963; M.A., University of North Dakota, 1964; Ph.D., University of Oklahoma, 1968; taught economics at the University of Montana, 1964-1965; assistant professor, West Texas State University, 1967-1968; assistant professor, Austin College, 1968-1972; associate professor, North Texas State University, 1972-1977, and chairman of the economics department, 1977-1983; also served as an economic consultant and adviser; Distinguished Fellow of the Fisher Institute, Dallas, Tex.; elected as a Republican to the Ninety-ninth and to the five succeeding Congresses (January 3, 1985-January 3, 1997); majority leader (One Hundred Fourth Congress); is a resident of Flower Mound, Tex.

**ARMFIELD, Robert Franklin,** a Representative from North Carolina; born near Greensboro, Guilford County, N.C., July 9, 1829; attended the common schools and was graduated from Trinity College, Durham, N.C.; studied law; was admitted to the bar in 1845 and began practice in Yadkinville, N.C.; enlisted in the Confederate Army in 1861; served as lieutenant and later as lieutenant colonel of the Thirty-eighth Regiment of North Carolina State troops during the Civil War; moved to Statesville, N.C., and continued the practice of law; State solicitor for the sixth district in 1862 while on furlough from the Army; member of the State senate in 1874 and 1875, serving as president in 1874; Lieutenant Governor of North Carolina in 1875 and 1876; elected as a Democrat to the Forty-sixth and Forty-seventh Congresses (March 4, 1879-March 3, 1883); was not a candidate for renomination in 1882; resumed the practice of law; appointed and subsequently elected judge of the superior court and served from 1889 until January 1, 1895, when he retired; died in Statesville, Iredell County, N.C., November 9, 1898; interment in Oakwood Cemetery.

**ARMSTRONG, David Hartley,** a Senator from Missouri; born in Nova Scotia, Canada, October 21, 1812; attended Maine Wesleyan Seminary; taught school in New Bedford, Mass., 1833-1837; moved to St. Louis, Mo., in 1837, and then to Lebanon, Ill., where he taught at McKendree College; returned to Missouri and was principal of the public school at Benton 1838-1847; comptroller of St. Louis 1847-1850; postmaster of St. Louis 1854-1858; member of the board of police commissioners 1873-1876; served as a member of the board of freeholders which framed the charter of St. Louis in 1876; was appointed as a Democrat to the United States Senate to fill the vacancy caused by the death of Lewis V. Bogy, and served from September 29, 1877, to January 26, 1879, when a successor was elected and qualified; was not a candidate for election in 1879; died in St. Louis, Mo., March 18, 1893; interment in Bellefontaine Cemetery.

**ARMSTRONG, James** (son of John Armstrong [1717-1795] and brother of John Armstrong, Jr., [1758-1843]), a Representative from Pennsylvania; born in Carlisle, Cumberland County, Pa., August 29, 1748; attended the Philadelphia Academy and the College of New Jersey (now Princeton University); studied medicine in Dr. John Morgan's School in Philadelphia and was graduated from the University of Pennsylvania at Philadelphia in 1769; commenced the practice of medicine in Winchester, Frederick County, Va.; was a medical officer during the Revolutionary War; pursued medical studies in London, England, for three years; returned to Carlisle, Pa., in 1788; moved to Mifflin County, Pa., and practiced medicine there for twelve years; was appointed an associate judge; elected to the Third Congress (March 4, 1793-March 3, 1795); was not a candidate for renomination in 1794 to. the Fourth Congress; returned to Carlisle in 1796 and continued the practice of his profession; appointed as an associate judge of the Cumberland County Court and served from September 12, 1808, until his death in Carlisle, Pa., May 6, 1828; interment in the Old Carlisle Cemetery.

**ARMSTRONG, John** (father of James Armstrong and John Armstrong, Jr. [1758-1843]), a Delegate from Pennsylvania; born in Brookbor, County Fermanagh, Ireland, October 13, 1717; attended school in Ireland, and became a civil engineer; immigrated to the United States and settled in Carlisle, Cumberland County, Pa.; was presented a medal by the city of Philadelphia for destroying the Kittanning Indian towns, September 8, 1756; rendered distinguished service in the Continental Army, was commissioned a brigadier general in 1776, and served until April 4, 1777; appointed a major general of the Pennsylvania Militia and served throughout the Revolutionary War, with the exception of the term of his congressional service; Member of the Continental Congress 1779-1780; died in Carlisle, Pa., March 9, 1795; interment in Old Carlisle Cemetery.

**Bibliography:** Crist, Robert G. "John Armstrong, Sr.: Proprietary Man." Ph.D. dissertation, Pennsylvania State University, 1981.

**ARMSTRONG, John, Jr.** (son of John Armstrong and brother of James Armstrong), a Delegate from Pennsylvania and a Senator from New York; born in Carlisle, Cumberland County, Pa., November 25, 1758; attended Princeton College but left college to enter the Revolutionary Army; secretary of state of Pennsylvania from 1783 until 1787; adjutant general for several years; Member of the Continental Congress, 1787-1788; moved to Dutchess County, N.Y., in 1789 and settled near Lexington Manor; elected to the United States Senate to fill the vacancy in the term ending March 3, 1801, caused by the resignation of John Laurance; reelected in 1801, and served from November 6, 1800, to February 5, 1802, when he resigned; was next appointed to the Senate to fill the vacancy caused by the resignation of De Witt Clinton in the term ending March 3, 1807, subsequently elected to fill the vacancy in the term ending March 3, 1809, caused by the resignation of Theodorus Bailey, and served from November 10, 1803, until June 30, 1804, when he again resigned to enter the diplomatic service; appointed Minister to France on June 30, 1804 and served until September 1810; also acted as Minister to Spain in 1806; during the War of 1812 was commissioned brigadier general; appointed Secretary of War in the Cabinet of President James Madison, and served from January 13, 1813 until his resignation on September 27, 1814; engaged in literary pursuits; died in Red Hook, Dutchess County, N.Y., April 1, 1843; interment in Rhinebeck Cemetery, Rhinebeck, N.Y.

**Bibliography:** *DAB*; Skeen, C. Edward. *John Armstrong, Jr., 1758-1843; A Biography.* Syracuse, N.Y.: Syracuse University Press, 1981.

**ARMSTRONG, Moses Kimball,** a Delegate from the Territory of Dakota; born in Milan, Erie County, Ohio, September 19, 1832; attended Huron Institute and Western Reserve College, Cleveland, Ohio; moved to the Territory of Minnesota in 1856; elected surveyor of Mower County, and assigned to survey the United States lands in 1858; moved to Yankton, then a small Indian village, in Dakota Territory, when Minnesota Territory was admitted as a State; was a member of the first Territorial house of representatives in 1861; reelected in 1862 and 1863, serving as speaker in 1863; edited the Dakota Union in 1864; appointed clerk of the supreme court in 1865; elected to the Territorial council in 1866 and in 1867 was chosen president; acted as secretary of the Indian peace commission in 1867; established the great meridian and standard lines for United States surveys in southern Dakota and in the northern Red River Valley; again elected to the Territorial council, in 1869; elected as a Democrat a Delegate to the Forty-second and Forty-third Congresses (March 4, 1871-March 3, 1875); unsuccessful candidate for reelection in 1874 to the Forty-fourth Congress; moved to St. James, Watonwan County, Minn., and engaged in banking and in the real estate business; died in Albert Lea, Freeborn County, Minn., January 11, 1906; interment in Lakewood Cemetery, Minneapolis, Minn.

**Bibliography:** Fleetwood, Mary. "Moses K. Armstrong." *North Dakota History* 28 (Winter 1961): 13-22.

**ARMSTRONG, Orland Kay,** a Representative from Missouri; born in Willow Springs, Howell County, Mo., October 2, 1893; Drury College, Springfield, Mo., A.B., 1916; Cumberland University Law School, Lebanon, Tenn., LL.B., 1922; University of Missouri School of Journalism at Columbia, bachelor of journalism, M.A. in journalism, 1925; was admitted to the bar in 1922, but did not practice; teacher of English and public speaking at Southwest Baptist College, Bolivar, Mo., in 1916 and 1917; during the First World War served from private to lieutenant in the United States Army Air Corps 1917-1919; Y.M.C.A. welfare representative in France in 1919 and 1920; established department of journalism at University of Florida at Gainesville in 1925 and served as director 1925-1928; author, magazine writer, and newspaper correspondent; secretary of Missouri Century of Progress Commission 1930, 1932; delegate to Republican State conventions, 1932-1945, 1950, 1952, and 1966; delegate to Republican National Conventions in 1944 and 1952; member of the State house of representatives 1932-1936 and 1942-1944; member of editorial staff of Reader's Digest from 1944 until his death; member of the staff of the United States Senate Committee on Post Office and Civil Service in 1947 and 1948; elected as a Republican to the Eighty-second Congress (January 3, 1951-January 3, 1953); was not a candidate for renomination in 1952; was a resident of Springfield, Mo., until his death there April 15, 1987; interment in Greenlawn Cemetery.

**ARMSTRONG, William,** a Representative from Virginia; born in Lisburn, County Antrim, Ireland, December 23, 1782; immigrated to the United States in 1792 with his parents, who settled in Virginia; studied law in Winchester; United States tax collector in 1818 and 1819; member of the Virginia house of delegates in 1822 and 1823; elected to the Nineteenth and to the three succeeding Congresses (March 4, 1825-March 3, 1833); engaged in the tavern business in Romney, W.Va., until 1862; died in Keyser, W.Va., May 10, 1865; interment in Indian Mound Cemetery, Romney, W.Va.

**ARMSTRONG, William Hepburn,** a Representative from Pennsylvania; born in Williamsport, Lycoming County, Pa., September 7, 1824; attended the common schools, and was graduated from Princeton College in 1847; studied law; was admitted to the Pennsylvania bar and commenced practice in Williamsport, Pa.; served in the Pennsylvania house of representatives in 1860 and 1861; declined a commission as president judge of the twenty-sixth judicial circuit of Pennsylvania in 1862; elected as a Republican to the Forty-first Congress (March 4, 1869-March 3, 1871); unsuccessful candidate for reelection in 1870 to the Forty-second Congress; declined the office of commissioner of Indian affairs tendered by President Ulysses S. Grant; commissioner of railroads 1882-1885; resumed the practice of law in Washington, D.C., and Philadelphia, Pa., until 1898, when he retired from active business pursuits; moved to Wilmington, Del., where he died on May 14, 1919; interment in Wilmington and Brandywine Cemetery.

**ARMSTRONG, William Lester,** a Representative and a Senator from Colorado; born in Fremont, Dodge County, Nebr., March 16, 1937; attended the public schools; attended Tulane University, 1954-1955, and the University of Minnesota, 1956; served in the United States Army National Guard, 1957-1963; president of a radio station in Aurora, Colo.; banker; Colorado State representative, 1963-1964; Colorado State senator, 1965-1972, serving as majority leader, 1969-1972; elected as a Republican to the Ninety-third and to the two succeeding Congresses (January 3, 1973-January 3, 1979); was not a candidate in 1978 for reelection to the House of Representatives, but was elected to the United States Senate; reelected in 1984, and served from January 3, 1979 to January 3, 1991; was not a candidate for reelection in 1990; chairman, Republican Policy Committee (Ninety-ninth through One Hundred First Congresses); is a resident of Denver, Colo.

**ARNELL, Samuel Mayes,** a Representative from Tennessee; born at Zion Settlement, near Columbia, Maury County, Tenn., May 3, 1833; attended Amherst (Mass.) College; studied law; was admitted to the bar and commenced practice in Columbia; member of the constitutional convention of Tennessee in 1865; served in the Tennessee State house of representatives in 1865 and 1866; upon the readmission of the State of Tennessee to representation was elected as an Unconditional Unionist to the Thirty-ninth Congress; reelected as a Republican to the Fortieth and Forty-first Congresses, and served from July 24, 1866 to March 3, 1871; chairman, Committee on Expenditures in the Department of State (Fortieth Congress), Committee on Education and Labor (Forty-first Congress); was not a candidate for renomination in 1870 to the Forty-second Congress; resumed the practice of law in Washington, D.C.; returned to Columbia, Tenn.; postmaster of Columbia, 1879-1884; superintendent of schools, 1884-1886; died in Johnson City, Washington County, Tenn., July 20, 1903; interment in Monte Vista Cemetery.

**Bibliography:** Zebley, Kathleen R. "Unconditional Unionist: Samuel Mayes Arnell and Reconstruction in Tennessee." *Tennessee Historical Quarterly* 53 (Winter 1994): 246-259.

**ARNOLD, Benedict** (brother-in-law of Matthias J. Bovee), a Representative from New York; born in Amsterdam, Montgomery County, N.Y., October 5, 1780; attended the common schools; engaged in mercantile pursuits and also was an extensive landowner and philanthropist; supervisor of Amsterdam 1813-1816; member of the State assembly in 1816 and 1817; elected to the Twenty-first Congress (March 4, 1829-March 3, 1831); was not a candidate for reelection in 1830; president of the board of trustees of the village of Amsterdam in 1832; did not resume active business pursuits, but lived in retirement until his death in Amsterdam, N.Y., March 3, 1849; interment in Green Hill Cemetery.

**ARNOLD, Isaac Newton,** a Representative from Illinois; born in Hartwick, Otsego County, N.Y., November 30, 1815; attended the district and select schools and Hartwick Seminary; taught school in Otsego County from 1832 until 1835; studied law; was admitted to the bar in 1835 and commenced practice in Cooperstown, Otsego County, N.Y.; moved to Chicago, Ill., in 1836 and continued the practice of law; was elected city clerk of Chicago in 1837, but had served only a short time when he resigned to devote his entire efforts to his law practice; delegate to the Democratic State convention in 1842; member of the Illinois State house of

representatives in 1842 and 1843; presidential elector on the Democratic ticket in 1844; delegate to the Free-Soil National Convention at Buffalo in 1848; again a member of the State house of representatives in 1855, and was an unsuccessful candidate for speaker; unsuccessful candidate for nomination in 1858 to the Thirty-sixth Congress; elected as a Republican to the Thirty-seventh and Thirty-eighth Congresses (March 4, 1861-March 3, 1865); chairman, Committee on Roads and Canals (Thirty-eighth Congress); declined to be a candidate for renomination in 1864 to the Thirty-ninth Congress; during the Civil War acted as aide to Colonel Hunter at the Battle of Bull Run, July 21, 1861; served as Sixth Auditor of the United States Treasury, Washington, D.C., from April 29, 1865, to September 29, 1866, when he resigned; resumed the practice of law and also engaged in literary pursuits; died in Chicago, Ill., April 24, 1884; interment in Graceland Cemetery.

**Bibliography:** *DAB*.

**ARNOLD, Jonathan** (father of Lemuel Hastings Arnold and great-great-grandfather of Theodore Francis Green), a Delegate from Rhode Island; born in Providence, R.I., December 3, 1741; studied medicine and practiced; member of the general assembly of Rhode Island from Providence in 1776; served in the Revolutionary Army as surgeon; director of the Army hospital in Providence; Member of the Continental Congress 1782-1783; moved to St. Johnsbury, Vt., in 1787 and engaged in agricultural pursuits; appointed a member of the Governor's council; was appointed judge of Orange County and served until his death in St. Johnsbury, Caledonia County, Vt., February 1, 1793; interment in Mount Pleasant Cemetery.

**Bibliography:** *DAB*.

**ARNOLD, Laurence Fletcher,** a Representative from Illinois; born in Newton, Jasper County, Ill., June 8, 1891; attended the public and high schools of his native city and the University of Chicago, Chicago, Ill.; studied law; engaged in banking and in the wholesale hay and grain business at Newton, Ill., in 1916; served in the State house of representatives 1923-1927 and 1933-1937; delegate to the Democratic National Convention at New York in 1924; elected as a Democrat to the Seventy-fifth, Seventy-sixth, and Seventy-seventh Congresses (January 3, 1937-January 3, 1943); unsuccessful candidate for reelection in 1942 to the Seventy-eighth Congress and for election in 1950 to the Eighty-second Congress; resumed former business interests; president, Peoples State Bank; died in Newton, Ill., December 6, 1966; interment in Westlawn Memorial Park Cemetery.

**ARNOLD, Lemuel Hastings** (son of Jonathan Arnold and great-great-uncle of Theodore Francis Green), a Representative from Rhode Island; born in St. Johnsbury, Vt., January 29, 1792; was graduated from Dartmouth College, Hanover, N.H., in 1811; studied law; was admitted to the bar in 1814 and commenced practice in Providence, R.I.; engaged in manufacturing and mercantile pursuits in 1821; member of the Rhode Island State house of representatives, 1826-1831; elected Governor of Rhode Island in 1831, reelected in 1832, and served from May 4, 1831 to May 1, 1833; unsuccessful candidate for reelection in 1833; member of the executive council during Dorr's Rebellion of 1842, directed against the government of Rhode Island for its failure to enact constitutional reforms; unsuccessful candidate for United States Senator in 1845; elected as a Whig to the Twenty-ninth Congress (March 4, 1845-March 3, 1847); was not a candidate for renomination in 1846; moved to South Kingston in 1847 and continued the practice of law until his death on June 27, 1852; interment in Swan Point Cemetery, Providence, R.I.

**ARNOLD, Marshall,** a Representative from Missouri; born at Cook Settlement, near Farmington, St. Francois County, Mo., October 21, 1845; attended the common schools; professor at Arcadia

College in 1870 and 1871; deputy clerk of the circuit, county, and probate courts of St. Francois County, Mo.; studied law; was admitted to the bar in 1872 and commenced practice in Commerce, Scott County, Mo.; prosecuting attorney of Scott County 1873-1876; member of the State house of representatives 1877-1879; elected as a Democrat to the Fifty-second and Fifty-third Congresses (March 4, 1891-March 3, 1895); unsuccessful candidate for reelection in 1894 to the Fifty-fourth Congress; resumed the practice of law in Benton, Scott County, Mo., and died there June 12, 1913; interment in Benton Cemetery.

**ARNOLD, Peleg,** a Delegate from Rhode Island; born in Smithfield, R.I., June 10, 1751; attended the common schools and Brown University, Providence, R.I.; studied law; was admitted to the bar and practiced; elected deputy to the general assembly of Rhode Island, serving from October 1777 to October 1778, and from May 1782 to May 1783; colonel of the Second Regiment of Providence County Militia in 1780; Member of the Continental Congress, 1787-1788; keeper of the "Peleg Arnold Tavern," at Smithfield, R.I.; assistant governor of Rhode Island in 1790; incorporator of the Providence Society for the Abolition of Slavery in 1790; unsuccessful Anti-Federalist candidate for election to the Fourth Congress in 1794, and also an unsuccessful Republican candidate for election to the same Congress to fill the vacancy caused by the resignation of Benjamin Bourne in 1796; chief justice of the supreme court of Rhode Island from June 1795 to June 1809, and again from May 1810 to May 1812; president of the Smithfield Union Bank in 1803; president of Smithfield Academy in 1810; again served as deputy to the general assembly of Rhode Island from October 1817 to May 1819; died in Smithfield, R.I., February 13, 1820; interment in Union Cemetery, opposite the Friends Meeting House, in Union Village, near Woonsocket, R.I.

**ARNOLD, Samuel,** a Representative from Connecticut; born in Haddam, Conn., June 1, 1806; attended the local academy at Plainfield, Conn., and Westfield Academy, Massachusetts; devoted most of his life to agricultural pursuits; acquired a controlling interest in a stone quarry and became owner of a line of schooners operating between New York and Philadelphia; was, also, for a number of years, president of the Bank of East Haddam; member of the State house of representatives in 1839, 1842, 1844, and again in 1851; elected as a Democrat to the Thirty-fifth Congress (March 4, 1857-March 3, 1859); declined to be a candidate for renomination in 1858; resumed agricultural pursuits and quarrying; died in Haddam, Middlesex County, Conn., May 5, 1869; interment in a mausoleum on his estate near Haddam.

**ARNOLD, Samuel Greene** (granduncle of Theodore Francis Green), a Senator from Rhode Island; born in Providence, R.I., April 12, 1821; received his early education under private tutors; was graduated from Brown University, Providence, R.I., in 1841 and from the law department of Harvard University in 1845; was admitted to the bar in 1845; lawyer and historian; trustee of Brown University, 1848-1880; elected lieutenant governor of Rhode Island in 1852; member of the peace commission held at Washington, D.C., in 1861 in an effort to devise means to prevent the impending war; again elected lieutenant governor in 1861 and 1862; during the Civil War organized a company of light artillery which went to Washington, D.C., and was mustered into the Union Army; elected as a Republican to the United States Senate to fill the vacancy caused by the resignation of James F. Simmons, and served from December 1, 1862 to March 3, 1863; returned to historical research; president of the Rhode Island Historical Society, 1868-1880; died in Providence, R.I., February 14, 1880; interment in Swan Point Cemetery.

Bibliography: *DAB.*

**ARNOLD, Samuel Washington,** a Representative from Missouri; born on a farm near Downing, Schuyler County, Mo., September 21, 1879; attended the Coffey, Mo., rural schools and was graduated from Kirksville (Mo.) State Teachers College in 1902; taught school in the Coffey, Mo., school district in 1896; superintendent of the public schools in Middletown, Mo., in 1901 and 1902 and in Atlanta, Mo., in 1903; employed in the St. Louis, Mo., internal revenue office in 1904; engaged in the retail lumber business at Atlanta, Mo., 1905-1908; moved to Kirksville, Mo., in 1908 and organized the Arnold Lumber Co.; elected as a Republican to the Seventy-eighth, Seventy-ninth, and Eightieth Congresses (January 3, 1943-January 3, 1949); unsuccessful candidate for reelection in 1948 to the Eighty-first Congress, for election in 1950 to the Eighty-second Congress, and in 1952 to the Eighty-third Congress; retired from political and business activities in 1952; died in Kirksville, Mo., December 18, 1961; interment in Maple Hills Cemetery.

**ARNOLD, Thomas Dickens,** a Representative from Tennessee; born in Spotsylvania County, Va., May 3, 1798; moved with his parents to Knox County, Tenn., in 1808; was tutored privately; at the age of fourteen enlisted as a drummer boy in the War of 1812; taught school in Knox and Grainger Counties; studied law; was admitted to the bar in 1820 and commenced practice in Knoxville, Tenn.; elected as an Anti-Jacksonian to the Twenty-second Congress (March 4, 1831-March 3, 1833); an attempt was made by Morgan A. Heard to assassinate him on May 14, 1832, as he descended the west steps of the Capitol; was made brigadier general of the Tennessee Militia in 1836; moved to Greeneville, Tenn.; elected as a Whig to the Twenty-seventh Congress (March 4, 1841-March 3, 1843); chairman, Committee on Claims (Twenty-seventh Congress); was not a candidate for reelection to the Twenty-eighth Congress; resumed the practice of law in Greeneville; died while attending court in Jonesboro, Washington County, Tenn., May 26, 1870; interment in Oak Grove Cemetery, Greeneville, Tenn.

**ARNOLD, Warren Otis,** a Representative from Rhode Island; born in Coventry, Kent County, R.I., June 3, 1839; attended the common schools; engaged in mercantile pursuits at Coventry from 1857 to 1864; was a manufacturer of cotton goods in Chepachet and Westerly, R.I., until 1866, when he began the manufacture of woolen goods; elected as a Republican to the Fiftieth and Fifty-first Congresses (March 4, 1887-March 3, 1891); was a candidate for reelection in 1890 to the Fifty-second Congress, but as neither candidate received a majority the general assembly ordered a new election, in which he declined to be a participant; elected to the Fifty-fourth Congress (March 4, 1895-March 3, 1897); declined to be a candidate for renomination in 1896; continued his former manufacturing pursuits until his death in Westerly, Washington County, R.I., April 1, 1910; interment in Acotes Hill Cemetery, Chepachet, R.I.

**ARNOLD, William Carlile,** a Representative from Pennsylvania; born in Luthersburg, Clearfield County, Pa., July 15, 1851; attended the public schools and Phillips Academy, Andover, Mass.; studied law; was admitted to the bar in Clearfield County, Pa., June 18, 1875, and practiced in Curwensville and Du Bois, Clearfield County, Pa.; elected as a Republican to the Fifty-fourth and Fifty-fifth Congresses (March 4, 1895-March 3, 1899); unsuccessful candidate for reelection in 1898 to the Fifty-sixth Congress; resumed the practice of law in Clearfield County, Pa.; died in Muskegon, Mich., while on a business trip to that city, March 20, 1906; interment in Oak Hill Cemetery, Curwensville, Pa.

**ARNOLD, William Wright,** a Representative from Illinois; born in Oblong, Crawford County, Ill., October 14, 1877; attended the country schools of his native county and Austin College, Effingham, Ill.; was graduated from the law department of the University of Illinois at Urbana in 1901; was admitted to the bar the same year and commenced the practice of law in Robinson, Crawford County, Ill.; was continuously engaged in the practice of his chosen profession until elected to Congress; elected as a Democrat to the Sixty-eighth and to the six succeeding Congresses and served from March 4, 1923, until his resignation, effective September 16, 1935, having been appointed July 29, 1935, a member of the United States Board of Tax Appeals (now the Tax Court of the United States); reappointed in 1944 and served until his retirement June 30, 1950; owned and operated two large farms; director of the Second National Bank, Farmers and Producers Bank, and the First National Bank of Robinson; died in Robinson, Ill., November 23, 1957; interment in New Cemetery.

**ARNOT, John, Jr.,** a Representative from New York; born in Elmira, Chemung County, N.Y., March 11, 1831; educated at private schools in his native city; entered Yale College, but left before graduation to enter business; upon the death of his father became engaged in banking in Elmira; president of the village 1859-1864; president of the board of trustees of the village of Elmira in 1859, 1860, and 1864; during the Civil War served as Army paymaster with the rank of major in Elmira; when the village of Elmira was chartered as a city, was elected mayor in 1864, 1870, and 1874; declined the proffered nomination as Democratic candidate for Congress in 1882, but accepted nomination at a subsequent convention; elected as a Democrat to the Forty-eighth and Forty-ninth Congresses and served from March 4, 1883, until his death in Elmira, N.Y., November 20, 1886; interment in Woodlawn Cemetery.

**ARRINGTON, Archibald Hunter** (uncle of Archibald Hunter Arrington Williams), a Representative from North Carolina; born near Nashville, Nash County, N.C., November 13, 1809; attended the local academy at Hilliardston and Louisburg (N.C.) College; studied law; was a large landowner, extensively engaged in planting; elected as a Democrat to the Twenty-seventh and Twenty-eighth Congresses (March 4, 1841-March 3, 1845); unsuccessful candidate for reelection in 1844 to the Twenty-ninth Congress; was a supporter of the Confederacy and a member of the secession convention in 1861; member of the First Confederate Congress in 1861; unsuccessful candidate for reelection in 1863 to the Second Confederate Congress; delegate to the Union National Convention at Philadelphia in 1866; chairman of the court of common pleas and quarter sessions for Nash County in 1866 and 1867; county commissioner in 1868; engaged in the management of his estate; died at his country home near Nashville, Nash County, N.C., July 20, 1872; interment in the family graveyard on his plantation.

**ARTHUR, Chester Alan,** a Vice President and 21st President of the United States; born in Fairfield, Franklin County, Vt., October 5, 1829; attended the public schools and was graduated from Union College, Schenectady, N.Y., in July 1848; became principal of an academy in North Pownal, Vt., in 1851, and of an academy in Cohoes, N.Y., in 1852; studied law; was admitted to the bar in May 1854 and commenced practice in New York City; took an active part in the reorganization of the State militia; during the Civil War, served as acting quartermaster general of the State in 1861; commissioned inspector general, appointed quartermaster general with the rank of brigadier general, and served until 1862; resumed the practice of law in New York City; appointed by President Ulysses S. Grant as collector of the New York Customhouse, and served from December 1, 1871 until suspended by President Rutherford B. Hayes on July 11, 1878; resumed the practice of law in New York City; elected Vice President of the United States, November 2, 1880, on the Republican ticket with James A. Garfield for the term beginning March 4, 1881; upon the death of President Garfield, became President of the United States on September 20, 1881, and served until March 3, 1885; returned to New York City, where he

died on November 18, 1886; interment in the Rural Cemetery Albany, N.Y.

**Bibliography:** *DAB*; Howe, George. *Chester A. Arthur, a Quarter-century of Machine Politics. 1935.* Reprint. New York: F. Ungar and Co., 1957; Reeves, Thomas C. *Gentleman Boss: The Life of Chester Alan Arthur.* New York: Knopf, 1975.

**ARTHUR, William Evans,** a Representative from Kentucky; born in Cincinnati, Ohio, March 3, 1825; moved with his parents to Covington, Ky., where he received instruction from private tutors and also in private schools; studied law; was admitted to the bar in 1850 and commenced practice in Covington; Commonwealth attorney for the ninth judicial district of Kentucky 1856-1862; presidential elector on the Democratic ticket of Breckinridge and Lane in 1860; appointed judge of the ninth judicial circuit in 1866 and served until 1868, when he resigned; elected as a Democrat to the Forty-second and Forty-third Congresses (March 4, 1871-March 3, 1875); was not a candidate for renomination in 1874; resumed the practice of law in Covington; became judge of the twelfth judicial circuit of Kentucky in 1886 and served until 1893, when he resigned; engaged in the practice of law until his death in Covington, Ky., May 18, 1897; interment in Linden Grove Cemetery.

**ASH, Michael Woolston,** a Representative from Pennsylvania; born in Philadelphia, Pa., March 5, 1789; studied law; was admitted to the bar June 21, 1811, and commenced practice in Philadelphia; served as a first lieutenant and lieutenant colonel in the First Regular Pennsylvania Volunteers during the War of 1812; at the close of the war went into partnership with James Buchanan, who subsequently was a President of the United States, and continued the practice of his profession in Philadelphia; elected as a Jacksonian to the Twenty-fourth Congress (March 4, 1835-March 3, 1837); was not a candidate for reelection in 1836 to the Twenty-fifth Congress; again engaged in the practice of his profession until his death in Philadelphia, Pa., December 14, 1858; interment in Christ Church Burial Ground, located at Fifth and Arch Streets.

**ASHBROOK, Jean Spencer** (wife of John Milan Ashbrook), a Representative from Ohio; born in Cincinnati, Hamilton County, Ohio, September 21, 1934; attended Central School, Newark, Ohio; graduated, Newark High School, 1952; B.S., Ohio State University, Columbus, 1956; elected as a Republican to the Ninety-seventh Congress, by special election, June 29, 1982, to fill the vacancy caused by the death of her husband, John Milan Ashbrook, and served from July 12, 1982, until January 3, 1983; is a resident of Newark, Ohio.

**ASHBROOK, John Milan** (son of William Albert Ashbrook and husband of Jean Spencer Ashbrook), a Representative from Ohio; born in Johnstown, Licking County, Ohio, September 21, 1928; graduated from Johnstown High School in 1946; served in the United States Navy, 1946-1948; member of the Byrd Antarctic Expedition, 1946-1947; A.B., Harvard University, 1952; J.D., Ohio State University Law School, 1955; was admitted to the bar in 1955 and commenced the practice of law in Johnstown, Ohio; publisher of the Johnstown Independent, a weekly newspaper; member, Ohio State house of representatives, 1957-1961; national chairman of Young Republican Clubs, 1957-1959; delegate to the Republican National Conventions of 1964 and 1968; elected as a Republican to the Eighty-seventh and to the ten succeeding Congresses, and served from January 3, 1961 until his death in Johnstown, Ohio, on April 24, 1982; cremated and ashes interred at Green Hill Cemetery.

**ASHBROOK, William Albert** (father of John Milan Ashbrook), a Representative from Ohio; born near Johnstown, Licking County, Ohio, July 1, 1867; attended the public schools, and Bartlett's Business College, Lansing, Mich.; in 1885 engaged in the newspaper publishing business in Johnstown, Ohio; also engaged in banking; served as postmaster of Johnstown from 1893 to 1897, when his successor was appointed; secretary of the National Editorial Association, 1902-1906; member, Ohio State house of representatives, 1904-1905; elected as a Democrat to the Sixtieth and to the six succeeding Congresses (March 4, 1907-March 3, 1921); chairman, Committee on Expenditures in the Post Office Department (Sixty-second Congress), Committee on Coinage, Weights, and Measures (Sixty-fourth and Sixty-fifth Congresses); unsuccessful candidate for reelection in 1920 to the Sixty-seventh Congress; resumed the newspaper publishing business and banking in Johnstown, Ohio; elected to the Seventy-fourth and to the two succeeding Congresses, and served from January 3, 1935 until his death in Johnstown, Ohio, January 1, 1940; interment in Green Hill Cemetery.

**ASHCROFT, John David,** a Senator from Missouri; born in Chicago, Ill., May 9, 1942; graduated Hillcrest High School Springfield, Mo.; A.B., Yale University, 1964, J.D., University of Chicago School of Law, 1967; unsuccessful candidate in 1972 for election to the Ninety-third Congress; Missouri State auditor, 1973-1975; Missouri State assistant attorney general, 1975-1976; elected Missouri State attorney general in 1976 and served from 1976 to 1985; elected Governor of Missouri in 1984, reelected in 1988, and served from January 14, 1985 to January 11, 1993; elected as a Republican to the United States Senate in 1994 for the term ending January 3, 2001; is a resident of Ballwin, Mo.

**ASHE, John Baptista** (uncle of John Baptista Ashe [1810-1857], Thomas Samuel Ashe, and William Shepperd Ashe), a Delegate and a Representative from North Carolina; born in Rocky Point, N.C., in 1748; was privately tutored at home; engaged in agricultural pursuits; served throughout the Revolutionary War and attained the rank of colonel in command of North Carolina troops at Valley Forge, and at the Battle of Eutaw Springs, S.C., September 9, 1781; member of the State house of commons 1784-1786, serving as speaker of the house in 1786; Member of the Continental Congress in 1787 and served until November 1, 1787, when he resigned; served as chairman of the committee of the whole in the State convention of 1789 that ratified the Constitution of the United States; member of the State senate in 1789; elected to the First and Second Congresses and served from March 24, 1790, until March 3, 1793; resumed agricultural pursuits; again served in the State senate in 1795; elected Governor of North Carolina in 1802, but died in Halifax, N.C., November 27, 1802, before being inaugurated; interment in the Churchyard Cemetery, Halifax, N.C.

**Bibliography:** *DAB.*

**ASHE, John Baptista** (brother of William Shepperd Ashe, nephew of John Baptista Ashe [1748-1802], and cousin of Thomas Samuel Ashe), a Representative from Tennessee; born in Rocky Point, Pender County, N.C., in 1810; attended Fayetteville Academy and was graduated from Trinity College, Hartford, Conn., in 1830; studied law; was admitted to the bar in 1832; moved to Tennessee and commenced practice in Brownsville; elected as a Whig to the Twenty-eighth Congress (March 4, 1843-March 3, 1845); moved to Galveston County, Tex., and settled near Galveston; continued the practice of his chosen profession until his death in Galveston, Tex., December 29, 1857; interment in a cemetery near Galveston.

**ASHE, Thomas Samuel** (nephew of John Baptista Ashe of North Carolina and cousin of John Baptista Ashe of Tennessee and of William Shepperd Ashe), a Representative from North Carolina; born in Hawfields, near Graham, Alamance County (then a part of Orange County), N.C., July 19, 1812; attended Bingham's Academy, Hillsboro, N.C., and was graduated from the University of North Carolina at Chapel Hill in 1832; studied law; was admitted to the bar in 1834 and commenced practice in Wadesboro, Anson County, in 1835; member of the North Carolina State house of commons in 1842; solicitor of the fifth judicial district of North Carolina, 1847-1851; elected to the State senate in 1854; Member of the

Confederate house of representatives, 1861-1864; elected to the Confederate senate in 1864, but did not serve due to the termination of the Civil War; served as State councilor in 1866; unsuccessful Conservative candidate for Governor of North Carolina in 1868; elected as a Democrat to the Forty-third and Forty-fourth Congresses (March 4, 1873-March 3, 1877); declined to be a candidate for renomination in 1876 to the Forty-fifth Congress; resumed the practice of law at Wadesboro; elected associate justice of the State supreme court in 1878; reelected in 1886 for a term of eight years, and served until his death in Wadesboro, Anson County, N.C., on February 4, 1887; interment in East View Cemetery.

**Bibliography:** *DAB.*

**ASHE, William Shepperd** (brother of John Baptista Ashe of Tennessee, nephew of John Baptista Ashe of North Carolina and cousin of Thomas Samuel Ashe), a Representative from North Carolina; born in Rocky Point, N.C., September 14, 1814; attended school at Fayetteville, N.C., and pursued classical studies in Trinity College, Hartford, Conn.; engaged in the cultivation of rice; studied law; was admitted to the North Carolina bar in 1836 and commenced the practice of law in New Hanover County, N.C., the same year; presidential elector of the Democratic ticket in 1844; member of the North Carolina State senate, 1846-1848; elected as a Democrat to the Thirty-first and to the two succeeding Congresses (March 4, 1849-March 3, 1855); chairman, Committee on Elections (Thirty-second Congress); was not a candidate for renomination in 1854 to the Thirty-fourth Congress; served as president of the Wilmington and Weldon Railroad Company from 1854 until his death; again a member of the North Carolina State senate, 1859-1861; delegate to the Democratic National Convention at Charleston in 1860; member of the North Carolina Constitutional Convention in 1861; during the Civil War served as a major in the Confederate Army, in charge of all transportation from the South to Virginia; killed in a railroad accident near Wilmington, N.C., September 14, 1862; interment in the family burying ground at "The Neck," near Ashton, Pender County, N.C.

**Bibliography:** *DAB.*

**ASHLEY, Chester,** a Senator from Arkansas; born in Massachusetts, June 1, 1790; moved with his parents to Hudson, N.Y.; attended the common schools and was graduated from Williams College, Williamstown, Mass., and the Litchfield (Conn.) Law School; was admitted to the bar in 1817 and commenced the practice of law in Hudson, N.Y.; moved to Little Rock, Ark., in 1820; elected as a Democrat to the United States Senate in 1844 to fill the vacancy caused by the death of William S. Fulton; reelected in 1846, and served from November 8, 1844, until his death in Washington, D.C., April 29, 1848; chairman, Committee on the Judiciary (Twenty-ninth and Thirtieth Congresses); interment in Mt. Holly Cemetery, Little Rock, Ark.

**ASHLEY, Delos Rodeyn,** a Representative from Nevada; born at The Post, Ark., February 19, 1828; received an academic education; studied law; was admitted to the bar in 1849 and practiced; moved to California in 1849 and continued the practice of law in Monterey in 1850; district attorney, 1851-1853; member of the California State house of representatives in 1854 and 1855; served in the State senate in 1856 and 1857; State treasurer of California in 1862 and 1863; moved to Virginia City, Storey County, Nev., in 1864 and continued the practice of law; elected as a Republican to the Thirty-ninth and Fortieth Congresses (March 4, 1865-March 3, 1869); was not a candidate for renomination in 1868 to the Forty-first Congress; moved to Pioche, Lincoln County, Nev., in 1871 and resumed the practice of law; due to failing health moved to San Francisco, Calif., in 1872, and lived in retirement until his death there on July 18, 1873; interment in Calvary Cemetery.

**ASHLEY, Henry,** a Representative from New York; born in Winchester, Cheshire County, N.H., February 19, 1778; attended the common schools; clerk of Winchester village in 1811; justice of the peace in 1817; engaged in the manufacture of leather in Catskill, Greene County, N.Y.; chairman of the tanners' association in 1825; elected to the Nineteenth Congress (March 4, 1825-March 3, 1827); was not a candidate for reelection in 1826; resumed his former business pursuits; president of the board of trustees of the village of Catskill in 1828; trustee of the apprentices' library in 1828; died in Catskill, N.Y., January 14, 1829; interment in Thomson Street Cemetery.

**ASHLEY, James Mitchell** (great-grandfather of Thomas William Ludlow Ashley), a Representative from Ohio; born near Pittsburgh, Pa., November 14, 1824; instructed himself in elementary subjects while employed as a clerk on boats operating on the Ohio and Mississippi Rivers; editor of the Dispatch, and afterwards of the Democrat, in Portsmouth, Ohio; studied law; was admitted to the bar in 1849 but never practiced; moved to Toledo, Ohio, and engaged in the wholesale drug business; elected as a Republican to the Thirty-sixth and to the four succeeding Congresses (March 4, 1859-March 3, 1869); chairman, Committee on Territories (Thirty-seventh through Fortieth Congresses); unsuccessful candidate for reelection in 1868 to the Forty-first Congress; delegate to the Philadelphia Loyalists' Convention in 1866; Governor of the Territory of Montana in 1869; constructed the Toledo, Ann Arbor and Northern Railroad, and served as president from 1877 to 1893; died in Alma, Gratiot County, Mich., September 16, 1896; interment in Woodlawn Cemetery, Toledo, Ohio.

**Bibliography:** *DAB*; Horowitz, Robert F. *The Great Impeacher: A Political Biography of James M. Ashley.* New York: Brooklyn College Press, 1979; Kahn, Maxine B. "Congressman Ashley in the Post-Civil War Years." *Northwest Ohio Quarterly* 36 (1964): 116-33, 194-210.

**ASHLEY, Thomas William Ludlow (Lud)** (great-grandson of James Mitchell Ashley), a Representative from Ohio; born in Toledo, Lucas County, Ohio, January 11, 1923; attended the Monroe and Glenwood elementary schools, and Kent School, Kent, Conn., 1939-1942; during the Second World War served in the United States Army as a corporal with service in the Pacific Theater of Operations, 1943-1945; B.A., Yale University, 1948; associated with Toledo Publicity and Efficiency Commission in 1948; studied law in evening classes at the University of Toledo Law School; LL.B., Ohio State University Law School, Columbus, 1951; was admitted to the bar in 1951 and commenced the practice of law in Whitehouse and Toledo, Ohio; in 1952 joined the staff of Radio Free Europe, serving in Europe as codirector of the press section and later as assistant director of special projects, resigning March 1, 1954; elected as a Democrat to the Eighty-fourth and to the twelve succeeding Congresses (January 3, 1955-January 3, 1981); chairman, Select Committee on Energy (Ad Hoc) (Ninety-fifth Congress), Committee on Merchant Marine and Fisheries (Ninety-sixth Congress); unsuccessful candidate for reelection in 1980 to the Ninety-seventh Congress; founder and since 1981 president of a legal and congressional consulting firm in Washington, D.C.; is a resident of Washington, D.C.

**ASHLEY, William Henry,** a Representative from Missouri; born in Powhatan County, Va., in 1778; attended the common schools; moved to St. Genevieve, Mo. (then Upper Louisiana), in 1803; engaged in the manufacture of saltpeter; became a merchant and later a surveyor; moved to St. Louis, Mo., in 1808; brigadier general of militia during the War of 1812; traded with the Indians and dealt in furs; unsuccessful candidate for governor in 1824; founded an organization which in 1830 became the Rocky Mountain Fur Co., and conducted trading and exploring expeditions to the headwaters of the Missouri River; elected as the first lieutenant governor of

Missouri and served from 1820 to 1824; elected as a Jacksonian to the Twenty-second Congress to fill the vacancy caused by the death of Spencer D. Pettis; reelected to the Twenty-third and Twenty-fourth Congresses and served from October 31, 1831, to March 3, 1837; did not seek renomination in 1836 to the Twenty-fifth Congress, but was an unsuccessful candidate for election for Governor of Missouri; died near Boonville, Mo., March 26, 1838; interment in an Indian mound overlooking the Missouri River, near his home, on the Lamine River, in Cooper County, Mo.

**Bibliography:** *DAB*; Ashley, William H. "The Diary of William H. Ashley." Edited by Dale L. Morgan. *Bulletin of the Missouri Historical Society* 11 (1954-55): 9-40, 158-86, 279-302; Clokey, Richard M. *William H. Ashley: Enterprise and Politics in the Trans-Mississippi West.* Norman: University of Oklahoma Press, 1980.

**ASHMORE, John Durant** (cousin of Robert Thomas Ashmore), a Representative from South Carolina; born in Greenville District, S.C., August 18, 1819; attended the common schools; studied law; was admitted to the bar but never practiced; engaged in agricultural pursuits; member of the State house of representatives 1848-1853; comptroller general of the State 1853-1857; elected as a Democrat to the Thirty-sixth Congress and served from March 4, 1859 until December 21, 1860, when he joined other secessionist members of the South Carolina delegation in withdrawing from the Thirty-sixth Congress; chairman, Committee on Mileage (Thirty-sixth Congress); during the Civil War was elected colonel of the Fourth South Carolina Regiment, but resigned before the regiment was called into service; engaged in mercantile pursuits in Greenville, S.C.; died in Sardis, Miss., December 5, 1871; interment in Black Jack Cemetery, near Sardis, in Panola County.

**ASHMORE, Robert Thomas** (cousin of John Durant Ashmore), a Representative from South Carolina; born on a farm near Greenville, S.C., February 22, 1904; attended the public schools of Greenville; was graduated from Furman University Law School, Greenville, S.C., in 1927; while a student engaged in agricultural work, retail sales, and as a substitute rural mail carrier; was admitted to the bar in January 1928 and engaged in the practice of law in Greenville, S.C.; solicitor of Greenville County Court 1930-1934; solicitor of the thirteenth judicial circuit of South Carolina 1936-1953; during the Second World War, while on official leave from duties as solicitor, volunteered for service in the United States Army in December 1942, serving in this country and overseas until discharged from active duty in May 1946, as a lieutenant colonel in the United States Army Reserve; promoted to colonel in 1955; elected as a Democrat to the Eighty-third Congress to fill the vacancy caused by the death of Joseph R. Bryson; reelected to the Eighty-fourth and to the six succeeding Congresses (June 2, 1953-January 3, 1969); was not a candidate for reelection in 1968 to the Ninety-first Congress; resumed the practice of law; member of the board, South Carolina Appalachian Regional Planning and Development Commission (later South Carolina Appalachian Council of Governments), and chairman, 1970-1972; was a resident of Greenville, S.C.; died October 5, 1989.

**ASHMUN, Eli Porter** (father of George Ashmun), a Senator from Massachusetts; born in a small village north of Albany on the Hudson River, June 24, 1770; attended the village school; member of the Massachusetts house of representatives 1803-1804; graduated from Middlebury College, Middlebury, Vt., in 1807; studied law; was admitted to the bar and commenced practice in Blandford; moved to Northampton, Mass., in 1807 and continued the practice of law; member, Massachusetts senate 1808-1810, 1813; member, Governor's council 1816; elected to the United States Senate to fill the vacancy caused by the resignation of Christopher Gore and served from June 12, 1816, to May 10, 1818, when he resigned; died in

Northampton, Mass., May 10, 1819; interment in Bridge Street Cemetery.

**ASHMUN, George** (son of Eli Porter Ashmun), a Representative from Massachusetts; born in Blandford, Hampden County, Mass., December 25, 1804; moved to Northampton with his parents in 1807; attended the local schools; was graduated from Yale College in 1823; studied law; was admitted to the bar and commenced practice in Springfield in 1828; member of the Massachusetts house of representatives in 1833, 1835, 1836, 1838, and 1841, serving as speaker in 1841; member of the Massachusetts senate in 1838 and 1839; elected as a Whig to the Twenty-ninth, Thirtieth, and Thirty-first Congresses (March 4, 1845-March 3, 1851); was not a candidate for renomination in 1850; resumed the practice of law in Springfield; chairman of the Republican National Convention at Chicago in 1860; director of the Union Pacific Railroad Co.; delegate to the Union National Convention at Philadelphia in 1866; died in Springfield, Hampden County, Mass., July 16, 1870; interment in Springfield Cemetery.

**Bibliography:** *DAB.*

**ASHURST, Henry Fountain,** a Senator from Arizona; born in Winnemucca, Humboldt County, Nev., September 13, 1874; moved with his parents to Arizona in 1875 and settled near the present town of Flagstaff, Coconino County; attended the public schools of Flagstaff and was graduated from the Stockton (Calif.) Business College in 1896; studied law and political economy at the University of Michigan at Ann Arbor; was admitted to the bar in 1897 and commenced practice in Williams, Ariz.; member of the Territorial house of representatives in 1897 and 1899, serving as speaker in 1899; served in the Territorial senate in 1903; district attorney of Coconino County 1905-1908; moved to Prescott, Ariz., in 1909 and continued the practice of law; upon the admission of Arizona as a State was elected as a Democrat to the United States Senate on March 27, 1912; reelected in 1916, 1922, 1928, and again in 1934, and served from March 27, 1912, to January 3, 1941; unsuccessful candidate for renomination in 1940; chairman, Committee on Indian Affairs (Sixty-third through Sixty-fifth Congresses), Committee on Industrial Expositions (Sixty-third Congress), Committee to Investigate Trespassers on Indian Land (Sixty-sixth Congress), Committee on the Judiciary (Seventy-third through Seventy-sixth Congresses); appointed a member of the Board of Immigration Appeals in the Department of Justice on April 8, 1941, and served until February 28, 1943, when he retired; died in Washington, D.C., May 31, 1962; interment in Sacred Heart Cemetery, Prescott, Ariz.

**Bibliography:** *DAB;* Ashurst, Henry F. *A Many-Colored Toga.* Tucson: University of Arizona Press, 1962.

**ASPER, Joel Funk,** a Representative from Missouri; born in Adams County, Pa., April 20, 1822; moved to Ohio with his parents, who settled in Trumbull County in 1827; attended the public schools and the local college in Warren, Ohio; studied law; was admitted to the bar in 1844 and commenced practice in Warren, Ohio; justice of the peace in 1846; prosecuting attorney of Geauga County in 1847; delegate to the Buffalo Free-Soil Convention in 1848; editor of the Western Reserve Chronicle in 1849; moved to Iowa in 1850 and published the Chardon Democrat; raised a company for the Civil War in 1861 and served as its captain; was wounded in the Battle of Winchester, Va.; promoted to the rank of lieutenant colonel in 1862; mustered out of the service in 1863 because of wounds received in action; moved to Chillicothe, Livingston County, Mo., in 1864 and resumed the practice of law; founded the Spectator in 1866; delegate to the Republican National Convention in 1868; elected as a Republican to the Forty-first Congress (March 4, 1869-March 3, 1871); was not a candidate for renomination in 1870 to the Forty-second Congress; practiced law until his death; died in Chillicothe, Mo., October 1, 1872; interment in Edgewood Cemetery.

**ASPIN, Leslie,** a Representative from Wisconsin; born in Milwaukee, Wis., July 21, 1938; graduated from Shorewood High School, Milwaukee; B.A., Yale University, 1960; M.A., Oxford University, England, 1962; Ph.D., economics, Massachusetts Institute of Technology, 1965; systems analyst to the Secretary of Defense while serving in the United States Army, captain, 1966-68; staff member to Senator William Proxmire in 1960, and was director of his 1964 campaign for reelection; staff assistant to Walter Heller, chairman of President John F. Kennedy's Council of Economic Advisers, 1963; unsuccessful candidate for nomination for Wisconsin State Treasurer, 1968; professor of economics, Marquette University, Milwaukee, Wis., 1969-70; elected as a Democrat to the Ninety-second and to the eleven succeeding Congresses, and served from January 3, 1971 until his resignation January 20, 1993, to become Secretary of Defense in the Cabinet of President William J. Clinton; served as Secretary of Defense until his resignation on January 20, 1994; chairman, Committee on Armed Services (Ninety-ninth through One Hundred Second Congresses); professor of international policy, Washington Center for Government, Marquette University; served as chair of the Foreign Intelligence Advisory Board, and of the Commission on the Roles and Capabilities of the United States Intelligence Community from August 1994 until his death in Washington, D.C. on May 21, 1995.

**ASPINALL, Wayne Norviel,** a Representative from Colorado; born in Middleburg, Logan County, Ohio, April 3, 1896; moved with his parents to Palisade, Mesa County, Colo., in 1904; attended the public schools; studied at the University of Denver until the First World War, then enlisted in the Air Service of the Signal Corps and served as a corporal and staff sergeant until discharged as a flying cadet; A.B., University of Denver, 1919; taught school in Palisade, Colo., 1919-1921; president of the Mount Lincoln School District School Board, 1920-1922; LL.B., University of Denver Law School, 1925; was admitted to the bar the same year and commenced practice in Palisade, Colo.; also engaged in the peach orchard industry; again taught school, 1925-1933; member of Palisade Board of Trustees, 1926-1934; district counsel of the Home Owners Loan Corporation in western Colorado, 1933-1934; member, Colorado State house of representatives, 1931-1934, and 1937-1938, serving as Democratic whip in 1933, and as speaker in 1937 and 1938; served in the State senate, 1939-1948, and was Democratic whip in 1939, majority floor leader in 1941, and minority floor leader, 1943-1947; during the Second World War was commissioned a captain in Military Government in 1943, serving overseas as a legal expert with the American and British forces; participated in the Normandy drive with the British Second Army; was discharged on December 14, 1944; elected as a Democrat to the Eighty-first and to the eleven succeeding Congresses (January 3, 1949-January 3, 1973); chairman, Committee on Interior and Insular Affairs (Eighty-sixth through Ninety-second Congresses); unsuccessful candidate for renomination in 1972 to the Ninety-third Congress; resumed the practice of law; was a resident of Palisade, Colo., until his death there on October 9, 1983; cremated; ashes interred at Orchard Mesa Municipal Cemetery, Grand Junction, Colo.

**Bibliography:** Edmonds, Carol. *Wayne Aspinall: Mr. Chairman.* Lakewood, Colo.: Crown Point, Inc., Publisher, 1980.

**ASWELL, James Benjamin,** a Representative from Louisiana; born near Vernon, Jackson Parish, La., December 23, 1869; attended the public schools; was graduated from Peabody Normal College, Nashville, Tenn., in 1892 and from the University of Nashville in 1893; taught in country schools and high schools, and later attended Chicago University; State institution conductor 1897-1900; president of the Louisiana Polytechnic Institute 1900-1904; State superintendent of public education 1904-1908, and while serving in that capacity reorganized the public-school system of Louisiana; president of the Louisiana State Normal College at Natchitoches 1908-1911; elected as a Democrat to the Sixty-third and to the nine succeeding Congresses and served from March 4, 1913, until his death in Washington, D.C., March 16, 1931; interment in Rock Creek Cemetery.

**ATCHISON, David Rice,** a Senator from Missouri; born in Frogtown, Ky., August 11, 1807; attended Transylvania University, Lexington, Ky.; studied law; was admitted to the bar and commenced practice in Liberty, Clay County, Mo., in 1829; also engaged in agricultural pursuits; member of the Missouri State house of representatives in 1834, and again in 1838; appointed judge of the Platte County circuit court in 1841; appointed and subsequently elected in 1843 as a Democrat to the United States Senate to fill the vacancy caused by the death of Lewis F. Linn; reelected in 1849, and served from October 14, 1843, to March 3, 1855; served as President pro tempore of the Senate during the Twenty-ninth through Thirty-third Congresses; chairman, Committee on the Militia (Twenty-ninth Congress), Committee on Indian Affairs (Thirtieth through Thirty-second Congresses); resumed the practice of law; died at his home near Gower, Clinton County, Mo., January 26, 1886; interment in Greenlawn Cemetery, Plattsburg, Mo.

Bibliography: *DAB*; Atchison, Theodore. "David R. Atchison, A Study in American Politics." *Missouri Historical Review* 24 (July 1930): 502-15; Parrish, William E. *David Rice Atchison of Missouri.* Columbia: University of Missouri Press, 1961.

**ATHERTON, Charles Gordon** (son of Charles Humphrey Atherton), a Representative and a Senator from New Hampshire; born in Amherst, Hillsborough County, N.H., July 4, 1804; was graduated from Harvard University in 1822; studied law; was admitted to the bar in 1825 and commenced practice in Dunstable (now Nashua), N.H.; member of the State house of representatives 1830 and 1833-1835, serving as speaker 1833-1835; elected as a Democrat to the Twenty-fifth and the two succeeding Congresses (March 4, 1837-March 3, 1843); did not seek reelection in 1842, having become a candidate for Senator; elected to the United States Senate as a Democrat in 1843, and served from March 4, 1843, to March 3, 1849; chairman, Committee on Printing (Twenty-ninth Congress), Committee on Roads and Canals (Twenty-ninth Congress), Committee on Finance (Thirtieth Congress); resumed the practice of law in Nashua; again elected to the United States Senate in 1852 for the term beginning March 4, 1853, but never qualified, having suffered a stroke; died in Manchester, N.H., November 15, 1853; interment in Nashua Cemetery, Nashua, N.H.

Bibliography: *DAB*.

**ATHERTON, Charles Humphrey** (father of Charles Gordon Atherton), a Representative from New Hampshire; born in Amherst, Hillsborough County, N.H., August 14, 1773; attended the common schools and was graduated from Harvard University in 1794; studied law; was admitted to the bar in 1797 and commenced practice in Amherst; register of probate 1798-1807; elected as a Federalist to the Fourteenth Congress (March 4, 1815-March 3, 1817); declined to be a candidate for renomination in 1816; member of the State house of representatives 1823-1839; resumed the practice of law; died in Amherst, N.H., January 8, 1853; interment in the Old Cemetery.

**ATHERTON, Gibson,** a Representative from Ohio; born near Newark, Licking County, Ohio, January 19, 1831; attended Denison University, Granville, Ohio, and was graduated from Miami University, Oxford, Ohio, in 1853; principal of the local academy at Osceola, Mo., in 1853 and 1854; studied law; was admitted to the bar in 1855 and commenced practice in Newark, Ohio; president of the board of education of Newark for fifteen years; elected prosecuting attorney of Licking County in 1857 and reelected in 1859 and 1861; mayor of Newark 1860-1864; unsuccessful Democratic candidate for the State senate in 1863 and for judge of the court of common pleas

in 1866; member of the city council of Newark for two years; delegate to the Democratic National Convention of 1876; elected as a Democrat to the Forty-sixth and Forty-seventh Congresses (March 4, 1879-March 3, 1883); did not seek renomination in 1882 to the Forty-eighth Congress, but was an unsuccessful candidate for election as judge of the supreme court of Ohio; appointed to that position by Governor George Hoadly the same year and served until the election of his successor six months later; resumed the practice of law; died in Newark, Ohio, November 10, 1887; interment in Cedar Hill Cemetery.

**ATKESON, William Oscar,** a Representative from Missouri; born on a farm near Buffalo, Putnam County, Va. (now West Virginia), August 24, 1854; attended the public schools and the University of Kentucky at Lexington; taught school in Mason County, W.Va., in 1874 and at New Haven, W.Va., in 1875; was graduated from Fairmont (W.Va.) Normal School in 1875; moved to Point Pleasant, W.Va., in 1876 and edited and published the West Virginia Monitor; studied law; was admitted to the bar in 1877 and commenced practice in Council Grove, Kans.; moved to Rich Hill, Bates County, Mo., in 1882 and to Butler, Bates County, Mo., in 1889, and continued to practice law; prosecuting attorney of Bates County, Mo., 1891-1893; unsuccessful candidate for circuit judge of the twenty-ninth judicial circuit in 1892; owner and editor of the Butler Free Press 1894-1902; unsuccessful candidate for election in 1906 to the Sixtieth Congress and in 1908 to the Sixty-first Congress; served as deputy State hotel inspector in 1910 and 1911 and as deputy State labor commissioner 1911-1913; owner and editor of the Bates County Record 1915-1918; elected as a Republican to the Sixty-seventh Congress (March 4, 1921-March 3, 1923); unsuccessful candidate for reelection in 1922 to the Sixty-eighth Congress; served as State warehouse commissioner in Kansas City, Mo., from July 1, 1923, until February 5, 1925, when he resigned; resumed the practice of law and also engaged in literary pursuits; died in Butler, Mo., October 16, 1931; interment in Oak Hill Cemetery.

**ATKINS, Chester Greenough,** a Representative from Massachusetts; born in Geneva, Switzerland, April 14, 1948; was graduated from Concord-Carlisle High School, Concord, Mass., in 1966; B.A., Antioch College, Yellow Springs, Ohio, 1970; founder and co-director, Brandeis Institute for State and Local Government, 1975; member of the Massachusetts house of representatives, 1970-1971, and the Massachusetts senate, 1972-1984; chairman of the Massachusetts Democratic Committee, 1977-1990; member, Democratic National Committee; elected as a Democrat to the Ninety-ninth and to the three succeeding Congresses (January 3, 1985-January 3, 1993); unsuccessful candidate for renomination in 1992 to the One Hundred Third Congress; owns and runs A.D.S. Ventures, Inc.; is a resident of Concord, Mass.

Bibliography: Atkins, Chester G., with Barry Hock and Bob Martin. *Getting Elected: A Guide to Winning State and Local Office.* Boston: Houghton Mifflin, 1973.

**ATKINS, John DeWitt Clinton,** a Representative from Tennessee; born near Manly's Chapel, Henry County, Tenn., June 4, 1825; attended a private school in Paris, Tenn., and was graduated from the East Tennessee University at Knoxville in 1846; studied law; was admitted to the bar but did not practice; engaged in agricultural pursuits; member of the State house of representatives 1849-1851; served in the State senate 1855-1857; elected as a Democrat to the Thirty-fifth Congress (March 4, 1857-March 3, 1859); unsuccessful candidate for reelection in 1858 to the Thirty-sixth Congress; during the Civil War served as lieutenant colonel of the Fifth Tennessee Regiment in the Confederate Army in 1861; elected to the Confederate Provisional Congress in August and November 1861 and in November 1863; elected as a Democrat to the Forty-third and to the four succeeding Congresses (March 4,

1873-March 3, 1883); chairman, Committee on Appropriations (Forty-fifth and Forty-sixth Congresses); was not a candidate for renomination in 1882 to the Forty-eighth Congress; engaged in agricultural pursuits near Paris, Henry County, Tenn.; appointed United States Commissioner of Indian Affairs by President Grover Cleveland on March 21, 1885, and served until June 13, 1888, when he resigned; was an unsuccessful candidate in 1888 for nomination to the United States Senate; again engaged in agricultural pursuits; retired from active pursuits in 1898 and moved to Paris, Tenn., where he lived in retirement until his death on June 2, 1908; interment in the City Cemetery.

**ATKINSON, Archibald,** a Representative from Virginia; born in Isle of Wight County, Va., September 15, 1792; received a liberal education; attended the law department of William and Mary College, Williamsburg, Va.; served during the War of 1812; was admitted to the bar and commenced practice in Smithfield, Isle of Wight County, Va.; member of the Virginia house of delegates 1815-1817 and 1828-1831; served in the Virginia senate 1839-1843; elected as a Democrat to the Twenty-eighth, Twenty-ninth, and Thirtieth Congresses (March 4, 1843-March 3, 1849); was not a candidate for renomination in 1848 to the Thirty-first Congress; served as prosecuting attorney for Isle of Wight County; died in Smithfield, Va., on January 7, 1872; interment in the graveyard of Old St. Luke's Church, four miles southeast of Smithfield, Va.

**ATKINSON, Eugene Vincent,** a Representative from Pennsylvania; born in Aliquippa, Beaver County, Pa., April 5, 1927; graduated from Aliquippa High School in 1945; master's degree program, University of Pittsburgh; served in United States Navy construction battalions (Seabees); owned and operated an insurance agency; appointed director of customs, Port of Pittsburgh, 1962-1969; Beaver County Commissioner, 1972-1978; elected as a Democrat to the Ninety-sixth and Ninety-seventh Congresses (January 3, 1979-January 3, 1983); announced his affiliation with the Republican Party on October 14, 1981, and continued in office during the Ninety-seventh Congress as a Republican; unsuccessful candidate for reelection in 1982 to the Ninety-eighth Congress; is a resident of Washington, D.C.

**ATKINSON, George Wesley,** a Representative from West Virginia; born near Charleston, Kanawha County, Va. (now West Virginia), June 29, 1845; attended the public schools of Charleston and was graduated from the Ohio Wesleyan University at Delaware in 1870; was graduated from Mount Union College, Alliance, Ohio, and Howard University Law School, Washington, D.C.; collector of tolls on the Kanawha River Board 1869-1871; postmaster of Charleston 1871-1877; was admitted to the bar in 1875 and commenced practice in Charleston; later attended lectures on law at Columbia University; moved to Wheeling, Ohio County, W.Va., in 1877; editor of the Wheeling Standard in 1877 and 1878; internal revenue agent of the Treasury Department 1879-1881; United States marshal for the district of West Virginia 1881-1885; successfully contested as a Republican the election of John O. Pendleton to the Fifty-first Congress and served from February 26, 1890, to March 3, 1891; declined to be a candidate for reelection in 1890 to the Fifty-second Congress; resumed the practice of law in Wheeling, W.Va.; editor of the West Virginia Journal 1891-1896; elected Governor of West Virginia in 1896 and served from March 4, 1897 to March 4, 1901; served as United States district attorney for the southern district of West Virginia from July 1, 1901, to April 18, 1905; appointed associate judge of the Court of Claims at Washington, D.C., on April 15, 1905, and served until April 16, 1916, when he retired; died in Charleston, W.Va., April 4, 1925; interment in Spring Hill Cemetery.

**Bibliography:** *DAB*.

**ATKINSON, Louis Evans,** a Representative from Pennsylvania; born in Delaware Township, Juniata County, Pa., April 16, 1841; attended the common schools and Airy View and Milnwood Academies; studied medicine and was graduated from the medical department of the College of the City of New York March 4, 1861; during the Civil War entered the medical department of the United States Army on September 5, 1861; served as assistant surgeon in the First Pennsylvania Reserve Cavalry and as surgeon of the One Hundred and Eighty-eighth Pennsylvania Volunteer Infantry, until mustered out in December 1865; was disabled while in the Army and, being unable to practice medicine, studied law; was admitted to the bar in September 1870 and commenced practice in Mifflintown, Pa.; elected as a Republican to the Forty-eighth and to the four succeeding Congresses (March 4, 1883-March 3, 1893); chairman, Committee on Expenditures in the Department of the Treasury (Fifty-first Congress); became a candidate for renomination in 1892 to the Fifty-third Congress, but ultimately withdrew; resumed the practice of law in Mifflintown, Pa.; appointed president judge of the forty-first Pennsylvania district and served one year; died in Mifflintown, Juniata County, Pa., February 5, 1910; interment in Presbyterian Cemetery.

**ATKINSON, Richard Merrill,** a Representative from Tennessee; born in Nashville, Davidson County, Tenn., February 6, 1894; attended the public schools; was graduated from Wallace University School, Nashville, Tenn., in 1912, from Vanderbilt University, Nashville, Tenn., in 1916, and from the law department of Cumberland University, Lebanon, Tenn., in 1917; was admitted to the bar in 1917 and commenced the practice of law in Nashville, Tenn., in 1920; during the First World War served from June 30, 1917 until honorably discharged on August 29, 1919, as a member of the Forty-seventh Company, United States Marines, Second Division, serving in France with the American Expeditionary Forces; attorney general of the tenth judicial circuit of Tennessee from September 1, 1926, to September 1, 1934; State commissioner of Smoky Mountain National Park, 1931-1933; elected as a Democrat to the Seventy-fifth Congress (January 3, 1937-January 3, 1939); unsuccessful candidate for renomination in 1938 to the Seventy-sixth Congress; engaged in the practice of law in Nashville, Tenn., until his death there on April 29, 1947; interment in Spring Hill Cemetery.

**ATLEE, Samuel John,** a Delegate from Pennsylvania; born in Trenton, N.J., in 1739, during the temporary residence of his parents at that place; moved with his mother to Lancaster, Pa., in 1745; educated by a private tutor and subsequently commenced the study of law, but abandoned it to enter the Army; during the French and Indian War at the age of sixteen was placed in command of a company of the provincial service from Lancaster County, Pa.; commissioned ensign in Col. William Clapham's Augusta regiment on April 23, 1756, and promoted to lieutenant December 7, 1757; served in the Forbes campaign and participated in a battle near Fort Duquesne, September 15, 1758; was commissioned captain May 13, 1759; appointed colonel of the Pennsylvania Musketry Battalion on March 21, 1776; during the Revolutionary War was captured by the British on August 27, 1776, at the Battle of Long Island and held as a prisoner until October 1, 1778, when he was exchanged; Member of the Continental Congress 1778-1782; served in the general assembly in 1782, 1785, and 1786; elected supreme executive councilor for Lancaster County in 1783; appointed a member of the board of commissioners to treat with the Indians in 1784 for the unpurchased lands in Pennsylvania; one of the charter members of the Society of the Cincinnati; died in Philadelphia, Pa., November 25, 1786, while attending a session of the assembly; interment in Christ Churchyard.

**ATWATER, John Wilbur,** a Representative from North Carolina; born near Rialto (now Fearington), Chatham County, N.C., December 27, 1840; attended the common schools and the old William Closs Academy; engaged in agricultural pursuits; during the Civil War enlisted in the Confederate Army and served in Company D, First Regiment, North Carolina Volunteer Infantry, and was with the army of General Robert E. Lee until the surrender at Appomattox; joined the Farmers' Alliance in 1887; first president of Chatham County Alliance; elected to the North Carolina State senate in 1890 as an Alliance Democrat, and also in 1892 and 1896 as a Populist; elected as an Independent Populist to the Fifty-sixth Congress (March 4, 1899-March 3, 1901); was an unsuccessful candidate for reelection in 1900 to the Fifty-seventh Congress; resumed agricultural pursuits; died in Fearington, N.C., on July 4, 1910; interment in Mount Pleasant Church Cemetery, near Pittsboro, N.C.

**ATWOOD, David,** a Representative from Wisconsin; born in Bedford, N.H., December 15, 1815; attended the public schools; moved to Hamilton, N.Y., in 1832; apprenticed as a printer and subsequently became publisher of the Hamilton Palladium; moved to Freeport, Ill., in 1845 and engaged in agricultural pursuits; moved to Madison, Wis., in 1847 and for forty-two years was editor and publisher of the State Journal, Madison, Wis.; was commissioned major general in the Wisconsin Militia in 1858; member of the State assembly in 1861; United States assessor for four years; mayor of Madison in 1868 and 1869; elected as a Republican to the Forty-first Congress to fill the vacancy caused by the death of Benjamin F. Hopkins and served from February 23, 1870, until March 3, 1871; declined to be a candidate for renomination in 1870; resumed his former newspaper activities; United States Centennial Exposition commissioner, representing the State of Wisconsin, 1872-1876; delegate to the Republican National Convention at Philadelphia in 1872 and at Cincinnati in 1876; died in Madison, Wis., December 11, 1889; interment in Forest Hill Cemetery.

Bibliography: *DAB*.

**ATWOOD, Harrison Henry,** a Representative from Massachusetts; born at the home of his grandmother in North Londonderry, Vt., August 26, 1863; attended the public schools of Boston, Mass.; studied architecture and engaged in that profession in Boston, Mass.; member of the Massachusetts house of representatives 1887-1889; city architect of Boston in 1889 and 1890; member of the Massachusetts Republican committee 1887-1889; member and secretary of the Boston Republican city committee 1888-1894; delegate to the Republican National Conventions in 1888 and 1892; elected as a Republican to the Fifty-fourth Congress (March 4, 1895-March 3, 1897); unsuccessful candidate for renomination in 1896 to the Fifty-fifth Congress; resumed his former profession in Boston; again a member of the Massachusetts house of representatives in 1915, 1917, 1918, 1923, 1924, 1927, and 1928; was an unsuccessful candidate for election in 1918 to the Sixty-sixth Congress; resumed his profession as an architect in Boston, Mass.; moved to Wellesley Hills, Mass., in April 1938; died in Boston, Mass., October 22, 1954; interment in Forest Hills Cemetery.

**AUCHINCLOSS, James Coats,** a Representative from New Jersey; born in New York City, January 19, 1885; attended Cutler School, New York City, and Groton School, Groton, Mass.; was graduated from Yale University in 1908; engaged in financial and stock brokerage business in New York City 1908-1940; a governor of the New York Stock Exchange, 1921-1938; served in the Seventh Regiment, New York National Guard, 1909-1913; during the First World War served as captain, Military Intelligence; deputy police commissioner of New York City; founder, treasurer, president, and chairman of the board of the New York Better Business Bureau; member of the borough council, Rumson, N.J., 1930-1937; mayor of Rumson, N.J., 1938-1943; elected as a Republican to the Seventy-eighth and to the ten succeeding Congresses (January 3, 1943-January 3, 1965); was not a candidate for reelection in 1964 to the Eighty-ninth Congress; died in Alexandria, Va., October 2, 1976; interment in Woodlawn Cemetery, Bronx, N.Y.

**AuCOIN, Les,** a Representative from Oregon; born in Portland, Multnomah County, Oreg., October 21, 1942; attended public schools in Redmond, Oreg.; graduated, Redmond Union High School, 1960; attended Portland State University, 1961, 1965-1966; B.A., Pacific University, Forest Grove, 1969; worked as a newsman and public information director; served in the United States Army, 1961-1964; served in the Oregon house of representatives, 1971-1974, and served as majority leader, 1973-1974; elected as a Democrat to the Ninety-fourth and to the eight succeeding Congresses (January 3, 1975-January 3, 1993); was not a candidate for reelection in 1992 to the House of Representatives, but was an unsuccessful candidate for election to the United States Senate; is a resident of Forest Grove, Oreg.

**AUF DER HEIDE, Oscar Louis,** a Representative from New Jersey; born in New York City, December 8, 1874; attended the public schools; moved with his parents to West New York, Hudson County, N.J., in 1887; engaged in the real estate business; member of the town council 1899-1902; member and president of the board of education in 1903 and 1904; member of the State house of assembly 1908-1911; served on the board of assessors of West New York in 1912 and 1913; mayor of West New York 1914-1917; elected a member and subsequently a director of the Board of Chosen Freeholders of Hudson County and served from 1915 to 1924; elected as a Democrat to the Sixty-ninth and to the four succeeding Congresses (March 4, 1925-January 3, 1935); was not a candidate for renomination in 1934 to the Seventy-fourth Congress; resumed the real estate and insurance business; died in West New York, N.J., March 29, 1945; interment in Hoboken Cemetery, North Bergen, N.J.

**AUSTIN, Albert Elmer** (stepfather of Clare Boothe Luce), a Representative from Connecticut; born in Medway, Norfolk County, Mass., November 15, 1877; attended the public schools and was graduated from Amherst (Mass.) College in 1899 and from Jefferson Medical College, Philadelphia, Pa., in 1905; member of the faculty of Attleboro (Mass.) High School 1899-1900; practicing physician in Old Greenwich, Conn., 1907-1939; health officer of Greenwich, Conn., 1917-1937; engaged in banking in Old Greenwich, Conn., 1926-1942; during the First World War served as regimental surgeon in the Two Hundred and Fourteenth Engineers, Fourteenth (Wolverine) Division, 1918-1919; member of the State house of representatives 1917-1919 and 1921-1923; elected as a Republican to the Seventy-sixth Congress (January 3, 1939-January 3, 1941); unsuccessful candidate for reelection in 1940 to the Seventy-seventh Congress; continued his former professional pursuits until his death in Greenwich, Conn., January 26, 1942; interment in Ferncliff Cemetery, Hartsdale, Westchester County, N.Y.

**AUSTIN, Archibald,** a Representative from Virginia; born near Buckingham, Buckingham County, Va., August 11, 1772; studied law; was admitted to the bar and commenced practice in Buckingham County; member of the Virginia house of delegates 1815-1817; elected as a Republican to the Fifteenth Congress (March 4, 1817-March 3, 1819); was not a candidate for renomination in 1818; resumed the practice of his profession; presidential elector on the Democratic ticket in 1832 and 1836; again a member of the Virginia house of delegates 1835-1837; died near Buckingham Court House, Buckingham County, Va., October 16, 1837; interment in the family cemetery on his estate.

AUSTIN, Richard Wilson, a Representative from Tennessee; born in Decatur, Morgan County, Ala., August 26, 1857; attended the common schools, Loudon High School, and the University of Tennessee at Knoxville in 1873; studied law; was admitted to the bar in 1878 and commenced practice in Knoxville, Tenn.; clerk in the Post Office Department at Washington, D.C., 1879-1881; Assistant Doorkeeper of the House of Representatives, 1881-1883; special agent of the War Department, 1883-1885; engaged in newspaper work in Knoxville, Tenn., in 1885; returned to Decatur, Ala., and continued the practice of law; private secretary to Representative Leonidas C. Houk of Tennessee in 1888; served as city attorney of Decatur, Ala.; unsuccessful candidate for election in 1890 to the Fifty-second Congress; delegate to the Republican National Convention of 1892; returned to Knoxville, Tenn., in 1893 and edited the Knoxville Republican; United States marshal for the eastern district of Tennessee 1897-1906; appointed United States consul at Glasgow, Scotland, and served from July 1906 to November 1907, when he resigned; elected as a Republican to the Sixty-first and to the four succeeding Congresses (March 4, 1909-March 3, 1919); unsuccessful candidate for renomination in 1918 to the Sixty-sixth Congress; died in Washington, D.C., April 20, 1919; interment in the Old Gray Cemetery, Knoxville, Tenn.

AUSTIN, Warren Robinson, a Senator from Vermont; born in Highgate Center, Franklin County, Vt., November 12, 1877; attended the public schools; was graduated from Brigham Academy, Bakersfield, Vt., in 1895 and from the University of Vermont, at Burlington, in 1899; studied law; was admitted to the bar in 1902 and commenced practice at St. Albans, Vt.; served as State's attorney of Franklin County, Vt., 1904-1906; United States commissioner 1907-1915; chairman of the Republican State Convention in 1908; mayor of St. Albans in 1909; delegate to the Congress of the Mint in 1912; trustee of the University of Vermont 1914-1941; special counsel for Vermont in the boundary-line dispute between Vermont and New Hampshire in 1925-1937; member of the United States Court for China in 1917; elected as a Republican to the United States Senate on March 31, 1931, to fill the vacancy caused by the death of Frank L. Greene; reelected in 1934 and 1940 and served from April 1, 1931, until his resignation on August 2, 1946, to become United States representative on the Security Council of the United Nations, serving until his retirement January 25, 1953; was a resident of Burlington, Vt., until his death on December 25, 1962; interment in Lake View Cemetery.

Bibliography: DAB; Mazuzan, George. "Warren R. Austin: Republican Internationalist and U.S. Foreign Policy." Ph.D. dissertation, Kent State University, 1969; Porter, David L. "Senator Warren Austin and the Neutrality Act of 1939." Vermont History 42 (Summer 1974): 228-38.

AVERETT, Thomas Hamlet, a Representative from Virginia; born near Halifax, Halifax County, Va., July 10, 1800; attended the common schools; served as a drummer boy in the War of 1812; studied medicine; was graduated from Jefferson Medical College, Philadelphia, Pa., and practiced in Halifax and the adjacent counties; served in the Virginia senate in 1848 and 1849; unsuccessful candidate for election in 1846 to the Thirtieth Congress; elected as a Democrat to the Thirty-first and Thirty-second Congresses (March 4, 1849-March 3, 1853); unsuccessful candidate for renomination in 1852; resumed the practice of medicine in Halifax County; died near Halifax Court House, Va., June 30, 1855; interment in the family burial ground near Halifax Court House, Va.

AVERILL, John Thomas, a Representative from Minnesota; born in Alna, Lincoln County, Maine, March 1, 1825; attended the common schools; moved with his parents to Montville, Maine, in 1838; was graduated from the Maine Wesleyan Seminary at Readfield in 1846; taught school for a short time, and subsequently engaged in lumbering for one year; moved to Winthrop, Maine, and engaged in mercantile pursuits for three years; moved to northern Pennsylvania in 1852 and again engaged in lumbering until 1857, when he settled in Lake City, Minn.; engaged in mercantile pursuits and the grain business; member of the State senate 1858-1860; commissioned lieutenant colonel of the Sixth Regiment, Minnesota Volunteer Infantry, August 22, 1862; promoted to colonel on November 22, 1864; honorably mustered out on September 28, 1865; moved to St. Paul, Minn., in 1866 and engaged in the wholesale paper and stationery business; member of the Republican National Committee 1868-1880; elected as a Republican to the Forty-second and Forty-third Congresses (March 4, 1871-March 3, 1875); chairman, Committee on Indian Affairs (Forty-third Congress); was not a candidate for renomination in 1874 to the Forty-fourth Congress; resumed his business activities in St. Paul, Minn., where he died on October 3, 1889; interment in Oakland Cemetery.

AVERY, Daniel, a Representative from New York; born in Groton, Conn., September 18, 1766; attended the common schools; appointed ensign in the Sixth Company, Eighth Regiment of the Connecticut Militia, and served as lieutenant and captain until May 1794; moved to Aurora, N.Y., in 1795 and subsequently became the owner of a large tract of land which was farmed by tenants; elected as a Republican to the Twelfth and Thirteenth Congresses (March 4, 1811-March 3, 1815); elected to the Fourteenth Congress to fill the vacancy caused by the resignation of Enos T. Throop and served from September 30, 1816, to March 3, 1817; resumed the management of his estate; connected with the land office at Albany, N.Y., for twenty years; died in Aurora, Cayuga County, N.Y., January 30, 1842; interment in Oak Glen Cemetery.

AVERY, John, a Representative from Michigan; born in Watertown, Jefferson County, N.Y., February 29, 1824; moved with his parents to Michigan in 1836; attended the common schools; entered Grass Lake Academy, Jackson, Mich., where he studied medicine for two years; was graduated from the Cleveland Medical College in 1850 and commenced the practice of medicine in Ionia, Mich.; moved to Otsego, Mich., in 1852 and continued the practice of his profession; during the Civil War was assistant surgeon and surgeon of the Twenty-first Regiment, Michigan Volunteer Infantry; served in the Army of the Cumberland in Kentucky and Tennessee; was with General William Tecumseh Sherman on his march to the sea, November-December 1864; settled in Greenville, Mich., in 1868 and again engaged in the practice of medicine; member of the Michigan State house of representatives in 1869 and 1870; appointed a member of the State board of health in 1880, and reappointed in 1886; elected as a Republican to the Fifty-third and Fifty-fourth Congresses (March 4, 1893-March 3, 1897); was not a candidate for renomination in 1896 to the Fifty-fifth Congress; engaged in the practice of medicine in Greenville, Mich., where he died on January 21, 1914; interment in Forest Home Cemetery.

AVERY, William Henry, a Representative from Kansas; born in Wakefield, Clay County, Kans., August 11, 1911; attended the public schools; A.B., University of Kansas, Lawrence, 1934; engaged in business as a farmer and stockman near Wakefield, Kans., since 1935; director of the Wakefield Rural High School Board of Education since 1946; served in the Kansas State house of representatives from 1951 until elected to Congress; member of legislative council of Kansas, 1953-1955; elected as a Republican to the Eighty-fourth and to the four succeeding Congresses (January 3, 1955-January 3, 1965); was not a candidate for renomination in 1964 to the Eighty-ninth Congress, but was elected Governor of Kansas, and served from January 11, 1965 to January 9, 1967; unsuccessful candidate for reelection in 1966; president, Real Petroleum Company; retired since 1977; is a resident of Wakefield, Kans.

**AVERY, William Tecumsah,** a Representative from Tennessee; born in Hardeman County, Tenn., November 11, 1819; attended the common schools and was graduated from old Jackson College near Columbia, Maury County, Tenn.; studied law; was admitted to the bar; moved to Memphis, Tenn., in 1840 and engaged in the practice of law; member of the Tennessee State house of representatives in 1843; elected as a Democrat to the Thirty-fifth and Thirty-sixth Congresses (March 4, 1857-March 3, 1861); was not a candidate for renomination in 1860 to the Thirty-seventh Congress; during the Civil War served as lieutenant colonel in the Confederate Army; clerk of the criminal court of Shelby County, 1870-1874; resumed the practice of law in Memphis, Tenn.; accidentally drowned in Ten Mile Bayou, Crittenden County, Ark., opposite Memphis, Tenn., May 22, 1880; interment in Elmwood Cemetery, Memphis, Tenn.

**AVIS, Samuel Brashear,** a Representative from West Virginia; born in Harrisonburg, Rockingham County, Va., February 19, 1872; attended the public schools and Staunton (Va.) Military Academy; was graduated from the law department of Washington and Lee University, Lexington, Va.; was admitted to the bar in 1893 and commenced practice in Charleston, W.Va.; commissioned senior captain of Company A, Second West Virginia Volunteer Infantry, during the Spanish-American War in 1898; served until 1899, when he was honorably discharged; prosecuting attorney of Kanawha County, W.Va., from January 1, 1900 to December 31, 1912; assistant United States attorney for the southern district of West Virginia from August 22 to November 15, 1904; elected as a Republican to the Sixty-third Congress (March 4, 1913-March 3, 1915); unsuccessful candidate for reelection in 1914 to the Sixty-fourth Congress; resumed the practice of law; was killed by lightning in Charleston, W.Va., June 8, 1924; interment in Spring Hill Cemetery, Spring Hill, W.Va.

**AXTELL, Samuel Beach,** a Representative from California; born near Columbus, Franklin County, Ohio, October 14, 1819; attended the local schools and Oberlin College; was graduated from Western Reserve College, Hudson, Ohio; studied law; was admitted to the bar in 1843 and commenced practice in Mount Clemens, Mich.; went to California in 1851 and engaged in mining in Amador County; prosecuting attorney of Amador County, 1854-1860; moved to San Francisco in 1860 and practiced law; elected as a Democrat to the Fortieth and Forty-first Congresses (March 4, 1867-March 3, 1871); was not a candidate for renomination in 1870 to the Forty-second Congress; affiliated with the Republican Party during the administration of President Ulysses S. Grant; appointed Governor of Utah Territory on January 6, 1875, and in July 1875 transferred to the office of Governor of the Territory of New Mexico; Governor of New Mexico Territory from July 30, 1875 until he was suspended by Secretary of the Interior Carl Schurz on September 4, 1878; chief justice of the supreme court of the Territory of New Mexico from August 1882 until his resignation May 25, 1885; engaged in the practice of law in Santa Fe, N.Mex.; at the time of his death was counsel of the Southern Pacific Railroad Co. and chairman of the Republican Territorial committee; died while on a visit to Morristown, Morris County, N.J., August 6, 1891; interment in First Presbyterian Church Cemetery.
**Bibliography:** *DAB.*

**AYCRIGG, John Bancker,** a Representative from New Jersey; born in New York City July 9, 1798; studied medicine; was graduated from the College of Physicians and Surgeons (now the medical department of Columbia University), New York City, in 1818 and was admitted to practice in New York; moved to New Jersey and located at Paramus; elected as a Whig to the Twenty-fifth Congress (March 4, 1837-March 3, 1839); presented credentials as a Member-elect to the Twenty-sixth Congress but was not permitted to qualify; elected to the Twenty-seventh Congress (March 4, 1841-March 3, 1843); was not a candidate for renomination in 1842 to the Twenty-eighth Congress; resumed the practice of medicine in Paramus; moved to Passaic, N.J., and died there November 8, 1856; interment in Paramus Church Cemetery, Ridgewood, N.J.

**AYER, Richard Small,** a Representative from Virginia; born in Montville, Waldo County, Maine, October 9, 1829; attended the common schools; was engaged for a number of years in agricultural and mercantile pursuits; during the Civil War enlisted in 1861 in the Union Army as a private in Company A, Fourth Regiment, Maine Volunteer Infantry; subsequently promoted to first lieutenant and was mustered out as a captain on March 22, 1863, for disability; settled in Virginia in 1865 and located near Warsaw; delegate to the Virginia constitutional convention in 1867-1868; upon the readmission of Virginia to representation was elected as a Republican to the Forty-first Congress and served from January 31, 1870, until March 3, 1871; was not a candidate for renomination in 1870; engaged in agricultural pursuits; returned to Montville, Maine; member of the Virginia house of representatives in 1888; died in Liberty, Waldo County, Maine, December 14, 1896; interment in Mount Repose Cemetery, Montville, Maine.

**AYERS, Roy Elmer,** a Representative from Montana; born on a ranch near Lewistown, Fergus County, Mont., November 9, 1882; attended the rural schools and Lewistown High School; was graduated from the law department of Valparaiso (Ind.) University in 1903; was admitted to the bar the same year and commenced practice in Lewistown, Mont.; also became engaged in ranching and the raising of livestock; served as attorney of Fergus County, Mont., 1905-1909; member of the Montana Board of Education 1908-1912; judge of the tenth judicial district of Montana 1913-1921 and justice of the State supreme court from January 1922 until his resignation on November 22, 1922, when he resumed the private practice of law in Lewistown, Mont.; during the First World War served as chairman of the Fergus County Exemption Board; delegate to the Democratic National Conventions of 1920 and 1940, and to every State Democratic Convention from 1906 to 1940; elected as a Democrat to the Seventy-third and Seventy-fourth Congresses (March 4, 1933-January 3, 1937); was not a candidate for renomination in 1936 to the Seventy-fifth Congress, but was elected Governor of Montana and served from January 4, 1937 until January 6, 1941; resumed his ranching activities; died in Lewistown, Mont., May 23, 1955; interment in Lewistown City Cemetery.

**AYRES, Steven Beckwith,** a Representative from New York; born in Fort Dodge, Iowa, October 27, 1861; moved with his parents to Elmira, N.Y., in 1866; attended the grammar school; moved to Penn Yan, N.Y., in 1873; attended the Penn Yan Academy and was graduated from Syracuse (N.Y.) University, in 1882; engaged in the publishing business at Penn Yan and was editor of the Yates County Chronicle; delegate to the Republican State convention in 1884; moved to New York City in 1893 and engaged in the advertising business; declined the Democratic nomination as candidate for the New York State assembly in 1910; elected as an Independent Democrat to the Sixty-second Congress (March 4, 1911-March 3, 1913); unsuccessful candidate for reelection as an Independent Democrat in 1912 to the Sixty-third Congress; author of several books and many historical articles; lecturer in the New York University Summer School in 1914; engaged in the cultivation of oranges at Clearwater, Fla., in winter and in the real estate business at Woodstock, N.Y., during the summer; died in New York City, June 1, 1929; interment in the Clearwater Cemetery, Clearwater, Fla.

**AYRES, William Augustus,** a Representative from Kansas; born in Elizabethtown, Hardin County, Ill., April 19, 1867; moved with his parents to Sedgwick County, Kans., in 1881; attended the common schools and Garfield University (now Friends University),

Wichita, Kans.; was admitted to the bar in 1893 and commenced practice in Wichita, Kans.; clerk of the Court of Appeals of Kansas 1897-1901; prosecuting attorney of Sedgwick County 1906-1910; elected as a Democrat to the Sixty-fourth, Sixty-fifth, and Sixty-sixth Congresses (March 4, 1915-March 3, 1921); unsuccessful candidate for reelection in 1920 to the Sixty-seventh Congress; elected to the Sixty-eighth and to the five succeeding Congresses and served from March 4, 1923, until his resignation effective August 22, 1934, having been appointed a member of the Federal Trade Commission on June 30, 1934, in which capacity he served until his death in Washington, D.C., February 17, 1952; interment in Old Mission Cemetery, Wichita, Kans.

Bibliography: *DAB*.

**AYRES, William Hanes,** a Representative from Ohio; born in Eagle Rock, Botetourt County, Va., February 5, 1916; moved with his parents to West Virginia and later to Lorain County, Ohio; attended the Weller Township High School; was graduated from Western Reserve University, Cleveland, Ohio, in 1936; salesman for heating equipment in Akron, Ohio, from 1936 until 1944; during the Second World War served as a private in the United States Army until discharged on December 17, 1945; president of the Ayres Heating and Insulation Co., Akron, Ohio, since 1946; elected as a Republican to the Eighty-second and to the nine succeeding Congresses (January 3, 1951-January 3, 1971); unsuccessful candidate for reelection in 1970 to the Ninety-second Congress; is a resident of Columbia, Md.

# B

**BABBITT, Clinton,** a Representative from Wisconsin; born in Westmoreland, Cheshire County, N.H., November 16, 1831; attended the common schools and was graduated from Keene (N.H.) Academy; moved to Wisconsin in 1853 and settled near Beloit, Rock County; engaged in agricultural pursuits; elected alderman and was a member of the first city council of Beloit; unsuccessful candidate for election in 1880 to the Forty-seventh Congress; appointed postmaster of Beloit by President Grover Cleveland on August 2, 1886, and served until August 17, 1889, when a successor was appointed; appointed secretary of the State agricultural society of Wisconsin in 1885 and served until 1899; elected as a Democrat to the Fifty-second Congress (March 4, 1891-March 3, 1893); unsuccessful candidate for reelection in 1892 to the Fifty-third Congress; retired from public life and active business pursuits and resided in Beloit, Wis., until his death there on March 11, 1907; interment in the Protestant Cemetery.

**BABBITT, Elijah,** a Representative from Pennsylvania; born in Providence, R.I., July 29, 1795; moved with his parents to New York State in 1805; received an academic education; moved to Milton, Northumberland County, Pa., in 1816; studied law; was admitted to the bar in March 1824 and commenced practice in Milton; moved to Erie, Pa., in 1826 and continued the practice of law; served as attorney for the borough and subsequently for the city of Erie; prosecuting attorney for Erie County in 1833; deputy attorney general for the State in 1834 and 1835; member of the Pennsylvania house of representatives in 1836 and 1837; served in the Pennsylvania senate 1843-1846; elected as a Republican to the Thirty-sixth and Thirty-seventh Congresses (March 4, 1859-March 3, 1863); was not a candidate for reelection in 1862 to the Twenty-eighth Congress; resumed the practice of his profession; died in Erie, Pa., January 9, 1887; interment in Erie Cemetery.

**BABCOCK, Alfred,** a Representative from New York; born in Hamilton, Madison County, N.Y., April 15, 1805; attended the local schools and Gaines (N.Y.) Academy; studied medicine; moved to Gaines, Orleans County, N.Y., where he practiced his profession; elected a member of the board of trustees of the village of Gaines at its first election on May 28, 1839; elected as a Whig to the Twenty-seventh Congress (March 4, 1841-March 3, 1843); resumed the practice of medicine in Gaines, N.Y.; moved to Illinois in 1850 and settled in Galesburg, Knox County, where he continued the practice of his profession until his death on May 16, 1871; interment in Hope Cemetery.

**BABCOCK, Joseph Weeks** (grandson of Joseph Weeks), a Representative from Wisconsin; born in Swanton, Franklin County, Vt., March 6, 1850; moved to Linn County, Iowa, with his parents, who settled near Mount Vernon in 1855; attended the common schools of Mount Vernon and Cedar Falls; moved to Necedah, Juneau County, Wis., in 1872 and engaged in the lumber business; member of the Wisconsin State assembly 1889-1893; chairman of the Republican National Congressional Committee in 1894 and 1902; delegate at large to the Republican National Convention at Chicago in 1904; elected as a Republican to the Fifty-third and to the six succeeding Congresses (March 4, 1893-March 3, 1907); chairman, Committee on District of Columbia (Fifty-fourth through Fifty-ninth Congresses); declined to be a candidate for renomination in 1906; retired and resided in Washington, D.C., until his death there on April 27, 1909; remains were cremated and the ashes deposited in the monument on the family plot in Rock Creek Cemetery.

Bibliography: *DAB*.

**BABCOCK, Leander,** a Representative from New York; born in Paris, Oneida County, N.Y., March 1, 1811; was graduated from Union College, Schenectady, N.Y., in 1830; studied law; was admitted to the bar in 1834; moved to Oswego, N.Y., and commenced the practice of law; district attorney for Oswego County 1841-1843; mayor of Oswego in 1850 and 1851; elected as a Democrat to the Thirty-second Congress (March 4, 1851-March 3, 1853); president of the board of education in 1853 and 1855; died in Richfield Springs, N.Y., August 18, 1864; interment in Riverside Cemetery, Oswego, N.Y.

**BABCOCK, William,** a Representative from New York; born in Hinsdale, Westmoreland County, N.H., in 1785; moved to Penn Yan, N.Y., in 1813 and engaged in mercantile pursuits; upon the formation of Yates County was appointed by the Governor as the first county treasurer; elected as an Anti-Masonic candidate to the Twenty-second Congress (March 4, 1831-March 3, 1833); resumed mercantile pursuits and also was engaged as a hotel keeper; died in Penn Yan, Yates County, N.Y., October 20, 1838; interment in City Hill Cemetery in Torrey Township, near Penn Yan.

**BABKA, John Joseph,** a Representative from Ohio; born in Cleveland, Ohio, March 16, 1884; attended the public schools; was graduated from the Cleveland Law School in 1908; was admitted to the bar the same year and commenced practice in Cleveland, Ohio; special counsel to the attorney general of Ohio in 1911 and 1912; assistant prosecuting attorney of Cuyahoga County 1912-1919; elected as a Democrat to the Sixty-sixth Congress (March 4, 1919-March 3, 1921); unsuccessful candidate for reelection in 1920 to the Sixty-seventh Congress; resumed the practice of law; delegate to the Democratic National Conventions in 1920 and 1932; at the time of his death was acting as liquidating attorney for the division of savings and loan associations of the department of commerce of Ohio; died at Cleveland, Ohio, March 22, 1937; interment in Calvary Cemetery.

**BACCHUS, James,** a Representative from Florida; born in Nashville, Tenn., June 21, 1949; graduated, Lyman High School, Longwood, Fla., 1967; B.A., Vanderbilt University, 1971; M.A., Yale University, 1973; J.D., Florida State University, 1978; admitted to the Florida bar in 1978; journalist, Orlando Sentinel; aide and adviser to Governor Reubin Askew of Florida; special assistant, United States International Trade Negotiator; general counsel, Florida Comprehensive Plan Committee; practicing attorney;

elected as a Democrat to the One Hundred Second and One Hundred Third Congresses (January 3, 1991-January 3, 1995); was not a candidate for reelection in 1994 to the One Hundred Fourth Congress; is a resident of Merritt Island, Fla.

**BACHARACH, Isaac,** a Representative from New Jersey; born in Philadelphia, Pa., January 5, 1870; moved to New Jersey in 1881 with his parents, who settled in Atlantic City; attended the public schools; entered the real-estate business and also became interested in the lumber business and in banking; member of the council of Atlantic City, N.J., 1905-1910; member of the State house of assembly in 1911; delegate to the Republican National Convention at Chicago in 1920; elected as a Republican to the Sixty-fourth and to the ten succeeding Congresses (March 4, 1915-January 3, 1937); unsuccessful candidate for reelection in 1936 to the Seventy-fifth Congress; engaged in the real-estate and insurance business in Atlantic City, N.J., until his death there on September 5, 1956; interment in Mount Sinai Cemetery, Philadelphia, Pa.

**BACHMAN, Nathan Lynn,** a Senator from Tennessee; born in Chattanooga, Tenn., August 2, 1878; attended the public schools, Baylor Preparatory School for Boys, Chattanooga, Tenn., Southwestern Presbyterian University, Clarksville, Tenn., Central University, Danville, Ky., Washington and Lee University, Lexington, Va., and the University of Chattanooga Law School, Chattanooga, Tenn.; was graduated from the law department of the University of Virginia at Charlottesville in 1903, admitted to the bar in 1903, and began practice in Chattanooga, Tenn., in the same year; city attorney of Chattanooga 1906-1908; served as judge of the circuit court of Hamilton County, Tenn., 1912-1918; served as associate justice of the Supreme Court of Tennessee from 1918 until his resignation in 1924; unsuccessful candidate for nomination for United States Senator in 1924; resumed the practice of law the same year; appointed and subsequently elected as a Democrat to the United States Senate to fill the vacancy caused by the resignation of Cordell Hull; reelected in 1936 and served from February 28, 1933, until his death in Washington, D.C., April 23, 1937; interment in Forest Hills Cemetery, Chattanooga, Tenn.

**BACHMAN, Reuben Knecht,** a Representative from Pennsylvania; born in Williams Township, Northampton County, Pa., August 6, 1834; attended the common schools; taught school for several years; entered the mercantile and milling business in Durham, Bucks County, Pa.; elected as a Democrat to the Forty-sixth Congress (March 4, 1879-March 3, 1881); was not a candidate for renomination in 1880; delegate to the Democratic National Convention at Chicago in 1884; engaged in the lumber business and the manufacture of builders' millwork at Riegelsville, Pa., and Phillipsburg, N.J.; died in Easton, Pa., September 19, 1911; interment in Durham Cemetery, near Durham, Bucks County, Pa.

**BACHMANN, Carl George,** a Representative from West Virginia; born in Wheeling, Ohio County, W.Va., May 14, 1890; attended the public schools; was graduated from Linsly Institute, Wheeling, W.Va., in 1908; attended Washington and Jefferson College, Washington, Pa., for two years; was graduated from West Virginia University at Morgantown in 1913 and from its law department in 1915; was admitted to the bar in 1915 and commenced practice in Wheeling; appointed assistant prosecuting attorney of Ohio County in January 1917; was subsequently elected prosecuting attorney in January 1921 and served until January 1925; elected as a Republican to the Sixty-ninth and to the three succeeding Congresses (March 4, 1925-March 3, 1933); minority whip (Seventy-second Congress); unsuccessful candidate for reelection in 1932 to the Seventy-third Congress and for election in 1934 to the Seventy-fourth Congress; resumed the practice of law in Wheeling, W.Va.; managed the campaign of Senator William E. Borah for the Republican presidential nomination in 1936; served on the city council of Wheeling, W.Va., 1939-1941; member of the West

Virginia State liquor control commission, 1941-1944; executive director of civilian defense for State of West Virginia, 1942-1944; elected mayor of Wheeling in 1947 for the term ending June 30, 1951; engaged in banking and the practice of law; was a resident of Wheeling, W.Va., where he died January 22, 1980; interment in Greenwood Cemetery, Wheeling W.Va.

**BACHUS, Spencer T., III,** a Representative from Alabama; born in Rocky Ridge, Ala., December 28, 1947; B.A., Auburn (Ala.) University, 1969; J.D., University of Alabama School of Law, 1972; attorney; factory owner; member, Alabama State senate, 1983-1984; member, Alabama house of representatives, 1984-1987; member, Alabama Board of Education, 1987-1991; candidate for Alabama attorney general, 1990; chairman, Alabama Republican Party, 1991-1992; elected as a Republican to the One Hundred Third and One Hundred Fourth Congresses (January 3, 1993-January 3, 1997); is a resident of Birmingham, Ala.

**BACON, Augustus Octavius** (cousin of William S. Howard), a Senator from Georgia; born in Bryan County, Ga., October 20, 1839; attended the common schools in Liberty and Troup Counties; was graduated from the literary department of the University of Georgia at Athens in 1859, and from its law department in 1860; was admitted to the bar in 1860 and commenced practice in Atlanta, Ga.; entered the Confederate Army at the beginning of the Civil War, and served during the campaigns of 1861 and 1862 as adjutant of the Ninth Georgia Regiment in the Army of Northern Virginia; subsequently commissioned captain in the Provisional Army of the Confederacy and assigned to general staff duty; at the close of the war resumed the practice of law in Macon, Ga.; member, Georgia State house of representatives, 1871-1886, serving as speaker pro tempore for two terms and as speaker for eight years; president of the Democratic State convention in 1880; elected as a Democrat to the United States Senate in 1894; reelected in 1900, 1906 and again in 1913, and served from March 4, 1895 until his death in Washington, D.C., February 14, 1914; served as President pro tempore during the Sixty-second Congress; chairman, Committee on Engrossed Bills (Sixtieth and Sixty-first Congresses), Committee on Private Land Claims (Sixty-first and Sixty-second Congresses), Committee on Foreign Relations (Sixty-third Congress); funeral services were held in the Chamber of the United States Senate; interment in Rose Hill Cemetery, Macon, Ga.

**Bibliography:** *DAB*; Steelman, Lola Carr. "The Public Career of Augustus Octavius Bacon." Ph.D. dissertation, University of North Carolina, 1950.

**BACON, Ezekiel** (son of John Bacon and father of William Johnson Bacon), a Representative from Massachusetts; born in Boston, Mass., September 1, 1776; received a liberal schooling and was graduated from Yale College in 1794; attended the Litchfield Law School and afterwards studied with Nathan Dane in Beverly; was admitted to the bar in 1800 and commenced practice in Stockbridge, Mass.; member of the Massachusetts house of representatives in 1805 and 1806; elected as a Republican to the Tenth Congress to fill the vacancy caused by the resignation of Barnabas Bidwell; reelected to the Eleventh and Twelfth Congresses and served from September 16, 1807, to March 3, 1813; chairman, Committee on Ways and Means (Twelfth Congress); chief justice of the court of common pleas for the western district of Massachusetts 1811-1814; First Comptroller of the United States Treasury from February 11, 1814, to February 28, 1815, when he resigned; moved to Utica, Oneida County, N.Y., in 1816; appointed associate justice of the court of common pleas in 1818; member of the Massachusetts assembly in 1819; delegate to the Massachusetts constitutional convention in 1821; unsuccessful candidate for election in 1824 to the Nineteenth Congress; at time of his death he was the oldest surviving Member of Congress and the last representative of the administration of President James Madison; died in Utica, N.Y., October 18, 1870; interment in Forest Hill Cemetery.

**Bibliography:** Barlow, William, and David O. Powell. "Congressman Ezekiel Bacon of Massachusetts and the Coming of the War of 1812." *Historical Journal of Western Massachusetts* 6 (Spring 1978): 28-41.

**BACON, Henry,** a Representative from New York; born in Brooklyn, N.Y., March 14, 1846; attended the Mount Pleasant Academy in Sing Sing, the Episcopal Academy in Cheshire, Conn., and was graduated from Union College in 1865; studied law; was admitted to the bar in 1866 and commenced practice in Goshen, N.Y.; elected as a Democrat to the Forty-ninth Congress to fill the vacancy caused by the death of Lewis Beach; reelected to the Fiftieth Congress and served from December 6, 1886, until March 3, 1889; chairman, Committee on Manufactures (Fiftieth Congress); unsuccessful candidate for reelection in 1888 to the Fifty-first Congress; elected to the Fifty-second Congress (March 4, 1891-March 3, 1893); chairman, Committee on Banking and Currency (Fifty-second Congress); unsuccessful candidate for renomination in 1892; resumed the practice of law in Goshen; delegate to the Democratic National Convention at Chicago in 1892; corporation counsel of Goshen 1909-1915; died in Goshen, N.Y., on March 25, 1915; interment in Slate Hill Cemetery.

**BACON, John** (father of Ezekiel Bacon and grandfather of William Johnson Bacon), a Representative from Massachusetts; born in Canterbury, Conn., April 5, 1738; was graduated from Princeton College in 1765; studied theology; had charge of the Old South Church, Boston, from September 25, 1771, until dismissed February 8, 1775, owing to differences of opinion; located in Stockbridge; studied law; was admitted to the bar and practiced; served on the committee of correspondence, inspection, and safety in 1777; member of the Massachusetts constitutional convention in 1779 and 1780; member of the Massachusetts house of representatives 1780, 1783, 1784, 1786, 1789-1791, and in 1793; member of the Massachusetts senate 1781, 1782, 1794-1796, 1798, and 1803-1806, serving as president in 1806; elected as a Republican to the Seventh Congress (March 4, 1801-March 3, 1803); chairman, Committee on Elections (Seventh Congress); presiding judge of the court of common pleas; chief justice of the Massachusetts supreme court in 1809; died in Stockbridge, Berkshire County, Mass., October 25, 1820; interment in Stockbridge Cemetery.

**Bibliography:** *DAB*.

**BACON, Mark Reeves,** a Representative from Michigan; born in Phillipstown, White County, Ill., February 29, 1852; attended the public schools of his native city; taught school at Bolivar (Mo.) Academy in 1871; studied law; was admitted to the bar on July 4, 1876, and commenced practice in Fairfield, Wayne County, Ill.; city attorney of Fairfield, Ill.; delegate to several State conventions; moved to Orlando, Fla., in 1882 and to Jacksonville, Fla., in 1886 and engaged in the abstract business; moved to Wyandotte, Wayne County, Mich., in 1895 and became associated with the Michigan Alkali Co.; presented credentials as a Republican Member-elect to the Sixty-fifth Congress and served from March 4 until December 13, 1917, when he was succeeded by Samuel W. Beakes, who contested his election; was not a candidate for renomination in 1918; retired in 1918 and resided in Wyandotte, Mich.; died at his winter home in Pasadena, Calif., August 20, 1941; interment in San Gabriel Cemetery, San Gabriel, Calif.

**BACON, Robert Low,** a Representative from New York; born in Jamaica Plain, Boston, Mass., July 23, 1884; attended the public schools; was graduated from Harvard University in 1907 and from its law school in 1910; was an employee of the United States Treasury Department in 1910 and 1911; moved to Old Westbury, N.Y., in 1911 and engaged in the banking business in New York City,

1911-1922; delegate to several State conventions; delegate to the Republican National Convention of 1920; attended the business men's training camp at Plattsburgh, N.Y. in 1915; served on the Texas border with the New York National Guard in 1916; during the First World War served with the United States military forces from April 24, 1917, to January 2, 1919, attaining the rank of major; awarded the Distinguished Service Medal; commissioned in the United States Officers' Reserve Corps with the rank of lieutenant colonel in 1919; promoted to colonel in January 1923 and served until his death; elected as a Republican to the Sixty-eighth and to the seven succeeding Congresses, and served from March 4, 1923 until his death at Lake Success, Long Island, N.Y., en route from a visit to New York City, September 12, 1938; interment in Arlington National Cemetery, Va.

**BACON, William Johnson** (son of Ezekiel Bacon and grandson of John Bacon), a Representative from New York; born in Williamstown, Mass., February 18, 1803; moved with his parents to Utica, N.Y., in 1815; was graduated from Hamilton College, Clinton, N.Y., in 1822; studied law and was graduated from the Litchfield Law School in 1824; was admitted to the bar the same year and commenced practice in Utica, Oneida County, N.Y.; appointed city attorney in 1837; member of the Massachusetts assembly in 1850; elected trustee of Hamilton College in 1851; elected judge of the Massachusetts supreme court of the fifth district in 1854 and served until 1870; elected as a Republican to the Forty-fifth Congress (March 4, 1877-March 3, 1879); was not a candidate for renomination in 1878; resumed the practice of law; died in Utica, N.Y., July 3, 1889; interment in Forest Hill Cemetery.

**BADGER, De Witt Clinton,** a Representative from Ohio; born near London, Madison County, Ohio, August 7, 1858; attended the country schools in Madison County and Mount Union College, Alliance, Ohio; taught school from 1875 to 1880; studied law; was admitted to the bar in 1881 and commenced practice in London, Ohio; prosecuting attorney of Madison County 1882-1885; moved to Columbus, Ohio, and was elected judge of the court of common pleas in 1893; reelected in 1897 and served until 1903, when he resigned, having been elected to Congress; elected as a Democrat to the Fifty-eighth Congress (March 4, 1903-March 3, 1905); declined to be a candidate for renomination in 1904; resumed the practice of law in Columbus, Ohio; mayor of Columbus 1906-1908; died in Columbus, Ohio, May 20, 1926; interment in Greenlawn Cemetery.

**BADGER, George Edmund,** a Senator from North Carolina; born in New Bern, N.C., April 17, 1795; instructed by private teachers and attended preparatory school at New Bern; attended Yale College in 1810 and 1811; studied law; was admitted to the bar in 1814 and commenced practice in New Bern; member of the house of commons of North Carolina in 1816; elected judge of the superior court in 1820 and served until 1825, when he resigned; moved to Raleigh, N.C.; appointed Secretary of the Navy in the Cabinet of President William Henry Harrison, March 5, 1841, reappointed by President John Tyler, and served until September 11, 1841, when he resigned to resume the practice of law; elected as a Whig to the United States Senate in 1846 to fill the vacancy caused by the resignation of William H. Haywood; reelected in 1849 and served from November 25, 1846, to March 3, 1855; was not a candidate for reelection; chairman, Committee on Enrolled Bills (Thirty-first Congress); nominated by President Millard Fillmore on January 10, 1853, as an Associate Justice of the United States Supreme Court, but the nomination was postponed by the Senate on February 11, 1853 and not taken up again; returned to Raleigh and resumed the practice of law; member of the North Carolina State convention in 1861; died in Raleigh, N.C., May 11, 1866; interment in Oakwood Cemetery.

**Bibliography:** *DAB*; London, Lawrence F. "The Public Career of George E. Badger." Ph.D. dissertation, University of North Carolina, 1936.

**BADGER, Luther,** a Representative from New York; born in Partridgefield (now Peru), Mass., April 10, 1785; moved with his father to New York in 1786; attended Hamilton College in 1807; studied law; was admitted to the bar in 1812 and commenced practice in Jamesville, Onondaga County, N.Y.; judge advocate of the Twenty-seventh Brigade, New York Militia, 1819-1827; elected to the Nineteenth Congress (March 4, 1825-March 3, 1827); resumed the practice of his profession; moved to Broome County in 1832; examiner in chancery 1833-1847; appointed commissioner of United States loans in 1840, and served until 1843; elected district attorney of Broome County and served from July 5, 1847, until his resignation in November 1849; resumed the practice of law in Jordan, Onondaga County, N.Y., where he died in 1869; interment in Jordan Cemetery.

**BADHAM, Robert Edward,** a Representative from California; born in Los Angeles, Calif., June 9, 1929; attended the public schools of Beverly Hills, Calif.; graduated, Beverly Hills High School, 1947; attended Occidental College, Eagle Rock, Calif., 1947-1948; B.A., Stanford (Calif.) University, 1951; business executive; served on active duty with the United States Naval Reserve, 1951-1954; director, officer, Hoffman Hardware Co., Los Angeles, 1952-1969; served in California assembly, 1963-1976; delegate to California State Republican conventions, 1962-1976; delegate to the Republican National Conventions of 1964, 1968, 1972, 1980 and 1984; elected as a Republican to the Ninety-fifth and to the five succeeding Congresses (January 3, 1977-January 3, 1989); was not a candidate for reelection in 1988 to the One Hundred First Congress; is a resident of Newport Beach, Calif.

**BADILLO, Herman,** a Representative from New York; born in Caguas, P.R., August 21, 1929; attended the New York City public schools; B.B.A., City College of New York, 1951; LL.B., Brooklyn Law School, 1954; admitted to the New York bar in 1955 and commenced practice in New York City; certified public accountant, 1956; commissioner, New York City Department of Relocation, 1962-1965; elected Bronx, N.Y., borough president, 1965-1969; delegate to New York State Constitutional convention, 1967; delegate to the Democratic National Conventions of 1968, 1972 and 1976; unsuccessful candidate for the Democratic nomination for mayor of New York City, 1969, 1973 and 1977; elected as a Democrat to the Ninety-second and to the three succeeding Congresses, and served from January 3, 1971 until his resignation on December 31, 1977, to become a deputy mayor of New York City for the term commencing in January 1978, and served in that capacity until his resignation in September 1979; resumed the practice of law in New York City; chairman, Board of Directors of the State of New York Mortgage Agency, February 1984-May 1986; unsuccessful candidate for New York State comptroller in 1986; unsuccessful Republican-Liberal Fusion candidate for New York City comptroller in 1993; appointed by Mayor Rudolph W. Giuliani as Special Counsel for the Fiscal Oversight of Education, and as a member of the Mayor's Judiciary Committee; is a resident of the Bronx, N.Y.

**BAER, George, Jr.,** a Representative from Maryland; born in Frederick, Md., in 1763; attended the common schools; engaged in mercantile pursuits; member of the State house of delegates in 1794; elected as a Federalist to the Fifth and Sixth Congresses (March 4, 1797-March 3, 1801); again a member of the State house of delegates, in 1808 and 1809; judge of the orphans' court of Frederick County in 1813; elected as a Federalist to the Fourteenth Congress (March 4, 1815-March 3, 1817); resumed his former mercantile pursuits; mayor of Frederick in 1820; died in Frederick, Md., April 3, 1834; interment in Mount Olivet Cemetery.

**BAER, John Miller,** a Representative from North Dakota; born at Black Creek, Outagamie County, Wis., March 29, 1886; attended the public schools; was graduated from Lawrence University, Appleton, Wis., in 1909; moved to Beach, Golden Valley County, N.Dak., in 1909; engaged as a civil engineer and in agricultural pursuits from 1909 until 1915; furnished cartoons and articles to newspapers from 1909 to 1917; postmaster of Beach, N.Dak., 1909-1915; elected as a Republican to the Sixty-fifth Congress to fill the vacancy caused by the death of Henry T. Helgesen; reelected to the Sixty-sixth Congress and served from July 10, 1917, to March 3, 1921; chairman, Committee on Expenditures in the Department of Agriculture (Sixty-sixth Congress); unsuccessful candidate for reelection in 1920 to the Sixty-seventh Congress; resumed activities as a cartoonist and journalist; died in Washington, D.C., February 18, 1970; interment in Gate of Heaven Cemetery, Silver Spring, Md.

**Bibliography:** Reid, Bill G. "John Miller Baer: Nonpartisan League Cartoonist and Congressman." *North Dakota History* 44 (Winter 1977): 4-13.

**BAESLER, Henry Scott (Scotty),** a Representative from Kentucky; born in Athens, Ky., July 9, 1941; B.S., University of Kentucky, 1963; J.D., University of Kentucky School of Law, 1966; attorney; administrator, Fayette County Legal Aid; vice mayor of Lexington, Ky.; Fayette County district judge; unsuccessful candidate in 1991 for nomination for Governor of Kentucky; mayor of Lexington, 1981-1993; elected as a Democrat to the One Hundred Third and One Hundred Fourth Congresses (January 3, 1993-January 3, 1997); is a resident of Lexington, Ky.

**BAFALIS, Louis Arthur (Skip),** a Representative from Florida; born in Boston, Suffolk County, Mass., September 28, 1929; attended the public schools in Manchester, N.H.; A.B., St. Anselm's College, Manchester, N.H., 1952; served in the United States Army as private and rose to rank of captain, 1953-1956; investment banker; member, Florida house of representatives, 1964; Florida senate, 1966-1970; unsuccessful candidate for nomination for Governor of Florida in 1970; elected as a Republican to the Ninety-third Congress and to the four succeeding Congresses (January 3, 1973-January 3, 1983); was not a candidate for reelection in 1982 to the Ninety-eighth Congress, but was an unsuccessful candidate for election for Governor of Florida; governmental affairs consultant in Washington, D.C., and Florida; is a resident of Palm Beach, Fla.

**BAGBY, Arthur Pendleton,** a Senator from Alabama; born in Louise County, Va., in 1794; studied law; was admitted to the bar in 1819 and commenced practice in Claiborne, Ala.; member of the State house of representatives in 1821, 1822, 1824, and 1834-1836, serving as speaker in 1822 and 1836; served in the State senate in 1825; elected Governor of Alabama in 1837, reelected in 1839, and served from November 21, 1837 to November 22, 1841; elected as a Democrat to the United States Senate to fill the vacancy caused by the resignation of Clement C. Clay and served from November 24, 1841, until June 16, 1848, when he resigned to become Minister to Russia; chairman, Committee on Territories (Twenty-eighth and Twenty-ninth Congresses), Committee on Claims (Twenty-ninth Congress), Committee on Indian Affairs (Twenty-ninth Congress); appointed United States Minister to Russia on June 15, 1848 and served until May 1849; member of the commission to codify the State laws of Alabama in 1852; moved to Mobile, Ala., in 1856, where he died on September 21, 1858; interment in Magnolia Cemetery, Mobile, Ala.

**Bibliography:** *DAB*; Martin, John M. "The Senatorial Career of Arthur Pendleton Bagby." *Alabama Historical Quarterly* 42 (Fall/Winter 1980): 124-56.

**BAGBY, John Courts,** a Representative from Illinois; born in Glasgow, Ky., January 24, 1819; attended the public schools; was graduated as a civil engineer from Bacon College, Harrodsburg, Ky., in June 1840; studied law; was admitted to the bar in March 1845 and commenced practice in Rushville, Schuyler County, Ill., in April 1846; elected as a Democrat to the Forty-fourth Congress (March 4, 1875-March 3, 1877); was not a candidate for renomination in 1876; resumed the practice of his profession in Rushville, Ill.; judge of Schuyler County 1882-1885; judge of the sixth judicial circuit court of Illinois 1885-1891; resumed the practice of law; died in Rushville, Ill., April 4, 1896; interment in Rushville Cemetery.

**BAGLEY, George Augustus,** a Representative from New York; born in Watertown, Jefferson County, N.Y., July 22, 1826; received an academic training; studied law; was admitted to the New York bar in 1847 and commenced practice in Watertown, N.Y.; retired from the practice of his profession in 1853 to engage in the manufacture of iron; president of the village of Watertown in 1866; supervisor of the town 1865-1868; elected as a Republican to the Forty-fourth and Forty-fifth Congresses (March 4, 1875-March 3, 1879); resumed the manufacture of iron; died in Watertown, N.Y., May 12, 1915; interment in Brookside Cemetery.

**BAGLEY, John Holroyd, Jr.,** a Representative from New York; born in Hudson, Columbia County, N.Y., November 26, 1832; attended the common schools; went to California in 1851 and engaged in mining and other pursuits; returned to New York and engaged in steamboating on the Hudson River; settled in Catskill, Greene County, N.Y., and engaged in mercantile pursuits and the manufacture of leather; supervisor of the town of Catskill 1860-1864; elected as a Democrat to the Forty-fourth Congress (March 4, 1875-March 3, 1877); was not a candidate for renomination in 1876; resumed his former mercantile pursuits; elected to the Forty-eighth Congress (March 4, 1883-March 3, 1885); chairman, Committee on Manufactures (Forty-eighth Congress); was not a candidate for renomination in 1884; engaged in banking and the insurance business and also served as vice president of the Catskill Mountain Railway Co.; trustee of the village of Catskill; member of the State assembly in 1888; unsuccessful candidate for election in 1896 to the Fifty-fifth Congress; died in Catskill, N.Y., October 23, 1902; interment in the Village Cemetery.

**BAILEY, Alexander Hamilton,** a Representative from New York; born in Minisink, N.Y., August 14, 1817; was graduated from Princeton College in 1837; studied law; was admitted to the bar and commenced practice; examiner in chancery of Greene County 1840-1842; justice of the peace of the town of Catskill for four years; member of the State assembly in 1849; judge of Greene County 1851-1855; moved to Rome, Oneida County, N.Y., in 1856 and continued the practice of law; served in the State senate 1861-1864; elected as a Republican to the Fortieth Congress to fill the vacancy caused by the resignation of Roscoe Conkling; reelected to the Forty-first Congress and served from November 30, 1867, to March 3, 1871; chairman, Committee on Expenditures in the Department of State (Forty-first Congress); was not a candidate for renomination in 1870; elected judge of the Oneida County Court in 1871 and served until his death in Rome, Oneida County, N.Y., April 20, 1874; interment in Rome Cemetery.

**BAILEY, Cleveland Monroe,** a Representative from West Virginia; born on a farm near St. Marys, Pleasants County, W.Va., July 15, 1886; attended the public schools, and West Liberty State College, West Liberty, W.Va.; was graduated from Geneva College, Beaver Falls, Pa., in 1908; high school principal at Clarksburg, W.Va., in 1917 and 1918; district supervisor of schools 1919-1922; councilman of Clarksburg, W.Va., 1921-1923; Associated Press editor in Clarksburg, W.Va., 1923-1933; assistant State auditor 1933-1941; State budget director 1941-1944; delegate to the Democratic National Convention at Chicago in 1932; elected as a Democrat to the Seventy-ninth Congress (January 3, 1945-January 3, 1947); unsuccessful candidate for reelection in 1946 to the Eightieth Congress; State tax statistician in 1947 and 1948; elected to the Eighty-first and to the six succeeding Congresses (January 3, 1949-January 3, 1963); unsuccessful candidate for reelection in 1962 to the Eighty-eighth Congress; was a resident of Clarksburg, W.Va.; died in Charleston, W.Va., July 13, 1965; interment in Greenlawn Cemetery, Clarksburg, W.Va.

**BAILEY, David Jackson,** a Representative from Georgia; born in Lexington, Ga., March 11, 1812; educated by a private tutor; moved to Jackson, Butts County, in 1829; studied law; was admitted to the bar in 1831 and practiced; elected to the State legislature before he was twenty-one, but was not permitted to take his seat because he was not of legal age; served as captain of a company through the Seminole and Creek Wars; served in the State house of representatives in 1835 and 1847; member of the State senate in 1838, 1849, and 1850; delegate to the Democratic county conventions in 1839 and 1850; secretary of the State senate 1839-1841; elected as a State Rights candidate to the Thirty-second Congress and as a Democrat to the Thirty-third Congress (March 4, 1851-March 3, 1855); unsuccessful candidate for reelection in 1854 to the Thirty-fourth Congress; again a member of the State senate, in 1855 and 1856, and served as president; resumed the practice of law in Jackson, Ga.; member of the secession convention in 1861; entered the Confederate Army during the Civil War and became colonel of the Thirtieth Regiment, Georgia Infantry; moved to Griffin, Spalding County, Ga., in 1861, where he died June 14, 1897; interment in Oak Hill Cemetery.

**BAILEY, Donald Allen,** a Representative from Pennsylvania; born in Pittsburgh, Pa., July 21, 1945; attended the public schools of Allegheny and Westmoreland Counties; graduated, Greensburg (Pa.) High School, 1963; B.A., University of Michigan, Ann Arbor, 1967; J.D., Duquesne University School of Law, Pittsburgh, Pa., 1976; served in the United States Army, first lieutenant, Vietnam, 1967-1970; admitted to the Pennsylvania bar in 1976 and commenced practice in Greensburg, Pa., and before the Supreme Court of Pennsylvania; laborer, painter, plant security, and assembly line worker, J. and L. Steel Corp.; administrative head and registration chairman, Pennsylvania Democratic Committee; elected as a Democrat to the Ninety-sixth and Ninety-seventh Congresses (January 3, 1979-January 3, 1983); unsuccessful candidate for renomination in 1982 to the Ninety-eighth Congress; elected auditor general of Pennsylvania in 1984; was an unsuccessful candidate for nomination to the United States Senate in 1986; is a resident of Greensburg, Pa.

**BAILEY, Goldsmith Fox,** a Representative from Massachusetts; born in Westmoreland, Cheshire County, N.H., July 17, 1823; attended the public schools of Fitchburg, Mass.; editor and publisher of the Bellows Falls (Vt.) Gazette in 1844; studied law; was admitted to the bar in 1848 and commenced practice in Fitchburg, Mass.; served on the school committee 1849-1854; appointed postmaster of Fitchburg on May 3, 1851 and served until May 4, 1853, when his successor was appointed; member of the Massachusetts house of representatives in 1857; served in the Massachusetts senate 1858-1860; elected as a Republican to the Thirty-seventh Congress and served from March 4, 1861, until his death in Fitchburg, Worcester County, Mass., May 8, 1862; interment in Laurel Hill Cemetery.

**BAILEY, James Edmund,** a Senator from Tennessee; born in Montgomery County, Tenn., August 15, 1822; attended the Clarksville Academy and the University of Nashville; studied law; was admitted to the Tennessee bar in 1843 and commenced practice in Clarksville, Montgomery County; elected as a Whig to the Tennessee house of representatives in 1853; during the Civil War served in the

Confederate Army as colonel of the Forty-ninth Tennessee Regiment; was appointed a member of the court of arbitration by Governor John C. Brown of Tennessee in 1874; elected as a Democrat to the United States Senate to fill the vacancy caused by the death of Andrew Johnson and served from January 19, 1877, to March 3, 1881; was an unsuccessful candidate for reelection in 1880; chairman, Committee on Education and Labor (Forty-sixth Congress); resumed the practice of law; died in Clarksville, Tenn., December 29, 1885; interment in Greenwood Cemetery.

**Bibliography:** McCord, Franklin. "J.E. Bailey: A Gentleman of Clarksville." *Tennessee Historical Quarterly* 23 (September 1964): 246-268.

**BAILEY, Jeremiah,** a Representative from Maine; born in Little Compton, R.I., May 1, 1773; attended the common schools and was graduated from Brown University, Providence, R.I., in 1794; studied law; was admitted to the bar and commenced practice in Wiscasset, Maine (until 1820 a district of Massachusetts), in 1798; presidential elector on the Federalist ticket in 1808; member of the general court 1811-1814; judge of probate 1816-1834; elected as a Whig to the Twenty-fourth Congress (March 4, 1835-March 3, 1837); unsuccessful candidate for reelection in 1836 to the Twenty-fifth Congress; collector of customs of Wiscasset 1849-1853; died in Wiscasset, Lincoln County, Maine, July 6, 1853; interment in Evergreen Cemetery.

**BAILEY, John,** a Representative from Massachusetts; born in 1786 in that part of Stoughton, Norfolk County, Mass., which in 1797 was set apart and named Canton; was graduated from Brown University, Providence, R.I., in 1807; tutor and librarian at Providence, R.I., 1807-1814; member of the Massachusetts house of representatives 1814-1817; clerk in the Department of State in Washington, D.C., 1817-1823; presented credentials as a Member-elect to the Eighteenth Congress, but the election was contested on the ground that he was not a resident of the district he purported to represent, and by resolution of March 18, 1824, the House declared he was not entitled to the seat; returned to Canton, Mass., and was subsequently elected to fill the vacancy thus caused in this Congress; reelected to the Nineteenth and to the two succeeding Congresses and served from December 13, 1824, to March 3, 1831; chairman, Committee on Expenditures in the Department of State (Nineteenth Congress); was not a candidate for renomination in 1830 to the Twenty-second Congress; member of the State senate in 1831 and 1834; unsuccessful Anti-Masonic candidate for election in 1834 for Governor; died in Dorchester, Mass., June 26, 1835; interment in Oak Grove Cemetery.

**BAILEY, John Mosher,** a Representative from New York; born in Bethlehem, N.Y., August 24, 1838; attended the public schools, and Hudson River Institute at Claverack, N.Y.; was graduated from Union College, Schenectady, N.Y., in 1861; during the Civil War entered the Union Army as a first lieutenant and adjutant of the One Hundred and Seventy-seventh Regiment, New York Volunteer Infantry, and served in the Department of the Gulf in 1862; graduated from the Albany Law School in 1864; was admitted to the bar the same year and commenced practice in Albany, N.Y.; assistant district attorney of Albany County 1865-1867; collector of internal revenue 1871-1874; district attorney of Albany County 1874-1877; elected as a Republican to the Forty-fifth Congress to fill the vacancy caused by the death of Terence J. Quinn; reelected to the Forty-sixth Congress and served from November 5, 1878, to March 3, 1881; was not a candidate for renomination in 1880 to the Forty-seventh Congress; United States consul to Hamburg, Germany, by appointment of President James A. Garfield from 1881 to 1885; delegate to the Republican National Convention of 1888; appointed by President Benjamin Harrison as surveyor of customs at Albany, N.Y., and served from 1889 to 1894; resumed the practice

of law; died in Albany, N.Y., February 21, 1916; interment in Elmwood Cemetery, Bethlehem, N.Y.

**BAILEY, Joseph,** a Representative from Pennsylvania; born in Pennsbury Township, Chester County, Pa., March 18, 1810; attended the common schools; learned the trade of a hatter, which he carried on in Parkersville; served in the Pennsylvania house of representatives in 1840; member of the Pennsylvania senate in 1843; moved to Perry County in 1845; again a member of the Pennsylvania senate 1851-1853; treasurer of Pennsylvania in 1854; studied law; was admitted to the bar in 1860; elected as a Democrat to the Thirty-seventh and Thirty-eighth Congresses (March 4, 1861-March 3, 1865); member of the Pennsylvania constitutional convention in 1872; died at Bailey Station, Perry County, Pa., on August 26, 1885; interment in Bloomfield Cemetery, New Bloomfield, Pa.

**BAILEY, Joseph Weldon** (father of Joseph Weldon Bailey, Jr.), a Representative and a Senator from Texas; born near Crystal Springs, Copiah County, Miss., October 6, 1862; attended the common schools; studied law; was admitted to the bar in 1883 and commenced practice in Hazlehurst, Miss.; moved to Gainesville, Tex., in 1885 and continued the practice of law; elected as a Democrat to the Fifty-second and to the four succeeding Congresses (March 4, 1891-March 3, 1901); was not a candidate for renomination in 1900 to the Fifty-seventh Congress; elected to the United States Senate in 1901, reelected in 1907, and served from March 4, 1901, until January 3, 1913, when he resigned; chairman, Committee on Revolutionary Claims (Sixty-first Congress), Committee on Woman Suffrage (Sixty-first Congress), Committee on Additional Accomodations for the Library (Sixty-second Congress); resumed the practice of law in Washington, D.C.; subsequently moved to Dallas, Tex., in 1921 and continued the practice of law; was an unsuccessful candidate for nomination in 1920 for Governor of Texas; died in a courtroom in Sherman, Tex., on April 13, 1929; interment in Gainesville Cemetery, Gainesville, Tex.

**Bibliography:** *DAB*; Acheson, Sam Hanna. *Joe Bailey, The Last Democrat.* 1932. Reprint. Freeport, N.Y.: Books For Libraries Press, 1970; Holcomb, Bob Charles. "Senator Joe Bailey, Two Decades of Controversy." Ph.D. dissertation, Texas Tech University, 1968.

**BAILEY, Joseph Weldon, Jr.** (son of Joseph Weldon Bailey), a Representative from Texas; born in Gainesville, Cooke County, Tex., December 15, 1892; attended the public schools in Gainesville, Tex., and Washington, D.C.; was graduated from Princeton University in 1915, and from the University of Virginia at Charlottesville in 1919; during the First World War served as a first lieutenant in the Three Hundred and Fourteenth Regiment of Field Artillery from August 15, 1917 to March 24, 1919; studied law; was admitted to the bar in 1920 and commenced practice in Fort Worth, Tex.; moved to Dallas, Tex., the same year and continued the practice of his profession; elected as a Democrat to the Seventy-third Congress (March 4, 1933-January 3, 1935); was not a candidate in 1934 for renomination to the House of Representatives, but was an unsuccessful candidate for nomination to the United States Senate; resumed the practice of law in Dallas, Tex.; during the Second World War served as a captain in the Marine Corps from May 13, 1942, until his death in an Army hospital at Gainesville, Tex., July 17, 1943; interment in Gainesville Cemetery.

**BAILEY, Josiah William,** a Senator from North Carolina; born in Warrenton, Warren County, N.C., September 14, 1873; moved with his parents to Raleigh, N.C., in 1877; attended the public schools and Raleigh Male Academy; was graduated from Wake Forest College in 1893; editor of the Biblical Recorder 1893-1907; member of the State board of agriculture 1896-1900; studied law; was admitted to the bar in 1908 and commenced practice in Raleigh, N.C.; United States collector of internal revenue for North Carolina

1913-1921; member of the North Carolina Constitutional Commission in 1915; trustee of the University of North Carolina 1930; elected as a Democrat to the United States Senate in 1930; reelected in 1936 and again in 1942 and served from March 4, 1931, until his death in Raleigh, N.C., on December 15, 1946; chairman, Committee on Claims (Seventy-third through Seventy-fifth Congresses), Committee on Commerce (Seventy-sixth through Seventy-ninth Congresses); interment in Oakwood Cemetery.

**Bibliography:** *DAB*; Marcello, Ronald. "Senator Josiah Bailey, Harry Hopkins, and the WPA: A Prelude to the Conservative Coalition." *Southern Studies* 22 (Winter 1983): 321-329; Moore, John R. *Senator Josiah William Bailey of North Carolina: A Political Biography*. Durham: Duke University Press, 1968.

**BAILEY, Ralph Emerson,** a Representative from Missouri; born in Cainsville, Harrison County, Mo., July 14, 1878; moved to Illinois with his parents, who settled in Benton, Franklin County, in 1880; attended the graded and high schools at Benton; moved to Bloomfield, Stoddard County, Mo., in 1897; was graduated from the Southeast Missouri Teachers' College at Cape Girardeau in 1901; afterwards took a special course in the University of Missouri at Columbia; studied law; was admitted to the bar in 1907 and commenced practice in Bloomfield, Mo.; moved to Sikeston, Scott County, Mo., in 1910 and continued the practice of law; city attorney 1912-1914 and again 1918-1922; served as a member of the board of regents of the Southeast Missouri Teachers' College; elected as a Republican to the Sixty-ninth Congress (March 4, 1925-March 3, 1927); was not a candidate for renomination in 1926 to the Seventieth Congress; resumed the practice of law in Sikeston, Mo.; died in Cape Girardeau, Mo., April 8, 1948; interment in the City Cemetery, Sikeston, Mo.

**BAILEY, Theodorus,** a Representative and a Senator from New York; born near Fishkill, Dutchess County, N.Y., October 12, 1758; attended the rural schools; studied law; was admitted to the bar in 1778 and commenced practice in Poughkeepsie, N.Y.; served with the New York Militia during the Revolutionary War; served in the State militia 1786-1805 and attained the rank of brigadier general; elected to the Third and Fourth Congresses (March 4, 1793-March 3, 1797); elected to the Sixth Congress (March 4, 1799-March 3, 1801); elected to the Seventh Congress to fill the vacancy caused by the resignation of Thomas Tillotson and served from October 6, 1801, to March 3, 1803; simultaneously served in the New York State assembly in 1802; elected to the United States Senate and served from March 4, 1803, to January 16, 1804, when he resigned to accept the position of postmaster of the city of New York, which he held until his death on September 6, 1828; interment in the Dutch Burying Ground; reinterment in the Rural Cemetery, Poughkeepsie, N.Y., January 8, 1864.

**BAILEY, Warren Worth,** a Representative from Pennsylvania; born in New Winchester, Hendricks County, Ind., January 8, 1855; moved to Illinois with his parents, who settled in Edgar County in 1863; attended the country schools; became a telegrapher, at which he worked until 1875, when he joined the Kansas (Ill.) News and learned the printing trade; engaged in the publishing business with his brother at Carlisle, Ind., in 1877; subsequently they purchased the Vincennes News, which they published until 1887; moved to Chicago in 1887 and became a member of the staff of the Daily News and later of the Evening Mail; moved to Johnstown, Pa., in 1893 and published the Daily Democrat, devoted to the single-tax principle; unsuccessful Democratic candidate for election in 1906 to the Sixtieth Congress; delegate at large to the Democratic National Convention of 1912; elected as a Democrat to the Sixty-third and Sixty-fourth Congresses (March 4, 1913-March 3, 1917); chairman, Committee on Mileage (Sixty-third Congress), Committee on Expenditures in the Department of Justice (Sixty-fourth Congress); unsuccessful candidate for reelection in 1916 to the Sixty-fifth

Congress; unsuccessful candidate for election in 1920 to the Sixty-seventh Congress, in 1922 to the Sixty-eighth Congress, and in 1926 to the Seventieth Congress; unsuccessfully contested the election of Anderson H. Walters to the Sixty-ninth Congress; resumed journalism in Johnstown, Cambria County, Pa., where he died on November 9, 1928; interment in Grandview Cemetery.

**BAILEY, Wendell,** a Representative from Missouri; born in Willow Springs, Howell County, Mo., July 30, 1940; attended public schools in Willow Springs; B.S., Southwest Missouri State University, Springfield, 1962; automobile dealer; member, Willow Springs City council, 1969-1971; mayor of Willow Springs, 1971-1972; member, Missouri State house of representatives, 1972-1980; elected as a Republican to the Ninety-seventh Congress (January 3, 1981-January 3, 1983); was an unsuccessful candidate for reelection in 1982 to the Ninety-eighth Congress; resumed business interests; elected Missouri State treasurer in 1984 for the four-year term beginning in January 1985; is a resident of Willow Springs, Mo.

**BAILEY, Willis Joshua,** a Representative from Kansas; born near Mount Carroll, Carroll County, Ill., October 12, 1854; attended the common schools, Mount Carroll High School, and the University of Illinois at Urbana; moved to Nemaha County, Kans., in 1879; engaged in agricultural pursuits, stock raising, and banking; founded the town of Baileyville, Kans.; member of the Kansas house of representatives 1888-1890; president of the Republican State League in 1893; member of the Kansas State Board of Agriculture 1895-1899; elected as a Republican to the Fifty-sixth Congress (March 4, 1899-March 3, 1901); was not a candidate for renomination in 1900 to the Fifty-seventh Congress; elected Governor of Kansas in 1902 and served from January 12, 1903 to January 9, 1905; moved to Atchison, Kans., in 1907 and engaged in the banking business; elected a director of the Federal Reserve Bank of Kansas City, Mo., in 1914, governor in 1922, and served until his death in Mission Hills, Johnson County, Kans., May 19, 1932; interment in Mount Vernon Cemetery, Atchison, Kans.

**BAIRD, David** (father of David Baird, Jr.), a Senator from New Jersey; born in Londonderry, County Derry, Ireland, April 7, 1839; attended the common schools; immigrated to the United States in 1856 and entered the lumber business in Port Deposit, Md.; moved in 1860 to Camden, N.J., where he continued in the lumber business and also engaged in banking; member of the board of chosen freeholders of Camden County 1876-1880; sheriff of Camden County 1887-1889 and 1895-1897; member of the State board of assessors in 1895 and 1901-1909; unsuccessful candidate for election to the United States Senate in 1910; appointed and subsequently elected as a Republican to the United States Senate to fill the vacancy caused by the death of William Hughes and served from February 23, 1918, to March 3, 1919; was not a candidate for renomination in 1918; resumed his former business pursuits in Camden, N.J., where he died on February 25, 1927; interment in Harleigh Cemetery.

**BAIRD, David, Jr.** (son of David Baird), a Senator from New Jersey; born in Camden, N.J., October 10, 1881; attended the Raymond Academy at Camden and Penn Charter School in Philadelphia, Pa.; was graduated from Lawrenceville (N.J.) School in 1899 and from Princeton University in 1903; engaged in a lumber business and banking in Camden, N.J., from 1903 to 1929; appointed as a Republican to the United States Senate to fill the vacancy caused by the resignation of Walter E. Edge and served from November 30, 1929, to December 2, 1930, when a duly elected successor qualified; was not a candidate for election to the vacancy in 1930; unsuccessful candidate for election in 1931 for Governor of New Jersey; resumed former business pursuits; was appointed by the Governor to the Delaware River Joint Commission to fill an unexpired term in 1938; engaged in insurance brokerage business; died in Camden, N.J., February 28, 1955; interment in Harleigh Cemetery.

**BAIRD, Joseph Edward,** a Representative from Ohio; born at Perrysburg, Wood County, Ohio, November 12, 1865; attended the public schools; was graduated from the Perrysburg High School in 1885 and from the law department of the University of Michigan at Ann Arbor in 1893; was admitted to the bar in 1893 but did not practice; moved to Bowling Green, Ohio, in 1894 and served as county clerk of Wood County, 1894-1900; engaged as a dealer in oil and farm lands from 1900 to 1921; served as mayor of Bowling Green, 1902-1905, and as postmaster, 1910-1914; secretary of the Ohio Public Utilities Commission, 1921-1923; served as assistant secretary of state, 1923-1929; elected as a Republican to the Seventy-first Congress (March 4, 1929-March 3, 1931); unsuccessful candidate for reelection in 1930 to the Seventy-second Congress; retired from active business pursuits and political activities; died in Bowling Green, Ohio, June 14, 1942; interment in Oak Grove Cemetery.

**BAIRD, Samuel Thomas,** a Representative from Louisiana; born in Oak Ridge, Morehouse Parish, La., May 5, 1861; educated under private tutors and attended the Vincennes (Ind.) University; studied law; was admitted to the bar in 1882 and commenced practice in Bastrop, Morehouse Parish, La.; district attorney of the sixth judicial district 1884-1888; district judge of the sixth judicial district 1888-1892; resumed the practice of law in Bastrop; member of the State senate in 1896; delegate to the Democratic National Convention at Chicago in 1896; elected as a Democrat to the Fifty-fifth and Fifty-sixth Congresses and served from March 4, 1897, until his death in Washington, D.C., April 22, 1899; interment in Christ Church Cemetery, Bastrop, La.

**BAKER, Caleb,** a Representative from New York; born in Providence, R.I., in 1762; moved to New York in 1790 and resided in the towns of Chemung, Ashland, and Newtown, Tioga County, from 1790 to 1836, and in Southport, Chemung County, from 1836 until his death; studied law; was admitted to the bar and practiced; assessor of the town of Chemung in 1791; taught school in Wellsburg, Chemung County, in 1803 and 1804; appointed surrogate of Tioga County on April 7, 1806, April 13, 1825, and again in 1829; appointed judge of common pleas in 1810; member of the State assembly in 1814, 1815, and again in 1829; justice of the peace of the town of Chemung in 1816; elected to the Sixteenth Congress (March 4, 1819-March 3, 1821); died in Southport (now a part of Elmira), Chemung County, N.Y., June 26, 1849; interment in Fitzsimmons Cemetery.

**BAKER, Charles Simeon,** a Representative from New York; born in Churchville, Monroe County, N.Y., February 18, 1839; attended the common schools, Cary Collegiate Institute of Oakfield, and the New York Seminary at Lima; taught school; studied law; was admitted to the bar in December 1860 and commenced practice in Rochester, N.Y.; served in the Union Army during the Civil War as first lieutenant, Company E, Twenty-seventh Regiment, New York Volunteer Infantry; disabled in the first Battle of Bull Run, July 21, 1861, and honorably discharged; member of the New York State assembly, 1879-1882; served in the State senate, 1884-1885; elected as a Republican to the Forty-ninth and to the two succeeding Congresses (March 4, 1885-March 3, 1891); chairman, Committee on Commerce (Fifty-first Congress); resumed the practice of law in Rochester, N.Y.; died in Washington, D.C., April 21, 1902; interment in Mount Hope Cemetery, Rochester, N.Y.

**BAKER, David Jewett,** a Senator from Illinois; born in East Haddam, Conn., September 7, 1792; moved with his parents to Ontario County, N.Y.; attended the common schools and was graduated from Hamilton College, Clinton, N.Y., in 1816; studied law; was admitted to the Illinois bar in 1819 and commenced the practice of law in Kaskaskia, Ill.; probate judge of Randolph County from August 1827 until December 6, 1830, when he resigned to become Senator; appointed as a Democrat to the United States Senate to fill the vacancy caused by the death of John McLean and served from November 12, 1830, to December 11, 1830, when a successor was elected and qualified; was not a candidate for election in 1830 to fill the vacancy; appointed United States district attorney for the district of Illinois in 1833 and served until 1841; resumed the practice of law; died in Alton, Madison County, Ill., August 6, 1869; interment in City Cemetery.

**BAKER, E. LaMar,** a Representative from Tennessee; born in Chattanooga, Hamilton County, Tenn., December 29, 1915; attended the Chattanooga public schools; attended David Lipscomb College, Nashville, Tenn., 1936-1938; B.S., Harding College, Searcy, Ark., 1940; Army Air Corps, 1942-1946; with European Theater of Operations, serving as group executive officer and adjutant; discharged with rank of major; member of the Tennessee State general assembly, 1967-1968; Tennessee State senator, 1969-1970; owner, Commercial Janitors, Inc., 1964-1978; delegate to Tennessee State Republican conventions, 1964-1972; delegate to the Republican National Conventions of 1972, 1980 and 1988; elected as a Republican to the Ninety-second and Ninety-third Congresses (January 3, 1971-January 3, 1975); unsuccessful candidate for reelection in 1974 to the Ninety-fourth Congress, and for election in 1976 to the Ninety-fifth Congress; Regional representative to the Secretary, United States Department of Transportation, 1981-1985; is a resident of Nashville, Tenn.

**BAKER, Edward Dickinson,** a Representative from Illinois and a Senator from Oregon; born in London, England, February 24, 1811; immigrated to the United States in 1815 with his parents, who settled in Philadelphia, Pa.; moved to Illinois in 1825; studied law; was admitted to the bar in 1830 and commenced practice in Springfield; member of the Illinois State house of representatives in 1837; member, State senate, 1840-1844; elected as a Whig to the Twenty-ninth Congress, and served from March 4, 1845 until his resignation on December 24, 1846, to take effect on January 15, 1847; commissioned colonel of the Fourth Regiment, Illinois Volunteer Infantry, on July 4, 1846, and served until he was honorably mustered out on May 29, 1847; participated in the siege of Vera Cruz in March 1847, and commanded a brigade at Cerro Gordo, April 18, 1847; after the Mexican War moved to Galena, Ill.; elected as a Whig to the Thirty-first Congress (March 4, 1849-March 3, 1851); was not a candidate for renomination in 1850 to the Thirty-second Congress; moved to San Francisco, Calif., in 1851 and resumed the practice of law; moved to Oregon in 1860; elected as a Republican to the United States Senate to fill the vacancy in the term beginning March 4, 1859, and served from October 2, 1860, until his death on the battlefield; raised a regiment in New York City and Philadelphia during the Civil War; commissioned brigadier general of United States Volunteers on May 17, 1861, but declined; commissioned colonel of the Seventy-first Regiment, Pennsylvania Volunteer Infantry, on June 22, 1861; offered the rank of major general of United States Volunteers on September 21, 1861, he had not accepted at the time of his death; killed in the Battle of Balls Bluff, Va., October 21, 1861; interment in San Francisco National Cemetery, San Francisco, Calif.

**Bibliography:** *DAB*; Blair, Harry, and Tarshis, Rebecca. *Colonel Edward D. Baker: Lincoln's Constant Ally.* Portland: Oregon Historical Society, 1960; Braden, Gayle Anderson. "The Public Career of Edward Dickinson Baker." Ph.D. dissertation, Vanderbilt University, 1960; Vandenhoff, Anne. *Edward Dickinson Baker: Western Gentleman, Frontier Lawyer, American Statesman.* Auburn, Calif.: Pony Express Printers, 1979.

**BAKER, Ezra,** a Representative from New Jersey; born in Tuckerton, N.J.; moved with his parents to the Province of East Jersey about 1765; educated for the medical profession and commenced practice; moved to Absecon, N.J., in 1799; served as collector of customs at the port of Great Egg Harbor, N.J., from

February 18, 1813, to March 1, 1815; elected as a Republican to the Fourteenth Congress (March 4, 1815-March 3, 1817); moved westward to the "Wabash country" with his sons in 1818 and engaged in the culture of castor beans for the New Orleans market; died in the "Wabash country."

**BAKER, Henry Moore,** a Representative from New Hampshire; born in Bow, near Concord, N.H., January 11, 1841; attended the common schools, Pembroke, Tilton, and Hopkinton Academies, New Hampshire; was graduated from the New Hampshire Conference Seminary in 1859, Dartmouth College, Hanover, N.H., in 1863, and the law school of Columbian (now George Washington) University, Washington, D.C., in 1866; was admitted to the bar in 1866; clerk in the War and Treasury Departments 1864-1874; commenced the practice of law in Washington, D.C., in 1874; judge advocate general of the National Guard of New Hampshire in 1886 and 1887 with rank of brigadier general; member of the State senate in 1891 and 1892; elected as a Republican to the Fifty-third and Fifty-fourth Congresses (March 3, 1893-March 3, 1897); was not a candidate for renomination in 1896; resumed the practice of his profession in Washington, D.C., but retained his legal residence in Bow, N.H.; member of the New Hampshire house of representatives 1905-1909; died in Washington, D.C., May 30, 1912; interment in Alexander Cemetery, Bow, N.H.

**BAKER, Howard Henry** (husband of Irene Bailey Baker and father of Howard Henry Baker, Jr.), a Representative from Tennessee; born in Somerset, Pulaski County, Ky., January 12, 1902; moved with his parents to Huntsville, Scott County, Tenn.; attended the public schools of Scott and Knox Counties, Tenn.; was graduated from the University of Tennessee at Knoxville in 1922 and from its law school in 1924; was admitted to the Tennessee bar in 1923 and commenced the practice of law in Huntsville, Tenn.; publisher of a weekly newspaper in Huntsville, Tenn.; served in the Tennessee house of representatives in 1929 and 1930; member of Scott County Board of Education in 1931 and 1932; attorney general of the nineteenth judicial circuit of Tennessee, 1934-1948; vice president and general counsel of the Oneida and Western Railroad Co., in 1945; member of the board of directors, First National Bank of Oneida, Tenn.; unsuccessful Republican candidate for election in 1938 for Governor of Tennessee; unsuccessful candidate for election in 1940 to the United States Senate; delegate to the Republican National Conventions of 1940, 1948, 1952 and 1956; elected as a Republican to the Eighty-second and to the six succeeding Congresses and served from January 3, 1951 until his death in Knoxville, Tenn., January 7, 1964; interment in Sherwood Memorial Gardens.

**BAKER, Howard Henry, Jr.** (son of Howard Henry Baker, stepson of Irene Bailey Baker, and son-in-law of Everett Dirksen), a Senator from Tennessee; born in Huntsville, Scott County, Tenn., November 15, 1925; attended Tulane University, New Orleans, La., and the University of the South, Sewanee, Tenn.; LL.B., University of Tennessee Law College, 1949; served in the United States Navy, 1943-1946; admitted to the Tennessee bar in 1949 and commenced practice; elected as a Republican to the United States Senate in 1966; reelected in 1972 and again in 1978, and served from January 3, 1967 to January 3, 1985; delivered keynote address at the Republican National Convention of 1976; was not a candidate for reelection in 1984; minority leader (Ninety-fifth and Ninety-sixth Congresses); majority leader (Ninety-seventh and Ninety-eighth Congresses); lawyer in Washington, D.C.; chief of staff to President Ronald Reagan, 1987 to 1988; is a resident of Washington, D.C., and Huntsville, Tenn.

**Bibliography:** Annis, J. Lee, Jr. *Howard Baker: Conciliator in An Age of Crisis.* Lanham, Md.: Madison Books, 1995.

**BAKER, Irene Bailey** (wife of Howard Henry Baker and stepmother of Howard Henry Baker, Jr.), a Representative from Tennessee; born November 17, 1901, in Sevierville, Sevier County, Tenn., attended the public schools of Sevierville and Maryville; studied music; deputy county court clerk, 1918-1922; deputy clerk and master, Chancery Court, Sevierville, Tenn., 1922-1924; Republican National Committeewoman for Tennessee 1960-1964; elected as a Republican to the Eighty-eighth Congress to fill the vacancy caused by the death of her husband, Howard H. Baker, serving from March 10, 1964, to January 3, 1965; was not a candidate in 1964 for renomination to the Eighty-ninth Congress; director, Public Welfare, city of Knoxville, 1965-1971; was a resident of Knoxville, Tenn.; died April 2, 1994.

**BAKER, Jacob Thompson,** a Representative from New Jersey; born near Cowan, Union County, Pa., April 13, 1847; attended the public schools and Bucknell University, Lewisburg, Pa.; studied law; was admitted to the bar in 1870 and commenced practice in Lewisburg, Pa.; chairman of the Democratic State convention in 1905; moved to New Jersey and was one of the founders of Wildwood and the borough of Wildwood Crest; first mayor of the consolidated city of Wildwood in 1911 and 1912; delegate to the Democratic National Convention in 1912; elected as a Democrat to the Sixty-third Congress (March 4, 1913-March 3, 1915); unsuccessful candidate for reelection in 1914 to the Sixty-fourth Congress; resumed real-estate activities in Wildwood, N.J.; died in Philadelphia, Pa., December 7, 1919; interment in Cold Spring Cemetery, Cold Spring, Cape May County, N.J.

**BAKER, Jehu,** a Representative from Illinois; born near Lexington, Fayette County, Ky., November 4, 1822; moved with his father to Lebanon, Ill., in 1829; attended the common schools and McKendree College at Lebanon; studied law; was admitted to the bar in 1846 and commenced practice at Belleville, St. Clair County, Ill.; master in chancery of St. Clair County 1861-1865; elected as a Republican to the Thirty-ninth and Fortieth Congresses (March 4, 1865-March 3, 1869); chairman, Committee on Expenditures in the Post Office Department (Thirty-ninth Congress), Committee on Education and Labor (Fortieth Congress); served as United States Minister to Venezuela from March 4, 1878 to September 5, 1881, and from May 16, 1882 to June 20, 1885, being Minister Resident and consul general for a time during the latter portion of his service; elected as a Republican to the Fiftieth Congress (March 4, 1887-March 3, 1889); unsuccessful candidate for reelection in 1888 to the Fifty-first Congress; continued the practice of law; elected as a Democrat to the Fifty-fifth Congress (March 4, 1897-March 3, 1899); declined to be a candidate for renomination in 1898 to the Fifty-sixth Congress; resumed the practice of law; died in Belleville, Ill., on March 1, 1903; interment in Walnut Hill Cemetery.

**Bibliography:** *DAB.*

**BAKER, John,** a Representative from Virginia; born in Frederick County, Md.; attended Washington College (now Washington and Lee University), Lexington, Va., for three years; studied law; was admitted to the bar and began practice in Berkeley County, Va. (now Jefferson County, W.Va.); member of the Virginia house of delegates 1798-1799; one of the lawyers who defended Aaron Burr when he was tried for treason in 1807; elected as a Federalist to the Twelfth Congress (March 4, 1811-March 3, 1813); resumed the practice of law; Commonwealth attorney for Jefferson County; died in Shepherdstown, Jefferson County, Va. (now West Virginia), August 18, 1823; interment in the Old Episcopal Church Cemetery.

**BAKER, John Harris** (brother of Lucien Baker), a Representative from Indiana; born in Parma Township, Monroe County, N.Y., February 28, 1832; moved with his parents to the present county of Fulton, Ohio; attended the public schools; taught school; attended the Wesleyan University in Delaware, Ohio, two years; studied law in Adrian, Mich.; was admitted to the bar in 1857 and commenced practice in Goshen, Ind.; member of the State senate in 1862, but, being a notary public at the time, was unseated because the State constitution forbid the simultaneous holding of two lucrative offices; elected as a Republican to the Forty-fourth, Forty-fifth, and Forty-sixth Congresses (March 4, 1875-March 3, 1881); declined to be a candidate for renomination in 1880 to the Forty-seventh Congress; resumed the practice of law in Goshen, Ind.; delegate to the Republican National Convention in 1888; appointed judge of the United States District Court for Indiana by President Harrision in 1892 and served until his retirement in 1904; resided in Goshen, Elkhart County, Ind., until his death on October 21, 1915; interment in Oak Ridge Cemetery.

**BAKER, Lucien** (brother of John Harris Baker), a Senator from Kansas; born near Cleveland, Fulton County, Ohio, June 8, 1846; moved with his parents to Morenci, Mich.; attended the public schools and was graduated from Adrian College, Michigan, and from the law department of the University of Michigan at Ann Arbor; was admitted to the bar in 1868 and commenced practice in Leavenworth, Kans., in 1869; city attorney of Leavenworth 1872-1874; member of the State senate 1893-1895; elected as a Republican to the United States Senate and served from March 4, 1895, to March 3, 1901; unsuccessful candidate for renomination; chairman, Committee on Civil Service and Retrenchment (Fifty-sixth Congress); resumed the practice of law in Leavenworth, Kans., where he died on June 21, 1907; interment in Mount Muncie Cemetery.

**BAKER, Osmyn,** a Representative from Massachusetts; born in Amherst, Mass., May 18, 1800; attended Amherst Academy; was graduated from Yale College in 1822; studied law; was admitted to the bar and commenced practice in Amherst in 1825; member of the Massachusetts house of representatives 1833, 1834, 1836, and 1837; county commissioner of Hampshire County 1834-1837; elected as a Whig to the Twenty-sixth Congress to fill the vacancy caused by the death of James C. Alvord; reelected to the Twenty-seventh and Twenty-eighth Congresses and served from January 14, 1840, to March 3, 1845; chairman, Committee on Accounts (Twenty-seventh Congress); was not a candidate for renomination in 1844 to the Twenty-ninth Congress; resumed the practice of law at Northampton in 1845; first president of Smith Charities 1860-1870; died in Northampton, Mass., February 9, 1875; interment in Bridge Street Cemetery.

**BAKER, Richard Hugh,** a Representative from Louisiana; born in New Orleans, La., May 22, 1948; attended public schools; graduated, University High School; Louisiana State University, Baton Rouge; real estate broker; member, Louisiana State house of representatives, 1972-1986; elected as a Republican to the One Hundredth and to the four succeeding Congresses (January 3, 1987-January 3, 1997); is a resident of Baton Rouge, La.

**BAKER, Robert,** a Representative from New York; born at Bury St. Edmunds, England, in April 1862; attended the common schools; immigrated to the United States in 1882 and settled in Albany, N.Y.; moved to Brooklyn, N.Y., in 1889; unsuccessful candidate for election to the State assembly in 1894; auditor of New York City in 1902; elected as a Democrat to the Fifty-eighth Congress (March 4, 1903-March 3, 1905); unsuccessful candidate for reelection in 1904 to the Fifty-ninth Congress and for election in 1906 to the Sixtieth Congress; became secretary of the New York City Department of Docks and Ferries in 1906; engaged in stone paving and in the general real-estate business in Brooklyn, N.Y., until his death there on June 15, 1943; interment in Evergreen Cemetery.

**BAKER, Stephen,** a Representative from New York; born in New York City, August 12, 1819; attended the common schools; engaged as importer and jobber in woolen goods; moved to Poughkeepsie, Dutchess County, N.Y., in 1850; elected as a Republican to the Thirty-seventh Congress (March 4, 1861-March 3,

1863); abandoned active business pursuits and lived in retirement until his death, while en route to California for his health, on a train near Ogden, Utah, June 9, 1875; interment in the Rural Cemetery, Poughkeepsie, N.Y.

**BAKER, William,** a Representative from Kansas; born near Centerville, Washington County, Pa., April 29, 1831; attended the public schools and was graduated from the Waynesboro College in 1856; taught school; moved to Iowa in 1859 and became principal of the public schools in Council Bluffs; studied law and was admitted to the bar in 1860 but never practiced; returned to Bealsville, Washington County, Pa., in 1865; engaged in mercantile pursuits 1865-1878; moved to Lincoln County, Kans., in 1878; engaged in agricultural pursuits and stock raising; elected as a Populist to the Fifty-second, Fifty-third, and Fifty-fourth Congresses (March 4, 1891-March 3, 1897); was not a candidate for renomination in 1896 to the Fifty-fifth Congress; resumed agricultural pursuits; died in Lincoln, Kans., February 11, 1910; interment in Lincoln Center Cemetery.

**BAKER, William Benjamin,** a Representative from Maryland; born near Aberdeen, Harford County, Md., July 22, 1840; attended the common schools and was privately tutored; engaged in agricultural pursuits until 1872, when he became interested in the canning industry, and later in banking; delegate to several State and congressional conventions; member of the State house of delegates in 1881; served in the State senate in 1893; elected as a Republican to the Fifty-fourth and to the two succeeding Congresses (March 4, 1895-March 3, 1901); was not a candidate for renomination in 1900 to the Fifty-seventh Congress; resumed the canning business; died in Aberdeen, Md., May 17, 1911; interment in Baker's Cemetery.

**BAKER, William Henry,** a Representative from New York; born in Lenox Township, Madison County, N.Y., January 17, 1827; moved with his parents to Oswego County in 1829; attended the common schools and Red Creek and Mexico Academies; studied law; was admitted to the bar in Syracuse, N.Y., in November 1851 and commenced practice in Cleveland, N.Y.; moved to Constantia, Oswego County, N.Y., in 1853; served as district attorney for Oswego County from January 1863 to January 1870; elected as a Republican to the Forty-fourth and Forty-fifth Congresses (March 4, 1875-March 3, 1879); declined to be a candidate for renomination in 1878 to the Forty-sixth Congress; delegate to the State constitutional convention in 1884; engaged in agricultural pursuits; died in Constantia, N.Y., November 25, 1911; interment in Trinity Church Cemetery.

**BAKER, William Pond,** a Representative from California; born in Oakland, Calif., June 14, 1940; graduated, Oakland High School; attended Oakland Junior College; B.S., San Jose State College, 1963; graduate study in international marketing research, Long Beach State College; United States Coast Guard Reserve service, 1957-1965; member, California State assembly, 1980-1992; budget analyst, California State department of finance; executive vice president, Contra Costa Taxpayers Association; elected as a Republican to the One Hundred Third and One Hundred Fourth Congresses (January 3, 1993-January 3, 1997); is a resident of Danville, Calif.

**BAKEWELL, Charles Montague,** a Representative from Connecticut; born in Pittsburgh, Pa., April 24, 1867; attended the public schools and the preparatory department of Western University of Pennsylvania (now the University of Pittsburgh); was graduated from the University of California at Berkeley in 1889 and from Harvard University, Cambridge, Mass., in 1894; attended the Universities of Berlin, Strassburg, and Paris 1894-1896; instructor in philosophy at Harvard University in 1896 and 1897 and at the University of California in 1897 and 1898; associate professor at Bryn Mawr College 1898-1900; associate professor and professor at the University of California 1900-1905; professor of philosophy at Yale University 1905-1933; president of the American Philosophical Association in 1910; during the First World War served as inspector and historian, with rank of major and deputy commissioner, under the Italian Commission of the American Red Cross in Italy; served in the State senate 1920-1924; served as chairman of the commission to revise and codify the educational laws of the State of Connecticut 1921-1923; also engaged as an author and editor; elected as a Republican to the Seventy-third Congress (March 4, 1933-January 3, 1935); unsuccessful candidate for reelection in 1934 to the Seventy-fourth Congress; died in New Haven, Conn., September 19, 1957; interment in Grove Street Cemetery.

**BAKEWELL, Claude Ignatius,** a Representative from Missouri; born in St. Louis, Mo., August 9, 1912; attended the St. Louis University High School; was graduated from Georgetown University, Washington, D.C., in 1932 and from St. Louis University School of Law in 1935; was admitted to the bar in 1935 and commenced practice in St. Louis; member of the board of aldermen of St. Louis, 1941-1945; during the Second World War served in the United States Navy as lieutenant (jg) with service in the South Pacific, and at the Philadelphia Navy Base from October 1944 to April 1946; elected as a Republican to the Eightieth Congress (January 3, 1947-January 3, 1949); unsuccessful candidate for reelection in 1948 to the Eighty-first Congress; elected to the Eighty-second Congress to fill the vacancy caused by the death of John B. Sullivan, and served from March 9, 1951, to January 3, 1953; unsuccessful candidate for reelection in 1952 to the Eighty-third Congress; resumed the practice of law; postmaster of the city of St. Louis since September 30, 1958; was a resident of St. Louis, Mo., until his death in University City, Mo., March 18, 1987; interment in Calvary Cemetery.

**BALDACCI, John Elias,** a Representative from Maine; born in Bangor, Penobscot County, Maine, January 30, 1955; graduated Bangor High School, 1973; B.A., University of Maine, Orono, 1986; worked at family business, Momma Baldacci's Restaurant, Bangor; Bangor City council, 1978-1981; member, Maine State senate, 1982-1994; elected as a Democrat to the One Hundred Fourth Congress (January 3, 1995-January 3, 1997); is a resident of Bangor, Maine.

**BALDRIGE, Howard Malcolm,** a Representative from Nebraska; born in Omaha, Nebr., June 23, 1894; attended the public schools and was graduated from the Omaha High School; attended Phillips Academy, Andover, Mass., and was graduated from Yale University in 1918; during the First World War served as captain of Battery F, Three Hundred and Thirty-eighth Field Artillery; was graduated from the Nebraska Law School, at Lincoln, in 1921; was admitted to the bar the same year and commenced practice in Omaha, Nebr.; served in the State house of representatives in 1923; delegate to the Republican National Conventions in 1924 and 1928; elected as a Republican to the Seventy-second Congress (March 4, 1931-March 3, 1933); unsuccessful candidate for reelection in 1932 to the Seventy-third Congress; resumed the practice of law; during the Second World War entered the Army on June 10, 1942, as a major in the Air Corps and was discharged as a colonel on October 25, 1945; resumed the practice of law with offices in New York City, and Washington, D.C.; was a resident of Washington, Conn., until his death, January 19, 1985, in Southbury, Conn.

**BALDUS, Alvin James,** a Representative from Wisconsin; born in Garner, Hancock County, Iowa, April 27, 1926; graduated, Elkton (Minn.) High School; A.A., Austin (Minn.) Junior College, 1946-1948; worked as an investment broker and a manufacturer's agent for farm machinery; served in the United States Merchant Marine, 1944-1946, and in the United States Army, 1951-1953, recipient of Bronze Star; served in the Wisconsin State general assembly,

1966-1975, assistant majority leader, 1973-1974; delegate, Wisconsin State Democratic conventions, 1966-1987; elected as a Democrat to the Ninety-fourth through the Ninety-sixth Congresses (January 3, 1975-January 3, 1981); unsuccessful candidate for reelection in 1980 to the Ninety-seventh Congress; member, Wisconsin State assembly, District 29, 1988 to present; is a resident of Menomonie, Wis.

**BALDWIN, Abraham,** a Delegate, a Representative, and a Senator from Georgia; born in North Guilford, Conn., November 22, 1754; moved with his father to New Haven, Conn., in 1769; attended private schools; was graduated from Yale College in 1772; subsequently studied theology at the college and was licensed to preach in 1775; served as a tutor in that institution 1775-1779, when he resigned to enter the Army; chaplain in the Second Connecticut Brigade, Revolutionary Army, from 1777 until 1783, when the troops disbanded; studied law during his service in the Army; was admitted to the bar in 1783 and practiced at Fairfield; moved to Augusta, Ga., in 1784 and continued the practice of law; member of the State house of representatives in 1785; originator of the plan for, and author of, the charter of the University of Georgia and served as president 1786-1801; member of the Continental Congress in 1785, 1787, and 1788; member of the United States Constitutional Convention in 1787; elected to the First and to the four succeeding Congresses (March 4, 1789-March 3, 1799); elected to the United States Senate in 1799; reelected in 1805 and served from March 4, 1799, until his death on April 4, 1807; served as President pro tempore of the Senate during the Seventh Congress; died in Washington, D.C.; interment in Rock Creek Cemetery.

**Bibliography:** *DAB*; Furlong, Patrick J. "Abraham Baldwin: A Georgia Yankee as Old-Congress Man." *Georgia Historical Quarterly* 56 (Spring 1972): 51-71; White, Henry C. *Abraham Baldwin, One of the Founders of the Republic, and Father of the University of Georgia, the First of America's State Universities.* Athens, Ga.: The McGregor Co., 1926.

**BALDWIN, Augustus Carpenter,** a Representative from Michigan; born in Salina (now Syracuse), Onondaga County, N.Y., December 24, 1817; attended the public schools; moved to Oakland County, Mich., in 1837 and taught school; studied law; was admitted to the bar in 1842 and commenced practice in Milford, Oakland County; member of the State house of representatives 1844-1846, serving as speaker pro tempore in 1846; moved to Pontiac, Mich., in March 1849; prosecuting attorney for Oakland County 1853 and 1854; delegate to the Democratic National Conventions at Charleston and Baltimore in 1860; elected as a Union Democrat to the Thirty-eighth Congress (March 4, 1863-March 3, 1865); unsuccessfully contested the election of Rowland E. Trowbridge to the Thirty-ninth Congress; delegate to the peace convention at Philadelphia in 1866; member of the Pontiac School Board 1868-1886; mayor of Pontiac in 1874; judge of the sixth judicial circuit court of Michigan from 1875 until April 15, 1880, when he resigned and resumed the practice of law; member of the board of trustees of the Eastern Michigan Asylum; died in Pontiac, Oakland County, Mich., January 21, 1903; interment in Oak Hill Cemetery.

**BALDWIN, Harry Streett,** a Representative from Maryland; born in Baldwin, Baltimore County, Md., August 21, 1894; attended the public and high schools, and the University of Maryland at College Park, Md.; owner and operator of a large truck farm; served in the State house of delegates in 1931; member of the board of county commissioners 1934-1942, serving as president 1938-1942; elected as a Democrat to the Seventy-eighth and Seventy-ninth Congresses (January 3, 1943-January 3, 1947); was not a candidate for renomination in 1946 to the Eightieth Congress, but was an unsuccessful Democratic candidate for the gubernatorial nomination; resumed agricultural pursuits; again elected to the board of county commissioners in 1950 and was serving as chairman at time of death; died in Baltimore, Md., October 19, 1952; interment in Chestnut Grove Cemetery, Jacksonville, Md.

**BALDWIN, Henry,** a Representative from Pennsylvania; born in New Haven, Conn., January 14, 1780; was graduated from Hopkins Grammar School in 1793 and from Yale College in 1797; studied law; was admitted to the Philadelphia bar in 1798 and commenced practice in Pittsburgh, Pa., in 1801; moved to Meadville, Crawford County, Pa.; elected to the Fifteenth, Sixteenth, and Seventeenth Congresses and served from March 4, 1817, until his resignation on May 8, 1822; chairman, Committee on Manufactures (Sixteenth and Seventeenth Congresses); engaged in the manufacture of iron at Bear Creek, Butler County, Pa.; resumed the practice of law in Pittsburgh, Pa.; nominated an Associate Justice of the United States Supreme Court by President Andrew Jackson on January 4, 1830; was confirmed by the Senate on January 6, 1830 and served until his death in Philadelphia, Pa., April 21, 1844; interment in Greendale Cemetery, Meadville, Pa.

**Bibliography:** *DAB.*

**BALDWIN, Henry Alexander,** a Delegate from the Territory of Hawaii; born in Paliuli, Maui County, Hawaii, January 12, 1871; attended Haiku School in Haiku, and Punahou School in Honolulu; was graduated from Phillips Academy in Andover, Mass., in 1889 and from Massachusetts Institute of Technology, Boston, Mass., in 1894; engaged in sugar planting; member of the Territorial senate 1913-1921; served as a lieutenant colonel and later as colonel in the Third Regiment of the Hawaii National Guard 1915-1917; elected as a Republican to the Sixty-seventh Congress to fill the vacancy caused by the death of J. Kuhio Kalanianaole and served from March 25, 1922, to March 3, 1923; declined to be a candidate for renomination in 1922; resumed his former business pursuits and was also interested in banking; served in the Hawaii house of representatives in 1933; member of the Hawaii senate 1934-1937, serving as president during the 1937 session; died at Paia, Maui County, Hawaii, October 8, 1946; interment in Makawao Cemetery, Makawao, Hawaii.

**BALDWIN, Henry Porter,** a Senator from Michigan; born in Coventry, R.I., February 22, 1814; attended the common schools; moved to Detroit, Mich., and established wholesale business in boots and shoes in 1838; member of the convention that met under the oaks at Jackson, Mich., July 6, 1854, at the organization of the Republican Party in Michigan; director of the Michigan State Bank and president of the Second National Bank of Detroit from 1863 until 1887; member, Michigan State senate, 1861-1862; elected Governor of Michigan in 1868, reelected in 1870, and served from January 6, 1869 to January 1, 1873; appointed and subsequently elected as a Republican to the United States Senate to fill the vacancy caused by the death of Zachariah Chandler and served from November 17, 1879 to March 3, 1881; was not a candidate for reelection; resumed his former business pursuits; president of the Detroit National Bank, 1883-1887; died in Detroit, Mich., December 31, 1892; interment in Elmwood Cemetery.

**Bibliography:** *DAB.*

**BALDWIN, John,** a Representative from Connecticut; born in Mansfield, Conn., April 5, 1772; attended the common schools; was graduated from Brown University, Providence, R.I., in 1797; studied law; was admitted to the bar in 1800 and commenced practice in Windham, Conn.; probate judge of Windham County 1818-1824; elected to the Nineteenth and Twentieth Congresses (March 4, 1825-March 3, 1829); affiliated with the Whig Party after its formation; resumed the practice of law; died in Windham, Windham County, Conn., March 27, 1850; interment in Windham Cemetery.

**BALDWIN, John Denison,** a Representative from Massachusetts; born in North Stonington, Conn., September 28, 1809; moved with his parents to Chenango County, N.Y., in 1816; returned to North Stonington in 1823; attended schools in Chenango County, N.Y., and in North Stonington, Conn.; studied law for a time but discontinued the study for theology; was graduated from the Yale Divinity School in 1834; was licensed to preach and assumed Congregational pastorates in West Woodstock, Conn., 1834-1837, in North Branford 1838-1845, and in North Killingly 1846-1849; member of the Massachusetts house of representatives 1847-1852; engaged in newspaper work in Hartford, Conn., 1849-1852, in Boston, Mass., 1852-1859, and was connected with the Worcester Spy from 1859 until his death; delegate to the Republican National Convention in 1860; elected as a Republican to the Thirty-eighth, Thirty-ninth, and Fortieth Congresses (March 4, 1863-March 3, 1869); was not a candidate for reelection in 1868; resumed his newspaper interests; died in Worcester, Mass., July 8, 1883; interment in the Rural Cemetery.

**Bibliography:** *DAB.*

**BALDWIN, John Finley, Jr.,** a Representative from California; born in Oakland, Alameda County, Calif., June 28, 1915; graduated from San Ramon Valley Union High School in Danville, Calif., and from the University of California at Berkeley in 1935, majoring in accounting and finance; assistant manager of South-Western Publishing Co., of San Francisco, 1936-1941; enlisted as a private in the United States Army in April 1941; served as director of training, Army Finance School, in 1943 and 1944; Chief of Foreign Fiscal Affairs Branch, Office of Fiscal Director, War Department, in 1945, and executive officer, Office of Fiscal Director, Mediterranean Theater, in 1946; discharged as a lieutenant colonel in October 1946; decorated by Italian Government for work in the devaluation of the lira currency in 1946; graduated from the University of California Boalt Hall School of Law in Berkeley in 1949; was admitted to the bar in 1950 and commenced the practice of law in Martinez, Calif.; elected as a Republican to the Eighty-fourth and to the five succeeding Congresses, serving from January 3, 1955, until his death in Washington, D.C., on March 9, 1966; interment in Oakmont Memorial Park, Pleasant Hill, Calif.

**BALDWIN, Joseph Clark,** a Representative from New York; born in New York City, January 11, 1897; attended private schools; was graduated from St. Paul's School, Concord, N.H., in 1916 and from Harvard University, Cambridge, Mass., in 1920; enlisted in the Navy in 1917 and was transferred to the Army in 1918, serving overseas as a private in the Machine Gun Company of the Three Hundred and Fifth Infantry; received a commission and commanded the First Platoon, Machine Gun Company, Thirty-ninth Infantry; officer of the French Legion of Honor; political reporter for the New York Tribune and later associate editor for the North Westchester Times 1922-1930; established a public relations firm in 1930; served as a member of the board of aldermen of New York City 1929-1934; member of the State senate 1934-1936; delegate to the New York State constitutional convention in 1938; member of the New York City council 1937-1941; elected as a Republican to the Seventy-seventh Congress to fill the vacancy caused by the death of Kenneth F. Simpson; reelected to the Seventy-eighth and Seventy-ninth Congresses and served from March 11, 1941, to January 3, 1947; unsuccessful candidate for renomination in 1946 to the Eightieth Congress; became a representative for United Dye and Chemical Corp., and William Recht Co., Inc.; died in New York City, October 27, 1957; interment in Woodlawn Cemetery.

**Bibliography:** Baldwin, Joseph Clark. *Flowers for the Judge.* New York: Coward-McCann, 1950.

**BALDWIN, Melvin Riley,** a Representative from Minnesota; born near Chester, Windsor County, Vt., April 12, 1838; moved with his parents to Oshkosh, Winnebago County, Wis., in 1847; attended the common schools; entered Lawrence University, Appleton, Wis., in 1855; studied law but adopted civil engineering as a profession; engaged on the Chicago and North Western Railway until April 19, 1861, when he enlisted as a private in Company E, Second Regiment, Wisconsin Volunteer Infantry; commissioned captain of his company; was captured at Gettysburg and confined in Libby Prison, Richmond, Va., at Macon, Ga., and at Charleston and Columbia, S.C., being prisoner for eighteen months; after the war engaged in operative railway work in Kansas; general superintendent for four years; moved to Duluth, St. Louis County, Minn., in 1885; elected as a Democrat to the Fifty-third Congress (March 4, 1893-March 3, 1895); unsuccessful candidate for reelection in 1894 to the Fifty-fourth Congress; chairman of the Chippewa Indian Commission, 1894-1897; went to Alaska in November 1897; died in Seattle, Wash., April 15, 1901; interment in Forest Hill Cemetery, Duluth, Minn.

**BALDWIN, Raymond Earl,** a Senator from Connecticut; born in Rye, Westchester County, N.Y., August 31, 1893; moved to Middletown, Conn., in 1903 and attended the public schools; graduated from Wesleyan University, Middletown, Conn., in 1916; entered Yale University in 1916 but enlisted as a seaman in the United States Navy when war was declared; was assigned to officers' training school, commissioned an ensign in February 1918, and promoted to lieutenant (jg) in September 1918; resigned from the Navy in August 1919 and returned to Yale University Law School, graduating in 1921; was admitted to the bar in 1921 and practiced in New Haven and Bridgeport, Conn.; prosecutor of Stratford Town Court, 1927-1930; judge of Stratford Town Court, 1931-1933; member of the Connecticut State house of representatives, 1931-1933, serving as majority leader in 1933; resumed the practice of law from 1933 until 1938; town chairman of Stratford, Conn., 1935-1937; elected Governor of Connecticut in 1938, and served from January 4, 1939 to January 8, 1941; unsuccessful candidate for reelection in 1940; again elected Governor in 1942, reelected in 1944, and served from January 6, 1943 until his resignation on December 27, 1946, having been elected United States Senator; elected as a Republican to the United States Senate in 1946 to fill the vacancy in the term ending January 3, 1947, caused by the death of Francis T. Maloney, and at the same time was elected for the term commencing January 3, 1947, and served from December 27, 1946, until his resignation on December 16, 1949; associate justice of the Connecticut Supreme Court of Errors; appointed chief justice in 1959 and served until his retirement in 1963; chairman, Connecticut Constitutional Convention 1965; died in Fairfield, Conn., October 4, 1986; interment in Indian Hill Cemetery, Middletown, Conn.

**Bibliography:** Baldwin, Raymond. *Let's Go Into Politics.* New York: Macmillan, 1952; Johnson, Curtis. *Raymond E. Baldwin: Connecticut Statesman.* Chester, Conn.: Pequot Press, 1972.

**BALDWIN, Roger Sherman** (son of Simeon Baldwin), a Senator from Connecticut; born in New Haven, Conn., January 4, 1793; attended the common schools and the Hopkins Grammar School; was graduated from Yale College in 1811; studied law in his father's office and in 1812 entered the Litchfield Law School; was admitted to the bar in 1814 and commenced practice in New Haven, Conn.; member, Connecticut State senate, 1837-1838; member, State house of representatives, 1840-1841; unsuccessful candidate for election in 1843 for Governor; elected Governor of Connecticut in 1844, reelected in 1845, and served from May 1844 until May 6, 1846; appointed and subsequently elected as a Whig to the United States Senate to fill the vacancy caused by the death of Jabez W. Huntington and served from November 11, 1847, to March 3, 1851; member of the peace convention held in Washington, D.C., in 1861 in an effort to devise means to prevent the impending war; died in New Haven, Conn., February 19, 1863; interment in the Grove Street Cemetery.

**Bibliography:** *DAB.*

**BALDWIN, Simeon** (father of Roger Sherman Baldwin), a Representative from Connecticut; born in Norwich, Conn., December 14, 1761; completed preparatory studies; was graduated from Yale College in 1781; was preceptor of the academy at Albany in 1782; tutor at Yale College from October 1783 until his resignation in September 1786; studied law; was admitted to the bar in 1786 and commenced practice in New Haven, Conn., the same year; elected city clerk in 1789 and served until June 1800; in 1790 was appointed clerk of the District and Circuit Courts of the United States for the District of Connecticut and served until November 1803, when he resigned, having been elected to Congress; elected as a Federalist to the Eighth Congress (March 4, 1803-March 3, 1805); declined to be a candidate for reelection in 1804; again appointed to his former clerkship, but was removed by Judge Edwards in 1806; associate judge of the superior court and of the supreme court of errors 1806-1817; president of the board of commissioners that located the Farmington Canal 1822-1830, when he resigned; mayor of New Haven in 1826; died in New Haven, Conn., May 26, 1851; interment in the Grove Street Cemetery.

**Bibliography:** *DAB*; Baldwin, Simeon E. *Life and Letters of Simeon Baldwin.* New Haven, Conn.: The Tuttle, Morehouse and Taylor Co., 1919.

**BALL, Edward,** a Representative from Ohio; born in Fairfax County, near Falls Church, Va., November 6, 1811; attended the village school; moved to Ohio and located near Zanesville; engaged in agricultural pursuits; deputy sheriff of Muskingum County in 1837 and 1838 and sheriff 1839-1843; member of the State house of representatives 1845-1849; became editor of the Zanesville Courier in 1849; elected as a Whig to the Thirty-third Congress and reelected as a Republican to the Thirty-fourth Congress (March 4, 1853-March 3, 1857); chairman, Committee on Public Buildings and Grounds (Thirty-fourth Congress); was not a candidate for renomination in 1856; studied law; was admitted to the bar in 1860 and commenced practice in Zanesville; delegate to the Republican National Convention at Chicago in 1860; Sergeant at Arms of the House of Representatives in the Thirty-seventh Congress 1861-1863; resumed the practice of law; again a member of the State house of representatives 1868-1870; accidentally killed by a railroad train near Zanesville, Ohio, on November 22, 1872; interment in Greenwood Cemetery.

**BALL, Joseph Hurst,** a Senator from Minnesota; born in Crookston, Polk County, Minn., November 3, 1905; attended the public schools; student at Antioch College, Yellow Springs, Ohio, 1922-1924, Eau Claire (Wis.) Normal School in 1925, and the University of Minnesota at Minneapolis in 1926 and 1927; journalist and writer, 1927-1940; appointed as a Republican to the United States Senate to fill the vacancy caused by the death of Ernest Lundeen for the term ending January 2, 1943, and served from October 14, 1940, to November 17, 1942, when a duly elected successor qualified; elected in 1942 for the term commencing January 3, 1943, and served from January 3, 1943, to January 3, 1949; unsuccessful candidate for reelection in 1948; chairman, Joint Committee on Labor-Management Relations (Eightieth Congress); resumed journalistic activities; shipping executive; resided on a farm near Front Royal, Va; died December 18, 1993.

**Bibliography:** Finney, Nathaniel S. "Joseph H. Ball: A Liberal Dose of Candor." In *Public Men In and Out of Office.* pp. 297-310. Edited by John T. Salter. Chapel Hill: University of North Carolina Press, 1946.

**BALL, Lewis Heisler,** a Representative and a Senator from Delaware; born near Stanton, New Castle County, Del., September 21, 1861; attended the common schools and Rugby Academy at Wilmington; was graduated from Delaware College, Newark, Del., in 1882 and from the medical department of the University of Pennsylvania, Philadelphia, Pa., in 1885; commenced the practice of medicine at Brandywine Springs, Del., in 1887; State treasurer of Delaware 1899-1901; elected as a Republican to the Fifty-seventh Congress and served from March 4, 1901, to March 3, 1903, when he resigned to become Senator; unsuccessful candidate for reelection in 1902 to the Fifty-eighth Congress; elected to the United States Senate on March 2, 1903, to fill the vacancy in the term commencing March 4, 1899, caused by the failure of the legislature to elect, and served from March 3, 1903, to March 3, 1905; resumed the practice of medicine at Brandywine Springs, Del.; again elected to the United States Senate and served from March 4, 1919, to March 3, 1925; unsuccessful candidate for renomination in 1924; chairman, Committee on Enrolled Bills (Sixty-sixth Congress), Committee on the District of Columbia (Sixty-seventh and Sixty-eighth Congresses); appointed a member of the rent commission of Washington, D.C., in 1925; resumed the practice of medicine; died in Faulkland, Del., October 18, 1932; interment in St. James Cemetery, Stanton, Del.

**BALL, Thomas Henry,** a Representative from Texas; born in Huntsville, Walker County, Tex., January 14, 1859; attended private schools; was graduated from Austin College, Sherman, Tex., in 1876; studied law at the University of Virginia at Charlottesville; was admitted to the bar in 1886 and commenced practice in Huntsville, Tex.; mayor of Huntsville 1887-1893; chairman of the Democratic executive committee of Walker County 1884-1896; delegate to all State conventions from 1886 to 1924, with three exceptions; delegate to the Democratic National Conventions in 1892, 1924, and 1928; elected as a Democrat to the Fifty-fifth and to the three succeeding Congresses and served from March 4, 1897, to November 16, 1903, when he resigned; resumed the practice of his profession; unsuccessful candidate for the Democratic gubernatorial nomination in 1914; general counsel for the State council of defense during the First World War; general counsel for the port commission of the Houston Harbor and Ship Channel from May 1922 to August 1931, when he retired; died in Houston, Tex., May 7, 1944; interment in Forest Park Cemetery.

**BALL, Thomas Raymond,** a Representative from Connecticut; born in New York City, February 12, 1896; attended the public schools, Anglo-Saxon School, Paris, France, Heathcote School, Harrison, N.Y., and the Art Students League, New York City; engaged as a designer in 1916; during the First World War served in the Depot Battalion, Seventh New York Infantry, in 1917, and overseas with the Camouflage Section, Fortieth United States Engineers, 1918-1919; after the war located in Old Lyme, Conn., and engaged in architectural pursuits; member of the board of education 1926-1938, and also served as selectman of Old Lyme, Conn.; served in the State house of representatives 1927-1937; elected as a Republican to the Seventy-sixth Congress (January 3, 1939-January 3, 1941); unsuccessful candidate for reelection in 1940 to the Seventy-seventh Congress; resumed his former pursuits at Old Lyme, Conn.; died in Old Lyme, Conn., June 16, 1943; interment in Duck River Cemetery.

**BALL, William Lee,** a Representative from Virginia; born in Lancaster County, Va., January 2, 1781; received a liberal schooling; served in the Virginia house of delegates, 1805-1806 and 1810-1814, and in the Virginia senate, 1814-1817; served as a paymaster in the War of 1812 and was assigned to the Ninety-second Virginia Regiment; elected as a Republican to the Fifteenth Congress; reelected to the three succeeding Congresses, and served from March 4, 1817 until his death in Washington, D.C., February 28, 1824; interment in the Congressional Cemetery.

**BALLENGER, Cass** (great-great-grandson of Lewis Cass), a Representative from North Carolina; born in Hickory, N.C., December 6, 1926; graduated from Episcopal High School, Alexan-

dria, Va., 1944; attended the University of North Carolina, Chapel Hill, 1944-1945; B.A., Amherst (Mass.) College, 1948; served in the United States Naval Air Corps, 1944-1945; founder and president of a packaging company; member, North Carolina State house of representatives, 1974-1976; member, North Carolina State senate, 1976-1986; elected as a Republican to the Ninety-ninth Congress, November 4, 1986, to complete the unexpired term of James Broyhill, and at the same time was elected to the One Hundredth Congress; reelected to the One Hundred First and to the three succeeding Congresses, and served from November 4, 1986 to January 3, 1997; is a resident of Hickory, N.C.

**BALLENTINE, John Goff,** a Representative from Tennessee; born in Pulaski, Giles County, Tenn., May 20, 1825; was graduated from Wurtemberg Academy in 1841, from the University of Nashville in 1845, and from the law department of Harvard University in 1848; was a member of the faculty of Livingston Law School in New York; commenced the practice of law in Pulaski; moved to Mississippi about 1854; continued the practice of law and engaged in agricultural pursuits; settled in Memphis, Tenn., in 1860; served as a colonel in the Confederate Army during the Civil War; returned to Pulaski, Tenn.; elected as a Democrat to the Forty-eighth and Forty-ninth Congresses (March 4, 1883-March 3, 1887); declined to be a candidate for renomination in 1886; retired from active pursuits; died in Pulaski, Tenn., on November 23, 1915; interment in the New Pulaski Cemetery.

**BALLOU, Latimer Whipple,** a Representative from Rhode Island; born in Cumberland, R.I., March 1, 1812; attended the public schools and the local academies in his native town; moved to Cambridge, Mass., in 1828 and learned the art of printing at the University Press; was instrumental in establishing the Cambridge Press in 1835 and continued in the printing business until 1842, when he moved to Woonsocket, R.I.; engaged in banking in 1850; was active in the organization of the Republican Party in 1856; delegate to the Republican National Convention at Philadelphia in 1872; elected as a Republican to the Forty-fourth, Forty-fifth and Forty-sixth Congresses (March 4, 1875-March 3, 1881); declined to be a candidate for renomination in 1880; engaged in his former business pursuits until his death in Woonsocket, Providence County, R.I., May 9, 1900; interment in Oak Hill Cemetery.

**BALTZ, William Nicolas,** a Representative from Illinois; born in Millstadt, St. Clair County, Ill., February 5, 1860; attended the public schools; engaged in agricultural pursuits, milling, and banking; member of the Millstadt Board of Education and served as president 1892-1917; member of the St. Clair County Board of Supervisors 1897-1913, serving as presiding officer from 1908 to 1911; member of the Democratic county central committee 1905-1913; elected as a Democrat to the Sixty-third Congress (March 4, 1913-March 3, 1915); unsuccessful candidate for reelection in 1914 to the Sixty-fourth Congress; mayor of Millstadt six years; resumed agricultural and industrial pursuits at Millstadt, Ill., until his death there August 22, 1943; interment in Mount Evergreen Cemetery.

**BANDSTRA, Bert Andrew,** a Representative from Iowa; born on a farm between Eddyville and Albia, Monroe County, Iowa, January 25, 1922; in 1925 moved to a farm in Mahaska County near Taintor; attended Taintor Independent School and New Sharon High School; enlisted as a seaman in the United States Navy in March 1942, served in the Solomon Islands and Okinawa campaigns, and was honorably discharged as a second-class petty officer in December 1945; received the Presidential Unit Citation; resumed education and graduated from Central College at Pella in 1950 and from the University of Michigan at Ann Arbor in 1953; was admitted to the bar in 1953 and began the practice of law in Pella, Iowa; service as Marion County attorney, January 1955 to June 1959; assistant to Representative Neal Smith, January 1959 to February 1964; elected as a Democrat to the Eighty-ninth Congress

(January 3, 1965-January 3, 1967); unsuccessful candidate for reelection in 1966 to the Ninetieth Congress; resumed the practice of law in Knoxville, Iowa; was a resident of Pella, Iowa; died October 23, 1995.

**BANISTER, John,** a Delegate from Virginia; born at "Hatcher's Run," near Petersburg, Dinwiddie County, Va., December 26, 1734; attended a private school at Wakefield, England, and was graduated in law from the Temple in London; returned to Virginia and commenced the practice of law in Petersburg; also engaged as a planter; member of the Virginia House of Burgesses in 1765, 1766-1774, and 1775; member of the conventions of 1775 and 1776; served in the Virginia house of delegates in 1776, 1777, and 1781-1783; Member of the Continental Congress in 1778; one of the framers and signers of the Articles of Confederation; during the Revolutionary War served as major and lieutenant colonel of the Virginia Militia; died on his estate, "Hatcher's Run," near Petersburg, Dinwiddie County, Va., on September 30, 1788; interment in the family burying ground on his estate.

Bibliography: *DAB.*

**BANKHEAD, John Hollis** (father of John Hollis Bankhead II and William Brockman Bankhead, and grandfather of Walter Will Bankhead), a Representative and a Senator from Alabama; born in Moscow, Marion (now Lamar) County, Ala., September 13, 1842; attended the common schools; planter; served in the Confederate Army during the Civil War as a captain in the Alabama Infantry; member, Alabama State house of representatives, 1865-1867, and again in 1880 and 1881; Alabama State senator, 1876-1877; warden of the State penitentiary at Wetumpka, Elmore County, Ala., 1881-1885; moved to Fayette, Ala., in 1885 and resumed planting; in 1912 moved to Jasper, Ala.; elected as a Democrat to the Fiftieth and to the nine succeeding Congresses (March 4, 1887-March 3, 1907); chairman, Committee on Public Buildings and Grounds (Fifty-second and Fifty-third Congresses); unsuccessful candidate for renomination in 1906 to the Sixtieth Congress; appointed a member of the Inland Waterways Commission in 1907; appointed and subsequently elected to the United States Senate in 1907 to fill the vacancy caused by the death of John T. Morgan; reelected in 1912 and 1918, and served from June 18, 1907 until his death in Washington, D.C., on March 1, 1920; chairman, Committee on Standards, Weights, and Measures (Sixty-second Congress), Committee on Post Office and Post Roads (Sixty-third through Sixty-fifth Congresses), Committee on Expenditures in the Department of Interior (Sixty-sixth Congress); interment in Oak Hill Cemetery, Jasper, Ala.

**BANKHEAD, John Hollis II** (son of John Hollis Bankhead, brother of William Brockman Bankhead, and father of Walter Will Bankhead), a Senator from Alabama; born on a farm near Old Moscow, Lamar County, Ala., July 8, 1872; attended the public schools; was graduated from the University of Alabama at Tuscaloosa in 1891, and from the law department of Georgetown University, Washington, D.C., in 1893; was admitted to the bar in 1893 and commenced practice in Jasper, Ala.; served in the Alabama National Guard with the rank of major, 1901-1903; member, Alabama State house of representatives, 1904-1905; president of the Bankhead Coal Co., 1911-1925; trustee of the University of Alabama, 1917-1919, and 1931-1946; elected as a Democrat to the United States Senate in 1930; reelected in 1936 and 1942, and served from March 4, 1931 until his death in the United States Naval Hospital, Bethesda, Md., on June 12, 1946; chairman, Committee on Irrigation and Reclamation (Seventy-fifth through Seventy-ninth Congresses); interment in Oak Hill Cemetery, Jasper, Ala.

Bibliography: Johnson, Evans C. "John H. Bankhead 2d: Advocate of Cotton." *Alabama Review* 41 (January 1988): 430-458; Key, Jack Brien. "John H. Bankhead, Jr. of Alabama: The

Conservative as Reformer." Ph.D. dissertation, Johns Hopkins University, 1966.

**BANKHEAD, Walter Will** (son of John Hollis Bankhead II, grandson of John Hollis Bankhead, and nephew of William Brockman Bankhead), a Representative from Alabama; born in Jasper, Walker County, Ala., July 21, 1897; attended the public schools; was graduated from Marion (Ala.) Military Institute in 1916, from the University of Alabama at Tuscaloosa in 1919, and from the law department of the same university in 1920; was admitted to the bar in 1920 and commenced practice in Jasper, Ala.; delegate to the Democratic National Convention of 1940; elected as a Democrat to the Seventy-seventh Congress, and served from January 3, 1941 until February 1, 1941, when he resigned; resumed the practice of law; chairman of the board of Bankhead Mining Co., Inc., and Bankhead Development Co., Inc.; president of Mammoth Packing Co. and Bankhead Broadcasting Co., Inc.; vice chairman, board of directors, First National Bank of Jasper; was a resident of Jasper, Ala., until his death on November 24, 1988; interment in Oak Hill Cemetery, Jasper, Ala.

**BANKHEAD, William Brockman** (son of John Hollis Bankhead, brother of John Hollis Bankhead II, and uncle of Walter Will Bankhead), a Representative from Alabama; born in Moscow, Lamar County, Ala., April 12, 1874; attended the country schools; was graduated from the University of Alabama at Tuscaloosa in 1893, and from the Georgetown University Law School at Washington, D.C., in 1895; was admitted to the bar the same year and commenced practice in Huntsville, Ala.; member, Alabama State house of representatives, 1900-1901; city attorney of Huntsville, 1898-1902; moved to Jasper, Ala., in 1905 and continued the practice of law; solicitor of the fourteenth judicial circuit of Alabama, 1910-1914; unsuccessful candidate for nomination in 1914 to the Sixty-fourth Congress; delegate to the Democratic National Convention of 1940; elected as a Democrat to the Sixty-fifth and to the eleven succeeding Congresses, and served from March 4, 1917 until his death in Washington, D.C., September 15, 1940; chairman, Committee on Rules (Seventy-third Congress); majority leader (Seventy-fourth Congress), elected Speaker of the House of Representatives on June 4, 1936 to fill the vacancy caused by the death of Speaker Joseph W. Byrns; reelected Speaker in the Seventy-fifth and Seventy-sixth Congresses; funeral services were held in the Hall of the House of Representatives; interment in Oak Hill Cemetery, Jasper, Ala.

Bibliography: *DAB*; Heacock, Walter J. "William Brockman Bankhead: A Biography." Ph.D. dissertation, University of Wisconsin, 1952; Heacock, Walter J. "William B. Bankhead and the New Deal." *Journal of Southern History* 21 (August 1955): 347-59.

**BANKS, John,** a Representative from Pennsylvania; born near Lewisburg, Juniata County, Pa., October 17, 1793; received a liberal education; studied law; was admitted to the bar and commenced practice in Juniata County in 1819; moved to Mercer County and continued the practice of law; elected as an Anti-Masonic candidate to the Twenty-second, Twenty-third, and Twenty-fourth Congresses and served from March 4, 1831, until his resignation in 1836; judge of the Berks judicial district from 1836 until he resigned to accept a State position; State treasurer of Pennsylvania in 1847; resumed the practice of law in Reading, Pa., where he died April 3, 1864; interment in Charles Evans Cemetery.

**BANKS, Linn,** a Representative from Virginia; born in Madison (then Culpeper) County, Va., January 23, 1784; studied law; was admitted to the bar in Madison County April 10, 1809; member of the Virginia house of delegates, 1812-1838, and served as speaker, 1817-1838; elected as a Democrat to the Twenty-fifth Congress to fill the vacancy caused by the resignation of John M. Patton; reelected to the Twenty-sixth Congress and served from April 28, 1838, to March 3, 1841; presented credentials as a Member-elect to the

Twenty-seventh Congress and served from March 4, 1841, until December 6, 1841, when he was succeeded by William Smith, who contested the election; was not a candidate for renomination in 1842; resumed the practice of law; served as a colonel in the Virginia Militia; was drowned while attempting to ford the Conway River near Wolftown, Madison County, Va., January 13, 1842; interment in the family burying ground on his estate, Vale Evergreen, near Graves Mill, Madison County, Va.

**BANKS, Nathaniel Prentice,** a Representative from Massachusetts; born in Waltham, Mass., January 30, 1816; attended the common schools; a machinist by trade; editor of a weekly paper in Waltham, Mass.; clerk in the customhouse in Boston, Mass.; studied law; was admitted to the Suffolk County bar and commenced practice in Boston; member of the Massachusetts house of representatives from 1849 until 1852, for two years serving as speaker; member of the Massachusetts constitutional convention of 1853; elected as a Democrat to the Thirty-third Congress, as the candidate of the American Party to the Thirty-fourth Congress, and as a Republican to the Thirty-fifth Congress and served from March 4, 1853, until he resigned December 24, 1857, to become Governor; Speaker of the House of Representatives (Thirty-fourth Congress); elected Governor of Massachusetts in 1857, reelected in 1858 and 1859, and served from January 7, 1858 until January 3, 1861; moved to Chicago, Ill.; vice president of the Illinois Central Railroad; entered the Union Army as a major general of Volunteers May 16, 1861; assumed command of the Fifth Corps in March 1862; commanded the military district of Washington, September 12 to October 27, 1862; commanded the Union Department and Army of the Gulf during the Red River campaign of 1864; honorably mustered out August 24, 1865; returned to Massachusetts; elected as a Union Republican to the Thirty-ninth Congress to fill the vacancy caused by the resignation of Daniel W. Gooch; reelected as a Republican to the Fortieth, Forty-first, and Forty-second Congresses and served from December 4, 1865, to March 3, 1873; chairman, Committee on Foreign Affairs (Thirty-ninth through Forty-second Congresses); unsuccessful Liberal and Democratic candidate for reelection in 1872 to the Forty-third Congress; member of the Massachusetts senate in 1874; elected as an Independent to the Forty-fourth Congress and as a Republican to the Forty-fifth Congress (March 4, 1875-March 3, 1879); unsuccessful candidate for renomination in 1878 to the Forty-sixth Congress; appointed United States marshal on March 11, 1879, and served until April 23, 1888; elected as a Republican to the Fifty-first Congress (March 4, 1889-March 3, 1891); chairman, Committee on Expenditures in the Department of the Interior (Fifty-first Congress); unsuccessful candidate for renomination in 1890 to the Fifty-second Congress; died in Waltham, Middlesex County, Mass., September 1, 1894; interment in Grove Hill Cemetery.

Bibliography: *DAB*; Harrington, Fred Harvey. *Fighting Politician, Major General N.P. Banks.* Philadelphia: University of Pennsylvania Press, 1948.

**BANNING, Henry Blackstone,** a Representative from Ohio; born in Bannings Mills, Ohio, November 10, 1836; attended the Clinton district school, Mount Vernon Academy, and Kenyon College, Gambier, Ohio; studied law; was admitted to the bar in 1857 and commenced practice in Mount Vernon, Ohio; during the Civil War enlisted April 1861 in the Union Army as a private; commissioned captain of the Fourth Regiment, Ohio Volunteer Infantry, June 5, 1861; colonel of the Eighty-seventh Regiment, Ohio Volunteer Infantry, June 25, 1862; honorably mustered out on October 4, 1862; commissioned lieutenant colonel of the One Hundred and Twenty-fifth Regiment, Ohio Volunteer Infantry, on January 1, 1863; transferred to the One Hundred and Twenty-first Regiment, Ohio Volunteer Infantry, April 5, 1863; appointed colonel on November 10, 1863; brevetted brigadier general and major general of Volunteers on March 13, 1865; resigned his commission

January 21, 1865; member, Ohio State house of representatives, 1866-1867; moved to Cincinnati, Ohio, in 1869 and resumed the practice of law; elected as a Liberal Republican to the Forty-third Congress, and as a Democrat to the Forty-fourth and Forty-fifth Congresses (March 4, 1873-March 3, 1879); chairman, Committee on Military Affairs (Forty-fourth and Forty-fifth Congresses); unsuccessful candidate for renomination in 1878 to the Forty-sixth Congress, and for election in 1880 to the Forty-seventh Congress; resumed the practice of law; died in Cincinnati, Ohio, December 10, 1881; interment in Spring Grove Cemetery.

**BANNON, Henry Towne,** a Representative from Ohio; born near Portsmouth, Scioto County, Ohio, June 5, 1867; attended the public schools of Portsmouth, Ohio State University at Columbus in 1885 and 1886, and was graduated from the University of Michigan at Ann Arbor in 1889; studied law; was admitted to the Ohio bar in 1891 and practiced in Portsmouth, Ohio; prosecuting attorney of Scioto County 1897-1902; elected as a Republican to the Fifty-ninth and Sixtieth Congresses (March 4, 1905-March 3, 1909); was not a candidate for renomination in 1908; resumed the practice of law; delegate to the Republican National Conventions in 1924, 1928, 1932, 1936, and 1940; served as a director of the First National Bank, National Bank of Portsmouth, Oak Hill Savings Bank, and the Selby Shoe Co.; also engaged in literary pursuits; died in Portsmouth, Ohio, September 6, 1950; interment in Greenlawn Cemetery.

**BANTA, Parke Monroe,** a Representative from Missouri; born in Berryman, Crawford County, Mo., November 21, 1891; attended the public schools, and William Jewell College at Liberty, Mo.; was graduated from Northwestern University Law School at Evanston-Chicago, Ill., in 1914; was admitted to the bar in 1913 and practiced at Potosi, Mo., 1914-1925 and at Ironton, Mo., 1925-1941; prosecuting attorney of Washington County, Mo., in 1917 and 1918; during the First World War served in the United States Army as a private and through the ranks to first lieutenant from April 1918 to August 1919; member of the board of trustees of Arcadia, Mo., in 1928 and 1929; member of Ironton-Arcadia School Board in 1932 and 1933; administrator of the Missouri State Social Security Commission 1941-1945; elected as a Republican to the Eightieth Congress (January 3, 1947-January 3, 1949); unsuccessful candidate for reelection in 1948 to the Eighty-first Congress and for election in 1950 to the Eighty-second Congress; resumed the practice of law in Ironton, Mo.; general counsel for Department of Health, Education, and Welfare, Washington, D.C., from April 11, 1953, until January 20, 1961; retired; died in Cape Girardeau, Mo., May 12, 1970; interment in New Masonic Cemetery, Potosi, Mo.

**BARBER, Hiram, Jr.,** a Representative from Illinois; born in Queensbury, Warren County, N.Y., March 24, 1835; moved to Horicon, Dodge County, Wis., in 1846; attended the University of Wisconsin at Madison; studied law in Albany, N.Y.; was admitted to the bar in 1856 and commenced practice at Juneau, Wis.; prosecuting attorney of Jefferson County, Wis., in 1861 and 1862; assistant attorney general of Wisconsin in 1865 and 1866; moved to Chicago, Ill., and resumed the practice of law in 1866; elected as a Republican to the Forty-sixth Congress (March 4, 1879-March 3, 1881); unsuccessful candidate for renomination in 1880; receiver of the land office at Mitchell, S.Dak., 1881-1888; returned to Chicago and continued the practice of law; served as master in chancery of the Cook County Superior Court from 1891 to 1914; retired from public life and active business pursuits; died at Lake Geneva, Wis., August 5, 1924; interment in Juneau Cemetery, Juneau, Wis.

**BARBER, Isaac Ambrose,** a Representative from Maryland; born near Salem, Salem County, N.J., January 26, 1852; attended the common schools, and studied medicine in Hahnemann Medical College, Philadelphia, Pa., from which he was graduated in 1872; commenced practice in Woodstown, N.J.; moved to Easton, Talbot

County, Md., in 1873 and continued the practice of medicine for fifteen years; engaged in the milling business; member of the Maryland State house of delegates in 1895; president of the Farmers and Merchants' National Bank of Easton; elected as a Republican to the Fifty-fifth Congress (March 4, 1897-March 3, 1899); resumed the milling business, and also engaged in agricultural pursuits; chairman of the Republican State central committee, 1900-1904; died in Easton, Md., March 1, 1909; interment in Spring Hill Cemetery.

**BARBER, Joel Allen,** a Representative from Wisconsin; born in Georgia (near St. Albans), Franklin County, Vt., January 17, 1809; attended the common schools, Georgia Academy, and the University of Vermont, Burlington, Vt.; studied law; was admitted to the bar in 1834 in Prince Georges County, Md., where he was teaching school, and commenced practice in Fairfield, Vt.; moved to Wisconsin in 1837 and settled in Lancaster, Grant County, and continued the practice of his profession; county clerk for four years and district attorney for three terms; member of the first constitutional convention of Wisconsin in 1846; elected to the Wisconsin State assembly in 1852, 1853, 1863, and 1864, serving as speaker in 1864; member of the Wisconsin State senate in 1856 and 1857; founded Lancaster Academy; elected as a Republican to the Forty-second and Forty-third Congresses (March 4, 1871-March 3, 1875); was not a candidate for renomination in 1874 to the Forty-fourth Congress; resumed the practice of law; died in Lancaster, Wis., June 17, 1881; interment in Hillside Cemetery.

**BARBER, Laird Howard,** a Representative from Pennsylvania; born on a farm near Mifflinburg, Union County, Pa., October 25, 1848; prepared for college in the Mifflinburg Academy, and was graduated from Lafayette College, Easton, Pa., in 1871; taught school at Mount Carmel and was principal of the Mauch Chunk Public Schools from 1875 to 1880; studied law; was admitted to the bar in Carbon County June 20, 1881, and commenced practice at Mauch Chunk; elected in 1890 a director of the Mauch Chunk School Board and served as president and treasurer; also served as secretary of the town council; unsuccessful candidate for election in 1896 to the Fifty-fifth Congress; elected as a Democrat to the Fifty-sixth Congress (March 4, 1899-March 3, 1901); was not a candidate for renomination in 1900 to the Fifth-seventh Congress; resumed the practice of law in Mauch Chunk; elected president judge of the fifty-sixth judicial district of Pennsylvania in 1913; reelected in 1923 and served from January 5, 1914, until his death in Mauch Chunk, Carbon County, Pa., February 16, 1928; interment in Evergreen Cemetery, East Mauch Chunk, Pa.

**BARBER, Levi,** a Representative from Ohio; born in Simsbury, Hartford County, Conn., October 16, 1777; moved to Ohio; was a surveyor in the employ of the Federal Government; member of the State house of representatives in 1806; was commissioned receiver of the United States land office in Marietta, Ohio, on April 1, 1807; aide to Governor Return Jonathan Meigs during the War of 1812; elected as a Republican to the Fifteenth Congress (March 4, 1817-March 3, 1819); unsuccessful candidate for reelection in 1818 to the Sixteenth Congress; elected to the Seventeenth Congress (March 4, 1821-March 3, 1823); unsuccessful candidate for reelection in 1822 to the Eighteenth Congress; clerk of the court of common pleas and the court of Washington County; justice of the peace; president of the Bank of Marietta; died in Harmar (now a part of Marietta), Ohio, April 23, 1833; interment in Harmar Cemetery.

**BARBER, Noyes** (uncle of Edwin Barbour Morgan and Christopher Morgan), a Representative from Connecticut; born in Groton, New London County, Conn., April 28, 1781; attended the common schools; engaged in mercantile pursuits; major of the Eighth Connecticut Regiment in the War of 1812; detailed to defend the coast towns during the blockade by the British Fleet; member of the State house of representatives in 1818; elected to the Seventeenth and to the six succeeding Congresses (March 4, 1821-March 3, 1835); unsuccessful candidate for reelection in 1834 to the Twenty-fourth Congress; resumed mercantile pursuits; member of all Whig State conventions from 1836; died in Groton, Conn., January 3, 1844; interment in Starr Cemetery.

**BARBOUR, Henry Ellsworth,** a Representative from California; born in Ogdensburg, St. Lawrence County, N.Y., March 8, 1877; attended the public schools of his native city, the local Free Academy at Ogdensburg, Union College at Schenectady, N.Y., and the law department of George Washington University, Washington, D.C.; was admitted to the New York bar in 1901; moved to Fresno, Fresno County, Calif., in 1902 and engaged in the practice of law; elected as a Republican to the Sixty-sixth and to the six succeeding Congresses (March 4, 1919-March 3, 1933); unsuccessful candidate for reelection in 1932 to the Seventy-third Congress; resumed the practice of his profession in Fresno, Calif., where he died on March 21, 1945; interment in Belmont Memorial Cemetery.

**BARBOUR, James** (brother of Philip Pendleton Barbour and cousin of John Strode Barbour), a Senator from Virginia; born at "Frascati," near Gordonsville, Orange County, Va., June 10, 1775; attended the common schools; deputy sheriff of Orange County; studied law; was admitted to the bar in 1794 at Orange Court House; served several terms in the Virginia house of delegates between 1796 and 1812, serving as speaker from 1809 to 1812; elected Governor of Virginia by the General Assembly, and served from January 3, 1812 to December 1, 1814; elected as an Anti-Democrat and State Rights candidate to the United States Senate in 1814 for the term commencing March 4, 1815; subsequently elected to fill the vacancy in the term ending March 3, 1815, caused by the death of Richard Brent; reelected in 1821 and served from January 2, 1815, to March 7, 1825, when he resigned to accept a Cabinet portfolio; served as President pro tempore of the Senate during the Fifteenth and Sixteenth Congresses; chairman, Committee on Foreign Relations (Fifteenth, Sixteenth, and Eighteenth Congresses), Committee on the District of Columbia (Seventeenth Congress); appointed Secretary of War by President John Quincy Adams, and served from March 7, 1825 to May 23, 1828, when he resigned to accept a diplomatic position; appointed United States Minister to Great Britain on May 23, 1828 and served until October 1829; chairman of the Whig National Convention in 1839; founder of the Orange County Humane Society, established for the advancement of education; died in Barboursville, Orange County, Va., June 7, 1842; interment in the family cemet

**Bibliography:** *DAB*; Lowery, Charles D. "James Barbour, Politician and Planter of Antebellum Virginia." Ph.D. dissertation, University of Virginia, 1966.

**BARBOUR, John Strode** (father of John Strode Barbour, Jr., cousin of James Barbour and Philip Pendleton Barbour), a Representative from Virginia; born at "Fleetwood," near Brandy Station, Culpeper County, Va., August 8, 1790; attended private schools; was graduated from the College of William and Mary, Williamsburg, Va., in 1808; studied law; was admitted to the bar in 1811 and commenced practice in Culpeper, Va.; served in the War of 1812 as aide-de-camp to General Madison; member of the Virginia house of delegates, 1813-1816, 1820-1823, 1833, and 1834; elected to the Eighteenth and Nineteenth Congresses, and elected as a Jacksonian to the Twentieth and to the two succeeding Congresses (March 4, 1823-March 3, 1833); was not a candidate for renomination in 1832 to the Twenty-third Congress; member of the Virginia constitutional conventions in 1829 and 1830; chairman of the Democratic National Convention of 1852; resumed the practice of law; died on his estate, "Fleetwood," near Culpeper, Va., on January 12, 1855; interment in the family burying ground on his estate.

**BARBOUR, John Strode, Jr.** (son of the John Strode Barbour), a Representative and a Senator from Virginia; born at "Catalpa," near Culpeper, Culpeper County, Va., December 29, 1820; attended the common schools and was graduated from the law department of the University of Virginia at Charlottesville; was admitted to the bar in 1841 and commenced practice in Culpeper; member of the Virginia house of delegates, 1847-1851; president of the Orange and Alexandria Railroad Co., 1852-1881; elected as a Democrat to the Forty-seventh and the two succeeding Congresses (March 4, 1881-March 3, 1887); chairman, Committee on the District of Columbia (Forty-eighth and Forty-ninth Congresses); declined to be a candidate for renomination in 1886 to the Fiftieth Congress; elected as a Democrat to the United States Senate, and served from March 4, 1889 until his death in Washington, D.C., May 14, 1892; interment in the burial ground at "Poplar Hill," Prince Georges County, Md.

**BARBOUR, Lucien** a Representative from Indiana; born in Canton, Hartford County, Conn., March 4, 1811; was graduated from Amherst (Mass.) College in 1837; moved to Indiana the same year and settled in Madison, Jefferson County; studied law; was admitted to the bar and commenced practice in Indianapolis, Ind., in 1839; acted a number of times as arbitrator between the State of Indiana and private corporations; appointed United States district attorney for the district of Indiana by President James K. Polk; member of the commission to codify the laws of Indiana in 1852; elected as a Republican to the Thirty-fourth Congress (March 4, 1855-March 3, 1857); was not a candidate for renomination in 1856 to the Thirty-fifth Congress; affiliated with the Republican Party in 1860; practiced law in Indianapolis, Ind., until his death in that city on July 19, 1880; interment in Crown Hill Cemetery.

**BARBOUR, Philip Pendleton** (brother of James Barbour and cousin of John Strode Barbour), a Representative from Virginia; born at "Frascati," near Gordonsville, Orange County, Va., May 25, 1783; attended common and private schools; was graduated from the College of William and Mary, Williamsburg, Va., in 1799; studied law; was admitted to the bar in 1800 and commenced practice in Bardstown, Ky.; returned to Virginia in 1801 and practiced law in Gordonsville, Orange County; member of the Virginia house of delegates 1812-1814; elected as a Republican to the Thirteenth Congress to fill the vacancy caused by the death of John Dawson; reelected to the Fourteenth and to the four succeeding Congresses and served from September 19, 1814, to March 3, 1825; Speaker of the House of Representatives (Seventeenth Congress); was not a candidate for renomination in 1824 to the Nineteenth Congress; offered the professorship of law in the University of Virginia in 1825, but declined; appointed a judge of the general court of Virginia and served for two years, resigning in 1827; elected to the Twentieth Congress and reelected as a Jacksonian to the Twenty-first Congress and served from March 4, 1827, until his resignation on October 15, 1830; chairman, Committee on the Judiciary (Twentieth Congress); president of the Virginia constitutional convention in 1829; appointed by President Andrew Jackson, June 1, 1830, judge of the United States Circuit Court for the Eastern District of Virginia, declining the chancellorship and the post of attorney general; refused nominations for judge of the court of appeals, for Governor, and for United States Senator; nominated an Associate Justice of the United States Supreme Court by President Jackson on December 28, 1835; was confirmed by the Senate on March 15, 1836 and served until his death in Washington, D.C., on February 25, 1841; interment in Congressional Cemetery.

Bibliography: *DAB.*

**BARBOUR, William Warren,** a Senator from New Jersey; born in Monmouth Beach, Monmouth County, N.J., July 31, 1888; attended the public schools and was graduated from the Browning School, New York City, N.Y., in 1906; also attended Princeton University; amateur heavyweight boxing champion of the United States and Canada in 1910 and 1911; member of the New York National Guard for ten years, serving on the Mexican border in 1916, attained the rank of captain; member of the Rumson (N.J.) Borough Council in 1922; served as mayor of Rumson, N.J., 1923-1928; moved to Locust, Monmouth County, N.J., in 1930; engaged in the thread manufacturing business and other industrial enterprises; appointed and subsequently elected as a Republican to the United States Senate to fill the vacancy caused by the death of Dwight W. Morrow and served from December 1, 1931, to January 3, 1937; unsuccessful candidate for reelection in 1936; resumed his former pursuits; member of the New Jersey Unemployment Compensation Commission in 1937; again elected to the United States Senate to fill the vacancy caused by the resignation of A. Harry Moore, reelected in 1940, and served from November 9, 1938 until his death in Washington, D.C., on November 22, 1943; interment in Cedar Lawn Cemetery, Paterson, N.J.

**BARCA, Peter William,** a Representative from Wisconsin; born in Kenosha, Wis., August 7, 1955; graduated from Mary D. Bradford High School; B.S., University of Wisconsin, Milwaukee, 1977, and M.A., 1982; graduate work at Harvard University; employment specialist; teacher of emotionally disturbed; director of camp for handicapped children; distribution manager; member, Wisconsin State assembly, 1985-1993; Kenosha County Democratic Party, chair; elected as a Democrat to the One Hundred Third Congress, May 4, 1993, by special election to fill the vacancy caused by the resignation of Leslie Aspin, and served from May 4, 1993 to January 3, 1995; unsuccessful candidate for reelection in 1994 to the One Hundred Fourth Congress; Midwest regional director, United States Small Business Administration, Chicago, Ill., 1995 to present; is a resident of Kenosha, Wis.

**BARCHFELD, Andrew Jackson,** a Representative from Pennsylvania; born in Pittsburgh, Pa., May 18, 1863; attended the public schools and the Pittsburgh Central High School; was graduated from Jefferson Medical College, Philadelphia, Pa., in 1884; commenced the practice of medicine in Pittsburgh, and was for many years president of the South Side Hospital; member of the common council of Pittsburgh 1886 and 1887; delegate to the Pennsylvania Republican conventions of 1886, 1894, and 1901; for many years a member of the Pennsylvania Republican committee; unsuccessful candidate for election in 1902 to the Fifty-eighth Congress; elected as a Republican to the Fifty-ninth and to the five succeeding Congresses (March 4, 1905-March 3, 1917); unsuccessful candidate for reelection in 1916 to the Sixty-fifth Congress; delegate to the peace congress at Brussels in 1905; member of the commission to the Philippine Islands in 1910 and of the Panama Canal Commission in 1912; continued to reside in Washington, D.C., after leaving Congress and was killed in the Knickerbocker Theater disaster in that city on January 28, 1922; interment in South Side Cemetery, Pittsburgh, Pa.

**BARCIA, James A.,** a Representative from Michigan; born in Bay City, Bay County, Mich., February 25, 1952; B.A., Saginaw Valley State University, University Center, Mich., 1974; member, Michigan State senate, 1983-1993; elected as a Democrat to the One Hundred Third and One Hundred Fourth Congresses (January 3, 1993-January 3, 1997); is a resident of Bay City, Mich.

**BARCLAY, Charles Frederick,** a Representative from Pennsylvania; born in Owego, Tioga County, N.Y., May 9, 1844; moved with his parents to Pennsylvania in 1845; attended Painted Post (N.Y.) High School and Coudersport (Pa.) Academy; taught school for several years; during the Civil War enlisted as a private in Company K, One Hundred and Forty-ninth Regiment, Pennsylvania Volunteer Infantry, in 1862 and served until 1865, when he was mustered out with the rank of captain; attended Belfast Seminary, New York, and subsequently studied law at the University of Michigan at Ann

Arbor, but never practiced; with an elder brother was engaged extensively in the lumber business in Sinnamahoning, Pa.; delegate to the Republican National Convention at Philadelphia in 1900; elected as a Republican to the Sixtieth and Sixty-first Congresses (March 4, 1907-March 3, 1911); was not a candidate for renomination in 1910 to the Sixty-second Congress; engaged in business in Washington, D.C., until his death March 9, 1914; interment in Wyside Cemetery, Sinnamahoning, Cameron County, Pa.

**BARCLAY, David,** a Representative from Pennsylvania; born in Punxsutawney, Jefferson County, Pa., in 1823; attended Washington (now Washington and Jefferson) College, Washington, Pa.; studied law in Pittsburgh; was admitted to the bar and practiced in Punxsutawney, Brookville, and Kittanning, Pa.; one of the editors and publishers of the Pittsburgh Union and Legal Journal 1850-1855; while a resident of Brookville was elected as a Democrat to the Thirty-fourth Congress (March 4, 1855-March 3, 1857); resumed the practice of law; died in Freeport, Armstrong County, Pa., September 10, 1889; interment in Freeport Cemetery.

**BARD, David,** a Representative from Pennsylvania; born at "Carroll's Delight," Adams County, Pa., in 1744; was graduated from Princeton College, New Jersey, in 1773; studied theology and was licensed to preach by the Donegal Presbytery in 1777; was ordained to the Presbyterian ministry at Lower Conotheague in 1779; missionary in Virginia and west of the Allegheny Mountains; pastor at Bedford, Pa., 1786-1789, and later at Frankstown (now Hollidaysburg), Blair County, Pa.; elected as a Republican to the Fourth and Fifth Congresses (March 4, 1795-March 3, 1799); elected to the Eighth and to the six succeeding Congresses and served from March 4, 1803, until his death in Alexandria, Huntingdon County, Pa., March 12, 1815; interment in Sinking Valley Cemetery, near Arch Spring, Blair County, Pa.

**BARD, Thomas Robert,** a Senator from California; born in Chambersburg, Franklin County, Pa., December 8, 1841; attended the common schools, and was graduated from the Chambersburg Academy in 1858; studied law, but before completing his studies secured a position with the Pennsylvania Railroad Co., later becoming assistant to the superintendent of the Cumberland Valley Railroad; engaged in the grain business at Hagerstown, Md.; during the early part of the Civil War served as a volunteer Union scout during the invasions of Maryland and Pennsylvania by the Confederates; moved to Ventura County, Calif., in 1864; member of the board of supervisors of Santa Barbara County 1868-1873; laid out the town of Hueneme; one of the commissioners appointed to organize Ventura County in 1871; director of the State board of agriculture in 1886 and 1887; elected as a Republican to the United States Senate to fill the vacancy in the term beginning March 4, 1899, and served from February 7, 1900, to March 3, 1905; unsuccessful candidate for reelection in 1904; chairman, Committee on Fisheries (Fifty-seventh Congress), Committee on Irrigation (Fifty-eighth Congress); died at his home, "Berylwood," in Hueneme, Ventura County, Calif., March 5, 1915; interment in the family cemetery on his estate.

**Bibliography:** Hutchinson, William Henry. *Oil, Land, and Politics: The California Career of Thomas R. Bard.* 2 vols. Norman: University of Oklahoma Press, 1965.

**BARDEN, Graham Arthur,** a Representative from North Carolina; born in Turkey Township, Sampson County, N.C., September 25, 1896; moved to Burgaw, Pender County, N.C., in 1908; attended the public schools; during the First World War served as a seaman in the United States Navy in 1918 and 1919; was graduated from the law department of the University of North Carolina at Chapel Hill in 1920; was admitted to the bar the same year and commenced practice in New Bern, N.C.; teacher in the New Bern (N.C.) High School in 1920; judge of the county court of Craven County, N.C., 1920-1924; member of the State house of representatives in 1933; elected as a Democrat to the Seventy-fourth and to the twelve succeeding Congresses (January 3, 1935-January 3, 1961); chairman, Committee on Education (Seventy-eighth and Seventy-ninth Congresses), Committee on Education and Labor (Eighty-first, Eighty-second, and Eighty-fourth through Eighty-sixth Congresses); was not a candidate for renomination in 1960; died in New Bern, N.C., January 29, 1967; interment in Cedar Grove Cemetery.

**Bibliography:** Puryear, Elmer L. *Graham A. Barden, Conservative Carolina Congressman.* Buie's Creek, N.C.: Campbell University Press, 1979.

**BARHAM, John All,** a Representative from California; born on a farm in Cass County, Mo., July 17, 1843; moved to California in 1849 with his parents, who settled in Woodland; attended the common schools and Hesperian College in Woodland, Calif.; taught in the public schools 1864-1876; studied law; was admitted to the bar in 1865 and commenced practice in Watsonville, San Francisco, and Santa Rosa; elected as a Republican to the Fifty-fourth, Fifty-fifth, and Fifty-sixth Congresses (March 4, 1895-March 3, 1901); chairman, Committeee on Mileage (Fifty-fifth and Fifty-sixth Congresses); was not a candidate for renomination in 1900; engaged in the practice of law until his death in Santa Rosa, Sonoma County, Calif., January 22, 1926; interment in Rural Cemetery.

**BARING, Walter Stephan, Jr.,** a Representative from Nevada; born in Goldfield, Esmeralda County, Nev., September 9, 1911; graduated from Reno High School in 1929 and from the University of Nevada at Reno, B.A. and B.S., 1934; holder of high school teacher's certificate; elected chairman of the Democratic Central Committee of Washoe County, Nev., in 1936; elected assemblyman from Washoe County to the State assembly in 1936, reelected in 1942, and served until his resignation to enlist in the United States Navy; served in the Navy from September 26, 1942, until May 31, 1945; engaged in the furniture business at Reno, Nev., 1945-1948; member of the Reno City Council in 1947 and 1948; elected as a Democrat to the Eighty-first and Eighty-second Congresses (January 3, 1949-January 3, 1953); unsuccessful candidate for reelection in 1952 to the Eighty-third Congress; delegate to the Democratic National Conventions in 1952, 1956, 1960, 1964, and 1968; engaged in the insurance business; unsuccessful candidate for election in 1954 to the Eighty-fourth Congress; elected to the Eighty-fifth and to the seven succeeding Congresses (January 3, 1957-January 3, 1973); unsuccessful candidate for renomination in 1972; returned to his home in Reno, Nev.; died in Los Angeles, Calif., July 13, 1975; cremated; ashes entombed in a mausoleum at Masonic Memorial Gardens, Reno, Nev.

**BARKER, Abraham Andrews,** a Representative from Pennsylvania; born in Lovell, Oxford County, Maine, March 30, 1816; attended the common schools; engaged in agricultural pursuits and also in the shook business; moved to Carrolltown, Pa., in 1854 and to Ebensburg, Cambria County, Pa., where he continued the shook business; also engaged in the mercantile business in 1858 and later in the lumber business; delegate to the Republican National Convention in 1860; served in Company E, Fourth Regiment, Pennsylvania Emergency Troops, during the Civil War; elected as a Union Republican to the Thirty-ninth Congress (March 4, 1865-March 3, 1867); unsuccessful candidate for renomination in 1866 and for election as a Republican in 1872 to the Forty-third Congress; reengaged in the lumber and shook business until 1880, when he retired from active pursuits; died in Altoona, Pa., while on a visit for medical treatment March 18, 1898; interment in Lloyd Cemetery, Ebensburg, Pa.

**BARKER, David, Jr.,** a Representative from New Hampshire; born in Stratham, N.H., January 8, 1797; attended Phillips Exeter Academy, Exeter, N.H., and was graduated from Harvard University in 1815; studied law; was admitted to the bar in 1819 and commenced practice in Rochester, N.H.; member of the State house of representatives in 1823, 1825, and 1826; elected to the Twentieth Congress (March 4, 1827-March 3, 1829); resumed the practice of law; was an original member of the New Hampshire Historical Society; died in Rochester, N.H., April 1, 1834; interment in the Old Rochester Cemetery.

**BARKER, Joseph,** a Representative from Massachusetts; born in Branford, Conn., October 19, 1751; attended the common schools in Branford, Harvard College for two years, and was graduated from Yale College in 1771; studied theology; licensed to preach January 3, 1775; ordained to the ministry December 5, 1781, and was installed as pastor of the First Congregational Church of Middleboro, Plymouth County, Mass.; elected as a Republican to the Ninth and Tenth Congresses (March 4, 1805-March 3, 1809); was not a candidate for renomination in 1808; member of the Massachusetts house of representatives in 1812 and 1813; continued in the ministry at Middleboro, Mass., until his death, July 5, 1815; interment in Green Cemetery.

**BARKLEY, Alben William,** a Representative and a Senator from Kentucky and a Vice President of the United States; born near Lowes, Graves County, Ky., November 24, 1877; attended the public schools and was graduated from Marvin College, Clinton, Ky., in 1897; attended Emory College, Oxford, Ga., and the University of Virginia Law School, Charlottesville, Va.; was admitted to the bar in 1901 and commenced practice in Paducah, McCracken County, Ky.; prosecuting attorney for McCracken County, Ky., 1905-1909; judge of the McCracken County Court from 1909 until 1913; elected as a Democrat to the Sixty-third and to the six succeeding Congresses (March 4, 1913-March 3, 1927); was not a candidate in 1926 for renomination to the House of Representatives, but was elected to the United States Senate; reelected in 1932, 1938, and again in 1944, and served from March 4, 1927 until his resignation on January 19, 1949; majority leader (Seventy-fifth through Seventy-ninth Congresses), minority leader (Eightieth Congress); elected Vice President of the United States on the Democratic ticket with President Harry S Truman in 1948, and was inaugurated January 20, 1949, for the term ending January 20, 1953; again elected to the United States Senate, and served from January 3, 1955 until his death in Lexington, Va., April 30, 1956; interment in Mount Kenton Cemetery, on Lone Oak Road, near Paducah, Ky.

**Bibliography:** *DAB*; Barkley, Alben. *That Reminds Me.* Garden City, N.Y.: Doubleday, 1954; Libbey, James K. *Dear Alben: Mr. Barkley of Kentucky.* Lexington: University Press of Kentucky, 1979; Ritchie, Donald A. "Alben W. Barkley: The President's Man." In *First Among Equals: Outstanding Senate Majority Leaders of the Twentieth Century,* edited by Richard A. Baker and Roger H. Davidson, pp. 127-162. Washington: Congressional Quarterly, Inc., 1991.

**BARKSDALE, Ethelbert** (brother of William Barksdale), a Representative from Mississippi; born in Smyrna, Rutherford County, Tenn., January 4, 1824; moved to Jackson, Hinds County, Miss.; adopted journalism as a profession; edited the official journal of the State 1854-1861 and 1876-1883; member of the Confederate Congress 1861-1865; delegate to the Democratic National Conventions in 1860, 1868, 1872, and 1880; chairman of the Democratic State executive committee 1877-1879; elected as a Democrat to the Forty-eighth and Forty-ninth Congresses (March 4, 1883-March 3, 1887); unsuccessful candidate for renomination in 1886; engaged in agricultural pursuits in Yazoo County; died in Yazoo City, Miss., February 17, 1893; interment in Greenwood Cemetery, Jackson, Miss.

**Bibliography:** Peterson, Owen M. "Ethelbert Barksdale in the Democratic National Convention of 1860." *Journal of Mississippi History* 14 (October 1952): 257-278.

**BARKSDALE, William** (brother of Ethelbert Barksdale), a Representative from Mississippi; born in Rutherford County, Tenn., August 21, 1821; attended the University of Nashville; studied law; was admitted to the bar in 1839 and commenced practice in Columbus, Lowndes County, Miss.; for a time was editor of the Columbus Democrat; served in the Mexican War as quartermaster of the Mississippi Volunteers; delegate to the Democratic National Convention of 1852; elected as a Democrat to the Thirty-third and to the three succeeding Congresses and served from March 4, 1853, until January 12, 1861, when he joined other secessionist members of the Mississippi delegation in withdrawing from the Thirty-sixth Congress; entered the Confederate Army during the Civil War as colonel of the Thirteenth Regiment of Mississippi Volunteers; promoted to the rank of brigadier general on August 12, 1862; commanded a Mississippi brigade in Longstreet's corps; wounded in the Battle of Gettysburg, Pa., and died as a result of his wounds the following day, July 3, 1863; interment in Greenwood Cemetery, Jackson, Miss.

**Bibliography:** *DAB*; McKee, James W. "William Barksdale and the Congressional Election of 1853." *Journal of Mississippi History* 34 (May 1972): 129-58; Tyson, Raymond W. "William Barksdale and the Brooks-Sumner Assault." *Journal of Mississippi History* 26 (May 1964): 135-40.

**BARLOW, Bradley,** a Representative from Vermont; born in Fairfield, Franklin County, Vt., May 12, 1814; attended the common schools; engaged in mercantile pursuits in Philadelphia until 1858, when he moved to St. Albans, Vt.; delegate to the State constitutional conventions in 1843, 1850, and 1857, acting as assistant secretary in 1843; member of the Vermont State house of representatives in 1845, 1850-1852, 1864, and 1865; engaged in banking and in the railroad business from 1860 until 1883; chairman of the school committee in St. Albans; president of the village corporation and treasurer of Franklin County, 1860-1867; served in the State senate, 1866-1868; elected as a Greenbacker to the Forty-sixth Congress (March 4, 1879-March 3, 1881); was not a candidate for renomination in 1880 to the Forty-seventh Congress; died in Denver, Colo., on November 6, 1889; interment in Greenwood Cemetery, St. Albans, Vt.

**BARLOW, Charles Averill,** a Representative from California born in Cleveland, Ohio, March 17, 1858; attended the common schools; engaged in agricultural and commercial pursuits; moved to Ventura, Calif., in 1875 and to San Luis Obispo County in 1889, engaging in wheat farming; member of the State assembly in 1892 and 1893; chairman of the People's Party State convention in 1896; elected as a Populist to the Fifty-fifth Congress (March 4, 1897-March 3, 1899); was not a candidate for renomination in 1898 to the Fifty-sixth Congress; moved to Kern County in 1901 and engaged in mining, fruit growing, and the production of oil; delegate to the Democratic National Conventions of 1912 and 1920; died in Bakersfield, Calif., on October 3, 1927; interment in Union Cemetery.

**BARLOW, Stephen,** a Representative from Pennsylvania; born in Redding, Fairfield County, Conn., June 13, 1779; attended the common schools and Yale College; moved to Meadville, Pa., in 1816; studied law; was admitted to the bar and commenced practice in Meadville, Crawford County, Pa.; elected to the Twentieth Congress (March 4, 1827-March 3, 1829); unsuccessful candidate for reelection in 1828 to the Twenty-first Congress; resumed the practice of his profession; served in the Pennsylvania house of representatives, 1829-1831; appointed as an associate judge of Crawford County in January 1831 and served until his death in Meadville, Pa., on August 24, 1845; interment in Greendale Cemetery.

**BARLOW, Thomas Jefferson, III,** a Representative from Kentucky; born in Washington, D.C., August 7, 1940; B.A., Haverford (Pa.) College, 1962; assistant vice president, Fidelity

Bank; Natural Resource Defense Council, Washington, D.C.; director of sales, Central Service, Kevil, Ky.; unsuccessful candidate for nomination in 1986 to the One Hundredth Congress; elected as a Democrat to the One Hundred Third Congress (January 3, 1993-January 3, 1995); unsuccessful candidate for reelection in 1994 to the One Hundred Fourth Congress; unsuccessful candidate in 1996 for nomination to the United States Senate; is a resident of Paducah, Ky.

**BARNARD, Daniel Dewey,** a Representative from New York; born in Sheffield, Berkshire County, Mass., July 16, 1797; attended the common schools and was graduated from Williams College, Williamstown, Mass., in 1818; studied law; was admitted to the bar in 1821 and began practice in Rochester, N.Y.; prosecuting attorney of Monroe County in 1826; elected to the Twentieth Congress (March 4, 1827-March 3, 1829); unsuccessful candidate for reelection in 1828 to the Twenty-first Congress; traveled in Europe in 1831; moved to Albany, N.Y., in 1832 and continued the practice of law; member of the State assembly in 1838; elected as a Whig to the Twenty-sixth, Twenty-seventh, and Twenty-eighth Congresses (March 4, 1839-March 3, 1845); chairman, Committee on the Judiciary (Twenty-seventh Congress); was not a candidate for reelection in 1844; appointed Minister to Prussia on September 3, 1850 and served until September 21, 1853; retired from active business pursuits in 1853 and engaged in literary pursuits; died in Albany, N.Y., April 24, 1861; interment in Albany Rural Cemetery.

Bibliography: *DAB*; Penney, Sherry. "Dissension in the Whig Ranks: Daniel Dewey Barnard versus Thurlow Weed." *New-York Historical Society Quarterly* 59 (January 1975): 71-92; Penney, Sherry. *Patrician in Politics: Daniel Dewey Barnard of New York.* Port Washington, New York: Kennikat Press, 1974.

**BARNARD, Druie Douglas, Jr.,** a Representative from Georgia; born in Augusta, Richmond County, Ga., March 20, 1922; attended the Richmond County public schools; graduated, Academy of Richmond County, Augusta, Ga., 1939; attended Augusta (Ga.) College, 1939-1940; A.B., Mercer University, Macon, Ga., 1943; entered the United States Army in 1943, and was released in 1945 as a technical sergeant following service with the 57th Financial Distribution Unit in Europe; LL.B., Walter F. George School of Law, Mercer University, 1948; engaged in the banking profession, 1948-1962; executive secretary to Governor Carl E. Sanders of Georgia, 1963-1966; board member, Georgia State Department of Transportation, 1966-1976; delegate to Georgia State Democratic convention, 1962; delegate to the Democratic National Convention of 1964; elected as a Democrat to the Ninety-fifth and to the seven succeeding Congresses (January 3, 1977-January 3, 1993); was not a candidate for reelection in 1992 to the One Hundred Third Congress; is a resident of Augusta, Ga.

**BARNARD, Isaac Dutton,** a Senator from Pennsylvania; born in Aston Township, Delaware County, Pa., July 18, 1791; moved with his parents to a farm near Chester, Pa.; attended the public schools; moved to Philadelphia, where he remained until 1811, when he returned to Chester; while studying law was appointed captain and major in the Fourteenth Regiment, United States Infantry, and served during the War of 1812; resumed his legal studies; was admitted to the bar in 1816 and commenced practice in West Chester, Chester County, Pa.; deputy attorney general for Chester County, 1817-1821; member of the Pennsylvania senate, 1820-1826; served as Pennsylvania secretary of State in 1826; elected as a Jacksonian to the United States Senate, and served from March 4, 1827 until December 6, 1831, when he resigned; chairman, Committee on Militia (Twenty-first and Twenty-second Congresses); died in West Chester, Pa., February 28, 1834; interment in Oakland's Cemetery, near West Chester, Pa.

**BARNARD, William Oscar,** a Representative from Indiana; born near Liberty, Union County, Ind., October 25, 1852; moved with his parents to Dublin, Wayne County, Ind., in 1854, to Fayette County in 1856, and to Henry County in 1866; attended the common schools, and Spiceland Academy, Spiceland, Ind.; taught school for five years in Henry and Wayne Counties; studied law; was admitted to the bar in 1876 and commenced practice in Newcastle, Ind.; prosecuting attorney of the eighteenth and fifty-third judicial circuits 1887-1893; judge of the fifty-third judicial circuit court of Indiana 1896-1902; resumed the practice of law in Newcastle; elected as a Republican to the Sixty-first Congress (March 4, 1909-March 3, 1911); unsuccessful candidate for reelection in 1910 to the Sixty-second Congress; resumed the practice of law in Newcastle, Ind., until his death there on April 8, 1939; interment in Southmound Cemetery.

**BARNES, Demas,** a Representative from New York; born in Gorham Township, Ontario County, N.Y., April 4, 1827; attended the public schools; engaged in mercantile pursuits; moved to New York City in 1849 and engaged in the drug business; crossed the continent in a wagon and studied the mineral resources of Colorado, Nevada, and California; returned to New York City and wrote articles and published works concerning his experiences; elected as a Democrat to the Fortieth Congress (March 4, 1867-March 3, 1869); was not a candidate for renomination in 1868; established and edited the Brooklyn Argus in 1873 and was also engaged in the real-estate business; member of the board of education; one of the original trustees of the Brooklyn Bridge when it was a private enterprise; died in New York City May 1, 1888; interment in Greenwood Cemetery.

**BARNES, George Thomas,** a Representative from Georgia; born in a suburb (now called Summerville) of Augusta, Richmond County, Ga., August 14, 1833; attended private schools, Richmond Academy, and Franklin College; was graduated from the University of Georgia at Athens in 1853; studied law; was admitted to the bar in 1855 and commenced practice in Augusta; during the Civil War served in the Confederate Army in the Washington Light Artillery Company of Augusta, Ga., as second lieutenant and major brevet; member of the State house of representatives 1860-1865; member of the Democratic National Committee 1876-1884; elected as a Democrat to the Forty-ninth, Fiftieth, and Fifty-first Congresses (March 4, 1885-March 3, 1891); unsuccessful candidate for reelection in 1890 to the Fifty-second Congress; resumed the practice of law; died in Augusta, Ga., October 24, 1901; interment in the City Cemetery.

**BARNES, James Martin,** a Representative from Illinois; born in Jacksonville, Morgan County, Ill., January 9, 1899; attended the public schools; during the First World War served overseas as a private in the United States Marine Corps in 1918 and 1919; was graduated from Illinois College at Jacksonville in 1921 and from the law department of Harvard University in 1924; was admitted to the bar in 1924 and commenced the practice of law in Jacksonville, Ill.; served as county judge of Morgan County, Ill., 1926-1934; resumed the practice of law 1934-1939; elected as a Democrat to the Seventy-sixth and Seventy-seventh Congresses (January 3, 1939-January 3, 1943); unsuccessful candidate for reelection in 1942 to the Seventy-eighth Congress; appointed administrative assistant to President Franklin D. Roosevelt on March 1, 1943, and served until July 15, 1945; resumed the practice of law in Washington, D.C., where he died June 8, 1958; interment in Arlington National Cemetery, Va.

**BARNES, Lyman Eddy,** a Representative from Wisconsin; born in Weyauwega, Waupaca County, Wis., June 30, 1855; attended the public schools and the law department of Columbia College, New York City; was admitted to the bar in 1876 and commenced practice in Appleton, Outagamie County, Wis., the same year; moved to

Rockledge, Brevard County, Fla., in 1882, where he remained about five years and continued the practice of law; returned to Appleton, Wis., and was elected district attorney of Outagamie County; elected as a Democrat to the Fifty-third Congress (March 4, 1893-March 3, 1895); unsuccessful candidate for reelection in 1894 to the Fifty-fourth Congress; resumed the practice of his profession; died in Appleton, Wis., on January 16, 1904; interment in Riverside Cemetery.

**BARNES, Michael Darr,** a Representative from Maryland; born in Washington, D.C., September 3, 1943; attended Landon School, Bethesda, Md.; graduated, Principia High School, St. Louis, Mo., 1961; B.A., University of North Carolina, Chapel Hill, 1965; Institute of Higher International Studies, Geneva, Switzerland, 1965-1966; served in United States Marine Corps, corporal, 1967-1969; J.D., George Washington University, 1972; admitted to the Washington, D.C. Bar in 1972 and commenced practice with Covington & Burling; private practice, 1972-1975; commissioner, Maryland Public Service Commission, 1975-1978; elected as a Democrat to the Ninety-sixth and to the three succeeding Congresses (January 3, 1979-January 3, 1987); was not a candidate in 1986 for reelection to the House of Representatives, but was an unsuccessful candidate for nomination to the United States Senate; resumed the practice of law in Washington, D.C. with Arent, Fox, Kintner, Plotkin and Kahn; is a resident of Kensington, Md.

**BARNETT, William,** a Representative from Georgia; born in Amherst County, Va., March 4, 1761; moved to Georgia with his father, who settled in Columbia County; at the outbreak of the Revolutionary War returned to Virginia with his brother and joined a military company from Amherst County under the leadership of the Marquis de Lafayette and was present at the surrender of Cornwallis at Yorktown; returned to Georgia at the close of the war and settled on Broad River, Elbert County; sheriff of Elbert County for several years; member of the State senate and served as pesident of that body; elected as a Republican to the Twelfth Congress to fill the vacancy caused by the resignation of Howell Cobb; reelected to the Thirteenth Congress and served from October 5, 1812, to March 3, 1815; appointed commissioner to establish the boundaries of the Creek Indian Reservation in 1815; moved to Montgomery County, Ala., and engaged in planting; died in Montgomery County, Ala., April 1832; interment in the Gilmer-Christian-Barnett Cemetery, near Mathews Station, Montgomery County, Ala.

**BARNEY, John,** a Representative from Maryland; born in Baltimore, Md., January 18, 1785; appointed a captain and assistant district quartermaster general in the United States Army August 15, 1814, and served until June 15, 1815, when he was honorably discharged; unsuccessful candidate for election in 1822 to the Eighteenth Congress; elected to the Nineteenth and Twentieth Congresses (March 4, 1825-March 3, 1829); unsuccessful candidate for reelection in 1828 to the Twenty-first Congress; engaged in literary pursuits until his death in Washington, D.C., January 26, 1857; interment in Greenmount Cemetery, Baltimore, Md.

**BARNEY, Samuel Stebbins,** a Representative from Wisconsin; born in Hartford, Washington County, Wis., January 31, 1846; attended the public schools and Lombard University, Galesburg, Ill.; taught in the high school at Hartford for four years; studied law in West Bend, Wis.; was admitted to the bar in 1873 and commenced practice in West Bend; superintendent of schools of Washington County 1876-1880; delegate to the Republican National Convention at Chicago in 1884; unsuccessful candidate for election in 1884 to the Forty-ninth Congress; elected as a Republican to the Fifty-fourth and to the three succeeding Congresses (March 4, 1895-March 3, 1903); was not a candidate for renomination in 1902; appointed associate justice of the court of claims, Washington, D.C., in 1904 and served until 1919; died in Milwaukee, Wis., December 31, 1919; interment in Union Cemetery, West Bend, Washington County, Wis.

**BARNHART, Henry A.,** a Representative from Indiana; born near Twelve Mile, Cass County, Ind., September 11, 1858; attended the common schools, Amboy Academy, and Wabash Normal Training School; taught school; moved to Liberty Township, Fulton County, in 1881 and engaged in agricultural pursuits until 1884; moved to Rochester, Ind., in 1885 and served as surveyor of Fulton County, 1885-1887; owner and editor of the Rochester Sentinel, 1886-1924; president and manager of the Rochester Telephone Co., 1895-1934; president of the Indiana Telephone Association; president of the National Telephone Association; director of the United States Bank & Trust Co.; appointed a director of the Indiana State Prison in 1893 and a trustee of the State hospital for the insane in 1903; elected as a Democrat to the Sixtieth Congress to fill the vacancy caused by the death of Abram L. Brick, reelected to the Sixty-first and to the four succeeding Congresses and served from November 3, 1908, to March 3, 1919; unsuccessful candidate for reelection in 1918 to the Sixty-sixth Congress; resumed his activities in the newspaper publishing business and in the telephone business; also engaged as a lecturer and in agricultural pursuits; died in Rochester, Ind., March 26, 1934; interment in the Mausoleum.

**BARNITZ, Charles Augustus,** a Representative from Pennsylvania; born in York, York County, Pa., September 11, 1780; attended York County Academy, York, Pa.; studied law; was admitted to the bar in 1811 and commenced practice in York; member of the Pennsylvania senate, 1815-1819; from 1820 until his death served as agent of the heirs of William Penn for their interests in Springettsbury Manor, the center of which is now the city of York; elected as an Anti-Masonic candidate to the Twenty-third Congress (March 4, 1833-March 3, 1835); was not a candidate for reelection in 1834 to the Twenty-fourth Congress; resumed the practice of law at York, Pa.; also engaged in banking and served as president of the York Bank; member of the Pennsylvania constitutional convention in 1838; delegate to the Whig National Conventions at Harrisburg in 1840 and at Baltimore in 1844; died in York, Pa., January 8, 1850; interment in the First Presbyterian Churchyard.

**BARNUM, William Henry,** a Representative and a Senator from Connecticut; born in Boston Corner, Columbia County, N.Y., September 17, 1818; attended the common schools; apprenticed to the trade of iron founder and subsequently admitted to partnership by his father, who was engaged in the iron business at Lime Rock, Conn.; member, State house of representatives in 1851-1852; elected as a Democrat to the Fortieth and to the four succeeding Congresses and served from March 4, 1867, until May 18, 1876, when he resigned to become Senator; elected to the United States Senate to fill the vacancy caused by the death of Orris S. Ferry and served from May 18, 1876, to March 3, 1879; chairman of the Democratic National Committee 1876-1889; resumed his former manufacturing pursuits; died at Lime Rock, Litchfield County, Conn., April 30, 1889; interment in the Lime Rock Cemetery.

**BARNWELL, Robert** (father of Robert Woodward Barnwell), a Delegate and a Representative from South Carolina; born in Beaufort, S.C., December 21, 1761; educated in the common schools and by private teachers; volunteered for service in the Revolutionary War when sixteen years of age; received seventeen wounds in the battle on Johns Island, S.C.; finally recovered and served as lieutenant with his company at the siege of Charleston in 1780; at the fall of that city was sent aboard the prison ship *Pack Horse*, but was released in the general exchange of prisoners in June 1781; was for many years president of the board of trustees of Beaufort College; Member of the Continental Congress in 1789; member of the convention of South Carolina for the adoption of the Federal Constitution in 1788; elected to the Second Congress (March 4, 1791-March 3, 1793); declined to be a candidate for renomination in

1792 to the Third Congress; member of the South Carolina house of representatives 1787-1788, 1790-1791, and 1794-1801, serving as speaker in 1795; member of the South Carolina senate in 1805 and 1806, serving as president in 1805; died in Beaufort, Beaufort County, S.C., October 24, 1814; interment in St. Helena's Churchyard.

**BARNWELL, Robert Woodward** (son of Robert Barnwell), a Representative and a Senator from South Carolina; born in Beaufort, Beaufort County, S.C., August 10, 1801; attended private schools in Beaufort and Charleston, S.C., and was graduated from Harvard University in 1821; studied law; was admitted to the bar and commenced practice in Beaufort, S.C., in 1824; member, State house of representatives 1826-1828; elected to the Twenty-first and Twenty-second Congresses (March 4, 1829-March 3, 1833); was not a candidate for renomination in 1832; president of South Carolina College (now the University of South Carolina) at Columbia 1835-1841, when he resigned; appointed to the United States Senate to fill the vacancy caused by the death of Franklin H. Elmore and served from June 4 to December 8, 1850, when a successor was elected and qualified; was not a candidate for election; member of the Nashville convention in 1850; commissioner to the Federal Government from South Carolina regarding the secession of that State in December 1860; delegate to the convention of the seceding States in Montgomery, Ala., his being the deciding vote in the South Carolina delegation which carried the State for Jefferson Davis and made him President of the Southern Confederacy; member of the Confederate States Senate 1861-1865; chairman of the faculty of the University of South Carolina 1866-1873; conducted a private girls school in Columbia, S.C.; died in Columbia, Richland County, S.C., November 5, 1882; interment in St. Helena's Churchyard, Beaufort, S.C.

Bibliography: *DAB*; Barnwell, John, ed. "'In the Hands of Compromisers': Letters of Robert W. Barnwell to James H. Hammond." *Civil War History* 29 (June 1983): 154-68; Barnwell, John, ed. "Hamlet to Hotspur: Letters of Robert Woodward Barnwell to Robert Barnwell Rhett." *South Carolina Historical Magazine* 77 (October 1976): 236-37, 247.

**BARR, Bob,** a Representative from Georgia; born in Iowa City, Johnson County, Iowa, November 5, 1948; graduated, Community High School, Tehran, Iran, 1966; B.A., University of Southern California, 1970; M.A., George Washington University, 1972; J.D., Georgetown University School of Law, 1977; United States attorney, 1986-1990; Central Intelligence Agency, 1970-1978; anti-drug coordinator for Department of Justice, Southeastern United States, 1986-1990; head, Public Corruption Subcommittee for United States Attorney General, 1987-1988; president, Southeastern Legal Foundation, 1990-1991; unsuccessful candidate in 1992 for Republican nomination to the United States Senate; elected as a Republican to the One Hundred Fourth Congress (January 3, 1995-January 3, 1997); is a resident of Smyrna, Ga.

**BARR, Joseph Walker,** a Representative from Indiana; born in Bicknell, Knox County, Ind., January 17, 1918; graduated from DePauw University in 1939 and from Harvard University in 1941; served in the United States Navy, 1942-1945, with subchaser duty in the Mediterranean and Atlantic; received Bronze Star for sinking submarine off Anzio Beach; engaged in the operation of grain elevators, theaters, real-estate, and publishing business; elected as a Democrat to the Eighty-sixth Congress (January 3, 1959-January 3, 1961); unsuccessful candidate for reelection in 1960 to the Eighty-seventh Congress; appointed assistant for congressional relations to Secretary of the Treasury Douglas Dillon, 1961; appointed Chairman of the Federal Deposit Insurance Corporation in 1963; Under Secretary of the Treasury, 1965-1968; appointed by President Lyndon B. Johnson as Secretary of the Treasury, and served from December 21, 1968 to January 20, 1969; president and

chairman, American Security and Trust Company, 1969-1974; chairman, Federal Home Loan Bank of Atlanta, 1977-1981; was a resident of Hume, Va.; died in Playa del Carman, Mexico, February 23, 1996, while on a vacation.

**BARR, Samuel Fleming,** a Representative from Pennsylvania; born near Coleraine, County Antrim, Ireland, June 15, 1829; immigrated to the United States in 1831 with his parents, who settled in Harrisburg, Pa.; attended the common schools; freight agent of the Pittsburgh, Fort Wayne & Chicago Railroad in 1855 and 1856; early in the Civil War was employed upon government railways in and about Washington, D.C.; editor of the Harrisburg Telegraph 1873-1878; elected as a Republican to the Forty-seventh and Forty-eighth Congresses (March 4, 1881-March 3, 1885); declined to be a candidate for renomination in 1884 to the Forty-ninth Congress; lived in retirement until his death, residing in San Diego, Calif., in the winter and in Seal Harbor, Maine, during the summer season; died in San Diego, Calif., May 29, 1919; interment in Odd Fellows Cemetery.

**BARR, Thomas Jefferson,** a Representative from New York; born in New York City in 1812; attended the public schools; moved to Scotch Plains, N.J., in 1835 and conducted a roadhouse; returned to New York City in 1842; assistant alderman of the sixth ward in 1849 and 1850 and alderman in 1852 and 1853; served in the State senate in 1854 and 1855; elected on January 6, 1859, as an Independent Democrat to the Thirty-fifth Congress to fill the vacancy caused by the resignation of John Kelly; reelected to the Thirty-sixth Congress and served from January 17, 1859, to March 3, 1861; was not a candidate for renomination in 1860 to the Thirty-seventh Congress; appointed a police commissioner of New York City in 1870 and served until 1873, when the police board was abolished; was subsequently employed in the customhouse; died in New York City, March 27, 1881; interment in Calvary Cemetery, Long Island, N.Y.

**BARRERE, Granville** (nephew of Nelson Barrere), a Representative from Illinois; born in New Market, near Hillsboro, Highland County, Ohio, July 11, 1829; attended the common schools, Augusta College, Augusta, Ky., and was graduated from Marietta College, Marietta, Ohio; studied law; was admitted to the bar in Chillicothe, Ross County, Ohio, in 1853 and commenced practice in Marion, Crittenden County, Ark.; moved to Bloomington, McLean County, Ill., in 1855, and then to Canton, Fulton County, Ill., the same year, and continued the practice of his profession; member of the city board of education; member of the board of supervisors of Canton; elected as a Republican to the Forty-third Congress (March 4, 1873-March 3, 1875); unsuccessful candidate for renomination in 1874; resumed the practice of law; died in Canton, Fulton County, Ill., January 13, 1889; interment in Greenwood Cemetery.

**BARRERE, Nelson** (uncle of Granville Barrere), a Representative from Ohio; born in New Market, near Hillsboro, Highland County, Ohio, April 1, 1808; attended the common schools, and Hillsboro High School in 1827; was graduated from Augusta (Ky.) College in 1830; studied law; was admitted to the bar in 1833 and commenced practice in Hillsboro; moved to West Union, Adams County, Ohio, in 1834 and continued the practice of law; in 1846 returned to Hillsboro, where he resided until his death; member of the State house of representatives in 1837 and 1838; elected as a Whig to the Thirty-second Congress (March 4, 1851-March 3, 1853); unsuccessful candidate for reelection in 1852 to the Thirty-third Congress; resumed the practice of law; died in Hillsboro, Highland County, Ohio, August 20, 1883; interment in Presbyterian Cemetery, New Market, Ohio.

**BARRET, John Richard,** a Representative from Missouri; born in Greensburg, Green County, Ky., August 21, 1825; attended the common schools and Centre College, Danville, Ky.; moved to St. Louis, Mo., in 1839; was graduated from the St. Louis University in

1843; studied law and practiced; elected to the State house of representatives in 1852 and served four terms; became identified with the St. Louis Agricultural Society and organized its exhibitions; presented credentials as a Democratic Member-elect to the Thirty-sixth Congress and served from March 4, 1859, to June 8, 1860, when he was succeeded by Francis P. Blair, Jr., who contested his election; subsequently elected to the same Congress to fill the vacancy caused by the resignation of Francis P. Blair, Jr., and served from December 3, 1860, to March 3, 1861; unsuccessful for reelection in 1860 to the Thirty-seventh Congress; moved to New York City and engaged in numerous occupations; died in New York City on November 2, 1903; interment in Cave Hill Cemetery, Louisville, Ky.

**BARRETT, Frank Aloysius,** a Representative and a Senator from Wyoming; born in Omaha, Douglas County, Nebr., November 10, 1892; attended the public schools; was graduated from Creighton University, Omaha, Nebr., in 1913 and from its law department in 1916; during the First World War served as a sergeant in the Balloon Corps, United States Army 1917-1919; was admitted to the bar in 1919 and commenced practice in Lusk, Wyo.; also a rancher; county attorney of Niobrara County, Wyo., 1923-1932; member, State senate 1933-1935; member of the board of trustees of the University of Wyoming; elected as a Republican to the Seventy-eighth and to the three succeeding Congresses and served from January 3, 1943, until his resignation December 31, 1950, having been elected Governor of Wyoming; served as Governor from January 1, 1951 until his resignation on January 3, 1953, having been elected a Senator; elected as a Republican to the United States Senate and served from January 3, 1953, to January 3, 1959; unsuccessful candidate for reelection in 1958; general counsel, Department of Agriculture, Washington, D.C., and member of board of directors of Commodity Credit Corporation 1959-1960; unsuccessful candidate for the Republican nomination for United States Senator in 1960; died in Cheyenne, Wyo., May 30, 1962; interment in Lusk Cemetery, Lusk, Wyo.

Bibliography: *DAB.*

**BARRETT, Thomas Mark,** a Representative from Wisconsin; born in Milwaukee, Wis., December 8, 1953; B.A., University of Wisconsin, Madison, 1976; J.D., University of Wisconsin School of Law, 1980; admitted to Wisconsin bar; law clerk to Judge Robert Warren, United States District Court for the Eastern District of Wisconsin; attorney, Milwaukee, Wis.; member, Wisconsin State house of representatives, 1984-1989; member, Wisconsin State senate, 1989-1993; elected as a Democrat to the One Hundred Third and One Hundred Fourth Congresses (January 3, 1993-January 3, 1997); is a resident of Milwaukee, Wis.

**BARRETT, William Aloysius,** a Representative from Pennsylvania; born in Philadelphia, Pa., August 14, 1896; was graduated from Brown Preparatory School in Philadelphia, Pa., and from St. Joseph's College, Philadelphia, Pa.; took a law course at South Jersey Law School in Camden, N.J.; engaged in the real-estate business; member of the Board of Mercantile Appraisers, Philadelphia, Pa., for four years; member of the Democratic city committee; elected as a Democrat to the Seventy-ninth Congress (January 3, 1945-January 3, 1947); unsuccessful candidate for reelection in 1946 to the Eightieth Congress; elected to the Eighty-first Congress; reelected to the thirteen succeeding Congresses and served from January 3, 1949, until his death April 12, 1976, in Philadelphia, Pa.; interment in Holy Cross Cemetery, Yeadon, Pa.

**BARRETT, William E.,** a Representative from Nebraska; born in Lexington, Dawson County, Nebr., February 9, 1929; graduate of Lexington High School; B.A., Hastings (Nebr.) College, 1952; entered active duty, United States Navy in 1951; released in 1952; real estate and insurance business; Barrett-Housel and Associates, Inc.; member, Nebraska State legislature, 1979-1990, speaker of the Nebraska legislature, 1987-1990; elected as a Republican to the One

Hundred Second and to the two succeeding Congresses (January 3, 1991-January 3, 1997); is a resident of Lexington, Nebr.

**BARRETT, William Emerson,** a Representative from Massachusetts; born in Melrose, Middlesex County, Mass., December 29, 1858; attended the public schools; was graduated from Dartmouth College, Hanover, N.H., in 1880; assistant editor of the St. Albans Daily Messenger; joined the staff of the Boston Daily Advertiser in 1882; Washington correspondent of the Boston Advertiser 1882-1886; recalled to Boston to become editor in chief and in 1888 became chief proprietor and manager of the Boston Daily Advertiser and the Boston Evening Record; member of the Massachusetts house of representatives 1887-1892 and served as speaker the last five years; elected as a Republican to the Fifty-fourth and Fifty-fifth Congresses (March 4, 1895-March 3, 1899); declined to be a candidate for renomination in 1898 to the Fifty-sixth Congress; returned to Boston and resumed active management of his newspaper interests; president of the Union Trust Co. of Boston; died in Newton, Mass., February 12, 1906; interment in Newton Cemetery.

**BARRINGER, Daniel Laurens** (uncle of Daniel Moreau Barringer), a Representative from North Carolina; born at "Poplar Grove," Cabarrus County, N.C., October 1, 1788; studied law; was admitted to the bar and commenced practice in Raleigh, Wake County, N.C.; member of the State house of commons in 1813, 1814, and 1819-1822; elected to the Nineteenth Congress to fill the vacancy caused by the resignation of Willie P. Mangum; reelected to the Twentieth and to the three succeeding Congresses and served from December 4, 1826, to March 3, 1835; unsuccessful candidate for reelection in 1834 to the Twenty-fourth Congress; moved to Bedford County, Tenn., about 1830 and settled in Shelbyville, where he continued the practice of law; member and speaker of the State house of representatives 1843-1845; presidential elector on the Whig ticket in 1844; died in Shelbyville, Bedford County, Tenn., October 16, 1852; interment in Willow Mount Cemetery.

**BARRINGER, Daniel Moreau** (nephew of Daniel Laurens Barringer), a Representative from North Carolina; born at "Poplar Grove," near Concord, Cabarrus County, N.C., July 30, 1806; was graduated from the University of North Carolina at Chapel Hill in 1826; studied law in Hillsboro; was admitted to the bar and commenced practice in Concord, N.C., in 1829; member of the State house of commons 1829-1834, 1840, and 1842; member of the State constitutional convention in 1835; elected as a Whig to the Twenty-eighth, Twenty-ninth, and Thirtieth Congresses (March 4, 1843-March 3, 1849); chairman, Committee on Expenditures in the Department of State (Thirtieth Congress), Committee on Indian Affairs (Thirtieth Congress); declined a renomination; appointed by President Zachary Taylor and reappointed by President Millard Fillmore Minister to Spain and served from June 18, 1849, until September 4, 1853; again elected to the State house of commons in 1854; delegate to the peace convention held in Washington, D.C., in 1861 in an effort to devise means to prevent the impending war; delegate to the Union National Convention at Philadelphia in August 1866; chairman of the Democratic State committee in 1872; died at White Sulphur Springs, Greenbrier County, Va., September 1, 1873; interment in Greenmount Cemetery, Baltimore, Md.

Bibliography: *DAB.*

**BARROW, Alexander,** a Senator from Louisiana; born near Nashville, Tenn., March 27, 1801; attended the United States Military Academy, West Point, N.Y., 1816-1818; studied law; was admitted to the bar in 1822 and commenced practice in Nashville, Tenn.; moved soon afterward to Louisiana and settled in Feliciana Parish and continued the practice of law, which he later abandoned to become a planter; member of the State house of representatives for several terms; elected in 1840 as a Whig to the United States Senate and served from March 4, 1841, until his death in Baltimore,

Md., December 29, 1846; chairman, Committee on Public Buildings (Twenty-seventh Congress), Committee on Militia (Twenty-seventh and Twenty-eighth Congresses); interment in a private cemetery at Afton Villa plantation, near Bayou Sara, La.

**BARROW, Middleton Pope** (grandson of Wilson Lumpkin), a Senator from Georgia; born near Antioch (now Stephens), Oglethorpe County, Ga., August 1, 1839; attended a private academy; was graduated from the law department of the University of Georgia at Athens in 1860; was admitted to the bar in 1860 and commenced practice in Athens, Clarke County, Ga.; during the Civil War entered the Confederate service in 1861 and served throughout the war; resumed the practice of law in Athens; member of the State constitutional convention in 1877; member, State house of representatives 1880-1881; elected as a Democrat to the United States Senate in 1882 to fill the vacancy caused by the death of Benjamin H. Hill and served from November 15, 1882, to March 3, 1883; was not a candidate for reelection; resumed the practice of law in Athens, Ga.; judge of the eastern judicial circuit of Georgia from January 6, 1902, until his death in Savannah, Ga., December 23, 1903; interment in a private cemetery on the family plantation in Oglethorpe County, Ga.

**BARROW, Washington,** a Representative from Tennessee; born in Davidson County, Tenn., October 5, 1807; received a classical education; studied law; was admitted to the bar in 1827 and commenced practice in Nashville, Tenn.; appointed Minister to Portugal on August 16, 1841 and served until February 24, 1844; editor of the Nashville Republican Banner 1845-1847; elected as a Whig to the Thirtieth Congress (March 4, 1847-March 3, 1849); was not a candidate for renomination in 1848 to the Thirty-first Congress; president of the Nashville Gas Company in 1848; member of the Tennessee State senate in 1860 and 1861; prominently identified with the Confederacy during the Civil War and was arrested by order of Governor Andrew Johnson on March 28, 1862, and imprisoned in Nashville; released the following week by order of President Lincoln; resumed newspaper interests; died in St. Louis, Mo., October 19, 1866; interment in the vault of Doctor John Shelby on a private estate in East Nashville, Tenn.
Bibliography: *DAB.*

**BARROWS, Samuel June,** a Representative from Massachusetts; born in New York City May 26, 1845; after attending primary school was graduated from the Harvard Divinity School in the fall of 1871; while at Harvard University was the Boston correspondent of the New York Tribune; went with the Yellowstone Expedition of 1873, under the command of General Stanley, and with the Black Hills Expedition in 1874, commanded by General Custer; in 1873 took part in the Battles of Tongue River and the Big Horn; pastor of the first parish, Dorchester (Boston), Mass., from 1876-1881, when he resigned to become editor of the Christian Register, which position he held for 16 years; American representative to the International Prison Congress of 1895, 1900, and 1905, at which he was elected to serve as president of the 1910 congress; elected as a Republican to the Fifty-fifth Congress (March 4, 1897-March 3, 1899); unsuccessful candidate for reelection in 1898 to the Fifty-sixth Congress; secretary of the New York Prison Association 1899-1909; died in New York City April 21, 1909; remains were cremated and the ashes placed in a private burying ground near Georgeville, Quebec, Canada.
Bibliography: *DAB.*

**BARRY, Alexander Grant,** a Senator from Oregon; born in Astoria, Clatsop County, Oreg., August 23, 1892; attended the public schools of Astoria and Portland, Oreg., the University of Washington at Seattle, the University of Oregon Law School, and Northwest College of Law at Portland, Oreg.; was admitted to the bar in 1917 and commenced practice in Portland, Oreg.; during the First World War was commissioned a second lieutenant and served in the artillery until February 1919; member of the Oregon Relief Committee in 1932, the Oregon Relief Commission in 1933, and the Oregon Liquor Control Commission, 1933-1935; chairman of School District No. 1 Civil Service Board in 1937 and 1938; elected as a Republican to the United States Senate to fill the vacancy caused by the resignation of Frederick Steiwer, and served from November 9, 1938 to January 3, 1939; was not a candidate for election to the full term; resumed the practice of law; member, Oregon State house of representatives, 1945-1950; died in Portland, Oreg., December 28, 1952; interment in Willamette National Cemetery.

**BARRY, Frederick George,** a Representative from Mississippi; born in Woodbury, Cannon County, Tenn., January 12, 1845; received a limited education; served as a private in Company E, Eighth Confederate Cavalry, Col. William B. Wade's regiment, during the Civil War; studied law; was admitted to the bar and commenced practice in Aberdeen, Monroe County, Miss.; moved to West Point, Miss., in 1873 and continued the practice of law; member of the State senate 1875-1879; elected as a Democrat to the Forty-ninth and Fiftieth Congresses (March 4, 1885-March 3, 1889); was not a candidate for renomination in 1888; resumed the practice of law in West Point, Clay County, Miss., where he died May 7, 1909; interment in Odd Fellows Rest Cemetery, Aberdeen, Miss.

**BARRY, Henry W.,** a Representative from Mississippi; born in Schoharie County, N.Y., in April 1840; self-educated; principal of Locust Grove Academy in Kentucky; during the Civil War enlisted in the Union Army; organized the first regiment of African-American troops in Kentucky; commissioned first lieutenant of the Tenth Regiment, Kentucky Volunteer Infantry, November 21, 1861, and served until his resignation November 17, 1862; appointed colonel of the Eighth United States Colored Artillery on April 28, 1864; brevetted brigadier general of Volunteers, March 13, 1865; mustered out on May 11, 1866; was graduated from the law department of Columbian College (now George Washington University), Washington, D.C., in 1867; was admitted to the bar the same year and commenced practice in Columbus, Lowndes County, Miss.; delegate to the State constitutional convention in 1867; member of the Mississippi State senate in 1868; upon the readmission of the State of Mississippi to representation was elected as a Republican to the Forty-first and to the two succeeding Congresses, and served from February 23, 1870 to March 3, 1875; chairman, Committee on Expenditures in the Post Office Department (Forty-second and Forty-third Congresses); died in Washington, D.C., June 7, 1875; interment in Oak Hill Cemetery.

**BARRY, Robert Raymond,** a Representative from New York; born in Omaha, Nebr., May 15, 1915; received early education in the public schools of Evanston, Ill.; attended Hamilton College, Clinton, N.Y., 1933-1936, and the Tuck School of Business Administration at Dartmouth College in 1937; studied law and finance at New York University Graduate School in 1938; engaged in investment banking with Kidder, Peabody & Co., in 1937 and 1938 and commercial banking with Manufacturers Trust Co., in 1938 and 1939; executive of Bendix Aviation Corp., 1940-1943 and Yale & Towne Manufacturing Co., 1945-1950; also engaged in farming, mining, and real-estate development; during the Second World War served in the office of the Under Secretary of the Navy; served on the political staffs of Wendell L. Willkie and Governor Thomas E. Dewey, and of Presidents Dwight D. Eisenhower and Richard M. Nixon; chairman of the United Nations Committee to Build World House at the United Nations; engaged in mining operations at Portola, Calif., and land development at Salton Sea, Calif.; United States delegate to several conferences of NATO parliamentarians; United States delegate to the United Nations Educational, Scientific and Cultural Organization; elected as a Republican to the Eighty-sixth Congress and to the two succeeding Congresses (January 3, 1959-January 3,

1965); unsuccessful candidate for reelection in 1964 to the Eighty-ninth Congress, and for nomination in 1972 to the Ninety-third Congress; was a resident of Woodside, Calif., until his death in Redwood City, Calif., on June 14, 1988.

**BARRY, William Bernard,** a Representative from New York; born in County Mayo, Ireland, July 21, 1902; immigrated to the United States in 1907 with his parents, who settled in Queens County, N.Y.; attended the public schools; was graduated from New York University at New York City in 1925 and from its law school in 1929; was admitted to the bar in 1929 and commenced practice in New York City; assistant district attorney of Queens County, N.Y., in 1932 and 1933; special United States attorney for the Department of Justice 1933-1935; member of the Democratic executive committee of Queens County 1930-1935; elected as a Democrat to the Seventy-fourth Congress to fill the vacancy caused by the resignation of William F. Brunner; reelected to the Seventy-fifth and to the four succeeding Congresses and served from November 5, 1935, until his death; had been renominated to the Eightieth Congress; died in New York City, on October 20, 1946; interment in Mount St. Mary's Cemetery, Flushing, N.Y.

**BARRY, William Taylor,** a Representative and a Senator from Kentucky; born near Lunenburg, Lunenburg County, Va., February 5, 1784; moved to Fayette County, Ky., in 1796 with his parents; attended the common schools, Pisgah Academy and Kentucky Academy in Woodford County, Ky., Transylvania University at Lexington, Ky., and was graduated from the College of William and Mary, Williamsburg, Va., in 1803; studied law; was admitted to the bar in 1805 and commenced practice at Lexington, Ky.; appointed Commonwealth attorney; member, Kentucky house of representatives 1807; elected as a Republican to the Eleventh Congress to fill the vacancy caused by the resignation of Benjamin Howard and served from August 8, 1810, to March 3, 1811; served in the military during the War of 1812; member, Kentucky house of representatives 1814 and was chosen speaker; elected as a Republican to the United States Senate to fill the vacancy caused by the resignation of George M. Bibb and served from December 16, 1814, until his resignation effective May 1, 1816, having been appointed to a judicial position; appointed judge of the circuit court for the eleventh district of Kentucky 1816-1817; member, Kentucky senate 1817-1821; elected lieutenant governor of Kentucky in 1820; professor of law and politics at Transylvania University 1822; secretary of Commonwealth of Kentucky 1824; appointed chief justice of the Kentucky court of appeals 1825; unsuccessful Democratic candidate for election in 1828 for Governor of Kentucky; appointed Postmaster General by President Andrew Jackson on March 9, 1829, and served until April 10, 1835, when he resigned; appointed Envoy Extraordinary and Minister Plenipotentiary to Spain on April 10, 1835; died in Liverpool, England, August 30, 1835, while in route to Madrid, Spain; interment in England; reinterment in the State Cemetery at Frankfort, Ky., 1854.

**Bibliography:** *DAB.*

**BARRY, William Taylor Sullivan,** a Representative from Mississippi; born in Columbus, Lowndes County, Miss., December 10, 1821; was graduated from Yale College in 1841; studied law; was admitted to the bar in 1844 and commenced practice in Columbus; also engaged in planting; member of the State house of representatives 1849-1851; elected as a Democrat to the Thirty-third Congress (March 4, 1853-March 3, 1855); again a member of the State house of representatives and served as speaker in 1855; president of the State secession convention in 1861; member of the Provisional Confederate Congress; during the Civil War entered the Confederate Army and raised the Thirty-fifth Regiment of Mississippi Infantry, at times acting as brigade commander; captured at Mobile April 12, 1865; resumed the practice of law in Columbus, Miss., where he died January 29, 1868; interment in Odd Fellows Cemetery.

**Bibliography:** *DAB.*

**BARSTOW, Gamaliel Henry,** a Representative from New York; born in Sharon, Litchfield County, Conn., July 20, 1784; moved to Tioga County, N.Y., in 1812; worked on his father's farm and taught school; studied medicine in Barrington, Mass., and practiced; member of the State assembly 1815-1819; appointed first judge of the Tioga County Court in 1818 and served until 1823; served in the State senate 1819-1822; again a member of the State assembly 1823-1826; State treasurer 1825-1828 and again in 1838; supervisor of Nichols, N.Y., in 1830; elected as an Anti-Masonic candidate to the Twenty-second Congress (March 4, 1831-March 3, 1833); continued the practice of medicine and engaged in agricultural pursuits in Nichols, N.Y., until his death there March 30, 1865; interment in Ashbury Cemetery, near Nichols, N.Y.

**BARSTOW, Gideon,** a Representative from Massachusetts; born in Mattapoisett, Plymouth County, Mass., September 7, 1783; attended the common schools and Brown University, Providence, R.I., 1799-1801; studied medicine; was admitted to practice and settled in Salem, Essex County, Mass.; member of the Massachusetts constitutional convention in 1820; elected to the Seventeenth Congress (March 4, 1821-March 3, 1823); was not a candidate for renomination in 1822; member of the Massachusetts house of representatives in 1823, 1829, 1833, and 1837; served in the Massachusetts senate in 1827 and 1834; presidential elector on the Whig ticket of Clay and Sergeant in 1832; because of ill health moved to St. Augustine, St. Johns County, Fla., and engaged in mercantile pursuits; died in St. Augustine, Fla., March 26, 1852; interment in Huguenot Cemetery.

**BARTHOLDT, Richard,** a Representative from Missouri; born in Schleiz, Germany, November 2, 1855; attended the public schools and Schleiz College (Gymnasium); immigrated to the United States in April 1872 and settled in Brooklyn, N.Y.; learned the printing trade and became a newspaper writer and publisher; moved to Missouri and settled in St. Louis in 1877; was connected with several papers as reporter, legislative correspondent, and editor, and at the time of his election to Congress was editor in chief of the St. Louis Tribune; member of the St. Louis Board of Education from 1888 to 1892, serving as president from 1890 to 1892; elected as a Republican to the Fifty-third and to the ten succeeding Congresses (March 4, 1893-March 3, 1915); was not a candidate for renomination in 1914 to the Sixty-fourth Congress; chairman, Committee on Immigration and Naturalization (Fifty-fourth Congress), Committee on Levees and Improvements of the Mississippi River (Fifty-fifth through Fifty-eighth Congresses), Committee on Public Buildings and Grounds (Fifty-ninth through Sixty-first Congresses); in 1911 was appointed by President William Howard Taft as a special envoy to the German Emperor to present a statue of Baron Steuben as a gift from Congress and the American people; engaged in literary pursuits; served as chairman of the Republican State convention at St. Joseph, Mo., in 1896; elected president of the Interparliamentary Union at the conference held in St. Louis in 1904, and for many years was president of the arbitration group in Congress, which he founded in 1903; died in St. Louis, Mo., March 19, 1932; his body was cremated and the ashes interred in Concordia Cemetery.

**Bibliography:** *DAB.*

**BARTINE, Horace Franklin,** a Representative from Nevada; born in New York City March 21, 1848; moved with his parents to New Jersey in 1858; attended the common schools until fifteen years of age, when he enlisted as a private in the Eighth Regiment, New Jersey Volunteer Infantry, in July 1863 and served during the last two years of the Civil War; was severely wounded at the Battle of the Wilderness; participated in many of the engagements of the Army of the Potomac and was present at the surrender of the Confederate forces at Appomattox Court House; returned to New Jersey and engaged in agricultural pursuits; moved to Carson City,

Nev., in 1869; from 1869 to 1876 engaged in the manufacture of copper sulphate for milling purposes; studied law; was admitted to the bar in 1880 and practiced in the courts of Nevada; served as district attorney of Ormsby County 1880-1882; elected as a Republican to the Fifty-first and Fifty-second Congresses (March 4, 1889-March 3, 1893); was not a candidate for renomination in 1892; editor of the National Bimetallist, published in Chicago, Ill., and Washington, D.C.; returned to Carson City, Nev., in 1902; appointed State tax examiner in 1904; appointed railroad commissioner in March 1907 and served as chief commissioner and chairman of the commission until his death in Winnemucca, Humboldt County, Nev., August 27, 1918; interment in Lone Mountain Cemetery, Carson City, Ormsby County, Nev.

**BARTLETT, Bailey,** a Representative from Massachusetts; born in Haverhill, Essex County, Mass., January 29, 1750; attended the common schools; engaged in mercantile pursuits until 1789; member of the Massachusetts house of representatives 1781-1784 and in 1788; member of the convention which adopted the Constitution of the United States in 1788; served in the Massachusetts senate in 1789; appointed high sheriff of Essex County by Governor John Hancock and served from July 1, 1789, until December 5, 1811; elected as a Federalist to the Fifth Congress to fill the vacancy caused by the resignation of Theophilus Bradbury; reelected to the Sixth Congress and served from November 27, 1797, to March 3, 1801; was not a candidate for renomination in 1800 to the Seventh Congress; served as treasurer of Essex County in 1812; again appointed high sheriff of Essex County on June 20, 1812, and served until his death; delegate to the Massachusetts constitutional convention in 1820; died in Haverhill, Mass., September 9, 1830; interment in Pentucket Cemetery.

**BARTLETT, Charles Lafayette,** a Representative from Georgia; born in Monticello, Jasper County, Ga., January 31, 1853; attended private schools in Monticello and was graduated from the University of Georgia at Athens in 1870; studied law at the University of Virginia at Charlottesville, and was graduated from the law department of the University of Georgia in 1872; was admitted to the bar the same year and commenced practice in Monticello in August 1872; moved to Macon, Ga., in 1875 and continued the practice of law; appointed solicitor general for the Macon Judicial Court on January 31, 1877, and served in that capacity until January 31, 1881; member of the State house of representatives 1882-1885; city attorney of Macon 1887-1892; served in the State senate in 1888 and 1889; appointed judge of the superior court of the Macon circuit in October 1892, and elected to the same office January 1, 1893, serving until May 1, 1894, when he resigned; elected as a Democrat to the Fifty-fourth and to the nine succeeding Congresses (March 4, 1895-March 3, 1915); was not a candidate for renomination in 1914 to the Sixty-fourth Congress; delegate to the Democratic National Convention of 1916; resumed the practice of law in Macon, Ga., also engaged in banking; died in Macon, Ga., April 21, 1938; interment in Rose Hill Cemetery.

**BARTLETT, Dewey Follett,** a Senator from Oklahoma; born in Marietta, Washington County, Ohio, March 28, 1919; educated in Marietta, Ohio, public schools and Lawrenceville Preparatory School, Lawrenceville, N.J.; graduated from Princeton University in 1942; during the Second World War served in the United States Marine Corps as a dive bomber pilot in the South Pacific Theater 1943-1945; moved to Oklahoma; oilman, farmer, and rancher; member, Oklahoma State senate, 1963-1966; elected Governor of Oklahoma in 1966, and served from January 9, 1967 to January 11, 1971; unsuccessful candidate for reelection in 1970 for Governor; elected as a Republican to the United States Senate in 1972 and served from January 3, 1973, to January 3, 1979; was not a candidate for reelection in 1978 due to ill health; died in Tulsa, Okla., March 1, 1979; interment in Calvary Cemetery.

**Bibliography:** *DAB.*

**BARTLETT, Edward Lewis (Bob),** a Delegate from the Territory of Alaska and a Senator from Alaska; born in Seattle, King County, Wash., April 20, 1904; attended the University of Washington, 1922-1924, and the University of Alaska, 1924-1925; reporter, Fairbanks (Alaska) Daily News-Miner, 1925-1933; secretary to Delegate Anthony J. Dimond of Alaska, 1933-1934; gold miner in Alaska, 1936-1939; chairman of the Unemployment Compensation Commission of Alaska, 1937-1939; appointed secretary of Alaska by President Franklin D. Roosevelt on January 30, 1939, and served until his resignation on February 6, 1944, to become a candidate for Delegate to Congress; member of the Alaska War Council, 1942-1944; elected as a Democrat a Delegate to the Seventy-ninth and to the six succeeding Congresses (January 3, 1945-January 3, 1959); was not a candidate in 1958 for renomination to the House of Representatives, having become a candidate for the United States Senate; elected as a Democrat to the United States Senate on November 25, 1958, and upon the admission of Alaska as a State into the Union on January 3, 1959, drew the two-year term beginning on that day and ending January 3, 1961; reelected in 1960 and again in 1966, and served from January 3, 1959 until his death in Cleveland, Ohio, December 11, 1968; interment in Northern Lights Memorial Park, Fairbanks, Alaska.

**Bibliography:** Naske, Claus-M. "Bob Bartlett and the Alaska Mental Health Act." *Pacific Northwest Quarterly* 71 (January 1980): 31-39; *Edward Louis "Bob" Bartlett of Alaska: A Life in Politics.* Fairbanks: University of Alaska Press, 1979.

**BARTLETT, Franklin,** a Representative from New York; born in Worcester County, Mass., September 10, 1847; was graduated from the Brooklyn Polytechnic Institute in 1865 and from Harvard University in 1869; attended Columbia College Law School in 1869; was admitted to the bar in 1870; attended Exeter College, Oxford University, England, in 1870 and 1871; concluded the course at Columbia College Law School in 1873; served as a member of the constitutional commission of the State of New York in 1890; delegate to the Democratic National Convention at Chicago in 1892; elected as a Democrat to the Fifty-third and Fifty-fourth Congresses (March 4, 1893-March 3, 1897); unsuccessful candidate for reelection in 1896 to the Fifty-fifth Congress; colonel of Volunteers in the war with Spain in 1898; died in New York City on April 23, 1909; interment in Greenwood Cemetery, Brooklyn, N.Y.

**BARTLETT, George Arthur,** a Representative from Nevada; born in San Francisco, Calif., November 30, 1869; moved with his parents to Eureka, Eureka County, Nev.; attended the common schools; was graduated from the law department of Georgetown University, Washington, D.C., in 1894; was admitted to the bar the same year and commenced the practice of law in the courts of Nevada; district attorney of Eureka County, Nev., in 1889 and 1890; elected as a Democrat to the Sixtieth and Sixty-first Congresses (March 4, 1907-March 3, 1911); was not a candidate for renomination in 1910; resumed the practice of law in Reno, Nev.; appointed United States assistant district attorney for the district of Nevada on March 3, 1915, and served until March 30, 1918, when he resigned; appointed judge of the second judicial district court of Nevada on April 1, 1918, in which capacity he served, with the exception of about two years, until January 1931, when he resumed the private practice of law; author of several books; died in Reno, Nev., June 1, 1951; interment in Mountain View Cemetery.

**BARTLETT, Harry Stephen (Steve),** a Representative from Texas; born in Los Angeles, Calif., September 19, 1947; attended public schools of Lockhart, Tex.; graduated, Kimball High School, Dallas, Tex., 1966; B.A., University of Texas, Austin, 1971; businessman; president and founder of manufacturing company; member, city council, Dallas, Tex., 1977-1981; delegate, Texas State Republican conventions, 1972-1982; elected as a Republican to the

Ninety-eighth and to the four succeeding Congresses, and served from January 3, 1983 until his resignation on March 11, 1991; elected mayor of Dallas, and served until June 5, 1995; was not a candidate for reelection; is a resident of Dallas, Tex.

**BARTLETT, Ichabod,** a Representative from New Hampshire; born in Salisbury, N.H., July 24, 1786; received a classical education and was graduated from Dartmouth College, Hanover, N.H., in 1808; studied law; was admitted to the bar in 1811 and commenced practice in Durham, Strafford County, N.H.; moved to Portsmouth in 1816 and continued the practice of law; clerk of the State senate in 1817 and 1818; State solicitor for Rockingham County, 1819-1821; member of the New Hampshire State house of representatives, 1819-1821; served as speaker in 1821; elected to the Eighteenth and to the two succeeding Congresses (March 4, 1823-March 3, 1829); declined the appointment as chief justice of the court of common pleas in 1825; again a member of the State house of representatives in 1830, 1838, 1851, and 1852; unsuccessful candidate for election in 1831 and 1832 for Governor of New Hampshire; member of the State constitutional convention in 1850; died in Portsmouth, N.H., October 19, 1853; interment in Harmony Grove Cemetery.

**Bibliography:** *DAB.*

**BARTLETT, Josiah** (father of Josiah Bartlett, Jr.), a Delegate from New Hampshire; born in Amesbury, Mass., November 21, 1729; attended the public schools; studied medicine, and commenced practice in Kingston, N.H., in 1750; was medical agent to General John Stark at the Battle of Bennington; member of the colonial legislature of New Hampshire, 1765-1775; Member of the Continental Congress in 1775, 1776 and 1778; signer of the Articles of Confederation and second signer of the Declaration of Independence; chief justice of the court of common pleas in 1778; became justice of the superior court in 1784, and chief justice in 1788; member of the convention which framed the Federal Constitution in 1787; in 1789 was elected to the United States Senate from New Hampshire, but declined, and at the same time resigned as chief justice; unsuccessful candidate for election for Governor in 1789; elected Governor of New Hampshire in 1790, reelected in 1792 and 1793, and served from June 5, 1790 to June 5, 1794; member of the constitutional convention of 1792, which changed the title of chief executive of New Hampshire from "president" to "Governor"; died in Kingston, N.H., May 19, 1795; interment in the Plains Cemetery, in rear of the Universalist Church.

**Bibliography:** *DAB*; Bartlett, Josiah. *The Papers of Josiah Bartlett.* Edited by Frank C. Mevers. Hanover, N.H.: University Press of New England, 1979; Page, Elwin L. "Josiah Bartlett and the Federation." *Historical New Hampshire* 2 (Oct. 1947): 1-6.

**BARTLETT, Josiah, Jr.** (son of Josiah Bartlett), a Representative from New Hampshire; born in Kingston, N.H., August 29, 1768; attended the common schools and was graduated from Exeter Academy, Exeter, N.H.; studied medicine and commenced practice in Stratham, Rockingham County, N.H.; member of the State senate in 1809 and 1810; elected as a Republican to the Twelfth Congress (March 4, 1811-March 3, 1813); resumed the practice of medicine; treasurer of Rockingham County; again elected to the State senate, in 1824, and served as president; presidential elector in 1824 and supported John Quincy Adams; resumed the practice of medicine; died in Stratham, N.H., April 16, 1838; interment in the Old Congregational Cemetery.

**BARTLETT, Roscoe Gardner,** a Representative from Maryland; born in Moreland, Jefferson County, Ky., June 3, 1926; B.S., Columbia Union College, Takoma Park, Md., 1947; M.S., University of Maryland, 1948, and Ph.D., 1952; instructor, University of Maryland, 1948-1952; assistant professor, Loma Linda (Calif.) Medical School, 1952-1954; assistant professor, Howard Medical School, 1954-1956; physiologist, National Institutes of Health,

Bethesda, Md., 1956-1959; physiologist, teacher, Navy School of Aviation Medicine, Pensacola, Fla., 1959-1962; engineer, manager, Applied Physics Laboratory, Johns Hopkins University, Fulton, Md., 1962-1967; engineer, manager, IBM, Gaithersburg, Md., 1967-1975; professor, Frederick (Md.) Community College, 1975-1987; director, Roscoe Bartlett and Associates, Frederick, Md., 1975-1987; farmer in Frederick, Md.; holder of twenty patents; unsuccessful candidate for election in 1982 to the Ninety-eighth Congress; elected as a Republican to the One Hundred Third and One Hundred Fourth Congresses (January 3, 1993-January 3, 1997); is a resident of Frederick, Md.

**BARTLETT, Thomas, Jr.,** a Representative from Vermont; born in Sutton, Caledonia County, Vt., June 18, 1808; attended the common schools; studied law; was admitted to the bar in 1833 and commenced practice in Groton, Vt.; moved to Lyndon, Vt., in 1836 and continued the practice of law; State's attorney for Caledonia County 1839-1842; member of the State senate in 1841 and 1842; served in the State house of representatives in 1849, 1850, 1854, and 1855; delegate to the State constitutional conventions in 1850 and 1857; elected as a Democrat to the Thirty-second Congress (March 4, 1851-March 3, 1853); chairman, Committee on Expenditures on Public Buildings (Thirty-second Congress); unsuccessful candidate for reelection in 1852 to the Thirty-third Congress; resumed the practice of law; died in Lyndon, Vt., September 12, 1876; interment in Lyndon Town Cemetery, Lyndon Center, Vt.

**BARTLEY, Mordecai,** a Representative from Ohio; born in Fayette County, Pa., December 16, 1783; attended school in Virginia; moved to Ohio in 1809 and settled in Jefferson County; served in the War of 1812 as captain and was promoted to adjutant; settled on a farm in Richland County in 1814 and engaged in agricultural pursuits; member of the State senate in 1817 and 1818; elected register of the land office of Virginia military district school lands in 1818 and served until his resignation in 1823, having been elected to Congress; elected to the Eighteenth and to the three succeeding Congresses (March 4, 1823-March 3, 1831); declined to be a candidate for renomination in 1830 to the Twenty-second Congress; resumed agricultural pursuits; moved to Mansfield in 1834 and engaged in mercantile pursuits; Governor of Ohio from April 15 until December 3, 1844; declined reelection and again engaged in agricultural pursuits; died in Mansfield, Richland County, Ohio, October 10, 1870; interment in Mansfield Cemetery.

**Bibliography:** *DAB.*

**BARTON, Bruce,** a Representative from New York; born in Robbins, Scott County, Tenn., August 5, 1886; educated in the public schools of Ohio, Massachusetts, and Illinois; graduated from Amherst (Mass.) College in 1907; moved to Chicago, Ill., in 1900 and engaged in literary and editorial pursuits; moved to New York City in 1912 and continued literary work; also engaged in the magazine and advertising business; elected as a Republican to the Seventy-fifth Congress to fill the vacancy caused by the death of Theodore A. Peyser; reelected to the Seventy-sixth Congress and served from November 2, 1937, to January 3, 1941; was not a candidate for renomination but was an unsuccessful candidate for election in 1940 to the United States Senate; delegate to the Republican State convention in 1938 and to the Republican National Convention at Philadelphia in 1940; resumed advertising business in New York City; died in New York City, on July 5, 1967; interment in Rock Hill Cemetery, Foxboro, Mass.

**Bibliography:** Nuechterlein, James A. "Bruce Barton and the Business Ethos of 1920's." *South Atlantic Quarterly* 76 (Summer 1977): 293-308.

**BARTON, David,** a Senator from Missouri; born near Greeneville, N.C. (now Tennessee), December 14, 1783; read law; was admitted to the Tennessee bar; moved to the Territory of Missouri in

1809; elected attorney general of the Territory in 1813; first circuit judge of Howard County in 1815 and presiding judge in 1816; member, Territorial house of representatives 1818 and served as speaker; member and president of the convention which formed the State constitution in 1820; upon the admission of Missouri as a State into the Union was elected to the United States Senate; reelected in 1825, and served from August 10, 1821, to March 3, 1831; unsuccessful candidate for reelection in 1830; chairman, Committee on Public Lands (Eighteenth through Twenty-first Congresses); member, State senate 1834-1835; died in Boonville, Mo., on September 28, 1837; interment in Walnut Grove Cemetery.

**Bibliography:** *DAB*; Shoemaker, Floyd C. "David Barton, John Rice Jones, and Edward Bates: Three Missouri State and Statehood Founders." *Missouri Historical Review* 65 (July 1971): 527-543; Van Ravensway, Charles. "The Tragedy of David Barton." *Missouri Historical Society Bulletin* 7 (October 1950): 35-56.

**BARTON, Joe Linus,** a Representative from Texas; born in Waco, McLennan County, Tex., September 15, 1949; attended Travis Elementary School, Bryan, Tex.; was graduated from Waco High School in 1968; B.S., Texas A&M University, College Station, Tex., 1972; M.S., Purdue University, West Lafayette, Ind., 1973; plant manager, assistant to the vice president, Ennis Business Forms, Inc., 1973-1981; awarded White House Fellowship, 1981-1982; served as aide to Secretary of Energy James B. Edwards; member, Natural Gas Decontrol Task Force in the Office of Planning Policy and Analysis; worked with the Department of Energy task force in support of the President's Private Sector Survey on Cost Control; natural gas decontrol and project cost control consultant, Atlantic Richfield Co.; vice president, Houston County Industrial Development Authority, 1980; chairman, Crockett Parks and Recreation Board, 1979-1980; elected as a Republican to the Ninety-ninth and to the five succeeding Congresses (January 3, 1985-January 3, 1997); is a resident of Ennis, Tex.

**BARTON, Richard Walker,** a Representative from Virginia; born at "Shady Oak," near Winchester, Frederick County, Va., in 1800; pursued academic studies; studied law; was admitted to the bar and commenced practice in Winchester, Va.; member of the Virginia assembly in 1823-1824, 1832-1835 and 1839; elected as a Whig to the Twenty-seventh Congress (March 4, 1841-March 3, 1843); unsuccessful candidate for reelection in 1842 to the Twenty-eighth Congress; resumed the practice of his profession in Winchester, Va.; died on his estate, "Springdale," near Winchester, Frederick County, Va., March 15, 1859; interment in the family burying ground at "Springdale."

**BARTON, Samuel,** a Representative from New York; born in New Dorp, Richmond County, N.Y., July 27, 1785; attended the common schools; agent for Commodore Vanderbilt's steamship lines; served in the State militia as a major in 1818 and as a colonel in 1833; member of the State assembly in 1821 and 1822; served on the Andrew Jackson reception committee in 1833; elected as a Jacksonian to the Twenty-fourth Congress (March 4, 1835-March 3, 1837); was not a candidate for renomination in 1836; resumed his former pursuits in the steamship business; director of the Tompkinsville Lyceum in 1842; died in New Dorp, Richmond County, N.Y., January 29, 1858; interment in Moravian Cemetery.

**BARTON, Silas Reynolds,** a Representative from Nebraska; born in New London, Henry County, Iowa, May 21, 1872; moved to Hamilton County, Nebr., in 1873 with his parents; was graduated from the Aurora High School and attended the Peru (Nebr.) State Normal School; engaged in agricultural pursuits and taught school; deputy treasurer of Hamilton County 1898-1901; grand recorder of the Ancient Order of United Workmen of Nebraska 1901-1908; president for two terms of the Grand Recorders' Association of the United States; State auditor 1909-1913; during his two terms as auditor and insurance commissioner was a member of the National Executive Committee of Insurance Commissioners; elected as a Republican to the Sixty-third Congress (March 4, 1913-March 3, 1915); was a candidate for election to the Sixty-fifth Congress, but died before election day in Grand Island, Hall County, Nebr., November 7, 1916; interment in Aurora Cemetery, Aurora, Hamilton County, Nebr.

**BARTON, William Edward** (cousin of Courtney Walker Hamlin), a Representative from Missouri; born in Pickens District (now County), S.C., April 11, 1868; in 1869 moved to Missouri with his parents, who settled in Crawford County, near Bourbon; attended the public schools and the Steelville Normal and Business Institute, Steelville, Mo.; employed as a farm hand, miner, and in a railroad office; taught school near Bourbon, Mo., 1889-1892; graduated from the law department of the Missouri University at Columbia in 1894; was admitted to the bar the same year and commenced practice in Houston, Mo.; delegate to the State judicial conventions in 1896 and 1906; during the Spanish-American War served as a sergeant in Company M, Second Regiment, Missouri Volunteer Infantry; prosecuting attorney of Texas County in 1901 and 1902; judge of the nineteenth judicial circuit 1923-1928; elected as a Democrat to the Seventy-second Congress (March 4, 1931-March 3, 1933); unsuccessful candidate for renomination in 1932 to the Seventy-third Congress; again elected judge of the nineteenth judicial circuit of Missouri and served from 1934 to 1946; resumed the private practice of law; died in Houston, Mo., July 29, 1955; interment in Houston Cemetery.

**BARWIG, Charles,** a Representative from Wisconsin; born in Hesse-Darmstadt, Germany, March 19, 1837; immigrated to the United States in 1845 with his parents, who settled in Milwaukee, Wis.; attended the public schools and was graduated from the Spencerian Business College at Milwaukee in 1857; moved to Mayville in 1865 and engaged in the wholesale liquor business; mayor of Mayville 1886-1888; elected as a Democrat to the Fifty-first, Fifty-second, and Fifty-third Congresses (March 4, 1889-March 3, 1895); chairman, Committee on Expenditures in the Department of the Treasury (Fifty-third Congress); unsuccessful candidate for reelection in 1894 to the Fifty-fourth Congress; engaged in the real estate business; died in Mayville, Wis., on February 15, 1912; interment in Graceland Cemetery.

**BASHFORD, Coles,** a Delegate from the Territory of Arizona; born near Cold Spring, Putnam County, N.Y., January 24, 1816; attended the Wesleyan Seminary (now Genesee College), Lima, N.Y.; studied law; was admitted to the bar in 1842; district attorney for Wayne County 1847-1850; resigned in 1850 and moved to Oshkosh, Wis.; member of the Wisconsin senate in 1853 and 1855; successfully contested the reelection of William A. Barstow as Governor of Wisconsin in 1855, and served as Governor from March 25, 1856 until January 1858; declined to be a candidate for renomination; moved to Arizona in 1863; first attorney general of Arizona 1864-1866; presiding officer of first Territorial Council in 1865; elected as an Independent to the Fortieth Congress (March 4, 1867-March 3, 1869); secretary of state of Arizona 1869-1876; resigned and moved to Prescott, Ariz., in 1876, where he engaged in business; died in Prescott, Ariz., April 25, 1878; interment in Mountain View Cemetery, Oakland, Calif.

**Bibliography:** *DAB*.

**BASS, Charles Foster** (son of Perkins Bass), a Representative from New Hampshire; born in Boston, Mass., January 8, 1952; graduated, Holderness School, Plymouth, N.H., 1970; A.B., Dartmouth College, Hanover, N.H., 1974; vice president, High Standard, Inc., Dublin, N.H.; chair, Columbia Architectural Products, Beltsville, Md.; field worker for Representative William S. Cohen of Maine, 1974; legislative assistant, 1975-1976, then chief of staff, 1976-1979, both with Representative David F. Emery of Maine;

unsuccessful candidate for nomination in 1980 to the Ninety-seventh Congress; delegate to New Hampshire constitutional convention, 1984; member, New Hampshire General Court, 1982-1988; member, New Hampshire State senate, 1988-1992; elected as a Republican to the One Hundred Fourth Congress (January 3, 1995-January 3, 1997); is a resident of Peterborough, N.H.

**BASS, Lyman Kidder,** a Representative from New York; born in the town of Alden, Erie County, N.Y., November 13, 1836; attended the common schools and was graduated from Union College, Schenectady, N.Y., in 1856; studied law; was admitted to the bar in 1858 and commenced practice in Buffalo, N.Y.; district attorney for Erie County 1865-1872; renominated in 1871, but declined to accept; unsuccessful Republican candidate for election in 1870 to the Forty-second Congress; elected as a Republican to the Forty-third and Forty-fourth Congresses (March 4, 1873-March 3, 1877); because of ill health declined to be a candidate for renomination in 1876; moved to Colorado Springs, Colo., in 1877 and continued the practice of law; served as general counsel for the Denver & Rio Grande Railroad Co., from 1878 to 1884; died in New York City, while on a visit, May 11, 1889; interment in Forest Lawn Cemetery, Buffalo, N.Y.

**BASS, Perkins** (father of Charles Foster Bass), a Representative from New Hampshire; born in East Walpole, Norfolk County, Mass., October 6, 1912; graduated from Dartmouth College, Hanover, N.H., in 1934 and from Harvard Law School in 1938; was admitted to the New Hampshire bar in 1938 and commenced the practice of law in Manchester, N.H.; law clerk to Judge Woodbury of First Circuit Court of Appeals in 1941 and 1942; entered military service April 9, 1942, and served as air combat intelligence officer with General Chennault's Fourteenth Air Force in China from 1943 until discharged with rank of major in 1945; awarded the Bronze Star Medal and from the Nationalist Government of China received the Yun-Ma Medal for distinguished and meritorious service; resumed practice of law in Manchester and Peterborough, N.H.; member of the New Hampshire house of representatives 1939, 1941, 1947, and 1951; served in the State senate 1949-1951 as president; director and member of the executive committee of Bird & Son, Inc., East Walpole, Mass., 1948-1984; elected as a Republican to the Eighty-fourth and to the three succeeding Congresses (January 3, 1955-January 3, 1963); was not a candidate for renomination in 1962 to the House of Representatives, but was an unsuccessful candidate for election to the United States Senate; Republican National Committeeman from New Hampshire, 1964-1968; selectman of Peterborough, N.H., 1972-1976; is a resident of Peterborough, N.H.

**BASS, Ross,** a Representative and a Senator from Tennessee; born on a farm in Giles County, near Pulaski, Tenn., March 17, 1918; attended the public schools in Middle, Tenn.; graduated from Martin College, Pulaski, Tenn., 1941; served during the Second World War as a captain in the Air Corps; owner of a soft drink bottling plant, florist and nurseryman, 1946-1947; postmaster of Pulaski, Tenn., 1947-1954; elected as a Democrat to the Eighty-fourth and to the four succeeding Congresses, serving from January 3, 1955 until his resignation on November 3, 1964; elected as a Democrat to the United States Senate, November 3, 1964, to fill the vacancy caused by the death of Estes Kefauver, and served from November 4, 1964 to January 2, 1967; unsuccessful candidate for renomination in 1966; owner of consulting firm in Washington, D.C.; unsuccessful candidate for election in 1976 to the Ninety-fifth Congress; was a resident of Miami Shores, Fla.; died January 1, 1993.

**BASSETT, Burwell,** a Representative from Virginia; born in New Kent County, Va., March 18, 1764; attended the College of William and Mary, Williamsburg, Va.; member of the Virginia house of delegates 1787-1789; served in the Virginia senate 1794-1805; unsuccessfully contested the election of John Clopton to the Fourth Congress; elected as a Republican to the Ninth and to the three succeeding Congresses (March 4, 1805-March 3, 1813); chairman, Committee on Claims (Twelfth Congress), Committee on Revisal and Unfinished Business (Twelfth Congress); unsuccessful candidate for reelection in 1812 to the Thirteenth Congress; elected as a Republican to the Fourteenth and Fifteenth Congresses (March 4, 1815-March 3, 1819); again a member of the State house of delegates 1819-1821; elected to the Seventeenth and to the three succeeding Congresses (March 4, 1821-March 3, 1829); unsuccessful candidate for reelection in 1828 to the Twenty-first Congress; died in New Kent County, Va., February 26, 1841.

**BASSETT, Edward Murray,** a Representative from New York; born in Brooklyn, N.Y., February 7, 1863; attended the public schools in Brooklyn and Watertown, N.Y., and Hamilton College, Clinton, N.Y., in 1881 and 1882; was graduated from Amherst (Mass.) College in 1884 and from Columbia Law School, New York City, in 1886; was admitted to the New York State bar in 1886 and commenced practice in Buffalo, N.Y.; moved to New York City in 1892 and continued the practice of law; member of the Brooklyn School Board 1899-1903; elected as a Democrat to the Fifty-eighth Congress (March 4, 1903-March 3, 1905); declined to be a candidate for renomination in 1904 to the Fifty-ninth Congress; resumed the practice of law; member of the New York Public Service Commission 1907-1911; chairman of the Heights of Buildings Commission 1913-1915; chairman of the Zoning Commission in 1916 and 1917; appointed by Secretary Herbert Hoover in 1922 as a member of the Department of Commerce, Advisory Committee on Zoning; writer on bankruptcy, eminent domain, and police power; died in Brooklyn, N.Y., October 27, 1948; interment in Ashfield Plains Cemetery, Ashfield, Mass.

**Bibliography:** *DAB.*

**BASSETT, Richard** (grandfather of Richard Henry Bayard and James Asheton Bayard, Jr.), a Senator from Delaware; born in Cecil County, Md., April 2, 1745; pursued preparatory studies; studied law; was admitted to the bar and practiced in Delaware; captain of a Delaware troop during the Revolutionary War; member of the State constitutional conventions in 1776 and 1792; member, State senate 1782; member, State house of representatives 1786; delegate to the convention which framed the Constitution of the United States in 1787; member of the Delaware convention which ratified the Federal Constitution in 1787; elected to the United States Senate and served from March 4, 1789, to March 3, 1793; chief justice of the court of common pleas 1793-1799; elected Governor of Delaware in 1798 and served from January 1799 to March 1801; appointed United States circuit judge by President John Adams in 1801; died on his estate, "Bohemia Manor," in Cecil County, Md., August 15, 1815; interment Brandywine Cemetery, Wilmington, Del.

**Bibliography:** *DAB*; Pattison, Robert E. *The Life and Character of Richard Bassett.* Wilmington, Del.: The Delaware Historical Society, 1900.

**BATE, William Brimage,** a Senator from Tennessee; born near Castalian Springs, Sumner County, Tenn., October 7, 1826; completed an academic course of study; served as a private in Louisiana and Tennessee regiments throughout the Mexican War; member, State house of representatives 1849-1851; graduated from the law department of Lebanon University, Lebanon, Tenn., in 1852; was admitted to the bar and commenced practice in Gallatin, Tenn.; elected attorney general for the Nashville district in 1854; during the Civil War served in the Confederate army, attained the rank of major general February 23, 1864, and surrendered with the Army of the Tennessee in 1865; after the war returned to Tennessee and resumed the practice of law at Gallatin; elected Governor of Tennessee in 1882, reelected in 1884, and served from January 15, 1883 to January 17, 1887; elected as a Democrat to the United States Senate in 1887; reelected in 1893, 1899, and again in 1905, and served from March 4, 1887, until his death in Washington, D.C., March 9, 1905; chairman, Committee on the Improvement of the Mississippi River and Its Tributaries (Fifty-third Congress), Committee on Military Affairs (Fifty-third Congress), Committee on Public Health and National Quarantine (Fifty-eighth and Fifty-ninth Congresses); funeral services were held in the Chamber of the United States Senate; interment in Mount Olivet Cemetery, Nashville, Tenn.

**Bibliography:** *DAB*; Marshall, Park. *A Life of William B. Bate, Citizen, Soldier, and Statesman.* Nashville: The Cumberland Press, 1908.

**BATEMAN, Ephraim,** a Representative and a Senator from New Jersey; born in Cedarville, N.J., July 9, 1780; attended the local schools and Nathaniel Ogden's Latin school; apprenticed as a tailor in 1796; taught in the local school 1799-1801; studied medicine with a physician in 1801 and at the University of Pennsylvania at Philadelphia in 1802 and 1803; practiced in Cedarville; member, State house of assembly 1808-1809, 1811, and 1813, serving as speaker in 1813; elected to the Fourteenth and to the three succeeding Congresses (March 4, 1815-March 3, 1823); member, State council 1826 and served as president; elected to the United States Senate to fill the vacancy caused by the death of Joseph McIlvaine and served from November 10, 1826, to January 12, 1829, when he resigned because of failing health; chairman, Committee on Agriculture (Twentieth Congress); died in Cedarville, Cumberland County, N.J., January 28, 1829; interment in Old Stone Church Cemetery, Fairfield Township, N.J.

**BATEMAN, Herbert Harvell,** a Representative from Virginia; born in Perquimans County, N.C., August 7, 1928; attended public schools of Virginia; graduated, Newport News High School, Newport News, Va., 1945; B.A., College of William and Mary, Williamsburg, Va., 1949; LL.B., Georgetown University Law Center, Washington, D.C., 1956; served, United States Air Force, 1951-1953; teacher; admitted to the Virginia bar, 1956; law clerk, United States Circuit Court of Appeals, District of Columbia Circuit, 1956-1957; partner, private law practice; member of Virginia senate, 1968-1983; delegate, Virginia Republican conventions, 1976-1982; elected as a Republican to the Ninety-eighth and to the six succeeding Congresses (January 3, 1983-January 3, 1997); is a resident of Newport News, Va.

**BATES, Arthur Laban** (nephew of John Milton Thayer), a Representative from Pennsylvania; born in Meadville, Crawford County, Pa., June 6, 1859; studied under tutors and was graduated from Allegheny College, Meadville, Pa., in 1880; studied law; was admitted to the bar in 1882; attended Oxford University, England, in 1882 and 1883; commenced the practice of law in Meadville, Pa., in 1884; also engaged in the newspaper publishing business in 1899; city solicitor of Meadville 1889-1896; elected as a Republican to the Fifty-seventh and to the five succeeding Congresses (March 4, 1901-March 3, 1913); declined to be a candidate for renomination in 1912 to the Sixty-third Congress; delegate to the International Peace Conference at Brussels in 1905 and at Rome in 1911; resumed the practice of law and the publishing business in Meadville; also engaged in banking; delegate to the Republican National Convention of 1924; died in Meadville, Pa., August 26, 1934; interment in Greendale Cemetery.

**BATES, Edward** (brother of James Woodson Bates), a Representative from Missouri; born in Belmont, Goochland County, Va., September 4, 1793; attended Charlotte Hall Academy, Maryland; acted as sergeant in a volunteer brigade during the War of 1812; moved to St. Louis, Mo., in 1814; studied law; was admitted to the bar in 1817 and practiced; circuit prosecuting attorney in 1818; member of the State constitutional convention in 1820; State's attorney in 1820; member of the Missouri State house of representatives in 1822; United States district attorney from 1821

until 1826; elected to the Twentieth Congress (March 4, 1827-March 3, 1829); unsuccessful candidate for reelection in 1828 to the Twenty-first Congress; resumed the practice of law; member of the Missouri State senate in 1830; again a member of the State house of representatives in 1834; declined the appointment as Secretary of War in 1850 in the Cabinet of President Millard Fillmore; judge of the St. Louis land court, 1853-1856; presided at the Whig National Convention in 1856; appointed by President Lincoln as Attorney General of the United States, and served from March 5, 1861 to November 24, 1864; died in St. Louis, Mo., March 25, 1869; interment in Bellefontaine Cemetery; removed from Bellefontaine Cemetery, place of reinterment not known.

**Bibliography:** *DAB*; Bates, Edward. *The Diary of Edward Bates, 1859-1866.* Edited by Howard Kennedy Beale. Washington, D.C.: Government Printing Office, 1933; Cain, Marvin R. *Lincoln's Attorney General: Edward Bates of Missouri.* Columbia: University of Missouri Press, 1965.

**BATES, George Joseph** (father of William Henry Bates), a Representative from Massachusetts; born in Salem, Essex County, Mass., February 25, 1891; attended the public schools; member of the Massachusetts house of representatives 1918-1924; served as mayor of Salem, Mass., 1924-1937; elected as a Republican to the Seventy-fifth and to the six succeeding Congresses and served from January 3, 1937, until his death in an airplane accident at the Washington (D.C.) National Airport on November 1, 1949; interment in St. Mary's Cemetery, Salem, Mass.

**BATES, Isaac Chapman,** a Representative and a Senator from Massachusetts; born in Granville, Mass., January 23, 1779; tutored privately; was graduated from Yale College in 1802; was admitted to the bar and commenced the practice of law in Northampton, Hampshire County, Mass., in 1808; member, Massachusetts house of representatives 1808-1809; elected to the Twentieth and to the three succeeding Congresses (March 4, 1827-March 3, 1835); chairman, Committee on Military Pensions (Twenty-first Congress); declined to be a candidate for renomination in 1834; elected as a Whig to the United States Senate to fill the vacancy in the term ending March 3, 1841, caused by the resignation of John Davis and on the same day elected for the term commencing March 4, 1841, and served from January 13, 1841, until his death in Washington, D.C., March 16, 1845; chairman, Committee on Pensions (Twenty-seventh and Twenty-eighth Congresses); interment in Bridge Street Cemetery, Northampton, Mass.

**BATES, James,** a Representative from Maine; born in Greene, Lincoln (now Kennebec) County, Maine, September 24, 1789; attended the common schools; studied medicine at Harvard Medical University; served as a surgeon during the War of 1812 and was present at the surrender of Fort Erie; was in charge of the general military hospital near Buffalo, N.Y., until his resignation in May 1815; practiced medicine in Hallowell, Maine, 1815-1819; moved to Norridgewock in 1819 and continued practice; elected as a Jacksonian to the Twenty-second Congress (March 4, 1831-March 3, 1833); superintendent of the State hospital for the insane 1845-1851; resumed the practice of medicine in Gardiner and Fairfield, Maine; moved to Yarmouth, Cumberland County, Maine, in 1858 and engaged in practice until his death there February 25, 1882; interment in what is now known as the Old Oak Cemetery, Norridgewock, Somerset County, Maine.

**Bibliography:** *DAB*.

**BATES, James Woodson** (brother of Edward Bates), a Delegate from the Territory of Arkansas; born in Goochland County, Va., August 25, 1788; attended Yale College and was graduated from Princeton College in 1807; studied law; was admitted to the bar and commenced practice in Virginia; moved to St. Louis, Mo., in 1816, and thence to the Post of Arkansas in 1819; elected as first Delegate from Arkansas to the Sixteenth and Seventeenth Congresses and served from December 21, 1819, to March 3, 1823; unsuccessful candidate for reelection in 1822 to the Eighteenth Congress; resumed the practice of law in Batesville, Ark.; judge of the fourth judicial circuit of Arkansas Territory 1824-1828; judge of the superior court of Arkansas 1828-1832; delegate to the State constitutional convention in 1835; judge of the probate court of Crawford County in 1836; register of the land office in Clarksville 1841-1845; died in Van Buren, Crawford County, Ark., December 26, 1846; interment in the family burying ground at Moores Rock, Crawford (now Sebastian) County, Ark.

**BATES, Jim,** a Representative from California; born in Denver, Colo., July 21, 1941; graduated, East Denver High School, Denver, 1959; B.A., San Diego State University, 1975; corporal, United States Marine Corps, 1959-1963; banker and aerospace business-man, 1963-1970; city councilman, San Diego, 1971-1974; chairman, board of supervisors, San Diego, 1975-1982; elected as a Democrat to the Ninety-eighth and to the three succeeding Congresses (January 3, 1983-January 3, 1991); unsuccessful candidate for reelection in 1990 to the One Hundred Second Congress; is a resident of Homedale, Idaho.

**BATES, Joseph Bengal,** a Representative from Kentucky; born in Republican, Ky., October 29, 1893; attended the public schools and the Mountain Training School at Hindman, Ky.; was graduated from Eastern Kentucky State Teachers College at Richmond in 1916; studied law; taught in the rural schools of Knott County, Ky., 1912-1915; high school superintendent at Raceland, Ky., 1917-1919; county clerk of Greenup County, Ky., 1922-1938; elected as a Democrat to the Seventy-fifth Congress to fill the vacancy caused by the resignation of Fred M. Vinson; reelected to the Seventy-sixth and to the six succeeding Congresses and served from June 4, 1938, to January 3, 1953; unsuccessful candidate for renomination in 1952, and was unsuccessful for the Democratic nomination in 1956 for the United States Senate; engaged in the practice of law and was a resident of Greenup, Ky.; died in Ashland, Ky., September 10, 1965; interment in Bellefonte Memorial Gardens, Flatwoods, Ky.

**BATES, Martin Waltham,** a Senator from Delaware; born in Salisbury, Conn., February 24, 1786; attended the common schools; moved to Delaware and taught school for several years; studied medicine and later studied law; was admitted to the bar in 1822 and commenced practice in Dover, Kent County, Del.; member, State house of representatives 1826; delegate to the State constitutional convention 1852; elected as a Democrat to the United States Senate to fill the vacancy caused by the death of John M. Clayton and served from January 14, 1857, to March 3, 1859; unsuccessful candidate for reelection in 1858; resumed the practice of law until his death in Dover, Del., January 1, 1869; interment in the Old Methodist Cemetery.

**BATES, William Henry** (son of George Joseph Bates), a Representative from Massachusetts; born in Salem, Essex County, Mass., April 26, 1917; attended the public schools; was graduated from Worcester Academy in 1936, from Brown University, Providence, R.I., in 1940, and from Harvard Graduate School of Business Administration, Boston, Mass., in 1947; enlisted in the United States Navy in July 1940 and served until February 14, 1950, resigning his commission as lieutenant commander after being elected to Congress; elected as a Republican to the Eighty-first Congress to fill the vacancy caused by the death of his father, George J. Bates; reelected to the Eighty-second and to the nine succeeding Congresses and served from February 14, 1950, until his death in Bethesda, Md., June 22, 1969; chairman, Select Committee to Conduct Investigation and Study of Benefits for Survivors of Deceased Members and Former Members of the Armed Forces (Eighty-third Congress); interment in St. Marys Cemetery, Salem, Mass.

**BATHRICK, Elsworth Raymond,** a Representative from Ohio; born near Pontiac, Oakland County, Mich., January 6, 1863; attended the country schools and was graduated from the Pontiac High School; moved to New York City in 1890 and engaged in the importation of edible oils; moved to Akron, Ohio, in 1900 and engaged in the real estate business; elected as a Democrat to the Sixty-second and Sixty-third Congresses (March 4, 1911-March 3, 1915); unsuccessful candidate for reelection in 1914 to the Sixty-fourth Congress; resumed his former business pursuits; elected to the Sixty-fifth Congress and served from March 4, 1917, until his death in Akron, Summit County, Ohio, December 23, 1917; interment in Glendale Cemetery.

**BATTIN, James Franklin,** a Representative from Montana; born in Wichita, Sedgwick County, Kans., February 13, 1925; moved with his parents to Montana in November 1929; educated in the public schools of Billings, Mont.; graduated from high school in 1942; enlisted in the United States Navy and served for three years, two and a half years of which were in the Pacific theater; B.A., Eastern Montana College, Billings, 1948; J.D., George Washington University School of Law, 1951; was admitted to the bar in 1951 and practiced law in Washington, D.C., 1951-1952; practiced law in Billings, Mont., 1953-1960; deputy Yellowstone County attorney, 1953-1955; secretary-counsel for the Billings-Yellowstone City-County Planning Board, 1955; Billings assistant city attorney, 1955-1957, and city attorney, 1957-1958; member, Montana State house of representatives, 1958-1959; delegate to the Republican National Conventions of 1964 and 1968; elected as a Republican to the Eighty-seventh and to the four succeeding Congresses, and served from January 3, 1961, until his resignation February 27, 1969; appointed by President Richard M. Nixon, February 27, 1969, as United States district judge for the District of Montana; became chief judge, District of Montana on November 16, 1978, and took senior status February 13, 1990; was a resident of Billings, Mont., until his death there on September 27, 1996.

**BATTLE, Laurie Calvin,** a Representative from Alabama; born in Wilsonville, Shelby County, Ala., May 10, 1912; attended the elementary school at Inglenook, Jefferson County, Ala.; moved to Tuscumbia in 1926; was graduated from Deshler High School in 1930; A.B., Birmingham-Southern College, 1934; attended Vanderbilt University and Scarritt College, Nashville, Tenn., in 1934 and 1935; M.A., Ohio State University, Columbus, 1939; worked for a dairy company, Cleveland, Ohio, 1937-1938; laborer and district clerk for the Southern Natural Gas Co., Birmingham, Ala., 1940-1941; sociology teacher at Ohio State University night school in 1940; during the Second World War served in the United States Army Air Corps as a private and through the ranks to major, with service in the Asiatic-Pacific theater from February 19, 1942, until discharged on March 6, 1946; awarded the Bronze Star Medal; retired from the military reserve, May 1972; student at the University of Alabama in 1946; elected as a Democrat to the Eightieth and to the three succeeding Congresses (January 3, 1947-January 3, 1955); was not a candidate in 1954 for renomination to the House of Representatives, but was an unsuccessful candidate for nomination for the United States Senate; engaged in the insurance business in Birmingham, Ala.; government relations representative and legislative consultant in Washington, D.C.; served as staff director and counsel of House of Representatives Rules Committee, 1966-1976; special adviser, United States League of Savings Associations, Washington, D.C., 1976-1988; retired; is a resident of Alexandria, Va.

**BAUCUS, Max Sieben,** a Representative and a Senator from Montana; born in Helena, Lewis and Clark County, Mont., December 11, 1941; graduated, Helena High School, 1959; attended the public schools of Missoula and Helena, Mont.; attended Carleton College, Northfield, Minn., 1959-1960; B.A., Stanford (Calif.)

University, 1964; LL.B., Stanford University Law School, 1967; admitted to the District of Columbia Bar in 1969; admitted to the Montana Bar in 1972; commenced practice in Washington, D.C., with the Civil Aeronautics Board, 1967-1968, and the Securities and Exchange Commission, 1968-1971; returned to Montana and practiced law in Missoula; served in the Montana State house of representatives, 1973-1974; elected as a Democrat to the Ninety-fourth and Ninety-fifth Congresses and served from January 3, 1975, until his resignation December 14, 1978; was not a candidate in 1978 for reelection to the House of Representatives, but was elected to the United States Senate for the six-year term commencing January 3, 1979; subsequently appointed by the Governor, December 15, 1978, to fill the vacancy caused by the resignation of Paul Hatfield for the term ending January 3, 1979; reelected in 1984 and again in 1990 for the term ending January 3, 1997; chairman, Committee on Environment and Public Works (One Hundred Third Congress); is a resident of Missoula, Mont.

**BAUMAN, Robert Edmund,** a Representative from Maryland; born in Bryn Mawr, Montgomery County, Pa., April 4, 1937; attended Catholic and public schools including Easton (Maryland) High School until 1953; graduated, Capitol Page School, Library of Congress, Washington, D.C., 1955; B.S., international affairs, School of Foreign Service, Georgetown University, Washington, D.C., 1959; J.D., Georgetown University Law Center, 1964; admitted to the Maryland Bar in 1964 and to the District of Columbia bar and commenced practice in Easton; delegate to the Republican National Conventions of 1964, 1974, 1978 and 1980; member, Federal Hospital Council of the United States Department of Health, Education, and Welfare, 1970-1973; member, Maryland State senate, 1971-1973; elected as a Republican, by special election, August 21, 1973, to the Ninety-third Congress to fill the vacancy caused by the death of William O. Mills; reelected to the three succeeding Congresses, and served from August 21, 1973 to January 3, 1981; unsuccessful candidate for reelection in 1980 to the Ninety-seventh Congress; was a candidate for nomination in 1982 to the Ninety-eighth Congress, but withdrew his candidacy before the election; resumed the practice of law in Washington, D.C.; is a resident of Washington, D.C.

Bibliography: Bauman, Robert E. *The Gentleman From Maryland; The Conscience of a Gay Conservative.* New York: Arbor House, 1986.

**BAUMHART, Albert David, Jr.,** a Representative from Ohio; born in Vermilion, Erie County, Ohio, June 15, 1908; attended the public schools; A.B. and M.A., Ohio University, Athens, 1931; publishing house representative at Vermilion, Ohio, 1932-1939; Ohio State senator, 1937-1940; elected as a Republican to the Seventy-seventh Congress, and served from January 3, 1941 until his resignation on September 2, 1942, to accept a commission in the United States Navy, in which he served until discharged as a lieutenant commander on January 17, 1946; member of the public relations staff of Owens-Corning Fiberglas Corp., Toledo, Ohio, 1946-1953; director, Republican National Committee, 1953-1954; elected as a Republican to the Eighty-fourth and to the two succeeding Congresses (January 3, 1955-January 3, 1961); was not a candidate for renomination in 1960 to the Eighty-seventh Congress; delegate to the Republican National Convention of 1968; engaged as public relations consultant; is a resident of Lorain, Ohio.

**BAXTER, Portus,** a Representative from Vermont; born in Brownington, Orleans County, Vt., December 4, 1806; attended the common schools, Norwich Military Academy, and the University of Vermont at Burlington; moved to Derby Line, Orleans County, Vt., in 1828; presidential elector on the Whig ticket in 1852 and on the Republican ticket in 1856; elected as a Republican to the Thirty-seventh, Thirty-eighth, and Thirty-ninth Congresses (March 4, 1861-March 3, 1867); chairman, Committee on Expenditures in

the Department of the Navy (Thirty-eighth Congress); declined to be a candidate for renomination in 1866; died in Washington, D.C., March 4, 1868; interment in Strafford Cemetery, Strafford, Orange County, Vt.

**BAY, William Van Ness,** a Representative from Missouri; born in Hudson, N.Y., November 23, 1818; attended the public schools; studied law; was admitted to the bar; moved to Union, Franklin County, Mo., in 1836 and commenced the practice of law; member of the Missouri State house of representatives, 1844-1848; elected as a Democrat to the Thirty-first Congress (March 4, 1849-March 3, 1851); resumed the practice of law; appointed judge of the State supreme court in 1862; elected to this position in 1863 and served until removed by Governor Thomas Clement Fletcher in 1865; moved to St. Louis, Mo., and again resumed the practice of law; retired in 1886 and moved to Eureka, Mo., where he died February 10, 1894; interment in Oak Hill Cemetery, Kirkwood, St. Louis County, Mo.

**BAYARD, James Asheton, Jr.** (son of James Asheton Bayard, Sr., brother of Richard Henry Bayard, grandson of Richard Bassett, father of Thomas Francis Bayard, Sr., and grandfather of Thomas Francis Bayard, Jr.), a Senator from Delaware; born in Wilmington, Del., November 15, 1799; pursued classical studies; studied law; was admitted to the bar and commenced practice in Wilmington; United States district attorney for Delaware 1838-1843; elected as a Democrat to the United States Senate in 1851; reelected in 1857 and 1863 and served from March 4, 1851, to January 29, 1864, when he resigned; chairman, Committee on Engrossed Bills (Thirty-second Congress), Committee on Public Buildings (Thirty-third and Thirty-fourth Congresses), Committee on Judiciary (Thirty-fifth and Thirty-sixth Congresses), Committee on Public Buildings and Grounds (Thirty-fifth Congress); resumed the practice of law in Wilmington; appointed in 1867 to the United States Senate to fill the vacancy caused by the death of George Read Riddle; was subsequently elected as a Democrat to that position and served from April 5, 1867, to March 3, 1869; was not a candidate for reelection; again resumed the practice of law; died in Wilmington, Del., June 13, 1880; interment in the Old Swedes Burial Ground.

Bibliography: *DAB.*

**BAYARD, James Asheton, Sr.** (father of Richard Henry Bayard and James Asheton Bayard, Jr., nephew of John Bubenheim Bayard, grandfather of Thomas Francis Bayard, Sr., and great-grandfather of Thomas Francis Bayard, Jr.), a Representative and a Senator from Delaware; born in Philadelphia, Pa., July 28, 1767; was graduated from Princeton College in 1784; studied law; was admitted to the bar in 1787 and commenced practice in Wilmington, Del.; declined the appointment as Minister to France tendered by President John Adams in 1801; elected as a Federalist to the Fifth, Sixth, and Seventh Congresses (March 4, 1797-March 3, 1803); unsuccessful candidate for reelection in 1802; one of the managers appointed by the House of Representatives in 1798 to conduct the impeachment proceedings against William Blount, a Senator from Tennessee; elected as a Federalist to the United States Senate in 1804 to fill the vacancy caused by the resignation of William Hill Wells; reelected in 1805 and 1811 and served from November 13, 1804, to March 3, 1813, when he resigned; appointed a member of the commission to negotiate peace with Great Britain in 1813; aided in negotiating the Treaty of Ghent, signed on December 24, 1814; declined the appointment as Minister to Russia tendered by President James Madison in 1815; died in Wilmington, Del., August 6, 1815; interment at Bohemia Manor, Cecil County, Md.; reinterment about 1842 in Wilmington and Brandywine Cemetery, Wilmington, Del.

Bibliography: *DAB*; Borden, Morton. *The Federalism of James A. Bayard.* 1955. Reprint. New York: AMS Press, 1968; Donnan, Elizabeth. *Papers of James Asheton Bayard, 1796-1815.* 1915. Reprint. New York: Da Capo Press, 1971.

**BAYARD, John Bubenheim** (uncle of James Asheton Bayard, Sr.), a Delegate from Pennsylvania; born at Bohemia Manor, Cecil County, Md., August 11, 1738; moved to Pennsylvania in 1756 and settled in Philadelphia, where he became one of the leading merchants; member of the general assembly 1776-1779 and in 1784, serving several terms as speaker; member of the council of safety in 1776 and 1777; during the Revolutionary War was colonel of the Second Regiment of Philadelphia Volunteers and served in the Battles of Brandywine, Germantown, and Princeton; Member of the Continental Congress 1785-1786; moved to New Brunswick, N.J., in 1788; city mayor in 1790 and, later, judge of the court of common pleas; died in New Brunswick, N.J., January 7, 1807; interment in the First Presbyterian Churchyard.

**Bibliography:** *DAB.*

**BAYARD, Richard Henry** (son of James Asheton Bayard, Sr., brother of James Asheton Bayard, Jr., and grandson of Richard Bassett), a Senator from Delaware; born in Wilmington, Del., September 26, 1796; was graduated from Princeton College in 1814; studied law; was admitted to the bar in New Castle, Del., in 1818 and commenced practice in Wilmington; first mayor of Wilmington in 1832; elected as a Whig to the United States Senate to fill the vacancy caused by the resignation of Arnold Naudain, and served from June 17, 1836 to September 19, 1839, when he resigned to become chief justice of Delaware; chairman, Committee on Private Land Claims (Twenty-seventh Congress), Committee on District of Columbia (Twenty-seventh Congress), Committee on Naval Affairs (Twenty-seventh and Twenty-eighth Congresses); served as chief justice of Delaware from 1839 until 1841, when he resigned; elected again to the United States Senate to fill the vacancy which had existed since his own resignation in 1839, and served from January 12, 1841 to March 3, 1845; was not a candidate for reelection in 1845; appointed Chargé d'Affaires to Belgium on December 10, 1850 and served until September 1853; died in Philadelphia, Pa., March 4, 1868; interment in the Wilmington and Brandywine Cemetery, Wilmington, Del.

**Bibliography:** *DAB.*

**BAYARD, Thomas Francis, Jr.** (son of Thomas Francis Bayard, Sr., and grandson of James Asheton Bayard, Jr.), a Senator from Delaware; born in Wilmington, Del., June 4, 1868; attended the common schools of Wilmington and St. Paul's School, Concord, N.H.; was graduated from Yale University in 1890; was a student at the Yale Law School in 1890 and 1891; was admitted to the Delaware bar in 1893 and commenced practice in Wilmington; moved to New York City, and was appointed an assistant corporation counsel in 1897; practiced law in New York until September 1901, when he returned to Wilmington, Del., to practice law; served as chairman of the Democratic State committee, 1906-1916; solicitor of the city of Wilmington, 1917-1919; elected on November 7, 1922, as a Democrat to the United States Senate to fill the vacancy caused by the resignation of Josiah O. Wolcott; on the same day was also elected for the full term commencing March 4, 1923, and served from November 8, 1922 to March 3, 1929; unsuccessful candidate for reelection in 1928; resumed the practice of law in Wilmington, Del.; unsuccessful Democratic candidate for election to the United States Senate in 1930; died in Wilmington, Del., July 12, 1942; interment in Old Swedes Cemetery.

**BAYARD, Thomas Francis, Sr.** (son of James Asheton Bayard, Jr., and father of Thomas Francis Bayard, Jr.), a Senator from Delaware; born in Wilmington, Del., October 29, 1828; attended Doctor Hawkes' school in Flushing, N.Y.; studied law; was admitted to the bar in 1851 and commenced practice in Wilmington, Del.; appointed United States district attorney for Delaware in 1853, but resigned in 1854; moved to Philadelphia and practiced law; returned to Wilmington in 1858; at the expiration of his father's Senate term in 1869 was elected as a Democrat to the United States Senate;

reelected in 1875 and 1881 and served from March 4, 1869, to March 6, 1885, when he resigned to become Secretary of State; served as President pro tempore of the Senate during the Forty-seventh Congress; chairman, Committee on Engrossed Bills (Forty-third through Forty-fifth Congresses), Committee on Finance (Forty-sixth Congress), Committee on Private Land Claims (Forty-seventh and Forty-eighth Congresses); was appointed a member of the Electoral Commission created by the act of Congress approved on January 29, 1877, to decide the contests in various States in the presidential election of 1876; appointed Secretary of State in the Cabinet of President Grover Cleveland, and served from March 6, 1885 to March 6, 1889; appointed Ambassador to Great Britain on March 30, 1893 and served until March 1897; died in Dedham, Mass., September 28, 1898; interment in Old Swedes Cemetery, Wilmington, Del.

**Bibliography:** *DAB;* Tansill, Charles. *The Congressional Career of Thomas F. Bayard.* Washington, D.C.: Georgetown University Press, 1946.

**BAYH, Birch Evan,** a Senator from Indiana; born in Terre Haute, Vigo County, Ind., January 22, 1928; attended the public schools; served in the United States Army, 1946-1948; B.S., Purdue University School of Agriculture, Lafayette, Ind., 1951; attended Indiana State University, Terre Haute, 1952-1953; J.D., Indiana University School of Law, Bloomington, 1960; was admitted to the Indiana bar in 1961 and commenced practice in Terre Haute; farmer and lawyer; member, Indiana State house of representatives, 1954-1962, serving as minority leader in 1957 and 1961, and as speaker in 1959; elected as a Democrat to the United States Senate in 1962; reelected in 1968 and 1974, and served from January 3, 1963 to January 3, 1981; unsuccessful candidate for reelection in 1980; unsuccessful candidate for the Democratic presidential nomination in 1976; chairman, Select Committee on Intelligence (Ninety-fifth and Ninety-sixth Congresses); lawyer practicing in Washington, D.C.

**Bibliography:** Bayh, Birch. *One Heartbeat Away: Presidential Disability and Succession.* Indianapolis: Bobbs Merrill, 1968.

**BAYLIES, Francis** (brother of William Baylies), a Representative from Massachusetts; born in Taunton, Mass., October 16, 1783; studied law; was admitted to the bar in 1810 and commenced practice in Taunton, Mass.; register of probate for Bristol County, 1812-1820; unsuccessful candidate for election in 1818 to the Sixteenth Congress; elected to the three succeeding Congresses (March 4, 1821-March 3, 1827); unsuccessful candidate for reelection in 1826 to the Twentieth Congress; member of the Massachusetts house of representatives, 1827-1832; appointed United States Chargé d'Affaires to the Republic of Buenos Aires (Argentina) on January 3, 1832, and served until September 1832; again elected to the Massachusetts house of representatives in 1835; engaged in literary pursuits; unsuccessful Native American Party candidate for Governor of Massachusetts in 1846 and 1847; died in Taunton, Bristol County, Mass., October 28, 1852; interment in the Old Plain Cemetery.

**Bibliography:** *DAB;* Rezneck, Samuel. "Letters from a Massachusetts Federalist to a New York Democrat, 1823-1839." *New York History* 48 (July 1967): 255-274.

**BAYLIES, William** (brother of Francis Baylies), a Representative from Massachusetts; born in Dighton, Mass., September 15, 1776; was graduated from Brown University, Providence, R.I., in 1795; studied law; was admitted to the bar and commenced practice in Bridgewater (west parish) in 1799; member of the Massachusetts house of representatives in 1808, 1809, 1812, and 1813; served in the Massachusetts senate in 1825 and 1826; presented credentials as a Federalist to the Eleventh Congress and served from March 4,

1809, until June 28, 1809, when he was succeeded by Charles Turner, Jr., who contested the election; elected to the Thirteenth and Fourteenth Congresses (March 4, 1813-March 3, 1817); again a member of the Massachusetts house of representatives in 1820 and 1821; again served in the Massachusetts senate in 1830 and 1831; elected as an Anti-Jacksonian to the Twenty-third Congress (March 4, 1833-March 3, 1835); unsuccessful candidate for reelection in 1834 to the Twenty-fourth Congress; resumed the practice of his profession; died in Taunton, Bristol County, Mass., on September 27, 1865; interment in the Old Cemetery, Dighton, Mass.

**BAYLOR, Robert Emmett Bledsoe** (nephew of Jesse Bledsoe), a Representative from Alabama; born in Lincoln County, Ky., May 10, 1793; served in the War of 1812; studied law; was admitted to the bar and practiced; member of the Kentucky house of representatives in 1819, but resigned and moved to Alabama in 1820, continuing the practice of law; studied theology, was licensed to preach, and was ordained to the Baptist ministry; member of the Alabama house of representatives in 1824; elected as a Jacksonian to the Twenty-first Congress (March 4, 1829-March 3, 1831); unsuccessful candidate for election in 1830 to the Twenty-second Congress; commanded an Alabama regiment during the Creek War; moved to Texas in 1839; elected judge of the district and supreme courts of the Republic; member of the convention that framed the State constitution of Texas in 1845; district judge for twenty-five years; one of the founders of Baylor University at Independence, Tex. (now located at Waco, Tex.), and Baylor Female College at Belton, Tex.; professor of law in Baylor University; died at Gay Hill, Washington County, Tex., on January 6, 1874; interment in the Baylor University grounds; later the remains were removed to the campus of Baylor Female College at Belton, Tex.

Bibliography: *DAB*.

**BAYLY, Thomas,** a Representative from Maryland; born at "Wellington," near Quantico, Somerset (now Wicomico) County, Md., September 13, 1775; attended private schools and was graduated from Princeton College in 1797; studied law; was admitted to the bar and practiced in Somerset and Worcester Counties, Md.; member of the State house of delegates 1804-1814; elected as a Federalist to the Fifteenth Congress and reelected to the Sixteenth and Seventeenth Congresses (March 4, 1817-March 3, 1823); resumed the practice of law; died at his home, "Wellington," near Quantico, Md., in 1829; interment in the family cemetery on the grounds of his estate.

**BAYLY, Thomas Henry** (son of Thomas Monteagle Bayly), a Representative from Virginia; born at "Mount Custis," the family estate, near Drummondtown, Accomac County, Va., December 11, 1810; attended the common schools and was graduated from the University of Virginia at Charlottesville in 1829; studied law; was admitted to the bar in 1830 and commenced practice in Accomac County; also engaged in agricultural pursuits; served in the Virginia house of delegates, 1836-1842; appointed brigadier general of the Twenty-first Brigade, Virginia Militia, in 1837 and served until 1842; elected judge of the superior court of law and chancery in 1842 and served until 1844; elected as a Democrat to the Twenty-eighth Congress to fill the vacancy caused by the resignation of Henry A. Wise; reelected to the Twenty-ninth and to the five succeeding Congresses and served from May 6, 1844, until his death on his estate, "Mount Custis," near Drummondtown, Accomac County, Va., June 23, 1856; chairman, Committee on Ways and Means (Thirty-first Congress), Committee on Foreign Affairs (Thirty-second and Thirty-third Congress); interment in the family burying ground on his estate.

Bibliography: *DAB*.

**BAYLY, Thomas Monteagle** (father of Thomas Henry Bayly), a Representative from Virginia; born at Hills Farm, near Drummondtown, Accomac County, Va., on March 26, 1775; attended Washington Academy, Maryland, and was graduated from Princeton College in 1794; studied law; was admitted to the bar about 1796 and commenced practice in Accomac County; also engaged in planting; member of the Virginia house of delegates 1798-1801; member of the Virginia senate 1801-1809; served during the War of 1812 as colonel of militia; elected as a Federalist to the Thirteenth Congress (March 4, 1813-March 3, 1815); was not a candidate for renomination in 1814; resumed agricultural pursuits and the practice of law; again a member of the Virginia house of delegates 1819, 1820, and 1828-1831; delegate to the Virginia constitutional convention in 1829 and 1830; died on his plantation, "Mount Custis," near Accomac, Accomac County, Va., January 7, 1834; interment in the family cemetery on his estate, "Mount Custis."

**BAYNE, Thomas McKee,** a Representative from Pennsylvania; born in Bellevue, Allegheny County, Pa., June 14, 1836; attended the public schools and Westminster College, New Wilmington, Pa.; studied law; during the Civil War entered the Union Army in July 1862 as colonel of the One Hundred and Thirty-sixth Regiment, Pennsylvania Volunteer Infantry; took part in the Battles of Fredericksburg and Chancellorsville; resumed the study of law in 1865; was admitted to the bar of Allegheny County in April 1866; elected district attorney for Allegheny County in October 1870 and held the office until January 1, 1874; unsuccessful candidate for election in 1874 to the Forty-fourth Congress; elected as a Republican to the Forty-fifth and to the six succeeding Congresses (March 4, 1877-March 3, 1891); was renominated as a candidate for reelection to the Fifty-second Congress, but declined to accept the nomination, retiring from public life and active business pursuits; died in Washington, D.C., on June 16, 1894; interment in Uniondale Cemetery, Pittsburgh, Pa.

**BEACH, Clifton Bailey,** a Representative from Ohio; born in Sharon, Medina County, Ohio, September 16, 1845; moved to Cleveland with his parents in 1857; attended the common schools and was graduated from Western Reserve College, Hudson, Ohio, in 1871; studied law; was admitted to the bar in 1872 and commenced practice in Cleveland; served as deputy collector of customs at Cleveland; retired from the practice of law in 1884 and engaged in the manufacture of wire nails, staples, and rods; elected as a Republican to the Fifty-fourth and Fifty-fifth Congresses (March 4, 1895-March 3, 1899); was not a candidate for renomination in 1898; resumed his former manufacturing pursuits in Cleveland; died at Rocky River, Cuyahoga County, Ohio, November 15, 1902; interment in Lake View Cemetery, Cleveland, Ohio.

**BEACH, Lewis,** a Representative from New York; born in New York City March 30, 1835; was graduated from the Yale Law School in 1856; was admitted to the bar the same year and commenced practice in New York; took up residence in Orange County, N.Y., in 1861; member and treasurer of the Democratic State central committee 1877-1879; elected as a Democrat to the Forty-seventh, Forty-eighth, and Forty-ninth Congresses and served from March 4, 1881, until his death at his home, "Knoll View," Cornwall, Orange County, N.Y., August 10, 1886; chairman, Committee on Expenditures on Public Buildings (Forty-ninth Congress); interment in Greenwood Cemetery, Brooklyn, N.Y.

**BEAKES, Samuel Willard,** a Representative from Michigan; born in Burlingham, Sullivan County, N.Y., January 11, 1861; attended Wallkill Academy, Middletown, N.Y.; was graduated from the law department of the University of Michigan at Ann Arbor in 1883; was admitted to the bar the same year and commenced practice in Westerville, Ohio; editor and proprietor of the Westerville Review in 1884, of the Adrian (Mich.) Daily Record 1884-1886, and of the Ann Arbor (Mich.) Argus 1886-1905; mayor of Ann Arbor

1888-1890; postmaster of Ann Arbor 1894-1898; city treasurer 1891-1893 and 1903-1905; city assessor 1906-1913; delegate to the Democratic National Convention at St. Louis in 1916; elected as a Democrat to the Sixty-third and Sixty-fourth Congresses (March 4, 1913-March 3, 1917); successfully contested the election of Mark R. Bacon to the Sixty-fifth Congress and served from December 13, 1917, to March 3, 1919; unsuccessful candidate for reelection in 1918 to the Sixty-sixth Congress; after his service in Congress located in Washington, D.C.; assistant chief of the industrial cooperation service of the United States Department of Commerce from April to July 1919; staff member of the United States Veterans' Bureau from 1919 until his death in Washington, D.C., February 9, 1927; interment in Forest Hill Cemetery, Ann Arbor, Mich.

**BEALE, Charles Lewis,** a Representative from New York; born in Canaan, Columbia County, N.Y., March 5, 1824; was graduated from Union College, Schenectady, N.Y., in 1844; studied law; was admitted to the bar in 1849 and commenced practice in Canaan, N.Y.; moved to Kinderhook, N.Y., in 1852 and continued the practice of law; elected as a Republican to the Thirty-sixth Congress (March 4, 1859-March 3, 1861); unsuccessful candidate for reelection in 1860 to the Thirty-seventh Congress; delegate to the Union National Convention at Philadelphia in 1866; resumed the practice of law; died in Hudson, N.Y., on January 29, 1900; interment in Kinderhook Cemetery, Kinderhook, N.Y.

**BEALE, James Madison Hite,** a Representative from Virginia; born in Mount Airy, Shenandoah County, Va., February 7, 1786; pursued preparatory studies; engaged in agricultural pursuits; member, Virginia house of delegates, 1818-1819; elected as a Jacksonian to the Twenty-third and Twenty-fourth Congresses (March 4, 1833-March 3, 1837); chairman, Committee on Invalid Pensions (Twenty-fourth Congress); resumed agricultural pursuits; elected as a Democrat to the Thirty-first and Thirty-second Congresses (March 4, 1849-March 3, 1853); chairman, Committee on Expenditures on Public Buildings (Thirty-first Congress), Committee on Manufactures (Thirty-second Congress); declined to be a candidate for renomination in 1852; resumed agricultural pursuits; died in Putnam County, W.Va., August 2, 1866; interment in Beale Cemetery, near Gallipolis Ferry, Mason County, W.Va.

**BEALE, Joseph Grant,** a Representative from Pennsylvania; born in Allegheny County, near Freeport, Armstrong County, Pa., March 26, 1839; attended the common schools; was graduated from Caton Academy, Turtle Creek, Pa., and from Iron City Commercial College, Pittsburgh, Pa.; during the Civil War enlisted in the Friend Rifles for three months, and later served as captain of Company C, Ninth Regiment, Pennsylvania Reserves, for three years; was taken prisoner and confined in Libby Prison, Richmond, Va., until released on parole; studied law; served as major in the Pennsylvania Militia; discontinuing the study of law, he engaged in the coal business in the suburbs of Pittsburgh; moved to Leechburg, Armstrong County, in the spring of 1868 and actively engaged in the iron and steel business; president of the Leechburg Banking Co.; elected as a Republican to the Sixtieth Congress (March 4, 1907-March 3, 1909); unsuccessful candidate for renomination in 1908 to the Sixty-first Congress; resumed his former business pursuits; died in Leechburg, Pa., May 21, 1915; interment in Evergreen Cemetery.

**BEALE, Richard Lee Turberville,** a Representative from Virginia; born in Hickory Hill, Westmoreland County, Va., May 22, 1819; attended private schools in Westmoreland County, Northumberland Academy and Rappahannock Academy, Virginia, and Dickinson College, Carlisle, Pa.; studied law; was graduated from the University of Virginia at Charlottesville in 1837; was admitted to the bar in 1839 and commenced practice at Hague, Westmoreland County, Va.; elected as a Democrat to the Thirtieth Congress (March 4, 1847-March 3, 1849); declined to be a candidate for renomination in 1848 to the Thirty-first Congress; member of the Virginia

constitutional convention in 1850-1851; member of the Virginia senate 1858-1860; commissioned first lieutenant in Lee's Legion in May 1861, and rose through a series of promotions to brigadier general in the Confederate Army on February 6, 1865; elected to the Forty-fifth Congress to fill the vacancy caused by the death of Beverly B. Douglas; reelected to the Forty-sixth Congress and served from January 23, 1879, to March 3, 1881; resumed the practice of law; died near Hague, Westmoreland County April 21, 1893; interment in Hickory Hill Cemetery.

**Bibliography:** *DAB.*

**BEALES, Cyrus William,** a Representative from Pennsylvania; born on a farm near York Spring, Adams County, Pa., December 16, 1877; attended the common schools; at the age of thirteen, upon the death of his father, took over the operation of his father's farm; was graduated from the pharmaceutical department of the Ohio Northern University at Ada in 1899; settled at York Springs and was employed as a pharmacist; moved to Gettysburg, Pa., in 1903 upon his appointment as mercantile appraiser of Adams County; clerk to the county commissioners in 1904 and 1905; engaged in the drug, banking, manufacturing, and printing businesses; postmaster of Gettysburg from April 1, 1910 to May 8, 1914; elected as a Republican to the Sixty-fourth Congress (March 4, 1915-March 3, 1917); was not a candidate for renomination in 1916; member of the State senate 1917-1921; engaged in the drug business in Gettysburg, and died there on November 14, 1927; interment in the family plot in Evergreen Cemetery.

**BEALL, James Andrew (Jack),** a Representative from Texas; born on a farm near Midlothian, Ellis County, Tex., October 25, 1866; attended the country schools; taught school in 1884 and 1885; was graduated from the law department of the University of Texas at Austin in 1890; was admitted to the bar the same year and commenced practice in Waxahachie, Ellis County, Tex.; member of the State house of representatives 1892-1895; served in the State senate 1895-1899; elected as a Democrat to the Fifty-eighth and to the five succeeding Congresses (March 4, 1903-March 3, 1915); chairman, Committee on Expenditures in the Department of Justice (Sixty-second Congress); was not a candidate for renomination in 1914 to the Sixty-fourth Congress; moved to Dallas, Tex., in 1914 and resumed the practice of law; also engaged in banking; served as president of the Texas Electric Railway Co., from 1921 until his death in Dallas, Tex., on February 12, 1929; interment in Oakland Cemetery.

**BEALL, James Glenn** (father of John Glenn Beall, Jr.), a Representative and a Senator from Maryland; born in Frostburg, Allegany County, Md., June 5, 1894; attended the public schools and Gettysburg College; during the First World War served in the Ordnance Corps, United States Army, 1918-1919, being discharged as a sergeant; engaged in the insurance and real-estate business; member of the Allegany County Road Commission, 1923-1930; Maryland State senator, 1930-1934; member and chairman of the Maryland State Road Commission, 1938-1939; elected as a Republican to the Seventy-eighth and to the four succeeding Congresses (January 3, 1943-January 3, 1953); was not a candidate in 1952 for reelection to the House of Representatives, but was elected to the United States Senate; reelected in 1958, and served from January 3, 1953 to January 3, 1965; unsuccessful candidate for reelection in 1964; returned to Frostburg, Md., and resumed his insurance business; died in Frostburg, Md., January 14, 1971; interment in Frostburg Memorial Park.

**BEALL, John Glenn, Jr.** (son of James Glenn Beall), a Representative and a Senator from Maryland; born in Cumberland, Allegany County, Md., June 19, 1927; A.B., Yale University, 1950; served in the United States Navy, 1945-1946; member of the general insurance firm of Beall, Garner & Geare, Inc.; member, Maryland State house of delegates, 1963-1968, serving as minority floor leader,

1963-1968; elected as a Republican to the Ninety-first Congress (January 3, 1969-January 3, 1971); was not a candidate for reelection in 1970 to the House of Representatives, but was elected to the United States Senate, and served from January 3, 1971 to January 3, 1977; unsuccessful candidate for reelection in 1976; unsuccessful candidate for election in 1978 for Governor of Maryland; resumed the insurance business in Cumberland, Md.; is a resident of Frostburg, Md.

**BEALL, Reasin,** a Representative from Ohio; born in Montgomery County, Md., December 3, 1769; received a limited schooling; served as an officer under General Josiah Harmar in 1790; appointed ensign in the United States Army March 7, 1792, and battalion quartermaster in 1793, and served under General Anthony Wayne in the campaign against the Indians; moved to New Lisbon, Ohio, in 1803; was commissioned brigadier general of Volunteers in 1812; moved to Wooster, Ohio, in 1815; elected as a Republican to the Thirteenth Congress to fill the vacancy caused by the death of John S. Edwards and served from April 20, 1813, until his resignation on June 7, 1814; served as register of the land offices at Canton and Wooster, Ohio, from 1814 to 1824; presided over the Whig mass convention held at Columbus, Ohio, on February 22, 1840; presidential elector on the Whig ticket in 1840; died in Wooster, Wayne County, Ohio, February 20, 1843; interment in Wooster Cemetery.

**BEAM, Harry Peter,** a Representative from Illinois; born in Peoria Ill., November 23, 1892; moved with his parents to Chicago, Ill., in 1899; attended St. Mary's School, Marshalltown, Iowa, and Holy Family School, Chicago, Ill., was graduated from St. Ignatius College, Chicago, Ill., in 1912 and from the law department of Loyola University, Chicago, Ill., in 1916; was admitted to the bar the same year and commenced practice in Chicago, Ill.; during the First World War served as a seaman, first class, in the United States Navy from May 1918 to December 1918; assistant corporation counsel of Chicago 1923-1927; elected as a Democrat to the Seventy-second and to the five succeeding Congresses and served from March 4, 1931, until his resignation on December 6, 1942; chairman, Committee on Memorials (Seventy-seventh Congress); elected as a judge of the municipal court of Chicago in 1942, reelected in 1948, 1954, and 1960; engaged in legal practice and retired in 1964; was a resident of Chicago, Ill., until his death there on December 31, 1967; interment in Holy Sepulchre Cemetery.

**BEAMAN, Fernando Cortez,** a Representative from Michigan; born in Chester, Vt., June 28, 1814; moved with his parents to a farm in Franklin County, N.Y., in 1819; attended the district schools and Malone (N.Y.) Academy; taught school; moved to Rochester, N.Y., in 1836; studied law; moved to Manchester, Mich., in 1838; was admitted to the bar and commenced practice in 1839; moved to Tecumseh in 1841 and practiced law there and in Clinton; moved to Adrian in 1843, having been appointed prosecuting attorney for Lenawee County, and served until 1850; city attorney of Adrian; member of the convention that met under the oaks at Jackson, Mich., July 6, 1854, at the organization of the Republican Party in Michigan; delegate to the first Republican National Convention, at Philadelphia in 1856; mayor of Adrian in 1856; judge of the probate court of Lenawee County, 1856-1860; elected as a Republican to the Thirty-seventh and to the four succeeding Congresses (March 4, 1861-March 3, 1871); chairman, Committee on Roads and Canals (Thirty-ninth Congress); declined to be a candidate for renomination in 1870 to the Forty-second Congress; returned to Adrian and resumed the practice of law; appointed judge of probate of Lenawee County in 1871, elected to the same position in 1872, and reelected in 1876; appointed United States Senator to fill the vacancy caused by the death of Zachariah Chandler in 1879, but declined the appointment owing to ill health; declined appointments to the State supreme court and as United States Commissioner of Indian Affairs;

died in Adrian, Lenawee County, Mich., September 27, 1882; interment in Oakwood Cemetery.

**BEAMER, John Valentine,** a Representative from Indiana; born on a farm in Wabash County, Ind., November 17, 1896; attended the public schools of Roann, Ind.; was graduated from Wabash College, Crawfordsville, Ind., in 1918; during the First World War served in the Field Artillery; employed with Service Motor Truck Co., Wabash, Ind., 1919-1921; representative for the Century Co., school textbook publisher, New York and Chicago, 1921-1928; vice president and general manager, Wabash (Ind.) Baking Powder & Chemical Co., 1928-1941; vice president and sales manager, Union Rock Wool Corp., Wabash, Ind., 1935-1942; owner and operator of a farm near Wabash, Ind.; served in the State house of representatives in 1949 and 1950; elected as a Republican to the Eighty-second and to the three succeeding Congresses (January 3, 1951-January 3, 1959); unsuccessful candidate for reelection in 1958 to the Eighty-sixth Congress; member of the National Selective Service Appeal Board from March 1960 until his resignation September 1, 1961; died in Anderson, Ind., September 8, 1964; interment in Falls Cemetery, Wabash, Ind.

**BEAN, Benning Moulton,** a Representative from New Hampshire; born in Moultonboro, Carroll County, N.H., on January 9, 1782; attended the public schools of Moultonboro and received private tutoring; engaged in teaching and in agricultural pursuits; selectman of Moultonboro 1811-1829 and 1832-1838; justice of the peace in 1816; trustee of Sandwich Academy in 1824; member of the State house of representatives 1815-1823; served in the State senate 1824-1826; again a member of the State house of representatives in 1827; member of the Governor's council in 1829; again served in the State senate in 1831 and 1832, being president the latter year; elected as a Jacksonian to the Twenty-third and Twenty-fourth Congresses (March 4, 1833-March 3, 1837); declined to be a candidate for renomination in 1836; resumed teaching and agricultural pursuits in Moultonboro, Carroll County, N.H., where he died February 6, 1866; interment in Bean Cemetery.

**BEAN, Curtis Coe,** a Delegate from the Territory of Arizona; born in Tamworth, Carroll County, N.H., January 4, 1828; upon the death of his father moved with his mother to Gilmanton, Belknap County, N.H., in 1837; attended Gilmanton Academy, Phillips Exeter Academy, Exeter, N.H., and Union College, Schenectady, N.Y.; moved to New York City in the early fifties and was employed in the United States customhouse; also engaged in the brokerage business; studied law; was admitted to the bar but did not practice extensively; moved to Tennessee in 1864 and settled in Columbia and later in Nashville; member of the State house of representatives in 1867 and 1868; moved to Arizona Territory and settled in Prescott in June 1868; engaged in mining; unsuccessful candidate for election in 1876 to the Forty-fifth Congress; member of the Territorial senate in 1879; elected as a Republican to the Forty-ninth Congress (March 4, 1885-March 3, 1887); unsuccessful candidate for reelection in 1886 to the Fiftieth Congress; returned to Arizona and resumed mining operations; moved to New York City in 1889 but maintained his citizenship and business interests in Arizona; died in New York City on February 1, 1904; interment in Greenwood Cemetery, Brooklyn, N.Y.

**BEARD, Edward Peter,** a Representative from Rhode Island; born in Providence, R.I., January 20, 1940; attended Assumption Elementary School and Hope High School, Providence; served in the Rhode Island National Guard from 1960 until 1966, where he completed high school as well as a college-level course in agriculture; worked as painter; served in the Rhode Island house of representatives, 1972-1974; delegate to the Democratic National Convention of 1976; elected as a Democrat to the Ninety-fourth and to the two succeeding Congresses (January 3, 1975-January 3, 1981); unsuccessful candidate for reelection in 1980 to the

Ninety-seventh Congress; owned and operated a tavern; unsuccessful candidate for nomination in 1990 to the One Hundred Second Congress; director of senior affairs, City of Providence, 1986 to present; is a resident of Providence, R.I.

**BEARD, Robin Leo, Jr.,** a Representative from Tennessee; born in Knoxville, Knox County, Tenn., August 21, 1939; attended Montgomery Bell Academy, Nashville, Tenn.; B.A., Vanderbilt University, Nashville, 1961; served in the United States Marine Corps, first lieutenant, 1962-1965; retired from the Reserves with the rank of colonel; Tennessee State commissioner of personnel, 1970-1972; delegate to Tennessee State Republican convention, 1972; delegate to the Republican National Convention of 1972; elected as a Republican to the Ninety-third and to the four succeeding Congresses (January 3, 1973-January 3, 1983); was not a candidate in 1982 for reelection to the House of Representatives, but was an unsuccessful candidate for election to the United States Senate; Assistant Secretary General, North Atlantic Treaty Organization (NATO), Brussels, 1984-1987; president of import-export company in Washington, D.C., 1987-1992; reappointed in 1992 as Assistant Secretary General to NATO, and served until 1995; chairman, Hughes Electronics Corporation, Europe.

**BEARDSLEY, Samuel,** a Representative from New York; born in Hoosick, Rensselaer County, N.Y., February 6, 1790; pursued academic studies; taught school; studied law in Rome, N.Y.; served as a lieutenant in the War of 1812 and took part in the defense of Sackets Harbor in 1813; was admitted to the bar in 1815 and commenced practice in Watertown; judge advocate in the State militia; returned to Rome in 1816 and continued the practice of law; prosecuting attorney in 1821; member of the State senate in 1823; moved to Utica, Oneida County, in 1823; United States attorney for the northern district of New York 1823-1830; elected as a Jacksonian to the Twenty-second, Twenty-third, and Twenty-fourth Congresses and served from March 4, 1831, to March 29, 1836, when he resigned; chairman, Committee on the Judiciary (Twenty-fourth Congress); appointed circuit judge in 1836; attorney general of the State of New York 1836-1838; elected as a Democrat to the Twenty-eighth Congress and served from March 4, 1843, to February 29, 1844, when he resigned to accept a judicial appointment; served as associate judge of the New York Supreme Court from 1844 to 1847, and was appointed chief justice in the latter year; declined another term of service and resumed the practice of law; died in Utica, N.Y., May 6, 1860; interment in Forest Hill Cemetery.

**Bibliography:** *DAB.*

**BEATTY, John,** a Delegate and a Representative from New Jersey; born in Neshaminy, Bucks County, Pa., December 10, 1749; was graduated from the College of New Jersey (now Princeton University) in 1769; studied medicine in Philadelphia and practiced in Bucks County; entered the Revolutionary Army in 1775 and had attained the rank of major when he was made prisoner at the surrender of Fort Washington; after his exchange was appointed commissary general of prisoners with the rank of colonel May 28, 1778; resigned March 31, 1780, and resumed the practice of medicine in Princeton, N.J.; member of the State council 1781-1783; Member of the Continental Congress in 1784-1785; appointed by Richard Henry Lee, president of the Continental Congress, as one of the special committee to receive and take leave of General Lafayette in the name of the Continental Congress while it was in session at Trenton on December 11, 1784; member of the State convention that adopted the Federal Constitution in 1787; member of the State general assembly in 1789 and 1790, serving as speaker; elected to the Third Congress (March 4, 1793-March 3, 1795); brigadier general of the Somerset Militia 1793-1796; secretary of state of New Jersey 1795-1805; served as trustee of the College of New Jersey from 1787 until 1802; president of the Trenton Banking Co., from

1815 to 1826; died in Trenton, N.J., May 30, 1826; interment in First Presbyterian Church Cemetery.

**Bibliography:** *DAB.*

**BEATTY, John,** a Representative from Ohio; born near Sandusky, Erie County, Ohio, December 16, 1828; attended the common schools; entered the banking business in 1852, and subsequently, with his brother, conducted a bank in Cardington, Morrow County, Ohio; at the beginning of the Civil War volunteered as a private in the Third Regiment, Ohio Volunteer Infantry; was commissioned lieutenant colonel on April 27, 1861; promoted to colonel February 12, 1862 and took a prominent part in the campaigns in the Southwest; commanded a regiment at Perryville, Ky., October 8, 1862, and a brigade at Stone's River, Tenn., December 30, 1862-January 2, 1863; commissioned brigadier general on November 29, 1862, and commanded a brigade at Tullahoma, Chickamauga, and Marion Ridge; resigned his commission on January 28, 1864; elected as a Republican to the Fortieth Congress to fill the vacancy caused by the death of Cornelius S. Hamilton; reelected to the Forty-first and Forty-second Congresses, and served from February 5, 1868 to March 3, 1873; chairman, Committee on Enrolled Bills (Forty-first Congress), Committee on Public Buildings and Grounds (Forty-first Congress); moved to Columbus, Ohio, in 1873 and organized the Citizens Savings Bank, serving as its president until 1903, when he retired from active business pursuits; unsuccessful candidate for nomination in 1882 for Governor of Ohio; member of the State board of charities, 1886-1887; died in Columbus, Ohio, December 21, 1914; interment in Oakland Cemetery, Sandusky, Ohio.

**Bibliography:** *DAB.*

**BEATTY, William,** a Representative from Pennsylvania; born in Stewartstown, County Tyrone, Ireland, in 1787; immigrated to the United States in 1807 and settled in Butler, Butler County, Pa.; was a sergeant in Captain Thompson's company in the War of 1812; sheriff of Butler County 1823-1826; elected as a Democrat to the the Twenty-fifth and Twenty-sixth Congresses (March 4, 1837-March 3, 1841); member of the State house of representatives 1840-1842; appointed deputy sheriff of Butler County; died in Butler, Pa., April 12, 1851; interment in the Old Butler Cemetery.

**BEATY, Martin,** a Representative from Kentucky; born in Abingdon, Va.; operated an iron furnace; moved to Wayne County, Ky., in 1817 and engaged in drilling wells for brine and in the manufacture of salt at Saltville, Ky.; member of the Kentucky senate 1824-1828 and in 1832; presidential elector on the tickets of Clay and Sergeant in 1832 and Harrison and Granger in 1836; was an unsuccessful candidate for election in 1828 to the Twenty-first Congress and in 1830 to the Twenty-second Congress; elected as an Anti-Jacksonian to the Twenty-third Congress (March 4, 1833-March 3, 1835); unsuccessful candidate for reelection in 1834 to the Twenty-fourth Congress; member of the Kentucky house of representatives in 1848; moved to a farm near Belmont, Tex., in 1856 and engaged in agricultural pursuits and cattle raising; died in Southfork, Owsley County, Ky.; interment in Belmont Cemetery.

**BEAUMONT, Andrew,** a Representative from Pennsylvania; born in Lebanon, New London County, Conn., January 24, 1790; moved to Pennsylvania in 1808; studied law but never practiced; collector of revenue in 1814; prothonotary and clerk of the courts of Luzerne County, Pa., 1816-1819; member of the Pennsylvania house of representatives in 1821, 1822, and 1826; postmaster of Wilkes-Barre 1826-1832; elected as a Jacksonian to the Twenty-third and Twenty-fourth Congresses (March 4, 1833-March 3, 1837); was not a candidate for renomination; commissioner of public buildings in Washington, D.C., from November 5, 1846, to March 3, 1847; again a member of the State house of representatives, in 1849;

died in Wilkes-Barre, Pa., September 30, 1853; interment in Hollenback Cemetery.

**BECERRA, Xavier,** a Representative from California; born in Sacramento, Calif., January 26, 1958; graduated McClatchy High School, Sacramento, 1976; A.B., Stanford University, Calif., 1980; J.D., Stanford University School of Law, 1984; attorney; deputy attorney general, California State department of justice, 1987-1990; member, California State assembly, 1990-1993; elected as a Democrat to the One Hundred Third and One Hundred Fourth Congresses (January 3, 1993-January 3, 1997); is a resident of Montebello, Calif.

**BECK, Erasmus Williams,** a Representative from Georgia; born in McDonough, Henry County, Ga., October 21, 1833; attended the local schools of his native county, a private school, and Mercer University, Macon, Ga., for two years; in 1855, on account of ill health, returned to McDonough and began the study of law; moved to Griffin, Ga., in 1856 and continued his law studies; was admitted to the bar in 1856 and commenced practice in Griffin, Ga.; served for a short period in the Confederate Army during the Civil War, but was invalided home on account of ill health; during the war was solicitor general of the Flint circuit; elected as a Democrat to the Forty-second Congress to fill the vacancy caused by the death of Thomas J. Speer and served from December 2, 1872, to March 3, 1873; was not a candidate for renomination in 1872; resumed the practice of his profession at Griffin, Ga.; judge of the city court of Griffin from 1890 until his death in that city on July 22, 1898; interment in Oak Hill Cemetery.

**BECK, James Burnie,** a Representative and a Senator from Kentucky; born in Dumfriesshire, Scotland, February 13, 1822; received an academic education; immigrated to the United States in 1838 and settled in Wyoming County, N.Y.; moved to Lexington, Ky., in 1843 and was graduated from Transylvania University, Lexington, Ky., in 1846; was admitted to the bar and commenced the practice of law in Lexington; elected as a Democrat to the Fortieth and to the three succeeding Congresses (March 4, 1867-March 3, 1875); appointed in May 1876 a member of the commission to define the boundary line between Maryland and Virginia; elected to the United States Senate in 1876; reelected in 1882, again in 1888, and served from March 4, 1877, until his death in Washington, D.C., on May 3, 1890; chairman, Committee on Transportation Routes to the Seaboard (Forty-sixth Congress); interment in Lexington Cemetery, Lexington, Ky.

**BECK, James Montgomery,** a Representative from Pennsylvania; born in Philadelphia, Pa., July 9, 1861; attended the public schools and was graduated from Moravian College, Bethlehem, Pa., in 1880; employed as clerk for a railway company in 1880 and studied law at night; was admitted to the bar in 1884 and commenced practice in Philadelphia; admitted to the bar of New York City in 1903, and to the bar of England in 1922; served as assistant United States attorney for the eastern district of Pennsylvania 1888-1892 and as United States attorney 1896-1900; appointed by President William McKinley as assistant to the Attorney General of the United States in 1900 and served until his resignation in 1903; continued the practice of law in Philadelphia, New York City, and Washington from 1903 to 1921; was elected a bencher of Gray's Inn in 1914, being the first foreigner in six hundred years to receive that distinction; also received decorations from France and Belgium; author of several books and articles on the First World War and on the Constitution of the United States; appointed by President Warren G. Harding as Solicitor General of the United States in 1921 and served until his resignation in 1925; resumed the practice of law; elected as a Republican to the Seventieth Congress to fill the vacancy caused by the resignation of James M. Hazlett; reelected to the Seventy-first and to the two succeeding Congresses and served from November 8, 1927, until his

resignation on September 30, 1934; resumed the practice of law and was also engaged as an author; died in Washington, D.C., April 12, 1936; interment in Rock Creek Cemetery.

**Bibliography:** *DAB*; Keller, Morton. *In Defense of Yesterday; James M. Beck and the Politics of Conservatism, 1861-1936.* New York: Coward-McCann, 1958.

**BECK, Joseph David,** a Representative from Wisconsin; born near Bloomingdale, Vernon County, Wis., March 14, 1866; attended the common schools; taught in the public schools of the State for twelve years; was graduated from the State Normal School, Stevens Point, Wis., in 1897 and from the University of Wisconsin at Madison in 1903; clerk of the State bureau of statistics of Wisconsin in 1901; deputy commissioner of statistics in 1902; chief of the department of labor statistics 1903-1913; president of the International Association of Labor Bureau Officials 1911-1913; chairman of the Industrial Commission of Wisconsin 1913-1917; engaged in agricultural pursuits and in stock raising near Viroqua, Vernon County, in 1917; elected as a Republican to the Sixty-seventh and to the three succeeding Congresses (March 4, 1921-March 3, 1929); was not a candidate for renomination in 1928 to the Seventy-first Congress, but was an unsuccessful candidate for nomination for Governor of Wisconsin; resumed agricultural pursuits; appointed a member of the State department of agriculture and markets in 1931 and served until his death in Madison, Wis., November 8, 1936; interment in Viroqua Cemetery, Viroqua, Wis.

**BECKER, Frank John,** a Representative from New York; born in Brooklyn, N.Y., August 27, 1899; moved with his parents to Lynbrook, Nassau County, L.I., in November 1905; attended the public schools of Lynbrook and Brown's Business College, Jamaica, L.I.; during the First World War enlisted in the United States Army July 22, 1918, and served overseas in France and England; was discharged from the service on September 22, 1919; engaged in the insurance business in Lynbrook, N.Y.; member of the State assembly of New York 1945-1953; director and later chairman of board of Suburbia Federal Savings & Loan Association; delegate to each Republican National Convention from 1952 to 1964; elected as a Republican to the Eighty-third and to the five succeeding Congresses (January 3, 1953-January 3, 1965); was not a candidate for renomination in 1964 to the Eighty-ninth Congress; president of a real-estate and insurance company; resided in Lynbrook, N.Y., where he died September 4, 1981; interment in Pine Lawn National Cemetery, Pinelawn, N.Y.

**BECKHAM, John Crepps Wickliffe** (grandson of Charles Anderson Wickliffe and cousin of Robert Charles Wickliffe), a Senator from Kentucky; born in Wickland, near Bardstown, Nelson County, Ky., August 5, 1869; attended the Roseland Academy at Bardstown and Central University, Richmond, Ky.; high school principal; studied law; was admitted to the bar in 1889 and commenced practice in Bardstown in 1893; member, Kentucky house of representatives 1894-1898, serving as speaker in 1898; lieutenant governor of Kentucky in 1899, becoming chief executive of Kentucky on February 3, 1900, upon the death of Governor William Goebel; subsequently elected Governor for the unexpired term ending December 8, 1903, and reelected in 1903 for the term ending December 10, 1907; elected as a Democrat to the United States Senate in 1914 and served from March 4, 1915 to March 3, 1921; unsuccessful candidate for reelection in 1920; chairman, Committee on Expenditures in the Department of Labor (Sixty-fourth and Sixty-fifth Congresses); resumed the practice of law in Louisville, Ky.; unsuccessful candidate for election in 1927 for Governor of Kentucky; unsuccessful candidate in 1936 for nomination to the United States Senate; died in Louisville, Ky., January 9, 1940; interment in Frankfort Cemetery, Frankfort, Ky.

**Bibliography:** Finch, Glenn. "The Election of United States Senators in Kentucky: The Beckham Period." *Filson Club History Quarterly* 44 (January 1970): 38-50.

**BECKNER, William Morgan,** a Representative from Kentucky; born in Moorefield, Nichols County, Ky., June 19, 1841; attended the public schools, Rand and Richeson Seminary, Maysville, Ky., and Centre College, Danville, Ky.; worked on a farm and was subsequently a clerk in a country store at Bethel, Bath County, Ky.; became a private tutor and taught school for two years in Orangeburg and Maysville; studied law; was admitted to the bar in 1864 and commenced practice in Winchester, Ky.; city judge in 1865; served as prosecuting attorney in 1866 and 1867; was elected judge of Clark County in 1870; established the Clark County Democrat in 1867, which he owned and edited for a number of years; appointed State prison commissioner in 1880; served as Kentucky railroad commissioner from 1882 until 1884, when he resigned; president of the interstate educational conventions held in Louisville in 1883 and 1885; member of the Kentucky constitutional convention in 1890; member of the Kentucky house of representatives in 1893; chairman of the Kentucky Democratic convention in 1893; elected as a Democrat to the Fifty-third Congress to fill the vacancy caused by the death of Marcus C. Lisle, and served from December 3, 1894 to March 3, 1895; unsuccessful candidate for renomination in 1894 to the Fifty-fourth Congress; resumed the practice of law; died in Winchester, Ky., March 14, 1910; interment in Winchester Cemetery.

**BECKWITH, Charles Dyer,** a Representative from New Jersey; born near Coveville, Saratoga County, N.Y., October 22, 1838; attended private schools in Troy, N.Y., Philadelphia, Pa., Worcester, Mass., and a military institution in New Haven, Conn.; moved to Paterson, Passaic County, N.J., in 1860 and engaged in the manufacture of iron; member of the board of aldermen in 1882; mayor of Paterson, N.J., 1885-1889; elected as a Republican to the Fifty-first Congress (March 4, 1889-March 3, 1891); unsuccessful candidate for reelection in 1890 to the Fifty-second Congress; resumed manufacturing pursuits; returned to the State of New York and settled on a farm in the town of Chatham, Columbia County, in 1897 and engaged in the management of his farm until his death near Chatham Center, Columbia County, N.Y., on March 27, 1921; interment in Chatham Center Rural Cemetery.

**BECKWORTH, Lindley Garrison, Sr.,** a Representative from Texas; born on a farm in the South Bouie community near Mabank, Kaufman County, Tex., June 30, 1913; attended the rural schools, Abilene Christian College, East Texas State Teachers College, Commerce, Tex., Sam Houston State Teachers College, Huntsville, Tex., and Southern Methodist University, Dallas, Tex.; taught school in Upshur County, Tex, for three years; attended the law department of Baylor University, Waco, Tex., and the University of Texas at Austin; was admitted to the bar in 1937 and commenced practice in Gilmer, Tex.; member of the State house of representatives 1936-1938; elected as a Democrat to the Seventy-sixth and to the six succeeding Congresses (January 3, 1939-January 3, 1953); was not a candidate for renomination in 1952, but was unsuccessful for the Democratic nomination for United States Senator; resumed the practice of law in Longview, Tex.; elected to the Eighty-fifth and to the four succeeding Congresses (January 3, 1957-January 3, 1967); unsuccessful candidate for renomination in 1966; judge, United States Custom Court, New York City, 1967-1968; resumed the practice of law; was a resident of Upshur County, Gladewater, Tex. until his death at Tyler, March 9, 1984; interment in Rose Hill Cemetery, Tyler, Tex.

**BEDE, James Adam,** a Representative from Minnesota; born on a farm in North Eaton Township, Lorain County, Ohio, January 13, 1856; attended the public schools of Ohio, Oberlin (Ohio) College, and Tabor (Iowa) College; read law while learning the printing trade; taught school in Iowa, Ohio, and Arkansas; editor and publisher of several newspapers and periodicals; served as a representative for several western newspapers in Washington, D.C.,

1888-1891; engaged in newspaper work at Pine City, Pine County, Minn.; served as United States marshal for the district of Minnesota in 1894 during the great railway strike; elected as a Republican to the Fifty-eighth, Fifty-ninth, and Sixtieth Congresses (March 4, 1903-March 3, 1909); unsuccessful candidate for renomination in 1908 to the Sixty-first Congress; returned to Pine City; engaged as a publisher and lecturer; moved to Duluth, Minn., in 1927 and engaged in his former pursuits; also was interested in the St. Lawrence inland waterway project; died in Duluth, Minn., April 11, 1942; interment in Birchwood Cemetery, Pine City, Minn.

**BEDELL, Berkley Warren,** a Representative from Iowa; born in Spirit Lake, Dickinson County, Iowa, March 5, 1921; educated in Spirit Lake public schools; graduated, Spirit Lake High School, 1939; attended Iowa State University, Ames, 1940-1942; engaged in fishing tackle business; founder and chairman of Berkley & Co., Spirit Lake; served in United States Army, first lieutenant, 1942-1945; member, Spirit Lake Board of Education, 1957-1962; unsuccessful candidate for election in 1972 to the Ninety-third Congress; delegate to Iowa State Democratic conventions, 1972-1974; elected as a Democrat to the Ninety-fourth and to the five succeeding Congresses (January 3, 1975-January 3, 1987); was not a candidate for reelection in 1986 to the One Hundredth Congress; is a resident of Spirit Lake, Iowa.

**BEDFORD, Gunning** (cousin of Gunning Bedford, Jr.), a Delegate from Delaware; born in Philadelphia, Pa., April 7, 1742; became a major in the Continental Army in 1775; lieutenant colonel in Haslet's Regiment, being wounded in the Battle of White Plains, N.Y., October 28, 1776; subsequently appointed muster-master-general in 1776; was admitted to the bar in 1779; member of the Delaware general assembly from New Castle County 1784-1786; elected a Member of the Continental Congress for the term 1786-1787 but declined to serve and resigned January 15, 1787; member of the Delaware convention in 1787 which ratified the Federal Constitution; elected Governor of Delaware in 1796, and served from January 13, 1796 until his death in New Castle, Del., September 28, 1797; interment in Immanuel Churchyard.

**Bibliography:** *DAB*.

**BEDFORD, Gunning, Jr.** (cousin of Gunning Bedford), a Delegate from Delaware; born in Philadelphia, Pa., in 1747; was graduated from Princeton College in 1771; studied law in Philadelphia; was admitted to the Delaware bar in 1779 and commenced practice in Dover, Del.; moved to Wilmington, Del.; Member of the Continental Congress 1783-1785; appointed attorney general of the State on April 26, 1784, and served until September 26, 1789; appointed a commissioner to the convention held at Annapolis, Md., in September 1786 but did not attend; member of the Federal constitutional convention at Philadelphia in 1787 and signed the Constitution; delegate to the State convention that ratified the Federal Constitution in 1787; member of the State senate in 1788; appointed on September 24, 1789, by President Washington as United States judge for the district of Delaware, which position he held until his death in Wilmington, Del., March 30, 1812; interment in First Presbyterian Churchyard; reinterment at the Masonic Home of Delaware, on Lancaster Pike, two miles west of Wilmington, Del.

**Bibliography:** *DAB*.

**BEDINGER, George Michael** (uncle of Henry Bedinger), a Representative from Kentucky; born in Hanover, York County, Pa., December 10, 1756; attended an English school; moved to Virginia about 1762 and to Kentucky in 1779 and settled at Boonesborough; adjutant in the expedition against Chillicothe in May 1779; major in the Battle of Blue Licks, August 19, 1782; major in Drake's Regiment in 1791; major commanding the Winchester Battalion of

Sharpshooters in the St. Clair expedition in 1791; major commanding the Third Sublegion of the United States Infantry from April 11, 1792, to February 28, 1793; member of the house of representatives of the first legislature of Kentucky in 1792; served in the Kentucky senate in 1800 and 1801; elected as a Republican to the Eighth and Ninth Congresses (March 4, 1803-March 3, 1807); engaged in agricultural pursuits; died at Blue Licks Springs, Ky., December 7, 1843; interment in the family cemetery on his farm near Lower Blue Licks Springs, Ky.

Bibliography: *DAB*; Talbert, Charles G. "George Michael Bedinger 1756-1843." *Register of the Kentucky Historical Society* 65 (January 1967): 28-46.

**BEDINGER, Henry** (nephew of George Michael Bedinger), a Representative from Virginia; born near Shepherdstown, Jefferson County, Va. (now West Virginia), February 3, 1812; attended the common schools; studied law; was admitted to the bar in 1832 and commenced practice in Shepherdstown; moved to Charlestown, Va., and continued the practice of law; elected as a Democrat to the Twenty-ninth and Thirtieth Congresses (March 4, 1845-March 3, 1849); was an unsuccessful candidate for reelection in 1848 to the Thirty-first Congress; resumed the practice of law; appointed Chargé d'Affaires to Denmark on May 24, 1853, and Minister Resident June 29, 1854, in which capacity he served until he presented his recall on August 10, 1858; had been nominated as Envoy Extraordinary and Minister Plenipotentiary on February 25, 1856, but his nomination was withdrawn before the Senate could act upon it; died in Shepherdstown, W.Va., November 26, 1858; interment in Elmwood Cemetery.

Bibliography: Levin, Alexandra Lee. "Henry Bedinger of Virginia: First United States Minister to Denmark." *Virginia Cavalcade* 29 (Spring 1980): 184-191.

**BEE, Carlos** (great-grandson of Thomas Bee), a Representative from Texas; born in Saltillo, Mexico, July 8, 1867, where his parents had moved after the collapse of the Confederacy; returned with his parents to San Antonio, Tex., in 1874; attended the public schools and the Agricultural and Mechanical College; studied law while working as a railway mail clerk; was admitted to the bar in 1893 and commenced practice in San Antonio, Tex.; United States commissioner for the western district of Texas in 1893; district attorney of the thirty-seventh judicial district 1898-1905; chairman of the Democratic State convention in 1904; delegate to the Democratic National Convention in 1904 and 1908; served as a member of the city school board of San Antonio 1906-1908; president of the county school board of Bexar County, Tex., 1912-1914; member of the State senate 1915-1919; elected as a Democrat to the Sixty-sixth Congress (March 4, 1919-March 3, 1921); unsuccessful candidate for reelection in 1920 to the Sixty-seventh Congress; engaged in the practice of law in San Antonio, Tex., until his death there on April 20, 1932; interment in the Confederate Cemetery.

**BEE, Thomas** (great-grandfather of Carlos Bee), a Delegate from South Carolina; born in Charleston, S.C., in 1725; educated in Charleston, and later at Oxford University, England; studied law; was admitted to the bar at Charleston, S.C., January 27, 1761, and practiced there; also engaged in planting; member of Commons House, Province of South Carolina, for St. Pauls, 1762-1764, for St. Peters in 1765, and for St. Andrews, 1772-1776; justice of the peace in 1775; Delegate to the First and Second Provincial Congresses in 1775 and 1776; member of the South Carolina State house of representatives, 1776-1779, and 1782, serving as speaker from 1777 to 1779; took an active part in the Revolution and was a member of the council of safety in 1775 and 1776; law judge, 1776-1778; member of the State legislative council, 1776-1778; lieutenant governor of South Carolina in 1779 and 1780; Member of the Continental Congress, 1780-1782; appointed judge of the United States Court for the District of South Carolina by President

Washington on June 14, 1790; published reports of the district court of South Carolina in 1810; died in Pendleton, S.C., February 18, 1812; interment in Woodstock Cemetery, Goose Creek, S.C.

**BEEBE, George Monroe,** a Representative from New York; born in New Vernon, Orange County, N.Y., October 28, 1836; attended the common schools, and Walkill Academy, Middletown, N.Y.; studied law and was graduated from the Albany Law University in 1857; was admitted to the bar the same year and commenced practice in Monticello, Sullivan County, N.Y.; moved to Peoria, Ill., in 1857 and became editor of the Central Illinois Democrat; moved to Troy, Doniphan County, Territory of Kansas, in 1858 and continued the practice of law; member of the Territorial council in 1858 and 1859; appointed by President James Buchanan as secretary of the Territory in 1859; Acting Governor in 1860 and 1861; moved to St. Joseph, Mo., in 1861 and to Virginia City, Nev., in 1863, continuing the practice of his profession; unsuccessful candidate for associate judge of the State supreme court in 1865; returned to Monticello, N.Y., and became editor of the Republican Watchman in 1866; unsuccessful candidate for the State senate in 1871; member of the State assembly in 1872 and 1873; commissioned by Governor John A. Dix as chief of artillery with the rank of colonel in the Fifth Division, National Guard of New York, in 1873; resigned in 1874 to enter Congress; elected as a Democrat to the Forty-fourth and Forty-fifth Congresses (March 4, 1875-March 3, 1879); chairman, Committee on Expenditures in the Department of the Navy (Forty-fourth Congress), Committee on Mines and Mining (Forty-fifth Congress); unsuccessful candidate for reelection in 1878 to the Forty-sixth Congress; resumed his former newspaper pursuits; delegate to the Democratic National Conventions of 1876, 1880 and 1892; member of the State court of claims from 1883 until 1900; resided at Monticello until 1892 when he moved to Ellenville, N.Y.; retired from active business pursuits in 1900; died in Ellenville, Ulster County, N.Y., on March 1, 1927; interment in Woodlawn Cemetery, Newburgh, N.Y.

**BEECHER, Philemon,** a Representative from Ohio; born in Kent, Litchfield County, Conn., in 1775; received a classical education; studied law; was admitted to the bar and practiced; moved to Lancaster, Ohio, in 1801 and continued the practice of law; member of the State house of representatives in 1803 and 1805-1807, serving as speaker in 1807; unsuccessful candidate in 1807 for election to the United States Senate, and also as judge of the Ohio Supreme Court; major general in the State militia; elected to the Fifteenth and Sixteenth Congresses (March 4, 1817-March 3, 1821); unsuccessful candidate for reelection in 1820 to the Seventeenth Congress; elected to the Eighteenth, Nineteenth, and Twentieth Congresses (March 4, 1823-March 3, 1829); unsuccessful candidate for reelection in 1828 to the Twenty-first Congress; engaged in the practice of law in Lancaster, Fairfield County, Ohio, until his death there November 30, 1839; interment in Elmwood Cemetery.

**BEEDY, Carroll Lynwood,** a Representative from Maine; born in Phillips, Franklin County, Maine, August 3, 1880; attended the public schools of Lewiston, Androscoggin County, Maine; was graduated from Bates College, Lewiston, Maine, in 1903 and from the law department of Yale University in 1906; was admitted to the bar in 1907 and commenced practice in Portland, Maine; prosecuting attorney of Cumberland County 1917-1921; elected as a Republican to the Sixty-seventh and to the six succeeding Congresses (March 4, 1921-January 3, 1935); chairman, Committee on Mileage (Sixty-eighth and Sixty-ninth Congresses), Committee on Expenditures in the Department of Labor (Sixty-ninth Congress), Committee on Elections No. 1 (Seventieth and Seventy-first Congresses); unsuccessful candidate for reelection in 1934 to the Seventy-fourth Congress; engaged in the practice of law in

Washington, D.C., until his death there August 30, 1947; interment in Evergreen Cemetery, Portland, Maine.

**BEEKMAN, Thomas,** a Representative from New York; born in Wayne County, N.Y.; town clerk of Smithfield, N.Y., in 1824; elected to the Twenty-first Congress (March 4, 1829-March 3, 1831); died in Peterboro, N.Y.

**BEEMAN, Joseph Henry,** a Representative from Mississippi; born near Gatesville, Gates County, N.C., November 17, 1833; moved with his parents to Morgan County, Ala., in 1847 and to Mississippi in 1849; received an academic education; taught school for several years; engaged in mercantile pursuits; served as a lieutenant in the Confederate Army during the Civil War; member of the State house of representatives 1883-1891; connected with the Farmers' Alliance and served as chairman of its executive committee; delegate to several State conventions; elected as a Democrat to the Fifty-second Congress (March 4, 1891-March 3, 1893); was not a candidate for reelection in 1892; engaged in agricultural pursuits until his death near Lena, Scott County, Miss., July 31, 1909; interment in Beeman Cemetery, Lena, Miss.

**BEERMANN, Ralph Frederick,** a Representative from Nebraska; born near Dakota City, Dakota County, Nebr., August 13, 1912; attended public schools, South Sioux City, Nebr.; Morningside College, Sioux City, Iowa, and Army specialist schools; during the Second World War served in the United States Army for three years in African-European Theaters in the Six Hundred and First Ordnance Battalion, Three Hundred and First Ordnance Regiment; engaged in partnership with six brothers (Beermann Bros.) in farming, cattle feeding, and alfalfa dehydrating in Dakota County, Nebr.; chairman of Dakota County Republican Central Committee for ten years; organized Dakota County Young Republicans; elected as a Republican to the Eighty-seventh and to the Eighty-eighth Congresses (January 3, 1961-January 3, 1965); unsuccessful candidate in 1964 for reelection to the Eighty-ninth Congress; resumed business pursuits; died in an airplane crash at Sioux City Municipal Airport, Iowa, February 17, 1977; interment in Dakota City Cemetery, Dakota City, Nebr.

**BEERS, Cyrus,** a Representative from New York; born in Newtown, Conn., June 21, 1786; moved with his parents to New York City; obtained a limited education in the public schools; engaged in mercantile pursuits and also in the lumber business; moved to Ithaca, N.Y., in 1821 and engaged in the mercantile business; delegate to the Democratic State convention at Herkimer in 1830; appointed commissioner of deeds at Ithaca in 1837; elected as a Democrat to the Twenty-fifth Congress to fill the vacancy caused by the death of Andrew D. W. Bruyn and served from December 3, 1838, to March 3, 1839; was not a candidate for renomination in 1838; delegate to the New York and Erie Railroad Convention at Ithaca in 1839; resumed his former business pursuits in Ithaca, Tompkins County, N.Y., where he died June 5, 1850, interment in the City Cemetery.

**BEERS, Edward McMath,** a Representative from Pennsylvania; born in Nossville, Huntingdon County, Pa., May 27, 1877; attended the public schools; moved with his parents to Mount Union, Pa., in 1889; was graduated from Mount Union High School in 1895; upon the death of his father, succeeded him in the hotel business in 1895; also interested in agricultural pursuits; delegate to the Pennsylvania Republican convention at Harrisburg in 1898; mayor of Mount Union 1910-1914; member of the board of directors of the First National Bank of Mount Union and of the Grange Trust Co. of Huntingdon, Pa.; associate judge of Huntingdon County 1914-1923; elected as a Republican to the Sixty-eighth and to the four succeeding Congresses and served from March 4, 1923, until his death in Washington, D.C., on April 21, 1932; interment in the Odd Fellows' Cemetery, Mount Union, Pa.

**BEESON, Henry White,** a Representative from Pennsylvania; born in Uniontown, Fayette County, Pa., September 14, 1791; attended the public schools; engaged in agricultural pursuits; colonel in the Fayette County Militia; elected as a Democrat to the Twenty-seventh Congress to fill the vacancy caused by the resignation of Enos Hook and served from May 31, 1841, to March 3, 1843; unsuccessful candidate for reelection in 1842 to the Twenty-eighth Congress; resumed agricultural pursuits; died in North Union Township, near Uniontown, Pa., October 28, 1863; interment in Oak Hill Cemetery.

**BEGG, James Thomas,** a Representative from Ohio; born on a farm near Lima, Allen County, Ohio, February 16, 1877; attended the public and high schools of Columbus Grove, and Lima (Ohio) College; was graduated from the Wooster (Ohio) University in 1903; taught school; superintendent of public schools at Columbus Grove 1905-1910, at Ironton, Ohio, 1910-1913, and at Sandusky, Ohio, 1913-1917; employed as a campaign director and lectured throughout the United States for the American City Bureau of New York in chamber of commerce work 1917-1919; elected as a Republican to the Sixty-sixth and to the four succeeding Congresses (March 4, 1919-March 3, 1929); was not a candidate for renomination in 1928 to the Seventy-first Congress; engaged in the banking business; unsuccessful candidate for election in 1942 to the Seventy-eighth Congress; business consultant and dairy farmer; moved to Oklahoma City, Okla., in 1959, where he resided until his death on March 26, 1963; interment in Garfield-Lakeview Cemetery, Cleveland, Ohio.

**BEGICH, Nicholas Joseph,** a Representative from Alaska; born in Eveleth, Saint Louis County, Minn., April 6, 1932; attended the Eveleth public schools and Eveleth Junior College; B.A., St. Cloud (Minn.) State College, 1952; M.A., University of Minnesota, Minneapolis, 1954; doctoral work at the Universities of Colorado and North Dakota; high school instructor, counselor and director, student personnel, 1952-1959; principal and superintendent, Fort Richardson Schools, Alaska, 1959-1968; part-time instructor, University of Alaska, Anchorage branch, 1956-1968; builder and manager of apartment houses in Anchorage, beginning in 1968; Alaska State senator, 1963-1971, serving as minority whip from 1967; elected as a Democrat to the Ninety-second and Ninety-third Congresses; disappeared while on a campaign flight from Anchorage to Juneau, Alaska, October 16, 1972; served from January 3, 1971, until December 29, 1972, at which time a presumptive death certificate was recorded in the State of Alaska.

**BEGOLE, Josiah Williams,** a Representative from Michigan; born in Groveland, Livingston County, N.Y., January 20, 1815; attended the public schools in Mount Morris and Temple Hill Academy, Geneseo, N.Y.; moved to Flint, Genesee County, Mich., in August 1836; taught school in 1837 and 1838; engaged in agricultural pursuits from 1839 to 1856; school inspector; justice of the peace and township treasurer; county treasurer 1856-1864; engaged in the lumber business in 1863; member of the State senate in 1870 and 1871; member of the city council for three years; delegate to the Republican National Convention of 1872; elected as a Republican to the Forty-third Congress (March 4, 1873-March 3, 1875); was an unsuccessful candidate for reelection in 1874 to the Forty-fourth Congress; resumed the lumber business and later engaged in the manufacture of wagons; also engaged in banking; elected Governor of Michigan in 1882 and served from January 1, 1883 to January 1, 1885; unsuccessful candidate for reelection in 1884 for Governor; resumed his former business activities; died in Flint, Mich., on June 5, 1896; interment in Glenwood Cemetery.

**BEIDLER, Jacob Atlee,** a Representative from Ohio; born in Tredyffrin Township, near Valley Forge, Chester County, Pa., November 2, 1852; attended the country schools, and Locke's Seminary, Norristown, Pa.; moved to Ohio and settled in Willoughby,

Lake County, in 1873; engaged in business as a coal dealer and later as an operator; elected a member of the city council of Willoughby in 1881; moved to his farm, "Belle Vernon," near Willoughby, in 1881 and engaged in raising dairy cattle; president of the Belle Vernon-Mapes Dairy Co.; vice president of the Cleveland, Painesville & Eastern Railroad Co.; elected as a Republican to the Fifty-seventh, Fifty-eighth, and Fifty-ninth Congresses (March 4, 1901-March 3, 1907); owing to ill health declined to be a candidate for renomination in 1906 to the Sixtieth Congress; resumed his former business activities; president of the Rhodes & Beidler Coal Co.; member of the State board of agriculture; died at "Belle Vernon," near Willoughby, Lake County, Ohio, September 13, 1912; interment in Lake View Cemetery, Cleveland, Ohio.

**BEILENSON, Anthony Charles,** a Representative from California; born in New Rochelle, Westchester County, N.Y., October 26, 1932; attended schools in Mt. Vernon, N.Y.; graduated, Phillips Academy, Andover, Mass., 1950; B.A., Harvard University, 1954; LL.B., Harvard University Law School, 1957; admitted to the California Bar in 1957 and commenced practice in Beverly Hills; counsel, California State assembly Committee on Finance and Insurance, 1960; served in California State assembly, 1963-1966; California State senate, 1967-1976; elected as a Democrat to the Ninety-fifth and to the nine succeeding Congresses (January 3, 1977-January 3, 1997); chairman, Permanent Select Committee on Intelligence (One Hundred First Congresss); was not a candidate for reelection in 1996 to the One Hundred Fifth Congress; is a resident of Woodland Hills, Calif.

**BEIRNE, Andrew,** a Representative from Virginia; born Andrew O'Beirne in Dangan, County Roscommon, Ireland, in 1771; received a classical education and was graduated from Trinity University, Dublin, Ireland; immigrated to the United States in 1793 and settled in Union, Monroe County, Va.; engaged in mercantile and agricultural pursuits; member of the Virginia house of delegates in 1807 and 1808; during the War of 1812 served as captain of a rifle company and as colonel of the Monroe County Militia; delegate to the Virginia constitutional convention in 1829 and 1830; member of the Virginia senate, 1831-1836; elected as a Democrat to the Twenty-fifth and Twenty-sixth Congresses (March 4, 1837-March 3, 1841); was not a candidate for reelection in 1840 to the Twenty-seventh Congress; resumed his former business activities; died while on a visit in Gainesville, Sumter County, Ala., March 16, 1845; interment in the family burying ground at Union, Monroe County, Va. (now West Virginia).
**Bibliography:** White, Edward T. "Andrew and Oliver Beirne of Monroe County." *West Virginia History* 20 (October 1958): 14-23.

**BEITER, Alfred Florian,** a Representative from New York; born in Clarence, Erie County, N.Y., July 7, 1894; attended elementary schools, Williamsville (N.Y.) High School, and Niagara University, Niagara Falls, N.Y.; moved to Williamsville, N.Y., and engaged in the general merchandising business from 1915 to 1929; supervisor of the town of Amherst, N.Y., 1930-1934; elected as a Democrat to the Seventy-third and to the two succeeding Congresses (March 4, 1933-January 3, 1939); chairman, Committee on War Claims (Seventy-fifth Congress); unsuccessful candidate for reelection in 1938 to the Seventy-sixth Congress; assistant to Secretary of the Interior Harold L. Ickes, 1939-1940; elected to the Seventy-seventh Congress (January 3, 1941-January 3, 1943); unsuccessful candidate for reelection in 1942 to the Seventy-eight Congress; owned and operated a hatchery and feed business in Buffalo, N.Y., 1944-1948; president of the National Customs Service Association, 1949-1961; Deputy Commissioner of Customs, Treasury Department, Washington, D.C., 1961-1964; retired and resided in Boca Raton, Fla., where he died on March 11, 1974; interment in Boca Raton Cemetery.

**BELCHER, Hiram,** a Representative from Maine; born in Hallowell, Maine, February 23, 1790; attended the rural schools and the local academy at Hallowell 1805-1807; studied law; was admitted to the bar and commenced practice in Farmington, Kennebec County, Maine, in 1812; elected town clerk of Farmington and served from 1814 to 1819; member of the State house of representatives in 1822, 1829, and 1832; served in the State senate in 1838 and 1839; elected as a Whig to the Thirtieth Congress (March 4, 1847-March 3, 1849); chairman, Committee on Mileage (Thirtieth Congress); was not a candidate for reelection in 1848 to the Thirty-first Congress; engaged in the practice of his profession until his death in Farmington, Maine, May 6, 1857; interment in Center Meeting House Cemetery.

**BELCHER, Nathan,** a Representative from Connecticut; born in Preston (now a part of Griswold), Conn., June 23, 1813; completed academic studies; was graduated from Amherst (Mass.) College in 1832; studied law at the Cambridge Law School; was admitted to the bar in 1836 and commenced practice in Clinton, Conn.; moved in 1841 to New London, where he engaged in manufacturing tools, hardware, and kitchen utensils; member of the State house of representatives 1846 and 1847; served in the State senate in 1850; elected as a Democrat to the Thirty-third Congress (March 4, 1853-March 3, 1855); was not a candidate for renomination in 1854; resumed his former manufacturing pursuits; also engaged in banking; died in New London, New London County, Conn., June 2, 1891; interment in Cedar Grove Cemetery.

**BELCHER, Page Henry,** a Representative from Oklahoma; born in Jefferson, Grant County, Okla., April 21, 1899, on the claim his father took in the opening of the Cherokee Strip; attended high school at Jefferson and Medford, Okla.; student at Friends University, Wichita, Kans., and the University of Oklahoma at Norman; veteran of the First World War; court clerk of Garfield County, Okla., 1934-1938; studied law, was admitted to the bar in 1936 and commenced the practice of law in Enid, Okla.; municipal judge, Enid, Okla., in 1938; eighth district chairman, ten years; State executive secretary of Republican Party; secretary to Representative Ross Rizley in 1941; member of Enid Board of Education; elected as a Republican to the Eighty-second and to the ten succeeding Congresses (January 3, 1951-January 3, 1973); was not a candidate for renomination in 1972 to the Ninety-third Congress; was a resident of Midwest City, Okla., where he died August 2, 1980; interment in Memorial Park Cemetery, Enid, Okla.

**BELDEN, George Ogilvie,** a Representative from New York; born in Norwalk, Conn., March 28, 1797; attended the public schools; studied law with Charles Baker, of Bloomingburg, N.Y.; was admitted to the bar and practiced in Monticello, Sullivan County, N.Y.; elected to the Twentieth Congress (March 4, 1827-March 3, 1829); resumed the practice of law; served as general of the Twenty-third Brigade of Infantry of the State of New York in 1831; died in Monticello, Sullivan County, N.Y., October 9, 1833; interment in the Old Cemetery on St. John Street.

**BELDEN, James Jerome,** a Representative from New York; born in Fabius, Onondaga County, N.Y., September 30, 1825; attended the common schools; engaged in the banking business at Syracuse, N.Y., in 1880; also interested in the construction of railroads and public works; served as mayor of Syracuse, N.Y., in 1877 and 1878; elected as a Republican to the Fiftieth Congress to fill the vacancy caused by the resignation of Frank Hiscock; reelected to the Fifty-first, Fifty-second, and Fifty-third Congresses and served from November 8, 1887, to March 3, 1895; was not a candidate for renomination in 1894; elected to the Fifty-fifth Congress (March 4, 1897-March 3, 1899); was not a candidate for renomination in 1898; died in Syracuse, Onondaga County, N.Y., January 1, 1904; interment in Oakwood Cemetery.

**BELFORD, James Burns** (cousin of Joseph McCrum Belford), a Representative from Colorado; born in Lewistown, Mifflin County, Pa., September 28, 1837; attended the common schools and Dickinson College, Carlisle, Pa.; studied law; was admitted to the bar in 1859; moved to California, Moniteau County, Mo., and commenced practice; moved to La Porte, La Porte County, Ind., in 1860; member of the State house of representatives in 1867; appointed an associate justice of the supreme court of Colorado in 1870 and moved to Central City; moved to Denver in 1883; upon the admission of Colorado as a State into the Union was elected as a Republican to the Forty-fourth Congress and served from October 3, 1876, until March 3, 1877; presented credentials as a Member-elect to the Forty-fifth Congress and served from March 4, 1877, until December 13, 1877, when he was succeeded by Thomas M. Patterson, who contested his election; elected to the Forty-sixth, Forty-seventh, and Forty-eighth Congresses (March 4, 1879-March 3, 1885); chairman, Committee on Expenditures in the Department of the Treasury (Forty-seventh Congress); unsuccessful candidate for renomination in 1884; engaged in the practice of law in Denver, Colo., until his death there January 10, 1910; interment in Riverside Cemetery.

**BELFORD, Joseph McCrum** (cousin of James Burns Belford), a Representative from New York; born in Mifflintown, Juniata County, Pa., August 5, 1852; attended Dickinson Seminary, Williamsport, Pa., and was graduated from Dickinson College, Carlisle, Pa., in 1871; moved to Long Island, N.Y., in 1884 and engaged in teaching at the Franklinville and Riverhead Academies; studied law; was admitted to the bar in 1889 and commenced the practice of law in Riverhead, Long Island, N.Y.; served as secretary and chairman of the Suffolk County Republican committee; clerk of the surrogate court; elected as a Republican to the Fifty-fifth Congress (March 4, 1897-March 3, 1899); was not a candidate for renomination in 1898 to the Fifty-sixth Congress; delegate to the Republican National Convention at Philadelphia in 1900; resumed the practice of his chosen profession in Riverhead, Suffolk County, Long Island, N.Y.; also engaged in the banking business; served as surrogate of Suffolk County from 1904 to 1910; died suddenly in Grand Central Station, New York City, May 3, 1917; interment in Riverhead Cemetery, Riverhead, Long Island, N.Y.

**BELKNAP, Charles Eugene,** a Representative from Michigan; born in Massena, St. Lawrence County, N.Y., October 17, 1846; moved with his parents to Grand Rapids, Mich., in 1855; attended the common schools; left school August 14, 1862, and enlisted in the Twenty-first Regiment, Michigan Volunteer Infantry; received a captain's commission January 8, 1864; brevet major August 1864; brevet lieutenant colonel June 1865; served until June 1865 with the Army of the Cumberland; engaged in the manufacture of wagons and sleighs in 1871; member of the board of education of Grand Rapids 1871-1878; served on the board of aldermen 1880-1882; elected mayor of Grand Rapids in 1884; trustee of the State institution for the deaf 1885-1891; president of the State hospital board 1905-1915; elected as a Republican to the Fifty-first Congress (March 4, 1889-March 3, 1891); was not a candidate for renomination in 1890, but was subsequently nominated and elected to the Fifty-second Congress to fill the vacancy caused by the death of Melbourne H. Ford and served from November 3, 1891, to March 3, 1893; unsuccessfully contested the election of George F. Richardson to the Fifty-third Congress; resumed the manufacture of wagons and sleighs; served on staff duty at Fort Oglethorpe during the Spanish-American War; died in Grand Rapids, Mich., January 16, 1929; interment in the Greenwood Cemetery.

**BELKNAP, Hugh Reid,** a Representative from Illinois; born in Keokuk, Lee County, Iowa, September 1, 1860; attended the public schools, Adams Academy, Quincy, Mass., and Phillips Academy, Andover, Mass.; at the age of eighteen entered the service of the Baltimore & Ohio Railroad Co. and worked in various capacities until he retired in 1892 to become superintendent of the South Side Rapid Transit Railroad of Chicago; successfully contested as a Republican the election of Lawrence E. McGann to the Fifty-fourth Congress; reelected to the Fifty-fifth Congress and served from December 27, 1895, to March 3, 1899; unsuccessful candidate for reelection in 1898 to the Fifty-sixth Congress; resided in Chicago, Ill., until 1901; appointed a paymaster in the United States Army with the rank of major and served from February 2, 1901, until his death in Calamba, Laguna, P.I., November 12, 1901; interment in Arlington National Cemetery, Va.

**BELL, Alphonzo,** a Representative from Calfornia; born in Los Angeles, Calif., September 19, 1914; attended Hawthorne Grammar and Webb schools; B.A., Occidental College, Los Angeles, Calif., 1938; served in the Army Air Corps, 1942-1945; engaged in ranching, real-estate and petroleum interests; president of Bell Petroleum Co., 1947-1960; chairman of the board of Bell Petroleum Co., since 1960; chairman of the Republican State Central Committee of California and member of the Republican National Committee, 1956-1959; chairman of the Republican Central Committee of Los Angeles County, 1958-1960; elected as a Republican to the Eighty-seventh and to the seven succeeding Congresses (January 3, 1961-January 3, 1977); was not a candidate in 1976 for reelection to the House of Representatives, but was an unsuccessful candidate for nomination to the United States Senate; owner and president of Bar-Bell Farms, Inc.; is a resident of Fallon, Nev.

**BELL, Charles Henry** (nephew of Samuel Bell and cousin of James Bell), a Senator from New Hampshire; born in Chester, Rockingham County, N.H., November 18, 1823; was graduated from Dartmouth College, Hanover, N.H., in 1844; studied law; was admitted to the bar and practiced in Chester, Great Falls, and Exeter, N.H.; county solicitor for ten years; member, State house of representatives 1858-1860, serving as speaker in 1860; member, State senate 1863-1864, serving as president in 1864; appointed as a Republican to the United States Senate to fill the vacancy in the term beginning March 4, 1879, and served from March 13, 1879, to June 18, 1879, when a successor was elected; was not a candidate for election to the Senate in 1879; resumed the practice of law at Exeter and also engaged in literary pursuits; elected Governor of New Hampshire in 1880 and served from June 2, 1881 to June 7, 1883; president of the State constitutional convention in 1889; president of the New Hampshire Historical Society 1868-1887; died in Exeter, Rockingham County, N.H., November 11, 1893; interment in Exeter Cemetery.

**Bibliography:** *DAB.*

**BELL, Charles Jasper,** a Representative from Missouri; born in Lake City, Hinsdale County, Colo., January 16, 1885; attended the country schools in Jackson County, Mo., Lees Summit (Mo.) High School, and the University of Missouri at Columbia; was graduated from Kansas City (Mo.) School of Law in 1913; was admitted to the bar the same year and commenced practice in Kansas City, Mo.; member of the city council of Kansas City 1926-1930; member of the committee to draft the administrative code which comprises the general law of Kansas City, Mo.; judge of the circuit court of Jackson County, Mo., from 1931 until his resignation in 1934; elected as a Democrat to the Seventy-fourth and to the six succeeding Congresses (January 3, 1935-Januray 3, 1949); chairman, Committee on Elections No. 1 (Seventy-sixth and Seventy-seventh Congresses), Committee on Insular Affairs (Seventy-eighth and Seventy-ninth Congresses); member of the Filipino Rehabilitation Commission in 1945 and 1946; was not a candidate for reelection in 1948 to the Eighty-first Congress; resumed the practice of law; managing private investments; died in Kansas City, Mo., January 21, 1978; interment in Blue Springs Cemetery, Blue Springs, Mo.

**BELL, Charles Keith** (nephew of Reese Bowen Brabson), a Representative from Texas; born in Chattanooga, Tenn., April 18, 1853; attended the public schools and Sewanee (Tenn.) College; moved to Texas in 1871; studied law; was admitted to the bar in 1874 and commenced practice in Hamilton, Tex.; prosecuting attorney of Hamilton County in 1876; district attorney 1880-1882; delegate to the Democratic National Convention in 1884; member of the State senate 1884-1888; judge of the twenty-ninth judicial district of Texas 1888-1890; elected as a Democrat to the Fifty-third and Fifty-fourth Congresses (March 4, 1893-March 3, 1897); was not a candidate for renomination in 1896; resumed the practice of law in Fort Worth, Tex.; attorney general of Texas 1901-1904; again resumed the practice of law in Fort Worth, where he died April 21, 1913; interment in East Oakwood Cemetery.

**BELL, Charles Webster,** a Representative from California; born in Albany, N.Y., June 11, 1857; attended the public schools; moved to California in 1877 and settled in Pasadena, Los Angeles County; engaged in fruit growing and the real estate business; county clerk of Los Angeles County 1899-1903; member of the State senate 1907-1912; elected as a Progressive Republican to the Sixty-third Congress (March 4, 1913-March 3, 1915); unsuccessful candidate for reelection in 1914 to the Sixty-fourth Congress; resumed his former business pursuits in Pasadena, Calif.; served as secretary of the Pasadena Mercantile Finance Corporation; died in Pasadena, Calif., April 19, 1927; interment in Mountain View Cemetery.

**BELL, Hiram,** a Representative from Ohio; born in Salem, Vt., April 22, 1808; attended the public schools of his native city; moved with his parents to Hamilton, Ohio, in 1826; studied law; was admitted to the bar in 1829 and commenced practice in Greenville, Darke County, Ohio; auditor of Darke County in 1829 and 1834; member of the State house of representatives in 1836, 1837, and 1840; elected as a Whig to the Thirty-second Congress (March 4, 1851-March 3, 1853); was not a candidate for renomination in 1852; engaged in the practice of his profession until his death in Greenville, Ohio, December 21, 1855; interment in the Greenville Cemetery.

**BELL, Hiram Parks,** a Representative from Georgia; born near Jefferson, Jackson County, Ga., January 19, 1827; attended the public schools at Cumming, Forsyth County, Ga.; taught school for two years, during which time he studied law; was admitted to the bar in 1849 and commenced practice in Cumming; member of the secession convention in 1861 and opposed the secession ordinance; commissioner from Georgia to solicit the cooperation of Tennessee in the formation of a southern confederacy; member of the State senate in 1861, but resigned to enter the Confederate Army; during the Civil War was commissioned captain and later promoted to lieutenant colonel and colonel of the Forty-third Georgia Regiment; member of the Second Confederate Congress in 1864 and 1865; member of the Democratic State executive committee 1868-1871; elected as a Democrat to the Forty-third Congress (March 4, 1873-March 3, 1875); delegate to the Democratic National Convention of 1876; was chosen a member of the Democratic National Committee from the State at large; elected to the Forty-fifth Congress to fill the vacancy caused by the resignation of Benjamin H. Hill and served from March 13, 1877, to March 3, 1879; unsuccessful candidate for renomination in 1878; member of the State house of representatives in 1898 and 1899; served in the State senate in 1900 and 1901; died in Atlanta, Ga., August 17, 1907; interment in Cumming Cemetery, Cumming, Ga.

**BELL, James** (son of Samuel Bell, uncle of Samuel Newell Bell, and cousin of Charles Henry Bell), a Senator from New Hampshire; born in Francistown, Hillsboro County, N.H., November 13, 1804; attended Phillips Academy, Andover, Mass., and was graduated from Bowdoin College, Brunswick, Maine, in 1822; studied law at Litchfield Law School, Litchfield, Conn.; was admitted to the bar in 1825 and commenced practice in Gilmanton, N.H.; moved to Exeter in 1831 and to Gilford in 1846; member, New Hampshire house of representatives 1846-1850; delegate to the State constitutional convention in 1850; unsuccessful candidate for election in 1853, 1854 and 1855 for Governor of New Hampshire; elected as a Republican to the United States Senate for the term beginning March 4, 1855, and served from July 30, 1855, until his death in Laconia, Belknap County, N.H., May 26, 1857; interment in Exeter Cemetery, Exeter, N.H.

**BELL, James Martin,** a Representative from Ohio; born in Huntingdon County, Pa., October 16, 1796; attended the public schools; studied law in Steubenville, Ohio; was admitted to the bar in 1817 and commenced practice in Cambridge, Guernsey County, Ohio; served as major general of the Fifteenth Division, Ohio Militia; prosecuting attorney of Guernsey County 1818-1832; member of the State house of representatives 1826-1831, serving as speaker in 1830 and 1831; master commissioner in 1827; justice of the peace in 1830; county school examiner in 1830; elected as an Anti-Jacksonian to the Twenty-third Congress (March 4, 1833-March 3, 1835); unsuccessful candidate for reelection in 1834 to the Twenty-fourth Congress; resumed the practice of law; served as mayor of Cambridge from 1838 to 1840; died in Cambridge, Ohio, on April 4, 1849; interment in Founders' Burial Ground.

**BELL, John,** a Representative from Ohio; born in Pennsboro, Lycoming County, Pa., June 19, 1796; received a limited education; moved to Ohio in 1810 with his parents, who settled in Greene County, near Xenia; moved to Lower Sandusky in 1823; city mayor in 1830; probate judge of Sandusky County several terms; commissioned major general of State militia in 1834; commanded Ohio forces in the Toledo war in 1835; served as postmaster of Lower Sandusky from November 14, 1838, to May 3, 1841; member of the State house of representatives in 1844 and 1845; mayor of Fremont, Ohio, in 1845 and 1846; elected as a Whig to the Thirty-first Congress to fill the vacancy caused by the death of Amos E. Wood and served from January 7 to March 3, 1851; probate judge 1852-1855 and 1858-1863; died in Fremont, Sandusky County, Ohio, May 4, 1869; interment in Oakwood Cemetery.

**BELL, John,** a Representative and a Senator from Tennessee; born near Nashville, Tenn., February 15, 1797; was graduated from the University of Nashville in 1814; studied law; was admitted to the bar in 1816 and commenced practice in Franklin, Tenn.; member, State senate 1817; declined to be a candidate for reelection and moved to Nashville; elected to the Twentieth, and to the six succeeding Congresses (March 4, 1827-March 3, 1841); Speaker of the House of Representatives (Twenty-third Congress); chairman, Committee on Indian Affairs (Twenty-first through Twenty-sixth Congresses, except for Twenty-third), Committee on Judiciary (Twenty-second and Twenty-third Congresses); appointed by President William Henry Harrison as Secretary of War on March 5, 1841, and served until September 13, 1841, when he resigned; member, State house of representatives in 1847; elected as a Whig to the United States Senate in 1847; reelected in 1853, and served from November 22, 1847, to March 3, 1859; unsuccessful candidate in 1860 for President of the United States on the Constitutional Union ticket; investor in ironworks at Cumberland Furnace in Chattanooga, Tenn.; died at his home on the banks of the Cumberland River, near Cumberland Furnace, September 10, 1869; interment in Mount Olivet Cemetery, near Nashville, Tenn.

**Bibliography:** *DAB*; Parks, Joseph H. *John Bell Of Tennessee.* Baton Rouge: Louisiana State University Press, 1950.

**BELL, John Calhoun,** a Representative from Colorado; born near Sewanee, Franklin County, Tenn., December 11, 1851; attended public and private schools in Franklin County; studied law in Winchester, Tenn., and was admitted to the bar in 1874; moved to

Colorado in 1874 and commenced practice in Del Norte, moving to Saguache, Colo., the same year; county attorney of Saguache County, Colo., from 1874 until May 1876; moved to Lake City, Colo., in 1876; elected county clerk of Hinsdale County in 1878; mayor of Lake City in 1885; moved to Montrose, Colo., in 1886 and continued the practice of law; served as judge of the seventh judicial district of Colorado from 1889 until his resignation in 1892, having been elected to Congress; elected as a Populist to the Fifty-third and to the four succeeding Congresses (March 4, 1893-March 3, 1903); unsuccessful candidate for reelection in 1902 to the Fifty-eighth Congress; member of the United States Industrial Commission in 1900 and 1901; resumed the practice of law in Montrose, Colo.; judge of the Court of Appeals of Colorado, 1913-1915; again resumed the practice of law; member of the Colorado State board of agriculture, 1931-1933; died in Montrose, Colo., August 12, 1933; interment in the Cedar Cemetery.

**BELL, John Junior,** a Representative from Texas; born in Cuero, De Witt County, Tex., May 15, 1910; attended the public schools; was graduated from the University of Texas at Austin in 1932 and from its law school in 1936; was admitted to the bar in 1936 and commenced the practice of law in Cuero, Tex.; served in the State house of representatives 1937-1947; president of a company operating compresses in Victoria, Shiner, Cuero, and Taft, Tex.; during the Second World War served as a private in the United States Army from May 1944 to March 1945; member of the State senate 1947-1954; delegate to the Democratic National Conventions in 1948 and 1952; elected as a Democrat to the Eighty-fourth Congress (January 3, 1955-January 3, 1957); unsuccessful candidate for renomination in 1956; lawyer, rancher, and farmer; was a resident of Cuero, Tex., until his death January 24, 1963; interment in Hillside Cemetery.

**BELL, Joshua Fry,** a Representative from Kentucky; born in Danville, Boyle County, Ky., November 26, 1811; attended the public schools; was graduated from Centre College, Danville, Ky., in 1828; studied law in Lexington, Ky.; traveled in Europe for several years before admission to the bar; commenced practice in Danville, Boyle County, Ky.; elected as a Whig to the Twenty-ninth Congress (March 4, 1845-March 3, 1847); declined to be a candidate for renomination in 1846 to the Thirtieth Congress; secretary of state of Kentucky in 1849; chosen by the legislature as one of six commissioners to the peace convention of 1861 held in Washington, D.C., in an effort to devise means to prevent the impending war; delegate to the Border State convention in 1861; nominated in 1863 by the Union Democrats for Governor of Kentucky, but declined to accept the nomination; member of the Kentucky house of representatives 1862-1867; died in Danville, Ky., August 17, 1870; interment in Bellevue Cemetery.

**BELL, Peter Hansbrough,** a Representative from Texas; born in Spotsylvania County, Va., May 12, 1812; attended the public schools; moved to Texas in 1836 during the war for Texan independence; participated in the Battle of San Jacinto, April 21, 1836; assistant adjutant general of the Texan forces in 1837 and inspector general in 1839; served in the Mexican War as captain of the Texas Volunteer Rangers in 1845 and 1846 and as lieutenant colonel of mounted volunteers; colonel of a Texan volunteer regiment in 1848 and 1849; elected Governor of Texas in 1849, reelected in 1851, and served from December 21, 1849 until November 23, 1853, when he resigned; elected as a Democrat to the Thirty-third and Thirty-fourth Congresses (March 4, 1853-March 3, 1857); was not a candidate for renomination in 1856 to the Thirty-fifth Congress; moved to North Carolina in 1857 and settled in Halifax County; died in Littleton, Halifax County, N.C., March 8, 1898; interment in City Cemetery.

**Bibliography:** *DAB.*

**BELL, Samuel** (father of James Bell, grandfather of Samuel Newell Bell, and uncle of Charles Henry Bell), a Senator from New Hampshire; born in Londonderry, N.H., February 9, 1770; attended the common schools and New Ipswich Academy; graduated from Dartmouth College, Hanover, N.H., in 1793; studied law; was admitted to the bar in 1796 and commenced practice in Francestown, N.H.; moved to Amherst, N.H., in 1810 and to Chester, N.H., in 1812 and continued the practice of law; member, New Hampshire State house of representatives, 1804-1807, serving as speaker from 1805 until 1807; member, State senate, serving as president of that body from 1807 to 1809; member, State executive council, 1809-1811; judge of the State supreme court from 1816 until 1819; elected Governor of New Hampshire in 1819, reelected in 1820, 1821, and 1822, and served from June 3, 1819 to June 5, 1823; elected to the United States Senate in 1823; reelected in 1829, and served from March 4, 1823, to March 3, 1835; was not a candidate for reelection in 1834; chairman, Committee on Claims (Twenty-third Congress); affiliated with the Whig Party upon its formation in 1834; retired to his farm; died in Chester, N.H., on December 23, 1850; interment in the Village Cemetery.

**Bibliography:** *DAB.*

**BELL, Samuel Newell** (grandson of Samuel Bell and nephew of James Bell), a Representative from New Hampshire; born in Chester, Rockingham County, N.H., March 25, 1829; attended school in Francestown, N.H., and Phillips Academy, Andover, Mass.; was graduated from Dartmouth College, Hanover, N.H., in 1847; studied law; was admitted to the bar in 1849 and commenced practice in Meredith, Belknap County, N.H.; elected as a Democrat to the Forty-second Congress (March 4, 1871-March 3, 1873); unsuccessful candidate for reelection in 1872 to the Forty-third Congress; elected to the Forty-fourth Congress (March 4, 1875-March 3, 1877); was not a candidate for reelection in 1876 to the Forty-fifth Congress; resumed the practice of law in Meredith; also interested in large real estate holdings; served as president of several railroads and vice president of the New Hampshire Fire Insurance Co.; appointed chief justice of the superior court of New Hampshire, but declined to accept; retired from public life; died while on a visit in North Woodstock, N.H., February 8, 1889; interment in the Valley Cemetery, Manchester, N.H.

**BELL, Theodore Arlington,** a Representative from California; born in Vallejo, Solano County, Calif., July 25, 1872; moved with his parents to St. Helena, Napa County, in 1876; attended the common schools; studied law; was admitted to the bar in 1893 and commenced practice at Napa, Calif.; district attorney of Napa County 1895-1903; elected as a Democrat to the Fifty-eighth Congress (March 4, 1903-March 3, 1905); unsuccessful candidate for reelection in 1904 to the Fifty-ninth Congress; moved to San Francisco in 1906 and continued the practice of his profession; unsuccessful candidate for election for Governor of California in 1906, 1910 and 1918; delegate to the Democratic National Convention of 1908, serving as temporary chairman, and to the Convention of 1912; announced his affiliation with the Republican Party in March 1922; was killed in an automobile accident near Fairfax, Marin County, Calif., on September 4, 1922; interment in Odd Fellows Cemetery, St. Helena, Calif.

**BELL, Thomas Montgomery,** a Representative from Georgia; born in Nacoochee Valley, near Cleveland, White County, Ga., March 17, 1861; attended the common schools, a private school in Cleveland, Ga., and Moore's Business University at Atlanta; taught in the public schools of Cleveland in 1878 and 1879; in the following year became employed as a traveling salesman and was connected with many wholesale business houses at Atlanta, Ga., and Baltimore, Md.; moved to Gainesville, Ga., in 1885 and continued his former pursuits; elected clerk of the superior court of Hall County in 1898; reelected in 1900 and again in 1902 and served until 1904; elected as a Democrat to the Fifty-ninth and to the twelve succeeding Congresses (March 4, 1905-March 3, 1931); majority whip (Sixty-third Congress); unsuccessful candidate for renomination in 1930; employed as a representative of a marble company; died in Gainesville, Ga., March 18, 1941; interment in Alta Vista Cemetery.

**BELLAMY, John Dillard,** a Representative from North Carolina; born in Wilmington, N.C., March 24, 1854; attended the common schools and Cape Fear Military Academy; was graduated from Davidson College, Davidson, N.C., in 1873 and from the University of Virginia at Charlottesville in 1875; was admitted to the bar in 1875 and commenced the practice of law in Wilmington, N.C.; city attorney of Wilmington 1892-1894; member of the State senate 1900-1902; delegate at large to the Democratic National Conventions of 1892, 1908, and 1920; elected as a Democrat to the Fifty-sixth and Fifty-seventh Congresses (March 4, 1899-March 3, 1903); unsuccessful candidate for renomination in 1902 to the Fifty-eighth Congress; resumed the practice of law in Wilmington, N.C.; also engaged as an author; district counsel for the Seaboard Air Line Railway Co., the Southern Bell Telephone Co., and the Western Union Telegraph Co.; also connected with the street railway company and cotton mills in Wilmington, N.C.; appointed by Governor Angus W. McLean as a commissioner from North Carolina to the celebration of the two-hundredth anniversary of the birth of George Washington, held in Washington, D.C., in 1932; died in Wilmington, N.C., September 25, 1942; interment in Oakdale Cemetery.

**BELLINGER, Joseph,** a Representative from South Carolina; born at Bellinger Plantation in Saint Bartholomew Parish, Ashepoo, Colleton County, S.C., in 1773; planter and owner of "Aeolian Lawn" plantation; member of the State house of representatives 1802-1809 and of the State senate from Barnwell District 1810-1813; elected as a Republican to the Fifteenth Congress (March 4, 1817-March 3, 1819); was not a candidate for reelection to the Sixteenth Congress; died at Charleston, S.C., January 10, 1830; interment in the Bellinger private burial ground, Poco Sabo Plantation, Ashepoo, S.C.

**BELLMON, Henry Louis,** a Senator from Oklahoma; born on a farm near Tonkawa, Kay County, Okla., September 3, 1921; educated in the public schools of Noble County; B.S., Oklahoma State University (then Oklahoma A.&M. College), 1942; served in United States Marine Corps, 1942-1946; farmer and rancher; served in Oklahoma State house of representatives, 1946-1948; State Republican chairman in 1960; elected Governor of Oklahoma in 1962, and served from January 14, 1963 to January 9, 1967; while in office, chairman, Interstate Oil Compact Commission, and member, executive committee, National Governors Conference; elected as a Republican to the United States Senate in 1968; reelected in 1974 and served from January 3, 1969, to January 3, 1981; was not a candidate for reelection in 1980; co-founder and co-chairman of the Committee for a Responsible Federal Budget; appointed director of the Oklahoma Department of Human Services, 1983; elected Governor of Oklahoma in 1986, and served from January 12, 1987 to January 14, 1991; is a resident of Red Rock, Okla.

**Bibliography:** Bellmon, Henry, with Pat Bellmon. *The Life and Times of Henry Bellmon.* Tulsa, Okla.: Council Oak Books, 1992.

**BELMONT, Oliver Hazard Perry** (brother of Perry Belmont), a Representative from New York; born in New York City November 12, 1858; attended St. Paul's School, Concord, N.H., and was graduated from the United States Naval Academy, Annapolis, Md., June 10, 1880; was commissioned as a midshipman and served until June 1, 1881, when he resigned; at one time a member of the banking firm of August Belmont & Co., New York City; became publisher of the Verdict, a weekly paper; delegate to the Democratic National Convention in 1900; elected as a Democrat to the Fifty-seventh Congress (March 4, 1901-March 3, 1903); was not a

candidate for renomination in 1902; died in Hempstead, N.Y., on June 10, 1908; interment in Woodlawn Cemetery, New York City.

**BELMONT, Perry** (brother of Oliver Hazard Perry Belmont), a Representative from New York; born in New York City December 28, 1851; attended Everest Military Academy, Hamden, Conn., and was graduated from Harvard University in 1872; studied civil law at the University of Berlin; was graduated from the Columbia Law School, New York City, in 1876; was admitted to the bar the same year and commenced practice in New York City; elected as a Democrat to the Forty-seventh and to the three succeeding Congresses and served from March 4, 1881, to December 1, 1888, when he resigned to accept a diplomatic position; chairman, Committee on Expenditures on Public Buildings (Forty-eighth Congress), Committee on Foreign Affairs (Forty-ninth and Fiftieth Congresses); declined to be a candidate for renomination in 1888 to the Fifty-first Congress; appointed United States Minister to Spain on November 17, 1888 and served until May 1, 1889; delegate to the Democratic National Conventions in 1892, 1896, 1904, and 1912; during the Spanish-American War served as major and inspector general of the First Division, Second Army Corps, United States Volunteers; in 1905 successfully initiated and organized the movement for the Federal and State campaign-publicity legislation, which was enacted into law in 1911, and was elected president of the National Association for Campaign Publicity Law; during the First World War was commissioned a captain in the remount service; resumed the practice of law in New York City in 1920; author of a number of books pertaining to national and political affairs; went abroad in 1932 for three years, residing mostly at Paris, France; returned, and made Newport, R.I., his permanent residence; died at Newport, R.I., May 25, 1947; interment in Island Cemetery.

**Bibliography:** Belmont, Perry. *An American Democrat; The Recollections of Perry Belmont.* 1941. Reprint. New York: AMS Press, 1967.

**BELSER, James Edwin,** a Representative from Alabama; born in Charleston, S.C., December 22, 1805; attended the public schools; in 1820 moved with his parents to Sumter District, S.C., where he continued his schooling under a private tutor; moved to Alabama in 1825 and settled in Montgomery; studied law; was admitted to the bar and commenced practice in Montgomery; elected clerk of the county court; member of the State house of representatives in 1828; edited the Planters Gazette for several years; appointed solicitor of Montgomery County in 1828 and later elected to that position; appointed by Governor Benjamin Fitzpatrick in 1842 as a commissioner of the State to procure a settlement of the claims against the Federal Government for money advanced in the Indian War of 1836; elected as a Democrat to the Twenty-eighth Congress (March 4, 1843-March 3, 1845); declined to be a candidate for renomination in 1844 to the Twenty-ninth Congress; resumed the practice of law in Montgomery; affiliated with the Whig Party in 1848; again elected a member of the State house of representatives in 1853 and reelected in 1857; died in Montgomery, Ala., January 16, 1859; interment in Oakwood Cemetery.

**BELTZHOOVER, Frank Eckels,** a Representative from Pennsylvania; born in Silver Spring Township, Cumberland County, Pa., November 6, 1841; attended Big Spring Academy, Newville; was graduated from Pennsylvania College at Gettysburg in 1862; studied law; was admitted to the bar in 1864 and commenced practice in Carlisle, Pa.; chairman of the Democratic committee of Cumberland County 1868 and 1873; district attorney 1874-1877; delegate to the Democratic National Convention of 1876; elected as a Democrat to the Forty-sixth and Forty-seventh Congresses (March 4, 1879-March 3, 1883); was not a candidate for renomination in 1882 to the Forty-eighth Congress; elected to the Fifty-second and Fifty-third Congresses (March 4, 1891-March 3, 1895); chairman,

Committee on War Claims (Fifty-second and Fifty-third Congresses); was not a candidate for renomination in 1894 to the Fifty-fourth Congress; resumed the practice of law in Carlisle, Pa.; discontinued the practice of his profession in 1910 and moved to Los Angeles, Calif., where he lived in retirement until his death on June 2, 1923; interment in Ashland Cemetery, Carlisle, Pa.

**BENDER, George Harrison,** a Representative and a Senator from Ohio; born in Cleveland, Ohio, September 29, 1896; attended the public schools; owner of an insurance business; in 1934 founder, editor and publisher of the National Republican magazine; member, State senate 1920-1930; unsuccessful candidate for election to the United States House of Representatives in 1930, 1932, 1934, and 1936; elected as a Republican to the Seventy-sixth and to the four succeeding Congresses (January 3, 1939-January 3, 1949); unsuccessful candidate for reelection in 1948 to the Eighty-first Congress; elected to the Eighty-second and Eighty-third Congresses and served from January 3, 1951, until his resignation effective December 15, 1954; elected as a Republican to the United States Senate to fill the vacancy in the term ending January 3, 1957, caused by the death of Robert A. Taft, and served from December 16, 1954, to January 3, 1957; unsuccessful candidate for reelection in 1956; special assistant to Secretary of the Interior Frederick A. Seaton, Washington, D.C., 1957-1958; died in Chagrin Falls, Ohio, June 18, 1961; interment in Knollwood Cemetery, Mayfield Heights, Cleveland, Ohio.

Bibliography: *DAB*; Bender, George. *The Challenge of 1940.* New York: G.P. Putnam's Sons, 1940.

**BENEDICT, Charles Brewster,** a Representative from New York; born in Attica Township, Wyoming County, N.Y., February 7, 1828; attended the public schools and Oberlin College, Oberlin, Ohio; taught school and also engaged in agricultural pursuits; studied law; was admitted to the bar in 1856 and commenced practice in Attica, N.Y.; justice of the peace 1854-1860; engaged in banking in 1859; member of the board of supervisors of Wyoming County 1869-1871 and 1873-1875, serving a part of the time as chairman; member of the Democratic State committee in 1875; elected as a Democrat to the Forty-fifth Congress (March 4, 1877-March 3, 1879); was not a candidate for renomination in 1878 to the Forty-sixth Congress; resumed banking in Attica, N.Y.; one of the organizers of the First National Bank at Moorhead, Minn., and also operated farming lands extensively in that vicinity; died in Attica, N.Y., October 3, 1901; interment in Forest Hill Cemetery.

**BENEDICT, Cleveland Keith,** a Representative from West Virginia; born in Harrisburg, Dauphin County, Pa., March 21, 1935; attended the public schools; graduated, The Hill School, Pottstown, Pa., 1953; B.A., Princeton University, 1959; graduated, Graham School for Cattlemen, Graham, Kans., 1962; dairy farmer; chairman, West Virginia Board of Probation and Parole, 1974-1975; commissioner, finance and administration, State of West Virginia, 1975-1977; chairman, West Virginia State Republican Executive Committee, 1977-1980; delegate, West Virginia State Republican conventions, 1964-1976; delegate to the Republican National Convention of 1984; elected as a Republican to the Ninety-seventh Congress (January 3, 1981-January 3, 1983); was not a candidate for reelection in 1982 to the House of Representatives, but was an unsuccessful candidate for election to the United States Senate; unsuccessful candidate in 1984 for election to the Ninety-ninth Congress; deputy assistant secretary, Department of Energy, 1983; chairman, R.S.M., Inc., Washington, D.C., 1985-1986; is a resident of Lewisburg, W.Va.

**BENEDICT, Henry Stanley,** a Representative from California; born in Boonville, Cooper County, Mo., February 20, 1878; moved with his parents to Los Angeles, Calif., in 1888; attended the grammar schools and high school; attended the University of Southern California College of Law, Los Angeles, Calif.; was admitted to the bar in 1910 and commenced practice in Los Angeles, Calif.; member, California State house of representatives, 1910-1914; served in the State senate, 1914-1916; elected as a Republican to the Sixty-fourth Congress to fill the vacancy caused by the resignation of William D. Stephens, and served from November 7, 1916 to March 3, 1917; was nominated by the Progressive Party in 1916 for the Sixty-fifth Congress, but withdrew in behalf of Henry Z. Osborne, the Republican nominee; continued the practice of law and also engaged in banking; member of the State department of finance of California (State board of control) from 1919 to 1921; served as a member of the California State Railroad Commission from 1921 to 1923; resumed the practice of law in Los Angeles, Calif., until his death while on a visit in London, England, July 10, 1930; interment in Forest Lawn Memorial Park, Glendale, Calif.

**BENET, Christie,** a Senator from South Carolina; born in Abbeville, Abbeville County, S.C., December 26, 1879; attended the common schools, the College of Charleston, the University of South Carolina at Columbia, and the University of Virginia at Charlottesville; studied law; was admitted to the bar and commenced practice in Columbia, Richland County, S.C., in 1903; solicitor of the fifth judicial circuit in 1908; attorney for the city of Columbia 1910-1912; three times secretary of the Democratic State committee; appointed as a Democrat to the United States Senate to fill the vacancy caused by the death of Benjamin R. Tillman and served from July 6 to November 5, 1918, when a successor was elected; unsuccessful candidate for election in 1918 to the Senate to fill the vacancy; chairman, Committee on National Banks (Sixty-fifth Congress); resumed the practice of law; member and later chairman of the board of regents of South Carolina State Hospital 1915-1946; during the Second World War served as chairman of the War Finance Committee for South Carolina and was serving as chairman of the Alien Enemy Hearing Board for the eastern district of South Carolina at time of death; died in Columbia, S.C., March 30, 1951; interment in Elmwood Cemetery.

**BENHAM, John Samuel,** a Representative from Indiana; born on a farm near Benham, Ripley County, Ind., October 24, 1863; attended the public schools, a business college in Delaware, Ohio, and a normal school in Brookville, Ind.; taught school in the winter and attended college in the summer, being engaged as a teacher in various places in Indiana from 1882 to 1907; was graduated from Indiana State Normal School at Terre Haute, Ind., in 1893 and from Indiana University at Bloomington, Ind., in 1903; specialized in history at the University of Chicago for several terms; superintendent of schools for Ripley County for fourteen years; returned to Benham, Ind., in 1907 and engaged in the timber, milling, and contracting business; also followed agricultural pursuits; delegate to the Republican National Convention in 1916; elected as a Republican to the Sixty-sixth and Sixty-seventh Congresses (March 4, 1919-March 3, 1923); chairman, Committee on Expenditures on Public Buildings (Sixty-seventh Congress); unsuccessful candidate for reelection in 1922 to the Sixty-eighth Congress; moved to Batesville, Ripley County, Ind., in 1923 and engaged as a building contractor; again superintendent of schools for Ripley County, Ind., 1924-1929; retired from active business pursuits in 1931 and resided in Batesville, Ind., until his death there on December 11, 1935; interment in Benham Church Cemetery, near Benham, Ind.

**BENITEZ, Jaime,** a Resident Commissioner from Puerto Rico; born in Vieques, P.R., October 29, 1908; educated in the public schools of Puerto Rico; Georgetown University, Washington, D.C., B.L., 1930, M.L., 1931; M.A., University of Chicago, 1938; author; instructor and associate professor of social and political sciences, University of Puerto Rico, 1931-1942; chancellor of the University of Puerto Rico, 1942-1966; president, University System of Puerto Rico, 1966-1971; member, Constitutional Convention of Puerto Rico and chairman, Committee on Bill of Rights, 1951-1952; member,

United States National Commission for the United Nations Educational, Scientific and Cultural Organization (UNESCO), 1948-1954; United States delegate to the University Convention, Utrecht, Netherlands, 1948, and to the National Conventions of UNESCO in Paris, 1950, and in Havana, 1952; president, National Association of State Universities, 1957-1958; contributor and director, La Torre, University of Puerto Rico Literary Review, 1956-1971; delegate to the Democratic National Convention of 1976; elected as a Popular Democrat to the United States House of Representatives, November 7, 1972, for a four-year term ending January 3, 1977, unsuccessful candidate for reelection in 1976 for a four-year term ending January 3, 1981; professor, Inter-American University of Puerto Rico, 1980-1986; professor of government, American College, Bayamón, Puerto Rico, 1984 to present; is a resident of San Juan, P.R.

**BENJAMIN, Adam, Jr.,** a Representative from Indiana; born in Gary, Lake County, Ind., August 6, 1935; attended the public elementary schools of Gary; graduated, Kemper Military (high) School, Boonville, Mo., 1952; B.S., United States Military Academy, West Point, N.Y., 1958; J.D., Valparaiso (Ind.) Law School, 1966; admitted to the Indiana Bar in 1966 and commenced practice in Gary; served in United States Marine Corps, corporal, 1952-1954; United States Army, first lieutenant, 1958-1961; teacher, Edison High School, Gary, 1961; employed as computer analyst, Chicago, Ill., 1962; served as zoning administrator, Gary, 1964-1965; executive secretary to the mayor of Gary, 1965-1967; served in Indiana house of representatives, 1967-1971; Indiana senate, 1971-1976; elected as a Democrat to the Ninety-fifth, Ninety-sixth, and Ninety-seventh Congresses; served from January 3, 1977, until his death on September 7, 1982, in Washington, D.C.; interment at Calumet Park Cemetery, Merrillville, Ind.

**BENJAMIN, John Forbes,** a Representative from Missouri; born in Cicero, Onondaga County, N.Y., January 23, 1817; attended the public schools; moved to Texas in 1845 and to Missouri in 1848; studied law; was admitted to the bar and commenced practice in Shelbyville, Shelby County, Mo., in 1848; member of the State house of representatives 1850-1852; presidential elector on the Democratic ticket of in 1856; entered the Union Army as a private in 1861 and was subsequently promoted to the ranks of captain, major, lieutenant colonel, and brigadier general; provost marshal of the Eighth District of Missouri in 1863 and 1864; delegate to the Republican National Convention in 1864; elected as a Republican to the Thirty-ninth, Fortieth, and Forty-first Congresses (March 4, 1865-March 3, 1871); chairman, Committee on Invalid Expenditures (Forty-first Congress); was not a candidate for renomination in 1870; resumed the practice of law in Shelbyville; unsuccessful candidate for election in 1872 to the Forty-third Congress; moved to Washington, D.C., in 1874 and engaged in banking; died in Washington, D.C., March 8, 1877; interment in a private cemetery at Shelbina, Shelby County, Mo.

**BENJAMIN, Judah Philip,** a Senator from Louisiana; born on the Island of St. Croix, Danish West Indies (now Virgin Islands), August 6, 1811; immigrated to Savannah, Ga., in 1816 with his parents, who later settled in Wilmington, N.C.; attended the Fayetteville Academy, Fayetteville, N.C., and Yale College; moved to New Orleans, La., in 1828 and taught school; studied law; was admitted to the bar in 1832 and commenced practice in New Orleans; elected to the lower house of the state legislature in 1842 and served until 1844; member of the State constitutional convention in 1845; elected as a Whig to the United States Senate in 1853; reelected as a Democrat in 1859 and served from March 4, 1853, to February 4, 1861, when he withdrew with other secessionist Senators; his seat was declared vacant and his name omitted from the roll by a resolution of March 14, 1861; chairman, Committee on Private Land Claims (Thirty-fourth through Thirty-sixth Con-

gresses); appointed Attorney General under the provisional government of the Confederate States on February 21, 1861; appointed Secretary of War of the Confederate States on September 17, 1861; served in this capacity until March 24, 1862, when he resigned to accept the appointment as Secretary of State in the Cabinet of President Jefferson Davis, in which capacity he served until the end of the war; moved to Great Britain in August 1865; studied English law at Lincoln's Inn, London, was admitted to the bar in that city in June 1866, and practiced law there; engaged in newspaper and magazine work; received the appointment of Queen's counsel in 1872; retired in 1883 from active practice and public life; moved to Paris, France, and died there May 6, 1884; interment in Père la Chaise Cemetery.

**Bibliography:** *DAB*; Evans, Eli N. *Judah P. Benjamin: The Jewish Confederate.* New York: The Free Press, 1988; Osterweis, R.G. *Judah P. Benjamin, Statesman of the Lost Cause.* New York: G.P. Putnam's Sons, 1933.

**BENNER, George Jacob,** a Representative from Pennsylvania; born in Gettysburg, Adams County, Pa., April 13, 1859; attended the public schools and was graduated from Pennsylvania College at Gettysburg in 1878; taught school for several years; studied law; was admitted to the Adams County bar in 1881 and commenced practice in Gettysburg; delegate to the Democratic State convention in 1886; elected as a Democrat to the Fifty-fifth Congress (March 4, 1897-March 3, 1899); was not a candidate for renomination in 1898 to the Fifty-sixth Congress; resumed the practice of law in Gettysburg, Pa.; unsuccessful candidate for election as president judge of the thirty-first judicial district in 1925; died in Gettysburg, Pa., December 30, 1930; interment in Evergreen Cemetery.

**BENNET, Augustus Witschief,** (son of William Stiles Bennet), a Representative from New York; born in New York City October 7, 1897; attended the public schools of New York City and Washington, D.C., and was graduated from Amherst (Mass.) College in 1918; during the First World War served in the United States Naval Reserve Flying Corps with the rating of chief quartermaster from June 8, 1918 to January 19, 1919; was graduated from the Columbia University Law School at New York City in 1921; was admitted to the bar the same year and commenced practice in Newburgh, N.Y.; United States referee in bankruptcy from 1923 until 1944; elected as a Republican to the Seventy-ninth Congress (January 3, 1945-January 3, 1947); unsuccessful candidate for renomination in 1946 to the Eightieth Congress; resumed the practice of law; resided in Laguna Hills, Calif. until his death in Concord, Mass. on June 5, 1983; cremated; ashes interred at Cedar Hills Mausoleum, Newburgh, N.Y.

**BENNET, Benjamin,** a Representative from New Jersey; born in Bucks County, Pa., October 31, 1764; attended the common schools; studied theology; was ordained as a minister in Middletown, Monmouth County, N.J., in 1793 and served as pastor of a Baptist church in that city; also engaged in agricultural pursuits; elected as a Republican to the Fourteenth and Fifteenth Congresses (March 4, 1815-March 3, 1819); resumed agricultural pursuits; died on his farm near Middletown, N.J., October 8, 1840; interment in the Baptist Cemetery, Holmdel, N.J.

**BENNET, Hiram Pitt,** a Delegate from the Territory of Colorado; born in Carthage, Franklin County, Maine, September 2, 1826; moved to Ohio with his parents, who settled in Richland County in 1831; attended public and private schools and the Ohio Wesleyan University at Delaware; taught school in northwestern Missouri in 1850; studied law; was admitted to the bar in 1851 and practiced in western Iowa and later at Glenwood, Iowa; judge of the circuit court of Iowa in 1852; moved to Nebraska Territory in 1854, settled in Nebraska City, and continued the practice of law; unsuccessfully contested in 1855 as a Republican the election of Bird B. Chapman to the Thirty-fourth Congress; member of the

Territorial council in 1856; member of the Territorial house of representatives in 1858 and served as speaker; moved to Denver, Colo., in 1859 and continued the practice of law; upon the admission of the Territory to representation was elected as a Conservative Republican, a Delegate to the Thirty-seventh Congress; reelected to the Thirty-eighth Congress and served from August 19, 1861, to March 3, 1865; was not a candidate for renomination in 1864; secretary of state of Colorado in 1867; appointed postmaster of Denver, Colo., on March 26, 1869, and served until May 27, 1874, when a successor was appointed; member of the first State senate in 1876; appointed "State agent" in 1888, and served until 1895 in recovering lands belonging to the State of Colorado which had been wrongfully disposed of; retired in 1899 and resided in Denver, Colo., until his death, November 11, 1914; interment in Riverside Cemetery.

**Bibliography:** Silverman, Jason H. "Making Brick Out of Straw: Delegate Hiram P. Bennet." *Colorado Magazine* 53 (Fall 1976): 309-327.

**BENNET, William Stiles** (father of Augustus Witschief Bennet), a Representative from New York; born in Port Jervis, Orange County, N.Y., November 9, 1870; attended the common schools; was graduated from Port Jervis Academy in 1889 and from Albany Law School in 1892; was admitted to the bar in 1892 and commenced practice the same year; official reporter of the Orange County Board of Supervisors in 1892 and 1893; member of the State assembly in 1901 and 1902; justice of the municipal court of New York City in 1903; member of the United States Immigration Commission 1907-1910; delegate to the Republican National Conventions in 1908 and 1916; elected as a Republican to the Fifty-ninth, Sixtieth, and Sixty-first Congresses (March 4, 1905-March 3, 1911); unsuccessful candidate for reelection in 1910 to the Sixty-second Congress; resumed the practice of law in New York City; elected to the Sixty-fourth Congress to fill the vacancy caused by the death of Joseph A. Goulden and served from November 2, 1915, to March 3, 1917; unsuccessful candidate for reelection in 1916 to the Sixty-fifth Congress; resumed the practice of law in New York City; official parliamentarian of the Republican National Convention at Chicago in 1916; moved to Chicago in 1920 and continued the practice of law; American delegate to the Seventeenth International Congress Against Alcoholism held at Copenhagen in 1923; general counsel and vice president of the Edward Hines associated lumber, coal, and railroad organizations 1920-1932; returned to New York City in 1933 and resumed the practice of law; unsuccessful candidate for election in 1936 to the Seventy-fifth Congress; served as a delegate to the State constitutional convention in 1938; unsuccessful candidate at a special election in 1944 to fill a vacancy in the Seventy-eighth Congress; was a resident of Mont Vernon, Westchester County, N.Y., until his death in Falkirk Hospital, Central Valley, N.Y., December 1, 1962; remains were cremated and the ashes interred in Laurel Grove Cemetery, Port Jervis, N.Y.

**BENNETT, Charles Edward,** a Representative from Florida; born in Canton, St. Lawrence County, N.Y., December 2, 1910; moved with his parents to Tampa, Fla., in 1913 and to Jacksonville, Fla., in 1932; attended the Tampa schools; A.B., J.D., University of Florida, Gainesville, 1934; was admitted to the bar the same year and commenced the practice of law in Jacksonville, Fla.; member of the Florida State house of representatives in 1941; during the Second World War enlisted in the United States Army on March 13, 1942, and discharged as a captain of infantry on January 13, 1947; served overseas in New Guinea and the Philippines, including guerrilla fighting on Luzon; awarded the Silver Star, Bronze Star, and Combat Infantry Badge; elected as a Democrat to the Eighty-first and to the twenty-one succeeding Congresses (January 3, 1949-January 3, 1993); chairman, Committee on Standards of Official Conduct (Ninety-sixth Congress); was not a candidate for reelection in 1992 to the One Hundred Third Congress; professor of government, Jacksonville University; is a resident of Jacksonville, Fla.

**BENNETT, Charles Goodwin,** a Representative from New York; born in Brooklyn, N.Y., December 11, 1863; attended the public schools; was graduated from the Brooklyn High School and from the New York Law School in 1882; was admitted to the bar in 1882 and commenced practice in Brooklyn, N.Y.; unsuccessful candidate for election in 1892 to the Fifty-third Congress; elected as a Republican to the Fifty-fourth and Fifty-fifth Congresses (March 4, 1895-March 3, 1899); unsuccessful candidate for reelection in 1898 to the Fifty-sixth Congress; Secretary of the United States Senate from January 29, 1900, to March 3, 1913, when a successor was elected; returned to Brooklyn, N.Y., discontinued active business pursuits, and lived in retirement until his death on May 25, 1914; interment in Evergreen Cemetery.

**BENNETT, David Smith,** a Representative from New York; born on a farm near Camillus, Onondaga County, N.Y., May 3, 1811; attended the common schools and the local academy in Onondaga; engaged in agricultural pursuits; moved to Syracuse and engaged in the produce business, afterwards extending his business to New York City; moved to Buffalo in 1853 and built and operated several grain elevators; also purchased the original Dart grain elevator; elected a member of the State senate in 1865; elected as a Republican to the Forty-first Congress (March 4, 1869-March 3, 1871); declined to be a candidate for renomination in 1870; resumed his former business pursuits in Buffalo, N.Y., where he died November 6, 1894; interment in Oakwood Cemetery, Syracuse, N.Y.

**BENNETT, Granville Gaylord,** a Delegate from the Territory of Dakota; born near Bloomingburg, Fayette County, Ohio, October 9, 1833; moved to Illinois in 1849 with his parents, who settled in Fulton County, and to Washington, Iowa, in 1855; attended Howe's Academy, Mount Pleasant, Iowa, and Washington College, Iowa; studied law; was admitted to the bar in 1859 and commenced practice in Washington, Iowa; during the Civil War served in the Union Army as a commissioned officer from July 1861 to August 1865 and was assigned to the Seventh and Nineteenth Regiments of Iowa Volunteer Infantry; returned to Washington, Iowa; member of the State house of representatives 1865-1867; served in the State senate 1867-1871; appointed associate justice of the supreme court of the Territory of Dakota on February 24, 1875, and served until August 23, 1878, when he resigned, having been nominated for Congress; elected as a Republican to the Forty-sixth Congress (March 4, 1879-March 3, 1881); was not a candidate for reelection in 1880 to the Forty-seventh Congress; resumed the practice of law in Deadwood, S.Dak.; elected judge of the probate court of Lawrence County and served three terms; died at Hot Springs, Fall River County, S.Dak., June 28, 1910; interment in Mount Moriah Cemetery, Deadwood, S.Dak.

**BENNETT, Hendley Stone,** a Representative from Mississippi; born near Franklin, Williamson County, Tenn., April 7, 1807; attended the public schools in West Point, Miss.; studied law; was admitted to the bar in 1830 and commenced practice in Columbus, Miss.; judge of the circuit court 1846-1854; elected as a Democrat to the Thirty-fourth Congress (March 4, 1855-March 3, 1857); unsuccessful candidate for renomination in 1856; resumed the practice of law in Columbus; moved to Paris, Tex., in 1859 and continued the practice of law; served as a captain in Company G, Thirty-second Regiment, Texas Cavalry, Confederate States Army, from August 5, 1861, to August 31, 1862; resumed the practice of law; in 1886 returned to Tennessee and settled in Franklin, Williamson County, and continued the practice of his profession; died in Franklin, Tenn., December 15, 1891; interment in Mount Hope Cemetery.

**BENNETT, Henry,** a Representative from New York; born in New Lisbon, Otsego County, N.Y., September 29, 1808; attended the public schools; studied law; was admitted to the bar in 1832 and commenced practice in New Berlin, Chenango County, N.Y.; served as clerk of the town of New Berlin in 1846; elected as a Whig to the Thirty-first through Thirty-fourth Congresses and as a Republican to the Thirty-fifth Congress (March 4, 1849-March 3, 1859); chairman, Committee on Public Lands (Thirty-fourth Congress); unsuccessful candidate for renomination in 1858 to the Thirty-sixth Congress; resumed the practice of law in New Berlin, N.Y., until his death there on May 10, 1868; interment in St. Andrews' Cemetery.

**BENNETT, John Bonifas,** a Representative from Michigan; born in Garden, Delta County, Mich., January 10, 1904; attended the public schools; was graduated from Watersmeet (Mich.) High School, from Marquette University Law School, Milwaukee, Wis., in 1925; took a postgraduate course at Chicago (Ill.) University Law School in 1926; was admitted to the Wisconsin bar in 1925, and to the Michigan bar in 1926; practiced law in Ontonagon, Mich., from 1926 until 1942; prosecuting attorney of Ontonagon County, 1929-1934; deputy commissioner of the Michigan Department of Labor and Industry, 1935-1937; elected as a Republican to the Seventy-eighth Congress (January 3, 1943-January 3, 1945); unsuccessful candidate for reelection in 1944 to the Seventy-ninth Congress; resumed the practice of law; elected to the Eightieth and to the eight succeeding Congresses and served from January 3, 1947, until his death in Chevy Chase, Md., August 9, 1964; interment in Gate of Heaven Cemetery, Silver Spring, Md.

**BENNETT, Joseph Bentley,** a Representative from Kentucky; born in Greenup County, Ky., April 21, 1859; attended the common schools and Greenup Academy, Greenup, Ky.; taught in the public schools; studied law; was admitted to the bar in 1878 and commenced practice in 1880; entered the mercantile business in 1885; judge of Greenup County 1894-1897; reelected in 1897 and served until 1901; member of the Kentucky Republican central committee in 1900 and 1904; elected as a Republican to the Fifty-ninth, Sixtieth, and Sixty-first Congresses (March 4, 1905-March 3, 1911); unsuccessful candidate for reelection in 1910 to the Sixty-second Congress; continued the practice of his profession until his death in Greenup, Greenup County, Ky., November 7, 1923; interment in Riverview Cemetery.

**BENNETT, Marion Tinsley** (son of Philip Allen Bennett), a Representative from Missouri; born in Buffalo, Dallas County, Mo., June 6, 1914; attended the public schools of Buffalo, Jefferson City, and Springfield, Mo.; A.B., Southwest Missouri State College, Springfield, Mo., 1935; LL.B., Washington University School of Law, St. Louis, Mo., 1938; was admitted to the bar in 1938 and commenced practice in Springfield, Mo.; served as secretary to his father, Representative Philip A. Bennett, 1941-1943; colonel in United States Air Force Reserve until 1974; member of the Greene County (Mo.) Republican central committee 1938-1942; delegate to Missouri State Conventions, 1938, 1940, 1944, 1946, and 1948; elected as a Republican to the Seventy-eighth Congress to fill the vacancy caused by the death of his father, Philip Allen Bennett; reelected to the Seventy-ninth and Eightieth Congresses and served from January 12, 1943, to January 3, 1949; congressional delegate to inspect atrocity camps in Germany, 1945; was an unsuccessful candidate for reelection in 1948 to the Eighty-first Congress; commissioner, United States Court of Claims, Washington, D.C., January 4, 1949, to September 11, 1964, when he became chief commissioner and served until July 6, 1972; judge, United States Court of Claims, July 7, 1972 to September 30, 1982; assumed office as judge, United States Court of Appeals for the Federal circuit, on October 1, 1982; assumed senior status on March 1, 1986; is a resident of Fort Belvoir, Va.

**BENNETT, Philip Allen** (father of Marion Tinsley Bennett), a Representative from Missouri; born on a farm near Buffalo, Dallas County, Mo., March 5, 1881; attended the public schools and Buffalo (Mo.) High School; was graduated from Springfield (Mo.) Normal and Business College in 1902; taught school at Independence, Mo., in 1899 and at Boyd, Mo., in 1900; purchased the Buffalo (Mo.) Reflex, which he edited and published 1904-1921; chairman of the Dallas County (Mo.) Republican committee for eight years; delegate to the Republican National Convention of 1912; served in the State senate 1921-1925; moved to Springfield, Mo., in 1922 and engaged in the real estate and loan business; Federal land bank appraiser 1923-1925; lieutenant governor of Missouri 1925-1929; unsuccessful candidate for nomination in 1928 for Governor; engaged in the insurance and loan business; unsuccessful candidate for election in 1938 to the Seventy-sixth Congress; elected as a Republican to the Seventy-seventh Congress and served from January 3, 1941, until his death in Washington, D.C., December 7, 1942; had been reelected to the Seventy-eighth Congress; interment in Hazelwood Cemetery, Springfield, Mo.

**BENNETT, Risden Tyler,** a Representative from North Carolina; born in Wadesboro, Anson County, N.C., June 18, 1840; attended the common schools and Anson Institute; was graduated from Cumberland University and from Lebanon Law School, Tennessee, in 1859; during the Civil War enlisted in the Confederate Army as a private on April 30, 1861, and left the service as colonel of the Fourteenth North Carolina Troops, having been wounded on three occasions; solicitor of Anson County in 1866 and 1867; member of the State house of representatives 1872-1874; delegate to the State constitutional convention in 1875; judge of the superior court from 1880 until his resignation in 1882; elected as a Democrat to the Forty-eighth and Forty-ninth Congresses (March 4, 1883-March 3, 1887); chairman, Committee on Expenditures in the Department of State (Forty-ninth Congress); engaged in the practice of law in Wadesboro, N.C., and died there July 21, 1913; interment in the family cemetery near Wadesboro, N.C.

**BENNETT, Robert Foster** (son of Wallace Foster Bennett), a Senator from Utah; born in Salt Lake City, Utah, September 18, 1933; B.A., University of Utah, 1957; head Congressional liaison, United States Department of Transportation; chief executive officer, The Franklin Institute, 1984-1992; chair, Education Strategic Planning Commission, Utah Board of Education; elected as a Republican to the United States Senate in 1992 for the term ending January 3, 1999; is a resident of Salt Lake City, Utah.

**BENNETT, Thomas Warren,** a Delegate from the Territory of Idaho; born in Union County, Ind., February 16, 1831; attended the common schools and was graduated from the law department of the Indiana Asbury (now De Pauw) University in July 1854; was admitted to the bar in 1855 and commenced practice in Liberty, Union County, Ind.; elected a member of the Indiana State senate in 1858 and resigned in 1861, upon the outbreak of the Civil War, to enter the Union Army; was commissioned a captain in the Fifteenth Regiment, Indiana Volunteer Infantry, in April 1861; became major of the Thirty-sixth Regiment on October 23, 1861; commissioned colonel of the Sixty-ninth Regiment on November 1, 1862, and was brevetted brigadier general on March 5, 1865; returned to Richmond, Ind.; again elected a member of the Indiana State senate, in October 1864, and served until March 1867; mayor of the city of Richmond, Ind., in 1869 and 1870; appointed Governor of the Territory of Idaho by President Ulysses S. Grant on October 24, 1871, and served until December 4, 1875, when he resigned, having been elected to Congress; presented credentials as an Independent Member-elect to the Forty-fourth Congress and served from March 4, 1875, to June 23, 1876, when he was succeeded by Stephen S. Fenn, who contested his election; was not a candidate for renomination in 1876 to the Forty-fifth Congress; resumed the practice of law in Richmond, Ind.; again served as the mayor of Richmond, 1877-1883, and 1885-1887; died in Richmond, Wayne County, Ind., February 2, 1893; interment in Earlham Cemetery.

**BENNETT, Wallace Foster** (father of Robert Foster Bennett), a Senator from Utah; born in Salt Lake City, Utah, November 13, 1898; attended the public schools; A.B., University of Utah, 1919; during the First World War, served as a member of the University of Utah Reserve Officers' Training Corps, and as a second lieutenant of Infantry; principal, San Luis Stake Academy, Manassa, Colo., 1919-1920; businessman and paint manufacturer; vice president, National Paint, Varnish and Lacquer Association, 1935-1936; president of the National Association of Manufacturers in 1949; elected as a Republican to the United States Senate in 1950; reelected in 1956, 1962, and again in 1968 and served from January 3, 1951, until his resignation December 20, 1974; was not a candidate for reelection in 1974; resumed business pursuits; was a resident of Salt Lake City, Utah, until his death there on December 19, 1993; interment in Salt Lake City Cemetery.

**Bibliography:** Bennett, Wallace F. *Faith and Freedom: The Pillars of American Democracy.* New York: Scribner, 1950; Bennett, Wallace F. *Why I Am A Mormon.* New York: T. Nelson, 1958.

**BENNY, Allan,** a Representative from New Jersey; born in Brooklyn, N.Y., July 12, 1867; attended the public schools of Bayonne, Hudson County, N.J.; studied law; was admitted to the bar in 1889 and commenced practice in Bayonne; member of the city council 1892-1894; member of the State house of assembly 1898-1900; prosecuting attorney of Bayonne from 1900 to 1903, when he resigned, having been elected to Congress; elected as a Democrat to the Fifty-eighth Congress (March 4, 1903-March 3, 1905); unsuccessful candidate for reelection in 1904 to the Fifty-ninth Congress; resumed the practice of his chosen profession; and was assistant librarian of the law library in the courthouse at Jersey City until his death; died in Bayonne, N.J., November 6, 1942; interment in Moravian Cemetery, Staten Island, N.Y.

**BENSON, Alfred Washburn,** a Senator from Kansas; born in Poland, Chautauqua County, N.Y., July 15, 1843; moved to Jamestown, N.Y., in 1860; attended Jamestown and Randolph Academies; during the Civil War enlisted in 1862 as a private in the One Hundred and Fifty-fourth Regiment, New York Volunteer Infantry, and at the close of the war held a commission as major; studied law; was admitted to the bar in Buffalo, N.Y., in 1866 and commenced practice in Sherman, N.Y.; moved to Ottawa, Franklin County, Kans., in 1869; held various local offices; member, State senate 1881-1885; judge of the fourth judicial district of Kansas 1885-1897; appointed as a Republican to the United States Senate to fill the vacancy caused by the resignation of Joseph R. Burton and served from June 11, 1906, to January 23, 1907, when a successor was elected; unsuccessful candidate for election in 1907 to fill this vacancy; appointed and subsequently elected associate justice of the supreme court of Kansas and served from 1907 to 1915, when he resigned; retired from public life; died in Topeka, Kans., January 1, 1916; interment in Highland Cemetery, Ottawa, Kans.

**BENSON, Carville Dickinson,** a Representative from Maryland; born near Halethorpe, Baltimore County, Md., August 24, 1872; attended the public schools of Baltimore, preparatory schools, and Lehigh University, Bethlehem, Pa., in 1890; was graduated from the law department of Baltimore University in 1893; was admitted to the bar the same year and commenced practice in Baltimore; member of the State house of representatives 1904-1910 and again in 1918, serving as speaker in 1906; member of the State senate 1912-1914; elected as a Democrat to the Sixty-fifth Congress to fill the vacancy caused by the death of Joshua F. C. Talbott; reelected to the Sixty-sixth Congress and served from November 5, 1918, to March 3, 1921; unsuccessful candidate for reelection in 1920 to the Sixth-seventh Congress; resumed the practice of law in

Baltimore, Md., and resided in Halethorpe, Md.; appointed State insurance commissioner of Maryland in 1924 and served until his death in Baltimore, Md., February 8, 1929; interment in Cedar Hill Cemetery, Brooklyn Station, Baltimore, Md.

**BENSON, Egbert,** a Delegate and a Representative from New York; born in New York City June 21, 1746; was graduated from Kings (now Columbia) College in 1765; studied law; was admitted to the bar and commenced practice in New York City; deputy to the provincial convention in 1775; member of the council of safety in 1777 and 1778; in 1777 was appointed the first attorney general of New York and served until 1789; member of the State assembly 1777-1781 and again in 1788; in 1783 was appointed one of the three commissioners to direct the embarkation of the Tory refugees for the loyal British provinces; associate judge of the supreme court of New York 1784-1801; Member of the Continental Congress in 1784, 1787 and 1788; member of the State constitutional convention in 1788, which ratified the Federal Constitution; elected to the First and Second Congresses (March 4, 1789-March 3, 1793); regent of the New York University 1789-1802; appointed judge of the United States Circuit Court, second circuit, February 20, 1801; served as the first president of the New-York Historical Society from 1804 to 1816; elected as a Federalist to the Thirteenth Congress and served from March 4, 1813, to August 2, 1813, when he resigned; died in Jamaica, Long Island, N.Y., August 24, 1833; interment in Prospect Cemetery.

**Bibliography:** *DAB.*

**BENSON, Elmer Austin,** a Senator from Minnesota; born in Appleton, Swift County, Minn., September 22, 1895; attended the public schools; was graduated from the St. Paul (Minn.) College of Law in 1918; during the First World War served as a private in the United States Army 1918-1919; was admitted to the bar but did not practice; engaged in banking and retail clothing business; State commissioner of securities in 1933 and State commissioner of banks 1933-1935; appointed as a Farmer-Laborite to the United States Senate to fill the vacancy caused by the death of Thomas D. Schall, and served from December 27, 1935 until November 3, 1936, when a successor was elected; was not a candidate for election to fill the vacancy; elected Governor of Minnesota in 1936, and served from January 4, 1937 to January 2, 1939; unsuccessful candidate for reelection in 1938 for Governor; unsuccessful candidate for election to the United States Senate in 1940 and 1942; engaged in agricultural pursuits; died in Minneapolis, Minn., March 13, 1985; interment in Appleton Cemetery, Appleton, Minn.

**Bibliography:** Benson, Elmer A. "Politics in My Lifetime." *Minnesota History* 47 (Winter 1980): 154-160; Shields, James M. *Mr. Progressive: A Biography of Elmer Austin Benson.* Minneapolis: Denison, 1971.

**BENSON, Samuel Page,** a Representative from Maine, born in Winthrop, Maine, November 28, 1804; received instruction from private teachers and attended the Monmouth (Maine) Academy; was graduated from Bowdoin College, Brunswick, Maine, in 1825; studied law; was admitted to the Kennebec County bar in 1828 and commenced practice in Unity, Maine; returned to Winthrop and practiced law until 1850; railroad builder; secretary of the Androscoggin & Kennebec (later Maine Central) Railroad; member of the State house of representatives in 1833 and 1834; served in the State senate in 1836 and 1837; secretary of state 1838-1841; overseer of Bowdoin College 1838-1876 and president of the board for sixteen years; chairman of the board of selectmen 1844-1848; elected as a Whig to the Thirty-third Congress and as a Republican to the Thirty-fourth Congress (March 4, 1853-March 3, 1857); chairman, Committee on Naval Affairs (Thirty-fourth Congress); was not a candidate for reelection in 1856; resumed the practice of law; died in Yarmouth, Cumberland County, Maine, August 12, 1876; interment in Maple Cemetery, Winthrop, Maine.

**BENTLEY, Alvin Morell,** a Representative from Michigan; born in Portland, Maine, August 30, 1918; graduated from Southern Pines (N.C.) High School in 1934, Asheville (N.C.) Prep School in 1936, and the University of Michigan in 1940; attended Turner's Diplomatic School, Washington, D.C., to qualify for diplomatic service; served as vice consul and secretary with the United States Diplomatic Corps in Mexico in May 1942, then going to Colombia, Hungary, and Italy; returned to Washington, D.C., March 15, 1950, for work in the State Department; resigned from the diplomatic service in 1950; returned to Owosso, Mich.; delegate to Republican State conventions in 1950, 1951, and 1952; vice president, Lake Huron Broadcasting Co., Saginaw, Mich., 1952; director of Mitchell-Bentley Corp.; elected as a Republican to the Eighty-third and to the three succeeding Congresses (January 3, 1953-January 3, 1961); wounded March 1, 1954 when three Puerto Rican Nationalists fired about thirty shots into a crowd of Representatives on the floor of the House; was not a candidate for renomination in 1960 to the House of Representatives, but was an unsuccessful candidate for election to the United States Senate; unsuccessful candidate in 1962 for election to the Eighty-eighth Congress; appointed by Governor George Romney in 1966 to the board of regents of the University of Michigan, a position he held at the time of his death in Tucson, Ariz., April 10, 1969; interment in Oak Hill Cemetery, Owosso, Mich.

**BENTLEY, Helen Delich,** a Representative from Maryland; born in Ruth, White Pine County, Nev., November 28, 1923; was graduated from the University of Missouri School of Journalism in 1944; recipient of several honorary degrees; reporter and maritime editor for the Baltimore Sun from 1945 until 1969; television producer, 1950-1965; appointed chairman of the Federal Maritime Commission, 1969-1975; international business consultant, 1975-1984; unsuccessful candidate for election in 1980 to the Ninety-seventh Congress, and for election in 1982 to the Ninety-eighth Congress; elected as a Republican to the Ninety-ninth and to the four succeeding Congresses (January 3, 1985-January 3, 1995); was not a candidate in 1994 for renomination to the One Hundred Fourth Congress, but was an unsuccessful candidate for nomination for Governor of Maryland; is a resident of Lutherville, Md.

**BENTLEY, Henry Wilbur,** a Representative from New York; born in DeRuyter, Madison County, N.Y., September 30, 1838; moved with his parents to Morrisville, N.Y.; attended Union School, Yates Polytechnic Institute at Chittenango, and Judd's private school at Berkshire; taught school for several years; studied law; was admitted to the bar in 1861 and commenced practice in Boonville, N.Y.; chairman of the Oneida County Building Commission; president of Boonville in 1874, 1889-1891, and 1899; elected as a Democrat to the Fifty-second Congress (March 4, 1891-March 3, 1893); unsuccessful candidate for reelection in 1892 to the Fifty-third Congress; continued the practice of law in Boonville, Oneida County, N.Y., until his death there on January 27, 1907; interment in Boonville Cemetery.

**BENTON, Charles Swan,** a Representative from New York; born in Fryeburg, Oxford County, Maine, July 12, 1810; pursued preparatory studies; moved to Herkimer County, N.Y., in 1824 to live with an elder brother; attended Lowville Academy, Lowville, N.Y.; learned the tanner's trade; editor of the Mohawk Courier and the Little Falls Gazette 1830-1832; studied law; was admitted to the bar in 1835 and commenced practice at Little Falls, N.Y.; surrogate of Herkimer County in 1837; judge advocate of the State militia; elected as a Democrat to the Twenty-eighth and Twenty-ninth Congresses (March 4, 1843-March 3, 1847); was not a candidate for renomination in 1846; clerk of the court of appeals 1847-1849; moved to Milwaukee, Wis., in 1855 and subsequently became editor of the Milwaukee News; appointed by President Franklin Pierce in 1856 as register of the United States land office at La Crosse, Wis., and served until 1861; was an unsuccessful candidate for election in

1862 to the Thirty-eighth Congress; engaged in agricultural pursuits near West Salem, Wis., and later, in 1865, at Galesburg, Ill.; returned to La Crosse, Wis., in 1869; judge of La Crosse County 1874-1881; died in La Crosse, Wis., May 4, 1882; interment in Oak Grove Cemetery.

**BENTON, Jacob,** a Representative from New Hampshire; born in Waterford, Caledonia County, Vt., August 19, 1814; attended the common schools, Lyndon (Vt.) Academy, and Randolph (Vt.) Academy, and was graduated from Burr and Burton Seminary at Manchester in 1839; taught school for several years; moved to Lancaster, Coos County, N.H., in 1842; studied law; was admitted to the bar in 1843 and commenced practice in Lancaster; member of the State house of representatives 1854-1856; delegate to the Republican National Convention in 1860; brigadier general, commanding State Volunteers; elected as a Republican to the Fortieth and Forty-first Congresses (March 4, 1867-March 3, 1871); declined to be a candidate for renomination in 1870; resumed the practice of law; died in Lancaster, Coos County, N.H., September 29, 1892; interment in the Summer Street Cemetery.

**BENTON, Lemuel** (great-grandfather of George William Dargan), a Representative from South Carolina; born in Granville County, N.C., in 1754; as a young man moved to that section of Cheraw District which is now Darlington County, S.C.; engaged as a planter and subsequently became an extensive landowner; elected major of the Cheraw Regiment in 1777 and served throughout the Revolutionary War, being promoted to the rank of colonel in 1781; resigned his commission in 1794; member of the State house of representatives 1782-1788; county court justice of Darlington County in 1785 and 1791; escheator of Cheraw District (composed of what is now Chesterfield, Darlington, and Marlboro Counties) in 1787; delegate to the State convention at Charleston that ratified the Federal Constitution in 1788; sheriff of Cheraw District in 1789 and 1791; delegate to the State constitutional convention at Columbia in 1790; elected to the Third Congress and reelected as a Republican to the Fourth and Fifth Congresses (March 4, 1793-March 3, 1799); unsuccessful candidate for reelection in 1798 to the Sixth Congress; resumed agricultural pursuits; died in Darlington, Darlington County, S.C., May 18, 1818; interment on his estate, "Stony Hill," near Darlington, S.C.

**BENTON, Maecenas Eason,** a Representative from Missouri; born near Dyersburg, Obion County, Tenn., January 29, 1848; attended two west Tennessee academies and St. Louis University; was graduated from the law department of Cumberland University, Lebanon, Tenn., in 1870; served in the Confederate Army during the Civil War; was admitted to the bar and commenced practice in Neosho, Newton County, Mo.; prosecuting attorney of Newton County 1878-1884; United States attorney from March 1885 to July 1889; delegate to the Democratic National Convention in 1896; elected as a Democrat to the Fifty-fifth, Fifty-sixth, Fifty-seventh, and Fifty-eighth Congresses (March 4, 1897-March 3, 1905); unsuccessful candidate for reelection in 1904 to the Fifty-ninth Congress; resumed the practice of law in Neosho, Mo.; member of the State constitutional conventions in 1922 and 1924; died in Springfield, Greene County, Mo., April 27, 1924; interment in the Odd Fellows Cemetery, Neosho, Mo.

**BENTON, Thomas Hart** (father-in-law of John C. Fremont), a Senator and a Representative from Missouri; born at Harts Mill, near Hillsboro, N.C., March 14, 1782; attended Chapel Hill College (now the University of North Carolina) and the law department of William and Mary College, Williamsburg, Va.; was admitted to the bar at Nashville, Tenn., in 1806 and commenced practice in Franklin, Williamson County, Tenn.; member, Tennessee State senate, 1809-1811; served as aide-de-camp to General Andrew Jackson; colonel of a regiment of Tennessee volunteers, 1812-1813; lieutenant colonel of the Thirty-ninth United States Infantry,

1813-1815; moved to St. Louis, Mo., where he edited the Missouri Inquirer and continued the practice of law; upon the admission of Missouri as a State into the Union, was elected in 1821 as a Democrat to the United States Senate; reelected in 1827, 1833, 1839, and 1845 and served from August 10, 1821, to March 3, 1851; chairman, Committee on Indian Affairs (Eighteenth through Twentieth Congresses), Committee on Military Affairs (Twentieth through Twenty-sixth and Twenty-ninth and Thirtieth Congresses), Committee on Foreign Relations (Thirtieth Congress); author of the January 1837 resolution to expunge from the Senate Journal the March 28, 1834 resolution of censure on President Andrew Jackson for his removal of public deposits from the Second Bank of the United States in October 1833; unsuccessful candidate for reelection to the Senate in 1850; censure proceedings were initiated against him in 1850, arising from an incident of disorderly conduct on April 17, 1850, on the Chamber floor when he threatened Senator Henry S. Foote of Mississippi following heated debate on the Compromise of 1850; Senator Foote drew his pistol in response but was restrained by other members before he could fire; the Senate took no action; elected as a Democrat to the Thirty-third Congress (March 4, 1853-March 3, 1855); chairman, Committee on Military Affairs (Thirty-third Congress); unsuccessful candidate for reelection in 1854 to the Thirty-fourth Congress; unsuccessful candidate for election in 1856 for Governor of Missouri; engaged in literary pursuits in Washington, D.C., until his death there on April 10, 1858; interment in Bellefontaine Cemetery, St. Louis, Mo.

**Bibliography:** *DAB*; Benton, Thomas H. *Thirty Years View: Or A History of the American Government for Thirty Years From 1820-1850.* 2 vols. 1854, 1856. Reprint. New York: Greenwood Press, 1968; Smith, Elbert B. *Magnificent Missourian: Thomas Hart Benton.* Philadelphia: Lippincott, 1957.

**BENTON, William,** a Senator from Connecticut; born in Minneapolis, Hennepin County, Minn., April 1, 1900; attended Shattuck Military Academy, Faribault, Minn., and Carleton College, Northfield, Minn., in 1917 and 1918; graduated from Yale University in 1921; worked for advertising agencies in New York and Chicago until 1929, and then co-founded his own advertising agency in New York; moved to Norwalk, Conn., in 1932; part-time vice president of the University of Chicago, 1937-1945; Assistant Secretary of State for Public Affairs, Washington, D.C., September 14, 1945, to September 30, 1947, during which time he was active in organizing the United Nations; member of and delegate to numerous United Nations and international conferences and commissions; chairman of the board and publisher of Encyclopedia Britannica, 1943-1973; trustee of several schools and colleges; appointed to the United States Senate, December 17, 1949, and subsequently elected as a Democrat to fill the vacancy caused by the resignation of Raymond E. Baldwin to the term ending January 3, 1953 and served from December 17, 1949, to January 3, 1953; unsuccessful candidate for election for the full term in 1952; United States Permanent Representative to the United Nations Educational, Scientific and Cultural Organization in Paris, 1963-1968; died in New York City, March 18, 1973; cremated; ashes scattered at family estate, Southport, Conn.

**Bibliography:** Hyman, Sidney. *The Lives of William Benton.* Chicago: University of Chicago Press, 1969.

**BENTSEN, Kenneth E., Jr.** (nephew of Lloyd Millard Bentsen), a Representative from Texas; born in Houston, Harris County, Tex., June 3, 1959; graduated, Deerfield Academy, 1977; B.A., University of St. Thomas, Houston, 1982; M.P.A., American University, Washington, D.C., 1985; former Harris County, Tex. Democratic chair; staff member, House Committee on Appropriations for Representative Ronald D. Coleman of Texas, 1983-1987; partner in Houston investment banking firm, 1987-1994; elected as a Democrat to the One Hundred Fourth Congress (January 3, 1995-January 3, 1997); is a resident of Houston, Tex.

**BENTSEN, Lloyd Millard, Jr.** (uncle of Kenneth E. Bentsen, Jr.), a Representative and a Senator from Texas; born in Mission, Hidalgo County, Tex., February 11, 1921; attended the public schools; LL.B., University of Texas Law School, Austin, 1942; admitted to the bar in 1942; served in the United States Army Air Corps, 1942-1945; entered the private practice of law in McAllen, Tex., in 1945; county judge of Hidalgo County, 1946-1948; elected as a Democrat in November 1948 to the Eighty-first Congress and, at a special election in December 1948, to fill the vacancy in the Eightieth Congress caused by the death of Milton H. West; reelected to the Eighty-second and Eighty-third Congresses, and served from December 4, 1948 to January 3, 1955; was not a candidate for renomination in 1954 to the Eighty-fourth Congress; founded and operated a financial holding company in Texas; elected in 1970 to the United States Senate; reelected in 1976, 1982, and 1988, and served from January 3, 1971 until his resignation on January 20, 1993; chairman, Joint Economic Committee (Ninety-eighth Congress), Democratic Senatorial Campaign Committee (Ninety-eighth Congress), Committee on Finance (One Hundredth through One Hundred Second Congresses); unsuccessful candidate for Vice President of the United States in 1988 on the Democratic ticket headed by Michael S. Dukakis; appointed Secretary of the Treasury in the Cabinet of President William J. Clinton, and served from January 22, 1993 until his resignation December 22, 1994; is a resident of Houston, Tex.

**BERESFORD, Richard,** a Delegate from South Carolina; born near Charleston, St. Thomas and St. Denis Parish, Berkeley County, S.C., in 1755; educated in South Carolina and in England; studied law at the Middle Temple in London; was admitted to the bar in 1773 and practiced in Charleston, S.C.; engaged in planting, with extensive estates in Berkeley and Colleton Counties, S.C., and in England; took an active part in the Revolution, serving under General Isaac Huger in the Georgia campaign in 1778; was captured at the fall of Charleston in 1780 and imprisoned at St. Augustine until 1781, when he was exchanged; member of the South Carolina State house of representatives in 1781; elected by the State general assembly a member of the privy council in 1782; elected Lieutenant Governor in January 1783, but resigned shortly afterward, having been elected to Congress; Member of the Continental Congress in 1783 and 1784; resumed planting; later engaged in literary pursuits; published the Vigil in Charleston in 1798; died in Charleston, S.C., February 6, 1803.

**BEREUTER, Douglas Kent,** a Representative from Nebraska; born in York, York County, Nebr., October 6, 1939; attended St. Paul's Lutheran School, Utica, Nebr.; graduated, Utica High School, 1957; B.A., University of Nebraska, Lincoln, 1961; M.C.P., Harvard University, 1963; M.P.A., Harvard University, 1973; attended Eagleton Institute of Politics, 1976; urban planner and economic development consultant in surrounding States; interest in family retail automotive, petroleum business; officer and counter-intelligence agent, First Infantry Division, United States Army, 1963-1965; State senator (Nebraska Unicameral Legislature), 1975-1978; chaired the Washington-based Urban Development Committee on the National Conference of State Legislatures, 1977-1978; division director, Nebraska Department of Economic Development, 1966-1968; director, State Office of Planning and Programming, 1968-1971; Federal-State Relations Coordinator for Nebraska State Government, 1967-1971; member, Nebraska Crime Commission, 1969-1971; elected as a Republican to the Ninety-sixth and to the eight succeeding Congresses (January 3, 1979-January 3, 1997); is a resident of Lincoln, Nebr.

**BERGEN, Christopher Augustus,** a Representative from New Jersey; born in Bridge Point, Somerset County, N.J., August 2, 1841; attended Harlingen School and Edge Hill Classical School and was graduated from Princeton College in 1863; studied law; was licensed by the supreme court of New Jersey in 1866 as an attorney and commenced practice in Camden, N.J.; licensed as a counselor in 1869; elected as a Republican to the Fifty-first and Fifty-second Congresses (March 4, 1889-March 3, 1893); unsuccessful candidate for renomination in 1892; resumed the practice of law; in 1903 moved to Haverford, Montgomery County, Pa., where he died on February 18, 1905; interment in Evergreen Cemetery, Camden, N.J.

**BERGEN, John Teunis** (second cousin of Teunis Garret Bergen), a Representative from New York; born in Gowanus, Brooklyn, N.Y., in 1786; completed preparatory studies; appointed a lieutenant in the New York State Militia in 1812 and promoted to captain in 1815; served in the War of 1812; sheriff of Kings County, N.Y., 1821-1825 and again from 1828 until 1831, when he resigned; purchased the Long Island Patriot in 1829, the name of which was subsequently changed to the Brooklyn Advocate, and which ultimately became the Brooklyn Daily Eagle; elected as a Jacksonian to the Twenty-second Congress (March 4, 1831-March 3, 1833); chairman, Committee on Accounts (Twenty-second Congress); was not a candidate for renomination in 1832; engaged in agricultural pursuits near Bay Ridge, New Utrecht, N.Y.; moved to Brooklyn, N.Y., and engaged in the grocery business; in 1837, with his sons, conducted a planing mill in New York City; moved to Genesee County and engaged in agricultural pursuits; died in Batavia, Genesee County, N.Y., on March 9, 1855; interment in Batavia Cemetery.

**BERGEN, Teunis Garret** (second cousin of John Teunis Bergen), a Representative from New York; born in Brooklyn, N.Y., October 6, 1806; attended the common schools and Erasmus Hall Academy, Flatbush, N.Y.; engaged in agricultural pursuits and surveying; supervisor of New Utrecht, Kings County, N.Y., 1836-1859; member of the State constitutional conventions in 1846, 1867, and 1868; delegate to the Democratic National Conventions at Baltimore and Charleston in 1860; elected as a Democrat to the Thirty-ninth Congress (March 4, 1865-March 3, 1867); was not a candidate for renomination in 1866; resumed agricultural pursuits and surveying near New Utrecht; also engaged in literary and historical work; served as ensign, captain, adjutant, lieutenant colonel, and colonel of the Two Hundred and Forty-first Regiment, New York State Militia, known as Kings County Troop; died in Brooklyn, N.Y., April 24, 1881; interment in Greenwood Cemetery.

**BERGER, Victor Luitpold,** a Representative from Wisconsin; born in Nieder Rebbach, Austria-Hungary, February 28, 1860; attended the Gymnasia at Leutschau and the universities at Budapest and Vienna; immigrated to the United States in 1878 with his parents, who settled near Bridgeport, Conn.; moved to Milwaukee, Wis., in 1880; taught school from 1880 until 1890; editor of the Milwaukee Daily Vorwaerts, 1892-1898; editor of the Wahrheit, the Social Democratic Herald, and the Milwaukee Leader, being publisher of the last named at the time of his death; delegate to the People's Party Convention at St. Louis in 1896; one of the organizers of the Social Democracy in 1897 and of the Social Democratic Party in 1898, known since 1900 as the Socialist Party; unsuccessful candidate of the Socialist Party for election in 1904 to the Fifty-ninth Congress; elected a member of the charter convention of Milwaukee in 1907, and alderman at large in 1910; elected as a Socialist to the Sixty-second Congress (March 4, 1911-March 3, 1913); presented credentials as a Member-elect to the Sixty-sixth Congress, but the House by a resolution adopted on November 10, 1919, declared him not entitled to take the oath of office as a Representative or to hold a seat as such; having been opposed to the entrance of the United States in the First World War and having written articles expressing his opinion on that question, he was indicted in various places in the Federal courts, tried in Chicago, found guilty, and sentenced by Judge Kenesaw M. Landis on February 20, 1919 to serve twenty years in the Federal penitentiary; this judgment was reversed by the United States Supreme Court on January 31, 1921, whereupon the Government withdrew all cases against him in 1922; his election to the Sixty-sixth Congress was unsuccessfully contested by Joseph P. Carney and the seat was declared vacant; presented credentials as a Member-elect to fill the vacancy caused by the action of the House and on January 10, 1920, the House again decided that he was not entitled to a seat in the Sixty-sixth Congress and declined to permit him to take the oath or qualify as a Representative; Henry H. Bodenstab unsuccessfully contested this election, and on February 25, 1921, the House again declared the seat vacant; elected as a Socialist to the Sixty-eighth and to the two succeeding Congresses (March 4, 1923-March 3, 1929); unsuccessful candidate for reelection in 1928 to the Seventy-first Congress; resumed his editorial work; died in Milwaukee, Wis., August 7, 1929; interment in Forest Home Cemetery.

**Bibliography:** *DAB*; Miller, Sally M. *Victor Berger and the Promise of Constructive Socialism, 1910-1920.* Westport, Conn.: Greenwood Press, 1973; Stevens, Michael E., and Ellen D. Goldlust-Gingrich, eds. *The Family Letters of Victor and Meta Berger, 1894-1929.* Madison: State Historical Society of Wisconsin, 1995.

**BERGLAND, Robert Selmer,** a Representative from Minnesota; born in Roseau, Minn., July 22, 1928; attended the Roseau public schools; University of Minnesota School of Agriculture, St. Paul, Minn., 1948; farmer; chairman, Minnesota Agriculture Stabilization and Conservation Service, March 1961-January 1963; midwest director, United States Department of Agriculture, January 1963 to May 1968; unsuccessful candidate for election in 1968 to the Ninety-first Congress; elected as a Democrat to the Ninety-second and to the three succeeding Congresses and served from Janaury 3, 1971, until his resignation January 22, 1977; appointed Secretary of Agriculture in the Cabinet of President Jimmy Carter, and served from January 23, 1977 until January 23, 1981; president, Farmland World Trade, March 1981-September 1982; vice president and general manager, National Rural Electric Cooperatives Association, Washington, D.C., September 1982 to present; is a resident of Annandale, Va.

**BERLIN, William Markle,** a Representative from Pennsylvania; born on a farm near Delmont, Westmoreland County, Pa., March 29, 1880; attended the public schools; was graduated from the Laird Institute at Murrysville, Pa., in 1896; moved to Greensburg, Pa., in 1916 and engaged as an automobile distributor, in the wholesale oil and gas business, and in coal mining; chairman of the Democratic County Committee in 1916; elected as a Democrat to the Seventy-third and Seventy-fourth Congresses (March 4, 1933-January 3, 1937); unsuccessful candidate for renomination in 1936 to the Seventy-fifth Congress; clerk of the court of Westmoreland County, Pa., 1937-1941; resumed the mining of coal in Pennsylvania and West Virginia in 1941; delegate to the Democratic National Convention of 1944; unsuccessful candidate for the Republican nomination in 1950 to the Eighty-second Congress; assistant librarian, United States House of Representatives, February 1, 1957, until 1961 when promoted to librarian, and served in that capacity until his death in Greensburg, Pa., October 14, 1962; interment in Westmoreland County Memorial Park.

**BERMAN, Howard Lawrence,** a Representative from California; born in Los Angeles, Calif., April 15, 1941; graduated, Hamilton High School, Los Angeles, 1959; B.A., University of California at Los Angeles, 1962; LL.B., University of California at Los Angeles School of Law, 1965; admitted to the California bar, 1966; attorney specializing in labor law, 1967-1973; Volunteers in Service to America volunteer, 1966-1967; elected to California State assembly, 1973-1982, majority leader, 1974-1975; delegate, Democratic National Convention, 1968, 1976, and 1984; past president, California

Federation of Young Democrats; elected as a Democrat to the Ninety-eighth and to the six succeeding Congresses (January 3, 1983-January 3, 1997); is a resident of Sherman Oaks, Calif.

**BERNARD, John Toussaint,** a Representative from Minnesota; born in Bastia, Island of Corsica, France, March 6, 1893; in 1907 immigrated to the United States with his parents, who settled in Eveleth, St. Louis County, Minn.; attended public schools in France and in Eveleth, Minn.; employed as an iron-ore miner 1910-1917 and as city fireman 1920-1936; served in the United States Army during the First World War as a corporal in the One Hundred and Twenty-fifth Field Artillery, and also as a civilian employee in the Army and Navy Intelligence 1917-1919, serving overseas fifteen months; delegate to the State Farmer-Labor Party conventions in 1936, 1938, and 1940; elected as a Farmer-Labor candidate to the Seventy-fifth Congress (January 3, 1937-January 3, 1939); unsuccessful candidate for reelection in 1938 to the Seventy-sixth Congress and for election in 1940 to the Seventy-seventh Congress; engaged as a labor organizer, legislative director and civil rights activist; moved to Long Beach, Calif., where he lived until his death there on August 6, 1983.

**Bibliography:** *"A Common Man's Courage: The Story of John Bernard."* 1977. Produced by University Community Video, Minneapolis, Minn. 29 minutes.

**BERNHISEL, John Milton,** a Delegate from the Territory of Utah; born at Sandy Hill, Tyrone Township, near Harrisburg, Cumberland County, Pa., July 23, 1799; attended the common schools; was graduated from the medical department of the University of Pennsylvania at Philadelphia; commenced the practice of medicine in New York City; moved to Nauvoo, Hancock County, Ill., in 1843, and thence to the Territory of Utah; settled in Salt Lake City in 1848 and continued the practice of medicine; elected as a Whig to the Thirty-second and to the three succeeding Congresses (March 4, 1851-March 3, 1859); was not a candidate for renomination in 1858 to the Thirty-sixth Congress; resumed the practice of medicine; elected to the Thirty-seventh Congress (March 4, 1861-March 3, 1863); was not a candidate for renomination in 1862 to the Thirty-eighth Congress; resumed the practice of his profession; served as regent of the University of Utah; died in Salt Lake City September 28, 1881; interment in Salt Lake City Cemetery.

**Bibliography:** Barrett, Gwynn W. "John M. Bernhisel: Mormon Elder in Congress." Ph.D. dissertation, Brigham Young University, 1968.

**BERRIEN, John Macpherson,** a Senator from Georgia; born at Rocky Hill, near Princeton, N.J., August 23, 1781; moved with his parents to Savannah, Ga., in 1782; was graduated from Princeton College in 1796; studied law in Savannah; was admitted to the bar and began practice in Louisville, then the capital of Georgia, in 1799; returned to Savannah; elected solicitor of the eastern judicial circuit of Georgia in 1809; judge of the same circuit from 1810 until January 30, 1821, when he resigned; captain of the Georgia Hussars, a Savannah volunteer company, in the War of 1812; member, Georgia State senate, 1822-1823; elected as a Jacksonian to the United States Senate and served from March 4, 1825, until March 9, 1829; resigned to accept the position of Attorney General in the Cabinet of President Andrew Jackson, and served from March 9, 1829 until June 22, 1831, when he resigned; resumed the practice of law; again elected, as a Whig, to the United States Senate and served from March 4, 1841, until May 1845, when he again resigned to accept an appointment to the Georgia State supreme court; again elected in 1845 to the United States Senate to fill the vacancy caused by his second resignation; reelected in 1846, and served from November 13, 1845 until May 28, 1852, when he resigned for the third time; chairman, Committee on Judiciary (Twentieth, Twenty-sixth, and Twenty-seventh Congresses); president of the American

Party convention at Milledgeville in 1855; died in Savannah, Ga., January 1, 1856; interment in Laurel Grove Cemetery.

**Bibliography:** *DAB*; Govan, Thomas P. "John Macpherson Berrien and the Administration of Andrew Jackson." *Journal of Southern History* 5 (November 1939): 447-67; McCrary, Royce, Jr. "John Macpherson Berrien of Georgia: A Political Biography." Ph.D. dissertation, University of Georgia, 1971.

**BERRY, Albert Seaton,** a Representative from Kentucky; born in Fairfield (now Dayton), Campbell County, Ky., May 13, 1836; attended the public schools; was graduated from Miami University, Oxford, Ohio, in 1855 and from the Cincinnati Law School in 1858; was admitted to the bar and practiced; prosecuting attorney of Newport, Ky., in 1859; served in the Confederate Army throughout the Civil War; mayor of Newport in 1870 and served five terms; member of the Kentucky senate in 1878 and 1884; elected as a Democrat to the Fifty-third and to the three succeeding Congresses (March 4, 1893-March 3, 1901); unsuccessful candidate for renomination in 1900; resumed the practice of law; appointed and subsequently elected judge of the seventeenth judicial district of Kentucky and served from 1905 until his death in Newport, Campbell County, Ky., January 6, 1908; interment in Evergreen Cemetery.

**BERRY, Campbell Polson** (cousin of James Henderson Berry), a Representative from California; born in Jackson County, Ala., November 7, 1834; moved to Arkansas in 1841 with his parents, who settled in Berryville; attended the grammar school; moved to California in 1857 and settled near Yuba City; was graduated from the Pacific Methodist College, Vacaville, Solano County, Calif., in 1865; served as supervisor of Sutter County 1866-1869; engaged in agricultural pursuits and for a short time, in 1872, was also in the mercantile business; member of the State assembly in 1869, 1871, 1873, 1875, 1877, and 1878, serving as speaker in 1877 and 1878; elected as a Democrat to the Forty-sixth and Forty-seventh Congresses (March 4, 1879-March 3, 1883); declined to be a candidate for renomination in 1882; subtreasurer of the United States at San Francisco, Calif., 1894-1898; died in Wheatland, Yuba County, Calif., on January 8, 1901; interment in Fairview Cemetery, Sutter County, Calif.

**BERRY, Ellis Yarnal,** a Representative from South Dakota; born in Larchwood, Lyon County, Iowa, October 6, 1902; attended Philip (S.Dak.) High School; student in Morningside College, Sioux City, Iowa, 1920-1922; was graduated from the law school of the University of South Dakota at Vermillion in 1927; was admitted to the bar the same year and commenced the practice of law in Kennebec, Lyman County, S.Dak., and at McLaughlin, Corson County, in 1929; served as State's attorney, mayor of McLaughlin, and judge of Probate Court, Corson County, 1931-1939; publisher of the McLaughlin Messenger since 1938, McIntosh News and Morristown World since 1952; delegate to State Republican Conventions in 1934, 1936, and 1938; editor of the State Bar Association Journal from 1938 until 1950; member of the State senate in the 1939 and 1941 legislative sessions, and legislative assistant to Governor Merrell Q. Sharpe during the 1943 session; member of the Missouri River States Committee, 1940-1943; member of the State Board of Regents of Education, 1946-1950; elected as a Republican to the Eighty-second and to the nine succeeding Congresses (January 3, 1951-January 3, 1971); was not a candidate for reelection in 1970 to the Ninety-second Congress; is a resident of Rapid City, S.Dak.

**Bibliography:** Sculte, Steven C. "Removing the Yoke of Government: E.Y. Berry and the Origins of Indian Termination Policy." *South Dakota History* 14 (Spring 1984): 48-67.

**BERRY, George Leonard,** a Senator from Tennessee; born in Lee Valley, Hawkins County, Tenn., September 12, 1882; attended the common schools; employed as a pressman from 1891 to 1907 in various cities; served during the First World War in the American Expeditionary Forces, with the rank of major, in the Railroad Transportation Engineers 1918-1919; president of the International Pressmen and Assistants' Union of North America 1907-1948; also engaged in agricultural pursuits and banking; delegate to many national and international labor conventions; appointed as a Democrat to the United States Senate to fill the vacancy caused by the death of Nathan L. Bachman and served from May 6, 1937, to November 8, 1938, when a successor was elected; unsuccessful candidate for nomination in 1938 to fill the vacancy; resumed the presidency of the International Pressmen and Assistants' Union of North America, and also his agricultural pursuits at Pressmen's Home, Tenn., until his death on December 4, 1948; interment in Pressmen's Home Cemetery.

**Bibliography:** *DAB.*

**BERRY, James Henderson** (cousin of Campbell Polson Berry), a Senator from Arkansas; born in Jackson County, Ala., May 15, 1841; moved to Arkansas with his parents, who settled in Carroll County in 1848; attended a private school in Berryville, Ark.; entered the Confederate Army in 1861 as a second lieutenant, Sixteenth Regiment, Arkansas Infantry; lost a leg in the Battle of Corinth, Miss., October 1862; studied law; was admitted to the bar in 1866 and commenced practice in Berryville, Carroll County, Ark.; elected to the Arkansas State house of representatives in 1866; reelected in 1872, and served as speaker in 1874; moved to Bentonville, Ark., in 1869 and continued the practice of law; chairman of the Democratic State convention in 1876; judge of the circuit court from 1878 until 1882; elected Governor of Arkansas in 1882, and served from January 13, 1883 to January 17, 1885; elected as a Democrat to the United States Senate in 1885 to fill the vacancy caused by the resignation of Augustus H. Garland; reelected in 1889, 1895, and 1901, and served from March 20, 1885, to March 3, 1907; unsuccessful candidate for reelection in 1906; chairman, Committee on Public Lands (Fifty-third Congress), Committee on Engrossed Bills (Fifty-ninth Congress); died in Bentonville, Benton County, Ark., January 30, 1913; interment in the Knights of Pythias Cemetery.

**Bibliography:** *DAB;* Berry, James. *An Autobiography of James Berry.* Bentonville, Ark.: Democrat Press, 1913.

**BERRY, John,** a Representative from Ohio; born near Carey, in that portion of Crawford County which is now Wyandot County, Ohio, April 26, 1833; attended the public schools, and Ohio Wesleyan University at Delaware; was graduated from the law department of Cincinnati College, Ohio, in 1857; was admitted to the bar in April 1857 and commenced practice in Upper Sandusky; elected prosecuting attorney of Wyandot County in 1862; reelected in 1864; mayor of Upper Sandusky, Ohio, in 1864; elected as a Democrat to the Forty-third Congress (March 4, 1873-March 3, 1875); declined to be a candidate for renomination in 1874; resumed the practice of law in Upper Sandusky, Ohio, where he died May 18, 1879; interment in Oak Hill Cemetery, near Upper Sandusky, Ohio.

**BESHLIN, Earl Hanley,** a Representative from Pennsylvania; born in Conewango Township, Warren County, Pa., April 28, 1870; was raised on a farm; attended the public schools and was graduated from Warren High School; studied law; was admitted to the bar of Warren County in 1893 and commenced practice in Warren, Warren County, Pa.; elected burgess of Warren County in 1906 for a term of three years; served as borough solicitor from 1914 to 1918; elected as a Democrat and Prohibitionist to the Sixty-fifth Congress to fill the vacancy caused by the resignation of Orrin D. Bleakley and served from November 8, 1917, to March 3, 1919; unsuccessful candidate for reelection in 1918 to the Sixty-sixth

Congress; member and later chairman, Board of Education, Warren County, 1919-1935; member and chairman, Warren State Hospital, 1935-1939; resumed and continued the practice of law until his death in Warren, Pa., on July 12, 1971; interment in Oakland Mausoleum.

**BETHUNE, Edwin Ruthvin, Jr.,** a Representative from Arkansas; born in Pocahontas, Randolph County, Ark., December 19, 1935; attended the public schools of Little Rock, Ark.; graduated, Pocahontas High School, 1953; B.A., University of Arkansas, Fayetteville, 1961; J.D., University of Arkansas School of Law, 1963; admitted to the Arkansas Bar in 1963 and commenced practice in Pocahontas; admitted to practice before the United States Supreme Court, 1972; served in United States Marine Corps, sergeant, 1954-1957, with service in Korea; deputy prosecuting attorney, Randolph County, Ark., 1963-1964; special agent, Federal Bureau of Investigation, 1964-1968; private practice of law in Searcy, Ark., 1968-1978; prosecuting attorney, first judicial district of Arkansas, 1970-1971; chairman, Ninth District Federal Home Loan Bank Board, 1973-1976; elected as a Republican to the Ninety-sixth and to the two succeeding Congresses (January 3, 1979-January 3, 1985); was not a candidate for reelection in 1984 to the House of Representatives, but was an unsuccessful candidate for election to the United States Senate; resumed the practice of law in Washington, D.C.; is a resident of Arlington, Va.

**BETHUNE, Lauchlin,** a Representative from North Carolina; born near Fayetteville, Cumberland County, N.C., April 15, 1785; attended private schools and the Lumberton (N.C.) Male Academy; engaged in agricultural pursuits; member of the North Carolina State senate in 1817, 1818, 1822-1825, and 1827; elected as a Jacksonian to the Twenty-second Congress (March 4, 1831-March 3, 1833); unsuccessful candidate for reelection in 1832 to the Twenty-third Congress; unsuccessful candidate for election in 1834 to the Twenty-fourth Congress, and for election in 1836 to the Twenty-fifth Congress; returned to his plantation near Fayetteville, N.C., and continued agricultural pursuits until his death on October 10, 1874; interment in the Presbyterian Cemetery, Aberdeen, Moore County, N.C.

**BETHUNE, Marion,** a Representative from Georgia; born near Greensboro, Greene County, Ga., April 8, 1816; attended private schools and De Hagan's Academy; moved with his widowed mother to Talbotton, Talbot County, Ga., in 1829; engaged in mercantile pursuits; studied law; was admitted to the bar in 1842, and commenced practice at Talbotton; probate judge of Talbot County from 1852 until 1868, when he voluntarily retired; member of the constitutional convention of Georgia at the time of the repeal of the ordinance of secession; member of the Georgia State house of representatives, 1867-1871; elected as a Republican to the Forty-first Congress to fill the vacancy caused by the House declaring that William P. Edwards was not entitled to the seat, and served from December 22, 1870 to March 3, 1871; unsuccessful candidate for reelection in 1870 to the Forty-second Congress; resumed the practice of law; unsuccessful candidate for election in 1872 to the Forty-third Congress; United States census supervisor in 1890; died in Talbotton, Ga., February 20, 1895; interment in Oakhill Cemetery.

**BETTON, Silas,** a Representative from New Hampshire; born in Londonderry, N.H., August 26, 1768; studied under a private tutor, and was graduated from Dartmouth College, Hanover, N.H., in 1787; studied law; was admitted to the bar and commenced practice in Salem, Rockingham County, N.H., in 1790; member of the State house of representatives 1797-1799; member of the State senate 1801-1803; elected as a Federalist to the Eighth and Ninth Congresses (March 4, 1803-March 3, 1807); resumed the practice of law; again a member of the State house of representatives in 1810 and 1811; served as high sheriff of Rockingham County 1813-1818;

died in Salem, N.H., January 22, 1822; interment in Old Parish Cemetery, Center Village, Salem, N.H.

**BETTS, Jackson Edward,** a Representative from Ohio; born in Findlay, Hancock County, Ohio, May 26, 1904; attended the public schools of Findlay, Ohio; A.B., Kenyon College, Gambier, Ohio, 1926; LL.B., Yale University Law School, New Haven, Conn., 1929; was admitted to the bar in 1930, and commenced the practice of law in Findlay, Ohio; prosecuting attorney of Hancock County, Ohio, 1933-1937; member of the Ohio State house of representatives, 1937-1947, serving as speaker in 1945 and 1946; elected as a Republican to the Eighty-second and to the ten succeeding Congresses (January 3, 1951-January 3, 1973); was not a candidate for reelection in 1972 to the Ninety-third Congress; part-time teacher at Findlay College, 1973-1983; acting judge, Findlay Municipal Court; was a resident of Findlay, Ohio; died August 13, 1993.

**BETTS, Samuel Rossiter,** a Representative from New York; born in Richmond, Berkshire County, Mass., June 8, 1787; was graduated from Williams College, Williamstown, Mass., in 1806; studied law in Hudson, N.Y.; was admitted to the bar in 1807 and commenced practice in Monticello, Sullivan County, N.Y.; served as judge advocate of Volunteers in the War of 1812; elected as a Republican to the Fourteenth Congress (March 4, 1815-March 3, 1817); was not a candidate for renomination in 1816 to the Fifteenth Congress; moved to Newburgh, Orange County, N.Y., where he continued the practice of law; appointed circuit judge under the new State constitution in 1823; appointed and subsequently elected judge of the United States District Court for the Southern District of New York and served from 1826 until 1867, when he resigned; died in New Haven, Conn., November 2, 1868; interment in Woodlawn Cemetery, New York City.

**Bibliography:** *DAB*.

**BETTS, Thaddeus,** a Senator from Connecticut; born in Norwalk, Conn., February 4, 1789; completed preparatory studies; was graduated from Yale College in 1807; studied law; was admitted to the bar in 1810 and commenced practice in Norwalk; member of the Connecticut State house of representatives in 1815 and 1830; member of the State senate in 1831; elected lieutenant governor of Connecticut in 1832 and 1836; elected as a Whig to the United States Senate, and served from March 4, 1839 until his death in Washington, D.C., April 7, 1840; interment in Union Cemetery, Norwalk, Conn.

**BEVERIDGE, Albert Jeremiah,** a Senator from Indiana; born near Sugar Tree Ridge, Concord Township, Highland County, Ohio, October 6, 1862; attended the common schools; was graduated from Indiana Asbury (now DePauw) University, Greencastle, Ind., in 1885; studied law; was admitted to the bar in 1887 and commenced practice in Indianapolis, Ind.; elected as a Republican to the United States Senate in 1899, reelected in 1905, and served from March 4, 1899, until March 3, 1911; unsuccessful candidate for reelection in 1910; chairman, Committee on Forest Reservations and Game Protection (Fifty-sixth Congress), Committee on Territories (Fifty-seventh through Sixty-first Congresses), Committee on Indian Depredations (Fifty-ninth Congress); returned to Indianapolis and engaged in literary and historical pursuits; unsuccessful Progressive candidate for election in 1912 for Governor of Indiana; chairman of the National Progressive Convention at Chicago in 1912; unsuccessful candidate as a Progressive in 1914 and as a Republican in 1922 for election to the United States Senate; died in Indianapolis, Ind., April 27, 1927; interment in Crown Hill Cemetery.

**Bibliography:** *DAB*; Bowers, Claude. *Beveridge and the Progressive Era*. Boston: Houghton-Mifflin Company, 1932; Braeman, John. *Albert J. Beveridge: American Nationalist*. Chicago: University of Chicago Press, 1971.

**BEVERIDGE, John Lourie,** a Representative from Illinois; born in Greenwich, Washington County, N.Y., July 6, 1824; attended the public schools; moved with his parents to De Kalb, Ill., in 1842; attended the Rock River Seminary, Mount Morris, Ill.; moved to Tennessee in 1845 and taught school until 1851; studied law; was admitted to the bar and practiced; moved to Sycamore, Ill., in 1851 and continued the practice of law; moved to Evanston in 1854 and practiced law in Chicago; during the Civil War served in the Union Army; appointed major of the Eighth Illinois Cavalry September 18, 1861; colonel of the Seventeenth Illinois Cavalry January 28, 1864; brevetted brigadier general and mustered out February 7, 1866; elected sheriff of Cook County, Ill., in 1866; member of the State senate in 1871; resigned, having been elected as a Republican to the Forty-second Congress to fill the vacancy caused by the resignation of John A. Logan and served from November 7, 1871, until January 4, 1873, when he resigned; elected Lieutenant Governor of Illinois in 1872; upon the resignation of Governor Richard J. Oglesby in 1873 became Governor, and served from January 23, 1873 to January 8, 1877; United States subtreasurer at Chicago 1877-1881; moved to California in 1895 and resided in Hollywood, until his death on May 3, 1910; interment in Rose Hill Cemetery, Chicago, Ill.

**BEVILL, Tom,** a Representative from Alabama; born in Townley, Walker County, Ala., March 27, 1921; graduated from Walker County High School in 1939; B.S., University of Alabama School of Commerce and Business Administration, 1943; LL.B., University of Alabama School of Law, 1948; admitted to Alabama Bar in 1949; entered the United States Army in 1943 and served in the European theater of operations; released as Captain in 1946; practiced law in Jasper, Ala.; elected to the Alabama State house of representatives in 1958 and reelected in 1962; Democratic National Convention, committee on rules, 1976, platform committee, 1984; elected as a Democrat to the Ninetieth and to the fourteen succeeding Congresses (January 3, 1967-January 3, 1997); was not a candidate for reelection in 1996 to the One Hundred Fifth Congress; is a resident of Jasper, Ala.

**BIAGGI, Mario,** a Representative from New York; born in New York City October 26, 1917; graduated from P.S. 171 and Harren High School, New York City; LL.B., New York Law School, 1963; admitted to the bar of the State of New York; senior partner of Biaggi, Ehrich & Lang, New York City; served as community relations specialist with the New York State Division of Housing and assistant to the secretary of state, New York State, 1961-1965; member of the New York City Police Department, 1942-1965; retired on line of duty disability as lieutenant; holds police department's Medal of Honor plus twenty-seven other decorations; also holds Medal of Honor for Valor from National Police Officers Association of America, and is included in Association's Hall of Fame; elected president, National Police Officers Association of America, 1967; unsuccessful Democratic candidate for nomination for mayor of New York City in 1973; elected as a Democrat to the Ninety-first and to the nine succeeding Congresses, and served from January 3, 1969 until his resignation August 5, 1988; consultant; is a resident of the Bronx, N.Y.

**BIBB, George Mortimer,** a Senator from Kentucky; born in Prince Edward County, Va., October 30, 1776; pursued preparatory studies; was graduated from Hampden-Sidney (Va.) College and from The College of William and Mary, Williamsburg, Va., in 1792; studied law; was admitted to the bar and practiced for a short time in Virginia; moved to Lexington, Ky., in 1798; elected to the Kentucky house of representatives in 1806, 1810, and 1817; appointed judge of the Kentucky Court of Appeals in 1808 and served as chief justice of that court from 1809 until 1810, when he resigned; elected to the United States Senate and served from March 4, 1811, to August 23, 1814, when he resigned; resumed the practice of law in Lexington; moved to Frankfort in 1816; was again appointed chief justice of the court of appeals, 1827-1828, when he again resigned; elected to the United States Senate as a Jacksonian and served from March 4, 1829, to March 3, 1835; chairman, Committee on Post Office and Post Roads (Twenty-first Congress); chancellor of the Louisville chancery court, 1835-1844; appointed Secretary of the Treasury in the Cabinet of President John Tyler, and served from June 15, 1844 to March 4, 1845; resumed the practice of law in Washington, D.C., and was an assistant in the office of the Attorney General; died in Washington, D.C., April 14, 1859; interment in the State Cemetery, Frankfort, Ky.

**Bibliography:** *DAB*; Goff, John. "The Last Leaf: George Mortimer Bibb." *Register of the Kentucky Historical Society* 59 (1961): 331-42.

**BIBB, William Wyatt,** a Representative and a Senator from Georgia; born in Amelia County, Va., October 2, 1781; pursued an academic course; attended William and Mary College, Williamsburg, Va., and was graduated from the medical department of the University of Pennsylvania at Philadelphia in 1801; moved to Petersburg, Elbert County, Ga., and began the practice of medicine; member, State house of representatives 1803-1805; resumed the practice of medicine; elected as a Republican to the Ninth Congress to fill the vacancy caused by the resignation of Thomas Spalding; reelected to the Tenth and to the three succeeding Congresses and served from January 26, 1807, until his resignation November 6, 1813, having been elected Senator; elected as a Republican to the United States Senate to fill the vacancy caused by the resignation of William H. Crawford and served from November 6, 1813, to November 9, 1816, when he resigned; moved to Alabama Territory and was appointed the first Territorial Governor; elected as the first Governor under the State Constitution and served from March 1817 until his death near Coosada Station, Elmore County, Ala., July 9, 1820; interment in the family cemetery, Coosada Station, Ala.

**Bibliography:** *DAB*.

**BIBIGHAUS, Thomas Marshal,** a Representative from Pennsylvania; born in Philadelphia, Pa., March 17, 1817; attended the common schools; studied law; was admitted to the bar in 1839 and commenced practice in Lebanon, Pa.; elected as a Whig to the Thirty-second Congress (March 4, 1851-March 3, 1853); was not a candidate for renomination in 1852 to the Thirty-third Congress owing to ill health; resumed the practice of law in Lebanon, Lebanon County, Pa., and died there June 18, 1853; interment in Mount Lebanon Cemetery.

**BIBLE, Alan Harvey,** a Senator from Nevada; born in Lovelock, Pershing County, Nev., November 20, 1909; A.B., University of Nevada, Reno, 1930; LL.B., Georgetown University Law School, Washington, D.C., 1934; was admitted to the Nevada bar in 1935 and commenced the practice of law in Reno, Nev.; district attorney of Storey County, 1935-1938; appointed deputy attorney general of Nevada in 1938; State attorney, 1942-1950; resumed private practice of law; elected as a Democrat to the United States Senate, November 2, 1954, to fill the vacancy caused by the death of Patrick A. McCarran for the term ending January 3, 1957; reelected in 1956, 1962, and again in 1968, and served from December 2, 1954 until his resignation on December 17, 1974; was not a candidate for reelection in 1974; chairman, Committee on District of Columbia (Eighty-fifth through Ninetieth Congresses), Joint Committee on Washington Metropolitan Problems (Eighty-fifth and Eighty-sixth Congresses), Select Committee on Small Business (Ninety-first through Ninety-third Congresses); lawyer; was a resident of Reno, Nev.; died September 12, 1988.

**Bibliography:** Elliott, Gary E. *Senator Alan Bible and the Politics of the New West.* Reno: University of Nevada Press, 1994.

**BICKNELL, Bennet,** a Representative from New York; born in Mansfield, Conn., November 14, 1781; attended the public schools; moved to Morrisville, N.Y., in 1808; served in the War of 1812; member of the State assembly in 1812; served in the State senate 1814-1818; clerk of Madison County, N.Y., 1821-1825; editor of the Madison Observer; elected as a Democrat to the Twenty-fifth Congress (March 4, 1837-March 3, 1839); unsuccessful candidate for reelection in 1838 to the Twenty-sixth Congress; died in Morrisville, Madison County, N.Y., September 15, 1841; interment in Morrisville Rural Cemetery.

**BICKNELL, George Augustus,** a Representative from Indiana; born in Philadelphia, Pa., February 6, 1815; was graduated from the University of Pennsylvania at Philadelphia in 1831; attended Yale Law School one year; completed the study of law; was admitted to the bar in 1836 and commenced practice in New York City; moved to Lexington, Scott County, Ind., in 1846; elected prosecuting attorney of Scott County in 1848; circuit prosecutor in 1850; moved to New Albany in 1851; judge of the second judicial circuit of Indiana 1852-1876; professor of law at the University of Indiana 1861-1870; elected as a Democrat to the Forty-fifth and Forty-sixth Congresses (March 4, 1877-March 3, 1881); unsuccessful candidate for renomination in 1880; appointed commissioner of appeals in the supreme court of Indiana in 1881, which office he held until the completion of its work in 1885; resumed the practice of law; elected judge of the circuit court of Indiana in 1889 and held that office until his death, April 11, 1891, in New Albany, Floyd County, Ind.; interment in Fairview Cemetery.

**BIDDLE, Charles John** (nephew of Richard Biddle), a Representative from Pennsylvania; born in Philadelphia, Pa., April 30, 1819; was graduated from Princeton College in 1837; studied law; was admitted to the bar and commenced practice in Philadelphia in 1840; served in the Mexican War and was brevetted major for meritorious services; resumed the practice of law in Philadelphia; entered the Union Army in 1861 as colonel of a regiment of the Pennsylvania Reserve Corps; elected as a Democrat to the Thirty-seventh Congress to fill the vacancy caused by the resignation of E. Joy Morris and served from July 2, 1861, to March 3, 1863; unsuccessful candidate for reelection in 1862 to the Thirty-eighth Congress; chairman of the Pennsylvania Democratic central committee in 1863; one of the proprietors and editor in chief of the Philadelphia Age until his death in Philadelphia September 28, 1873; interment in Old St. Peter's Church Cemetery.

**BIDDLE, Edward** (uncle of Richard Biddle), a Delegate from Pennsylvania; born in Philadelphia, Pa., in 1738; entered the provincial army as an ensign in 1754, promoted to lieutenant and captain, and served until 1763, when he resigned; studied law; was admitted to the bar and commenced practice in Reading, Pa.; member of the Pennsylvania assembly 1767-1775, serving as speaker in 1774; member of the provincial convention held at Philadelphia in 1775; again a member of the Pennsylvania assembly in 1778; Member of the Continental Congresses in 1774 and 1775; died at Chatsworth, near Baltimore, Md., September 5, 1779; interment in St. Paul's Churchyard, Baltimore, Md.

**BIDDLE, John,** a Delegate from the Territory of Michigan; born in Philadelphia, Pa., March 2, 1792; attended the common schools and Princeton College; enlisted in the War of 1812; appointed a second lieutenant in the Third Artillery on July 6, 1812, first lieutenant on March 13, 1813, and captain in the Forty-second Infantry, October 1, 1813; assistant inspector general with the rank of major from June 19, 1817 until June 1, 1821; attached to the staff of General Scott on the Niagara frontier; paymaster and Indian agent at Green Bay, Wis., 1821-1822; register of the land at Detroit, Territory of Michigan, 1823-1837; commissioner for determining the ancient land claims at Detroit, Mackinaw, Sault Ste. Marie, Green Bay, and Prairie du Chien; mayor of Detroit, 1827-1828; elected a

Delegate from the Territory of Michigan to the Twenty-first Congress, and served from March 4, 1829 until February 21, 1831, when he resigned; president of the convention that framed the State constitution for Michigan in 1835; president of the Michigan Central Railroad Company in 1835; unsuccessful candidate for election in 1835 to the United States Senate; unsuccessful candidate for election in 1835 for Governor of Michigan; member of the State house of representatives in 1841, and served as speaker; retired from public life and active pursuits, and resided on his farm near Wyandotte, Mich.; later spent much time on his estate near St. Louis, Gratiot County, Mich.; went to White Sulphur Springs, Va., for the summer, and died there on August 25, 1859; interment in Elmwood Cemetery, Detroit, Mich.

**BIDDLE, Joseph Franklin,** a Representative from Pennsylvania; born near Bedford, Bedford County, Pa., September 14, 1871; educated in the public schools; was graduated from Millersville State Teachers' College at Millersville, Pa., in 1894 and from the law department of Dickinson College, Carlisle, Pa., in 1897; was admitted to the bar in 1897 and commenced practice in Bedford, Pa.; moved to Everett, Pa., in 1903 and engaged in the practice of law and in newspaper publishing; moved to Huntingdon, Pa., in 1918 and engaged in the printing and publishing business and in banking; member of the Pennsylvania Publishers' Association 1924-1936; director of the National Editorial Association 1926-1936; member of the Pennsylvania Republican committee 1932-1936; elected as a Republican to the Seventy-second Congress to fill the vacancy caused by the death of Edward M. Beers and served from November 8, 1932, to March 3, 1933; was not a candidate for election to the Seventy-third Congress in 1932; resumed the printing and newspaper publishing business in Huntingdon, Pa., where he died on December 3, 1936; interment in Trinity Churchyard, Friends' Cove, near Bedford, Pa.

**BIDDLE, Richard** (nephew of Edward Biddle and uncle of Charles John Biddle), a Representative from Pennsylvania; born in Philadelphia, Pa., March 25, 1796; pursued classical studies; was graduated from the University of Pennsylvania at Philadelphia in 1811; served as a volunteer in the Washington Guards during the War of 1812; studied law; was admitted to the bar in Philadelphia in 1817 and commenced practice in Pittsburgh the same year; went to Great Britain in 1827, remained there three years, and published works upon American discovery and travel; elected as an Anti-Masonic candidate to the Twenty-fifth and Twenty-sixth Congresses and served from March 4, 1837, until his resignation in 1840; resumed the practice of law in Pittsburgh, Pa., where he died on July 6, 1847; interment in Allegheny Cemetery.

**BIDEN, Joseph Robinette, Jr.,** a Senator from Delaware; born in Scranton, Lackawanna County, Pa., November 20, 1942; educated at St. Helena's School, Wilmington, Del., and Archmere Academy, Claymont, Del.; B.A., University of Delaware, Newark, 1965; J.D., Syracuse (N.Y.) University College of Law, 1968; admitted to the Delaware bar in 1968 and commenced practice in Wilmington; served on the New Castle County Council, 1970-1972; elected as a Democrat to the United States Senate in 1972 for the term commencing January 3, 1973; reelected in 1978, 1984, and 1990 for the term ending January 3, 1997; chairman, Committee on the Judiciary (One Hundredth through One Hundred Third Congresses); is a resident of Wilmington, Del.

**BIDLACK, Benjamin Alden,** a Representative from Pennsylvania; born in Paris, Oneida County, N.Y., September 8, 1804; moved to Wilkes-Barre, Pa.; attended the public schools; was graduated from the Wilkes-Barre Academy; studied law; was admitted to the bar in 1825 and commenced practice in Wilkes-Barre; elected district attorney of Luzerne County in 1825; moved to Milford, Pike County, Pa., in 1830; served as Pike County treasurer in 1834; returned to Wilkes-Barre; member, Pennsylvania house of

representatives, 1835-1836; editor of the Republican Farmer and the Democratic Journal, Wilkes-Barre; elected as a Democrat to the Twenty-seventh and Twenty-eighth Congresses (March 4, 1841-March 3, 1845); appointed Chargé d'Affaires to New Grenada (Colombia) on May 14, 1845; successfully negotiated and signed, December 12, 1846, a "treaty of peace, amity, and navigation" with New Grenada and secured for the United States the right to build a canal or railroad across the Isthmus of Panama; died in Bogota, Colombia, February 6, 1849; interment in the English Cemetery.

**Bibliography:** *DAB.*

**BIDWELL, Barnabas,** a Representative from Massachusetts; born in Tyringham (now Monterey), Mass., August 23, 1763; was graduated from Yale College in 1785; studied law at Brown University, Providence, R.I.; was admitted to the bar in 1805 and commenced practice in Stockbridge, Mass.; served in the Massachusetts senate 1801-1804; member of the Massachusetts house of representatives 1805-1807; elected as a Republican to the Ninth and Tenth Congresses and served from March 4, 1805, until his resignation on July 13, 1807; attorney general of Massachusetts from June 15, 1807, to August 30, 1810; moved to Canada about 1815 and settled near Kingston; became interested in political affairs and engaged in the practice of law; died in Kingston, Ontario, Canada, July 27, 1833; interment in Cataraqui Cemetery, Cataraqui, Ontario.

**Bibliography:** *DAB.*

**BIDWELL, John,** a Representative from California; born in Chautauqua County, N.Y., August 5, 1819; moved with his parents to Erie, Pa., in 1829 and to Ashtabula County, Ohio, in 1831; attended the country schools and Kingsville Academy, Ashtabula, Ohio; taught school in Ohio; spent two years in Missouri and taught school; crossed the Rockies and Sierras with the first overland expedition, arriving in the Sacramento Valley, California on November 4, 1841; secured employment on the ranch of John A. Sutter; later engaged in mining; served in the War with Mexico, attaining the rank of major; member of the State senate in 1849; supervisor in California of the United States census in 1850 and in 1860; delegate to the Democratic National Convention at Charleston in 1860; was appointed brigadier general of the California Militia in 1863; delegate to the Republican National Convention in 1864; elected as a Republican to the Thirty-ninth Congress (March 4, 1865-March 3, 1867); chairman, Committee on Agriculture (Thirty-ninth Congress); was not a candidate for renomination in 1866 to the Fortieth Congress; engaged extensively in agricultural pursuits; unsuccessful candidate for Governor of California in 1875 on the Anti-Monopoly ticket; presided over the Prohibition State convention in 1888 and was the unsuccessful candidate of that party for Governor of California in 1890, and for President of the United States in 1892; died in Chico, Butte County, Calif., April 4, 1900; interment in Chico Cemetery.

**Bibliography:** *DAB;* Hunt, Rockwell D. *John Bidwell; Prince of California Pioneers.* Caldwell, Idaho: The Caxton Printers, 1942; Royce, C. C. *John Bidwell; Pioneer Statesman, Philanthropist: A Biographical Sketch.* Chico, California, 1906.

**BIEMILLER, Andrew John,** a Representative from Wisconsin; born in Sandusky, Erie County, Ohio, July 23, 1906; attended the public schools; was graduated from Cornell University, Ithaca, N.Y., A.B., 1926, and was also engaged in graduate work at the University of Pennsylvania; taught history at Syracuse (N.Y.) University, 1926-1928, and at the University of Pennsylvania at Philadelphia, 1929-1931; moved to Milwaukee, Wis., in 1932; organizer from the Wisconsin State Federation of Labor (A. F. of L.); member of the Wisconsin State assembly, 1937-1941, serving as party floor leader, 1939-1941; assistant to Joseph D. Keenan, vice chairman for labor production, War Production Board, Washington, D.C., 1941-1944; elected as a Democrat to the Seventy-ninth Congress (January 3,

1945-January 3, 1947); unsuccessful candidate for reelection in 1946 to the Eightieth Congress; engaged as a public relations counselor; delegate to the Democratic National Convention of 1948; elected to the Eighty-first Congress (January 3, 1949-January 3, 1951); unsuccessful candidate for reelection in 1950 to the Eighty-second Congress; special assistant to Secretary of the Interior Oscar L. Chapman, 1951-1952; public relations counselor and lobbyist for the AFL-CIO, Washington, D.C., 1953-1979; resided in Bethesda, Md., until his death there on April 3, 1982; interment in Ellicott Family Cemetery, Ellicott City, Md.

**BIERMANN, Frederick Elliott,** a Representative from Iowa; born in Rochester, Olmstead County, Minn., March 20, 1884; moved to Decorah, Iowa, in 1888; attended the public and high schools of Decorah, Iowa, and the University of Minnesota at Minneapolis; was graduated from Columbia University, New York City, in 1905 and later attended Valder's Business College, Decorah, Iowa, and Harvard Law School; homesteaded in North Dakota in 1906 and 1907; editor and publisher of the Decorah (Iowa) Journal 1908-1931; volunteered for service in the United States Army during the First World War; was commissioned a second lieutenant August 15, 1917, and a first lieutenant on December 31, 1917, in the Eighty-eighth Division; served from April 1917 until June 1919, being overseas ten months; postmaster of Decorah, Iowa, 1913-1923; served as park commissioner of Decorah beginning in 1922; delegate to the Democratic National Conventions in 1928, 1940, and 1956; delegate to the Interparliamentary Union Conference at Paris in 1937; elected as a Democrat to the Seventy-third, Seventy-fourth, and Seventy-fifth Congresses (March 4, 1933-January 3, 1939); unsuccessful candidate for reelection in 1938 to the Seventy-sixth Congress; appointed United States Marshal for northern Iowa in October 1940, in which capacity he served until 1953; died in La Crosse, Wis., July 1, 1968; interment in Phelps Cemetery, Decorah, Iowa.

**BIERY, James Soloman,** a Representative from Pennsylvania; born on a farm near Emlenton, Venango County, Pa., March 2, 1839; attended the district schools, a select school of the county, and Emlenton (Pa.) Academy; taught school for three years in the oil regions of Pennsylvania; moved to Allentown, Lehigh County, Pa., in 1861 and continued teaching for eight years; studied theology for two years; subsequently studied law; was admitted to the bar in 1868 and commenced practice in Allentown; member of the Pennsylvania house of representatives in 1869; elected as a Republican to the Forty-third Congress (March 4, 1873-March 3, 1875); was not a candidate for renomination in 1874; resumed the practice of law at Allentown and also engaged in literary pursuits; died in Allentown, Pa., December 3, 1904; interment in Fairview Cemetery.

**BIESTER, Edward George, Jr.,** a Representative from Pennsylvania; born in Trevose, Bucks County, Pa., January 5, 1931; attended the Doylestown (Pa.) public schools and graduated from the George School in 1948; B.A., Wesleyan University, 1952; LL.B., Temple University School of Law, 1955; admitted to Pennsylvania bar in 1956; assistant district attorney, Bucks County, 1958-1964; elected as a Republican to the Ninetieth and to the four succeeding Congresses (January 3, 1967-January 3, 1977); was not a candidate for reelection in 1976 to the Ninety-fifth Congress; attorney general, Commonwealth of Pennsylvania, 1979-1980; judge, court of common pleas of Bucks County, seventh judicial district, 1980 to present; is a resident of Furlong, Pa.

**BIGBY, John Summerfield,** a Representative from Georgia; born near Newnan, Coweta County, Ga., February 13, 1832; attended the common schools; was graduated from Emory College, Oxford, Ga., in 1853; studied law; was admitted to the bar in 1856 and commenced practice in Newnan, Coweta County, Ga.; member of the State constitutional conventions of 1867-1868; solicitor

general of the Tallapoosa circuit from August 1867 to September 22, 1868; judge of the superior court of the same circuit from September 22, 1868, to March 3, 1871; elected as a Republican to the Forty-second Congress (March 4, 1871-March 3, 1873); unsuccessful candidate for reelection in 1872 to the Forty-third Congress; resumed the practice of law in Atlanta, Ga.; delegate to the Republican National Convention of 1876; became president of the Atlanta & West Point Railroad in 1876; died in Atlanta, Ga., March 28, 1898; interment in West View Cemetery.

**BIGELOW, Abijah,** a Representative from Massachusetts; born in Westminster, Mass., on December 5, 1775; attended Leicester (Mass.) Academy and an academy at New Ipswich, N.H.; was graduated from Dartmouth College, Hanover, N.H., in 1795; studied law in Groton, Mass.; was admitted to the bar in 1798 and commenced practice in Leominster, Mass., in the same year; town clerk of Leominster 1803-1809; member of the Massachusetts house of representatives 1807-1809; justice of the peace 1809-1860 and justice of the quorum 1812-1860; elected as a Federalist to the Eleventh Congress to fill the vacancy caused by the resignation of William Stedman; reelected to the Twelfth and Thirteenth Congresses and served from October 8, 1810, to March 3, 1815; moved to Worcester in 1817; clerk of the courts of Worcester County 1817-1833; resumed the practice of law; served as trustee of Leicester Academy in 1819 and 1820 and as treasurer 1820-1853; appointed a master in chancery in 1838; died in Worcester, Worcester County, Mass., April 5, 1860; interment in the Rural Cemetery.

**Bibliography:** Scotti, N. David. "An Addition to the Letters of Abijah Bigelow." *American Antiquarian Society, Proceedings* 79, Pt. 2 (October 1969): 245-252.

**BIGELOW, Herbert Seely,** a Representative from Ohio; born in Elkhart, Ind., January 4, 1870; attended the public schools and Oberlin (Ohio) College; was graduated from Western Reserve University, Cleveland, Ohio, in 1894; moved to Cincinnati, Ohio, and studied in Lane Theological Seminary; ordained as a Congregational minister in 1895 and became pastor of the Vine Street Congregational Church in Cincinnati, Ohio; delegate to the fourth constitutional convention of Ohio in 1912, serving as president; member of the Ohio State house of representatives in 1913 and 1914; served on the Cincinnati City Council in 1936; elected as a Democrat to the Seventy-fifth Congress (January 3, 1937-January 3, 1939); unsuccessful candidate for reelection in 1938 to the Seventy-sixth Congress; member of the Cincinnati city council in 1940 and 1941; resumed his duties as pastor of the Vine Street Congregational Church (Peoples Church), Cincinnati, Ohio, where he died on November 11, 1951; remains were cremated and the ashes scattered over his farm near Forestville, Hamilton County, Ohio.

**Bibliography:** Beaver, Daniel R. *A Buckeye Crusader: A Sketch of the Political Career of Herbert Seely Bigelow, Preacher, Prophet, Politician.* Privately Printed in Cincinnati, Ohio, 1957.

**BIGELOW, Lewis,** a Representative from Massachusetts; born in Petersham, Worcester County, Mass., August 18, 1785; was graduated from Williams College, Williamstown, Mass., in 1803; studied law; was admitted to the bar and commenced practice in Petersham; member of the Massachusetts senate 1819-1821; editor of the first seventeen volumes of Massachusetts Reports and of a digest of six volumes of Pickering's Reports; elected as a Federalist to the Seventeenth Congress (March 4, 1821-March 3, 1823); moved to Peoria, Ill., in 1831 and continued the practice of law; interested in the real estate business and in the operation of ferry boats; served as justice of the peace; appointed clerk of the circuit court of Peoria County, November 26, 1835, and served until his death in Peoria, Ill., October 2, 1838; interment presumed to be in the Old Centre Cemetery, Petersham, Mass.

**BIGGS, Asa,** a Representative and a Senator from North Carolina; born in Williamston, Martin County, N.C., February 4, 1811; attended the common schools; pursued classical studies; studied law; was admitted to the bar in 1831 and commenced practice in Williamston, N.C.; member of the State constitutional convention in 1835; member, State house of commons 1840-1842; member, State senate 1844-1845; elected as a Democrat to the Twenty-ninth Congress (March 4, 1845-March 3, 1847); unsuccessful candidate for reelection in 1846 to the Thirtieth Congress; member of a commission to codify the State laws in 1851; elected as a Democrat to the United States Senate and served from March 4, 1855, until May 5, 1858, when he resigned, having been appointed United States judge for the district of North Carolina by President James Buchanan; served as judge of the district court until 1861; member of the secession convention of North Carolina in 1861; Confederate judge 1861-1865; resumed the practice of law in Tarboro, Edgecombe County, N.C., in 1865; moved to Norfolk, Va., in 1869 and continued the practice of law until his death in that city on March 6, 1878; interment in Elmwood Cemetery.

Bibliography: *DAB*; Biggs, Asa. *Autobiography of Asa Biggs, Including a Journal of a Trip from North Carolina to New York in 1832*. Edited by Robert D. W. Connor. North Carolina Historical Commission Publications. Bulletin No. 19. Raleigh: Edwards and Broughton Printing Company, 1915.

**BIGGS, Benjamin Thomas,** a Representative from Delaware; born near Summit Bridge, New Castle County, Del., October 1, 1821; attended the public schools and Pennington Seminary in New Jersey; taught school for a short time and later attended the Wesleyan University, Middletown, Conn.; engaged in agricultural pursuits; member of the State constitutional convention in 1853; became interested in railroad operations and was a director of the Kent & Queen Annes Railroad; unsuccessful candidate for election in 1860 to the Thirty-seventh Congress; elected as a Democrat to the Forty-first and Forty-second Congresses (March 4, 1869-March 3, 1873); was not a candidate for renomination in 1872 to the Forty-third Congress; delegate to the Democratic National Convention of 1872; elected Governor of Delaware in 1886 and served from January 1887 to January 1891; died in Middletown, New Castle County, Del., December 25, 1893; interment in Bethel Cemetery, near Chesapeake City, Cecil County, Md.

**BIGGS, Marion,** a Representative from California; born near Curryville, Pike County, Mo., May 2, 1823; attended the common schools; moved to California in 1850; returned to Missouri; was elected sheriff of Monroe County, Mo., in 1852 and reelected in 1854; returned to California in 1864; was a cattle buyer and was also engaged in agricultural pursuits; elected to the State assembly from Sacramento County in 1867 and from Butte County in 1869; elected to the State constitutional convention from the State at large in 1878; elected as a Democrat to the Fiftieth and Fifty-first Congresses (March 4, 1887-March 3, 1891); was not a candidate for renomination in 1890 to the Fifty-second Congress; commissioner to attend the centennial celebration of the inauguration of George Washington as President of the United States, in 1889; resided in Gridley, Butte County, Calif., and lived in retirement until his death there on August 2, 1910; interment in Helvetia Cemetery, Sacramento, Calif.

**BIGLER, William,** a Senator from Pennsylvania; born in Shiremanstown, Cumberland County, Pa., on January 1, 1814; attended the public schools; in 1829 was apprenticed to the printing trade; moved to Clearfield, Clearfield County, Pa., in 1833 and established the Clearfield Democrat; engaged in the lumber business; member, State senate 1841-1847, twice serving as speaker; elected Governor in 1851 and served from January 20, 1852 to January 16, 1855; unsuccessful candidate for reelection in 1854; elected as a Democrat to the United States Senate to fill the vacancy in the term commencing March 4, 1855, caused by failure of the legislature to elect and served from January 14, 1856, to March 3, 1861; unsuccessful candidate for reelection; chairman, Committee on Engrossed Bills (Thirty-sixth Congress), Committee on Patents and Patent Office (Thirty-sixth Congress); member of the constitutional convention of Pennsylvania; member of the board of finance of the Centennial Exposition in 1876; president of the Philadelphia & Erie Railroad; died in Clearfield, Pa., August 9, 1880; interment in Hillcrest Cemetery.

Bibliography: *DAB*.

**BILBO, Theodore Gilmore,** a Senator from Mississippi; born on a farm near Poplarville, Pearl River County, Miss., October 13, 1877; attended the public schools, Peabody College, Nashville, Tenn., the law department of Vanderbilt University, Nashville, Tenn., and the University of Michigan at Ann Arbor; teacher in the district and high schools of Mississippi for five years; was admitted to the bar in 1908 and commenced practice in Poplarville, Miss.; Mississippi State senator, 1908-1912; elected lieutenant governor of Mississippi, and served from January 17, 1912 until January 17, 1916; elected Governor of Mississippi in 1915, and served from January 18, 1916 to January 20, 1920; elected Governor in 1927, and served from January 17, 1928 to January 19, 1932; elected as a Democrat to the United States Senate in 1934, 1940, and again in 1946, and served from January 3, 1935 until his death in New Orleans, La., on August 21, 1947; did not take the oath of office in 1947 at the beginning of the Eightieth Congress; chairman, Committee on District of Columbia (Seventy-eighth and Seventy-ninth Congresses), Committee on Pensions (Seventy-eighth Congress); interment in Juniper Grove Cemetery, near Poplarville, Miss.

Bibliography: *DAB*; Morgan, Chester M. *Redneck Liberal: Theodore G. Bilbo and the New Deal*. Baton Rouge: Louisiana State University Press, 1985; Smith, Charles P. "Theodore G. Bilbo's Senatorial Career, The Final Years: 1941-1947." Ph.D. dissertation, University of Southern Mississippi, 1983.

**BILBRAY, Brian P.,** (nephew of James Hubert Bilbray), a Representative from California; born at North Island Naval Air Station, Coronado, San Diego County, Calif., January 28, 1951; graduated Mar Vista High School; attended Southwestern College, Chula Vista, Calif., 1970-1974; mayor of Imperial Beach, Calif.; owner, Bilbray Tax Service; member, San Diego County Board of Supervisors, 1984-1994; elected as a Republican to the One Hundred Fourth Congress (January 3, 1995-January 3, 1997); is a resident of Imperial Beach, Calif.

**BILBRAY, James Hubert,** (uncle of Brian P. Bilbray), a Representative from Nevada; born in Las Vegas, Nev., May 19, 1938; attended public schools, Brigham Young University and the University of Nevada-Las Vegas; B.A., American University, Washington, D.C., 1962; J.D., American University Law School, 1964; served in the United States Army Reserve in Nevada National Guard, 1955-1963; practiced law in Las Vegas; deputy district attorney, Clark County, Nev., 1965-1967; chief legal counsel, Clark County juvenile court, 1967-1968; alternate judge, City of Las Vegas, 1978-1980; member, Nevada State senate, 1980-1986; elected as a Democrat to the One Hundredth and to the three succeeding Congresses (January 3, 1987-January 3, 1995); unsuccessful candidate for reelection in 1994 to the One Hundred Fourth Congress; resumed the practice of law; is a resident of Las Vegas, Nev.

**BILIRAKIS, Michael,** a Representative from Florida; born in Tarpon Springs, Pinellas County, Fla., July 16, 1930; raised in western Pennsylvania; attended public schools in Clairton, Pa.; Douglas Business College, McKeesport, Pa., 1949; B.S., University of Pittsburgh, Pittsburgh, Pa., 1959; attended George Washington University, Washington, D.C., 1960; J.D., University of Florida,

Gainesville, Fla., 1963; served, United States Air Force, 1950-1954; Federal regulatory engineer, 1959-61; admitted to the Florida bar, 1964; government contract negotiator, 1963-68; attorney, 1968-1982, judge, Pasco County, 1970-1972; elected as a Republican to the Ninety-eighth and to the six succeeding Congresses (January 3, 1983-January 3, 1997); is a resident of Palm Harbor, Fla.

**BILLINGHURST, Charles,** a Representative from Wisconsin; born in Brighton, Franklin County, N.Y., July 27, 1818; attended the common schools; studied law; was admitted to the bar in 1847 and commenced practice in Rochester, N.Y.; moved to Wisconsin the same year and settled in Juneau, Dodge County; continued the practice of his profession; elected as a member of the first State legislature of Wisconsin in 1848; was elected a presidential elector on the Democratic ticket in 1852; elected as a Republican to the Thirty-fourth and Thirty-fifth Congresses (March 4, 1855-March 3, 1859); unsuccessful candidate for reelection in 1858 to the Thirty-sixth Congress; resumed the practice of law in Juneau, Wis., where he died August 18, 1865; interment in Juneau Cemetery.

**BILLMEYER, Alexander,** a Representative from Pennsylvania; born in Liberty Township, Montour County, Pa., January 7, 1841; attended the common schools; engaged in agricultural pursuits; interested in the manufacture of lumber; director of a national bank in Washingtonville, Montour County, Pa.; elected as a Democrat to the Fifty-seventh Congress to fill the vacancy caused by the death of Rufus K. Polk and served from November 4, 1902, to March 3, 1903; was not a candidate for renomination in 1902; resumed agricultural pursuits in Montour County, Pa.; died near Washingtonville, Pa., May 24, 1924; interment in Odd Fellows Cemetery, Danville, Pa.

**BINDERUP, Charles Gustav,** a Representative from Nebraska; born in Horsens, Denmark, March 5, 1873; when six months old immigrated to the United States with his parents, who settled on a farm near Hastings, Adams County, Nebr.; attended the county schools and Grand Island (Nebr.) Business College; engaged in agricultural pursuits near Hastings and Minden, Nebr., and also in the mercantile and creamery business at Minden, Nebr.; elected as a Democrat to the Seventy-fourth and Seventy-fifth Congresses (January 3, 1935-January 3, 1939); was an unsuccessful candidate for reelection in 1938 to the Seventy-sixth Congress and for election as an Independent in 1940 to the Seventy-seventh Congress; organized and was active in the Constitutional Money League of America in Minden, Nebr., until his death; died in Minden, Nebr., August 19, 1950; interment in Minden Cemetery.

**BINES, Thomas,** a Representative from New Jersey; born in Trenton, N.J.; attended the common schools; appointed coroner for Salem County on October 16, 1802; elected sheriff of Salem County in 1808 and served until 1810; elected as a Republican to the Thirteenth Congress to fill the vacancy caused by the death of Jacob Hufty and served from November 2, 1814, to March 3, 1815; was not a candidate for renomination in 1814 to the Fourteenth Congress; elected justice of the peace of Lower Penns Neck Township in 1822 and served in this capacity until 1826; died in Lower Penns Neck Township, Salem County, April 9, 1826.

**BINGAMAN, Jesse Francis, Jr. (Jeff),** a Senator from New Mexico; born in El Paso, Tex., October 3, 1943; attended public schools of Silver City, N.Mex.; graduated Western High School, 1961; B.A., Harvard University, 1965; J.D., Stanford (Calif.) University Law School, 1968; served in the United States Army Reserve, 1968-1974; admitted to the New Mexico bar in 1968; assistant New Mexico attorney general, 1969; counsel to the State constitutional convention of 1969; commenced the private practice of law in 1970; elected New Mexico attorney general, 1979-1982; elected as a Democrat to the United States Senate in 1982 for the term commencing January 3, 1983; reelected in 1988, and again in 1994 for the term ending January 3, 2001; chairman, Senate Impeachment Trial Committee (One Hundred First Congress); is a resident of Santa Fe, N.Mex.

**BINGHAM, Henry Harrison,** a Representative from Pennsylvania; born in Philadelphia, Pa., December 4, 1841; was graduated from Jefferson College, Canonsburg, Pa., in 1862 and from the law department of Washington and Jefferson College, Washington, Pa.; during the Civil War entered the Union Army as a first lieutenant in the One Hundred and Fortieth Regiment, Pennsylvania Volunteer Infantry, August 22, 1862; commissioned captain September 9, 1862; major and judge advocate September 20, 1864; brevetted major of Volunteers August 1, 1864; brevetted lieutenant colonel of Volunteers April 9, 1865; colonel and brigadier general of Volunteers April 9, 1865; honorably mustered out of service July 2, 1866; awarded a Congressional Medal of Honor August 26, 1893, for actions at the Battle of the Wilderness, Virginia, May 6, 1864; appointed postmaster of Philadelphia in March 1867 and served until December 1872, when he resigned to accept the clerkship of the courts of oyer and terminer and quarter sessions of the peace in Philadelphia, having been elected by the people; reelected clerk of courts in 1875; delegate to the Republican National Conventions 1872-1900; elected as a Republican to the Forty-sixth and to the sixteen succeeding Congresses and served from March 4, 1879, until his death in Philadelphia March 22, 1912; chairman, Committee on the Post Office and Post Roads (Forty-seventh and Fifty-first Congresses), Committee on Expenditures in the Post Office Department (Fifty-fourth Congress); interment in Laurel Hill Cemetery.

**BINGHAM, Hiram** (father of Jonathan Brewster Bingham), a Senator from Connecticut; born in Honolulu, Hawaii, November 19, 1875; educated at Punahou School and Oahu College, Hawaii, 1882-1892, Phillips Academy, Andover, Mass., 1892-1894, Yale University, 1894-1898, University of California at Berkeley, 1899-1900, and Harvard University, 1900-1905; professor of history and politics at Harvard and then Princeton Universities; South American explorer, credited with discovering, in 1911, the ruins of an ancient Inca city on an Andean mountain at Machu Picchu, northwest of Cuzco, Peru; delegate to the First Pan American Scientific Congress at Santiago, Chile, in 1908; captain, Connecticut National Guard, 1916; became an aviator in the spring of 1917; organized the United States Schools of Military Aeronautics in May 1917; served in the Aviation Section, Signal Corps, and attained the rank of lieutenant colonel; commanded the flying school at Issoudun, France, from August to December 1918; lieutenant governor of Connecticut, 1922-1924; elected Governor of Connecticut on November 4, 1924, but served only from January 7 to January 8, 1925, when he resigned, having been elected Senator; elected as a Republican to the United States Senate on December 16, 1924, to fill the vacancy caused by the death of Frank B. Brandegee in the term ending March 3, 1927; reelected in 1926 and served from December 17, 1924, to March 3, 1933; unsuccessful candidate for reelection in 1932; chairman, Committee on Printing (Seventieth Congress), Committee on Territories and Insular Possessions (Seventieth through Seventy-second Congresses); censured by the Senate on November 4, 1929 for temporarily hiring Charles L. Eyanson as his principal clerk while Eyanson was also employed by the Manufacturers' Association of Connecticut; appointed a member of the President's Aircraft Board by President Calvin Coolidge in 1925; engaged in banking and literary work in Washington, D.C.; lectured at naval training schools during the Second World War, 1942-1943; chairman of the Civil Service Commission's Loyalty Review Board, 1951-1953; died in Washington, D.C., June 6, 1956; interment in Arlington National Cemetery, Va.

**Bibliography:** *DAB*; Bingham, Alfred M. *Portrait of an Explorer: Hiram Bingham, Discoverer of Machu Picchu.* Ames: Iowa State University Press, 1989; Bingham, Woodbridge. *Hiram Bingham: A Personal History.* Boulder, Colo.: Bin Lan Zhen Publishers, 1989.

**BINGHAM, John Armor,** a Representative from Ohio; born in Mercer, Mercer County, Pa., January 21, 1815; pursued academic studies; apprentice in a printing office for two years; attended Franklin College, Ohio; studied law; was admitted to the bar in 1840 and commenced practice in New Philadelphia, Tuscarawas County, Ohio; district attorney for Tuscarawas County, Ohio, 1846-1849; elected as a Republican to the Thirty-fourth and to the three succeeding Congresses (March 4, 1855-March 3, 1863); unsuccessful candidate for reelection in 1862 to the Thirty-eighth Congress; appointed by President Lincoln as judge advocate of the Union Army with the rank of major in 1864; later appointed solicitor of the court of claims; special judge advocate in the trial of the conspirators against the life of President Lincoln; elected to the Thirty-ninth and to the three succeeding Congresses (March 4, 1865-March 3, 1873); chairman, Committee on Claims (Fortieth Congress), Committee on the Judiciary (Forty-first and Forty-second Congresses); unsuccessful candidate for renomination in 1872 to the Forty-third Congress; one of the managers appointed by the House of Representatives in 1862 to conduct the impeachment proceedings against West H. Humphreys, United States judge for the several districts of Tennessee, and in 1868 in the proceedings against Andrew Johnson; appointed Minister to Japan on May 31, 1873 and served until July 2, 1885; died in Cadiz, Harrison County, Ohio, March 19, 1900; interment in Cadiz Cemetery.

Bibliography: *DAB*; Beauregard, Erving E. *Bingham of the Hills: Politician and Diplomat Extraordinary*. New York: Peter Lang, 1989; Riggs, C. Russell. "The Ante-Bellum Career of John A. Bingham: A Case Study in the Coming of the Civil War." Ph.D. dissertation, New York University, 1959.

**BINGHAM, Jonathan Brewster,** (son of Hiram Bingham), a Representative from New York; born in New Haven, Conn., April 24, 1914; attended Groton (Mass.) School; B.A., Yale University, 1936; newspaper correspondent, 1935-1938; LL.B., Yale University Law School, 1939; commenced practice in New York City; admitted to the New York bar in 1940; enlisted as a private in the United States Army in April 1943, and was discharged as a captain in October 1945 with War Department Staff Citation; special assistant to the Assistant Secretary of State in 1945 and 1946; deputy administrator, Technical Cooperation Administration (Point Four program), 1951-1953; secretary to Governor Averell Harriman of New York, 1955-1958; unsuccessful candidate in 1958 for the New York State senate; United States representative on United Nations Trusteeship Council with rank of Minister in 1961 and 1962 and serving as president in 1962; United States representative on United Nations Economic and Social Council with the rank of Ambassador, 1963-1964; United States delegate to four United Nations General Assemblies; elected as a Democrat to the Eighty-ninth and to the eight succeeding Congresses (January 3, 1965-January 3, 1983); was not a candidate for reelection in 1982 to the Ninety-eighth Congress; was a resident of the Bronx, N.Y., until his death in New York City on July 3, 1986.

Bibliography: Bingham, Jonathan B. *Shirt-Sleeve Diplomacy: Point Four in Action*. 1954. Reprint. Freeport, N.Y.: Books for Libraries Press, 1970.

**BINGHAM, Kinsley Scott,** a Representative and a Senator from Michigan; born in Camillus, Onondaga County, N.Y., December 16, 1808; attended the common schools; studied law in Syracuse, N.Y.; moved to Green Oak, Mich., in 1833; admitted to the bar and practiced law; engaged in agricultural pursuits; held a number of local offices, including those of justice of the peace, postmaster, and first judge of probate of Livingston County; member of the Michigan State house of representatives in 1837; reelected four times and served as speaker for three terms; elected as a Democrat to the Thirtieth and Thirty-first Congresses (March 4, 1847-March 3, 1851); chairman, Committee on Expenditures in the Department of State (Thirty-first Congress); was not a candidate for reelection in

1850; resumed agricultural pursuits; elected Governor of Michigan in 1854, reelected in 1856, and served from January 3, 1855 to January 5, 1859; instrumental in establishing the Michigan Agricultural College and other educational institutions; elected as a Republican to the United States Senate, and served from March 4, 1859 until his death on October 5, 1861; chairman, Committee on Enrolled Bills (Thirty-seventh Congress); died in Green Oak, Livingston County, Mich.; interment in Old Village Cemetery, Brighton, Livingston County, Mich.

**BINGHAM, William,** a Delegate and a Senator from Pennsylvania; born in Philadelphia, Pa., March 8, 1752; was graduated from Philadelphia College in 1768; agent of the Continental Congress at Martinique, and afterwards consul at St. Pierre, in the West Indies 1777-1780; Member of the Continental Congress 1786-1788; member, Pennsylvania house of representatives 1790-1791, serving as speaker in 1791; served in, and was president of, the Pennsylvania senate 1794-1795; elected as a Federalist to the United States Senate and served from March 4, 1795, to March 3, 1801; was not a candidate for reelection; served as President pro tempore of the Senate during the Fourth Congress; withdrew from public life and engaged in the management of his extensive estates; moved in 1801 to Bath, England, and resided with his daughter until his death in that city on February 7, 1804; interment in Bath Abbey, Bath, England.

Bibliography: *DAB*; Alberts, Robert. *The Golden Voyage: The Life and Times of William Bingham*. New York: Houghton Mifflin, 1969.

**BINNEY, Horace,** a Representative from Pennsylvania; born in Philadelphia, Pa., January 4, 1780; attended a classical school in Bordentown, N.J., three years; was graduated from Harvard University in 1797; studied law; was admitted to the bar and commenced practice in Philadelphia in 1800; member of the Pennsylvania house of representatives in 1806 and 1807; between 1807 and 1814 prepared and published six volumes of reported decisions of the supreme court of Pennsylvania; director of the United States Bank; elected as an Anti-Jacksonian to the Twenty-third Congress (March 4, 1833-March 3, 1835); was not a candidate for renomination in 1834; except for his appearance before the supreme court in 1844 as counsel for Philadelphia in the Girard will case, he retired from his practice in the courts and confined himself to giving written opinions; died in Philadelphia, Pa., August 12, 1875; interment in St. James the Less Cemetery, Falls of the Schuylkill (now a part of Philadelphia), Pa.

Bibliography: *DAB*; Binney, Charles Chauncy. *Life of Horace Binney, with Selections from His Letters*. Philadelphia: Lippincott, 1903.

**BIRCH, William Fred,** a Representative from New Jersey; born in Newark, N.J., August 30, 1870; moved with his parents to Phillipsburg, N.J., in 1872 and to Dover, Morris County, N.J., in 1874; attended the public schools and was graduated from the New Jersey State Model School at Trenton and from Coleman's Business College at Newark in 1887; engaged in the manufacture of boilers and smokestacks at Dover; member of the Dover Common Council for several years; city recorder 1904-1909; member of the State house of assembly 1910-1912; elected as a Republican to the Sixty-fifth Congress to fill the vacancy caused by the death of John H. Capstick and served from November 5, 1918, to March 3, 1919; was not a candidate for renomination in 1918; resumed his former manufacturing pursuits; also engaged in the fire-insurance and automobile businesses and was interested in banking; retired from business activities in 1941; died in Glen Ridge, N.J., January 25, 1946; interment in Orchard Street Cemetery, Dover, N.J.

**BIRD, John,** a Representative from New York; born in Litchfield, Conn., November 22, 1768; pursued classical studies; was graduated from Yale College in 1786; studied law; was admitted to the bar and commenced practice in Litchfield, Conn.; moved to Troy, N.Y., in 1793 and engaged in the practice of law; member of the State assembly 1796-1798; elected as a Federalist to the Sixth and Seventh Congresses and served from March 4, 1799, to July 25, 1801, when he resigned; again resumed the practice of his profession; died in Troy, N.Y., on February 2, 1806; interment in Mount Ida Cemetery.

**BIRD, John Taylor,** a Representative from New Jersey; born in Bloomsbury, Hunterdon County, N.J., August 16, 1829; attended the public schools, and a classical academy at Hackettstown, N.J.; studied law; was admitted to the bar in 1855 and commenced practice in Bloomsbury, N.J.; moved to Clinton in 1858; prosecutor of the pleas for Hunterdon County 1862-1867; moved to Flemington in 1865; elected as a Democrat to the Forty-first and Forty-second Congresses (March 4, 1869-March 3, 1873); was not a candidate for renomination in 1872; resumed the practice of law in Flemington, N.J.; member of the New Jersey constitutional convention in 1876; moved to Trenton, N.J., in 1882; vice chancellor of New Jersey 1882-1896; master in chancery 1900-1909; died in Trenton, N.J., May 6, 1911; interment in Riverview Cemetery.

**BIRD, Richard Ely,** a Representative from Kansas; born in Cincinnati, Ohio, November 4, 1878; moved with his parents to Wichita, Sedgwick County, Kans., in 1887; attended the public schools and was graduated from Wichita High School in 1898; studied law; was admitted to the bar in 1901 and commenced practice in Wichita; judge of the district court of the eighteenth judicial district of Kansas 1916-1921; elected as a Republican to the Sixty-seventh Congress (March 4, 1921-March 3, 1923); unsuccessful candidate for reelection in 1922 to the Sixty-eighth Congress; resumed the practice of law; United States referee in bankruptcy, Wichita, Kans., 1925-1927; retired from public life in 1937 and moved to Long Beach, Calif., where he died January 10, 1955; interment in Maplegrove Cemetery, Wichita, Kans.

**BIRDSALL, Ausburn,** a Representative from New York; born in Otego, Otsego County, N.Y.; moved to Binghamton, Broome County, N.Y.; studied law; was admitted to the bar and practiced; district attorney of Broome County; elected as a Democrat to the Thirtieth Congress (March 4, 1847-March 3, 1849); appointed United States naval storekeeper in New York City; returned to Binghamton, N.Y., and resumed the practice of law until 1890, when he retired and moved to New York City, where he resided until his death July 10, 1903; interment in Woodlawn Cemetery, New York City.

**BIRDSALL, Benjamin Pixley,** a Representative from Iowa; born in Weyauwega, Waupaca County, Wis., October 26, 1858; attended the common schools of Iowa and Iowa State University, Iowa City; studied law; was admitted to the bar in 1878 and practiced; served as district judge of the eleventh judicial district of Iowa from January 1893 to October 1900; elected as a Republican to the Fifty-eighth, Fifty-ninth, and Sixtieth Congresses (March 4, 1903-March 3, 1909); resumed the practice of law in Clarion, Wright County, Iowa, where he died May 26, 1917; interment in Evergreen Cemetery.

**BIRDSALL, James,** a Representative from New York; born in that State in 1783; studied law; was admitted to the bar in 1806 and was the first lawyer to settle in Norwich, Chenango County, N.Y.; surrogate of Chenango County, N.Y., in 1811; elected as a Republican to the Fourteenth Congress (March 4, 1815-March 3, 1817); member of the State assembly in 1827; one of the incorporators of the Bank of Chenango; moved to Fenton, Genesee County, Mich., in 1839 and later to Flint, Mich., where he died July 20, 1856; interment in Glenwood Cemetery.

**BIRDSALL, Samuel,** a Representative from New York; born in Hillsdale, Columbia County, N.Y., May 14, 1791; attended the common schools; studied law in the office of Martin Van Buren; was admitted to the bar in 1812 and commenced practice in Cooperstown, N.Y.; master in chancery in 1815; moved to Waterloo, N.Y., in 1817; division judge advocate with rank of colonel in 1819; counselor in the supreme court and solicitor in chancery in 1823; surrogate of Seneca County 1827-1837; bank commissioner in 1832; elected as a Democrat to the Twenty-fifth Congress (March 4, 1837-March 3, 1839); was not a candidate for renomination in 1838; admitted to practice before the United States Supreme Court in 1838; district attorney of Seneca County in 1846; postmaster of Waterloo, Seneca County, N.Y., 1853-1863; died in Waterloo, N.Y., February 8, 1872; interment in Maple Grove Cemetery.

**BIRDSEYE, Victory,** a Representative from New York; born in Cornwall, Conn., December 25, 1782; attended the public schools, and was graduated from Williams College, Williamstown, Mass., in 1804; studied law; was admitted to the bar in 1807 and commenced practice in Pompey Hill, Onondaga County, N.Y.; elected as a Republican to the Fourteenth Congress (March 4, 1815-March 3, 1817); was not a candidate for renomination in 1816; postmaster of Pompey Hill 1817-1838; district attorney of Onondaga County 1818-1833; master of chancery of Onondaga County 1818-1822; delegate to the State constitutional convention in 1821; member of the State assembly 1823 and 1838-1840; served in the State senate in 1827; unsuccessful candidate for election in 1838 to the Twenty-sixth Congress; elected as a Whig to the Twenty-seventh Congress (March 4, 1841-March 3, 1843); was not a candidate for renomination in 1842 to the Twenty-eighth Congress; resumed the practice of law; died in Pompey, Onondaga County, N.Y., September 16, 1853; interment in Pompey Hill Cemetery.

**BISBEE, Horatio, Jr.,** a Representative from Florida; born in Canton, Oxford County, Maine, May 1, 1839; attended the public schools, and was graduated from Tufts College, Medford, Mass., in 1863; during the Civil War served as a private for three months in the Fifth Regiment, Massachusetts Volunteer Infantry; mustered out the middle of July 1861; appointed captain in the Ninth Regiment, Maine Volunteer Infantry, in September 1861; promoted to the rank of lieutenant colonel and afterwards to the rank of colonel; honorably mustered out of the service with the latter rank in March 1863; moved to Illinois in 1863; studied law; was admitted to the bar in Chicago in 1864 and commenced practice in Jacksonville, Fla., in 1865; United States attorney for the northern district of Florida 1869-1873 and for a short period filled the office of attorney general of the State; presented credentials as a Republican Member-elect to the Forty-fifth Congress and served from March 4, 1877, to February 20, 1879, when he was succeeded by Jesse J. Finley, who contested the election; successfully contested the election of Noble A. Hull to the Forty-sixth Congress and served from January 22, 1881, to March 3, 1881; successfully contested the election of Jesse J. Finley to the Forty-seventh Congress and served from June 1, 1882, to March 3, 1883; reelected to the Forty-eighth Congress (March 4, 1883-March 3, 1885); unsuccessful candidate for reelection in 1884 to the Forty-ninth Congress; resumed the practice of his profession; died in Dixfield, Oxford County, Maine, March 27, 1916; interment in Greenwood Cemetery.

**Bibliography:** Klingman, Peter D. "Inside the Ring: Bisbee-Lee Correspondence, February-April 1880." *Florida Historical Quarterly* 57 (October 1978): 187-204.

**BISHOP, Cecil William (Runt),** a Representative from Illinois; born on a farm near West Vienna, Johnson County, Ill., June 29, 1890; attended the public schools, and Union Academy, Anna, Ill.; learned the tailoring trade; worked as coal miner, telephone lineman, professional football and baseball player and manager; engaged in the cleaning-tailoring business 1910-1922; city clerk of

Carterville, Ill., 1915-1918; postmaster at Carterville, Ill., 1923-1933; elected as a Republican to the Seventy-seventh and to the six succeeding Congresses (January 3, 1941-January 3, 1955); chairman, Special Committee on Campaign Expenditures (Eighty-third Congress); unsuccessful candidate for reelection in 1954 to the Eighty-fourth Congress; congressional liaison assistant, Post Office Department, Washington, D.C., 1955-1957; superintendent of Division of Industrial Planning and Development, State of Illinois, in 1957 and 1958; Department of Labor conciliator for State of Illinois, 1958-1960; retired; died in Marion, Ill., September 21, 1971; interment in Oakwood Cemetery, Carterville, Ill.

**BISHOP, James,** a Representative from New Jersey; born in New Brunswick, N.J., May 11, 1816; attended Spaulding School and Rutgers College Preparatory School, New Brunswick, N.J.; engaged in mercantile pursuits in New Brunswick; member of the State house of assembly in 1849 and 1850; elected as a Whig to the Thirty-fourth Congress (March 4, 1855-March 3, 1857); unsuccessful candidate for reelection in 1856 to the Thirty-fifth Congress; prominent in the rubber trade in New York City; chief of the bureau of labor statistics of New Jersey 1878-1893 and a resident of Trenton; died at Kemble Hall, near Morristown, Morris County, N.J., May 10, 1895; interment in Elmwood Cemetery, New Brunswick, Middlesex County, N.J.

**BISHOP, Phanuel,** a Representative from Massachusetts; born in Rehoboth, Mass., September 3, 1739; attended the common schools; was an innkeeper; served in the Massachusetts senate 1787-1791; member of the Massachusetts house of representatives in 1792, 1793, 1797, and 1798; elected as a Republican to the Sixth through Ninth Congresses (March 4, 1799-March 3, 1807); died in Rehoboth, Mass., January 6, 1812; interment in Old Cemetery, Rumford, East Providence, R.I.

**BISHOP, Roswell Peter,** a Representative from Michigan; born in Sidney, Delaware County, N.Y., January 6, 1843; attended Unadilla Academy, Cooperstown Seminary, and Walton Academy, New York; taught school several years; during the Civil War enlisted as a private in Company C, Forty-third Regiment, New York Volunteer Infantry, in 1861 and was discharged in December 1862 because of a wound which necessitated the amputation of his right arm; entered the University of Michigan, Ann Arbor, in September 1868 where he remained until December 1872; studied law; was admitted to the bar in Ann Arbor in May 1875 and commenced practice in Ludington, Mason County, Mich.; elected prosecuting attorney of Mason County in 1876, 1878, and 1884; member of the Michigan State house of representatives in 1882 and 1892; elected as a Republican to the Fifty-fourth and to the five succeeding Congresses (March 4, 1895-March 3, 1907); chairman, Committee on Ventilation and Acoustics (Fifty-seventh through Fifty-ninth Congresses); unsuccessful candidate for renomination in 1906 to the Sixtieth Congress; resumed the practice of law in Ludington, Mich.; served as a member of the Michigan constitutional convention in 1907; was appointed a member of the Spanish Treaty Claims Commission in December 1907, and served until the work of the commission was completed; moved to Hollister, Calif., in 1910 and engaged in fruit growing; died at Pacific Grove, Monterey County, Calif., March 4, 1920; interment in the El Carmelo Cemetery.

**BISHOP, Sanford Dixon, Jr.,** a Representative from Georgia; born in Mobile, Ala., February 4, 1947; attended Mobile County public schools; B.A., Morehouse College, Atlanta, Ga., 1968; J.D., Emory University School of Law, Atlanta, 1971; attorney; member, Georgia State house of representatives, 1977-1991; member, Georgia State senate, 1991-1993; elected as a Democrat to the One Hundred Third and One Hundred Fourth Congresses (January 3, 1993-January 3, 1997); is a resident of Columbus, Ga.

**BISHOP, William Darius,** a Representative from Connecticut; born in Bloomfield, Essex County, N.J., September 14, 1827; pursued preparatory studies; was graduated from Yale College in 1849; studied law; was admitted to the bar but did not practice, instead carrying on his father's railroad enterprises which involved the construction of the Naugatuck and the New York and New Haven Railroads in Connecticut and the railroad between Saratoga Springs and Whitehall in New York; founder of the Eastern Railroad Association and its president until the time of his death; elected as a Democrat to the Thirty-fifth Congress (March 4, 1857-March 3, 1859); chairman, Committee on Manufactures (Thirty-fifth Congress); unsuccessful candidate for reelection in 1858 to the Thirty-sixth Congress; commissioner of patents from May 23, 1859, to January 1860; vice president and president of the New York, New Haven & Hartford Railroad Co.; member of the State house of representatives in 1866 and 1871; served in the State senate in 1877 and 1878; died in Bridgeport, Conn., Feb. 4, 1904; interment in Mountain Grove Cemetery.

**Bibliography:** *DAB.*

**BISSELL, William Harrison,** a Representative from Illinois; born in Hartwick, Otsego County, N.Y., on April 25, 1811; attended the public schools, and was graduated from the Philadelphia Medical College in 1835; moved to Monroe County, Ill., in 1837; taught school and practiced medicine until 1840; member of the Illinois State house of representatives, 1840-1842; studied law; was admitted to the bar and commenced practice in Belleville, St. Clair County, Ill.; prosecuting attorney of St. Clair County in 1844; served in the Mexican War as colonel of the Second Regiment, Illinois Volunteer Infantry; elected as a Democrat to the Thirty-first and Thirty-second Congresses, and as an Independent Democrat to the Thirty-third Congress (March 4, 1849-March 3, 1855); chairman, Committee on Military Affairs (Thirty-second and Thirty-third Congresses); was not a candidate for renomination in 1854 to the Thirty-fourth Congress; elected Governor of Illinois in 1856, and served from January 12, 1857 until his death in Springfield, Sangamon County, Ill., March 18, 1860; interment in Oak Ridge Cemetery.

**Bibliography:** *DAB*; Tingley, Donald Fred. "The Jefferson Davis-William H. Bissell Duel." *Mid-America* 38 (July 1956): 146-155.

**BIXLER, Harris Jacob,** a Representative from Pennsylvania; born in New Buffalo, Perry County, Pa., September 16, 1870; attended the public schools and Lock Haven State Normal School; taught school in the country districts in Perry and Clinton Counties 1878-1892; attended Potts Business College, Williamsport, Pa.; moved to Johnsonburg, Elk County, Pa., in 1892 and worked as a shipping clerk; later was engaged in banking and manufacturing; director of the Johnsonburg National Bank; served as president of the city council 1900-1904 and as president of the board of education 1904-1910; mayor of Johnsonburg 1908-1912; sheriff of Elk County, Pa., 1916-1920; chairman of the Republican county committee 1916-1925; treasurer of Elk County 1920-1922; elected as a Republican to the Sixty-seventh, Sixty-eighth, and Sixty-ninth Congresses (March 4, 1921-March 3, 1927); unsuccessful candidate for renomination in 1926 to the Seventieth Congress; engaged in business as a freight contractor and also interested in agricultural pursuits; died in Johnsonburg, Pa., on March 29, 1941; interment in Duncannon Cemetery, Duncannon, Pa.

**BLACK, Edward Junius** (father of George Robison Black), a Representative from Georgia; born in Beaufort, S.C., October 30, 1806; attended the common schools and was graduated from Richmond Academy, Augusta, Ga.; studied law; was admitted to the bar in 1827 and commenced practice in Augusta, Ga.; member of the State house of representatives 1829-1831; moved to Screven County, Ga., in 1832; elected as a Whig to the Twenty-sixth Congress (March

4, 1839-March 3, 1841); unsuccessful Democratic candidate for reelection in 1840 to the Twenty-seventh Congress; subsequently elected as a Democrat to the Twenty-seventh Congress to fill in part the vacancies caused by the resignations of Julius C. Alford, William C. Dawson, and Eugenius A. Nisbet; reelected to the Twenty-eighth Congress and served from January 3, 1842, to March 3, 1845; unsuccessful candidate for reelection in 1844 to the Twenty-ninth Congress; resumed the practice of law; died in Millettville, Barnwell District, S.C., September 1, 1846; interment in the family burying ground near Millettville, Allendale County, S.C.

**BLACK, Eugene,** a Representative from Texas; born near Blossom, Lamar County, Tex., July 2, 1879; attended the public schools of Blossom; taught school in Lamar County 1898-1900; employed in the post office at Blossom; was graduated from the law department of Cumberland University, Lebanon, Tenn., in 1905; was admitted to the bar the same year and commenced practice in Clarksville, Red River County, Tex.; was also engaged in the wholesale grocery business; elected as a Democrat to the Sixty-fourth and to the six succeeding Congresses (March 4, 1915-March 3, 1929); unsuccessful candidate for renomination in 1928 to the Seventy-first Congress; appointed by President Herbert Hoover to the United States Board of Tax Appeals (now the United States Tax Court) on November 5, 1929 to fill an unexpired term; reappointed in 1932 and again in 1944 by President Franklin D. Roosevelt for a term of twelve years and served until his retirement November 30, 1953; recalled December 1, 1953, to perform further judicial service with the United States Tax Court until March 31, 1966; resided in Washington, D.C., until his death there on May 22, 1975; interment in Cedar Hill Cemetery, Suitland, Md.

**BLACK, Frank Swett,** a Representative from New York; born near Limington, York County, Maine, March 8, 1853; attended the district schools, and was graduated from Lebanon Academy, West Lebanon, Maine, in 1871; taught school for several years; was graduated from Dartmouth College, Hanover, N.H., in 1875; editor of the Johnstown (N.Y.) Journal; moved to Troy, N.Y., and engaged in newspaper work; studied law; was admitted to the bar in 1879 and commenced practice in Troy; elected as a Republican to the Fifty-fourth Congress, and served from March 4, 1895 to January 7, 1897, when he resigned to become Governor; elected Governor of New York in 1896, and served from January 1, 1897 to January 1, 1899; resumed the practice of law in New York City; died in Troy, N.Y., March 22, 1913; the remains were cremated and placed in a sepulchre on his farm near Freedom, Carroll County, N.H.

**Bibliography:** *DAB.*

**BLACK, George Robison** (son of Edward Junius Black), a Representative from Georgia; born on his father's plantation near Jacksonboro, Screven County, Ga., March 24, 1835; attended the common schools, the University of Georgia at Athens, and the University of South Carolina at Columbia; studied law; was admitted to the bar in 1857 and commenced practice in Savannah, Ga.; during the Civil War entered the Confederate service as first lieutenant of the Phoenix Riflemen and afterwards was promoted to lieutenant colonel of the Sixty-third Georgia Regiment; delegate to the State constitutional convention in 1865; delegate to the Democratic National Convention in 1872; member of the State senate 1874-1877; vice president of the Georgia State Agricultural Society; elected as a Democrat to the Forty-seventh Congress (March 4, 1881-March 3, 1883); was an unsuccessful candidate for renomination in 1882 to the Forty-eighth Congress; died in Sylvania, Screven County, Ga., November 3, 1886; interment in Sylvania Cemetery.

**BLACK, Henry,** a Representative from Pennsylvania; born near the borough of Somerset, Somerset County, Pa., February 25, 1783; attended the common schools; engaged in agricultural pursuits; member of the Pennsylvania house of representatives 1816-1818;

justice of the peace; associate judge of Somerset County, Pa., 1820-1840; elected as a Whig to the Twenty-seventh Congress to fill the vacancy caused by the death of Charles Ogle and served from June 28, 1841, until his death in Somerset, Pa., on November 28, 1841; interment in the family cemetery, Stony Creek Township, Somerset County, Pa.

**BLACK, Hugo Lafayette,** a Senator from Alabama; born near Ashland, Clay County, Ala., February 27, 1886; attended the public schools and Ashland College, Ashland, Ala.; was graduated from the law department of the University of Alabama at Tuscaloosa in 1906; was admitted to the Alabama bar the same year and commenced practice in Ashland, Ala.; moved to Birmingham, Ala., in 1907 and continued the practice of law; during the First World War served as a captain of the Eighty-first Field Artillery and as company regimental adjutant in the Nineteenth Artillery Brigade, 1917-1918; police court judge in Birmingham, Ala.; prosecuting attorney of Jefferson County, Ala.; elected as a Democrat to the United States Senate in 1926; reelected in 1932 and served from March 4, 1927, until his resignation on August 19, 1937, having been nominated by President Franklin D. Roosevelt on August 12 as an Associate Justice of the United States Supreme Court; chairman, Committee on Education and Labor (Seventy-fourth and Seventy-fifth Congresses); was confirmed by the Senate on August 17, 1937, took his seat as an Associate Justice on October 4, 1937 and served until his resignation on September 17, 1971; died in Bethesda, Md., on September 25, 1971; interment in Arlington National Cemetery, Va.

**Bibliography:** Ball, Howard. *Hugo L. Black: Cold Steel Warrior.* New York: Oxford University Press, 1996. Dunne, Gerald T. *Hugo Black and the Judicial Revolution.* New York: Simon and Schuster, 1977; Hamilton, Virginia. *Hugo Black: The Alabama Years.* Baton Rouge: Louisiana State University Press, 1972.

**BLACK, James,** a Representative from Pennsylvania; born in Newport, Perry County, Pa., March 6, 1793; attended the common schools; engaged in mercantile pursuits; member of the Pennsylvania house of representatives in 1830 and 1831; elected as a Jacksonian to the Twenty-fourth Congress to fill the vacancy caused by the resignation of Jesse Miller and served from December 5, 1836, to March 3, 1837; associate judge of Perry County in 1842 and 1843; elected as a Democrat to the Twenty-eighth and Twenty-ninth Congresses (March 4, 1843-March 3, 1847); Pennsylvania collector of tolls on the Juniata Canal; died in New Bloomfield, Perry County, Pa., on June 21, 1872; interment in New Bloomfield Cemetery.

**BLACK, James Augustus,** a Representative from South Carolina; born on his father's plantation in Ninety Six District, near Abbeville, S.C., in 1793; attended the common schools on his father's plantation; during the War of 1812 was appointed a second lieutenant in the Eighth Infantry March 12, 1812; promoted to first lieutenant December 2, 1813, and was honorably discharged June 15, 1815; engaged in the mining of iron ore on what is now the present site of Cherokee Falls, S.C.; moved to Georgia and settled in Savannah; engaged in cotton dealing; served as tax collector of Chatham County, Ga.; returned to South Carolina and settled in Columbia; cashier of the State (branch) bank; member of South Carolina house of representatives, 1826-1828 and 1832-1835; elected as a Democrat to the Twenty-eighth, Twenty-ninth, and Thirtieth Congresses and served from March 4, 1843, until his death in Washington, D.C., on April 3, 1848; chairman, Committee on the Militia (Twenty-ninth Congress); interment in the graveyard of the First Presbyterian Church, Columbia, S.C.

**BLACK, James Conquest Cross,** a Representative from Georgia; born in Stamping Ground, Scott County, Ky., May 9, 1842; attended the common schools and the high school at Newcastle, Ky., and was graduated from Georgetown College, Kentucky, in 1862; during the Civil War enlisted as a private in Company A, Ninth Kentucky Cavalry, in the Confederate Army; moved to Augusta, Ga., in 1865; studied law; was admitted to the bar in 1866 and commenced practice in Augusta, Ga.; member of the State house of representatives 1873-1877; served as president of the Augusta Orphan Asylum 1879-1886; member of the city council; served as city attorney; elected as a Democrat to the Fifty-third and Fifty-fourth Congresses and served from March 4, 1893, to March 4, 1895, when he resigned; subsequently elected to fill the vacancy caused by his own resignation and served from October 2, 1895, to March 3, 1897; was not a candidate for renomination in 1896; resumed the practice of law in Augusta, Ga., until his death there on October 1, 1928; interment in Magnolia Cemetery.

**BLACK, John,** a Senator from Mississippi; born in Massachusetts, but date of birth is unknown; engaged in teaching; studied law; commenced practice in Louisiana; moved to Mississippi; elected judge of the fourth circuit and supreme court, 1826-1832; appointed to the United States Senate to fill the vacancy caused by the resignation of Powhatan Ellis, and served from November 12, 1832 to March 3, 1833; elected as a Whig to the United States Senate to fill the vacancy in the term commencing March 4, 1833, and served from November 22, 1833 to January 22, 1838, when he resigned; chairman, Committee on Private Lands (Twenty-third and Twenty-fourth Congresses); resumed the practice of law in Winchester, Va., and died there on August 29, 1854; interment in Mount Hebron Cemetery.

**BLACK, John Charles,** a Representative from Illinois; born in Lexington, Holmes County, Miss., January 27, 1839; moved to Danville, Vermilion County, Ill., in 1847; attended the common schools and Wabash College, Crawfordsville, Ind., but was not graduated until after the close of the Civil War; served in the Union Army from April 14, 1861, to August 15, 1865; entered as a private, and was successively sergeant major, major, lieutenant colonel, and colonel; brevetted brigadier general for service in the storming of Fort Blakeley, Ala., on April 9, 1865; received the Congressional Medal of Honor October 31, 1893 for valor during the Battle of Prairie Grove, Ark., on December 7, 1862; studied law in Chicago, Ill.; was admitted to the bar in 1867 and commenced practice in Danville, Ill.; appointed United States Commissioner of Pensions by President Grover Cleveland and served from March 17, 1885, to March 27, 1889; elected as a Democrat to the Fifty-third Congress and served from March 4, 1893, to January 12, 1895, when he resigned; United States attorney for the northern district of Illinois 1895-1899; department commander of the Loyal Legion of Illinois 1895-1897; department commander of the Illinois department, Grand Army of the Republic, in 1898; commander in chief of the Grand Army of the Republic in 1903 and 1904; member of the United States Civil Service Commission 1904-1913 and served as its president; resigned and returned to Chicago, Ill., where he died August 17, 1915; interment in Spring Hill Cemetery, Danville, Ill.

**Bibliography:** *DAB.*

**BLACK, Loring Milton, Jr.,** a Representative from New York; born in New York City, May 17, 1886; attended the public schools and was graduated from Fordham University, New York City, in 1907; studied law at Columbia University, New York City; was admitted to the bar in 1909 and commenced practice in New York City; member of the State senate in 1911 and 1912; resumed the practice of his profession in New York City; again a member of the State senate in 1919 and 1920; elected as a Democrat to the Sixty-eighth and to the five succeeding Congresses (March 4, 1923-January 3, 1935); chairman, Committee on Claims (Seventy-second and Seventy-third Congresses); was not a candidate for renomination in 1934; resumed the practice of law in New York City and Washington, D.C.; died in Washington, D.C., May 21, 1956; interment in Fort Lincoln Cemetery.

**BLACKBURN, Benjamin Bentley,** a Representative from Georgia; born in Atlanta, Fulton County, Ga., February 14, 1927; attended the public schools in Atlanta, Ga.; B.A., University of North Carolina, 1947; LL.B., Emory University School of Law, 1954; during the Second World War served in the United States Navy, 1944-1946; during the Korean conflict again served in the United States Navy, 1950-1952; was retired as a lieutenant commander in the United States Naval Reserve; served in the State attorney general's office, 1955-1957; admitted to the bar in 1954 and commenced private practice in Atlanta, Ga., after service with the State attorney general; elected as a Republican to the Ninetieth and to the three succeeding Congresses (January 3, 1967-January 3, 1975); was an unsuccessful candidate for reelection in 1974 to the Ninety-fourth Congress; is a resident of Atlanta, Ga.

**BLACKBURN, Edmond Spencer,** a Representative from North Carolina; born near Boone, Watauga County, N.C., September 22, 1868; attended the common schools and academies of his native State; studied law; was admitted to the bar in 1890 and commenced practice in Jefferson, Ashe County, N.C.; reading clerk of the State senate in 1894 and 1895; member of the State house of representatives in 1896 and 1897, serving as speaker pro tempore the latter year; assistant United States attorney in 1898; elected as a Republican to the Fifty-seventh Congress (March 4, 1901-March 3, 1903); unsuccessful candidate for reelection in 1902 to the Fifty-eighth Congress; elected to the Fifty-ninth Congress (March 4, 1905-March 3, 1907); was not a candidate for renomination in 1906; resumed the practice of law in Greensboro, N.C.; died in Elizabethton, Carter County, Tenn., March 10, 1912; interment in Old Hopewel Cemetery, near Boone, N.C.

**BLACKBURN, Joseph Clay Stiles,** a Representative and a Senator from Kentucky; born near Spring Station, Woodford County, Ky., October 1, 1838; attended Sayres Institute, Frankfort, Ky., and was graduated from Centre College, Danville, Ky., in 1857; studied law in Lexington, Ky.; was admitted to the bar in 1858 and practiced in Chicago, Ill., until 1860, when he returned to Woodford County, Ky.; entered the Confederate Army as a private in 1861 and was promoted to the rank of lieutenant colonel before the close of the Civil War; settled in Arkansas in 1865, where he was engaged as lawyer and planter in Desha County until 1868, when he returned to Kentucky and opened law offices in Versailles; member, Kentucky house of representatives, 1871-1875; elected as a Democrat to the Forty-fourth and to the four succeeding Congresses (March 4, 1875-March 3, 1885); chairman, Committee on the District of Columbia (Forty-fifth Congress), Committee on Expenditures in the Department of War (Forty-fifth and Forty-sixth Congresses); elected as a Democrat to the United States Senate in 1885; reelected in 1890, and served from March 4, 1885 to March 3, 1897; unsuccessful candidate for reelection in 1896; chairman, Committee on Rules (Fifty-third Congress); again elected to the United States Senate, and served from March 4, 1901 to March 3, 1907; unsuccessful candidate for reelection in 1907; Democratic caucus chairman 1906-1907; appointed Governor of the Canal Zone, Isthmus of Panama, by President Theodore Roosevelt on April 1, 1907; resigned in November 1909 and returned to his estate in Woodford County, Ky.; died in Washington, D.C., September 12, 1918; interment in the State Cemetery, Frankfort, Ky.

**Bibliography:** *DAB*; Schlup, Leonard. "Joseph Blackburn of Kentucky and the Panama Question." *The Filson Club Quarterly* 51 (October 1977): 350-62.

**BLACKBURN, Robert E. Lee,** a Representative from Kentucky; born on a farm near Furnace, Estill County, Ky., April 9, 1870; as an infant moved with his parents to Stanton, Powell County, Ky.; attended the county schools, and Elliott Academy at Kirksville, Madison County, Ky.; traveling salesman for an oil company 1891-1900; during the Spanish-American War served as a second lieutenant in Company C, Fourth Infantry, United States Volunteers; engaged in general merchandising at Stanton, Ky., and in agricultural pursuits 1900-1907; member of the Kentucky house of representatives in 1904 and 1905; served as clerk of the court of Powell County 1906 to 1910; was engaged in the insurance and stock brokerage business 1910-1919; moved to Lexington, Ky., in 1919 and continued the insurance and brokerage business; also engaged in the oil-development business; appointed a member of the Kentucky board of agriculture in 1926 and served until 1928; elected as a Republican to the Seventy-first Congress (March 4, 1929-March 3, 1931); unsuccessful candidate for reelection in 1930 to the Seventy-second Congress and for election in 1932 to the Seventy-third Congress; resumed his former activities in the oil business and resided in Lexington, Ky., until his death there on September 20, 1935; interment in Stanton Cemetery, Stanton, Ky.

**BLACKBURN, William Jasper,** a Representative from Louisiana; born on the Fourche de Mau, Randolph County, Ark., on July 24, 1820; received his early education from his mother; moved to Batesville in 1839 and learned the printer's trade; moved to Little Rock in 1845, to Fort Smith in 1846, and to Minden, La., in 1849, where he established the Minden Herald; moved to Homer, La., and established the Homer Iliad in 1859; member of the State constitutional convention in 1867; county judge of Claiborne Parish, La., for four years; upon the readmission of the State of Louisiana to representation was elected as a Republican to the Fortieth Congress and served from July 18, 1868, to March 3, 1869; was not a candidate for renomination in 1868; member of the State senate 1874-1878; returned to Little Rock, Ark., in 1880; published the Arkansas Republican from 1881 to 1884 and the Free South from 1885 to 1892; died in Little Rock, Ark., November 10, 1899; interment in Mount Holly Cemetery.

**BLACKLEDGE, William** (father of William Salter Blackledge), a Representative from North Carolina; born in Craven County, N.C.; member of the State house of commons 1797-1799 and again in 1809; elected as a Republican to the Eighth, Ninth, and Tenth Congresses (March 4, 1803-March 3, 1809); one of the managers appointed by the House of Representatives in 1804 to conduct the impeachment proceedings against John Pickering, judge of the United States District Court for New Hampshire; unsuccessful candidate for reelection in 1808 to the Eleventh Congress; elected to the Twelfth Congress (March 4, 1811-March 3, 1813); unsuccessful candidate for reelection in 1812 to the Thirteenth Congress; died at Spring Hill, Craven County, N.C., October 19, 1828.

**BLACKLEDGE, William Salter** (son of William Blackledge), a Representative from North Carolina; born in Pitt County, N.C., in 1793; moved to Craven County, N.C., and settled in New Bern; graduated from the University of North Carolina at Chapel Hill in 1813; member of the State house of commons in 1820; elected to the Sixteenth Congress to fill the vacancy caused by the death of Jesse Slocumb; reelected to the Seventeenth Congress and served from February 7, 1821, until March 3, 1823; died in New Bern, Craven County, N.C., March 21, 1857; interment in New Bern Cemetery.

**BLACKMAR, Esbon,** a Representative from New York; born in Freehold, Greene County, N.Y., June 19, 1805; attended the district schools and was graduated from the high school; engaged in the general merchandise business; member of the State senate in 1838 and 1841; elected as a Whig to the Thirtieth Congress to fill the vacancy caused by the death of John M. Holley and served from December 4, 1848, to March 3, 1849; resumed his former business activities; died in Newark, Wayne County, N.Y., on November 19, 1857; interment in Willow Avenue Cemetery.

**BLACKMON, Fred Leonard,** a Representative from Alabama; born at Lime Branch, Polk County, Ga., September 15, 1873; moved with his parents to Calhoun County, Ala., in 1883; attended the public schools in Dearmanville and Choccolocco, the State normal college at Jacksonville, Ala., Douglasville (Ga.) College, and Mountain City Business College, Chattanooga, Tenn.; was graduated from the law department of the University of Alabama at Tuscaloosa in 1894; was admitted to the bar in the same year and commenced practice in Anniston, Calhoun County, Ala.; city attorney for Anniston 1898-1902; member of the State senate 1900-1910; chairman of the congressional committee for the fourth Alabama district from 1906 until 1910, when he resigned; elected as a Democrat to the Sixty-second and to the four succeeding Congresses and served from March 4, 1911, until his death; had also been reelected to the Sixty-seventh Congress; died in Bartow, Polk County, Fla., on February 8, 1921; interment in the Hillside Cemetery, Anniston, Ala.

**BLACKNEY, William Wallace,** a Representative from Michigan; born in Clio, Genesee County, Mich., August 28, 1876; attended the public schools, Olivet College, Olivet, Mich., and Ferris School, Big Rapids, Mich.; moved to Flint, Mich., in 1904; served as county clerk of Genesee County 1905-1912; was graduated from the law department of the University of Michigan at Ann Arbor in 1912; was admitted to the bar the same year and commenced practice in Flint, Mich.; served as assistant prosecuting attorney of Genesee County 1913-1917; member of the Flint School Board 1924-1934; member of the Republican State central committee 1925-1930; instructor in the General Motors Co. technical night school for sixteen years; elected as a Republican to the Seventy-fourth Congress (January 3, 1935-January 3, 1937); unsuccessful candidate for reelection in 1936 to the Seventy-fifth Congress; elected to the Seventy-sixth and to the six succeeding Congresses (January 3, 1939-January 3, 1953); was not a candidate for renomination in 1952; retired to Flint, Mich., until his death there March 14, 1963; interment in Woodlawn Cemetery, Clio, Mich.

**BLACKWELL, Julius W.,** a Representative from Tennessee; born in Virginia; attended the public schools; moved to Tennessee and settled in Athens, McMinn County; elected as a Democrat to the Twenty-sixth Congress (March 4, 1839-March 3, 1841); unsuccessful candidate for reelection in 1840 to the Twenty-seventh Congress; elected to the Twenty-eighth Congress (March 4, 1843-March 3, 1845); unsuccessful candidate for reelection in 1844 to the Twenty-ninth Congress.

**BLACKWELL, Lucien Edward,** a Representative from Pennsylvania; born in Philadelphia, Fayette County, Pa., August 1, 1931; attended Philadelphia, Pa., public schools; United States Army service during Korean conflict, 1952-1954, 25th Infantry Division; laborer, foreman, trustee, vice president, business agent, president (eighteen years), all with Local 1332, International Longshoremen's Association, AFL-CIO; Philadelphia City councilman, seventeen years; candidate for mayor, 1991; former chairman, Philadelphia Gas Commission; member, Pennsylvania house of representatives; former commissioner, Delaware Port Authority; elected as a Democrat to the One Hundred Second Congress, November 5, 1991, by special election to fill the vacancy caused by the resignation of William H. Gray III; reelected to the One Hundred Third Congress, and served from November 5, 1991 to January 3, 1995; unsuccessful candidate for renomination in 1994 to the One Hundred Fourth Congress; is a resident of Philadelphia, Pa.

**BLAINE, James Gillespie,** a Representative and a Senator from Maine; born in West Brownsville, Washington County, Pa., January 31, 1830; was graduated from Washington College, Washington, Pa., in 1847; taught at the Western Military Institute, Blue Lick Springs, Ky.; returned to Pennsylvania; studied law; taught at the Pennsylvania Institution for the Blind in Philadelphia from 1852 until 1854; moved in 1854 to Maine, where he edited the Portland Advertiser and the Kennebec Journal; member, Maine State house of representatives, 1859-1862, serving the last two years as speaker; elected as a Republican to the Thirty-eighth and to the six succeeding Congresses, and served from March 4, 1863 to July 10, 1876, when he resigned; Speaker of the House of Representatives (Forty-first through Forty-third Congresses); chairman, Committee on Rules (Forty-third through Forty-fifth Congresses); unsuccessful candidate for the Republican presidential nomination in 1876 and 1880; appointed and subsequently elected as a Republican to the United States Senate to fill the vacancy caused by the resignation of Lot M. Morrill; reelected and served from July 10, 1876 to March 5, 1881, when he resigned to become Secretary of State; chairman, Committee on Civil Service and Retrenchment (Forty-fifth Congress), Committee on Rules (Forty-fifth Congress); Secretary of State in the Cabinets of Presidents James A. Garfield and Chester A. Arthur from March 5 to December 12, 1881; nominated by the Republican Party for President of the United States on June 7, 1884, but was unsuccessful in the general election; Secretary of State in the Cabinet of President Benjamin Harrison from March 5, 1889 until his resignation on June 4, 1892; aided in organizing and was the first president of the Pan American Conference in Washington, D.C., October 1889-April 1890; died in Washington, D.C., January 27, 1893; interment in Oak Hill Cemetery; reinterment at the request of the State of Maine in the Blaine Memorial Park, Augusta, Maine, in June 1920.

**Bibliography:** *DAB*; Blaine, James G. *Twenty Years of Congress: From Lincoln to Garfield.* 2 vols. Norwich, Conn.: The Henry Bill Publishing Company, 1884-1886; Muzzey, David S. *James G. Blaine: A Political Idol of Other Days.* 1943. Reprint. Port Washington, N.Y.: Kennikat Press, 1963.

**BLAINE, John James,** a Senator from Wisconsin; born on a farm in Wingville Township, Grant County, Wis., May 4, 1875; attended the common schools; was graduated from the law department of Valparaiso (Ind.) University in 1896; was admitted to the bar in 1896 and commenced practice in Montford; moved to Boscobel in 1897 and continued the practice of law; mayor of Boscobel, 1901-1904, 1906-1907; member of the Grant County Board of Supervisors, 1901-1904; member, Wisconsin State senate, 1909-1913; unsuccessful independent candidate for election in 1914 for Governor; attorney general of the State of Wisconsin, 1919-1921; elected Governor of Wisconsin in 1920, reelected in 1922 and 1924, and served from January 3, 1921 until January 3, 1927; elected as a Republican to the United States Senate for the term beginning March 4, 1927, and served from March 4, 1927, to March 3, 1933; unsuccessful candidate for renomination in 1932; resumed the practice of law at Boscobel; appointed a director of the Reconstruction Finance Corporation in 1933 and served until his death in Boscobel, Wis., April 16, 1934; interment in Hillside Cemetery.

**Bibliography:** *DAB*; O'Brien, Patrick. "Senator John J. Blaine: An Independent Progressive During 'Normalcy'." *Wisconsin Magazine of History* 60 (Autumn 1976): 25-41.

**BLAIR, Austin,** a Representative from Michigan; born in Caroline, Tompkins County, N.Y., February 8, 1818; attended the common schools, Cazenovia Seminary, and Hamilton College, Clinton, N.Y.; was graduated from Union College, Schenectady, N.Y., in 1837; studied law in Oswego; was admitted to the bar in Tioga County, N.Y., in 1841; moved to Michigan and settled in Eaton Rapids, where he commenced the practice of his profession in 1842; county clerk of Eaton County; moved to Jackson, Mich., in 1844; elected to the Michigan State house of representatives in 1845; delegate to the Free-Soil National Convention at Buffalo, N.Y., in 1848; elected prosecuting attorney of Jackson County in 1852; elected to the State senate in 1854; member of the convention that met under the oaks at Jackson, Mich., July 6, 1854, at the organization of the Republican Party in Michigan, and was a

member of the platform committee; delegate to the Republican National Convention at Chicago in 1860; elected Governor of Michigan in 1860, reelected in 1862, and served from January 2, 1861 to January 4, 1865; elected as a Republican to the Fortieth and to the two succeeding Congresses (March 4, 1867-March 3, 1873); chairman, Committee on Private Land Claims (Forty-first and Forty-second Congresses); was not a candidate for renomination in 1872 to the Forty-third Congress, but was an unsuccessful Liberal Republican candidate for election for Governor; resumed the practice of law in Jackson, Mich., and died there on August 6, 1894; interment in Mount Evergreen Cemetery.

**Bibliography:** *DAB*; Crofts, Daniel W. "The Blair Bill and the Elections Bill: The Congressional Aftermath to Reconstruction." Ph.D. dissertation, Yale University, 1968; Harris, Robert C. "Austin Blair of Michigan: A Political Biography." Ph.D. dissertation, Michigan State University, 1969.

**BLAIR, Bernard,** a Representative from New York; born in Williamstown, Mass., May 24, 1801; attended the public schools and pursued preparatory studies; was graduated from Williams College, Williamstown, Mass., in 1825; moved to Salem, Washington County, N.Y., in 1825; studied law; was admitted to the bar in 1828 and commenced practice in Salem, subsequently being admitted as counselor and solicitor in chancery; elected as a Whig to the Twenty-seventh Congress (March 4, 1841-March 3, 1843); discontinued the practice of his profession and engaged in business pursuits; died in Salem, Washington County, N.Y., May 7, 1880; interment in Evergreen Cemetery.

**BLAIR, Francis Preston, Jr.,** a Representative and a Senator from Missouri; born in Lexington, Ky., on February 19, 1821; as a child moved with his father to Washington, D.C.; attended private schools and the University of North Carolina at Chapel Hill; was graduated from Princeton College in 1841; studied law at Transylvania University, Lexington, Ky.; was admitted to the bar in 1842 and commenced practice in St. Louis in 1843; enlisted as a private during the Mexican War; served as attorney general of the Territory of New Mexico; resumed the practice of law in St. Louis; member, Missouri State house of representatives, 1852-1856; elected as a Republican to the Thirty-fifth Congress (March 4, 1857-March 3, 1859); successfully contested the election of John R. Barret to the Thirty-sixth Congress and served from June 8 to June 25, 1860, when he resigned; unsuccessful candidate for reelection to the Thirty-sixth Congress to fill the vacancy caused by his own resignation; elected to the Thirty-seventh Congress and served from March 4, 1861, until his resignation in July 1862 to become a colonel in the Union Army; chairman, Committee on Military Affairs (Thirty-seventh Congress); presented credentials as a Member-elect to the Thirty-eighth Congress and served from March 4, 1863, to June 10, 1864, when he was succeeded by Samuel Knox, who contested the election; nominated as revenue collector in St. Louis, and as United States Minister to Austria, but the Senate refused to confirm both nominations; unsuccessful candidate for Vice President of the United States in 1868 on the Democratic ticket headed by Horatio Seymour; member, Missouri State house of representatives, 1870; elected as a Democrat to the United States Senate to fill the vacancy caused by the resignation of Charles D. Drake and served from January 20, 1871, to March 3, 1873; was not a candidate for reelection; State superintendent of insurance from November 1, 1874 until his death in St. Louis, Mo., July 8, 1875; interment in Bellefontaine Cemetery.

**Bibliography:** *DAB*; Smith, William E. *The Francis Preston Blair Family in Politics.* 2 vols. New York: Macmillan, 1933.

**BLAIR, Henry William,** a Representative and a Senator from New Hampshire; born in Campton, Grafton County, N.H., December 6, 1834; attended the common schools and private academies; studied law; was admitted to the bar in 1859 and commenced practice in Plymouth, N.H.; appointed prosecuting attorney for Grafton County 1860; during the Civil War served in the Union Army as lieutenant colonel of the Fifteenth Regiment, New Hampshire Volunteer Infantry; member, State house of representatives 1866; member, State senate 1867-1868; elected as a Republican to the Forty-fourth and Forty-fifth Congresses (March 4, 1875-March 3, 1879); was not a candidate for renomination in 1878 to the Forty-sixth Congress; elected as a Republican to the United States Senate on June 17, 1879, for the vacancy in the term ending March 3, 1885, and served from June 20, 1879, to March 3, 1885; the State legislature not being in session, he was appointed on March 5, 1885, and elected on June 17, 1885, to fill the vacancy in the term beginning March 4, 1885, and served from March 10, 1885, to March 3, 1891; unsuccessful candidate for renomination in 1891; chairman, Committee on Education and Labor (Forty-seventh through Fifty-first Congresses); declined an appointment as judge of the district court for the district of New Hampshire tendered by President Benjamin Harrison in 1891; appointed Envoy Extraordinary and Minister Plenipotentiary to China on February 27, 1891, he was objected to by the Chinese Government as being persona non grata; subsequently tendered his resignation which was accepted October 6, 1891; elected as a Republican to the Fifty-third Congress (March 4, 1893-March 3, 1895); was not a candidate for reelection in 1894; engaged in the practice of law in Washington, D.C., until his death on March 14, 1920; interment in Campton Cemetery, Campton, N.H.

**Bibliography:** *DAB.*

**BLAIR, Jacob Beeson,** a Representative from Virginia and from West Virginia; born in Parkersburg, Wood County, Va. (now West Virginia), April 11, 1821; attended the public schools; studied law; was admitted to the bar in 1844 and commenced practice at Harrisville, Ritchie County, Va. (now West Virginia); prosecuting attorney of Ritchie County for several years; returned to Parkersburg in 1856; elected as a Unionist from Virginia to the Thirty-seventh Congress to fill the vacancy caused by the resignation of John S. Carlile and served from December 2, 1861, to March 3, 1863; upon the admission of West Virginia as a State into the Union was elected as an Unconditional Unionist to the Thirty-eighth Congress and served from December 7, 1863, to March 3, 1865; appointed United States Minister to Costa Rica on July 25, 1868 and served until June 30, 1873; associate justice of the supreme court of Wyoming 1876-1888; moved to Utah in 1888; probate judge for Salt Lake County, Utah, 1892-1895; surveyor general of Utah from 1897 until his death in Salt Lake City on February 12, 1901; interment in Mount Olivet Cemetery.

**BLAIR, James,** a Representative from South Carolina; born in the Waxhaw settlement, Lancaster County, S.C., about 1790; engaged in planting; sheriff of Lancaster District; elected to the Seventeenth Congress and served from March 4, 1821, to May 8, 1822, when he resigned; elected as a Jacksonian to the Twenty-first through Twenty-third Congresses and served from March 4, 1829, until his death in Washington, D.C., April 1, 1834; interment in Congressional Cemetery.

**BLAIR, James Gorrall,** a Representative from Missouri; born near Blairville, Ky., January 1, 1825; was self-educated, having attended the public schools only three months; moved to Monticello, Lewis County, Mo., in 1840 and engaged in agricultural pursuits; elected circuit clerk in 1848 and served until 1854; studied law; was admitted to the bar and commenced practice in Canton, Mo., in 1854; delegate to the Republican State convention in 1870; elected as a Liberal Republican to the Forty-second Congress (March 4, 1871-March 3, 1873); was not a candidate for renomination in 1872; resumed the practice of law and also engaged in agricultural pursuits; died in Monticello, Lewis County, Mo., March 1, 1904; interment in Forest Grove Cemetery, Canton, Mo.

**BLAIR, John,** a Representative from Tennessee; born at Blairs Mill, near Jonesborough (now Jonesboro), Washington County, Tenn., September 13, 1790; attended Martain Academy, and was graduated from Washington (Tenn.) College in 1809; studied law; was admitted to the bar in 1813 and practiced; member of the State house of representatives 1815-1817; served in the State senate 1817-1821; elected to the Eighteenth Congress; reelected to the Nineteenth Congress and reelected as a Jacksonian to the Twentieth through Twenty-third Congresses (March 4, 1823-March 3, 1835); chairman, Committee on Expenditures in the Department of State (Twentieth Congress); unsuccessful candidate for reelection in 1834 to the Twenty-fourth Congress; retired to private life; again a member of the State house of representatives, in 1849 and 1850; resumed the practice of law; died in Jonesboro, Tenn., July 9, 1863; interment in the Old Cemetery.

**BLAIR, Samuel Steel,** a Representative from Pennsylvania; born in Indiana, Indiana County, Pa., December 5, 1821; attended the public schools and was graduated from Jefferson College, Canonsburg, Pa., in 1838; studied law; was admitted to the bar in 1845 and commenced practice in Hollidaysburg, Blair County, Pa., in 1846; delegate to the Republican National Convention in 1856; elected as a Republican to the Thirty-sixth and Thirty-seventh Congresses (March 4, 1859-March 3, 1863); chairman, Committee on Private Lands (Thirty-seventh Congress); unsuccessful candidate for reelection in 1862 to the Thirty-eighth Congress; resumed the practice of law; unsuccessful candidate for election in 1874 to the Forty-fourth Congress; died in Hollidaysburg, Pa., December 8, 1890; interment in the Presbyterian Cemetery.

**BLAISDELL, Daniel,** a Representative from New Hampshire; born in Amesbury, Mass., January 22, 1762; attended the public schools; served in the Revolutionary War from August 1776 to August 1777; moved to Canaan, N.H., in 1780; taught school and also acquired some legal knowledge; engaged in agricultural pursuits; held several local offices; member of the State house of representatives in 1793, 1795, and 1799; served as a member of the executive council 1803-1808; moderator of Canaan in 1808, 1809, 1812, 1822, 1824, 1826, and 1830; elected as a Federalist to the Eleventh Congress (March 4, 1809-March 3, 1811); served in the War of 1812; again a member of the State house of representatives, in 1812, 1813, 1824, and 1825; served as selectman of Canaan in 1813, 1815, and 1818; resumed agricultural pursuits; member of the State senate in 1814 and 1815; chief justice of the court of sessions in 1822; died in Canaan, N.H., January 10, 1833; interment in Wells Cemetery.

**BLAKE, Harrison Gray Otis,** a Representative from Ohio; born in Newfane, Windham County, Vt., March 17, 1818; moved to Salem, N.Y., and in 1830 to Guilford, Medina County, Ohio; attended the public schools; studied medicine at Seville for one year; moved to Medina in 1836 and engaged in mercantile pursuits; also studied law; was admitted to the bar and commenced practice in Medina; member of the Ohio State house of representatives in 1846 and 1847; member of the State senate in 1848 and 1849, serving as its president; elected as a Republican to the Thirty-sixth Congress to fill the vacancy caused by the death of Cyrus Spink; reelected to the Thirty-seventh Congress, and served from October 11, 1859 to March 3, 1863; was not a candidate for renomination in 1862 to the Thirty-eighth Congress; entered the Union Army in 1864 as colonel of the One Hundred and Sixty-sixth Regiment; declined the appointment of Governor of Idaho Territory; resumed the practice of law; also interested in banking and mercantile pursuits; delegate to the Loyalist Convention at Philadelphia in 1866; died in Medina, Medina County, Ohio, April 16, 1876; interment in Spring Grove Cemetery.

**BLAKE, John, Jr.,** a Representative from New York; born in Ulster County, N.Y., December 5, 1762; attended the public schools; during the Revolutionary War served in the New York State Militia; appointed deputy sheriff of Ulster County in 1793; member of the State assembly 1798-1800; sheriff of Orange County 1803-1805; elected as a Republican to the Ninth and Tenth Congresses (March 4, 1805-March 3, 1809); again a member of the State assembly in 1812 and 1813; judge of the court of common pleas for Orange County 1815-1818; again served in the State assembly in 1819; supervisor of the town of Montgomery fifteen terms; died in Montgomery, Orange County, N.Y., January 13, 1826; interment in the Berea Churchyard, near Newburgh, N.Y.

**BLAKE, John Lauris,** a Representative from New Jersey; born in Boston, Mass., March 25, 1831; received a classical education; moved to Orange, N.J., in 1846; studied law; was admitted to the bar in 1852 and commenced practice in Orange, N.J.; member of the State house of assembly in 1857; delegate to the Republican National Convention in 1876; elected as a Republican to the Forty-sixth Congress (March 4, 1879-March 3, 1881); declined to be a candidate for renomination in 1880; resumed the practice of his profession in Orange; became president of the Citizens' Gas Light Co. of Newark, N.J., in 1893; died in West Orange, Essex County, N.J., October 10, 1899; interment in Rosedale Cemetery, Orange, N.J.

Bibliography: *DAB*.

**BLAKE, Thomas Holdsworth,** a Representative from Indiana; born in Calvert County, Md., June 14, 1792; attended the public schools; studied law in Washington, D.C.; member of the militia of the District of Columbia which took part in the Battle of Bladensburg in 1814; moved to Kentucky and thence to Indiana; was admitted to the bar and commenced practice in Terre Haute, Ind.; prosecuting attorney and judge of the circuit court; abandoned the practice of law to engage in business; member of the State house of representatives; elected to the Twentieth Congress (March 4, 1827-March 3, 1829); was an unsuccessful candidate for reelection in 1828 to the Twenty-first Congress; was appointed Commissioner of the General Land Office by President Tyler on May 19, 1842, and served until April 1845; chosen president of the Erie & Wabash Canal Co.; visited England as financial agent of the State of Indiana and, while returning, died in Cincinnati, Ohio, November 28, 1849; interment in Woodlawn Cemetery, Terre Haute, Ind.

**BLAKENEY, Albert Alexander,** a Representative from Maryland; born in Riderwood, Baltimore County, Md., September 28, 1850; attended private schools; learned the business of cotton manufacturing and established the large cotton-duck mills located in Franklinville, Md.; commissioner of Baltimore County 1895-1899; elected as a Republican to the Fifty-seventh Congress (March 4, 1901-March 3, 1903); declined to be a candidate for renomination in 1902; resumed his former business activities in Franklinville, Md.; elected to the Sixty-seventh Congress (March 4, 1921-March 3, 1923); unsuccessful candidate for reelection in 1922 to the Sixty-eighth Congress; died in Baltimore, Md., October 15, 1924; interment in the Baltimore Cemetery.

**BLAKLEY, William Arvis,** a Senator from Texas; born in Miami Station, Saline County, Mo., November 17, 1898; moved with his parents to Arapaho, Custer County, Okla.; during the First World War served in the United States Army; admitted to the bar in 1933 and commenced practice in Dallas, Tex.; appointed as a Democrat by the Governor to the United States Senate on January 15, 1957, to fill the vacancy caused by the resignation of Price Daniel and served from January 15, 1957, to April 28, 1957; declined to be a candidate for election to the vacancy; unsuccessful candidate for the Democratic nomination for a full term to the United States Senate in 1958; again appointed by the Governor on January 3, 1961, to the United States Senate to fill the vacancy caused by the resignation of Lyndon B. Johnson and served from January 3, 1961, to June 14, 1961; was unsuccessful for election to fill the vacancy; resumed former business interests; died in Dallas, Tex., January 5, 1976; interment in Restland Memorial Park.

**BLANCHARD, George Washington,** a Representative from Wisconsin; born in Colby, Marathon County, Wis., January 26, 1884; attended the graded and high schools; was graduated from the University of Wisconsin at Madison in 1906 and from its law department in 1910; was admitted to the bar in 1910 and commenced practice in Edgerton, Rock County, Wis.; city attorney of Edgerton from 1912 until his resignation in 1932, having been elected to Congress; member of the Wisconsin State assembly, 1925-1927; served in the State senate, 1927-1933; elected as a Republican to the Seventy-third Congress (March 3, 1933-January 3, 1935); was renominated in 1934 to the Seventy-fourth Congress, but withdrew his candidacy on September 29, 1934; practiced law in Edgerton, Wis., until his death there on October 2, 1964; interment in Fassett Cemetery.

**BLANCHARD, James Johnston,** a Representative from Michigan; born in Detroit, Wayne County, Mich., August 8, 1942; attended the public schools of Ferndale, Mich.; B.A., Michigan State University, East Lansing, 1964; M.B.A., Michigan State University, 1965; J.D., University of Minnesota Law School, Minneapolis, 1968; admitted to the Michigan bar in 1968 and commenced practice in Lansing; legal adviser to Michigan Secretary of State, 1968-1969; assistant attorney general of Michigan, 1969-1974; administrative assistant to the attorney general, 1970-1971; assistant deputy attorney general, 1971-1972; elected as a Democrat to the Ninety-fourth and to the three succeeding Congresses (Janaury 3, 1975-January 3, 1983); was not a candidate for reelection in 1982 to the Ninety-eighth Congress, but was elected Governor of Michigan; reelected in 1986, and served from January 1, 1983 to January 1, 1991; unsuccessful candidate for reelection in 1990; nominated as Ambassador to Canada on July 13, 1993, and was confirmed by the Senate on July 30, 1993; is a resident of Pleasant Ridge, Mich.

**BLANCHARD, John,** a Representative from Pennsylvania; born in Peacham Township, Cadedonia County, Vt., September 30, 1787; attended the common schools; taught school; was graduated from Dartmouth College, Hanover, N.H., in 1812; moved to Pennsylvania in 1812 and settled in York, where he again taught school; studied law; was admitted to the bar on March 31, 1815, and commenced practice in Lewistown, Mifflin County, Pa.; moved to Bellefonte the same year and continued the practice of law; elected as a Whig to the Twenty-ninth and Thirtieth Congresses (March 4, 1845-March 3, 1849); was not a candidate for renomination in 1848 to the Thirty-first Congress; died in Columbia, Lancaster County, Pa., en route from Washington, D.C., to his home, March 9, 1849; interment in Union Cemetery, Bellefonte, Centre County, Pa.

**BLANCHARD, Jonathan,** a Delegate from New Hampshire; born in Dunstable, N.H., September 18, 1738; attended the public schools; chosen a member of the council of twelve in 1775; delegate to the Fifth Provincial Congress in 1775; served in the first house of representatives of the State in 1776; appointed State attorney general in 1777; member of the committee of safety in 1777 and 1778; one of the commissioners from New Hampshire to the convention at New Haven, Conn., in 1778 to regulate prices; Member of the Continental Congress in 1784; first judge of probate under the State constitution of 1784; brigadier general of militia 1784-1788; died in Dunstable, N.H., July 16, 1788; interment in the Old South Burying Ground at Dunstable, now merged into the town of Nashua, N.H.

**BLANCHARD, Newton Crain,** a Representative and a Senator from Louisiana; born in Rapides Parish, La., January 29, 1849; completed academic studies; studied law in Alexandria, La., in 1868 and was graduated from the law department of the University of Louisiana in 1870; was admitted to the bar and commenced practice in Shreveport, La., in 1871; delegate to the State constitutional convention in 1879; elected as a Democrat to the Forty-seventh and to the six succeeding Congresses and served from March 4, 1881, until his resignation, effective March 12, 1894; chairman, Committee on Rivers and Harbors (Fiftieth through Fifty-third Congresses); appointed and subsequently elected as a Democrat to the United States Senate to fill the vacancy caused by the resignation of Edward D. White and served from March 12, 1894, to March 3, 1897; was not a candidate for reelection; chairman, Committee on Improvement of the Mississippi River and its Tributaries (Fifty-third Congress); elected associate justice of the supreme court of Louisiana and served from 1897 to 1903, when he resigned; elected Governor of Louisiana in 1904, and served from May 10, 1904 to May 12, 1908; resumed the practice of law in Shreveport, La.; member of the State constitutional convention in 1913 and served as president; died in Shreveport, La., June 22, 1922; interment in Greenwood Cemetery.

Bibliography: *DAB.*

**BLAND, Oscar Edward,** a Representative from Indiana; born near Bloomfield, Green County, Ind., November 21, 1877; attended the public schools, Valparaiso University, Valparaiso, Ind., and the University of Indiana at Bloomington; taught school for three years; studied law; was admitted to the bar in 1901 and commenced practice in Linton, Ind.; member of the State senate 1907-1909; unsuccessful Republican candidate for election to Congress in 1910, 1912, and 1914; elected as a Republican to the Sixty-fifth, Sixty-sixth, and Sixty-seventh Congresses (March 4, 1917-March 3, 1923); chairman, Committee on Industrial Arts and Expositions (Sixty-sixth and Sixty-seventh Congresses); unsuccessful candidate for reelection in 1922 to the Sixty-eighth Congress; appointed by President Warren G. Harding as associate judge of the United States Court of Customs Appeals (now the United States Court of Customs and Patent Appeals) on March 4, 1923, and served until his resignation on December 1, 1949; resumed the private practice of law in Washington, D.C., where he died August 3, 1951; interment in Fort Lincoln Cemetery.

**BLAND, Richard** (uncle of Theodorick Bland), a Delegate from Virginia; born in Orange County, Va., May 6, 1710; completed preparatory studies; attended the College of William and Mary; member of the Virginia House of Burgesses 1742-1775; member of the Virginia committee of correspondence in 1773; Member of the Continental Congress in 1774 and 1775; again chosen, but declined to serve; member of the Virginia Revolutionary conventions of 1775 and 1776; elected to the Virginia House of Delegates in 1776; died in Williamsburg, Va., October 26, 1776; interment in a private cemetery on the Jordan Point plantation, on the James River.

Bibliography: *DAB*; Detweiler, Robert C. "Richard Bland: Conservator of Self-government in Eighteenth-century Viriginia." Ph.D. dissertation, University of Washington, 1968; Rossiter, Clinton L. "Richard Bland: The Whig in America." *William and Mary Quarterly* 3rd ser., 10 (January 1953): 33-79.

**BLAND, Richard Parks,** a Representative from Missouri; born near Hartford, Ohio County, Ky., August 19, 1835; received an academic education; moved to Missouri in 1855, thence to California, and later to that portion of Utah which is now the State of Nevada; taught school for several years; studied law; was admitted to the bar and commenced practice in Virginia City; also interested in mining; treasurer of Carson County from 1860 until the organization of the State government of Nevada; returned to Missouri in 1865 and continued the practice of law in Rolla; moved to Lebanon, Laclede County, in August 1869; elected as a Democrat to the Forty-third and to the ten succeeding Congresses (March 4, 1873-March 3, 1895); chairman, Committee on Mines and Mining (Forty-fourth Congress), Committee on Coinage, Weights, and Measures (Forty-eighth through Fiftieth Congresses and Fifty-second and Fifty-third Congresses); co-sponsor of the Bland-Allison Silver Purchase Act of 1878, requiring the Federal government to encourage bimetallism and assist silver producers by making monthly purchases of silver bullion; unsuccessful candidate for reelection in 1894 to the Fifty-fourth Congress; unsuccessful candidate for the Democratic presidential nomination in 1896; elected to the Fifty-fifth and Fifty-sixth Congresses, and served from March 4, 1897 until his death in Lebanon, Mo., June 15, 1899; interment in Lebanon Cemetery.

Bibliography: *DAB*; Byars, William V. *"An American Commoner": The Life and Times of Richard Parks Bland.* Columbia, Mo.: E. W. Stephens, 1900; Haswell, Harold A., Jr. "The Public Life of Congressman Richard Parks Bland." Ph.D. dissertation, University of Missouri-Columbia, 1951.

**BLAND, Schuyler Otis,** a Representative from Virginia; born near Gloucester, Gloucester County, Va., May 4, 1872; attended private schools, Gloucester (Va.) Academy, and the College of William and Mary, Williamsburg, Va.; taught school in Accomac and Northampton Counties for several years; studied law; was admitted to the bar in 1900 and commenced practice in Newport News, Va.; elected as a Democrat to the Sixty-fifth Congress to fill the vacancy caused by the death of William A. Jones; reelected to the Sixty-sixth and to the fifteen succeeding Congresses and served from July 2, 1918, until his death at the naval hospital, Bethesda, Md., February 16, 1950; chairman, Committee on Merchant Marine and Fisheries (Seventy-third through Seventy-ninth Congresses and Eighty-first Congress); interment in Greenlawn Cemetery, Newport News, Va.

**BLAND, Theodorick** (nephew of Richard Bland), a Delegate and a Representative from Virginia; born at Cawsons, on the Appomattox River, near Petersburg, Prince George County, Va., March 21, 1742; was sent to England to be educated; studied medicine in Edinburgh and was admitted to practice; returned to his home in 1759 and engaged in extensive practice; took an active part in the Revolutionary War; entered the Continental Army as captain of the First Troop of Virginia Cavalry; Member of the Continental Congress, 1780-1783; appointed by Governor Patrick Henry as lieutenant of the Prince George County Militia in 1785; member, Virginia house of delegates, 1786-1788; member of the Virginia convention of 1788 on the adoption of the Federal Constitution and was one of the minority which opposed its ratification; elected to the First Congress and served from March 4, 1789, until his death in New York City, June 1, 1790; interment in Trinity Churchyard; reinterred in the Congressional Cemetery, Washington, D.C., August 31, 1828.

Bibliography: *DAB.*

**BLAND, William Thomas** (grandson of John George Jackson and cousin of James Monroe Jackson), a Representative from Missouri; born in Weston, Lewis County, Va. (now West Virginia), January 21, 1861; was graduated from the University of West Virginia at Morgantown in 1883 and from the law department of that university in 1884; took a special course in law at the University of Virginia at Charlottesville in 1885; was admitted to the bar and commenced practice in Weston, W.Va.; moved to Atchison, Kans., in 1887; prosecuting attorney of Atchison County, Kans., 1890-1892; mayor of Atchison in 1894; elected judge of the second Kansas district in 1896; reelected in 1900, and served until 1901, when he resigned; entered the wholesale drug business in 1901; moved to Kansas City, Mo., in 1904 and continued in business until 1917 when he engaged in banking; chairman of the Kansas City River and Harbor Improvement Commission 1909-1918;

director of the National Rivers and Harbors Congress; vice president of the Mississippi Valley Waterway Association; elected to the Kansas City Board of Education in 1912 for a six-year term and served as vice president and president; elected as a Democrat to the Sixty-sixth Congress (March 4, 1919-March 3, 1921); unsuccessful candidate for reelection in 1920 to the Sixty-seventh Congress, moved to Florida and settled in Orlando in 1921; engaged in banking; served as a member of the Orlando Utilities Commission for three years; died in Orlando, Orange County, Fla., January 15, 1928; interment in Greenwood Cemetery.

**BLANTON, Leonard Ray,** a Representative from Tennessee; born on a farm in Hardin County, Tenn., April 10, 1930; attended the public schools of Hardin County; University of Tennessee at Knoxville, B.S., 1951; in 1954, with his father and brother, organized the B & B Construction Co.; in 1964, elected to Tennessee house of representatives from McNairy and Chester Counties; elected as a Democrat to the Ninetieth and to the two succeeding Congresses (January 3, 1967-January 3, 1973); was not a candidate for reelection in 1972 to the House of Representatives, but was an unsuccessful candidate for election to the United States Senate; elected Governor of Tennessee in 1974, and served from January 18, 1975 to January 17, 1979; was not a candidate for reelection in 1978 for Governor; is a resident of Jackson, Tenn.

**BLANTON, Thomas Lindsay,** a Representative from Texas; born in Houston, Harris County, Tex., October 25, 1872; educated in the public schools; was graduated from the law department of the University of Texas at Austin in 1897, with three years in the academic department; was admitted to the bar in 1897 and commenced practice in Cleburne, Tex.; moved to Albany, Tex., and continued the practice of law until 1908, when he was elected judge of the forty-second judicial district of Texas; reelected in 1912 and served in that capacity from 1908 until elected to Congress; elected as a Democrat to the Sixty-fifth and to the five succeeding Congresses (March 4, 1917-March 3, 1929); censured by the House of Representatives on October 24, 1921, for abuse of leave to print; was not a candidate for renomination in 1928 but was an unsuccessful candidate for nomination to the United States Senate; subsequently elected on May 20, 1930, to the Seventy-first Congress to fill the vacancy caused by the death of Robert Q. Lee; reelected to the Seventy-second, Seventy-third, and Seventy-fourth Congresses and served from May 20, 1930, to January 3, 1937; unsuccessful candidate for renomination in 1936; engaged in the practice of law in Washington, D.C., in 1937 and 1938; returned to Albany, Tex., in 1938, and continued practicing law; also engaged in the raising of Hereford cattle; died in Albany, Tex., August 11, 1957; interment in Albany Cemetery.

**BLATNIK, John Anton,** a Representative from Minnesota; born in Chisholm, St. Louis County, Minn., August 17, 1911; attended the public schools and was graduated from Chisholm High School in June 1929; taught a one-room rural school in St. Louis County in 1930 and 1931; B.E., State Teachers College, Winona, Minn., 1935; also attended the University of Chicago during summer of 1938, and the University of Minnesota at Minneapolis in 1941 and 1942; engaged in Civilian Conservation Corps work in the Superior National Forest in Minnesota 1935-1937; taught chemistry in high school at Chisholm, Minn., 1937-1939; assistant county superintendent of schools of St. Louis County, Minn., 1939-1941; member of the Minnesota State senate 1941-1946; served with the United States Army Air Corps and the Office of Strategic Services from August 1942 until his discharge as a captain on January 1946 with eighteen months' service overseas; awarded the Bronze Star Medal with Oak Leaf Cluster and the Air Medal; elected as a Democrat to the Eightieth and to the thirteen succeeding Congresses and served from January 3, 1947, until his resignation December 31, 1974; chairman, Committee on Public Works

(Ninety-second and Ninety-third Congresses); was not a candidate for reelection in 1974 to the Ninety-fourth Congress; became a part-time consultant for shippers; environmental and economic development consultant; was a resident of Chisholm, Minn.; died December 17, 1991.

**BLAZ, Ben Garrido,** a Delegate from Guam; born in Agana, Guam, February 14, 1928; lived on the island during the three years of Japanese occupation during World War II; was graduated from the University of Notre Dame, South Bend, Ind., in 1951; M.A., George Washington University, Washington, D.C., 1963; was graduated from the Naval War College, Newport, R.I., in 1971; LL.D., University of Guam, 1973; commissioned a second lieutenant in the United States Marine Corps in 1951; twice awarded the Legion of Merit and the Navy Commendation Medal; also awarded the Bronze Medal with Combat "V," and the Vietnamese Cross of Gallantry; retired with the rank of brigadier general in 1980; professor at the University of Guam, 1983-1984; elected as a Republican to the Ninety-ninth and to the three succeeding Congresses (January 3, 1985-January 3, 1993); unsuccessful candidate for reelection in 1992 to the One Hundred Third Congress; is a resident of Ordot, Guam.

**BLEAKLEY, Orrin Dubbs,** a Representative from Pennsylvania; born in Franklin, Venango County, Pa., May 15, 1854; attended the common schools, the local academy of his native city, and the University of Bonn, in Prussia; engaged in banking with his father until 1876; interested in the production of oil from 1876 to 1883; organized the Franklin Trust Company in the latter year, and became its president; delegate at large to the Republican National Convention in 1904; served as chairman of the Venango County Republican committee; elected as a Republican to the Sixty-fifth Congress and served from March 4 to April 3, 1917, when he resigned without having qualified; resumed banking in Franklin, Pa.; died in Robinson, Ill., December 3, 1927; interment in Franklin Cemetery, Franklin, Pa.

**BLEASE, Coleman Livingston,** a Senator from South Carolina; born near Newberry, Newberry County, S.C., October 8, 1868; attended the common schools; was graduated from the law department of Georgetown University, Washington, D.C., in 1889; was admitted to the bar the same year and commenced practice in Newberry, S.C.; member, South Carolina State house of representatives, 1890-1894, 1899, and 1900, serving as speaker pro tempore 1892-1894; mayor of Helena, S.C., in 1897; city attorney of Newberry in 1901 and 1902; member of the State senate from 1905 until 1909, serving as president pro tempore in 1906 and 1907; mayor of Newberry in 1910; elected Governor of South Carolina in 1910, reelected in 1912, and served from January 17, 1911 until his resignation on January 14, 1915; elected as a Democrat to the United States Senate and served from March 4, 1925, to March 3, 1931; unsuccessful candidate for renomination in 1930; unsuccessful candidate for the gubernatorial nomination in 1934 and 1938; elected a member of the State unemployment compensation commission for a four-year term beginning in 1941; died in Columbia, S.C., January 19, 1942; interment in Rosemont Cemetery, Newberry, S.C.

Bibliography: *DAB*; Burnside, Ronald D. "The Governorship of Coleman Livingston Blease of S.C." Ph.D. dissertation, Indiana University, 1963; Hollis, Daniel W. "Cole Blease and the Senate Campaign of 1924." *Proceedings of the South Carolina Historical Association* 48 (1978): 53-68; Simon, Bryant. "The Appeal of Cole Blease of South Carolina: Race, Class, and Sex in the New South." *Journal of Southern History* 62 (February 1996): 57-86.

**BLEDSOE, Jesse** (uncle of Robert Emmett Bledsoe Baylor), a Senator from Kentucky; born in Culpeper County, Va., April 6, 1776; when quite young moved with an elder brother to Kentucky; attended Transylvania Seminary and Transylvania University,

Lexington Ky.; studied law in Lexington; was admitted to the bar about 1800 and commenced practice; appointed secretary of state 1808; member, Kentucky house of representatives 1812; elected as a Republican to the United States Senate and served from March 4, 1813, until his resignation on December 24, 1814; member, State senate 1817-1820; judge of the Lexington circuit in 1822; settled in Lexington and was professor of law in Transylvania University; minister in the Disciples Church; moved to Mississippi in 1833 and to Texas in 1835; died near Nacogdoches, Nacogdoches County, Tex., June 25, 1836.

**BLEECKER, Harmanus,** a Representative from New York; born in Albany, N.Y., October 9, 1779; studied law; was admitted to the bar in 1801 and commenced practice in Albany; elected as a Federalist to the Twelfth Congress (March 4, 1811-March 3, 1813); was not a candidate for renomination in 1812 to the Thirteenth Congress; resumed the practice of law in Albany, N.Y.; member of the State assembly in 1814 and 1815; regent of the University of the State of New York 1822-1834; appointed Chargé d'Affaires to the Netherlands on May 15, 1839, and served until August 1842; retired from public life and business pursuits; died in Albany, N.Y., July 19, 1849; interment in the Rural Cemetery.

**BLILEY, Thomas Jerome, Jr.,** a Representative from Virginia; born in Chesterfield County, Va., January 28, 1932; attended private schools; graduated, Benedictine High School, Richmond, 1948; B.A., Georgetown University, Washington, D.C., 1952; served in the United States Navy, lieutenant, 1952-1955; president, Joseph W. Bliley Co. Funeral Home; vice-mayor, Richmond, 1968-1970; mayor, Richmond, 1970-1977; elected as a Republican to the Ninety-seventh and to the seven succeeding Congresses (January 3, 1981-January 3, 1997); chairman, Committee on Commerce (One Hundred Fourth Congress); is a resident of Richmond, Va.

**BLISS, Aaron Thomas,** a Representative from Michigan; born in Peterboro, Madison County, N.Y., May 22, 1837; attended the common schools; employed as a clerk in a store in Morrisville, N.Y., in 1853 and 1854; attended a select school in Munnsville, N.Y., in 1854; moved to Bouckville, N.Y., in 1855 and engaged in mercantile pursuits; enlisted as a private in the Tenth Regiment, New York Volunteer Cavalry, October 1, 1861; served three years, being confined six months of this time in the prisons of Andersonville, Charleston, Macon, and Columbia; rose while in the service from private to captain; moved to Saginaw, Mich., in December 1865 and engaged in the manufacture of lumber; member of the Michigan State senate in 1882; appointed aide-de-camp on the staff of Governor Russell A. Alger in 1885; held the same position on the staff of the commander in chief of the Grand Army of the Republic in 1888; elected as a Republican to the Fifty-first Congress (March 4, 1889-March 3, 1891); unsuccessful candidate for reelection in 1890 to the Fifty-second Congress; resumed the lumber business and also engaged in banking; department commander of the Grand Army of the Republic in Michigan in 1897; elected Governor of Michigan in 1900, reelected in 1902, and served from January 1, 1901 until January 1, 1905; died in Milwaukee, Wis., September 16, 1906, while on a visit for medical treatment; interment in Forest Lawn Cemetery, Saginaw, Mich.

**Bibliography:** *DAB.*

**BLISS, Archibald Meserole,** a Representative from New York; born in Brooklyn, N.Y., January 25, 1838; attended the common schools; alderman of Brooklyn, N.Y., 1864-1867, serving as president of the board of aldermen in 1866; unsuccessful Republican candidate for mayor of Brooklyn in 1867; delegate to the Republican National Convention in 1864 and 1868, to the Liberal National Convention in 1872, and to the Democratic National Conventions in 1876, 1880, 1884, and 1888; member of the board of water commissioners of Brooklyn in 1871 and 1872; president and vice president of the Bushwick Railroad Co., 1868-1878; director of the New York & Long Island Bridge Co.; elected as a Democrat to the Forty-fourth and to the three succeeding Congresses (March 4, 1875-March 3, 1883); was not a candidate for renomination in 1882 to the Forty-eighth Congress; elected to the Forty-ninth and Fiftieth Congresses (March 4, 1885-March 3, 1889); chairman, Committee on Pensions (Fiftieth Congress); was not a candidate for renomination in 1888 to the Fifty-first Congress; engaged in the real estate business in Washington, D.C., until his death there on March 19, 1923; interment in Cypress Hills Cemetery, Brooklyn, N.Y.

**BLISS, George,** a Representative from Ohio; born in Jericho, Vt., January 1, 1813; attended Granville College; studied law; was admitted to the bar in 1841 and commenced practice in Akron, Ohio; appointed presiding judge of the eighth judicial district in 1850 and served until the office was discontinued, owing to a change in the constitution; elected as a Democrat to the Thirty-third Congress (March 4, 1853-March 3, 1855); was a candidate for renomination in 1854 to the Thirty-fourth Congress, but subsequently withdrew; moved to Wooster, Ohio, and continued the practice of law; elected to the Thirty-eighth Congress (March 4, 1863-March 3, 1865); unsuccessful candidate for reelection in 1864 to the Thirty-ninth Congress; delegate to the Union National Convention at Philadelphia in 1866; died in Wooster, Ohio, October 24, 1868; interment in Oak Hill Cemetery.

**Bibliography:** *DAB.*

**BLISS, Philemon,** a Representative from Ohio; born in Canton, Conn., July 28, 1813; attended Fairfield Academy and Hamilton College; studied law; was admitted to the bar in 1840 and commenced practice at Cuyahoga Falls, Ohio; later practiced in Elyria, Ohio; presiding judge of the fourteenth judicial circuit of Ohio 1848-1851; elected as a Republican to the Thirty-fourth and Thirty-fifth Congresses (March 4, 1855-March 3, 1859); was not a candidate for renomination in 1858; appointed chief justice of the supreme court of the Territory of Dakota by President Lincoln in 1861; subsequently moved to St. Joseph, Mo.; associate justice of the supreme court of Missouri 1868-1872; dean of the law division of the State University of Missouri at Columbia 1872-1889; died in St. Paul, Minn., August 25, 1889; interment in the Columbia Cemetery, Columbia, Mo.

**Bibliography:** *DAB.*

**BLITCH, Iris Faircloth,** a Representative from Georgia; born in Toombs County, near Vidalia, Ga., April 25, 1912; attended the public schools of Vidalia, Douglas, Fitzgerald, and Homerville, Ga., and graduated from high school in Hagerstown, Md.; student at the University of Georgia at Athens in 1929, and attended South Georgia College at Douglas in 1949; associated with her husband in drug business, naval stores operations, and farming in Homerville, Ga.; Georgia State senator, District 5, 1947-1948 and 1953-1954; member of the State house of representatives from Clinch County, 1949-1950; Democratic national committeewoman for Georgia, 1948-1956; elected as a Democrat to the Eighty-fourth and to the three succeeding Congresses (January 3, 1955-January 3, 1963); was not a candidate for renomination in 1962 to the Eighty-eighth Congress; announced her affiliation with the Republican Party in August 1964; was a resident of St. Simons Island, Ga; moved in 1988 to San Diego, Calif., where she died on August 19, 1993; interment in Pinelawn Cemetery, Homerville, Ga.

**BLODGETT, Rufus,** a Senator from New Jersey; born in Dorchester, N.H., October 9, 1834; attended the common schools and Wentworth (N.H.) Academy; learned the machinist's trade; moved to New Jersey in 1866 and settled in Long Branch; builder of railroad equipment; president of the Long Branch City Bank; member, New Jersey State assembly, 1878-1879; superintendent of the New York and Long Branch Railroad from 1884 to 1910; elected as a Democrat to the United States Senate, and served from March 4, 1887 to

March 3, 1893; was not a candidate for reelection; mayor of Long Branch, 1893-1898; engaged in the railroad business and in banking; died in Long Branch, Monmouth County, N.J., October 3, 1910; interment in Village Cemetery, Wentworth, N.H.

**BLOODWORTH, Timothy,** a Delegate, a Representative, and a Senator from North Carolina; born in New Hanover County, N.C., in 1736; teacher; in 1776 was employed in making muskets and bayonets for the Continental Army; member, State house of commons 1778-1779; treasurer of Wilmington District 1781-1782; appointed commissioner of confiscated property in 1783; Member of the Continental Congress in 1786; member, State senate 1788-1789; elected to the First Congress and served from April 6, 1790, to March 3, 1791; member, State house of representatives 1793-1794; elected to the United States Senate and served from March 4, 1795, to March 3, 1801; collector of customs at Wilmington; died in Wilmington, N.C., August 24, 1814.

**Bibliography:** *DAB*.

**BLOOM, Isaac,** a Representative from New York, born in Jamaica, Queens County, N.Y., about 1716; moved to Dutchess County about 1740; captain of minutemen of Charlotte precinct, Dutchess County, in 1775; was engaged in mercantile pursuits in 1784; member of the State assembly 1788-1792; delegate to the State convention in 1801; served in the State senate 1800-1802; elected to the Eighth Congress and served from March 4, 1803, until his death in Clinton, Dutchess County, N.Y., April 26, 1803; interment probably in Jamaica.

**BLOOM, Sol,** a Representative from New York; born in Pekin, Tazewell County, Ill., March 9, 1870; moved with his parents to San Francisco, Calif., in 1873; attended the public schools; engaged in the newspaper, theatrical, and music publishing businesses; superintendent of construction of the Midway Plaisance at the World's Columbian Exposition at Chicago in 1893; moved to New York City in 1903 and engaged in the real estate and construction business; captain in the New York Naval Reserve in 1917; director of the United States George Washington Bicentennial Commission; director general of the United States Constitution Sesquicentennial Commission; chairman of the Committee on Celebration of the One Hundred and Fiftieth Anniversary of the United States Supreme Court; director and United States Commissioner, New York World's Fair, 1939; elected as a Democrat to the Sixty-eighth Congress, January 30, 1923, by special election to fill the vacancy caused by the death of Representative-elect Samuel Marx; reelected to the Sixty-ninth and to the twelve succeeding Congresses, and served from March 4, 1923 until his death in Washington, D.C., March 7, 1949; chairman, Committee on Foreign Affairs (Seventy-sixth through Seventy-ninth Congresses and Eighty-first Congress), Special Committee on Chamber Improvements (Eighty-first Congress); interment in Mount Eden Cemetery, Westchester Hills, N.Y.

**Bibliography:** *DAB*; Bloom, Sol. *The Autobiography of Sol Bloom*. New York: Putnam's, 1948.

**BLOOMFIELD, Joseph,** a Representative from New Jersey; born in Woodbridge, Middlesex County, N.J., October 18, 1753; educated at Rev. Enoch Green's school in Deerfield, N.J.; studied law; was admitted to the bar in 1775 and commenced practice in Bridgeton, N.J.; entered the Revolutionary Army as captain of the Third New Jersey Regiment on February 9, 1776; attained the rank of major; resumed the practice of law in Burlington, N.J.; registrar of the admiralty court 1779-1783; State attorney general from 1783 to 1792, when he resigned; trustee of Princeton College from 1793 until his resignation in 1801; chosen Governor of New Jersey by the legislature of the State and served from October 31, 1801 to October 28, 1802, and from October 29, 1803 to October 29, 1812; commissioned brigadier general on March 13, 1812, and served until June 15, 1815; elected as a Republican to the Fifteenth Congress and reelected to the Sixteenth Congress (March 4, 1817-March 3, 1821); unsuccessful candidate for reelection in 1820 to the Seventeenth Congress; died in Burlington, N.J., on October 3, 1823; interment in St. Mary's Episcopal Churchyard.

**Bibliography:** *DAB*.

**BLOUIN, Michael Thomas,** a Representative from Iowa; born in Jacksonville, Duval County, Fla., November 7, 1945; attended the elementary and secondary schools of Miami Shores, Fla., and Chicago, Ill.; B.A., Loras College, Dubuque, Iowa, 1966; taught in the elementary schools of Dubuque, Iowa, and later worked as advertising consultant; member, Iowa State house of representatives, 1968-1972; Iowa State senator, 1972-1974; delegate to Iowa State Democratic conventions, 1966-1973; elected as a Democrat to the Ninety-fourth and Ninety-fifth Congresses (January 3, 1975-January 3, 1979); unsuccessful candidate for reelection in 1978 to the Ninety-sixth Congress; director, Information Security Oversight Office, 1979; assistant director for community action, Community Services Administration, 1980-1981; executive director of foundations and grants, Kirkwood Community College, Cedar Rapids, Iowa, 1981-1987; director of economic development, Cedar Rapids Area Chamber of Commerce, 1987-1993, and president and chief executive officer, 1993 to present; is a resident of Cedar Rapids, Iowa.

**BLOUNT, James Henderson,** a Representative from Georgia; born near Clinton, Jones County, Ga., September 12, 1837; attended private schools in Clinton, Ga., and Tuscaloosa, Ala.; was graduated from the University of Georgia at Athens in 1858; studied law; was admitted to the bar in 1859 and commenced practice in Clinton, Jones County, Ga.; moved to Macon, Ga., in 1872 and continued the practice of law; during the Civil War served in the Confederate Army as a private in the Second Georgia Battalion, Floyd Rifles, for two years, and was later lieutenant colonel for two years; delegate to the State constitutional convention in 1865; elected as a Democrat to the Forty-third and to the nine succeeding Congresses (March 4, 1873-March 3, 1893); chairman, Committee on Expenditures in the Department of Justice (Forty-sixth Congress), Committee on the Post Office and Post Roads (Forty-ninth and Fiftieth Congresses), Committee on Foreign Affairs (Fifty-second Congress); was not a candidate for renomination in 1892 to the Fifty-third Congress; appointed by President Grover Cleveland commissioner to the Hawaiian Islands on March 20, 1893; retired from that position in 1893 and devoted his time to his plantation interests; died in Macon, Ga., March 8, 1903; interment in Rose Hill Cemetery.

**Bibliography:** *DAB*.

**BLOUNT, Thomas** (brother of William Blount and uncle of William Grainger Blount), a Representative from North Carolina; born at "Blount Hall," Craven (now Pitt) County, N.C., May 10, 1759; educated at home; at the age of sixteen years entered the Continental Army; was captured and sent to Great Britain as a prisoner of war; after the Revolutionary War engaged in the mercantile business in Tarboro, Edgecombe County, N.C.; member of the North Carolina State house of commons in 1788; elected to the Third Congress, and as a Republican to the Fourth and Fifth Congresses (March 4, 1793-March 3, 1799); unsuccessful candidate for election in 1802 to the Eighth Congress; elected to the Ninth and Tenth Congresses (March 4, 1805-March 3, 1809); unsuccessful candidate for reelection in 1808 to the Eleventh Congress; elected to the Twelfth Congress, and served from March 4, 1811 until his death in Washington, D.C., February 7, 1812; interment in the Congressional Cemetery.

**Bibliography:** *DAB*; Keith, Alice Barnwell. "John Gray and Thomas Blount, Merchants, 1783-1800." *North Carolina Historical Review* 25 (April 1948): 194-205.

**BLOUNT, William** (father of William Grainger Blount and brother of Thomas Blount), a Delegate from North Carolina and a Senator from Tennessee; born near Windsor, Bertie County, N.C., March 26, 1749; pursued preparatory studies in New Bern, N.C.; paymaster of the Continental troops, North Carolina Line, in 1777; member, North Carolina State house of commons, 1780-1784; Member of the Continental Congress in 1782, 1783, 1786, and 1787; delegate to the convention that framed the Federal Constitution in 1787; member, North Carolina State senate, 1788-1790; appointed Governor of the Territory South of the Ohio river by President Washington on June 8, 1790; Superintendent of Indian Affairs, 1790-1796; chairman of the convention which framed the first State constitution of Tennessee in 1796; upon the admission of Tennessee as a State into the Union was elected to the United States Senate and served from August 2, 1796, until he was found guilty "of a high misdemeanor, entirely inconsistent with his public trust and duty as a Senator," because he had been active in a plan to incite the Creek and Cherokee Indians to aid the British in conquering the Spanish territory of West Florida; expelled from the Senate on July 8, 1797; impeachment proceedings were instituted but dismissed; during the trial was elected to the State senate of Tennessee and chosen its president; died in Knoxville, Tenn., March 21, 1800; interment in the First Presbyterian Church Cemetery.

**Bibliography:** *DAB*; Masterson, William. *William Blount.* 1954. Reprint. New York: Greenwood Press, 1969.

**BLOUNT, William Grainger** (son of William Blount and nephew of Thomas Blount), a Representative from Tennessee; born near New Bern, Craven County, N.C., in 1784; attended the New Bern Academy; moved with his parents to Knoxville, Tenn., in 1792; studied law; was admitted to the bar in 1805 and commenced practice in Knoxville; also engaged in agricultural pursuits; member of State house of representatives in 1811; secretary of state of Tennessee 1811-1815; elected as a Republican to the Fourteenth Congress to fill the vacancy caused by the death of John Sevier; reelected to the Fifteenth Congress and served from December 8, 1815, to March 3, 1819; declined to be a candidate for renomination; resumed the practice of his profession in Knoxville; moved to Paris, Henry County, Tenn., in 1826 and continued the practice of law until his death on May 21, 1827; interment in the City Cemetery.

**BLOW, Henry Taylor,** a Representative from Missouri; born in Southampton County, Va., July 15, 1817; moved to St. Louis, Mo., in 1830; attended St. Louis University in 1830 and 1831; engaged in the paint and oil business and later became especially interested in lead mines; member of the State senate 1854-1858; served as Minister Resident at Venezuela from June 8, 1861, to February 22, 1862; elected as an Unconditional Unionist to the Thirty-eighth Congress and as a Republican to the Thirty-ninth Congress (March 4, 1863-March 3, 1867); was not a candidate for renomination in 1866 to the Fortieth Congress; resumed his former business pursuits; appointed United States Minister to Brazil on May 1, 1869 and served until November 1870; was a member of the Board of Commissioners of the District of Columbia in 1874 and 1875; died in Saratoga, Saratoga County, N.Y., September 11, 1875; interment in Bellefontaine Cemetery, St. Louis, Mo.

**Bibliography:** *DAB.*

**BLUE, Richard Whiting,** a Representative from Kansas; born near Parkersburg, Wood County, Va. (now West Virginia), September 8, 1841; worked on a farm in the summertime and studied in the select schools of that locality during the winter season; attended Monongalia Academy, Morgantown, Va., in 1859 and Washington (Pa.) College until his enlistment, on June 29, 1863, as a private in Company A, Third Regiment, West Virginia Volunteer Infantry, during the Civil War; became second and then first lieutenant of the company; honorably discharged May 22, 1866, at Leavenworth, Kans., when he returned to Grafton, W.Va.; taught school; studied

law; was admitted to the bar in Virginia, and commenced practice in Linn County, Kans., in 1871; probate judge of Linn County 1872-1876; county attorney 1876-1880; member of the State senate 1880-1888; elected as a Republican to the Fifty-fourth Congress (March 4, 1895-March 3, 1897); unsuccessful candidate for reelection in 1896 to the Fifty-fifth Congress; engaged in the practice of law until his death in Bartlesville, Washington County, Okla., January 28, 1907; interment in Pleasanton Cemetery, Pleasanton, Linn County, Kans.

**BLUMENAUER, Earl,** a Representative from Oregon; born in Portland, Oreg., August 16, 1949; attended the public schools of Portland, and graduated from Centennial High School in 1966; B.A., Lewis and Clark College, 1970, and J.D., 1976; chair of the Oregon "Go 19" campaign in 1969; assistant to the president of Portland State University; member, Oregon State house of representatives, 1972-1978; member of the Multnomah County (Oreg.) Commission, 1978-1987; served on the Governor's Commission on Higher Education, 1990-1991; member, Portland City council, 1987-1996; elected as a Democrat to the One Hundred Fourth Congress, May 21, 1996, by special election to fill the vacancy caused by the resignation of Ronald L. Wyden, and served from May 21, 1996 to January 3, 1997; is a resident of Portland, Oreg.

**BLUTE, Peter Ignatius,** a Representative from Massachusetts; born in Worcester, Mass., January 28, 1956; graduated St. John's Preparatory, Shrewsbury, Mass., 1974; B.A., Boston College, 1978; worked for Boston Red Sox baseball club; founder, sports promotion and marketing firm; marketing representative, Burdett School, Boston, Mass.; Senate campaign staff of former United States Attorney General Elliot L. Richardson, 1984; adviser to Massachusetts Civic Interest Council and Citizens for Limited Taxation; member, Massachusetts house of representatives, 1988-1993; elected as a Republican to the One Hundred Third and One Hundred Fourth Congresses (January 3, 1993-January 3, 1997); is a resident of Shrewsbury, Mass.

**BOARDMAN, Elijah** (father of William Whiting Boardman), a Senator from Connecticut; born in New Milford, Conn., March 7, 1760; educated under private tutors; served in the Revolutionary War; employed as clerk in a mercantile establishment; engaged in mercantile pursuits 1781-1812; member, State house of representatives 1803-1805 and again in 1816; member, State upper house 1817-1819; member, State senate 1819-1821; elected as a Democrat to the United States Senate and served from March 4, 1821, until his death while on a visit to Boardman, Ohio, August 18, 1823; interment in the Center Cemetery, New Milford, Conn.

**BOARDMAN, William Whiting** (son of Elijah Boardman), a Representative from Connecticut; born in New Milford, Conn., October 10, 1794; attended Bacon Academy, Colchester, Conn.; was graduated from Yale College in 1812; studied law in Cambridge and Litchfield Law Schools and commenced the practice of his profession in New Haven in 1819; clerk of the State senate in 1820; judge of probate; member of the State house of representatives 1836-1839, serving as speaker in 1836 and 1839; elected as a Whig to the Twenty-sixth Congress to fill the vacancy caused by the resignation of William L. Storrs; reelected to the Twenty-seventh Congress and served from December 7, 1840, to March 3, 1843; chairman, Committee on Public Buildings and Grounds (Twenty-seventh Congress); was not a candidate for renomination in 1842 to the Twenty-eighth Congress; member of the State house of representatives in 1845, 1849, and 1851, serving as speaker in 1845; resumed the practice of law; died in New Haven, Conn., August 27, 1871; interment in Grove Street Cemetery.

**BOARMAN, Alexander (Aleck),** a Representative from Louisiana; born in Yazoo City, Miss., December 10, 1839; lost his parents in infancy and was raised by relatives in Shreveport, Caddo Parish, La.; attended the common schools of Shreveport, La., and Kentucky Military Institute at Frankfort; was graduated from the University of Kentucky at Lexington in 1860; at the outbreak of the Civil War enlisted in the Confederate Army and served as lieutenant of the Caddo Rifles; was subsequently promoted to the rank of captain and served throughout the war; studied law; was admitted to the bar in 1866 and commenced practice in Shreveport, La.; mayor of Shreveport from May 7, 1866, to August 8, 1867; city attorney of Shreveport 1868-1872; unsuccessful candidate for election as secretary of state in 1872; elected as a Liberal Republican to the Forty-second Congress to fill the vacancy caused by the death of Representative-elect James McCleery and served from December 3, 1872, to March 3, 1873; unsuccessful candidate for renomination in 1872 to the Forty-third Congress; resumed the practice of law in Shreveport, La.; judge of the tenth judicial district court, Caddo Parish, La., 1877-1880; appointed on May 18, 1881, by President James A. Garfield as United States judge for the western district of Louisiana, and served until his death, while on a visit, at Loon Lake, Franklin County, N.Y., August 30, 1916; interment in Oakland Cemetery, Shreveport, La.

**BOATNER, Charles Jahleal,** a Representative from Louisiana; born in Columbia, Caldwell Parish, La., January 23, 1849; completed preparatory studies; studied law; was admitted to the bar in 1870 and practiced; member of the State senate from 1876 until May 1878; elected as a Democrat to the Fifty-first and to the two succeeding Congresses (March 4, 1889-March 3, 1895); presented credentials as a Member-elect to the Fifty-fourth Congress, but on March 20, 1896, the House declared the seat vacant, the election having been contested by Alexis Benoit; elected to fill the vacancy caused by the House declaring the seat vacant and served from June 10, 1896, to March 3, 1897; declined to be a candidate for reelection in 1896 to the Fifty-fifth Congress; moved to New Orleans and resumed the practice of law; died in New Orleans, La., on March 21, 1903; interment in Monroe Cemetery, Monroe, La.

**BOCKEE, Abraham,** a Representative from New York; born in Shekomeko, Dutchess County, N.Y., February 3, 1784; attended the public schools; was graduated from Union College, Schenectady, N.Y., 1803; studied law in Poughkeepsie; was admitted to the bar in 1806 and practiced in Poughkeepsie until 1815, when he returned to Shekomeko; engaged in agricultural pursuits; member of the State assembly in 1820; elected as a Jacksonian to the Twenty-first Congress (March 4, 1829-March 3, 1831); elected to the Twenty-third and Twenty-fourth Congresses (March 4, 1833-March 3, 1837); chairman, Committee on Agriculture (Twenty-third and Twenty-fourth Congresses); served in the State senate 1840-1844; elected judge of the court of errors in 1843; first judge of the Dutchess County Court in 1846; died in Shekomeko, N.Y., June 1, 1865; interment on his estate near Shekomeko.

**BOCOCK, Thomas Stanley,** a Representative from Virginia; born at Buckingham Court House, Buckingham (now Appomattox) County, Va., May 18, 1815; educated by private tutors; was graduated from Hampden-Sydney (Va.) College in 1838; studied law; was admitted to the bar in 1840 and commenced practice at Buckingham Court House; member of the Virginia house of delegates, 1842-1844; served as prosecuting attorney of Appomattox County in 1845 and 1846; elected as a Democrat to the Thirtieth and to the six succeeding Congresses (March 4, 1847-March 3, 1861); chairman, Committee on Naval Affairs (Thirty-third and Thirty-fifth Congresses); elected a Representative to the Confederate Congress in 1861, being chosen speaker of that body on February 18, 1862; again served as a member of the Virginia house of delegates, 1877-1879; was a delegate to the Democratic National Conventions of 1868, 1876 and 1880; died in Appomattox County, Va., on August 5, 1891; interment in Old Bocock Cemetery (private burying ground), near Wildway, Va.

**Bibliography:** *DAB.*

**BODEN, Andrew,** a Representative from Pennsylvania; born in Carlisle, Cumberland County, Pa.; attended the public schools; studied law; was admitted to the bar and practiced; also engaged in the real estate business; elected as a Republican to the Fifteenth Congress and reelected to the Sixteenth Congress (March 4, 1817-March 3, 1821); resumed the practice of law; died in Carlisle, Pa., December 20, 1835.

**BODINE, Robert Nall,** a Representative from Missouri; born near Paris, Monroe County, Mo., December 17, 1837; attended Paris Academy and was graduated from the University of Missouri at Columbia in 1859; principal of the Paris public schools; studied law; was admitted to the bar and began practice in Paris, Mo.; prosecuting attorney of Monroe County; delegate to the State convention in 1890; member of the State house of representatives 1895-1897; elected as a Democrat to the Fifty-fifth Congress (March 4, 1897-March 3, 1899); unsuccessful candidate for renomination in 1898; resumed the practice of law in Paris, Mo., and died there March 16, 1914; interment in Walnut Grove Cemetery.

**BODLE, Charles,** a Representative from New York; born near Poughkeepsie, Dutchess County, N.Y., in 1787; was a wagon maker by trade; justice of the peace; held several political offices in Bloomingburg, Sullivan County; elected as a Jacksonian to the Twenty-third Congress (March 4, 1833-March 3, 1835); died in New York City October 31, 1835; interment in Bloomingburg Cemetery, Bloomingburg, N.Y.

**BOEHLERT, Sherwood Louis,** a Representative from New York; born in Utica, Oneida County, N.Y., September 28, 1936; attended Roosevelt Elementary School, Utica, N.Y.; graduated, Whitesboro Central High School, 1954; A.B., Utica College, 1961; served, United States Army, 1956-1958; chief of staff to Representative Alexander Pirnie of New York, 1964-1972; chief of staff to Representative Donald J. Mitchell of New York, 1973-79; county executive, Oneida County, N.Y., 1979-1982; delegate, New York State Republican Convention, 1980; delegate, Republican National Convention, 1980; elected as a Republican to the Ninety-eighth and to the six succeeding Congresses (January 3, 1983-January 3, 1997); is a resident of New Hartford, N.Y.

**BOEHNE, John William, Jr.,** (son of John William Boehne), a Representative from Indiana; born in Evansville, Vanderburgh County, Ind., March 2, 1895; attended the public and parochial schools; was graduated from the University of Wisconsin at Madison in 1918; during the First World War served as a private and sergeant in the Detached Service, Ordnance, United States Army, from January 9, 1918, to April 8, 1919; secretary and treasurer of the Indiana Stove Works at Evansville, Ind., 1920-1931; elected as a Democrat to the Seventy-second Congress; reelected to the five succeeding Congresses (March 4, 1931-January 3, 1943); unsuccessful candidate for reelection in 1942 to the Seventy-eighth Congress; corporation tax counselor in Washington, D.C., 1943-1957; retired; died in Irvington, Md., July 5, 1973; interment in Rock Creek Cemetery, Washington, D.C.

**BOEHNER, John Andrew,** a Representative from Ohio; born in Cincinnati, Ohio, November 17, 1949; graduated, Moeller High School, Cincinnati, 1968; B.S., B.A., Xavier University, Cincinnati, 1977; businessman; manager, Merrell-Dow Pharmaceuticals, Inc., 1972-1976; president, Nucite Sales, Inc. (plastics and packaging), 1976-1990; Union Township Trustee, 1982-1984; member, Ohio State house of representatives, 1985-1990; elected as a Republican to the One Hundred Second and to the two succeeding Congresses (January 3, 1991-January 3, 1997); is a resident of West Chester, Ohio.

**BOEN, Haldor Erickson,** a Representative from Minnesota; born in Sondre Aurdal, Valders, Norway, January 2, 1851; immigrated to the United States in 1868 and settled in Mower County, Minn.; attended the St. Cloud Normal School in 1869 and 1870; located near Fergus Falls, Ottertail County, January 1, 1871; employed in the auditor's office in 1872, computing the first taxes levied in Ottertail County; taught in the common schools of that county 1874-1879; justice of the peace 1875-1900; elected county commissioner in 1880; register of deeds 1888-1892; elected as a Populist to the Fifty-third Congress (March 4, 1893-March 3, 1895); unsuccessful candidate for reelection in 1894 to the Fifty-fourth Congress; editor of the Fergus Falls Globe; resumed agricultural pursuits in Ottertail County, Minn.; died in Aurdal Township, Ottertail County, Minn., July 23, 1912; interment in Aurdal Cemetery, near Fergus Falls, Minn.

**BOERUM, Simon,** a Delegate from New York; born in New Lots (now Brooklyn), Long Island, N.Y., February 29, 1724; attended the Dutch school at Flatbush, N.Y., from which he was graduated; engaged in agricultural pursuits and milling; appointed county clerk of Kings County by Governor Clinton in 1750; also became clerk of the board of supervisors and held both positions until his death; member of the colonial assembly, 1761-1775; deputy to the provincial convention in April 1775; Member of the Continental Congress in 1774 and 1775; died in Brooklyn, N.Y., July 11, 1775; interment in Glenwood Cemetery.

**BOGGS, Corinne Claiborne (Lindy),** (wife of Thomas Hale Boggs, Sr., great, great grandniece of John Francis Hamtramck Claiborne, great, great, great grandniece of Nathaniel Herbert Claiborne and William Charles Cole Claiborne, and great, great, great grandniece of Thomas Claiborne [1749-1812]), a Representative from Louisiana; born on Brunswick Plantation, Pointe Coupee Parish, La., March 13, 1916; graduated from St. Joseph's Academy, New Roads, La., 1931; B.A., Sophie Newcomb College, Tulane University, New Orleans, La., 1935; teacher; president, Woman's National Democratic Club, 1958-1959, and Democratic Congressional Wives Forum, 1962; president, The Congressional Club, 1971-1972; cochairman of the inaugural balls for President John F. Kennedy, 1961, and President Lyndon B. Johnson, 1965; chair of Democratic National Convention in 1976; elected as a Democrat to the Ninety-third Congress, March 20, 1973, by special election to fill the vacancy caused by the disappearance of her husband, Thomas Hale Boggs, Sr., in an airplane in October 1972; reelected to the eight succeeding Congresses, and served from March 20, 1973 to January 3, 1991; chairman, Joint Committee on Bicentennial Arrangements (Ninety-fourth Congress), Commission on the Bicentenary of the United States House of Representatives (Ninety-ninth through One Hundred First Congresses); was not a candidate for reelection in 1990 to the One Hundred Second Congress; is a resident of New Orleans, La.

Bibliography: Boggs, Lindy, with Katherine Hatch. *Washington Through a Purple Veil: Memoirs of a Southern Woman.* New York: Harcourt Brace and Co., 1994; Ferrell, Thomas H., and Judith Haydel. "Hale and Lindy Boggs: Louisiana's National Democrats." *Louisiana History* 35 (Fall 1994): 389-402.

**BOGGS, James Caleb,** a Representative and a Senator from Delaware; born in Cheswold, Kent County, Del., May 15, 1909; attended the rural schools; was graduated from the University of Delaware at Newark in 1931 and from Georgetown University Law School, Washington, D.C., in 1937; was admitted to the bar in 1938 and commenced practice in Dover, Del.; served during the Second World War in the United States Army, 1941-1946; deputy judge of the family court of New Castle County, Del., 1946; elected as a

Republican to the Eightieth and to the two succeeding Congresses (January 3, 1947-January 3, 1953); was not a candidate for renomination in 1952 to the Eighty-third Congress, but was elected Governor of Delaware; reelected in 1956, and served from January 20, 1953 until his resignation on December 30, 1960, having been elected United States Senator; elected as a Republican to the United States Senate in 1960; reelected in 1966 and served from January 3, 1961, to January 3, 1973; unsuccessful candidate for reelection in 1972; practiced law in Wilmington, Del.; was a resident of Wilmington, Del.; died March 26, 1993.

**BOGGS, Thomas Hale, Sr.** (husband of Corinne Claiborne Boggs), a Representative from Louisiana; born in Long Beach, Harrison County, Miss., February 15, 1914; attended the public and parochial schools of Jefferson Parish, La.; was graduated from Tulane University, New Orleans, La., in 1935 and from the law department of the same university in 1937; was admitted to the bar in 1937 and commenced practice in New Orleans, La.; elected as a Democrat to the Seventy-seventh Congress (January 3, 1941-January 3, 1943); unsuccessful candidate for renomination in 1942 to the Seventy-eighth Congress; resumed the practice of law in New Orleans, La.; enlisted in the United States Naval Reserve in November 1943; was commissioned an ensign and attached to the Potomac River Naval Command and the United States Maritime Service until separated in January 1946; again elected as a Democrat to the Eightieth and to the thirteen succeeding Congresses; chairman, Special Committee on Campaign Expenditures (Eighty-second Congress); majority whip (Eighty-seventh through Ninety-first Congresses), majority leader (Ninety-second Congress); disappeared while on a campaign flight from Anchorage to Juneau, Alaska, October 16, 1972; served from January 3, 1947, until January 3, 1973, when he was presumed dead pursuant to House Resolution 1, Ninety-third Congress.

Bibliography: Balias, Scott E. "The Courage of His Convictions: Hale Boggs and Civil Rights." Ph.D. dissertation, Tulane University, 1993; Ferrell, Thomas H., and Judith Haydel. "Hale and Lindy Boggs: Louisiana's National Democrats." *Louisiana History* 35 (Fall 1994): 389-402; Kirn, Dorothy Nelson. "Hale Boggs: A Southern Spokesman for the Democratic Party." Ph.D. dissertation, Louisiana State University, 1980.

**BOGY, Lewis Vital,** a Senator from Missouri; born in Ste. Genevieve, Mo., April 9, 1813; attended the public schools; employed as clerk in a mercantile establishment; studied law in Illinois; was graduated from Transylvania University, Lexington, Ky., in 1835 and commenced practice in St. Louis; served in the Black Hawk War; member of the board of aldermen of St. Louis in 1838; member, State house of representatives 1840-1841, 1854-1855; Commissioner of Indian Affairs in 1867 and 1868; president of the city council of St. Louis in 1872; one of the founders of the St. Louis & Iron Mountain Railway, acting as president for two years; elected as a Democrat to the United States Senate and served from March 4, 1873, until his death in St. Louis, Mo., September 20, 1877; interment in Calvary Cemetery.

**BOHN, Frank Probasco,** a Representative from Michigan; born in Charlottesville, Hancock County, Ind., July 14, 1866; attended the common and high schools and the Danville (Ind.) Normal College; was graduated from the Medical College of Indiana, Indianapolis, Ind., in 1890; moved to Seney, Mich., in 1890 and engaged in the practice of medicine; moved to Newberry, Luce County, Mich., in 1898 and practiced his profession until 1923; also engaged in banking in 1905; served as village president of Newberry 1904 to 1919; member of the Newberry School Board 1908-1914; member of the State senate 1923-1926; elected as a Republican to the Seventieth, Seventy-first and Seventy-second Congresses (March 4, 1927-March 3, 1933); unsuccessful candidate for reelection in 1932 to the Seventy-third Congress; resumed banking activities in Newberry, Mich.; member of the Michigan State Hospital Commission 1935-1937; died in Newberry, Mich., June 1, 1944; interment in Forest Home Cemetery.

**BOIES, William Dayton,** a Representative from Iowa; born on a farm in Boone County, Ill., January 3, 1857; moved with his parents to Buchanan County, Iowa, in 1873 and settled near Quasqueton; attended country schools and the public schools of Belvidere, Ill.; was graduated in law from the State University of Iowa at Iowa City in 1880; was admitted to the bar in 1881 and commenced practice in Sanborn, O'Brien County, Iowa; moved to Sheldon, Iowa, in 1887 and continued the practice of law; unsuccessful candidate for election as judge of the district court in 1890; member of the school board of the independent school district of Sheldon 1900-1912; appointed judge of the district court of the fourth judicial district of Iowa January 1, 1913; on a division of this district became judge of the twenty-first judicial district of the State and in 1914 was elected for a term of four years, which position he resigned on March 31, 1918, to become a candidate for the Republican nomination for Congress; elected as a Republican to the Sixty-sixth and to the four succeeding Congresses (March 4, 1919-March 3, 1929); one of the managers appointed by the House of Representatives in 1926 to conduct the impeachment proceedings against George W. English, judge of the United States District Court for the Eastern District of Illinois; was not a candidate for renomination in 1928; died in Sheldon, Iowa, May 31, 1932; interment in Eastlawn Cemetery.

**BOILEAU, Gerald John,** a Representative from Wisconsin; born in Woodruff, Oneida County, Wis., January 15, 1900; moved to Minocqua, Oneida County, Wis., in 1909; attended the public and high schools; during the First World War enlisted in the United States Army on February 25, 1918, as a private in the Eleventh Field Artillery, Battery D, and was honorably discharged as a corporal on July 16, 1919; LL.B., Marquette University, Milwaukee, Wis., 1923; was admitted to the bar the same year and commenced practice in Wausau, Marathon County, Wis.; served as district attorney of Marathon County, Wis., 1926-1931; delegate to the Republican National Convention of 1928; elected as a Republican to the Seventy-second and Seventy-third Congresses, and as a Progressive to the Seventy-fourth and Seventy-fifth Congresses (March 4, 1931-January 3, 1939); unsuccessful candidate for reelection in 1938 to the Seventy-sixth Congress, and for election in 1940 to the Seventy-seventh Congress; resumed the practice of law; elected circuit judge of the sixteenth judicial circuit of Wisconsin in 1942; reelected in 1945, 1951, 1957, and again in 1963 for a six-year term; retired in 1970; appointed to serve as temporary circuit judge in Milwaukee County in 1970, for an unexpired term ending in 1974; resided in Wausau, Wis., until his death on January 30, 1981; interment in Restlawn Memorial Park.

**Bibliography:** Lorence, James J. *Gerald J. Boileau and the Progressive-Farmer-Labor Alliance: Politics of the New Deal.* Columbia: University of Missouri Press, 1994.

**BOKEE, David Alexander,** a Representative from New York; born in New York City, October 6, 1805; attended the public schools; engaged in mercantile pursuits; studied law; was admitted to the bar and practiced; president of the Brooklyn Board of Aldermen 1840-1843 and 1845-1848; member of the State senate 1846-1849; trustee of the New York Life Insurance Co., 1848-1860; elected as a Whig to the Thirty-first Congress (March 4, 1849-March 3, 1851); appointed by President Fillmore as naval officer of customs of the port of New York and served from 1851 to 1853; engaged as a shipping merchant; died in Washington, D.C., March 15, 1860; interment in Greenwood Cemetery, Brooklyn, N.Y.

**BOLAND, Edward Patrick,** a Representative from Massachusetts; born in Springfield, Hampden County, Mass., October 1, 1911; educated in Central High School, Bay Path Institute; attended Boston College Law School; member of the Massachusetts house of representatives 1935-1940; register of deeds for Hampden County 1941-1952; enlisted in May 1942 as a private in the United States Army and served through the ranks until his discharge as a captain in 1946, serving eleven months overseas in the Philippines; elected as a Democrat to the Eighty-third and to the seventeen succeeding Congresses (January 3, 1953-January 3, 1989); chairman, Select Committee on Intelligence (Ninety-fifth through Ninety-eighth Congresses); was not a candidate for reelection in 1988 to the One Hundred First Congress; is a resident of Springfield, Mass.

**BOLAND, Patrick Joseph** (husband of Veronica G. Boland), a Representative from Pennsylvania; born in Scranton, Lackawanna County, Pa., January 6, 1880; attended the parochial schools and St. Thomas College, Scranton, Pa.; began work as a carpenter; member of the firm of Boland Brothers, general building contractors; also associated with a sewer and paving contract company; member of the city council of Scranton, Pa., 1905-1906; served on the school board of Scranton, 1907-1909; county commissioner of Lackawanna County, Pa., 1915-1919; elected as a Democrat to the Seventy-second and to the five succeeding Congresses, and served from March 4, 1931 until his death in Scranton, Pa., May 18, 1942; majority whip (Seventy-fourth through Seventy-seventh Congresses); interment in Cathedral Cemetery.

**BOLAND, Veronica Grace** (wife of Patrick J. Boland), a Representative from Pennsylvania; born in Scranton, Lackawanna County, Pa., March 18, 1899; attended the public schools and Scranton Technical High School; elected as a Democrat to the Seventy-seventh Congress to fill the vacancy caused by the death of her husband, Patrick J. Boland, and served from November 19, 1942, to January 3, 1943; was not a candidate for reelection to the Seventy-eighth Congress; was a resident of Scranton, Pa., until her death there on June 19, 1982; interment in Cathedral Cemetery.

**BOLES, Thomas,** a Representative from Arkansas; born near Clarksville, Johnson County, Ark., July 16, 1837; attended the common schools; taught school for several years; sheriff of Yell County in 1858; deputy clerk of the circuit court of Yell County in 1859 and 1860; studied law; was admitted to the bar in 1860 and commenced practice in Danville, Ark.; during the Civil War served as captain of Company E, Third Regiment, Arkansas Volunteer Cavalry; judge of the fourth judicial circuit from 1865 to April 20, 1868, when he resigned; upon the readmission of Arkansas to representation was elected as a Republican to the Fortieth Congress; reelected to the Forty-first Congress and served from June 22, 1868, until March 3, 1871; successfully contested the election of John Edwards to the Forty-second Congress and served from February 9, 1872, until March 3, 1873; was not a candidate for renomination in 1872 to the Forty-third Congress; resumed the practice of law at Dardanelle, Ark.; served many years as school director and alderman; appointed receiver of the land office at Dardanelle by President Rutherford B. Hayes in February 1878; United States marshal for the western district of Arkansas 1881-1889; delegate to every Republican State convention from the organization of the party until his death; clerk of the United States Circuit Court for the Eighth Judicial Circuit from September 1897 until his death in Fort Smith, Sebastian County, Ark., March 13, 1905; interment in Brealey Cemetery, Dardanelle, Ark.

**BOLLES, Stephen,** a Representative from Wisconsin; born in Springboro, Crawford County, Pa., June 25, 1866; attended the public schools; was graduated from the State Normal School of Pennsylvania at Slippery Rock, Pa., in 1888 and from the law department of Milton College, Milton, Wis.; served as reporter, correspondent, managing editor, and publisher of newspapers in Ohio, Pennsylvania, and New York, 1893-1901; chairman of the congressional committee of the Eleventh Ohio District and secretary of the Republican city committee of Toledo in 1894; chairman of the congressional committee of the Twenty-sixth Pennsylvania District and secretary of the Pennsylvania Republican League of Clubs in 1896; superintendent of the press department of the Pan American Exposition at Buffalo, N.Y., in 1901; managing editor of the Buffalo (N.Y.) Enquirer, 1902-1903; superintendent of graphic arts of the St. Louis (Mo.) Exposition, 1903-1905; director of publicity of the Jamestown (Va.) Exposition in 1907; engaged as a special writer and also in private business, including the brokerage business, in Atlanta, Ga., 1907-1919; moved to Janesville, Wis., in 1920 and again engaged as a newspaper editor until elected to Congress; delegate to the Republican National Convention of 1928; elected as a Republican to the Seventy-sixth and Seventy-seventh Congresses, and served from January 3, 1939 until his death in Washington, D.C., July 8, 1941; interment in Oak Hill Cemetery, Janesville, Wis.

**BOLLING, Richard Walker** (great-great-grandson of John Williams Walker and great-great-nephew of Percy Walker), a Representative from Missouri; born in New York City, May 17, 1916; attended grade schools and Phillips Exeter Academy, Exeter, N.H.; at the age of fifteen, upon his father's death, returned to his home in Huntsville, Ala.; B.A., 1937, M.A., 1939, University of the South, Sewanee, Tenn.; graduate studies, Vanderbilt University, Nashville, Tenn., 1939-1940; taught at Sewanee Military Academy in 1938 and 1939; served as assistant to the head of the Department of Education, Florence State Teachers College, in Alabama, in 1940; educational administrator by profession; entered the United States Army as a private in April 1941, and served until discharged as a lieutenant colonel in July 1946, with four years' overseas service in Australia, New Guinea, Philippines, and in Japan as assistant to chief of staff to General Douglas MacArthur; awarded the Legion of Merit and Bronze Star Medal; veterans' adviser at the University of Kansas City in 1946 and 1947; elected as a Democrat to the Eighty-first and to the sixteen succeeding Congresses (January 3, 1949-January 3, 1983); chairman, Select Committee on Committees of the House (Ninety-third Congress), Joint Economic Committee (Ninety-fifth Congress); Committee on Rules (Ninety-sixth and Ninety-seventh Congresses); was not a candidate for reelection in 1982 to the Ninety-eighth Congress; was a resident of Crumpton, Md.; died April 21, 1991.

**Bibliography:** Bolling, Richard. *House Out of Order*. New York: Dutton, 1965; Bolling, Richard. *Power in the House: A History of the Leadership of the House of Representatives*. New York: Capricorn Books, 1974.

**BOLTON, Chester Castle** (husband of Frances P. Bolton and father of Oliver P. Bolton), a Representative from Ohio; born in Cleveland, Ohio, September 5, 1882; attended the public schools; was graduated from the University School, Clevland, Ohio, in 1901 and from Harvard University in 1905; employed in the steel industry in Cleveland 1905-1917; member of the Ohio National Guard 1905-1915; commissioned a captain in the Reserve Corps and ordered into active service in March 1917; detailed first to the War Industries Board, then served as aide to the Assistant Secretary of War; transferred to the General Staff in 1917; promoted to the rank of lieutenant colonel and detailed to the One Hundred and First Division as Assistant Chief of Staff; discharged in December 1918; returned to Cleveland, Ohio, and served as a director of several large business corporations; also engaged in raising and breeding cattle; member of the Lyndhurst Village Council 1918-1921; served in the State senate 1923-1928, serving as president pro tempore in 1927 and 1928; delegate to the Republican National Convention of 1928; elected as a Republican to the Seventy-first and to the three succeeding Congresses (March 4, 1929-January 3, 1937); unsuccessful candidate for reelection in 1936 to the Seventy-fifth Congress; served as chairman of the Republican Congressional Campaign Committee in 1934 and 1936; resumed his former business pursuits; elected to the Seventy-sixth Congress and served from January 3,

1939, until his death in Cleveland, Ohio, October 29, 1939; interment in Lake View Cemetery.

**BOLTON, Frances Payne** (wife of Chester C. Bolton, granddaughter of Henry B. Payne, and mother of Oliver P. Bolton), a Representative from Ohio; born March 29, 1885, in Cleveland, Ohio; attended private schools in United States and France; active in public health, nursing education and other social service, education, and philanthropic work; vice regent for Ohio of the Mount Vernon Ladies' Association; member of the Republican State central committee, 1937-1940; delegate to Republican National Conventions and member of Resolutions Committee, 1956, 1960, 1964, and 1968; first woman appointed as congressional delegate to United Nations General Assembly, 1953; elected as a Republican by special election, February 27, 1940, to the Seventy-sixth Congress to fill the vacancy caused by the death of her husband, Chester C. Bolton; reelected to the fourteen succeeding Congresses and served from February 27, 1940, to January 3, 1969; unsuccessful candidate for reelection in 1968 to the Ninety-first Congress; resided in Lyndhurst, Ohio, where she died March 9, 1977; interment in Lake View Cemetery, Cleveland, Ohio.

**Bibliography:** Loth, David. *A Long Way Forward: The Biography of Congresswoman Frances P. Bolton*. New York: Longmans, Green, 1957.

**BOLTON, Oliver Payne** (son of Chester Castle Bolton and Frances Payne Bolton and great-grandson of Henry B. Payne), a Representative from Ohio; born in Cleveland, Ohio, February 22, 1917; graduated from Milton (Mass.) Academy in 1935, Harvard College in 1939, and Western Reserve University Law School in 1947; was admitted to the bar in 1947 and began practice in Cleveland, Ohio; member of the One Hundred and Seventieth Cavalry, Ohio National Guard, 1939-1941; spent five years in the service, 1941-1946, one of which was in the Pacific Theater on the staff of C-2 section of Fifth Amphibious Corps; chairman of Ohio Young Republicans, 1948-1949; Young Republicans national committeeman from Ohio, 1950-1951; publisher of Lake County News Herald, Willoughby, Ohio, and the Daily Reporter, Dover, Ohio, 1952-1963; elected as a Republican to the Eighty-third and to the Eighty-fourth Congresses (January 3, 1953-January 3, 1957); was not a candidate for renomination in 1956 to the Eighty-fifth Congress; director of commerce, State of Ohio, from February 4 to August 2, 1957; elected to the Eighty-eighth Congress (January 3, 1963-January 3, 1965); unsuccessful candidate for reelection in 1964 to the Eighty-ninth Congress; partner, Prescott, Merrill, Turben & Co., investment bankers, 1965-1972; died in Palm Beach, Fla., December 13, 1972; interment in Lake View Cemetery, Cleveland, Ohio.

**BOLTON, William P.,** a Representative from Maryland; born near Whiteford, Harford County, Md., July 2, 1885; attended the public schools and St. Francis Parochial School in Baltimore County, Md.; was graduated from the Baltimore University Law School in 1909; was admitted to the bar in 1909 and commenced the practice of law in Towson, Md.; served as trial magistrate 1941-1946; member of the State senate 1946-1948; elected as a Democrat to the Eighty-first Congress (January 3, 1949-January 3, 1951); was an unsuccessful candidate for reelection in 1950 to the Eighty-second Congress; resumed the practice of law in Towson, Md.; appointed Baltimore County Civil Defense director in January 1951; died in Union Memorial Hospital, Baltimore, Md., November 22, 1964; interment in Mount Maria Cemetery, Towson, Md.

**BOND, Charles Grosvenor** (nephew of Charles Henry Grosvenor), a Representative from New York; born in Columbus, Franklin County, Ohio, May 29, 1877; attended the public schools; was graduated from the law department of Ohio State University at Columbus in 1899; was admitted to the bar the same year and commenced the practice of law in Columbus, Ohio; moved to New

York City in 1903 and continued the practice of his profession; elected as a Republican to the Sixty-seventh Congress (March 4, 1921-March 3, 1923); unsuccessful candidate for reelection in 1922 to the Sixty-eighth Congress; resumed the practice of law; also interested in banking; unsuccessful Republican candidate for president of the borough of Brooklyn in 1926; delegate to the Republican National Convention of 1936; member of the New York City Alcoholic Beverage Control Board, 1934-1970, chairman, 1960-1970; retired; died in Bound Brook, N.J., January 10, 1974; cremated; ashes interred at West Union Cemetery, Athens, Ohio.

**BOND, Christopher Samuel (Kit),** a Senator from Missouri; born in St. Louis, Mo., March 6, 1939; attended public schools; B.A., Woodrow Wilson School of Public and International Affairs, Princeton University, 1960; J.D., University of Virginia Law School, 1963; law clerk, United States Court of Appeals, Fifth Circuit, 1963-1964; practiced law in Washington, D.C., 1965-1968, and returned to Missouri in 1968; assistant attorney general of Missouri, 1969-1970; Missouri State auditor, 1971-1973; elected Governor of Missouri in 1972, and served from January 8, 1973 to January 10, 1977; unsuccessful candidate for reelection in 1976; president, Great Plains Legal Foundation, 1978-1981; again elected Governor in 1980, and served from January 12, 1981 to January 14, 1985; elected as a Republican to the United States Senate in 1986 for the term beginning January 3, 1987; reelected in 1992 to the term ending January 3, 1999; chairman, Committee on Small Business (One Hundred Fourth Congress); is a resident of Mexico, Mo.

**BOND, Shadrack,** a Delegate from Illinois Territory; born in Frederick, Md., November 24, 1773; received a common-school education; moved to Kaskaskia, Ill. (then Indiana Territory), in 1794 and engaged in agricultural pursuits; member of the legislative council of Indiana Territory, 1805-1808; when Illinois Territory was formed was elected a Delegate to Congress on October 10, 1812, and served from December 3, 1812, to August 2, 1813; served as receiver of public moneys in the general land office at Kaskaskia, Ill., 1814-1818; upon the admission of Illinois as a State into the Union was elected its first Governor in 1818, and served from October 6, 1818 to December 5, 1822; appointed register of the land office for the district of Kaskaskia on January 28, 1823, and served until his death in Kaskaskia, Randolph County, Ill., April 12, 1832; interment in Evergreen Cemetery, Chester, Randolph County, Ill.

**Bibliography:** *DAB.*

**BOND, William Key,** a Representative from Ohio; born in St. Marys County, Md., October 2, 1792; attended the schools at Litchfield, Conn., where he also studied law at the Litchfield Law School; moved to Chillicothe, Ohio, in 1812; was admitted to the bar in 1813 and commenced practice in Chillicothe; elected as a Whig to the Twenty-fourth, Twenty-fifth, and Twenty-sixth Congresses (March 4, 1835-March 3, 1841); chairman, Committee on Public Expenditures (Twenty-sixth Congress); declined to be a candidate for renomination in 1840; moved to Cincinnati in 1841 and continued the practice of his profession; appointed surveyor of the port of Cincinnati by President Fillmore May 2, 1849, and served until September 28, 1853; became interested in the development of railroads in the west; died in Cincinnati, Ohio, February 17, 1864; interment in Spring Grove Cemetery.

**BONE, Homer Truett,** a Senator from Washington; born in Franklin, Johnson County, Ind., January 25, 1883; attended the public schools; employed in the postal service and in the accounting and credit department of a furniture company; was graduated from the Tacoma (Wash.) Law School in 1911; was admitted to the bar the same year and commenced practice in Tacoma, Wash.; special deputy prosecuting attorney of Pierce County, Wash., 1912; corporation counsel of the port of Tacoma, Wash., 1918-1932; member, State house of representatives 1923-1924; unsuccessful

candidate for the Republican nomination in 1928 to the Seventy-first Congress; elected as a Democrat to the United States Senate in 1932; reelected in 1938 and served from March 4, 1933, until his resignation on November 13, 1944; chairman, Committee on Patents (Seventy-sixth through Seventy-eighth Congresses); appointed a judge of the United States Circuit Court of Appeals for the Ninth Judicial Circuit 1944-1956; resumed the practice of law in San Francisco and sat on the bench occasionally until 1968; returned to Tacoma, Wash., where he died on March 11, 1970; cremated and ashes interred in Oakwood Cemetery.

**BONER, William Hill,** a Representative from Tennessee; born in Nashville, Davidson County, Tenn., February 14, 1945; attended Warner public school, 1953-1959; graduated, East Nashville Senior High School, 1963; B.S., Middle Tennessee State University, Murfreesboro, 1967; M.A., George Peabody College, Nashville, 1969; served in the Tennessee house of representatives, 1970-1972, 1974-1976; engaged in banking profession, 1972-1976; law clerk, 1976-1977; served in Tennessee State senate, 1976-1978; J.D., YMCA Night Law School, Nashville, 1978; elected as a Democrat to the Ninety-sixth and to the four succeeding Congresses and served from January 3, 1979, until his resignation on October 5, 1987; elected mayor of Nashville, Tenn., on September 22, 1987, for a term beginning October 5, 1987; is a resident of Nashville, Tenn.

**BONHAM, Milledge Luke,** a Representative from South Carolina; born near Red Bank (now Saluda), Edgefield District, S.C., December 25, 1813; attended private schools in Edgefield District and at Abbeville, S.C.; was graduated from South Carolina College (now the University of South Carolina) at Columbia in 1834; studied law; was admitted to the bar and commenced practice in Edgefield, S.C. in 1837; served as major and adjutant general of the South Carolina Brigade in the Seminole War in Florida in 1836; during the Mexican War was lieutenant colonel and colonel of the Twelfth Regiment, United States Infantry; major general of the South Carolina Militia; member of the South Carolina State house of representatives, 1840-1843; solicitor of the southern circuit of South Carolina, 1848-1857; elected as a Democrat to the Thirty-fifth and Thirty-sixth Congresses and served from March 4, 1857, until December 21, 1860, when he joined other secessionist members of the South Carolina delegation in withdrawing from the Thirty-sixth Congress; appointed major general and commander of the Army of South Carolina by Governor Francis W. Pickens in February 1861; appointed brigadier general in the Confederate Army on April 23, 1861; resigned his commission January 29, 1862, to enter the Confederate Congress; chosen Governor of South Carolina by the legislature of the State and served from December 1862 until December 1864; appointed brigadier general of Cavalry in the Confederate Army on February 20, 1865; again a member of the State house of representatives, 1865-1866; delegate to the Democratic National Convention of 1868; member of the South Carolina taxpayers' convention in 1871 and 1874; resumed the practice of law in Edgefield, engaged in planting, and also conducted an insurance business in Edgefield, S.C., and Atlanta, Ga., 1865-1878; appointed State railroad commissioner in 1878 and served until his death at White Sulphur Springs, N.C., August 27, 1890; interment in Elmwood Cemetery, Columbia, S.C.

**Bibliography:** *DAB.*

**BONILLA, Henry,** a Representative from Texas; born in San Antonio, Tex., January 2, 1954; graduated South San Antonio High School, 1972; B.A., University of Texas, Austin, 1976; executive producer for public affairs, KENS-TV, San Antonio; executive news producer, KENS-TV, San Antonio; elected as a Republican to the One Hundred Third and One Hundred Fourth Congresses (January 3, 1993-January 3, 1997); is a resident of San Antonio, Tex.

**BONIN, Edward John,** a Representative from Pennsylvania; born in Hazleton, Luzerne County, Pa., December 23, 1904; attended the parochial and public schools of Hazleton; served in the United States Navy 1922-1926; graduated from Wyoming Seminary, Kingston, Pa., in 1929, Dickinson College, Carlisle, Pa., in 1933, and Temple University, Philadelphia, Pa., in 1937; studied law; was admitted to the bar in February 1938 and began practice in Hazleton, Pa.; served in the United States Army 1942-1944; resumed law practice; assistant district attorney of Luzerne County 1949-1952; mayor of Hazleton, Pa., 1951-1953; elected as a Republican to the Eighty-third Congress (January 3, 1953-January 3, 1955); was an unsuccessful candidate for reelection in 1954 to the Eighty-fourth Congress; assistant to Philadelphia regional director, Post Office Department, from February 1955 to March 1963; general attorney, Post Office Department, Washington, D.C., from March 1963 to December 1966; resumed the practice of law; was a resident of Hazleton, Pa.; died December 20, 1990.

**BONIOR, David Edward,** a Representative from Michigan; born in Detroit, Wayne County, Mich., June 6, 1945; attended the parochial schools; graduated, Notre Dame High School, 1963; B.A., University of Iowa, Iowa City, 1967; M.A., Chapman College, Orange, California, 1972; served in United States Air Force, staff sergeant, 1968-1972; member, Michigan State house of representatives, 1973-1977; delegate to Michigan State Democratic conventions, 1972-1977; elected as a Democrat to the Ninety-fifth and to the nine succeeding Congresses (January 3, 1977-January 3, 1997); majority whip (One Hundred Second and One Hundred Third Congresses), minority whip (One Hundred Fourth Congress); is a resident of Mount Clemens, Mich.

**BONKER, Don Leroy,** a Representative from Washington; born in Denver, Colo., March 7, 1937; attended the public schools in Westminister, Colo.; A.A., Clark College, Vancouver, Wash., 1962; B.A., Lewis and Clark College, Portland, Oreg., 1964; engaged in graduate work at American University, Washington, D.C., 1964; served in United States Coast Guard, first class yeoman, 1955-1959; Clark County auditor, Vancouver, Wash., 1966-1970; unsuccessful candidate for Washington secretary of state, 1972; delegate to Washington State Democratic conventions, 1968-1970; elected as a Democrat to the Ninety-fourth and to the six succeeding Congresses (January 3, 1975-January 3, 1989); was not a candidate in 1988 for reelection to the House of Representatives, but was an unsuccessful candidate for nomination to the United States Senate; is a resident of Vancouver, Wash.

**BONNER, Herbert Covington,** a Representative from North Carolina; born in Washington, Beaufort County, N.C., May 16, 1891; attended a private school; was graduated from Graham School, Warrenton, N.C.; engaged as a salesman and in agricultural pursuits; during the First World War served as sergeant in Company I, Three Hundred and Twenty-second Infantry, with overseas service in the Eighty-first Division; secretary to Congressman Lindsay C. Warren 1924-1940; elected as a Democrat on November 5, 1940, to the Seventy-sixth Congress to fill the vacancy caused by the resignation of Lindsay C. Warren and on the same day was elected to the Seventy-seventh Congress; reelected to the Seventy-eighth and to the eleven succeeding Congresses and served from November 5, 1940, until his death November 7, 1965, at Walter Reed Army Hospital, Washington, D.C.; chairman, Committee on Election of President, Vice President, and Representatives (Seventy-ninth Congress), Committee on Merchant Marine and Fisheries (Eighty-fourth through Eighty-ninth Congresses); interment in Oakdale Cemetery, Washington, N.C.

**BONO, Sonny,** a Representative from California; born in Detroit, Wayne County, Mich., February 16, 1935; graduated, Inglewood (Calif.) High School, 1952; restauranteur in Hollywood, Calif., Houston, Tex., and Palm Springs, Calif.; entertainer, songwriter, and producer; mayor of Palm Springs, Calif., 1988-1994; unsuccessful candidate in 1992 for the Republican nomination to the United States Senate; elected as a Republican to the One Hundred Fourth Congress (January 3, 1995-January 3, 1997); is a resident of Palm Springs, Calif.

**BONYNGE, Robert William,** a Representative from Colorado; born in New York City September 8, 1863; attended the public schools; was graduated from the College of the City of New York in 1882 and from the law department of Columbia College, New York City, in 1885; was admitted to the bar in 1885 and commenced practice in New York City; moved to Denver, Colo., in 1888 and continued the practice of law; member of the State house of representatives in 1893 and 1894; unsuccessful candidate for election in 1900 to the Fifty-seventh Congress; contested the election to the Fifty-eighth Congress of John F. Shafroth, who in an address before the House of Representatives conceded his defeat and withdrew from the contest; reelected as a Republican to the Fifty-ninth and Sixtieth Congresses and served from February 16, 1904, until March 3, 1909; unsuccessful candidate for reelection in 1908 to the Sixty-first Congress; member of the National Monetary Commission 1908-1912; resumed the practice of law in Denver, Colo.; moved to New York City in November 1912 and continued the practice of law; chief counsel of the New York State Industrial Commission 1916-1918; appointed United States agent before the Mixed Claims Commission (United States and Germany) in 1923 and before the Tripartite Claims Commission (United States, Austria, and Hungary) in 1927; died in New York City, September 22, 1939; interment in Woodlawn Cemetery.

**BOODY, Azariah,** a Representative from New York; born in Stanstead County, Province of Quebec, Canada, April 21, 1815; moved to Massachusetts with his parents, who settled in Lowell; attended the common schools; moved to Rochester, N.Y., in 1850 and engaged in agricultural pursuits; trustee of the University of Rochester 1853-1865; elected as a Whig to the Thirty-third Congress and served from March 4, 1853 until his resignation in October 1853, before the convening of Congress; moved to New York City in 1855 and engaged in the construction of railroads, canals, and bridges; served as president of the Wabash Railroad Co.; retired from active business pursuits in 1875, retaining his residence in New York City, where he died on November 18, 1885; interment in Mount Hope Cemetery, Rochester, N.Y.

**BOODY, David Augustus,** a Representative from New York; born in Jackson, Waldo County, Maine, August 13, 1837; attended the common schools and Phillips Academy, Andover, Mass.; studied law; was admitted to the bar in 1860 at Belfast, Maine, and commenced practice in Camden, Maine; moved to Brooklyn, N.Y., in 1862 and engaged in the banking and brokerage business; unsuccessful candidate for election in 1882 to the Forty-eighth Congress; delegate to the Democratic National Conventions in 1884 and 1892; president of Berkeley Institute, Brooklyn, N.Y., 1886-1922; elected as a Democrat to the Fifty-second Congress and served from March 4 to October 13, 1891, when he resigned, having become a candidate for mayor; mayor of Brooklyn in 1892 and 1893; resumed his former banking and brokerage business; served as president of the board of trustees of the Brooklyn Public Library from 1897 until his death; was a member of the New York Stock Exchange but retired in 1926, and resided in Brooklyn, N.Y., until his death there on January 20, 1930; interment in Greenwood Cemetery.

**BOOHER, Charles Ferris,** a Representative from Missouri; born on a farm near East Groveland, Livingston County, N.Y., January 31, 1848; attended the common schools and the Geneseo Academy, Geneseo, N.Y.; taught school and studied law; was admitted to the bar in 1871 and commenced practice in Rochester, Mo.; moved to Savannah, Mo., in 1875, having been appointed prosecuting attorney of Andrew County, in which capacity he served until 1877, and again from 1883 to 1885; resumed the practice of law in Savannah, Mo., and also, in 1888, engaged in the loan and real estate business; mayor of Savannah, Mo., 1886-1890; elected as a Democrat to the Fiftieth Congress to fill the vacancy caused by the death of James N. Burnes and served from February 19 to March 3, 1889; was not a candidate for election for the full term; elected to the Sixtieth and to the six succeeding Congresses and served from March 4, 1907, until his death; was not a candidate for renomination in 1920; died in Savannah, Andrew County, Mo., January 21, 1921; interment in City Cemetery.

**BOOKER, George William,** a Representative from Virginia; born near Stuart, Patrick County, Va., December 5, 1821; attended the public schools; taught school; studied law; was admitted to the bar in 1846 and commenced practice in Patrick County; elected a justice of the peace in Henry County; member and presiding justice of the county court from August 1856 to February 1868; member of the Virginia house of delegates in 1865-1867 and 1871-1873; nominated by the Republican Party and elected attorney general in 1868, but resigned in 1869; upon the readmission of Virginia to representation was elected as a Conservative to the Forty-first Congress and served from January 26, 1870, to March 3, 1871; resumed the practice of law in Martinsville, Henry County, Va., where he died June 4, 1883; interment in the family cemetery.

**BOON, Ratliff,** a Representative from Indiana; born in Franklin County, N.C., January 18, 1781; moved with his parents to Warren County, Ky.; attended the public schools; moved to Danville, Ky., and learned the gunsmith's trade; moved to what is now Boon Township, Warrick County, Ind., in 1809; on the organization of Warrick County was appointed its first treasurer in 1813; member of the State house of representatives in 1816 and 1817; served in the State senate in 1818; elected lieutenant governor of Indiana in 1819; upon the resignation of Jonathan Jennings became Acting Governor of Indiana and served from September 12 to December 5, 1822; reelected Lieutenant Governor in August 1822 and served until January 30, 1824, when he resigned to become a candidate for Congress; elected to the Nineteenth Congress (March 4, 1825-March 3, 1827); unsuccessful candidate for reelection in 1826 to the Twentieth Congress; elected as a Jacksonian to the Twenty-first through Twenty-fourth Congresses and as a Democrat to the Twenty-fifth Congress (March 4, 1829-March 3, 1839); chairman, Committee on Public Lands (Twenty-fourth and Twenty-fifth Congresses); unsuccessful candidate for election to the United States Senate in 1836; moved to Pike County, Mo., in 1839; died in Louisiana, Mo., on November 20, 1844; interment in Riverview Cemetery.

**BOONE, Andrew Rechmond,** a Representative from Kentucky; born in Davidson County, Tenn., April 4, 1831; moved with his parents to Mayfield, Graves County, Ky., in 1833; attended the public schools; studied law; was admitted to the bar in 1852 and practiced in Mayfield; elected judge of the Graves County court in 1854; reelected in 1858 and served until 1861, when he resigned; member of the Kentucky house of representatives in 1861; circuit judge for the first judicial district of Kentucky 1868-1874; elected as a Democrat to the Forty-fourth and Forty-fifth Congresses (March 4, 1875-March 3, 1879); was not a candidate for reelection in 1878; chairman of the State railroad commission 1882-1886; died in Mayfield, Ky., January 26, 1886; interment in Mayfield Cemetery.

**BOOTH, Newton,** a Senator from California; born in Salem, Washington County, Ind., December 30, 1825; attended the common schools, and was graduated from Asbury (later DePauw) University, Greencastle, Ind., in 1846; studied law in Terre Haute, Ind.; was admitted to the bar in 1850; moved the same year to California, where he temporarily engaged in the wholesale grocery business at Sacramento; returned to Terre Haute in 1857 and engaged in the

practice of law until 1860, when he returned to Sacramento, Calif., and again engaged in mercantile pursuits; member of the California State senate in 1863; elected Governor of California in 1871, and served from December 8, 1871 until February 27, 1875, when he resigned, having been elected Senator; elected as an Anti-Monopolist to the United States Senate and served from March 4, 1875, to March 3, 1881; was not a candidate for reelection in 1880; chairman, Committee on Manufacturers (Forty-fifth Congress), Committee on Patents (Forty-fifth Congress); engaged in the wholesale mercantile business in Sacramento, Calif., where he died on July 14, 1892; interment in the City Cemetery.

**Bibliography:** *DAB*; Booth, Newton. *Newton Booth of California, His Speeches and Addresses.* New York: G.P. Putnam's Sons, 1894.

**BOOTH, Walter,** a Representative from Connecticut; born in Woodbridge, Conn., December 8, 1791; attended the common schools; settled in Meriden and engaged in manufacturing; colonel of the Tenth Regiment, Second Battalion of Militia, 1825-1827, brigadier general in 1827 and 1828, and major general of the First Division 1831-1834; judge of the county court in 1834; member of the State house of representatives in 1838; elected as a Free-Soiler to the Thirty-first Congress (March 4, 1849-March 3, 1851); unsuccessful candidate for reelection in 1850 to the Thirty-second Congress; resumed his former manufacturing pursuits; died in Meriden, New Haven County, Conn., April 30, 1870; interment in East Cemetery.

**BOOTHMAN, Melvin Morella,** a Representative from Ohio; born near Bryan, Williams County, Ohio, October 16, 1846; attended the public schools; engaged in agricultural pursuits; enlisted in Company H, Thirty-eighth Regiment, Ohio Volunteer Infantry, January 4, 1864; served through the Atlanta campaign; was graduated from the law department of Michigan University at Ann Arbor in 1871; was admitted to the bar and commenced practice in Bryan, Ohio; elected treasurer of Williams County in 1871 and reelected in 1873; elected as a Republican to the Fiftieth and Fifty-first Congresses (March 4, 1887-March 3, 1891); was not a candidate for renomination in 1890 to the Fifty-second Congress; resumed the practice of law in Bryan, Ohio, and died there March 5, 1904; interment in Fountain City Cemetery.

**BOOZE, William Samuel,** a Representative from Maryland; born in Baltimore, Md., January 9, 1862; attended the public schools; was graduated from Baltimore City College in 1879 and afterwards attended the University of Maryland School of Medicine; was graduated in medicine from the College of Physicians and Surgeons, New York City, in 1882 and practiced his profession in Baltimore until 1896, when he was elected to Congress; unsuccessfully contested the election of Harry Welles Rusk to the Fifty-fourth Congress; elected as a Republican to the Fifty-fifth Congress (March 4, 1897-March 3, 1899); was not a candidate for renomination in 1898; engaged in banking and in the brokerage business in Baltimore, Md., until 1915, when he again engaged in the practice of medicine; delegate to the Republican National Conventions in 1904 and 1908; died in Wilmington, Del., December 6, 1933, while en route to his home from a trip to South America; interment in Loudoun Park Cemetery, Baltimore, Md.

**BORAH, William Edgar,** a Senator from Idaho; born on a farm near Fairfield, Wayne County, Ill., June 29, 1865; attended the common schools of Wayne County and the Cumberland Presbyterian Academy at Enfield; moved to Lyons, Kans. in 1883 and attended the Rice County Normal Institute; taught school; attended the University of Kansas at Lawrence, 1885-1889; studied law; was admitted to the Kansas bar on September 16, 1887, and commenced practice in Lyons; served as city attorney of Lyons during 1889-1890; moved to Boise, Idaho, in 1890; admitted to the Idaho bar on February 19, 1891, and practiced law; unsuccessful candidate on the Silver Republican ticket for election in 1896 to the Fifty-fifth

Congress; unsuccessful candidate in 1903 for nomination to the United States Senate; elected as a Republican to the United States Senate in 1907; reelected in 1913, 1918, 1924, 1930, and again in 1936, and served from March 4, 1907 until his death in Washington, D.C. on January 19, 1940; chairman, Committee on Education and Labor (Sixty-first, Sixty-second, Sixty-seventh, and Sixty-eighth Congresses), Committee on Indian Depredations (Sixty-third and Sixty-fourth Congresses), Committee on Expenditures in the Department of Justice (Sixty-fifth Congress), Committee on Inter-oceanic Canals (Sixty-sixth and Sixty-seventh Congresses), Committee on Foreign Relations (Sixty-eighth through Seventy-second Congresses); unsuccessful candidate for the Republican presidential nomination in 1936; funeral services were held in the Chamber of the United States Senate; interment in Morris Hill Cemetery, Boise, Idaho.

**Bibliography:** *DAB*; Ashby, Leroy. *The Spearless Leader, Senator Borah and the Progressive Movement in the 1920's.* Urbana: University of Illinois Press, 1972; McKenna, Marian C. *Borah.* Ann Arbor: University of Michigan Press, 1961.

**BORCHERS, Charles Martin,** a Representative from Illinois; born in Lockville, Fairfield County, Ohio, November 18, 1869; moved to Illinois with his parents, who settled in Macon County in 1875; attended the common schools; taught school in Macon County for seven years; studied law; was admitted to the bar in 1897 and commenced practice in Decatur, Macon County, Ill.; mayor of Decatur 1909-1911; elected as a Democrat to the Sixty-third Congress (March 4, 1913-March 3, 1915); unsuccessful candidate for reelection in 1914 to the Sixty-fourth Congress; resumed the practice of law; again served as mayor of Decatur 1919-1923; unsuccessful candidate in 1924 for Governor; died in Decatur, Ill., December 2, 1946; interment in Frantz Cemetery, Macon County, Ill.

**BORDEN, Nathaniel Briggs,** a Representative from Massachusetts; born in Fall River, Mass., April 15, 1801; attended the district school and Plainfield (Conn.) Academy; organized the Pocasset Manufacturing Co., in Fall River, Mass.; member of the Massachusetts house of representatives in 1831 and 1834; elected as a Jacksonian to the Twenty-fourth Congress and reelected as a Democrat to the Twenty-fifth Congress (March 4, 1835-March 3, 1839); unsuccessful Whig candidate for reelection to the Twenty-sixth Congress in 1838; elected as a Whig to the Twenty-seventh Congress (March 4, 1841-March 3, 1843); member of the Massachusetts senate from 1845 to 1848; served in the Massachusetts house of representatives in 1851; elected mayor of Fall River in 1856 and reelected in 1857; again a member of the Massachusetts house of representatives in 1864; engaged in banking and served as president of the Fall River Savings Bank and of the Fall River Union Bank; was president also of the Fall River Railroad Co.; died in Fall River, Bristol County, Mass., April 10, 1865; interment in Oak Grove Cemetery.

**BOREING, Vincent,** a Representative from Kentucky; born near Jonesboro, Washington County, Tenn., November 24, 1839; moved with his father to Laurel County, Ky., in 1847; attended Laurel Seminary, London, Ky., and Tusculum College, Greenville, Tenn.; enlisted as a private in the Union Army in Company A, Twenty-fourth Regiment, Kentucky Volunteer Infantry, November 1, 1861; for meritorious conduct was commissioned first lieutenant; county superintendent of public schools 1868-1872; established the Mountain Echo at London, Ky., in 1875, the first Republican newspaper published in southeastern Kentucky; county judge in 1886; president of the Cumberland Valley Land Co. in 1887; president of the First National Bank of London in 1888; department commander of the Grand Army of the Republic in Kentucky in 1889; elected as a Republican to the Fifty-sixth, Fifty-seventh, and Fifty-eighth Congresses and served from March 4, 1899, until his

death in London, Laurel County, Ky., September 16, 1903; interment in Pine Grove Cemetery.

**BOREMAN, Arthur Inghram,** a Senator from West Virginia; born in Waynesburg, Pa., July 24, 1823; moved to Virginia with his parents, who settled in Middlebourne, Tyler County, in 1827, and in Moundsville, Marshall County, in 1840; attended the public schools; studied law; was admitted to the bar in 1843 and commenced practice in Parkersburg; member, Virginia house of delegates 1855-1861; presided over the convention of supporters of the Union of the northwestern counties of Virginia held at Wheeling on June 19, 1861, to form the new State of West Virginia; elected judge of the circuit court, nineteenth circuit of Virginia 1861-1863; elected the first Governor of West Virginia in 1863, reelected in 1864 and 1866, and served from June 20, 1863 until February 26, 1869, when he resigned to accept the nomination as United States Senator; elected as a Republican to the United States Senate and served from March 4, 1869, to March 3, 1875; was not a candidate for reelection in 1874; chairman, Select Committee on the Removal of Political Disabilities (Forty-second Congress), Committee on Territories (Forty-third Congress); resumed the practice of law in Parkersburg, W.Va.; elected judge of the circuit court for the fifth judicial circuit of West Virginia in 1888 and served until his death in Parkersburg, Wood County, W.Va., April 19, 1896; interment in the Odd Fellows Cemetery.

**Bibliography:** *DAB*; Woodward, Isaiah Alfonso. "Arthur Inghram Boreman: A Biography." Ph.D. dissertation, West Virginia University, 1970.

**BOREN, David Lyle** (son of Lyle H. Boren), a Senator from Oklahoma; born in Washington, D.C., April 21, 1941; attended the public schools of Seminole, Okla., and Bethesda, Md.; B.A., Yale University, 1963; attended Oxford University, England, as a Rhodes Scholar and received a graduate degree in 1965; J.D., University of Oklahoma College of Law, Norman, Okla., 1968; admitted to the Oklahoma bar in 1968 and commenced practice in Seminole; captain in the Oklahoma National Guard 1968-1974; chairman, department of government, Oklahoma Baptist University, Shawnee, Okla., 1970-1974; member of the Oklahoma State house of representatives, 1967-1975; elected Governor of Oklahoma in 1974, and served from January 13, 1975 to January 3, 1979; elected as a Democrat to the United States Senate in 1978; reelected in 1984 and again in 1990, and served from January 3, 1979 until his resignation on November 15, 1994 to become president of the University of Oklahoma; chairman, Select Committee on Intelligence (One Hundredth through One Hundred Second Congresses), Joint Committee on the Organization of Congress (One Hundred Third Congress); is a resident of Norman, Okla.

**BOREN, Lyle H.** (father of David Lyle Boren), a Representative from Oklahoma; born near Waxahachie, Ellis County, Tex., May 11, 1909; moved to Lawton, Okla., in 1917; attended the public schools; was graduated from the East Central College at Ada, Okla., in 1930 and from Oklahoma Agricultural and Mechanical College at Stillwater; teacher in the schools at Wolf, Okla., 1930-1935; served as a deputy procurement officer of the United States Treasury Department; engaged in agricultural pursuits and also was interested in the mercantile business; author; lieutenant commander in the United States Naval Reserve; elected as a Democrat to the Seventy-fifth and to the four succeeding Congresses (January 3, 1937-January 3, 1947); unsuccessful candidate for renomination in 1946 to the Eightieth Congress; resumed former mercantile business and agricultural pursuits; president of a petroleum corporation; representative of the Association of Western Railroads, 1954-1970; assistant to the Insurance Commissioner, State of Oklahoma; was a resident of Oklahoma City, Okla.; died July 2, 1992.

**BORLAND, Charles, Jr.,** a Representative from New York; born in Minisink, Orange County, N.Y., June 29, 1786; pursued preparatory studies; was graduated from Union College, Schenectady, N.Y., in 1811; studied law; was admitted to the bar and practiced; president of the board of trustees of Montgomery for ten years; member of the State assembly in 1820 and 1821; elected to the Seventeenth Congress to fill the vacancy caused by the death of Selah Tuthill and served from November 8, 1821, to March 3, 1823; district attorney of Orange County 1835-1841; again a member of the State assembly, in 1836; died in Wardsbridge, N.Y., February 23, 1852; interment in Riverside Cemetery, Montgomery, N.Y.

**BORLAND, Solon,** a Senator from Arkansas; born near Suffolk, Nansemond County, Va., September 21, 1808; attended preparatory schools in North Carolina; studied medicine and afterwards practiced; settled in Little Rock, Ark.; served throughout the Mexican War as a major in the Arkansas Volunteer Cavalry; was appointed and subsequently elected as a Democrat to the United States Senate to fill the vacancy caused by the resignation of Ambrose H. Sevier and served from March 30, 1848, to April 3, 1853, when he resigned; chairman, Committee on Printing (Thirty-first and Thirty-second Congresses), Committee on Public Lands (Thirty-third Congress); appointed United States Minister to Nicaragua and to the other Central American Republics on April 18, 1853 and served until April 1854; declined an appointment as Governor of the Territory of New Mexico; returned to Arkansas and resumed the practice of medicine in Little Rock until 1861; during the Civil War raised a brigade of troops for the Confederate Army; later was appointed a brigadier general in the Confederate Army; died near Houston, Tex., on January 1, 1864; interment in City Cemetery, Houston, Tex.

Bibliography: *DAB.*

**BORLAND, William Patterson,** a Representative from Missouri; born in Leavenworth, Kans., October 14, 1867; attended the public schools; was graduated from the law department of the University of Michigan at Ann Arbor in 1892; was admitted to the bar and commenced the practice of law in Kansas City, Mo., the same year; assisted in the organization of the Kansas City School of Law and served as dean 1895-1909; member of the board of freeholders directed to draft a charter for Kansas City in 1898; also engaged as an author on law subjects; elected as a Democrat to the Sixty-first and to the four succeeding Congresses and served from March 4, 1909, until his death; unsuccessful candidate for renomination in 1918 to the Sixty-sixth Congress; died near Coblenz, Germany, while on a Masonic mission abroad, on February 20, 1919; interment in Elmwood Cemetery, Kansas City, Mo.

**BORSKI, Robert Anthony, Jr.,** a Representative from Pennsylvania; born in Philadelphia, Pa., October 20, 1948; attended St. Joan of Arc, Philadelphia, Pa.; graduated, Frankford High School, Philadelphia, 1966; B.A., University of Baltimore, 1971; stockbroker; elected, Pennsylvania house of representatives, 1976-1982; elected as a Democrat to the Ninety-eighth and to the six succeeding Congresses (January 3, 1983-January 3, 1997); is a resident of Philadelphia, Pa.

**BORST, Peter I.,** a Representative from New York; born in Middleburg, Schoharie County, N.Y., April 24, 1797; attended the common schools; served as an officer of State troops and on the staff of Governor William C. Bouck; held various local positions; elected as a Jacksonian to the Twenty-first Congress (March 4, 1829-March 3, 1831); served as a member of the committee appointed by the county board of supervisors to oversee the building of the first county almshouse in 1838; died in Middleburg, N.Y., November 14, 1848; interment in the family burying ground on his estate, "The Hook," in Schoharie County.

**BOSCH, Albert Henry,** a Representative from New York; born in New York City, October 30, 1908; attended the public schools; LL.B., St. Johns College School of Law, 1933; was admitted to the bar in 1938 and commenced the practice of law in New York City; also admitted to practice before the Treasury Department and the Supreme Court of the United States; trustee of Hamburg Savings Bank, Ridgewood, N.Y.; elected as a Republican to the Eighty-third and to the three succeeding Congresses and served from January 3, 1953, until his resignation December 31, 1960, having been elected judge of county court of Queens, and served until September 1, 1962; elected justice, supreme court of New York State, eleventh judicial district, and served until his retirement, December 31, 1974; is a resident of Whiting, N.J.

**BOSCHWITZ, Rudolph Eli (Rudy),** a Senator from Minnesota; born in Berlin, Germany, November 7, 1930; attended the public schools in New Rochelle, N.Y., and Pennington, N.J.; attended Johns Hopkins University, Baltimore, Md.; B.S., New York University, 1950; LL.B., New York University Law School, 1953; admitted to the New York bar in 1954 and the Wisconsin bar in 1959, and commenced practice in New York City in 1956; served in the United States Army Signal Corps, 1954-1955; founder and chairman of Home Value, Inc., a plywood firm, 1963-1995; elected as a Republican to the United States Senate in 1978 for the term commencing January 3, 1979; subsequently appointed by the Governor, December 30, 1978, to fill the vacancy caused by the resignation of Wendell R. Anderson for the term ending January 3, 1979; reelected in 1984 for the term ending January 3, 1991; unsuccessful candidate for reelection in 1990; candidate for election to the United States Senate in 1996; is a resident of Plymouth, Minn.

**BOSCO, Douglas Harry,** a Representative from California; born in Brooklyn, Kings County, N.Y., July 28, 1946; attended Homestead High School, Sunnyvale, Calif.; graduated, Capitol Page School, Washington, D.C., 1963; B.A., Willamette University, Salem, Oreg., 1968; J.D., Willamette University School of Law, 1971; admitted to the California bar in 1971 and commenced practice in San Rafael; director, Department of Human Relations, Marin County, Calif., 1973; executive director, Marin County Housing Authority, 1974; served in the California legislature, 1979-1982; delegate, California State Democratic convention, 1982; delegate to the Democratic National Convention of 1980; elected as a Democrat to the Ninety-eighth and to the three succeeding Congresses (January 3, 1983-January 3, 1991); unsuccessful candidate for reelection in 1990 to the One Hundred Second Congress; is a resident of Occidental, Calif.

**BOSONE, Reva Zilpha Beck,** a Representative from Utah; born in American Fork, Utah County, Utah, April 2, 1895; attended the public schools; graduated from Westminster Junior College in 1917; B.A., University of California, Berkeley, 1919; taught high school English and speech in American Fork, Delta, and Ogden, Utah, 1920-1927; graduated from the University of Utah College of Law at Salt Lake City in 1930 and was admitted to the bar the same year; practiced law in Helper, Utah, 1931-1933, and Salt Lake City, 1933-1936; member of the Utah State house of representatives, 1933-1935, serving as floor leader in 1935; elected Salt Lake City police and traffic court judge in 1936 and served until elected to Congress; during the Second World War was chairman of Women's Army Corps Civilian Advisory Committee of the Ninth Service Command; official observer at the founding conference of the United Nations at San Francisco in 1945; first director of the Utah State Board for Education on Alcoholism in 1947 and 1948; elected as a Democrat to the Eighty-first and Eighty-second Congresses (January 3, 1949-January 3, 1953); unsuccessful candidate for reelection in 1952 to the Eighty-third Congress, and for election in 1954 to the Eighty-fourth Congress; delegate to Democratic National Conventions of 1952 and 1956; resumed the practice of law in Salt Lake City, 1953-1957; legal counsel to the Safety and Compensation Subcommittee of House Committee on Education and Labor, 1957-1960; judicial officer, United States Post Office Department, and chair of the Post Office Contract Board of Appeals from 1961 until her retirement in January 1968; was a resident of Vienna, Va., until her death there July 21, 1983.

**Bibliography:** Clopton, Beverly B. *Her Honor, the Judge: The Story of Reva Beck Bosone*. Ames: Iowa State University Press, 1980.

**BOSS, John Linscom, Jr.,** a Representative from Rhode Island; born in Charleston, S.C., September 7, 1780; completed preparatory studies; studied law; was admitted to the bar and commenced practice in Newport, R.I.; held many important local offices; member of the State house of representatives from 1806 to 1815; elected as a Federalist to the Fourteenth and Fifteenth Congresses (March 4, 1815-March 3, 1819); died in Newport, R.I., August 1, 1819; interment in the Common Burial Ground.

**BOSSIER, Pierre Evariste John Baptiste,** a Representative from Louisiana; born in Natchitoches, La., March 22, 1797; received a classical education; engaged as a sugar and cotton planter; member of the State senate 1833-1843; elected as a Democrat to the Twenty-eighth Congress and served from March 4, 1843, until his death in Washington, D.C., on April 24, 1844; interment in the Congressional Cemetery, Washington, D.C.; reinterment in the Catholic Cemetery, Natchitoches, La.

**BOTELER, Alexander Robinson,** a Representative from Virginia; born in Shepherdstown, Jefferson County, Va. (now West Virginia), May 16, 1815; was graduated from Princeton College in 1835; engaged in agriculture and literary pursuits; elected as the candidate of the Opposition Party to the Thirty-sixth Congress (March 4, 1859-March 3, 1861); during the Civil War entered the Confederate Army and was a member of General Thomas J. Jackson's staff; chosen by the Virginia convention as Representative to the Confederate Provisional Congress on November 19, 1861; elected from Virginia to the Confederate Congress, serving from February 1862 to February 1864; appointed a member of the Centennial Commission in 1876; appointed a member of the Tariff Commission by President Chester A. Arthur, and subsequently made pardon clerk in the Department of Justice by Attorney General Benjamin H. Brewster; died in Shepherdstown, Jefferson County, W.Va., May 8, 1892; interment in Elmwood Cemetery.

**Bibliography:** *DAB*.

**BOTKIN, Jeremiah Dunham,** a Representative from Kansas; born near Atlanta, Logan County, Ill., April 24, 1849; attended the country schools; spent one year at De Pauw University, Greencastle, Ind.; pursued theological studies, and entered the Methodist ministry in 1870; unsuccessful Prohibition candidate for Governor of Kansas in 1888; unsuccessful candidate for election in 1894 to the Fifty-fourth Congress; chaplain of the Kansas senate in 1897; elected as a Populist to the Fifty-fifth Congress (March 4, 1897-March 3, 1899); unsuccessful candidate for reelection in 1898 to the Fifty-sixth Congress; resumed ministerial duties; unsuccessful Democratic candidate for election in 1908 for Governor; warden of the State penitentiary, Lansing, Kans., 1913-1915; again resumed his ministerial duties; became a Chautauqua lecturer in 1921; died in Liberal, Seward County, Kans., December 29, 1921; interment in Winfield Cemetery, Winfield, Cowley County, Kans.

**BOTTS, John Minor,** a Representative from Virginia; born in Dumfries, Va., September 16, 1802; attended the common schools in Richmond, Va.; studied law; was admitted to the bar in 1830 and commenced practice in Richmond, Va.; moved to Henrico County and engaged in agricultural pursuits; member of the Virginia house of delegates 1833-1839; elected as a Whig to the Twenty-sixth and

Twenty-seventh Congresses (March 4, 1839-March 3, 1843); unsuccessful candidate for reelection in 1842 to the Twenty-eighth Congress; elected to the Thirtieth Congress (March 4, 1847-March 3, 1849); chairman, Committee on Military Affairs (Thirtieth Congress); unsuccessful candidate for reelection in 1848 and 1850 to the Thirty-first and Thirty-second Congresses, respectively; member, State constitutional convention, 1850-1851; resumed the practice of law in Richmond, Va., in 1852; delegate to the Southern Loyalists' Convention in 1866; died in Richmond, Va., January 8, 1869; interment in Shockoe Hill Cemetery.

**Bibliography:** *DAB*.

**BOTTUM, Joseph H.,** a Senator from South Dakota; born in Faulkton, Faulk County, S.Dak., August 7, 1903; attended the public schools of Faulkton; attended Yankton College and the University of South Dakota 1920-1921; graduated from the law school of the University of South Dakota at Vermillion in 1927; was admitted to the bar in 1927 and commenced the practice of law in St. Paul, Minn., in 1928; state's attorney at Faulkton 1932-1936; State director of taxation 1937-1943; unsuccessful candidate for nomination in 1942 for Governor of South Dakota; unsuccessful candidate for nomination in 1950 to the Eighty-second Congress; lieutenant governor of South Dakota 1960-1962; appointed as a Republican to the United States Senate July 9, 1962, to fill the vacancy caused by the death of Francis Case and served until January 3, 1963; unsuccessful candidate in 1962 for election to the vacancy; circuit judge of Seventh Judicial Circuit; was a resident of Rapid City, S.Dak. until his death there on July 4, 1984; interment in Pine Lawn Cemetery, Rapid City, S.Dak.

**Bibliography:** Clem, Alan. *The Nomination of Joe Bottum: Analysis of a Committee Decision to Nominate a United States Senator*. Vermillion: Govermental Research Bureau, University of South Dakota, 1963.

**BOUCHER, Frederick C.,** a Representative from Virginia; born in Abingdon, Washington County, Va., August 1, 1946; graduated from Abingdon High School in 1964; B.A., Roanoke College, 1968; J.D., University of Virginia School of Law, 1971; associate, Milbank, Tweed, Hadley & McCloy, New York City; partner, Boucher & Boucher, Abingdon, Va.; elected to the Virginia senate in 1975 and reelected in 1979; elected as a Democrat to the Ninety-eighth and to the six succeeding Congresses (January 3, 1983-January 3, 1997); is a resident of Abingdon, Va.

**BOUCK, Gabriel** (nephew of Joseph Bouck), a Representative from Wisconsin; born in Fultonham, Schoharie County, N.Y., December 16, 1828; was graduated from Union College, Schenectady, N.Y., in 1847; studied law; moved to Oshkosh, Winnebago County, Wis., in 1848; was admitted to the bar the same year and commenced practice in Oshkosh; attorney general of the State in 1858 and 1859; member of the State assembly in 1860 and 1874, serving the last year as speaker; served in the Union Army as captain of Company E, Second Regiment, Wisconsin Volunteer Infantry, from July 11, 1861, to April 21, 1862, and as colonel of the Eighteenth Regiment, Wisconsin Volunteer Infantry, from April 22, 1862, to January 4, 1864; delegate to the Democratic National Conventions in 1868 and 1872; unsuccessful Democratic candidate for election in 1874 to the Forty-fourth Congress; elected as a Democrat to the Forty-fifth and Forty-sixth Congresses (March 4, 1877-March 3, 1881); unsuccessful candidate for reelection in 1880 to the Forty-seventh Congress; resumed the practice of law in Oshkosh, Wis., and died there on February 21, 1904; interment in the Riverside Cemetery.

**BOUCK, Joseph** (uncle of Gabriel Bouck), a Representative from New York; born on Bouck's Island, near Fultonham, Schoharie County, N.Y., July 22, 1788; attended the rural schools of his native county; engaged in agricultural pursuits for many years in

Schoharie County until his change of residence to Middleburgh; served as inspector of turnpike roads in Schoharie County in 1828; elected as a Jacksonian to the Twenty-second Congress (March 4, 1831-March 3, 1833); resided in Middleburgh, N.Y., until his death on March 30, 1858; interment in his son's plot in Middleburgh Cemetery.

**BOUDE, Thomas,** a Representative from Pennsylvania; born in Lancaster, Pa., May 17, 1752; attended private schools; during the Revolutionary War served as a lieutenant under General Anthony Wayne with the Second, Fourth, and Fifth Pennsylvania Battalions from January 5, 1776, to November 3, 1783, and was promoted to captain and brevet major; engaged in business as a lumber dealer in Columbia, Lancaster County, Pa.; member and one of the organizers of the Society of the Cincinnati; member of the Pennsylvania house of representatives from 1794 until 1796; elected as a Federalist to the Seventh Congress (March 4, 1801-March 3, 1803); unsuccessful candidate for reelection in 1802 to the Eighth Congress; resumed his former business as a lumber dealer; died in Columbia, Pa., October 24, 1822; interment in that part of Mount Bethel Cemetery known as the "Brick Graveyard."

**BOUDINOT, Elias,** a Delegate and a Representative from New Jersey; born in Philadelphia, Pa., May 2, 1740; received a classical education; studied law; was admitted to the bar in 1760 and commenced practice in Elizabethtown, N.J.; member of the board of trustees of Princeton College from 1772 until 1821; member of the committee of safety in 1775; commissary general of prisoners in the Revolutionary Army, 1776-1779; Member of the Continental Congress in 1778, 1781, 1782, and 1783, serving as President in 1782 and 1783, and signing the Treaty of Paris, which brought about peace with Great Britain; resumed the practice of law; elected to the First, Second, and Third Congresses (March 4, 1789-March 3, 1795); was not a candidate for renomination in 1794 to the Fourth Congress; Director of the United States Mint from October 1795 to July 1805, when he resigned; elected first president of the American Bible Society in 1816; died in Burlington, N.J., October 24, 1821; interment in St. Mary's Protestant Episcopal Church Cemetery.

Bibliography: *DAB*; Boudinot, Elias. *The Life, Public Services, Addresses, and Letters of Elias Boudinot*. 2 vols. 1896. Reprint. New York: Da Capo Press, 1971; Boyd, George Adams. *Elias Boudinot: Patriot and Statesman, 1740-1821*. Princeton, N.J.: Princeton University Press, 1952.

**BOULDIN, James Wood** (brother of Thomas Tyler Bouldin), a Representative from Virginia; born in Charlotte County, Va., in 1792; attended the common schools; studied law; was admitted to the bar April 12, 1813, and commenced practice at Charlotte Court House, Va.; member, Virginia house of delegates, 1825-1826; elected as a Jacksonian to the Twenty-third Congress to fill the vacancy caused by the death of Thomas T. Bouldin; reelected to the Twenty-fourth Congress and reelected as a Democrat to the Twenty-fifth Congress and served from March 15, 1834, to March 3, 1839; chairman, Committee on District of Columbia (Twenty-fifth Congress); resumed the practice of law and also engaged in agricultural pursuits; died at his country home, "Forest Hill," Charlotte County, Va., March 30, 1854; interment in the private burial ground on his estate.

**BOULDIN, Thomas Tyler** (brother of James Wood Bouldin), a Representative from Virginia; born near Charlotte Court House, Charlotte County, Va., in 1781; attended the country schools; studied law; was admitted to the Virginia bar December 6, 1802, and commenced practice at Charlotte Court House, Va.; appointed judge of the circuit court; elected as a Jacksonian to the Twenty-first and Twenty-second Congresses (March 4, 1829-March 3, 1833); unsuccessful candidate for reelection to the Twenty-third Congress; subsequently elected to the Twenty-third Congress to fill the vacancy caused by the death of John Randolph and served from August 26, 1833, until his death in Washington, D.C., February 11, 1834, while addressing the House of Representatives; interment in a private cemetery on his farm, "Golden Hills," near Drakes Branch, Charlotte County, Va.

**BOULIGNY, Charles Dominique Joseph** (uncle of John Edward Bouligny), a Senator from Louisiana; born in New Orleans, La., August 22, 1773; was educated by private tutors; served as ensign in his father's Spanish Regiment; commissioner of the municipal council in 1800; assumed American citizenship when the United States acquired Louisiana through the Louisiana Purchase in 1803; studied law; was admitted to the bar and practiced in New Orleans; member, Louisiana Territorial house of representatives 1806; appointed justice of the peace in New Orleans 1807; served on the committee on public defense during the British invasion in 1814 and 1815; elected to the United States Senate to fill the vacancy caused by the resignation of Henry Johnson and served from November 19, 1824, to March 3, 1829; died in New Orleans, La., on March 4, 1833; interment in St. Louis Cemetery No. 1.

Bibliography: *DAB*.

**BOULIGNY, John Edward** (nephew of Charles Joseph Dominique Bouligny), a Representative from Louisiana; born in New Orleans, La., February 5, 1824; attended the public schools; studied law; was admitted to the bar and commenced practice in New Orleans; held several local offices; elected as the candidate of the American Party to the Thirty-sixth Congress (March 4, 1859-March 3, 1861); was strongly opposed to secession and was the only Louisiana Member to retain his seat after the State seceded on January 26, 1861; retired to private life and remained in the North during the Civil War; died in Washington, D.C., February 20, 1864; interment in the Congressional Cemetery.

**BOULTER, Eldon Beau,** a Representative from Texas; born in El Paso, El Paso County, Tex., February 23, 1942; was graduated from Levelland High School in 1960, the University of Texas in 1965, and the Baylor University Law School, Waco, Tex., in 1968; admitted to the bar in 1968 and practiced law in Amarillo, Tex.; member of the Amarillo City Commission 1981-1983; unsuccessful candidate for nomination to the Ninety-eighth Congress in 1982; elected as a Republican to the Ninety-ninth and One Hundredth Congresses (January 3, 1985-January 3, 1989); was not a candidate in 1988 for reelection to the House of Representatives, but was an unsuccessful candidate for election to the United States Senate; is a resident of Amarillo, Tex.

**BOUND, Franklin,** a Representative from Pennsylvania; born in Milton, Northumberland County, Pa., April 9, 1829; attended the common schools and old Milton Academy; studied law at Easton, Pa.; was admitted to the bar in 1853 and commenced practice in Milton; member of the Pennsylvania senate 1860-1863; delegate to the Republican National Convention in 1868; served as a private in one of the emergency regiments called for the defense of Pennsylvania; was mustered into the United States service and discharged with his regiment; elected as a Republican to the Forty-ninth and Fiftieth Congresses (March 4, 1885-March 3, 1889); was not a candidate for renomination in 1888; resumed the practice of law; died in Milton, Pa., on August 8, 1910; interment in Milton Cemetery.

**BOUQUARD, Marilyn Lloyd,** a Representative from Tennessee. (*See* LLOYD, Marilyn Laird.)

**BOURNE, Benjamin,** a Representative from Rhode Island; born in Bristol, R.I., September 9, 1755; was graduated from Harvard College in 1775; studied law; was admitted to the bar and commenced practice in Providence; held several public offices; quartermaster of the Second Rhode Island Regiment in 1776; member of the general assembly in 1789 and 1790; upon the ratification of the Constitution by the State of Rhode Island was elected to the First through Third Congresses and as a Federalist to the Fourth and Fifth Congresses and served from August 31, 1790, until his resignation in 1796, before the close of the Fourth Congress; appointed judge of the United States District Court for the District of Rhode Island in 1801 and, later, judge of the United States Circuit Court for the Eastern Circuit; died in Bristol, R.I., September 17, 1808; interment in Juniper Hill Cemetery.

**BOURNE, Jonathan, Jr.,** a Senator from Oregon; born in New Bedford, Bristol County, Mass., February 23, 1855; attended private schools and Harvard University; settled in Portland 1878; studied law; was admitted to the bar in 1881 and practiced in Portland 1881-1886; interests in mining, farming, cotton mills, and commercial enterprises; member, Oregon house of representatives 1887-1899; elected as a Republican to the United States Senate and served from March 4, 1907, to March 3, 1913; unsuccessful candidate for renomination in 1912; chairman, Committee on Fisheries (Sixtieth and Sixty-first Congresses), Committee on Post Offices and Post Roads (Sixty-second Congress); president of the National Republican Progressive League; resumed his former pursuits in Oregon and Massachusetts; engaged in newspaper work in Washington, D.C., until his death there on September 1, 1940; interment in Cedar Hill Cemetery.

**Bibliography:** *DAB*; Pike, Albert Jr. "Jonathan Bourne Jr., Progressive." Ph.D. dissertation, University of Oregon, 1957.

**BOURNE, Shearjashub,** a Representative from Massachusetts; born in Barnstable, Mass., June 14, 1746; was graduated from Harvard College in 1764; studied law; was admitted to the bar and commenced practice in Boston; member of the Massachusetts house of representatives 1782-1785 and 1788-1790; member of the convention in 1788 which ratified the Constitution; elected to the Second and Third Congresses (March 4, 1791-March 3, 1795); served as justice of the court of common pleas of Suffolk County from 1799 until his death in Boston, Mass., March 11, 1806.

**BOUTELL, Henry Sherman,** a Representative from Illinois; born in Boston, Mass., March 14, 1856; moved to Chicago, Ill., in 1863; pursued academic studies; was graduated from Northwestern University, Evanston, Ill., in 1874, and from Harvard University in 1876; studied law; was admitted to the bar in 1879 and commenced practice in Chicago, Ill.; member of the Illinois State house of representatives in 1884 and 1885; elected as a Republican to the Fifty-fifth Congress to fill the vacancy caused by the death of Edward D. Cooke; reelected to the Fifty-sixth and to the five succeeding Congresses, and served from November 23, 1897 to March 3, 1911; chairman, Committee on Expenditures in the Department of the Navy (Sixtieth and Sixty-first Congresses); unsuccessful candidate for reelection in 1910 to the Sixty-second Congress; trustee of Northwestern University, 1899-1911; delegate to the Republican National Convention of 1908; appointed Envoy Extraordinary and Minister Plenipotentiary to Portugal on March 2, 1911, but did not proceed to his post; appointed Envoy Extraordinary and Minister Plenipotentiary to Switzerland on April 24, 1911, and served until July 1913, when he resigned; professor of constitutional law at Georgetown University, Washington, D.C., 1914-1923; died while on a trip in San Remo, Italy, March 11, 1926; interment in Pine Grove Cemetery, Westboro, Worcester County, Mass.

**Bibliography:** *DAB*.

**BOUTELLE, Charles Addison,** a Representative from Maine; born in Damariscotta, Lincoln County, Maine, February 9, 1839; attended the public schools at Brunswick and the Yarmouth Academy; adopted the profession of shipmaster; in the spring of 1862 volunteered and was appointed acting master in the United States Navy; served in the North and South Atlantic and West Gulf Squadrons; promoted to lieutenant, May 5, 1864; participated in the capture of Mobile and in receiving surrender of the Confederate Fleet; afterwards assigned to command of naval forces in Mississippi Sound; honorably discharged January 14, 1866; engaged in business in New York; became managing editor of the Bangor (Maine) Whig and Courier in 1870 and purchased controlling ownership in 1874; delegate to the Republican National Convention at Cincinnati in 1876; elected as a Republican to the Forty-eighth and to the nine succeeding Congresses and served from March 4, 1883, until his resignation, March 3, 1901, before the commencement of the Fifty-seventh Congress, to which he had been reelected; chairman, Committee on Naval Affairs (Fifty-first Congress and Fifty-fourth through Fifty-sixth Congresses); by joint resolution of Congress on January 16, 1901, was placed on the retired list of the Navy, with the rank of captain; died in Waverley, Middlesex County, Mass., May 21, 1901; interment in Mount Hope Cemetery, Bangor, Maine.

**Bibliography:** *DAB*.

**BOUTWELL, George Sewall,** a Representative and a Senator from Massachusetts; born in Brookline, Mass., January 28, 1818; attended the public schools; taught school in Shirley, Mass.; engaged in mercantile pursuits in Groton, Mass., in 1841, and in that same year was appointed postmaster of Groton; studied law; member, Massachusetts house of representatives, 1842-1844, 1847-1850; unsuccessful Democratic candidate for election in 1844 to the Twenty-ninth Congress, in 1846 to the Thirtieth Congress, and in 1848 to the Thirty-first Congress; unsuccessful candidate for Governor of Massachusetts in 1849; Massachusetts bank commissioner, 1849-1851; elected Governor of Massachusetts by the Legislature in 1850, and served 1851-1852; member of the Massachusetts constitutional convention in 1853; secretary of the Massachusetts board of education, 1855-1861; member of the board of overseers of Harvard University, 1850-1860; member of the peace convention of 1861 held in Washington, D.C., in an effort to devise means to prevent the impending war; served on the military commission under the War Department in 1862; first Commissioner of Internal Revenue in 1862 and 1863; elected as a Republican to the Thirty-eighth and to the three succeeding Congresses, and served from March 4, 1863 to March 12, 1869, when he resigned; one of the managers appointed by the House of Representatives in 1868 to conduct the impeachment proceedings against President Andrew Johnson; appointed Secretary of the Treasury by President Ulysses S. Grant, and served from March 11, 1869 until March 17, 1873, when he resigned; elected as a Republican to the United States Senate to fill the vacancy caused by the resignation of Henry Wilson, and served from March 17, 1873 until March 3, 1877; chairman, Committee on the Revision of the Laws of the United States (Forty-fourth Congress); appointed by President Rutherford B. Hayes as commissioner to codify and edit the Statutes at Large in 1877; United States counsel before the French and American Claims Commission in 1880; declined appointment as Secretary of the Treasury in 1884; practiced law in Washington, D.C.; counsel for Haiti in 1885, for Hawaii in 1886, and for Chile in 1893 and 1894; president of the Anti-Imperialist League from 1898 until 1905; died in Groton, Mass., February 27, 1905; interment in Groton Cemetery.

**Bibliography:** *DAB*; Boutwell, George S. *Reminiscences of Sixty Years in Public Affairs*. 1902. Reprint. New York: Greenwood Press, 1968; Brown, Thomas H. *George Sewall Boutwell: Human Rights Advocate*. Groton, Mass.: Groton Historical Society, 1989.

**BOVEE, Matthias Jacob,** a Representative from New York; born in Amsterdam, Montgomery County, N.Y., July 24, 1793; attended the rural school until the death of his father in 1807; taught school in winter and worked the family farm in summer; engaged in mercantile pursuits in 1815; chairman of the town of Amsterdam; member of the county board of supervisors; elected a member of the State assembly in 1826; trustee of the village of

Amsterdam in 1831; elected as a Jacksonian to the Twenty-fourth Congress (March 4, 1835-March 3, 1837); returned to Amsterdam and resumed mercantile pursuits; moved to Milwaukee, Wis., in June 1843 and two months later settled near Eagle, Waukesha County, and engaged in agricultural pursuits; justice of the peace for ten years; died in Eagle, Wis., September 12, 1872; interment in Oak Ridge Cemetery.

**BOW, Frank Townsend,** a Representative from Ohio; born in Canton, Stark County, Ohio, February 20, 1901; attended the public schools in Canton and Plain Township, Stark County, Ohio, the University School, Cleveland, Ohio, and Culver Military Academy, Culver, Ind.; attended the law school of Ohio Northern University at Ada in 1921; engaged in postgraduate work at Columbia University, New York City; was admitted to the bar in 1923 and commenced the practice of law in Canton, Ohio; assistant attorney general of Ohio, 1929-1932; during the Second World War became news editor of radio station WHBC, Canton, Ohio, and in 1945 was selected to serve as a war correspondent with Ohio's Thirty-seventh Division in the Philippines; general counsel to Subcommittee on Expenditures, and to the Select Committee To Investigate the Federal Communications Commission, 1947-1949; legislative assistant to Senator Andrew F. Schoeppel, 1949-1951; elected as a Republican to the Eighty-second and to the ten succeeding Congresses, and served from January 3, 1951 until his death in Bethesda, Md., on November 13, 1972; had announced in January 1972 that he would not be a candidate for reelection to the Ninety-third Congress; interment in West Lawn Cemetery, Canton, Ohio.

**BOWDEN, George Edwin** (nephew of Lemuel Jackson Bowden), a Representative from Virginia; born in Williamsburg, James City County, Va., July 6, 1852; attended a private school; studied law; was admitted to the bar but never practiced; engaged in banking; collector of customs for the port of Norfolk from September 1879 until May 1885; elected as a Republican to the Fiftieth and Fifty-first Congresses (March 4, 1887-March 3, 1891); unsuccessful candidate for reelection in 1890 to the Fifty-second Congress; again collector of customs for the port of Norfolk; clerk of the United States Court for the Eastern District of Virginia from March 10, 1899, until his death in Norfolk, Va., January 22, 1908; interment in Elmwood Cemetery.

**BOWDEN, Lemuel Jackson** (uncle of George Edwin Bowden), a Senator from Virginia; born in Williamsburg, James City County, Va., January 16, 1815; graduated from William and Mary College, Williamsburg, Va.; studied law; was admitted to the bar in 1838 and commenced practice in Williamsburg; member, Virginia house of delegates 1841-1846; delegate to the Virginia constitutional conventions in 1849 and 1851; elected as a Republican to the United States Senate and served from March 4, 1863, until his death in Washington, D.C., on January 2, 1864; interment in Congressional Cemetery.

**BOWDLE, Stanley Eyre,** a Representative from Ohio; born in Clifton, Hamilton County, Ohio, September 4, 1868; attended the public schools until fifteen years of age; served an apprenticeship of three years in the machine shops of Cramp's shipyard, Philadelphia, Pa.; studied law, and was graduated from the Cincinnati Law School in 1889; was admitted to the bar the same year and commenced practice in Cincinnati; because of ill health, moved to Colorado and later to Mexico, where he resided from 1897 to 1900; returned to Cincinnati and resumed his profession; member of the State constitutional convention in 1912; elected as a Democrat to the Sixty-third Congress (March 4, 1913-March 3, 1915); unsuccessful candidate for reelection in 1914 to the Sixty-fourth Congress and in 1916 to the Sixty-fifth Congress; mayor of Clifton, Ohio; engaged in the practice of law in Cincinnati, Ohio, until his death there April 6, 1919; interment in Spring Grove Cemetery.

**BOWDON, Franklin Welsh** (uncle of Sydney Johnston Bowie), a Representative from Alabama; born in Chester District, S.C., February 17, 1817; attended the common schools and was graduated from the University of Alabama at Tuscaloosa in 1836; studied law; was admitted to the bar and commenced practice in Talladega, Ala.; member of the State house of representatives in 1844 and 1845; elected as a Democrat to the Twenty-ninth Congress to fill the vacancy caused by the death of Felix G. McConnell; reelected to the Thirtieth and Thirty-first Congresses and served from December 7, 1846, to March 3, 1851; chairman, Committee on Public Buildings and Grounds (Thirty-first Congress); was not a candidate for renomination in 1850; moved to Henderson, Rusk County, Tex., in 1852, where he resumed the practice of his profession; died in Henderson, Tex., June 8, 1857; interment in the City Cemetery.

**BOWEN, Christopher Columbus,** a Representative from South Carolina; born in Providence, R.I., January 5, 1832; attended the public schools; moved to Georgia in 1850; engaged in agricultural pursuits; studied law; was admitted to the bar in 1862 and commenced practice in Charleston, S.C.; during the Civil War enlisted in the Confederate Army and served throughout the war as a captain in the Coast Guard; resumed the practice of law in Charleston, S.C.; member of the Republican State convention at Charleston in May 1867; first chairman of the Republican State central committee; delegate to the State constitutional convention in November 1867; upon the readmission of South Carolina to representation was elected as a Republican to the Fortieth and Forty-first Congresses and served from July 20, 1868, to March 3, 1871; unsuccessful candidate for reelection in 1870 to the Forty-second Congress; member of South Carolina house of representatives, 1871-1872; elected sheriff of Charleston in November 1872; died in New York City, June 23, 1880; interment in St. Laurence Cemetery, Charleston, S.C.

**BOWEN, David Reece,** a Representative from Mississippi; born in Houston, Chickasaw County, Miss., October 21, 1932; graduated from Cleveland (Miss.) High School in 1950; attended the University of Missouri, 1950-1952; A.B., Harvard University, 1954; M.A., Oxford University, Oxford, England, 1956; served in the United States Army, private first class, 1957-1958; assistant professor of political science and history, Mississippi College, Clinton, 1958-1959, and Millsaps College, Jackson, Miss., 1959-1964; employed by the United States Office of Economic Opportunity, 1966-1967; United States Chamber of Commerce, 1967-1968; first coordinator of federal-state programs, State of Mississippi, 1968-1972; elected as a Democrat to the Ninety-third and to the four succeeding Congresses (January 3, 1973-January 3, 1983); was not a candidate for reelection in 1982 to the Ninety-eighth Congress; visiting lecturer, Mississippi State University, 1985-1987; is a resident of Jackson, Miss.

**BOWEN, Henry** (son of Rees Tate Bowen, nephew of John Warfield Johnston, and cousin of William Bowen Campbell), a Representative from Virginia; born at "Maiden Springs," near Tazewell, Tazewell County, Va., December 26, 1841; attended the public schools and Emory and Henry College, Emory, Va.; engaged in agricultural pursuits; entered the Confederate Army in 1861 as a captain of Cavalry in Payne's brigade, Lee's division, Army of Northern Virginia, and served until December 21, 1864, when he was captured by Sheridan's cavalry at Lacy Springs, Va.; released June 19, 1865; returned to his native county and resumed farming; member of the Virginia house of delegates 1869-1873; elected as a Readjuster to the Forty-eighth Congress (March 4, 1883-March 3, 1885); unsuccessful candidate for renomination in 1884 to the Forty-ninth Congress; elected as a Republican to the Fiftieth Congress (March 4, 1887-March 3, 1889); unsuccessful candidate for reelection in 1888 to the Fifty-first Congress; delegate to the Republican National Convention in 1892; resumed agricultural interests and stock raising in Tazewell County, Va.; died at his home, "Maiden Springs," in Tazewell County, April 29, 1915; interment in Jeffersonville Cemetery, Tazewell, Va.

**BOWEN, John Henry,** a Representative from Tennessee; born in Washington County, Va., in September 1780; attended the schools of Lexington, Ky.; studied law; was admitted to the bar and commenced practice in Gallatin, Tenn.; elected as a Republican to the Thirteenth Congress (March 4, 1813-March 3, 1815); engaged in the practice of law in Gallatin, Cherokee County, Tenn., until his death there September 25, 1822.

**BOWEN, Rees Tate** (father of Henry Bowen), a Representative from Virginia; born at "Maiden Springs," near Tazewell, Tazewell County, Va., January 10, 1809; attended Abingdon Academy, Virginia; engaged in agricultural pursuits; appointed brigadier general of the Virginia militia; member of the Virginia house of delegates 1863-1865; magistrate of Tazewell County for several years prior to the war and presiding justice of the county court a portion of that time; elected as a Democrat to the Forty-third Congress (March 4, 1873-March 3, 1875); was not a candidate for renomination in 1874 to the Forty-fourth Congress; resumed agricultural pursuits; died at his home, "Maiden Springs," in Tazewell County, Va., August 29, 1879; interment in the family burying ground on his estate, "Maiden Springs."

**BOWEN, Thomas Mead,** a Senator from Colorado; born near the present site of Burlington, Iowa, October 26, 1835; attended the public schools and the academy at Mount Pleasant, Iowa; studied law; was admitted to the bar in 1853 and practiced; moved to Wayne County, Iowa, in 1856; member, Iowa State house of representatives, 1856; moved to Kansas in 1858; during the Civil War served in the Union Army as a captain of Nebraska and Kansas cavalry units, then as a colonel, September 20, 1862; brevetted brigadier general on February 13, 1865; located in Arkansas after the war; member and president of the constitutional convention of Arkansas in 1866; justice of the supreme court of Arkansas, 1867-1871; appointed Governor of Idaho Territory by President Ulysses S. Grant on April 19, 1871; resigned on September 15, 1871 and returned to Arkansas; moved to Colorado in 1875 and resumed the practice of law; upon the organization of the State government was elected judge of the fourth judicial district, 1876-1880; member, Colorado State house of representatives, 1882; resigned, having been elected as a Republican to the United States Senate, and served from March 4, 1883, to March 3, 1889; chairman, Committee on Mining (Forty-eighth Congress), Committee on Enrolled Bills (Forty-ninth and Fiftieth Congresses); engaged in mining in Colorado, with residence in Pueblo, Colo., where he died December 30, 1906; interment in Roselawn Cemetery.

Bibliography: *DAB.*

**BOWER, Gustavus Miller,** a Representative from Missouri; born near Culpeper, Culpeper County, Va., December 12, 1790; attended the public schools; studied medicine in Philadelphia, Pa.; moved to Kentucky prior to 1812 and resided near Nicholasville; enlisted during the War of 1812 as a surgeon-dresser; was one of the few survivors of the massacre at Frenchtown, near Detroit, January 23, 1813; moved to Monroe County, Mo., in 1833, settled near Paris, and engaged in the practice of medicine and also in agricultural pursuits; elected as a Democrat to the Twenty-eighth Congress (March 4, 1843-March 3, 1845); resumed the practice of medicine; died near Paris, Monroe County, Mo., November 17, 1864; interment in the family burying ground north of Paris, Mo.

**BOWER, William Horton,** a Representative from North Carolina; born near Wilkesboro, Wilkes County, N.C., June 6, 1850; attended the Finley High School at Lenoir, N.C.; studied law; was admitted to the bar in 1870 and commenced practice in Lenoir; moved to California in 1876 and taught school there four years;

returned to Lenoir, N.C., in 1881; member of the State house of representatives in 1882; served in the State senate in 1884; solicitor of the tenth judicial district of North Carolina in 1885 and 1886; unsuccessful candidate for Congress in 1890; elected as a Democrat to the Fifty-third Congress (March 4, 1893-March 3, 1895); unsuccessful candidate for reelection in 1894 to the Fifty-fourth Congress; resumed the practice of law in Lenoir, Caldwell County, N.C., and died there May 11, 1910; interment in Elkville Cemetery, Caldwell County, N.C.

**BOWERS, Eaton Jackson,** a Representative from Mississippi; born in Canton, Madison County, Miss., June 17, 1865; attended the public schools, and Mississippi Military Institute at Pass Christian; studied law; was admitted to the bar in 1883 at the age of seventeen and practiced in Canton until August 1884, when he moved to Bay St. Louis; engaged in the practice of law and in newspaper work; editor and proprietor of the Gulf Coast Progress at Bay St. Louis; member of the Democratic State executive committee 1886-1900; retired from the newspaper business in 1890; member of the State senate in 1896; served in the State house of representatives in 1900; delegate to the Democratic National Conventions in 1900 and 1916; elected as a Democrat to the Fifty-eighth and to the three succeeding Congresses (March 4, 1903-March 3, 1911); was not a candidate for renomination in 1910 to the Sixty-second Congress; resumed the practice of law in Bay St. Louis, Hancock County, Miss.; moved to New Orleans, La., and continued the practice of law until his death there October 26, 1939; interment in Cedar Rest Cemetery, Bay St. Louis, Miss.

**BOWERS, George Meade,** a Representative from West Virginia; born in Gerrardstown, Berkeley County, W.Va., September 13, 1863; educated by private tutors and attended high school; engaged in banking; member of the State house of delegates 1883-1887; supervisor of the United States census for West Virginia in 1890; delegate to the Republican National Convention in 1892; member and treasurer of the board of World's Fair commissioners for West Virginia in 1893; Commissioner of Fisheries from 1898 to 1913, when he resigned; elected as a Republican to the Sixty-fourth Congress to fill the vacancy caused by the death of William G. Brown, Jr.; reelected to the Sixty-fifth, Sixty-sixth, and Sixty-seventh Congresses and served from May 9, 1916, to March 3, 1923; unsuccessful candidate for reelection in 1922 to the Sixty-eighth Congress; president of the People's Trust Co.; died in Martinsburg, W.Va., December 7, 1925; interment in the Presbyterian Cemetery, Gerrardstown, W.Va.

**BOWERS, John Myer,** a Representative from New York; born in Boston, Mass., September 25, 1772; attended the common schools and was graduated from Columbia College, New York City; studied law; was admitted to the bar in 1802 and commenced practice in Cooperstown, N.Y.; moved to his country home, "Lakelands," near Cooperstown, in 1805; presented credentials as a Federalist Member-elect to the Thirteenth Congress to fill the vacancy caused by the death of Representative-elect William Dowse and served from May 26, 1813, to December 20, 1813, when he was succeeded by Isaac William, Jr., who contested the election; resumed the practice of law in Cooperstown, Otsego County, N.Y., where he died February 24, 1846; interment in Lakewood Cemetery.

**BOWERS, William Wallace,** a Representative from California; born in Whitestown, Oneida County, N.Y., October 20, 1834; attended the common schools; moved to Wisconsin in 1854; enlisted as a private in Company I, First Wisconsin Cavalry, February 22, 1862; discharged from the service as second sergeant February 22, 1865; moved to San Diego, Calif., in 1869; engaged in ranching; member of the State assembly in 1873 and 1874; appointed collector of customs of the port of San Diego, Calif., September 25, 1874, and served until his resignation on February 3, 1879; owned and operated a hotel in San Diego 1884-1891; member of the State senate 1887-1889; elected as a Republican to the Fifty-second, Fifty-third, and Fifty-fourth Congresses (March 4, 1891-March 3, 1897); chairman, Committee on Revision of the Laws (Fifty-fourth Congress); unsuccessful candidate for reelection in 1896 to the Fifty-fifth Congress; again appointed collector of customs of the port of San Diego, Calif., on March 15, 1902, and served until March 4, 1906; resided in San Diego, Calif., in retirement until his death there on May 2, 1917; interment in the Masonic Cemetery.

**BOWERSOCK, Justin De Witt,** a Representative from Kansas; born near Columbiana, Columbiana County, Ohio, September 19, 1842; moved to Iowa City, Iowa, in 1860 and engaged in mercantile pursuits and grain shipping; moved to Lawrence, Kans., in 1877 and engaged in banking and in the manufacture of flour, paper, and barbed wire; mayor of Lawrence 1881-1885; elected to the Kansas house of representatives in 1887; member of the State senate in 1895; elected as a Republican to the Fifty-sixth and to the three succeeding Congresses (March 4, 1899-March 3, 1907); was not a candidate for renomination in 1906; interested in banking and manufactures in Lawrence, Kans., until his death there on October 27, 1922; interment in Oak Hill Cemetery.

**BOWIE, Richard Johns,** a Representative from Maryland; born in Georgetown, D.C., June 23, 1807; attended the public schools and Brookville Academy; studied law and was graduated from the Georgetown Law School in 1826; commenced practice in Washington, D.C., in 1826; admitted to practice before the Supreme Court in 1829; moved to Rockville, Md., and engaged in agricultural pursuits and also practiced law; member of the State house of delegates 1835-1837; served in the State senate 1837-1841; delegate to the Whig National Convention at Harrisburg, Pa., in 1840; State's attorney for Montgomery County 1844-1849; elected as a Whig to the Thirty-first and Thirty-second Congresses (March 4, 1849-March 3, 1853); unsuccessful candidate for election in 1853 for Governor of Maryland; resumed the practice of his profession in Rockville; chief judge of the court of appeals of Maryland 1861-1867; chief judge of the sixth judicial circuit, and as such also an associate judge of the court of appeals of Maryland, from November 7, 1871, until his death near Rockville, Montgomery County, Md., March 12, 1881; interment in Rockville Cemetery.

**Bibliography:** *DAB.*

**BOWIE, Sydney Johnston** (nephew of Franklin Welsh Bowdon), a Representative from Alabama; born in Talladega, Talladega County, Ala., July 26, 1865; attended private schools, and was graduated from the law department of the University of Alabama at Tuscaloosa in 1885; was admitted to the bar June 1, 1885, and commenced practice in Talladega, Ala.; city clerk of Talladega in 1885 and 1886; member of the board of aldermen in 1891; member of the Democratic State executive committee 1894-1899; moved to Anniston, Ala., in 1899; elected as a Democrat to the Fifty-seventh, Fifty-eighth, and Fifty-ninth Congresses (March 4, 1901-March 3, 1907); declined to be a candidate for renomination in 1906; moved to Birmingham and continued the practice of law until 1919, when he engaged in business there as an automobile dealer; member of the Southern Education Board in 1908 and 1909; member of the Birmingham Board of Education 1915-1919; chairman of the State educational commission in 1920; delegate at large to the Democratic National Convention in 1920; president of the Alabama Tuberculosis Commission 1920-1922; member of the State harbor commission in 1922 and 1923; died in Birmingham, Ala., May 7, 1928; interment in Elmwood Cemetery.

**BOWIE, Thomas Fielder** (grandnephew of Walter Bowie and brother-in-law of Reverdy Johnson), a Representative from Maryland; born in Queen Anne, Prince Georges County, Md., April 7, 1808; attended Charlotte Hall Academy in St. Marys County, Md., and Princeton College, Princeton, N.J.; was graduated from Union College, Schenectady, N.Y., in 1827; studied law; was admitted to the bar in 1829 and commenced practice in Upper Marlboro, Md.; deputy attorney general for Prince Georges County 1833-1842; member of the State house of delegates 1842-1846; unsuccessful candidate for Governor in 1843; unsuccessful candidate for election in 1850 to the Thirty-second Congress; member of the State constitutional convention in 1851; member of the judicial committee assisting in framing the State's new constitution; presidential elector on the Whig ticket in 1852; elected as a Democrat to the Thirty-fourth and Thirty-fifth Congresses (March 4, 1855-March 3, 1859); was an unsuccessful candidate for renomination in 1858 to the Thirty-sixth Congress; resumed the practice of his profession; died in Upper Marlboro, Md., October 30, 1869; interment in the Waring family burying ground at Mount Pleasant, near Upper Marlboro, Md.

**BOWIE, Walter** (granduncle of Thomas Fielder Bowie), a Representative from Maryland; born in Mattaponi, near Nottingham, Prince Georges County, Md., in 1748; attended Rev. John Eversfield's School, near Nottingham, the common schools in Annapolis, and Craddock's School, near Baltimore, Md.; engaged in agricultural pursuits, was a large landowner, and also was interested in shipping; member of the State constitutional convention in 1776; captain and, later, major of a Prince Georges County company during the Revolution; member of the State house of delegates 1780-1800; served in the State senate 1800-1802; elected as a Republican to the Seventh Congress to fill the vacancy caused by the resignation of Richard Sprigg, Jr.; reelected to the Eighth Congress and served from March 24, 1802, to March 3, 1805; declined to be a candidate for renomination in 1804 to the Ninth Congress; died near Collington, Prince Georges County, Md., November 9, 1810; interment in the family burying ground on his estate.

**BOWLER, James Bernard,** a Representative from Illinois; born in Chicago, Ill., February 5, 1875; attended the parochial and public schools; professional bicycle rider and racer; member of the Chicago City Council 1906-1923; served as commissioner of compensation for the city of Chicago 1923-1927; public vehicle license commissioner for the city of Chicago in 1934; again served as a member in the city council 1928-1953, serving as president pro tempore for eight years; engaged in the insurance business; elected as a Democrat to the Eighty-third Congress to fill the vacancy caused by the death of Adolph J. Sabath; reelected to the Eighty-fourth and Eighty-fifth Congresses and served from July 7, 1953, until his death in Chicago, Ill., July 18, 1957; interment in All Saints Cemetery, Des Plaines, Ill.

**BOWLES, Chester Bliss,** a Representative from Connecticut; born in Springfield, Hampden County, Mass., April 5, 1901; graduated from Choate School, Wallingford, Conn., in 1919 and from Yale University in 1924; businessman in Springfield, Mass., and New York City, 1924-1929; cofounder Benton and Bowles, Inc., an advertising agency, New York City, in 1929 and was chairman of the board, 1936-1941; Connecticut State rationing administrator in 1942, State director in 1942 and 1943, and general manager July-October 1943; administrator, Office of Price Administration, 1943-1946; member, War Production Board and Petroleum Board for War, 1943-1946; chairman, Economic Stabilization Board, 1946; delegate to the United Nations Economic, Scientific and Cultural Organization Conference at Paris in 1946; elected Governor of Connecticut in 1948, and served from January 5, 1949 to January 3, 1951; unsuccessful candidate for reelection in 1950; appointed Ambassador to India and Nepal on October 10, 1951 and served until March 1953; author and lecturer; trustee of the Rockefeller Foundation, the Woodrow Wilson Foundation, and the Franklin D. Roosevelt Foundation; delegate to the Democratic National Conventions of 1940, 1948, and 1956; chairman of the platform committee for the Democratic National Convention of 1960; elected as a

Democrat to the Eighty-sixth Congress (January 3, 1959-January 3, 1961); was not a candidate for renomination in 1960 to the Eighty-seventh Congress; Under Secretary of State from January 24 to December 3, 1961; Presidential Special Representative and Adviser on African, Asian and Latin American Affairs, December 1961 to June 1963; appointed United States Ambassador to India on May 3, 1963 and served until April 1969; retired from public life; was a resident of Essex, Conn., until his death there on May 25, 1986.

**Bibliography:** Bowles, Chester. *Promises to Keep: My Years in Public Life, 1941-1969*. New York: Harper and Row, 1971; Schaffer, Howard B. *Chester Bowles: New Dealer in the Cold War*. Cambridge, Mass.: Harvard University Press, 1993.

**BOWLES, Henry Leland,** a Representative from Massachusetts; born in Athens, Windham County, Vt., January 6, 1866; attended the district schools at Kendricks Corner and Vermont Academy at Saxtons River, Vt.; at the age of eighteen moved to Osage, Iowa, and engaged in agricultural pursuits; later moved to California, where for four years he worked as lumberjack, rancher, and farmer; returned east and settled in Massachusetts, working in Waltham, Salem, and Lynn at various businesses; trustee of the Vermont Academy; moved to Springfield, Mass., in 1898 and operated a chain of restaurants; member of the Governor's council in 1913, 1918, and 1919; delegate to the Republican National Conventions of 1920 and 1924; elected as a Republican to the Sixty-ninth Congress to fill the vacancy caused by the death of George B. Churchill; reelected to the Seventieth Congress and served from September 29, 1925, to March 3, 1929; was not a candidate for renomination in 1928 to the Seventy-first Congress; resumed his former business pursuits; died in Springfield, Mass., May 17, 1932; the remains were cremated and the ashes interred in Springfield Cemetery.

**BOWLIN, James Butler,** a Representative from Missouri; born near Fredericksburg, Spotsylvania County, Va., January 16, 1804; apprenticed to a trade, but abandoned it to teach school; received a classical education; moved to Lewisburg, Greenbrier County, Va., in 1825; studied law; was admitted to the bar in 1826 and commenced practice in Greenbrier County; moved to St. Louis, Mo., in 1833 and continued the practice of law; established the Farmers and Mechanics' Advocate; chief clerk of the State house of representatives in 1836; member of the State house of representatives in 1836 and 1837; appointed district attorney for St. Louis in 1837; unsuccessful candidate for the State house of representatives in 1838; elected judge of the criminal court in 1839 and served until his resignation in 1842; elected as a Democrat to the Twenty-eighth and to the three succeeding Congresses (March 4, 1843-March 3, 1851); chairman, Committee on Private Land Claims (Twenty-ninth Congress), Committee on Public Lands (Thirty-first Congress); unsuccessful candidate for reelection in 1850 to the Thirty-second Congress; appointed Minister Resident to New Granada (Colombia) by President Franklin Pierce on December 13, 1854 and served until May 1857; appointed commissioner to Paraguay by President James Buchanan on September 9, 1858, and served until February 10, 1859; resumed the practice of law; died in St. Louis, Mo., July 19, 1874; interment in Bellefontaine Cemetery.

**BOWLING, William Bismarck,** a Representative from Alabama; born near Iron City, Calhoun County, Ala., September 24, 1870; attended the common schools, and was graduated from the State normal school, Jacksonville, Ala., in 1892; taught in the public schools of Montgomery, Ala., 1893-1895 and of Columbus, Ga., 1896-1899; moved to Lafayette, Chambers County, Ala.; studied law; was admitted to the bar in 1900 and commenced practice in Lafayette; solicitor of the fifth judicial circuit of Alabama 1905-1920; member of the board of trustees of Alabama Polytechnic Institute at Auburn; elected as a Democrat to the Sixty-sixth Congress to fill the vacancy caused by the resignation of J. Thomas Heflin; reelected to the Sixty-seventh and to the three succeeding Congresses and served from December 14, 1920, until his resignation effective August 16, 1928, having been appointed judge for the fifth judicial circuit of Alabama, in which capacity he served until his death; died in Lafayette, Ala., on December 27, 1946; interment in Lafayette Cemetery.

**BOWMAN, Charles Calvin,** a Representative from Pennsylvania; born in Troy, Rensselaer County, N.Y., November 14, 1852; attended the public schools and Lansingburg Academy, Troy, N.Y.; learned the woodworking trade; was graduated in civil engineering from Union College, Schenectady, N.Y., in 1875; engaged in civil engineering work for the State of Massachusetts at Danvers in 1875; organized the western shipping department of the Pennsylvania Coal Co., Pittston, Pa., in 1876, which he managed until 1883; served as general manager of the Florence Coal Co., in 1883 and 1884, later operating as an independent miner and shipper of anthracite coal; mayor of the city of Pittston in 1886; also served as a member of the city council for sixteen terms; delegate to the Independent Republican Pennsylvania convention in 1890 and to the Republican Pennsylvania convention in 1898; presented credentials as a Republican Member-elect to the Sixty-second Congress and served from March 4, 1911, to December 12, 1912, when the seat was declared vacant; unsuccessful candidate for election in 1912 to the Sixty-third Congress; resumed the coal business; died in Pittston, Pa., July 3, 1941; interment in Pittston Cemetery.

**BOWMAN, Frank Llewellyn,** a Representative from West Virginia; born in Masontown, Fayette County, Pa., January 21, 1879; attended the public schools; moved with his parents to Morgantown, W.Va.; was graduated from the University of West Virginia at Morgantown in 1902; teller in a bank at Morgantown from 1902 until 1904, when he resigned to take up the study of law; was admitted to the bar in 1905 and commenced practice in Morgantown, W.Va.; was also interested in coal mining; appointed postmaster of Morgantown on May 25, 1911, and served until April 14, 1915, when a successor was appointed; city mayor in 1916 and 1917; declined renomination for mayor; elected as a Republican to the Sixty-ninth and to the three succeeding Congresses (March 4, 1925-March 3, 1933); unsuccessful candidate for reelection in 1932 to the Seventy-third Congress; organized a coal company in Washington, D.C., and served as president until appointed a member of the Board of Veterans Appeals of the Veterans' Administration in 1935, and served until his death in Washington, D.C., on September 15, 1936; interment in Oak Grove Cemetery, Morgantown, W.Va.

**BOWMAN, Selwyn Zadock,** a Representative from Massachusetts; born in Charlestown, Middlesex County, Mass., May 11, 1840; attended the Charlestown public schools; moved to Somerville, Mass., with his parents in 1855; was graduated from Harvard University in 1860 and from its law school in 1863; was admitted to the bar in 1863 and commenced practice in Boston, Mass., and continued his residence in Somerville, Mass.; member of the Massachusetts house of representatives in 1870, 1871, and again in 1875; city solicitor of Somerville, Mass., in 1872 and 1873; served in the Massachusetts senate in 1876 and 1877; elected as a Republican to the Forty-sixth and Forty-seventh Congresses (March 4, 1879-March 3, 1883); unsuccessful candidate for reelection in 1882 to the Forty-eighth Congress; returned to Somerville, Mass., and resumed the practice of law in Boston, Mass.; again served as city solicitor of Somerville, Mass., 1888-1897; moved to Cohasset, Mass., in 1914, and continued the practice of law in Boston, Mass.; died in Framingham, Mass., September 30, 1928; interment in Mount Auburn Cemetery, Cambridge, Mass.

**BOWMAN, Thomas,** a Representative from Iowa; born in Wiscasset, Lincoln County, Maine, May 25, 1848; moved to Council Bluffs, Iowa, in 1868; engaged in mercantile pursuits; elected treasurer of Pottawattamie County in 1875, and reelected in 1877 and 1879; mayor of Council Bluffs in 1882; appointed postmaster in 1885 and served until 1889, when he resigned; purchased controlling ownership of the Council Bluffs Globe in 1883; elected as a Democrat to the Fifty-second Congress (March 4, 1891-March 3, 1893); was not a candidate for renomination in 1892; again postmaster of Council Bluffs 1904-1908; engaged in railroad contracting; died in Council Bluffs, Iowa, December 1, 1917; interment in Pine Grove Cemetery, Dresden Mills, Maine.

**BOWNE, Obadiah,** a Representative from New York; born near Richmond, Richmond County, Staten Island, N.Y., May 19, 1822; attended private schools, and was a student at Princeton College 1838-1840; held several local offices; elected as a Whig to the Thirty-second Congress (March 4, 1851-March 3, 1853); declined to be a candidate for renomination in 1852; quarantine commissioner 1857-1859; presidential elector on the Republican ticket in 1864; died in Richmond Village, Staten Island, N.Y., April 27, 1874; interment in St. Andrew's Cemetery.

**BOWNE, Samuel Smith,** a Representative from New York; born in New Rochelle, Westchester County, N.Y., April 11, 1800; moved to Otsego County with his parents, who settled near Morris, N.Y.; attended the common schools; engaged in agricultural pursuits; moved to Laurens, Otsego County, in 1825; studied law; was admitted to the bar in 1832 and commenced practice in Laurens; moved to Cooperstown, N.Y.; member of the State assembly in 1834; elected as a Democrat to the Twenty-seventh Congress (March 4, 1841-March 3, 1843); was not a candidate for renomination in 1842; moved to Rochester, N.Y., in 1846 and continued the practice of his profession; judge of Otsego County 1851-1855; resumed the practice of law; died on his farm near Morris, Otsego County, N.Y., July 9, 1865; interment in Friends Burying Ground.

**BOWRING, Eva Kelly,** a Senator from Nebraska; born in Nevada, Vernon County, Mo., January 9, 1892; cattle rancher near Merriman, Nebr.; vice chair, Nebraska Republican Central Committee, 1946-1954; director of the Women's Division of the Republican Party in Nebraska, 1946-1954; appointed as a Republican to the United States Senate, April 16, 1954, to fill the vacancy caused by the death of Dwight P. Griswold, and served from April 26 to November 7, 1954; was not a candidate for election to fill the vacancy; member of the National Advisory Council, National Institutes of Health 1954-1958, and 1960-1961; member, Board of Parole, Department of Justice, 1956-1964; died in Gordon, Nebr., January 8, 1985; interment in Gordon Cemetery.

**Bibliography:** Donovan, R.G. "Lady from the Sand Hills." *Independent Woman* 33 (June 1954): 204-206.

**BOX, John Calvin,** a Representative from Texas; born near Crockett, Houston County, Tex., March 28, 1871; attended the country schools, and Alexander Collegiate Institute (later Lon Morris College), Kilgore, Tex.; studied law; was admitted to the bar in 1893 and commenced practice in Lufkin, Tex.; moved to Jacksonville, Cherokee County, Tex., in 1897 and continued the practice of his profession; also a licensed Methodist minister; judge of the Cherokee County Court 1898-1901; mayor of Jacksonville 1902-1905; member of the Democratic State committee 1908-1910; member of the board of education and served as chairman 1913-1918; elected as a Democrat to the Sixty-sixth and to the five succeeding Congresses (March 4, 1919-March 3, 1931); unsuccessful candidate for renomination in 1930; resumed the practice of law in Jacksonville, Tex., until his death there May 17, 1941; interment in the City Cemetery.

**BOXER, Barbara,** a Representative and a Senator from California; born in Brooklyn, Kings County, N.Y., November 11, 1940; attended public schools of Brooklyn; graduated, Wingate High School, 1958; B.A., Brooklyn College, 1962; stockbroker, 1962-1965; newspaper editor, 1972-1974; aide to Representative John L. Burton, 1974-1976; elected member, board of supervisors, Marin County, Calif., 1976-1982, president, 1980-1981; delegate, California State Democratic convention, 1983; elected as a Democrat to the Ninety-eighth and to the four succeeding Congresses (January 3, 1983-January 3, 1993); was not a candidate in 1992 for reelection to the House of Representatives, but was elected to the United States Senate for the term ending January 3, 1999; is a resident of Los Angeles, Calif.

**BOYCE, William Henry,** a Representative from Delaware; born at Peppers Mills, near Laurel, Sussex County, Del., November 28, 1855; attended the public schools and Laurel Academy; was principal of the public schools at Laurel, 1875-1880, and at Oxford, Md., 1880-1881; recorder of deeds for Sussex County at Georgetown, Del., 1881-1886; studied law; was admitted to the bar in 1887 and practiced in Georgetown, Del., until 1897; president of the board of education, 1883-1886; captain of Company G, Delaware National Guard, 1887-1890; president of the town commissioners, 1895-1897; chairman of the Sussex County Democratic committee, 1893-1897; delegate to the Democratic National Conventions of 1896 and 1924; appointed Delaware secretary of state on January 19, 1897, and served until June 17, 1897, when he resigned; associate judge of the Delaware Supreme Court, 1897-1921, and ex officio judicial reporter, 1909-1921; retired on June 15, 1921; elected as a Democrat to the Sixty-eighth Congress (March 4, 1923-March 3, 1925); unsuccessful candidate for reelection in 1924 to the Sixty-ninth Congress; resumed the practice of law until his retirement in 1936; died in Dover, Del., February 6, 1942; interment in Christ Church Cemetery.

**BOYCE, William Waters,** a Representative from South Carolina; born in Charleston, S.C., October 24, 1818; attended South Carolina College (now the University of South Carolina) at Columbia, and the University of Virginia at Charlottesville; studied law; was admitted to the bar in 1839 and practiced in Winnsboro, S.C.; member of the South Carolina State house of representatives, 1846-1847; elected as a Democrat to the Thirty-third and to the three succeeding Congresses, and served from March 4, 1853 until his retirement on December 21, 1860; chairman, Committee on Elections (Thirty-fifth Congress); appointed a delegate for South Carolina to the Confederate Provisional Congress, January 4, 1861; member of the First and Second Confederate Congresses, 1862-1864; moved to Washington, D.C., in 1866 and practiced law until his retirement a few years before his death; died at his country home, "Ashland," in Fairfax County, Va., February 3, 1890; interment in the Episcopal Cemetery, Winnsboro, Fairfield County, S.C.

**BOYD, Adam,** a Representative from New Jersey; born in Mendham, N.J., March 21, 1746; moved to Bergen County about 1770 and to Hackensack a few years later; member of the board of freeholders and justices in 1773, 1784, 1791, 1794, and 1798; sheriff of Bergen County 1778-1781 and again in 1789; member of the State house of assembly in 1782, 1783, 1787, 1794, and 1795; judge of the court of common pleas of Bergen County 1803-1805; elected as a Republican to the Eighth Congress (March 4, 1803-March 3, 1805); elected to the Tenth Congress to fill the vacancy caused by the death of Ezra Darby; reelected to the Eleventh and Twelfth Congresses and served from March 8, 1808, to March 3, 1813; again judge of the court of common pleas 1813-1833; died in Hackensack, Bergen County, N.J., August 15, 1835; interment in the First Reformed Church Cemetery.

**BOYD, Alexander,** a Representative from New York; born in Albany, N.Y., September 14, 1764; moved to Middleburg, Schoharie County, N.Y., and engaged in agricultural pursuits; elected as a Federalist to the Thirteenth Congress (March 4, 1813-March 3, 1815); died in the town of Esperence, Schoharie County, N.Y., April 8, 1857; interment in Schoharie Cemetery, Schoharie, N.Y.

**BOYD, John Frank,** a Representative from Nebraska; born in Connellsville, Fayette County, Pa., August 8, 1853; moved with his parents to Henry County, Ill., in 1857; attended the public schools and Abingdon (Ill.) College; studied law; was admitted to the bar in 1878 and commenced practice in Galva, Ill.; moved to Nebraska in 1883 and settled in Oakdale, Antelope County; prosecuting attorney of Antelope County, Nebr., 1888-1894; judge of the Ninth Judicial District Court of Nebraska 1900-1907; moved to Neligh, Antelope County, Nebr., in 1901; elected as a Republican to the Sixtieth Congress (March 4, 1907-March 3, 1909); unsuccessful candidate for reelection in 1908 to the Sixty-first Congress; resumed the practice of law in Neligh, Nebr., until 1929, when he retired and moved to Los Angeles, Calif.; died in Los Angeles, Calif., May 28, 1945; interment in Forest Lawn Cemetery.

**BOYD, John Huggins,** a Representative from New York; born in Salem, N.Y., July 31, 1799; attended the common schools, and was graduated from Washington Academy, Salem, N.Y., in 1818; studied law; was admitted to the bar in 1823 and commenced practice in Salem, N.Y., but shortly afterward moved to Whitehall, N.Y.; elected justice of the peace in 1828 and served for many years; member of the State assembly in 1840; supervisor of Whitehall in 1845, 1848, and 1849; elected as a Whig to the Thirty-second Congress (March 4, 1851-March 3, 1853); special surrogate of Washington County 1857-1859; elected president of the village; resumed the practice of law; died in Whitehall, Washington County, N.Y., on July 2, 1868; interment in Evergreen Cemetery, Salem, N.Y.

**BOYD, Linn,** a Representative from Kentucky; born in Nashville, Tenn., November 22, 1800; pursued preparatory studies; moved with his parents to New Design, Trigg County, Ky.; engaged in agricultural pursuits in Calloway County; member of the Kentucky house of representatives, 1827-1832; returned to Trigg County in 1834; elected as a Jacksonian to the Twenty-fourth Congress (March 4, 1835-March 3, 1837); unsuccessful candidate for reelection in 1836 to the Twenty-fifth Congress; elected as a Democrat to the Twenty-sixth and to the seven succeeding Congresses (March 4, 1839-March 3, 1855); chairman, Committee on Accounts (Thirtieth Congress), Committee on Territories (Thirty-first Congress); Speaker of the House of Representatives (Thirty-second and Thirty-third Congresses); moved to Paducah, Ky., in 1852; elected Lieutenant Governor of Kentucky in 1859, but when the senate convened was too ill to preside over its deliberations; died in Paducah, Ky., December 17, 1859; interment in Oak Grove Cemetery.

Bibliography: Hamilton, Holman. "Kentucky's Linn Boyd and the Dramatic Days of 1850." *Register of the Kentucky Historical Society* 55 (July 1957): 185-195.

**BOYD, Sempronius Hamilton,** a Representative from Missouri; born near Nashville, Williamson County, Tenn., May 28, 1828; moved to Missouri in 1840 with his parents, who settled on a farm near Springfield, Greene County; educated by private tutors; moved to California in 1849, where he prospected for gold and taught school; returned to Missouri in 1854; clerk of the court of Greene County 1854-1856; studied law; was admitted to the bar in 1856 and commenced practice in Springfield, Mo.; mayor of Springfield in 1856; during the Civil War raised the Twenty-fourth Missouri Infantry and served as colonel until his election to Congress; elected as an Unconditional Unionist to the Thirty-eighth Congress (March 4, 1863-March 3, 1865); chairman, Committee on Revisal and Unfinished Business (Thirty-eighth Congress); appointed judge of

the court of the fourteenth judicial district in 1865; member of the Republican National Committee 1864-1868; delegate to the Republican National Convention of 1864; interested in building and operating the Southwest Pacific Railroad 1867-1874; elected as a Republican to the Forty-first Congress (March 4, 1869-March 3, 1871); chairman, Committee on Revolutionary Claims (Forty-first Congress); operated a wagon factory from 1874 to 1876; resumed the practice of law; appointed Minister Resident and consul general to Siam by President Benjamin Harrison on October 1, 1890, and served until October 26, 1892; died in Springfield, Greene County, Mo., June 22, 1894; interment in the Hazelwood Cemetery.

**BOYD, Thomas Alexander,** a Representative from Illinois; born near Bedford, Adams County, Pa., June 25, 1830; attended the public schools; was graduated from Marshall College, Mercersburg, Pa., in 1848; studied law in Chambersburg, Pa.; was admitted to the bar and commenced practice in Bedford, Pa.; moved to Lewistown, Ill., in 1856 and engaged in the practice of law until 1861; during the Civil War enlisted in the Seventeenth Regiment, Illinois Infantry, in 1861 and obtained the commission of captain; member of the State senate in 1866 and was reelected in 1870; elected as a Republican to the Forty-fifth and Forty-sixth Congresses (March 4, 1877-March 3, 1881); was not a candidate for renomination in 1880; resumed the practice of law; died in Lewistown, Fulton County, Ill., May 28, 1897; interment in Oak Hill Cemetery.

**BOYDEN, Nathaniel,** a Representative from North Carolina; born in Conway, Mass., August 16, 1796; attended the common schools; served in the War of 1812; was graduated from Union College, Schenectady, N.Y., in 1821; moved to Stokes County, N.C., in 1822; taught school for several years; studied law; was admitted to the bar and practiced; member of the State house of commons in 1838 and 1840; moved to Salisbury, N.C., in 1842 and continued the practice of law; served in the State senate in 1844; elected as a Whig to the Thirtieth Congress (March 4, 1847-March 3, 1849); was not a candidate for renomination in 1848; resumed the practice of law; member of the State constitutional convention of 1865; upon the readmission of North Carolina to representation was elected as a Conservative to the Fortieth Congress and served from July 13, 1868, to March 3, 1869; unsuccessfully contested the election of Francis E. Shober to the Forty-first Congress; resumed the practice of law until elected associate justice of the supreme court of North Carolina in 1872 and served until his death in Salisbury, N.C., November 20, 1873; interment in the Lutheran Cemetery.

**BOYER, Benjamin Markley,** a Representative from Pennsylvania; born in Pottstown, Montgomery County, Pa., January 22, 1823; attended the common schools, and was graduated from the University of Pennsylvania at Philadelphia in 1841; studied law; was admitted to the bar in 1844 and practiced; deputy attorney general of Montgomery County 1848-1850; elected as a Democrat to the Thirty-ninth and Fortieth Congresses (March 4, 1865-March 3, 1869); was not a candidate for renomination in 1868; appointed judge of Montgomery County Court in 1882 and served until his death in Norristown, Pa., August 16, 1887; interment in West Laurel Hill Cemetery, Philadelphia, Pa.

**BOYER, Lewis Leonard,** a Representative from Illinois; born on a farm near Richfield, Richfield Township, Adams County, Ill., May 19, 1886; attended the rural schools; taught school at Douglas, Franklin, Pin Oak, and Liberty, Ill., 1904-1915, and, while teaching, studied civil engineering; moved to Quincy, Ill., in 1915 and engaged in engineering as county superintendent of highways of Adams County, Ill., from March 1915 until December 1936; elected as a Democrat to the Seventy-fifth Congress (January 3, 1937-January 3, 1939); unsuccessful candidate for reelection in 1938 to the Seventy-sixth Congress; unsuccessful candidate for the State senate in 1940 and 1942; died in Quincy, Ill., March 12, 1944; interment in Zander Cemetery, Liberty, Ill.

**BOYKIN, Frank William,** a Representative from Alabama; born in Bladon Springs, Choctaw County, Ala., February 21, 1885; attended the public schools; moved to Fairford, Ala., in 1890 and was employed as a clerk in a store and later as store manager; moved to Malcolm, Ala., in 1905 and engaged in the manufacture of railroad cross ties; moved to Mobile, Ala., in 1915 and was occupied with real estate, farming, livestock, timber, lumber, and naval stores in southern Alabama; during the First World War served as an official in shipbuilding companies; elected as a Democrat to the Seventy-fourth Congress to fill the vacancy caused by the resignation of John McDuffie; reelected to the Seventy-fifth and to the twelve succeeding Congresses and served from July 30, 1935, to January 3, 1963; chairman, Committee on Patents (Seventy-eighth and Seventy-ninth Congresses); unsuccessful candidate for renomination in 1962 to the Eighty-eighth Congress; returned to his many business activities; died in Washington, D.C., March 12, 1969; interment in Pine Crest Cemetery, Mobile, Ala.

**Bibliography:** Boykin, Edward. *Everything's Made for Love in This Man's World; Vignettes from the Life of Frank W. Boykin.* Privately Printed in Mobile, Alabama, 1973.

**BOYLAN, John Joseph,** a Representative from New York; born in New York City, September 20, 1878; attended the public schools, Cathedral School, De La Salle Institute, and Manhattan College, all in New York City; employed as a postal clerk and afterward engaged in the real estate business; member of the New York State assembly, 1909-1913; served in the New York State senate, 1913-1922; elected as a Democrat to the Sixty-eighth and to the seven succeeding Congresses and served from March 4, 1923, until his death in New York City on October 5, 1938; had declined to be a candidate for renomination to the Seventy-sixth Congress due to failing health; chairman, Thomas Jefferson Memorial Commission; interment in Calvary Cemetery, Long Island City, N.Y.

**BOYLE, Charles Augustus,** a Representative from Illinois; born in Spring Lake, Ottawa County, Mich., August 13, 1907; after leaving the farm of his parents he graduated from Mount Carmel High School, Chicago, Ill., in 1925; worked for the Chicago Motor Coach Co. while a student; was graduated from Loyola University, Chicago, Ill., in 1930 and from Loyola Law School in 1933; was admitted to the Illinois bar in 1934 and commenced the practice of law in Chicago, Ill.; zone attorney for the Federal Housing Administration in 1937 and 1938; elected as a Democrat to the Eighty-fourth, Eighty-fifth, and Eighty-sixth Congresses and served from January 3, 1955, until his death in an automobile accident in Chicago, Ill., November 4, 1959; interment in All Saints Cemetery, Des Plaines, Ill.

**BOYLE, Charles Edmund,** a Representative from Pennsylvania; born in Uniontown, Fayette County, Pa., February 4, 1836; attended the common schools, and Waynesburg College, Waynesburg, Greene County, Pa.; studied law; was admitted to the bar in December 1861 and practiced; elected district attorney for Fayette County in 1862; member of the Pennsylvania house of representatives in 1865 and 1866; president of the Democratic State convention in 1867 and 1871; delegate to the Democratic National Convention in 1876 and 1880; elected as a Democrat to the Forty-eighth and Forty-ninth Congresses (March 4, 1883-March 3, 1887); was not a candidate for renomination in 1886; appointed judge of the Territory of Washington in September 1888 and served until his death in Seattle, Wash., December 15, 1888; interment in Oak Grove Cemetery, Uniontown, Pa.

**BOYLE, John,** a Representative from Kentucky; born at "Castle Woods," near Tazewell, Botetourt County, Va., October 28, 1774; moved with his father to Whitleys Station, Ky., in 1779; educated by private tutors and in private schools; studied law; was admitted to the bar in 1797 and commenced practice in Lancaster, Ky.; member of the Kentucky house of representatives in 1800; elected as a Republican to the Eighth and to the two succeeding Congresses (March 4, 1803-March 3, 1809); one of the managers appointed by the House of Representatives, in January 1804, to conduct the impeachment proceedings against John Pickering, and, in December of the same year, against Samuel Chase; chairman, Committee on Public Land Claims (Ninth and Tenth Congresses); appointed Governor of Illinois Territory in 1809, but declined; judge of the Court of Appeals of Kentucky from April 1809 to April 1810, serving as chief justice from April 1810 to November 8, 1826, when he resigned; appointed on December 13, 1826, by President John Quincy Adams as United States judge for the district of Kentucky, and served until his death near Danville, Boyle County, Ky., February 28, 1835; interment in Bellevue Cemetery, Bellevue, Ky.

**BRABSON, Reese Bowen** (uncle of Charles Keith Bell), a Representative from Tennessee; born at Brabsons Ferry, near Knoxville, Tenn., September 16, 1817; attended the Dandridge Academy, Dandridge, Tenn.; was graduated from Maryville College, Maryville, Tenn., in 1840; studied law; was admitted to the bar in 1848 and commenced practice in Chattanooga, Tenn.; also engaged in agricultural pursuits; member of the State house of representatives in 1851 and 1852; elected as a candidate of the Opposition Party to the Thirty-sixth Congress (March 4, 1859-March 3, 1861); was not a candidate for renomination in 1860; engaged in the practice of his profession until his death in Chattanooga, Tenn., August 16, 1863; interment in the Citizens Cemetery.

**BRACE, Jonathan,** a Representative from Connecticut; born in Harwinton, Conn., November 12, 1754; pursued preparatory studies; was graduated from Yale College in 1779; studied law; was admitted to the bar in Bennington, Vt., in 1779 and commenced practice in Pawlet, Vt.; moved to Manchester, Vt., in 1782 and continued the practice of law; member of the council of censors to revise the constitution; prosecuting attorney for Bennington County 1784-1785; moved to Glastonbury, Conn., in January 1786 but was not admitted to the Connecticut bar until 1790; member of the general assembly 1788 and 1791-1794 and was chosen assistant in the council in May 1798; moved to Hartford, Conn., in 1794; judge of the city court from 1797 until 1815, with the exception of two years; elected as a Federalist to the Fifth Congress to fill the vacancy caused by the death of Joshua Coit; reelected to the Sixth Congress and served from December 3, 1798, until his resignation in 1800; assistant in the council of the State 1802-1818; appointed prosecuting attorney for Hartford County in December 1807 and served until May 1809, when he resigned; appointed judge of the county court and of probate in May 1809; continued as judge of the county court until 1821 and as judge of probate until 1824; mayor of Hartford 1815-1824; member of the State senate in 1819 and 1820; died in Hartford, Conn., August 26, 1837; interment in the Old North Cemetery.

**BRACKENRIDGE, Henry Marie,** a Representative from Pennsylvania; born in Pittsburgh, Pa., May 11, 1786; instructed by his father and private tutors; attended a French academy at St. Genevieve, La.; studied law; was admitted to the bar in 1806 and practiced in Somerset, Pa., until 1810; appointed deputy attorney general of the Territory of Orleans (Louisiana) in 1811; district judge of Louisiana in 1812; appointed secretary of a mission to South America in 1817; judge for the western district of Florida from 1821 until 1832; returned to Pennsylvania in 1832, and became owner of a large tract of land in Allegheny County upon which he founded the town of Tarentum, Pa.; elected as a Whig to the Twenty-sixth Congress to fill the vacancy caused by the resignation of Richard Biddle, and served from October 13, 1840 to March 3, 1841; unsuccessful candidate for renomination in 1840 to the Twenty-seventh Congress; member of the commission under the treaty with Mexico in 1841; engaged in literary pursuits until his death in

Pittsburgh, Pa., January 18, 1871; interment in Prospect Cemetery, Brackenridge, Pa.

**Bibliography:** *DAB*; Keller, William F. *The Nation's Advocate: Henry Marie Brackenridge and Young America*. Pittsburgh: University of Pittsburgh Press, 1956.

**BRADBURY, George,** a Representative from Massachusetts; born in Falmouth, Mass., October 10, 1770; was graduated from Harvard University in 1789; studied law; was admitted to the bar and commenced practice in Portland, Maine (until 1820 a district of Massachusetts); member of the Massachusetts house of representatives 1806-1812; elected as a Federalist to the Thirteenth and Fourteenth Congresses (March 4, 1813-March 3, 1817); unsuccessful candidate for renomination in 1816; resumed the practice of law; associate clerk of the Portland Court 1817-1820; member of the State senate in 1820; died in Portland, Maine, November 7, 1823; interment in Eastern Cemetery.

**BRADBURY, James Ware,** a Senator from Maine; born in Parsonsfield, Maine, June 10, 1802; attended the common schools and Gorham Academy; was graduated from Bowdoin College, Brunswick, Maine, in 1825; principal of Hallowell Academy and founder of the first normal school in New England, at Effingham, N.H., in 1829; studied law; was admitted to the bar and commenced practice in Augusta, Maine, in 1830; prosecuting attorney 1834-1838; elected as a Democrat to the United States Senate and served from March 4, 1847, until March 3, 1853; declined to be a candidate for reelection; chairman, Committee on Printing (Thirtieth Congress), Committee on Retrenchment (Thirty-first and Thirty-second Congresses); trustee of Bowdoin College 1861; president of the Maine Historical Society 1867-1887; practiced law in Augusta, Maine; died in Augusta, Maine, January 6, 1901; interment in Forest Grove Cemetery.

**Bibliography:** *DAB*.

**BRADBURY, Theophilus,** a Representative from Massachusetts; born in Newbury, Mass., November 13, 1739; was graduated from Harvard College in 1757; taught school and studied law in Portland, Maine; was admitted to the bar and commenced practice in Portland in 1761; moved to Newburyport, Mass., in 1764 and continued the practice of law; member of the Massachusetts senate 1791-1794; elected as a Federalist to the Fourth and Fifth Congresses and served from March 4, 1795, until July 24, 1797, when he resigned; appointed judge of the supreme court of Massachusetts in 1797, which position he held until his death; member of the electoral college in 1800; died in Newburyport, Mass., September 6, 1803; interment in Newburyport Cemetery.

**Bibliography:** *DAB*.

**BRADEMAS, John,** a Representative from Indiana; born in Mishawaka, Saint Joseph County, Ind., March 2, 1927; graduate of Central High School, South Bend, Ind.; served in the United States Navy in 1945 and 1946; B.A., Harvard University, 1949; D.Phil., Oxford University (Rhodes Scholar for Indiana), 1954; legislative assistant to Senator Patrick V. McNamara of Michigan in 1955; administrative assistant to Representative Thomas L. Ashley of Ohio in 1955; executive assistant to Adlai E. Stevenson in 1955 and 1956; assistant professor of political science, Saint Mary's College, Notre Dame, Ind., in 1957 and 1958; member of congressional delegation to First Inter-American Conference, Lima, Peru, in 1959; unsuccessful candidate for election in 1954 to the Eighty-fourth Congress, and for election in 1956 to the Eighty-fifth Congress; elected as a Democrat to the Eighty-sixth and to the ten succeeding Congresses (January 3, 1959-January 3, 1981); majority whip (Ninety-fifth and Ninety-sixth Congresses); unsuccessful candidate for reelection in 1980 to the Ninety-seventh Congress; president, New York University, New York City; chair, President's Committee on Arts and the Humanities; is a resident of New York City.

**Bibliography:** Brademas, John. *Washington, D.C. to Washington Square*. New York: Weidenfield and Nicolson, 1986.

**BRADFORD, Allen Alexander,** a Delegate from the Territory of Colorado; born in Friendship, Maine, July 23, 1815; moved to Missouri in 1841; studied law; was admitted to the bar and practiced; clerk of the circuit court of Atchison County, Mo., 1845-1851; moved to Iowa and was judge of the sixth judicial district 1852-1855; moved to the Territory of Nebraska; served as a member of the Territorial house of representatives in 1856, 1857, and 1858; moved to the Territory of Colorado in 1860; appointed judge of the supreme court of the Territory by President Lincoln on June 6, 1862; elected as a Republican to the Thirty-ninth Congress (March 4, 1865-March 3, 1867); resumed the practice of law; elected to the Forty-first Congress (March 4, 1869-March 3, 1871); engaged in the practice of law in Pueblo, Colo., until his death there March 12, 1888; interment in the City Cemetery.

**BRADFORD, Taul,** a Representative from Alabama; born in Talladega, Talladega County, Ala., January 20, 1835; attended the local school; was graduated from the University of Alabama at Tuscaloosa in 1854; studied law; was admitted to the bar in 1855 and commenced practice in Talladega, Ala.; served in the Confederate Army as major of the Tenth Regiment, Alabama Infantry, and subsequently became lieutenant colonel of the Thirtieth Regiment, Alabama Infantry; member of the Alabama State house of representatives in 1871 and 1872; elected as a Democrat to the Forty-fourth Congress (March 4, 1875-March 3, 1877); was not a candidate for renomination in 1876 to the Forty-fifth Congress; continued the practice of law in Talladega, Ala., until his death on October 28, 1883; interment in Oak Hill Cemetery, Talladega, Ala.

**BRADFORD, William,** a Senator from Rhode Island; born in Plympton, Plymouth County, Mass., November 4, 1729; studied medicine in Hingham, Mass., and afterwards practiced in Warren, R.I.; moved to Bristol, R.I.; abandoned the profession of medicine and studied law; was admitted to the Rhode Island bar in 1767 and commenced practice in Bristol; member of the Rhode Island house of representatives for several terms between 1761 and 1803, serving as speaker on several occasions; member of the Rhode Island Committee of Correspondence in 1773; deputy governor of Rhode Island, 1775-1778; elected as a Delegate to the Continental Congress in 1776, but did not attend; elected to the United States Senate, and served from March 4, 1793 until his resignation in October 1797; served as President pro tempore of the Senate during the Fifth Congress; retired to his home in Bristol, R.I., and died there on July 6, 1808; interment in East Burial Ground.

**BRADLEY, Edward,** a Representative from Michigan; born in East Bloomfield, Ontario County, N.Y., in April 1808; attended the common schools and the local academy in Canandaigua; associate judge of the common pleas court of Ontario County, N.Y., in 1836; moved to Detroit, Mich., in 1839; studied law; was admitted to the bar in 1841 and commenced practice in Marshall, Calhoun County, Mich.; prosecuting attorney of Calhoun County in 1842; member of the State senate in 1842 and 1843; elected as a Democrat to the Thirtieth Congress and served from March 4, 1847, until his death on August 5, 1847, in New York City while en route to Washington, D.C., before the assembling of Congress; interment in the Congressional Cemetery, Washington, D.C.

**BRADLEY, Frederick Van Ness,** a Representative from Michigan; born in Chicago, Ill., April 12, 1898; moved to Rogers City, Mich., in 1910; attended the public schools, Rogers City (Mich.) High School, and Montclair (N.J.) Academy; served in the Student Army Training Corps at Plattsburgh, N.Y., in 1918; was graduated from Cornell University, Ithaca, N.Y., in 1921; salesman with the Michigan Limestone and Chemical Co., Buffalo, N.Y., 1921-1923, and purchasing agent, 1928-1938; also purchasing agent, Bradley

Transportation Co., Rogers City, Mich., 1924-1938; elected as a Republican to the Seventy-sixth and to the four succeeding Congresses and served from January 3, 1939, until his death on May 24, 1947, at New London, Conn., while there as a member of the Board of Visitors to the Coast Guard Academy; chairman, Committee on Merchant Marine and Fisheries (Eightieth Congress); interment in Rogers City Memorial Park, Rogers City, Mich.

**BRADLEY, Michael Joseph,** a Representative from Pennsylvania; born in Philadelphia, Pa., May 24, 1897; attended the parochial and public high schools; engaged as a telegrapher from 1914 until 1917; during the First World War served overseas as a chief radio electrician in the United States Navy, 1917-1919; engaged in the security and brokerage business in Philadelphia, Pa., 1921-1935; deputy insurance commissioner of Pennsylvania, 1935-1937; unsuccessful candidate for election in 1934 to the Seventy-fourth Congress; elected as a Democrat to the Seventy-fifth and to the four succeeding Congresses (January 3, 1937-January 3, 1947); was not a candidate for renomination in 1946 to the Eightieth Congress; chairman of the Democratic county executive committee of Philadelphia, 1946-1948; collector of customs for district No. 11, Port of Philadelphia, 1948-1953; deputy managing director, city of Philadelphia, 1953-1955; member of Pennsylvania Navigation Commission for the Delaware River, 1954-1964; chairman, Board of Fair Labor Standards, city of Philadelphia, 1954-1962; became a member of the Philadelphia Board of Revision of Taxes in April 1955; retired in 1976; resided in Philadelphia, Pa., where he died on November 27, 1979; interment in Holy Cross Cemetery, Yeadon, Pa.

**BRADLEY, Nathan Ball,** a Representative from Michigan; born in Lee, Berkshire County, Mass., May 28, 1831; moved with his parents to Lorain County, Ohio, in 1835; attended the common schools; moved to Wisconsin in 1849; employed in a sawmill in the pine region; returned to Ohio in 1850 and built and operated a sawmill until 1852, when he moved to Lexington, Mich., and engaged in the manufacture of lumber; moved to St. Charles, in the Saginaw Valley, in 1855 and engaged in the lumber industry; purchased a mill in Bay City, Mich., which he operated from 1858 to 1864; engaged in the salt industry in Bay City; justice of the peace three terms, a supervisor one term, an alderman three terms, and the first mayor of Bay City after it obtained its charter in 1865; member of the State senate 1866-1868; engaged in banking in 1867; vice president of the First National Bank of Bay City; elected as a Republican to the Forty-third and Forty-fourth Congresses (March 4, 1873-March 3, 1877); was not a candidate for renomination in 1876 to the Forty-fifth Congress; again engaged in the lumber business in Bay City and also was instrumental in establishing the first beet-sugar factory in the State; died in Bay City, Bay County, Mich., November 8, 1906; interment in Elm Lawn Cemetery.

**BRADLEY, Stephen Row** (father of William Czar Bradley), a Senator from Vermont; born in Wallingford, Conn., February 20, 1754; was graduated from Yale College in 1775; studied law; was admitted to the bar in 1779 and commenced practice in Westminster, Vt.; captain of a volunteer company during the Revolutionary War; State's attorney for Cumberland County 1780; register of probate for Westminster 1782; appointed judge of Windham County 1783; member, State house of representatives 1785, serving as speaker; appointed associate judge of the superior court of Vermont 1788; member of the city council of Westminster 1798; upon the admission of Vermont as a State into the Union was elected to the United States Senate and served from October 17, 1791, to March 3, 1795; unsuccessful candidate for reelection in 1795; again elected to the United States Senate in 1801 to fill the vacancy caused by the resignation of Elijah Paine; reelected in 1807, and served from October 15, 1801, to March 3, 1813; served as President pro tempore of the Senate during the Seventh and Tenth Congresses; retired from public life and returned to Westminster; moved to Walpole,

N.H., in 1818 and died there December 9, 1830; interment in the Old Cemetery, Westminster, Vt.

Bibliography: *DAB.*

**BRADLEY, Thomas Joseph,** a Representative from New York; born in New York City January 2, 1870; attended the public schools; was graduated from the College of the City of New York in 1887; taught in the public schools of New York City from 1887 until 1891; was graduated from the law department of the University of New York, New York City, in 1889; was admitted to the bar in 1891 and commenced practice in New York City; deputy assistant district attorney of the county of New York 1892-1895; resumed the practice of law; elected as a Democrat to the Fifty-fifth and Fifty-sixth Congresses (March 4, 1897-March 3, 1901); was not a candidate for renomination in 1900; continued the practice of law until his death in New York City April 1, 1901; interment in Calvary Cemetery.

**BRADLEY, Thomas Wilson,** a Representative from New York; born in Yorkshire, England, April 6, 1844; emigrated to the United States in 1846 with his parents, who settled in Walden, Orange County, N.Y.; attended school until nine years of age; during the Civil War entered the Union Army as a private; promoted to captain in the One Hundred and Twenty-fourth Regiment, New York Volunteer Infantry; was aide-de-camp to Major General Mott, Third Division, Second Army Corps; awarded the Congressional Medal of Honor "for gallantry at Chancellorsville"; was brevetted major of United States Volunteers; member of the State house of assembly in 1876; delegate to the Republican National Conventions of 1892, 1896, and 1900; elected as a Republican to the Fifty-eighth and to the four succeeding Congresses (March 4, 1903-March 3, 1913); was not a candidate for renomination in 1912 to the Sixty-third Congress; engaged in banking; president and treasurer of the New York Knife Co.; died in Walden, N.Y., May 30, 1920; interment in Wallkill Valley Cemetery.

**BRADLEY, William Czar** (son of Stephen Row Bradley), a Representative from Vermont; born in Westminster, Vt., March 23, 1782; received his early education in the schools of Cheshire, Conn., and Charlestown, N.H., and for a short time attended Yale College, New Haven, Conn.; studied law; was admitted to the bar in 1802 and commenced practice in Westminster; prosecuting attorney for Windham County, 1804-1811; member of the Vermont State house of representatives in 1806, 1807, and 1819; member of the Governor's council in 1812; elected as a Republican to the Thirteenth Congress (March 4, 1813-March 3, 1815); agent of the United States under the Treaty of Ghent to fix the boundary line between Maine and Canada, 1815-1820; elected to the Eighteenth and Nineteenth Congresses (March 4, 1823-March 3, 1827); resumed the practice of law; unsuccessful Democratic candidate for election in 1834, 1835, 1836, 1837 and 1838 for Governor of Vermont; again a member of the State house of representatives in 1850; presidential elector on the Republican ticket in 1856; member of the State constitutional convention in 1857; retired from the practice of his profession in 1858; died in Westminster, Windham County, Vt., March 3, 1867; interment in the Old Cemetery.

Bibliography: *DAB.*

**BRADLEY, William O'Connell,** a Senator from Kentucky; born near Lancaster, Garrard County, Ky., March 18, 1847; educated by private tutors and at a private school in Somerset, Ky.; during the Civil War entered the Union Army at the age of fifteen, but because of his youth served only a short time; studied law and was licensed to practice in 1865; prosecuting attorney of Garrard County in 1870; unsuccessful candidate in 1887 for election for Governor of Kentucky; appointed Minister to Korea on March 30, 1889, but declined appointment; member of the Republican National Committee, 1890-1896; elected Governor of Kentucky in 1895, and served from December 1895 to December 12, 1899; elected as a Republican to the United States Senate, and served from March 4, 1909 until his death in Washington, D.C., May 23, 1914; chairman, Committee on Expenditures in the Department of Justice (Sixty-first and Sixty-second Congresses), Committee to Investigate Trespassers upon Indian Land (Sixty-first Congress), Committee on Revolutionary Claims (Sixty-third Congress); interment in State Cemetery, Frankfort, Ky.

**BRADLEY, William Warren (Bill),** a Senator from New Jersey; born in Crystal City, Jefferson County, Mo., July 28, 1943; attended Crystal City Public Schools; graduated Crystal City High School, 1961; B.A., Princeton University, 1965; M.A., Oxford University, England, 1968; member of the United States Olympic Team in 1964; served in the United States Air Force Reserve from 1967 until 1978; author; professional basketball player, New York Knicks, 1967-1977; elected as a Democrat to the United States Senate in 1978; reelected in 1984 and 1990, and served from January 3, 1979 to January 3, 1997; was not a candidate for reelection in 1996; is a resident of Denville, N.J.

**Bibliography:** Bradley, Bill. *Time Present, Time Past: A Memoir.* New York: Alfred A. Knopf, 1996.

**BRADLEY, Willis Winter,** a Representative from California; born in Ransomville, Niagara County, N.Y., June 28, 1884; moved with his parents to Milnor, N.Dak., in July 1884 and to Forman, N.Dak., in 1891; attended the public schools, and Hamlin University, St. Paul, Minn.; deputy registrant of deeds of Sargent County, N.Dak., in 1902 and 1903; was graduated from the United States Naval Academy in 1906; during the First World War served as gunnery officer and as chief of the Explosives Section, Bureau of Ordnance, Navy Department; awarded the Congressional Medal of Honor; Governor of Guam, 1929-1931; captain of the Pearl Harbor Navy Yard, 1933-1935; attached to the Board of Inspection and Survey, Pacific Coast Section, 1940-1946; in 1946 retired from the United States Navy because of physical incapacity incurred in the line of duty; took up residence in Long Beach, Calif., in 1931; elected as a Republican to the Eightieth Congress (January 3, 1947-January 3, 1949); was an unsuccessful candidate for reelection in 1948 to the Eighty-first Congress; assistant to the president of the Pacific Coast Steamship Co., 1949-1952; member of the California State assembly from 1952 until his death in Santa Barbara, Calif., August 27, 1954; interment in Fort Rosecrans National Cemetery, San Diego, Calif.

**BRADSHAW, Samuel Carey,** a Representative from Pennsylvania; born in Plumstead, Bucks County, Pa., June 10, 1809; attended the public schools; was graduated from Pennsylvania Medical College in 1833 and practiced in Quakertown, Bucks County, Pa.; elected as a Whig to the Thirty-fourth Congress (March 4, 1855-March 3, 1857); unsuccessful candidate for reelection in 1856 to the Thirty-fifth Congress; died in Quakertown, Pa., June 9, 1872; interment in Friends Burial Ground.

**BRADY, James Dennis,** a Representative from Virginia, born in Portsmouth, Va., April 3, 1843; moved to New York City when twelve years of age; attended the public schools; engaged in mercantile pursuits; during the Civil War enlisted as a private in the Thirty-seventh New York Volunteers and was successively promoted to the grades of lieutenant and adjutant, captain, major, and lieutenant colonel of the Sixty-third New York Volunteers, holding the latter rank when mustered out of service in July 1865; returned to Portsmouth, Va., after the war and was elected clerk of the corporation court of Portsmouth, which position he held until June 1877; appointed collector of internal revenue for the second district of Virginia and served from June 1877 until his death, with the exception of eight years (1885-1889, 1893-1897) under the two administrations of President Grover Cleveland; delegate to the Republican National Conventions of 1880, 1888, and 1896; elected as a Republican to the Forty-ninth Congress (March 4, 1885-March 3, 1887); was not a candidate for renomination in 1886 to the

Fiftieth Congress; member of the Republican National Committee 1888-1892; studied law; was admitted to the bar in 1892 and commenced practice in Washington, D.C.; died in Petersburg, Dinwiddie County, Va., November 30, 1900; interment in St. Joseph's Cemetery.

**BRADY, James Henry,** a Senator from Idaho; born in Indiana County, Pa., June 12, 1862; moved with his parents to Johnson County, Kans., in 1865; attended the public schools and Leavenworth Normal College; taught school; edited a newspaper in Enterprise, Kans.; engaged in the real estate business at Abilene, Kans.; moved to Chicago, Ill., in 1890 and engaged in the sale of Texas lands; moved to Idaho in 1895 and became interested in the development of water power and in irrigation projects; chairman of the Republican State central committee, 1904-1908; president of the Trans-Mississippi Commercial Congress; vice president of the National Irrigation Congress, 1904-1906; elected Governor of Idaho in 1908 and served from January 4, 1909 to January 2, 1911; unsuccessful candidate for reelection in 1910; elected as a Republican to the United States Senate in 1913 to fill the vacancy caused by the death of Weldon B. Heyburn; reelected in 1914, and served from February 6, 1913, until his death in Washington, D.C., January 13, 1918; chairman, Committee on National Banks (Sixty-second Congress), Committee on Disposition of Useless Executive Papers (Sixty-fifth Congress); was cremated and the ashes deposited in the James H. Brady Memorial Chapel in Mountain View Cemetery, Pocatello, Bannock County, Idaho.

**BRADY, Jasper Ewing,** a Representative from Pennsylvania; born in Sunbury, Northumberland County, Pa., March 4, 1797; attended the common schools; learned the hatter's trade; taught school in Franklin County, Pa.; studied law; was admitted to the bar in 1827 and commenced practice in Chambersburg, Franklin County, Pa.; served as treasurer of Franklin County for three years; member of the Pennsylvania house of representatives in 1844 and 1845; elected as a Whig to the Thirtieth Congress (March 4, 1847-March 3, 1849); unsuccessful candidate for reelection in 1848 to the Thirty-first Congress; moved to Pittsburgh, Pa., in September 1849 and resumed the practice of law; clerk in the office of the paymaster general in the War Department, Washington, D.C., 1861-1869; retired from active business pursuits in 1869 and resided in Washington, D.C., until his death in that city on January 26, 1871; interment in City Cemetery, Sunbury, Northumberland County, Pa.; reinterment in Rock Creek Cemetery, Washington, D.C., in 1893.

**BRADY, Nicholas Frederick,** a Senator from New Jersey; born in New York City, April 11, 1930; graduated from St. Mark's School, Southboro, Mass., 1948; B.A., Yale University, 1952; M.B.A., Harvard University Business School, 1954; investment banker; chairman, Dillon, Read and Co., Inc.; appointed as a Republican to the United States Senate on April 12, 1982, to fill the vacancy caused by the resignation of Harrison A. Williams, Jr., and served from April 12, 1982 until his resignation on December 27, 1982; declined to be a candidate for election in 1982 to a full term; resumed banking and business interests in New York City; chairman of the Presidential Task Force on Market Mechanisms ("Brady Commission"), 1987; served as Secretary of the Treasury in the Cabinet of President Ronald Reagan, and in the Cabinet of President George Bush, September 15, 1988 to January 1993; chairman, Darby Overseas Investments, Ltd.; is a resident of Trappe, Md.

**BRAGG, Edward Stuyvesant,** a Representative from Wisconsin; born in Unadilla, Otsego County, N.Y., February 20, 1827; attended the district schools, the local academy, and Geneva (later Hobart) College at Geneva, N.Y.; studied law; was admitted to the bar in 1848 and commenced practice in Unadilla; moved to Fond du Lac, Wis., in 1850 and continued the practice of law; elected district attorney in 1853; delegate to the Democratic National Convention at Charleston in 1860; entered the Union Army as a captain in the Sixth Regiment, Wisconsin Volunteer Infantry, July 16, 1861; major September 17, 1861; lieutenant colonel June 21, 1862; colonel March 24, 1863; brigadier general of Volunteers June 25, 1864; mustered out of the service October 9, 1865; appointed postmaster of Fond du Lac by President Andrew Johnson in 1866; member of the State senate in 1868 and 1869; delegate to the Democratic National Conventions of 1872, 1880 and 1896; unsuccessful candidate for election to the United States Senate in 1874; elected as a Democrat to the Forty-fifth and to the two succeeding Congresses (March 4, 1877-March 3, 1883); chairman, Committee on Expenditures in the Department of Justice (Forty-fifth Congress), Committee on War Claims (Forty-sixth Congress); was not a candidate for renomination in 1882 to the Forty-eighth Congress; elected to the Forty-ninth Congress (March 4, 1885-March 3, 1887); chairman, Committee on Military Affairs (Forty-ninth Congress); was not a candidate for renomination in 1886 to the Fiftieth Congress; resumed the practice of law in Fond du Lac, Wis.; appointed Envoy Extraordinary and Minister Plenipotentiary to Mexico January 16, 1888, and served from March 5, 1888, to May 27, 1889; appointed consul general at Habana, Cuba, May 19, 1902, and assumed charge June 30, 1902; appointed consul general at Hong Kong, China, September 15, 1902, and assumed his duties March 1, 1903; resigned, effective May 1, 1906; died in Fond du Lac, Wis., June 20, 1912; interment in the Rienzi Cemetery.

**Bibliography:** *DAB*; Hardgrove, J.G. "General Edward S. Bragg's Reminiscences." *Wisconsin Magazine of History* 33 (March 1950): 281-309.

**BRAGG, John,** a Representative from Alabama; born near Warrenton, Warren County, N.C., January 14, 1806; attended the local academy at Warrenton, and was graduated from the University of North Carolina at Chapel Hill in 1824; studied law; was admitted to the bar in 1830 and commenced practice in Warrenton; member of the State house of commons of North Carolina 1830-1834; moved to Mobile, Ala., in 1836 and continued the practice of law; was appointed judge of the tenth judicial circuit in 1842; member of the State house of representatives; elected as a Democrat to the Thirty-second Congress (March 4, 1851-March 3, 1853); declined to be a candidate for reelection in 1852; resumed the practice of his profession; delegate from Mobile to the State constitutional convention in 1861; died in Mobile, Ala., August 10, 1878; interment in Magnolia Cemetery.

**BRAGG, Thomas,** a Senator from North Carolina; born in Warrenton, Warren County, N.C., November 9, 1810; attended the Warrenton Academy; was graduated from Captain Partridge's Military Academy, Middletown, Conn.; studied law; was admitted to the bar in 1833 and commenced practice in Jackson, Northampton County, N.C.; member, North Carolina State house of commons, 1842-1843; prosecuting attorney for Northampton County; elected Governor of North Carolina in 1854, reelected in 1856, and served from January 1, 1855 to January 1, 1859; elected as a Democrat to the United States Senate and served from March 4, 1859, until March 6, 1861, when he joined other secessionist Senators and withdrew; expelled from the Senate by a resolution of July 11, 1861, for support of the Confederacy; appointed Attorney General of the Confederate States of America on November 21, 1861, and served until March 18, 1862; resumed the practice of law; died in Raleigh, N.C., January 21, 1872; interment in Oakwood Cemetery.

**Bibliography:** *DAB*; Cowper, Pulaski. "Thomas Bragg." In *Lives of Distinguished North Carolinians.* pp. 306-32. Edited by William Peele. Raleigh: North Carolina Publishing Society, 1898.

**BRAINERD, Lawrence,** a Senator from Vermont; born in East Hartford, Conn., March 16, 1794; went to Troy, N.Y., in 1803 to reside with an uncle and in 1808 moved with him to St. Albans, Vt.; completed preparatory studies; taught school; employed as a clerk in a mercantile establishment until 1816; engaged in mercantile, banking, navigation, and railroad enterprises; elected to the state legislature in 1834; affiliated with the Whig Party until 1840, when he became a member of the Liberty Party; unsuccessful Free-Soil candidate for election in 1846, 1847, 1852 and 1853 for Governor of Vermont; elected as a member of the Free-Soil Party to the United States Senate to fill the vacancy caused by the death of William Upham and served from October 14, 1854, to March 3, 1855; was not a candidate for reelection; nonimated for Governor but declined; resumed business activities; died in St. Albans, Franklin County, Vt., May 9, 1870; interment in Greenwood Cemetery.

**Bibliography:** *DAB*.

**BRAINERD, Samuel Myron,** a Representative from Pennsylvania; born in Albion, Erie County, Pa., November 13, 1842; attended the public schools, Edinboro Normal School, and Ann Arbor (Mich.) Law School; was admitted to the bar in 1869 and commenced practice in North East, Erie County, Pa.; district attorney of Erie County 1872-1875; moved to Erie, Pa., in 1874 and continued the practice of law; chairman of the Republican county committee in 1880; elected as a Republican to the Forty-eighth Congress (March 4, 1883-March 3, 1885); unsuccessful candidate for renomination in 1884; resumed the practice of law in Erie, Pa., and died there November 21, 1898; interment in the City Cemetery.

**BRAMBLETT, Ernest King,** a Representative from California; born in Fresno, Calif., April 25, 1901; attended the public schools; was graduated from Stanford University in 1925; engaged in graduate work at Stanford, Fresno State, San Jose State, and the University of Southern California; engaged in the insurance and automobile business, 1925-1928, and in educational work from 1928 until 1946; mayor of Pacific Grove, 1939-1947; coordinator of Monterey County schools, 1943-1946; member of the Republican Central Committee, 1944-1946; elected as a Republican to the Eightieth and to the three succeeding Congresses (January 3, 1947-January 3, 1955); was not a candidate for renomination in 1954 to the Eighty-fourth Congress; engaged as a consultant in southern California, 1955-1966; was a resident of Woodland Hills, Calif., until his death on December 27, 1966.

**BRANCH, John** (uncle of Lawrence O'Bryan Branch and great-uncle of William Augustus Blount Branch), a Senator and a Representative from North Carolina; born in Halifax, Halifax County, N.C., November 4, 1782; appointed commissioner for valuation of lands and dwellings and enumeration of slaves, third district of North Carolina 1799; was graduated from the University of North Carolina at Chapel Hill in 1801; studied law; was admitted to the bar; member, State senate 1811-1817, 1822, serving as speaker 1815-1817; Governor of North Carolina 1817-1820; appointed Federal judge for the western district of Florida by President James Monroe in 1822; elected to the United States Senate in 1822; reelected in 1829, and served from March 4, 1823, to March 9, 1829, when he resigned; chairman, Committee on Agriculture (Twentieth Congress); appointed Secretary of the Navy by President Andrew Jackson and served from March 9, 1829, until his resignation, effective May 12, 1831, having been elected to Congress; elected as a Democrat to the Twenty-second Congress and served from May 12, 1831, to March 3, 1833; was not a candidate for renomination in 1832 to the Twenty-third Congress; member of the State constitutional convention in 1835; appointed Governor of Florida Territory by President John Tyler and served from June 21, 1844, until the election of a Governor under the State constitution in 1845; died in Enfield, Halifax County, N.C., January 3, 1863; interment in the family burial ground.

**Bibliography:** *DAB*.

BRANCH, Lawrence O'Bryan (father of William Augustus Blount Branch and nephew of John Branch), a Representative from North Carolina; born in Enfield, Halifax County, N.C., November 28, 1820; pursued a preparatory course under a private teacher in Washington, D.C., and at the Bingham Military Academy in North Carolina; attended the University of North Carolina at Chapel Hill for a short time and was graduated from Princeton College in 1838; studied law at Nashville, Tenn., and owned and edited a newspaper there; moved to Tallahassee, Fla., in 1840; was admitted to the bar in Florida in 1840 by a special act of the legislature and commenced practice in Tallahassee; fought in the Seminole War in 1841; moved to Raleigh, N.C., in 1852 and continued the practice of law; president of the Raleigh & Gaston Railroad Co.; elected as a Democrat to the Thirty-fourth, Thirty-fifth, and Thirty-sixth Congresses (March 4, 1855-March 3, 1861); was not a candidate for renomination in 1860 to the Thirty-seventh Congress; appointed Secretary of the Treasury by President James Buchanan on December 2, 1860, but declined; entered the Confederate Army and was appointed brigadier general on November 16, 1861; senior brigadier general in A.P. Hill's Light Division, Stonewall Jackson's corps; killed in the Battle of Antietam, Md., while in command of the Fourth Brigade, North Carolina Troops, September 17, 1862; interment in Old City Cemetery, Raleigh, N.C.

BRANCH, William Augustus Blount (son of Lawrence O'Bryan Branch and great-nephew of John Branch), a Representative from North Carolina; born in Tallahassee, Fla., February 26, 1847; moved with his father to Raleigh, N.C., in 1852; attended Lovejoy's Academy, Raleigh, N.C., Bingham Military Academy near Mebane, N.C., the University of North Carolina at Chapel Hill, and Virginia Military Institute at Lexington; joined the Confederate Army and served as a courier on the staff of General Robert F. Hoke; surrendered with General Joseph E. Johnston's army in 1865; studied law but never practiced; in 1867 took charge of his landed estate near Washington, Beaufort County, N.C., and engaged in agricultural pursuits; elected as a Democrat to the Fifty-second and Fifty-third Congresses (March 4, 1891-March 3, 1895); unsuccessful candidate for reelection in 1894 to the Fifty-fourth Congress; again engaged in agricultural pursuits on his estate; member of the North Carolina State house of representatives in 1896; died in Washington, N.C., November 18, 1910; interment in Oakdale Cemetery.

BRAND, Charles, a Representative from Ohio; born in Urbana, Champaign County, Ohio, November 1, 1871; attended the graded schools of his native city and Ohio Wesleyan University, Delaware, Ohio; engaged in agricultural pursuits, manufacturing, and banking at Urbana; member and president of the Urbana City Council 1911-1912; member of the State senate in 1921 and 1922; served as a member of the advisory committee of the War Finance Corporation in 1921; elected as a Republican to the Sixty-eighth and to the four succeeding Congresses (March 4, 1923-March 3, 1933); was not a candidate for renomination in 1932; resumed former business pursuits until his retirement; died in Melbourne Beach, Fla., May 23, 1966; interment in Melbourne Cemetery.

BRAND, Charles Hillyer, a Representative from Georgia; born in Loganville, Walton County, Ga., April 20, 1861; attended the common schools, and was graduated from the University of Georgia at Athens in 1881; was admitted to the bar in 1882 and commenced practice in Lawrenceville, Gwinnett County, Ga.; member of the State senate in 1894 and 1895 and served as president pro tempore; served as president and director of the Brand Banking Co., Lawrenceville, Ga., and director of the Georgia National Bank and of the American State Bank, Athens, Ga.; solicitor general for the western judicial circuit of Georgia 1896-1904; judge of the superior court 1906-1917; elected as a Democrat to the Sixty-fifth Congress to fill the vacancy caused by the death of Representative-elect Samuel J. Tribble; reelected to the Sixty-sixth and to the seven succeeding Congresses and served from March 4, 1917, until his death in Athens, Ga., on May 17, 1933; interment in Shadow Lawn Cemetery, Lawrenceville, Ga.

BRANDEGEE, Augustus (father of Frank Bosworth Brandegee), a Representative from Connecticut; born in New London, Conn., July 15, 1828; pursued preparatory studies; was graduated from Yale College in 1849 and from the Yale Law School in 1851; was admitted to the bar in 1851 and commenced practice in New London; member of the State house of representatives 1854, 1858, 1859, and 1861, and served as speaker the last term; elected as a Republican to the Thirty-eighth and Thirty-ninth Congresses (March 4, 1863-March 3, 1867); was not a candidate for reelection in 1866; delegate to the Republican National Convention in 1864, the Loyalist Convention at Philadelphia in 1866, and the Republican National Conventions in 1880 and 1884; resumed the practice of law; corporation counsel of New London in 1897 and 1898; died in New London, Conn., November 10, 1904; interment in Cedar Grove Cemetery.

BRANDEGEE, Frank Bosworth (son of Augustus Brandegee), a Representative and a Senator from Connecticut; born in New London, Conn., July 8, 1864; attended the common schools, and was graduated from Yale College in 1885; studied law; was admitted to the bar in 1888 and practiced in New London; member, State house of representatives 1888; corporation counsel of New London 1889-1893, 1894-1897, when he resigned; member, State house of representatives 1899, and served as speaker; again elected corporation counsel of New London 1901-1902, when he resigned to become a Member of Congress; chairman of the Republican State convention in 1904; elected as a Republican to the Fifty-seventh Congress to fill the vacancy caused by the death of Charles A. Russell; reelected to the Fifty-eighth and Fifty-ninth Congresses and served from November 5, 1902, until May 10, 1905, when he resigned, having been elected a United States Senator to fill the vacancy caused by the death of Orville H. Platt; reelected in 1908, 1914, and 1920, and served from May 10, 1905, until his death in Washington, D.C., October 14, 1924; served as President pro tempore during the Sixty-second Congress; chairman, Committee on Forest Reservations and Game Protection (Fifty-ninth through Sixty-first Congresses), Committee on Interoceanic Canals (Sixty-second Congress), Committee on Panama (Sixty-second Congress), Committee on Pacific Railroads (Sixty-third through Sixty-fifth Congresses), Committee on Library (Sixty-sixth and Sixty-seventh Congresses), Committee on Judiciary (Sixty-eighth Congress); interment in Cedar Grove Cemetery, New London, Conn.

**Bibliography:** *DAB*; Janick, Herbert. "Senator Frank B. Brandegee and the Election of 1920." *Historian* 35 (May 1973): 434-451.

BRANTLEY, William Gordon, a Representative from Georgia; born in Blackshear, Pierce County, Ga., September 18, 1860; attended the public schools, and the University of Georgia at Athens; studied law; was admitted to the bar in 1881 and commenced practice in Blackshear, Pierce County, Ga.; member, Georgia State house of representatives, 1884-1885; served in the State senate in 1886 and 1887; solicitor general (prosecuting attorney) of the Brunswick Circuit Court of Georgia, 1888-1896; moved to Brunswick in 1889 and continued the practice of law; elected as a Democrat to the Fifty-fifth and to the seven succeeding Congresses (March 4, 1897-March 3, 1913); was not a candidate for renomination in 1912 to the Sixty-third Congress; delegate to the Democratic National Convention of 1912; moved from Brunswick, Ga., to Washington, D.C., in 1913 and resumed the practice of law; died in Washington, D.C., September 11, 1934; interment in Blackshear Cemetery, Blackshear, Ga.

**BRASCO, Frank James,** a Representative from New York; born in Brooklyn, N.Y., October 15, 1932; educated in St. Michael's High School; B.A., Brooklyn College, 1955; LL.B., Brooklyn Law School, 1957; staff attorney, Legal Aid Society, 1957-1961; assistant district attorney and assistant chief of Rackets Bureau, Kings County, 1961-1966; captain, United States Army Reserve, Judge Advocate General department, Fourth Judge Advocate General Corps; Speakers Bureau of the district attorney's office, Kings County; elected as a Democrat to the Ninetieth and to the three succeeding Congresses (January 3, 1967-January 3, 1975); was not a candidate for reelection in 1974 to the Ninety-fourth Congress; resumed the practice of law in New York City; is a resident of Woodmere, N.Y.

**BRATTON, John,** a Representative from South Carolina; born in Winnsboro, Fairfield County, S.C., March 7, 1831; attended the Academy of Mount Zion Institute in Winnsboro; was graduated from South Carolina College at Columbia in 1850 and from South Carolina Medical College at Charleston in 1853; engaged in the practice of medicine in Winnsboro from 1853 to 1861; also engaged as a planter; volunteered in the Confederate Army as a private and served throughout the Civil War, attaining the rank of brigadier general; member of the State constitutional convention in 1865; served in the State senate in 1866; chairman of the South Carolina delegation in the Democratic National Convention in 1876; delegate to the Democratic National Convention in 1880; elected comptroller general of South Carolina by the legislature, to fill a vacancy, in 1881; elected to the Forty-eighth Congress to fill the vacancy caused by the death of John H. Evins and served from December 8, 1884, to March 3, 1885; was not a candidate for renomination in 1884; retired from active politics and again engaged in planting at "Farmington," near Winnsboro; died in Winnsboro, S.C., January 12, 1898; interment in the Episcopal Cemetery.

**Bibliography:** *DAB*.

**BRATTON, Robert Franklin,** a Representative from Maryland; born in Barren Creek Springs, Somerset (now Wicomico) County, Md., May 13, 1845; was graduated from Washington College, Chestertown, Md., in 1864; deputy register of wills for Somerset County; admitted to the bar in 1867; member of the State convention of 1865 which sent delegates to a peace convention held in Philadelphia in the following year; member of several State and congressional conventions; member of the State house of representatives in 1869; served in the State senate in 1873, 1879, 1887, and 1890; elected president of the senate in 1890; engaged in the practice of law in Princess Anne, Somerset County, Md.; elected as a Democrat to the Fifty-third Congress and served from March 4, 1893, until his death in Princess Anne, Md., May 10, 1894; interment in St. Andrew's Cemetery.

**BRATTON, Sam Gilbert,** a Senator from New Mexico; born in Kosse, Limestone County, Tex., August 19, 1888; attended the public schools; graduated from State Normal School and taught school for several years at Claude and Hereford, Tex.; studied law; was admitted to the bar in 1909 and commenced practice in Farwell, Parmer County, Tex.; moved to Clovis, N.Mex., in 1915 and continued the practice of law; judge of the district court for the fifth judicial district of New Mexico 1919-1921, when, this district being divided, he became judge of the ninth judicial district 1921-1923; associate justice of the supreme court of New Mexico 1923-1924, when he resigned to accept the nomination for Senator; elected as a Democrat to the United States Senate in 1924; reelected in 1930 and served from March 4, 1925, until his resignation, effective June 24, 1933; chairman, Committee on Irrigation and Reclamation (Seventy-third Congress); resigned to accept an appointment as circuit judge of the United States Circuit Court of Appeals for the Tenth Judicial Circuit 1933-1961; died in Albuquerque, N.Mex., September 22, 1963; interment in Fairview Park Cemetery.

**BRAWLEY, William Huggins** (cousin of John James Hemphill and great-uncle of Robert Witherspoon Hemphill), a Representative from South Carolina; born in Chester, Chester County, S.C., May 13, 1841; attended the common schools, and was graduated from South Carolina College at Columbia in 1860; enlisted as a private in Company F, Sixth Regiment, South Carolina Infantry, Confederate States Army, April 11, 1861; lost an arm in the Battle of Seven Pines, Va., 1862, and was retired from service; traveled and studied in Europe in 1864 and 1865; studied law; was admitted to the bar in 1866 and commenced practice at Chester, S.C.; elected solicitor of the sixth judicial circuit of South Carolina in 1868 and served until his resignation in 1874; moved to Charleston and continued the practice of his profession; member of the State house of representatives 1882-1890; elected as a Democrat to the Fifty-second and Fifty-third Congresses and served from March 4, 1891, until February 12, 1894, when he resigned to accept a position on the bench; appointed January 18, 1894, United States district judge of the district of South Carolina and served from February 12, 1894, until his resignation June 14, 1911; lived in retirement until his death in Charleston, S.C., November 15, 1916; interment in Magnolia Cemetery.

**Bibliography:** *DAB*; Brawley, William H. *Journal of William H. Brawley, 1864-1865.* Edited with an introduction by Frances Poe Brawley. Charlottesville, Va.: 1970.

**BRAXTON, Carter** (great-grandfather of Elliott Muse Braxton), a Delegate from Virginia; born at "Newington," on the Mattaponi River, near King and Queen Court House, Va., September 16, 1736; was graduated from the College of William and Mary, Williamsburg, Va., in 1755; spent three years in England and attended Cambridge University; member of the Virginia House of Burgesses 1761-1771 and 1775-1776; elected a Member of the Continental Congress to fill the vacancy caused by the death of Peyton Randolph and served from February to August 1776, when Virginia reduced her representation from seven to five; a signer of the Declaration of Independence; member, Virginia house of delegates, 1776-1783, 1785-1786, and 1790-1794; member of the Virginia Council of State 1786-1791 and from 1794 until his death in Richmond, Va., October 10, 1797; interment on his estate, "Chericoke," King William County, Va.

**Bibliography:** *DAB*; Dill, Alonzo T. *Carter Braxton; Last Virginia Signer.* Richmond, Va.: Virginia Independence Bicentennial Commission, 1976; Dill, Alonzo T. *Carter Braxton, Virginia Signer: A Conservative in Revolt.* Lanham, Md.: University Press of America, 1983.

**BRAXTON, Elliott Muse** (great-grandson of Carter Braxton), a Representative from Virginia; born in Matthews, Matthews County, Va., October 8, 1823; attended the common schools; studied law; was admitted to the bar in 1849 and commenced practice in Richmond, Va.; subsequently moved to Richmond County; member of the Virginia senate from 1852 until 1856; moved to Fredericksburg, Spotsylvania County, in 1860 and continued the practice of law; during the Civil War raised a company for the Confederate Army and was elected its captain; subsequently commissioned a major and served on the staff of General John R. Cooke; elected a member of the common council of Fredericksburg in 1866; elected as a Democrat to the Forty-second Congress (March 4, 1871-March 3, 1873); unsuccessful candidate for reelection in 1872 to the Forty-third Congress; resumed the practice of law in Fredericksburg, Va., where he died on October 2, 1891; interment in Confederate Cemetery.

**BRAY, William Gilmer,** a Representative from Indiana; born on a farm near Mooresville, Morgan County, Ind., June 17, 1903; attended the public schools of Mooresville, Ind.; was graduated from Indiana University Law School at Bloomington in 1927 and was admitted to the bar the same year; prosecuting attorney of the fifteenth judicial district of Indiana, Martinsville, Ind., 1926-1930; commenced the private practice of law in Martinsville, Ind., in 1930; called from the Army Reserve June 21, 1941, with the rank of captain and served with a tank company throughout the Pacific campaign, receiving the Silver Star; after the war was transferred to Military Government and served nine months in Korea as deputy property custodian; released from active duty in November 1946 with the rank of colonel; returned to private law practice in Martinsville, Ind.; elected as a Republican to the Eighty-second and to the eleven succeeding Congresses (January 3, 1951-January 3, 1975); unsuccessful candidate for reelection in 1974 to the Ninety-fourth Congress; resumed the practice of law; named to be a commissioner to the American Battle Monuments Commission by President Gerald R. Ford, 1975-1978; resided in Martinsville, Ind., where he died June 4, 1979; interment in White Lick Cemetery, Mooresville, Ind.

**BRAYTON, William Daniel,** a Representative from Rhode Island; born in Warwick, Kent County, R.I., November 6, 1815; attended Kent Academy in East Greenwich and Kingston Academy; spent two years in Brown University, Providence, R.I.; engaged in mercantile pursuits; major of the Fourth Regiment of Rhode Island Militia in the Dorr Rebellion; town clerk of Warwick in 1844; member of the town council; member of the State house of representatives in 1841 and 1851; served in the State senate in 1848 and 1853; elected as a Republican to the Thirty-fifth and Thirty-sixth Congresses (March 4, 1857-March 3, 1861); chairman, Committee on Expenditures on Public Buildings (Thirty-sixth Congress); unsuccessful candidate for reelection in 1860 to the Thirty-seventh Congress; appointed collector of internal revenue for the second district of Rhode Island in 1862 and served until 1871, when he resigned; delegate to the Republican National Convention in 1872; for a number of years in charge of the money-order division of the Providence post office; died in Providence, R.I., June 30, 1887; interment in Brayton Cemetery, Apponaug, R.I.

**BREAUX, John Berlinger,** a Representative and a Senator from Louisiana; born in Crowley, La., March 1, 1944; graduated St. Michael's High School, 1961; B.A., University of Southwestern Louisiana, Lafayette, 1964; J.D., Louisiana State University Law School, Baton Rouge, 1967; admitted to Louisiana bar in 1967; practiced law, 1967-1968; assistant to Representative Edwin W. Edwards of Louisiana, 1968-1972; elected as a Democrat to the Ninety-second Congress, September 30, 1972, by special election to fill the vacancy caused by the resignation of Edwin W. Edwards; reelected to the seven succeeding Congresses and served from September 30, 1972, to January 3, 1987; was not a candidate in 1986 for reelection to the House of Representatives, but was elected to the United States Senate for the term beginning January 3, 1987; reelected in 1992 for the term ending January 3, 1999; chairman, Democratic Senatorial Campaign Committee (One Hundred First Congress); is a resident of Crowley, La.

**BREAZEALE, Phanor,** a Representative from Louisiana; born in Natchitoches Parish, La., December 29, 1858; attended private schools; moved to Natchitoches, La., in 1877; clerked in a mercantile establishment for two years; studied law; clerk in the supreme court of the State; was graduated from the law department of Tulane University, New Orleans, in 1881; was admitted to the bar the same year and commenced practice in Natchitoches; also engaged in newspaper work, 1882-1884; president of the school board of Natchitoches Parish, 1888-1891; district attorney for the tenth judicial district from 1892 to 1900; member of the State constitutional convention in 1898; elected as a Democrat to the Fifty-sixth and to the two succeeding Congresses (March 4, 1899-March 3, 1905); unsuccessful candidate for renomination in 1904 to the Fifty-ninth Congress; resumed the practice of law in Natchitoches, La.; appointed in October 1908 as a member of a commission to

codify the criminal laws of Louisiana, and to prepare a code of criminal procedure; member of the Democratic State central committee, beginning in 1908, and a member of the executive committee; delegate to the Democratic National Conventions of 1908 and 1916; member of the convention to frame a constitution for the State of Louisiana in 1921; died in Natchitoches, La., April 29, 1934; interment in the Catholic Cemetery.

**BRECK, Daniel** (brother of Samuel Breck), a Representative from Kentucky; born in Topsfield, Essex County, Mass., February 12, 1788; attended the local school; taught school; was graduated from Dartmouth College, Hanover, N.H., in 1812; studied law; was admitted to the bar in 1814 and commenced practice in Richmond, Madison County, Ky., in October of the same year; judge of the Richmond County Court; member of the Kentucky house of representatives 1824-1827 and again in 1834; president of the Richmond branch of the State Bank of Kentucky 1835-1843; appointed associate judge of the supreme court of Kentucky April 7, 1843, and served until 1849; elected as a Whig to the Thirty-first Congress (March 4, 1849-March 3, 1851); returned to Richmond, Ky., and again served as president to the Richmond branch of the State bank; died in Richmond, Ky., February 4, 1871; interment in Richmond Cemetery.

**BRECK, Samuel** (brother of Daniel Breck), a Representative from Pennsylvania; born in Boston, Mass., July 17, 1771; attended the Royal Military School of Loreze, France; moved to Pennsylvania and settled in Philadelphia in 1792, where he engaged in business as a merchant; served as corporal during the Whisky Rebellion; member of the Pennsylvania house of representatives 1817-1820; served in the State senate 1832-1834; elected to the Eighteenth Congress (March 4, 1823-March 3, 1825); withdrew from active business pursuits and lived in retirement until his death in Philadelphia, Pa., August 31, 1862; interment in St. Peter's Churchyard.

**Bibliography:** *DAB*; Wainwright, Nicholas B. "The Diary of Samuel Breck, 1814-1835, 1838." *Pennsylvania Magazine of History and Biography* 102 (October 1978): 469-508; 103 (1979): 85-113, 222-51, 356-82.

**BRECKINRIDGE, Clifton Rodes** (son of John Cabell Breckinridge and great-grandson of John Breckinridge), a Representative from Arkansas; born near Lexington, Ky., November 22, 1846; attended the rural schools; served in the Confederate Army and was a midshipman in the Navy; after the Civil War he attended Washington College (now Washington and Lee University), Lexington, Va., for three years; settled near Pine Bluff, Ark., in 1870 and engaged in cotton planting and in the commission business for 13 years; elected as a Democrat to the Forty-eighth and to the two succeeding Congresses (March 4, 1883-March 3, 1889); presented credentials as a Member-elect to the Fifty-first Congress and served from March 4, 1889, until September 5, 1890, when John M. Clayton was declared to have been duly elected, but, owing to the death of Mr. Clayton while the contest was pending, the seat was declared vacant; subsequently elected to the Fifty-first Congress to fill the vacancy thus caused; reelected to the Fifty-second and Fifty-third Congresses and served from November 4, 1890, to August 14, 1894, when he resigned to accept a consular position; unsuccessful candidate for renomination in 1894 to the Fifty-fourth Congress; appointed Minister to Russia by President Grover Cleveland on July 20, 1894, and served until December 13, 1897, when he returned to Pine Bluff, Ark.; member of the Dawes Commission, 1900-1905; engaged in banking at Fort Smith, Ark., serving as president of the Arkansas Valley Trust Co.; member of the State constitutional convention in 1917; was a resident of Fort Smith, Ark., until 1925, when he moved to Wendover, Leslie County, Ky., where he died on December 3, 1932; interment in Old Lexington Cemetery, Lexington, Ky.

**Bibliography:** Bolin, James Duane. "Clifton Rodes Breckinridge: 'The Little Arkansas Giant.'" *Arkansas Historical Quarterly* 53 (Winter 1994): 407-427.

**BRECKINRIDGE, James** (brother of John Breckinridge, great-great-great-uncle of John Bayne Breckinridge, and cousin of John Brown of Virginia and Kentucky, James Brown, and Francis Preston), a Representative from Virginia; born near Fincastle, Botetourt County, Va., March 7, 1763; studied under private tutors; during the Revolutionary War served in Colonel Preston's rifle regiment under General Greene; attended Washington College (now Washington and Lee University), Lexington, Va., and was graduated from the College of William and Mary, Williamsburg, Va., in 1785; studied law; was admitted to the bar and practiced in Fincastle; member of the Virginia house of delegates 1789-1802, 1806-1808, 1819-1821 and 1823-1824; took a special interest in the construction of the Chesapeake & Ohio Canal; elected as a Federalist to the Eleventh and to the three succeeding Congresses (March 4, 1809-March 3, 1817); was an associate of Thomas Jefferson in the establishment of the University of Virginia, Charlottesville, Va.; served as brigadier general in the War of 1812; resumed the practice of law; died at his country home, "Grove Hill," Botetourt County, Va., May 13, 1833; interment in the family burial plot on his estate near Fincastle, Va.

**BRECKINRIDGE, James Douglas,** a Representative from Kentucky; born in Woodville, near Louisville, Jefferson County, Ky.; attended Washington College (now Washington and Lee University), Lexington, Va., 1800-1803; studied law; was admitted to the bar and commenced practice in Louisville, Ky.; member of the Kentucky house of representatives 1809-1811; appointed judge by Governor Robert Desha in April 1826, but declined to serve; elected to the Seventeenth Congress to fill the vacancy caused by the death of Wingfield Bullock and served from November 21, 1821, to March 3, 1823; unsuccessful candidate for reelection in 1822 to the Eighteenth Congress; resumed the practice of law; died in Louisville, Ky., May 6, 1849; interment in St. John's Cemetery; reinterment in St. Louis Catholic Cemetery at Louisville in 1867.

**BRECKINRIDGE, John** (brother of James Breckinridge, grandfather of John Cabell Breckinridge and William Campbell Preston Breckinridge, great-grandfather of Clifton Rodes Breckinridge, great-great-grandfather of John Bayne Breckinridge, cousin of John Brown, James Brown, and Francis Preston), a Senator from Kentucky; born near Staunton, Augusta County, Va., December 2, 1760; educated at Augusta Academy, near Staunton (now Washington and Lee University, Lexington, Va.), and at the College of William and Mary, Williamsburg, Va.; elected a member of the Virginia house of burgesses in 1780 when nineteen years of age, but being under age was not allowed to take his seat until elected the third time; served as subaltern in the Virginia Militia during the Revolutionary War; studied law; was admitted to the bar in 1785 and commenced practice in Charlottesville, Va.; elected as a Democrat to the Third Congress, but resigned in 1792 before the commencement of the congressional term; moved to Kentucky in 1793 and resumed the practice of law in Lexington; unsuccessful candidate for election to the United States Senate in 1794; appointed attorney general of Kentucky in 1795 and served until November 30, 1797, when he resigned; member, Kentucky house of representatives, 1798-1800, serving as speaker in 1799 and 1800; member of the Kentucky constitutional convention in 1799; elected as a Republican to the United States Senate and served from March 4, 1801, until August 7, 1805, when he resigned to accept the position of Attorney General in the Cabinet of President Thomas Jefferson; served in this capacity from August 7, 1805 until his death at "Cabell's Dale," near Lexington, Ky., December 14, 1806; interment in Lexington Cemetery, Lexington, Ky.

**Bibliography:** *DAB*; Harrison, Lowell. *John Breckinridge, Jeffersonian Republican.* Louisville: Filson Club, 1969; Klotter, James C. *The Breckinridges of Kentucky: Two Centuries of Leadership.* Lexington: The University Press of Kentucky, 1986.

**BRECKINRIDGE, John Bayne** (great-great-grandson of John Breckinridge, great-great-great-nephew of James Breckinridge, and great-nephew of William Campbell Preston Breckinridge), a Representative from Kentucky; born in Washington, D.C., November 29, 1913; attended various Lexington schools, Massie Preparatory, Versailles, Ky., Tome Preparatory, Port Deposit, Md.; A.B., University of Kentucky, 1937, and LL.B., 1939; admitted to the Kentucky Bar in 1940 and commenced practice in Lexington; special attorney, Anti-Trust Division, United States Department of Justice, 1940-1941; served in the United States Army, 1941-1946, and attained the rank of lieutenant colonel; engaged in the private practice of law from 1946 to 1972; member, Kentucky house of representatives, 1956-1960; attorney general of Kentucky, 1960-1964, and 1968-1972; corporation counsel, city of Lexington, 1964; commissioner, National Conference of Commissioners on Uniform State Law, 1960-1964; delegate to the Democratic National Convention of 1960; elected as a Democrat to the Ninety-third and to the two succeeding Congresses (January 3, 1973-January 3, 1979); unsuccessful candidate for renomination in 1978 to the Ninety-sixth Congress; resumed the practice of law in Lexington, Ky., where he died on July 29, 1979; cremated; ashes interred at Lexington Cemetery.

**Bibliography:** Klotter, James C. *The Breckinridges of Kentucky, 1760-1981.* Lexington: The University Press of Kentucky, 1986.

**BRECKINRIDGE, John Cabell** (grandson of John Breckinridge, father of Clifton Rodes Breckinridge, and cousin of Henry Donnel Foster), a Representative and a Senator from Kentucky and a Vice President of the United States; born at "Cabell's Dale," near Lexington, Ky., January 15, 1821; attended Pisgah Academy, Woodford County, Ky.; was graduated from Centre College, Danville, Ky., in 1839; later attended the College of New Jersey (now Princeton University); studied law in the Transylvania Institute, Lexington, Ky.; was admitted to the bar in 1840; moved to Burlington, Iowa, but soon returned and began practice in Lexington, Ky.; major of the Third Kentucky Volunteers during the Mexican War in 1847 and 1848; member, Kentucky house of representatives, 1849; elected as a Democrat to the Thirty-second and Thirty-third Congresses (March 4, 1851-March 3, 1855); was not a candidate for renomination in 1854 to the Thirty-fourth Congress; was tendered the mission to Spain by President Franklin Pierce, but declined; elected Vice President of the United States in 1856 on the Democratic ticket headed by James Buchanan; was inaugurated on March 4, 1857, and served until March 4, 1861; unsuccessful Southern Democratic candidate for election for President of the United States in 1860; elected to the United States Senate and served from March 4, 1861 until expelled by resolution of December 4, 1861, for support of the Confederacy; entered the Confederate Army during the Civil War; appointed brigadier general on November 2, 1861, and was commissioned major general April 14, 1862; Secretary of War in the Cabinet of the Confederate States from February 4, 1865 until April 1865; resided in Europe until 1868; returned to Lexington, Ky., and resumed the practice of law; vice president of the Elizabethtown, Lexington and Big Sandy Railroad Company; died in Lexington, Ky., May 17, 1875; interment in Lexington Cemetery.

**Bibliography:** *DAB*; Davis, William. *John C. Breckinridge: Statesman, Soldier, Symbol.* Baton Rouge: Louisiana State University Press, 1974; Heck, Frank. *Proud Kentuckian, John C. Breckinridge, 1821-1875.* Lexington: The University Press of Kentucky, 1976.

**BRECKINRIDGE, William Campbell Preston** (grandson of John Breckinridge, uncle of Levin Irving Handy, and great-uncle of John Bayne Breckinridge), a Representative from Kentucky; born in

Baltimore, Md., August 28, 1837; attended the common schools, Jefferson College, Chambersburg, Pa., and Pisgah Academy, Woodford County, Ky.; was graduated from Centre College, Danville, Ky., in 1855 and from the law department of the University of Louisville in 1857; was admitted to the bar in 1857 and commenced practice in Lexington, Ky.; entered the Confederate Army in 1861 as captain and was subsequently promoted to the rank of colonel in the Ninth Kentucky Cavalry; was in command of the Kentucky cavalry designated to act as bodyguard for President Jefferson Davis and the members of his cabinet at the close of the Civil War; returned to Lexington, Ky., and was attorney for Fayette County; edited the Lexington (Ky.) Observer and Reporter, 1866-1868; professor of equity and jurisprudence in the University of Kentucky at Lexington; delegate to the Democratic National Conventions of 1876 and 1888; elected as a Democrat to the Forty-ninth and to the four succeeding Congresses (March 4, 1885-March 3, 1895); unsuccessful candidate for election in 1896 to the Fifty-fifth Congress; resumed the practice of law and also edited the Lexington Herald; died in Lexington, Ky., November 18, 1904; interment in Lexington Cemetery.

**Bibliography:** *DAB*; Klotter, James C. *The Breckinridges of Kentucky, 1760-1981*. Lexington: The University Press of Kentucky, 1986.

**BREEDING, James Floyd,** a Representative from Kansas; born near Robinson, Brown County, Kans., September 28, 1901; educated in grade schools, Moonlight, Dickinson County, Kans., and Berryton High School in Shawnee County, Kans.; attended Kansas State College at Manhattan in 1921 and 1922; moved to Rolla, Kans., in 1928; farmer-stockman near Rolla, Morton County, 1928-1956; member of State house of representatives 1947-1949, serving as minority leader in 1949 session; Democratic candidate for election for lieutenant governor of Kansas in 1950; president of the Western Kansas Development Association in 1951; delegate to the Democratic National Conventions of 1960 and 1964; elected as a Democrat to the Eighty-fifth and to the two succeeding Congresses (January 3, 1957-January 3, 1963); unsuccessful candidate for reelection in 1962 to the Eighty-eighth Congress; appointed by President John F. Kennedy as assistant to Secretary of Agriculture, Grain and Feed Division, 1963-1966; unsuccessful candidate in 1966 for election to the United States Senate; died in Dodge City, Kans., October 17, 1977; interment in Rolla Cemetery, Rolla, Kans.

**BREEN, Edward G.,** a Representative from Ohio; born in Dayton, Montgomery County, Ohio, June 10, 1908; attended Corpus Christi Grammar School; graduated from the University of Dayton and attended the Ohio State University; engaged in the hotel business in Dayton; during the Second World War served as a major in the United States Air Force in North Africa and Italy until released from active service as a lieutenant colonel in the Infantry Reserve; mayor of Dayton, Ohio, from November 1945 until his resignation in April 1948 to seek nomination to Congress; elected as a Democrat to the Eighty-first and Eighty-second Congresses and served from January 3, 1949, until his resignation October 1, 1951, due to ill health; member of the Montgomery County Board of Commissioners, 1955-1960; engaged in the real-estate and insurance business; was a resident of Dayton, Ohio; died May 8, 1991.

**BREESE, Sidney,** a Senator from Illinois; born in Whitesboro, N.Y., July 15, 1800; attended Hamilton College, Clinton, N.Y., and was graduated from Union College, Schenectady, N.Y., in 1818; moved to Illinois; studied law; was admitted to the bar in 1820 and commenced practice in Kaskaskia; appointed postmaster of Kaskaskia in 1821; prosecuting attorney of the third judicial circuit 1822-1826; United States district attorney for Illinois 1827-1829; was the first reporter of the proceedings of the State supreme court in 1831; held several commissions in the militia and served as a lieutenant colonel of Volunteers in the Black Hawk War in 1832;

circuit judge of the second district 1835-1841; judge of the State supreme court in 1841-1842; elected as a Democrat to the United States Senate and served from March 4, 1843, to March 3, 1849; unsuccessful candidate for renomination in 1849; chairman, Committee on District of Columbia (Twenty-ninth Congress), Committee on Public Lands (Twenty-ninth and Thirtieth Congresses); member, State house of representatives 1851-1852, serving as speaker in the former year; judge of the circuit court of Illinois 1855-1857; judge of the supreme court of Illinois from 1857 until his death; served as chief justice 1867-1870, 1873, and 1874; died in Pinkneyville, Perry County, Ill., June 27, 1878; interment in Carlyle Cemetery, Carlyle, Ill.

**Bibliography:** *DAB*; McNulty, John W. "Sidney Breese: His Early Career in Law and Politics in Illinois." *Journal of the Illinois State Historical Society* 61 (Summer 1968): 164-181.

**BREHM, Walter Ellsworth,** a Representative from Ohio; born in Somerset, Perry County, Ohio, May 25, 1892; attended the public schools, Boston (Mass.) University, and Ohio Wesleyan University at Delaware, Ohio; was graduated from the Ohio State University Dental School at Columbus in 1917; worked in steel mills, rubber factories, and oil fields after graduation from high school; member of Company D, Seventh Regiment, Ohio Infantry, 1908-1913; engaged in the practice of dentistry in Logan, Ohio, 1921-1942; treasurer of the Republican executive committee of Hocking County, Logan City Council, 1936-1938; served in the State house of representatives 1938-1942; elected as a Republican to the Seventy-eighth and to the four succeeding Congresses (January 3, 1943-January 3, 1953); was not a candidate for reelection in 1952 to the Eighty-third Congress; resumed the practice of dentistry and affiliated with a dental supply company after retirement from active practice; resided in Columbus, Ohio, until his death there August 24, 1971.

**BREITUNG, Edward,** a Representative from Michigan; born in Schalkau, Duchy of Saxe-Meiningen, Germany, November 10, 1831; attended the College of Mining, Meiningen, Germany, in 1849; after the revolution in Germany immigrated to the United States and settled in Kalamazoo County, Mich.; moved to Detroit in 1851 and became a clerk in a mercantile house; moved to Marquette, Mich., and engaged in mercantile pursuits until 1859, when he went to Negaunee, Marquette County; sold his mercantile business to engage exclusively in iron mining operations in 1864; explored the iron range in Marquette and Menominee Counties from 1864 to 1867, locating several profitable mines; later became interested in gold and silver mining in Colorado; member of the Michigan State house of representatives, 1873-1874; member of the State senate, 1877-1878; served as mayor of Negaunee, Mich., in 1879, 1880, and 1882; elected as a Republican to the Forty-eighth Congress (March 4, 1883-March 3, 1885); declined to be a candidate for renomination in 1884 to the Forty-ninth Congress; died in Negaunee, Marquette County, Mich., March 3, 1887; interment in Park Cemetery, Marquette, Mich.

**BREMNER, Robert Gunn,** a Representative from New Jersey; born in Keiss, Caithness, Scotland, December 17, 1874; immigrated with his parents to Canada; attended the public schools; moved to the United States, and was employed as a carpenter and electrician in New York City in 1894 and 1895; became a newspaper reporter in Paterson, N.J., in 1895; served as a private in Company C, Second Regiment, New Jersey Volunteer Infantry, during the Spanish-American War; resumed newspaper work in Paterson; editor and publisher of the Daily Herald, Passaic, N.J., 1902-1914; elected as a Democrat to the Sixty-third Congress and served from March 4, 1913, until his death in a hospital in Baltimore, Md., February 5, 1914; interment in Laurel Grove Cemetery, Totowa Borough, N.J.

**BRENGLE, Francis,** a Representative from Maryland; born in Frederick, Md., November 26, 1807; completed academic studies; studied law; was admitted to the bar and practiced in Frederick,

Md.; member of the State house of delegates 1832, 1834, and 1836; elected as a Whig to the Twenty-eighth Congress (March 4, 1843-March 3, 1845); died in Frederick, Frederick County, Md., December 10, 1846; interment in Mount Olivet Cemetery.

**BRENNAN, Joseph Edward,** a Representative from Maine; born in Portland, Maine, November 2, 1934; attended public schools; B.S., Boston College, 1958; LL.B., University of Maine Law School, 1963; member, Maine State house of representatives, 1965-1971; Maine State senator, 1973-1975; Maine State attorney general, 1975-1977; elected Governor of Maine in 1978, reelected in 1982, and served from January 3, 1979 to January 7, 1987; elected as a Democrat to the One Hundredth and One Hundred First Congresses (January 3, 1987-January 3, 1991); was not a candidate for reelection in 1990 to the One Hundred Second Congress, but was an unsuccessful candidate for election for Governor; candidate in 1996 for election to the United States Senate; is a resident of Portland, Maine.

**BRENNAN, Martin Adlai,** a Representative from Illinois; born in Bloomington, McLean County, Ill., September 21, 1879; attended parochial schools; employed as a reporter for the Bloomington Bulletin; was graduated from the Wesleyan College of Law, Bloomington, Ill., in 1902; was admitted to the bar the same year and commenced practice in Bloomington, Ill.; served as presiding judge of the Illinois Court of Claims, 1913-1917; served as census supervisor for McLean County, Ill., in 1920; member of the Illinois State house of representatives, 1921-1923; delegate to the Democratic National Convention of 1924; elected as a Democrat to the Seventy-third and Seventy-fourth Congresses (March 4, 1933-January 3, 1937); was not a candidate for renomination in 1936 to the Seventy-fifth Congress; resumed the practice of law in Bloomington, Ill., until his death there on July 4, 1941; interment in St. Mary's Cemetery.

**BRENNAN, Vincent Morrison,** a Representative from Michigan; born in Mount Clemens, Macomb County, Mich., April 22, 1890; moved with his parents to Detroit in 1895; was graduated from SS. Peter and Paul's Parochial School, from Detroit College in 1909, from the law department of Harvard University in 1912, and from the University of Detroit in 1914; was admitted to the bar in 1912 and commenced practice in Detroit; legal adviser to the Michigan State Labor Department, 1912-1913; assistant corporation counsel for the city of Detroit, 1915-1920; Michigan State senator, 1919-1920; drafted the automobile traffic ordinance of Detroit, used as a model for many other cities; elected as a Republican to the Sixty-seventh Congress (March 4, 1921-March 3, 1923); was not a candidate for reelection in 1922 to the Sixty-eighth Congress; elected judge of the circuit court of Wayne County, Mich., for the term commencing in January 1924; reelected for six successive terms, and served until his resignation on December 31, 1954; practiced law; died in Detroit, Mich., February 4, 1959; interment in Holy Sepulchre Cemetery, Birmingham, Mich.

**BRENNER, John Lewis,** a Representative from Ohio; born in Wayne Township, Montgomery County, Ohio, February 2, 1832; attended the common schools and Springfield (Ohio) Academy; engaged in agricultural pursuits until 1862, interested in the nursery business until 1872, and then engaged in the production of tobacco; moved to Dayton, Ohio, in 1866; member of the board of police commissioners 1885-1887; elected as a Democrat to the Fifty-fifth and Fifty-sixth Congresses (March 4, 1897-March 3, 1901); unsuccessful candidate for renomination in 1900; resumed his former occupation as a dealer in leaf tobacco; died in Dayton, Montgomery County, Ohio, November 1, 1906; interment in Woodland Cemetery.

**BRENT, Richard** (uncle of William Leigh Brent and nephew of Daniel Carroll), a Representative and a Senator from Virginia; born at "Richland," on the Potomac River, at Aquia Creek, Stafford County, Va., in 1757; studied law; was admitted to the bar and practiced; member of the Virginia house of delegates from Stafford County in 1788 and from Prince William County in 1793, 1794, 1800, and 1801; elected to the Fourth and Fifth Congresses (March 4, 1795-March 3, 1799); elected again to the Seventh Congress (March 4, 1801-March 3, 1803); member, Virginia senate 1808-1810; elected to the United States Senate and served from March 4, 1809, until his death in Washington, D.C., on December 30, 1814; interment in the family burial ground at "Richland," on the Potomac River, at Aquia Creek.

**BRENT, William Leigh** (nephew of Richard Brent), a Representative from Louisiana; born at Port Tobacco, Charles County, Md., February 20, 1784; studied law and was admitted to the bar; moved to Louisiana about 1809 and commenced practice; appointed by President James Madison as deputy attorney general for the western district of the Territory of Orleans; elected to the Eighteenth and to the two succeeding Congresses (March 4, 1823-March 3, 1829); affiliated with the Whig Party upon its formation; resumed the practice of law in Louisiana, and in Washington, D.C.; died in St. Martinsville, La., July 7, 1848; interment in St. Martin's Catholic Cemetery.

**BRENTANO, Lorenzo,** a Representative from Illinois; born in Manneheim, Grand Duchy of Baden, Germany, November 4, 1813; studied jurisprudence in the Universities of Heidelberg and Freiburg and was graduated; practiced before the supreme court of Baden; elected to the Chamber of Deputies and in 1848 to the Frankfort Parliament; president of the provisional republic established by the revolutionists in 1849; sentenced to imprisonment for life after the failure of the revolution, but sought refuge in the United States; settled in Kalamazoo County, Mich., and engaged in agricultural pursuits; moved to Chicago in 1859; was admitted to the bar in 1859 and commenced practice in Chicago, Ill; became editor in chief and principal proprietor of the Illinois Staats-Zeitung; member of the State house of representatives in 1862; member of the Chicago Board of Education 1862-1868; delegate to the Republican National Convention in 1864; appointed United States consul at Dresden in 1872 and served until April 1876; elected as a Republican to the Forty-fifth Congress (March 4, 1877-March 3, 1879); unsuccessful candidate for renomination in 1878; engaged in literary pursuits; died in Chicago, Ill., September 18, 1891; interment in Graceland Cemetery.

**Bibliography:** *DAB.*

**BRENTON, Samuel,** a Representative from Indiana; born in Gallatin County, Ky., November 22, 1810; attended the public schools; was ordained to the Methodist ministry in 1830 and served as a minister; located at Danville, Ind., in 1834 because of ill health, and studied law; member of the Indiana State house of representatives, 1838-1841; returned to the ministry in 1841 and served at Crawfordsville, Perryville, Lafayette, and finally at Fort Wayne, where he suffered a paralytic stroke in 1848 and was compelled to abandon his ministerial duties; appointed register of the land office at Fort Wayne, Ind., on May 2, 1849, and served until July 31, 1851, when he resigned; elected as a Whig to the Thirty-second Congress (March 4, 1851-March 3, 1853); unsuccessful candidate for reelection in 1852 to the Thirty-third Congress; elected as a Republican to the Thirty-fourth and Thirty-fifth Congresses, and served from March 4, 1855 until his death in Fort Wayne, Ind., March 29, 1857; interment in Lindenwood Cemetery.

**BRENTS, Thomas Hurley,** a Delegate from the Territory of Washington; born near Florence, Pike County, Ill., December 24, 1840; attended the common schools, Portland (Oreg.) Academy, Baptist Seminary, Oregon City, Oreg., and McMinnville (Oreg.)

College; justice of the peace in 1862; engaged in the general mercantile business at Canyon City, Oreg., 1863-1866; postmaster of Canyon City in 1863 and 1864; clerk of Grant County, Oreg., 1864-1866; delegate to the Union-Republican convention of Oregon in 1866; member of the State house of representatives in 1866; studied law; was admitted to the bar in 1866 and commenced practice in San Francisco, Calif., in 1867; moved to Walla Walla, Wash., in 1870; city attorney of Walla Walla in 1871 and 1872; presided over the Republican Territorial convention at Vancouver in 1874; elected as a Republican to the Forty-sixth, Forty-seventh, and Forty-eighth Congresses (March 4, 1879-March 3, 1885); unsuccessful candidate for renomination in 1884; resumed the practice of law; judge of the superior court of Walla Walla 1896-1913; died in Walla Walla, Wash., October 23, 1916; interment in Blue Mountain Cemetery.

**BRETZ, John Lewis,** a Representative from Indiana; born near Huntingburg, Dubois County, Ind., September 21, 1852; attended the country schools and Huntingburg High School; taught school 1876-1880; studied law, and was graduated from the Cincinnati Law School in 1880; was admitted to the bar and commenced practice in Jasper, Ind.; prosecuting attorney of the eleventh judicial circuit 1884-1890; elected as a Democrat to the Fifty-second and Fifty-third Congresses (March 4, 1891-March 3, 1895); unsuccessful candidate for reelection in 1894 to the Fifty-fourth Congress; judge of the circuit court of Pike and Dubois Counties from 1895 until his death; delegate to the Democratic National Convention in 1900; died in Jasper, Dubois County, Ind., December 25, 1920; interment in Fairmount Cemetery, Huntingburg, Ind.

**BREVARD, Joseph,** a Representative from South Carolina; born in Iredell, Iredell County, N.C., July 19, 1766; entered the Continental Army when still a boy; was commissioned lieutenant in the North Carolina Line in 1782 and served throughout the Revolutionary War; moved to Camden, S.C.; sheriff of Camden District 1789-1791; commissioner in equity October 14, 1791; studied law; was admitted to the bar in 1792 and commenced practice in Camden, S.C.; engaged in the compilation of the law reports which bear his name 1793-1815; member of South Carolina house of representatives, 1796-1799; elected judge of the State supreme court December 17, 1801, and served until December 1815, when he resigned; resumed the practice of law in Camden; elected to the Sixteenth Congress (March 4, 1819-March 3, 1821); was not a candidate for renomination in 1820; unsuccessful candidate for Congress at a special election held in 1821; died in Camden, Kershaw County, S.C., October 11, 1821; interment in the Quaker Cemetery.

**BREWER, Francis Beattie,** a Representative from New York; born in Keene, Cheshire County, N.H., October 8, 1820; attended the Barnet (Vt.) public schools, Newbury (Vt.) Seminary, and Kimball Union Academy at Meriden, N.H.; was graduated from Dartmouth College, Hanover, N.H., in 1843 and from the medical department of the same institution in 1846; practiced medicine in Barnet, Vt., Plymouth, Mass., and Titusville, Pa., from 1849 to 1861; pioneer oil operator and lumberman in Titusville, Pa.; moved to Westfield, N.Y., in 1861 and engaged in banking, manufacturing, and agricultural pursuits; State military agent with rank of major during the Civil War; member of the board of supervisors of Chautauqua County, N.Y., 1868-1879; delegate to the Republican National Convention in 1872; member of the State assembly in 1873 and 1874; Government director of the Union Pacific Railroad four years under Presidents Grant and Hayes; appointed manager of the State insane asylum, Buffalo, N.Y., in 1881; elected as a Republican to the Forty-eighth Congress (March 4, 1883-March 3, 1885); was not a candidate for reelection in 1884; resumed the practice of medicine; died in Westfield, Chautauqua County, N.Y., July 29, 1892; interment in Allegheny Cemetery, Pittsburgh, Pa.

**BREWER, John Hart,** a Representative from New Jersey; born in Hunterdon County, N.J., March 29, 1844; attended the Lawrenceville schools and Trenton Academy; was graduated from the Delaware Literary Institution, Franklin, Delaware County, N.Y., in 1862; moved to Trenton, N.J., in 1865 and engaged in the manufacture of pottery; member of the State house of assembly in 1876; president of the National Potters' Association in 1879; elected as a Republican to the Forty-seventh and Forty-eighth Congresses (March 4, 1881-March 3, 1885); resumed the manufacture of pottery until 1895, when he engaged in the insurance business; appointed assistant appraiser of merchandise at the port of New York City by President William McKinley and served until his death in Trenton, N.J., December 21, 1900; interment in Riverview Cemetery.

**BREWER, Mark Spencer,** a Representative from Michigan; born in Addison Township, Oakland County, Mich., October 22, 1837; attended the rural schools and Romeo and Oxford Academies; studied law; was admitted to the bar in 1864 and commenced practice in Pontiac, Mich.; city attorney of Pontiac in 1866 and 1867; circuit court commissioner for Oakland County 1866-1869; member of the State senate 1872-1874; elected as a Republican to the Forty-fifth and Forty-sixth Congresses (March 4, 1877-March 3, 1881); appointed consul general to Berlin on June 30, 1881, by President James A. Garfield and served from August 29, 1881, until June 7, 1885; elected to the Fiftieth and Fifty-first Congresses (March 4, 1887-March 3, 1891); declined to be a candidate for renomination in 1890 to the Fifty-second Congress; resumed the practice of law in Pontiac, Mich.; delegate to the Republican National Convention of 1896; appointed a member of the United States Civil Service Commission by President William McKinley on January 18, 1898, and served until his death in Washington, D.C., March 18, 1901; interment in Oak Hill Cemetery, Pontiac, Mich.

**Bibliography:** *DAB.*

**BREWER, Willis,** a Representative from Alabama; born near Livingston, Sumter County, Ala., March 15, 1844; attended the common schools; entered the Confederate Army at the age of eighteen years; journalist, author, and planter; studied law; was admitted to the bar in 1870 and commenced practice at Haynesville, Ala.; treasurer of Lowndes County in 1871; State auditor 1876-1880; member of the State house of representatives 1880-1882; served in the State senate 1882-1890; again a member of the State house of representatives 1890-1894; again served in the State senate 1894-1897; elected as a Democrat to the Fifty-fifth and Fifty-sixth Congresses (March 4, 1897-March 3, 1901); unsuccessful candidate for renomination in 1900; resumed the practice of law and continued his work as an author until his death in Montgomery, Ala., on October 30, 1912; interment in the family mausoleum on Cedars plantation, near Montgomery, Ala.

**BREWSTER, Daniel Baugh,** a Representative and a Senator from Maryland; born in Baltimore County, Md., November 23, 1923; educated at Gilman School, Baltimore, Md., St. Paul's School, Concord, N.H., Princeton University, and Johns Hopkins University; during the Second World War enlisted as a private in the United States Marine Corps in 1942; commissioned as a second lieutenant in 1943 and served until 1946; graduated from the University of Maryland Law School in 1949; was admitted to the bar in 1949 and commenced practice in Towson, Md.; member, Maryland State house of delegates, 1950-1958; elected as a Democrat to the Eighty-sixth and Eighty-seventh Congresses (January 3, 1959-January 3, 1963); was not a candidate for renomination in 1962 to the House of Representatives, but was elected to the United States Senate, and served from January 3, 1963, to January 3, 1969; unsuccessful candidate for reelection in 1968; farmer; is a resident of Glyndon, Md.

**BREWSTER, David P.,** a Representative from New York; born in Cairo, Greene County, N.Y., June 15, 1801; attended the common schools, and was graduated from Union College, Schenectady, N.Y., in 1823; moved to New York City; studied law; was admitted to the bar in 1825 and commenced practice in Oswego, N.Y.; trustee of the village of Oswego in 1828, 1836, and 1845; prosecuting attorney of Oswego County from 1829 until 1833; treasurer of the village of Oswego, 1832-1834, and served as its president in 1837; judge of the court of common pleas, 1833-1841; elected as a Democrat to the Twenty-sixth and Twenty-seventh Congresses (March 4, 1839-March 3, 1843); appointed postmaster of Oswego, N.Y., on July 21, 1845, and served until January 10, 1849, when his successor was appointed; resumed the practice of law; also engaged in agricultural pursuits; member of the excise board commission, and served as president, 1870-1873; died in Oswego, N.Y., February 20, 1876; interment in Riverside Cemetery.

**BREWSTER, Henry Colvin,** a Representative from New York; born in Rochester, N.Y., September 7, 1845; attended the public schools; became a clerk in the Traders' National Bank in 1863; employed as cashier from 1868 until 1894, as president from 1907 to 1917, and as chairman of the board from 1917 until 1923; vice president of the New York State League of Republican Clubs and president of the Monroe County League; president of the Rochester Chamber of Commerce in 1893 and 1902; one of the organizers of the New York State Bankers' Association, serving as vice president in 1894 and president in 1899; elected as a Republican to the Fifty-fourth and Fifty-fifth Congresses (March 4, 1895-March 3, 1899); chairman, Committee on Alcoholic Liquor Traffic (Fifty-fifth Congress); was not a candidate for renomination in 1898 to the Fifty-sixth Congress; vice president of the National League of Republican Clubs in 1897; resumed banking and other business activities; delegate to the Republican National Convention of 1900; retired in 1923; died January 29, 1928, in Canandaigua, N.Y., while on a visit; interment in Mount Hope Cemetery, Rochester, N.Y.

**BREWSTER, Ralph Owen,** a Representative and a Senator from Maine; born in Dexter, Penobscot County, Maine, February 22, 1888; attended the public schools; was graduated from Bowdoin College, Brunswick, Maine, in 1909, and from the law department of Harvard University in 1913; high school principal 1910; was admitted to the bar in 1913 and commenced practice in Portland, Maine; member of the Portland school committee from 1915 until 1923; member, Maine State house of representatives, 1917-1918, but resigned to enter military service; served successively as private, second lieutenant, captain, and regimental adjutant, Third Infantry, Maine National Guard; member, State house of representatives, 1921-1923; member of the State senate, 1923-1925; elected Governor of Maine in 1924, reelected in 1926, and served from January 8, 1925 to January 2, 1929; unsuccessful candidate for election in 1932 to the Seventy-third Congress; elected as a Republican to the Seventy-fourth and to the two succeeding Congresses (January 3, 1935-January 3, 1941); was not a candidate in 1940 for reelection to the House of Representatives, but was elected to the United States Senate; reelected in 1946, and served from January 3, 1941, until his resignation December 31, 1952; unsuccessful candidate for renomination in 1952; chairman, Special Committee on National Defense (Eightieth Congress); died in Boston, Mass., December 25, 1961; interment in Mount Pleasant Cemetery, Dexter, Maine.

Bibliography: *DAB.*

**BREWSTER, William K.,** a Representative from Oklahoma; born in Ardmore, Carter County, Okla., November 8, 1941; graduated, Petrolia, Tex., high school, 1959; B.S., Southwestern Oklahoma State University, Weatherford, 1968; United States Army Reserve service; pharmacist; rancher; owner-operator, Colleyville (Tex.) Drug Inc., 1964-1977; Brewster Angus Farms, 1968 to present; member, Oklahoma State house of representatives, 1983-1990; elected as a Democrat to the One Hundred Second and to the two succeeding Congresses (January 3, 1991-January 3, 1997); was not a candidate for reelection in 1996 to the One Hundred Fifth Congress; is a resident of Marietta, Okla.

**BRICE, Calvin Stewart,** a Senator from Ohio; born in Denmark, Ashtabula County, Ohio, September 17, 1845; attended Miami University, Oxford, Ohio; during the Civil War enlisted in the university company in April 1861 and served in West Virginia; was graduated from Miami University in June 1863; recruited a company, reentered the Civil War as captain of that company and served until July 1865, attaining the rank of lieutenant colonel; studied law at the University of Michigan at Ann Arbor; was admitted to the Cincinnati bar in 1866 and commenced practice in Lima, Allen County, Ohio; member of the Democratic National Committee, serving as chairman in 1889; elected as a Democrat to the United States Senate and served from March 4, 1891, to March 3, 1897; was not a candidate for reelection; chairman, Committee on Pacific Railroads (Fifty-third Congress); died in New York City, December 15, 1898; interment in Woodlawn Cemetery, Lima, Ohio.

Bibliography: *DAB*; Havighurst, Walter. "The World of Calvin Brice." In *Men of Old Miami, 1809-1873*. pp. 209-24. New York: G.P. Putnam's Sons, 1974.

**BRICK, Abraham Lincoln,** a Representative from Indiana; born on his father's farm, near South Bend, St. Joseph County, Ind., May 27, 1860; attended the common schools and was graduated from the South Bend High School; later attended Cornell and Yale Colleges, and was graduated from the law department of the University of Michigan at Ann Arbor in 1883; was admitted to the bar the same year and commenced practice in South Bend, St. Joseph County, Ind.; prosecuting attorney for the counties of St. Joseph and La Porte in 1886; delegate to the Republican National Convention in 1896; elected as a Republican to the Fifty-sixth and to the four succeeding Congresses and served from March 4, 1899, until his death in Indianapolis, Ind., April 7, 1908; interment in Riverview Cemetery, South Bend, Ind.

**BRICKER, John William,** a Senator from Ohio; born on a farm near Mount Sterling, Madison County, Ohio, September 6, 1893; attended the country schools; graduated from Ohio State University at Columbus in 1916 and from its law department in 1920; was admitted to the bar in 1917 and commenced practice in Columbus, Ohio, in 1920; during the First World War served as first lieutenant and chaplain in the United States Army in 1917 and 1918; solicitor for Grandview Heights, Ohio, 1920-1928; assistant attorney general of Ohio from 1923 until 1927; member of the Public Utilities Commission of Ohio, 1929-1932; attorney general of Ohio, 1933-1937; unsuccessful Republican candidate for election for Governor in 1936; elected Governor of Ohio in 1938, reelected in 1940 and 1942, and served from January 9, 1939 to January 8, 1945; unsuccessful Republican candidate for Vice President in 1944 on the ticket headed by Thomas E. Dewey; elected as a Republican to the United States Senate in 1946, reelected in 1952, and served from January 3, 1947 to January 3, 1959; as Bricker entered the Senate subway on July 12, 1947, he was fired upon but not wounded by William L. Kaiser, who had formerly been connected with a failed building and loan association in Ohio; unsuccessful candidate for reelection in 1958; chairman, Committee on Interstate and Foreign Commerce (Eighty-third Congress); sponsor of the proposed "Bricker Amendment" to the Constitution, restricting the authority of the President to negotiate international treaties and agreements; resumed the practice of law; died in Columbus, Ohio, March 22, 1986; interment in Greenlawn Cemetery.

Bibliography: Davies, Richard O. *Defender of the Old Guard: John Bricker and American Politics*. Columbus: Ohio State

University Press, 1993; Tanantaum, Duane. "The Bricker Amendment Controversy: The Interaction Between Domestic and Foreign Affairs." Ph.D. dissertation, Columbia University, 1980; Zahniser, Marvin R., ed. "John W. Bricker Reflects Upon the Fight for the Bricker Amendment." *Ohio History* 87 (Summer 1978): 322-33.

**BRICKNER, George H.,** a Representative from Wisconsin; born in Anspach, Bavaria, Germany, January 21, 1834; immigrated to the United States in 1840 with his parents, who settled in Seneca County, Ohio; attended the public schools; engaged in mercantile pursuits in Tiffin, Ohio, 1850-1855; moved to Cascade, Wis., in 1855 and again engaged in mercantile pursuits; operated a flour mill until 1868, when he engaged in the manufacture of woolens at Sheboygan Falls, Wis.; established a glass factory in Tiffin, Ohio, in 1889; elected as a Democrat to the Fifty-first, Fifty-second, and Fifty-third Congresses (March 4, 1889-March 3, 1895); chairman, Committee on Expenditures in the Department of the Treasury (Fifty-second Congress); was not a candidate for reelection in 1894 to the Fifty-fourth Congress; lived in retirement in Sheboygan Falls, Sheboygan County, Wis., until his death on August 12, 1904; interment in St. Mary's Cemetery.

**BRIDGES, George Washington,** a Representative from Tennessee; born in Charleston, Bradley County, Tenn., October 9, 1825; attended East Tennessee University at Knoxville; studied law; was admitted to the bar in 1848 and commenced practice in Athens, McMinn County, Tenn.; also engaged in agricultural pursuits; attorney general of Tennessee 1849-1860; elected as a Unionist to the Thirty-seventh Congress, but was arrested by Confederate troops while en route to Washington, D.C., taken back to Tennessee, and held as a prisoner for more than a year; finally made his escape and went to Washington, D.C., and assumed his duties; qualified and took his seat in the House of Representatives on February 25, 1863, and served until March 3, 1863; enlisted in the Union Army as a captain on August 25, 1863; mustered in as a lieutenant colonel in the Tenth Tennessee Volunteer Cavalry February 23, 1864, and was discharged December 29, 1864; elected circuit judge of the fourth judicial district of Tennessee in 1866 and served about one year; died in Athens, Tenn., March 16, 1873; interment in Cedar Grove Cemetery.

**BRIDGES, Henry Styles,** a Senator from New Hampshire; born in West Pembroke, Washington County, Maine, September 9, 1898; attended the public schools; was graduated from the University of Maine at Orono in 1918; instructor at Sanderson Academy, Ashfield, Mass., 1918-1919; member of the extension staff of the University of New Hampshire at Durham, 1921-1922; secretary of the New Hampshire Farm Bureau Federation, 1922-1923; editor of the Granite Monthly Magazine, 1924-1926; director and secretary of the New Hampshire Investment Co., 1924-1929; member of the New Hampshire Public Service Commission, 1930-1934; lieutenant in the United States Army Reserve Corps from 1925 until 1937; elected Governor of New Hampshire in 1934 and served from January 3, 1935 to January 7, 1937; member of the Commission on Organization of the Executive Branch of the Government (Hoover Commission); elected as a Republican to the United States Senate in 1936, 1942, 1948, 1954, and again in 1960, and served from January 3, 1937, until his death in East Concord, N.H., on November 26, 1961; minority leader (Eighty-second Congress); served as President pro tempore of the Senate during the Eighty-third Congress; chairman, Joint Committee on Foreign Economic Cooperation (Eightieth Congress), Joint Committee on Inaugural Arrangements (Eighty-second and Eighty-fourth Congresses), Committee on Appropriations (Eightieth and Eighty-third Congresses), Republican Policy Committee (Eighty-fourth through Eighty-seventh Congresses); interment in Pine Grove Cemetery.

**BRIDGES, Samuel Augustus,** a Representative from Pennsylvania; born in Colchester, Conn., January 27, 1802; pursued an academic course, and was graduated from Williams College, Williamstown, Mass., in 1826; studied law; was admitted to the bar in 1829 and commenced practice in Doylestown, Pa.; moved to Allentown, Lehigh County, Pa., in 1830, where he continued the practice of law; town clerk 1837-1842; deputy attorney general of Pennsylvania for Lehigh County 1837-1844; delegate to the Pennsylvania Democratic convention in 1841; elected as a Democrat to the Thirtieth Congress to fill the vacancy caused by the death of John W. Hornbeck and served from March 6, 1848, to March 3, 1849; was not a candidate for renomination in 1848 to the Thirty-first Congress; elected to the Thirty-third Congress (March 4, 1853-March 3, 1855); unsuccessful candidate for reelection in 1854 to the Thirty-fourth Congress; resumed the practice of law; elected to the Forty-fifth Congress (March 4, 1877-March 3, 1879); was not a candidate for renomination in 1878 to the Forty-sixth Congress; continued the practice of law in Allentown, Pa., where he died January 14, 1884; interment in Union Cemetery.

**BRIDGES, Styles,** a Senator from New Hampshire. (*See* BRIDGES, Henry Styles.)

**BRIGGS, Clay Stone,** a Representative from Texas; born in Galveston, Tex., January 8, 1876; attended private and public schools, the University of Texas at Austin, and Harvard Unversity; was graduated from the law department of Yale University in 1899; was admitted to the bar the same year and commenced the practice of law in Galveston, Tex.; member of the State house of representatives 1906-1908; served as judge of the tenth judicial district of Texas from June 15, 1909, until February 1, 1919, when he resigned, having been elected to Congress; elected as a Democrat to the Sixty-sixth and to the seven succeeding Congresses and served from March 4, 1919, until his death in Washington, D.C., April 29, 1933; interment in Oakwood Cemetery, Syracuse, N.Y.

**BRIGGS, Frank Obadiah** (son of James Frankland Briggs), a Senator from New Jersey; born in Concord, N.H., August 12, 1851; attended the public schools, Francestown (N.H.) Academy, and Phillips Academy, Exeter, N.H.; was graduated from the United States Military Academy at West Point in 1872; served in the Second Regiment, United States Infantry, as second lieutenant until 1877, when he resigned from the Army; moved to Trenton, N.J., in 1877 and engaged in the manufacture of wire and wire products; member of the Trenton School Board 1884-1892; mayor of Trenton 1899-1902; member of the State board of education in 1901 and 1902; State treasurer 1902-1907; chairman of the Republican State committee 1904-1911; elected as a Republican to the United States Senate and served from March 4, 1907, to March 3, 1913; unsuccessful candidate for reelection; chairman, Committee on Geological Survey (Sixty-first Congress), Committee to Audit and Control the Contingent Expense (Sixty-second Congress); resumed his former business pursuits in Trenton, N.J., where he died May 8, 1913; interment in Riverview Cemetery.

**BRIGGS, Frank Parks,** a Senator from Missouri; born in Armstrong, Howard County, Mo., February 25, 1894; attended Armstrong and Fayette schools and Central College at Fayette, Mo., 1911-1914; was graduated from the University of Missouri at Columbia in 1915; engaged in the newspaper business in 1915 and in the publishing business at Macon, Mo., in 1925; mayor of Macon, Mo., 1930-1932; member, Missouri State senate, 1933-1944; appointed as a Democrat to the United States Senate to fill the vacancy caused by the resignation of Harry S Truman and served from January 18, 1945, to January 3, 1947; unsuccessful candidate for election to the United States Senate in 1946; resumed the newspaper publishing business; chairman, Missouri State Conservation Commission, 1955-1956; Assistant Secretary of the Interior for Fish and Wildlife, 1961-1965; was a resident of Macon, Mo.; died September 23, 1992.

**BRIGGS, George,** a Representative from New York; born near Broadalbin, Fulton County, N.Y., May 6, 1805; moved to Vermont, in 1812 with his parents, who settled in Bennington; attended the public schools; engaged in business as a dealer in hardware; member of the Vermont house of representatives in 1837; returned to New York, settled in New York City in 1838, and continued in the hardware business; elected as a Whig to the Thirty-first and Thirty-second Congresses (March 4, 1849-March 3, 1853); declined to be a candidate for renomination in 1852; elected as a Republican to the Thirty-sixth Congress (March 4, 1859-March 3, 1861); chairman, Committee on Revolutionary Claims (Thirty-sixth Congress); declined to be a candidate for renomination in 1860 and retired; delegate to the Union National Convention at Philadelphia in 1866; died at his summer home, "Woodlawn," at Saratoga Springs, N.Y., June 1, 1869; interment in Greenwood Cemetery, New York City.

**BRIGGS, George Nixon,** a Representative from Massachusetts; born in Adams, Mass., April 12, 1796; when seven years of age moved with his parents to Manchester, Vt., and, two years later, to White Creek, N.Y.; attended the public schools; moved to Lanesboro, Mass., in 1814; apprenticed to the hatter's trade; studied law; was admitted to the bar in 1818 and commenced practice in Lanesboro; register of deeds for Berkshire County 1824-1831; elected town clerk in 1824; appointed chairman of the board of commissioners of highways in 1826; elected as an Anti-Jacksonian to the Twenty-second and Twenty-third Congresses, and as a Whig to the Twenty-fourth through Twenty-seventh Congresses (March 4, 1831-March 3, 1843); chairman, Committee on Public Expenditures (Twenty-sixth Congress), Committee on the Post Office and Post Roads (Twenty-seventh Congress); was not a candidate for renomination in 1842 to the Twenty-eighth Congress; moved to Pittsfield in 1843; elected Governor of Massachusetts in 1843, reelected every year from 1844 through 1850, and served from January 1844 to January 11, 1851; resumed the practice of law in Pittsfield; member of the Massachusetts constitutional convention in 1853; judge of the court of common pleas 1853-1858; appointed in 1861 as a member of a commission to adjust differences between the United States and New Granada (Colombia); accidentally killed in Pittsfield, Berkshire County, Mass., on September 11, 1861; interment in the Pittsfield Cemetery.

Bibliography: *DAB.*

**BRIGGS, James Frankland** (father of Frank Obadiah Briggs), a Representative from New Hampshire; born in Bury, Lancashire, England, October 23, 1827; immigrated to the United States in 1829 with his parents, who settled in Holderness (now Ashland), N.H.; attended the common schools and Newbury Academy; studied law; was admitted to the bar in 1851 and practiced in Hillsboro, N.H., until 1871; moved to Manchester, N.H.; member of the New Hampshire State house of representatives, 1856-1858, and in 1874; during the Civil War served as major of the Eleventh Regiment, New Hampshire Volunteer Infantry; served in the New Hampshire State senate in 1876; elected as a Republican to the Forty-fifth and to the two succeeding Congresses (March 4, 1877-March 3, 1883); chairman, Committee on Expenditures in the Department of War (Forty-seventh Congress); was not a candidate for renomination in 1882 to the Forty-eighth Congress; resumed the practice of law; again a member of the State house of representatives in 1883, 1891, and 1897, serving as speaker in 1897; delegate to the State constitutional convention in 1889; died in Manchester, N.H., January 21, 1905; interment in Green Grove Cemetery, Ashland, Grafton County, N.H.

**BRIGHAM, Elbert Sidney,** a Representative from Vermont; born in St. Albans, Franklin County, Vt., October 19, 1877; attended the graded schools; was graduated from St. Albans High School in 1898 and from Middlebury (Vt.) College in 1903; engaged in agricultural pursuits and the breeding of dairy cattle; auditor for the town of St. Albans in 1911 and 1912; State commissioner of agriculture 1913-1924; member of the National Agricultural Advisory Committee and of the United States Food Administration, Washington, D.C., in 1918; trustee of Middlebury College 1922-1960; director, National Life Insurance Co., in 1925; elected as a Republican to the Sixty-ninth, Seventieth, and Seventy-first Congresses (March 4, 1925-March 3, 1931); was not a candidate for renomination in 1930; member of Reconstruction Finance Corporation in 1932; chairman of Vermont Advisory Banking Board, 1933-1936; president, National Life Insurance Co., Montpelier, Vt., 1937-1948; president, Franklin County Savings Bank & Trust Co., St. Albans, Vt., 1944-1957 and chairman of the board 1957-1962; died in St. Albans City, Vt., July 5, 1962; interment in St. Albans Bay Cemetery, St. Albans Town, Vt.

**BRIGHAM, Elijah,** a Representative from Massachusetts; born in Westboro (now Northboro), Mass., July 7, 1751; was graduated from Dartmouth College, Hanover, N.H., in 1778; studied law, but did not practice; engaged in mercantile pursuits at Westboro; member of the Massachusetts house of representatives 1791-1793; justice of the court of common pleas 1795-1811; served in the Massachusetts senate in 1796, 1798, 1801-1805, and 1807-1810; Massachusetts councilor in 1799, 1800, and 1806; elected as a Federalist to the Twelfth, Thirteenth, and Fourteenth Congresses and served from March 4, 1811, until his death in Washington, D.C., February 22, 1816; interment in the Congressional Cemetery.

**BRIGHAM, Lewis Alexander,** a Representative from New Jersey; born at New York Mills, Oneida County, N.Y., January 2, 1831; attended the district schools and Whitestown Seminary, Whitesboro, N.Y.; was graduated from Hamilton College, Clinton, N.Y., in 1849; studied law; was admitted to the bar in 1855 and commenced practice in New York City; superintendent of public schools, Bergen, N.J., 1866-1870; member of the board of police commissioners of Jersey City 1874-1876; member of the State house of assembly in 1877; elected as a Republican to the Forty-sixth Congress (March 4, 1879-March 3, 1881); unsuccessful candidate for reelection in 1880 to the Forty-eighth Congress; resumed the practice of law in New York City; died in Jersey City, N.J., February 19, 1885; interment in Old Bergen Church Cemetery.

**BRIGHT, Jesse David,** a Senator from Indiana; born in Norwich, Chenango County, N.Y., December 18, 1812; moved with his parents to Madison, Ind., in 1820; attended the public schools; studied law; was admitted to the bar in 1831 and commenced practice in Madison, Jefferson County, Ind.; elected judge of the probate court of Jefferson County in 1834; United States marshal for the district of Indiana, 1840-1841; member, Indiana State senate, 1841-1843; Lieutenant Governor of Indiana, 1843-1845; elected as a Democrat to the United States Senate in 1845; reelected in 1850 and 1856, and served from March 4, 1845 to February 5, 1862, when he was expelled for acknowledging Jefferson Davis as "President of the Confederation of States" in a letter of March 1861, and for disloyalty to the Union; served as President pro tempore of the Senate during the Thirty-third, Thirty-fourth and Thirty-sixth Congresses; chairman, Committee on Enrolled Bills (Twenty-ninth Congress), Committee on Public Buildings (Twenty-ninth Congress), Committee on Revolutionary Claims (Thirtieth Congress), Committee on Roads and Canals (Thirty-first through Thirty third Congresses), Committee on Public Buildings and Grounds (Thirty-fifth and Thirty-sixth Congresses); unsuccessful candidate for election in 1863 to the United States Senate to fill the vacancy caused by his expulsion; moved to Carrollton, Ky., in 1863 and then to Covington, Ky.; member of the State house of representatives in 1866; president of the Raymond City Coal Co., 1871-1875; moved to Baltimore, Md. in 1874; died in Baltimore on May 20, 1875; interment in Greenmount Cemetery.

Bibliography: *DAB*; Cooney, Charles F. "Treason or Tyranny? The Great Senate Purge of '62." *Civil War Times Illustrated* 18 (July 1979): 30-31; Murphy, Charles. "The Political Career of Jesse Bright." *Indiana Historical Society Publications* 10 (1931): 101-45; Van Der Weele, Wayne J. "Jesse David Bright: Master Politician from the Old Northwest." Ph.D. dissertation, Indiana University, 1958.

**BRIGHT, John Morgan,** a Representative from Tennessee; born in Fayetteville, Lincoln County, Tenn., January 20, 1817; attended the schools of Fayetteville and Bingham's School, Hillsboro, N.C.; was graduated from Nashville (Tenn.) University in September 1839 and from the law department of Transylvania University, Lexington, Ky., in March 1841; was admitted to the bar in 1841 and commenced practice in Fayetteville, Tenn.; member of the State house of representatives in 1847 and 1848; served as general on the staff of Governor Isham G. Harris 1861-1865; elected as a Democrat to the Forty-second and to the four succeeding Congresses (March 4, 1871-March 3, 1881); chairman, Committee on Claims (Forty-fourth through Forty-sixth Congresses), Committee on Expenditures in the Department of the Treasury (Forty-fourth Congress); unsuccessful candidate for reelection in 1880 to the Forty-seventh Congress; resumed the practice of law; died in Fayetteville, Tenn., October 3, 1911; interment in the Presbyterian Churchyard.

**BRINKERHOFF, Henry Roelif** (cousin of Jacob Brinkerhoff), a Representative from Ohio; born in Adams County, Pa., September 23, 1787; moved with his parents to Cayuga County, N.Y., in 1793; attended the country schools; commanded a company of militia in the War of 1812, distinguishing himself in the Battle of Queenstown Heights, Canada, October 13, 1812; engaged in agricultural pursuits; member of the State assembly in 1828 and 1829; senior major general of the New York State Militia in 1824; commanded the military escort which accompanied General Lafayette in his progress through the State; moved to Huron County, Ohio, in 1837; elected as a Democrat to the Twenty-eighth Congress and served from March 4, 1843, until his death in Huron County, Ohio, April 30, 1844; interment in the Pioneer Cemetery, Plymouth, Richland County, Ohio.

**BRINKERHOFF, Jacob** (cousin of Henry Roelif Brinkerhoff), a Representative from Ohio; born in Niles, Cayuga County, N.Y., August 31, 1810; attended the public schools and Plattsburgh Academy, Steuben County, N.Y.; studied law; was admitted to the bar in 1837 and commenced practice in Mansfield, Richland County, Ohio; moved to Plymouth, Ohio; prosecuting attorney of Richland County, Ohio, 1839-1843; elected as a Democrat to the Twenty-eighth and Twenty-ninth Congresses (March 4, 1843-March 3, 1847); chairman, Committee on Invalid Pensions (Twenty-eighth Congress); resumed the practice of law in Mansfield, Ohio; affiliated with the Republican Party on its formation in 1856; delegate to numerous Republican National Conventions; justice of the supreme court of Ohio, 1856-1871; died in Mansfield, Ohio, July 19, 1880; interment in Mansfield Cemetery.

Bibliography: *DAB*.

**BRINKLEY, Jack Thomas,** a Representative from Georgia; born in Faceville, Decatur County, Ga., December 22, 1930; attended the public schools of Faceville, Ga.; B.A., Young Harris (Ga.) College, 1949; taught school, 1949-1951; served as a pilot in the United States Air Force, 1951-1956, with service during the Korean conflict; J.D., University of Georgia School of Law, 1959; was admitted to the bar and commenced practice in Columbus, Ga., in 1959; member,

Georgia State house of representatives, 1965-1966; elected as a Democrat to the Ninetieth and to the seven succeeding Congresses (January 3, 1967-January 3, 1983); was not a candidate for reelection in 1982 to the Ninety-eighth Congress; is a resident of Columbus, Ga.

**BRINSON, Samuel Mitchell,** a Representative from North Carolina; born in New Bern, Craven County, N.C., March 20, 1870; attended private and public schools, and was graduated from Wake Forest College, North Carolina, in 1891; taught school in New Bern one year; was graduated from the law department of the University of North Carolina at Chapel Hill in 1895; was admitted to the North Carolina bar in 1896 and commenced the practice of law in New Bern, N.C.; served as county superintendent of public instruction in Craven County 1902-1919; president of the Atlantic & North Carolina Railroad Company in 1918; elected as a Democrat to the Sixty-sixth and Sixty-seventh Congresses and served from March 4, 1919, until his death in New Bern, N.C., April 13, 1922; interment in Cedar Grove Cemetery.

**BRISBIN, John,** a Representative from Pennsylvania; born in Sherburne, Chenango County, N.Y., July 13, 1818; taught school; studied law; was admitted to the bar and commenced practice in Tunkhannock, Wyoming County, Pa., about 1843; elected as a Democrat to the Thirty-first Congress to fill the vacancy caused by the death of Chester Butler and served from January 13 to March 3, 1851; president of the Delaware, Lackawanna & Western Railway Co. 1863-1867 and member of the board of managers and general counsel from 1867 until his death in Newark, N.J., February 3, 1880; interment in Evergreen Cemetery, Elizabeth, N.J.

**BRISTOW, Francis Marion,** a Representative from Kentucky; born in Clark County, Ky., August 11, 1804; pursued preparatory studies; studied law; was admitted to the bar and commenced practice in Elkton; member of the Kentucky house of representatives 1831-1833; served in the Kentucky senate in 1846; delegate to the Kentucky constitutional convention in 1849; elected as a Whig to the Thirty-third Congress to fill the vacancy caused by the death of Presley Underwood Ewing and served from December 4, 1854, to March 3, 1855; elected as a candidate of the Opposition Party to the Thirty-sixth Congress (March 4, 1859-March 3, 1861); was not a candidate for reelection in 1860; resumed the practice of law; member of the House Committee of Thirty-three appointed by the Speaker in December 1860 to consider compromise proposals to avert civil war, and also attended the peace convention of 1861 held in Washington, D.C., in an effort to devise means to prevent the impending war; died in Elkton, Todd County, Ky., June 10, 1864; interment in the family burying ground.

Bibliography: Webb, Ross A. "Francis Marion Bristow, A Study in Unionism." *Filson Club History Quarterly* 37 (April 1963): 142-58.

**BRISTOW, Henry,** a Representative from New York; born in St. Michael, Azores Islands, June 5, 1840; immigrated to the United States with his parents, who settled in Brooklyn, N.Y.; attended public and private schools; engaged in mercantile pursuits until 1896; served as a private in Company B, Seventh Regiment, New York State Militia, from April 26, 1861, to June 3, 1861; appointed city magistrate in 1896; member of the board of education of Brooklyn 1880-1889; elected as a Republican to the Fifty-seventh Congress (March 4, 1901-March 3, 1903); unsuccessful candidate for reelection in 1902 to the Fifty-eighth Congress; appointed public administrator of Brooklyn, N.Y., in 1904 and served until his death in that city October 11, 1906; interment in Greenwood Cemetery.

**BRISTOW, Joseph Little,** a Senator from Kansas; born near Hazel Green, Wolf County, Ky., July 22, 1861; moved with his father to Fredonia, Kans., in 1873; attended the country schools, and was graduated from Baker University, Baldwin, Kans., in 1886; clerk of the district court of Douglas County, 1886-1890; in 1890 bought the

Salina (Kans.) Daily Republican, which he edited for five years; elected secretary of the Republican State committee in 1894; private secretary to Governor Edmund N. Morrill, 1895-1897; purchased the Ottawa (Kans.) Herald, which he owned for more than ten years; again elected secretary of the Republican State committee in 1898; Fourth Assistant Postmaster General, 1897-1905; purchased the Salina Daily Republican-Journal in 1903; appointed a special commissioner of the Panama Railroad in 1905; elected as a Republican to the United States Senate and served from March 4, 1909, to March 3, 1915; was an unsuccessful candidate for reelection in 1914; chairman, Committee on Expenditures in the Post Office Department (Sixty-first and Sixty-second Congresses), Committee on Cuban Relations (Sixty-third Congress); temporarily engaged in agricultural pursuits with his son near Fairfax, Va.; chairman of the Kansas Utilities Commission, 1915-1918; engaged in agricultural pursuits on his estate, "Ossian Hall," near Fairfax, Va., from 1918 until his death there July 14, 1944; interment in Gypsum Hill Cemetery, Salina, Kans.

**Bibliography:** *DAB*; Sageser, A. Bower. *Joseph L. Bristow: Kansas Progressive.* Lawrence: University Press of Kansas, 1968.

**BRITT, Charles Robin,** a Representative from North Carolina; born in San Antonio, Bexar County, Tex., June 29, 1942; educated in Asheville, N.C. schools; graduated, Enka High School, Asheville, N.C., 1959; B.A., University of North Carolina, Chapel Hill, 1963; J.D., same university, 1973; LL.M., New York University, New York City, 1976; admitted to the North Carolina bar, 1973, and commenced practice in Greensboro; United States Naval Reserve, 1963-1984; chairman, Guilford County Democratic Party, 1979-1981; delegate, North Carolina State Democratic convention, 1980; delegate, Democratic National Convention, 1980; elected as a Democrat to the Ninety-eighth Congress (January 3, 1983-January 3, 1985); unsuccessful candidate for reelection in 1984 to the Ninety-ninth Congress; president and director, Project Uplift, Greensboro; is a resident of Greensboro, N.C.

**BRITT, James Jefferson,** a Representative from North Carolina; born in Unico County, near Johnson City, Tenn., March 4, 1861; attended the common schools and studied under private tutors; principal of Burnsville (N.C.) Academy, 1886-1893; superintendent of the public schools of Mitchell County, 1894-1896; headmaster of Bowman Academy, Bakersville, N.C., 1895-1896; deputy collector of internal revenue at Asheville, N.C., 1896-1899; studied law at the University of North Carolina at Chapel Hill; was admitted to the bar in 1900 and commenced practice in Asheville, N.C.; delegate to the Republican National Convention of 1904; unsuccessful candidate for election in 1906 to the Sixtieth Congress; special assistant United States attorney in 1906 and 1907; member of the North Carolina State senate, 1909-1911; special counsel to the Post Office Department from July 1, 1909 to December 1, 1910; special assistant to the Attorney General from July 13 to December 1, 1910; appointed Third Assistant Postmaster General by President William Howard Taft on December 1, 1910, and served until March 17, 1913; elected as a Republican to the Sixty-fourth Congress (March 4, 1915-March 3, 1917); successfully contested the election of Zebulon Weaver to the Sixty-fifth Congress, and served from March 1 to March 3, 1919; unsuccessful candidate for reelection in 1918 to the Sixty-sixth Congress; resumed the practice of law in Asheville, N.C.; served as chief counsel for the Bureau of Prohibition, Treasury Department, 1922-1932; was an unsuccessful candidate for chief justice of the supreme court of North Carolina in 1926; resumed the practice of law in 1933; died in Asheville, N.C., on December 26, 1939; interment in Riverside Cemetery.

**BRITTEN, Frederick Albert,** a Representative from Illinois; born in Chicago, Ill., November 18, 1871; attended the public schools, and Healds Business College at San Francisco, Calif.; engaged in general building construction work in Chicago in 1893;

member of the Chicago City Council 1908-1912; member of the city civil service committee in 1909, serving as chairman; member of the executive committee of the American group of the Interparliamentary Union 1923-1934; became a member of the Republican National Congressional Committee in 1926; delegate to the Republican National Convention in 1936; elected as a Republican to the Sixty-third and to the ten succeeding Congresses (March 4, 1913-January 3, 1935); chairman, Committee on Naval Affairs (Seventieth and Seventy-first Congress); unsuccessful candidate for reelection in 1934 to the Seventy-fourth Congress; corporation executive in Chicago and New York; retired from public life and resided in Washington, D.C., until his death in Bethesda, Md., on May 4, 1946; interment in Abbey Mausoleum (adjoining Arlington National Cemetery), Arlington, Va.

**BROADHEAD, James Overton,** a Representative from Missouri; born in Charlottesville, Va., May 29, 1819; attended the high school in Albemarle County and the University of Virginia at Charlottesville; moved to Missouri in 1837; studied law; was admitted to the bar in 1842 and commenced practice in Bowling Green, Pike County, Mo.; delegate to the State constitutional conventions in 1845, 1861, 1863, and 1875; member of the Missouri State house of representatives, 1846-1847; served in the State senate, 1850-1853; moved to St. Louis in 1859 and continued the practice of law; appointed United States attorney for the eastern district of Missouri in 1861; commissioned by President Lincoln as lieutenant colonel of Volunteers and appointed provost marshal general of Missouri in 1863; delegate to the Democratic National Conventions of 1868 and 1872; appointed by President Ulysses S. Grant as special United States attorney to assist in the prosecution of the so-called "Whiskey Ring" at St. Louis in 1876; president of the American Bar Association in 1878; elected as a Democrat to the Forty-eighth Congress (March 4, 1883-March 3, 1885); was not a candidate for renomination in 1884 to the Forty-ninth Congress; appointed a special commissioner on French spoliation claims by President Grover Cleveland in 1885; appointed Minister to Switzerland on April 7, 1893, and served until November 1895; died in St. Louis, Mo., August 7, 1898; interment in Bellefontaine Cemetery.

**Bibliography:** *DAB*.

**BROCK, Lawrence,** a Representative from Nebraska; born in Platte County, near Columbus, Nebr., August 16, 1906; graduated from Leigh High School and from the University of Nebraska College of Pharmacy at Lincoln, Nebr., in 1929; engaged as a pharmacist in Madison, Nebr.; cattle feeder and farmer; former president of Nebraska Livestock Feeders Association, Cornbelt Livestock Feeders Association, and Northeast Nebraska Rural Electric Association; member Nebraska Highway Advisory Commission; delegate to the Democratic National Convention in 1956; elected as a Democrat to the Eighty-sixth Congress (January 3, 1959-January 3, 1961); was an unsuccessful candidate for reelection in 1960 to the Eighty-seventh Congress; appointed assistant administrator, Farmers Home Administration, Washington, D.C., in February 1961; died in Zion, Ill., on August 28, 1968; interment in the Wakefield Cemetery, Wakefield, Nebr.

**BROCK, William Emerson** (grandfather of William Emerson Brock III), a Senator from Tennessee; born near Mocksville, Davie County, N.C., March 14, 1872; attended the public schools; engaged in agricultural pursuits until 1894; moved to Winston-Salem, N.C., in 1894 and was employed as a clerk in a general store until 1896; tobacco salesman 1896-1901; moved to Chattanooga, Tenn., in 1909 and became engaged in the manufacture of candy; also was interested in banking and various other business enterprises and was director in a life and accident insurance company; served as trustee of the University of Chattanooga, Emory and Henry College, and Martha Washington College for Girls; appointed and subsequently elected as a Democrat to the United States Senate to fill the vacancy caused by the death of Lawrence D. Tyson and served from September 2, 1929, to March 3, 1931; was not a candidate for election to the full term; resumed the candy manufacturing business until his death in Chattanooga, Tenn., August 5, 1950; interment in Forest Hills Cemetery.

Bibliography: *DAB.*

BROCK, William Emerson, III (grandson of William Emerson Brock), a Representative and a Senator from Tennessee; born in Chattanooga, Hamilton County, Tenn., November 23, 1930; attended schools in Lookout Mountain and Chattanooga Tenn.; graduated from Washington and Lee University, Lexington, Va., 1953; served in the United States Navy 1953-1956; employed by the Brock Candy Co., becoming vice president of marketing; member of the board of directors of the Brock Candy Company; elected as a Republican to the Eighty-eighth and to the three succeeding Congresses (January 3, 1963-January 3, 1971); was not a candidate in 1970 for reelection to the House of Representatives, but was elected to the United States Senate, and served from January 3, 1971 to January 3, 1977; unsuccessful candidate for reelection in 1976; chairman, Republican National Committee, 1977-1981; United States Trade Representative, 1981-1985; appointed Secretary of Labor by President Ronald Reagan, and served from April 29, 1985 until October 31, 1987; consultant in Washington, D.C.; unsuccessful candidate in 1994 for election to the United States Senate from Maryland; is a resident of Annapolis, Md.

BROCKENBROUGH, William Henry, a Representative from Florida; born in Virginia February 23, 1812; studied law; was admitted to the bar and settled in Tallahassee, Fla.; member of the State house of representatives in 1837; served in the State senate 1840-1844, being its president in 1842; United States district attorney 1841-1843; upon the admission of Florida as a State into the Union successfully contested as a Democrat the election of Edward C. Cabell to the Twenty-ninth Congress and served from January 24, 1846, to March 3, 1847; died in Tallahassee, Fla., January 28, 1850; interment in the Episcopal Cemetery.

BROCKSON, Franklin, a Representative from Delaware; born in Blackbird Hundred, Newcastle County, Del., August 6, 1865; attended the public schools; was graduated from the Wilmington Conference Academy at Dover, Del., in 1890; engaged in mercantile pursuits; teacher and principal in the public schools at Port Penn and Marshallton, Del.; was graduated from the law department of Washington and Lee University, Lexington, Va., in 1896; was admitted to the bar September 21, 1896, and commenced practice in Wilmington, Del.; member of the State house of representatives 1908-1910; elected as a Democrat to the Sixty-third Congress (March 4, 1913-March 3, 1915); unsuccessful candidate for reelection in 1914 to the Sixty-fourth Congress; resumed the practice of law in Clayton, and Wilmington, Del.; died in Clayton, Del., March 16, 1942; interment in Odd Fellows Cemetery, Smyrna, Del.

BROCKWAY, John Hall, a Representative from Connecticut; born in Ellington, Tolland County, Conn., January 31, 1801; pursued preparatory studies and was graduated from Yale College, New Haven, Conn., in 1820; taught school; studied law; was admitted to the bar in 1823 and commenced practice in Ellington; member of the State house of representatives 1832-1838; served in the State senate in 1834; elected as a Whig to the Twenty-sixth and Twenty-seventh Congresses (March 4, 1839-March 3, 1843); prosecuting attorney for Tolland County from 1849 to 1867, when he resigned; died in Ellington, Conn., July 29, 1870; interment in Ellington Center Cemetery.

BRODBECK, Andrew R., a Representative from Pennsylvania; born in Jefferson (now Codorus), York County, Pa., April 11, 1860; attended the public schools; engaged in agricultural pursuits; taught in the public schools of York County 1878-1880; moved to Hanover, Pa., in 1880 and engaged in the farm implement and fertilizer business until 1896; sheriff of York County, Pa., 1896-1899; member of the board of directors of various business enterprises; unsuccessful candidate for election in 1910 to the Sixty-second Congress; elected as a Democrat to the Sixty-third Congress (March 4, 1913-March 3, 1915); unsuccessful candidate for reelection in 1914 to the Sixty-fourth Congress; elected to the Sixty-fifth Congress (March 4, 1917-March 3, 1919); unsuccessful candidate for reelection in 1918 to the Sixty-sixth Congress; delegate at large to the Democratic National Convention in 1920; retired in 1920; died in Hanover, Pa., February 27, 1937; interment in Mount Olivet Cemetery.

BRODERICK, Case (cousin of David Colbreth Broderick and Andrew Kennedy), a Representative from Kansas; born near Marion, Grant County, Ind., September 23, 1839; attended the common schools; moved to Holton, Jackson County, Kans., in 1858 and engaged in agricultural pursuits; during the Civil War enlisted as a private in the Second Kansas Battery in 1862 and was mustered out at Leavenworth in August 1865; studied law; was admitted to the bar in 1870 and commenced practice in Holton, Kans.; mayor of Holton in 1874 and 1875; prosecuting attorney of Jackson County 1876-1880; member of the State senate 1880-1884; appointed by President Chester A. Arthur as an associate justice of the supreme court of the Territory of Idaho in March 1884 and took up his residence in Boise City, Idaho; served until the fall of 1888, when he returned to Holton, Kans., and resumed the practice of law; elected as a Republican to the Fifty-second and to the three succeeding Congresses (March 4, 1891-March 3, 1899); unsuccessful candidate for renomination in 1898 to the Fifty-sixth Congress; again engaged in the practice of law in Holton, Kans.; retired from the practice of law and devoted his time to farming and livestock interests; died in Holton, Kans., April 1, 1920; interment in Holton Cemetery.

BRODERICK, David Colbreth (cousin of Andrew Kennedy and Case Broderick), a Senator from California; born in Washington, D.C., February 4, 1820, his father having emigrated from Ireland to work as a stonecutter on the Capitol; moved with his parents to New York City in 1823; attended the common schools; apprenticed to a stonecutter in early youth; unsuccessful candidate for election in 1846 to the Thirtieth Congress; moved to California in 1849 and engaged in smelting and assaying gold; member, California State senate, 1850-1851, serving as president in 1851; elected as a Democrat to the United States Senate, and served from March 4, 1857 until mortally wounded September 12, 1859 in a duel with David S. Terry, former chief justice of the supreme court of California; died near San Francisco, Calif., September 16, 1859; interment under a monument erected by the people of the State in Lone Mountain Cemetery, San Francisco.

Bibliography: *DAB*; Lynch, Jeremiah. *The Life of David C. Broderick: A Senator of the Fifties.* New York: The Baker and Taylor Co., 1911; Quinn, Arthur. *The Rivals: William Gwin, David Broderick, and the Birth of California.* New York: Crown Publishers, 1994; Williams, David. *David C. Broderick: A Political Portrait.* San Marino: Huntington Library, 1969.

BRODHEAD, John, a Representative from New Hampshire; born in Lower Smithfield, Pa., October 5, 1770; attended the common schools and Stroudsburg (Pa.) Academy; studied theology; was ordained a minister and active in ministerial service for forty-four years; moved in 1796 to New England, where he became supervisor of Methodist societies in the Connecticut Valley; settled in Canaan, N.H., in 1801; moved to Newfields Village, Newmarket,

N.H., in 1809; member of the New Hampshire State senate from 1817 until 1827; officiated as chaplain of the New Hampshire State house of representatives in 1825; elected as a Jacksonian to the Twenty-first and Twenty-second Congresses (March 4, 1829-March 3, 1833); declined to be a candidate for renomination in 1832 to the Twenty-third Congress, and resumed his ministerial duties; died in Newfields, Rockingham County, N.H., April 7, 1838; interment in Locust Cemetery.

**BRODHEAD, John Curtis,** a Representative from New York; born in Modena, Ulster County, N.Y., October 27, 1780; attended the district schools; engaged in mercantile and agricultural pursuits; sheriff of Ulster County 1825-1828; elected as a Jacksonian to the Twenty-second Congress (March 4, 1831-March 3, 1833); was not a candidate for reelection in 1832; elected as a Democrat to the Twenty-fifth Congress (March 4, 1837-March 3, 1839); chairman, Committee on Expenditures in the Department of the Navy (Twenty-fifth Congress); declined to be a candidate for renomination in 1838; resumed mercantile and agricultural pursuits; died in Modena, Ulster County, N.Y., January 2, 1859; interment in Modena Rural Cemetery.

**BRODHEAD, Joseph Davis** (son of Richard Brodhead), a Representative from Pennsylvania; born in Easton, Northampton County, Pa., January 12, 1859; attended the public schools; studied law; was admitted to the bar in 1881 and commenced practice in Stroudsburg, Monroe County, Pa.; elected district attorney of Northampton County in 1889; delegate to the Democratic National Conventions of 1892 and 1904; elected to the Sixtieth Congress (March 4, 1907-March 3, 1909); unsuccessful candidate for renomination in 1908 to the Sixty-first Congress; resumed the practice of law in South Bethlehem, Northampton County, Pa.; appointed judge of the courts of record of Northampton County in 1914; died in Washington, D.C., April 23, 1920; interment in Easton Cemetery, Easton, Pa.

**BRODHEAD, Richard** (father of Joseph Davis Brodhead), a Representative and a Senator from Pennsylvania; born in Lehman Township, Pike County, Pa., January 5, 1811; moved to Easton in 1830; studied law; was admitted to the bar in 1836 and commenced practice in Easton; member, Pennsylvania house of representatives, 1837-1839; appointed treasurer of Northampton County in 1841; elected as a Democrat to the Twenty-eighth and to the two succeeding Congresses (March 4, 1843-March 3, 1849); chairman, Committee on Revolutionary Pensions (Twenty-ninth Congress); was not a candidate for renomination in 1848 to the Thirty-first Congress; elected as a Democrat to the United States Senate and served from March 4, 1851, to March 3, 1857; chairman, Committee on Claims (Thirty-second and Thirty-third Congresses), Committee on Revolutionary Claims (Thirty-second Congress); died in Easton, Pa., September 16, 1863; interment in Easton Cemetery.

**BRODHEAD, William McNulty,** a Representative from Michigan; born in Cleveland, Cuyahoga County, Ohio, September 12, 1941; attended the elementary and secondary schools of Cleveland; attended John Carroll University, Cleveland, 1959-1960, and the University of Detroit, 1960-1963; A.B., Wayne State University, Detroit, Mich., 1965; J.D., University of Michigan Law School, Ann Arbor, 1967; admitted to the Michigan Bar in 1968 and commenced practice in Detroit; member, Michigan State house of representatives, 1971-1975; elected as a Democrat to the Ninety-fourth and to the three succeeding Congresses (January 3, 1975-January 3, 1983); was not a candidate for reelection in 1982 to the Ninety-eighth Congress; resumed the practice of law; is a resident of West Bloomfield, Mich.

**BROGDEN, Curtis Hooks,** a Representative from North Carolina; born in Goldsboro, Wayne County, N.C., November 6, 1816; pursued academic studies; member of the North Carolina State house of representatives, 1840-1850; comptroller of the State, 1857-1867; appointed collector of internal revenue in 1869; member of the North Carolina State senate, 1868-1872; lieutenant governor of North Carolina in 1872; became Governor upon the death of Governor Tod R. Caldwell on July 11, 1874, and served until January 1, 1877; elected as a Republican to the Forty-fifth Congress (March 4, 1877-March 3, 1879); again a member of the State house of representatives, 1886-1888; represented North Carolina at the centennial celebration in Philadelphia, Pa., in 1876; died in Goldsboro, N.C., January 5, 1901; interment in Willowdale Cemetery.

**BROMBERG, Frederick George,** a Representative from Alabama; born in New York City, June 19, 1837; moved with his parents to Mobile, Ala., in February 1838; attended the public schools; was graduated from Harvard University in 1858; studied chemistry at Harvard University from 1861 until 1863; tutor of mathematics at Harvard University, 1863-1865; appointed treasurer of the city of Mobile in July 1867 by Major General John Pope, who commanded the department, and served until January 19, 1869; member of the Alabama State senate, 1868-1872; appointed postmaster of Mobile in July 1869 but was removed in June 1871; chairman of the Alabama delegation to the Liberal Republican Convention at Cincinnati in 1872; elected as a Liberal Republican to the Forty-third Congress (March 4, 1873-March 3, 1875); unsuccessfully contested the election of Jeremiah Haralson to the Forty-fourth Congress; studied law; was admitted to the bar in 1877 and commenced practice in Mobile, Ala.; Alabama commissioner of the World's Columbian Exposition at Chicago in 1893; president of the Alabama State bar association in 1906; died in Mobile, Ala., on September 4, 1930; interment in Magnolia Cemetery.

Bibliography: Sizemore, Margaret Davidson. "Frederick G. Bromberg of Mobile: An Illustrious Character, 1837-1928." *The Alabama Review* 29 (April 1976): 104-12.

**BROMWELL, Henry Pelham Holmes,** a Representative from Illinois; born in Baltimore, Md., August 26, 1823; moved with his parents to Cincinnati, Ohio, in 1824, and thence to Cumberland, Ill., in 1836; attended private schools in Ohio and Illinois, and Marshall Academy, Marshall, Ill.; becoming an instructor in that academy in 1844; studied law; was admitted to the bar in 1853 and commenced practice in Vandalia, Ill.; edited his father's newspaper for several years; judge of Fayette County, 1853-1857; took an active part in the founding and building of the Republican Party; moved to Charleston, Coles County, Ill., in 1857; delegate to the State constitutional convention in 1870; elected as a Republican to the Thirty-ninth and Fortieth Congresses (March 4, 1865-March 3, 1869); unsuccessful candidate for renomination in 1868 to the Forty-first Congress; moved to Denver, Colo., in 1870 and continued the practice of law; president of the Denver School Board, 1871-1874; member of the Territorial council in 1874; delegate to the constitutional convention of Colorado in 1875; declined the office as judge of Arapahoe County in 1878 and the appointment as chief justice of Utah Territory in 1879; appointed by the Governor in 1879 to compile the general statutes of Colorado; died in Denver, Colo., January 7, 1903; interment in Riverside Cemetery.

**BROMWELL, Jacob Henry,** a Representative from Ohio; born in Cincinnati, Ohio, May 11, 1848; resided during his boyhood in Newport, Ky.; attended the public schools of Cincinnati and was graduated from Hughes High School in 1864; taught in the public schools of southern Indiana and of Cincinnati for twenty-three years; was graduated from Cincinnati Law College in 1870; was admitted to the bar of Hamilton County in 1888 and commenced practice in Cincinnati; mayor of Wyoming, Hamilton County, Ohio,

1880-1886; assistant county solicitor of Hamilton County 1888-1892; elected as a Republican to the Fifty-third Congress to fill the vacancy caused by the resignation of John A. Caldwell; reelected to the Fifty-fourth and to the three succeeding Congresses and served from December 3, 1894, to March 3, 1903; was not a candidate for renomination in 1902; resumed the practice of law in Cincinnati; judge of the court of common pleas of Hamilton County 1907-1913; declined to be a candidate for renomination; again engaged in the practice of law; died in Wyoming, Ohio, June 4, 1924; interment in Spring Grove Cemetery, Cincinnati, Ohio.

**BROMWELL, James Edward,** a Representative from Iowa; born in Cedar Rapids, Linn County, Iowa, March 26, 1920; attended Johnson School; graduated from Franklin High School in 1938 and from the University of Iowa in 1942; during the Second World War entered the United States Army as a private, was assigned to the European theater with Headquarters Information and Education Division, served four years, and was discharged as a captain; graduated from the Harvard University School of Business Administration in 1947; returned to the University of Iowa to study law and was graduated in 1950; was admitted to the bar and began practice in Cedar Rapids; elected as a Republican to the Eighty-seventh and Eighty-eighth Congresses (January 3, 1961-January 3, 1965); unsuccessful candidate in 1964 for reelection to the Eighty-ninth Congress; unsuccessful candidate for the Republican nomination for United States Senator in 1968; resumed the practice of law until 1974, and practiced again from 1979 to 1986; is a resident of Cedar Rapids, Iowa.

**BRONSON, David,** a Representative from Maine; born in Suffield, Conn., February 8, 1800; was graduated from Dartmouth College, Hanover, N.H., in 1819; studied law; was admitted to the bar in 1823 and commenced practice in North Anson, Maine; member of the State house of representatives in 1832 and 1834; justice of the peace; elected as a Whig to the Twenty-seventh Congress to fill the vacancy caused by the resignation of George Evans and served from May 31, 1841, to March 3, 1843; moved to Augusta, Maine, in 1843 and resumed the practice of law; member of the State senate in 1846; moved to Bath, Maine, in 1850 and served as collector of customs until 1853; judge of probate for Sagadahoc County 1854-1857; unsuccessful candidate for election in 1856 to the Thirty-fifth Congress; died in St. Michaels, Talbot County, Md., November 20, 1863; interment in the Episcopal Cemetery of St. Michael's Parish.

**BRONSON, Isaac Hopkins,** a Representative from New York; born in Rutland, Jefferson County, N.Y., October 16, 1802; attended the public schools; studied law; was admitted to the bar in 1822 and commenced practice in Watertown, Jefferson County, N.Y.; elected as a Democrat to the Twenty-fifth Congress (March 4, 1837-March 3, 1839); chairman, Committee on Territories (Twenty-fifth Congress); unsuccessful candidate for reelection in 1838 to the Twenty-sixth Congress; appointed judge of the fifth judicial district of New York, April 18, 1838; moved to St. Augustine, Fla., and a number of years later moved to Palatka, Putnam County, Fla.; appointed on March 14, 1840, by President Martin Van Buren as United States judge for the eastern district of Florida; upon the admission of Florida as a State into the Union in March 1845 was unanimously chosen as judge for the eastern circuit; appointed on August 8, 1846, by President James K. Polk as United States judge for the district of Florida; when the State was divided he retained the judgeship of the northern district and served until his death in Palatka, Fla., on August 13, 1855; interment in the Episcopal Church Cemetery.

**BROOCKS, Moses Lycurgus,** a Representative from Texas; born near San Augustine, San Augustine County, Tex., November 1, 1864; attended the common schools; was graduated from the law department of the University of Texas at Austin in 1891 and commenced practice at San Augustine; member of the State house of

representatives in 1892; moved to Beaumont, Jefferson County, Tex.; elected district attorney of the first judicial district of Texas in 1896 and served one term; elected as a Democrat to the Fifty-ninth Congress (March 4, 1905-March 3, 1907); resumed the practice of law in San Augustine, Tex., and died there May 27, 1908; interment in Old Broocks Cemetery, about four miles east of San Augustine, Tex.

**BROOKE, Edward William, III,** a Senator from Massachusetts; born in Washington, D.C., October 26, 1919; attended the public schools of Washington, D.C.; B.S., Howard University, Washington, D.C., 1941; LL.B., Boston University Law School, 1948, LL.M., 1950; entered the United States Army in 1942 as a second lieutenant and served with the Three Hundred Sixty-sixth Infantry Regiment in the European theater of operations, and with partisans in Italy; released as a captain in 1945; unsuccessful candidate in 1960 for election as secretary of the Commonwealth of Massachusetts; chairman of Finance Commission, city of Boston 1961-1962; elected attorney general of the Commonwealth of Massachusetts in 1962; reelected in 1964; elected as a Republican to the United States Senate in 1966; reelected in 1972 and served from January 3, 1967, to January 3, 1979; unsuccessful candidate for reelection in 1978; lawyer; is a resident of Warrenton, Va.

**Bibliography:** Brooke, Edward. *The Challenge of Change: Crisis in Our Two-Party System.* Boston: Little Brown, 1966; Cutler, John Henry. *Ed Brooke: Biography of a Senator.* New York: Bobbs-Merrill Company, 1972.

**BROOKE, Walker,** a Senator from Mississippi; born at Page Brooke, near Winchester, Clarke County, Va., December 25, 1813; attended the public schools in Richmond, Va., and Georgetown, D.C.; was graduated from the University of Virginia at Charlottesville in 1835; studied law; was admitted to the bar in 1838 and commenced practice in Lexington, Miss.; member of the Mississippi State house of representatives in 1848; member, State senate, 1850-1852; elected as a Whig to the United States Senate to fill the vacancy caused by the resignation of Henry S. Foote, and served from February 18, 1852 to March 3, 1853; was not a candidate for reelection; resumed the practice of law; moved to Vicksburg, Miss., in 1857 and continued the practice of law; delegate to the State constitutional convention in 1861; became affiliated with the Democratic Party in 1861; elected a member of the Provisional Confederate Congress from Mississippi in 1861 and served one year; appointed a member of the permanent military court of the Confederate States; died in Vicksburg, Miss., February 18, 1869; interment in Vicksburg Cemetery.

**BROOKHART, Smith Wildman,** a Senator from Iowa; born near Arbela, Scotland County, Mo., February 2, 1869; attended the country schools in Missouri and Bloomfield, Iowa: graduated from the Southern Iowa Normal and Scientific Institute at Bloomfield in 1889; taught school for five years at Keosauqua; studied law; was admitted to the bar in 1892 and commenced practice in Washington, Iowa; attorney of Washington County, 1895-1901; during the Spanish-American War served as second lieutenant; resumed the practice of law and also engaged in agricultural pursuits; chairman of the Republican State Convention in 1912; major and lieutenant colonel during the First World War; president of the National Rifle Association, 1921-1925; elected as a Progressive Republican to the United States Senate to fill the vacancy caused by the resignation of William S. Kenyon, and served from November 7, 1922 to March 3, 1925; presented credentials as a Republican Senator-elect for the term commencing March 4, 1925, and served until April 12, 1926, when he was succeeded by Daniel F. Steck, who contested his election; again elected as a Republican in 1926, and served from March 4, 1927 to March 3, 1933; unsuccessful candidate for renomination in 1932 and for election as an independent candidate;

foreign-trade adviser in the Agricultural Adjustment Administration, 1933-1935; unsuccessful Republican candidate in 1936 for nomination to the United States Senate; practiced law in Washington, D.C., until 1943; died in Whipple, Ariz., November 15, 1944; interment in Elm Grove Cemetery, Washington, Iowa.

**Bibliography:** *DAB*; McDaniel, George William. *Smith Wildman Brookhart: Iowa's Renegade Republican.* Ames: Iowa State University Press, 1995; Neprash, Jerry. *The Brookhart Campaigns in Iowa 1920-1926: A Study in the Motivation of Political Attitudes.* 1932. Reprint. New York: AMS Press, 1968.

**BROOKS, Charles Wayland,** a Senator from Illinois; born in West Bureau, Ill., March 8, 1897; attended the public schools at Wheaton, Ill., the University of Illinois at Urbana, and Northwestern University, Chicago, Ill.; during the First World War served as a first lieutenant in the United States Marines, 1917-1919; wounded several times; was graduated from the law department of Northwestern University in 1926; was admitted to the bar the same year and commenced practice in Chicago, Ill.; instructor of law at Northwestern University in 1926 and 1927; assistant State's attorney, 1926-1932; unsuccessful Republican candidate for Governor in 1936; elected as a Republican to the United States Senate to fill the vacancy caused by the death of James Hamilton Lewis, reelected in 1942, and served from November 22, 1940, to January 3, 1949; unsuccessful candidate for reelection in 1948; chairman, Committee on Rules and Administration (Eightieth Congress), Joint Committee on the Library (Eightieth Congress), Joint Committee on Inaugural Arrangements (Eightieth Congress); resumed the practice of law in Chicago, Ill.; Republican National Committeeman for Illinois in 1952; died in Chicago, Ill., January 14, 1957; interment in Pleasant View Cemetery, Kewanee, Ill.

**BROOKS, David,** a Representative from New York; born in Philadelphia, Pa., in 1756; attended the public schools; during the Revolutionary War entered the Continental Army as a lieutenant in the Pennsylvania Battalion of the Flying Camp in 1776; was captured at Fort Washington, November 16, 1776, and exchanged in January 1780; appointed assistant clothier general; studied law; was admitted to the bar and practiced; after the war settled in New York County, N.Y.; member of the New York State assembly, 1787 and 1788; moved to Dutchess County, N.Y.; member of the New York State assembly, 1794-1796, and 1810; judge of Dutchess County, 1795-1807; elected as a Federalist to the Fifth Congress (March 4, 1797-March 3, 1799); unsuccessful candidate for reelection in 1798 to the Sixth Congress, and in 1800 to the Seventh Congress; appointed commissioner to negotiate a treaty with the Seneca Indians; clerk of Dutchess County, June 5, 1807, to January 25, 1809, and from February 9, 1810, to February 14, 1811, and again from February 23, 1813, to February 13, 1815; appointed an officer in the United States Customs Service; an original member of the Society of the Cincinnati; died in Poughkeepsie, Dutchess County, N.Y., August 30, 1838; interment probably in the Old Rural Cemetery.

**BROOKS, Edward Schroeder,** a Representative from Pennsylvania; born in York, Pa., June 14, 1867; attended the public schools, York County Academy, York, Pa., and York (Pa.) Collegiate Institute; engaged as a banker, manufacturer of steel forgings, and as a contractor; member of the city council from 1897 to 1902; treasurer of York County, 1903-1905; member of the Pennsylvania Republican committee in 1917 and 1918; elected as a Republican to the Sixty-sixth and Sixty-seventh Congresses (March 4, 1919-March 3, 1923); was not a candidate for renomination in 1922 to the Sixty-eighth Congress; acting postmaster of York, Pa., from September 30, 1925, until February 23, 1926, and postmaster, 1926-1931; engaged in the clothing business from 1937 until his retirement; died in York, Pa., July 12, 1957; interment in Prospect Hill Cemetery.

**BROOKS, Edwin Bruce** (cousin of Edmund Howard Hinshaw), a Representative from Illinois; born in Newton, Jasper County, Ill., September 20, 1868; attended the public schools, and was graduated from Valparaiso (Ind.) University in 1892; superintendent of schools at Newman, 1894-1897, at Newton 1897-1903, at Greenville 1903-1905, and at Paris 1905-1912; engaged in banking at Newton, Ill., 1912-1914; county superintendent of schools of Jasper County, 1914-1918; elected as a Republican to the Sixty-sixth and Sixty-seventh Congresses (March 4, 1919-March 3, 1923); unsuccessful candidate for reelection in 1922 to the Sixty-eighth Congress; superintendent of charities for the State of Illinois from 1924 until 1930; assistant attorney general, 1930-1932; died in Newton, Ill., September 18, 1933; interment in River Side Cemetery.

**BROOKS, Franklin Eli,** a Representative from Colorado; born in Sturbridge, Worcester County, Mass., November 19, 1860; attended the public schools; was graduated from Southbridge High School in 1879, and from Brown University, Providence, R.I., in 1883; taught school for several years; attended the law school of Boston University in 1887 and 1888; was admitted to the bar in 1888 and commenced practice in Boston, Mass.; moved to Colorado Springs, El Paso County, Colo., in 1891, where he continued the practice of law; delegate to the Republican State conventions in 1900 and 1907, serving as chairman the latter year; elected as a Republican to the Fifty-eighth and Fifty-ninth Congresses (March 4, 1903-March 3, 1907); was not a candidate for renomination in 1906 to the Sixtieth Congress; resumed the practice of law in Colorado Springs, Colo., but devoted himself principally to land development, being president of the Costilla Estates Development Company; appointed a member of the Colorado State board of agriculture and trustee of the State agricultural college, Fort Collins, Colo., in 1907; trustee of Brown University; died in St. Augustine, Fla., February 7, 1916; interment in Evergreen Cemetery, Colorado Springs, Colo.

**BROOKS, George Merrick,** a Representative from Massachusetts; born in Concord, Mass., July 26, 1824; attended an academy in Concord and a boarding school at Waltham; was graduated from Harvard University in 1844; studied law; was admitted to the bar in 1847 and commenced practice in Concord; member of the Massachusetts house of representatives in 1858; served in the Massachusetts senate in 1859; elected as a Republican to the Forty-first Congress to fill the vacancy caused by the resignation of George S. Boutwell; reelected to the Forty-second Congress and served from November 2, 1869, to May 13, 1872, when he resigned, having been appointed to a judicial position; judge of probate for Middlesex County, and served until his death in Concord, Mass., September 22, 1893; interment in Sleepy Hollow Cemetery.

**BROOKS, Jack Bascom,** a Representative from Texas; born in Crowley, Acadia Parish, La., December 18, 1922; moved with his family to Beaumont, Tex., in 1927; attended public schools; A.A., Lamar Junior College, Beaumont, Tex., 1941; B.J., University of Texas, Austin, 1943; enlisted as a private in the United States Marine Corps on November 7, 1942, serving overseas twenty-three and one-half months on Guadalcanal, Guam, Okinawa, and in North China, and discharged as a first lieutenant on April 23, 1946; colonel in the United States Marine Corps Reserve, 1946-1972; member of the Texas State house of representatives, 1946-1950; J.D., University of Texas School of Law, 1949; was admitted to the bar the same year and commenced the practice of law in Beaumont, Tex.; owns and operates a farm; elected as a Democrat to the Eighty-third and to the twenty succeeding Congresses (January 3, 1953-January 3, 1995); unsuccessful candidate for reelection in 1994 to the One Hundred Fourth Congress; chairman, Joint Committee on Congressional Operations (Ninety-second and Ninety-fourth Congresses), Committee on Government Operations (Ninety-fourth through One Hundredth Congresses), Committee on the Judiciary (One Hundred

First through One Hundred Third Congresses); is a resident of Beaumont, Tex.

**BROOKS, James,** a Representative from New York; born in Portland, Maine, November 10, 1810; attended the public schools; attended the academy at Monmouth, Maine; taught school at sixteen years of age in Lewiston; was graduated from Waterville (Maine) College in 1831; studied law and also edited the Portland Advertiser, and in 1832 was its Washington correspondent; member of the Maine State house of representatives in 1835; unsuccessful candidate for election in 1836 to the Twenty-fifth Congress; moved to New York City in 1836 and established the New York Daily Express, of which he was editor in chief the remainder of his life; served in the New York State assembly in 1847; elected as a Whig to the Thirty-first and Thirty-second Congresses (March 4, 1849-March 3, 1853); unsuccessful candidate for reelection in 1852 to the Thirty-third Congress; resumed his editorial pursuits; elected as a Democrat to the Thirty-eighth Congress (March 4, 1863-March 3, 1865); presented credentials as a Member-elect to the Thirty-ninth Congress, and served from March 4, 1865 to April 7, 1866, when he was succeeded by William E. Dodge, who contested the election; appointed a Government director of the Union Pacific Railroad in October 1867; member of the New York State constitutional convention in 1867; elected to the Fortieth and to the three succeeding Congresses, and served from March 4, 1867 until his death in Washington, D.C., April 30, 1873; censured by the House of Representatives on February 27, 1873, for attempted bribery in connection with the construction by the Crédit Mobilier of America of a portion of the Union Pacific Railroad; interment in Greenwood Cemetery, Brooklyn, N.Y.

Bibliography: *DAB*.

**BROOKS, Joshua Twing,** a Representative from Pennsylvania; born in Edgeworth (now Sewickley), Allegheny County, Pa., February 27, 1884; attended the public schools and was graduated from the Sheffield Scientific School of Yale University in 1908; engaged in the steel industry; during the First World War served in the Quartermaster Division in Washington, D.C., purchasing steel products for the Army; returned to Sewickley, Pa., and continued in the steel industry; later established his own business, being a distributor of railway supplies and steel products; elected as a Democrat to the Seventy-third and Seventy-fourth Congresses (March 4, 1933-January 3, 1937); unsuccessful candidate for renomination in 1936 to the Seventy-fifth Congress; member of the Pennsylvania Liquor Board at Harrisburg, Pa., 1937-1939; assistant director of aviation for Allegheny County, Pa., 1940-1948; manager of the Allegheny County Airport, 1949-1956; died in Sewickley, Pa., February 7, 1956; interment in Sewickley Cemetery.

**BROOKS, Micah,** a Representative from New York; born in Brooksvale, near Cheshire, Conn., May 14, 1775; received his early education from his father; a pioneer and one of the earliest surveyors of western New York; justice of the peace in 1806; member of the State assembly in 1808 and 1809; colonel on the frontier and at Fort Erie, 1812-1814; major general of the New York State Infantry, 1828-1830; elected as a Republican to the Fourteenth Congress (March 4, 1815-March 3, 1817); engaged in agricultural pursuits; delegate from Ontario County to the New York State constitutional convention in 1821; presidential elector on the John Quincy Adams ticket in 1824; died in Fillmore, Allegany County, N.Y., on July 7, 1857; interment in Nunda Cemetery, Nunda, Livingston County, N.Y.

**BROOKS, Overton** (nephew of John Holmes Overton), a Representative from Louisiana; born near Baton Rouge, East Baton Rouge Parish, La., December 21, 1897; attended the public schools; during the First World War served overseas as an enlisted man in the Sixth Field Artillery, First Division, Regular Army, in 1918 and 1919; was graduated from the law department of Louisiana State University at Baton Rouge in 1923; was admitted to the bar the same year and commenced practice in Shreveport, La.; served as United States Commissioner from 1925 until 1935; elected as a Democrat to the Seventy-fifth and to the twelve succeeding Congresses and served from January 3, 1937, until his death in Bethesda, Md., September 16, 1961; chairman, Committee on Science and Astronautics (Eighty-sixth and Eighty-seventh Congresses); interment in Forest Hills Cemetery, Shreveport, La.

Bibliography: *DAB*.

**BROOKS, Preston Smith,** a Representative from South Carolina; born in Edgefield District, S.C., August 5, 1819; attended the common schools and was graduated from South Carolina College (now the University of South Carolina) at Columbia in 1839; studied law; was admitted to the bar in 1845 and commenced practice in Edgefield, S.C.; member of the South Carolina State house of representatives in 1844; served in the Mexican War as captain in the Palmetto Regiment of South Carolina Volunteers; elected as a Democrat to the Thirty-third and Thirty-fourth Congresses and served from March 4, 1853, until July 15, 1856, when he resigned, even though the attempt to expel him for his assault upon Senator Charles Sumner of Massachusetts on May 22, 1856, had failed through lack of the necessary two-thirds vote; chairman, Committee on Expenditures in the Department of State (Thirty-fourth Congress); reelected to the Thirty-fourth Congress to fill the vacancy caused by his own resignation and served from August 1, 1856, until his death in Washington, D.C., January 27, 1857; had been reelected to the Thirty-fifth Congress; interment in Willow Brook Cemetery, Edgefield, S.C.

Bibliography: *DAB*; U.S. Congress. *House Select Committee on Assault upon Senator Sumner*. Thirty-fourth Congress, report no. 182. Washington, 1856.

**BROOKSHIRE, Elijah Voorhees,** a Representative from Indiana; born near Ladoga, Montgomery County, Ind., August 15, 1856; attended the common schools, and was graduated from Central Indiana Normal College at Ladoga in August 1878; taught in the common schools of Montgomery County, Ind. 1879-1882; also engaged in agricultural pursuits; studied law; was admitted to the bar in 1883 and commenced practice in Crawfordsville the same year; elected as a Democrat to the Fifty-first, Fifty-second, and Fifty-third Congresses (March 4, 1889-March 3, 1895); unsuccessful candidate for reelection in 1894 to the Fifty-fourth Congress; resumed the practice of law in Washington, D.C., and was admitted to practice before the United States Supreme Court in 1894; moved to Los Angeles, Calif., in 1925, and to Seattle, Wash., in 1935, having retired from active law practice in 1925; died in Seattle, Wash., April 14, 1936; interment in Harshbarger Cemetery, near Ladoga, Montgomery County, Ind.

**BROOM, Jacob** (son of James Madison Broom), a Representative from Pennsylvania; born in Baltimore, Md., July 25, 1808; received a classical education; moved to Philadelphia, Pa., with his parents in 1819; studied law; was admitted to the bar in 1832 and commenced practice in Philadelphia, Pa.; appointed deputy auditor of Pennsylvania in 1840; clerk of the Philadelphia orphans' court 1848-1852; nominated by the Native American Party in 1852 for President of the United States; elected as a candidate of the American Party to the Thirty-fourth Congress (March 4, 1855-March 3, 1857); chairman, Committee on Revolutionary Pensions (Thirty-fourth Congress); unsuccessful candidate for renomination in 1856 and for election to the Thirty-sixth Congress in 1858; died in Washington, D.C., November 28, 1864; interment in Congressional Cemetery.

**BROOM, James Madison** (father of Jacob Broom), a Representative from Delaware; born near Wilmington, Del., in 1776; was graduated from Princeton College in 1794; studied law; was admitted to the bar in 1801 and practiced in New Castle and Wilmington, Del., and Baltimore, Md.; elected as a Federalist to the Ninth and Tenth Congresses and served from March 4, 1805, until his resignation in 1807, before the assembling of the Tenth Congress; moved to Philadelphia, Pa., in 1819 and resumed the practice of law; member of the Pennsylvania house of representatives in 1824; died in Philadelphia, Pa., January 15, 1850; interment in St. Mary's Churchyard, Hamilton Village (now a part of Philadelphia), Pa.

**BROOMALL, John Martin,** a Representative from Pennsylvania; born in Upper Chichester Township, Delaware County, Pa., January 19, 1816; attended private schools; taught school for several years; studied law; was admitted to the bar in 1840 and commenced practice in Chester, Pa.; member of the Pennsylvania house of representatives in 1851 and 1852; served on the Pennsylvania revenue board in 1854; unsuccessful candidate for election in 1854 to the Thirty-fourth Congress and in 1858 to the Thirty-sixth Congress; delegate to the Republican National Convention in 1860; moved to Media in 1860 and continued the practice of law; served in the Union Army as captain of Company C, Twenty-ninth Regiment, Pennsylvania Emergency Men, from June 18 to August 1, 1863; elected as a Republican to the Thirty-eighth, Thirty-ninth, and Fortieth Congresses (March 4, 1863-March 3, 1869); chairman, Committee on Accounts (Fortieth Congress); was not a candidate for renomination in 1868; resumed the practice of law; delegate to the Pennsylvania constitutional convention in 1874; appointed judge of the courts of Delaware County in March 1874 and served until January 1875, being an unsuccessful candidate for election to succeed himself; again resumed the practice of law in Media, Delaware County, Pa.; died in Philadelphia, Pa., June 3, 1894; interment in Media Cemetery, Media, Pa.

**BROOMFIELD, William S.,** a Representative from Michigan; born in Royal Oak, Oakland County, Mich., April 28, 1922; graduated from high school in 1940; B.A., Michigan State College (now Michigan State University), East Lansing, 1951; during the Second World War served in the United States Army Air Corps; engaged in the real-estate and property-management business; member of the Michigan State house of representatives, 1949-1954, serving as speaker pro tempore in 1953; served in the State senate in 1955 and 1956; member of the United States delegation to the Twenty-second General Assembly of the United Nations, 1967-1968; elected as a Republican to the Eighty-fifth and to the seventeen succeeding Congresses (January 3, 1957-January 3, 1993); was not a candidate for reelection in 1992 to the One Hundred Third Congress; is a resident of Birmingham, Mich.

**BROPHY, John Charles,** a Representative from Wisconsin; born in Eagle, Walworth County, Wis., October 8, 1901; attended the public and parochial schools of Milwaukee, Wis.; was graduated from St. Patrick's and Marquette Academy; enlisted in the United States Navy during the First World War and served as a seaman from August 1919 until honorably discharged in May 1921; worked as a mechanic 1922-1938; alderman of the city of Milwaukee from April 1939 to December 1946; unsuccessful candidate for election in 1942 to the Seventy-eighth Congress; elected as a Republican to the Eightieth Congress (January 3, 1947-January 3, 1949); unsuccessful candidate for reelection in 1948 to the Eighty-first Congress and for election in 1950 to the Eighty-second Congress; engaged in sales and public relations until retirement in 1969; resided in Milwaukee, Wis., where he died December 26, 1976; interment in Mount Olivet Cemetery.

**BROSIUS, Marriott,** a Representative from Pennsylvania; born in Colerain Township, Lancaster County, Pa., March 7, 1843; attended the common schools and Thomas Baker's Academy in Colerain Township; enlisted as a private in Company K, Ninety-seventh Regiment, Pennsylvania Volunteers, in October 1861, for

three years, and reenlisted May 20, 1864; honorably discharged December 28, 1864, and on February 28, 1865, was commissioned a second lieutenant for bravery on the field of battle; after the war attended the Pennsylvania normal school at Millersville and the law department of the University of Michigan at Ann Arbor; was admitted to the bar in 1868 and commenced practice in Lancaster, Lancaster County, Pa.; elected as a Republican to the Fifty-first and to the six succeeding Congresses and served from March 4, 1889, until his death in Lancaster, Pa., March 16, 1901; chairman, Committee on Reform in the Civil Service (Fifty-fourth and Fifty-fifth Congresses), Committee on Banking and Currency (Fifty-sixth Congress); interment in Greenwood Cemetery.

**BROTZMAN, Donald Glenn,** a Representative from Colorado; born on a farm in Logan County, Colo., near Sterling, Colo., June 28, 1922; educated in Logan County schools; B.B.S., University Colorado School of Business at Boulder, 1949; LL.B., University of Colorado School of Law, 1949; was admitted to the bar in 1950 and began practice in Boulder, Colo.; served as a first lieutenant with the Eighty-first Infantry Division in the South Pacific, 1945-1946; served in the State house of representatives, 1952-1954, and in the State senate, 1954-1956; Republican caucus leader in 1956; unsuccessful candidate for election for Governor in 1954 and in 1956; appointed United States attorney for Colorado by President Dwight D. Eisenhower and served from 1959 to 1961; elected as a Republican to the Eighty-eighth Congress (January 3, 1963-January 3, 1965); unsuccessful candidate for reelection in 1964 to the Eighty-ninth Congress; elected to the Ninetieth and to the three succeeding Congresses (January 3, 1967-January 3, 1975); unsuccessful candidate for reelection in 1974 to the Ninety-fourth Congress; Assistant Secretary of the Army for Manpower and Reserve Affairs, 1975-1977; president of Rubber Manufacturers Association and National Rubber Shippers Association; chairman, Industry Safety Council, Washington, D.C.; is a resident of Fort Washington, Md.

**BROUGHTON, Joseph Melville,** a Senator from North Carolina; born in Raleigh, Wake County, N.C., November 17, 1888; attended the public schools; was graduated from Hugh Morson Academy in 1906 and Wake Forest (N.C.) College in 1910; taught school in Bunn, N.C., 1910-1912; reporter on a newspaper in Winston-Salem, N.C., in 1912; attended Harvard University Law School in 1912 and 1913; was admitted to the bar in 1914 and commenced practice in Raleigh, N.C., the same year; also engaged in agricultural pursuits; member, North Carolina State senate, 1927-1929; elected Governor of North Carolina in 1940 and served from January 9, 1941 to January 4, 1945; served as a member of the board of trustees of Wake Forest College and of the University of North Carolina; elected as a Democrat to the United States Senate on November 2, 1948, to fill the vacancy in the term ending January 3, 1949, caused by the death of Josiah W. Bailey and at the same time was elected for the full term commencing January 3, 1949; served from December 31, 1948, until his death in Washington, D.C., March 6, 1949; interment in Montlawn Memorial Park, Raleigh, N.C.

**BROUSSARD, Edwin Sidney** (brother of Robert Foligny Broussard), a Senator from Louisiana; born near Loreauville, Iberia Parish, La., December 4, 1874; attended the public schools, and was graduated from the Louisiana State University and Agricultural and Mechanical College at Baton Rouge in 1896; taught in the public schools of Iberia and St. Martin Parishes, 1896-1898; at the outbreak of the Spanish-American War volunteered for service and served as a captain in Cuba, 1898-1899; accompanied William Howard Taft's Commission to the Phillippine Islands in 1899, and served as an assistant secretary; returned to the United States in 1900; was graduated from the law department of Tulane University, New Orleans, La., in 1901; was admitted to the bar the same year, and commenced practice in New Iberia, La.; prosecuting attorney for the nineteenth district of Louisiana, 1903-1908; unsuccessful candidate for lieutenant governor in 1916; elected as a Democrat to the United States Senate in 1920; reelected in 1926, and served from March 4, 1921 to March 3, 1933; unsuccessful candidate for renomination in 1932; resumed the practice of law in New Iberia, La., where he died on November 19, 1934; interment in St. Peters Cemetery.

**Bibliography:** Wakefield, Ann. "The Broussard Papers of the University of Southwestern Louisiana: New Light on Louisiana Progressivism." *Louisiana History* 31 (Summer 1990): 293-300.

**BROUSSARD, Robert Foligny** (brother of Edwin Sidney Broussard), a Representative and a Senator from Louisiana; born on the "Mary Louise" plantation, near New Iberia, Iberia Parish, La., August 17, 1864; attended public and private schools; attended Georgetown University, Washington, D.C., 1879-1882; night inspector of customs in New Orleans, 1885-1888, and served as assistant weigher and statistician, 1888-1889; studied law at Tulane University, New Orleans, La., and was graduated in 1889; was admitted to the bar the same year and commenced practice in New Iberia; elected prosecuting attorney of the nineteenth judicial district, 1892-1897; elected as a Democrat to the Fifty-fifth and to the eight succeeding Congresses (March 4, 1897-March 3, 1915); chairman, Committee on Expenditures in the Department of Justice (Sixty-third Congress); did not seek renomination in 1914 to the House of Representatives, having become a candidate for Senator; elected as a Democrat in 1914 to the United States Senate, and served from March 4, 1915 until his death in New Iberia, La., April 12, 1918; chairman, Committee on National Banks (Sixty-fourth and Sixty-fifth Congresses); interment in the Catholic Cemetery.

**Bibliography:** Wakefield, Ann. "The Broussard Papers of the University of Southwestern Louisiana: New Light on Louisiana Progressivism." *Louisiana History* 31 (Summer 1990): 293-300.

**BROWDER, John Glen,** a Representative from Alabama; born in Sumter, S.C., January 15, 1943; graduated, Edmunds High School, Sumter, 1961; B.A., Presbyterian College, Clinton, S.C., 1965; M.A., Emory University, Atlanta, Ga., and Ph.D., political science, 1971; assistant in public relations for alumni affairs, Presbyterian College, 1965; sports writer, Atlanta Journal, 1966; investigator, United States Civil Service Commission, 1966-1968; professor of political science, Jacksonville (Ala.) State University, 1971-1987; member, Alabama State house of representatives, 1982-1986; Alabama secretary of state, 1987-1989; elected as a Democrat to the One Hundred First Congress, April 4, 1989, by special election to fill the vacancy caused by the death of William F. Nichols; reelected to the One Hundred Second and to the two succeeding Congresses, and served from April 4, 1989 to January 3, 1997; was not a candidate in 1996 for reelection to the House of Representatives, but was an unsuccessful candidate for nomination to the United States Senate; is a resident of Jacksonville, Ala.

**BROWER, John Morehead,** a Representative from North Carolina; born in Greensboro, Guilford County, N.C., July 19, 1845; moved to Surry County, N.C., with his parents, who settled in Mount Airy in 1845; educated by private tutors and attended the Mount Airy Male Academy; engaged in agricultural pursuits, the raising and processing of tobacco, and mercantile pursuits; delegate to all Republican State conventions from 1872 to 1896; member of the State senate 1876-1878; elected as a Republican to the Fiftieth and Fifty-first Congresses (March 4, 1887-March 3, 1891); chairman, Committee on Expenditures in the Post Office Department (Fifty-first Congress); unsuccessful candidate for reelection in 1890 to the Fifty-second Congress; member of the State house of representatives 1896-1898; resumed his former agricultural and business pursuits; moved to Oklahoma and settled in Boswell, Choctaw County, in 1907 and engaged in the manufacture of lumber,

agricultural pursuits, and stock raising; died in Paris, Lamar County, Tex., August 5, 1913; interment in Oakdale Cemetery, Mount Airy, N.C.

**BROWN, Aaron Venable,** a Representative from Tennessee; born in Brunswick County, Va., August 15, 1795; attended Westrayville Academy, North Carolina, and was graduated from the University of North Carolina at Chapel Hill in 1814; moved to Nashville, Tenn., in 1815; studied law; was admitted to the bar in 1817 and commenced practice in Nashville; moved to Giles County in 1818 and continued the practice of law; became the partner of James K. Polk; served in the Tennessee State senate, 1821-1825; member of the State house of representatives, 1831-1833; elected as a Democrat to the Twenty-sixth and to the two succeeding Congresses (March 4, 1839-March 3, 1845); chairman, Committee on Territories (Twenty-eighth Congress); was not a candidate for reelection in 1844 to the Twenty-ninth Congress; elected Governor of Tennessee in 1845, and served from October 14, 1845 to October 17, 1847; unsuccessful candidate for reelection in 1847; delegate to the Democratic National Convention of 1852; appointed Postmaster General in the Cabinet of President James Buchanan on March 6, 1857, and served until his death in Washington, D.C., on March 8, 1859; interment in Mount Olivet Cemetery, Nashville, Tenn.

**Bibliography:** *DAB*.

**BROWN, Albert Gallatin,** a Representative and a Senator from Mississippi; born in Chester District, S.C., May 31, 1813; moved with his parents to Copiah County, Miss., in 1823; attended Mississippi College, Clinton, Miss., and Jefferson College, Washington, Miss.; studied law; was admitted to the bar in 1833 and commenced practice in Gallatin, Miss.; member, Mississippi State house of representatives, 1835-1839; elected as a Democrat to the Twenty-sixth Congress (March 4, 1839-March 3, 1841); declined to be a candidate for renomination in 1840 to the Twenty-seventh Congress; judge of the circuit superior court, 1842-1843; elected Governor of Mississippi in 1843, reelected in 1845, and served from January 10, 1844 to January 10, 1848; elected to the Thirtieth and to the two succeeding Congresses (March 4, 1847-March 3, 1853); chairman, Committee on the District of Columbia (Thirty-first Congress); was not a candidate for reelection in 1852 to the Thirty-third Congress; elected to the United States Senate in 1854 to fill the vacancy in the term beginning March 4, 1853; reelected in 1859, and served from January 7, 1854 until January 12, 1861, when he withdrew with other secessionist Senators; his seat was declared vacant and his name omitted from the roll by a resolution of March 14, 1861; chairman, Committee on the District of Columbia (Thirty-fourth through Thirty-sixth Congresses), Committee on Enrolled Bills (Thirty-sixth Congress); during the Civil War entered the Confederate Army as a captain; elected a member of the Confederate Senate in 1862 and served in the First and Second Confederate Congresses; engaged in agricultural pursuits; died near Terry, Hinds County, Miss., June 12, 1880; interment in Greenwood Cemetery, Jackson, Miss.

**Bibliography:** *DAB*; McCutchen, Samuel. "The Political Career of Albert Gallatin Brown." Ph.D. dissertation, University of Chicago, 1930; Ranck, James B. *Albert Gallatin Brown: Radical Southern Nationalist.* New York: Appleton-Century Company, 1937.

**BROWN, Anson,** a Representative from New York; born in Charlton, Saratoga County, N.Y., in 1800; attended the public schools, and was graduated from Union College, Schenectady, N.Y., in 1819; studied law; was admitted to the bar and commenced practice in Ballston Spa; one of the first directors of the Ballston Spa State Bank (later the Ballston Spa National Bank), which was organized in 1830; elected as a Whig to the Twenty-sixth Congress and served from March 4, 1839, until his death in Ballston Spa, N.Y., June 14, 1840; interment in the cemetery of the Ballston Spa Cemetery Association.

**BROWN, Arthur,** a Senator from Utah; born near Kalamazoo, Kalamazoo County, Mich., March 8, 1843; attended the common schools and was graduated from Antioch College, Yellow Springs, Ohio, in 1862; engaged in graduate work at the University of Michigan at Ann Arbor; was graduated from the law department of the University of Michigan in 1864; was admitted to the bar and commenced practice in Kalamazoo; moved to Salt Lake City, Utah, in 1879; upon the admission of Utah as a State into the Union was elected as a Republican to the United States Senate, and served from January 22, 1896 until March 3, 1897; was not a candidate for renomination; resumed the practice of law in Salt Lake City; shot and killed in Washington, D.C. by a woman who claimed to be the mother of his children on December 12, 1906; interment in Mount Olivet Cemetery, Salt Lake City, Utah.

**Bibliography:** Thatcher, Linda. "The 'Gentile Polygamist': Arthur Brown, Ex-Senator from Utah." *Utah Historical Quarterly* 52 (Summer 1984): 231-245.

**BROWN, Bedford,** a Senator from North Carolina; born in Caswell County, N.C., near Greensboro, June 6, 1795; was graduated from the University of North Carolina at Chapel Hill in 1813; studied law; was admitted to the bar in 1815 but did not practice; planter; elected to the house of commons of North Carolina in 1815, 1816, 1817, and 1823; member, State senate 1828-1829; elected in 1829 as a Democrat to the United States Senate to fill the vacancy caused by the resignation of John Branch; reelected in 1835 and served from December 9, 1829, until November 16, 1840, when he resigned, because he would not obey the instructions of the general assembly of North Carolina; chairman, Committee on Agriculture (Twenty-third and Twenty-fourth Congresses), Committee on Revolutionary Claims (Twenty-fourth and Twenty-fifth Congresses), Committee to Audit and Control the Contingent Expense (Twenty-fifth Congress); again elected to the State senate in 1842; unsuccessful candidate for election to the United States Senate in 1842; moved to Missouri in 1843; subsequently moved to Virginia; returned to North Carolina and engaged in agricultural pursuits; member, State senate 1858-1860; delegate to the reconstruction convention in 1865; again elected to the State senate in 1868, but was not permitted to take his seat; died at "Rose Hill," Caswell County, N.C., near Greensboro, December 6, 1870; interment in the family cemetery at "Rose Hill."

**Bibliography:** *DAB*; Jones, Houston. *Bedford Brown: States Rights Unionist.* Carrolton, Ga.: West Georgia College, 1955.

**BROWN, Benjamin** (nephew of John Brown), a Representative from Massachusetts; born in Swansea, Mass., September 23, 1756; pursued academic studies; studied medicine and commenced practice in Waldoboro, Maine (until 1820 a district of Massachusetts); surgeon in 1778 on the American frigate *Boston,* commanded by Commodore Tucker, which conveyed John Adams as American commissioner to France; with Commander Tucker, was captured in 1781 on the American warship *Thorne* at the mouth of the St. Lawrence River and imprisoned on Prince Edward Island; escaped in an open boat and reached Boston, Mass.; member of the Massachusetts house of representatives in 1809, 1811, 1812, and again in 1819; elected as a Federalist to the Fourteenth Congress (March 4, 1815-March 3, 1817); resumed the practice of medicine; died in Waldoboro, Lincoln County, Maine, September 17, 1831; interment in Waldoboro Cemetery.

**BROWN, Benjamin Gratz** (grandson of John Brown of Virginia and Kentucky [1757-1837], a Senator from Missouri; born in Lexington, Ky., May 28, 1826; completed preparatory studies; was graduated from Transylvania University, Lexington, Ky., in 1845 and from Yale College in 1847; studied law in Louisville, Ky.; was admitted to the bar in 1849 and commenced practice in St. Louis, Mo.; member, State house of representatives 1852-1858; one of the founders of the Missouri Democrat and its chief editor in 1854; unsuccessful candidate for election in 1857 for Governor of Missouri; took an active part in preventing the secession of Missouri in 1861; during the Civil War enlisted in the Union Army; raised a regiment and commanded it; elected as an Unconditional Unionist to the United States Senate to fill the vacancy caused by the expulsion of Waldo P. Johnson and served from November 13, 1863 to March 3, 1867; chairman, Committee on Public Buildings and Grounds (Thirty-ninth Congress), Committee to Audit and Control the Contingent Expense (Thirty-ninth Congress); elected Governor of Missouri in 1870 and served from January 9, 1871 to January 8, 1873; unsuccessful Democratic candidate for Vice President of the United States on the ticket with Horace Greeley in 1872; resumed the practice of law; died in Kirkwood, near St. Louis, Mo., December 13, 1885; interment in Oak Hill Cemetery, Kirkwood, Mo.

**Bibliography:** *DAB*; Peterson, Norma L. *Freedom and Franchise: The Political Career of Benjamin Gratz Brown.* Columbia: University of Missouri Press, 1968.

**BROWN, Charles,** a Representative from Pennsylvania; born in Philadelphia, Pa., September 23, 1797; attended the public schools; in early boyhood moved with his father to Cumberland County, N.J., and resided near Bridgeton; officer in the Pennsylvania militia 1817-1819; town clerk of Dover Township 1819; taught school at Dividing Creek in 1820 and 1821; returned to Philadelphia in 1823 and engaged in the cordwood business; appointed a director of the Philadelphia public schools in 1828; member of the Philadelphia City Council in 1830 and 1831; served in the Pennsylvania house of representatives 1830-1833; delegate to the convention to revise the constitution of Pennsylvania 1834-1838; served in the Pennsylvania senate 1838-1841; elected as a Democrat to the Twenty-seventh Congress (March 4, 1841-March 3, 1843); was not a candidate for reelection in 1842; president of the Pennsylvania convention to nominate candidates for the board of canal commissioners in 1843; member of the board of commissioners, Northern Liberties Township, in 1843; elected to the Thirtieth Congress (March 4, 1847-March 3, 1849); was not a candidate for reelection in 1848; member of the board of inspectors of the Eastern State Penitentiary 1851-1853; collector of customs at the port of Philadelphia 1853-1857; member of the board of guardians of the poor of Philadelphia in 1860; moved to Dover, Del., in 1861 and engaged in agricultural pursuits; town commissioner of Dover in 1864 and 1865; delegate to the Union National Convention at Philadelphia in 1866; president of the board of trustees of the Dover public schools 1871-1878; died at Dover, Del., September 4, 1883; interment in Laurel Hill Cemetery, Philadelphia, Pa.

**BROWN, Charles Elwood,** a Representative from Ohio; born in Cincinnati, Ohio, July 4, 1834; attended the common schools and Greenfield Academy, and was graduated from Miami University, Oxford, Ohio, in 1854; went south and, while serving as tutor at Baton Rouge, La., studied law; was admitted to the bar in 1859 and commenced practice in Chillicothe, Ohio; prosecuting attorney of Ross County in 1859 and 1860; enlisted as a private in Company B, Sixty-third Regiment, Ohio Volunteers, September 2, 1861, and was commissioned captain October 23, 1861; promoted through the ranks to colonel June 6, 1865, and brevetted brigadier general March 13, 1865; mustered out July 8, 1865; resumed the practice of law in Chillicothe, Ross County, Ohio; postmaster of Chillicothe 1866-1872; commissioned pension agent at Cincinnati in 1872, which position he held until President Rutherford B. Hayes' administration; elected as a Republican to the Forty-ninth and Fiftieth Congresses (March 4, 1885-March 3, 1889); was not a candidate for renomination in 1888 to the Fifty-first Congress; resumed the practice of law; member of the State senate in 1900 and 1901; died at College Hill, Hamilton County, Ohio, on May 22, 1904; interment in Spring Grove Cemetery, Cincinnati, Ohio.

**BROWN, Charles Harrison,** a Representative from Missouri; born in Coweta, Wagoner County, Okla., October 22, 1920; attended the public schools in Humansville and Republic, Mo., and high school in Springfield, Mo.; attended Drury College, Springfield, Mo., in 1937, 1938, and 1940, and George Washington University, Washington, D.C., in 1939; program director for a radio station in Springfield, Mo., in 1937 and 1938; radio publicity director for Missouri Conservation Commission in 1940; account executive for an advertising company in St. Louis, Mo., 1943-1945; founder and president of Brown Radio-TV Productions, Inc., Springfield, Mo.; partner, Brown Brothers Advertising Agency, Nashville, St. Louis, and Springfield; delegate to Democratic State and National Conventions in 1956, 1960, and 1964; elected as a Democrat to the Eighty-fifth and Eighty-sixth Congresses (January 3, 1957-January 3, 1961); unsuccessful candidate for reelection in 1960 to the Eighty-seventh Congress; public relations consultant in Washington, D.C., and Los Angeles; senior vice president of an oil refining company in Los Angeles, 1973-1979; is a resident of Incline Village, Nev.

**BROWN, Clarence J.** (father of Clarence J. Brown, Jr.) a Representative from Ohio; born in Blanchester, Clinton County, Ohio, July 14, 1893; attended the Blanchester public schools and the law school of Washington and Lee University, Lexington, Va., 1913-1915; State statistician in 1915 and 1916; engaged in newspaper work at Blanchester, Ohio, in 1917 and was publisher of several country newspapers; president of the Brown Publishing Co., Blanchester, Ohio; also owned and operated several large farms; Lieutenant Governor of Ohio, 1919-1923; secretary of state of Ohio, 1927-1933; Republican candidate for election for Governor in 1934; delegate to the Republican National Conventions of 1936, 1940, 1944, and 1948; member of the Republican National Committee; member, Commission on Organization of the Executive Branch of the Government (Hoover Commission); elected as a Republican to the Seventy-sixth and to the thirteen succeeding Congresses and served from January 3, 1939, until his death in Washington, D.C., August 23, 1965; chairman, Select Committee on Newsprint (Eightieth Congress); interment in I.O.O.F. Cemetery, Blanchester, Ohio.

Bibliography: *DAB.*

**BROWN, Clarence J., Jr.** (son of Clarence J. Brown), a Representative from Ohio; born in Columbus, Ohio, June 18, 1927; attended the public schools in Blanchester, Ohio; also attended Stoddard Elementary, Gordon Junior High, and Western High School in Washington, D.C.; B.A., Duke University, 1947; M.B.A., Harvard University Business School, 1949; served in the United States Navy, 1944-1947 (V-12 Program); again served in the Navy with Command Amphibious Forces Pacific in 1950-1952 in the Korean conflict; released as a lieutenant (jg) after sea duty; worked for Brown Publishing Co. and newspaper business from youth to 1953, and from 1957 to present, serving as president, 1965-1976, and chairman of the board, 1972 to present; editor, Blanchester, Ohio, Star Republican, 1949-1953; editor and co-owner of Franklin, Ohio, Chronicle, 1953-1959; editor of Urbana, Ohio, Daily Citizen, 1957-1965, and publisher, 1959-1969; farm owner; general manager of radio station WCOM in Urbana, Ohio, 1963-1965; delegate to the Republican National Conventions of 1968, 1972, 1976 and 1984; elected as a Republican to the Eighty-ninth Congress, November 2, 1965, by special election to fill the vacancy caused by the death of his father, Clarence J. Brown; reelected to the eight succeeding Congresses, and served from November 2, 1965 to January 3, 1983; was not a candidate for reelection in 1982 to the Ninety-eighth Congress, but was an unsuccessful candidate for election for Governor of Ohio; deputy Secretary of Commerce, 1983-1988; board member, Overseas Private Investment Corp., 1989-1991; chairman, C.J. Brown Consulting, 1989-1992; president, United States Capitol

Historical Society, 1992 to present; is a resident of Urbana, Ohio, and Washington, D.C.

**BROWN, Corrine,** a Representative from Florida; born in Jacksonville, Fla., November 11, 1946; B.S., Florida Agricultural and Mechanical University, Tallahassee, 1969; Ed.S., University of Florida, 1974; educator; member, Florida State house of representatives, 1983-1993; elected as a Democrat to the One Hundred Third and One Hundred Fourth Congresses (January 3, 1993-January 3, 1997); is a resident of Jacksonville, Fla.

**BROWN, Elias,** a Representative from Maryland; born near Baltimore, Md., on May 9, 1793; attended the common schools; presidential elector on the ticket of Monroe and Tompkins in 1820 and on the ticket of Adams and Rush in 1828; elected as a Jacksonian to the Twenty-first Congress (March 4, 1829-March 3, 1831); member of the State house of representatives in 1834 and 1835; member of the State senate 1836-1838; presidential elector on the ticket of Harrison and Tyler in 1836; delegate to the State constitutional convention in 1836; died near Baltimore, Md., July 7, 1857; interment in a private cemetery near Eldersburg, Carroll County, Md.

**BROWN, Ernest S.,** a Senator from Nevada; born in Alturas, Modoc County, Calif., September 25, 1903; moved with his family to Reno, Nev., in 1906; attended the public schools; graduated from the University of Nevada at Reno in 1926; studied law; was admitted to the bar in 1927 and commenced practice in Reno, Nev.; member, State assembly 1933; district attorney of Washoe County 1935-1941, resigning in December 1941 to enter active service in the United States Army as a second lieutenant; commissioned a colonel and discharged in December 1945; returned to Reno and resumed the practice of law; appointed as a Republican to the United States Senate October 1, 1954, to fill the vacancy caused by the death of Pat McCarran, and served until December 1, 1954; was unsuccessful for election to the vacancy; resumed the practice of law; died in Reno, Nev., July 23, 1965; interment in Masonic section of Mountain View Cemetery.

**BROWN, Ethan Allen,** a Senator from Ohio; born in Darien, Conn., July 4, 1776; pursued academic studies; studied law under Alexander Hamilton; was admitted to the bar in 1802; moved to Cincinnati in 1804, where he began the practice of law; associate judge of the supreme court of Ohio 1810-1818; Governor of Ohio from December 14, 1818 until January 4, 1822, when he resigned to become a Senator; elected to the United States Senate to fill the vacancy caused by the death of William A. Trimble and served from January 3, 1822, to March 3, 1825; unsuccessful candidate for reelection in 1825; canal commissioner of Ohio 1825-1830; appointed Chargé d'Affaires to Brazil on May 26, 1830 and served until April 1834; commissioner of the General Land Office in Washington 1835-1836; moved to Rising Sun, Ohio County, Ind., 1836; member, Indiana house of representatives 1842; died in Indianapolis, Ind., February 24, 1852; interment in Cedar Hedge Cemetery, Rising Sun, Ind.

Bibliography: *DAB.*

**BROWN, Foster Vincent** (father of Joseph Edgar Brown), a Representative from Tennessee; born near Sparta, White County, Tenn., December 24, 1852; attended the common schools; was graduated from Burritt College, Spencer, Van Buren County, Tenn., in 1871 and from the law department of Cumberland University, Lebanon, Tenn., in 1873; was admitted to the bar and commenced practice in Jasper, Tenn., in 1874; delegate to the Republican National Conventions in 1884, 1896, 1900, and 1916; attorney general of the fourth judicial district 1886-1894; moved to Chattanooga, Tenn., in May 1890 and continued the practice of law; elected as a Republican to the Fifty-fourth Congress (March 4, 1895-March 3, 1897); declined to be a candidate for renomination in

1896; resumed the practice of law; appointed attorney general of Puerto Rico on May 10, 1910, and served until April 20, 1912, when he resigned; resumed the practice of law in Chattanooga, Tenn., until his death there on March 26, 1937; interment in Forest Hills Cemetery.

**BROWN, Fred Herbert,** a Senator from New Hampshire; born in Ossipee, Carroll County, N.H., April 12, 1879; attended the public schools and Dow Academy, Franconia, N.H., Dartmouth College, Hanover, N.H., and Boston (Mass.) University School of Law; was admitted to the bar in 1907 and commenced practice in Somersworth, N.H.; city solicitor 1910-1914; delegate to the State constitutional convention in 1912; mayor of Somersworth, N.H., 1914-1922; United States attorney for the district of New Hampshire 1914-1922; elected Governor of New Hampshire in 1922 and served from January 4, 1923 to January 1, 1925; unsuccessful candidate for reelection in 1924; member of the New Hampshire Public Service Commission 1925-1933; elected as a Democrat to the United States Senate in 1932 and served from March 4, 1933, to January 3, 1939; unsuccessful candidate for reelection in 1938; appointed Comptroller General of the United States by President Franklin D. Roosevelt in April 1939 and served until his resignation on June 19, 1940; served as a member of the United States Tariff Commission 1940-1941; retired from public and political activities; died in Somersworth, N.H., on February 3, 1955; interment in Ossipee Cemetery, Ossipee, N.H.

**BROWN, Garry Eldridge,** a Representative from Michigan; born in Schoolcraft, Kalamazoo County, Mich., August 12, 1923; served in the Twenty-fourth Infantry Division as second lieutenant in Japan, 1946-1947; B.A., Kalamazoo College, 1951; LL.B., George Washington University Law School, 1954; admitted to the bar in 1954 and commenced practice in Kalamazoo, Mich.; commissioner of the United States District Court for the western district of Michigan, 1957-1962; delegate to the Michigan constitutional convention of 1961-1962; served in the Michigan State senate, 1962-1966, minority floor leader and chairman of the Republican senate policy committee; elected as a Republican to the Ninetieth and to the five succeeding Congresses (January 3, 1967-January 3, 1979); unsuccessful candidate for reelection in 1978 to the Ninety-sixth Congress; resumed the practice of law; is a resident of Washington, D.C.

**BROWN, George Edward, Jr.,** a Representative from California; born in Holtville, Imperial County, Calif., March 6, 1920; attended the public schools of Holtville; graduated from Holtville Union High School in 1935; El Centro Junior College, 1938; B.A., University of California at Los Angeles, 1946; entered active duty, U.S. Army in 1942, released in 1946; employed by the city of Los Angeles in personnel and engineering for twelve years between 1940 and 1957; management consultant, 1957-1962; mayor and city councilman of Monterey Park, 1954-1958; member of the California State assembly, 1959-1962; elected as a Democrat to the Eighty-eighth and to the three succeeding Congresses (January 3, 1963-January 3, 1971); was not a candidate for reelection in 1970 to the House of Representatives, but was an unsuccessful candidate for nomination to the United States Senate; elected to the Ninety-third and to the eleven succeeding Congresses (January 3, 1973-January 3, 1997); chairman, Committee on Science, Space and Technology (One Hundred Second and One Hundred Third Congresses); is a resident of San Bernardino, Calif.

**BROWN, George Hanks (Hank),** a Representative and a Senator from Colorado; born in Denver, Colo., February 12, 1940; attended the public schools; graduated, Menlo-Atherton High School, 1957; B.S., University of Colorado, Boulder, 1961; J.D., University of Colorado School of Law, 1969; LL.M. (tax), George Washington University School of Law, 1986; served in the United States Navy as a lieutenant from 1962 until his release in 1966 after

service in Vietnam; admitted to the Colorado bar in 1969; vice president, Monfort of Colorado, 1969-1980; member, Colorado State senate, 1972-1976, assistant majority leader, 1974-1976; became Certified Public Accountant, 1988; elected as a Republican to the Ninety-seventh and to the four succeeding Congresses (January 3, 1981-January 3, 1991); was not a candidate in 1990 for reelection to the House of Representatives, but was elected to the United States Senate and served from January 3, 1991 to January 3, 1997; was not a candidate for reelection in 1996; is a resident of Greeley, Colo.

**BROWN, George Houston,** a Representative from New Jersey; born in Lawrenceville, N.J., February 12, 1810; attended the common schools and Lawrenceville Academy and was graduated from Princeton College in 1828; teacher in Lawrenceville Academy 1828-1830; studied law at Yale College for one year and also in a law office in Somerville, N.J.; was admitted to the bar in 1835 and commenced practice in Somerville; member of the State council 1842-1845; delegate to the State constitutional convention in 1844; elected as a Whig to the Thirty-second Congress (March 4, 1851-March 3, 1853); was not a candidate for renomination in 1852; resumed the practice of law; associate justice of the supreme court of New Jersey from 1861 until his death in Somerville, Somerset County, N.J., August 1, 1865; interment in the Old Cemetery.

**BROWN, James** (brother of John Brown of Virginia and Kentucky [1757-1837], cousin of John Breckinridge, James Breckinridge, and Francis Preston), a Senator from Louisiana; born near Staunton, Va., September 11, 1766; attended Washington College (now Washington and Lee University), Lexington, Va., and William and Mary College, Williamsburg, Va.; studied law; was admitted to the bar and commenced practice in Frankfort, Ky.; commanded a company of sharpshooters in an expedition against the Indians in 1789; secretary to Governor Isaac Shelby in 1792; soon after the cession of the Territory of Louisiana moved to New Orleans and was appointed as secretary of the Territory in 1804; subsequently became United States district attorney for the Territory; elected to the United States Senate on December 1, 1812, to fill the vacancy caused by the resignation of John N. Destréhan, and served from February 5, 1813 to March 3, 1817; unsuccessful candidate for reelection; again elected to the United States Senate in 1819, and served from March 4, 1819 until December 10, 1823, when he resigned; chairman, Committee on Foreign Relations (Sixteenth Congress); appointed United States Minister to France on December 9, 1823 and served until June 1829; returned to the United States and settled in Philadelphia, Pa., where he died on April 7, 1835.

**Bibliography:** *DAB*; Padgett, James A., ed. "Letters of James Brown to Henry Clay, 1804-1835." *Louisiana Historical Quarterly* 24 (1941): 921-1177.

**BROWN, James Sproat,** a Representative from Wisconsin; born in Hampden, Penobscot County, Maine, February 1, 1824; attended the public schools; moved to Cincinnati, Ohio, in 1840; studied law; was admitted to the bar in 1843 and commenced practice in Milwaukee, Wis., in 1844; elected prosecuting attorney for Milwaukee County in 1846; attorney general of Wisconsin in 1848 and 1849; mayor of Milwaukee in 1861; elected as a Democrat to the Thirty-eighth Congress (March 4, 1863-March 3, 1865); unsuccessful candidate for reelection in 1864 to the Thirty-ninth Congress; in 1865 went to Europe to recuperate his health; returned to the United States in 1873; resumed the practice of law in Milwaukee, Wis.; died on April 15, 1878, in Chicago, Ill.; interment in Forest Home Cemetery, Milwaukee, Wis.

**BROWN, James W.** (son-in-law of Thomas Marshall Howe); a Representative from Pennsylvania; born in Pittsburgh, Pa., July 14, 1844; attended the common schools of Allegheny County and also private schools; became interested in the iron and steel industry and served as vice president of the Crucible Steel Co.; also engaged in banking and was trustee of the Dollar Savings Bank; elected as an

Independent Republican to the Fifty-eighth Congress (March 4, 1903-March 3, 1905); declined to be a candidate for renomination in 1904; resumed his former business pursuits and served as president of the Colonial Steel Co.; died at Point Mouille, Mich., on October 23, 1909; interment in Allegheny Cemetery, Pittsburgh, Pa.

**BROWN, Jason Brevoort,** a Representative from Indiana; born in Dillsboro, Dearborn County, Ind., February 26, 1839; attended the common schools and Wilmington Academy, Dearborn County, Ind.; studied law; was admitted to the bar in 1860 and commenced practice in Brownstown, Ind.; member of the State house of representatives 1862-1866; member of the State senate in 1870; secretary of the Territory of Wyoming 1873-1875; moved to Seymour, Ind., in 1875; again a member of the State senate 1880-1883; elected as a Democrat to the Fifty-first, Fifty-second, and Fifty-third Congresses (March 4, 1889-March 3, 1895); chairman, Committee on Elections (Fifty-third Congress); unsuccessful candidate for renomination in 1894; resumed the practice of law in Seymour, Jackson County, Ind., and died there March 10, 1898; interment in Riverview Cemetery.

**BROWN, Jeremiah,** a Representative from Pennsylvania; born in Little Britain (now Fulton) Township, Lancaster County, Pa., April 14, 1785; engaged in milling and agricultural pursuits; member of the Pennsylvania house of representatives in 1826; delegate to the convention to revise the Pennsylvania constitution in 1836; elected as a Whig to the Twenty-seventh and Twenty-eighth Congresses (March 4, 1841-March 3, 1845); was not a candidate for renomination in 1844 to the Twenty-ninth Congress; first associate judge for Lancaster and served from 1851 to 1856; died in Goshen, Fulton Township, Lancaster County, Pa., March 2, 1858; interment in the cemetery adjoining Penn Hill Quaker Meeting House, Little Britain (later Fulton) Township, Pa.

**BROWN, John,** a Representative from Maryland; member of the State house of delegates in 1807 and 1808; elected as a Republican to the Eleventh and Twelfth Congresses and served from March 4, 1809, until his resignation in 1810, before the close of the Eleventh Congress, to accept an appointment as clerk of the court of Queen Annes County, Md., which office he held until his death in Centerville, Queen Annes County, December 13, 1815; interment in Chesterfield Cemetery.

**BROWN, John,** a Representative from Pennsylvania; born in Kishacoquillas Valley, near Lewistown, Mifflin County, Pa., August 12, 1772; attended the common schools; moved to Lewistown, Pa., in 1800; engaged in the gristmill and sawmill business; member of the State house of representatives 1809-1813; elected to the Seventeenth and Eighteenth Congresses (March 4, 1821-March 3, 1825); resumed his former business pursuits; moved to Limestone, Buncombe County, N.C., in 1827 and engaged in agricultural pursuits and in the real estate business; died in a section of Buncombe County, N.C., then called Limestone, near Skyland, on October 12, 1845; interment in Riverside Cemetery, Asheville, N.C.

**BROWN, John** (uncle of Benjamin Brown and grandfather of John Brown Francis), a Representative from Rhode Island; born in Providence, R.I., January 27, 1736; engaged in mercantile pursuits; one of the party which destroyed the British sloop of war *Gaspee* in Narragansett Bay June 17, 1772; sent in irons to Boston for trial, but released through the efforts of his brother Moses; laid the cornerstone of the first building of the College of Rhode Island (now Brown University) May 14, 1770; trustee of Brown University, Providence, R.I., 1774-1803; treasurer 1775-1796; member of the State house of representatives 1782-1784; chosen as a Delegate to the Continental Congress in 1784 and 1785, but did not serve; elected as a Federalist to the Sixth Congress (March 4, 1799-March 3, 1801); resumed his former business pursuits; died in Providence, R.I., September 20, 1803; interment in the North Burial Ground.

**Bibliography:** *DAB*.

**BROWN, John** (brother of James Brown and grandfather of Benjamin Gratz Brown, cousin of John Breckinridge, James Breckinridge, and Francis Preston), a Delegate and a Representative from Virginia and a Senator from Kentucky; born in Staunton, Va., September 12, 1757; attended Washington College (now Washington and Lee University), Lexington, Va., and Princeton College; enlisted in the Revolutionary Army and served until the close of the war; completed his studies at William and Mary College, Williamsburg, Va.; taught school for several years; studied law; was admitted to the bar in 1782 and commenced practice in Frankfort, Ky.; member, Virginia senate from the district of Kentucky 1784-1788; Delegate from the Kentucky district of Virginia to the Continental Congress in 1787 and 1788; elected from Virginia to the First and Second Congresses and served from March 4, 1789, to June 1, 1792, when that portion of Virginia which is now Kentucky was admitted into the Union; elected on June 18, 1792, to the United States Senate from Kentucky for the term ending March 3, 1793; reelected on December 11, 1792, and again in 1799 and served from June 18, 1792, to March 3, 1805; served as President pro tempore of the Senate during the Eighth Congress; resumed the practice of law; died in Frankfort, Ky., August 29, 1837, being the last survivor of the Continental Congress; interment in Frankfort Cemetery.

**Bibliography:** *DAB*; Sprague, Stuart S. "Senator John Brown of Kentucky, 1757-1837: A Political Biography." Ph.D. dissertation, New York University, 1972; Warren, Elizabeth. "John Brown and His Influence on Kentucky Politics: 1784-1805." Ph.D. dissertation, Northwestern University, 1937.

**BROWN, John Brewer,** a Representative from Maryland; born in Philadelphia, Pa., May 13, 1836; attended Centerville (Maryland) Academy and Dickinson College, Carlisle, Pa.; studied law; was admitted to the bar in 1857 and practiced in Centerville, Queen Annes County, Md.; member of the State house of delegates in 1870; served in the State senate 1888-1892; elected as a Democrat to the Fifty-second Congress to fill the vacancy caused by the resignation of Henry Page and served from November 8, 1892, to March 3, 1893; declined to be a candidate for renomination in 1892; resumed the practice of law; died in Centerville May 16, 1898; interment in Chesterfield Cemetery.

**BROWN, John Robert,** a Representative from Virginia; born near Snow Creek, Franklin County, Va., January 14, 1842; attended private schools in Franklin and Henry Counties; entered the Confederate Army in 1861 as a private in Company D, Twenty-fourth Regiment, Virginia Volunteers; formed a partnership with his father in the tobacco business at Shady Grove in 1870; moved to Martinsville, Henry County, in 1882 and continued in the tobacco business; also engaged in banking; mayor of Martinsville 1884-1888; elected as a Republican to the Fiftieth Congress (March 4, 1887-March 3, 1889); unsuccessfully contested the election of Claude A. Swanson to the Fifty-fifth Congress; reengaged in the tobacco business; retired from active business pursuits; died in Martinsville August 4, 1927; interment in Oakwood Cemetery.

**BROWN, John W.,** a Representative from New York; born in Dundee, Scotland, October 11, 1796; immigrated to the United States in 1802 with his father, who settled in Newburgh, N.Y.; attended the public schools; studied law; was admitted to the New York bar in 1818 and commenced the practice of law in Newburgh, N.Y.; elected justice of the peace in 1820; elected as a Jacksonian to the Twenty-third and Twenty-fourth Congresses (March 4, 1833-March 3, 1837); resumed the practice of law; elected judge of the supreme court for the second judicial district of New York in 1849; reelected in 1857, and served until 1865; resumed the practice of law; died in Newburgh September 6, 1875; interment in Cedar Hill Cemetery.

**BROWN, John Young** (nephew of Bryan Rust Young and William Singleton Young), a Representative from Kentucky; born in Claysville, Hardin County, Ky., June 28, 1835; was graduated from Centre College, Danville, Ky., in 1855; studied law; was admitted to the bar in 1857 and commenced practice in Elizabethtown, Ky.; elected as a Democrat to the Thirty-sixth Congress (March 4, 1859-March 3, 1861), but because he had not attained the age required by the Constitution he did not take his seat until the second session began December 3, 1860; member of the Douglas National Committee in 1860; elected to the Fortieth Congress, but his seat was declared vacant because of alleged disloyalty; elected to the Forty-third and Forty-fourth Congresses (March 4, 1873-March 3, 1877); censured by the House of Representatives on February 4, 1875, for the use of unparliamentary language; resumed the practice of law in Louisville; elected Governor of Kentucky in 1891, and served from September 1891 to December 1895; returned to Louisville, where he practiced law until his death in Henderson, Henderson County, Ky., January 11, 1904; interment in Fernwood Cemetery.

**Bibliography:** *DAB.*

**BROWN, John Young,** a Representative from Kentucky; born on a farm near Geigers Lake, Union County, Ky., February 1, 1900; attended the county schools and the high school at Sturgis, Ky.; Centre College, Danville, Ky., A.B., 1921, and from the law department of the University of Kentucky at Lexington, LL.B., 1926; was admitted to the bar the same year and commenced practice in Lexington, Ky.; also engaged in agricultural pursuits; city representative of Lexington, Ky., in 1930; county representative of Fayette County, Ky., in 1932 and again in 1946; member of the Kentucky house of representatives 1930 to 1932, serving as speaker in 1932; elected as a Democrat to the Seventy-third Congress (March 4, 1933-January 3, 1935); unsuccessful candidate for renomination in 1934 to the Seventy-fourth Congress; resumed the practice of law; unsuccessful candidate in 1946 for election to the United States Senate; member of the Kentucky legislature in 1953 and 1954; unsuccessful candidate in 1960 for nomination to the United States Senate; member, Kentucky house of representatives, 1962-1963, and 1966-1967, during which time he served as majority floor leader; returned to law practice in Lexington and Louisville; died in Louisville, Ky., June 16, 1985; interment at Lexington Cemetery, Lexington, Ky.

**BROWN, Joseph Edgar** (son of Foster Vincent Brown), a Representative from Tennessee; born in Jasper, Marion County, Tenn., February 11, 1880; attended Baylor's Preparatory School, Chattanooga, Tenn., and was graduated from Cumberland University, Lebanon, Tenn., in 1902; studied law; was admitted to the Tennessee bar in 1904 and commenced practice in Jasper, Tenn.; moved to Chattanooga, Tenn., in 1907 and continued the practice of law; elected as a Republican to the Sixty-seventh Congress (March 4, 1921-March 3, 1923); was not a candidate for renomination in 1922; served as chairman of the Republican State executive committee 1922-1924; resumed the practice of law in Chattanooga, Tenn.; delegate to the Republican National Convention in 1924; died in Chattanooga June 13, 1939; interment in Forest Hills Cemetery.

**BROWN, Joseph Emerson,** a Senator from Georgia; born in the Pickens District of South Carolina April 15, 1821; moved to Georgia; attended Calhoun Academy in South Carolina; taught school; studied law; was admitted to the bar in 1845 and later was graduated from the Yale Law School; returned to Georgia and commenced practice in 1846; member, State senate 1849; judge of the superior court of the Blue Ridge circuit in 1855; Governor of Georgia from November 6, 1857 until June 17, 1865, when he resigned; chief justice of the supreme court of Georgia 1865-1870, when he resigned and accepted the presidency of the Western & Atlantic Railroad Co.; appointed and subsequently elected in 1880 as a Democrat to the United States Senate to fill the vacancy caused by the resignation of John B. Gordon; reelected in 1885 and served from May 26, 1880, until March 3, 1891; died in Atlanta, Ga., November 30, 1894; interment in Oakland Cemetery.

**Bibliography:** *DAB;* Parks, Joseph. *Joseph E. Brown of Georgia.* Baton Rouge: Louisiana State University Press, 1977; Roberts, Derrell C. *Joseph E. Brown and the Politics of Reconstruction.* University, Ala.: University of Alabama Press, 1973.

**BROWN, Lathrop,** a Representative from New York; born in New York City February 26, 1883; was graduated from Groton School, Massachusetts, in 1900 and from Harvard University in 1903; engaged in the real estate business; served in Squadron A, National Guard of New York, for five years; elected as a Democrat to the Sixty-third Congress (March 4, 1913-March 3, 1915); unsuccessfully contested the election of Frederick C. Hicks to the Sixty-fourth Congress; special assistant to Secretary of the Interior Franklin K. Lane from March 1917 to October 1918; served as a private in the Tank Corps during the First World War; joint secretary of President Woodrow Wilson's Industrial Conference in 1919; delegate to the Democratic National Conventions of 1920, 1924, and 1936; studied monetary theory at the Graduate School of Harvard University 1928-1932; moved to California in 1946 and settled on a cattle ranch; elected to the sheriff's posse of Monterey County in 1947; member of committee to supervise Graduate School of Public Administration of Harvard University in 1954 and 1955; died in Fort Myers, Fla., November 28, 1959; cremated; ashes interred in Abbey of the Light, Manasota Memorial Park, Sarasota, Fla.

**BROWN, Milton,** a Representative from Tennessee; born in Lebanon, Ohio, February 28, 1804; moved to Nashville, Tenn.; studied law; was admitted to the bar and commenced practice in Paris, Tenn.; later moved to Jackson, Tenn.; became judge of the chancery court of west Tennessee in 1835 and held this position until elected as a Whig to the Twenty-seventh Congress; reelected to the two succeeding Congresses (March 4, 1841-March 3, 1847); resumed the practice of law; one of the founders of Southwestern University (later Union University) and of Lambuth College, both in Jackson, Madison County, Tenn.; president of the Mississippi Central & Tennessee Railroad Co., 1854-1856; president of the Mobile & Ohio Railroad Co., 1856-1871; died in Jackson, Tenn., on May 15, 1883; interment in Riverside Cemetery.

**BROWN, Norris,** a Senator from Nebraska; born in Maquoketa, Jackson County, Iowa, May 2, 1863; attended the common schools; was graduated from the law department of the University of Iowa at Iowa City in 1883; was admitted to the bar in 1884 and commenced practice in Perry, Dallas County, Iowa; moved to Kearney, Buffalo County, Nebr., in 1888 and continued the practice of law; prosecuting attorney of Buffalo County 1892-1896; deputy attorney general of Nebraska 1900-1904; attorney general of Nebraska 1904-1906; elected as a Republican to the United States Senate and served from March 4, 1907, to March 3, 1913; unsuccessful candidate for renomination 1912; chairman, Committee on Patents (Sixty-first and Sixty-second Congresses); resumed the practice of law in Omaha, Nebr., 1913-1942; retired and moved to Seattle, Wash., where he died January 5, 1960; interment in Forest Lawn Cemetery, Omaha, Nebr.

**BROWN, Paul,** a Representative from Georgia; born near Hartwell, Hart County, Ga., March 31, 1880; attended the public schools; was graduated in 1901 from the Lumpkin Law School, University of Georgia, at Athens; was admitted to the bar the same year and practiced law in Lexington, Ga., until 1920; also engaged in agricultural pursuits; mayor of Lexington, Ga., 1908-1914; member of the State house of representatives in 1907 and 1908; moved to Elberton, Ga., in 1920; county attorney of Elbert County 1928-1933; delegate to the Democratic National Convention in 1932; elected as a Democrat to the Seventy-third Congress to fill the vacancy caused by the death of Charles H. Brand; reelected to the Seventy-fourth and to the twelve succeeding Congresses and served from July 5, 1933, to January 3, 1961; chairman, Joint Committee on Defense Production (Eighty-fourth and Eighty-sixth Congresses); was not a candidate for renomination in 1960; died in Elberton, Ga., September 24, 1961; interment in Elmhurst Cemetery.

**BROWN, Prentiss Marsh,** a Representative and a Senator from Michigan; born in St. Ignace, Mackinac County, Mich., June 18, 1889; attended the public schools, and the University of Illinois at Urbana; was graduated from Albion (Mich.) College in 1911; studied law; was admitted to the bar in 1914 and commenced practice in St. Ignace, Mich.; prosecuting attorney of Mackinac County 1914-1926; city attorney of St. Ignace 1916-1928; unsuccessful candidate for election in 1924 to the Sixty-ninth Congress and for election in 1928 as justice of the Michigan Supreme Court; member of the State board of law examiners 1930-1942; elected as a Democrat to the Seventy-third Congress; reelected to the Seventy-fourth Congress and served from March 4, 1933, until his resignation, effective November 18, 1936; elected as a Democrat on November 3, 1936, to the United States Senate for the term beginning January 3, 1937, but was subsequently appointed to the United States Senate to fill the vacancy caused by the death of James Couzens for the term ending January 3, 1937, and served from November 19, 1936, to January 3, 1943; unsuccessful candidate for reelection in 1942; chairman, Committee on Claims (Seventy-seventh Congress); administrator in the Office of Price Administration 1943; resumed the practice of law in Washington, D.C., and Detroit, Mich.; chairman of the Mackinac Bridge Authority until his death; interested in atomic reactor company; resided in St. Ignace, Mich., where he died December 19, 1973; interment in Lakeside Cemetery.

**BROWN, Robert,** a Representative from Pennsylvania; born in Weaversville, East Allen Township, Northampton County, Pa., December 25, 1744; attended the common schools and was apprenticed to the blacksmith trade; at the beginning of the Revolutionary War was commissioned first lieutenant in the Pennsylvania "Flying Camp" on September 10, 1776; captured at the surrender of Fort Washington, N.Y. on November 16, 1776; worked at the blacksmith trade while a prisoner; later put aboard the prison ship *Judith* and subsequently imprisoned in the old city hall, New York City; paroled on board ship, December 10, 1777; member of the Pennsylvania senate, 1783-1787; elected as a Republican to the Fifth Congress to fill the vacancy caused by the resignation of Samuel Sitgreaves; reelected to the Sixth and to the seven succeeding Congresses, and served from December 4, 1798 to March 3, 1815; was not a candidate for renomination in 1814 to the Fourteenth Congress; retired from public life and lived on his farm; died near Weaversville, Northampton County, Pa., February 26, 1823; interment in East Allen Presbyterian Churchyard.

**BROWN, Seth W.,** a Representative from Ohio; born near Waynesville, Warren County, Ohio, January 4, 1841; attended the public schools; during the Civil War served in Company H, Seventy-ninth Regiment, Ohio Volunteer Infantry; engaged in the newspaper business; studied law; was admitted to the bar in 1873 and commenced practice in Waynesville, Ohio; prosecuting attorney for Warren County 1880-1883; resumed the practice of law in Lebanon, Ohio; member of the State house of representatives 1883-1887; elected as a Republican to the Fifty-fifth and Fifty-sixth Congresses (March 4, 1897-March 3, 1901); unsuccessful candidate for renomination in 1900; resumed the practice of law in Lebanon and Cincinnati, Ohio; writer on political and governmental subjects; died in Lebanon, Warren County, Ohio, February 24, 1923; interment in Miami Cemetery, Waynesville, Ohio.

**BROWN, Sherrod Campbell,** a Representative from Ohio; born in Mansfield, Richland County, Ohio, November 9, 1952; B.A., Yale University, 1974; M.A., Ohio State University, 1979, and M.A.,

1981; political science instructor, Ohio State University, 1979-1980; faculty associate, Mershon Center, Ohio State University, 1991-1993; Sherrod Brown Elections Enterprises, Inc.; member, Ohio State house of representatives, 1975-1983; Ohio secretary of state, 1983-1991; elected as a Democrat to the One Hundred Third and One Hundred Fourth Congresses (January 3, 1993-January 3, 1997); is a resident of Chippewa Lake, Ohio.

**BROWN, Titus,** a Representative from New Hampshire; born in Alstead, Cheshire County, N.H., February 11, 1786; was graduated from Middlebury (Vt.) College in 1811; studied law; was admitted to the bar and commenced practice in Reading, Vt., in 1814; moved to Francestown, N.H., in 1817 and continued the practice of law; member of the State house of representatives 1820-1825; solicitor of Hillsborough County 1823-1825 and 1829-1834; elected to the Nineteenth and Twentieth Congresses (March 4, 1825-March 3, 1829); was not a candidate for reelection in 1828; member of the State senate and served as its president in 1842; chairman of the boards of bank and railroad commissioners at the time of his death; died in Francestown, N.H., January 29, 1849; interment in Mill Village Cemetery.

**BROWN, Webster Everett,** a Representative from Wisconsin; born near Peterboro village, Madison County, N.Y., July 16, 1851; moved with his parents to Wisconsin in 1857; resided for a time in Newport, Columbia County, and then in Hull and Stockton, Portage County; attended the common schools; completed a preparatory course at Lawrence University, Appleton, Wis., and later, in 1870, a business course at the Spencerian Business College, Milwaukee, Wis.; was graduated from the University of Wisconsin at Madison in 1874; engaged in the logging and lumber business at Stevens Point, Wis., in 1875; moved to Rhinelander, Oneida County, Wis., in 1882 and continued in the logging and lumber business; also engaged in manufacture of paper; mayor of Rhinelander in 1894 and 1895; elected as a Republican to the Fifty-seventh, Fifty-eighth, and Fifty-ninth Congresses (March 4, 1901-March 3, 1907); chairman, Committee on Mines and Mining (Fifty-eighth and Fifty-ninth Congresses); was not a candidate for renomination in 1906; resumed his former business and manufacturing pursuits in Rhinelander, Wis.; died in Chicago, Ill., while on a visit for medical treatment, December 14, 1929; interment in Forest Home Cemetery, Rhinelander, Wis.

**BROWN, William,** a Representative from Kentucky; born in Frederick County, Va., April 19, 1779; attended the common schools; moved with his father to Bourbon County, Ky., in 1784 and to Cynthiana, Harrison County, Ky., about 1795; studied law; was admitted to the bar and practiced; served as a colonel in the War of 1812; member of the Kentucky house of representatives; elected to the Sixteenth Congress (March 4, 1819-March 3, 1821); moved to Jacksonville, Morgan County, Ill., in 1832, where he died October 6, 1833.

**BROWN, William Gay** (father of William Gay Brown, Jr.), a Representative from Virginia and from West Virginia; born in Kingwood, Preston County, Va. (now West Virginia), September 25, 1800; attended the public schools; studied law; was admitted to the bar in 1823 and commenced practice in Kingwood, Va.; member of the Virginia house of delegates in 1832 and 1840-1843; elected as a Democrat to the Twenty-ninth and Thirtieth Congresses (March 4, 1845-March 3, 1849); delegate to the Virginia constitutional conventions in 1850 and 1861; delegate to the Democratic National Conventions at Charleston and Baltimore in 1860; elected as a Unionist to the Thirty-seventh Congress (March 4, 1861-March 3, 1863); upon the admission of West Virginia as a State into the Union was elected as an Unconditional Unionist to the Thirty-eighth Congress and served from December 7, 1863, to March 3, 1865; died in Kingwood, W.Va., April 19, 1884; interment in Maplewood Cemetery.

**BROWN, William Gay, Jr.** (son of William Gay Brown), a Representative from West Virginia; born in Kingwood, Preston County, Va. (now West Virginia), April 7, 1856; attended the common schools; was graduated from the University of West Virginia at Morgantown in 1877; studied law; was admitted to the bar in 1877 and commenced practice in Preston County, W.Va.; also engaged in banking; elected as a Democrat to the Sixty-second, Sixty-third, and Sixty-fourth Congresses and served from March 4, 1911, until his death in Washington, D.C., March 9, 1916; interment in Kingwood Cemetery, Kingwood, W.Va.

**BROWN, William John,** a Representative from Indiana; born near Washington, Mason County, Ky., August 15, 1805; moved to Clermont County, Ohio, in 1808 with his parents, who settled near New Richmond; attended the common schools and Franklin Academy in Clermont County; moved to Rushville, Rush County, Ind., in 1821; studied law; was admitted to the bar in 1826 and commenced practice in Rushville; member of the Indiana State house of representatives, 1829-1832; prosecuting attorney, 1831-1835; secretary of state of Indiana, 1836-1840; moved to Indianapolis, Ind., in 1837; again a member of the State house of representatives, 1841-1843; elected as a Democrat to the Twenty-eighth Congress (March 4, 1843-March 3, 1845); appointed Second Assistant Postmaster General by President James K. Polk and served from 1845 until 1849; elected to the Thirty-first Congress (March 4, 1849-March 3, 1851); unsuccessful candidate for renomination in 1850 to the Thirty-second Congress; chief editor of the Indianapolis Sentinel, 1850-1855; many times chairman of the Democratic State central committee of Indiana; appointed by President Franklin Pierce as special agent of the Post Office Department for Indiana and Illinois, which position he held from 1853 until his death near Indianapolis, Ind., March 18, 1857; interment in Crown Hill Cemetery.

**BROWN, William Ripley,** a Representative from Kansas; born in Buffalo, N.Y., July 16, 1840; was prepared for college in Phillips Exeter Academy, Exeter, N.H., and was graduated from Union College, Schenectady, N.Y., in 1862; went immediately to Kansas and settled in Emporia; studied law; was admitted to the bar in 1864 and commenced practice in Emporia, Lyon County, Kans.; judge of the ninth judicial district of Kansas 1867-1877; elected as a Republican to the Forty-fourth Congress (March 4, 1875-March 3, 1877); unsuccessful candidate for renomination in 1876; resumed the practice of law in Hutchinson, Kans.; register of the United States land office in Larned, Kans., 1883-1885; moved to El Reno, Okla., in 1892; probate judge of Canadian County 1894-1898; died in Kansas City, Mo., March 3, 1916; interment in Lawrence Cemetery, Lawrence, Douglas County, Kans.

**BROWN, William Wallace,** a Representative from Pennsylvania; born in Summer Hill, Cayuga County, N.Y., April 22, 1836; moved with his parents to Elk County, Pa., in 1838; attended the common schools and Smethport Academy; was graduated from Alfred University, Allegany County, N.Y., in 1861; enlisted in the Twenty-third New York Volunteers in 1861; transferred to the First Pennsylvania Rifles on December 18, 1861; appointed recorder of deeds of McKean County, Pa. in 1864 and its superintendent of schools in 1866; studied law; was admitted to the bar in 1866 and practiced; elected district attorney of McKean County the same year; moved in 1869 to Corry, Erie County, Pa., where he served three years as city attorney and two years in the city council; member of the State house of representatives 1872-1876; appointed aide-de-camp to Governor John F. Hartranft in 1876 and was associated with the National Guard of Pennsylvania; moved to Bradford, Pa., in 1878 and continued the practice of law; elected as a Republican to the Forty-eighth and Forty-ninth Congresses (March 4, 1883-March 3, 1887); unsuccessful candidate for renomination in 1886 to the Fiftieth Congress; resumed the practice of law; city solicitor of

Bradford 1892-1897; auditor for the War Department 1897-1899; auditor for the Navy Department 1899-1907; appointed by President Theodore Roosevelt in 1907, and served until 1910, as Assistant Attorney General, in charge of defense of Spanish treaty claims; resumed the practice of law in Bradford, Pa., where he died November 4, 1926; interment in Alfred Cemetery, Alfred, Allegany County, N.Y.

**BROWNBACK, Samuel Dale,** a Representative from Kansas; born in Garnett, Anderson County, Kans., September 12, 1956; graduated Prairie View High School, 1974; B.S., Kansas State University, Manhattan, 1978; J.D., University of Kansas, Lawrence, 1982; administrator; farm broadcaster, station KKSU; partner in Manhattan, Kans., law firm; teacher of agricultural law, Kansas State University; city attorney for Ogden and Leonardville; White House Fellow with United States Trade Representative Carla Hills and Intergovernmental Advisory Committee to the United States Trade Representative; Kansas secretary of agriculture, 1986-1993; elected as a Republican to the One Hundred Fourth Congress (January 3, 1995-January 3, 1997); was not a candidate in 1996 for renomination to the House of Representatives, but was a candidate for election to the United States Senate for the remainder of the term ending January 3, 1999; is a resident of Topeka, Kans.

**BROWNE, Charles,** a Representative from New Jersey; born in Philadelphia, Pa., September 28, 1875; attended private schools in Philadelphia; was graduated from Princeton University in 1896; studied medicine, and was graduated from the University of Pennsylvania at Philadelphia in 1900; attended the University of Berlin in 1902 and 1903; overseer of the poor, Princeton, N.J., 1912-1914; mayor of Princeton 1914-1923; served as first lieutenant and captain in the Medical Corps from March 1917 to April 1919; resumed the practice of his profession in Princeton; elected as a Democrat to the Sixty-eighth Congress (March 4, 1923-March 3, 1925); unsuccessful candidate for reelection in 1924 to the Sixty-ninth Congress; member of the Board of Public Utility Commissioners of New Jersey 1925-1931; served in the New Jersey house of assembly 1937-1939, and again in 1941 and 1942; adviser in the department of politics at Princeton University; died in Princeton, August 17, 1947; remains were cremated and the ashes interred in the grounds of his home in Princeton.

**BROWNE, Edward Everts,** a Representative from Wisconsin; born in Waupaca, Waupaca County, Wis., February 16, 1868; attended the public schools and Waupaca High School; was graduated from the University of Wisconsin at Madison in 1890 and from the law department of the same university in 1892; was admitted to the bar in 1892 and commenced practice in Waupaca, Wis.; district attorney of Waupaca County 1898-1905; delegate to the Republican State conventions in 1902, 1904, and 1906; member of the board of regents of the University of Wisconsin in 1905 and 1906; member of the State senate 1907-1912; elected as a Republican to the Sixty-third and to the eight succeeding Congresses (March 4, 1913-March 3, 1931); unsuccessful candidate for renomination in 1930; resumed the practice of law; member of the State conservation commission 1936-1941; died in Evanston, Ill., November 23, 1945; interment in Lakeside Cemetery, Waupaca, Wis.

**BROWNE, George Huntington,** a Representative from Rhode Island; born in Gloucester, R.I., January 6, 1811; attended the public schools and was graduated from Brown University in 1840; studied law; was admitted to the bar in 1843 and commenced practice in Providence, R.I.; elected a representative to the "Charter" General Assembly of Rhode Island in 1842; at the same time was elected a representative to what was termed the "Suffrage" legislature and attended the latter; member of the general assembly under the constitution, 1849-1852; appointed United States district attorney in 1852, and served until 1861 when he resigned; delegate to the Democratic National Conventions held in Charleston and Baltimore in 1860; delegate to the peace convention held in Washington, D.C., in 1861 in an effort to devise means to prevent the impending war; elected as a candidate of the Democratic and Constitutional Union Parties to the Thirty-seventh Congress (March 4, 1861-March 3, 1863); unsuccessful candidate for reelection in 1862 to the Thirty-eighth Congress; declined the appointment as Governor of the Territory of Arizona in 1861; entered the Union Army as colonel of the Twelfth Regiment, Rhode Island Volunteer Infantry, October 13, 1862, and served throughout the Civil War; member of the Rhode Island State senate in 1872 and 1873; elected chief justice of the supreme court of Rhode Island in May 1874, but declined the office; died in Providence, R.I., September 26, 1885; interment in Swan Point Cemetery.

**BROWNE, Thomas Henry Bayly,** a Representative from Virginia; born at Accomac Court House, Accomac County, Va., February 8, 1844; instructed by private tutors; attended Hanover and Bloomfield Academies in Virginia; during the Civil War enlisted as a private in Company F, Thirty-ninth Regiment, Virginia Volunteer Infantry, Confederate Army; afterwards served as a private in Chew's battery of the Stuart Horse Artillery; was surrendered with the Army of Northern Virginia in April 1865; was graduated from the law department of the University of Virginia at Charlottesville in 1867; admitted to the bar in 1868 and commenced practice in Accomac, Va.; elected prosecuting attorney for Accomac County in 1873; elected as a Republican to the Fiftieth and Fifty-first Congresses (March 4, 1887-March 3, 1891); unsuccessful candidate for reelection in 1890 to the Fifty-second Congress; resumed the practice of law; died in Accomac, Va., August 27, 1892; interment in Mount Curtis Cemetery.

**BROWNE, Thomas McLelland,** a Representative from Indiana; born in New Paris, Preble County, Ohio, April 19, 1829; moved to Indiana in January 1844; attended the common schools; moved to Winchester, Randolph County, Ind., in 1848; studied law; was admitted to the bar in 1849 and commenced practice in Winchester; elected prosecuting attorney for the thirteenth judicial circuit in 1855; reelected in 1857 and 1859; secretary of the Indiana State senate in 1861; member of the State senate in 1863; assisted in organizing the Seventh Regiment, Indiana Volunteer Cavalry of the Union Army, and went to the field with that regiment as captain of Company B, August 28, 1863; commissioned lieutenant colonel on October 1, 1863; promoted to colonel on October 10, 1865, and subsequently commissioned by President Lincoln as brigadier general by brevet, March 13, 1865; mustered out on February 18, 1866; appointed United States attorney for the district of Indiana in April 1869 and served until his resignation on August 1, 1872; unsuccessful candidate in 1872 for election for Governor of Indiana; delegate to the Republican National Convention in 1876; elected as a Republican to the Forty-fifth and to the six succeeding Congresses (March 4, 1877-March 3, 1891); chairman, Committee on Invalid Pensions (Forty-seventh Congress), Committee on Revision of the Laws (Fifty-first Congress); was not a candidate for renomination in 1890 to the Fifty-second Congress; died in Winchester, Ind., July 17, 1891; interment in Fountain Park Cemetery.

**BROWNING, Gordon Weaver,** a Representative from Tennessee; born near Atwood, Carroll County, Tenn., November 22, 1889; attended the public schools; B.S., Valparaiso (Ind.) University, 1913; graduated from Cumberland University Law School in 1915; was admitted to the bar and commenced practice in Huntingdon, Tenn., in 1915; enlisted in the National Guard in June 1917, and commissioned a second lieutenant of the First Tennessee Field Artillery, afterwards the One Hundred and Fourteenth Field Artillery, Thirtieth Division; promoted to first lieutenant and to captain, and served in France; was discharged from the service in 1919 and resumed the practice of law in Huntingdon, Tenn.; unsuccessful candidate for election in 1920 to the Sixty-seventh

Congress; elected as a Democrat to the Sixty-eighth and to the five succeeding Congresses (March 4, 1923-January 3, 1935); was not a candidate in 1934 for renomination to the House of Representatives, but was an unsuccessful candidate for nomination to the United States Senate; one of the managers appointed by the House of Representatives in 1933 to conduct the impeachment proceedings against Harold Louderback, judge of the United States District Court for the Northern District of California; resumed the practice of law; elected Governor of Tennessee in 1936, and served from January 15, 1937 to January 16, 1939; unsuccessful candidate for renomination in 1938; chancellor of the Eighth Tennessee Chancery Division, 1942-1949; was appointed a captain in the United States Army on February 17, 1943; attended the School of Military Government at Charlottesville, Va.; advanced through the ranks to lieutenant colonel; acted as deputy head of the Belgium-Luxembourg missions until January 1946; was attached to the Allied military government in Germany for one year, serving as civil-affairs adviser on the supreme commander's staff; elected Governor of Tennessee in 1948, reelected in 1950, and served from January 17, 1949 to January 15, 1953; unsuccessful candidate for renomination in 1952, and for nomination as governor in 1954; engaged in the practice of law and in the operation of a dairy farm; president of an insurance firm before retirement; resided in Huntingdon, Tenn., where he died on May 23, 1976; interment in Oak Hill Cemetery.

**Bibliography:** Adams, J.W. "Governor Gordon Browning, Campaigner Extraordinary–The 1936 Election for Governor." *West Tennessee Historical Society Papers* 30 (1976): 5-23; Majors, William R. *The End of Arcadia: Gordon Browning and Tennessee Politics.* Memphis, Tenn.: Memphis State University Press, 1982.

**BROWNING, Orville Hickman,** a Senator from Illinois; born in Cynthiana, Harrison County, Ky., February 10, 1806; attended Augusta College; studied law; was admitted to the bar in 1831; moved to Quincy, Ill., in 1831 and practiced; served in the Illinois Volunteers during the Black Hawk War 1832; member, Illinois State senate, 1836-1843; unsuccessful candidate for election as a Whig in 1850 to the Thirty-second Congress, and in 1852 to the Thirty-third Congress; delegate to the anti-Nebraska convention held at Bloomington, Ill., in May 1856, which helped lay the foundations of the Republican Party; appointed as a Republican to the United States Senate to fill the vacancy caused by the death of Stephen A. Douglas, and served from June 26, 1861 to January 12, 1863, when a successor was elected; was not a candidate for election in 1863; chairman, Committee on Enrolled Bills (Thirty-seventh Congress); appointed Secretary of the Interior in the Cabinet of President Andrew Johnson, and served from September 1, 1866 to March 3, 1869, also discharging the duties of Attorney General from March 13 to July 14, 1868; delegate to the State constitutional convention in 1869; resumed the practice of law; died in Quincy, Adams County, Ill., August 10, 1881; interment in Woodland Cemetery.

**Bibliography:** *DAB*; Baxter, Maurice. *Orville H. Browning: Lincoln's Friend and Critic.* Bloomington: Indiana University Press, 1957; Browning, Orville. *The Diary of Orville H. Browning, 1850-1881.* Edited by Theodore C. Pease and James G. Randall. Springfield: Trustees of the Illinois State Historical Society, 1925-1931.

**BROWNING, William John,** a Representative from New Jersey; born in Camden, N.J., April 11, 1850; attended the Friends' School; at an early age engaged in the wholesale dry goods business in Camden; member of the Camden Board of Education and of the city council; appointed postmaster of Camden on June 18, 1889, and served until June 1, 1894, when his successor was appointed; Chief Clerk of the House of Representatives of the United States 1895-1911; elected as a Republican to the Sixty-second Congress to fill the vacancy caused by the death of Henry C. Loudenslager; reelected to the Sixty-third and to the three succeeding Congresses and served from November 7, 1911, until his death in the Capitol Building, Washington, D.C., March 24, 1920; interment in Harleigh Cemetery, Camden, N.J.

**BROWNLOW, Walter Preston** (nephew of William Gannaway Brownlow), a Representative from Tennessee; born in Abingdon, Washington County, Va., March 27, 1851; attended the common schools; employed as a telegraph messenger boy when only ten years of age; became an apprentice in the tinning business at the age of fourteen and later became a locomotive engineer; entered upon newspaper work as a reporter for the Knoxville Whig and Chronicle in 1876; in the same year purchased the Herald and Tribune in Jonesboro, Tenn.; delegate to the Republican National Conventions in 1880, 1884, 1896, 1900, and 1904; appointed postmaster at Jonesboro in March 1881; resigned in the following December to accept the position of Doorkeeper of the House of Representatives in the Forty-seventh Congress and served in that capacity from 1881 to 1883; member of the Republican National Committee in 1884, 1896, and 1900; elected as a Republican to the Fifty-fifth and to the six succeeding Congresses and served from March 4, 1897, until his death; member of the Board of Managers for the National Soldiers' Home for Disabled Volunteer Soldiers 1902-1910; died at the National Soldiers' Home, Johnson City, Washington County, Tenn., July 8, 1910; interment in the Soldiers' Home Cemetery.

**BROWNLOW, William Gannaway** (uncle of Walter Preston Brownlow), a Senator from Tennessee; born near Wytheville, Wythe County, Va., August 29, 1805; attended the common schools; entered the Methodist ministry in 1826; moved to Elizabethton, Tenn., in 1828 and continued his ministerial duties; published and edited a newspaper called the Whig at Elizabethton in 1839; moved the paper to Jonesboro, Tenn., in 1840 and to Knoxville, Tenn., in 1849 and from his caustic and trenchant editorials became widely known as "the fighting parson"; unsuccessful candidate for election in 1842 to the Twenty-eighth Congress; appointed by President Millard Fillmore in 1850 as a member of the Tennessee River Commission for the Improvement of Navigation; delegate to the constitutional convention which reorganized the State government of Tennessee in 1864; elected Governor of Tennessee in 1865, reelected in 1867, and served from April 5, 1865 until his resignation in October 1867; elected as a Republican to the United States Senate, and served from March 4, 1869 to March 3, 1875; was not a candidate for reelection; chairman, Committee on Revolutionary Claims (Forty-third Congress); returned to journalism in Knoxville, Tenn., until his death there on April 29, 1877; interment in the Old Grey Cemetery.

**Bibliography:** *DAB*; Coulter, E. Merton. *William G. Brownlow: Fighting Parson of the Southern Highlands.* 1937. Reprint. Knoxville: University of Tennesee, 1971; Humphrey, Steven. *That D....d Brownlow.* Boone, N.C.: Appalachian Consortium Press, 1978.

**BROWNSON, Charles Bruce,** a Representative from Indiana; born in Jackson, Mich., February 5, 1914; moved with his parents to Flint, Mich., in 1916; attended the public schools; was graduated from the University of Michigan at Ann Arbor in 1935; entered Infantry Reserve training in 1935; moved to Indianapolis, Ind., in October 1936 and established the Central Wallpaper and Paint Corp.; entered on active duty as a first lieutenant in the Infantry Reserve, February 10, 1941; served as Assistant Chief of Staff, G-1, Eighty-third Infantry Division, in 1943; executive officer to Assistant Chief of Staff G-1, First Army, during invasion planning in England and combat in Europe until V-E Day; transferred with the First Army Planning Headquarters to Canlubang, Philippine Islands, August 5, 1945; released from active duty on February 27, 1946, as a lieutenant colonel, Army Reserve, and retired as a colonel in 1974; Legion of Merit, Bronze Star, and French Medaille de Reconnaissance; chairman of the Marion County Juvenile Court Advisory Council in 1948 and 1949; elected as a Republican to the Eighty-second and to the three succeeding Congresses (January 3, 1951-January 3, 1959); unsuccessful candidate for reelection in 1958 to the Eighty-sixth Congress; assistant administrator for public affairs and congressional liaison, Housing and Home Finance Agency, Washington, D.C., 1959-1964; editor and publisher of Congressional Staff Directory; engaged in public relations in Washington, D.C., 1961-1985; was a resident of Coral Gables, Fla., and Mount Vernon, Va., until his death in Alexandria, Va., on August 4, 1988; interment in Arlington National Cemetery, Va.

**BROWNSON, Nathan,** a Delegate from Georgia; born in Woodbury, Conn., May 14, 1742; was graduated from Yale College in 1761; studied medicine and practiced in Woodbury; moved to Liberty County, Ga., about 1764; member of the Provincial Congress in 1775; surgeon in the Revolutionary Army; Member of the Continental Congress in 1777; member of the Georgia State house of representatives in 1781, and served as speaker; chosen by that body as Governor of Georgia in 1782; again elected to the State house of representatives in 1788, and served as speaker; delegate to the State convention to ratify the Federal Constitution in 1788 and to the State constitutional convention in 1789; member of the State senate, 1789-1791 and served as president of that body; died on his plantation near Riceboro, Liberty County, Ga., November 6, 1796; interment in the Old Midway Burial Ground.

**BROYHILL, James Thomas,** a Representative and a Senator from North Carolina; born in Lenoir, Caldwell County, N.C., August 19, 1927; attended the public schools; B.S., University of North Carolina, Chapel Hill, 1950; employed with the Broyhill Furniture Factories of Lenoir from 1945 until 1962 in a variety of capacities; member of the Planning and Zoning Commission and the Recreation Commission of Lenoir; served on the board of directors of the Northwest North Carolina Forestry Association and as vice chairman of the Furniture, Plywood, and Veneer Council; member of the North Carolina Development Association; elected as a Republican to the Eighty-eighth and to the eleven succeeding Congresses, and served from January 3, 1963 until his resignation on July 14, 1986; appointed to the United States Senate, July 3, 1986, to fill the vacancy caused by the death of John East, and served from July 14, 1986 to November 10, 1986, when a successor was elected; unsuccessful candidate for election in 1986 to the full Senate term ending January 3, 1993; chairman, North Carolina Economic Development Board, 1987-1989; North Carolina Secretary of Commerce, 1989-1991; board member, North Carolina Air Cargo Airport Authority, 1991-1993; appointed in 1993 by Governor James B. Hunt, Jr. as chairman of the statewide Coordinating Committee seeking passage of five State bond issues to assist higher education, water treatment, and economic development; co-chairman of the 1994 campaign of Representative Richard Burr of North Carolina; member of the finance committee, Forsyth County Republican Party; is a resident of Winston-Salem, N.C.

**BROYHILL, Joel Thomas,** a Representative from Virginia; born in Hopewell, Prince George County, Va., November 4, 1919; attended the public schools, Fork Union Military Academy, Fork Union, Va., and George Washington University, Washington, D.C., 1939-1941, engaged in the building business in the firm of M. T. Broyhill and Sons since 1945; entered the United States Army in February 1942 as an enlisted man; served in European Theater as a captain in One Hundred and Sixth Infantry Division and was taken prisoner during the Battle of the Bulge, December 1944; after six months in German prison camps escaped and rejoined advancing American forces; after four years of service was released from active duty on November 1, 1945, as a captain of Infantry; resumed real estate pursuits; president, Arlington County Chamber of Commerce; chairman, Arlington County Planning Commission; elected as a Republican to the Eighty-third and to the ten succeeding Congresses, and served from January 3, 1953 until his resignation on December 31, 1974; unsuccessful candidate for reelection in 1974 to the Ninety-fourth Congress; resumed business interests in the building and construction industries; is a resident of Arlington, Va.

**BRUCE, Blanche Kelso,** a Senator from Mississippi; born into slavery near Farmville, Prince Edward County, Va., March 1, 1841; was tutored by his master's son; worked as a field hand and printer's apprentice in Virginia, Mississippi and Missouri; escaped from slavery at the beginning of the Civil War and attempted to enlist in the Union Army, but his application was refused; attended Oberlin College, Ohio, and worked as a steamboat porter on the Mississippi River; settled in Hannibal, Mo., in 1864 and taught school; after the war became a landowner in Mississippi; served as registrar of voters in Tallahatchie County, Miss., and as tax assessor of Bolivar County, Miss.; member of the Mississippi Levee Board; sheriff and tax collector of Bolivar County 1872-1875; elected as a Republican to the United States Senate and served from March 4, 1875, to March 3, 1881; was the first black person to serve a full term in the United States Senate; declined appointment as United States Minister to Brazil; appointed Registrar of the Treasury by President James A. Garfield in 1881 and served until 1885; lecturer and author of magazine articles; superintendent of an exhibit at the World's Cotton Exposition in New Orleans 1884-1885; recorder of deeds for the District of Columbia 1889-1893; trustee of the public schools of Washington, D.C.; again Registrar of the Treasury from 1897 until his death in Washington, D.C., on March 17, 1898; interment in Woodlawn Cemetery.

**Bibliography:** *DAB*; Mann, Kenneth Eugene. "Blanche Kelso Bruce: United States Senator Without a Constituency." *Journal of Mississippi History* 38 (May 1976): 183-98; St. Clair, Sadie. "The National Career of Blanche Kelso Bruce." Ph.D. dissertation, New York University, 1948.

**BRUCE, Donald Cogley,** a Representative from Indiana; born in Troutville, Clearfield County, Pa., April 27, 1921; graduated from high school in Allentown, Pa., and attended Muskingum College in New Concord, Ohio; engaged in the radio broadcasting industry, serving as program director, business manager, and general manager, 1941-1960; elected as a Republican to the Eighty-seventh and Eighty-eighth Congresses (January 3, 1961-January 3, 1965); was not a candidate in 1964 for renomination to the Eighty-ninth Congress, but was an unsuccessful candidate for nomination for United States Senator in primary election; on leaving Congress, he helped form the American Conservative Union, a political action group; created a management and political consulting firm, Bruce Enterprises in Round Hill, Va.; died in Round Hill, Va., August 31, 1969; interment in Ebenezer Cemetery near Round Hill.

**BRUCE, Phineas,** a Representative from Massachusetts; born in Mendon, Mass., June 7, 1762; received a classical education and was graduated from Yale College in 1786; studied law; was admitted to the bar in 1790 and commenced practice in Machias, Maine (then a district of Massachusetts); member of the Massachusetts house of representatives 1791-1798 and in 1800; elected as a Federalist to the Eighth Congress commencing March 4, 1803, but was prevented by illness from qualifying; died in Uxbridge, Mass., October 4, 1809; interment in the Old Burying Ground; reinterment in Prospect Hill Cemetery.

**BRUCE, Terry L.,** a Representative from Illinois; born in Olney, Richland County, Ill., March 25, 1944; was graduated from East Richland High School, Olney, 1962; B.S., University of Illinois, Urbana, 1966; J.D., University of Illinois Law School, 1969; was admitted to the bar in 1969; Illinois State senator, District 54, 1971-1984, and assistant majority leader, 1975-1984; unsuccessful candidate for election in 1978 to the Ninety-sixth Congress; elected as a Democrat to the Ninety-ninth and to the three succeeding Congresses (January 3, 1985-January 3, 1993); unsuccessful candidate in 1992 for renomination to the One Hundred Third

Congress; senior legislative adviser, Fleishman-Hillard, Washington, D.C.; is a resident of Olney, Ill.

**BRUCE, William Cabell,** a Senator from Maryland; born in Staunton Hill, Charlotte County, Va., March 12, 1860; received an academic education at Norwood High School and College, Nelson County, Va.; attended the University of Virginia at Charlottesville; was graduated from the University of Maryland Law School at Baltimore in 1882; was admitted to the Maryland bar the same year and commenced practice in Baltimore, Md.; lawyer and writer; received the Pulitzer Prize in 1917 for his biography of Benjamin Franklin; member, State senate 1894-1896, serving as president in 1896; head of the city law department of Baltimore 1903-1908; member, Baltimore Charter Commission 1910; general counsel to the Public Service Commission of Maryland 1910-1922, when he resigned; unsuccessful candidate for the Democratic nomination for United States Senator in 1916; elected as a Democrat to the United States Senate and served from March 4, 1923, to March 3, 1929; unsuccessful candidate for reelection in 1928; resumed the practice of law in Baltimore until 1937, when he retired; died in Ruxton, Baltimore County, Md., May 9, 1946; interment in St. Thomas' Episcopal Church Cemetery, Garrison, Md.

**Bibliography:** *DAB*; Bruce, William C. *Recollections*. Baltimore: King Brothers, Inc., 1936.

**BRUCKER, Ferdinand,** a Representative from Michigan; born in Bridgeport, Saginaw County, Mich., January 8, 1858; attended the common schools; member of the State militia 1878-1881; was graduated from the law department of the University of Michigan at Ann Arbor in 1881; was admitted to the bar the same year and commenced practice in Saginaw, Mich.; alderman of East Saginaw 1882-1884; judge of the probate court of Saginaw County 1888-1896; delegate to the Democratic National Convention in 1896; elected as a Democrat to the Fifty-fifth Congress (March 4, 1897-March 3, 1899); was an unsuccessful candidate for reelection in 1898 to the Fifty-sixth Congress; resumed the practice of law; died in Saginaw, Mich., on March 3, 1904; interment in Bridgeport Cemetery, Bridgeport, Mich.

**BRUCKNER, Henry,** a Representative from New York; born in New York City, June 17, 1871; attended the common and high schools in New York; became engaged in the manufacture of mineral waters in 1892; member of the State assembly in 1901; commissioner of public works for the Borough of the Bronx, New York City, 1902-1905; elected as a Democrat to the Sixty-third, Sixty-fourth, and Sixty-fifth Congresses and served from March 4, 1913, until December 31, 1917, when he resigned; chairman, Committee on Railways and Canals (Sixty-fifth Congress); resumed his former business pursuits in New York City; also interested in banking; president of the Borough of the Bronx 1918-1933; died in New York City on April 14, 1942; interment in Woodlawn Cemetery.

**BRUMBAUGH, Clement Laird,** a Representative from Ohio; born on a farm near Pikeville, Darke County, Ohio, February 28, 1863; attended the district schools and the Greenville (Ohio) High School; taught school, worked on a farm, and tutored; was graduated from National Normal University, Lebanon, Ohio, in 1887; founded and conducted the Van Buren Academy 1887-1891; attended Ohio Wesleyan University, Delaware, Ohio, 1891-1893; was graduated from Harvard University in 1894; taught school in Washington, D.C., 1894-1896; superintendent of schools in Greenville, Ohio, 1896-1900; studied law; was admitted to the bar in 1900 and commenced practice in Columbus, Ohio; member of the State house of representatives 1900-1904, serving as minority leader; elected as a Democrat to the Sixty-third and to the three succeeding Congresses (March 4, 1913-March 3, 1921); chairman, Committee on Railways and Canals (Sixty-fifth Congress); was not a candidate for renomination in 1920; lived in retirement in Columbus, Ohio, until his death there on September 28, 1921; interment in Greenville Cemetery, Greenville, Ohio.

**BRUMBAUGH, David Emmert,** a Representative from Pennsylvania; born in Martinsburg, Blair County, Pa., October 8, 1894; attended the public schools of North Woodbury Township, Pa., and the summer normal school at Martinsburg, Pa.; student of the International Correspondence School of Scranton, Pa.; in 1914 became interested in banking at Claysburg, Pa.; during the First World War was a private in the Thirty-third Division, Fifty-eighth Brigade Headquarters, serving overseas in 1918 and 1919; in 1921 became interested in the lumber business and later established an insurance agency; trustee of the Pennsylvania Industrial School, Huntingdon, Pa., 1939-1943; elected as a Republican to the Seventy-eighth Congress to fill the vacancy caused by the resignation of James E. Van Zandt; reelected to the Seventy-ninth Congress and served from November 2, 1943, to January 3, 1947; was not a candidate for renomination in 1946 to the Eightieth Congress; secretary of banking of the Commonwealth of Pennsylvania, Harrisburg, Pa., 1947-1951; resumed banking interests as president of the First National Bank of Claysburg; served in Pennsylvania senate 1963-1967; resided in Claysburg, Pa., where he died April 22, 1977; interment in Fairview Cemetery, Martinsburg, Pa.

**BRUMM, Charles Napoleon** (father of George Franklin Brumm), a Representative from Pennsylvania; born in Pottsville, Schuylkill County, Pa., June 9, 1838; attended the common schools and Pennsylvania College, Gettysburg, Pa.; studied law for two years; under the first call of President Lincoln for three-months' men enlisted as a private and was elected first lieutenant of Company I, Fifth Regiment, Pennsylvania Volunteer Infantry; reenlisted September 15, 1861, for three years and was elected first lieutenant of Company K, Seventy-sixth Regiment, Pennsylvania Volunteer Infantry, November 18, 1861; detailed on the staff of General William B. Barton as assistant quartermaster and aide-de-camp, which position he held under General Barton and General Galusha Pennypacker until the expiration of his term of service in 1871; resumed the study of law; was admitted to the bar in 1871 and commenced practice in Pottsville; unsuccessful candidate for election in 1878 to the Forty-sixth Congress; elected as a Greenbacker to the Forty-seventh and Forty-eighth Congresses and as a Republican to the Forty-ninth and Fiftieth Congresses (March 4, 1881-March 3, 1889); unsuccessful candidate for reelection in 1888 to the Fifty-first Congress; delegate to the Republican National Convention of 1884; elected as a Republican to the Fifty-fourth and Fifty-fifth Congresses (March 4, 1895-March 3, 1899); chairman, Committee on Claims (Fifty-fourth and Fifty-fifth Congresses); unsuccessful candidate for renomination in 1898 to the Fifty-sixth Congress; elected to the Fifty-ninth Congress to fill the vacancy caused by the death of George R. Patterson; reelected to the Sixtieth Congress and served from November 6, 1906, to January 4, 1909, when he resigned, having been elected judge of the court of common pleas of Schuylkill County, in which capacity he served until his death at Minersville, Pa., January 11, 1917; chairman, Committee on Mileage (Sixtieth Congress); interment in Charles Baber Cemetery, Pottsville, Pa.

**BRUMM, George Franklin** (son of Charles Napoleon Brumm), a Representative from Pennsylvania; born in Minersville, Schuylkill County, Pa., January 24, 1880; attended the common schools of Minersville, Washington, and Pottsville; was graduated from the University of Pennsylvania at Philadelphia in 1901 and from its law school in 1907; was admitted to the bar of Pennsylvania in 1908 and commenced practice in Pottsville, Pa.; served in 1916 as a private and corporal in Company C, Pennsylvania Engineers, on the Mexican border; appointed by Governor Martin G. Brumbaugh in 1918 as election commissioner for Texas to take the vote of servicemen at cantonments; during the First World War was attorney for the conscription board; unsuccessful candidate in 1918 for nomination to the Sixty-sixth Congress, and in 1920 for nomination to the Sixty-seventh Congress; elected as a Republican to the Sixty-eighth and Sixty-ninth Congresses (March 4, 1923-March 3, 1927); chairman, Committtee on Expenditures in the Department of the Navy (Sixty-ninth Congress); unsuccessful candidate for renomination in 1926 to the Seventieth Congress; resumed the practice of law in Minersville, Pa.; elected to the Seventy-first, Seventy-second, and Seventy-third Congresses and served from March 4, 1929, until his death in the Methodist Hospital, Philadelphia, Pa., May 29, 1934; interment in Charles Baber Cemetery, Pottsville, Pa.

**BRUNDIDGE, Stephen, Jr.,** a Representative from Arkansas; born in Searcy, White County, Ark., January 1, 1857; educated by private tutors and in the public schools in his native city; studied law; was admitted to the bar in 1879 and commenced practice in Newport, Ark.; returned to Searcy, Ark., in 1880 and continued the practice of law; elected prosecuting attorney of the first judicial district of Arkansas in 1886; reelected in 1888 and served until 1890; resumed the practice of law; member of the Democratic State central committee 1890-1892; elected as a Democrat to the Fifty-fifth and to the five succeeding Congresses (March 4, 1897-March 3, 1909); was not a candidate for renomination in 1908, but was an unsuccessful candidate for Governor that year; resumed the practice of law in Searcy, Ark.; unsuccessful candidate for election to the United States Senate in 1918; died in Searcy, Ark., January 14, 1938; interment in Oak Grove Cemetery.

**BRUNNER, David B.,** a Representative from Pennsylvania; born in Amity, Berks (now Washington) County, Pa., March 7, 1835; attended the common schools; learned the carpenter's trade; taught school from 1853 to 1856, during which time he studied the classics; was graduated from Dickinson College, Carlisle, Pa., in 1860; principal of the Reading (Pa.) Classical Academy, 1860-1869; established the Reading Business College in 1880; elected as a Democrat to the Fifty-first and Fifty-second Congresses (March 4, 1889-March 3, 1893); was not a candidate for renomination in 1892 to the Fifty-third Congress; taught at the Reading Business College; died in Reading, Pa., on November 29, 1903; interment in Amityville Cemetery, Berks County, Pa.

**BRUNNER, William Frank,** a Representative from New York; born in Woodhaven, Queens County, N.Y., September 15, 1887; attended the public schools, the high school at Far Rockaway, N.Y., and Packard Commercial School at New York City; moved to Rockaway Park, Queens County, N.Y., in 1901; engaged in the trucking, general insurance, and real-estate businesses; professional basketball player with the New York Nationals; served in the United States Navy as a yeoman first class, 1917-1919; member of the New York State assembly, 1922-1928; elected as a Democrat to the Seventy-first and to the three succeeding Congresses, and served from March 4, 1929 until his resignation on September 27, 1935, having been elected sheriff of Queens County, N.Y.; served as sheriff from 1935 until his resignation in 1936; president of the board of aldermen of New York City, 1936-1938; resumed the insurance and real-estate business; commissioner of borough works, Queens County, N.Y., from July 1 to December 31, 1941; unsuccessful candidate for the Democratic nomination in 1942 and for election on the American Labor ticket to the Seventy-eighth Congress; president of Rockaway Beach Hospital (later named Peninsula General Hospital) from 1946 until his retirement on April 12, 1965; died in Edgemere, Queens, N.Y., April 23, 1965; interment in St. John's Cemetery, Middle Village, N.Y.

**BRUNSDALE, Clarence Norman,** a Senator from North Dakota; born in Sherbrooke, Steele County, N.Dak., July 9, 1891; resided on a farm near Hatton, N.Dak., until 1899, when his family moved to Portland, N.Dak.; attended private and public schools; graduated from Luther College, Decorah, Iowa, in 1913; taught business at Portland, N.Dak., 1913-1914; also a farmer and businessman; member, North Dakota State senate, 1927-1935, 1940-1951, serving as president pro tempore in 1943 and majority floor leader in 1945, 1947, and 1949; elected Governor of North Dakota in 1950, reelected in 1952 and 1954, and served from January 3, 1951 to January 9, 1957; appointed as a Republican to the United States Senate, November 19, 1959, to fill the vacancy caused by the death of William Langer and served from November 19, 1959, to August 7, 1960; was not a candidate for election to the vacancy; resumed agricultural pursuits until retirement in 1968; resided in Mayville, N.Dak., where he died on January 27, 1978; interment in Mayville Cemetery.

**BRUSH, Henry,** a Representative from Ohio; born in Dutchess County, N.Y., in June 1778; completed preparatory studies; studied law; was admitted to the bar in 1803 and commenced practice in Chillicothe, Ohio; member of the State house of representatives in 1810; served in the State senate in 1814; moved to London, Ohio; elected to the Sixteenth Congress (March 4, 1819-March 3, 1821); chairman, Committee on Expenditures in the Department of War (Sixteenth Congress); unsuccessful candidate for reelection in 1820 to the Seventeenth Congress; judge of the supreme court of Ohio in 1828; retired to his farm near London, Madison County, Ohio, where he died January 19, 1855; interment in Oak Hill Cemetery.

**BRUYN, Andrew DeWitt,** a Representative from New York; born in Warwarsing, Ulster County, N.Y., November 18, 1790; attended Kingston Academy, Kingston, N.Y., and was graduated from Princeton College in 1810; studied law; was admitted to the bar in 1814 and commenced practice in Ithaca, Tompkins County, N.Y.; justice of the peace in 1817; first surrogate of Tompkins County 1817-1821; member of the State assembly in 1818; appointed trustee of Ithaca in 1821; president of the village in 1822; unsuccessful candidate for election to the State senate in 1825; county supervisor in 1825; treasurer of the village 1826-1828; judge of the court of common pleas 1826-1836; served as a director of the Ithaca & Owego Railroad in 1828; also interested in banking; elected as a Democrat to the Twenty-fifth Congress and served from March 4, 1837, until his death in Ithaca, Tompkins County, N.Y., on July 27, 1838; interment in Ithaca City Cemetery.

**BRYAN, Guy Morrison,** a Representative from Texas; born in Herculaneum, Jefferson County, Mo., January 12, 1821; moved to the Mexican State of Texas in 1831 with his parents, who settled near San Felipe; attended private schools; joined the Texas Army at San Jacinto in 1836; was graduated from Kenyon College, Gambier, Ohio, in 1842; studied law, but never practiced; engaged in planting; served as a private in the Brazoria company, under the command of Captain Ballowe, during the Mexican War with the Texas Volunteers on the eastern bank of the Rio Grande; member of the Texas State house of representatives, 1847-1853; served in the Texas State senate, 1853-1857; delegate to the Democratic National Convention of 1856; chairman of the Texas delegation in the Democratic National Convention at Baltimore in 1860; elected as a Democrat to the Thirty-fifth Congress (March 4, 1857-March 3, 1859); was not a candidate for renomination in 1858 to the Thirty-sixth Congress; during the Civil War served as volunteer aide-de-camp on the staff of General Herbert and afterwards as assistant adjutant general, with the rank of major, of the trans-Mississippi Department; established a cotton bureau in Houston, Tex., in order to escape the blockade along the Gulf; moved to Galveston, Tex., in 1872; again a member of the State house of representatives in 1873, 1879, and 1887-1891, and served as speaker in 1873; moved to Quintana, Tex., in 1890 and to Austin, Travis County, Tex., in 1898; elected president of the Texas Veterans

Association in 1892 and served until his death in Austin, Tex., June 4, 1901; interment in the State Cemetery.

**BRYAN, Henry Hunter,** (brother of Joseph Hunter Bryan) a Representative from Tennessee; born in Martin County, N.C., February 23, 1786; attended grammar and high schools; moved to Tennessee and held several local offices; elected to the Sixteenth Congress (March 4, 1819-March 3, 1821); had been reelected to the Seventeenth Congress, but did not qualify; died in Montgomery County, Tenn., May 7, 1835.

**BRYAN, James Wesley,** a Representative from Washington; born in Lake Charles, Calcasieu Parish, La., March 11, 1874; attended the public schools and Lake Charles College at Lake Charles, La.; was graduated from Baylor University, Waco, Tex., in 1895 and from Yale University in 1897; studied law; was admitted to the bar in 1898 and commenced practice at Lake Charles, La.; moved to Bremerton, Wash., in 1905 and continued the practice of law; city attorney in 1907, 1908, and again in 1911; member of the State senate 1908-1912; elected as a Progressive to the Sixty-third Congress (March 4, 1913-March 3, 1915); was an unsuccessful candidate for renomination in 1914 to the Sixty-fourth Congress; owned and published the Navy Yard American from 1915 to 1917; resumed the practice of law; prosecuting attorney of Kitsap County 1926-1930; president of the Bremerton Port Commission 1933-1936; practiced law in Bremerton, Wash., until his death there on August 26, 1956; interment in Forest Lawn Cemetery.

**BRYAN, John Heritage,** a Representative from North Carolina; born in New Bern, N.C., November 4, 1798; studied under private teachers and attended New Bern Academy; was graduated from the University of North Carolina in 1815; studied law; was admitted to the bar in 1819 and commenced practice in New Bern, N.C.; member of the State senate in 1823 and 1824; trustee of the University of North Carolina at Chapel Hill 1823-1868; elected to the Nineteenth and Twentieth Congresses (March 4, 1825-March 3, 1829); was not a candidate for renomination in 1828; resumed the practice of law in New Bern; moved to Raleigh in 1839 and continued the practice of law; died in Raleigh, N.C., May 19, 1870; interment in Oakwood Cemetery.

**BRYAN, Joseph,** a Representative from Georgia; born in Savannah, Ga., August 18, 1773; was educated by private tutors and attended Oxford University in England; traveled in France during the Revolutionary War; engaged in agricultural pursuits on Wilmington Island, Ga.; elected as a Republican to the Eighth and Ninth Congresses and served from March 4, 1803, until his resignation in 1806; engaged in planting; died on his estate, "Nonchalance," Wilmington Island, near Savannah, Ga., on September 12, 1812; interment in the family burial ground on his estate.

**BRYAN, Joseph Hunter,** (brother of Henry Hunter Bryan) a Representative from North Carolina; born in Martin County, N.C., April 9, 1782; member of the State house of commons 1804, 1805, and 1807-1809; trustee of the University of North Carolina at Chapel Hill, 1809-1817, and was sent to Tennessee on behalf of the university to secure from the general assembly of Tennessee its claims to escheated lands; elected as a Republican to the Fourteenth and Fifteenth Congresses (March 4, 1815-March 3, 1819); died at La Grange, Fayette County, Tenn., December 28, 1839; interment in Elmwood Cemetery, Memphis, Tenn.

**BRYAN, Nathan,** a Representative from North Carolina; born in Craven (now Jones) County, N.C., in 1748; member of the house of commons of North Carolina in 1787 and 1791-1794; elected as a Republican to the Fourth and Fifth Congresses and served from March 4, 1795, until his death in Philadelphia, Pa., June 4, 1798; interment in the Baptist burial ground on Second Street; reinterred at an unknown location when the burial ground was used as a building site.

**BRYAN, Nathan Philemon** (brother of William James Bryan), a Senator from Florida; born near Fort Mason, Orange (now Lake) County, Fla., April 23, 1872; attended the common schools; was graduated from Emory College, Oxford, Ga. (now Emory University, Atlanta, Ga.), in 1893 and from the law department of Washington and Lee University, Lexington, Va., in 1895; was admitted to the bar in 1895 and commenced practice in Jacksonville, Fla.; chairman of the board of control of the Florida State institutions of higher education 1905-1909; appointed on February 22, 1911, the legislature having failed to elect, and subsequently elected as a Democrat to the United States Senate and served from March 4, 1911, to March 3, 1917; unsuccessful candidate for renomination in 1916; chairman, Committee on Claims (Sixty-third and Sixty-fourth Congresses); resumed the practice of law; declined the appointment as Governor General of the Philippine Islands by President Woodrow Wilson in 1917; trustee of Emory University; judge of the United States Circuit Court of Appeals of the Fifth Judicial Circuit from April 1920 until his death in Jacksonville, Fla., on August 8, 1935; interment in Evergreen Cemetery.

**BRYAN, Richard Hudson,** a Senator from Nevada; born in Washington, D.C., July 16, 1937; attended Las Vegas (Nev.) High School, 1951-1955; A.B., University of Nevada, 1959; LL.B., University of California, Hastings College of Law, 1963; entered active duty, United States Army in 1959, released in 1960; United States Army reserve service; attorney; deputy district attorney, Clark County, Nev., 1964-1966; public defender, 1966-1968; counsel to juvenile court, 1968-1969; member, Nevada State assembly, 1969-1973; member, Nevada State senate, 1973-1979; Nevada attorney general, 1979-1983; elected Governor of Nevada in 1982, reelected in 1986, and served from January 3, 1983 until his resignation January 3, 1989, having been elected Senator; elected as a Democrat to the United States Senate in 1988 for the term commencing January 3, 1989; reelected in 1994 for the term ending January 3, 2001; chairman, Select Committee on Ethics (One Hundred Third Congress); is a resident of Las Vegas, Nev.

**BRYAN, William James** (brother of Nathan Philemon Bryan), a Senator from Florida; born near Fort Mason, Orange (now Lake) County, Fla., October 10, 1876; attended the public schools; was graduated from Emory College, Oxford, Ga., (now Emory University, Atlanta, Ga.) in 1896 and from the law department of Washington and Lee University, Lexington, Va., in 1899; was admitted to the bar in 1899 and commenced practice in Jacksonville, Fla.; solicitor of the Duval County Criminal Court of Record, 1902-1907; appointed as a Democrat to the United States Senate to fill the vacancy caused by the death of Stephen R. Mallory, and served from December 26, 1907 until his death in Washington, D.C., March 22, 1908; interment in Evergreen Cemetery, Jacksonville, Fla.

**BRYAN, William Jennings** (father of Ruth Bryan Owen), a Representative from Nebraska; born in Salem, Marion County, Ill., March 19, 1860; attended the public schools and Whipple Academy, Jacksonville, Ill.; was graduated from Illinois College, Jacksonville, Ill., in 1881; studied law at Union College in Chicago; was graduated in 1883 and commenced practice at Jacksonville, Ill., in 1883; moved to Lincoln, Nebr., in 1887 and continued the practice of law; elected as a Democrat to the Fifty-second and Fifty-third Congresses (March 4, 1891-March 3, 1895); declined to be a candidate for reelection in 1894 to the House of Representatives, but was an unsuccessful candidate for election to the United States Senate; delegate to the Democratic National Conventions of 1896, 1904, 1912, 1920, and 1924; nominated by the Democratic Party for President of the United States in 1896, 1900, and 1908, but was unsuccessful for election; was endorsed by the Populist and Silver Republican Parties in the first and second campaigns; during the Spanish-American War raised the Third Regiment, Nebraska Volunteer Infantry, in May 1898 and was commissioned colonel; established a newspaper, The Commoner, at Lincoln, Nebr., in 1901; engaged in editorial writing and delivering Chautauqua lectures; Secretary of State in the Cabinet of President Woodrow Wilson from March 4, 1913 until June 9, 1915, when he resigned; resumed his former pursuits of lecturing and writing; established his home in Miami, Fla., in 1921; died while attending court in Dayton, Tenn., July 26, 1925; interment in Arlington National Cemetery, Va.

**Bibliography:** *DAB*; Bryan, William Jennings, and Mary Baird Bryan. *Memoirs of William Jennings Bryan, by Himself and his Wife.* 2 vols. 1925. Reprint. Port Washington, N.Y.: Kennikat, 1971; Coletta, Paolo E. *William Jennings Bryan.* 3 vols. Lincoln: University of Nebraska Press, 1964-1969.

**BRYANT, Edward,** a Representative from Tennessee; born in Jackson, Madison County, Tenn., September 7, 1948; graduated, Jackson High School; B.A., University of Mississippi, 1970, and J.D., 1972; entered active duty, United States Army in 1970; released as captain in 1978 after service in Judge Advocate General's Corps; instructor, United States Military Academy, West Point, N.Y.; United States Attorney for the Western District of Tennessee, 1991-1993; practicing attorney, Jackson, Tenn.; elected as a Republican to the One Hundred Fourth Congress (January 3, 1995-January 3, 1997); is a resident of Henderson, Tenn.

**BRYANT, John Wiley,** a Representative from Texas; born in Lake Jackson, Brazoria County, Tex., February 22, 1947; attended Lake Jackson Elementary School; graduated, Brazosport High School, Freeport, Tex., 1965; B.A., Southern Methodist University, Dallas, Tex., 1969; J.D., Southern Methodist University School of Law, 1972; admitted to the Texas bar in 1972 and commenced practice in Dallas; served as counsel to the Subcommittee on Consumer Affairs, Texas State senate, 1972-1973; member, Texas State house of representatives, 1974-1982; delegate to the Democratic National Conventions of 1976, 1984, 1988 and 1992; elected as a Democrat to the Ninety-eighth and to the six succeeding Congresses (January 3, 1983-January 3, 1997); was not a candidate in 1996 for reelection to the House of Representatives, but was an unsuccessful candidate for nomination to the United States Senate; is a resident of Dallas, Tex.

**BRYCE, Lloyd Stephens,** a Representative from New York; born in Flushing, Queens County, N.Y., September 4, 1851; attended the public schools and Georgetown University, Washington, D.C.; was graduated from Oxford University, England, in 1869; studied law at Columbia Law School, New York City; paymaster general for the State of New York in 1886 and 1887; elected as a Democrat to the Fiftieth Congress (March 4, 1887-March 3, 1889); unsuccessful candidate for reelection in 1888 to the Fifty-first Congress; editor of the North American Review 1889-1896; appointed Envoy Extraordinary and Minister Plenipotentiary to the Netherlands on August 12, 1911 and served until September 10, 1913; died in Flushing, N.Y., April 2, 1917; interment in Greenwood Cemetery, Brooklyn, N.Y.

**Bibliography:** *DAB*.

**BRYSON, Joseph Raleigh,** a Representative from South Carolina; born in Brevard, Transylvania County, N.C., January 18, 1893; moved, with his parents, to Greenville, Greenville County, S.C., in 1900; attended the public schools; was graduated from Furman University, Greenville, S.C., in 1917 and from the law department of the University of South Carolina at Columbia in 1920; enlisted on September 28, 1915, as a private in Company A, First Infantry, South Carolina National Guard, and served until discharged on August 9, 1916; reenlisted on August 3, 1917, in the Medical Reserve Corps, being discharged as a second lieutenant of Infantry on December 12, 1918; was admitted to the bar in 1920 and commenced practice in Greenville, S.C.; member of the State house of representatives 1921-1924; served in the State senate 1929-1932; elected as a Democrat to the Seventy-sixth and to the seven succeeding Congresses, and served from January 3, 1939, until his death in the naval hospital at Bethesda, Md., March 10, 1953; interment in Woodlawn Memorial Park, Greenville, S.C.

**BUCHANAN, Andrew,** a Representative from Pennsylvania; born in Chester County, Pa., April 8, 1780; was graduated from Dickinson College, Carlisle, Pa.; studied law; was admitted to the bar in 1798 and commenced practice in York, Pa.; located in Waynesburg, Greene County, Pa., in 1803; member of the Pennsylvania house of representatives; served in the Pennsylvania senate; elected as a Jacksonian to the Twenty-fourth Congress, and as a Democrat to the Twenty-fifth Congress (March 4, 1835-March 3, 1839); chairman, Committee on Elections (Twenty-fifth Congress); resumed the practice of his profession until his death in Waynesburg, Pa., on December 2, 1848; interment in Greene Mount Cemetery.

**BUCHANAN, Frank,** a Representative from Illinois; born on a farm near Madison, Jefferson County, Ind., June 14, 1862; attended the rural schools of the county; engaged in agricultural pursuits at home and subsequently became a bridge builder and structural iron worker in Chicago; served as business agent for the Bridge and Structural Iron Worker's Union and was elected president of the International Structural Iron Worker's Union in 1901; unsuccessful candidate for election in 1906 to the Sixtieth Congress and again in 1908 to the Sixty-first Congress; elected as a Democrat to the Sixty-second, Sixty-third, and Sixty-fourth Congresses (March 4, 1911-March 3, 1917); unsuccessful candidate for reelection in 1916 to the Sixty-fifth Congress; resumed his former business pursuits as a structural iron worker; died in Chicago, Ill., April 18, 1930; interment in Irving Park Boulevard Cemetery.

**BUCHANAN, Frank** (husband of Vera Daerr Buchanan), a Representative from Pennsylvania; born in McKeesport, Allegheny County, Pa., December 1, 1902; attended the public schools and was graduated from the University of Pittsburgh in 1925; teacher in high schools of Homestead and McKeesport, Pa., 1924-1928 and 1931-1942; automobile dealer 1928-1931; economic consultant 1928-1946; served as mayor of McKeesport, Pa., 1942-1946; elected as a Democrat to the Seventy-ninth Congress to fill the vacancy caused by the resignation of Samuel A. Weiss; reelected to the Eightieth, Eighty-first and Eighty-second Congresses and served from May 21, 1946, until his death in Bethesda, Md., April 27, 1951; chairman, Select Committee on Lobbying Activities (Eighty-first Congress); interment in Mount Vernon Cemetery, Elizabeth Township (near McKeesport), Pa.

**BUCHANAN, Hugh,** a Representative from Georgia; born in Argyleshire, Scotland, September 15, 1823; immigrated to the United States and settled in Vermont; attended the public schools of that State; studied law; was admitted to the bar in 1845 and commenced practice in Newnan, Coweta County, Ga., in 1846; member of the State senate in 1855 and 1857; delegate to the Democratic National Conventions in 1856 and 1868; presidential elector on the Democratic ticket of Breckinridge and Lane in 1860; during the Civil War enlisted in the Confederate Army in June 1861 and served until 1865; elected to the Thirty-ninth Congress, but his credentials were not presented to the House as the State had not been readmitted to representation; appointed judge of the superior court of the Coweta circuit in August 1872 and served until September 1880; delegate to the State constitutional convention of 1877; elected as a Democrat to the Forty-seventh and Forty-eighth Congresses (March 4, 1881-March 3, 1885); was not a candidate for renomination in 1884; died in Newnan, Ga., June 11, 1890; interment in Oak Hill Cemetery.

**BUCHANAN, James,** a Representative from New Jersey; born in Ringoes, Hunterdon County, N.J., June 17, 1839; attended the public schools and Clinton Academy; studied law at Albany University; was admitted to the bar in 1864 and commenced practice in Trenton, N.J.; reading clerk of the New Jersey House of Assembly in 1866; member of the Trenton Board of Education in 1868 and 1869; presiding judge of Mercer County 1872-1877; delegate to the Republican National Convention in 1872; appointed a member of the board of trustees of Peddie Institute, Hightstown, N.J., in 1875; member of the Common Council of Trenton 1883-1885; elected as a Republican to the Forty-ninth and to the three succeeding Congresses (March 4, 1885-March 3, 1893); chairman, Committee on Manufactures (Fifty-first Congress); declined to be a candidate for renomination in 1892; resumed the practice of law in Trenton; elected city solicitor of Trenton May 7, 1900, and served until his death; trustee of Bucknell College, Lewisburg, Pa.; died in Trenton, N.J., on October 30, 1900; interment in Mountain View Cemetery, Cherryville, Hunterdon County, N.J.

**BUCHANAN, James,** a Representative and a Senator from Pennsylvania and 15th President of the United States; born at Cove Gap, near Mercersburg, Franklin County, Pa., April 23, 1791; moved to Mercersburg, Pa., with his parents in 1799; was privately tutored and then attended the village academy; was graduated from Dickinson College, Carlisle, Pa., in 1809; moved to Lancaster, Pa., the same year; studied law; was admitted to the bar in 1812 and practiced in Lancaster; was one of the first volunteers in the War of 1812 and served in the defense of Baltimore; member, Pennsylvania house of representatives, 1814-1815; elected to the Seventeenth and to the four succeeding Congresses (March 4, 1821-March 3, 1831); chairman, Committee on the Judiciary (Twenty-first Congress); was not a candidate for renomination in 1830 to the Twenty-second Congress; one of the managers appointed by the House of Representatives in 1830 to conduct the impeachment proceedings against James H. Peck, judge of the United States District Court for the District of Missouri; appointed Minister to Russia by President Andrew Jackson on January 4, 1832 and served until August 5, 1833; elected as a Democrat to the United States Senate to fill the vacancy caused by the resignation of William Wilkins; reelected in 1837 and 1843 and served from December 6, 1834, until he resigned on March 5, 1845, to accept a Cabinet portfolio; chairman, Committee on Foreign Relations (Twenty-fourth through Twenty-sixth Congresses); Secretary of State in the Cabinet of President James K. Polk from March 6, 1845 to March 7, 1849; appointed Minister to Great Britain by President Franklin Pierce on April 11, 1853 and served until March 15, 1856; elected as a President of the United States on the Democratic ticket in 1856 and served from March 4, 1857, to March 4, 1861; retired to his home, "Wheatland," near Lancaster, Pa., where he died on June 1, 1868; interment in Woodward Hill Cemetery, Lancaster, Pa.

**Bibliography:** *DAB*; Buchanan, James. *The Works of James Buchanan.* Edited by John B. Moore. 12 vols. Philadelphia: Lippincott Company, 1908-1911; Klein, Philip. *President James Buchanan: A Biography.* University Park: Pennsylvania State University Press, 1962.

**BUCHANAN, James Paul** (cousin of Edward William Pou), a Representative from Texas; born in Midway, Orangeburg County, S.C., April 30, 1867; moved to Texas in 1867 with his parents, who settled near Chapel Hill, Washington County; attended the district school; was graduated from the law department of the University of Texas at Austin in 1889; was admitted to the bar and commenced practice in Brenham, Washington County, Tex.; justice of the peace of Washington County 1889-1892; prosecuting attorney 1892-1899; district attorney for the twenty-first judicial district of Texas 1899-1906; served as a member of the State house of representatives 1906-1913; elected as a Democrat to the Sixty-third Congress to fill the vacancy caused by the resignation of Albert Sidney Burleson;

reelected to the Sixty-fourth and to the eleven succeeding Congresses and served from April 5, 1913, until his death in Washington, D.C., February 22, 1937; chairman, Committee on Appropriations (Seventy-third through Seventy-fifth Congresses); interment in Prairie Lea Cemetery, Brenham, Tex.

**BUCHANAN, John Alexander,** a Representative from Virginia; born near Groseclose, Smyth County, Va., October 7, 1843; attended the "old field" school and the local academies at Chatham Hill and Marion, Va.; during the Civil War served as a private in Company D, Virginia Infantry, Stonewall Brigade, of the Confederate Army; was captured at the Battle of Gettysburg on July 3, 1863, and remained a prisoner until February 1865; attended Emory and Henry College, Emory, Va., from 1865 until 1870, and was graduated in June 1870; studied law at the University of Virginia at Charlottesville in 1870 and 1871; was admitted to the bar in 1872 and commenced practice in Abingdon, Va.; member of the Virginia house of delegates, 1885-1887; elected as a Democrat to the Fifty-first and Fifty-second Congresses (March 4, 1889-March 3, 1893); declined to be a candidate for renomination in 1892 to the Fifty-third Congress; returned to the practice of law; elected associate judge of the court of appeals of Virginia on January 1, 1895, and served until January 1915; retired from political activities and engaged in agricultural pursuits; died near Emory, Washington County, Va., on September 2, 1921; interment in the Old Glade Spring Presbyterian Cemetery, Glade Spring, Va.

**BUCHANAN, John Hall, Jr.,** a Representative from Alabama; born in Paris, Henry County, Tenn., March 19, 1928; served in the United States Navy, 1945-1946; A.B., Samford University, Birmingham, Ala., 1949; engaged in graduate work in economics at the University of Virginia, 1950-1951; Th.B., Southern Theological Seminary, Louisville, Ky., 1957; served as pastor of churches in Tennessee, Virginia, and Alabama from 1952 until 1962; unsuccessful candidate for election in 1962 to the Eighty-eighth Congress; served as a supply pastor in the Birmingham, Ala., area and as director of finance for the Alabama Republican Party, 1962-1964; elected as a Republican to the Eighty-ninth and to the seven succeeding Congresses (January 3, 1965-January 3, 1981); unsuccessful candidate for renomination in 1980 to the Ninety-seventh Congress; member, United States delegation to the United Nations, 1973 and 1984; member, United States delegation, United Nations Human Rights Committee, 1978-1980; chairman, Fund for the Improvement of Post-Secondary Education in the Department of Education, 1981-1983; chairman, People for the American Way, 1982 to present; is a resident of Bethesda, Md.

**BUCHANAN, Vera Daerr** (wife of Frank Buchanan), a Representative from Pennsylvania; born in Wilson (later a part of Clairton), Allegheny County, Pa., July 20, 1902; moved to Duquesne, Pa., and attended the public and parochial schools; elected as a Democrat to the Eighty-second Congress to fill the vacancy caused by the death of her husband, Frank Buchanan; reelected to the Eighty-third and Eighty-fourth Congresses, and served from July 24, 1951 until her death in McKeesport, Pa., November 26, 1955; interment in Mount Vernon Cemetery, in Elizabeth Township (near McKeesport), Pa.

**BUCHER, John Conrad,** a Representative from Pennsylvania; born in Harrisburg, Pa., December 28, 1792; attended the public schools; studied law; was admitted to the bar and commenced practice in Harrisburg; clerk of the land department of Pennsylvania in 1813; member of the borough council of Harrisburg; member of the board of school directors; elected as a Jacksonian to the Twenty-second Congress (March 4, 1831-March 3, 1833); trustee of Harrisburg Academy, Franklin College, Lancaster, Pa., and Marshall College, Mercersburg, Pa.; by appointment of Governor Porter was an associate judge of Dauphin County from 1839 until his death

in Harrisburg, Pa., October 15, 1851; interment in the City Cemetery.

**BUCK, Alfred Eliab,** a Representative from Alabama; born in Foxcroft, Piscataquis County, Maine, February 7, 1832; was graduated from Waterville (Maine) College (now Colby College) in 1859; during the Civil War entered the Union Army as captain of Company C, Thirteenth Regiment, Maine Volunteer Infantry; appointed lieutenant colonel of the Ninety-first United States Colored Troops in August 1863; transferred to the Fifty-first United States Colored Troops in October 1864; brevetted colonel of Volunteers for gallant conduct; mustered out of the service at Baton Rouge, La., in June 1866; delegate to the constitutional convention of Alabama in 1867; clerk of the circuit court of Mobile County, 1867-1868; elected as a Republican to the Forty-first Congress (March 4, 1869-March 3, 1871); appointed president of the city council of Mobile in 1873; served as clerk of the United States circuit and district courts in Atlanta, Ga., 1874-1889; United States marshal for the northern district of Georgia, 1889-1893; appointed Minister to Japan by President William McKinley on April 13, 1897, and served until his death in Tokyo, Japan, on December 4, 1902; interment in Arlington National Cemetery, Va.

Bibliography: Bhurtel, Shyam Krishna. "Alfred Eliab Buck: Carpetbagger in Alabama and Georgia." Ph.D. dissertation, Auburn University, 1981.

**BUCK, Charles Francis,** a Representative from Louisiana; born in Durrheim, Grand Duchy of Baden, Germany, November 5, 1841; immigrated to the United States in 1852 with his parents, who settled in New Orleans, La.; was graduated from the high school of New Orleans in 1861; attended Louisiana State Seminary and Military Academy at Alexandria; studied law; was admitted to the bar in 1867 and commenced practice in New Orleans, La.; member of the school board of New Orleans for many years; city attorney of New Orleans 1880-1884; elected as a Democrat to the Fifty-fourth Congress (March 4, 1895-March 3, 1897); declined to be a candidate for reelection in 1896; resumed the practice of law; unsuccessful candidate for mayor of New Orleans in 1896 and again 1904; member of the supreme court board of examiners for admission to the bar 1898-1900; died in New Orleans, La., January 19, 1918; interment in the Metairie Cemetery.

**BUCK, Clayton Douglass** (great-grandnephew of John M. Clayton), a Senator from Delaware; born at "Buena Vista," the family estate, in New Castle County, Del., March 21, 1890; was graduated from Friends School, Wilmington, Del., and for two years attended the University of Pennsylvania Engineering School at Philadelphia; engaged in road building and engineering work in Delaware; chief engineer of the Delaware State Highway Department from 1922 until 1929; elected Governor of Delaware in 1928, reelected in 1932, and served from January 15, 1929 to January 19, 1937; engaged in the banking business; member of the Republican National Committee, 1930-1937; elected as a Republican to the United States Senate in 1942 and served from January 3, 1943, to January 3, 1949; unsuccessful candidate for reelection in 1948; chairman, Committee on the District of Columbia (Eightieth Congress); resumed the banking business; tax commissioner of Delaware, 1953-1957; was a resident of "Buena Vista," New Castle County, Del., until his death on January 27, 1965; interment in family plot in Immanuel Episcopal Church Grounds, New Castle, Del.

**BUCK, Daniel** (father of Daniel Azro Ashley Buck), a Representative from Vermont; born in Hebron, Conn., November 9, 1753; studied law; was admitted to the bar in 1783 and practiced in Thetford, Vt.; prosecuting attorney of Orange County 1783-1785; clerk of the court in 1783 and 1784; moved to Norwich, Vt., in 1785; delegate to the State constitutional convention in 1791; member of the State house of representatives in 1793 and 1794 and served as speaker; elected as a Federalist to the Fourth Congress (March 4, 1795-March 3, 1797); unsuccessful candidate for renomination in 1796; attorney general of Vermont in 1802 and 1803; moved to Chelsea, Vt., about 1805; again a member of the State house of representatives in 1806 and 1807; resumed the practice of law in Chelsea, Vt., where he died August 16, 1816; interment in the Old Cemetery.

**Bibliography:** *DAB.*

**BUCK, Daniel Azro Ashley** (son of Daniel Buck), a Representative from Vermont; born in Norwich, Vt., April 19, 1789; moved with his parents to Chelsea; was graduated from Middlebury College in 1807 and from the United States Military Academy at West Point in 1808; commissioned a lieutenant in the Engineer Corps of the United States Army in the latter year; resigned in 1811 and studied law; appointed a second lieutenant in the Third Artillery in 1811; raised a volunteer company of rangers in 1813 and served until 1815; appointed a captain of the Thirty-first Infantry in 1813; was honorably discharged June 15, 1815; was admitted to the bar in 1814 and commenced the practice of law in Chelsea, Vt.; member of the State house of representatives 1816-1826, 1828-1830, and 1833-1835, and served as speaker of the house 1820-1822, 1825, 1826, and 1829; State's attorney for Orange County 1819-1822 and 1830-1834; elected to the Eighteenth Congress (March 4, 1823-March 3, 1825); elected to the Twentieth Congress (March 4, 1827-March 3, 1829); unsuccessful candidate for renomination in 1828; was a clerk in the War Department 1835-1839; clerk in the Treasury Department in 1840; died in Washington, D.C., December 24, 1841; interment in the Congressional Cemetery.

**BUCK, Ellsworth Brewer,** a Representative from New York; born in Chicago, Ill., July 3, 1892; attended the public schools in Chicago and Morgan Park (Ill.) Academy; was graduated from Dartmouth College, Hanover, N.H., in 1914; engaged in the chewing gum industry 1914-1917; enlisted in the United States Naval Reserve on July 5, 1917; attended Naval Aviation Ground School, Massachusetts Institute of Technology; commissioned an ensign and assigned as instructor in meteorology and as custodian of meteorological instruments at the United States Naval Observatory, Washington, D.C., in 1918; moved to Staten Island, N.Y., in 1919 and became associated with L.A. Dreyfus Co., serving as chairman of the board 1932-1957; chairman of the Chewing Gum Code Authority, under N.R.A., in 1934 and 1935; member of the board of education of New York City 1935-1944, serving as vice president, 1938-1942, and as president 1942-1944; elected as a Republican to the Seventy-eighth Congress to fill the vacancy caused by the death of James A. O'Leary; reelected to the Seventy-ninth and Eightieth Congresses and served from June 6, 1944, to January 3, 1949; was not a candidate for renomination in 1948; delegate to the Republican National Convention in 1952; director, Office of Trade Investment and Monetary Affairs, Foreign Operations Administration, in 1954; public adviser, United States delegation to United Nations Economic and Social Council, Geneva, Switzerland, in 1955; died at his summer home at Thunder Mountain Ranch, Township of Stephenson, Marinette County, Wis., August 14, 1970; cremated; ashes placed in Burial Stone at Thunder Mountain Ranch Cemetery.

**BUCK, Frank Henry,** a Representative from California; born on a ranch near Vacaville, Solano County, Calif., September 23, 1887; attended the public schools; was graduated from the University of California at Berkeley in 1908 and from the law department of Harvard University in 1911; was admitted to the bar the same year and commenced practice in San Francisco, Calif.; fruit grower and farmer at Vacaville, Calif.; also engaged in the lumber business and in oil refining; delegate to the Democratic National Conventions in 1928, 1936, and 1940; elected as a Democrat to the Seventy-third and to the four succeeding Congresses and served from March 4,

1933, until his death in Washington, D.C., September 17, 1942; interment in Vacaville-Elmira Cemetery, Vacaville, Calif.

**BUCK, John Ransom,** a Representative from Connecticut; born in Glastonbury, Hartford County, Conn., December 6, 1835; attended the common schools, Wilbraham (Mass.) Academy, and Wesleyan University, Middletown, Conn.; taught school; studied law; was admitted to the bar in 1862 and practiced in Hartford; assistant clerk of the State house of representatives in 1864 and clerk in 1865; clerk of the senate in 1866; president of the Hartford Court of Common Council in 1868; city attorney 1871-1873; treasurer of Hartford County 1873-1881; member of the State senate in 1880 and 1881; elected as a Republican to the Forty-seventh Congress (March 4, 1881-March 3, 1883); unsuccessful candidate for reelection in 1882 to the Forty-eighth Congress; elected to the Forty-ninth Congress (March 4, 1885-March 3, 1887); unsuccessful candidate for reelection in 1886 to the Fiftieth Congress; resumed the practice of law in Hartford, Conn., where he died February 6, 1917; interment in Cedar Hill Cemetery.

**BUCKALEW, Charles Rollin,** a Senator and a Representative from Pennsylvania; born in Fishing Creek Township, Columbia County, Pa., December 28, 1821; was graduated from Harford Academy, Susquehanna County, Pa.; studied law; was admitted to the bar in 1843 and commenced practice in Bloomsburg, Pa., in 1844; prosecuting attorney for Columbia County, 1845-1847; member of the Pennsylvania senate in 1850-1853, 1857-1858, and in 1869; commissioner to exchange ratifications of a treaty with Paraguay in 1854; chairman of the Pennsylvania Democratic committee in 1857; appointed one of the commissioners to revise the penal code of Pennsylvania in 1857; appointed Minister Resident to Ecuador on June 14, 1858, and served until July 1861; elected as a Democrat to the United States Senate, and served from March 4, 1863 to March 3, 1869; unsuccessful candidate in 1872 for election for Governor of Pennsylvania; delegate to the constitutional convention of 1873; elected as a Democrat to the Fiftieth and Fifty-first Congresses (March 4, 1887-March 3, 1891); resumed the practice of his profession in Bloomsburg, Columbia County, Pa., where he died on May 19, 1899; interment in Rosemont Cemetery.

**Bibliography:** *DAB*; Hummel, William W. "Charles R. Buckalew: Democratic Statesman in a Republican Era." Ph.D. dissertation, University of Pittsburgh, 1964.

**BUCKBEE, John Theodore,** a Representative from Illinois; born on a farm near Rockford, Winnebago County, Ill., August 1, 1871; attended the public schools of Rockford; studied agriculture and horticulture in Austria, France, Denmark, Sweden, Belgium, Italy, Great Britain, and the Netherlands; established and engaged in a seed business in Rockford, Ill.; elected as a Republican to the Seventieth and to the four succeeding Congresses, and served from March 4, 1927, until his death in Rockford, Ill., April 23, 1936; was not a candidate for renomination in 1936 to the Seventy-fifth Congress; interment in Greenwood Cemetery.

**BUCKINGHAM, William Alfred,** a Senator from Connecticut; born in Lebanon, Conn., May 28, 1804; attended the common schools and Bacon Academy, Colchester, Conn.; engaged in mercantile pursuits and in manufacturing; mayor of Norwich, Conn., 1849-1850, 1856-1857; elected Governor of Connecticut in 1858, reelected every year from 1859 through 1865, and served from May 5, 1858 to May 2, 1866; resumed his former business pursuits; elected as a Republican to the United States Senate and served from March 4, 1869, until his death in Norwich, Conn., on February 5, 1875; chairman, Committee on Engrossed Bills (Forty-first and Forty-second Congresses), Committee on Investigation and Retrenchment (Forty-second Congress), Committee on Indian Affairs (Forty-third Congress); interment in Yantic Cemetery, Norwich, Conn.

**Bibliography:** *DAB*; Buckingham, Samuel. *The Life of William A. Buckingham, the War Governor of Connecticut.* Springfield, Mass.: W.F. Adams Co., 1894.

**BUCKLAND, Ralph Pomeroy,** a Representative from Ohio; born in Leyden, Mass., January 20, 1812; moved with his parents to Ravenna, Ohio, the same year; attended the country schools, Tallmadge (Ohio) Academy, and Kenyon College, Gambier, Ohio; studied law; was admitted to the bar in 1837 and commenced practice in Fremont, Ohio; mayor of Fremont 1843-1845; delegate to the Whig National Convention in 1848; member of the State senate 1855-1859; entered the Union Army as colonel of the Seventy-second Regiment, Ohio Volunteer Infantry, January 10, 1862; commissioned brigadier general of Volunteers November 29, 1862; resigned from the Army on January 6, 1865; brevetted major general March 13, 1865; elected as a Republican to the Thirty-ninth and Fortieth Congresses (March 4, 1865-March 3, 1869); was not a candidate for renomination in 1868 to the Forty-first Congress; resumed the practice of law; delegate to the Philadelphia Loyalists' Convention in 1866 and to the Pittsburgh Soldiers' Convention; delegate to the Republican National Convention of 1876; Government director of the Union Pacific Railroad 1877-1880; died in Fremont, Sandusky County, Ohio, May 27, 1892; interment in Oakwood Cemetery.

**Bibliography:** *DAB.*

**BUCKLER, Richard Thompson,** a Representative from Minnesota; born on a farm near Oakland, Coles County, Ill., October 27, 1865; attended the public schools; engaged in agricultural pursuits in Cole County, Ill.; moved to Andover Township, Polk County, Minn., in 1904 and continued agricultural pursuits; active in Farm Bureau and Farmers' Union organizations; held numerous township and local school district offices; served in the State senate 1915-1919, 1923-1927, and 1931-1933; elected on the Farmer-Labor ticket to the Seventy-fourth and to the three succeeding Congresses (January 3, 1935-January 3, 1943); was not a candidate for renomination in 1942; resumed agricultural pursuits; died in Crookston, Minn., January 23, 1950; interment in Oakdale Cemetery.

**BUCKLEY, Charles Anthony,** a Representative from New York; born in New York City, June 23, 1890; attended the public schools; contractor and builder in New York City, beginning in 1914; member of the board of aldermen of New York City, 1918-1923; New York State tax appraiser, 1923-1929; appointed chamberlain of New York City on January 3, 1929, and served until his resignation on October 8, 1933; elected as a Democrat to the Seventy-fourth and to the fourteen succeeding Congresses (January 3, 1935-January 3, 1965); chairman, Committee on Pensions (Seventy-eighth and Seventy-ninth Congresses), Committee on Public Works (Eighty-second Congress and Eighty-fourth through Eighty-eighth Congresses); unsuccessful candidate for renomination in 1964 to the Eighty-ninth Congress; Bronx County Democratic leader from 1953 until his death in New York City, January 22, 1967; interment in Gate of Heaven Cemetery, Valhalla, N.Y.

**BUCKLEY, Charles Waldron,** a Representative from Alabama; born in Unadilla, Otsego County, N.Y., February 18, 1835; attended the public schools in Unadilla and Freeport, Ill., where his parents moved in 1846; was graduated from Beloit College, Wisconsin, in 1860 and from the Union Theological Seminary in New York City in 1863; entered the Union Army on February 9, 1864, and served as chaplain of the Forty-seventh Regiment, United States Colored Volunteer Infantry, and of the Eighth Regiment, Louisiana Colored Infantry, until January 5, 1866, when he was mustered out; Alabama superintendent of education for the bureau of refugees and freedmen in 1866 and 1867, and resided in Montgomery; delegate to the Alabama constitutional convention in 1867; engaged in agricultural pursuits, banking, the fire insurance business, and mining; upon the readmission of the State of Alabama to representation was elected as a Republican to the Fortieth Congress; reelected to the Forty-first and Forty-second Congresses, and served from July 21, 1868 to March 3, 1873; was not a candidate

for renomination in 1872 to the Forty-third Congress; probate judge of Montgomery County, 1874-1878; resumed banking and also engaged in the fire insurance business; postmaster of Montgomery, 1881-1885, 1890-1893, and 1897-1906; delegate to the Republican National Convention of 1896; died in Montgomery, Ala., on December 4, 1906; interment in Woodlawn Cemetery, New York City.

**BUCKLEY, James Lane,** a Senator from New York; born in New York City, March 9, 1923; received secondary education at the Millbrook (N.Y.) School; B.A., Yale University, 1943; enlisted in the United States Navy in 1942 and was discharged with rank of lieutenant (jg) in 1946; attended Columbia University Law School, 1947; LL.B., Yale University Law School, 1949; admitted to the Connecticut bar in 1950 and commenced practice in New Haven; joined The Catawba Corporation of New York as a vice president and director, 1953-1970; elected as the candidate of the Conservative Party of New York State to the United States Senate in 1970, and served from January 3, 1971 to January 3, 1977; unsuccessful candidate for reelection in 1976, and for election to the United States Senate from Connecticut in 1980; Under Secretary of State for International Security Affairs, February 28, 1981 to August 20, 1982; Counselor for the Department of State, September 9 to September 26, 1982; president, Radio Free Europe/Radio Liberty, Inc., 1982-1985; nominated by President Ronald Reagan as judge, United States Court of Appeals for the District of Columbia Circuit, October 16, 1985; entered on duty December 17, 1985; took senior status September 1, 1996; is a resident of Washington, D.C.

**Bibliography:** Buckley, James Lane. *If Men Were Angels: A View From the Senate.* New York: G.P. Putnam's Sons, 1975.

**BUCKLEY, James Richard,** a Representative from Illinois; born in Chicago, Ill., November 18, 1870; attended the public and parochial schools and Christian Brothers' Commercial Academy; engaged in mercantile pursuits; permit clerk of the department of public works, 1893-1897; deputy city gas inspector from 1897 until 1910; unsuccessful Democratic candidate for clerk of the supreme court of Cook County, Ill., in 1908; member of the Chicago Board of Aldermen, 1910-1912; delegate to the Democratic National Conventions of 1908, 1912 and 1916; chief deputy criminal court clerk from 1912 to 1918; manager of the State personal property tax collection department, 1918-1923; elected as a Democrat to the Sixty-eighth Congress (March 4, 1923-March 3, 1925); unsuccessful candidate for reelection in 1924 to the Sixty-ninth Congress; vice president of the Universal Granite Quarries; was serving as chief drain inspector at the time of his death in Chicago, Ill., on June 22, 1945; interment in Calvary Cemetery, Evanston, Ill.

**BUCKLEY, James Vincent,** a Representative from Illinois; born on a farm in Saginaw County, Mich., May 15, 1894; attended the public schools of Saginaw County, Mich.; moved to Chicago, Ill., at an early age and worked in the automobile industry; engaged in the real estate and building business in the Calumet region of Cook County, Ill., and Lake County, Ind.; during the Second World War was active in war-plant production service and was elected president of Local Union 714, United Automobile Workers; elected as a Democrat to the Eighty-first Congress (January 3, 1949-January 3, 1951); unsuccessful candidate for reelection in 1950 to the Eighty-second Congress; engaged in the real estate and building business at Calumet City, Ill., from 1951 until his death in Hammond, Ind., July 30, 1954; interment in Calvary Cemetery, Gary, Ind.

**BUCKMAN, Clarence Bennett,** a Representative from Minnesota; born in Doylestown, Bucks County, Pa., April 1, 1851; attended the public and normal schools; moved to Minnesota in 1872 and settled in what is now known as Buckman; engaged in agricultural pursuits and in the lumber business; appointed justice of the peace in 1873; member of the State house of representatives 1881-1883; served in the State senate 1887-1891 and 1899-1903; elected as a Republican to the Fifty-eighth and Fifty-ninth Congresses (March 4, 1903-March 3, 1907); unsuccessful candidate for renomination in 1906; deputy United States marshal 1912-1917; resumed the lumber business in Little Falls, Morrison County, Minn.; died in Battle Creek, Mich., March 1, 1917; interment in Oakland Cemetery, Little Falls, Minn.

BUCKNER, Alexander, a Senator from Missouri; born in Jefferson County, Ky., in 1785; studied law; moved to Charleston, Clark County, Ind., in 1812; moved to Missouri in 1818 and settled near Jackson, Cape Girardeau County; practiced law and also engaged in agricultural pursuits; appointed by the Territorial Governor as circuit attorney for the Cape Girardeau district; president of the State constitutional convention in 1820; member, State senate 1822-1826; elected to the United States Senate and served from March 4, 1831, until his death in Cape Girardeau County, Mo., June 6, 1833; interment on his farm in Cape Girardeau County; reinterment in City Cemetery, Cape Girardeau, Mo., in 1897.

BUCKNER, Aylett Hawes (nephew of Aylett Hawes and cousin of Richard Hawes and Albert Gallatin Hawes), a Representative from Missouri; born in Fredericksburg, Va., December 14, 1816; attended Georgetown College, Washington, D.C., and the University of Virginia at Charlottesville; engaged in teaching for several years; moved to Palmyra, Mo., in 1837; served as deputy sheriff; studied law; was admitted to the bar in 1838 and commenced practice in Bowling Green, Mo.; became editor of the Salt River Journal; elected clerk of the Pike County Court in 1841; moved to St. Louis, Mo., in 1850 and continued the practice of law; attorney for the Bank of the State of Missouri in 1852; appointed commissioner of public works in 1854 and served until 1855; returned to Pike County and settled on a farm near Bowling Green; elected judge of the third judicial circuit in 1857; delegate to the convention held in Washington, D.C., in 1861 in an effort to devise means to prevent the impending war; moved to St. Charles, Mo., in 1862 and became interested in the manufacture of tobacco in St. Louis; also engaged in mercantile pursuits; moved to Mexico, Audrain County; member of the Democratic central committee in 1868; delegate to the Democratic National Convention in 1872; elected as a Democrat to the Forty-third and to the five succeeding Congresses (March 4, 1873-March 3, 1885); chairman, Committee on District of Columbia (Forty-fourth Congress), Committee on Banking and Currency (Forty-fifth, Forty-sixth, and Forty-eighth Congresses); declined to be a candidate for reelection in 1884 and retired from public life; died in Mexico, Mo., February 5, 1894; interment in Elmwood Cemetery.

BUCKNER, Aylette (son of Richard Aylett Buckner), a Representative from Kentucky; born in Greensburg, Green County, Ky., July 21, 1806; attended the New Athens Seminary; studied law; was admitted to the bar and commenced practice in Greensburg; member of the Kentucky house of representatives in 1842 and 1843; elected as a Whig to the Thirtieth Congress (March 4, 1847-March 3, 1849); unsuccessful candidate in 1848 for reelection to the Thirty-first Congress; moved to St. Louis, Mo., and continued the practice of his profession; returned to Lexington, Ky., in 1864, where he died July 3, 1869; interment in Lexington Cemetery.

BUCKNER, Richard Aylett (father of Aylette Buckner), a Representative from Kentucky; born in Fauquier County, Va., July 16, 1763; received a liberal education; moved to Green County, Ky., in 1803; studied law; was admitted to the bar; taught school; moved to Greensburg in 1811 and practiced law; county attorney and Commonwealth's attorney of Green County; member of the Kentucky house of representatives in 1813 and 1815; elected to the Eighteenth and to the two succeeding Congresses (March 4,

1823-March 3, 1829); chairman, Committee on Private Land Claims (Nineteenth and Twentieth Congresses); unsuccessful candidate for reelection in 1828 to the Twenty-first Congress; appointed associate judge of the court of appeals December 31, 1831, but resigned shortly afterwards; unsuccessful candidate for Governor of Kentucky in 1832; again a member of the Kentucky house of representatives, 1837-1839; presidential elector on the William Henry Harrison tickets in 1836 and 1840; circuit judge in 1845; judge of the Court of Appeals of Kentucky; died in Greensburg, Ky., December 8, 1847; interment in the family graveyard at the ancestral home, "Buckner's Hill."

BUDD, James Herbert, a Representative from California; born in Janesville, Rock County, Wis., May 18, 1851; moved to California in 1859 with his parents, who settled in Stockton; attended the public schools in Stockton, and Brayton College, Oakland, in 1869; was graduated from the University of California at Berkeley in 1873; served as lieutenant colonel on the staff of Governor Newton Booth in 1873 and 1874; deputy district attorney in 1873 and 1874; studied law; was admitted to the bar in 1874 and commenced practice in Stockton; served as first lieutenant in the California National Guard and was promoted to major of the line; elected as a Democrat to the Forty-eighth Congress (March 4, 1883-March 3, 1885); declined to be a candidate for reelection in 1884 to the Forty-ninth Congress; appointed police and fire commissioner of Stockton in 1889; member of the board for drafting the city charter in 1889; elected Governor of California in 1894, and served from January 11, 1895 to January 3, 1899; resumed the practice of law in San Francisco; died in Stockton, Calif., July 30, 1908; interment in Rural Cemetery.

BUDGE, Hamer Harold, a Representative from Idaho; born in Pocatello, Bannock County, Idaho, November 21, 1910; attended the public schools of Boise, Idaho; graduated from Boise High School in 1928, and attended the College of Idaho at Caldwell, 1928-1930; A.B., Stanford University, 1933; LL.B., University of Idaho School of Law, Moscow, Idaho, 1936; was admitted to the bar in 1936 and commenced the practice of law in Boise; member from Ada County in the Idaho State house of representatives, 1939-1941, serving as assistant Republican floor leader; served in the United States Navy from 1942 until discharged in 1945 as a lieutenant commander, United States Naval Reserve; again a member of the State house of representatives in 1949, serving as Republican floor leader; elected as a Republican to the Eighty-second and to the four succeeding Congresses (January 3, 1951-January 3, 1961); unsuccessful candidate for reelection in 1960 to the Eighty-seventh Congress; judge of the Third Judicial District of Idaho, 1961-1964; appointed to the Securities and Exchange Commission by President Lyndon B. Johnson in 1964, became chairman in 1969, and served until his resignation, January 2, 1971; president and chief executive officer of The Mutual Funds Complex (IDS) in Minneapolis, Minn., until 1978; is a resident of Palm Desert, Calif.

BUECHNER, John William (Jack), a Representative from Missouri; born in Kirkwood, Mo., June 4, 1940; attended parochial schools; A.B., Benedictine College, Atchison, Kans., 1962; J.D., St. Louis University Law School, 1965; admitted to the Missouri bar in 1965 and commenced practice in St. Louis County; real estate developer; member, Missouri State house of representatives, 1972-1982; elected as a Republican to the One Hundredth and One Hundred First Congresses (January 3, 1987-January 3, 1991); unsuccessful candidate for reelection in 1990 to the One Hundred Second Congress; president, International Republican Institute, 1991-1993; partner, Manatt, Phelps and Phillips, Washington, D.C.; is a resident of McLean, Va.

BUEL, Alexander Woodruff, a Representative from Michigan; born in Castleton, Vt., December 13, 1813; attended the public schools in Poultney, Vt., and was graduated from Middlebury

College, Vermont, in 1830; taught school and studied law; moved to Detroit, Mich., in 1834; was admitted to the bar in 1835 and commenced practice in Detroit, Mich.; city attorney in 1837; member of the State house of representatives in 1838 and 1848, serving as speaker the latter year; prosecuting attorney for Wayne County 1843-1846; elected as a Democrat to the Thirty-first Congress (March 4, 1849-March 3, 1851); unsuccessful candidate for reelection in 1850 to the Thirty-second Congress; resumed the practice of law; again a member of the State house of representatives, in 1859 and 1860; appointed postmaster of Detroit on September 28, 1860, and served until March 18, 1861; died in Detroit, Mich., April 19, 1868; interment in Elmwood Cemetery.

**BUELL, Alexander Hamilton,** a Representative from New York; born in Fairfield, Herkimer County, N.Y., July 14, 1801; attended the district schools and Fairfield Academy; engaged in mercantile pursuits in Fairfield, N.Y., and maintained general stores in other cities; served as a member of the State assembly in 1845; elected as a Democrat to the Thirty-second Congress and served from March 4, 1851, until his death in Washington, D.C., on January 29, 1853; interment in the Episcopal Cemetery, Fairfield, N.Y.

**BUFFETT, Howard Homan,** a Representative from Nebraska; born in Omaha, Douglas County, Nebr., August 13, 1903; attended the public schools, and was graduated from the University of Nebraska at Lincoln in 1925; engaged in the investment business in 1926; member of the Omaha Board of Education 1939-1942; elected as a Republican to the Seventy-eighth, Seventy-ninth, and Eightieth Congresses (January 3, 1943-January 3, 1949); unsuccessful candidate for reelection in 1948 to the Eighty-first Congress; elected to the Eighty-second Congress (January 3, 1951-January 3, 1953); was not a candidate for renomination in 1952; resumed former business pursuits; was a resident of Omaha, Nebr., until his death there on April 30, 1964; interment in Forest Lawn Memorial Park.

**BUFFINGTON, James,** a Representative from Massachusetts; born in Fall River, Mass., March 16, 1817; attended the common schools, and Friends College, Providence, R.I.; studied medicine but never practiced; engaged in mercantile pursuits in Fall River; mayor of Fall River in 1854 and 1855; elected as a candidate of the American Party to the Thirty-fourth Congress and as a Republican to the three succeeding Congresses (March 4, 1855-March 3, 1863); chairman, Committee on Accounts (Thirty-seventh Congress), Committee on Military Affairs (Thirty-seventh Congress); was not a candidate for renomination in 1862; was mustered into the service April 24, 1861, and was discharged June 15, 1861; special agent of the United States Treasury and internal revenue collector for the district of Massachusetts 1867-1869; elected as a Republican to the Forty-first and to the three succeeding Congresses and served from March 4, 1869, until his death in Fall River, Mass., March 7, 1875; chairman, Committee on Accounts (Forty-second and Forty-third Congresses); interment in Oak Grove Cemetery.

**BUFFINGTON, Joseph,** a Representative from Pennsylvania; born in West Chester, Pa., November 27, 1803; attended the common schools and Western University, Pittsburgh, Pa.; moved to Butler County, Pa., and edited a weekly newspaper; studied law; was admitted to the bar in 1826 and commenced practice in Butler; moved to Kittanning, Pa., in 1827 and continued the practice of law; elected as a Whig to the Twenty-eighth and Twenty-ninth Congresses (March 4, 1843-March 3, 1847); was not a candidate for renomination in 1846; appointed president judge of the eighteenth district in 1849 and served until 1851; declined the appointment as chief justice of the Territory of Utah tendered by President Fillmore in 1852; judge of the tenth district of Pennsylvania from 1855 until his retirement in 1871; died in Kittanning, Pa., February 3, 1872; interment in Kittanning Cemetery.

**BUFFUM, Joseph, Jr.,** a Representative from New Hampshire; born in Fitchburg, Mass., September 23, 1784; attended the public schools and the local academy; was graduated from Dartmouth College, Hanover, N.H., in 1806; studied law and practiced in Westmoreland and Keene, N.H.; elected to the Sixteenth Congress (March 4, 1819-March 3, 1821); appointed judge of the court of common pleas on January 21, 1825; engaged in agricultural pursuits; died in Westmoreland, Cheshire County, N.H., February 24, 1874; interment in South Village Cemetery.

**BUGG, Robert Malone,** a Representative from Tennessee; born in Boydton, Mecklenburg County, Va., January 20, 1805; attended the public schools; moved to Tennessee and settled in Williamson County in 1825, where he taught school for several years; moved to Giles County and engaged in agricultural pursuits; justice of the peace in 1840; member of the State house of representatives in 1851 and 1852; elected as a Whig to the Thirty-third Congress (March 4, 1853-March 3, 1855); declined to be a candidate for renomination in 1854; resumed agricultural pursuits; served in the State senate in 1871 and 1872; died in Lynnville, Giles County, Tenn., February 18, 1887; interment in McLaurine Cemetery, near Lynnville, Tenn.

**BULKELEY, Morgan Gardner** (cousin of Edwin Denison Morgan), a Senator from Connecticut; born in East Haddam, Middlesex County, Conn., December 26, 1837; attended the district schools; moved with his parents to Hartford, Conn., in 1846; engaged in mercantile pursuits in Brooklyn, N.Y., from 1852 until 1872; member of the Republican general committee of Kings County; during the Civil War enlisted in the Thirteenth Regiment, New York National Guard, and served at Baltimore and at Suffolk, Va.; returned to Hartford, Conn., in 1872; engaged in the life insurance business and served as president of the Aetna Life Insurance Co.; served in the Hartford city council in 1874; member of the board of aldermen in 1875 and 1876; first president of the National League of Professional Baseball Clubs in 1876; mayor of Hartford, 1880-1888; elected Governor of Connecticut in 1888, and served from January 10, 1889 to January 4, 1893; remained in office for an additional term since the gubernatorial election of 1890 was in dispute, the Legislature being unable to declare which candidate was the victor; elected commander of the Department of Connecticut, Grand Army of the Republic, in 1903; elected as a Republican to the United States Senate, and served from March 4, 1905 to March 3, 1911; unsuccessful candidate for reelection; chairman, Committee to Examine Branches of the Civil Service (Fifty-ninth Congress), Committee on Railroads (Sixtieth and Sixty-first Congresses); resumed his former business pursuits; died in Hartford, Conn., on November 6, 1922; interment in Cedar Hill Cemetery; inducted in 1937 into the National Baseball Hall of Fame, Cooperstown, N.Y.

**Bibliography:** *DAB.*

**BULKLEY, Robert Johns,** a Representative and a Senator from Ohio; born in Cleveland, Cuyahoga County, Ohio, October 8, 1880; attended the University School, Cleveland, Ohio, and was graduated from Harvard University in 1902; studied at Harvard Law School; was admitted to the bar in 1906 and commenced practice in Cleveland, Ohio; elected as a Democrat to the Sixty-second and Sixty-third Congresses (March 4, 1911-March 3, 1915); during the First World War served as chief of the legal section of the War Industries Board 1917-1918; resumed the practice of law; elected as a Democrat to the United States Senate on November 4, 1930, to fill the vacancy caused by the death of Theodore E. Burton; reelected in 1932 and served from December 1, 1930, to January 3, 1939; unsuccessful candidate for reelection in 1938; chairman, Committee on Manufactures (Seventy-third through Seventy-fifth Congresses); engaged in banking; resumed the practice of law; during the Second World War served as a member of the board of appeals in visa cases; died in Cleveland, Ohio, July 21, 1965; interment in Lakeview Cemetery.

**Bibliography:** Jenkins, William D. "Robert Bulkley: Progressive Profile." Ph.D. dissertation, Case Western Reserve, 1969; Stegh, Leslie J. "A Paradox of Prohibition: Election of Robert J. Bulkley as Senator from Ohio, 1930." *Ohio History* 83 (Summer 1974): 57-72.

**BULL, John,** a Representative from Missouri; born in Virginia in 1803; studied medicine in Baltimore, Md.; moved to Howard County, Mo., and settled near Glasgow; engaged in the practice of medicine; studied theology; was ordained to the ministry and became a Methodist minister in that locality; presidential elector on the ticket of Andrew Jackson and John C. Calhoun in 1828; unsuccessful candidate in 1832 for Governor of Missouri; elected to the Twenty-third Congress (March 4, 1833-March 3, 1835); resumed his ministerial duties and also the practice of medicine; died near Rothville, Chariton County, Mo., in February 1863; interment in Hutcheson Cemetery, a family burial ground, near Rothville, Mo.

**BULL, John,** a Delegate from South Carolina; born in Prince William's Parish, South Carolina, about 1740; justice of the peace of Greenville County; member of the Provincial house of commons in 1772; deputy secretary of the Province in 1772; delegate to the First and Second provincial congresses in 1775 and 1776; member of the first general assembly in 1776; served in the State house of representatives 1778-1781 and in 1784; Member of the Continental Congress 1784-1787; served in the State senate in 1798; died in South Carolina in 1802; interment in Prince William's Parish Churchyard, Beaufort County, S.C.

**BULL, Melville,** a Representative from Rhode Island; born in Newport, R.I., September 29, 1854; attended Phillips Exeter Academy, Exeter, N.H., and was graduated from Harvard University in 1877; engaged in agricultural pursuits near Newport; member of the Rhode Island house of representatives, 1883-1885; served in the State senate, 1885-1892; member of the Republican State central committee; delegate to the Republican National Convention of 1888; lieutenant governor of Rhode Island, 1892-1894; elected as a Republican to the Fifty-fourth and to the three succeeding Congresses (March 4, 1895-March 3, 1903); chairman, Committee on Accounts (Fifty-sixth and Fifty-seventh Congresses); unsuccessful candidate for reelection in 1902 to the Fifty-eighth Congress; lived in Middletown, Newport County, R.I., until his death on July 5, 1909; interment in Island Cemetery, Newport, R.I.

**BULLARD, Henry Adams,** a Representative from Louisiana; born in Pepperell, Mass., September 9, 1788; was graduated from Harvard University in 1807; studied law in Boston and Philadelphia; was admitted to the bar about 1812; accompanied General José Álvarez Toledo as military secretary on his revolutionary expedition into Texas in 1813; moved to Natchitoches, La., and commenced the practice of law; appointed district judge in 1822, but resigned after a few years' service, returning to the bench later for another period of service; elected as an Anti-Jacksonian to the Twenty-second and Twenty-third Congresses and served from March 4, 1831, until January 4, 1834, when he resigned, having been appointed judge; judge of the supreme court of Louisiana from 1834 to 1846; acted as secretary of state of Louisiana in 1839; resumed the practice of law in New Orleans, La.; appointed professor of civil law in the Law School of Louisiana in 1847; served as a member of the Louisiana State house of representatives in 1850; elected as a Whig to the Thirty-first Congress to fill the vacancy caused by the resignation of Charles M. Conrad and served from December 5, 1850, to March 3, 1851; died in New Orleans on April 17, 1851; interment in Girod Street Cemetery.

**Bibliography:** *DAB*; Bonquois, Dora J. "The Career of Henry Adams Bullard, Louisiana Jurist, Legislator, and Educator." *Louisiana Historical Quarterly* 23 (October 1940): 999-1106.

**BULLOCH, Archibald** (father of William Bellinger Bulloch and great-great-grandfather of Theodore Roosevelt), a Delegate from Georgia; born in Charleston, S.C., about 1730; completed preparatory studies; studied law, was admitted to the bar and practiced; commissioned lieutenant in a South Carolina regiment in 1757; moved to Savannah, Ga., about 1762; appointed a member of the committee to correspond with Benjamin Franklin for redress of grievances in 1768 and of the committee to sympathize with the citizens of Boston; elected speaker of the Georgia Royal assembly in 1772; president of the Georgia provincial congress in 1775 and 1776; Member of the Continental Congress in 1775; led a company to clear Tybee Island of the enemy; elected by the provincial congress president and commander in chief of Georgia and served from June 20, 1776, to February 5, 1777, when the State government was adopted; signed the first constitution of Georgia; died in Savannah, Ga., February 22, 1777; interment in Colonial Cemetery.

**Bibliography:** *DAB*.

**BULLOCH, William Bellinger** (son of Archibald Bulloch), a Senator from Georgia; born in Savannah, Ga., in 1777; studied law; was admitted to the bar and commenced practice in Savannah in 1797; appointed United States district attorney in 1804; mayor of Savannah in 1812 and alderman in 1814; during the War of 1812 served in the Savannah Heavy Artillery; solicitor general of the State; collector of customs 1849-1850; member, State house of representatives; member, State senate; appointed as a Republican to the United States Senate to fill the vacancy caused by the resignation of William H. Crawford and served from April 8, 1813, until November 6, 1813, when a successor was elected; one of the founders of the State Bank of Georgia and served as its president 1816-1843; died in Savannah, Ga., May 6, 1852; interment in Laurel Grove Cemetery.

**BULLOCK, Robert,** a Representative from Florida; born in Greenville, Pitt County, N.C., December 8, 1828; attended the common schools; moved to Florida in 1844 and settled at Fort King, then a United States Government post, near the present city of Ocala; taught in the first school in Sumter County; clerk of the circuit court of Marion County from November 13, 1849, to November 11, 1855; commissioned by Governor James E. Broome in 1856 a captain to raise a mounted company of volunteers for the suppression of Indian hostilities; the company was mustered into the service of the United States and served eighteen months, until the cessation of hostilities; entered the Confederate Army as captain in the Seventh Regiment Florida Volunteers in 1862 and served until the close of the war; promoted to lieutenant colonel in 1863, and to brigadier general on November 29, 1864; studied law; was admitted to the bar in 1866 and began practice in Marion County; judge of probate court, 1866-1868; member of the Florida State house of representatives in 1879; again clerk of the circuit court of Marion County from 1881 to 1889; elected as a Democrat to the Fifty-first and Fifty-second Congresses (March 4, 1889-March 3, 1893); was not a candidate for renomination in 1892 to the Fifty-third Congress; engaged in agricultural pursuits; elected judge of Marion County in 1903, and served until his death in Ocala, Marion County, Fla., July 27, 1905; interment in Evergreen Cemetery.

**BULLOCK, Stephen,** a Representative from Massachusetts; born in Rehoboth, Mass., October 10, 1735; attended the common schools; taught school; during the Revolutionary War was captain of the Sixth Company in Col. Thomas Carpenter's Regiment, and was in the Battle of Rhode Island in 1778; delegate to the first Massachusetts constitutional convention in 1780; member of the Massachusetts house of representatives in 1783, 1785, 1786, 1795, and 1796; elected as a Federalist to the Fifth Congress (March 4, 1797-March 3, 1799); judge of the court of common pleas for Bristol County; member of the Governor's council 1803-1805; died in Rehoboth, Bristol County, Mass., February 2, 1816; interment in Burial Place Hill.

**BULLOCK, Wingfield,** a Representative from Kentucky; born in Spotsylvania, Va.; studied law; moved to Kentucky; member of the Kentucky senate from Shelby County, 1812-1814; elected to the Seventeenth Congress, and served from March 4, 1821 until his death in Shelbyville, Shelby County, Ky., October 13, 1821; interment in an old burying ground near Shelbyville.

**BULOW, William John,** a Senator from South Dakota; born on a farm near Moscow, Clermont County, Ohio, January 13, 1869; attended the public schools in Moscow, Ohio, and was graduated from the law department of the University of Michigan at Ann Arbor in 1893; was admitted to the bar the same year and commenced practice in Beresford, Union County, S.Dak., in 1894; member of the South Dakota State senate in 1899; served as city attorney of Beresford, S.Dak., 1902-1912, and 1913-1927; mayor of Beresford in 1912 and 1913; county judge of Union County, S.Dak., 1918; unsuccessful candidate in 1924 for election for Governor; elected Governor of South Dakota in 1926, reelected in 1928, and served from January 4, 1927 to January 6, 1931; elected as a Democrat to the United States Senate in 1930; reelected in 1936, and served from March 4, 1931, to January 3, 1943; unsuccessful candidate for renomination in 1942; chairman, Committee on the Civil Service (Seventy-third through Seventy-seventh Congresses); retired and resided in Washington, D.C., until his death there on February 26, 1960; interment in St. John's Catholic Cemetery, Beresford, S.Dak.

**BULWINKLE, Alfred Lee,** a Representative from North Carolina; born in Charleston, S.C., April 21, 1883; moved with his parents to Dallas, N.C., in 1891; attended the common schools; studied law at the University of North Carolina at Chapel Hill; was admitted to the bar in 1904 and commenced practice in Dallas, Gaston County, N.C.; prosecuting attorney for the municipal court of Gastonia 1913-1916; captain in Company B, First Infantry, North Carolina National Guard, 1909-1917; served on the Mexican border in 1916 and 1917; during the First World War served as a major in command of the Second Battalion, One Hundred and Thirteenth Field Artillery, Fifty-fifth Brigade, Thirtieth Division, American Expeditionary Forces; elected as a Democrat to the Sixty-seventh and to the three succeeding Congresses (March 4, 1921-March 3, 1929); unsuccessful candidate for reelection in 1928 to the Seventy-first Congress; elected to the Seventy-second and to the nine succeeding Congresses and served from March 4, 1931, until his death; chairman, Committee on Memorials (Seventy-sixth Congress); delegate to the International Aviation Conference at Chicago, Ill., in 1944; United States adviser, International Civil Aviation Organization at Montreal, Canada, and Geneva, Switzerland, in 1947; died in Gastonia, N.C., August 31, 1950; interment in Oakwood Cemetery.

**BUMPERS, Dale,** a Senator from Arkansas; born in Charleston, Franklin County, Ark., August 12, 1925; attended the public schools of Arkansas and the University of Arkansas, Fayetteville; J.D., Northwestern University Law School, Chicago, Ill., 1951; admitted to the Arkansas bar in 1952 and commenced practice in Charleston; entered the United States Marine Corps in 1943, released as a staff sergeant in 1946 after service during the Second World War; president of Charleston Hardware and Furniture Company, 1951-1956; Charleston city attorney from 1952 until 1970; cattle farmer, 1966-1970; special justice, Arkansas Supreme Court, 1968; elected Governor of Arkansas in 1970, reelected in 1972, and served from January 12, 1971 until his resignation on January 3, 1975, having been elected Senator; elected as a Democrat to the United States Senate in 1974 for the term commencing January 3, 1975; reelected in 1980, 1986, and again in 1992 for the term ending January 3, 1999; chairman, Committee on Small Business (One Hundredth through One Hundred Third Congresses); is a resident of Charleston, Ark.

**BUNCH, Samuel,** a Representative from Tennessee; born in Grainger County, Tenn., December 4, 1786; attended the public schools; engaged in agricultural pursuits; served in the Creek War as captain of a company of mounted riflemen under General Andrew Jackson, and participated in the attack on Hillibeetown on November 18, 1813; sheriff of Grainger County for several years; elected as a Jacksonian to the Twenty-third Congress and reelected as a White supporter to the Twenty-fourth Congress (March 4, 1833-March 3, 1837); resumed agricultural pursuits; died on his farm near Rutledge, Grainger County, Tenn., September 5, 1849; interment in a private cemetery on his farm near Rutledge.

**BUNDY, Hezekiah Sanford,** a Representative from Ohio; born in Marietta, Ohio, August 15, 1817; moved with his parents to Athens County in 1819; attended the public schools; engaged in agricultural pursuits; studied law; was admitted to the bar in 1850 and practiced until 1860, when he became engaged in the iron business; member of the State house of representatives in 1848 and 1850; served in the State senate in 1855; unsuccessful candidate for election in 1862 to the Thirty-eighth Congress; elected as a Republican to the Thirty-ninth Congress (March 4, 1865-March 3, 1867); declined to be a candidate for renomination in 1866; elected to the Forty-third Congress (March 4, 1873-March 3, 1875); chairman, Committee on Mileage (Forty-third Congress); unsuccessful candidate for reelection in 1874 to the Forty-fourth Congress; moved to Wellston, Jackson County, in 1887 and resumed the practice of law; elected to the Fifty-third Congress to fill the vacancy caused by the death of William H. Enochs and served from December 4, 1893, to March 3, 1895; died in Wellston, Jackson County, Ohio, December 12, 1895; interment in the City Cemetery.

**BUNDY, Solomon,** a Representative from New York; born in Oxford, Chenango County, N.Y., May 22, 1823; attended the common schools and Oxford (N.Y.) Academy; taught school for several years; engaged in mercantile pursuits; studied law; was admitted to the bar in 1859 and commenced practice in Oxford; while studying law served as justice of the peace and clerk of the Board of Supervisors of Chenango County; district attorney of Chenango County 1862-1865; elected as a Republican to the Forty-fifth Congress (March 4, 1877-March 3, 1879); was not a candidate for renomination in 1878; resumed the practice of law; died in Oxford, N.Y., January 13, 1889; interment in Riverview Cemetery.

**BUNKER, Berkeley Lloyd,** a Senator and a Representative from Nevada; born in what was then St. Thomas, Clark County, Nev., August 12, 1906; attended the public schools; engaged in the tire and oil business in Las Vegas, Nev., in 1934; member of the Nevada State assembly from 1936 to 1941, serving as speaker in 1939; appointed as a Democrat in 1940 to the United States Senate to fill the vacancy caused by the death of Key Pittman for the term ending January 3, 1941, and also for the term beginning January 3, 1947, and served from November 27, 1940, until December 6, 1942, when a duly elected successor qualified; unsuccessful candidate for nomination in 1942 for the vacancy; engaged in the life insurance business in Las Vegas, Nev.; elected as a Democrat to the Seventy-ninth Congress (January 3, 1945-January 3, 1947); was not a candidate for renomination in 1946 to the House of Representatives, but was an unsuccessful candidate for election to the United States Senate; investment broker and president of a management and equity company; is a resident of Las Vegas, Nev.

**BUNN, Benjamin Hickman,** a Representative from North Carolina; born on a farm in Nash County, near Rocky Mount, N.C., October 19, 1844; attended the local schools; during the Civil War enlisted in the Confederate Army as a second lieutenant in Company A, Forty-seventh North Carolina Regiment; promoted successively and became captain of the Fourth Company of Sharpshooters, MacRae's brigade, Army of Northern Virginia, 1861-1865; studied law; was admitted to the bar in 1866 and commenced practice in Rocky Mount, N.C.; elected mayor of Rocky Mount in 1867; delegate to the State constitutional convention in 1875 and to the Democratic National Convention of 1880; member of the State house of representatives 1883-1885; elected as a Democrat to the Fifty-first and to the two succeeding Congresses (March 4, 1889-March 3, 1895); chairman, Committee on Claims (Fifty-second and Fifty-third Congresses); was not a candidate for renomination in 1894 to the Fifty-fourth Congress; postmaster of Rocky Mount, N.C., from April 23, 1895, until the appointment of his successor on July 27, 1897; resumed the practice of law; died in Nash County, near Rocky Mount, N.C., August 25, 1907; interment in Pineview Cemetery.

**BUNN, James Lee,** a Representative from Oregon; born in McMinnville, Yamhill County, Oreg., December 12, 1956; graduated Dayton (Oreg.) Union High School, 1975; A.A., Chemeketa Community College, Salem, Oreg., 1977; B.A., Northwest Nazarene College, Nampa, Idaho, 1979; Oregon National Guard Reserve service as second lieutenant; member, County search and rescue; County sheriff's reserve deputy; member, Oregon State senate, 1987-1994; farmer; delegate, Republican National Convention, platform committee, 1992; Oregon Republican executive director and treasurer; County Republican chair; County chair, Reagan-Bush campaign and Bush-Quayle campaign; elected as a Republican to the One Hundred Fourth Congress (January 3, 1995-January 3, 1997); is a resident of McMinnville, Oreg.

**BUNNELL, Frank Charles,** a Representative from Pennsylvania; born in Washington Township, Luzerne County, Pa., March 19, 1842; attended the district rural school and Wyoming Seminary, Kingston, Pa., until he enlisted as a private in Company B, Fifty-second Regiment, Pennsylvania Volunteers, in September 1861; promoted and served as quartermaster sergeant of his regiment during the peninsular campaign under General George B. McClellan; discharged from the service April 2, 1863, on a surgeon's certificate of disability; engaged in mercantile pursuits 1864-1869; moved to Tunkhannock and engaged in agricultural pursuits and in banking; unsuccessful candidate for nomination in 1872 to the Forty-third Congress; subsequently elected to the Forty-second Congress to fill the vacancy caused by the resignation of Ulysses Mercur and served from December 24, 1872, to March 3, 1873; president of the Wyoming County Agricultural Society for over twenty years; elected burgess and borough treasurer of Tunkhannock, Wyoming County, in 1884; elected as a Republican to the Forty-ninth and Fiftieth Congresses (March 4, 1885-March 3, 1889); was not a candidate for renomination in 1888 to the Fifty-first Congress; died in Philadelphia, Pa., September 11, 1911; interment in Gravel Hill Cemetery, Tunkhannock, Pa.

**BUNNER, Rudolph,** a Representative from New York; born in Savannah, Wayne County, N.Y., August 17, 1779; was graduated from Columbia College, at New York City, in 1798; studied law; was admitted to the bar and practiced in Newburgh, Orange County, N.Y., from 1819 until 1822; moved to Oswego, Oswego County, N.Y., in October 1822; engaged in manufacturing and served as a director in the Oswego Cloth & Carpet Manufacturing Co.; also was an extensive landowner; member of the first board of directors of the Oswego Canal Co.; elected to the Twentieth Congress (March 4, 1827-March 3, 1829); died in Oswego, N.Y., July 16, 1837; interment in Riverside Cemetery.

**BUNNING, James Paul David,** a Representative from Kentucky; born in Southgate, Ky., October 23, 1931; attended parochial schools in Southgate and Cincinnati, Ohio; graduated St. Xavier High School, Cincinnati, 1949; B.S., Xavier University, Cincinnati, 1953; professional baseball pitcher with major league teams in Detroit, Philadelphia, Pittsburgh and Los Angeles, 1955-1969; investment broker and agent, 1960 to present; member, Fort Thomas (Ky.) City Council, 1977-1979; member, Kentucky senate, 1979-1983; unsuccessful candidate in 1983 for election for Governor of Kentucky; elected as a Republican to the One Hundredth and to the four succeeding Congresses (January 3, 1987-January 3, 1997); inducted in 1996 into the National Baseball Hall of Fame, Cooperstown, N.Y.; is a resident of Southgate, Ky.

**BUNTING, Thomas Lathrop,** a Representative from New York; born in Eden, Erie County, N.Y., April 24, 1844; was educated in the common schools and the Griffith Institute, Springville, N.Y.; taught school in winters and attended the academy in summer months; illness having interrupted his preparation for college, he moved to Hamburg, N.Y., in 1868 and later established a general mercantile store; engaged in the canning business; elected as a Democrat to the Fifty-second Congress (March 4, 1891-March 3, 1893); declined to be a candidate for renomination in 1892; resumed the canning business and also became interested in farming, dairying, and stock raising; died in Buffalo, N.Y., December 27, 1898; interment in Forest Lawn Cemetery at Hamburg, Erie County, N.Y.

**BURCH, John Chilton,** a Representative from California; born in Boone County, Mo., February 1, 1826; attended the Bonne Femme Academy and Kemper College; studied law in Jefferson City; was admitted to the bar and practiced; deputy clerk of Cole County; assistant adjutant general of Missouri; moved to California in 1850 and worked in the mines until 1851; elected clerk of the newly organized Trinity County; appointed district attorney in 1853; member of the State assembly in 1856; served in the State senate 1857-1859; elected as a Democrat to the Thirty-sixth Congress (March 4, 1859-March 3, 1861); resumed the practice of law in San Francisco; appointed a code commissioner and served four years; declined to be a candidate for judge of the supreme court of California; died in San Francisco, Calif., August 31, 1885; interment in the City Cemetery, Sacramento, Calif.

**BURCH, Thomas Granville,** a Representative and a Senator from Virginia; born on a farm near Dyer's Store, in Henry County, Va., July 3, 1869; attended the public schools; engaged in agricultural pursuits and in the tobacco manufacturing business; moved to Martinsville, Va., in 1886 and engaged in the banking business; also interested in the insurance and real estate businesses; member of the Virginia board of agriculture 1910-1913; mayor of Martinsville, Va., 1912-1914; United States marshal for the western district of Virginia 1914-1921; member of the commission in 1927 to simplify and reorganize the Virginia government; served with the Virginia transportation and public utility advisory commission in 1929; member of the Virginia board of education in 1930 and 1931; elected as a Democrat to the Seventy-second Congress and to the seven succeeding Congresses and served from March 4, 1931, to May 31, 1946, when he resigned; chairman, Committee on Post Office and Post Roads (Seventy-eighth and Seventy-ninth Congresses); appointed to the United States Senate to fill the vacancy caused by the death of Carter Glass and served from May 31, 1946, until November 5, 1946, when a duly elected successor qualified; was not a candidate for election to the vacancy in 1946; chairman of Governor's Commission on Reorganization of the Virginia Government in 1947; resumed his business pursuits; died in Martinsville, Va., March 20, 1951; interment in Oakwood Cemetery.

**BURCHARD, Horatio Chapin,** a Representative from Illinois; born in Marshall, Oneida County, N.Y., September 22, 1825; attended the public schools and private preparatory schools; was graduated from Hamilton College, Clinton, N.Y., in 1850; studied law; was admitted to the bar in 1854 and commenced practice in Freeport, Ill.; member of the Illinois State house of representatives

1863-1866; elected as a Republican to the Forty-first Congress to fill the vacancy caused by the resignation of Elihu B. Washburne; reelected to the Forty-second and to the three succeeding Congresses and served from December 6, 1869, to March 3, 1879; unsuccessful candidate for renomination in 1878; director of the United States Mint 1879-1885; resumed the practice of law in Freeport, Ill.; member of the commission to revise the State revenue laws in 1885 and 1886; was placed in charge of the jury of awards of the mining department of the World's Columbian Exposition at Chicago in 1893; died in Freeport, Ill., May 14, 1908; interment in Oakland Cemetery.

**BURCHARD, Samuel Dickinson,** a Representative from Wisconsin; born in Leyden, N.Y., July 17, 1836; moved with his father to Beaver Dam, Wis., in 1845; attended Madison (now Colgate) University, Hamilton, N.Y.; engaged in the wool manufacturing business in Beaver Dam; during the Civil War entered the Union Army as a lieutenant in the Missouri Militia; appointed assistant quartermaster of United States Volunteers with the rank of captain; was stationed at New York; was mustered out with the rank of major; member of the Wisconsin senate 1872-1874; elected as a Democrat to the Forty-fourth Congress (March 4, 1875-March 3, 1877); engaged in agricultural pursuits; died in Greenwood, Wise County, Tex., September 1, 1901; interment in Greenwood Cemetery.

**BURCHILL, Thomas Francis,** a Representative from New York; born in New York City August 3, 1882; attended St. Francis Xavier High School in New York City and Niagara University, Niagara Falls, N.Y., A.B.; auctioneer, appraiser, and also interested in the insurance business in New York City after 1900; member of the State assembly 1919-1924; served in the State senate 1924-1938; appointed a member of the New York World's Fair Commission in 1938; elected as a Democrat to the Seventy-eighth Congress (January 3, 1943-January 3, 1945); was not a candidate for renomination in 1944; resumed his former business pursuits in New York City; consultant; alien property custodian; died in New York City March 28, 1960; interment in Gate of Heaven Cemetery, Valhalla, N.Y.

**BURD, George,** a Representative from Pennsylvania; born in 1793; studied law; was admitted to the bar in 1810 at Carlisle, Cumberland County, Pa., and practiced; elected to the Twenty-second and Twenty-third Congresses (March 4, 1831-March 3, 1835); moved to Mercer County in 1843; died in Bedford, Bedford County, Pa., on January 13, 1844; interment in Bedford Cemetery.

**BURDETT, Samuel Swinfin,** a Representative from Missouri; born at Sutton-in-the-Elms, Leicestershire, England, February 21, 1836; when twelve years of age immigrated to the United States; worked on a farm in Lorain County, Ohio, and attended the common schools; studied law at Oberlin College, Ohio, was admitted to the bar in 1858 and commenced practice in Dewitt, Iowa; entered the Union Army as a private in the First Regiment, Iowa Volunteer Cavalry, in May 1861; promoted to the rank of lieutenant, later becoming captain, and served until August 1864; assistant provost marshal general from March 1 until August 1, 1864; moved to Osceola, St. Clair County, Mo., in December 1865; attorney for the seventh circuit in 1868 and 1869; delegate to the Republican National Convention in 1868; elected as a Republican to the Forty-first and Forty-second Congresses (March 4, 1869-March 3, 1873); chairman, Committee on Manufactures (Forty-second Congress); unsuccessful candidate in 1872 for reelection to the Forty-third Congress; resumed the practice of law in Osceola, Mo.; appointed Commissioner of the General Land Office in 1874; engaged in the practice of law in Washington, D.C., residing at Glencarlyn, Va., during his last years; commander in chief of the Grand Army of the Republic in 1885 and 1886; died at Sutton-in-the-Elms, Leicestershire, England, September 24, 1914; interment in Arlington National Cemetery, Va.

**BURDICK, Clark,** a Representative from Rhode Island; born in Newport, R.I., January 13, 1868; attended the public schools; was a student at the Harvard Law School 1893-1895; was admitted to the bar in 1894 and commenced practice in Newport; also interested in banking and served as president of the Newport Trust Co.; member of the First Division, Rhode Island Naval Militia, in 1896 and 1897; member of the city school board 1899-1901; city solicitor of Newport in 1901, 1902, and again in 1907 and 1908; member of the State house of representatives 1906-1908; delegate to the Republican National Convention in 1912; member of the Newport representative council 1906-1916, serving as chairman; served in the State senate in 1915 and 1916; awarded the third class order of the Sacred Treasury of Japan for services rendered the representatives of the Emperor of Japan in 1917; mayor of Newport in 1917 and 1918; elected as a Republican to the Sixty-sixth and to the six succeeding Congresses (March 4, 1919-March 3, 1933); unsuccessful candidate for reelection in 1932 to the Seventy-third Congress; reengaged in the practice of law and also in his banking interests in Newport, R.I., until his death on August 27, 1948; interment in St. Mary's Episcopal Cemetery, Portsmouth, R.I.

**BURDICK, Jocelyn Birch** (wife of Quentin Northrop Burdick), a Senator from North Dakota; born in Fargo, Cass County, N.Dak., February 6, 1922; graduated from Fargo Central High School in 1939; attended Principia College, Elsah, Ill.; Bachelor's Degree, Northwestern University, Evanston, Ill., 1943; worked as a radio reporter and announcer in Moorhead, Minn. for two years; founding member, Democratic Women Plus, Fargo, N.Dak.; appointed as a Democrat to the United States Senate, September 12, 1992, to fill the vacancy caused by the death of her husband, Quentin N. Burdick, and served from September 16 until December 14, 1992, her successor, Kent Conrad, having won in a special election; was not a candidate for reelection in 1992 for the term ending January 3, 1995; is a resident of Fargo, N.Dak.

**BURDICK, Quentin Northrop** (son of Usher Lloyd Burdick), a Representative and a Senator from North Dakota; born in Munich, Cavalier County, N.Dak., June 19, 1908; attended the public schools; B.A., University of Minnesota, 1931; LL.B., University of Minnesota School of Law, 1932; was admitted to the bar in 1932 and commenced practice in Fargo, N.Dak.; unsuccessful candidate in 1934 and 1940 for election for Cass County state's attorney; unsuccessful candidate in 1936 for nomination to the North Dakota State senate, and in 1942 for election for lieutenant governor; unsuccessful candidate in 1946 for election for Governor; unsuccessful candidate in 1956 for election to the United States Senate; elected as a Democrat to the Eighty-sixth Congress and served from January 3, 1959, until his resignation August 8, 1960; elected to the United States Senate on June 28, 1960, to fill the vacancy caused by the death of William Langer; reelected in 1964, 1970, 1976, 1982, and 1988; served from August 8, 1960 until his death September 8, 1992; chairman, Committee on Environment and Public Works (One Hundreth through One Hundred Second Congresses).

**Bibliography:** Burdick, Quentin. "Impressions of Congress." *North Dakota Quarterly* 27 (Spring 1959): 29-32.

**BURDICK, Theodore Weld,** a Representative from Iowa; born in Evansburg, Crawford County, Pa., October 7, 1836; attended the common schools; moved with his parents to Decorah, Iowa, in 1853 and engaged in banking; deputy treasurer and recorder of Winneshiek County 1854-1857; treasurer and recorder from 1858 to 1862, when he resigned to recruit a company for the Union Army; was commissioned as captain and assigned to the Sixth Regiment, Iowa Volunteer Cavalry, in which he served for three years in the Department of the Northwest; after the regiment was mustered out in 1865 he returned to Decorah and became cashier of the First National Bank; elected as a Republican to the Forty-fifth Congress (March 4, 1877-March 3, 1879); declined to be a candidate for renomination in 1878 to the Forty-sixth Congress; resumed banking at Decorah, Iowa, and Sault Ste. Marie, Mich.; member of the State senate in 1886 and 1887; died in Decorah, Iowa, July 16, 1898; interment in Phelps Cemetery.

**BURDICK, Usher Lloyd** (father of Quentin Northrop Burdick and father-in-law of Robert W. Levering), a Representative from North Dakota; born in Owatonna, Steele County, Minn., February 21, 1879; moved with his parents to Dakota Territory in 1882; raised among the Sioux Indians; was graduated from the State normal school at Mayville, N.Dak., in 1900; deputy superintendent of schools of Benson County, N.Dak., 1900-1902; was graduated from the law department of the University of Minnesota at Minneapolis in 1904, teaching school in a business college while attending the university; was admitted to the bar in 1904 and commenced practice in Munich, N.Dak.; member, North Dakota State house of representatives, 1907-1911, serving as speaker in 1909; moved to Williston, N.Dak., in 1910 and continued the practice of law; Lieutenant Governor of North Dakota, 1911-1913; State's attorney of Williams County, 1913-1915; assistant United States district attorney for North Dakota, 1929-1932; unsuccessful candidate in 1932 for the Republican nomination to the Seventy-third Congress; also engaged in livestock breeding and farming; author; elected as a Republican to the Seventy-fourth and to the four succeeding Congresses (January 3, 1935-January 3, 1945); was not a candidate in 1944 for renomination to the House of Representatives, but was an unsuccessful candidate for nomination to the United States Senate; unsuccessful Independent candidate for election in 1944 to the Seventy-ninth Congress; elected as a Republican to the Eighty-first and to the four succeeding Congresses (January 3, 1949-January 3, 1959); was not a candidate for renomination in 1958 to the Eighty-sixth Congress; died in Washington, D.C., August 19, 1960; interment on his ranch at Williston, N.Dak.

Bibliography: *DAB*.

**BURGENER, Clair Walter,** a Representative from California; born in Vernal, Uintah County, Utah, December 5, 1921; attended the public schools of Salt Lake City, Utah; A.B., California State University, San Diego, 1950; served in the United States Army Air Corps, 1943-1946; attained the rank of second lieutenant; awarded Air Medal, 1945; recalled for duty with the United States Air Force during the Korean Conflict, 1951; president, Clair W. Burgener Co., realtors, San Diego, Calif.; elected councilman, city of San Diego, 1953-1957; vice mayor of San Diego, 1955-1956; member, California State assembly, 1962-1966; State senator, 1967-1972; president, California Association for Retarded Children, 1959-1961; vice president, National Association for Retarded Children, 1961-1962; vice chairman, President's Committee on Mental Retardation, 1970-1973; delegate to the Republican National Conventions of 1960 and 1964; elected as a Republican to the Ninety-third and to the four succeeding Congresses (January 3, 1973-January 3, 1983); was not a candidate for reelection in 1982 to the Ninety-eighth Congress; member, board of directors, Board for International Broadcasting, 1983-1988; chairman, Board of Regents, University of California, 1995-1996; is a resident of Rancho Santa Fe, Calif.

**BURGES, Dempsey,** a Representative from North Carolina; born in Shiloh, Camden County, N.C., in 1751; member of the Provincial Congress in 1775 and 1776; took an active part in the Revolutionary War, serving first as major of the Pasquotank Minutemen and later as lieutenant colonel of Gregory's Continental Regiment; elected as a Republican to the Fourth and Fifth Congresses (March 4, 1795-March 3, 1799); died in Camden County, N.C., January 13, 1800; interment in Shiloh Baptist Churchyard.

**BURGES, Tristam** (great-great-uncle of Theodore Francis Green), a Representative from Rhode Island; born in Rochester, Mass., February 26, 1770; attended the common schools; studied medicine at a school in Wrentham; upon the death of his father he abandoned the study of medicine; was graduated from Rhode Island College (now Brown University), Providence, R.I., in 1796; studied law; was admitted to the bar in 1799 and commenced practice in Providence, R.I.; member of the State house of representatives in 1811 and was prominent as a member of the Federal Party; appointed chief justice of the supreme court of Rhode Island in May 1815; unsuccessful candidate for election to the same in 1816; professor of oratory in Brown University; elected to the Ninteenth through Twenty-first Congresses and elected as an Anti-Jacksonian to the Twenty-second and Twenty-third Congresses (March 4, 1825-March 3, 1835); chairman, Committee on Revolutionary Pensions (Nineteenth Congress), Committee on Military Pensions (Nineteenth and Twentieth Congresses), Committee on Revolutionary Claims (Twenty-first Congress), Committee on Invalid Pensions (Twenty-second and Twenty-third Congresses); unsuccessful candidate for reelection; unsuccessful Whig candidate for Governor in 1836; resumed the practice of law; died on his estate, "Watchemoket Farm" (now a part of East Providence, R.I.), October 13, 1853; interment in North Burial Ground, Providence, R.I.

**BURGESS, George Farmer,** a Representative from Texas; born in Wharton, Wharton County, Tex., September 21, 1861; attended the common schools; moved with his mother to Fayette County in 1880 and engaged in agricultural pursuits near Flatonia; was later employed as a clerk in a country store; studied law; was admitted to the bar in 1882 and commenced practice in La Grange, Tex.; moved to Gonzales in 1884; prosecuting attorney of Gonzales County from 1886 to 1889, when he resigned; elected as a Democrat to the Fifty-seventh and to the seven succeeding Congresses (March 4, 1901-March 3, 1917); unsuccessful candidate for the Democratic nomination of United States Senator in 1916; resumed the practice of law at Gonzales, Tex., where he died December 31, 1919; interment in the Masonic Cemetery.

**BURGIN, William Olin,** a Representative from North Carolina; born on a farm near Marion, McDowell County, N.C., July 28, 1877; moved with his parents to Rutherfordton, N.C., where he attended the public schools and Rutherfordton Military Institute; also attended the Law School of the University of North Carolina at Chapel Hill; engaged as a clerk in a general store in Rutherfordton in 1893 and later as a traveling salesman and merchant; moved to Thomasville and engaged in the mercantile business; was admitted to the bar; mayor of Thomasville, N.C., 1906-1910; moved to Lexington, N.C., and continued the practice of law; president and attorney of the Industrial Bank of Lexington; director in a number of business enterprises in Lexington; served in the State house of representatives in 1931; member of the State senate in 1933; elected as a Democrat to the Seventy-sixth and to the three succeeding Congresses and served from January 3, 1939, until his death in Washington, D.C., on April 11, 1946; interment in Lexington Cemetery, Lexington, N.C.

**BURK, Henry,** a Representative from Pennsylvania; born in Wurttemberg, Germany, September 26, 1850; immigrated to the United States in 1854 with his parents, who settled in Philadelphia, Pa.; attended the public schools about three years; became a repairer of shoemaking machinery and subsequently engaged in supplying this machinery to the trade; engaged in the manufacture of leather and in 1887 invented the alum and sumac process, which revolutionized the industry; president of the Manufacturers' National Association in 1895; elected as a Republican to the Fifty-seventh and Fifty-eighth Congresses and served from March 4, 1901, until his death in Philadelphia, Pa., December 5, 1903; interment in Holy Sepulchre Cemetery.

**BURKE, Aedanus,** a Representative from South Carolina; born in Galway, Ireland, June 16, 1743; attended the theological college at St. Omer, France; visited the West Indies; immigrated to the American Colonies and settled in Charles Town (now Charleston),

S.C.; served in the militia forces of South Carolina during the Revolutionary War; appointed a judge of the State circuit court in 1778 and served until the enemy overran the State; member of the South Carolina house of representatives 1779-1788; again served in the Revolutionary Army 1780-1782; when the courts were reestablished resumed his seat on the bench, and in 1785 was appointed one of three commissioners to prepare a digest of the State laws; member of the convention in 1788 called to consider ratification of the Constitution of the United States, which he opposed; elected to the First Congress (March 4, 1789-March 3, 1791); declined to be a candidate for reelection in 1790 to the Second Congress, the legislature having passed a law prohibiting a State judge from leaving the State; elected a chancellor of the courts of equity in 1799 and served until his death in Charleston, S.C., March 30, 1802; interment in the cemetery of the Chapel of Ease of St. Bartholomew's Parish, near Jacksonboro, Colleton County, S.C.

**Bibliography:** *DAB*; Meleney, John C. *The Public Life of Aedanus Burke: Revolutionary Republican in Post-Revolutionary South Carolina.* Columbia: University of South Carolina Press, 1989.

**BURKE, Charles Henry,** a Representative from South Dakota; born on a farm near Batavia, Genesee County, N.Y., April 1, 1861; attended the public schools of Batavia, N.Y.; moved to the Territory of Dakota in 1882 and settled on a homestead in Beadle County; moved to Hughes County in 1883; studied law; was admitted to the bar in 1886; engaged in the real estate investment business in Pierre, S.Dak.; member of the South Dakota State house of representatives in 1895 and 1897; elected as a Republican to the Fifty-sixth and to the three succeeding Congresses (March 4, 1899-March 3, 1907); unsuccessful candidate for renomination in 1906 to the Sixtieth Congress; elected to the Sixty-first and to the two succeeding Congresses (March 4, 1909-March 3, 1915); chairman, Committee on Indian Affairs (Sixty-first Congress); minority whip (Sixty-third Congress); was not a candidate in 1914 for renomination to the House of Representatives, but was an unsuccessful candidate for election to the United States Senate; resumed the investment business; appointed Commissioner of Indian Affairs on April 1, 1921, and served until his resignation on June 30, 1929; engaged in the real estate and loan business in Pierre S. Dak., and also worked in the interest of Indians in Washington, D.C.; died in Washington, D.C., April 7, 1944; interment in Riverside Cemetery, Pierre, S.Dak.

**Bibliography:** Flynn, Sean J. "Western Assimilationist: Charles H. Burke and the Burke Act." *Midwest Review* 11 (1989): 1-15.

**BURKE, Edmund,** a Representative from New Hampshire; born in Westminster, Vt., January 23, 1809; attended the public schools; studied law; was admitted to the bar in 1826 and commenced practice in Colebrook, N.H.; moved to Claremont, N.H., in 1833 and assumed editorial management of the New Hampshire Argus; moved to Newport in 1834 and united the Argus with the Spectator of that place, continuing as editor for several years; commissioned as adjutant in the State militia in 1837 and as brigade inspector in 1838; elected as a Democrat to the Twenty-sixth and to the two succeeding Congresses (March 4, 1839-March 3, 1845); was not a candidate for renomination in 1844 to the Twenty-ninth Congress; appointed Commissioner of Patents by President James K. Polk and served from May 5, 1846, to September 3, 1850; resumed the practice of law in Newport, N.H.; delegate to the Democratic National Conventions of 1844 and 1852; delegate to the Democratic State convention in 1867, and served as presiding officer; member of the State board of agriculture in 1871; died in Newport, Sullivan County, N.H., January 25, 1882; interment in Maple Grove Cemetery.

**BURKE, Edward Raymond,** a Representative and a Senator from Nebraska; born at Running Water, Bon Homme County, S.Dak., November 28, 1880; moved with his parents to Sparta, Monroe County, Wis., in 1880; educated in the public schools of Sparta, Wis.; moved to Beloit, Rock County, in 1902; was graduated from Beloit (Wis.) College in 1906; taught school in Chadron, Nebr., 1906-1908; was graduated from the law department of Harvard University in 1911; was admitted to the bar the same year and commenced practice in Omaha, Nebr.; during the First World War enlisted and was commissioned a second lieutenant in the Air Service 1917-1919; president of the board of education of Omaha 1927-1930; elected as a Democrat to the Seventy-third Congress (March 4, 1933-January 3, 1935); did not seek renomination in 1934, having become a candidate for United States Senator; elected to the United States Senate in 1934 and served from January 3, 1935, to January 3, 1941; unsuccessful candidate for renomination in 1940; chairman, Committee on Claims (Seventy-sixth Congress); resumed the practice of law in Omaha, Nebr.; moved to Washington, D.C., in 1942 and served as president of Southern Coal Producers Association until 1947; Washington representative and general counsel for Hawaiian Statehood Commission until 1950; retired and resided in Kensington, Md., until his death there on November 4, 1968; interment in Fort Lincoln Mausoleum.

**BURKE, Frank Welsh,** a Representative from Kentucky; born in Louisville, Jefferson County, Ky., June 1, 1920; educated in the parochial schools of Louisville, and St. Xavier High School; attended the University of Southern California; Ph.B., Xavier University, Cincinnati, Ohio, 1942; J.D., University of Louisville, 1948; was admitted to the bar in 1948 and commenced the practice of law in Louisville, Ky.; served in the United States Army, 1942-1946; assistant city attorney of Louisville, 1950-1951; director of public safety of Louisville, 1952; executive assistant to Mayor Charles R.P. Farnsley of Louisville, 1952-1953; member of the Kentucky house of representatives, 1957-1958; elected as a Democrat to the Eighty-sixth and Eighty-seventh Congresses (January 3, 1959-January 3, 1963); unsuccessful candidate in 1962 for reelection to the Eighty-eighth Congress; served as mayor of Louisville, 1969-1973; is a resident of Louisville, Ky.

**BURKE, J. Herbert,** a Representative from Florida; born in Chicago, Ill., January 14, 1913; attended the public schools of Chicago; A.A., Central Y.M.C.A. College, Chicago, 1936; LL.B., Northwestern University, 1940; J.D., Kent College of Law, Chicago, 1940; served in the United States Army in the European Theater 1942-1945, was awarded the Purple Heart, Bronze Star, the European Theater Medal, and the American Theater Ribbon, and was discharged with the rank of captain; admitted to the bar in 1940 and practiced law in Chicago, 1940-1949; moved to Florida in 1949 and practiced law in Hollywood until 1968; member, Broward County (Fla.) Commission, 1952-1967, commission chairman, 1956-1958; Republican State committeeman, 1954-1958; delegate to Republican National Convention, 1968; member, Republican Platform Committee, 1968; appointed by President Dwight D. Eisenhower to Southeastern Advisory Board of Small Business in 1956; appointed by the National Republican Party as adviser to the National Rivers and Harbors Congress in 1957; elected as a Republican to the Ninetieth and to the five succeeding Congresses; (January 3, 1967-January 3, 1979); unsuccessful candidate for reelection in 1978 to the Ninety-sixth Congress; was a resident of Falls Church, Va., and Fern Park, Fla., until his death in Fern Park on June 16, 1993; interment in Arlington National Cemetery, Va.

**BURKE, James Anthony,** a Representative from Massachusetts; born in Boston, Mass., March 30, 1910; educated in the Boston public schools and Lincoln Preparatory School; attended Suffolk University, Boston; registrar of vital statistics for the city of Boston; during the Second World War was special agent in the Counterintelligence, attached to the Seventy-seventh Infantry Division in the South Pacific; member of the Massachusetts general court for ten years; member of the Massachusetts house of representatives for four years, serving as assistant majority leader; vice chairman of the Massachusetts Democratic State committee for four years; elected as a Democrat to the Eighty-sixth and to the nine succeeding Congresses (January 3, 1959-January 3, 1979); was not a candidate for reelection in 1978 to the Ninety-sixth Congress; was a resident of Milton, Mass. until his death in Boston, Mass., on October 13, 1983; interment at Milton Cemetery, Milton, Mass.

**BURKE, James Francis,** a Representative from Pennsylvania; born in Petroleum Center, Venango County, Pa., October 21, 1867; attended the public schools, and was graduated from the law department of the University of Michigan at Ann Arbor in 1892; was admitted to the bar the same year and commenced practice in Pittsburgh, Pa.; secretary of the Republican National Committee in 1892, resigning during the same year to devote his entire time to his duties as president of the American Republican College League; appointed by President Benjamin Harrison to codify the navigation laws of the United States; officer of, or a delegate to, the Republican National Conventions from 1892 to 1924, with the exception of the year 1912; appointed a delegate to the Parliamentary Peace Conference at Brussels in 1905; elected as a Republican to the Fifty-ninth and to the four succeeding Congresses (March 4, 1905-March 3, 1915); chairman, Committee on Education (Sixty-first Congress); was not a candidate for renomination in 1914 to the Sixty-fourth Congress; United States Government director of War Savings during the First World War; resumed the practice of law; elected general counsel of the Republican National Committee in December 1927 and served until his death; parliamentarian of the Republican National Convention at Kansas City, Mo., in 1928; died in Washington, D.C., August 8, 1932; interment in Calvary Cemetery, Pittsburgh, Pa.

**BURKE, John Harley,** a Representative from California; born in Excelsior, Richland County, Wis., June 2, 1894; moved to Milaca, Minn., with his parents in 1897, to San Pedro, Calif., in 1900, and to Long Beach, Calif., in 1909; attended the public schools; attended the University of Santa Clara and the law department of the University of Southern California at Los Angeles; was admitted to the bar in 1917 and commenced practice in Long Beach, Calif.; during the First World War served as a private, first class, in the Twelfth Training Battery, Field Artillery, Camp Taylor, Ky.; in 1921 engaged in the oil business as an independent producer; elected as a Democrat to the Seventy-third Congress (March 4, 1933-January 3, 1935); was not a candidate for renomination in 1934 to the Seventy-fourth Congress; engaged in the real estate business in Long Beach, Calif., until his death there on May 14, 1951; interment in Calvary Cemetery, Los Angeles, Calif.

**BURKE, Michael Edmund,** a Representative from Wisconsin; born at Beaver Dam, Dodge County, Wis., October 15, 1863; attended the public schools and was graduated from the Wayland Academy at Beaver Dam in 1884; studied law at the University of Wisconsin at Madison in 1886 and 1887; was admitted to the bar in 1888 and commenced practice at Beaver Dam; town clerk 1887-1889; member of the State assembly 1891-1893; served in the State senate 1895-1899; city attorney of Beaver Dam 1893-1908; delegate to the Democratic National Convention in 1904; elected mayor of Beaver Dam and served from 1908 to 1910; elected as a Democrat to the Sixty-second, Sixty-third, and Sixty-fourth Congresses (March 4, 1911-March 3, 1917); unsuccessful candidate for reelection in 1916; died at Beaver Dam, Wis., December 12, 1918; interment in St. Patrick's Cemetery.

**BURKE, Raymond Hugh,** a Representative from Ohio; born in Nicholsville, Clermont County, Ohio, November 4, 1881; attended Jackson School; worked on a farm and in the village while studying

to teach in rural schools; taught at Pendleton School near Point Pleasant in 1899 and 1900; student at Oberlin Academy and College 1900-1905; was graduated from the University of Chicago in 1906; taught in Miami University at Oxford, Ohio, 1906-1915; personnel and employment manager 1918-1923; secretary-treasurer of an automobile agency 1923-1926; special representative for an insurance company at Hamilton, Ohio, 1926-1954; mayor of Hamilton 1928-1940 and councilman 1928-1942; member of the State senate 1942-1946; elected as a Republican to the Eightieth Congress (January 3, 1947-January 3, 1949); unsuccessful candidate for reelection in 1948 to the Eighty-first Congress; lecturer in the finance department of Miami University in 1949 and 1950; died in Hamilton, Ohio, August 18, 1954; interment in Greenwood Cemetery.

**BURKE, Robert Emmet,** a Representative from Texas; born near Dadeville, Tallapoosa County, Ala., August 1, 1847; attended the public schools of his native city; volunteered as a private in Company D, Tenth Georgia Cavalry, Confederate Army, at the age of sixteen and served throughout the Civil War; moved to Jefferson, Tex., in 1866; studied law; was admitted to the bar in November 1870 and commenced practice in Dallas, Tex., in 1871; judge of Dallas County from 1878 until 1888; judge of the fourteenth judicial district of Texas, 1888-1896; elected as a Democrat to the Fifty-fifth and to the two succeeding Congresses and served from March 4, 1897, until his death in Dallas, Tex., June 5, 1901; interment in Greenwood Cemetery.

**BURKE, Thomas,** a Delegate from North Carolina; born in Galway, Ireland, about 1747; studied medicine; immigrated to America in 1764, settled in Accomac County, Va., and practiced; studied law; was admitted to the bar and commenced practice in Norfolk, Va.; moved to Hillsboro, N.C., in 1771; delegate to the State convention at New Bern and Hillsboro in 1775 and at Halifax in 1776; member of the State house of commons in 1777; Member of the Continental Congress from 1777 to 1781; elected Governor of North Carolina in June 1781; captured in Hillsboro, N.C., September 12, 1781, by Loyalists under the command of Colonel David Fanning; held as a hostage in Wilmington, N.C. and on Sullivan's Island, Charleston harbor, until January 16, 1782, when he succeeded in escaping; resumed his duties as Governor on February 1, 1782 and served until April 22, 1782; died at "Tyaquin," near Hillsboro, Orange County, N.C., December 2, 1783; interment in Mars Hill Churchyard, near Hillsboro, N.C.

**Bibliography:** *DAB*; Sanders, Jennings B. "Thomas Burke in the Continental Congress." *North Carolina Historical Review* 9 (January 1932): 22-37; Watterson, John S. "Thomas Burke, Paradoxical Patriot." *Historian* 41 (August 1979): 664-681.

**BURKE, Thomas A.,** a Senator from Ohio; born in Cleveland, Cuyahoga County, Ohio, October 30, 1898; attended parochial schools; was graduated from Holy Cross College, Worcester, Mass., in 1920, and Western Reserve University Law School, Cleveland, Ohio, in 1923; during the First World War served in the United States Army; was admitted to the bar in 1923 and commenced practice in Cleveland, Ohio; assistant prosecutor of Cuyahoga County, 1930-1936; special counsel to the Ohio attorney general in 1937; director of law for the city of Cleveland, 1942-1945; mayor of Cleveland from 1945 until 1953; president of the National Conference of Mayors in 1953; appointed as a Democrat to the United States Senate on October 12, 1953, to fill the vacancy caused by the death of Robert A. Taft, and served from November 10, 1953 to December 2, 1954; unsuccessful candidate for election to the vacancy in 1954; resumed the practice of law; died in Cleveland, Ohio, December 5, 1971; interment in Calvary Cemetery.

**BURKE, Thomas Henry,** a Representative from Ohio; born in Toledo, Lucas County, Ohio, May 6, 1904; attended St. Patrick's grade school and St. John's College in Toledo, Ohio; served in the

United States Navy as a pharmacist's mate, 1923-1927, and in the Naval Fleet Reserve, 1927-1939; worked for the Dana Corporation, Toledo, Ohio, 1928-1937; official of United Automobile Workers' Union from 1938 until 1948; member of the Ohio State house of representatives in 1941 and 1942; member of the Toledo city council, 1944-1948; vice mayor of Toledo in 1948; elected as a Democrat to the Eighty-first Congress (January 3, 1949-January 3, 1951); unsuccessful candidate for reelection in 1950 to the Eighty-second Congress; labor and manpower adviser in the National Production Authority in 1951; unsuccessful candidate for election in 1952 to the Eighty-third Congress; moved to Alexandria, Va.; legislative representative, United Automobile Workers' Union; died in Arlington, Va., September 12, 1959; interment in Arlington National Cemetery.

**BURKE, William Joseph,** a Representative from Pennsylvania; born near London, England, September 25, 1862; immigrated to the United States in 1866 with his parents, who settled in Reynoldsville, Jefferson County, Pa.; attended the public schools; employed in the coal mines at the age of twelve; entered the railroad service in 1878 with residence in Pittsburgh, Pa.; was a member of the Allegheny Common Council for four years, and from 1906 to 1910 was a member of the greater city council of Pittsburgh; became extensively interested in the production of oil near Callery, Butler County, in 1904; identified with organized labor as chairman of the general committee of adjustment, Order of Railroad Conductors, of the Baltimore & Ohio Railroad system; elected a member of the Pennsylvania senate in 1914 and served until January 1, 1918, when he resigned to become a member of the Pittsburgh City Council, serving until January 1919, when he resigned, having been elected to Congress; elected as a Republican to the Sixty-sixth and Sixty-seventh Congresses (March 4, 1919-March 3, 1923); did not seek renomination, but was an unsuccessful candidate for election as United States Senator in 1922; resumed activities with organized labor and served as chairman of the general committee of the Brotherhood of Railroad Conductors; also engaged in agricultural pursuits and in the production of oil; died at his summer home in Callery Junction, Butler County, near Pittsburgh November 7, 1925; interment in Calvary Cemetery, Pittsburgh, Pa.

**BURKE, Yvonne Brathwaite,** a Representative from California; born in Los Angeles, Calif., October 5, 1932; attended the public schools in Los Angeles; B.A., University of California, Los Angeles, 1953; J.D., University of Southern California School of Law, Los Angeles, 1956; admitted to the California bar in 1956 and commenced practice in Los Angeles; served as deputy corporation commissioner, hearing officer for Los Angeles Police Commission, and attorney on the staff of the McCone Commission; elected to California State legislature, 1967-1972; delegate to the Democratic National Convention of 1972; elected as a Democrat to the Ninety-third and to the two succeeding Congresses (January 3, 1973-January 3, 1979); was not a candidate for reelection in 1978 to the Ninety-sixth Congress, but was an unsuccessful Democratic candidate for State Attorney General of California; appointed by Governor Edmund G. Brown, Jr. to the Los Angeles County Board of Supervisors, and served from June 1979 until December 1980; resumed the practice of law in Los Angeles; member of the Los Angeles County Board of Supervisors; is a resident of Los Angeles, Calif.

Bibliography: Gray, Pamela Lee. "Yvonne Brathwaite Burke: The Congressional Career of California's First Black Congresswoman, 1972-1978." Ph.D. dissertation, University of Southern California, 1987.

**BURKETT, Elmer Jacob,** a Representative and a Senator from Nebraska; born on a farm near Glenwood, Mills County, Iowa, December 1, 1867; attended the public schools; was graduated from Tabor (Iowa) College in 1890 and from the law department of the University of Nebraska at Lincoln in 1893; principal of the Leigh, Nebr., public schools 1890-1892; was admitted to the bar in 1893 and commenced practice in Lincoln, Nebr.; trustee of Tabor College 1895-1905; member, State house of representatives 1896-1898; elected as a Republican to the Fifty-sixth and to the two succeeding Congresses (March 4, 1899-March 3, 1905); reelected in 1904 to the Fifty-ninth Congress, but resigned, effective March 4, 1905, to become Senator; elected as a Republican to the United States Senate and served from March 4, 1905, to March 3, 1911; unsuccessful candidate for renomination in 1910; chairman, Committee on Indian Depredations (Fifty-ninth Congress); Committee on Pacific Railroads (Fifty-ninth through Sixty-first Congresses); resumed the practice of law in Lincoln, Nebr.; declined the nomination for Governor of Nebraska in 1912; unsuccessful candidate in 1912 for the Republican vice presidential nomination; died in Lincoln, Nebr., May 23, 1935; interment in the Wyuka Cemetery.

**BURKHALTER, Everett Glen,** a Representative from California; born in Heber Springs, Cleburne County, Ark., Janruay 19, 1897; attended the public schools in Arkansas, Indiana, Colorado, and California; electrical and illuminating engineer in the motion picture industry; enlisted in the United States Navy, 1918, honorable discharge 1919, active reserve until 1921; member, California State assembly, 1942-1952; delegate to the electoral college, 1946; appointed to the California State legislative commission, American Legion; elected to the Los Angeles City Council, and served three terms, 1952-1962; elected as a Democrat to the Eighty-eighth Congress (January 3, 1963-January 3, 1965); was not a candidate for renomination in 1964 to the Eighty-ninth Congress; retired and resided in North Hollywood, Calif.; died in Duarte, Calif., May 24, 1975; interment in Forest Lawn Memorial Park, Hollywood Hills, Los Angeles, Calif.

**BURLEIGH, Edwin Chick,** a Representative and a Senator from Maine; born in Linneus, Aroostook County, Maine, November 27, 1843; attended the common schools and was graduated from the Houlton (Maine) Academy; taught school; clerk in the adjutant general's office; surveyor and farmer; clerk in the State land office at Bangor, 1870-1876; moved to Augusta in 1876; State land agent, 1876-1878; assistant clerk in the Maine State house of representatives in 1878; clerk in the office of the State treasurer from 1880 until 1884; State treasurer, 1884-1888; became principal owner of the Kennebec Journal in 1887; elected Governor of Maine in 1888, reelected in 1890, and served from January 2, 1889 to January 4, 1893; elected as a Republican to the Fifty-fifth Congress in 1897 to fill the vacancy caused by the death of Seth L. Milliken; reelected to the Fifty-sixth and to the five succeeding Congresses and served from June 21, 1897, to March 3, 1911; unsuccessful candidate for reelection in 1910 to the Sixty-second Congress; resumed newspaper publishing in Augusta, Maine, and the management of timberlands; elected as a Republican to the United States Senate and served from March 4, 1913, until his death in Augusta, Maine, on June 16, 1916; interment in Forest Grove Cemetery.

**BURLEIGH, Henry Gordon,** a Representative from New York; born in Canaan, Grafton County, N.H., June 2, 1832; attended the common schools; moved to New York in 1846 with his parents, who settled in Ticonderoga, Essex County; engaged in the mining of iron ore and in the lumber, coal, and transportation business; supervisor of the town of Ticonderoga in 1864 and 1865; moved to Whitehall, Washington County, N.Y., in 1867; member of the State assembly in 1876; delegate to the Republican National Conventions of 1880, 1884, 1888, 1892, and 1896; elected as a Republican to the Forty-eighth and Forty-ninth Congresses (March 4, 1883-March 3, 1887); unsuccessful candidate for reelection in 1886 to the Fiftieth Congress; died in Whitehall, N.Y., August 10, 1900; interment in Mount Hope Cemetery, Ticonderoga, N.Y.

**BURLEIGH, John Holmes** (son of William Burleigh), a Representative from Maine; born in South Berwick, York County, Maine, October 9, 1822; attended the local academy; became a sailor when sixteen years of age and commanded a ship on foreign voyages from 1846 until 1853 when he engaged in woolen manufacturing at South Berwick, Maine; also engaged in banking; member of the State house of representatives in 1862, 1864, 1866, and again in 1872; delegate to the Republican National Convention of 1864; elected as a Republican to the Forty-third and Forty-fourth Congresses (March 4, 1873-March 3, 1877); was an unsuccessful candidate for renomination in 1876 to the Forty-fifth Congress; resumed his former manufacturing pursuits; died in South Berwick, Maine, December 5, 1877; interment in the Portland Street Cemetery.

**BURLEIGH, Walter Atwood,** a Delegate from the Territory of Dakota; born in Waterville, Kennebec County, Maine, October 25, 1820; attended the public schools; served as a private in the Aroostook War in 1839; studied medicine in Burlington, Vt., and New York City, and commenced practice in Richmond, Maine; moved to Kittanning, Pa., in 1852; continued the practice of medicine and studied law; Indian agent at Greenwood, Dak., 1861-1865; elected as a Republican to the Thirty-ninth and Fortieth Congresses (March 4, 1865-March 3, 1869); unsuccessful candidate for reelection in 1868 to the Forty-first Congress; member of the Dakota Territorial council in 1877; engaged as a contractor and in agricultural pursuits; moved to Miles City, Mont., in 1879 and practiced law; member of the special session of the Montana Territorial council in 1887; delegate to the State convention that framed the constitution of Montana in 1889; member of the first State house of representatives; prosecuting attorney of Custer County in 1889 and 1890; returned to South Dakota in 1893; served in the State senate in 1893; resumed the practice of law; died in Yankton, Yankton County, S.Dak., March 7, 1896; interment in Yankton Cemetery.

**Bibliography:** Wilson, Wesley C. "Doctor Walter A. Burleigh: Dakota Territorial Delegate to 39th and 40th Congress: Politician, Extraordinary." *North Dakota History* 33 (Spring 1966): 93-103.

**BURLEIGH, William** (father of John Holmes Burleigh), a Representative from Maine; born in Northwood, Rockingham County, N.H., October 24, 1785; moved with his parents to Gilmanton, N.H., in 1788; attended the common schools and taught for several years; studied law; was admitted to the bar in 1815 and commenced practice in South Berwick, Maine; elected to the Eighteenth, Nineteenth, and Twentieth Congresses and served from March 4, 1823, until his death in South Berwick, York County, Maine, July 2, 1827; chairman, Committee on Expenditures in the Department of the Treasury (Nineteenth Congress); interment in Portland Street Cemetery.

**BURLESON, Albert Sidney,** a Representative from Texas; born in San Marcos, Hays County, Tex., June 7, 1863; attended the public schools and Coronal Institute, San Marcos, Tex., and the Agricultural and Mechanical College, College Station, Tex.; was graduated from Baylor University, Waco, Tex., in 1881 and from the law department of the University of Texas at Austin in 1884; was admitted to the bar in 1884 and commenced practice in Austin, Travis County, Tex., in 1885; assistant city attorney of Austin, 1885-1890; served as district attorney of the twenty-sixth judicial district, 1891-1898; elected as a Democrat to the Fifty-sixth and to the seven succeeding Congresses, and served from March 4, 1899 until March 6, 1913, when he resigned to accept a Cabinet portfolio; Postmaster General in the Cabinet of President Woodrow Wilson from March 7, 1913 to March 4, 1921, when he retired from public life; chairman of the United States Telegraph and Telephone Administration in 1918; chairman of the United States Commission to the International Wire Communication Conference in 1920; returned to Austin, Tex., and engaged in banking; also interested in

agricultural pursuits and the raising of livestock; died in Austin, Tex., November 24, 1937; interment in Oakwood Cemetery.

**Bibliography:** *DAB*; Anderson, Adrian N. "Albert Sidney Burleson: A Southern Politician in the Progressive Era." Ph.D. dissertation, Texas Tech University, 1967; Anderson, Adrian N. "President Wilson's Politician: Albert Sidney Burleson of Texas." *Southwestern Historical Quarterly* 77 (January 1974): 339-54.

**BURLESON, Omar Truman,** a Representative from Texas; born in Anson, Jones County, Tex., March 19, 1906; attended the public schools, Abilene Christian College, and Hardin-Simmons University at Abilene, Tex.; was graduated from Cumberland University, Lebanon, Tenn., in 1929; was admitted to the bar the same year and commenced practice in Gorman, Tex.; county attorney of Jones County, Tex., 1931-1934; judge of Jones County, Tex., 1934-1940; special agent of the Federal Bureau of Investigation in 1940 and 1941; secretary to Representative Sam Russell of Texas in 1941 and 1942; general counsel for the Housing Authority, District of Columbia, in 1942; served in the United States Navy from December 1942 to April 1946, with service in the South Pacific Theater; elected as a Democrat to the Eightieth Congress; reelected to the fifteen succeeding Congresses and served from January 3, 1947, until his resignation December 31, 1978; chairman, Committee on House Administration (Eighty-fourth through Ninetieth Congresses), Joint Committee on the Library (Eighty-fourth through Ninetieth Congresses), Joint Committee on Printing (Eighty-fourth Congress); was not a candidate for reelection in 1978 to the Ninety-sixth Congress; was a resident of Abilene, Tex.; died May 14, 1991.

**BURLINGAME, Anson,** a Representative from Massachusetts; born in New Berlin, N.Y., November 14, 1820; moved with his parents to Seneca County, Ohio, in 1823, and to Detroit, Mich., in 1833; attended private schools and the Detroit branch of the University of Michigan; was graduated from the law department of Harvard University in 1846; was admitted to the bar and commenced practice in Boston; served in the Massachusetts senate in 1852; member of the Massachusetts constitutional convention in 1853; elected as a candidate of the American Party to the Thirty-fourth Congress, and as a Republican to the Thirty-fifth and Thirty-sixth Congresses (March 4, 1855-March 3, 1861); unsuccessful candidate for reelection in 1860 to the Thirty-seventh Congress; appointed Minister to Austria on March 22, 1861, but was not accepted by the Austrian Government because of certain opinions he was known to entertain regarding Hungary and Sardinia; Minister to China from June 14, 1861, to November 21, 1867; appointed December 1, 1867, by the Chinese Government its ambassador to negotiate treaties with foreign powers; died in St. Petersburg, Russia, February 23, 1870; interment in Mount Auburn Cemetery, Cambridge, Mass.

**Bibliography:** *DAB*; Anderson, David L. "Anson Burlingame: Reformer and Diplomat." *Civil War History* 25 (December 1979): 293-308; Williams, Frederick Wells. *Anson Burlingame and the First Chinese Mission to Foreign Powers.* New York: Russell and Russell, 1972.

**BURLISON, William Dean,** a Representative from Missouri; born in Wardell, Pemscot County, Mo., March 15, 1933; B.A., Southeast Missouri State University, Cape Girardeau, Mo., 1953, and B.S., 1959; M.Ed. and LL.B., University of Missouri, 1956; admitted to practice before United States Supreme Court, United States Court of Military Appeals, United States District Court, and all Missouri courts; president, Missouri Prosecuting Attorneys Association; assistant attorney general of Missouri, 1960-1962; prosecuting attorney of Cape Girardeau County, 1963-1968; Head General Courts-Martial Trial Counsel, Second Marine Division, United States Marine Corps.; instructor in business law, Southeast Missouri State College; delegate to the Democratic National

Convention of 1964; elected as a Democrat to the Ninety-first and to the five succeeding Congresses (January 3, 1969-January 3, 1981); unsuccessful candidate for reelection in 1980 to the Ninety-seventh Congress; resumed the practice of law; is a resident of Crofton, Md.

**BURNELL, Barker,** a Representative from Massachusetts; born in Nantucket, Mass., January 30, 1798; member of the Massachusetts house of representatives in 1819; member of the Massachusetts Constitutional convention in 1820; served in the Massachusetts senate in 1824 and 1825; delegate to the Whig National Convention in 1840; elected as a Whig to the Twenty-seventh and Twenty-eighth Congresses and served from March 4, 1841, until his death in Washington, D.C., June 15, 1843; interment in Congressional Cemetery; reinterment in Prospect Hill Cemetery, Nantucket, Mass., in 1844.

**BURNES, Daniel Dee,** a Representative from Missouri; born in Ringgold, Platte County, Mo., January 4, 1851; received his early schooling at Weston, Mo.; was graduated from St. Louis University, St. Louis, Mo., in 1873 and from the law department of Harvard University in 1874; went to Germany and studied at Heidelberg University; returned to the United States and settled in St. Joseph, Mo., where he engaged in the practice of law; elected as a Democrat to the Fifty-third Congress (March 4, 1893-March 3, 1895); declined to be a candidate for reelection in 1894; resumed the practice of law; died on his estate, "Ayr Lawn," at St. Joseph, Buchanan County, Mo., November 2, 1899; interment in Mount Mora Cemetery.

**BURNES, James Nelson,** a Representative from Missouri; born in Marion County, Ind., August 22, 1827; moved with his parents to Platte County, Mo., in 1837; attended the common schools; was graduated from the Harvard Law School in 1853; was admitted to the bar and commenced practice in Missouri; attorney of the district of Missouri in 1856; judge of the court of common pleas 1868-1872; engaged in banking and the construction of railroads; served as president of the Missouri Valley Railroad Co.; principal owner and president of the St. Joseph Waterworks Co.; elected as a Democrat to the Forty-eighth, Forty-ninth, and Fiftieth Congresses and served from March 4, 1883, until his death; had been reelected to the Fifty-first Congress, but died in Washington, D.C. on January 23, 1889, before the commencement of the congressional term; interment in Mount Mora Cemetery, St. Joseph, Buchanan County, Mo.

**BURNET, Jacob** (son of William Burnet), a Senator from Ohio; born in Newark, N.J., February 22, 1770; pursued preparatory studies; was graduated from the College of New Jersey (now Princeton University) in 1791; studied law; was admitted to the bar in 1796 and commenced practice in Cincinnati, Ohio; one of three judges appointed to hold court in Cincinnati, Vincennes, and Detroit; member, Territorial councils of Ohio 1799-1802; member, State house of representatives 1814-1816; appointed judge of the Ohio Supreme Court in 1821 and served until his resignation in December 1828; elected to the United States Senate to fill the vacancy caused by the resignation of William H. Harrison and served from December 10, 1828, to March 3, 1831; was not a candidate for renomination in 1831; member of the commission appointed in 1831 by the States of Virginia and Kentucky to settle their controversy over the statute of limitation passed by Kentucky; resumed the practice of law; president of the Cincinnati College and the Medical College of Ohio; president of the Cincinnati branch of the United States Bank; died in Cincinnati, Ohio, on May 10, 1853; interment in Spring Grove Cemetery.

**Bibliography:** *DAB.*

**BURNET, William** (father of Jacob Burnet), a Delegate from New Jersey; born in Newark, N.J., December 2, 1730; was graduated from Princeton College in 1749; studied medicine in New York and commenced practice in Newark; chairman of the committee of public safety in Newark in 1775; superintendent of a military hospital in Newark in 1775; surgeon general of the eastern district of the United States 1776-1783; returned to Newark and engaged in agricultural pursuits; appointed presiding judge of the court of common pleas by the State legislature in 1776; Member of the Continental Congress from December 11, 1780, to April 1, 1781, when he resigned; first judge of Essex County in 1781; president of the State medical society in 1787; died in Newark, N.J., October 7, 1791; interment in the First Presbyterian Churchyard.

**Bibliography:** *DAB.*

**BURNETT, Edward,** a Representative from Massachusetts; born in Boston, Mass., March 16, 1849; attended St. Paul's School; was graduated from St. Mark's School, Southboro, Mass., in 1867 and from Harvard University in 1871; engaged in agricultural pursuits near Southboro, Mass.; elected as a Democrat to the Fiftieth Congress (March 4, 1887-March 3, 1889); unsuccessful candidate for reelection in 1888 to the Fifty-first Congress; general manager of Flosham Farms, Madison, N.J., 1892-1900; became engaged as a farm architect in New York City from 1900 to 1925; died in Milton, Mass., November 5, 1925; interment in St. Mark's Churchyard, Southboro, Mass.

**BURNETT, Henry Cornelius,** a Representative from Kentucky; born in Essex County, Va., October 5, 1825; moved with his parents to Kentucky in early childhood; attended the common schools and an academy at Hopkinsville, Christian County; studied law; was admitted to the bar in 1847 and commenced practice in Cadiz, Ky.; clerk of the Trigg County circuit court, 1851-1853; elected as a Democrat to the Thirty-fourth and to the three succeeding Congresses, and served from March 4, 1855 to December 3, 1861, when he was expelled for support of the Confederacy; colonel of the Eighth Regiment, Kentucky Infantry, in the Confederate Army during the Civil War; president of the Kentucky Southern Conference in Russellville, October 29, 1861, and of the sovereignty convention in Russellville, November 18, which passed an ordinance of secession and organized a State government; Representative from Kentucky to the Provisional Confederate Congress, and served from November 18, 1861 to February 17, 1862; elected as a Senator from Kentucky to the First and Second Confederate Congresses, and served from February 19, 1862 to February 18, 1865; resumed the practice of law; died in Hopkinsville, Ky., October 1, 1866; interment in East End Cemetery, Cadiz, Trigg County, Ky.

**Bibliography:** Craig, Berry F. "Henry Cornelius Burnett: Champion of Southern Rights." *Register of the Kentucky Historical Society* 77 (Autumn 1979): 266-74.

**BURNETT, John Lawson,** a Representative from Alabama; born in Cedar Bluff, Cherokee County, Ala., January 20, 1854; attended the common schools of the county, Wesleyan Institute, Cave Spring, Ga., and the local high school at Gaylesville, Ala.; studied law and was graduated from Vanderbilt University, Nashville, Tenn.; was admitted to the bar in Cherokee County, Ala., in 1876 and commenced practice in Gadsden; served in the Alabama State house of representatives in 1884; member of the State senate in 1886; moved to Gadsden, Etowah County, Ala. in 1893; member of the United States Immigration Commission, 1907-1910; elected as a Democrat to the Fifty-sixth and to the ten succeeding Congresses, and served from March 4, 1899 until his death in Gadsden, Ala., May 13, 1919; chairman, Committee on Immigration and Naturalization (Sixty-second through Sixty-fifth Congresses); interment in Forest Cemetery.

**Bibliography:** Johnson, Timothy D. "Anti-War Sentiment and Representative John Lawson Burnett of Alabama." *Alabama Review* 39 (July 1986): 187-195.

**BURNEY, William Evans,** a Representative from Colorado; born in Hubbard, Hill County, Tex., September 11, 1893; attended the public schools in Texas and the University of New Mexico at Albuquerque; during the First World War served in the United States Navy; moved to Pueblo, Colo., in 1924 and engaged in the life insurance business until 1942; member of the Pueblo board of education 1937-1943; member of the United States Army Reserve Corps 1924-1942, serving in all grades up to major; elected as a Democrat to the Seventy-sixth Congress to fill the vacancy caused by the death of John A. Martin and served from November 5, 1940, to January 3, 1941; was not a candidate for election to the full term in the Seventy-seventh Congress; was called to active duty in the Army as a major in January 1942 and was promoted to the rank of lieutenant colonel in October 1942; returned to the United States from India and took command of Camp Ross in May 1945; left the service in December 1945 with the rank of colonel; resumed the life insurance business until his retirement; died in Denver, Colo., January 29, 1969; interment in Fairmount Cemetery.

**BURNHAM, Alfred Avery,** a Representative from Connecticut; born in Windham, Windham County, Conn., on March 8, 1819; completed a preparatory course and attended college one year; studied law; was admitted to the bar in 1843 and commenced practice in Windham; member of the State house of representatives in 1844, 1845, 1850, and 1858, serving as speaker in 1858; clerk of the State senate in 1847; Lieutenant Governor in 1857; elected as a Republican to the Thirty-sixth and Thirty-seventh Congresses (March 4, 1859-March 3, 1863); was not a candidate for renomination in 1862; again a member of the State house of representatives in 1870 and served as speaker; died in Windham, Conn., April 11, 1879; interment in Windham Cemetery, Windham Center, Conn.

**BURNHAM, George,** a Representative from California; born in London, England, December 28, 1868; attended the public schools; immigrated in 1881 to the United States with his parents, who settled in Spring Valley, Minn.; employed as a clerk 1884-1886; moved to Jackson, Minn., in 1887 and engaged in the retail shoe business until 1901, when he moved to Spokane, Wash., and engaged in the real-estate business and in ranching; moved to San Diego, Calif., in 1903 and continued in the real estate business until 1917 when he took up banking; one of the organizers of the Panama-California Exposition in 1909, serving as vice president from 1909 to 1916; member of the Honorary Commercial Commission to China in 1910; member of the San Diego Library Commission 1926-1932 and of the San Diego Scientific Library 1926-1932; elected as a Republican to the Seventy-third and Seventy-fourth Congresses (March 4, 1933-January 3, 1937); was not a candidate for renomination in 1936 to the Seventy-fifth Congress; vice president of the California-Pacific International Exposition 1935-1936; retired and resided in San Diego, Calif., until his death there on June 28, 1939; interment in Greenwood Cathedral Mausoleum, Greenwood Memorial Park.

**BURNHAM, Henry Eben,** a Senator from New Hampshire; born in Dunbarton, Merrimack County, N.H., November 8, 1844; attended the public schools and Kimball Union Academy; was graduated from Dartmouth College, Hanover, N.H., in 1865; studied law; was admitted to the bar in 1868 and commenced practice in Manchester; was engaged in banking and insurance; member, State house of representatives 1873-1874; treasurer of Hillsboro County 1875-1877; judge of probate for Hillsboro County 1876-1879; member of the constitutional convention of 1889; chairman of the Republican State convention in 1888; served as ballot-law commissioner 1892-1900; elected as a Republican to the United States Senate in 1901; reelected in 1907 and served from March 4, 1901, to March 3, 1913; was not a candidate for reelection; chairman, Committee on Cuban Relations (Fifty-eighth through Sixtieth Congresses), Committee on Claims (Sixty-first Congress), Commit-

tee on Agriculture and Forestry (Sixty-second Congress); resumed the practice of law; died in Manchester, N.H., February 8, 1917; interment in Pine Grove Cemetery.

**BURNS, Conrad R.,** a Senator from Montana; born in Gallatin, Davies County, Mo., January 25, 1935; graduated, Gallatin High School, 1952; attended the University of Missouri at Columbia, 1952-1954; entered active duty, United States Marine Corps in 1955; released as corporal in 1957; radio and television broadcaster; founder, Northern Ag-Network, 1975-1986; Yellowstone (Mont.) County Commissioner, 1987-1988; former manager, Northern International Livestock Exposition and Rodeo and Riverton (Wyo.) Livestock Auction; elected as a Republican to the United States Senate in 1988 for the term commencing January 3, 1989; reelected in 1994 for the term ending January 3, 2001; is a resident of Billings, Mont.

**BURNS, John Anthony,** a Delegate from the Territory of Hawaii; born Harry John Burns in Fort Assinneboine, Mont., March 30, 1909; resident of Hawaii beginning on May 30, 1913; attended school in Honolulu, and in Kansas from 1925 to 1927; received diploma from St. Louis College (high school) in Hawaii, 1930; attended the University of Hawaii in 1930 and 1931; police officer, city and county of Honolulu, 1934-1945; chairman, Traffic Safety Commission, city and county of Honolulu, 1950-1954; president of Burns & Co., Ltd., real-estate broker; Honolulu Civil Defense Administrator, 1951-1955; delegate to the Democratic National Conventions of 1952, 1956, 1960, 1964, and 1968; chairman of Honolulu County Democratic Committee, 1948-1952; chairman of Territorial Democratic Central Committee, 1952-1956; elected as a Democrat a Delegate to the Eighty-fifth and to the Eighty-sixth Congresses and served from January 3, 1957, to August 21, 1959, when Hawaii became a State in the Union; unsuccessful candidate for election for Governor of the State of Hawaii in 1959; real-estate broker; elected Governor of Hawaii in 1962, reelected in 1966 and 1970, and served from December 3, 1962 to December 2, 1974; died in Honolulu, Hawaii, April 5, 1975; interment in Punchbowl National Cemetery.

**Bibliography:** Burns, Sheenagh M. "Jack Burns: A Daughter's Portrait." *Hawaiian Journal of History* 24 (1990): 163-183; Crowningburg-Amalu, Samuel. *Jack Burns: A Portrait in Transition.* Honolulu: The Mamalahoa Foundation, 1974.

**BURNS, Joseph,** a Representative from Ohio; born in Waynesboro, Augusta County, Va., March 11, 1800; moved to Ohio with his parents, who settled in New Philadelphia in 1815, and near Coshocton, Coshocton County, in 1816; attended the rural schools; engaged in agricultural pursuits; auditor of Coshocton County 1821-1838; member of the State house of representatives 1838-1840; county clerk 1843-1851; served as a major general in the State militia; elected as a Democrat to the Thirty-fifth Congress (March 4, 1857-March 3, 1859); unsuccessful candidate for reelection in 1858 to the Thirty-sixth Congress; engaged in the drug business in Coshocton, Ohio; probate judge of Coshocton County; died in Coshocton, Ohio, May 12, 1875; interment in Oak Ridge Cemetery.

**BURNS, Robert,** a Representative from New Hampshire; born in Hudson, Hillsboro County, N.H., December 12, 1792; moved with his parents in childhood to Rumney, Grafton County; studied medicine in Warren; taught school; attended Dartmouth Medical School in 1815; returned to Warren and commenced the practice of medicine; moved to Hebron, Grafton County, in 1818 and continued the practice of his profession until 1835; fellow of the New Hampshire Medical Society in 1824; member of the State senate in 1831; elected as a Jacksonian to the Twenty-third and Twenty-fourth Congresses (March 4, 1833-March 3, 1837); continued the practice of medicine in Plymouth, N.H., until his death June 26, 1866; interment in the churchyard of Trinity Church, Holderness, Grafton County, N.H.

**BURNSIDE, Ambrose Everett,** a Senator from Rhode Island; born in Liberty, Union County, Ind., May 23, 1824; attended a seminary at Liberty and Beach Grove Academy; was graduated from the United States Military Academy at West Point in 1847; served in the Mexican and Indian wars; resigned in 1853 to manufacture a breech-loading rifle of his own invention; moved to Illinois, and was appointed treasurer of the Illinois Central Railroad in 1858; during the Civil War entered the Union Army in 1861 as colonel, First Rhode Island Volunteers; commanded a brigade at the first Battle of Bull Run, July 21, 1861; commissioned brigadier general August 6, 1861, and major general March 18, 1862; commanded the Ninth Corps at Antietam; placed in command of the Army of the Potomac on November 9, 1862, and served until January 26, 1863; took command of the department of the Ohio, March 25, 1863; returned to the eastern theater as commander of the Ninth Corps; resigned his commission April 15, 1865; elected Governor of Rhode Island in 1866, reelected in 1867 and 1868, and served from May 29, 1866 to May 25, 1869; during a visit to Europe in 1870 acted as mediator between the French and the Germans then at war; elected as a Republican to the United States Senate in 1874; reelected in 1880, and served from March 4, 1875, until his death in Bristol, R.I., September 13, 1881; chairman, Committee on Education and Labor (Forty-fifth Congress), Committee on Foreign Relations (Forty-seventh Congress); interment in Swan Point Cemetery, Providence, R.I.

Bibliography: *DAB*; Marvel, William. *Burnside.* Chapel Hill: University of North Carolina Press, 1991; Morton, Julia Jenkins. "Trusting to Luck: Ambrose E. Burnside and the American Civil War." Ph.D. dissertation, Kent State University, 1992; Poore, Benjamin Perley. *Life and Public Service of Ambrose Burnside.* Providence, R.I.: J.A. and R.A. Reid, 1882.

**BURNSIDE, Maurice Gwinn,** a Representative from West Virginia; born near Columbia, Richland County, S.C., August 23, 1902; attended the public schools of South Carolina; student at The Citadel, Charleston, S.C., 1920-1922; graduated from Furman University Law School, Greenville, S.C., in 1926; M.A. in Latin American relations, University of Texas at Austin, 1928; studied and traveled in Europe and Asia, 1928-1931; Ph.D., Duke University, 1937; instructor in Greenville (S.C.) High School, 1931-1932; purchaser of rare documents for Duke University Library, Durham, N.C., 1933-1935; instructor in Alabama Polytechnic Institute at Auburn in 1936 and 1937; professor of political science at Marshall University, Huntington, W.Va., 1937-1948; member of Parole and Probation Examination Board of West Virginia 1939-1941; chairman of Workers Education for West Virginia 1942-1945; elected as a Democrat to the Eighty-first and Eighty-second Congresses (January 3, 1949-January 3, 1953); unsuccessful candidate for reelection in 1952 to the Eighty-third Congress; with the National Security Agency, Washington, D.C., from February 20 to March 27, 1953; elected to the Eighty-fourth Congress (January 3, 1955-January 3, 1957); unsuccessful candidate for election in 1956 to the Eighty-fifth Congress; president of Tri-State Tobacco Warehouses, Inc., beginning in 1957; legislative representative in Washington, D.C., for the National Education Association, 1959-1961; legislative liaison, Department of Defense, 1961-1968; author; is a resident of Wilson, N.C.

**BURNSIDE, Thomas,** a Representative from Pennsylvania; born near Newton Stewart, County Tyrone, Ireland, July 28, 1782; immigrated to the United States with his father's family, who settled in Norristown, Montgomery County, Pa., in 1793; studied law; was admitted to the bar in 1804 and commenced practice in Bellefonte; appointed deputy attorney general January 12, 1809; served in the Pennsylvania senate in 1811 and 1812; elected as a Republican to the Fourteenth Congress to fill the vacancy caused by the death of David Bard and served from October 10, 1815, to April 1816, when he resigned; appointed president judge of the Luzerne district courts in 1815, and resigned in 1819; again a member of the State senate and its presiding officer in 1823; president judge of the fourth judicial district 1826-1841 and later presided in the same capacity over the seventh judicial district; appointed an associate justice of the supreme court of Pennsylvania in 1845, which office he held until his death in Germantown, Pa., March 25, 1851; interment in Union Cemetery, Bellefonte, Centre County, Pa.

**BURR, Aaron** (cousin of Theodore Dwight), a Senator from New York and a Vice President of the United States; born in Newark, N.J., February 6, 1756; was graduated from the College of New Jersey (now Princeton University) in 1772; studied theology but soon abandoned it for the law; during the Revolutionary War entered the Continental Army and served from 1775 until 1779; was admitted to the bar in 1782 and practiced in Albany, N.Y.; moved to New York City in 1783; member, New York State assembly, 1784-1785, 1798-1799; attorney general of New York, 1789-1790; commissioner of Revolutionary claims in 1791; elected as a Democrat to the United States Senate and served from March 4, 1791, to March 3, 1797; unsuccessful candidate for reelection; president of the New York constitutional convention in 1801; in the presidential election of 1800, Burr and Thomas Jefferson each had seventy-three electoral votes, and the House of Representatives on the thirty-sixth ballot, February 17, 1801, elected Jefferson President and Burr Vice President; unsuccessful candidate for election in 1804 for Governor of New York; challenged and mortally wounded Alexander Hamilton in a duel fought at Weehawken, N.J., July 11, 1804; the coroner's jury returned a verdict of murder, Burr escaped to South Carolina, then returned to Washington and completed his term of service as Vice President March 4, 1805; arrested February 19, 1807, tried for treason in Richmond, Va. for attempting to form a republic in the Southwest of which he was to be the head, and was acquitted on September 1, 1807; went abroad in July 1808; returned to New York City in June 1812 and resumed the practice of law; died in Port Richmond, Staten Island, N.Y., September 14, 1836; interment in the President's lot, Princeton Cemetery, Princeton, N.J.

Bibliography: *DAB*; Burr, Aaron. *The Political Correspondence and Public Papers of Aaron Burr.* Edited by Mary-Jo Kline. 2 vols. Princeton, N.J.: Princeton University Press, 1983; Lomask, Milton. *Aaron Burr: The Years from Princeton to Vice President 1756-1805.* New York: Farrar, Straus and Giroux, 1979; Lomask, Milton. *Aaron Burr: The Conspiracy and Years of Exile 1805-1836.* New York: Farrar, Straus and Giroux, 1982.

**BURR, Albert George,** a Representative from Illinois; born near Batavia, Genesee County, N.Y., November 8, 1829; moved to Illinois with his mother, who settled near Springfield, Sangamon County, in 1830; completed preparatory studies; taught school for several years at Vandalia, Ill.; moved to Winchester, Scott County, in 1850 and engaged in mercantile pursuits; studied law; was admitted to the bar in 1856 and commenced practice in Winchester; member of the State house of representatives 1861-1864; moved to Carrollton, Greene County, in 1868 and continued the practice of law; member of the State constitutional convention in 1870; elected as a Democrat to the Fortieth and Forty-first Congresses (March 4, 1867-March 3, 1871); was not a candidate for renomination in 1870 to the Forty-second Congress; resumed the practice of law in Carrollton, Ill.; elected circuit judge of the seventh judicial circuit in 1877 and served until his death; died in Carrollton, Ill., June 10, 1882; interment in the Carrollton Cemetery.

**BURR, Richard M.,** a Representative from North Carolina; born in Charlottesville, Va., November 30, 1955; graduated Reynolds High School, Winston-Salem, N.C., 1974; B.A., Wake Forest University, Winston-Salem, N.C., 1978; sales and marketing of consumer goods at Carswell Distributing; unsuccessful candidate for election in 1992 to the One Hundred Third Congress; elected as a

Republican to the One Hundred Fourth Congress (January 3, 1995-January 3, 1997); is a resident of Winston-Salem, N.C.

**BURRELL, Orlando,** a Representative from Illinois; born in Newton, Bradford County, Pa., July 26, 1826; moved with his parents to White County, Ill., in 1834; attended the common schools; engaged in agricultural pursuits; during the Civil War raised a company of Cavalry in June 1861, was elected its captain, and was attached to the First Regiment, Illinois Volunteer Cavalry; judge of White County 1873-1881; sheriff of White County 1892-1894; delegate to the Republican National Convention at Minneapolis in 1892; elected as a Republican to the Fifty-fourth Congress (March 4, 1895-March 3, 1897); unsuccessful candidate for reelection in 1896 to the Fifty-fifth Congress; retired from public life and resumed his agricultural pursuits; died in Carmi, White County, Ill., June 7, 1921; interment in Maple Ridge Cemetery.

**BURRILL, James, Jr.** (great-grandfather of Theodore Francis Green), a Senator from Rhode Island; born in Providence, R.I., April 25, 1772; was graduated from Rhode Island College (now Brown University) at Providence in 1788; studied law; was admitted to the bar in 1791 and commenced practice in Providence; attorney general of Rhode Island 1797-1814; member, State house of representatives 1813-1816 and served as speaker 1814-1816; chief justice of the State supreme court in 1816; elected to the United States Senate and served from March 4, 1817, until his death in Washington, D.C., December 25, 1820; chairman, Committee on Judiciary (Fifteenth Congress); funeral services were held in the Chamber of the United States Senate; interment in Congressional Cemetery.

**Bibliography:** *DAB.*

**BURROUGHS, Sherman Everett,** a Representative from New Hampshire; born in Dunbarton, Merrimack County, N.H., February 6, 1870; attended the public schools, and was graduated from Dartmouth College, Hanover, N.H., in 1894; private secretary to Representative Henry M. Baker of New Hampshire, 1894-1897; was graduated from the law school of Columbian College (now George Washington University), Washington, D.C., in 1896; was admitted to the bar in 1896 and commenced practice in Manchester, N.H., in 1897; member of the State house of representatives in 1901 and 1902; member of the State board of charities and corrections 1901-1907; member of the State board of equalization in 1909 and 1910; elected as a Republican to the Sixty-fifth Congress on May 29, 1917, to fill the vacancy caused by the death of Cyrus A. Sulloway; reelected to the Sixty-sixth and Sixty-seventh Congresses and served from June 7, 1917, until his death; declined to be a candidate for reelection in 1922 to the Sixty-eighth Congress; died in Washington, D.C., January 27, 1923; interment in Valley Cemetery, Manchester, N.H.

**BURROUGHS, Silas Mainville,** a Representative from New York; born in Ovid, N.Y., July 16, 1810; completed a preparatory course; village clerk of Medina, Orleans County, N.Y., in 1835; village trustee in 1836 and 1839-1843; studied law; was admitted to the bar in Orleans County in 1840 and commenced practice in Medina; again trustee of Medina 1845-1847; village attorney 1845-1847; served as brigadier general in the New York State Militia 1848-1858; member of the State assembly in 1837, 1850, 1851, and 1853; elected as a Republican to the Thirty-fifth and Thirty-sixth Congresses and served from March 4, 1857, until his death in Medina, N.Y., June 3, 1860; interment in Boxwood Cemetery.

**BURROWS, Daniel** (uncle of Lorenzo Burrows), a Representative from Connecticut; born at Fort Hill, Groton, Conn., October 26, 1766; pursued preparatory studies; engaged in the manufacture of carriages and wagons at New London, Conn.; studied theology; was ordained as a minister of the Methodist Church; member of the State house of representatives 1816-1820 and in 1826; delegate to

the State constitutional convention in 1818; one of the commissioners to establish the boundary line between the States of Connecticut and Massachusetts; elected to the Seventeenth Congress (March 4, 1821-March 3, 1823); was not a candidate for renomination in 1822; resident of Middletown, Conn., 1823-1854; surveyor and inspector of customs for the port of Middletown 1823-1847; died in Mystic, New London County, Conn., January 23, 1858; interment in Elm Grove Cemetery.

**BURROWS, Joseph Henry,** a Representative from Missouri; born in Manchester, England, May 15, 1840; immigrated to the United States with his parents, who settled in Quincy, Ill.; attended the common schools at Quincy, Ill., and Keokuk, Iowa; engaged in mercantile pursuits and later in agricultural pursuits; moved to Cainsville, Harrison County, Mo., in 1862; was ordained as a minister in Cainsville in 1867; member of the State house of representatives 1870-1874 and 1878-1880; elected as a Greenbacker to the Forty-seventh Congress (March 4, 1881-March 3, 1883); unsuccessful candidate for reelection in 1882 to the Forty-eighth Congress; resumed ministerial duties and also engaged in agricultural pursuits; died in Cainsville, Mo., April 28, 1914; interment in Oak Lawn Cemetery, near Cainsville.

**BURROWS, Julius Caesar,** a Representative and a Senator from Michigan; born in North East, Erie County, Pa., January 9, 1837; moved with his parents to Ashtabula County, Ohio; attended district school, Kingsville Academy, and Grand River Institute, Austinburg, Ohio; studied law; was admitted to the bar at Jefferson, Ohio, in 1859; moved to Richland, Kalamazoo County, Mich., in 1860; principal of the Richland Seminary; commenced the practice of law in Kalamazoo in 1861; raised an infantry company in 1862; served as its captain until the fall of 1863; elected circuit court commissioner in 1864; prosecuting attorney for Kalamazoo County, 1866-1870; declined appointment as supervisor of internal revenue for Michigan and Wisconsin in 1868; elected as a Republican to the Forty-third Congress (March 4, 1873-March 3, 1875); chairman, Committee on Expenditures in the Department of the Navy (Forty-third Congress); unsuccessful candidate for reelection in 1874 to the Forty-fourth Congress; elected to the Forty-sixth and Forty-seventh Congresses (March 4, 1879-March 3, 1883); chairman, Committee on Territories (Forty-seventh Congress); unsuccessful candidate for reelection in 1882 to the Forty-eighth Congress; elected a Republican to the Forty-ninth and to the five succeeding Congresses, and served from March 4, 1885 until his resignation on January 23, 1895, having been elected Senator; chairman, Committee on Levees and Improvements of Mississippi River (Fifty-first Congress); elected as a Republican to the United States Senate to fill the vacancy caused by the death of Francis B. Stockbridge; reelected in 1899 and 1905, and served from January 24, 1895 to March 3, 1911; unsuccessful candidate for renomination; chairman, Committee on Revision of the Laws of the United States (Fifty-fourth through Fifty-sixth Congresses), Committee on Privileges and Elections (Fifty-seventh through Sixty-first Congresses); member of the National Monetary Commission, and its vice chairman, 1908-1912; retired from active business pursuits and political life; died in Kalamazoo, Mich., November 16, 1915; interment in Mountain Home Cemetery.

**Bibliography:** *DAB*; Holsinger, M. Paul. "J.C. Burrows and the Fight Against Mormonism, 1903-1907." *Michigan History* 52 (Fall 1968): 181-95; Orcutt, Dana. *Burrows of Michigan and the Republican Party.* New York: Longmans, Green and Company, 1917.

**BURROWS, Lorenzo** (nephew of Daniel Burrows), a Representative from New York; born in Groton, Conn., March 15, 1805; attended the academies at Plainfield, Conn., and Westerly, R.I.; moved to New York and settled in Albion, Orleans County, in 1824; employed as a clerk until 1826, when he engaged in mercantile pursuits; assisted in establishing the Bank of Albion in 1839, and served as cashier; treasurer of Orleans County in 1840; assignee in bankruptcy for Orleans County in 1841; supervisor of the town of Barre in 1845; elected as a Whig to the Thirty-first and Thirty-second Congresses (March 4, 1849-March 3, 1853); comptroller of the State of New York 1855-1857; director and president of the Niagara Falls International Bridge Co.; chosen a regent of the University of New York in 1858 and appointed one of the commissioners of Mount Albion Cemetery in 1862, serving in both of these capacities at the time of his death in Albion, Orleans County, N.Y., March 6, 1885; interment in Mount Albion Cemetery.

**BURSUM, Holm Olaf,** a Senator from New Mexico; born at Fort Dodge, Webster County, Iowa, February 10, 1867; attended the public schools; moved to New Mexico in 1881; settled near Socorro, Socorro County, and engaged in stock raising; member, Territorial senate 1899-1900; chairman of the Territorial central committee in 1905 and 1911; member of the State constitutional convention in 1910; unsuccessful candidate in 1916 for election for Governor of New Mexico; member of the Republican National Committee 1920-1924; appointed, and subsequently elected as a Republican to the United States Senate to fill the vacancy caused by the resignation of Albert B. Fall and served from March 11, 1921, to March 3, 1925; unsuccessful candidate for reelection in 1924; chairman, Committee on Pensions (Sixty-seventh and Sixty-eighth Congresses) engaged in the newspaper business in Washington, D.C., and subsequently returned to Socorro, N.Mex., and resumed his former business interests until his death in Colorado Springs, Colo., August 7, 1953; interment in Socorro Protestant Cemetery, Socorro, N.Mex.

**Bibliography:** Moorman, Donald R. "A Political Biography of Holm O. Bursum, 1899-1924." Ph.D. dissertation, University of New Mexico, 1962.

**BURT, Armistead,** a Representative from South Carolina; born at Clouds Creek, near Edgefield, Edgefield District, S.C., November 13, 1802; moved with his parents to Pendleton, S.C.; completed preparatory studies; studied law; was admitted to the bar in 1823 and practiced in Pendleton; moved to Abbeville, S.C., in 1828 and continued the practice of law; also engaged in agricultural pursuits; member of the South Carolina house of representatives, 1834-1835, and 1838-1841; elected as a Democrat to the Twenty-eighth and to the four succeeding Congresses (March 4, 1843-March 3, 1853); chairman, Committee on Military Affairs (Thirty-first and Thirty-second Congresses); served as Speaker pro tempore of the House of Representatives during the absence of Speaker Winthrop in 1848; was not a candidate for renomination in 1852; resumed the practice of law in Abbeville; delegate to the Democratic National Convention in 1868; died in Abbeville, S.C., October 30, 1883; interment in Episcopal Cemetery.

**BURTNESS, Olger Burton,** a Representative from North Dakota; born on a farm near Mekinock, Grand Forks County, N.Dak., March 14, 1884; attended the country school; was graduated from the academic department of the University of North Dakota at Grand Forks in 1906 and from its law department in 1907; was admitted to the bar the same year and commenced practice in Grand Forks; prosecuting attorney of Grand Forks County 1911-1916; delegate to the Republican National Conventions in 1916, 1936, and 1948; member of the State house of representatives in 1919 and 1920; elected as a Republican to the Sixty-seventh and to the five succeeding Congresses (March 4, 1921-March 3, 1933); unsuccessful candidate for renomination in 1932; resumed the practice of law; city attorney of Grand Forks, N.Dak., in 1936 and 1937; judge of the first judicial district of North Dakota from November 1950 until his death; died in Grand Forks, N.Dak., January 20, 1960; interment in Memorial Park Cemetery.

**BURTON, Charles Germman,** a Representative from Missouri; born in Cleveland, Ohio, April 4, 1846; moved to Warren, Ohio, and attended the public schools; enlisted as a private September 7, 1861, in Company C, Nineteenth Regiment, Ohio Volunteer Infantry, and served with the regiment until discharged October 29, 1862; corporal in Company A, One Hundred and Seventy-first Regiment, Ohio National Guard, during the "one hundred days" campaign of 1864; studied law; was admitted to the bar in Warren, Ohio, in 1867; moved to Virgil City, Mo., in 1868, to Erie, Kans., in 1869, and Nevada, Vernon County, Mo., in 1871, where he practiced law; circuit attorney and judge of the twenty-fifth circuit; delegate to the Republican National Conventions of 1884 and 1904; elected as a Republican to the Fifty-fourth Congress (March 4, 1895-March 3, 1897); unsuccessful candidate for reelection in 1896 to the Fifty-fifth Congress; resumed the practice of law; collector of internal revenue at Kansas City, Mo., 1907-1915; commander in chief of the Grand Army of the Republic in 1908; died in Kansas City, Mo., February 25, 1926; interment in Deepwood Cemetery, Nevada, Mo.

**BURTON, Clarence Godber,** a Representative from Virginia; born in Providence, R.I., December 14, 1886; moved with his parents to Lynchburg, Campbell County, Va., at an early age; attended the public schools; was graduated from Piedmont Business College, Lynchburg, Va.; engaged in the hosiery manufacturing industry, becoming treasurer of a firm in 1907 and president in 1921; also engaged in cattle raising and banking; member of the Lynchburg School Board, 1938-1943, serving as vice chairman; member of the Lynchburg City Council, 1942-1948, serving as mayor from 1946 to 1948; elected as a Democrat to the Eightieth Congress on November 2, 1948, to fill the vacancy caused by the resignation of J. Lindsay Almond, Jr., and at the same time was elected to the Eighty-first Congress; reelected to the Eighty-second Congress, and served from November 2, 1948 to January 3, 1953; unsuccessful candidate for reelection in 1952 to the Eighty-third Congress; chairman of board of Lynchburg Hosiery Mills, Inc.; member, Lynchburg Board of Zoning Appeals, 1957-1977; director, American Federal Savings and Loan Association, 1924-1968, and chairman until 1980; resided in Lynchburg, Va., until his death there on January 18, 1982; interment in Spring Hill Cemetery.

**BURTON, Danny Lee,** a Representative from Indiana; born in Indianapolis, Marion County, Ind., June 21, 1938; attended Indianapolis public schools; graduated, Shortridge High School, Indianapolis, 1956; attended Indiana University, Indianapolis, 1958; Cincinnati Bible College, Cincinnati, Ohio, 1959-1960; businessman; served, United States Army, 1957-1958; elected, Indiana State house of representatives, 1967-1968 and 1977-1980; member, Indiana State senate, 1969-1972 and 1981-1982; unsuccessful candidate for the United States Congress in 1970; elected as a Republican to the Ninety-eighth and to the six succeeding Congresses (January 3, 1983-January 3, 1997); is a resident of Indianapolis, Ind.

**BURTON, Harold Hitz,** a Senator from Ohio; born in Jamaica Plain, Mass., June 22, 1888; attended the public schools; A.B., Bowdoin College, Brunswick, Maine, 1909; LL.B., Harvard University School of Law, 1912; was admitted to the bar in 1912 and commenced practice in Cleveland, Ohio; assistant attorney for a power company in Salt Lake City, Utah, 1914-1916 and attorney for a power company in Boise, Idaho, 1916-1917; during the First World War served in the army as lieutenant, and later as captain, in 1917 and 1918; resumed the practice of law in Cleveland, Ohio, in 1919; instructor in Western Reserve University, Cleveland, Ohio, 1923-1925; member of the board of education of East Cleveland in 1928 and 1929; member of the Ohio State house of representatives in 1929; director of law of Cleveland, 1929-1932; served as acting mayor of Cleveland from November 1931 to February 1932; mayor of Cleveland, 1935-1940; elected as a Republican to the United States

Senate in 1940, and served from January 3, 1941 until his resignation on September 30, 1945; nominated on September 19, 1945 by President Harry S Truman as an Associate Justice of the United States Supreme Court; was confirmed by the Senate on the same day, and served until October 13, 1958, when he retired due to ill health; died in Washington, D.C., October 28, 1964; cremated at Highland Park Cemetery, Cleveland, Ohio.

**Bibliography:** *DAB*; Hudon, Edward. *The Occasional Papers of Mr. Justice Burton*. Brunswick, Maine: Bowdoin College, 1969.

**BURTON, Hiram Rodney,** a Representative from Delaware; born in Lewes, Sussex County, Del., November 13, 1841; attended the public schools and St. Peter's Academy at Lewes; taught for two years in the schools of Sussex County; engaged in the dry goods business in Washington, D.C., 1862-1865; was graduated from the medical department of the University of Pennsylvania at Philadelphia in 1868, and practiced in Frankford, Del., from 1868 until 1872, when he moved to Lewes, Del.; deputy collector of customs for the port of Lewes, 1877-1888; acting assistant surgeon in the United States Marine Hospital Service, 1890-1893, stationed at Lewes; unsuccessful candidate for the Delaware State senate in 1898; delegate to the Republican National Conventions of 1896, 1900, and 1908; elected as a Republican to the Fifty-ninth and Sixtieth Congresses (March 4, 1905-March 3, 1909); unsuccessful candidate for renomination in 1908 to the Sixty-first Congress; resumed the practice of medicine in Lewes, Del.; director of the Lewes National Bank; died in Lewes, Del., June 17, 1927; interment in St. Paul's Episcopal Churchyard, Georgetown, Sussex County, Del.

**BURTON, Hutchins Gordon** (nephew of Robert Burton), a Representative from North Carolina; born in Virginia in 1782; when three years of age his father died and he was sent to Granville County, where he was reared by his uncle, Colonel Robert Burton; moved to Mecklenburg County, N.C., in 1803; studied law; was admitted to the bar in 1806 and practiced; member of the North Carolina State house of commons in 1809; elected attorney general of North Carolina in 1810 and served until his resignation in November 1816; moved to Halifax, N.C., in 1816, and again elected a member of the North Carolina State house of commons in 1817; elected to the Sixteenth and to the two succeeding Congresses and served from December 6, 1819, until March 23, 1824, when he resigned; Governor of North Carolina from December 7, 1824 to December 8, 1827; resumed the practice of law in Halifax; was the host of General Lafayette when the latter visited Raleigh during his tour of the United States in 1825; died while on a visit to relatives in Iredell County, N.C., April 21, 1836; interment in Unity Churchyard, Beattys Ford, Lincoln County, N.C.

**Bibliography:** *DAB*.

**BURTON, John Lowell,** (brother of Phillip Burton and brother-in-law of Sala Burton), a Representative from California; born in Cincinnati, Ohio, December 15, 1932; moved with his parents to Detroit, Mich. in 1934, to Milwaukee, Wis. in 1936, and to San Francisco, Calif. in June 1941; attended the public schools of San Francisco; A.B., San Francisco State College, 1954; LL.B., University of San Francisco Law School, 1960; served in the United States Army, 1954-1956; admitted to the California bar in 1961 and commenced practice in San Francisco; member, California State assembly, 1965-1974; chairman, California State Democratic Party, 1973-1974; co-chairman of the California delegation to the Democratic National Convention of 1972; elected as a Democrat to the Ninety-third Congress, June 4, 1974, by special election to fill the vacancy caused by the resignation of William S. Mailliard; reelected to the four succeeding Congresses and served from June 4, 1974, to January 3, 1983; was not a candidate for reelection in 1982 to the Ninety-eighth Congress; resumed the practice of law; member of the California State assembly, District 12, April 1988 to present; is a resident of San Francisco, Calif.

**BURTON, Joseph Ralph,** a Senator from Kansas; born near Mitchell, Lawrence County, Ind., November 16, 1852; attended the common schools, Franklin (Ind.) College, and DePauw University at Greencastle; studied law; was admitted to the bar in 1875 and commenced practice in Princeton, Ind.; moved to Abilene, Dickinson County, Kans., in 1878; member, Kansas State house of representatives, 1882-1886; appointed a member of the World's Fair Columbian Commission at Chicago in 1893, representing Kansas; elected as a Republican to the United States Senate, and served from March 4, 1901 until June 4, 1906, when he resigned; chairman, Committee on Forest Reservations and Game Protection (Fifty-seventh and Fifty-eighth Congresses); returned to Abilene, Kans., and engaged in the newspaper business; died in Los Angeles, Calif., February 27, 1923; was cremated and the ashes deposited in the columbarium of the Los Angeles Crematory Association.

**BURTON, Laurence Junior,** a Representative from Utah; born in Ogden, Weber County, Utah, October 30, 1926; graduated from Ogden High School in 1944; enlisted in the United States Navy Air Corps and served from January 1945 to July 1946; graduated from Weber College at Ogden, Utah, in 1948; B.S., University of Utah, Salt Lake City, 1951; M.S., Utah State University, Logan, 1956; engaged in postgraduate work at Georgetown and George Washington Universities, Washington, D.C., 1957-1958; public relations director and athletic manager at Weber College, 1948-1956; regional director, American College Public Relations Association, 1954-1955; editor of the National Junior College Athletic Association magazine, 1951-1961; legislative assistant to Representative Henry A. Dixon of Utah, 1957-1958; assistant professor of political science at Weber College, 1958-1960; administrative assistant to Governor George D. Clyde of Utah, 1960-1962; delegate to the Republican National Convention of 1968; elected as a Republican to the Eighty-eighth and to the three succeeding Congresses (January 3, 1963-January 3, 1971); was not a candidate in 1970 for reelection to the House of Representatives, but was an unsuccessful candidate for election to the United States Senate; is a resident of Ogden, Utah.

**BURTON, Phillip** (brother of John Lowell Burton and husband of Sala Burton), a Representative from California; born in Cincinnati, Hamilton County, Ohio, June 1, 1926; moved with his parents to Detroit, Mich. in 1934, to Milwaukee, Wis. in 1936, and to San Francisco, Calif. in June 1941; attended the public schools and graduated from Washington High School, San Francisco, in January 1944; enlisted in Navy V-12 program and attended the University of Southern California, Los Angeles, as an apprentice seaman from January 1944 until March 1945; B.A., University of Southern California, Los Angeles, 1947; worked as a janitor and salesman of gasoline station leases while studying law; LL.B., Golden Gate Law School, San Francisco, 1952; admitted to California bar the same year; engaged as an attorney at law; admitted to practice before the United States Supreme Court in 1956; during the Korean conflict served in the Air Force as a first lieutenant in the office of the Judge Advocate General, Camp Parks, Calif.; unsuccessful candidate for nomination in 1954 to the California State assembly from District 23; member of the California State assembly, District 20, 1957-1964; represented the United States at the Atlantic Treaty Association Conference in France in 1959; delegate, California State Democratic convention, 1968-1982; delegate to the Democratic National Convention of 1968; elected as a Democrat to the Eighty-eighth Congress, February 18, 1964, by special election to fill the vacancy caused by the resignation of John F. Shelley; reelected to the ten succeeding Congresses, and served from February 18, 1964 until his death in San Francisco, Calif., April 10, 1983; cremated; ashes interred in the National Cemetery of the Presidio of San Francisco.

**Bibliography:** Jacobs, John. *A Rage for Justice: The Passion and Politics of Philip Burton*. Berkeley: University of California Press, 1995; Robinson, Judith. *"You're in Your Mother's Arms": The Life and Legacy of Congressman Phil Burton*. San Francisco: M.J. Robinson, 1994.

**BURTON, Robert** (uncle of Hutchins Gordon Burton), a Delegate from North Carolina; born near Chase City, Mecklenburg County, Va., October 20, 1747; attended private schools; moved to Granville County, N.C., in 1775; engaged as a planter; served in the Revolutionary Army and as quartermaster general attained the rank of colonel; member of the Governor's council in 1783 and 1784; Member of the Continental Congress in 1787; member of the commission to establish the boundary line between the States of North Carolina, South Carolina, and Georgia in 1801; died in Granville (now Vance) County, N.C., May 31, 1825; interment on his estate, "Montpelier," at Williamsboro (now Henderson), Vance County, N.C.

**BURTON, Sala,** (wife of Phillip Burton and sister-in-law of John Lowell Burton), a Representative from California; born in Bialystok, Poland, April 1, 1925; attended public schools in San Francisco and San Francisco University; associate director, California Public Affairs Institute, 1948-1950; vice president, California Democratic Council, 1951-1954; president, San Francisco Democratic Women's Forum, 1957-1959; delegate to the Democratic National Conventions of 1956, 1976, 1980, and 1984; elected as a Democrat to the Ninety-eighth Congress, June 21, 1983, by special election to fill the vacancy caused by the death of her husband, Representative Phillip Burton; reelected to the two succeeding Congresses, and served from June 21, 1983 until her death in Washington, D.C., February 1, 1987; was a resident of San Francisco; interment in the Presidio of San Francisco.

**BURTON, Theodore Elijah,** a Representative and a Senator from Ohio; born in Jefferson, Ashtabula County, Ohio, December 20, 1851; attended the public schools, Grand River Institute, Austinburg, Ohio, and Iowa College, Grinnell, Iowa; was graduated from Oberlin (Ohio) College in 1872; studied law; was admitted to the bar in 1875 and commenced practice in Cleveland, Ohio; elected as a Republican to the Fifty-first Congress (March 4, 1889-March 3, 1891); unsuccessful candidate for reelection in 1890 to the Fifty-second Congress; declined to be a candidate for in 1892 to the Fifty-third Congress; elected to the Fifty-fourth and to the seven succeeding Congresses, and served from March 4, 1895 until his resignation, effective March 3, 1909, having been elected United States Senator; chairman, Committee on Rivers and Harbors (Fifty-sixth through Sixtieth Congresses); chosen a member of the American group of the Interparliamentary Union in 1904; appointed by President Theodore Roosevelt as chairman of the Inland Waterways Commission, 1907-1908, and of the National Waterways Commission, 1908-1912; member of the National Monetary Commission, 1908-1912; elected as a Republican to the United States Senate, and served from March 4, 1909 to March 3, 1915; was not a candidate for renomination in 1914; chairman, Committee on Expenditures in the Treasury Department (Sixty-first and Sixty-second Congresses); engaged in banking in New York City; elected as a Republican to the Sixty-seventh and to the three succeeding Congresses, and served from March 4, 1921 until his resignation on December 15, 1928; did not seek renomination, having become a candidate for Senator; appointed by President Warren G. Harding as a member of the World War Debt Funding Commission in 1922; chairman of the United States delegation to the conference for the control of international traffic in arms at Geneva, Switzerland, in 1925; elected as a Republican to the United States Senate to fill the vacancy caused by the death of Frank B. Willis, and served from December 15, 1928 until his death in Washington, D.C., October 28, 1929; funeral services were held in the Chamber of the United States Senate; interment in Lake View Cemetery, Cleveland, Ohio.

Bibliography: *DAB*; Crissey, Forrest. *Theodore E. Burton, American Statesman.* Cleveland: World Publishing Company, 1956; Stay, Clarence. "Theodore E. Burton on Navigation and Conservation: His Role as Chairman of the Committee on Rivers and Harbors, 1898-1909." Ph.D. dissertation, Case Western Reserve University, 1975.

**BURWELL, William Armisted,** a Representative from Virginia; born near Boydton, Mecklenburg County, Va., on March 15, 1780; was graduated from the College of William and Mary, Williamsburg, Va.; moved to Franklin County in 1802; member of the Virginia house of delegates, 1804-1806; private secretary to President Thomas Jefferson; elected as a Republican to the Ninth Congress to fill the vacancy caused by the resignation of Christopher Clark; reelected to the Tenth and to the six succeeding Congresses and served from December 1, 1806, until his death in Washington, D.C., February 16, 1821; interment in Congressional Cemetery.

**BUSBEY, Fred Ernst,** a Representative from Illinois; born in Tuscola, Douglas County, Ill., February 8, 1895; attended the public schools, Armour Institute of Technology, Chicago, Ill., and Northwestern University, Evanston, Ill.; during the First World War enlisted September 24, 1917, in the United States Regular Army and served overseas as a sergeant until after the Armistice, when he was made a battalion sergeant major in the One Hundred and Twenty-fourth Field Artillery, Thirty-third Division, being discharged June 8, 1919; in 1930 engaged in the investment brokerage business in Chicago, Ill.; elected as a Republican to the Seventy-eighth Congress (January 3, 1943-January 3, 1945); unsuccessful candidate for reelection in 1944 to the Seventy-ninth Congress; elected in 1946 to the Eightieth Congress (January 3, 1947-January 3, 1949); unsuccessful candidate for reelection in 1948 to the Eighty-first Congress; elected to the Eighty-second and Eighty-third Congresses (January 3, 1951-January 3, 1955); unsuccessful candidate for reelection in 1954 to the Eighty-fourth Congress; resumed the investment brokerage business until his retirement in 1958; resided in Cocoa Beach, Fla., until his death there on February 11, 1966; interment in Mount Hope Cemetery, Chicago, Ill.

**BUSBY, George Henry,** a Representative from Ohio; born in Davistown, Pa., June 10, 1794; attended the public schools; moved to Ohio in 1810 with his father, who settled in Royalton, Fairfield County; engaged in the general mercantile business; major of militia in the War of 1812; moved to Marion County in 1823 and helped organize the town of Marion, where he continued mercantile pursuits; clerk of the Marion County courts and clerk of the supreme court 1824-1828; recorder of deeds 1831-1835; elected as a Democrat to the Thirty-second Congress (March 4, 1851-March 3, 1853); was not a candidate for renomination in 1852; resumed mercantile pursuits; member of the State senate 1853-1855; probate judge of Marion County from 1866 until his death in Marion, Ohio, August 22, 1869; interment in Marion Cemetery.

**BUSBY, Thomas Jefferson,** a Representative from Mississippi; born near Short, Tishomingo County, Miss., July 26, 1884; attended the common schools of his native city, Oakland College, Yale, Miss., and Iuka Normal College at Iuka, Miss.; taught in the public schools of Tishomingo, Alcorn, and Chickasaw Counties, Miss., 1903-1908; was graduated from the George Robertson Christian College, Henderson, Tenn., in 1905 and from the law department of the University of Mississippi at Oxford in 1909; was admitted to the bar in 1909 and commenced practice of law at Houston, Miss.; prosecuting attorney of Chickasaw County 1912-1920; elected as a Democrat to the Sixty-eighth and to the five succeeding Congresses (March 4, 1923-January 3, 1935); unsuccessful candidate for renomination in 1934; resumed the practice of law in Houston, Miss., until his death there on October 18, 1964; interment in Houston Cemetery.

**BUSEY, Samuel Thompson,** a Representative from Illinois; born in Greencastle, Putnam County, Ind., November 16, 1835; moved with his parents to Urbana, Ill.; attended the public schools; studied law; attended commercial college and law lectures in 1859 and 1860; during the Civil War served as first sergeant and then first lieutenant of the Urbana Zouaves in 1861 and 1862; town collector in 1862; second lieutenant in the recruiting service in June 1862 and helped to organize the Seventy-sixth Regiment, Illinois Volunteer Infantry; captain of Company B of that regiment June 22, 1862; lieutenant colonel August 22, 1862; colonel January 7, 1863; brevetted brigadier general of Volunteers April 9, 1865; mustered out of the service July 22, 1865, in Chicago, Ill.; engaged in banking from 1867 to 1888; mayor of Urbana 1880-1889; elected as a Democrat to the Fifty-second Congress (March 4, 1891-March 3, 1893); unsuccessful candidate for reelection in 1892 to the Fifty-third Congress; again engaged in banking; died in Urbana, Ill., August 12, 1909; interment in Woodlawn Cemetery.

**BUSH, Alvin Ray,** a Representative from Pennsylvania; born on a farm in Boggs Township, Clearfield County, Pa., June 4, 1893; attended the public schools; at the age of thirteen started work as a laborer in Pennsylvania coal mines and later was an apprentice in a machine shop; during the First World War served overseas as a corporal with the Five Hundred and Forty-first Motor Truck Company; established an automobile repair business in Philipsburg, Pa.; purchased a bus line serving Philipsburg and neighboring communities, later becoming president and general manager of the Williamsport Transportation Co.; operated a dairy farm in Lycoming County, Pa.; director of Lowry Electric Co. and Muncy Valley Hospital; elected as a Republican to the Eighty-second and to the four succeeding Congresses, and served from January 3, 1951 until his death in Williamsport, Pa., November 5, 1959; interment in Twin Hills Cemetery, near Montoursville, Pa.

**BUSH, George Herbert Walker** (son of Prescott Sheldon Bush), a Representative from Texas and a Vice President of the United States and 41st President of the United States; born in Milton, Suffolk County, Mass., June 12, 1924; graduated, Phillips Academy, Andover, Mass., 1942; B.A., Yale University, 1948; served as a lieutenant (junior grade) in the United States Navy, 1942-1945; formed Bush-Overby Oil Development, Inc., Midland, Tex., 1951; helped organize Zapata Petroleum Corp., Midland, Tex., 1953, and first president of Zapata Off-Shore Co., Midland, Tex., 1954; unsuccessful candidate in 1964 for election to the United States Senate; elected as a Republican to the Ninetieth and Ninety-first Congresses (January 3, 1967-January 3, 1971); was not a candidate for reelection in 1970 to the House of Representatives, but was an unsuccessful candidate for election to the United States Senate; appointed United States Ambassador to the United Nations on February 16, 1971 and served until January 1973; chairman, Republican National Committee, 1973-1974; appointed chief United States liaison officer, People's Republic of China, on September 26, 1974 and served until December 1975; director, Central Intelligence Agency, 1976-1977; elected Vice President of the United States on the Republican ticket headed by Ronald Reagan, November 4, 1980; inaugurated January 20, 1981; reelected in 1984 for the term ending January 20, 1989; elected President of the United States on November 8, 1988, and was inaugurated January 20, 1989; was an unsuccessful candidate for reelection in 1992; is a resident of Houston, Tex.

**Bibliography:** King, Nicholas. *George Bush: A Biography.* New York: Dodd, Mead, 1980.

**BUSH, Prescott Sheldon** (father of George Herbert Walker Bush), a Senator from Connecticut; born in Columbus, Franklin County, Ohio, May 15, 1895; attended the Douglas School of Columbus, Ohio, and St. George's School, Newport, R.I., 1908-1913; graduated from Yale University in 1917; enlisted in Connecticut National Guard in 1916, and served as captain of Field Artillery in American Expeditionary Forces, 1917-1919; engaged in hardware business as a warehouse clerk in St. Louis, Mo.; moved to Greenwich, Conn., in 1924; engaged in banking business in New York City 1926; moderator, Greenwich Representative Town Meeting, 1935-1952; trustee, Yale University; unsuccessful Republican candidate for the United States Senate in 1950; elected as a Republican to the United States Senate to fill the vacancy caused by the death of Brien McMahon; reelected in 1956, and served from November 4, 1952 to January 2, 1963; was not a candidate for reelection in 1962; resumed his career in the banking and investment field; died in New York City, October 8, 1972; interment in Putnam Cemetery, Greenwich, Conn.

**BUSHFIELD, Harlan John** (husband of Vera C. Bushfield), a Senator from South Dakota; born in Atlantic, Cass County, Iowa, August 6, 1882; moved with his parents to South Dakota in 1883; attended the public schools in Miller, S.Dak., and Dakota Wesleyan University, Mitchell, S.Dak., 1899-1901; was graduated from the Minnesota University Law School at Minneapolis in 1904; was admitted to the bar the same year and commenced practice in Miller, S.Dak.; elected Governor of South Dakota in 1938, reelected in 1940, and served from January 3, 1939 to January 5, 1943; elected as a Republican to the United States Senate in 1942 and served from January 3, 1943, until his death in Miller, S.Dak., September 27, 1948; interment in the G. A. R. Cemetery.

**BUSHFIELD, Vera Cahalan** (wife of Harlan J. Bushfield), a Senator from South Dakota; born in Miller, Hand County, S.Dak., August 9, 1889; attended the public schools; graduated from the Stout Institute, Menominee, Wis., in 1912; also attended Dakota Wesleyan University and the University of Minnesota; appointed as a Republican to the United States Senate to fill the vacancy caused by the death of her husband, Harlan J. Bushfield, and served from October 6, 1948 until her resignation on December 26, 1948; died in Fort Collins, Colo., April 16, 1976; interment in the G. A. R. Cemetery, Miller, S.Dak.

**BUSHNELL, Allen Ralph,** a Representative from Wisconsin; born in Hartford, Trumbull County, Ohio, July 18, 1833; attended the public schools and the academies of Oberlin and Hiram, Ohio; moved to Wisconsin in 1854 and settled in Platteville; studied law; was admitted to the bar in 1857 and commenced practice in Platteville; elected district attorney of Grant County in 1860; resigned to enter the Union Army in August 1861; served as first lieutenant and afterwards as captain of Company C, Seventh Regiment, Wisconsin Volunteer Infantry; member of the Iron Brigade; moved to Lancaster, Wis., in 1864; district attorney of Grant County in 1864; member of the State assembly in 1872; elected first mayor of Lancaster in 1875; United States district attorney for the western district of Wisconsin 1886-1890; moved to Madison, Wis., in 1891; elected as a Democrat to the Fifty-second Congress (March 4, 1891-March 3, 1893); was not a candidate for renomination in 1892; resumed the practice of law in Madison, Wis., and died there March 29, 1909; interment in Hillside Cemetery, Lancaster.

**BUSHONG, Robert Grey** (grandson of Anthony Ellmaker Roberts), a Representative from Pennsylvania; born in Reading, Berks County, Pa., June 10, 1883; attended Phillips Academy, Andover, Mass.; was graduated from Yale University in 1903, and from the law school of Columbia University, New York City, in 1906; was admitted to the bar in 1906 and commenced practice in Reading, Pa.; member of the Pennsylvania house of representatives in 1908 and 1909; president judge of the orphans' court of Berks County, 1914-1915; delegate to the Republican National Conventions of 1916 and 1924; elected as a Republican to the Seventieth Congress (March 4, 1927-March 3, 1929); was not a candidate for renomination in 1928 to the Seventy-first Congress; resumed the practice of law in Reading, Pa., and resided in Sinking Springs, Pa.; died in Reading, Pa., April 6, 1951; interment in Charles Evans Cemetery.

**BUSTAMANTE, Albert Garza,** a Representative from Texas; born in Asherton, Dimmit County, Tex., April 8, 1935; attended the public schools and was graduated from Asherton High School in 1954; paratrooper in the United States Army, 1954-1956; studied a liberal arts course at San Antonio College, 1956-1958; B.A., Sul Ross State College, Alpine, Tex., 1961; school teacher and coach, 1961-1968; assistant to Representative Henry B. Gonzalez, 1968-1971; member of the Bexar County Commission, 1973-1978; Bexar County judge, 1979-1984; elected as a Democrat to the Ninety-ninth and to the three succeeding Congresses (January 3, 1985-January 3, 1993); unsuccessful candidate for reelection in 1992 to the One Hundred Third Congress; is a resident of San Antonio, Tex.

**BUTLER, Andrew Pickens** (son of William Butler and uncle of Matthew Calbraith Butler), a Senator from South Carolina; born in Edgefield, S.C., November 18, 1796; attended Doctor Waddell's Academy at Willington, Abbeville County, S.C., and was graduated from South Carolina College (now the University of South Carolina) at Columbia in 1817; studied law; was admitted to the bar in 1818 and practiced in Columbia, Edgefield, Lexington, Barnwell, and Newberry; member, State house of representatives; member, State senate 1824-1833; aide on the staff of Governor John Lyde Wilson in 1824; appointed judge of the session court in 1833; judge of the State court of common pleas 1835-1846; appointed and subsequently elected as a States Rights Democrat to the United States Senate to fill the vacancy caused by the resignation of George McDuffie; reelected in 1848 and again in 1854 as a Democrat and served from December 4, 1846, until his death near Edgefield, S.C., May 25, 1857; chairman, Committee on Judiciary (Thirtieth through Thirty-fifth Congress); interment in Big Creek Butler Churchyard, Edgefield, S.C.

**Bibliography:** *DAB.*

**BUTLER, Benjamin Franklin** (grandfather of Butler Ames and father-in-law of Adelbert Ames), a Representative from Massachusetts; born in Deerfield, N.H., November 5, 1818; moved with his mother to Lowell, Mass., in 1828; attended high school and Exeter Academy, and was graduated from Waterville College (now Colby College), Waterville, Maine, in 1838; studied law; was admitted to the bar in 1840 and commenced practice in Lowell, Mass.; member of the Massachusetts house of representatives in 1853; served in the Massachusetts senate in 1859; delegate to the Democratic National Conventions at Charleston and Baltimore in 1860; entered the Union Army on April 17, 1861, as a brigadier general of the Massachusetts militia; promoted to major general on May 16, 1861, and assigned to the command of Fort Monroe and the Department of Eastern Virginia; military governor of New Orleans, La., from May 1, 1862 until his removal on December 16, 1862; commander of the Department of Virginia and North Carolina; relieved of command on January 8, 1865; resigned his commission November 30, 1865; elected as a Republican to the Fortieth and to the three succeeding Congresses (March 4, 1867-March 3, 1875); chairman, Committee on Revision of the Laws (Forty-second Congress), Committee on the Judiciary (Forty-third Congress); one of the managers appointed by the House of Representatives in 1868 to conduct the impeachment proceedings against Andrew Johnson, President of the United States; unsuccessful candidate for the Republican nomination for Governor in 1871 and 1872, and for reelection in 1874 to the Forty-fourth Congress; elected to the Forty-fifth Congress (March 4, 1877-March 3, 1879); declined to be a candidate for renomination in 1878 to the Forty-sixth Congress; unsuccessful candidate for Governor as an Independent in 1878, and as a Democrat in 1879; elected Governor in 1882 by the combined efforts of the Greenback and Democratic Parties, and served from January 4, 1883 to January 3, 1884; unsuccessful candidate for reelection in 1883; unsuccessful candidate for President of the United States on the Greenback and Anti-Monopolist ticket in 1884;

died while attending court in Washington, D.C., January 11, 1893; interment in Hildreth Cemetery, Lowell, Mass.

**Bibliography:** *DAB*; Butler, Benjamin F. *Autobiography and Personal Reminiscences.* Boston: A. M. Thayer, 1892; Trefousse, Hans L. *Ben Butler: The South Called Him Beast!* 1957. Reprint. New York: Octagon Books, 1974.

**BUTLER, Chester Pierce,** a Representative from Pennsylvania; born in Wilkes-Barre, Luzerne County, Pa., March 21, 1798; attended Wilkes-Barre Academy and was graduated from Princeton College in 1817; trustee of Wilkes-Barre Academy 1818-1838 and served as secretary; studied law at Litchfield Law School; was admitted to the bar in 1820 and commenced practice in Wilkes-Barre; register and recorder of Luzerne County 1821-1824; member of the Pennsylvania house of representatives in 1832, 1838, 1839, and again in 1843; elected as a Whig to the Thirtieth and Thirty-first Congresses and served from March 4, 1847, until his death in Philadelphia, Pa., October 5, 1850; interment in Hollenbeck Cemetery, Wilkes-Barre, Pa.

**BUTLER, Ezra,** a Representative from Vermont; born in Lancaster, Worcester County, Mass., September 24, 1763; moved with his parents to West Windsor, Vt., in 1770; engaged in agricultural pursuits in Claremont, N.H.; served in the Revolutionary War for a short time; moved to Waterbury, Vt., in 1785; studied law; was admitted to the bar and commenced practice in Waterbury, Vt., in 1786; town clerk in 1790; one of the first three town selectmen; member of the Vermont State house of representatives, 1794-1797, 1799-1804, 1807, and 1808; served in the executive council for fifteen years; first judge of the Chittenden County Court, 1803-1806; chief justice from 1806 until 1811; when Jefferson County (which has since become Washington County) was formed in 1812 he was elected chief justice and held the position continuously, with the exception of his congressional service, until 1825; elected as a Republican to the Thirteenth Congress (March 4, 1813-March 3, 1815); member of the State constitutional convention in 1822; elected Governor of Vermont in 1826, reelected in 1827, and served from October 13, 1826 to October 10, 1828; died in Waterbury, Washington County, Vt., July 12, 1838; interment in Waterbury Cemetery.

**Bibliography:** *DAB.*

**BUTLER, Hugh Alfred,** a Senator from Nebraska; born on a farm near Missouri Valley, Harrison County, Iowa, February 28, 1878; attended the public schools and was graduated from Doane College at Crete, Nebr., in 1900; construction engineer with the Chicago, Burlington & Quincy Railroad 1900-1908; member of the city board of Curtis, Nebr., 1908-1913; engaged in the flour-milling and grain business 1908-1940; member of the board of education of Omaha, Nebr.; Republican National committeeman for Nebraska 1936-1940; elected as a Republican to the United States Senate in 1940; reelected in 1946 and again in 1952 and served from January 3, 1941, until his death in the naval hospital at Bethesda, Md., July 1, 1954; chairman, Committee on Public Lands (Eightieth Congress), Committee on Interior and Insular Affairs (Eighty-third Congress); interment in Forest Lawn Cemetery, Omaha, Nebr.

**Bibliography:** Paul, Justis F. *Senator Hugh Butler and Nebraska Republicanism.* Lincoln: Nebraska State Historical Society, 1976.

**BUTLER, James Joseph,** a Representative from Missouri; born in St. Louis, Mo., August 29, 1862; attended the public schools; served an apprenticeship as a blacksmith, and worked at that trade for several years; was graduated from St. Louis (Mo.) University in 1881; studied law at Washington University, St. Louis, Mo.; was admitted to the bar in 1884 and commenced practice in St. Louis, Mo.; served as city attorney of St. Louis, 1886-1894; presented credentials as a Democratic Member-elect to the Fifty-seventh

Congress, and served from March 4, 1901 until June 28, 1902, when the seat was declared vacant; subsequently presented credentials as a Member-elect to fill the vacancy thus caused, and served from November 4, 1902 until February 26, 1903, when he was succeeded by George C. R. Wagoner, who contested his election; elected to the Fifty-eighth Congress (March 4, 1903-March 3, 1905); delegate to the Democratic National Conventions of 1904 and 1908; resumed the practice of law in St. Louis, Mo., and died there on May 31, 1917; interment in Calvary Cemetery.

**BUTLER, John Cornelius,** a Representative from New York; born in Buffalo, Erie County, N.Y., July 2, 1887; attended the public schools and Old Central High School, Buffalo, N.Y.; from boyhood was employed in waterfront industries in Buffalo; held many offices in longshoremen's, grain elevator employees', and electrical workers' unions; elected as a Republican to the Seventy-seventh Congress to fill the vacancy caused by the death of Pius L. Schwert; reelected to the Seventy-eighth, Seventy-ninth, and Eightieth Congresses and served from April 22, 1941, to January 3, 1949; unsuccessful candidate for reelection in 1948 to the Eighty-first Congress; sales manager of Fire Equipment Sales Co., and estimator for Beacon Electrical Engineering and Construction Co., Buffalo, N.Y.; elected to the Eighty-second Congress (January 3, 1951-January 3, 1953); unsuccessful candidate for renomination in 1952; died in Buffalo, N.Y., August 13, 1953; interment in Forest Lawn Cemetery.

**BUTLER, John Marshall,** a Senator from Maryland; born in Baltimore, Md., July 21, 1897; attended the public schools; during the First World War enlisted in the United States Army 1917-1919; student, Johns Hopkins University 1919 and 1921, and graduated from the University of Maryland Law School in 1926; was admitted to the bar in 1926 and commenced the practice of law in Baltimore, Md.; member of City Service Commission of Baltimore 1947-1949; elected as a Republican in 1950 to the United States Senate; reelected in 1956 and served from January 3, 1951, to January 2, 1963; was not a candidate for reelection in 1962; resided in Baltimore, Md., until his death in Rocky Mount, N.C., March 14, 1978; interment in Druid Ridge Cemetery, Pikesville, Md.

**BUTLER, Josiah,** a Representative from New Hampshire; born in Pelham, N.H., December 4, 1779; attended the Londonderry and Atkinson Academies and was instructed by private tutors; was graduated from Harvard University in 1803; taught school in Virginia for three years; studied law; was admitted to the bar of Virginia in 1807; returned to Pelham, N.H., and commenced practice in 1807; moved to Deerfield in 1809; sheriff of Rockingham County 1810-1813; clerk of the court of common pleas; unsuccessful candidate for election in 1812 to the Thirteenth Congress; member of the State house of representatives in 1815 and 1816; elected as a Republican to the Fifteenth Congress and reelected to the Sixteenth and Seventeenth Congresses (March 4, 1817-March 3, 1823); chairman, Committee on Agriculture (Seventeenth Congress); associate justice of the State court of common pleas 1825-1835; died in Deerfield, Rockingham County, N.H., October 27, 1854; interment in Granite Cemetery, South Deerfield, N.H.

**BUTLER, Manley Caldwell,** a Representative from Virginia; born in Roanoke, Va., June 2, 1925; attended the public schools of Roanoke, Va.; A.B., University of Richmond (Va.), 1948; LL.B., University of Virginia Law School, Charlottesville, 1950; ensign, United States Navy, 1942-1946; admitted to the Virginia Bar in 1950 and commenced practice in Roanoke; elected to Virginia house of delegates from Roanoke, 1962-1971, serving as chairman of the joint Republican caucus, 1964-1966, and as minority leader, 1966-1971; elected as a Republican to the Ninety-second Congress, November 7, 1972, by special election, to fill the vacancy caused by the resignation of Richard H. Poff and at the same time elected to the Ninety-third Congress; reelected to the four succeeding Congresses and served from November 7, 1972, to January 3, 1983;

was not a candidate for reelection in 1982 to the Ninety-eighth Congress; resumed the practice of law in Roanoke; member, National Bankruptcy Review Commission, December 1994 to present; is a resident of Roanoke, Va.

**BUTLER, Marion,** a Senator from North Carolina; born near Clinton, Sampson County, N.C., May 20, 1863; was graduated from the University of North Carolina at Chapel Hill in 1885; taught school for three years; moved to Clinton, N.C., in 1888 and became editor and publisher of the Clinton Caucasian; moved to Raleigh in 1894, but continued the publication of the paper; elected to the State senate in 1890; president of the National Farmers' Alliance and Industrial Union in 1894 and 1895; chairman of the People's Party State committee in 1894; trustee and member of the executive committee of the University of North Carolina 1891-1899; studied law; was admitted to the bar in 1899 and commenced practice in Raleigh, N.C.; elected as a Populist to the United States Senate and served from March 4, 1895, to March 3, 1901; unsuccessful candidate for reelection in 1901; chairman, Committee on Organization, Conduct, and Expenditures of Executive Departments (Fifty-fourth and Fifty-fifth Congresses); chairman of the Populist National Executive Committee 1896-1904; affiliated with the Republican Party in 1904; assisted in organizing the Cotton and Tobacco Cooperative Marketing Association of the South in 1923 and 1924; resumed the practice of law in Washington, D.C.; died in Takoma Park, Md., June 3, 1938; interment in Clinton Cemetery, Clinton, N.C.

**Bibliography:** *DAB*; Hunt, James. "The Making of a Populist: Marion Butler, 1863-1865." *North Carolina Historical Review* 62 (January 1985): 53-77, 62 (April 1985): 179-202, 62 (July 1985): 317-43.

**BUTLER, Matthew Calbraith** (son of William Butler (1759-1821) and nephew of Andrew Pickens Butler), Senator from South Carolina; born near Greenville, Greenville County, S.C., March 8, 1836; attended the local academy in Edgefield, S.C., and South Carolina College at Columbia; studied law; was admitted to the bar in 1857 and commenced practice in Edgefield; elected to the State house of representatives in 1860; entered the Confederate Army as captain in June 1861 and attained the rank of colonel in August 1862; lost a foot in the Battle of Brandy Station, Va., June 9, 1863; upon his return to active duty was commissioned brigadier general September 1, 1863; appointed major general September 17, 1864; again elected to the State house of representatives in 1866; unsuccessful candidate for lieutenant governor of South Carolina in 1870; elected as a Democrat to the United States Senate in 1876; reelected in 1882 and again in 1888 and served from March 4, 1877, until March 3, 1895; unsuccessful candidate for reelection; chairman, Committee on Civil Service and Retrenchment (Forty-sixth Congress), Committee on Interstate Commerce (Fifty-third Congress); resumed the practice of law in Washington, D.C.; during the Spanish-American War was appointed major general of United States Volunteers, and was one of the commissioners appointed to supervise the evacuation of Cuba by the Spanish forces in 1898; returned to Edgefield, S.C., and resumed the practice of law; died in Columbia, S.C., April 14, 1909; interment in Willow Brook Cemetery, Edgefield, S.C.

**Bibliography:** *DAB*.

**BUTLER, Mounce Gore,** a Representative from Tennessee; born in Gainesboro, Jackson County, Tenn., May 11, 1849; attended the common schools, Old Philomath Academy, and the law department of Cumberland University, Lebanon, Tenn.; was admitted to the bar in 1871 and commenced the practice of law in Gainesboro; delegate to all Democratic State conventions from 1872 to 1916; attorney general for the fifth judicial circuit of Tennessee 1894-1902; elected as a Democrat to the Fifty-ninth Congress

(March 4, 1905-March 3, 1907); unsuccessful candidate for renomination in 1906; resumed the practice of his profession in Gainesboro, Jackson County, Tenn., and died there February 13, 1917; interment in Gainesboro Cemetery.

**BUTLER, Pierce,** a Delegate and a Senator from South Carolina; born in County Carlow, Ireland, July 11, 1744; pursued preparatory studies; came to America in 1758 as an officer in the British Army; resigned his commission prior to the Revolutionary War and settled in Charles Town (now Charleston), S.C.; planter; aided the American cause during the Revolutionary War; delegate to the Continental Congress in 1787; member of the convention which framed the Federal Constitution in 1787; elected to the United States Senate in 1789 for the term ending March 3, 1793; reelected December 5, 1792, and served from March 4, 1789, to October 25, 1796, when he resigned; again elected to the United States Senate to fill the vacancy caused by the death of John Ewing Colhoun and served from November 4, 1802, until his resignation November 21, 1804; died in Philadelphia, Pa., February 15, 1822; interment in Christ Churchyard, Philadelphia, Pa.

Bibliography: *DAB*; Coglan, Francis. "Pierce Butler, 1744-1822, First Senator from South Carolina." *South Carolina Historical Magazine* 78 (April 1977): 104-19.

**BUTLER, Robert Reyburn** (grandson of Roderick Randum Butler), a Representative from Oregon; born in Butler, Johnson County, Tenn., September 24, 1881; attended the public schools and Holly Springs College; was graduated from the law department of Cumberland University, Lebanon, Tenn., in 1903; was admitted to the bar and commenced practice in Mountain City, Tenn.; moved to Condon, Oreg., in 1906 and resumed the practice of law; mayor of Condon, Oreg.; appointed circuit judge for the eleventh judicial district of Oregon and served from February 1909 until his retirement in January 1911; moved to The Dalles in 1911 and resumed the practice of law; member of the State senate 1913-1917 and 1925-1929; elected on November 6, 1928, as a Republican to the Seventieth Congress to fill the vacancy caused by the resignation of Nicholas J. Sinnott and on the same day was elected to the Seventy-first Congress; reelected to the Seventy-second Congress and served until his death; unsuccessful candidate for reelection in 1932 to the Seventy-third Congress; died in Washington, D.C., January 7, 1933; interment in the Odd Fellows Cemetery, The Dalles, Oreg.

**BUTLER, Roderick Randum** (grandfather of Robert Reyburn Butler), a Representative from Tennessee; born in Wytheville, Va., April 9, 1827; bound as an apprentice and learned the tailor's trade; moved to Taylorsville (now Mountain City), Tenn.; attended night school; studied law; was admitted to the bar in 1853 and commenced practice in Taylorsville; appointed postmaster of Taylorsville by President Fillmore; major of the First Battalion of Tennessee Militia; member of the Tennessee State senate, 1859-1863; during the Civil War served in the Union Army as lieutenant colonel of the Thirteenth Regiment, Tennessee Volunteer Cavalry, from November 5, 1863, until April 25, 1864, when he was honorably discharged; delegate to the Republican National Conventions of 1864, 1872 and 1876; delegate to the State constitutional convention in 1865; county judge and judge of the first judicial circuit of Tennessee in 1865; chairman of the first State Republican executive committee of Tennessee; delegate to the Baltimore Border State Convention; elected as a Republican to the Fortieth and to the three succeeding Congresses (March 4, 1867-March 3, 1875); chairman, Committee on the Militia (Forty-third Congress); censured by the House of Representatives on March 16, 1870, for corruption in regard to an appointment to West Point; unsuccessful candidate for reelection in 1874 to the Forty-fourth Congress; president of the Republican State conventions in 1869 and 1882; member of the Tennessee State house of representatives, 1879-1885; elected to the Fiftieth Congress

(March 4, 1887-March 3, 1889); was not a candidate for renomination in 1888 to the Fifty-first Congress; resumed the practice of law; again a member of the State senate, 1893-1901; died in Mountain City, Johnson County, Tenn., August 18, 1902; interment in Mountain View Cemetery.

**BUTLER, Sampson Hale,** a Representative from South Carolina; born near Ninety Six, Edgefield District, S.C., January 3, 1803; attended the country schools and South Carolina College (now the University of South Carolina) at Columbia; studied law; was admitted to the bar in 1825 and commenced practice in Edgefield, S.C.; moved to Barnwell, S.C., and continued the practice of law; sheriff of Barnwell County 1832-1839; member of the State house of representatives 1832-1835; elected as a Democrat to the Twenty-sixth and Twenty-seventh Congresses and served from March 4, 1839, until September 27, 1842, when he resigned; resumed the practice of law; moved to Florida; died in Tallahassee, Fla., March 16, 1848; interment in a cemetery in that city.

**BUTLER, Thomas,** a Representative from Louisiana; born near Carlisle, Cumberland County, Pa., April 14, 1785; attended the common schools and received a college education in Pittsburgh, Pa.; studied law; was admitted to the bar in 1806 and commenced practice at Pittsburgh, Pa.; moved to Mississippi Territory about 1807; admitted to the bar there in 1808; captain of a Cavalry troop in the Mississippi Territory Militia in 1810; purchased land in the parish of Feliciana, Orleans Territory and settled there in 1811; appointed parish judge on December 14, 1812; appointed judge of the third district by Governor William C.C. Claiborne of Louisiana on March 4, 1813; elected as a Republican to the Fifteenth Congress to fill the vacancy caused by the resignation of Thomas B. Robertson; reelected to the Sixteenth Congress and served from November 16, 1818, to March 3, 1821; unsuccessful candidate for renomination in 1820 to the Seventeenth Congress; appointed special judge of the third judicial district in 1822 and again in 1840; member of the Whig Party and afterwards affiliated with the American Party; owing to ill health declined to be a candidate in 1844 for the Twenty-ninth Congress; owner of sugar and cotton plantations; president of the board of trustees of the Louisiana College, Jackson, La.; died in St. Louis, Mo., August 7, 1847; interment on his plantation, "The Cottage," near St. Francisville, West Feliciana Parish, La.

**BUTLER, Thomas Belden,** a Representative from Connecticut; born in Wethersfield, Conn., August 22, 1806; attended the common schools; was graduated from the medical department of Yale University in 1828 and commenced practice in Norwalk, Conn.; member of the State house of representatives 1832-1846; studied law; was admitted to the bar in 1837 and commenced practice in Norwalk; served in the State senate in 1847 and 1848; elected as a Whig to the Thirty-first Congress (March 4, 1849-March 3, 1851); unsuccessful candidate for reelection in 1850 to the Thirty-second Congress; judge of the superior court in 1855; appointed associate justice of the State supreme court in 1861 and became chief justice of the same court in 1870; died in Norwalk, Conn., June 8, 1873; interment in Norwalk Cemetery.

Bibliography: *DAB*.

**BUTLER, Thomas Stalker,** a Representative from Pennsylvania; born in Uwchland Township, Chester County, Pa., November 4, 1855; attended the common schools, West Chester State Normal School, and Wyer's Academy, West Chester, Pa.; studied law; was admitted to the bar in 1877 and commenced practice in West Chester, Pa.; served as trustee of the West Chester State Normal School 1885-1889 and again in 1927 and 1928; appointed judge of the fifteenth judicial district of Pennsylvania in 1888; unsuccessful candidate for reelection in 1889; delegate to the Republican National Convention in 1892; elected as an Independent Republican to the Fifty-fifth Congress and as a Republican to the fifteen succeeding

Congresses and served from March 4, 1897, until his death in Washington, D.C., May 26, 1928; chairman, Committee on Pacific Railroads (Fifty-ninth through Sixty-first Congresses), Committee on Naval Affairs (Sixty-sixth through Seventieth Congresses); interment in Oaklands Cemetery, West Chester, Pa.

**BUTLER, Walter Halben,** a Representative from Iowa; born in Springboro, Crawford County, Pa., February 13, 1852; moved to Minnesota in 1868 with his parents, who settled in Mankato, Blue Earth County; attended public and private schools, and was graduated from the University of Wisconsin at Madison in 1875; studied law; was admitted to the bar in 1875 and commenced practice in Princeton, Green Lake County, Wis.; moved to Iowa in 1876 and taught school at La Porte City until 1878 and at Manchester until 1880; moved to West Union, Iowa, in 1883 and became owner and publisher of the Fayette County Union; served as superintendent of the tenth division, railway mail service, at St. Paul, Minn., 1885-1889; returned to West Union, Iowa, and resumed his former newspaper pursuits; elected as a Democrat to the Fifty-second Congress (March 4, 1891-March 3, 1893); was an unsuccessful candidate for reelection in 1892 to the Fifty-third Congress; moved to Des Moines, Iowa, in 1897 and to Kansas City, Mo., in 1907; engaged in the real estate and loan business and, later, in banking; died in Kansas City, Mo., April 24, 1931; interment in Forest Hill Cemetery.

**BUTLER, William** (father of William Butler [1790-1850] and Andrew Pickens Butler and grandfather of Matthew Calbraith Butler), a Representative from South Carolina; born in Prince William County, Va., December 17, 1759; attended grammar schools; moved to South Carolina; served in the Snow Campaign under Colonel Richard Richardson in December 1775, and in General Andrew Williamson's expedition against the Cherokee Indians in 1776; lieutenant in Casimir Pulaski's legion, under General Benjamin Lincoln, in 1779; served under General Andrew Pickens at the siege of Augusta in September 1780, as captain under General Henderson in 1781, and as captain of Mounted Rangers under General Pickens in 1782; member of the State convention which adopted the Federal Constitution; member of the State house of representatives in 1787-1795; sheriff of the Ninety-sixth District in 1791; elected major general of the upper division of State militia in 1796; elected as a Republican to the Seventh and to the five succeeding Congresses (March 4, 1801-March 3, 1813); was not a candidate for reelection in 1812 to the Thirteenth Congress; major general commanding the troops raised for the defense of South Carolina during the War of 1812; retired to his plantation on the Saluda River, near Mount Willing, Edgefield County, S.C., and died there November 15, 1821; interment in the family burial ground at Butler Methodist Church, near Saluda, Edgefield (now Saluda) County, S.C.

**Bibliography:** *DAB.*

**BUTLER, William** (son of William Butler [1759-1821], brother of Andrew Pickens Butler, and father of Matthew Calbraith Butler), a Representative from South Carolina; born in the Edgefield District, S.C., near the present town of Saluda, February 1, 1790; attended the common schools, and was graduated from South Carolina College at Columbia in 1810; studied medicine and was licensed to practice; served as a surgeon in the Battle of New Orleans during the War of 1812; continued his service in the Navy until June 6, 1820, when he resigned; elected as a Whig to the Twenty-seventh Congress (March 4, 1841-March 3, 1843); agent of the Cherokee Indians from May 29, 1849, until his death in Fort Gibson, Indian Territory (now Oklahoma), September 25, 1850; interment near Van Buren, Ark.

**BUTLER, William Morgan,** a Senator from Massachusetts; born in New Bedford, Mass., January 29, 1861; attended the public schools; studied law; was admitted to the bar in 1883; was graduated from the law department of Boston University in 1884; practiced law in New Bedford until 1895; member, Massachusetts house of representatives 1890-1891; member, State senate 1892-1895, serving as president in 1894 and 1895; moved to Boston, Mass., in 1895 and continued the practice of law until 1912, when he engaged in the manufacture of cotton goods; member of the commission to revise the statutes of Massachusetts 1896-1900; chairman of the Republican National Committee in 1924; appointed as a Republican to the United States Senate to fill the vacancy caused by the death of Henry Cabot Lodge and served from November 13, 1924, to December 6, 1926, when a successor was elected; unsuccessful candidate for election to fill the vacancy; chairman, Committee on Patents (Sixty-ninth Congress); resumed his manufacturing interests; resided in Boston, until his death there on March 29, 1937; interment in Forest Hills Cemetery.

**BUTLER, William Orlando,** a Representative from Kentucky; born in Jessamine County, Ky., April 19, 1791; moved with his parents to Maysville, Ky.; pursued preparatory studies; was graduated from Transylvania University, Lexington, Ky., in 1812; studied law at Lexington; during the War of 1812 served as captain, and was brevetted major for distinguished service in the Battle of New Orleans, January 8, 1815; aide to General Andrew Jackson in 1816 and 1817; was admitted to the bar in 1817 and commenced practice at Carrollton, Ky.; member of the Kentucky house of representatives in 1817 and 1818; elected as a Democrat to the Twenty-sixth and Twenty-seventh Congresses (March 4, 1839-March 3, 1843); was not a candidate for reelection in 1842 to the Twenty-eighth Congress; during the war with Mexico was commissioned major general of Volunteers June 29, 1846; received the thanks of Congress and a sword for gallantry for his part in the storming of Monterey, Mexico on September 25, 1846; unsuccessful Democratic candidate for Vice President of the United States on the ticket headed by Lewis Cass in 1848; declined appointment as Governor of Nebraska Territory in 1855; delegate to the peace convention held in Washington, D.C., in 1861 in an effort to devise means to prevent the impending war; died in Carrollton, Ky., August 6, 1880; interment in a private burying ground at the foot of Butlers Hill, near Carrollton, Ky.

**Bibliography:** Blair, Francis Preston. *Biographical Sketch of General William O. Butler.* Washington: Printed at the Congressional Globe office, 1848.

**BUTMAN, Samuel,** a Representative from Maine; born in Worcester, Worcester County, Mass., in 1788; moved to Maine in 1804, and settled in Dixmont, Penobscot County; engaged in agricultural pursuits; served as a captain in the War of 1812; member of the State constitutional convention in 1820; member of the house of representatives of Maine in 1822, 1826, and 1827; elected to the Twentieth and Twenty-first Congresses (March 4, 1827-March 3, 1831); county commissioner of Penobscot County in 1846; served in the State senate and was its president in 1853; died in Plymouth, Maine, October 9, 1864.

**BUTTERFIELD, Martin,** a Representative from New York; born in Westmoreland, N.H., December 8, 1790; attended the common schools; moved to Palmyra, Wayne County, N.Y., in 1828 and engaged in the hardware business and also in the manufacture of rope and cordage; presidential elector on the Whig ticket in 1848; elected as a Republican to the Thirty-sixth Congress (March 4, 1859-March 3, 1861); chairman, Committee on Agriculture (Thirty-sixth Congress); declined to be a candidate for renomination in 1860; resumed his former business pursuits; died in Palmyra, N.Y., August 6, 1866; interment in the Village Cemetery.

**BUTTERWORTH, Benjamin,** a Representative from Ohio; born near Maineville, Warren County, Ohio, October 22, 1837; attended the common schools of Warren County, the academy in Maineville, Ohio, and Ohio University in Athens; studied law; was admitted to the bar in 1861 and commenced practice in Cincinnati, Ohio; appointed assistant United States district attorney in 1868; member of the State senate in 1874 and 1875; elected as a Republican to the Forty-sixth and Forty-seventh Congresses (March 4, 1879-March 3, 1883); unsuccessful candidate for reelection in 1882 to the Forty-eighth Congress; delegate to the Republican National Convention of 1880; Regent of the Smithsonian Institution; appointed a commissioner of the Northern Pacific Railroad by President Chester A. Arthur in 1883; special Government counsel to prosecute the South Carolina election cases in 1883; elected to the Forty-ninth and to the two succeeding Congresses (March 4, 1885-March 3, 1891); chairman, Committee on Patents (Fifty-first Congress); was not a candidate for renomination in 1890 to the Fifty-second Congress; resumed the practice of his profession in Washington, D.C.; served as Commissioner of Patents from 1896 until his death in Thomasville, Ga., January 16, 1898; interment in Rock Creek Cemetery, Washington, D.C.

**Bibliography:** *DAB.*

**BUTTON, Daniel Evan,** a Representative from New York; born in Dunkirk, Chautauqua County, N.Y., November 1, 1917; B.A., University of Delaware, 1938; M.A., Columbia University, 1939; author; assistant to the president of the State University of New York, 1952-1958; also on staffs of University of Delaware and Rensselaer Polytechnic Institute; worked with newspapers in Wilmington, Del., and the Associated Press in New York City, 1939-1947; executive editor of the Albany Times-Union, 1960-1966; co-moderator of the television program, "Speak for Yourself," 1963-1966; elected as a Republican to the Ninetieth and Ninety-first Congresses (January 3, 1967-January 3, 1971); unsuccessful candidate for reelection in 1970 to the Ninety-second Congress; served as president of the National Arthritis Foundation, and as editor of Science Digest magazine; worked as an independent journalist; is a resident of Delmar, N.Y.

**BUTTZ, Charles Wilson,** a Representative from South Carolina; born in Stroudsburg, Monroe County, Pa., November 16, 1837; moved with his parents to Buttzville, N.J., in 1839; completed academic studies; studied law in Belvidere, N.J.; entered the Union Army in 1861 as second lieutenant in the Eleventh Pennsylvania Cavalry; was promoted to first lieutenant in 1862; was wounded in 1863; resigned on account of impaired health in October 1863; received two brevet ranks from the President, one as captain and the other as major, both dating May 1865; was admitted to the bar in 1863 and commenced the practice of law in Norfolk, Va.; delegate to the Republican National Convention in 1864; appointed director of the Exchange Bank of Virginia in 1864; Commonwealth attorney for King William County in 1866; moved to Charleston, S.C., in 1870; solicitor of the first judicial circuit 1872-1880; contested as a Republican the election of Edmund W. M. Mackey to the Forty-fourth Congress, but the House decided that neither was entitled to the seat; subsequently elected to fill the vacancy caused by the decision of the House and served from November 7, 1876, to March 3, 1877; was not a candidate for renomination in 1876; moved to Fargo, N.Dak., in 1878; procured the official organization of Ransom County in 1882, and established his residence in what is now known as Buttzville, N.Dak.; State's attorney 1884-1886; member of the State house of representatives 1903-1909; died in Lisbon, Ransom County, N.Dak., July 20, 1913; interment in Oakwood Cemetery.

**BUYER, Stephen Earle,** a Representative from Indiana; born in Rensselaer, Jasper County, Ind., November 26, 1958; graduated from North White High School in 1976; B.S., The Citadel, Charleston, S.C., 1980; J.D., Valparaiso (Ind.) University School of Law, 1984; entered active duty, United States Army as officer in Medical Service Corps; returned to active duty and assigned as special assistant to the United States Attorney in Virginia; recalled

for service as legal counsel for Twenty-second Theater Army in Operations Desert Shield and Desert Storm, 1990; deputy to Indiana attorney general; counsel, Indiana Licensing Agency; attorney, 1988 to present; vice chair, White County Republican party; elected as a Republican to the One Hundred Third and One Hundred Fourth Congresses (January 3, 1993-January 3, 1997); is a resident of Monticello, Ind.

**BYNUM, Jesse Atherton,** a Representative from North Carolina; born in Halifax County, N.C., May 23, 1797; attended Princeton College in 1818 and 1819; studied law; was admitted to the bar and commenced practice in Halifax, N.C.; member of the house of commons of North Carolina in 1823, 1824, and 1827-1830; elected as a Jacksonian to the Twenty-third and Twenty-fourth Congresses and as a Democrat to the two succeeding Congresses (March 4, 1833-March 3, 1841); moved to Alexandria, Rapides Parish, La., where he engaged in agricultural pursuits; died in Alexandria, La., September 23, 1868; interment in Rapides Cemetery, Pineville, La.

**BYNUM, William Dallas,** a Representative from Indiana; born near Newberry, Greene County, Ind., June 26, 1846; attended the country schools, and was graduated from the University of Indiana at Bloomington in 1869; studied law; was admitted to the bar in 1872 and commenced practice in Washington, Ind.; served as the first city clerk; city attorney of Washington 1871-1875; mayor of Washington 1875-1879; moved from Daviess County to Indianapolis in 1880; member of the State house of representatives 1881-1885, and served as speaker in 1885; elected as a Democrat to the Forty-ninth and to the four succeeding Congresses (March 4, 1885-March 3, 1895); served for some time as whip of the Democratic minority; censured by the House of Representatives on May 17, 1890, for the use of unparliamentary language; unsuccessful candidate for reelection in 1894 to the Fifty-fourth Congress; was active in the organization of the National (Gold-Standard) Democratic Party in 1896, and was chairman of its national committee 1896-1898; settled in Washington, D.C.; appointed by President William McKinley in 1900 a member of the commission to codify the United States criminal laws and served until 1906; retired from the practice of law; died in Indianapolis, Ind., October 21, 1927; interment in Oak Grove Cemetery, Washington, Ind.

**BYRD, Adam Monroe,** a Representative from Mississippi; born in Sumter County, Ala., July 6, 1859; moved to Neshoba County, Miss.; attended the common schools and Cooper Institute in Daleville; was graduated from the law department of Cumberland University, Lebanon, Tenn., in 1884; was admitted to the bar in 1885 and commenced practice in Philadelphia, Neshoba County, Miss.; superintendent of education for Neshoba County, 1887-1889; member of the Mississippi State senate, 1889-1896; served in the State house of representatives in 1896 and 1897, when he resigned; prosecuting attorney for the tenth judicial district in 1897; judge of the sixth chancery district from 1897 until his resignation in 1903; elected as a Democrat to the Fifty-eighth and to the three succeeding Congresses (March 4, 1903-March 3, 1911); unsuccessful candidate for renomination in 1910 to the Sixty-second Congress; resumed the practice of law in Philadelphia, Miss.; died at Hot Springs, Ark., June 21, 1912; interment in Town Cemetery, Philadelphia, Miss.

**BYRD, Harry Flood** (father of Harry Flood Byrd, Jr., and nephew of Henry De La Warr Flood and Joel West Flood), a Senator from Virginia; born in Martinsburg, Berkeley County, W.Va., June 10, 1887; moved with his parents to Winchester, Va., in 1887; attended the public schools and Shenandoah Valley Academy at Winchester, Va.; entered the newspaper publishing business in 1903 and became publisher of the Winchester (Va.) Star; also engaged extensively in agricultural pursuits near Berryville, Va., in 1906, specializing in growing and storing apples and peaches; president of the Valley Turnpike Co., 1908-1918; member, Virginia senate, 1915-1925; Virginia fuel commissioner in 1918; was elected chairman of the Virginia Democratic committee in 1922; elected Governor of Virginia in 1925, and served from February 1, 1926 to January 15, 1930; Democratic National committeeman from 1928 until 1940; was appointed March 4, 1933, and subsequently elected as a Democrat to the United States Senate to fill the vacancy caused by the resignation of Claude A. Swanson; was reelected in 1934, 1940, 1946, 1952, 1958, and 1964, and served from March 4, 1933, until his resignation November 10, 1965; chairman, Committee on Rules (Seventy-seventh through Seventy-ninth Congresses), Committee on Finance (Eighty-fourth through Eighty-ninth Congresses), Joint Committee on the Reduction of Nonessential Federal Expenditures (Eightieth through Eighty-ninth Congresses), Joint Committee on Internal Revenue Taxation (Eighty-fourth through Eighty-ninth Congresses); died in Berryville, Va., October 20, 1966; interment in Mount Hebron Cemetery, Winchester, Va.

**Bibliography:** Hawkes, Robert T., Jr. "The Career of Harry Flood Byrd, Sr., to 1933." Ph.D. dissertation, University of Virginia, 1975; Heinemann, Ronald L. *Harry Byrd of Virginia.* Charlottesville: University Press of Virginia, 1996; Wilkinson, J. Harvie. *Harry Byrd and the Changing Face of Virginia Politics, 1945-1966.* Charlottesville: University Press of Virginia, 1968.

**BYRD, Harry Flood, Jr.** (son of Harry Flood Byrd, Sr.), a Senator from Virginia; born in Winchester, Va., December 20, 1914; educated at Virginia Military Institute and the University of Virginia; newspaper editor and fruit grower; member of the Virginia Democratic central committee from 1940 until 1965; during the Second World War, served in the United States Naval Reserve as a lieutenant commander; member of the Virginia senate from 1948 to 1965; appointed as a Democrat to the United States Senate on November 12, 1965, to fill the vacancy caused by the resignation of his father, Harry Flood Byrd, and was subsequently elected on November 8, 1966, to fill the unexpired term ending January 3, 1971; announced on March 17, 1970 that he would be a candidate for reelection as an Independent; reelected as an Independent in 1970 and in 1976, and served from November 12, 1965 to January 2, 1983; was not a candidate for reelection in 1982; is a resident of Winchester, Va.

**BYRD, Robert Carlyle,** a Representative and a Senator from West Virginia; born in North Wilkesboro, Wilkes County, N.C., November 20, 1917; attended West Virginia public schools; student at Beckley College, Concord College, Morris Harvey College, and Marshall College, all in West Virginia, and George Washington University Law School, Washington, D.C.; J.D., American University Law School, Washington, D.C., 1963; member of the West Virginia house of delegates, 1947-1950; member of the West Virginia senate, 1951-1952, resigning when elected to Congress; elected as a Democrat to the Eighty-third and to the two succeeding Congresses (January 3, 1953-January 3, 1959); was not a candidate in 1958 for reelection to the House of Representatives, but was elected to the United States Senate for the term commencing January 3, 1959; reelected in 1964, 1970, 1976, 1982, 1988, and in 1994 for the term ending January 3, 2001; Secretary, Senate Democratic Conference 1967-1971; Democratic whip 1971-1977; majority leader, (Ninety-fifth and Ninety-sixth Congresses, One Hundredth Congress), minority leader, (Ninety-seventh through Ninety-ninth Congresses), President pro tempore (One Hundred First through One Hundred Third Congresses), chairman, Committee on Appropriations (One Hundred First through One Hundred Third Congresses); is a resident of Sophia, W.Va.

**BYRNE, Emmet Francis,** a Representative from Illinois; born in Chicago, Ill., December 6, 1896; educated in the public and parochial schools of Chicago and graduated from St. Ignatius Academy; attended Loyola University in 1916; veteran of the First

World War; graduated from De Paul University Law School, Chicago, Ill., in 1920; was admitted to the bar in 1919 and commenced the practice of law in Chicago, Ill.; assistant corporation counsel for city of Chicago from June 1921 to June 1923; assistant State's attorney for Cook County, Ill., from June 1, 1923, to December 1, 1928; unsuccessful candidate for election as judge of the municipal court of Chicago in 1934 and again in 1936; hearing officer for Illinois Commerce Commission in 1947 and 1948 and again in 1955 and 1956; elected as a Republican to the Eighty-fifth Congress (January 3, 1957-January 3, 1959); unsuccessful candidate for reelection in 1958 to the Eighty-sixth Congress; resumed law practice; appointed by Secretary of Commerce Maurice H. Stans to the Chicago Regional Export Expansion Council, April 17, 1970; resided in Evanston, Ill., where he died on September 25, 1974; interment in Holy Sepulchre Cemetery, Worth, Ill.

**BYRNE, James Aloysius,** a Representative from Pennsylvania; born in Philadelphia, Pa., June 22, 1906; attended the parochial school, St. Joseph's Preparatory School, public high school, and St. Joseph's College in Philadelphia; engaged in business as a mortician from 1937 until 1950; county registrar, Bureau of Vital Statistics, 1934-1939; chief deputy United States marshal, 1940-1943, and United States marshal for eastern district of Pennsylvania, 1943-1945; senior disbursing officer of the Pennsylvania Treasury, 1945-1950; delegate to the Democratic National Convention of 1936; member, Pennsylvania house of representatives, 1951-1952; elected as a Democrat to the Eighty-third and to the nine succeeding Congresses (January 3, 1953-January 3, 1973); unsuccessful candidate for renomination in 1972 to the Ninety-third Congress; was a resident of Philadelphia, Pa., where he died on September 3, 1980; interment in Holy Sepulchre Cemetery, Wyndmoor, Pa.

**BYRNE, Leslie Larkin,** a Representative from Virginia; born in Salt Lake City, Utah, October 27, 1946; graduated, Olympus High School, Salt Lake City; attended the University of Utah; co-founder and president, Quintech Associates, Inc.; member, Virginia house of Delegates, 1986-1993; elected as a Democrat to the One Hundred Third Congress (January 3, 1993-January 3, 1995); unsuccessful candidate for reelection in 1994 to the One Hundred Fourth Congress; was a candidate for nomination in 1996 to the United States Senate until she withdrew from the race; nominated as director, Office of Consumer Affairs, Department of Health and Human Services, August 15, 1996; is a resident of Annandale, Va.

**BYRNE, William Thomas,** a Representative from New York; born in the town of Florida, Montgomery County, N.Y., March 6, 1876; attended the public schools; was graduated from Albany (N.Y.) Law School (branch of Union College) in 1904; was admitted to the bar the same year and commenced practice in Albany, N.Y.; taught public speaking at Albany Law School and the Albany Railroad Y.M.C.A. for many years; director of the Home Savings Bank of Albany; represented Albany County in the New York State senate, 1923-1936; elected as a Democrat to the Seventy-fifth and to the seven succeeding Congresses, and served from January 3, 1937 until his death in Troy, N.Y., January 27, 1952; interment in St. John's Cemetery, West Albany, Town of Colonie, N.Y.

**BYRNES, James Francis,** a Representative and a Senator from South Carolina; born in Charleston, S.C., May 2, 1882; attended the public schools; official court reporter for the second circuit of South Carolina, 1900-1908; editor of the Journal and Review, Aiken, S.C., 1903-1907; studied law; was admitted to the bar in 1903 and commenced practice in Aiken, S.C.; solicitor for the second circuit of South Carolina, 1908-1910; elected as a Democrat to the Sixty-second Congress, reelected to the six succeeding Congresses (March 4, 1911-March 3, 1925); was not a candidate for renomination in 1924 to the House of Representatives, but was an unsuccessful candidate for nomination to the United States Senate; resumed the practice of law in Spartanburg, S.C.; elected as a

Democrat to the United States Senate on November 4, 1930; reelected in 1936, and served from March 4, 1931 until his resignation on July 8, 1941 to accept a judicial position; chairman, Committee to Audit and Control the Contingent Expense (Seventy-third through Seventy-seventh Congresses); nominated on June 12, 1941 by President Franklin D. Roosevelt as an Associate Justice of the United States Supreme Court; was confirmed by the Senate the same day and served until his resignation on October 3, 1942, to head the wartime Office of Economic Stabilization until May 1943; director of the Office of War Mobilization, May 1943 until his resignation in April 1945; Secretary of State in the Cabinet of President Harry S Truman, July 2, 1945 to January 21, 1947; resumed the practice of law in Washington, D.C.; elected Governor of South Carolina in 1950 and served from January 16, 1951 to January 18, 1955; retired and resided in Columbia, S.C., where he died April 9, 1972; interment in Trinity Episcopal Church Cemetery.

**Bibliography:** Byrnes, James F. *All in One Lifetime.* New York: Harper, 1958; Moore, Winfred B. "New South Statesman: The Political Career of James Francis Byrnes, 1911-1941." Ph.D. dissertation, University of California, Berkeley, 1975; Robertson, David. *Sly and Able: A Political Biography of James F. Byrnes.* New York: Norton, 1994.

**BYRNES, John William,** a Representative from Wisconsin; born in Green Bay, Brown County Wis., June 12, 1913; attended the public and parochial schools; was graduated from the University of Wisconsin at Madison in 1936 and from the law school of the same university in 1938; was admitted to the bar in 1938 and commenced practice in Green Bay, Wis.; served as a special deputy commissioner of banking for the State of Wisconsin from 1938 until his resignation in 1940 to assume his duties as State senator; member of the State senate 1940-1944, serving as majority floor leader in 1943; elected as a Republican to the Seventy-ninth and to the thirteen succeeding Congresses (January 3, 1945-January 3, 1973); was not a candidate for reelection in 1972 to the Ninety-third Congress; returned to the practice of law in Washington, D.C.; was a resident of Arlington, Va., until his death in Marshfield, Wis., on January 12, 1985.

**BYRNS, Joseph Wellington,** (father of Joseph Wellington Byrns, Jr.) a Representative from Tennessee; born near Cedar Hill, Robertson County, Tenn., July 20, 1869; attended the common schools; was graduated from Nashville High School in 1887, and from the law department of Vanderbilt University, Nashville, Tenn., in 1890; was admitted to the bar in 1890 and commenced the practice of law in Nashville; member of the Tennessee State house of representatives, 1895-1901; State senator, 1901-1903; unsuccessful candidate for district attorney general of Davidson County in 1902; chairman of the Democratic National Congressional Campaign Committee, 1928-1930; elected as a Democrat to the Sixty-first and to the thirteen succeeding Congresses, and served from March 4, 1909 until his death in Washington, D.C., June 4, 1936; was a candidate for reelection to the Seventy-fifth Congress at the time of his death; chairman, Committee on Appropriations (Seventy-second Congress); majority leader (Seventy-third Congress), Speaker of the House of Representatives (Seventy-fourth Congress); funeral services were held in the Hall of the House of Representatives; interment in Mount Olivet Cemetery, Nashville, Tenn.

**Bibliography:** *DAB*; Galloway, Jewell M. "Speaker Joseph W. Byrns: Party Leader in the New Deal." *Tennessee Historical Quarterly* 25 (Spring 1966): 63-76.

**BYRNS, Joseph Wellington, Jr.** (son of Joseph Wellington Byrns), a Representative from Tennessee; born in Nashville, Davidson County, Tenn., August 15, 1903; attended the public schools; was graduated from Emerson Institute at Washington, D.C., in 1922 and from the law department of Vanderbilt University at Nashville, Tenn., in 1928; was admitted to the bar in 1928 and commenced practice in Nashville; member of the Air Corps Reserve

from 1930 to 1938, with the rank of captain; elected as a Democrat to the Seventy-sixth Congress (January 3, 1939-January 3, 1941); unsuccessful candidate for reelection in 1940 to the Seventy-seventh Congress; resumed the practice of law; served in the United States Army from June 23, 1942 to August 17, 1945, with two and one-half years overseas in the European Theater of Operations; retired; resided in Daytona Beach, Fla., where he died on March 8, 1973; interment in Mount Olivet Cemetery, Nashville, Tenn.

**BYRNS, Samuel,** a Representative from Missouri; born on a farm in Jefferson County, Mo., March 4, 1848; studied law; was admitted to the bar in 1872 and commenced practice in Hillsboro, Mo.; collector of revenue for Jefferson County in 1872; member, Missouri State house of representatives, 1876-1877; served in the State senate in 1878; member of the Democratic State central committee, 1886-1888; elected as a Democrat to the Fifty-second Congress (March 4, 1891-March 3, 1893); was an unsuccessful candidate for renomination in 1892 to the Fifty-third Congress; resumed the practice of his chosen profession in De Soto, Jefferson County, Mo., where he died on July 9, 1914; interment in Hillsboro Cemetery, Hillsboro, Mo.

**BYRON, Beverly Barton Butcher,** (wife of Goodloe Edgar Byron and daughter-in-law of William Devereux Byron and Katharine Edgar Byron), a Representative from Maryland; born in Baltimore, Md., July 27, 1932; graduated, National Cathedral School, Washington, D.C., 1950; attended Hood College, Frederick, Md., 1963-1964; treasurer, Maryland Young Democrats, 1962 and 1965; active in the political career of her husband, Goodloe E. Byron; elected as a Democrat to the Ninety-sixth and to the six succeeding Congresses (January 3, 1979-January 3, 1993); unsuccessful candidate for renomination in 1992 to the One Hundred Third Congress; is a resident of Frederick, Md.

**BYRON, Goodloe Edgar** (husband of Beverly Barton Butcher Byron, son of Katharine Edgar Byron and William Devereux Byron, and great-grandson of Louis Emery McComas), a Representative from Maryland; born in Williamsport, Washington County, Md., June 22, 1929; attended the Williamsport public schools and St. Albans School of Washington, D.C.; B.A., University of Virginia at Charlottesville, 1951; J.D., George Washington University, Washington, D.C., 1953; commissioned first lieutenant, United States Army, with judge advocate general's office, 1954, serving as legal officer with Third Armored Division in Germany; discharged with rank of captain, 1957; subsequently joined Maryland National Guard, serving as aide-de-camp to Major General William Purnell, commander, Twenty-ninth Infantry Division; admitted to the Maryland bar in 1953 and commenced practice in Frederick, 1958; Frederick County attorney, 1959-1961; chairman, Maryland State Planning and Zoning Law Study commission, 1966-1970; member, Maryland house of delegates, 1963-1967; member, Maryland senate, 1967-1971; elected as a Democrat to the Ninety-second and to the three succeeding Congresses and served from January 3, 1971, until his death in Hagerstown, Md., on October 11, 1978; had been renominated to the Ninety-sixth Congress; interment in Antietam National Cemetery, Sharpsburg, Md.

**BYRON, Katharine Edgar** (wife of William Devereux Byron, mother of Goodloe Edgar Byron, granddaughter of Louis Emory McComas and mother-in-law of Beverly Barton Butcher Byron), a Representative from Maryland; born in Detroit, Mich., October 25, 1903; attended the public schools, Westover School, Middlebury, Conn., and Holton Arms School, Washington, D.C.; moved to Williamsport, Md., in 1922; chairman of Red Cross flood disaster committee of Williamsport in 1936; town commissioner of Williamsport 1938-1940; elected as a Democrat to the Seventy-seventh Congress, by special election, May 27, 1941, to fill the vacancy caused by the death of her husband, William D. Byron, and served from May 27, 1941, to January 3, 1943; was not a candidate for reelection in 1942 to the Seventy-eighth Congress; retired and resided in Washington, D.C., where she died December 28, 1976; interment in Riverview Cemetery, Williamsport, Md.

**BYRON, William Devereux** (husband of Katharine Edgar Byron, father of Goodloe Edgar Byron and father-in-law of Beverly Barton Butcher Byron), a Representative from Maryland; born in Danville, Pittsylvania County, Va., May 15, 1895; moved to Williamsport, Washington County, Md. with his parents in 1899; attended the public schools, Phillips Exeter Academy, Exeter, N.H., and Pratt Institute, Brooklyn, N.Y.; during the First World War enlisted as a private in the Aviation Corps; commissioned a first lieutenant, and was assigned as an instructor in flying and in aerial gunnery; engaged in the leather manufacturing business in 1919; served as mayor of Williamsport 1926-1930; member of the State senate 1930-1934; member of the Maryland Roads commission in 1934 and 1935; elected as a Democrat to the Seventy-sixth and Seventy-seventh Congresses and served from January 3, 1939, until his death in an airplane crash at Jonesboro, Ga., February 27, 1941; interment in Riverview Cemetery, Williamsport, Md.

# C

**CABANISS, Thomas Banks** (cousin of Thomas Chipman McRae), a Representative from Georgia; born in Forsyth, Monroe County, Ga., August 31, 1835; attended private schools and Penfield College; was graduated from the University of Georgia at Athens in 1853; studied law; was admitted to the bar in 1861; entered the Confederate Army April 1, 1861, and served throughout the Civil War; returned to Forsyth, Ga., and commenced the practice of law; member of the State house of representatives 1865-1867; appointed assistant secretary of the State senate in 1870 and secretary in 1873; resigned to become solicitor general of the Flint circuit, which office he held until 1877; served in the State senate 1878-1880 and 1884-1886; elected as a Democrat to the Fifty-third Congress (March 4, 1893-March 3, 1895); unsuccessful candidate for renomination in 1894; appointed a member of the Dawes Commission to adjust affairs in the Indian Territory; mayor of Forsyth, Ga., in 1910; judge of the city court in 1913 and 1914; died in Forsyth, Ga., August 14, 1915; interment in Oakland Cemetery.

**CABELL, Earle,** a Representative from Texas; born on a farm, south of Trinity River in Dallas County, Tex., October 27, 1906; graduated from North Dallas High School in 1925; attended Texas A. & M. and Southern Methodist University; in 1932 with two brothers organized Cabell's, Inc. (dairies and convenience stores) and became president and chairman of the board; engaged in banking and investments; elected mayor of Dallas May 1961 and reelected in 1963, serving until his resignation February 3, 1964, to be a candidate for Congress; elected as a Democrat to the Eighty-ninth and to the three succeeding Congresses (January 3, 1965-January 3, 1973); unsuccessful candidate for reelection in 1972 to the Ninety-third Congress; retired and returned to Dallas where he died September 24, 1975; interment in Restland Memorial Park.

**CABELL, Edward Carrington,** a Representative from Florida; born in Richmond, Va., February 5, 1816; attended Washington College (now Washington and Lee University), Lexington, Va., in 1832 and 1833 and Reynolds' Classical Academy in 1833 and 1834; was graduated from the University of Virginia at Charlottesville in 1836; moved to Florida in 1837 and engaged in agricultural pursuits near Tallahassee; delegate to the Territorial convention to form a State constitution in 1838; returned to Virginia; studied law; was admitted to the bar in 1840; returned to Tallahassee, Fla.; upon the admission of Florida as a State into the Union presented credentials as a Member-elect to the Twenty-ninth Congress, and served from October 6, 1845, to January 24, 1846, when he was succeeded by William H. Brockenbrough, who contested the election; elected as a Whig to the Thirtieth and to the two succeeding Congresses (March 4, 1847-March 3, 1853); chairman, Committee on Expenditures on

Public Buildings (Thirtieth-Congress); unsuccessful candidate for reelection in 1852 to the Thirty-third Congress; resumed the practice of law in Tallahassee; moved to St. Louis, Mo., in 1859; during the Civil War served in the Confederate Army with rank of lieutenant colonel; engaged in the practice of law in New York City from 1868 to 1872, and subsequently in St. Louis, Mo.; member of the Missouri State senate from 1878 until 1882; died in St. Louis, Mo., February 28, 1896; interment in Bellefontaine Cemetery.

**CABELL, George Craighead,** a Representative from Virginia; born in Danville, Pittsylvania County, Va., January 25, 1836; attended the Danville Academy, and the law school of the University of Virginia at Charlottesville in 1857; was admitted to the bar and commenced practice in Danville in 1858; edited the Republican and later the Democratic Appeal in Danville; elected Commonwealth attorney for Danville in September 1858, and served until April 23, 1861, when he volunteered as a private in the Confederate Army; commissioned major in June 1861 and was assigned to the Eighteenth Regiment, Virginia Infantry; promoted to the rank of colonel and served until the close of the Civil War; resumed the practice of his profession; elected as a Democrat to the Forty-fourth and to the five succeeding Congresses (March 4, 1875-March 3, 1887); chairman, Committee on Railways and Canals (Forty-fifth and Forty-sixth Congresses); unsuccessful candidate for reelection in 1886 to the Fiftieth Congress; resumed the practice of law in Danville, Va.; died in Baltimore, Md., June 23, 1906; interment in Green Hill Cemetery, Danville, Va.

**CABELL, Samuel Jordan,** a Representative from Virginia; born in Albemarle (now Nelson) County, Va., December 15, 1756; attended the College of William and Mary, Williamsburg, Va.; left school to enter the Revolutionary Army; appointed captain of Amherst County Volunteers in 1776; assigned to the Sixth Virginia Regiment; promoted to the rank of major for gallantry at Saratoga in 1777; served in Washington's army, 1778-1779 and attained the rank of lieutenant colonel; was taken prisoner by the British on May 12, 1780, at the capture of Charleston; after the war returned to Virginia and engaged in planting; member of the Virginia house of delegates 1785-1792; member of ratification convention in 1788; elected as a Republican to the Fourth and to the three succeeding Congresses (March 4, 1795-March 3, 1803); was not a candidate for reelection in 1802; died on his estate "Soldiers' Joy," near New Market (now Norwood), Nelson County, Va., August 4, 1818; interment in the family burying ground.

**Bibliography:** *DAB.*

**CABLE, Benjamin Taylor,** a Representative from Illinois; born in Georgetown, Scott County, Ky., August 11, 1853; moved with his parents to Rock Island, Ill., in September 1856; attended the public schools and Racine College, Racine, Wis.; was graduated from the University of Michigan at Ann Arbor in 1876; engaged in agricultural pursuits and also became interested in various manufacturing enterprises; chairman of the western branch of the Democratic National Committee in 1892; chairman of the Democratic executive committee in 1902; delegate to the Democratic National Convention in 1904; elected as a Democrat to the Fifty-second Congress (March 4, 1891-March 3, 1893); declined to be a candidate for renomination in 1892; engaged in agricultural pursuits as joint owner of a ranch near San Antonio, Tex.; died in Rock Island, Ill., on December 13, 1923; interment in Chippiannock Cemetery.

**CABLE, John Levi** (great-grandson of Joseph Cable), a Representative from Ohio; born in Lima, Allen County, Ohio, April 15, 1884; attended the public schools; Kenyon College, Gambier, Ohio, LL.B., 1906 and from the law department of George Washington University, Washington, D.C., J.D., 1909; was admitted to the bar in 1909 and commenced practice in Lima, Ohio; prosecuting attorney of Allen County 1917-1921; elected as a

Republican to the Sixty-seventh and Sixty-eighth Congresses (March 4, 1921-March 3, 1925); chairman, Committee on Alcoholic Liquor Traffic (Sixty-eighth Congress); was not a candidate for renomination in 1924; resumed the practice of law; again elected to the Seventy-first Congress; reelected to the Seventy-second Congress (March 4, 1929-March 3, 1933); unsuccessful candidate for reelection in 1932 to the Seventy-third Congress; resumed the practice of law; special assistant to attorney general of Ohio 1933-1937; special counsel to the Reconstruction Finance Corporation in the liquidation of the Lima First American Bank & Trust Co.; appointed Government appeal agent of Selective Service Board No. 2, Lima, Ohio, 1948-1960; author and publisher; died in Lima, Ohio, September 15, 1971; entombment in a niche in St. Boniface Episcopal Church, Sarasota, Fla.

**CABLE, Joseph** (great-grandfather of John Levi Cable), a Representative from Ohio; born in Jefferson County, then in the Terrritory Northwest of the River Ohio (now in the State of Ohio), April 17, 1801; attended the public schools; studied law; was admitted to the bar and commenced practice in Jefferson County; established and published the Jeffersonian and Democrat at Steubenville, Ohio, in 1831 and later the Ohio Patriot at New Lisbon, Ohio; elected as a Democrat to the Thirty-first and Thirty-second Congresses (March 4, 1849-March 3, 1853); was not a candidate for renomination in 1852; moved to Sandusky, Ohio, in 1853 and published the Daily Sandusky Minor; in 1857 established the American and later the Bulletin at Van Wert, Ohio; moved to Wauseon, Ohio, and established the Wauseon Republican; subsequently moved to Paulding, where he published the Political Review; died in Paulding, Ohio, May 1, 1880; interment in Live Oak Cemetery.

**CABOT, George** (great-grandfather of Henry Cabot Lodge), a Senator from Massachusetts; born in Salem, Mass., December 3, 1752; received a classical education and attended Harvard College; member of the Massachusetts provincial congress in 1775; delegate to the Massachusetts constitutional convention in 1777 and to the convention that ratified the Constitution of the United States in 1787; elected to the United States Senate and served from March 4, 1791, to June 9, 1796, when he resigned; appointed the first Secretary of the Navy in the Cabinet of President John Adams in 1798, but declined; member, executive council of Massachusetts in 1808; delegate to the Hartford convention of December 1814-January 1815, and served as its presiding officer; died in Boston, Mass., April 18, 1823; interment in the Granary Burial Ground, Boston, Mass.; reinterment in Mount Auburn Cemetery, Cambridge, Mass.

Bibliography: *DAB*; Lodge, Henry C. *Life and Letters of George Cabot.* 1877. Reprint. New York: Da Capo Press, 1974.

**CADMUS, Cornelius Andrew,** a Representative from New Jersey; born at Dundee Lake, Bergen County, N.J., October 7, 1844; attended the public schools; engaged in the feed and grain business in Paterson, N.J.; member of the State house of assembly in 1884 and 1885; sheriff of Passaic County 1887-1890; elected as a Democrat to the Fifty-second and Fifty-third Congresses (March 4, 1891-March 3, 1895); was not a candidate for renomination in 1894; member of the board of inspectors of the State prison; resumed his former business pursuits; died in Paterson, N.J., January 20, 1902; interment in Cedar Lawn Cemetery, near Paterson, N.J.

**CADWALADER, John,** a Representative from Pennsylvania; born in Philadelphia, Pa., April 1, 1805; was graduated from the University of Pennsylvania at Philadelphia in 1821; studied law; was admitted to the bar in 1825 and commenced practice in Philadelphia; solicitor for the Bank of the United States in 1830; captain of a military company during the riots of 1844 in Philadelphia; elected as a Democrat to the Thirty-fourth Congress (March 4, 1855-March 3, 1857); declined to be a candidate for renomination in 1856; resumed the practice of law in Philadelphia; appointed judge of the United States District Court for the Eastern District of Pennsylvania in 1858 and served until his death in Philadelphia, Pa., January 26, 1879; interment in Christ Churchyard.

Bibliography: *DAB*.

**CADWALADER, Lambert,** a Delegate and a Representative from New Jersey; born near Trenton, N.J., in 1742; attended Dr. Allison's Academy, and the University of Pennsylvania at Philadelphia in 1760; member of the common council of Philadelphia at the beginning of the Revolution; signed the nonimportation agreement in 1765; delegate to the provincial convention in Pennsylvania in 1775 and to the State constitutional convention in 1776; entered the Revolutionary Army and commanded a regiment of "The Greens"; lieutenant colonel of the Third Pennsylvania Battalion in 1776; colonel of the Fourth Pennsylvania Line; after being taken a prisoner at Fort Washington on the Hudson resigned from the Army; Member of the Continental Congress in 1785, 1786 and 1787; elected to the First Congress (March 4, 1789-March 3, 1791); elected to the Third Congress (March 4, 1793-March 3, 1795); died on his estate, "Greenwood," near Trenton, N.J., September 13, 1823; interment in the Friends Burying Ground, Trenton, N.J.

Bibliography: *DAB*.

**CADY, Claude Ernest,** a Representative from Michigan; born in Lansing, Ingham County, Mich., May 28, 1878; attended the common schools and the high school of his native city; engaged in the wholesale and retail grocery business from 1899 to 1913; was active in the amusement business, being owner of three theaters in Lansing, and also had financial interests in other Michigan cities 1914-1925; in the wholesale candy and fountain supplies business from 1925 to 1932; served as a member of the board of aldermen 1910-1917; member of the Lansing Police and Fire Commission 1918-1928; elected as a Democrat to the Seventy-third Congress (March 4, 1933-January 3, 1935); unsuccessful candidate for reelection in 1934 to the Seventy-fourth Congress; served as postmaster at Lansing, Mich., 1935-1943; retired from political and business life; died in Lansing, Mich., November 30, 1953; interment in Mount Hope Cemetery.

**CADY, Daniel** (uncle of John Watts Cady), a Representative from New York; born in Canaan, Columbia County, N.Y., April 29, 1773; attended the public schools; studied law in Albany, N.Y.; was admitted to the bar in 1795 and commenced practice in Florida, N.Y.; moved to Johnstown (then in Montgomery County), N.Y., and continued the practice of law; member of the State assembly 1808-1813; village trustee in 1808 and supervisor in 1809 and 1810; district attorney of the fifth district in 1813; elected as a Federalist to the Fourteenth Congress (March 4, 1815-March 3, 1817); was not a candidate for renomination in 1816; resumed the practice of law; served as justice of the State supreme court, fourth district, from June 7, 1847, to January 1, 1855, when he resigned; served as judge of the court of appeals in 1853; presidential elector on the Republican ticket in 1856 and served as president of the State electoral college; died in Johnstown, N.Y., October 31, 1859; interment in Johnstown Cemetery.

Bibliography: *DAB*.

**CADY, John Watts** (nephew of Daniel Cady), a Representative from New York; born in Florida, Montgomery County, N.Y., June 28, 1790; attended school at the Old Stone Manse at Fort Hunter, and was graduated from Union College, Schenectady, N.Y., in 1808; studied law; was admitted to the bar and commenced practice in Johnstown (then in Montgomery County), N.Y.; town clerk of Johnstown 1814, 1816, and 1817; county supervisor 1818-1822 and 1826-1829; member of the State assembly in 1822; elected to the Eighteenth Congress (March 4, 1823-March 3, 1825); was not a candidate for renomination in 1824; resumed the practice of law at Johnstown, N.Y.; district attorney of Fulton County 1840-1846; justice of the peace of Johnstown in 1853; died in Johnstown, N.Y., January 5, 1854; interment in Johnstown Cemetery.

**CAFFERY, Donelson** (grandfather of Patrick Thomson Caffery), a Senator from Louisiana; born near Franklin, St. Mary Parish, La., September 10, 1835; attended private schools in Franklin, St. Mary's College, Baltimore, Md., and Louisiana University at New Orleans; studied law; during the Civil War served as a lieutenant in the Thirteenth Louisiana Regiment; served as clerk of court in 1866; was admitted to the bar in 1867 and commenced the practice of law in Franklin, La.; sugar planter; delegate to the State constitutional convention in 1879; member, State senate 1892-1893; appointed and subsequently elected as a Democrat to the United States Senate in 1894 to fill the vacancy caused by the death of Randall Lee Gibson and served from December 31, 1892, to March 3, 1901; was not a candidate for reelection in 1900; chairman, Committee on Enrolled Bills (Fifty-third Congress), Committee on Corporations Organized in the District of Columbia (Fifty-sixth Congress); resumed the practice of law; died in New Orleans, La., on December 30, 1906; interment in Franklin Cemetery, Franklin, La.

**Bibliography:** *DAB.*

**CAFFERY, Patrick Thomson** (grandson of Donelson Caffery), a Representative from Louisiana; born near Franklin, St. Mary Parish, La., July 6, 1932; attended public schools of Franklin and Hanson Memorial High School; B.A., University of Southwestern Louisiana, 1955; J.D., Louisiana State University Law School, 1956; associate and managing editor, Louisiana Law Review, 1955-1956; was admitted to the bar in 1956 and commenced practice in New Iberia, La.; assistant district attorney, sixteenth judicial district of Louisiana, 1958-1962; member, Louisiana State house of representatives, 1964-1968; elected as a Democrat to the Ninety-first and Ninety-second Congresses (January 3, 1969-January 3, 1973); was not a candidate for reelection in 1972 to the Ninety-third Congress; resumed the practice of law; is a resident of New Iberia, La.

**CAGE, Harry,** a Representative from Mississippi; born at Cages Bend of the Cumberland River, Sumner County, Tenn.; moved to Wilkinson County, Miss., in early youth; studied law; was admitted to the bar and commenced practice in Woodville, Miss.; judge of the supreme court of Mississippi 1829-1832; elected as a Jacksonian to the Twenty-third Congress (March 4, 1833-March 3, 1835); retired from the practice of law and settled on Woodlawn plantation in the parish of Terrebonne, near the town of Houma, in Louisiana; died while on a visit to New Orleans, La., in 1859; interment in the cemetery of the Stewart family in Wilkinson County, Miss.

**CAHILL, William Thomas,** a Representative from New Jersey; born in Philadelphia, Pa., June 25, 1912; moved with his parents to Camden, N.J. in 1919; graduated from Camden (N.J.) Catholic High School in 1929; B.A., St. Joseph's College, 1933; LL.B., South Jersey Law School (now Rutgers University School of Law), 1937; special agent of the Federal Bureau of Investigation, 1937-1938; was admitted to the bar in 1939 and commenced the practice of law in Camden, N.J.; city prosecutor of Camden, N.J., 1944-1945; first assistant prosecutor of Camden County, 1948-1951; special deputy attorney general of New Jersey in 1951; member of the New Jersey State general assembly, 1951-1953; elected as a Republican to the Eighty-sixth and to the five succeeding Congresses, and served from January 3, 1959 until his resignation on January 19, 1970, having been elected Governor; elected Governor of New Jersey in 1969, and served from January 20, 1970 to January 15, 1974; unsuccessful candidate for renomination in 1973; senior fellow, Woodrow Wilson School, Princeton University, 1974-1978; resumed the practice of law with the firm of Wilinski and Cahill; was a resident of Haddonfield, N.J., until his death there on July 1, 1996; interment in Calvary Cemetery, Cherry Hill, N.J.

**CAHOON, William,** a Representative from Vermont; born in Providence, R.I., January 12, 1774; attended the common schools; moved with his parents to Lyndon, Vt., in 1791 and engaged in milling and agricultural pursuits; member of the State house of representatives 1802-1810; succeeded his father as town clerk in 1808; presidential elector in 1808 and voted for James Madison and John Langdon; county judge 1811-1819; appointed major general in the militia in 1808 and served during the War of 1812; delegate to the State constitutional conventions in 1814 and 1828; member of the executive council 1815-1820; lieutenant governor of Vermont in 1820 and 1821; elected on the Anti-Masonic ticket to the Twenty-first and Twenty-second Congresses (March 4, 1829-March 3, 1833); unsuccessful candidate in 1832 for reelection to the Twenty-third Congress; died in Lyndon, Vt., on May 30, 1833; interment in Lyndon Town Cemetery, Lyndon Center, Vt.

**CAIN, Harry Pulliam,** a Senator from Washington; born in Nashville, Davidson County Tenn., January 10, 1906; moved with his parents to Tacoma, Pierce County, Wash., in 1911; attended the public schools and Hill Military Academy at Portland, Oreg.; graduated, University of the South, Sewanee, Tenn., 1929; pursued graduate study in England and Germany; engaged in newspaper work in Portland, Oreg., 1924-1925, and in the banking business at Tacoma, Wash., from 1929 until 1939; elected mayor of Tacoma, Wash., in 1940, and again in 1942 for a four-year term; took leave of absence in May 1943 to enter the United States Army as a major; served in the United States Army in the European theater, 1943-1945; resumed his duties as mayor of Tacoma until June 15, 1946; elected as a Republican to the United States Senate on November 5, 1946, for the term commencing January 3, 1947; subsequently appointed on December 26, 1946, to fill the vacancy in the term ending January 3, 1947, caused by the resignation of Hugh B. Mitchell, and served from December 26, 1946 to January 3, 1953; unsuccessful candidate for reelection in 1952; member of the Subversive Activities Control Board, Washington, D.C., 1953-1956; moved to Florida in 1957 and resumed banking business; also involved in civic work; resided in Miami Lakes, Fla., where he died on March 3, 1979; cremated; ashes scattered on a golf course in Bethesda, Md.

**Bibliography:** *DAB.*

**CAIN, Richard Harvey,** a Representative from South Carolina; born in Greenbrier County, Va., April 12, 1825; moved with his family to Gallipolis, Ohio, in 1831 and attended school while working on steamboats along the Ohio River; entered the ministry of the Methodist Episcopal Church in Hannibal, Mo., 1844; affiliated with the African Methodist Episcopal Church in 1848 and was a pastor in Muscatine, Iowa; attended Wilberforce University, Ohio; was a pastor in Brooklyn, N.Y., from 1861 to 1865; moved to South Carolina in 1865 and settled in Charleston; delegate to the constitutional convention of South Carolina in 1868; member of the State senate 1868-1870; editor and publisher of the South Carolina Leader (later renamed the Missionary Record) 1866-1872; elected as a Republican to the Forty-third Congress (March 4, 1873-March 3, 1875); was not a candidate for renomination in 1874 to the Forty-fourth Congress; elected to the Forty-fifth Congress (March 4, 1877-March 3, 1879); was not a candidate for renomination in 1878 to the Forty-sixth Congress; elected a bishop of the African Methodist Episcopal Church in 1880 and served the Texas-Louisiana conference; assisted in the establishment of Paul Quinn College, Waco, Tex., and served as its president until July 1884; bishop of the New Jersey conference of the African Methodist Episcopal Church from 1884 until his death in Washington, D.C., January 18, 1887; interment in Graceland Cemetery.

**Bibliography:** *DAB*; Mann, Kenneth E. "Richard Harvey Cain,

Congressman, Minister and Champion for Civil Rights." *Negro History Bulletin* 35 (March 1972): 64-66.

**CAINE, John Thomas,** a Delegate from the Territory of Utah; born in the parish of Kirk Patrick, Isle of Man, January 8, 1829; attended the common schools in Douglas, Isle of Man; immigrated to the United States in 1846 and lived in New York City until 1848, when he went to St. Louis; settled in the Territory of Utah in 1852 and taught school; served as secretary of the Territorial council during the sessions of 1856, 1857, 1859, and 1860; one of the founders of the Salt Lake Herald in 1870, serving as managing editor and president; delegate to the constitutional conventions in 1872 and 1882; member of the Territorial council in 1874, 1876, 1880, and 1882; recorder of Salt Lake City in 1876, 1878, 1880, and 1882; elected as a Democrat to the Forty-seventh Congress to fill the vacancy caused by the action of the House declaring the Delegate-elect ineligible; reelected as a Democrat to the Forty-eighth, Forty-ninth, and Fiftieth Congresses and on the People's Party ticket to the Fifty-first and Fifty-second Congresses and served from November 7, 1882, to March 3, 1893; was not a candidate for renomination in 1892; was an unsuccessful Democratic candidate for Governor of Utah in 1895; member of the State senate in 1896; resumed the management of the Salt Lake Herald; died in Salt Lake City, Utah, September 20, 1911; interment in Salt Lake City Cemetery.

**CAKE, Henry Lutz,** a Representative from Pennsylvania; born near Northumberland, Northumberland County, Pa., on October 6, 1827; attended the common and private schools; learned the art of printing, and published the Pottsville (Pa.) Mining Record until the Civil War; entered the Union Army April 17, 1861, as a second lieutenant, and was elected colonel of the Twenty-fifth Regiment, Pennsylvania Volunteer Infantry, in Washington, D.C., May 1, 1861; reorganized the regiment after three months' service; commanded the Ninety-sixth Regiment, Pennsylvania Volunteer Infantry, from September 23, 1861, to March 12, 1863, when he resigned and settled in Tamaqua, Schuylkill County, Pa.; engaged in the mining and shipping of anthracite coal; elected as a Republican to the Fortieth and Forty-first Congresses (March 4, 1867-March 3, 1871); chairman, Committee on Accounts (Forty-first Congress); unsuccessful candidate for renomination in 1870; resumed the mining and shipping of coal; died in Northumberland, Pa., August 26, 1899; interment in Riverview Cemetery.

**CALDER, William Musgrave,** a Representative and a Senator from New York; born in Brooklyn, N.Y., March 3, 1869; attended the public schools of Brooklyn; apprenticed to the carpenter's trade and studied at the evening school of Cooper Institute, New York City; engaged in building construction in 1893; building commissioner of the Borough of Brooklyn 1902-1903; elected as a Republican to the Fifty-ninth and to the four succeeding Congresses (March 4, 1905-March 3, 1915); was not a candidate for reelection in 1914; elected as a Republican to the United States Senate and served from March 4, 1917, to March 3, 1923; unsuccessful candidate for reelection in 1922; chairman, Committee to Audit and Control the Contingent Expense (Sixty-sixth and Sixty-seventh Congresses); again engaged in building construction and was also a director in many Brooklyn financial institutions; died in Brooklyn, N.Y., March 3, 1945; interment in Greenwood Cemetery.

**CALDERHEAD, William Alexander,** a Representative from Kansas; born on a farm near New Lexington, Perry County, Ohio, September 26, 1844; received private schooling and also attended the common schools and Franklin College, New Athens, Ohio; during the Civil War enlisted in August 1862 as a private in Company H, One Hundred and Twenty-sixth Regiment, Ohio Volunteer Infantry; was transferred to Company D, Ninth Veteran Reserves, for disability incurred in service and discharged June 27, 1865; moved to Harvey County, Kans., in 1868 and engaged in

agricultural pursuits near Newton; moved to Newton, Kans., in 1872 and taught school and studied law; was admitted to the bar in 1875; moved to Atchison, Kans., and continued to study law; also engaged in teaching; settled in Marysville, Marshall County, Kans., in 1879 and commenced the practice of law; served as prosecuting attorney of Marshall County 1889-1891; elected as a Republican to the Fifty-fourth Congress (March 4, 1895-March 3, 1897); unsuccessful candidate for reelection in 1896 to the Fifty-fifth Congress; elected to the Fifty-sixth and to the five succeeding Congresses (March 4, 1899-March 3, 1911); chairman, Committee of Expenditures in the Department of Justice (Fifty-eighth and Fifty-ninth Congresses); unsuccessful candidate for renomination in 1910; resumed the practice of law in Marysville, Kans., until 1920, when he retired from active business pursuits and moved to Enid, Okla., where he died on December 18, 1928; interment in Marysville Cemetery, Marysville, Kans.

**CALDWELL, Alexander,** a Senator from Kansas; born at Drakes Ferry, Huntingdon County, Pa., March 1, 1830; attended the public schools; enlisted in 1847 as a private in the Mexican War; moved to Columbia, Pa., in 1848; employed in a bank and subsequently went into business for himself; moved to Leavenworth, Kans., in 1861 and engaged in the transportation of military supplies to the various posts on the plains; engaged in the building of railroads, especially the Missouri River and Kansas Central Railroad; elected as a Republican to the United States Senate and served from March 4, 1871, to March 24, 1873, when he resigned; manufactured wagons and carriages 1877-1897; president of the First National Bank of Leavenworth 1897-1915; died in Kansas City, Mo., May 19, 1917; interment in Mount Muncie Cemetery, Leavenworth, Kans.

**Bibliography:** *DAB.*

**CALDWELL, Andrew Jackson,** a Representative from Tennessee; born in Montevallo, Shelby County, Ala., July 22, 1837; moved to Tennessee in 1844 with his parents, who settled near Nashville; attended the common schools; was graduated from Franklin College, Tennessee, in 1854; taught school in Nashville 1854-1857; moved to Trenton in 1857 and studied law; during the Civil War served in the Confederate Army as a private and regimental quartermaster in the First Regiment, Tennessee Cavalry; resumed his law studies; was admitted to the Tennessee bar in 1867 and commenced the practice of law in Nashville, Tenn.; attorney general for the district of Davidson and Rutherford Counties, Tenn., 1870-1878; served as a member of the State house of representatives in 1880 and 1882; elected as a Democrat to the Forty-eighth and Forty-ninth Congresses (March 4, 1883-March 3, 1887); was not a candidate for reelection to the Fiftieth Congress; resumed the practice of law; died in Nashville, Tenn., November 22, 1906; interment in Mount Olivet Cemetery.

**CALDWELL, Ben Franklin,** a Representative from Illinois; born near Carrollton, Greene County, Ill., August 2, 1848; moved to Illinois in April 1853 with his parents, who settled near Chatham, Ill.; attended the public schools; engaged in agricultural pursuits; member of the Board of Supervisors of Sangamon County in 1877 and 1878; member of the Illinois State house of representatives, 1882-1886; served in the Illinois State senate, 1890-1894; upon his election to Congress in 1898 he resigned the presidency of the Farmers' National Bank of Springfield, which office he had held since 1885; president of the Caldwell State Bank of Chatham; elected as a Democrat to the Fifty-sixth and to the two succeeding Congresses (March 4, 1899-March 3, 1905); unsuccessful candidate for reelection in 1904 to the Fifty-ninth Congress; elected to the Sixtieth Congress (March 4, 1907-March 3, 1909); was not a candidate for renomination in 1908 to the Sixty-first Congress; again engaged in banking in Chatham, Ill.; died in Springfield, Ill., on December 29, 1924; interment in Oak Ridge Cemetery.

**CALDWELL, Charles Pope,** a Representative from New York; born near Bastrop, Bastrop County, Tex., June 18, 1875; attended the public schools; was graduated from the law department of the University of Texas at Austin in 1898 and the law department of Yale University in 1899; was admitted to the bar in Austin, Tex., in 1898, and later in New York City, where he commenced practice in 1900; appointed by the Governor as a delegate to the Atlantic Deeper Water Ways Convention in 1910; delegate to the Democratic National Convention of 1912; elected as a Democrat to the Sixty-fourth and to the two succeeding Congresses (March 4, 1915-March 3, 1921); declined to be a candidate for renomination in 1920 to the Sixty-seventh Congress; resumed the practice of law in New York City; appointed associate justice of the court of special sessions of New York City January 1, 1926, and served until December 1935; resumed the practice of law in Long Island, N.Y.; died in Sunnyside, Queens County, N.Y., July 31, 1940; remains were cremated and the ashes scattered over his ancestral estate in Bastrop County, Tex.

**CALDWELL, George Alfred,** a Representative from Kentucky; born in Columbia, Adair County, Ky., October 18, 1814; attended the common schools; studied law; was admitted to the bar in 1837 and commenced practice in Adair County; member of the Kentucky house of representatives in 1839 and 1840; elected as a Democrat to the Twenty-eighth Congress (March 4, 1843-March 3, 1845); chairman, Committee on Expenditures in the Department of the Treasury (Twenty-eighth Congress); commissioned major and quartermaster of Volunteers in the war with Mexico June 26, 1846; major of Infantry March 3, 1847, and major of voltigeurs April 9, 1847; brevetted lieutenant colonel September 13, 1847 for service in the Battle of Chapultepec, Mexico; honorably mustered out August 25, 1848; elected to the Thirty-first Congress (March 4, 1849-March 3, 1851); chairman, Committee on Expenditures in the Department of the Treasury (Thirty-first Congress); was not a candidate for reelection in 1850 to the Thirty-second Congress; resumed the practice of law in Louisville; delegate to the Union National Convention at Philadelphia in 1866; died in Louisville, Ky., September 17, 1866; interment in Cave Hill Cemetery.

**CALDWELL, Greene Washington,** a Representative from North Carolina; born in Belmont, Gaston County, N.C., April 13, 1806; pursued academic studies; was graduated from the medical department of the University of Pennsylvania at Philadelphia in 1831 and practiced; assistant surgeon in the United States Army 1832; studied law; was admitted to the bar and practiced in Charlotte, N.C.; member of the State house of commons 1836-1841; elected as a Democrat to the Twenty-seventh Congress (March 4, 1841-March 3, 1843); was not a candidate for renomination in 1842; appointed superintendent of the United States Mint at Charlotte in 1844; participated in the war with Mexico as captain of Infantry; commissioned captain of the Third Dragoons April 9, 1847, and was mustered out July 20, 1848; member of the State senate in 1849; unsuccessful candidate for election in 1850 to the Thirty-second Congress; resumed the practice of medicine; died in Charlotte, N.C., July 10, 1864; interment in the Old Cemetery.

**CALDWELL, James,** a Representative from Ohio; born in Baltimore, Md., November 30, 1770; moved with his father to Virginia (now West Virginia) in 1772 and settled on what is now the site of the city of Wheeling; received a liberal schooling; moved to St. Clairsville, Ohio, in 1799; engaged in mercantile pursuits and later in banking; delegate to the convention which framed the first constitution of Ohio; clerk of the court of Belmont County, Ohio, 1806-1810; captain in an Ohio regiment in the War of 1812; member of the State senate 1809-1812; elected as a Republican to the Thirteenth and Fourteenth Congresses (March 4, 1813-March 3, 1817); resumed banking and mercantile business in St. Clairsville,

Ohio; died in Wheeling, Va. (now West Virginia), in May 1838; interment in Episcopal Cemetery, St. Clairsville, Belmont County, Ohio.

**CALDWELL, John Alexander,** a Representative from Ohio; born in Fairhaven, Preble County, Ohio, April 21, 1852; educated in the common schools of his native county and also by private teachers; taught school for several years; was graduated from the Cincinnati Law College in 1876; was admitted to the bar the same year; again engaged in teaching; commenced the practice of law in Cincinnati, Ohio, in 1878; prosecuting attorney of the Cincinnati police court 1881-1885; elected judge of the city police court in 1887; elected president of the Ohio League of Republican Clubs in 1887; elected as a Republican to the Fifty-first, Fifty-second, and Fifty-third Congresses and served from March 4, 1889, until May 4, 1894, when he resigned; mayor of Cincinnati 1894-1897; lieutenant governor of Ohio 1899-1901; elected judge of the court of common pleas in 1902, and served until his death in Cincinnati, Ohio, May 24, 1927; interment in Spring Grove Cemetery.

**CALDWELL, John Henry,** a Representative from Alabama; born in Huntsville, Ala., April 4, 1826; attended the common schools of Huntsville and Bacon College, Harrodsburg, Ky.; taught school in Limestone County, Ala., four years; moved to Jacksonville, Ala., in 1848; was principal of the Jacksonville Female Academy 1848-1852 and of the Jacksonville Male Academy 1853-1857; edited the Jacksonville Republican in 1851 and 1852 and assumed the editorship of the Sunny South in 1855; member of the State house of representatives in 1857 and 1858; studied law; was admitted to the bar in 1859 and commenced practice in Jacksonville, Ala.; during the Civil War enlisted in the Confederate Army and organized Company A of the Tenth Alabama Regiment, from St. Clair and Calhoun Counties, and served throughout the war; promoted to major and then to lieutenant colonel; served in the Army of Virginia; elected solicitor for the tenth judicial circuit in 1863 but was deposed by the Provisional Governor in 1865; reelected the same year, and in 1867 was removed from office for refusing to obey military orders; elected as a Democrat to the Forty-third and Forty-fourth Congresses (March 4, 1873-March 3, 1877); chairman, Committee on Agriculture (Forty-fourth Congress); was not a candidate for renomination in 1876; resumed the practice of law; died in Jacksonville, Ala., September 4, 1902; interment in Jacksonville Cemetery.

**CALDWELL, John William,** a Representative from Kentucky; born in Russellville, Logan County, Ky., January 15, 1837; attended the common schools and Bethel College; moved with his uncle to Texas in 1850, where he worked on a farm; engaged as a clerk and as a surveyor; returned to Kentucky and studied law in the Louisville University; was admitted to the bar in 1858 and commenced practice in Russellville, Ky.; volunteered as a private in the Confederate Army in 1861 and was immediately elected captain of the "Logan Grays"; promoted to major, lieutenant colonel, and colonel of the Ninth Regiment, Kentucky Infantry; resumed the practice of law in Russellville in 1865; elected judge of the Logan County Court in 1866 and reelected in 1870; elected as a Democrat to the Forty-fifth, Forty-sixth, and Forty-seventh Congresses (March 4, 1877-March 3, 1883); declined to be a candidate for reelection; president of the Logan County Bank; died in Russellville, Ky., July 4, 1903; interment in Maple Grove Cemetery.

**CALDWELL, Joseph Pearson,** a Representative from North Carolina; born near Olin, Iredell County, N.C., March 5, 1808; attended Bethany Academy, near Statesville, N.C.; studied law; was admitted to the bar and commenced practice in Statesville, N.C.; served in the State senate in 1833 and 1834; member of the State house of commons 1838-1844; elected as a Whig to the Thirty-first and Thirty-second Congresses (March 4, 1849-March 3, 1853); was not a candidate for renomination in 1852; died in Statesville, N.C., June 30, 1853; interment in Old Statesville Cemetery.

**CALDWELL, Millard Fillmore,** a Representative from Florida; born in Beverly, Tenn., February 6, 1897; attended the public schools, Carson-Newman College, Jefferson City, Tenn., the University of Mississippi at Oxford, and the University of Virginia at Charlottesville; during the First World War enlisted in the United States Army on April 3, 1918, was commissioned a second lieutenant in the Field Artillery, and was discharged on January 11, 1919; studied law; was admitted to the bar in 1922 and commenced practice in Milton, Fla., in 1925; served as prosecuting attorney and county attorney of Santa Rosa County, Fla., 1926-1932; member of the Florida State house of representatives from Santa Rosa County, 1929-1932; elected as a Democrat to the Seventy-third and to the three succeeding Congresses (March 4, 1933-January 3, 1941); was not a candidate for renomination in 1940 to the Seventy-seventh Congress; resumed the practice of law; elected Governor of Florida in 1944, and served from January 2, 1945 to January 4, 1949; chairman of the National Governors Conference in 1946 and 1947; chairman, Regional Board of Control for Southern Regional Education, 1948-1950; Administrator, Federal Civil Defense Administration, 1950-1952; appointed a justice of the Supreme Court of Florida on February 14, 1962, and served as chief justice from September 5, 1967 until his retirement on January 7, 1969; engaged in farming and banking; counsel to a law firm in Tallahassee until his retirement in 1979; resided in Tallahassee, Fla., until his death there on October 23, 1984.

**CALDWELL, Patrick Calhoun,** a Representative from South Carolina; born near Newberry, S.C., March 10, 1801; was graduated from South Carolina College (now the University of South Carolina) at Columbia in 1820; studied law; was admitted to the bar in 1822 and commenced practice in South Carolina; member of the State house of representatives 1838-1839; elected as a Democrat to the Twenty-seventh Congress (March 4, 1841-March 3, 1843); unsuccessful candidate for reelection to the Twenty-eighth Congress; served in the State senate in 1848; died in South Carolina November 22, 1855.

**CALDWELL, Robert Porter,** a Representative from Tennessee; born in Adair County, Ky., December 16, 1821; moved with his parents to Henry County, Tenn.; a few years later moved to Obion County; attended the public schools at Troy and Lebanon; studied law at Troy; was admitted to the bar and commenced practice in Trenton in 1845; member of the State house of representatives in 1847 and 1848; served in the State senate in 1855 and 1856; elected attorney general for the sixteenth judicial circuit of Tennessee in 1858; during the Civil War was a major in the Twelfth Regiment, Tennessee Infantry, of the Confederate Army; elected as a Democrat to the Forty-second Congress (March 4, 1871-March 3, 1873); unsuccessful candidate for renomination in 1872 to the Forty-third Congress; resumed the practice of law in Trenton, Tenn.; died in Trenton March 12, 1885; interment in Oakland Cemetery.

**CALDWELL, William Parker,** a Representative from Tennessee; born in Christmasville, Carroll County, Tenn., November 8, 1832; attended school at McLemoresville, Tenn., and at Princeton, Ky.; studied law at Cumberland University, Lebanon, Tenn.; was admitted to the bar in 1853 and practiced in Dresden and Union City, Tenn.; member of the State house of representatives 1857-1859; presidential elector on the Democratic ticket of Douglas and Johnson in 1860; delegate to the Democratic National Convention in 1868; elected as a Democrat to the Forty-fourth and Forty-fifth Congresses (March 4, 1875-March 3, 1879); was not a candidate for reelection to the Forty-sixth Congress in 1878; resumed the practice of law in Gardner, Tenn.; member of the State senate 1891-1893; died in Gardner, Tenn., June 7, 1903; interment in the Caldwell Cemetery.

**CALE, Thomas,** a Delegate from the Territory of Alaska; born in Underhill, Chittenden County, Vt., September 17, 1848; attended the district schools and Bell Academy, Underhill Flats, Vt.; moved to Fort Edward, Washington County, N.Y., in 1866; taught school near Underhill Center, Vt., in 1867 and 1868; moved to Fond du Lac, Wis., in 1869; taught school in several districts in Fond du Lac County and then engaged in agricultural pursuits near Eden, Wis.; town clerk of Eden 1881-1884; member of the board of commissioners of Fond du Lac County 1884-1886; returned to Fond du Lac and served as undersheriff of Fond du Lac County 1886-1888; county sheriff 1888-1890; engaged as a salesman of farm machinery; moved to Fairbanks, Alaska, in 1898 and engaged in mining; elected as an Independent to the Sixtieth Congress (March 4, 1907-March 3, 1909); was not a candidate for renomination in 1908; engaged in farming near McLaughlin, S.Dak., 1910-1915 and near Stevens Point, Wis., 1915-1920; retired from active pursuits in 1920 and resided in Fond du Lac, Wis., until his death in that city on February 3, 1941; interment in Calvary Cemetery.

**CALHOON, John,** a Representative from Kentucky; born in Henry County, Ky., in 1797; studied law; was admitted to the bar and practiced; member of the Kentucky house of representatives in 1820, 1821, 1829, and 1830; unsuccessful candidate for election to the Twentieth Congress; received the credentials of an election to the Twentieth Congress, held November 5-7, 1827, to fill the vacancy caused by the death of William S. Young, but, in order to avoid a contest, resigned and, together with his opponent, Thomas Chilton, petitioned the Governor for a new election; was again unsuccessful; elected as a Whig to the Twenty-fourth and Twenty-fifth Congresses (March 4, 1835-March 3, 1839); was not a candidate for reelection to the Twenty-sixth Congress; moved to St. Louis, Mo., in 1839; resumed the practice of law; returned to Kentucky; appointed judge of the fourteenth judicial district in January 1842.

**CALHOUN, John Caldwell** (cousin of John Ewing Colhoun and Joseph Calhoun), a Representative and a Senator from South Carolina and a Vice President of the United States; born near Calhoun Mills, Abbeville District (now Mount Carmel, McCormick County), S.C., March 18, 1782; attended the common schools and private academies; was graduated from Yale College in 1804; studied law, was admitted to the bar in 1807, and commenced practice in Abbeville, S.C.; also engaged in agricultural pursuits; member, South Carolina State house of representatives, 1808-1809; elected as a Republican to the Twelfth and to the three succeeding Congresses, and served from March 4, 1811 to November 3, 1817, when he resigned; appointed Secretary of War in the Cabinet of President James Monroe on October 8, 1817 and served until March 7, 1825; elected Vice President of the United States in 1824, and served under John Quincy Adams; reelected in 1828 with Andrew Jackson, and served from March 4, 1825 to December 28, 1832, when he resigned, having been elected to the United States Senate on December 12, 1832, to fill the vacancy caused by the resignation of Robert Y. Hayne; reelected in 1834 and 1840, and served from December 29, 1832 until his resignation, effective March 3, 1843; appointed Secretary of State in the Cabinet of President John Tyler on March 6, 1844 and served until March 10, 1845; again elected to the United States Senate to fill the vacancy caused by the resignation of Daniel E. Huger; reelected in 1846, and served from November 26, 1845 until his death in Washington, D.C., March 31, 1850; chairman, Committee on Finance (Twenty-ninth Congress); interment in St. Philip's Churchyard, Charleston, S.C.

**Bibliography:** *DAB*; Bartlett, Irving H. *John C. Calhoun: A Biography.* New York: W.W. Norton and Co., 1993; Calhoun, John C. *The Papers of John C. Calhoun.* Edited by Robert Meriwether, W. Edwin Hemphill, and Clyde N. Wilson. 22 vols. to date. Columbia: University of South Carolina Press, 1959-; Wiltse, Charles M. *John C. Calhoun.* 3 vols. Indianapolis: Bobbs-Merrill, 1944-1951. Reprint. New York: Russell and Russell, 1968.

**CALHOUN, Joseph** (cousin of John Caldwell Calhoun and John Ewing Colhoun), a Representative from South Carolina; born in Staunton, Augusta County, Va., October 22, 1750; moved with his father to South Carolina in 1756 and settled in Granville District, on Little River, near the present town of Abbeville; received a limited education; engaged in agricultural pursuits; served as a member of the South Carolina house of representatives in 1804 and 1805; colonel of State militia; elected as a Republican to the Tenth Congress to fill the vacancy caused by the death of Levi Casey; reelected to the Eleventh Congress and served from June 2, 1807, to March 3, 1811; declined to be a candidate for reelection in 1810 to the Twelfth Congress; resumed agricultural pursuits and engaged in milling; died in Calhoun Mills, Abbeville District (now Mount Carmel, McCormick County), April 14, 1817; interment in the family burying ground near his home.

**CALHOUN, William Barron,** a Representative from Massachusetts; born in Boston, Mass., December 29, 1796; was graduated from Yale College in 1814; studied law; was admitted to the bar and commenced practice in Springfield; member of the Massachusetts house of representatives 1825-1834, serving as speaker 1828-1834; elected as a Whig to the Twenty-fourth and to the three succeeding Congresses (March 4, 1835-March 3, 1843); chairman, Committee on Private Land Claims (Twenty-sixth Congress); was not a candidate for renomination in 1842; member of the Massachusetts senate in 1846 and 1847, serving as its president; secretary of state of the Commonwealth of Massachusetts 1848-1851; Massachusetts bank commissioner 1853-1855; mayor of Springfield in 1859; again a member of the Massachusetts house of representatives in 1861 and 1862; died in Springfield, Mass., November 8, 1865; interment in Springfield Cemetery.

Bibliography: *DAB.*

**CALKIN, Hervey Chittenden,** a Representative from New York; born in Malden, Ulster County, N.Y., March 23, 1828; attended the public schools; moved to New York City in 1847; employed in the Morgan Iron Works for five years; in 1852 commenced business as a dealer in metals and identified with the shipping interests of the country; school officer in his ward; elected as a Democrat to the Forty-first Congress (March 4, 1869-March 3, 1871); was not a candidate for reelection in 1870; resumed his former business pursuits in New York City until 1904, when he retired; died in the Bronx, New York City, April 20, 1913; interment in Woodlawn Cemetery.

**CALKINS, William Henry,** a Representative from Indiana; born in Pike County, Ohio, February 18, 1842; studied law; was admitted to the bar and practiced; during the Civil War served in the Union Army from May 1861 to December 1865, except three months in 1863, attached to the Fourteenth Iowa Infantry and the Twelfth Indiana Cavalry; took up his residence in La Porte, Ind.; State's attorney for the ninth Indiana judicial circuit 1866-1870; member of the State house of representatives in 1871; elected as a Republican to the Forty-fifth and to the three succeeding Congresses and served from March 4, 1877, to October 20, 1884, when he resigned; chairman, Committee on Elections (Forty-seventh Congress); moved to Tacoma, Wash., and resumed the practice of law; appointed United States associate justice of the Territory of Washington in April 1889 and served until November 11, 1889, when the Territory was admitted as a State into the Union; died in Tacoma, Wash., on January 29, 1894; interment in Tacoma Cemetery.

**CALL, Jacob,** a Representative from Indiana; born in Kentucky; was graduated from an academy in Kentucky; studied law; was admitted to the bar and practiced in Vincennes and Princeton, Ind.; judge of the Knox County Circuit Court in 1817, 1818, and 1822-1824; elected to the Eighteenth Congress to fill the vacancy caused by the death of William Prince and served from December 23, 1824, to March 3, 1825; died in Frankfort, Ky., April 20, 1826.

**CALL, Richard Keith** (uncle of Wilkinson Call), a Delegate from the Territory of Florida; born near Petersburg, Va., October 24, 1792; attended the common schools and Mount Pleasant Academy; in 1814 entered the United States Army as first lieutenant in the Forty-fourth Infantry; special aide to Major General Andrew Jackson in the Battle of New Orleans, January 8, 1815; promoted to captain in July 1818 and resigned May 1, 1822; settled in the Territory of Florida; studied law; was admitted to the bar and practiced in Pensacola; member of the Territorial council in 1822; brigadier general of the West Florida Militia in 1823; elected to the Eighteenth Congress (March 4, 1823-March 3, 1825); receiver of the land office of the Territory of Florida; appointed Governor of Florida Territory by President Jackson on March 16, 1836, and served until removed from office by President Martin Van Buren in December 1839; again appointed Governor of the Territory by President William Henry Harrison on March 19, 1841, and served until 1844; unsuccessful candidate of the Whig Party for Governor of the new State in 1845; died in Tallahassee, Fla., September 14, 1862; interment in a private cemetery on his estate.

Bibliography: *DAB;* Doherty, Herbert J. *Richard Keith Call, Southern Unionist.* Gainesville: University of Florida Press, 1961.

**CALL, Wilkinson** (nephew of Richard Keith Call and cousin of James David Walker), a Senator from Florida; born in Russellville, Logan County, Ky., January 9, 1834; attended the common schools; moved to Jacksonville, Fla.; studied law; was admitted to the bar and practiced; served as adjutant general in the Confederate Army during the Civil War; elected to the United States Senate on December 29, 1865, but was not permitted to take the seat; member of the Democratic National Executive Committee; practiced law in Jacksonville; elected as a Democrat to the United States Senate in 1879; reelected in 1885 and 1891 and served from March 4, 1879, to March 3, 1897; chairman, Committee on Civil Service and Retrenchment (Fifty-third Congress), Committee on Patents (Fifty-third Congress); retired and resided in Washington, D.C., until his death on August 24, 1910; interment in Oak Hill Cemetery.

**CALLAHAN, Herbert Leon (Sonny),** a Representative from Alabama; born in Mobile, Mobile County, Ala., September 11, 1932; attended grade school in Mobile and was graduated from McGill Institute (high school), Mobile, in 1950; served in the United States Navy, 1952-1954; attended the University of Alabama (night school) in Mobile, 1959-1960; businessman with the Finch Companies, 1964-1984; served as a Democrat in the Alabama State house of representatives, 1971-1979 and in the Alabama State senate, 1979-1983; unsuccessful candidate for the Democratic nomination for lieutenant governor in 1982; elected as a Republican to the Ninety-ninth and to the five succeeding Congresses (January 3, 1985-January 3, 1997); is a resident of Mobile, Ala.

**CALLAHAN, James Yancy,** a Delegate from the Territory of Oklahoma; born on a farm near Salem, Dent County, Mo., December 19, 1852; attended the common schools; entered the ministry in 1880; engaged in agricultural pursuits, saw-milling, and mining; moved to Stanton County, Kans., in 1885; elected register of deeds in 1886; reelected in 1888 and served until December 1889, when he resigned; returned to Dent County, Mo.; moved to Oklahoma in 1892 and settled near Kingfisher, Kingfisher County, and engaged in agricultural pursuits; elected on the Free Silver ticket to the Fifty-fifth Congress (March 4, 1897-March 3, 1899); was not a candidate for renomination in 1898; published the Jacksonian at Enid, Garfield County, Okla., until January 1, 1913; retired from active business pursuits and resided in Enid, Okla., until his death there on May 3, 1935; interment in Enid Cemetery.

**CALLAN, Clair Armstrong,** a Representative from Nebraska; born in Odell, Gage County, Nebr., March 29, 1920; attended the public schools; graduated from Peru State College; during the Second World War served as an officer in the United States Navy on a destroyer in the Pacific Theater, served on the Odell (Nebr.) Village Board, Odell School Board, Gage County School Reorganization Board, Gage County Fair Board, Gage County Extension Board; chairman of the Governor's Committee on State Government Reorganization Board, and chairman of the Nebraska Power Review Board; engaged as a farmer, stockman, and in the hardware and farm supply business; elected as a Democrat to the Eighty-ninth Congress (January 3, 1965-January 3, 1967); unsuccessful candidate for reelection in 1966 to the Ninetieth Congress, and in 1970 to the Ninety-second Congress; deputy administrator of the Rural Electrification Administration, 1967-1968; served as president, Allied Industries International, Inc., and Agri-Tech in Nashville, Tenn.; is a resident of Fairbury, Nebr.

**CALLAWAY, Howard Hollis (Bo),** a Representative from Georgia; born in LaGrange, Troup County, Ga., April 2, 1927; attended the public schools of LaGrange and Hamilton in Georgia; graduated from Episcopal High School, Alexandria, Va., in 1944; attended Georgia Institute of Technology, Atlanta, Ga., in 1944 and 1945; graduated from the United States Military Academy, West Point, N.Y. in June 1949; served in Korea as an Infantry platoon leader in 1950 and 1951, and as an instructor in tactics at Infantry School, Fort Benning, Ga., 1951-1952; president of Callaway Gardens, 1953-1970, and the Ida Cason Callaway Foundation, 1956-1970; director of Georgia Power Co., Atlanta, Ga., 1960-1964, and the Trust Co. of Georgia, Atlanta, Ga., 1958-1964; chairman, Freedom's Foundation at Valley Forge, Pa., 1966-1973; elected as a Republican to the Eighty-ninth Congress (January 3, 1965-January 3, 1967); was not a candidate for reelection in 1966 to the Ninetieth Congress, but was an unsuccessful candidate for election for Governor of Georgia; member, executive committee, Republican National Committee; National Committeeman for Georgia, 1968-1973; appointed Secretary of the Army by President Richard M. Nixon and served from May 15, 1973 until July 3, 1975; campaign manager for President Gerald R. Ford, July 1975-April 1976; unsuccessful candidate for nomination to the United States Senate from Colorado in 1980; chairman, Colorado Republican Party, 1981-1987; chairman, Callaway Gardens; is a resident of Pine Mountain, Ga.

**CALLAWAY, Oscar,** a Representative from Texas; born in Harmony Hill (Nip-and-Tuck), Rusk County, Tex., October 2, 1872; moved with his parents to Comanche County in 1876; attended the public schools, and was graduated from the Comanche High School in 1894; taught school from 1894 to 1897; attended the University of Texas at Austin, 1897-1899, and was graduated from the law department of that university in 1900; was admitted to the bar the same year and commenced practice in Comanche, Tex.; prosecuting attorney of Comanche County, 1900-1902; delegate to Democratic State conventions in 1896, 1898, 1900-1916, and 1920-1926; elected as a Democrat to the Sixty-second and to the two succeeding Congresses (March 4, 1911-March 3, 1917); unsuccessful candidate for renomination in 1916 to the Sixty-fifth Congress; returned to his ranch near Comanche, Tex., where he engaged in agricultural pursuits and stock raising, and also in the practice of law in Comanche; died in Comanche, Tex., January 31, 1947; interment in Oakwood Cemetery.

**CALLIS, John Benton,** a Representative from Alabama; born in Fayetteville, Cumberland County, N.C., January 3, 1828; moved to Tennessee in 1834 with his parents, who settled in Carroll County, and thence, in 1840, to Lancaster, Grant County, Wis.; attended the common schools; studied medicine for three years, but then abandoned its further study; went to Minnesota in 1849; moved to California in 1851 and engaged in mining and the mercantile business; went to Central America in 1853; returned to Lancaster, Wis., in the fall of that year and again engaged in mercantile pursuits; entered the Union Army as a lieutenant, and was promoted to captain in the Seventh Regiment, Wisconsin Volunteer Infantry, August 30, 1861; major January 5, 1863; appointed by President Lincoln military superintendent of the War Department at Washington, D.C., in 1864; promoted to lieutenant colonel February 11, 1865; settled in Huntsville, Ala., in 1865; resigned his commission in the Army on February 4, 1868; upon the readmission of the State of Alabama to representation was elected as a Republican to the Fortieth Congress and served from July 21, 1868, to March 3, 1869; was not a candidate for renomination in 1868 to the Forty-first Congress; returned to Lancaster, Wis., and engaged in the real-estate business; member of the State assembly in 1874; retired from active pursuits; died in Lancaster, Wis., on September 24, 1898; interment in Hillside Cemetery.

**CALVERT, Charles Benedict,** a Representative from Maryland; born in Riverdale, Prince Georges County, Md., August 24, 1808; completed preparatory studies at Bladensburg Academy, Md.; was graduated from the University of Virginia at Charlottesville in 1827; engaged in agricultural pursuits and stock breeding; member of the State house of delegates in 1839, 1843, and 1844; president of the Prince Georges County Agricultural Society and the Maryland State Agricultural Society; vice president of the United States Agricultural Society; founded the first agricultural research college in America (later the Maryland Agricultural College at College Park), chartered in 1856; one of the early advocates for the establishment of the United States Department of Agriculture; elected as a Unionist to the Thirty-seventh Congress (March 4, 1861-March 3, 1863); was not a candidate for renomination in 1862 to the Thirty-eighth Congress; resumed agricultural pursuits; died in Riverdale, Prince Georges County, Md., May 12, 1864; interment in Calvert Cemetery.

**Bibliography:** *DAB.*

**CALVERT, Ken,** a Representative from California; born in Corona, Riverside County, Calif., June 8, 1953; A.A., Chaffey College, Rancho Cucamonga, Calif., 1973; B.A., San Diego State University, 1975; general manager, Jolly Fox Restaurant, Corona, 1975-1979; Mareus W. Meairs Co., Corona, 1979-1981; president and general manager, Ken Calvert Real Properties, 1981 to present; aide to Representative Victor V. Veysey of California; youth chair, Thirty-eighth Congressional District, 1970, and Forty-third Congressional District, 1972; chair, Corona-Norco Youth for Nixon, 1968 and 1972; worked for the Reagan-Bush campaign of 1980; chair, Riverside County Republican Party, 1984-1988; unsuccessful candidate for nomination in 1982 to the Ninety-eighth Congress; co-chaired the senatorial campaigns of Pete Wilson (1982, 1988); co-chaired the gubernatorial campaigns of George Deukmejian (1982, 1986), and Pete Wilson (1990); Corona-Norco Republican Assembly; elected as a Republican to the One Hundred Third and One Hundred Fourth Congresses (January 3, 1993-January 3, 1997); is a resident of Corona, Calif.

**CALVIN, Samuel,** a Representative from Pennsylvania; born in Washingtonville, Pa., July 30, 1811; attended the common schools and Milton Academy; taught in Huntingdon Academy; studied law; was admitted to the bar in 1836 and commenced practice in Hollidaysburg, Pa.; elected as a Whig to the Thirty-first Congress (March 4, 1849-March 3, 1851); declined to be a candidate for renomination in 1850; resumed the practice of law; director of the Hollidaysburg School Board for thirty years; member of the Pennsylvania revenue board; member of the Pennsylvania constitutional convention in 1873; died in Hollidaysburg, Blair County, Pa., on March 12, 1890; interment in Presbyterian Cemetery.

**CAMBRELENG, Churchill Caldom,** a Representative from New York; born in Washington, Beaufort County, N.C., October 24, 1786; attended school in New Bern, N.C.; moved to New York City in 1802, where he became a clerk and subsequently engaged in the mercantile business; elected to the Seventeenth through Twentieth Congresses, elected as a Jacksonian to the Twenty-first through Twenty-fourth Congresses, and elected as a Democrat to the Twenty-fifth Congress (March 4, 1821-March 3, 1839); chairman, Committee on Commerce (Twentieth through Twenty-second Congresses), Committee on Foreign Affairs (Twenty-third Congress), Committee on Ways and Means (Twenty-fourth and Twenty-fifth Congresses); unsuccessful candidate for reelection in 1838 to the Twenty-sixth Congress; appointed United States Minister to Russia by President Martin Van Buren and served from May 20, 1840, to July 13, 1841; member of the State constitutional convention in 1846; died at his residence near Huntington, Suffolk County, N.Y., April 30, 1862; interment in Greenwood Cemetery, Brooklyn, N.Y.

Bibliography: *DAB.*

**CAMDEN, Johnson Newlon** (father of Johnson Newlon Camden, Jr.), a Senator from West Virginia; born in Collins Settlement, Lewis County, Va. (now West Virginia), March 6, 1828; attended school in Sutton, Va. (now West Virginia); appointed as a cadet to the United States Military Academy at West Point from 1846 until 1848, when he resigned; studied law; was admitted to the bar and commenced practice in Sutton in 1851; appointed the same year prosecuting attorney for Braxton County; elected prosecuting attorney for Nicholas County in 1852; engaged in the development of petroleum and in manufacturing in Parkersburg, Va. (now West Virginia) in 1858; president of the First National Bank of Parkersburg at its organization in 1862; unsuccessful Democratic candidate for Governor in 1868 and again in 1872; elected as a Democrat to the United States Senate, and served from March 4, 1881 to March 3, 1887; resumed the practice of law at Parkersburg; again elected as a Democrat to the United States Senate to fill the vacancy caused by the death of John E. Kenna, and served from January 25, 1893 to March 3, 1895; chairman, Committee to Audit and Control the Contingent Expense (Fifty-third Congress), Committee on Railroads (Fifty-third Congress); continued former business pursuits; died in Baltimore, Md., April 25, 1908; interment in Odd Fellows Cemetery, Parkersburg, W.Va.

Bibliography: *DAB*; Summers, Festus. *Johnson Newlon Camden: A Study in Individualism.* New York: G.P. Putnam's Sons, 1937.

**CAMDEN, Johnson Newlon, Jr.** (son of the Johnson Newlon Camden), a Senator from Kentucky; born in Parkersburg, Wood County, W.Va., January 5, 1865; attended Episcopal High School, Alexandria, Va., Phillips Academy, Andover, Mass., Virginia Military Institute, Lexington, Va., Columbia Law School, New York City, and the law school of the University of Virginia at Charlottesville; was admitted to the bar in 1888 but never practiced; moved to Spring Hill Farm, near Versailles, Woodford County, Ky., in 1890; engaged in farming and horsebreeding; also interested in the opening and development of the coal fields of eastern Kentucky; appointed and subsequently elected as a Democrat to the United States Senate to fill the vacancy caused by the death of William O. Bradley and served from June 16, 1914, to March 3, 1915; was not a candidate for renomination in 1914; resumed agricultural pursuits on a farm near Paris, Ky., until his death on August 16, 1942; interment in Frankfort Cemetery, Frankfort, Ky.

**CAMERON, Angus,** a Senator from Wisconsin; born in Caledonia, Livingston County, N.Y., July 4, 1826; attended the public schools and the Genesee Wesleyan Seminary, Lima, N.Y.; taught school; studied law in Buffalo, N.Y.; was graduated from the National Law School, Ballston Spa, N.Y., in 1853; was admitted to the bar the same year and commenced practice in Buffalo, N.Y.; engaged in banking for a year; moved to La Crosse, Wis., in 1857 and resumed the practice of law; member, State senate 1863-1864, 1871-1872; member, State assembly in 1866-1867, and served as speaker in 1867; regent of the University of Wisconsin 1866-1875; elected as a Republican to the United States Senate on February 3, 1875, and served from March 4, 1875, until March 3, 1881; was not a candidate for reelection in 1881; elected March 10, 1881, to fill the vacancy caused by the death of Matthew H. Carpenter and took his seat March 14, 1881, and served until March 3, 1885; was not a candidate for reelection; chairman, Committee on Claims (Forty-seventh and Forty-eighth Congresses); resumed the practice of law in La Crosse, Wis., and died there March 30, 1897; interment in Oak Grove Cemetery.

**CAMERON, James Donald** (son of Simon Cameron), a Senator from Pennsylvania; born in Middletown, Dauphin County, Pa., May 14, 1833; was graduated from Princeton College in 1852, and received a graduate degree in 1855; bank clerk and cashier; president of the Northern Central Railway Company of Pennsylvania, 1866-1874; appointed Secretary of War in the Cabinet of President Ulysses S. Grant on May 22, 1876 and served until March 3, 1877; chairman of the Republican National Committee in 1880; elected as a Republican to the United States Senate, March 5, 1877, to fill the vacancy caused by the resignation of his father, Simon Cameron; reelected in 1879, 1885, and 1890, and served from March 20, 1877 to March 3, 1897; chairman, Committee on Naval Affairs (Forty-seventh through Fifty-second and Fifty-fourth Congresses), Committee on Revolutionary Claims (Fifty-third Congress); was not a candidate for reelection; engaged in several business enterprises in Harrisburg, Pa.; died at his country home, "Donegal," in Lancaster County, Pa., August 30, 1918; interment in the Harrisburg Cemetery, Harrisburg, Pa.

Bibliography: *DAB*; Harrison, Robert. "Blaine and the Camerons: A Study in the Limits of Machine Power." *Pennsylvania History* 49 (July 1982): 157-175.

**CAMERON, Ralph Henry,** a Delegate and a Senator from Arizona; born in Southport, Lincoln County, Maine, October 21, 1863; attended the common schools; emigrated to the West and became interested in mining and stock raising; locator and builder of the Bright Angel trail into the Grand Canyon of the Colorado River in Arizona; moved to the Territory of Arizona in 1883; sheriff of Coconino County in 1891 and 1894-1898; member of the board of supervisors of Coconino County 1905-1907 and served as chairman; elected as a Republican Delegate to the Sixty-first and Sixty-second Congresses and served from March 4, 1909, to February 18, 1912, when Arizona was admitted as a State into the Union; resumed mining pursuits at Phoenix, Ariz.; elected as a Republican to the United States Senate in 1920 and served from March 4, 1921, to March 3, 1927; unsuccessful candidate for reelection in 1926 and for election in 1928; engaged in mica mining in North Carolina and Georgia and in gold mining in California; resided in Los Angeles, Calif., and Yuma, Ariz., until his death in Washington, D.C., while on a business trip, February 12, 1953; interment in the American Legion Cemetery, Grand Canyon, Ariz.

Bibliography: Lamb, Blaine. "A Many Checkered Toga: Arizona Senator Ralph H. Cameron, 1921-1927." *Arizona and the West* 19 (Spring 1977): 47-64.

**CAMERON, Ronald Brooks,** a Representative from California; born in Kansas City, Jackson County, Mo., August 16, 1927; educated in the public schools of Kansas, Missouri, and Ohio; served in the United States Marine Corps, 1945-1946; attended Case Western Reserve University, Cleveland, Ohio, 1946-1947, and the University of California at Los Angeles, 1949-1953; J.D., Pepperdine University School of Law, 1973; admitted to practice as a certified public accountant in 1954; elected to the California State assembly in 1958 and reelected in 1960; delegate to the Democratic National Conventions of 1960 and 1964; elected as a Democrat to the

Eighty-eighth and Eighty-ninth Congresses (January 3, 1963-January 3, 1967); unsuccessful candidate for reelection in 1966 to the Ninetieth Congress; resumed practice as a certified public accountant and attorney; Democratic candidate for election for California State Comptroller in 1970; is a resident of Whittier, Calif.

**CAMERON, Simon** (father of James Donald Cameron), a Senator from Pennsylvania; born in Maytown, Lancaster County, Pa., March 8, 1799; apprenticed as a printer; newspaper owner and editor; cashier of a bank, president of two railroad companies, and adjutant general of Pennsylvania; elected to the United States Senate to fill the vacancy caused by the resignation of James Buchanan, and served from March 13, 1845, to March 3, 1849; elected as a Republican to the United States Senate and served from March 4, 1857, to March 4, 1861, when he resigned, having been appointed Secretary of War; chairman, Committee on Patents and the Patent Office (Twenty-ninth Congress), Committee on Public Buildings (Twenty-ninth Congress), Committee on District of Columbia (Twenty-ninth and Thirtieth Congresses), Committee on Printing (Thirtieth Congress); unsuccessful candidate for the Republican presidential nomination in 1860; served as Secretary of War in the Cabinet of President Abraham Lincoln from March 5, 1861 until January 14, 1862; appointed United States Minister to Russia on January 17, 1862 and served until September 1862; was again elected as a Republican to the United States Senate in 1867; reelected in 1873, and served from March 4, 1867, until his resignation, effective March 12, 1877; chairman, Committee on Agriculture (Fortieth and Forty-first Congresses), Committee on Foreign Relations (Forty-second through Forty-fifth Congresses), Committee on Public Buildings and Grounds (Forty-second Congress); retired from active business pursuits and traveled extensively in Europe and the West Indies; died near Maytown, Lancaster County, Pa., June 26, 1889; interment in Harrisburg Cemetery, Harrisburg, Pa.

**Bibliography:** *DAB*; Bradley, Erwin. *Simon Cameron, Lincoln's Secretary of War: A Political Biography*. Philadelphia: University of Pennsylvania Press, 1966; Crippen, Lee. *Simon Cameron, Antebellum Years*. 1942. Reprint. New York: Da Capo Press, 1972.

**CAMINETTI, Anthony,** a Representative from California; born in Jackson, Amador County, Calif., July 30, 1854; attended the public schools of his native county, the grammar schools in San Francisco, and the University of California at Berkeley; studied law; was admitted to the bar in 1877 and commenced practice in Jackson, Calif.; district attorney of Amador County 1878-1882; served in the State assembly in 1883-1885; member of the State senate 1885-1887; elected as a Democrat to the Fifty-second and Fifty-third Congresses (March 4, 1891-March 3, 1895); unsuccessful candidate in 1894 for reelection to the Fifty-fourth Congress; delegate to the Democratic National Convention in 1896; again a member of the State assembly 1896-1900; in April 1897 was appointed code commissioner and served until July 31, 1899; member of the State senate 1907-1913; served as United States commissioner of immigration from 1913 to 1921; in 1917 was appointed a member of the War Industries Board and after the war was sent to Europe to investigate conditions there; engaged in the practice of law in Jackson, Amador County, Calif., until his death, November 17, 1923; interment in the Protestant Cemetery.

**Bibliography:** Giovinco, Joseph P. "The California Career of Anthony Caminetti, Italian-American Politician." Ph.D. dissertation, University of California at Berkeley, 1973.

**CAMP, Albert Sidney,** a Representative from Georgia; born on a farm near Moreland, Coweta County, Ga., July 26, 1892; attended the public schools, and was graduated from the law department of the University of Georgia at Athens in 1915; was admitted to the bar the same year and commenced practice at Newnan, Ga.; during the First World War served overseas as a member of Headquarters Detachment of the Eighty-second Division 1917-1919; delegate to the Democratic National Convention in 1924; member of the State house of representatives 1923-1928; assistant United States attorney for the northern district of Georgia 1934-1939; elected as a Democrat to the Seventy-sixth Congress to fill the vacancy caused by the death of Emmett M. Owen; reelected to the Seventy-seventh and to the six succeeding Congresses and served from August 1, 1939, until his death in Bethesda, Md., July 24, 1954; interment in Oak Hill Cemetery, Newnan, Ga.

**CAMP, David Lee,** a Representative from Michigan; born in Midland, Mich., July 9, 1953; graduated, H.H. Dow High School, Midland, 1971; B.A., Albion (Mich.) College, 1975; University of Sussex, Brighton, England, 1973-1974; J.D., University of San Diego School of Law, 1978; admitted to Michigan bar, 1978; practicing attorney; member, Midland County Republican Executive Committee; special assistant Attorney General, 1980-1984; administrative assistant to Representative Bill Schuette of Michigan, 1984-1987; member, Michigan State house of representatives, 1989-1990, assistant minority whip; elected as a Republican to the One Hundred Second and to the two succeeding Congresses (January 3, 1991-January 3, 1997); is a resident of Midland, Mich.

**CAMP, John Henry,** a Representative from New York; born in Ithaca, Tompkins County, N.Y., April 4, 1840; attended the common schools, and was graduated from the Albany Law School in 1860; was admitted to the bar the same year and commenced practice in Lyons, N.Y.; clerk of the surrogate court in 1863; prosecuting attorney of Wayne County 1867-1870; elected as a Republican to the Forty-fifth and to the two succeeding Congresses (March 4, 1877-March 3, 1883); was not a candidate for reelection in 1882 to the Forty-eighth Congress; resumed the practice of law in Lyons, Wayne County, N.Y., where he died October 12, 1892; interment in Grove Cemetery, Trumansburg, N.Y.

**CAMP, John Newbold Happy,** a Representative from Oklahoma; born in Enid, Garfield County, Okla., May 11, 1908; attended elementary and high schools in Blackwell, Douglas, and Waukomis, Okla.; attended Phillips University, Enid, Okla.; engaged in the business of banking; president, Waukomis State Bank; member, State of Oklahoma Legislature, 1942-1962; chairman, Oklahoma State Board of Public Affairs, 1967-1968; served as Republican Party precinct chairman, Garfield County Young Republican chairman, and Oklahoma committee member; elected as a Republican to the Ninety-first and to the two succeeding Congresses (January 3, 1969-January 3, 1975); unsuccessful candidate for reelection in 1974 to the Ninety-fourth Congress; was a resident of Waukomis, Okla., until his death in Enid, Okla., on September 27, 1987; interment in Waukomis Cemetery.

**CAMPBELL, Albert James,** a Representative from Montana; born in Pontiac, Oakland County, Mich., December 12, 1857; attended the common schools and the Michigan Agricultural College at Lansing; taught school for several years; studied law; was admitted to the bar in 1881 and commenced practice in Oxford, Mich.; moved to Clarke, Mich., in 1882, and resumed the practice of law; prosecuting attorney of Lake County, Mich., from 1886 to 1888 when he resigned; moved to Butte, Mont., on November 16, 1889, and continued the practice of his profession; member of the State house of representatives in 1897; elected as a Democrat to the Fifty-sixth Congress (March 4, 1899-March 3, 1901); declined to be a candidate for renomination in 1900; resumed the practice of law in Butte, Mont.; died in New York City, August 9, 1907; interment in Mount Moriah Cemetery, Butte, Mont.

**CAMPBELL, Alexander,** a Representative from Illinois; born on a farm near Concord, Franklin County, Pa., October 4, 1814; attended the public schools; became a clerk in an iron works and was subsequently promoted to superintendent, continuing in the business of managing iron works in Pennsylvania, Kentucky, and Missouri until 1850, when he moved to La Salle, Ill., and became interested in the coal fields; mayor of La Salle in 1852 and 1853; member of the State house of representatives in 1858 and 1859; delegate to the State constitutional convention in 1862; elected as an Independent to the Forty-fourth Congress (March 4, 1875-March 3, 1877); unsuccessful candidate for reelection in 1876 to the Forty-fifth Congress; retired from public life; died in La Salle, Ill., August 8, 1898; interment in Oakwood Cemetery.

**CAMPBELL, Alexander,** a Senator from Ohio; born in Frederick County, Va., in 1779; moved with his parents to east Tennessee and later to Kentucky, settling near Lexington, and later in Woodford County, Ky.; educated at Pisgah Academy, Woodford County, Ky.; studied medicine at Transylvania University and commenced practice in Cynthiana, Ky., in 1801; member, Kentucky house of representatives 1803; moved to Adams County in 1804, and later to Brown County, Ohio, where he continued the practice of medicine; also engaged in mercantile pursuits; member, Ohio State house of representatives 1807; reelected in 1808 and 1809, and served as speaker in 1808 and 1809; unsuccessful candidate for United States Senator in 1808; elected as a Republican to the United States Senate to fill the vacancy caused by the resignation of Edward Tiffin and served from December 11, 1809, to March 3, 1813; resumed the practice of medicine; moved to Staunton (now Ripley), Ohio, in 1815; member, Ohio State house of representatives 1819, and served as speaker pro tempore; member, Ohio State senate 1822-1824; unsuccessful candidate for Governor in 1826; member, Ohio State house of representatives 1832-1833; served as vice president of the first general antislavery society of Ohio in 1835; mayor of Ripley 1838-1840; died in Ripley, Brown County, Ohio, November 5, 1857; interment in Maplewood Cemetery.

**CAMPBELL, Ben Nighthorse,** a Representative and a Senator from Colorado; born in Auburn, Calif., April 13, 1933; attended public schools; B.A., San Jose (Calif.) State University, 1957; attended Meiji University, Tokyo, Japan, 1960-1964; served in the United States Air Force in Korea, 1951-1954; jewelry designer; rancher; served in the Colorado State Legislature, 1983-1986; elected as a Democrat to the One Hundredth and to the two succeeding Congresses (January 3, 1987-January 3, 1993); was not a candidate for reelection to the House of Representatives in 1992, but was elected to the United States Senate for the term ending January 3, 1999; announced his affiliation with the Republican Party on March 3, 1995; is a resident of Ignacio, Colo.

**CAMPBELL, Brookins,** a Representative from Tennessee; born in Washington County, Tenn., in 1808; attended the rural schools and was graduated from Washington College (now Washington and Lee University) at Lexington; studied law; was admitted to the bar and practiced; member of the State house of representatives 1835-1839, 1841-1846, and 1851-1853, and served as speaker in 1845; during the Mexican War was appointed by President Polk in 1846 an assistant quartermaster to the Army with the rank of major; elected as a Democrat to the Thirty-third Congress and served from March 4, 1853, until his death in Washington, D.C., December 25, 1853, without having qualified; interment in Providence Presbyterian Churchyard, Greene County, Tenn.

**CAMPBELL, Carroll Ashmore, Jr.,** a Representative from South Carolina; born in Greenville, Greenville County, S.C., July 24, 1940; attended the public schools of Greenville, McCallie School, Chattanooga, Tenn., and the University of South Carolina; real estate broker, farmer, and businessman; served in the South Carolina State house of representatives, 1970-1974; appointed executive assistant by Governor James Edwards, 1975; served in the South Carolina senate, 1976-1978; delegate to the Republican National Convention of 1976; elected as a Republican to the Ninety-sixth and to the three succeeding Congresses (January 3,

1979-January 3, 1987); was not a candidate for reelection in 1986 to the One Hundredth Congress, but was elected Governor of South Carolina; reelected in 1990, and served from January 7, 1987 to January 11, 1995; president and chief executive officer, American Council of Life Insurance; member, National Commission on Economic Growth and Tax Reform, 1995-1996; is a resident of Fountain Inn, S.C.

**CAMPBELL, Courtney Warren,** a Representative from Florida; born in Chillicothe, Livingston County, Mo., April 29, 1895; educated in Westminster College, Fulton, Mo., and the University of Missouri at Columbia, Mo.; during the First World War served as a second lieutenant in the United States Army; studied law; was admitted to the bar in Missouri and Florida in 1924 and practiced in Tampa, Fla., 1924-1928; farmer, citrus grower, banker, and land developer; assistant attorney general of the State of Florida; member, Florida State Road Board, 1942-1947; member, Florida War Labor Relations Board, 1941-1946; elected as a Democrat to the Eighty-third Congress (January 3, 1953-January 3, 1955); unsuccessful candidate for reelection in 1954 to the Eighty-fourth Congress; returned to his extensive business and civic interests and resided in Clearwater, Fla.; died in Dunedin, Fla., December 22, 1971; interment in Sylvan Abbey Memorial Park, Pinellas County, Fla.

**CAMPBELL, Ed Hoyt,** a Representative from Iowa; born in Battle Creek, Ida County, Iowa, March 6, 1882; attended the public schools of his native city, and was graduated from the law department of the State University of Iowa at Iowa City in 1906; was admitted to the bar the same year and commenced practice in Battle Creek; mayor of Battle Creek 1908-1911; member of the State house of representatives 1911-1913; during the First World War served as a private in Company Six, First Officers Training School, Fort Snelling, Minn.; member of the State senate 1920-1928, serving as president pro tempore 1924-1926; elected as a Republican to the Seventy-first and Seventy-second Congresses (March 4, 1929-March 3, 1933); unsuccessful candidate for reelection in 1932 to the Seventy-third Congress; resumed the practice of law; died in Battle Creek, Iowa, April 26, 1969; interment in Mount Hope Cemetery.

**CAMPBELL, Felix,** a Representative from New York; born in Brooklyn, N.Y., February 28, 1829; attended the common schools; became a manufacturer of iron pipe and a consulting engineer; president of the board of supervisors in 1858; appointed by Governor Samuel J. Tilden a member of the board of commissioners from New York to the Centennial Exhibition at Philadelphia in 1876; elected as a Democrat to the Forty-eighth and to the three succeeding Congresses (March 4, 1883-March 3, 1891); declined to be a candidate for renomination in 1890 to the Fifty-second Congress; died in Brooklyn, N.Y., November 8, 1902; interment in Holy Cross Cemetery.

**CAMPBELL, George Washington,** a Representative and a Senator from Tennessee; born in the parish of Tongue, Sutherland-shire, Scotland, February 9, 1769; immigrated with his parents to North Carolina in 1772; taught school; was graduated from the College of New Jersey (now Princeton University) in 1794; studied law while teaching; was admitted to the bar in North Carolina and commenced practice in Knoxville, Tenn.; elected as a Republican to the Eighth and to the two succeeding Congresses (March 4, 1803-March 3, 1809); chairman, Committee on Ways and Means (Tenth Congress); one of the managers appointed by the House of Representatives in January 1804 to conduct the impeachment proceedings against John Pickering, judge of the United States District Court for New Hampshire, and in December of the same year against Samuel Chase, Associate Justice of the United States Supreme Court; judge of the State supreme court of errors and appeals, 1809-1811; elected as a Republican to the United States Senate to fill the vacancy caused by the resignation of Jenkin

Whiteside, and served from October 8, 1811 to February 11, 1814, when he resigned; appointed Secretary of the Treasury in the Cabinet of President James Madison, and served from February 9 to September 4, 1814, when he resigned because of ill health; again elected as a Republican to the United States Senate and served from October 10, 1815, until his resignation, effective April 20, 1818; chairman, Committee on Finance (Fifteenth Congress); appointed Minister to Russia on April 16, 1818 and served until July 1820; member of the French Spoliation Claims Commission in 1831; died in Nashville, Tenn., February 17, 1848; interment in the City Cemetery.

**Bibliography:** *DAB*; Jordan, Weymouth. *George Washington Campbell of Tennessee, Western Statesman.* Tallahassee: Florida State University Press, 1955.

**CAMPBELL, Guy Edgar,** a Representative from Pennsylvania; born in Fetterman, Taylor County, W.Va., October 9, 1871; attended the grammar and high schools; moved to Pennsylvania with his parents, who located in Pittsburgh in 1889, and in Crafton Borough, Allegheny County, in 1893; attended Iron City Business College at Pittsburgh; was employed as a clerk in the offices of the Baltimore & Ohio Railroad at Pittsburgh, Pa., until June 1896, when he resigned; was engaged in the general insurance business in Pittsburgh until 1903; was interested in the production of oil and gas in Pennsylvania and West Virginia; elected as a Democrat to the Sixty-fifth, Sixty-sixth, and Sixty-seventh Congresses, and as a Republican to the Sixty-eighth and to the four succeeding Congresses (March 4, 1917-March 3, 1933); chairman, Committee on Expenditures in the Department of Labor (Sixty-eighth Congress); unsuccessful candidate for reelection in 1932 to the Seventy-third Congress; engaged in an advisory capacity in Washington, D.C.; died at Willoughby, Ohio, February 17, 1940; interment in Mount Union Cemetery, Robinson Township, Allegheny County, Pa.

**CAMPBELL, Howard Edmond,** a Representative from Pennsylvania; born in Pittsburgh, Allegheny County, Pa., January 4, 1890; attended the public schools and the University of Pittsburgh; engaged in the real estate and insurance business in Pittsburgh in 1922; president of the Pittsburgh Real Estate Board in 1943 and 1944; elected as a Republican to the Seventy-ninth Congress (January 3, 1945-January 3, 1947); was not a candidate for renomination in 1946 to the Eightieth Congress; resumed the real estate and insurance business; president of East Liberty Chamber of Commerce in 1954 and 1955; resided in Pittsburgh until his death there January 6, 1971; interment in Homewood Cemetery.

**CAMPBELL, Jacob Miller,** a Representative from Pennsylvania; born at "White Horse," near Somerset, Allegheny Township, Somerset County, Pa., November 20, 1821; moved with his parents to Allegheny City, Pa., in 1826; attended the public schools; learned the art of printing in the office of the Somerset Whig; later was connected with a magazine publishing company in Pittsburgh and with leading newspapers in New Orleans, La.; engaged in steamboating on the lower Mississippi River 1814-1847 and in gold mining in California in 1851; aided in the building of the Cambria Iron Works in Johnstown, Pa., in 1853, and was employed by that company until 1861, when he resigned; delegate to the first Republican National Convention at Philadelphia in 1856; served in the Union Army as first lieutenant and quartermaster of Company G, Third Regiment, Pennsylvania Volunteer Infantry; recruited the Fifty-fourth Regiment of Infantry and was commissioned its colonel February 27, 1862; brevetted brigadier general March 13, 1865; returned to Johnstown, Pa.; surveyor general (later secretary of internal affairs) of Pennsylvania 1865-1871; declined a renomination; engaged in mechanical and other industrial pursuits; elected as a Republican to the Forty-fifth Congress (March 4, 1877-March 3, 1879); unsuccessful candidate for reelection in 1878 to the Forty-sixth Congress; elected to the Forty-seventh, Forty-eighth,

and Forty-ninth Congresses (March 4, 1881-March 3, 1887); chairman, Committee on Manufactures (Forty-seventh Congress); unsuccessful candidate for renomination in 1886 to the Fiftieth Congress; financially interested in banking and in the manufacture of steel; chairman of the Pennsylvania Republican convention in 1887; died in Johnstown, Cambria County, Pa., September 27, 1888; interment in Grand View Cemetery.

**CAMPBELL, James Edwin** (nephew of Lewis Davis Campbell), a Representative from Ohio; born in Middletown, Butler County, Ohio, July 7, 1843; attended the public schools and Miami University, Oxford, Ohio; entered the Union Army as a member of the Mississippi Squadron, November 29, 1863, and served until honorably discharged September 24, 1864; studied law; was admitted to the bar in 1865; deputy collector of internal revenue, third district; commenced the practice of law in Hamilton, Ohio, in 1867; prosecuting attorney of Butler County 1876-1880; successfully contested as a Democrat the election of Henry L. Morey to the Forty-eighth Congress; reelected to the Forty-ninth and Fiftieth Congresses and served from June 20, 1884, to March 3, 1889; chairman, Committee on Alcoholic Liquor Traffic (Forty-ninth Congress); was not a candidate for renomination in 1888 to the Fifty-first Congress; elected Governor of Ohio in 1889 and served from January 13, 1890 to January 11, 1892; unsuccessful candidate for reelection in 1891, and for election for Governor in 1895; delegate to the Democratic National Conventions of 1892, 1920, and 1924; served on the commission to codify the State laws 1908-1911; resumed the practice of law in Columbus, Ohio, and died there on December 18, 1924; interment in Greenlawn Cemetery.

**Bibliography:** Doyle, James T. "James Edwin Campbell: Conservative Democratic Congressman, Governor and Statesman." Ph.D. dissertation, Ohio State University, 1967.

**CAMPBELL, James Hepburn,** a Representative from Pennsylvania; born in Williamsport, Lycoming County, Pa., February 8, 1820; attended the common schools, and was graduated from the law department of Dickinson College, Carlisle, Pa., in 1841; was admitted to the bar the same year and commenced practice in Pottsville, Pa.; delegate to the Whig National Convention in 1844; elected as a Whig to the Thirty-fourth Congress (March 4, 1855-March 3, 1857); unsuccessful candidate for reelection in 1856 to the Thirty-fifth Congress; elected to the Thirty-sixth and Thirty-seventh Congresses (March 4, 1859-March 3, 1863); was not a candidate for renomination in 1862 to the Thirty-eighth Congress; during the Civil War served as major of the Twenty-fifth Regiment of Pennsylvania Infantry; appointed Minister to Sweden by President Lincoln on May 18, 1864, and served until March 1867; appointed Minister to Colombia on November 16, 1866, but declined the mission; located in Philadelphia, Pa., in 1867 and continued the practice of law; died on his estate "Aeola," near Wayne, Delaware County, Pa., April 12, 1895; interment in Woodlands Cemetery, Philadelphia, Pa.

**Bibliography:** *DAB*.

**CAMPBELL, James Romulus,** a Representative from Illinois; born near McLeansboro, Hamilton County, Ill., May 4, 1853; attended the public schools and the University of Notre Dame, Notre Dame, Ind.; studied law; was admitted to the bar in 1877 and commenced practice in McLeansboro, Ill.; owned and edited the McLeansboro Times 1870-1898; member of the State house of representatives 1884-1888; served in the State senate 1888-1896; elected as a Democrat to the Fifty-fifth Congress (March 4, 1897-March 3, 1899); was not a candidate for reelection to the Fifty-sixth Congress in 1898; served in the war with Spain in the Ninth Regiment, Illinois Volunteer Infantry; commissioned colonel June 28, 1898; after the muster out of that regiment was appointed lieutenant colonel of the Thirtieth Regiment, United States Volunteers, on July 5, 1899, and assigned to service in the

Philippine Islands; commissioned brigadier general of Volunteers January 3, 1901, and was honorably discharged March 25, 1901; engaged in milling and banking in McLeansboro, Ill., and died there August 12, 1924; interment in Odd Fellows Cemetery.

**CAMPBELL, John,** a Representative from Maryland; born near Port Tobacco, Charles County, Md., September 11, 1765; studied law; was admitted to the bar and practiced; held several local offices; member of the State senate for three years; elected as a Federalist to the Seventh and to the four succeeding Congresses (March 4, 1801-March 3, 1811); judge of the orphans' court of Charles County; died at "Charleston" farm, Charles County, Md., June 23, 1828; interment in the private burying ground on the estate of Daniel Jenifer.

**CAMPBELL, John** (brother of Robert Blair Campbell), a Representative from South Carolina; born near Brownsville, Marlboro County, S.C.; was graduated from South Carolina College (now the University of South Carolina) at Columbia in 1819; studied law; was admitted to the bar and commenced practice in Brownsville, S.C.; moved to Parnassus, Marlboro District, and continued the practice of law; elected as a Jacksonian to the Twenty-first Congress (March 4, 1829-March 3, 1831); elected as a Nullifier to the Twenty-fifth Congress and as a Democrat to the three succeeding Congresses (March 4, 1837-March 3, 1845); chairman, Committee on Elections (Twenty-sixth Congress), Committee on District of Columbia (Twenty-eighth Congress); died in Parnassus (now Blenheim), Marlboro County, S.C., on May 19, 1845; interment in a private cemetery near Blenheim, S.C.

**CAMPBELL, John Goulder,** a Delegate from the Territory of Arizona; born in Glasgow, Scotland, June 25, 1827; immigrated to the United States in 1841 and settled in the State of New York; attended the public and high schools; moved to California in 1849 and engaged in numerous occupations; moved to Prescott, Ariz., in 1863 and engaged in mercantile pursuits and stock raising; member of the Territorial house of representatives 1868-1874; county supervisor of Yavapai County; elected as a Democrat to the Forty-sixth Congress (March 4, 1879-March 3, 1881); resumed his former business pursuits; also engaged in the hotel business and in stock raising; died in Prescott, Ariz., December 22, 1903; interment in Mountain View Cemetery.

**CAMPBELL, John Hull,** a Representative from Pennsylvania; born in York, York County, Pa., October 10, 1800; studied law; was admitted to the bar in Philadelphia, Pa., in 1823 and commenced practice in that city; member of the Pennsylvania house of representatives in 1831; elected as a candidate of the American Party to the Twenty-ninth Congress (March 4, 1845-March 3, 1847); declined to be a candidate for renomination in 1846; resumed the practice of law; died in Philadelphia, Pa., on January 19, 1868; interment in Monument Cemetery.

**CAMPBELL, John Pierce, Jr.,** a Representative from Kentucky; born near Hopkinsville, Christian County, Ky., December 8, 1820; pursued an academic course; studied law; was admitted to the bar in 1841 and commenced practice in Lexington, Mo.; member of the Missouri house of representatives 1848-1852; returned to Hopkinsville, Ky., and engaged in agricultural pursuits; elected as a candidate of the American Party to the Thirty-fourth Congress (March 4, 1855-March 3, 1857); declined to be a candidate for reelection; president of the Henderson & Nashville Railroad in 1870; organized the Mastodon Coal & Iron Co., which was succeeded by the St. Bernard Coal Co.; devoted the latter years of his life to his large landed estates; died in Hopkinsville, Ky., October 29, 1888; interment in Riverside Cemetery.

**CAMPBELL, John Wilson,** a Representative from Ohio; born near Miller's Iron Works, Augusta County, Va., February 23, 1782; attended the common schools; taught school; studied law; was admitted to the bar in 1808 and commenced practice in West Union, Ohio; justice of the peace of Tiffin Township, Adams County, 1809-1815; prosecuting attorney of Adams County in 1809; member of the State house of representatives in 1810, 1813, and 1815; elected as a Republican to the Fifteenth Congress and reelected to the four succeeding Congresses (March 4, 1817-March 3, 1827); chairman, Committee on Private Land Claims (Sixteenth through Nineteenth Congresses); declined to be a candidate for renomination in 1826; judge of the United States Court for the District of Ohio from 1829 until his death in Delaware, Delaware County, Ohio, September 24, 1833; interment in the Old North Cemetery, Columbus, Ohio.

**Bibliography:** *DAB.*

**CAMPBELL, Lewis Davis** (uncle of James Edwin Campbell), a Representative from Ohio; born in Franklin, Warren County, Ohio, August 9, 1811; attended the public schools; apprenticed to learn the art of printing, 1828-1831; published a Clay Whig newspaper in Hamilton, Ohio, 1831-1835; studied law; was admitted to the bar in 1835 and practiced in Hamilton until 1850; engaged in agricultural pursuits; unsuccessful candidate for election in 1840 to the Twenty-seventh Congress, in 1842 to the Twenty-eighth Congress, and 1844 to the Twenty-ninth Congress; elected as a Whig to the Thirty-first, Thirty-second, and Thirty-third Congresses and as an American Party candidate on a Fusion ticket to the Thirty-fourth Congress (March 4, 1849-March 3, 1857); chairman, Committee on Ways and Means (Thirty-fourth Congress); presented credentials as a Republican Member-elect to the Thirty-fifth Congress, and served from March 4, 1857 to May 25, 1858, when he was succeeded by Clement L. Vallandigham, who successfully contested the election; was an unsuccessful candidate for election in 1858 to the Thirty-sixth Congress; served in the Union Army as colonel of the Sixty-ninth Regiment, Ohio Volunteer Infantry, in 1861 and 1862; appointed by President Andrew Johnson as Envoy Extraordinary and Minister Plenipotentiary to Mexico on May 4, 1866; arrived in Mexico but did not present his credentials, and resigned on June 16, 1867; elected to the Ohio State senate in 1869 and resigned in 1870; elected as a Democrat to the Forty-second Congress (March 4, 1871-March 3, 1873); was not a candidate for reelection in 1872 to the Forty-third Congress; delegate to the third State constitutional convention in 1873; resumed agricultural pursuits; died in Hamilton, Butler County, Ohio, on November 26, 1882; interment in Greenwood Cemetery.

**Bibliography:** *DAB*; Van Horne, William E. "Lewis D. Campbell and the Know-Nothing Party in Ohio." *Ohio History* 76 (Autumn 1967): 202-21.

**CAMPBELL, Philip Pitt,** a Representative from Kansas; born in Cape Breton, Nova Scotia, Canada, April 25, 1862; moved with his parents to Neosho County, Kans., in 1867; attended the common schools, and was graduated from Baker University, Baldwin, Kans., in 1888; studied law; was admitted to the bar in 1889 and commenced practice in Pittsburg, Kans.; elected as a Republican to the Fifty-eighth and to the nine succeeding Congresses (March 4, 1903-March 3, 1923); chairman, Committee on Levees and Improvements of the Mississippi River (Sixty-first Congress), Committee on Rules (Sixty-sixth and Sixty-seventh Congresses); unsuccessful candidate for reelection in 1922 to the Sixty-eighth Congress; parliamentarian of the Republican National Convention in 1924; resumed the practice of law in Washington, D.C., with residence in Arlington, Va.; died in Washington, D.C., May 26, 1941; interment in Abbey Mausoleum (near Arlington National Cemetery), Arlington, Va.

**CAMPBELL, Robert Blair** (brother of John Campbell of South Carolina), a Representative from South Carolina; born in Marlboro County, S.C.; educated by a private tutor; attended school in Fayetteville, N.C., and was graduated from South Carolina College (now the University of South Carolina) at Columbia in 1809; engaged in agricultural pursuits; commissioned captain in South Carolina Militia in 1814; unsuccessful candidate in 1820 for election to the Seventeenth Congress; served in the State senate 1821-1823; elected to the Eighteenth Congress (March 4, 1823-March 3, 1825); unsuccessful candidate for reelection in 1824 to the Nineteenth Congress and for election in 1826 to the Twentieth Congress and in 1830 to the Twenty-second Congress; elected to the State senate in 1830; elected as a Nullifier to the Twenty-third Congress to fill the vacancy caused by the death of Thomas B. Singleton; reelected to the Twenty-fourth Congress and served from February 27, 1834, to March 3, 1837; in 1833 during the nullification movement was commissioned general of South Carolina troops; moved to Lowndes County, Ala., about 1840; member of the State house of representatives in 1840; appointed on September 28, 1842, consul at Habana, Cuba, and served until July 22, 1850; moved to San Antonio, Tex.; was appointed on March 16, 1853, a commissioner for the United States to aid in settlement of the disputed boundary line between Texas and Mexico; appointed consul at London, England, and served from August 3, 1854, to March 1861, when he was recalled; moved to Ealing, London, England, where he died July 12, 1862; interment in the crypt of Kensington Church.

**CAMPBELL, Samuel,** a Representative from New York; born in Mansfield, Conn., July 11, 1773; attended the common schools; moved to Columbus, N.Y., and engaged in agricultural pursuits; supervisor of the town of Columbus in 1807, 1808, 1821, and 1840; member of the New York State assembly in 1808, 1809, 1812, and 1820; served on the staff of Major General Nathaniel King as division quartermaster in the War of 1812; associate judge of Chenango County Court in 1814; justice of the peace in Columbus for twenty-five years; sheriff of Chenango County from 1815 until 1819; elected to the Seventeenth Congress (March 4, 1821-March 3, 1823); affiliated with the Whig Party after its formation; resumed agricultural pursuits; died in Columbus, near Sherburne, Chenango County, N.Y., June 2, 1853; interment in Lambs Corners Cemetery.

**CAMPBELL, Thomas J.,** a Representative from California; born in Chicago, August 14, 1952; graduated, St. Ignatius High School, Chicago, 1969; B.A. and M.A., University of Chicago, 1973; J.D., Harvard University Law School, 1976; Ph.D., University of Chicago, 1980; admitted to Illinois and District of Columbia bars, 1976; law clerk to Justice Byron R. White, United States Supreme Court, 1977-1978; co-founder, California Legal Reform Project; White House fellow in office of chief of staff and White House counsel, 1981; director, Bureau of Competition, Federal Trade Commission, 1981-1983; professor, Stanford University Law School, 1983-1988; elected as a Republican to the One Hundred First and One Hundred Second Congresses (January 3, 1989-January 3, 1993); was not a candidate for reelection in 1992 to the House of Representatives, but was an unsuccessful candidate for nomination to the United States Senate; member, California State senate, District 11, 1993-1995; elected to the One Hundred Fourth Congress, December 12, 1995, by special election to fill the vacancy caused by the resignation of Norman Y. Mineta, and served from December 12, 1995 to January 3, 1997; is a resident of Campbell, Calif.

**CAMPBELL, Thomas Jefferson,** a Representative from Tennessee; born in Rhea County, Tenn., in 1786; attended the public schools; assistant inspector general to Major General Cole's division of the East Tennessee Militia from September 25, 1813, to March 12, 1814; clerk of the Tennessee State house of representatives, 1817-1819, 1821, and 1825-1831, and a member of that body from 1833 until 1837; elected as a Whig to the Twenty-seventh Congress (March 4, 1841-March 3, 1843); unsuccessful candidate for reelection in 1842 to the Twenty-eighth Congress; Clerk of the House of Representatives in the Thirtieth and Thirty-first Congresses and served from December 7, 1847, until his death in Washington, D.C., on April 13, 1850; interment at Calhoun, McMinn County, Tenn.

**CAMPBELL, Thompson,** a Representative from Illinois; born in Ireland in 1811; immigrated to the United States with his parents, who settled in Chester County, Pa.; attended the public schools; studied law; was admitted to the bar in Pittsburgh, Pa.; moved to Galena, Ill., and engaged in mining; secretary of state of Illinois from 1843 until he resigned in 1846; delegate to the State constitutional convention in 1847; elected as a Democrat to the Thirty-second Congress (March 4, 1851-March 3, 1853); unsuccessful candidate for reelection in 1852 to the Thirty-third Congress; delegate to the Democratic National Convention of 1852; appointed United States land commissioner for California by President Franklin Pierce in 1853 and served until he resigned in 1855; returned to Illinois; delegate to the Democratic National Convention at Charleston in 1860; elector at large on the Southern Democratic ticket of John C. Breckinridge and Joseph Lane in 1860; returned to California and served in the California house of representatives as a member of the Union Party in 1863 and 1864; delegate to the Republican National Convention of 1864; died in San Francisco, Calif., December 6, 1868; interment in Laurel Hill Cemetery.

**CAMPBELL, Timothy John,** a Representative from New York; born in County Cavan, Ireland, January 8, 1840; immigrated with his parents to the United States in 1845; attended the public schools of New York City; learned the printer's trade; studied law; was admitted to the bar in 1869 and commenced practice in New York City; member of the State assembly 1868-1873, 1875, and 1883; justice of the fifth district civil court in New York City 1875-1883; served in the State senate in 1884 and 1885; elected as a Democrat to the Forty-ninth Congress to fill the vacancy caused by the resignation of Samuel S. Cox; reelected to the Fiftieth Congress and served from November 3, 1885, to March 3, 1889; chairman, Committee on Expenditures on Public Buildings (Fiftieth Congress); unsuccessful candidate for reelection in 1888 to the Fifty-first Congress; elected to the Fifty-second and Fifty-third Congresses (March 4, 1891-March 3, 1895); unsuccessful candidate in 1894 for reelection to the Fifty-fourth Congress; resumed the practice of his profession in New York City where he died on April 7, 1904; interment in Calvary Cemetery, Long Island City, N.Y.

**CAMPBELL, William Bowen** (cousin of Henry Bowen), a Representative from Tennessee; born near Hendersonville, Sumner County, Tenn., February 1, 1807; attended private schools; studied law in Abingdon and Winchester, Va.; was admitted to the bar in 1829 and commenced practice in Carthage, Smith County, Tenn.; also engaged in agricultural pursuits and banking; elected district attorney in 1831; member, Tennessee State house of representatives, 1835-1836; captain of a company in Trousdale's regiment of Tennessee Mounted Volunteers in the Seminole War; mustered out on January 14, 1837; elected as a Whig to the Twenty-fifth and to the two succeeding Congresses (March 4, 1837-March 3, 1843); declined to be a candidate for reelection in 1842 to the Twenty-eighth Congress; elected colonel of the First Tennessee Volunteers in the Mexican War on June 3, 1846, and was mustered out May 25, 1847; unanimously elected judge of the fourth circuit of Tennessee and served from 1847 to 1850; elected Governor of Tennessee in 1851, and served from October 16, 1851 to October 17, 1853; declined to be a candidate in 1853 for renomination for Governor; elected judge of the circuit court in 1857; appointed by President Lincoln as a brigadier general of Volunteers on June 30, 1862; resigned January 26, 1863, on account of ill health; upon the readmission of the State of Tennessee to representation was elected as a Unionist to the Thirty-ninth Congress, and served from July 24, 1866 to March 3, 1867; resumed banking and agricultural pursuits; died near Lebanon, Wilson County, Tenn., August 19, 1867; interment in Cedar Grove Cemetery.

Bibliography: *DAB*.

CAMPBELL, William W., a Representative from New York; born in Cherry Valley, N.Y., June 10, 1806; attended the common schools; was graduated from Union College, Schenectady, N.Y., in 1827; studied law; was admitted to the bar in 1831 and commenced practice in New York City; was appointed master in chancery in 1841; commissioner in bankruptcy; elected as a candidate of the American Party to the Twenty-ninth Congress (March 4, 1845-March 3, 1847); was not a candidate for renomination in 1846; justice of the superior court of New York City 1849-1855; returned to Cherry Valley in December 1855; judge of the supreme court for the sixth district of New York 1857-1865; author and engaged in historical work; died in Cherry Valley, Otsego County, N.Y., September 7, 1881; interment in Cherry Valley Cemetery.

Bibliography: *DAB*.

CAMPBELL, William Wildman, a Representative from Ohio; born in Rochester, Windsor County, Vt., April 2, 1853; attended the public schools, Goddard Seminary, Barre, Vt., and Tufts College, Medford, Mass.; studied law; was admitted to the bar in 1878 and commenced practice at Napoleon, Henry County, Ohio; served as prosecuting attorney for Henry County, 1893-1896; elected as a Republican to the Fifty-ninth Congress (March 4, 1905-March 3, 1907); unsuccessful candidate for reelection in 1906 to the Sixtieth Congress and for election in 1908 to the Sixty-first Congress; resumed the practice of law in Napoleon, Ohio; member of the State constitutional convention of 1911 and 1912; died in Napoleon, Ohio, August 13, 1927; interment in Forest Hill Cemetery.

CANADY, Charles Terrance, a Representative from Florida; born in Lakeland, Polk County, Fla., June 22, 1954; B.A., Haverford (Pa.) College, 1976; J.D., Yale University School of Law, 1979; attorney, Lakeland, 1979 to present; member, Florida State house of representatives, 1984-1990; elected as a Republican to the One Hundred Third and One Hundred Fourth Congresses (January 3, 1993-January 3, 1997); is a resident of Lakeland, Fla.

CANBY, Richard Sprigg, a Representative from Ohio; born in Lebanon, Ohio, September 30, 1808; completed preparatory studies; attended Miami University, Oxford, Ohio, 1826-1828; engaged in mercantile pursuits and while thus employed studied law; was admitted to the bar about 1840 and commenced practice in Bellefontaine, Ohio; member of the State house of representatives in 1845 and 1846; elected as a Whig to the Thirtieth Congress (March 4, 1847-March 3, 1849); engaged in agricultural pursuits; upon its formation in 1856 affiliated with the Republican Party; moved to Olney, Richland County, Ill., in 1863, where he resumed the practice of law; elected judge of the second judicial circuit court of Illinois in 1867 and served for several years; again resumed the practice of his profession in Olney; discontinued active business pursuits in 1882, and lived in retirement until his death; died in Olney, Ill., July 27, 1895; interment in Haven Hill Cemetery.

CANDLER, Allen Daniel (cousin of Ezekiel Samuel Candler, Jr., and Milton Anthony Candler), a Representative from Georgia; born in Homer, Banks County, Ga., November 4, 1834; attended country schools, and was graduated from Mercer University, Macon, Ga., in 1859; studied law; entered the Confederate Army as a private in Company H, Thirty-fourth Regiment of Georgia Infantry on May 12, 1862; was elected first lieutenant May 17, 1862; promoted to captain October 26, 1862; appointed lieutenant colonel May 16, 1864; promoted to colonel December 27, 1864; engaged in agricultural pursuits; member of the Georgia State house of representatives, 1873-1877; served in the State senate during 1878

and 1879; engaged in manufacturing and was president of a railroad; elected as a Democrat to the Forty-eighth and to the three succeeding Congresses (March 4, 1883-March 3, 1891); chairman, Committee on Education (Fiftieth Congress); was not a candidate for reelection in 1890 to the Fifty-second Congress; secretary of state of Georgia from May 28, 1894, until March 1, 1898, when he resigned; elected Governor of Georgia in 1898, reelected in 1900, and served from October 29, 1898 to October 25, 1902; compiler of the records of the State of Georgia from 1903 until his death in Atlanta, Ga., October 26, 1910; interment in Alta Vista Cemetery, Gainesville, Ga.

Bibliography: *DAB*.

CANDLER, Ezekiel Samuel, Jr. (nephew of Milton A. Candler and cousin of Allen Daniel Candler), a Representative from Mississippi; born in Belleville, Hamilton County, Fla., January 18, 1862; moved with his parents to Tishomingo County, Miss., in 1870; attended the common schools and Iuka (Miss.) Male Academy; was graduated from the law department of the University of Mississippi at Oxford in 1881; was admitted to the bar the same year and commenced practice in Iuka, Miss.; chairman of the Democratic executive committee of Tishomingo County in 1884; moved to Corinth in 1887 and continued the practice of law; member of the Democratic executive committee of Alcorn County for several years; elected as a Democrat to the Fifty-seventh and to the nine succeeding Congresses (March 4, 1901-March 3, 1921); chairman, Committee on Alcoholic Liquor Traffic (Sixty-seventh Congress); unsuccessful candidate for renomination in 1920; resumed the practice of his profession; mayor of Corinth, Miss., 1933-1937; died in Corinth, Miss., December 18, 1944; interment in Henry Cemetery.

CANDLER, John Wilson, a Representative from Massachusetts; born in Boston, Mass., February 10, 1828; attended the Marblehead Academy and Dummer Academy, Byfield, Mass.; entered a countingroom in Boston in 1845; merchant, engaged in shipping and commerce with the East and West Indies and South America; served as a member of the Massachusetts house of representatives in 1866; chairman of the commissioners of prisons of Massachusetts; president of the Boston Board of Trade and of the Commercial Club of Boston; elected as a Republican to the Forty-seventh Congress (March 4, 1881-March 3, 1883); unsuccessful candidate for reelection in 1882 to the Forty-eighth Congress; elected to the Fifty-first Congress (March 4, 1889-March 3, 1891); unsuccessful candidate for reelection in 1890 to the Fifty-second Congress; engaged in mercantile pursuits until his retirement in 1893; died in Providence, R.I., March 16, 1903; interment in Mount Auburn Cemetery, Cambridge, Mass.

CANDLER, Milton Anthony (uncle of Ezekiel Samuel Candler Jr., and cousin of Allen Daniel Candler), a Representative from Georgia; born near Campbellton, Campbell County, Ga., January 11, 1837; attended private schools; was graduated from the University of Georgia at Athens in 1854; studied law; was admitted to the bar in 1856 and commenced practice in Cassville, Bartow County, Ga.; moved to Decatur in 1857; member of the State house of representatives 1861-1863; delegate to the State constitutional convention in 1865; served in the State senate 1868-1872; delegate to the Democratic National Convention in 1872 and 1876; elected as a Democrat to the Forty-fourth and Forty-fifth Congresses (March 4, 1875-March 3, 1879); was a candidate for renomination in 1878 to the Forty-sixth Congress, but withdrew because of the adoption of a free-silver plank by the district convention; resumed the practice of law; died in Decatur, De Kalb County, Ga., August 8, 1909; interment in Decatur Cemetery.

CANFIELD, Gordon, a Representative from New Jersey; born in Salamanca, Cattaraugus County, N.Y., April 15, 1898; attended the public schools of Binghamton, N.Y.; served as a private in the Signal Corps, United States Army, in 1917 and 1918; reporter in

Passaic, N.J., 1919-1923; studied law at New Jersey Law School in Newark; George Washington University Law School, Washington, D.C., LL.B., 1926; was admitted to the District of Columbia bar in 1927; served as secretary to Representative George N. Seger 1923-1940; elected as a Republican to the Seventy-seventh and to the nine succeeding Congresses (January 3, 1941-January 3, 1961); served during the Congressional recess in 1944 as an ordinary seaman, North Atlantic tanker duty, United States Merchant Marine; was not a candidate for renomination in 1960 to the Eighty-seventh Congress; director, National Housing Conference, and First Federal Savings and Loan Association of Paterson; remained active in civic affairs until his death in Hawthorne, N.J., June 20, 1972; interment in Laurel Grove Memorial Park, Totowa Borough, N.J.

**CANFIELD, Harry Clifford,** a Representative from Indiana; born near Moores Hill, Dearborn County, Ind., November 22, 1875; attended the public schools, Moores Hill College, Central Normal College, Danville, Ind., and Vorhies Business College, Indianapolis, Ind.; taught school in Dearborn County 1896-1898; moved to Batesville, Ripley County, in 1899 and engaged in the manufacture of furniture; also interested in the jobbing of furniture, and in farming and banking; elected as a Democrat to the Sixty-eighth and to the four succeeding Congresses (March 4, 1923-March 3, 1933); unsuccessful candidate for renomination in 1932; resumed the furniture manufacturing business in Batesville, Ind., where he died February 9, 1945; interment in the First Methodist Episcopal Cemetery.

**CANNON, Arthur Patrick,** a Representative from Florida; born in Powder Springs, Cobb County, Ga., May 22, 1904; moved to Laurens County, S.C.; attended the public schools, Wofford College, Spartanburg, S.C., and John B. Stetson University, De Land, Fla.; was graduated from the law college of the University of Miami, Miami, Fla., in 1931; was admitted to the bar the same year and commenced practice in Miami; elected as a Democrat to the Seventy-sixth and to the three succeeding Congresses (January 3, 1939-January 3, 1947); unsuccessful candidate for renomination in 1946 to the Eightieth Congress; resumed the practice of law; elected circuit judge of Dade County, Fla., in 1952, reelected in 1954, and again in 1960 for a six-year term; was a resident of Miami, Fla., until his death there on January 23, 1966; interment in Woodlawn Park Cemetery, Miami, Fla.

**CANNON, Clarence Andrew,** a Representative from Missouri; born in Elsberry, Lincoln County, Mo., April 11, 1879; was graduated from La Grange Junior College, Hannibal, Mo., in 1901, from William Jewell College, Liberty, Mo., in 1903, and from the law department of the University of Missouri at Columbia in 1908; professor of history, Stephens College, Columbia, Mo., 1904-1908; was admitted to the bar in 1908 and commenced practice in Troy, Mo.; in 1911 became a clerk in the office of the Speaker of the House; parliamentarian of the House of Representatives in the Sixty-fourth, Sixty-fifth, and Sixty-sixth Congresses, 1915-1920; parliamentarian of the Democratic National Conventions 1920-1960; author of A Synopsis of the Procedure of the House, Procedure in the House of Representatives, and Cannon's Procedure, subsequent editions of the latter being published periodically by resolutions of the House until 1963; editor and compiler of Precedents of the House of Representatives by act of Congress; regent of the Smithsonian Institution 1935-1964; elected as a Democrat to the Sixty-eighth and to the twenty succeeding Congresses and served from March 4, 1923, until his death in Washington, D.C., May 12, 1964; chairman, Committee on Appropriations (Seventy-seventh through Seventy-ninth Congresses, Eighty-first and Eighty-second Congresses, and Eighty-fourth through Eighty-eighth Congresses); interment in Elsberry City Cemetery, Elsberry, Mo.

**Bibliography:** *DAB*; Fulkerson, William M. "A Rhetorical Study of the Appropriations Speaking of Clarence Andrew Cannon in the House of Representatives, 1923-1964." Ph.D. dissertation, Michigan State University, 1969.

**CANNON, Frank Jenne** (son of George Quayle Cannon), a Delegate from the Territory of Utah and a Senator from Utah; born in Salt Lake City, Utah, January 25, 1859; attended the public schools, and was graduated from the University of Utah at Salt Lake City in 1878; newspaper writer; moved to San Francisco, Calif., in 1880 and worked as a newspaper reporter; moved to Ogden, Utah, in 1882, and served as deputy county clerk and recorder; elected county recorder in 1884; became editor of the Ogden Herald in 1887 and established the Ogden Standard in 1888; unsuccessful candidate for election in 1892 to the Fifty-third Congress; interested in the building of the Ogden Canyon electric power plant in 1893; elected as a Republican to the Fifty-fourth Congress and served from March 4, 1895, to January 4, 1896, when the Territory was admitted as a State into the Union; was then elected as a Republican to the United States Senate and served from January 22, 1896, to March 3, 1899; unsuccessful candidate for reelection in 1898; affiliated with the Democratic Party in 1900 and served as State chairman from 1902 until 1904; again became interested in newspaper publishing and established the Daily Utah State Journal at Ogden in 1903; moved to Denver, Colo., in 1909 and engaged in newspaper work and mining; died in Denver, Colo., July 25, 1933; interment in Ogden City Cemetery, Ogden, Utah.

**Bibliography:** Schlup, Leonard. "Utah Maverick: Frank J. Cannon and the Politics of Conscience in 1896." *Utah Historical Quarterly* 62 (Fall 1994): 335-348.

**CANNON, George Quayle** (father of Frank Jenne Cannon), a Delegate from the Territory of Utah; born in Liverpool, England, January 11, 1827; attended the common schools; immigrated to the United States in 1842 with his parents, who settled in Nauvoo, Ill.; moved to Great Salt Lake (then Mexican territory), Utah, in 1847; went to California in 1849 and a year later to the Hawaiian Islands as a missionary; returned to Salt Lake City in 1854; learned the art of printing; editor of the Western Standard in 1856 and 1857 and of the Deseret News 1867-1874 and 1877-1879; member of the Territorial council 1865, 1866, and 1869-1872; member of the board of regents of the Deseret University (now the University of Utah) and later chancellor; elected by the constitutional convention in 1872 a delegate to present the constitution and memorial to Congress for admission of the Territory as a State into the Union; elected as a Republican to the Forty-third and to the three succeeding Congresses (March 4, 1873-March 3, 1881); contested the election of Allen G. Campbell to the Forty-seventh Congress, but the House, on April 20, 1882, decided that neither was entitled to the seat; returned to Salt Lake City; director of the Union Pacific Railroad and a member of the board of directors of several financial and industrial enterprises at the time of his death; died in Monterey, Monterey County, Calif., April 12, 1901; interment in Salt Lake City Cemetery, Salt Lake City, Utah.

**Bibliography:** *DAB*; Cannon, Mark W. "The Mormon Issue in Congress 1872-1882: Drawing on the Experience of Territorial Delegate George Q. Cannon." Ph.D. dissertation, Harvard University, 1961.

**CANNON, Howard Walter,** a Senator from Nevada; born in St. George, Washington County, Utah, January 26, 1912; B.E., Arizona State Teachers College, 1933; LL.B., University of Arizona Law School, 1937; was admitted to the bar in Arizona in 1937, Utah in 1938, and Nevada in 1946; reference attorney for the Utah State senate in 1939; elected county attorney of Washington County, Utah, in 1940; during the Second World War served in the United States Army in 1941 and the United States Army Air Corps 1942-1946, attaining the rank of lieutenant colonel; served in the Air Force Reserve and retired as a major general; elected city attorney of Las

Vegas, Nev., in 1949 and served for four consecutive terms; elected as a Democrat to the United States Senate in 1958; reelected in 1964, 1970 and 1976 and served from January 3, 1959 to January 3, 1983; unsuccessful candidate for reelection in 1982; chairman, Joint Committee on Inaugural Arrangements (Ninety-second Congress), Select Committee on Standards and Conduct (Ninety-third and Ninety-fourth Congresses), Committee on Rules and Administration (Ninety-third through Ninety-fifth Congresses), Joint Committee on Inaugural Ceremonies (Ninety-fourth Congress), Joint Committee on the Library (Ninety-fifth Congress), Joint Committee on Printing (Ninety-fifth Congress), Committee on Commerce, Science, and Transportation (Ninety-fifth and Ninety-sixth Congresses); is a resident of Las Vegas, Nev.

**Bibliography:** Fenno, Richard F. "The Changing Senate in the Cannon Years." *Halcyon* 11 (1989): 65-84; Titus, A. Constandina. "Howard Cannon, the Senate and Civil Rights Legislation, 1959-1968." *Nevada Historical Society Quarterly* 33 (Winter 1990): 13-29.

**CANNON, Joseph Gurney,** a Representative from Illinois; born in Guilford, Guilford County, N.C., May 7, 1836; moved with his parents to Bloomingdale, Ind., in 1840; completed preparatory studies; studied law at the Cincinnati Law School; was admitted to the bar in 1858 and commenced practice in Terre Haute, Ind., in 1858; moved to Tuscola, Ill., in 1859; State's attorney for the twenty-seventh judicial district of Illinois from March 1861 to December 1868; elected as a Republican to the Forty-third and to the eight succeeding Congresses (March 4, 1873-March 3, 1891); chairman, Committee on Expenditures in the Post Office Department (Forty-seventh Congress), Committee on Appropriations (Fifty-first Congress); moved to Danville, Ill., in 1878; unsuccessful candidate for reelection in 1890 to the Fifty-second Congress; elected to the Fifty-third and to the nine succeeding Congresses (March 4, 1893-March 3, 1913); chairman, Committee on Appropriations (Fifty-fourth through Fifty-seventh Congresses), Committee on Rules (Fifty-eighth through Sixty-first Congresses); Speaker of the House of Representatives (Fifty-eighth through Sixty-first Congresses); received fifty-eight votes for the presidential nomination at the Republican National Convention of 1908; unsuccessful candidate for reelection in 1912 to the Sixty-third Congress; again elected to the Sixty-fourth and to the three succeeding Congresses (March 4, 1915-March 3, 1923); declined to be a candidate for renomination in 1922 to the Sixty-eighth Congress; retired from public life; died in Danville, Vermilion County, Ill., November 12, 1926; interment in Spring Hill Cemetery.

**Bibliography:** *DAB*; Bolles, Blair. *Tyrant From Illinois; Uncle Joe Cannon's Experiment With Personal Power.* New York: Norton, 1951; Cannon, Joseph G. *Uncle Joe Cannon: The Story of a Pioneer American, as told to L. White Busbey.* 1927. Reprint. St. Clair Shores, Mich.: Scholarly Press, 1970; Rager, Scott William. "The Fall of the House of Cannon: Uncle Joe and His Enemies, 1903-1910." Ph.D. dissertation, University of Illinois, Urbana-Champaign, 1991.

**CANNON, Marion,** a Representative from California; born near Morgantown, Va. (now West Virginia), October 30, 1834; attended the district school; learned the blacksmith trade; moved to California in 1852 and engaged in mining in Nevada County for twenty-one years; elected county recorder of Nevada County in 1869 and served two years; moved to Ventura County, Calif., and settled near Ventura in 1874; engaged in agricultural pursuits; elected first State president of the Farmers' Alliance on November 20, 1890, and reelected October 22, 1891; organized the People's Party of California on October 20, 1891; chosen a representative to the supreme council in Indianapolis, November 1891; selected by that body to represent California in the industrial conference at St. Louis on February 22, 1892; delegate to the People's Party National Convention in 1892; elected as Populist to the Fifty-third Congress (March 4, 1893-March 3, 1895); was not a candidate for renomination in 1894 to the Fifty-fourth Congress; resumed agricultural

pursuits until his death at "Ranch Home," near Ventura, August 27, 1920; interment in Ivy Lawn Cemetery, Ventura, Calif.

**CANNON, Newton,** a Representative from Tennessee; born in Guilford County, N.C., May 22, 1781; attended the common schools; moved to Tennessee at an early age and settled near Nashville, Williamson County; engaged in agricultural pursuits; member of the Tennessee State house of representatives in 1811 and 1812; enlisted in the War of 1812 and became colonel of a regiment of Tennessee Mounted Rifles; elected as a Republican to the Thirteenth Congress to fill the vacancy caused by the resignation of Felix Grundy; reelected to the Fourteenth Congress and served from September 16, 1814, to March 3, 1817; chairman, Committee on Expenditures in the Post Office Department (Fourteenth Congress); appointed by President James Monroe a commissioner to negotiate a treaty with the Chickasaw Indians in 1819; elected to the Sixteenth and Seventeenth Congresses (March 4, 1819-March 3, 1823); resumed agricultural pursuits; elected Governor of Tennessee in 1835, reelected in 1837, and served from October 12, 1835 to October 14, 1839; unsuccessful candidate for reelection in 1839; died in Nashville, September 16, 1841; interment in a cemetery on his estate near Allisona, Williamson County, Tenn.

**Bibliography:** *DAB*; Cassell, Robert. "Newton Cannon and State Politics, 1835-1839." *Tennessee Historical Quarterly* 15 (December 1956): 306-321; Harkins, John E. "Newton Cannon, Jackson Nemesis." *Tennessee Historical Quarterly* 43 (Winter 1984): 355-375.

**CANNON, Raymond Joseph,** a Representative from Wisconsin; born in Ironwood, Gogebic County, Mich., August 26, 1894; his parents having died when he was six months old, he spent his early life in a home for dependent children; attended the public schools; taught school at Minocqua, Wis., in 1910 and 1911; professional baseball player 1908-1922; attended the law department of Marquette University, Milwaukee, Wis., for two years; was admitted to the bar in 1914 and commenced practice in Milwaukee; unsuccessful candidate for election as associate justice of the Wisconsin Supreme Court in 1930; elected as a Democrat to the Seventy-third and to the two succeeding Congresses (March 4, 1933-January 3, 1939); chairman, Committee on Revision of the Laws (Seventy-fourth and Seventy-fifth Congresses); was an unsuccessful candidate in 1938 for renomination as a Democrat, and for reelection as an Independent to the Seventy-sixth Congress; resumed the practice of law; unsuccessful candidate for the Democratic gubernatorial nomination in 1940 and 1942; unsuccessful candidate for the Democratic nomination in 1944 to the Seventy-ninth Congress; died in Milwaukee, Wis., November 25, 1951; interment in Holy Cross Cemetery.

**CANTOR, Jacob Aaron,** a Representative from New York; born in New York City December 6, 1854; attended the public schools; reporter on the New York World for several years; was graduated from the law department of the College of the City of New York in 1875; was admitted to the bar and commenced practice in New York City; served in the State assembly 1885-1887; member of the State senate 1887-1898 and served as president in 1893 and 1894; elected president of the Borough of Manhattan in 1901; declined to be a candidate for renomination; elected as a Democrat to the Sixty-third Congress to fill the vacancy caused by the resignation of Francis Burton Harrison and served from November 4, 1913, to March 3, 1915; unsuccessfully contested the election of Isaac Siegel to the Sixty-fourth Congress; resumed the practice of law in New York City; president of the Tax Commission Board of New York City at the time of his death there on July 2, 1921; interment in Mount Hope Cemetery, Mount Hope, Westchester County, N.Y.

**CANTRILL, James Campbell,** a Representative from Kentucky; born in Georgetown, Scott County, Ky., July 9, 1870; attended the common schools, Georgetown (Ky.) College, and the University of

Virginia at Charlottesville; engaged in agricultural pursuits until his death; chairman of the Scott County Democratic committee in 1895; elected a member of the Kentucky house of representatives in 1897, and again in 1899; served in the Kentucky senate, 1901-1905; was nominated in 1904 to the Fifty-ninth Congress, but declined; delegate to the Democratic National Convention of 1904; elected president of the American Society of Equity for Kentucky, an organization of farmers, in 1908; elected as a Democrat to the Sixty-first and to the seven succeeding Congresses, and served from March 4, 1909 until his death in Louisville, Ky., September 2, 1923, during his campaign as the Democratic nominee for Governor of Kentucky; chairman, Committee on Industrial Arts and Expositions (Sixty-fourth and Sixty-fifth Congresses); interment in Georgetown Cemetery, Georgetown, Ky.

**CANTWELL, Maria E.,** a Representative from Washington; born in Indianapolis, Ind., October 13, 1958; graduated, Manual High School, Indianapolis, 1973; B.A., Miami University, Oxford, Ohio, 1981; public relations consultant, Cantwell and Associates; member, Washington State house of representatives, 1987-1993; elected as a Democrat to the One Hundred Third Congress (January 3, 1993-January 3, 1995); unsuccessful candidate for reelection in 1994 to the One Hundred Fourth Congress; is a resident of Mountlake Terrace, Wash.

**CAPEHART, Homer Earl,** a Senator from Indiana; born in Algiers, Pike County, Ind., June 6, 1897; attended the public schools; during the First World War enlisted as a private in the United States Army; promoted to sergeant and served in the Twelfth Infantry, 1917-1919; engaged in farming and the radio, phonograph, and television manufacturing business; elected as a Republican to the United States Senate in 1944; reelected in 1950 and 1956, and served from January 3, 1945 to January 3, 1963; unsuccessful candidate for reelection in 1962; chairman, Joint Committee on Defense Production (Eighty-third Congress), Committee on Banking and Currency (Eighty-third Congress); engaged in farming, manufacturing, and investment pursuits; retired; resided in Indianapolis, Ind., until his death there on September 3, 1979; interment in Crown Hill Cemetery.

Bibliography: *DAB*; Pickett, William B. *Homer E. Capehart: A Senator's Life, 1897-1979.* Indianapolis: Indiana Historical Society, 1990; Taylor, John. "Homer E. Capehart: United States Senator, 1944-1962." Ph.D. dissertation, Ball State University, 1977.

**CAPEHART, James,** a Representative from West Virginia; born in Point Pleasant, Mason County, Va. (now West Virginia), March 7, 1847; attended the public schools and Marietta College, Ohio; studied at Duff's Commercial College, Pittsburgh, Pa.; clerk and bookkeeper in his father's store; engaged in agricultural pursuits and stock breeding from 1867 until 1903; president of Mason County Court in 1871, 1872, and again from 1880 to 1885; delegate to the Democratic National Convention of 1888; elected as a Democrat to the Fifty-second and Fifty-third Congresses (March 4, 1891-March 3, 1895); was not a candidate for reelection in 1894 to the Fifty-fourth Congress; president of the Point Pleasant National Bank in 1901; after 1903 he became interested in fruit growing in Brevard County, Fla.; resided in Cocoa, Fla., until his death on April 28, 1921; interment in Lone Oak Cemetery, Point Pleasant, W.Va.

**CAPERTON, Allen Taylor** (son of Hugh Caperton), a Senator from West Virginia; born near Union, Monroe County, Va. (now West Virginia), November 21, 1810; attended the public schools of Virginia and Huntsville, Ala., and the University of Virginia at Charlottesville; was graduated from Yale College in 1832; studied law in Staunton, Va.; was admitted to the bar and practiced; member, Virginia house of delegates 1841-1842; member, State senate 1844-1848; delegate to the State constitutional conventions in 1850 and 1861; member, State house of delegates 1857-1861; elected by the legislature of Virginia a member of the Confederate

States Senate and served until 1865; elected as a Democrat to the United States Senate from West Virginia and served from March 4, 1875, until his death in Washington, D.C., July 26, 1876; interment in Green Hill Cemetery, Union, W.Va.

**CAPERTON, Hugh** (father of Allen Taylor Caperton), a Representative from Virginia; born in Greenbrier County, Va. (now West Virginia), April 17, 1781; was a planter and also engaged in mercantile pursuits; moved to Monroe County; sheriff of Monroe County in 1805; member of the State house of delegates 1810-1813 and 1826-1830; elected as a Federalist to the Thirteenth Congress (March 4, 1813-March 3, 1815); resumed agricultural and mercantile pursuits; died on his estate, "Elmwood," in Monroe County, near Union, Va. (now West Virginia), February 9, 1847; interment in Green Hill Cemetery, Union, W.Va.

**CAPOZZOLI, Louis Joseph,** a Representative from New York; born in Cosenza, Italy, March 6, 1901; immigrated to the United States in 1906; attended the public schools in New York City; was graduated from the law department of Fordham University, New York City in 1922; was admitted to the bar in 1923 and commenced practice in New York City; assistant district attorney of New York County 1930-1937; member of the State assembly in 1939 and 1940; elected as a Democrat to the Seventy-seventh and Seventy-eighth Congresses (January 3, 1941-January 3, 1945); was not a candidate for renomination in 1944; resumed the practice of law; elected a justice of the New York City Court in 1946 and served from 1947 to 1950; elected to the Court of General Sessions, County of New York, in 1950, and served until January 1957; appointed and served as a judge of the New York Supreme Court from January 21, 1957, to December 31, 1957; elected to the New York Supreme Court for a fourteen-year term; appointed as associate justice of the Appellate Division of New York State Supreme Court, First Judicial Department, April 29, 1966; was a resident of New York City until his death there on October 8, 1982.

**CAPPER, Arthur,** a Senator from Kansas; born in Garnett, Anderson County, Kans., July 14, 1865; attended the common schools; learned the art of printing and subsequently became a newspaper reporter; owner and publisher of the Topeka (Kans.) Daily Capital, Capper's Weekly, Capper's Farmer, the Household Magazine, and other publications; owner of two radio stations; president of the board of regents, Kansas Agricultural College 1910-1913; unsuccessful candidate for Governor of Kansas in 1912; elected Governor of Kansas in 1914, reelected in 1916, and served from January 11, 1915 to January 13, 1919; elected as a Republican to the United States Senate in 1918; reelected in 1924, 1930, 1936, and again in 1942 and served from March 4, 1919, to January 3, 1949; was not a candidate for renomination in 1948; chairman, Committee on Expenditures in the Department of Agriculture (Sixty-sixth Congress), Committee on Claims (Sixty-seventh and Sixty-eighth Congresses), Committee on District of Columbia (Sixty-ninth through Seventy-second Congresses), Committee on Agriculture and Forestry (Eightieth Congress); returned to Topeka and continued in the publishing business; died in Topeka, Kans., December 19, 1951; interment in Topeka Cemetery.

Bibliography: Capper, Arthur. *The Agricultural Bloc.* New York: Harcourt, Brace, and Co., 1922; Socolofsky, Homer E. *Arthur Capper, Publisher, Politician, and Philanthropist.* Lawrence: University of Kansas Press, 1962.

**CAPRON, Adin Ballou,** a Representative from Rhode Island; born in Mendon, Worcester County, Mass., January 9, 1841; attended the Woonsocket High School and Westbrook Seminary, near Portland, Maine; settled in Stillwater, Providence County, R.I., and engaged in milling and dealing in grain; enlisted as a sergeant in the Second Regiment, Rhode Island Volunteer Infantry, in May 1861; promoted to the rank of sergeant major July 11, 1861; commissioned lieutenant in September 1861; served in the Signal

Corps until the close of the Civil War, having been commissioned first lieutenant on March 3, 1863, and subsequently promoted to the rank of captain and major by brevet; member of the State house of representatives 1887-1892 and served as speaker in 1891 and 1892; unsuccessful candidate for election in 1892 to the Fifty-third Congress; elected as a Republican to the Fifty-fifth and to the six succeeding Congresses (March 4, 1897-March 3, 1911); was not a candidate for renomination in 1910; resumed his former business activities in Stillwater, Providence County, R.I., where he died March 17, 1911; interment in Swan Point Cemetery, Providence, R.I.

**CAPSTICK, John Henry,** a Representative from New Jersey; born in Lawrence, Mass., September 2, 1856; attended the public schools of Lawrence; moved with his parents to Providence, R.I., in 1868; attended a business college; member of the Rhode Island Militia in 1870 and 1871; moved to Montville, N.J., in 1883, and engaged in the manufacture of textile fabrics the same year; member of the State sewerage commission 1905-1908; president of the State board of health 1908-1914; elected as a Republican to the Sixty-fourth and Sixty-fifth Congresses and served from March 4, 1915, until his death in Montville, Morris County, N.J., March 17, 1918; interment in Greenwood Cemetery, Boonton, N.J.

**CAPUTO, Bruce Faulkner,** a Representative from New York; born in New York City, August 7, 1943; graduated from Deerfield (Mass.) Academy, 1961; B.A., 1965, M.B.A., 1967, Harvard University; J.D., Georgetown Law School, Washington, D.C., 1971; employed in Office of the Secretary, United States Department of Defense, 1967-1969; member, New York State assembly, 1973-1976; elected as a Republican to the Ninety-fifth Congress (January 3, 1977-January 3, 1979); was not a candidate for reelection in 1978 to the Ninety-sixth Congress, but was an unsuccessful candidate for nomination for lieutenant governor of New York; resumed the practice of law in New York City; is a resident of Bronxville, N.Y.

**CARAWAY, Hattie Wyatt** (wife of Thaddeus Horatius Caraway), a Senator from Arkansas; born in Bakerville, Humphreys County, Tenn., February 1, 1878; attended the public schools and was graduated from Dickson (Tenn.) Normal College in 1896; thereafter located in Jonesboro, Ark.; appointed as a Democrat on November 13, 1931, and subsequently elected on January 12, 1932, to the United States Senate to fill the vacancy in the term ending March 3, 1933, caused by the death of her husband, Thaddeus H. Caraway; reelected in 1932 and again in 1938, and served from November 13, 1931 to January 2, 1945; unsuccessful candidate for renomination in 1944; first woman elected to the United States Senate; chairman, Committee on Enrolled Bills (Seventy-third through Seventy-eighth Congresses); member of the United States Employees' Compensation Commission, 1945-1946; member of the Employees' Compensation Appeals Board from July 1946 until her death in Falls Church, Va., December 21, 1950; interment in West Lawn Cemetery, Jonesboro, Ark.

**Bibliography:** *DAB*; Kincaid, Diane D., ed. *Silent Hattie Speaks: The Personal Journal of Senator Hattie Caraway.* Westport, Conn.: Greenwood Press, 1979; Towns, Stuart. "A Louisiana Medicine Show: The King Fish Elects an Arkansas Senator." *Arkansas Historical Quarterly* 25 (Summer 1966): 117-27.

**CARAWAY, Thaddeus Horatius** (husband of Hattie Wyatt Caraway), a Representative and a Senator from Arkansas; born on a farm near Springhill, Stoddard County, Mo., October 17, 1871; attended the common schools; moved to Arkansas in 1883 with his parents, who settled in Clay County; was graduated from Dickson (Tenn.) College in 1896; taught in country schools from 1896 to 1899; studied law; was admitted to the bar in 1900 and commenced practice in Osceola, Ark.; moved to Lake City, Craighead County, Ark., in 1900, and to Jonesboro, Ark., in 1901, and continued the practice of law; prosecuting attorney for the second judicial circuit of Arkansas, 1908-1912; elected as a Democrat to the Sixty-third and

to the three succeeding Congresses (March 4, 1913-March 3, 1921); was not a candidate in 1920 for renomination to the House of Representatives, but was elected to the United States Senate; reelected in 1926, and served from March 4, 1921 until his death in Little Rock, Ark., November 6, 1931; interment in West Lawn Cemetery, Jonesboro, Ark.

**Bibliography:** *DAB*; Adams, Horace. "Thaddeus H. Caraway in the United States Senate." Ph.D. dissertation, George Peabody College for Teachers, 1935.

**CARDEN, Cap Robert,** a Representative from Kentucky; born on a farm near Munfordville, Hart County, Ky., December 17, 1866; attended the rural schools and Bowling Green (Ky.) Business and Normal School; studied law; was admitted to the bar in 1895 and commenced practice in Munfordville, Hart County, Ky.; also engaged in agricultural pursuits and in banking; sheriff of Hart County 1887-1890; was elected county attorney of Hart County in 1890 and served from 1891 to 1894; served as master commissioner of the circuit court of Hart County 1900-1915; elected as a Democrat to the Seventy-second, Seventy-third, and Seventy-fourth Congresses and served from March 4, 1931, until his death in Louisville, Ky., on June 13, 1935; interment in Munfordville Cemetery, Munfordville, Ky.

**CARDIN, Benjamin Louis,** a Representative from Maryland; born in Baltimore, October 5, 1943; attended public schools; graduated Baltimore City College, 1961; B.A., University of Pittsburgh, Pa., 1964; J.D., University of Maryland, 1967; admitted to the Maryland State bar in 1967 and began practice in Baltimore; chair, Maryland Legal Services Corp.; member, Maryland State house of delegates, 1966-1986, and served as speaker, 1979-1986; elected as a Democrat to the One Hundredth and to the four succeeding Congresses (January 3, 1987-January 3, 1997); is a resident of Baltimore, Md.

**CAREW, John Francis** (nephew of Thomas Francis Magner), a Representative from New York; born in Williamsburg, Brooklyn, N.Y., April 16, 1873; attended the public schools of Brooklyn and New York City and the College of the City of New York; was graduated from Columbia College in 1893 and from Columbia University Law School in New York City in 1896; was admitted to the bar in 1897 and commenced practice in New York City; member of the State assembly in 1904; delegate to all Democratic State conventions from 1912 to 1924; delegate to the Democratic National Conventions in 1912 and 1924; elected as a Democrat to the Sixty-third and to the eight succeeding Congresses; served from March 4, 1913, until his resignation on December 28, 1929, having been appointed a justice of the New York State Supreme Court; was subsequently elected to the same office in November 1930 for a fourteen-year term, but retired December 31, 1943, due to age limitation; served as official referee of the New York Supreme Court; died in Rockville Centre, N.Y., April 10, 1951; interment in Calvary Cemetery, Queens County, N.Y.

**CAREY, Hugh Leo,** a Representative from New York; born in Brooklyn, Kings County, N.Y., April 11, 1919; graduated from St. John's College and from the law school of the same college, LL.B., 1951; admitted to the bar in 1951 and commenced the practice of law in Brooklyn, N.Y.; during the Second World War entered the United States Army as an enlisted man in the One Hundred First Cavalry, New York National Guard, serving in Europe as a major of infantry in the One Hundred Fourth Division; decorated with Bronze Star, Croix de Guerre, and Combat Infantry Award; State chairman, Young Democrats of New York, 1946; director and officer in several industrial companies; elected as a Democrat to the Eighty-seventh and to the six succeeding Congresses and served from January 3, 1961, until his resignation on December 31, 1974; was not a candidate for reelection in 1974 to the Ninety-fourth Congress, but was elected Governor of New York; reelected in 1978, and served from January 1, 1975 to January 1, 1983; resumed the practice of law in New York City; is a resident of New York City.

**Bibliography:** Kramer, Daniel C. *The Days of Wine and Roses Are Over: Governor Hugh Carey and New York State*. Lanham, Md.: University Press of America, 1996.

**CAREY, John,** a Representative from Ohio; born in Monongalia County, Va. (now West Virginia), April 5, 1792; moved with his parents to the Northwest Territory in 1798; served under General William Hull in the War of 1812; associate judge from 1825 until 1832; appointed Indian agent at the Wyandotte Reservation in 1829; member of the Ohio State house of representatives in 1828, 1836, and 1843; promoter and first president of the Mad River Railroad, from Sandusky to Dayton, about 1845; established the town of Carey, Wyandot County, Ohio; elected as a Republican to the Thirty-sixth Congress (March 4, 1859-March 3, 1861); died in Carey, Ohio, March 17, 1875; interment in the family burial ground on the home farm; reinterment in 1919 in Spring Grove Cemetery, Carey, Ohio.

**Bibliography:** Kinney, Muriel. "John Carey, An Ohio Pioneer." *Ohio State Archaeological and Historical Quarterly* 46 (April 1937): 166-98.

**CAREY, Joseph Maull** (father of Robert Davis Carey), a Delegate from the Territory of Wyoming and a Senator from Wyoming; born in Milton, Sussex County, Del., January 19, 1845; attended the common schools, Fort Edward Collegiate Institute, and Union College, New York; was graduated from the law department of the University of Pennsylvania at Philadelphia in 1864; was admitted to the bar in 1867 and commenced practice in Philadelphia; United States attorney for the Territory of Wyoming, 1869-1871; associate justice of the supreme court of the Territory of Wyoming, 1871-1876; retired from the bench and engaged in the cattle and ranching business; member of the United States Centennial Commission, 1872-1876; member of the Republican National Committee, 1876-1897; mayor of Cheyenne, Wyo., 1881-1885; elected as a Republican to the Forty-ninth and to the two succeeding Congresses, and served from March 4, 1885 until July 10, 1890, when the Territory became a State; elected as a Republican to the United States Senate, and served from November 15, 1890 until March 3, 1895; unsuccessful candidate for reelection in 1895; chairman, Committee on Education and Labor (Fifty-second Congress); resumed the practice of law in Cheyenne, Wyo.; elected Governor of Wyoming in 1910, and served from January 2, 1911 to January 4, 1915; one of the organizers of the Progressive Party in 1912; vice president of the Federal Land Bank; member of the board of trustees of the University of Wyoming at Laramie; died in Cheyenne, Wyo., February 5, 1924; interment in Lakeview Cemetery.

**Bibliography:** *DAB*; Peters, Betsy R. "Joseph M. Carey and The Progressive Movement in Wyoming." Ph.D. dissertation, University of Wyoming, 1971.

**CAREY, Robert Davis** (son of Joseph Maull Carey), a Senator from Wyoming; born in Cheyenne, Laramie County, Wyo., August 12, 1878; attended the public schools, and Hill School in Pottstown, Pa.; was graduated from Yale University 1900; moved to Careyhurst, Converse County, Wyo., in 1900; engaged in the raising of livestock and agricultural pursuits; also interested in banking; member of the Progressive National Committee for Wyoming 1912-1916; chairman of the Wyoming State Highway Commission 1917-1918; president of the Wyoming Stock Growers' Association 1917-1921; elected Governor of Wyoming in 1918 and served from January 6, 1919 to January 1, 1923; appointed by President Calvin Coolidge in 1924 as chairman of the agricultural conference to investigate the agricultural situation in the United States; elected as a Republican to the United States Senate on November 4, 1930, to fill the vacancy caused by the death of Francis E. Warren and on the same day was also elected for the term commencing March 4, 1931, and served from December 1, 1930, to January 3, 1937; unsuccessful candidate for reelection in 1936; resumed agricultural pursuits and ranching; died in Cheyenne, Wyo., January 17, 1937; interment in Lakeview Cemetery.

**CARLETON, Ezra Child,** a Representative from Michigan; born in St. Clair, St. Clair County, Mich., September 6, 1838; attended the common schools, and was graduated from the Port Huron High School in 1859; engaged in business as a hardware merchant in Port Huron, St. Clair County; mayor of Port Huron in 1881 and 1882; elected as a Democrat to the Forty-eighth and Forty-ninth Congresses (March 4, 1883-March 3, 1887); engaged in his former mercantile pursuits in Port Huron, until his death there July 24, 1911, interment in Lakeside Cemetery.

**CARLETON, Peter,** a Representative from New Hampshire; born in Haverhill, Mass., September 19, 1755; attended the public schools; engaged in agricultural pursuits; served in a Massachusetts regiment during the Revolutionary War; moved to Landaff, Grafton County, N.H., about 1789; member of the State constitutional convention in 1790; member of the State house of representatives in 1803 and 1804; served in the State senate in 1806 and 1807; elected as a Republican to the Tenth Congress (March 4, 1807-March 3, 1809); died in Landaff, N.H., on April 29, 1828; interment in the City Cemetery.

**CARLEY, Patrick J.,** a Representative from New York; born in County Roscommon, Ireland, February 2, 1866; immigrated to the United States with his parents at an early age; attended the public schools; engaged in the building and construction business; also interested in banking; director of the Bay Ridge Memorial Hospital; elected as a Democrat to the Seventieth and to the three succeeding Congresses (March 4, 1927-January 3, 1935); chairman, Committee on Election of President, Vice President, and Representatives (Seventy-second and Seventy-third Congresses); was not a candidate for renomination in 1934; resumed the building and construction business until his retirement; died in Brooklyn, N.Y., February 25, 1936; interment in Calvary Cemetery, Queens County, N.Y.

**CARLILE, John Snyder,** a Representative and a Senator from Virginia; born in Winchester, Va., on December 16, 1817; educated by his mother; clerked in a store and commenced business for himself in 1834; studied law; was admitted to the bar in 1840 and commenced practice in Beverly, Va. (now West Virginia) in 1842; moved to Philippi and later to Clarksburg and continued the practice of law; member, Virginia senate 1847-1851; delegate to the Virginia constitutional convention in 1850; elected as the candidate of the American Party to the Thirty-fourth Congress (March 4, 1855-March 3, 1857); delegate to the Virginia secession convention in February 1861; elected as a Unionist to the Thirty-seventh Congress and served from March 4, 1861, until July 9, 1861, when he resigned to become Senator; elected as a Unionist to the United States Senate to fill the vacancy caused by the retirement of Robert M.T. Hunter and served from July 9, 1861, to March 3, 1865; member of the convention that submitted the new Virginia ordinance in August 1861; died in Clarksburg, Harrison County, W.Va., October 24, 1878; interment in Odd Fellows Cemetery.

**Bibliography:** *DAB*.

**CARLIN, Charles Creighton,** a Representative from Virginia; born in Alexandria, Va., April 8, 1866; attended the public schools and Alexandria Academy; was graduated from National University Law School, Washington, D.C.; was admitted to the bar in 1891 and commenced practice in Alexandria, Va.; postmaster at Alexandria, Va., 1893-1897; served as delegate to Democratic National Conventions for forty years; elected as a Democrat to the Sixtieth Congress to fill the vacancy caused by the death of John F. Rixey; reelected to the Sixty-first and to the five succeeding Congresses and served from November 5, 1907, to March 3, 1919, when he resigned before the commencement of the Sixty-sixth Congress, to which he had been reelected; resumed the practice of law in Alexandria, Va., and Washington, D.C.; also engaged in the newspaper publishing business at Alexandria, Va.; moved to Washington, D.C., in 1936 and continued the practice of law; died in Washington, D.C., October 14, 1938; interment in Ivy Hill Cemetery, Alexandria, Va.

**CARLISLE, John Griffin,** a Representative and a Senator from Kentucky; born in Campbell (now Kenton) County, Ky., September 5, 1835; attended the common schools; taught school in Covington and elsewhere for five years; studied law; was admitted to the bar in 1858 and commenced practice in Covington, Ky.; member, Kentucky house of representatives, 1859-1861; member, Kentucky senate, 1866-1871; lieutenant governor of Kentucky from 1871 to 1875; editor of the Louisville Daily Ledger in 1872; elected as a Democrat to the Forty-fifth and to the six succeeding Congresses and served from March 4, 1877, to May 26, 1890, when he resigned, having been elected Senator; Speaker of the House of Representatives (Forty-eighth, Forty-ninth, and Fiftieth Congresses); chairman, Committee on Rules (Forty-eighth through Fiftieth Congresses); elected as a Democrat to the United States Senate to fill the vacancy caused by the death of James B. Beck, and served from May 26, 1890 until February 4, 1893, when he resigned to accept a Cabinet portfolio; appointed Secretary of the Treasury in the Cabinet of President Grover Cleveland, and served from March 4, 1893 to March 4, 1897; moved to New York City and resumed the practice of law; died in New York City, July 31, 1910; interment in Linden Grove Cemetery, Covington, Ky.

**Bibliography:** *DAB*; Barnes, James. *John G. Carlisle, Financial Statesman.* 1931. Reprint. Gloucester, Mass.: P. Smith Company, 1967.

**CARLSON, Cliffard Dale,** a Representative from Illinois; born in Aurora, Kane County, Ill., December 30, 1915; educated in the public schools of Aurora, Ill., and North Central College, Naperville, Ill.; B.A., University of New Mexico, 1939; served in the United States Naval Reserve as a lieutenant (jg), Pacific Theater, during the Second World War; delegate to the Republican National Conventions of 1960, 1964, and 1968; Republican State Central Committeeman; involved in manufacturing; elected as a Republican, by special election, April 4, 1972, to the Ninety-second Congress to fill the vacancy caused by the resignation of Charlotte T. Reid, and served from April 4, 1972, to January 3, 1973; was not a candidate in 1972 for reelection to the Ninety-third Congress; unsuccessful candidate for election in 1974 to the Ninety-fourth Congress; died at the family farm near Dixon, Ill., August 28, 1977; interment in Oak Hill Cemetery, Geneva, Ill.

**CARLSON, Frank,** a Representative and a Senator from Kansas; born in Concordia, Cloud County, Kans., January 23, 1893; attended the public schools, Concordia (Kans.) Normal and Business College, and Kansas State College at Manhattan; during the First World War served as a private in the United States Army, 1918-1919; engaged in agricultural pursuits and stock raising; member, Kansas State house of representatives, 1929-1933; chairman of the Republican State committee, 1932-1934; elected as a Republican to the Seventy-fourth and to the five succeeding Congresses (January 3, 1935-January 3, 1947); was not a candidate for renomination in 1946 to the Eightieth Congress; elected Governor of Kansas in 1946, reelected in 1948, and served from January 13, 1947 until his resignation on November 28, 1950, having been elected a Senator; chairman of the Interstate Oil Compact Commission in 1949; chairman of the National Governors Conference in 1950; elected as a Republican to the United States Senate in 1950 to fill the vacancy caused by the death of Clyde M. Reed for the term ending January 3, 1951, and also for the full term commencing January 3, 1951; reelected in 1956, and again in 1962,

and served from November 29, 1950, to January 3, 1969; was not a candidate for reelection in 1968; chairman, Committee on Post Office and Civil Service (Eighty-third Congress); died in Concordia, Kans., May 30, 1987; interment in Pleasant Hill Cemetery.

**CARLTON, Henry Hull,** a Representative from Georgia; born in Athens, Ga., May 14, 1835; attended the public schools and the University of Georgia at Athens for two years; was graduated in medicine and surgery from Jefferson Medical College, Philadelphia, Pa., in 1857, and practiced until 1872; during the Civil War served four years in the Confederate Army under General Robert E. Lee, holding the ranks of lieutenant, captain, and major of artillery; member of the Georgia State house of representatives from 1873 until 1877, serving as speaker pro tempore in 1877; editor and proprietor of the Athens Banner (Banner Watchman) until 1880; studied law; was admitted to the bar in 1881 and commenced practice in Athens, Ga.; city attorney of Athens in 1881 and 1882; member and president of the Georgia State senate in 1884 and 1885; elected as a Democrat to the Fiftieth and Fifty-first Congresses (March 4, 1887-March 3, 1891); again a member of the State house of representatives in 1899; declined to be a candidate for reelection; volunteered for service in the Spanish-American War and was made inspector general with the rank of major; engaged in the insurance business; died in Athens, Ga., October 26, 1905; interment in Oconee Cemetery.

**CARLYLE, Frank Ertel,** a Representative from North Carolina; born in Lumberton, Robeson County, N.C., April 7, 1897; educated in the schools of Robeson County, N.C., and Wilson Memorial Academy, Nyack, N.Y.; graduated from the University of North Carolina at Chapel Hill; during the First World War served in the United States Navy; licensed to practice law on January 31, 1921, and commenced practice in Lumberton, N.C.; elected solicitor of the ninth judicial district of North Carolina in 1938, 1942, and 1946, and served until elected to Congress; elected as a Democrat to the Eighty-first and to the three succeeding Congresses (January 3, 1949-January 3, 1957); unsuccessful for renomination in 1956; died in Lumberton, N.C., October 2, 1960; interment in Meadowbrook Cemetery.

**CARMACK, Edward Ward,** a Representative and a Senator from Tennessee; born near Castalian Springs, Sumner County, Tenn., November 5, 1858; attended Webb's School, Culleoka, Tenn.; studied law; was admitted to the bar in 1879 and practiced in Columbia, Tenn.; city attorney of Columbia in 1881; elected to the Tennessee General Assembly from Maury and Williamson Counties in 1884; joined the editorial staff of the Nashville Daily American in 1886; editor in chief of the Nashville Democrat in 1888, and became editor in chief of the Daily American when the newspapers were merged; editor of the Memphis Commercial in 1892; elected as a Democrat to the Fifty-fifth and Fifty-sixth Congresses (March 4, 1897-March 3, 1901); elected as a Democrat to the United States Senate, and served from March 4, 1901 to March 3, 1907; unsuccessful candidate for reelection in 1906; resumed the practice of law; unsuccessful candidate for nomination for Governor in 1908; appointed editor in chief of the Nashville Tennessean on August 31, 1908; died in a gun fight with Colonel Duncan B. Cooper in Nashville, Tenn., November 9, 1908; interment in Rose Hill Cemetery, Columbia, Tenn.

**Bibliography:** *DAB*; Faries, Clyde J. "Carmack Versus Patterson: The Genesis of a Political Feud." *Tennessee Historical Quarterly* 38 (Fall 1979): 332-47; Majors, William R. *Editorial Wild Oats: Edward Ward Carmack and Tennessee Politics.* Macon, Ga.: Mercer University Press, 1984.

**CARMAN, Gregory Wright,** a Representative from New York; born in Farmingdale, Nassau County, N.Y., January 31, 1937; attended the public schools; attended the University of Paris, France, L'institut d'Etudes Politique, 1956-1957; B.A., St. Lawrence

University, Canton, N.Y., 1958; J.D., St. John's University, Jamaica, N.Y., 1961; graduated, University of Virginia Law School, J.A.G. School, 1962; served in the United States Army as a captain, Second Infantry Division, 1958-1964; admitted to the New York State bar in 1961 and commenced practice in Farmingdale, 1964; member, Town Board of Oyster Bay, N.Y., 1972-1980; elected as a Republican to the Ninety-seventh Congress (January 3, 1981-January 3, 1983); was not a candidate for reelection in 1982 to the Ninety-eighth Congress; confirmed, United States Judge, United States Court of International Trade, March 2, 1983; is a resident of Farmingdale, N.Y.

**CARMICHAEL, Archibald Hill,** a Representative from Alabama; born near Sylvan Grove in Dale County, Ala., June 17, 1864; attended the public schools; was graduated from the law department of the University of Alabama at Tuscaloosa in 1886; was admitted to the bar the same year and commenced practice in Tuscumbia, Ala.; served as solicitor of the eighth judicial district of Alabama 1890-1894; delegate to the State constitutional convention in 1901; member of the State house of representatives 1907-1911 and 1915-1919, serving as speaker in 1907 and 1911; delegate at large to the Democratic National Conventions in 1916, 1928, and 1932; served in the State senate 1919-1923; member of the State Board of Education 1919-1947 and of the Tuscumbia Board of Education 1920-1947; trustee of the University of Alabama 1924-1947; elected as a Democrat to the Seventy-third Congress to fill the vacancy caused by the death of Edward B. Almon; reelected to the Seventy-fourth Congress and served from November 14, 1933, to January 3, 1937; was not a candidate for renomination in 1936; resumed the practice of law and was also interested in banking until his death in Tuscumbia, Ala., on July 15, 1947; interment in Oakwood Cemetery.

**CARMICHAEL, Richard Bennett** (grandnephew of William Carmichael), a Representative from Maryland; born in Centerville, Queen Annes County, Md., December 25, 1807; attended the academy at Centerville, and Dickinson College, Carlisle, Pa.; was graduated from Princeton College in 1828; studied law; was admitted to the bar in 1830 and commenced practice in Centerville, Queen Annes County, Md.; member of the State house of delegates in 1831 and 1841-1866; elected as a Jacksonian to the Twenty-third Congress (March 4, 1833-March 3, 1835); resumed the practice of law; delegate to the Democratic National Conventions in 1856, 1864, 1868, and 1876; judge of the circuit court 1858-1864; presiding judge of the county court of Queen Annes County in 1861; member and president of the State constitutional convention in 1867; died at "Wye," near Carmichael, Queen Annes County, Md., October 21, 1884; interment in the family burying ground at "Wye."

**CARMICHAEL, William** (granduncle of Richard Bennett Carmichael), a Delegate from Maryland; born at "Round Top," in Queen Annes County, Md., near Chestertown, Md.; studied law; was admitted to the bar and practiced in Centerville, Md.; was in London, England, at the beginning of the Revolution; assistant to Silas Deane, secret agent of Congress, at Paris in 1776; went to Berlin to represent American interests in 1776; named secretary to the American commissioners in France in 1777, but did not serve, returning to the United States in May 1778; Member of the Continental Congress, 1778-1779; went to Spain in September 1779 and served as secretary of the legation; appointed Chargé d'Affaires at Madrid, Spain, April 20, 1782, and served until May 1794; died in Madrid on February 9, 1795; interment in a lot adjoining the Roman Catholic Cemetery.

**Bibliography:** *DAB.*

**CARNAHAN, Albert Sidney Johnson,** a Representative from Missouri; born on a farm near Ellsinore, Carter County, Mo., January 9, 1897; attended public schools in Ellsinore and Cape Girardeau, Mo.; was graduated from State Teachers College at Cape Girardeau in 1926, and from the University of Missouri at Columbia

in 1934; taught school, served as high school principal for one year, and held school administrative positions in Carter, Reynolds, and Shannon Counties from 1920 until 1944; served overseas in the United States Navy as a yeoman third class with a naval aviation unit in 1918 and 1919; elected as a Democrat to the Seventy-ninth Congress (January 3, 1945-January 3, 1947); unsuccessful candidate for reelection in 1946 to the Eightieth Congress; superintendent of schools at Ellsinore, Mo.; elected to the Eighty-first and to the five succeeding Congresses (January 3, 1949-January 3, 1961); unsuccessful candidate for renomination in 1960 to the Eighty-seventh Congress; appointed Ambassador to Sierra Leone on May 11, 1961 and served until July 1963; retired to Crites Corner, west of Ellsinore; died in Rochester, Minn., on March 24, 1968, interment in Carson Hill Cemetery, northeast of Ellsinore, Mo.

**CARNES, Thomas Petters,** a Representative from Georgia; born in Maryland in 1762; completed preparatory studies; studied law; was admitted to the bar and practiced in Milledgeville, Ga.; member of the State house of representatives 1786, 1787, 1789, and 1797; solicitor general for the western circuit of Georgia; attorney general of Georgia from December 1789 until December 1792, when he resigned; elected to the Third Congress (March 4, 1793-March 3, 1795); resumed the practice of law; judge of the western circuit court of Georgia from January 1798 until May 1803, when he resigned, and from December 1809 to November 1810; member of the State constitutional convention in 1798; appointed one of the commissioners to settle the boundary disputes between the States of Georgia and North Carolina in 1806; again a member of the State house of representatives in 1807 and 1808; died on his farm in Franklin (now Hart) County, Ga., May 5, 1822; interment in the garden on his estate.

**CARNEY, Charles Joseph,** a Representative from Ohio; born in Youngstown, Mahoning County, Ohio, April 17, 1913; attended schools in Youngstown and Campbell, Ohio; attended Youngstown State University; member, Ohio State senate, 1950-1970, serving as minority leader from 1969 to 1970; staff member, vice-president, and president, United Rubber Workers Union Local 102, 1934-1950; staff representative, United Steelworkers of America, 1950-1968; served as vice-president of Mahoning County CIO Industrial Council; elected as a Democrat to the Ninety-first Congress, November 3, 1970, by special election, to fill the vacancy caused by the death of Michael Kirwan and at the same time elected to the Ninety-second Congress; reelected to the three succeeding Congresses, and served from November 3, 1970, to January 3, 1979; unsuccessful candidate for reelection in 1978 to the Ninety-sixth Congress; was a resident of Youngstown, Ohio, until his death there on October 7, 1987; interment in Calvary Cemetery.

**CARNEY, William,** a Representative from New York; born in Brooklyn, Kings County, N.Y., July 1, 1942; received preliminary education at St. Catherine of Genoa, Brooklyn; graduated from Delahanty High School, Queens, 1960; attended Florida State University, Tallahassee, Fla., 1960-1961; served in the United States Army Medical Corps, 1961-1964; sales representative for a heavy equipment firm, 1972-1976; member, Suffolk County, N.Y., legislature, 1976-1979; elected as a Republican to the Ninety-sixth and to the three succeeding Congresses (January 3, 1979-January 3, 1987); was not a candidate for reelection in 1986 to the One Hundredth Congress; is a resident of Hauppauge, N.Y.

**CARPENTER, Cyrus Clay,** a Representative from Iowa; born near Harford, Susquehanna County, Pa., November 24, 1829; attended the common schools, and was graduated from Harford Academy in 1853; moved to Iowa in 1854 and engaged in teaching and afterwards in land surveying; studied law but never practiced; county surveyor of Webster County in 1856; member of the Iowa State house of representatives, 1858-1860; during the Civil War was appointed captain of Volunteers on March 24, 1862, lieutenant colonel on September 26, 1864, and brevet colonel of Volunteers on July 12, 1865; registrar of the State land office, 1866-1868; elected Governor of Iowa in 1871, reelected in 1873, and served from January 11, 1872 to January 13, 1876; Second Comptroller of the Treasury from January 1876 to September 1877; appointed railroad commissioner of Iowa on March 26, 1878; elected as a Republican to the Forty-sixth and Forty-seventh Congresses (March 4, 1879-March 3, 1883); was not a candidate for renomination in 1882 to the Forty-eighth Congress; again served in the State house of representatives, 1884-1886; postmaster of Fort Dodge, 1889-1893; engaged in the management of his farm and in the real-estate business; died in Fort Dodge, Iowa, May 29, 1898; interment in Oakland Cemetery.

Bibliography: *DAB*; Throne, Mildred. *Cyrus Clay Carpenter and Iowa Politics, 1854-1898.* Iowa City: State Historical Society of Iowa, 1974.

CARPENTER, Davis, a Representative from New York; born in Walpole, Cheshire County, N.H., December 25, 1799; studied medicine; was graduated from Middlebury (Vt.) College in 1824; studied law; was admitted to the bar and commenced practice in Brockport, Monroe County, N.Y.; elected as a Whig to the Thirty-third Congress to fill the vacancy caused by the resignation of Azariah Boody and served from November 8, 1853, to March 3, 1855; unsuccessful candidate for reelection in 1854 to the Thirty-fourth Congress; engaged in the practice of medicine in Brockport, N.Y., and died there October 22, 1878; interment in High Street Cemetery.

CARPENTER, Edmund Nelson, a Representative from Pennsylvania; born in Wilkes-Barre, Pa., June 27, 1865; attended the public schools in Wilkes-Barre and the Wyoming Seminary, Kingston, Pa.; interested in mining and the manufacture of sheet-metal products; enlisted as a private in 1893 and attained the rank of major in the Pennsylvania National Guard; during the Spanish-American War served as first lieutenant and quartermaster in the Ninth Regiment, Pennsylvania Volunteer Infantry, from April 27, 1898, to October 29, 1898; unsuccessful candidate for election in 1918 to the Sixty-sixth Congress; elected as a Republican to the Sixty-ninth Congress (March 4, 1925-March 3, 1927); unsuccessful candidate for reelection in 1926 to the Seventieth Congress; resumed his manufacturing interests; died in Philadelphia, Pa., November 4, 1952; interment in Hollenback Cemetery, Wilkes-Barre, Pa.

CARPENTER, Levi D., a Representative from New York; born in Waterville, Oneida County, N.Y., August 21, 1802; attended the public schools; studied law; was admitted to the bar and commenced practice in Waterville, N.Y.; supervisor of the town of Sangerfield in 1835; elected as a Democrat to the Twenty-eighth Congress to fill the vacancy caused by the resignation of Samuel Beardsley and served from November 5, 1844, to March 3, 1845; was not a candidate for reelection in 1844 to the Twenty-ninth Congress; resumed the practice of law in Waterville, N.Y., and died there October 27, 1856; interment in the City Cemetery.

CARPENTER, Lewis Cass, a Representative from South Carolina; born in Putnam, Conn., February 20, 1836; attended the public schools; moved to New Jersey, where he taught school; appointed State inspector of public schools in New Jersey in 1863; at an early age began writing for the press, and was connected with the New York papers for several years; went to Washington, D.C., in 1864 and was employed in the Treasury Department; studied law at Columbian (now George Washington) University; was admitted to the bar and practiced; Washington newspaper correspondent; moved to Charleston, S.C., in 1867 and became editor of the Charleston Courier; assisted in establishing the Charleston Republican in 1868; secretary to Senator William H. Buckingham, of Connecticut, 1868-1873; elected as a Republican to the Forty-third Congress to fill the vacancy caused by the resignation of Robert B. Elliott and served from November 3, 1874, to March 3, 1875; unsuccessful candidate for election to the Forty-fifth Congress; moved to Denver, Colo., in 1878, and thence, in 1879, to Leadville, where he edited a newspaper; appointed supervisor of the census for Colorado in 1880; appointed United States post-office inspector in 1881 and resigned in 1883; engaged in the insurance business 1883-1890; resumed the practice of law; died in Denver, Colo., March 6, 1908; interment in Fairmount Cemetery.

CARPENTER, Matthew Hale, a Senator from Wisconsin; born Decatur Merritt Hammond Carpenter in Moretown, Washington County, Vt., December 22, 1824; attended the common schools; entered the United States Military Academy at West Point in 1843 and remained two years; studied law; was admitted to the bar in 1847 and practiced in Boston, Mass.; moved to Beloit, Wis., in 1848 and became known as Matthew Hale Carpenter; district attorney of Rock County 1850-1854; moved to Milwaukee in 1858; until the commencement of the Civil War belonged to the Douglas wing of the Democratic Party; elected as a Republican to the United States Senate and served from March 4, 1869, to March 3, 1875; unsuccessful candidate for reelection in 1875; served as President pro tempore of the Senate during the Forty-third Congress; chairman, Committee on Enrolled Bills (Forty-second Congress), Committee to Audit and Control the Contingent Expense (Forty-second and Forty-third Congresses); resumed the practice of law in Washington and in Milwaukee; again elected as a Republican to the United States Senate and served from March 4, 1879, until his death in Washington, D.C., February 24, 1881; interment in Forest Home Cemetery, Milwaukee, Wis.

Bibliography: *DAB*; Deutsch, Herman J. "Carpenter and the Senatorial Election of 1875 in Wisconsin." *Wisconsin Magazine of History* 16 (September 1932): 26-46; Thompson, E. Bruce. *Matthew Hale Carpenter.* Madison: State Historical Society of Wisconsin, 1954.

CARPENTER, Terry McGovern, a Representative from Nebraska; born in Cedar Rapids, Linn County, Iowa, March 28, 1900; attended the public schools of Cedar Rapids; moved to Scottsbluff, Nebr., in 1916 and was employed in various positions with a railroad company; was engaged in the wholesale candy and tobacco business in 1922 and 1923; moved to Long Beach, Calif., in 1923 and was employed as manager of the municipal gas and water department; returned to Scottsbluff, Nebr., in 1927 and worked in the garage business and the retail coal business; unsuccessful candidate for mayor in 1931; elected as a Democrat to the Seventy-third Congress (March 4, 1933-January 3, 1935); was not a candidate for renomination in 1934 to the Seventy-fourth Congress; unsuccessful candidate for nomination for Governor in 1934, for election to the United States Senate in 1936, for election for Lieutenant Governor in 1938, for election for Governor in 1940, for nomination to the United States Senate in 1942, for election to the United States Senate in 1948, for nomination for Governor in 1950, for nomination to the United States Senate in 1954, for nomination for Governor in 1960, for nomination to the United States Senate in 1972, and for Lieutenant Governor in 1974; major, United States Air Corps, 1942-1945; changed political affiliation five times; delegate to the Republican National Convention in 1956; served in the State legislature in 1953, 1957-1959, 1963-1974; engaged in operating Terry Carpenter, Inc., in Terrytown, Nebr.; resided in Scottsbluff, Nebr., where he died April 27, 1978; interment in Fairview Cemetery.

CARPENTER, William Randolph, a Representative from Kansas; born in Marion, Marion County, Kans., April 24, 1894; attended public and high schools; was graduated from the law department of the University of Michigan at Ann Arbor in 1917; was admitted to the bar the same year and commenced practice in

Marion, Kans.; also interested in agricultural pursuits; organized Company M, Third Regiment Infantry, Kansas National Guard, serving as second lieutenant; during the First World War was transferred to Company M, One Hundred and Thirty-ninth Infantry, Thirty-fifth Division; was promoted to first lieutenant during the Argonne offensive, and served until his discharge on May 8, 1919; member of the Marion Board of Education 1925-1933; served in the State house of representatives 1929-1933; elected as a Democrat to the Seventy-third and Seventy-fourth Congresses (March 4, 1933-January 3, 1937); was not a candidate for renomination in 1936; resumed the practice of law; United States attorney for the district of Kansas 1945-1948; unsuccessful Democratic candidate for Governor in 1948; member of the United States Motor Carrier Claims Commission 1950-1952; died in Topeka, Kans., July 26, 1956; interment in Highland Cemetery, Marion, Kans.

**CARPER, Thomas Richard,** a Representative from Delaware; born in Beckley, Raleigh County, W.Va., January 23, 1947; attended public schools; graduated, Whetstone High School, Columbus, Ohio, 1964; B.A., Ohio State University, Columbus, 1968; M.B.A., University of Delaware, Newark, 1975; served as a flight officer in the United States Navy, 1968-1973; Naval Reserve, commander, 1973 to present; industrial development specialist, Delaware Division of Economic Development; Delaware State treasurer, 1976-1982; elected as a Democrat to the Ninety-eighth and to the four succeeding Congresses (January 3, 1983-January 3, 1993); was not a candidate for reelection in 1992 to the One Hundred Third Congress, but was elected Governor of Delaware for the term beginning January 19, 1993; is a resident of Wilmington, Del.

**CARR, Francis** (father of James Carr), a Representative from Massachusetts; born in Newbury, Mass., December 6, 1751; attended the common schools; engaged in the mercantile business; member of the State house of representatives from Haverhill 1791-1795 and 1801-1803, and from Orrington, Maine (then Massachusetts), 1806-1808; served in the Massachusetts senate 1809-1811; elected as a Republican to the Twelfth Congress to fill the vacancy caused by the resignation of Barzillai Gannett and served from April 6, 1812, to March 3, 1813; unsuccessful candidate for reelection in 1812 to the Thirteenth Congress; resumed mercantile pursuits; died in Bangor, Maine, October 6, 1821; interment in Mount Hope Cemetery.

**CARR, James** (son of Francis Carr), a Representative from Massachusetts; born in Bangor, Maine (then a part of Massachusetts), September 9, 1777; attended Exeter and Byfield Academies; clerk on the U.S.S. *Crescent;* appointed as secretary to the United States consul at Algiers and served two years; engaged in mercantile pursuits in Orrington, Maine (then Massachusetts); member of the Massachusetts house of representatives 1806-1811; elected as a Federalist to the Fourteenth Congress (March 4, 1815-March 3, 1817); was drowned in the Ohio River August 24, 1818; memorial headstone placed in Mount Hope Cemetery, Bangor, Maine.

**CARR, John,** a Representative from Indiana; born in Uniontown, Perry County, Ind., April 9, 1793; moved with his parents to Clark County, Ind., in 1806; attended the public schools; fought in the Battle of Tippecanoe, November 7, 1811; appointed lieutenant in a company of United States Rangers, authorized by an act of Congress for defense of western frontiers, in 1812; brigadier general and major general of the Indiana Militia until his death; county clerk 1824-1830; presidential elector for Jackson and Calhoun in 1824; elected as a Jacksonian to the Twenty-second and to the two succeeding Congresses (March 4, 1831-March 3, 1837); chairman, Committee on Private Land Claims (Twenty-fourth Congress); unsuccessful candidate in 1836 for reelection to the Twenty-fifth Congress; elected as a Democrat to the Twenty-sixth Congress (March 4, 1839-March 3, 1841); died in Charlestown, Clark County, Ind., January 20, 1845; interment in the Old Cemetery.

**CARR, Milton Robert (Bob),** a Representative from Michigan; born in Janesville, Rock County, Wis., March 27, 1943; educated in public schools of Janesville; B.S., University of Wisconsin, Madison, 1965; J.D., University of Wisconsin Law School, Madison, 1968; engaged in graduate work at Michigan State University, East Lansing; admitted to the Wisconsin bar, 1968, and the Michigan bar, 1969, and commenced practice in Lansing, Mich.; Michigan assistant attorney general, 1970-1972; elected as a Democrat to the Ninety-fourth and to the two succeeding Congresses (January 3, 1975-January 3, 1981); unsuccessful candidate for reelection in 1980 to the Ninety-seventh Congress; elected to the Ninety-eighth and to the five succeeding Congresses (January 3, 1983-January 3, 1995); was not a candidate in 1994 for reelection to the House of Representatives, but was an unsuccessful candidate for election to the United States Senate; vice chairman, The Jefferson Group, Inc.; is a resident of Orchard Lake, Mich., and Washington, D.C.

**CARR, Nathan Tracy,** a Representative from Indiana; born in Corning, Steuben County, N.Y., December 25, 1833; attended the common schools, and was graduated from Starkey Academy in 1851; moved to Midland County, Mich.; studied law; was admitted to the Midland County bar in 1858 and commenced practice at Vassar, Mich.; member of the State house of representatives 1858-1860; recorder of Midland County in 1861 and 1862; served as a lieutenant in the Second Regiment, Michigan Volunteer Infantry, in 1862; moved to Columbus, Ind., in 1867; prosecuting attorney for Bartholomew, Shelby, Jackson, and Brown Counties in 1870; elected as a Democrat to the Forty-fourth Congress to fill the vacancy caused by the death of Michael C. Kerr and served from December 5, 1876, to March 3, 1877; unsuccessful candidate for renomination in 1876; resumed the practice of law in Columbus, Bartholomew County, Ind.; appointed judge of the ninth judicial circuit court of Indiana in 1878; died in Columbus, Ind., May 28, 1885; interment in the City Cemetery.

**CARR, Wooda Nicholas,** a Representative from Pennsylvania; born in Allegheny City (now a part of Pittsburgh), Pa., February 6, 1871; attended the public schools and Madison College; was graduated from Monongahela College, Pennsylvania, in 1891; editor of the Uniontown (Pa.) News and the Uniontown Democrat in 1892; studied law; was admitted to the Pennsylvania bar in 1895 and commenced practice in Uniontown; delegate to the Pennsylvania Democratic conventions in 1898, 1899, 1900, and 1904; elected as a Democrat to the Sixty-third Congress (March 4, 1913-March 3, 1915); was an unsuccessful candidate for reelection in 1914 to the Sixty-fourth Congress; resumed the practice of law; was appointed postmaster of Uniontown, Pa., on August 2, 1934, and served until his retirement in 1947; died in Uniontown, Pa., on June 28, 1953; interment in Oak Grove Cemetery.

**CARRIER, Chester Otto,** a Representative from Kentucky; born on a farm near Brownsville, Edmonson, County, Ky., May 5, 1897; attended the public schools of Grayson County, Ky., the University of West Virginia at Morgantown, and was graduated from the law department of the University of Louisville at Louisville, Ky., in 1924; engaged in ranching in Wyoming for one year; took up railroading in Pennsylvania in 1920; was admitted to the bar in 1923 and commenced practice in Leitchfield, Grayson County, Ky.; county attorney of Grayson County, 1925-1943; elected as a Republican to the Seventy-eighth Congress to fill the vacancy caused by the death of Edward W. Creal and served from November 30, 1943, to January 3, 1945; unsuccessful candidate for reelection in 1944 to the Seventy-ninth Congress; resumed the practice of law in Leitchfield; retired to North Seminole, Fla., where he died September 24, 1980; interment in Clarkson Baptist Cemetery, Clarkson, Ky.

**CARRIGG, Joseph Leonard,** a Representative from Pennsylvania; born in Susquehanna, Pa., February 23, 1901; attended Laurel Hill Academy, Susquehanna, Pa., was graduated from Niagara University, Niagara Falls, N.Y., in 1922, Albany Law School, Albany, N.Y., in 1924, and Dickinson Law School, Carlisle, Pa., in 1925; was admitted to the bar in 1926 and commenced the practice of law in Susquehanna, Pa.; district attorney of Susquehanna County, Pa., 1936-1948; burgess of borough of Susquehanna 1948-1951; elected as a Republican to the Eighty-second Congress to fill the vacancy caused by the death of Wilson D. Gillette; reelected to the Eighty-third, Eighty-fourth, and Eighty-fifth Congresses and served from November 6, 1951, to January 3, 1959; unsuccessful candidate for reelection in 1958 to the Eighty-sixth Congress; director of practice, Internal Revenue Service, Washington, D.C., 1959-1960; secretary to Representative William W. Scranton of Pennsylvania in 1961; manager, Pennsylvania Workmen's Insurance Fund, 1963; was a resident of Scranton, Pa.; died February 6, 1989.

**CARRINGTON, Edward,** a Delegate from Virginia; born in Goochland County, Va., February 11, 1748; member of the county committee in 1775 and 1776; served in the Revolutionary Army; commissioned lieutenant colonel of Artillery November 30, 1776; served as quartermaster general on the staff of General Greene; commanded the Artillery at the Battle of Hobkirks Hill, N.C., April 25, 1781, and at Yorktown; Member of the Continental Congress 1786-1788; appointed by President Washington marshal of Virginia in 1789; foreman of the jury during the trial of Aaron Burr for treason in 1807; died in Richmond, Va., October 28, 1810; interment in St. John's Cemetery.

**CARROLL, Charles (Barrister)** (cousin of Charles Carroll of Carrollton and Daniel Carroll), a Delegate from Maryland; born in Annapolis, Md., March 22, 1723; received his education at the English House, West Lisbon, Portugal, at Eton, and Cambridge University in England, and studied law in the Middle Temple, Garden Court; returned to Annapolis, Md., in 1746 and commenced the practice of law; elected to the Maryland lower house of assembly in 1755 to fill the vacancy caused by the death of his father, Doctor Charles Carroll; framed the "Declaration of Rights" adopted by the convention of Maryland on November 3, 1776; became a member of the Council of Safety in August 1775; elected a Delegate to the Continental Congress on November 10, 1776, to succeed his cousin, Charles Carroll of Carrollton, serving until February 15, 1777; was elected in 1777 to the first State senate, having previously declined the position of chief judge of the general court of Maryland; was reelected in 1781 and held that office until his death at his residence, Mount Clare, near Baltimore, Md., March 23, 1783.

**CARROLL, Charles (of Carrollton)** (cousin of Charles Carroll, the "Barrister," and Daniel Carroll), a Delegate and a Senator from Maryland; born in Annapolis, Md., September 19, 1737; attended the Jesuits' College of Bohemia at Hermans Manor, Md., and the College of St. Omer in France; studied civil law at the College of Louis le Grand in Rheims, and common law in London; returned to Annapolis, Md., in 1765; delegate to the revolutionary convention of Maryland in 1775; Continental commissioner to Canada in 1776; member of the Board of War 1776-1777; Delegate to the Continental Congress 1776-1778; again elected to the Continental Congress in 1780, but declined to serve; was a signer of the Declaration of Independence; member, State senate 1777-1800; elected to the United States Senate in 1789; reelected in 1791 and served from March 4, 1789, to November 30, 1792, when, preferring to remain a State senator, he resigned because of a law passed by the Maryland legislature disqualifying the members of the State senate who held seats in Congress; retired to private life in 1801; involved in establishing the Baltimore & Ohio Railroad Company in 1828; died in Baltimore, Md., November 14, 1832; at the time of his death was the last surviving signer of the Declaration of Independence; interment in the chapel of Doughoregan Manor, near Ellicott City, Howard County, Md.

**Bibliography:** *DAB*; Hanley, Thomas O'Brien. *Charles Carroll of Carrollton: The Making of a Revolutionary Gentleman.* Washington, D.C.: Catholic University of America Press, 1970; Smith, Ellen H. *Charles Carroll of Carrollton.* 1942. Reprint. New York: Russell and Russell, 1971.

**CARROLL, Charles Holker,** a Representative from New York; born at Belle Vue, Hagerstown, Md., May 4, 1794; was graduated from St. Mary's College, Baltimore, Md., in 1813; moved to Livingston County, N.Y.; studied law but never practiced; engaged in agricultural pursuits; land agent; supervisor of Groveland, Livingston County, in 1817, 1818, 1822, 1840, and 1848; county judge 1823-1829; served in the State senate in 1827 and 1828; member of the State assembly in 1836; elected as a Whig to the Twenty-eighth and Twenty-ninth Congresses (March 4, 1843-March 3, 1847); was not a candidate for renomination in 1846; managed his large landed estate near Groveland, N.Y.; presidential elector on the American Party ticket in 1856; died in Groveland, N.Y., June 8, 1865; interment in Williamsburgh Cemetery.

**Bibliography:** Robert F. McNamara. "In Search of the Carrolls of Belle Vue." *Maryland Historical Magazine* 80 (Spring 1985): 99-113.

**CARROLL, Daniel** (uncle of Richard Brent, cousin of Charles Carroll of Carrollton, and Charles Carroll "Barrister"), a Delegate and a Representative from Maryland; born in Upper Marlboro, Prince Georges County, Md., July 22, 1730; educated at the Jesuit School at Bohemia Manor, Md., and at St. Omer's College, France; returned to Maryland in 1748; Member of the Continental Congress 1781-1783, signing the Articles of Confederation on March 1, 1781; appointed a delegate on May 26, 1787, to the convention that framed the Federal Constitution; member of the first State senate of Maryland and up to the time of his death was a member of the senate of Maryland, or the executive council of Maryland; elected to the First Congress (March 4, 1789-March 3, 1791); took an active part in fixing the seat of government for the United States; appointed by President Washington on January 22, 1791, as one of the commissioners to locate the District of Columbia and the Federal City and served until July 25, 1795, when he resigned; engaged in agricultural pursuits, his farm being the site of the present city of Washington; died at Rock Creek (Forest Glen), near Washington, D.C., May 7, 1796.

**Bibliography:** *DAB*; Geiger, Mary V. "Daniel Carroll, A Framer of the Constitution." Ph.D. dissertation, Catholic University of America, 1943.

**CARROLL, James,** a Representative from Maryland; born in Baltimore, Md., December 2, 1791; was graduated from old St. Mary's College at Baltimore in 1808; studied law but did not practice; settled on a farm on West River; returned to Baltimore, Md., in 1831; judge of the orphans' court; trustee of the poor; served as a director of the Baltimore & Ohio Railroad Company and the Chesapeake & Ohio Canal Company; elected as a Democrat to the Twenty-sixth Congress (March 4, 1839-March 3, 1841); was not a candidate for renomination in 1840 to the Twenty-seventh Congress; unsuccessful Democratic candidate for Governor of Maryland in 1844; retired from political life; died in Baltimore, Md., January 16, 1873; interment in St. Paul's Burying Ground.

**CARROLL, John Albert,** a Representative and a Senator from Colorado; born in Denver, Colo., July 30, 1901; attended the public schools; during the First World War served in the United States Army, 1918-1919; was graduated from Westminster Law School, Denver, Colo., in 1929; was admitted to the bar the same year and commenced practice in Denver, Colo.; assistant United States district attorney in 1933 and 1934; district attorney of Denver, 1937-1941; regional attorney for the Office of Price Administration, 1942-1943; served in the Second World War as a commissioned officer in the United States Army, 1943-1945; resumed the practice of law; elected as a Democrat to the Eightieth and Eighty-first Congresses (January 3, 1947-January 3, 1951); was not a candidate in 1950 for renomination to the House of Representatives, but was an unsuccessful candidate for election to the United States Senate; unsuccessful candidate for election to the United States Senate in 1954; special assistant to President Harry S Truman, 1951-1952; elected as a Democrat to the United States Senate in 1956, and served from January 3, 1957 to January 3, 1963; unsuccessful candidate for reelection in 1962; was a resident of Denver, Colo. until his death on August 31, 1983; interment at Ft. Logan National Cemetery, Denver, Colo.

**CARROLL, John Michael,** a Representative from New York; born in Springfield, Otsego County, N.Y., April 27, 1823; attended the public schools; was graduated from Fairfield Seminary, Fairfield, N.Y., and from Union College, Schenectady, N.Y., in 1846; studied law; was admitted to the bar in 1848 and commenced practice in Broadalbin, Fulton County, N.Y.; prosecuting attorney of Fulton County 1859-1862; moved to Johnstown, N.Y., in 1862 and continued the practice of law; elected as a Democrat to the Forty-second Congress (March 4, 1871-March 3, 1873); declined to be a candidate for renomination in 1872; engaged in the practice of law in Johnstown, Fulton County, N.Y., until his death there on May 8, 1901; interment in Johnstown Cemetery.

**CARSON, Henderson Haverfield,** a Representative from Ohio; born on a farm near Cadiz, Harrison County, Ohio, October 25, 1893; attended the public and high schools; Cleveland (Ohio) Law School and Baldwin-Wallace College at Berea, Ohio, LL.B., 1919; became affiliated with the legal department of the Pennsylvania Railroad Co. in 1915; enlisted in the Field Artillery in 1918; was transferred to Base Hospital, One Hundred and Nineteenth Unit, Camp Zachary Taylor, Ky., and served there until honorably discharged in 1919 as a corporal; was admitted to the bar in 1919 and commenced practice in Canton, Ohio, in 1922; member of the faculty of McKinley Law School 1926-1942, where he received his J.D. degree; elected as a Republican to the Seventy-eighth Congress (January 3, 1943-January 3, 1945); unsuccessful candidate for reelection in 1944 to the Seventy-ninth Congress; elected to the Eightieth Congress (January 3, 1947-January 3, 1949); was an unsuccessful candidate for reelection in 1948 to the Eighty-first Congress; resumed the practice of law in Canton, Ohio, and Washington, D.C.; resided in Canton, Ohio, where he died October 5, 1971; interment in West Lawn Cemetery.

**CARSON, Samuel Price,** a Representative from North Carolina; born in Pleasant Gardens, N.C., January 22, 1798; studied under private tutors in Pleasant Gardens; engaged in agricultural pursuits; member of the State senate 1822-1824; elected to the Nineteenth and to the three succeeding Congresses (March 4, 1825-March 3, 1833); unsuccessful candidate in 1833 for reelection to the Twenty-third Congress; again elected to the State senate in 1834; delegate to the State constitutional convention in 1835; moved to Texas in 1836; member of the Texas convention that adopted the constitution of that Republic in 1836; appointed Secretary of State for the Republic of Texas in September 1836 and served until 1838; sent as a commissioner to Washington, D.C., to intercede for the recognition of the independence of Texas in 1836; died at Hot Springs, Ark., November 2, 1838; interment in the Government Cemetery, Hot Springs, Ark.

**CARSS, William Leighton,** a Representative from Minnesota; born in Pella, Marion County, Iowa, February 15, 1865; moved with his parents to Des Moines, Iowa, in 1867; attended the public schools; studied civil and mechanical engineering and followed that

profession for a number of years; moved to St. Louis County, Minn., in 1893 and settled in Proctor; engaged as a locomotive engineer; elected as a Union Labor candidate to the Sixty-sixth Congress (March 4, 1919-March 3, 1921); unsuccessful candidate for reelection as a Democrat in 1920 to the Sixty-seventh Congress and for election in 1922 to the Sixty-eighth Congress; elected on the Farmer-Labor ticket to the Sixty-ninth and Seventieth Congresses (March 4, 1925-March 3, 1929); unsuccessful candidate for reelection in 1928 to the Seventy-first Congress and for election in 1930 to the Seventy-second Congress; moved to Duluth, Minn., in 1929; resumed his position as locomotive engineer at Proctor, Minn.; died in Duluth, Minn., May 31, 1931; interment in Oneota Cemetery.

**CARTER, Albert Edward,** a Representative from California; born in Lemoncove, near Visalia, Tulare County, Calif., July 5, 1881; attended the public schools; was graduated from San Jose State Normal School in 1903; taught school six years; was graduated from the law department of the University of California at Berkeley in 1913; was admitted to the bar the same year and commenced practice in Oakland, Calif.; representative of the United States War Department Commission on Training Camps 1917-1919; attorney for the California State Board of Pharmacy in 1920 and 1921; commissioner of public works of Oakland 1921-1925 and in 1923 initiated the plan for a comprehensive development of the harbor on the east side of San Francisco Bay; president of the Pacific Coast Association of Port Authorities; elected as a Republican to the Sixty-ninth and to the nine succeeding Congresses (March 4, 1925-January 3, 1945); unsuccessful candidate for reelection in 1944 to the Seventy-ninth Congress; resumed the practice of law in California and Washington, D.C.; died in Oakland, Calif., August 8, 1964; interment in Home of Peace Cemetery, Porterville, Calif.

**CARTER, Charles David,** a Representative from Oklahoma; born near Boggy Depot, Choctaw Nation, Indian Territory (now Oklahoma), August 16, 1868; moved with his father to Mill Creek, a stage stand on the western frontier of the Chickasaw Nation, in April 1876; attended the Indian day schools and Chickasaw Manual Training Academy at Tishomingo; employed on a ranch from 1887 to 1889 and in a mercantile establishment in Ardmore, Okla., from 1889 to 1892; auditor of public accounts of the Chickasaw Nation 1892-1894; member of the Chickasaw Council in 1895; superintendent of schools of the Chickasaw Nation in 1897; appointed mining trustee of Indian Territory by President William McKinley in November 1900 and served four years; secretary of the first Democratic executive committee of the proposed State of Oklahoma from June to December 1906; upon the admission of Oklahoma as a State into the Union was elected as a Democrat to the Sixtieth and to the nine succeeding Congresses and served from November 16, 1907, to March 3, 1927; chairman, Committee on Indian Affairs (Sixty-fifth Congress); unsuccessful candidate for renomination in 1926 to the Seventieth Congress; member of the State highway commission 1927-1929; died in Ardmore, Okla., April 9, 1929; interment in Rose Hill Cemetery.

**CARTER, John,** a Representative from South Carolina; born on the Black River, near Camden, Sumter District, S.C., September 10, 1792; was graduated from South Carolina College (now the University of South Carolina) at Columbia in 1811; studied law; was admitted to the bar in 1814 and commenced practice in Camden, S.C.; served as commissioner in equity 1814-1820; elected to the Seventeenth Congress to fill the vacancy caused by the resignation of James Blair; reelected to the Eighteenth and Nineteenth Congresses and reelected as a Jacksonian to the Twentieth Congresses and served from December 11, 1822, to March 3, 1829; resumed the practice of law in Camden, S.C.; moved to Georgetown, D.C., in 1836, and died there June 20, 1850.

**CARTER, Luther Cullen,** a Representative from New York; born in Bethel, Maine, February 25, 1805; moved to New York City and engaged in mercantile pursuits; member of the Board of Education of New York City in 1853; retired from business and moved to Long Island City, where he engaged in agricultural pursuits; elected as a Republican to the Thirty-sixth Congress (March 4, 1859-March 3, 1861); chairman, Committee on District of Columbia (Thirty-sixth Congress); unsuccessful candidate for reelection in 1860 to the Thirty-seventh Congress; died in New York City January 3, 1875; interment in Greenwood Cemetery, Brooklyn, N.Y.

**CARTER, Steven V.,** a Representative from Iowa; born in Carterville, Utah, October 8, 1915; at the age of 14 years moved with his parents to Lamoni, Decatur County, Iowa, and attended the public schools; graduated from Graceland College, Lamoni, Iowa, in 1934, University of Iowa in 1937, and State University of Iowa College of Law in 1939; was admitted to the bar in 1939 and commenced the practice of law in Leon, Iowa; county attorney, Decatur County, 1940-1944; served as a supply officer in the United States Navy 1943-1946, with service in the South Pacific Theater; city attorney, Leon, Iowa, 1946-1948; unsuccessful Democratic candidate for election to the Eighty-fifth Congress in 1956, and later unsuccessfully contested the election; elected as a Democrat to the Eighty-sixth Congress and served from January 3, 1959, until his death in Bethesda, Md., November 4, 1959; interment in Leon Cemetery, Leon, Iowa.

**CARTER, Thomas Henry,** a Delegate, a Representative, and a Senator from Montana; born near Portsmouth, Scioto County, Ohio, October 30, 1854; moved with his parents to Pana, Ill.; attended the common schools in Illinois; engaged in farming, school teaching, and railroading; at the same time studied law and was admitted to the bar; in 1882 moved from Burlington, Iowa, to Helena, Mont.; elected as a Republican Delegate to the Fifty-first Congress, and served from March 4, 1889 to November 7, 1889, when the Territory was admitted as a State into the Union; elected as its first Representative, and served from November 8, 1889 to March 3, 1891; chairman, Committee on Mines and Mining (Fifty-first Congress); unsuccessful candidate for reelection in 1890 to the Fifty-second Congress; Commissioner of the General Land Office from 1891 until 1892, when he was elected chairman of the Republican National Committee; elected as a Republican to the United States Senate, and served from March 4, 1895 until March 3, 1901; chairman, Committee on Relations with Canada (Fifty-fourth Congress), Committee on the Census (Fifty-fifth and Fifty-sixth Congresses); appointed by President William McKinley a member of the board of commissioners of the Louisiana Purchase Exposition and served as its president; again elected as a Republican to the United States Senate, and served from March 4, 1905 to March 3, 1911; chairman, Committee on Organization, Conduct, and Expenditures of Executive Departments (Fifty-ninth and Sixtieth Congresses), Committee on Expenditures in the Department of State (Sixtieth Congress), Committee on Irrigation and Reclamation of Arid Lands (Sixty-first Congress); chairman of the United States section of the International Joint Commission created to prevent disputes regarding the use of boundary waters between the United States and Canada from March 1911 until his death in Washington, D.C., September 17, 1911; interment in Mount Olivet Cemetery.

**Bibliography:** Roeder, Richard B. "Thomas H. Carter, Spokesman for Western Development." *Montana* 39 (Spring 1989): 23-29.

**CARTER, Tim Lee,** a Representative from Kentucky; born in Tompkinsville, Monroe County, Ky., September 2, 1910; attended the public schools, graduated from Western Kentucky State College in 1934 and from the University of Tennessee in 1937; studied medicine; volunteered for military service during the Second World War and served forty-two months as a combat medic as captain in the Thirty-eighth Infantry Division; practicing physician in Tompkinsville, Ky., 1940-1964; elected as a Republican to the Eighty-ninth and to the seven succeeding Congresses (January 3, 1965-January 3, 1981); was not a candidate for reelection in 1980 to the Ninety-seventh Congress; was a resident of Tompkinsville, Ky. until his death in Glasgow, Ky. on March 27, 1987; interment in Evans-Oak Hill Cemetery, Tompkinsville.

**CARTER, Timothy Jarvis,** a Representative from Maine; born in Bethel, in the Maine district of Massachusetts, August 18, 1800; attended the town schools of Bethel; studied law at Northampton, Mass., was admitted to the bar in 1826 and commenced practice in Rumford, Oxford County, Maine; moved to Paris, Oxford County, Maine, in 1827 and continued the practice of law; secretary of the State senate of Maine in 1833; county attorney 1833-1837; elected as a Democrat to the Twenty-fifth Congress and served from September 4, 1837, until his death in Washington, D.C., March 14, 1838; interment in the Congressional Cemetery.

**CARTER, Vincent Michael,** a Representative from Wyoming; born in St. Clair, Schuylkill County, Pa., November 6, 1891; moved with his parents to Pottsville, Pa., in 1893; attended public schools, the United States Naval Academy Preparatory School, Annapolis, Md., and Fordham University, New York City; was graduated from the law department of Catholic University, Washington, D.C., in 1915; was admitted to the bar in 1919 and commenced practice in Casper, Wyo., the same year; moved to Kemmerer, Wyo., in 1929 and continued the practice of law; during the First World War served in the Marine Corps as a lieutenant in the Eighth Regiment, Third Brigade; captain in the State militia 1919-1921; deputy attorney general of Wyoming 1919-1923; State auditor 1923-1929; elected as a Republican to the Seventy-first and to the two succeeding Congresses (March 4, 1929-January 3, 1935); was not a candidate for renomination in 1934, but was an unsuccessful candidate for election to the United States Senate; resumed the practice of law in Cheyenne, Wyo., retiring in 1965; delegate to the Republican National Conventions in 1936 and 1940; died in Albuquerque, N.Mex., December 30, 1972; interment in Mt. Calvary Cemetery.

**CARTER, William Blount,** a Representative from Tennessee; born in Elizabethton, Carter County, Tenn., October 22, 1792; attended the public schools; during the War of 1812 served as a colonel; member of the State house of representatives; served in the State senate; delegate to the State constitutional convention in 1834 and served as its presiding officer; elected as a White supporter to the Twenty-fourth Congress and as a Whig to the Twenty-fifth and Twenty-sixth Congresses (March 4, 1835-March 3, 1841); died in Elizabethton, Tenn., April 17, 1848; interment in Carter Cemetery.

**CARTER, William Henry,** a Representative from Massachusetts; born at Needham Heights, Norfolk County, Mass., June 15, 1864; attended public schools; was graduated from Comers Commercial College, Boston, Mass.; worked in several capacities at the knit-underwear manufacturing plant of the William Carter Co.; member of the Massachusetts house of representatives in 1906; member of the Massachusetts Republican committee in 1907 and 1908; elected as a Republican to the Sixty-fourth and Sixty-fifth Congresses (March 4, 1915-March 3, 1919); was not a candidate for reelection in 1918; interested in real-estate development; was elected president of the William Carter Co. in 1918 and continued manufacturing activities until his death; died in Needham, Mass., April 23, 1955; interment in Needham Cemetery.

**CARTTER, David Kellogg,** a Representative from Ohio; born in Jefferson County, N.Y., in June 22, 1812; pursued preparatory studies; studied law in Rochester, N.Y.; was admitted to the bar in 1832 and commenced practice in Rochester, N.Y.; four years later moved to Akron, Ohio, and then to Massillon, Ohio, and continued the practice of law; elected as a Democrat to the Thirty-first and

Thirty-second Congresses (March 4, 1849-March 3, 1853); chairman, Committee on Patents (Thirty-second Congress); moved to Cleveland, Ohio, in 1856 and continued law practice; delegate to the Republican National Convention of 1860; appointed Minister Resident to Bolivia on March 27, 1861, and served until October 1862; appointed chief justice of the Supreme Court of the District of Columbia in 1863, and served until his death in Washington, D.C., on April 16, 1887; interment in Lakeview Cemetery, Cleveland, Ohio.

**CARTWRIGHT, Wilburn,** a Representative from Oklahoma; born on a farm near Georgetown, Meigs County, Tenn., January 12, 1892; moved with his parents to the Chickasaw Nation, Indian Territory, in 1903; attended the public schools at Wapanucka and Ada, Okla., and State Teachers College at Durant, Okla.; taught in the schools of Coal, Atoka, Bryan, and Pittsburg Counties, Okla., 1914-1926; member of the Oklahoma State house of representatives, 1914-1918; studied law; was admitted to the bar in 1917 and commenced practice in McAlester, Okla.; served as a private in the Student Army Training Corps, 1917-1918; member of the State senate, 1918-1922; was graduated from the law department of the University of Oklahoma at Norman in 1920; engaged in postgraduate work at the University of Chicago, Ill.; vocational adviser for disabled veterans at McAlester, Okla., 1921-1922; unsuccessful candidate for the Democratic nomination in 1922 to the Sixty-eighth Congress, and in 1924 to the Sixty-ninth Congress; superintendent of schools at Krebs, Okla., 1922-1926; elected as a Democrat to the Seventieth and to the seven succeeding Congresses (March 4, 1927-January 3, 1943); chairman, Committee on Roads (Seventy-third through Seventy-seventh Congresses); unsuccessful candidate for renomination in 1942 to the Seventy-eighth Congress; served as a major in the United States Army, Allied Military Government, with service in Africa and Europe from 1943 until injured; returned to the United States as an instructor at Fort Custer, Mich., in 1945; employed with the Veterans' Administration at Muskogee, Okla., in 1945 and 1946; elected secretary of state of Oklahoma for four-year term in 1946; elected State auditor for four-year term in 1950; elected State corporation commissioner for six-year term in 1954, and reelected in 1960 and 1966; was a resident of Oklahoma City, Okla. until his death there on March 14, 1979; interment in I.O.O.F. Cemetery, Norman, Okla.

**CARUTH, Asher Graham,** a Representative from Kentucky; born in Scottsville, Allen County, Ky., on February 7, 1844; attended the public schools; was graduated from the high school of Louisville in June 1864 and from the law department of the University of Louisville, Kentucky, in March 1866; was admitted to the bar and commenced practice in Hopkinsville, Christian County, Ky.; established the Kentucky Weekly New Era; moved to Louisville in 1871 and continued the practice of law; attorney of the board of trustees of the public schools of Louisville from 1873 to 1880; elected Commonwealth attorney for the ninth judicial district of Kentucky in 1880 for six years and reelected in August 1886; resigned the office in March 1887; elected as a Democrat to the Fiftieth and to the three succeeding Congresses (March 4, 1887-March 3, 1895); unsuccessful candidate for renomination in 1894; resumed the practice of law in Louisville, Ky.; judge of the criminal division of the Jefferson County Circuit Court in 1902; commissioner of the St. Louis Exposition in 1904; died in Louisville, Ky., November 25, 1907; interment in Cave Hill Cemetery.

**CARUTHERS, Robert Looney,** a Representative from Tennessee; born in Smith County, Tenn., July 31, 1800; engaged in mercantile pursuits 1817-1819; attended Woodward's Academy, near Columbia, Tenn., and Greenville College in 1820 and 1821; studied law; was admitted to the bar in 1823; clerk of the State house of representatives in 1824; clerk of the chancery court of Smith County and editor of the Tennessee Republican; moved to Lebanon, Wilson

County, Tenn., in 1826; State's attorney 1827-1832; member of the State house of representatives in 1835; was the founder of Cumberland University, Lebanon, Tenn., in 1842 and of its law department in 1847; elected as a Whig to the Twenty-seventh Congress (March 4, 1841-March 3, 1843); appointed judge of the supreme court of Tennessee in 1852 to fill a vacancy and elected to the position in 1854, which he held until the beginning of the Civil War; member of the peace convention of 1861 held in Washington, D.C., in an effort to devise means to prevent the impending war; elected Governor in 1862, but because of the occupation of the State by Federal forces never assumed the duties of the office; at the close of the Civil War became professor of law in Cumberland University and served in that capacity until his death in Lebanon, Tenn., October 2, 1882; interment in Cedar Grove Cemetery.

**CARUTHERS, Samuel,** a Representative from Missouri; born in Madison County, Mo., October 13, 1820; was graduated from Cumberland University, Lebanon, Tenn.; studied law; was admitted to the bar and commenced practice in Fredericktown, Madison County, Mo.; moved to Cape Girardeau, Mo., in 1844; held several local offices; elected as a Whig to the Thirty-third and Thirty-fourth Congresses (March 4, 1853-March 3, 1857); reelected as a Democrat to the Thirty-fifth Congress (March 4, 1857-March 3, 1859); died in Cape Girardeau, Cape Girardeau County, Mo., July 20, 1860.

**CARVILLE, Edward Peter,** a Senator from Nevada; born in Mound Valley, Nev., May 14, 1885; attended the public schools in Elko County, Nev.; graduated from the University of Notre Dame, South Bend, Ind., in 1909; admitted to the bar in 1909 and commenced practice in Elko, Nev.; district attorney of Elko County, Nev., 1912-1918; district judge of Elko County from 1928 until 1934; United States attorney for Nevada, 1934-1938; elected Governor of Nevada in 1938, reelected in 1942, and served from January 2, 1939 until his resignation July 24, 1945 to accept appointment as United States Senator; appointed July 24, 1945, as a Democrat to the United States Senate to fill the vacancy caused by the death of James G. Scrugham and served from July 25, 1945, until January 3, 1947; unsuccessful candidate for renomination in 1946; resumed the practice of law in Reno, Nev., until his death on June 27, 1956; interment in Nevada Memorial Park Mausoleum, Reno, Nev.

**CARY, George,** a Representative from Georgia; born near Allens Fresh, Charles County, Md., August 7, 1789; received a classical education; studied law; was admitted to the bar and commenced practice in Frederick, Md.; also engaged in agricultural pursuits; moved to Appling, Ga.; member of the State house of representatives 1819-1821; elected to the Eighteenth and Nineteenth Congresses (March 4, 1823-March 3, 1827); engaged in the newspaper business and edited the Hickory Nut; again a member of the State house of representatives in 1834; died in Thomaston, Upson County, Ga., September 10, 1843; interment in the Methodist Churchyard.

**CARY, George Booth,** a Representative from Virginia; born at "Bonny Doon," near Courtland, Southampton County, Va., in 1811; received a liberal education; engaged in planting; elected as a Democrat to the Twenty-seventh Congress (March 4, 1841-March 3, 1843); resumed agricultural pursuits; died in Bethlehem, Va., March 5, 1850; interment in the family cemetery on his estate, "Bonny Doon," near Courtland, Southampton County, Va.

**CARY, Glover H.,** a Representative from Kentucky; born in Calhoun, McLean County, Ky., May 1, 1885; attended public and private schools, and Centre College, Danville, Ky.; employed as deputy clerk, bank cashier, and newspaper editor; studied law; was admitted to the bar in June 1909 and commenced practice in Calhoun, Ky.; member of the Kentucky house of representatives 1914-1917; prosecuting attorney of McLean County 1918-1922; served as Commonwealth's attorney for the sixth judicial district from 1922 until his resignation on February 28, 1931, having been elected to Congress; moved to Owensboro, Ky., in 1926; elected as a Democrat to the Seventy-second, Seventy-third, and Seventy-fourth Congresses and served from March 4, 1931, until his death; had been reelected to the Seventy-fifth Congress; delegate to the Democratic National Convention in 1932; died in Cincinnati, Ohio, on December 5, 1936; interment in Calhoun Cemetery, Calhoun, Ky.

**CARY, Jeremiah Eaton,** a Representative from New York; born in Coventry, R.I., April 30, 1803; attended the public schools; moved to Cherry Valley, N.Y., in 1820; studied law; was admitted to the bar in 1829 and commenced practice in New York City; elected as a Democrat to the Twenty-eighth Congress (March 4, 1843-March 3, 1845); resumed the practice of law in New York City; moved to Plainfield, N.J., in 1860, where he continued the practice of law; died in June 1888 while on a visit at Rockville Center, Long Island, N.Y.; interment in Grace Episcopal Church Cemetery, Plainfield, N.J.

**CARY, Samuel Fenton,** a Representative from Ohio; born in Cincinnati, Ohio, February 18, 1814; attended public schools; was graduated from Miami University, Oxford, Ohio, in 1835 and from the Cincinnati Law School in 1837; was admitted to the bar in the latter year and commenced practice in Cincinnati; elected judge of the Ohio State supreme court but declined; continued the practice of his profession until 1845, when he devoted himself to temperance and other reforms; delegate to the Republican National Convention of 1864; served as paymaster general for the State of Ohio under Governors Thomas W. Bartley and William Bebb; collector of internal revenue for the first district of Ohio in 1865; elected as an Independent Republican to the Fortieth Congress to fill the vacancy caused by the resignation of Rutherford B. Hayes, and served from November 21, 1867 to March 3, 1869; chairman, Committee on Education and Labor (Fortieth Congress); unsuccessful candidate for reelection in 1868 to the Forty-first Congress; unsuccessful candidate for lieutenant governor of Ohio in 1875; nominated by the Greenback National Convention in 1876 as a candidate for Vice President of the United States on the ticket headed by Peter Cooper; writer and lecturer for twenty years; died at the Cary homestead in College Hill, Cincinnati, Ohio, September 29, 1900; interment in Spring Grove Cemetery.

**CARY, Shepard,** a Representative from Maine; born in New Salem, Mass., July 3, 1805; attended the common schools; moved with his parents to Houlton, Maine, in 1822; engaged in extensive lumber operations and also in agricultural and mercantile pursuits; member of the State house of representatives in 1832, 1833, 1839-1842, 1848, 1849, and 1862; served in the State senate in 1843 and 1850-1853; elected as a Democrat to the Twenty-eighth Congress; took his seat May 10, 1844, and served until March 3, 1845; candidate of the Liberty Party for Governor in 1854; died in Houlton, Aroostook County, Maine, August 9, 1866; interment in Evergreen Cemetery.

**CARY, William Joseph,** a Representative from Wisconsin; born in Milwaukee, Wis., March 22, 1865; educated in the public schools and St. John's Academy; was left an orphan at the age of eleven, when he became a messenger boy; studied telegraphy and was employed as a telegraph operator 1883-1895; engaged in the brokerage business 1895-1905; elected a member of the board of aldermen of Milwaukee in 1900 and was reelected in 1902 for the term ending in 1904; served as sheriff of Milwaukee County 1904-1906; elected as a Republican to the Sixtieth and to the five succeeding Congresses (March 4, 1907-March 3, 1919); unsuccessful candidate for renomination in 1918 to the Sixty-sixth Congress; served as county clerk of Milwaukee County 1921-1933; died in Milwaukee, Wis., January 2, 1934; interment in Calvary Cemetery.

**CASE, Charles** a Representative from Indiana; born in Austinburg, Ohio, December 21, 1817; studied law; was admitted to the bar and commenced practice in Fort Wayne, Ind.; elected as a Republican to the Thirty-fifth Congress to fill the vacancy caused by the death of Samuel Brenton; reelected to the Thirty-sixth Congress and served from December 7, 1857, to March 3, 1861; unsuccessful candidate for reelection in 1860 to the Thirty-seventh Congress; during the Civil War served as first lieutenant and adjutant of the Forty-fourth Regiment, Indiana Volunteer Infantry; subsequently became a major in the Third Regiment, Indiana Volunteer Cavalry, and served from November 26, 1861, to August 15, 1862; resumed the practice of his profession in Washington, D.C.; died in Brighton, Washington County, Iowa, June 30, 1883; interment in the Congressional Cemetery, Washington, D.C.

**CASE, Clifford Philip,** a Representative and a Senator from New Jersey; born in Franklin Park, Somerset County, N.J., April 16, 1904; attended the public schools of Poughkeepsie, N.Y.; was graduated from Rutgers University, New Brunswick, N.J., in 1925 and from Columbia University Law School, New York City, in 1928; was admitted to the bar in 1928 and commenced practice in New York City; member of the Rahway (N.J.) Common Council 1938-1942; member, New Jersey house of assembly 1943-1944; trustee of Rutgers University; elected as a Republican to the Seventy-ninth and to the four succeeding Congresses, and served from January 3, 1945, until his resignation August 16, 1953; president of The Fund for the Republic 1953-1954; elected as a Republican to the United States Senate in 1954; reelected in 1960, 1966, and again in 1972 and served from January 3, 1955, to January 3, 1979; unsuccessful candidate for renomination in 1978; resumed the practice of law; lecturer at Rutgers University's Eagleton Institute of Politics; resided in Rahway, N.J., until his death in Washington, D.C., on March 5, 1982; interment at New Cemetery, Somerville, N.J.

**Bibliography:** Case, Clifford. "Changing Role of Congress: The Growing Concern with the Legislative Process." *George Washington Law Review* 32 (June 1964): 929-31; Case, Clifford. "Congress and the Double Standard." *Federal Bar Journal* 24 (Summer 1964): 257-63.

**CASE, Francis Higbee,** a Representative and a Senator from South Dakota; born in Everly, Clay County, Iowa, December 9, 1896; moved with his parents to Sturgis, S.Dak., in 1909; attended the public schools; graduated from Dakota Wesleyan University, Mitchell, S.Dak., in 1918, and from Northwestern University, Evanston, Ill., in 1920; during the First World War served as a private in the United States Marine Corps in 1918; served in both the United States Army and the United States Marine Corps Reserves; assistant editor, Epworth Herald, Chicago, Ill., 1920-1922; telegraph editor and editorial writer on the Rapid City (S.Dak.) Daily Journal, 1922-1925; editor and publisher of the Hot Springs (S.Dak.) Star, 1925-1931; editor and publisher of the Custer (S.Dak.) Chronicle, 1931-1946; member of the State regents of education, 1931-1933; unsuccessful candidate for election in 1934 to the Seventy-fourth Congress; elected as a Republican to the Seventy-fifth and to the six succeeding Congresses (January 3, 1937-January 3, 1951); elected to the United States Senate in 1950; reelected in 1956 and served from January 3, 1951, until his death in the naval hospital at Bethesda, Md., June 22, 1962; chairman, Committee on the District of Columbia (Eighty-third Congress); interment in Mountain View Cemetery, Rapid City, S.Dak.

**Bibliography:** Chenoweth, Richard. "Francis Case: A Political Biography." Ph.D. dissertation, University of Nebraska, 1977; Pressler, Larry. "Francis H. Case." In *U.S. Senators from the Prairie*, pp. 140-149. Vermillion, S.Dak: Dakota Press, 1982.

**CASE, Walter,** a Representative from New York; born in Pleasant Valley, Dutchess County, N.Y., in 1776; educated by private tutors; attended Newburgh Academy, and was graduated from Union College, Schenectady, N.Y., in 1799; studied law; was admitted to the bar in 1802 and commenced practice in Newburgh; elected to the Sixteenth Congress (March 4, 1819-March 3, 1821); affiliated with the Whig Party after its formation; resumed the practice of law; moved to New York City in 1844 and continued the practice of law until 1848, when he retired; died in Fishkill, Dutchess County, N.Y., October 7, 1859; interment in Fishkill Rural Cemetery.

**CASEY, John Joseph,** a Representative from Pennsylvania; born in Wilkes-Barre Township, Luzerne County, Pa., May 26, 1875; attended the public schools and St. Mary's parochial school; member of Pennsylvania house of representatives 1907-1909; elected as a Democrat to the Sixty-third and Sixty-fourth Congresses (March 4, 1913-March 3, 1917); unsuccessful candidate for reelection in 1916 to the Sixty-fifth Congress; appointed a member of the advisory council to the Secretary of Labor in 1918; appointed labor adviser and executive of the labor adjustment division, Emergency Fleet Corporation, United States Shipping Board, during the First World War; elected to the Sixty-sixth Congress (March 4, 1919-March 3, 1921); unsuccessful candidate for reelection in 1920 to the Sixty-seventh Congress; elected to the Sixty-eighth Congress (March 4, 1923-March 3, 1925); unsuccessful candidate for reelection in 1924 to the Sixty-ninth Congress; business agent for the Plumbers and Steam Fitters' Union; elected to the Seventieth and Seventy-first Congresses and served from March 4, 1927, until his death at Balboa, Canal Zone, May 5, 1929; interment in St. Mary's Cemetery, Hanover Township, Luzerne County, Pa.

**CASEY, Joseph,** a Representative from Pennsylvania; born at Ringgold Manor, Washington County, Md., December 17, 1814; studied law in Carlisle, Pa.; was admitted to the bar in 1838 and commenced practice in Bloomfield, Perry County, Pa.; moved to New Berlin, Pa., and resumed the practice of law; elected as a Whig to the Thirty-first Congress (March 4, 1849-March 3, 1851); declined to be a candidate for renomination in 1850; again engaged in the practice of his profession; in 1856 was appointed reporter of the decisions of the supreme court of Pennsylvania, which position he held until 1861; was appointed in 1861 by President Lincoln one of the judges of the court of claims; upon the reorganization of that court in 1863 was appointed chief justice and was the first person to serve in that capacity, holding the position until December 1870, when he resigned; engaged in the practice of law in Washington, D.C., until his death, February 10, 1879; interment in Oak Hill Cemetery.

Bibliography: *DAB.*

**CASEY, Joseph Edward,** a Representative from Massachusetts; born in Clinton, Worcester County, Mass., December 27, 1898; attended the public schools; served as a private in the United States Army at Camp Lee, Va., in 1918; was graduated from the law department of Boston University, Boston, Mass., in 1920; was admitted to the bar in 1920 and commenced practice in Clinton, Mass.; delegate to the Democratic National Conventions in 1924, 1932, 1936, 1940, and 1944; elected as a Democrat to the Seventy-fourth and to the three succeeding Congresses (January 3, 1935-January 3, 1943); was not a candidate for renomination in 1942 to the Seventy-eighth Congress, but was an unsuccessful candidate for election to the United States Senate; resumed the practice of law in Boston, Mass., and in Washington, D.C., where he resided until his death on September 1, 1980; interment in Arlington National Cemetery, Va.

**CASEY, Levi,** a Representative from South Carolina; born in that State about 1752; served in the Continental Army during the Revolutionary War; elected brigadier general of militia; justice of Newberry County Court in 1785; member of the State senate in 1781 and 1782 and 1800-1802; member of the State house of representatives 1786-1788, 1792-1795 and 1798-1799; elected as a Republican to the Eighth and Ninth Congresses and served from March 4, 1803, until his death, before the close of the Ninth Congress; had been reelected to the Tenth Congress; died in Washington, D.C., February 3, 1807; interment in the Congressional Cemetery.

**CASEY, Lyman Rufus,** a Senator from North Dakota; born in York, Livingston County, N.Y., May 6, 1837; moved with his parents to Ypsilanti, Mich., in 1853; received a classical education; engaged in the hardware business for many years; moved to Carrington, Foster County, Territory of Dakota, in 1882 and became a rancher; chairman of the North Dakota Committee on Irrigation; commissioner of Foster County in 1887; upon the admission of North Dakota as a State into the Union was elected as a Republican to the United States Senate and served from November 25, 1889, to March 3, 1893; unsuccessful candidate for renomination in 1892; chairman, Committee on Railroads (Fifty-second Congress); moved to New York City; returned to Washington, D.C., and died there January 26, 1914; interment in Greenmount Cemetery, Baltimore, Md.

**CASEY, Robert Randolph,** a Representative from Texas; born in Joplin, Jasper County, Mo., July 27, 1915; moved with his parents to Houston, Tex., in 1930 and graduated from San Jacinto High School; student at the University of Houston, also the South Texas School of Law 1934-1940; was admitted to the Texas bar in 1940 and commenced the practice of law in Alvin, Tex.; served as city attorney of Alvin, Tex., in 1942 and 1943; member of the school board; in 1943 returned to Houston as an assistant district attorney in Harris County in charge of the civil department; in 1948 was elected to the State house of representatives and served in the regular and special sessions of the fifty-first legislature; elected county judge of Harris County in 1950, 1952, and again in 1954 for a four-year term; member of board of regents of the South Texas College of Law, board of directors of the Speech and Hearing Center, and director of the South Texas Law Journal, Inc.; elected as a Democrat to the Eighty-sixth and to the eight succeeding Congresses and served from January 3, 1959, until his resignation January 22, 1976, to become a Commissioner on the Federal Maritime Commission; was a resident of Houston, Tex.; died in Houston April 17, 1986.

**CASEY, Samuel Lewis,** a Representative from Kentucky; born near Caseyville, Union County, Ky., February 12, 1821; attended the country schools; engaged in mercantile pursuits; member of the Kentucky house of representatives 1860-1862; elected as a Unionist to the Thirty-seventh Congress to fill the vacancy caused by the expulsion of Henry C. Burnett and served from March 10, 1862, to March 3, 1863; retired from active business pursuits; died in St. Joseph, Mo., August 25, 1902; the remains were cremated and the ashes interred in Caseyville Cemetery, Caseyville, Ky.

**CASEY, Zadoc,** a Representative from Illinois; born in Greene County, Ga., March 7, 1796; attended the common schools; moved to Illinois in 1819 and settled near the present site of Mount Vernon, Jefferson County; member of the Illinois State house of representatives, 1822-1826; served in the Illinois State senate, 1826-1830; elected Lieutenant Governor of Illinois in 1830; volunteer in the Black Hawk War in 1832; elected as a Jacksonian to the Twenty-third and Twenty-fourth Congresses, as a Democrat to the Twenty-fifth and Twenty-sixth Congresses, and as an Independent Democrat to the Twenty-seventh Congress (March 4, 1833-March 3, 1843); chairman, Committee on Public Lands (Twenty-fifth Congress), Committee on Private Land Claims (Twenty-sixth Congress); unsuccessful candidate for reelection in 1842 to the Twenty-eighth Congress; delegate to the State constitutional conventions in 1848 and 1860; again a member of the State house of representatives, 1848-1852, and served as speaker in 1852; again served in the State senate, 1860-1862; retired to his farm, "Elm Hill," near Mount

Vernon, Ill.; died September 4, 1862, in Caseyville, St. Clair County, Ill., which was named after him; interment in old Union Cemetery, near Mount Vernon, Ill.

**CASKIE, John Samuels,** a Representative from Virginia; born in Richmond, Va., November 8, 1821; was graduated from the University of Virginia at Charlottesville in 1842; studied law; was admitted to the bar about 1842 and practiced in Richmond; prosecuting attorney of the city of Richmond 1842-1846; judge of the Richmond and Henrico circuits 1846-1849; elected as a Democrat to the Thirty-second and to the three succeeding Congresses (March 4, 1851-March 3, 1859); unsuccessful candidate for renomination in 1858; resumed the practice of law; died in Richmond, Va., December 16, 1869; interment in Hollywood Cemetery.

**CASON, Thomas Jefferson,** a Representative from Indiana; born near Brownsville, Union County, Ind., September 13, 1828; moved to Boone County with his parents, who settled on a farm near Thorntown in 1832; attended the common schools; taught school in Boone County for several years; studied law in Crawfordsville; was admitted to the bar in 1850 and commenced practice in Lebanon, Ind.; member of the State house of representatives 1861-1864; member of the State senate 1864-1867; appointed by Governor Conrad Baker common pleas judge of Boone County in April 1867, and was subsequently elected to the same office in October 1867 for a term of four years; declined reelection and resumed the practice of law; elected as a Republican to the Forty-third and Forty-fourth Congresses (March 4, 1873-March 3, 1877); unsuccessful candidate for renomination in 1876 to the Forty-fifth Congress; resumed the practice of law in Lebanon, Ind.; retired in 1897 and moved to Washington, D.C., where he died July 10, 1901; interment in Oak Hill Cemetery, Lebanon, Boone County, Ind.

**CASS, Lewis** (great-great-grandfather of Cass Ballenger), a Senator from Michigan; born in Exeter, N.H., October 9, 1782; attended Exeter Academy; moved with his parents to Wilmington, Del., in 1799 and taught school there; moved to the Northwest Territory in 1801 and settled on a farm near Zanesville, Ohio; studied law and was admitted to the bar in 1802; member, Ohio State house of representatives, 1806; United States marshal for the district of Ohio, 1807-1812, when he resigned to enlist in the Army; served in the United States Army, 1813-1814, attained the rank of brigadier general; appointed military and civil Governor of Michigan Territory by President James Madison on October 29, 1813, and served until his resignation on July 20, 1831, to accept a Cabinet portfolio; appointed Secretary of War by President Andrew Jackson and served from August 1, 1831 to October 5, 1836, when he resigned, having been appointed to a diplomatic post; appointed Envoy Extraordinary and Minister Plenipotentiary to France on October 4, 1836 and served until November 1842; elected as a Democrat to the United States Senate and served from March 4, 1845, until May 29, 1848, when he resigned, having been nominated for President of the United States; chairman, Committee on Military Affairs (Thirtieth Congress); unsuccessful candidate for President on the Democratic ticket in 1848; again elected to the United States Senate on January 20, 1849, to fill the vacancy caused by his own resignation; was reelected, and served from March 4, 1849 to March 3, 1857; served as President pro tempore of the Senate during the Thirty-third Congress; appointed Secretary of State by President James Buchanan on March 6, 1857, and served until his resignation on December 14, 1860; returned to Detroit, Mich., and engaged in literary pursuits; died in Detroit, Mich., June 17, 1866; interment in Elmwood Cemetery.

**Bibliography:** *DAB*; Klunder, Willard Carl. *Lewis Cass and the Politics of Moderation.* Kent, Ohio: Kent State University Press, 1996; McLaughlin, Andrew Cunningham. *Lewis Cass.* 1899. Reprint. New York: Chelsea House, 1980; Woodford, Frank B. *Lewis Cass: The Last Jeffersonian.* New Brunswick: Rutgers University Press, 1950.

**CASSEDY, George,** a Representative from New Jersey; born in Hackensack, Bergen County, N.J., September 16, 1783; attended the common schools; studied law; was admitted to the bar in 1809 and commenced practice in Hackensack; postmaster of Hackensack from June 10, 1805, to January 1, 1806; elected to the Seventeenth, Eighteenth, and Nineteenth Congresses (March 4, 1821-March 3, 1827); died in Hackensack, December 31, 1842; interment in the cemetery of the First Reformed Church.

**CASSEL, Henry Burd,** a Representative from Pennsylvania; born in Marietta, Lancaster County, Pa., October 19, 1855; attended the public schools of Marietta and Columbia Classical Institute; engaged in the wholesale and retail lumber business; member of the Republican county committee in 1881; chairman of the county committee in 1893; delegate to the Republican National Convention in 1896; member of the Pennsylvania house of representatives in 1898 and 1900; elected as a Republican to the Fifty-seventh Congress to fill the vacancy caused by the death of Marriott Brosius; reelected to the Fifty-eighth, Fifty-ninth, and Sixtieth Congresses and served from November 5, 1901, to March 3, 1909; chairman, Committee on Accounts (Fifty-ninth Congress); engaged in business as a manufacturer and contractor; died in Marietta, Pa., April 28, 1926; interment in Marietta Cemetery.

**CASSERLY, Eugene,** a Senator from California; born in Mullingar, County Westmeath, Ireland, November 13, 1820; immigrated to the United States in 1822 with his parents, who settled in New York; prepared for college by his father; was graduated from Georgetown College, Washington, D.C.; studied law; was admitted to the bar in 1844 and commenced practice in New York City; editor of the Freeman's Journal and contributor to newspapers in other cities; corporation counsel of New York City 1846-1847; moved to San Francisco, Calif., in 1850 and published the Public Balance, the True Balance, and the Standard; elected State printer in 1851; retired from journalism and resumed the practice of law; elected as a Democrat to the United States Senate and served from March 4, 1869, until November 29, 1873, when he resigned; chairman, Committee on Engrossed Bills (Forty-second and Forty-third Congresses), Committee on Pacific Railroads (Forty-second Congress); again engaged in the practice of law in San Francisco, Calif.; member of the constitutional convention of California in 1878 and 1879; died in San Francisco June 14, 1883; interment in Calvary Cemetery.

**CASSIDY, George Williams,** a Representative from Nevada; born near Paris, Bourbon County, Ky., April 25, 1836; attended the public schools and was educated by private tutors; studied law but never practiced; moved to Eureka, Nev., in 1870; engaged in newspaper work; member of the State senate 1872-1879 and served as president during the session of 1879; elected as a Democrat to the Forty-seventh and Forty-eighth Congresses (March 4, 1881-March 3, 1885); chairman, Committee on Pacific Railroads (Forty-eighth Congress); unsuccessful candidate for reelection in 1884 to the Forty-ninth Congress; appointed national bank examiner for Nevada, Utah, California, and Colorado by President Grover Cleveland and served from 1886 to 1890; unsuccessful candidate for election in 1888 to the Fifty-first Congress, and in 1890 to the Fifty-second Congress; delegate to the Democratic National Convention of 1892; nominated as a candidate for election to the Fifty-third Congress, but died in Reno, Nev., June 24, 1892, before the election; interment in Hillside Cemetery.

**CASSIDY, James Henry,** a Representative from Ohio; born in Cleveland, Ohio, October 28, 1869; attended the public schools; studied law at the Cleveland Law School; was admitted to the bar in 1899 and commenced practice in Cleveland, Ohio; served as clerk of the Committee on Rivers and Harbors, House of Representatives, from December 1901 until January 11, 1909, when he resigned; elected as a Republican to the Sixty-first Congress to fill the vacancy caused by the resignation of Theodore E. Burton, and served from April 20, 1909, to March 3, 1911; was an unsuccessful candidate for reelection in 1910 to the Sixty-second Congress; resumed the practice of his profession in Cleveland, Ohio; appointed as receiver of the Cleveland & Pittsburgh Coal Co.; moved to New York in 1915 and engaged in the brokerage business; president of an express company; died in Forest Hills Gardens, N.Y., August 23, 1926; interment in Maple Grove Cemetery, Kew Gardens, Long Island, N.Y.

**CASSINGHAM, John Wilson,** a Representative from Ohio; born in Coshocton, Coshocton County, Ohio, June 22, 1840; attended the public schools; deputy county treasurer 1857-1868; engaged in the mercantile business from 1868 to 1875 and in the mining of coal in 1875; later also engaged in the manufacture of paper and in banking; county auditor 1880-1887; trustee of the public library of Coshocton; member of the board of education; president of the Coshocton Board of Trade; delegate to the Democratic National Convention in 1896; elected as a Democrat to the Fifty-seventh and Fifty-eighth Congresses (March 4, 1901-March 3, 1905); declined to be a candidate for reelection in 1904 to the Fifty-ninth Congress; reengaged in his former business interests in Coschoton, Ohio, until 1915, when he retired from active pursuits; died in Coshocton, Ohio, March 14, 1930; interment in South Lawn Cemetery.

**CASTELLOW, Bryant Thomas,** a Representative from Georgia; born on a farm near Georgetown, Quitman County, Ga., July 29, 1876; attended the local school, high schools at Eufaula, Ala., and Coleman, Ga., and Mercer University, Macon, Ga.; was graduated from the law department of the University of Georgia, at Athens in 1897; was admitted to the bar in 1897 and commenced practice in Fort Gaines, Ga., in 1898; superintendent of the public schools in Coleman, Ga., in 1897 and 1898; captain of Company D, Fourth Infantry, Georgia State Troops, 1899-1902; solicitor of Clay County court in 1900 and 1901; judge of Clay County court 1901-1905; moved to Cuthbert, Randolph County, Ga., in 1906 and served as referee in bankruptcy for the western division of the northern district of Georgia 1906-1912; solicitor general of the Pataula judicial circuit from 1913 until his resignation in 1932, having been nominated for Congress; elected on November 8, 1932, as a Democrat to the Seventy-second Congress to fill the vacancy caused by the resignation of Charles R. Crisp and on the same day was elected to the Seventy-third Congress; reelected to the Seventy-fourth Congress and served from November 8, 1932, to January 3, 1937; was not a candidate for renomination in 1936; retired from public life and the practice of law; died in Cuthbert, Ga., July 23, 1962; interment in Rosedale Cemetery.

**CASTLE, Curtis Harvey,** a Representative from California; born near Galesburg, Knox County, Ill., October 4, 1848; attended the public schools and Knox College, Galesburg, Ill.; was graduated from Northwestern University, Evanston, Ill., in 1872; served as principal of the Washington, Tex., public schools 1872-1876; was graduated from the College of Physicians and Surgeons, Keokuk, Iowa, in 1878; practiced in Fulton County, Ill., and in Wayland, Henry County, Iowa, until 1882; moved to Point Arena, Calif., in 1882 and to Merced, Merced County, Calif., in 1888, and continued the practice of medicine; served from 1894 to 1896 as a member of the American Academy of Medicine, as chairman of the Populist executive committee of Merced County, and as a member of the State executive committee; elected as a Populist to the Fifty-fifth Congress (March 4, 1897-March 3, 1899); unsuccessful candidate for reelection in 1898 to the Fifty-sixth Congress; resumed the practice of medicine in Merced, Calif.; lived in retirement in Santa Barbara, Calif., until his death on July 12, 1928; remains were cremated and

the ashes deposited in the mausoleum of the Santa Barbara Cemetery and Crematory.

**CASTLE, James Nathan,** a Representative from Minnesota; born in Shefford, Quebec, Canada, May 23, 1836; attended the public schools; studied law; moved to Afton, Washington County, Minn., in 1862 and taught school; completed his law studies; was admitted to the bar and practiced; moved to Stillwater, Washington County, Minn., in 1865 and continued the practice of law; elected county attorney in 1866 to fill the unexpired term of his deceased brother; city attorney in 1868; elected to the State senate in 1868 and 1878, and again in 1882; elected as a Democrat to the Fifty-second Congress (March 4, 1891-March 3, 1893); chairman, Committee on Mileage (Fifty-second Congress); unsuccessful candidate for reelection in 1892 to the Fifty-third Congress; engaged in the practice of law until his death in Stillwater, Minn., January 2, 1903; interment in Fairview Cemetery.

**CASTLE, Michael Newbold,** a Representative from Delaware; born in Wilmington, Del., July 2, 1939; graduate of Tower Hill School, 1957; B.S., Hamilton College, Clinton, N.Y., 1961; J.D., Georgetown University School of Law, Washington, D.C., 1964; practicing attorney, 1964-1980; deputy attorney general for Delaware, 1965-1966; member, Delaware State general assembly, 1966-1967; member, Delaware State senate, 1968-1976; Lieutenant Governor of Delaware, 1981-1984; elected Governor of Delaware in 1984, reelected in 1988, and served from January 1, 1985 until his resignation on December 31, 1992, having been elected to Congress; elected as a Republican to the One Hundred Third and One Hundred Fourth Congresses (January 3, 1993-January 3, 1997); is a resident of Dover, Del.

**CASTOR, George Albert,** a Representative from Pennsylvania; born in Holmesburg (a part of the city of Philadelphia), Pa., August 6, 1855; attended the public schools; entered a cloth house early in life and subsequently became a merchant tailor with large establishments in New York City, Boston, and Philadelphia; retired from active business pursuits in 1875; unsuccessful candidate in 1892 for nomination to the Fifty-third Congress; member of the Republican city committee for fifteen years; elected as a Republican to the Fifty-eighth Congress to fill the vacancy caused by the death of Henry Burk; reelected to the Fifty-ninth Congress and served from February 16, 1904, until his death in Philadelphia, Pa., February 19, 1906; interment in Emanuel Prostestant Episcopal Cemetery, Holmesburg, Pa.

**CASWELL, Lucien Bonaparte,** a Representative from Wisconsin; born in Swanton, Franklin County, Vt., November 27, 1827; moved to Wisconsin in 1837 with his parents, who settled near Lake Koshkonong, in Rock County; attended the common schools, Milton Academy, and Beloit College; studied law; was admitted to the bar in 1851 and commenced practice in Fort Atkinson, Wis.; district attorney of Jefferson County in 1855 and 1856; served on the local school board for nearly sixty-five years; organized the First National Bank of Fort Atkinson in 1863, the Northwestern Manufacturing Co. in 1866, and the Citizens' State Bank in 1885; member of the State assembly in 1863, 1872, and 1874; during the Civil War served as commissioner of the second district board of enrollment from September 1863 to May 5, 1865; delegate to the Republican National Convention in 1868; elected as a Republican to the Forty-fourth and to the three succeeding Congresses (March 4, 1875-March 3, 1883); unsuccessful candidate for renomination in 1882; elected to the Forty-ninth, Fiftieth, and Fifty-first Congresses (March 4, 1885-March 3, 1891); chairman, Committee on Private Land Claims (Fifty-first Congress); unsuccessful candidate for renomination in 1890; resumed the practice of law in Fort Atkinson, Jefferson County, Wis.; died in Fort Atkinson, Wis., April 26, 1919; interment in Evergreen Cemetery.

**CASWELL, Richard,** a Delegate from North Carolina; born in Harford (now Baltimore) County, Md., August 3, 1729; moved to North Carolina in 1746; appointed deputy surveyor of the colony in 1750; clerk of the court of Orange County, 1752-1754; studied law; was admitted to the bar in 1754 and commenced practice in Hillsboro, N.C.; member of the colonial house of delegates, 1754-1771, and served as speaker the last two years; commanded the right wing of Governor William Tryon's army at the Battle of Alamance in 1771; served in the Revolutionary Army; Member of the Continental Congress, 1774-1775; commanded the patriots at the Battle of Moores Creek Bridge, N.C., February 23, 1776; appointed brigadier general of the New Bern District by the Provincial Congress in 1776; delegate to the North Carolina constitutional convention and its president in 1776; elected Governor of North Carolina by the General Assembly and served from December 1776 until April 1780; commanded the North Carolina troops at the Battle of Camden, S.C., August 16, 1780; comptroller general in 1782; member of the North Carolina State senate, 1782-1784 and served as speaker; again elected Governor by the General Assembly and served from December 1785 until December 1787; appointed delegate from North Carolina to the convention that framed the Federal Constitution in 1787, but did not attend; member of the State convention at Fayetteville, N.C., that adopted the Federal Constitution in 1789; member and speaker of the State house of commons in 1789 and served until his death in Fayetteville, N.C., November 10, 1789; interment in the family cemetery on his estate near Kinston, Lenoir County, N.C.

**Bibliography:** *DAB.*

**CATCHINGS, Thomas Clendinen,** a Representative from Mississippi; born near Brownsville, Hinds County, Miss., January 11, 1847; was tutored at home; attended the University of Mississippi at Oxford in 1859 and Oakland College in 1861; entered the Confederate Army in 1861 and served as a private in Company A, Eighteenth Mississippi Infantry, and subsequently in Company C, Eleventh (Perrin's) Mississippi Cavalry; studied law; was admitted to the bar in 1866 and commenced practice in Vicksburg; elected to the Mississippi State senate in 1875, but resigned in 1877; elected attorney general of Mississippi in 1877; reelected in 1881 and served until February 16, 1885; elected as a Democrat to the Forty-ninth and to the seven succeeding Congresses (March 4, 1885-March 3, 1901); chairman, Committee on Levees and Improvements of the Mississippi River (Fiftieth Congress), Committee on Railways and Canals (Fifty-second and Fifty-third Congresses), Committee on Rivers and Harbors (Fifty-third Congress); resumed the practice of law; also served as division counsel for the Southern Railway Company; member of the Mississippi Code Commission by appointment of Governor James Kimble Vardaman; died in Vicksburg, Miss., December 24, 1927; interment in the City Cemetery.

**Bibliography:** Schlup, Leonard. "Bourbon Democrat: Thomas C. Catchings and the Repudiation of Silver Monometallism." *Journal of Mississippi History* 57 (Fall 1995): 207-223.

**CATE, George Washington,** a Representative from Wisconsin; born in Montpelier, Washington County, Vt., September 17, 1825; attended the common schools; studied law and was admitted to the bar at Montpelier in 1845; moved to Wisconsin the same year and commenced the practice of law in Plover, Portage County; member of the State assembly in 1852 and 1853; moved to Stevens Point; elected judge of the circuit court in April 1854 and served in that capacity until March 4, 1875, when he resigned, having been elected to Congress; elected as a Democrat to the Forty-fourth Congress (March 4, 1875-March 3, 1877); unsuccessful candidate for reelection in 1876 to the Forty-fifth Congress; resumed the practice of law in Stevens Point, Portage County, Wis., and died there March 7, 1905; interment in Forest Cemetery.

**CATE, William Henderson,** a Representative from Arkansas; born near Murfreesboro, Rutherford County, Tenn., November 11, 1839; attended the common schools, and an academy at Abingdon, Va.; was graduated from the University of Tennessee at Knoxville in 1857; taught school in the south and west; served in the Confederate Army during the Civil War and was promoted to captain; moved to Jonesboro, Craighead County, Ark., in 1865; studied law; was admitted to the Arkansas bar in 1866 and commenced practice in Jonesboro; member of the Arkansas house of representatives 1871-1873 and during the extra session of 1874; elected prosecuting attorney in 1878; was appointed and subsequently elected judge of the second judicial circuit of Arkansas in 1884; organized the Bank of Jonesboro in 1887; presented credentials as a Democratic Member-elect to the Fifty-first Congress and served from March 4, 1889, to March 5, 1890, when he was succeeded by Lewis P. Featherstone, who contested the election; elected to the Fifty-second Congress (March 4, 1891-March 3, 1893); declined to be a candidate for renomination in 1892 to the Fifty-third Congress; resumed the practice of law in Jonesboro, Ark.; died while on a visit in Toledo, Ohio, August 23, 1899; interment in the City Cemetery, Jonesboro, Ark.

**CATHCART, Charles William,** a Representative and a Senator from Indiana; born July 24, 1809, in Funchal, Island of Madeira, where his father was the United States consul; travelled to Spain with his parents; attended private schools; returned to the United States in 1819 and went to sea; moved to Washington, D.C., in 1830, and was a clerk in the General Land Office; moved to Indiana; justice of the peace at New Durham Township, Ind., in 1833; engaged in agricultural pursuits near La Porte, Ind., in 1837; United States land surveyor; member, State senate 1837-1840; elected as a Democrat to the Twenty-ninth and Thirtieth Congresses (March 4, 1845-March 3, 1849); appointed as a Democrat to the United States Senate to fill the vacancy caused by the death of James Whitcomb and served from December 6, 1852, to March 3, 1853; unsuccessful candidate for election in 1860 to the Thirty-seventh Congress; engaged in agricultural pursuits; died on his farm near La Porte, La Porte County, Ind., August 22, 1888; interment in Pine Lake Cemetery.

**CATLIN, George Smith,** a Representative from Connecticut; born in Harwinton, Conn., August 24, 1808; attended the common schools, Amherst (Mass.) College, and the Litchfield (Conn.) Law School; was admitted to the bar in 1828 and practiced in Windham, Conn., 1829-1851; member of the Connecticut State house of representatives in 1831 and again in 1846; secretary to Governor John S. Peters, 1831-1833; prosecuting attorney for Windham County in 1842 and 1843; elected as a Democrat to the Twenty-eighth Congress (March 4, 1843-March 3, 1845); unsuccessful Democratic candidate for Governor of Connecticut in 1848; served in the State senate in 1850; judge of the Windham County Court in 1850 and 1851; died in Windham, Conn., December 26, 1851; interment in Windham Cemetery.

**CATLIN, Theron Ephron,** a Representative from Missouri; born in St. Louis, Mo., May 16, 1878; attended private schools; was graduated from Harvard University in 1899 and from the law department of the same institution in 1902; was admitted to the bar in 1903 and commenced practice in St. Louis, Mo.; member of the State house of representatives 1907-1909; presented credentials as a Republican Member-elect to the Sixty-second Congress and served from March 4, 1911, to August 12, 1912, when he was succeeded by Patrick F. Gill, who contested the election; unsuccessful for election in 1912 to the Sixty-third Congress; resumed the practice of law; member of the board of directors of St. Louis Union Trust Co.; died in St. Louis, Mo., March 19, 1960; interment in Bellefontaine Cemetery.

**CATRON, Thomas Benton,** a Delegate and a Senator from New Mexico; born near Lexington, Lafayette County, Mo., October 6, 1840; attended the common schools, and was graduated from the University of Missouri at Columbia in 1860; served four years in the Confederate Army during the Civil War; moved to New Mexico in 1866; studied law; was admitted to the bar in 1867 and commenced practice in Las Cruces, N.Mex.; district attorney of the third district 1866-1868; in 1869 was appointed attorney general of the Territory; resigned to take the position of United States attorney, to which he had been appointed by President Ulysses Grant; member, Territorial council 1884, 1888, 1890, 1899, 1905, and 1909; unsuccessful candidate for election in 1892 to Congress; elected as a Republican Delegate to the Fifty-fourth Congress (March 4, 1895-March 3, 1897); unsuccessful candidate for reelection in 1896; resumed the practice of law in Santa Fe, N.Mex.; upon the admission of New Mexico as a State into the Union was elected as a Republican to the United States Senate and served from March 27, 1912, to March 3, 1917; was not a candidate for renomination in 1916; chairman, Committee on Expenditures in the Interior Department (Sixty-second Congress); retired to Santa Fe, N.Mex., where he died on May 15, 1921; interment in Fairview Cemetery.

**Bibliography:** Duran, Tobias. "Francisco Chavez, Thomas B. Catron, and Organized Political Violence in Santa Fe in the 1890s." *New Mexico Historical Review* 59 (July 1984): 291-310; Westphall, Victor. *Thomas Benton Catron and His Era.* Tucson: University of Arizona Press, 1973.

**CATTELL, Alexander Gilmore,** a Senator from New Jersey; born in Salem, N.J., February 12, 1816; received an academic education; engaged in mercantile pursuits in Salem, N.J. until 1846; elected to the New Jersey general assembly in 1840, and served as clerk 1842-1844; member of the State constitutional convention in 1844; moved to Philadelphia in 1846 and engaged in business and banking; member of the Philadelphia Common Council 1848-1854; organized the Corn Exchange Bank and was president 1858-1871; moved to Merchantville, N.J., in 1863; elected as a Republican to the United States Senate to succeed John P. Stockton, whose seat was declared vacant, and served from September 19, 1866, to March 3, 1871; was not a candidate for reelection; chairman, Committee on the Library (Forty-first Congress); appointed by President Ulysses S. Grant a member of the first United States Civil Service Commission and served two years, resigning to accept the position of United States financial agent in London, serving in 1873 and 1874; member of New Jersey Board of Tax Assessors 1884-1891, and was president 1889-1891; appointed member of the State board of education in 1891 for a term of three years; died in Jamestown, Chautauqua County, N.Y., April 8, 1894; interment in Colestown Cemetery, near Merchantville, Camden County, N.J.

**Bibliography:** *DAB.*

**CAULFIELD, Bernard Gregory,** a Representative from Illinois; born in Alexandria, Va., October 18, 1828; received a classical education; was graduated from Georgetown College, Washington, D.C., in 1848 and from the law department of the University of Pennsylvania at Philadelphia in 1850; was admitted to the bar in 1850 and commenced the practice of law in Lexington, Ky.; moved to Chicago, Ill., in 1853 and continued the practice of his profession; elected as a Democrat to the Forty-third Congress to fill the vacancy caused by the death of John B. Rice; reelected to the Forty-fourth Congress and served from February 1, 1875, to March 3, 1877; chairman, Committee on Expenditures in the Department of Justice (Forty-fourth Congress); was not a candidate for renomination in 1876; resumed the practice of law; moved to Dakota Territory in 1878 and settled in Deadwood; continued the practice of law and became a large landowner; died in Deadwood, Territory of Dakota (now South Dakota), December 19, 1887; interment in Calvary Cemetery, St. Louis, Mo.

**CAULFIELD, Henry Stewart,** a Representative from Missouri; born in St. Louis, Mo., December 9, 1873; attended the St. Louis public schools and St. Charles (Mo.) College; was graduated from the law department of Washington University, St. Louis, Mo., in 1895; was admitted to the bar the same year and commenced practice in St. Louis; unsuccessful candidate for election in 1904 to the Fifty-ninth Congress; elected as a Republican to the Sixtieth Congress (March 4, 1907-March 3, 1909); was not a candidate for renomination in 1908 to the Sixty-first Congress; excise commissioner of St. Louis in 1909 and 1910; judge of the St. Louis Court of Appeals 1910-1912; city counselor in 1921 and 1922; chairman of the board of freeholders to merge the city of St. Louis and St. Louis County, 1925-1926; elected Governor of Missouri in 1928 and served from January 14, 1929 to January 9, 1933; unsuccessful candidate in 1938 for election to the United States Senate; director of public welfare of St. Louis from June 2, 1941, to April 21, 1949; resumed the practice of law; member of the State Reorganization Commission of Missouri; died in St. Louis, Mo., May 11, 1966; interment in Oak Grove Cemetery.

**CAUSEY, John Williams,** a Representative from Delaware; born in Milford, Kent County, Del., September 19, 1841; attended a private school and Albany Academy, New York, and was graduated from the Pennsylvania Agricultural College; engaged in agricultural pursuits; member of the State senate 1875-1877; delegate to the Democratic National Convention of 1884; appointed internal revenue collector for Delaware by President Grover Cleveland in 1885 and served until 1887; elected as a Democrat to the Fifty-second and Fifty-third Congresses (March 4, 1891-March 3, 1895); was not a candidate for renomination in 1894 to the Fifty-fourth Congress; resumed agricultural pursuits; president of an insurance company; died in Milford, Del., October 1, 1908; interment in Odd Fellows Cemetery.

**CAUSIN, John M.S.,** a Representative from Maryland; born in St. Marys County, Md., in 1811; studied law; was admitted to the bar in Prince Georges County about 1836; returned to St. Marys County and commenced the practice of law in Leonardtown, Md.; member of the State house of representatives in 1837 and again 1843; elected as a Whig to the Twenty-eighth Congress (March 4, 1843-March 3, 1845); moved to Annapolis, Md., delegate to the State constitutional convention; moved to Chicago, Ill., in 1858 and resumed the practice of law; died in Cairo, Alexander County, Ill., January 30, 1861; interment in the City Cemetery (now Lincoln Park), Chicago.

**CAVALCANTE, Anthony,** a Representative from Pennsylvania; born in Vanderbilt, Fayette County, Pa., February 6, 1897; attended public schools; served overseas with Company D, One Hundred and Tenth Infantry, Twenty-eighth Division, from May 3, 1918, to May 6, 1919; awarded the Purple Heart Medal; student at Bucknell University, Lewisburg, Pa., in 1920 and 1921 and Pennsylvania State College in 1921; graduated from the law school of Dickinson College, Carlisle, Pa., in 1924; was admitted to the bar the same year and commenced the practice of law in Uniontown, Pa.; member of the Pennsylvania senate 1935-1943; chief counsel for United Mine Workers of America, District Four of German Township School District, German Township Road Supervisors, and South Union Township Road Supervisors; elected as a Democrat to the Eighty-first Congress (January 3, 1949-January 3, 1951); unsuccessful candidate for reelection in 1950 to the Eighty-second Congress; engaged in the practice of law; died in Uniontown, Pa., October 29, 1966; interment in Sylvan Heights Cemetery.

**CAVANAUGH, James Michael,** a Representative from Minnesota and a Delegate from the Territory of Montana; born in Springfield, Mass., July 4, 1823; received an academic education; engaged in newspaper work; studied law; was admitted to the bar in 1854 and began practice in Davenport, Iowa; moved to Chatfield, Fillmore County, Minn., in 1854 and continued the practice of law;

upon the admission of Minnesota as a State into the Union was elected as a Democrat to the Thirty-fifth Congress and served from May 11, 1858, to March 3, 1859; unsuccessful candidate for reelection in 1858 to the Thirty-sixth Congress; moved to Colorado in 1861 and resumed the practice of law; also engaged in mining; member of the State constitutional convention in 1865; moved to Montana in 1866; elected as a Democrat a Delegate to the Fortieth and Forty-first Congresses (March 4, 1867-March 3, 1871); unsuccessful candidate for renomination in 1870; engaged in the practice of law in New York City; returned to Colorado in 1879 and settled in Leadville, where he died October 30, 1879; interment in Greenwood Cemetery, New York City.

**CAVANAUGH, John Joseph,** a Representative from Nebraska; born in Omaha, Douglas County, Nebr., August 1, 1945; graduated from Creighton Preparatory School, Omaha, in 1963; B.A., Regis College, Denver, Colo., 1967; J.D., Creighton University School of Law, Omaha, 1972; admitted to the Nebraska bar in 1972 and commenced practice in Omaha; served in United States Army, 1968-1970; served in the Nebraska State legislature, 1973-1977; elected as a Democrat to the Ninety-fifth and to the Ninety-sixth Congresses (January 3, 1977-January 3, 1981); was not a candidate for reelection in 1980 to the Ninety-seventh Congress; resumed the practice of law in Omaha; is a resident of Omaha, Nebr.

**CAVICCHIA, Peter Angelo,** a Representative from New Jersey; born in Roccamandolfi, Province of Campobasso, Italy, May 22, 1879; immigrated to the United States in 1888 with his parents, who settled in Newark, N.J.; attended the public schools; was graduated from the American International (formerly French-American) College, Springfield, Mass., in 1906 and from the law department of the New York University, New York City, in 1908; was admitted to the bar in 1909 and commenced practice in Newark, N.J.; also served as director and counsel for several building and loan associations; appointed supervisor of inheritance tax of Essex County in 1917; member of the Newark Board of Education 1917-1931, serving as president 1924-1926; professor of law and trustee of Mercer Beasley School of Law (now part of Rutgers University), Newark, N.J., 1925-1931; elected as a Republican to the Seventy-second, Seventy-third, and Seventy-fourth Congresses (March 4, 1931-January 3, 1937); unsuccessful candidate for reelection in 1936 to the Seventy-fifth Congress; resumed the practice of law and again served as supervisor of inheritance tax for Essex County, N.J., 1937-1956; chairman of Central Planning Board of Newark, 1946-1957; died in Belleville, N.J., September 11, 1967; interment in Fairmount Cemetery, Newark, N.J.

**CEDERBERG, Elford Albin,** a Representative from Michigan; born in Bay City, Bay County, Mich., March 6, 1918; attended the public schools and Bay City Junior College 1935-1937; entered the United States Army in April 1941, commissioned a second lieutenant in July 1942, a captain in 1943, and assigned to the Eighty-third Infantry; participated in the Normandy invasion and fought in France and Germany; manager of Nelson Manufacturing Co. of Bay City, Mich., 1946-1952; mayor of Bay City 1949-1953; elected as a Republican to the Eighty-third and to the twelve succeeding Congresses and served from January 3, 1953, until his resignation December 31, 1978; unsuccessful candidate for reelection in 1978 to the Ninety-sixth Congress; is a resident of Alexandria, Va.

**CELLER, Emanuel,** a Representative from New York; born in Brooklyn, N.Y., May 6, 1888; attended the public schools; was graduated from Columbia College, New York City, in 1910, and from Columbia University Law School, New York City, in 1912; was admitted to the bar in 1912 and commenced practice in New York City; Government appeal agent on the draft board during the First World War; delegate to the Democratic State conventions from 1922 until 1932; delegate and member of Platform Committee of Democratic National Conventions from 1942 through 1964; elected as a Democrat to the Sixty-eighth and to the twenty-four succeeding Congresses (March 4, 1923-January 3, 1973); chairman, Committee on the Judiciary (Eighty-first, Eighty-second, and Eighty-fourth through Ninety-second Congresses), Special Committee on Seating of Adam Clayton Powell (Ninetieth Congress); unsuccessful candidate for renomination in 1972 to the Ninety-third Congress; member of the Commission on Revision of the Federal Appellate Court System, 1973-1975; resumed the practice of law; resided in Brooklyn, N.Y. where he died January 15, 1981; interment in Mount Neboh Cemetery, Cypress Hills, N.Y.

**Bibliography:** Celler, Emanuel. *You Never Leave Brooklyn: The Autobiography of Emanuel Celler.* New York: John Day Co., 1953.

**CESSNA, John,** a Representative from Pennsylvania; born near Bedford County, Pa., June 29, 1821; attended the common schools and Hall's Military Academy, Bedford, Pa.; was graduated from Marshall College, Mercersburg, Pa., in 1842; taught school; studied law; was admitted to the bar in 1845 and commenced practice in Bedford; member of the Pennsylvania house of representatives in 1850, 1851, 1862, and 1863, and served as speaker of the house in 1850 and 1863; delegate to the Democratic National Convention at Cincinnati in 1856 and at Charleston and Baltimore in 1860; affiliated with the Republican Party in 1863; chairman of the Pennsylvania Republican convention in 1865; elected chairman of the Pennsylvania Republican central committee in 1865; delegate to the Republican National Conventions in 1868, 1876, and 1880; elected as a Republican to the Forty-first Congress (March 4, 1869-March 3, 1871); unsuccessful candidate for reelection in 1870 to the Forty-second Congress; elected to the Forty-third Congress (March 4, 1873-March 3, 1875); was not a candidate for renomination in 1874; again a member of the Pennsylvania house of representatives in 1892; resumed the practice of law in Bedford, Pa., where he died December 13, 1893; interment in Bedford Cemetery.

**CHABOT, Steven J.,** a Representative from Ohio; born in Cincinnati, Ohio, January 22, 1953; attended LaSalle High School, Cincinnati; B.A., College of William and Mary, Williamsburg, Va., 1975; J.D., Salmon P. Chase College of Law, Northern Kentucky University, 1978; Cincinnati Recreation Commission, Millvale Community Center; teacher, St. Joseph School, Cincinnati; investigator, Holbrook, Jonson, Bressler and Houser, Hamilton, Ohio; practicing attorney, Westwood, Ohio; Cincinnati City Council, 1985-1991; member, Hamilton County Board of Commissioners, 1990-1991, president, 1991; elected as a Republican to the One Hundred Fourth Congress (January 3, 1995-January 3, 1997); is a resident of Cincinnati, Ohio.

**CHACE, Jonathan,** a Representative and a Senator from Rhode Island; born at Fall River, Mass., July 22, 1829; attended the public schools and Friends' School at Providence, R.I.; moved to Central Falls, R.I.; engaged in cotton manufacturing; member, State senate 1876-1877; elected as a Republican to the Forty-seventh and Forty-eighth Congresses and served from March 4, 1881, to January 26, 1885, when he resigned; elected as a Republican to the United States Senate to fill the vacancy caused by the death of Henry B. Anthony; reelected in 1888 and served from January 20, 1885, to April 9, 1889, when he resigned; chairman, Committee on Civil Service and Retrenchment (Fiftieth and Fifty-first Congresses); president of the Phoenix National Bank of Providence, R.I., and interested in several manufacturing enterprises; died in Providence, R.I., June 30, 1917; interment in the North Burial Ground.

**CHADWICK, E. Wallace,** a Representative from Pennsylvania; born in Vincennes, Knox County, Ind., January 17, 1884; moved with his parents to Chester, Delaware County, Pa., in 1890; was graduated from Chester High School, from the University of Pennsylvania in 1906, and from the law school of the same university in 1910; was admitted to the bar in 1910 and commenced practice in Chester, Pa.; also interested in the banking business; president judge of the Delaware County Orphans' Court in 1945; elected as a Republican to the Eightieth Congress (January 3, 1947-January 3, 1949); unsuccessful candidate for renomination in 1948 to the Eighty-first Congress; resumed the practice of law in Chester, Pa.; in 1954 was named chief counsel of special Senate committee to study censure charges against Senator Joseph R. McCarthy; died in Chester, Pa., August 18, 1969; interment in Union United Methodist Church Cemetery, Rose Valley, Wallingford, Pa.

**CHAFEE, John Hubbard,** a Senator from Rhode Island; born in Providence, R.I., October 22, 1922; graduated, Deerfield (Mass.) Academy, 1940; B.A., Yale University, 1947; LL.B., Harvard University Law School, 1950; admitted to the Rhode Island bar in 1950 and commenced practice in Providence; entered the United States Marine Corps as a second lieutenant in 1942, released in 1945 after service at Guadalcanal and Okinawa during the Second World War; served as captain of a rifle company during the Korean conflict, 1951-1953; served in the Rhode Island State house of representatives from 1957 until 1963, minority leader, 1959-1963; elected Governor of Rhode Island in 1962, reelected in 1964 and 1966, and served from January 1, 1963 to January 7, 1969; unsuccessful candidate for reelection in 1968; appointed Secretary of the Navy in the Cabinet of President Richard M. Nixon, and served from January 31, 1969 to May 4, 1972; unsuccessful candidate for election to the United States Senate in 1972; elected as a Republican to the United States Senate in November 1976 for the term commencing January 3, 1977; subsequently appointed by the Governor, December 29, 1976, to fill the vacancy caused by the resignation of John O. Pastore for the term ending January 3, 1977; reelected in 1982, 1988, and again in 1994 for the term ending January 3, 2001; chairman, Republican Conference (Ninety-ninth through One Hundred First Congresses), Committee on Environment and Public Works (One Hundred Fourth Congress); is a resident of Warwick, R.I.

**CHAFFEE, Calvin Clifford,** a Representative from Massachusetts; born at Saratoga Springs, N.Y., on August 28, 1811; attended the common schools; studied medicine, and was graduated from the medical school of Middlebury College, Middlebury, Vt., in 1835; settled in Springfield, Mass., where he began the practice of his profession; elected on the American Party ticket to the Thirty-fourth Congress and as a Republican to the Thirty-fifth Congress (March 4, 1855-March 3, 1859); was not a candidate for renomination in 1858; librarian of the House of Representatives 1860-1862; settled in Washington, D.C., and engaged in the practice of medicine until 1876, when he moved to Springfield, Mass.; president of the Union Relief Association 1880-1893; died in Springfield, Hampden County, Mass., on August 8, 1896; interment in Springfield Cemetery.

**CHAFFEE, Jerome Bunty,** a Delegate from the Territory of Colorado and a Senator from Colorado; born in Niagara County, N.Y., April 17, 1825; attended the public schools of Lockport, N.Y.; moved to Adrian, Mich., in 1844, where he taught school and clerked in a store; moved in 1852 to St. Joseph, Mo., and later to Elmwood, Kans., where he engaged in banking and the real-estate business; moved to the Territory of Colorado in 1860 and engaged in mining and stamp-mill operations at Lake Gulch, Gilpin County; member, Territorial house of representatives, 1861-1863, and served in 1863 as speaker of the house; one of the founders of the city of Denver; president of the First National Bank of Denver from 1865 until 1880; elected as a Republican Delegate to the Forty-second and Forty-third Congresses (March 4, 1871-March 3, 1875); upon the admission of Colorado as a State into the Union was elected as a Republican to the United States Senate, and served from November 15, 1876 to March 3, 1879; was not a candidate for reelection;

chairman of the Republican State executive committee in 1884; died in Salem Center, Westchester County, N.Y., March 9, 1886; interment in Adrian Cemetery, Adrian, Lenawee County, Mich.

**Bibliography:** *DAB*; West, Elliott. "Jerome B. Chaffee and the McCook-Elbert Fight." *Colorado Magazine* 46 (Spring 1969): 145-165.

**CHALMERS, James Ronald** (son of Joseph Williams Chalmers), a Representative from Mississippi; born near Lynchburg, Halifax County, Va., January 12, 1831; moved with his parents in 1835 to Jackson, Tenn., and in 1839 to Holly Springs, Miss.; attended St. Thomas Hall, Holly Springs, Miss., and was graduated from South Carolina College (now the University of South Carolina) at Columbia in 1851; studied law; was admitted to the bar in 1853 and commenced practice at Holly Springs; delegate to the Democratic National Convention in 1852; district attorney for the seventh judicial district of Mississippi in 1858; member of the secession convention of Mississippi in 1861; entered the Confederate Army as a captain in March 1861; elected colonel of the Ninth Mississippi Regiment in April 1861; promoted to the rank of brigadier general in February 1862; transferred to the Cavalry service in 1863; in command of the first division of Forrest's cavalry corps; surrendered in May 1865; member of the State senate in 1876 and 1877; elected as a Democrat to the Forty-fifth and Forty-sixth Congresses (March 4, 1877-March 3, 1881); presented credentials as a Member-elect to the Forty-seventh Congress and served from March 4, 1881, to April 29, 1882, when he was succeeded by John R. Lynch, who contested the election; elected as an Independent to the Forty-eighth Congress and, after a contest with Van H. Manning as to the legality of his election, took his seat June 25, 1884, and served until March 3, 1885; unsuccessful candidate for reelection in 1884 to the Forty-ninth Congress; resumed the practice of law in Memphis, Tenn., where he died April 9, 1898; interment in Elmwood Cemetery.

**Bibliography:** *DAB*; Halsell, Willie D. "James R. Chalmers and 'Mahoneism' in Mississippi." *Journal of Southern History* 10 (February 1944): 37-58.

**CHALMERS, Joseph Williams** (father of James Ronald Chalmers), a Senator from Mississippi; born in Halifax County, Va., 1807; studied law in the University of Virginia at Charlottesville, and in Richmond; was admitted to the bar and practiced; moved to Jackson, Tenn., in 1835 and to Holly Springs, Miss., in 1839, practicing law in both places; vice chancellor of the northern Mississippi district in 1842 and 1843; appointed and subsequently elected as a Democrat to the United States Senate to fill the vacancy caused by the resignation of Robert J. Walker and served from November 3, 1845, to March 3, 1847; chairman, Committee on Engrossed Bills (Twenty-ninth Congress); engaged in the practice of law in Holly Springs, Marshall County, Miss., until his death on June 16, 1853; interment in Hill Crest Cemetery.

**CHALMERS, William Wallace,** a Representative from Ohio; born in Strathroy, Ontario, Canada, November 1, 1861; moved with his parents to Kent County, near Grand Rapids, Mich., in 1865; attended the public schools, and Michigan State Normal School; was graduated from the University of Michigan at Ann Harbor in 1887, from Eureka (Ill.) College in 1889, and from Heidelberg University, Tiffin, Ohio, in 1904; teacher and principal of schools until 1890; superintendent of schools in Grand Rapids, Mich., 1890-1898 and in Toledo, Ohio, 1898-1905; president of Toledo University in 1904; engaged at different periods in farming, lumbering and, in the real-estate and insurance business at Toledo, Ohio; elected as a Republican to the Sixty-seventh Congress (March 4, 1921-March 3, 1923); unsuccessful candidate for reelection in 1922 to the Sixty-eighth Congress; elected to the Sixty-ninth, Seventieth, and Seventy-first Congresses (March 4, 1925-March 3, 1931); unsuccessful candidate for renomination in 1930; died in Indianapolis, Ind., on October 1, 1944; interment in Crown Hill Cemetery.

**CHAMBERLAIN, Charles Ernest,** a Representative from Michigan; born on a farm in Locke Township, Ingham County, Mich., July 22, 1917, attended Lansing, Mich., public schools; B.S., University of Virginia, 1941; LL.B., University of Virginia Law School, 1949; admitted to the Virginia and Michigan bars in 1949 and commenced practice in Lansing, Mich., in 1950; served in the United States Coast Guard from February 1942 to February 1946 and attained the rank of lieutenant commander; captain, United States Coast Guard Reserves, 1946-1977; Internal Revenue agent, Treasury Department, in 1946 and 1947; assistant prosecutor of Ingham County in 1950; city attorney of East Lansing and legal counsel to the Michigan State senate judiciary committee in 1953 and 1954; prosecuting attorney of Ingham County in 1955 and 1956; elected as a Republican to the Eighty-fifth and to the eight succeeding Congresses and served from January 3, 1957, until his resignation December 31, 1974; was not a candidate for reelection in 1974 to the Ninety-fourth Congress; resumed the practice of law in Washington, D.C.; is a resident of Waterford, Va.

**CHAMBERLAIN, Ebenezer Mattoon,** a Representative from Indiana; born in Orrington, Maine, August 20, 1805; attended the public schools; employed in his father's shipyard; studied law; moved to Connersville, Ind., where he completed his studies; was admitted to the bar in 1832 and commenced practice in Elkhart County in 1833; member of the State house of representatives 1835-1837; served in the State senate 1839-1842; elected prosecuting attorney of the ninth judicial circuit in 1842; elected president judge of the ninth judicial district in 1843, reelected in 1851 and served until he resigned, having been elected to Congress; delegate to the Democratic National Convention in 1844; elected as a Democrat to the Thirty-third Congress (March 4, 1853-March 3, 1855); engaged in the practice of law in Goshen, Elkhart County, Ind., until his death there March 14, 1861; interment in Oak Ridge Cemetery.

**CHAMBERLAIN, George Earle,** a Senator from Oregon; born on a plantation near Natchez, Adams County, Miss., January 1, 1854; attended private and public schools in Natchez; clerk in a general merchandise store in Natchez from 1870 until 1872; was graduated from Washington and Lee University, Lexington, Va., in 1876; moved to Oregon in 1876 and taught school in Linn County; deputy clerk of Linn County from 1877 to 1879, when he resigned; was admitted to the bar in 1879 and commenced the practice of law in Albany, Linn County, Oreg.; member, Oregon State house of representatives, 1880-1882; district attorney for the third judicial district, 1884-1886; appointed and subsequently elected attorney general of Oregon, 1891-1894; continued the practice of law in Portland; district attorney for the fourth judicial district, 1900-1902; elected Governor of Oregon in 1902, reelected in 1906, and served from January 14, 1903 until his resignation March 1, 1909, having been elected Senator; elected in 1908 as a Democrat to the United States Senate; reelected in 1914 and served from March 4, 1909, to March 3, 1921; unsuccessful candidate for reelection in 1920; chairman, Committee on Geological Survey (Sixty-second Congress), Committee on Military Affairs (Sixty-third through Sixty-fifth Congresses), Committee on Public Lands (Sixty-third Congress), Committee on Expenditures in the War Department (Sixty-sixth Congress); member of the United States Shipping Board, 1921-1923; engaged in the practice of law in Washington, D.C., and died there on July 9, 1928; interment in Arlington National Cemetery, Va.

**Bibliography:** *DAB*; Robert, Frank. "The Public Speaking of George Earle Chamberlain, A Study of the Utilization of Speech by a Prominent Politician." Ph.D. dissertation, Stanford University, 1955.

**CHAMBERLAIN, Jacob Payson,** a Representative from New York; born in Dudley, Mass., August 1, 1802; moved with his parents to Seneca Falls, N.Y., in 1807; attended the public schools; operated flour mills, malt houses, and woolen mills; organized the first savings bank of the village; supervisor of Seneca Falls; member of the board of education; member of the State assembly 1859-1861; elected as a Republican to the Thirty-seventh Congress (March 4, 1861-March 3, 1863); was not a candidate for renomination; resumed the flour-milling business; died at Seneca Falls, Seneca County, N.Y., October 5, 1878; interment in Restvale Cemetery.

**CHAMBERLAIN, John Curtis,** a Representative from New Hampshire; born in Worcester, Mass., June 5, 1772; was graduated from Harvard College in 1793; studied law; was admitted to the bar in 1796 and commenced practice in Alstead, Cheshire County, N.H.; member of the State house of representatives 1802-1804; moved to Charlestown, N.H., in 1804; elected as a Federalist to the Eleventh Congress (March 4, 1809-March 3, 1811); resumed the practice of law; again a member of the State house of representatives in 1818; moved to Honeoye Falls, Monroe County, N.Y., in 1826, and thence to Utica, N.Y., where he died December 8, 1834.

**CHAMBERLAIN, William,** a Representative from Vermont; born in Hopkinton, Mass., April 27, 1755; attended the common schools; moved with his father to Loudon, N.H., in 1774; served as a sergeant during the Revolutionary War; engaged in land surveying and farming; moved to Peacham, Vt., in 1780; clerk of the proprietors of the town the same year; town clerk, 1785-1797; town representative twelve years; member of the Vermont State house of representatives, 1785, 1787-1796, 1805, and 1808; justice of the peace, 1786-1796; delegate to the State constitutional convention in 1791; brigadier general of State militia in 1794; major general in 1799; assistant judge of Orange County in 1795 and chief judge of Caledonia County, 1796-1803; secretary of the board of trustees of the Caledonia County Grammar School, 1795-1812, and president, 1813-1828; State councilor, 1796-1803; Federalist presidential elector in 1800; elected as a Federalist to the Eighth Congress (March 4, 1803-March 3, 1805); elected to the Eleventh Congress (March 4, 1809-March 3, 1811); lieutenant governor of Vermont, 1813-1815; delegate to the State constitutional convention in 1814; died in Peacham, Caledonia County, Vt., September 27, 1828, interment in Peacham Cemetery.

**CHAMBERS, David,** a Representative from Ohio; born in Allentown, Pa., November 25, 1780; tutored by his father; was a confidential express rider for President Washington during the Whiskey Rebellion in 1794; learned the art of printing; moved to Zanesville, Ohio, in 1810, where he established a newspaper and was elected State printer; volunteer aide-de-camp to General Lewis Cass in the War of 1812; served as recorder and mayor of Zanesville; member of the State house of representatives in 1814, 1828, 1836-1838, 1841, and 1842; clerk of the Ohio State senate in 1817; clerk of the court of common pleas of Muskingum County 1817-1821; unsuccessful candidate for election in 1820 to the Seventeenth Congress; subsequently elected to the Seventeenth Congress to fill the vacancy caused by the resignation of Representative-elect John C. Wright and served from October 9, 1821, to March 3, 1823; was not a candidate for renomination in 1822 to the Eighteenth Congress; affiliated with the Whig Party after its formation; member of the State senate in 1843 and 1844; president of the senate in 1844; delegate to the State constitutional convention of 1850; engaged in agricultural pursuits until 1856; died in Zanesville, Muskingum County, Ohio, August 8, 1864; interment in Greenwood Cemetery.

**CHAMBERS, Ezekiel Forman,** a Senator from Maryland; born in Chestertown, Kent County, Md., February 28, 1788; was graduated from Washington College at Chestertown in 1805; studied law; was admitted to the bar in 1808 and commenced practice in Chestertown, Md.; served in the War of 1812, attaining the rank of brigadier general; member, State senate 1822; elected to the United States Senate to fill the vacancy caused by the resignation of Edward Lloyd; reelected in 1831 and served from January 24, 1826, until his resignation on December 20, 1834; chairman, Committee on District of Columbia (Twenty-first through Twenty-third Congresses); presiding judge of the second judicial circuit of Maryland and judge of the court of appeals 1834-1851; unsuccessful Democratic candidate for Governor in 1864; died in Chestertown, Md., January 30, 1867; interment in Chester Cemetery.

**Bibliography:** *DAB*.

**CHAMBERS, George,** a Representative from Pennsylvania; born in Chambersburg, Pa., February 24, 1786; received a classical education and attended the Chambersburg Academy; was graduated from Princeton College in 1804; studied law; was admitted to the bar in 1807 and commenced practice in Chambersburg; elected as an Anti-Masonic candidate to the Twenty-third and Twenty-fourth Congresses (March 4, 1833-March 3, 1837); resumed the practice of law; member of the Pennsylvania constitutional convention in 1837; appointed a justice of the Pennsylvania Supreme Court April 12, 1851, which position he held until it was vacated by constitutional provision; died in Chambersburg, Franklin County, Pa., March 25, 1866; interment in Falling Spring Presbyterian Churchyard.

**Bibliography:** *DAB*.

**CHAMBERS, Henry H.,** a Senator from Alabama; born near Kenbridge, Lunenburg County, Va., October 1, 1790; was graduated from William and Mary College, Williamsburg, Va., in 1808 and from the medical department of the University of Pennsylvania at Philadelphia in 1811; moved to Madison, Ala., in 1812 and engaged in the practice of medicine; served in the Indian wars as a surgeon; returned to Alabama and settled in Huntsville; member of the State constitutional convention in 1819; member, State house of representatives 1820; unsuccessful candidate for Governor in 1821 and 1823; elected to the United States Senate and served from March 4, 1825, until his death near Kenbridge, Lunenburg County, Va., January 24, 1826, while en route to Washington, D.C.; interment in the family burial ground near Kenbridge, Va.

**CHAMBERS, John,** a Representative from Kentucky; born at Bromley Bridge, Somerset County, N.J., October 6, 1780; attended the public schools and the Transylvania Seminary, Lexington, Ky.; moved with his father to Washington, Mason County, Ky., in 1794; studied law; was admitted to the bar in 1800 and commenced practice in Washington, Ky.; served as aide-de-camp to General William Henry Harrison in the War of 1812 and was at the Battle of the Thames, October 5, 1813; member of the Kentucky house of representatives in 1812, 1815, 1830, and 1831; appointed judge of the court of appeals in 1825; resigned in 1827; elected to the Twentieth Congress to fill the vacancy caused by the resignation of Thomas Metcalfe and served from December 1, 1828, to March 3, 1829; elected as a Whig to the Twenty-fourth and Twenty-fifth Congresses (March 4, 1835-March 3, 1839); chairman, Committee on Claims (Twenty-fifth Congress); appointed Governor of the Territory of Iowa by President William Henry Harrison on March 25, 1841, and served until November 1845; commissioner to negotiate a treaty with the Sioux Indians in 1849; died near Paris, Bourbon County, Ky., September 21, 1852; interment in the family burial ground at Washington, Mason County, Ky.

**Bibliography:** *DAB*.

**CHAMBLISS, Saxby,** a Representative from Georgia; born in Warrenton, Warren County, N.C., November 10, 1943; attended C.E. Byrd High School, Shreveport, La.; B.A., University of Georgia, 1966; J.D., University of Tennessee College of Law, 1968; admitted to Georgia bar; attorney, Moultrie, Ga.; elected as a Republican to the One Hundred Fourth Congress (January 3, 1995-January 3, 1997); is a resident of Moultrie, Ga.

**CHAMPION, Edwin Van Meter,** a Representative from Illinois; born in Mansfield, Piatt County, Ill., September 18, 1890; attended the public schools; was graduated from the law department of the University of Illinois at Urbana, 1912; was admitted to the bar the same year and commenced practice in Peoria, Ill.; during the First World War entered the Officers' Training Camp at Fort Sheridan, Ill., on May 15, 1917; commissioned second lieutenant and assigned to service overseas with the Three Hundred and Forty-first Infantry, Company C, Eighty-sixth Division; discharged with rank of captain on February 6, 1919; served as assistant State's attorney of Peoria County, Ill., in 1919 and 1920 and as State's attorney 1932-1936; president of the Illinois State's Atorneys' Association in 1935; elected as a Democrat to the Seventy-fifth Congress (January 3, 1937-January 3, 1939); was not a candidate for renomination in 1938 to the Seventy-sixth Congress; resumed the practice of law in Peoria, Ill., where he died February 11, 1976; entombment in Springdale Mausoleum.

**CHAMPION, Epaphroditus,** a Representative from Connecticut; born in Westchester parish, Colchester, Conn., April 6, 1756; educated by private tutors and in the common schools; served during the Revolutionary War; moved to East Haddam, Conn., in 1782; served as captain in the Twenty-fourth Regiment of State militia 1784-1792, as major 1793 and 1794, as lieutenant colonel 1795-1798, and as brigadier general of the Seventh Brigade 1800-1803; merchant, shipowner, exporter, and importer; member of the State assembly 1791-1806; elected as a Federalist to the Tenth and to the four succeeding Congresses (March 4, 1807-March 3, 1817); resumed his former business activities, but soon retired to private life; died in East Haddam, Conn., December 22, 1834; interment in Riverview Cemetery.

**CHAMPLIN, Christopher Grant,** a Representative and a Senator from Rhode Island; born in Newport, R.I., April 12, 1768; completed preparatory studies; was graduated from Harvard College in 1786 and continued his studies at the College of St. Omer in France; elected as a Federalist to the Fifth and Sixth Congresses (March 4, 1797-March 3, 1801); engaged in mercantile pursuits; elected as a Federalist to the United States Senate to fill the vacancy caused by the death of Francis Malbone and served from June 26, 1809, to October 2, 1811, when he resigned; president of the Rhode Island Bank until a short time before his death in Newport, Newport County, R.I., March 18, 1840; interment in Common Burial Ground.

**CHANDLER, Albert Benjamin (Happy),** a Senator from Kentucky; born in Corydon, Henderson County, Ky., July 14, 1898; attended the public schools; attended Harvard University; served as a private in the United States Army, 1918-1919; graduated from Transylvania College, Lexington, Ky., in 1921, and from the law department of the University of Kentucky at Lexington in 1924; was admitted to the bar in 1925 and commenced practice in Versailles, Ky.; master commissioner of the Woodford circuit in 1928; member, Kentucky senate, 1930-1931; receiver of the Inter-Southern Life Insurance Co., in 1932; lieutenant governor, 1931-1935; elected Governor of Kentucky in 1935, and served from December 10, 1935 until his resignation October 9, 1939; appointed as a Democrat and subsequently elected to the United States Senate to fill the vacancy caused by the death of Marvel Mills Logan; reelected in 1942 and served from October 10, 1939, until his resignation; resigned from the Senate on November 1, 1945 to become commissioner of major league baseball, and served in that capacity until July 15, 1951; engaged in the practice of law, raising of tobacco, and the publication of a weekly newspaper; elected Governor of Kentucky in 1955, and served from December 13, 1955 to December 9, 1959; unsuccessful gubernatorial candidate in 1963; named to the Kentucky Sports Hall of Fame in 1957; commissioner, Continental Professional Football League, 1965; trustee of the Ty Cobb Foundation, the

University of Kentucky, and Transylvania college; served as Democratic National Committeeman from Kentucky; inducted in 1982 into the National Baseball Hall of Fame, Cooperstown, N.Y.; died June 14, 1991.

**Bibliography:** Chandler, Happy, with Vance H. Trimble. *Heroes, Plain Folks, and Skunks: The Life and Times of Happy Chandler: An Autobiography.* Chicago: Bonus Books, 1989; Roland, Charles P. "Happy Chandler." *Register of the Kentucky Historical Society* 85 (Spring 1987): 138-161.

**CHANDLER, John** (brother of Thomas Chandler and uncle of Zachariah Chandler), a Representative from Massachusetts and a Senator from Maine; born in Epping, N.H., February 1, 1762; self-educated; served in the Revolutionary War; moved to the Maine district of Massachusetts and settled on a farm near Monmouth; member, Massachusetts senate 1803-1805; elected as a Republican to the Ninth and Tenth Congresses (March 4, 1805-March 3, 1809); was not a candidate for renomination in 1808 to the Eleventh Congress; appointed sheriff of Kennebec County the same year; during the War of 1812 served in the Maine Militia 1812-1815, attained the rank of brigadier general; member of the Massachusetts General Court in 1819; first president of the Maine senate; member of the Maine constitutional convention 1819-1820; upon the admission of Maine as a State into the Union was elected to the United States Senate in 1820; reelected in 1823 and served from June 14, 1820, to March 3, 1829; was not a candidate for renomination; chairman, Committee on Militia (Eighteenth through Twentieth Congresses); collector of customs at Portland 1829-1837; died in Augusta, Kennebec County, Maine, September 25, 1841; interment in Mount Pleasant Cemetery.

**Bibliography:** *DAB.*

**CHANDLER, Joseph Ripley,** a Representative from Pennsylvania; born in Kingston, Mass., August 22, 1792; attended the common schools; engaged in commercial work in Boston; moved to Philadelphia, Pa., in 1815; founded a young ladies' seminary; editor of the United States Gazette 1822-1847; member of the Philadelphia city council 1832-1848; member of the Pennsylvania constitutional convention in 1837; elected as a Whig to the Thirty-first, Thirty-second, and Thirty-third Congresses (March 4, 1849-March 3, 1855); unsuccessful candidate for reelection in 1854 to the Thirty-fourth Congress; appointed by President James Buchanan as Minister to the Two Sicilies and served from June 15, 1858 until November 1860; president of the board of directors of Girard College; interested in prison reform and was a delegate to the International Prison Congress held at London in 1872; died in Philadelphia, Pa., July 10, 1880; interment in New Cathedral Cemetery.

**Bibliography:** *DAB*; Gerrity, Frank. "The Disruption of the Philadelphia Whigocracy: Joseph R. Chandler, Anti-Catholicism, and the Congressional Election of 1854." *Pennsylvania Magazine of History and Biography* 111 (April 1987): 161-194.

**CHANDLER, Rod Dennis** (great-great-grandnephew of Zachariah Chandler), a Representative from Washington; born in La Grande, Union County, Oreg., July 13, 1942; attended public schools; attended Eastern Oregon College, La Grande, 1961; B.S., Oregon State University, Corvallis, 1968; public relations consultant and television news correspondent; served in Oregon National Guard, 1959-1964; elected to the Washington house of representatives, 1974-1982; served on the King County Metro Council, 1974-1975; delegate, Washington State Republican conventions, 1976, 1978, and 1980; elected as a Republican to the Ninety-eighth and to the four succeeding Congresses (January 3, 1983-January 3, 1993); was not a candidate for reelection in 1992 to the House of Representatives, but was an unsuccessful candidate for election to the United States Senate; is a resident of Redmond, Wash.

**CHANDLER, Thomas** (brother of John Chandler and uncle of Zachariah Chandler), a Representative from New Hampshire; born in Bedford, N.H., August 10, 1772; attended the public schools; justice of the peace in 1808; captain of militia in 1815; member of the State house of representatives in 1818 and again in 1827; elected as a Jacksonian to the Twenty-first and Twenty-second Congresses (March 4, 1829-March 3, 1833); innkeeper and also engaged in agricultural pursuits; died in Bedford, N.H., January 28, 1866; interment in Bedford Cemetery.

**CHANDLER, Thomas Alberter,** a Representative from Oklahoma; born near Eucha, Delaware County, Indian Territory (now Oklahoma), July 26, 1871; attended the public schools, Worcester Academy, Vinita, Indian Territory, in 1888, and, later, Drury College, Springfield, Mo.; appointed a Cherokee revenue collector in 1891; Cherokee town-site commissioner 1895-1898; United States deputy clerk of the court for the northern district of Indian Territory 1900-1907; studied law; was admitted to the bar in 1907 and commenced practice in Vinita, Indian Territory; delegate to the Republican National Convention in 1908; member of the first Board of Public Affairs for the State of Oklahoma in 1909 and 1910; resumed the practice of law; also engaged in the production of oil, in agricultural pursuits, and in the real-estate business; elected as a Republican to the Sixty-fifth Congress (March 4, 1917-March 3, 1919); unsuccessful candidate for reelection in 1918 to the Sixty-sixth Congress; elected to the Sixty-seventh Congress (March 4, 1921-March 3, 1923); unsuccessful candidate for reelection in 1922 to the Sixty-eighth Congress; resumed the practice of law; died in Vinita, Okla., June 22, 1953; interment in Fairview Cemetery.

**CHANDLER, Walter (Clift),** a Representative from Tennessee; born in Jackson, Madison County, Tenn., October 5, 1887; attended the public schools and was graduated from the law department of the University of Tennessee at Knoxville in 1909; admitted to the bar the same year and commenced practice in Memphis, Tenn.; assistant district attorney general in 1916; member of the State house of representatives in 1917; served in the State senate 1921-1923; city attorney of Memphis 1928-1934; served as a captain in the One Hundred and Fourteenth Field Artillery, Thirtieth Division, American Expeditionary Forces, from July 25, 1917, to April 19, 1919; delegate to the Democratic National Conventions in 1940 and 1944; elected as a Democrat to the Seventy-fourth, Seventy-fifth, and Seventy-sixth Congresses and served from January 3, 1935, until his resignation on January 2, 1940, having been elected mayor of Memphis; reelected mayor in 1943 and served until September 1, 1946; resumed the practice of law; temporary president, Tennessee constitutional convention, in 1953; mayor of Memphis in 1955 for unexpired term; resided in Memphis, Tenn., until his death there on October 1, 1967; interment in Forest Hill Cemetery.

**CHANDLER, Walter Marion,** a Representative from New York; born near Yazoo City, Yazoo County, Miss., December 8, 1867; attended the public schools, the University of Virginia at Charlottesville, and the University of Mississippi at Oxford; taught school; was graduated from the University of Michigan at Ann Arbor in 1897; studied history and jurisprudence at the Universities of Berlin and Heidelberg, Germany; was admitted to the bar in 1897 and commenced the practice of law in Dallas, Tex.; moved to New York City in 1900 and continued the practice of law; also engaged in writing and lecturing; elected as a Progressive to the Sixty-third and Sixty-fourth Congresses and as a Republican to the Sixty-fifth Congress (March 4, 1913-March 3, 1919); unsuccessful candidate for reelection in 1918 to the Sixty-sixth Congress; elected as a Republican to the Sixty-seventh Congress (March 4, 1921-March 3, 1923); unsuccessful candidate for reelection in 1922 to the Sixty-eighth Congress and also unsuccessfully contested the election of Sol Bloom to fill a vacancy in the Sixty-eighth Congress;

unsuccessful candidate for election in 1924 to the Sixty-ninth Congress; member of the faculty and lecturer at the American Expeditionary Forces University at Beaune, France, during the First World War; resumed the practice of law in New York City; died in New York City on March 16, 1935; interment in the West Evergreen Cemetery, Jacksonville, Fla.

**CHANDLER, William Eaton,** a Senator from New Hampshire; born in Concord, N.H., December 28, 1835; attended the common schools and the academies in Thetford, Vt., and Pembroke, N.H.; was graduated from Harvard Law School in 1854; was admitted to the bar in 1855 and commenced practice in Concord, N.H.; appointed reporter of the decisions of the supreme court of New Hampshire in 1859; member, New Hampshire State house of representatives, 1862-1864, and served as speaker during the last two years; appointed by President Abraham Lincoln solicitor and judge advocate general of the Navy Department in 1865; served as First Assistant Secretary of the Treasury from 1865 until 1867, when he resigned; newpaper publisher and editor in New Hampshire during the 1870s and 1880s; member of the State constitutional convention in 1876; member of the New Hampshire State house of representatives in 1881; appointed by President Chester A. Arthur as Secretary of the Navy, and served from April 16, 1882 to March 6, 1885; elected as a Republican to the United States Senate to fill the vacancy caused by the death of Austin F. Pike and served from June 14, 1887, to March 3, 1889; subsequently elected for the term beginning March 4, 1889; reelected in 1895 and served from June 18, 1889, to March 3, 1901; unsuccessful candidate for renomination; chairman, Committee on Immigration (Fifty-first and Fifty-second Congresses), Committee on Census (Fifty-fourth Congress), Committee on Privileges and Elections (Fifty-fifth and Fifty-sixth Congresses); appointed by President William McKinley as president of the Spanish Claims Treaty Commission, 1901-1908; resumed the practice of law in Concord, N.H., and Washington, D.C.; died in Concord, N.H., November 30, 1917; interment in Blossom Hill Cemetery.

**Bibliography:** *DAB*; Richardson, Leon B. *William E. Chandler, Republican.* New York: Dodd, Mead and Company, 1940.

**CHANDLER, Zachariah** (nephew of John Chandler and Thomas Chandler, grandfather of Frederick Hale and great-great-granduncle of Rod Dennis Chandler), a Senator from Michigan; born in Bedford, N.H., December 10, 1813; attended the common schools; taught school; moved to Detroit, Mich., in 1833 and engaged in mercantile pursuits; served as mayor of Detroit in 1851; unsuccessful Whig candidate for Governor in 1852; was prominent in the organization of the Republican Party in 1854; elected as a Republican to the United States Senate in 1857; reelected in 1863 and again in 1869, and served from March 4, 1857 to March 3, 1875; unsuccessful candidate for reelection in 1874; chairman, Committee on Commerce (Thirty-seventh through Forty-third Congresses); appointed Secretary of the Interior by President Ulysses S. Grant, and served from October 9, 1875 to March 11, 1877; chairman of the Republican National Committee from 1868 to 1876; again elected in 1879 to the United States Senate to fill the vacancy caused by the resignation of Isaac P. Christiancy, and served from February 22, 1879 until his death in Chicago, Ill., on November 1, 1879; interment in Elmwood Cemetery, Detroit, Mich.

**Bibliography:** *DAB*; George, Mary K. *Zachariah Chandler: A Political Biography.* East Lansing: Michigan State University Press, 1969; Harris, W.C. *Public Life of Zachariah Chandler, 1851-1875.* East Lansing: Michigan Historical Commission, 1917.

**CHANEY, John,** a Representative from Ohio; born in Washington County, Md., January 12, 1790; moved with his parents to Pennsylvania; received a limited schooling; moved to Ohio in 1810 and settled in Bloom Township, Fairfield County; engaged in agricultural pursuits; justice of the peace in 1821, 1824, and 1827;

trustee of Bloom Township for twenty-three years; major, colonel, and paymaster in the Ohio State Militia; member of the State house of representatives 1828-1830; elected associate judge of Fairfield County in 1831; elected as a Jacksonian to the Twenty-third and Twenty-fourth Congresses and as a Democrat to the Twenty-fifth Congress (March 4, 1833-March 3, 1839); returned to Ohio and settled in Canal Winchester, Franklin County; again a member of the State house of representatives in 1842 and served as speaker; member of the village council; served in the State senate in 1844 and 1845; again a member of the State house of representatives in 1855; served as a delegate to the Maryland constitutional convention in 1851; died at Canal Winchester, Ohio, April 10, 1881; interment in Union Grove Cemetery.

**CHANEY, John Crawford,** a Representative from Indiana; born near New Lisbon, Columbiana County, Ohio, February 1, 1853; in 1854 moved to Lafayette Township, Allen County, Ind., with his parents, who settled on a farm near Fort Wayne; attended the common schools; was graduated from Ascension Seminary, Farmersburg, Sullivan County, Ind., in 1874 and later from the Terre Haute Commercial College; taught school and served as superintendent of schools for five years; was graduated from the law school of Cincinnati University in June 1882; was admitted to the bar in 1883 and commenced practice in Sullivan, Sullivan County, Ind.; member of the State central committee from the second district in 1884 and 1885; appointed by President Benjamin Harrison as assistant to Attorney General William H.H. Miller in July 1889, which position he filled until August 1893, when he resigned and resumed the practice of law; elected as a Republican to the Fifty-ninth and Sixtieth Congresses (March 4, 1905-March 3, 1909); unsuccessful candidate for reelection in 1908 to the Sixty-first Congress; continued the practice of law in Sullivan, Ind.; died in Sullivan, Ind., April 26, 1940; interment in Center Ridge Cemetery.

**CHANLER, John Winthrop** (father of William Astor Chanler), a Representative from New York; born in New York City September 14, 1826; received his early education from private tutors, and was graduated from Columbia College, New York, in 1847; attended the University of Heidelberg, Germany; studied law; was admitted to the bar and practiced; member of the State assembly in 1858 and 1859; was nominated as a candidate for State senator in 1860 but declined; unsuccessful candidate for election in 1860 to the Thirty-seventh Congress; elected as a Democrat to the Thirty-eighth and to the two succeeding Congresses (March 4, 1863-March 3, 1869); censured by the Thirty-ninth Congress on May 14, 1866, for an insult to the House of Representatives; died at "Rokeby," Barrytown, N.Y., October 19, 1877; interment in Trinity Cemetery, New York.

**CHANLER, William Astor** (son of John Winthrop Chanler), a Representative from New York; born in Newport, R.I., June 11, 1867; attended St. John's School, Ossining, N.Y., Phillips Academy, Exeter, N.H., and Harvard University for two years; Fellow of the Royal Geographic Society of London; in 1889 explored territory in northeastern Tanzania in the vicinity of Mount Kilimanjaro; delegate to the State Republican convention at Saratoga in 1896; member of the State assembly in 1897; during the Spanish-American War was appointed captain and assistant adjutant general of Volunteers on May 10, 1898; served as acting ordnance officer, Cavalry Division, Fifth Army Corps, from May 23 to August 23, 1898; participated in the Battle of Santiago; elected as a Democrat to the Fifty-sixth Congress (March 4, 1899-March 3, 1901); was not a candidate for renomination in 1900 to the Fifty-seventh Congress; traveler, author, and explorer; moved to Europe in 1920; died in Menton, France, on March 4, 1934; interment in Trinity Church Cemetery, New York City.

**CHAPIN, Alfred Clark** (grandfather of Hamilton Fish, Jr., [1926-1996]), a Representative from New York; born in South Hadley, Hampshire County, Mass., March 8, 1848; resided in Springfield, Mass., in Keene, N.H., and in Rutland, Vt.; attended the public and private schools; was graduated from Williams College, Williamstown, Mass., in 1869 and from Harvard Law School in 1871; was admitted to the bar in 1872 and commenced practice in New York City with residence in Brooklyn, N.Y.; member of the State assembly in 1882 and 1883, serving as speaker in the latter year; State comptroller 1884-1887; mayor of Brooklyn 1888-1891; elected as a Democrat to the Fifty-second Congress to fill the vacancy caused by the resignation of David A. Boody and served from November 3, 1891, to November 16, 1892, when he resigned; served as railroad commissioner of New York State 1892-1897; continued the practice of law and was also financially interested in various enterprises; died while on a visit in Montreal, Canada, October 2, 1936; interment in Woodlawn Cemetery, the Bronx, New York City.

**CHAPIN, Chester Williams,** a Representative from Massachusetts; born in Ludlow, Mass., December 16, 1798; attended the common schools and Westfield Academy, Westfield, Mass.; engaged in mercantile pursuits; mail contractor, running post coaches and steamboats; member of the constitutional convention of Massachusetts in 1853; president and director of the Western Railroad Corporation 1854-1867; president of the Boston & Albany Railroad Co. 1868-1878, and one of the directors 1868-1880; elected as a Democrat to the Forty-fourth Congress (March 4, 1875-March 3, 1877); unsuccessful candidate for reelection in 1876 to the Forty-fifth Congress; died in Springfield, Hampden County, Mass., on June 10, 1883; interment in Springfield Cemetery.

Bibliography: *DAB.*

**CHAPIN, Graham Hurd,** a Representative from New York; born in Salisbury, Conn., February 10, 1799; moved to Lyons, Wayne County, N.Y., in 1817; was graduated from Yale College in 1819; studied law; was admitted to the bar in 1823 and practiced in Lyons; surrogate of Wayne County 1826-1833; district attorney of Wayne County in 1829 and 1830; moved to Rochester, N.Y., in 1833 and continued the practice of law; elected as a Jacksonian to the Twenty-fourth Congress (March 4, 1835-March 3, 1837); died in Mount Morris, Livingston County, N.Y., September 8, 1843.

**CHAPMAN, Andrew Grant** (son of John Grant Chapman), a Representative from Maryland; born in La Plata, Charles County, Md., January 17, 1839; after being tutored at home attended the Charlotte Hall Academy, St. Marys County, Md.; was graduated from St. John's College, Annapolis, Md., in 1858 and from the law department of the University of Virginia at Charlottesville in 1860; moved to Baltimore, Md., in 1860; was admitted to the bar the same year and commenced practice in that city; moved to Port Tobacco, Md., in 1864 and continued the practice of law; also engaged in agricultural pursuits; member of the State house of delegates in 1867, 1868, 1870, 1872, 1879, and 1885; appointed aide and inspector with rank of brigadier general in 1874 on the staff of Governor James B. Groome and reappointed by Governor John Lee Carroll; elected as a Democrat to the Forty-seventh Congress (March 4, 1881-March 3, 1883); unsuccessful candidate for reelection in 1882 to the Forty-eighth Congress; resumed the practice of law; appointed deputy collector of internal revenue in 1885 and collector in 1888; delegate to the Democratic National Convention of 1888; died at his home, "Normandy," near La Plata, Md., September 25, 1892; interment in Mount Rest Cemetery, La Plata, Md.

**CHAPMAN, Augustus Alexandria,** a Representative from Virginia; born in Union, Monroe County, Va. (now West Virginia), March 9, 1803; studied law; was admitted to the bar in 1825 and commenced practice in Union; member, Virginia house of delegates, 1835-1841; elected as a Democrat to the Twenty-eighth and Twenty-ninth Congresses (March 4, 1843-March 3, 1847); member, Virginia constitutional convention, 1850-1851; again a member of the Virginia house of delegates, 1857-1861; at the outbreak of the Civil War was a brigadier general of the Virginia militia and as such took the field with his command in 1861, serving with the Confederate Army in the Kanawha Valley; resumed the practice of law in Union, W.Va., and also engaged in agricultural pursuits; died in Hinton, Summers County, W.Va., June 7, 1876, while en route to attend the Democratic State convention at Charleston; interment in Green Hill Cemetery, Union, Monroe County, W.Va.

**CHAPMAN, Bird Beers,** a Delegate from the Territory of Nebraska; born in Salisbury, Litchfield County, Conn., August 24, 1821; attended the public schools; studied law; was admitted to the bar and commenced practice in Elyria, Lorain County, Ohio; moved to the Territory of Nebraska and settled in Omaha; was editor of the Omaha Nebraskan from 1855 until 1859; elected as a Democrat to the Thirty-fourth Congress (March 4, 1855-March 3, 1857); unsuccessfully contested the election of Fenner Ferguson to the Thirty-fifth Congress; died at Put in Bay, Ottawa County, Ohio, September 21, 1871; interment in Ridgelawn Cemetery, Elyria, Ohio.

**CHAPMAN, Charles,** a Representative from Connecticut; born in Newtown, Conn., June 21, 1799; pursued academic studies; studied law at the Litchfield (Conn.) Law School; was admitted to the bar in 1820 and commenced practice in New Haven, Conn., in 1827; moved to Hartford in 1832 and became editor of the New England Review; member of the Connecticut State house of representatives in 1840, 1847, and 1848; United States attorney for the district of Connecticut from 1841 until 1848; unsuccessful candidate for election in 1848 to the Thirty-first Congress; elected as a Whig to the Thirty-second Congress (March 4, 1851-March 3, 1853); unsuccessful candidate for Governor of Connecticut as a Temperance candidate in 1854; elected as a Democrat to the State house of representatives in 1862 and 1864; resumed the practice of law; died in Hartford, Conn., on August 7, 1869; interment in Cedar Hill Cemetery.

**CHAPMAN, Henry,** a Representative from Pennsylvania; born in Newtown, Pa., February 4, 1804; attended Doylestown Academy and Doctor Gummere's private boys' school near Burlington, N.J.; studied law; was admitted to the bar in 1825 and commenced practice in Doylestown; member of the Pennsylvania senate in 1843; judge of the fifteenth judicial district from 1845 until 1849; elected as a Democrat to the Thirty-fifth Congress (March 4, 1857-March 3, 1859); declined to be a candidate for renomination in 1858 to the Thirty-sixth Congress; judge of the Bucks County Court in 1861; retired in 1871; died at "Frosterley," near Doylestown, Bucks County, Pa., April 11, 1891; interment in the graveyard of Doylestown Presbyterian Church.

**CHAPMAN, Jim,** a Representative from Texas; born in Washington, D.C., March 8, 1945; attended public schools in Sulphur Springs, Tex.; B.A., University of Texas, Austin, 1968; J.D., Southern Methodist University School of Law, Dallas, 1970; admitted to the Texas State bar in 1970 and commenced practice in Sulphur Springs, Tex., district attorney, Eighth Judicial District, 1977-1984; elected as a Democrat to the Ninety-ninth Congress, August 3, 1985, by special election to fill the vacancy caused by the resignation of Sam B. Hall, Jr.; reelected to the five succeeding Congresses, and served from August 3, 1985 to January 3, 1997; was not a candidate in 1996 for reelection to the House of Representatives, but was an unsuccessful candidate for nomination to the United States Senate; is a resident of Sulphur Springs, Tex.

**CHAPMAN, John,** a Representative from Pennsylvania; born in Wrightstown Township, Bucks County, Pa., October 18, 1740; commissioned justice of the peace on February 25, 1779, and was one of the justices commissioned judge of the court of common pleas of Bucks County the same year; moved to Upper Makefield, Pa., prior to 1776; member of the Pennsylvania assembly from 1787 until 1796; elected as a Federalist to the Fifth Congress (March 4, 1797-March 3, 1799); died in Upper Makefield, Pa., January 27, 1800; interment in the Friends' Burying Ground, Wrightstown, Pa.

**CHAPMAN, John Grant** (father of Andrew Grant Chapman), a Representative from Maryland; born in La Plata, Charles County, Md., July 5, 1798; was tutored at home; attended a college in Pennsylvania in 1812 and 1813, and was graduated from Yale College in 1817; studied law; was admitted to the bar in 1819 and commenced practice at Port Tobacco, Charles County, Md.; also interested in agricultural pursuits; member of the Maryland State house of delegates from 1824 to 1832, and from 1843 to 1844, serving as speaker 1826-1829, and again in 1844; member, State senate, 1832-1836, serving as president of that body from 1833 to 1836; served in the State militia; unsuccessful candidate for Governor of Maryland in 1844; elected as a Whig to the Twenty-ninth and Thirtieth Congresses (March 4, 1845-March 3, 1849); chairman, Committee on District of Columbia (Thirtieth Congress); resumed the practice of law at Port Tobacco, Md.; president of the State constitutional convention in 1851; died on his sister's estate, "Waverly," on the Wicomico River, Charles County, Md., on December 10, 1856; interment at St. Johns, a family estate; reinterment in Mount Rest Cemetery, La Plata, Md.

**CHAPMAN, Pleasant Thomas,** a Representative from Illinois; born on a farm near Vienna, Johnson County, Ill., October 8, 1854; attended the public schools, and was graduated from McKendree College, Lebanon, Ill., in June 1876; taught school; served as superintendent of public schools of Johnson County from 1877 until 1882; studied law; was admitted to the bar at Mount Vernon, Ill., in 1878 and commenced practice in Vienna, Ill.; also engaged in banking and in agricultural pursuits; judge of Johnson County, 1882-1890; member of the Illinois State senate, 1890-1902; elected as a Republican to the Fifty-ninth and to the two succeeding Congresses (March 4, 1905-March 3, 1911); unsuccessful candidate for reelection in 1910 to the Sixty-second Congress; resumed the practice of law in Vienna, Ill., and also engaged in banking and agricultural pursuits; delegate to the Republican National Convention of 1924; died in Vienna, Ill., January 31, 1931; interment in Fraternal Cemetery.

**CHAPMAN, Reuben,** a Representative from Alabama; born in Bowling Green, Caroline County, Va., July 15, 1799; attended an academy in Virginia; studied law; was admitted to the bar in 1825 and commenced practice in Somerville, Morgan County, Ala.; member of the Alabama State senate, 1832-1835; elected as a Jacksonian to the Twenty-fourth Congress, and as a Democrat to the five succeeding Congresses (March 4, 1835-March 3, 1847); was not a candidate for renomination in 1846 to the Thirtieth Congress, having become a gubernatorial candidate; elected Governor of Alabama in 1847, and served from December 16, 1847 to December 17, 1849; member of the State house of representatives in 1855; delegate to the Democratic Convention at Baltimore in 1860; was a representative of the Confederacy to France from 1862 until 1865; resumed the practice of law; died in Huntsville, Madison County, Ala., May 16, 1882; interment in Maple Hill Cemetery.

**Bibliography:** *DAB.*

**CHAPMAN, Virgil Munday,** a Representative and a Senator from Kentucky; born in Middleton, Simpson County, Ky., on March 15, 1895; attended the public schools of Franklin, Ky.; studied law; was admitted to the bar in 1917; was graduated from the law department of the University of Kentucky at Lexington in 1918, and commenced practice at Irvine, Estill County, Ky., in 1918; city attorney of Irvine, 1918-1920; moved to Paris, Ky., in 1920 and continued the practice of law; assisted in organizing the tobacco growers of Kentucky and nearby States into cooperative marketing associations from 1921 until 1923; elected as a Democrat to the Sixty-ninth and Seventieth Congresses (March 4, 1925-March 3, 1929); unsuccessful candidate for reelection in 1928 to the Seventy-first Congress; elected as a Democrat to the Seventy-second and to the eight succeeding Congresses (March 4, 1931-January 3, 1949); was not a candidate in 1948 for reelection to the House of Representatives, but was elected to the United States Senate and served from January 3, 1949, until his death in the naval hospital at Bethesda, Md., March 8, 1951; interment in Paris Cemetery, Paris, Ky.

**CHAPMAN, William Williams,** a Delegate from the Territory of Iowa; born in Clarksburg, Marion County, Va. (now West Virginia), August 11, 1808; attended the common schools; studied law while serving as clerk of the court; was admitted to the bar and commenced practice in Middleton; was one of the first settlers in Burlington, Iowa (then Michigan Territory), in 1835; prosecuting attorney of Michigan Territory in 1836; first district attorney when Wisconsin Territory was organized in July 1836; after the Territory of Iowa was granted representation he was elected as a Democrat to the Twenty-fifth and Twenty-sixth Congresses, and served from September 10, 1838, to October 27, 1840, when his term expired by law; moved to Agency City, an Indian village, in Wapello County, Iowa, in 1843; elected from that county as a delegate to the first constitutional convention in Iowa City in 1844; started across the plains to become a pioneer of Oregon in 1847; went to California in 1848; returned to Oregon; member of the Oregon territorial house of representatives; was one of the founders of the Oregonian, the first newspaper established in the Territory; surveyor general in 1858; died in Portland, Oreg., on October 18, 1892; interment in the Lone Fir Cemetery.

**Bibliography:** Colton, Kenneth E. "W.W. Chapman, Delegate to Congress from Iowa Territory." *Annals of Iowa* 3rd Series, 21 (April 1938): 283-95.

**CHAPPELL, Absalom Harris** (cousin of Lucius Quintus Cincinnatus Lamar), a Representative from Georgia; born at Mount Zion, Hancock County, Ga., December 18, 1801; attended the local academy at Mount Zion, and was graduated from the law department of the University of Georgia at Athens in 1821; was admitted to the bar the same year and commenced practice in Sandersville, Washington County, Ga.; moved to Forsyth, Ga., in 1824 and practiced; member of the State senate in 1832 and 1833; served in the State house of representatives 1834-1839; moved to Macon, Ga., in 1836 and continued the practice of law; delegate to the Knoxville convention in 1836; promoter of the Monroe Railroad; appointed on the board of commissioners to arrange a State finance system in 1839; elected as a Whig to the Twenty-eighth Congress to fill the vacancy caused by the resignation of Representative-elect John B. Lamar and served from October 2, 1843, to March 3, 1845; was not a candidate for renomination in 1844 to the Twenty-ninth Congress; member of the State senate in 1845, serving as president; resumed the practice of law; moved to Columbus, Ga., in 1857 and continued the practice of law; also engaged in literary pursuits; affiliated with the Democratic Party; delegate to the State constitutional convention in 1865 and again in 1877; also a delegate to the Conservative convention at Macon in 1867; died in Columbus, Muscogee County, Ga., December 11, 1878; interment in Linwood Cemetery.

**Bibliography:** *DAB.*

**CHAPPELL, John Joel,** a Representative from South Carolina, born on Little River, near Columbia, Fairfield District, S.C., where the family was on a visit, January 19, 1782; as an infant was taken by his parents to their home on the Congaree River, Richland District, S.C.; attended the common schools and was graduated from the law department of South Carolina College (now the University of South Carolina) at Columbia; was admitted to the bar in 1805 and commenced practice in Columbia, Richland County, S.C.; appointed adjutant of the Thirty-third South Carolina Regiment in 1805 and elected captain and then colonel of the same regiment in 1808; member of the State house of representatives 1808-1812; appointed trustee of South Carolina College in 1809; served in the War of 1812; elected as a Republican to the Thirteenth and Fourteenth Congresses (March 4, 1813-March 3, 1817); chairman, Committee on Pensions and Revolutionary Claims (Thirteenth and Fourteenth Congresses); resumed the practice of law until 1837; director of the Columbia branch of the State Bank of South Carolina 1830-1858; moved to Lowndes County, Ala., and became a cotton planter; died in Lowndes County, Ala., May 23, 1871; interment in First Baptist Church Cemetery, Columbia, S.C.

**CHAPPELL, William Venroe, Jr.,** a Representative from Florida; born in Kendrick, Marion County, Fla., February 3, 1922; B.A., University of Florida, 1947; LL.B., University of Florida School of Law, 1949, and J.D., 1967; served in the United States Navy, aviator, 1942-1946; retired as a captain from United States Naval Reserve in 1983; Marion County prosecuting attorney, 1950-1954; served in the Florida State house of representatives, 1954-1964, speaker, 1961-1963; did not seek reelection in 1964 but was elected again in 1966; member of the law firm of Chappell and Rowland, Ocala, Fla.; elected as a Democrat to the Ninety-first and to the nine succeeding Congresses (January 3, 1969-January 3, 1989); unsuccessful candidate for reelection in 1988 to the One Hundred First Congress; was a resident of Ocala, Fla.; died March 30, 1989; interment in Kendrick, Fla.

**CHAPPIE, Eugene A.,** a Representative from California; born in Sacramento, Sacramento County, Calif., March 28, 1920; attended the public schools; graduated from Sacramento High School, 1938; served in the United States Army, Armored Force South Pacific Service, captain, 1942-1947; Korea, 1950; rancher; El Dorado County Supervisor, 1950-1964; served in the California State legislature, 1964-1980; delegate, California State Republican conventions, 1968-1972; delegate to the Republican National Conventions of 1968 and 1972; elected as a Republican to the Ninety-seventh and to the two succeeding Congresses (January 3, 1981-January 3, 1987); was not a candidate for reelection in 1986 to the One Hundredth Congress; was a resident of Georgetown, Calif.; died May 31, 1992.

**CHARLES, William Barclay,** a Representative from New York; born in Glasgow, Scotland, April 3, 1861; attended private schools and high schools in Stirling and Glasgow, Scotland; immigrated to the United States in 1884; spent two years ranching in Texas and Mexico; settled in Amsterdam, N.Y., in 1886 and engaged in textile manufacturing; member of the State assembly 1904-1906; director of the Amsterdam First National Bank; elected as a Republican to the Sixty-fourth Congress (March 4, 1915-March 3, 1917); was not a candidate for renomination in 1916; reengaged in the textile business until his retirement; died in Amsterdam, N.Y., November 25, 1950; interment in Green Hill Cemetery.

**CHARLTON, Robert Milledge,** a Senator from Georgia; born in Savannah, Ga., January 19, 1807; studied law; was admitted to the bar and commenced practice in Savannah; member, State house of representatives; United States district attorney; elected a judge of the superior court in 1832; appointed as a Democrat to the United States Senate to fill the vacancy caused by the resignation of John Macpherson Berrien and served from May 31, 1852, to March 3, 1853; mayor of Savannah; died in Savannah, Chatham County, Ga., January 18, 1854; interment in Laurel Grove Cemetery.

**CHASE, Dudley** (uncle of Salmon Portland Chase and Dudley Chase Denison), a Senator from Vermont; born in Cornish, N.H., December 30, 1771; attended the common schools, and was graduated from Dartmouth College, Hanover, N.H., in 1791; studied law; was admitted to the bar in 1793 and practiced in Randolph, Vt.; prosecuting attorney for Orange County 1803-1812; member, State house of representatives 1805-1812, and served as speaker 1808-1812; delegate to the State constitutional conventions in 1814 and 1822; elected as a Jeffersonian Democrat to the United States Senate and served from March 4, 1813, to November 3, 1817, when he resigned; chairman, Committee on Judiciary (Fourteenth Congress); chief justice of the supreme court of Vermont 1817-1821; member, State house of representatives 1823-1824; elected as a Republican to the United States Senate and served from March 4, 1825, to March 3, 1831; engaged in agricultural pursuits; died in Randolph Center, Vt., February 23, 1846; interment in Randolph Cemetery.

**CHASE, George William,** a Representative from New York; born in the town of Maryland, Otsego County, N.Y.; attended the common schools; engaged in agricultural pursuits; also engaged in mercantile and milling pursuits at Schenevus, Otsego County, N.Y.; elected as a Whig to the Thirty-third Congress (March 4, 1853-March 3, 1855); resumed his former agricultural and business pursuits; died in Chaseville, Maryland Township, N.Y., April 17, 1867; interment in the Chase vault in Schenevus Cemetery, Schenevus, N.Y.

**CHASE, Jackson Burton,** a Representative from Nebraska; born in Seward, Nebr., August 19, 1890; in early life lived in California and Illinois; worked for the Burlington Railroad; graduated from high school in Omaha, Nebr., in 1907; employed by John Deere Plow Co., 1907-1910; attended the University of Nebraska 1910-1912; LL.B., University of Michigan Law School, 1913; was admitted to the bar the same year and commenced practice in Chicago, Ill.; during the First World War served with the Field Artillery, United States Army; assistant attorney general of Nebraska in 1921 and 1922; engaged in the practice of law in Omaha, Nebr., 1923-1942; legal adviser to Omaha Welfare Board in 1930 and 1931; member of the State house of representatives in 1933 and 1934; owner and manager of farmland in Nebraska and Iowa; served as a major, Judge Advocate General's Department, 1942-1945; chairman of Nebraska Liquor Control Commission in 1945 and 1946; judge of the fourth judicial district court of Nebraska, 1946-1954; elected as a Republican to the Eighty-fourth Congress (January 3, 1955-January 3, 1957); was not a candidate for renomination in 1956 to the Eighty-fifth Congress; again elected judge of the fourth judicial district court of Nebraska 1956-1960; died in Atlanta, Ga., May 4, 1974; interment in Hillcrest Cemetery, Omaha, Nebr.

**CHASE, James Mitchell,** a Representative from Pennsylvania; born in Glen Richey, Clearfield County, Pa., December 19, 1891; attended the public schools, the high school at Clearfield, Pa., and was graduated from the law department of Dickinson College, Carlisle, Pa., in 1916; was admitted to the bar in 1919 and commenced practice in Clearfield, Pa.; enlisted in the Air Service and served with the American Expeditionary Forces 1917-1919; commander of the American Legion, Department of Pennsylvania, in 1924 and 1925; elected as a Republican to the Seventieth, Seventy-first, and Seventy-second Congresses (March 4, 1927-March 3, 1933); unsuccessful candidate for renomination in 1932; resumed the practice of law; died in Clearfield, Pa., January 1, 1945; interment in Hillcrest Cemetery.

**CHASE, Jeremiah Townley,** a Delegate from Maryland; born in Baltimore, Md., May 23, 1748; was a member of the committees of observation and correspondence in 1774; delegate to the Maryland constitutional convention of 1776; moved to Annapolis in 1779;

member of the Governor's council 1780-1784 and 1786-1788; mayor of Annapolis in 1783; Member of the Continental Congress in 1783 and 1784; an Anti-Federalist member of the convention of ratification of the United States Constitution in 1788; judge of the general court in 1789, and chief justice of the court of appeals until his resignation in 1824; died in Annapolis, Md., May 11, 1828; interment in the City Cemetery.

**CHASE, Lucien Bonaparte,** a Representative from Tennessee; born in Derby Line, Vt., December 5, 1817; moved to Dover, Tenn., about 1838 and taught school; studied law; was admitted to the bar and commenced practice in Charlotte, Dickson County, Tenn.; moved to Clarksville, Tenn., and resumed the practice of law; elected as a Democrat to the Twenty-ninth and Thirtieth Congresses (March 4, 1845-March 3, 1849); declined to be a candidate for reelection in 1848; moved to New York City in 1849; resumed the practice of law; died in Derby Line, Orleans County, Vt., December 4, 1864; interment in Greenwood Cemetery, Brooklyn, N.Y.

**CHASE, Ray P.,** a Representative from Minnesota; born in Anoka County, Minn., March 12, 1880; attended the public schools; was graduated from the University of Minnesota at Minneapolis in 1903; attended the law department of the University of Minnesota in 1904, 1905, 1915, and 1916; engaged in the publishing and printing business at Anoka, Minn., 1904-1914; municipal judge of Anoka, Minn., 1911-1916; deputy State auditor and land commissioner of Minnesota 1916-1920; was graduated from the St. Paul (Minn.) College of Law in 1919; was admitted to the bar the same year, but did not practice; State auditor and land commissioner of Minnesota 1921-1931; unsuccessful candidate in 1930 for election for Governor of Minnesota; elected as a Republican to the Seventy-third Congress (March 4, 1933-January 3, 1935); unsuccessful candidate for renomination in 1934 to the Seventy-fourth Congress; practiced law, specializing in legal research, 1935-1943; member of the Minnesota Railroad and Warehouse Commission 1944-1948; died in Anoka, Minn., on September 18, 1948; interment in Forest Hill Cemetery.

**CHASE, Salmon Portland** (nephew of Dudley Chase and cousin of Dudley Chase Denison), a Senator from Ohio; born in Cornish, N.H., January 13, 1808; attended schools at Windsor, N.H., Worthington, Ohio, and the Cincinnati (Ohio) College; was graduated from Dartmouth College, Hanover, N.H., in 1826; taught school; studied law in Washington, D.C.; was admitted to the bar in 1829; commenced practice in Cincinnati, Ohio, in 1830; elected as a Whig to the Cincinnati City Council in 1840; identified himself in 1841 with the Liberty Party, and later with the Free-Soil Party; elected to the United States Senate as a Free-Soil candidate and served from March 4, 1849, to March 3, 1855; elected Governor of Ohio in 1855 as a Free-Soil Democrat, reelected in 1857 as a Republican, and served from January 14, 1856 to January 9, 1860; elected as a Republican to the United States Senate in 1860; took his seat March 4, 1861, but resigned two days later to become Secretary of the Treasury under President Abraham Lincoln; served as Secretary of the Treasury until June 3, 1864, when he resigned; member of the peace convention of 1861 held in Washington, D.C., in an effort to devise means to prevent the impending war; nominated by President Lincoln as Chief Justice of the United States on December 6, 1864; was confirmed by the Senate the same day and served until his death; presided at the impeachment trial of President Andrew Johnson in 1868; died in New York City on May 7, 1873; interment in Oak Hill Cemetery, Washington, D.C.; reinterment in Spring Grove Cemetery, Cincinnati, Ohio.

**Bibliography:** *DAB;* Blue, Frederick J. *Salmon P. Chase: A Life in Politics.* Kent, Ohio: Kent State University Press, 1987; Chase, Salmon P. *The Salmon P. Chase Papers.* Volume 1: *Journals, 1829-1872;* Volume 2: *Correspondence, 1823-1857.* Edited by John Niven, James P. McClure and Patrick Delana. Kent, Ohio: Kent

State University Press, 1993- ; Niven, John. *Salmon P. Chase: A Biography.* New York: Oxford University Press, 1995.

**CHASE, Samuel,** a Delegate from Maryland; born in Princess Anne, Somerset County, Md., April 17, 1741; was tutored privately and pursued an academic course; studied law; was admitted to the bar in 1761 and commenced practice in Annapolis, Md.; member of the General Assembly of Maryland 1764-1784; Member of the Continental Congress 1774-1778; sent on a special mission to Canada in 1776 to induce the Canadians to join in the revolution against Great Britain; a signer of the Declaration of Independence; went to England in 1783 as agent for the State of Maryland to recover the stock in the Bank of England which had been purchased when the State was a colony of Great Britain; moved to Baltimore, Md., in 1786; judge of the Baltimore criminal court in 1788; appointed judge of the general court of Maryland in 1791; nominated by President Washington as an Associate Justice of the United States Supreme Court on January 26, 1796, and was confirmed by the Senate the following day; articles of impeachment were filed against him in 1804 on charges of malfeasance in office because of his conduct, five years earlier during the trials of John Fries and James T. Callender for sedition, and for a more recent address to a Maryland grand jury; tried by the Senate, he was acquitted of all charges on March 1, 1805; resumed his seat on the bench, and retained it until his death in Washington, D.C., on June 19, 1811; interment in Old St. Paul's Cemetery, Baltimore, Md.

**Bibliography:** *DAB.*

**CHASE, Samuel,** a Representative from New York; born in Cooperstown, N.Y.; district attorney of Otsego County 1821-1829; elected to the Twentieth Congress (March 4, 1827-March 3, 1829); died in Richfield, Otsego County, N.Y., August 3, 1838.

**CHASTAIN, Elijah Webb,** a Representative from Georgia; born near Pickens, Pickens County, S.C., September 25, 1813; moved with his parents to Habersham, Ga., in 1821; attended the common schools; served as captain and colonel in the Seminole Indian War; located on a farm in Union County, Ga.; served in the State senate 1840-1850; studied law; was admitted to the bar in 1849 and practiced in Blairsville, Union County, Ga.; elected as a Unionist to the Thirty-second Congress and as a Democrat to the Thirty-third Congress (March 4, 1851-March 3, 1855); chairman, Committee on Militia (Thirty-third Congress); delegate to the secession convention at Milledgeville, Ga., in 1860; during the Civil War served in the Confederate Army as lieutenant colonel of the First Georgia Regiment; State's attorney for the Western & Atlantic Railroad in 1860 and 1861; died near Dalton, Murray County, Ga., April 9, 1874; interment in the family cemetery near Morganton, Fannin County, Ga.

**CHATHAM, Richard Thurmond,** a Representative from North Carolina; born in Elkin, Surry County, N.C., August 16, 1896; educated in the public schools; attended the University of North Carolina at Chapel Hill in 1915 and 1916 and Yale University in 1916 and 1917; served in the United States Navy from May 1917 until discharged as an ensign in June 1919; in July 1919 started working in the textile mills of Chatham Manufacturing Co. at Winston-Salem, N.C., and retired in 1955 as chairman of the board of directors; also owned and operated a farm near Elkin, N.C.; member of the Woolen Wage and Hour Board, Washington, D.C., in 1939; served as a member of the State Board of Conservation and Development and as county commissioner of Forsyth County; served in the Navy from February 14, 1942, to November 25, 1945, with combat duty in the Southwest Pacific; unsuccessful candidate for the Democratic nomination in 1946 to the Eightieth Congress; elected as a Democrat to the Eighty-first and to the three succeeding Congresses (January 3, 1949-January 3, 1957); unsuccessful candidate for renomination in 1956; died in Durham, N.C., February 5, 1957; interment in Salem Cemetery, Winston-Salem, N.C.

**Bibliography:** Christian, Ralph J. "The Folger-Chatham Congressional Primary of 1946." *The North Carolina Historical Review* 53 (Winter 1976): 25-53.

**CHAVES, Jose Francisco,** a Delegate from the Territory of New Mexico; born in Los Padillas, Mexico (now New Mexico), June 27, 1833; attended schools in St. Louis, Mo., New York City, and Fishkill, N.Y.; studied medicine at the New York College of Physicians and Surgeons; returned to New Mexico in 1852 and engaged in the stock-raising business; major of the First New Mexico Infantry in the Union Army during the Civil War; promoted to the rank of lieutenant colonel; took part in the Battle of Valverde, N.Mex., February 21, 1862; elected as a Republican to the Thirty-ninth Congress (March 4, 1865-March 3, 1867); successfully contested the election of Charles P. Clever to the Fortieth Congress; reelected to the Forty-first Congress, and served from February 20, 1869 to March 3, 1871; unsuccessful candidate for reelection in 1870 to the Forty-second Congress; engaged in farming and stock raising; district attorney of the second judicial district, 1875-1877; elected a member of the Territorial council from Valencia County in 1875 and served until his death; member and president of the State constitutional convention in 1889; State superintendent of public instruction from March 1901 until his death; appointed State historian of New Mexico in 1903, but died before his term of service began; assassinated at the home of Juan Dios de Salas in Pinos Wells, Valencia County, N.Mex., November 26, 1904; interment in the United States National Cemetery, Santa Fe, N.Mex.

**Bibliography:** Duran, Tobias. "Francisco Chaves, Thomas B. Catron, and Organized Political Violence in Santa Fe in the 1890s." *New Mexico Historical Review* 59 (July 1984): 291-310.

**CHAVEZ, Dennis,** a Representative and a Senator from New Mexico; born in Los Chavez, Valencia County, N.Mex., April 8, 1888; attended the public schools; worked as a grocer's clerk as a boy and later in the engineering department of the city of Albuquerque; travelled to Washington in 1917 with Senator Andrieus A. Jones, and served as clerk in the office of the Secretary of the United States Senate, 1917-1920; was graduated from the law department of Georgetown University, Washington, D.C., in 1920; was admitted to the bar in 1920 and commenced practice in Albuquerque, N.Mex.; member, New Mexico State house of representatives, 1923-1924; elected as a Democrat to the Seventy-second and Seventy-third Congresses (March 4, 1931-January 3, 1935); chairman, Committee on Irrigation and Reclamation (Seventy-third Congress); was not a candidate in 1934 for renomination to the House of Representatives, but was an unsuccessful candidate for United States Senator; appointed as a Democrat on May 11, 1935, and elected on November 3, 1936, to the United States Senate to fill the vacancy caused by the death of Bronson M. Cutting; reelected in 1940, 1946, 1952, and again in 1958, and served from May 11, 1935 until his death in Washington, D.C., November 18, 1962; chairman, Committee on Post Office and Post Roads (Seventy-ninth Congress), Committee on Public Works (Eighty-first through Eighty-seventh Congresses); interment in Mount Calvary Cemetery, Albuquerque, N.Mex.

**Bibliography:** *DAB*; Crouch, Barry. "Dennis Chavez and Roosevelt's 'Court-Packing Plan.'" *New Mexico Historical Review* 42 (October 1967): 261-280; Lujan, Joe Roy. "Dennis Chavez and the Roosevelt Era, 1933-1945." Ph.D. dissertation, University of New Mexico, 1987; Pickens, William H. "Bronson Cutting vs. Dennis Chavez: Battle of the Patrones in New Mexico, 1934." *New Mexico Historical Review* 46 (January 1971): 5-36.

**CHEADLE, Joseph Bonaparte,** a Representative from Indiana; born in Perrysville, Vermillion County, Ind., August 14, 1842; attended the common schools; entered Asbury (now De Pauw) University, Greencastle, Ind., but upon the organization of the Seventy-first Regiment, Indiana Volunteer Infantry, enlisted as a private in Company K and served until the close of the Civil War; returned home and entered upon the study of law; was graduated from the Indianapolis Law College in 1867; was admitted to the bar and commenced practice in Newport, Ind.; continued in practice until 1873, when he entered upon newspaper work; elected as a Republican to the Fiftieth and Fifty-first Congresses (March 4, 1887-March 3, 1891); unsuccessful candidate for renomination in 1890 to the Fifty-second Congress; unsuccessful candidate for nomination in 1892 to the Fifty-third Congress, and in 1894 to the Fifty-fourth Congress; affiliated with the Democratic Party in 1896; unsuccessful Democratic and Populist candidate for election in 1896 to the Fifty-fifth Congress; unsuccessful Democratic candidate for election in 1898 to the Fifty-sixth Congress; editor of the American Standard in 1896; died in Frankfort, Clinton County, Ind., May 28, 1904; interment in Greenlawn Cemetery.

**CHEATHAM, Henry Plummer,** a Representative from North Carolina; born into slavery near Henderson, Granville (now Vance) County, N.C., December 27, 1857; attended the public schools and the normal school of Shaw University, Raleigh, N.C., 1875-1878; A.B., Shaw University, 1882; principal in 1883 and 1884 of the State normal school for black students at Plymouth, N.C.; moved to Henderson, N.C., and served as register of deeds of Vance County, 1884-1888; studied law but did not practice; one of the founders, incoporators, and directors of the North Carolina Colored Orphanage at Oxford in 1887; delegate to the State convention at Raleigh in 1892; delegate to the Republican National Conventions of 1892 and 1900; elected as a Republican to the Fifty-first and Fifty-second Congresses (March 4, 1889-March 3, 1893); unsuccessful candidate for reelection in 1892 to the Fifty-third Congress, and for election in 1894 to the Fifty-fourth Congress; appointed by President William McKinley as recorder of deeds of the District of Columbia, 1897-1901; moved to Oxford, N.C., in 1907; president of the Negro Association of North Carolina; also engaged in agricultural pursuits and lecturing; superintendent of the North Carolina Colored Orphanage from 1907 until his death in Oxford, N.C., November 29, 1935; interment in Harrisburg Cemetery.

**Bibliography:** Reid, George W. "Four in Black: North Carolina's Black Congressmen, 1874-1901." *Journal of Negro History* 64 (Summer 1979): 229-243.

**CHEATHAM, Richard,** a Representative from Tennessee; born in Springfield, Robertson County, Tenn., February 20, 1799; pursued preparatory studies; engaged in mercantile pursuits, stock raising, and operation of a cotton gin; member of the State house of representatives in 1833; member of the State constitutional convention which met at Nashville from May 19 To August 30, 1834; served as general in the State militia; unsuccessful candidate for election to the Twenty-second, Twenty-third, and Twenty-fourth Congresses; elected as a Whig to the Twenty-fifth Congress (March 4, 1837-March 3, 1839); unsuccessful candidate for reelection to the Twenty-sixth and Twenty-seventh Congresses; resumed his former pursuits; died while visiting at White's Creek Springs, near Springfield, Tenn., September 9, 1845; interment in Old City Cemetery.

**CHELF, Frank Leslie,** a Representative from Kentucky; born on a farm near Elizabethtown, Hardin County, Ky., September 22, 1907; attended the public schools, Centre College at Danville, Ky., and St. Mary's (Ky.) College; was graduated from the law school of Cumberland University, Lebanon, Tenn., in 1931; was admitted to the bar in 1931 and commenced practice in Lebanon, Ky.; attorney of Marion County, Ky., 1933-1944; took leave of absence from his official duties on August 1, 1942, to volunteer in the United States Army; commissioned a first lieutenant in the Air Corps and saw active service; served as chief code designator, Intelligence Division, Air Transport Command, and later as executive officer, Plans and Liaison Division, and as assistant chief of Air Staff Training; discharged on August 10, 1944, due to physical disability, with rank of major in the Air Corps; delegate to the Democratic National Convention in 1936; elected as a Democrat to the Seventy-ninth and to the ten succeeding Congresses (January 3, 1945-January 3, 1967); unsuccessful candidate for reelection in 1966 to the Ninetieth Congress; resumed the practice of law; legislative consultant; resident of Lebanon, Ky., until his death there on September 1, 1982; interment at Ryder Cemetery.

**Bibliography:** Baird, Nancy Disher. "'To Hear Their Beefs and Squaks': A Kentucky Congressman Visits Postwar Europe." *Filson Club History Quarterly* 68 (October 1994): 445-464.

**CHENEY, Person Colby,** a Senator from New Hampshire; born in Holderness (now Ashland), N.H., February 25, 1828; attended academies in Peterborough and Hancock, N.H., and in Parsonfield, Maine; engaged in the manufacture of paper in Peterborough until 1866; member of the New Hampshire State house of representatives in 1854; during the Civil War was first lieutenant and regimental quartermaster in the Thirteenth Regiment, New Hampshire Volunteer Infantry, 1862-1863; State railroad commissioner, 1864-1867; moved to Manchester, N.H., in 1867 and engaged in business as a dealer in paper stock and continued the manufacture of paper at Goffstown, N.H.; also engaged in agricultural pursuits; elected mayor of Manchester in 1871; elected Governor of New Hampshire in 1875, reelected in 1876, and served from June 10, 1875 to June 6, 1877; appointed as a Republican to the United States Senate to fill the vacancy caused by the death of Austin F. Pike and served from November 24, 1886, to June 14, 1887, when a successor was elected and qualified; was not a candidate for election to fill the vacancy; resumed his former manufacturing pursuits; appointed Envoy Extraordinary and Minister Plenipotentiary to Switzerland on December 13, 1892 and served until January 1893; died in Dover, Strafford County, N.H., on June 19, 1901; interment in Pine Grove Cemetery, Manchester, N.H.

**Bibliography:** *DAB*.

**CHENEY, Richard Bruce,** a Representative from Wyoming; born in Lincoln, Lancaster County, Nebr., January 30, 1941; attended public schools in Lincoln and Casper, Wyo.; attended Yale University, 1959-1960, and Casper College, Casper, Wyo., 1963; B.A., University of Wyoming, Laramie, 1965, and M.A., 1966; Ph.D. candidate, University of Wisconsin, Madison, 1968; congressional fellow, 1968-1969; special assistant to the Director of the Office of Economic Opportunity, 1969-1970; White House staff assistant, 1971; assistant director, Cost of Living Council, 1971-1973; vice president, Bradley, Woods and Co., 1973-1974; Deputy Assistant to President Gerald R. Ford, 1974-1975; Assistant to the President and White House Chief of Staff, 1975-1977; elected as a Republican to the Ninety-sixth and to the five succeeding Congresses, and served from January 3, 1979 until his resignation on March 17, 1989; Secretary of Defense in the Cabinet of President George Bush from March 21, 1989 to January 20, 1993; president and chief executive officer, Halliburton Company, 1995-1996, and chairman of the board since January 2, 1996; is a resident of Dallas, Tex.

**CHENOWETH, Helen P.,** a Representative from Idaho; born in Topeka, Kans., January 27, 1938; graduated, Grants Pass (Oreg.) High School; attended Whitworth College, Spokane, Wash., 1955-1958; self-employed medical and legal office manager, 1964-1975; manager, Northside Medical Center, Orofino, Idaho; state executive director, Idaho State Republican Party, 1975-1977; chief of staff then campaign manager to Representative Steven D. Symms of Idaho; founding partner and vice president, Consulting Associates, Inc.; guest lecturer at University of Idaho Law School; elected as a Republican to the One Hundred Fourth Congress (January 3, 1995-January 3, 1997); is a resident of Boise, Idaho.

**CHENOWETH, John Edgar,** a Representative from Colorado; born in Trinidad, Las Animas County, Colo., August 17, 1897; attended the public and high schools, and the University of Colorado at Boulder; engaged in railroading and in the mercantile business from 1916 until 1925; studied law; was admitted to the bar in 1925 and commenced practice in Trinidad in 1926; assistant district attorney for the third judicial district, 1929-1933; county judge of Las Animas County, Colo., 1933-1941; member, Advisory Board of Colorado Women's College (now Temple Buell); elected as a Republican to the Seventy-seventh and to the three succeeding Congresses (January 3, 1941-January 3, 1949); unsuccessful candidate for reelection in 1948 to the Eighty-first Congress; elected to the Eighty-second and to the six succeeding Congresses (January 3, 1951-January 3, 1965); unsuccessful candidate for reelection in 1964 to the Eighty-ninth Congress; resumed the practice of law; was a resident of Trinidad, Colo., until his death there on January 2, 1986; interment in Odd Fellows Cemetery.

**Bibliography:** Mehls, Carol J. "Into the Frying Pan: J. Edgar Chenoweth and the Frying Pan-Arkansas Reclamation Project." Ph.D. dissertation, University of Colorado at Boulder, 1986.

**CHESNEY, Chester Anton,** a Representative from Illinois; born in Chicago, Cook County, Ill., March 9, 1916; attended St. Hyacinth and Lane Technical High School; was graduated from the De Paul University, Chicago, Ill., in 1938; played professional football with the Chicago Bears in 1939 and 1940; entered the United States Air Force in June 1941 as a private and was discharged as a major in 1946 with service in the Pacific and European Theaters; assistant chief of special service, Veterans Administration, Hines, Ill., in 1946 and 1947; engaged in graduate work at Northwestern University Graduate Commerce School in 1947; executive with Montgomery Ward and Company in 1948 and 1949; elected as a Democrat to the Eighty-first Congress (January 3, 1949-January 3, 1951); unsuccessful candidate for reelection in 1950 to the Eighty-second Congress; delegate to the 1968 Democratic National Convention; vice-president and director of Avondale Savings & Loan Association; was a resident of Marco Island, Fla., until his death there September 20, 1986; interment in St. Adalbert Cemetery, Niles, Ill.

**CHESNUT, James, Jr.,** a Senator from South Carolina; born near Camden, S.C., January 18, 1815; was graduated from the law department of the College of New Jersey (now Princeton University) in 1837; was admitted to the bar the same year and commenced practice in Camden, S.C.; member, South Carolina State house of representatives, 1842-1854; delegate to the southern convention at Nashville in 1850; served in the State senate, 1854-1858; elected as a Democrat to the United States Senate to fill the vacancy caused by the death of Josiah J. Evans, and served from December 3, 1858 until November 10, 1860, when he withdrew with other secessionist Senators; expelled from the Senate by a resolution of July 11, 1861, for support of the Confederacy; delegate to the Confederate Provisional Congress in 1861; during the Civil War served as colonel in the Confederate Army; appointed brigadier general on April 23, 1864, and was placed in command of the reserve forces of South Carolina; resumed the practice of law in Camden, Kershaw County, S.C., and died there on February 1, 1885; interment in Knights Hill Cemetery, near Camden, S.C.

**Bibliography:** *DAB*; Chesnut, Mary B. *Mary Chesnut's Civil War.* Edited by C. Vann Woodward. New Haven: Yale University Press, 1981.

**CHETWOOD, William,** a Representative from New Jersey; born in Elizabeth, N.J., June 17, 1771; was graduated from Princeton College in 1792; studied law; was admitted to the bar in 1796 and commenced practice in Elizabeth, N.J.; served as prosecutor of the pleas for Essex County; member of the State Council of New Jersey; was a major of militia and served in the

Whiskey Rebellion of 1794 as aide-de-camp to Major General Henry Lee; elected as a Whig to the Twenty-fourth Congress to fill the vacancy caused by the resignation of Philemon Dickerson and served from December 5, 1836, to March 3, 1837; resumed the practice of law; died in Elizabeth, N.J., December 17, 1857; interment in Evergreen Cemetery.

**CHEVES, Langdon,** a Representative from South Carolina; born September 17, 1776, in Bulltown Fort, near Rocky River, Ninety-sixth District (now Abbeville County), S.C., where the settlers had taken refuge from the onslaught of the Cherokee Indians; received his early education at his home and Andrew Weed's School near Abbeville, S.C.; joined his father in Charleston, S.C., in 1786 and continued his schooling in that city; studied law; was admitted to the bar October 14, 1797, and commenced practice in Charleston; city alderman in 1802; member of the State house of representatives 1802-1804 and 1806-1808; elected attorney general of the State in 1808; elected as a Republican to the Eleventh Congress to fill the vacancy caused by the resignation of Robert Marion, having previously been elected to the Twelfth Congress; reelected to the Thirteenth Congress, and served from December 31, 1810, to March 3, 1815; succeeded Henry Clay as Speaker of the House of Representatives on January 19, 1814, during the second session of the Thirteenth Congress; chairman, Committee on Ways and Means (Twelfth Congress), Committee on the Naval Establishment (Twelfth Congress); declined to be a candidate for reelection in 1814 to the Fourteenth Congress, and also the position of Secretary of the Treasury tendered by President James Madison; resumed the practice of law; elected associate justice of law and appeal in December 1816; resigned in 1819; declined to accept an appointment as Associate Justice of the Supreme Court of the United States; elected president of the Second Bank of the United States March 6, 1819, and held this office until 1822, when he resigned; chief commissioner of claims under the Treaty of Ghent; resided in Philadelphia, Pa. and Washington, D.C., 1819-1826, and in Lancaster, Pa., 1826-1829; returned to South Carolina in 1829; engaged extensively in the cultivation of rice in South Carolina and Georgia; tendered an appointment by Governor Whitmarsh B. Seabrook to the United States Senate to fill the vacancy caused by the death of John C. Calhoun, but declined; delegate to the Southern convention at Nashville, Tenn., in 1850 and to the State convention at Columbia, S.C., in 1852; died in Columbia, S.C., June 26, 1857; interment in Magnolia Cemetery, Charleston, S.C.

Bibliography: *DAB*; Huff, Archie Vernon. *Langdon Cheves of South Carolina.* Tricentennial Studies, No. 11. Columbia: University of South Carolina Press, 1977; Wright, David McCord. "Langdon Cheves and Nicholas Biddle: New Data for a New Interpretation." *Journal of Economic History* 13 (Summer 1953): 305-19.

**CHICKERING, Charles Addison,** a Representative from New York; born in Harrisburg, Lewis County, N.Y., November 26, 1843; attended the common schools and Lowville Academy and was for some time a teacher in that institution; engaged in business as a hardware merchant; served as school commissioner of Lewis County 1865-1875; member of the New York assembly 1879-1881 and as clerk of the assembly 1884-1890; served as chairman of the Lewis County Republican committee; member of the Republican State committee, serving as secretary, and as a member of its executive committee; elected as a Republican to the Fifty-third and to the three succeeding Congresses and served from March 4, 1893, until his accidental death from injuries received in a fall from a window of the Grand Union Hotel in New York City while on a business trip February 13, 1900; chairman, Committee on Railways and Canals (Fifty-fourth through Fifty-sixth Congresses); interment in Riverside Cemetery, Copenhagen, Lewis County, N.Y.

**CHILCOTT, George Miles,** a Delegate from the Territory of Colorado and a Senator from Colorado; born near Cassville, Huntingdon County, Pa., January 2, 1828; moved with his parents to Jefferson County, Iowa, in 1844; studied medicine until 1850; sheriff of Jefferson County in 1853; moved to the Territory of Nebraska in 1856; member, Territorial house of representatives 1856; moved to the Territory of Colorado in 1859; member, Territorial council 1861-1862; studied law; was admitted to the bar in 1863; register of the United States land office 1863-1867; elected as a Republican Delegate to the Fortieth Congress (March 4, 1867-March 3, 1869); member, Territorial council 1872-1874; member, State house of representatives 1878; appointed to the United States Senate to fill the vacancy caused by the resignation of Henry M. Teller and served from April 17, 1882, to January 27, 1883; died in St. Louis, Mo., March 6, 1891; interment in Masonic Cemetery, Pueblo, Colo.

**CHILD, Thomas, Jr.,** a Representative from New York; born in Bakersfield, near St. Albans, Vt., March 22, 1818; attended the common schools and entered the University of Vermont at Burlington at the age of fourteen; member of the State constitutional convention in 1838; studied law; was admitted to the bar in September 1839 and commenced practice in East Berkshire, Vt.; justice of the peace in 1840; moved to New York City about 1848 and engaged in the distilling business; elected as a Whig to the Thirty-fourth Congress on March 4, 1855, but never qualified or attended a session owing to illness; by resolution adopted on March 3, 1857, the House resolved that his salary be computed and paid to him from August 18, 1856, to March 3, 1857, as "though he had been in regular attendance at the sittings of the House"; moved to Port Richmond, Staten Island, N.Y., in 1857 and retired from active business; supervisor of the town of Northfield, N.Y., in 1865 and 1866; member of the State assembly in 1866; died in Port Richmond, Staten Island, N.Y., March 9, 1869; interment in Greenwood Cemetery, Brooklyn, N.Y.

**CHILDS, Robert Andrew,** a Representative from Illinois; born in Malone, Franklin County, N.Y., March 22, 1845; moved to Illinois with his parents, who settled near Belvidere, Boone County, in 1852; attended the common schools; during the Civil War enlisted in General Stephen A. Hurlbut's company, which subsequently became a part of the Fifteenth Regiment, Illinois Volunteer Infantry, and served throughout the war; graduated from the Illinois State Normal University in 1870; principal and superintendent of the public schools in Amboy from 1871 until 1873; studied law; was admitted to the bar in 1872 and commenced practice in Belvidere, Ill.; settled in Hinsdale, a suburb of Chicago, in July 1873; member of the village board of trustees and president of the school board; elected as a Republican to the Fifty-third Congress (March 4, 1893-March 3, 1895); was not a candidate for renomination in 1894 to the Fifty-fourth Congress; resumed the practice of law in Chicago; died in Hinsdale, Ill., December 19, 1915; interment in Bronswood Cemetery.

**CHILDS, Timothy,** a Representative from New York; born in Pittsfield, Mass., in 1785; moved to Rochester, N.Y.; was graduated from Williams College, Williamstown, Mass., in 1811; studied law; was admitted to the bar and practiced in Rochester, N.Y.; prosecuting attorney of Monroe County 1821-1831; member of the State assembly in 1828 and again in 1833; elected as an Anti-Masonic candidate to the Twenty-first Congress (March 4, 1829-March 3, 1831); resumed the practice of law; elected as a Whig to the Twenty-fourth and Twenty-fifth Congresses (March 4, 1835-March 3, 1839); chairman, Committee on Expenditures in the Post Office Department (Twenty-fifth Congress); elected to the Twenty-seventh Congress (March 4, 1841-March 3, 1843); died in Santa Cruz, N.Mex., November 8, 1847.

**CHILES, Lawton Mainor, Jr.,** a Senator from Florida; born in Lakeland, Polk County, Fla., April 3, 1930; attended the Lakeland public schools; B.S., University of Florida, Gainesville, 1952; LL.B., University of Florida School of Law, 1955; served in the United States Army as artillery officer during the Korean Conflict, 1953-1954; admitted to the Florida bar in 1955 and commenced practice in Lakeland; member, Florida State house of representatives, 1958-1966; member, Florida State senate, 1966-1970; businessman, banker, and industrial developer; chairman, Florida Law Revision Commission, 1968-1970; elected as a Democrat to the United States Senate in 1970; reelected in 1976 and again in 1982, and served from January 3, 1971 to January 3, 1989; chairman, Special Committee on Aging (Ninety-Sixth Congress), Committee on the Budget (One Hundredth Congress); was not a candidate for reelection in 1988; elected Governor of Florida in 1990, reelected in 1994, and served from January 8, 1991 to present; is a resident of Tallahassee, Fla.

**CHILTON, Horace** (grandson of Thomas Chilton), a Senator from Texas; born near Tyler, Smith County, Tex., December 29, 1853; received private instruction; attended the local schools in Texas and Lynnland Institute, Glendale, Ky.; learned the printing business and published a tri-weekly newspaper in Tyler; studied law; was admitted to the bar in 1872 and commenced practice in Tyler, Tex.; appointed assistant attorney general of Texas 1881-1883; appointed as a Democrat to the United States Senate to fill the vacancy caused by the resignation of John H. Reagan and served from June 10, 1891, to March 22, 1892, when a successor was elected; unsuccessful candidate for election to this vacancy; elected as a Democrat to the United States Senate in 1894 and served from March 4, 1895, to March 3, 1901; withdrew as a candidate for reelection; resumed the practice of law in Tyler and Beaumont, Tex.; moved to Dallas, Tex., in 1906 and continued the practice of law; died in Dallas, Tex., June 12, 1932; interment in Oakwood Cemetery, Tyler, Tex.

**CHILTON, Samuel,** a Representative from Virginia; born near Warrenton, Fauquier County, Va., September 7, 1804; moved to Missouri with his parents; attended private school; studied law; was admitted to the bar in 1826 and practiced in Warrenton; elected as a Whig to the Twenty-eighth Congress (March 4, 1843-March 3, 1845); resumed the practice of law in Warrenton, Va., and in Washington, D.C.; delegate to the Virginia constitutional convention of 1850-1851; appointed to defend John Brown at Harpers Ferry, but was dismissed by his client because he advocated that the defendant advance a plea of insanity as his defense; died in Warrenton, Va., January 14, 1867; interment in Warrenton Cemetery.

**CHILTON, Thomas** (grandfather of Horace Chilton), a Representative from Kentucky; born near Lancaster, Garrard County, Ky., July 30, 1798; attended the common schools in Paris, Ky.; studied law; was admitted to the bar and commenced practice in Owingsville, Bath County, Ky.; member of the Kentucky house of representatives in 1819; moved to Elizabethtown, Ky.; was a candidate for election to the Twentieth Congress to fill the vacancy caused by the death of William S. Young, but owing to an irregularity the votes of one county were eliminated and the credentials were issued to his opponent, John Calhoon; subsequently both candidates renounced all claim to the seat and petitioned the Governor for a new election; was duly elected to fill the resulting vacancy; reelected to the Twenty-first Congress and served from December 22, 1827, to March 3, 1831; unsuccessful candidate for reelection in 1830 to the Twenty-second Congress; resumed the practice of law in Elizabethtown; presidential elector for Clay and Sergeant in 1832; elected as an Anti-Jacksonian to the Twenty-third Congress (March 4, 1833-March 3, 1835); declined to be a candidate for renomination in 1834; moved to Talladega, Ala., and resumed the practice of law; was pastor of a church in Hopkinsville, Ky.; president of the Alabama Baptist State Convention in 1841; abandoned the practice of law and became general agent of the Alabama convention; continued his ministerial duties in Montgomery, Greensboro, and Newbern, Ala.; moved to Houston, Tex., in 1851 and served as pastor of a Baptist church; died in Montgomery, Montgomery County, Tex., August 15, 1854; interment in the Old Cemetery.

**Bibliography:** Hannum, Sharon Elaine. "Thomas Chilton-Lawyer, Politician, Preacher." *Filson Club Historical Quarterly* 38 (April 1964): 97-114.

**CHILTON, William Edwin,** a Senator from West Virginia; born in Colesmouth (now St. Albans), Kanawha County, W.Va. (then Virginia), March 17, 1858; attended public and private schools and was graduated from Shelton College, St. Albans, W.Va.; taught school; studied law; was admitted to the bar in 1880 and commenced practice in Charleston, W.Va., in 1882; also engaged in the newspaper publishing business; prosecuting attorney of Kanawha County in 1883; chairman of the Democratic State executive committee in 1892; secretary of state of West Virginia 1893-1897; elected as a Democrat to the United States Senate and served from March 4, 1911, to March 3, 1917; chairman, Committee on Census (Sixty-third and Sixty-fourth Congresses), Committee on Printing (Sixty-fourth Congress); unsuccessfully contested the election of Howard Sutherland to the United States Senate for the term commencing March 4, 1917; resumed the practice of law and the newspaper publishing business in Charleston, W.Va.; was an unsuccessful candidate for election to the United States Senate in 1924 and again in 1934; died in Charleston, W.Va., November 7, 1939; interment in Teay's Hill Cemetery, St. Albans, W.Va.

**CHINDBLOM, Carl Richard,** a Representative from Illinois; born in Chicago, Ill., December 21, 1870; attended the public schools; was graduated from Augustana College, Rock Island, Ill., in 1890 and from the Kent College of Law (Lake Forest University) at Chicago in 1898; teacher in Martin Luther College in Chicago 1893-1896; was admitted to the bar in 1900 and commenced the practice of law in Chicago, Ill.; delegate to the Republican State conventions in 1904, 1908, 1912, and 1916; attorney for the Illinois State Board of Health in 1905 and 1906; member of the Cook County Board of Commissioners 1906-1910; county attorney of Cook County 1912-1914; master in chancery of the circuit court of Cook County 1916-1918; elected as a Republican to the Sixty-sixth and to the six succeeding Congresses (March 4, 1919-March 3, 1933); unsuccessful candidate for renomination in 1932; resumed the practice of law in Chicago, Ill., until his death; referee in bankruptcy in the United States District Court for the Northern District of Illinois 1934-1942; died in Chicago, Ill., September 12, 1956; interment in Ridgewood Cemetery, Des Plaines, Ill.

**CHINN, Joseph William,** a Representative from Virginia; born at "Epping Forest," near Nuttsville, Lancaster County, Va., on November 16, 1798; was graduated from Union College, Schenectady, N.Y., in 1819; studied law at Needham, Va.; was admitted to the bar in 1821 and practiced in Lancaster County, Va.; member of the Virginia house of delegates 1826-1828; served in the Virginia senate 1829-1831; elected as a Jacksonian to the Twenty-second and Twenty-third Congresses (March 4, 1831-March 3, 1835); chairman, Committee on District of Columbia (Twenty-third Congress); moved to Richmond, Va., where he resumed the practice of his profession; died on his estate, "Wilna," near Richmond, Va., on December 5, 1840; interment in the family burying ground at "Wilna."

**CHINN, Thomas Withers** (cousin of Robert Enoch Withers), a Representative from Louisiana; born near Cynthiana, Harrison County, Ky., November 22, 1791; attended the rural schools of his community and was also tutored by his father; served as a private in the First Rifles of the Kentucky Militia Volunteers from August 15, 1812, to October 14, 1812; clerked in a general store in Cynthiana until 1813; moved to Woodville, Miss., and engaged in mercantile pursuits; studied medicine and commenced the practice of his profession in St. Francisville, West Feliciana Parish, La., about 1817; studied law; was admitted to the bar in 1825 and commenced practice in St. Francisville; appointed judge of West Feliciana Parish in 1826; moved to Cypress Hall plantation, near Baton Rouge, in West Baton Rouge Parish, La., in 1831; continued the practice of law and also engaged in sugarcane planting; elected as a Whig to the Twenty-sixth Congress (March 4, 1839-March 3, 1841); was not a candidate for renomination in 1840 to the Twenty-seventh Congress; appointed by President Zachary Taylor as Minister to the Two Sicilies on June 5, 1849, but did not assume his duties because of ill health; died at his plantation in West Baton Rouge Parish, La., on May 22, 1852; interment at Grosse Tete, La., near Rosedale, La.

**CHIPERFIELD, Burnett Mitchell** (father of Robert Bruce Chiperfield), a Representative from Illinois; born in Dover, Bureau County, Ill., June 14, 1870; attended the public schools of Illinois and Hamline University, St. Paul, Minn.; studied law; was admitted to the bar in 1891 and commenced practice at Canton, Ill.; prosecuting attorney of Fulton County, Ill., 1896-1900; member of the State house of representatives 1903-1913; secretary and trustee of the Western Illinois State Normal School at Macomb, Ill., 1904-1909; was connected with the Illinois National Guard for twenty years; organized a regiment for service in the Spanish-American War; unsuccessful candidate for election in 1912 to the Sixty-third Congress; elected as a Republican to the Sixty-fourth Congress (March 4, 1915-March 3, 1917); did not seek renomination, having become a candidate for the Republican nomination as United States Senator but was unsuccessful; during the First World War served as judge advocate with several divisions in France and occupied Germany, 1917-1919; resumed the practice of law and also engaged in banking; delegate to the Republican National Conventions in 1920 and 1936; appointed lieutenant colonel in the Judge Advocate General's Department, Officers' Reserve Corps, February 5, 1921, and served until his retirement in 1934 with the rank of brigadier general; elected to the Seventy-first and Seventy-second Congresses (March 4, 1929-March 3, 1933); unsuccessful candidate for reelection in 1932 to the Seventy-third Congress and for election in 1934 to the Seventy-fourth Congress; reengaged in the practice of law in Canton, Ill., until his death there on June 24, 1940; interment in Greenwood Cemetery.

**CHIPERFIELD, Robert Bruce** (son of Burnett Mitchell Chiperfield), a Representative from Illinois; born in Canton, Fulton County, Ill., November 20, 1899; educated in the public schools of Canton, Ill., Washington, D.C., and at Phillips Exeter Academy, Exeter, N.H.; served as a private during the First World War; attended Knox College, Galesburg, Ill.; was graduated from Harvard College in 1922 and from the law department of Boston University in 1925; was admitted to the bar in 1925 and commenced practice in Canton, Ill.; city attorney of Canton, Ill.; elected as a Republican to the Seventy-sixth and to the eleven succeeding Congresses (January 3, 1939-January 3, 1963); chairman, Committee on Foreign Affairs (Eighty-third Congress); was not a candidate for renomination in 1962 to the Eighty-eighth Congress; resided in Canton, Ill., until his death there, April 9, 1971; interment in Greenwood Cemetery.

**CHIPMAN, Daniel** (brother of Nathaniel Chipman), a Representative from Vermont; born in Salisbury, Conn., on October 22, 1765; was graduated from Dartmouth College, Hanover, N.H., in 1788; studied law; was admitted to the bar and practiced in Rutland, Vt., 1790-1794; was a member of the State constitutional conventions in 1793, 1814, 1836, 1843, and 1850; moved to Middlebury, Vt., in 1794; member of the State house of representatives 1798-1808, 1812-1814, 1818, and 1821, and served as speaker during the sessions of 1813 and 1814; professor of law at Middlebury College 1806-1818; member of the Governor's council in 1808; elected as a

Federalist to the Fourteenth Congress and served from March 4, 1815, to May 5, 1816, when he resigned; appointed reporter of the superior court in 1824; moved to Ripton, Vt., in 1828 and continued the practice of law; engaged in literary pursuits; died in Ripton, Addison County, Vt., April 23, 1850; interment in West Cemetery, Middlebury, Vt.

**Bibliography:** *DAB*.

**CHIPMAN, John Logan** (grandson of Nathaniel Chipman), a Representative from Michigan; born in Detroit, Mich., on June 5, 1830; attended the public schools of that city and the University of Michigan at Ann Arbor 1843-1845; engaged in the Lake Superior region as explorer for the Montreal Mining Co. in 1846; assistant clerk of the State house of representatives in 1853; studied law; was admitted to the bar in 1854 and practiced in the Lake Superior region; returned to Detroit; city attorney of Detroit 1857-1860; member of the State house of representatives in 1865 and 1866; unsuccessful Democratic candidate for election in 1866 to the Fortieth Congress; attorney of the police board of Detroit 1867-1879; elected judge of the superior court of Detroit May 1, 1879; reelected in 1885 and served until 1887, when he resigned, having been elected to Congress; elected as a Democrat to the Fiftieth and to the three succeeding Congresses and served from March 4, 1887, until his death in Detroit, Mich., on August 17, 1893; interment in Elmwood Cemetery, Detroit, Mich.

**CHIPMAN, John Smith,** a Representative from Michigan; born in Shoreham, Addison County, Vt., on August 10, 1800; attended the rural schools and was graduated from Middlebury College in Vermont in 1823; studied law; was admitted to the bar and practiced in Addison County, Vt., and Essex County, N.Y.; moved to Centerville, Mich., in 1838, where he held several local offices; member of the State house of representatives in 1842; elected as a Democrat to the Twenty-ninth Congress (March 4, 1845-March 3, 1847); moved to Niles, Berrien County, Mich., and later, in 1850, to San Francisco, Calif., where he resumed the practice of law; moved to San Jose, Santa Clara County, Calif., in 1869 and lived in retirement until his death there on July 27, 1869; interment in Oak Hill Cemetery.

**CHIPMAN, Nathaniel** (brother of Daniel Chipman and grandfather of John Logan Chipman), a Senator from Vermont; born in Salisbury, Conn., November 15, 1752; privately tutored; received his degree from Yale College in 1777 while in the Army; served as a lieutenant in the Revolutionary War; studied law; was admitted to the bar in 1779 and commenced practice in Tinmouth, Vt.; member, State house of representatives 1784-1785; elected as judge of the State supreme court in 1786 and chosen chief justice in 1789; judge of the United States District Court 1791-1794; again elected chief justice of the State supreme court in 1796; elected as a Federalist to the United States Senate to fill the vacancy caused by the resignation of Isaac Tichenor and served from October 17, 1797, until March 3, 1803; unsuccessful candidate for reelection; member, State house of representatives 1806-1811; chief justice of Vermont 1813-1815; died in Tinmouth, Vt., February 13, 1843; interment in the Tinmouth Cemetery.

**Bibliography:** *DAB*; Chipman, Daniel. *Life of Honorable Nathaniel Chipman with Selections from His Miscellaneous Papers.* Boston: C.C. Little and J. Brown, 1846; Chipman, Nathaniel. *Principles of Government, A Treatise on Free Institutions Including the Constitution of the United States.* 1833. Reprint. New York: Da Capo Press, 1970.

**CHIPMAN, Norton Parker,** a Delegate from the District of Columbia; born in Milford Center, Union County, Ohio, March 7, 1836; attended the public schools; moved to Iowa in 1845 and entered Washington College; afterwards attended the law school in Cincinnati; returned to Washington, Iowa; was admitted to the bar and commenced practice in that city; entered the Union Army; commissioned major of the Second Iowa Infantry on September 23, 1861, and commissioned colonel on April 17, 1862; brevetted brigadier general of Volunteers, March 13, 1865; settled in Washington, D.C.; upon the establishment of a Territorial form of government for the District of Columbia was appointed secretary, and subsequently was elected as a Republican a Delegate to the Forty-second and Forty-third Congresses, and served from April 21, 1871 until March 3, 1875; moved to California in 1876 and engaged in the lumber business; member of the California State Board of Trade, and its president, 1895-1906; appointed a commissioner of the supreme court of California in April 1897; appointed presiding justice of the district court of appeals for the third district in 1905; elected in November 1906, and served until his resignation on December 18, 1922; died in San Francisco, Calif., February 1, 1924; interment in Cypress Lawn Cemetery.

**CHISHOLM, Shirley Anita,** a Representative from New York; born Shirley Anita St. Hill, November 30, 1924, in Brooklyn, Kings County, N.Y.; first black woman elected to Congress; as a young girl lived with her grandparents in Barbados, and attended the Vauxhall Coeducational School; attended the public schools of Brooklyn, N.Y.; B.A., Brooklyn College, 1946; M.A., Columbia University, 1952; nursery school teacher, Mount Calvary Child Care Center, New York City, 1946-1953; director, Hamilton-Madison Child Care Center, New York City, 1953-1959; educational consultant, New York City Division of Day Care, 1959-1964; member, New York State assembly, District 55, 1964-1968; elected as a Democrat to the Ninety-first and to the six succeeding Congresses (January 3, 1969-January 3, 1983); was not a candidate for reelection in 1982 to the Ninety-eighth Congress; is a resident of Williamsville, N.Y.

**Bibliography:** Brownmiller, Susan. *Shirley Chisholm.* Garden City, N.Y.: Doubleday, 1970; Chisholm, Shirley. *Unbought and Unbossed.* Boston: Houghton Mifflin, 1970.

**CHITTENDEN, Martin,** a Representative from Vermont; born in Salisbury, Conn., March 12, 1763; moved with his parents to Williston, Vt., in 1776; attended Mares School, and was graduated from Dartmouth College, Hanover, N.H., in 1789; engaged in agricultural and mercantile pursuits in Jericho, Vt.; appointed justice of the peace in October 1789; delegate to the State convention that ratified the Federal Constitution; aide-de-camp to Lieutenant Governor Olcott in 1790; clerk of the county court of Chittenden County 1790-1793; member of the State house of representatives 1790-1796; judge of the Chittenden County Court 1793-1795, and chief justice 1796-1813; captain of the First Militia in Jericho in 1793; lieutenant colonel commanding the First Regiment, Seventh Division, Vermont Militia, in 1794; brigadier general in 1799; major general 1799-1803; first collector of the census for Chittenden County; elected as a Federalist to the Eighth and to the four succeeding Congresses (March 4, 1803-March 3, 1813); Governor of Vermont from October 23, 1813 to October 14, 1815; judge of probate 1821-1823; died in Williston, Chittenden County, Vt., September 5, 1840; interment in the Old Cemetery.

**Bibliography:** *DAB.*

**CHITTENDEN, Simeon Baldwin,** a Representative from New York; born in Guilford, New Haven County, Conn., March 29, 1814; attended Guilford Academy; engaged in mercantile pursuits in New Haven 1829-1842; moved to New York City and engaged in mercantile pursuits in 1842; unsuccessful candidate for election in 1866 to the Fortieth Congress; vice president of the New York City Chamber of Commerce 1867-1869; elected as an Independent Republican to the Forty-third Congress to fill the vacancy caused by the resignation of Stewart L. Woodford; reelected as an Independent Republican to the Forty-fourth Congress and as a Republican to the Forty-fifth and Forty-sixth Congresses and served from November 3, 1874, to March 3, 1881; unsuccessful candidate for reelection in

1880 to the Forty-seventh Congress; retired from public life; died in Brooklyn, N.Y., on April 14, 1889; interment in Greenwood Cemetery.

**Bibliography:** *DAB.*

**CHITTENDEN, Thomas Cotton,** a Representative from New York; born in Stockbridge, Berkshire County, Mass., on August 30, 1788; moved to Adams, Jefferson County, N.Y.; studied law; was admitted to the bar in 1813 and commenced practice in Adams, N.Y.; elected as a Whig to the Twenty-sixth and Twenty-seventh Congresses (March 4, 1839-March 3, 1843); appointed judge of Jefferson County in 1840, serving for five years; after entering upon his judicial duties, moved to Watertown, N.Y., the county seat; resumed the practice of law in Watertown; also engaged in banking; died in Watertown, N.Y., August 22, 1866; interment in Brookside Cemetery.

**CHOATE, Rufus,** a Representative and a Senator from Massachusetts; born in Essex, Mass., on October 1, 1799; was graduated from Dartmouth College, Hanover, N.H., in 1819; studied law; was admitted to the bar and commenced practice in Danvers, Mass., in 1823; member, Massachusetts house of representatives, 1825; member of the Massachusetts senate in 1826; moved to Salem, Mass. in 1828; elected as a Whig to the Twenty-second and Twenty-third Congresses, and served from March 4, 1831 to June 30, 1834, when he resigned; moved to Boston in 1834; elected to the United States Senate to fill the vacancy caused by the resignation of Daniel Webster, and served from February 23, 1841 to March 3, 1845; retired from political life to devote his time to law; member of the Massachusetts constitutional convention in 1853; attorney general of Massachusetts in 1853; died in Halifax, Nova Scotia, on July 13, 1859; interment in Mount Auburn Cemetery, Cambridge, Mass.

**Bibliography:** *DAB*; Choate, Rufus. *The Works of Rufus Choate: With A Memoir of His Life.* Edited by Samuel Gilman Brown. 2 vols. 1862. Reprint. New York: AMS Press, 1972; Matthews, Jean. *Rufus Choate, the Law and Civic Virtue.* Philadelphia: Temple University Press, 1980; Neilson, Joseph. *Memories of Rufus Choate.* 1884. Reprint. Littleton, Colo.: Fred B. Rothman and Co., 1985.

**CHRISMAN, James Stone,** a Representative from Kentucky; born in Monticello, Wayne County, Ky., September 14, 1818; attended the common schools; engaged in agricultural pursuits; studied law; was admitted to the bar in 1849 and commenced practice in Monticello, Wayne County, Ky.; unsuccessful candidate for election to the Kentucky house of representatives in 1845 and 1847; delegate to the Kentucky constitutional convention in 1849; elected as a Democrat to the Thirty-third Congress (March 4, 1853-March 3, 1855); unsuccessfully contested the election of William C. Anderson to the Thirty-sixth Congress; Representative from Kentucky to the First and Second Confederate Congresses 1862-1865; member of the Kentucky house of representatives 1869-1871; resumed the practice of law in Monticello, Ky., where he died July 29, 1881; interment in a private cemetery on his farm.

**CHRISTENSEN, Jon Lynn,** a Representative from Nebraska; born in St. Paul, Howard County, Nebr., February 20, 1963; attended St. Paul High School; B.A., Midland Lutheran College, Fremont, Nebr., 1985; J.D., South Texas College of Law, Houston, 1989; beef lugger, Monfort Beef (now division of ConAgra Corp.); clerk with Vinson and Elkins law firm, 1986-1989; intern at Windle Turley, P.C., Dallas, Tex. and banking divisions of Chamberlain, Hrdlicka tax firm; vice president of corporate division of COMREP, Inc., 1989-1991; marketing director, Connecticut Mutual Insurance Co.; formed The Aquila Group, Inc.; elected as a Republican to the One Hundred Fourth Congress (January 3, 1995-January 3, 1997); is a resident of Omaha, Nebr.

**CHRISTGAU, Victor Laurence August,** a Representative from Minnesota; born in Dexter Township, Mower County, near Austin, Minn., September 20, 1894; attended the rural schools and the high school at Austin; was graduated from the school of agriculture of the University of Minnesota at St. Paul in 1917 and from its college of agriculture in 1923; engaged in agricultural pursuits; during the First World War served overseas in the United States Army as a sergeant in the Thirty-third Regiment of Engineers; member of the State senate from 1927 until his resignation in 1929; elected as a Republican to the Seventy-first and Seventy-second Congresses (March 4, 1929-March 3, 1933); unsuccessful candidate for renomination in 1932 to the Seventy-third Congress; resumed agricultural pursuits; appointed executive assistant to the director of production, Division of Agricultural Adjustment Administration, in June 1933, and director of the Production Division and assistant administrator in January 1934, serving until February 1935; was appointed State administrator of the Minnesota Works Progress Administration in June 1935 and served until June 1938; State director of the Minnesota division of employment and security at St. Paul, Minn., 1939-1954; president of the Interstate Conference Employment Security Agencies in 1947 and 1948; Director, Bureau of Old Age and Survivors Insurance, Social Security Adminstration, 1954-1963, and executive director of the Social Security Administration from January 1963 to March 1967; was a resident of Washington, D.C.; died October 10, 1991.

**CHRISTIANCY, Isaac Peckham,** a Senator from Michigan; born near Johnstown, Fulton County, N.Y., March 12, 1812; attended the common schools and Johnstown and Ovid Academies; taught school; studied law; moved to Monroe, Mich., in 1836; was admitted to the bar and practiced in Monroe from 1838 until 1858; prosecuting attorney for Monroe County, 1841-1846; unsuccessful Free Soil candidate for Governor in 1852; member, Michigan State senate, 1850-1852; aided in the organizing of the Republican Party in 1854; editor and proprietor of the Monroe Commercial in 1857; associate judge of the Michigan supreme court, 1857-1875, and served as chief justice from 1872 to 1874; was elected as a Republican to the United States Senate, and served from March 4, 1875 to February 10, 1879, when he resigned to accept a diplomatic position; chairman, Committee on Revision of the Laws (Forty-fifth Congress); appointed Minister to Peru on February 11, 1879 and served until August 1881; returned to Lansing and resumed the practice of law; died in Lansing, Mich., September 8, 1890; interment in Woodlawn Cemetery, Monroe, Monroe County, Mich.

Bibliography: *DAB.*

**CHRISTIANSON, Theodore,** a Representative from Minnesota; born on a farm near Lac qui Parle, Minn., September 12, 1883; attended the rural schools and Dawson (Minn.) High School; was graduated from the arts college of the University of Minnesota at Minneapolis in 1906 and from its law school in 1909; principal of the public school at Robbindale, Minn., 1906-1909; was admitted to the bar in 1909 and commenced practice in Dawson, Lac qui Parle County, Minn.; also owner and publisher of the Dawson Sentinel from 1909 until 1925; president of the village council at Dawson, Minn., in 1910 and 1911; member of the Minnesota State house of representatives, 1915-1925; elected Governor of Minnesota in 1924, reelected in 1926 and 1928, and served from January 6, 1925 to January 6, 1931; manufacturing executive in Minneapolis, Minn., in 1931 and 1932; elected as a Republican to the Seventy-third and Seventy-fourth Congresses (March 4, 1933-January 3, 1937); was not a candidate for renomination in 1936 to the House of Representatives, but was an unsuccessful candidate for election to the United States Senate; served as secretary-manager of the National Association of Retail Grocers, 1937-1939, and as public relations counsel for the National Association of Retail Druggists, 1939-1945; editor of the National Association of Retail Druggists

Journal from 1945 until his death in Dawson, Minn., on December 9, 1948; interment in Sunset Memorial Cemetery, Minneapolis, Minn.

**CHRISTIE, Gabriel,** a Representative from Maryland; born in Perryman, Harford County, Md., in 1755; during the Revolutionary War was a member of a company of militia organized September 12, 1775, by the provincial convention held at Annapolis on July 26, 1775; member of the State house of delegates; appointed by Governor William Smallwood one of the commissioners to "straighten and amend the post road from Havre de Grace to Baltimore town" by authority of the act of 1787; elected to the Third and Fourth Congresses (March 4, 1793-March 3, 1797); elected as a Republican to the Sixth Congress (March 4, 1799-March 3, 1801); one of the commissioners of Havre de Grace in 1800 and 1801, and again in 1806; appointed collector of the port of Baltimore and served until his death in Baltimore, Md., April 1, 1808; interment in Spesutia Churchyard, Perryman, Harford County, Md.

**CHRISTOPHER, George Henry,** a Representative from Missouri; born on a farm in Bates County, near Butler, Mo., December 9, 1888; attended the public schools of Bates County, Mo.; was graduated from Hill's Business College, Sedalia, Mo., in 1907; lived on a farm in Calhoun County, Ill., and in Craig County, near Vinita, Okla; owned and operated a farm in Bates County, Mo.; elected as a Democrat to the Eighty-first Congress (January 3, 1949-January 3, 1951); unsuccessful candidate for reelection in 1950 to the Eighty-second Congress; assistant to the director, Agricultural Conservation Program, Department of Agriculture, from January 1951 to September 1952; elected to the Eighty-fourth and to the two succeeding Congresses, and served from January 3, 1955 until his death in Washington, D.C., January 23, 1959; interment in Oak Hill Cemetery, Butler, Mo.

**CHRISTOPHERSON, Charles Andrew,** a Representative from South Dakota; born in Amherst Township, Fillmore County, Minn., July 23, 1871; attended the public schools of Amherst Township, Minn., and Sioux Falls (S.Dak.) Business College and Normal School; moved to Sioux Falls, S.Dak., in 1890; studied law; was admitted to the bar in 1893 and commenced practice in Sioux Falls, S.Dak.; member of the board of education of Sioux Falls 1908-1918, serving as president 1911-1915; member of the board of directors of the Union Savings Association in 1912 and was subsequently elected president; member of the State house of representatives 1912-1916, serving as speaker during his last term; elected as a Republican to the Sixty-sixth and to the six succeeding Congresses (March 4, 1919-March 3, 1933); unsuccessful candidate for reelection in 1932 to the Seventy-third Congress and for election in 1934 to the Seventy-fourth Congress; reengaged in the practice of law in Sioux Falls, S.Dak., until September 1936, and was also interested in the banking business; delegate to the Republican National Convention of 1944; served as State administrator of the War Savings staff in 1941-1943; executive manager of the State war finance committee; in 1944 became chairman of the Advisory Committee of the United States Savings Bond Division; died in Sioux Falls, S.Dak., November 2, 1951; interment in Woodlawn Cemetery.

**CHRYSLER, Richard R.,** a Representative from Michigan; born in St. Paul, Ramsey County, Minn., April 29, 1942; attended Brighton (Mich.) High School; assembly line worker, Willow Run Plant, Ypsilanti, Mich.; sweeper, vice president then owner, Hurst Performance; owner, Cars and Concepts; owner, RCI, Brighton, Mich., 1993 to present; unsuccessful candidate in 1986 for nomination for Governor of Michigan, and in 1992 for election to the One Hundred Third Congress; elected as a Republican to the One Hundred Fourth Congress (January 3, 1995-January 3, 1997); is a resident of Brighton, Mich.

**CHUDOFF, Earl,** a Representative from Pennsylvania; born in Philadelphia, Pa., November 15, 1907; attended the public schools; graduated from the Wharton School, University of Pennsylvania, in economics in 1929 and from the law school of the University of Pittsburgh in 1932; was admitted to the bar in 1933 and commenced the practice of law in Philadelphia, Pa.; building and loan examiner, Pennsylvania State Department of Banking, 1936-1939; served as chief boatswain's mate in the United States Coast Guard Reserve from December 1942 to September 1945; member of the Pennsylvania house of representatives 1941-1948; elected as a Democrat to the Eighty-first and to the four succeeding Congresses and served from January 3, 1949, until his resignation January 5, 1958, having been elected judge of the Philadelphia Court of Common Pleas No. 1, for the term ending in 1968; reelected for the term ending in 1978; was a resident of Philadelphia; died May 17, 1993.

**CHURCH, Denver Samuel,** a Representative from California; born in Folsom City, Sacramento County, Calif., December 11, 1862; attended the common schools; was graduated from Healdsburg (Calif.) College in 1885; studied law; was admitted to the bar in 1893 and commenced practice in Fresno, Fresno County, Calif.; district attorney of Fresno County 1907-1913; delegate to the Democratic National Convention of 1916; elected as a Democrat to the Sixty-third and to the two succeeding Congresses (March 4, 1913-March 3, 1919); was not a candidate for renomination in 1918 to the Sixty-sixth Congress; resumed the practice of law in Fresno, Calif.; superior judge of Fresno County 1924-1930; elected to the Seventy-third Congress (March 4, 1933-January 3, 1935); was not a candidate for renomination in 1934 to the Seventy-fourth Congress; resumed the practice of law; died in Fresno, Calif., February 21, 1952; interment in Belmont Memorial Cemetery.

**CHURCH, Frank Forrester, III,** a Senator from Idaho; born in Boise, Ada County, Idaho, July 25, 1924; graduated from Boise High School in 1942; enlisted in the United States Army on December 7, 1942, and was commissioned a second lieutenant in the infantry in July 1944; assigned to Military Intelligence in India, Burma, and Kunming, China, and served until discharged as a first lieutenant, June 11, 1946; B.A., Stanford University, 1947; attended Harvard University Law School, 1947-1948; LL.B., Stanford University Law School, 1950, and was admitted to the bar the same year; legal counsel, Idaho Office of Price Stabilization, 1950-1951; commenced the practice of law in Boise in 1951; president, Idaho Young Democrats, 1952-1954; elected as a Democrat to the United States Senate in 1956; reelected in 1962, 1968, and again in 1974, and served from January 3, 1957 to January 3, 1981; delivered keynote address at the Democratic National Convention of 1960; unsuccessful candidate for reelection in 1980; chairman, Special Committee on Aging (Ninety-second through Ninety-fifth Congresses), Special Committee on Termination of the National Emergency (Ninety-second through Ninety-fourth Congresses), Select Committee on Government Intelligence Activities (Ninety-fourth Congress), Committee on Foreign Relations (Ninety-sixth Congress); unsuccessful candidate for the Democratic presidential nomination in 1976; United States delegate to the twenty-first General Assembly of the United Nations; resumed the practice of law; was a resident of Bethesda, Md., until his death there on April 7, 1984; interment in Morris Hill Cemetery, Boise, Idaho.

Bibliography: Ashby, LeRoy, and Rod Gramer. *Fighting the Odds: The Life of Senator Frank Church.* Pullman: Washington State University Press, 1994; Church, F. Forrester. *Father and Son: A Personal Biography of Senator Frank Church by his Son.* New York: Harper and Row, 1985.

**CHURCH, Marguerite Stitt** (wife of Ralph Edwin Church), a Representative from Illinois; born in New York City September 13, 1892; attended St. Agatha School in New York City; Wellesley (Mass.) College, A.B., 1914 and Columbia University, New York City, A.M., 1917; teacher at Wellesley College in 1915; consulting psychologist of State Charities Aid Association in New York City during the First World War; lecturer and writer; participant, through Presidential invitation, in the 1960 White House Conference on children and youth; elected as a Republican to the Eighty-second and to the five succeeding Congresses (January 3, 1951-January 3, 1963); was not a candidate for renomination in 1962 to the Eighty-eighth Congress; member of the United States delegation to the fifteenth General Assembly of the United Nations in 1961; member, National Board of Directors, Girl Scouts of America; was a resident of Evanston, Ill.; died May 26, 1990.

**CHURCH, Ralph Edwin** (husband of Marguerite Stitt Church), a Representative from Illinois; born on a farm near Catlin, Vermilion County, Ill., on May 5, 1883; attended the public schools; was graduated from the University of Michigan at Ann Arbor in 1907 and from the law department of Northwestern University, Evanston, Ill., in 1909; was admitted to the bar in 1909 and commenced practice in Chicago, Ill.; elected to the Illinois State house of representatives in 1916, resigning during the First World War to attend the Reserve Officers' Training Camp; again a member of the State house of representatives, serving from 1917 until 1932; lieutenant commander in the United States Naval Reserve, 1938-1941; elected as a Republican to the Seventy-fourth and to the two succeeding Congresses (January 3, 1935-January 3, 1941); was not a candidate for renomination in 1940 to the House of Representatives, but was an unsuccessful candidate for nomination to the United States Senate; delegate to the Interparliamentary Conference at Oslo, Norway, in 1939; again elected to the Seventy-eighth and to the three succeeding Congresses and served from January 3, 1943, until his death on March 21, 1950, while appearing before the Committee on Expenditures in the Executive Departments, in the House Office Building, Washington, D.C.; interment in Memorial Park, Skokie, Ill.

**CHURCHILL, George Bosworth,** a Representative from Massachusetts; born in Worcester, Mass., October 24, 1866; attended the grammar and high schools, and was graduated from Amherst (Mass.) College in 1889; taught in the Worcester High School until 1892; moved to Philadelphia and taught in the William Penn Charter School, and at the same time took a postgraduate course at the University of Pennsylvania 1892-1894; went to Europe and studied in the University of Strassburg, Germany, in 1894 and 1895, and then attended the University of Berlin, Germany, 1895-1897; returned to the United States and became assistant editor of the Cosmopolitan Magazine in 1897 and 1898; member of the faculty of Amherst College 1898-1925; moderator of Amherst 1905-1925; member of the Massachusetts senate 1917-1919; delegate to the Massachusetts constitutional conventions in 1917 and 1919; elected as a Republican to the Sixty-ninth Congress and served from March 4, 1925, until his death in Amherst, Mass., July 1, 1925; interment in Wildwood Cemetery.

**CHURCHILL, John Charles,** a Representative from New York; born in Mooers, Clinton County, N.Y., January 17, 1821; attended the Burr Seminary, Manchester, Vt., and was graduated from Middlebury College, Vermont, in 1843; teacher of languages in the Castleton Seminary, Vermont, and a tutor in Middlebury College; attended the Dane Law School of Harvard University; was admitted to the bar in 1847 and commenced practice in Oswego, Oswego County, N.Y., in 1848; member of the Oswego Board of Education, 1853-1856; member of the board of supervisors of Oswego County in 1854 and 1855; prosecuting attorney, 1857-1860; judge of Oswego County, 1860-1864; appointed by Governor Edwin D. Morgan as commissioner to superintend the draft for Oswego County in 1862 and 1863; elected as a Republican to the Fortieth and Forty-first Congresses (March 4, 1867-March 3, 1871); chairman, Committee on Expenditures on Public Buildings (Forty-first Congress); delegate to the Republican National Convention of 1876; unsuccessful candidate for secretary of state of New York in 1877; again a member of the Oswego Board of Education, and president of the board in 1879 and 1880; appointed associate justice of the supreme court of New York to fill a vacancy January 17, 1881; was subsequently elected, and served until the expiration of his term by age limit on December 31, 1891; died in Oswego, N.Y., June 4, 1905; interment in Riverside Cemetery.

**CHURCHWELL, William Montgomery,** a Representative from Tennessee; born near Knoxville, Knox County, Tenn., February 20, 1826; attended private schools and Emory and Henry College, Emory, Va., 1840-1843; studied law; was admitted to the bar and commenced practice in Knoxville; one of the judges for Knox County; elected as a Democrat to the Thirty-second and Thirty-third Congresses (March 4, 1851-March 3, 1855); chairman, Committee on Revolutionary Pensions (Thirty-third Congress); provost marshal for the district of east Tennessee; during the administration of President James Buchanan was sent on a secret mission to Mexico; during the Civil War served in the Confederate Army as colonel of the Fourth Tennessee Regiment; died in Knoxville, Tenn., August 18, 1862; interment in the Old Gray Cemetery.

**CILLEY, Bradbury** (uncle of Jonathan Cilley and Joseph Cilley), a Representative from New Hampshire; born in Nottingham, Rockingham County, N.H., on February 1, 1760; attended the common schools; engaged in agricultural pursuits; appointed by President John Adams as United States marshal for the district of New Hampshire on March 19, 1798, and served until May 3, 1802; elected as a Federalist to the Thirteenth and Fourteenth Congresses (March 4, 1813-March 3, 1817); colonel and aide on the staff of Governor John T. Gilman from 1814 until 1816; retired from public life; died in Nottingham, N.H., December 17, 1831; interment in the General Joseph Cilley Burying Ground in Nottingham Square.

**CILLEY, Jonathan** (nephew of Bradbury Cilley and brother of Joseph Cilley), a Representative from Maine; born in Nottingham, Rockingham County, N.H., July 2, 1802; attended Atkinson Academy, New Hampshire; was graduated from New Hampton Academy and later, in 1825, from Bowdoin College, Brunswick, Maine; studied law; was admitted to the bar in 1828 and commenced practice in Thomaston, Knox County, Maine; editor of the Thomaston Register, 1829-1831; member of the Maine State house of representatives, 1831-1836, and served as speaker in 1835 and 1836; elected as a Democrat to the Twenty-fifth Congress and served from March 4, 1837, until February 24, 1838, when he was killed in a duel on the Marlboro Pike, Md., near Washington, D.C., by Representative William J. Graves of Kentucky; this duel prompted passage of a congressional act of February 20, 1839, prohibiting the giving or accepting, within the District of Columbia, of challenges to a duel; interment in Cilley Cemetery, Thomaston, Maine.

**CILLEY, Joseph** (nephew of Bradbury Cilley and brother of Jonathan Cilley), a Senator from New Hampshire; born in Nottingham, Rockingham County, N.H., January 4, 1791; attended the common schools and was graduated from Atkinson Academy, New Hampshire; engaged in agricultural pursuits; served in the New Hampshire Regiment, United States Infantry 1812-1816, attained the brevetted rank of captain; quartermaster of New Hampshire in 1817; division inspector in 1821; aide-de-camp to the Governor in 1827; elected as a Democrat to the United States Senate to fill the vacancy caused by the resignation of Levi Woodbury and served from June 13, 1846, until March 3, 1847; unsuccessful candidate for reelection in 1846; retired to his farm in Nottingham, N.H., and died there September 16, 1887; interment in the General Joseph Cilley Burying Ground in Nottingham Square.

**Bibliography:** Scales, John. *Life of General Joseph Cilley.* New Hampshire: Standard Book Company, 1921.

**CITRON, William Michael,** a Representative from Connecticut; born in New Haven, Conn., August 29, 1896; moved with his parents to Middletown, Middlesex County, Conn., in 1899; attended the grammar and high schools; was graduated from Wesleyan University, Middletown, Conn., in 1918 and from the law department of Harvard University in 1921; was commissioned a second lieutenant of Field Artillery on September 16, 1918, and was in training until discharged on December 14, 1918; was admitted to the bar in 1922 and commenced practice in Middletown, Conn.; member of the State house of representatives 1927-1929 and 1931-1933, serving as minority leader during two sessions; unsuccessful candidate for election in 1928 to the Seventy-first Congress and in 1932 to the Seventy-third Congress; city corporation counsel 1928-1934; served as a member of the Connecticut Old Age Pension Commission in 1932 and 1933; clerk of the State senate 1933-1935; elected as a Democrat to the Seventy-fourth Congress; reelected to the Seventy-fifth Congress (January 3, 1935-January 3, 1939); unsuccessful candidate for reelection in 1938 to the Seventy-sixth Congress; chairman of the Housing Authority of Middletown, Conn., 1940-1942; entered the military service of the United States as captain, Corps of Military Police, on July 16, 1942, and was subsequently promoted to major on April 16, 1943; served in Africa from October 1942 until retired for physical incapacity on March 3, 1944; resumed the practice of law; member of the Connecticut Veterans Reemployment and Advisory Commission in 1948 and 1949; commander, Connecticut Disabled American Veterans, 1947-1948; unsuccessful candidate in 1952 for election to the Eighty-third Congress; died in Titusville, Fla., June 7, 1976; interment in Congregation Adath Israel Cemetery, Middletown, Conn.

**CLAFLIN, William,** a Representative from Massachusetts; born in Milford, Mass., March 6, 1818; attended the public schools, and Brown University, Providence, R.I.; engaged in the shoe and leather business in St. Louis, Mo., and afterward in Boston, Mass.; member of the Massachusetts house of representatives, 1849-1852; moved to Newton, Mass., in 1855 and continued his business activity in Boston; served in the Massachusetts senate in 1860 and 1861, being president of that body in the latter year; member of the Republican National Executive Committee from 1864 until 1875, serving as chairman, 1868-1872; Lieutenant Governor of Massachusetts, 1866-1868; elected Governor of Massachusetts in 1868, reelected in 1869 and 1870, and served from January 7, 1869 to January 4, 1872; elected as a Republican to the Forty-fifth and Forty-sixth Congresses (March 4, 1877-March 3, 1881); was not a candidate for renomination in 1880 to the Forty-seventh Congress; resumed his former business pursuits; died in Newton, Middlesex County, Mass., January 5, 1905; interment in Newton Cemetery, Newtonville, Mass.

**Bibliography:** *DAB.*

**CLAGETT, Clifton,** a Representative from New Hampshire; born in Portsmouth, N.H., December 3, 1762; studied law; was admitted to the bar and commenced practice in Litchfield in 1787; elected as a Federalist to the Eighth Congress (March 4, 1803-March 3, 1805); appointed a justice of the peace and quorum in 1808; appointed judge of probate for Hillsborough County in 1810 and served until his resignation in 1812, having been appointed to a judicial position; moved to Amherst in 1812; appointed a judge of the supreme court in 1812; member of the State house of representatives in 1816; elected as a Republican to the Fifteenth Congress and reelected to the Sixteenth Congress (March 4, 1817-March 3, 1821); appointed judge of probate August 5, 1823, and held the office until his death in Amherst, Hillsborough County, New Hampshire, January 25, 1829.

**CLAGETT, William Horace** (uncle of Samuel Barrett Pettengill), a Delegate from the Territory of Montana; born in Upper Marlboro, Prince Georges County, Md., September 21, 1838; moved with his father to Keokuk, Iowa, in 1850; attended the public schools; studied law in Keokuk and at the law school in Albany, N.Y.; was admitted to the bar in 1858 and commenced practice in Keokuk; moved to Carson City, Nev., in 1861 and Humboldt, Nev., in 1862 and continued the practice of law; member of the Territorial house of representatives in 1862 and 1863 and of the State house of representatives in 1864 and 1865; practiced law in Virginia City, Nev., Helena, Mont., and Deer Lodge, Mont.; elected as a Republican a Delegate from Montana to the Forty-second Congress (March 4, 1871-March 3, 1873); unsuccessful candidate for reelection in 1872 to the Forty-third Congress; resumed the practice of law in Deer Lodge, Mont., Denver, Colo., Deadwood, Dakota Territory, Portland, Oreg., and Coeur d'alene, Idaho; president of the constitutional convention of Idaho in 1889; unsuccessful candidate for election to the United States Senate from Idaho in 1891 and again in 1895; moved to Spokane, Wash., resumed the practice of law, and died there August 3, 1901; interment in Greenwood Cemetery.

**CLAGUE, Frank,** a Representative from Minnesota; born in Warrensville, Cuyahoga County, Ohio, July 13, 1865; attended the common schools; moved to Minnesota in 1881; attended the State normal school at Mankato 1882-1885; taught school at Springfield, Minn., 1886-1890; studied law; was admitted to the bar in 1891 and commenced practice in Lamberton, Redwood County, Minn., the same year; prosecuting attorney of Redwood County, Minn., 1895-1903; member of the State house of representatives from January 1, 1903, to January 1, 1907, serving as speaker in the 1905 session; served in the State senate from January 1, 1907, to December 31, 1915; judge of the ninth judicial district of Minnesota from January 1, 1919, to March 1, 1920, when he resigned; elected as a Republican to the Sixty-seventh and to the five succeeding Congresses (March 4, 1921-March 3, 1933); was not a candidate for renomination in 1932; resumed the practice of law and also engaged in agricultural pursuits until his retirement; died in Redwood Falls, Minn., March 25, 1952; interment in Redwood Falls Cemetery.

**CLAIBORNE, James Robert,** a Representative from Missouri; born in St. Louis, Mo., June 22, 1882; attended the public schools; was graduated from the law department of the University of Missouri at Columbia in 1907; was admitted to the bar the same year and commenced practice in St. Louis, Mo.; lecturer in the law school at St. Louis University for several years; unsuccessful candidate for judge of the circuit court of the eighth judicial district in 1924; elected as a Democrat to the Seventy-third and Seventy-fourth Congresses (March 4, 1933-January 3, 1937); unsuccessful candidate for renomination in 1936 to the Seventy-fifth Congress; engaged in the practice of law in St. Louis, Mo., until his death there, February 16, 1944; interment in Oak Grove Cemetery.

**CLAIBORNE, John** (son of Thomas Claiborne [1749-1812] and brother of Thomas Claiborne [1780-1856]), a Representative from Virginia; born in Brunswick County, Va., in 1777; pursued academic studies; was graduated from the medical department of the University of Pennsylvania at Philadelphia in 1798 and practiced; elected as a Republican to the Ninth and Tenth Congresses and served from March 4, 1805, until his death in Brunswick County, Va., on October 9, 1808; interment in the family burying ground of Parson Jarratt, Dinwiddie, Va.

**CLAIBORNE, John Francis Hamtramck** (nephew of William Charles Cole Claiborne and Nathaniel Herbert Claiborne, grand-nephew of Thomas Claiborne [1749-1812], great-grandfather of Herbert Claiborne Pell, Jr., great-great-grandfather of Claiborne de Borda Pell, and great-great granduncle of Corinne Claiborne Boggs), a Representative from Mississippi; born in Natchez, Adams County, Miss., April 24, 1807; attended school in Virginia; studied law; was admitted to the bar in 1825 and commenced practice at Natchez, Miss.; member of the State house of representatives 1830-1834; moved to Madison County, Miss.; elected as a Jacksonian to the Twenty-fourth Congress (March 4, 1835-March 3, 1837); presented credentials as a Member-elect to the Twenty-fifth Congress and served from July 18, 1837, until February 5, 1838, when the seat was declared vacant; engaged in newspaper work in Natchez, Miss.; moved to New Orleans, La., in 1844 and resumed newspaper interests; appointed United States timber agent for Louisiana and Mississippi in 1853; author of several historical works; returned to his estate, "Dumbarton," near Natchez, Miss., and died there on May 17, 1884; interment in Trinity Churchyard, Natchez, Miss.

**Bibliography:** *DAB*; Williams, Frederich D. "The Career of J.F.H. Claiborne, States' Rights Unionist." Ph.D. dissertation, Indiana University, 1953.

**CLAIBORNE, Nathaniel Herbert** (brother of William Charles Cole Claiborne, nephew of Thomas Claiborne [1749-1812], uncle of John Francis Hamtramck Claiborne, and great-great-great grand-uncle of Corinne Claiborne Boggs), a Representative from Virginia; born in Chesterfield, Sussex County, Va., November 14, 1777; attended a local academy; engaged in agricultural pursuits; member of the Virginia house of delegates 1810-1812; served in the Virginia senate 1821-1825; an executive councilor; elected to the Nineteenth and Twentieth Congresses, elected as a Jacksonian to the Twenty-first through Twenty-third Congresses, and elected as an Anti-Jacksonian to the Twenty-fourth Congress (March 4, 1825-March 3, 1837); chairman, Committee on Elections (Twenty-second through Twenty-fourth Congresses); unsuccessful candidate in 1836 for reelection to the Twenty-fifth Congress; resumed agricultural pursuits; died near Rocky Mount, Franklin County, Va., August 15, 1859; interment in the family cemetery of his Claibrook estate near Rocky Mount, Va.

**Bibliography:** *DAB*.

**CLAIBORNE, Thomas** (son of Thomas Claiborne [1749-1812] and brother of John Claiborne), a Representative from Tennessee; born near Petersburg, Brunswick County, Va., May 17, 1780; attended the common schools in Virginia; served as major on the staff of General Andrew Jackson in the Creek War; studied law; was admitted to the bar and commenced practice in Nashville, Tenn., in 1807; served for some years in the general assembly of Tennessee; elected as a Republican to the Fifteenth Congress (March 4, 1817-March 3, 1819); resumed the practice of law in Nashville, where he died on January 7, 1856; interment in Nashville City Cemetery.

**CLAIBORNE, Thomas** (father of John Claiborne and Thomas Claiborne [1780-1856], uncle of Nathaniel Herbert Claiborne and William Charles Cole Claiborne, granduncle of John Francis Hamtramck Claiborne, and great-great-great-great granduncle of Corinne Claiborne Boggs), a Representative from Virginia; born in Brunswick County, Va., February 1, 1749; member of the Virginia house of delegates 1783-1788; served as colonel in command of the Brunswick County Militia in 1789; sheriff of Brunswick County 1789-1792; member of the Virginia senate 1790-1792; elected to the Third Congress; reelected as a Republican to the Fourth and Fifth Congresses (March 4, 1793-March 3, 1799); unsuccessful candidate for reelection in 1798 to the Sixth Congress; again elected as a Republican to the Seventh and Eighth Congresses (March 4, 1801-March 3, 1805); died on his estate in Brunswick County, Va., in 1812.

**CLAIBORNE, William Charles Cole** (brother of Nathaniel Herbert Claiborne, nephew of Thomas Claiborne [1749-1812], uncle of John Francis Hamtramck Claiborne, and great-great-great granduncle of Corinne Claiborne Boggs), a Representative from Tennessee and a Senator from Louisiana; born in Sussex County,

Va., in 1775; moved in early youth to New York City; studied law in Richmond, Va.; was admitted to the bar and commenced practice in Sullivan County, Tenn.; delegate to the State constitutional convention from Sullivan County in 1796; appointed judge of the superior court in 1796; elected as a Republican from Tennessee to the Fifth and Sixth Congresses, and served from November 23, 1797, to March 3, 1801, in spite of the fact that he was still initially under the constitutional age requirement of twenty-five years; appointed Governor of the Territory of Mississippi by President Thomas Jefferson on May 25, 1801, and served until 1805; appointed in October 1803 one of the commissioners to take possession of Louisiana when purchased from France; appointed Governor of the Territory of Orleans by President Jefferson on August 30, 1804 and served until 1812; elected Governor of Louisiana in 1812, and served from July 30, 1812 to December 16, 1816; elected as a Democrat from Louisiana to the United States Senate and served from March 4, 1817, until his death, before the assembling of Congress, in New Orleans, La., November 23, 1817; interment in Basin St. Louis Cemetery; reinterment in Metairie Cemetery.

Bibliography: *DAB*; Hatfield, Joseph T. *William Claiborne: Jeffersonian Centurion in the American Southwest.* Lafayette: University of Southwest Louisiana Press, 1976; Winters, John D. "William C.C. Claiborne: Profile of a Democrat." *Louisiana History* 10 (Summer 1969): 189-210.

CLANCY, Donald Daniel, a Representative from Ohio; born in Cincinnati, Hamilton County, Ohio, July 24, 1921; graduated from Elder High School; attended Xavier University, Cincinnati, 1939-1943, LL.B., University of Cincinnati Law School, 1948; was admitted to the bar in 1948 and commenced the practice of law in Cincinnati; member, Cincinnati city council, 1952-1960; mayor of Cincinnati, 1958-1960; chairman of Cincinnati Planning Commission, 1958-1960; elected as a Republican to the Eighty-seventh and to the seven succeeding Congresses (January 3, 1961-January 3, 1977); unsuccessful candidate for reelection in 1976 to the Ninety-fifth Congress; resumed the practice of law; is a resident of Cincinnati, Ohio.

CLANCY, John Michael, a Representative from New York; born in County Queens, Ireland, May 7, 1837; immigrated with his parents to the United States and settled in New York City; attended the public schools of Brooklyn; engaged in the real-estate business; served as an alderman of the city of Brooklyn 1868-1875; member of the State assembly 1878-1881; elected as a Democrat to the Fifty-first, Fifty-second, and Fifty-third Congresses (March 4, 1889-March 3, 1895); was not a candidate for renomination in 1894; resumed the real-estate business in New York City; unsuccessful candidate for election in 1896 to the Fifty-fifth Congress; died in Butte, Mont., while returning from a visit to Yellowstone Park, July 25, 1903; interment in Holy Cross Cemetery, Brooklyn, N.Y.

CLANCY, John Richard, a Representative from New York; born in Syracuse, N.Y., March 8, 1859; attended the public schools; engaged in the manufacture of theatrical rigging in 1885 and later in the manufacture of hardware specialties; vice president of the board of trustees of the New York State College of Forestry; member of the Central New York State Park Commission; executive with several banks; elected as a Democrat to the Sixty-third Congress (March 4, 1913-March 3, 1915); unsuccessful candidate for reelection in 1914 to the Sixty-fourth Congress; resumed manufacturing interests in Syracuse, N.Y.; during the First World War served on the Governor's committee of public safety, on the committee on armories of the State, and had charge of stampings and forgings for five central New York counties under the War Production Board; died in Syracuse, N.Y., April 21, 1932; interment in St. Agnes Cemetery.

CLANCY, Robert Henry, a Representative from Michigan; born in Detroit, Mich., March 14, 1882; attended the public schools; was graduated from the literary department of the University of Michigan at Ann Arbor in 1907; later studied law there one year; reporter on Detroit newspapers for four years; secretary to Representative Frank E. Doremus of Michigan, 1911-1913; secretary to Assistant Secretary of Commerce Edwin F. Sweet, 1913-1917; United States customs appraiser for Michigan, 1917-1922; during the First World War was manager of the War Trade Board at Detroit, chief inspector of purchases in Michigan for the Medical Corps of the War Department, and recruiting officer of the aviation division in Detroit; elected as a Democrat to the Sixty-eighth Congress (March 4, 1923-March 3, 1925); unsuccessful candidate for reelection in 1924 to the Sixty-ninth Congress; affiliated with the Republican Party in 1926; engaged in the real-estate business; elected as a Republican to the Seventieth and to the two succeeding Congresses (March 4, 1927-March 3, 1933); unsuccessful candidate for reelection in 1932 to the Seventy-third Congress; engaged in executive capacity with a manufacturing company until his retirement in 1948; died in Detroit, Mich., April 23, 1962; interment in Mount Olivet Cemetery.

CLAPP, Asa William Henry, a Representative from Maine; born in Portland, Maine, March 6, 1805; was graduated from the Norwich (Vt.) Military Academy in 1823; engaged as a merchant in foreign and domestic commerce at Portland; elected as a Democrat to the Thirtieth Congress (March 4, 1847-March 3, 1849); was not a candidate for renomination in 1848; delegate to the Democratic National Convention in 1848 and 1852; resumed his former business pursuits; served as a director of the Maine General Hospital and of the Portland Public Library until his death in Portland, Maine, on March 22, 1891; interment in Evergreen Cemetery.

CLAPP, Moses Edwin, a Senator from Minnesota; born in Delphi, Carroll County, Ind., May 21, 1851; moved with his parents to Hudson, Wis., in 1857; attended the common schools; was graduated from the law department of the University of Wisconsin at Madison in 1873; was admitted to the bar in 1874 and commenced practice in Hudson, St. Croix County, Wis.; prosecuting attorney of St. Croix County, Wis., 1878-1880; moved to Fergus Falls, Minn., in 1881 and continued the practice of law; attorney general of Minnesota, 1887-1893; moved to St. Paul, Minn., in 1891 and continued the practice of law; unsuccessful candidate for the Republican nomination for Governor of Minnesota in 1896; elected as a Republican to the United States Senate in 1901 to fill the vacancy caused by the death of Cushman K. Davis; reelected in 1905 and 1911, and served from January 23, 1901 to March 3, 1917; unsuccessful candidate for renomination in 1916; chairman, Committee to Examine Branches of the Civil Service (Fifty-seventh through Fifty-ninth Congresses), Committee on Indian Affairs (Fifty-ninth through Sixty-first Congresses), Committee on Interstate Commerce (Sixty-second Congress), Committee on Standards, Weights, and Measures (Sixty-third and Sixty-fourth Congresses); practiced law in Washington, D.C., 1918-1923; became vice president and general counsel of the North American Development Corporation in Washington, D.C., in 1923; died at his country home, "Union Farm," near Accotink, Va., on March 6, 1929; interment in Fort Lincoln Cemetery, Washington, D.C.

CLARDY, John Daniel, a Representative from Kentucky; born in Smith County, Tenn., August 30, 1828; moved with his parents to Christian County, Ky., in 1831; attended the county schools, and was graduated from Georgetown (Ky.) College in 1848; taught school one year; studied medicine at the University of Louisville, Kentucky, for one year, and was graduated from the University of Pennsylvania at Philadelphia in 1851; practiced his profession for a number of years, and then abandoned it to devote his time to scientific agriculture and stock raising; delegate to the Kentucky constitutional convention in 1890; appointed as one of the Kentucky commissioners to the Columbian Exposition at Chicago in 1893; elected as a Democrat to the Fifty-fourth and Fifty-fifth Congresses (March 4, 1895-March 3, 1899); was not a candidate for renomination in 1898; retired from public life; died at his home, "Oakland," near Hopkinsville, Christian County, Ky., on August 20, 1918; interment in Clardy's County Cemetery, Bells, Christian County, Ky.

**CLARDY, Kit Francis,** a Representative from Michigan; born in Butler, Bates County, Mo., June 17, 1892; moved with his family to Kansas City and then to a farm near Liberty, Mo., in 1907; attended schools in Butler, Kansas City, and Liberty, Mo., and the William Jewel College, Liberty, Mo.; was graduated from the University of Michigan Law School at Ann Arbor in 1925; admitted to the bar in 1925 and practiced in Ionia, Mich., 1925-1927; assistant attorney general, State of Michigan, 1927-1931; member and chairman of the Michigan Public Utilities commission 1931-1934; reentered private practice of law in 1934; elected as a Republican to the Eighty-third Congress (January 3, 1953-January 3, 1955); unsuccessful candidate for reelection in 1954 to the Eighty-fourth Congress; in 1956 moved to Palos Verdes Estates, Calif., where he died September 5, 1961; interment in Forest Lawn Memorial Park, Glendale, Calif.

**CLARDY, Martin Linn,** a Representative from Missouri; born in Ste. Genevieve County, near Farmington, Mo., April 26, 1844; attended the St. Louis University and the University of Mississippi at Oxford; was graduated from the University of Virginia at Charlottesville; served in the Confederate Army until the close of the Civil War and retired with the rank of major; studied law; was admitted to the bar and commenced the practice of law in Farmington, St. Francois County, Mo.; elected as a Democrat to the Forty-sixth and to the four succeeding Congresses (March 4, 1879-March 3, 1889); chairman, Committee on Mines and Mining (Forty-ninth Congress), Committee on Commerce (Fiftieth Congress); was an unsuccessful candidate for reelection in 1888 to the Fifty-first Congress; served as a delegate to the Democratic National Convention in 1884; resumed the practice of his profession in Farmington, Mo.; moved to St. Louis, Mo., in 1894, having been appointed general attorney for the Missouri Pacific and St. Louis & Iron Mountain Railway companies, and was elected vice president and general solicitor in 1909 and served until his death in St. Louis, Mo., on July 5, 1914; interment in Bellefontaine Cemetery.

**CLARK, Abraham,** a Delegate and a Representative from New Jersey; born near Elizabethtown (now Elizabeth), N.J., February 15, 1726; attended private schools; studied law but never practiced; sheriff of Essex County; member of the New Jersey provincial congress from May 23, 1775, to June 22, 1776, and was appointed assistant secretary October 9, 1775; Member of the Continental Congress 1776-1778, 1780-1783 and 1786-1788; a signer of the Declaration of Independence; delegate to the State conventions of 1786 and 1787; member of the State general assembly in 1776 and 1783-1785; member of the legislative council in 1778; elected to the Second and Third Congresses and served from March 4, 1791, until his death in Rahway, N.J., on September 15, 1794; interment in Rahway Cemetery.

Bibliography: *DAB*; Bogin, Ruth. *Abraham Clark and the Quest for Equality in the Revolutionary Era, 1774-1794.* Rutherford, N.J.: Fairleigh Dickinson University Press, 1982; Bogin, Ruth. "New Jersey's True Policy: The Radical Republican Vision of Abraham Clark." *William and Mary Quarterly* 3rd ser., 35 (January 1978): 100-09.

**CLARK, Alvah Augustus** (cousin of James Nelson Pidcock), a Representative from New Jersey; born in Lebanon, Hunterdon County, N.J., September 13, 1840; attended public and private schools; studied law; was admitted to the bar in 1863 and commenced practice in New Germantown, N.J.; licensed as a

counselor in 1867; moved to Somerville, Somerset County, in 1867 and continued the practice of law; elected as a Democrat to the Forty-fifth and Forty-sixth Congresses (March 4, 1877-March 3, 1881); was not a candidate for renomination in 1880; resumed the practice of law; appointed postmaster at Somerville on May 26, 1896, and served until his successor was appointed on June 15, 1899; again resumed the practice of law until his death in Somerville, N.J., on December 27, 1912; interment in Somerville Cemetery.

**CLARK, Ambrose Williams,** a Representative from New York; born near Cooperstown, N.Y., on February 19, 1810; attended the public schools; publisher of the Otsego Journal 1831-1836, of the Northern Journal in Lewis County 1836-1844, and of the Northern New York Journal at Watertown 1844-1860; surrogate for five years; elected as a Republican to the Thirty-seventh and Thirty-eighth Congresses (March 4, 1861-March 3, 1865); appointed consul at Valparaiso by President Lincoln and served from 1865 to 1869; acted as Chargé d'Affaires in Chile in the absence of the Minister in 1869; died in Watertown, N.Y., October 13, 1887; interment in Brookside Cemetery.

**CLARK, Amos, Jr.,** a Representative from New Jersey; born in Brooklyn, N.Y., November 8, 1828; engaged in business in New York City, with residence in Elizabeth, where he was largely interested in real estate; member of the city council of Elizabeth in 1865 and 1866; served in the State senate 1866-1869; elected as a Republican to the Forty-third Congress (March 4, 1873-March 3, 1875); unsuccessful candidate for reelection in 1874 to the Forty-fourth Congress; retired to his residence in Norfolk County, Mass., but retained business interests in Elizabeth, N.J.; died in Boston, Mass., October 31, 1912; interment in Evergreen Cemetery, Elizabeth, N.J.

**CLARK, Champ,** a Representative from Missouri. (*See* Clark, James Beauchamp.)

**CLARK, Charles Benjamin,** a Representative from Wisconsin; born in Theresa, Jefferson County, N.Y., August 24, 1844; attended the common schools; moved to Wisconsin in 1855 with his widowed mother, who settled in Neenah, Winnebago County; enlisted in Company I, Twenty-first Regiment, Wisconsin Volunteer Infantry, at its organization, and served with the same during the Civil War; engaged in mercantile pursuits, banking, and the manufacture of paper; mayor of Neenah 1880-1883; member of the city council of Neenah 1883-1885; member of the State assembly in 1885; elected as a Republican to the Fiftieth and Fifty-first Congresses (March 4, 1887-March 3, 1891); unsuccessful candidate for reelection in 1890 to the Fifty-second Congress; died in Watertown, Jefferson County, N.Y., while on a visit to his old home, September 10, 1891; interment in Oak Hill Cemetery, Neenah, Wis.

**CLARK, Charles Nelson,** a Representative from Missouri; born in Cortland County, N.Y., on August 21, 1827; attended Hamilton College, Clinton, N.Y.; moved to Illinois in 1859; when the Civil War broke out he assisted in raising a company of cavalry, which was made Company G, Third Illinois Cavalry, August 6, 1861, and went directly into service; became disabled and left the Army in 1863; settled in Hannibal, Marion County, Mo., in April 1865; became interested in the Mississippi River bottom lands in Illinois and undertook their reclamation; elected as a Republican to the Fifty-fourth Congress (March 4, 1895-March 3, 1897); engaged in agricultural pursuits; died in Hannibal, Mo., October 4, 1902; interment in Wauseon Cemetery, Wauseon, Fulton County, Ohio.

**CLARK, Christopher Henderson** (brother of James Clark and uncle of John Bullock Clark), a Representative from Virginia; born in Albemarle County, Va., in 1767; attended Washington College (now Washington and Lee University), Lexington, Va.; studied law in the office of Patrick Henry; was admitted to the bar in 1788 and commenced practice in New London (now Bedford Springs), Va.;

member of the Virginia house of delegates in 1790; elected as a Republican to the Eighth Congress to fill the vacancy caused by the death of John Trigg; reelected to the Ninth Congress and served from November 5, 1804, to July 1, 1806, when he resigned; resumed the practice of law; died near New London, Va., November 21, 1828; interment in a private cemetery at Old Lawyers Station, near Lynchburg, Va.

**CLARK, Clarence Don,** a Representative and a Senator from Wyoming; born in Sandy Creek, Oswego County, N.Y., April 16, 1851; attended the common schools and the University of Iowa at Iowa City; studied law; was admitted to the bar in 1874; taught school and practiced law in Manchester, Delaware County, Iowa, until 1881, when he moved to Evanston, Wyo., and continued the practice of law; prosecuting attorney of Uinta County 1882-1884; delegate to the State constitutional convention in 1889; upon the admission of Wyoming as a State into the Union was elected as a Republican to the Fifty-first Congress; reelected to the Fifty-second Congress (December 1, 1890, to March 3, 1893); unsuccessful candidate for reelection in 1892; elected as a Republican to the United States Senate in 1895 to fill the vacancy in the term beginning March 4, 1893, caused by the failure of the legislature to elect; reelected in 1899, 1905, and again in 1911 and served from January 23, 1895, to March 3, 1917; unsuccessful candidate for reelection in 1916; chairman, Committee on Railroads (Fifty-fourth through Fifty-ninth Congresses), Committee on Judiciary (Fifty-ninth through Sixty-second Congresses), Committee on Geological Survey (Sixty-third and Sixty-fourth Congresses); resumed the practice of law in Washington, D.C.; appointed a member of the International Joint Commission created to adjust disputes between the United States and Canada in 1919, chairman 1923-1929; retired from active pursuits and resided in Evanston, Wyo., until his death on November 18, 1930; interment in the Masonic Cemetery.

**CLARK, Daniel,** a Senator from New Hampshire; born in Stratham, N.H., October 24, 1809; attended the common schools, Hampton Academy, and Union College, Schenectady, N.Y.; was graduated from Dartmouth College, Hanover, N.H., in 1834; studied law; was admitted to the bar in 1837 and commenced practice in Epping, N.H.; moved to Manchester in 1839; member, State house of representatives 1842-1843, 1846, 1854-1855; elected as a Republican to the United States Senate to fill the vacancy caused by the death of James Bell; reelected in 1861, and served from June 27, 1857, to July 27, 1866, when he resigned; served as President pro tempore of the Senate during the Thirty-eighth Congress; chairman, Committee on Claims (Thirty-seventh through Thirty-ninth Congresses); United States district judge from 1866 until his death; president of the New Hampshire constitutional convention in 1876; died in Manchester, N.H., on January 2, 1891; interment in Valley Cemetery.

**Bibliography:** *DAB.*

**CLARK, Daniel,** a Delegate from the Territory of Orleans; born in Sligo, Ireland, about 1766; educated at Eton and other colleges in England; immigrated to the United States in 1786 and settled in New Orleans, La.; engaged in land speculation and banking; appointed a member of the first legislative council for the Territory of Orleans, but declined; elected to the Ninth and Tenth Congresses and served from December 1, 1806, to March 3, 1809; was an unsuccessful candidate for renomination in 1808 to the Eleventh Congress; died in New Orleans, La., August 16, 1813; interred in St. Louis Cemetery No. 1.

**Bibliography:** *DAB;* Wohl, Michael S. "A Man in the Shadow: The Life of Daniel Clark." Ph.D. dissertation, Tulane University, 1984.

**CLARK, David Worth,** a Representative and a Senator from Idaho; born in Idaho Falls, Bonneville County, Idaho, April 2, 1902; attended the public schools; was graduated from the University of Notre Dame, South Bend, Ind., in 1922 and from the law department of Harvard University in 1925; was admitted to the bar in 1925 and commenced practice in Pocatello, Idaho; assistant attorney general of Idaho 1933-1935; elected as a Democrat to the Seventy-fourth and Seventy-fifth Congresses (January 3, 1935-January 3, 1939); did not seek renomination in 1938, having become a candidate for United States Senator; elected as a Democrat to the United States Senate in 1938 and served from January 3, 1939, to January 3, 1945; unsuccessful candidate for renomination in 1944; resumed the practice of law in Boise, Idaho, and Washington, D.C.; moved to Los Angeles, Calif., in November 1954; also interested in broadcasting and banking; died in Los Angeles, Calif., June 19, 1955; interment in Holy Cross Cemetery, Culver City, Calif.

**CLARK, Ezra, Jr.,** a Representative from Connecticut; born in Brattleboro, Vt., September 12, 1813; moved with his parents to Hartford, Conn., in 1819; attended the public schools; engaged in business as an iron merchant; member of the common council and the board of aldermen; president of the National Screw Co. of Hartford, later consolidated with the American Screw Co. of Providence, R.I.; judge of the municipal court; elected as the candidate of the American Party to the Thirty-fourth Congress and as a Republican to the Thirty-fifth Congress (March 4, 1855-March 3, 1859); chairman, Committee on Manufactures (Thirty-fourth Congress); unsuccessful candidate for reelection to the Thirty-sixth Congress; president of the Hartford Board of Water Commissioners 1882-1895; president of the Young Men's Institute of Hartford for many years; died in Hartford, Conn., September 26, 1896; interment in Spring Grove Cemetery.

**CLARK, Frank,** a Representative from Florida; born in Eufaula, Barbour County, Ala., March 28, 1860; attended the common schools of Alabama and Georgia; studied law; was admitted to the bar in 1881 and commenced practice in Newnan, Coweta County, Ga.; moved to Florida in 1884 and settled in Polk County; city attorney of Bartow, Fla., in 1885 and 1886; member of the State house of representatives 1889-1891 and in 1899; assistant United States attorney in 1893; United States attorney for the southern district of Florida 1894-1897; moved to Jacksonville in 1895 and continued the practice of law; chairman of the Democratic State committee in 1900; delegate to the Democratic National Convention of 1920; elected as a Democrat to the Fifty-ninth and to the nine succeeding Congresses (March 4, 1905-March 3, 1925); chairman, Committee on Public Buildings and Grounds (Sixty-third through Sixty-fifth Congresses); unsuccessful candidate for renomination in 1924 to the Sixty-ninth Congress; resumed the practice of law in Miami, Fla.; appointed by President Calvin Coolidge as a Democratic member of the United States Tariff Commission, serving from April 12, 1928, to September 16, 1930; resumed the practice of law in Washington, D.C.; served as attorney for the Bureau of Internal Revenue, Treasury Department, from November 16, 1933, until his death in Washington, D.C., April 14, 1936; interment in Wildwood Cemetery, Bartow, Fla.

**CLARK, Franklin,** a Representative from Maine; born in Wiscasset, Lincoln County, Maine, August 2, 1801; attended the common schools; engaged in the lumber and shipping business in Wiscasset; member of the State senate in 1847; elected as a Democrat to the Thirtieth Congress (March 4, 1847-March 3, 1849); engaged in the manufacture of lumber; an executive councilor in 1855; died in Brooklyn, N.Y., on August 24, 1874; interment in Greenwood Cemetery.

**CLARK, Frank Monroe,** a Representative from Pennsylvania; born in Bessemer, Lawrence County, Pa., December 24, 1915; attended the public schools; also attended Pittsburgh Institute of

Aeronautics; enlisted in the United States Army Air Corps in 1942, and served in Europe as a flight officer until discharged in 1945; major in Air Force Reserve; while still in the service was appointed chief of police of Bessemer, serving in that capacity until November 1954; unsuccessful candidate for election in 1952 to the Eighty-third Congress; delegate to the North Atlantic Treaty Organization Conference, 1956-1974, to the Interparliamentary Conference in Germany in 1957, to the Christian Leadership for Peace Conference at The Hague in 1958, and to International Roads Conference in 1959, 1962-1968; elected as a Democrat to the Eighty-fourth and to the nine succeeding Congresses, and served from January 3, 1955 until his resignation on December 31, 1974; unsuccessful candidate for reelection in 1974 to the Ninety-fourth Congress; unsuccessful candidate for nomination in 1976 to the Ninety-fifth Congress, and in 1978 to the Ninety-sixth Congress; is a resident of Bessemer, Pa.

**CLARK, Henry Alden,** a Representative from Pennsylvania; born in Harborcreek Township, Erie County, Pa., January 7, 1850; attended the common schools and the Erie Academy in 1864, the State normal school, Edinboro, Pa., in 1865 and 1866, and Willoughby Collegiate Institute, Willoughby, Ohio, in 1866 and 1867; taught school; was graduated from the Erie Central High School in 1870, from Harvard University in 1874, and from Harvard Law School in 1877; was admitted to the bar in Fall River, Mass., in March 1878; subsequently associated with the Edison electric light interests in New York; moved to Erie, Pa., in 1882, continuing with the Edison corporation until 1887; was admitted to the Pennsylvania bar May 9, 1884; member of the common council of Erie in 1888; bought and edited the Erie Gazette 1890-1892; chairman of the Republican city and county committees in 1890; city solicitor of Erie from July 11, 1896, until April 30, 1899; served in the Pennsylvania senate in 1911, 1913, and 1915; elected as a Republican to the Sixty-fifth Congress (March 4, 1917-March 3, 1919); was not a candidate for renomination in 1918 to the Sixty-sixth Congress; resumed the practice of his profession; judge of the orphans' court for Erie County 1921-1931; died in Erie, Pa., on February 15, 1944; interment in Erie Cemetery.

**CLARK, Henry Selby,** a Representative from North Carolina; born near Leechville, Beaufort County, N.C., September 9, 1809; attended the common schools, and was graduated from the University of North Carolina at Chapel Hill in 1828; studied law; was admitted to the bar and commenced practice in Washington, Beaufort County, N.C.; member of the State house of commons 1834-1836; solicitor for the district in 1842; elected as a Democrat to the Twenty-ninth Congress (March 4, 1845-March 3, 1847); moved to Greenville, Pitt County, N.C., and resumed the practice of law; died in Greenville, N.C., January 8, 1869; interment at his country home near Leechville, N.C.

**CLARK, Horace Francis,** a Representative from New York; born in Southbury, Conn., November 29, 1815; was graduated from Williams College, Williamstown, Mass., in 1833; studied law; was admitted to the bar and commenced practice in New York City in 1837, where he was prominent in financial, political, and railroad circles; elected as a Democrat to the Thirty-fifth Congress and reelected as an Anti-Lecompton Democrat to the Thirty-sixth Congress (March 4, 1857-March 3, 1861); became director of the New York & Harlem Railroad, and subsequently was president of the Union Pacific, the Michigan Southern, and many other railroads; active manager of the Western Union Telegraph Co. and president of the Union Trust Co.; died in New York City on June 19, 1873; interment in Woodlawn Cemetery.

**Bibliography:** *DAB.*

**CLARK, James** (brother of Christopher Henderson Clark and uncle of John Bullock Clark), a Representative from Kentucky; born near the Peaks of Otter in Bedford County, Va., January 16, 1770; moved with his parents to Clark County, Ky., in 1794; was educated by private tutors; attended Pisgah Academy, Woodford County, Ky.; studied law; was admitted to the bar and commenced practice in Winchester, Ky., in 1797; member of the Kentucky house of representatives in 1807 and 1808; appointed judge of the court of appeals in 1810; elected as a Republican to the Thirteenth and Fourteenth Congresses and served from March 4, 1813, until his resignation in 1816; judge of the circuit court from 1817 until 1824; elected to the Nineteenth Congress to fill the vacancy caused by the resignation of Henry Clay; reelected to the Twentieth and Twenty-first Congresses and served from August 1, 1825, to March 3, 1831; chairman, Committee on Territories (Twenty-first Congress); member of the Kentucky senate, 1831-1835; elected, as a Whig, Governor of Kentucky in 1836, and served from June 1, 1836 until his death in Frankfort, Ky., September 27, 1839; interment in the private burial ground of the old Clark home at Winchester, Clark County, Ky.

**Bibliography:** *DAB.*

**CLARK, James Beauchamp (Champ)** (father of Joel Bennett Clark), a Representative from Missouri; born near Lawrenceburg, Anderson County, Ky., March 7, 1850; attended the common schools and Kentucky University at Lexington; was graduated from Bethany (W.Va.) College in 1873 and from Cincinnati Law School in 1875; president of Marshall College, Huntington, W.Va., in 1873 and 1874; admitted to the bar in 1875; edited a country newspaper and practiced law; moved to Bowling Green, Pike County, Mo., in 1876; city attorney of Louisiana, Mo., and Bowling Green, Mo., 1878-1881; deputy prosecuting attorney and prosecuting attorney of Pike County from 1885 until 1889; member of the Missouri State house of representatives in 1889 and 1891; delegate to the Trans-Mississippi Congress at Denver in May 1891; elected as a Democrat to the Fifty-third Congress (March 4, 1893-March 3, 1895); unsuccessful candidate for reelection in 1894 to the Fifty-fourth Congress; elected to the Fifty-fifth and to the eleven succeeding Congresses and served from March 4, 1897, until his death in Washington, D.C., March 2, 1921; minority leader (Sixtieth and Sixty-first Congresses), Speaker of the House of Representatives (Sixty-second through Sixty-fifth Congresses), minority leader (Sixty-sixth Congress); unsuccessful candidate for reelection in 1920 to the Sixty-seventh Congress; unsuccessful candidate for the Democratic presidential nomination in 1912; chairman of the Democratic National Convention of 1904; funeral services were held in the Hall of the House of Representatives; interment in City Cemetery, Bowling Green, Mo.

**Bibliography:** *DAB*; Clark, Champ. *My Quarter Century of American Politics.* 2 vols. New York: Harper, 1920; Morrison, Geoffrey F. "A Political Biography of Champ Clark." Ph.D. dissertation, St. Louis University, 1972.

**CLARK, James West,** a Representative from North Carolina; born in Bertie County, N.C., October 15, 1779; was graduated from Princeton College in 1797; member of the North Carolina State house of commons in 1802, 1803, and 1811; presidential elector on the James Madison ticket in 1812; member of the North Carolina State senate, 1812-1814; elected as a Republican to the Fourteenth Congress (March 4, 1815-March 3, 1817); appointed chief clerk of the Navy Department by Secretary John Branch and served from 1829 to 1831; died in Tarboro, Edgecomb County, N.C., December 20, 1843.

**CLARK, Jerome Bayard,** a Representative from North Carolina; born on Phoebus Plantation near Elizabethtown, Bladen County, N.C., April 5, 1882; attended the public schools, Davidson (N.C.) College, and the University of North Carolina at Chapel Hill; studied law; was admitted to the bar in 1906 and commenced practice in Elizabethtown, N.C.; president of the Bank of Elizabethtown 1910-1922; served in the State house of representatives in 1915; moved to Fayetteville, N.C., in 1920 and continued the practice of law; member of the State Democratic committee

1909-1919; member of the North Carolina State Judicial Conference 1924-1928; elected as a Democrat to the Seventy-first and to the nine succeeding Congresses (March 4, 1929-January 3, 1949); chairman, Committee on Elections No. 1 (Seventy-second and Seventy-third Congresses); was not a candidate for renomination in 1948; resumed the practice of law; died in Fayetteville, N.C., August 26, 1959; interment in Cross Creek Cemetery No. 3.

**CLARK, Joel Bennett** (son of James Beauchamp Clark), a Senator from Missouri; born in Bowling Green, Mo., January 8, 1890; attended the public schools at Bowling Green, Mo., and at Washington, D.C.; graduated from the University of Missouri at Columbia in 1912, and from the law department of George Washington University, Washington, D.C., in 1914; parliamentarian of the United States House of Representatives 1913-1917; was admitted to the Missouri bar in 1914; during the First World War served in the United States Army 1917-1919, attained the rank of colonel; commenced the practice of law in St. Louis, Mo., in 1919; author and compiler of several manuals on parliamentary law; elected as a Democrat to the United States Senate in 1932 for the term commencing March 4, 1933, and was subsequently appointed to the Senate to fill the vacancy caused by the resignation of Harry B. Hawes for the term ending March 3, 1933; reelected in 1938 and served from February 3, 1933, to January 3, 1945; unsuccessful candidate for renomination in 1944; chairman, Committee on Interoceanic Canals (Seventy-fifth through Seventy-eighth Congresses); member of the Board of Regents, Smithsonian Institution 1940-1944; associate justice of the United States Court of Appeals for the District of Columbia from 1945 until his death in Gloucester, Mass., July 13, 1954; interment in Arlington National Cemetery, Va.

**Bibliography:** *DAB*; Spencer, Thomas T. "Bennett Champ Clark and the 1936 Presidential Campaign." *Missouri Historical Review* 75 (January 1981): 197-213.

**CLARK, John Bullock** (father of John Bullock Clark, Jr., and nephew of Christopher Henderson Clark and James Clark), a Representative from Missouri; born in Madison County, Ky., April 17, 1802; attended the country schools; studied law; was admitted to the bar in 1824 and practiced in Fayette, Mo.; clerk of the Howard County courts 1824-1834; colonel of Missouri Mounted Volunteers in the Black Hawk War in 1832; major general of militia in 1848; member of the State house of representatives 1850 and 1851; elected as a Democrat to the Thirty-fifth Congress to fill the vacancy caused by the resignation of James S. Green; reelected to the Thirty-sixth and Thirty-seventh Congresses and served from December 7, 1857, until July 13, 1861, when he was expelled for having taken up arms against the union; brigadier general of Missouri Confederate State troops; a Senator from Missouri in the First Confederate Congress and a Representative in the Second Confederate Congress; practiced law until his death in Fayette, Howard County, Mo., October 29, 1885; interment in Fayette Cemetery.

**CLARK, John Bullock, Jr.** (son of John Bullock Clark), a Representative from Missouri; born in Fayette, Howard County, Mo., January 14, 1831; attended Fayette Academy, and the University of Missouri at Columbia; spent two years in California for travel and adventure; returned to the East, and was graduated from the law department of Harvard University in 1854; was admitted to the bar and practiced in Fayette, Mo., from 1855 until the commencement of the Civil War, when he entered the Confederate Army as a lieutenant; promoted successively to the rank of captain, major, colonel, and brigadier general; resumed the practice of law in Fayette, Mo.; elected as a Democrat to the Forty-third and to the four succeeding Congresses (March 4, 1873-March 3, 1883); chairman, Committee on the Post Office and Post Roads (Forty-fourth Congress); unsuccessful candidate for renomination in 1882 to the Forty-eighth Congress; clerk of the House of Representatives 1883-1889; engaged in the practice of law

in Washington, D.C., until his death there, September 7, 1903; interment in Rock Creek Cemetery.

**CLARK, John Chamberlain,** a Representative from New York; born in Pittsfield, Mass., January 14, 1793; pursued preparatory studies; was graduated from Williams College, Williamstown, Mass., in 1811; was admitted to the bar and commenced practice in Hamilton, N.Y.; moved to Bainbridge, Chenango County, about 1818; district attorney 1823-1827; elected to the Twentieth Congress (March 4, 1827-March 3, 1829); elected as a Democrat to the Twenty-fifth Congress (March 4, 1837-March 3, 1839), but changed his politics on the appearance of President Martin Van Buren's message in 1837 favoring an independent Treasury; reelected as a Whig to the Twenty-sixth and Twenty-seventh Congresses (March 4, 1839-March 3, 1843); served as First Auditor of the Treasury from August 2 to October 31, 1849; moved to Chemung County, N.Y., and engaged in the lumber business; died in Elmira, Chemung County, N.Y., October 25, 1852; interment in St. Peter's Churchyard, Bainbridge, N.Y.

**CLARK, Joseph Sill,** a Senator from Pennsylvania; born in Philadelphia, Pa., October 21, 1901; attended the Chestnut Hill Academy and was graduated from Middlesex School in 1919; B.S., Harvard University, 1923; LL.B., University of Pennsylvania Law School, 1926; was admitted to the bar in 1926 and commenced the practice of law in Philadelphia; unsuccessful candidate in 1934 for election to the Philadelphia city council; entered the United States Army Air Corps in August 1941 as a captain, and was released in 1945 as a colonel following service in the China-Burma-India theater; city controller of Philadelphia, 1950-1952; mayor of Philadelphia, 1952-1956; member of the board of overseers, Harvard University, 1953-1958; elected as a Democrat to the United States Senate in 1956; reelected in 1962 and served from January 3, 1957, to January 3, 1969; unsuccessful candidate for reelection in 1968; professor, Temple University, 1969; president, World Federalists, U.S.A., 1969-1971; chairman, Coalition on National Priorities and Military Policy; died January 12, 1990.

**Bibliography:** Clark, Joseph S. *The Senate Establishment*. New York: Hill and Wang, 1963; Clark, Joseph S. *Congress: The Sapless Branch*. New York: Harper and Row, 1964.

**CLARK, Lincoln,** a Representative from Iowa; born in Conway, Franklin County, Mass., August 9, 1800; attended the district and private schools; was graduated from Amherst (Mass.) College in 1825; studied law; was admitted to the bar in 1831 and commenced practice in Pickensville, Pickens County, Ala.; member of the State house of representatives in 1834, 1835, and 1845; moved to Tuscaloosa in 1836; elected attorney general by the legislature in 1839; appointed circuit judge by Governor Benjamin Fitzpatrick in 1846; moved to Dubuque, Iowa, in 1848; elected as a Democrat to the Thirty-second Congress (March 4, 1851-March 3, 1853); unsuccessful candidate in 1852 for reelection to the Thirty-third Congress, and in 1854 for election to the Thirty-fourth Congress; resumed the practice of law in Chicago, Ill.; appointed United States register in bankruptcy in 1866; retired from active business and returned to Conway, Mass., in 1869; died in Conway, Mass., September 16, 1886; interment in Howland Cemetery.

**CLARK, Linwood Leon,** a Representative from Maryland; born in Aberdeen, Harford County, Md., on March 21, 1876; attended the public schools; was graduated from Milton Academy, Baltimore, Md., in 1899, from the American University of Harriman, Tenn., in 1902, and from the law department of the University of Maryland in 1904; was admitted to the bar in 1904 and commenced practice in Baltimore, Md.; completed a LaSalle Extension University course in railway transportation in 1919; unsuccessful candidate for election in 1926 to the Seventieth Congress; elected as a Republican to the Seventy-first Congress (March 4, 1929-March 3, 1931); unsuccessful candidate for reelection in 1930 to the Seventy-second Congress;

resumed the practice of law in Baltimore, Md.; judge of the circuit court of Maryland, fifth judicial district, 1935-1938; practiced law in Annapolis, Md., and was a resident of Horn Point, near Annapolis, Md.; died in Annapolis, Md., November 18, 1965; interment in Woodlawn Cemetery, Baltimore, Md.

**CLARK, Lot,** a Representative from New York; born in Hillsdale, Columbia County, N.Y., May 23, 1788; moved with his parents to Otsego County in 1796; pursued academic studies; studied law; was admitted to the bar on June 11, 1816, and practiced in Norwich, N.Y.; district attorney of Chenango County in 1822 and 1823; elected to the Eighteenth Congress (March 4, 1823-March 3, 1825); appointed postmaster of Norwich on April 29, 1825, and served until April 12, 1828; again served as district attorney of Chenango County in 1828 and 1829; moved to Lockport, N.Y., in 1829 and continued the practice of law; became president of the Lockport Bank in 1829; member and agent of the so-called Albany Co., owners of all the unsold lands in Niagara and Orleans Counties and in the northern parts of Genesee and Erie Counties; moved to Buffalo, N.Y., in 1835; projector of the first wire-cable bridge over the Niagara chasm; president of the Suspension Bridge Company until his death; member of the State assembly in 1846; died in Buffalo, N.Y., Dec. 18, 1862; interment in Greenwood Cemetery, Brooklyn, N.Y.

**CLARK, Richard Clarence (Dick),** a Senator from Iowa; born in Paris, Linn County, Iowa, September 14, 1928; attended the public schools; attended the University of Maryland, Wiesbaden, Germany, 1950-1952, and the University of Frankfurt, Germany, 1951-1952; served in the United States Army, 1950-1952; B.A., Upper Iowa University, Fayette, 1953; M.A., University of Iowa, Iowa City, 1956; teaching assistant and professor of history and political science, 1956-1964; chairman of the Iowa Civil Defense Administration and the Iowa Office of Emergency Planning, 1963-1965; administrative assistant to Representative John C. Culver of Iowa, 1965-1972; elected as a Democrat to the United States Senate in 1972, and served from January 3, 1973 to January 3, 1979; unsuccessful candidate for reelection in 1978; appointed by President Jimmy Carter to be Ambassador at Large and United States Coordinator for Refugee Affairs, 1979; Director, Congressional Program, The Aspen Institute, 1980 to present; is a resident of Washington, D.C.

**CLARK, Robert,** a Representative from New York; born in Washington County, N.Y., on June 12, 1777; was tutored privately; studied medicine in the office of his brother; commenced practice in Galway, Washington County, N.Y., in 1799; moved to Stamford, Delaware County, and later settled near Delhi, Delaware County, where he continued the practice of his profession; member of the State assembly 1812-1815; elected to the Sixteenth Congress (March 4, 1819-March 3, 1821); delegate to the State constitutional convention in 1821; moved to Monroe County, Mich., and settled on a farm near the village of Monroe, where he again engaged in the practice of his profession and was also interested in the scientific cultivation of fruits and grasses and the subject of drainage; appointed register of the land office for the second land district of Michigan Territory on May 26, 1823, and served until March 25, 1831; died October 1, 1837.

**CLARK, Rush,** a Representative from Iowa; born in Schellsburg, Bedford County, Pa., October 1, 1834; attended the common schools, the local academy at Ligonier, Pa., and was graduated from Jefferson College, Canonsburg, Pa., in 1853; studied law; was admitted to the bar in 1853 and commenced practice in Iowa City, Iowa; member of the Iowa house of representatives 1860-1864, serving as speaker in 1863 and 1864; served on the staff of Governor Samuel J. Kirkwood of Iowa in 1861 and 1862, and aided in the organization of volunteer regiments from Iowa during the Civil War; trustee of Iowa University at Iowa City 1862-1866; again served in the State house of representatives in 1876; elected as a Republican to the Forty-fifth and Forty-sixth Congresses and served from March 4, 1877, until his death in Washington, D.C., April 29, 1879; interment in Oakland Cemetery, Iowa City, Iowa.

**CLARK, Samuel,** a Representative from New York and a Representative from Michigan; born in Clarksville, Cayuga County, N.Y., in January 1800; attended Hamilton College, Clinton, N.Y.; studied law in Auburn, N.Y.; was admitted to the bar and commenced the practice of law in Waterloo, N.Y., in 1826; elected as a Jacksonian from New York to the Twenty-third Congress (March 4, 1833-March 3, 1835); moved to Kalamazoo, Mich., in 1842 and resumed the practice of law; member of the State constitutional convention in 1850; elected as a Democrat from Michigan to the Thirty-third Congress (March 4, 1853-March 3, 1855); unsuccessful candidate for reelection in 1854 to the Thirty-fourth Congress; assisted in locating and inaugurating a land office at Buchanan, situated at the head of Lake Superior; discontinued the practice of his profession and retired from political activities; became greatly interested in agricultural pursuits; died in Kalamazoo, Kalamazoo County, Mich., on October 2, 1870; interment in Mountain Home Cemetery.

**CLARK, Samuel Mercer,** a Representative from Iowa; born near Keosauqua, Van Buren County, Iowa, October 11, 1842; attended the public schools and the Des Moines Valley College, West Point, Iowa; studied law; was admitted to the bar in 1864, but did not engage in extensive practice; editor of the Keokuk Daily Gate City for thirty-one years; delegate to the Republican National Conventions in 1872, 1876, and 1880; appointed commissioner of education to the Paris Exposition in 1889; postmaster of Keokuk from 1879-1885; member of the Keokuk Board of Education 1879-1894, serving as president 1882-1894; elected as a Republican to the Fifty-fourth and Fifty-fifth Congresses (March 4, 1895-March 3, 1899); was not a candidate for renomination in 1898 to the Fifty-sixth Congress; resumed editorial duties; died in Keokuk, Lee County, Iowa, on August 11, 1900; interment in Oakland Cemetery.

**CLARK, William,** a Representative from Pennsylvania; born in Dauphin, Pa., February 18, 1774; captain of militia in Dauphin County in 1793 and 1795; went to Crawford County, Pa., early in life; was associate judge of Crawford County 1803-1818; brigade inspector of the western district of Pennsylvania 1800-1817; participated in the War of 1812; was on board the flagship *Lawrence* in her first engagement with the British fleet on Lake Erie; secretary of the Pennsylvania land office 1818-1821; Pennsylvania treasurer 1821-1827; Treasurer of the United States from June 4, 1828, to November 1829; elected as an Anti-Masonic candidate to the Twenty-third and Twenty-fourth Congresses (March 4, 1833-March 3, 1837); member of the Pennsylvania constitutional revision commission in 1837; engaged in agricultural pursuits; died near Dauphin, Pa., March 28, 1851; interment in English Presbyterian Cemetery.

**CLARK, William Andrews,** a Senator from Montana; born near Connellsville, Fayette County, Pa., January 8, 1839; attended the common schools and the Laurel Hill Academy; in 1856 moved with his parents to Iowa, where he taught school; while teaching, studied law at the Iowa Wesleyan University at Mount Pleasant; worked in the quartz mines near Central City, Gilpin County, Colo., in 1862; went to Montana in 1863 and settled in Bannack, Beaverhead County, and engaged in placer mining for two years; engaged in various mercantile pursuits in Blackfoot and Helena and in banking at Deer Lodge; major of a battalion that pursued Chief Joseph and his band in the Nez Perces invasion of 1877; president of the State constitutional convention in 1884 and of the second constitutional convention in 1889; elected as a Democrat to the United States Senate for the term commencing March 4, 1899; took his seat December 4, 1899, and vacated his seat on May 15, 1900 before a resolution declaring his election void because of election fraud could be adopted; appointed to fill the vacancy caused by his own resignation, but did not qualify; again elected as a Democrat to the United States Senate in 1901 and served from March 4, 1901, to March 3, 1907; was not a candidate for reelection; resumed his copper mining, banking, and railroad interests; resident of New York City until his death there on March 2, 1925; interment in Woodlawn Cemetery.

**Bibliography:** *DAB*; Foot, Forrest L. "The Senatorial Aspirations of William A. Clark, 1898-1901: A Study In Montana Politics." Ph.D. dissertation, University of California, 1941; Mangam, William. *The Clarks, An American Phenomenon.* New York: Silver Bow Press, 1941.

**CLARK, William Thomas,** a Representative from Texas; born in Norwalk, Conn., June 29, 1831; self-educated; taught school in Norwalk, Conn., in 1846; studied law in New York City; was admitted to the bar in 1855 and commenced practice in Davenport, Iowa, the same year; during the Civil War served in the Union Army; commissioned first lieutenant and adjutant of the Thirteenth Iowa Infantry on November 2, 1861; successively commissioned captain and assistant adjutant general, major and adjutant general, and lieutenant colonel and assistant adjutant general; brevetted brigadier general of volunteers (July 22, 1864), and major general (November 24, 1865); engaged in banking in Galveston, Tex.; upon the readmission of the State of Texas to representation was elected as a Republican to the Forty-first Congress, and served from March 31, 1870 to March 3, 1871; presented credentials as a Member-elect to the Forty-second Congress, and served from March 4, 1871 to May 13, 1872, when he was succeeded by De Witt C. Giddings, who contested his election; postmaster of Galveston from June 19, 1872 to May 7, 1874; employed in various offices of the Government at Washington from 1876 until April 12, 1880, when he became chief clerk of the Internal Revenue Department, serving until June 30, 1883; moved to Fargo, N.Dak. in 1883 and continued the practice of law; also served as assistant editor of the Fargo Daily Argus; moved to Denver, Colo., in 1890 and practiced law; went to Washington, D.C., in 1898 and was employed in the Internal Revenue Service as a special inspector, and served until his death in New York City, October 12, 1905; interment in Arlington National Cemetery, Va.

**Bibliography:** *DAB*.

**CLARKE, Archibald Smith** (brother of Staley Nichols Clarke), a Representative from New York; born on a plantation in Prince Georges County, Md., in 1788; attended grammar and high schools; studied law; was admitted to the bar and practiced in Niagara County, N.Y.; surrogate of Niagara County in 1808 and 1809; member of the State assembly 1809-1811; served in the State senate 1813-1816; county clerk in 1815 and 1816; elected as a Republican to the Fourteenth Congress to fill the vacancy caused by the resignation of Peter B. Porter and served from December 2, 1816, to March 3, 1817; died in Clarence, Erie County, N.Y., December 4, 1821.

**CLARKE, Bayard,** a Representative from New York; born in New York City on March 17, 1815; was graduated from Geneva College in 1835; studied law; was admitted to the bar; attaché to General Lewis Cass, United States Minister to France, 1836-1840; student in the Royal Cavalry School; appointed second lieutenant in the Eighth Infantry, March 3, 1841; transferred to the Second Dragoons in September 1841, and resigned on December 15, 1843; settled in Westchester County, N.Y.; unsuccessful candidate for election in 1852 to the Thirty-third Congress; elected as a Whig to the Thirty-fourth Congress (March 4, 1855-March 3, 1857); died in Schroon Lake, Essex County, N.Y., June 20, 1884; interment in a vault at Newtown, Long Island, N.Y.

**CLARKE, Beverly Leonidas,** a Representative from Kentucky; born in Winterfield, Chesterfield County, Va., February 11, 1809; attended the common schools; moved to Kentucky in 1823; studied law in Franklin, Ky., and was graduated from the Lexington Law School in 1831; was admitted to the bar in 1833 and commenced practice in Franklin, Ky.; member of the Kentucky house of representatives, 1841-1842; delegate to the Kentucky constitutional convention in 1849; elected as a Democrat to the Thirtieth Congress (March 4, 1847-March 3, 1849); delegate to the Kentucky constitutional convention in 1849; unsuccessful Democratic candidate for election for Governor in 1855; appointed by President James Buchanan as Minister to Guatemala, and was also accredited to Honduras, and served from January 7, 1858, until his death in Guatemala, March 17, 1860; interment in the State Cemetery, Frankfort, Ky.

**CLARKE, Charles Ezra,** a Representative from New York; born in Saybrook, Conn., April 8, 1790; completed preparatory studies and was graduated from Yale College in 1809; studied law; was admitted to the bar in 1815 and commenced practice in Watertown, N.Y.; moved to Great Bend, Jefferson County, N.Y., in 1840; member of the State assembly in 1839 and 1840; elected as a Whig to the Thirty-first Congress (March 4, 1849-March 3, 1851); resumed the practice of law; also built and operated a gristmill and engaged in agricultural pursuits; died in Great Bend, N.Y., December 29, 1863; interment in Brookside Cemetery, Watertown, N.Y.

**CLARKE, Frank Gay,** a Representative from New Hampshire; born in Wilton, Hillsborough County, N.H., September 10, 1850; attended Kimball Union Academy, Meriden, N.H., and Dartmouth College, Hanover, N.H.; studied law; was admitted to the bar in 1876 and commenced practice in Peterboro; member of the New Hampshire State house of representatives in 1885; appointed colonel on the military staff of Governor Samuel W. Hale, and served in that capacity from 1885 to 1887; served in the State senate in 1889; elected to the State house of representatives in 1891 and chosen speaker of that body; elected as a Republican to the Fifty-fifth and Fifty-sixth Congresses, and served from March 4, 1897 until his death in Peterboro, Hillsborough County, N.H., January 9, 1901; interment in Pine Hill Cemetery.

**CLARKE, Freeman,** a Representative from New York; born in Troy, N.Y., March 22, 1809; attended the common schools; went into business for himself at the age of fifteen; began his financial career as cashier of the Bank of Orleans, Albion, N.Y.; moved to Rochester, N.Y., in 1845; became director and president of numerous banks, railroads, and telegraph and trust companies of Rochester and New York City; delegate to the Whig National Convention at Baltimore in 1852; vice president of the first Republican State convention of New York in 1854; appointed Comptroller of the Currency in 1865; delegate to the State constitutional convention in 1867; elected as a Republican to the Thirty-eighth Congress (March 4, 1863-March 3, 1865); was not a candidate for renomination in 1864; Comptroller of the Currency from March 9, 1865, to February 6, 1867; again elected to the Forty-second and Forty-third Congresses (March 4, 1871-March 3, 1875); resumed his former business pursuits; died in Rochester, N.Y., on June 24, 1887; interment in Mount Hope Cemetery.

**CLARKE, James McClure,** a Representative from North Carolina; born in Manchester, Bennington County, Vt., June 12, 1917; attended the public schools of Manchester, Vt., and Buncombe County, N.C.; graduated from Asheville (N.C.) School, 1935; A.B., Princeton University, 1939; worked for Farmers Federation Cooperative, Asheville, N.C., 1939-1959; served in the United States Navy, lieutenant, 1942-1945; associate editor, Asheville Citizen Times, 1960-1968; assistant to the president, Warren Wilson College, Asheville, 1969-1982; chairman, Buncombe County Board of Education, 1969-1976; member, North Carolina State house of representatives, 1977-1980; North Carolina State senator, 1981-1982; elected as a Democrat to the Ninety-eighth Congress (January 3, 1983-January 3, 1985); unsuccessful candidate for reelection in 1984 to the Ninety-ninth Congress; elected to the One Hundredth and One Hundred First Congresses (January 3, 1987-January 3, 1991); unsuccessful candidate for reelection in 1990 to the One Hundred Second Congress; dairy farmer and apple orchardist; is a resident of Fairview, N.C.

**CLARKE, James Paul,** a Senator from Arkansas; born in Yazoo City, Yazoo County, Miss., August 18, 1854; attended the public schools and Professor Tutwilder's Academy, Greenbrier, Ala.; was graduated from the law department of the University of Virginia at Charlottesville in 1878; was admitted to the bar in 1879 and commenced practice in Helena, Phillips County, Ark.; member, Arkansas State house of representatives, 1886-1888; member of the State senate from 1888 until 1892, serving as president in 1891 and ex officio lieutenant governor; attorney general of Arkansas, 1892-1894; declined to be a candidate for renomination; elected Governor of Arkansas in 1894, and served from January 1895 to January 12, 1897; moved to Little Rock, Ark., in 1897 and resumed the practice of law; elected as a Democrat to the United States Senate in 1903; reelected in 1909 and again in 1915, and served from March 4, 1903, until his death on October 1, 1916; served as President pro tempore of the Senate during the Sixty-third and Sixty-fourth Congresses; chairman, Committee on Disposition of Useless Executive Papers (Sixty-first and Sixty-second Congresses), Committee on Commerce (Sixty-third and Sixty-fourth Congresses); died in Little Rock, Ark.; interment in Oakland Cemetery.

**Bibliography:** *DAB.*

**CLARKE, John Blades,** a Representative from Kentucky; born near Augusta, Bracken County, Ky., on April 14, 1833; attended the common schools and Augusta (Ky.) College; taught school in the winters of 1851 and 1852; studied law in Augusta, Ky.; was admitted to the bar on April 20, 1854, and commenced practice in Rockport, Ind., in January 1885; moved to Brooksville, Ky., in December 1855 and continued the practice of law; prosecuting attorney of Bracken County 1858-1862; member of the Kentucky senate 1867-1870; elected as a Democrat to the Forty-fourth and Forty-fifth Congresses (March 4, 1875-March 3, 1879); declined to be a candidate for renomination in 1878; resumed the practice of his profession; died in Brooksville, Bracken County, Ky., May 23, 1911; interment in Mount Zion Cemetery, near Brooksville, Ky.

**CLARKE, John Davenport** (husband of Marian Williams Clarke), a Representative from New York; born in Hobart, Delaware County, N.Y., January 15, 1873; attended the common schools and was graduated from Lafayette College, Easton, Pa., in 1898; took postgraduate courses in economics and history in Colorado College at Colorado Springs; studied law in the New York Law School, and was graduated from the Brooklyn Law School in 1911; was admitted to the bar in 1912 and commenced practice in New York City; engaged in work with the mining department of the Carnegie Steel Co.; assistant to the secretary of mines of the United States Steel Corporation 1901-1907; secretary and treasurer of other mining interests; moved to Delaware County in 1915 and engaged in agricultural pursuits; elected as a Republican to the Sixty-seventh and Sixty-eighth Congresses (March 4, 1921-March 3, 1925); unsuccessful candidate for reelection in 1924 to the Sixty-ninth Congress; resumed agricultural pursuits; elected to the Seventieth and to the three succeeding Congresses and served from March 4, 1927, until his death, the result of an automobile collision near Delhi, N.Y., November 5, 1933; interment in Locust Hill Cemetery, Hobart, N.Y.

**CLARKE, John Hopkins,** a Senator from Rhode Island; born in Elizabeth, N.J., April 1, 1789; moved to Providence, R.I., where he studied under a private teacher; was graduated from Brown University, Providence, R.I., in 1809; studied law; was admitted to the bar and commenced practice in Providence in 1812; clerk of the supreme court of Providence County in 1813; proprietor of a distillery in Cranston, R.I., until 1824, when he became a cotton manufacturer in Providence, Pontiac, and Woonsocket; member, State house of representatives 1836-1842, 1845-1847; elected as a Whig to the United States Senate and served from March 4, 1847, to March 3, 1853; resumed his former manufacturing pursuits; died in Providence, R.I., November 23, 1870; interment in the North Burial Ground.

**CLARKE, Marian Williams** (wife of John Davenport Clarke), a Representative from New York; born at Standing Stone, Bradford County, Pa., July 29, 1880; moved with her parents to Cheyenne, Wyo., in 1881; attended the public schools and spent one year in the art school of the University of Nebraska at Lincoln; was graduated from Colorado College at Colorado Springs in 1902; resided in seven different States from 1881 to 1918; moved to Delaware County, N.Y., in 1918 and settled on a farm near Fraser; elected as a Republican to the Seventy-third Congress to fill the vacancy caused by the death of her husband, John Davenport Clarke, and served from December 28, 1933 to January 3, 1935; was a candidate for renomination in 1934 to the Seventy-fourth Congress, but withdrew her name before the primary election; returned to her farm, "Arbor Hill," near Delhi, N.Y., where she resided until 1950; died in Cooperstown, N.Y., April 8, 1953; interment in Locust Hill Cemetery, Hobart, N.Y.

**CLARKE, Reader Wright,** a Representative from Ohio; born in Bethel, Ohio, May 18, 1812; learned the art of printing; studied law; was admitted to the bar in 1836 and commenced practice in Batavia, Ohio; published a Whig paper in Shawneetown, Ill., for a few years; returned to Batavia, Ohio; member of the State house of representatives 1840-1842; presidential elector on the Whig ticket in 1844; clerk of the court of Clermont County 1846-1852; elected as a Republican to the Thirty-ninth and Fortieth Congresses (March 4, 1865-March 3, 1869); third auditor of the Treasury from March 26, 1869, to March 26, 1870; appointed collector of internal revenue in Ohio; died in Batavia, Clermont County, Ohio, May 23, 1872; interment in Union Cemetery.

**CLARKE, Richard Henry,** a Representative from Alabama; born in Dayton, Marengo County, Ala., February 9, 1843; attended Green Springs Academy and was graduated from the University of Alabama at Tuscaloosa in July 1861; during the Civil War served in the Confederate Army as a lieutenant in the First Battalion of Alabama Artillery; studied law; was admitted to the bar in 1867 and commenced practice in Dayton, Ala.; moved to Demopolis, Marengo County, Ala., and continued the practice of law; State solicitor for Marengo County 1872-1876; prosecuting attorney of the seventh judicial circuit in 1876 and 1877; resumed the practice of law in Mobile, Ala.; elected as a Democrat to the Fifty-first and to the three succeeding Congresses (March 4, 1889-March 3, 1897); was not a candidate for renomination, but was an unsuccessful candidate for Governor in 1896; resumed the practice of law; member of the State house of representatives in 1900 and 1901; died in St. Louis, Mo., September 26, 1906; interment in Magnolia Cemetery, Mobile, Ala.

**CLARKE, Sidney,** a Representative from Kansas; born in Southbridge, Worcester County, Mass., October 16, 1831; attended the public schools; publisher of the Southbridge Press in 1854; settled in Lawrence, Kans., in 1859; enlisted as a volunteer during the Civil War; appointed assistant adjutant general of Volunteers by President Lincoln February 9, 1863; captain and assistant provost marshal general for Kansas, Nebraska, Colorado, and Dakota; elected as a Republican to the Thirty-ninth, Fortieth, and Forty-first Congresses (March 4, 1865-March 3, 1871); chairman, Committee on Indian Affairs (Forty-first Congress); unsuccessful candidate in 1870 for reelection to the Forty-second Congress; member of the State house of representatives in 1879 and served as speaker; moved to

Oklahoma City, Oklahoma County, Okla., in 1889 and engaged in railroad building; chairman of the statehood executive committee in 1891; member of the Territorial council 1898-1902; died in Oklahoma City, Okla., on June 18, 1909; interment in Fairlawn Cemetery.

**CLARKE, Staley Nichols** (brother of Archibald Smith Clarke), a Representative from New York; born in Prince Georges County, Md., May 24, 1794; moved to Buffalo, N.Y., in 1815; employed as a clerk in the Bank of Niagara; clerk in the office of the Holland Land Co., Batavia, N.Y., from 1819 to January 1822, when he was transferred as their agent for the county of Cattaraugus to Ellicottville, N.Y.; treasurer of Cattaraugus County for seventeen years; elected as a Whig to the Twenty-seventh Congress (March 4, 1841-March 3, 1843); declined to be a candidate for renomination in 1842 to the Twenty-eighth Congress; died in Ellicottville, Cattaraugus County, N.Y., October 14, 1860; interment in Jefferson Street Cemetery.

**CLARKSON, Matthew,** a Delegate from Pennsylvania; born in New York City in April 1733; moved to Philadelphia, Pa.; was justice of the court of common pleas, quarter sessions of the peace, and of the Philadelphia orphans' court in 1771 and 1772; elected to the Continental Congress in 1785, but did not serve; member of the board of aldermen in 1789; mayor of Philadelphia 1792-1796; died in Philadelphia, Pa., October 5, 1800; interment in Christ Church Burying Ground.

**Bibliography:** *DAB.*

**CLASON, Charles Russell,** a Representative from Massachusetts; born in Gardiner, Kennebec County, Maine, September 3, 1890; attended the public schools; Bates College, Lewiston, Maine, A.B., 1911 and LL.D., 1914; Georgetown University, Washington, D.C., LL.B. and J.D., 1914; Oxford University, England, M.A. and B.A., 1917; connected with the Interstate Commerce Commission and the Department of Education, Washington, D.C., in 1913 and 1914; member of the commission for relief in Belgium in 1914 and 1915 and was decorated with the Medaille du Roi Albert; was admitted to the bar in 1917 and commenced practice in Boston, Mass.; during the First World War served as a sergeant major in the Coast Artillery, United States Army; instructor in law at Northeastern University, Springfield, Mass., 1920-1937; assistant district attorney of the western district of Massachusetts 1922-1926 and district attorney 1927-1930; elected as a Republican to the Seventy-fifth and to the five succeeding Congresses (January 3, 1937-January 3, 1949); unsuccessful candidate for reelection in 1948 to the Eighty-first Congress; resumed the practice of law; delegate to the Republican National Conventions in 1952, 1956, and 1960; dean, Western New England College School of Law, 1952-1970; was a resident of Springfield, Mass., until his death there July 7, 1985; interment in Longmeadow Cemetery.

**CLASSON, David Guy,** a Representative from Wisconsin born in Oconto, Oconto County, Wis., September 27, 1870; attended the public schools, and was graduated from the law department of the University of Wisconsin at Madison in 1891; was admitted to the bar the same year and commenced practice in Oconto, Wis.; judge of Oconto County 1894-1898; mayor of Oconto 1898-1900; city attorney 1900-1906; president of the board of education in 1912 and 1913; president of the board of fire and police commissioners in 1915 and 1916; elected as a Republican to the Sixty-fifth, Sixty-sixth, and Sixty-seventh Congresses (March 4, 1917-March 3, 1923); declined to be a candidate for renomination in 1922; resumed the practice of law in Oconto, Wis.; served as circuit judge of the twentieth judicial circuit 1928-1930; died in Oconto, Wis., September 6, 1930; interment in Evergreen Cemetery.

**CLAUSEN, Donald Holst,** a Representative from California; born in Ferndale, Humboldt County, Calif., April 27, 1923; graduated from the elementary and high schools of Ferndale; attended San Jose (Calif.) State College, Weber College, Ogden, Utah, and St. Mary's (Calif.) College; completed United States Navy V-5 Program: California Polytechnic, San Luis Obispo, Calif.; graduated as United States Naval officer and aviator; established an insurance business, Clausen Associates, and an air ambulance service, Clausen Flying Service, both in Crescent City, Calif.; served as a carrier pilot in the Asiatic-Pacific Theater, 1944-1945; member, board of supervisors, Del Norte County, 1955-1962; elected as a Republican to the Eighty-eighth Congress to fill the vacancy caused by the death of Clement W. Miller (who had been elected posthumously), and to the nine succeeding Congresses, serving from January 22, 1963 to January 3, 1983; unsuccessful candidate for reelection in 1982 to the Ninety-eighth Congress; appointed by President Ronald Reagan as a special assistant to the administrator, and director of special programs, Federal Aviation Administration, 1983-1990; member, Technical Advisory Committee on Aeronautics, California Transportation Commission; is a resident of Santa Rosa and of Ferndale, Calif.

**CLAWSON, Delwin Morgan,** a Representative from California; born in Thatcher, Graham County, Ariz., January 11, 1914; attended the public schools of Pima and Safford, Ariz.; attended Gila College, Thatcher, Ariz., in 1933 and 1934; various employment, 1934-1940; interviewer with the United States Employment Service, 1941; with the Federal Public Housing Authority in Arizona and California, 1942-1947; manager of the Mutual Housing Association of Compton, Calif., 1947-1963; member of the city council of Compton, 1953-1957; mayor of Compton, 1957-1961 and reelected in 1961 for another four-year term; director of three Los Angeles County Sanitation Districts 1957-1963; elected as a Republican to the Eighty-eighth Congress to fill the vacancy caused by the death of Clyde G. Doyle; reelected to the seven succeeding Congresses and served from June 11, 1963, until his resignation December 31, 1978; was not a candidate for reelection in 1978 to the Ninety-sixth Congress; was a resident of Downey, Calif.; died May 5, 1992.

**CLAWSON, Isaiah Dunn,** a Representative from New Jersey; born in Woodstown, Salem County, N.J., March 30, 1822; attended Delaware College, Newark, Del., and Lafayette College, Easton, Pa.; was graduated from Princeton College in 1840 and from the medical department of the University of Pennsylvania at Philadelphia in 1843; commenced the practice of medicine in Woodstown, N.J.; member of the State house of assembly in 1854; elected as a Whig to the Thirty-fourth Congress and reelected as a Republican to the Thirty-fifth Congress (March 4, 1855-March 3, 1859); was not a candidate for renomination in 1858 to the Thirty-sixth Congress; resumed the practice of medicine in Woodstown, N.J., where he died on October 9, 1879; interment in the Baptist Cemetery.

**CLAY, Alexander Stephens,** a Senator from Georgia; born near Powder Springs, Cobb County, Ga., September 25, 1853; attended the common schools; was graduated from Hiawassee (Tenn.) College in 1875; studied law; was admitted to the bar in 1877 and commenced practice in Marietta, Ga.; member of the city council in 1880 and 1881; member, State house of representatives 1884-1887, 1889-1890; served as speaker pro tempore in 1886-1887, 1889-1890; member, State senate 1892-1894, serving as president for two years; elected in 1896 as a Democrat to the United States Senate; reelected in 1902 and again in 1908 and served from March 4, 1897, until his death in Atlanta, Ga., on November 13, 1910; chairman, Committee on Revolutionary Claims (Fifty-ninth Congress), Committee on Woman Suffrage (Sixty-first Congress); interment in the City Cemetery, Marietta, Ga.

**CLAY, Brutus Junius,** a Representative from Kentucky; born in Richmond, Madison County, Ky., July 1, 1808; attended the common schools and was graduated from Centre College, Danville, Ky.; engaged in agricultural pursuits and stock raising; moved to Bourbon County in 1837 and continued former pursuits; member of Kentucky house of representatives in 1840; elected president of Bourbon County Agricultural Association in 1840 and served thirty years; president of the Kentucky Agricultural Association 1853-1861; again a member of the Kentucky house of representatives in 1860; elected as a Unionist to the Thirty-eighth Congress (March 4, 1863-March 3, 1865); chairman, Committee on Agriculture (Thirty-eighth Congress); was not a candidate for reelection; resumed former pursuits; died near Paris, Ky., October 11, 1878; interment in the family burial ground at "Auvergne," near Paris, Ky.

**Bibliography:** Hood, James Larry. "The Union and Slavery: Congressman Brutus J. Clay of the Bluegrass." *Register of the Kentucky Historical Society* 75 (July 1977): 214-21.

**CLAY, Clement Claiborne, Jr.** (son of Clement Comer Clay), a Senator from Alabama; born in Huntsville, Ala., December 13, 1816; was graduated from the University of Alabama at Tuscaloosa in 1834 and from the law department of the University of Virginia at Charlottesville in 1839; was admitted to the bar and commenced practice in Huntsville, Ala., in 1840; member of the Alabama State house of representatives in 1842, 1844, and 1845; judge of the county court of Madison County, 1846-1848; unsuccessful candidate for election in 1850 to the Thirty-second Congress; elected as a Democrat to the United States Senate to fill the vacancy in the term commencing March 4, 1853, caused by the failure of the legislature to elect; reelected in 1858, and served from November 29, 1853 to January 21, 1861, when he withdrew with other secessionist Senators; his seat was declared vacant and his name omitted from the roll by a resolution of March 14, 1861; chairman, Committee on Commerce (Thirty-fifth and Thirty-sixth Congresses): member of the Confederate Senate, 1861-1863; was a diplomatic agent of the Confederate States; arrested and imprisoned in Fortress Monroe, Va. in 1865; after the war settled on his plantation in Jackson County, Ala., and devoted himself to agricultural pursuits and to the practice of law; died at "Wildwood," near Gurley, Madison County, Ala., January 3, 1882; interment in Maple Hill Cemetery, Huntsville, Ala.

**Bibliography:** *DAB*; Clay-Clopton, Virginia. *A Belle of the Fifties.* 1904. Reprint. New York: Da Capo Press, 1969; Nueremberger, Ruth Anna. *The Clays of Alabama.* Lexington: University of Kentucky Press, 1958.

**CLAY, Clement Comer** (father of Clement Claiborne Clay, Jr.), a Representative and a Senator from Alabama; born in Halifax County, Va., December 17, 1789; moved with his parents to a farm near Knoxville, Tenn.; attended the public schools and was graduated from the East Tennessee University in 1807; studied law; was admitted to the bar in 1809; moved to Huntsville, Ala., in 1811, and commenced practice; served in the war against the Creek Indians in 1813; member, Territorial council of Alabama, 1817-1818; elected a judge of the circuit court in 1819, and chief justice in 1820; resigned in 1823 and resumed the practice of law; member, Alabama State house of representatives, 1827-1828, and served as speaker; elected to the Twenty-first and to the two succeeding Congresses (March 4, 1829-March 3, 1835); chairman, Committee on Public Lands (Twenty-third Congress); elected Governor of Alabama in 1835, and served from November 21, 1835 to July 17, 1837; elected as a Democrat to the United States Senate to fill the vacancy caused by the resignation of John McKinley, and served from June 19, 1837 until his resignation on November 15, 1841; chairman, Committee on Engrossed Bills (Twenty-fifth Congress), Committee on Militia (Twenty-fifth and Twenty-sixth Congresses); associate judge of the State supreme court in 1843; codified the laws of Alabama in 1842

and 1843; died in Huntsville, Ala., September 7, 1866; interment in Maple Hill Cemetery.

**Bibliography:** *DAB*; Nueremberger, Ruth Anna. *The Clays of Alabama.* Lexington: University of Kentucky Press, 1958.

**CLAY, Henry** (father of James Brown Clay), a Senator and a Representative from Kentucky; born in the district known as "the Slashes," Hanover County, Va., April 12, 1777; attended the public schools; studied law in Richmond, Va.; was admitted to the bar in 1797 and commenced practice in Lexington, Ky.; member of the Kentucky house of representatives in 1803; elected to the United States Senate to fill the vacancy caused by the resignation of John Adair, and served from November 19, 1806 to March 3, 1807, despite being younger than the constitutional age limit of thirty years; member, Kentucky house of representatives, 1808-1809, and served as speaker in 1809; again elected to the United States Senate to fill the vacancy caused by the resignation of Buckner Thruston, and served from January 4, 1810 to March 3, 1811; elected as a Republican to the Twelfth and Thirteenth Congresses, and served from March 4, 1811 to January 19, 1814, when he resigned; Speaker of the House of Representatives (Twelfth and Thirteenth Congresses); appointed one of the commissioners to negotiate the treaty of peace with Great Britain in 1814; elected as a Republican to the Fourteenth, Fifteenth, and Sixteenth Congresses (March 4, 1815-March 3, 1821); Speaker of the House of Representatives (Fourteenth, Fifteenth and Sixteenth Congresses); elected to the Eighteenth and Nineteenth Congresses, and served from March 3, 1823 to March 6, 1825, when he resigned; again served as Speaker of the House of Representatives (Eighteenth Congress); appointed Secretary of State by President John Quincy Adams and served from March 7, 1825 to March 3, 1829; elected as a Whig to the United States Senate on November 10, 1831, to fill the vacancy in the term commencing March 4, 1831; reelected in 1836 and served from November 10, 1831 until March 31, 1842, when he resigned; chairman, Committee on Foreign Relations (Twenty-third and Twenty-fourth Congresses), Committee on Finance (Twenty-seventh Congress); unsuccessful presidential candidate of the Democratic-Republican Party in 1824, of the National Republican Party in 1832, and of the Whig Party in 1844; again elected to the United States Senate, and served from March 4, 1849 until his death in Washington, D.C., June 29, 1852; funeral services held in the Chamber of the Senate; interment in Lexington Cemetery, Lexington, Ky.

**Bibliography:** *DAB*; Clay, Henry. *The Papers of Henry Clay, 1797-1824.* Edited by James F. Hopkins, Mary W.M. Hargreaves, Robert Seager II, and Melba Porter Hay et al. 10 vols. and supplement. Lexington: University Press of Kentucky, 1959-1992; Van Deusen, Glyndon G. *The Life of Henry Clay.* 1937. Reprint. Westport, Conn.: Greenwood Press, 1979.

**CLAY, James Brown** (son of Henry Clay), a Representative from Kentucky; born in Washington, D.C., November 9, 1817; pursued preparatory studies; attended Transylvania University, Lexington, Ky., and Kenyon College, Gambier, Ohio; clerk in a countinghouse in Boston 1832-1834; studied law at Lexington Law School; was admitted to the bar and practiced with his father in Lexington; Chargé d'Affaires to Portugal from August 1, 1849, to July 19, 1850; was a resident of Missouri in 1851 and 1852, when he returned to Lexington, Ky.; elected as a Democrat to the Thirty-fifth Congress (March 4, 1857-March 3, 1859); was not a candidate for renomination in 1858; declined the appointment by President Buchanan to a mission to Germany; member of the peace convention of 1861 held in Washington, D.C., in an effort to devise means to prevent the impending war; during the Civil War identified himself with the Confederacy; died in Montreal, Canada, January 26, 1864, where he had gone for his health; interment in Lexington Cemetery, Lexington, Kentucky.

**CLAY, James Franklin,** a Representative from Kentucky; born in Henderson, Henderson County, Ky. October 29, 1840; attended public and private schools at Henderson; was graduated from Georgetown College, Kentucky, in June 1860; studied law; was admitted to the bar in 1862 and commenced practice in Henderson, Ky.; member of the Kentucky senate in 1870; elected as a Democrat to the Forty-eighth Congress (March 4, 1883-March 3, 1885); unsuccessful candidate for renomination in 1884; resumed the practice of his profession in Henderson, Ky.; served as city attorney and as attorney for the St. Louis & Southern Railroad and the Ohio Valley Railway Co.; died in Henderson, Ky., on August 17, 1921; interment in Fernwood Cemetery.

**CLAY, Joseph** (grandfather of William Henry Stiles), a Delegate from Georgia; born in Beverly, Yorkshire, England, October 16, 1741; immigrated to the United States and in 1760 settled in Savannah, Ga., where he engaged in the general commission business; elected a member of the council of safety June 22, 1775; delegate to the Provisional Congress which met in Savannah July 4, 1775; major in the Georgia Line of the Continental Army during the Revolutionary War; appointed by the Continental Congress deputy paymaster general in Georgia with the rank of colonel August 6, 1777; elected to the Continental Congress in 1778, but did not attend; original trustee of Franklin College, Athens, Ga.; elected treasurer of Georgia in July 1782; judge of the United States Court for the District of Georgia 1786-1801; died in Savannah, Ga., November 15, 1804; interment in Colonial Park Cemetery.

**Bibliography:** *DAB.*

**CLAY, Joseph,** a Representative from Pennsylvania; born in Philadelphia, Pa., July 24, 1769; elected as a Republican to the Eighth, Ninth, and Tenth Congresses, and served from March 4, 1803, to 1808, when he resigned to engage in banking; chairman, Committee on Ways and Means (Ninth Congress); one of the managers appointed by the House of Representatives in 1804 to conduct the impeachment proceedings against John Pickering, judge of the United States District Court for New Hampshire; became cashier of the the Farmers & Mechanics' Bank of Philadelphia; died in Philadelphia, Pa., on August 27, 1811; interment in Christ Church Burying Ground.

**CLAY, Matthew,** a Representative from Virginia; born in Halifax County, near Danville, Va., March 25, 1754; during the Revolutionary War entered the Ninth Virginia Regiment October 1, 1776, transferred to the First Virginia Regiment in 1778 and to the Fifth Virginia Regiment in 1781, being successively promoted to first lieutenant, captain, and quartermaster; mustered out 1783; member of the State house of delegates 1790-1794; elected as a Republican to the Fifth and to the seven succeeding Congresses (March 4, 1797-March 3, 1813); chairman, Committee on Militia (Tenth Congress); unsuccessful candidate for reelection in 1813 to the Thirteenth Congress; elected to the Fourteenth Congress and served from March 4, 1815, until his death at Halifax Court House, Va., May 27, 1815; interment in the old family burying ground in Pittsylvania County, Va.

**CLAY, William Lacy, Sr.,** a Representative from Missouri; born in St. Louis, Mo., April 30, 1931; B.S., St. Louis University, 1953; real estate broker; manager, life insurance company, 1959-1961; alderman, Twenty-sixth Ward, St. Louis, Mo., 1959-1964; business representative, city employees union, 1961-1964; education coordinator, Steamfitters Local No. 562, 1966-1967; elected as a Democrat to the Ninety-first and to the thirteen succeeding Congresses (January 3, 1969-January 3, 1997); chairman, Committee on the Post Office and Civil Service (One Hundred Second and One Hundred Third Congresses); is a resident of St. Louis, Mo.

**CLAYPOOL, Harold Kile** (son of Horatio Clifford Claypool and cousin of John Barney Peterson), a Representative from Ohio; born in Bainbridge, Ross County, Ohio, June 2, 1886; attended the public schools and Ohio State University at Columbus; engaged in the publishing business at Columbus, Ohio, and published Hunter and Trader Magazine; deputy probate judge of Ross County, Ohio; elected as a Democrat to the Seventy-fifth, Seventy-sixth, and Seventy-seventh Congresses (January 3, 1937-January 3, 1943); unsuccessful candidate for reelection in 1942 to the Seventy-eighth Congress; resumed the publishing and office supply business; United States marshal for the southern district of Ohio 1944-1953; died in Chillicothe, Ohio, August 2, 1958; interment in Grandview Cemetery.

**CLAYPOOL, Horatio Clifford** (father of Harold Kile Claypool and cousin of John Barney Peterson), a Representative from Ohio; born in McArthur, Vinton County, Ohio, February 9, 1859; attended the common schools, and was graduated from the normal school at Lebanon, Ohio, in 1880; studied law; was admitted to the bar in 1882 and commenced practice in Chillicothe, Ohio; prosecuting attorney of Ross County 1899-1903; probate judge of the county 1905-1910; elected as a Democrat to the Sixty-second and Sixty-third Congresses (March 4, 1911-March 3, 1915); unsuccessful candidate for reelection in 1914 to the Sixty-fourth Congress; elected to the Sixty-fifth Congress (March 4, 1917-March 3, 1919); unsuccessful candidate for reelection in 1918 to the Sixty-sixth Congress; resumed the practice of law in Chillicothe, Ohio; died in Columbus, Ohio, January 19, 1921; interment in Grandview Cemetery, Chillicothe, Ross County, Ohio.

**CLAYTON, Augustin Smith,** a Representative from Georgia; born in Fredericksburg, Va., November 27, 1783; moved with his parents to Richmond County, Ga., in 1784; attended Richmond Academy, and was graduated from Franklin College, Athens, Ga., in 1804; studied law; was admitted to the bar in 1806 and commenced practice in Carnesville, Franklin County; moved to Athens; selected by the legislature in 1810 to compile the statutes of Georgia from 1800; member of the State house of representatives 1810-1812; clerk of the State house of representatives 1813-1815; served in the State senate in 1826 and 1827; judge of the superior court 1819-1825 and 1828-1831; elected as a Jacksonian to the Twenty-second Congress to fill the vacancy caused by the resignation of Wilson Lumpkin; reelected to the Twenty-third Congress and served from January 21, 1832, to March 3, 1835; resumed the practice of law in Athens, Ga., and died there June 21, 1839; interment in Oconee Cemetery.

**Bibliography:** *DAB.*

**CLAYTON, Bertram Tracy** (brother of Henry De Lamar Clayton), a Representative from New York; born on the Clayton estate near Clayton, Barbour County, Ala., October 19, 1862; attended the University of Alabama at Tuscaloosa; was graduated from the United States Military Academy at West Point in 1886 and appointed a second lieutenant in the Eleventh Regiment, United States Infantry; served until April 30, 1888, when he resigned to go into business as a civil engineer in Brooklyn; during the Spanish-American War was mustered into the United States volunteer service as captain of Troop C, New York Volunteers, May 20, 1898; was later placed in command of Troops A, B, and C of the New York Cavalry, and served throughout the Puerto Rican campaign; elected as a Democrat to the Fifty-sixth Congress (March 4, 1899-March 3, 1901); unsuccessful candidate in 1900 for reelection to the Fifty-seventh Congress; appointed a captain in the United States Regular Army on April 17, 1901; quartermaster in the United States Army in the Philippine Islands 1901-1904; quartermaster and disbursing officer of the United States Military Academy, West Point, N.Y., 1911-1914; during the First World War was appointed colonel in the Quartermaster Corps of the American Army March 15, 1918; quartermaster of the First Division in

France; killed in action at Noyer, Department of the Oise, France, May 30, 1918; interment in Arlington National Cemetery, Va.

**CLAYTON, Charles,** a Representative from California; born in Devonshire, England, October 5, 1825; attended the public schools; immigrated to the United States and settled in Wisconsin in 1842; went to Oregon in 1847 and in the following year to San Francisco, Calif.; alcalde of Santa Clara in 1849 and 1850; built the Santa Clara flour mills in 1852; returned to San Francisco in 1853 and engaged in the grain and flour business; member of the State assembly 1863-1866; member of the board of supervisors of San Francisco, Calif., 1864-1869; appointed surveyor of customs of the port and district of San Francisco by President Ulysses S. Grant on March 16, 1870; elected as a Republican to the Forty-third Congress (March 4, 1873-March 3, 1875); was not a candidate for renomination in 1874 to the Forty-fourth Congress; California State prison director in 1881 and 1882; died in Oakland, Calif., October 4, 1885; interment in Mountain View Cemetery.

**CLAYTON, Eva M.,** a Representative from North Carolina; born in Savannah, Ga., September 16, 1934; B.S., Johnson C. Smith University, Charlotte, N.C., 1955; M.S., North Carolina Central University, Durham, 1963; attended North Carolina Central University and University of North Carolina Law School; director, North Carolina Health Manpower Development Programs, University of North Carolina; executive director, Soul City Foundation; Assistant Secretary for Community Development, North Carolina Department of Natural Resources and Community Development, 1977-1981; president and owner, Technical Resources International, Ltd., 1981 to present; member, Warren County Commission, 1983-1993; adjunct assistant professor, health education, School of Public Health, University of North Carolina (Chapel Hill); unsuccessful candidate for nomination in 1968 to the Ninety-first Congress; elected as a Democrat to the One Hundred Second Congress, November 3, 1992, by special election to fill the vacancy caused by the death of Walter B. Jones, and at the same time elected to the One Hundred Third Congress; reelected to the One Hundred Fourth Congress, and served from November 3, 1992 to January 3, 1997; is a resident of Littleton, N.C.

**CLAYTON, Henry De Lamar** (brother of Bertram Tracy Clayton), a Representative from Alabama; born near Clayton, Barbour County, Ala., February 10, 1857; attended the common schools and Emory and Henry College, Emory, Va.; A.B., University of Alabama, Tuscaloosa, 1877; LL.B., University of Alabama School of Law, 1878; was admitted to the bar in 1878 and commenced practice in Clayton, Ala.; moved to Eufaula, Ala., in 1880 and continued the practice of law; member of the State house of representatives in 1890 and 1891; United States district attorney for the middle district of Alabama 1893-1896; permanent chairman of the Democratic National Convention of 1908; elected as a Democrat to the Fifty-fifth and to the eight succeeding Congresses and served from March 4, 1897, until May 25, 1914, when he resigned; moved to Montgomery, Ala., to accept appointment by President Woodrow Wilson as United States judge for the middle and northern district of Alabama, in which capacity he served until his death; chairman, Committee on the Judiciary (Sixty-second and Sixty-third Congresses); sponsor of the Clayton Anti-Trust Act of 1914, prohibiting corporate purchases of stock in competitive businesses or contracts in which a buyer was not allowed to do business with the seller's competitors, making interlocking corporate directorships illegal, exempting labor unions from prosecution under the anti-trust laws, and recognizing labor's right to strike and picket; one of the managers appointed by the House of Representatives in 1905 to conduct the impeachment proceedings against Charles Swayne, judge of the United States District Court for the Northern District of Florida, and in 1912 against Robert W. Archbald, judge of the United States Commerce Court; appointed to the United States Senate by Governor Emmet O'Neal, August 12, 1913, to fill the vacancy caused by the death of Joseph Forney Johnston, but his appointment was challenged and his credentials withdrawn October 21, 1913; died in Montgomery, Ala., December 21, 1929; interment in Fairview Cemetery, Eufaula, Ala.

**Bibliography:** *DAB*; Rodabaugh, Karl. "Congressman Henry D. Clayton and the Dothan Post Office Fight: Patronage and Politics in the Progressive Era." *Alabama Review* 33 (April 1980): 125-49; Rodabaugh, Karl. "Congressman Henry D. Clayton, Patriarch in Politics: A Southern Congressman During the Progressive Era." *Alabama Review* 31 (April 1978): 110-20.

**CLAYTON, John Middleton** (nephew of Joshua Clayton, cousin of Thomas Clayton, and great-granduncle of C. Douglass Buck), a Senator from Delaware; born in Dagsboro, Sussex County, Del., July 24, 1796; pursued preparatory studies at academies in Berlin, Md., and Milford, Del., and was graduated from Yale College in 1815; studied law at the Litchfield Law School; was admitted to the bar in 1819 and commenced practice in Dover; member, State house of representatives 1824; secretary of State of Delaware 1826-1828; elected to the United States Senate in 1829; reelected in 1835 and served from March 4, 1829, until December 29, 1836, when he resigned; chairman, Committee on the Judiciary (Twenty-third and Twenty-fourth Congresses); chief justice of Delaware 1837-1839; elected as a Whig to the United States Senate and served from March 4, 1845, until February 23, 1849, when he resigned to accept a Cabinet position; appointed Secretary of State in the Cabinet of President Zachary Taylor and served from March 7, 1849 until July 22, 1850; while Secretary of State negotiated the Clayton-Bulwer treaty with Great Britain; elected as a Whig to the United States Senate and served from March 4, 1853, until his death in Dover, Del., November 9, 1856; interment in Presbyterian Cemetery.

**Bibliography:** *DAB*; Comegys, Joseph. *Memoir of John M. Clayton.* Wilmington: The Historical Society of Delaware, 1882; Wire, Richard. "John M. Clayton and the Search for Order: A Study in Whig Politics and Diplomacy." Ph.D. dissertation, University of Maryland, 1971.

**CLAYTON, Joshua** (father of Thomas Clayton and uncle of John Middleton Clayton), a Senator from Delaware; born at Bohemia Manor, Cecil County, Md., July 20, 1744; studied medicine in Philadelphia and practiced in Middletown, Del.; during the Revolutionary War served as major in the Bohemia battalion of the Maryland Line, and was an aide on the staff of General George Washington at the Battle of the Brandywine, September 11, 1777; delegate to the Provincial Congress 1782-1784; member, State house of representatives 1785, and 1787; judge of the court of appeals; elected State treasurer in 1786; served as the first Governor of Delaware, June 2, 1789 to January 13, 1796; elected to the United States Senate to fill the vacancy caused by the resignation of John Vining, and served from January 19, 1798, until his death in Philadelphia, August 11, 1798; interment in Bethel Cemetery, Cecil County, Md.

**Bibliography:** *DAB*.

**CLAYTON, Powell,** a Senator from Arkansas; born in Bethel, Delaware County, Pa., August 7, 1833; attended the common schools and Partridge Military Academy, Bristol, Pa.; studied civil engineering in Wilmington, Del.; moved to Leavenworth, Kans., where he practiced his profession; appointed city engineer in 1857; at the outbreak of the Civil War entered the Union Army, attaining the rank of brigadier general August 1, 1864; following his discharge August 24, 1865 he moved to Arkansas and became a planter on land near Pine Bluff, Jefferson County; Governor of Arkansas from July 2, 1868 until his resignation on March 17, 1871, having been elected Senator; elected as a Republican to the United States Senate and served from March 4, 1871, to March 3, 1877; chairman, Committee on Enrolled Bills (Forty-third Congress), Committee on

Civil Service Retrenchment (Forty-fourth Congress); moved to Little Rock, Ark.; member of the Republican National Committee; appointed Ambassador to Mexico on March 22, 1897 and served until May 1905; lived in retirement until his death in Washington, D.C., on August 25, 1914; interment in Arlington National Cemetery, Va.

**Bibliography:** *DAB*; Burnside, William H. *The Honorable Powell Clayton.* Conway, Ark.; UCA Press, 1991.

**CLAYTON, Thomas** (son of Joshua Clayton and cousin of John Middleton Clayton), a Representative and a Senator from Delaware; born in Masseys Cross Roads, Md., in July 1777; received a classical education at Newark Academy; studied law; was admitted to the bar in 1799 and commenced practice in New Castle; clerk of the Delaware State house of representatives in 1800, and a member of that body from 1802 until 1806, and in 1810, 1812 and 1813; secretary of State of Delaware, 1808-1810; member of the State senate in 1808; State attorney general, 1810-1815; elected as a Federalist to the Fourteenth Congress (March 4, 1815-March 3, 1817); member of the State senate in 1821; elected to the United States Senate to fill the vacancy caused by the resignation of Caesar A. Rodney, and served from January 8, 1824 to March 3, 1827; chief justice of the court of common pleas of Delaware in 1828; chief justice of the superior court of the State in 1832; elected as a Whig to the United States Senate to fill the vacancy caused by the resignation of John M. Clayton; reelected in 1841, and served from January 9, 1837 to March 3, 1847; chairman, Committee on Printing (Twenty-seventh Congress), Commmittee on Revolutionary Claims (Twenty-ninth Congress); moved to New Castle and retired from public life; died in New Castle, Del., August 21, 1854; interment in Presbyterian Church Cemetery, Dover, Del.

**Bibliography:** *DAB*.

**CLEARY, William Edward,** a Representative from New York; born in Ellenville, Ulster County, N.Y., July 20, 1849; attended the public schools and the Ellenville Academy; moved to Brooklyn in 1879 and engaged in water transportation; vice president of the New York Board of Trade and Transportation; was a founder, and served as president, of the Victory Memorial Hospital; elected as a Democrat to the Sixty-fifth Congress to fill the vacancy caused by the resignation of Daniel J. Griffin; reelected to the Sixty-sixth Congress and served from March 5, 1918, to March 3, 1921; unsuccessful candidate for reelection in 1920 to the Sixty-seventh Congress; elected to the Sixty-eighth and Sixty-ninth Congresses (March 4, 1923-March 3, 1927); was not a candidate for reelection in 1926; resumed his former business interests; died in Brooklyn, N.Y., December 20, 1932; interment in Holy Cross Cemetery.

**CLEMENS, Jeremiah,** a Senator from Alabama; born in Huntsville, Ala., December 28, 1814; attended La Grange College and was graduated from the University of Alabama at Tuscaloosa in 1833; studied law at Transylvania University, Lexington, Ky.; was admitted to the bar in 1834 and practiced in Huntsville; appointed United States district attorney for the northern district of Alabama in 1838; member, State house of representatives 1839-1841; raised a company of riflemen in 1842 and served in the Texas War of Independence; member, State house of representatives 1843-1844; served in the United States Army during the Mexican War, attained the rank of lieutenant colonel; unsuccessful candidate for election in 1848 to the Thirty-first Congress; elected as a Democrat to the United States Senate to fill the vacancy caused by the death of Dixon H. Lewis and served from November 30, 1849, to March 3, 1853; novelist; moved to Memphis, Tenn., in 1858 and became editor of the Memphis Eagle and Enquirer in 1859; returned to Alabama; delegate to the convention in 1861 in which Alabama voted to secede from the Union; held office under the Confederacy, but became a strong Union supporter in 1864; died in Huntsville, Madison County, Ala., May 21, 1865; interment in Maple Hill Cemetery.

**Bibliography:** *DAB*; Martin, John. "The Senatorial Career of Jeremiah Clemens, 1849-1853." *Alabama Historical Quarterly* 43 (Fall 1981): 186-235.

**CLEMENS, Sherrard,** a Representative from Virginia; born in Wheeling, Va. (now West Virginia), on April 28, 1820; appointed a cadet to the United States Military Academy at West Point, but resigned after six months; was graduated in law from Washington (now Washington and Jefferson) College, Washington, Pa.; was admitted to the bar in 1843 and commenced practice in Wheeling; elected as a Democrat to the Thirty-second Congress to fill the vacancy caused by the resignation of George W. Thompson and served from December 6, 1852, to March 3, 1853; elected to the Thirty-fifth and Thirty-sixth Congresses (March 4, 1857-March 3, 1861); was not a candidate for renomination in 1860; member, Virginia convention, 1861; resumed the practice of law in Wheeling, W.Va.; moved to St. Louis, Mo., and continued the practice of law; died in St. Louis, Mo., June 30, 1881; interment in Calvary Cemetery.

**CLEMENT, Robert Nelson,** a Representative from Tennessee; born in Nashville, Tenn., September 23, 1943; attended public schools in Nashville; graduated Hillsboro High School, Nashville, 1958; B.S., University of Tennessee, 1967; M.A., Memphis State University, 1968; entered U.S. Army in 1969; released in 1971; and in the Tennessee Army National Guard Reserve, 1971 to present; member of the Tennessee Public Service Commission, 1973-1979; unsuccessful candidate for nomination for Governor of Tennessee in 1978; member, board of directors, Tennessee Valley Authority, 1979-1981; unsuccessful candidate for election in 1982 to the Ninety-eighth Congress; president, Cumberland University, 1983-1987; elected as a Democrat to the One Hundredth Congress, by special election, January 19, 1988, to fill the vacancy caused by the resignation of William Hill Boner; reelected to the One Hundred First and to the three succeeding Congresses and served from January 19, 1988, to January 3, 1997; is a resident of Nashville, Tenn.

**CLEMENTE, Louis Gary,** a Representative from New York; born in New York City June 10, 1908; attended St. Ann's Academy in New York City and LaSalle Military Academy, Oakdale, N.Y.; received a Reserve officer's certificate at Plattsburgh, N.Y., in 1925 and a Reserve commission in 1929; was graduated from Georgetown University Law School, Washington, D.C., in 1931; admitted to the District of Columbia bar in 1931 and commenced the practice of law in Washington, D.C.; admitted to the New York State bar and also to the Supreme Court bar; entered the United States Army as a second lieutenant in 1941 and served until released from active duty as a lieutenant colonel in 1946; member of the New York City Council, 1946-1949; elected as a Democrat to the Eighty-first and Eighty-second Congresses (January 3, 1949-January 3, 1953); unsuccessful candidate for reelection in 1952 to the Eighty-third Congress; executive vice president of Unexcelled Chemical Corp., Ohio Bronze Corp., Premier Chemical Corp., and Modene Paint Corp.; died in Jamaica, N.Y., May 13, 1968; interment in St. John's Cemetery, Flushing, N.Y.

**CLEMENTS, Andrew Jackson,** a Representative from Tennessee; born in Clementsville, Clay County, Tenn., December 23, 1832; attended a private school and Burritt College, Sparta, Tenn.; studied medicine and commenced practice in Lafayette, Tenn.; during the Civil War served as surgeon with the First Regiment, Tennessee Mounted Volunteer Infantry; elected as a Unionist to the Thirty-seventh Congress (March 4, 1861-March 3, 1863); member of the State house of representatives, 1866-1867; resumed the practice of his profession; established a school on his estate for the people of that section of the Cumberland highlands; died in Glasgow, Barren County, Ky.; November 7, 1913; interment in Glasgow Cemetery.

**CLEMENTS, Earle C.,** a Representative and a Senator from Kentucky; born in Morganfield, Union County, Ky., October 22, 1896; attended the public schools and the University of Kentucky at Lexington; during the First World War served in the United States Army, attained the rank of captain; engaged in agricultural pursuits; sheriff of Union County, 1922-1925; clerk of Union County, 1926-1933; judge of Union County, 1934-1941; member of the Kentucky senate, 1942-1944, serving as majority floor leader in 1944; elected as a Democrat to the Seventy-ninth and Eightieth Congresses, and served from January 3, 1945 until his resignation on January 6, 1948, having been elected Governor; elected Governor of Kentucky in 1947, and served from December 9, 1947 until his resignation on November 27, 1950, having been elected to the United States Senate to fill the vacancy caused by the resignation of Alben W. Barkley; at the same time was elected for a six-year term, and served from November 27, 1950 to January 3, 1957; unsuccessful candidate for reelection in 1956; Democratic whip, 1953-1957; director of the United States Senate Democratic Campaign Committee, 1957-1959; highway commissioner of Kentucky in 1960; consultant for the American Merchant Marine Institute, 1961-1963; consultant to tobacco industry and president of the Tobacco Institute, Inc., 1964-1976; died in Morganfield, Ky., March 12, 1985; interment in Morganfield Independent Order of Odd Fellows Cemetery.

**Bibliography:** Syvertsen, Thomas H. "Earle Chester Clements and the Democratic Party, 1920-1950." Ph.D. dissertation, University of Kentucky, 1982.

**CLEMENTS, Isaac,** a Representative from Illinois; born near Brookville, Franklin County, Ind., March 31, 1837; attended the common schools; was graduated from the Indiana Asbury College (now De Pauw University), Greencastle, Ind., in 1859; studied law in Greencastle; moved to Illinois and taught school; entered the Union Army in July 1861 and served as second lieutenant of Company G, Ninth Regiment, Illinois Volunteer Infantry; remained in the service over three years; was twice promoted; appointed register in bankruptcy in June 1867; elected as a Republican to the Forty-third Congress (March 4, 1873-March 3, 1875); unsuccessful candidate for reelection in 1874 to the Forty-fourth Congress; appointed a United States penitentiary commissioner in 1877; United States pension agent at Chicago, Ill., from March 18, 1890, until November 4, 1893; moved to Normal, Ill., in 1899; superintendent of the Soldiers' Orphans' Home at Normal, Ill.; died in Danville, Vermilion County, Ill., May 31, 1909; interment in Home Cemetery.

**CLEMENTS, Judson Claudius,** a Representative from Georgia; born near Villanow, Walker County, Ga., February 12, 1846; attended the common schools; served in the Confederate Army during the Civil War as a first lieutenant in the First Regiment, Georgia State Troops, Stovall's brigade; was wounded at Atlanta July 22, 1864; studied law at Cumberland University, Lebanon, Tenn.; was admitted to the bar in 1869 and commenced practice in La Fayette, Walker County, Ga.; served as school commissioner of Walker County in 1871 and 1872; member of the State house of representatives 1872-1876; served in the State senate 1877-1880; elected as a Democrat to the Forty-seventh and to the four succeeding Congresses (March 4, 1881-March 3, 1891); was not a candidate for renomination in 1890; appointed on March 17, 1892, a member, and in 1911 became chairman, of the Interstate Commerce Commission and served until his death in Washington, D.C., June 18, 1917; interment in Cave Hill Cemetery, Louisville, Ky.

**CLEMENTS, Newton Nash,** a Representative from Alabama; born in Tuscaloosa County, Ala., December 23, 1837; was graduated from the University of Alabama at Tuscaloosa in 1858; entered Harvard University in 1859; studied law but never practiced; during the Civil War entered the Confederate Army as a captain in the Twenty-sixth Alabama Regiment, afterward the Fiftieth Alabama

Regiment; successively promoted to major, lieutenant colonel, and colonel; member of the State house of representatives 1870-1872 and 1874-1878, serving as speaker in 1876, 1877, and 1878; elected as a Democrat to the Forty-sixth Congress to fill the vacancy caused by the resignation of Burwell B. Lewis and served from December 8, 1880, to March 3, 1881; unsuccessful candidate for renomination in 1880; largely interested in planting and cotton manufactures; died in Tuscaloosa, Ala., February 20, 1900; interment in Evergreen Cemetery.

**CLENDENIN, David,** a Representative from Ohio; moved from Harford County, Md., to near Struthers in the Mahoning Valley, Ohio, about 1806; was a pioneer in the iron and steel industry; lived in Trumbull County, Ohio; served as first lieutenant of Capt. James Hazlep's company of artillery attached to a regiment of the Ohio Militia in the War of 1812; also as lieutenant paymaster in the Second Regiment, Ohio Militia, from August 26, 1812, until January 19, 1813; assistant district paymaster in the United States Army from April 19, 1814, to December 19, 1814; elected as a Republican to the Thirteenth Congress to fill the vacancy caused by the resignation of Reasin Beall; reelected to the Fourteenth Congress and served from October 11, 1814, to March 3, 1817.

**CLEVELAND, Chauncey Fitch,** a Representative from Connecticut; born in Canterbury, Conn., February 16, 1799; attended the common schools; taught school from the age of fifteen to twenty; studied law; was admitted to the bar in 1819 and commenced practice in Hampton; member of the Connecticut State house of representatives, 1826-1829, 1832, 1835, 1836, 1838, 1847, and 1848; served as speaker in 1836 and 1838; State's attorney in 1832, and as State bank commissioner in 1838; moved to Norwich, Conn., in 1841; elected Governor of Connecticut in 1842, reelected in 1843, and served from May 4, 1842 to May 1844; unsuccessful candidate for reelection in 1844; resumed the practice of law in Hampton; elected as a Democrat to the Thirty-first and Thirty-second Congresses (March 4, 1849-March 3, 1853); became affiliated with the Republican Party upon its organization; delegate to the Republican National Conventions of 1856 and 1860; member of the peace convention of 1861 held in Washington, D.C., in an effort to devise means to prevent the impending war; again a member of the State house of representatives in 1863 and 1866 and served as speaker in the former year; engaged in agricultural pursuits and the practice of law; died in Hampton, Windham County, Conn., June 6, 1887; interment in South Cemetery.

**Bibliography:** *DAB.*

**CLEVELAND, James Colgate,** a Representative from New Hampshire; born in Montclair, Essex County, N.J., June 13, 1920; attended public schools and Deerfield Academy; B.A., Colgate University, Hamilton, N.Y., 1941; LL.B., Yale University Law School, 1948; enlisted in United States Army in December 1941, served forty months overseas in the Pacific in the Fortieth Infantry Division, and was discharged as a captain of Field Artillery in February 1946; was recalled to overseas duty in the Korean conflict from June 1951 to November 1952; awarded the Bronze Star for valor; after graduation from Yale in 1948 served briefly in the office of Senator Styles Bridges of New Hampshire; was admitted to the bar in 1948 and began the practice of law in Concord and New London, N.H., in January 1949; chairman, Merrimack County Republican Party, 1950-1951; organizer, incorporator, officer, and director of New London Trust Co.; member of the New Hampshire State senate, 1951-1963, and twice served as majority floor leader; elected as a Republican to the Eighty-eighth and to the eight succeeding Congresses (January 3, 1963-January 3, 1981); was not a candidate for reelection in 1980 to the Ninety-seventh Congress; chaired the New Hampshire campaign of President Gerald R. Ford in 1976; resumed the practice of law; was a resident of New London, N.H., until his death there on December 3, 1995.

**CLEVELAND, Jesse Franklin,** a Representative from Georgia; born in Greenville, S.C., October 25, 1804; attended the local schools; moved to Georgia; member of the Georgia State senate from 1831 until 1834; elected as a Jacksonian to the Twenty-fourth Congress to fill the vacancy caused by the resignation of William Schley; reelected as a Democrat to the Twenty-fifth Congress and served from October 5, 1835, to March 3, 1839; moved to Charleston, S.C., in 1839 and engaged in the mercantile business; served as a director of the Bank of South Carolina until his death in Charleston, S.C., on June 22, 1841; interment in St. Michael's Church Burial Ground.

**CLEVELAND, Orestes,** a Representative from New Jersey; born in Duanesburg, Schenectady County, N.Y., March 2, 1829; attended the common schools; moved to Jersey City, N.J., in 1845 and became involved in the manufacture of black lead, stove polish, and pencils; member of the board of aldermen of Jersey City in 1861 and 1862, serving as its president in the latter year; mayor of Jersey City from 1864 until 1866; elected as a Democrat to the Forty-first Congress (March 4, 1869-March 3, 1871); unsuccessful candidate for reelection in 1870 to the Forty-second Congress; engaged in business with the Forbes Fibre Co. of Jersey City; unsuccessful candidate for the nomination for Governor on the Democratic ticket in 1880; again mayor of Jersey City from 1886 to 1891; was one of the organizers of the board of trade of Jersey City in 1888, and its first president; moved to Tenafly in 1892 and thence to Engelwood, N.J.; died March 30, 1896, in Norwich, Windsor County, Vt., where he had gone in search of health; interment in Fairview Cemetery.

**CLEVENGER, Cliff,** a Representative from Ohio; born on a ranch near Long Pine, Brown County, Nebr., August 20, 1885; moved in 1895 with his parents to Lacona, Warren County, Iowa, where he attended the public and high schools; engaged in the mercantile business at Marengo, Iowa, 1901-1903 and at Appleton, Wis., 1904-1914; president of the Clevenger Stores, Bowling Green, Ohio, 1915-1926; manager of the F. W. Uhlman Stores, Bryan, Ohio, 1927-1938; also interested in agricultural pursuits, stock raising, and stock feeding; elected as a Republican to the Seventy-sixth and to the nine succeeding Congresses (January 3, 1939-January 3, 1959); was not a candidate for renomination in 1958; died in Tiffin, Ohio, December 13, 1960; interment in Oak Hill Cemetery, Neenah, Wis.

**CLEVENGER, Raymond Francis,** a Representative from Michigan; born in Chicago, Cook County, Ill., June 6, 1926; attended the Oak Park, Ill., schools; graduated from high school in 1944; served in the United States Army Medical Corps, July 1944 to July 1946; resumed education and attended Roosevelt University in Chicago and the London School of Economics and Political Science; graduated from Roosevelt University in 1949 and from the University of Michigan Law School in 1952; began the practice of law in Sault Ste. Marie in 1953; delegate to Democratic State conventions, 1954-1964; delegate to the Democratic National Convention of 1956; admitted to practice law in Michigan, Illinois, and before the Federal courts; Chippewa County Circuit Court Commissioner, 1958-1960; member of the Democratic State central committee, 1958-1960; Michigan Corporation and Securities Commissioner, 1961-1963; elected as a Democrat to the Eighty-ninth Congress (January 3, 1965-January 3, 1967); unsuccessful candidate for reelection in 1966 to the Ninetieth Congress; appointed by President Lyndon B. Johnson as chairman, Great Lakes Basin Commission, 1967-1968; resumed the practice of law; is a resident of Ann Arbor, Mich.

**CLEVER, Charles P.,** a Delegate from the Territory of New Mexico; born in Cologne, Prussia, February 23, 1830; attended the gymnasium of Cologne and the University of Bonn; immigrated to the United States in 1848 and settled in Santa Fe, N.Mex., in 1850; engaged in trade from 1855 to 1862; appointed United States marshal for New Mexico in 1857; became one of the owners of the Santa Fe Weekly Gazette, a paper published in English and Spanish, in 1858; studied law; was admitted to the bar in 1861 and commenced practice in Santa Fe, N.Mex.; appointed United States marshal and census enumerator in 1861; served as adjutant on the staff of General Edward R.S. Canby at the Battle of Valverde, N.Mex., February 21, 1862; adjutant general of New Mexico 1861-1865 and in 1867 and 1868; attorney general 1862-1867; presented credentials as a Democratic Delegate-elect to the Fortieth Congress and served from September 2, 1867 (date of election), to February 20, 1869, when he was succeeded by Jose Francisco Chaves, who contested the election; appointed one of the incorporators of the Centennial Exposition in 1869; served as a commissioner to revise and codify the laws of New Mexico; engaged in the practice of law until his death in Tome, Valencia County, N.Mex., on July 8, 1874; interment in the National Cemetery, Santa Fe, N.Mex.

**CLIFFORD, Nathan,** a Representative from Maine; born in Rumney, Grafton County, N.H., August 18, 1803; attended the public schools of Rumney, the Haverhill (N.H.) Academy, and New Hampton Literary Institute; taught school and gave vocal lessons; studied law in New York; was admitted to the bar and commenced practice in Newfield, York County, Maine, in 1824; member of the Maine State house of representatives, 1830-1834, and served as speaker the last two years; attorney general, 1834-1838; elected as a Democrat to the Twenty-sixth and Twenty-seventh Congresses (March 4, 1839-March 3, 1843); was not a candidate for renomination in 1842 to the Twenty-eighth Congress; appointed Attorney General in the Cabinet of President James K. Polk, and served from October 17, 1846 to March 17, 1848; commissioner to Mexico, with the rank of Envoy Extraordinary and Minister Plenipotentiary, from March 18, 1848 to September 6, 1849; through him the treaty was arranged with the Mexican Government by which California became a part of the United States; resumed the practice of law in Portland, Maine; nominated as an Associate Justice of the Supreme Court of the United States by President James Buchanan on December 9, 1857; was confirmed by the Senate on January 12, 1858, and served until his death; president of the commission established by Congress in 1877 to allocate disputed electoral votes in the Hayes-Tilden presidential contest; died in Cornish, Maine, on July 25, 1881; interment in Evergreen Cemetery, Portland, Maine.

**Bibliography:** *DAB*; Clifford, Philip G. *Nathan Clifford, Democrat, 1803-1881.* New York: G.P. Putnam's Sons, 1922.

**CLIFT, Joseph Wales,** a Representative from Georgia; born in North Marshfield, Plymouth County, Mass., September 30, 1837; attended the common schools and Phillips Exeter Academy, Exeter, N.H.; was graduated from the medical school of Harvard University in 1862; entered the Union Army and was acting surgeon from July 13, 1862, to August 7, 1865; served in the Army of the Potomac until November 18, 1866; practiced medicine in Savannah, Ga.; appointed registrar of the city of Savannah by Major General Pope under the reconstruction acts; upon the readmission of Georgia to representation was elected as a Republican to the Fortieth Congress and served from July 25, 1868, to March 3, 1869; presented credentials as a Member-elect to the Forty-first Congress, but was not permitted to qualify; died in Rock City Falls, Saratoga County, N.Y., May 2, 1903; interment in the cemetery adjoining the Clift estate, North Marshfield, Mass.

**CLINCH, Duncan Lamont,** a Representative from Georgia; born at "Ard-Lamont," Edgecombe County, N.C., April 6, 1787; entered the United States Army as first lieutenant of the Third Infantry on July 1, 1808; promoted to captain December 31, 1810; appointed lieutenant colonel of the Forty-Third Regiment, United States Infantry, on August 4, 1813; appointed colonel of the Eighth Regiment, United States Infantry, April 20, 1819; attained the rank of brigadier general on April 20, 1829; commanded at the Battle of

Ouithlacoochee against the Seminole Indians on December 31, 1835; resigned September 21, 1836, and settled on a plantation near St. Marys, Ga.; elected as a Whig to the Twenty-eighth Congress to fill the vacancy caused by the death of John Millen and served from February 15, 1844, to March 3, 1845; died in Macon, Ga., November 27, 1849; interment in Bonaventure Cemetery, Savannah, Ga.

**Bibliography:** Patrick, Rembert Wallace. *Aristocrat in Uniform, General Duncan L. Clinch*. Gainesville: University of Florida Press, 1963.

**CLINE, Cyrus,** a Representative from Indiana; born near Mansfield, Richland County, Ohio, July 12, 1856; moved to Steuben County, Ind., in 1858 with his parents, who settled near Angola; attended the Angola High School, and was graduated from Hillsdale College, Michigan, in 1876; superintendent of the schools of Steuben County 1877-1883; studied law; was admitted to the bar and began practice in Angola, Ind., in 1884; elected as a Democrat to the Sixty-first and to the three succeeding Congresses (March 4, 1909-March 3, 1917); chairman, Committee on Expenditures on Public Buildings (Sixty-second Congress); unsuccessful candidate for reelection in 1916; resumed the practice of law in Angola, Ind., and died there on October 5, 1923; interment in Circle Hill Cemetery.

**CLINGAN, William,** a Delegate from Pennsylvania; born probably near Wagontown, West Colen Township, Chester County, Pa.; justice of the peace 1757-1786; Member of the Continental Congress 1777-1779; one of the first signers of the Articles of Confederation in 1778; president of the county courts 1780-1786; died on May 9, 1790; interment in Upper Octorara Burial Grounds, Chester County, Pa.

**CLINGER, William Floyd, Jr.,** a Representative from Pennsylvania; born in Warren, Pa., April 4, 1929; attended the public schools of Warren; graduated from The Hill School, Pottstown, Pa., 1947; B.A., Johns Hopkins University, Baltimore, Md., 1951; LL.B., University of Virginia, Charlottesville, 1965; served in the United States Navy, lieutenant, 1951-1955; associated with the New Process Co., Warren, Pa., 1955-1962; admitted to the Pennsylvania bar in 1965 and commenced practice in Warren; delegate, Pennsylvania constitutional convention, 1967-1968; delegate to the Republican National Convention of 1972; chief counsel, Economic Development Administration, 1975-1977; elected as a Republican to the Ninety-sixth and to the eight succeeding Congresses (January 3, 1979-January 3, 1997); chairman, Committee on Government Reform and Oversight (One Hundred Fourth Congress); was not a candidate for reelection in 1996 to the One Hundred Fifth Congress; is a resident of Warren, Pa.

**CLINGMAN, Thomas Lanier,** a Representative and a Senator from North Carolina; born in Huntsville, N.C., July 27, 1812; educated by private tutors and in the public schools in Iredell County, N.C.; was graduated from the University of North Carolina at Chapel Hill in 1832; studied law; was admitted to the bar in 1834 and began practice in Huntsville, N.C.; elected to the North Carolina State house of commons in 1835; moved to Asheville, Buncombe County, N.C., in 1836; member of the State senate in 1840; elected as a Whig to the Twenty-eighth Congress (March 4, 1843-March 3, 1845); unsuccessful candidate for reelection in 1844 to the Twenty-ninth Congress; elected as a Whig to the Thirtieth and to the five succeeding Congresses, and served from March 4, 1847 to May 7, 1858, when he resigned to become Senator; chairman, Committee on Public Expenditures (Thirtieth Congress), Committee on Foreign Affairs (Thirty-fifth Congress); appointed as a Democrat to the United States Senate on May 6, 1858, to fill the vacancy caused by the resignation of Asa Biggs; reelected in 1861, and served from May 7, 1858 to March 28, 1861, when he withdrew; expelled from the Senate on July 11, 1861 for support of the Confederacy; chairman, Committee on Revolutionary Claims

(Thirty-fifth Congress); appointed a brigadier general in the Confederate Army on May 17, 1862; severely wounded during operations in Virginia in August 1864, and was unable to rejoin his command until shortly before the close of the war; delegate to the Democratic National Convention of 1868; explored and measured mountain peaks in the range of the Appalachians along the boundary between North Carolina and Tennessee, and was instrumental in developing the mining of mineral silicates in that region; died in Morganton, Burke County, N.C., November 3, 1897; interment in Riverside Cemetery, Asheville, N.C.

**Bibliography:** *DAB*; Inscoe, John C. "Thomas Clingman, Mountain Whiggery, and the Southern Cause." *Civil War History* 33 (March 1987): 42-62; Jeffrey, Thomas. "Thunder From the Mountains: Thomas Lanier Clingman and the End of Whig Supremacy in North Carolina." *North Carolina Historical Review* 56 (October 1979): 366-395; Kruman, Marc. "Thomas L. Clingman and the Whig Party: A Reconsideration." *North Carolina Historical Review* 64 (January 1987): 1-18.

**CLINTON, De Witt** (half brother of James Graham Clinton, nephew of George Clinton [1739-1812] and cousin of George Clinton [1771-1809]), a Senator from New York; born in Napanock, Ulster County, N.Y., March 2, 1769; was graduated from Columbia College in 1786; studied law; was admitted to the bar in 1790 and commenced practice in New York City; private secretary to the Governor, 1790-1795; member of the New York State assembly in 1798; member, New York State senate, 1798-1802, 1806-1811; delegate to the State constitutional convention in 1801; member of the council of appointments in 1801, 1802, 1806, and 1807; elected as a Republican to the United States Senate to fill the vacancy caused by the resignation of John Armstrong and served from February 9, 1802, to November 4, 1803, when he resigned; mayor of New York City, 1803-1807, 1810, 1811, 1813, and 1814; while mayor he organized the Historical Society of New York in 1804 and was its president; also organized the Academy of Fine Arts in 1808; lieutenant governor of New York, 1811-1813; unsuccessful candidate of the Peace Party for President of the United States in 1812; regent of the University of New York, 1808-1825; in 1809 was a member of the commission to explore a route for a canal between Lake Erie and the Hudson River, broke ground for that canal while Governor, and served several years as canal commissioner; elected Governor of New York in 1817, reelected in 1820, and served from July 1, 1817 to January 1, 1823; elected Governor in 1824, reelected in 1826, and served from January 1, 1825 until his death in Albany, N.Y., on February 11, 1828; interment in Green-Wood Cemetery, Brooklyn, N.Y.

**Bibliography:** *DAB*; Bobbe, Dorothie. *De Witt Clinton*. New York: Minton, Balch and Company, 1933; McBain, Howard. *De Witt Clinton and the Origin of the Spoils System in New York*. New York: AMS Press, 1967.

**CLINTON, George** (father of George Clinton [1771-1809] and uncle of De Witt Clinton and James Graham Clinton), a Delegate from New York and a Vice President of the United States; born in Little Britain, Ulster (now Orange) County, N.Y., July 26, 1739; completed preparatory studies; served as lieutenant of rangers in the expedition against Fort Frontenac; studied law; was admitted to the bar and commenced practice in Little Britain; clerk of the court of common pleas in 1759 and district attorney in 1765; surveyor of New Windsor; member of the State assembly in 1768; served on the New York Committee of Correspondence in 1774; Member of the Continental Congress from May 15, 1775, to July 8, 1776, when he was ordered to take the field as brigadier general of militia; appointed brigadier general by Congress in March 1777; Governor of New York from July 9, 1777 to July 1, 1795; president of the State convention which ratified the Federal Constitution; elected Governor of New York in 1801, and served from July 1, 1801 to July 1, 1804; elected Vice President of the United States in 1804 as a

Republican and served four years under President Thomas Jefferson; reelected in 1808 and served under President James Madison until his death in office; died in Washington, D.C., April 20, 1812; interment in the Congressional Cemetery; reinterment in the First Dutch Reformed Church Cemetery, Kingston, N.Y., in May 1908.

**Bibliography:** *DAB*; Pagano, Frances B. "An Historical Account of the Military and Political Career of George Clinton, 1739-1812." Ph.D. dissertation, St. John's University, 1956; Spaulding E. Wilder. *His Excellency, George Clinton: Critic of the Constitution.* 1938. Reprint. Port Washington, N.Y.: I.J. Friedman, 1964.

**CLINTON, George** (son of George Clinton [1739-1812] and cousin of De Witt Clinton and James Graham Clinton), a Representative from New York; born in New York City June 6, 1771; delegate to the State constitutional convention in 1801; member of the State assembly 1804 and 1805; elected as a Republican to the Eighth and Ninth Congresses to fill the vacancies caused by the resignation of Samuel L. Mitchill (who had been reelected to the Ninth Congress); reelected to the Tenth Congress and served from February 14, 1805, to March 3, 1809; died in New York City September 16, 1809.

**CLINTON, James Graham** (half brother of De Witt Clinton, nephew of George Clinton [1739-1812] and cousin of George Clinton [1771-1809]), a Representative from New York; born in Little Britain, Orange County, N.Y., January 2, 1804; attended the common schools and Newburgh (N.Y.) Academy; studied law; was admitted to the bar in 1823 and practiced in Newburgh; master in chancery of Orange County; judge of the court of common pleas of Orange County; director of the old Newburgh Whaling Co. and of the Delaware & Hudson Railroad project; colonel in the State militia; elected as a Democrat to the Twenty-seventh and Twenty-eighth Congresses (March 4, 1841-March 3, 1845); chairman, Committee on Public Expenditures (Twenty-eighth Congress); was not a candidate for reelection in 1844; died in New York City May 28, 1849; interment in the family cemetery at Little Britain, New Windsor Township, N.Y., reinterment in Woodlawn Cemetery, New Windsor, N.Y.

**CLIPPINGER, Roy,** a Representative from Illinois; born in Fairfield, Wayne County, Ill., January 13, 1886; attended the public schools; learned the printer's trade and engaged in the newspaper business; publisher and editor 1909-1961; founder and president of the Board of Greater Weeklies, New York City; president of the Carmi, Ill., Hospital Association 1945-1948; manager of the White County, Ill., Bridge Commission 1941-1961; engaged in the furniture business 1947-1950; elected as a Republican to the Seventy-ninth Congress to fill the vacancy caused by the death of James V. Heidinger; reelected in 1946 to the Eightieth Congress and served from November 6, 1945, to January 3, 1949; was not a candidate for renomination in 1948; resumed his former business pursuits; was a resident of Carmi, Ill., where he died on December 24, 1962; interment in I.O.O.F. Cemetery, McLeansboro, Ill.

**CLOPTON, David,** a Representative from Alabama; born in Putnam County, near Milledgeville, Ga., September 29, 1820; attended the county schools and Edenton (Ga.) Academy; was graduated from Randolph-Macon College, Boydton, Va., in 1840; studied law; was admitted to the bar in 1841 and commenced practice in Milledgeville, Ga.; moved to Tuskegee, Ala., in 1844, and continued the practice of his profession; elected as a Democrat to the Thirty-sixth Congress and served from March 4, 1859, to January 21, 1861, when he joined other secessionist members of the Alabama delegation in withdrawing from the Thirty-sixth Congress; during the Civil War enlisted as a private in the Confederate Army in the Twelfth Alabama Infantry for one year; elected as a Representative to the First and Second Confederate Congresses and served from 1862 to 1864; appointed judge of the supreme court of Alabama October 30, 1884, and served until his death; died in Montgomery, Ala., February 5, 1892; interment in Oakwood Cemetery.

**Bibliography:** *DAB.*

**CLOPTON, John,** a Representative from Virginia; born in St. Peter's parish, near Tunstall, New Kent County, Va., February 7, 1756; was graduated from the College of Philadelphia (now the University of Pennsylvania) in 1776; studied law; was admitted to the bar and practiced; served as first lieutenant and as captain in the Revolutionary War; wounded at the Battle of Brandywine; member of the Virginia house of delegates 1789-1791; elected as a Republican to the Fourth and Fifth Congresses (March 4, 1795-March 3, 1799); member of the Virginia privy council 1799-1801; elected to the Seventh and to the seven succeeding Congresses and served from March 4, 1801, until his death near Tunstall, Va., September 11, 1816; chairman, Committee on Revisal and Unfinished Business (Tenth Congress); interment in the family burying ground on his plantation.

**Bibliography:** *DAB.*

**CLOUSE, Wynne F.,** a Representative from Tennessee; born in Goffton, near Cookeville, Putnam County, Tenn., August 29, 1883; attended the public schools; was graduated from Cleveland Hill Academy, Pleasant Hill, Tenn., in 1898 and from Cumberland University, Lebanon, Tenn., in 1911; studied law; was admitted to the bar in 1911 and commenced practice in Cookeville, Tenn., in 1912; delegate to the Republican National Conventions in 1916 and 1924; elected as a Republican to the Sixty-seventh Congress (March 4, 1921-March 3, 1923); unsuccessful candidate for reelection in 1922 to the Sixty-eighth Congress; resumed the practice of law in the city of Nashville; was appointed receiver of the Tennessee Central Railroad Co.; served as special assistant to the Attorney General of the United States in 1924; appointed referee in bankruptcy for the Nashville division of the middle district of Tennessee and served until his resignation in January 1940; died in Franklin, Tenn., February 19, 1944; interment in Mount Hope Cemetery.

**CLOVER, Benjamin Hutchinson,** a Representative from Kansas; born near Jefferson, Franklin County, Ohio, December 22, 1837; attended the common schools; moved to Kansas in 1871 and located in Cambridge; engaged in agricultural pursuits; member of the board of school commissioners 1873-1888; twice president of the Kansas State Farmers' Alliance and Industrial Union and twice vice president of the national organization of that order; elected as a Populist to the Fifty-second Congress (March 4, 1891-March 3, 1893); was not a candidate for renomination in 1892; resumed agricultural pursuits; died in Douglas, Butler County, Kans., on December 30, 1899; interment in Douglas Cemetery.

**CLOWNEY, William Kennedy,** a Representative from South Carolina; born in Union County, S.C., March 21, 1797; attended private schools and an academy; was graduated from South Carolina College at Columbia in 1818; taught in the public schools of Unionville and in the University of South Carolina; member of the State house of representatives 1830-1831; studied law; was admitted to the bar and began practice in Union; commissioner in equity of South Carolina 1830-1833; elected as a Nullifier to the Twenty-third Congress (March 4, 1833-March 3, 1835); elected as a Nullifier to the Twenty-fifth Congress (March 4, 1837-March 3, 1839); chairman, Committee on Expenditures in the Department of War (Twenty-fifth Congress); member of the State senate in 1840; lieutenant governor of South Carolina; died in Union, S.C., March 12, 1851; interment in Fairforest Cemetery, Union County, S.C.

**CLUETT, Ernest Harold,** a Representative from New York; born in Troy, N.Y., July 13, 1874; attended the public schools; was graduated from Albany (N.Y.) Academy in 1892 and from Williams College, Williamstown, Mass., in 1896; also studied at Oxford

University in England; treasurer of Cluett, Peabody & Co. 1900-1916, vice president 1916-1929, and chairman of the board of directors 1929-1937; head of the employment division of the Watervliet (N.Y.) Government Arsenal in 1918; served on a special mission to France for the Y.M.C.A. in 1918; member of the National War Work Council; unsuccessful candidate for election to the United States Senate in 1934; elected as a Republican to the Seventy-fifth and to the two succeeding Congresses (January 3, 1937-January 3, 1943); was not a candidate for renomination in 1942 to the Seventy-eighth Congress; retired from public life and resided in Palm Beach, Fla., and Troy, N.Y.; died in Troy, N.Y., February 4, 1954; interment in Oakwood Cemetery.

**CLUNIE, Thomas Jefferson,** a Representative from California; born in St. John's, Newfoundland, March 25, 1852, while his parents were on a visit there from Massachusetts; moved with his parents to California in 1854; returned to the East and settled in Maine, and then went back to California in 1861; attended the public schools; studied law; was admitted to the bar in 1868 and commenced practice in Sacramento in 1870; member of the State assembly in 1875; delegate to the Democratic National Convention in 1884; served in the State senate 1887-1889; took an active part in the State militia, and was retired as brigadier general; elected as a Democrat to the Fifty-first Congress (March 4, 1889-March 3, 1891); was an unsuccessful candidate for reelection in 1890 to the Fifty-second Congress; resumed the practice of his profession; died in San Francisco, Calif., on June 30, 1903; interment in the City Cemetery, Sacramento, Calif.

**CLYBURN, James Enos,** a Representative from South Carolina; born in Sumter, S.C., July 21, 1940; graduated, Mather Academy, Camden, S.C., 1957; B.S., South Carolina State University, Orangeburg, 1962; attended University of South Carolina Law School, 1972-1974; public school teacher; executive director, South Carolina Commission for Farm Workers, 1968; staff of Governor John C. West, 1970-1974; South Carolina State human affairs commissioner, 1974-1993; elected as a Democrat to the One Hundred Third and One Hundred Fourth Congresses (January 3, 1993-January 3, 1997); is a resident of Columbia, S.C.

**CLYMER, George,** a Delegate and a Representative from Pennsylvania; born in Philadelphia, Pa., March 16, 1739; engaged in mercantile pursuits in Philadelphia; captain of a volunteer company at the outbreak of hostilities with Great Britain and a member of the committee of safety; Member of the Continental Congress, 1776-1777, and 1780-1782; a signer of the Declaration of Independence; member of the Pennsylvania house of representatives, 1785-1788; delegate to the convention which framed the Federal Constitution in 1787; elected to the First Congress (March 4, 1789-March 3, 1791); chairman, Committee on Elections (First Congress); was not a candidate for renomination in 1790 to the Second Congress; appointed collector of excise duties in 1791, but resigned after the Whiskey Rebellion of 1794; appointed one of the commissioners to negotiate a treaty with the Cherokees and the Creeks, June 29, 1796; died at his home, "Sommerseat," Morrisville, Pa., January 23, 1813; interment in Friends Meeting House Burial Ground, Trenton, N.J.

Bibliography: *DAB*; Grundfest, Jerry. "George Clymer, Philadelphia Revolutionary, 1739-1813." Ph.D. dissertation, Columbia University, 1973; Mohr, Walter H. "George Clymer." *Pennsylvania History* 5 (October 1932): 282-85.

**CLYMER, Hiester** (nephew of William Hiester and cousin of Isaac Ellmaker Hiester), a Representative from Pennsylvania; born near Morgantown, Caernarvon Township, Berks County, Pa., November 3, 1827; attended primary schools at Reading and was graduated from Princeton College in 1847; studied law; was admitted to the bar of Berks County April 6, 1849, and practiced in Reading and Berks County until 1851, when he moved to Pottsville,

Schuylkill County; returned to Reading in 1856; represented Berks County on the board of revenue commissioners of Pennsylvania in January 1860; delegate to the Democratic National Conventions at Charleston and at Baltimore in 1860; member of the Pennsylvania senate from October 1860 until March 1866, when he resigned; unsuccessful Democratic candidate for election for Governor in 1866; delegate to the Democratic National Convention of 1868; member of the Pennsylvania board of charities in 1870; elected as a Democrat to the Forty-third and to the three succeeding Congresses (March 4, 1873-March 3, 1881); chairman, Committee on Expenditures in the Department of War (Forty-fourth Congress), Committee on Appropriations (Forty-fourth Congress), Committee on Expenditures in the Department of State (Forty-sixth Congress); was not a candidate for renomination in 1880 to the Forty-seventh Congress; after his retirement from Congress was vice president of the Union Trust Co. of Philadelphia and president of the Clymer Iron Co.; died in Reading, Pa., on June 12, 1884; interment in the Charles Evans Cemetery.

Bibliography: Joachim, Walter. "Heister Clymer and the Belknap Case." *Historical Review of Berks County* 36 (Winter 1970-1971): 24-31.

**COAD, Merwin,** a Representative from Iowa; born in Cawker City, Mitchell County, Kans., September 28, 1924; in 1932 moved with his parents to a farm near Auburn, Nebr.; graduated from high school in Auburn, Nebr., in 1941; student at Peru (Nebr.) State Teachers College in 1941 and 1942, and Phillips University, Enid, Okla., 1942-1944; graduated from Texas Christian University at Fort Worth in 1945; also studied at Drake University, Des Moines, Iowa; ordained to the ministry of Disciples of Christ Church, Boone, Iowa, in 1945; associate minister St. Joseph, Mo., in 1948 and 1949; minister at Lenox, Iowa, 1949-1951, and Boone, Iowa, 1951-1956; elected as a Democrat to the Eighty-fifth and reelected to the two succeeding Congresses (January 3, 1957-January 3, 1963); was not a candidate for renomination in 1962 to the Eighty-eighth Congress; engaged in residential and commercial construction; is a resident of Washington, D.C., and Harpers Ferry, W.Va.

**COADY, Charles Pearce,** a Representative from Maryland; born in Baltimore, Md., February 22, 1868; attended the public schools, and was graduated from Baltimore City College in 1886; engaged in mercantile pursuits; studied law; was admitted to the bar in 1894 and commenced practice in Baltimore, Md., in the same year; member of the State senate for the term 1908-1912; reelected for the four-year term ending in 1916, but resigned in 1913, having been nominated as a candidate for Congress; elected as a Democrat to the Sixty-third Congress to fill the vacancy caused by the death of George Konig; reelected to the Sixty-fourth, Sixty-fifth, and Sixty-sixth Congresses and served from November 4, 1913, to March 3, 1921; unsuccessful candidate for reelection in 1920 to the Sixty-seventh Congress; resumed the practice of law; Baltimore City collector and manager of the bureau of receipts 1922-1925; died in Baltimore, Md., February 16, 1934; interment in New Cathedral Cemetery.

**COATS, Daniel Ray,** a Representative and a Senator from Indiana; born in Jackson, Mich., May 16, 1943; attended the public schools; graduated from Jackson High School, 1961; B.A., Wheaton College, Wheaton, Ill., 1965; J.D., Indiana University School of Law, Indianapolis, 1971; admitted to the Indiana bar in 1972 and commenced practice in Fort Wayne; served in the United States Army, 1966-1968; assistant vice president and counsel, Mutual Security Life Insurance Co., 1972-1976; district assistant to Representative Dan Quayle, 1976-1980; elected as a Republican to the Ninety-seventh and to the four succeeding Congresses, and served from January 3, 1981 until his resignation January 3, 1989; appointed to the United States Senate, December 27, 1988, to fill vacancy caused by the election of J. Danforth Quayle as Vice

President of the United States, and took his seat January 3, 1989; reelected November 6, 1990 by special election to complete the remainder of the term ending January 3, 1993; reelected in 1992 to the term ending January 3, 1999; is a resident of Fort Wayne, Ind.

**COBB, Amasa,** a Representative from Wisconsin; born in Crawford County, Ill., September 27, 1823; attended the public schools; moved to the Territory of Wisconsin in 1842 and engaged in lead mining; served in the Mexican War as a private in the United States Army; studied law; was admitted to the bar and commenced practice in Mineral Point, Iowa County, Wis.; district attorney 1850-1854; member of the State senate in 1855 and 1856; adjutant general of Wisconsin 1855-1858; member of the State assembly in 1860 and 1861 and served as speaker during the last year; entered the Union Army as colonel of the Fifth Wisconsin Infantry July 12, 1861; became colonel of the Forty-third Wisconsin Infantry on September 29, 1864; brevetted brigadier general March 13, 1865; elected as a Republican to the Thirty-eighth and to the three succeeding Congresses (March 4, 1863-March 3, 1871); moved to Lincoln, Nebr., and continued the practice of law; appointed mayor of Lincoln, Nebr., in 1873; associate justice of the State supreme court 1878-1892 and served as chief justice for four years; died in Los Angeles, Calif., July 5, 1905; interment in Evergreen Cemetery, Lincoln, Nebr.

**Bibliography:** Nelson, Meredith K. "Amasa Cobb." *Nebraska Law Bulletin* 14 (November 1935): 197-213.

**COBB, Clinton Levering,** a Representative from North Carolina; born in Elizabeth City, Pasquotank County, N.C., August 25, 1842; attended the common schools and was graduated from the University of North Carolina at Chapel Hill; studied law; was admitted to the bar in 1867 and commenced practice in Elizabeth City, N.C.; engaged in the mercantile business; elected as a Republican to the Forty-first, Forty-second, and Forty-third Congresses (March 4, 1869-March 3, 1875); chairman, Committee on the Freedman's Bureau (Forty-second and Forty-third Congresses); unsuccessful candidate for reelection in 1874 to the Forty-fourth Congress; resumed the practice of law in Elizabeth City, N.C., and died there on April 30, 1879; interment in Episcopal Cemetery.

**COBB, David,** a Representative from Massachusetts; born in Attleboro, Mass., September 14, 1748; was graduated from Harvard College in 1766; studied medicine in Boston and afterward practiced in Taunton, Mass.; member of the Provincial Congress in 1775; lieutenant colonel of Jackson's regiment in 1777 and 1778, serving in Rhode Island and New Jersey; was aide-de-camp on the staff of General Washington; appointed major general of militia in 1786 and rendered conspicuous service during Shays' Rebellion; judge of the Bristol County court of common pleas 1784-1796; member of the Massachusetts house of representatives 1789-1793 and served as speaker; elected to the Third Congress (March 4, 1793-March 3, 1795); moved to the district of Maine in 1796 and engaged in agricultural pursuits; elected to the Massachusetts senate from the eastern district of Maine in 1802 and served as president; elected to the Massachusetts council in 1808; Lieutenant Governor in 1809; member of the board of military defense in 1812; chief justice of the Hancock County court of common pleas; returned in 1817 to Taunton, Mass., where he died April 17, 1830; interment in Plain Cemetery.

**Bibliography:** *DAB.*

**COBB, George Thomas,** a Representative from New Jersey; born in Morristown, N.J., October 13, 1813; became an orphan when six years of age and received very little schooling; employed at an early age as a clerk in a store at Denville, N.J., and later employed at the iron works at Powerville and Boonton, N.J.; transferred to a store in New York City; engaged in foreign trade; retired from active business pursuits after having amassed a fortune; returned to New

Jersey; elected as a Democrat to the Thirty-seventh Congress (March 4, 1861-March 3, 1863); declined to be a candidate for renomination in 1862; affiliated with the Republican Party in 1863 and as such was elected a member of the State senate in 1865 and again in 1868; mayor of Morristown 1865-1869; became a trustee of Drew Theological Seminary in 1868 and served until his death; unsuccessful candidate for election to the United States Senate in 1869; president of the Sabbath School Association of Morris County; was killed in an accident on the Chesapeake & Ohio Railroad at Jerrys Run, near White Sulphur Springs, Va., August 12, 1870; interment in Evergreen Cemetery, Morristown, N.J.

**COBB, Howell** (uncle of Howell Cobb [1815-1868]), a Representative from Georgia; born in Granville County, N.C., August 3, 1772; moved to Georgia and settled near Louisville, Jefferson County, where he engaged in agricultural pursuits; served in the United States Army as ensign and lieutenant in the Second Sub Legion and as captain in the Artillerists and Engineers from February 23, 1793 until January 31, 1806, when he resigned; elected as a Republican to the Tenth and to the two succeeding Congresses, and served from March 4, 1807 until 1812, when he resigned; returned to his plantation in Jefferson County, Ga., and resumed agricultural pursuits; died on his plantation, "Cherry Hill," nine miles northwest of Louisville, Jefferson County, Ga., May 26, 1818; interment in the family cemetery on his estate.

**COBB, Howell** (nephew of Howell Cobb [1772-1818]), a Representative from Georgia; born at "Cherry Hill," Jefferson County, Ga., September 7, 1815; moved with his father to Athens, Ga., in childhood; was graduated from Franklin College (then a part of the University of Georgia), at Athens in 1834; studied law; was admitted to the bar and commenced practice in Athens, Ga., in 1836; solicitor general of the western judicial circuit of Georgia, 1837-1841; elected as a Democrat to the Twenty-eighth and to the three succeeding Congresses (March 4, 1843-March 3, 1851); chairman, Committee on Mileage (Twenty-eighth Congress); Speaker of the House of Representatives (Thirty-first Congress); elected Governor of Georgia in 1851, and served from November 5, 1851 to November 9, 1853; elected to the Thirty-fourth Congress (March 4, 1855-March 3, 1857); appointed Secretary of the Treasury in the Cabinet of President James Buchanan, and served from March 6, 1857 to December 10, 1860, when he resigned; chairman of the convention of delegates from the seceded States which assembled in Montgomery, Ala., on February 24, 1861, to form a Confederate Government; appointed a brigadier general in the Confederate Army February 13, 1862, and promoted to major general September 9, 1863; surrendered at Macon, Ga., April 20, 1864; died in New York City October 9, 1868; interment in Oconee Cemetery, Athens, Clarke County, Ga.

**Bibliography:** *DAB*; Simpson, John E. *Howell Cobb: The Politics of Ambition.* Chicago: Adams Press, 1973; Toombs, Robert. *The Correspondence of Robert Toombs, Alexander H. Stephens, and Howell Cobb.* Edited by Ulrich Bonnel Phillips. 1913. Reprint. New York: DaCapo Press, 1970.

**COBB, James Edward,** a Representative from Alabama; born in Thomaston, Upson County, Ga., October 5, 1835; attended the public schools, and was graduated from Emory College, Oxford, Ga., in June 1856; studied law; was admitted to the bar and practiced; moved to Texas in 1857; entered the Confederate Army in 1861 as lieutenant in Company F, Fifth Texas Regiment, and served in the Army of Northern Virginia until he was made prisoner at the Battle of Gettysburg, July 1863; after his release settled in Tuskegee, Ala., and practiced law until 1874; circuit judge from 1874 to 1886; reelected in 1886, but before qualifying was elected to Congress; elected to the Fiftieth and to the three succeeding Congresses (March 4, 1887-March 3, 1895); presented credentials as a Member-elect to the Fifty-fourth Congress and served from March 4,

1895, to April 21, 1896, when he was succeeded by Albert T. Goodwyn, who contested his election; resumed the practice of law in Tuskegee, Macon County, Ala.; delegate to the State constitutional convention in 1901; died in East Las Vegas, San Miguel County, N.Mex., June 2, 1903; interment in Evergreen Cemetery, Tuskegee, Ala.

**COBB, Seth Wallace,** a Representative from Missouri; born near Petersburg, Va., December 5, 1838; attended the common schools; joined a volunteer company from his native county in 1861 and served throughout the Civil War in the Army of Northern Virginia; moved to St. Louis, Mo., in 1867 and was employed as a clerk in a grain commission house for three years; in 1870 became engaged in the same business on his own account; president of the Merchants' Exchange in 1886; president of the corporation which built the Merchants' Bridge across the Mississippi River at St. Louis; elected as a Democrat to the Fifty-second, Fifty-third, and Fifty-fourth Congresses (March 4, 1891-March 3, 1897); was not a candidate for renomination in 1896; resumed the grain commission business in St. Louis; vice president of the Louisiana Purchase Exposition at St. Louis in 1904; died in St. Louis, Mo., May 22, 1909; interment in Calvary Cemetery.

**COBB, Stephen Alonzo,** a Representative from Kansas; born in Madison, Somerset County, Maine, June 17, 1833; attended the common schools; moved with his father to Minnesota in 1850; studied languages and prepared for college; entered Beloit College, Beloit, Wis., in 1854, where he was a student for two years; was graduated from Brown University, Providence, R.I., in 1858; settled in Wyandotte, Wyandotte County, Kans., in 1859 and commenced the practice of law; entered the Union Army in 1862; became captain and commissary sergeant of Volunteers on May 18, 1864; brevetted major August 16, 1865, and honorably discharged on September 23, 1865; mayor of Wyandotte in 1862 and again in 1868; served in the State senate in 1862, 1869, and 1870; member of the State house of representatives in 1872 and served as speaker; elected as a Republican to the Forty-third Congress (March 4, 1873-March 3, 1875); unsuccessful candidate for reelection in 1874 to the Forty-fourth Congress; died in Wyandotte (now a part of Kansas City), Kans., August 24, 1878; interment in Oak Grove Cemetery, Kansas City, Kans.

**COBB, Thomas Reed,** a Representative from Indiana; born in Springville, Lawrence County, Ind., July 2, 1828; attended Indiana University, Bloomington, Ind.; studied law; was admitted to the bar in 1851 and commenced practice in Bedford, Ind.; commissioned major of Indiana Militia in 1852; moved to Vincennes, Ind., in 1867; member of the State senate 1858-1866; president of the Democratic State convention in 1876; delegate to the Democratic National Convention in 1876; elected as a Democrat to the Forty-fifth and to the four succeeding Congresses (March 4, 1877-March 3, 1887); chairman, Committee on Mileage (Forty-fifth and Forty-sixth Congresses), Committee on Public Lands (Forty-eighth and Forty-ninth Congresses); was not a candidate for renomination in 1886; resumed the practice of law and also engaged in agricultural pursuits; died in Vincennes, Knox County, Ind., June 23, 1892; interment in Old Vincennes Cemetery.

**COBB, Thomas Willis,** a Representative and a Senator from Georgia; born in Columbia County, Ga., in 1784; pursued preparatory studies; studied law; was admitted to the bar and practiced in Lexington, Ga.; moved to Greensboro, Greene County; elected to the Fifteenth and Sixteenth Congresses (March 4, 1817-March 3, 1821); unsuccessful candidate for reelection to the Seventeenth Congress; elected to the Eighteenth Congress and served from March 4, 1823, to December 6, 1824, when he resigned, having been elected Senator; chairman, Committee on Public Expenditures (Eighteenth Congress); elected to the United States Senate to fill the vacancy caused by the death of Nicholas Ware and served from December 6, 1824, until his resignation in 1828; judge of the superior court of Georgia; died in Greensboro, Ga., February 1, 1830.

**COBB, Williamson Robert Winfield,** a Representative from Alabama; born in Rhea County, Tenn., June 8, 1807; moved in 1809 to Bellefontaine, Madison County, Ala., with his father, who settled on a plantation and engaged in the raising of cotton; received a limited education; was a clock peddler for a short time and subsequently entered the mercantile business in Bellefontaine; member of the State house of representatives in 1845 and 1846; located on a plantation in Madison County and engaged in cotton raising; elected as a Democrat to the Thirtieth and to the six succeeding Congresses and served from March 4, 1847, to January 30, 1861, when he joined other secessionist members of the Alabama delegation in withdrawing from the Thirty-sixth Congress; chairman, Committee on Revisal and Unfinished Business (Thirty-first through Thirty-third Congresses), Committee on Public Lands (Thirty-fifth Congress); unsuccessful candidate for election to the Confederate House of Representatives in 1861; resumed agricultural pursuits in Madison County; elected in 1863 to the Confederate House of Representatives, but did not take his seat when the new Congress met, whereupon his fidelity was suspected and subsequently he was expelled by a unanimous vote; was killed by the accidental discharge of his own pistol while putting up a fence on his plantation near Bellefontaine, Ala., on November 1, 1864; interment in the plot of the Cobb family estate near Cobb's Bridge in Madison County, Ala.

**Bibliography:** Atkins, Leah. "Williamson R.W. Cobb and the Graduation Act of 1854." *The Alabama Review* 28 (January 1975): 16-31.

**COBEY, William Wilfred, Jr.,** a Representative from North Carolina; born in Washington, D.C., May 13, 1939; attended high school in Hyattsville, Md.; B.A., Emory University, Atlanta, Ga., 1962; M.B.A., University of Pennsylvania, 1964; worked as a bank administrative assistant, 1964-1965, and as a chemical salesman, 1965-1966; M.Ed., University of Pittsburgh, 1968; physical education instructor 1967-1968, academic counselor and assistant athletic business manager 1968-1971, assistant athletic director 1971-1976, and director of athletics at the University of North Carolina at Chapel Hill, 1976-1980; unsuccessful candidate in 1980 for lieutenant governor of North Carolina; chairman of the Taxpayers Educational Coalition, 1980-1982; unsuccessful candidate for election in 1982 to the Ninety-eighth Congress; president of Cobey & Associates, 1982-1984; elected as a Republican to the Ninety-ninth Congress (January 3, 1985-January 3, 1987); unsuccessful candidate for reelection in 1986 to the One Hundredth Congress; deputy secretary, North Carolina State department of transportation, 1987-1989; North Carolina State secretary of environment, health and natural resources, 1989-1993; town manager, Town of Morrisville, N.C., 1993-1996; co-chairman, Richard Petty for Secretary of State (North Carolina), 1996; is a resident of Orange County, N.C.

**COBLE, Howard,** a Representative from North Carolina; born in Greensboro, Guilford County, N.C., March 18, 1931; attended the public schools of Guilford County and Appalachian State University, Boone, N.C., 1949-1950; A.B., Guilford College, Greensboro, N.C., 1958; J.D., the University of North Carolina School of Law, Chapel Hill, N.C., in 1962; enlisted in the United States Coast Guard in 1952, served on active duty 1952-1956 and 1977-1978, reserve duty as Captain, 1960-1982; admitted to the North Carolina bar in 1966; field claim representative and superintendent for automobile insurance, 1961-1967; member, North Carolina State house of representatives in 1969 and 1979-1983; Assistant United States Attorney for the Middle District of North Carolina, 1969-1973; secretary, North Carolina Department of Revenue, 1973-1977; attorney, Turner, Enochs and Sparrow, Greensboro, 1979-1984; elected as a Republican to the Ninety-ninth and to the five succceeding Congresses (January 3, 1985-January 3, 1997); is a resident of Greensboro, N.C.

**COBURN, Frank Potter,** a Representative from Wisconsin; born on a farm near West Salem, La Crosse County, Wis., December 6, 1858; attended the public schools; engaged in agricultural pursuits near West Salem; also engaged in the banking business in West Salem; was an unsuccessful Democratic candidate for election in 1888 to the Fifty-first Congress; elected as a Democrat to the Fifty-second Congress (March 4, 1891-March 3, 1893); was an unsuccessful candidate for reelection in 1892 to the Fifty-third Congress; resumed banking interests and agricultural pursuits near West Salem, Wis.; member of the county board of supervisors, 1894-1903, serving as chairman in 1902 and 1903; jury commissioner from 1897 until 1932; trustee of the county asylum, 1907-1932; member of the board of review of income taxes for the county, 1912-1926; died in La Crosse, Wis., on November 2, 1932; interment in Hamilton Cemetery, West Salem, Wis.

**COBURN, John,** a Representative from Indiana; born in Indianapolis, Ind., October 27, 1825; attended the public schools and was graduated from Wabash College, Crawfordsville, Ind., in 1846; studied law; was admitted to the bar in 1849 and commenced practice in Indianapolis; member of the State house of representatives in 1850; judge of the court of common pleas from 1859 to 1861, when he resigned to enter the Union Army; became colonel of the Thirty-third Regiment, Indiana Volunteer Infantry, September 16, 1861, and was mustered out September 20, 1864; brevetted brigadier general of Volunteers March 13, 1865; appointed as the first secretary of the Territory of Montana in March 1865 but resigned at once; elected judge of the fifth judicial circuit of Indiana in October 1865 and resigned in July 1866; elected as a Republican to the Fortieth and to the three succeeding Congresses (March 4, 1867-March 3, 1875); chairman, Committee on Public Expenditures (Forty-first Congress), Committee on Military Affairs (Forty-second and Forty-Third Congresses); was an unsuccessful candidate for reelection in 1874 to the Forty-fourth Congress; was appointed a justice of the supreme court of the Territory of Montana on February 19, 1884, and served until December 1885; returned to Indianapolis, and resumed the practice of law; died in Indianapolis, Ind., on January 28, 1908; interment in Crown Hill Cemetery.

**COBURN, Stephen,** a Representative from Maine; born in Bloomfield (now Skowhegan), Maine, on November 11, 1817; attended Waterville and China Academies; was graduated from Waterville (now Colby) College, Waterville, Maine, in 1839; taught a plantation school in Tarboro, N.C., 1839-1840; principal of Bloomfield (Maine) Academy, 1840-1844; studied law at the Harvard Law School; was admitted to the bar in 1845 and commenced practice in Skowhegan; member of the Maine State board of education, 1849-1850; delegate to several Republican State conventions; elected as a Republican to the Thirty-sixth Congress on November 6, 1860, to fill the vacancy caused by the resignation of Israel Washburn, Jr., and served from January 2 to March 3, 1861; was not a candidate for the Thirty-seventh Congress, that election having been held in September 1860, previous to his election to the Thirty-sixth Congress; member of the peace convention of 1861 held in Washington, D.C., in an effort to devise means to prevent the impending war; resumed the practice of law; postmaster of Skowhegan from July 25, 1868 to January 23, 1877; was drowned in the Kennebec River, at Skowhegan, Maine, July 4, 1882; interment in South Cemetery, Skowhegan, Maine.

**COBURN, Thomas Allen,** a Representative from Oklahoma; born in Casper, Natrona County, Wyo., March 14, 1948; raised in Muskogee, Okla.; graduated, Central High School, Muskogee, 1966; B.S., Oklahoma State University, 1970; M.D., University of Oklahoma Medical School, 1983; manufacturing manager, Ophthalmic Division of Coburn Optical Industries, Colonial Heights,

Va., 1970-1978; intern in general surgery, St. Anthony's Hospital, Oklahoma City, Okla.; family practice residency, University of Arkansas, Fort Smith; physician, Muskogee, Okla.; past chair, Muskogee Regional Medical Center; participant in medical mission trips to Haiti, 1985 and Iraq, 1992; elected as a Republican to the One Hundred Fourth Congress (January 3, 1995-January 3, 1997); is a resident of Muskogee, Okla.

**COCHRAN, Alexander Gilmore,** a Representative from Pennsylvania; born in Allegheny City (now a part of Pittsburgh), Pa., March 20, 1846; attended private and public schools of that city, Phillips Academy, Andover, Mass., and Columbia Law School, New York City; was admitted to the bar in 1866 and commenced practice in Pittsburgh, Pa.; elected as a Democrat to the Forty-fourth Congress (March 4, 1875-March 3, 1877); unsuccessful candidate for reelection in 1876 to the Forty-fifth Congress; resumed the practice of law at Pittsburgh; moved to St. Louis, Mo., in 1879, where he continued the practice of law, and for more than twenty years was general solicitor for the Missouri Pacific Railway Co. and head of its legal department in the West; also served as vice president of the Missouri Pacific and Iron Mountain Railway; served as judge advocate with rank of lieutenant colonel in the Missouri National Guard; died in St. Louis, Mo., May 1, 1928; interment in Bellefontaine Cemetery.

**COCHRAN, Charles Fremont,** a Representative from Missouri; born in Kirksville, Adair County, Mo., September 27, 1846; moved to Atchison, Kans., in 1860; attended public and private schools; apprenticed to the printer's trade; editor and publisher of the Atchison Patriot in 1868 and 1869; studied law; was admitted to the bar in 1873 and practiced until 1885; prosecuting attorney of Atchison County, Kans., 1880-1884; returned to Missouri in 1885 and settled in St. Joseph; engaged in the newspaper business and edited the St. Joseph (Mo.) Gazette; served in the State senate 1890-1894; elected as a Democrat to the Fifty-fifth and to the three succeeding Congresses (March 4, 1897-March 3, 1905); was a contestant for renomination in 1904 to the Fifty-ninth Congress, but finally withdrew as a candidate; founded the Observer, a weekly newspaper, of which he served as editor until his death in St. Joseph, Mo., on December 19, 1906; interment in Mount Vernon Cemetery, Atchison, Kans.

**COCHRAN, James,** a Representative from New York; born in Albany, N.Y., on February 11, 1769; was graduated from Columbia College, New York City, in 1788; studied law; was admitted to the bar; commissioned major in the Army by President John Adams; regent of the University of the State of New York 1796-1820; elected as a Federalist to the Fifth Congress (March 4, 1797-March 3, 1799); member of the State senate 1814-1818; moved to Oswego, N.Y., in 1826; postmaster of Oswego from September 27, 1841, to July 21, 1845; editor of the Oswego Democratic Gazette for several years; died in Oswego, N.Y., November 7, 1848; interment in Riverside Cemetery.

**COCHRAN, James** (grandfather of James Cochrane Dobbin), a Representative from North Carolina; born near Mount Tirzah Township, Person County, N.C., about 1767; attended the public schools; engaged in agricultural pursuits near Helena, N.C.; member of the State house of commons 1802-1806; served in the State senate in 1807; elected as a Republican to the Eleventh and Twelfth Congresses (March 4, 1809-March 3, 1813); died in Roxboro, Person County, N.C., April 7, 1813; interment in the burial ground at Leas Chapel, five miles west of Roxboro, N.C.

**COCHRAN, John Joseph,** a Representative from Missouri; born in Webster Groves, St. Louis County, Mo., August 11, 1880; attended the public schools; employed in the editorial department of various St. Louis newspapers for several years; assistant to the election commissioners of St. Louis 1911-1913; secretary to

Representative William L. Igoe of Missouri, 1913-1917, 1918-1921; private secretary to United States Senator William J. Stone of Missouri and clerk to the Committee on Foreign Relations of the United States Senate in 1917 and 1918; studied law; was admitted to the bar in 1921 at St. Louis, Mo., but did not engage in extensive practice; secretary to Representative Harry B. Hawes of Missouri, 1921-1926; elected as a Democrat to the Sixty-ninth Congress to fill the vacancy caused by the resignation of Harry B. Hawes and at the same time was elected to the Seventieth Congress; reelected to the Seventy-first and to the two succeeding Congresses; did not seek renomination in 1934 to the House of Representatives, but was an unsuccessful candidate for nomination to the United States Senate; subsequently was nominated by convention and elected to the Seventy-fourth Congress; reelected to the Seventy-fifth and to the four succeeding Congresses; served from November 2, 1926, to January 3, 1947; chairman, Committee on Expenditures in Executive Departments (Seventy-second through Seventy-sixth Congresses), Committee on Accounts (Seventy-sixth through Seventy-ninth Congresses); was not a candidate for renomination in 1946 to the Eightieth Congress; died in St. Louis, Mo., March 6, 1947; interment in Calvary Cemetery.

**COCHRAN, Thomas Cunningham,** a Representative from Pennsylvania; born in Sandy Creek Township, near Sheakleyville, Mercer County, Pa., November 30, 1877; moved with his parents to Mercer, Pa., in 1879; attended the public schools; was graduated from the Mercer High School in 1896 and from Westminster College, New Wilmington, Pa., in 1901; member of the faculty of Mercer Academy in 1902 and 1903; studied law; was admitted to the bar in 1903 and commenced practice in Mercer, Pa.; district attorney of Mercer County 1906-1909; trustee of Westminster College; elected as a Republican to the Seventieth and to the three succeeding Congresses (March 4, 1927-January 3, 1935); was not a candidate for renomination in 1934; delegate to the Interparliamentary Union conferences in Paris in 1927, Berlin in 1928, Geneva in 1929, London in 1930, and Istanbul in 1934, and as an observer in Oslo in 1939, Istanbul in 1951, and Washington in 1953; resumed the practice of law; died in Mercer, Pa., December 10, 1957; interment in Mercer Citizens Cemetery.

**COCHRAN, William Thad,** a Representative and a Senator from Mississippi; born in Pontotoc, Pontotoc County, Miss., December 7, 1937; educated in the public schools of Mississippi; graduated Byram High School, 1955; B.A., University of Mississippi, Oxford, 1959; studied international law and jurisprudence at Trinity College, University of Dublin, Ireland, 1963-1964; J.D., University of Mississippi Law School, 1965; served in the United States Navy from 1959 until 1961; admitted to the Mississippi bar in 1965 and commenced practice in Jackson; elected as a Republican to the Ninety-third and to the two succeeding Congresses and served from January 3, 1973, until his resignation, December 26, 1978; was not a candidate in 1978 for reelection to the House of Representatives, but was elected to the United States Senate for the term commencing January 3, 1979; subsequently appointed by the Governor, December 27, 1978, to fill the vacancy caused by the resignation of James O. Eastland for the term ending January 3, 1979; reelected in 1984 and again in 1990 for the term ending January 3, 1997; chairman, Senate Republican Conference (One Hundred Second through One Hundred Fourth Congresses); is a resident of Jackson, Miss.

**COCHRANE, Aaron Van Schaick** (nephew of Isaac Whitbeck Van Schaick), a Representative from New York; born in Coxsackie, Greene County, N.Y., March 14, 1858; attended the common schools and the Hudson River Institute at Claverack, N.Y.; was graduated from Yale College in 1879; moved to Hudson, N.Y., in 1879; studied law; was admitted to the bar in 1881 and commenced practice in Hudson, N.Y.; city judge of Hudson in 1887 and 1888; district attorney of Columbia County, 1889-1892; elected as a Republican to

the Fifty-fifth and Fifty-sixth Congresses (March 4, 1897-March 3, 1901); was not a candidate for renomination in 1900 to the Fifty-seventh Congress, but was elected associate justice of the supreme court of New York in 1901; reelected in 1915 for the term ending in 1928, designated by Governor Nathan L. Miller presiding justice of the appellate division of the New York State supreme court in 1922; retired from the bench in 1928 but served as official referee until 1941; died in Hudson, N.Y., September 7, 1943; interment in Riverside Cemetery, Coxsackie, N.Y.

**COCHRANE, Clark Betton,** a Representative from New York; born in New Boston, N.H., May 31, 1815; moved to Montgomery County, N.Y.; was graduated from Union College, Schenectady, N.Y., in 1841; studied law; was admitted to the bar in 1841 and practiced in Amsterdam 1841-1851, Schenectady 1851-1855, and Albany, N.Y., from 1855 until his death; elected as a Democrat a member of the State assembly in 1844; trustee of Union College 1853-1867; elected as a Republican to the Thirty-fifth and Thirty-sixth Congresses (March 4, 1857-March 3, 1861); was not a candidate for renomination in 1860; resumed the practice of law in Albany; delegate to the Republican National Convention in 1864; again a member of the State assembly in 1866; died in Albany, N.Y., on March 5, 1867; interment in Green Hill Cemetery, Amsterdam, Montgomery County, N.Y.

**COCHRANE, John,** a Representative from New York; born in Palatine, N.Y., August 27, 1813; pursued preparatory studies, attended Union College, Schenectady, N.Y., and was graduated from Hamilton College, Clinton, N.Y., in 1831; studied law; was admitted to the bar in 1834 and practiced in Palatine, Oswego, and Schenectady, N.Y.; moved to New York City in 1846; surveyor of the port of New York 1853-1857; elected as a Democrat to the Thirty-fifth and Thirty-sixth Congresses (March 4, 1857-March 3, 1861); chairman, Committee on Commerce (Thirty-fifth Congress); unsuccessful candidate in 1860 for reelection to the Thirty-seventh Congress; delegate to the Democratic National Conventions at Charleston and Baltimore in 1860; entered the Union Army as colonel of the Sixty-fifth New York Infantry on June 11, 1861; became brigadier general July 17, 1862, and served until his resignation on February 25, 1863, on account of physical disability; chairman of the Radical Democratic Party convention, which nominated him for Vice President May 31, 1864, on the ticket with John Charles Frémont for President, but withdrew, with General Frémont, on September 22; attorney general of New York 1863-1865; collector of internal revenue for the sixth district of New York in 1869; declined the position of United States Minister to Uruguay and Paraguay tendered by President Ulysses S. Grant in 1869; delegate to the Liberal Republican National Convention at Cincinnati in 1872; member of the board of aldermen and served as president in 1872 and again a member in 1883; appointed police justice of New York May 22, 1889, but resigned after serving a few weeks; died in New York City February 7, 1898; interment in Rural Cemetery, Albany, N.Y.

**Bibliography:** *DAB*.

**COCKE, John** (son of William Cocke and uncle of William Michael Cocke), a Representative from Tennessee; born in Brunswick, Nottoway County, Va., in 1772; moved with his parents to Tennessee, where he attended the public schools; studied law; was admitted to the bar in 1793 and practiced in Hawkins County; member of the Tennessee State house of representatives in 1796, 1797, 1807, 1809, 1812, and again in 1837, and served as speaker in 1812 and 1837; served in the Tennessee State senate, 1799-1801; served as major general of Tennessee Volunteers in the Creek War in 1813 and as colonel of a regiment of Tennessee riflemen, under General Andrew Jackson, at New Orleans; elected to the Sixteenth and to the three succeeding Congresses (March 4, 1819-March 3, 1827); chairman, Committee on Indian Affairs (Eighteenth and

Nineteenth Congresses); engaged in agricultural pursuits; founded a school for deaf mutes in Knoxville, Tenn.; again a member of the State senate in 1843; died in Rutledge, Grainger County, Tenn., February 16, 1854; interment in the Methodist Church Cemetery.

**COCKE, William** (father of John Cocke and grandfather of William Michael Cocke), a Senator from Tennessee; born in Amelia County, Va., in 1748; pursued preparatory studies; studied law; was admitted to the bar and practiced; in company with Daniel Boone explored the territory of eastern Tennessee and western Kentucky; successfully led four companies of Virginians against hostile Indians in 1776 in Tennessee; member of the Virginia house of burgesses and a colonel of militia; moved to Tennessee in 1776; member of the Tennessee constitutional convention in 1796; upon the admission of Tennessee as a State into the Union was elected to the United States Senate and served from August 2, 1796, to March 3, 1797; was appointed his own successor, as there had been no election by the legislature, and served under this appointment from April 22, 1797, to September 26, 1797, when a successor was elected; again elected to the United States Senate as a Republican and served from March 4, 1799, to March 3, 1805; appointed judge of the first circuit in 1809; moved to Mississippi, and was elected to the Mississippi territorial legislature in 1813; served under General Andrew Jackson in the War of 1812; was appointed by President James Madison as Indian agent for the Chickasaw Nation in 1814; died in Columbus, Miss., on August 22, 1828, and was interred in that city.

Bibliography: *DAB*.

**COCKE, William Michael** (grandson of William Cocke and nephew of John Cocke), a Representative from Tennessee; born in Rutledge, Grainger County, Tenn., July 16, 1815; pursued classical studies and was graduated from the East Tennessee College at Knoxville; studied law; was admitted to the bar and practiced in Rutledge and Nashville; member of the State house of representatives; elected as a Whig to the Twenty-ninth and Thirtieth Congresses (March 4, 1845-March 3, 1849); chairman, Committee on Revolutionary Pensions (Thirtieth Congress); was not a candidate for reelection in 1848; held many local and State offices; died in Nashville, Tenn., February 6, 1896; interment in Mount Olivet Cemetery.

**COCKERILL, Joseph Randolph,** a Representative from Ohio; born in Loudoun County, Va., January 2, 1818; moved to Scott Township, Adams County, Ohio, in 1837 and settled in Youngstown; attended the public schools; taught school; county surveyor in 1840; studied law; was admitted to the bar in 1851 and commenced practice in West Union, Adams County, Ohio; clerk of the court of common pleas; member of the State house of representatives in 1853 and 1854; elected as a Democrat to the Thirty-fifth Congress (March 4, 1857-March 3, 1859); entered the Union Army during the Civil War and served as colonel of the Seventieth Ohio Volunteer Infantry; brevetted brigadier general of Volunteers March 13, 1865; again a member of the State house of representatives 1868-1871; resumed the practice of law; died in West Union, Ohio, October 23, 1875; interment in West Union Cemetery.

**COCKRAN, William Bourke,** a Representative from New York; born in County Sligo, Ireland, February 28, 1854; was educated in France and in his native country; immigrated to the United States when seventeen years of age; teacher in a private academy and principal of a public school in Westchester County, N.Y.; studied law; was admitted to the bar in 1876 and commenced practice in Mount Vernon, N.Y.; two years later moved to New York City and continued the practice of law; elected as a Democrat to the Fiftieth Congress (March 4, 1887-March 3, 1889); was not a candidate for renomination in 1888 to the Fifty-first Congress; delegate to the Democratic National Conventions of 1884, 1892, 1904, and 1920; member of the commission to revise the judiciary article of the constitution of the State of New York in 1890; elected to the Fifty-second Congress to

fill the vacancy caused by the death of Francis B. Spinola; reelected to the Fifty-third Congress and served from November 3, 1891, to March 3, 1895; was not a candidate for renomination in 1894 to the Fifty-fourth Congress; opposed the free-silver platform of William Jennings Bryan in 1896 and campaigned for William McKinley; in 1900 returned to the Democratic Party and supported Bryan; elected as a Democrat to the Fifty-eighth Congress to fill the vacancy caused by the resignation of George B. McClellan; reelected to the Fifty-ninth and Sixtieth Congresses and served from February 23, 1904, to March 3, 1909; declined to be a candidate for renomination in 1908 to the Sixty-first Congress; resumed the practice of law in New York City; unsuccessful candidate for election in 1912 to the Sixty-third Congress; elected as a Democrat to the Sixty-seventh Congress and served from March 4, 1921, until his death in Washington, D.C., March 1, 1923; had been reelected to the Sixty-eighth Congress; interment in Gate of Heaven Cemetery, Mount Hope, Westchester, N.Y.

Bibliography: *DAB*; Bloom, Florence Teicher. "The Political Career of William Bourke Cockran." Ph.D. dissertation, City University of New York, 1970; McGurrin, James. *Bourke Cockran; A Free Lance in American Politics.* New York: Charles Scribner's Sons, 1948.

**COCKRELL, Francis Marion** (brother of Jeremiah Vardaman Cockrell), a Senator from Missouri; born in Warrensburg, Johnson County, Mo., October 1, 1834; attended the common schools; was graduated from Chapel Hill College, Lafayette County, Mo., in July 1853; studied law; was admitted to the bar in 1855 and practiced in Warrensburg, Mo.; served in the Confederate Army as a captain and brigade commander; appointed brigadier general July 18, 1863; captured at Fort Blakeley, Ala., in April 1865 and paroled in May 1865; at the close of the Civil War resumed the practice of law; elected as a Democrat to the United States Senate in 1874; reelected four times and served from March 4, 1875, to March 3, 1905; chairman, Committee on Claims (Forty-sixth Congress), Committee on Engrossed Bills (Fifty-first through Fifty-eighth Congresses, except for Fifty-third), Committee on Appropriations (Fifty-third Congress); appointed by President Theodore Roosevelt a member of the Interstate Commerce Commission 1905-1910; appointed in 1911 a United States commissioner to reestablish the boundary line between Texas and New Mexico; civilian member of the board of ordnance in the War Department, which position he held until his death in Washington, D.C., December 13, 1915; interment in Warrensburg Cemetery, Warrensburg, Mo.

Bibliography: *DAB*; Cockrell, Francis. *The Senator From Missouri, The Life and Times of Francis Marion Cockrell.* New York: Exposition Press, 1962; Williamson, Hugh P. "Correspondence of Senator Francis Marion Cockrell: December 23, 1885-March 24, 1888." *Bulletin of the Missouri Historical Society* 28 (July 1969): 296-305.

**COCKRELL, Jeremiah Vardaman** (brother of Francis Marion Cockrell), a Representative from Texas; born near Warrensburg, Johnson County, Mo., May 7, 1832; attended the common schools and Chapel Hill College, Lafayette County, Mo.; went to California in 1849; returned to Missouri in 1853; engaged in agricultural pursuits and studied law; entered the Confederate Army as a lieutenant and served throughout the Civil War, attaining the rank of colonel; at the close of the war he settled in Sherman, Grayson County, Tex., and engaged in the practice of law; chief justice of Grayson County in 1872; delegate to the Democratic State conventions in 1878 and 1880; moved to Jones County; appointed judge of the thirty-ninth judicial district court in 1885, to which position he was elected in 1886 and reelected in 1890; elected as a Democrat to the Fifty-third and Fifty-fourth Congresses (March 4, 1893-March 3, 1897); was not a candidate for renomination in 1896; engaged in farming and stock raising in Jones County, Tex.; died in

Abilene, Tex., on March 18, 1915; interment in the Masonic Cemetery.

**COCKS, William Willets** (brother of Frederick Cocks Hicks), a Representative from New York; born in Old Westbury, Long Island, N.Y., July 24, 1861; attended private schools and Swarthmore College, Swarthmore, Pa.; engaged in agricultural pursuits; elected commissioner of highways of the town of North Hempstead in 1894; reelected in 1896 and again in 1898; served in the State senate in 1901 and 1902; member of the State assembly in 1904; delegate to the Republican National Convention in 1908; elected as a Republican to the Fifty-ninth, Sixtieth, and Sixty-first Congresses (March 4, 1905-March 3, 1911); unsuccessful candidate for reelection in 1910 to the Sixty-second Congress; again engaged in agricultural pursuits; member of the board of managers of Swarthmore College; president of the Friends Academy, Locust Valley, Nassau County; vice president of the Roslyn Savings Bank; a director of the Bank of Westbury and the Bank of Hicksville; elected mayor of the village of Old Westbury, Long Island, N.Y., in 1924 and served until his death there on May 24, 1932; interment in Friends Cemetery, Westbury, Long Island, N.Y.

**CODD, George Pierre,** a Representative from Michigan; born in Detroit, Mich., December 7, 1869; attended the public schools and was graduated from the University of Michigan at Ann Arbor in 1891; studied law; was admitted to the bar in 1892 and commenced practice in Detroit in 1893; assistant city attorney 1894-1897; member of the board of aldermen 1902-1904; mayor of Detroit in 1905 and 1906; unsuccessful candidate for reelection; delegate to the Republican National Convention of 1908; circuit judge of Wayne County 1911-1921; regent of the University of Michigan in 1910 and 1911; elected as a Republican to the Sixty-seventh Congress (March 4, 1921-March 3, 1923); declined to be a candidate for renomination in 1922 to the Sixty-eighth Congress; resumed the practice of law; again elected circuit judge of Wayne County in 1924 and served until his death in Detroit, Mich., on February 16, 1927; interment in Elmwood Cemetery.

**CODDING, James Hodge,** a Representative from Pennsylvania; born in Pike Township, Bradford County, Pa., July 8, 1849; moved to Towanda, Pa., in 1854; attended the Susquehanna Collegiate Institute, Towanda, Pa., and Dartmouth College, Hanover, N.H.; engaged in the hardware business at Towanda in 1868; studied law; was admitted to the bar and commenced practice in Towanda, Pa., in 1879; elected as a Republican to the Fifty-fourth Congress to fill the vacancy caused by the death of Myron B. Wright; reelected to the Fifty-fifth Congress and served from November 5, 1895, to March 3, 1899; was not a candidate for reelection in 1898; resumed the practice of law in Towanda; moved to New York City in 1903; grand secretary general of the northern Masonic jurisdiction for the Scottish Rite bodies from 1902 until his death in Brooklyn, N.Y., September 12, 1919; interment in Oak Hill Cemetery, Towanda, Bradford County, Pa.

**COELHO, Anthony Lee,** a Representative from California; born in Los Banos, Merced County, Calif., June 15, 1942; attended the public schools in Dos Palos; B.A., Loyola University, Los Angeles, 1964; member of the staff of Representative B. F. Sisk, 1965-1978, became administrative assistant in 1970; staff director, Subcommittee on Cotton, House Agriculture Committee, 1971-1972; consultant, House Parking Committee, 1971-1974; staff coordinator, House Subcommittee on Broadcasting, House Rules Committee, and House Select Committee on Professional Sports, 1965-1976; delegate, California State Democratic convention, 1977 to present; delegate to the Democratic National Conventions of 1976, 1980, 1984 and 1988; elected as a Democrat to the Ninety-sixth and to the five succeeding Congresses and served from January 3, 1979, until his resignation June 15, 1989; majority whip (One Hundredth and One Hundred First Congresses); is a resident of Merced, Calif.

**COFFEE, Harry Buffington,** a Representative from Nebraska; born near Harrison, Sioux County, Nebr., March 16, 1890; attended the public schools at Chadron, Nebr.; University of Nebraska at Lincoln, A.B., 1913; engaged in the real estate and insurance business in Chadron, Nebr., 1914-1939; served as a second lieutenant in the Air Service in 1917 and 1918; organized the Coffee Cattle Co., Inc., in 1915 with extensive ranch holdings in Sioux County, Nebr.; also engaged in agricultural pursuits; elected as a Democrat to the Seventy-fourth and to the three succeeding Congresses (January 3, 1935-January 3, 1943); was not a candidate for renomination in 1942 to the House of Representatives, but was an unsuccessful candidate for nomination to the United States Senate; president of a stockyard company and also of a terminal railway company from 1943 until 1961 when he was named chairman of the board; died in Omaha, Nebr., October 3, 1972; interment in Forest Lawn Cemetery.

**COFFEE, John,** a Representative from Georgia; born in Prince Edward County, Va., December 3, 1782; moved with his father to a plantation near Powelton, Hancock County, Ga., in 1800; settled in Telfair County in 1807 and engaged in agricultural pursuits; general of the State militia during the Creek War; cut a road through the State of Georgia (called Coffee Road) to carry munitions of war to Florida Territory to fight the Indians; member of the State senate 1819-1827; elected as a Jacksonian to the Twenty-third and Twenty-fourth Congresses and served from March 4, 1833, until his death; was reelected to the Twenty-fifth Congress on October 3, 1836, announcement of his death not having been received; died on his plantation near Jacksonville, Telfair County, Ga., on September 25, 1836; interment on his plantation near Jacksonville, Ga.; reinterment in McRae Cemetery, McRae, Ga., in 1921.

**COFFEE, John Main,** a Representative from Washington; born in Tacoma, Wash., January 23, 1897; attended Stadium High School; A.B. and LL.B., University of Washington at Seattle, 1920; J.D., Yale University School of Law, 1921; was admitted to the bar in 1922 and commenced practice in Tacoma, Wash.; trust officer, Puget Sound National Bank; secretary to United States Senator Clarence C. Dill in 1923 and 1924; secretary of the advisory board of the National Recovery Administration 1933-1935; appraiser and examiner of Pierce County for the Washington State Inheritance Tax and Escheat Division 1933-1936; civil service commissioner for Tacoma, Wash., in 1936; elected as a Democrat to the Seventy-fifth and to the four succeeding Congresses (January 3, 1937-January 3, 1947); unsuccessful candidate for reelection in 1946 to the Eightieth Congress, for election in 1950 to the Eighty-second Congress, and in 1958 to the Eighty-sixth Congress; practicing attorney in Tacoma and Seattle, Wash.; was a resident of Tacoma, Wash.; died June 3, 1983.

**Bibliography:** Libby, Justin H. "Anti-Japanese Sentiment in the Pacific Northwest: Senator Schwellenbach and Congressman Coffee Attempt to Embargo Japan, 1937-1941." *Mid-America* 58 (October 1976): 167-174.

**COFFEEN, Henry Asa,** a Representative from Wyoming; born near Gallipolis, Gallia County, Ohio, February 14, 1841; moved with his parents to Indiana, and thence to Homer, Champaign County, Ill., in 1853; attended the country schools and was graduated from the scientific department of Abingdon College (afterwards consolidated with Eureka College), Illinois; engaged in teaching; member of the faculty of Hiram College, Ohio; moved to Sheridan, Sheridan County, Wyo., in 1884; delegate from Wyoming to the World's Fair Congress of Bankers and Financiers at Chicago in June 1893; member of the constitutional convention that framed the constitution of the new State of Wyoming in 1889; elected as a Democrat to the Fifty-third Congress (March 4, 1893-March 3, 1895); unsuccessful candidate for reelection in 1894 to the Fifty-fourth Congress;

engaged in literary pursuits until his death in Sheridan, Wyo., December 9, 1912; interment in Sheridan Cemetery.

**Bibliography:** Schlup, Leonard. "'I'm Not a Cuckoo Democrat!': The Congressional Career of Henry Coffeen." *Wyoming Annals* 66 (Fall 1994): 30-47.

**COFFEY, Robert Lewis, Jr.,** a Representative from Pennsylvania; born in Chattanooga, Hamilton County, Tenn., October 21, 1918; moved with his parents in early boyhood to Pennsylvania, and graduated from the Ferndale High School in 1935; also attended the University of Pittsburgh and Penn State College; employed in coal mines in all positions from coal loader to engineer; appointed a flying cadet on September 23, 1939; commissioned a second lieutenant in June 1940; promoted to first lieutenant on November 1, 1941, and served in the United States Army Air Force during the Second World War; military air attaché, United States Embassy, Santiago, Chile, from October 1945 to April 1948; resigned his commission as a lieutenant colonel September 1, 1948, to pursue a political candidacy; commissioned a colonel, Air Force Reserve, September 2, 1948; elected as a Democrat to the Eighty-first Congress, and served from January 3, 1949 until his death in an airplane accident in Albuquerque, N.Mex., April 20, 1949; interment in Arlington National Cemetery, Va.

**COFFIN, Charles Dustin,** a Representative from Ohio; born in Newburyport, Mass., September 9, 1805; attended the public schools; moved with his parents to New Lisbon, Columbiana County, Ohio; studied law; was admitted to the bar in September 1823 and commenced practice in New Lisbon; clerk of the courts of Columbiana County in 1828; was elected as a Whig to the Twenty-fifth Congress to fill the vacancy caused by the resignation of Andrew W. Loomis and served from December 20, 1837, to March 3, 1839; declined to be a candidate for renomination in 1838 to the Twenty-sixth Congress; resumed the practice of law and engaged in banking; president of the Columbiana Bank of New Lisbon; moved to Cincinnati, Ohio, in 1842 and continued the practice of law; elected judge of the superior court in 1845 and served seven years; was appointed to the same position by Governor William Dennison, Jr. in 1861; died in Cincinnati, Ohio, February 28, 1880; interment in Spring Grove Cemetery.

**COFFIN, Charles Edward,** a Representative from Maryland; born in Boston, Mass., July 18, 1841; attended the Boston grammar and high schools; moved to Maryland in 1863 and settled in Muirkirk, Prince Georges County, where he took charge of the ironworks; member of the State house of delegates in 1884; served in the State senate 1890-1894; delegate to the Republican National Convention in 1892; elected as a Republican to the Fifty-third Congress to fill the vacancy caused by the resignation of Barnes Compton; reelected on the same day to the Fifty-fourth Congress and served from November 6, 1894, to March 3, 1897; engaged in the manufacture of charcoal pig iron, and subsequently became the owner of the Muirkirk blast furnaces; died in Muirkirk, Md., May 24, 1912; interment in St. John's Protestant Episcopal Church Cemetery, Beltsville, Md.

**COFFIN, Frank Morey,** a Representative from Maine; born in Lewiston, Androscoggin County, Maine, July 11, 1919; educated in Lewiston public schools; A.B., Bates College, Lewiston, Maine, 1940; I.A., Harvard University Business School, 1943; LL.B., Harvard University Law School, 1947; served in the Pacific Theater with the United States Navy as an ensign and later as a lieutenant, 1943-1946; was admitted to the bar and commenced the practice of law in Lewiston, Maine in 1947; law clerk for Federal judge, district of Maine, 1947-1949; chairman of the Maine Democratic State committee, 1954-1956; elected as a Democrat to the Eighty-fifth and Eighty-sixth Congresses (January 3, 1957-January 3, 1961); was not a candidate for renomination in 1960 to the Eighty-seventh Congress, but was an unsuccessful candidate in a special election for

Governor of Maine; managing director of the United States Department of State Development Loan Fund until October 1961, when he became deputy administrator of the Agency for International Development and served until 1964; United States Representative to the Development Assistance Committee of the Organization for Economic Cooperation and Development, Paris, 1964-1965; appointed by President Lyndon B. Johnson to the United States Court of Appeals for the First Circuit, October 2, 1965, and served as chief judge of that court from 1972 to 1983; chairman, United States Judicial Conference Committee on the Judicial Branch, 1984 to present; is a resident of South Portland, Maine.

**COFFIN, Howard Aldridge,** a Representative from Michigan; born in Middleboro, Plymouth County, Mass., June 11, 1877; attended the Vermont Academy at Saxtons River; was graduated from Brown University, Providence, R.I., in 1901; teacher in Friends School, Providence, R.I., in 1901; representative for Ginn & Co., book publishers, 1901-1911; controller, Warren Motor Car Co., Detroit, Mich., 1911-1913; manager, Firestone Tire & Rubber Co., of Michigan, 1913-1918; secretary, Detroit Pressed Steel Co., 1918-1921; assistant to president, Cadillac Motor Co., of Detroit, 1921-1925; vice president and later president, White Star Refining Co., 1925-1933; general manager, Socony-Vacuum Oil Co., 1933-1946; elected as a Republican to the Eightieth Congress (January 3, 1947-January 3, 1949); unsuccessful candidate for reelection in 1948 to the Eighty-first Congress; organized the Industrial Service Bureau in Washington, D.C., and was a business consultant until his retirement in 1954; died in Washington, D.C., February 28, 1956; interment in Woodlawn Cemetery, Detroit, Mich.

**COFFIN, Peleg, Jr.,** a Representative from Massachusetts; born in Nantucket, Mass., November 3, 1756; completed academic studies; president of the New England Marine Insurance Co.; member of the Massachusetts house of representatives in 1783, 1784, and 1789; served in the Massachusetts senate in 1785, 1786, 1790-1792, 1795, 1796, and 1802; elected to the Third Congress (March 4, 1793-March 3, 1795); Massachusetts treasurer 1797-1802; died in Boston, Mass., March 6, 1805; interment probably in Friends Burial Grounds; reinterment in Mount Auburn Cemetery in 1833.

**COFFIN, Thomas Chalkley,** a Representative from Idaho; born in Caldwell, Canyon County, Idaho, October 25, 1887; moved to Boise, Ada County, Idaho, with his parents in 1898; attended the public schools of Caldwell and Boise, Idaho, and was graduated from the Phillips-Exeter Academy at Exeter, N.H., in 1906; attended Yale Sheffield Scientific School and was graduated from the law department Yale University in 1910; was admitted to the bar in 1911 and commenced the practice of law in Boise, Idaho; served as assistant attorney general of Idaho 1913-1915; moved to Pocatello, Idaho, in 1917 and continued the practice of law; during the First World War served in the aviation branch of the United States Navy; mayor of Pocatello 1931-1933; elected as a Democrat to the Seventy-third Congress and served from March 4, 1933, until his death in Washington, D.C., on June 8, 1934; interment in Mountainview Cemetery, Pocatello, Idaho.

**COFFROTH, Alexander Hamilton,** a Representative from Pennsylvania; born in Somerset, Somerset County, Pa., May 18, 1828; attended the public schools and Somerset Academy; published a Democratic paper in Somerset for five years; studied law in the law office of Hon. Jeremiah S. Black; was admitted to the bar in February 1851 at Somerset, Pa., where he practiced his profession; delegate to several Pennsylvania Democratic conventions; delegate to the Democratic National Conventions which assembled in Charleston and Baltimore in 1860; an assessor of internal revenue in 1867; delegate to the Democratic National Convention in 1872; elected as a Democrat to the Thirty-eighth Congress (March 4, 1863-March 3, 1865); claimed reelection to the Thirty-ninth Congress; was seated on February 19, 1866, and served until July

18, 1866, when he was succeeded by William H. Koontz, who contested the election; elected to the Forty-sixth Congress (March 4, 1879-March 3, 1881); chairman, Committee on Invalid Pensions (Forty-sixth Congress); was not a candidate for renomination in 1880; resumed the practice of law in Somerset, Pa.; he was the last surviving pallbearer who had served at the funeral of President Lincoln; died in Markleton, Somerset County, Pa., September 2, 1906; interment in Union Cemetery, Somerset, Pa.

**COGHLAN, John Maxwell,** a Representative from California; born in Louisville, Ky., December 8, 1835; moved with his parents to Illinois in 1847, and in 1850 they moved to California and settled in Suisun City; studied law; was admitted to the bar and practiced in Suisun City; member of the State assembly in 1865 and 1866; elected as a Republican to the Forty-second Congress (March 4, 1871-March 3, 1873); unsuccessful candidate for reelection in 1872 to the Forty-third Congress; engaged in the practice of law until his death in Oakland, Calif., March 26, 1879; interment in Mountain View Cemetery.

**COGSWELL, William,** a Representative from Massachusetts; born in Bradford, Mass., August 23, 1838; attended Phillips Academy, Andover, Mass., and Dartmouth College, Hanover, N.H.; was graduated from the Dane Law School, Harvard University, in 1860; was admitted to the bar and commenced practice in Salem; was commissioned a captain in the Second Regiment, Massachusetts Volunteer Infantry, May 11, 1861; lieutenant colonel October 23, 1862; colonel June 25, 1863; brevetted brigadier general of Volunteers December 15, 1864; mustered out July 24, 1865; resumed the practice of his profession; mayor of Salem 1867-1869, 1873, and 1874; member of the Massachusetts house of representatives 1870, 1871, and 1881-1883; served in the Massachusetts senate in 1885 and 1886; delegate to the Republican National Convention in 1892; elected as a Republican to the Fiftieth and to the four succeeding Congresses and served from March 4, 1887, until his death in Washington, D.C., May 22, 1895; interment in Harmony Grove Cemetery, Salem, Mass.

**COHELAN, Jeffery,** a Representative from California; born in San Francisco, Calif., June 24, 1914; attended the public schools and San Mateo Junior College; A.B., University of California School of Economics; Fulbright research scholar at Leeds and Oxford Universities in England in 1953 and 1954; secretary-treasurer Milk Drivers and Dairy Employees, Local 302, Alameda and Contra Costa Counties, 1942-1958; consultant, University of California Institute of Industrial Relations; member of the Berkeley, Calif., Welfare Commission, 1949-1953, and the Berkeley City Council, 1955-1958; former member of San Francisco Council on Foreign Relations; elected as a Democrat to the Eighty-sixth and to the five succeeding Congresses (January 3, 1959-Janaury 3, 1971); unsuccessful candidate for renomination in 1970 to the Ninety-second Congress; executive director, Group Health Association of America to 1979; is a resident of Washington, D.C.

**COHEN, John Sanford,** a Senator from Georgia; born in Augusta, Ga., February 26, 1870; educated at private schools in Augusta, Richmond (Va.) Academy, and Shenandoah Valley Academy at Winchester, Va.; also attended the United States Naval Academy at Annapolis in 1885 and 1886; became a newspaper reporter for the New York World in 1886; secretary to Secretary of the Interior Hoke Smith, 1893-1896; member of the press galleries of Congress, 1893-1897; during the Spanish-American War served as a war correspondent for the Atlanta Journal;, subsequently enlisted and served in the Third Georgia Volunteer Infantry, attaining the rank of major; member of the army of occupation in Cuba; president and editor of the Atlanta Journal, 1917-1935; originator of the plan for the national highway from New York City to Jacksonville, Fla.; vice chairman of the Democratic National Committee, 1932-1935; appointed as a Democrat to the United

States Senate to fill the vacancy caused by the death of William J. Harris, and served from April 25, 1932 to January 11, 1933, when a successor was duly elected and qualified; was not a candidate in 1932 for election to fill the vacancy; continued in his former business activities until his death in Atlanta, Ga., May 13, 1935; interment in West View Cemetery, Atlanta, Ga.

**COHEN, William Sebastian,** a Representative and a Senator from Maine; born in Bangor, Penobscot County, Maine, August 28, 1940; attended the public schools; graduated Bangor High School, 1958; B.A., Bowdoin College, Brunswick, Maine, 1962; LL.B., Boston University Law School, 1965; admitted to the Maine bar in 1965 and commenced practice in Bangor; instructor, University of Maine, 1968-1972; assistant county attorney, Penobscot County, 1968-1970; member, Bangor City Council, 1969-1972; member, Bangor School Board, 1970-1971; mayor of Bangor, 1971-1972; author; elected as a Republican to the Ninety-third and to the two succeeding Congresses (January 3, 1973-January 3, 1979); was not a candidate in 1978 for reelection to the House of Representatives, but was elected to the United States Senate; reelected in 1984 and again in 1990, and served from January 3, 1979 to January 3, 1997; chairman, Select Committee on Indian Affairs (Ninety-seventh Congress), Special Committee on Aging (One Hundred Fourth Congress); was not a candidate for reelection in 1996; is a resident of Bangor, Maine.

**COHEN, William Wolfe,** a Representative from New York; born in Brooklyn, N.Y., September 6, 1874; attended the public schools; became associated with his father in the shoe manufacturing business until 1903, when he engaged in the banking and brokerage business; vice chairman of the Public Schools Athletic League; honorary deputy chief of the New York fire department; member of the New York Stock Exchange and director of the New York Cotton Exchange; elected as a Democrat to the Seventieth Congress (March 4, 1927-March 3, 1929); was not a candidate for renomination in 1928; resumed his former business pursuits in New York City until his death there on October 12, 1940; interment in Mount Neboh Cemetery, Brooklyn, N.Y.

**COIT, Joshua,** a Representative from Connecticut; born in New London, Conn., October 7, 1758; attended the common schools, and was graduated from Harvard College in 1776; studied law; was admitted to the bar and commenced practice in New London in 1779; member of the State house of representatives in 1784, 1785, 1789, 1790, 1792, and 1793; served as clerk during several terms and as speaker in 1793; elected to the Third Congress; reelected as a Federalist to the Fourth and Fifth Congresses and served from March 4, 1793, until his death in New London, Conn., September 5, 1798; chairman, Committee on Elections (Fifth Congress); interment in Cedar Grove Cemetery.

**Bibliography:** Destler, Chester McArthur. *Joshua Coit, American Federalist, 1758-1798.* Middletown, Conn.: Wesleyan University Press, 1962.

**COKE, Richard** (nephew of Richard Coke, Jr.), a Senator from Texas; born in Williamsburg, James City County, Va., March 13, 1829; attended the common schools and was graduated from William and Mary College, Williamsburg, Va., in 1849; studied law; was admitted to the bar in 1850 and commenced practice in Waco, McLennan County, Tex.; entered the Confederate Army as a private; was promoted to the rank of captain and served throughout the Civil War; appointed district judge in June 1865; elected judge of the State supreme court in 1866 and served one year before being removed as "an impediment to reconstruction"; resumed the practice of law in Waco, Tex.; elected Governor of Texas in 1873, reelected in 1875, and served from January 15, 1874 until December 1, 1876, when he resigned; elected as a Democrat to the United States Senate in 1877; reelected in 1883 and again in 1889 and served from March 4, 1877, to March 3, 1895; was not a candidate for renomination; chairman, Committee on Indian Affairs (Forty-sixth Congress), Committee on Revolutionary Claims (Fiftieth through Fifty-second Congresses), Committee on Fisheries (Fifty-third Congress); died in Waco, Tex., May 14, 1897; interment in Oakwood Cemetery.

**Bibliography:** *DAB*; Fett, B.J. "Early Life of Richard Coke." *Texana* 4 (1972): 310-20.

**COKE, Richard, Jr.** (uncle of Richard Coke [1829-1897]), a Representative from Virginia; born in Williamsburg, Va., November 16, 1790; completed preparatory studies, and was graduated from the College of William and Mary, Williamsburg, Va.; studied law; was admitted to the bar and commenced practice in Gloucester County, Va.; elected as a Jacksonian to the Twenty-first and Twenty-second Congresses (March 4, 1829-March 3, 1833); died on his plantation, "Abingdon Place," in Gloucester County, Va., March 31, 1851; interment in the family burying ground on the estate.

**COLCOCK, William Ferguson,** a Representative from South Carolina; born in Beaufort, S.C., November 5, 1804; attended Hulburt's School, Charleston, S.C., and was graduated from South Carolina College (now the University of South Carolina) at Columbia in 1823; studied law; was admitted to the bar in 1825 and commenced practice in Coosawhatchie, Jasper County, S.C.; also engaged in planting; member of the State house of representatives 1830-1847; elected as a Democrat to the Thirty-first and Thirty-second Congresses (March 4, 1849-March 3, 1853); a Regent of the Smithsonian Institution 1850-1853; collector of the port of Charleston 1853-1865, serving first under the United States Government and subsequently under the Confederate States Government; delegate to the Democratic National Convention at Charleston in 1860; resumed the practice of law; died in McPhersonville, Hampton County, S.C., on June 13, 1889; interment in Stoney Creek Cemetery, Beaufort County, S.C.

**COLDEN, Cadwallader David,** a Representative from New York; born in Springhill, near Flushing, N.Y., April 4, 1769; prepared for college by a private tutor and pursued classical studies at Jamaica, N.Y., and in London, England; returned to the United States in 1785; studied law; was admitted to the bar in 1791 and commenced practice in New York City; moved to Poughkeepsie in 1793, and in 1796 relocated in New York City; appointed district attorney in 1798 and again in 1810; colonel of Volunteers in the War of 1812; member of the State assembly in 1818; mayor of the city of New York in 1819; successfully contested the election of Peter Sharpe to the Seventeenth Congress and served from December 12, 1821, to March 3, 1823; member of the State senate 1824-1827; moved to Jersey City, N.J.; devoted much time to the completion of the Morris Canal; died in Jersey City, N.J., on February 7, 1834.

**Bibliography:** *DAB*.

**COLDEN, Charles J.,** a Representative from California; born on a farm in Peoria County, Ill., August 24, 1870; moved to Nodaway County, Mo., with his parents in 1880; attended the rural schools, Stanberry (Mo.) Normal School, and Shenandoah College, Shenandoah, Iowa; taught school in Missouri and Iowa 1889-1896; editor and publisher of the Parnell Sentinel 1896-1900 and of the Nodaway Forum, at Maryville, 1900-1908; member of the Missouri house of representatives 1901-1905; president of the board of regents of Northwest Missouri Teachers College 1905-1908; moved to Kansas City, Mo., in 1908 and engaged in the real-estate business and in the building of residences; moved to San Pedro, Calif., in 1912 and continued in the real estate and building business; president of the San Pedro Chamber of Commerce 1922-1924; member and president of the Los Angeles Harbor commission 1923-1925; member of the Los Angeles city council 1925-1929; elected as a Democrat to the Seventy-third and to the two succeeding Congresses and served

from March 4, 1933, until his death in Washington, D.C., April 15, 1938; interment in Roosevelt Memorial Park Cemetery, Gardena, Calif.

**COLE, Albert McDonald,** a Representative from Kansas; born in Moberly, Randolph County, Mo., October 13, 1901; moved to Topeka, Kans., in 1909; attended the grade schools of Topeka, Kans., Sabetha (Kans.) High School, and Washburn College, Topeka, Kans.; LL.B., University of Chicago, 1925; was admitted to the bar in 1926 and commenced practice in Holton, Kans.; county attorney of Jackson County 1927-1931; member and president of the Holton School Board 1931-1943; member of the Kansas State senate 1941-1945; elected as a Republican to the Seventy-ninth and to the three succeeding Congresses (January 3, 1945-January 3, 1953); unsuccessful candidate for reelection in 1952 to the Eighty-third Congress; administrator, Housing and Home Finance Agency, Washington, D.C., from March 1953 to January 1959; vice president of Reynolds Aluminum Service Corp. 1959-1961, president, Reynolds Metals Development Corp., 1961-1967, and director 1967-1970; resident counsel, McKenna and Fitting law office, 1968-1981; consultant, Reynolds Metals Development Corporation; was a resident of Washington, D.C.; died June 5, 1994.

**COLE, Cornelius,** a Representative and a Senator from California; born in Lodi, Seneca County, N.Y., September 17, 1822; attended the common schools, Ovid Academy at Ovid, Lima Seminary at Lima, and Hobart College at Geneva, N.Y.; was graduated from Wesleyan University, Middletown, Conn., in 1847; studied law; was admitted to the bar in Auburn, N.Y., in 1848; went to California in 1849, and after working a year in the gold mines commenced the practice of law in San Francisco in 1850; moved to Sacramento in 1851; district attorney of Sacramento City and County 1859-1862; member of the Republican National Committee 1856-1860; moved to Santa Cruz in 1862; during the Civil War was commissioned as a captain in the Union Army in 1863; elected as a Union Republican to the Thirty-eighth Congress (March 4, 1863-March 3, 1865); elected as a Republican to the United States Senate and served from March 4, 1867, to March 3, 1873; chairman, Committee on Appropriations (Forty-second Congress); resumed the practice of law; moved to Colegrove, Los Angeles County, Calif., in 1880, and retired from active practice; died in Hollywood, Calif., November 3, 1924; interment in Hollywood Cemetery.

**Bibliography:** Cole, Cornelius. *Memoirs of Cornelius Cole*. New York: McLaughlin Brothers, 1908; Phillips, Catherine. *Cornelius Cole, California Pioneer and U.S. Senator*. San Francisco: Nash, 1927.

**COLE, Cyrenus,** a Representative from Iowa; born on a farm near Pella, Marion County, Iowa, January 13, 1863; attended the public schools, and was graduated from Central University, Pella, Iowa, in 1887; engaged in newspaper work, and was connected with the Des Moines Register from 1887 to 1898, serving seven years as editorial writer; acquired an interest in the Cedar Rapids Republican in 1898, and was connected with that paper until 1921, during which period he founded the Times as an evening edition of the Republican; author of many publications; elected as a Republican to the Sixty-seventh Congress to fill the vacancy caused by the resignation of James W. Good; reelected to the Sixty-eighth and to the four succeeding Congresses, and served from July 19, 1921 to March 3, 1933; was not a candidate for renomination in 1932 to the Seventy-third Congress; engaged as an author and resided in Washington, D.C., until his death there on November 14, 1939; interment in First Dutch Reform Church Cemetery near Pella, Marion County, Iowa.

**Bibliography:** Cole, Cyrenus. *I Remember, I Remember: A Book of Recollections*. Iowa City: State Historical Society of Iowa, 1936.

**COLE, George Edward,** a Delegate from the Territory of Washington; born in Trenton (now Trenton Falls), Oneida County, N.Y., December 23, 1826; attended the public schools and Hobart Hall Institute; employed as clerk in a country store; moved to Illinois, thence to California in 1849, and later to Oregon in 1850; member of the Oregon house of representatives in 1852 and 1853; engaged in mercantile pursuits and steamboat transportation on the Willamette River; clerk of the United States District Court of Oregon in 1859 and 1860; moved to Walla Walla, Wash., in 1860; elected as a Democrat to the Thirty-eighth Congress (March 4, 1863-March 3, 1865); was not a candidate for renomination in 1864 to the Thirty-ninth Congress; appointed Governor of Washington Territory by President Andrew Johnson on November 21, 1866 and served until March 4, 1867, the Senate having refused to confirm the appointment; returned to Portland, Oreg., in 1867; engaged in railroad construction 1869-1872; postmaster of Portland, Oreg., 1873-1881; moved to Spokane, Wash., in 1889; treasurer of Spokane County, 1890-1892; had extensive interests in mining, manufacturing, and farming; died in Portland, Oreg., December 3, 1906; interment in Lone Fir Cemetery.

**COLE, Nathan,** a Representative from Missouri; born in St. Louis, Mo., July 26, 1825; attended the common schools and took a partial course at Shurtleff College, Alton, Ill.; engaged in mercantile pursuits in St. Louis; a director of the Bank of Commerce for forty-three years, most of which time he was vice president; director in a number of insurance and other corporations; mayor of St. Louis 1869-1871; president of the Merchants' Exchange in 1876; elected as a Republican to the Forty-fifth Congress (March 4, 1877-March 3, 1879); unsuccessful candidate for reelection in 1878 to the Forty-sixth Congress; resumed his former business activities in St. Louis, Mo., where his death occurred March 4, 1904; interment in Bellefontaine Cemetery.

**COLE, Orsamus,** a Representative from Wisconsin; born in Cazenovia, Madison County, N.Y., August 23, 1819; attended the common schools and was graduated from Union College, Schenectady, N.Y., in 1843; studied law; was admitted to the bar in 1845 and commenced practice in Chicago, Ill.; moved to Potosi, Grant County, Wis., the same year and continued the practice of law; member of the State constitutional convention in 1847; elected as a Whig to the Thirty-first Congress (March 4, 1849-March 3, 1851); unsuccessful candidate for reelection in 1850 to the Thirty-second Congress; resumed the practice of law in Potosi until 1855; associate justice of the State supreme court 1855-1880, and chief justice from April 1881 to January 4, 1892; resumed the practice of law; retired in Milwaukee, Wis., where he died on May 5, 1903; interment in Forest Hill Cemetery, Madison, Wis.

**COLE, Ralph Dayton** (brother of Raymond Clinton Cole), a Representative from Ohio; born in Vanlue, Hancock County, Ohio, November 30, 1873; attended the common schools; was graduated from Findlay College, Findlay, Ohio, in 1896 and from Ohio Northern University, Ada, Ohio, in 1900; deputy clerk of Hancock County 1897-1899; studied law; was admitted to the bar in 1900 and commenced practice in Findlay, Hancock County, Ohio; member of the State house of representatives 1900-1904; elected as a Republican to the Fifty-ninth, Sixtieth, and Sixty-first Congresses (March 4, 1905-March 3, 1911); unsuccessful candidate for renomination in 1910 to the Sixty-second Congress; resumed the practice of law in Findlay, Toledo, and Columbus, Ohio; legal adviser to the Comptroller of the Currency in 1912 and 1913; chairman of the speakers' bureau, Republican National Committee, in 1916; delegate to the Republican National Conventions in 1916, 1924, and 1928; enlisted in the United States Army June 6, 1917, serving overseas as major and lieutenant colonel in the Thirty-seventh Infantry Division, taking part in many major engagements; was honorably discharged from the service April 6, 1919; one of the founders of the American Legion at Paris February 16, 1919; resumed the practice of his profession; sustained serious injuries in an automobile accident near Parkman, Geauga County, Ohio, from which he died in Warren, Trumbull County, Ohio, on October 15, 1932; interment in Maple Grove Cemetery, Findlay, Ohio.

**COLE, Raymond Clinton** (brother of Ralph Dayton Cole), a Representative from Ohio; born in Biglick Township, near Findlay, Hancock County, Ohio, August 21, 1870; attended the common schools and Findlay College, Findlay, Ohio; taught school nine years; was graduated from the law department of Ohio Northern University at Ada in 1900; was admitted to the Ohio bar the same year and commenced practice in Findlay, Ohio, in 1901; member of the National Guard 1903-1913; served as city solicitor 1912-1916; elected as a Republican to the Sixty-sixth, Sixty-seventh, and Sixty-eighth Congresses (March 4, 1919-March 3, 1925); chairman, Committee on Elections No. 1 (Sixty-eighth Congress); was an unsuccessful candidate for reelection in 1924 to the Sixty-ninth Congress; resumed the practice of law; died in Findlay, Ohio, on February 8, 1957; interment in Bright Cemetery.

**COLE, William Clay,** a Representative from Missouri; born on a farm near Fillmore, Andrew County, Mo., August 29, 1897; attended the public schools; served ten months as a mounted scout on the Mexican border with the Missouri forces in 1916; during the First World War served fourteen months in the war zone; was graduated from St. Joseph (Mo.) Law School in 1928; was admitted to the bar the same year and commenced practice in St. Joseph, Mo.; member of the State house of representatives at a special session in 1942; elected as a Republican to the Seventy-eighth, Seventy-ninth, and Eightieth Congresses (January 3, 1943-January 3, 1949); unsuccessful candidate for reelection in 1948 to the Eighty-first Congress and for election in 1950 to the Eighty-second Congress; elected to the Eighty-third Congress (January 3, 1953-January 3, 1955); unsuccessful candidate for reelection in 1954 to the Eighty-fourth Congress; member, Board of Veterans Appeals, Washington, D.C., from January 21, 1955, to July 31, 1960; resumed the practice of law in St. Joseph, Mo., where he resided until his death September 23, 1965; interment in Fillmore Cemetery, Fillmore, Mo.

**COLE, William Hinson,** a Representative from Maryland; born in Baltimore, Md., January 11, 1837; attended a private school; studied medicine, and then studied law; was admitted to the bar and commenced practice in Baltimore in 1857; moved to Kansas City, Kans., and continued the practice of law; member of the Territorial house of representatives; graduated from the University of Louisiana in 1860; enlisted in the Confederate Army and was appointed surgeon of Bartow's Eighth Georgia Regiment; served in the Battle of Gettysburg, July 1863, then took charge of the wounded in Longstreet's corps; prisoner in Fort McHenry, Baltimore, for six months; returned South and acted as surgeon on the staff of General Bradley Johnson, of Maryland, until the close of the war; was appointed deputy register of Baltimore in 1870; resigned when elected chief clerk of the first branch of the Baltimore City council; served as a reading clerk of the Maryland State house of delegates 1874-1878; became a reporter on the Baltimore Evening Commercial, and later its proprietor; later connected with the Baltimore Gazette, and afterward with its successor, The Day, continuing with the press until his election to Congress in 1884; elected as a Democrat to the Forty-ninth Congress and served from March 4, 1885, until his death in Washington, D.C., on July 8, 1886; interment in Bonnie Brae Cemetery, Baltimore, Md.

**COLE, William Purington, Jr.,** a Representative from Maryland; born in Towson, Baltimore County, Md., May 11, 1889; attended the public schools; was graduated as a civil engineer from Maryland Agricultural College (now University of Maryland) in 1910; studied law at the University of Maryland at Baltimore; was admitted to the bar in 1912 and commenced practice the same year;

commissioned as first lieutenant November 1917 and was assigned to the Three Hundred and Sixteenth Regiment of Infantry, Seventy-ninth Division, Camp Meade, Md.; served overseas; resumed the practice of law in 1919 at Towson, Md.; elected as a Democrat to the Seventieth Congress (March 4, 1927-March 3, 1929); unsuccessful candidate for reelection in 1928 to the Seventy-first Congress; resumed the practice of law in Towson Md.; again elected to the Seventy-second and to the five succeeding Congresses and served from March 4, 1931, until his resignation on October 26, 1942, to become a judge of the United States customs court, in which capacity he served until 1952; member of the Board of Regents of the Smithsonian Institution 1940-1943; named a member of the Board of Regents of the University of Maryland in 1931 and became chairman of the board in 1944; appointed judge of the United States Court of Customs and Patent Appeals by President Harry S Truman on July 10, 1952, and served until his death in Baltimore, Md., September 22, 1957; interment in Arlington National Cemetery, Va.

**COLE, William Sterling,** a Representative from New York; born in Painted Post, Steuben County, N.Y., April 18, 1904; attended the public schools; A.B., Colgate University, Hamilton, N.Y., 1925; Albany Law School of Union University, Schenectady, N.Y., LL.B., 1929; teacher in the public schools, Corning Free Academy, Corning, N.Y., in 1925 and 1926; was admitted to the New York Bar in 1929 and commenced practice in Bath, N.Y., in 1930; employed with investment firm, Albany, N.Y., 1929-1930; unsuccessful candidate for the Republican nomination in 1932 to the Seventy-third Congress; elected as a Republican to the Seventy-fourth Congress; reelected to the eleven succeeding Congresses and served from January 3, 1935, until his resignation December 1, 1957, to become Director General of the International Atomic Energy Agency with headquarters in Vienna, Austria, 1957-1961; chairman, Joint Committee on Atomic Energy (Eighty-third Congress); resumed the practice of law in Washington, D.C.; was a resident of Arlington, Va., until his death in Washington, D.C., March 15, 1987; interment in Bath, N.Y.

**COLEMAN, Earl Thomas,** a Representative from Missouri; born in Kansas City, Jackson County, Mo., May 29, 1943; attended public schools; B.A., William Jewell College, Liberty, Mo., 1965; M.P.A., New York University, New York City, 1969; J.D., Washington University, St. Louis, Mo., 1969; admitted to the Missouri bar in 1969 and commenced practice in Kansas City; served as State assistant attorney general, 1969-1972; member, Missouri State house of representatives, 1972-1976; elected as a Republican to the Ninety-fourth Congress, November 2, 1976, by special election to fill the vacancy caused by the death of Jerry L. Litton, and at the same time elected to the Ninety-fifth Congress; reelected to the seven succeeding Congresses, and served from November 2, 1976 to January 3, 1993; unsuccessful candidate for reelection in 1992 to the One Hundred Third Congress; is a resident of Gladstone, Mo.

**COLEMAN, Hamilton Dudley,** a Representative from Louisiana; born in New Orleans, La., May 12, 1845; attended public and private schools; enlisted in 1861 as a private in the Washington Artillery, Army of Northern Virginia, and served throughout the Civil War, surrendering at Appomattox with General Robert E. Lee; manufacturer and dealer in plantation machinery at New Orleans; one of the organizers of the first electric lighting company established in New Orleans in 1880, serving as vice president and in 1881 as president of the company; active in the organization of the World's Industrial and Cotton Centennial Exposition in 1884 and 1885; member of the Republican State central committee in 1884; election commissioner in 1886; president of the New Orleans chamber of commerce in 1887 and 1888; one of the vice presidents of the National Board of Trade in 1888 and 1889; vice president of the New Orleans Board of Trade in 1889; elected as a Republican to the

Fifty-first Congress (March 4, 1889-March 3, 1891); unsuccessful candidate for reelection in 1890 to the Fifty-second Congress, and for election in 1894 to the Fifty-fourth Congress; unsuccessful candidate for Governor in 1890 and 1894, and for Lieutenant Governor in 1892; delegate to the Republican League Convention at Cleveland, Ohio, in 1895; appointed melter and refiner of the United States mint at New Orleans in 1899 and served until March 1, 1905; served as a member of the United States Assay Commission in 1912; died in Biloxi, Harrison County, Miss., March 16, 1926; interment in Metairie Cemetery, New Orleans, La.

**COLEMAN, Nicholas Daniel,** a Representative from Kentucky; born in Cynthiana, Ky., April 22, 1800; attended the grammar and high schools; was graduated from Transylvania College, Lexington, Ky.; studied law; was admitted to the bar and practiced; member of the Kentucky house of representatives in 1824 and 1825; elected as a Jacksonian to the Twenty-first Congress (March 4, 1829-March 3, 1831); moved to Vicksburg, Miss., where he resumed the practice of law; postmaster of Vicksburg 1841-1844; again resumed the practice of law; died in Vicksburg, Miss., on May 11, 1874; interment in Cedar Hill Cemetery.

**COLEMAN, Ronald D'Emory,** a Representative from Texas; born in El Paso, Tex., November 29, 1941; attended the public schools of El Paso; graduated Austin High School, El Paso, 1959; B.A., University of Texas at El Paso, 1963; J.D., University of Texas School of Law, 1967; attended the University of Kent, Canterbury, England, 1982; served in the United States Army, captain, 1967-1969; teacher, Texas School for the Deaf, 1963; teacher, El Paso public schools, 1967; legislative assistant, Texas State house and senate, 1965-1967; admitted to the Texas bar, 1969 and commenced practice in El Paso; assistant county attorney, El Paso County, Texas, 1969; first assistant county attorney, 1971; attorney, 1969-1982; vice president, Del Paso Energy Corp., 1980-1982; elected to the Texas State house of representatives, 1973-1982; delegate, Texas constitutional convention, 1974; elected as a Democrat to the Ninety-eighth and to the six succeeding Congresses (January 3, 1983-January 3, 1997); was not a candidate for reelection in 1996 to the One Hundred Fifth Congress; is a resident of El Paso, Tex.

**COLEMAN, William Henry,** a Representative from Pennsylvania; born in North Versailles Township, Allegheny County, Pa., December 28, 1871; attended the public schools; was graduated from Columbian University (now George Washington University) Law School; mayor of McKeesport, 1906-1909; clerk of courts, Allegheny County, 1909-1915; delegate to the Republican National Convention in 1912; was admitted to the bar on November 10, 1913, and commenced practice in Pittsburgh, Pa.; elected as a Republican to the Sixty-fourth Congress (March 4, 1915-March 3, 1917); unsuccessful candidate for reelection in 1916 to the Sixty-fifth Congress; resumed the practice of his profession; died in McKeesport, Pa., June 3, 1943; interment in Richland Cemetery, Dravosburg, Pa.

**COLERICK, Walpole Gillespie,** a Representative from Indiana; born in Fort Wayne, Ind., August 1, 1845; attended the public schools; studied law; was admitted to the bar in 1872 and commenced practice at Fort Wayne, Ind.; elected as a Democrat to the Forty-sixth and Forty-seventh Congresses (March 4, 1879-March 3, 1883); supreme court commissioner from 1883 to 1885; again engaged in the practice of law at Fort Wayne, Ind., until his death there on January 11, 1911; interment in Lindenwood Cemetery.

**COLES, Isaac** (father of Walter Coles), a Representative from Virginia; born in Richmond, Va., March 2, 1747; educated at the College of William and Mary, Williamsburg, Va.; served as a colonel of militia during the Revolutionary War; member of the Virginia house of delegates 1780-1781 and 1783-1788; member of the convention which met in Richmond, Va., in June 1788 to ratify the new Federal Constitution, which he opposed; during his political career lived on a plantation on Staunton River at Coles Ferry, Halifax County; moved to Pittsylvania County in 1798; elected to the First Congress (March 4, 1789-March 3, 1791); elected to the Third Congress and reelected as a Republican to the Fourth Congress (March 4, 1793-March 3, 1797); died on his plantation, "Coles Hill," near Chatham, Pittsylvania County, Va., June 3, 1813; interment in the family cemetery on his plantation.

**COLES, Walter** (son of Isaac Coles), a Representative from Virginia; born at Coles Ferry, Halifax County, Va., December 8, 1790; moved with his parents to Pittsylvania County, Va., in 1798; attended Hampden-Sidney College, Prince Edward County, Va., and Washington College (now Washington and Lee University), Lexington, Va.; served as a second lieutenant in the Second Regiment of Light Dragoons in the War of 1812; promoted to the rank of captain of riflemen on the northern frontier; was honorably discharged in 1815 and returned to Virginia, where he engaged in agricultural pursuits; justice of the peace; member of the Virginia house of delegates 1817, 1818, 1833, and 1834; elected as a Jacksonian to the Twenty-fourth Congress and reelected as a Democrat to the four succeeding Congresses (March 4, 1835-March 3, 1845); was not a candidate for renomination in 1844; resumed agricultural pursuits; died at his home, "Coles Hill," near Chatham, Va., on November 9, 1857; interment in the family burying ground at "Coles Hill."

**COLFAX, Schuyler,** a Representative from Indiana and a Vice President of the United States; born in New York City, March 23, 1823; attended the common schools; in 1836 moved with his parents to New Carlisle, Ind.; appointed deputy auditor of Joseph County, Ind., in 1841; became a legislative correspondent for the Indiana State Journal; purchased an interest in the South Bend Free Press and changed its name in 1845 to the St. Joseph Valley Register, the Whig organ of northern Indiana; delegate to the Whig National Convention of 1848; member of the Indiana State constitutional convention in 1850; unsuccessful Whig candidate for election in 1851 to the Thirty-second Congress; elected as a Republican to the Thirty-fourth and to the six succeeding Congresses (March 4, 1855-March 3, 1869); was not a candidate for renomination in 1868 to the Forty-first Congress, having become the Republican candidate for Vice President; Speaker of the House of Representatives (Thirty-eighth, Thirty-ninth, and Fortieth Congresses); elected Vice President of the United States on the Republican ticket headed by Ulysses S. Grant in 1868, was inaugurated March 4, 1869, and served until March 3, 1873; unsuccessful candidate for renomination in 1872, owing to charges of corruption in connection with the Crédit Mobilier of America scandal; lecturer; died at the Omaha railway station in Mankato, Blue Earth County, Minn., January 13, 1885; interment in City Cemetery, South Bend, Ind.

**Bibliography:** *DAB*; Hollister, Ovando. *Life of Schuyler Colfax.* New York: Funk and Wagnalls, 1886; Smith, Willard H. *Schuyler Colfax: The Changing Fortunes of a Political Idol.* Indianapolis: Indiana Historical Bureau, 1952.

**COLHOUN, John Ewing** (cousin of John Caldwell Calhoun and Joseph Calhoun), a Senator from South Carolina; born in Staunton, Augusta County, Va., around 1749; attended the common schools and was graduated from the College of New Jersey (now Princeton University) in 1774; member, South Carolina State house of representatives, 1778-1800; studied law; was admitted to the bar in 1783 and commenced practice in Charleston, S.C.; farmer; elected a member of the privy council and also a commissioner of confiscated estates in 1785; member of the State senate in 1801; member of the committee which was instructed to report a modification of the judiciary system of the United States; elected as a Republican to the United States Senate, and served from March 4, 1801 until his death in Pendleton, S.C., October 26, 1802; interment in the family cemetery, Old Pendleton District, now Pickens County, South Carolina.

**COLLAMER, Jacob,** a Representative and a Senator from Vermont; born in Troy, N.Y., January 8, 1791; moved with his father to Burlington, Vt.; attended the common schools, and was graduated from the University of Vermont at Burlington in 1810; served in the War of 1812; studied law; was admitted to the bar in 1813 and practiced in Woodstock, Vt., from 1813 to 1833; member, Vermont State house of representatives, 1821-1822, 1827-1828; State's attorney for Windsor County, 1822-1824; judge of the superior court, 1833-1842; elected as a Whig to the Twenty-eighth and to the two succeeding Congresses (March 4, 1843-March 3, 1849); chairman, Committee on Manufactures (Twenty-eighth Congress), Committee on Public Lands (Thirtieth Congress); appointed Postmaster General by President Zachary Taylor, and served from March 8, 1849 to July 22, 1850; again judge of the superior court of Vermont, 1850-1854; elected in 1855 as a Republican to the United States Senate; reelected in 1861, and served from March 4, 1855 until his death in Woodstock, Windsor County, Vt., November 9, 1865; chairman, Committee on Engrossed Bills (Thirty-fourth Congress), Committee on Post Office and Post Roads (Thirty-seventh through Thirty-ninth Congresses), Committee on Library (Thirty-eighth and Thirty-ninth Congresses); interment in River Street Cemetery.

**COLLIER, Harold Reginald,** a Representative from Illinois; born in Lansing, Ingham County, Mich., December 12, 1915; graduated from J. Sterling Morton High School in 1932; attended Morton Junior College, Cicero, Ill., 1932-1933; entered Lake Forest (Ill.) College in 1934 and left in 1937 to become editor of the Berwyn (Ill.) Beacon; columnist, Berwyn Life, 1938-1941; worked in the sales department and as personnel manager of the Match Corporation of America, Chicago, Ill., 1941-1951; alderman, Berwyn city council, 1951; advertising and public relations director, McAlear Manufacturing Co., Chicago, Ill., 1952-1956; unsuccessful candidate for nomination for Illinois secretary of state in 1952; township supervisor of Berwyn, 1953-1956; secretary-treasurer, Cook County Supervisors Association, 1953-1956; president of Berwyn Public Health Board, 1953-1956; chairman of the first senatorial district Republican committee, 1954-1974; secretary, third legislative district, Republican committee, 1954-1974; elected as a Republican to the Eighty-fifth and to the eight succeeding Congresses (January 3, 1957-January 3, 1975); was not a candidate for reelection in 1974 to the Ninety-fourth Congress; is a resident of Boynton Beach, Fla.

**COLLIER, James William,** a Representative from Mississippi; born in Warren County, Miss., on the Glenwood plantation near Vicksburg, September 28, 1872; attended the graded and high schools; was graduated from the law department of the University of Mississippi at Oxford in 1894; was admitted to the bar the same year and commenced practice in Vicksburg; member of the Mississippi State house of representatives, 1896-1899; circuit clerk of Warren County from 1900 until 1909; elected as a Democrat to the Sixty-first and to the eleven succeeding Congresses (March 4, 1909-March 3, 1933); chairman, Commitee on Ways and Means (Seventy-second Congress); declined to become a candidate for reelection in 1932 to the Seventy-third Congress, after a controversy over whether candidates should run at large or by districts; appointed a member of the United States Tariff Commission by President Franklin D. Roosevelt, and served from March 28, 1933 until his death in Washington, D.C., September 28, 1933; interment in Cedar Hill Cemetery, Vicksburg, Miss.

**COLLIER, John Allen** (great-grandfather of Edwin Arthur Hall), a Representative from New York; born in Litchfield, Conn., November 13, 1787; attended Yale College in 1803; studied law in the Litchfield Law School; was admitted to the bar at Troy, N.Y., in 1809 and commenced practice in Binghamton, Broome County, N.Y.; district attorney of Broome County June 11, 1818, to February 25,

1822; elected as an Anti-Masonic candidate to the Twenty-second Congress (March 4, 1831-March 3, 1833); unsuccessful candidate for reelection in 1832 to the Twenty-third Congress; comptroller of the State of New York January 27, 1841, to February 7, 1842; unsuccessful candidate for election in 1844 to the Twenty-ninth Congress; appointed a commissioner to revise the statutes in 1847; presidential elector on the Whig ticket in 1848; resumed his law practice; died in Binghamton, N.Y., March 24, 1873; interment in Spring Forest Cemetery.

**Bibliography:** Philp, Kenneth R. "John Collier and the Indians of the Americas: The Dream and the Reality." *Prologue* 11 (Spring 1979): 5-21.

**COLLIN, John Francis,** a Representative from New York; born in Hillsdale, N.Y., April 30, 1802; attended the common schools and Lenox Academy, Massachusetts; engaged in agricultural pursuits; member of the State assembly in 1834; supervisor of Hillsdale; elected as a Democrat to the Twenty-ninth Congress (March 4, 1845-March 3, 1847); chairman, Committee on Expenditures in the Department of the Navy (Twenty-ninth Congress); resumed agricultural pursuits; died in Hillsdale, Columbia County, N.Y., September 16, 1889; interment in Hillsdale Rural Cemetery.

**COLLINS, Barbara-Rose,** a Representative from Michigan; born in Detroit, Mich., April 13, 1939; graduated Detroit public school system; attended Wayne State University, Detroit; member, Detroit public school board, 1971-1973; member, Michigan State house of representatives, 1975-1981; vice chair, Michigan Democratic caucus; member, Detroit City Council, 1982-1990; chair, Detroit City Council Task Force on Teenage Violence and Juvenile Crime, 1985; unsuccessful candidate for nomination in 1988 to the One Hundred First Congress; elected as a Democrat to the One Hundred Second and to the two succeeding Congresses (January 3, 1991-January 3, 1997); unsuccessful candidate for renomination in 1996 to the One Hundred Fifth Congress; is a resident of Detroit, Mich.

**COLLINS, Cardiss,** (wife of George Washington Collins), a Representative from Illinois; born in St. Louis, Mo., September 24, 1931; at the age of ten moved to Detroit, Mich., and attended the public schools; graduated Detroit High School of Commerce; attended Northwestern University; began her career as a stenographer with the Illinois State department of labor, promoted to secretary with Illinois State department of revenue, then accountant, and eventually moved into the position of revenue auditor and served in this capacity until announcing her candidacy for the House of Representatives; committeewoman of Chicago's twenty-fourth ward; elected as a Democrat to the Ninety-third Congress, June 5, 1973, by special election to fill the vacancy caused by the death of her husband, George W. Collins; reelected to the eleven succeeding Congresses and served from June 5, 1973, to January 3, 1997; was not a candidate for reelection in 1996 to the One Hundred Fifth Congress; is a resident of Chicago, Ill.

**COLLINS, Ela** (father of William Collins), a Representative from New York; born in Meriden, Conn., February 14, 1786; attended Clinton Academy; studied law; was admitted to the bar and commenced practice in Lowville, N.Y., in 1807; member of the State assembly in 1815; district attorney for Lewis, Jefferson, and St. Lawrence Counties 1815-1818, and for Lewis County from June 11, 1818, to March 24, 1840; delegate to the State constitutional convention in 1821; elected to the Eighteenth Congress (March 4, 1823-March 3, 1825); resumed the practice of law; died in Lowville, Lewis County, N.Y., November 23, 1848; interment in Jackson Street Cemetery.

**COLLINS, Francis Dolan,** a Representative from Pennsylvania; born in Saugerties, Ulster County, N.Y., March 5, 1841; attended St. Joseph's College, near Montrose, Susquehanna County; moved with his parents to Dinsmore, Lackawanna County, Pa.; attended Wyoming Seminary at Kingston, Pa.; studied law; was admitted to the bar in 1866 and commenced practice in Scranton, Pa.; elected district attorney of the mayor's court district in 1869; served in the Pennsylvania senate 1872-1874; elected as a Democrat to the Forty-fourth and Forty-fifth Congresses (March 4, 1875-March 3, 1879); resumed the practice of his profession; died in Scranton, Lackawanna County, Pa., November 21, 1891; interment in Cathedral Cemetery, Hyde Park (Scranton).

**COLLINS, George Washington** (husband of Cardiss Collins), a Representative from Illinois; born in Chicago, Ill., March 5, 1925; graduated from Waller High School and studied business law at Northwestern University; served with Army Engineers in the South Pacific during the Second World War before his discharge as a sergeant in 1946; graduated from Central Y.M.C.A. College; worked as a clerk with the Chicago Municipal Court; graduated from Northwestern University, 1957; deputy sheriff of Cook County, Ill., 1958-1961; secretary to Alderman Benjamin Lewis of the Twenty-fourth Ward; administrative assistant, Chicago Board of Health; alderman, Chicago city council, Twenty-fourth Ward, 1964-1970; elected as a Democrat to the Ninety-first Congress, November 3, 1970, by special election, to fill the vacancy caused by the death of Daniel J. Ronan and at the same time elected to the Ninety-second Congress; reelected to the Ninety-third Congress, and served from November 3, 1970, until his death December 8, 1972, in an air crash during landing approach to Midway Airport, Chicago, Ill.; interment in Burr Oak Cemetery.

**COLLINS, James Mitchell,** a Representative from Texas; born in Hallsville, Dallas County, Tex., April 29, 1916; attended high school in Dallas, Tex.; Southern Methodist University, B.S.C., 1937; Northwestern University, M.B.A., 1938; American College, C.L.U. degree in life insurance, 1940; Harvard Business School, M.B.A., 1943; three and one-half years in the United States Army; completed service as captain, United States Army Engineers; one and one-half years in the European Theater from Omaha Beach through France, Belgium, and Germany; president: Consolidated Industries, Inc., 1954-1968, International Industries, Inc., 1961-1968, All Products Co., 1965-1968, Fidelity Union Life Insurance Co., 1954-1965, president: Pacific Industries, 1983-1989; White House Conference on Youth, regional chairman, 1955; delegate, Republican National Convention, 1968; elected as a Republican to the Ninetieth Congress, by special election, August 24, 1968, to fill the vacancy caused by the death of Joseph R. Pool; reelected to seven succeeding Congresses and served from August 24, 1968, to January 3, 1983; was not a candidate for reelection in 1982 to the House of Representatives, but was an unsuccessful candidate for election to the United States Senate; was a resident of Dallas, Tex.; died July 21, 1989.

**COLLINS, John,** a Delegate from Rhode Island; born in Newport, R.I., June 8, 1717; member of the committee sent by the general assembly in September 1776 to inform General Washington of the condition of the colony and obtain his views upon the best method to adopt for its defense; Member of the Continental Congress 1778-1780 and 1782-1783; Governor of Rhode Island 1786-1790; as Governor he cast the deciding vote in the senate, thereby assuring the calling of a convention to decide upon the acceptance of the Constitution of the United States; elected to the First Congress, but did not take his seat; died in Newport, R.I., March 4, 1795; interment on his farm, "Brenton Neck," near Newport, R.I.

**Bibliography:** *DAB.*

**COLLINS, Michael Allen (Mac),** a Representative from Georgia; born in Jackson, Butts County, Ga., September 15, 1944; graduated, Jackson High School, 1962; owner, Collins Trucking Company, Inc.; member, Georgia State senate, 1989-1993; member, Butts County Commission, chair, 1976; chair, Butts County Republican Party; elected as a Republican to the One Hundred Third and One Hundred Fourth Congresses (January 3, 1993-January 3, 1997); is a resident of Jackson, Ga.

**COLLINS, Patrick Andrew,** a Representative from Massachusetts; born near Fermoy, County Cork, Ireland, March 12, 1844; immigrated to the United States with his parents, who settled in Chelsea, Mass., in 1848; attended the common schools; learned the upholstery trade; member of the Massachusetts house of representatives in 1868 and 1869; served in the Massachusetts senate in 1870 and 1871; studied law at the Harvard Law School and in Boston; was admitted to the bar in 1871 and practiced in Boston; judge advocate general of Massachusetts in 1875; delegate to the Democratic National Conventions of 1876, 1880, 1888, and 1892; elected as a Democrat to the Forty-eighth and to the two succeeding Congresses (March 4, 1883-March 3, 1889); was not a candidate for renomination in 1888 to the Fifty-first Congress; resumed the practice of law; consul general at London from May 6, 1893, to May 17, 1897, under President Grover Cleveland's administration; again engaged in the practice of his profession, served as mayor of Boston 1902-1905; died while on a visit to Hot Springs, Va., on September 13, 1905; interment in Holyhood Cemetery, Brookline, Norfolk County, Mass.

**Bibliography:** *DAB*; Curran, Michael P. *Life of Patrick A. Collins.* Norwood, Mass.: Norwood Press, 1906.

**COLLINS, Ross Alexander,** a Representative from Mississippi; born in Collinsville, Lauderdale County, Miss., April 25, 1880; attended the public schools of Meridian, Miss., and Mississippi Agricultural and Mechanical College; was graduated from the University of Kentucky at Lexington in 1900 and from the law department of the University of Mississippi at Oxford in 1901; was admitted to the bar in 1901 and commenced practice in Meridian, Miss.; attorney general of Mississippi 1912-1920; unsuccessful candidate for Governor of Mississippi in 1919; elected as a Democrat to the Sixty-seventh and to the six succeeding Congresses (March 4, 1921-January 3, 1935); was not a candidate in 1934 for renomination to the House of Representatives, but was an unsuccessful candidate for nomination to the United States Senate; elected to the Seventy-fifth and to the two succeeding Congresses (January 3, 1937-January 3, 1943); unsuccessful candidate for the United States Senate in a special election in 1941; was not a candidate in 1942 for renomination to the House of Representatives, but was an unsuccessful candidate for nomination to the United States Senate; resumed the practice of law; died in Meridian, Miss., July 14, 1968; interment in Magnolia Cemetery.

**COLLINS, Samuel LaFort,** a Representative from California; born in Fortville, Hancock County, Ind., on August 6, 1895; attended the public schools of Indiana and California and was graduated from Chaffey Union High School of Ontario, Calif., in 1915; enlisted as a private in the Hospital Corps, Seventh Infantry, California National Guard, on June 21, 1916, served on the Mexican border, and was discharged on November 11, 1916; served in the United States Army from September 18, 1917, until discharged on April 29, 1919, being overseas as a sergeant in Company C, Three Hundred and Sixty-fourth Infantry, Ninety-first Division; studied law; was admitted to the bar in 1921 and commenced practice in Fullerton, Calif.; assistant district attorney of Orange County, Calif., 1926-1930 and district attorney 1930-1932; elected as a Republican to the Seventy-third and Seventy-fourth Congresses (March 4, 1933-January 3, 1937); unsuccessful candidate for reelection in 1936 to the Seventy-fifth Congress; member of the State assembly 1940-1952, serving as speaker 1947-1952; resumed the practice of law; died in Fullerton, Calif., June 26, 1965; interment in Loma Vista Memorial Park.

**COLLINS, William** (son of Ela Collins), a Representative from New York; born in Lowville, Lewis County, N.Y., February 22, 1818; studied law; was admitted to the bar and commenced practice in Lowville; district attorney for Lewis County 1845-1847; elected as a Democrat to the Thirtieth Congress (March 4, 1847-March 3, 1849); declined to be a candidate for renomination in 1848; moved to Cleveland, Ohio, in 1853 and continued the practice of law; also engaged in banking; served as a director of the Lake Shore Railroad and East Cleveland Railroad; affiliated with the Republican Party upon its organization in 1856; died in Cleveland, Ohio, June 18, 1878; interment in Lake View Cemetery.

**COLMER, William Meyers,** a Representative from Mississippi; born in Moss Point, Jackson County, Miss., February 11, 1890; attended the public schools and Millsaps College at Jackson, Miss.; taught school at Lumberton, Miss., 1914-1917; studied law; was admitted to the bar in 1917; during the First World War served as a private in the Quartermaster Corps, advancing through the ranks to regimental sergeant major, and served from July 24, 1918, to March 17, 1919; commenced the practice of law in Pascagoula, Miss., in 1919; county attorney of Jackson County, Miss., 1921-1927; district attorney of the second district of Mississippi from 1928 until his resignation in 1933, having been elected to Congress; elected as a Democrat to the Seventy-third and to the nineteen succeeding Congresses (March 4, 1933-January 3, 1973); chairman, Committee on Rules (Ninetieth through Ninety-second Congresses); unsuccessful candidate for the Democratic nomination for the United States Senate in 1947; was not a candidate for reelection in 1972 to the Ninety-third Congress; was a resident of Pascagoula, Miss., where he died September 9, 1980; interment in Machpelah Cemetery, Pascagoula, Miss.

**Bibliography:** Schlauch, Wolfgang. "Representative William M. Colmer and Senator James O. Eastland and the Reconstruction of Germany, 1945." *Journal of Mississippi History* 34 (August 1972): 193-214.

**COLORADO, Antonio J.,** a Resident Commissioner from Puerto Rico; born in New York City, September 8, 1939; B.S., Boston University, 1962; J.D., University of Puerto Rico School of Law, 1965; LL.M., Harvard University Law School, 1966; legal adviser to administrator, Administration of Economic Development (Puerto Rico); professor of taxation, University of Puerto Rico and Inter-American University; administrator, Economic Development Administration, 1985; Secretary of State for Puerto Rico, 1990-1992; appointed as a Democrat by the Governor to the One Hundred Second Congress, February 21, 1992, to fill the vacancy caused by the resignation of Jaime B. Fuster, and served from March 4, 1992 until January 3, 1993; unsuccessful candidate for reelection in 1992 to the One Hundred Third Congress; is a resident of San Juan, P.R.

**COLQUITT, Alfred Holt** (son of Walter Terry Colquitt), a Representative and a Senator from Georgia; born in Monroe, Walton County, Ga., April 20, 1824; attended school in Monroe and was graduated from Princeton College in 1844; studied law; was admitted to the bar in 1846 and commenced practice in Monroe, Ga.; served as a staff officer with the rank of major during the Mexican War; elected to the Thirty-third Congress (March 4, 1853-March 3, 1855); was not a candidate for renomination in 1854 to the Thirty-fourth Congress; member of the Georgia State house of representatives in 1859; member of the State secession convention in 1861; entered the Confederate Army and was commissioned colonel on May 27, 1861; appointed brigadier general on September 1, 1862; elected Governor of Georgia in 1876, reelected in 1880, and served from January 12, 1877 to November 4, 1882; elected as a

Democrat to the United States Senate in 1883; reelected in 1888 and served from March 4, 1883, until his death in Washington, D.C., March 26, 1894; chairman, Committee on Post Office and Post Roads (Fifty-third Congress); interment in Rose Hill Cemetery, Macon, Bibb County, Ga.

**Bibliography:** *DAB*; Wynne, Lewis. "The Bourbon Triumverate [Alfred H. Colquitt, John B. Gordon, Joseph E. Brown]: A Reconsideration." *Atlanta Historical Journal* 24 (Summer 1980): 39-56.

**COLQUITT, Walter Terry** (father of Alfred Holt Colquitt), a Representative and a Senator from Georgia; born in Halifax County, Va., December 27, 1799; moved with his parents to Mount Zion, Carroll County, Ga.; attended the common schools and Princeton College; studied law; was admitted to the bar in 1820 and commenced practice in Sparta, Hancock County, Ga.; moved to Cowpens, Ga.; elected judge of the Chattahoochee circuit in 1826 and reelected in 1829; was licensed a Methodist preacher in 1827; member, State senate 1834, 1837; elected as a Whig to the Twenty-sixth Congress and served from March 4, 1839, to July 21, 1840, when he resigned; elected as a Van Buren Democrat to the Twenty-seventh Congress to fill in part vacancies caused by the resignations of Julius C. Alford, William C. Dawson, and Eugenius A. Nisbet, and served from January 3, 1842, to March 3, 1843; elected as a Democrat to the United States Senate and served from March 4, 1843, until his resignation in February 1848; chairman, Committee on District of Columbia (Twenty-ninth Congress), Committee on Patents and Patent Office (Twenty-ninth Congress); member of the Nashville convention in 1850; died in Macon, Ga., May 7, 1855; interment in Linnwood Cemetery, Columbus, Ga.

**COLSON, David Grant,** a Representative from Kentucky; born in Yellow Creek (now Middlesboro), Knox (now Bell) County, Ky., April 1, 1861; attended the common schools and the academies at Tazewell and Mossy Creek, Tenn.; studied law at the University of Kentucky at Lexington in 1879 and 1880; was admitted to the bar and commenced practice in Pineville; examiner and special examiner in the Pension Bureau of the Department of the Interior, Washington, D.C., from September 1882 to June 1886; returned to Kentucky in 1887; member of the Kentucky house of representatives in 1887 and 1888; mayor of Middlesboro 1893-1895; elected as a Republican to the Fifty-fourth and Fifty-fifth Congresses (March 4, 1895-March 3, 1899); chairman, Committee on Expenditures on Public Buildings (Fifty-fifth Congress); colonel of a Kentucky regiment during the Spanish-American War; died in Middlesboro, Ky., September 27, 1904; interment in Colson Cemetery.

**COLSTON, Edward,** a Representative from Virginia; born near Winchester, Va., December 25, 1786; studied under private teachers, and was graduated from Princeton College in 1806; studied law; was admitted to the bar and practiced; served in the War of 1812; member of the Virginia house of delegates 1812-1814, 1816-1817, 1823-1828, and 1833-1835; high sheriff of Berkeley County 1844 and 1845; elected as a Federalist to the Fifteenth Congress (March 4, 1817-March 3, 1819); died at "Honeywood," Berkeley County, Va. (now West Virginia), April 23, 1852; interment in the family burying ground on his estate, "Honeywood," near Hedgesville, Berkeley County, W.Va.

**COLT, LeBaron Bradford,** a Senator from Rhode Island; born in Dedham, Dedham County, Mass., June 25, 1846; attended the public schools and Williston Seminary; was graduated from Yale University in 1868 and from the law department of Columbia College, New York City, in 1870; devoted a year to European travel; upon his return to the United States in 1871 was admitted to the bar and commenced practice in Chicago, Ill.; moved to Bristol, R.I., in 1875 and practiced law in Providence, R.I.; member, State house of representatives 1879-1881; appointed by President James Garfield United States district judge for the first judicial district

1881-1884, when he was appointed by President Chester Arthur presiding judge of the United States Circuit Court of Appeals for the first circuit; elected in 1913 as a Republican to the United States Senate; reelected in 1919 and served from March 4, 1913, until his death in Bristol, R.I., August 18, 1924; chairman, Committee on Conservation of Natural Resources (Sixty-fifth Congress), Committee on Immigration (Sixty-sixth through Sixty-eighth Congresses); interment in Juniper Hill Cemetery.

**Bibliography:** *DAB*; Schlup, Leonard. "A Senator of Principle: Some Correspondence Between LeBaron Bradford Colt and William Howard Taft." *Rhode Island History* 42 (February 1983): 3-16.

**COLTON, Don Byron,** a Representative from Utah; born near Mona, Juab County, Utah, September 15, 1876; moved with his parents to Uintah County, Utah, in 1879; attended the public schools and the Uintah Academy, Vernal, Utah; was graduated from the commercial department of Brigham Young University, Provo, Utah, in 1896; engaged in teaching in 1898, 1901, and 1902; member of the State house of representatives in 1903; was graduated from the law department of the University of Michigan at Ann Arbor in 1905; was admitted to the bar the same year and commenced practice in Vernal, Utah; also engaged in ranching, sheep raising, and other business enterprises; receiver of the United States land office at Vernal 1905-1914; delegate to the Republican State conventions 1914-1924; member of the State senate 1915-1917; delegate to the Republican National Conventions in 1904, 1924, and 1928; elected as a Republican to the Sixty-seventh and to the five succeeding Congresses (March 4, 1921-March 3, 1933); chairman, Committee on Elections No. 1 (Sixty-ninth and Seventieth Congresses), Committee on Public Lands (Seventieth and Seventy-first Congresses); unsuccessful candidate for reelection in 1932 to the Seventy-third Congress; resumed the practice of law in Vernal, Utah; unsuccessful candidate for United States Senator in 1934; moved to Salt Lake City in 1937 and continued the practice of law; also engaged in farming and stock raising; unsuccessful candidate for Governor in 1940; died in Salt Lake City, Utah, August 1, 1952; interment in Wasatch Lawn Cemetery.

**COMBEST, Larry Ed,** a Representative from Texas; born in Memphis, Hall County, Tex., March 20, 1945; graduated from Panhandle High School, 1963; B.B.A., West Texas State University, Canyon, 1969; engaged in farming; Director of Agriculture Stabilization and Conservation Service of the United States Department of Agriculture, 1971; legislative assistant to Senator John G. Tower of Texas, 1971-1978; owner of Combest Distributing Company, an electronic equipment business, 1978-1984; elected as a Republican to the Ninety-ninth and to the five succeeding Congresses (January 3, 1985-January 3, 1997); chairman, Permanent Select Committee on Intelligence (One Hundred Fourth Congress); is a resident of Lubbock, Tex.

**COMBS, George Hamilton, Jr.,** a Representative from Missouri; born in Kansas City, Mo., May 2, 1899; attended the Kansas City public schools, the University of Missouri at Columbia, and the University of Michigan at Ann Arbor; served in the United States Navy in 1918; was graduated from the Kansas City School of Law in 1921; was admitted to the bar the same year and commenced practice in Kansas City, Mo.; assistant prosecuting attorney of Jackson County, Mo., 1922-1924; unsuccessful candidate for election in 1924 to the Sixty-ninth Congress; elected as a Democrat to the Seventieth Congress (March 4, 1927-March 3, 1929); was not a candidate for renomination in 1928; delegate to the Democratic National Convention of 1928; moved to New York City in 1929 and continued the practice of law; special assistant to the attorney general of the State of New York in 1931; attorney for the Triborough Bridge Authority in 1933 and 1934; associate counsel to the New York State Joint Legislative Committee to Investigate Public Utilities 1934-1936; appointed by President Franklin D.

Roosevelt as New York State director of the National Emergency Council in 1936; radio news analyst, war correspondent, and writer 1937-1951; special United States attorney, Office of Price Stabilization for southern district of New York, in 1951 and 1952; television and radio news commentator, 1952-1961; chief United Nations correspondent and news commentator for the Mutual Broadcasting System, 1961-1971; died in West Palm Beach, Fla., November 29, 1977.

**COMBS, Jesse Martin,** a Representative from Texas; born in Center, Shelby County, Tex., July 7, 1889; attended the public schools; was graduated from Southwest Texas State Teachers' College in 1912; was admitted to the bar in 1918 and commenced practice in Kountze, Tex.; county judge of Hardin County, Tex., in 1919 and 1920; district judge of the seventy-fifth district 1923-1925; associate justice of the ninth court of civil appeals 1933-1943; member and president of the board of trustees of South Park Schools 1926-1940; president of the board of trustees of Lamar College 1940-1944; elected as a Democrat to the Seventy-ninth and to the three succeeding Congresses (January 3, 1945-January 3, 1953); was not a candidate for renomination in 1952; returned to Beaumont, Tex., where he died August 21, 1953; interment in Magnolia Cemetery.

**COMEGYS, Joseph Parsons,** a Senator from Delaware; born in "Cherbourg," Kent County, near Dover, Del., December 29, 1813; attended the old academy at Dover; studied law; was admitted to the bar in 1835 and commenced practice in Dover; member, State house of representatives 1842, 1848; member of the commission to revise the State statutes in 1852; appointed as a Whig to the United States Senate to fill the vacancy caused by the death of John M. Clayton and served from November 19, 1856, to January 14, 1857, when a successor was elected; declined renomination; resumed the practice of law in Dover; appointed chief justice of the State supreme court in 1876 and served until 1893, when he resigned owing to ill health; died in Dover, Del., February 1, 1893; interment in the Presbyterian Cemetery.

**COMER, Braxton Bragg,** a Senator from Alabama; born in Spring Hill, Barbour (now Mobile) County, Ala., November 7, 1848; attended the common schools, the University of Alabama at Tuscaloosa, and the University of Georgia at Athens; was graduated from Emory and Henry College, Emory, Va., in 1869; engaged as a planter, merchant, banker, and cotton manufacturer; member of the commissioners' court of Barbour County, Ala., 1874-1880; moved to Anniston, Ala., and to Birmingham, Ala., in 1890; continued in his agricultural and business pursuits; president of the Railroad Commission of Alabama, 1905-1906; elected Governor of Alabama in 1906, and served from January 14, 1907 to January 17, 1911; appointed as a Democrat to the United States Senate to fill the vacancy caused by the death of John H. Bankhead and served from March 5, 1920, to November 2, 1920, when a successor was elected; resumed his former business pursuits in Birmingham, Ala., and died there August 15, 1927; interment in Elmwood Cemetery.

Bibliography: *DAB.*

**COMINGO, Abram,** a Representative from Missouri; born near Harrodsburg, Mercer County, Ky., January 9, 1820; attended the common and high schools and was graduated from Centre College, Danville, Ky.; studied law; was admitted to the bar in Harrodsburg, Ky., in 1847; moved to Independence, Mo., in 1848 and commenced the practice of law; delegate to the Missouri State convention in February 1861; appointed provost marshal of the sixth district of Missouri in May 1863; elected recorder of deeds of Jackson County in 1868; elected as a Democrat to the Forty-second and Forty-third Congresses (March 4, 1871-March 3, 1875); was not a candidate for renomination in 1874 to the Forty-fourth Congress; resumed the practice of law in Independence, Mo.; appointed by President Ulysses S. Grant in 1876 a member of the commission to arbitrate

with the Sioux Indians for the possession of Sioux lands in Dakota bordering on the Black Hills; moved to Kansas City, Mo., in 1881; retired from public life; died in Kansas City, Mo., November 10, 1889; interment in Elmwood Cemetery.

**COMINS, Linus Bacon,** a Representative from Massachusetts; born in Charlton, Mass., November 29, 1817; attended the common schools at Brookfield, Mass., and was graduated from Worcester County Manual Training High School; engaged in manufacturing in Roxbury, Mass.; member of the Roxbury city council 1846-1848 and served as its president in 1847 and 1848; mayor of Roxbury in 1854; elected as a candidate of the American Party to the Thirty-fourth Congress and as a Republican to the Thirty-fifth Congress (March 4, 1855-March 3, 1859); resumed manufacturing pursuits; delegate to the Republican National Convention in 1860; died in Jamaica Plain, Mass., October 14, 1892; interment in Forest Hills Cemetery, Boston, Mass.

**COMPTON, Barnes** (great-grandson of Philip Key), a Representative from Maryland; born in Port Tobacco, Charles County, Md., November 16, 1830; attended Charlotte Hall Academy, St. Marys County, Md., and was graduated from Princeton College in June 1851; engaged in agricultural pursuits and as a planter; member of the State house of delegates in 1860 and 1861; member of the State senate in 1867, 1868, 1870, and 1872, and served as president in 1868 and 1870; State tobacco inspector in 1873 and 1874; State treasurer 1874-1885; moved to Laurel, Prince Georges County, Md., in 1880; elected as a Democrat to the Forty-ninth and Fiftieth Congresses (March 4, 1885-March 3, 1889); presented credentials as Member-elect to the Fifty-first Congress and served from March 4, 1889, to March 20, 1890, when he was succeeded by Sydney Mudd, who contested the election; elected to the Fifty-second and Fifty-third Congresses and served from March 4, 1891, until his resignation, effective May 15, 1894; appointed by President Grover Cleveland naval officer at Baltimore, Md., and served from 1894 to 1898; died in Laurel, Md., December 4, 1898; interment in Loudon Park Cemetery, Baltimore, Md.

**COMPTON, C.H. Ranulf,** a Representative from Connecticut; born in Poe, Allen County, Ind., September 16, 1878; attended the public schools at Indianapolis, Ind.; was graduated from the Howe Military School, Howe, Ind., in 1899, and attended Harvard University; engaged in banking and finance in New York and Connecticut; served as captain of Infantry, New York National Guard, 1912-1916; captain of Infantry, United States Army, July 1916-March 1918; captain and major in the Tank Corps April 1918-August 1919; went overseas with the A.E.F. on December 12, 1917; decorated with the Purple Heart and the French Legion of Honor; retired from the United States Army on August 8, 1919, with rank of major; military secretary to Governor Nathan L. Miller of New York in 1920; deputy secretary of state of New York in 1921 and 1922; executive secretary and treasurer of the Hudson River Regulating District, Albany, N.Y., 1923-1929; served as aide-de-camp to Governor Raymond E. Baldwin of Connecticut in 1940 and 1941; elected as a Republican to the Seventy-eighth Congress (January 3, 1943-January 3, 1945); unsuccessful candidate for reelection in 1944 to the Seventy-ninth Congress; president and owner of South Jersey Broadcasting Company from 1945 until his retirement in 1968; resided in Madison, Conn., until his death there January 26, 1974; interment in West Cemetery.

**COMSTOCK, Charles Carter,** a Representative from Michigan; born in Sullivan, Cheshire County, N.H., March 5, 1818; attended the common schools; moved to Grand Rapids, Mich., in 1853; engaged in agricultural pursuits, lumbering, and the manufacture of furniture and woodenware; mayor of Grand Rapids in 1863 and 1864; unsuccessful Democratic candidate for Governor in 1870; unsuccessful candidate for election in 1873 to the Forty-third Congress; elected as a Democrat to the Forty-ninth

Congress (March 4, 1885-March 3, 1887); declined to be a candidate for renomination in 1886; died in Grand Rapids, Mich., February 20, 1900; interment in Fulton Street Cemetery.

**COMSTOCK, Daniel Webster,** a Representative from Indiana; born in Germantown, Montgomery County, Ohio, December 16, 1840; attended the common schools, and was graduated from the Ohio Wesleyan University, Delaware, Ohio, in 1860; studied law; was admitted to the bar in 1861 and commenced practice in New Castle, Ind.; district attorney in 1862; during the Civil War enlisted in the Ninth Indiana Cavalry and was successively promoted to regimental sergeant major, first lieutenant, captain, and acting assistant adjutant general in the military division of Mississippi; settled in Richmond, Ind., in 1866; city attorney in 1866; prosecuting attorney of the Wayne circuit court 1872-1874; member of the State senate in 1878; judge of the seventeenth judicial circuit 1886-1895; judge of the appellate court 1896-1911; resumed the practice of law; elected as a Republican to the Sixty-fifth Congress and served from March 4, 1917, until his death in Washington, D.C., May 19, 1917; interment in Earlham Cemetery, Richmond, Wayne County, Ind.

**COMSTOCK, Oliver Cromwell,** a Representative from New York; born in Warwick, R.I., March 1, 1780; moved with his parents to Schenectady, N.Y., when a child; received a liberal schooling; studied medicine and practiced in Trumansburg, N.Y.; member of the State assembly 1810-1812; first judge of common pleas for Seneca County, N.Y., 1812-1815; elected as a Republican to the Thirteenth, Fourteenth, and Fifteenth Congresses (March 4, 1813-March 3, 1819); was not a candidate for renomination in 1818; first judge of court of common pleas for Tompkins County in 1817 and 1818; abandoned the practice of medicine and studied theology; was licensed to preach and ordained to the Baptist ministry; installed as pastor of the First Baptist Church, Rochester, N.Y., and served in that capacity from 1825 to 1834; elected Chaplain of the House of Representatives on December 20, 1836, and served until March 3, 1837; moved to Michigan and resumed ministerial duties at Detroit in 1839; was a regent of the University of Michigan at Ann Arbor 1841-1843; State superintendent of public instruction 1843-1845; died in Marshall, Calhoun County, Mich., January 11, 1860; interment in Oakridge Cemetery.

**COMSTOCK, Solomon Gilman,** a Representative from Minnesota; born in Argyle, Penobscot County, Maine, May 9, 1842; moved to Passadumkeag, Maine, with his parents in 1845; attended the rural schools, East Corinth (Maine) Academy, Maine Wesleyan Academy at Kents Hill, and Hampden (Maine) Academy; studied law in Bangor, Maine, and later, in 1868 and 1869, continued his studies at the University of Michigan at Ann Arbor; moved to Nebraska in 1869 and settled in Omaha, where he was admitted to the bar the same year and commenced practice; moved to Minneapolis, Minn., in 1870, and to Moorhead, Clay County, Minn., in 1871, where he continued the practice of his profession; prosecuting attorney for Clay County 1872-1878; member of the State house of representatives in 1875, 1876, 1878, and 1881; served in the State senate 1882-1888; unsuccessful candidate for election as State attorney general in 1882 and as Lieutenant Governor in 1884; retired from law practice in 1884 and engaged in the real-estate business; elected as a Republican to the Fifty-first Congress (March 4, 1889-March 3, 1891); unsuccessful candidate for reelection in 1890 to the Fifty-second Congress; delegate to the Republican National Convention in 1892; resumed the real-estate business in Moorhead, Minn.; also engaged in the manufacture of farm implements in 1893; member of the State normal school board 1897-1905; retired from business pursuits and resided in Moorhead, Minn., until his death there June 3, 1933; interment in Prairie Home Cemetery.

**CONABLE, Barber Benjamin, Jr.,** a Representative from New York; born in Warsaw, Wyoming County, N.Y., November 2, 1922; attended the Warsaw public schools; A.B., Cornell University, Ithaca, N.Y., 1942; enlisted in the United States Marine Corps, served on Iwo Jima and in the occupation forces in Japan; LL.B., Cornell University Law School, 1948; began the practice of law in Buffalo, N.Y.; recalled to duty during the Korean conflict; colonel in the Marine Corps Reserve; established a law firm in Batavia, N.Y., in 1952; member of the New York State senate in 1963 and 1964; elected as a Republican to the Eighty-ninth and to the nine succeeding Congresses (January 3, 1965-January 3, 1985); was not a candidate for reelection in 1984 to the Ninety-ninth Congress; appointed president of the International Bank for Reconstruction and Development (World Bank) in July 1986 and served until September 1991; is a resident of Alexander, N.Y.

**Bibliography:** Conable, Barber B., Jr., with A.L. Singleton. *Congress and the Income Tax.* Norman: University of Oklahoma Press, 1989.

**CONARD, John,** a Representative from Pennsylvania; born in Chester Valley, Chester County, Pa., in November 1773; educated at the Friends School; moved to Germantown about 1795; studied law; was admitted to the bar and practiced; professor of mathematics at the local academy in Germantown; elected as a Republican to the Thirteenth Congress (March 4, 1813-March 3, 1815); declined to be a candidate for renomination in 1814; associate judge of the district court; appointed United States marshal for the eastern district of Pennsylvania by President James Monroe; reappointed by President John Quincy Adams and served two years under President Andrew Jackson; retired from public life in 1832; moved to Maryland about 1834 and settled in Cecil County near Port Deposit, where he lived until 1851, when he moved to Philadelphia; died in Philadelphia, Pa., May 9, 1857; interment in St. Ann's Protestant Episcopal Churchyard, North East, Cecil County, Md.

**CONDICT, Lewis** (nephew of Silas Condict), a Representative from New Jersey; born in Morristown, Morris County, N.J., March 3, 1772; attended the common schools; was graduated from the medical department of the University of Pennsylvania at Philadelphia in 1794 and commenced practice in Morristown; sheriff of Morris County, N.J., 1801-1803; member of the commission for adjusting the boundary line between the States of New York and New Jersey in 1804; member of the State house of assembly 1805-1809 and served as speaker the last two years; elected as a Republican to the Twelfth, Thirteenth, and Fourteenth Congresses (March 4, 1811-March 3, 1817); president of the State medical society in 1816 and 1819; elected to the Seventeenth and to the five succeeding Congresses (March 4, 1821-March 3, 1833); chairman, Committee on Revisal and Unfinished Business (Fourteenth Congress), Committee on Expenditures on Public Buildings (Fourteenth Congress); declined to be a candidate for renomination in 1832; elected trustee of Princeton College in 1827, and served in this capacity until 1861, when he resigned; one of the incorporators of the Morris & Essex Railroad Co. and became its first president in 1835; again a member of the State house of assembly in 1837 and 1838 and served as speaker; presidential elector on the Whig ticket in 1840; died in Morristown, N.J., May 26, 1862; interment in the cemetery of the Presbyterian Church.

**CONDICT, Silas** (uncle of Lewis Condict and great-grandfather of Augustus William Cutler), a Delegate from New Jersey; born in Morristown, Morris County, N.J., March 7, 1738; completed preparatory studies; was a large landholder in Morristown and vicinity; member of the State council from its organization in 1776 until 1780; member of the committee of safety; Member of the Continental Congress 1781-1783; served in the State general assembly 1791-1794, 1796-1798, and 1800, and served as speaker

1792-1794 and again in 1797; died in Morristown, N.J., September 6, 1801; interment in the cemetery of the First Presbyterian Church.

**CONDIT, Gary Adrian,** a Representative from California; born in Salina, Mayes County, Okla., April 21, 1948; attended Modesto (Calif.) Junior College; B.A., California State University, Stanislaus, 1972; member, Ceres City Council, 1972-1976; member, Stanislaus County Board of Supervisors, 1976-1982, chair, 1980; member, California State assembly, 1983-1989; elected as a Democrat to the One Hundred First Congress, September 12, 1989, by special election to fill the vacancy caused by the resignation of Anthony L. Coelho; reelected to the One Hundred Second and to the two succeeding Congresses, and served from September 12, 1989 to January 3, 1997; is a resident of Ceres, Calif.

**CONDIT, John** (father of Silas Condit), a Representative and a Senator from New Jersey; born in Orange, N.J., July 8, 1755; attended the public schools; studied medicine; served as a surgeon in the Revolutionary War; one of the founders and a trustee of the Orange Academy in 1785; member, State general assembly 1788-1789; elected as a Republican to the Sixth and Seventh Congresses (March 4, 1799-March 3, 1803); appointed as a Republican to the United States Senate to fill the vacancy in the term beginning March 4, 1803, caused by the failure of the legislature to elect; subsequently elected and served from September 1, 1803, to March 3, 1809; again appointed to the United States Senate to fill the vacancy caused by the resignation of Aaron Kitchell; subsequently elected and served from March 21, 1809, to March 3, 1817; elected to the Sixteenth Congress and served from March 4 to November 4, 1819, when he resigned to accept a Treasury position; appointed assistant collector of the port of New York 1819-1830; died in Orange Township, N.J., May 4, 1834; interment in the Old Graveyard, Orange, Essex County, N.J.

**Bibliography:** *DAB*.

**CONDIT, Silas** (son of John Condit), a Representative from New Jersey; born in Orange, N.J., August 18, 1778; was graduated from Princeton College, New Jersey, in 1795; engaged in mercantile pursuits in Orange; moved to Newark, N.J.; clerk of Essex County 1804-1811; sheriff of Essex County 1813-1816; member of the State general assembly in 1812, 1813, and 1816; served in the State council 1819-1822; president of the Newark Banking Co. 1820-1842; elected as an Anti-Jacksonian to the Twenty-second Congress (March 4, 1831-March 3, 1833); engaged in banking; delegate to the State constitutional convention in 1844; died in Newark, N.J., November 29, 1861; interment in the cemetery of the First Presbyterian Church.

**CONDON, Francis Bernard,** a Representative from Rhode Island; born in Central Falls, Providence County, R.I., November 11, 1891; attended the public schools; was graduated from Georgetown University Law School, Washington, D.C., in 1916; was admitted to the bar in 1916 and commenced practice in Pawtucket, R.I.; served as a sergeant in the One Hundred and Fifty-second Regiment, Depot Brigade, Twenty-third Company, from May 1918 to June 1919; member of the State house of representatives 1921-1926, serving as Democratic floor leader 1923-1926; member of the Democratic State committee 1924-1926 and 1928-1930, serving as a member of the executive committee 1928-1930; unsuccessful candidate in 1928 for lieutenant governor of Rhode Island; Rhode Island department commander of the American Legion in 1927 and 1928; elected as a Democrat to the Seventy-first Congress to fill the vacancy caused by the resignation of Jeremiah E. O'Connell and at the same time was elected to the Seventy-second Congress; reelected to the Seventy-third and Seventy-fourth Congresses and served from November 4, 1930, until his resignation on January 10, 1935, having been appointed an associate justice of the Rhode Island supreme court, in which capacity he served until January 1958; appointed chief justice of the Rhode Island supreme court January 7, 1958 and served until

his death in Boston, Mass., on November 23, 1965; interment in Mount St. Mary's Cemetery, East Providence, R.I.

**CONDON, Robert Likens,** a Representative from California; born in Berkeley, Alameda County, Calif., November 10, 1912; attended the public schools; was graduated from the University of California at Berkeley in 1934 and from the law college of the same university in 1938; editor in chief of the California Law Review in 1938; admitted to the California bar in 1938; attorney for National Labor Relations Board 1938-1942; with the Office of Price Administration in 1942 as chief enforcement attorney for northern California and later as regional investigator for five Western States; entered the United States Army as a private in December 1942; served overseas in the European Theater with Company G, Three Hundred and Tenth Infantry Regiment, Seventy-eighth Division, in France, Belgium, and Germany; discharged in February 1946 as a staff sergeant; decorated with two battle stars and the Silver Star; engaged in private practice of law in 1946 in Martinez, Calif.; member of California State assembly 1948-1952; elected as a Democrat to the Eighty-third Congress (January 3, 1953-January 3, 1955); unsuccessful candidate for reelection in 1954 to the Eighty-fourth Congress; resumed law practice in Martinez, Calif.; died in Walnut Creek, Calif., June 3, 1976; cremated; ashes scattered at sea, three miles beyond the Golden Gate Bridge, San Francisco, Calif.

**CONGER, Edwin Hurd,** a Representative from Iowa; born in Knox County, Ill., March 7, 1843; was graduated from Lombard University, Galesburg, Ill., in 1862; during the Civil War enlisted as a private in Company I, One Hundred and Second Regiment, Illinois Volunteer Infantry, and served until the close of the war; attained the rank of captain and received the brevet of major; studied law and was graduated from the Albany Law School in 1866; was admitted to the bar and practiced in Galesburg, Ill., until 1868; moved to Dexter, Dallas County, Iowa, in 1868 and engaged in stock growing, banking, and agricultural pursuits; elected treasurer of Dallas County in 1877 and reelected in 1879; elected Iowa State treasurer in 1880, and reelected in 1882; elected as a Republican to the Forty-ninth and to the two succeeding Congresses, and served from March 4, 1885 to October 3, 1890, when he resigned to accept a diplomatic mission; chairman, Committee on Coinage, Weights, and Measures (Fifty-first Congress); appointed Minister to Brazil on September 27, 1890 and served until September 1893; again appointed Minister to Brazil on May 27, 1897 and served until February 1898; appointed Minister to China on January 19, 1898, and served until his resignation on March 8, 1905, on which day he was appointed as Ambassador to Mexico, and served until his resignation on October 18, 1905; died in Pasadena, Calif., May 18, 1907; interment in Mountain View Cemetery.

**Bibliography:** *DAB*.

**CONGER, Harmon Sweatland,** a Representative from New York; born in Freeport, Cortland County, N.Y., April 9, 1816; attended the local academy at Cortland in 1833; studied law; was admitted to the bar in 1844 and commenced practice in Cortland, N.Y.; editor and owner of the Cortland County Whig 1840-1845; elected as a Whig to the Thirtieth and Thirty-first Congresses (March 4, 1847-March 3, 1851); resumed the practice of law in Cortland, N.Y.; moved to Janesville, Wis., in 1855 and continued the practice of law; elected judge of the circuit court in 1870; reelected in 1877 and served until his death in Janesville, Rock County, Wis., October 22, 1882; interment in Oak Hill Cemetery.

**CONGER, James Lockwood,** a Representative from Michigan; born in Trenton, N.J., February 18, 1805; moved to New York in 1809 with his parents, who settled in Canandaigua, Ontario County; attended the district schools and Canandaigua Academy; studied medicine; moved to Lancaster, Ohio, in 1822; taught school for several years; studied law; was admitted to the bar in 1825 and commenced practice in Lancaster, Ohio; moved to Cleveland, Ohio, and continued the practice of law from 1826 to 1837, when he moved to Macomb County, Mich., and laid out the town of Belvidere; engaged in banking and mercantile pursuits until 1850; moved to Mount Clemens, Mich.; elected as a Whig to the Thirty-second Congress (March 4, 1851-March 3, 1853); declined to be a candidate for renomination in 1852; resumed his former business pursuits; owing to ill health retired from active business pursuits; died in St. Clair, St. Clair County, Mich., April 10, 1876; interment in Greenlawn Cemetery, Columbus, Ohio.

**CONGER, Omar Dwight,** a Representative and a Senator from Michigan; born in Cooperstown, Otsego County, N.Y., April 1, 1818; moved with his father to Huron County, Ohio, in 1824; pursued academic studies at Huron Institute, Milan, Ohio, and was graduated from Western Reserve College, Hudson, Ohio, in 1841; engaged in mineral explorations of the Lake Superior copper and iron regions in connection with the Michigan State Geological Survey 1845-1847; engaged in the practice of law in Port Huron, Mich., in 1848; elected judge of the St. Clair county court in 1850; member, State senate 1855-1859, and served as President pro tempore in 1859; member of the State military board during the Civil War, holding the rank of colonel; member of the State constitutional convention in 1866; elected as a Republican to the Forty-first and to the five succeeding Congresses and served from March 4, 1869, until March 3, 1881, when he resigned to become Senator; chairman, Committee on Expenditures in the Department of State (Forty-second Congress), Committee on Patents (Forty-third Congress); elected in 1881 as a Republican to the United States Senate and served from March 4, 1881, to March 3, 1887; unsuccessful candidate for renomination; chairman, Committee on Manufactures (Forty-seventh Congress), Committee on Revision of the Laws (Forty-eighth Congress), Committee on Post Office and Post Roads (Forty-ninth Congress); engaged in the practice of law in Washington, D.C.; died in Ocean City, Worcester County, Md., July 11, 1898; interment in Lakeside Cemetery, Port Huron, Mich.

**Bibliography:** Rubenstein, Bruce A. "Omar D. Conger: Michigan's Forgotten Favorite Son." *Michigan History* 66 (September/October 1982): 32-39.

**CONKLING, Alfred** (father of Frederick Augustus Conkling and Roscoe Conkling), a Representative from New York; born in Amagansett, N.Y., October 12, 1789; was graduated from Union College, Schenectady, N.Y., in 1810; studied law; was admitted to the bar in 1812 and commenced practice in Canajoharie; prosecuting attorney for Montgomery County, 1818-1821; elected to the Seventeenth Congress (March 4, 1821-March 3, 1823); moved to Albany, N.Y., about 1824 and to Auburn, N.Y., in 1839; appointed United States district judge for the northern district of New York, and served from 1825 to 1852; appointed United States Minister to Mexico on August 6, 1852, and served until August 1853; settled in Omaha, Nebr., and practiced law until 1861, when he resided successively in Rochester, Geneseo, and Utica, N.Y., moving to the latter city in 1872; devoted much time to literary pursuits; died in Utica, Oneida County, N.Y., on February 5, 1874; interment in Forest Hill Cemetery.

**Bibliography:** *DAB*; Jonas, Harold J. "Alfred Conkling, Jurist and Gentleman." *New York History* 20 (July 1939): 295-305.

**CONKLING, Frederick Augustus** (son of Alfred Conkling and brother of Roscoe Conkling), a Representative from New York; born in Canajoharie, Montgomery County, N.Y., August 22, 1816; pursued classical studies and attended the Albany Academy; engaged in mercantile pursuits in New York City; member of the State assembly in 1854, 1859, and 1860; organized the Eighty-fourth Regiment, New York Volunteers, in June 1861 and became its colonel; served throughout the Shenandoah campaign; one of the organizers of the West Side Savings Bank of New York City and served as its president for many years; subsequently he became president of the Aetna Fire Insurance Co., of Hartford, Conn., and served until its dissolution in 1880; elected as a Republican to the Thirty-seventh Congress (March 4, 1861-March 3, 1863); unsuccessful candidate for reelection in 1862 to the Thirty-eighth Congress; was an unsuccessful Republican candidate for mayor of New York City in 1868; author of numerous pamphlets on political, commercial, and scientific subjects; died in New York City, on September 18, 1891; interment in Greenwood Cemetery, Brooklyn, N.Y.

**CONKLING, Roscoe** (son of Alfred Conkling and brother of Frederick Augustus Conkling), a Representative and a Senator from New York; born in Albany, N.Y., October 30, 1829; moved with his parents to Auburn, N.Y., in 1839; completed an academic course; studied law; was admitted to the bar in 1850 and commenced practice in Utica, N.Y.; district attorney for Oneida County in 1850; mayor of Utica 1858; elected as a Republican to the Thirty-sixth and Thirty-seventh Congresses (March 4, 1859-March 3, 1863); chairman, Committee on District of Columbia (Thirty-seventh Congress); unsuccessful candidate in 1862 for reelection; elected to the Thirty-ninth and Fortieth Congresses and served from March 4, 1865, until he resigned to become Senator, effective March 4, 1867; elected in 1867 as a Republican to the United States Senate; reelected in 1873 and again in 1879 and served from March 4, 1867, until May 16, 1881, when he resigned as a protest against the federal appointments made in New York State; was an unsuccessful candidate for reelection to the United States Senate to fill the vacancy caused by his own resignation; chairman, Committee on Revision of the Laws of the United States (Fortieth through Forty-third Congresses), Committee on Commerce (Forty-fourth, Forty-fifth, and Forty-seventh Congresses), Committee on Engrossed Bills (Forty-sixth and Forty-seventh Congresses); resumed the practice of law in New York City; declined to accept a nomination to the United States Supreme Court in 1882; died in New York City, on April 18, 1888; interment in Forest Hill Cemetery, Utica, N.Y.

**Bibliography;** *DAB*; Chidsey, Donald B. *The Gentleman from New York: A Life of Roscoe Conkling*. New Haven: Yale University Press, 1935; Jordan, David M. *Roscoe Conkling: Voice in the Senate*. Ithaca: Cornell University Press, 1971.

**CONLAN, John Bertrand,** a Representative from Arizona; born in Oak Park, Cook County, Ill., September 17, 1930; attended Illinois public schools; B.S., Northwestern University, Evanston, Ill., 1951; LL.B., Harvard University Law School, 1954; Fulbright Scholarship, University of Cologne, Germany, 1954-1955; studied at The Hague Academy of International Law; admitted to the Illinois bar in 1954 and commenced practice in Chicago; served in the United States Army, captain, 1956-1961; former member of political science faculties at the University of Maryland and Arizona State University; practiced law in Phoenix, Ariz.; Arizona State senator, 1965-1972; delegate, Arizona State Republican conventions, 1962-1972; elected as a Republican to the Ninety-third and Ninety-fourth Congresses (January 3, 1973-January 3, 1977); was not a candidate in 1976 for reelection to the House of Representatives, but was an unsuccessful candidate for nomination to the United States Senate; is a resident of Phoenix, Ariz.

**CONN, Charles Gerard,** a Representative from Indiana; born in Phelps, Ontario County, N.Y., January 29, 1844; moved with his parents to Elkhart, Ind., in 1851; attended the common schools; enlisted in the Union Army on May 18, 1861, and served as a private in the band of Company B, Fifteenth Regiment, Indiana Volunteer Infantry; discharged on September 10, 1862; reenlisted in Company G, First Michigan Sharpshooters, November 18, 1862; was wounded and taken prisoner, being released from Columbia (S.C.) prison camp at the close of hostilities; engaged in the grocery and bakery business and, in 1877, in the manufacture of band instruments at Elkhart, Ind.; mayor of Elkhart, 1880-1883; member of the Indiana

State house of representatives in 1889; established the Elkhart Daily Truth in 1890; was owner of the Washington (D.C.) Times during part of his congressional term; elected as a Democrat to the Fifty-third Congress (March 4, 1893-March 3, 1895); was not a candidate for renomination in 1894 to the Fifty-fourth Congress; resumed the manufacture of band instruments at Elkhart, Ind.; in 1916 retired and moved to Los Angeles, Calif., where he died on January 5, 1931; interment in Grace Lawn Cemetery, Elkhart, Ind.

**CONNALLY, Thomas Terry (Tom),** a Representative and a Senator from Texas; born near Hewitt, McLennan County, Tex., August 19, 1877; attended the public schools; was graduated from Baylor University, Waco, Tex., in 1896 and from the law department of the University of Texas at Austin in 1898; was admitted to the bar in 1898 and commenced practice in Waco, Tex.; moved to Marlin, Falls County, Tex., in 1899 and continued the practice of law; served as sergeant major in the Second Regiment, Texas Volunteer Infantry, during the Spanish-American War; member, Texas State house of representatives, 1901-1904; prosecuting attorney of Falls County, Tex., 1906-1910; during the First World War became captain and adjutant of the Twenty-second Infantry Brigade, Eleventh Division, United States Army, in 1918; permanent chairman of Texas Democratic State convention in 1938; elected as a Democrat to the Sixty-fifth and to the five succeeding Congresses (March 4, 1917-March 3, 1929); did not seek renomination in 1928 to the House of Representatives, having become a candidate for Senator; elected as a Democrat to the United States Senate in 1928; reelected in 1934, 1940, and again in 1946, and served from March 4, 1929 to January 3, 1953; was not a candidate for renomination in 1952; chairman, Committee on Public Buildings and Grounds (Seventy-third through Seventy-seventh Congresses), Committee on Foreign Relations (Seventy-seventh through Seventy-ninth and Eighty-first and Eighty-second Congresses); member and vice chairman of the United States delegation to the United Nations Conference on International Organization at San Francisco in 1945; representative of the United States to the first session of the General Assembly of the United Nations at London, and to the second session at New York in 1946; engaged in the practice of law in Washington, D.C., where he died on October 28, 1963; interment in Calvary Cemetery, Marlin, Tex.

**Bibliography:** Connally, Thomas Terry. *My Name is Tom Connally.* New York: Crowell, 1954; Gulick, Merle L. "Tom Connally as a Founder of the United Nations." Ph.D. dissertation, Georgetown University, 1955; Smyrl, Frank Herbert. "Tom Connally and the New Deal." Ph.D. dissertation, University of Oklahoma, 1968.

**CONNELL, Charles Robert** (son of William Connell), a Representative from Pennsylvania; born in Scranton, Lackawanna County, Pa., September 22, 1864; attended the public schools, and was graduated from Williston Academy, Easthampton, Mass., in 1884; engaged in mercantile pursuits with his father; also engaged in banking; became interested in the Lackawanna Mills and subsequently served as president and treasurer of the Scranton Button Co. from 1888 until his death; also interested in other manufacturing enterprises and banking; elected as a Republican to the Sixty-seventh Congress and served from March 4, 1921, until his death in Scranton, Pa., September 26, 1922; interment in Forest Hill Cemetery.

**CONNELL, Richard Edward,** a Representative from New York; born in Poughkeepsie, Dutchess County, N.Y., November 6, 1857; attended St. Peter's Parochial School and the public schools of Poughkeepsie; reporter and editor on the Poughkeepsie News Press 1887-1910; police commissioner of Poughkeepsie in 1892; unsuccessful candidate for election to the Fifty-fifth Congress in 1896; unsuccessful candidate for member of the State assembly in 1898 and 1900; inheritance tax appraiser 1907-1909; delegate to the Democratic National Convention in 1900 and 1904; elected as a Democrat to the Sixty-second Congress and served from March 4, 1911, until his death; had been nominated in 1912 as the Democratic candidate for reelection to the Sixty-third Congress; died in Poughkeepsie, N.Y., on October 30, 1912; interment in St. Peter's Cemetery.

**CONNELL, William** (father of Charles Robert Connell), a Representative from Pennsylvania; born in Sidney, Cape Breton, Nova Scotia, September 10, 1827; received a limited schooling; moved with his parents to Hazleton, Luzerne County, Pa., in 1844; worked in the coal mines; in 1856 was appointed superintendent of the mines of the Susquehanna & Wyoming Valley Railroad & Coal Company, with offices in Scranton; upon the expiration of that company's charter in 1870 he purchased its property and became one of the largest independent coal operators in the Wyoming region; one of the founders of the Third National Bank of Scranton in 1872, and in 1879 was chosen its president; was also identified with many other industries and commercial enterprises of Scranton; was a delegate to the Republican National Convention in 1896; member of the Pennsylvania Republican committee; elected as a Republican to the Fifty-fifth, Fifty-sixth, and Fifty-seventh Congresses (March 4, 1897-March 3, 1903); successfully contested the election of George Howell to the Fifty-eighth Congress and served from February 10, 1904, to March 3, 1905; died in Scranton, Lackawanna County, Pa., on March 21, 1909; interment in Forest Hill Cemetery.

**CONNELL, William James,** a Representative from Nebraska; born in Cowansville, Province of Quebec, Canada, July 6, 1846; moved to Schroon Lake, N.Y., in 1857 and to Vermont in 1862; completed a preparatory course; moved to Omaha, Nebr., in 1867; studied law; was admitted to the bar in 1869 and engaged in practice; district attorney of the third judicial district of Nebraska 1872-1876; city attorney of Omaha 1883-1887; elected as a Republican to the Fifty-first Congress (March 4, 1889-March 3, 1891); unsuccessful candidate for reelection in 1890 to the Fifty-second Congress; reappointed city attorney of Omaha, Nebr., in 1892; resumed the practice of his profession; died in Atlantic City, N.J., August 16, 1924; interment in Prospect Hill Cemetery, Omaha, Douglas County, Nebr.

**CONNELLY, John Robert,** a Representative from Kansas; born near Mount Sterling, Brown County, Ill., February 27, 1870; moved to Thayer County, Nebr., with his parents in 1883; attended the common schools and Salina (Kans.) Normal University; moved to Thomas County, Kans., in 1888; homesteaded there in 1892; began teaching school when nineteen years of age; superintendent of schools for Thomas County 1894-1898; owner and editor of the Colby Free Press 1897-1919; served as mayor of Colby and as a member of the city council; unsuccessful Democratic candidate for election in 1908 to the Sixty-first Congress; elected as a Democrat to the Sixty-third, Sixty-fourth, and Sixty-fifth Congresses (March 4, 1913-March 3, 1919); unsuccessful candidate for reelection in 1918 to the Sixty-sixth Congress; resumed his former business pursuits; delegate to the Democratic National Conventions in 1908, 1920, and 1928; unsuccessful candidate for election in 1924 to the Sixty-ninth Congress; engaged in the real-estate business at Colby, Thomas County, Kans.; died in Concordia, Kans., September 9, 1940; interment in Beulah Cemetery, Colby, Kans.

**CONNER, James Perry,** a Representative from Iowa; born in Delaware County, Ind., January 27, 1851; attended the Upper Iowa University, Fayette, Iowa, and was graduated from the law department of the University of Iowa at Iowa City in 1873; was admitted to the bar and practiced; district attorney of the thirteenth judicial district of Iowa, 1880-1884; circuit judge of the thirteenth judicial district in 1884; district judge of the sixteenth judicial district in 1886; delegate to the Republican National Convention of 1892; elected as a Republican to the Fifty-sixth Congress to fill the vacancy caused by the resignation of Jonathan P. Dolliver; reelected to the Fifty-seventh and to the three succeeding Congresses, and served from December 4, 1900 to March 3, 1909; unsuccessful candidate for reelection in 1908 to the Sixty-first Congress; resumed the practice of law in Denison, Crawford County, Iowa, where he died on March 19, 1924; interment in Oakland Cemetery.

**CONNER, John Coggswell,** a Representative from Texas; born in Noblesville, Hamilton County, Ind., October 14, 1842; attended the Noblesville public schools and Wabash College, Crawfordsville, Ind.; admitted to the United States Naval Academy, Annapolis, Md., September 20, 1861, and remained during the academic year, 1861-1862; commissioned a second lieutenant in the Sixty-third Regiment, Indiana Volunteer Infantry, on August 30, 1862, and a first lieutenant on September 3, 1862; honorably discharged June 20, 1864; unsuccessful candidate for election to the Indiana house of representatives in 1866; commissioned a captain in the Forty-first Regiment, United States Infantry, on July 28, 1866, and served in Texas until November 29, 1869, when he resigned, having received the nomination for Congress; upon the readmission of Texas to representation was elected as a Democrat to the Forty-first Congress; reelected to the Forty-second Congress and served from March 31, 1870, to March 3, 1873; owing to failing health was not a candidate for renomination in 1872; died in Washington, D.C., December 10, 1873; interment in the Old Cemetery, Noblesville, Ind.

**CONNER, Samuel Shepard,** a Representative from Massachusetts; born in Exeter, N.H., about 1783; attended Phillips Exeter Academy, Exeter, N.H., in 1794; was graduated from Yale College in 1806; studied law; was admitted to the bar and commenced practice in Waterville, Maine (at that time a district of Massachusetts), in 1810; served in the War of 1812 as major of the Twenty-first Infantry; promoted to lieutenant colonel of the Thirteenth Infantry March 12, 1813; resigned July 14, 1814; resumed the practice of law in Waterville, Maine; elected as a Republican to the Fourteenth Congress (March 4, 1815-March 3, 1817); appointed surveyor general of the Ohio land district in 1819; died in Covington, Ky., December 17, 1820.

**CONNERY, Lawrence Joseph** (brother of William Patrick Connery, Jr.), a Representative from Massachusetts; born in Lynn, Essex County, Mass., October 17, 1895; attended the local parochial and public schools, and St. Mary's College, St. Marys, Kans.; employed as a reporter for the Lynn Item; served on the Mexican border in 1916 with Company A, Ninth Massachusetts Infantry; served with Company A, One Hundred and First Regiment, Twenty-sixth Division, from March 25, 1917, until honorably discharged on March 24, 1919, with nineteen months service in France; employed as chief purser aboard a United Fruit Co. liner 1919-1923; secretary to his brother, Representative William P. Connery, Jr., 1923-1937; was graduated from the law department of Georgetown University, Washington, D.C., in 1926; engaged in the office-supplies and printing business in 1934 in Lynn, Mass.; elected as a Democrat to the Seventy-fifth Congress to fill the vacancy caused by the death of his brother, William P. Connery, Jr.; reelected to the Seventy-sixth and Seventy-seventh Congresses and served from September 28, 1937, until his death in Arlington, Va., October 19, 1941; interment in St. Mary's Cemetery, Lynn, Mass.

**CONNERY, William Patrick, Jr.** (brother of Lawrence Joseph Connery), a Representative from Massachusetts; born in Lynn, Mass., August 24, 1888; attended St. Mary's School at Lynn, Montreal College in Canada 1902-1904, and Holy Cross College, Worcester, Mass., 1904-1908; entered the theatrical profession as an actor 1908-1916; engaged as a theater manager in 1916 and 1917; during the First World War enlisted as a private in the One Hundred and First Regiment, United States Infantry, and served nineteen months in France; electric company employee 1919-1921; engaged in the manufacture of candy in 1921; secretary to the mayor of Lynn from January 1, 1922, to February 25, 1923; elected as a

Democrat to the Sixty-eighth and to the seven succeeding Congresses and served from March 4, 1923, until his death; chairman, Committee on Labor (Seventy-second through Seventy-fifth Congresses); studied law; was admitted to the bar October 10, 1934, but did not practice extensively; died in Washington, D.C., June 15, 1937; interment in St. Mary's Cemetery, Lynn, Mass.

**CONNESS, John,** a Senator from California; born in Abbey, County Galway, Ireland, September 22, 1821; immigrated to the United States in 1833; learned the art of pianoforte making in New York; moved to California in 1849 and engaged in mining and mercantile pursuits; member, California State assembly, 1853-1854, 1860-1861; unsuccessful candidate in 1861 for election for Governor of California; elected as a Douglas Democrat to the United States Senate, afterwards changed party affiliation to a Union Republican, and served from March 4, 1863 to March 3, 1869; chairman, Committee on Mining (Thirty-ninth and Fortieth Congresses); moved to Boston, Mass., in 1869; retired from active business pursuits; died in Jamaica Plain, Mass., January 10, 1909; interment in Cedar Grove Cemetery, Dorchester, Mass.

**CONNOLLY, Daniel Ward,** a Representative from Pennsylvania; born in Cochecton, Sullivan County, N.Y., April 24, 1847; moved with his parents to Scranton, Pa., in 1849; attended the public schools; studied law; was admitted to the bar in June 1870 and commenced practice in Scranton; elected president judge of Lackawanna County in 1878 but did not serve because the Pennsylvania supreme court held that there was no vacancy; unsuccessful candidate for election in 1880 to the Forty-seventh Congress; elected as a Democrat to the Forty-eighth Congress (March 4, 1883-March 3, 1885); unsuccessful candidate for reelection in 1884 to the Forty-ninth Congress; appointed postmaster of Scranton, Pa., on May 2, 1885, and served until March 29, 1889; died in Scranton, Pa., December 4, 1894; interment in Forest Hill Cemetery.

**CONNOLLY, James Austin,** a Representative from Illinois; born in Newark, N.J., March 8, 1843; moved to Chesterville, Ohio, with his parents in 1850; attended the common schools and Selby Academy, Chesterville, Ohio; assistant clerk of the State senate in 1858 and 1859; studied law; was admitted to the bar in 1859 and practiced in Mount Gilead, Ohio; moved to Charleston, Ill., in 1861; enlisted in the Union Army as a private in the One Hundred and Twenty-third Regiment, Illinois Volunteer Infantry, in 1862 and was afterwards captain, major, and brevet lieutenant colonel; member of the State house of representatives 1872-1876; United States attorney for the southern district of Illinois from 1876 to 1885 and again from 1889 to 1893; unsuccessful candidate for election in 1886 to the Fiftieth Congress; again nominated in 1888 but declined to run; elected as a Republican to the Fifty-fourth and Fifty-fifth Congresses (March 4, 1895-March 3, 1899); was not a candidate for renomination in 1898; resumed the practice of law in Springfield, Ill., where he died December 15, 1914; interment in Oak Ridge Cemetery.

**Bibliography:** Connolly, James Austin. *Three Years in the Army of the Cumberland; The Letters and Diary of Major James A. Connolly.* Edited by Paul M. Angle. Bloomington: Indiana University Press, 1959.

**CONNOLLY, James Joseph,** a Representative from Pennsylvania; born in Philadelphia, Pa., September 24, 1881; attended the high schools of that city; member of the Republican State committee; served as financial secretary of the Republican city committee of Philadelphia; elected as a Republican to the Sixty-seventh and to the six succeeding Congresses (March 4, 1921-January 3, 1935); unsuccessful candidate for reelection in 1934 to the Seventy-fourth Congress and for election in 1936 to the Seventy-fifth Congress; engaged in the real-estate business; also vice president of Philadelphia Transportation Co. and Transit Investment Corp.; died in Philadelphia, Pa., December 10, 1952; interment in Holy Sepulchre Cemetery, Township of Cheltenham, Montgomery County, Pa.

**CONNOLLY, Maurice,** a Representative from Iowa; born in Dubuque, Iowa, March 13, 1877; attended the common schools; was graduated from Cornell University, Ithaca, N.Y., in 1897 and from the law department of New York University, New York City, in 1898; was admitted to the bar in 1899; engaged in postgraduate work at Balliol College, Oxford, England, and the University of Heidelberg, Germany; engaged in the insurance business and banking; elected as a Democrat to the Sixty-third Congress (March 4, 1913-March 3, 1915); was not a candidate in 1914 for renomination to the House of Representatives, but was an unsuccessful candidate for election to the United States Senate; chairman of the Iowa State Democratic convention in 1914; was a delegate to the Democratic National Convention of 1916; major in the Aviation Corps during the First World War; died in an airplane accident near Indian Head, Md., May 28, 1921; interment in Mount Olivet Cemetery, Dubuque, Iowa.

**CONNOR, Henry William,** a Representative from North Carolina; born near Amelia Court House, Prince George County, Va., August 5, 1793; was graduated from South Carolina College (now the University of South Carolina) at Columbia in 1812; served as aide-de-camp to Brigadier General Joseph Graham with the rank of major in the expedition against the Creek Indians in 1814; settled in Falls Town, Iredell County, N.C.; engaged in planting; elected to the Seventeenth through Twenty-second Congresses, elected as a Jacksonian to the Twenty-third and Twenty-fourth Congresses, and elected as a Democrat to the Twenty-fifth and Twenty-sixth Congresses (March 4, 1821-March 3, 1841); chairman, Committee on the Post Office and Post Roads (Twenty-second through Twenty-fifth Congresses); was not a candidate for renomination in 1840 to the Twenty-seventh Congress; member of the State senate 1848-1850; died at Beatties Ford, Lincoln County, N.C., January 6, 1866; interment in Rehoboth Methodist Church Cemetery, near Sherrills Ford, Catawba County, N.C.

**CONOVER, Simon Barclay,** a Senator from Florida; born in Middlesex County, N.J., September 23, 1840; attended an academy in Trenton, N.J.; studied medicine at the University of Pennsylvania at Philadelphia; was graduated from the medical department of the University of Nashville, Tenn., in 1864; during the Civil War served in the medical department of the Union Army; appointed acting assistant surgeon in 1866, assigned to Lake City, Fla; resigned from the medical department of the Army upon readmission of the State of Florida into the Union; delegate to the State constitutional convention in 1868; was appointed State treasurer in 1868, serving one term; member, Republican National Committee, 1868-1872; member of the Florida State house of representatives in 1873, and served as speaker; elected as a Republican to the United States Senate, and served from March 4, 1873 to March 3, 1879; was not a candidate for reelection; chairman, Committee on Enrolled Bills (Forty-fourth and Forty-fifth Congresses); resumed the practice of his profession; unsuccessful candidate in 1880 for election for Governor; delegate to the State constitutional convention in 1885; appointed United States surgeon at Port Townsend, Wash., in 1889; became president of the board of regents of the Agricultural College and School of Sciences of the State of Washington in 1891; practiced medicine in Port Townsend, Wash., until his death on April 19, 1908; interment in the Masonic Cemetery.

**CONOVER, William Sheldrick, II,** a Representative from Pennsylvania; born in Richmond, Va., August 27, 1928; graduated from Lake Forest (Ill.) High School, 1946; B.S., Northwestern University, Evanston, Ill., 1950; served in the United States Navy, lieutenant (jg), 1952-1954; president, Mt. Lebanon Young Republicans, 1959-1960; president, Upper St. Clair Republican Club, 1965-1966; president and owner, Conover & Associates, Inc.,

insurance brokers, Pittsburgh, Pa.; elected as a Republican to the Ninety-second Congress, April 25, 1972, by special election to fill the vacancy caused by the death of James G. Fulton, and served from April 25, 1972 to January 3, 1973; unsuccessful candidate for nomination in 1972 to the Ninety-third Congress; resumed business interests; is a resident of Pittsburgh, Pa.

**CONRAD, Charles Magill,** a Senator and a Representative from Louisiana; born in Winchester, Frederick County, Va., December 24, 1804; moved with his father to Mississippi, and then to the Teche country in Louisiana; educated in a private school in New Orleans; studied law; was admitted to the bar in 1828 and commenced practice in New Orleans, La.; member, State house of representatives; elected as a Whig to the United States Senate to fill the vacancy caused by the resignation of Alexander Mouton, and served from April 14, 1842 to March 3, 1843; chairman, Committee on Engrossed Bills (Twenty-seventh Congress); delegate to the State constitutional convention in 1844; elected as a Whig to the Thirty-first Congress and served from March 4, 1849, to August 17, 1850, when he resigned; appointed Secretary of War by President Millard Fillmore on August 15, 1850 and served until March 7, 1853; delegate from Louisiana to the Provisional Confederate Congress at Montgomery, Ala., in 1861; delegate to the First and Second Confederate Congresses, 1862-1864; after the war resumed the practice of law; died in New Orleans, La., February 11, 1878; interment in Girod Street Cemetery.

**Bibliography:** *DAB.*

**CONRAD, Frederick,** a Representative from Pennsylvania; born near Worcester Township, Montgomery County, Pa., in 1759; attended the common schools; was elected to the Pennsylvania assembly in 1798, 1800, and 1802; paymaster of the Fifty-first Regiment of Pennsylvania Militia in 1804 and 1805; elected as a Republican to the Eighth and Ninth Congresses (March 4, 1803-March 3, 1807); chairman, Committee on Accounts (Ninth Congress); appointed justice of the peace 1807; appointed prothonotary and clerk of the courts in 1821, and reappointed in 1824; resided near Center Point and was interested in agricultural pursuits; moved to Norristown, and died there August 3, 1827; interment in Wentz's Reformed Church Cemetery, Center Point, Montgomery County, Pa.

**CONRAD, Kent,** a Senator from North Dakota; born in Bismarck, N.Dak., March 12, 1948; attended the public schools of Bismarck; graduated Wheelus High School, Tripoli, Libya, 1966; attended the University of Missouri, Columbia, 1967; B.A., Stanford University, Stanford, Calif., 1971; M.B.A., George Washington University, Washington, D.C., 1975; assistant to the North Dakota tax commissioner, Bismarck, 1974-1980; tax commissioner, State of North Dakota, 1981-1986; elected as a Democrat to the United States Senate in 1986, and served from January 3, 1987 until his resignation December 14, 1992; elected December 4, 1992 by special election to fill the vacancy in the term ending January 3, 1995 caused by the resignation of Jocelyn B. Burdick, and took the oath of office December 14, 1992; reelected in 1994 for the term ending January 3, 2001; is a resident of Bismarck, N.Dak.

**CONRY, Joseph Aloysius,** a Representative from Massachusetts; born in Brookline, Mass., September 12, 1868; attended the common schools; studied law; was admitted to the bar and commenced practice in Boston; president of the Boston Common Council in 1896 and 1897; chairman of the board of aldermen in 1898; elected as a Democrat to the Fifty-seventh Congress (March 4, 1901-March 3, 1903); unsuccessful candidate for reelection in 1902 to the Fifty-eighth Congress; resumed the practice of his profession in Boston, Mass.; recognized as consul of Russia in September 1912 and served until 1919; decorated by Nicholas II, the Czar of Russia, and made a member of the Knights of St. Anne; director of the port of Boston, Mass., 1911-1916; resumed the practice of law in Boston;

special attorney for the Maritime Commission in Washington, D.C., in 1938 and 1939; practiced law in Washington, D.C., until his death June 22, 1943; interment in Mount Olivet Cemetery.

**CONRY, Michael Francis,** a Representative from New York; born in Shenandoah, Schuylkill County, Pa., April 2, 1870; employed in the coal mines until crippled for life; attended the public schools; engaged in teaching for seven years; was graduated from the law department of the University of Michigan at Ann Arbor in 1896; was admitted to the bar and commenced practice in Scranton, Pa.; unsuccessful candidate for election in 1900 to the Fifty-seventh Congress; moved to New York City and resumed the practice of law; served two years as assistant corporation counsel of the city of New York; elected as a Democrat to the Sixty-first and to the three succeeding Congresses and served from March 4, 1909, until his death; had been reelected to the Sixty-fifth Congress; died in Washington, D.C., March 2, 1917; interment in Calvary Cemetery, New York City.

**CONSTABLE, Albert,** a Representative from Maryland; born near Charlestown, Md., June 3, 1805; studied law; was admitted to the bar in 1829 and settled in Bel Air, Harford County, Md.; moved to Baltimore and practiced law; later moved to Perryville, Cecil County, Md.; elected as a Democrat to the Twenty-ninth Congress (March 4, 1845-March 3, 1847); judge of the circuit court of Maryland in 1851; died in Camden, N.J., September 18, 1855.

**CONTE, Silvio Otto,** a Representative from Massachusetts; born in Pittsfield, Berkshire County, Mass., November 9, 1921; attended the public schools and graduated from Pittsfield Vocational High School in 1940; machinist at the General Electric Co., Pittsfield, in 1940 and 1941, and at the Berkshire Evening Eagle, Pittsfield, in 1941 and 1942; served with United States Navy construction battalions (Seabees) from 1942 to 1944 in the Southwest Pacific; LL.B., Boston College and Boston College Law School, 1949; was admitted to the bar in 1949 and commenced the practice of law in Pittsfield; member of the Massachusetts senate from the Berkshire District, 1951-1958; parliamentarian, Massachusetts Republican conventions in 1956 and 1958; delegate to the Republican National Conventions of 1960, 1964 and 1968, also serving on the platform committee in those years; was a resident of Pittsfield, Mass.; elected as a Republican to the Eighty-sixth and to the sixteen succeeding Congresses, and served from January 3, 1959 until his death in the naval hospital at Bethesda, Md., February 8, 1991; interment in St. Joseph's Cemetery, Pittsfield, Mass.

**CONTEE, Benjamin** (uncle of Alexander Contee Hanson and granduncle of Thomas Contee Worthington), a Delegate and a Representative from Maryland; born at "Brookefield," near Nottingham, Prince Georges County, Md., in 1755; attended a private school; served in the Revolutionary War as lieutenant and captain in the Third Maryland Battalion; member of the State house of delegates 1785-1787; Member of the Continental Congress in 1788; elected to the First Congress (March 4, 1789-March 3, 1791); was not a candidate for renomination in 1790; traveled in various European countries, and studied theology; continued theological study on his return to the United States, and was ordained a minister of the Episcopal Church in 1803; was pastor of the Episcopal Church at Port Tobacco, Charles County; was serving as presiding judge of the Charles County Orphans' Court at the time of his death; died in Charles County, Md., November 30, 1815; interment at "Bromont," his former home, near Port Tobacco, Md.

**CONVERSE, George Leroy,** a Representative from Ohio; born in Georgesville, Franklin County, Ohio, June 4, 1827; attended the common schools and Central College, Ohio, and was graduated from Denison University, Granville, Ohio, in 1849; studied law; was admitted to the bar in 1851 and commenced practice in Columbus, Ohio, in 1852; prosecuting attorney of Franklin County in 1857;

member of the State house of representatives 1860-1863 and 1874-1876 and speaker of the house in 1874; member of the State senate in 1864 and 1865; elected as a Democrat to the Forty-sixth, Forty-seventh, and Forty-eighth Congresses (March 4, 1879-March 3, 1885); chairman, Committee on Public Lands (Forty-sixth Congress); was not a candidate for renomination in 1884 to the Forty-ninth Congress; resumed the practice of his profession; delegate to the Nicaraguan Canal Convention in 1892, and made chairman of this and the subsequent convention held in New Orleans; died in Columbus, Ohio, March 30, 1897; interment in Greenlawn Cemetery.

**CONWAY, Henry Wharton** (cousin of Ambrose Hendley Sevier), a Delegate from the Territory of Arkansas; born near Greeneville, Greene County, Tenn., March 18, 1793; educated by private tutors; enlisted as an ensign in the War of 1812 and was promoted to lieutenant in 1813; clerk in the Treasury Department, Washington, D.C., in 1817; moved to Missouri Territory in 1818 and to Arkansas Territory in 1820; receiver of public moneys in 1820 and 1821; elected a Delegate to the Eighteenth, Nineteenth, and Twentieth Congresses and served from March 4, 1823, until his death near Arkansas Post, Ark., then the Territorial seat of government, November 9, 1827; interment in Arkansas Post Cemetery.

**CONWAY, Martin Franklin,** a Representative from Kansas; born at "Bretons Hill," near Fallston, Harford County, Md., November 19, 1827; received a liberal schooling; moved to Baltimore, Md., in 1843; learned the art of printing and became an organizer of the National Typographical Union; studied law; was admitted to the bar in 1852 and commenced practice in Baltimore; moved to Kansas in 1853 and continued the practice of law; also an agent in Kansas for the Massachusetts Abolition Society; member of the first legislative council July 2, 1854; member of the Kansas Free State convention in 1855; chief justice of the supreme court under the Topeka constitution of provisional government in 1856 and 1857; president of the Leavenworth constitutional convention of 1858; upon the admission of Kansas as a State into the Union was elected as a Republican to the Thirty-sixth and Thirty-seventh Congresses and served from January 29, 1861, to March 3, 1863; member of the peace convention of 1861 held in Washington, D.C., in an effort to devise means to prevent the impending war; appointed by President Andrew Johnson United States consul at Marseilles, France, on June 10, 1866, and served until April 16, 1869, when he retired from public life because of ill health; returned to Washington, D.C., where he died February 15, 1882; interment in Rock Creek Cemetery.

**Bibliography:** *DAB.*

**CONYERS, John, Jr.,** a Representative from Michigan; born in Detroit, Wayne County, Mich., May 16, 1929; attended Detroit public schools; served as an officer in the Corps of Engineers, United States Army; B.A., Wayne State University, Detroit, 1957; LL.B., Wayne State Law School, 1958; was admitted to the Michigan bar in 1959; attorney, Detroit, Mich., 1959-1961; legislative assistant to Representative John D. Dingell of Michigan, 1958-1961; general counsel for three labor locals in Detroit, 1959-1964; referee, Michigan Workmen's Compensation Department, 1961-1963; elected as a Democrat to the Eighty-ninth and to the fifteen succeeding Congresses (January 3, 1965-January 3, 1997); chairman, Committee on Government Operations (One Hundred First through One Hundred Third Congresses); is a resident of Detroit, Mich.

**COOK, Burton Chauncey,** a Representative from Illinois; born in Pittsford, Monroe County, N.Y., May 11, 1819; attended the Collegiate Institute, Rochester, N.Y.; studied law; in 1835 moved to Ottawa, Ill., where he commenced the practice of law in 1840; elected by the legislature in 1846 State's attorney for the ninth judicial district for two years; reelected by the people in 1848 for four years; member of the State senate 1852-1860; delegate to the Republican National Convention in 1860 and 1864; member of the peace convention of 1861 held in Washington, D.C., in an effort to devise means to prevent the impending war; elected as a Republican to the Thirty-ninth and to the three succeeding Congresses and served from March 4, 1865, to August 26, 1871, when he resigned; chairman, Committee on Roads and Canals (Fortieth Congress), Committee on District of Columbia (Forty-first Congress); resumed the practice of his profession in Evanston, Cook County, Ill., and died there August 18, 1894; interment in Oakwood Cemetery, Chicago, Ill.

**COOK, Daniel Pope,** a Representative from Illinois; born in Scott County, Ky., in 1794; attended the common schools; studied law; was admitted to the bar and commenced practice in Kaskaskia, Ill., in 1815; moved to Edwardsville, Ill., in 1816 and engaged in newspaper work; editor of the Illinois Intelligencer; auditor of public accounts in 1816; judge of the western circuit; appointed the first attorney general of Illinois and served from March 15 to October 15, 1819; unsuccessful candidate for election in 1818 to the Fifteenth Congress; elected to the Sixteenth and to the three succeeding Congresses (March 4, 1819-March 3, 1827); unsuccessful candidate for reelection in 1826 to the Twentieth Congress; directed in 1827 by President John Quincy Adams to proceed to Cuba and report on political conditions; died in Scott County, Ky., October 16, 1827; the county of Cook, Illinois, was named for him.

**Bibliography:** De Love, Sidney L. *Cook County and Daniel Pope Cook: Their Story*. Chicago: Independence Hall, 1968.

**COOK, George Washington,** a Representative from Colorado; born in Bedford, Lawrence County, Ind., November 10, 1851; at the age of eleven ran away from home and enlisted in the Fifteenth Regiment, Indiana Volunteer Infantry, in the Union Army and served as a drummer boy; was transferred to the One Hundred and Forty-fifth Regiment, Indiana Volunteer Infantry, and served as chief regimental clerk; at the close of the Civil War attended the public schools, Bedford Academy, and the Indiana University at Bloomington; moved to Chicago in 1880 and entered the employ of the Louisville, New Albany & Chicago Railway; moved to Leadville, Colo., in 1880 and became division superintendent of the Denver & Rio Grande Railroad; mayor of Leadville 1885-1887; moved to Denver in 1888 and became general sales agent for the Colorado Fuel & Iron Co.; department commander of the Grand Army of the Republic for Colorado and Wyoming in 1891 and 1892; became an independent mining operator in 1893; senior vice commander in chief of the Grand Army of the Republic in 1905 and 1906; organized and commanded the Cook Drum Corps, of Denver; elected as a Republican to the Sixtieth Congress (March 4, 1907-March 3, 1909); was not a candidate for renomination in 1908; resumed mining operations in Colorado; died in Pueblo, Colo., December 18, 1916; interment in Fairmount Cemetery, Denver, Colo.

**COOK, Joel,** a Representative from Pennsylvania; born in Philadelphia, Pa., March 20, 1842; attended the public schools and was graduated from the Central High School of Philadelphia in 1859; studied law at the University of Pennsylvania at Philadelphia; was admitted to the bar in 1863 and practiced; correspondent with the Army of the Potomac and a Washington correspondent during the Civil War; on the editorial staff of the Philadelphia Public Ledger from 1865 to 1882; financial editor 1883-1907; president of the board of wardens for the port of Philadelphia 1891-1907; president of the board of trade and of the Vessel Owners and Captains' Association; member of the Union League of Philadelphia; elected as a Republican to the Sixtieth Congress to fill the vacancy caused by the resignation of John E. Reyburn; reelected to the Sixty-first Congress and served from November 5, 1907, until his death in Philadelphia, Pa., December 15, 1910; interment in North Laurel Hill Cemetery.

**COOK, John Calhoun,** a Representative from Iowa; born in Seneca, Seneca County, Ohio, December 26, 1846; attended the common schools; studied law; was admitted to the bar in 1867 and commenced practice in Newton, Jasper County, Iowa; judge of the sixth judicial district of Iowa in 1878; successfully contested as a Democrat the election of Marsena E. Cutts to the Forty-seventh Congress and took his seat March 3, 1883, the closing day of the Congress; elected to the Forty-eighth Congress to fill the vacancy caused by the death of Marsena E. Cutts and served from October 9, 1883, to March 3, 1885; resumed the practice of law in Newton, Iowa; moved to Webster City, Iowa, where he became attorney for a railroad company; died in Algona, Kossuth County, Iowa, June 7, 1920; interment in Riverview Cemetery.

**COOK, John Parsons,** a Representative from Iowa; born in Whitestown, Oneida County, N.Y., August 31, 1817; moved with his father to Davenport, Iowa, in 1836; studied law; was admitted to the bar in 1842 and commenced practice in Tipton, Cedar County, Iowa; member of the Iowa Territorial council 1842-1845; served in the State senate 1848-1851; returned to Davenport, Iowa, in 1851 and continued the practice of law; unsuccessful candidate in 1850 for election to the Thirty-second Congress; elected as a Whig to the Thirty-third Congress (March 4, 1853-March 3, 1855); was not a candidate for renomination in 1854; continued the practice of law and also engaged in banking in Davenport until his death there April 17, 1872; interment in Oakdale Cemetery.

**COOK, Marlow Webster,** a Senator from Kentucky; born in Akron, Erie County, N.Y., on July 27, 1926; entered the United States Navy at seventeen and served in the submarine service in the Atlantic and Pacific during the Second World War; LL.B., University of Louisville Law School, 1950; practiced law in Louisville, Kentucky; member, Kentucky house of representatives, 1957-1961; judge of Jefferson County, Ky., 1961-1968; elected in 1968 as a Republican to the United States Senate; subsequently was appointed on December 17, 1968, to fill the unexpired term caused by the resignation of Thruston B. Morton, and served from December 17, 1968 until his resignation on December 27, 1974; unsuccessful candidate for reelection in 1974; resumed the practice of law in Washington, D.C.; is a resident of Washington, D.C.

**COOK, Orchard,** a Representative from Massachusetts; born in Salem, Mass., March 24, 1763; attended the public schools; engaged in mercantile pursuits; assessor of Pownal Borough in 1786; town clerk of New Milford, district of Maine, 1795-1797; justice of the peace; judge of the court of common pleas for Lincoln County 1799-1810; appointed assistant assessor of the twenty-fifth district in November 1798; overseer of Bowdoin College, Brunswick, Maine, 1800-1805; elected as a Republican to the Ninth, Tenth, and Eleventh Congresses (March 4, 1805-March 3, 1811); was not a candidate for renomination in 1810; sheriff of Lincoln County in 1811; postmaster of Wiscasset, Lincoln County, Maine, from 1811 until his death there August 12, 1819; interment in Evergreen Cemetery.

**COOK, Philip,** a Representative from Georgia; born in Twiggs County, Ga., July 30, 1817; was graduated from Oglethorpe University, Georgia, and from the law department of the University of Virginia at Charlottesville in 1840; practiced in Forsyth, Ga., in 1841 and 1842; moved successively to Sumter, Lanier, and Oglethorpe Counties, and continued the practice of law until 1869; served in the State senate in 1859, 1860, 1863, and 1864; entered the Confederate Army in 1861 as a private, Macon County (Ga.) Volunteers; attained the ranks of first lieutenant and lieutenant colonel; commissioned colonel November 1, 1862; commissioned brigadier general August 5, 1864; wounded at Fort Stedman, Va., March 25, 1865, and captured in the hospital at Petersburg, Va., in April; member of the State convention in 1865; moved to Americus, Sumter County, Ga., in 1885; elected as a Democrat to the

Forty-third and to the four succeeding Congresses (March 4, 1873-March 3, 1883); chairman, Committee on Public Buildings and Grounds (Forty-fifth and Forty-sixth Congresses); resumed the practice of law in Americus, Ga.; State capitol commissioner 1883-1889; elected secretary of state of Georgia in 1890 and served until his death in Atlanta, Ga., May 24, 1894; interment in Rose Hill Cemetery, Macon, Ga.

**Bibliography:** *DAB.*

**COOK, Robert Eugene,** a Representative from Ohio; born in Kent, Portage County, Ohio, May 19, 1920; attended Brimfield Elementary School, and graduated from Kent State High School in 1938; served in the United States Air Force as a warrant officer, 1942-1946; graduated from Kent State University in 1947, and from William and Mary Law School, Williamsburg, Va., in 1950; was admitted to the Ohio bar in 1950 and commenced the practice of law in Ravenna; elected prosecuting attorney of Portage County, Ohio, in 1952, reelected in 1956, and served until January 1, 1959; elected as a Democrat to the Eighty-sixth and Eighty-seventh Congresses (January 3, 1959-January 3, 1963); unsuccessful candidate for reelection in 1962 to the Eighty-eighth Congress; judge, Court of Common Pleas, Portage County, Ohio, 1963-1969; member of the eleventh district Court of Appeals of Ohio from February 9, 1969 to November 1988; deceased.

**COOK, Samuel Andrew,** a Representative from Wisconsin; born in Ontario, Canada, January 28, 1849; moved with his parents to Calumet County, Wis., in 1856; attended the common schools in Fond du Lac and Calumet Counties; enlisted as a private in Company A, Second Wisconsin Cavalry, under General George A. Custer, and served until the end of the Civil War; lived on a farm in Calumet County until 1872, when he located in Marathon County and engaged in business; moved to Neenah, Winnebago County, in 1881; elected mayor of Neenah in 1889; member of the Wisconsin State assembly in 1891 and 1892; delegate to the Republican National Convention of 1892; elected as a Republican to the Fifty-fourth Congress (March 4, 1895-March 3, 1897); declined to be a candidate for renomination in 1896 to the Fifty-fifth Congress; was an unsuccessful candidate for United States Senator in 1897 and again in 1907; commander of the Grand Army of the Republic for the Department of Wisconsin in 1915 and 1916; became a manufacturer of print paper at Menasha, Wis., with residence in Neenah, Wis.; president of the Alexandria Paper Company at Alexandria, Ind.; died in Neenah, Wis., on April 4, 1918; interment in Oak Hill Cemetery.

**COOK, Samuel Ellis,** a Representative from Indiana; born on a farm in Huntington County, Ind., September 30, 1860; attended the common schools in Whitley County and the normal schools at Columbia City, Ind., and Ada, Ohio; taught school and engaged in agricultural pursuits; studied law; was graduated from the law department of Valparaiso University, Indiana, in 1888; was admitted to the bar the same year and commenced practice in Huntington, Ind.; prosecuting attorney for Huntington County 1892-1894; delegate to the Democratic National Convention in 1896; editorial writer for the Huntington News-Democrat 1896-1900; judge of the Huntington circuit court for the fifty-sixth judicial district 1906-1918; elected as a Democrat to the Sixty-eighth Congress (March 4, 1923-March 3, 1925); unsuccessful candidate for reelection in 1924 to the Sixty-ninth Congress; resumed the practice of law in Huntington, Ind., where he died February 22, 1946; interment in Mount Hope Cemetery.

**COOK, Zadock,** a Representative from Georgia; born in Virginia February 18, 1769; moved to Hancock County, Ga., in early life, and was one of the first settlers in Clark County; self-educated; ensign in the Washington County Militia in 1793; captain of the Eleventh Company, Hancock County Militia, in 1796; member of the State house of representatives in 1806, 1807, and again in 1822; served in the State senate 1810-1814, 1823, and 1824; elected as a Republican to the Fourteenth Congress to fill the vacancy caused by the resignation of Alfred Cuthbert; reelected to the Fifteenth Congress and served from December 2, 1816, to March 3, 1819; retired from public life and settled on his plantation near Watkinsville, Ga., and engaged in agricultural pursuits until his death on August 3, 1863; interment in Jackson Cemetery, Clark (now Oconee) County, Ga.

**COOKE, Bates,** a Representative from New York; born in Wallingford, Conn., December 23, 1787; attended the public schools; moved to Lewiston, N.Y.; studied law; was admitted to the bar about 1815 and commenced practice in Lewiston; participated in the War of 1812; supervisor of the town of Cambria in 1814; elected as an Anti-Masonic candidate to the Twenty-second Congress (March 4, 1831-March 3, 1833); was not a candidate for renomination in 1832; elected comptroller of the State of New York in February 1839; served as bank commissioner from May 14, 1840, until his death in Lewiston, Niagara County, N.Y., May 31, 1841; interment in Oak Wood Cemetery.

**COOKE, Edmund Francis,** a Representative from New York; born in Prescott, Yavapai County, Ariz., April 13, 1885; moved with his parents to Alden, Erie County, N.Y., in 1887; attended the public schools; studied law; was admitted to the bar in 1910 and commenced practice in Alden, N.Y.; served as a member of the New York assembly 1923-1928; elected as a Republican to the Seventy-first and Seventy-second Congresses (March 4, 1929-March 3, 1933); unsuccessful candidate for reelection in 1932 to the Seventy-third Congress; resumed the practice of law in Buffalo, N.Y.; was a resident of Alden, N.Y., until his death there on May 13, 1967; interment in Evergreen Cemetery.

**COOKE, Edward Dean,** a Representative from Illinois; born in Cascade, Dubuque County, Iowa, October 17, 1849; attended the common schools, the local academy, and the high school at Dubuque; studied law at Dubuque and in the law department of Columbian (now George Washington) University, Washington, D.C., and was graduated from that institution in 1873; was admitted to the bar in the same year and commenced practice in Chicago, Ill.; member of the State house of representatives in 1883; elected as a Republican to the Fifty-fourth and Fifty-fifth Congresses and served from March 4, 1895, until his death in Washington, D.C., June 24, 1897; interment in Rosehill Cemetery, Chicago, Ill.

**COOKE, Eleutheros,** a Representative from Ohio; born in Granville, Washington County, N.Y., December 25, 1787; attended the country schools; studied law; was admitted to the bar and commenced practice in Granville; moved to Indiana in 1817, and thence to Sandusky, Erie County, Ohio, in 1819; member of the State house of representatives in 1822, 1823, and 1825; obtained from the Ohio Legislature in 1826 the first charter granted to a railroad in the United States–the Mad River & Lake Erie Railroad–and ground was broken for it in 1832; elected as an Anti-Jacksonian to the Twenty-second Congress (March 4, 1831-March 3, 1833); was an unsuccessful candidate for reelection to the Twenty-third Congress; resumed the practice of his profession; again a member of the State house of representatives in 1840; died in Sandusky, Ohio, on December 27, 1864; interment in St. Paul's Episcopal churchyard, Elkins Park, Pa.

**Bibliography:** *DAB.*

**COOKE, Joseph Platt,** a Delegate from Connecticut; born in Stratford (now Bridgeport), Conn., on January 4, 1730; was graduated from Yale College in 1750; from 1763 to 1783 he represented the town in about thirty sessions of the general assembly; justice of the peace in 1764; appointed colonel of the Sixteenth Regiment of Militia in 1771; during the Revolutionary War accompanied General Wolcott's forces to New York in 1776; was in command of Continental forces when the British burned Danbury on April 26 and 27, 1777; resigned his colonelcy early in 1778; member of the council of safety in 1778; member of the State house of representatives in 1776, 1778, 1780-1782, and 1784; Member of the Continental Congress 1784-1785 and 1787-1788; judge of the probate court for Danbury district 1776-1813; served as one of the Governor's council in 1803; died in Danbury, Conn., on February 3, 1816; interment in North Main Street Cemetery.

**COOKE, Thomas Burrage,** a Representative from New York; born in Wallingford, Conn., November 21, 1778; moved to New York about 1802 and settled in Catskill; engaged in mercantile pursuits; elected as a Republican to the Twelfth Congress (March 4, 1811-March 3, 1813); elected president of what is now the Catskill National Bank in 1813; took the oath of office as justice of the peace September 2, 1818; engaged in the water freighting business in 1823 and also interested in agricultural pursuits; became one of the incorporators of the Catskill & Canajoharie Railway on April 19, 1830; member of the State assembly in 1838 and 1839; died in Catskill, N.Y., on November 20, 1853; interment in the Village Cemetery.

**COOLEY, Harold Dunbar,** a Representative from North Carolina; born in Nashville, Nash County, N.C., July 26, 1897; attended the public schools, the University of North Carolina at Chapel Hill, and the law school of Yale University; was admitted to the bar in 1918 and commenced practice in Nashville, N.C.; served in the Naval Aviation Flying Corps in 1918; delegate to the Interparliamentary Conferences held at Cairo, Egypt, in 1947 and at Rome, Italy, in 1948 and served as president of the American group for two four-year terms; elected as a Democrat to the Seventy-third Congress, by special election, July 7, 1934, to fill the vacancy caused by the death of Edward W. Pou; reelected to the sixteen succeeding Congresses and served from July 7, 1934, to January 3, 1967; chairman, Committee on Agriculture (Eighty-first and Eighty-second Congresses and Eighty-fourth through Eighty-ninth Congresses); unsuccessful candidate for reelection in 1966 to the Ninetieth Congress; resumed the practice of law; died in Wilson, N.C., January 15, 1974; interment in Forest Hill Cemetery, Nashville, N.C.

**COOLEY, Wester,** a Representative from Oregon; born in Los Angeles, Calif., March 28, 1932; B.S., University of Southern California, 1958; United States Army Special Forces service in Korea; assistant to the president, chair of the board, division manager, director of drug regulatory affairs and vice president of Viratek, division of ICN Pharmaceuticals; cattle rancher; founder and co-owner of Rose Laboratories, Inc.; member, Oregon State senate, 1992-1994; elected as a Republican to the One Hundred Fourth Congress (January 3, 1995-January 3, 1997); was not a candidate for reelection in 1996 to the One Hundred Fifth Congress; is a resident of Powell Butte, Oreg.

**COOLIDGE, Calvin,** a Vice President and 30th President of the United States; born John Calvin Coolidge in Plymouth, Windsor County, Vt., July 4, 1872, but dropped John from his name upon graduating from college; attended the public schools, Black River Academy, Ludlow, Vt., and St. Johnsbury Academy; was graduated from Amherst College, Massachusetts, in 1895; studied law; was admitted to the bar in 1897 and commenced practice in Northampton, Mass.; member of the city council in 1899; city solicitor, 1900-1902; clerk of courts in 1904; member, Massachusetts house of representatives, 1907-1908; resumed the practice of his profession in Northampton; elected mayor of Northampton in 1910 and 1911; member, Massachusetts senate, 1912-1915, and served as president of that body in 1914 and 1915; Lieutenant Governor of Massachusetts, 1916-1918; elected Governor of Massachusetts in 1918, reelected in 1919, and served from January 2, 1919 to January 6, 1921; elected Vice President of the United States November 2, 1920,

on the Republican ticket headed by Warren G. Harding; was inaugurated on March 4, 1921, and served until August 3, 1923; upon the death of President Warren G. Harding became President of the United States on August 3, 1923; elected President of the United States in 1924 for the term expiring March 3, 1929; was not a candidate for renomination in 1928; served as chairman of the Nonpartisan Railroad Commission and as honorary president of the Foundation of the Blind; died at "The Beeches," Northampton, Mass., January 5, 1933; interment in Notch Cemetery, Plymouth, Vt.

**Bibliography:** *DAB*; Coolidge, Calvin. *The Autobiography of Calvin Coolidge.* New York: Cosmopolitan Book Corp., 1929; McCoy, Donald. *Calvin Coolidge: The Quiet President.* New York: Macmillan, 1967.

**COOLIDGE, Frederick Spaulding** (father of Marcus Allen Coolidge), a Representative from Massachusetts; born in Westminster, Worcester County, Mass., December 7, 1841; attended the common schools; became manager of the Boston Chair Manufacturing Co. and of the Leominster Rattan Works; selectman of his native town for three years; member of the Massachusetts Democratic central committee; member of the Massachusetts house of representatives in 1875; elected as a Democrat to the Fifty-second Congress (March 4, 1891-March 3, 1893); unsuccessful candidate for reelection in 1892 to the Fifty-third Congress; retired from active business pursuits; died in Fitchburg, Mass., on June 8, 1906; interment in Mount Pleasant Cemetery, Westminster, Mass.

**COOLIDGE, Marcus Allen** (son of Frederick Spaulding Coolidge), a Senator from Massachusetts; born in Westminster, Worcester County, Mass., October 6, 1865; attended the public schools and Bryant & Stratton Commercial College at Boston, Mass.; employed by his father in the manufacture of chairs and rattan; moved to Fitchburg, Mass., in 1895; engaged in the contracting business, building street railways, water works, and bridges 1883-1905, and in the manufacture of machine tools in 1905; mayor of Fitchburg 1916; appointed in 1919 by President Woodrow Wilson as special envoy to Poland representing the Peace Commission; chairman of the Massachusetts Democratic convention in 1920; trustee and president of Cushing Academy at Ashburnham, Mass.; elected as a Democrat to the United States Senate and served from March 4, 1931, to January 3, 1937; was not a candidate for renomination in 1936; chairman, Committee on Immigration (Seventy-third and Seventy-fourth Congresses); resumed his former business pursuits and resided in Fitchburg, Mass.; died at Miami Beach, Fla., January 23, 1947; interment in Mount Pleasant Cemetery, Westminster, Mass.

**COOMBS, Frank Leslie,** a Representative from California; born in Napa, Napa County, Calif., December 27, 1853; attended the public schools in California; attended the Dorchester High School, Boston, Mass., and was graduated from the law department of Columbian (now George Washington) University, Washington, D.C., in 1875; was admitted to the bar in 1875 and commenced practice in Napa, Calif.; district attorney of Napa County, Calif., 1880-1885; member of the California State assembly, 1887-1889, and 1891-1897; served as speaker in 1891 and again in 1897; appointed United States Minister to Japan to fill the vacancy caused by the death of John F. Swift, and served from April 20, 1892 to July 1893; State librarian of California from April 1, 1898 to April 1, 1899; United States attorney for the northern district of California from April 1, 1899 to March 1, 1901; elected as a Republican to the Fifty-seventh Congress (March 4, 1901-March 3, 1903); unsuccessful candidate for reelection in 1902 to the Fifty-eighth Congress; resumed the practice of law in Napa, Calif.; again a member of the State assembly, 1921-1923, and 1925-1927; died in Napa, Calif., October 5, 1934; interment in Tulocay Cemetery.

**COOMBS, William Jerome,** a Representative from New York; born in Jordan, Onondaga County, N.Y., December 24, 1833; attended the Jordan Academy, Jordan, N.Y.; moved to New York City in 1850, and in 1855 took up his residence in Brooklyn; in 1856 entered upon the business of exporting American goods and continued in this business for thirty-seven years; unsuccessful candidate for election in 1888 to the Fifty-first Congress; elected as a Democrat to the Fifty-second and Fifty-third Congresses (March 4, 1891-March 3, 1895); unsuccessful candidate for reelection in 1894 to the Fifty-fourth Congress; appointed a director of the Union Pacific Railroad by President Grover Cleveland in 1894, with special commission to collect the debts due the United States Government from the various Pacific railroads; president of the Manufacturers' Terminal Co., later consolidated with the Title Guarantee & Trust Co. of Brooklyn; in 1904 became president of the South Brooklyn Savings Bank, in which capacity he served until his death in Brooklyn, N.Y., January 12, 1922; interment in Greenwood Cemetery.

**COON, Samuel Harrison,** a Representative from Oregon; born in Boise, Ada County, Idaho, April 15, 1903; attended public schools in Cambridge and Boise, Idaho; graduated from the University of Idaho at Moscow in 1925; worked as a wool grader, bank clerk, foreman of a sheep ranch, and as an office manager for a mining concern; owned and operated a cattle ranch near Keating, Baker County, Oreg., 1929-1950; supervisor, Keating Soil Conservation District, 1941-1945; engaged in the real estate business in 1951 and 1952; served in the Oregon State senate in 1951 and 1952; elected as a Republican to the Eighty-third and Eighty-fourth Congresses (January 3, 1953-January 3, 1957); was an unsuccessful candidate for reelection in 1956 to the Eighty-fifth Congress; served as Deputy Director for the International Cooperation Administration in Lima, Peru, from February 26, 1957 until March 20, 1959; resided in Laguna Hills, Calif., until his death there on May 8, 1980; cremated; ashes scattered at sea.

**Bibliography:** Swanson, Bert E., and Deborah Rosenfield. "The Coon-Neuberger Debates of 1955: 'Ten Dam Nights in Oregon'." *Pacific Northwest Quarterly* 55 (April 1964): 55-66.

**COONEY, James,** a Representative from Missouri; born in County Limerick, Ireland, July 28, 1848; immigrated to the United States in 1852 with his parents, who settled near Troy, N.Y.; moved to Missouri where he attended the public schools and the University of Missouri at Columbia; taught school in Illinois for several years; in 1875 settled in Marshall, Mo.; studied law; was admitted to the bar and engaged in the practice of law; elected probate judge in 1880 and prosecuting attorney of Saline County in 1882 and 1884; elected as a Democrat to the Fifty-fifth, Fifty-sixth, and Fifty-seventh Congresses (March 4, 1897-March 3, 1903); unsuccessful candidate for renomination in 1902; resumed the practice of law; died in Marshall, Saline County, Mo., November 16, 1904; interment in Ridge Park Cemetery.

**COOPER, Allen Foster,** a Representative from Pennsylvania; born in Franklin Township, Fayette County, Pa., June 16, 1862; attended the public schools of his native township, and was graduated from the Pennsylvania normal school, California, Pa., in 1882; attended Mount Union College, Alliance, Ohio, in 1883; taught school for six years; was graduated from the law department of the University of Michigan at Ann Arbor in 1888; was admitted to the bar December 4, 1888, and commenced practice in Uniontown, Fayette County, Pa.; elected as a Republican to the Fifty-eighth and to the three succeeding Congresses (March 4, 1903-March 3, 1911); resumed business and the practice of law in Uniontown, Pa.; died in Uniontown April 20, 1917; interment in Oak Grove Cemetery.

**COOPER, Charles Merian,** a Representative from Florida; born in Athens, Clarke County, Ga., January 16, 1856; moved with his parents to Florida in 1864; pursued academic studies at Gainesville Academy; studied law; was admitted to the bar in 1877 and commenced practice in St. Augustine, Fla.; member of the State house of representatives in 1880; served in the State senate in 1884; attorney general of Florida 1885-1889; appointed in 1889 one of the three commissioners to revise the statutes of the State; elected as a Democrat to the Fifty-third and Fifty-fourth Congresses (March 4, 1893-March 3, 1897); was not a candidate for renomination; resumed the practice of law in Jacksonville, Fla., until his death there November 14, 1923; interment in St. Mary's Cemetery.

**COOPER, Edmund** (brother of Henry Cooper), a Representative from Tennessee; born in Franklin, Williamson County, Tenn., September 11, 1821; was graduated from Jackson (Tenn.) College in 1839; studied law at Harvard University; was admitted to the bar and commenced practice in Shelbyville, Bedford County, Tenn., in 1841; member of the State house of representatives in 1849; presidential elector on the Constitutional Union ticket in 1860; Union delegate to the State constitutional convention of 1861; again elected to the State house of representatives but in 1865 resigned; upon the readmission of the State of Tennessee to representation was elected as a Unionist to the Thirty-ninth Congress and served from July 24, 1866, to March 3, 1867; unsuccessful candidate for reelection in 1866 to the Fortieth Congress; appointed by President Andrew Johnson Assistant Secretary of the Treasury November 20, 1867, and served until March 20, 1869; resumed the practice of law at Shelbyville, and died there on July 21, 1911; interment in Willow Mount Cemetery.

**COOPER, Edward,** a Representative from West Virginia; born in Treverton, Northumberland County, Pa., February 26, 1873; moved with his parents to Fayette County, W.Va., in 1875; attended public and private schools; was graduated from Washington and Lee University, Lexington, Va., in 1892, and subsequently from the law department of the same university; was admitted to the bar in 1894 and practiced law for three years in Bramwell, Mercer County, W.Va.; member of the town council for eight years; on the death of his father abandoned the practice of law and engaged in the development of coal properties in West Virginia; delegate to the Republican National Convention in 1912; elected as a Republican to the Sixty-fourth and Sixty-fifth Congresses (March 4, 1915-March 3, 1919); unsuccessful candidate for reelection in 1918 to the Sixty-sixth Congress; again engaged in the production of coal in Mercer and McDowell Counties, W.Va., and served as a director in several coal companies; died in Bluefield, W.Va., March 1, 1928; interment in Hollywood Cemetery, Richmond, Va.

**COOPER, George Byran,** a Representative from Michigan; born at Long Hill, Morris County, N.J., June 6, 1808; attended the public schools; moved to Ann Arbor, Mich., in 1830, and later, in 1835, to Jackson, Mich., where he engaged in mercantile pursuits; postmaster of Jackson from 1836 to 1846; member of the Michigan State senate in 1837 and 1838; established an iron foundry at Jackson in 1840; served in the State house of representatives in 1842; State treasurer of Michigan from March 17, 1846, to March 13, 1850; engaged in banking at Jackson in 1851; presented credentials as a Democratic Member-elect to the Thirty-sixth Congress and served from March 4, 1859, to May 15, 1860, when he was succeeded by William A. Howard, who successfully contested his election; resided in New Bedford, Wall Township, Monmouth County, until his death on August 29, 1866; interment probably at Shark River, N.J.

**COOPER, George William,** a Representative from Indiana; born near Columbus, Bartholomew County, Ind., May 21, 1851; attended the country schools, and was graduated in the academic and law courses from the Indiana University at Bloomington in 1872; was admitted to the bar and commenced practice in Columbus, Ind.; prosecuting attorney of Columbus in 1872; mayor of Columbus in 1877; city attorney of Columbus 1879-1883; elected as a Democrat to the Fifty-first, Fifty-second, and Fifty-third Congresses (March 4, 1889-March 3, 1895); chairman, Committee on Irrigation of Arid Lands (Fifty-third Congress); unsuccessful candidate for reelection in 1894 to the Fifty-fourth Congress; resumed the practice of law in Columbus, Ind.; died in Chicago, Ill., November 27, 1899; interment in Garland Brook Cemetery, Columbus, Ind.

**COOPER, Henry** (brother of Edmund Cooper), a Senator from Tennessee; born in Columbia, Maury County, Tenn., on August 22, 1827; attended Dixon Academy, Shelbyville, Tenn., and was graduated from Jackson (Tenn.) College in 1847; studied law; was admitted to the bar in 1850 and commenced practice in Shelbyville; member, State house of representatives 1853-1855, 1857-1859; appointed judge of the seventh judicial circuit of Tennessee in April 1862 and resigned in January 1866; professor in the law school at Lebanon, Tenn. 1866-1867; moved to Nashville where he resumed the practice of law; member, State senate 1869-1870; elected as a Democrat to the United States Senate and served from March 4, 1871, to March 3, 1877; was not a candidate for renomination in 1876; was killed by bandits in Tierra Blanca, Guadelupe y Calvo, Mexico, on February 4, 1884, where he was engaged in mining operations; interment in Tierra Blanca.

**COOPER, Henry Allen,** a Representative from Wisconsin; born in Spring Prairie, Walworth County, Wis., September 8, 1850; moved with his parents to Burlington, Wis., in 1851; attended the common schools; was graduated from Burlington High School in June 1869, from Northwestern University, Evanston, Ill., in 1873, and from Union College of Law (then the legal department of Northwestern University and of the old University of Chicago) in 1875; was admitted to the bar and commenced practice at Burlington, Wis.; elected district attorney of Racine County in November 1880; moved to the city of Racine in January 1881; reelected district attorney without opposition in 1882 and 1884; delegate to the Republican National Conventions in 1884, 1908, and 1924; member of the State senate 1887-1889 and author of the bill which became the law first establishing the Australian secret ballot system in the State of Wisconsin; unsuccessful candidate for election in 1890 to the Fifty-second Congress; elected as a Republican to the Fifty-third and to the twelve succeeding Congresses (March 4, 1893-March 3, 1919); chairman, Committee on Rivers and Harbors (Fifty-fifth Congress), Committee on Insular Affairs (Fifty-sixth through Sixtieth Congresses); unsuccessful candidate for reelection in 1918 to the Sixty-sixth Congress; again elected to the Sixty-seventh and to the four succeeding Congresses and served from March 4, 1921, until his death; had been reelected to the Seventy-second Congress; died in Washington, D.C., March 1, 1931; interment in Mound Cemetery, Racine, Wis.

**COOPER, James,** a Representative and a Senator from Pennsylvania; born in Frederick County, Md., May 8, 1810; pursued academic studies, and was graduated from Washington (now Washington and Jefferson) College, Washington, Pa., in 1832; studied law; was admitted to the bar in 1834 and commenced practice in Gettysburg, Pa.; elected as a Whig to the Twenty-sixth and Twenty-seventh Congresses (March 4, 1839-March 3, 1843); chairman, Committee on Indian Affairs (Twenty-seventh Congress); member, Pennsylvania house of representatives, 1843-1844, 1846, 1848, and served as speaker one term; moved to Pottsville, Pa.; attorney general of Pennsylvania in 1848; elected to the United States Senate and served from March 4, 1849, to March 3, 1855; moved to Philadelphia; authorized by President Abraham Lincoln to raise a brigade of loyal Marylanders, and commissioned brigadier general in 1861; served in West Virginia under General John C. Frémont; appointed commandant at Camp Chase, near Columbus, Ohio, and died there on March 28, 1863; interment in Mount Olivet Cemetery, Frederick, Md.

**Bibliography:** *DAB.*

**COOPER, James Hayes Shofner,** a Representative from Tennessee; born in Shelbyville, Bedford County, Tenn., June 19, 1954; graduated from Groton School, Groton, Mass., 1972; B.A., University of North Carolina (Morehead Scholar), Chapel Hill, 1975; M.A., Oxford University (Rhodes Scholar), Oxford, England, 1977; J.D., Harvard Law School, 1980; admitted to the Tennessee bar, 1980, and commenced practice in Nashville; elected as a Democrat to the Ninety-eighth and to the five succeeding Congresses (January 3, 1983-January 3, 1995); was not a candidate in 1994 for reelection to the House of Representatives, but was an unsuccessful candidate for election to the United States Senate; managing director, Investment Banking, Equitable Securities Corporation, Nashville, Tenn., April 3, 1995 to present; is a resident of Shelbyville, Tenn.

**COOPER, Jere,** a Representative from Tennessee; born on a farm near Dyersburg, Dyer County, Tenn., July 20, 1893; attended the public schools; was graduated from the law department of Cumberland University, Lebanon, Tenn., in 1914; was admitted to the bar in 1915 and commenced practice in Dyersburg, Tenn.; in 1917 enlisted in the Second Tennessee Infantry, National Guard and was commissioned a first lieutenant; transferred with his company to Company K, One Hundred and Nineteenth Infantry, Thirtieth Division, and served in France and Belgium; on July 9, 1918, was promoted to captain and served as regimental adjutant until discharged from the Army on April 2, 1919; after the war resumed the practice of law in Dyersburg, Tenn.; member of city council and city attorney 1920-1928; elected State commander of the American Legion of Tennessee in 1921; elected as a Democrat to the Seventy-first and to the fourteen succeeding Congresses and served from March 4, 1929, until his death in Bethesda, Md., December 18, 1957; chairman, Committee on Ways and Means (Eighty-fourth and Eighty-fifth Congresses), Joint Committee on Internal Revenue Taxation (Eighty-fifth Congress); interment in Fairview Cemetery, Dyersburg, Tenn.

**Bibliography:** *DAB.*

**COOPER, John,** a Delegate from New Jersey; born near Woodbury, Gloucester County, N.J., February 5, 1729; received a liberal education; member of the committee of correspondence for Gloucester County in 1774; member of the Provincial Congress in 1775 and 1776 and served on the committee that drafted the first constitution of New Jersey; appointed by the Provincial Congress treasurer of the western division of New Jersey and served from October 28, 1775, to August 31, 1776; served on the legislative council from Gloucester County 1776-1780 and 1784; elected to the Continental Congress in 1776, but did not attend; member of the State council of safety in 1778; elected judge of the pleas for Gloucester County courts on December 25, 1779; reelected in 1784, and served until his death in Woodbury, N.J., April 1, 1785; interment in Quaker Cemetery.

**COOPER, John Gordon,** a Representative from Ohio; born in Wigan, England, April 27, 1872; immigrated to the United States in 1880 with his parents, who settled in Youngstown, Ohio; attended the public schools; began work in the steel mills in 1885; entered the service of the Pennsylvania Railroad Company in 1896 and was employed as a locomotive fireman 1896-1900 and as an engineer 1900-1915; member of the Republican county committee in 1906; was a delegate to the Republican State convention in 1910; member of the State house of representatives 1910-1912; elected as a Republican to the Sixty-fourth and to the ten succeeding Congresses (March 4, 1915-January 3, 1937); was an unsuccessful candidate for reelection in 1936 to the Seventy-fifth Congress; served as chairman of the Board of Claims, Ohio Industrial Commission, 1937-1945; retired from public and political activities in 1947 and resided in Youngstown, Ohio; died in Hagerstown, Md., January 7, 1955; interment in Lake Park Cemetery, Youngstown, Ohio.

**COOPER, John Sherman,** a Senator from Kentucky; born in Somerset, Pulaski County, Ky., August 23, 1901; attended the public schools at Somerset and Centre College, Danville, Ky.; A.B., Yale College, 1923; attended Harvard Law School, 1923-1925; was admitted to the bar in 1928 and commenced practice in Somerset, Ky.; member, Kentucky house of representatives, 1928-1930; judge of Pulaski County, Ky., 1930-1938; member of the board of trustees of the University of Kentucky, 1935-1946; served during the Second World War in the United States Army 1942-1946, attaining the rank of captain; elected circuit judge of the twenty-eighth judicial district of Kentucky in 1945 and served until his resignation in November 1946; elected as a Republican to the United States Senate to fill the vacancy caused by the resignation of Albert B. Chandler and served from November 6, 1946, to January 3, 1949; unsuccessful candidate for reelection in 1948; resumed the practice of law; delegate to the General Assembly of the United Nations in 1949, and alternate delegate in 1950 and 1951; served as adviser to the Secretary of State at the London and Brussels meetings of the Council of Ministers of the North Atlantic Treaty Organization in 1950; elected as a Republican to the United States Senate to fill the vacancy caused by the death of Virgil M. Chapman and served from November 5, 1952, to January 3, 1955; unsuccessful candidate for reelection in 1954; appointed Ambassador to India and Nepal on February 4, 1955 and served until April 1956; delegate to the United Nations General Assembly of 1968; elected as a Republican to the United States Senate in 1956 to fill the vacancy caused by the death of Alben W. Barkley; reelected in 1960, and again in 1966 and served from November 7, 1956, to January 3, 1973; was not a candidate for reelection in 1972; appointed the first United States Ambassador to the German Democratic Republic on September 19, 1974, and served until September 1976; resumed the practice of law in Washington, D.C., and was a resident of Somerset, Ky., and Washington, D.C.; died February 21, 1991.

**Bibliography:** Mitchiner, Clarice J. *Senator John Sherman Cooper.* New York: Arno Press, 1982; Schulman, Robert. *John Sherman Cooper: The Global Kentuckian.* Lexington: University of Kentucky Press, 1976; Smoot, Richard C. "John Sherman Cooper: The Early Years, 1901-27." *Register of the Kentucky Historical Society* 93 (Spring 1995): 133-158.

**COOPER, Mark Anthony** (cousin of Eugenius Aristides Nisbet), a Representative from Georgia; born near Powellton, Hancock County, Ga., on April 20, 1800; was graduated from South Carolina College (now the University of South Carolina) at Columbia in 1819; studied law; was admitted to the bar in 1821 and commenced practice in Eatonton, Putnam County, Ga.; moved to Columbus, Ga.; served in the campaign against the Seminole Indians in Florida in 1825, and again in 1836; member of the State house of representatives in 1833; elected as a Whig to the Twenty-sixth Congress (March 4, 1839-March 3, 1841); unsuccessful candidate for reelection in 1840 to the Twenty-seventh Congress, but was later elected as a Democrat to fill the vacancy caused by the resignation of William C. Dawson; reelected as a Democrat to the Twenty-eighth Congress and served from January 3, 1842, to June 26, 1843, when he resigned to become a candidate for Governor, but was unsuccessful; president of the Etowah Manufacturing & Mining Co. of Etowah, Ga., in 1859; died at his home, "Glen Holly," near Cartersville, Bartow County, Ga., March 17, 1885; interment on his estate.

**Bibliography:** *DAB.*

**COOPER, Richard Matlack,** a Representative from New Jersey; born in Gloucester County, N.J., February 29, 1768; completed a preparatory course of studies; engaged in banking; coroner 1795-1799; judge and justice of Gloucester County courts 1803-1823; member of the State general assembly 1807-1810; president of the State Bank of New Jersey at Camden 1813-1842; elected to the Twenty-first and Twenty-second Congresses (March 4,

1829-March 3, 1833); declined to be a candidate for reelection in 1832 to the Twenty-third Congress; died in Camden, N.J., March 10, 1843; interment in the Newton Burying Ground.

**COOPER, Samuel Bronson,** a Representative from Texas; born near Eddyville, Caldwell County, Ky., May 30, 1850; moved with his parents to Texas the same year and located in Woodville, Tyler County; attended the common schools; studied law; was admitted to the bar in 1871 and commenced practice in Woodville in January 1872; prosecuting attorney of Tyler County 1876-1880; member of the State senate 1880-1884; appointed collector of internal revenue for the first district of Texas by President Grover Cleveland in 1885 and served until 1888; unsuccessful candidate for district judge in 1888; elected as a Democrat to the Fifty-third and to the five succeeding Congresses (March 4, 1893-March 3, 1905); unsuccessful candidate for reelection in 1904 to the Fifty-ninth Congress; elected to the Sixtieth Congress (March 4, 1907-March 3, 1909); unsuccessful candidate for reelection in 1908 to the Sixty-first Congress; appointed a member of the United States Board of General Appraisers at the port of New York City by President William Howard Taft in 1910; died in New York City on August 21, 1918; interment in Magnolia Cemetery, Beaumont, Tex.

**COOPER, Thomas,** a Representative from Delaware; born in Little Creek Hundred, Sussex County, Del., in 1764; completed preparatory studies; member of the State house of representatives 1803-1808; studied law; was admitted to the bar in 1805 and practiced; served in the State senate in 1808; elected as a Federalist to the Thirteenth and Fourteenth Congresses (March 4, 1813-March 3, 1817); resumed the practice of law in Georgetown, Del., where he died in 1829; interment in the Cooper family cemetery, near Laurel, Del.

**COOPER, Thomas Buchecker,** a Representative from Pennsylvania; born in Coopersburg, Pa., December 29, 1823; attended the public schools and Pennsylvania College at Gettysburg; was graduated from the medical department of the University of Pennsylvania at Philadelphia in 1843 and commenced practice in Coopersburg; elected as a Democrat to the Thirty-seventh Congress and served from March 4, 1861, until his death in Coopersburg, Pa., on April 4, 1862; interment in Woodland Cemetery.

**COOPER, William,** a Representative from New York; born in Philadelphia, Pa., December 2, 1754; was apprenticed to the trade of manufacturing and repairing horse-drawn vehicles; lived in Burlington, N.J., where he owned a store; moved in 1789 to Otsego County, N.Y., where he established the town of Cooperstown; appointed the first judge of the court of common pleas for Otsego County on February 17, 1791; elected as a Federalist to the Fourth Congress (March 3, 1795-March 3, 1797); unsuccessful candidate for reelection in 1796 to the Fifth Congress; again elected to the Sixth Congress (March 4, 1799-March 3, 1801); father of James Fenimore Cooper; died in Albany, N.Y., on December 22, 1809; interment in Christ Churchyard, Cooperstown, N.Y.

**Bibliography:** *DAB;* Taylor, Alan. *William Cooper's Town: Power and Persuasion on the Frontier of the Early American Republic.* New York: Alfred A. Knopf, 1995.

**COOPER, William Craig,** a Representative from Ohio; born in Mount Vernon, Knox County, Ohio, on December 18, 1832; attended the public schools and Mount Vernon Academy; studied law; was admitted to the bar in 1852 and commenced practice in Mount Vernon, Ohio; prosecuting attorney of Knox County 1859-1863; mayor of Mount Vernon 1862-1864; member of the State house of representatives 1872-1874; judge advocate general of Ohio 1879-1884; member and president of the board of education of Mount Vernon; elected as a Republican to the Forty-ninth, Fiftieth, and Fifty-first Congresses (March 4, 1885-March 3, 1891); was not a candidate for renomination in 1890 to the Fifty-second Congress;

resumed the practice of law in Mount Vernon, Ohio, where he died on August 29, 1902; interment in Mound View Cemetery.

**COOPER, William Raworth,** a Representative from New Jersey; born near Bridgeport, Gloucester County, N.J., February 20, 1793; attended the local schools; engaged in agricultural pursuits; member of the State general assembly 1839-1841; elected as a Democrat to the Twenty-sixth Congress (March 4, 1839-March 3, 1841); resumed agricultural pursuits until his death near Bridgeport, N.J., on September 22, 1856; interment in the Cooper family burying ground, near Bridgeport, N.J.

**COPELAND, Oren Sturman,** a Representative from Nebraska; born on a farm near Huron, Beadle County, S.Dak., March 16, 1887; moved with his parents to Pender, Nebr., in 1891; attended the public schools at Pender; attended the University of Nebraska at Lincoln 1904-1907; engaged in newspaper work at Lincoln, Nebr., in 1910 and in the fuel business in 1913; served as city commissioner, department of public safety, 1935-1937; mayor of Lincoln from 1937 until his resignation in 1940; elected as a Republican to the Seventy-seventh Congress (January 3, 1941-January 3, 1943); unsuccessful candidate for renomination in 1942; resumed the retail fuel business; died in Lincoln, Nebr., April 10, 1958; interment in Wyuka Cemetery.

**COPELAND, Royal Samuel,** a Senator from New York; born in Dexter, Washtenaw County, Mich., on November 7, 1868; attended the public schools and Michigan State Normal School, Ypsilanti, Mich.; was graduated from the medical department of the University of Michigan at Ann Arbor in 1889; took postgraduate courses in Europe; house surgeon in the University of Michigan Hospital, 1889-1890; practiced medicine in Bay City, Mich., 1890-1895; professor in the medical school of the University of Michigan, 1895-1908; mayor of Ann Arbor, Mich., 1901-1903; president of the park board in 1905 and 1906, and president of the Ann Arbor board of education in 1907 and 1908; member of the Michigan State tuberculosis board of trustees, 1900-1908; moved to New York City in 1908; dean of the New York Flower Hospital and Medical College, 1908-1918; member of the United States pension examining board in 1917; commissioner of public health and president of the New York Board of Health, 1918-1923; nationally known for his writings and radio broadcasts on health problems; unsuccessful candidate for nomination as mayor of New York City in 1937; elected as a Democrat to the United States Senate in 1922; reelected in 1928 and 1934, and served from March 4, 1923 until his death in Washington, D.C., June 17, 1938; chairman, Committee on Rules (Seventy-third Congress), Committee on Commerce (Seventy-fourth and Seventy-fifth Congresses); interment in Mahwah Cemetery, Mahwah, N.J.

**Bibliography:** *DAB*; Potter, Raymond. "Royal Samuel Copeland, 1868-1938: A Physician in Politics." Ph.D. dissertation, Case Western Reserve University, 1967.

**COPLEY, Ira Clifton** (nephew of Richard Henry Whiting), a Representative from Illinois; born near Galesburg, Knox County, Ill., October 25, 1864; moved with his parents to Aurora, Ill., in 1867; attended the public schools and Jennings Seminary at Aurora; was graduated from Yale University in 1887 and from the Union College of Law at Chicago in 1889; became connected with the gas and electric business in Aurora, Ill., in 1889; owner and publisher of the Beacon-News at Aurora in 1905, the Courier-News at Elgin in 1908, and the Herald-News at Joliet in 1913; elected as a Republican to the Sixty-second and Sixty-third Congresses; reelected as a Progressive to the Sixty-fourth Congress and as a Republican to the Sixty-fifth through Sixty-seventh Congresses (March 4, 1911-March 3, 1923); was not a candidate for renomination in 1922; continued the development and publishing of daily newspapers, acquiring the Illinois State Journal at Springfield, the Union and the Tribune at San Diego, Calif., and eleven other dailies in southern California;

died in Aurora, Ill., November 1, 1947; interment in Spring Lake Cemetery.

**Bibliography:** *DAB*.

**COPPERSMITH, Sam,** a Representative from Arizona; born in Johnstown, Cambria County, Pa., May 22, 1955; graduated, Westmont Hilltop High School, Johnstown, 1972; A.B., Harvard University, 1976; J.D., Yale University School of Law, 1982; foreign service officer, United States Department of State, 1977-1979; admitted to Arizona bar and California bar; director, Arizona Community Service Legal Assistance Foundation, 1986-1992; elected as a Democrat to the One Hundred Third Congress (January 3, 1993-January 3, 1995); was not a candidate in 1994 for renomination to the House of Representatives, but was an unsuccessful candidate for election to the United States Senate; resumed the practice of law; is a resident of Phoenix, Ariz.

**CORBETT, Henry Winslow,** a Senator from Oregon; born in Westboro, Mass., February 18, 1827; moved with his parents to White Creek, Washington County, N.Y., in 1831; attended the common schools; engaged in mercantile pursuits in Cambridge, N.Y., in 1840 and attended Cambridge Academy; moved to New York City in 1843 and was employed in the mercantile business until 1851; went with a stock of goods around Cape Horn to Portland, Oreg., in 1851, and engaged in a general merchandising business, later changing to wholesale hardware; became largely interested in banking, railroads, building, and investments; city treasurer of Portland, member of the city council, and chairman of the Republican State central committee; elected as a Republican to the United States Senate and served from March 4, 1867, to March 3, 1873; was not a candidate for reelection in 1873; resumed business interests; appointed to the United States Senate March 6, 1897, to fill the vacancy in the term beginning March 4, 1897, the legislature having failed to elect, but was not permitted to qualify; unsuccessful candidate for election to the United States Senate in 1901; died in Portland, Oreg., March 31, 1903; interment in Riverview Cemetery.

**Bibliography:** *DAB*.

**CORBETT, Robert James,** a Representative from Pennsylvania; born in Avalon (Pittsburgh), Pa., August 25, 1905; attended the public schools; was graduated from Allegheny College, Meadville, Pa., in 1927 and from the University of Pittsburgh, Pittsburgh, Pa., in 1929; senior high-school instructor at Coraopolis, Pa., 1929-1938; instructor in the Pittsburgh (Pa.) Academy Evening School in 1938; elected as a Republican to the Seventy-sixth Congress (January 3, 1939-January 3, 1941); unsuccessful candidate for reelection in 1940 to the Seventy-seventh Congress; served on the staff of Senator James J. Davis in Pittsburgh; sheriff of Allegheny County, Pa., 1942-1944; elected to the Seventy-ninth and to the thirteen succeeding Congresses, and served from January 3, 1945 until his death in Pittsburgh, Pa., April 25, 1971; interment in Union Dale Cemetery.

**CORCORAN, Thomas Joseph,** a Representative from Illinois; born in Ottawa, LaSalle County, Ill., May 23, 1939; attended the parochial schools of Ottawa and Peru, Ill.; B.A., University of Notre Dame, South Bend, Ind., 1961; engaged in graduate work at the University of Illinois, 1962; University of Chicago, 1963; Northwestern University, 1967; served in the United States Army, 1963-1965; director, State of Illinois Office, Washington, D.C., 1969-1972; served as administrative assistant to the State senate president, 1973-1974; vice president, Chicago-North Western Transportation Co., 1974-1976; elected as a Republican to the Ninety-fifth and to the three succeeding Congresses (January 3, 1977-January 3, 1985); was not a candidate for reelection in 1984 to the House of Representatives, but was an unsuccessful candidate for nomination to the United States Senate; owner of a consulting and financial services corporation in Washington, D.C., and Chicago, 1985 to present; is a resident of Chicago, Ill., and McLean, Va.

**CORDON, Guy,** a Senator from Oregon; born in Cuero, De Witt County, Tex., April 24, 1890; moved to Roseburg, Oreg., and attended the public schools; deputy assessor 1909-1916; county assessor of Douglas County, Oreg., 1917-1920; during the First World War served as a private in the Field Artillery of the United States Army; was admitted to the bar in 1920 and commenced practice in Roseburg, Oreg.; district attorney of Douglas County 1923-1935; appointed and subsequently elected as a Republican to the United States Senate to fill the vacancy caused by the death of Charles L. McNary; reelected in 1948 and served from March 4, 1944, to January 3, 1955; unsuccessful candidate for reelection in 1954; chairman, Committee on Interior and Insular Affairs (Eighty-third Congress); engaged in the practice of law in Washington, D.C., until his retirement in 1962; died in Washington, D.C., June 8, 1969; interment in Roseburg Memorial Gardens, Roseburg, Oreg.

**CORDOVA, Jorge Luis,** a Resident Commissioner from Puerto Rico, born in Manatí, P.R., April 20, 1907; A.B., Catholic University of America, 1928; LL.B., Harvard University, 1931; judge, Superior Court of San Juan, 1940-1945; justice, Supreme court of Puerto Rico, 1945-1946; lawyer; elected as a New Progressive to be Resident Commissioner of Puerto Rico to the United States House of Representatives, November 5, 1968, for a four-year term ending January 3, 1973; unsuccessful candidate for reelection in 1972; resumed the practice of law in San Juan until 1984; president of the Puerto Rico American Insurance Company until 1984 and chairman of the board, 1984 to present; is a resident of San Juan, P.R.

**CORKER, Stephen Alfestus,** a Representative from Georgia; born near Waynesboro, Burke County, Ga., May 7, 1830; attended the common schools; studied law; was admitted to the bar and commenced practice in Waynesboro, Ga.; also engaged in agricultural pursuits; entered the Confederate Army in 1861, and served as captain of Company A, Third Georgia Regiment; resumed the practice of law in Waynesboro, Ga.; member of the State house of representatives; elected as a Democrat to the Forty-first Congress to fill the vacancy caused by the House declaring Charles H. Prince not entitled to the seat and served from December 22, 1870, to March 3, 1871; resumed the practice of law in Waynesboro, Ga., and died there on October 18, 1879; interment in the Old Cemetery, Waynesboro, Ga.

**CORLETT, William Wellington,** a Delegate from the Territory of Wyoming; born in Concord, Ohio, April 10, 1842; attended the district schools, and was graduated from the Willoughby (Ohio) Collegiate Institute in 1861; enlisted in the Union Army in 1862 and served in the Twenty-eighth Regiment, Ohio Volunteer Infantry and the Eighty-seventh Regiment, Ohio Volunteer Infantry; captured with the command at Harpers Ferry September 15, 1862; was paroled and returned to Ohio, where he taught school in Kirkland and Painesville; reentered the Army with the Twenty-fifth Ohio Battery; was later placed on detached service with the Third Iowa Battery; returned to Ohio in 1865; attended the law school of the University of Michigan at Ann Arbor, and was graduated from Union Law College, Cleveland, Ohio, in July 1866; was admitted to the bar the same year; professor in elementary law at the State University and Law College and lecturer at several commercial colleges in Cleveland; settled in Cheyenne, Wyo., August 20, 1867, and engaged in the practice of law; unsuccessful Republican candidate for Delegate to the Forty-first Congress in 1869; postmaster of Cheyenne in 1870; member of the Territorial senate in 1871; prosecuting attorney of Laramie County 1872-1876; elected as a Republican a Delegate to the Forty-fifth Congress (March 4, 1877-March 3, 1879); was not a candidate for renomination in 1878; resumed the practice of law; declined the appointment as chief

justice of Wyoming Territory in 1879; member of the legislative council 1880-1882; died in Cheyenne, Wyo., July 22, 1890; interment in Lakeview Cemetery.

**CORLEY, Manuel Simeon,** a Representative from South Carolina; born in Lexington County, S.C., February 10, 1823; was a student in Lexington Academy four years; engaged in business in 1838; opposed the first attempt at secession of South Carolina in 1852, when an effort was made to expel him from the State; editor of the South Carolina Temperance Standard in 1855 and 1856; entered the Confederate Army in 1863; captured by Union troops at Petersburg, Va., April 2, 1865; took the oath of allegiance June 5, 1865; delegate to the constitutional convention of South Carolina in 1867; upon the readmission of South Carolina to representation was elected as a Republican to the Fortieth Congress and served from July 25, 1868, to March 3, 1869; special agent of the United States Treasury in 1869; commissioner of agricultural statistics of South Carolina in 1870; treasurer of Lexington County in 1874; died in Lexington, S.C., November 20, 1902; interment in St. Stephen's Lutheran Cemetery.

**CORLISS, John Blaisdell,** a Representative from Michigan; born in Richford, Vt., June 7, 1851; attended the common schools and Fairfax (Vt.) Preparatory School; was graduated from the Vermont Methodist University at Montpelier in 1871 and from the law department of Columbian College (now George Washington University), Washington, D.C., in 1875; settled in Detroit, Mich., in 1875; was admitted to the bar the same year and commenced practice in that city; city attorney of Detroit 1882-1886; prepared the first complete charter for Detroit which was passed by the legislature in 1884; elected as a Republican to the Fifty-fourth and to the three succeeding Congresses (March 4, 1895-March 3, 1903); chairman, Committee on Election of President, Vice President, and Representatives (Fifty-fifth through Fifty-seventh Congresses); unsuccessful candidate for reelection in 1902 to the Fifty-eighth Congress; reengaged in the practice of law in Detroit, Mich., until his death there on December 24, 1929; interment in Woodlawn Cemetery.

**CORMAN, James Charles,** a Representative from California; born in Galena, Cherokee County, Kans., October 20, 1920; moved with his family to Los Angeles, Calif., in 1933; attended the public schools of Los Angeles; B.A., University of California at Los Angeles, 1942; LL.B., University of Southern California Law School, 1948; served as a lieutenant in the United States Marine Corps with the Third Marine Division, 1942-1946, and was in the Bougainville, Guam, and Iwo Jima actions; also served in the United States Marine Corps during the Korean Conflict, 1950-1952; was admitted to the bar in 1949 and engaged in the practice of law in Van Nuys, Calif.; member of Los Angeles city council, 1957-1960; member, President's National Advisory Commission on Civil Disorders, 1967-1968; elected as a Democrat to the Eighty-seventh and to the nine succeeding Congresses (January 3, 1961-January 3, 1981); unsuccessful candidate for reelection in 1980 to the Ninety-seventh Congress; is a resident of Arlington, Va.

**CORNELL, Ezekiel,** a Delegate from Rhode Island; born in Scituate, R.I., in 1732; attended the public schools; employed as a mechanic; appointed lieutenant colonel in Hitchcock's Rhode Island Regiment in 1775; was present at the siege of Boston; became deputy adjutant general on October 1, 1776; appointed brigadier general of State troops in 1776 and served until March 16, 1780; Member of the Continental Congress 1780-1782; retired to his farm at Scituate; died in Milford, Mass., April 25, 1800.
**Bibliography:** *DAB.*

**CORNELL, Robert John,** a Representative from Wisconsin; born in Gladstone, Delta County, Mich., December 16, 1919; attended parochial schools in Green Bay, Wis.; B.A., St. Norbert College, DePere, Wis., 1941; M.A. and Ph.D., history, Catholic University of America, Washington, D.C., 1957; ordained a Roman Catholic priest, Norbertine Order, 1944; teacher of social sciences in parochial schools of Philadelphia, Pa., 1941-1947; professor of history and political science, St. Norbert College, 1947-1974; chairman, Eighth Congressional District Democratic Party of Wisconsin, 1969-1974; member, State Administrative Committee of the Democratic Party of Wisconsin, 1969-1974; elected as a Democrat to the Ninety-fourth and Ninety-fifth Congresses (January 3, 1975-January 3, 1979); unsuccessful candidate for reelection in 1978 to the Ninety-sixth Congress; professor of political science and history, St. Norbert College, 1979 to present; is a resident of DePere, Wis.

**CORNELL, Thomas,** a Representative from New York; born in White Plains, N.Y., January 27, 1814; attended the public schools; engaged in the steamboat transportation business between Rondout and New York City in 1843, and also in the railroad business and banking; commissioned major in the New York Militia during the Civil War; elected as a Republican to the Fortieth Congress (March 4, 1867-March 3, 1869); unsuccessful candidate for reelection in 1868 to the Forty-first Congress; again elected to the Forty-seventh Congress (March 4, 1881-March 3, 1883); was not a candidate for renomination in 1882 to the Forty-eighth Congress; resumed the transportation business and banking in Kingston, N.Y.; delegate to the Republican National Convention of 1884; died in Kingston, N.Y., March 30, 1890; interment in Montrepose Cemetery.

**CORNING, Erastus** (grandfather of Parker Corning), a Representative from New York; born in Norwich, Conn., December 14, 1794; moved to Troy, N.Y., and thence, in 1814, to Albany, where he established himself in iron manufacturing; served in the State senate 1842-1845; alderman of Albany; mayor 1834-1837; elected as a Democrat to the Thirty-fifth Congress (March 4, 1857-March 3, 1859); unsuccessful candidate for reelection to the Thirty-sixth Congress; member of the peace conference of 1861; elected to the Thirty-seventh and Thirty-eighth Congresses and served from March 4, 1861, to October 5, 1863, when he resigned; delegate to the State constitutional convention in 1867; died in Albany, N.Y., April 9, 1872; interment in Rural Cemetery.

Bibliography: *DAB*; Neu, Irene Dorothy. *Erastus Corning, Merchant and Financier, 1794-1872.* Ithaca, N.Y.: Cornell University Press, 1960.

**CORNING, Parker** (grandson of Erastus Corning), a Representative from New York; born in Albany, N.Y., January 22, 1874; attended the public schools, the Boys' Academy in Albany, and St. Paul's School, Concord, N.H.; was graduated from Yale University in 1895; engaged in the manufacture of steel and woolens; also interested in banking; elected as a Democrat to the Sixty-eighth and to the six succeeding Congresses (March 4, 1923-January 3, 1937); was not a candidate for renomination in 1936; resumed his former pursuits; died in Albany, N.Y., May 24, 1943; interment in the Rural Cemetery, Menands, Albany County, N.Y.

**CORNISH, Johnston,** a Representative from New Jersey; born in Bethlehem Township, Hunterdon County, N.J., June 13, 1858; attended the common schools; moved with his parents to Washington, N.J., in 1870; was graduated from the Easton (Pa.) Business College; engaged in the manufacture of pianos and organs; elected mayor of Washington, N.J., in 1884, and reelected in 1885 and 1886; declined renomination in 1887 and in 1888; member of the State senate 1891-1893; elected as a Democrat to the Fifty-third Congress (March 4, 1893-March 3, 1895); unsuccessful candidate for reelection in 1894; again a member of the State senate 1900-1902 and 1906-1911; president of the Cornish Piano Co. in 1910; member of

the Democratic State Committee; president of the First National Bank, the Washington Water Co., and the Warren County Bankers' Association at the time of his death in Washington, N.J., June 26, 1920; interment in the Cornish family plot in Washington Cemetery.

**CORNWELL, David Lance,** a Representative from Indiana; born in Paoli, Orange County, Ind., June 14, 1945; attended Paoli public schools, Culver (Ind.) Military Academy, Phillips Andover (Mass.) Academy; graduated from Park High School, Indianapolis, Ind., 1964; attended Hillsdale (Mich.) College, 1964, American College of Monaco, 1969, and Indiana University, 1974; secretary, Board of Directors, Cornwell Co., Inc., Paoli; served in the United States Army in Vietnam, 1966-1968; unsuccessful candidate for nomination in 1974 to the Ninety-fourth Congress; elected as a Democrat to the Ninety-fifth Congress (January 3, 1977-January 3, 1979); unsuccessful candidate for reelection in 1978 to the Ninety-sixth Congress; works in governmental and international relations; is a resident of Falls Church, Va.

**CORRADA-del RIO, Baltasar,** a Resident Commissioner from Puerto Rico; born in Morovis, P.R., April 10, 1935; attended Morovis Public Elementary School; graduated from Colegio Ponceno de Varones High School, 1952; B.A., University of Puerto Rico, 1956; J.D., University of Puerto Rico Law School, 1959; admitted to the Puerto Rico bar in 1959 and commenced practice in San Juan; appointed to the Civil Rights Commission of Puerto Rico, 1969; columnist, El Mundo newspaper; member, Puerto Rico Human Rights Review, 1971-1972; elected as a New Progressive to the United States House of Representatives, November 2, 1976, for a four-year term commencing January 3, 1977; reelected in 1980; did not seek reelection in 1984; mayor of San Juan, P.R., 1984-1989; elected president, New Progressive Party, 1986; is a resident of Rio Piedras, P.R.

**CORWIN, Franklin** (nephew of Moses Bledso Corwin and Thomas Corwin), a Representative from Illinois; born in Lebanon, Warren County, Ohio, January 12, 1818; attended private schools; studied law; was admitted to the bar in 1839 and practiced in Wilmington, Ohio; member of the Ohio house of representatives in 1846 and 1847; served in the State senate 1847-1849; moved to Peru, La Salle County, Ill., in 1857; member of the Illinois house of representatives and served as speaker; elected as a Republican to the Forty-third Congress (March 4, 1873-March 3, 1875); was an unsuccessful candidate for reelection in 1874 to the Forty-fourth Congress; resumed the practice of his profession in Peru, Ill., until his death there on June 15, 1879.

**CORWIN, Moses Bledso** (brother of Thomas Corwin and uncle of Franklin Corwin), a Representative from Ohio; born in Bourbon County, Ky., January 5, 1790; spent the early part of his life on a farm; attended the rural schools; studied law; was admitted to the bar in 1812 and commenced practice in Urbana, Champaign County, Ohio; member of the State house of representatives in 1838 and 1839; elected as a Whig to the Thirty-first Congress (March 4, 1849-March 3, 1851); again elected to the Thirty-third Congress (March 4, 1853-March 3, 1855); engaged in the practice of law until his death in Urbana, Ohio, April 7, 1872; interment in Oak Dale Cemetery.

**CORWIN, Thomas** (brother of Moses Bledso Corwin and uncle of Franklin Corwin), a Representative and a Senator from Ohio; born in Bourbon County, Ky., July 29, 1794; moved with his parents to Lebanon, Warren County, Ohio, in 1798; studied law; was admitted to the bar in 1817 and commenced practice in Lebanon, Ohio; prosecuting attorney of Warren County 1818-1828; member, Ohio State house of representatives, 1822-1823, 1829; elected as a Whig to the Twenty-second and to the four succeeding Congresses, and served from March 4, 1831 until his resignation, effective May 30, 1840, having become a candidate for Governor; chairman,

Committee on Public Lands (Twenty-sixth Congress); elected Governor of Ohio in 1840, and served from December 16, 1840 to December 14, 1842; unsuccessful candidate for reelection in 1842; declined to be a candidate for the gubernatorial nomination in 1844; president of the Ohio Whig convention in 1844; elected as a Whig to the United States Senate, and served from March 4, 1845 to July 20, 1850, when he resigned to enter the Cabinet; appointed Secretary of the Treasury by President Millard Fillmore, and served from July 23, 1850 to March 6, 1853; elected as a Republican to the Thirty-sixth and Thirty-seventh Congresses, and served from March 4, 1859 to March 12, 1861, when he resigned to enter the diplomatic service; chairman, Committee on Foreign Affairs (Thirty-sixth Congress); appointed by President Lincoln as Minister to Mexico on March 22, 1861, and served until April 1864, when he resigned; settled in Washington, D.C., and practiced law until his death on December 18, 1865; interment in Lebanon Cemetery, Lebanon, Ohio.

**Bibliography:** *DAB*; Morrow, Josiah. *Life and Speeches of Thomas Corwin: Orator, Lawyer, Statesman.* Cincinnati: W.H. Anderson and Company, 1896; Pendergraft, Daryl. "The Public Career of Thomas Corwin." Ph.D. dissertation, State University of Iowa, 1943.

**COSDEN, Jeremiah,** a Representative from Maryland; born in 1768; presented credentials as a Member-elect to the Seventeenth Congress and served from March 4, 1821, to March 19, 1822, when he was succeeded by Philip Reed, who contested his election; died in Baltimore, Md., December 5, 1824.

**COSGROVE, John,** a Representative from Missouri; born near Alexandria Bay, Jefferson County, N.Y., September 12, 1839; attended the district schools and the Redwood (N.Y.) School; studied law in Watertown; was admitted to the bar in October 1863 and commenced practice in New York; moved to Boonville, Mo., in 1865 and continued the practice of law; city attorney of Boonville in 1870 and 1871; elected prosecuting attorney of Cooper County in 1872; delegate to the Democratic National Conventions of 1872 and 1920; again city attorney of Boonville from April 1877 to April 1878, and from April 1879 to April 1881; elected as a Democrat to the Forty-eighth Congress (March 4, 1883-March 3, 1885); was renominated in 1884 to the Forty-ninth Congress, but withdrew before election day; resumed the practice of law in Boonville, Mo., where he died August 15, 1925; interment in Walnut Grove Cemetery.

**COSTELLO, Jerry Francis,** a Representative from Illinois; born in East St. Louis, St. Clair County, Ill., September 29, 1949; attended parochial schools; graduated Assumption High School, 1968; A.A., Belleville (Ill.) Area College, 1970; B.A., Maryville College of the Sacred Heart, St. Louis, Mo., 1972; county bailiff, Illinois 20th judicial circuit; deputy sheriff, St. Clair County, Ill.; director of court services and probation, Illinois 20th judicial district; chief investigator, Illinois State Attorney's office of St. Clair County; elected County board chairman, St. Clair County, and served from November 18, 1980, to August 11, 1988; elected as a Democrat to the One Hundredth Congress, by special election, August 9, 1988, to fill the vacancy caused by the death of Charles Melvin Price; reelected to the One Hundred First and to the three succeeding Congresses and served from August 9, 1988, to January 3, 1997; is a resident of Belleville, Ill.

**COSTELLO, John Martin,** a Representative from California; born in Los Angeles, Calif., January 15, 1903; attended the public schools; was graduated from the law department of Loyola University, Los Angeles, Calif., in 1924; was admitted to the bar the same year and commenced practice in Los Angeles; teacher in Los Angeles secondary schools in 1924 and 1925; unsuccessful candidate for election to the Seventy-third Congress in 1932; elected as a Democrat to the Seventy-fourth and to the four succeeding Congresses (January 3, 1935-January 3, 1945); unsuccessful

candidate for renomination in 1944 to the Seventy-ninth Congress; general counsel and manager of the Washington office of the Los Angeles Chamber of Commerce, 1945-1947; engaged in the practice of law in Washington, D.C., 1947-1976; died in Las Vegas, Nev., August 28, 1976; interment in Calvary Cemetery, Los Angeles, Calif.

**COSTELLO, Peter Edward,** a Representative from Pennsylvania; born in Boston, Mass., June 27, 1854; attended the public schools of Boston; moved to Philadelphia, Pa., in 1877; engaged in various manufacturing industries, also general construction work and real estate development; member of the common council of Philadelphia, 1895-1903; director of the department of public works of Philadelphia, 1903-1905; again a member of the common council, 1908-1915; elected as a Republican to the Sixty-fourth and to the two succeeding Congresses (March 4, 1915-March 3, 1921); was not a candidate for renomination in 1920 to the Sixty-seventh Congress; continued in the real-estate and investment brokerage business in Philadelphia, Pa., until his death there on October 23, 1935; interment in West Laurel Hill Cemetery.

**COSTIGAN, Edward Prentiss,** a Senator from Colorado; born near Beaulahville, King William County, Va., July 1, 1874; moved to Colorado in 1877 with his parents, who settled in Ouray, Ouray County; attended the public schools; studied law; was admitted to the bar in Salt Lake City, Utah, in 1897; was graduated from Harvard University in 1899; commenced the practice of law in Denver, Colo., in 1900; began his political life as a Republican; one of the founders of the Progressive Party in Colorado in 1912; unsuccessful Progressive candidate in 1912 and 1914 for election for Governor of Colorado; appointed a member of the United States Tariff Commission by President Woodrow Wilson in 1917; and served until his resignation in March 1928; resumed the practice of law in Denver, Colo.; affiliated with the Democratic Party in 1930; elected as a Democrat to the United States Senate in 1930 and served from March 4, 1931, to January 3, 1937; was not a candidate for renomination in 1936; retired from professional and political activities and resided in Denver, Colo., until his death there on January 17, 1939; interment in Fairmount Cemetery.

**Bibliography:** *DAB*; Costigan, Edward. *Public Ownership of Government: Collected Papers of Edward P. Costigan.* 1940. Reprint. New York: Kennikat Press, 1968; Greenbaum, Fred. *Fighting Progressive: A Biography of Edward P. Costigan.* Washington, D.C.: Public Affairs Press, 1971.

**COTHRAN, James Sproull,** a Representative from South Carolina; born near Abbeville, Abbeville County, S.C., August 8, 1830; attended the country schools; was graduated from the University of Georgia at Athens in 1852; studied law; was admitted to the bar in 1853 and commenced practice in Abbeville, S.C.; entered the Confederate service as a private at the beginning of the Civil War and was with his company at the surrender of the Army of Northern Virginia at Appomattox, having attained the rank of captain; resumed the practice of law in Abbeville; elected solicitor of the eighth judicial circuit in 1876 and 1880; appointed to the judgeship of that circuit to fill a vacancy caused by the death of Judge Thomson in 1881; elected by the legislature to the same office the following winter, and reelected in 1885; elected as a Democrat to the Fiftieth and Fifty-first Congresses (March 4, 1887-March 3, 1891); was not a candidate for renomination in 1890; again resumed the practice of law in Abbeville and Greenville, S.C.; died in a sanitarium in New York City, December 5, 1897; interment in Upper Long Cane Cemetery, Abbeville, S.C.

**COTTER, William Ross,** a Representative from Connecticut; born in Hartford, Conn., July 18, 1926; attended the Hartford public schools; B.A., Trinity College, Hartford, Conn., 1949; member, court of common council, city of Hartford, 1953; aide to Governor Abraham Ribicoff, 1955-1957; deputy insurance commissioner, State of Connecticut, 1957-1964, and insurance commissioner, 1964-1970;

delegate to Connecticut State Democratic conventions, 1954-1970; delegate to Democratic National Conventions, 1964, 1968; elected as a Democrat to the Ninety-second and to the five succeeding Congresses and served from January 3, 1971, until his death in East Lyme, Conn., September 8, 1981; was a resident of Hartford, Conn.; interment in Mount Saint Benedict Cemetery, Bloomfield, Conn.

**COTTMAN, Joseph Stewart,** a Representative from Maryland; born near Allen, Somerset (now Wicomico) County, Md., August 16, 1803; completed preparatory studies; attended Princeton College in 1821 and Yale College in 1822 and 1823; studied law; was admitted to the bar in 1826 and commenced practice in Princess Anne, Md.; member of the State house of delegates in 1831, 1832, and again in 1839; served in the State senate in 1837; elected as an Independent Whig to the Thirty-second Congress (March 4, 1851-March 3, 1853); unsuccessful candidate for reelection in 1852 to the Thirty-third Congress; resumed the practice of law; also engaged in agricultural and literary pursuits; died on his farm "Mortherton," near Allen, Wicomico County, Md., January 28, 1863; interment in St. Andrew's Episcopal Churchyard, Princess Anne, Md.

**COTTON, Aylett Rains,** a Representative from Iowa; born in Austintown, Ohio, November 29, 1826; attended the local public schools and Cottage Hill Academy, Ellsworth, Ohio, in 1842 and 1843; taught school; moved to Iowa with his father, who settled near Dewitt, Clinton County, in 1844; attended Allegheny College, Meadville, Pa., in 1845; taught school at Union Academy, Fayette County, Tenn., 1845-1847; returned to Iowa in 1847; studied law; was admitted to the Clinton County bar in 1848 and practiced; went to California in 1849 and engaged in mining on the Feather River; returned to Iowa in 1851 and settled in Lyons; county judge of Clinton County 1851-1853; prosecuting attorney of Clinton County in 1854; mayor of Lyons 1855-1857; member of the State constitutional convention in 1857; member of the State house of representatives 1868-1870, and served as speaker during the last term; elected as a Republican to the Forty-second and Forty-third Congresses (March 4, 1871-March 3, 1875); was not a candidate for renomination in 1874 to the Forty-fourth Congress; returned to California in 1883 and engaged in the practice of law in San Francisco, Calif., where he died October 30, 1912; interment in Woodlawn Cemetery, San Mateo County, Calif.

**COTTON, Norris H.,** a Representative and a Senator from New Hampshire; born on a farm in Warren, Grafton County, N.H., May 11, 1900; attended Phillips Exeter Academy at Exeter, N.H.; was graduated from Wesleyan University, Middletown, Conn., in 1923; editor of the Granite Monthly; clerk of the New Hampshire State senate; aide to Senator George Moses of New Hampshire, 1924-1928; attended the law school of George Washington University, Washington, D.C.; was admitted to the bar in 1928 and commenced practice in Lebanon, N.H.; member, New Hampshire State house of representatives, 1923, 1943, 1945, serving as majority leader in 1943, and speaker in 1945; elected as a Republican to the Eightieth and to the three succeeding Congresses, and served from January 3, 1947 until his resignation on November 7, 1954, having been elected to the United States Senate; elected in 1954 to the United States Senate to complete the unexpired term caused by the death of Charles W. Tobey for the term ending January 3, 1957; reelected in 1956, 1962, and again in 1968, and served from November 8, 1954 until his resignation on December 31, 1974; was not a candidate for reelection in 1974; chairman, Republican Conference (Ninety-third Congress); subsequently appointed to the seat on August 8, 1975, to fill the vacancy caused by the contested election of November 5, 1974, and served from August 8, 1975 until September 18, 1975; died February 24, 1989.

**Bibliography:** Bixby, Roland. *Standing Tall: The Life Story of Senator Norris Cotton.* Crawfordsville, Ind.: Lakeside Press, 1988;

Cotton, Norris. *In the Senate: Amidst the Conflict and the Turmoil.* New York: Dodd, Mead and Company, 1978.

**COTTRELL, James La Fayette,** a Representative from Alabama; born near King William, King William County, Va., August 25, 1808; completed preparatory studies; studied law; was admitted to the bar in 1830 and commenced practice in Hayneville, Ala.; member of the Alabama house of representatives in 1834, 1836, and 1837; served in the State senate 1838-1841, and was president of that body in 1840; elected as a Democrat to the Twenty-ninth Congress to fill the vacancy caused by the resignation of William L. Yancey and served from December 7, 1846, to March 3, 1847; moved to Florida in 1854; served in the Florida senate 1865-1885; appointed collector of customs at Cedar Keys, Levy County, Fla., and served until his death in that city September 7, 1885; interment in Old Town Cemetery, Old Town, Dixie County, Fla.

**COUDERT, Frederic René, Jr.,** a Representative from New York; born in New York City May 7, 1898; attended Browning and Morristown Schools in New York City; was graduated from Columbia University in 1918, and from its law school in 1922; served as a first lieutenant in the One Hundred and Fifth United States Infantry, Twenty-seventh Division, with overseas service, in 1917 and 1918; was admitted to the bar in 1923 and commenced practice in New York City; assistant United States attorney for the southern district of New York in 1924 and 1925; unsuccessful Republican candidate for district attorney of New York County in 1929; delegate to the Republican State conventions from 1930 to 1948; delegate to the Republican National Conventions of 1936, 1940, 1944, and 1948; member of the New York State senate, 1939-1946; elected as a Republican to the Eightieth and to the five succeeding Congresses (January 3, 1947-January 3, 1959); was not a candidate for renomination in 1958 to the Eighty-sixth Congress; engaged in the practice of law in New York City; member of State Commission on Governmental Operations of the city of New York, 1959-1961; retired from the practice of law due to ill health and resided in New York City, where he died on May 21, 1972; interment in Memorial Cemetery, Cold Spring Harbor, N.Y.

**Bibliography:** Coudert, Paula M., Paul B. Jones, and Lawrence Klepp. *Frederic R. Coudert, Jr.: A Biography.* With an introduction by William F. Buckley, Jr. N.p.: Paula M. Coudert, 1985.

**COUDREY, Harry Marcy,** a Representative from Missouri; born in Brunswick, Chariton County, Mo., February 28, 1867; moved with his parents to St. Louis, Mo., in 1878; attended the public schools of Brunswick and St. Louis and was graduated from the Manual Training School at St. Louis in 1886; elected a member of the municipal house of delegates of St. Louis and served from 1897 to 1899, inclusive; became interested in various business enterprises in St. Louis; successfully contested as a Republican the election of Ernest E. Wood in the Fifty-ninth Congress; reelected to the Sixtieth and Sixty-first Congresses and served from June 23, 1906, to March 3, 1911; was not a candidate for renomination in 1910 to the Sixty-second Congress; moved to New York City in 1911; engaged in the real estate, insurance, and publishing businesses; died in Norfolk, Va., July 5, 1930; interment in Bellefontaine Cemetery, St. Louis, Mo.

**COUGHLIN, Clarence Dennis** (uncle of Robert Lawrence Coughlin), a Representative from Pennsylvania; born in Kingston, Luzerne County, Pa., July 27, 1883; attended the public schools of Wilkes-Barre, Pa., Wesleyan College, Middletown, Conn., and Harvard College; taught in the Wilkes-Barre High School from 1906 to 1910; studied law; was admitted to the bar in 1910 and practiced law in Luzerne County, 1910-1920; engaged in manufacturing, banking, and the development of real estate in Wilkes-Barre and Scranton; member of the committee of public safety of Pennsylvania and county in 1918; served six years as a member of the commission to revise the penal code of Pennsylvania; chairman of the

Republican county committee of Luzerne County, 1915-1917; elected as a Republican to the Sixty-seventh Congress (March 4, 1921-March 3, 1923); chairman, Committee on Expenditures in the Department of Commerce (Sixty-seventh Congress); unsuccessful candidate for reelection in 1922 to the Sixty-eighth Congress; appointed judge of the court of common pleas of Luzerne County on October 6, 1925, to fill an unexpired term caused by the death of Judge Woodward; elected in November 1927 for a ten-year term and served until 1937; died in Wilkes-Barre, Pa., December 15, 1946; interment in Mount Greenwood Cemetery, Trucksville, Pa.

**COUGHLIN, Robert Lawrence** (nephew of Clarence Dennis Coughlin), a Representative from Pennsylvania; born in Wilkes-Barre, Luzerne County, Pa., April 11, 1929; A.B., Yale University, 1950; M.B.A., Harvard University Graduate School of Business Administration, 1954; LL.B., Temple University Evening Law School, 1958; admitted to the Pennsylvania bar in 1958; attorney, 1958-1969; manufacturer; captain, United States Marine Corps, 1950-1952, aide-de-camp to General Lewis B. Puller; member, Pennsylvania house of representatives, 1965-1966; member, Pennsylvania senate, 1967-1968; elected as a Republican to the Ninety-first and to the eleven succeeding Congresses (January 3, 1969-January 3, 1993); was not a candidate for reelection in 1992 to the One Hundred Third Congress; is a resident of Plymouth Meeting, Pa.

**COULTER, Richard,** a Representative from Pennsylvania; born in Westmoreland County, Pa., in March 1788; attended Jefferson College; studied law; was admitted to the bar in 1811 and commenced the practice of his profession in Greensburg, Westmoreland County, Pa.; member of the Pennsylvania house of representatives 1816-1820; elected to the Twentieth Congress and reelected as a Jacksonian to the Twenty-first through Twenty-third Congresses (March 4, 1827-March 3, 1835); unsuccessful candidate for reelection in 1834 to the Twenty-fourth Congress; elected judge of the supreme court of Pennsylvania and served from 1846 until his death on April 21, 1852, in Greensburg, Pa.; interment in St. Clair Cemetery.

**COURTER, James Andrew,** a Representative from New Jersey; born in Montclair, Essex County, N.J., October 14, 1941; educated in public and private schools; graduated from Montclair Academy, Montclair, 1959; B.A., Colgate University, Hamilton, N.Y., 1963; J.D., Duke University Law School, Durham, N.C., 1966; Peace Corps volunteer in Venezuela, 1966-1968; admitted to the New Jersey bar in 1971 and Washington, D.C., bar in 1966 and commenced practice in Washington, D.C., 1969; founder and partner of law firm in Hackettstown, N.J., in 1972; assistant corporation counsel for Washington, D.C., 1969-1970; Union County Legal Services, 1970-1971; first assistant, Warren County Prosecutor, 1973-1977; co-founder, Warren County Legal Services, 1975; attorney for municipalities in Warren and Sussex Counties; elected as a Republican to the Ninety-sixth and to the five succeeding Congresses (January 3, 1979-January 3, 1991); unsuccessful candidate for election in 1989 for Governor of New Jersey; was not a candidate for reelection in 1990 to the One Hundred Second Congress; is a resident of Hackettstown, N.J.

**COURTNEY, William Wirt,** a Representative from Tennessee; born in Franklin, Williamson County, Tenn., September 7, 1889; was graduated from Battle Ground Academy, Franklin, Tenn., in 1907; attended Vanderbilt University, Nashville, Tenn., and the Faculté de Droit of the Sorbonne, Paris, France; studied law; was admitted to the bar in 1911 and commenced practice in Franklin, Tenn.; city judge 1915-1917; enlisted in the United States Army as a private in the One Hundred and Seventeenth Infantry, Thirtieth Division, in September 1917, and was honorably discharged as a first lieutenant in June 1919; resumed the practice of law in Franklin, Tenn.; adjutant general of Tennessee in 1932; member of the Tennessee

National Guard in 1933 with rank of brigadier general; served as circuit judge and chancellor of the seventeenth judicial circuit of Tennessee 1933-1939; elected as a Democrat to the Seventy-sixth Congress to fill the vacancy caused by the death of Clarence W. Turner; reelected to the Seventy-seventh and to the three succeeding Congresses and served from May 11, 1939, to January 3, 1949; unsuccessful candidate for renomination in 1948 to the Eighty-first Congress; resumed the practice of law; died in Franklin, Tenn., April 6, 1961; interment in Mount Hope Cemetery.

**COUSINS, Robert Gordon,** a Representative from Iowa; born on a farm, "Indian Lodge," near Tipton, Cedar County, Iowa, January 31, 1859; attended the common schools, and was graduated from Cornell College, Mount Vernon, Iowa, in 1881; studied law; was admitted to the bar in 1882 and engaged in practice in Tipton, Iowa; member of the State house of representatives in 1886; elected by the State house of representatives as one of the managers to conduct the impeachment proceedings of John L. Brown before the State senate in 1886; prosecuting attorney of Cedar County 1888-1890; elected as a Republican to the Fifty-third and to the seven succeeding Congresses (March 4, 1893-March 3, 1909); chairman, Committee on Expenditures in the Department of the Treasury (Fifty-fifth through Fifty-ninth Congresses), Committee on Foreign Affairs (Sixtieth Congress); declined to be a candidate for renomination in 1908; resumed the practice of law at Tipton, Iowa; also engaged as a writer and as a Chautauqua lecturer; died June 20, 1933, in Iowa City, Iowa; interment in Red Oak Cemetery, five miles northwest of Tipton, Iowa.

**Bibliography:** Swisher, Jacob A. *Robert Gordon Cousins*. Iowa City: State Historical Society of Iowa, 1938.

**COUZENS, James,** a Senator from Michigan; born in Chatham, Province of Ontario, Canada, August 26, 1872; attended the public schools of Chatham; moved to Detroit, Mich., in 1890; railroad car checker from 1890 to 1897; clerk in the coal business, 1897-1903; was associated with the Ford Motor Co. in the manufacture of automobiles, 1903-1919; president of the Bank of Detroit and director of the Detroit Trust Co.; commissioner of street railways, 1913-1915; commissioner of the metropolitan police department, 1916-1918; mayor of Detroit, 1919-1922; appointed November 29, 1922, as a Republican to the United States Senate, and elected on November 4, 1924 to fill the vacancy caused by the resignation of Truman H. Newberry, and on the same day was elected for the term commencing March 4, 1925; reelected in 1930, and served from November 29, 1922 until his death in Detroit, Mich. on October 22, 1936; unsuccessful candidate for renomination in 1936; chairman, Committee on Civil Service (Sixty-ninth Congress), Committee on Education and Labor (Sixty-ninth and Seventieth Congresses), Committee on Interstate Commerce (Seventy-first and Seventy-second Congresses); interment in Woodlawn Cemetery, Detroit, Mich.

**Bibliography:** *DAB*; Barnard, Harry. *Independent Man: The Life of Senator James Couzens*. New York: Charles Scribner's Sons, 1958.

**COVERDELL, Paul D.,** a Senator from Georgia; born in Des Moines, Iowa, January 20, 1939; graduated Lee's Summit (Mo.) High School, 1957; B.A., University of Missouri, 1961; United States Army service as captain; president, insurance marketing firm; member, Georgia State senate, 1970-1989, minority leader, 1974-1989; chair, Georgia Republican Party, 1985-1987; chair, Southern Steering Committee, George Bush for President, 1987-1988; director, Peace Corps, 1989-1991; elected as a Republican to the United States Senate, November 24, 1992, for the term ending January 3, 1999; is a resident of Atlanta, Ga.

**COVERT, James Way,** a Representative from New York; born at Oyster Bay, Long Island, N.Y., September 2, 1842; attended the public schools and received an academic education in Locust Valley, N.Y.; studied law; was admitted to the bar in 1863 and commenced practice in Flushing, Long Island, N.Y.; district school commissioner 1867-1870; assistant prosecuting attorney of Queens County; surrogate of Queens County 1870-1874; unsuccessful candidate for election in 1872 to the Forty-third Congress; elected as a Democrat to the Forty-fifth and Forty-sixth Congresses (March 4, 1877-March 3, 1881); chairman, Committee on Agriculture (Forty-sixth Congress); member of the State senate in 1882 and 1883; elected to the Fifty-first, Fifty-second, and Fifty-third Congresses (March 4, 1889-March 3, 1895); chairman, Committee on Patents (Fifty-third Congress); moved to Brooklyn, N.Y., in 1896 and resumed the practice of law; died in Brooklyn, N.Y., May 16, 1910; interment in Mount Olivet Cemetery, Maspeth, N.Y.

**COVINGTON, George Washington,** a Representative from Maryland; born in Berlin, Worcester County, Md., September 12, 1838; attended the common schools, Buckingham Academy, and the law school of Harvard University; was admitted to the bar in 1861 and practiced in Berlin and Snow Hill, Md.; member of the State constitutional convention in 1867; elected as a Democrat to the Forty-seventh and Forty-eighth Congresses (March 4, 1881-March 3, 1885); chairman, Committee on Accounts (Forty-eighth Congress); was not a candidate for renomination in 1884; resumed the practice of law in Snow Hill, Worcester County, Md.; died in New York City April 6, 1911; interment in All Hallows Cemetery, Snow Hill, Md.

**COVINGTON, James Harry,** a Representative from Maryland; born in Easton, Talbot County, Md., May 3, 1870; received an academic training in the public schools of Talbot County and the Maryland Military Academy at Oxford; entered the law department of the University of Pennsylvania at Philadelphia in 1891, attending at the same time special lectures in history, literature, and economics, and was graduated from that institution in 1894; commenced the practice of law in Easton, Md.; unsuccessful Democratic candidate for election to the Kentucky senate in 1901; State's attorney for Talbot County, 1903-1908; elected as a Democrat to the Sixty-first and to the two succeeding Congresses, and served from March 4, 1909 until his resignation on September 30, 1914, to accept a judicial position; chief justice of the Supreme Court of the District of Columbia from October 1, 1914 to June 1, 1918, when he resigned to practice law in Washington, D.C.; professor of law in Georgetown University, Washington, D.C., 1914-1919; appointed by President Woodrow Wilson as a member of the United States Railroad Commission in January 1918; practiced law in Washington, D.C., where he died on February 4, 1942; interment in Spring Hill Cemetery, Easton, Md.

**COVINGTON, Leonard,** a Representative from Maryland; born in Aquasco, Md., October 30, 1768; received a liberal schooling; entered the United States Army as a cornet of Cavalry March 14, 1792; commissioned lieutenant of Dragoons in 1793, and joined the Army under General Anthony Wayne; distinguished himself at Fort Recovery and the Battle of Miami; promoted to a captaincy, and resigned September 12, 1795; engaged in agricultural pursuits; member of the State house of delegates for many years; elected as a Republican to the Ninth Congress (March 4, 1805-March 3, 1807); appointed lieutenant colonel of Light Dragoons on January 9, 1809, and colonel February 15, 1809; was in command at Fort Adams on the Mississippi in 1810 and took possession of Baton Rouge and a portion of West Florida; was ordered to the northern frontier in 1813, and appointed brigadier general August 1, 1813; mortally wounded at the Battle of Chryslers Field, November 11, 1813, and died at Frenchs Mills, N.Y., on November 14, 1813; remains were removed to Sackets Harbor, Jefferson County, N.Y., August 13, 1820; place of burial now known as Mount Covington.

**COVODE, John,** a Representative from Pennsylvania; born near West Fairfield, Westmoreland County, Pa., March 17, 1808; attended the public schools; engaged in agricultural pursuits, manufacturing, and transportation; largely interested in the coal trade; elected as a Whig to the Thirty-fourth Congress and as a Republican to the Thirty-fifth, Thirty-sixth, and Thirty-seventh Congresses (March 4, 1855-March 3, 1863); chairman, Committee on Public Expenditures (Thirty-seventh Congress); delegate to the Union National Convention at Philadelphia in 1866; elected to the Fortieth Congress (March 4, 1867-March 3, 1869); chairman, Committee on Public Buildings and Grounds (Fortieth Congress); contested with Henry D. Foster the election to the Forty-first Congress, neither being sworn pending the contest, as no credentials were issued by the Governor; on February 9, 1870, the House declared him duly elected, whereupon he qualified and served until his death; was not a candidate for reelection in 1870; died in Harrisburg, Pa., January 11, 1871; interment in Methodist Episcopal Cemetery, West Fairfield, Pa.

Bibliography: *DAB*; Chester, Edward W. "The Impact of the Covode Congressional Investigation." *Western Pennsylvania Historical Magazine* 42 (December 1959): 343-50.

**COWAN, Edgar,** a Senator from Pennsylvania; born in Westmoreland County, Pa., September 19, 1815; was graduated from Franklin College, Ohio, in 1839; became a raftsman, boat builder, schoolmaster, and a student of medicine; studied law; was admitted to the bar and commenced practice in Greensburg, Westmoreland County, Pa., in 1842; elected as a Republican to the United States Senate, and served from March 4, 1861 to March 3, 1867; unsuccessful candidate for reelection; chairman, Committee on Patents and the Patent Office (Thirty-seventh through Thirty-ninth Congresses); appointed by President Andrew Johnson as Minister to Austria in January 1867, but was not confirmed by the Senate; resumed the practice of law; died in Greensburg, Pa., August 31, 1885; interment in St. Clair Cemetery.

Bibliography: *DAB*.

**COWAN, Jacob Pitzer,** a Representative from Ohio; born in Florence, Washington County, Pa., March 20, 1823; attended the common schools; moved with his parents to Steubenville, Ohio, in 1835; engaged in the manufacture of woolens until 1843; studied medicine; in 1846 moved to Ashland County, Ohio, where he commenced the practice of his profession; was graduated from Starling Medical College, Columbus, Ohio, March 6, 1855; member of the State house of representatives 1855-1857; resumed the practice of medicine in 1859; elected as a Democrat to the Forty-fourth Congress (March 4, 1875-March 3, 1877); chairman, Committee on Militia (Forty-fourth Congress); unsuccessful candidate for renomination in 1876; again engaged in the practice of medicine in Ashland, Ohio, where he died July 9, 1895; interment in Ashland Cemetery.

**COWEN, Benjamin Sprague,** a Representative from Ohio; born in Washington County, N.Y., September 27, 1793; attended the common schools; studied medicine; served in the War of 1812 as a private; in 1820 moved to Moorefield, Ohio, where he practiced medicine and studied law; was admitted to the bar in 1829 and commenced practice in St. Clairsville, Ohio; edited the Belmont Chronicle 1836-1840; delegate to the Whig National Convention at Harrisburg, Pa., in 1839; elected as a Whig to the Twenty-seventh Congress (March 4, 1841-March 3, 1843); member of the State house of representatives in 1845 and 1846; presiding judge of the court of common pleas in 1847; died in St. Clairsville, Belmont County, Ohio, September 27, 1860.

**COWEN, John Kissig,** a Representative from Maryland; born near Millersburg, Holmes County, Ohio, October 28, 1844; attended the public schools and the local academies at Fredericksburg and

Hayesville, Ohio; was graduated from Princeton College in 1866 and from the law department of the University of Michigan at Ann Arbor; was admitted to the bar of Ohio in 1868 and commenced practice in Mansfield, Richland County, Ohio; prosecuting attorney of Holmes County; moved to Baltimore, Md., in February 1872 and was appointed counsel of the Baltimore & Ohio Railroad Co.; from 1876 to 1896 was general counsel of the Baltimore & Ohio Railroad Co.; elected as a Democrat to the Fifty-fourth Congress (March 4, 1895-March 3, 1897); was not a candidate for renomination in 1896 to the Fifty-fifth Congress; president of the Baltimore & Ohio Railroad Co. from January 1896 to June 1901; died in Chicago, Ill., April 26, 1904; interment in Oak Hill Cemetery, Millersburg, Holmes County, Ohio.

**Bibliography:** *DAB*.

**COWGER, William Owen,** a Representative from Kentucky; born in Hastings, Adams County, Nebr., January 1, 1922; attended Hastings High School; one year at Texas A.&M.; graduated from Carleton College, Northfield, Minn.; three years of postgraduate study in political science at the University of Louisville and American University; graduated from Navy Midshipmen's School at Columbia University, New York City; served twenty months in the Atlantic and Pacific theaters during the Second World War; president Thompson & Cowger Co., a mortgage loan company; in 1953 elected president of the Louisville Junior Chamber of Commerce; president, Kentucky Municipal League, 1963; president, Inter-American Municipal Organization, 1964-1965; in 1961, elected mayor of Louisville, Ky., on the Republican ticket; served for many years as the third district Republican congressional chairman and also as a member of the Kentucky central committee; elected as a Republican to the Ninetieth and to the Ninety-first Congresses (January 3, 1967-January 3, 1971); unsuccessful candidate for reelection in 1970 to the Ninety-second Congress; returned to his business career in Louisville, Ky., where he died, October 2, 1971; interment in Cave Hill Cemetery.

**COWGILL, Calvin,** a Representative from Indiana; born in Clinton County, Ohio, January 7, 1819; attended the common schools; moved with his parents to Indiana in 1836; studied law in Winchester, Randolph County; moved to Wabash County, Ind., in 1846; was admitted to the bar and commenced practice in Wabash; member of the Indiana State house of representatives in 1851 and again during the special session of 1865; treasurer of Wabash County, 1855-1859; provost marshal of the eleventh district of Indiana, 1862-1865; elected as a Republican to the Forty-sixth Congress (March 4, 1879-March 3, 1881); was not a candidate for renomination in 1880 to the Forty-seventh Congress; resumed the practice of his profession in Wabash, Ind., where he died on February 10, 1903; interment in Falls Cemetery.

**COWHERD, William Strother,** a Representative from Missouri; born near Lees Summit, Jackson County, Mo., September 1, 1860; attended the public schools in the town of Lees Summit and was graduated from the literary department of the University of Missouri at Columbia in 1881 and from the law department of the same institution in 1882; was admitted to the bar and commenced practice in Kansas City, Mo.; appointed assistant prosecuting attorney of Jackson County in 1885, and served four years; appointed first assistant city counselor of Kansas City in 1890; mayor of Kansas City in 1892; elected as a Democrat to the Fifty-fifth and to the three succeeding Congresses (March 4, 1897-March 3, 1905); unsuccessful candidate for reelection in 1904 to the Fifty-ninth Congress; resumed the practice of law in Kansas City, Mo.; unsuccessful Democratic candidate for Governor in 1908; moved to Pasadena, Calif., and continued the practice of his profession; died in Pasadena June 20, 1915; interment in Lees Summit Cemetery, near Lees Summit, Mo.

**COWLES, Charles Holden** (nephew of William Henry Harrison Cowles), a Representative from North Carolina; born in Charlotte, N.C., July 16, 1875; moved with his parents to Wilkesboro, Wilkes County, December 26, 1885; attended Charlotte graded school, private schools, Wilkesboro Academy, and completed a commercial college course; member of the board of aldermen of Wilkesboro in 1897 and again in 1914; deputy clerk of the United States Court at Statesville and Charlotte, 1899-1901; private secretary to Representative Edmond S. Blackburn of North Carolina, 1901-1903; member of the North Carolina State house of representatives, 1904-1908, 1920-1924, 1928-1930, and 1932-1934; delegate to the Republican National Conventions of 1904, 1908, 1912, and 1916; elected as a Republican to the Sixty-first Congress (March 4, 1909-March 3, 1911); unsuccessful candidate for reelection in 1910 to the Sixty-second Congress; nominated in 1916 by the Progressive Republicans for the United States Senate but declined the nomination; established and published the Wilkes Patriot, Wilkesboro, N.C., 1906-1919; during the First World War served as a member of the Wilkes County council of defense; was a member of the North Carolina State senate, 1938-1940; served as chairman of War Price and Rationing Board No. 1 for Wilkes County from January 7, 1942, to September 15, 1945; appointed deputy clerk of the United States Court in Wilkesboro on April 1, 1941, and served until his retirement in October 1956; died in Mocksville, N.C., October 2, 1957; interment in Episcopal Church Cemetery, Wilkesboro, N.C.

**COWLES, George Washington,** a Representative from New York; born in Otisco, Onondaga County, N.Y., December 6, 1823; attended the common schools, and was graduated from Hamilton College, Clinton, N.Y., in 1845; taught school until 1853; studied law; was admitted to the bar in 1854 and commenced practice in Clyde, Wayne County, N.Y.; judge of the Wayne County court from January 1, 1864, to October 30, 1869; elected as a Republican to the Forty-first Congress (March 4, 1869-March 3, 1871); was not a candidate for renomination in 1870; resumed the practice of law; again judge of Wayne County court from January 1, 1874, to January 1, 1880, and from January 1, 1886, until his death in Clyde, N.Y., January 20, 1901; interment in Maple Grove Cemetery.

**COWLES, Henry Booth,** a Representative from New York; born in Hartford, Conn., March 18, 1798; moved with his father to Dutchess County, N.Y., in 1809; was graduated from Union College, Schenectady, N.Y., in 1816; studied law; was admitted to the bar and commenced practice in Putnam County; member of the State assembly 1826-1828; elected to the Twenty-first Congress (March 4, 1829-March 3, 1831); moved to New York City in 1834 and practiced law until his death there on May 17, 1873; interment in Rhinebeck Cemetery, Rhinebeck, Dutchess County, N.Y.

**COWLES, William Henry Harrison** (uncle of Charles Holden Cowles), a Representative from North Carolina; born in Hamptonville, Yadkin County, N.C., April 22, 1840; attended the common schools and academies of his native county; entered the Confederate service as a private in Company A, First North Carolina Cavalry, and served from the spring of 1861 to the close of the war with the Army of Northern Virginia, holding successively the ranks of captain, major, and lieutenant colonel of his regiment; entered upon the study of law in Richmond Hill, Yadkin County, in 1866; obtained a county court license in January 1867 and a superior court license in January 1868; moved to Wilkesboro, Wilkes County, where he commenced the practice of law; reading clerk of the State senate of North Carolina 1872-1874; elected solicitor of the tenth judicial district in 1874 and served for four years; member of the Democratic State executive committee for eight years; elected as a Democrat to the Forty-ninth and to the three succeeding Congresses (March 4, 1885-March 3, 1893); chairman, Committee on Expenditures in the Department of Justice (Fiftieth Congress), Committee on Mines and

Mining (Fifty-second Congress); was not a candidate for renomination in 1892; engaged in agricultural pursuits and also interested in other business activities; died in Wilkesboro, N.C., December 30, 1901; interment in Presbyterian Cemetery.

**COX, Charles Christopher,** a Representative from California; born in St. Paul, Ramsey County, Minn., October 16, 1952; graduated, St. Thomas Academy, St. Paul, 1970; B.A., University of Southern California, 1973; M.B.A., Harvard University Business School, 1977; J.D., Harvard University Law School, 1977; admitted to California bar, 1978; District of Columbia bar, 1980; law clerk to Judge Herbert Y.C. Choy, United States Court of Appeals for the Ninth Circuit, 1977-1978; attorney, Newport Beach, Calif.; lecturer on business administration, Harvard Business School, 1982-1983; co-founder, Context Corp., St. Paul, 1984-1986; senior associate counsel to President Ronald Reagan, 1986-1988; elected as a Republican to the One Hundred First and to the three succeeding Congresses (January 3, 1989-January 3, 1997); is a resident of Newport Beach, Calif.

**COX, Edward Eugene,** a Representative from Georgia; born near Camilla, Mitchell County, Ga., April 3, 1880; attended the grade schools, Camilla High School, the academic department of Mercer University, Macon, Ga., for nearly four years, and was graduated from the law department of that university in 1902; was admitted to the bar the same year and commenced practice at Camilla, Ga.; mayor of Camilla, 1904-1906; delegate to the Democratic National Convention of 1908; appointed and subsequently elected judge of the superior court of the Albany circuit and served from 1912 until he resigned in 1916, having become a candidate for Congress; unsuccessful candidate for election in 1916 to the Sixty-fifth Congress; elected as a Democrat to the Sixty-ninth and to the thirteen succeeding Congresses, and served from March 4, 1925 until his death in Bethesda, Md., December 24, 1952; had been reelected to the Eighty-third Congress; chairman, Select Committee on Tax Exempt Foundations (Eighty-second Congress); interment in Oakview Cemetery, Camilla, Ga.

Bibliography: *DAB*.

**COX, Isaac Newton,** a Representative from New York; born in Fallsburg, Sullivan County, N.Y., August 1, 1846; moved to Ellenville in 1864 and engaged in the lumber business; supervisor of the town of Wawarsing in 1875 and during 1883-1886, and served as chairman of the board during the last year; served four years on the Democratic State committee; appointed by President Grover Cleveland chairman of the commission to examine and report upon the condition of the Northern Pacific Railroad in 1886; elected as a Democrat to the Fifty-second Congress (March 4, 1891-March 3, 1893); unsuccessful candidate for reelection in 1892 to the Fifty-third Congress; appointed a member of the State commission on fisheries, and served from 1894 to 1899; engaged in mercantile pursuits, lumbering, and banking in Ellenville, Ulster County, N.Y., where he died September 28, 1916; interment in Fantinekill Cemetery.

**COX, Jacob Dolson,** a Representative from Ohio; born in Montreal, Canada, October 27, 1828; moved with his parents to New York City in 1829; attended private schools; moved to Lorain, Ohio, in 1846; was graduated from Oberlin (Ohio) College in 1851; studied law; was admitted to the bar in 1853 and commenced practice in Warren, Trumbull County, Ohio; member of the Ohio State senate, 1860-1861; entered the Union Army as brigadier general of Ohio Volunteers on May 17, 1861; commissioned major general of volunteers, October 6, 1862; resigned on January 1, 1866, having been elected Governor of Ohio in October 1865; served as Governor from January 8, 1866 to January 13, 1868; moved to Cincinnati, Ohio, and resumed the practice of law; Secretary of the Interior in the Cabinet of President Ulysses S. Grant from March 5, 1869 until November 1, 1870, when he resigned; resumed the practice of law in Cincinnati; president of the Wabash Railroad, 1873-1878; moved to Toledo, Ohio, in 1874; elected as a Republican to the Forty-fifth Congress (March 4, 1877-March 3, 1879); declined to be a candidate for renomination in 1878 to the Forty-sixth Congress; returned to Cincinnati in 1878; dean of the Cincinnati Law School, 1881-1897; president of the University of Cincinnati, 1885-1889; was an author and writer on Civil War subjects; died in Magnolia, near Gloucester, Mass., August 4, 1900; interment in Spring Grove Cemetery, Cincinnati, Ohio.

Bibliography: *DAB*; Cox, Jacob Dolson. *Military Reminiscences of the Civil War.* 2 vols. New York: Scribner's Sons, 1900; Losson, Christopher Thomas. "Jacob Dolson Cox: A Military Biography." Ph.D. dissertation, University of Mississippi, 1993; Schmiel, Eugene D. "The Career of Jacob Dolson Cox, 1828-1900." Ph.D. dissertation, Ohio State University, 1969.

**COX, James,** a Representative from New Jersey; born in Monmouth, N.J., June 14, 1753; attended the public schools; commanded a company of militia at the Battles of Germantown, Pa., October 4, 1777, and of Monmouth, N.J., June 28, 1778, attaining the rank of brigadier general; member of the State general assembly 1801-1807, and served as speaker 1804-1807; elected as a Republican to the Eleventh Congress and served from March 4, 1809, until his death in Monmouth, N.J., September 12, 1810; interment in the Yellow Meeting House Cemetery, Upper Freehold Township, N.J.

**COX, James Middleton,** a Representative from Ohio; born on a farm near Jacksonburg, Butler County, Ohio, March 31, 1870; attended Butler County schools and Amanda (Ohio) High School; after two years of high school passed the teacher's examination, and at the age of sixteen years began teaching school; commenced his newspaper career as a reporter on the Middletown (Ohio) Signal and in 1892 went to work on the Cincinnati Enquirer; secretary to Representative Paul J. Sorg of Ohio, 1894-1897; became owner and publisher of the Dayton Daily News in 1898, of the Springfield Daily News in 1903, of the Miami (Fla.) News in 1923, of the Atlanta (Ga.) Journal in 1939, of the Dayton Journal and Herald in 1949, and of the Atlanta (Ga.) Constitution in 1950; elected as a Democrat to the Sixty-first and Sixty-second Congresses and served from March 4, 1909, until January 12, 1913, when he resigned, having been elected Governor; elected Governor of Ohio in 1912, and served from January 13, 1913 to January 11, 1915; unsuccessful candidate for reelection in 1914; elected Governor in 1916, reelected in 1918, and served from January 8, 1917 to January 10, 1921; unsuccessful Democratic candidate for election as President of the United States in 1920; vice chairman of the United States delegation to the World Economic Conference at London in 1933 and president of its monetary commission; declined appointment to the United States Senate by Governor Frank Lausche in 1946; retired from political life, but continued his activities as a newspaper publisher and owner of several radio and television stations; died in Dayton, Ohio, July 15, 1957; interment in Woodland Cemetery.

Bibliography: *DAB*; Cebula, James E. *James M. Cox: Journalist and Politician.* New York: Garland, 1985; Cox, James M. *Journey Through My Years.* New York: Simon and Schuster, 1946.

**COX, John W., Jr.,** a Representative from Illinois; born in Hazel Green, Grant County, Wis., July 10, 1947; B.S., University of Wisconsin, 1969; J.D., John Marshall School of Law, Chicago, Ill., 1975; admitted to the Illinois bar in 1975; United States Army service, 1969-1970; practicing attorney; special assistant attorney general, Illinois Department of Public Aid, 1984-1987; city attorney, Galena, Ill., 1989-1990; elected as a Democrat to the One Hundred Second Congress (January 3, 1991-January 3, 1993); unsuccessful candidate for reelection in 1992 to the One Hundred Third Congress; is a resident of Galena, Ill.

**COX, Leander Martin,** a Representative from Kentucky; born in Cumberland County, Va., May 7, 1812; completed academic studies; studied law; was admitted to the bar and practiced; moved to Flemingsburg, Fleming County, Ky.; member of the Kentucky house of representatives 1843-1845; captain in the Third Kentucky Volunteers in the Mexican War in 1847; elected as a Whig to the Thirty-third Congress and as a candidate of the American Party to the Thirty-fourth Congress (March 4, 1853-March 3, 1857); unsuccessful candidate for reelection in 1856 to the Thirty-fifth Congress; resumed the practice of law; died in Flemingsburg, Ky., March 19, 1865; interment in Fleming County Cemetery.

**COX, Nicholas Nichols,** a Representative from Tennessee; born in Bedford County, Tenn., January 6, 1837; went to Seguin, Tex., in early childhood; attended the common schools; served on the Mexican frontier; was graduated from Lebanon (Tenn.) Law School in 1858; was admitted to the bar the same year and commenced practice at Linden, Tenn.; was a colonel in the Tenth Tennessee Cavalry of the Confederate Army during the Civil War, serving principally with General Nathan Bedford Forrest; settled in Franklin, Williamson County, Tenn., in 1866; engaged in agricultural pursuits; presidential elector on the Democratic ticket of John C. Breckinridge and Joseph Lane in 1860; elected as a Democrat to the Fifty-second and to the four succeeding Congresses (March 4, 1891-March 3, 1901); declined to be a candidate for renomination in 1900 to the Fifty-seventh Congress; resumed the practice of law and engaged in banking in Franklin, Tenn., where he died on May 2, 1912; interment in Mount Hope Cemetery.

**COX, Samuel Sullivan,** a Representative from Ohio and from New York; born in Zanesville, Muskingum County, Ohio, September 30, 1824; attended the Ohio University at Athens, and was graduated from Brown University, Providence, R.I., in 1846; studied law; was admitted to the bar and commenced practice in Zanesville in 1849; owner and editor of the Columbus (Ohio) Statesman in 1853 and 1854; secretary of the legation at Lima, Peru, in 1855; delegate to the Democratic National Conventions of 1864 and 1868; elected as a Democrat from Ohio to the Thirty-fifth and to the three succeeding Congresses (March 4, 1857-March 3, 1865); chairman, Committee on Revolutionary Claims (Thirty-fifth Congress); unsuccessful candidate for reelection in 1864 to the Thirty-ninth Congress; moved to New York City on March 4, 1865, and resumed the practice of law; elected from New York to the Forty-first and Forty-second Congresses (March 4, 1869-March 3, 1873); unsuccessful candidate of the Democrats and Liberal Republicans for reelection in 1872 as Representative at large to the Forty-third Congress; subsequently elected to the Forty-third Congress to fill the vacancy caused by the death of James Brooks; reelected to the Forty-fourth and to the five succeeding Congresses and served from November 4, 1873, to May 20, 1885, when he resigned, having accepted a diplomatic position; chairman, Committee on Banking and Currency (Forty-fourth Congress), Committee on the Census (Forty-sixth Congress), Committee on Foreign Affairs (Forty-sixth Congress), Committee on Naval Affairs (Forty-eighth Congress); elected Speaker pro tempore of the House on February 17, May 12, and June 19, 1876, and appointed to that office on May 1 and June 7, 1876; appointed Envoy Extraordinary and Minister Plenipotentiary to Turkey by President Grover Cleveland and served from May 21, 1885, to October 22, 1886, when he resigned; was again elected to the Forty-ninth Congress to fill the vacancy caused by the resignation of Joseph Pulitzer; reelected to the Fiftieth and Fifty-first Congresses and served from November 2, 1886, until his death in New York City September 10, 1889; interment in Greenwood Cemetery, Brooklyn, N.Y.

Bibliography: *DAB*; Lindsey, David. *"Sunset" Cox: Irrepressible Democrat.* Detroit: Wayne State University Press, 1959.

**COX, William Elijah,** a Representative from Indiana; born on a farm near Birdseye, Dubois County, Ind., September 6, 1861; attended the common and high schools of Huntingburg and Jasper, Ind.; was graduated from Lebanon University, Tenn., in 1888 and from the law department of the University of Michigan at Ann Arbor in 1889; was admitted to the bar July 10, 1889, and commenced practice at Rockport, Spencer County, Ind., moving to Jasper, Ind., later in the same year; prosecuting attorney for the eleventh judicial district of Indiana 1892-1898; elected as a Democrat to the Sixtieth and to the five succeeding Congresses (March 4, 1907-March 3, 1919); chairman, Committee on Expenditures in the Department of the Treasury (Sixty-second Congress); unsuccessful candidate for reelection in 1918 to the Sixty-sixth Congress; resumed the practice of law and also was engaged with a desk-manufacturing company, serving as president at the time of his death; died in Jasper, Ind., March 11, 1942; interment in Fairmount Cemetery, Huntingburg, Ind.

**COX, William Ruffin,** a Representative from North Carolina; born in Scotland Neck, Halifax County, N.C., March 11, 1831; attended Vine Hill Academy in his native town; moved with his mother to Nashville, Tenn.; was graduated from Franklin College in 1851 and from the Lebanon College Law School in 1853; was admitted to the bar in 1853 and practiced in Nashville, Tenn., 1853-1857; returned to North Carolina in 1857 and engaged in agricultural pursuits in Edgecombe County; moved to Raleigh, N.C., in 1859; early in the Civil War entered the Confederate Army as major of the Second North Carolina State Troops; became brigadier general; resumed the practice of law at Raleigh, N.C., in 1865; solicitor of the sixth district 1866-1870; delegate to the Democratic National Convention in 1868; judge of the superior court for the sixth district in 1877 and 1878, when he resigned; chairman of the Democratic State committee 1875-1877; elected as a Democrat to the Forty-seventh, Forty-eighth, and Forty-ninth Congresses (March 4, 1881-March 3, 1887); unsuccessful candidate for renomination; elected Secretary of the United States Senate April 6, 1893, qualified August 7, 1893, and served until January 31, 1900; resumed agricultural pursuits, with residence at Penelo, Edgecombe County, N.C.; president of the State agricultural society in 1900 and 1901; died in Richmond, Va., on December 26, 1919; interment in Oakwood Cemetery, Raleigh, N.C.

Bibliography: *DAB*.

**COXE, Tench,** a Delegate from Pennsylvania; born in Philadelphia, Pa., May 22, 1755; received a liberal schooling; engaged in mercantile pursuits; resigned from the Pennsylvania Militia in 1776, turned Loyalist, and joined the British Army under Howe in 1777; was arrested, paroled, and joined the patriot cause; commissioner to the Federal Convention at Annapolis in 1786; Member of the Continental Congress in 1789; was appointed Assistant Secretary of the Treasury on September 11, 1789, and served until the office was abolished on May 8, 1792; was appointed revenue commissioner June 30, 1792, and served until removed by President Adams; was appointed by President Jefferson purveyor of public supplies and served from 1803 to 1812; was a writer on political and economic subjects; died in Philadelphia, Pa., July 17, 1824; interment in Christ Church Burying Ground.

Bibliography: *DAB*; Cooke, Jacob E. *Tench Coxe and the Early Republic.* Chapel Hill: University of North Carolina Press, 1978.

**COXE, William, Jr.,** a Representative from New Jersey; born in Burlington, N.J., May 3, 1762; served as a member of the State general assembly 1796-1804, 1806-1809, and again in 1816 and 1817; served as speaker 1798-1800 and again in 1802; elected as a Federalist to the Thirteenth Congress (March 4, 1813-March 3, 1815); author; died in Burlington, Burlington County, N.J., on February 25, 1831; interment in St. Mary's Churchyard.

Bibliography: *DAB*.

**COYLE, William Radford,** a Representative from Pennsylvania; born in Washington, D.C., July 10, 1878; attended the public schools, and Columbian College (now George Washington University), Washington, D.C., in 1898 and 1899; field assistant in the United States Geological Survey 1896-1899; attended the Naval War College, Newport, R.I., in 1900; served in the United States Marine Corps as second lieutenant, first lieutenant, and captain 1900-1906; attended the law department of the University of Pennsylvania at Philadelphia in 1906 and 1907; moved to Germantown, Pa., in 1906 and to Bethlehem, Pa., in 1908; school director of Bethlehem, Pa., 1912-1918; captain of the Fourth Regiment, National Guard of Pennsylvania, in 1913; was commissioned a captain in the United States Marine Corps in 1918, and later the same year, a major; promoted to lieutenant colonel in 1932; president of the American Wholesale Coal Association in 1921 and 1922; trustee to settle the affairs of the Tidewater Coal Exchange 1922-1925; elected as a Republican to the Sixty-ninth Congress (March 4, 1925-March 3, 1927); unsuccessful candidate for reelection in 1926 to the Seventieth Congress; elected to the Seventy-first and Seventy-second Congresses (March 4, 1929-March 3, 1933); unsuccessful candidate for reelection in 1932 to the Seventy-third Congress, for election in 1936 to the Seventy-fifth Congress, and for election in 1942 to the Seventy-eighth Congress; delegate to the Republican National Conventions in 1936 and 1944; chairman of civilian defense in Bethlehem, Pa., 1941-1945; vice president of Weston Dodson & Co., Inc., 1932-1954; chairman of Bethlehem Redevelopment Authority 1953-1959; died in Bethlehem, Pa., January 30, 1962; interment in Nisky Hill Cemetery.

**COYNE, James Kitchenman, III,** a Representative from Pennsylvania; born in Farmville, Prince Edward County, Va., November 17, 1946; attended the public schools of Abington, Pa.; graduated from Abington High School, 1964; B.S., Yale University, 1968; M.B.A., Harvard University Business School, 1970; lecturer, Wharton School, University of Pennsylvania, 1974-1979; president, Coyne Chemical Corp., 1971-1981; founder and president, Rechem Co., 1976; founder and chairman, Energy Management Services, 1977-1978; supervisor, Upper Makefield Township, Pa., 1979-1980; elected as a Republican to the Ninety-seventh Congress (January 3, 1981-January 3, 1983); unsuccessful candidate for reelection in 1982 to the Ninety-eighth Congress; director, White House Office of Private Sector Initiatives, 1983-1985; chief executive officer, American Consulting Engineers Council, 1985-1986; president, American Tort Reform Association, 1986-1988; is a resident of Newtown, Pa.

**COYNE, William Joseph,** a Representative from Pennsylvania; born in Pittsburgh, Pa., August 24, 1936; attended private schools; graduated from Central Catholic High School, Pittsburgh, 1954; B.S., Robert Morris College, Pittsburgh, 1965; served in the United States Army, corporal, 1955-1957; accountant; corporation manager; served in the Pennsylvania Legislature, 1970-1972; Pittsburgh city councilman, 1974-1980; elected as a Democrat to the Ninety-seventh and to the seven succeeding Congresses (January 3, 1981-January 3, 1997); is a resident of Pittsburgh, Pa.

**CRABB, George Whitfield,** a Representative from Alabama; born in Botetourt County, Va., February 22, 1804; attended the public schools; moved to Tuscaloosa, Ala.; elected assistant secretary of the State senate and comptroller of public accounts in 1829; served in the Florida Indian War of 1836 and was lieutenant colonel of the Alabama Volunteers; member of the State house of representatives in 1836 and 1837; served in the State senate in 1837 and 1838; major general of militia; elected as a Whig to the Twenty-fifth Congress to fill the vacancy caused by the death of Joab Lawler; reelected to the Twenty-sixth Congress and served from September 4, 1838, to March 3, 1841; unsuccessful candidate for reelection in 1840 to the Twenty-seventh Congress; appointed judge

of the county court of Mobile in 1846; died in Philadelphia, Pa., August 15, 1846; interment in Greenwood Cemetery, Tuscaloosa, Ala.

**CRABB, Jeremiah,** a Representative from Maryland; born in Montgomery County, Md., in 1760; served in the Revolutionary War as second lieutenant in the First Maryland Regiment; promoted to the rank of first lieutenant on December 15, 1777, and served as such until April 1, 1778, when he resigned because of ill health occasioned by the winter hardships endured at Valley Forge; was an extensive landowner in Montgomery County; served as general with General Harry Lee in Pennsylvania during the Whiskey Rebellion of 1794; elected as a Federalist to the Fourth Congress and served from March 4, 1795, until his resignation in 1796; returned to his home near Rockville, Montgomery County, Md., and died there in 1800; interment in the family burying ground near Derwood, Montgomery County, Md.

**CRADDOCK, John Durrett,** a Representative from Kentucky; born in Munfordville, Hart County, Ky., October 26, 1881; attended the public schools of Hart County; during the Philippine Insurrection and also during the Boxer Uprising in China served as a corporal and sergeant in Troop F, Third United States Cavalry; employed as a railroad engineer with the Isthmian Canal Commission, Panama Canal Zone, 1904-1910; returned to Munfordville, Ky., in 1910 and engaged in banking and agricultural pursuits; member of the board of trustees of Munfordville, 1910-1925; assisted in organizing the Burley Tobacco Growers Association in 1922, and served as director from 1922 to 1941; member, Kentucky Mammoth Cave National Park Commission, 1922-1928; elected as a Republican to the Seventy-first Congress (March 4, 1929-March 3, 1931); unsuccessful candidate for reelection in 1930 to the Seventy-second Congress; field man, Federal Farm Board, Washington, D.C., 1931-1932; agent of the Kentucky Blue Grass Cooperative Association, Winchester, Ky., 1933-1934; treasurer of Hart County at Munfordville, Ky., 1934-1935; resumed his former pursuits; served as a member of the Kentucky Agricultural Adjustment Administration Committee from 1939 until his death in Louisville, Ky., May 20, 1942; interment in New Munfordville Cemetery, Munfordville, Ky.

**CRADLEBAUGH, John,** a Delegate from the Territory of Nevada; born in Circleville, Pickaway County, Ohio, February 22, 1819; attended the common schools, Kenyon College, Gambier, Ohio, and Oxford (Ohio) University; studied law; was admitted to the bar in 1840; appointed United States associate justice for the district of Utah on June 4, 1858; moved to Carson City, Nev.; upon the formation of the Territory of Nevada was elected a Delegate to the Thirty-seventh Congress and served from December 2, 1861, to March 3, 1863; colonel of the One Hundred and Fourteenth Regiment, Ohio Volunteer Infantry, and served from April 27, 1862, until honorably discharged October 20, 1863, on tender of resignation; wounded at Vicksburg; returned to Nevada and settled in Eureka; engaged in the mining business until his death in Eureka, Nev., February 22, 1872; interment in Forest Cemetery, Circleville, Ohio.

**CRAFTS, Samuel Chandler,** a Representative and a Senator from Vermont; born in Woodstock, Conn., October 6, 1768; was graduated from Harvard College in 1790; moved in 1791 to Vermont with his father, who founded the town of Craftsbury; town clerk 1799-1829; delegate to the Vermont constitutional convention 1793; member, State house of representatives 1796, 1800-1803, 1805, and clerk of the house 1798-1799; register of probate 1796-1815; assistant judge of the Orleans County Court 1800-1810, 1825-1828; made an extensive botanical reconnaissance of the Mississippi Valley in 1802; member, State council 1809-1813; chief judge of the Orleans County Court 1810-1816; elected to the Fifteenth and to the three succeeding Congresses (March 4, 1817-March 3, 1825); again served as State councilor in 1825 and 1826; Governor of Vermont from October 10, 1828 to October 18, 1831; member of the Vermont constitutional convention of 1829 and served as president; clerk of Orleans County 1836-1839; appointed and subsequently elected to the United States Senate to fill the vacancy caused by the resignation of Samuel Prentiss and served from April 23, 1842, until March 3, 1843; retired to his farm in Craftsbury, Orleans County, Vt., where he died November 19, 1853; interment in North Craftsbury Cemetery, North Craftsbury, Vt.

**CRAGIN, Aaron Harrison** a Representative and a Senator from New Hampshire; born in Weston, Windsor County, Vt., February 3, 1821; completed preparatory studies; studied law; was admitted to the bar in Albany, N.Y., in 1847 and commenced practice in Lebanon, N.H.; member, New Hampshire house of representatives 1852-1855; elected by the American Party to the Thirty-fourth Congress and as a Republican to the Thirty-fifth Congress (March 4, 1855-March 3, 1859); chairman, Committee on Expenditures in the Department of War (Thirty-fourth Congress); resumed the practice of law; member, State house of representatives 1859; elected as a Republican to the United States Senate in 1864; reelected in 1870 and served from March 4, 1865, to March 3, 1877; chairman, Committee on Engrossed Bills (Thirty-ninth Congress), Committee to Audit and Control the Contingent Expense (Fortieth and Forty-first Congresses), Committee on Naval Affairs (Forty-first and Forty-third Congresses), Committee on Railroads (Forty-third and Forty-fourth Congresses); appointed by President Rutherford Hayes one of the commissioners for the purchase of the Hot Springs Reservation in Arkansas and served as chairman 1877-1879; died in Washington, D.C., May 10, 1898; interment in School Street Cemetery, Lebanon, N.H.

**CRAGO, Thomas Spencer,** a Representative from Pennsylvania; born in Carmichaels, Greene County, Pa., August 8, 1866; attended Greene Academy and Waynesburg College; was graduated from Princeton College in 1893; studied law; was admitted to the bar of Greene County in 1894 and commenced practice in Waynesburg, Pa.; served as captain of Company K in the Tenth Pennsylvania Volunteer Infantry during the Spanish-American War and the Philippine Insurrection; after the war helped to reorganize the Pennsylvania National Guard and was elected major and later lieutenant colonel of the Tenth Infantry; resigned his commission while in Congress, but was later retired with the rank of colonel; delegate to the Republican National Convention of 1904; elected as a Republican to the Sixty-second Congress (March 4, 1911-March 3, 1913); unsuccessful candidate for reelection in 1912 to the Sixty-third Congress; commander in chief of the Veterans of Foreign Wars in 1914 and 1915; elected to the Sixty-fourth, Sixty-fifth, and Sixty-sixth Congresses (March 4, 1915-March 3, 1921); was not a candidate for renomination in 1920, but was subsequently elected to the Sixty-seventh Congress to fill the vacancy caused by the death of Mahlon M. Garland and served from September 20, 1921, to March 3, 1923; was not a candidate for renomination in 1922 to the Sixty-eighth Congress; appointed special assistant to the Attorney General of the United States on March 7, 1923, and assigned to the War Frauds Division, resigned August 15, 1924; vice president of the Union Deposit and Trust Co. of Waynesburg; died in Waynesburg, Pa., September 12, 1925; interment in Green Mount Cemetery.

**CRAIG, Alexander Kerr,** a Representative from Pennsylvania; born near Claysville, Buffalo Township, Washington County, Pa., February 21, 1828; attended the common schools and was educated by a private tutor; became a teacher at the age of sixteen; began the study of law, but devoted himself to agricultural pursuits; taught school in winter months and subsequently became principal of the Claysville public schools; enlisted in February 1865 in the Eighty-seventh Regiment, Pennsylvania Volunteer Infantry; resumed agricultural pursuits near Claysville; school director and justice of the peace; successfully contested as a Democrat the

election of Andrew Stewart to the Fifty-second Congress and served from February 26, 1892, until his death in Claysville, Pa., July 29, 1892; interment in Claysville Cemetery.

**CRAIG, George Henry,** a Representative from Alabama; born in Cahaba, Dallas County, Ala., December 25, 1845; attended the Cahaba Academy; entered the Confederate Army as a private in Colonel Byrd's regiment, Alabama Volunteers, at Mobile, in 1862; attended the University of Alabama at Tuscaloosa as a cadet in 1863; promoted to first lieutenant of Infantry, and in 1863 again entered the Confederate service and remained until the end of the war; resumed his studies at the University of Alabama in 1865; studied law; was admitted to the bar in December 1867 and commenced practice in Selma, Ala.; elected solicitor of Dallas County in 1868; appointed sheriff of Dallas County in March 1869; elected as judge of the criminal court of Dallas County in March 1870; appointed by Governor David P. Lewis in July 1874 judge of the first judicial circuit to fill an unexpired term, was elected to this position on November 4, 1874, and served until 1880; resumed the practice of law in Selma, Ala.; successfully contested as a Republican the election of Charles M. Shelley to the Forty-eighth Congress and served from January 9, 1885, to March 3, 1885; unsuccessful candidate for reelection in 1884 to the Forty-ninth Congress; appointed United States attorney for the middle and northern districts of Alabama by President Chester A. Arthur; was appointed by President Grover Cleveland a member of the Board of Visitors to the United States Military Academy at West Point in 1894; resumed the practice of law in Selma, Ala., and died there January 26, 1923; interment in Live Oak Cemetery.

**CRAIG, Hector,** a Representative from New York; born in Paisley, Scotland, in 1775; immigrated to the United States and settled in Orange County, N.Y., in 1790; founded the town of Craigsville, where he built a paper mill, grist mill, and saw mill; elected to the Eighteenth Congress (March 4, 1823-March 3, 1825); elected as a Jacksonian to the Twenty-first Congress and served from March 4, 1829, to July 12, 1830, when he resigned; appointed surveyor of the port of New York by President Andrew Jackson in 1830; United States Commissioner of Insolvency in 1832; surveyor of customs in New York 1833-1839; died in Craigsville, N.Y., January 31, 1842; interment in a private cemetery on the Caldwell estate in Blooming Grove, N.Y.

**CRAIG, James,** a Representative from Missouri; born in Washington County, Pa., February 28, 1818; attended the public schools; moved to Mansfield, Ohio, in 1821; studied law; and was admitted to the bar in New Philadelphia, Ohio, in 1839; moved to St. Joseph, Mo., in 1844, where he commenced the practice of law; captain of a volunteer company in the Mexican War and served until 1848; State's attorney for the twelfth judicial circuit 1852-1856; member of the State house of representatives in 1856 and 1857; elected as a Democrat to the Thirty-fifth and Thirty-sixth Congresses (March 4, 1857-March 3, 1861); unsuccessful candidate for renomination in 1860 to the Thirty-seventh Congress; resumed the practice of law; was commissioned brigadier general of Volunteers by President Lincoln on March 21, 1862, and commanded the district of Nebraska in the Union department of Kansas; resigned his commission June 4, 1863; member of the Missouri State militia from May 19, 1864 to January 2, 1865; was the first president of the Hannibal & St. Joseph Railroad and the first comptroller of the city of St. Joseph; died in St. Joseph, Mo., October 22, 1888; interment in Mount Mora Cemetery.

**CRAIG, Larry Edwin,** a Representative and a Senator from Idaho; born in Council, Adams County, Idaho, July 20, 1945; attended the Midvale public schools; B.A., University of Idaho, Moscow, Idaho, 1969; graduate work at George Washington University, Washington, D.C., 1970; U.S. Army National Guard

Service, 1970-1974; Washington County Republican Central Committee, chair, 1971-1972; farmer-rancher; member, Idaho State senate, 1974-1980; Young Republican League of Idaho, president, 1976-1977; delegate and member, executive committee, Idaho State Republican conventions, 1976-1978; elected as a Republican to the Ninety-seventh and to the four succeeding Congresses (January 3, 1981-January 3, 1991); was not a candidate for renomination in 1990 to the House of Representatives, but was elected to the United States Senate for the term commencing January 3, 1991 and ending January 3, 1997; chairman, Republican Committee on Committees, chair, Senate Republican Policy Committee (One Hundred Fourth Congress); is a resident of Boise, Idaho.

**CRAIG, Robert,** a Representative from Virginia; born near Christiansburg, Montgomery County, Va., in 1792; attended the rural schools, Washington College (now Washington and Lee University), Lexington, Va., and was graduated from Lewisburg Academy in Greenbrier County; engaged in planting; served in the Virginia house of delegates in 1817, 1818, and again in 1825-1829; member of the Virginia Board of Public Works, 1820-1823; elected as a Jacksonian to the Twenty-first and Twenty-second Congresses (March 4, 1829-March 3, 1833); unsuccessful candidate for reelection in 1832 to the Twenty-third Congress; resumed agricultural pursuits; elected as a Jacksonian to the Twenty-fourth Congress and reelected as a Democrat to the Twenty-fifth and Twenty-sixth Congresses (March 4, 1835-March 3, 1841); chairman, Committee on Revolutionary Claims (Twenty-fifth and Twenty-sixth Congresses); was not a candidate for renomination in 1840 to the Twenty-seventh Congress; moved to Roanoke County, Va., in 1842 and engaged in agricultural pursuits; again a member of the Virginia house of delegates, 1850-1852; died on his estate, "Green Hill," near Salem, Roanoke County, Va., November 25, 1852; interment in the family burying ground at "Green Hill."

**CRAIG, Samuel Alfred,** a Representative from Pennsylvania; born in Brookville, Jefferson County, Pa., November 19, 1839; attended the common schools of his native town and Washington and Jefferson College, Canonsburg, Pa.; learned the printer's trade and taught school; enlisted in the Union Army as a private April 19, 1861; promoted successively to second lieutenant, first lieutenant, and captain of Company B, One Hundred and Fifth Regiment, Pennsylvania Volunteer Infantry; commissioned captain in the Veteran Reserve Corps, United States Army, and served continuously four years and three months; studied law; was admitted to the bar in 1876 and commenced practice in Brookville, Pa.; elected district attorney of Jefferson County in 1878; elected as a Republican to the Fifty-first Congress (March 4, 1889-March 3, 1891); unsuccessful candidate for renomination in 1890 to the Fifty-second Congress; resumed the practice of law in Brookville, Pa., where he died March 17, 1920; interment in Brookville Cemetery.

**CRAIG, William Benjamin,** a Representative from Alabama; born in Selma, Dallas County, Ala., November 2, 1877; attended the public and high schools of Selma and was graduated from the law department of Cumberland University, Lebanon, Tenn.; was admitted to the bar in 1898 and commenced practice in Selma, Ala.; served an apprenticeship as a machinist in the shops of the Southern Railway at Selma from 1893 to 1897; served in the Alabama National Guard as a private, noncommissioned officer, and captain; member of the State senate 1903-1907; elected as a Democrat to the Sixtieth and Sixty-first Congresses (March 4, 1907-March 3, 1911); declined to be a candidate for renomination in 1910 to the Sixty-second Congress; resumed the practice of law in Selma, Ala.; died in Selma, Ala., November 27, 1925; interment in Live Oak Cemetery.

**CRAIGE, Francis Burton,** a Representative from North Carolina; born near Salisbury, Rowan County, N.C., March 13, 1811; attended a private school in Salisbury, and was graduated from the University of North Carolina at Chapel Hill in 1829; editor and proprietor of the Western Carolinian 1829-1831; studied law; was admitted to the bar in 1832 and commenced practice in Salisbury; one of the last borough representatives in the State house of representatives 1832-1834; elected as a Democrat to the Thirty-third and to the three succeeding Congresses (March 4, 1853-March 3, 1861); chairman, Committee on Public Buildings and Grounds (Thirty-third Congress); delegate to the State secession convention in 1861 and introduced the ordinance of secession in the form in which it was adopted; delegate to the Provisional Congress of the Confederate States which met in Richmond, Va., in July 1861; died in Concord, Cabarrus County, N.C., while attending the courts of that county, December 30, 1875; interment in Old English Cemetery, Salisbury, N.C.

**CRAIK, William,** a Representative from Maryland; born near Port Tobacco, Md., October 31, 1761; attended Delameve School in Frederick County; studied law; was admitted to the bar and commenced practice in Port Tobacco and Leonardtown; moved to Baltimore; was appointed chief justice of the fifth judicial district of Maryland January 13, 1793, and served until his resignation in 1796; elected as a Federalist to the Fourth Congress to fill the vacancy caused by the resignation of Jeremiah Crabb; reelected to the Fifth and Sixth Congresses and served from December 5, 1796, to March 3, 1801; again appointed chief justice of the fifth judicial district of Maryland and served from October 20, 1801, to January 28, 1802; resided in Frederick, Md.; died prior to 1814.

**CRAIL, Joe,** a Representative from California; born in Fairfield, Jefferson County, Iowa, December 25, 1877; attended the public schools and was graduated from Drake University, Des Moines, Iowa, in 1898; during the Spanish-American War enlisted as a private in the Twelfth Company, United States Volunteer Signal Corps; promoted to corporal and served in the American Army of Occupation in Cuba until its withdrawal; studied law at Iowa College of Law, Des Moines, Iowa; was admitted to the bar in 1903 and commenced practice in Fairfield, Iowa; moved to California in 1913, settled in Los Angeles, and practiced law until elected to Congress; served as chairman of the Republican State central committee for southern California 1918-1920; elected as a Republican to the Seventieth, Seventy-first, and Seventy-second Congresses (March 4, 1927-March 3, 1933); was not a candidate for renomination in 1932, but was an unsuccessful candidate for nomination as United States Senator; resumed the practice of law; also engaged in banking; died in Los Angeles, Calif., March 2, 1938; interment in Inglewood Park Mausoleum, Inglewood, Calif.

**CRAIN, William Henry,** a Representative from Texas; born in Galveston, Tex., November 25, 1848; attended the Christian Brothers' School, New York City, until the age of fourteen, and was graduated from St. Francis Xavier's College, New York City, in 1867; returned to Texas and lived on a ranch for two years; studied law in Indianola, Tex., while teaching school; was admitted to the bar in 1871 and commenced practice in Indianola, Tex.; member of the State senate 1876-1878; district attorney of the twenty-third judicial district of Texas 1872-1876; elected as a Democrat to the Forty-ninth and to the five succeeding Congresses and served from March 4, 1885, until his death in Washington, D.C., February 10, 1896; chairman, Committee on Expenditures on Public Buildings (Fifty-third Congress); interment in Hillside Cemetery, Cuero, Tex.

**CRALEY, Nathaniel Neiman, Jr.,** a Representative from Pennsylvania; born in Red Lion, York County, Pa., November 17, 1927; attended public schools and York Collegiate Institute; graduated from the Taft School, Watertown, Conn., in 1946 and from Gettysburg College in 1950; engaged in furniture manufacturing from 1950 until 1965; treasurer of the York County Planning Commission, 1959-1965; director and first vice president of the York County Council of Community Services, 1960-1964; director of the York County Council for Human Relations, 1960-1963; chairman of the York County Democratic committee, 1962-1964; instructor in economics and history at York Junior College, 1958-1959; elected as a Democrat to the Eighty-ninth Congress (January 3, 1965-January 3, 1967); unsuccessful candidate for reelection in 1966 to the Ninetieth Congress; Commissioner for Public Affairs, Trust Territory of the Pacific Islands, 1967-1972; special assistant to the High Commissioner, 1972-1976; executive director, Plebiscite Commission, Northern Mariana Islands, 1975; special assistant to the Resident Commissioner, Commonwealth of Northern Mariana Islands, 1976-1978; director for administration, Trust Territory of the Pacific Islands, 1978-1981; special assistant to the High Commissioner, 1981-1985; chairman, York County Democratic Committee, 1990-1993; is a resident of York County, Pa.

**CRAMER, John,** a Representative from New York; born in Waterford, N.Y., May 17, 1779; attended the rural schools and was graduated from Union College, Schenectady, N.Y., in 1801; studied law; was admitted to the bar and commenced practice in Waterford, N.Y.; presidential elector on the ticket of Jefferson and Clinton in 1804; appointed a master in chancery in 1805; member of the State assembly in 1806 and 1811; served in the State senate 1823-1825; delegate to the State constitutional convention in 1821; elected as a Jacksonian to the Twenty-third and Twenty-fourth Congresses (March 4, 1833-March 3, 1837); again a member of the State assembly in 1842; died in Waterford, Saratoga County, N.Y., June 1, 1870; interment in Waterford Rural Cemetery.

**CRAMER, Robert E., Jr. (Bud),** a Representative from Alabama; born in Huntsville, Madison County, Ala., August 22, 1947; graduated, Huntsville High School, 1965; B.A., University of Alabama, 1969; J.D., University of Alabama School of Law, 1972; admitted to Alabama bar in 1972; practicing attorney; Madison County district attorney, 1981-1990; elected as a Democrat to the One Hundred Second and to the two succeeding Congresses (January 3, 1991-January 3, 1997); is a resident of Huntsville, Ala.

**CRAMER, William Cato,** a Representative from Florida; born in Denver, Colo., August 4, 1922; moved with his parents to St. Petersburg, Fla., in 1925; attended the public schools; attended St. Petersburg Junior College, 1941-1943; enlisted in the Naval Reserve in 1943 and served as a gunnery officer until discharged as a lieutenant in 1946; was cited for his activities during the invasion of southern France; A.B., University of North Carolina, Chapel Hill, 1946; LL.B., Harvard University Law School, 1948; was admitted to the Florida bar in 1948 and commenced the practice of law in St. Petersburg, Fla.; served in the Florida State house of representatives, 1950-1952, and served as minority leader in 1951; unsuccessful candidate for election in 1952 to the Eighty-third Congress; delegate or alternate delegate to the Republican National Conventions, 1952-1984; Republican National Committeeman from Florida, 1964-1984; county attorney for Pinellas County in 1953 and 1954; elected as a Republican to the Eighty-fourth and to the seven succeeding Congresses (January 3, 1955-January 3, 1971); was not a candidate in 1970 for reelection to the House of Representatives, but was an unsuccessful candidate for election to the United States Senate; is a resident of St. Petersburg, Fla.

**Bibliography:** Hathorn, Billy B. "Cramer v. Kirk: The Florida Republican Schism of 1970." *Florida Historical Quarterly* 68 (April 1990): 403-426.

**CRAMTON, Louis Convers,** a Representative from Michigan; born in Hadley Township, Lapeer County, Mich., December 2, 1875; attended the common schools of the county; was graduated from the Lapeer High School in 1893 and from the law department of the University of Michigan at Ann Arbor in 1899; was admitted to the bar in 1899 and commenced practice in Lapeer, Mich.; discontinued the practice of his profession in 1905 and published the Lapeer County Clarion from 1905 until 1923; law clerk of the State senate for three terms; deputy commissioner of railroads of Michigan in 1907; secretary of the Michigan Railroad Commission from September 1907 to January 1, 1909; member of the State house of representatives in 1909 and 1910; elected as a Republican to the Sixty-third and to the eight succeeding Congresses (March 4, 1913-March 3, 1931); unsuccessful candidate for renomination in 1930 to the Seventy-second Congress; special assistant to Secretary of the Interior Ray L. Wilbur in 1931 and 1932; circuit judge of the fortieth judicial circuit from November 21, 1934, to December 31, 1941; delegate to the Republican National Convention of 1940; resumed the practice of law; member, Michigan State house of representatives, 1948-1960; died in Saginaw, Mich., June 23, 1966; interment in Mt. Hope Cemetery, Lapeer, Mich.

**CRANE, Daniel Bever** (brother of Philip Miller Crane), a Representative from Illinois; born in Chicago, Ill., January 10, 1936; attended the public schools of Chicago; A.B., Hillsdale (Mich.) College, 1958; D.D.S., Indiana University, 1963; engaged in graduate work at the University of Michigan, 1964-1965; dentist; served in the United States Army, captain, 1967-1970; elected as a Republican to the Ninety-sixth and to the two succeeding Congresses (January 3, 1979-January 3, 1985); unsuccessful candidate for reelection in 1984 to the Ninety-ninth Congress; resumed the practice of dentistry; is a resident of Danville, Ill.

**CRANE, Joseph Halsey** (grandson of Stephen Crane), a Representative from Ohio; born in Elizabethtown (now Elizabeth), N.J., August 31, 1782; was a student at Princeton College; studied law; was admitted to the bar of New Jersey in 1802 and practiced; moved to Dayton, Ohio, in 1804 and continued the practice of law; member of the Ohio State house of representatives in 1809; prosecuting attorney of Montgomery County, 1813-1816; elected president judge of the court of common pleas in 1817; elected to the Twenty-first and Twenty-second Congresses, elected as an Anti-Jacksonian to the Twenty-third Congress, and elected as a Whig to the Twenty-fourth Congress (March 4, 1829-March 3, 1837); declined to be a candidate for renomination in 1836 to the Twenty-fifth Congress; resumed the practice of his profession in Dayton; associate justice of the supreme court of Ohio at the time of his death in Dayton, Ohio, on November 13, 1851; interment in Woodland Cemetery.

**CRANE, Philip Miller** (brother of Daniel B. Crane), a Representative from Illinois; born in Chicago, Cook County, Ill., November 3, 1930; attended DePauw University, 1948-1950; University of Michigan, 1952-1954; the University of Vienna, 1953-1956; B.A., Hillsdale College, Hillsdale, Mich., 1952; M.A., Indiana University, Bloomington, Ind., 1961, and Ph.D., 1963; LL.D., Grove City College (PA), 1975; served with the United States Army, 1954-1956; taught at Indiana University, 1959-1962; assistant professor of history, Bradley University, 1963-1967; public relations, Republican Party, 1962; director of research for the Illinois presidential campaign of Barry M. Goldwater in 1964; director of schools, Westminster Academy, Northbrook, Ill., 1967-1968; at the request of Richard M. Nixon, served as one of his advisers and researchers on political and national issues from 1964-1968; director, Intercollegiate Studies Institute since 1968; president, American Public Affairs Educational Fund, Washington, D.C., since 1965; elected as a Republican to the Ninety-first Congress, by special election, November 25, 1969, to fill the vacancy caused by the resignation of Donald H. Rumsfeld; reelected to the thirteen succeeding Congresses and served from November 25, 1969, to January 3, 1997; is a resident of Mount Prospect, Ill.

**CRANE, Stephen** (grandfather of Joseph Halsey Crane), a Delegate from New Jersey; born in Elizabethtown (now Elizabeth), N.J., in July 1709; sheriff of Essex County; was chosen by the Elizabethtown Associates to go to England and lay a petition before King George II in 1743; member of the town committee in 1750; judge of the court of common pleas during the agitation over the stamp act; member of the New Jersey general assembly, 1766-1773, and served as speaker in 1771; mayor of Elizabethtown, 1772-1774; was appointed chairman of the county committee of New Brunswick in 1774; Member of the Continental Congress, 1774-1776; chairman of the town committee in 1776; member of the State council in 1776, 1777, and 1779; died in Elizabeth, N.J., on July 1, 1780; interment in the First Presbyterian Church Cemetery.

**CRANE, Winthrop Murray,** a Senator from Massachusetts; born in Dalton, Mass., April 23, 1853; attended the public schools of Dalton, Wilbraham Academy, Wilbraham, Mass., and Williston Seminary, Easthampton, Mass.; engaged in the manufacture of paper at Dalton; Lieutenant Governor of Massachusetts, 1897-1899; elected Governor of Massachusetts in 1899, reelected in 1900 and 1901, and served from January 4, 1900 to January 8, 1903; appointed Secretary of the Treasury by President Theodore Roosevelt in 1902, but declined; appointed and subsequently elected as a Republican to the United States Senate to fill the vacancy caused by the death of George F. Hoar; reelected in 1907 and served from October 12, 1904, to March 3, 1913; declined to be a candidate for reelection in 1912; chairman, Committee on Canadian Relations (Fifty-ninth and Sixtieth Congresses), Committee on Rules (Sixty-first and Sixty-second Congresses); resumed his former business pursuits; died in Dalton, Mass., October 2, 1920; interment in Dalton Cemetery.

Bibliography: *DAB*; Griffin, Solomon B. *W. Murray Crane, A Man and Brother.* Boston: Little, Brown and Company, 1926; Johnson, Carolyn. *Winthrop Murray Crane: Republican Leadership, 1892-1920.* Northampton, Mass.: Smith College, 1967.

**CRANFORD, John Walter,** a Representative from Texas; born near Grove Hill, Clarke County, Ala., in 1862; attended the common and high schools of Alabama and finished preparatory studies under a private tutor; moved to Texas about 1880 and settled at Sulphur Springs; studied law; was admitted to the bar and commenced practice in Texas; member of the State senate 1888-1896; elected president pro tempore of the twenty-second senate; elected as a Democrat to the Fifty-fifth Congress and served from March 4, 1897, until his death in Washington, D.C., March 3, 1899; interment in the City Cemetery, Sulphur Springs, Tex.

**CRANSTON, Alan MacGregor,** a Senator from California; born in Palo Alto, Santa Clara County, Calif., June 19, 1914; attended the public schools in Los Altos, Calif., Pomona College, 1932-1933, and the University of Mexico, 1933; A.B., Stanford University, Palo Alto, Calif., 1936; correspondent for the International News Service, covering Great Britain, Germany, Italy, and Ethiopia during 1937-1938; chief, foreign language division, Office of War Information, 1940-1944; enlisted in the United States Army in 1944 and served until the conclusion of the Second World War; national president, United World Federalists, 1949-1952; founder and president of the California Democratic Council, 1953-1957; elected State controller of California in 1958, and reelected in 1962; unsuccessful candidate in 1964 for nomination to the United States Senate, and in 1966 for reelection as State controller; pursued a business career in land investment and home construction; elected as a Democrat to the United States Senate in 1968; reelected in 1974, 1980, and again in 1986, and served from January 3, 1969 to January 3, 1993; was not a candidate for reelection in 1992; Democratic whip (Ninety-fifth through One Hundred Second Congresses); chairman, Committee on Veterans' Affairs (Ninety-fifth, Ninety-sixth, One Hundredth through One Hundred Second

Congresses); chairman, Gorbachev Foundation, USA; president, United States-Kyrgyz Business Council; senior international adviser, Schooner Capital Corp.; is a resident of Los Angeles, Calif.

**CRANSTON, Henry Young** (brother of Robert Bennie Cranston), a Representative from Rhode Island; born in Newport, R.I., October 9, 1789; attended the public schools; engaged in mercantile pursuits in New Bedford, Mass.; moved to Newport, R.I., in 1810, and engaged in the commission business until 1815; studied law; was admitted to the bar in 1819 and commenced practice in Newport; clerk of the court of common pleas, 1818-1833; member of the Rhode Island State house of representatives, 1827-1843; member and vice president of the convention that framed the State constitution in 1842; elected as a Law and Order candidate to the Twenty-eighth Congress; reelected as a Whig to the Twenty-ninth Congress (March 4, 1843-March 3, 1847); again a member of the State house of representatives, 1847-1854, and served three years as speaker; died in Newport, R.I., February 12, 1864; interment in Island Cemetery.

**CRANSTON, Robert Bennie** (brother of Henry Young Cranston), a Representative from Rhode Island; born in Newport, R.I., January 14, 1791; attended the public schools; employed in the collection of internal revenue from 1812 to 1815; sheriff of Newport County, 1818-1827; postmaster of Newport in 1827; elected as a Whig to the Twenty-fifth and to the two succeeding Congresses (March 4, 1837-March 3, 1843); member of the Rhode Island State house of representatives, 1843-1847, and served one year as speaker; served in the State senate; elected as a Whig to the Thirtieth Congress (March 4, 1847-March 3, 1849); was elected the first mayor of Newport on June 9, 1853, and resigned the same day; presidential elector on the Republican ticket in 1864; died in Newport, R.I., January 27, 1873; interment in Common Burial Ground.

**CRAPO, Michael Dean,** a Representative from Idaho; born in Idaho Falls, Bonneville County, Idaho, May 20, 1951; graduated, Idaho Falls High School, 1969; B.A., Brigham Young University, Provo, Utah, 1973; J.D., Harvard University School of Law, 1977; attorney; member, Idaho State senate, 1985-1993; elected as a Republican to the One Hundred Third and One Hundred Fourth Congresses (January 3, 1993-January 3, 1997); is a resident of Idaho Falls, Idaho.

**CRAPO, William Wallace,** a Representative from Massachusetts; born in Dartmouth, Mass., May 16, 1830; moved with his parents to New Bedford, Mass., in 1832; attended private and public schools of New Bedford, and was graduated from the local high school in 1845; attended Phillips Academy, Andover, Mass., and later the Friends' Academy at New Bedford; was graduated from the latter institution in 1848 and from Yale College in 1852; studied law at Harvard Law School for one year; was admitted to the bar in 1855 and commenced practice in New Bedford; city solicitor of New Bedford 1855-1867; member of the Massachusetts house of representatives in 1857; elected to the Forty-fourth Congress to fill the vacancy caused by the death of James Buffington; reelected as a Republican to the Forty-fifth, Forty-sixth, and Forty-seventh Congresses and served from November 2, 1875, to March 3, 1883; chairman, Committee on Banking and Currency (Forty-seventh Congress); was not a candidate for renomination in 1882 to the Forty-eighth Congress; resumed the practice of law and also engaged in banking and in the manufacture of fine cotton goods; member of the Republican National Committee in 1884; appointed by Governor Roger Wolcott in 1897 a member of the commission to revise street railway regulations; died in New Bedford, Mass., February 28, 1926; interment in the Rural Cemetery.

**CRARY, Isaac Edwin,** a Representative from Michigan; born in Preston, New London County, Conn., October 2, 1804; attended the public schools, and was graduated from Trinity College, Hartford, Conn., in its first class in 1827; studied law; was admitted to the bar and commenced practice in Marshall, Mich., in 1833; delegate to the State constitutional convention in 1835; upon the admission of Michigan as a State into the Union was elected as a Jacksonian to the Twenty-fourth Congress and as a Democrat to the Twenty-fifth and Twenty-sixth Congresses and served from January 26, 1837, to March 3, 1841; regent of the University of Michigan 1837-1844; founded the public-school system of Michigan; member of the State board of education 1850-1852; editor of the Marshall Expounder for several years; member of the State house of representatives 1842-1846, and speaker of the house in 1846; died in Marshall, Calhoun County, Mich., on May 8, 1854; interment in Oakridge Cemetery.

**Bibliography:** *DAB*.

**CRAVENS, James Addison** (second cousin of James Harrison Cravens), a Representative from Indiana; born in Rockingham County, Va., November 4, 1818; moved with his father to Indiana in 1820 and settled near Hardinsburg, Madison Township, Washington County; attended the public schools; engaged in agricultural pursuits and stock raising; served in the war with Mexico as major of the Second Indiana Volunteers in 1846 and 1847; member of the Indiana State house of representatives in 1848 and 1849; served in the State senate, 1850-1853; commissioned brigadier general of militia in 1854; elected as a Democrat to the Thirty-seventh and Thirty-eighth Congresses (March 4, 1861-March 3, 1865); was not a candidate for renomination in 1864 to the Thirty-ninth Congress; delegate to the Union National Convention of Conservatives at Philadelphia in 1866, and to the Democratic National Convention of 1868; resumed agricultural pursuits; died in Hardinsburg, Washington County, Ind., June 20, 1893; interment in the Hardin Cemetery.

**CRAVENS, James Harrison** (second cousin of James Addison Cravens), a Representative from Indiana; born in Harrisonburg, Rockingham County, Va., August 2, 1802; studied law; was admitted to the bar in 1823 and commenced practice in Harrisonburg, Va.; moved to Franklin, Pa., in 1823 and resumed the practice of law; moved to Madison, Ind., in 1829 and engaged in agricultural pursuits; member of the State house of representatives in 1831 and 1832; moved to Ripley County, Ind., in 1833, where he practiced law and managed a farm; member of the State senate in 1839; elected as a Whig to the Twenty-seventh Congress (March 4, 1841-March 3, 1843); unsuccessful candidate of the Free-Soil Party for Governor of Indiana in 1852, member of the State house of representatives in 1856; unsuccessful candidate for election to the attorney generalship of the State in 1856; lieutenant colonel of the Eighty-third Regiment, Indiana Volunteer Infantry, in the Civil War; he and his soldiers were taken captive during John Hunt Morgan's July 1863 raid in Indiana; died in Osgood, Ripley County, Ind., December 4, 1876; interment in Versailles Cemetery, Versailles, Ind.

**CRAVENS, Jordan Edgar** (cousin of William Ben Cravens), a Representative from Arkansas; born in Fredericktown, Madison County, Mo., November 7, 1830; moved with his father to Arkansas the following year; attended the common schools, and was graduated from the Cane Hill Academy at Boonsboro (now Canehill), Washington County, Ark., in 1850; studied law; was admitted to the bar in 1854 and commenced practice in Clarksville, Ark.; member of the Arkansas State house of representatives in 1860; entered the Confederate Army in 1861 as a private, promoted to colonel in 1862, and continued in the service until the close of the Civil War; returned to Clarksville; prosecuting attorney of Johnson County, 1865-1866; Arkansas State senator, 1866-1868; elected as an Independent Democrat to the Forty-fifth Congress; reelected as a Democrat to the Forty-sixth and Forty-seventh Congresses (March

4, 1877-March 3, 1883); was an unsuccessful candidate for renomination in 1882 to the Forty-eighth Congress; resumed the practice of law in Clarksville, Ark.; judge of the circuit court, 1890-1894; died in Fort Smith, Ark., April 8, 1914; interment in Oakland Cemetery, Clarksville, Ark.

**CRAVENS, William Ben** (father of William Fadjo Cravens and cousin of Jordan Edgar Cravens), a Representative from Arkansas; born in Fort Smith, Sebastian County, Ark., January 17, 1872; attended the common schools, Louisville (Ky.) Military Academy, and Staunton (Va.) Military Academy; was graduated from the law department of the University of Missouri at Columbia in 1893; was admitted to the Arkansas bar the same year and commenced practice in Fort Smith, Ark.; city attorney of Fort Smith, 1898-1902; served as prosecuting attorney for the twelfth judicial district of Arkansas 1902-1908; elected as a Democrat to the Sixtieth and to the two succeeding Congresses (March 4, 1907-March 3, 1913); was not a candidate for reelection in 1912 to the Sixty-third Congress; resumed the practice of law; elected to the Seventy-third and to the three succeeding Congresses, and served from March 4, 1933 until his death in Washington, D.C., on January 13, 1939; interment in Oak Cemetery, Fort Smith, Ark.

**CRAVENS, William Fadjo** (son of William Ben Cravens), a Representative from Arkansas; born in Fort Smith, Sebastian County, Ark., February 15, 1899; attended the public schools, the University of Arkansas at Fayetteville, the University of Pittsburgh, Pittsburgh, Pa., and was graduated from the law school of Washington and Lee University, Lexington, Va., in 1920; was admitted to the bar in 1920 and commenced practice at Fort Smith, Ark.; during the First World War served as a seaman in the United States Navy; city attorney of Fort Smith, Ark., for ten years; elected as a Democrat to the Seventy-sixth Congress, September 12, 1939, by special election to fill the vacancy caused by the death of his father, William Ben Cravens; reelected to the four succeeding Congresses, and served from September 12, 1939 to January 3, 1949; was not a candidate for renomination in 1948 to the Eighty-first Congress; died in Fort Smith, Ark., April 16, 1974; interment in Forest Park.

**CRAWFORD, Coe Isaac,** a Senator from South Dakota; born near Volney, Allamakee County, Iowa, January 14, 1858; attended the common schools and was instructed by a private tutor; was graduated from the law department of the University of Iowa at Iowa City in 1882; was admitted to the bar and commenced practice at Independence, Iowa; moved to Pierre, Territory of Dakota, in 1883 and continued the practice of law; prosecuting attorney of Hughes County in 1887 and 1888; member, Territorial council 1889; upon the admission of South Dakota as a State was elected as a member of the first State senate; attorney general of South Dakota 1892-1896; unsuccessful Republican candidate in 1896 for Representative at Large to the Fifty-fifth Congress; attorney for the Chicago & North Western Railway Co. for the area around South Dakota 1897-1903, when he resigned; moved to Huron in 1897; elected Governor of South Dakota in 1906 and served from January 8, 1907 to January 5, 1909; elected as a Republican to the United States Senate and served from March 4, 1909, to March 3, 1915; unsuccessful candidate for renomination in 1914; chairman, Committee on Expenditures in the Interior Department (Sixty-first Congress), Committee on Claims (Sixty-second Congress); resumed the practice of law in Huron, S.Dak., until 1934, when he retired from active business and political life; died in Yankton, S.Dak., April 25, 1944; interment in Municipal Cemetery, Iowa City, Iowa.

**Bibliography:** Armin, Calvin. "Coe I. Crawford and the Progressive Movement in South Dakota." Ph.D. dissertation, University of Colorado, 1957; Meyer, Edward L. "Coe I. Crawford and the Persuasion of Progressive Movement in South Dakota." Ph.D. dissertation, University of Minnesota, 1975.

**CRAWFORD, Fred Lewis,** a Representative from Michigan; born in Dublin, Erath County, Tex., May 5, 1888; attended the public schools, business college at Peniel, Tex., and the University of Michigan at Ann Arbor; engaged in accountancy at Des Moines, Iowa, and Detroit, Mich., 1914-1917; built, financed, and operated beet sugar mills in various sections of the United States 1917-1935; also engaged in manufacturing, ranching, and overland transportation; director of the Michigan National Bank and the Refiners Transport & Petroleum Corp. of Detroit, Mich., at time of death; elected as a Republican to the Seventy-fourth and to the eight succeeding Congresses and served from January 3, 1935, to January 3, 1953; unsuccessful candidate for renomination in 1952; retired to his farm at Allentown, Prince Georges County, Md.; died in Washington, D.C., April 13, 1957; interment in Cedar Hill Cemetery.

**CRAWFORD, George Washington,** a Representative from Georgia; born in Columbia County, Ga., December 22, 1798; was graduated from Princeton College in 1820; studied law; was admitted to the bar in 1822 and commenced practice in Augusta, Ga.; attorney general of Georgia, 1827-1831; member of the Georgia State house of representatives, 1837-1842; elected as a Whig to the Twenty-seventh Congress to fill the vacancy caused by the death of Richard W. Habersham and served from January 7, 1843, to March 3, 1843; elected Governor of Georgia in 1843, reelected in 1845, and served from November 8, 1843 to November 3, 1847; appointed Secretary of War in the Cabinet of President Zachary Taylor, and served from March 8, 1849 to July 23, 1850; presided over the State secession convention in 1861; died on his estate, "Bel Air," near Augusta, Ga., July 27, 1872; interment in Summerville Cemetery.

**Bibliography:** *DAB*; Cleveland, Len G. "George W. Crawford of Georgia, 1798-1872." Ph.D. dissertation, University of Georgia, 1974.

**CRAWFORD, Joel,** a Representative from Georgia; born in Columbia County, Ga., June 15, 1783; completed preparatory studies; studied law at the Litchfield Law School; was admitted to the bar and commenced practice in Sparta in 1808; moved to Milledgeville, Ga., in 1811; served in the war against the Creek Indians as second lieutenant and aide-de-camp to Brigadier General Floyd in 1813 and 1814; resumed the practice of law in Milledgeville; member of the State house of representatives 1814-1817; elected as a Republican to the Fifteenth Congress and reelected to the Sixteenth Congress (March 4, 1817-March 3, 1821); returned to Sparta, Hancock County, in 1828; member of the State senate in 1827 and 1828; appointed a commissioner to run the boundary line between Alabama and Georgia in 1826; unsuccessful candidate for Governor of Georgia in 1828 and 1831; delegate to the International Improvement Convention in 1831; elected in 1837 a State commissioner to locate and construct the Western & Atlantic Railroad; died near Blakely, Early County, Ga., April 5, 1858; interment in the family burying ground on his plantation in Early County, Ga.

**CRAWFORD, Martin Jenkins,** a Representative from Georgia; born in Jasper County, Ga., March 17, 1820; attended Brownwood Institute and Mercer University, Macon, Ga.; studied law; was admitted to the bar in 1839 and practiced in Hamilton, Ga.; also engaged in agricultural pursuits; member of the State house of representatives 1845-1847; moved to Columbus, Ga., in 1849; delegate to the Southern convention at Nashville in May 1850; judge of the superior courts of the Chattahoochee circuit from February 1, 1854, to November 1854; elected as a Democrat to the Thirty-fourth and to the two succeeding Congresses and served from March 4, 1855, until January 23, 1861, when he joined other secessionist members of the Georgia delegation in withdrawing from the Thirty-sixth Congress; elected to the Confederate Provisional Congress and served from January 1861 to February 22, 1862; appointed by Jefferson Davis a special commissioner to the

Government of the United States; raised the Third Georgia Cavalry Regiment in May 1862; served with it one year, and was then placed on the staff with Major General Howell Cobb, where he served until the close of the Civil War; appointed judge of the superior court of the Chattahoochee circuit to fill a vacancy caused by the resignation of Judge James Johnson on October 1, 1875; reappointed in 1877 and served until February 9, 1880, when he resigned; appointed February 10, 1880, to the supreme court of Georgia to fill a vacancy; reappointed, and served until his death in Columbus, Ga., July 23, 1883; interment in Linnwood Cemetery.

**Bibliography:** *DAB*.

**CRAWFORD, Thomas Hartley,** a Representative from Pennsylvania; born in Chambersburg, Franklin County, Pa., November 14, 1786; was graduated from Princeton College in 1804; studied law; was admitted to the bar in 1807 and commenced practice in Chambersburg; elected as a Jacksonian to the Twenty-first and Twenty-second Congresses (March 4, 1829-March 3, 1833); member of the Pennsylvania house of representatives in 1833 and 1834; appointed a commissioner to investigate alleged frauds in the sale of the Creek Reservation in 1836; appointed Commissioner of Indian Affairs by President Martin Van Buren and served from October 22, 1838, to October 30, 1845; appointed by President James K. Polk as judge of the criminal court of the District of Columbia in 1845 and served until 1861, when the court was reorganized; died in Washington, D.C., on January 27, 1863; interment in the Congressional Cemetery.

**CRAWFORD, William,** a Representative from Pennsylvania; born in Paisley, Scotland, in 1760; received a liberal schooling; studied medicine at the University of Edinburgh, and in 1781 received his degree; immigrated to the United States and settled near Gettysburg, Adams County, Pa.; purchased a farm on Marsh Creek in 1785, where he spent the rest of his life practicing medicine; associate judge for Adams County 1801-1808; elected as a Republican to the Eleventh and to the three succeeding Congresses (March 4, 1809-March 3, 1817); again resumed the practice of medicine near Gettysburg, Pa., where he died on October 23, 1823; interment in Evergreen Cemetery, Gettysburg, Pa.

**CRAWFORD, William Harris,** a Senator from Georgia; born in Nelson County, Va., February 24, 1772; moved with his father to Edgefield District, S.C., in 1779 and to Columbia County, Ga., in 1783; pursued classical studies in a private school and in Richmond Academy, Augusta, Ga.; studied law; was admitted to the bar and commenced practice in Lexington, Ga., in 1799; appointed to prepare a digest of the laws of Georgia in 1799; member, State house of representatives 1803-1807; elected to the United States Senate to fill the vacancy caused by the death of Abraham Baldwin and served from November 7, 1807, to March 23, 1813, when he resigned; served as President pro tempore of the Senate during the Twelfth Congress; declined the portfolio of Secretary of War tendered by President James Madison in 1813; appointed Minister to France in April 1813 and served until April 1815; returned home to act as agent for the sale of the land donated by Congress to the Marquis de Lafayette; appointed Secretary of War by President Madison on August 1, 1815; transferred to the Treasury Department on October 22, 1816 and served under Presidents Madison and James Monroe until March 7, 1825; unsuccessful Democratic candidate for President of the United States in 1824; due to illness refused the tender of President John Quincy Adams that he remain Secretary of the Treasury; returned to Georgia and was appointed judge of the northern circuit court in 1827, which position he held until his death in Oglethorpe County, Ga., September 15, 1834; interment on his estate, "Woodlawn," near Crawford, Oglethorpe County, Ga.

**Bibliography:** *DAB*; Green, Philip. *The Life of William Crawford.* Chapel Hill: University of North Carolina Press, 1965; Mooney, Chase. *William H. Crawford, 1772-1834.* Lexington: University of Kentucky Press, 1974.

**CRAWFORD, William Thomas,** a Representative from North Carolina; born near Waynesville, Haywood County, N.C., June 1, 1856; attended the public schools and Waynesville Academy; member of the State house of representatives 1884-1888; engrossing clerk of the State house of representatives in 1889; was graduated from the law department of the University of North Carolina at Chapel Hill in 1890; was admitted to the bar in 1891 and commenced practice in Waynesville; elected as a Democrat to the Fifty-second and Fifty-third Congresses (March 4, 1891-March 3, 1895); delegate to the American Bimetallic League in Washington, D.C., in 1893; unsuccessful candidate for reelection in 1894 to the Fifty-fourth Congress; presented credentials as a Member-elect to the Fifty-sixth Congress and served from March 4, 1899, to May 10, 1900, when he was succeeded by Richmond Pearson, who contested the election; unsuccessful candidate for election in 1900 to the Fifty-seventh Congress; delegate to the Democratic State conventions 1900-1912; delegate to the gubernatorial convention in 1908; elected as a Democrat to the Sixtieth Congress (March 4, 1907-March 3, 1909); unsuccessful candidate for reelection in 1908 to the Sixty-first Congress; resumed the practice of law in Waynesville, N.C., where he died November 16, 1913; interment in Green Hill Cemetery.

**CREAGER, Charles Edward,** a Representative from Oklahoma; born near Dayton, Montgomery County, Ohio, April 28, 1873; attended the public schools of Ohio, and Northern Indiana University; engaged in the newspaper business; enlisted as sergeant major in the Fourth Ohio Volunteer Infantry during the Spanish-American War and served under Major General Nelson D. Miles in the Puerto Rican campaign; city editor of the Columbus Press-Post 1899-1901; editor of the Daily Leader, Marietta, Ohio, 1902-1904; moved to Muskogee, Indian Territory (now Oklahoma) in November 1904 and engaged in the newspaper business, later becoming publisher and editor of several Oklahoma newspapers; elected as a Republican to the Sixty-first Congress (March 4, 1909-March 3, 1911); unsuccessful candidate for reelection in 1910 to the Sixty-second Congress; employed in the United States Indian Service and later engaged in oil production until 1934, when he retired; was a resident of Muskogee, Okla., until his death there on January 11, 1964; interment in Greenhill Cemetery.

**CREAL, Edward Wester,** a Representative from Kentucky; born in a log house near Mount Sherman, Larue County, Ky., November 20, 1883; attended the public schools of Hart and Larue Counties, Ky.; taught school for nine years in Larue County and between teaching terms attended Southern Normal School at Bowling Green, Ky., and East Lynn College at Buffalo, Ky.; was graduated from the law department of Centre College, Danville, Ky., in 1906; was admitted to the bar in 1904 and commenced practice in Hodgenville, Ky., in 1910; county superintendent of schools of Larue County, Ky., 1910-1918; county attorney 1918-1928; Commonwealth attorney 1929-1936; owner and publisher of a weekly newspaper in Hodgenville, Ky., from 1918 until the time of his death; member of the Kentucky Democratic executive committee 1924-1940; elected as a Democrat to the Seventy-fourth Congress to fill the vacancy caused by the death of Cap R. Carden; reelected to the Seventy-fifth and to the three succeeding Congresses and served from November 5, 1935, until his death in Hodgenville, Ky., on October 13, 1943; interment in Red Hill Cemetery.

**CREAMER, Thomas James,** a Representative from New York; born near Garadice Lake, Ireland, May 26, 1843; immigrated to the United States and took up his residence in New York City; attended the public schools; shipping clerk in a dry-goods house in 1860; studied law; was admitted to the bar and practiced; member of the State assembly 1865-1867; served in the State senate 1868-1871; city tax commissioner for five years; acted as counsel for State commissions to revise the tax laws; elected as a Democrat to the

Forty-third Congress (March 4, 1873-March 3, 1875); was not a candidate for renomination in 1874; elected to the Fifty-seventh Congress (March 4, 1901-March 3, 1903); was not a candidate for renomination in 1902; resumed the practice of law in New York City, and died there August 4, 1914; interment in Greenwood Cemetery.

**CREBS, John Montgomery,** a Representative from Illinois; born in Middleburg, Loudoun County, Va., April 9, 1830; moved to Illinois in 1837 with his parents, who settled in White County; attended the public schools; studied law; was admitted to the bar in 1852 and commenced practice in White County, Ill.; served in the Union Army, and was commissioned lieutenant colonel, Eighty-seventh Regiment, Illinois Infantry, in 1862; took part in the Mississippi, Vicksburg, and Arkansas campaigns; commanded a brigade of Cavalry in the Department of the Gulf; after the close of the war resumed the practice of law; elected as a Democrat to the Forty-first and Forty-second Congresses (March 4, 1869-March 3, 1873); unsuccessful candidate for renomination in 1872 to the Forty-third Congress; engaged in the practice of his profession until his death in Carmi, White County, Ill., June 26, 1890; interment in Maple Ridge Cemetery.

**CREELY, John Vaudain,** a Representative from Pennsylvania; born in Philadelphia, Pa., November 14, 1839; received a classical education; studied law; was admitted to the bar in 1862 and practiced in Philadelphia; during the Civil War served with the Union Army as an officer of Light Artillery; member of the Philadelphia city council for four years; elected as an Independent Republican to the Forty-second Congress (March 4, 1871-March 3, 1873); before his term of service had expired he mysteriously disappeared, and upon the application of his sister, Adelaide G. Creely, to whom was awarded his estate, he was declared legally dead on September 28, 1900, by the orphans' court of Philadelphia.

**CREIGHTON, William, Jr.,** a Representative from Ohio; born in Berkeley County, Va., October 29, 1778; was graduated from Dickinson College, Carlisle, Pa.; studied law; was admitted to the bar in 1798 and commenced practice in Chillicothe, Ohio; secretary of state 1803-1808; member of the State house of representatives in 1810; elected as a Republican to the Thirteenth Congress to fill the vacancy caused by the resignation of Duncan McArthur; reelected to the Fourteenth Congress and served from May 4, 1813, to March 3, 1817; unsuccessful candidate for election in 1815 to the United States Senate; president of the branch bank of the United States at Chillicothe; elected to the Twentieth Congress and served from March 4, 1827, until his resignation in 1828; was appointed during the recess of Congress and nominated by President John Quincy Adams on December 11, 1828, as a United States judge of the district court, but the Senate on February 16, 1829, passed a resolution that it was "not expedient to fill the vacancy at the present session of Congress"; reelected to the Twenty-first and Twenty-second Congresses (March 4, 1829-March 3, 1833); was not a candidate for renomination in 1832 to the Twenty-third Congress; resumed the practice of law; died in Chillicothe, Ross County, Ohio, October 1, 1851; interment in Grandview Cemetery.

**Bibliography:** *DAB.*

**CREMEANS, Frank A.,** a Representative from Ohio; born in Cheshire, Gallia County, Ohio, April 5, 1943; graduated from Kyger Creek Local, 1961; B.A., University of Rio Grande, Ohio, 1966; M.A., Ohio University, Athens, 1969; teacher; assistant superintendent of schools for Gallia County, Ohio, then superintendent for Kyger Creek Local School District; owner of concrete, crane and rigging business; elected as a Republican to the One Hundred Fourth Congress (January 3, 1995-January 3, 1997); is a resident of Gallipolis, Ohio.

**CRESWELL, John Angel James,** a Representative and a Senator from Maryland; born at Creswells Ferry (now Port Deposit), Cecil County, Md., November 18, 1828; attended the local academy at Port Deposit; was graduated from Dickinson College, Carlisle, Pa., in 1848; studied law; was admitted to the bar in Baltimore in 1850 and commenced practice in Elkton, Md.; unsuccessful candidate for election on the Whig ticket in 1850 to the Reform State Convention; member of the Maryland State house of delegates in 1861; affiliated with the Republican Party in 1861; adjutant general of Maryland, 1862-1863; elected as a Republican to the Thirty-eighth Congress (March 4, 1863-March 3, 1865); unsuccessful candidate for reelection in 1864 to the Thirty-ninth Congress; elected to the United States Senate to fill the vacancy caused by the death of Thomas H. Hicks, and served from March 9, 1865 to March 3, 1867; chairman, Committee on Library (Thirty-ninth Congress); was elected secretary of the United States Senate in 1868, but declined to serve; appointed Postmaster General by President Ulysses S. Grant, and served from March 5, 1869 to July 6, 1874, when he resigned; served as counsel of the United States before the Alabama Claims Commission, 1874-1876; resumed the practice of law; president of two banks; died near Elkton, Cecil County, Md., December 23, 1891; interment in Elkton Presbyterian Cemetery.

**Bibliography:** *DAB*; Friedenberg, Robert V. "John A.J. Creswell of Maryland: Reformer in the Post Office." *Maryland Historical Magazine* 64 (Summer 1969): 133-143.

**CRETELLA, Albert William,** a Representative from Connecticut; born in New Haven, Conn., April 22, 1897; attended the public schools of New Haven; graduated from Yale University in 1917; entered Yale University Law School, but interrupted his studies and enlisted in the United States Navy on June 18, 1918; was in officers training school when the Armistice was signed; reentered Yale Law School and graduated in 1921; was admitted to the Connecticut bar the same year and began practice in New Haven; moved to North Haven in 1926 and served as prosecuting attorney, 1931-1945, and town counsel, 1931-1970, excluding the years 1946 and 1947; member of the Connecticut State house of representatives, 1947-1952; elected as a Republican to the Eighty-third and to the two succeeding Congresses (January 3, 1953-January 3, 1959); unsuccessful candidate for reelection in 1958 to the Eighty-sixth Congress, and for election in 1960 to the Eighty-seventh Congress; engaged in the practice of law; died in New Haven, Conn., May 24, 1979; interment in St. Lawrence Cemetery, West Haven, Conn.

**CRIPPA, Edward David,** a Senator from Wyoming; born in Rock Springs, Sweetwater County, Wyo., April 8, 1899; attended the public schools; during the First World War served as a private in the United States Army; councilman of Rock Springs, 1926-1928; president of Union Mercantile Company in 1930; owner and manager of Crippa Motor Company, Rock Springs, Wyo.; president of North Side State Bank and director of the Rock Springs Fuel Company in 1940; Wyoming State highway commissioner, 1941-1947; appointed as a Republican to the United States Senate to fill the vacancy caused by the death of Lester C. Hunt, and served from June 24, 1954 to November 28, 1954; was not a candidate for election to fill the vacancy; resumed his business activities; died in Rock Springs, Wyo., October 20, 1960; interment in St. Josephs Cemetery.

**CRISFIELD, John Woodland,** a Representative from Maryland; born near Chestertown, Kent County, Md., November 8, 1806; was educated at Washington College, Chestertown; studied law; was admitted to the bar in 1830 and commenced practice in Princess Anne, Somerset County; member of the State house of representatives in 1836; elected as a Whig to the Thirtieth Congress (March 4, 1847-March 3, 1849); delegate to the State constitutional convention in 1850; member of the peace conference of 1861 held in Washington, D.C., in an effort to devise means to prevent the impending war;

elected as a Unionist to the Thirty-seventh Congress (March 4, 1861-March 3, 1863); unsuccessful candidate for reelection in 1862 to the Thirty-eighth Congress; resumed the practice of law; delegate to the Union National Convention at Philadelphia in 1866; located and founded the town of Crisfield, Somerset County, Md., in 1866; instrumental in building the Eastern Shore Railroad and served as president; died in Princess Anne, Md., on January 12, 1897; interment in Manokin Presbyterian Cemetery.

**CRISP, Charles Frederick** (father of Charles Robert Crisp), a Representative from Georgia; born in Sheffield, England, January 29, 1845; later in that year his parents immigrated to the United States and settled in Georgia; attended the common schools of Savannah and Macon, Ga.; entered the Confederate Army in May 1861; commissioned lieutenant in Company K, Tenth Regiment, Virginia Infantry, and served with that regiment until May 12, 1864, when he became a prisoner of war; upon his release from Fort Delaware in June 1865 joined his parents at Ellaville, Schley County, Ga.; studied law at Americus, Ga.; was admitted to the bar in 1866 and commenced practice in Ellaville; appointed solicitor general of the southwestern judicial circuit in 1872, and reappointed in 1873 for a term of four years; appointed judge of the superior court of the same circuit in June 1877; elected by the general assembly to the same office in 1878; reelected judge for a term of four years in 1880; resigned that office in September 1882 to accept nomination for Congress; president of the Democratic gubernatorial convention at Atlanta in April 1883; elected as a Democrat to the Forty-eighth and to the six succeeding Congresses, and served from March 4, 1883 until his death in Atlanta, Ga., October 23, 1896; chairman, Committee on Elections (Fiftieth Congress), Committee on Rules (Fifty-second and Fifty-third Congress); Speaker of the House of Representatives (Fifty-second and Fifty-third Congresses); had been nominated for United States Senator in the Georgia primary of 1896; interment in Oak Grove Cemetery, Atlanta, Ga.

**Bibliography:** *DAB*; Malone, Preston St. Clair. "The Political Career of Charles Frederick Crisp." Ph.D. dissertation, University of Georgia, 1962; Martin, S. Walter. "Charles F. Crisp: Speaker of the House." *Georgia Review* 8 (Summer 1954): 167-77; Schlup, Leonard. "Mr. Speaker: Charles F. Crisp and American Politics, 1891-1896." *Journal of Southwest Georgia History* 10 (Fall 1995): 1-22.

**CRISP, Charles Robert** (son of Charles Frederick Crisp), a Representative from Georgia; born in Ellaville, Schley County, Ga., October 19, 1870; attended the public schools of Americus, Ga.; clerk in the Interior Department, Washington, D.C., 1889-1891; parliamentarian of the House of Representatives, 1891-1895; studied law; was admitted to the bar in 1895 and commenced practice in Americus, Sumter County, Ga.; elected as a Democrat to the Fifty-fourth Congress to fill the vacancy caused by the death of his father, Charles F. Crisp, and served from December 19, 1896 to March 3, 1897; was not a candidate for renomination in 1896 to the Fifty-fifth Congress; resumed the practice of law in Americus, Ga.; judge of the city court of Americus, 1900-1912; again parliamentarian of the House of Representatives in the Sixty-second Congress, 1911-1913; parliamentarian of the Democratic National Convention of 1912; elected to the Sixty-third and to the nine succeeding Congresses, and served from March 4, 1913 until October 7, 1932, when he resigned to become a member of the United States Tariff Commission, in which capacity he served until December 30, 1932; was not a candidate in 1932 for renomination to the House of Representatives, but was an unsuccessful candidate for nomination to the United States Senate to fill the vacancy caused by the death of William J. Harris; member of the American World War Debt Funding Commission; resumed the practice of his chosen profession in Washington, D.C.; died in Americus, Ga., February 7, 1937; interment in Oak Grove Cemetery.

**CRIST, Henry,** a Representative from Kentucky; born in Fredericksburg, Spotsylvania County, Va., October 20, 1764; moved with his father to Pennsylvania, where he attended the public schools; moved to Kentucky and engaged in the surveying of lands; moved to Bullitt County, Ky., in 1788 and engaged in the manufacture of salt; member of the Kentucky house of representatives in 1795 and 1806; served in the Kentucky senate 1800-1804; elected as a Republican to the Eleventh Congress (March 4, 1809-March 3, 1811); was a Whig after the organization of that party; died near Shepherdsville, Bullitt County, Ky., August 11, 1844; interment in State Cemetery, Frankfort, Ky.

**CRITCHER, John,** a Representative from Virginia; born at Oak Grove, Westmoreland County, Va., on March 11, 1820; attended Brent's Preparatory School; was graduated from the University of Virginia at Charlottesville in 1839, and later pursued higher studies in France for three years; studied law; was admitted to the bar in 1842 and commenced practice in Westmoreland County, Va.; served in the State senate 1861 and 1874-1877; member of the Virginia secession convention in 1861; served as lieutenant colonel of Cavalry in the Confederate Army during the Civil War; appointed judge of the eighth judicial circuit of Virginia, but was removed under the resolution of Congress dated February 18, 1869, which provided that anyone who had borne arms against the United States should be dismissed from office within thirty days; elected as a Democrat to the Forty-second Congress (March 4, 1871-March 3, 1873); died in Alexandria, Va., September 27, 1901; interment in the Episcopal Cemetery.

**CRITTENDEN, John Jordan** (uncle of Thomas Theodore Crittenden), a Senator and a Representative from Kentucky; born near Versailles, Woodford County, Ky., September 10, 1786; completed preparatory studies; attended Pisgah Academy, Woodford County, Ky., Washington College (now Washington and Lee University), Lexington, Va., and was graduated from the College of William and Mary, Williamsburg, Va., in 1806; studied law; was admitted to the bar and commenced practice in Woodford County, Ky., in 1807; attorney general of Illinois Territory, 1809-1810; served in the War of 1812 as aide to the Governor; resumed the practice of law in Russellville, Ky.; member, Kentucky house of representatives, 1811-1817, and served as speaker the last term; elected to the United States Senate and served from March 4, 1817, to March 3, 1819, when he resigned; chairman, Committee on Judiciary (Fifteenth Congress); moved to Frankfort, Ky., in 1819; member, Kentucky house of representatives, 1825, 1829-1832; appointed and was confirmed as United States district attorney in 1827, but was removed by President Andrew Jackson in 1829; nominated on December 17, 1828 by President John Quincy Adams as an Associate Justice of the United States Supreme Court, but the nomination was postponed by the Senate on February 12, 1829, and not taken up again; elected to the United States Senate as a Whig, and served from March 4, 1835 to March 3, 1841; appointed Attorney General in the Cabinet of President William Henry Harrison, and served from March 5 to September 13, 1841; appointed and subsequently elected to the United States Senate to fill the vacancy caused by the resignation of Henry Clay, and served from March 31, 1842 to June 12, 1848, when he resigned; chairman, Committee on Military Affairs (Twenty-seventh and Twenty-eighth Congresses); elected Governor of Kentucky in 1848, and served from June 1, 1848 until his resignation on July 31, 1850; again appointed Attorney General by President Millard Fillmore, and served from July 22, 1850 until March 7, 1853; again elected to the United States Senate, and served from March 4, 1855 to March 3, 1861; chairman, Committee on Revolutionary Claims (Thirty-sixth Congress); sponsor of the "Crittenden Compromise" of 1860-1861, a series of constitutional amendments and supplementary resolutions designed to avert possible civil war; elected as a Unionist to the Thirty-seventh Congress (March 4, 1861-March 3, 1863); was a candidate for reelection at the time of his death; died in Frankfort, Ky., July 26, 1863; interment in State Cemetery, Frankfort, Ky.

**Bibliography:** *DAB*; Kirwan, Albert D. *John J. Crittenden: The Struggle for Union.* Lexington: Kentucky University Press, 1962; Ledbetter, Patsy S. "John J. Crittenden and the Compromise Debacle." *Filson Club History Quarterly* 51 (April 1977): 125-42.

**CRITTENDEN, Thomas Theodore** (nephew of John Jordan Crittenden), a Representative from Missouri; born near Shelbyville, Shelby County, Ky., January 1, 1832; attended the primary schools at Cloverport, Ky.; was graduated from Centre College, Danville, Ky., in 1855; served as registrar of Franklin County in 1856; studied law in Frankfort, Ky.; was admitted to the bar in 1858 and commenced practice in Lexington, Mo.; served in the Union Army, being commissioned captain April 19, 1861, and colonel April 27, 1861; commissioned brigadier general United States Volunteers, April 28, 1862; captured at Murfreesboro, Tenn., on July 13, 1862, he later returned to active duty and resigned his commission May 5, 1863; moved to Warrensburg, Johnson County, Mo. in 1865 and continued the practice of law; appointed attorney general of Missouri by Governor Willard P. Hall in 1864 to fill out the unexpired term of Aikman Welch, deceased; elected as a Democrat to the Forty-third Congress (March 4, 1873-March 3, 1875); was not a candidate for renomination in 1874 to the Forty-fourth Congress; elected to the Forty-fifth Congress (March 4, 1877-March 3, 1879); elected Governor of Missouri in 1880 and served from January 10, 1881 to January 12, 1885; moved to Kansas City in 1885 and continued the practice of law; United States consul general at Mexico City from April 5, 1893, to 1897; referee in bankruptcy from 1898 until his death in Kansas City, Mo., May 29, 1909; interment in Forest Hill Cemetery.

**Bibliography:** *DAB*; Powers, P. Joseph. "'Yours Very Truly, Thos. T. Crittenden': A Missouri Democrat's Observations of the Election of 1896." *Missouri Historical Review* 68 (January 1974): 186-203; Scholes, Walter V. "Mexico in 1896 as Viewed by an American Consul." *Hispanic American Historical Review* 30 (May 1950): 250-57.

**CROCHERON, Henry** (brother of Jacob Crocheron), a Representative from New York; born on Staten Island, Richmond County, N.Y., December 26, 1772; attended the common schools; engaged in mercantile pursuits in Northfield; supervisor of Northfield 1808-1814; elected as a Republican to the Fourteenth Congress (March 4, 1815-March 3, 1817); captain of militia in 1818; died in New Springville, Richmond County, N.Y., on November 8, 1819; interment in St. Andrew's Churchyard, Richmond County, Staten Island, N.Y.

**CROCHERON, Jacob** (brother of Henry Crocheron), a Representative from New York; born on Staten Island, Richmond County, N.Y., August 23, 1774; engaged in agricultural pursuits; sheriff of Richmond County in 1802, 1811, and again in 1821; elected as a Jacksonian to the Twenty-first Congress (March 4, 1829-March 3, 1831); died in Richmond County, Staten Island, on December 27, 1849; interment in St. Andrew's Churchyard, Staten Island, N.Y.

**CROCKER, Alvah,** a Representative from Massachusetts; born in Leominster, Mass., October 14, 1801; attended the public schools and Groton Academy; proprietor of paper manufactories at Fitchburg; president of the Boston & Fitchburg Railroad; member of the Hoosac Tunnel Commission; member of the Massachusetts house of representatives in 1836, 1842, and 1843; served in the Massachusetts senate for two terms; elected as a Republican to the Forty-second Congress to fill the vacancy caused by the resignation of William B. Washburn; reelected to the Forty-third Congress and served from January 2, 1872, until his death in Fitchburg, Mass., December 26, 1874; interment in Laurel Hill Cemetery.

**Bibliography:** *DAB*; Wheelwright, William Bond. *Life and Times of Alvah Crocker.* 1923. Reprint. New York: Arno Press, 1981.

**CROCKER, Samuel Leonard,** a Representative from Massachusetts; born in Taunton, Mass., March 31, 1804; was graduated from Brown University, Providence, R.I., in 1822; engaged in manufacturing; member of the executive council of Massachusetts in 1849; elected as a Whig to the Thirty-third Congress (March 4, 1853-March 3, 1855); unsuccessful candidate for reelection in 1854 to the Thirty-fourth Congress; president of the Taunton Copper Manufacturing Co.; died in Boston, Mass., February 10, 1883; interment in Mount Pleasant Cemetery, Taunton, Bristol County, Mass.

**CROCKETT, David** (father of John Wesley Crockett), a Representative from Tennessee; born at the confluence of Limestone Creek and Noli-Chuckey River in the State of Franklin, which a few years later became Greene County, Tenn., August 17, 1786; attended the common schools for a short time; moved to Lincoln County about 1808 and to what is now Gibson County in 1822; commanded a battalion of mounted riflemen under General Andrew Jackson in the Creek campaign in 1813 and 1814; member, Tennessee State house of representatives, 1821-1823; unsuccessful candidate for election in 1825 to the Nineteenth Congress; elected to the Twentieth and Twenty-first Congresses (March 4, 1827-March 3, 1831); unsuccessful candidate for reelection in 1830 to the Twenty-second Congress; elected as an Anti-Jacksonian to the Twenty-third Congress (March 4, 1833-March 3, 1835); unsuccessful candidate for reelection in 1834 to the Twenty-fourth Congress; went to Texas in 1836 to aid the Texans in their struggle for independence from Mexico; joined a band of one hundred eighty-six men in the defense of the Alamo, San Antonio de Bexar, and was among those killed in that battle which terminated on March 6, 1836; his body destroyed by pyre at the Alamo.

Bibliography: *DAB*; Crockett, David. *A Narrative of the Life of David Crockett of the State of Tennessee.* Edited by James A. Shackford and Stanley J. Folmsbee. Knoxville: University of Tennessee Press, 1973; Derr, Mark. *The Frontiersman: The Real Life and the Many Legends of Davy Crockett.* New York: William Morrow and Co., 1993; Shackford, James Atkins. *David Crockett: The Man and the Legend.* 1986. Reprint. Edited by John B. Shackford. Introduction by Michael A. Lofaro. Lincoln: University of Nebraska Press, 1994.

**CROCKETT, George William, Jr.,** a Representative from Michigan; born in Jacksonville, Duval County, Fla., August 10, 1909; attended the public schools; A.B., Morehouse College, Atlanta, Ga., 1931; J.D., University of Michigan Law School, Ann Arbor, 1934; admitted to the Florida bar in 1934 and commenced practice in Jacksonville; senior attorney, United States Department of Labor, 1939-1943; hearing officer, Federal Fair Employment Practices Commission, 1943; moved to Detroit, Mich. in 1944 and served as director of the Fair Employment Practices Department of the United Automobile Workers; senior member of a law firm in Detroit, 1950-1966; elected judge, recorder's court, Detroit, 1967-1979; acting corporation counsel, city of Detroit, 1980; elected as a Democrat to the Ninety-sixth Congress, November 4, 1980, by special election to fill the vacancy caused by the resignation of Charles C. Diggs, Jr., and at the same time elected to the Ninety-seventh Congress; reelected to the four succeeding Congresses, and served from November 4, 1980 to January 3, 1991; was not a candidate for reelection in 1990 to the One Hundred Second Congress; is a resident of Detroit, Mich.

**CROCKETT, John Wesley** (son of David Crockett), a Representative from Tennessee; born in Trenton, Tenn., July 10, 1807; attended the public schools; studied law; was admitted to the bar and commenced practice in Paris, Tenn.; held various local and State offices; was elected as a Whig to the Twenty-fifth and Twenty-sixth Congresses (March 4, 1837-March 3, 1841); elected by the State legislature attorney general for the ninth district of

Tennessee, and served from 1841 to 1843; moved to New Orleans in 1843 and engaged in business as a commission merchant; became editor of the National on May 22, 1848, and established the Crescent in 1850; moved to Memphis, Tenn., in 1852, where he died on November 24, 1852; interment in the Old City Cemetery, Paris, Tenn.

**CROFT, George William** (father of Theodore Gaillard Croft), a Representative from South Carolina; born in Newberry County, S.C., December 20, 1846; attended the common schools in Greenville, S.C.; entered the South Carolina Military Academy at Charleston in 1863; the cadets of that institution were mustered into the Confederate Army in 1864 and served until the close of the Civil War; attended the University of Virginia at Charlottesville in 1866 and 1867; studied law; was admitted to the bar in 1869 and commenced practice in Aiken, S.C., in 1870; president of the State bar association; member of the State house of representatives, 1882-1883 and 1901-1902; served in the State senate; elected as a Democrat to the Fifty-eighth Congress and served from March 4, 1903, until his death in Washington, D.C., on March 10, 1904; interment in St. Thaddeus' Episcopal Churchyard, Aiken, S.C.

**CROFT, Theodore Gaillard** (son of George William Croft), a Representative from South Carolina; born in Aiken, Aiken County, S.C., November 26, 1874; attended the common schools; was graduated from Bethel Military Academy, Warrenton, Va., in 1895 and from the law department of the University of South Carolina at Columbia in 1897; was admitted to the bar the same year and commenced practice in Aiken, S.C.; elected as a Democrat to the Fifty-eighth Congress to fill the vacancy caused by the death of his father, George W. Croft, and served from May 17, 1904 to March 3, 1905; was not a candidate for renomination in 1904 to the Congress; resumed the practice of law in Aiken, S.C.; member of the South Carolina State house of representatives, 1907-1908; served in the State senate, 1909-1912; enlisted in the United States Army on October 29, 1918; was assigned to duty as a private in the Field Artillery Central Officers' Training School, Camp Zachary Taylor, and served until December 5, 1918, when he was honorably discharged; resumed the practice of law; died in Aiken, S.C., March 23, 1920; interment in St. Thaddeus' Episcopal Churchyard.

**CROLL, William Martin,** a Representative from Pennsylvania; born in Upper Macungie Township, Lehigh County, Pa., April 9, 1866; attended the public schools and Keystone State Normal School, Kutztown, Pa.; was graduated from Eastman Business College at Poughkeepsie, N.Y.; taught school; moved to Maxatawny in 1889 and engaged in the general merchandise business; moved to Reading, Pa., in 1897 and engaged in the retail clothing business and in banking; treasurer of Berks County 1909-1912; served as naval officer, port of Philadelphia, from 1913 to 1918; delegate to the Democratic National Conventions in 1912 and 1920; elected as a Democrat to the Sixty-eighth Congress (March 4, 1923-March 3, 1925); unsuccessful candidate for reelection in 1924 to the Sixty-ninth Congress; resumed mercantile pursuits; died in Reading, Pa., October 21, 1929; interment in Laureldale Cemetery, Laureldale, Pa.

**CROMER, George Washington,** a Representative from Indiana; born near Anderson, Madison County, Ind., May 13, 1856; attended the common schools and Wittenberg College, Springfield, Ohio, and was graduated from the Indiana University at Bloomington in 1882; became editor of the Muncie (Ind.) Times in 1883; studied law; was admitted to the bar in 1886 and commenced practice in Muncie, Delaware County, Ind.; prosecuting attorney for the forty-sixth judicial circuit of Indiana 1886-1890; member of the State Republican committee in 1892 and 1894; mayor of Muncie 1894-1898; elected as a Republican to the Fifty-sixth and to the three succeeding Congresses (March 4, 1899-March 3, 1907); unsuccessful candidate for reelection in 1906 to the Sixtieth

Congress; resumed the practice of his profession in Muncie, Ind., until his death in that city November 8, 1936; interment in Beech Grove Cemetery.

**CRONIN, Paul William,** a Representative from Massachusetts; born in Boston, Suffolk County, Mass., March 14, 1938; B.A., Boston University, 1962; M.P.A., John F. Kennedy Graduate School of Government, Harvard University, 1969; elected selectman, town of Andover at age 23; Massachusetts house of representatives, 1967-1969; chief assistant to Representative F. Bradford Morse in Washington, D.C.; delegate to Massachusetts State Republican conventions, 1962-1972; delegate to the Republican National Conventions of 1968 and 1972; elected as a Republican to the Ninety-third Congress (January 3, 1973-January 3, 1975); unsuccessful candidate for reelection in 1974 to the Ninety-fourth Congress; president, Sunsav Inc., 1975-1986; president, Highline Industries, Inc., 1986 to present; is a resident of Andover, Mass.

**CROOK, Thurman Charles,** a Representative from Indiana; born on a farm near Peru, Miami County, Ind., July 18, 1891; attended the Cass County schools, Logansport High School, Indiana State Normal, Purdue University, Indiana University, and graduated from Valparaiso University in 1930; learned the carpentry and cement trades; taught departmental work and coached athletics in Indiana high schools 1913-1948; member of the State house of representatives 1939-1943; served in the State senate 1943-1947; fruit grower near Logansport, Ind., 1924-1947; unsuccessful for the Democratic nomination in 1946 to the Eightieth Congress; elected as a Democrat to the Eighty-first Congress (January 3, 1949-January 3, 1951); unsuccessful candidate for reelection in 1950 to the Eighty-second Congress and for election in 1956 to the Eighty-fifth Congress; farmer, horticulturist, and sheep raiser; was a resident of Macy, Ind., until his death in Rochester, Ind., on October 23, 1981.

**CROOKE, Philip Schuyler,** a Representative from New York; born in Poughkeepsie, N.Y., March 2, 1810; was graduated from Dutchess Academy in Poughkeepsie; studied law; was admitted to the bar in 1831 and commenced practice in Brooklyn, N.Y.; moved to Flatbush in 1838; member of the Board of Supervisors of Kings County 1844-1852 and 1858-1870, and chairman of the board in 1861, 1862, 1864, and 1865; presidential elector on the Democratic ticket in 1852; elected a member of the general assembly as a Republican in 1863; served forty years in the National Guard of the State of New York, from private to brigadier general, and during the Civil War commanded the Fifth Brigade, National Guard, in Pennsylvania in June and July 1863; elected as a Republican to the Forty-third Congress (March 4, 1873-March 3, 1875); was not a candidate for renomination in 1874 to the Forty-fourth Congress; resumed the practice of law; died in Flatbush, N.Y., March 17, 1881; interment in Greenwood Cemetery, Brooklyn, N.Y.

**CROSBY, Charles Noel,** a Representative from Pennsylvania; born September 29, 1876, in a farming settlement named Cherry Valley, near Andover, Ashtabula County, Ohio; attended preparatory schools, New Lyme (Ohio) Institute, and Allegheny College, Meadville, Pa.; was graduated from Western Reserve University, Cleveland, Ohio, in 1897; moved to Linesville, Pa., in 1901, engaging in the manufacture of silos and in the lumber business; engaged in agricultural pursuits in 1914; member of the Linesville and Meadville (Pa.) Boards of Education 1920-1929; president of the Meadville Chamber of Commerce 1922-1924; elected as a Democrat to the Seventy-third and to the two succeeding Congresses (March 4, 1933-January 3, 1939); unsuccessful candidate for renomination in 1938 to the Seventy-sixth Congress; moved to Montgomery County, Md., in 1940 and operated a large dairy farm near Clarksburg; died in Frederick, Md., January 26, 1951; interment in Columbia Gardens Cemetery, Arlington, Va.

**CROSBY, John Crawford,** a Representative from Massachusetts; born in Sheffield, Berkshire County, Mass., on June 15, 1859; attended the public schools of Pittsfield; was graduated from Eastman Business College, Poughkeepsie, N.Y., and from Boston University Law School, Boston, Mass.; was admitted to the bar in 1882 and commenced practice in Pittsfield, Berkshire County, Mass.; member of the school committee of Pittsfield 1884-1890; served in the Massachusetts house of representatives in 1886 and 1887; member of the Massachusetts senate in 1888 and 1889; director of a bank and of fire and life insurance companies; elected as a Democrat to the Fifty-second Congress (March 4, 1891-March 3, 1893); unsuccessful candidate for reelection in 1892 to the Fifty-third Congress; mayor of Pittsfield, Mass., in 1894 and 1895; delegate to the Democratic National Convention in 1896; city solicitor 1896-1900; appointed justice of the superior court on January 25, 1905, and served until December 31, 1913, when he was appointed justice of the Massachusetts Supreme Judicial Court, in which capacity he served until his retirement on October 1, 1937; died in Pittsfield, Mass., on October 14, 1943; interment in Pittsfield Cemetery.

**CROSS, Edward,** a Representative from Arkansas; born in Hawkins City, Tenn., November 11, 1798; attended the public schools; studied law; was admitted to the bar and practiced; moved to Arkansas in 1826; appointed on May 26, 1830, by President Andrew Jackson as United States judge for the Territory of Arkansas; served as United States surveyor general for Arkansas from April 30, 1836, until September 1, 1838; elected as a Democrat to the Twenty-sixth and to the two succeeding Congresses (March 4, 1839-March 3, 1845); chairman, Committee on Private Land Claims (Twenty-eighth Congress); was not a candidate for renomination in 1844 to the Twenty-ninth Congress; judge of the State supreme court from July 1845 to 1855; president of the Cairo and Fulton (later the St. Louis, Iron Mountain and Southern) Railway 1855-1862; appointed attorney general of Arkansas in 1874; died at his country residence, "Marlbrook," near Washington, Hempstead County, Ark., April 6, 1887; interment on his estate.

**Bibliography:** *DAB.*

**CROSS, Oliver Harlan,** a Representative from Texas; born in Eutaw, Greene County, Ala., July 13, 1868; attended the public schools and was graduated from the University of Alabama at Tuscaloosa in 1891; teacher in the public schools at Union Springs, Ala., in 1891 and 1892; studied law; was admitted to the bar in 1893 and commenced practice in Deming, N.Mex.; moved to McGregor, Tex., in 1894 and continued the practice of law; served as city attorney of McGregor in 1895 and 1896; moved to Waco, Tex., in 1896 and continued the practice of law; assistant attorney of McLennan County 1898-1902; member of the State house of representatives in 1900; district attorney of McLennan County 1902-1906; retired from law practice in 1917 and assumed agricultural pursuits; elected as a Democrat to the Seventy-first and to the three succeeding Congresses (March 4, 1929-January 3, 1937); was not a candidate for renomination in 1936; engaged in agricultural pursuits and in real-estate activities; died in Waco, Tex., April 24, 1960; interment in Hearne Cemetery, Hearne, Tex.

**CROSSER, Robert,** a Representative from Ohio; born in Holytown, Lanarkshire, Scotland, June 7, 1874; immigrated to the United States in 1881 with his parents and settled in Cleveland, Ohio; moved to Salineville, Ohio, the same year and attended the public schools; was graduated from Kenyon College, Gambier, Ohio, in 1897; studied law at Columbia University in New York City and was graduated from Cincinnati Law School in 1901; was admitted to the bar in 1901 and commenced practice in Cleveland, Ohio; taught at the Baldwin-Wallace Law School, 1904-1905; member, Ohio State house of representatives, 1911-1912; member of the fourth constitutional convention in 1912; elected as a Democrat to the Sixty-third and to the two succeeding Congresses (March 4, 1913-March 3, 1919); chairman, Committee on Expenditures in the Department of Commerce (Sixty-fifth Congress); unsuccessful candidate for renomination in 1918 to the Sixty-sixth Congress, and for election in 1920 to the Sixty-seventh Congress; elected to the Sixty-eighth and to the fifteen succeeding Congresses (March 4, 1923-January 3, 1955); chairman, Committee on Interstate and Foreign Commerce (Eighty-first and Eighty-second Congresses); unsuccessful candidate for renomination in 1954 to the Eighty-fourth Congress; resided in Bethesda, Md., until his death there on June 3, 1957; interment in Highland Park Cemetery, Warrensville, Ohio.

Bibliography: *DAB*; Tribe, Henry Franklin. "Disciple of 'Progress and Poverty': Robert Crosser and Twentieth Century Reform." Ph.D. dissertation, Bowling Green State University, 1990.

**CROSSLAND, Edward,** a Representative from Kentucky; born in Hickman County, Ky., June 30, 1827; completed preparatory studies; studied law; was admitted to the bar in 1852 and began practice at Clinton, Hickman County, Ky.; sheriff of Hickman County in 1851 and 1852; member of the Kentucky house of representatives in 1857 and 1858; during the Civil War enlisted as captain in the First Kentucky Regiment, Confederate Army; was elected colonel of the Seventh Kentucky Regiment and served until the end of the war; elected judge of the court of common pleas of the first judicial district of Kentucky in August 1867 for six years, but resigned November 1, 1870; elected as a Democrat to the Forty-second and Forty-third Congresses (March 4, 1871-March 3, 1875); resumed the practice of law in Mayfield, Graves County, Ky.; elected judge of the circuit court for the first judicial district of Kentucky in August 1880 and served until his death in Mayfield, Ky., September 11, 1881; interment in Maplewood Cemetery.

**CROUCH, Edward,** a Representative from Pennsylvania; born at Walnut Hill, near Highspire, Paxtang Township, Lancaster (now Dauphin) County, Pa., on November 9, 1764; attended the common schools; at the age of seventeen enlisted during the Revolutionary War; commanded a company in the Whiskey Rebellion of 1794; engaged in mercantile pursuits at Walnut Hill; member of the Pennsylvania house of representatives, 1804-1806; appointed associate judge of Dauphin County on April 16, 1813, but resigned upon election to Congress; elected as a Republican to the Thirteenth Congress to fill the vacancy caused by the resignation of John Gloninger, and served from October 12, 1813 until March 3, 1815; was not a candidate for renomination in 1814 to the Fourteenth Congress; returned to Walnut Hill, Paxtang Township, Dauphin County, Pa., and resided there until his death on February 2, 1827; interment in Paxtang Cemetery.

**CROUNSE, Lorenzo,** a Representative from Nebraska; born in Sharon, Schoharie County, N.Y., January 27, 1834; attended a seminary at Charlotteville, N.Y.; taught school; moved to Fort Plain, N.Y., in 1855; studied law; was admitted to the bar in 1857; during the Civil War raised a battery of light artillery in 1861 and entered the Army as its captain; wounded, and resigned after a year's service; moved to Nebraska Territory in 1864; member of the Territorial house of representatives in 1866; delegate to the State constitutional convention in 1866; elected associate justice of the State supreme court in 1867; at the expiration of his term was elected as a Republican to the Forty-third and Forty-fourth Congresses (March 4, 1873-March 3, 1877); declined to be a candidate for reelection in 1876 to the Forty-fifth Congress; collector of internal revenue for the district of Nebraska from March 15, 1879, to March 30, 1883; appointed Assistant Secretary of the United States Treasury on April 27, 1891, and served until his resignation on October 31, 1892; elected Governor of Nebraska in 1892, and served from January 1893 to January 1895; died in Omaha, Nebr., May 13, 1909; interment in City Cemetery, Fort Calhoun, Washington County, Nebr.

Bibliography: *DAB*.

**CROUSE, George Washington,** a Representative from Ohio; born in Tallmadge, Summit County, Ohio, November 23, 1832; attended the common schools; taught school for five years; moved to Akron, Ohio; deputy in offices of county auditor and treasurer 1855-1858; auditor of Summit County 1858-1863; served as county treasurer in 1863; manager in 1863 of the Akron branch of C. Altman & Co., dealers in farming implements; upon the organization of Altman, Miller & Co. in 1865, as a separate corporation, became secretary and treasurer, and later its president; during the Civil War served as sergeant in Company F, One Hundred and Sixty-fourth Regiment, Ohio Volunteer Infantry, and served in fortifications around Washington in 1864; member and president of the city council for four years and of the board of education of the city of Akron four years; served as commissioner of Summit County in 1874 and 1875; member of the State senate 1885-1887; elected as a Republican to the Fiftieth Congress (March 4, 1887-March 3, 1889); declined to be a candidate for renomination in 1888; resumed former business activities; died in Akron, Ohio, January 5, 1912; interment in Glendale Cemetery.

**CROW, Charles Augustus,** a Representative from Missouri; born on a farm near Sikeston, Scott County, Mo., March 31, 1873; attended the common schools; moved to a farm near Bernie, Stoddard County, Mo., in August 1896 and engaged in agricultural pursuits; moved to Caruthersville, Pemiscot County, in 1901 and engaged in the real estate and insurance business; postmaster of Caruthersville from May 19, 1902, to January 14, 1909; elected as a Republican to the Sixty-first Congress (March 4, 1909-March 3, 1911); unsuccessful candidate for reelection in 1910 to the Sixty-second Congress; moved to Campbell, Dunklin County, Mo., in 1911 and resumed agricultural pursuits; also engaged in the real estate and insurance business; died in Campbell, Mo., March 20, 1938; interment in Woodlawn Cemetery.

**CROW, William Evans** (father of William J. Crow), a Senator from Pennsylvania; born in German Township, Fayette County, Pa., March 10, 1870; attended the public schools; was graduated from the Southwestern State Normal School in 1890, and also attended Waynesburg College; engaged in newspaper work for three years; studied law; was admitted to the bar in 1895 and commenced practice in Uniontown, Pa.; appointed assistant district attorney in 1896; was elected district attorney in 1898 and served three years; member, Pennsylvania senate 1907-1921, when he resigned, having been appointed United States Senator; president pro tempore of the Pennsylvania senate in 1909 and 1911; appointed as a Republican to the United States Senate on October 17, 1921, to fill the vacancy caused by the death of Philander C. Knox, and served from October 24, 1921, until his death at his home, "Chalk Hill," near Uniontown, Fayette County, Pa., August 2, 1922; interment in Uniontown Cemetery.

**CROW, William Josiah** (son of William Evans Crow), a Representative from Pennsylvania; born in Uniontown, Fayette County, Pa., January 22, 1902; attended the public schools; was graduated from Pennsylvania Military College at Chester in 1922 and from Dickinson School of Law, Carlisle, Pa., in 1925; was admitted to the bar in 1926 and commenced practice in Uniontown, Pa.; assistant district attorney of Fayette County 1928-1932; elected mayor of Uniontown in 1938 and reelected in 1940 for a four-year term and served until called into active service from the Reserves as major of Ordnance June 4, 1941, being forty-one months overseas, in the Pacific theater; elected as a Republican to the Eightieth Congress (January 3, 1947-January 3, 1949); unsuccessful candidate for reelection in 1948 to the Eighty-first Congress; resumed the practice of law; recalled to active duty with the Ordnance Corps in 1951 and served as chief of legislative coordination branch until 1956; became regional administrator, Securities and Exchange

Commission, Washington, D.C., in January 1957; moved to Carlisle, Cumberland County, Pa., after retiring in 1964, and served on the Zoning Board and the Parks Commission; died in Carlisle, Pa., October 13, 1974; interment in Oak Grove Cemetery, Uniontown, Pa.

**CROWE, Eugene Burgess,** a Representative from Indiana; born near Jeffersonville, Clark County, Ind., January 5, 1878; attended the rural schools and Borden (Ind.) Academy; taught in county schools 1894-1896; moved to Bedford, Ind., in 1899 and engaged in the retail furniture business, real estate, and banking; delegate to the Democratic State conventions 1908-1960; delegate to the Democratic National Conventions in 1928, 1944, 1948, 1952, 1956, and 1960; delegate to the Interparliamentary Union Congress at Oslo, Norway, in 1939; elected as a Democrat to the Seventy-second and to the four succeeding Congresses (March 4, 1931-January 3, 1941); unsuccessful candidate for reelection in 1940 to the Seventy-seventh Congress; resumed his former business interests; president of Stone City National Bank and Greystone Hotel; director of Wabash Fire and Casualty Insurance Co.; remained active in business and civic affairs until his death in Indianapolis, Ind., May 12, 1970; interment in Green Hill Cemetery, Bedford, Ind.

**CROWELL, John,** a Delegate from Alabama Territory and a Representative from Alabama; born in Halifax County, N.C., September 18, 1780; attended the public schools; moved to Alabama in 1815, having been appointed as agent of the Government to the Muscogees; settled in St. Stephens, Ala., in 1817; elected as a Delegate to the Fifteenth Congress and served from January 29, 1818, to March 3, 1819; upon the admission of Alabama as a State into the Union was elected a Representative to the Sixteenth Congress and served from December 14, 1819, until March 3, 1821; in 1821 was appointed agent for the Creek Indians, then inhabiting western Georgia and eastern Alabama, and occupied that position until they were moved to the Indian Territory in 1836; died at Fort Mitchell, Ala., June 25, 1846; interment in a private cemetery.

**CROWELL, John,** a Representative from Ohio; born in East Haddam, Middlesex County, Conn., September 15, 1801; moved to Ohio in 1806 with his parents, who settled in Rome, Ashtabula County; attended the district school; moved to Warren, Ohio, in 1822; attended Warren Academy 1822-1825; studied law; was admitted to the bar in 1827 and commenced practice in Warren; was also part owner and editor of the Western Reserve Chronicle at Warren; member of the State senate in 1840; elected as a Whig to the Thirtieth and Thirty-first Congresses (March 4, 1847-March 3, 1851); was not a candidate for renomination in 1850; moved to Cleveland, Ohio, in 1852 and resumed the practice of law; served in the State militia for twenty years, holding the rank of brigadier general and subsequently that of major general; became editor of the Western Law Monthly, published in Cleveland, and a member of the faculty of the Homeopathic Medical College; president of the Ohio State and Union Law College of Cleveland from 1862 to 1876, when he retired; died in Cleveland, Ohio, March 8, 1883; interment in Lake View Cemetery.

**CROWLEY, Joseph Burns,** a Representative from Illinois; born in Coshocton, Coshocton County, Ohio, July 19, 1858; moved with his parents to a farm near St. Marie, Jasper County, Ill., in 1860 and to Robinson, Ill., in 1872; attended the common schools; engaged in mercantile pursuits 1876-1880; studied law; was admitted to the bar in May 1883 and began practice at Robinson, Crawford County, Ill.; president of the Robinson city school board 1884-1888; master in chancery 1886-1890; elected judge of Crawford County in November 1886, and reelected in 1890; appointed United States special Treasury agent in charge of the seal fisheries of Alaska in April 1893 and served until his resignation in April 1898; elected as a Democrat to the Fifty-sixth, Fifty-seventh, and Fifty-eighth Congresses

(March 4, 1899-March 3, 1905); declined to be a candidate for renomination in 1904; resumed the practice of law in Robinson, Ill.; served as State's attorney of Crawford County 1912-1916; died in Robinson, Ill., June 25, 1931; interment in the old Robinson Cemetery.

**CROWLEY, Miles,** a Representative from Texas; born in Boston, Mass., February 22, 1859; attended the common schools; employed as a longshoreman; moved to Galveston in the seventies; assistant chief of the Galveston Fire Department; studied law; was admitted to the bar in 1892 and commenced practice; member of the State house of representatives in 1892; served in the State senate in 1893 and 1894; elected as a Democrat to the Fifty-fourth Congress (March 4, 1895-March 3, 1897); was not a candidate for reelection in 1896; resumed the practice of law in Galveston, Tex.; prosecuting attorney of Galveston County 1904-1912; elected judge of Galveston County Court in 1920, in which capacity he was serving at the time of his death in Galveston, Tex., on September 22, 1921; interment in Calvary Cemetery.

**CROWLEY, Richard,** a Representative from New York; born in Pendleton, near Lockport, Niagara County, N.Y., December 14, 1836; attended the public schools and Lockport Union School; studied law; was admitted to the bar in 1860 and commenced practice in Lockport; city attorney of Lockport in 1865 and 1866; admitted to practice before the Supreme Court of the United States in 1865; member of the State senate 1866-1870; appointed United States district attorney for the northern district of New York by President Ulysses S. Grant on March 23, 1871; reappointed March 3, 1875, and served in that capacity until March 3, 1879; elected as a Republican to the Forty-sixth and Forty-seventh Congresses (March 4, 1879-March 3, 1883); chairman, Committee on Claims (Forty-seventh Congress); unsuccessful candidate for election in 1888 to the Fifty-first Congress; resumed the practice of law in Lockport, N.Y.; appointed by Governor Levi P. Morton in 1896 as counsel for the State of New York in Civil War claims cases, in which capacity he was serving at the time of his death at Olcott Beach, near Lockport, N.Y., July 22, 1908; interment in Glenwood Cemetery.

**CROWNINSHIELD, Benjamin Williams** (brother of Jacob Crowninshield), a Representative from Massachusetts; born in Salem, Mass., December 27, 1772; prepared for college; engaged in mercantile pursuits in Salem, Mass.; member of the Massachusetts house of representatives in 1811; served in the Massachusetts senate in 1812; appointed Secretary of the Navy by President James Madison on December 19, 1814; reappointed by President James Monroe and served in this capacity until October 1, 1818, when he resigned; again a member of the Massachusetts house of representatives in 1821; elected to the Eighteenth and to the three succeeding Congresses (March 4, 1823-March 3, 1831); chairman, Committee on Naval Affairs (Eighteenth Congress); unsuccessful candidate for reelection in 1830 to the Twenty-second Congress; again a member of the Massachusetts house of representatives in 1833; resumed his former business pursuits; died in Boston, Mass., February 3, 1851; interment in Mount Auburn Cemetery, Cambridge, Mass.

Bibliography: *DAB.*

**CROWNINSHIELD, Jacob** (brother of Benjamin Williams Crowninshield), a Representative from Massachusetts; born in Salem, Mass., March 31, 1770; engaged in mercantile pursuits; unsuccessful candidate for election in 1798 to the Sixth Congress to fill the vacancy caused by the resignation of Dwight Foster; member of the Massachusetts senate in 1801; was tendered the position of Secretary of the Navy by President Jefferson, but never entered upon his duties on account of ill health; elected as a Republican to the Eighth and to the two succeeding Congresses and served from March 4, 1803 until his death in Washington, D.C., on April 15,

1808; chairman, Committee on Commerce and Manufactures (Ninth Congress); interment in Harmony Grove Cemetery, Salem, Mass.

**Bibliography:** *DAB*; Reinoehl, John H., ed. "Some Remarks on the American Trade: Jacob Crowninshield to James Madison, 1806." *William and Mary Quarterly* 3rd ser., 16 (January 1959): 83-118.

**CROWTHER, Frank,** a Representative from New York; born in Liverpool, England, July 10, 1870; immigrated to the United States in 1872 with his parents, who settled in Canton, Mass.; attended the public schools; was graduated from the Lowell School of Design, a branch of the Massachusetts Institute of Technology, in 1888; designer of fabrics, carpets, and rugs for seven years; was graduated from Harvard Dental School in 1898 and commenced practice in Boston, Mass.; moved to Perth Amboy, N.J., in 1901 and continued the practice of dentistry; member of the New Jersey house of assembly in 1904 and 1905; member of the Middlesex County Board of Taxation 1906-1909; moved to Schenectady, N.Y., in 1912 and continued the practice of his profession until elected to Congress; president of the common council of Schenectady in 1917 and 1918; elected as a Republican to the Sixty-sixth and to the eleven succeeding Congresses (March 4, 1919-January 3, 1943); chairman, Committee on Memorials (Seventy-first Congress); was not a candidate for renomination in 1942 to the Seventy-eighth Congress; moved to Pueblo, Colo., in 1943 and engaged in violin study, landscape painting, and public speaking; died in Pueblo, Colo., July 20, 1955; interment in Roselawn Cemetery.

**CROWTHER, George Calhoun,** a Representative from Missouri; born in Lancashire, England, on January 26, 1849; immigrated to the United States in 1855 with his parents, who settled in Dakota City, Nebr.; attended the public schools until his tenth year, when he became a printer's apprentice at Sioux City, Iowa; entered the Union Army in 1862, and was mustered out of the service July 14, 1865; moved to Kansas in 1866 and engaged in newspaper work until 1873; elected secretary of the Kansas State senate in January 1869, and reelected in 1871 and 1873; again engaged in the printing and publishing of a newspaper 1875-1886; moved to St. Joseph, Mo., in 1877; appointed deputy sheriff of Buchanan County, Mo., in 1887; elected city treasurer of St. Joseph in 1888 and reelected in 1890; unsuccessful candidate for election in 1892 to the Fifty-third Congress; elected as a Republican to the Fifty-fourth Congress (March 4, 1895-March 3, 1897); unsuccessful candidate for reelection in 1896 to the Fifty-fifth Congress; unsuccessful candidate for mayor of St. Joseph in 1904; engaged in the manufacture of iron and steel in St. Joseph, Mo., until his death there March 18, 1914; interment in Oakland Cemetery.

**CROXTON, Thomas,** a Representative from Virginia; born in Tappahannock, Essex County, Va., March 8, 1822; attended the primary schools and the Tappahannock and Rappahannock Academies; was graduated from the law department of the University of Virginia at Charlottesville in 1842; was admitted to the bar and commenced practice in Tappahannock, Essex County, Va.; served as attorney for the Commonwealth from 1852 to 1865, when he resigned; during the Civil War served on the staff of General George E. Pickett; elected as a Democrat to the Forty-ninth Congress (March 4, 1885-March 3, 1887); unsuccessful candidate for reelection in 1886 to the Fiftieth Congress; resumed the practice of law; also engaged in agricultural pursuits; elected judge of Essex County, Va., and served from 1892 until his resignation in 1901; died in Tappahannock, Va., July 3, 1903; interment in St. John's Episcopal Churchyard.

**CROZIER, John Hervey,** a Representative from Tennessee; born in Knoxville, Tenn., February 10, 1812; attended the public schools; was graduated from the University of Tennessee at Knoxville in 1829; studied law; was admitted to the Tennessee bar and practiced in Knoxville; member of the State house of representatives 1837-1839; elected as a Whig to the Twenty-ninth and Thirtieth Congresses (March 4, 1845-March 3, 1849); chairman, Committee on Expenditures in the Department of War (Thirtieth Congress); resumed the practice of his profession in Knoxville; affiliated with the Democratic Party in 1856; retired from active practice about 1866 and engaged in literary pursuits and historical research; died in Knoxville, Tenn., October 25, 1889; interment in the Old Gray Cemetery.

**CROZIER, Robert,** a Senator from Kansas; born in Cadiz, Harrison County, Ohio, October 13, 1827; attended the public schools and an academy; studied law in Carrollton, Ohio, and was admitted to the bar in 1848; prosecuting attorney of Carroll County 1848-1850; moved to Leavenworth, Kans., in 1856, where he established the Leavenworth Daily Times and also engaged in the practice of law; member, Territorial council 1857-1858; appointed United States attorney for the district of Kansas by President Abraham Lincoln 1861-1864, when he resigned; chief justice of Kansas supreme court 1864-1867; cashier and manager of the First National Bank of Leavenworth; appointed as a Republican to the United States Senate to fill the vacancy caused by the resignation of Alexander Caldwell and served from November 24, 1873, to February 12, 1874, when a successor was elected; was not a candidate for election; resumed the practice of his profession in Leavenworth, Kans.; district judge of the first judicial district of Kansas 1876-1892; member of the board of directors of the Kansas Historical Society 1886-1889; died in Leavenworth, Leavenworth County, Kans., October 2, 1895; interment in Mount Muncie Cemetery.

**CRUDUP, Josiah,** a Representative from North Carolina; born in Wakelon, Wake County, N.C., January 13, 1791; attended a private school in Louisburg, N.C., and Columbian College (now George Washington University), Washington, D.C.; studied theology; was ordained as a Baptist minister and, excepting the service in Congress, continued in the ministry until his death; engaged in farming; served in the State senate in 1820; member of the State house of representatives 1821-1823; elected to the Seventeenth Congress (March 4, 1821-March 3, 1823); unsuccessful candidate for reelection in 1822 to the Eighteenth Congress; resumed agricultural pursuits; delegate to the State constitutional convention in 1835; died near Kittrell, Vance County, N.C., May 20, 1872; interment in the family burial ground at his home near Kittrell, N.C.

**CRUGER, Daniel,** a Representative from New York; born in Sunbury, Pa., December 22, 1780; attended the public schools; learned the printer's trade; published the Owego Democrat at Owego, N.Y.; studied law; was admitted to the bar in 1805, and commenced practice in Bath, N.Y.; served as major in the War of 1812; member of the State assembly 1814-1816 and again in 1826 and served as speaker in 1816; elected as a Republican to the Fifteenth Congress (March 4, 1817-March 3, 1819); district attorney of the seventh district of New York 1815-1818, and of Steuben County 1818-1821; resumed the practice of law; moved to Wheeling, Va. (now West Virginia); died in Wheeling July 12, 1843; interment in the Stone Church Cemetery.

**CRUMP, Edward Hull,** a Representative from Tennessee; born on a farm near Holly Springs, Marshall County, Miss., October 2, 1874; attended the public schools until the age of fourteen, when he was apprenticed as a printer; engaged in agricultural pursuits and as a bill clerk in a general store in Lula, Miss.; moved to Memphis, Tenn., in 1893; employed as a bookkeeper; engaged in the wholesale mercantile business and the manufacture of harness and buggies; delegate to the Democratic State conventions in 1902 and 1904; elected to the Memphis Board of Public Works in 1905 and served until his resignation in 1907; elected fire and police commissioner in 1907; elected mayor of Memphis in 1909, reelected in 1911 and 1915 and served from 1910 until his resignation February 22, 1916; delegate to the Democratic National Conventions of 1912, 1924,

1928, 1936, 1940, 1944 and 1948; county trustee of Shelby County 1917-1925; engaged in the banking, insurance, mortgage-loan, and real-estate businesses; also interested in farming; member of the Democratic State committee 1926-1930 and of the Democratic National Committee 1936-1945; elected as a Democrat to the Seventy-second and Seventy-third Congresses (March 4, 1931-January 3, 1935); was not a candidate for renomination in 1934 to the Seventy-fourth Congress; Regent of the Smithsonian Institution 1931-1935; elected mayor of Memphis in November 1939 but resigned January 1, 1940 to permit the city council to select a successor; resumed his business activities; died in Memphis, Tenn., October 16, 1954; interment in Elmwood Cemetery.

**Bibliography:** *DAB*; Miller, William D. *Mr. Crump of Memphis.* Baton Rouge: Louisiana State University Press, 1964.

**CRUMP, George William,** a Representative from Virginia; born in Powhatan County, Va., September 26, 1786; attended Washington College (now Washington and Lee University), Lexington, Va.; was graduated from Princeton College in 1805; studied medicine at the University of Pennsylvania, Philadelphia, Pa., 1806-1808; member of the State house of delegates 1817-1822 and 1825-1828; elected to the Nineteenth Congress to fill the vacancy caused by the resignation of John Randolph and served from January 21, 1826, to March 3, 1827; unsuccessful candidate for reelection in 1826 to the Twentieth Congress; was appointed by President Jackson as chief clerk of the Pension Bureau in 1832, which position he held until his death; moved to Powhatan County, Va., where he died on October 1, 1848; interment on his home grounds at "Log Castle" on Swift Creek, Chesterfield County, near Colonial House, Va.

**CRUMP, Rousseau Owen,** a Representative from Michigan; born in Pittsford, Monroe County, N.Y., May 20, 1843; attended the public schools in Pittsford and Rochester; moved to Plainwell, Mich., in 1869 and engaged in the lumber business in Allegan and Kalamazoo Counties; moved to West Bay City in 1881 and established a sawmill and box factory; member of the board of aldermen 1889-1892; mayor of West Bay City 1893-1895; member of the State house of representatives 1895-1901; elected as a Republican to the Fifty-fourth and to the three succeeding Congresses and served from March 4, 1895, until his death in West Bay City, Mich., May 1, 1901; chairman, Committee on Mines and Mining (Fifty-sixth Congress); interment in Elm Lawn Cemetery, Bay City, Bay County, Mich.

**CRUMPACKER, Edgar Dean** (father of Maurice Edgar Crumpacker and cousin of Shepard J. Crumpacker, Jr.), a Representative from Indiana; born in Westville, La Porte County, Ind., May 27, 1851; attended the common schools and Valparaiso Academy, Valparaiso, Ind.; studied law in the law department of Indiana University at Bloomington; was admitted to the bar in 1876 and commenced practice in Valparaiso, Ind.; prosecuting attorney for the thirty-first judicial district of Indiana 1884-1888; served as appellate judge, by appointment of Governor Hovey, from March 1891 to January 1, 1893; elected as a Republican to the Fifty-fifth and to the seven succeeding Congresses (March 4, 1897-March 3, 1913); chairman, Committee on the Census (Fifty-eighth through Sixty-first Congresses); unsuccessful candidate for reelection in 1912 to the Sixty-third Congress; resumed the practice of law in Valparaiso, Porter County, Ind., where he died May 19, 1920; interment in Graceland Cemetery.

**CRUMPACKER, Maurice Edgar** (son of Edgar Dean Crumpacker and cousin of Shepard J. Crumpacker, Jr.), a Representative from Oregon; born in Valparaiso, Porter County, Ind., December 19, 1886; attended the public schools of Valparaiso, Ind., and Washington, D.C.; was graduated from the Culver (Ind.) Military Academy in 1905 and from the University of Michigan at Ann Arbor in 1909; studied law at Harvard University; was admitted to the bar in 1912 and commenced practice in Portland, Oreg.; was commissioned

December 31, 1917, as first lieutenant in the aviation section of the Signal Reserve Corps; accepted appointment as captain in the Air Service (production), National Army, July 8, 1918, and served until December 27, 1918, when he was honorably discharged as captain in the Air Service (aircraft production); special deputy district attorney for Multnomah County, Oreg., in 1921; unsuccessful candidate for the Republican nomination for Congress in 1922; elected as a Republican to the Sixty-ninth and Seventieth Congresses and served from March 4, 1925, until his death in San Francisco, Calif., July 24, 1927; interment in Riverview Cemetery, Portland, Oreg.

**CRUMPACKER, Shepard J., Jr.** (cousin of Edgar Dean Crumpacker and Maurice Edgar Crumpacker), a Representative from Indiana; born in South Bend, St. Joseph County, Ind., February 13, 1917; attended the public schools; was graduated from Northwestern University, Evanston, Ill., in 1938, and from the law school of the University of Michigan at Ann Arbor in 1941; was admitted to the bar the same year and commenced the practice of law in South Bend, Ind.; entered the United States Army Air Corps as a private September 26, 1941, and advanced through the ranks to flight chief in a fighter squadron; commissioned a lieutenant in 1943 and assigned to heavy-bomber maintenance; relieved from active duty as a first lieutenant March 1, 1946; major in the Air Force Reserve; owned and operated a farm; delegate to Indiana State Republican convention 1958 through 1970; elected as a Republican to the Eighty-second, Eighty-third, and Eighty-fourth Congresses (January 3, 1951-January 3, 1957); did not seek renomination in 1956; practiced law until 1977; appointed judge of the St. Joseph Superior Court and served from 1977-1985; was a resident of South Bend, Ind., until his death there October 14, 1986; interment in Riverview Cemetery.

**CRUTCHFIELD, William,** a Representative from Tennessee; born in Greeneville, Greene County, Tenn., November 16, 1824; attended the common schools; moved to McMinn County, Tenn., in 1840 and remained there four years; settled in Jacksonville, Ala., in 1844 and engaged in agricultural pursuits; became a permanent resident of Chattanooga, Tenn. in 1850; during the Civil War never enlisted, but served in the Union Army as honorary captain in the Chickamauga campaign; was with General George H. Thomas during the siege of Chattanooga, and was an assistant to General James B. Steedman and other commanders until the close of the war; elected as a Republican to the Forty-third Congress (March 4, 1873-March 3, 1875); was not a candidate for renomination in 1874 to the Forty-fourth Congress; resumed agricultural pursuits; died in Chattanooga, Tenn., January 24, 1890; interment in the family lot in Old Citizens Cemetery.

**CUBIN, Barbara L.,** a Representative from Wyoming; born in Salinas, Monterey County, Calif., November 30, 1946; graduated, Natrona County (Wyo.) High School; B.S., Creighton University, Omaha, Nebr., 1969; substitute teacher in mathematics and science; social worker for State of Wyoming; Department of Labor and Ironworkers Union training minorities and Vietnam veterans; chemist, Wyoming Machinery Co.; manager of husband's medical office since 1975; member, Wyoming State house of representatives, 1987-1991; member, Wyoming State senate, 1992-1994; Natrona County Republican Women, state convention parliamentarian, 1992; elected as a Republican to the One Hundred Fourth Congress (January 3, 1995-January 3, 1997); is a resident of Casper, Wyo.

**CULBERSON, Charles Allen** (son of David Browning Culberson), a Senator from Texas; born in Dadeville, Tallapoosa County, Ala., June 10, 1855; moved to Texas with his parents, who settled first in Gilmer and later in Jefferson; attended the common schools and was graduated from the Virginia Military Institute at Lexington in 1874; studied law at the University of Virginia at Charlottesville in 1876 and 1877; was admitted to the bar in 1877 and commenced practice in Jefferson, Tex.; moved to Dallas, Tex., in 1887; attorney general of Texas, 1890-1894; elected Governor of Texas in 1894, reelected in 1896, and served from January 15, 1895 to January 17, 1899; elected as a Democrat to the United States Senate on January 25, 1899; reelected in 1905, 1911, and again in 1916, and served from March 4, 1899, to March 3, 1923; unsuccessful candidate for reelection in 1922; Democratic caucus chairman 1907-1909; chairman, Committee on Additional Accommodations for the Library (Sixty-first Congress), Committee on Public Health and National Quarantine (Sixty-second Congress), Committee on Judiciary (Sixty-third through Sixty-fifth Congresses), Committee on Private Land Claims (Sixty-sixth Congress); lived in retirement until his death in Washington, D.C., March 19, 1925; interment in East Oakwood Cemetery, Fort Worth, Tex.

**Bibliography:** *DAB*; Hughes, Pollyanna, and Harrison, Elizabeth. "Charles Culberson: Not a Shadow of Hogg." *East Texas Historical Journal* 11 (Fall 1973): 41-52; Madden, James. *Charles Allen Culberson, His Character and Public Service*. Austin, Tex.: Gammel's Book Store, 1929.

**CULBERSON, David Browning** (father of Charles Allen Culberson), a Representative from Texas; born in Troup County, Ga., September 29, 1830; pursued preparatory studies in Brownwood College, La Grange, Ga.; studied law; was admitted to the bar in 1851 and commenced practice in Dadeville, Ala.; moved to Texas in 1856; settled in Jefferson, Marion County, in 1861 and continued the practice of law; member of the Texas State house of representatives in 1859; during the Civil War entered the Confederate Army as a private; promoted to the rank of colonel of the Eighteenth Texas Infantry; assigned to duty in 1864 as adjutant general of the State of Texas with the rank of colonel; again a member of the State house of representatives in 1864; elected to the Texas State senate in 1873 and served until his resignation, having been elected to Congress; elected as a Democrat to the Forty-fourth and to the ten succeeding Congresses (March 4, 1875-March 3, 1897); chairman, Committee on the Judiciary (Fiftieth, Fifty-second, and Fifty-third Congresses); declined to be a candidate for renomination in 1896 to the Fifty-fifth Congress; appointed by President William McKinley on June 21, 1897, as one of the commissioners to codify the laws of the United States, and served in this capacity until his death in Jefferson, Tex., May 7, 1900; interment in Oaklawn Cemetery.

**Bibliography:** *DAB*.

**CULBERTSON, William Constantine,** a Representative from Pennsylvania; born in Edinboro, Erie County, Pa., November 25, 1825; attended the common schools of his native town; engaged in lumbering on the Allegheny River in Jefferson County, Pa.; also operated a mill and a factory at Covington, Ky.; moved to Girard, Pa., in 1863; purchased extensive tracts of timberland in Michigan, Wisconsin, and other States; later became interested in agricultural pursuits in Minnesota and in his native county; president of the Citizens' National Bank of Corry, Pa.; elected as a Republican to the Fifty-first Congress (March 4, 1889-March 3, 1891); unsuccessful candidate for renomination in 1890; resumed his former business activities; died in Girard, Erie County, Pa., on May 24, 1906; interment in Girard Cemetery.

**CULBERTSON, William Wirt,** a Representative from Kentucky; born near Lewistown, Mifflin County, Pa., September 22, 1835; moved with his parents to Kentucky; attended the common schools; engaged in the manufacture of iron; enlisted as a private in the Union Army in Company F, Twenty-seventh Regiment, Ohio Volunteer Infantry, July 16, 1861; promoted to the rank of captain August 2, 1861; resigned March 3, 1864; member of the Kentucky house of representatives in 1870; served in the Kentucky senate in 1873; delegate to the Republican National Convention in 1876, 1880, and 1884; mayor of Ashland, Ky., in 1882 and 1883 when he resigned; elected as a Republican to the Forty-eighth Congress

(March 4, 1883-March 3, 1885); died in Oxford, Butler County, Ohio, on October 31, 1911; interment in Ashland Cemetery, Ashland, Ky.

**CULBRETH, Thomas,** a Representative from Maryland; born in Kent County, Del., eight miles northeast of Greensboro, Md., April 13, 1786; attended the public schools and studied under private tutors; moved to Denton, Caroline County, Md., in 1806; was clerk in a store in Denton; member of the congressional committee at Hillsboro in 1810; member of the State house of delegates in 1812 and 1813; cashier of the State Bank at Denton in 1813; elected as a Republican to the Fifteenth Congress and reelected to the Sixteenth Congress (March 4, 1817-March 3, 1821); declined to be a candidate for reelection in 1820 to the Seventeenth Congress and for election in 1822 to the Eighteenth Congress; appointed chief judge of the Caroline County orphans' court in 1822; clerk of the executive council of Maryland 1825-1838, and resided in Annapolis, Md.; returned to Denton, Md., 1838 and engaged in mercantile pursuits; soon afterward moved to "Orrell Farm," near Greensboro, where he died April 16, 1843; interment in the family cemetery on the farm.

**CULKIN, Francis Dugan,** a Representative from New York; born in Oswego, Oswego County, N.Y., November 10, 1874; attended the public schools in Oswego and St. Andrew's College and the University of Rochester in Rochester, N.Y.; newspaper reporter in Rochester, N.Y., 1894-1902; studied law; was admitted to the bar in 1902 and commenced practice in Oswego, N.Y.; served as a private, Company D, Third New York Volunteers, in the Spanish-American War; captain in the New York National Guard 1901-1908; city attorney of Oswego, 1906-1910; district attorney of Oswego County, 1911-1921; judge of Oswego County, 1921-1928; member of the Thomas Jefferson Bicentennial Commission and the Thomas Jefferson Memorial Commission; elected as a Republican to the Seventieth Congress to fill the vacancy caused by the death of Thaddeus C. Sweet; reelected to the Seventy-first and to the seven succeeding Congresses and served from November 6, 1928, until his death in Oswego, N.Y., on August 4, 1943; interment in St. Paul's Cemetery.

**CULLEN, Elisha Dickerson,** a Representative from Delaware; born in Millsboro, Sussex County, Del., April 23, 1799; attended Princeton College; studied law; was admitted to the bar in 1821 and commenced practice in Georgetown, Del; elected as the candidate of the American Party to the Thirty-fourth Congress (March 4, 1855-March 3, 1857); was an unsuccessful candidate for reelection in 1856 to the Thirty-fifth Congress; resumed the practice of law; died in Georgetown, Del., on February 8, 1862; interment in the Presbyterian Churchyard, Lewes, Del.

**CULLEN, Thomas Henry,** a Representative from New York; born in Brooklyn, N.Y., March 29, 1868; attended the local parochial schools, and was graduated from St. Francis College, Brooklyn, N.Y., in 1880; became engaged in the marine insurance and shipping business; member of the Senate assembly 1896-1898; served in the State senate 1899-1918; delegate to the Democratic National Conventions from 1912 through 1932; elected as a Democrat to the Sixty-sixth and to the twelve succeeding Congresses and served from March 4, 1919, until his death in Washington, D.C., on March 1, 1944; interment in Holy Cross Cemetery, Brooklyn, N.Y.

**CULLEN, William,** a Representative from Illinois; born in County Donegal, Ireland, March 4, 1826; immigrated to the United States in 1832 with his parents, who settled in Pittsburgh, Pa.; attended the public schools and the Allegheny Academy at Pittsburgh; moved to Adams Township, La Salle County, Ill., in 1846 and engaged in agricultural pursuits; sheriff of La Salle County in 1864 and 1865; moved to Ottawa, La Salle County, Ill., in 1865; political editor of the Ottawa Republican 1871-1887; elected as a Republican to the Forty-seventh and Forty-eighth Congresses

(March 4, 1881-March 3, 1885); unsuccessful candidate for renomination in 1884; lived in retirement in Ottawa, Ill., until his death there January 17, 1914; interment in Ottawa Avenue Cemetery.

**CULLOM, Alvan** (brother of William Cullom and uncle of Shelby Moore Cullom), a Representative from Tennessee; born in Monticello, Ky., September 4, 1797; received a liberal schooling; studied law; was admitted to the bar in 1823 and commenced practice in Monroe, Overton County, Tenn.; member of the State house of representatives in 1835 and 1836; elected as a Democrat to the Twenty-eighth and Twenty-ninth Congresses (March 4, 1843-March 3, 1847); resumed the practice of law; circuit judge of the fourth judicial circuit of Tennessee 1850-1852; member of the peace convention of 1861 held in Washington, D.C., in an effort to devise means to prevent the impending war; died in Livingston, Overton County, Tenn., July 20, 1877; interment in Bethlehem Cemetery, near Livingston.

**CULLOM, Shelby Moore** (nephew of Alvan Cullom and William Cullom), a Representative and a Senator from Illinois; born in Wayne County, Ky., November 22, 1829; moved with his father to Tazewell County, Ill., in 1830; received an academic and university training; moved to Springfield, Ill., in 1853; studied law; was admitted to the bar in 1855 and commenced practice in Springfield; elected city attorney in 1855; member, Illinois State house of representatives, 1856, 1860-1861, and served as speaker of the house during the second year; elected as a Republican to the Thirty-ninth and to the two succeeding Congresses (March 4, 1865-March 3, 1871); chairman, Committee on Territories (Forty-first Congress); member, State house of representatives 1873-1874, and served as speaker in 1873; elected Governor of Illinois in 1876, reelected in 1880, and served from January 8, 1877 to February 8, 1883, when he resigned, having been elected Senator; elected as a Republican to the United States Senate in 1882; reelected in 1888, 1894, 1900, and 1906 and served from March 4, 1883, to March 3, 1913; Republican caucus chairman 1910-1913; chairman, Committee on Expenditures of Public Money (Forty-ninth Congress), Committee on Interstate Commerce (Fiftieth through Fifty-second, Fifty-fourth through Fifty-sixth, and Sixty-first Congresses), Committee on Foreign Relations (Fifty-seventh through Sixty-first Congresses), Republican Conference (Sixty-first and Sixty-second Congresses); Regent of the Smithsonian Institution 1885-1913; chairman and resident commissioner of the Lincoln Memorial Commission in 1913 and 1914; member of the commission appointed to prepare a system of laws for the Hawaiian Islands; died in Washington, D.C., January 28, 1914; interment in Oak Ridge Cemetery, Springfield, Ill.

Bibliography: *DAB*; Cullom, Shelby. *Fifty Years in Public Service: Personal Recollections*. 1911. Reprint. New York: Da Capo Press, 1967; Neilson, James. *Shelby M. Cullom: Prairie State Republican*. Urbana: University of Illinois Press, 1962.

**CULLOM, William** (brother of Alvan Cullom and uncle of Shelby Moore Cullom), a Representative from Tennessee; born near Monticello, Wayne County, Ky., June 4, 1810; attended the public schools; studied law in Lexington, Ky.; was admitted to the bar and practiced in the courts of Kentucky and Tennessee; moved to Carthage, Tenn.; member of the Tennessee general assemblies, 1843-1847; elected as a Whig to the Thirty-second and Thirty-third Congresses (March 4, 1851-March 3, 1855); unsuccessful candidate for reelection in 1854 to the Thirty-fourth Congress; appointed Clerk of the House of Representatives in the Thirty-fourth Congress and served from February 4, 1856, to December 6, 1857; resumed the practice of law; attorney general, sixteenth district, 1873-1878; died in Clinton, Tenn., December 6, 1896; interment in McAdoo Cemetery, Clinton, Tenn., and later reinterred in Mount Olivet Cemetery, Chattanooga, Tenn.

**CULLOP, William Allen,** a Representative from Indiana; born near Oaktown, Knox County, Ind., March 28, 1853; attended the common schools; was graduated from Hanover (Ind.) College in June 1878; professor for two years in Vincennes (Ind.) University; studied law; was admitted to the bar in 1881 and commenced practice in Vincennes, Ind.; prosecuting attorney of the twelfth judicial circuit 1883-1886; member of the State house of representatives 1891-1893; delegate to the Democratic National Conventions in 1892 and 1896; elected as a Democrat to the Sixty-first and to the three succeeding Congresses (March 4, 1909-March 3, 1917); unsuccessful candidate for renomination in 1916; unsuccessful candidate for the Democratic nomination as United States Senator in 1926; resumed the practice of law and was also interested in various business enterprises; died in Vincennes, Ind., October 9, 1927; interment in Greenlawn Cemetery.

**CULPEPPER, John,** a Representative from North Carolina; born near Wadesboro, Anson County, N.C., in 1761; attended the public schools; became a minister in the Baptist Church; presented credentials as a Federalist Member-elect to the Tenth Congress and served from March 4, 1807, until January 2, 1808, when the seat was declared vacant as the result of a contest on account of alleged irregularities; subsequently reelected to fill the vacancy declared by the House of Representatives and served from February 23, 1808, to March 3, 1809; elected as a Federalist to the Thirteenth and Fourteenth Congresses (March 4, 1813-March 3, 1817); unsuccessful candidate for reelection in 1816 to the Fifteenth Congress; elected to the Sixteenth Congress (March 4, 1819-March 3, 1821); unsuccessful candidate for reelection in 1820 to the Seventeenth Congress; elected to the Eighteenth Congress (March 4, 1823-March 3, 1825); unsuccessful candidate for reelection in 1824 to the Nineteenth Congress; elected to the Twentieth Congress (March 4, 1827-March 3, 1829); declined to be candidate for reelection in 1828 and retired from public life; died at the residence of his son in Darlington County, S.C. in January 1841; interment in the cemetery at Society Hill, S.C.

**CULVER, Charles Vernon,** a Representative from Pennsylvania; born in Logan, Hocking County, Ohio, September 6, 1830; received a liberal preparatory schooling and attended the Ohio Wesleyan University, Delaware, Ohio; moved to Pennsylvania and settled in Reno, Venango County, and engaged in mercantile pursuits; also became interested in the development of oil in Venango County, Pa., and the establishment of national banks in thirteen cities throughout the East; elected as a Republican to the Thirty-ninth Congress (March 4, 1865-March 3, 1867); was not a candidate for renomination in 1866 to the Fortieth Congress; while a Member of Congress became bankrupt and was imprisoned in 1866, but after a prolonged trial was acquitted; resumed operations in the oil business, with headquarters in Franklin, Venango County, Pa.; died in Philadelphia, Pa., January 10, 1909, while on a business trip; interment in Franklin Cemetery, Franklin, Pa.

**CULVER, Erastus Dean,** a Representative from New York; born in Champlain, Washington County, N.Y., on March 15, 1803; was graduated from the University of Vermont at Burlington in 1826; studied law; was admitted to the bar in 1831 and commenced practice in Fort Ann, N.Y.; moved to Greenwich, N.Y., in 1836; member of the New York State assembly, 1838-1840; elected as a Whig to the Twenty-ninth Congress (March 4, 1845-March 3, 1847); moved to Brooklyn, N.Y., in 1850; judge of the city court of Brooklyn, 1854-1861; appointed by President Lincoln as Minister Resident to Venezuela on July 12, 1862, and served in that capacity until May 1866; died in Greenwich, Washington County, N.Y., October 13, 1889; interment in the Culver vault in Greenwich Cemetery.

**CULVER, John Chester,** a Representative and a Senator from Iowa; born in Rochester, Olmsted County, Minn., August 8, 1932; attended Cedar Rapids public schools; A.B., Harvard University,

1954; attended Cambridge University, England, as a Harvard Scholar, 1954-1955; served in the United States Marine Corps, 1955-1958, and was discharged with rank of captain; served as dean of men of Harvard University Summer School in 1960; LL.B., Harvard University Law School, 1962; admitted to the bar in 1963 and commenced practice in Cedar Rapids, Iowa; elected as a Democrat to the Eighty-ninth and to the four succeeding Congresses (January 3, 1965-January 3, 1975); was not a candidate in 1974 for reelection to the House of Representatives, but was elected to the United States Senate, and served from January 3, 1975 to January 3, 1981; unsuccessful candidate for reelection in 1980; resumed the practice of law in Washington, D.C.; is a resident of Washington, D.C.

**Bibliography:** Drew, Elizabeth. *Senator*. New York: Simon and Schuster, 1979.

**CUMBACK, William,** a Representative from Indiana; born near Mount Carmel, Franklin County, Ind., March 24, 1829; attended the common schools and was graduated from Miami University, Oxford, Ohio; taught school two years; studied law at the Cincinnati Law School; was admitted to the bar and commenced practice in Greensburg, Ind., in 1853; elected as a Republican to the Thirty-fourth Congress (March 4, 1855-March 3, 1857); unsuccessful candidate for reelection in 1856 to the Thirty-fifth Congress; resumed the practice of law; appointed a paymaster in the Army and served throughout the Civil War; member of the State senate in 1866; lieutenant governor of Indiana in 1868; unsuccessful candidate for election to the United States Senate in 1869; United States revenue collector 1871-1883; trustee of De Pauw University, Greencastle, Ind.; unsuccessful candidate for nomination for Governor in 1896; died in Greensburg, Ind., July 31, 1905; interment in South Park Cemetery.

**CUMMING, Thomas William,** a Representative from New York; born in Frederick, Md., in 1814 or 1815; moved to Georgia; appointed a midshipman in the United States Navy May 19, 1832; was promoted to passed midshipman June 23, 1838, and served until February 23, 1841, when he resigned; while in the Navy was a member of the Wilkes expedition in 1838; moved to Brooklyn, N.Y.; became a druggist and importer of drugs in New York City and subsequently engaged in mercantile pursuits in Brooklyn, N.Y., 1843-1853; elected as a Democrat to the Thirty-third Congress (March 4, 1853-March 3, 1855); died in Brooklyn, N.Y., October 13, 1855; interment in Greenwood Cemetery.

**CUMMING, William,** a Delegate from North Carolina; born in Edenton, N.C.; studied law; was admitted to the bar and practiced; member of the North Carolina Provincial Congress in 1776; member of the State house of commons in 1781, 1783, 1784, and 1788; Member of the Continental Congress in 1785; nominated for judge in 1790.

**CUMMINGS, Amos Jay,** a Representative from New York; born in Conkling, Broome County, N.Y., May 15, 1841; attended the common schools; apprenticed to the printing trade when twelve years of age; was with William Walker in his last invasion of Nicaragua in October 1858; during the Civil War served as sergeant major of the Twenty-sixth New Jersey Regiment, Second Brigade, Sixth Corps, Army of the Potomac; awarded Congressional Medal of Honor; filled editorial positions on the New York Tribune under Horace Greeley, the New York Sun, and the New York Express; elected as a Democrat to the Fiftieth Congress (March 4, 1887-March 3, 1889); declined renomination in 1888, but was subsequently elected to the Fifty-first Congress to fill the vacancy caused by the death of Samuel S. Cox; reelected to the Fifty-second and Fifty-third Congresses and served from November 5, 1889, to November 21, 1894, when he resigned; chairman, Committee on Naval Affairs (Fifty-third Congress); elected to the Fifty-fourth Congress to fill the vacancy caused by the death of Representative-elect Andrew J. Campbell; reelected to the Fifty-fifth, Fifty-sixth, and Fifty-seventh Congresses and served from November 5, 1895, until his death in Baltimore, Md., May 2, 1902; interment in Clinton Cemetery, Irvington, N.J.

**Bibliography:** *DAB*.

**CUMMINGS, Elijah Eugene,** a Representative from Maryland; born in Baltimore, Md., January 18, 1951; attended the public schools; graduated, Baltimore City College High School, 1969; B.S., Howard University, Washington, D.C., 1973; J.D., University of Maryland School of Law, 1976; admitted to the Maryland bar in December 1976; chairman, Governor's Commission on Black Males, 1990 to present; chief judge, Maryland Moot Court Board; member, Maryland State house of delegates, District 39 (now District 44), 1983-1996, serving as Speaker Pro Tempore in 1995-1996; elected as a Democrat to the One Hundred Fourth Congress, April 16, 1996, by special election to fill the vacancy caused by the resignation of Kweisi Mfume; elected to the One Hundred Fifth Congress, and served from April 16, 1996 to January 3, 1999; is a resident of Baltimore, Md.

**CUMMINGS, Fred Nelson,** a Representative from Colorado; born on a farm near Groveton, Coos County, N.H., September 18, 1864; in 1865 moved with his parents to Clinton, Iowa, and in 1879 to a farm near West Union, Custer County, Nebr.; attended the rural schools; engaged in agricultural pursuits and the raising of livestock; studied law; was admitted to the bar in 1891 and commenced practice in Custer County, Nebr.; moved to Fort Collins, Colo., in 1906 and resumed agricultural pursuits; member of the city council of Fort Collins 1909-1913; elected as a Democrat to the Seventy-third and to the three succeeding Congresses (March 4, 1933-January 3, 1941); unsuccessful candidate for reelection in 1940 to the Seventy-seventh Congress; resumed his former pursuits; died in Fort Collins, Colo., November 10, 1952; interment in Grandview Cemetery.

**CUMMINGS, Henry Johnson Brodhead,** a Representative from Iowa; born in Newton, Sussex County, N.J., May 21, 1831; attended the public schools of Muncy, Pa.; edited a newspaper in Schuylkill County, Pa., in 1850; studied law, and was admitted to the bar at Williamsport, Pa., in 1855; moved to Iowa in 1856 and settled in Winterset, Madison County; prosecuting attorney of Madison County, 1856-1858; entered the Union Army in July 1861; was made captain of Company F, Fourth Regiment, Iowa Volunteer Infantry, on August 15, 1861; accepted the commission of colonel of the Thirty-ninth Regiment, Iowa Volunteer Infantry, September 12, 1862, and was honorably discharged on December 22, 1864; became editor and proprietor of the Winterset Madisonian in 1869; elected as a Republican to the Forty-fifth Congress (March 4, 1877-March 3, 1879); unsuccessful candidate for reelection in 1878 to the Forty-sixth Congress; died in Winterset, Iowa, April 16, 1909; interment in Winterset Cemetery.

**CUMMINGS, Herbert Wesley,** a Representative from Pennsylvania; born in West Chillisquaque Township, Northumberland County, Pa., July 13, 1873; attended the public schools; was graduated from the Lewisburg (Pa.) High School in 1890; studied law; was admitted to the bar May 7, 1897, and commenced practice in Sunbury, Pa.; district attorney of Northumberland County in 1901 and 1904-1908; elected judge of the common pleas court of Northumberland County in 1911 and served ten years as president judge; elected as a Democrat to the Sixty-eighth Congress (March 4, 1923-March 3, 1925); unsuccessful candidate for reelection in 1924 to the Sixty-ninth Congress; resumed the practice of law until November 18, 1935, when he was appointed judge of Northumberland County; subsequently elected and served until January 7, 1946; resumed the practice of law; died in Sunbury, Pa., March 4, 1956; interment in Pomsret Manor Cemetery.

**CUMMINS, Albert Baird,** a Senator from Iowa; born near Carmichaels, Greene County, Pa., February 15, 1850; attended the public schools, and a preparatory academy; graduated Waynesburg (Pa.) College in 1869; moved to Iowa; briefly engaged as a carpenter; clerked in the office of the recorder of Clayton County; assistant surveyor of Allen County; engaged in railroad building; studied law; was admitted to the bar in 1875 and commenced practice in Chicago; returned to Des Moines, Iowa, in 1878, where he continued the practice of law; member, Iowa State house of representatives, 1888-1890; unsuccessful candidate for election to the United States Senate in 1894 and 1900; member of the Republican National Committee, 1896-1900; elected Governor of Iowa in 1901, reelected in 1903 and 1906, and served from January 16, 1902 until November 24, 1908, when he resigned, having been elected Senator; elected as a Republican to the United States Senate in 1908 to fill the vacancy caused by the death of William B. Allison; reelected in 1909, 1914, and again in 1920, and served from November 24, 1908, until his death; unsuccessful candidate for renomination in 1926; served as President pro tempore of the Senate during the Sixty-sixth through the Sixty-ninth Congresses; chairman, Committee on Civil Service and Retrenchment (Sixty-first and Sixty-second Congresses), Committee on the Mississippi River and its Tributaries (Sixty-third through Sixty-fifth Congresses), Committee on Interstate Commerce (Sixty-sixth and Sixty-seventh Congresses), Committee on Judiciary (Sixty-eighth and Sixty-ninth Congresses); died in Des Moines, Iowa, July 30, 1926; interment in Woodland Cemetery.

**Bibliography:** Bray, Thomas. "The Cummins Leadership." *Annals of Iowa* 32 (April 1954): 241-96; Sayre, Ralph Mills. "Albert Baird Cummins and the Progressive Movement in Iowa." Ph.D. dissertation, Columbia University, 1958.

**CUMMINS, John D.,** a Representative from Ohio; born in Pennsylvania in 1791; attended the public schools, and was graduated from Jefferson College, Canonsburg, Pa., in 1834; studied law; was admitted to the bar and commenced practice in New Philadelphia, Ohio; prosecuting attorney of Tuscarawas County 1836-1841; elected as a Democrat to the Twenty-ninth and Thirtieth Congresses (March 4, 1845-March 3, 1849); died in Milwaukee, Wis., while attending a session of the circuit court, September 11, 1849.

**CUNNINGHAM, Francis Alanson,** a Representative from Ohio; born in Abbeville District, S.C., November 9, 1804; moved to Eaton, Ohio, in 1826; taught school; studied medicine and commenced practice in 1829; clerk of the court of Preble County in 1833; elected as a Democrat to the Twenty-ninth Congress (March 4, 1845-March 3, 1847); unsuccessful candidate for reelection in 1846 to the Thirtieth Congress; studied law; was admitted to the bar in 1847 and began practice in Eaton; appointed additional paymaster of Volunteers by President James K. Polk on December 30, 1847; was commissioned paymaster in the Regular Army on March 2, 1849, and was retired from active service August 27, 1863; died in Eaton, Preble County, Ohio, August 16, 1864; interment in Mount Hill Cemetery.

**CUNNINGHAM, Glenn Clarence,** a Representative from Nebraska; born in Omaha, Douglas County, Nebr., September 10, 1912; attended the public schools; A.B., University of Omaha, 1935; salesman for Aetna Life Insurance Co., Omaha, Nebr., 1935-1937; executive secretary of Omaha Junior Chamber of Commerce, 1936-1940, and president in 1945; manager of the convention bureau, Omaha Chamber of Commerce, in 1940 and 1941; manager of Omaha Safety Council, 1942-1947; member of Omaha Board of Education, 1946-1948; organized Glenn Cunningham & Co., an insurance agency, in 1947; member of Omaha City Council in 1947 and 1948; mayor of Omaha, 1949-1954; appointed Nebraska State Director, Savings Bonds Division, United States Treasury, in 1954 and served until April 1956; delegate to the Republican National Conventions of 1948 and 1952; elected as a Republican to the Eighty-fifth and to the six succeeding Congresses (January 3, 1957-January 3, 1971); unsuccessful candidate for renomination in 1970 to the Ninety-second Congress; is a resident of Omaha, Nebr.

**CUNNINGHAM, John Edward, III,** a Representative from Washington; born in Chicago, Ill., March 27, 1931; attended the public schools of Scituate, Mass.; attended the University of San Francisco and Seattle University; businessman, engaged in plastics manufacturing in Tacoma; served in United States Air Force Reserve, 1953-1954; member, Washington State house of representatives, 1973-1975; Washington State senator, 1975-1977; elected as a Republican to the Ninety-fifth Congress, May 17, 1977, by special election to fill the vacancy caused by the resignation of Brock Adams, and served from May 17, 1977 to January 3, 1979; unsuccessful candidate for reelection in 1978 to the Ninety-sixth Congress; is a resident of Zenith, Wash.

**CUNNINGHAM, Paul Harvey,** a Representative from Iowa; born on a farm in Indiana County, near Kent, Pa., June 15, 1890; attended the public schools; was graduated from State Teachers College, Indiana, Pa., in 1911, from the literary department of the University of Michigan at Ann Arbor in 1914, and from its law department in 1915; was admitted to the bar in 1915 and commenced practice in Grand Rapids, Mich.; during the First World War served as a first lieutenant of Infantry 1917-1919; moved to Des Moines, Iowa, in 1919 and continued the practice of law; member of the Iowa National Guard 1920-1923; member of the State house of representatives 1933-1937; elected as a Republican to the Seventy-seventh and to the eight succeeding Congresses (January 3, 1941-January 3, 1959); unsuccessful candidate for reelection in 1958 to the Eighty-sixth Congress; resumed the practice of law; died at his summer home on Gull Lake, Brainerd, Minn., July 16, 1961; interment in Masonic Cemetery, Des Moines, Iowa.

**CUNNINGHAM, Randy (Duke),** a Representative from California; born in Los Angeles, December 8, 1941; graduated, Shelbina (Mo.) High School; B.A., University of Missouri, 1964, and M.A., 1965; M.B.A., National University, San Diego, Calif., 1985; entered active duty, United States Navy in 1966; released as commander in 1988 after service as fighter pilot during Vietnam War; teacher, Hinsdale (Ill.) high school; elected as a Republican to the One Hundred Second and to the two succeeding Congresses (January 3, 1991-January 3, 1997); is a resident of San Diego, Calif.

**CURLEY, Edward Walter,** a Representative from New York; born in Easton, Northampton County, Pa., May 23, 1873; moved to New York City with his parents in 1874; attended the public schools and the College of the City of New York; engaged in the building industry 1892-1900, and in the builders' and contractors' machinery and equipment business 1900-1916; member of the New York City board of aldermen from January 1, 1916, until November 5, 1935, when he resigned, having been elected to Congress; elected as a Democrat to the Seventy-fourth Congress to fill the vacancy caused by the death of Anthony J. Griffin; reelected to the Seventy-fifth and Seventy-sixth Congresses and served from November 5, 1935, until his death in New York City on January 6, 1940; interment in Kensico Cemetery, Valhalla, Westchester County, N.Y.

**CURLEY, James Michael,** a Representative from Massachusetts; born in Boston, Mass., November 20, 1874; attended the public schools of Boston; salesman for Logan, Johnston & Co., a bakers' and confectioners' supply firm; engaged in the real-estate and insurance business; member of the Boston common council in 1900 and 1901; served in the State house of representatives in 1902 and 1903; member of the Boston board of aldermen 1904-1909; member of the Boston City Council in 1910 and 1911; elected as a Democrat to the Sixty-second and Sixty-third Congresses and served from March 4, 1911, until his resignation, effective February 4, 1914, having been elected mayor of Boston, in which capacity he served from 1914 to 1918; president of the Hibernia Savings Bank, Boston; unsuccessful candidate in 1918 for nomination to the Sixty-sixth Congress; again served as mayor, 1922-1926, and 1930-1934; unsuccessful candidate in 1924 for election for Governor; elected Governor of Massachusetts in 1934 and served from January 3, 1935 to January 7, 1937; unsuccessful candidate in 1936 for election to the United States Senate; unsuccessful candidate for mayor of Boston in 1937 and again in 1941; unsuccessful candidate in 1938 for election for Governor; member of the Democratic National Committee in 1941 and 1942; elected to the Seventy-eighth and Seventy-ninth Congresses (January 3, 1943-January 3, 1947); was not a candidate for renomination in 1946 to the Eightieth Congress; again elected mayor of Boston in 1945, and served until January 1950; unsuccessful candidate in 1949 for reelection as mayor, and for nomination for mayor in 1951 and again in 1955; appointed a member of the Massachusetts Labor Relations Commission in 1957; died in Boston, Mass., November 12, 1958; interment in Old Calvary Cemetery.

**Bibliography:** *DAB*; Beatty, Jack. *The Rascal King: The Life and Times of James Michael Curley*. Reading, Mass.: Addison-Wesley Publishing Co., 1993; Curley, James Michael. *I'd Do It Again; A Record of All My Uproarious Years*. Englewood Cliffs, N.J.: Prentice-Hall, 1957; Dinneen, Joseph F. *The Purple Shamrock; the Honorable James Michael Curley of Boston*. New York: Norton, 1949.

**CURLIN, William Prather, Jr.,** a Representative from Kentucky; born in Paducah, McCracken County, Ky., November 30, 1933; graduated from Frankfort High School; A.B., University of Kentucky, 1958; LL.B., University of Kentucky School of Law, 1962; entered private law practice in Frankfort, Ky.; attorney and assistant commissioner, Kentucky Department of Revenue, 1962-1964; elected to the Kentucky general assembly, 1967; reelected, 1969 and 1971; chairman, Appropriations and Revenue Committee, Kentucky general assembly, 1970; elected as a Democrat to the Ninety-second Congress, December 4, 1971, by special election to fill the vacancy caused by the death of John C. Watts, and served from December 4, 1971 to January 3, 1973; was not a candidate for reelection in 1972 to the Ninety-third Congress; is a resident of Woodford County, Ky.

**CURRIE, Gilbert Archibald,** a Representative from Michigan; born in Midland Township, Midland County, Mich., September 19, 1882; attended the district school, Midland (Mich.) High School, and was graduated from the law department of the University of Michigan at Ann Arbor in 1905; was admitted to the Michigan bar in 1905 and commenced practice in Midland; member of the State house of representatives 1909-1915, serving as speaker in 1913 and 1914; unsuccessful candidate for the Republican nomination in 1914 to the Sixty-fourth Congress; elected as a Republican to the Sixty-fifth and Sixty-sixth Congresses (March 4, 1917-March 3, 1921); unsuccessful candidate for renomination in 1920 to the Sixty-seventh Congress; resumed the practice of law and also engaged in the banking business until his death in Midland, Mich., June 5, 1960; interment in Midland Cemetery.

**CURRIER, Frank Dunklee,** a Representative from New Hampshire; born in Canaan, Grafton County, N.H., October 30, 1853; attended the common schools, Kimball Union Academy, Meriden, N.H., and Doctor Hixon's School, Lowell, Mass.; studied law; was admitted to the bar in 1874 and commenced practice in Canaan, N.H.; member of the State house of representatives in 1879; secretary of the Republican State committee 1882-1890; clerk of the State senate in 1883 and 1885; delegate to the Republican National Convention in 1884; member of the State senate in 1887 and served as president of that body; naval officer of customs at the port of Boston, Mass., 1890-1894; speaker of the State house of representatives in 1899; elected as a Republican to the Fifty-seventh

and to the five succeeding Congresses (March 4, 1901-March 3, 1913); chairman, Committee on Patents (Fifty-eighth through Sixty-first Congresses); unsuccessful candidate for reelection in 1912 to the Sixty-third Congress; retired from public life; died in Canaan, N.H., November 25, 1921; interment in Canaan Street Cemetery.

**CURRY, Charles Forrest** (father of Charles Forrest Curry, Jr.), a Representative from California; born in Naperville, Du Page County, Ill., March 14, 1858; attended the common schools and the Episcopal Academy, Mineral Point, Wis.; studied one year at the University of Washington at Seattle, and also was educated by a private tutor; moved with his parents to Seattle, Wash., in 1872, and thence to San Francisco, Calif., in 1873; engaged in agricultural pursuits and the cattle, lumber, and mining businesses; member of the State assembly in 1887 and 1888; was admitted to the bar of San Francisco in 1888; superintendent of Station B post office, San Francisco, 1890-1894; clerk of San Francisco city and county 1894-1898; secretary of state of California 1899-1910; unsuccessful candidate for the Republican nomination for Governor in 1910; appointed building and loan commissioner of California in 1911; representative to the Panama Pacific International Exposition for the Pacific Coast and Intermountain States in 1911; elected as a Republican to the Sixty-third and to the eight succeeding Congresses and served from March 4, 1913, until his death in Washington, D.C., October 10, 1930; chairman, Committee on Territories (Sixty-sixth through Seventy-first Congresses); interment in Abbey Mausoleum (near Arlington National Cemetery), Arlington, Va.

**CURRY, Charles Forrest, Jr.** (son of Charles Forrest Curry), a Representative from California; born in San Francisco, Calif., August 13, 1893; attended the public schools, Howe's Academy, Sacramento, Calif., and George Washington University and Georgetown University School of Law, Washington, D.C.; secretary to his father, Representative Charles F. Curry, 1913-1917; during the First World War enlisted in the Aviation Section, Signal Enlisted Reserve Corps, on August 15, 1917; commissioned a second lieutenant and served until May 22, 1919, with overseas service; clerk to the Committee on the Territories, House of Representatives, 1919-1930; was admitted to the bar in 1921; elected as a Republican to the Seventy-second Congress (March 4, 1931-March 3, 1933); unsuccessful candidate for reelection in 1932 to the Seventy-third Congress; engaged in the practice of law, and in mining and other business enterprises; resided in Long Beach, Calif., where he died October 7, 1972; interment in Westminster Memorial Park, Westminster, Calif.

**CURRY, George,** a Representative from New Mexico; born on Greenwood plantation, near Bayou Sara, La., April 3, 1861; attended the public schools; moved to the Territory of New Mexico in 1879 and worked on a cattle ranch until 1881; acted as post trader at Fort Stanton; engaged in the mercantile and stock business until 1886; deputy treasurer of Lincoln County in 1886 and 1887; elected county clerk in 1888, county assessor in 1890, and sheriff in 1892; member of the Territorial senate in 1894 and 1896, serving as president the latter year; lieutenant of the First Volunteer Cavalry, known as "Roosevelt's Rough Riders," in the Spanish-American War; sheriff of Otero County in 1899; resigned to join the Eleventh Volunteer Cavalry; lieutenant, provost marshal, and provost judge, with service in the Philippine Islands from December 16, 1899, to March 20, 1901; Governor of the Province of Camarines, Philippine Islands, in 1901; chief of police of the city of Manila, 1901; Governor of the Province of Isabela, 1903-1905; Governor of the Province of Samar from 1905 to 1907, when he resigned; appointed Governor of the Territory of New Mexico by President Theodore Roosevelt on April 1, 1907, and served until his resignation on February 28, 1910; upon the admission of New Mexico as a State into the Union was elected as a Republican to the Sixty-second Congress and served from January 8, 1912, to March 3, 1913; declined to be a candidate for renomination in 1912 to the Sixty-third Congress; engaged in the hotel business in Socorro, N.Mex.; private secretary to Senator Holm O. Bursum of New Mexico in 1921 and 1922; member of the International Boundary Commission, 1922-1927; moved to a ranch near Cutter, N.Mex.; served as State historian for New Mexico from 1945 until his death in Albuquerque, N.Mex., November 27, 1947; interment in National Cemetery, Santa Fe, N.Mex.

**Bibliography:** Curry, George. *George Curry, 1861-1947; An Autobiography*. edited by H.B. Hening. Albuquerque: University of New Mexico Press, 1958; Larson, Robert W. "Ballinger vs. Rough Rider George Curry: The Other Feud." *New Mexico Historical Review* 43 (October 1968): 271-90.

**CURRY, Jabez Lamar Monroe,** a Representative from Alabama; born near Double Branches, Lincoln County, Ga., June 5, 1825; moved with his father to Talladega County, Ala., in 1838; was graduated from the University of Georgia at Athens in 1843; studied law at Harvard University; was admitted to the bar and commenced practice in Talladega County in 1845; served in the war with Mexico as a private in the Texas Rangers in 1846, but resigned because of ill health; member of the Alabama State house of representatives in 1847, 1853, and 1855; elected as a Democrat to the Thirty-fifth and Thirty-sixth Congresses, and served from March 4, 1857 until January 21, 1861, when he joined other secessionist colleagues and withdrew; deputy from Alabama to the Provisional Confederate Congress and a Representative in the First Confederate Congress; during the Civil War served as lieutenant colonel of Cavalry in the Confederate Army; after the war became a Baptist preacher; chosen president of Howard College, Alabama, in 1865; professor in Richmond College, Virginia, 1868-1881; agent of the Peabody and States Funds from 1881 until his death; appointed Envoy Extraordinary and Minister Plenipotentiary to Spain on October 7, 1885, and served until July 1888; appointed Ambassador Extraordinary on special mission to Spain (the coming of age of King Alfonso XIII) on February 3, 1902; died in Victoria, near Asheville, N.C., February 12, 1903; interment in Hollywood Cemetery, Richmond, Va.

**Bibliography:** *DAB*; Alderman, Edwin A., and Armistead Gordon. *J.L.M. Curry: A Biography*. New York: The Macmillan Company, 1911; Rice, Jessie Pearl. *J.L.M. Curry, Southerner, Statesman and Educator*. New York: King's Crown Press, 1949.

**CURTIN, Andrew Gregg,** a Representative from Pennsylvania; born in Bellefonte, Pa., April 22, 1817; pursued preparatory studies in Milton (Pa.) Academy, and was graduated from Dickinson College, Carlisle, Pa., in 1837; studied law; was admitted to the bar in 1837 and commenced practice in Bellefonte; presidential elector on the Whig ticket in 1848 and in 1852; secretary of the Commonwealth of Pennsylvania and superintendent of public instruction; elected Governor of Pennsylvania in 1860, reelected in 1863, and served from January 15, 1861 to January 15, 1867; appointed Minister to Russia on April 16, 1869 and served until July 1872; delegate to the constitutional convention of Pennsylvania; elected as a Democrat to the Forty-seventh and to the two succeeding Congresses (March 4, 1881-March 3, 1887); chairman, Committee on Foreign Affairs (Forty-eighth Congress), Committee on Banking and Currency (Forty-ninth Congress); was not a candidate for renomination in 1886 to the Fiftieth Congress; resumed the practice of his profession; died in Bellefonte, Centre County, Pa., on October 7, 1894; interment in Union Cemetery.

**Bibliography:** *DAB*; Albright, Rebecca G. "The Civil War Career of Andrew Gregg Curtin, Governor of Pennsylvania." *Western Pennsylvania Historical Magazine* 47 (October 1964): 323-41; 48 (January 1965): 51-73.

**CURTIN, Willard Sevier,** a Representative from Pennsylvania; born in Trenton, Mercer County, N.J., November 28, 1905; moved to Morrisville, Bucks County, Pa., with his parents in 1911; attended the public schools; graduated from Pennsylvania State University in 1929, and from the University of Pennsylvania Law School in 1932; was admitted to the bar in 1932 and commenced practice in Morrisville, Pa.; co-founded the law firm of Curtin and Heefner in 1951; first assistant district attorney of Bucks County from 1938 until 1949, and district attorney, 1949-1956; county committeeman to the Pennsylvania Republican committee, 1954-1956; elected as a Republican to the Eighty-fifth and to the four succeeding Congresses (January 3, 1957-January 3, 1967); was not a candidate for reelection in 1966 to the Ninetieth Congress; was a resident of Ft. Myers, Fla., until his death there on February 4, 1996; cremated; ashes scattered at sea.

**CURTIS, Carl Thomas,** a Representative and a Senator from Nebraska; born near Minden, Kearney County, Nebr., March 15, 1905; attended the public schools, and Nebraska Wesleyan University at Lincoln; teacher in the Minden, Nebr., schools in 1927; studied law; was admitted to the bar in 1930 and commenced practice in Minden; county attorney of Kearney County, Nebr., 1931-1934; elected as a Republican to the Seventy-sixth and to the seven succeeding Congresses, and served from January 3, 1939 until his resignation on December 31, 1954; was not a candidate in 1954 for reelection to the House of Representatives, but was elected to the United States Senate for the six-year term commencing January 3, 1955; subsequently appointed by the Governor, January 1, 1955, to fill the vacancy caused by the resignation of Hazel H. Abel for the term ending January 3, 1955; reelected in 1960, 1966, and again in 1972, and served from January 1, 1955 to January 3, 1979; was not a candidate for reelection in 1978; chairman, Republican Conference (Ninety-fourth and Ninety-fifth Congresses); practices law in Lincoln, Nebr.; is a resident of Lincoln, Nebr.

**Bibliography:** Curtis, Carl T., and Regis Courtemanche. *Forty Years Against the Tide: Congress and the Welfare State*. Chicago: Regnery Gateway, 1986.

**CURTIS, Carlton Brandaga,** a Representative from Pennsylvania; born in Madison County, N.Y., December 17, 1811; pursued an academic course; moved to Mayville, N.Y.; studied law; moved to Erie, Pa., where he continued the study of law; was admitted to the bar in 1834; moved to Warren, Pa., the same year and commenced practice; member of the Pennsylvania house of representatives 1836-1838; elected as a Democrat to the Thirty-second and Thirty-third Congresses (March 4, 1851-March 3, 1855); chairman, Committee on Accounts (Thirty-third Congress); affiliated with the Republican Party in 1855; entered the Union Army on February 13, 1862, as lieutenant colonel of the Fifty-eighth Regiment, Pennsylvania Volunteer Infantry for a period of three years; promoted to colonel of that regiment May 23, 1863; because of illness was honorably discharged as colonel July 2, 1863; returned to Warren and practiced law; moved to Erie, Pa., in 1868 and continued the practice of law; also interested in banking and the production of oil, and was one of the originators and builders of the Dunkirk & Venango Railroad; elected as a Republican to the Forty-third Congress (March 4, 1873-March 3, 1875); was an unsuccessful candidate for reelection in 1874 to the Forty-fourth Congress; resumed the practice of law; died in Erie, Erie County, Pa., March 17, 1883; interment in Oakland Cemetery, Warren, Pa.

**CURTIS, Charles,** a Representative and a Senator from Kansas and a Vice President of the United States; born in Topeka, Kans., January 25, 1860; attended the common schools; studied law; was admitted to the bar in 1881 and commenced practice in Topeka; prosecuting attorney of Shawnee County, 1885-1889; elected as a Republican to the Fifty-third and to the six succeeding Congresses, and served from March 4, 1893 until January 28, 1907, when he resigned, having been elected Senator; chairman, Committee on Expenditures in the Department of the Interior (Fifty-fourth through Fifty-seventh Congresses); had been reelected to the Sixtieth Congress, but on January 23, 1907, was elected to the United States Senate as a Republican to fill the vacancy in the term ending March 3, 1907, caused by the resignation of Joseph R. Burton, and on the same day was reelected for the term commencing March 4, 1907; served from January 29, 1907 to March 3, 1913; unsuccessful candidate for reelection in 1912; served as President pro tempore of the Senate during the Sixty-second Congress; chairman, Committee on Indian Depredations (Fifty-ninth through Sixty-first Congresses), Committee on Coast Defenses (Sixty-second Congress), Republican Conference (Sixty-eighth through Seventieth Congresses); again elected to the United States Senate for the term commencing March 4, 1915; reelected in 1920 and 1926, and served from March 4, 1915 until his resignation on March 3, 1929, having been elected Vice President of the United States; Republican whip 1915-1924; majority leader (Sixty-eighth, Sixty-ninth, and Seventieth Congresses); elected Vice President of the United States, November 6, 1928, on the Republican ticket headed by Herbert Hoover; inaugurated on March 4, 1929, and served until March 3, 1933; unsuccessful candidate for reelection in 1932 for Vice President; resumed the practice of law in Washington, D.C., where he died on February 8, 1936; interment in Topeka Cemetery, Topeka, Kans.

**Bibliography:** *DAB*; Ewy, Martin. "Charles Curtis of Kansas, Vice-President of the United States, 1929-1933." *Emporia State Research Studies* 10 (December 1961); 5-58; Unrau, William E. *Mixed Bloods and Tribal Dissolution: Charles Curtis and the Quest for Indian Identity.* Lawrence: University Press of Kansas, 1989.

**CURTIS, Edward,** a Representative from New York; born in Windsor, Vt., October 25, 1801; was graduated from Union College, Schenectady, N.Y., in 1821; studied law; was admitted to the New York bar in 1824 and commenced the practice of law in New York City; member of the common council in 1834, and was elected president of the board of assistant aldermen; elected as a Whig to the Twenty-fifth and Twenty-sixth Congresses (March 4, 1837-March 3, 1841); chairman, Committee on Commerce (Twenty-sixth Congress); was not a candidate for renomination to the Twenty-seventh Congress; appointed collector of the port of New York City March 18, 1841, and served in that office until July 7, 1844; resumed the practice of law in Washington, D.C.; died in New York City on August 2, 1856; place of interment unknown.

**CURTIS, George Martin,** a Representative from Iowa; born near Oxford, Chenango County, N.Y., April 1, 1844; moved to Ogle County, Ill., in 1856 with his parents, who settled on a farm near Rochelle; attended the common schools and Rock River Seminary, Mount Morris, Ill.; was a clerk in Rochelle, Ill., 1863-1865, and subsequently for two years in Cortland, Ill.; moved to Clinton, Iowa, in 1867 and engaged in the manufacture of lumber; one of the incorporators of the City National Bank of Clinton and served as a director following its organization in 1880; elected vice president of the bank in 1890 and served in that capacity until his death; director in a number of lumber companies; member of the Iowa State house of representatives, 1888-1889; delegate to the Republican National Convention of 1892; elected as a Republican to the Fifty-fourth and Fifty-fifth Congresses (March 4, 1895-March 3, 1899); declined to be a candidate for renomination in 1898 to the Fifty-sixth Congress; resumed his former business activities in Clinton, Iowa, and died there on February 9, 1921; interment in Springdale Cemetery.

**CURTIS, Laurence,** a Representative from Massachusetts; born in Boston, Suffolk County, Mass., September 3, 1893; graduated from Groton School in 1912 and from Harvard University in 1916; served in the Foreign Diplomatic Service for one year; during the First World War entered the United States Navy and after a training crash, resulting in the loss of a leg, served out the rest of the war as a ground officer at Pensacola, Fla.; awarded Silver Star citation for war services; returned to Harvard Law School and graduated in 1921; admitted to the Massachusetts bar the same year and commenced practice in Boston; secretary to United States Supreme Court Justice Oliver Wendell Holmes in 1921 and 1922; assistant United States attorney in Boston 1923-1925; member of Boston City Council 1930-1933; member of the Massachusetts house of representatives 1933-1936; member of Massachusetts senate 1936-1941; Massachusetts treasurer in 1947 and 1948; delegate to the Republican National Convention of 1960; past State Commander and National Senior Vice Commander of the Disabled American Veterans; elected as a Republican to the Eighty-third and to the four succeeding Congresses (January 3, 1953-January 3, 1963); was not a candidate for renomination in 1962 to the House of Representatives, but was an unsuccessful candidate for nomination to the United States Senate; resumed the practice of law; unsuccessful candidate for election in 1970 to the Ninety-second Congress; was a resident of Newton, Mass.; died July 11, 1989.

**CURTIS, Newton Martin,** a Representative from New York; born in De Peyster, St. Lawrence County, N.Y., May 21, 1835; attended the common schools and Gouverneur Wesleyan Seminary; entered the Union Army as captain of Company G, Sixteenth Regiment, New York Infantry, May 15, 1861; lieutenant colonel of the One Hundred and Forty-second Regiment, New York Infantry, October 23, 1862; colonel January 21, 1863; brevetted brigadier general of Volunteers October 28, 1864; brigadier general January 15, 1865; brevetted major general of Volunteers March 13, 1865; awarded the Congressional Medal of Honor; appointed collector of customs, district of Oswegatchie, N.Y., in 1866; appointed special agent of the United States Treasury Department in 1867, which position he resigned in 1880; employed by the Department of Justice 1880-1882; member of the State assembly 1884-1890; elected as a Republican to the Fifty-second Congress to fill the vacancy caused by the resignation of Leslie W. Russell; reelected to the Fifty-third and Fifty-fourth Congresses and served from November 3, 1891, to March 3, 1897; chairman, Committee on Election of President, Vice President, and Representatives (Fifty-fourth Congress); was not a candidate for renomination in 1896; assistant inspector general of the National Home for Disabled Volunteer Soldiers 1910; died in New York City on January 8, 1910; interment in Ogdensburg Cemetery, Ogdensburg, N.Y.

**Bibliography:** *DAB.*

**CURTIS, Samuel Ryan,** a Representative from Iowa; born near Champlain, Clinton County, N.Y., February 3, 1805; moved to Ohio, where he attended the public schools; appointed a cadet in the United States Military Academy at West Point in 1827, and was graduated in July 1831, as brevet second lieutenant in the Seventh Infantry; resigned in June 1832; studied law; was admitted to the bar and commenced practice in Zanesville, Ohio; chief engineer of the Muskingum River improvements from April 1837 to May 1839; served in the war with Mexico as adjutant general of Ohio and colonel of the Third Regiment, Ohio Infantry; honorably discharged June 24, 1847; resumed the practice of law; elected as a Republican to the Thirty-fifth, Thirty-sixth, and Thirty-seventh Congresses and served from March 4, 1857, to August 4, 1861, when he resigned; member of the peace convention of 1861 held in Washington, D.C., in an effort to devise means to prevent the impending war; appointed colonel of the Second Regiment, Iowa Volunteer Infantry, June 1, 1861; brigadier general of Volunteers May 17, 1861; major general of Volunteers March 21, 1862; mustered out April 30, 1866; appointed United States peace commissioner to treat with the Indians in 1865; appointed commissioner to examine and report on the condition of the Union Pacific Railroad, and served from November 1865 to April

1866; died in Council Bluffs, Iowa, on December 25, 1866; interment in Oakland Cemetery, Keokuk, Iowa.

**Bibliography:** *DAB.*

**CURTIS, Thomas Bradford,** a Representative from Missouri; born in St. Louis, Mo., May 14, 1911; attended the public schools of Webster Groves, Mo.; A.B., Dartmouth College, Hanover, N.H., 1932, and M.A., 1951; LL.B., Washington University, St. Louis, Mo., 1935; J.D., Westminster College, 1964; was admitted to the bar in 1934 and commenced the practice of law in St. Louis; member of the Board of Election Commissioners of St. Louis County in 1942; served in the United States Navy from April 8, 1942, until discharged as a lieutenant commander December 21, 1945; member of the Missouri State Board of Law Examiners 1947-1950; elected as a Republican to the Eighty-second and to the eight succeeding Congresses (January 3, 1951-January 3, 1969); was not a candidate for reelection in 1968 to the House of Representatives but was an unsuccessful candidate for election to the United States Senate; delegate to the Republican National Conventions of 1964, 1976 and 1980; vice president and general counsel, Encyclopedia Britannica, 1969-1973; unsuccessful candidate in 1974 for election to the United States Senate; chairman, Corporation for Public Broadcasting, 1972-1973; chairman, Federal Election Commission from April 1975 to May 1976; consultant, National Association of Technical and Trade Schools; was a resident of Clayton, Mo.; died January 10, 1993.

**CUSACK, Thomas,** a Representative from Illinois; born in Kilrush, County Clare, Ireland, October 5, 1858; immigrated to the United States in 1861 with his parents, who settled in New York City; after the death of his parents moved to Chicago, Ill., in 1863; attended private and public schools; learned the sign-painting trade; organized an outdoor advertising company in 1875; member of the board of education 1891-1898 and served as vice president of the board 1896-1898; served as colonel on the staff of Governor John P. Altgeld 1893-1897; member of the Democratic State central committee 1896-1898; elected as a Democrat to the Fifty-sixth Congress (March 4, 1899-March 3, 1901); was not a candidate for renomination in 1900 to the Fifty-seventh Congress; resumed his former business pursuits in Chicago, Ill. where he died November 19, 1926; interment in Calvary Cemetery.

**CUSHING, Caleb,** a Representative from Massachusetts; born in Salisbury, Mass., January 17, 1800; was graduated from Harvard University in 1817; studied law; was admitted to the bar at Newburyport, Mass. in 1823; member of the Massachusetts house of representatives in 1825; served in the Massachusetts senate in 1827; again a member of the Massachusetts house of representatives in 1833 and 1834; unsuccessful candidate in 1833 for election to the Twenty-third Congress; elected as a Whig to the Twenty-fourth and to the three succeeding Congresses (March 4, 1835-March 3, 1843); chairman, Committee on Foreign Affairs (Twenty-seventh Congress); was not a candidate for renomination in 1842 to the Twenty-eighth Congress; appointed by President John Tyler as Envoy Extraordinary and Minister Plenipotentiary to China on May 8, 1843, and also commissioner on the same date, and served until his resignation on March 4, 1845; while serving as commissioner to China was empowered to negotiate a treaty of navigation and commerce with Japan; again a member of the Massachusetts house of representatives in 1845 and 1846; colonel of a Massachusetts regiment which served in the war with Mexico; appointed brigadier general by President James K. Polk on April 14, 1847; unsuccessful Democratic candidate for Governor in 1847 and again in 1848; again elected to the Massachusetts house of representatives in 1850; offered the position as attorney general of Massachusetts in 1851, but declined; mayor of Newburyport, Mass., in 1851 and 1852; appointed judge of the supreme court of Massachusetts in 1852; appointed Attorney General in the Cabinet of President Franklin

Pierce, and served from March 7, 1853 until March 3, 1857; chairman of the Democratic National Conventions at Baltimore and Charleston in 1860; appointed by President Andrew Johnson as a commissioner to codify the laws of the United States and served from 1866 to 1870; instructed on November 25, 1868, in concert with the Minister Resident to Colombia, to negotiate a treaty for a ship canal across the Isthmus; appointed in 1872 by President Ulysses S. Grant counsel for the United States before the Geneva Tribunal of Arbitration on the *Alabama* claims; nominated by President Grant on January 9, 1874 to be Chief Justice of the United States, but the nomination was withdrawn on January 13; Envoy Extraordinary and Minister Plenipotentiary to Spain from January 6, 1874, to April 9, 1877; died in Newburyport, Essex County, Mass., on January 2, 1879; interment in Highland Cemetery.

**Bibliography:** *DAB*; Baldasty, Gerald J. "Political Stalemate in Essex County: Caleb Cushing's Race for Congress, 1830-1832." *Essex Institute Historical Collections* 117 (January 1981): 54-70; Fuess, Claude M. *The Life of Caleb Cushing*. New York: Harcourt, Brace and Co., 1923.

**CUSHING, Thomas,** a Delegate from Massachusetts; born in Boston, Mass., March 24, 1725; attended Boston Latin School; was graduated from Harvard College in 1744; studied law; was admitted to the bar and commenced practice in Boston; member of the provincial assembly 1761-1774 and served as speaker; delegate to the Provincial Congress in 1774; Member of the Continental Congress 1774-1776; commissary general of Massachusetts in 1775; declined to be a candidate for election to the Continental Congress in 1779; lieutenant governor of Massachusetts 1780-1788 and Acting Governor in 1785; delegate to the Massachusetts constitutional convention which ratified the Federal Constitution in 1788; one of the founders of the American Academy of Arts and Sciences; died in Boston, Mass., February 28, 1788; interment in Granary Burial Ground.

**Bibliography:** *DAB.*

**CUSHMAN, Francis Wellington,** a Representative from Washington; born in Brighton, Washington County, Iowa, May 8, 1867; attended the public schools in Brighton and Pleasant Plain Academy in Pleasant Plain, Jefferson County, Iowa; moved to Albany County, Wyo., in 1885; employed as a ranch hand and as a teacher; studied law; was admitted to the bar in 1889 and commenced practice in Bassett, Rock County, Nebr.; moved to Tacoma, Wash., in 1891 and continued the practice of law; member of Troop B, First Cavalry, Washington National Guard, 1896-1903; elected as a Republican to the Fifty-sixth and to the five succeeding Congresses and served from March 4, 1899, until his death in New York City July 6, 1909; the remains were cremated and the ashes interred in Tacoma Cemetery, Tacoma, Wash.

**CUSHMAN, John Paine,** a Representative from New York; born in Pomfret, Conn., March 8, 1784; attended the common schools and Plainfield Academy, and was graduated from Yale College in 1807; studied law; was admitted to the bar in 1809 and commenced practice in Troy, N.Y.; elected as a Federalist to the Fifteenth Congress (March 4, 1817-March 3, 1819); was not a candidate for renomination in 1818; resumed the practice of law; regent of the State University from April 1830 until April 1834, when he resigned; trustee of Union College, Schenectady, N.Y., from 1833 until his death; recorder of Troy, N.Y., 1834-1838; judge of the circuit court of the third circuit 1838-1844; engaged in the real-estate business and was interested in civic improvements; died in Troy, N.Y., on September 16, 1848; interment in Oakwood Cemetery.

**CUSHMAN, Joshua,** a Representative from Massachusetts and from Maine; born in Halifax, Mass., April 11, 1761; served in the Revolutionary Army from April 1, 1777, until March 1780; was graduated from Harvard University in 1787; studied theology; was ordained to the ministry and licensed to preach; located in Winslow, Maine (then a district of Massachusetts), and was pastor of the Congregational Church for nearly twenty years; served in the Massachusetts senate in 1810; member of the Massachusetts house of representatives in 1811 and 1812; elected from Massachusetts to the Sixteenth Congress (March 4, 1819-March 3, 1821); when the State of Maine was separated from Massachusetts and admitted as a State into the Union was elected a Representative from Maine to the Seventeenth and Eighteenth Congresses (March 4, 1821-March 3, 1825); served in the Maine senate in 1828; member of the Maine house of representatives in 1834; died in Augusta, Maine, on January 27, 1834; interment in a tomb on the State grounds, Augusta, Maine.

**Bibliography:** *DAB.*

**CUSHMAN, Samuel,** a Representative from New Hampshire; born in Portsmouth, N.H., June 8, 1783; attended the common schools; studied law; was admitted to the bar and commenced practice in Portsmouth; served as judge of the Portsmouth police court; county treasurer 1823-1828; member of the State house of representatives 1833-1835; nominated by President Andrew Jackson to be United States attorney for the district of New Hampshire but was not confirmed; elected as a Jacksonian to the Twenty-fourth Congress and reelected as a Democrat to the Twenty-fifth Congress (March 4, 1835-March 3, 1839); chairman, Committee on Commerce (Twenty-fifth Congress); United States Navy officer at Portsmouth 1845-1849; died in Portsmouth, N.H., on May 20, 1851; interment in Proprietors' Burying Ground.

**CUTCHEON, Byron M.,** a Representative from Michigan; born in Pembroke, Merrimack County, N.H., May 11, 1836; attended the common schools and Pembroke Academy; taught school in Pembroke for several years; moved to Ypsilanti, Mich., in 1855; principal of Birmingham Academy, Oakland County, in 1857; attended Ypsilanti Seminary, and was graduated from the University of Michigan at Ann Arbor in 1861; professor of ancient languages in the Ypsilanti High School, 1861-1862; enlisted in the Union Army in 1862 and served in the Twentieth Regiment, Michigan Infantry, attaining the rank of lieutenant colonel; commissioned colonel of the Twenty-seventh Regiment, Michigan Infantry, on November 12, 1864; commanded the Second Brigade, Second Division, Ninth Army Corps, from October 16, 1864 until his resignation on March 6, 1865; awarded the Congressional Medal of Honor on June 29, 1891, "for distinguished gallantry at the Battle of Horseshoe Bend, Ky., May 10, 1863"; was graduated from the University of Michigan Law School in 1866; was admitted to the bar the same year and commenced practice in Ionia, Mich.; moved to Manistee, Mich., in 1867; member of the board of control of railroads of Michigan, 1867-1883; city attorney of Manistee, Mich., 1870-1873; prosecuting attorney of Manistee County, Mich., 1873-1874; regent of Michigan University, 1875-1881; postmaster of Manistee, Mich., 1877-1883; elected as a Republican to the Forty-eighth and to the three succeeding Congresses (March 4, 1883-March 3, 1891); chairman, Committee on Military Affairs (Fifty-first Congress); unsuccessful candidate for reelection in 1890 to the Fifty-second Congress; appointed a civilian member of the Board of Ordnance and Fortifications by President Benjamin Harrison in July 1891 and served until March 25, 1895; editorial writer for the Detroit Daily Tribune and Detroit Journal, 1895-1897; resumed the practice of law in Grand Rapids, Mich.; died in Ypsilanti, Washtenaw County, Mich., April 12, 1908; interment in Highland Cemetery.

**CUTHBERT, Alfred** (brother of John Alfred Cuthbert), a Representative and a Senator from Georgia; born in Savannah, Ga., December 23, 1785; instructed by private tutors and was graduated from Princeton College in 1803; studied law; was admitted to the bar about 1805 but did not practice; captain of a company of volunteer infantry in 1809; member, State house of representatives 1810-1813; elected as a Republican to the Thirteenth Congress to fill the vacancy caused by the resignation of William W. Bibb; reelected to the Fourteenth Congress and served from December 13, 1813, to November 9, 1816, when he resigned; member, State senate 1817-1819; elected to the Seventeenth, Eighteenth, and Nineteenth Congresses (March 4, 1821-March 3, 1827); was not a candidate for renomination in 1826; elected to the United States Senate to fill the vacancy caused by the resignation of John Forsyth; reelected in 1837, and served from January 12, 1835, to March 3, 1843; was not a candidate for reelection in 1843; retired from active business pursuits and lived on his estate near Monticello, Jasper County, Ga., until his death on July 9, 1856; interment in Summerville Cemetery, Augusta, Ga.

**CUTHBERT, John Alfred** (brother of Alfred Cuthbert), a Representative from Georgia; born in Savannah, Ga., June 3, 1788; was graduated from Princeton College in 1805; studied law; was admitted to the bar in 1809 and commenced practice in Eatonton, Ga.; member of the Georgia State house of representatives in 1811, 1813, and 1817; commanded a volunteer company during the War of 1812; served in the Georgia State senate in 1814 and 1815; elected to the Sixteenth Congress (March 4, 1819-March 3, 1821); appointed by President James Monroe a commissioner to treat with the Creek and Cherokee Indians in 1822; again a member of the State house of representatives in 1822; secretary of the State senate in 1830, 1833, and 1834; editor and subsequently proprietor of the Federal Union at Milledgeville, Ga., 1831-1837; moved to Mobile, Ala., in 1837 and practiced law; elected judge of the county court of Mobile County in 1840, and appointed by Governor Howell Cobb judge of the circuit court of the same county in 1852; retired from the bench and practiced law until his death at "Sans Souci," on Mon Luis Island, near Mobile, Ala., September 22, 1881; interment in a private burying ground on Mon Luis Island.

**CUTLER, Augustus William** (great-grandson of Silas Condict), a Representative from New Jersey; born in Morristown, Morris County, N.J., October 22, 1827; spent the early part of his life on a farm; attended the common schools and Yale College; studied law; was admitted to the bar in 1849 and commenced practice in Morristown, N.J.; prosecutor of the pleas for Morris County, 1856-1861; elected president of the board of education in 1870; member of the New Jersey State senate, 1871-1874; delegate to the State constitutional convention in 1873; elected as a Democrat to the Forty-fourth and Forty-fifth Congresses (March 4, 1875-March 3, 1879); chairman, Committee on Agriculture (Forty-fifth Congress); declined to be a candidate for renomination in 1878 to the Forty-sixth Congress; resumed the practice of law at Morristown; unsuccessful candidate for election in 1880 to the Forty-seventh Congress, and for election in 1896 to the Fifty-fifth Congress; died in Morristown, N.J., January 1, 1897; interment in Evergreen Cemetery.

**CUTLER, Manasseh,** a Representative from Massachusetts; born in Killingly, Conn., May 13, 1742; was prepared for college by a private teacher, and was graduated from Yale College in 1765; taught school in Dedham, Mass., for a short time; engaged in the whaling business at Edgartown, Martha's Vineyard, Mass.; studied law; was admitted to the bar in 1767 but did not practice; studied theology and was licensed to preach in 1770; ordained to the ministry by the Congregational Society at Hamilton, Mass., September 11, 1771; appointed chaplain of Colonel Francis' regiment on September 5, 1776, and of General Titcomb's brigade in 1778; began the study of medicine the same year and became a physician; taught navigation; held in esteem for his knowledge of botany and astronomy; one of the projectors of the Ohio Company in 1787, formed for the purpose of colonizing the new Territory; drafted the Ordinance of 1787; appointed judge of the United States Court for Ohio in 1795 by President Washington, but declined; member of the Massachusetts house of representatives in 1800; elected as a Federalist to the Seventh and Eighth Congresses (March 4, 1801-March 3, 1805); was not a candidate for renomination in 1804 to the Ninth Congress; engaged in literary pursuits; died in Hamilton, Mass., July 28, 1823; interment in Main Street Cemetery.

**Bibliography:** *DAB*; Cutler, W.P., and J.P. Cutler. *Life Journals and Correspondence of Rev. Manasseh Cutler.* 2 vols. Cincinnati: R. Clarke and Co., 1888; Potts, Louis W. "Manasseh Cutler, Lobbyist." *Ohio History* 96 (Summer/Autumn 1987): 101-23.

**CUTLER, William Parker,** a Representative from Ohio; born in Marietta, Ohio, July 12, 1812; attended the common schools and Ohio University at Athens; engaged in agricultural pursuits; member of the Ohio State house of representatives, 1844-1847, serving as speaker during the last term; trustee of Marietta College, 1845-1889; delegate to the State constitutional convention in 1850; president of the Marietta and Cincinnati Railroad from 1850 to 1860; elected as a Republican to the Thirty-seventh Congress (March 4, 1861-March 3, 1863); unsuccessful for reelection in 1862 to the Thirty-eighth Congress; resumed agricultural pursuits and also engaged in railroad building; died in Marietta, Ohio, April 11, 1889; interment in Oak Grove Cemetery.

**Bibliography:** Bogue, Allan G. "William Parker Cutler's Congressional Diary of 1862-63." *Civil War History* 33 (December 1987): 315-330.

**CUTTING, Bronson Murray,** a Senator from New Mexico; born in Oakdale, Long Island, N.Y., June 23, 1888; attended the common schools and Groton (Mass.) School; was graduated from Harvard University in 1910; becoming an invalid he moved to Santa Fe, N.Mex., in 1910 to restore his health; became a newspaper publisher in 1912 and published the Santa Fe New Mexican and El Nuevo Mexicano; served as president of the New Mexican Printing Company, 1912-1918, and of the Santa Fe New Mexican Publishing Corporation from 1920 until his death; during the First World War was commissioned captain and served as an assistant military attaché of the American Embassy in London, 1917-1918; regent of New Mexico Military Institute in 1920; served as chairman of the board of commissioners of the New Mexican State Penitentiary in 1925; appointed as a Republican to the United States Senate to fill the vacancy caused by the death of Andrieus A. Jones, and served from December 29, 1927 until December 6, 1928, when a duly elected successor qualified; was not a candidate for election to this vacancy; elected as a Republican in 1928 to the United States Senate; reelected in 1934, and served from March 4, 1929 until his death in an airplane crash near Atlanta, Mo., on May 6, 1935; interment in Greenwood Cemetery, Brooklyn, N.Y.

**Bibliography:** *DAB*; Lowitt, Richard. *Bronson M. Cutting: Progressive Politician.* Albuquerque: University of New Mexico Press, 1992; Pickens, William. "Bronson Cutting vs. Dennis Chavez: Battle of the Patrones in New Mexico, 1934." *New Mexico Historical Journal* 46 (January 1971): 5-36; Seligman, Gustav. "The Political Career of Senator Bronson M. Cutting." Ph.D. dissertation, University of Arizona, 1967.

**CUTTING, Francis Brockholst,** a Representative from New York; born in New York City August 6, 1804; attended Bensel School and was also tutored privately; studied law in the Litchfield (Conn.) Law School; was admitted to the bar in 1827 and commenced practice in New York City; member of the State assembly in 1836 and 1837; was not a candidate for reelection; unsuccessful candidate for election in 1836 to the Twenty-fifth Congress; member of the board of aldermen in 1843; city recorder; elected as a Democrat to the Thirty-third Congress (March 4, 1853-March 3, 1855); was not a candidate for renomination in 1854; resumed the practice of law; died in New York City June 26, 1870; interment in Greenwood Cemetery, Brooklyn, N.Y.

**CUTTING, John Tyler,** a Representative from California; born in Westport, Essex County, N.Y., September 7, 1844; was left an orphan at ten years of age, when he journeyed westward; resided in Wisconsin and Illinois from 1855 to 1860; worked on a farm; while employed as a clerk in a mercantile establishment attended the public schools of Illinois; enlisted in Taylor's Chicago Battery at the outbreak of the Civil War and served until July 20, 1862; reenlisted January 4, 1864, in the Chicago Mercantile Battery, in which he served until the close of the war; moved to California in 1877 and established a wholesale fruit and commission business; was a member of the National Guard of California, and subsequently assisted in the organization of the Coast Guard, of which he later became brigadier general in command of the Second Brigade; elected as a Republican to the Fifty-second Congress (March 4, 1891-March 3, 1893); declined to be a candidate for renomination in 1892; in 1894 settled in New York City, where he became interested in the automobile industry; retired to Westport, N.Y., in 1907; died in Toronto, Ontario, Canada, November 24, 1911; interment in Hillside Cemetery, Westport, N.Y.

**CUTTS, Charles,** a Senator from New Hampshire; born in Portsmouth, N.H., January 31, 1769; was graduated from Harvard University in 1789; studied law; was admitted to the bar in 1795 and practiced; member, State house of representatives 1803-1810, serving as speaker in 1807, 1808, and 1810; elected as a Federalist to the United States Senate to fill the vacancy caused by the resignation of Nahum Parker and served from June 21, 1810, to March 3, 1813; subsequently appointed to fill the vacancy occurring at the close of his term and served from April 2, 1813, to June 10, 1813, when a successor was elected; elected secretary of the United States Senate and served from October 11, 1814, to December 12, 1825; moved to Fairfax County, Va., and settled near Lewinsville, Va., where he died January 25, 1846; interment in a private cemetery near Lewinsville, Fairfax County, Va.

**CUTTS, Marsena Edgar,** a Representative from Iowa; born in Orwell, Addison County, Vt., May 22, 1833; attended the common schools of his native village and St. Lawrence Academy, Potsdam, N.Y.; moved to Sheboygan Falls, Wis., in 1853; taught school for two years, at the same time studying law; moved to Oskaloosa, Iowa, in June 1855 and completed his law studies; was admitted to the bar in August and commenced practice in Montezuma, Iowa; prosecuting attorney of Poweshiek County in 1857 and 1858; member of the State house of representatives at the extra session in May 1861; served in the State senate from January 1864 until August 1866, when he resigned and returned to Oskaloosa; again a member of the State house of representatives 1870-1872; attorney general of Iowa 1872-1877; presented credentials as a Republican Member-elect to the Forty-seventh Congress and served from March 4, 1881, to March 3, 1883 (the closing day of Congress), when he was succeeded by John C. Cook, who contested the election; elected to the Forty-eighth Congress and served from March 4, 1883, until his death in Oskaloosa, Mahaska County, Iowa, on September 1, 1883, before the assembling of the Congress; interment in Forest Cemetery.

**CUTTS, Richard,** a Representative from Massachusetts; born on Cutts Island, Saco, Mass. (now Maine), June 28, 1771; attended rural and private schools; was graduated from Harvard University in 1790; studied law; engaged extensively in navigation and commercial pursuits; member of the Massachusetts house of representatives in 1799 and 1800; elected as a Republican to the Seventh and the five succeeding Congresses (March 4, 1801-March 3, 1813); was an unsuccessful candidate for reelection in 1812 to the Thirteenth Congress; appointed superintendent general of military supplies and served from 1813 to 1817; appointed Second Comptroller of the United States Treasury on March 6, 1817, and served in this capacity until March 21, 1829; died in Washington, D.C., April 7, 1845; interment in St. John's Graveyard; reinterment in Oak Hill Cemetery in 1857.

# D

**DADDARIO, Emilio Quincy,** a Representative from Connecticut; born in Newton Center, Suffolk County, Mass., September 24, 1918; attended the public schools in Boston, Mass., Tilton (N.H.) Academy, and Newton (Mass.) Country Day School; graduated from Wesleyan University, Middletown, Conn., in 1939; attended Boston University Law School, 1939-1941; transferred to University of Connecticut and graduated in 1942; was admitted to the bar in Connecticut and Massachusetts in 1942 and commenced the practice of law in Middletown, Conn.; in February 1943 enlisted as a private in the United States Army; assigned to the Office of Strategic Services at Fort Meade, Md.; served overseas in the Mediterranean Theater; was separated from the service as a captain in September 1945; awarded the United States Legion of Merit and Italian Medaglia d'Argento medals; member of the Connecticut National Guard; mayor of Middletown, Conn., 1946-1948; appointed judge of the Middletown Municipal Court and served from 1948 to 1950 when he was called into active service with the Forty-third Division of the Connecticut National Guard during the Korean conflict; served as a major with the Far East Liaison Group in Korea and Japan until separated from the service as a major in 1952; resumed the practice of law in Hartford, Conn.; elected as a Democrat to the Eighty-sixth and to the five succeeding Congresses (January 3, 1959-January 3, 1971); was not a candidate for reelection in 1970 to the Ninety-second Congress, but was an unsuccessful candidate for election for Governor of Connecticut; Director, Office of Technology Assessment, 1973-1977; president, American Association for the Advancement of Science, 1977-1978; co-chairman, American Bar Association, Association for the Advancement of Sciences, Conference of Lawyers and Scientists, 1974-1985; member, National Institute of Medicine Committee on Health Sciences Policy; member, National Forum on Science and Technology Goals, 1995-1996; chairman of the board, Medical Technologies Software Corp., Louisville, Ky.; is a resident of Washington, D.C.

**DAGGETT, David,** a Senator from Connecticut; born in Attleboro, Mass., December 31, 1764; pursued preparatory studies and was graduated from Yale College in 1783; taught in a private school and also in the Hopkins Grammar School; studied law; was admitted to the bar in 1786 and commenced practice in New Haven, Conn.; member, State house of representatives 1791-1796, and served as speaker 1794-1796; member, State council or upper house 1797; member, State house of representatives 1805; again served in the State council 1809-1813; State's attorney for New Haven County 1811-1813; elected as a Federalist to the United States Senate to fill the vacancy caused by the resignation of Chauncey Goodrich and served from May 13, 1813, to March 3, 1819; was not a candidate for reelection; resumed the practice of law; associate instructor in the New Haven Law School in 1824; appointed in 1826 to the Kent professorship of law in Yale College, in which capacity he served until 1848; judge of the State supreme court 1826-1832, and then served as chief judge until 1834; mayor of New Haven in 1828; retired from public life; died in New Haven, Conn., on April 12, 1851; interment in Grove Street Cemetery.

Bibliography: *DAB*.

**DAGGETT, Rollin Mallory,** a Representative from Nevada; born in Richville, St. Lawrence County, N.Y., February 22, 1831; moved with his father to northwestern Ohio in 1837; attended school in Defiance, where he also learned the printing business; crossed the plains to the Pacific coast in 1849; followed mining until 1852, and in that year started the Golden Era at San Francisco; with others established the San Francisco Mirror in 1860, and united it with the San Francisco Herald; moved to Nevada in 1862 and settled in Virginia City; elected a member of the Territorial council in 1863;

became connected editorially in 1864 with the Territorial Enterprise; clerk of the United States district court 1867-1876; elected as a Republican to the Forty-sixth Congress (March 4, 1879-March 3, 1881); unsuccessful candidate for reelection in 1880 to the Forty-seventh Congress; appointed Minister Resident to Hawaii July 1, 1882, and served until April 10, 1885, when he resigned; engaged in editorial work in San Francisco, Calif., until his death there November 12, 1901; interment in Laurel Hill Cemetery.

Bibliography: Weisenburger, Francis Phelps. *Idol of the West; The Fabulous Career of Rollin Mallory Daggett*. Syracuse, N.Y.: Syracuse University Press, 1965.

**DAGUE, Paul Bartram,** a Representative from Pennsylvania; born in Whitford, Chester County, Pa., May 19, 1898; attended the public schools; took special studies at West Chester State Teachers College and studied electrical engineering at Drexel Institute, Philadelphia, Pa.; during the First World War served as a private in the United States Marine Corps from July 22, 1918, to June 30, 1919; assistant superintendent of the Pennsylvania Department of Highways 1925-1935; served as deputy sheriff of Chester County, Pa., 1936-1943 and as sheriff 1944-1946; elected as a Republican to the Eightieth and to the nine succeeding Congresses (January 3, 1947-January 3, 1967); was not a candidate for reelection in 1966 to the Ninetieth Congress; retired and resided in Downingtown, Pa.; died in West Chester, Pa., December 2, 1974; interment in Northwood Cemetery, Downingtown, Pa.

**DAHLE, Herman Bjorn,** a Representative from Wisconsin; born in Perry, Dane County, Wis., March 30, 1855; attended the public schools, and was graduated from the University of Wisconsin at Madison in 1877; moved to Mount Vernon, Wis., in 1877 and engaged in mercantile pursuits; moved to Mount Horeb, Wis., in 1887, where he continued in the mercantile business and also, in 1890, engaged in banking; elected as a Republican to the Fifty-sixth and Fifty-seventh Congresses (March 4, 1899-March 3, 1903); unsuccessful candidate for renomination in 1902 to the Fifty-eighth Congress; resumed mercantile pursuits and banking in Mount Horeb, Wis., where he died April 25, 1920; interment in the Lutheran Cemetery.

**DAILY, Samuel Gordon,** a Delegate from the Territory of Nebraska; born in Trimble County, Ky., in 1823; moved with his parents to Jefferson County, Ind., in 1824; attended the common schools and Hanover (Ind.) College; studied law; was admitted to the bar at Indianapolis and commenced practice in Madison, Ind.; unsuccessful candidate of the Free-Soil Party for election to the State legislature; moved to Indianapolis and engaged in the cooperage business; moved to Nebraska Territory in 1857 and settled in Peru, Nemaha County; built a sawmill on the Missouri River; member of the Territorial house of representatives in 1858; successfully contested as a Republican the election of Experience Estabrook to the Thirty-sixth Congress; reelected to the Thirty-seventh and Thirty-eighth Congresses and served from May 18, 1860, to March 3, 1865; appointed deputy collector of customs in New Orleans at the special request of President Lincoln in March 1865, which position he held until his death in New Orleans, La., August 15, 1866; interment in Mount Vernon Cemetery, Peru, Nebr.

**DALE, Harry Howard,** a Representative from New York; born in New York City December 3, 1868; moved with his parents to Brooklyn in 1870; attended the public schools of Brooklyn and New York Law School; was admitted to the New York bar May 14, 1891, and commenced practice in Brooklyn, N.Y.; member of the State assembly 1899-1904; served as attorney for the State comptroller in 1911 and 1912; elected as a Democrat to the Sixty-third, Sixty-fourth, and Sixty-fifth Congresses and served from March 4, 1913, to January 6, 1919, when he resigned having been appointed judge of the magistrate's court in 1919; reappointed in 1929 and served from January 7, 1919, to July 21, 1931; appointed judge for the court of special sessions on July 22, 1931, and served until his death in Bellmore, Nassau County, N.Y., on November 17, 1935; remains were cremated and the ashes deposited in Fresh Pond Road Crematory, Brooklyn, N.Y.

**DALE, Porter Hinman,** a Representative and a Senator from Vermont; born in Island Pond, Essex County, Vt., March 1, 1867; attended the public schools and Eastman Business College; studied in Philadelphia and Boston and spent two years in study with a Shakespearean scholar and actor; taught school in Green Mountain Seminary, Waterbury, Vt., and Bates College, Lewiston, Maine; studied law; was admitted to the bar in 1896 and commenced practice at Island Pond; chief deputy collector of customs at Island Pond 1897-1910, when he resigned; appointed judge of the Brighton municipal court in 1910; member, Vermont State senate, 1910-1914; served in the State militia and as colonel on the staff of the Governor; interested in the lumber, electric, and banking businesses; elected as a Republican to the Sixty-fourth and to the four succeeding Congresses, and served from March 4, 1915 until August 11, 1923, when he resigned to become a candidate for the United States Senate; chairman, Committee on Expenditures in the Department of the Treasury (Sixty-sixth and Sixty-seventh Congresses); elected as a Republican to the United States Senate on November 6, 1923, to fill the vacancy caused by the death of William P. Dillingham during the term ending March 3, 1927; reelected in 1926, and again in 1932, and served from November 7, 1923 until his death at his summer home in Westmore, Vt., October 6, 1933; chairman, Committee on Civil Service (Sixty-ninth through Seventy-second Congresses); interment in Lakeside Cemetery, Island Pond, Vt.

**DALE, Thomas Henry,** a Representative from Pennsylvania; born in Daleville, Lackawanna County, Pa., June 12, 1846; attended the public schools and Wyoming Seminary, Kingston, Pa.; during the Civil War enlisted in the Union Army in 1863; after discharge from the service engaged in business as a coal operator; also engaged in the wholesale beef business; interested in various other business enterprises in Scranton, Pa.; instrumental in organizing the Scranton Board of Trade and was its president for several terms; chairman of the Republican county committee for several years; prothonotary of Lackawanna County 1882-1892; delegate to the Republican National Convention of 1896; elected as a Republican to the Fifty-ninth Congress (March 4, 1905-March 3, 1907); unsuccessful candidate for reelection in 1906 to the Sixtieth Congress; president of the Anthracite Trust Co., Scranton, Pa.; died in Daleville, Pa., August 21, 1912; interment in Dunmore Cemetery, Scranton, Pa.

**D'ALESANDRO, Thomas, Jr.** (father of Nancy Pelosi), a Representative from Maryland; born in Baltimore, Md., August 1, 1903; attended the parochial schools and Calvert Business College; left school in 1916 to work in the insurance business; precinct runner in the First Legislative District of east Baltimore; member of the Maryland State house of delegates from 1926 until 1933, when he resigned to become internal revenue collector; general deputy collector of internal revenue, 1933-1934; member, Baltimore City council, 1935-1938; delegate to each Democratic National Convention from 1944 to 1968; elected as a Democrat to the Seventy-sixth and to the four succeeding Congresses, and served from January 3, 1939 until his resignation on May 16, 1947; mayor of Baltimore from May 1947 to May 1959; unsuccessful candidate for renomination for mayor; unsuccessful candidate for election to the United States Senate in 1958; appointed by President John F. Kennedy to the Federal Renegotiation Board, 1961-1969; insurance and real estate broker; appointed to the State Parole Board in 1971; was a resident of Baltimore, Md. until his death there on August 23, 1987; interment in New Cathedral Cemetery.

**DALLAS, George Mifflin** (great-great-granduncle of Claiborne Pell), a Senator from Pennsylvania and a vice president of the United States; born in Philadelphia, Pa., July 10, 1792; was graduated from the College of New Jersey (now Princeton University) in 1810; studied law; was admitted to the bar in 1813; private secretary to Albert Gallatin, Minister to Russia; returned in 1814 and commenced the practice of law in New York City; solicitor of the United States Bank, 1815-1817; returned to Philadelphia and was appointed deputy attorney general in 1817; mayor of Philadelphia in 1829; United States district attorney for the eastern district of Pennsylvania, 1829-1831; elected as a Democrat to the United States Senate to fill the vacancy caused by the resignation of Isaac D. Barnard, and served from December 13, 1831 to March 3, 1833; declined to be a candidate for reelection in 1832; chairman, Committee on Naval Affairs (Twenty-second Congress); resumed the practice of law; attorney general of Pennsylvania 1833-1835; appointed by President Martin Van Buren as Envoy Extraordinary and Minister Plenipotentiary to Russia on March 7, 1837 and served until July 1839, when he was recalled at his own request; elected Vice President of the United States on the Democratic ticket in 1844 with James K. Polk, and served from March 4, 1845 to March 3, 1849; appointed Envoy Extraordinary and Minister Plenipotentiary to Great Britain by President Franklin Pierce on February 4, 1856 and served until May 1861; returned to Philadelphia, and died there on December 31, 1864; interment in St. Peter's Churchyard.

**Bibliography:** *DAB*; Ambacher, Bruce. "George M. Dallas: Leader of the 'Family' Party." Ph.D. dissertation, Temple University, 1970; Belohlavek, John M. *George Mifflin Dallas: Jacksonian Patrician.* State College: Pennsylvania State University Press, 1977.

**DALLINGER, Frederick William,** a Representative from Massachusetts; born in Cambridge, Middlesex County, Mass., October 2, 1871; attended the public schools; was graduated from Cambridge Latin School in 1889, from Harvard University in 1893, and from Harvard University Law School in 1897; was admitted to the bar in 1897 and commenced practice in Boston; member of the Massachusetts house of representatives in 1894 and 1895; served in the Massachusetts senate 1896-1899; public administrator of Middlesex County 1897-1932; president of the Cambridge Chamber of Commerce; lecturer on government at Harvard University in 1912; elected as a Republican to the Sixty-fourth and to the four succeeding Congresses (March 4, 1915-March 3, 1925); chairman, Committee on Elections No. 1 (Sixty-sixth and Sixty-seventh Congresses), Committtee on Education (Sixty-eighth Congress); was not a candidate for renomination in 1924 to the House of Representatives, but was an unsuccessful candidate for nomination to the United States Senate; subsequently elected to the Sixty-ninth Congress to fill the vacancy caused by the death of Harry I. Thayer; reelected to the Seventieth and to the two succeeding Congresses and served from November 2, 1926, until his resignation effective October 1, 1932, having been appointed to the bench; judge of the United States Customs Court from October 2, 1932, until his resignation on October 2, 1942; engaged in agricultural pursuits; retired and resided in Center Lovell, Maine; died in North Conway, N.H., September 5, 1955; interment in Center Lovell Cemetery, Center Lovell, Maine.

**DALTON, Tristram,** a Senator from Massachusetts; born in Newburyport, Mass., May 28, 1738; attended Dummer Academy, Byfield, Mass., and was graduated from Harvard College in 1755; studied law; was admitted to the bar but did not practice; engaged in mercantile pursuits; delegate from Massachusetts to the convention of committees of New England Provinces which met in Providence, R.I., December 25, 1776; member, Massachusetts house of representatives 1782-1785, and served as speaker in 1784; elected to the Continental Congress in 1783 and 1784, but did not attend; member, State senate 1785-1788; elected to the United States Senate and served from March 4, 1789, to March 3, 1791; unsuccessful candidate for reelection in 1790; surveyor of the port of Boston from November 1814 until his death in Boston, Mass., May 30, 1817; interment in the churchyard of St. Paul's Episcopal Church, Newburyport, Essex County, Mass.

**Bibliography:** Stone, Eben. "A Sketch of Tristram Dalton." *Historical Collections of the Essex Institute* 25 (1888): 3-10.

**DALY, John Burrwood,** a Representative from Pennsylvania; born in Philadelphia, Pa., February 13, 1872; attended the public schools; was graduated from La Salle College, Philadelphia, Pa., in 1890 and from the University of Pennsylvania at Philadelphia in 1896; studied law; was admitted to the bar in 1896 and commenced practice in Philadelphia, Pa.; assistant city solicitor 1914-1922; member of the faculty of La Salle College 1923-1930; elected as a Democrat to the Seventy-fourth and to the two succeeding Congresses and served from January 3, 1935, until his death in Philadelphia, Pa., March 12, 1939; interment in St. Denis Cemetery, South Ardmore, Montgomery County, Pa.

**DALY, William Davis,** a Representative from New Jersey; born in Jersey City, N.J., June 4, 1851; attended the public schools; from the age of fourteen until he was nineteen was employed as an iron molder; studied law; was admitted to the bar in 1874 and commenced practice in Hudson County, N.J.; assistant United States attorney for New Jersey 1885-1888; member of the State house of assembly 1889-1891; judge of the district court of Hoboken from 1891 until his resignation in 1892; member of the State senate 1892-1898; delegate to the Democratic National Convention of 1896; chairman of the Democratic State convention in 1896 and member of the State committee 1896-1898; elected as a Democrat to the Fifty-sixth Congress and served from March 4, 1899, until his death in Hoboken, N.J., July 31, 1900; interment in New York Bay Cemetery.

**DALZELL, John,** a Representative from Pennsylvania; born in New York City April 19, 1845; moved with his parents to Pittsburgh, Pa., in 1847; attended the common schools and the Western University of Pennsylvania, Pittsburgh, Pa.; was graduated from Yale College with the class of 1865; studied law; was admitted to the bar in 1867 and commenced practice in Pittsburgh, Pa.; elected as a Republican to the Fiftieth and to the twelve succeeding Congresses (March 4, 1887-March 3, 1913); chairman, Committee on Pacific Railroads (Fifty-first Congress), Committee on Rules (Sixty-first Congress); unsuccessful candidate for renomination in 1912 to the Sixty-third Congress; delegate to the Republican National Conventions of 1904 and 1908; Regent of the Smithsonian Institution 1906-1913; retired in Washington, D.C.; died while on a visit to Altadena, Los Angeles County, Calif., October 2, 1927; interment in Allegheny Cemetery, Pittsburgh, Pa.

**Bibliography:** DAB.

**D'AMATO, Alfonse Marcello,** a Senator from New York; born in Brooklyn, Kings County, N.Y., August 1, 1937; raised on Long Island, N.Y., and graduated from Chaminade High School, Mineola, 1955; B.S., Syracuse University School of Business Administration, 1959; J.D., Syracuse University School of Law, 1961; admitted to the New York State bar in 1962; public administrator, Nassau County, N.Y., 1965-1968; tax assessor, Hempstead, N.Y., 1969; town supervisor, Hempstead, 1971-1977; presiding supervisor, Hempstead, and vice chairman, Nassau County Board of Supervisors, 1977-1980; elected as a Republican to the United States Senate in 1980 for the term commencing January 3, 1981; reelected in 1986 and again in 1992 for the term ending January 3, 1999; chairman, Committee on Banking, Housing, and Urban Affairs (One Hundred Fourth Congress); is a resident of Island Park, N.Y.

**D'AMOURS, Norman Edward,** a Representative from New Hampshire; born in Holyoke, Hampden County, Mass., October 14, 1937; attended parochial school in Holyoke, Mass., and high school in Worcester, Mass.; B.A., Assumption College, 1960; LL.B., Boston University Law School, 1963; served in the United States Army Reserves, 1964-1967; admitted to the Massachusetts bar in 1963 and to the New Hampshire bar in 1964; New Hampshire Assistant Attorney General, 1966-1969; Manchester City Prosecutor, 1970-1972; delegate to New Hampshire State Democratic conventions, 1970, 1972; delegate to Democratic National Convention, 1972; elected as a Democrat to the Ninety-fourth and to the four succeeding Congresses (January 3, 1975-January 3, 1985); was not a candidate for reelection in 1984 to the House of Representatives, but was an unsuccessful candidate for election to the United States Senate; returned to the practice of law in Washington, D.C.; nominated to be a member and the chairman of the National Credit Union Administration on October 25, 1993 for a term expiring in August 1999; confirmed by the Senate on November 22, 1993; is a resident of McLean, Va.

**DAMRELL, William Shapleigh,** a Representative from Massachusetts; born in Portsmouth, N.H., November 29, 1809; attended the public schools; learned the art of printing and became the proprietor of a large printing establishment in Boston; elected as the candidate of the American Party to the Thirty-fourth Congress and as a Republican to the Thirty-fifth Congress (March 4, 1855-March 3, 1859); suffered a paralytic stroke before the expiration of his term; was not a candidate for renomination in 1858 to the Thirty-sixth Congress; resumed business activities; died in Dedham, Norfolk County, Mass., May 17, 1860; interment in Forest Hills Cemetery.

**DANA, Amasa,** a Representative from New York; born in Wilkes-Barre, Pa., October 19, 1792; attended private schools and Dana Academy, Wilkes-Barre, Pa.; studied law in Owego, N.Y.; was admitted to the bar in 1817 and practiced; moved to Ithaca, N.Y., in 1821 and continued the practice of law; district attorney of Tompkins County 1823-1837; member of the State assembly in 1828 and 1829; president and trustee of the village of Ithaca in 1835, 1836, and 1839; elected judge of the court of common pleas of Tompkins County in 1837; elected as a Democrat to the Twenty-sixth Congress (March 4, 1839-March 3, 1841); was not a candidate for renomination in 1840; resumed the practice of law; elected to the Twenty-eighth Congress (March 4, 1843-March 3, 1845); chairman, Committee on Expenditures in the Department of the Navy (Twenty-eighth Congress); resumed the practice of his profession and also engaged in banking; died in Ithaca, Tompkins County, N.Y., on December 24, 1867; interment in Ithaca City Cemetery.

**DANA, Francis,** a Delegate from Massachusetts; born in Charlestown, Mass., June 13, 1743; was graduated from Harvard College in 1762; studied law; was admitted to the bar and commenced practice in Boston in 1767; delegate to the Provincial Congress in 1774; spent two years in England endeavoring to adjust differences between Great Britain and the American Colonies; State councilor 1776-1780; Member of the Continental Congress 1777-1778, and was one of the signers of the Articles of Confederation July 9, 1778; elected September 28, 1779, secretary to accompany John Adams, who was appointed a commissioner to negotiate a treaty of peace with Great Britain and a treaty of commerce with the Netherlands; appointed December 19, 1780, Minister Resident to Russia, but was never received as such, and left his post in September 1783; again a Member of the Continental Congress in 1784; judge of the supreme court of Massachusetts 1785-1791; appointed chief justice November 29, 1791, and served for fifteen years; member of the State convention which adopted the Federal Constitution in 1788; a founder of the American Academy of Arts and Sciences; died in Cambridge, Middlesex County, Mass., April 25, 1811; interment in Old Cambridge Cemetery.

**Bibliography:** *DAB.*

**DANA, Judah,** a Senator from Maine; born in Pomfret, Vt., April 25, 1772; attended the common schools, and was graduated from Dartmouth College, Hanover, N.H., in 1795; studied law; was admitted to the bar in 1798 and practiced in Fryeburg, Maine (at the time a district of Massachusetts); prosecuting attorney of Oxford County 1805-1811; judge of probate 1811-1822; judge of the court of common pleas 1811-1823; was also a circuit judge; delegate to the State constitutional convention in 1819 at which a committee was appointed to draw up a constitution for Maine; member of the Maine Executive Council in 1834; appointed as a Democrat to the United States Senate to fill the vacancy caused by the resignation of Ether Shepley and served from December 7, 1836, to March 3, 1837, when a successor was elected and qualified; died in Fryeburg, Oxford County, Maine, December 27, 1845; interment in Village Cemetery.

**Bibliography:** Spalding, James. "The School and College Life of Judah Dana." *The Dartmouth Alumni Magazine* 9 (February 1917): 155-66.

**DANA, Samuel,** a Representative from Massachusetts; born in Groton, Mass., June 26, 1767; attended the district school; studied law; was admitted to the bar in 1789 and commenced practice in Groton; appointed postmaster of Groton January 1, 1801; member of the Massachusetts house of representatives in 1803; attorney for Middlesex County 1807-1811; elected as a Republican to the Thirteenth Congress to fill the vacancy caused by the resignation of William M. Richardson and served from September 22, 1814, to March 3, 1815; unsuccessful candidate for reelection in 1814 to the Fourteenth Congress; member of the Massachusetts senate 1805-1812 and 1817 and served as its president in 1807, 1811, and 1812; chief justice of the court of common pleas in 1811 and 1812; delegate to the Massachusetts constitutional convention in 1820; again a member of the Massachusetts house of representatives 1825-1827; resumed the practice of his profession; died in Charlestown, Mass., November 20, 1835; interment in Groton Cemetery.

**DANA, Samuel Whittlesey,** a Representative and a Senator from Connecticut; born in Wallingford, Conn., February 13, 1760; pursued academic studies and was graduated from Yale College in 1775; studied law; was admitted to the bar in 1778 and practiced in Middletown, Conn.; member, State general assembly 1789-1796; elected to the Fourth Congress to fill the vacancy caused by the resignation of Uriah Tracy and to the seven succeeding Congresses and served from January 3, 1797, to May 10, 1810, when he resigned to become Senator; chairman, Committee on Elections (Sixth Congress); one of the managers appointed by the House of Representatives in 1798 to conduct the impeachment proceedings against William Blount, a Senator from Tennessee; elected as a Federalist in 1810 to the United States Senate to fill the vacancy caused by the resignation of James Hillhouse; reelected in 1815 and served from May 10, 1810, to March 3, 1821; mayor of Middletown, Conn., from 1822 until his death; presiding judge of the Middlesex County Court from 1825 until his death in Middletown on July 21, 1830; interment in Washington Street Cemetery.

**Bibliography:** *DAB.*

**DANAHER, John Anthony,** a Senator from Connecticut; born in Meriden, New Haven County, Conn., January 9, 1899; attended the local schools; during the First World War served in the Student's Army Training Corps at Yale College and in the Officers' Reserve Corps; was graduated from Yale College in 1920; studied law at Yale Law School; was admitted to the bar in 1922 and commenced practice in Hartford, Conn.; assistant United States attorney for the district of Connecticut, 1921-1935; member of the State Board of Finance and Control, 1933-1935; secretary of the State of Connecticut, 1935-1939; elected as a Republican in 1938 to the United States Senate and served from January 3, 1939, to January 3, 1945; unsuccessful candidate for reelection in 1944; resumed the practice of law in Hartford, Conn., and Washington, D.C.; appointed a circuit judge of the United States Court of Appeals for the District of Columbia Circuit, by President Dwight D. Eisenhower and took the oath of office November 20, 1953; became a senior United States circuit judge January 23, 1969; was a resident of West Hartford, Conn.; died September 22, 1990.

**Bibliography:** Clifford, J. Garry, and Robert Griffiths. "Senator John A. Danaher and the Battle Against American Intervention in World War II." *Connecticut History* 25 (1984): 39-63.

**DANE, Joseph,** a Representative from Maine; born in Beverly, Essex County, Mass., October 25, 1778; received his early education in Beverly, Mass.; attended Phillips Academy, Andover, Mass., and was graduated from Harvard University in 1799; studied law; was admitted to the bar in 1802 and commenced practice in Kennebunk, Maine (until 1820 a district of Massachusetts); a delegate to the Massachusetts constitutional conventions in 1816 and 1819; chosen a member of the executive council of Massachusetts in 1817, but declined the office; elected to the Sixteenth Congress to fill the vacancy caused by the resignation of John Holmes, a Representative from Massachusetts but residing in the new State of Maine, thus becoming the first Representative from Maine; reelected to the Seventeenth Congress and served from November 6, 1820, to March 3, 1823; was not a candidate for renomination in 1822; member of the Maine house of representatives in 1824, 1825, 1832, 1833, 1839, and 1840; served in the State senate in 1829; declined to serve as executive councilor of Maine in 1841; died in Kennebunk, York County, Maine, May 1, 1858; interment in Hope Cemetery, Hope, Knox County, Maine.

**DANE, Nathan,** a Delegate from Massachusetts; born in Ipswich, Mass., December 29, 1752; was graduated from Harvard College in 1778; taught school; studied law; was admitted to the bar and commenced practice in Beverly, Mass., in 1782; member of the Massachusetts house of representatives 1782-1785; Member of the Continental Congress 1785-1788; served in the Massachusetts senate in 1790, 1791, and 1794-1797; judge of the court of common pleas for Essex County in 1794; commissioner to codify the laws of Massachusetts in 1795; presidential elector on the Clinton ticket in 1812; was selected the same year to make a new publication of the statutes; member of the Hartford convention of 1814; elected delegate to the Massachusetts constitutional convention of 1820, but did not serve; died in Beverly, Essex County, Mass., February 15, 1835; interment in Central Cemetery.

**Bibliography:** *DAB.*

**DANFORD, Lorenzo,** a Representative from Ohio; born in Washington Township, Belmont County, Ohio, on October 18, 1829; attended the common schools and a college at Waynesburg, Pa., for two years; studied law; was admitted to the bar at St. Clairsville, Belmont County, Ohio, in September 1854, and commenced practice there; presidential elector on the American Party ticket in 1856; prosecuting attorney of Belmont County from 1857 to 1861, when he resigned to enlist in the Fifteenth Regiment, Ohio Volunteer Infantry, as a private; commissioned a lieutenant and later a captain, and served until honorably discharged in August 1864; resumed the practice of his profession in St. Clairsville; elected as a Republican to the Forty-third, Forty-fourth, and Forty-fifth Congresses (March 4, 1873-March 3, 1879); was not a candidate for renomination in 1878; resumed the practice of his profession; elected to the Fifty-fourth, Fifty-fifth, and Fifty-sixth Congresses and served from March 4, 1895, until his death in St. Clairsville, Ohio, June 19, 1899; chairman, Committee on Immigration and Naturalization (Fifty-fifth Congress); interment in the Methodist Episcopal Cemetery.

**DANFORTH, Henry Gold,** a Representative from New York; born in the town of Gates (now part of Rochester), Monroe County, N.Y., June 14, 1854; attended private schools in Rochester, N.Y., and Phillips Exeter Academy, Exeter, N.H.; was graduated from the collegiate department of Harvard University in 1877 and from the law department in 1880; was admitted to the bar in 1880 and commenced practice in Rochester; director of the Rochester General Hospital 1889-1918; member of the board of managers of the New York State Reformatory, Elmira, N.Y., 1900-1902; trustee of the Reynolds Library 1906-1918; elected as a Republican to the Sixty-second, Sixty-third, and Sixty-fourth Congresses (March 4, 1911-March 3, 1917); unsuccessful candidate for renomination in 1916; resumed the practice of law; died in Rochester, N.Y., April 8, 1918; interment in Mount Hope Cemetery.

**DANFORTH, John Claggett,** a Senator from Missouri; born in St. Louis, Mo., September 5, 1936; graduated, St. Louis County Day (High) School, 1954; A.B., Princeton University, 1958; LL.B., Yale University Law School, 1963; B.D., Yale University Divinity School, 1963; admitted to the New York bar in 1963 and commenced practice in New York City; ordained minister, Episcopal Church, 1963; attorney general of Missouri, 1969-1976; unsuccessful candidate in 1970 for nomination to the United States Senate; elected as a Republican to the United States Senate in 1976 for the term commencing January 3, 1977; subsequently appointed by the Governor to fill the vacancy caused by the resignation of Stuart Symington for the term ending January 3, 1977; reelected in 1982 and again in 1988 and served from December 27, 1976 to January 3, 1995; was not a candidate for reelection in 1994; chairman, Committee on Commerce, Science and Transportation (Ninety-ninth Congress); is a resident of Newburg, Mo.

**DANIEL, Charles Ezra,** a Senator from South Carolina; born in Elberton, Elbert County, Ga., November 11, 1895; moved with his family to Anderson, S.C., in 1898 and attended the public schools; student at The Citadel, Charleston, S.C., 1916-1918; during the First World War served as a lieutenant in the Infantry 1917-1919; businessman; interests in construction, banking, building supplies, telecommunications, insurance, and airlines; life trustee of Clemson College and member of the board of South Carolina Foundation of Independent Colleges; appointed as a Democrat to the United States Senate to fill the vacancy caused by the death of Burnet R. Maybank and served from September 6, 1954, until his resignation December 23, 1954; was not a candidate for election to fill the vacancy; resumed management of his business interests; died in Greenville, S.C., September 13, 1964; interment in Springwood Cemetery.

**DANIEL, Dan,** a Representative from Virginia. (*See* DANIEL, Wilbur Clarence.)

**DANIEL, Henry,** a Representative from Kentucky; born in Louisa County, Va., March 15, 1786; attended the public schools; moved to Kentucky; studied law; was admitted to the bar and commenced practice in Mount Sterling, Montgomery County, Ky.; member of the Kentucky house of representatives in 1812; served in the War of 1812 as captain of the Eighth Regiment, United States Infantry, 1813-1815; again a member of the Kentucky house of representatives in 1819 and 1826; elected as a Jacksonian to the Twentieth, Twenty-first, and Twenty-second Congresses (March 4, 1827-March 3, 1833); unsuccessful candidate for reelection in 1832 to the Twenty-third Congress; resumed the practice of law; died in Mount Sterling, Ky., October 5, 1873; interment in Macphelah Cemetery.

**DANIEL, John Reeves Jones,** a Representative from North Carolina; born near Halifax, Halifax County, N.C., January 13, 1802; instructed privately at home; was graduated from the University of North Carolina at Chapel Hill in 1821; studied law; was admitted to the North Carolina bar in 1823 and commenced the practice of law in Halifax, N.C.; member of the State house of commons 1832-1834; elected attorney general of North Carolina in 1834; elected as a Democrat to the Twenty-seventh and to the five succeeding Congresses (March 4, 1841-March 3, 1853); chairman, Committee on Claims (Twenty-ninth, Thirty-first, and Thirty-second Congresses); was not a candidate for renomination in 1852 to the Thirty-third Congress; resumed the practice of law; moved to Louisiana in 1860 and settled near Shreveport; continued the practice of law and also engaged in planting; died in Shreveport, Caddo Parish, La., June 22, 1868.

**DANIEL, John Warwick,** a Representative and a Senator from Virginia; born in Lynchburg, Va., September 5, 1842; attended private schools, Lynchburg College, and Dr. Gessner Harrison's University School; during the Civil War served in the Confederate Army 1861-1864, attained the rank of major; permanently crippled in the Battle of the Wilderness in May 1864; studied law at the University of Virginia at Charlottesville; was admitted to the bar in 1866 and commenced practice at Lynchburg, Va.; member, Virginia house of delegates 1869-1872; member, Virginia senate 1875-1881; unsuccessful candidate for Governor in 1881; elected as a Democrat to the Forty-ninth Congress (March 4, 1885-March 3, 1887); did not seek renomination in 1886 to the House of Representatives, having been elected Senator; elected in 1885 as a Democrat to the United States Senate; reelected in 1891, 1897, 1904, and 1910, and served from March 4, 1887, until his death on June 29, 1910; died before his credentials for the last election could be presented; chairman, Committee on Revision of the Laws of The United States (Fifty-third Congress), Committee on Corporations Organized in the District of Columbia (Fifty-fifth Congress), Committee on Public Health and National Quarantine (Sixtieth Congress), Committee on Private Land Claims (Sixty-first Congress); died in Lynchburg, Va.; interment in Spring Hill Cemetery.

Bibliography: *DAB*; Doss, Richard. "John Warwick Daniel: A Study in the Virginia Democracy." Ph.D. dissertation, University of Virginia, 1955.

**DANIEL, Price Marion,** a Senator from Texas; born in Dayton, Liberty County, Tex., October 10, 1910; attended the public schools of Liberty and Fort Worth, Tex.; reporter for the Fort Worth Star-Telegram, 1926-1927, and for the Waco News Tribune, 1929-1931; graduated from Baylor University, Waco, Tex., in 1931 and from the law school of the same university in 1932; admitted to the Texas bar in 1932 and began practice in Liberty, Tex.; co-owner and publisher of two weekly newspapers; member, Texas State house of representatives, 1939-1943, serving as speaker in 1943; enlisted as a private in the United States Army in 1943 and served in the Pacific Theater and in Japan until discharged as a captain in June 1946; attorney general of Texas, 1946-1953; elected as a Democrat to the United States Senate for the term beginning January 3, 1953, and served until his resignation January 14, 1957; elected Governor of Texas in 1956, reelected in 1958 and 1960, and served from January 14, 1957 to January 15, 1963; practiced law in Liberty and Austin, Tex., 1963-1967; appointed by President Lyndon B. Johnson as Director of the Office of Emergency Preparedness and Assistant to the President for Federal-State Relations, 1967-1969; also served on the National Security Council and as President Johnson's liaison with Governors; served as a member of the Texas State supreme court from January 1971 to December 1978; resumed the practice of law; died August 25, 1988.

Bibliography: Murph, David R. "Price Daniel: The Life of a Public Man, 1910-1956." Ph.D. dissertation, Texas Christian University, 1975.

**DANIEL, Robert Williams, Jr.,** a Representative from Virginia; born in Richmond, Va., March 17, 1936; educated at the Fay School, Southboro, Mass., 1946-1949; Woodberry Forest School, Woodberry Forest, Va., 1949-1954; B.A., University of Virginia, 1954-1958; M.B.A., Columbia University, 1960-1961; active duty as a United States Army Reserve officer, 1959; farmer; businessman; financial analyst; teacher; served with United States Central Intelligence Agency, 1964-1968; delegate to Virginia State Republican convention, 1972; delegate to the Republican National Convention of 1972; elected as a Republican to the Ninety-third and to the four succeeding Congresses (January 3, 1973-January 3, 1983); unsuccessful candidate for reelection in 1982 to the Ninety-eighth Congress; is a resident of Spring Grove, Va.

**DANIEL, Wilbur Clarence (Dan),** a Representative from Virginia; born in Chatham, Pittsylvania County, Va., May 12, 1914; grew up on a tobacco farm in Mecklenburg County, Va.; educated in Virginia schools; graduate of Dan River Textile School, Danville, Va.; associated with Dan River Mills, Inc., 1939-1968, except for period of service in the United States Navy during the Second World War; advanced through ranks to assistant to the board chairman; elected to the Virginia house of delegates, 1959-1968; elected State commander of American Legion, 1951, national commander, 1956; President of Virginia State Chamber of Commerce, 1968; permanent member, President's People-to-People Committee; elected as a Democrat to the Ninety-first and to the nine succeeding Congresses and served from January 3, 1969, until his death in Charlottesville, Va., on January 23, 1988; was a resident of Danville, Va; interment in Highland Burial Park, Danville.

**DANIELL, Warren Fisher,** a Representative from New Hampshire; born in Newton Lower Falls, Middlesex County, Mass., June 26, 1826; attended the common schools; moved with his parents to Franklin, Merrimack County, N.H., in 1834; continued his studies until fourteen years of age, when he entered his father's paper mill as an apprentice; constructed a paper mill at Waterville, Maine, in 1852, and in the following year managed a similar mill in Pepperell, Mass.; returned to Franklin, N.H., in 1854 and engaged in the manufacture of paper; also engaged in agricultural pursuits, the breeding of blooded stock, and banking; member of the State house of representatives in 1861, 1862, and 1870-1877; delegate to the Democratic National Convention in 1872; served in the State senate in 1873 and 1874; elected as a Democrat to the Fifty-second Congress (March 4, 1891-March 3, 1893); was not a candidate for renomination in 1892; continued his activities in the manufacture of paper at Franklin, N.H., until 1898, being interested in the Winnepesogee Paper Co.; died in Franklin, N.H., July 30, 1913; interment in Franklin Cemetery.

**DANIELS, Charles,** a Representative from New York; born in New York City March 24, 1825; at an early age he was taken to Toledo, Ohio, and learned his father's trade of shoemaker; moved to Buffalo, N.Y., in 1842, where he studied law; was admitted to the bar in 1847 and commenced practice in Buffalo; elected an associate justice of the New York Supreme Court in 1863; appointed by Governor Horatio Seymour to hold the office of justice of that court until January 1, 1864, when the term to which he had been elected commenced; twice reelected, and served until December 1891, when he reached the age limit and was retired; elected as a Republican to the Fifty-third and Fifty-fourth Congresses (March 4, 1893-March 3, 1897); chairman, Committee on Elections No. 1 (Fifty-fourth Congress); was not a candidate for renomination in 1896 to the Fifty-fifth Congress; died in Buffalo, N.Y., December 20, 1897; interment in Forest Lawn Cemetery.

**DANIELS, Dominick Vincent,** a Representative from New Jersey; born in Jersey City, Hudson County, N.J., October 18, 1908; educated in the Jersey City public schools; attended Fordham University, New York City; graduated from Rutgers University Law School, New Brunswick, N.J., in 1929; was admitted to the New Jersey bar in 1930 and commenced the practice of law in Jersey City, N.J.; appointed magistrate of the Jersey City Municipal Court in May 1952, reappointed in 1955, and subsequently was appointed presiding magistrate, in which capacity he served until March 1958; delegate, Democratic National Conventions, 1960, 1964, and 1968; elected as a Democrat to the Eighty-sixth and to the eight succeeding Congresses (January 3, 1959-January 3, 1977); was not a candidate for reelection in 1976 to the Ninety-fifth Congress; returned to the practice of law in Jersey City; was a resident of Union City, N.J., until his death in Jersey City on July 17, 1987; interment in Holy Cross Cemetery, North Arlington, N.J.

**DANIELS, Milton John,** a Representative from California; born in Cobleskill, Schoharie County, N.Y., April 18, 1838; attended the public schools; when a boy moved to Bradford County, Pa., and engaged with his father in the lumber business; moved to Rochester, Minn., in 1856; appointed deputy postmaster of Rochester in 1859; entered Middlebury Academy, Wyoming County, N.Y., in 1860; volunteered April 23, 1861, for service in the Civil War; returned to Minnesota and raised a company in August 1862, and was commissioned second lieutenant of Company F, Ninth Regiment, Minnesota Volunteers; took command of the Third Minnesota Mounted Infantry in the Indian war of 1862; joined his company at St. Louis in 1863, and was commissioned captain; in March 1865 was commissioned captain and commissary of subsistence by President Lincoln; engaged in banking; member of the State house of representatives 1882-1886; served in the State senate 1886-1890; president of the Minnesota State Board of Asylums for the Insane 1882-1888; moved to California in 1889 and located in Riverside; engaged in horticultural pursuits; elected as a Republican to the Fifty-eighth Congress (March 4, 1903-March 3, 1905); was not a candidate for renomination in 1904 to the Fifty-ninth Congress; resumed his occupation as horticulturist in Riverside, Calif., until his death there on December 1, 1914; interment in Evergreen Cemetery.

**DANIELSON, George Elmore,** a Representative from California; born in Wausa, Knox County, Nebr., February 20, 1915; attended the Wausa public schools, and Wayne State Teachers College, Wayne, Nebr., 1933-1935; B.A., University of Nebraska, 1937; J.D., University of Nebraska School of Law, 1939; special agent, Federal Bureau of Investigation, 1939-1944; served with the United States Naval Reserve in the Pacific Theater, 1944-1946, discharged with rank of lieutenant (jg); admitted to the Nebraska bar in 1941; admitted to the California bar in 1949 and commenced practice in Los Angeles; assistant United States attorney, 1949-1951; member, California State assembly, 1963-1967; California State senator, 1967-1971; delegate to California State Democratic conventions, 1960-1974; delegate to the Democratic National Convention of 1968; elected as a Democrat to the Ninety-second and to the five succeeding Congresses and served from January 3, 1971, until his resignation March 9, 1982, to be an associate justice of the California Court of Appeal, Second Appellate District, Division Three, Los Angeles, Calif.; is a resident of Monterey Park, Calif.

**DANNEMEYER, William Edwin,** a Representative from California; born in Long Beach, Los Angeles County, Calif., September 22, 1929; attended the Trinity Lutheran School, Los Angeles, 1943; graduated from Long Beach Poly High School, 1946; attended Santa Maria Junior College, 1947; B.A., Valparaiso University, Indiana, 1950; J.D., Hastings Law School, University of California, 1952; served in the United States Army, 1952-1954; admitted to the California bar in 1953 and commenced practice in Santa Barbara, 1955; deputy district attorney, 1955-1957; Fullerton assistant city attorney, 1959-1962; served in the California State assembly, 1963-1966 and 1977-1978; municipal and superior court judge pro tempore, 1966-1976; delegate to California State Republican conventions, 1972 and 1976-1978; elected as a Republican to the Ninety-sixth and to the six succeeding Congresses (January 3, 1979-January 3, 1993); was not a candidate for reelection in 1992 to the House of Representatives, but was an unsuccessful candidate for nomination to the United States Senate; is a resident of Fullerton, Calif.

**DANNER, Joel Buchanan,** a Representative from Pennsylvania; born in Liberty, Md., in 1804; engaged in the hardware business and carriage building at Gettysburg, Adams County, Pa.; justice of the peace; elected as a Democrat to the Thirty-first Congress to fill the vacancy caused by the death of Henry Nes, and served from December 2, 1850 to March 3, 1851; resumed his former business pursuits in Gettysburg, Pa., where he died on July 29, 1885; interment in Evergreen Cemetery.

**DANNER, Patsy Ann (Pat),** a Representative from Missouri; born in Louisville, Ky., January 13, 1934; public schools in Bevier, Mo.; B.A., Northeast Missouri State University, Kirksville, 1972; district assistant to Representative Jerry L. Litton of Missouri; Federal co-chair, Ozarks Regional Commission, 1977-1981; member, Missouri State senate, 1983-1993; elected as a Democrat to the One Hundred Third and One Hundred Fourth Congresses (January 3, 1993-January 3, 1997); is a resident of Smithville, Mo.

**DARBY, Ezra,** a Representative from New Jersey; born in Scotch Plains, N.J., June 7, 1768; attended the common schools; engaged in agricultural pursuits; held offices as chosen freeholder, assessor, and justice of the peace from 1800 to 1804; member of the State house of assembly 1802-1804; elected as a Republican to the Ninth and Tenth Congresses and served from March 4, 1805, until his death in Washington, D.C., January 27, 1808; interment in Congressional Cemetery.

**DARBY, Harry,** a Senator from Kansas; born in Kansas City, Wyandotte County, Kans., January 23, 1895; attended the public schools; was graduated from the University of Illinois in 1917 and 1929; during the First World War served in the United States Army 1917-1919, attaining the rank of captain; industrialist and farmer-stockman with business interests in railroads, steel, banking, insurance, retail sales, and utility companies; chairman, State highway commission 1933-1937; appointed as a Republican to the United States Senate to fill the vacancy caused by the death of Clyde M. Reed and served from December 2, 1949, to November 28, 1950, a successor having been elected; was not a candidate for election to fill the vacancy; resumed business and political activities; was a resident of Kansas City, Kans., until his death there on January 17, 1987; interment in Highland Park Cemetery.

**DARBY, John Fletcher,** a Representative from Missouri; born in Person County, N.C., December 10, 1803; attended the public schools; moved with his father to Missouri in 1818, where he worked on a farm; moved to Frankfort, Ky., in 1825; studied law; was admitted to the bar and afterward practiced in St. Louis, Mo.; mayor of St. Louis 1835-1841; member of the Missouri senate in 1838; elected as a Whig to the Thirty-second Congress (March 4, 1851-March 3, 1853); returned to St. Louis and engaged in banking; died near Pendleton Station, Warren County, Mo., May 11, 1882; interment in Calvary Cemetery, St. Louis, Mo.

Bibliography: Darby, John Fletcher. *Personal Recollections.* 1880. Reprint. New York: Arno Press, 1975.

**DARDEN, Colgate Whitehead, Jr.,** a Representative from Virginia; born on a farm near Franklin, Southampton County, Va., February 11, 1897; attended the public schools; was graduated from the University of Virginia at Charlottesville in 1922 and from Columbia University, New York City, in 1923; awarded a Carnegie Fellowship to Oxford University, England, in 1924; during the First World War served with the French Army in 1916 and 1917 and later as a lieutenant in the United States Marine Corps Air Service; studied law; was admitted to the bar in 1922 and commenced practice in Norfolk, Va.; member of the Virginia house of delegates 1930-1933; elected as a Democrat to the Seventy-third and Seventy-fourth Congresses (March 4, 1933-January 3, 1937); unsuccessful candidate for renomination in 1936 to the Seventy-fifth Congress; elected to the Seventy-sixth and Seventy-seventh Congresses and served from January 3, 1939, until his resignation on March 1, 1941, to become a candidate for Governor; elected Governor of Virginia in 1941 and served from January 21, 1942 to January 16, 1946; president of the University of Virginia at Charlottesville from June 23, 1947, to September 1, 1959; United States delegate to the Tenth General Assembly of the United Nations, 1955; member of the President's Commission on National Goals, 1960; chairman, Commission on Goals for Higher Education in the South, 1961; resided in Norfolk, Va., where he died June 9, 1981; interment on family estate, Southampton, Va.

**DARDEN, George (Buddy),** a Representative from Georgia; born in Hancock County, Ga., November 22, 1943; attended public schools, Sparta, Ga.; A.B., University of Georgia, Athens, 1965; J.D., University of Georgia, 1967; admitted to the Georgia bar, 1968 and commenced practice in Marietta; assistant district attorney, Cobb County, Ga., 1968-1972; district attorney, Cobb County, Ga., 1973-1976; Georgia State representative, District 20, 1980-1983; elected as a Democrat to the Ninety-eighth Congress, November 8, 1983, by special election to fill the vacancy caused by the death of Lawrence P. (Larry) McDonald; reelected to the Ninety-ninth and to the four succeeding Congresses (November 8, 1983-January 3, 1995); unsuccessful candidate for reelection in 1994 to the One Hundred Fourth Congress; is a resident of Marietta, Ga.

**DARGAN, Edmund Strother,** a Representative from Alabama; born near Wadesboro, Montgomery County, N.C., April 15, 1805; pursued preparatory studies at home; studied law; was admitted to the bar in Wadesboro in 1829; moved to Washington, Ala., where he commenced the practice of law and was for several years a justice of the peace; moved to Montgomery in 1833 and to Mobile in 1841; judge of the circuit court, Mobile district, in 1841 and 1842; served in the State senate in 1844; mayor of Mobile in 1844; elected as a Democrat to the Twenty-ninth Congress (March 4, 1845-March 3, 1847); was not a candidate for renomination in 1846 to the Thirtieth Congress; associate justice of the State supreme court in 1847, and in 1849 became chief justice; resigned in December 1852 and resumed the practice of law; delegate to the State convention in 1861 and voted for the ordinance of secession; member of the first Confederate House of Representatives; resumed the practice of law in Mobile, Ala., and died there on November 22, 1879; interment in Magnolia Cemetery.

**DARGAN, George William** (great-grandson of Lemuel Benton), a Representative from South Carolina; born at "Sleepy Hollow," near Darlington, S.C., May 11, 1841; attended the schools of Darlington County and the South Carolina Military Academy; served in the Confederate Army throughout the Civil War; studied law; was admitted to the bar in 1872 and practiced in Darlington, S.C.; elected to the State house of representatives in 1877; solicitor of the fourth judicial circuit of South Carolina in 1880; elected as a Democrat to the Forty-eighth and to the three succeeding Congresses (March 4, 1883-March 3, 1891); was not a candidate for renomination in 1890 to the Fifty-second Congress; resumed the practice of law; died in Darlington, S.C., June 29, 1898; interment in First Baptist Churchyard.

**DARLING, Mason Cook,** a Representative from Wisconsin; born in Amherst, Hampshire County, Mass., May 18, 1801; attended the public schools; taught school in the State of New York; studied medicine; was graduated from the Berkshire Medical College in 1824 and practiced medicine for thirteen years; moved to Wisconsin in 1837 and was one of the original settlers at Fond du Lac; member of the Territorial legislative assembly 1840-1846; member of the Territorial council in 1847 and 1848; upon the admission of Wisconsin as a State into the Union was elected as a Democrat to the Thirtieth Congress and served from June 9, 1848, to March 3, 1849; was not a candidate for renomination in 1848 to the Thirty-first Congress; was elected the first mayor of Fond du Lac in 1852; resumed the practice of medicine and was a dealer in real estate at Fond du Lac until 1864, when he moved to Chicago; died in Chicago, Ill., March 12, 1866; interment in Rienzi Cemetery, Fond du Lac, Wis.

**DARLING, William Augustus,** a Representative from New York; born in Newark, N.J., December 27, 1817; attended the public schools; moved to New York City, where he was employed as a clerk and afterwards engaged in the wholesale grocery business; director of the Mercantile Library Association; served eleven years as a private and officer in the New York National Guard; deputy receiver of taxes for the city of New York 1847-1854; served as president of the Third Avenue Railroad 1854-1865; elected as a Republican to the Thirty-ninth Congress (March 4, 1865-March 3, 1867); unsuccessful candidate for reelection in 1866 to the Fortieth Congress; unsuccessful candidate for mayor of New York City in 1866; served as collector of internal revenue for the ninth district of New York from April 26, 1869, to April 17, 1871, and as appraiser from April 18, 1871, to April 1, 1876; engaged in banking and served as president of the Murray Hill Bank; died in New York City May 26, 1895; interment in Trinity Cemetery.

**DARLINGTON, Edward** (cousin of Isaac Darlington and William Darlington), a Representative from Pennsylvania; born in West Chester, Chester County, Pa., September 17, 1795; moved in early youth with his parents to Delaware County; attended the common schools and was graduated from West Chester Academy; taught school 1817-1820; studied law; was admitted to the bar in 1821 and commenced practice in Chester, Pa.; deputy attorney general 1824-1830; elected as an Anti-Masonic candidate to the Twenty-third and to the two succeeding Congresses (March 4, 1833-March 3, 1839); chairman, Committee on Expenditures on Public Buildings (Twenty-fourth Congress); was not a candidate for renomination in 1838 to the Twenty-sixth Congress; resumed the practice of law; attorney for county commissioners 1846-1856; moved to Media, Pa., in 1851; district attorney of Delaware County 1851-1854; died in Media, Delaware County, Pa., November 21, 1884; interment in Chester Rural Cemetery, Chester, Pa.

**DARLINGTON, Isaac** (cousin of Edward Darlington and William Darlington), a Representative from Pennsylvania; born near West Chester, Chester County, Pa., December 13, 1781; attended Friends School at Birmingham, Chester County, Pa.; taught in the country schools; studied law; was admitted to the bar in 1801 and commenced practice in West Chester, Pa.; member of the Pennsylvania house of representatives 1807-1809; lieutenant and adjutant of the Second Regiment, Pennsylvania Volunteers, in 1814 and 1815; elected as a Federalist to the Fifteenth Congress (March 4, 1817-March 3, 1819); declined to be a candidate for renomination in 1818 to the Sixteenth Congress; was appointed deputy attorney general for Chester County in 1820; presiding judge of the judicial district comprising the counties of Chester and Delaware from May 1821 until the time of his death in West Chester, Chester County, Pa., April 27, 1839; interment in Friends Burying Ground, Birmingham, Chester County, Pa.

**DARLINGTON, Smedley** (second cousin of Edward Darlington, Isaac Darlington, and William Darlington), a Representative from Pennsylvania; born in Pocopson Township, Chester County, Pa., December 24, 1827; attended the common schools and the Friends' Central School, Philadelphia; teacher in the latter school for several years; while teaching he made stenographic reports of sermons, lectures, and speeches for the morning dailies of Philadelphia; established a school in Ercildoun in 1851 which he operated for twelve years; enlisted in the Civil War as a private and subsequently promoted to the rank of captain in Beaumont's independent company of cavalry, Pennsylvania Volunteer Emergency Militia; discharged with the company September 24, 1862; moved to West Chester, Pa. in 1864; conducted an extensive banking and brokerage business; delegate to the Liberal Republican National Convention of 1872 and the Republican National Convention of 1896; elected as a Republican to the Fiftieth and Fifty-first Congresses (March 4, 1887-March 3, 1891); was not a candidate for renomination in 1890 to the Fifty-second Congress; resumed the brokerage business and banking; died in West Chester, Chester County, Pa., June 24, 1899; interment in Oakland Cemetery near West Chester, Pa.

**DARLINGTON, William** (cousin of Edward Darlington and Isaac Darlington), a Representative from Pennsylvania; born in Birmingham, Chester County, Pa., April 28, 1782; attended Friends School at Birmingham; spent his youth on a farm; became a botanist at an early age; studied medicine; was graduated from the medical department of the University of Pennsylvania at Philadelphia in 1804; went to the East Indies as ship's surgeon in 1806; returned to West Chester in 1807 and was a practicing physician there for a number of years; raised a company of volunteers at the beginning of the War of 1812 and was major of a volunteer regiment; elected as a Republican to the Fourteenth Congress (March 4, 1815-March 3, 1817); elected to the Sixteenth and Seventeenth Congresses (March 4, 1819-March 3, 1823); appointed canal commissioner in 1825; president of the West Chester Railroad; established a natural history society in West Chester in 1826; published several works on botany and natural history; director and president of the National Bank of Chester County from 1830 until 1863; died in West Chester, Chester County, Pa., on April 23, 1863; interment in Oakland Cemetery.

**Bibliography:** *DAB*; Lansing, Dorothy I. *That Magnificent Cestrian: Dr. William Darlington, 1782-1863.* Paoli, Pa.: Serpentine Press, 1985.

**DARRAGH, Archibald Bard,** a Representative from Michigan; born in La Salle Township, Monroe County, Mich., December 23, 1840; attended the common schools and a private academy in Monroe, Mich.; entered the University of Michigan at Ann Arbor in 1857 and pursued a classical course for two years; moved to Claiborne County, Miss., and became a teacher; returned to Michigan upon the outbreak of the Civil War; enlisted in Company H, Eighteenth Regiment, Michigan Volunteer Infantry, in 1862; commissioned second lieutenant, Company D, Ninth Regiment, Michigan Volunteer Cavalry, in 1863; promoted to first lieutenant in 1864 and captain in 1865; superintendent of the public schools of Jackson in 1867; reentered the University of Michigan and was graduated in 1868; moved to St. Louis, Gratiot County, Mich., in 1870 and engaged in banking; elected treasurer of Gratiot County in 1872; member of the State house of representatives in 1882 and 1883; mayor of St. Louis, Mich., in 1893; member of the board of control of the State asylum; elected as a Republican to the Fifty-seventh and to the three succeeding Congresses (March 4, 1901-March 3, 1909); was not a candidate for renomination in 1908; again engaged in banking; died in St. Louis, Mich., on February 21, 1927; interment in Oak Grove Cemetery.

**DARRAGH, Cornelius,** a Representative from Pennsylvania; born in Pittsburgh, Pa., in 1809; attended the Western University of Pennsylvania, and was graduated with the class of 1826; studied law; was admitted to the bar in 1829 and commenced practice in Pittsburgh; member of the Pennsylvania senate 1836-1839; United States district attorney for the western district of Pennsylvania 1841-1844; elected as a Whig to the Twenty-eighth Congress to fill the vacancy caused by the resignation of William Wilkins; reelected to the Twenty-ninth Congress and served from March 26, 1844, to March 3, 1847; attorney general of Pennsylvania from January 4, 1849, to April 28, 1851; died in Pittsburgh, Pa., on December 22, 1854; interment in Allegheny Cemetery.

**DARRALL, Chester Bidwell,** a Representative from Louisiana; born near Addison, Somerset County, Pa., June 24, 1842; attended the common schools; studied medicine and was graduated from the Albany (N.Y.) Medical College; during the Civil War entered the Union Army as assistant surgeon of the Eighty-sixth Regiment, New York Volunteers, and later was promoted to surgeon; resigned from the Army while on duty in Louisiana in 1867 and engaged in mercantile pursuits and planting in Brashear (now Morgan City), La.; member of the State senate of Louisiana in 1868; delegate to the Republican National Convention in 1872 and 1876; elected as a Republican to the Forty-first and to the three succeeding Congresses (March 4, 1869-March 3, 1877); presented credentials as a Member-elect to the Forty-fifth Congress and served from March 4, 1877, to February 20, 1878, when he was succeeded by Joseph H. Acklen, who contested the election; was not a candidate for renomination in 1878; moved to Morgan City, St. Mary Parish, La.; elected to the Forty-seventh Congress (March 4, 1881-March 3, 1883); unsuccessful candidate for reelection in 1882 to the Forty-eighth Congress; register of the United States land office, New Orleans, La., 1883-1885; engaged in sugarcane planting; unsuccessful candidate for election in 1888 to the Fiftieth Congress; moved to Washington, D.C., where he died on January 1, 1908; interment in Glenwood Cemetery.

**DARROW, George Potter,** a Representative from Pennsylvania; born in Waterford, New London County, Conn., February 4, 1859; attended the common schools of New London, Conn.; was graduated from Alfred University, Alfred, N.Y., in 1880; moved to Philadelphia, Pa., in 1888 and engaged in banking, in the manufacture of paints, and in the insurance business; president of the Twenty-second Sectional School Board of Philadelphia 1906-1909; member of the Philadelphia Common Council 1910-1915; elected as a Republican to the Sixty-fourth and to the ten succeeding Congresses (March 4, 1915-January 3, 1937); unsuccessful candidate for reelection in 1936 to the Seventy-fifth Congress; elected to the Seventy-sixth Congress (January 3, 1939-January 3, 1941); was not a candidate for renomination in 1940 to the Seventy-seventh Congress; died in Philadelphia, Pa., June 7, 1943; interment in Ivy Hill Mausoleum.

**DASCHLE, Thomas Andrew,** a Representative and a Senator from South Dakota; born in Aberdeen, Brown County, S.Dak., December 9, 1947; attended private and public schools; B.A., South Dakota State University, 1969; served in the United States Air Force, 1969-1972; chief legislative assistant to Senator James Abourezk of S.Dak., 1973-1977; representative for financial investment firm; elected as a Democrat in 1978 to the Ninety-sixth Congress; reelected to the three succeeding Congresses (January 3, 1979-January 3, 1987); was not a candidate for renomination to the House of Representatives in 1986, but was elected to the United States Senate for the term beginning January 3, 1987; reelected in 1992 for the term ending January 3, 1999; co-chair, Democratic Policy Committee (One Hundred First through One Hundred Third Congresses), minority leader (One Hundred Fourth Congress); is a resident of Aberdeen, S.Dak.

**DAUB, Harold John, Jr. (Hal),** a Representative from Nebraska; born in Fort Bragg, Cumberland County, N.C., April 23, 1941; attended the public schools; B.S., Washington University, St. Louis, Mo., 1963; J.D., University of Nebraska, Lincoln, 1966; served in the United States Army Infantry, captain, 1966-1968; admitted to the Nebraska bar in 1966 and commenced practice in Omaha, 1968; vice president and general counsel for Standard Chemical Company, 1971-1981; delegate, Nebraska State Republican conventions, 1970 and 1980; elected as a Republican to the Ninety-seventh and to the three succeeding Congresses (January 3, 1981-January 3, 1989); was not a candidate in 1988 for reelection to the House of Representatives but was an unsuccessful candidate for nomination to the United States Senate; elected mayor of Omaha in 1994 to fill the remainder of a term expiring June 9, 1997, and took office on January 7, 1995; is a resident of Omaha, Nebr.

**DAUGHERTY, James Alexander,** a Representative from Missouri; born in Athens, McMinn County, Tenn., August 30, 1847, attended the common schools; moved to Missouri with his parents, who settled near Carterville, Jasper County, in 1867; active in all civic enterprises of the State and county; engaged in farming, stock raising, and mining; assisted in developing the lead and zinc fields of Missouri; associate judge for the western district of Jasper County, 1890-1892, and presiding judge, 1892-1896; member of the State house of representatives in 1897; served as president of the First National Bank of Carterville from 1907 to 1920; elected as a Democrat to the Sixty-second Congress (March 4, 1911-March 3, 1913); unsuccessful candidate for renomination in 1912 to the Sixty-third Congress; resumed his former business activities; appointed presiding judge of Jasper County on May 17, 1919, and served until his death in Carterville, Jasper County, Mo., on January 26, 1920; interment in Webb City Cemetery, Webb City, Mo.

**DAUGHTON, Ralph Hunter,** a Representative from Virginia; born in Washington, D.C., September 23, 1885; attended public and private schools in Washington, D.C., and Prince Georges County, Md.; was graduated from the law department of National University, Washington, D.C., in 1905; was admitted to the bar in 1907 and practiced law in Washington, D.C.; joined the investigative agency of the Department of Justice, which later became the Federal Bureau of Investigation, in 1910; moved to Norfolk, Va., in 1912, and served as chief of the F.B.I. for Virginia, North Carolina, West Virginia, and part of Maryland until after the First World War; commenced the private practice of law in Norfolk, Va.; served in the Virginia house of delegates 1933-1940; member of the Virginia senate 1940-1944; in 1938 was elected president of the Piedmont Baseball League and served for nine years; elected as a Democrat to the Seventy-eighth Congress to fill the vacancy caused by the resignation of Winder R. Harris and at the same time was elected to the Seventy-ninth Congress and served from November 7, 1944, to January 3, 1947; unsuccessful candidate for renomination in 1946 to the Eightieth Congress; resumed the practice of law until his death; died in Norfolk, Va., December 22, 1958; interment in Mount Olivet Cemetery, Washington, D.C.

**DAVEE, Thomas,** a Representative from Maine; born in Plymouth, Mass., December 9, 1797; attended the common schools; moved to Maine, where he engaged in mercantile pursuits; member of the State house of representatives in 1826 and 1827; served in the State senate 1830-1832; high sheriff of Somerset County in 1835; postmaster of Blanchard from November 6, 1833, to March 24, 1837; elected as a Democrat to the Twenty-fifth and Twenty-sixth Congresses (March 4, 1837-March 3, 1841); was not a candidate for renomination in 1840; resumed mercantile pursuits; again a member of the State senate in 1841 and served until his death in Blanchard, Piscataquis County, Maine, December 9, 1841; interment in the Village Cemetery, Monson, Maine.

**DAVENPORT, Franklin** (nephew of Benjamin Franklin), a Senator and a Representative from New Jersey; born in Philadelphia, Pa., in September 1755; received an academic education; studied law in Burlington, N.J.; was admitted to the bar in 1776 and commenced practice in Gloucester City, N.J.; clerk of Gloucester County Court in 1776; during the Revolutionary War enlisted as a private in the New Jersey Militia, later becoming brigade major, brigade quartermaster, and in 1778 assistant quartermaster for

Gloucester County; appointed colonel in the New Jersey Militia in 1779 and subsequently major general, which rank he held until his death; prosecutor of pleas in 1777; moved to Woodbury, N.J., in 1781 and continued the practice of law; appointed first surrogate of Gloucester County in 1785; member, New Jersey State general assembly, 1786-1789; colonel in the New Jersey Line during the Whiskey Rebellion of 1794; appointed brigadier general of the Gloucester County Militia in 1796; appointed to the United States Senate as a Federalist to fill the vacancy caused by the resignation of John Rutherfurd, and served from December 5, 1798, to March 3, 1799, when a successor was elected and qualified; elected to the Sixth Congress (March 4, 1799-March 3, 1801); was not a candidate for renomination in 1800 to the Seventh Congress; resumed the practice of law; appointed master in chancery in 1826; died in Woodbury, Gloucester County, N.J., July 27, 1832; interment in Presbyterian Cemetery, North Woodbury, N.J.

**DAVENPORT, Frederick Morgan,** a Representative from New York; born in Salem, Essex County, Mass., August 27, 1866; attended the public schools; moved with his parents to Pennsylvania in 1874 and settled in New Milford; moved to Yonkers, N.Y., in 1893; was graduated from Wesleyan University, Middletown, Conn., in 1889 and from Columbia University, New York City, in 1905; member of the faculty of political science of Hamilton College, Clinton, N.Y., 1904-1929; served in the New York State senate, 1909-1911; unsuccessful Progressive candidate for Lieutenant Governor of New York in 1912, and for Governor in 1914; again a member of the State senate, 1919-1925; chairman of the New York State Legislative Committee on Taxation and Retrenchment, 1919-1925; delegate to the Republican National Convention of 1924; elected as a Republican to the Sixty-ninth and to the three succeeding Congresses (March 4, 1925-March 3, 1933); unsuccessful candidate for reelection in 1932 to the Seventy-third Congress, and for election in 1934 to the Seventy-fourth Congress; president of the National Institute of Public Affairs, Washington, D.C., 1934-1949; chairman of the Federal Personnel Council, Washington, D.C., from 1939 until his retirement in 1953; died in Washington, D.C., December 26, 1956; interment in Woodlawn Cemetery, New York City.

**Bibliography:** Teti, Frank M. "Profile of a Progressive: The Life of Frederick Morgan Davenport." Ph.D. dissertation, Syracuse University, 1966.

**DAVENPORT, Harry James,** a Representative from Pennsylvania; born in Wilmerding, Allegheny County, Pa., August 22, 1902; attended St. Peter's Parochial School and McKeesport High School; newspaper publisher; unsuccessful candidate for nomination in 1946 to the Eightieth Congress; elected as a Democrat to the Eighty-first Congress (January 3, 1949-January 3, 1951); was an unsuccessful candidate for reelection in 1950 to the Eighty-second Congress and was also unsuccessful for nomination in 1960 to the Eighty-seventh Congress; lecturer and book salesman; resided in Millvale, Pa., where he died December 19, 1977; interment in New St. Joseph Cemetery, North Versailles, Pa.

**DAVENPORT, Ira,** a Representative from New York; born in Hornellsville, Steuben County, N.Y., June 28, 1841; moved with his father to Bath, N.Y., in 1847; attended Haverling Academy, Bath, N.Y., and Russell Collegiate School, New Haven, Conn.; upon the death of his father in 1868 assumed the management of the large estate and business affairs; member of the State senate 1878-1881; comptroller of the State of New York 1881-1883; unsuccessful candidate for reelection in 1883; unsuccessful Republican candidate for Governor of New York in 1885; elected as a Republican to the Forty-ninth and Fiftieth Congresses (March 4, 1885-March 3, 1889); was not a candidate for renomination in 1888 to the Fifty-first Congress; retired; died in Bath, Steuben County, N.Y., October 6,

1904; interment in the family cemetery on his estate, "Riverside," Bath, N.Y.

**DAVENPORT, James** (brother of John Davenport of Connecticut), a Representative from Connecticut; born in Stamford, Conn., October 12, 1758; was graduated from Yale College in 1777; served in the commissary department of the Continental Army in the Revolutionary War; judge of the court of common pleas; member of the State house of representatives 1785-1790; served in the State senate 1790-1797; judge of Fairfield County Court from 1792 until 1796; elected as a Federalist to the Fourth Congress to fill the vacancy caused by the resignation of James Hillhouse; reelected to the Fifth Congress and served from December 5, 1796, until his death in Stamford, Conn., August 3, 1797; interment in North Field (now Franklin Street) Cemetery.

**DAVENPORT, James Sanford,** a Representative from Oklahoma; born on a farm near Gaylesville, Cherokee County, Ala., September 21, 1864; moved with his parents to Conway, Faulkner County, Ark., in 1880; attended the common schools, Vilona (Ark.) High School, and Greenbrier (Ark.) Academy; studied law; was admitted to the bar of Faulkner County February 14, 1890, and commenced practice in Conway; in October of that year moved to Muskogee, Indian Territory (now Oklahoma), and in 1893 to Vinita, where he engaged in the practice of law; member of the Territorial council 1897-1901, serving as speaker the last two years of his term; one of the attorneys for the Cherokee Nation 1901-1907; mayor of Vinita in 1903 and 1904; elected as a Democrat to the Sixtieth Congress on September 17, 1907, and served from November 16, 1907, when Oklahoma was admitted as a State into the Union, until March 3, 1909; unsuccessful candidate for reelection in 1908 to the Sixty-first Congress; elected to the Sixty-second, Sixty-third, and Sixty-fourth Congresses (March 4, 1911-March 3, 1917); unsuccessful candidate for reelection in 1916 to the Sixty-fifth Congress; resumed the practice of law in Vinita; was elected judge of the criminal court of appeals of Oklahoma in November 1926; reelected in 1932 and served until his death in Oklahoma City, Okla., January 3, 1940; interment in Fairview Cemetery, Vinita, Okla.

**DAVENPORT, John** (brother of James Davenport), a Representative from Connecticut; born in Stamford, Conn., January 16, 1752; pursued academic studies; was graduated from Yale College in 1770; engaged in teaching there in 1773 and 1774; studied law; was admitted to the bar in 1773 and practiced in Stamford, Conn.; member of the State house of representatives 1776-1796; served in the commissary department of the Continental Army during the Revolutionary War, attaining the rank of major in 1777; elected as a Federalist to the Sixth and to the eight succeeding Congresses (March 4, 1799-March 3, 1817); chairman, Committee on Revisal and Unfinished Business (Seventh Congress); declined to be a candidate for reelection in 1816; died in Stamford, Fairfield County, Conn., November 28, 1830; interment in North Field (now Franklin Street) Cemetery.

**DAVENPORT, John,** a Representative from Ohio; born near Winchester, Jefferson County, Va., January 9, 1788; attended the common schools; moved to Ohio in 1818 and engaged in mercantile pursuits; member of the State house of representatives in 1824, 1827, and 1830; member of the State senate in 1825 and 1826; elected to the Twentieth Congress (March 4, 1827-March 3, 1829); unsuccessful candidate for reelection in 1828 to the Twenty-first Congress; twice elected by the legislature as judge of the Monroe judicial circuit; died in Woodsfield, Monroe County, Ohio, July 18, 1855; interment in Green Mount Cemetery, Barnesville, Ohio.

**DAVENPORT, Samuel Arza,** a Representative from Pennsylvania; born near Watkins, Schuyler County, N.Y., January 15, 1834; moved to Pennsylvania with his parents, who settled in Erie, Erie County, in 1839; attended the Erie Academy; studied law; was admitted to the bar in 1854; in 1855 was graduated from the Harvard Law School, and commenced the practice of his profession in Erie, Pa., the same year; elected district attorney for the county of Erie in 1860; owner and publisher of the Erie Gazette 1865-1890; delegate to the Republican National Conventions in 1888 and 1892; elected as a Republican to the Fifty-fifth and Fifty-sixth Congresses (March 4, 1897-March 3, 1901); was not a candidate for renomination in 1900; resumed the practice of law in the county, Pennsylvania, and Federal courts; also interested in the Erie Car Works, and in the manufacture of organs and boots and shoes; died in Erie, Erie County, Pa., on August 1, 1911; interment in Erie Cemetery.

**DAVENPORT, Stanley Woodward,** a Representative from Pennsylvania; born in Plymouth, Luzerne County, Pa., July 21, 1861; attended the public schools and Wyoming Seminary; was graduated from the Wesleyan University, Middletown, Conn., in 1884; studied law; was admitted to the bar in 1890 and commenced practice in Plymouth, Pa., in 1891; appointed a director of the poor for the central district of Luzerne County in 1893; secretary and treasurer of the poor district; register of wills of Luzerne County 1894-1897; elected as a Democrat to the Fifty-sixth Congress (March 4, 1899-March 3, 1901); unsuccessful candidate for renomination in 1900; resumed the practice of law in Plymouth, Luzerne County, Pa., and died in that city September 26, 1921; interment in Plymouth Cemetery.

**DAVENPORT, Thomas,** a Representative from Virginia; born in Cumberland County, Va.; completed preparatory studies; studied law; was admitted to the bar and commenced practice in Meadville, Va.; elected to the Nineteenth and Twentieth Congresses, elected as a Jacksonian to the Twenty-first and Twenty-second Congresses, and elected as an Anti-Jacksonian to the Twenty-third Congress (March 4, 1825-March 3, 1835); chairman, Committee on Public Expenditures (Twenty-third Congress); unsuccessful candidate for reelection in 1834 to the Twenty-fourth Congress; died near Meadville, Halifax County, Va., November 18, 1838.

**DAVEY, Martin Luther,** a Representative from Ohio; born in Kent, Portage County, Ohio, July 25, 1884; attended the public schools; was graduated from Oberlin Academy in 1906 and later attended Oberlin College; associated with his father in tree surgery in 1906; organized and became general manager of the Davey Tree Expert Co. (Inc.) in 1909 and became president in 1923; also became treasurer of the Davey Compressor Co. in 1929; also engaged in the real-estate business; mayor of Kent from 1913 until 1918; elected as a Democrat to the Sixty-fifth Congress to fill the vacancy caused by the death of Ellsworth R. Bathrick; reelected to the Sixty-sixth Congress and served from November 5, 1918, to March 3, 1921; unsuccessful candidate for reelection in 1920 to the Sixty-seventh Congress; resumed his former business pursuits; delegate at large to the Democratic National Conventions of 1932 and 1940; elected to the Sixty-eighth and to the two succeeding Congresses (March 4, 1923-March 3, 1929); was not a candidate for renomination in 1928 to the Seventy-first Congress, but was an unsuccessful candidate for election as governor; elected Governor of Ohio in 1934, reelected in 1936, and served from January 14, 1935 to January 9, 1939; unsuccessful candidate in 1940 for election for Governor; resumed his former business pursuits; died in Kent, Ohio, March 31, 1946; interment in Standing Rock Cemetery.

**Bibliography:** Vazzano, Frank P. "Harry Hopkins and Martin Davey: Federal Relief and Ohio Politics during the Great Depression." *Ohio History* 96 (Summer/Autumn 1987): 124-39; Vazzano, Frank P. "Martin Davey, John Bricker, and the Ohio Election of 1936." *Ohio History* 104 (Winter/Spring 1995): 5-23.

**DAVEY, Robert Charles,** a Representative from Louisiana; born in New Orleans, La., October 22, 1853; attended the public schools, and was graduated from St. Vincent's College, Cape Girardeau, Mo., in 1871; engaged in mercantile pursuits; elected to the State senate in 1879, 1884, and again in 1892; served as president pro tempore of the senate during the sessions of 1884 and 1886; judge of the first recorder's court in New Orleans 1880-1888; unsuccessful candidate for mayor of New Orleans in 1888; elected as a Democrat to the Fifty-third Congress (March 4, 1893-March 3, 1895); declined to be a candidate for renomination in 1894; elected to the Fifty-fifth and to the five succeeding Congresses and served from March 4, 1897, until his death; had been reelected to the Sixty-first Congress, but died in New Orleans, La., December 26, 1908, before the close of the Sixtieth Congress; interment in Metairie Cemetery.

**DAVIDSON, Alexander Caldwell,** a Representative from Alabama; born near Charlotte, Mecklenburg County, N.C., December 26, 1826; attended the public schools of Marengo County, Ala., and was graduated from the University of Alabama at Tuscaloosa July 11, 1848; studied law in Mobile, Ala., but never practiced; engaged in cotton planting near Uniontown, Perry County, Ala.; member of the State house of representatives in 1880 and 1881; served in the State senate 1882-1885; elected as a Democrat to the Forty-ninth and Fiftieth Congresses (March 4, 1885-March 3, 1889); unsuccessful candidate for renomination in 1888; resumed agricultural pursuits; died at "Westwood," near Uniontown, Ala., November 6, 1897; interment in the Holy Cross Cemetery of Davidson Memorial Church, Uniontown, Perry County, Ala.

**DAVIDSON, Irwin Delmore,** a Representative from New York; born in New York City January 2, 1906; attended the public schools; Washington Square College of New York University, B.S., 1927; New York University Law School, LL.B., 1928; was admitted to the bar in 1929 and commenced the practice of law in New York City; counsel for Legislative Bill Drafting Commission in 1935 and special counsel to New York State Mortgage Commission in 1936; attended the New York State Constitutional convention in 1938 and acted as secretary to the Democratic leader; elected to the State assembly in 1936 and resigned in 1948; justice of the Court of Special Sessions in New York City from 1948 until his resignation in 1954 to become a candidate for United States House of Representatives; elected as a Democrat-Liberal to the Eighty-fourth Congress and served from January 3, 1955, until his resignation on December 31, 1956; elected judge of the Court of General Sessions in the county of New York in 1956 for a fourteen-year term; New York State Supreme Court, 1963-1974; resided in New Rochelle, N.Y. until his death there on August 1, 1981; cremated; ashes scattered over the Long Island Sound by seaplane.

**DAVIDSON, James Henry,** a Representative from Wisconsin; born in Colchester, Delaware County, N.Y., June 18, 1858; attended the public schools and Walton (N.Y.) Academy; taught school in Delaware and Sullivan Counties, N.Y.; was graduated from the Albany Law School in 1884 and was admitted to the bar the same year; moved to Green Lake County, Wis., and commenced practice in Princeton in 1887; also taught school; elected district attorney of Green Lake County in 1888; chairman of the Republican congressional committee for the sixth district of Wisconsin in 1890; moved to Oshkosh, Wis., January 1, 1892, and continued the practice of law; appointed city attorney in May 1895 for two years; elected as a Republican to the Fifty-fifth and to the seven succeeding Congresses (March 4, 1897-March 3, 1913); chairman, Committee on Railways and Canals (Fifty-sixth through Sixty-first Congresses); unsuccessful candidate for reelection in 1912 to the Sixty-third Congress and for election in 1914 to the Sixty-fourth Congress; resumed the practice of his profession; elected to the Sixty-fifth Congress and served from March 4, 1917, until his death in Washington, D.C., August 6, 1918; interment in Riverside Cemetery, Oshkosh, Wis.

**DAVIDSON, Robert Hamilton McWhorta,** a Representative from Florida; born near Quincy, Gadsden County, Fla., September 23, 1832; attended the common schools and the Quincy Academy in

Quincy, Fla.; studied law at the University of Virginia, Charlottesville, Va.; was admitted to the bar in 1853 and commenced practice in Quincy, Fla.; member of the State house of representatives 1856-1859; served in the State senate 1860-1862; retired from the State senate in 1862 and served during the Civil War in the Confederate Army as captain of Infantry and later with rank of lieutenant colonel; member of the State constitutional convention in 1865; elected as a Democrat to the Forty-fifth and to the six succeeding Congresses (March 4, 1877-March 3, 1891); chairman, Committee on Railways and Canals (Forty-eighth through Fiftieth Congresses); unsuccessful candidate for renomination in 1890 to the Fifty-second Congress; member of the State railroad commission in 1897 and 1898; engaged in the practice of his profession until his death in Quincy, Fla., January 18, 1908; interment in Western Cemetery.

**DAVIDSON, Thomas Green,** a Representative from Louisiana; born at Coles Creek, Jefferson County, Miss., August 3, 1805; completed preparatory studies; studied law; was admitted to the bar and commenced practice in Greensburg, La.; appointed register of the United States land office; member of the State house of representatives 1833-1846; elected as a Democrat to the Thirty-fourth, Thirty-fifth, and Thirty-sixth Congresses (March 4, 1855-March 3, 1861); resumed the practice of his profession; president of the Democratic State convention in 1855; served again in the State house of representatives 1874-1878, 1880, and 1883; died in Springfield, Livingston Parish, La., September 11, 1883; interment in Springfield Cemetery.

**DAVIDSON, William,** a Representative from North Carolina; born in Charleston, S.C., on September 12, 1778; completed preparatory studies; moved with his parents to North Carolina in early youth and settled in Mecklenburg County; engaged extensively in planting; member of the State senate in 1813, 1815-1819, and 1825; moved to Charlotte, N.C., in 1820; elected as a Federalist to the Fifteenth Congress to fill the vacancy caused by the resignation of Daniel M. Forney; reelected to the Sixteenth Congress and served from December 2, 1818, to March 3, 1821; unsuccessful candidate for reelection in 1820 to the Seventeenth Congress; again elected a member of the State senate and served from 1827 to 1830; resumed his business pursuits; died in Charlotte, N.C., on September 16, 1857; interment in the Old Cemetery.

**DAVIES, Edward,** a Representative from Pennsylvania; born in Churchtown, Caernarvon Township, Lancaster County, Pa., in November 1779; attended the rural schools; engaged in agricultural and mercantile pursuits; member of the Pennsylvania house of representatives, 1834-1835; elected as an Anti-Masonic candidate to the Twenty-fifth and Twenty-sixth Congresses (March 4, 1837-March 3, 1841); resumed his former business activities; died in Churchtown, Pa., May 18, 1853; interment in the cemetery at Pottstown, Pa.

**DAVIES, John Clay,** a Representative from New York; born in Albany, N.Y., May 1, 1920; attended Camden (N.Y.) High School; attended the University of Alabama at Tuscaloosa, Ala., and Hamilton College, Clinton, N.Y.; editor of the Camden (N.Y.) Chronicle in 1940 and 1941; maintained a publicity office in Albany, 1941-1943; associated with the public relations department of Westinghouse Electric Corp., New York City, 1943-1946; vice president of the Earle Ferris Co., Inc., New York City, 1946-1948; partner in a public relations business, Utica, N.Y., 1948-1953; elected as a Democrat to the Eighty-first Congress (January 3, 1949-January 3, 1951); unsuccessful candidate for reelection in 1950 to the Eighty-second Congress; writer; public relations executive in San Juan; is a resident of San Juan, Puerto Rico.

**DAVILA, Felix Cordova,** a Resident Commissioner from Puerto Rico; born in Vega Baja, P.R., on November 20, 1878; attended the public schools at Manati; came to Washington, D.C., and was graduated from National University Law School; was admitted to the bar in 1903 and commenced practice in San Juan, P.R.; judge of the municipal court of Caguas in 1904; judge of the municipal court of Manati 1904-1908; renominated as judge, and also as candidate for the Puerto Rico house of representatives; declined both nominations; district attorney for the district of Aguadilla in 1908; judge of the district court of Guayama 1908-1910; judge of the district court of Arecibo in 1910 and 1911; judge of the district court of San Juan 1911-1917; elected as a Unionist a Resident Commissioner to the United States on July 16, 1917; reelected in 1920, 1924, and 1928 and served from August 7, 1917, until his resignation on April 11, 1932, having been appointed an associate justice of the supreme court of Puerto Rico, in which capacity he served until his death in Condado, San Juan County, P.R., on December 3, 1938; interment in Fournier Cemetery, San Juan, P.R.

**DAVIS, Alexander Mathews,** a Representative from Virginia; born in Old Mount Airy, Wythe County, Va., January 17, 1833; attended the old field schools and was privately tutored; was graduated from Emory and Henry College, Emory, Va.; studied law; was admitted to the bar in 1854 and commenced practice in Wytheville, Va.; moved to Independence, Grayson County, Va.; captain of Company C, Forty-fifth Virginia Infantry, Confederate Army, in 1861; major in 1862; lieutenant colonel in 1864; captured near the close of the war and held prisoner on Johnson's Island, Lake Erie; member of the Virginia senate 1869-1871; presented credentials as a Democratic Member-elect to the Forty-third Congress and served from March 4, 1873, to March 5, 1874, when he was succeeded by Christopher Y. Thomas, who contested his election; resumed the practice of law; died in Independence, Grayson County, Va., September 25, 1889; interment in the Davis family burial ground.

**DAVIS, Amos** (brother of Garrett Davis), a Representative from Kentucky; born in Mount Sterling, Ky., August 15, 1794; completed preparatory studies; studied law; was admitted to the bar and commenced practice in Mount Sterling; was sheriff of Montgomery County, Ky.; member of the Kentucky house of representatives in 1819, 1825, 1827, and 1828; unsuccessful candidate for election to the Twentieth and Twenty-second Congresses; elected as an Anti-Jacksonian to the Twenty-third Congress (March 4, 1833-March 3, 1835); was a candidate for reelection, but died in Owingsville, Ky., while campaigning, June 11, 1835; interment in the City Cemetery, Mount Sterling, Ky.

**DAVIS, Charles Russell,** a Representative from Minnesota; born in Pittsfield, Pike County, Ill., September 17, 1849; moved with his father to Le Sueur County, Minn., in 1854; attended the public schools and also instructed by private tutor; was graduated from a business college at St. Paul, Minn.; studied law; was admitted to the bar March 6, 1872, and commenced practice in St. Peter, Minn.; city attorney and city clerk of St. Peter 1878-1898; prosecuting attorney of Nicollet County 1879-1889 and 1901-1903; served as captain in the Minnesota National Guard; member of the State house of representatives in 1889 and 1890; served in the State senate 1891-1895; elected as a Republican to the Fifty-eighth and to the ten succeeding Congresses (March 4, 1903-March 3, 1925); chairman, Committee on Appropriations (Sixty-seventh Congress); unsuccessful candidate for renomination in 1924; resumed the practice of law in Washington, D.C., and St. Peter, Minn., died in Washington, D.C., July 29, 1930; interment in Woodlawn Cemetery, St. Peter, Minn.

**DAVIS, Clifford,** a Representative from Tennessee; born in Hazlehurst, Copiah County, Miss., November 18, 1897; moved with his parents to Memphis, Tenn., in 1911; attended the public schools of Memphis, and was graduated from the law department of the University of Mississippi at Oxford in 1918; was admitted to the bar in 1918 and commenced practice in Memphis, Tenn.; city judge of Memphis 1923-1927; vice mayor and commissioner of public safety of Memphis 1928-1940; elected as a Democrat to the Seventy-sixth Congress to fill the vacancy caused by the resignation of Walter C. Chandler; reelected to the Seventy-seventh and to the eleven succeeding Congresses and served from February 15, 1940, to January 3, 1965; chairman, Special Committee on Campaign Expenditures (Eighty-fourth through Eighty-eighth Congresses); unsuccessful candidate for renomination in 1964 to the Eighty-ninth Congress; returned to the practice of law in Washington, D.C., and practiced until his death there June 8, 1970; interment in Forest Hill Cemetery, Memphis, Tenn.

**DAVIS, Cushman Kellogg,** a Senator from Minnesota; born in Henderson, Jefferson County, N.Y., June 16, 1838; moved with his parents to Waukesha, Wis.; attended the public schools, Carroll College in Waukesha; graduated from the University of Michigan at Ann Arbor in 1857; studied law; was admitted to the bar in 1859 and commenced practice in Waukesha; during the Civil War served as first lieutenant in the Twenty-eighth Regiment, Wisconsin Volunteer Infantry, in 1861 and 1862; assistant adjutant general, 1862-1864; moved to St. Paul, Minn., in 1865; member of the Minnesota State house of representatives in 1867; United States district attorney from 1868 until 1873; elected Governor of Minnesota in 1873, and served from January 7, 1874 to January 7, 1876; elected as a Republican to the United States Senate in 1886; reelected in 1892 and again in 1898, and served from March 4, 1887, until his death in St. Paul, Minn. on November 27, 1900; chairman, Committee on Pensions (Fiftieth through Fifty-second Congresses), Committee on Territories (Fifty-fourth Congress), Committee on Foreign Relations (Fifty-fifth and Fifty-sixth Congresses); member of the commission which met in Paris in September 1898 to arrange terms of peace after the war between the United States and Spain; interment in Arlington National Cemetery, Va.

Bibliography: *DAB*; Coy, Richard. "Cushman K. Davis and American Foreign Policy, 1887-1900." Ph.D. dissertation, University of Minnesota, 1965; Kreuter, Kent. "The Presidency or Nothing: Cushman K. Davis and the Campaign of 1896." *Minnesota History* 41 (Fall 1969): 301-16.

**DAVIS, David** (cousin of Henry Winter Davis), a Senator from Illinois; born near Cecilton, Cecil County, Md., March 9, 1815; attended the public schools of Maryland and was graduated from Kenyon College, Ohio, in 1832; studied law in Lenox, Mass., and at the law school in New Haven; was admitted to the bar in 1835 and commenced practice in Pekin, Tazewell County, Ill.; moved to Bloomington, Ill., in 1836, and continued the practice of law; member, State house of representatives 1844; delegate to the State constitutional convention in 1847; judge of the eighth judicial circuit of Illinois 1848-1862; nominated by President Abraham Lincoln as an Associate Justice of the United States Supreme Court on December 1, 1862; was confirmed by the Senate on December 8, 1862 and served until March 7, 1877, when he resigned, having been elected Senator; nominated for President of the United States by the Labor Reform Party in 1872 but declined; elected as an Independent to the United States Senate and served from March 4, 1877, until March 3, 1883; was not a candidate for renomination in 1882; served as President pro tempore of the Senate during the Forty-seventh Congress; retired from public life; died in Bloomington, McLean County, Ill., June 26, 1886; interment in Evergreen Cemetery.

Bibliography: *DAB*; King, Willard. *Lincoln's Manager: David Davis.* Cambridge: Harvard University Press, 1960; Pratt, Harry. "David Davis, 1815-1886." Ph.D. dissertation, University of Illinois, 1930.

**DAVIS, Ewin Lamar,** a Representative from Tennessee; born in Bedford County, Tenn., February 5, 1876; attended the public schools, Webb School, Bell Buckle, Tenn., Woolwine School, Tullahoma, Tenn., and Vanderbilt University, Nashville, Tenn., 1895-1897; was graduated from Columbian (now George Washington) University Law School, Washington, D.C., in 1899; was admitted to the bar the same year and commenced practice in Tullahoma, Tenn.; delegate to all Democratic State conventions 1900-1910; judge of the seventh judicial circuit of Tennessee 1910-1918; chairman of the district exemption board for the middle district of Tennessee in 1917 and 1918; director of the Traders National Bank of Tullahoma 1903-1940; trustee of Tennessee College for Women 1906-1939; elected as a Democrat to the Sixty-sixth and to the six succeeding Congresses (March 4, 1919-March 3, 1933); chairman, Committee on Merchant Marine and Fisheries (Seventy-second Congress); was an unsuccessful candidate for renomination in 1932; member of the Federal Trade Commission from May 23, 1933, until his death, serving as chairman in 1935, 1940, and 1945; member of the American National Committee, Third World Power Conference, in 1936; died in Washington, D.C., on October 23, 1949; interment in Oakwood Cemetery, Tullahoma, Tenn.

**DAVIS, Garrett** (brother of Amos Davis), a Representative and a Senator from Kentucky; born in Mount Sterling, Ky., September 10, 1801; completed preparatory studies; employed in the office of the county clerk of Montgomery County and afterward of Bourbon County; studied law; was admitted to the bar in 1823 and commenced practice in Paris, Ky.; member, Kentucky house of representatives 1833-1835; elected as a Whig to the Twenty-sixth and to the three succeeding Congresses (March 4, 1839-March 3, 1847); chairman, Committee on Territories (Twenty-seventh Congress); declined to be a candidate for reelection in 1846; resumed the practice of law and also engaged in agricultural pursuits; declined the nomination for lieutenant governor in 1848; declined the American Party nomination for governor in 1855 and for the presidency in 1856; was opposed to secession and supported the Constitutional Union ticket in 1860; elected as a Unionist in 1861 to the United States Senate to fill the vacancy caused by the expulsion of John C. Breckinridge; reelected as a Democrat in 1867 and served from December 10, 1861, until his death in Paris, Bourbon County, Ky., September 22, 1872; chairman, Committee on Private Land Claims (Forty-second Congress); interment in Paris Cemetery.

Bibliography: *DAB*.

**DAVIS, George Royal,** a Representative from Illinois; born in Palmer, Hampden County, Mass., January 3, 1840; completed classical studies at Williston Seminary, Easthampton, Mass., and was graduated in 1860; studied law; entered the Union Army in July 1862 and served as captain in the Eighth Regiment, Massachusetts Volunteer Infantry, and as major in the Third Regiment, Rhode Island Volunteer Cavalry; engaged in manufacturing, the insurance business, and as financial agent at Chicago, Ill.; member of the State militia and senior colonel of the First Regiment, Illinois National Guard; elected as a Republican to the Forty-sixth, Forty-seventh, and Forty-eighth Congresses (March 4, 1879-March 3, 1885); was not a candidate for renomination in 1884; resumed his former business pursuits; served as treasurer of Cook County, Ill., 1886-1890; director general of the World's Columbian Exposition at Chicago in 1893; died in Chicago, Ill., November 25, 1899; interment in Rosehill Cemetery.

**DAVIS, George Thomas,** a Representative from Massachusetts; born in Sandwich, Mass., January 12, 1810; was graduated from Harvard University in 1829; studied law at Cambridge and Greenfield, Mass.; was admitted to the bar in 1832 and commenced practice in Greenfield, Franklin County; established the Franklin Mercury in 1833; member of the Massachusetts senate in 1839 and

1840; elected as a Whig to the Thirty-second Congress (March 4, 1851-March 3, 1853); was not a candidate for renomination in 1852; resumed the practice of law in Taunton and Greenfield, Mass.; member of the State house of representatives in 1861; moved to Portland, Maine, where he died June 17, 1877; interment in Green River Cemetery, Greenfield, Mass.

**DAVIS, Glenn Robert,** a Representative from Wisconsin; born on a farm in Vernon, Waukesha County, Wis., October 28, 1914; attended the rural schools and graduated from Mukwonago High School in 1930; B.Ed., Platteville (Wis.) State Teachers College, 1934; taught high school at Cottage Grove, 1934-1936, and at Waupun, 1936-1938; LL.B., University of Wisconsin Law School, Madison, 1940; was admitted to the bar in 1940 and commenced practice in Waukesha; elected to the Wisconsin State assembly in 1940 and served from January 6, 1941, until his resignation in June 1942 to enlist in the United States Navy; served thirty-two months aboard an aircraft carrier in the Pacific; discharged as a lieutenant on December 12, 1945; resumed the practice of law; Court Commissioner, Wisconsin; delegate, Wisconsin State Republican conventions, 1938-1942, 1946-1970; delegate to each Republican National Convention from 1952 until 1972; elected as a Republican to the Eightieth Congress to fill the vacancy caused by the death of Robert K. Henry; reelected to the Eighty-first and to the three succeeding Congresses and served from April 22, 1947, to January 3, 1957; was not a candidate for renomination in 1956 to the House of Representatives, but was an unsuccessful candidate for nomination to the United States Senate; was also unsuccessful for the senatorial nomination in 1957 to fill a vacancy; resumed the practice of law; elected as a Republican to the Eighty-ninth and to the four succeeding Congresses and served from January 3, 1965, until his resignation December 31, 1974; unsuccessful candidate for renomination in 1974 to the Ninety-fourth Congress; consultant, Potter International, Inc., 1975-1983; was a resident of Arlington, Va.; died September 21, 1988.

**Bibliography:** Smith, Kevin B. *The Iron Man: The Life and Times of Congressman Glenn R. Davis.* Lanham, Md.: University Press of America and Glenn Davis Charitable Foundation, Ltd., 1994.

**DAVIS, Henry Gassaway** (brother of Thomas Beall Davis and grandfather of Davis Elkins), a Senator from West Virginia; born near Woodstock, Howard County, Md., November 16, 1823; attended the country schools; worked on a farm until 1843; employed by the Baltimore & Ohio Railroad Co. for fourteen years as brakeman and conductor, and later had charge of the Piedmont terminal and shops; commenced the banking business and the mining of coal at Piedmont, W.Va., in 1858; engaged in railroad building and in the lumber business; elected to the house of delegates of West Virginia in 1865; member, West Virginia State senate, 1868, 1870; elected as a Democrat to the United States Senate in 1871; reelected in 1877, and served from March 4, 1871 to March 3, 1883; declined to be a candidate for renomination in 1882; chairman, Committee on Appropriations (Forty-sixth Congress); settled in Elkins, Randolph County, W.Va., where he resumed his banking and coal mining interests; represented the United States at the Pan American conferences of 1889 and 1901; unsuccessful candidate for Vice President of the United States in 1904 on the Democratic ticket headed by Alton B. Parker; chairman of the permanent Pan American Railway Committee, 1901-1916; died in Washington, D.C., March 11, 1916; interment in Maplewood Cemetery, Elkins, W.Va.

**Bibliography:** *DAB*; Pepper, Charles. *The Life and Times of Henry Gassaway Davis.* New York: The Century Co., 1920; Ross, Thomas Richard. *Henry Gassaway Davis: An Old-Fashioned Biography.* Parsons, W.Va.: McClain Printing Co., 1994; Williams, John Alexander. "Davis and Elkins of West Virginia: Businessmen in Politics." Ph.D. dissertation, Yale University, 1967.

**DAVIS, Henry Winter** (cousin of David Davis), a Representative from Maryland; born in Annapolis, Md., August 16, 1817; was tutored privately; lived in Alexandria, Va. and Wilmington; returned to Maryland in 1827 with his father, who settled in Anne Arundel County; attended Wilmington College in 1826 and 1827; St. John's College, Annapolis, Md., and Hampden-Sydney College, Virginia; was graduated from Kenyon College, Gambier, Ohio, in 1837; studied law at the University of Virginia, Charlottesville, Va.; was admitted to the bar and commenced practice in Alexandria, Va.; in 1850 moved to Baltimore, Md., where he continued the practice of law and also engaged in literary pursuits; elected as the candidate of the American Party to the Thirty-fourth through Thirty-sixth Congresses (March 4, 1855-March 3, 1861); unsuccessful candidate for reelection in 1860 to the Thirty-seventh Congress; elected as an Unconditional Unionist to the Thirty-eighth Congress (March 4, 1863-March 3, 1865); chairman, Committee on Foreign Affairs (Thirty-eighth Congress); co-sponsor of the Wade-Davis bill of 1864, establishing requirements (such as abolition of slavery and administration of loyalty oaths) for the readmission of former Confederate states into the Union; was not a candidate for renomination in 1864 to the Thirty-ninth Congress; died in Baltimore, Md., on December 30, 1865; interment in Greenmount Cemetery.

**Bibliography:** *DAB*; Belz, Herman. "Henry Winter Davis and the Origins of Congressional Reconstruction." *Maryland Historical Magazine* 67 (Summer 1972): 129-143; Henig, Gerald S. *Henry Winter Davis: Antebellum and Civil War Congressman From Maryland.* New York: Twayne, 1973; Luthin, Reinhard H. "A Discordant Chapter in Lincoln's Administration: The Davis-Blair Controversy." *Maryland Historical Magazine* 39 (March 1944): 25-48.

**DAVIS, Horace,** a Representative from California; born in Worcester, Mass., March 16, 1831; attended the public schools of Worcester, and Williams College, Williamstown, Mass.; was graduated from Harvard University in 1849; studied law in the Dane Law School of Harvard University, but did not engage in professional pursuits by reason of failing eyesight; moved to California in 1852 and engaged in mercantile pursuits; moved to San Francisco in 1860 and engaged in the flour-milling business; elected as a Republican to the Forty-fifth and Forty-sixth Congresses (March 4, 1877-March 3, 1881); unsuccessful candidate for reelection in 1880 to the Forty-seventh Congress; resumed his former business pursuits; member of the Republican National Committee 1880-1888; president of the Chamber of Commerce of San Francisco in 1883 and 1884; president of the board of trustees of Stanford University 1885-1916; president of the University of California at Berkeley 1887-1890; died in San Francisco, Calif., July 12, 1916; interment in Cypress Lawn Cemetery.

**Bibliography:** *DAB*.

**DAVIS, Jack D.,** a Representative from Illinois; born in Chicago, Ill., September 6, 1935; B.A., Southern Illinois University, 1956; served in the United States Navy, 1956-1959; operated a steel warehouse business from 1959 until 1978; served in the Illinois State house of representatives, 1976-1986; elected as a Republican to the One Hundredth Congress (January 3, 1987-January 3, 1989); unsuccessful candidate for reelection in 1988 to the One Hundred First Congress; Assistant Secretary for Manpower, Readiness and Resources, Department of the Air Force, 1990-1992; awarded Meritorious Service Medal for combat activity in northern Iraq and readiness-resource allocation during Operations Desert Shield and Desert Storm; is a resident of Cantrall, Ill.

**DAVIS, Jacob Cunningham,** a Representative from Illinois; born near Staunton, Augusta County, Va., September 16, 1820; attended the common schools and William and Mary College, Williamsburg, Va.; moved to Warsaw, Hancock County, Ill., in 1838;

studied law; was admitted to the bar and commenced practice in Warsaw; clerk of Hancock County; appointed circuit clerk in 1841; served in the State senate 1842-1848, and again from 1850 until his resignation in 1856, having been elected to Congress; elected as a Democrat to the Thirty-fourth Congress to fill the vacancy caused by the resignation of William A. Richardson and served from November 4, 1856, to March 3, 1857; was not a candidate to the Thirty-fifth Congress; resumed the practice of law in Clark County, Mo.; died in Alexandria, Clark County, Mo., December 25, 1883; interment in Mitchell Cemetery, near Alexandria, Mo.

**DAVIS, Jacob Erastus,** a Representative from Ohio; born in Beaver Village, Pike County, Ohio, October 31, 1905; attended the rural schools; was graduated from Beaver (Ohio) High School in 1923; A.B., Ohio State University, Columbus, 1927; J.D., Harvard University School of Law, 1930; was admitted to the bar in 1930 and commenced practice in Waverly, Ohio; prosecuting attorney of Pike County, Ohio, 1931-1935; member of the Ohio State house of representatives, 1935-1937, serving as speaker pro tempore and majority floor leader in 1937; common pleas judge of Pike County from 1937 until 1940; elected as a Democrat to the Seventy-seventh Congress (January 3, 1941-January 3, 1943); was an unsuccessful candidate for reelection in 1942 to the Seventy-eighth Congress; served as a special assistant to the Secretary of the Navy in 1943 and 1944; vice president, Kroger Company of Cincinnati, Ohio, 1945-1960, president, 1961-1970, and chairman of the board until his retirement in 1970; is a resident of Cincinnati, Ohio, and Naples, Fla.

**DAVIS, James Curran,** a Representative from Georgia; born in Franklin, Heard County, Ga., May 17, 1895; attended the public schools, Reinhardt College, Waleska, Ga., and Emory College, Oxford, Ga.; studied law; was admitted to the bar in 1919 and commenced practice in Atlanta, Ga.; during the First World War enlisted in the United States Marine Corps and served from December 24, 1917, until his discharge on January 11, 1919; served as a first lieutenant and captain in the Judge Advocate General's Department, Officers Reserve Corps; resumed the practice of law; member of the State house of representatives from De Kalb County 1924-1928; attorney for the Georgia Department of Industrial Relations 1928-1931 and for De Kalb County 1931-1934; judge of superior courts, Stone Mountain judicial circuit, 1934-1947; delegate to Democratic National Convention in 1948; elected as a Democrat to the Eightieth and to the seven succeeding Congresses (January 3, 1947-January 3, 1963); unsuccessful candidate for renomination in 1962 to the Eighty-eighth Congress; resumed the practice of law; publisher of the Atlanta (Ga.) Times, 1964-1965; member, boards of directors, Salem Campground and De Kalb Federal Savings and Loan Association, Atlanta, Ga., where he resided until his death there on December 18, 1981; interment in Oak Hill Cemetery, Newnan, Ga.

**DAVIS, James Harvey (Cyclone),** a Representative from Texas; born near Walhalla, Pickens District, S.C., December 24, 1853; moved to Texas with his parents, who settled in Wood County, near Winnsboro, in 1857; attended the common schools; taught school from 1875 to 1878; elected judge of Franklin County in 1878; studied law; was admitted to the bar in 1882 and commenced practice in Mount Vernon, Tex.; lecturer for the Farmers' Alliance for three years; engaged in the newspaper-publishing business; president of the Texas Press Association 1886-1888; unsuccessful Populist candidate for attorney general of Texas in 1892; was influential in the formation of the Populist Party and served as organizer and committeeman from 1892 to 1900; unsuccessful Populist candidate for election in 1894 to the Fifty-fourth Congress; declined the appointment as superintendent of agriculture for the Philippine Islands in 1914; elected as a Democrat to the Sixty-fourth Congress (March 4, 1915-March 3, 1917); unsuccessful candidate for

renomination in 1916 to the Sixty-fifth Congress; returned to his home in Sulphur Springs, Hopkins County, Tex., and engaged in agricultural pursuits and Chautauqua work; moved to Kaufman, Tex., in 1935, where he died on January 31, 1940; interment in the City Cemetery, Sulphur Springs, Tex.

**DAVIS, James John,** a Senator from Pennsylvania; was born in Tredegar, South Wales, October 27, 1873; immigrated to the United States in 1881 with his parents, who settled in Pittsburgh, Pa., and later moved to Sharon, Pa.; attended the public schools and Sharon (Pa.) Business College; apprenticed as a puddler in the steel industry when eleven years of age; moved to Elwood, Ind., in 1893 and worked in steel and tin-plate mills; held various offices in the Amalgamated Association of Iron, Steel, and Tin Workers of America; city clerk of Elwood, Ind., 1898-1902; recorder of Madison County, Ind., 1903-1907; moved to Pittsburgh, Pa., in 1907 and engaged in organizational work for the Loyal Order of Moose; chairman of the Loyal Order of Moose War Relief Commission in 1918 and visited the various camps in the United States, Canada, and Europe; appointed Secretary of Labor by President Warren G. Harding, reappointed by Presidents Calvin Coolidge and Herbert Hoover, and served from March 5, 1921 until December 9, 1930, when he resigned, having been elected Senator; elected as a Republican to the United States Senate to fill the vacancy caused by the refusal of the Senate to seat William S. Vare; reelected in 1932 and 1938, and served from December 2, 1930 to January 3, 1945; unsuccessful candidate for reelection in 1944; resumed educational and organizational work for the Loyal Order of Moose; died in Takoma Park, Md., November 22, 1947; interment in Uniondale Cemetery, Pittsburgh, Pa.

**Bibliography:** *DAB*; Chapple, Joseph. *"Our Jim": A Biography of James Davis.* Boston: Chapple Publishing Company, 1928; Davis, James John. *The Iron Puddler: My Life in the Rolling Mills and What Came of It.* Indianapolis: The Bobbs-Merrill Company, 1922.

**DAVIS, Jeff,** a Senator from Arkansas; born near Richmond, Little River County, Ark., May 6, 1862; attended school in Russellville, Ark., and was graduated from Vanderbilt University, Nashville, Tenn., in 1884; studied law; was admitted to the bar in Pope County, Ark., and commenced practice in Russellville, Ark.; prosecuting attorney of the fifth judicial district from 1892 until 1896; attorney general of Arkansas, 1898-1900; elected Governor of Arkansas in 1900, reelected in 1902 and 1904, and served from January 8, 1901 to January 8, 1907; continued the practice of law at Little Rock, Ark.; elected as a Democrat to the United States Senate and served from March 4, 1907, until his death in Little Rock, Ark., January 3, 1913; chairman, Committee on the Mississippi and its Tributaries (Sixty-second Congress); interment in Mount Holly Cemetery.

**Bibliography:** *DAB*; Arsenault, Raymond. *The Wild Ass of the Ozarks: Jeff Davis and the Social Bases of Southern Politics.* Knoxville: University of Tennessee Press, 1988; Jacobson, Charles. *The Life Story of Jeff Davis, the Stormy Petrel of Arkansas Politics.* Little Rock: Parke-Harper Publishers, 1925.

**DAVIS, Jefferson,** a Representative and a Senator from Mississippi; born in what is now Fairview, Todd County, Ky., June 3, 1808; moved with his parents to a plantation near Woodville, Wilkinson County, Miss.; attended the country schools, St. Thomas College, Washington County, Ky., Jefferson College, Adams County, Miss., Wilkinson County Academy, and Transylvania University, Lexington, Ky.; was graduated from the United States Military Academy, West Point, N.Y., in 1828; served in the Black Hawk War in 1832; promoted to the rank of first lieutenant in the First Dragoons in 1833, and served until June 30, 1835, when he resigned; moved to his plantation, "Brierfield," in Warren County, Miss., and engaged in cotton planting; elected as a Democrat to the Twenty-ninth Congress, and served from March 4, 1845 until June

1846, when he resigned to command the First Regiment of Mississippi Riflemen in the war with Mexico; appointed to the United States Senate to fill the vacancy caused by the death of Jesse Speight; subsequently was elected and served from August 10, 1847 until September 23, 1851, when he resigned; chairman, Committee on Military Affairs (Thirtieth through Thirty-second Congresses); unsuccessful candidate for Governor in 1851; appointed Secretary of War by President Franklin Pierce on March 7, 1853 and served until March 6, 1857; again elected as a Democrat to the United States Senate and served from March 4, 1857 until January 21, 1861, when he withdrew with other secessionist Senators; his seat was declared vacant and his name omitted from the roll by a resolution of March 14, 1861; chairman, Committee on Military Affairs and the Militia (Thirty-fifth and Thirty-sixth Congresses); commissioned major general of the State militia in January 1861; chosen President of the Confederacy by the Provisional Congress and inaugurated in Montgomery, Ala., February 18, 1861; elected President of the Confederacy for a term of six years and inaugurated in Richmond, Va., February 22, 1862; captured by Union troops in Irwinsville, Ga., May 10, 1865; imprisoned in Fortress Monroe, indicted for treason, and was paroled in the custody of the court in 1867; returned to Mississippi and spent the remaining years of his life writing; died in New Orleans, La., on December 6, 1889; interment in Metairie Cemetery, New Orleans, La.; reinterment on May 31, 1893, in Hollywood Cemetery, Richmond, Va.; the legal disabilities placed upon him were removed, and he was posthumously restored to the full rights of citizenship, effective December 25, 1868, pursuant to a Joint Resolution of the Ninety-fifth Congress (Public Law 95-466), approved on October 17, 1978.

**Bibliography:** *DAB*; Eaton, Clement. *Jefferson Davis.* New York: Macmillan, 1977; Davis, Jefferson. *The Papers of Jefferson Davis.* Edited by Haskell M. Monroe, James T. McIntosh, Lynda Lasswell Crist, and Mary Seaton Dix. 8 vols. to date. Baton Rouge: Louisiana State University Press, 1971-.

**DAVIS, John,** a Representative from Kansas; born near Springfield, Sangamon County, Ill., August 9, 1826; moved with his parents to Macon County in 1830; attended the country schools, Springfield Academy, and Illinois College, Jacksonville, Ill.; engaged in agricultural and horticultural pursuits near Decatur, Ill.; moved to Kansas in 1872 and located on a farm near Junction City; secretary of the Central Kansas Horticultural Society for many years; elected president of the first distinctive farmers' convention held in Kansas in 1873, out of which grew the Farmers' Cooperative Association, of which he was the first president; president of the Grange convention in 1874; became proprietor and editor of the Junction City Tribune in 1875; unsuccessful candidate of the Greenback Party for election in 1880 to the Forty-seventh Congress and in 1882 to the Forty-eighth Congress; elected as a Populist to the Fifty-second and Fifty-third Congresses (March 4, 1891-March 3, 1895); unsuccessful candidate for reelection in 1894 to the Fifty-fourth Congress; devoted his time to literary work until his death in Topeka, Kans., August 1, 1901; interment in Topeka Cemetery.

**DAVIS, John,** a Representative and a Senator from Massachusetts; born in Northboro, Mass., January 13, 1787; attended Leicester Academy, and was graduated from Yale College in 1812; studied law; was admitted to the bar and commenced practice in Worcester, Mass., in 1815; elected to the Nineteenth and to the four succeeding Congresses and served from March 4, 1825, to January 14, 1834, when he resigned, having been elected Governor; elected Governor of Massachusetts in 1833, reelected in 1834, and served from January 9, 1834 to March 1, 1835; elected as a Whig to the United States Senate and served from March 4, 1835, to January 5, 1841, when he resigned; chairman, Committee on Commerce (Twenty-fourth Congress); again elected Governor in 1840, reelected in 1841 and served from January 7, 1841 to January 17, 1843;

unsuccessful candidate for reelection in 1842; again elected in 1845 to the United States Senate to fill the vacancy caused by the death of Isaac C. Bates; reelected in 1847 and served from March 24, 1845, to March 3, 1853; declined to be a candidate for renomination in 1852, and retired from public life; died in Worcester, Mass., on April 19, 1854; interment in the Rural Cemetery.

**Bibliography:** *DAB.*

**DAVIS, John,** a Representative from Pennsylvania; born in Solebury Township, Bucks County, Pa., August 7, 1788; moved to Maryland and settled on a farm at Rock Creek Meeting House in 1795; attended the common schools; returned to Pennsylvania in 1812 and settled in what is now Davisville; engaged in agricultural and mercantile pursuits; served as captain in the War of 1812; rose to the rank of major general of militia; elected as a Democrat to the Twenty-sixth Congress (March 4, 1839-March 3, 1841); unsuccessful candidate for reelection in 1840 to the Twenty-seventh Congress; appointed surveyor of the port of Philadelphia by President James K. Polk and served from March 17, 1845, to March 18, 1849; resumed his former business activities; died in Davisville, Pa., April 1, 1878; interment in Davisville Baptist Church Cemetery, Bucks County, Pa.

**DAVIS, John Givan,** a Representative from Indiana; born near Flemingsburg, Fleming County, Ky., October 10, 1810; moved to Indiana with his parents, who settled in Rockville, Parke County, in 1819; attended the country schools; engaged in agricultural pursuits; sheriff of Parke County from 1830 to 1833, when he resigned; clerk of the county court 1833-1850; elected as a Democrat to the Thirty-second and Thirty-third Congresses (March 4, 1851-March 3, 1855); unsuccessful candidate for reelection in 1854 to the Thirty-fourth Congress; elected as a Democrat to the Thirty-fifth Congress and reelected as an Anti-Lecompton Democrat to the Thirty-sixth Congress (March 4, 1857-March 3, 1861); was not a candidate for renomination in 1860 to the Thirty-seventh Congress; engaged in mercantile pursuits and meat packing in Montezuma, Parke County, Ind.; moved to Terre Haute, Ind., and engaged in business as a dry-goods merchant; died in Terre Haute, Ind., on January 18, 1866; interment in Highland Lawn Cemetery.

**DAVIS, John James** (father of John William Davis), a Representative from West Virginia; born in Clarksburg, Va. (now West Virginia), May 7, 1835; attended the Northwestern Virginia Academy at Clarksburg, and was graduated from the Lexington Law School (now the law department of Washington and Lee University), Lexington, Va., in 1856; was admitted to the bar in 1856 and commenced practice in Clarksburg, Va.; member of the Virginia house of delegates in 1861; member of the first convention looking toward the formation of a new State loyal to the Union, from counties of western Virginia, held April 22, 1861; delegate from Harrison County to the Wheeling convention June 11, 1861; delegate to the Democratic National Conventions of 1868, 1876 and 1892; member of the West Virginia house of delegates in 1869 and 1870; elected as a Democrat to the Forty-second Congress and reelected as an Independent Democrat to the Forty-third Congress (March 4, 1871-March 3, 1875); was not a candidate for renomination in 1874 to the Forty-fourth Congress; resumed the practice of law in Clarksburg, W.Va.; died in Clarksburg, Harrison County, W.Va., March 19, 1916; interment in Odd Fellows Cemetery.

**Bibliography:** Ham, F. Gerald, ed. "The Mind of a Copperhead: Letters of John J. Davis on the Secession Crisis and Statehood Politics in Western Virginia 1860-1862." *West Virginia History* 24 (January 1963): 93-109.

**DAVIS, John Wesley,** a Representative from Indiana; born in New Holland, Lancaster County, Pa., April 16, 1799; moved to Cumberland County, Pa., with his parents, who settled near Shippensburg; completed preparatory studies; studied medicine;

was graduated from the Baltimore Medical College in 1821; moved to Carlisle, Ind., in 1823 and practiced medicine; surrogate of Sullivan County, 1829-1831; member of the Indiana State house of representatives, 1831-1833, and served as speaker in 1831; commissioner to negotiate an Indian treaty in 1834; elected as a Jacksonian to the Twenty-fourth Congress (March 4, 1835-March 3, 1837); declined to be a candidate for renomination in 1836 to the Twenty-fifth Congress because of ill health; elected as a Democrat to the Twenty-sixth Congress (March 4, 1839-March 3, 1841); unsuccessful candidate for reelection in 1840 to the Twenty-seventh Congress; again a member of the State house of representatives, 1841-1843, and served as speaker in 1841; elected as a Democrat to the Twenty-eighth and Twenty-ninth Congresses (March 4, 1843-March 3, 1847); chairman, Committee on Public Lands (Twenty-eighth Congress); Speaker of the House of Representatives (Twenty-ninth Congress); was not a candidate for renomination in 1846 to the Thirtieth Congress; appointed United States Commissioner to China by President James K. Polk on January 3, 1848 and served until May 1850; member of the State house of representatives in 1851, 1852, and again in 1857; delegate to the Democratic National Convention of 1852; appointed by President Franklin Pierce as Governor of Oregon Territory and served from December 2, 1853 until his resignation on August 1, 1854; member of the Board of Visitors to the United States Military Academy at West Point in 1858; died in Carlisle, Sullivan County, Ind., August 22, 1859; interment in the City Cemetery.

**Bibliography:** *DAB*.

**DAVIS, John William,** a Representative from Georgia; born in Rome, Floyd County, Ga., September 12, 1916; attended the public schools; A.B., University of Georgia, Athens, 1937; LL.B., University of Georgia School of Law, 1939; was admitted to the bar in 1939 and commenced practice in Rome, Ga.; served in the War Department Headquarters from July 1942 to December 1945, and was assigned to the Counter Intelligence Corps, serving for a time in South America; moved to Summerville, Ga., in 1946 and resumed the practice of law; solicitor general of the Rome Circuit from December 27, 1950 to January 1, 1953; elected judge of the Lookout Mountain Judicial Circuit for six years, and served from January 1, 1955, until his resignation December 31, 1960; elected as a Democrat to the Eighty-seventh and to the six succeeding Congresses (January 3, 1961-January 3, 1975); unsuccessful candidate for renomination in 1974 to the Ninety-fourth Congress; resumed the practice of law; was a resident of St. Simons Island, Ga.; died October 3, 1992.

**DAVIS, John William** (son of John James Davis), a Representative from West Virginia; born in Clarksburg, Harrison County, W.Va., April 13, 1873; attended various private schools; was graduated from the literary department of Washington and Lee University, Lexington, Va., in 1892; taught school; reentered the university and was graduated from its law department in 1895; was admitted to the bar the same year and commenced practice in Clarksburg, W.Va.; professor of law at Washington and Lee University in 1896 and 1897; resumed the practice of law in Clarksburg, W.Va., in 1897; member of the State house of delegates in 1899; delegate to the Democratic National Convention of 1904; president of the West Virginia Bar Association in 1906; appointed a member of the West Virginia Commission on Uniform State Laws in 1909; elected as a Democrat to the Sixty-second and Sixty-third Congresses and served from March 4, 1911, to August 29, 1913, when he resigned; one of the managers appointed by the House of Representatives in 1912 to conduct the impeachment proceedings against Robert W. Archbald, judge of the United States Commerce Court; Solicitor General of the United States 1913-1918; appointed Ambassador to Great Britain and served from November 21, 1918, to March 31, 1921; member of the American delegation for conference with Germany on the treatment and exchange of prisoners of war, held in Berne, Switzerland, in September 1918;

honorary bencher of the Middle Temple, London, England; nominated July 9, 1924 for president of the United States, on the one hundred third ballot, by the Democratic National Convention meeting in New York City, but was unsuccessful for election; delegate to the Democratic National Convention of 1932; was a resident of Nassau County, N.Y., and practiced law in New York City until his death; died in Charleston, S.C., March 24, 1955; interment in Locust Valley Cemetery, Glen Cove, Long Island, N.Y.

**Bibliography:** Harbaugh, William H. *Lawyer's Lawyer: The Life of John W. Davis.* 1973. Reprint. Charlottesville: University Press of Virginia, 1990.

**DAVIS, Joseph Jonathan,** a Representative from North Carolina; born near Louisburg, Franklin County, N.C., April 13, 1828; attended Louisburg Academy, Wake Forest (N.C.) College, and the College of William and Mary, Williamsburg, Va.; was graduated from the law department of the University of North Carolina at Chapel Hill in 1850; was admitted to the bar the same year and practiced in Oxford, N.C., and later in Louisburg, N.C.; served as captain of Company G, Forty-seventh Regiment, Confederate Army, during the Civil War; member of the State house of representatives 1868-1870; elected as a Democrat to the Forty-fourth, Forty-fifth, and Forty-sixth Congresses (March 4, 1875-March 3, 1881); resumed the practice of law; appointed a justice of the State supreme court in 1887, and subsequently elected in 1888; died in Louisburg, N.C., August 7, 1892; interment in Oaklawn Cemetery.

**DAVIS, Lowndes Henry,** a Representative from Missouri; born in Jackson, Cape Girardeau County, Mo., December 13, 1836; was graduated from Yale College in 1860 and from the Louisville University Law School in 1863; admitted to the bar and commenced practice in Jackson, Mo.; State attorney for the tenth judicial district of Missouri 1868-1872; member of the State constitutional convention in 1875; member of the State house of representatives 1876-1878; elected as a Democrat to the Forty-sixth, Forty-seventh, and Forty-eighth Congresses (March 4, 1879-March 3, 1885); chairman, Committee on Expenditures in the Department of the Treasury (Forty-eighth Congress); engaged in agricultural pursuits and in stock raising; died in Cape Girardeau, Mo., February 4, 1920; interment in Maple Hill Cemetery, Huntsville, Ala.

**DAVIS, Mendel Jackson,** a Representative from South Carolina; born in North Charleston, S.C., October 23, 1942; attended the North Charleston public schools; B.S., College of Charleston, 1966; J.D., University of South Carolina School of Law, 1970; admitted to the South Carolina bar in 1970; district assistant to Representative L. Mendel Rivers; elected as a Democrat to the Ninety-second Congress, April 27, 1971, by special election to fill the vacancy caused by the death of L. Mendel Rivers; reelected to the four succeeding Congresses, and served from April 27, 1971 to January 3, 1981; was not a candidate for reelection in 1980 to the Ninety-eighth Congress; resumed the practice of law; is a resident of Mount Pleasant, S.C.

**DAVIS, Noah,** a Representative from New York; born in Haverhill, N.H., September 10, 1818; moved with his parents to Albion, N.Y., in 1825; attended the common schools and Lima Seminary, Buffalo, N.Y.; studied law in Lewiston; was admitted to the bar and practiced in Gainesville and Buffalo; returned to Albion in February 1844, where he continued the practice of law until May 1858; appointed and subsequently twice elected judge of the supreme court for the eighth judicial district, and served from 1857 to 1868; resumed the practice of law; elected as a Republican to the Forty-first Congress and served from March 4, 1869, until July 15, 1870, when he resigned; appointed by President Ulysses S. Grant as United States attorney for the southern district of New York and served from July 20, 1870, until December 31, 1872, when he resigned, having been elected a judge of the supreme court of the State, in which position he served until 1887; resumed the practice of law in New York City; member of the council of the University of the City of New York (now New York University); died in New York City March 20, 1902; interment in Mount Albion Cemetery, Albion, Orleans County, N.Y.

**DAVIS, Reuben,** a Representative from Mississippi; born in Winchester, Tenn., January 18, 1813; moved with his parents to Alabama about 1818; attended the public schools; studied medicine, but practiced only a few years, when he abandoned the profession; studied law; was admitted to the bar in 1834 and commenced practice in Aberdeen, Miss.; prosecuting attorney for the sixth judicial district 1835-1839; unsuccessful Whig candidate for the Twenty-sixth Congress in 1838; judge of the high court of appeals in 1842, but after four months' service resigned; served as colonel of the Second Regiment of Mississippi Volunteers in the war with Mexico; member of the State house of representatives 1855-1857; elected as a Democrat to the Thirty-fifth and Thirty-sixth Congresses and served from March 4, 1857, to January 12, 1861, when he joined other secessionist members of the Mississippi delegation in withdrawing from the Thirty-sixth Congress; during the Civil War served in the Confederate Army as brigadier general; resumed the practice of law; unsuccessful Greenback candidate for election in 1878 to the Forty-sixth Congress; died in Huntsville, Ala., October 14, 1890; interment in Odd Fellows Cemetery, Aberdeen, Monroe County, Miss.

Bibliography: *DAB*; Davis, Reuben. *Recollections of Mississippi and Mississippians*. Rev. ed. Hattiesburg: University and College Press of Mississippi, 1972.

**DAVIS, Richard David,** a Representative from New York; born at Stillwater, Saratoga County, N.Y., in 1799; was graduated from Yale College in 1818; studied law; was admitted to the bar in 1821 and commenced practice in Poughkeepsie; elected as a Democrat to the Twenty-seventh and Twenty-eighth Congresses (March 4, 1841-March 3, 1845); chairman, Committee on Revolutionary Claims (Twenty-eighth Congress); was not a candidate for renomination in 1844 to the Twenty-ninth Congress; withdrew from political and professional life; engaged in agricultural pursuits in Waterford, Saratoga County, N.Y., where he died on June 17, 1871; interment in Waterford Rural Cemetery.

**DAVIS, Robert Lee,** a Representative from Pennsylvania; born in Philadelphia, Pa., October 29, 1893; educated in the public schools; employed with the Pennsylvania Railroad 1910-1932; during the First World War served as a junior lieutenant in the United States Navy; assistant executive director of the Republican central campaign committee of Philadelphia 1928-1932; director of the Republican city committee 1932-1935; elected as a Republican to the Seventy-second Congress to fill the vacancy caused by the resignation of George A. Welsh and served from November 8, 1932, to March 3, 1933; was not a candidate for election in 1932 to the Seventy-third Congress; paymaster and stock analyst with the Dupont Co. at Philadelphia, Pa., 1940-1946; real-estate broker in Ocean City, N.J.

**DAVIS, Robert Thompson,** a Representative from Massachusetts; born in County Down, Ireland, August 28, 1823; immigrated to the United States with his parents, who settled in Amesbury, Essex County, Mass., in 1826; attended the Amesbury Academy and the Friends' School in Providence, R.I.; was graduated from the medical department of Harvard University in 1847; dispensary physician in Boston; practiced medicine in Waterville, Maine; moved to Fall River, Mass., in 1850; member of the Massachusetts constitutional convention in 1853; served in the Massachusetts senate 1859-1861; delegate to the Republican National Conventions of 1860, 1876, and 1900; member of the Massachusetts board of charities when organized in 1863; appointed a member of the Massachusetts board of health upon its organization in 1869; mayor of Fall River in 1873; elected as a Republican to the Forty-eighth and to the two

succeeding Congresses (March 4, 1883-March 3, 1889); was not a candidate for renomination in 1888 to the Fifty-first Congress; resumed the practice of medicine at Fall River and also engaged in the cotton manufacturing industry; died at Fall River, Mass., October 29, 1906; interment in Oak Grove Cemetery.

**DAVIS, Robert William,** a Representative from Michigan; born in Marquette, Mich., July 31, 1932; attended the public schools of Mackinac County and graduated from LaSalle High School, St. Ignace, in 1950; attended Northern Michigan University, Marquette, 1950 and 1952, and Hillsdale (Mich.) College, 1951-1952; B.S., College of Mortuary Science, Wayne State University, 1954; funeral director, the Davis Funeral Home, St. Ignace, 1954-1966; member of the St. Ignace City Council, 1964-1966; Michigan State representative, 1966-1970; majority whip, Michigan State senate, 1970-1974; State Senate Republican leader, 1974-1978; delegate to Michigan State Republican conventions, 1966-1978; elected as a Republican to the Ninety-sixth and to the six succeeding Congresses (January 3, 1979-January 3, 1993); was not a candidate for reelection in 1992 to the One Hundred Third Congress; is a resident of Gaylord, Mich.

**DAVIS, Robert Wyche,** a Representative from Florida; born near Albany, Lee County, Ga., March 15, 1849; attended the common schools; enlisted in 1863 in the Fifth Georgia Regiment of the Confederate Army, and served until the surrender of his company on April 26, 1865; studied law; was admitted to the bar in 1869 and commenced practice in Blakeley, Ga.; moved to Florida in 1879 and practiced in Green Cove Springs, Clay County, then in Gainesville, Alachua County, and afterward in Palatka, Putnam County; member of the State house of representatives from Clay County in 1884 and 1885, serving as speaker the latter year; elected as a Democrat to the Fifty-fifth and to the three succeeding Congresses (March 4, 1897-March 3, 1905); was not a candidate for renomination in 1904 to the Fifty-ninth Congress; resumed the practice of law in Palatka, and Tampa, Fla.; moved to Gainesville, Fla., in 1914 and served as register of the United States land office at Gainesville 1914-1922; editor of the Gainesville Sun; served as mayor of Gainesville in 1924 and 1925; resumed the practice of law in 1928; died in Gainesville, Fla., September 15, 1929; interment in Evergreen Cemetery.

**DAVIS, Roger,** a Representative from Pennsylvania; born in Charlestown Village, Chester County, Pa., October 2, 1762; studied medicine at the University of Pennsylvania and commenced practice about 1785 in Charlestown; member of the Pennsylvania house of representatives 1809-1811; elected as a Republican to the Twelfth and Thirteenth Congresses (March 4, 1811-March 3, 1815); resumed the practice of medicine in Charlestown, where he died November 20, 1815; interment in Great Valley Presbyterian Churchyard.

**DAVIS, Samuel,** a Representative from Massachusetts; born in Bath, Maine (until 1820 a district of Massachusetts), in 1774; engaged in mercantile pursuits; became a shipowner in 1801; member of the Massachusetts house of representatives in 1803 and 1808-1812; overseer of Bowdoin College 1813-1818; president of the Lincoln Bank, Bath, Maine, in 1813; elected as a Federalist to the Thirteenth Congress (March 4, 1813-March 3, 1815); again a member of the Massachusetts house of representatives in 1815 and 1816; merchant in African and West Indian trade; died in Bath, Maine, April 20, 1831; interment in Maple Grove Cemetery.

**DAVIS, Thomas,** a Representative from Rhode Island; born in Dublin, Ireland, December 18, 1806; attended private schools; immigrated to the United States and located in Providence, R.I., in 1817; engaged in manufacturing jewelry; member of the State senate 1845-1853; elected as a Democrat to the Thirty-third Congress (March 4, 1853-March 3, 1855); unsuccessful candidate for reelection in 1854 to the Thirty-fourth Congress; resumed his former manufacturing pursuits; unsuccessful candidate for election to the

Thirty-sixth, Forty-second, Forty-third, and Forty-sixth Congresses; again served in the State senate in 1877 and 1878; member of the State house of representatives 1887-1890; member of the Providence school committee; died in Providence, R.I., July 26, 1895; interment in Swan Point Cemetery.

**DAVIS, Thomas Beall** (brother of Henry Gassaway Davis), a Representative from West Virginia; born in Baltimore, Md., April 25, 1828; moved to Howard County, Md., where he attended the common schools; moved to Piedmont, Va. (now West Virginia), in 1854 and entered the employ of the Baltimore & Ohio Railroad Co.; a few years later he moved to Keyser and engaged in the mercantile business, lumbering, banking, mining, and finally the building of railroads; member of the Democratic State executive committee 1876-1907; member of the State house of delegates 1898-1900; elected as a Democrat to the Fifty-ninth Congress to fill the vacancy caused by the resignation of Alston G. Dayton and served from June 6, 1905, to March 3, 1907; was not a candidate for reelection in 1906; resumed agricultural pursuits and coal mining; died in Keyser, Mineral County, W.Va., November 26, 1911; interment in Maplewood Cemetery, Elkins, W.Va.

**DAVIS, Thomas M., III,** a Representative from Virginia; born in Minot, Ward County, N.Dak., January 5, 1949; graduated United States Capitol Page School; B.A., Amherst (Mass.) College, 1971; J.D., University of Virginia, 1975; entered active duty, United States Army in 1971; released in 1972; United States Army Reserve service as first lieutenant, 1972-1979; legislative assistant, Virginia house of delegates; vice president and general counsel then corporate counsel and chair, PRC, Inc., Fairfax, Va.; member, Mason District Board of Supervisors, Fairfax, Va.; chair, Board of Supervisors, Fairfax County, Va.; elected as a Republican to the One Hundred Fourth Congress (January 3, 1995-January 3, 1997); is a resident of Springfield, Va.

**DAVIS, Thomas Terry,** a Representative from Kentucky; studied law; was admitted to the Kentucky bar on June 28, 1789, and commenced the practice of law in Mercer County, Ky.; served as deputy attorney for the Commonwealth and the first prosecuting attorney for his district; member of the Kentucky house of representatives 1795-1797; elected as a Republican to the Fifth and to the two succeeding Congresses (March 4, 1797-March 3, 1803); appointed on February 8, 1803, by President Jefferson as United States judge for the Territory of Indiana, and served as chancellor of Indiana Territory from March 1, 1806, until his death; died in Jeffersonville, Clark County, Ind., on November 15, 1807.

**DAVIS, Thomas Treadwell** (grandson of Thomas Tredwell), a Representative from New York; born in Middlebury, Addison County, Vt., August 22, 1810; moved to New York in 1817 with his parents, who settled in Clinton, Oneida County; attended the Clinton (N.Y.) Academy, and was graduated from Hamilton College, Clinton, N.Y., in 1831; moved to Syracuse, Onondaga County, in 1831; studied law; was admitted to the bar in 1833 and commenced practice in Syracuse; was also interested in railroading and coal mining; elected as a Unionist to the Thirty-eighth Congress and reelected as a Republican to the Thirty-ninth Congress (March 4, 1863-March 3, 1867); was not a candidate for renomination in 1866; resumed the practice of law in Syracuse; died in Washington, D.C., May 2, 1872; remains were cremated and the ashes deposited in Oakwood Cemetery.

**DAVIS, Timothy,** a Representative from Iowa; born in Newark, N.J., March 29, 1794; attended the public schools; moved to Kentucky in 1816; studied law; was admitted to the bar and practiced; moved to Missouri and engaged in the practice of law, and later, in 1837, moved to Dubuque, Iowa, and continued the practice of law; unsuccessful candidate for election in 1848 to the Thirty-first Congress; elected as a Republican to the Thirty-fifth Congress

(March 4, 1857-March 3, 1859); resumed the practice of his profession and also engaged in business activities in Dubuque; was also interested in merchant milling at Elkader, Iowa, Galesville, Wis., and Pickwick, Minn.; died in Elkader, Clayton County, Iowa, on April 27, 1872; interment in Elkader Cemetery.

**DAVIS, Timothy,** a Representative from Massachusetts; born in Gloucester, Mass., April 12, 1821; attended the public schools; served two years in a printing office; engaged in mercantile pursuits in Boston; member of the Massachusetts house of representatives in 1870 and 1871; elected as the candidate of the American Party to the Thirty-fourth Congress and as a Republican to the Thirty-fifth Congress (March 4, 1855-March 3, 1859); delegate to the Republican National Convention in 1860; appointed assistant appraiser in the Boston customhouse in 1861; engaged in the prosecution of claims against the Government; died in Boston, Mass., on October 23, 1888; interment in Oak Grove Cemetery.

**DAVIS, Warren Ransom,** a Representative from South Carolina; born in Columbia, S.C., May 8, 1793; pursued preparatory studies; was graduated from South Carolina College (now the University of South Carolina) at Columbia in 1810; studied law; was admitted to the bar in 1814 and practiced in Pendleton, S.C.; State solicitor of the western circuit 1818-1824; elected as a Jacksonian to the Twentieth and Twenty-first Congresses; reelected as a Nullifier to the Twenty-second through Twenty-fourth Congresses and served from March 4, 1827, until his death in Washington, D.C., on January 29, 1835, before the opening of the Twenty-fourth Congress; chairman, Committee on the Judiciary (Twenty-second Congress); interment in the Congressional Cemetery.

**DAVIS, William Morris,** a Representative from Pennsylvania; born in Keene Valley, Essex County, N.Y., August 16, 1815; moved to Pennsylvania and became a sugar refiner in Philadelphia; elected as a Republican to the Thirty-seventh Congress (March 4, 1861-March 3, 1863); died in Keene Valley, N.Y., August 5, 1891; interment in Friends Fair Hill Burial Ground, Germantown, Philadelphia, Pa.

**DAVISON, George Mosby,** a Representative from Kentucky; born in Stanford, Lincoln County, Ky., March 23, 1855; attended the common schools, Stanford Academy, and Meyers Academy; studied law; was admitted to the bar in 1879 and commenced practice in Stanford, Ky.; appointed collector of internal revenue for the sixth Kentucky district and served from July 20, 1885, to June 30, 1889; appointed master of chancery or commissioner of the Lincoln circuit court in 1886, and served until 1893, when he resigned; member of the Kentucky house of representatives 1886-1888; judge of the Lincoln County Court 1894-1896; elected as a Republican to the Fifty-fifth Congress (March 4, 1897-March 3, 1899); unsuccessful candidate for reelection in 1898 to the Fifty-sixth Congress; resumed the practice of law; assistant United States attorney for the eastern district of Kentucky 1900-1910; retired from public life; died in Stanford, Ky., December 18, 1912; interment in Buffalo Springs Cemetery.

**DAVY, John Madison,** a Representative from New York; born in Ottawa, Ontario, Canada, June 29, 1835; moved to New York with his parents, who settled near Rochester, Monroe County, in 1835; attended the common schools and the Monroe Academy, East Henrietta, N.Y.; served in the Union Army during the Civil War as a first lieutenant in Company G, One Hundred and Eighth Regiment, Volunteer Infantry, in 1862 and 1863; studied law in Rochester; was admitted to the bar in 1863 and commenced practice in Rochester, N.Y.; district attorney of Monroe County 1868-1872; collector of customs for the port of Genesee from 1872 until his resignation in 1875; elected as a Republican to the Forty-fourth Congress (March 4, 1875-March 3, 1877); unsuccessful candidate for reelection in 1876 to the Forty-fifth Congress; resumed the practice of law; elected justice of the supreme court of New York and served from

January 1, 1889, until his retirement in 1905; again resumed the practice of law; died in Atlantic City, N.J., April 21, 1909; interment in Mount Hope Cemetery, Rochester, N.Y.

**DAWES, Beman Gates** (son of Rufus Dawes and brother of Vice President Charles Gates Dawes), a Representative from Ohio; born in Marietta, Washington County, Ohio, January 14, 1870; attended the common schools and Marietta Academy and College, Marietta, Ohio; engaged in agricultural pursuits and engineering and became interested in public utilities; elected as a Republican to the Fifty-ninth and Sixtieth Congresses (March 4, 1905-March 3, 1909); after his retirement from Congress became interested in the production of oil and the building of electric railways; founder of the Dawes Arboretum, an endowed institution dedicated to the education of youth; in 1914 was elected president and chairman of the board of directors of the Pure Oil Co., and was a member of the executive committee at time of death; died in Newark, Ohio, May 15, 1953; interment in Dawes Mausoleum, Dawes Arboretum, Newark, Ohio.

**DAWES, Charles Gates** (son of Rufus Dawes and brother of Beman Gates Dawes), a Vice President of the United States; born in Marietta, Washington County, Ohio, August 27, 1865; attended the common schools; was graduated from Marietta College in 1884 and from the Cincinnati Law School in 1886; was admitted to the bar in 1886 and practiced in Lincoln, Nebr., 1887-1894; interested in public utilities and banking, 1894-1897; Comptroller of the Currency, United States Treasury Department, 1898-1901; unsuccessful candidate for the United States Senate in 1902; during the First World War was commissioned major, lieutenant colonel, and brigadier general of the Seventeenth Engineers; served with the American Expeditionary Forces as chief of supply procurement and was a member of the Liquidation Commission, War Department; resigned from the Army in 1919; upon the creation of the Bureau of the Budget was appointed its first Director in 1921; appointed to the Allied Reparations Commission in 1923; for his work on a program to enable Germany to restore and stabilize its economy, he shared the 1925 Nobel Peace Prize with Sir Austen Chamberlain of Great Britain; elected Vice President of the United States November 5, 1924, on the Republican ticket with President Calvin Coolidge and was inaugurated on March 4, 1925, for the term ending March 3, 1929; appointed by President Herbert Hoover as Ambassador to Great Britain, and served from April 16, 1929 until his resignation on February 2, 1932; chairman, Reconstruction Finance Corporation; resumed the banking business and was chairman of the board of the City National Bank and Trust Co., Chicago, Ill., from 1932 until his death in Evanston, Ill., April 23, 1951; interment in Rosehill Cemetery, Chicago, Ill.

**Bibliography:** *DAB*; Dawes, Charles. *Notes As Vice President, 1928-1929.* Boston: Little, Brown, 1935; Timmons, Bascom N. *Charles G. Dawes: Portrait of an American.* 1953. Reprint. New York: Garland Publishers, 1979.

**DAWES, Henry Laurens,** a Representative and a Senator from Massachusetts; born in Cummington, Mass., October 30, 1816; attended the common schools and received private instruction in preparatory studies; was graduated from Yale College in 1839; became a teacher and edited the Greenfield Gazette and the North Adams Transcript; studied law; was admitted to the bar in 1842 and commenced practice in North Adams, Mass.; member, Massachusetts house of representatives 1848-1849, 1852; member, Massachusetts senate 1850; member of the Massachusetts constitutional convention in 1853; district attorney for the western district of Massachusetts 1853-1857; elected to the Thirty-fifth and to the eight succeeding Congresses (March 4, 1857-March 3, 1875); chairman, Committee on Elections (Thirty-seventh through Fortieth Congresses), Committee on Appropriations (Forty-first Congress), Committee on Ways and Means (Forty-second and Forty-third Congresses); declined to be a candidate for reelection in 1874; elected as a Republican to the United States Senate in 1875; reelected in 1881 and again in 1887, and served from March 4, 1875, to March 3, 1893; declined to be a candidate for reelection in 1893; chairman, Committee on Public Buildings and Grounds (Forty-fifth Congress), Committee on Indian Affairs (Forty-seventh through Fifty-second Congresses); settled in Pittsfield, Mass.; chairman of the commission created to administer the tribal affairs of the Five Civilized Tribes of Indians in the Indian Territory 1893-1903; sponsor of the Dawes (General Allotment) Act of 1887, an unsuccessful effort to supplant the reservation system by granting trust land to certain individual Indians in allotments of forty, eighty or one hundred sixty acres; died in Pittsfield, Mass., February 5, 1903; interment in Pittsfield Cemetery.

**Bibliography:** *DAB*; Arcanti, Steven J. "To Secure the Party: Henry L. Dawes and the Politics of Reconstruction." *Historical Journal of Western Massachusetts* 5 (Spring 1977): 33-45; Carlson, Leonard A. *Indians, Bureaucrats, and Land: The Dawes Act and the Decline of Indian Farming.* Westport, Conn.: Greenwood Press, 1981; Nicklason, Fred H. "The Early Career of Henry L. Dawes, 1816-1871." Ph.D. dissertation, Yale University, 1967.

**DAWES, Rufus** (father of Charles Gates Dawes and Beman Gates Dawes), a Representative from Ohio; born in Malta, Morgan County, Ohio, July 4, 1838; attended the common schools, and was graduated from Marietta College, Ohio, in 1860; during the Civil War volunteered on April 25, 1861, and was chosen captain of Company K, Sixth Wisconsin Regiment, in the Army of the Potomac; appointed major on June 21, 1862, lieutenant colonel, March 24, 1863, colonel on July 6, 1864, and brevet brigadier general, March 13, 1865; after the close of the war engaged in the wholesale lumber business in Marietta, Ohio; elected as a Republican to the Forty-seventh Congress (March 4, 1881-March 3, 1883); unsuccessful candidate for reelection in 1882 to the Forty-eighth Congress; resumed the wholesale lumber business in Marietta, Washington County, Ohio, and died there on August 2, 1899; interment in Oak Grove Cemetery.

**DAWSON, Albert Foster,** a Representative from Iowa; born in Spragueville, Jackson County, Iowa, January 26, 1872; attended the public schools and the University of Wisconsin at Madison; engaged in newspaper work at Preston, Iowa, in 1891 and 1892 and at Clinton, Iowa, from 1892 to 1894; secretary to Representative George M. Curtis and Senator William B. Allison of Iowa, 1895-1905; studied finance at George Washington University, Washington, D.C.; elected as a Republican to the Fifty-ninth and to the two succeeding Congresses (March 4, 1905-March 3, 1911); declined to be a candidate for renomination in 1910 to the Sixty-second Congress; also declined an appointment as private secretary to President William Howard Taft tendered in 1910; president of the First National Bank of Davenport, Iowa, 1911-1929; executive secretary of the Republican National Senatorial Committee in 1930; public utility executive, 1931-1945; retired from business activities and resided in Highland Park, Ill., until his death March 9, 1949, on a train as it neared Cincinnati, Ohio; interment in Preston Cemetery, Preston, Iowa.

**DAWSON, John,** a Delegate and a Representative from Virginia; born in Virginia in 1762; was graduated from Harvard University in 1782; studied law; was admitted to the bar, and practiced; member of the Virginia house of delegates, 1786-1789; Member of the Continental Congress in 1788; delegate to the Virginia convention in 1788 that ratified the Federal Constitution; elected privy councilor on December 16, 1789; was the bearer of dispatches from President John Adams to the Government of France in 1801; served as aide to General Jacob Brown and to General Andrew Jackson in the War of 1812; elected as a Republican to the Fifth and to the eight succeeding Congresses, and served from

March 4, 1797 until his death in Washington, D.C., March 31, 1814; chairman, Committee on District of Columbia (Thirteenth Congress); interment in the Congressional Cemetery.

**Bibliography:** *DAB.*

**DAWSON, John Bennett,** a Representative from Louisiana; born near Nashville, Tenn., March 17, 1798; attended Centre College, Danville, Ky.; moved to Louisiana and became a planter and was also interested in the newspaper business; unsuccessful Democratic candidate for Governor of Louisiana in 1834; member of the Louisiana State house of representatives; elected brigadier general of militia and a few days afterward was elected major general; judge of the parish court; elected as a Democrat to the Twenty-seventh and to the two succeeding Congresses, and served from March 4, 1841 until his death in St. Francisville, La., on June 26, 1845; while a Member of the House was appointed postmaster at New Orleans, La., April 10, 1843, and served until his successor was appointed on December 19, 1843; interment in Grace Episcopal Churchyard.

**DAWSON, John Littleton,** a Representative from Pennsylvania; born in Uniontown, Fayette County, Pa., February 7, 1813; moved with his parents to Brownsville, Pa., in early youth; was graduated from Washington (Pa.) College in 1833; studied law; was admitted to the bar September 9, 1835, and commenced practice in Brownsville, Pa.; deputy attorney general of Fayette County in 1838; delegate to the Democratic National Conventions of 1844, 1848, 1860, and 1868; United States attorney for the western district of Pennsylvania 1845-1848; unsuccessful candidate for election in 1848 to the Thirty-first Congress; elected as a Democrat to the Thirty-second and Thirty-third Congresses (March 4, 1851-March 3, 1855); chairman, Committee on Agriculture (Thirty-third Congress); declined to be a candidate for renomination in 1854 to the Thirty-fourth Congress; appointed Governor of Kansas Territory by President Franklin Pierce, but declined the office; elected to the Thirty-eighth and Thirty-ninth Congresses (March 4, 1863-March 3, 1867); was not a candidate for renomination in 1866 to the Fortieth Congress; retired from public life and resided on his estate, "Friendship Hill," in Springfield Township, Fayette County, Pa., until his death there on September 18, 1870; interment in Christ Episcopal Churchyard, Brownsville, Fayette County, Pa.

**DAWSON, William,** a Representative from Missouri; born in New Madrid, New Madrid County, Mo., March 17, 1848; was graduated from Christian Brothers' College, St. Louis, Mo., in 1869; elected sheriff and collector of New Madrid County in 1870 and 1872; served as a member of the State house of representatives 1878-1884; elected as a Democrat to the Forty-ninth Congress (March 4, 1885-March 3, 1887); unsuccessful candidate for renomination in 1886; engaged in the land business in New Madrid, Mo.; served as clerk of the circuit court of New Madrid County 1915-1927; died in New Madrid, Mo., October 12, 1929; interment in Evergreen Cemetery.

**DAWSON, William Adams,** a Representative from Utah; born in Layton, Davis County, Utah, November 5, 1903; attended the public schools; was graduated from the law department of the University of Utah at Salt Lake City in 1926; was admitted to the bar the same year and commenced practice in Salt Lake City; county attorney of Davis County 1926-1934; mayor of Layton 1935-1939; member of the State senate 1940-1944; elected as a Republican to the Eightieth Congress (January 3, 1947-January 3, 1949); unsuccessful candidate for reelection in 1948 to the Eighty-first Congress; elected to the Eighty-third, Eighty-fourth, and Eighty-fifth Congresses (January 3, 1953-January 3, 1959); unsuccessful candidate for reelection in 1958 to the Eighty-sixth Congress; vice president of Zions First National Bank, 1959-1969; was a resident of Salt Lake City, Utah, until his death on November 7, 1981; interment in Kaysville Cemetery, Kaysville, Utah.

**DAWSON, William Crosby,** a Representative and a Senator from Georgia; born in Greensboro, Greene County, Ga., January 4, 1798; attended the common schools; was graduated from Franklin College, Athens, Ga., in 1816; studied law; was admitted to the bar in 1816 and commenced practice in Greensboro, Ga.; member, Georgia State house of representatives; elected as a State Rights candidate to the Twenty-fourth Congress to fill the vacancy caused by the death of John Coffee; reelected as a Whig to the Twenty-fifth and to the two succeeding Congresses, and served from November 7, 1836 to November 13, 1841, when he resigned; chairman, Committee on Mileage (Twenty-fifth Congress), Committee on Claims (Twenty-sixth Congress), Committee on Military Affairs (Twenty-seventh Congress); unsuccessful Whig candidate for Governor of Georgia in 1841; judge of the Ocmulgee circuit court in 1845; elected as a Whig to the United States Senate, and served from March 4, 1849 to March 3, 1855; chairman, Committee on Private Land Claims (Thirty-second Congress); presided over the Southern convention at Memphis in 1853; died in Greensboro, Ga., May 5, 1856; interment in Greensboro Cemetery.

**DAWSON, William Johnson,** a Representative from North Carolina; born near Edenton, Chowan County, N.C.; member of the State house of commons in 1791; served as a member of the committee appointed in 1791 to fix a permanent place for the seat of government of North Carolina; elected to the Third Congress (March 4, 1793-March 3, 1795); died in Bertie County, N.C., in 1798.

**DAWSON, William Levi,** a Representative from Illinois; born in Albany, Dougherty County, Ga., April 26, 1886; attended the public schools; was graduated from the Albany (Ga.) Normal School in 1905, and from Fisk University, Nashville, Tenn., in 1909; moved to Chicago, Ill. in 1912 and attended the Kent College of Law and Northwestern University Law School, Evanston, Ill.; during the First World War served overseas as a first lieutenant with the Three Hundred and Sixty-fifth Infantry 1917-1919; was admitted to the bar in 1920 and commenced practice in Chicago; unsuccessful candidate for nomination in 1928 to the Seventy-first Congress; Republican State central committeeman for the First Congressional District of Illinois 1930-1932; alderman for the Second Ward of Chicago 1933-1939; affiliated with the Democratic Party and became Democratic committeeman for the Second Ward in 1939; unsuccessful candidate for election in 1938 to the Seventy-sixth Congress; elected as a Democrat to the Seventy-eighth and to the thirteen succeeding Congresses and served from January 3, 1943, until his death in Chicago, Ill., November 9, 1970; chairman, Committee on Expenditures in Executive Departments (Eighty-first and Eighty-second Congresses), Committee on Government Operations (Eighty-fourth through Ninety-first Congresses); cremated; ashes placed in Columbarium in Griffin Funeral Home, Chicago, Ill.

**Bibliography:** Wilson, James Q. "Two Negro Politicians: An Interpretation." *Midwest Journal of Political Science* 4 (November 1960): 346-69.

**DAY, Rowland,** a Representative from New York; born in Chester, Mass., March 6, 1779; moved with his parents to Skaneateles, N.Y., in 1805, and from thence to Moravia, N.Y., in 1810; engaged in mercantile pursuits; served in the State assembly in 1816 and 1817; member of the convention to revise the constitution of the State of New York in 1821; held several local offices in Sempronius, where he resided; elected to the Eighteenth Congress (March 4, 1823-March 3, 1825); elected as a Jacksonian to the Twenty-third Congress (March 4, 1833-March 3, 1835); resumed mercantile pursuits; died in Moravia, Cayuga County, N.Y., December 23, 1853; interment in Indian Mound Cemetery.

**DAY, Stephen Albion,** a Representative from Illinois; born in Canton, Stark County, Ohio, July 13, 1882; attended the public schools at Canton, the University School at Cleveland, Ohio, and Asheville (N.C.) School; was graduated from the University of

Michigan at Ann Arbor in 1905; secretary to Chief Justice Melville W. Fuller of the Supreme Court of the United States 1905-1907; studied law at the University of Michigan; was admitted to the bar in 1907 and commenced practice in Cleveland, Ohio; moved to Evanston, Ill., in 1908 and continued the practice of law in Chicago, Ill.; special counsel to the Comptroller of the Currency 1926-1928; author; elected as a Republican to the Seventy-seventh and Seventy-eighth Congresses (January 3, 1941-January 3, 1945); unsuccessful candidate for reelection in 1944 to the Seventy-ninth Congress; resumed the practice of law in Evanston, Ill., where he died January 5, 1950; interment in Memorial Park, Skokie, Ill.

**DAY, Timothy Crane,** a Representative from Ohio; born in Cincinnati, Ohio, January 8, 1819; attended the public schools; printer and engraver 1838-1840; engaged in literary pursuits; became one of the editors and proprietors of the Cincinnati Enquirer in 1849; disposed of his interests in that paper in 1852 and made a tour of Europe; elected as a Republican to the Thirty-fourth Congress (March 4, 1855-March 3, 1857); declined renomination in 1856 because of ill health and retired from active business; died in Cincinnati, Ohio, April 15, 1869; interment in Spring Grove Cemetery.

**DAYAN, Charles,** a Representative from New York; born in Amsterdam, Montgomery County, N.Y., July 8, 1792; attended the common schools and was tutored privately; was graduated from Lowville Academy, Lewis County, N.Y.; engaged in teaching; commissioned a lieutenant colonel in the War of 1812; studied law; was admitted to the bar in 1817 and practiced in Lowville; member of the State senate in 1827 and 1828 and served as president pro tempore in the latter year; acting Lieutenant Governor from October 17 to December 31, 1828; supreme court commissioner 1830-1838; elected as a Jacksonian to the Twenty-second Congress (March 4, 1831-March 3, 1833); member of the State assembly in 1835 and 1836; master and examiner in chancery for several years, terminating in 1838; district attorney for Lewis County 1840-1845; retired from public life because of ill health, but continued the practice of law for a number of years; died in Lowville, Lewis County, N.Y., December 25, 1877; interment in Lowville Rural Cemetery.

**DAYTON, Alston Gordon,** a Representative from West Virginia; born in Philippi, Va. (now West Virginia), October 18, 1857; attended the public schools, and was graduated from the University of West Virginia at Morgantown in June 1878; studied law; was admitted to the bar in 1878 and commenced practice in Philippi; appointed to fill an unexpired term as prosecuting attorney of Upshur County, W.Va., in 1879; prosecuting attorney for Barbour County 1882-1886; elected as a Republican to the Fifty-fourth and to the five succeeding Congresses and served from March 4, 1895, until his resignation March 16, 1905, to accept a judicial position; appointed United States district judge for the northern district of West Virginia on March 5, 1905, and served until his death in Battle Creek, Mich., on July 30, 1920; interment in Fraternity Cemetery, Philippi, Barbour County, W.Va.

**DAYTON, Elias** (father of Jonathan Dayton), a Delegate from New Jersey; born in Elizabethtown (now Elizabeth), N.J., May 1, 1737; apprenticed as a mechanic; completed preparatory studies; lieutenant of militia March 19, 1756, and captain March 19, 1760; served in the "Jersey Blues" under General James Wolfe at Quebec, and against Pontiac near Detroit; proprietor of a general store at Elizabethtown, N.J.; alderman; member of committee to enforce measures recommended by Continental Congress, and on October 26, 1775, became one of Essex County's four muster-masters; commissioned a colonel of the third battalion of the New Jersey Line on January 10, 1776; elected to the Continental Congress December 12, 1778, in place of John Neilson, but declined May 25, 1779; was in active service until the discharge of the New Jersey Line on

November 3, 1783; promoted to brigadier general January 8, 1783; returned to Elizabethtown and operated a general store; major general of militia; recorder of Elizabethtown in 1789; member of State general assembly 1791-1792 and 1794-1796; mayor of Elizabethtown 1796-1805; president of the New Jersey Society of the Cincinnati; died in Elizabethtown (now Elizabeth), N.J., October 22, 1807; interment in a vault in the First Presbyterian Churchyard.

**DAYTON, Jonathan** (son of Elias Dayton), a Delegate, a Representative, and a Senator from New Jersey; born in Elizabethtown (now Elizabeth), N.J., October 16, 1760; was graduated from the College of New Jersey (now Princeton University) in 1776; studied law; was admitted to the bar; during the Revolutionary War served in the Third and later the Second New Jersey Regiment of the Continental Army 1776-1783, attaining the rank of captain; taken prisoner at Elizabethtown, N.J., and later exchanged; member, State general assembly 1786-1787, 1790, and served as speaker in 1790; delegate to the Federal Constitutional Convention in 1787 and signed the Constitution; Delegate to the Continental Congress 1787-1788; member, State council 1790; elected to the Second and to the three succeeding Congresses (March 4, 1791-March 3, 1799); Speaker of the House of Representatives (Fourth and Fifth Congresses); chairman, Committee on Elections (Third Congress); was not a candidate for renomination in 1798, having become a candidate for the United States Senate; elected as a Federalist to the United States Senate and served from March 4, 1799, to March 3, 1805; was arrested in 1807 on the charge of conspiring with Aaron Burr in treasonable projects; subsequently released and never brought to trial; member, New Jersey assembly 1814-1815; died in Elizabethtown, N.J., October 9, 1824; interment in a vault in St. John's Churchyard; the city of Dayton, Ohio, was named for him.

**Bibliography:** *DAB.*

**DAYTON, William Lewis,** a Senator from New Jersey; born in Basking Ridge, Somerset County, N.J., February 17, 1807; attended Trenton (N.J.) Academy and was graduated from the College of New Jersey (now Princeton University) in 1825; studied law; was admitted to the bar in 1830 and commenced practice in Freehold, N.J.; member, New Jersey State council, 1837-1838; associate judge of the State supreme court from 1838 until 1841, when he resigned; appointed and subsequently elected as a Whig to the United States Senate to fill the vacancy caused by the death of Samuel L. Southard; reelected in 1845, and served from July 2, 1842 to March 3, 1851; unsuccessful candidate for reelection; chairman, Committee on Public Buildings (Twenty-seventh and Twenty-eighth Congresses), Committee on Engrossed Bills (Twenty-eighth Congress); resumed the practice of law; nominated in 1856 by the Republican Party as its candidate for Vice President of the United States on the ticket with John C. Frémont; attorney general of New Jersey, 1857-1861; appointed Minister to France on March 18, 1861, and served until his death in Paris, December 1, 1864; interment in Riverview Cemetery, Trenton, N.J.

**Bibliography:** *DAB.*

**DEAL, John Nathan,** a Representative from Georgia; born in Millen, Jenkins County, Ga., August 25, 1942; graduated, Washington County High School, Sandersville, Ga., 1960; B.A. Mercer University, Macon, Ga., 1964; J.D., Mercer University School of Law, 1966; entered active duty, United States Army in 1966; released in 1968 after service with Judge Advocate General's Corps; assistant district attorney for Northeastern District of Georgia, 1970-1971; judge, juvenile court of Hall County, Ga., 1971-1972; attorney for Hall County; member, Georgia State senate, 1981-1993, president pro tempore, 1991; elected as a Democrat to the One Hundred Third and One Hundred Fourth Congresses (January 3, 1993-January 3, 1997); announced his affiliation with the Republican Party on April

10, 1995, and continued in office during the One Hundred Fourth Congress as a Republican; is a resident of Gainesville, Ga.

**DEAL, Joseph Thomas,** a Representative from Virginia; born near Surry, Va., November 19, 1860; attended the public schools; was graduated from Virginia Military Institute at Lexington in 1882; engaged in civil engineering and lumber manufacturing in Surry County in 1883; moved to Norfolk, Va., in 1891; chairman of the Improvement Board of Norfolk 1905-1910; delegate to the Democratic National Convention of 1908; member of the Virginia house of delegates 1910-1912; served in the Virginia senate in 1919; elected as a Democrat to the Sixty-seventh and to the three succeeding Congresses (March 4, 1921-March 3, 1929); was an unsuccessful candidate for reelection in 1928 to the Seventy-first Congress; resumed his activities in the lumber business until his death in Norfolk, Va., on March 7, 1942; interment in Forest Lawn Cemetery.

**DEAN, Benjamin,** a Representative from Massachusetts; born in Clitheroe, England, August 14, 1824; immigrated to the United States with his parents, who settled in Lowell, Mass.; attended Lowell schools, and Dartmouth College, Hanover, N.H.; studied law; was admitted to the bar in 1845 and commenced practice in Lowell; moved to Boston in 1852 and continued the practice of law; served in the State senate in 1862, 1863, and 1869; member of the common council 1865-1866 and 1872-1873; successfully contested as a Democrat the election of Walbridge A. Field to the Forty-fifth Congress and served from March 28, 1878, to March 3, 1879; was not a candidate for renomination in 1878 to the Forty-sixth Congress; resumed the practice of law in Boston; member of the board of park commissioners for several years and served as chairman; died in South Boston, Mass., April 9, 1897; interment in Lowell Cemetery, Lowell, Mass.

**DEAN, Ezra,** a Representative from Ohio; born in Hillsdale, Columbia County, N.Y., April 9, 1795; attended the common schools; in the War of 1812 was appointed ensign in the Eleventh Regiment of United States Infantry on April 17, 1814; commissioned lieutenant on October 1, 1814, for meritorious conduct at the sortie of Fort Erie; at the close of the war was placed in command of a revenue cutter on Lake Champlain; resigned to study law; was admitted to the bar in Plattsburgh, N.Y., in 1823; settled in Wooster, Ohio in 1824 and commenced the practice of law; postmaster of Wooster, 1828-1832; president judge of the court of common pleas, 1834-1841; elected as a Democrat to the Twenty-seventh and Twenty-eighth Congresses (March 4, 1841-March 3, 1845); chairman, Committee on the Militia (Twenty-eighth Congress); was not a candidate for renomination in 1844 to the Twenty-ninth Congress; resumed the practice of law in Wooster; moved to Ironton, Ohio, in 1867, and died there on January 25, 1872; interment in Woodland Cemetery.

**DEAN, Gilbert,** a Representative from New York; born in Pleasant Valley, Dutchess County, N.Y., August 14, 1819; attended the common schools and Amenia Seminary, Dutchess County, N.Y.; was graduated from Yale College in 1841; studied law; was admitted to the bar and commenced practice in Poughkeepsie, N.Y., in 1844; elected as a Democrat to the Thirty-second and Thirty-third Congresses and served from March 4, 1851, to July 3, 1854, when he resigned; appointed justice of the supreme court of New York on June 26, 1854, to fill a vacancy, and served until December 31, 1855; moved to New York City in 1856 and continued the practice of law; died in Poughkeepsie, N.Y., October 12, 1870; interment in the Presbyterian Cemetery, Pleasant Valley, N.Y.; reinterment in Portland Evergreen Cemetery, Brocton, Chautauqua County, N.Y.

**DEAN, Josiah,** a Representative from Massachusetts; born in Raynham, Mass., March 6, 1748; attended the common schools; engaged in the rolling-mill and shipbuilding business; selectman in 1781; town clerk in 1805; served in the Massachusetts senate 1804-1807; elected as a Republican to the Tenth Congress (March 4, 1807-March 3, 1809); member of the Massachusetts house of representatives in 1810 and 1811; resumed his former business pursuits; died in Raynham, Mass., October 14, 1818; interment in Pleasant Street Cemetery.

**DEAN, Sidney,** a Representative from Connecticut; born in Glastonbury, Conn., November 16, 1818; attended the common schools and Wilbraham and Suffield Academies; minister in the Methodist Episcopal Church from 1843 to 1853, when he retired from the ministry because of impaired health; engaged in manufacturing in Putnam, Conn.; member of the Connecticut house of representatives in 1854 and 1855; elected as the candidate of the American Party to the Thirty-fourth Congress and as a Republican to the Thirty-fifth Congress (March 4, 1855-March 3, 1859); chairman, Committee on Public Expenditures (Thirty-fourth Congress); declined to be a candidate for renomination in 1858; in 1860 reentered the ministry, with pastorates in Pawtucket, Providence, and finally in Warren, R.I.; during the period 1865-1880 engaged as editor of the Providence Press, Providence Star, and Rhode Island Press; served in the Rhode Island senate in 1870 and 1871; engaged in literary pursuits and lecturing; died in Brookline, Norfolk County, Mass., October 29, 1901; interment in South Cemetery, Warren, R.I.

**Bibliography:** *DAB.*

**DEANE, Charles Bennett,** a Representative from North Carolina; born in Ansonville Township, Anson County, N.C., November 1, 1898; attended Pee Dee Academy, Rockingham, N.C., and Trinity Park School, Durham, N.C., 1918-1920; was graduated from the law department of Wake Forest (N.C.) College in 1923; was admitted to the bar the same year and commenced practice in Rockingham, N.C.; register of deeds of Richmond County 1926-1934; attorney in the Wage and Hour Division, Department of Labor, Washington, D.C., in 1938 and 1939; in 1940 engaged in administrative law and in the general insurance business; served as chairman of the Richmond County Democratic executive committee 1932-1946; trustee of Wake Forest College; elected as a Democrat to the Eightieth and to the four succeeding Congresses (January 3, 1947-January 3, 1957); was an unsuccessful candidate for renomination in 1956 to the Eighty-fifth Congress; died in Rockingham, N.C., November 24, 1969; interment in Eastside Cemetery.

**DEANE, Silas,** a Delegate from Connecticut; born in Groton, Conn., December 24, 1737; received a classical training, and was graduated from Yale College, New Haven, Conn., in 1758; studied law; was admitted to the bar in 1761 and commenced practice in Wethersfield, Conn., afterward engaged in mercantile pursuits in the same town; deputy of the general assembly 1768-1775; Member of the Continental Congress 1774-1776; ordered to France in March 1776 as a secret political and financial agent, and in September was commissioned as Ambassador with Benjamin Franklin and Arthur Lee; negotiated and signed the treaty between France and the United States in Paris on February 6, 1778; personally secured the services of the Marquis de Lafayette, De Kalb, and other foreign officers; recalled in 1778 and investigated by Congress for financial misconduct; returned to Europe to secure documents for his defense; died on board ship sailing from Gravesend to Boston, September 23, 1789; interment in St. Leonard's Churchyard in Deal, on the Kentish coast, England; in 1842 Congress voted to pay his heirs a restitution.

**Bibliography:** *DAB*; James, Coy H. "The Revolutionary Career of Silas Deane." Ph.D. dissertation, Michigan State University, 1956; Deane, Silas. *The Deane Papers.* 5 vols. Edited by Charles Isham. New York: New-York Historical Society, 1886-90.

**DEAR, Cleveland,** a Representative from Louisiana; born in Sugartown, Beauregard Parish, La., August 22, 1888; attended the public schools; was graduated from Louisiana State University at Baton Rouge in 1910 and from its law department in 1914; was admitted to the bar in 1914 and commenced practice in Alexandria, Rapides Parish, La.; during the First World War was appointed a second lieutenant of Field Artillery on August 15, 1917; promoted to first lieutenant and served in the ammunition train of the Field Artillery in the Eighty-seventh and One Hundred and Eleventh Divisions until his discharge on December 14, 1918; served as district attorney of the ninth judicial district of Louisiana from 1920 until his resignation in 1933, having been elected to Congress; elected as a Democrat to the Seventy-third and Seventy-fourth Congresses (March 4, 1933-January 3, 1937); chairman, Committee on Elections No. 1 (Seventy-fourth Congress); was not a candidate for renomination in 1936, but was an unsuccessful candidate for the gubernatorial nomination; resumed the practice of law; appointed judge of the ninth judicial district court of Louisiana in 1941 to fill an unexpired term and was elected in 1942 and again in 1948 and served until his death in Alexandria, La., December 30, 1950; interment in Greenwood Memorial Park, Pineville, La.

**DEARBORN, Henry** (father of Henry Alexander Scammell Dearborn), a Representative from Massachusetts; born in North Hampton, N.H., February 23, 1751; attended the public schools; studied medicine; commenced practice in Nottingham Square in 1772; during the Revolutionary War was a captain in John Stark's Regiment and participated in the Battle of Bunker Hill, June 17, 1775; accompanied Benedict Arnold's expedition to Canada and took part in the attempt to storm the city of Quebec on December 31, 1775; was taken prisoner, but was released on parole in May 1776; joined General George Washington's staff in 1781 as deputy quartermaster general with rank of colonel, and served at the siege of Yorktown; moved to Monmouth, Mass. (now Maine), in June 1784; elected brigadier general of militia in 1787 and made major general in 1789; appointed United States marshal for the district of Maine in 1789; elected from a Maine district of Massachusetts to the Third Congress and reelected as a Republican to the Fourth Congress (March 4, 1793-March 3, 1797); appointed Secretary of War by President Thomas Jefferson and served from March 4, 1801 to March 7, 1809; appointed collector of the port of Boston by President James Madison in 1809, which position he held until January 27, 1812, when he was appointed senior major general in the United States Army; was in command at the capture of York (now Toronto), Canada, on April 27, 1813, and Fort George, May 27, 1813; recalled from the frontier on July 6, 1813, and placed in command of the city of New York; appointed Minister Plenipotentiary to Portugal by President James Monroe, and served from May 7, 1822 to June 30, 1824, when, by his own request, he was recalled; returned to Roxbury, Mass., where he died June 6, 1829; interment in Forest Hills Cemetery, Boston, Mass.

Bibliography: *DAB*; Erney, Richard A. "The Public Life of Henry Dearborn." Ph.D. dissertation, Columbia University, 1957.

**DEARBORN, Henry Alexander Scammell** (son of Henry Dearborn), a Representative from Massachusetts; born in Exeter, N.H., March 3, 1783; attended the common schools and Williams College, Williamstown, Mass., for two years; was graduated from the College of William and Mary, Williamsburg, Va., in 1803; studied law; was admitted to the bar and practiced in Salem, Mass., and Portland, Mass. (now Maine); collector of customs in Boston, 1812-1829; served as brigadier general commanding the Volunteers in the defenses of Boston Harbor in the War of 1812; member of the State constitutional convention in 1820; member of the Massachusetts house of representatives in 1829; served in the Massachusetts senate in 1830; elected as an Anti-Jacksonian to the Twenty-second Congress (March 4, 1831-March 3, 1833); was an unsuccessful candidate for reelection in 1832 to the Twenty-third Congress;

served as adjutant general of Massachusetts, 1834-1843; mayor of Roxbury, 1847-1851; president of the Massachusetts Horticultural Society; author of many books; died in Portland, Maine, July 29, 1851; interment in Forest Hills Cemetery, Roxbury, Mass.

Bibliography: *DAB*.

**DE ARMOND, David Albaugh,** a Representative from Missouri; born in Altoona, Blair County, Pa., on March 18, 1844; attended the public schools and Williamsport Dickinson Seminary; moved to Davenport, Iowa, in 1866; studied law; was admitted to the bar in 1867 and commenced practice in Davenport; moved to Missouri in 1869 and settled in Greenfield, Dade County; member of the State senate 1879-1883; Missouri Supreme Court commissioner in 1884; judge of the twenty-second judicial circuit of Missouri 1886-1890; elected as a Democrat to the Fifty-second and to the nine succeeding Congresses and served from March 4, 1891, until his death; one of the managers appointed by the House of Representatives in 1905 to conduct the impeachment proceedings against Charles Swayne, judge of the United States District Court for the Northern District of Florida; died in Butler, Bates County, Mo., November 23, 1909; interment in Oak Hill Cemetery.

**DEBERRY, Edmund,** a Representative from North Carolina; born in Lawrenceville (now Mount Gilead), Montgomery County, N.C., August 14, 1787; attended school at High Shoals; engaged in agricultural pursuits and also in the operation of cotton mills and flour mills; member of the State senate 1806-1811, 1813, 1814, 1820, 1821, and 1826-1828; served as justice of the peace; elected to the Twenty-first Congress (March 4, 1829-March 3, 1831); unsuccessful candidate for reelection in 1830 to the Twenty-second Congress; elected as an Anti-Jacksonian to the Twenty-third Congress and as a Whig to the Twenty-fourth through Twenty-eighth Congresses (March 4, 1833-March 3, 1845); chairman, Committee on Agriculture (Twenty-fifth through Twenty-eighth Congresses); was not a candidate for renomination in 1844; elected as a Whig to the Thirty-first Congress (March 4, 1849-March 3, 1851); was not a candidate for renomination in 1850; resumed his former agricultural and business pursuits; died at his home in Pee Dee Township, Montgomery County, N.C., December 12, 1859; interment in the family cemetery on his plantation near Mount Gilead.

**DEBOE, William Joseph,** a Senator from Kentucky; born in Crittenden County, Ky., June 30, 1849; attended the public schools and Ewing College, Illinois; studied law and medicine; was graduated from the medical department of the University of Louisville and practiced a few years, when his health failed; renewed the study of law; was admitted to the bar in 1889 and commenced practice in Marion, Crittenden County, Ky.; served as superintendent of schools of Crittenden County; unsuccessful candidate for election in 1892 to the Fifty-third Congress; member, Kentucky senate 1893-1898; elected as a Republican to the United States Senate and served from March 4, 1897, to March 3, 1903; was not a candidate for renomination in 1902; chairman, Committee on Indian Depredations (Fifty-sixth Congress), Committee to Establish the University of the United States (Fifty-seventh Congress); engaged in mining; postmaster of Marion 1923-1927; died in Marion, Crittenden County, Ky., on June 15, 1927; interment in Maple View Cemetery.

**DE BOLT, Rezin A.,** a Representative from Missouri; born near Basil, Fairfield County, Ohio, January 20, 1828; attended the common schools; employed as a tanner; studied law; was admitted to the bar in 1856 and commenced practice in Lancaster, Fairfield County, Ohio; moved to Trenton, Grundy County, Mo., in 1858 and continued the practice of his profession; appointed in 1859 and elected in 1860 commissioner of common schools for Grundy County; entered the Union Army as captain in the Twenty-third Regiment, Missouri Volunteers, in 1861; captured at the Battle of Shiloh, Tenn., April 6, 1862, and held as prisoner until the following

October; resigned his commission in 1863 because of impaired health; elected judge of the circuit court for the eleventh judicial circuit of Missouri in November 1863, which position he held by reelection until January 1, 1875; in 1864 again entered the United States service as major in the Forty-fourth Regiment, Missouri Volunteer Infantry; mustered out in August 1865; elected as a Democrat to the Forty-fourth Congress (March 4, 1875-March 3, 1877); was not a candidate for renomination in 1876 to the Forty-fifth Congress; resumed the practice of law; died in Trenton, Grundy County, Mo., October 30, 1891; interment in Odd Fellows Cemetery.

**DECKARD, Huey Joel,** a Representative from Indiana; born in Vandalia, Fayette County, Ill., March 7, 1942; attended public schools in Mount Vernon, Ind.; University of Evansville, 1962-1967; Indiana National Guard, 1966-1972; affiliated with broadcasting stations in southern Illinois and Indiana, 1959-1972; cable TV executive and legislative liaison for the Illinois-Indiana TV Association, 1974-1977; formed corporation involved in design and construction of energy-efficient and solar-heated homes and offices; member of Indiana house of representatives, 1966-1974; elected as a Republican to the Ninety-sixth and to the Ninety-seventh Congresses (January 3, 1979-January 3, 1983); unsuccessful candidate for reelection in 1982 to the Ninety-eighth Congress; is a resident of Evansville, Ind.

**DECKER, Perl D.,** a Representative from Missouri; born on a farm near Coolville, Athens County, Ohio, September 10, 1875; moved with his parents to a farm near Hollis, Cloud County, Kans., in 1879; attended the public schools of Cloud County, and Park College, Parkville, Mo., from which he was graduated in 1897; was graduated in law from the University of Kansas at Lawrence in 1899; was admitted to the bar in 1900 and commenced practice at Joplin, Jasper County, Mo.; served as city attorney 1900-1902; elected as a Democrat to the Sixty-third, Sixty-fourth, and Sixty-fifth Congresses (March 4, 1913-March 3, 1919); unsuccessful candidate for reelection in 1918 to the Sixty-sixth Congress; resumed the practice of law in Joplin, Mo.; delegate to the Democratic National Convention in 1932; died in Kansas City, Mo., August 22, 1934; interment in Mount Hope Cemetery, Joplin, Mo.

**DeCONCINI, Dennis Webster,** a Senator from Arizona; born in Tucson, Pima County, Ariz., May 8, 1937; attended the public schools of Tucson and Phoenix; B.A., University of Arizona, 1959; LL.B., University of Arizona School of Law, 1963; admitted to the Arizona bar in 1963 and commenced practice in Tucson; served in the United States Army 1959-1960; Army Reserve 1960-1967; member of Governor Sam Goddard's staff, 1965-1967; Pima County attorney, 1973-1976; elected as a Democrat to the United States Senate in 1976; reelected in 1982 and again in 1988, and served from January 3, 1977 to January 3, 1995; was not a candidate for reelection in 1994; chairman, Select Committee on Intelligence (One Hundred Third Congress); is a resident of Tucson, Ariz.

**DEEMER, Elias,** a Representative from Pennsylvania; born near Durham, Bucks County, Pa., January 3, 1838; attended public and private schools; engaged in mercantile pursuits in Lycoming County, Pa., and in Philadelphia in 1860; during the Civil War enlisted in July 1861 as a private in Company E, One Hundred and Fourth Regiment, Pennsylvania Volunteers, and served until the middle of May following, when he was discharged because of disabilities; moved to Milford, N.J., in 1862 and engaged in business; moved to Williamsport, Pa., in 1868 and engaged in the manufacture of lumber; president of the common council 1888-1890; president of the Williamsport National Bank 1893-1918; also interested in the publication of several newspapers at Williamsport; delegate to the Republican National Convention of 1896; elected as a Republican to the Fifty-seventh and to the two succeeding Congresses (March 4, 1901-March 3, 1907); unsuccessful candidate

for reelection in 1906 to the Sixtieth Congress, and for election in 1908 to the Sixty-first Congress; resumed lumber operations in Pennsylvania, and at Deemer, Miss., which town he founded and gave his name; died in Williamsport, Pa., March 29, 1918; interment in Wildwood Cemetery.

**DEEN, Braswell Drue,** a Representative from Georgia; born on a farm near Baxley, Appling County, Ga., June 28, 1893; attended public and high schools and South Georgia College at McRae; Appling County (Ga.) school superintendent from November 1916 until his resignation in August 1918; during the First World War served as a Young Men's Christian Association secretary at Fort Caswell, N.C.; B.P.H., Emory University, Atlanta, Ga., 1922; superintendent of schools at Tennille, Ga., 1922-1924; president of South Georgia Junior College, McRae, 1924-1927; engaged in farming and real estate development in 1927 and 1928; editor and proprietor of the Alma (Ga.) Times; also engaged in banking; elected as a Democrat to the Seventy-third and to the two succeeding Congresses (March 4, 1933-January 3, 1939); was not a candidate for renomination in 1938 to the Seventy-sixth Congress; insurance broker and cattle farmer; resided in Alma, Bacon County, Ga., until his death there on November 28, 1981; interment at Rose Hill Cemetery.

**DEERING, Nathaniel Cobb,** a Representative from Iowa; born in Denmark, Oxford County, Maine, September 2, 1827; attended the common schools and was graduated from North Bridgeton Academy; member of the State house of representatives from Penobscot County in 1855 and 1856; moved to Iowa, and settled in Osage, Mitchell County, in 1857; engaged in the lumber business and built and operated a sawmill; for several years a clerk in the United States Senate, but resigned in 1865; special agent of the Post Office Department for the district of Minnesota, Iowa, and Nebraska from 1865 to 1869, when he resigned; national-bank examiner for the State of Iowa 1872-1877; elected as a Republican to the Forty-fifth, Forty-sixth, and Forty-seventh Congresses (March 4, 1877-March 3, 1883); chairman, Committee on Expenditures in the Department of State (Forty-seventh Congress); unsuccessful candidate for renomination in 1882; engaged in agricultural pursuits; also interested in cattle raising in Montana, and at the time of his death served as president of a large cattle company in that territory; died in Osage, Mitchell County, Iowa, December 11, 1887; interment in Osage Cemetery.

**DeFAZIO, Peter Anthony,** a Representative from Oregon; born in Needham, Norfolk County, Mass., May 27, 1947; B.A., Tufts University, Medford, Mass., 1969; M.S., University of Oregon, 1977; entered active duty, U.S. Air Force in 1967; released in 1971; aide to Representative James Weaver of Oregon, 1977-1982; Lane County (Oreg.) Commissioner, 1983-1986, chairman, 1985-1986; elected as a Democrat to the One Hundredth and to the four succeeding Congresses (January 3, 1987-January 3, 1997); unsuccessful candidate for nomination to the United States Senate in a December 1995 special primary election; is a resident of Springfield, Oreg.

**DE FOREST, Henry Schermerhorn,** a Representative from New York; born in Schenectady, N.Y., February 16, 1847; attended the public schools of his native town and Eastman Business College, Poughkeepsie, N.Y.; engaged in the real-estate, banking, and contracting businesses; city recorder 1883-1885; mayor of Schenectady 1885-1887 and 1889-1891; elected as a Republican to the Sixty-second Congress (March 4, 1911-March 3, 1913); unsuccessful candidate for reelection in 1912 to the Sixty-third Congress; resumed the real-estate business and banking; unsuccessful candidate for nomination in 1914 to the Sixty-fourth Congress and for election in 1916 to the Sixty-fifth Congress; died in Schenectady, N.Y., February 13, 1917; interment in Vale Cemetery.

**DE FOREST, Robert Elliott,** a Representative from Connecticut; born in Guilford, New Haven County, Conn., February 20, 1845; attended the common schools; was graduated from Guilford Academy in 1863 and from Yale College in 1867; moved to Royalton, Vt., in 1867 and became an instructor in the Royalton Academy; studied law; was admitted to the bar in 1870 and commenced practice in Bridgeport, Conn.; prosecuting attorney for Bridgeport in 1872; judge of the court of common pleas for Fairfield County in 1874-1877; mayor of Bridgeport in 1878; member of the State house of representatives in 1880; served in the State senate in 1882; corporation counsel for Bridgeport; again elected mayor in 1889 and 1890; elected as a Democrat to the Fifty-second and Fifty-third Congresses (March 4, 1891-March 3, 1895); chairman, Committee on Reform in the Civil Service (Fifty-third Congress); unsuccessful candidate for reelection in 1894 to the Fifty-fourth Congress; served two terms as judge of the common pleas court; resumed the practice of law in Bridgeport, Conn., where he died October 1, 1924; interment in Mountain Grove Cemetery.

**DEFREES, Joseph Hutton,** a Representative from Indiana; born in Sparta, White County, Tenn., May 13, 1812; moved to Ohio with his parents, who settled in Piqua in 1819; attended the common schools; apprenticed to the blacksmith trade from 1826 until 1829; learned the art of printing; moved to Indiana and settled in South Bend in 1831, where he established the Northwestern Pioneer; moved to Goshen, Elkhart County, Ind., in 1833 and engaged in mercantile pursuits and later in banking; appointed county agent; sheriff of Elkhart County, 1835-1840; member of the Indiana State house of representatives in 1849, and again in 1872; served in the State senate, 1850-1854; elected as a Republican to the Thirty-ninth Congress (March 4, 1865-March 3, 1867); was not a candidate for renomination in 1866 to the Fortieth Congress; resumed his former business pursuits; also interested in milling, the manufacture of linseed oil, and the construction of the Goshen Hydraulic Works; director of the Cincinnati, Wabash and Michigan Railroad and served as its first president; died at Goshen, Ind., December 21, 1885; interment in Oak Ridge Cemetery.

**DEGENER, Edward,** a Representative from Texas; born in Brunswick, Germany, October 20, 1809; pursued an academic course in Germany and in Great Britain; twice a member of the legislative body in Anhalt-Dessau and a member of the first German National Assembly in Frankfurt am Main in 1848; immigrated to the United States in 1850 and located in Sisterdale, Kendall County, Tex.; engaged in agricultural pursuits; during the Civil War was court-martialed and imprisoned by the Confederates because of his devotion to the Union cause; after his release from imprisonment engaged in the wholesale grocery business in San Antonio; member of the Texas constitutional conventions in 1866 and 1868; upon the readmission of the State of Texas to representation was elected as a Republican to the Forty-first Congress and served from March 31, 1870, to March 3, 1871; unsuccessful for reelection in 1870 to the Forty-second Congress; member of the city council of San Antonio, Tex., 1872-1878; died in San Antonio, Texas, September 11, 1890; interment in the City Cemetery.

**DEGETAU, Federico,** a Resident Commissioner from Puerto Rico; born in Ponce, P.R., December 5, 1862; attended the common schools and Central College of Ponce; completed an academic course at Barcelona, Spain, and was graduated from the law department of Central University of Madrid; was admitted to the bar and commenced practice in Madrid, Spain; returned to Puerto Rico; one of the four commissioners sent by Puerto Rico to ask Spain for autonomy; settled in San Juan and continued the practice of law; member of the municipal council of San Juan in 1897; mayor of San Juan in 1898; deputy to the Spanish Cortes (Parliament) of 1898; appointed by General Henry secretary of the interior of the first American cabinet that was formed in Puerto Rico in 1899; appointed by General Davis a member of the insular board of charities; writer and author; first vice president of the municipal council of San Juan in 1899 and 1900; president of the board of education of San Juan in 1900 and 1901; elected as a Puerto Rican Republican a Resident Commissioner to the United States in 1900; reelected in 1902, and served from March 4, 1901, until March 3, 1905; was not a candidate for renomination in 1904; resumed the practice of law; died in Santurce, Puerto Rico, January 20, 1914; interment in the Cemetery of San Juan.

**DE GRAFF, John Isaac,** a Representative from New York; born in Schenectady, N.Y., October 2, 1783; attended the common schools and Union College, Schenectady, N.Y., in 1811; engaged in mercantile pursuits in Schenectady; served in the War of 1812; elected to the Twentieth Congress (March 4, 1827-March 3, 1829); mayor of Schenectady 1832-1834 and again in 1836; elected as a Democrat to the Twenty-fifth Congress (March 4, 1837-March 3, 1839); was not a candidate for renomination; engaged in mercantile pursuits; interested in the building of the Mohawk & Hudson Railroad; again served as mayor of Schenectady in 1842 and 1845; engaged in banking until his death in Schenectady, N.Y., July 26, 1848; interment in Vale Cemetery.

**DE GRAFFENREID, Reese Calhoun,** a Representative from Texas; born in Franklin, Williamson County, Tenn., May 7, 1859; attended the common schools of Franklin and the University of Tennessee at Knoxville; was graduated from the law department of Cumberland University, Lebanon, Tenn.; was admitted to the bar in 1879 and commenced practice in Franklin; moved to Chattanooga, Tenn., where he practiced his profession for one year, moving thence to Texas; helped in the construction of the Texas & Pacific Railroad; resumed the practice of law at Longview, Tex., in 1883; elected county attorney and resigned two months afterward; unsuccessful candidate for election in 1890 to the Fifty-second Congress; elected as a Democrat to the Fifty-fifth, Fifty-sixth, and Fifty-seventh Congresses and served from March 4, 1897, until his death in Washington, D.C., August 29, 1902; interment in Greenwood Cemetery, Longview, Gregg County, Tex.

**deGRAFFENRIED, Edward,** a Representative from Alabama; born in Eutaw, Greene County, Ala., June 30, 1899; attended the public schools in Greensboro, Ala.; was graduated from Gulf Coast Military Academy, Gulfport, Miss., in 1917; during the First World War served as a private in the United States Army and was discharged on December 5, 1918, at Camp Pike, Ark.; graduated from the law school of the University of Alabama at Tuscaloosa in 1921; was admitted to the bar in June 1921 and commenced the practice of law in Tuscaloosa, Ala.; solicitor of the sixth judicial circuit of Alabama from 1927 through 1934; unsuccessful for reelection in 1934 and for election in 1938; again elected solicitor and served from January 1943 to January 1947; was unsuccessful for the Democratic nomination in 1946 to the Eightieth Congress; elected as a Democrat to the Eighty-first and to the Eighty-second Congresses (January 3, 1949-January 3, 1953); unsuccessful candidate for renomination in 1952; resumed the practice of law; continued the practice of law until his retirement shortly before his death in Tuscaloosa, Ala., November 5, 1974; interment in Evergreen Cemetery.

**DE HART, John,** a Delegate from New Jersey; born in Elizabethtown (now Elizabeth), N.J., in 1728; completed preparatory studies; studied law; was admitted to the bar and practiced; was made a sergeant-at-law on September 11, 1770; was one of the signers of the Articles of Association in 1774; Member of the Continental Congress 1774-1776; member of the committee who prepared the draft for the New Jersey State constitution in June 1776; elected chief justice of the State supreme court September 4, 1776, and served until February 5, 1777; mayor of Elizabethtown under the revised charter and served from November 1789 until his death; died in Elizabethtown, N.J., June 1, 1795; interment in St. John's Churchyard.

**DE HAVEN, John Jefferson,** a Representative from California; born in St. Joseph, Buchanan County, Mo., March 12, 1849; moved to California in 1853 with his parents, who settled in Humboldt County; attended the common schools; became a printer, and pursued that vocation for four years; studied law; was admitted to the bar of the district court in Humboldt in 1866 and commenced practice at Eureka; elected district attorney of Humboldt County in 1867; member of the State house of representatives in 1869; served in the State senate 1871-1875; appointed city attorney of Eureka in 1878, and served two years; unsuccessful candidate for election in 1882 to the Forty-eighth Congress; elected judge of the superior court of Humboldt County in 1884; elected as a Republican to the Fifty-first Congress and served from March 4, 1889, until October 1, 1890, when he resigned; elected associate justice of the California Supreme Court to fill an unexpired term of four years; United States district judge for the northern district of California from June 8, 1897, until his death in Yountville, Napa County, Calif., January 26, 1913; interment in Mount Olivet Cemetery, San Francisco, Calif.

**DEITRICK, Frederick Simpson,** a Representative from Massachusetts; born in New Brighton, Beaver County, Pa., April 9, 1875; attended the public schools; was graduated from Geneva College, Beaver Falls, Pa., in 1895 and from Harvard Law School in 1898; was admitted to the bar in 1899 and commenced practice in Boston, Mass.; member of the board of aldermen of Cambridge in 1908 and 1909; member of the Massachusetts house of representatives 1902-1905; elected as a Democrat to the Sixty-third Congress (March 4, 1913-March 3, 1915); unsuccessful candidate for reelection in 1914 to the Sixty-fourth Congress; resumed the practice of law in Boston, Mass.; died in Middleton, Mass., May 24, 1948; interment in Mount Auburn Cemetery, Cambridge, Mass.

**DE JARNETTE, Daniel Coleman,** a Representative from Virginia; born at "Spring Grove Manor," near Bowling Green, Caroline County, Va., October 18, 1822; studied under a private teacher and attended Bethany College, Bethany, Va. (now West Virginia); engaged in agricultural pursuits; served in the State house of representatives 1853-1858; elected as an Independent Democrat to the Thirty-sixth Congress (March 4, 1859-March 3, 1861); reelected to the Thirty-seventh Congress, but did not present his credentials; Representative from Virginia to the First and Second Confederate Congresses 1862-1865; was an arbitrator in 1871 to define the boundary line between Maryland and Virginia; died at White Sulphur Springs, Greenbrier County, W.Va., August 20, 1881; interment in private burying ground on his estate, "Spring Grove," Caroline County, Va.

**de la GARZA, Eligio, II (Kika),** a Representative from Texas; born in Mercedes, Hidalgo County, Tex., September 22, 1927; educated at Mission (Tex.) High School, Edinburgh (Tex.) Junior College; LL.B., St. Mary's University, San Antonio, Tex., 1952; at age seventeen enlisted in the United States Navy and served from 1945 to 1946; served as an officer in the United States Army, Thirty-seventh Division Artillery, 1950-1952; graduated as a second lieutenant, St. Mary's Reserve Officer Training Corps, in 1951 and from the Artillery School, Fort Sill, Okla., in 1952; was admitted to the Texas bar in 1952 and began practice in Mission, Tex.; member of the Texas State house of representatives from 1952 until 1964; elected as a Democrat to the Eighty-ninth and to the fifteen succeeding Congresses (January 3, 1965-January 3, 1997); chairman, Committee on Agriculture (Ninety-seventh through One Hundred Third Congresses); was not a candidate for reelection in 1996 to the One Hundred Fifth Congress; is a resident of Mission, Tex.

**DE LA MATYR, Gilbert,** a Representative from Indiana; born in Pharsalia, Chenango County, N.Y., July 8, 1825; pursued an academic course; was a graduate of the theological course of the Methodist Episcopal Church in 1854; itinerant elder in that church; member of the general conference in 1868, and for one term filled the office of presiding elder; during the Civil War helped enlist the Eighth Regiment of New York Heavy Artillery in 1862, and was its chaplain for three years; after holding pastorates in several large cities he settled in Indianapolis, Ind., and continued his ministerial duties; elected as a Greenbacker to the Forty-sixth Congress (March 4, 1879-March 3, 1881); was not a candidate for renomination in 1880 to the Forty-seventh Congress; moved to Denver, Colo., in 1881 and again engaged in preaching; pastor of the First Methodist Episcopal Church of Akron, Ohio, from 1889 until his death in that city May 17, 1892; interment in Mount Albion Cemetery, Albion, N.Y.

**Bibliography:** Doolen, Richard M. "Pastor in Politics: The Congressional Career of Reverend Gilbert De La Matyr." *Indiana Magazine of History* 68 (June 1972): 103-24.

**DE LA MONTANYA, James,** a Representative from New York; born in New York City March 20, 1798; resided in Haverstraw, Rockland County, N.Y.; supervisor of Haverstraw in 1832 and 1833; member of the State assembly in 1833; elected as a Democrat to the Twenty-sixth Congress (March 4, 1839-March 3, 1841); died in New York City April 29, 1849; interment in the Barnes family burial ground, Stony Point, Rockland County, N.Y.

**DE LACY, Emerson Hugh,** a Representative from Washington; born in Seattle, King County, Wash., May 9, 1910; attended the Queen Anne public schools; was graduated from the University of Washington at Seattle, in 1932; received M.A. degree in 1932; taught English at the University of Washington 1933-1937; member of the city council of Seattle 1937-1940; employed as a shipyard machinist 1940-1944; elected as a Democrat to the Seventy-ninth Congress (January 3, 1945-January 3, 1947); unsuccessful candidate for reelection in 1946 to the Eightieth Congress; engaged in 1947 as editor of monthly Bulletin of Machinists' Union, Seattle, Wash.; State director of Progressive Party of Ohio, 1948-1950; worked as carpenter in Cleveland, Ohio, 1951-1958, except for employment during part of 1952 in the presidential campaign of the Progressive Party; continued in carpentry in Los Angeles, 1959-1960, and became a general building contractor until his retirement in 1967; pursued graduate studies in philosophy at San Fernando Valley State College; was a resident of Van Nuys, Calif. until his death in Santa Cruz, Calif. on August 19, 1986.

**DELANEY, John Joseph,** a Representative from New York; born in Brooklyn, N.Y., August 21, 1878; attended St. Ann's Parochial School and St. James' Academy, Brooklyn, N.Y., and Manhattan College, New York City; engaged in the diamond business in 1897; was graduated from the Brooklyn Law School of St. Lawrence University in 1914; admitted to the bar in 1915 and commenced practice in New York City; elected as a Democrat to the Sixty-fifth Congress to fill the vacancy caused by the resignation of John J. Fitzgerald and served from March 5, 1918, to March 3, 1919; declined to be a candidate for renomination in 1918; resumed his former business pursuits; delegate to the Democratic State conventions in 1922 and 1924; deputy commissioner of public markets of New York City 1924-1931; elected to the Seventy-second and to the eight succeeding Congresses and served from March 4, 1931, until his death; had been reelected to the Eighty-first Congress; died in Brooklyn, N.Y., November 18, 1948; interment in Holy Cross Cemetery.

**DELANO, Charles,** a Representative from Massachusetts; born in New Braintree, Worcester County, Mass., June 24, 1820; moved with his parents to Amherst, Mass., in 1833; attended the common schools and was graduated from Amherst College, Amherst, Mass., in 1840; studied law; was admitted to the bar in 1842 and commenced practice in Amherst, Mass.; moved to Northampton, Mass., in 1848 and continued the practice of law; treasurer of Hampshire County 1849-1858; elected as a Republican to the Thirty-sixth and Thirty-seventh Congresses (March 4, 1859-March 3, 1863); was not a candidate for renomination in 1862 to the Thirty-eighth Congress; resumed the practice of law; trustee of the Clarke School for the Education of the Deaf 1877-1883; appointed by Governor Alexander H. Rice in 1878 to act as special counsel for the Commonwealth of Massachusetts in matters relating to the Hoosac Tunnel and the Troy and Greenfield Railroad, and served in this capacity until his death in Northampton, Mass., January 23, 1883; interment in Bridge Street Cemetery.

**DELANO, Columbus,** a Representative from Ohio; born in Shoreham, Vt., June 4, 1809; moved with his parents to Mount Vernon, Knox County, Ohio, in 1817; pursued an academic course; studied law; was admitted to the bar in 1831 and commenced practice in Mount Vernon; elected as a Whig to the Twenty-ninth Congress (March 4, 1845-March 3, 1847); was not a candidate for renomination in 1846; unsuccessful candidate for the nomination for Governor at the Whig State convention in 1847; delegate to the Republican National Convention in 1860 and 1864; served as State commissary general of Ohio in 1861; unsuccessful candidate by two votes for the United States Senate in 1862; member of the State house of representatives in 1863; elected as a Republican to the Thirty-ninth Congress (March 4, 1865-March 3, 1867); chairman, Committee on Claims (Thirty-ninth Congress); successfully contested the election of George W. Morgan to the Fortieth Congress and served from June 3, 1868, to March 3, 1869; was not a candidate for renomination in 1868; Commissioner of Internal Revenue from March 11, 1869, to October 31, 1870; appointed Secretary of the Interior by President Ulysses S. Grant on November 1, 1870, which position he held until October 19, 1875, when he resigned; retired to his farm near Mount Vernon, Ohio; president of the First National Bank of Mount Vernon until his death in Mount Vernon, Ohio, October 23, 1896; interment in Mount View Cemetery.

Bibliography: *DAB*.

**DE LANO, Milton,** a Representative from New York; born in Wampsville, Madison County, N.Y., August 11, 1844; attended the common schools; settled in Canastota, N.Y., and engaged in mercantile pursuits for eight years; town clerk of Lenox 1867-1869; sheriff of Madison County, N.Y., 1873-1875 and 1879-1881; engaged in banking, the real-estate business, and in the manufacture of window glass; member of the Canastota Board of Education 1883-1905 and served as president 1893-1905; aided in the organization of the Canastota Northern Railroad Co.; delegate to the Republican National Convention in 1884; elected as a Republican to the Fiftieth and Fifty-first Congresses (March 4, 1887-March 3, 1891); chairman, Committee on Pensions (Fifty-first Congress); declined to be a candidate for renomination in 1890; resumed banking; receiver of the Hudson River Power Co. 1908-1912; became president of the State Bank of Canastota, N.Y., in 1912; died in Syracuse, N.Y., January 2, 1922; interment in Mount Pleasant Cemetery, Canastota, N.Y.

**DELAPLAINE, Isaac Clason,** a Representative from New York; born in New York City October 27, 1817; pursued an academic course; was graduated from Columbia College (now Columbia University), New York City, in 1834; studied law; was admitted to the bar about 1840 and commenced practice in New York City; elected as a Democrat to the Thirty-seventh Congress (March 4, 1861-March 3, 1863); died in New York City July 17, 1866; interment in Greenwood Cemetery, Brooklyn, N.Y.

**DE LARGE, Robert Carlos,** a Representative from South Carolina; born into slavery in Aiken, S.C., March 15, 1842; received such an education as was then attainable, and was graduated from the Wood High School, Charleston, S.C.; engaged in agricultural pursuits and worked as a tailor; agent for the Freedman's Bureau in South Carolina; chaired the credentials committee of the 1865 Colored People's Convention, held in Zion Church, Charleston; chaired the platform committee of the 1867 State Republican convention; delegate to the State constitutional convention in 1868, and served on the Committee on Franchise and Elections; member of the South Carolina State house of representatives, 1868-1870; was one of the State commissioners of the sinking fund (instituted to pay off the principal of the State's debt); elected State land commissioner in 1870 and served until elected to Congress; presented credentials as a Republican Member-elect to the Forty-second Congress, and served from March 4, 1871 until January 24, 1873, when the seat was declared vacant, the election having been contested by Christopher C. Bowen; declined to be a candidate for reelection in 1872 to the Forty-third Congress; served as a local magistrate until his death in Charleston, S.C., February 14, 1874; interment in Brown Fellowship Graveyard.

**DeLAURO, Rosa L.,** a Representative from Connecticut; born in New Haven, Conn., March 2, 1943; attended St. Louis Grammar School and graduated Laurelton Hall High School; B.A., Marymount College, Tarrytown, N.Y., 1964; attended the London School of Economics, 1962-1963; M.A., Columbia University, 1966; assistant director, National Urban Fellows, 1970-1975; executive assistant, Mayor of New Haven; campaign manager, Frank Logue for mayor, 1978; executive assistant to New Haven Development Administration, 1978-1979; campaign manager for Senator Christopher J. Dodd of Connecticut, 1979-1980; administrative assistant to Senator Dodd, 1981-1986; executive director, Countdown '87; executive director, Emily's List; elected as a Democrat to the One Hundred Second and to the two succeeding Congresses (January 3, 1991-January 3, 1997); is a resident of New Haven, Conn.

**DeLAY, Thomas Dale (Tom),** a Representative from Texas; born in Laredo, Webb County, Tex., April 8, 1947; spent much of his boyhood in Venezuela, where his father was an oil drilling contractor; graduated from Calallan High School, Corpus Christi, Tex., in 1965; attended Baylor University, Waco, Tex., 1967; B.S., University of Houston, Tex., 1970; opened a pest control business in 1973; member, Texas State house of representatives, 1979-1984; elected as a Republican to the Ninety-ninth and to the five succeeding Congresses (January 3, 1985-January 3, 1997); majority whip (One Hundred Fourth Congress); is a resident of Sugar Land, Tex.

**DELGADO, Francisco Afan,** a Resident Commissioner from the Philippine Islands; born in Bulacan Province, Philippine Islands, January 25, 1886; studied at San Juan de Letran, Ateneo de Manila, Colegio Filipino, Los Angeles (Calif.) High School, and Compton (Calif.) Union High School; Indiana University at Bloomington, LL.B., 1907 and Yale University, LL.M., 1909; was admitted to the bar in 1908 and commenced practice in Indianapolis, Ind.; returned to the Philippine Islands in 1908 and was employed with the Philippine Government as a law clerk and later as chief of the law division of the executive bureau until 1913, when he returned to the private practice of law; served in the Philippine National Guard in 1918; member of the National Council of Defense for the Philippines in 1918; served in the Philippine house of representatives 1931-1934; elected as a Nationalist a Resident Commissioner to the United States and served from January 3, 1935, until February 14, 1936, when a successor qualified in accordance with the new form of government of the Commonwealth of the Philippine Islands; appointed justice of the court of appeals February 1936-1937; resumed the practice of law; delegate to the International Committee of Jurists at Washington, D.C., and to the founding conference of the United Nations at San Francisco in 1945; member of the Philippine War Damage Commission from June 4,

1946, to March 31, 1951; member, Philippine senate, 1951-1957; Ambassador of the Philippines to the United Nations, September 29, 1958-January 1, 1962; returned to Philippines and resided in Bulacan Province; died in Manila, Republic of the Philippines, October 27, 1964.

**DELLAY, Vincent John,** a Representative from New Jersey; born in Union City, Hudson County, N.J., June 23, 1907; educated in West New York High School, New York Evening High School, and the American Institute of Banking; advanced from messenger to bookkeeper, Irving Trust Co., New York City, 1923-1929; assistant comptroller, Sterling National Bank & Trust Co., New York City, 1929-1936; auditor, New Jersey State Treasury Department, 1936-1956; served in the United States Navy as a petty officer from February 1944 until December 1945; chief warrant officer New Jersey National Guard 1949-1960; unsuccessful candidate for election in 1954 to the Eighty-fourth Congress; elected as a Republican to the Eighty-fifth Congress (January 3, 1957-January 3, 1959); announced his affiliation with the Democratic Party on October 29, 1957, and continued in office during the Eighty-fifth Congress as a Democrat; was unsuccessful for nomination as an Independent candidate in 1958 to the Eighty-sixth Congress; later reaffiliated with the Republican Party; engaged as supervising field auditor for New Jersey Treasury Department until his retirement in 1971; is a resident of Hasbrouck Heights, N.J.

**DELLENBACK, John Richard,** a Representative from Oregon; born in Chicago, Ill., November 6, 1918; B.S., Yale University, 1940; special work in Northwestern University School of Speech, summers of 1946 and 1949; J.D., University of Michigan Law School, 1949; commissioned an ensign in United States Naval Reserve; active duty, April 1942-1946, with rank of lieutenant; remained in Naval Reserve for several years, honorably discharged with rank of lieutenant commander; instructor and then assistant professor of business law at Oregon State College, 1949-1951; practiced law in Medford, Oreg., from 1951 until 1966; delegate to the Republican National Conventions of 1964, 1968, and 1972; representative from Jackson County in the Oregon State Legislature from 1960 until 1966; vice chairman of the Judicial Council of Oregon; elected as a Republican to the Ninetieth and to the three succeeding Congresses (January 3, 1967-January 3, 1975); unsuccessful candidate for reelection in 1974 to the Ninety-fourth Congress; director of the United States Peace Corps from April 1975 until May 1977; president, Christian College Coalition, 1977-1981; chairman of the board, World Vision U.S., 1988-1996; secretary, World Vision International, 1993 to present; is a resident of Medford, Oreg.

**DELLET, James,** a Representative from Alabama; born in Camden, N.J., February 18, 1788; moved to Columbia, S.C., with his parents in 1800; was graduated from the University of South Carolina at Columbia in 1810; studied law; was admitted to the bar in 1813 and practiced; moved to Alabama in 1818 and settled in Claiborne and continued the practice of law; elected to the first State house of representatives of Alabama under the State government in 1819 and served as its speaker; reelected in 1821 and 1825; unsuccessful as the Whig candidate for Congress in 1833; elected as a Whig to the Twenty-sixth Congress (March 4, 1839-March 3, 1841); elected to the Twenty-eighth Congress (March 4, 1843-March 3, 1845); resumed the practice of law and also engaged in agricultural pursuits; died in Claiborne, Monroe County, Ala., December 21, 1848; interment in a private cemetery at Claiborne, Ala.

**DELLUMS, Ronald Vernie,** a Representative from California; born in Oakland, Alameda County, Calif., November 24, 1935; attended the Oakland public schools; A.A., Oakland City College, 1958; B.A., San Francisco State College, 1960; M.S.W., University of California, 1962; entered active duty, United States Marine Corps,

1954-1956; psychiatric social worker, California Department of Mental Hygiene, 1962-1964; program director, Bayview Community Center, 1964-1965; associate director, then director, Hunters Point Youth Opportunity Center, 1965-1966; planning consultant, Bay Area Social Planning Council, 1966-1967; director, Concentrated Employment Program, San Francisco Economic Opportunity Council, 1967-1968; senior consultant, Social Dynamics, Inc. (manpower specialization programs), 1968-1970; part-time lecturer, San Francisco State College, University of California, and Berkeley Graduate School of Social Welfare; member, Berkeley City Council, 1967-1970; delegate to Democratic National Convention, 1972; elected as a Democrat to the Ninety-second and to the twelve succeeding Congresses (January 3, 1971-January 3, 1997); chairman, Committee on District of Columbia (Ninety-sixth through One Hundred Second Congresses), Committee on Armed Services (One Hundred Third Congress); is a resident of Oakland, Calif.

**de LUGO, Ron,** the first Delegate from the Territory of the Virgin Islands; born in Englewood, N.J., August 2, 1930; educated at Saints Peter and Paul School, St. Thomas, V.I., and Colegio San Jose, P.R.; served in the United States Army, 1948-1950; program director and announcer, Armed Forces Radio Service, 1948; WSTA radio, St. Thomas, V.I., 1950; WIVI radio, St. Croix, V.I., 1955; Virgin Islands territorial senator, 1956-1960, 1963-1966; served as minority leader, 1958-1966; Democratic National Committeeman, 1959; member, Democratic National Committee, 1960-1964; administrator for St. Croix, United States Virgin Islands, April 1961-August 1962; representative, Virgin Islands, Washington, D.C., 1968-1972; delegate to the Democratic National Conventions of 1956, 1960, 1964 and 1968; elected as a Democrat to the Ninety-third and to the two succeeding Congresses (January 3, 1973-January 3, 1979); was not a candidate for reelection in 1978 to the Ninety-sixth Congress, but was an unsuccessful candidate for election as Governor of the Virgin Islands; elected as a Democrat to the Ninety-seventh and to the six succeeding Congresses (January 3, 1981-January 3, 1995); was not a candidate for reelection in 1994 to the One Hundred Fourth Congress; is a resident of St. Thomas, V.I.

**DEMING, Benjamin F.,** a Representative from Vermont; born in Danville, Caledonia County, Vt., in 1790; pursued an academic course; engaged in mercantile pursuits; member of the Governor's council 1827-1832; clerk of the Caledonia County Court 1817-1833; county judge of probate 1821-1833; elected as an Anti-Masonic candidate to the Twenty-third Congress and served from March 4, 1833, until his death at Saratoga Springs, N.Y., en route home, July 11, 1834; interment in Danville Green Cemetery, Danville, Caledonia County, Vt.

**DEMING, Henry Champion,** a Representative from Connecticut; born in Colchester, New London County, Conn., May 23, 1815; pursued classical studies; was graduated from Yale College in 1836 and from the Harvard Law School in 1839; was admitted to the bar in 1839 and began practice in New York City but devoted his time chiefly to literary work; moved to Hartford, Conn., in 1847; member of the State house of representatives in 1849, 1850, and 1859-1861; member of the State senate in 1851; mayor of Hartford, Conn., 1854-1858 and 1860-1862; entered the Union Army in September 1861 as colonel of the Twelfth Regiment, Connecticut Volunteers; mayor of New Orleans under martial law from October 1862 to February 1863, when he resigned from the Army; elected as a Republican to the Thirty-eighth and Thirty-ninth Congresses (March 4, 1863-March 3, 1867); chairman, Committee on Expenditures in the Department of War (Thirty-eighth and Thirty-ninth Congresses); unsuccessful candidate for reelection in 1866 to the Fortieth Congress; appointed collector of internal revenue in 1869 and served until his death in Hartford, Conn., October 8, 1872; interment in Spring Grove Cemetery.

**Bibliography:** *DAB.*

**DE MOTT, John,** a Representative from New York; born in Readington, Hunterdon County, N.J., October 7, 1790; moved to Herkimer County, N.Y., in 1793 with his parents, who settled in what is now the town of Lodi, Seneca County; attended the common schools; pursued an academic course; major general of the Thirty-eighth Brigade of the State militia; supervisor in the town of Covert in 1823 and 1824 and of Lodi in 1826, 1827, 1829, and 1830; engaged in mercantile pursuits in Lodi, N.Y., for more than forty years; member of the State assembly in 1833; unsuccessful candidate for election in 1840 to the Twenty-seventh Congress; elected as a Democrat to the Twenty-ninth Congress (March 4, 1845-March 3, 1847); was not a candidate for renomination in 1846; resumed his former business pursuits and also engaged in the banking business; died in Lodi, Seneca County, N.Y., July 31, 1870; interment in Evergreen Cemetery, Ovid, N.Y.

**DE MOTTE, Mark Lindsey,** a Representative from Indiana; born in Rockville, Parke County, Ind., December 28, 1832; pursued preparatory studies; was graduated from the literary department of Indiana Asbury (now De Pauw) University, Greencastle, Ind., in 1853 and from the law department of the same university in 1855; was admitted to the bar and began practice in Valparaiso in 1855; elected prosecuting attorney of the sixty-seventh judicial district in 1856; served in the Union Army with the rank of first lieutenant in 1861; promoted to captain in 1862; at the close of the war moved to Lexington, Mo., and resumed the practice of law; editor and proprietor of the Lexington Register; unsuccessful Republican candidate for election to Congress in 1872 and 1876; delegate to the Republican National Convention in 1876; returned to Valparaiso, Ind., in 1877 and resumed the practice of law; organized the Northern Indiana Law School in 1879; elected as a Republican to the Forty-seventh Congress (March 4, 1881-March 3, 1883); unsuccessful candidate for reelection in 1882 to the Forty-eighth Congress; member of the State senate 1886-1890; appointed postmaster of Valparaiso March 24, 1890, and served until March 20, 1894; dean of the Northern Indiana Law School 1890-1908; died in Valparaiso, Porter County, Ind., September 23, 1908; interment in Maplewood Cemetery.

**DEMPSEY, John Joseph,** a Representative from New Mexico; born in White Haven, Luzerne County, Pa., June 22, 1879; attended the grade schools; engaged as a telegrapher; held various positions with the Brooklyn Union Elevator Co.; vice president of the Brooklyn Rapid Transit Co. until 1919; entered the oil business in Oklahoma in 1919 and was vice president of the Continental Oil & Asphalt Co.; moved to Santa Fe, N.Mex., in 1920 and was an independent oil operator; in 1928 became president of the United States Asphalt Co.; in 1932 was appointed a member and later president of the Board of Regents of the University of New Mexico; State director for the National Recovery Administration in 1933, then became State director of the Federal Housing Administration and the National Emergency Council; elected as a Democrat to the Seventy-fourth and to the two succeeding Congresses (January 3, 1935-January 3, 1941); was not a candidate for renomination in 1940 to the House of Representatives, but was an unsuccessful candidate for nomination to the United States Senate; member of the United States Maritime Commission in 1941; Under Secretary of the Interior from July 7, 1941 until his resignation on June 24, 1942; elected Governor of New Mexico in 1942, reelected in 1944, and served from January 1, 1943 to January 1, 1947; unsuccessful candidate in 1946 for nomination to the United States Senate; elected to the Eighty-second and to the three succeeding Congresses, and served from January 3, 1951 until his death in Washington, D.C., March 11, 1958; interment in Rosario Cemetery, Santa Fe, N.Mex.

**DEMPSEY, Stephen Wallace,** a Representative from New York; born in Hartland, Niagara County, N.Y., May 8, 1862; attended the district school of his native town, and was graduated from the De Veaux School, Niagara Falls, N.Y., in 1880; studied law; was admitted to the bar in 1886 and commenced practice in Lockport, Niagara County, N.Y.; assistant United States attorney, 1889-1907; special assistant to the Attorney General of the United States, 1907-1912, and was in charge of the prosecution of the Standard Oil Co. and certain railroads; elected as a Republican to the Sixty-fourth and to the seven succeeding Congresses (March 4, 1915-March 3, 1931); chairman, Committee on Rivers and Harbors (Sixty-seventh through Seventy-first Congresses); unsuccessful candidate for renomination in 1930 to the Seventy-second Congress; reengaged in the practice of law in Washington, D.C., until his death on March 1, 1949; interment in Rock Creek Cemetery.

**DE MUTH, Peter Joseph,** a Representative from Pennsylvania; born in Pittsburgh, Pa., January 1, 1892; attended the parochial and public schools; B.S., Carnegie Institute of Technology, Pittsburgh, Pa.; was a civil engineer from 1914 until his enlistment in the United States Navy as a chief machinist mate on July 15, 1918; returned to Pittsburgh, Pa., and was employed as a sales manager, 1919-1922; engaged in the real estate business and as a building contractor in 1922; elected as a Democrat to the Seventy-fifth Congress (January 3, 1937-January 3, 1939); unsuccessful candidate for reelection in 1938 to the Seventy-sixth Congress; resumed the real estate and building business in Pittsburgh, Pa., until June 1949; moved to Los Angeles, Calif., and continued his activities in the real estate, insurance, and building business; was a resident of Laguna Hills, Calif.; died April 3, 1993.

**DeNARDIS, Lawrence Joseph,** a Representative from Connecticut; born in New Haven, Conn., March 18, 1938; attended the public schools; B.A., Holy Cross College, Worcester, Mass., 1960; M.A., New York University, 1964 and Ph.D., 1968; served as a lieutenant in the United States Naval Reserve, 1960-1963; associate professor, Albertus Magnus College, New Haven, Conn., 1964-1979; President, Connecticut Conference of Independent Colleges, 1979-1980; served in the Connecticut State senate, 1970-1979; delegate, Connecticut State Republican conventions, 1966-1982; delegate to the Republican National Conventions of 1976 and 1980; elected as a Republican to the Ninety-seventh Congress (January 3, 1981-January 3, 1983); unsuccessful candidate for reelection in 1982 to the Ninety-eighth Congress, and for election in 1984 to the Ninety-ninth Congress; visiting professor of government, Connecticut College, New London, 1983-1984; assistant secretary, Department of Health and Human Services, 1985-1987; guest scholar, Woodrow Wilson International Center, Washington, D.C., 1987; resident of Hamden, Conn. and Washington, D.C.

**DENBY, Edwin** (grandson of Graham Newell Fitch), a Representative from Michigan; born in Evansville, Vanderburg County, Ind., February 18, 1870; attended the public schools; traveled to China in 1885 with his father, Charles Denby, who was United States Minister; employed in the Chinese imperial maritime customs service from 1887 until 1894; returned to the United States in 1894; was graduated from the law department of the University of Michigan at Ann Arbor in 1896; was admitted to the bar and commenced practice in Detroit in 1896; during the war with Spain served as a gunner's mate, third class, United States Navy, on the *Yosemite;* member of the Michigan State house of representatives in 1903; elected as a Republican to the Fifty-ninth and to the two succeeding Congresses (March 4, 1905-March 3, 1911); unsuccessful candidate for reelection in 1910 to the Sixty-second Congress; resumed the practice of law in Detroit; also engaged in banking and various other business enterprises; president of the Detroit Charter Commission, 1913-1914; president of the Detroit Board of Commerce, 1916-1917; enlisted as a private in the United States Marine Corps in 1917; retired as a major in the United States Marine Corps

Reserve in 1919; appointed chief probation officer in the recorder's court of the city of Detroit and in the circuit court of Wayne County in 1920; appointed Secretary of the Navy by President Warren G. Harding, and served from March 6, 1921 until March 10, 1924, when he resigned in the aftermath of the "Teapot Dome" scandal; again resumed the practice of law and various business enterprises; died in Detroit, Mich., February 8, 1929; interment in Elmwood Cemetery.

**Bibliography:** *DAB*.

**DENEEN, Charles Samuel,** a Senator from Illinois; born in Edwardsville, Madison County, Ill., May 4, 1863; raised in Lebanon, St. Clair County, Ill.; attended the public schools, and was graduated from McKendree College, Lebanon, Ill., in 1882; later studied law at the same college and at Union College of Law (later Northwestern University), Chicago, Ill.; was admitted to the bar in 1886 and commenced practice in Chicago; member of the Illinois State house of representatives in 1892; attorney for the Chicago Sanitary District, 1895-1896; State's attorney for Cook County, Ill., 1896-1904; elected Governor of Illinois in 1904, reelected in 1908, and served from January 9, 1905 to February 3, 1913; unsuccessful candidate for reelection in 1912; resumed the practice of law in Chicago; appointed as a Republican to the United States Senate on February 26, 1925, to fill the vacancy caused by the death of Medill McCormick in the term ending March 3, 1925; had been previously elected in 1924 for the term commencing March 4, 1925, and served from February 26, 1925, to March 3, 1931; unsuccessful candidate for renomination in 1930; chairman, Committee to Audit and Control the Contingent Expense (Seventieth and Seventy-first Congresses); resumed the practice of law; died in Chicago, Ill., February 5, 1940; interment in Oak Woods Cemetery.

**DENHOLM, Frank Edward,** a Representative from South Dakota; born in Scotland Township, Day County, S.Dak., November 29, 1923; educated in the public schools; B.S., South Dakota State University, Brookings, 1956; engaged in postgraduate work in public administration at the University of Minnesota, Minneapolis, in 1956; J.D., University of South Dakota, Vermillion, 1962; farmer; auctioneer of land and livestock; engaged in the business of interstate truck transportation, 1945-1953; sheriff of Day County, S.Dak., 1950-1952; agent, Federal Bureau of Investigation, 1956-1961; admitted to the South Dakota bar in 1962 and commenced practice in Brookings; corporate counsel for the cities of Arlington, Brookings, Clear Lake, Estelline, and Volga, S.Dak., 1962-1971; lecturer in law at South Dakota State University, 1962-1966; delegate to South Dakota State Democratic conventions, 1950-1952; delegate to the Democratic National Convention of 1968; elected as a Democrat to the Ninety-second and Ninety-third Congresses (January 3, 1971-January 3, 1975); unsuccessful candidate for reelection in 1974 to the Ninety-fourth Congress; resumed the practice of law with the firm of Denholm, Glover and Britzman, which he founded in 1962; is a resident of Brookings, S.Dak.

**DENISON, Charles** (nephew of George Denison), a Representative from Pennsylvania; born in Wyoming Valley, Pa., January 23, 1818; received a liberal education, and was graduated from Dickinson College, Carlisle, Pa., in 1838; studied law; was admitted to the bar in 1840 and commenced practice in Wilkes-Barre; elected as a Democrat to the Thirty-eighth, Thirty-ninth, and Fortieth Congresses and served from March 4, 1863, until his death in Wilkes-Barre, Pa., June 27, 1867; interment in Forty Fort Cemetery, Kingston, Pa.

**DENISON, Dudley Chase** (nephew of Dudley Chase and cousin of Salmon Portland Chase), a Representative from Vermont; born in Royalton, Vt., September 13, 1819; attended Royalton Academy, and was graduated from the University of Vermont at Burlington in 1840; studied law; was admitted to the bar in 1845 and commenced practice in Royalton; member of the State senate in 1853 and 1854;

State's attorney 1858-1860; served in the State house of representatives 1861-1863; United States district attorney for the district of Vermont 1865-1869; elected as an Independent Republican to the Forty-fourth Congress and reelected as a Republican to the Forty-fifth Congress (March 4, 1875-March 3, 1879); was not a candidate for renomination in 1878; resumed the practice of law; died in Royalton, Windsor County, Vt., February 10, 1905; interment in North Royalton Cemetery.

**DENISON, Edward Everett,** a Representative from Illinois; born in Marion, Williamson County, Ill., August 28, 1873; attended the public schools; was graduated from Baylor University, Waco, Tex., in 1895, from Yale University, in 1896, and from Columbian (now George Washington) University Law School, Washington, D.C., in 1899; was admitted to the bar in 1899 and commenced practice in Marion, Ill., in 1900; engaged in the banking business for one year; elected as a Republican to the Sixty-fourth and to the seven succeeding Congresses (March 4, 1915-March 3, 1931); unsuccessful candidate for reelection in 1930 to the Seventy-second Congress and for election in 1932 to the Seventy-third Congress; resumed the general practice of law in Marion, Ill.; unsuccessful candidate for circuit judge of the first judicial circuit of Illinois in 1939; died in Carbondale, Ill., June 17, 1953; interment in Maplewood Cemetery, Marion, Ill.

**DENISON, George** (uncle of Charles Denison), a Representative from Pennsylvania; born in Kingston, Luzerne County, Pa., February 22, 1790; engaged in mercantile pursuits; attended the Wilkes-Barre Academy; clerk of the Wilkes-Barre borough council 1811-1814, and member of the council for many years, serving as president in 1823 and 1824; recorder and registrar of Luzerne County 1812-1815; studied law; was admitted to the bar in 1813 and commenced practice in Luzerne County; member of the Pennsylvania house of representatives in 1815 and 1816; elected to the Sixteenth and Seventeenth Congresses (March 4, 1819-March 3, 1823); chairman, Committee on Expenditures in the Post Office Department (Seventeenth Congress); was not a candidate for renomination; resumed the practice of law; deputy attorney general for Luzerne County in 1824; again elected to the Pennsylvania house of representatives in 1827, and served until his death; burgess of Wilkes-Barre Borough in 1829 and 1830; died in Wilkes-Barre, Pa., August 20, 1831; interment in Hollenback Cemetery.

**DE NIVERNAIS, Edward James,** a Representative from California. (*See* LIVERNASH, Edward James.)

**DENNEY, Robert Vernon,** a Representative from Nebraska; born in Council Bluffs, Pottawattamie County, Iowa, April 11, 1916; graduated from Fairbury High School in 1933; attended Peru State Teachers College, and the University of Nebraska, 1933-1936; LL.B., Creighton University School of Law, 1939; practiced law in Fairbury, Nebr., 1939-1940; special agent for the Federal Bureau of Investigation, 1940-1941, serving in Washington, D.C., and Chicago, Ill.; enlisted in the United States Marine Corps, October 1942, with the First Armored Amphibian Battalion; remained active in United States Marine Corps Reserve until 1960, retired with rank of lieutenant colonel; resumed practice of law in Fairbury, Nebr. in 1945; Jefferson County attorney, 1947-1951; Fairbury city attorney, 1958-1966; Jefferson County Republican chairman, and chairman of the Nebraska Republican Party; elected as a Republican to the Ninetieth and Ninety-first Congresses (January 3, 1967-January 3, 1971); was not a candidate for reelection in 1970 to the Ninety-second Congress; appointed United States District Court Judge in 1971; resided in Omaha, Nebr., where he died on June 26, 1981; interment in Fairbury Cemetery, Fairbury, Nebr.

**DENNING, William,** a Representative from New York; born probably in St. John's, Newfoundland, in April 1740; moved to New York City in early youth and engaged in mercantile pursuits; member of the Committee of One Hundred in 1775; deputy to the New York Provincial congress 1775-1777; member of the convention of State representatives in 1776 and 1777; served in the State assembly 1784-1787 and in the State senate 1798-1808; member of the council of appointment in 1799; elected to the Eleventh Congress and served from March 4, 1809, until his resignation in 1810, never having qualified; died in New York City October 30, 1819; interment in St. Paul's Churchyard.

**DENNIS, David Worth,** a Representative from Indiana; born in Washington, D.C., June 7, 1912; graduated from Sidwell Friends School, Washington, D.C., 1929; A.B., Earlham College, Richmond, Ind., 1933; LL.B. (now J.D.), Harvard University Law School, 1936; admitted to the bar in 1935 and commenced practice in Richmond, Ind. in 1936; prosecuting attorney, Wayne County, Ind., 1939-1943; enlisted in the United States Army, 1944-1946, commissioned first lieutenant, Judge Advocate General department, and served in the Pacific; elected representative from Wayne County to the Indiana State general assembly, 1947-1949; joint State representative, Wayne and Union Counties, 1953-1959; elected as a Republican to the Ninety-first and to the two succeeding Congresses (January 3, 1969-January 3, 1975); unsuccessful candidate for reelection in 1974 to the Ninety-fourth Congress; resumed the practice of law in Richmond, Ind.; is a resident of Richmond, Ind.

**DENNIS, George Robertson,** a Senator from Maryland; born in Whitehaven, Somerset County, Md., April 8, 1822; was graduated from the Rensselaer Polytechnic Institute, Troy, N.Y., and entered the University of Virginia at Charlottesville; studied medicine at the University of Pennsylvania at Philadelphia; was graduated in 1843 and practiced in Kingston, Md., for many years; later devoted himself to agricultural pursuits; member, State senate 1854; member, State house of delegates 1867; member, State senate 1871; elected as a Democrat to the United States Senate and served from March 4, 1873, until March 3, 1879; died in Kingston, Somerset County, Md., on August 13, 1882; interment in St. Andrew's Churchyard, Princess Anne, Somerset County, Md.

**DENNIS, John** (father of John Dennis [1807-1859] and uncle of Littleton Purnell Dennis), a Representative from Maryland; born at "Beverly," Worcester County, Md., December 17, 1771; completed preparatory studies in Washington Academy; attended Yale College; studied law; was admitted to the bar in 1793 and commenced practice in Somerset County; served two terms in the State house of delegates; elected as a Federalist to the Fifth and to the three succeeding Congresses (March 4, 1797-March 3, 1805); one of the managers appointed by the House of Representatives in 1798 to conduct the impeachment proceedings against William Blount, a Senator from Tennessee; died in Philadelphia, Pa., August 17, 1806; interment in Old Christ Church Graveyard.

**DENNIS, John** (son of John Dennis [1771-1806] and cousin of Littleton Purnell Dennis), a Representative from Maryland; born at "Beckford," near Princess Anne, Somerset County, Md., in 1807; completed preparatory studies; studied law; was admitted to the bar and practiced; also engaged in agricultural pursuits; served in the State house of delegates; elected as a Whig to the Twenty-fifth and Twenty-sixth Congresses (March 4, 1837-March 3, 1841); delegate to the State constitutional convention in 1850; died at "Beckford," November 1, 1859.

**DENNIS, Littleton Purnell** (nephew of John Dennis [1771-1806] and cousin of John Dennis [1807-1859]), a Representative from Maryland; born at "Beverly," Worcester County, Md., July 21, 1786; attended Washington Academy, Somerset County, Md.; was graduated from Yale College in 1803; studied law; was admitted to the bar and practiced; member of the State house of delegates in 1815, 1816, and 1819-1827; member of the executive council of Maryland in 1829; an elector of the Maryland State senate in 1831; elected as an Anti-Jacksonian to the Twenty-third Congress and served from March 4, 1833, until his death in Washington, D.C., April 14, 1834; interment in the Congressional Cemetery.

**DENNISON, David Short,** a Representative from Ohio; born in Poland, Mahoning County, Ohio, July 29, 1918; educated in Warren, Ohio, public schools; graduated from Western Reserve Academy, Hudson, Ohio, in 1936, Williams College, Williamstown, Mass., in 1940, and Western Reserve University Law School in 1945; admitted to the bar in 1946 and commenced the practice of law in Warren, Ohio; served as a volunteer ambulance driver with American Field Service and assigned to British Eighth Army in Africa in 1942 and 1943; served as special counsel to the city of Warren in 1950 and 1951; special assistant in Trumbull County to Ohio State attorney general, 1953-1956; elected as a Republican to the Eighty-fifth Congress (January 3, 1957-January 3, 1959); unsuccessful candidate for reelection in 1958 to the Eighty-sixth Congress, and for election in 1960 to the Eighty-seventh Congress; admitted to District of Columbia bar in 1959; served as consultant to the Civil Rights Commission, Washington, D.C., in 1959; resumed the practice of law; member, Federal Trade Commission, 1970-1974; vice president, secretary, and general counsel, Wheeling-Pittsburgh Steel Corp., 1975-1978; resumed the practice of law in California in 1979; is a resident of Pebble Beach, Calif.

**DENNY, Arthur Armstrong,** a Delegate from the Territory of Washington; born in Salem, Washington County, Ind., June 20, 1822; moved with his parents to Greencastle, Putnam County, Ind. in 1823 and to Knox County, Ill. in 1834; surveyor of Knox County 1843-1851; moved to Oregon Territory in 1851 and settled at Alki Point on Elliott Bay; engaged in cutting timber and mercantile pursuits; served as county commissioner of Thurston County, Oreg., and King County, Wash.; first postmaster of Seattle 1853-1855; upon the organization of Washington Territory in 1853 was elected a member of the Territorial house of representatives and served until 1861; elected speaker in 1857; during the Indian war of 1855 served in the Volunteer Army for six months; register of the land office in Olympia 1861-1865; member of the Territorial council in 1862 and 1863; elected as a Republican a Delegate to the Thirty-ninth Congress (March 4, 1865-March 3, 1867); was not a candidate for renomination in 1866; entered the banking business in 1872; also engaged as an author; died in Seattle, Wash., on January 9, 1899; interment in Lakeview Cemetery.

**DENNY, Harmar** (great-grandfather of Harmar Denny Denny, Jr.), a Representative from Pennsylvania; born in Pittsburgh, Pa., May 13, 1794; was graduated from Dickinson College, Carlisle, Pa., in 1813; studied law; was admitted to the bar in 1816 and commenced practice in Pittsburgh, Pa.; member of the Pennsylvania house of representatives 1824-1829; elected as an Anti-Masonic candidate to the Twenty-first Congress to fill the vacancy caused by the resignation of William Wilkins; reelected to the Twenty-second through Twenty-fourth Congresses and served from December 15, 1829, to March 3, 1837; was not a candidate for renomination in 1836; resumed the practice of law in Pittsburgh, Pa.; delegate to the Pennsylvania constitutional convention in 1837; presidential elector on the Whig ticket in 1840; commissioner under act of incorporation of the Pennsylvania Railroad Co. April 13, 1846; incorporator of Ohio & Pennsylvania Railroad Co., 1848; declined the nomination to be a candidate for Congress in 1850; president of the Pittsburgh & Steubenville Railroad Co. in 1851 and 1852; trustee of the Western University of Pennsylvania and director of the Western Theological Seminary; died in Pittsburgh, Pa., January 29, 1852; interment in Allegheny Cemetery.

**Bibliography:** Backofen, Catherine. "Congressman Harmar Denny." *Western Pennsylvania Historical Magazine* 23 (June 1940): 65-78.

**DENNY, Harmar Denny, Jr**. (great-grandson of Harmar Denny), a Representative from Pennsylvania; born in Allegheny, Pa., July 2, 1886; attended Allegheny Preparatory School and St. Paul's School, Concord, N.H., in 1904; was graduated from Yale University in 1908, and from the law school of the University of Pittsburgh in 1911; was admitted to the bar in 1911 and commenced the practice of law in Pittsburgh, Pa.; during the First World War served in the United States Army Air Corps as a first lieutenant and bombing pilot; director of public safety, Pittsburgh, Pa., in 1933 and 1934; unsuccessful Republican candidate for mayor of Pittsburgh, Pa., in 1941; served as a lieutenant colonel in the United States Army Air Corps as assistant air inspector, Eastern Flying Training Command, 1942-1945; commissioned lieutenant colonel, Air Force, retired; elected as a Republican to the Eighty-second Congress (January 3, 1951-January 3, 1953); was an unsuccessful candidate for reelection in 1952 to the Eighty-third Congress; served as a member of Civil Aeronautics Board from April 7, 1953, to November 15, 1959; retired and resided in Pittsburgh, Pa.; died in Buxton, Derbyshire, England, January 6, 1966; interment in Allegheny Cemetery, Pittsburgh, Pa.

**DENNY, James William,** a Representative from Maryland; born in Frederick County, Va., November 20, 1838; attended the academy of the Reverend William Johnson, Berryville, Clarke County, Va.; was graduated from the University of Virginia at Charlottesville; principal of Osage Seminary, Osceola, St. Clair County, Mo.; during the Civil War he returned to his native State and enlisted in Company A, Thirty-ninth Virginia Battalion of Cavalry, Confederate Army, in which he served until 1863, when he was detailed for service at General Robert E. Lee's headquarters, where he continued until the surrender at Appomattox Court House, April 9, 1865; returned to Clarke County, Va., and began the study of law in Winchester, Va.; was admitted to the bar in Baltimore, Md., in 1868 and commenced practice in that city; elected to the first branch of the city council in 1881; reelected in 1882 and became its president; member, Maryland State house of delegates, 1888-1890; colonel on the staff of Governor Elihu E. Jackson; member of the Baltimore School Board for eight years; elected as a Democrat to the Fifty-sixth Congress (March 4, 1899-March 3, 1901); unsuccessful candidate for reelection in 1900 to the Fifty-seventh Congress; elected to the Fifty-eighth Congress (March 4, 1903-March 3, 1905); engaged in the practice of law until his death in Baltimore, Md., April 12, 1923; interment in Loudon Park Cemetery.

**DENNY, Walter McKennon,** a Representative from Mississippi; born in Moss Point, Jackson County, Miss., October 28, 1853; attended the common schools and Roanoke College, Salem, Va.; was graduated from the law department of the University of Mississippi at Oxford in 1874; was admitted to the bar and commenced practice in Pascagoula, Jackson County, Miss.; clerk of the circuit and chancery courts of Jackson County, Miss., from November 1883 until January 1, 1895; delegate to the State constitutional convention in 1890; elected as a Democrat to the Fifty-fourth Congress (March 4, 1895-March 3, 1897); unsuccessful candidate for renomination in 1896; joined the Republican Party in 1896; resumed the practice of law at Pascagoula, Miss., and for fifteen years was legal adviser to the Jackson County Board of Supervisors; died in Pascagoula November 5, 1926; interment in Machpelah Cemetery.

**DENOYELLES, Peter,** a Representative from New York; born in Haverstraw, Rockland County, N.Y., in 1766; completed preparatory studies; engaged in the manufacture of brick; member of the State assembly in 1802 and 1803; held several local offices; elected as a Republican to the Thirteenth Congress (March 4, 1813-March 3, 1815); resumed his former manufacturing pursuits; died in Haverstraw, Rockland County, N.Y., May 6, 1829; interment in Mount Repose Cemetery.

**DENSON, William Henry,** a Representative from Alabama; born in Uchee, Russell County, Ala., March 4, 1846; attended the common schools and the University of Alabama at Tuscaloosa; left the University of Alabama in 1863 to join the Confederate Army; worked on his father's farm and studied law; was admitted to the bar in 1868 and commenced practice in Union Springs, Ala.; moved to Lafayette, Chambers County, Ala., in October 1870; mayor of Lafayette in 1874; member of the State house of representatives in 1876; moved to Gadsden, Etowah County, in 1877 and continued the practice of his profession; appointed by President Grover Cleveland United States district attorney for the northern and middle districts of Alabama and served from June 30, 1885, to June 3, 1889; chairman of the Democratic State convention in 1890; elected as a Democrat to the Fifty-third Congress (March 4, 1893-March 3, 1895); was an unsuccessful candidate for renomination in 1894 to the Fifty-fourth Congress; moved to Birmingham, Ala., where he resumed the practice of law; died in Birmingham, Ala., September 26, 1906; interment in Elmwood Cemetery.

**Bibliography:** Harris, D. Alan. "Campaigning in the Bloody Seventh: The Election of 1894 in the Seventh Congressional District." *The Alabama Review* 27 (April 1974): 127-38.

**DENT, George,** a Representative from Maryland; born on his father's estate, "Windsor Castle," on the Mattawoman, Charles County, Md., in 1756; completed preparatory studies; during the Revolutionary War served as first lieutenant of militia of Charles and St. Marys Counties under Capt. Thomas H. Marshall, and as first lieutenant in the Third Battalion of the Flying Camp Regular Troops of Maryland in 1776; captain in the Twenty-sixth Battalion, Maryland Militia, in 1778; member of the Maryland House of Assembly 1782-1790, serving as speaker pro tempore in 1788 and as speaker in 1789 and 1790; justice of the Charles County Court in 1791 and 1792; member of the State senate in 1791 and 1792, serving as president during the latter year until his resignation on December 21, 1792; elected to the Third Congress and reelected as a Federalist to the Fourth through Sixth Congresses (March 4, 1793-March 3, 1801); chairman, Committee on Elections (Sixth Congress); Speaker pro tempore of the House at various times from 1797 to 1799; appointed by President Jefferson as United States marshal of the District Court for the Potomac District at Washington, D.C., April 4, 1801; moved to Georgia in 1802 and settled about twelve miles from Augusta, where he died December 2, 1813; interment on his plantation.

**DENT, John Herman,** a Representative from Pennsylvania; born in Johnetta, Armstrong County, Pa., March 10, 1908; educated in the public schools of Armstrong and Westmoreland Counties, the Great Lakes Naval Aviation Academy, and through correspondence school courses; member of the local council of United Rubber Workers 1923-1937, serving as president of Local 18759 and on the executive council; also member of the international council; Jeannette City Councilman, 1932-1934; served in the United States Marine Air Corps 1924-1928; member of the Pennsylvania house of representatives 1934-1936; elected to the Pennsylvania senate in 1936; reelected in 1940, 1944, 1948, 1952, and 1956, and served until elected to Congress; Democratic floor leader in Pennsylvania senate 1939-1958; operated the Kelden Coal & Coke Co. of Hunkers, Pa., and the Building & Transportation Co. of Trafford and Jeannette, Pa.; elected as a Democrat to the Eighty-fifth Congress, by special election, January 21, 1958, to fill the vacancy caused by the death of Augustine B. Kelly; reelected to the ten succeeding Congresses and served from January 21, 1958, to January 3, 1979; was not a candidate for reelection in 1978 to the Ninety-sixth Congress; was a resident of Greensburg, Pa., until his death in Jeannette, Pa., on April 9, 1988.

**DENT, Stanley Hubert, Jr.,** a Representative from Alabama; born in Eufaula, Barbour County, Ala., August 16, 1869; attended the common schools, and was graduated from Southern University (later known as Birmingham Southern College), Greensboro, Ala., in 1886; was graduated from the University of Virginia Law School at Charlottesville in 1889; was admitted to the bar the same year and practiced in Eufaula, Ala., until 1899; moved to Montgomery, Ala., in 1899 and continued the practice of his profession; delegate to the State constitutional convention in 1901; prosecuting attorney for Montgomery County 1902-1909; delegate to the Democratic National Convention in 1908; elected as a Democrat to the Sixty-first and to the five succeeding Congresses (March 4, 1909-March 3, 1921); chairman, Committee on Military Affairs (Sixty-fifth Congress); unsuccessful candidate for renomination in 1920; resumed the practice of law in Montgomery, Ala.; served as president of the State constitutional convention for repeal of the Eighteenth Amendment in 1933; died in Montgomery, Ala., on October 6, 1938; interment in Eufaula Cemetery, Eufaula, Ala.

**Bibliography:** Ward, Robert D. "Stanley Hubert Dent and American Military Policy, 1916-1920." *Alabama Historical Quarterly* 33 (Fall/Winter 1971): 177-89.

**DENT, William Barton Wade,** a Representative from Georgia; born in Bryantown, Charles County, Md., September 8, 1806; attended a private school in Charlotte Hall, St. Marys County, Md., and was graduated from Charlotte Hall Military Academy in 1823; moved to Mallorysville, Wilkes County, Ga., in 1824 and taught school; engaged in mercantile pursuits at Bullsboro, Ga., in 1827; took an active part in founding the city of Newnan, Ga., in 1828; subsequently engaged in agricultural pursuits and milling in Coweta, Carroll, and Heard Counties; became interested in large land holdings in Alabama, Georgia, Arkansas, Tennessee, and Texas; served as a colonel in the State militia during the Creek War; member of the State house of representatives in 1843; returned to Newnan in 1849 and served as judge of the inferior court of Coweta County; elected as a Democrat to the Thirty-third Congress (March 4, 1853-March 3, 1855); was not a candidate for renomination in 1854; died in Newnan, Coweta County, Ga., September 7, 1855; interment in Oak Hill Cemetery.

**DENTON, George Kirkpatrick** (father of Winfield K. Denton), a Representative from Indiana; born near Sebree, Webster County, Ky., November 17, 1864; attended the public schools and Van Horn Institute; was graduated from the Ohio Wesleyan University at Delaware in 1891 and from the law department of Boston (Mass.) University in 1893; was admitted to the bar in 1893 and commenced practice in Evansville, Ind.; served as counsel for the Intermediate Life Insurance Co.; elected as a Democrat to the Sixty-fifth Congress (March 4, 1917-March 3, 1919); unsuccessful candidate for reelection in 1918 to the Sixty-sixth Congress; resumed the practice of law in Evansville, Ind.; unsuccessful candidate in 1924 for judge of the Indiana Supreme Court; candidate for the Democratic nomination for United States Senator in 1926, but died before the primary election; died in Evansville, Ind., January 4, 1926; interment in Oak Hill Cemetery.

**DENTON, Jeremiah Andrew, Jr.,** a Senator from Alabama; born in Mobile, Ala., July 15, 1924; graduated from McGill Institute, Mobile, 1942; attended Spring Hill College, Mobile, 1942-1943; B.S., United States Naval Academy, Annapolis, Md., 1946; M.A., George Washington University, Washington, D.C., 1964; served in the United States Navy, attaining the rank of rear admiral 1946-1977; shot down, captured, and held prisoner in Vietnam for nearly eight years; consultant; elected as a Republican to the United States Senate in 1980 for the term commencing January 3, 1981; subsequently appointed by the Governor, January 2, 1981, to fill the vacancy caused by the resignation of Donald W. Stewart for the term ending January 3, 1981; served from January 2, 1981, to January 3,

1987; unsuccessful candidate for reelection in 1986; founder of Denton Associates, Mobile, Ala.; founder of the National Forum Foundation, Washington, D.C.; is a resident of Mobile, Ala.

**Bibliography:** Denton, Jeremiah. *When Hell Was in Session.* New York: Readers Digest Press, 1976.

**DENTON, Winfield Kirkpatrick** (son of George Kirkpatrick Denton), a Representative from Indiana; born in Evansville, Vanderburgh County, Ind., October 28, 1896; attended the public schools and De Pauw University, Greencastle, Ind., until the beginning of the First World War, when he enlisted as a private; later commissioned a second lieutenant as an aviator in the United States Army Air Corps and served until discharged in 1919 with overseas service; A.B., De Pauw University, 1919; J.D., Harvard Law School, 1922; was admitted to the bar in 1920 and commenced the practice of law in Evansville, Ind., in 1922; prosecuting attorney of Vanderburgh County, Ind., 1932-1936; member of the Indiana State Legislature 1937-1942, serving as caucus chairman in 1939 and as minority leader in 1941; member of the State budget committee 1940-1942; entered the service as a major in 1942; served in the Judge Advocate General's Department, Wright Field, Ohio, and was discharged as a lieutenant colonel in 1945; elected as a Democrat to the Eighty-first and Eighty-second Congresses (January 3, 1949-January 3, 1953); unsuccessful candidate for reelection in 1952 to the Eighty-third Congress; delegate to each Democratic National Convention from 1952 to 1964; elected to the Eighty-fourth and to the five succeeding Congresses (January 3, 1955-January 3, 1967); unsuccessful candidate for reelection in 1966 to the Ninetieth Congress; resumed the practice of law; died in Evansville, Ind., November 2, 1971; interment in Oak Hill Cemetery.

**DENVER, James William** (father of Matthew Rombach Denver), a Representative from California; born in Winchester, Va., October 23, 1817; attended the public schools; moved to Ohio in 1830 with his parents, who settled near Wilmington; taught school in Missouri in 1841; was graduated from the Cincinnati Law School in 1844; was admitted to the bar and commenced practice in Xenia, Ohio; also published the Thomas Jefferson; moved to Platte City, Mo., in 1845 and continued the practice of law; served as a captain in the Twelfth Regiment, United States Infantry, during the war with Mexico; moved to California in 1850; elected to the California State senate in 1851; appointed secretary of state of California in 1852; elected as a Democrat to the Thirty-fourth Congress (March 4, 1855-March 3, 1857); was not a candidate for renomination in 1856 to the Thirty-fifth Congress; appointed Commissioner of Indian Affairs on April 17, 1857; resigned on December 2, 1857 to become Governor of the Kansas Territory; appointed Governor of the Territory of Kansas by President James Buchanan on December 10, 1857 and took the oath of office on December 21; during his administration the present capital of Colorado (then Kansas Territory) was founded and named "Denver" for the chief executive; resigned as Governor on October 10, 1858; reappointed Commissioner of Indian Affairs on November 9, 1858, and served until his resignation on March 12, 1859; was commissioned brigadier general in the Union Army on August 14, 1861; commanded divisions in the Army of Tennessee; resigned from the Army on March 5, 1863; resumed the practice of his profession in Washington, D.C., and Wilmington, Ohio; delegate to the Democratic National Conventions of 1876, 1880, and 1884; died in Washington, D.C., August 9, 1892; interment in Sugar Grove Cemetery, Wilmington, Ohio.

**Bibliography:** *DAB*; Cook, Edward Magruder, ed. *Justified by Honor: Highlights in the Life of General James William Denver.* Falls Church, Va.: Higher Education Publications, 1988; Taylor, Edward T. "General James W. Denver–An Appreciation." *The Colorado Magazine* 17 (March 1940): 41-51.

**DENVER, Matthew Rombach** (son of James William Denver), a Representative from Ohio; born in Wilmington, Clinton County, Ohio, December 21, 1870; attended the public schools; was graduated from Georgetown University, Washington, D.C., in 1892; engaged in agricultural pursuits, banking, and manufacturing; delegate to the Democratic National Conventions in 1896, 1908, 1912, 1920, 1924, 1928, 1932, and 1936; member of the Democratic State committee 1896-1908; elected as a Democrat to the Sixtieth, Sixty-first, and Sixty-second Congresses (March 4, 1907-March 3, 1913); declined to be a candidate for reelection in 1912 to the Sixty-third Congress; returned to Wilmington, Ohio, and resumed banking pursuits; president of the Ohio Bankers' Association in 1918 and 1919; again elected a member of the Democratic State committee for the term 1926-1928; president of the Clinton County National Bank & Trust Co., from 1902 until his death in Wilmington, Ohio, May 13, 1954; interment in Sugar Grove Cemetery.

**DEPEW, Chauncey Mitchell,** a Senator from New York; born in Peekskill, N.Y., April 23, 1834; attended private schools; was graduated from the Peekskill Military Academy in 1852 and from Yale College in 1856; studied law; was admitted to the bar in 1858 and commenced practice at Peekskill, N.Y., in 1859; member, State assembly 1861-1862; secretary of State of New York 1863; appointed United States Minister to Japan by President Andrew Johnson on November 15, 1865, was confirmed by the Senate, but declined; unsuccessful candidate for election as lieutenant governor in 1872; colonel and judge advocate of the fifth division of the New York National Guard 1873-1881; unsuccessful Republican candidate for election to the United States Senate in 1881; appointed president of the New York Central & Hudson River Railroad Co. 1885-1899, and later became chairman of the board of directors of that railroad system; unsuccessful candidate for the Republican presidential nomination in 1888; elected as a Republican to the United States Senate in 1899; reelected in 1905 and served from March 4, 1899, to March 3, 1911; unsuccessful candidate for reelection in 1910; chairman, Committee on Revision of the Laws of the United States (Fifty-seventh through Sixtieth Congresses), Committee on Pacific Islands and Puerto Rico (Sixty-first Congress); resumed his legal and corporate business pursuits in New York City, where he died on April 5, 1928; interment in Hillside Cemetery, Peekskill, N.Y.

Bibliography: *DAB*; Depew, Chauncey. *My Memories of 80 Years*. New York: Scribner's Sons, 1922; Murphy, Arthur F. "The Political Personality of Chauncey Mitchell Depew." Ph.D. dissertation, Fordham University, 1959.

**DE PRIEST, Oscar Stanton,** a Representative from Illinois; born in Florence, Lauderdale County, Ala., March 9, 1871; moved to Kansas in 1878 with his parents, who settled in Salina; attended the public schools and Salina (Kans.) Normal School; moved to Chicago, Ill., in 1889; engaged as an apprentice plasterer, house painter and decorator, and became a real estate broker; member of the board of commissioners of Cook County, Ill., 1904-1908; member of the Chicago City Council, 1915-1917; elected as a Republican to the Seventy-first and to the two succeeding Congresses (March 4, 1929-January 3, 1935); unsuccessful candidate for reelection in 1934 to the Seventy-fourth Congress, and for election in 1936 to the Seventy-fifth Congress; resumed the real estate business; vice chairman of the Cook County Republican central committee, 1932-1934; delegate to the Republican National Convention of 1936; again a member of the City Council, 1943-1947; died in Chicago, Ill., May 12, 1951; interment in Graceland Cemetery.

Bibliography: *DAB*; Day, S. Davis. "Herbert Hoover and Racial Politics: The De Priest Incident." *Journal of Negro History* 65 (Winter 1980): 6-17; Rudwick, Elliott M. "Oscar De Priest and the Jim Crow Restaurant in the U.S. House of Representatives." *Journal of Negro Education* 35 (Winter 1966): 77-82.

**DE ROUEN, René Louis,** a Representative from Louisiana; born on a farm near Ville Platte, St. Landry Parish (now Evangeline Parish), January 7, 1874; attended private and public schools, and St. Charles College, Grand Coteau, La.; was graduated from Holy Cross College, New Orleans, La., in 1892; engaged in mercantile pursuits, banking, and farming; delegate to the State constitutional convention in 1921; elected as a Democrat to the Seventieth Congress to fill the vacancy caused by the death of Ladislas Lazaro; reelected to the Seventy-first and to the five succeeding Congresses and served from August 23, 1927, to January 3, 1941; chairman, Committee on Public Lands (Seventy-third through Seventy-sixth Congresses); was not a candidate for renomination in 1940; served in the State banking department in Baton Rouge, La., after his retirement from Congress until his death; died in Baton Rouge, La., March 27, 1942; interment in Catholic Cemetery, Ville Platte, La.

**DEROUNIAN, Steven Boghos,** a Representative from New York; born in Sofia, Bulgaria, April 6, 1918; brought to the United States at the age of three by his parents, who settled in Mineola, N.Y.; attended the public schools; graduated from New York University in 1938, and from the Fordham Law School in 1942; was admitted to the New York bar in 1942 and began practice in Mineola, N.Y., the same year; entered the United States Army as a private in July 1942; graduated from officers school as an Infantry officer and was assigned to the One Hundred and Third Infantry; served overseas from October 1944 to March 1946, and separated from the service as a captain in May 1946; awarded the Purple Heart and Bronze Star with oak leaf; councilman of town board of North Hempstead, N.Y., from January 1, 1948 to December 30, 1952; elected as a Republican to the Eighty-third and to the five succeeding Congresses (January 3, 1953-January 3, 1965); unsuccessful candidate for reelection in 1964 to the Eighty-ninth Congress; justice of the New York State supreme court, 1969-1981; is a resident of Austin, Tex.

**DERRICK, Butler Carson, Jr.,** a Representative from South Carolina; born in Springfield, Hampden County, Mass., September 30, 1936; attended the public schools in Mayesville, S.C., and Florence, S.C.; attended University of South Carolina, 1954-1958; LL.B., University of Georgia Law School, 1965; admitted to the South Carolina bar in 1965 and commenced practice in Edgefield; served in the South Carolina house of representatives, 1969-1974; delegate to South Carolina State Democratic conventions, 1972, 1974; delegate to the Democratic Mid-Term Convention, 1974; elected as a Democrat to the Ninety-fourth and to the nine succeeding Congresses (January 3, 1975-January 3, 1995); was not a candidate for reelection in 1994 to the One Hundred Fourth Congress; is a resident of Edgefield, S.C.

**DERSHEM, Franklin Lewis,** a Representative from Pennsylvania; born near New Columbia, Union County, Pa., March 5, 1865; attended the common schools; was graduated from Palm's National Business College at Philadelphia in 1887; appointed postmaster at Kelly Point, Union County, Pa., on March 9, 1888, and served until January 13, 1891; engaged in agricultural pursuits, and was also interested in the hardware business 1891-1913; member of the board of trustees of Albright College, Myerstown, Pa.; member of the Pennsylvania house of representatives in 1907, 1908, and again in 1911 and 1912; elected as a Democrat to the Sixty-third Congress (March 4, 1913-March 3, 1915); unsuccessful candidate for reelection in 1914 to the Sixty-fourth Congress; appointed as an auditor in the Philadelphia division of the United States Bureau of Internal Revenue October 1, 1915, in which capacity he served until March 31, 1935; was engaged as an auditor and income-tax specialist in Lewisburg, Pa., where he died February 14, 1950; interment in Lewisburg Cemetery.

**DERWINSKI, Edward Joseph,** a Representative from Illinois; born in Chicago, Ill., September 15, 1926; graduated from Mount Carmel High School in 1944; served in the United States Army as an infantryman with service in the Pacific Theater and with the Japanese Occupation Forces in 1945 and 1946; Loyola University in Chicago, B.S., 1951; president of the West Pullman Savings & Loan Association, 1950-1975; served one term in the Illinois State house of representatives, 1957-1958; elected as a Republican to the Eighty-sixth and to the eleven succeeding Congresses (January 3, 1959-January 3, 1983); unsuccessful candidate for renomination in 1982 to the Ninety-eighth Congress; chairman of the United States delegation to the Interparliamentary Union, 1970-1972, 1978-1980; member, Interparliamentary Union Executive Committee, 1968-1972 and 1976-1980; Counselor for the Department of State, March 23, 1983 to March 24, 1987; Under Secretary of State for International Security Affairs, March 24, 1987 to January 21, 1989; appointed Secretary of Veterans Affairs by President George Bush, and served from March 15, 1989 until his resignation on September 26, 1992; was the first person to hold that office; international consultant; is a resident of Falls Church, Va., and Chicago, Ill.

**DE SAUSSURE, William Ford,** a Senator from South Carolina; born in Charleston, S.C., February 22, 1792; was graduated from Harvard University in 1810; studied law; was admitted to the bar and practiced in Charleston and Columbia, S.C.; member, State house of representatives 1846; judge of the chancery court 1847; appointed and subsequently elected as a Democrat to the United States Senate to fill the vacancy caused by the resignation of R. Barnwell Rhett and served from May 10, 1852, to March 3, 1853; resumed the practice of law in Columbia; trustee of South Carolina College (now the University of South Carolina) at Columbia for many years; died in Columbia, Richland County, S.C., March 13, 1870; interment in Presbyterian Churchyard.

**DESHA, Joseph** (brother of Robert Desha), a Representative from Kentucky; born in Monroe County, Pa., December 9, 1768; pursued preparatory studies; moved to Kentucky with his parents, who settled in Fayette County in 1779, and later in 1782, they moved to Tennessee and settled near Gallatin, Sumner County; returned to Kentucky in 1792 and settled in Mason County; served in the Indian wars under General Anthony Wayne and General William Henry Harrison in 1794; returned to Kentucky and engaged in agricultural pursuits; member of the Kentucky house of representatives in 1797 and 1799-1802; served in the Kentucky senate 1803-1807; elected as a Republican to the Tenth and to the five succeeding Congresses (March 4, 1807-March 3, 1819); chairman, Committee on Public Expenditures (Fifteenth Congress); was not a candidate for renomination in 1818 to the Sixteenth Congress; unsuccessful candidate for Governor of Kentucky in 1820; served as major general of Volunteers under General William Henry Harrison at the Battle of the Thames, October 5, 1813; on his return to civil life he was elected Governor of Kentucky in 1824 and served from June 1, 1824 to June 1, 1828; lived on his farm in Harrison County until his death near Georgetown, Ky., October 11, 1842; interment in Georgetown Cemetery.

**Bibliography:** *DAB*; Desha, Joseph. "Joseph Desha, Letters and Papers." Edited by James A. Padgett. *Register of the Kentucky Historical Society* 51 (December 1953): 286-304; Doutrich, Paul E., III. "A Pivotal Decision: The 1824 Gubernatorial Election in Kentucky." *Filson Club History Quarterly* 56 (January 1982): 14-29.

**DESHA, Robert** (brother of Joseph Desha), a Representative from Tennessee; born near Gallatin, Sumner County, Tenn., January 14, 1791; attended the public schools; engaged in the mercantile business at Gallatin; appointed on March 12, 1812, a captain in the Twenty-fourth Regiment, United States Infantry, in the War of 1812; also served as brevet major; honorably discharged on June 15, 1815; elected as a Jacksonian to the Twentieth and Twenty-first

Congresses (March 4, 1827-March 3, 1831); declined to be a candidate for renomination in 1830 for the Twenty-second Congress; moved to Mobile, Ala., and continued mercantile pursuits until his death there February 6, 1849; interment in Magnolia Cemetery.

**DESTRÉHAN, Jean Noel,** a Senator from Louisiana; born in 1754 in that section of Louisiana which became the St. Charles Parish; engaged in mercantile pursuits and as a planter; member, legislative council of the Territory of Orleans and served as its president in 1806 and 1811; although opposed to the admission of the Territory to statehood, was a delegate to the convention and helped to draft the State constitution; member, State senate 1812-1817; upon the admission of Louisiana as a State into the Union was elected to the United States Senate on September 3, 1812, but resigned on October 1, 1812, without having qualified; resumed his former occupation as a planter; died in 1823; interment near Destréhan, La.

**DEUSTER, Peter Victor,** a Representative from Wisconsin; born near Aix la Chapelle, Rhenish Prussia, February 13, 1831; pursued an academic course; immigrated to the United States with his parents, who settled on a farm near Milwaukee, Wis., in May 1847; worked in a printing office; moved to Port Washington, Wis., in 1854 and edited a newspaper; also served simultaneously as postmaster, clerk of the circuit court, clerk of the land office, and notary public; returned to Milwaukee in 1856 and edited the Milwaukee See-Bote, a Democratic daily paper, until 1860, when he became proprietor; member of the State assembly in 1863; served in the State senate in 1870 and 1871; elected as a Democrat to the Forty-sixth, Forty-seventh, and Forty-eighth Congresses (March 4, 1879-March 3, 1885); chairman, Committee on Expenditures on Public Buildings (Forty-sixth Congress); unsuccessful candidate for reelection in 1884 to the Forty-ninth Congress; resumed newspaper interests; appointed chairman of a commission to diminish the Umatilla Indian Reservation in Oregon in 1887; appointed consul at Crefeld, Germany, February 19, 1896, and served until a successor was appointed October 15, 1897; died in Milwaukee, Wis., December 31, 1904; interment in Calvary Cemetery.

**DEUTSCH, Peter R.,** a Representative from Florida; born in the Bronx, New York City, April 1, 1957; graduated, Horace Mann School, New York City, 1975; B.A., Swarthmore (Pa.) College, 1979; J.D., Yale University School of Law, 1982; attorney; non-profit executive; member, Florida State house of representatives, 1983-1993; elected as a Democrat to the One Hundred Third and One Hundred Fourth Congresses (January 3, 1993-January 3, 1997); is a resident of Lauderhill, Fla.

**DEVEREUX, James Patrick Sinnott,** a Representative from Maryland; born in Cabana, Cuba, February 20, 1903; attended the public schools of Maryland, the Army and Navy Preparatory School in Washington, D.C., the Tome School at Port Deposit, Md., LaVilla in Lausanne, Switzerland, and Loyola College, Baltimore, Md.; enlisted in the United States Marine Corps in 1923; commissioned a second lieutenant in 1925 and advanced through grades to brigadier general in 1948; served in Nicaragua, Cuba and China; led a detachment of four hundred Marines who defended Wake Island from Japanese attack for fifteen days in December 1941; prisoner of war in from December 1941 to January 1945; retired from the service in 1948; engaged in farming near Glyndon, Md., in 1946; elected as a Republican to the Eighty-second and to the three succeeding Congresses (January 3, 1951-January 3, 1959); was not a candidate for renomination in 1958 to the Eighty-sixth Congress, but was an unsuccessful candidate for governor of Maryland; director of public safety for Baltimore County, December 1962 to 1966; was a resident of Ruxton, Md., until his death in Baltimore on August 5, 1988; interment in Arlington National Cemetery, Va.

**DE VEYRA, Jaime Carlos,** a Resident Commissioner from the Commonwealth of the Philippine Islands; born in Tanawan, Province of Leyte, Philippine Islands, November 4, 1873; attended public and private schools; was graduated from the College of San Juan de Letran in Manila in 1893; studied law, philosophy, and letters in the University of Santo Tomas at Manila 1895-1897; secretary to the Military Governor of Leyte in 1898 and 1899; engaged in newspaper work; member of the municipal council of Cebu; Governor of Leyte in 1906 and 1907; member of the Philippine house of representatives 1907-1909; member of the Philippine Commission 1913-1916; executive secretary of the Philippine Islands in 1916 and 1917; elected as a Nationalist a Resident Commissioner to the United States in 1917; reelected in 1920 and served from March 4, 1917, to March 3, 1923; declined to be a candidate for renomination in 1922; engaged in journalistic work during 1923; head of the department of Spanish, University of the Philippines at Manila, 1925-1936; director, Institute of National Language, 1936-1944; served as historical researcher in charge of manuscripts and publications, National Library; historical researcher, Office of the President, 1946; died in Manila, Philippine Islands, March 7, 1963; interment in La Loma Cemetery.

**DEVINE, Samuel Leeper,** a Representative from Ohio; born in South Bend, Saint Joseph County, Ind., December 21, 1915; moved to Columbus, Ohio, in 1920; attended the public schools in Columbus, Grandview, and Upper Arlington, Ohio; attended Colgate University in 1933 and 1934, Ohio State University 1934-1937; University of Notre Dame, LL.B., J.D., 1940; was admitted to the bar in 1940 and practiced law in Columbus, Ohio; in 1940 was appointed special agent, Federal Bureau of Investigation, United States Department of Justice, and served until his resignation in October 1945; resumed the private practice of law in Columbus, Ohio; member of the Ohio State house of representatives 1951-1955; prosecuting attorney, Franklin County, Ohio, 1955-1958; former chairman, Ohio Un-American Activities commission; college football official for twenty-seven years; elected as a Republican to the Eighty-sixth and to the ten succeeding Congresses (January 3, 1959-January 3, 1981); unsuccessful candidate for reelection in 1980 to the Ninety-seventh Congress; attorney and consultant; is a resident of Naples, Fla., and Columbus, Ohio.

**DEVITT, Edward James,** a Representative from Minnesota; born in St. Paul, Ramsey County, Minn., May 5, 1911; attended public and parochial schools; graduated from St. John's University, Collegeville, Minn., in 1932; LL.B., University of North Dakota School of Law, Grand Forks, 1935; was admitted to the bar in 1935 and commenced practice in East Grand Forks, Minn.; instructor in the law department of the University of North Dakota, 1935-1939; part-time municipal judge at East Grand Forks, Minn., 1935-1939; assistant attorney general of Minnesota, 1939-1942; member of faculty of St. Paul College of Law in 1945 and 1946; served as an intelligence officer in the United States Navy from October 1942 to February 1946, with service in Pacific area; awarded the Purple Heart; elected as a Republican to the Eightieth Congress (January 3, 1947-January 3, 1949); unsuccessful candidate for reelection in 1948 to the Eighty-first Congress; served in 1949 as special attorney to prosecute violations of the Minnesota Fair Trade Practices Act; probate judge, Ramsey County, Minn., from January 6, 1950, to December 20, 1954; United States judge for the district of Minnesota from December 20, 1954 until his retirement; member, board of directors, Federal Judicial Center; was a resident of St. Paul, Minn.; died March 2, 1992.

**DE VRIES, Marion,** a Representative from California; born on a ranch near Woodbridge, San Joaquin County, Calif., August 15, 1865; attended the public schools; was graduated from the San Joaquin Valley College, Woodbridge, Calif., in 1886 and from the law department of the University of Michigan at Ann Arbor in 1888; was admitted to the bar in 1887 and commenced practice in Stockton, Calif., in 1889; assistant district attorney of San Joaquin County from January 1893 to February 1897, when he resigned, having been elected to Congress; elected as a Democrat to the Fifty-fifth and Fifty-sixth Congresses and served from March 4, 1897, to August 20, 1900, when he resigned to accept a court position; appointed on June 9, 1900, a member of the Board of General Appraisers (now United States Customs Court) at New York City and served until his resignation effective April 1, 1910; was president of the board 1906-1910; associate judge of the United States Court of Customs Appeals from April 2, 1910, to June 30, 1921; served as presiding judge from July 1, 1921, until October 31, 1922, when he resigned; reengaged in the practice of law in Washington, D.C., and New York City, until 1939, when he retired to his ranch near Woodbridge, Calif., where he died on September 11, 1939; interment in the family plot on De Vries Ranch.

**DEWALT, Arthur Granville,** a Representative from Pennsylvania; born in Bath, Northampton County, Pa., October 11, 1854; attended the common schools; was graduated from Keystone State Normal School in 1870 and from Lafayette College, Easton, Pa., in 1874; studied law; was admitted to the bar in 1877 and commenced practice at Allentown, Pa., in 1878; district attorney of Lehigh County 1880-1883; member of the Pennsylvania senate 1902-1910; delegate to the Democratic National Convention in 1904 and 1908; chairman of the Pennsylvania Democratic committee in 1909 and 1910; adjutant of the Fourth Regiment of the Pennsylvania National Guard for ten years; elected as a Democrat to the Sixty-fourth, Sixty-fifth, and Sixty-sixth Congresses (March 4, 1915-March 3, 1921); declined to be a candidate for renomination in 1920; unsuccessful candidate for election in 1926 to the Seventieth Congress; resumed the practice of law at Allentown, Pa., where he died on October 26, 1931; interment in Fairview Cemetery.

**DEWART, Lewis** (father of William Lewis Dewart), a Representative from Pennsylvania; born in Sunbury, Pa., November 14, 1780; attended the common schools; was a clerk in his father's store for several years and later became a coal operator and banker; postmaster at Sunbury, 1806-1816; member of the Pennsylvania house of representatives, 1812-1820; elected to the Pennsylvania senate in 1823 and served three years; one of the organizers and builders of the Danville and Pottsville Railroad, and served as one of the first directors; elected as a Jacksonian to the Twenty-second Congress (March 4, 1831-March 3, 1833); again a member of the Pennsylvania house of representatives, 1835-1840, and served as speaker in 1840; chief burgess of Sunbury in 1837; member of the school board; unsuccessful candidate for the Democratic nomination for Governor of Pennsylvania in 1840; died in Sunbury, Northumberland County, Pa., April 26, 1852; interment in Sunbury Cemetery.

**D'EWART, Wesley Abner,** a Representative from Montana; born in Worcester, Mass., October 1, 1889; attended the public schools of Worcester, Mass., and Washington State College at Pullman; moved to Wilsall, Park County, Mont., in 1910 and engaged in the Forest Service; stockman, farmer, and businessman in Park County, Mont.; served in the State house of representatives 1937-1939; member of the State senate 1941-1945; elected as a Republican to the Seventy-ninth Congress, by special election, June 5, 1945, to fill the vacancy caused by the death of James F. O'Connor; reelected to the four succeeding Congresses and served from June 5, 1945, to January 3, 1955; was not a candidate for renomination in 1954, but was unsuccessful for election to the United States Senate; assistant to the Secretary of Agriculture, Washington, D.C., from January 1955 to September 1955; assistant secretary, Department of the Interior, from October 1955 to July 1956; special representative to Secretary of Agriculture from August 1956 to October 1958; unsuccessful candidate for the Republican nomination for Governor of Montana in 1960; member, Western States Water Council, 1966-1969; was a director of the National Water Resources Association; resided in Wilsall, Mont.; died in Livingston, Mont., September 2, 1973; interment in Mountain View Cemetery.

**DEWART, William Lewis** (son of Lewis Dewart), a Representative from Pennsylvania; born in Sunbury, Northumberland County, Pa., June 21, 1821; attended the common schools of Sunbury and Harrisburg, Pa.; was graduated from Dickinson Preparatory School, Carlisle, Pa., and from Princeton College in 1839; studied law; was admitted to the Northumberland County bar on January 3, 1843, and commenced practice in Sunbury, Pa.; chief burgess of Sunbury in 1845 and 1846; president of the school board; delegate to the Democratic National Conventions in 1852, 1856, 1860, and 1884; unsuccessful candidate for election in 1854 to the Thirty-fourth Congress; elected as a Democrat to the Thirty-fifth Congress (March 4, 1857-March 3, 1859); chairman, Committee on Revisal and Unfinished Business (Thirty-fifth Congress); unsuccessful candidate for reelection in 1858 to the Thirty-sixth Congress; resumed the practice of his profession in Sunbury, Pa.; died in Sunbury, Pa., on April 19, 1888; interment in the family vault in Sunbury Cemetery.

**DEWEESE, John Thomas,** a Representative from North Carolina; born in Van Buren, Crawford County, Ark., June 4, 1835; educated at home; studied law; was admitted to the bar in 1856 and commenced practice in Henderson, Ky.; resident of Denver, Colo., for some years; moved to Pike County, Ind., in 1860; entered the Union Army July 6, 1861, as second lieutenant of Company E, Twenty-fourth Regiment, Indiana Volunteer Infantry, and served with that command until February 15, 1862, when he resigned; mustered in as captain of Company F, Fourth Indiana Cavalry, August 8, 1862; successively promoted to rank of colonel; moved to North Carolina; upon the reorganization of the Army was appointed second lieutenant, Eighth United States Infantry, July 24, 1866; resigned August 14, 1867, having been elected to Congress; appointed register in bankruptcy for North Carolina in 1868; upon the readmission of North Carolina to representation was elected as a Republican to the Fortieth and Forty-first Congresses and served from July 6, 1868, to February 28, 1870, when he resigned, pending the investigation of certain appointments to the United States Military and Naval Academies; chairman, Committee on Expenditures in the Department of the Interior (Forty-first Congress), Committee on Revolutionary Pensions (Forty-first Congress); censured by the House of Representatives on March 1, 1870, for selling an appointment to the Naval Academy; delegate to the Democratic National Convention of 1876; resumed the practice of law; died in Washington, D.C., July 4, 1906; interment in Arlington National Cemetery, Va.

**DEWEY, Charles Schuveldt,** a Representative from Illinois; born in Cadiz, Harrison County, Ohio, November 10, 1880; moved in infancy to Chicago, Ill.; attended the public schools and St. Paul's School, Concord, N.H.; was graduated from Yale University in 1904; engaged in the real estate business in Chicago, Ill., 1905-1917; served in the United States Navy 1917-1919 and was honorably discharged with the rank of senior lieutenant; vice president of a trust company in Chicago, Ill., 1920-1924; Assistant Secretary of the Treasury in charge of fiscal affairs, 1924-1927; national treasurer of American National Red Cross in 1926 and 1927; served as financial adviser to the Polish Government and as director of the Bank of Poland, 1927-1930; returned to Chicago in 1931 and resumed banking; unsuccessful candidate for election in 1938 to the Seventy-sixth Congress; elected as a Republican to the Seventy-seventh and Seventy-eighth Congresses (January 3, 1941-January 3, 1945); unsuccessful candidate for reelection in 1944 to the Seventy-ninth Congress; resumed the banking business; in April 1948 was appointed agent general of the Joint Committee on Foreign Economic Cooperation and served until June 1952; chairman, District of Columbia Chapter of the American Red Cross, 1957-1961; resided in Washington, D.C., until his death on December 27, 1980; interment in Arlington National Cemetery, Va.

**DEWEY, Daniel,** a Representative from Massachusetts; born in Sheffield, Mass., January 29, 1766; attended Yale College; studied law; was admitted to the bar in 1787 and commenced practice in Williamstown, Mass.; treasurer of Williams College, Williamstown, Mass., 1798-1814; member of the Governor's council 1809-1812; elected as a Federalist to the Thirteenth Congress and served from March 4, 1813, until February 24, 1814, when he resigned, having been assigned to a judicial position; appointed by Governor Caleb Strong an associate judge of the supreme court of Massachusetts on February 24, 1814, and served until his death in Williamstown, Mass., May 26, 1815; interment in West Lawn Cemetery.

**DeWINE, Michael,** a Representative and a Senator from Ohio; born in Springfield, Ohio, January 5, 1947; attended the public schools in Yellow Springs, Ohio; B.S., Miami University, Oxford, Ohio, 1969; J.D., Ohio Northern University College of Law, Ada, Ohio, 1972; admitted to Ohio State bar in 1972, and commenced practice in Xenia, Ohio; assistant prosecuting attorney, Greene County, Ohio, 1973-1975; prosecuting attorney, Greene County, 1977-1981; elected to the Ohio State senate, 1981-1982; elected as a Republican to the Ninety-eighth and to the three succeeding Congresses (January 3, 1983-January 3, 1991); was not a candidate for reelection in 1990 to the One Hundred Second Congress; Ohio lieutenant governor, 1991-1995; elected to the United States Senate in 1994 for the term ending January 3, 2001; is a resident of Cedarville, Ohio.

**DE WITT, Alexander,** a Representative from Massachusetts; born in New Braintree, Mass., April 2, 1798; pursued an academic course; engaged in textile manufacturing in Oxford; member of the Massachusetts house of representatives 1830-1836; served in the Massachusetts senate in 1842, 1844, 1850, and 1851; member of the Massachusetts constitutional convention in 1853; elected as a Free-Soil candidate to the Thirty-third Congress and reelected as a candidate of the American Party to the Thirty-fourth Congress (March 4, 1853-March 3, 1857); unsuccessful candidate for reelection in 1856 to the Thirty-fifth Congress; resumed the manufacture of textiles; died in Oxford, Worcester County, Mass., January 13, 1879; interment in South Cemetery.

**DE WITT, Charles** (grandfather of Charles Gerrit De Witt), a Delegate from New York; born in Kingston, Ulster County, N.Y., in 1727; pursued classical studies; colonel of militia; member of the colonial assembly 1768-1776; delegate to the provisional convention in 1775; member of the Provisional Congress which approved the Declaration of Independence, 1775-1777; served on the constitutional committee in 1776, and on the committee of safety in 1777; Member of the Continental Congress from February to October 1784; editor of the Ulster Sentinel for several years; member of the State assembly in 1781, 1785, and 1786; member of the committee to draft the State constitution; died in Kingston, N.Y., August 27, 1787; interment in Dutch Reformed Cemetery, Hurley, N.Y.

**DE WITT, Charles Gerrit** (grandson of Charles De Witt), a Representative from New York; born in Greenhill, Ulster County, N.Y., November 7, 1789; studied law and practiced; clerk in the Navy Department; edited the Ulster Sentinel; elected as a Jackson supporter to the Twenty-first Congress (March 4, 1829-March 3, 1831); was not a candidate for renomination in 1830 to the Twenty-second Congress; resumed the practice of law; appointed Chargé d'Affaires to Central America on January 29, 1833; returned home in February 1839; died on board a river steamer opposite Newburgh, N.Y., April 12, 1839; interment in Dutch Reformed Cemetery, Hurley, N.Y.

**DE WITT, David Miller,** a Representative from New York; born in Paterson, Passaic County, N.J., November 25, 1837; moved to New York in 1845 with his parents, who settled in Brooklyn; attended the public schools of Brooklyn, a select school at Saugerties, and the local academy at Kingston; was graduated from Rutgers College, New Brunswick, N.J., in 1858; studied law; was admitted to the bar in 1858 and commenced practice in Kingston, N.Y.; principal of New Paltz Academy (later a State normal school) in 1861 and 1862; district attorney of Ulster County 1863-1870; unsuccessful candidate for reelection; elected as a Democrat to the Forty-third Congress (March 4, 1873-March 3, 1875); was not a candidate for renomination; resumed the practice of law and also engaged in literary pursuits; assistant corporation counsel of Brooklyn, N.Y., 1878-1881; member of the State assembly in 1883; corporation counsel of Kingston in 1884; surrogate of Ulster County from November 20, 1885, to December 31, 1886; again engaged in the practice of law; died in Kingston, N.Y., June 23, 1912; interment in Wiltwyck Rural Cemetery.

**DE WITT, Francis Byron,** a Representative from Ohio; born in Jackson County, Ind., March 11, 1849; moved with his parents in 1854 to a farm in Delaware County, Ohio; during the Civil War enlisted in the Forty-sixth Regiment, Ohio Volunteer Infantry, at the age of twelve; mustered out for temporary disability and reenlisted in 1862 in the One Hundred and Twenty-first Regiment, Ohio Volunteer Infantry, and served until the close of the war; prisoner of war in Salisbury, Danville, and Libby Prisons; attended the common schools and high school in Galena, Ohio, National Normal School, Lebanon, Ohio, and Ohio Wesleyan University, Delaware, Ohio; moved to Paulding, Ohio, in 1872 and taught school; studied law; was admitted to the bar in 1875 and practiced his profession in Paulding until 1891, when he engaged in agricultural pursuits; member of the State house of representatives 1892-1895; elected as a Republican to the Fifty-fourth Congress (March 4, 1895-March 3, 1897); unsuccessful candidate for reelection in 1896; resumed agricultural pursuits near Paulding, Ohio; moved to Standish, Arenac County, Mich., in 1903 and resumed the practice of law; served as register of deeds; member of the Michigan house of representatives 1920-1922; elected prosecuting attorney of Arenac County, Mich., in 1926; reelected in 1928 and served until his death in Standish, Mich., on March 21, 1929; interment in Live Oak Cemetery, Paulding, Ohio.

**DE WITT, Jacob Hasbrouck,** a Representative from New York; born in Marbletown, Ulster County, N.Y., October 2, 1784; attended the rural schools and Kingston (N.Y.) Academy; engaged in agricultural pursuits; served as adjutant in the War of 1812; elected to the Sixteenth Congress (March 4, 1819-March 3, 1821); was not a candidate for renomination in 1820; resumed agricultural pursuits; supervisor of Ulster County in 1827 and again in 1840; member of the State assembly in 1839 and again in 1847; died in Kingston, Ulster County, N.Y., January 30, 1867; interment in the Sharpe Cemetery, on Albany Avenue.

**DE WOLF, James,** a Senator from Rhode Island; born in Bristol, R.I., March 18, 1764; during the Revolutionary War shipped as a sailor on a private armed vessel; participated in several naval encounters and was twice captured by the enemy; before he was twenty years old became captain of a ship; engaged in extensive commercial ventures, principally trading in slaves, with Cuba and other West Indian islands; member, State house of representatives 1797-1801, 1803-1812; fitted out a privateer in the War of 1812; one of the pioneers in cotton manufacturing; built the Arkwright Mills in Coventry, R.I., in 1812; member, State house of representatives 1817-1821, and served as speaker 1819-1821; elected as a Republican to the United States Senate and served from March 4, 1821, to October 31, 1825, when he resigned; member, State house of representatives 1829-1837; died in New York City December 21, 1837; interment in the De Wolf private cemetery, Woodlawn Avenue, Bristol, R.I.

**DEXTER, Samuel,** a Representative and a Senator from Massachusetts; born in Boston, Mass., on May 14, 1761; was graduated from Harvard University in 1781; studied law; was admitted to the bar in 1784 and commenced practice in Lunenburg, Mass.; member, Massachusetts house of representatives, 1788-1790; elected to the Third Congress (March 4, 1793-March 3, 1795); elected as a Federalist to the United States Senate, and served from March 4, 1799 until May 30, 1800, when he resigned to accept a Cabinet portfolio; appointed Secretary of War by President John Adams and served from May 13, 1800 to January 31, 1801; served as Secretary of the Treasury from January 1 until March 6, 1801; resumed the practice of law in Washington, D.C.; moved to Boston, Mass., in 1805 and continued the practice of law; declined the appointment of Minister to Spain in 1815; unsuccessful candidate for Governor in 1816; died in Athens, Greene County, N.Y., May 4, 1816; interment in Mount Auburn Cemetery, Cambridge, Mass.

**Bibliography:** *DAB*; Sargent, Lucius. *Reminiscences of Samuel Dexter*. Boston: H.W. Dutton and Son, 1857.

**DEZENDORF, John Frederick,** a Representative from Virginia; born in Lansingburg, Rensselaer County, N.Y., August 10, 1834; pursued an academic course; learned the carpenter's trade; studied architecture and civil engineering; engaged in railroad and other building at Toledo and Cleveland, Ohio, 1850-1860, and later, from 1860 to 1862, in mercantile pursuits; moved to Norfolk, Va., in 1863 and engaged in the shipping business until 1866; surveyor of Norfolk City and County, 1866-1869; assistant assessor of the United States internal revenue from September 9, 1870 to August 6, 1872; appraiser of merchandise at the Norfolk custom house from August 7, 1872 until the position was abolished in 1877; delegate to the Republican National Convention of 1876; unsuccessful Republican candidate for election in 1878 to the Forty-sixth Congress; elected as a Republican to the Forty-seventh Congress (March 4, 1881-March 3, 1883); engaged in the construction business; died in Norfolk, Va., June 22, 1894; interment in Elmwood Cemetery.

**DIAL, Nathaniel Barksdale,** a Senator from South Carolina; born near Laurens, Laurens County, S.C., April 24, 1862, attended the common schools, Richmond (Va.) College, and Vanderbilt University, Nashville, Tenn.; studied law at the University of Virginia at Charlottesville; was admitted to the bar in 1883 and commenced practice in Laurens, S.C.; mayor of Laurens 1887-1891 and again in 1895; declined the office of consul to Zurich, Switzerland, tendered by President Grover Cleveland in 1893; engaged in banking and in various manufacturing enterprises; unsuccessful candidate for election to the United States Senate in 1912; elected in 1918 as a Democrat to the United States Senate and served from March 4, 1919, to March 3, 1925; unsuccessful candidate for reelection in 1924; member of the commission to report on the use of the nitrate plant at Muscle Shoals, Ala., 1925; resumed the practice of law in South Carolina and Washington, D.C., and also his former manufacturing enterprises in South Carolina; died in Washington, D.C., on December 11, 1940; interment in Laurens Cemetery, Laurens, S.C.

**Bibliography:** Slaunwhite, Jerry L. "The Public Career of Nathaniel Barksdale Dial." Ph.D. dissertation, University of South Carolina, 1979.

**DIAZ-BALART, Lincoln,** a Representative from Florida; born in Havana, Cuba, August 13, 1954; graduated, American School of Madrid, Spain, 1972; B.A., New College of the University of South Florida, Sarasota, 1976; J.D., Case Western Reserve University, Cleveland, Ohio, 1979; attorney; member, Florida State house of representatives, 1987-1989; member, Florida State senate, 1989-1993; elected as a Republican to the One Hundred Third and One

Hundred Fourth Congresses (January 3, 1993-January 3, 1997); is a resident of Miami, Fla.

**DIBBLE, Samuel,** a Representative from South Carolina; born in Charleston, S.C., September 16, 1837; pursued an academic course in Bethel, Conn., and Charleston, S.C.; attended the College of Charleston for two years, and was graduated from Wofford College, Spartanburg, S.C., in 1856; engaged in teaching 1856-1858; studied law; was admitted to the bar in 1859 and commenced practice in Orangeburg, S.C.; served in the Confederate Army throughout the Civil War; resumed the practice of law in Orangeburg, S.C.; also edited the Orangeburg News; member of the State house of representatives in 1877 and 1878; trustee of the University of South Carolina at Columbia in 1878; member of the Board of School Commissioners of Orangeburg County; delegate to the Democratic National Convention in 1880; presented credentials as a Democratic Member-elect to the Forty-seventh Congress to fill a vacancy thought to exist by reason of the death (pending a contest) of Michael P. O'Connor, and served from June 9, 1881, to May 31, 1882, when the seat was awarded to Edmund W.M. Mackey under the original election; elected to the Forty-eighth and to the three succeeding Congresses (March 4, 1883-March 3, 1891); chairman, Committee on Public Buildings and Grounds (Forty-ninth and Fiftieth Congresses); declined to be a candidate for reelection in 1890 to the Fifty-second Congress; engaged in banking and other business interests in Orangeburg, Orangeburg County, S.C.; died near Baltimore, Md., September 16, 1913; interment in Sunny Side Cemetery, Orangeburg.

**DIBRELL, George Gibbs,** a Representative from Tennessee; born in Sparta, White County, Tenn., April 12, 1822; attended the public schools, and was graduated from the East Tennessee University, Knoxville, Tenn., in 1843; studied law; was admitted to the bar in 1843 and practiced; engaged in agricultural and mercantile pursuits; justice of the peace and county court clerk of White County, Tenn., for many years; member, State house of representatives, 1861; volunteered in the Confederate Army and served from 1861 to 1865; rose from private to lieutenant colonel of Infantry and colonel of Cavalry, and was discharged as brigadier general; delegate to the State's constitutional convention in 1870; elected as a Democrat to the Forty-fourth and to the four succeeding Congresses (March 4, 1875-March 3, 1885); was not a candidate for renomination in 1884 to the Forty-ninth Congress; resumed agricultural and mercantile pursuits; died in Sparta, Tenn., May 9, 1888; interment in the Old Sparta Cemetery.

Bibliography: *DAB.*

**DICK, Charles William Frederick,** a Representative and a Senator from Ohio; born in Akron, Summit County, Ohio, November 3, 1858; attended the public schools; studied law; was admitted to the bar in 1894 and commenced practice in Akron, Ohio; served in the Eighth Regiment, Ohio Volunteer Infantry, in Cuba during the war with Spain; resumed the practice of law; auditor of Summit County, Ohio, 1886-1894; secretary of the Republican National Committee 1896-1900; elected as a Republican to the Fifty-fifth Congress to fill the vacancy caused by the death of Stephen A. Northway; reelected to three succeeding Congresses and served from November 8, 1898, to March 23, 1904, when he resigned, having been elected Senator; chairman, Committee on Militia (Fifty-seventh and Fifty-eighth Congresses); elected March 2, 1904, as a Republican to the United States Senate to fill the vacancy caused by the death of Marcus A. Hanna; on the same day also was elected for the ensuing term and served from March 23, 1904, to March 3, 1911; unsuccessful candidate for reelection in 1911; chairman, Committee on Indian Depredations (Fifty-eighth Congress), Committee on Mines and Mining (Fifty-ninth through Sixty-first Congresses); resumed the practice of law in Washington, D.C., and Akron, Ohio; unsuccessful candidate for the Republican

nomination for Senator in 1922; died in Akron, Ohio, March 13, 1945; interment in Glendale Cemetery.

**DICK, John** (father of Samuel Bernard Dick), a Representative from Pennsylvania; born in Pittsburgh, Pa., June 17, 1794; moved with his parents to Meadville, Pa., in December of that year; attended the common schools; major of the First Battalion in 1821; colonel of the First Regiment in 1825; brigadier general Second Brigade, Sixteenth Division, Pennsylvania Militia, in 1831; engaged in mercantile pursuits and banking; established the banking house of J.&J.R. Dick in 1850; associate judge of Crawford County in 1850; prominent in promoting the Atlantic & Great Western Railroad; trustee of Allegheny College, Meadville, Pa.; president of the Crawford Mutual Insurance Co.; elected as a Whig to the Thirty-third Congress and as a Republican to the Thirty-fourth and Thirty-fifth Congresses (March 4, 1853-March 3, 1859); was nominated as a candidate for reelection in 1858 to the Thirty-sixth Congress, but subsequently withdrew; resumed his former business pursuits; died in Meadville, Crawford County, Pa., May 29, 1872; interment in Greendale Cemetery.

**DICK, Samuel,** a Delegate from New Jersey; born in Nottingham, Prince Georges County, Md., November 14, 1740; received a classical education; studied medicine in Scotland, and commenced practice in Salem, N.J., in 1770; member of the New Jersey Provincial congress in 1776; was appointed colonel of the First Battalion, Salem County Militia, in 1776; assistant surgeon in the Continental Army in the Canadian campaign; member of the first State general assembly; appointed collector of customs for the western district of New Jersey in 1778; Member of the Continental Congress in 1784 and 1785; delegate to the New Jersey State convention in 1787 to ratify the Federal Constitution; surrogate of Salem County 1785-1804; died in Salem, Salem County, N.J., November 16, 1812; interment in St. John's Episcopal Churchyard.

**DICK, Samuel Bernard** (son of John Dick), a Representative from Pennsylvania; born in Meadville, Crawford County, Pa., October 26, 1836; attended the public schools and Allegheny College, Meadville, Pa.; engaged in banking; during the Civil War was in command of Company F, Ninth Regiment, Pennsylvania Reserve Corps; severely wounded in Dranesville, Va., December 20, 1861; subsequently served as colonel of the regiment until February 1863, when he resigned; commanded the Fifth Regiment, Pennsylvania Militia, and proceeded to Newcreek, W.Va., in July 1863; mayor of Meadville in 1870; elected as a Republican to the Forty-sixth Congress (March 4, 1879-March 3, 1881); was not a candidate for reelection in 1880 to the Forty-seventh Congress; president of the Pittsburgh, Bessemer & Lake Erie Railroad Co. until April 1900; president of Phoenix Iron Works Co.; died in Meadville, Pa., May 10, 1907; interment in Greendale Cemetery.

**DICKENS, Samuel,** a Representative from North Carolina; born near Roxboro, Person County, N.C.; pursued an academic course; member of the State house of commons 1813-1815; elected as a Republican to the Fourteenth Congress to fill the vacancy caused by the death of Richard Stanford and served from December 2, 1816, to March 3, 1817; again a member of the State house of commons in 1818; moved to Madison County, Tenn., in 1820; died in Madison County in 1840.

**DICKERMAN, Charles Heber,** a Representative from Pennsylvania; born in Harford, Susquehanna County, Pa., February 3, 1843; attended the public schools of his native village and was graduated from Harford University, Harford, Pa., in 1860; taught school for several years; studied law, but before qualifying for admission to the bar became bookkeeper for a large coal company at Beaver Meadow, Pa.; interested in the coal commission business and slate quarrying in 1868 at Bethlehem, Pa.; secretary and treasurer of a concern engaged in the manufacture of railroad equipment at Milton, Pa.,

1880-1899; chairman of Northumberland County Democratic committee for three years; delegate to the Pennsylvania constitutional convention in 1891; delegate to the Democratic National Convention in 1892; interested in banking at Mauch Chunk, Sunbury, and Bethlehem, and in 1897 became president of the First National Bank at Milton, in which capacity he served until his death; elected as a Democrat to the Fifty-eighth Congress (March 4, 1903-March 3, 1905); declined to be a candidate for renomination in 1904; appointed by President Theodore Roosevelt a delegate to the Brussels Peace Congress in 1905; again engaged in banking; died in Milton, Pa., December 17, 1915; interment in Milton Cemetery.

**DICKERSON, Mahlon** (brother of Philemon Dickerson), a Senator from New Jersey; born in Hanover, N.J., April 17, 1770; educated by private tutors and was graduated from the College of New Jersey (now Princeton University) in 1789; studied law; was admitted to the bar in 1793; during the Whiskey Rebellion served as a private in the Second Regiment Cavalry, New Jersey Detached Militia; settled in Philadelphia, Pa., and was admitted to practice in the Pennsylvania courts in 1797; Pennsylvania commissioner of bankruptcy in 1802; adjutant general of Pennsylvania, 1805-1808; recorder of the city, 1808-1810; moved to Morris County, N.J., in 1810; member, New Jersey State general assembly, 1811-1813; law reporter for the New Jersey State supreme court, 1813-1814; justice of the New Jersey State supreme court, 1813-1815; chosen Governor of New Jersey by the legislature of the State and served from October 26, 1815 to February 1, 1817, when he resigned; elected as a Republican to the United States Senate in 1816; reelected in 1823 and served from March 4, 1817, to January 30, 1829, when he resigned; immediately reelected to fill the vacancy caused by the resignation of Ephraim Bateman and served from January 30, 1829, to March 3, 1833; chairman, Committee on Library (Fifteenth Congress), Committee on Commerce and Manufactures (Sixteenth through Eighteenth Congresses), Committee on Manufactures (Nineteenth through Twenty-second Congresses); member of the New Jersey State council in 1833, and served as its vice president; declined appointment as Minister to Russia in 1834; appointed Secretary of the Navy by President Andrew Jackson; reappointed by President Martin Van Buren and served from July 1, 1834 to June 30, 1838; United States district judge for New Jersey in 1840; delegate to the State constitutional convention of 1844; died in Succasunna, Morris County, N.J., October 5, 1853; interment in the Presbyterian Cemetery.

Bibliography: *DAB*; Beckwith, Robert R. "Mahlon Dickerson of New Jersey, 1770-1853." Ph.D. dissertation, Columbia University, 1964.

**DICKERSON, Philemon** (brother of Mahlon Dickerson), a Representative from New Jersey; born in Succasunna, Morris County, N.J., January 11, 1788; pursued classical studies, and was graduated from the University of Pennsylvania at Philadelphia in 1808; studied law; was admitted to the bar in 1813 and commenced practice in Paterson, N.J., the same year; admitted as a counselor in 1817; member of the State general assembly from Essex County in 1821 and 1822; elected as a Jacksonian to the Twenty-third and Twenty-fourth Congresses and served from March 4, 1833, until November 3, 1836, when he resigned, having been chosen Governor by the legislature; served as Governor and ex officio chancellor from November 3, 1836, to October 27, 1837; appointed sergeant at law in 1834, being the last person in New Jersey to hold that title; elected as a Democrat to the Twenty-sixth Congress (March 4, 1839-March 3, 1841); unsuccessful candidate for reelection in 1840 to the Twenty-seventh Congress; appointed judge of the United States District Court for the District of New Jersey on March 2, 1841, and served until his death; president of the city council of Paterson, N.J., in 1851; died in Paterson, N.J., December 10, 1862; interment in Cedar Lawn Cemetery.

Bibliography: *DAB*.

**DICKERSON, William Worth,** a Representative from Kentucky; born in Sherman, Grant County, Ky., November 29, 1851; attended the public schools and the private academy of N.M. Lloyd in Crittenden, Ky.; studied law; was admitted to the bar in 1872 and commenced practice in Williamstown, Ky.; prosecuting attorney of Grant County 1872-1876; member of the Kentucky house of representatives 1885-1887; served in the Kentucky senate 1887-1891; elected as a Democrat to the Fifty-first Congress to fill the vacancy caused by the resignation of John G. Carlisle; reelected to the Fifty-second Congress and served from June 21, 1890, to March 3, 1893; unsuccessful candidate for renomination in 1892; resumed the practice of law in Williamstown, Grant County, Ky.; moved to Cincinnati, Ohio, in 1902 and continued the practice of his profession until his death January 31, 1923; remains were cremated and the ashes interred in the City Cemetery, Williamstown, Ky.

**DICKEY, Henry Luther,** a Representative from Ohio; born in South Salem, Ross County, Ohio, October 29, 1832; moved with his parents to Washington Court House, Ohio, in 1836; moved to Greenfield, Ohio, in 1847; attended Greenfield Academy; pursued the vocation of civil engineer, and in that capacity had charge of the construction of the Marietta & Cincinnati Railroad in Vinton County, Ohio; resigned in 1855; studied law; was admitted to the bar at Chillicothe, Ohio, in 1857; was graduated from the Cincinnati Law School in 1859; commenced practice in Greenfield; member of the State house of representatives in 1861; served in the State senate in 1868 and 1869; elected as a Democrat to the Forty-fifth and Forty-sixth Congresses (March 4, 1877-March 3, 1881); was not a candidate for renomination in 1880; resumed the practice of law; was admitted to practice before the Supreme Court of the United States in 1877; president of the Commercial Bank of Greenfield; died in Greenfield, Ohio, on May 23, 1910; interment in Greenfield Cemetery.

**DICKEY, Jay W., Jr.,** a Representative from Arkansas; born in Pine Bluff, Jefferson County, Ark., December 14, 1939; graduated, Pine Bluff High School; attended Hendrix College, Conway, Ark.; B.A., University of Arkansas, 1961; J.D., University of Arkansas School of Law, 1963; attorney, Pine Bluff; owner, Baskin-Robbins franchise, 1972; owner, two Taco Bell restaurants, Condray Sign and Advertising Co., and Adventure Travel; Pine Bluff city attorney, 1968-1970; member, Pine Bluff City Council; elected as a Republican to the One Hundred Third and One Hundred Fourth Congresses (January 3, 1993-January 3, 1997); is a resident of Pine Bluff, Ark.

**DICKEY, Jesse Column,** a Representative from Pennsylvania; born in New Castle, Lawrence County, Pa., February 27, 1808; moved with his parents to New London, Chester County, in 1812; attended the common schools, and was graduated from New London Academy; began teaching school at Hopewell Academy in 1828; engaged in agricultural pursuits; member of the Pennsylvania house of representatives 1842-1845; elected as a Whig to the Thirty-first Congress (March 4, 1849-March 3, 1851), unsuccessful candidate for reelection in 1850 to the Thirty-second Congress; resumed agricultural pursuits; quartermaster and later paymaster in the United States Army during the Civil War; continued agricultural pursuits; died in New London, Pa., February 19, 1890; interment in Presbyterian Cemetery.

**DICKEY, John** (father of Oliver James Dickey), a Representative from Pennsylvania; born in Greensburg, Westmoreland County, Pa., June 23, 1794; completed preparatory studies; appointed postmaster of Old Brighton, Pa., on April 11, 1818, and served until May 17, 1821; served as sheriff 1824-1827; member of the Pennsylvania senate in 1835 and 1837; elected as a Whig to the Twenty-eighth Congress (March 4, 1843-March 3, 1845); elected to the Thirtieth Congress (March 4, 1847-March 3, 1849); appointed United States marshal for the western district of Pennsylvania on

January 22, 1852; died in Beaver, Beaver County, Pennsylvania, on March 14, 1853; interment in the Old Cemetery.

**DICKEY, Oliver James** (son of John Dickey), a Representative from Pennsylvania; born in Old Brighton, Beaver County, Pa., April 6, 1823; completed preparatory studies; attended Beaver Academy and Dickinson College, Carlisle, Pa.; studied law; was admitted to the bar at Lancaster, Lancaster County, Pa., in 1844 and practiced; district attorney of Lancaster County 1856-1859; during the Civil War served as lieutenant colonel of the Tenth Regiment, Pennsylvania Volunteers; elected as a Republican to the Fortieth Congress to fill the vacancy caused by the death of Thaddeus Stevens and on the same day was elected to the Forty-first Congress; reelected to the Forty-second Congress and served from December 7, 1868, to March 3, 1873; was not a candidate for renomination in 1872; delegate to the Pennsylvania constitutional convention at Harrisburg in 1873; resumed the practice of law in Lancaster, Pa., and died there April 21, 1876; interment in Woodward Hill Cemetery.

**DICKINSON, Clement Cabell,** a Representative from Missouri; born at Prince Edward Court House, Prince Edward County, Va., December 6, 1849; tutored privately and also attended private schools; was graduated from Hampden-Sidney College, Virginia, in June 1869; taught school in Virginia and Kentucky, 1869-1872; moved to Clinton, Mo., in September 1872 and continued teaching; also studied law; was admitted to the bar in 1875 and commenced practice in Clinton, Mo.; prosecuting attorney of Henry County, Mo., 1877-1882; city attorney of Clinton, 1882-1884; member of the Missouri State house of representatives, 1900-1902; served in the State senate, 1902-1906; member of the board of regents of the State Normal School at Warrensburg, Mo., 1907-1913; elected as a Democrat to the Sixty-first Congress to fill the vacancy caused by the death of David A. De Armond; reelected to the Sixty-second and to the four succeeding Congresses, and served from February 1, 1910 to March 3, 1921; unsuccessful candidate for reelection in 1920 to the Sixty-seventh Congress; elected to the Sixty-eighth and to the two succeeding Congresses (March 4, 1923-March 3, 1929); unsuccessful candidate for reelection in 1928 to the Seventy-first Congress; elected to the Seventy-second and Seventy-third Congresses (March 4, 1931-January 3, 1935); unsuccessful candidate for renomination in 1934 to the Seventy-fourth Congress; resumed the practice of law at Clinton, Mo., where he died on January 14, 1938; interment in Englewood Cemetery.

**Bibliography:** Carney, George O. "Clement C. Dickinson: Rural Progressive." *Missouri Historical Society Bulletin* 25 (October 1968): 18-30.

**DICKINSON, Daniel Stevens,** a Senator from New York; born in Goshen, Conn., September 11, 1800; moved with his parents to Guilford, Chenango County, N.Y., in 1806; attended the common schools; was apprenticed to a clothier; taught school for several years; subsequently engaged in land surveying; studied law; was admitted to the bar in 1828 and commenced practice in Guilford, N.Y.; postmaster of Guilford, 1827-1832; moved to Binghamton, N.Y.; first president of the city of Binghamton in 1834; member, New York State senate, 1837-1840; Lieutenant Governor and ex officio president of the State senate and president of the court of errors, 1842-1844; appointed and subsequently elected in 1844 as a Democrat to the United States Senate to fill the vacancy caused by the resignation of Nathaniel P. Tallmadge; reelected in 1845, and served from November 30, 1844 to March 3, 1851; unsuccessful candidate for reelection; chairman, Committee on Finance (Thirty-first Congress), Committee on Manufactures (Twenty-ninth and Thirtieth Congresses), Committee on Private Land Claims (Thirty-first Congress); resumed the practice of law; appointed collector of the port of New York, but declined the position; elected attorney general of the State in 1861; appointed United States commissioner for the final settlement of the Hudson Bay and Puget Sound

agricultural claims in 1864; appointed by President Abraham Lincoln as United States attorney for the southern district of New York, and served in 1865 and 1866; died in New York City, April 12, 1866; interment in Spring Forest Cemetery, Binghamton, Broome County, N.Y.

**Bibliography:** *DAB*; Dickinson, Daniel S. *Speeches, Correspondence, etc. of the late Daniel Dickinson of New York.* Edited by John R. Dickinson. 2 vols. New York: G.P. Putnam and Sons, 1867; Hinman, Marjory Barnum. *Daniel S. Dickinson: Defender of the Constitution.* Windsor, N.Y.: M.B. Hinman, 1987.

**DICKINSON, David W.** (nephew of William Hardy Murfree), a Representative from Tennessee; born in Franklin, Tenn., June 10, 1808; completed preparatory studies and was graduated from the University of North Carolina at Chapel Hill; studied law; was admitted to the bar and practiced; elected as a Jacksonian to the Twenty-third Congress (March 4, 1833-March 3, 1835); elected as a Whig to the Twenty-eighth Congress (March 4, 1843-March 3, 1845); was unable to attend the last session of Congress on account of his failing health; died at "Grantland," his father's home, near Murfreesboro, Rutherford County, Tenn., on April 27, 1845; interment in the family burying ground on the estate.

**DICKINSON, Edward,** a Representative from Massachusetts; born in Amherst, Mass., January 1, 1803; attended the public schools and Amherst Academy; was graduated from Yale College in 1823; studied law in the law school of Northampton, Mass.; was admitted to the bar and commenced practice in Amherst in 1826; treasurer of Amherst College 1835-1873; member of the Massachusetts house of representatives in 1838 and 1839; served in the Massachusetts senate in 1842 and 1843; member of the Governor's council in 1846 and 1847; elected as a Whig to the Thirty-third Congress (March 4, 1853-March 3, 1855); declined to be a candidate for the Republican nomination of Lieutenant Governor in 1861; again elected a member of the Massachusetts house of representatives in 1873; father of Emily Dickinson; died in Boston, Mass., June 16, 1874; interment in West Cemetery, Amherst, Hampshire County, Mass.

**Bibliography:** Bingham, Millicent (Todd). *Emily Dickinson's Home; Letters of Edward Dickinson and His Family.* New York: Harper, 1955; Thomas, Owen. "Father and Daughter: Edward and Emily Dickinson." *American Literature* 40 (January 1969): 510-23.

**DICKINSON, Edward Fenwick,** a Representative from Ohio; born in Fremont, Sandusky County, Ohio, January 21, 1829; attended the public schools; was graduated from St. Xavier College, Cincinnati, Ohio; studied law; was admitted to the bar and commenced practice in Fremont, Ohio; prosecuting attorney of Sandusky County, Ohio, from 1852 until his resignation in 1854; during the Civil War served in the Union Army as a lieutenant; promoted to captain and served as regimental quartermaster of Company G, Eighth Regiment, Ohio Volunteer Infantry; served as probate judge of Sandusky County 1866-1869; elected as a Democrat to the Forty-first Congress (March 4, 1869-March 3, 1871); unsuccessful candidate for reelection in 1870 to the Forty-second Congress; resumed the practice of his profession; elected mayor of Fremont in 1871, 1873, and 1875; again served as probate judge of Sandusky County from 1877 to 1879 and from 1885 until his death; died in Fremont, Ohio, August 25, 1891; interment in Oakwood Cemetery.

**DICKINSON, John** (brother of Philemon Dickinson), a Delegate from Pennsylvania and from Delaware; born on his father's estate, "Crosiadoré," near Trappe, Talbot County, Md., November 8, 1732; moved with his parents in 1740 to Dover, Del., where he studied under a private teacher; studied law in Philadelphia and at the Middle Temple in London; was admitted to the bar in 1757 and commenced practice in Philadelphia; member of the Assembly of

"Lower Counties," as the State of Delaware was then called, in 1760; member of the Pennsylvania Assembly in 1762 and 1764; delegate to the Stamp Act Congress in 1765; Member from Pennsylvania to the Continental Congress 1774-1776 and from Delaware in 1779; brigadier general of Pennsylvania Militia; President of the State of Delaware in 1781; returned to Philadelphia and served as President of Pennsylvania 1782-1785; returned to Delaware; was a member of the Federal convention of 1787 which framed the Constitution and was one of the signers from Delaware; died in Wilmington, New Castle County, Del., on February 14, 1808; interment in Wilmington Friends Meetinghouse Burial Ground.

Bibliography: *DAB*; Dickinson, John. *The Political Writings of John Dickinson*, 1764-1774. Edited by Paul Leicester Ford. 1895. Reprint. New York: Da Capo Press, 1970; Flower, Milton E. *John Dickinson, Conservative Revolutionary*. Charlottesville: University Press of Virginia, 1983.

**DICKINSON, John Dean,** a Representative from New York; born in Middletown, Conn., June 28, 1767; completed preparatory studies, and was graduated from Yale College in 1785; moved to Lansingburg, Rensselaer County, N.Y., in 1790; was admitted to the bar in April 1791 and commenced the practice of law in Lansingburg; moved to Troy, N.Y.; served as president of the Farmers' Bank of Troy, N.Y., from its foundation in 1801 until his death; a director and founder of the Rensselaer & Saratoga Insurance Co. in 1814; member of the State assembly from November 1816 to April 1817; first president of the Troy Lyceum of Natural History in 1818; elected to the Sixteenth and Seventeenth Congresses (March 4, 1819-March 3, 1823); one of the original trustees of the Rensselaer Polytechnic Institute in 1824; member of the committee which received Lafayette on his visits to Troy in 1824 and 1825; elected to the Twentieth and Twenty-first Congresses (March 4, 1827-March 3, 1831); resumed the practice of law in Troy, N.Y., and died there January 28, 1841; interment in Oakwood Cemetery.

**DICKINSON, Lester Jesse** (cousin of Fred Dickinson Letts), a Representative and a Senator from Iowa; born in Derby, Lucas County, Iowa, October 29, 1873; attended the public schools; was graduated from Cornell College, Mount Vernon, Iowa, in 1898, and from the law department of the University of Iowa at Iowa City in 1899; was admitted to the bar in 1899 and commenced practice in Algona, Iowa; second lieutenant in the Fifty-second Infantry, Iowa National Guard, 1900-1902; city clerk of Algona 1900-1904; prosecuting attorney of Kossuth County 1909-1913; elected as a Republican to the Sixty-sixth and to the five succeeding Congresses (March 4, 1919-March 3, 1931); was not a candidate for renomination in 1930, having become a candidate for Senator; elected as a Republican to the United States Senate in 1930 and served from March 4, 1931, to January 3, 1937; unsuccessful candidate for reelection in 1936 and for election in 1938; resumed the practice of law in Des Moines, Iowa, where he died on June 4, 1968; interment in Algona Cemetery, Algona, Iowa.

**DICKINSON, Philemon** (brother of John Dickinson), a Delegate from Delaware and a Senator from New Jersey; born at "Crosiadoré," near Trappe, Talbot County, Md., April 5, 1739; moved with his parents to Dover, Del., in 1740, where he received his education from a private tutor, and was graduated in the first class of the University of Pennsylvania at Philadelphia in 1759; superintended his father's estates in Delaware until 1760; studied law in Philadelphia, was admitted to the bar, but never practiced; moved to Trenton, N.J., in 1767; delegate to the New Jersey Provincial Congress in 1776; served in the Revolutionary War; was commissioned brigadier general in 1776, and in 1777 major general commanding the New Jersey Militia, serving in the latter capacity throughout the Revolution; Member of the Continental Congress from Delaware 1782-1783; vice president of the Council of New Jersey 1783-1784; member of the commission to choose a site for the national capital in 1784; elected to the United States Senate from New Jersey to fill the vacancy caused by the resignation of William Paterson and served from November 23, 1790, to March 3, 1793; was not a candidate for renomination; devoted his time to the care of his estates; died at his home, "The Hermitage," near Trenton, N.J., February 4, 1809; interment in the Friends Meeting House Burying Ground, Trenton, N.J.

Bibliography: *DAB*.

**DICKINSON, Rodolphus,** a Representative from Ohio; born in Hatfield, Mass., December 28, 1797; attended the public schools and Williams College, Williamstown, Mass., 1818-1821; studied law; was admitted to the bar and commenced practice in Tiffin, Ohio; appointed prosecuting attorney for Seneca County in 1824, for Williams County in 1826, and for Sandusky County in 1827; moved to Lower Sandusky, Ohio, in 1826; served as a member of the Board of Public Works of Ohio 1836-1845; elected as a Democrat to the Thirtieth and Thirty-first Congresses and served from March 4, 1847, until his death in Washington, D.C., on March 20, 1849; interment in Washington, D.C.; reinterment in Oakwood Cemetery, Fremont, Sandusky County, Ohio.

**DICKINSON, William Louis,** a Representative from Alabama; born in Opelika, Lee County, Ala., June 5, 1925; attended the public schools of Opelika, Ala.; served in United States Navy, 1943-1946; major, United States Air Force Reserves; J.D., University of Alabama Law School, 1950; was admitted to the bar in 1950 and began practice in Opelika, Ala.; Opelika city judge, 1952-1954; judge of Lee County Court of Common Pleas and of Juvenile Court, 1954-1958; circuit judge, Fifth Judicial Circuit of Alabama, 1958-1962; assistant vice president of the Southern Railway System, 1962-1964; member of Opelika Board of Education, 1954-1962, and served as president in 1961; member and one of cofounders of the board of directors of Lee County Rehabilitation Center, 1960-1962; member of Governor's Industrial Development Committee of One Hundred, 1963; delegate, State Republican conventions, 1964, 1966, 1968, and 1970; delegate to the Republican National Convention of 1968; elected as a Republican to the Eighty-ninth and to the thirteen succeeding Congresses (January 3, 1965-January 3, 1993); was not a candidate for reelection in 1992 to the One Hundred Third Congress; is a resident of Montgomery, Ala.

**DICKS, Norman DeValois,** a Representative from Washington; born in Bremerton, Kitsap County, Wash., December 16, 1940; attended the public schools and graduated from West Bremerton High School in 1959; B.A., University of Washington, 1963; J.D., University of Washington School of Law, 1968; admitted to the Washington bar in 1968; served as legislative and administrative assistant to Senator Warren G. Magnuson of Washington, 1968-1976; elected as a Democrat to the Ninety-fifth and to the nine succeeding Congresses (January 3, 1977-January 3, 1997); is a resident of Bremerton, Wash.

**DICKSON, David,** a Representative from Mississippi; born in Georgia; moved to Mississippi; studied medicine and practiced extensively in Pike County; delegate to the State constitutional convention in 1817; brigadier general of militia in 1818; member of the Mississippi State senate in 1820 and 1821; lieutenant governor of Mississippi from January 7, 1822 until January 7, 1824; postmaster of Jackson, Miss., in 1822; unsuccessful candidate for Governor of Mississippi in 1823; delegate to the State constitutional convention in 1832, and was an unsuccessful candidate for president of the convention; secretary of the State senate in 1833; secretary of state in 1835; elected as a Whig to the Twenty-fourth Congress and served from March 4, 1835, until his death at Hot Springs, Ark., July 31, 1836.

**DICKSON, Frank Stoddard,** a Representative from Illinois; born in Hillsboro, Montgomery County, Ill., October 6, 1876; attended the public schools and was graduated from the high school at Decatur, Ill., in 1896; taught school at Ramsey, Ill.; served as a private in the Fourth Regiment, Illinois Infantry, during the war with Spain; again engaged in teaching at Ramsey, Ill.; elected as a Republican to the Fifty-ninth Congress (March 4, 1905-March 3, 1907); unsuccessful candidate for reelection in 1906 to the Sixtieth Congress; assistant adjutant general of Illinois 1908-1910; adjutant general of Illinois 1910-1922; assistant to the director of finance, United States Shipping Board and Emergency Fleet Corporation, 1922-1924; secretary to Senator Medill McCormick 1924-1926; associated with the National Board of Fire Underwriters in Chicago, Ill., and was general counsel at time of death; died in Washington, D.C., February 24, 1953; interment in Oak Ridge Cemetery, Springfield, Ill.

**DICKSON, John,** a Representative from New York; born in Keene, N.H., June 1, 1783; was graduated from Middlebury (Vt.) College in 1808; studied law; was admitted to the bar in 1812 and commenced practice in West Bloomfield, N.Y.; member of the State assembly in 1829 and 1830; elected as an Anti-Masonic candidate to the Twenty-second and Twenty-third Congresses (March 4, 1831-March 3, 1835); chairman, Committee on Revisal and Unfinished Business (Twenty-third Congress); resumed the practice of law in West Bloomfield, Ontario County, N.Y., where he died February 22, 1852; interment in Pioneer Cemetery.

**DICKSON, Joseph,** a Representative from North Carolina; born in Chester County, Pa., in April 1745; moved with his parents to Rowan County, N.C., and was reared and educated there; engaged in cotton and tobacco planting; member of the committee of safety of Rowan County in 1775; commissioned captain in the Colonial Army the same year; served under Colonel McDowell in 1780, and at the Battle of Kings Mountain, S.C., October 7, 1780, as major of the "Lincoln County Men"; clerk of Lincoln County Court in 1781; member of the State senate, 1788-1795, and during this time was appointed one of a commission to establish the University of North Carolina at Chapel Hill; elected as a Federalist to the Sixth Congress (March 4, 1799-March 3, 1801); moved to Tennessee in 1803 and settled in that portion of Davidson County which subsequently became Rutherford County; member of the State house of representatives, 1807-1811, and served as speaker the last two years; died in Rutherford County, Tenn., April 14, 1825; interment on his plantation northeast of Murfreesboro, Tenn.

**DICKSON, Samuel,** a Representative from New York; born in the town of Bethlehem (now New Scotland), Albany County, N.Y., March 29, 1807; completed preparatory studies; graduated from Union College, Schenectady, N.Y., in 1825; received a diploma from the Censors of the Medical Society of the State of New York in May 1829 and commenced the practice of his profession in New Scotland, N.Y.; elected as a Whig to the Thirty-fourth Congress (March 4, 1855-March 3, 1857); died in New Scotland, N.Y., on May 3, 1858; interment in New Scotland Presbyterian Church Cemetery.

**DICKSON, William,** a Representative from Tennessee; born in Duplin County, N.C., May 5, 1770; educated at Grove Academy, Kenansville, N.C.; moved with his parents to Tennessee in 1795; studied medicine and practiced in Nashville for many years; member of the State house of representatives 1799-1803 and served as speaker; elected as a Republican to the Seventh, Eighth, and Ninth Congresses (March 4, 1801-March 3, 1807); trustee of the University of Nashville 1806-1816; died in Nashville, Tenn., in February 1816; interment in a rural cemetery near Nashville.

**DICKSON, William Alexander,** a Representative from Mississippi; born in Centreville, Wilkinson County, Miss., July 20, 1861; attended private and public schools, Pleasant Grove School, Centenary College, Jackson, La., and Vanderbilt University, Nashville, Tenn.; engaged in agricultural pursuits; studied law but did not practice; supervisor 1886-1888; member of the State house of representatives 1887-1893; school commissioner of Wilkinson County; member of the board of trustees of the Agricultural and Mechanical College, Starkville, Miss., and of Edward Magehee College, Woodville, Miss., for five years; elected as a Democrat to the Sixty-first and Sixty-second Congresses (March 4, 1909-March 3, 1913); engaged in agricultural pursuits; elected supervisor of the third district of Wilkinson County and superintendent of its highways in 1927; died in Centreville, Miss., February 25, 1940; interment in Oaklawn Cemetery.

**DICKSTEIN, Samuel,** a Representative from New York; born near Vilna, Russia, February 5, 1885; immigrated to the United States in 1887 with his parents, who settled in New York City; attended public and private schools in New York City, the College of the City of New York, and was graduated from the New York City Law School in 1906; was admitted to the bar in 1908 and commenced the practice of law in New York City; special deputy attorney general of the State of New York 1911-1914; member of the board of aldermen in 1917; member of the State assembly 1919-1922; served as a member of the Democratic county committee; elected as a Democrat to the Sixty-eighth and to the eleven succeeding Congresses and served from March 4, 1923, until his resignation on December 30, 1945; chairman, Committee on Immigration and Naturalization (Seventy-second through Seventy-ninth Congresses); judge of the New York State Supreme Court until his death in New York City, April 22, 1954; interment in Union Field Cemetery, Queens County, Brooklyn, N.Y.

**DIEKEMA, Gerrit John,** a Representative from Michigan; born in Holland, Ottawa County, Mich., on March 27, 1859; attended the common schools; was graduated from Hope College, Holland, Mich., in 1881 and from the law department of the University of Michigan at Ann Arbor in 1883; was admitted to the bar and commenced practice in Holland in 1883; city attorney; member of the State house of representatives 1885-1891, serving as speaker in 1889; mayor of Holland in 1895; chairman of the Michigan Republican State central committee 1900-1910; delegate to the Republican National Convention of 1896; member of the Spanish Treaty Claims Commission from 1901 until he resigned in 1907; elected April 27, 1907, as a Republican to the Sixtieth Congress to fill the vacancy caused by the resignation of William Alden Smith; reelected to the Sixty-first Congress and served from March 17, 1908, to March 3, 1911; unsuccessful candidate for reelection in 1910 to the Sixty-second Congress; resumed the practice of law in Holland, Mich.; manager of the Republican Speakers' Bureau in Chicago in 1912; chairman of the Republican State central committee in 1927; appointed United States Minister to the Netherlands by President Herbert Hoover on August 20, 1929, and served until his death in The Hague, Netherlands, December 20, 1930; interment in Pilgrim Home Cemetery, Holland, Mich.

Bibliography: Schrier, William. *Gerrit J. Diekema, Orator; A Rhetorical Study of the Political and Occasional Addresses of Gerrit J. Diekema.* Grand Rapids, Mich.: Eerdmans, 1950; Vander Hill, Charles Warren. *Gerritt J. Diekema.* Grand Rapids, Mich.: Eerdmans, 1970.

**DIES, Martin** (father of Martin Dies, Jr.), a Representative from Texas; born in Jackson Parish, La., March 13, 1870; moved with his parents to Freestone County, Tex., in 1876; attended the common schools and was graduated from the law department of the University of Texas at Austin; was admitted to the bar in 1893 and commenced practice in Woodville, Tex.; edited a newspaper in

Freestone County; was county marshal; county judge of Tyler County in 1894; district attorney of the first judicial district of Texas 1898-1900; moved to Colorado, Tex., and engaged in the practice of law; moved to Beaumont, Tex., in 1902 and was employed as counsel for the Gulf Refining Co.; elected as a Democrat to the Sixty-first and to the four succeeding Congresses (March 4, 1909-March 3, 1919); chairman, Committee on Railways and Canals (Sixty-third and Sixty-fourth Congresses); was not a candidate for reelection in 1918; retired to his ranch on Turkey Creek, Tyler County, Tex.; moved to Kerrville, Tex., in 1921 and died there July 13, 1922; interment in Glenwood Cemetery, Houston, Tex.

**DIES, Martin, Jr.** (son of Martin Dies), a Representative from Texas; born in Colorado, Mitchell County, Tex., November 5, 1900; moved with his parents to Beaumont, Tex., in 1902; attended the public schools, Wesley College, Greenville, Tex., and Cluster Springs Academy, Cluster Springs, Va.; was graduated from the University of Texas at Austin in 1919 and from the law department of National University, Washington, D.C. (now George Washington University), LL.B., 1920; was admitted to the bar in 1920 and commenced practice in Marshall, Tex.; moved to Orange, Tex., in 1922 and continued the practice of law; also interested in ranching and agricultural pursuits at Jasper, Tex.; member of the faculty of East Texas Law School, Beaumont, Tex., in 1930; district judge; elected as a Democrat to the Seventy-second and to the six succeeding Congresses (March 4, 1931-January 3, 1945); chairman, Special Committee to Investigate Un-American Activities (Seventy-fifth through Seventy-eighth Congresses); unsuccessful candidate in 1941 for nomination to fill a vacancy in the United States Senate; did not seek renomination in 1944 to the Seventy-ninth Congress; elected to the Eighty-third and to the two succeeding Congresses (January 3, 1953-January 3, 1959); unsuccessful candidate in 1957 for nomination to fill a vacancy in the United States Senate; declined to be a candidate for renomination in 1958 to the Eighty-sixth Congress; resumed the practice of law; died in Lufkin, Tex., November 14, 1972; entombment in Garden of Memories Mausoleum.
    Bibliography: Dies, Martin. *Martin Dies' Story*. New York: Bookmailer, 1963; Gellermann, William. *Martin Dies*. 1944. Reprint. New York: Da Capo Press, 1972; McDaniel, Dennis Kay. "Martin Dies of Un-American Activities: His Life and Times." Ph.D. dissertation, University of Houston, 1988.

**DIETERICH, William Henry,** a Representative and a Senator from Illinois; born on a farm near Cooperstown, Brown County, Ill., March 31, 1876; attended the rural schools; was graduated from Kennedy Normal and Business College, Rushville, Ill., in 1897 and from Northern Indiana Law School, Valparaiso, Ind., in 1901; was admitted to the bar in 1901 and commenced practice in Rushville, Schuyler County, Ill., the same year; during the Spanish-American War served as a corporal in Company K, Anderson's Provisional Regiment; city attorney of Rushville, Ill., 1903-1907; treasurer of Rushville Union Schools 1906-1908; county judge of Schuyler County, Ill., 1906-1910; moved to Chicago, Ill., in 1911 and to Beardstown, Ill., in 1912, and continued the practice of law; special inheritance-tax attorney of Illinois 1913-1917; member, State house of representatives 1917-1921; elected as a Democrat to the Seventy-second Congress (March 4, 1931-March 3, 1933); did not seek renomination, having become a candidate for the United States Senate; elected as a Democrat to the United States Senate and served from March 4, 1933 to January 3, 1939; was not a candidate for renomination in 1938; resumed the practice of law; died in Springfield, Ill., on October 12, 1940, while on a business trip; interment in Rushville City Cemetery, Rushville, Ill.

**DIETRICH, Charles Elmer,** a Representative from Pennsylvania; born in Tunkhannock, Wyoming County, Pa., July 30, 1889; attended the public and high schools; was graduated from Wyoming Seminary, Kingston, Pa., in 1907; owned and operated a theater 1914-1942; engaged in agricultural pursuits 1924-1942; prothonotary and clerk of the courts of Wyoming County 1920-1935; delegate to the Democratic National Convention in 1932; elected as a Democrat to the Seventy-fourth Congress (January 3, 1935-January 3, 1937); unsuccessful candidate for reelection in 1936 to the Seventy-fifth Congress; resumed former business pursuits; died in Tunkhannock, Pa., May 20, 1942; interment in Sunnyside Cemetery.

**DIETRICH, Charles Henry,** a Senator from Nebraska; born in Aurora, Kane County, Ill., November 26, 1853; attended the public schools; employed as a clerk in a hardware store in St. Joseph, Mo.; moved to Chicago, Ill., and engaged in the hardware business; moved to Deadwood, Dakota Territory (now South Dakota), in 1875 and engaged in mercantile pursuits, delivering goods on pack animals through the Black Hills; located and owned the "Aurora" mine; settled in Hastings, Adams County, Nebr., in 1878 and engaged in mercantile pursuits and in banking; elected Governor of Nebraska in 1900 and served from January 3, 1901 until May 1, 1901, when he resigned, having been elected Senator; elected as a Republican to the United States Senate to fill the vacancy caused by the death of Monroe L. Hayward and served from March 28, 1901, to March 3, 1905; was not a candidate for reelection in 1904; retired in 1905; died in Hastings, Nebr., on April 10, 1924; interment in Parkview Cemetery.

**DIETZ, William,** a Representative from New York; born in Schoharie, N.Y., June 28, 1778; attended the district schools; engaged in agricultural pursuits; town clerk in 1804 and 1805; supervisor of Schoharie in 1812; served in the State assembly in 1814, 1815, and 1823; elected to the Nineteenth Congress (March 4, 1825-March 3, 1827); member of the State senate 1830-1833; resumed agricultural pursuits; colonel of the militia; died in Schoharie, Schoharie County, N.Y., on August 24, 1848; interment in St. Paul's Lutheran Cemetery.

**DIFENDERFER, Robert Edward,** a Representative from Pennsylvania; born in Lewisburg, Union County, Pa., June 7, 1849; attended the common schools; studied dentistry and practiced this profession for fourteen years in Lewisburg and Pottsville, Pa.; built and operated the first woolen mill at Tientsin, China; returned to the United States in August 1900; engaged in the wholesale lumber business and as a contractor at Jenkintown; elected as a Democrat to the Sixty-second and Sixty-third Congresses (March 4, 1911-March 3, 1915); unsuccessful candidate for renomination in 1914 to the Sixty-fourth Congress, in 1916 to the Sixty-fifth Congress, and in 1918 to the Sixty-sixth Congress; engaged in the retail confectionery business at Jenkintown; died in Philadelphia, Pa., April 25, 1923; interment in Westminster Cemetery.

**DIGGS, Charles Coles, Jr.,** a Representative from Michigan; born in Detroit, Wayne County, Mich., December 2, 1922; attended the public schools of Detroit and graduated from Miller High School in 1940; attended the University of Michigan, Ann Arbor, from September 1940 until June 1942; enrolled at Fisk University, Nashville, Tenn., in the fall of 1942 and while a student entered the United States Army as a private on February 19, 1943, commissioned a second lieutenant in 1944, and was discharged June 1, 1945; enrolled in Wayne College of Mortuary Science, Detroit, Mich., in September 1945 and graduated in June 1946; subsequently became a licensed mortician and board chairman of the House of Diggs, Inc.; attended the Detroit College of Law in 1951; Michigan State senator, 1951-1954; elected as a Democrat to the Eighty-fourth Congress; reelected to the twelve succeeding Congresses, and served from January 3, 1955 until his resignation on June 3, 1980; chairman, Committee on District of Columbia (Ninety-third through Ninety-fifth Congresses); founder and first chairman of the Congressional Black Caucus, 1969-1971; is a resident of Hillcrest Heights, Md.

**DILL, Clarence Cleveland,** a Representative and a Senator from Washington; born near Fredericktown, Knox County, Ohio, September 21, 1884; attended the public schools; engaged in teaching, 1901-1903; was graduated from Ohio Wesleyan University, Delaware, Ohio, 1907; newspaper reporter in Cleveland, Ohio, in 1907; taught in the high schools at Dubuque, Iowa, 1907-1908, and in Spokane, Wash., 1908-1910; studied law; was admitted to the bar in 1910 and commenced practice in Spokane, Wash.; deputy prosecuting attorney of Spokane County, 1911-1913; private secretary to Governor Ernest Lister in 1913; elected as a Democrat to the Sixty-fourth and Sixty-fifth Congresses (March 4, 1915-March 3, 1919); unsuccessful candidate for reelection in 1918 to the Sixty-sixth Congress; resumed the practice of law in Spokane, Wash.; elected as a Democrat to the United States Senate in 1922; reelected in 1928 and served from March 4, 1923, to January 3, 1935; was not a candidate for renomination in 1934; chairman, Committee on Interstate Commerce (Seventy-third Congress); engaged in the practice of law in Washington, D.C., and Spokane, Wash., 1935-1939; unsuccessful candidate in 1940 for election for Governor of Washington; unsuccessful candidate for election in 1942 to the Seventy-eighth Congress; member of the Columbia Basin Commission of the State of Washington, 1945-1948; special assistant to the United States Attorney General, 1946-1953; resumed the practice of law in Spokane, Wash., where he died January 14, 1978; interment in Fairmont Memorial Park.

**Bibliography:** *DAB*; Barkley, Frederick R. "Clarence Dill: The Hometown Boy Who Made Good." In *Sons of the Wild Jackass.* pp. 245-68. Boston: L.C. Page and Company, 1932; Dill, Clarence C. *How Congress Makes Laws.* Washington, D.C.: Ransdell, Inc., 1936; Irish, Kerry Eugene. "Clarence Dill: The Life of a Western Politician." Ph.D. dissertation, University of Washington, 1994.

**DILLINGHAM, Paul, Jr.** (father of William Paul Dillingham), a Representative from Vermont; born in Shutesbury, Mass., August 10, 1799; moved with his father to Waterbury, Vt., in 1805; attended the district school in Waterbury; studied law; was admitted to the bar in March 1823 and commenced practice in Waterbury, Vt.; justice of the peace from 1826 to 1844; town clerk of Waterbury, 1829-1844; member of the Vermont State house of representatives, 1833-1835, and 1837-1840; prosecuting attorney of Washington County, 1835-1838; delegate to the State constitutional conventions of 1836, 1857, and again in 1870; served in the State senate in 1841, 1842, and 1861; elected as a Democrat to the Twenty-eighth and Twenty-ninth Congresses (March 4, 1843-March 3, 1847); was not a candidate for renomination in 1846 to the Thirtieth Congress; Lieutenant Governor 1862-1865; elected Governor of Vermont in 1865, reelected in 1866, and served from October 13, 1865 to October 13, 1867; resumed the practice of law; retired in 1875; died at his home in Waterbury, Vt., on July 26, 1891; interment in the Village Cemetery.

**DILLINGHAM, William Paul** (son of Paul Dillingham, Jr.), a Senator from Vermont; born in Waterbury, Washington County, Vt., December 12, 1843; attended the public schools of Waterbury, Newbury Seminary, and Kimball Union Academy, Meriden, N.H.; studied law; was admitted to the bar in 1867 and commenced practice in Waterbury; prosecuting attorney of Washington County, 1872-1876; secretary of civil and military affairs, 1874-1876; member, Vermont State house of representatives, 1876, 1884; member, State senate 1878, 1880; State tax commissioner, 1882-1888; elected Governor of Vermont in 1888, and served from October 4, 1888 to October 2, 1890; president of the Waterbury National Bank, 1890-1923; trustee of the University of Vermont at Burlington; president of the board of trustees of Montpelier Seminary; elected in 1900 as a Republican to the United States Senate to fill the vacancy caused by the death of Justin S. Morrill; reelected in 1903, 1909, 1914, and 1920, and served from October 18, 1900 until his death in Montpelier, Vt., July 12, 1923; chairman, Committee on

Transportation Routes to the Seaboard (Fifty-seventh Congress), Committee on Immigration (Fifty-eighth through Sixty-first Congresses), Committee on Privileges and Elections (Sixty-second, Sixty-sixth, and Sixty-seventh Congresses), Committee to Establish the University of the United States (Sixty-third through Sixty-fifth Congresses); chairman of the United States Immigration Commission, 1907-1910; interment in the Village Cemetery, Waterbury, Vt.

**Bibliography:** *DAB*; Lund, John M. "Vermont Nativism: William Paul Dillingham and U.S. Immigration Legislation." *Vermont History* 63 (Winter 1995): 15-29.

**DILLON, Charles Hall,** a Representative from South Dakota; born near Jasper, Dubois County, Ind., December 18, 1853; attended the public schools; was graduated from the academic department of Indiana University at Bloomington in 1874 and from its law department in 1876; was admitted to the bar in 1876 and commenced practice in Jasper, Ind.; moved to Marion, Iowa, in 1881, to Mitchell, Dakota Territory (now South Dakota), in 1882 and to Yankton in 1894 and continued the practice of law; delegate to the Republican National Conventions in 1900 and 1908; member of the State senate 1903-1911; elected as a Republican to the Sixty-third, Sixty-fourth, and Sixty-fifth Congresses (March 4, 1913-March 3, 1919); was not a candidate for reelection in 1918; resumed the practice of law in Yankton; moved to Vermillion, S.Dak., in 1922, having been elected associate justice of the State supreme court, and served until November 15, 1926, when he resigned; unsuccessful candidate for nomination as United States Senator in 1924; retired in 1926; died in Vermillion, S.Dak., September 15, 1929; interment in Yankton Cemetery, Yankton, S.Dak.

**DILWEG, LaVern Ralph,** a Representative from Wisconsin; born in Milwaukee, Wis., November 1, 1903; attended the public schools; was graduated from the law department of Marquette University, Milwaukee, Wis., in 1927; was admitted to the bar in 1927 and commenced practice in Green Bay, Wis.; played professional football 1926-1934 and continued his connection with the game as an official in the Big Ten until 1943; connected with construction work and a number of business concerns in Green Bay, Wis.; in charge of Home Owners Loan Corporation, Green Bay, Wis., area 1934-1942; elected as a Democrat to the Seventy-eighth Congress (January 3, 1943-January 3, 1945); unsuccessful candidate for reelection in 1944 to the Seventy-ninth Congress; resumed the practice of law in Green Bay, Wis., and Washington, D.C.; confirmed as a member of the Foreign Claims Settlement Commission April 13, 1961; died in St. Petersburg, Fla., January 2, 1968; interment in Fort Howard Cemetery, Green Bay, Wis.

**DIMMICK, Milo Melankthon** (brother of William Harrison Dimmick), a Representative from Pennsylvania; born in Milford, Wayne (now Pike) County, Pa., October 30, 1811; pursued classical studies; studied law; was admitted to the bar in 1834 and commenced practice in Stroudsburg, Pa.; elected as a Democrat to the Thirty-first and Thirty-second Congresses (March 4, 1849-March 3, 1853); chairman, Committee on Expenditures in the Department of War (Thirty-first and Thirty-second Congresses); was not a candidate for renomination in 1852 to the Thirty-third Congress; resumed the practice of law; unsuccessful candidate for president judge of the twenty-second judicial district of Pennsylvania in 1853; moved to Mauch Chunk, Carbon County, Pa., in 1853 and continued the practice of law; also engaged in the banking business; died in Mauch Chunk, Pa., November 22, 1872; interment in Mauch Chunk Cemetery.

**DIMMICK, William Harrison** (brother of Milo Melankthon Dimmick), a Representative from Pennsylvania; born in Milford, Wayne (now Pike) County, Pa., December 20, 1815; attended private schools; studied law; was admitted to the bar in 1835 and commenced practice in Bethany, Pa.; moved to Honesdale, Pa., in 1842 and continued the practice of law; prosecuting attorney of

Wayne County in 1836 and 1837; member of the Pennsylvania senate 1845-1847; elected as a Democrat to the Thirty-fifth and Thirty-sixth Congresses (March 4, 1857-March 3, 1861); resumed the practice of law; died in Honesdale, Wayne County, Pa., August 2, 1861; interment in Glen Dyberry Cemetery.

**DIMOCK, Davis, Jr.,** a Representative from Pennsylvania; born in Exeter, near Wilkes-Barre, Luzerne County, Pa., September 17, 1801; attended the schools of the pioneer settlement of Montrose, Pa., and the Susquehanna County Academy at Montrose; studied law; was admitted to the bar in 1833 and commenced practice in Montrose; also engaged in editorial work; appointed county treasurer in 1834; elected as a Democrat to the Twenty-seventh Congress and served from March 4, 1841, until his death in Montrose, Pa., January 13, 1842; interment in Montrose Cemetery.

**DIMOND, Anthony Joseph,** a Delegate from the Territory of Alaska; born in Palatine Bridge, Montgomery County, N.Y., November 30, 1881; attended the public schools and St. Mary's Catholic Institute, Amsterdam, N.Y.; taught school in Montgomery County, N.Y., 1900-1903; prospector and miner in Alaska 1904-1912; studied law; was admitted to the bar in 1913 and commenced practice in Valdez, Alaska; United States Commissioner at Chisana, Alaska, in 1913 and 1914; special assistant United States attorney for the third judicial division of Alaska at Valdez in 1917; mayor of Valdez 1920-1922 and 1925-1932; member of the Alaska Territorial senate 1923-1926 and 1929-1932; elected as a Democrat a Delegate to the Seventy-third and to the five succeeding Congresses (March 4, 1933-January 3, 1945); was not a candidate for renomination, having been confirmed as district judge for the third division of Alaska, in which capacity he was serving at the time of death; died in Anchorage, Alaska, May 28, 1953; interment in Anchorage Cemetery.

**DINGELL, John David** (father of John David Dingell, Jr.), a Representative from Michigan; born in Detroit, Mich., February 2, 1894; newsboy, printer, and newspaperman; engaged in natural-gas pipeline construction; wholesale dealer in beef and pork products; organizer and trustee of Colorado Springs Labor College; elected as a Democrat to the Seventy-third and to the eleven succeeding Congresses and served from March 3, 1933, until his death in Washington, D.C., September 19, 1955; interment in Holy Sepulchre Mausoleum, Detroit, Mich.

**DINGELL, John David, Jr.** (son of John David Dingell), a Representative from Michigan; born in Colorado Springs, El Paso County, Colo., July 8, 1926; attended Capitol Page School, Washington, D.C., and Georgetown Preparatory School, Garrett Park, Md.; served as a page boy in the House of Representatives 1938-1943; B.S., Georgetown University, Washington, D.C., 1949; J.D., Georgetown University Law School, 1952; served as an infantryman in the Army of the United States from 1944 until discharged as a second lieutenant in 1946; admitted to the District of Columbia bar in 1952; admitted to the Michigan bar in 1953; park ranger, United States Department of the Interior, 1948-1952; commenced the practice of law in Detroit, Mich., in 1953; a research assistant to United States Circuit Judge Theodore Levin, 1952-1953; assistant prosecuting attorney of Wayne County, Mich., in 1954-1955; delegate to the Democratic National Conventions of 1956, 1960, 1968, 1980 and 1984; elected as a Democrat to the Eighty-fourth Congress, by special election, December 13, 1955, to fill the vacancy caused by the death of his father, John D. Dingell, Sr.; reelected to the twenty succeeding Congresses and served from December 13, 1955, to January 3, 1997; chairman, Committee on Energy and Commerce (Ninety-seventh through One Hundred Third Congresses); is a resident of Trenton, Mich.

**DINGLEY, Nelson, Jr.,** a Representative from Maine; born in Durham, Androscoggin County, Maine, February 15, 1832; attended the common schools at Unity, Maine, Waterville Seminary, and Waterville College; was graduated from Dartmouth College, Hanover, N.H., in 1855; studied law and was admitted to the bar, but left the profession and became proprietor and editor of the Lewiston (Maine) Journal in 1856; member of the Maine State house of representatives, 1862-1865, 1868, and again in 1873, and served as speaker in 1863 and 1864; elected Governor of Maine in 1873, reelected in 1874, and served from January 7, 1874 to January 5, 1876; delegate to the Republican National Conventions of 1876 and 1880; elected as a Republican to the Forty-seventh Congress to fill the vacancy caused by the resignation of William P. Frye; reelected to the Forty-eighth and to the seven succeeding Congresses, and served from September 12, 1881 until his death in Washington, D.C., January 13, 1899, before the close of the Fifty-fifth Congress; chairman, Committee on Ways and Means (Fifty-fourth and Fifty-fifth Congresses); had also been reelected to the Fifty-sixth Congress; interment in Oak Hill Cemetery, near Auburn, Maine.

**Bibliography:** *DAB*; Dingley, Edward N. *The Life and Times of Nelson Dingley, Jr.* Kalamazoo: Ihling Brothers and Everard, 1902.

**DINSMOOR, Samuel,** a Representative from New Hampshire; born in Windham, N.H., July 1, 1766; pursued classical studies; was graduated from Dartmouth College, Hanover, N.H., in 1789; studied law; was admitted to the bar and commenced practice in Keene, N.H.; elected as a Republican to the Twelfth Congress (March 4, 1811-March 3, 1813); unsuccessful candidate for reelection in 1812 to the Thirteenth Congress; State councilor in 1821; judge of probate of Cheshire County from 1823 until 1831; unsuccessful candidate for election in 1823 for Governor; member of the commission to establish the boundary line between the States of New Hampshire and Massachusetts in 1825; elected Governor of New Hampshire in 1831, reelected in 1832 and 1833, and served from June 2, 1831 to June 5, 1834; died in Keene, Cheshire County, N.H., March 15, 1835; interment in Washington Street Cemetery.

**Bibliography:** Tilly, Bette B. "The Jackson-Dinsmoor Feud: A Paradox in a Minor Key." *Journal of Mississippi History* 39 (May 1977): 117-131.

**DINSMORE, Hugh Anderson,** a Representative from Arkansas; born at Cave Springs, Benton County, Ark., on December 24, 1850; attended private schools in Benton and Washington Counties; studied law in Bentonville; appointed clerk of the circuit court for Benton County in 1873; was admitted to the bar in 1874; moved to Fayetteville, Washington County, in 1875 and pursued the practice of law; prosecuting attorney of the fourth judicial district 1878-1884; in January 1887 was appointed by President Cleveland as Minister Resident and consul general to the Kingdom of Korea and served until May 25, 1890; resumed the practice of law in Fayetteville, Ark.; elected as a Democrat to the Fifty-third and to the five succeeding Congresses (March 4, 1893-March 3, 1905); unsuccessful candidate for renomination in 1904 to the Fifty-ninth Congress; resumed the practice of law in Fayetteville, Ark., and in later years devoted most of his time to the management of his farming interests; member of the board of trustees of the University of Arkansas; died in St. Louis, Mo., on May 2, 1930; interment in Evergreen Cemetery, Fayetteville, Ark.

**DioGUARDI, Joseph J.,** a Representative from New York; born in New York City, September 20, 1940; attended Fordham Preparatory School, Bronx, N.Y.; B.S., Fordham University, Bronx, N.Y., 1962; served in the United States Army Reserves, 1963-1969; worked as a certified public accountant with Arthur Andersen & Co. in New York City from 1962 until 1984, becoming a partner in 1972; elected as a Republican to the Ninety-ninth and One Hundredth Congresses (January 3, 1985-January 3, 1989); unsuccessful candidate for reelection in 1988 to the One Hundred First Congress;

unsuccessful candidate for election in 1992 to the One Hundred Third Congress; unsuccessful candidate in 1994 for the Republican nomination to the One Hundred Fourth Congress, and for election to the One Hundred Fourth Congress as the nominee of the Conservative and Right-to-Life parties; unsuccessful candidate for nomination in 1996 to the One Hundred Fifth Congress; is a resident of the Town of Mount Pleasant, N.Y.

**DIRKSEN, Everett McKinley** (father-in-law of Howard Henry Baker, Jr.), a Representative and a Senator from Illinois; born in Pekin, Tazewell County, Ill., January 4, 1896; attended public schools and worked as a clerk in a grocery store; attended the University of Minnesota College of Law at Minneapolis, 1914-1917; during the First World War served overseas as a private and later as a second lieutenant of Field Artillery, 1918, and was also attached to the office of the military censor, 1918-1919; general manager of a dredging company, 1922-1925, and worked with his brothers in the grocery and wholesale bakery business; commissioner of finance of Pekin, Ill., 1927-1931; studied law; was admitted to the bar in 1936 and commenced practice in Pekin; elected as a Republican to the Seventy-third and to the seven succeeding Congresses (March 4, 1933-January 3, 1949); chairman, Committee on District of Columbia (Eightieth Congress); was not a candidate for renomination in 1948 to the Eighty-first Congress; elected as a Republican to the United States Senate in 1950; reelected in 1956, 1962, and again in 1968, and served from January 3, 1951 until his death in Washington, D.C., September 7, 1969; Republican whip (Eighty-fifth Congress), minority leader (Eighty-sixth through Ninetieth Congresses, Ninety-first Congress), chairman, Joint Committee on Inaugural Arrangements (Ninetieth Congress); interment in Glendale Memorial Gardens, Pekin, Ill.

Bibliography: Loomis, Burdett. "Everett McKinley Dirksen: The Consummate Minority Leader." In *First Among Equals: Outstanding Senate Leaders of the Twentieth Century*, edited by Richard A. Baker and Roger H. Davidson, pp. 236-263. Washington: Congressional Quarterly, Inc., 1991; MacNeil, Neil. *Dirksen: Portrait of a Public Man*. New York: World Publishing Company, 1970; Schapsmeier, Edward, and Frederick Schapsmeier. *Dirksen of Illinois: Senatorial Statesman*. Urbana: University of Illinois Press, 1985.

**DISNEY, David Tiernan,** a Representative from Ohio; born in Baltimore, Md., August 25, 1803; moved with his parents to Ohio in 1807; attended the common schools; studied law; was admitted to the bar and commenced practice in Cincinnati; became a writer for a newspaper in 1825; member of the State house of representatives in 1829, 1831, and 1832, and served as speaker in the last-named year; served in the State senate in 1833, 1834, 1843, and 1844, and was president of the senate in 1833; one of the commissioners to adjust the boundary line between the States of Ohio and Michigan in 1834; chairman of the commission to adjust taxes of the counties of Ohio in 1840; delegate to the Democratic National Convention of 1848; elected as a Democrat to the Thirty-first and to the two succeeding Congresses (March 4, 1849-March 3, 1855); chairman, Committee on Elections (Thirty-second Congress), Committee on Public Lands (Thirty-third Congress); unsuccessful candidate for renomination in 1854 to the Thirty-fourth Congress; died in Washington, D.C., March 14, 1857; interment in Spring Grove Cemetery, Cincinnati, Ohio.

**DISNEY, Wesley Ernest,** a Representative from Oklahoma; born in Richland, Shawnee County, Kans., October 31, 1883; attended the public schools of Kansas and was graduated from the law department of the University of Kansas at Lawrence in 1906; was admitted to the Kansas bar in 1906, the Oklahoma bar in 1908, and began practice in Muskogee, Okla., in 1908; county attorney of Muskogee County, Okla., 1911-1915; member of the Oklahoma State house of representatives 1919-1924; chairman of the board of

managers in the impeachment trial of Governor John C. Walton in 1923; elected as a Democrat to the Seventy-second and to the six succeeding Congresses (March 4, 1931-January 3, 1945); was not a candidate for renomination in 1944 to the House of Representatives, but was an unsuccessful candidate for nomination for United States Senator; engaged in the practice of law in Washington, D.C., and Tulsa, Okla., until his death in Washington, D.C., on March 26, 1961; interment in Memorial Park Cemetery, Tulsa, Okla.

**DITTER, John William,** a Representative from Pennsylvania; born in Philadelphia, Pa., September 5, 1888; attended the public schools and was graduated from the law department of Temple University, Philadelphia, Pa., in 1913; was admitted to the bar the same year; professor of history and commerce in the Philadelphia high schools 1912-1925; moved to Ambler, Pa., in 1925 and commenced the practice of law; served as workmen's compensation referee for eastern Pennsylvania in 1929; elected as a Republican to the Seventy-third and to the five succeeding Congresses and served from March 4, 1933, until his death in an airplane crash near Columbia, Lancaster County, Pa., on November 21, 1943; interment in Whitemarsh Memorial Cemetery, Prospectville, Montgomery County, Pa.

**DIVEN, Alexander Samuel,** a Representative from New York; born in Catharine (later Watkins), N.Y., February 10, 1809; attended the common schools and the academies in Penn Yan and Ovid, N.Y.; studied law; was admitted to the bar in 1831 and commenced practice in Elmira; member of the State senate in 1858; elected as a Republican to the Thirty-seventh Congress (March 4, 1861-March 3, 1863); was not a candidate for renomination in 1862; entered the Army on August 13, 1862, as lieutenant colonel of the One Hundred and Seventh Regiment, New York Volunteer Infantry; promoted to colonel on October 21, 1862; was granted leave of absence from the Army for ninety days to take his seat in Congress; honorably discharged as colonel May 11, 1863; brevetted brigadier general of Volunteers April 30, 1864; engaged in railroad building and operation 1865-1875; prominently identified with the Erie Railroad; died in Elmira, Chemung County, N.Y., June 11, 1896; interment in Woodlawn Cemetery.

Bibliography: *DAB*.

**DIX, John Adams** (son-in-law of John Jordan Morgan), a Senator from New York; born in Boscawen, N.H., July 24, 1798; completed preparatory studies; during the War of 1812 was appointed a cadet, promoted to ensign, and took part in the operations on the Canadian frontier; served in the United States Army until 1828, having attained the rank of captain; studied law and was admitted to the bar in Washington, D.C.; settled in Cooperstown, N.Y., and began the practice of law; moved to Albany in 1830, having been appointed adjutant general of the State and served from 1831 to 1833; canal commissioner; member of the New York State assembly in 1842; elected as a Democrat to the United States Senate to fill the vacancy caused by the resignation of Silas Wright, Jr., and served from January 27, 1845 to March 3, 1849; was not a candidate for reelection, having become a candidate for Governor; chairman, Committee on Pensions (Twenty-eighth and Twenty-ninth Congresses), Committee on Commerce (Twenty-ninth and Thirtieth Congresses); unsuccessful Free-Soil candidate for Governor in 1848; Assistant Treasurer of the United States at New York, 1853; appointed postmaster of the city of New York, 1860-1861; appointed Secretary of the Treasury by President James Buchanan, and served from January 15 until March 4, 1861; appointed major general of United States Volunteers by President Lincoln on May 16, 1861; commanded the departments of Annapolis, Pennsylvania, and Virginia, and the Middle Department and the Department of the East; resigned his commission November 30, 1865; appointed United States Minister to France on September 24, 1866 and served until May 23, 1869; elected Governor of New York in 1872, and served from January 1, 1873 to January 1, 1875; unsuccessful candidate for reelection in 1874; unsuccessful candidate for election as mayor of New York City in 1876; died in New York City April 21, 1879; interment in Trinity Cemetery.

Bibliography: *DAB*; Dix, John Adams. *Memoirs of John Adams Dix.* Edited by Morgan Dix. 2 vols. New York: Harper and Brothers, 1883; Lichterman, Martin. "John Adams Dix, 1798-1879." Ph.D. dissertation, Columbia University, 1952.

DIXON, Alan John, a Senator from Illinois; born in Belleville, St. Clair County, Ill., July 7, 1927; attended the public schools; B.S., University of Illinois, Urbana, 1949; LL.B., Washington University School of Law, St. Louis, Mo., 1949; served in the United States Navy Air Corps as a lieutenant (jg), 1945-1946; admitted to the Illinois bar in 1949 and commenced practice in Belleville; Belleville police magistrate, 1949; assistant state attorney, St. Clair County, Ill., 1950; member, Illinois State house of representatives, 1951-1963; member, Illinois State senate, 1963-1971, serving as a minority whip, 1964-1970; Illinois State treasurer, 1971-1977; Illinois secretary of State, 1977-1981; elected as a Democrat to the United States Senate in 1980; reelected in 1986, and served from January 3, 1981 to January 3, 1993; unsuccessful candidate for renomination in 1992; chair, Defense Base Closure and Realignment Commission, October 1994 to July 1995; is a resident of Belleville, Ill.

DIXON, Archibald, a Senator from Kentucky; born near Redhouse, Caswell County, N.C., April 2, 1802; moved with his parents to Henderson County, Ky., in 1805; educated by his mother and attended the common schools; studied law; was admitted to the bar in 1824 and commenced practice in Henderson, Ky.; member, Kentucky house of representatives, 1830, 1841; member of the Kentucky senate in 1836; lieutenant governor of Kentucky in 1843; member of the Kentucky constitutional convention in 1849; elected as a Whig to the United States Senate to fill the vacancy caused by the resignation of Henry Clay, and served from September 1, 1852 until March 3, 1855; was not a candidate for reelection in 1854; resumed the practice of law; also engaged as a planter; died in Henderson, Ky., April 23, 1876; interment in Fernwood Cemetery.

DIXON, Henry Aldous, a Representative from Utah; born in Provo, Utah County, Utah, June 29, 1890; attended the public schools; was graduated from Brigham Young University, Provo, Utah, in 1914, from the University of Chicago in 1917, and from the University of Southern California in 1937; instructor at Weber College, Ogden, Utah, 1914-1918, serving as president, 1919-1920, and 1937-1953; superintendent of Provo city schools, 1920-1924, and 1932-1937; managing vice president of Farmers & Merchants Bank, 1924-1932; member of the President's Commission on Higher Education, 1946-1948; member, board of directors, Salt Lake Branch of the Federal Reserve Bank of San Francisco, 1945-1951; director, Association of Junior Colleges, 1950-1954; president of Utah State University at Logan from August 1953 until December 1954; elected as a Republican to the Eighty-fourth and to the two succeeding Congresses (January 3, 1955-January 3, 1961); was not a candidate for renomination in 1960 to the Eighty-seventh Congress; instructor at Brigham Young University until 1965; died in Ogden, Utah, January 22, 1967; interment in Washington Heights Memorial Park.

DIXON, James, a Representative and a Senator from Connecticut; born in Enfield, Hartford County, Conn., August 5, 1814; pursued preparatory studies; was graduated from Williams College, Williamstown, Mass., in 1834; studied law; was admitted to the bar in 1834 and commenced practice in Enfield, Conn.; member, Connecticut State house of representatives, 1837-1838, 1844, and served as speaker in 1837; moved to Hartford, Conn., in 1839 and continued the practice of law; elected as a Whig to the Twenty-ninth and Thirtieth Congresses (March 4, 1845-March 3, 1849); member of the State house of representatives in 1854; declined the nomination for Governor of Connecticut in 1854; unsuccessful candidate for United States Senator in 1854; elected as a Republican to the United States Senate in 1856; reelected in 1863, and served from March 4, 1857 to March 3, 1869; chairman, Committee to Audit and Control the Contingent Expense (Thirty-seventh and Thirty-eighth Congresses), Committee on District of Columbia (Thirty-eighth and Thirty-ninth Congresses), Committee on Post Office and Post Roads (Thirty-ninth Congress); unsuccessful Democratic candidate for the United States Senate and the House of Representatives in 1868; appointed Minister to Russia in 1869 but declined; engaged in literary pursuits and extensive traveling until his death in Hartford, Conn., March 27, 1873; interment in Cedar Hill Cemetery.

Bibliography: *DAB*; Albright, Claude. "Dixon, Doolittle, and Norton: The Forgotten Republican Votes on Andrew Johnson's Impeachment." *Wisconsin Magazine of History* 59 (Winter 1975-1976): 91-100; Burr, Nelson B. "United States Senator James Dixon: 1814-1873, Episcopalian Anti-Slavery Statesman." *History Magazine of the Protestant Episcopal Church* 50 (March 1981): 29-72.

DIXON, Joseph, a Representative from North Carolina; born in Greene County, near Farmville, Pitt County, N.C., April 9, 1828; attended the public schools and was tutored privately; engaged in agricultural pursuits and also in the mercantile business; appointed colonel of the North Carolina State Militia soon after the Civil War; judge of the county court in 1864 and 1865; member of the State house of commons 1865-1867; elected as a Republican to the Forty-first Congress to fill the vacancy caused by the death of David Heaton; took his seat December 5, 1870, and served until March 3, 1871; was not a candidate for renomination in 1870; United States Commissioner of Claims in 1871 and 1872; resumed agricultural pursuits; delegate from Greene County to the State constitutional convention in 1875; died near Fountain Hill, Pitt County, N.C., March 3, 1883; interment in Edwards Chapel Cemetery in Lenoir County.

DIXON, Joseph Andrew, a Representative from Ohio; born in Cincinnati, Ohio, June 3, 1879; attended St. Patrick's School, Hughes High School, and St. Xavier University, Cincinnati, Ohio; clerk in a mercantile store 1893-1900; engaged in retail clothing business in Anderson, Ind., Hartford City, Ind., and Cincinnati; also was manager and owner of amateur and professional baseball teams; active in young men's welfare work; elected as a Democrat to the Seventy-fifth Congress (January 3, 1937-January 3, 1939); unsuccessful candidate for reelection in 1938 to the Seventy-sixth Congress and for election in 1940 to the Seventy-seventh Congress; resumed his former business pursuits in Cincinnati, Ohio, until his death there on July 4, 1942; interment in St. Joseph's Cemetery.

DIXON, Joseph Moore, a Representative and a Senator from Montana; born in Snow Camp, Alamance County, N.C., July 31, 1867; attended Earlham College, Richmond, Ind., and was graduated from Guilford College, North Carolina, in 1889; moved to Missoula, Missoula County, Mont., in 1891; studied law; was admitted to the bar in 1892; assistant prosecuting attorney of Missoula County 1893-1895; prosecuting attorney 1895-1897; member, State house of representatives 1900; elected as a Republican to the Fifty-eighth and Fifty-ninth Congresses (March 4, 1903-March 3, 1907); was not a candidate in 1906 for reelection to the House of Representatives, but was elected to the United States Senate and served from March 4, 1907, to March 3, 1913; unsuccessful candidate for reelection in 1912; chairman, Committee to Examine Branches of the Civil Service (Sixtieth Congress), Committee on the Conservation of Natural Resources (Sixty-first and Sixty-second Congresses); chairman of the National Progressive Convention in 1912; engaged in newspaper publishing and dairy farming; elected Governor of Montana in 1920 and served from January 3, 1921 to January 4, 1925; unsuccessful candidate for reelection in 1924; unsuccessful candidate for election to the United

States Senate in 1928; First Assistant Secretary of the Interior 1929-1933; died at Missoula, Mont., May 22, 1934; interment in Missoula Cemetery.

**Bibliography:** Karlin, Jules. *Joseph M. Dixon of Montana.* Missoula: University of Montana Publications, 1974.

**DIXON, Julian Carey,** a Representative from California; born in Washington, D.C., August 8, 1934; attended the public schools in Los Angeles; graduated Dorsey High School, 1953; B.S., California State University at Los Angeles, 1962; LL.B., Southwestern University, Los Angeles, 1967; served in United States Army, sergeant, 1957-1960; member of the California State assembly, 1972-1978; delegate to California State Democratic conventions, 1972-1978; delegate to Democratic National Convention, 1976; chairman, rules committee, Democratic National Convention, 1984; elected as a Democrat to the Ninety-sixth and to the eight succeeding Congresses (January 3, 1979-January 3, 1997); chairman, Committee on Standards of Official Conduct (Ninety-ninth through One Hundred First Congresses); is a resident of Los Angeles, Calif.

**DIXON, Lincoln,** a Representative from Indiana; born in Vernon, Jennings County, Ind., on February 9, 1860; attended Vernon Academy, and was graduated from Indiana University at Bloomington in 1880; employed as a clerk in the Department of the Interior at Washington, D.C., in 1881; returned to Vernon, Ind., and studied law; was admitted to the bar in 1882 and commenced practice in North Vernon; reading clerk of the State house of representatives in 1883; prosecuting attorney for the sixth judicial circuit 1884-1892; member of the Democratic State committee 1897-1904 and 1920-1927; elected as a Democrat to the Fifty-ninth and to the six succeeding Congresses (March 4, 1905-March 3, 1919); unsuccessful candidate for reelection in 1918 to the Sixty-sixth Congress; resumed the practice of law; delegate to the Democratic National Conventions of 1920 and 1924; in charge of the Democratic campaign in the West in 1924; appointed a member of the United States Tariff Commission by President Calvin Coolidge in 1927 and retired in 1930; reappointed by President Herbert Hoover on June 17, 1931, and served until his death, while on a visit, in Lyndon, Ky., September 16, 1932; interment in Vernon Cemetery, Vernon, Ind.

**DIXON, Nathan Fellows** (father of Nathan Fellows Dixon [1812-1881] and grandfather of Nathan Fellows Dixon [1847-1897]), Senator from Rhode Island; born in Plainfield, Conn., December 13, 1774; attended Plainfield Academy and was graduated from the College of Rhode Island (now Brown University) in 1799; studied law; was admitted to the bar in 1801 and commenced practice in New London County, Conn.; moved to Westerly, R.I., in 1802 and continued the practice of law; also engaged in banking, serving as president of the Washington Bank of Westerly from 1829 until his death; member, State house of representatives 1813-1830; served as a colonel in the State militia; elected as a Whig to the United States Senate and served from March 4, 1839, until his death in Washington, D.C., January 29, 1842; chairman, Committee on Revolutionary Claims (Twenty-seventh Congress); interment in River Bend Cemetery, Westerly, Washington County, R.I.

**DIXON, Nathan Fellows** (son of Nathan Fellows Dixon [1774-1842], and father of Nathan Fellows Dixon [1847-1897], a Representative from Rhode Island; born in Westerly, R.I., May 1, 1812; attended Plainfield (Conn.) Academy, and was graduated from Brown University, Providence, R.I., in 1833; later pursued the study of law at the Cambridge (Mass.) and New Haven (Conn.) Law Schools; was admitted to the bar in 1837 and commenced practice in Westerly, R.I.; also engaged in banking; member of the State house of representatives 1841-1849, 1851-1854, 1858-1862, and 1871-1877; appointed a member of the Governor's council in 1842; elected as a Whig to the Thirty-first Congress (March 4, 1849-March 3, 1851);

was not a candidate for renomination in 1850; elected as a Republican to the Thirty-eighth and to the three succeeding Congresses (March 4, 1863-March 3, 1871); chairman, Committee on Commerce (Forty-first Congress); declined to be a candidate for reelection in 1870 to the Forty-second Congress; delegate to the Union National Convention at Philadelphia in 1866; resumed the practice of law and banking; died in Westerly, Washington County, R.I., April 11, 1881; interment in River Bend Cemetery.

**DIXON, Nathan Fellows** (son of Nathan Fellows Dixon [1812-1881] and grandson of Nathan Fellows Dixon [1777-1842]), a Representative and a Senator from Rhode Island; born in Westerly, Washington County, R.I., August 28, 1847; attended the common schools of Westerly and Phillips Academy, Andover, Mass.; was graduated from Brown University, Providence, R.I., in 1869 and from Albany (N.Y.) Law School in 1871; was admitted to the bar in 1871 and commenced practice in Westerly, R.I.; United States attorney for the district of Rhode Island 1877-1885; elected as a Republican to the Forty-eighth Congress to fill the vacancy caused by the resignation of Jonathan Chace and served from February 12 to March 3, 1885; was not a candidate for renomination; member, State senate 1885-1889; elected as a Republican to the United States Senate to fill the vacancy caused by the resignation of Jonathan Chace and served from April 10, 1889, to March 3, 1895; was not a candidate for reelection; chairman, Committee on Patents (Fifty-second Congress); resumed the practice of law and engaged in banking; died in Westerly, R.I., November 8, 1897; interment in River Bend Cemetery.

**DIXON, William Wirt,** a Representative from Montana; born in Brooklyn, N.Y., June 3, 1838; moved to Illinois in 1843 and to Keokuk, Iowa, in 1849; pursued preparatory studies; studied law in Keokuk and was admitted to the bar in 1858; moved to Tennessee in 1860, in the same year to Arkansas, then to California in 1862, and thence to Humboldt County, Nev.; in 1866 moved to Montana and resided in Helena and later in Deer Lodge until 1879; member of the Territorial house of representatives in 1871 and 1872; spent two years in the Black Hills; returned to Montana in 1881, settled in Butte, and engaged in the practice of law; delegate to the constitutional conventions of Montana in 1884 and 1889; elected as a Democrat to the Fifty-second Congress (March 4, 1891-March 3, 1893); unsuccessful candidate for reelection to the Fifty-third Congress; resumed the practice of his profession; candidate for election to the United States Senate, but the legislature failed to make a choice; died in Los Angeles, Calif., November 13, 1910; interment in Calvary Cemetery; reinterment in Rock Creek Cemetery, Washington, D.C., March 15, 1911.

**DOAN, Robert Eachus,** a Representative from Ohio; born near Wilmington, Clinton County, Ohio, July 23, 1831; attended the common schools and completed an academic course; taught school three years in southern Ohio; was graduated from the Cincinnati Law School in 1857; was admitted to the bar the same year and commenced practice in Wilmington, Ohio; editor of the Wilmington Watchman in 1859 and 1860; prosecuting attorney of Clinton County in 1862; elected as a Republican to the Fifty-second Congress (March 4, 1891-March 3, 1893); unsuccessful candidate for renomination in 1892; resumed the practice of law in Washington, D.C.; died in Wilmington, Ohio, February 24, 1919; interment in Sugar Grove Cemetery.

**DOAN, William,** a Representative from Ohio; born in Maine April 4, 1792; attended the common schools; moved with his parents in 1812 to Ohio and settled near Lindale, Clermont County; studied medicine at New Richmond and commenced practice in 1818 at Withamsville, Clermont County; was graduated from the Ohio Medical College at Cincinnati in 1827; member of the State house of representatives in 1831 and 1832; served in the State senate in 1833 and 1834; elected as a Democrat to the Twenty-sixth and

Twenty-seventh Congresses (March 4, 1839-March 3, 1843); was not a candidate for renomination in 1842; resumed the practice of medicine; died in Withamsville, Clermont County, Ohio, June 22, 1847; interment in Union Township (Mount Moriah) Cemetery, Tobasco, Clermont County, Ohio.

**DOBBIN, James Cochrane** (grandson of James Cochran), a Representative from North Carolina; born in Fayetteville, N.C., January 17, 1814; attended the Fayetteville Academy and the William Bingham School, Hillsboro, N.C.; was graduated from the University of North Carolina at Chapel Hill in 1832; studied law; was admitted to the bar in 1835 and commenced practice in Fayetteville; elected as a Democrat to the Twenty-ninth Congress (March 4, 1845-March 3, 1847); declined to be a candidate for renomination in 1846 to the Thirtieth Congress; resumed the practice of law; member of the North Carolina State house of commons in 1848, 1850, and 1852, serving as speaker in 1850; delegate to the Democratic National Convention of 1852; appointed Secretary of the Navy in the Cabinet of President Franklin Pierce, and served from March 8, 1853 to March 6, 1857; died in Fayetteville, Cumberland County, N.C., August 4, 1857; interment in Cross Creek Cemetery.

**Bibliography:** *DAB.*

**DOBBINS, Donald Claude,** a Representative from Illinois; born on a farm near Dewey, Champaign County, Ill., March 20, 1878; attended the public schools, the University of Illinois at Urbana, Dixon (Ill.) Business College, and George Washington University, Washington, D.C.; taught school 1896-1899; stenographer and correspondent 1900-1906; United States post office inspector 1906-1909; studied law; was admitted to the bar in 1909 and commenced practice in Champaign, Ill.; delegate to the Democratic National Convention at Philadelphia in 1936; elected as a Democrat to the Seventy-third and Seventy-fourth Congresses (March 4, 1933-January 3, 1937); was not a candidate for renomination in 1936; resumed the practice of law; died in Champaign, Ill., February 14, 1943; interment in Mount Hope Cemetery.

**DOBBINS, Samuel Atkinson,** a Representative from New Jersey; born near Vincentown, Burlington County, N.J., April 14, 1814; attended private and public schools; engaged in agricultural pursuits; moved to Mount Holly, N.J., in 1838 and continued farming; high sheriff of Burlington County 1854-1857; member of the State house of assembly 1859-1861; delegate to the Republican National Convention in 1864; trustee of Pennington (N.J.) Seminary 1866-1886, serving as president of the board of trustees for ten years; elected as a Republican to the Forty-third and Forty-fourth Congresses (March 4, 1873-March 3, 1877); was not a candidate for renomination in 1876; resumed agricultural pursuits; died in Mount Holly, N.J., May 26, 1886; interment in Mount Holly Cemetery.

**DOCKERY, Alexander Monroe,** a Representative from Missouri; born near Gallatin, Daviess County, Mo., February 11, 1845; attended the common schools and Macon Academy, Macon, Mo.; studied medicine; was graduated from the St. Louis (Mo.) Medical College March 2, 1865, and commenced practice near Linneus, Linn County; attended lectures at Bellevue College, New York City, and Jefferson Medical College, Philadelphia, during the winter of 1865-1866; returned to Missouri and settled in Chillicothe, where he continued the practice of his profession for seven years; president of the board of education of Chillicothe, Mo., 1870-1872; served as county physician of Livingston County; in March 1874 returned to Gallatin, Mo., where he assisted in organizing the Farmers' Exchange Bank; chairman of the congressional committee of his district; member of the city council of Gallatin 1878-1881; mayor 1881-1883; delegate to and chairman of the Democratic State conventions in 1886 and 1901; elected as a Democrat to the Forty-eighth and to the seven succeeding Congresses (March 4, 1883-March 3, 1899); chairman, Committee on Expenditures in the Post Office Department (Fiftieth Congress); was not a candidate for renomination in 1898 to the Fifty-sixth Congress; elected Governor of Missouri in 1900, and served from January 14, 1901 to January 9, 1905; delegate to the Democratic National Convention of 1904; appointed Third Assistant Postmaster General on March 17, 1913, and served until his resignation on March 31, 1921; died in Gallatin, Mo., December 26, 1926; interment in Edgewood Cemetery, Chillicothe, Livingston County, Mo.

**DOCKERY, Alfred** (father of Oliver Hart Dockery), a Representative from North Carolina; born near Rockingham, Richmond County, N.C., December 11, 1797; attended the public schools; engaged in planting; member of the State house of commons in 1822; member of the State constitutional convention in 1835; served in the State senate 1836-1844; elected as a Whig to the Twenty-ninth Congress (March 4, 1845-March 3, 1847); declined to be a candidate for reelection in 1846 to the Thirtieth Congress; elected to the Thirty-second Congress (March 4, 1851-March 3, 1853); unsuccessful Whig candidate for Governor of North Carolina in 1854; died near Rockingham, Richmond County, N.C., on December 7, 1875; interment in the family cemetery.

**DOCKERY, Oliver Hart** (son of Alfred Dockery), a Representative from North Carolina; born near Rockingham, Richmond County, N.C., August 12, 1830; attended the public schools and Wake Forest (N.C.) College; was graduated from the University of North Carolina at Chapel Hill in 1848; studied law, but never practiced; engaged in agricultural pursuits; member of the State house of representatives in 1858 and 1859; served for a short time in the Confederate service, but withdrew and advocated sustaining the Federal Government; upon the readmission of North Carolina to representation was elected as a Republican to the Fortieth Congress; reelected to the Forty-first Congress and served from July 13, 1868, to March 3, 1871; chairman, Committee on the Freedmen's Bureau (Forty-first Congress); unsuccessful candidate for reelection in 1870 to the Forty-second Congress; again engaged in agricultural pursuits; member of the State constitutional convention in 1875; unsuccessful candidate for Governor in 1888; appointed United States consul general at Rio de Janeiro, Brazil, on June 14, 1889, and served until July 1, 1893; resumed agricultural pursuits; died in Baltimore, Md., March 21, 1906; interment in the family cemetery at Mangum, Richmond County, N.C.

**DOCKWEILER, John Francis,** a Representative from California; born in Los Angeles on September 19, 1895; attended parochial schools; was graduated from Loyola College, Los Angeles in 1918 and from the University of Southern California, Los Angeles in 1921; attended the law department of Harvard University; was admitted to the bar September 6, 1921, and commenced practice in Los Angeles in 1922; elected as a Democrat to the Seventy-third, Seventy-fourth, and Seventy-fifth Congresses (March 4, 1933-January 3, 1939); was not a candidate in 1938 for renomination to the Seventy-sixth Congress, but was an unsuccessful candidate for nomination for Governor; unsuccessful Independent candidate in 1938 for reelection to the Seventy-sixth Congress; resumed the practice of law; district attorney of Los Angeles County, 1940-1943; died in Los Angeles, Calif., January 31, 1943; interment in Calvary Cemetery.

**DODD, Christopher John** (son of Thomas Joseph Dodd), a Representative and a Senator from Connecticut; born in Willimantic, Windham County, Conn., May 27, 1944; graduated from Georgetown Preparatory School, Potomac, Md., 1962; B.A., Providence (R.I.) College, 1966; J.D., University of Louisville (Ky.) School of Law, 1972; served as a Peace Corps volunteer in the Dominican Republic from 1966 until 1968; admitted to the Connecticut bar in 1973 and commenced practice in New London; served in the United States Army, 1969-1975; elected as a Democrat to the Ninety-fourth and to the two succeeding Congresses (January 3, 1975-January 3,

1981); was not a candidate in 1980 for reelection to the House of Representatives, but was elected to the United States Senate for the term commencing January 3, 1981; reelected in 1986 and again in 1992 for the term ending January 3, 1999; general chairman, Democratic National Committee, January 1995 to present; is a resident of East Haddam, Conn.

**DODD, Edward,** a Representative from New York; born in Salem, Washington County, N.Y., August 25, 1805; attended the public schools; engaged in mercantile pursuits; moved to Argyle, N.Y., in 1835; county clerk of Washington County 1835-1844; delegate to the State constitutional convention in 1846; elected as a Whig to the Thirty-fourth Congress and reelected as a Republican to the Thirty-fifth Congress (March 4, 1855-March 3, 1859); chairman, Committee on District of Columbia (Thirty-fourth Congress); United States marshal for the northern district of New York from April 1863 to April 1869; editor of the County Post for thirty years; trustee of the Argyle Academy for fifty-one years; president of the village of Argyle for eight years; member of the Republican State committee for many years; died in Argyle, N.Y., March 1, 1891; interment in Prospect Hill Cemetery.

**DODD, Thomas Joseph** (father of Christopher John Dodd), a Representative and a Senator from Connecticut; born in Norwich, New London County, Conn., May 15, 1907; attended the public schools; graduated from St. Anselm's Preparatory School in 1926, Providence College in 1930, and Yale University Law School in 1933; special agent for Federal Bureau of Investigation, 1933-1934; Connecticut director of National Youth Administration, 1935-1938; assistant to five successive United States Attorneys General, 1938-1945; vice chairman, Board of Review, and later executive trial counsel, Office of the United States Chief of Counsel for the Prosecution of Axis Criminality at Nuremberg, Germany, in 1945 and 1946; engaged in private practice of law in Hartford, Conn., 1947-1953; elected as a Democrat to the Eighty-third and Eighty-fourth Congresses (January 3, 1953-January 3, 1957); declined to be a candidate for renomination in 1956 to the House of Representatives, but was an unsuccessful candidate for election to the United States Senate; elected as a Democrat to the United States Senate in 1958; reelected in 1964 and served from January 3, 1959, to January 2, 1971; unsuccessful candidate for reelection in 1970; censured by the Senate on June 23, 1967 for financial misconduct; was a resident of Old Lyme, Conn., until his death there, May 24, 1971; interment in St. Michael's New Cemetery, Pawcatuck, Conn.

Bibliography: Dodd, Thomas J. *Freedom and Foreign Policy.* New York: Bookmailer, 1962.

**DODDRIDGE, Philip,** a Representative from Virginia; born in Bedford County, Va., May 17, 1773; reared on a farm; moved to Brooke County, Va. (now West Virginia); attended school in Wellsburg (then Charleston), Va. (now West Virginia); studied law and was admitted to the bar in 1797; member of the Virginia senate, 1804-1809; member of the house of delegates of Virginia in 1815, 1816, 1822, 1823, 1828, and 1829; delegate to the Virginia constitutional convention in 1829; unsuccessful candidate for election in 1822 to the Eighteenth Congress, and in 1824 to the Nineteenth Congress; elected to the Twenty-first and Twenty-second Congresses, and served from March 4, 1829 until his death in Washington, D.C., November 19, 1832; chairman, Committee on District of Columbia (Twenty-first and Twenty-second Congresses); interment in the Congressional Cemetery.

Bibliography: *DAB*; Willey, Waitman Thomas. *A Sketch of the Life of Philip Doddridge.* Morgantown, W.Va.: Morgan and Hoffman, Printers, 1875.

**DODDS, Francis Henry,** a Representative from Michigan; born on a farm near Waddington, Louisville Township, St. Lawrence County, N.Y., June 9, 1858; attended the local schools; moved with his parents to Isabella County, Mich., in 1866; was graduated from Olivet (Mich.) College; taught school at Farwell and Mount Pleasant; was graduated from the law department of the University of Michigan at Ann Arbor in 1880; was admitted to the bar the same year and commenced the practice of law at Mount Pleasant, Mich.; served as city attorney of Mount Pleasant 1892-1894; member of the board of education 1894-1897; elected as a Republican to the Sixty-first and Sixty-second Congresses (March 4, 1909-March 3, 1913); unsuccessful candidate for renomination in 1912; resumed the practice of law in Mount Pleasant, Mich., until his death in that city on December 23, 1940; interment in Riverside Cemetery.

**DODDS, Ozro John,** a Representative from Ohio; born in Cincinnati, Ohio, March 22, 1840; attended the common schools, and Miami University, Oxford, Ohio, for four years; organized Captain Dodd's university company and enlisted on April 18, 1861, as captain of Company B, Twentieth Ohio Volunteer Regiment; captain of Company F, Eighty-first Ohio Volunteer Infantry from September 1, 1861, to January 1, 1863; became lieutenant colonel of the First Alabama Union Cavalry October 18, 1863; at the close of the war was given his degree from Miami University; studied law at Cincinnati Law School; was admitted to the bar in 1866 and commenced practice in Cincinnati; member of the State house of representatives in 1870 and 1871; elected as a Democrat to the Forty-second Congress to fill the vacancy caused by the resignation of Aaron F. Perry and served from October 8, 1872, to March 3, 1873; was not a candidate for renomination in 1872; resumed the practice of law at Cincinnati; died in Columbus, Ohio, April 18, 1882; interment in Spring Grove Cemetery, Cincinnati, Ohio.

**DODGE, Augustus Caesar** (son of Henry Dodge), a Delegate and a Senator from Iowa; born in Ste. Genevieve, Mo., January 2, 1812; self-educated; moved to Illinois in 1827, settled in Galena, and was employed there in various capacities in his father's lead mines; served in the Black Hawk and other Indian wars; moved to Burlington, Iowa, in 1837, where he served as register of the land office 1838-1840; elected as a Democratic Delegate to the Twenty-sixth Congress to fill the vacancy caused by the act of March 3, 1839; reelected to the Twenty-seventh and to the two succeeding Congresses and served from October 28, 1840, to December 28, 1846, when the Territory of Iowa was admitted as a State into the Union; was then elected as a Democrat to the United States Senate; reelected in 1849, and served from December 7, 1848, to February 22, 1855, when he resigned to accept a diplomatic post; chairman, Committee to Audit and Control the Contingent Expense (Thirty-first and Thirty-second Congresses), Committee on Pensions (Thirty-first Congress), Committee on Revolutionary Claims (Thirty-second Congress), Committee on Public Lands (Thirty-third Congress); appointed Minister to Spain on February 9, 1855 and served until March 1859; unsuccessful candidate for Governor of Iowa in 1859; mayor of Burlington 1874-1875; withdrew from political activities and engaged in lecturing at pioneer gatherings; died in Burlington, Des Moines County, Iowa, November 20, 1883; interment in Aspen Grove Cemetery.

Bibliography: *DAB*; Pelzer, Louis. *Augustus Caesar Dodge.* Iowa City: The State Historical Society of Iowa, 1908.

**DODGE, Grenville Mellen,** a Representative from Iowa; born in Danvers, Essex County, Mass., April 12, 1831; attended the Danvers public schools and Durham Academy, New Hampshire; was graduated as a civil engineer from Norwich University, Vermont, in 1851; moved to Iowa and settled in Council Bluffs; member of the city council of Council Bluffs in 1860; entered the Union Army as colonel of the Fourth Iowa Volunteer Infantry on July 6, 1861; promoted to brigadier general of Volunteers March 21, 1862, and major general June 7, 1864; resigned from the Army May 30, 1866; chief engineer of the Union Pacific Railroad 1866-1870; elected as a Republican to the Fortieth Congress (March 4, 1867-March 3, 1869); declined to be a candidate for renomination in 1868; delegate to the Republican National Convention in 1868, 1872, and 1876; settled in New York City; president of the commission to inquire into the management of the war with Spain; died in Council Bluffs, Iowa, January 3, 1916; interment in Walnut Hill Cemetery.

**Bibliography:** *DAB*; Farnham, Wallace D. "Grenville Dodge and the Union Pacific: A Study of Historical Legends." *Journal of American History* 51 (March 1965): 632-50; Hirshon, Stanley P. *Grenville M. Dodge: Soldier, Politician, Railroad Pioneer.* Bloomington: Indiana University Press, 1967.

**DODGE, Henry** (father of Augustus Caesar Dodge), a Delegate and a Senator from Wisconsin; born in Vincennes, Ind., October 12, 1782; received a limited schooling; moved to Missouri in 1796 and settled at Ste. Genevieve; sheriff of Cape Girardeau County in 1808; moved to Galena, Ill., and operated a lead mine; moved to Wisconsin in 1827, then part of Michigan Territory, and settled near the present site of Dodgeville; served in the Black Hawk and other Indian wars; was commissioned major of United States Rangers in 1832; left the Army as colonel of the First United States Dragoons, 1836; appointed Governor of the Territory of Wisconsin by President Andrew Jackson on April 30, 1836 and served until 1841; elected as a Democrat a Delegate to the Twenty-seventh and Twenty-eighth Congresses (March 4, 1841-March 3, 1845); was not a candidate for renomination in 1844 to the Twenty-ninth Congress, having accepted the appointment of Governor of the Territory of Wisconsin from President James K. Polk, and served from April 8, 1845 until the admission of Wisconsin as a State into the Union in 1848; elected in 1848 as a Democrat to the United States Senate; reelected in 1851 and served from June 8, 1848, to March 3, 1857; chairman, Committee on Commerce (Thirty-fourth Congress); declined the appointment of Governor of Washington Territory by President Franklin Pierce in 1857; retired to private life; died in Burlington, Des Moines County, Iowa, June 19, 1867; interment in Aspen Grove Cemetery.

**Bibliography:** *DAB*; Clark, James I. *Henry Dodge, Frontiersman; First Governor of Wisconsin Territory.* Madison: State Historical Society of Wisconsin, 1957; Pelzer, Louis. *Henry Dodge.* Iowa City: The State Historical Society of Iowa, 1911.

**DODGE, William Earle,** a Representative from New York; born in Hartford, Conn., September 4, 1805; completed preparatory studies; moved to New York City in 1818; became a clerk; in 1826 established the house of Phelps, Dodge & Co., of which he was the head for forty years; delegate to the peace convention of 1861 held in Washington, D.C., in an effort to devise means to prevent the impending war; successfully contested as a Republican the election of James Brooks to the Thirty-ninth Congress and served from April 7, 1866, to March 3, 1867; declined to be a candidate for renomination in 1866; resumed business interests; died in New York City February 9, 1883; interment in Woodlawn Cemetery.

**Bibliography:** *DAB*; Lowitt, Richard. *A Merchant Prince of the Nineteenth Century: William E. Dodge.* New York: Columbia University Press, 1954.

**DOE, Nicholas Bartlett,** a Representative from New York; born in New York City on June 16, 1786; was graduated from Phillips Exeter Academy, Exeter, N.H.; studied law; was admitted to the bar and practiced; settled in Saratoga County, N.Y.; elected as a Whig to the Twenty-sixth Congress to fill the vacancy caused by the death of Anson Brown; took his seat on December 7, 1840, and served until March 3, 1841; resumed the practice of law; trustee of the village of Waterford, Saratoga County, in 1841; died at Saratoga Springs, N.Y., December 6, 1856; interment in Greenridge Cemetery.

**DOGGETT, Lloyd Alton, II,** a Representative from Texas; born in Austin, Travis County, Tex., October 6, 1946; graduated, Austin High School; B.A., University of Texas, Austin, 1967; J.D., University of Texas School of Law, 1970; member, Texas State senate, 1973-1989; unsuccessful candidate in 1984 for election to the United States Senate; justice, Texas State supreme court, 1989-1994; adjunct professor, University of Texas School of Law; elected as a Democrat to the One Hundred Fourth Congress (January 3, 1995-January 3, 1997); is a resident of Austin, Tex.

**DOIG, Andrew Wheeler,** a Representative from New York; born in Salem, Washington County, N.Y., July 24, 1799; pursued an academic course; moved to Lowville, N.Y., and engaged in mercantile pursuits; town clerk of Lowville in 1825; county clerk of Lewis County 1825-1831; member of the State assembly in 1832; moved to Martinsburg, N.Y., in 1833; cashier of the Lewis County Bank in 1833 and 1834; returned to Lowville; surrogate of Lewis County 1835-1840; elected as a Democrat to the Twenty-sixth and Twenty-seventh Congresses (March 4, 1839-March 3, 1843); member of the board of directors and vice president of the Bank of Lowville 1843-1847; moved to California in 1849 and engaged in mining; returned in 1850 to Lowville, N.Y., where he resided until late in life; clerk in the customhouse, New York City, 1853-1857; died in Brooklyn, N.Y., July 11, 1875; interment in the Rural Cemetery, Lowville, N.Y.

**DOLE, Robert Joseph,** a Representative and a Senator from Kansas; born in Russell, Kans., July 22, 1923; attended Kansas University, 1941-1943, and the University of Arizona, 1948-1949; A.B., Washburn Municipal University, Topeka, Kans., 1952, LL.B., 1952; entered active duty, U.S. Army in 1943; during the Second World War served as a combat infantry officer in Italy; was wounded in April 1945 and hospitalized for thirty-nine months; admitted to the Kansas bar and commenced the practice of law in Russell, Kans., 1952; member, Kansas State house of representatives, 1951-1953; county attorney of Russell County from 1953 to 1961; elected as a Republican to the Eighty-seventh and to the three succeeding Congresses (January 3, 1961-January 3, 1969); unsuccessful Republican candidate for Vice President of the United States in 1976 on the ticket headed by President Gerald R. Ford; elected to the United States Senate in 1968; reelected in 1974, 1980, 1986 and again in 1992, and served from January 3, 1969 until his resignation on June 11, 1996; chairman, Committee on Finance (Ninety-seventh and Ninety-eighth Congresses), Special Committee on Security and Cooperation in Europe (Ninety-ninth Congress), minority leader (One Hundredth through One Hundred Third Congresses), majority leader (Ninety-ninth Congress, One Hundred Fourth Congress); unsuccessful candidate for the Republican presidential nomination in 1980 and 1988; Republican presidential nominee in 1996; is a resident of Russell, Kans.

**Bibliography:** Cramer, Richard Ben. *Bob Dole.* New York: Vintage Books, 1995; Thompson, Jake H. *Bob Dole: The Republicans' Man For All Seasons.* New York: D.I. Fine Books, 1996.

**DOLLINGER, Isidore,** a Representative from New York; born in New York City, November 13, 1903; BC.S., New York University, 1925; LL.B., New York Law School, 1928; was admitted to the bar in 1929 and commenced practice in New York City; served in the New York State assembly from 1937 to 1944; member of the New York State senate, 1945-1948; elected as a Democrat to the Eighty-first and to the five succeeding Congresses and served from January 3, 1949, until his resignation December 31, 1959; delegate to the Democratic National Conventions of 1956 and 1960; elected district attorney of Bronx County, N.Y., in November 1959 and took office January 1, 1960, for a four-year term; reelected district attorney in November 1963 and again in November 1967; resigned in 1968 when elected a justice of the New York State supreme court, First

Judicial District, and served from January 1, 1969, to December 31, 1975; is a resident of New York City.

**DOLLIVER, James Isaac** (nephew of Jonathan Prentiss Dolliver), a Representative from Iowa; born in Park Ridge, Cook County, Ill., August 31, 1894; attended the public schools in Hot Springs, S.Dak.; was graduated from Morningside College, Sioux City, Iowa, in 1915; taught school at Alta and Humboldt, Iowa, 1915-1917; during the First World War served in the United States Army as a private in the Third Service Company of the Signal Corps; was graduated from the University of Chicago Law School in 1921; was admitted to the bar the same year and commenced practice in Chicago; moved to Fort Dodge, Webster County, Iowa, in 1922; prosecuting attorney of Webster County, 1924-1929; member of the school board of Fort Dodge Independent School District 1938-1945; elected as a Republican to the Seventy-ninth and to the five succeeding Congresses (January 3, 1945-January 3, 1957); unsuccessful candidate for reelection in 1956 to the Eighty-fifth Congress; served as regional legal counsel for International Cooperation Administration in the Middle East, 1957-1959; retired in 1959; resided in Spirit Lake, Iowa; died in Rolla, Mo., December 10, 1978; interment in Oakland Cemetery, Fort Dodge, Iowa.

**DOLLIVER, Jonathan Prentiss** (uncle of James Isaac Dolliver), a Representative and a Senator from Iowa; born near Kingwood, Preston County, Va. (now West Virginia), February 6, 1858; attended the public schools and was graduated from the University of West Virginia at Morgantown in 1876; studied law; was admitted to the bar in 1878 and commenced practice in Fort Dodge, Iowa; city solicitor of Fort Dodge 1880-1887; elected as a Republican to the Fifty-first and to the five succeeding Congresses and served from March 4, 1889, to August 22, 1900, when he resigned to become Senator; chairman, Committee on Expenditures (Fifty-sixth Congress); appointed as a Republican to the United States Senate in 1900 to fill the vacancy in the term ending March 3, 1901, caused by the death of John H. Gear; reappointed and subsequently elected for the term beginning March 4, 1901; reelected in 1907 and served from August 22, 1900, until his death in Fort Dodge, Iowa, October 15, 1910; chairman, Committee on Pacific Railroads (Fifty-seventh through Fifty-ninth Congresses), Committee on Education and Labor (Fifty-ninth and Sixtieth Congresses), Committee on Agriculture and Forestry (Sixty-first Congress); interment in Oakland Cemetery.

**Bibliography:** *DAB*; Ross, Thomas R. *Jonathan Prentiss Dolliver: A Study in Political Integrity and Independence.* Iowa City: The State Historical Society of Iowa, 1958.

**DOLPH, Joseph Norton** (uncle of Frederick William Mulkey), a Senator from Oregon; born in Dolphsburg, Tompkins (now Schuyler) County, N.Y., October 19, 1835; attended the common schools and the Genesee Wesleyan Seminary, Lima, N.Y.; taught school and studied law; was admitted to the bar in Binghamton, N.Y., in 1861 and commenced practice in Schuyler County, N.Y.; in 1862 enlisted in the "Oregon Escort," a company raised under an act of Congress for the purpose of protecting emigrants crossing the Plains to the Pacific coast against hostile Indians; settled in Portland, Oreg., in 1862; city attorney 1864-1865; United States district attorney 1865-1868; member, State senate 1866, 1868, 1872, 1874; engaged in various enterprises; elected as a Republican to the United States Senate in 1882; reelected in 1888 and served from March 4, 1883, to March 3, 1895; unsuccessful candidate for reelection in 1894; chairman, Committee on Coast Defenses (Forty-ninth through Fifty-second Congresses), Committee on Public Lands (Fifty-second Congress); resumed the practice of law in Portland, Oreg., where he died on March 10, 1897; interment in Riverview Cemetery.

**Bibliography:** *DAB*.

**DOMENGEAUX, James,** a Representative from Louisiana; born in Lafayette, Lafayette Parish, La., January 6, 1907; attended Mount Carmel Academy, Cathedral High School, Southwestern Louisiana Institute at Lafayette, and Loyola University, New Orleans, La.; was graduated from the law department of Tulane University, New Orleans, La., in 1931; was admitted to the bar the same year and commenced practice in Lafayette, La.; member of the State house of representatives in 1940; elected as a Democrat to the Seventy-seventh Congress; reelected to the Seventy-eighth Congress and served from January 3, 1941, to April 15, 1944, when he resigned to join the armed forces of the United States; served as a private in the Combat Engineers until his medical discharge; was subsequently elected to fill the vacancy in the Seventy-eighth Congress caused by his own resignation; reelected to the Seventy-ninth and Eightieth Congresses and served from November 7, 1944, to January 3, 1949; chairman, Committee on Elections No. 1 (Seventy-eighth and Seventy-ninth Congresses); was not a candidate for renomination in 1948, but was an unsuccessful candidate for the Democratic nomination for United States Senator; resumed the practice of law; founder, Council for the Development of French in Louisiana, 1968; member, Governor's Committee on Tidelands; was a resident of Lafayette, La., until his death there on April 11, 1988; interment in St. John's Cemetery.

**DOMENICI, Pete Vichi,** a Senator from New Mexico; born in Albuquerque, Bernalillo County, N.Mex., May 7, 1932; graduated St. Mary's High School; B.S., University of New Mexico, 1954; LL.B., Denver University Law School, 1958; admitted to the New Mexico bar in 1958 and commenced practice in Albuquerque; elected to Albuquerque City Commission in 1966, and served as chairman (ex-officio mayor) in 1967; appointed to Governor's Policy Board for Law Enforcement and Middle Rio Grande Conference of Governments, 1968-1969; unsuccessful candidate in 1970 for election for Governor of New Mexico; elected as a Republican to the United States Senate in 1972 for the term commencing January 3, 1973; reelected in 1978, 1984, and again in 1990 for the term ending January 3, 1997; chairman, Committee on the Budget (Ninety-seventh through Ninety-ninth Congresses; One Hundred Fourth Congress); is a resident of Albuquerque, N.M.

**DOMINICK, Frederick Haskell,** a Representative from South Carolina; born in Peak, Newberry County, S.C., February 20, 1877; attended the public schools of Columbia, Newberry (S.C.) College, South Carolina College at Columbia, and the law school of the University of Virginia at Charlottesville; was admitted to the bar in 1898 and commenced practice in Newberry, S.C.; member of the State house of representatives 1901-1902; chairman of the Democratic county committee 1906-1914; assistant attorney general of South Carolina 1913-1916; delegate to the Democratic National Conventions of 1920 and 1924; elected as a Democrat to the Sixty-fifth and to the seven succeeding Congresses (March 4, 1917-March 3, 1933); unsuccessful candidate for renomination in 1932; one of the managers appointed by the House of Representatives in 1926 to conduct the impeachment proceedings against George W. English, judge of the United States District Court for the Eastern District of Illinois; during the Second World War served as assistant to the Attorney General, Department of Justice, Washington, D.C.; practiced law in Newberry, S.C., until his death there March 11, 1960; interment in Rosemont Cemetery.

**DOMINICK, Peter Hoyt** (nephew of Howard Alexander Smith), a Representative and a Senator from Colorado; born in Stamford, Fairfield County, Conn., July 7, 1915; attended public schools; graduated from St. Mark's School, Southborough, Mass., in 1933; A.B., Yale University, 1937; LL.B, Yale University Law School, 1940; during the Second World War entered the Army Air Corps in 1942 as an aviation cadet, and served until 1945 when he was discharged as a captain; engaged in law practice in New York City in 1940-1942 and in early 1946, and in Denver, Colo., 1946-1961; member, Colorado State house of representatives, 1957-1961; member of the National Commission for the United Nations Educational, Scientific, and Cultural Organization, 1960-1961; elected as a Republican to the Eighty-seventh Congress (January 3, 1961-January 3, 1963); was not a candidate in 1962 for reelection to the House of Representatives, but was elected to the United States Senate; reelected in 1968, and served from January 3, 1963 to January 2, 1975; unsuccessful candidate for reelection in 1974; appointed Ambassador to Switzerland on February 20, 1975, and served until July of that year; resided in Cherry Hills, Colo., until his death in Hobe Sound, Fla., March 18, 1981; interment in Fairmount Cemetery, Denver, Colo.

**DONAHEY, Alvin Victor,** a Senator from Ohio; born in Cadwallader, Tuscarawas County, Ohio, July 7, 1873; attended the public schools; learned the printer's trade; employed as a journeyman at New Philadelphia, Ohio, 1893-1905; clerk of Goshen Township, Tuscarawas County, Ohio, 1898-1903; county auditor from 1905 until 1909; member of the board of education of New Philadelphia, 1909-1911; delegate to the fourth Ohio constitutional convention in 1912; Ohio State auditor in 1912; unsuccessful candidate in 1920 for election for Governor; elected Governor of Ohio in 1922, reelected in 1924 and 1926, and served from January 8, 1923 to January 14, 1929; elected as a Democrat to the United States Senate in 1934 and served from January 3, 1935, to January 3, 1941; was not a candidate for renomination in 1940; engaged in the insurance business and in the manufacture of clay products in Columbus, Ohio; was also interested in banking; died in Columbus, Ohio, April 8, 1946; interment in East Avenue Cemetery, New Philadelphia, Ohio.

**DONDERO, George Anthony,** a Representative from Michigan; born in Greenfield Township, Wayne County, Mich., on December 16, 1883; attended the public schools; served as village clerk of Royal Oak in 1905 and 1906, as town treasurer in 1907 and 1908, and as village assessor in 1909; was graduated from the Detroit College of Law, Detroit, Mich., in 1910; was admitted to the bar the same year and commenced practice in Royal Oak, Mich.; village attorney 1911-1921; assistant prosecuting attorney for Oakland County, Mich., in 1918 and 1919; mayor of Royal Oak in 1921 and 1922; member of the board of education 1910-1928; elected as a Republican to the Seventy-third and to the eleven succeeding Congresses (March 4, 1933-January 3, 1957); chairman, Committee on Public Works (Eightieth and Eighty-third Congresses); was not a candidate for renomination in 1956; resumed the practice of law; died in Royal Oak, Mich., January 29, 1968; interment in Oakview Cemetery.

**DONLEY, Joseph Benton,** a Representative from Pennsylvania; born in Mount Morris, Greene County, Pa., on October 10, 1838; completed preparatory studies; was graduated from Waynesburg (Pa.) College in 1859; member of the faculty of Abingdon (Ill.) College 1860-1862; entered the Union Army as a captain in the Eighty-third Regiment, Illinois Volunteer Infantry, in 1862 and served throughout the war; was graduated from the Albany (N.Y.) Law School in 1866; was admitted to the bar in 1867 and commenced practice in Waynesburg, Pa.; referee in bankruptcy in 1867 and 1868; elected as a Republican to the Forty-first Congress (March 4, 1869-March 3, 1871); unsuccessful candidate for reelection in 1870 to the Forty-second Congress; resumed the practice of his profession in Waynesburg, Pa., and died there January 23, 1917; interment in Green Mount Cemetery.

**DONNAN, William G.,** a Representative from Iowa; born in West Charlton, N.Y., June 30, 1834; attended the district schools and Cambridge Academy; was graduated from Union College, New York, in 1856; moved to Independence, Iowa, in 1856; studied law; was admitted to the bar in 1856 and commenced practice at

Independence in 1857; served as treasurer and recorder of Buchanan County from 1857 until 1862; entered the Union Army as a private in Company H, Twenty-seventh Iowa Infantry, in 1862; promoted to the grade of first lieutenant and brevetted captain and major; was adjutant on the staff of General James J. Gilbert; member of the Iowa State senate in 1868 and 1870; elected as a Republican to the Forty-second and Forty-third Congresses (March 4, 1871-March 3, 1875); declined to be a candidate for reelection in 1874 to the Forty-fourth Congress; resumed the practice of law at Independence; delegate at large to the Republican National Convention of 1884; chairman of the Republican State central committee, 1884-1886; again a member of the State senate, 1884-1886; died in Independence, Buchanan County, Iowa, December 4, 1908; interment in Oakwood Cemetery.

**DONNELL, Forrest C.,** a Senator from Missouri; born in Quitman, Nodaway County, Mo., August 20, 1884; attended the public schools; was graduated from the University of Missouri at Columbia in 1904 and from its law school in 1907; was admitted to the bar in 1907 and commenced practice in St. Louis, Mo.; city attorney of Webster Groves, Mo.; elected Governor of Missouri in 1940, and served from January 13, 1941 to January 8, 1945; elected as a Republican to the United States Senate, and served from January 3, 1945 to January 3, 1951; was an unsuccessful candidate for reelection in 1950; resumed the practice of law in St. Louis, Mo., where he died on March 3, 1980; interment in Bellefontaine Cemetery.

**Bibliography:** *DAB.*

**DONNELL, Richard Spaight** (grandson of Richard Dobbs Spaight), a Representative from North Carolina; born in New Bern, N.C., September 20, 1820; attended New Bern Academy and Yale College; was graduated from the University of North Carolina at Chapel Hill in 1839; studied law; was admitted to the bar in 1840 and commenced practice in New Bern, N.C.; elected as a Whig to the Thirtieth Congress (March 4, 1847-March 3, 1849); was not a candidate for renomination in 1848 to the Thirty-first Congress; resumed the practice of law in Washington, N.C.; delegate to the State secession convention in 1861 and to the State constitutional convention in 1865; member of the State house of commons in 1862 and 1864, and served as speaker; died in New Bern, N.C., June 3, 1867; interment in Cedar Grove Cemetery.

**DONNELLY, Brian Joseph,** a Representative from Massachusetts; born in Boston, Mass., March 2, 1946; attended private schools in Suffolk County; graduated from Catholic Memorial High School, West Roxbury, 1963; B.S., Boston University, 1970; engaged in graduate work at Boston University, 1970; teacher and coach, Boston public schools, 1970-1972; member, Massachusetts legislature, 1973-1978; served as assistant majority leader, 1977-1978; elected as a Democrat to the Ninety-sixth and to the six succeeding Congresses (January 3, 1979-January 3, 1993); was not a candidate for reelection in 1992 to the One Hundred Third Congress; nominated as alternate representative to the Forty-eighth session of the United Nations General Assembly, October 29, 1993; nominated as Ambassador to Trinidad and Tobago on June 9, 1994 and was confirmed by the Senate on June 30, 1994; is a resident of Boston, Mass.

**DONNELLY, Ignatius,** a Representative from Minnesota; born in Philadelphia, Pa., November 3, 1831; attended the public schools; studied law; was admitted to the bar in 1852 and commenced practice in Philadelphia; moved to Minnesota in 1857 and settled in Nininger, Dakota County; engaged in literary pursuits; lieutenant governor of Minnesota, 1859-1863; elected as a Republican to the Thirty-eighth and to the two succeeding Congresses (March 4, 1863-March 3, 1869); unsuccessful candidate for reelection in 1868 to the Forty-first Congress, and for election in 1870 to the Forty-second Congress; member of the Minnesota State senate,

1874-1878; resumed the practice of law; also engaged in literary pursuits; unsuccessful candidate in 1900 for Vice President of the United States on the People's (Populist) Party ticket headed by Wharton Barker; died in Minneapolis, Minn., January 1, 1901; interment in Calvary Cemetery, St. Paul, Minn.

**Bibliography:** *DAB*; Hicks, John D. "The Political Career of Ignatius Donnelly." *Mississippi Valley Historical Review* 8 (June-September 1921): 80-132; Ridge, Martin. *Ignatius Donnelly: The Portrait of a Politician.* 1962. Reprint. St. Paul: Minnesota Historical Society Press, 1991.

**DONOHOE, Michael,** a Representative from Pennsylvania; born in Killeshandra, County Cavan, Ireland, February 22, 1864; attended the schools of Ireland and a private classical school; taught as principal of a national school from January 1885 until October 1886; immigrated to the United States and settled in Philadelphia, Pa., November 8, 1886; real-estate broker; engaged in banking and in the manufacture of glassware; elected as a Democrat to the Sixty-second and Sixty-third Congresses (March 4, 1911-March 3, 1915); unsuccessful candidate for reelection in 1914 to the Sixty-fourth Congress; director of Northwestern General Hospital 1893-1943; trustee of Temple University; real-estate assessor for the city of Philadelphia from April 15, 1919, to March 31, 1946, when he retired; died in Philadelphia, Pa., January 17, 1958; interment in Holy Sepulchre Cemetery.

**DONOHUE, Harold Daniel,** a Representative from Massachusetts; born in Worcester, Mass., June 18, 1901; attended the public schools; was graduated from Northeastern University School of Law, Worcester, Mass., in 1925; was admitted to the bar in February 1926 and commenced practice in Worcester, Mass.; councilman and alderman of Worcester, Mass., from January 1927 to December 1935; served with the United States Navy from December 1942 until December 1945, when he was separated from the service with the rank of lieutenant commander; elected as a Democrat to the Eightieth Congress; reelected to the thirteen succeeding Congresses and served from January 3, 1947, until his resignation December 31, 1974; was not a candidate for reelection in 1974 to the Ninety-fourth Congress; resided in Worcester, Mass., until his death November 4, 1984.

**DONOVAN, Dennis D.,** a Representative from Ohio; born near Texas, Henry County, Ohio, January 31, 1859; attended the common schools, and Northern Indiana Normal School, Valparaiso, Ind.; taught school; engaged in the mercantile and timber business; was graduated from the law department of Georgetown University, Washington, D.C., in 1895; was admitted to the bar the same year and commenced practice in Deshler, Ohio; appointed postmaster of Deshler by President Grover Cleveland on July 21, 1885, and served until January 27, 1888; member of the State house of representatives in 1887 and 1889; elected as a Democrat to the Fifty-second and Fifty-third Congresses (March 4, 1891-March 3, 1895); unsuccessful candidate for renomination in 1894 to the Fifty-fourth Congress; resumed the practice of law in Deshler, Ohio; moved to Napoleon, Henry County, Ohio, in 1897 and continued the practice of law; unsuccessful candidate for nomination for Governor of Ohio in 1898; died in Napoleon, Ohio, on April 21, 1941; interment in St. Augustine Cemetery.

**DONOVAN, James George,** a Representative from New York; born in Clinton, Worcester County, Mass., December 15, 1898, attended Massachusetts Institute of Technology at Cambridge in 1916 and 1917; during the First World War served in the United States Navy as a seaman in 1918; attended Harvard University, 1919-1921, and was graduated from the law school of Columbia University, New York City, in 1924; was admitted to the Massachusetts bar in 1923 and the New York bar in 1925; commenced the practice of law in New York City in 1925; under-sheriff of New York County 1934-1941; member of the State senate in 1943 and 1944;

elected as a Democrat to the Eighty-second, Eighty-third, and Eighty-fourth Congresses (January 3, 1951-January 3, 1957); unsuccessful candidate for reelection in 1956 to the Eighty-fifth Congress; resumed the practice of law; New York State Director, Federal Housing Administration, 1957; was a resident of New York City until his death there on April 6, 1987; interment in Woodlawn Cemetery.

**DONOVAN, Jeremiah,** a Representative from Connecticut; born in Ridgefield, Fairfield County, Conn., October 18, 1857; attended the public schools and was graduated from Ridgefield Academy; moved to South Norwalk in 1870 and engaged in the retail liquor business until 1898 when he retired; member of the city council; served as deputy sheriff; delegate to all Democratic National Conventions from 1896 to 1916, inclusive; member of the State house of representatives in 1903 and 1904; served in the State senate 1905-1909; elected as a Democrat to the Sixty-third Congress (March 4, 1913-March 3, 1915); unsuccessful candidate for reelection in 1914 to the Sixty-fourth Congress; mayor of the city of Norwalk, Conn., 1917-1921; retired from active pursuits; died in Norwalk, Conn., April 22, 1935; interment in St. John's Cemetery.

**DONOVAN, Jerome Francis,** a Representative from New York; born in New Haven Conn., February 1, 1872; attended the public schools; was graduated from the law department of Yale University in 1894; was admitted to the bar the same year and commenced practice in New Haven; captain of Company C, Second Regiment of the Connecticut National Guard, 1897-1903; member of the State assembly 1901-1903; auditor of the city of New Haven 1902-1904; secretary of the New Haven civil service commission 1904-1906; moved to New York City in 1910 and was admitted to the New York State bar the same year; special deputy attorney general of New York State 1911-1913; elected as a Democrat to the Sixty-fifth Congress to fill the vacancy caused by the resignation of Murray Hulbert; reelected to the Sixty-sixth Congress and served from March 5, 1918, to March 3, 1921; unsuccessful candidate for reelection in 1920 to the Sixty-seventh Congress; served as deputy attorney general in charge of the legal work of the New York State Labor Department in 1923 and 1924; resumed the practice of law in New York City until his retirement in 1936; moved to Stony Creek, Conn., where he died November 2, 1949; interment in St. Bernard's Cemetery, New Haven, Conn.

**DOOLEY, Calvin M.,** a Representative from California; born in Visalia, Tulare County, Calif., January 11, 1954; B.S., University of California, Davis, 1977; M.S., Stanford University, Calif., 1987; partner, Dooley Farms; aide to California State senator Rose Ann Vuich, 1987-1989; elected as a Democrat to the One Hundred Second and to the two succeeding Congresses (January 3, 1991-January 3, 1997); is a resident of Visalia, Calif.

**DOOLEY, Edwin Benedict,** a Representative from New York; born in Brooklyn, Kings County, N.Y., April 13, 1905; graduated from St. John's Prep School; Dartmouth College, Hanover, N.H., A.B., 1927, and Fordham University Law School, New York City, LL.B., 1930; feature writer, New York Sun, 1927-1938; radio broadcaster, New York City, 1936-1948; public relations executive, 1938-1955; during the Second World War served on Secretary of the Navy and Secretary of War food committees; trustee village of Mamaroneck, N.Y., 1942-1946; associated with Institute of Public Relations, 1946-1948; mayor of Mamaroneck, N.Y., 1950-1956; elected as a Republican to the Eighty-fifth, Eighty-sixth, and Eighty-seventh Congresses (January 3, 1957-January 3, 1963); unsuccessful for renomination in 1962 to the Eighty-eighth Congress; again engaged in public relations; chairman of the New York State Athletic Commission, 1966-1975; resident of Boca Raton, Fla., until his death there on January 25, 1982; cremated; ashes scattered at family gravesite at Gate of Heaven Cemetery, Hawthorne, N.Y.

**DOOLING, Peter Joseph,** a Representative from New York; born in New York City February 15, 1857; attended the public schools; engaged in the real-estate business; served as court officer in the court of general sessions 1887-1889; member of the board of aldermen of New York City in 1891 and 1892; deputy clerk of the court of special sessions 1893-1895; member of the aqueduct commission in 1898; deputy commissioner of the department of water supply, gas, and electricity 1898-1901; member of the State senate 1903-1905; clerk of the city and county of New York 1906-1909; elected as a Democrat to the Sixty-third and to the three succeeding Congresses (March 4, 1913-March 3, 1921); chairman, Committee on Expenditures in the Department of War (Sixty-fifth Congress); unsuccessful candidate for reelection in 1920 to the Sixty-seventh Congress; sheriff of New York County in 1924; commissioner of the department of purchases of New York City in 1926; reengaged in the real-estate business; died in New York City October 18, 1931; interment in Calvary Cemetery.

**DOOLITTLE, Dudley,** a Representative from Kansas; born at Cottonwood Falls, Chase County, Kans., June 21, 1881; attended the public schools and the University of Kansas at Lawrence, being graduated from its law department in 1903; was admitted to the bar the same year and commenced practice at Cottonwood Falls, Kans., in 1904; prosecuting attorney of Chase County 1908-1912; mayor of Strong City in 1912; elected as a Democrat to the Sixty-third, Sixty-fourth, and Sixty-fifth Congresses (March 4, 1913-March 3, 1919); unsuccessful candidate for reelection in 1918 to the Sixty-sixth Congress; representative of the United States Treasury Department to Italy in 1919; Federal Prohibition Director for Kansas in 1920; engaged in the practice of law in Strong City, Kans., Kansas City, Mo., and Washington, D.C., 1921-1934; elected a member of the Democratic National Committee in 1925; general agent of the ninth district, Farm Credit Administration, 1934-1938; member of the board of directors of the College of Emporia and served as its president 1938-1940; president of the Strong City State Bank and a director of the Exchange National Bank of Cottonwood Falls at time of death; died in Emporia, Kans., November 14, 1957; interment in Prairie Grove Cemetery, Cottonwood Falls, Kans.

**DOOLITTLE, James Rood,** a Senator from Wisconsin; born in Hampton, N.Y., January 3, 1815; attended the common schools and Middlebury (Vt.) Academy, and was graduated from Hobart College, Geneva, N.Y., in 1834; studied law; was admitted to the bar in 1837 and commenced practice in Rochester, N.Y.; moved to Warsaw, N.Y., in 1841; district attorney of Wyoming County, N.Y., 1847-1850; moved to Racine, Wis., in 1851; judge of the first judicial circuit of Wisconsin 1853-1856, when he resigned; the repeal of the Missouri Compromise caused him to leave the Democratic Party; elected as a Republican to the United States Senate in January 1857; reelected in 1863 and served from March 4, 1857, to March 3, 1869; chairman, Committee on Indian Affairs (Thirty-seventh through Thirty-ninth Congresses); left the Republican Party and was an unsuccessful candidate for Governor on the Democratic ticket in 1871; resumed the practice of law in Chicago, Ill., but retained his residence in Racine, Wis.; trustee of the University of Chicago, serving one year as its president, and was for many years a professor in its law school; died in Edgewood, Providence, R.I., July 23, 1897; interment in Mound Cemetery, Racine, Wis.

**Bibliography:** *DAB*; Albright, Claude. "Dixon, Doolittle and Norton: The Forgotten Republican Votes on Johnson's Impeachment." *Wisconsin Magazine of History* 59 (Winter 1975-1976): 91-100.

**DOOLITTLE, John Taylor,** a Representative from California; born in Glendale, Los Angeles County, Calif., October 30, 1950; graduated Cupertino (Calif.) High School, 1968; B.A., University of California, Santa Cruz, 1972; J.D., University of the Pacific, McGeorge School of Law, Stockton, Calif., 1978; admitted to the California bar, 1978; member, California State senate, 1981-1990, chair, Senate Republican caucus, 1987-1990; elected as a Republican to the One Hundred Second and to the two succeeding Congresses (January 3, 1991-January 3, 1997); is a resident of Rocklin, Calif.

**DOOLITTLE, William Hall,** a Representative from Washington; born near North East in Erie County, Pa., November 6, 1848; moved with his parents to Portage County, Wis., in 1859; attended the district school; early in 1865, enlisted as a private in the Ninth Wisconsin Battery; went to Pennsylvania in 1867 and pursued an academic course; studied law in Chautauqua County, N.Y., and was admitted to the bar in 1871; moved to Nebraska in 1872 and commenced practice in Tecumseh, Johnson County; member of the State house of representatives 1874-1876; assistant United States district attorney 1876-1880; moved to Washington Territory in 1880 and settled in Colfax, Whitman County; engaged in the practice of law; moved to Tacoma in 1888; elected as a Republican to the Fifty-third and Fifty-fourth Congresses (March 4, 1893-March 3, 1897); unsuccessful for reelection in 1896 to the Fifty-fifth Congress; resumed the practice of law; died in Tacoma, Wash., February 26, 1914; interment in Tacoma Cemetery.

**DOREMUS, Frank Ellsworth,** a Representative from Michigan; born in Venango County, Pa., August 31, 1865; attended the public schools of Portland, Mich., and was graduated from Detroit (Mich.) College of Law; established the Portland Review in 1885, editing it until 1899; member of the State house of representatives 1890-1892; postmaster of Portland 1895-1899; was admitted to the bar and commenced practice in Detroit in 1899; assistant corporation counsel of Detroit 1903-1907; city comptroller 1907-1910; elected as a Democrat to the Sixty-second and to the four succeeding Congresses (March 4, 1911-March 3, 1921); served as mayor of Detroit, Mich., in 1923 and 1924; resumed the practice of law in Fowlerville, Mich.; died in Howell, Mich., September 4, 1947; interment in Roseland Park, Detroit, Mich.

**DORGAN, Byron Leslie,** a Representative and a Senator from North Dakota; born in Dickinson, Stark County, N.Dak., May 14, 1942; attended the public schools; graduated Regent High School, 1961; B.S., University of North Dakota, Grand Forks, 1964; M.B.A., University of Denver, Denver, Colo., 1966; management development program, Martin Marietta Corp., 1966-1968; deputy tax commissioner, 1968-1969 then tax commissioner, State of North Dakota, 1969-1980; delegate, North Dakota State Democratic conventions, 1969-1981; elected as a Democrat to the Ninety-seventh and to the five succeeding Congresses and served from January 3, 1981 until his resignation December 14, 1992; elected to the United States Senate in 1992 to the term beginning January 3, 1993; appointed by the Governor to begin serving on December 14, 1992, to fill the vacancy caused by the resignation of Senator Kent Conrad, and served until January 3, 1993; elected November 3, 1992 for the term ending January 3, 1999; is a resident of Bismarck, N.Dak.

**DORN, Francis Edwin,** a Representative from New York; born in Brooklyn, N.Y., April 18, 1911; attended St. Augustine and Bishop McLaughlin Memorial High Schools; was graduated from Fordham University in 1932 and from the law school of the same university in 1935; also studied government at New York University in 1936; was admitted to the bar in 1936 and began practice in Brooklyn, N.Y.; elected to the New York State assembly in 1940, but resigned to enlist in the United States Navy in 1941; served four years overseas and was discharged in 1946 as a lieutenant commander in the Naval Reserve, later being promoted to commander; assistant attorney general, State of New York, 1946-1950; engaged in the private practice of law after 1950; elected as a Republican to the Eighty-third and to the three succeeding Congresses (January 3, 1953-January 3, 1961); unsuccessful candidate for reelection in 1960 to the Eighty-seventh Congress, and for election in 1962 to the

Eighty-eighth Congress; resumed the practice of law in Brooklyn; founder of the Appeal of Conscience Foundation; was a resident of Brooklyn until his death in New York City, September 17, 1987; interment in Greenwood Cemetery.

**DORN, William Jennings Bryan,** a Representative from South Carolina; born near Greenwood, Greenwood County, S.C., April 14, 1916; attended the public schools; engaged in agricultural pursuits; served in the South Carolina State house of representatives, 1939-1940; member of the State senate, 1941-1942; enlisted as a private in the Army Air Forces, and served from June 20, 1942 until discharged as a corporal on October 12, 1945, nineteen months of which were in the European Theater; elected as a Democrat to the Eightieth Congress (January 3, 1947-January 3, 1949); was not a candidate in 1948 for renomination to the House of Representatives, but was an unsuccessful candidate for nomination to the United States Senate; resumed agricultural pursuits; elected to the Eighty-second and to the eleven succeeding Congresses, and served from January 3, 1951 until his resignation on December 31, 1974; chairman, Committee on Veterans' Affairs (Ninety-third Congress); was not a candidate for reelection in 1974 to the Ninety-fourth Congress; was an unsuccessful candidate in 1974 for Governor; chairman, South Carolina Democratic Party, 1980-1984; is a resident of Greenwood, S.C.

**Bibliography:** Dorn, William Jennings Bryan, and Scott Derks. *Dorn: Of the People, A Political Way of Life.* Columbia and Orangeburg, S.C.: Bruccoli Clark Layman/Sandlapper Publishing, 1988.

**DORNAN, Robert Kenneth,** a Representative from California; born in New York City April 3, 1933; attended parochial schools; graduated from Loyola (Calif.) High School, 1950; attended Loyola University of Los Angeles, 1950-1953; served to captain in the United States Air Force, 1953-1958; Air Force Reserve, 1958-1975; commercial pilot; broadcaster-journalist; television producer; associated with KHJ-TV and KTLA-TV, 1967-1973; delegate to the Republican National Conventions of 1976, 1980, 1984 and 1988; co-chair, Bush for President, 1988; elected as a Republican to the Ninety-fifth and to the two succeeding Congresses (January 3, 1977-January 3, 1983); was not a candidate for reelection in 1982 to the House of Representatives, but was an unsuccessful candidate for nomination to the United States Senate; elected as a Republican to the Ninety-ninth and to the five succeeding Congresses (January 3, 1985-January 3, 1997); candidate for the Republican presidential nomination in 1996; is a resident of Garden Grove, Calif.

**DORR, Charles Phillips,** a Representative from West Virginia; born in Miltonsburg, Monroe County, Ohio, August 12, 1852; moved with his parents to Woodsfield, Ohio, in 1866; attended the common schools; taught school in Ohio and West Virginia; studied law; was admitted to the bar in 1874 and commenced practice in West Virginia the same year; member of the town council of Webster Springs, W.Va.; elected a member of the State house of delegates in 1884 and 1888; sergeant at arms of that body in 1887; elected as a Republican to the Fifty-fifth Congress (March 4, 1897-March 3, 1899); was not a candidate for renomination in 1898; resumed the practice of law at Webster Springs, W.Va.; died on his estate at Clover Lick, near Marlinton, Pocahontas County, W.Va., October 8, 1914; interment in Clover Lick Cemetery.

**DORSEY, Clement,** a Representative from Maryland; born near Oaklands in Anne Arundel County, Md., in 1778; attended St. John's College, Annapolis, Md.; studied law; was admitted to the bar and commenced practice; major in the Maryland Militia 1812-1818; elected to the Nineteenth, Twentieth, and Twenty-first Congresses (March 4, 1825-March 3, 1831); resumed the practice of law; unsuccessful candidate for election in 1832 to the Twenty-third Congress; judge of the fifth circuit court of Maryland until his death

in Leonardtown, St. Marys County, Md., August 6, 1848; interment in a private burial ground at "Summerseat," near Laurel Grove, Md.

**DORSEY, Frank Joseph Gerard,** a Representative from Pennsylvania; born in Philadelphia, Pa., April 26, 1891; attended grade and high schools; was graduated from the University of Pennsylvania at Philadelphia in 1917; served on the faculty of the University of Pennsylvania in 1916 and 1917; enlisted as a private in the Ordnance Department, United States Army, in July 1917 and was honorably discharged as a lieutenant on April 18, 1919; engaged in the manufacture of steel tools in 1919; also engaged in banking; elected as a Democrat to the Seventy-fourth and Seventy-fifth Congresses (January 3, 1935-January 3, 1939); unsuccessful candidate for reelection in 1938 to the Seventy-sixth Congress; member of the United States Sesquicentennial Constitution Commission in 1938; director, Region III, Wage and Hours and Public Contracts Division, United States Department of Labor, from 1939 until his death in Philadelphia, Pa., July 13, 1949; interment in St. Dominic's Cemetery.

**DORSEY, George Washington Emery,** a Representative from Nebraska; born in Loudoun County, Va., January 25, 1842; moved with his parents to Preston County, Va. (now West Virginia), in 1856; attended private schools and Oak Hill Academy; recruited a company and entered the Union Army in August 1861 as first lieutenant in the Sixth Regiment, West Virginia Infantry; promoted to captain and major, and was mustered out with the Army of the Shenandoah in August 1865; moved to Nebraska in 1866; studied law; was admitted to the bar and commenced practice in 1869; engaged in banking; vice president of the State board of agriculture; chairman of the Republican State central committee; elected as a Republican to the Forty-ninth, Fiftieth, and Fifty-first Congresses (March 4, 1885-March 3, 1891); chairman, Committee on Banking and Currency (Fifty-first Congress); unsuccessful candidate for reelection in 1890 to the Fifty-second Congress; engaged in mining enterprises in Nevada and Utah; died in Salt Lake City, Utah, June 12, 1911; interment in the City Cemetery, Fremont, Dodge County, Nebr.

**DORSEY, John Lloyd, Jr.,** a Representative from Kentucky; born in Henderson, Ky., August 10, 1891; educated in the public schools and at Bethel College, Russellville, Ky.; was graduated from Centre College, Danville, Ky., in 1912; studied law at Centre College; was admitted to the bar in 1913 and commenced practice in Henderson, Ky.; served as a private in Headquarters Company, One Hundred and Fifty-ninth Depot Brigade, in 1918; executive Democratic committeeman 1920-1924; city attorney of Henderson in 1926 and 1930; elected as a Democrat to the Seventy-first Congress to fill the vacancy caused by the resignation of David H. Kincheloe and served from November 4, 1930, to March 3, 1931; was not a candidate for election to the Seventy-second Congress in 1930; resumed the practice of law; again served as city attorney of Henderson in 1936 and 1937; continued the practice of law until his death in Henderson, Ky., March 22, 1960; interment in Fernwood Cemetery.

**DORSEY, Stephen Wallace,** a Senator from Arkansas; born in Benson, Rutland County, Vt., February 28, 1842; moved to Ohio and settled in Oberlin; attended the public schools; during the Civil War served in the Union Army until the close of the war; returned to Ohio and settled in Sandusky; was employed by the Sandusky Tool Co. and subsequently became its president; elected president of the Arkansas Railway Co.; moved to Arkansas and settled in Helena; elected as a Republican to the United States Senate and served from March 4, 1873, to March 3, 1879; was not a candidate for reelection; chairman, Committee on District of Columbia (Forty-fifth Congress); member of the Republican National Committee in 1880; engaged in cattle raising and mining in New Mexico and Colorado; subsequently moved to Los Angeles, Calif., and resided there until his death on March 20, 1916; interment in Fairmont Cemetery, Denver, Colo.

**Bibliography:** *DAB*; Caperton, Thomas J. *Rogue! Being an Account of the Life and High Times of Stephen W. Dorsey, United States Senator and New Mexico Cattle Baron.* Santa Fe: Museum of New Mexico Press, 1978; Lowry, Sharon K. "Portrait of an Age: The Political Career of Stephen W. Dorsey, 1868-1889." Ph.D. dissertation, North Texas State University, 1980.

**DORSHEIMER, William,** a Representative from New York; born in Lyons, Wayne County, N.Y., February 5, 1832; moved to Buffalo, N.Y., with his parents in 1836; attended the common schools, Phillips Academy, Andover, Mass., and Harvard University; studied law; was admitted to the bar in 1854 and commenced practice in Buffalo, N.Y.; was appointed a major in the United States Army in August 1861 and served as aide-de-camp on the staff of General John C. Frémont; United States attorney for the northern district of New York 1867-1871; delegate to the Liberal Republican Convention at Cincinnati in 1872; member of the first board of park commissioners of Buffalo; lieutenant governor of New York, 1875-1880; delegate to the Democratic National Convention of 1876; commissioner of the State survey in 1876 and president of the commission in 1883; moved to New York City in 1880 and continued the practice of law; appointed commissioner of the State reservation at Niagara, N.Y., in 1883; elected as a Democrat to the Forty-eighth Congress (March 4, 1883-March 3, 1885); declined to be a candidate for renomination in 1884 to the Forty-ninth Congress; appointed United States district attorney for the southern district of New York in 1885; resigned the same year, having become owner of the New York Star; died in Savannah, Ga., March 26, 1888, while en route to Florida for a visit; interment in Forest Lawn Cemetery, Buffalo, N.Y.

**Bibliography:** *DAB*.

**DOTY, James Duane** (cousin of Morgan Lewis Martin), a Delegate and a Representative from Wisconsin; born in Salem, Washington County, N.Y., November 5, 1799; attended the common schools; studied law; moved to Detroit, Mich., in 1818; was admitted to the bar in 1819 and commenced practice in Detroit; secretary of the legislative council and clerk of court of Michigan Territory; United States judge for northern Michigan, 1823-1832; member of the legislative council in 1834 and 1835; assisted in bringing about the division of Michigan Territory into the three Territories of Michigan, Wisconsin, and Iowa; preempted several tracts of Government land in the Territory of Wisconsin; laid out the capital of Wisconsin and named it Madison; successfully contested as a Democrat the election of George W. Jones as a Delegate to the Twenty-fifth Congress; reelected to the Twenty-sixth Congress, and served from January 14, 1839 to March 3, 1841; appointed Governor of the Territory of Wisconsin by President John Tyler on April 15, 1841 and served until the expiration of his term in June 1844; delegate to the first constitutional convention of 1846; elected as a Democrat a Representative to the Thirty-first Congress and as an Independent Democrat to the Thirty-second Congress (March 4, 1849-March 3, 1853); appointed superintendent of Indian affairs for Utah Territory in September 1861; appointed Governor of Utah Territory by President Lincoln on June 2, 1863 and served until his death in Salt Lake City, Utah, June 13, 1865; interment in Fort Douglas Cemetery.

**Bibliography:** *DAB*.

**DOUBLEDAY, Ulysses Freeman,** a Representative from New York; born in Otsego County, N.Y., December 15, 1792; received a limited schooling; learned the art of printing and worked as a printer in Cooperstown, Utica, and Albany, N.Y.; served at Sackets Harbor in the War of 1812; established the Saratoga Courier at Ballston Spa; moved to Auburn, N.Y., where he published the Cayuga Patriot 1819-1839; elected as a Jacksonian to the Twenty-second Congress (March 4, 1831-March 3, 1833); appointed

inspector of Auburn Prison in 1834; elected to the Twenty-fourth Congress (March 4, 1835-March 3, 1837); engaged in agricultural pursuits in Scipio, N.Y., 1837-1846; moved to New York City and engaged in mercantile pursuits 1846-1860; died in Belvidere, Boone County, Ill., March 11, 1866; interment probably in the North Street Cemetery, Auburn, N.Y.

**DOUGHERTY, Charles,** a Representative from Florida; born in Athens, Ga., October 15, 1850; attended the public schools of Athens and the University of Virginia at Charlottesville; followed the sea; moved to Florida in 1871 and settled near Port Orange; engaged in planting; member of the Florida State house of representatives from 1877 until 1885, and served as speaker in 1879; elected as a Democrat to the Forty-ninth and Fiftieth Congresses; (March 4, 1885-March 3, 1889); resumed agricultural pursuits; again a member of the State house of representatives in 1891, 1892, 1911, and 1912; served in the Florida State senate, 1895-1898; died at Daytona Beach, Volusia County, Fla., on October 11, 1915; interment in Pinewood Cemetery.

**DOUGHERTY, Charles Francis,** a Representative from Pennsylvania; born in Philadelphia June 26, 1937; attended St. Helena's School, 1951; graduated from St. Joseph's Preparatory School, 1955; served in the United States Marine Corps Reserve, 1957-1959 (active duty, 1959-1962, reserve duty, 1962-1977); B.S., St. Joseph's College, 1959; engaged in graduate work at the University of Pennsylvania, 1962-1964, and at Temple University, 1967; high school teacher, 1962-1965; special agent, Office of Naval Intelligence, Department of the Navy, 1965-1966; assistant dean of students and director of athletics, Community College of Philadelphia, 1966-1970; high school principal and coordinator of Federal programs, 1970-1972; served in the Pennsylvania senate, 1972-1978; elected as a Republican to the Ninety-sixth and Ninety-seventh Congresses (January 3, 1979-January 3, 1983); unsuccessful candidate for reelection in 1982 to the Ninety-eighth Congress; is a resident of Philadelphia, Pa.

**DOUGHERTY, John,** a Representative from Missouri; born in Iatan, Platte County, Mo., February 25, 1857; moved with his parents the same year to Liberty, Clay County, Mo.; attended the public schools and William Jewell College, Liberty, Mo,; studied law; was admitted to the bar in 1889 and commenced practice at Liberty, Mo.; elected city attorney of Liberty, Mo., in 1881 and served five years; editor and proprietor of the Liberty Tribune 1885-1888; elected prosecuting attorney of Clay County, Mo., in 1888 and served six years; unsuccessful candidate for nomination in 1896 to the Fifty-fifth Congress; elected as a Democrat to the Fifty-sixth, Fifty-seventh, and Fifty-eighth Congresses (March 4, 1899-March 3, 1905); unsuccessful candidate for renomination in 1904; resumed the practice of law; died in Liberty, Mo., August 1, 1905; interment in Fairview Cemetery.

**DOUGHTON, Robert Lee,** a Representative from North Carolina; born at Laurel Springs, Alleghany County, N.C., on November 7, 1863; was educated in the public schools at Laurel Springs and Sparta; engaged in agricultural pursuits and the raising of livestock at Laurel Springs; also interested in banking; member of the North Carolina State board of agriculture, 1903-1909; served in the State senate, 1908-1909; director of the State prison board, 1909-1911; became president of the Deposit & Savings Bank, North Wilkesboro, N.C., in 1911; elected as a Democrat to the Sixty-second and to the twenty succeeding Congresses (March 4, 1911-January 3, 1953); chairman, Committee on Expenditures in the Department of Agriculture (Sixty-third through Sixty-fifth Congresses), Committee on Ways and Means (Seventy-third through Seventy-ninth Congresses and Eighty-first and Eighty-second Congresses), Joint Committee on Internal Revenue Taxation (Eighty-first and Eighty-second Congresses); was not a candidate for renomination in 1952 to the Eighty-third

Congress; returned to Laurel Springs, N.C., where he died on October 1, 1954; interment in Laurel Springs Baptist Church Cemetery.

**Bibliography:** *DAB.*

**DOUGLAS, Albert,** a Representative from Ohio; born in Chillicothe, Ohio, April 25, 1852; attended the public schools of Chillicothe and a preparatory school; was graduated from Kenyon College, Gambier, Ohio, in 1872, and from the law department of Harvard University in 1874; was admitted to the bar in 1874 and commenced practice in Chillicothe, Ohio; prosecuting attorney of Ross County, 1877-1881; elected as a Republican to the Sixtieth and Sixty-first Congresses (March 4, 1907-March 3, 1911); unsuccessful candidate for reelection in 1910 to the Sixty-second Congress; resumed the practice of law in Chillicothe, Ohio; appointed Ambassador Extraordinary to represent the United States at the centennial of the independence of Peru in 1921; retired and resided in Washington, D.C., until his death in that city on March 14, 1935; interment in Grandview Cemetery, Chillicothe, Ohio.

**DOUGLAS, Beverly Browne,** a Representative from Virginia; born at Providence Forge, New Kent County, Va., December 21, 1822; attended Rumford Academy in King William County, the College of William and Mary, Williamsburg, Va., Yale College, and the University of Edinburgh, Scotland; upon his return to the United States reentered William and Mary, and was graduated from the law department in 1843; was admitted to the bar in 1844 and commenced practice in Norfolk, Va.; moved to King William County in 1846 and continued the practice of his profession; delegate to the Virginia constitutional convention in 1850 and 1851; member of the Virginia senate 1852-1865; presidential elector on the Democratic ticket of Breckinridge and Lane in 1860; during the Civil War entered the Confederate Army as first lieutenant in Lee's Rangers, and was successively promoted to the rank of major of the Fifth Virginia Cavalry; elected as a Democrat to the Forty-fourth and Forty-fifth Congresses and served from March 4, 1875, until his death in Washington, D.C., December 22, 1878; interment in the family burying ground at "Zoar," near Aylett, King William County, Va.

**DOUGLAS, Charles Gwynne, III,** a Representative from New Hampshire; born in Abington, Montgomery County, Pa., December 2, 1942; B.A., University of New Hampshire, 1965; LL.B., Boston University School of Law, 1968; New Hampshire Army National Guard service, 1968 to present, colonel; admitted to New Hampshire bar, 1968; Massachusetts bar, 1985; attorney, Manchester, N.H., 1968-1988; administrative assistant to majority leader of New Hampshire State house of representatives, 1965; legislative counsel to Governor Meldrim Thomson, Jr., of New Hampshire, 1973-1974; associate justice, New Hampshire State superior court, 1974-1976; associate justice, New Hampshire State supreme court, 1977-1983, senior associate justice, 1983-1985; elected as a Republican to the One Hundred First Congress (January 3, 1989-January 3, 1991); unsuccessful candidate for reelection in 1990 to the One Hundred Second Congress; is a resident of Concord, N.H.

**DOUGLAS, Emily Taft** (wife of Paul H. Douglas), a Representative from Illinois, born in Chicago, Ill., April 10, 1899; was graduated from the University of Chicago in 1920; engaged in the theatrical profession; organizer and chairman of the department of government and foreign policy for the Illinois League of Women Voters; secretary of the International Relations Center, Chicago, Ill.; elected as a Democrat to the Seventy-ninth Congress (January 3, 1945-January 3, 1947); unsuccessful candidate for reelection in 1946 to the Eightieth Congress; United States Representative to the United Nations Educational, Scientific and Cultural Organization, Paris; author; was a resident of White Plains, N.Y.; died January 28, 1994.

**Bibliography:** Douglas, Emily Taft. *Margaret Sanger; Pioneer of the Future.* New York: Holt, Rinehart, and Winston, 1970; Douglas, Emily Taft. *Remember the Ladies; The Story of Great Women Who Helped Shape America.* New York: G.P. Putnam's Sons, 1966.

**DOUGLAS, Fred James,** a Representative from New York; born in Clinton, Worcester County, Mass., September 14, 1869; moved with his parents to Little Falls, N.Y., in 1874; attended the public schools, and was graduated from the medical department of Dartmouth College, Hanover, N.H., in 1895; moved to Utica, N.Y., the same year and commenced the practice of medicine; member of the board of education of Utica 1910-1920; mayor of Utica 1922-1924; commissioner of public safety of Utica in 1928 and 1929; unsuccessful candidate for Lieutenant Governor of New York in 1934; elected as a Republican to the Seventy-fifth and to the three succeeding Congresses (January 3, 1937-January 3, 1945); unsuccessful candidate for renomination in 1944; resumed his former profession as a surgeon; died in Utica, N.Y., January 1, 1949; interment in Mount Olivet Cemetery, Whitesboro, N.Y.

**DOUGLAS, Helen Gahagan,** a Representative from California; born in Boonton, Morris County, N.J., November 25, 1900; attended the public schools, Berkeley School for Girls, Brooklyn, N.Y., Capen School for Girls, Northampton, Mass., and Barnard College, New York City; moved to Los Angeles, Calif., in 1931; engaged in the theatrical profession and also as an opera singer, 1922-1938; Democratic National committeewoman for California, 1940-1944; vice chairman of the Democratic State central committee and chairman of the women's division, 1940-1944; member of the national advisory committee of the Works Progress Administration, and of the State committee of the National Youth Administration, 1939-1940; member of the board of governors of the California Housing and Planning Association in 1942 and 1943; appointed by President Franklin D. Roosevelt as a member of the Voluntary Participation Committee, Office of Civilian Defense; appointed by President Harry S Truman as alternate United States Delegate to the United Nations Assembly; elected as a Democrat to the Seventy-ninth and to the two succeeding Congresses (January 3, 1945-January 3, 1951); was not a candidate for renomination in 1950 to the House of Representatives, but was an unsuccessful candidate for election to the United States Senate; lecturer and author; appointed by President Lyndon B. Johnson as Special Ambassador to head United States delegation to inauguration ceremonies of President William V.S. Tubman of Liberia in 1964; resided in New York City until her death on June 28, 1980.

**Bibliography:** *DAB*; Douglas, Helen Gahagan. *A Full Life.* Garden City, N.Y.: Doubleday, 1982; Scobie, Ingrid Winther. *Center Stage: Helen Gahagan Douglas, A Life.* New York: Oxford University Press, 1992.

**DOUGLAS, Lewis Williams,** a Representative from Arizona; born in Bisbee, Cochise County, Ariz., July 2, 1894; attended the public schools and Montclair (N.J.) Academy; was graduated from Amherst (Mass.) College in 1916; attended the Massachusetts Institute of Technology in 1916; commissioned as a second lieutenant on August 15, 1917, and assigned to the Three Hundred and Forty-seventh Regiment, Field Artillery; promoted to first lieutenant and served overseas as assistant, G-3 staff, Ninety-first Division, until discharged on February 18, 1919; instructor of history at Amherst College in 1920; engaged in mining and general business; member of the Arizona State house of representatives, 1923-1925; elected as a Democrat to the Seventieth and to the three succeeding Congresses, and served from March 4, 1927 until his resignation on March 4, 1933, before the commencement of the Seventy-third Congress; appointed Director of the Budget by President Franklin D. Roosevelt; took the oath of office on March 7, 1933 and served until August 31, 1934, when he resigned; vice president and member of the board, American Cyanamid Co.,

1934-1938; principal and vice chancellor of McGill University, Montreal, Canada, from January 1938 to December 1939; president of the Mutual Life Insurance Co. of New York from 1940-1947, and chairman of the board on leave of absence, 1947-1959; deputy administrator of the War Shipping Administration from May 1942 to March 1944; appointed Ambassador to Great Britain on March 6, 1947 and served until November 1950; director, General Motors Corporation, 1944-1965; chairman and director, Southern Arizona Bank & Trust Company, 1949-1966; appointed to head Government Study of Foreign Economic Problems and their Relation to the United States, 1953; member, President's Task Force on American Indians, 1966-1967; died in Tucson, Ariz., March 7, 1974; remains cremated.

Bibliography: Browder, Robert Paul, and Thomas G. Smith. *Independent: A Biography of Lewis W. Douglas.* New York: Alfred A. Knopf, 1986; Smith, Thomas G. "Lewis Douglas, Arizona Politics and the Colorado River Controversy." *Arizona and the West* 22 (Summer 1980): 125-62.

DOUGLAS, Paul Howard (husband of Emily Taft Douglas), a Senator from Illinois; born in Salem, Essex County, Mass., March 26, 1892; attended the public schools of Newport, Maine; graduated from Bowdoin College in 1913, and from Columbia University in 1915; studied at Harvard University, 1915-1916; economist, author and college professor; taught economics at University of Illinois, 1916-1917, and at Reed College, Portland, Oreg., 1917-1918; engaged in industrial relations work with Emergency Fleet Corporation, 1918-1919; resumed teaching at the University of Washington, 1919-1920; professor of industrial relations, University of Chicago, 1920-1949; between 1930 and 1939 served on many state and national commissions and committees; alderman, Chicago city council, 1939-1942; unsuccessful candidate for nomination in 1942 to the United States Senate; during the Second World War served in the United States Marine Corps, 1942-1945; enlisted as a private and rose to the rank of lieutenant colonel; elected as a Democrat to the United States Senate in 1948; reelected in 1954 and again in 1960, and served from January 3, 1949 to January 3, 1967; unsuccessful candidate for reelection in 1966; chairman, Joint Committee on the Economic Report (Eighty-fourth Congress), Joint Economic Committee (Eighty-sixth and Eighty-eighth Congresses); chairman of the President's Committee on Urban Affairs, 1967-1968; chairman, Committee on Tax Reform, 1969; resided in Washington, D.C., until his death there on September 24, 1976; cremated; ashes scattered in the wooded area in Jackson Park, Chicago, Ill.

Bibliography: *DAB*; Anderson, Jerry M. "Paul H. Douglas: Insurgent Senate Spokesman for Humane Causes, 1949-1963." Ph.D. dissertation, Michigan State University, 1964; Douglas, Paul H. *In the Fullness of Time: The Memoirs of Paul H. Douglas.* New York: Harcourt Brace Jovanovich, 1972.

DOUGLAS, Stephen Arnold, a Representative and a Senator from Illinois; born in Brandon, Rutland County, Vt., April 23, 1813; educated in the common schools and completed preparatory studies in Brandon Academy; moved to Middlebury, Vt. in 1828 and learned the cabinetmaker's trade; moved with his family to a farm near Clifton Springs, N.Y. in December 1830; entered Canandaigua Academy in 1832 and studied law; settled in Winchester, Ill., in December 1833, where he taught school until June 1834 and resumed the study of law; was admitted to the bar in March 1834 and commenced practice in Jacksonville, Morgan County, Ill.; elected State's attorney for the Morgan circuit in 1835; member, Illinois State house of representatives, 1836-1837; appointed by President Martin Van Buren register of the land office at Springfield, Ill., March 9, 1837, and served until his resignation on March 2, 1840; unsuccessful Democratic candidate for election in 1838 to the Twenty-sixth Congress; appointed secretary of the State of Illinois on November 30, 1840; elected as one of the judges of the State supreme court, February 15, 1841, and served until his

resignation on June 28, 1843; elected as a Democrat to the Twenty-eighth and to the two succeeding Congresses and served from March 4, 1843, until his resignation on March 3, 1847, at the close of the Twenty-ninth Congress; elected as a Democrat to the United States Senate in 1847; reelected in 1853 and again in 1859, and served from March 4, 1847 until his death; chairman, Committee on Territories (Thirtieth through Thirty-fifth Congresses); unsuccessful candidate for the Democratic presidential nomination in 1852 and 1856; nominated for President of the United States on June 23, 1860, by the Democratic National Convention which had reassembled in Baltimore, but was unsuccessful in the general election; died in Chicago, Ill., June 3, 1861; interment in Douglas Monument Park.

Bibliography: *DAB*; Douglas, Stephen A. *The Letters of Stephen A. Douglas.* Edited by Robert W. Johannsen. Urbana: University of Illinois Press, 1961; Johannsen, Robert W. *Stephen A. Douglas.* New York: Oxford University Press, 1973.

DOUGLAS, William Harris, a Representative from New York; born in New York City December 5, 1853; attended private schools and the College of the City of New York; entered the exporting and importing trade; elected as a Republican to the Fifty-seventh and Fifty-eighth Congresses (March 4, 1901-March 3, 1905); declined to be a candidate for renomination in 1904; resumed his former business pursuits; delegate to the Republican National Conventions in 1908, 1912, and 1916; died in New York City on January 27, 1944; interment in Sleepy Hollow Cemetery, Tarrytown, N.Y.

DOUGLASS, John Joseph, a Representative from Massachusetts; born in East Boston, Suffolk County, Mass., February 9, 1873; attended the public schools; was graduated from Boston College in 1893, and from the law department of Georgetown University, Washington, D.C., in 1896; was admitted to the bar in 1897 and commenced practice in Boston; member of the Massachusetts house of representatives in 1899, 1900, 1906, and again in 1913; delegate to the Massachusetts constitutional convention in 1917 and 1918; author and playwright; delegate to the Democratic National Conventions in 1928 and 1932; elected as a Democrat to the Sixty-ninth and to the four succeeding Congresses (March 4, 1925-January 3, 1935); chairman, Committee on Education (Seventy-second and Seventy-third Congresses); unsuccessful candidate for renomination in 1934; resumed the practice of law; served as commissioner of penal institutions of Boston from 1935 until his death in West Roxbury, Suffolk County, Mass., April 5, 1939; interment in St. Joseph's Cemetery.

DOUTRICH, Isaac Hoffer, a Representative from Pennsylvania; born on a farm near Middletown, Dauphin County, Pa., December 19, 1871; moved to Elizabethtown, Pa., with his parents in 1880; attended the rural schools, the public schools in Elizabethtown, Pa., and Keystone State Normal School (now State Teachers College), Kutztown, Pa.; worked in the retail clothing business in Middletown and Harrisburg, Pa.; also interested in banking and other businesses; member of the Harrisburg city council 1924-1927; elected as a Republican to the Seventieth and to the four succeeding Congresses (March 4, 1927-January 3, 1937); unsuccessful for reelection in 1936 to the Seventy-fifth Congress; reengaged in the retail clothing business in Harrisburg, Pa., until his death May 28, 1941; interment in the East Harrisburg Cemetery.

DOVENER, Blackburn Barrett, a Representative from West Virginia; born in Tays Valley, Cabell County, Va. (now West Virginia), April 20, 1842; attended the common schools; taught school from 1858 to 1861; at the age of nineteen raised a company and served as captain of Company A, Fifteenth Regiment, West Virginia Volunteer Infantry; became captain of an Ohio River steamboat in 1867; studied law; was admitted to the bar in 1873 and commenced practice in Wheeling, W.Va.; member of the State house of delegates in 1883 and 1884; unsuccessful candidate in 1890 for election to the Fifty-second Congress; elected as a Republican to the Fifty-fourth and to the five succeeding Congresses (March 4, 1895-March 3, 1907); unsuccessful candidate for renomination in 1906 to the Sixtieth Congress; resumed the practice of law in Wheeling; lived in retirement at Glen Echo, Md., until his death on May 9, 1914; interment in Arlington National Cemetery, Va.

**DOW, John Goodchild,** a Representative from New York; born in New York City on May 6, 1905; attended the public schools of Canton, Mass.; A.B., Harvard University, 1927; M.A., Columbia University, 1937; systems analyst for large corporations, 1929-1964; director of civil defense in Grand View, N.Y., 1950-1964; chairman of the Zoning Board of Appeals in Grand View, 1964; chairman of the Democratic committee in Orangetown, N.Y., 1957-1962; candidate for the New York State legislature in 1954 and 1956; elected as a Democrat to the Eighty-ninth and Ninetieth Congresses (January 3, 1965-January 3, 1969); unsuccessful candidate for reelection in 1968 to the Ninety-first Congress; delegate to Democratic National Convention of 1968; staff assistant, United States Congress; elected to the Ninety-second Congress (January 3, 1971-January 3, 1973); unsuccessful candidate for reelection in 1972 to the Ninety-third Congress, and for election in 1974 to the Ninety-fourth Congress; assistant director, New York State comprehensive employment training act program, 1976-1982; founder, Americans Against Nuclear War, 1980; unsuccessful candidate for nomination in 1982 to the Ninety-eighth Congress; is a resident of Grand View, N.Y.

**DOWD, Clement,** a Representative from North Carolina; born at Richland Creek, near Carthage, Moore County, N.C., August 27, 1832; attended the common schools; was graduated from the University of North Carolina at Chapel Hill in 1856; engaged in teaching in 1857 and 1858; studied law; was admitted to the bar in 1859 and commenced practice in Charlotte, N.C.; during the Civil War served in the Confederate Army; after the war resumed the practice of law; mayor of Charlotte 1869-1871; president of the Merchants & Farmers' National Bank 1871-1874; president of the Commercial National Bank of Charlotte, N.C., 1874-1880; delegate to the Democratic State convention in 1881; elected as a Democrat to the Forty-seventh and Forty-eighth Congresses (March 4, 1881-March 3, 1885); was not a candidate for renomination in 1884 to the Forty-ninth Congress; State bank examiner in 1885 and 1886; collector of internal revenue for the district of North Carolina in 1886 and 1887; again engaged in the practice of law; died in Charlotte, N.C., April 15, 1898; interment in Elmwood Cemetery.

**DOWDELL, James Ferguson,** a Representative from Alabama; born near Monticello, Jasper County, Ga., November 26, 1818; completed preparatory studies and in 1840 was graduated from Randolph-Macon College, Ashland, Va.; studied law; was admitted to the bar in 1841 and commenced practice in Greenville, Ga.; moved to Chambers County, Ala., in 1846 and engaged in agricultural pursuits; unsuccessful candidate for election to the State house of representatives in 1849 and 1851; elected as a Democrat to the Thirty-third, Thirty-fourth, and Thirty-fifth Congresses (March 4, 1853-March 3, 1859); during the Civil War served as colonel of the Thirty-seventh Regiment, Alabama Volunteer Infantry, under General Price from 1862 until the close of the war; president of the East Alabama College at Auburn 1868-1870; died near Auburn, Lee County, Ala., September 6, 1871; interment in City Cemetery.

**DOWDNEY, Abraham,** a Representative from New York; born in Youghal, Ireland, October 31, 1841; immigrated to the United States with his parents, who settled in New York City; attended private schools; engaged in the building and contracting business; served in the Civil War as captain in the One Hundred and Thirty-second Regiment, New York Volunteer Infantry, in 1862 and 1863; chairman of the public-school trustees of New York City 1882-1885; elected as a Democrat to the Forty-ninth Congress and

served from March 4, 1885, until his death in New York City December 10, 1886; interment in Calvary Cemetery, Long Island City, N.Y.

**DOWDY, Charles Wayne,** a Representative from Mississippi; born in Fitzgerald, Ben Hill County, Georgia, July 27, 1943; attended the public schools; graduated from Gulfport (Miss.) High School, 1961; B.A., Millsaps College, Jackson, Miss., 1965; LL.B., Jackson School of Law, Jackson, Miss., 1968; admitted to the Mississippi bar in 1969 and commenced practice in McComb; city judge, McComb, 1970-1974; mayor of McComb, 1978-1981; elected as a Democrat to the Ninety-seventh Congress, July 7, 1981, by special election to fill the vacancy caused by the resignation of Jon C. Hinson; reelected to the three succeeding Congresses, and served from July 7, 1981 to January 3, 1989; was not a candidate in 1988 for reelection to the House of Representatives, but was an unsuccessful candidate for election to the United States Senate; is a resident of McComb, Miss.

**DOWDY, John Vernard,** a Representative from Texas; born in Waco, McLennan County, Tex., February 11, 1912; spent early years of his youth in Rusk, Tex.; graduated from high school in Henderson, Tex., in 1928; attended the College of Marshall (now East Texas Baptist University) 1929-1931, and undertook the private study of law; official court reporter for the One Hundred Twenty-third Judicial District, Center, Tex., 1931-1936, and for the Third Judicial District, Athens, Tex., 1937-1944; admitted to the bar in 1940 and began practice in Athens, Tex.; district attorney, third judicial district of Texas, 1945-1952; elected as a Democrat to the Eighty-second Congress, by special election, September 23, 1952, to fill the vacancy caused by the resignation of Tom Pickett; reelected to the ten succeeding Congresses and served from September 23, 1952, to January 3, 1973; was not a candidate for reelection in 1972 to the Ninety-third Congress; was a resident of Athens, Tex., until his death there on April 12, 1995; interment in Oaklawn Memorial Park.

**DOWELL, Cassius Clay,** a Representative from Iowa; born on a farm near Summerset, Warren County, Iowa, February 29, 1864; attended the public schools, Baptist College at Des Moines, Iowa, and Simpson College, Indianola, Iowa; was graduated from the liberal arts department of Drake University, Des Moines, Iowa, in 1886 and from its law department in 1887; was admitted to the bar in 1888 and commenced practice in Des Moines; member of the State house of representatives 1894-1898; served in the State senate 1902-1912; elected as a Republican to the Sixty-fourth and to the nine succeeding Congresses (March 4, 1915-January 3, 1935); chairman, Committee on Elections No. 3 (Sixty-sixth and Sixty-seventh Congresses), Committee on Roads (Sixty-eighth through Seventy-first Congresses); unsuccessful candidate for reelection in 1934 to the Seventy-fourth Congress; resumed the practice of law in Des Moines; elected to the Seventy-fifth and Seventy-sixth Congresses and served from January 3, 1937, until his death in Washington, D.C., February 4, 1940; interment in Woodland Cemetery, Des Moines, Iowa.

**DOWNEY, Sheridan** (son of Stephen Wheeler Downey), a Senator from California; born in Laramie, Albany County, Wyo., March 11, 1884; attended the public schools; was graduated from the law department of the University of Michigan at Ann Arbor in 1907; was admitted to the bar the same year and commenced practice in Laramie, Wyo.; served as district attorney of Albany County; moved to Sacramento, Calif., in 1912 and continued the practice of law; elected as a Democrat to the United States Senate in 1938; reelected in 1944 and served from January 3, 1939, until his resignation November 30, 1950, due to ill health; was not a candidate for renomination in 1950; chairman, Committee on Civil Service (Seventy-eighth and Seventy-ninth Congresses); resumed the practice of law until his retirement in 1955; died in San

Francisco, Calif., October 25, 1961; body willed to the University of California Medical Center.

**Bibliography:** *DAB*; Downey, Sheridan. *Onward America.* Sacramento: Larkin Printing Co., 1933; Downey, Sheridan. *They Would Rule the Valley.* San Francisco: n.p., 1947.

**DOWNEY, Stephen Wheeler** (father of Sheridan Downey), a Delegate from the Territory of Wyoming; born in Western Port, Allegany County, Md., July 25, 1839; pursued an academic course; enlisted as a private in Company C, Third Regiment, Potomac Home Brigade, Maryland Infantry, October 31, 1861; successively promoted to first lieutenant, lieutenant colonel, and colonel; studied law; was admitted to the bar in Washington, D.C., in 1863; moved to the Territory of Wyoming in 1869 and practiced law in Laramie; prosecuting attorney of Albany County, 1869-1870; elected a member of the Territorial council in 1871, 1875, and 1877; treasurer of the Territory, 1872-1875; auditor of the Territory, 1877-1879; elected as a Republican to the Forty-sixth Congress (March 4, 1879-March 3, 1881); declined to be a candidate for renomination in 1880 to the Forty-seventh Congress; elected a member of the Territorial house of representatives in 1886, and again in 1890; trustee of the University of Wyoming at Laramie, 1891-1897, and served as its president; member of the Wyoming State house of representatives in 1893 and 1895, and served as speaker in the latter year; member of the State constitutional convention in 1889; again prosecuting attorney of Albany County from 1899 until his death in Denver, Colorado, August 3, 1902; interment in Green Hill Cemetery, Laramie, Albany County, Wyo.

**DOWNEY, Thomas Joseph,** a Representative from New York; born in Ozone Park, Queens County, N.Y., January 28, 1949; attended public schools in West Islip, N.Y.; B.S., Cornell University, Ithaca, N.Y., 1970; attended St. John's University Law School, Brooklyn, N.Y., 1972-1974; J.D., American University School of Law, 1979; served as Suffolk County (N.Y.) legislator, 1972-1974; delegate to the Democratic National Convention of 1972; elected as a Democrat to the Ninety-fourth and to the eight succeeding Congresses (January 3, 1975-January 3, 1993); unsuccessful candidate for reelection in 1992 to the One Hundred Third Congress; chairman, Downey Chandler, Inc., Washington, D.C.; is a resident of Washington, D.C.

**DOWNING, Charles,** a Delegate from Florida; born in Virginia; studied law; was admitted to the bar and practiced in St. Augustine, Fla.; member of the legislative council of the Territory of Florida in 1837; elected to the Twenty-fifth and Twenty-sixth Congresses (March 4, 1837-March 3, 1841); died in St. Augustine, Fla., in 1845.

**DOWNING, Finis Ewing,** a Representative from Illinois; born in Virginia, Cass County, Ill., August 24, 1846; attended public and private schools; engaged in mercantile pursuits in Virginia, Ill., and Butler, Mo., 1864-1880; member of the board of aldermen, Virginia, Ill., 1876-1878; mayor 1878-1880; clerk of the circuit court of Cass County 1880-1892; studied law; was admitted to the bar in December 1887 and commenced practice at Virginia, Ill.; engaged in the newspaper business 1891-1897; secretary of the State senate in 1892 and 1893; presented credentials as a Democratic Member-elect to the Fifty-fourth Congress and served from March 4, 1895, to June 5, 1896, when he was succeeded by John I. Rinaker, who contested his election; unsuccessful candidate for renomination in 1896; unsuccessful Democratic candidate for secretary of state of Illinois in 1896; resumed the practice of law in Virginia, Ill., and also engaged in the real-estate business; died in Virginia, Ill., March 8, 1936; interment in Walnut Ridge Cemetery.

**DOWNING, Thomas Nelms,** a Representative from Virginia; born in Newport News, Va., February 1, 1919; attended the public schools; B.S., Virginia Military Institute, Lexington, 1940; LL.B., University of Virginia, 1948; was admitted to the bar in 1948 and commenced the practice of law in Warwick and Hampton, Va.; served as a troop commander of Mechanized Cavalry with Third United States Army, 1942-1946, and commanded the first troops in the Third Army to invade Germany; substitute judge of the municipal court for the city of Warwick (now Newport News) Va., 1953-1958; elected as a Democrat to the Eighty-sixth and to the eight succeeding Congresses (January 3, 1959-January 3, 1977); chairman, Select Committee on Assassinations (Ninety-fourth Congress); was not a candidate for reelection in 1976 to the Ninety-fifth Congress; is a resident of Newport News, Va.

**DOWNS, Le Roy Donnelly,** a Representative from Connecticut; born in Danbury, Fairfield County, Conn., April 11, 1900; attended the public schools of his native city; enlisted on August 27, 1917, and served as a corporal in United States Army, with four months' service in France, being discharged on December 21, 1918; engaged as a newspaper publisher in South Norwalk, Conn., in 1923; chairman and member of the Veterans' Home Building Commission 1931-1938; city clerk of Norwalk, Conn., 1933-1940; elected as a Democrat to the Seventy-seventh Congress (January 3, 1941-January 3, 1943); unsuccessful for reelection in 1942 to the Seventy-eighth Congress; resumed the newspaper publishing business; comptroller of the city of Norwalk, Conn., 1943-1944; War Manpower Director for southwestern Connecticut 1944-1946; served as regional representative for the Veterans' Administration in New York, New Jersey, and Pennsylvania from 1961 until his death, January 18, 1970, in Norwalk, Conn.; interment in Riverside Cemetery.

**DOWNS, Solomon Weathersbee,** a Senator from Louisiana; born in Montgomery County, Tenn., in 1801; pursued classical studies and was graduated from the Transylvania University, Lexington, Ky., in 1823; studied law; was admitted to the bar in 1826 and commenced practice in Bayou Sara, West Feliciana Parish, La.; moved to Ouachita, La., and then to New Orleans, La., in 1845, where he engaged in the practice of law; United States attorney for the district of Louisiana 1845-1847; member of the State constitutional convention; elected as a Democrat to the United States Senate and served from March 4, 1847, to March 3, 1853; chairman, Committee on Engrossed Bills (Thirtieth Congress), Committee on Private Land Claims (Thirtieth through Thirty-second Congresses); appointed by President Franklin Pierce collector of the port of New Orleans in 1853; died in Crab Orchard Springs, Lincoln County, Ky., August 14, 1854; interment in Old City Cemetery, Monroe, Ouachita Parish, La.

**DOWSE, Edward,** a Representative from Massachusetts; born in Charlestown, Mass., October 22, 1756; moved to Dedham, Mass.; after the Revolution was a shipmaster and engaged in the East Indian and China carrying trade; elected to the Sixteenth Congress and served from March 4, 1819, until May 26, 1820, when he resigned; died in Dedham, Mass., September 3, 1828; interment in the Old Cemetery.

**DOX, Peter Myndert** (grandson of John Nicholas), a Representative from Alabama; born in Geneva, Ontario County, N.Y., September 11, 1813; attended Geneva Academy and was graduated from Hobart College at Geneva in 1833; studied law; was admitted to the bar and commenced practice at Geneva, N.Y.; member of the State assembly in 1842; judge of the Ontario County Courts from November 1855 until his resignation on March 18, 1856; moved to Alabama in the same year and settled in Madison County; engaged in agricultural pursuits; member of the State constitutional convention in 1865; elected as a Democrat to the Forty-first and Forty-second Congresses (March 4, 1869-March 3, 1873); retired from public life; died in Huntsville, Madison County, Ala., April 2, 1891; interment in Maple Hill Cemetery.

**DOXEY, Charles Taylor,** a Representative from Indiana; born in Tippecanoe County, Ind., July 13, 1841; moved with his mother to Minnesota in 1855 and worked on a farm; later moved to Fairbury, Ill., where he attended the public schools; moved to Anderson, Ind.; entered the service as first sergeant of Company A, Nineteenth Regiment, Indiana Volunteer Infantry, in July 1861; promoted to second lieutenant, subsequently resigned, and then became captain of Company K, Sixteenth Indiana Infantry; engaged in the manufacture of staves and headings; member of the State senate in 1876; member of the board of directors in the first natural-gas companies of Anderson; elected as a Republican to the Forty-seventh Congress to fill the vacancy caused by the death of Godlove S. Orth and served from January 17 to March 3, 1883; unsuccessful candidate for election in 1884 to the Forty-ninth Congress; resumed former business activities; died in Anderson, Ind., April 30, 1898; interment in Maplewood Cemetery.

**DOXEY, Wall,** a Representative and a Senator from Mississippi; born in Holly Springs, Marshall County, Miss., August 8, 1892; attended the public schools; was graduated from the University of Mississippi at Oxford in 1913 and from its law department in 1914; was admitted to the bar in 1914 and commenced practice in Holly Springs, Miss.; prosecuting attorney of Marshall County, Miss., 1915-1923; district attorney for the third judicial district of Mississippi 1923-1929; elected as a Democrat to the Seventy-first and to the six succeeding Congresses and served from March 4, 1929, until September 28, 1941; elected as a Democrat to the United States Senate on September 23, 1941, to fill the vacancy caused by the death of Pat Harrison and served from September 29, 1941, to January 3, 1943; unsuccessful candidate for renomination to the United States Senate in 1942; elected Sergeant at Arms of the United States Senate 1943-1947; engaged as a hearing examiner with the United States Department of Agriculture, Washington, D.C., 1947; resumed the practice of law in Holly Springs, Miss., until his retirement in 1948; died in Memphis, Tenn., March 2, 1962; interment in Hill Crest Cemetery, Holly Springs, Miss.

**DOYLE, Clyde Gilman,** a Representative from California; born in Oakland, Alameda County, Calif., July 11, 1887; attended public schools in Oakland, Calif., Seattle, Wash., Los Angeles and Long Beach, Calif.; was graduated from the College of Law of the University of Southern California at Los Angeles in 1917; was admitted to the bar in 1916 and commenced practice in Long Beach, Calif.; member and president of the Board of Freeholders, Long Beach, Calif., 1921-1922; member of the California State Board of Education; elected as a Democrat to the Seventy-ninth Congress (January 3, 1945-January 3, 1947); unsuccessful candidate for reelection in 1946 to the Eightieth Congress; elected to the Eighty-first and to the seven succeeding Congresses, and served from January 3, 1949 until his death in Arlington, Va., on March 14, 1963.

**DOYLE, Michael F.,** a Representative from Pennsylvania; born in Swissvale, Allegheny County, Pa., August 5, 1953; graduated from Swissvale Area High School, 1971; B.S., Pennsylvania State University, 1975; executive director, Turtle Creek Valley Citizens Union, 1977-1979, 1983 to present; chief of staff to Pennsylvania senator Frank Pecora, 1979-1983; owner of insurance business, Pittsburgh, Pa.; elected as a Democrat to the One Hundred Fourth Congress (January 3, 1995-January 3, 1997); is a resident of Swissvale, Pa.

**DOYLE, Thomas Aloysius,** a Representative from Illinois; born in Chicago, Ill., January 9, 1886; attended the public schools of his native city; engaged in the real-estate and insurance business and, after 1926, in the automobile business; member of the Chicago city council 1914-1918; member of the State house of representatives 1918-1923; commissioner on the Chicago Board of Local Improvements in 1923; elected as a Democrat to the Sixty-eighth Congress

to fill the vacancy caused by the death of John W. Rainey; reelected to the Sixty-ninth, Seventieth, and Seventy-first Congresses and served from November 6, 1923, to March 3, 1931; was not a candidate for renomination in 1930; in 1931 again became a member of the Chicago city council and served until his death in Chicago, Ill., January 29, 1935; interment in Mount Olivet Cemetery.

**DRAKE, Charles Daniel,** a Senator from Missouri; born in Cincinnati, Ohio, April 11, 1811; attended St. Joseph's College, Bardstown, Ky., in 1823 and 1824, and Patridge's Military Academy, Middletown, Conn., in 1824 and 1825; appointed midshipman in the United States Navy in 1825 and served four years, when he resigned; studied law; was admitted to the bar in Cincinnati in 1833; moved to St. Louis, Mo., in 1834 and continued the practice of law; member, State house of representatives 1859-1860; member of the State constitutional convention in 1865; elected as a Republican to the United States Senate and served from March 4, 1867, to December 19, 1870, when he resigned to accept a judicial position; chairman, Committee on Education (Forty-first Congress); appointed chief justice of the Court of Claims 1870-1885, when he retired; died in Washington, D.C., April 1, 1892; remains were cremated and the ashes interred in Bellefontaine Cemetery, St. Louis, Mo.

**Bibliography:** *DAB*; March, David. "The Life and Times of Charles Daniel Drake." Ph.D. dissertation, University of Missouri, 1949.

**DRAKE, John Reuben,** a Representative from New York; born in Pleasant Valley, Dutchess County, N.Y., November 28, 1782; completed preparatory studies; engaged in mercantile and agricultural pursuits; supervisor of the town of Owego in 1813; first judge of Broome County 1815-1823; member of the State assembly 1817-1819; elected as a Republican to the Fifteenth Congress (March 4, 1817-March 3, 1819); judge of the court of common pleas for Tioga County 1833-1838; member of the State assembly in 1834; president of Owego village 1841-1845; died in Owego, Tioga County, N.Y., on March 21, 1857; interment in Evergreen Cemetery.

**DRANE, Herbert Jackson,** a Representative from Florida; born in Franklin, Simpson County, Ky., June 20, 1863; attended the public schools of Louisville, Ky., and Brevards Academy at Franklin, Ky.; moved to Macon, Ga., in 1881, and to Lakeland (of which he was one of the founders), Polk County, Fla., in November 1883; engaged in the real-estate and insurance business, railway construction, and in the growing of citrus fruits; mayor of Lakeland 1888-1892; county commissioner of Polk County 1896-1899; chief engrossing clerk of the State house of representatives 1889-1901; member of the State house of representatives 1903-1905; served in the State senate 1913-1917, being its president from 1913 to 1915; elected as a Democrat to the Sixty-fifth and to the seven succeeding Congresses (March 4, 1917-March 3, 1933); unsuccessful candidate for renomination in 1932; member of the Federal Power Commission 1933-1937; resumed the real estate and insurance businesses, property management, and the growing of citrus fruits; died in Lakeland, Fla., on August 11, 1947; interment in Roselawn Cemetery.

**DRAPER, Joseph,** a Representative from Virginia; born in Draper Valley, Wythe (now Pulaski) County, Va., December 25, 1794; attended private schools; studied law; was admitted to the bar in 1818 and commenced practice in Wytheville, Wythe County, Va.; served as a private in the War of 1812; member of the Virginia senate 1828-1830; elected as a Jacksonian to the Twenty-first Congress to fill the vacancy caused by the death of Alexander Smyth and served from December 6, 1830, to March 3, 1831; unsuccessfully contested the election of Charles C. Johnston to the Twenty-second Congress; subsequently elected to the Twenty-second Congress to fill the vacancy caused by the death of Charles C. Johnston and served from December 6, 1832, to March 3, 1833; was not a candidate for renomination; resumed the practice of law until his death in Wytheville, Va., June 10, 1834; interment in a private cemetery known as Oglesbies Cemetery, Drapers Valley, Va.

**DRAPER, William Franklin,** a Representative from Massachusetts; born in Lowell, Middlesex County, Mass., April 9, 1842; attended public, private, and high schools; studied mechanical engineering and cotton manufacturing; enlisted as a private in the Twenty-fifth Regiment, Massachusetts Volunteer Infantry on September 9, 1861; promoted through the ranks to lieutenant colonel; brevetted colonel and brigadier general of Volunteers; became a manufacturer of cotton machinery at Hopedale, Worcester County, and patented many improvements; delegate to the Republican National Convention of 1876; colonel on the staff of Governor John Davis Long from 1880 to 1883; elected as a Republican to the Fifty-third and Fifty-fourth Congresses (March 4, 1893-March 3, 1897); chairman, Committee on Patents (Fifty-fourth Congress); was not a candidate for renomination in 1896 to the Fifty-fifth Congress; president of the Draper Co. upon its incorporation in 1896; appointed Ambassador and Minister Plenipotentiary to Italy on April 5, 1897 and served until June 1900; died in Washington, D.C., on January 28, 1910; interment in Village Cemetery, Hopedale, Mass.

**Bibliography:** *DAB*.

**DRAPER, William Henry,** a Representative from New York; born in Rochdale, Worcester County, Mass., June 24, 1841; moved with his parents to Troy, N.Y., in 1847; attended the public schools until 1856; engaged in mercantile pursuits; trustee of the village of Lansingburgh for ten years; commissioner of jurors for Rensselaer County 1896-1900; elected as a Republican to the Fifty-seventh and to the five succeeding Congresses (March 4, 1901-March 3, 1913); was not a candidate for reelection in 1912; engaged in the manufacture of cordage and twine and was president of the W.H. Draper & Sons (Inc.); died in Troy, N.Y., December 7, 1921; interment in Oakwood Cemetery.

**DRAYTON, William,** a Representative from South Carolina; born in St. Augustine, Fla., December 30, 1776; attended preparatory schools in England; returned to the United States in 1790 and settled in Charleston, S.C.; studied law; was admitted to the bar December 12, 1797, and commenced practice in Charleston; member of the State house of representatives 1806-1808; entered the United States Army as lieutenant colonel of the Tenth Infantry March 12, 1812; became colonel of the Eighteenth Infantry July 25, 1812; inspector general August 1, 1814, and served throughout the War of 1812; resumed the practice of law in Charleston; recorder of Charleston 1819-1824; elected to the Nineteenth Congress to fill the vacancy caused by the resignation of Joel R. Poinsett; reelected as a Jacksonian to the Twentieth and to the two succeeding Congresses and served from May 17, 1825, to March 3, 1833; chairman, Committee on Military Affairs (Twentieth through Twenty-second Congresses); declined appointment as Secretary of War in the Cabinet of President Andrew Jackson, and also appointment as Minister to Great Britain; opposed nullification in 1830; moved to Philadelphia, Pa., in August 1833; president of the Bank of the United States in 1840 and 1841; died in Philadelphia, Pa., May 24, 1846; interment in Laurel Hill Cemetery.

**Bibliography:** *DAB*.

**DRAYTON, William Henry,** a Delegate from South Carolina; born at Drayton Hall, on Ashley River, S.C., in September 1742; pursued classical studies; attended Westminister School and Balliol College, Oxford, England; returned to South Carolina in 1764; studied law and was admitted to the bar; visited England again in 1770 and was appointed by King George III privy councilor for the Province of South Carolina; while on his way home was appointed assistant judge, but took such an active part in the pre-Revolutionary movement that he was deprived of both positions; president of the council of safety in 1775, and in 1776 was chief justice; Member of the Continental Congress in 1778 and served until his death in Philadelphia, Pa., on September 3, 1779; interment in Christ Church Cemetery.

**Bibliography:** *DAB*; Dabney, William M., and Marion Dargan. *William Henry Drayton and the American Revolution*. Albuquerque, N.M.: University of New Mexico Press, 1962; Dabney, William M. "Drayton and Laurens in the Continental Congress." *South Carolina Historical Magazine* 60 (April 1959): 74-82.

**DREIER, David Timothy,** a Representative from California; born in Kansas City, Jackson County, Mo., July 5, 1952; attended the Principia Middle and Upper Schools in St. Louis, Mo.; B.A., Claremont McKenna College, Claremont, Calif., 1975; M.A., Claremont Graduate School, 1976; director, corporate relations, Claremont McKenna College, 1975-1979; delegate, California State Republican conventions, 1978-1980; delegate, Republican National Conventions, 1976-1980; vice president, Dreier Development Co., Kansas City, Mo., 1979-1980; unsuccessful candidate in 1978 for election to the Ninety-sixth Congress; elected as a Republican to the Ninety-seventh and to the seven succeeding Congresses (January 3, 1981-January 3, 1997); is a resident of LaVerne, Calif.

**DRESSER, Solomon Robert,** a Representative from Pennsylvania; born in Litchfield, Hillsdale County, Mich., February 1, 1842; attended the common schools and Hillsdale College; engaged in agricultural pursuits until 1865; became an inventor of oil and gas well equipment; moved to Pennsylvania in 1872 and engaged in the production of oil and gas; founder and president of the S.R. Dresser Manufacturing Co.; elected as a Republican to the Fifty-eighth and Fifty-ninth Congresses (March 4, 1903-March 3, 1907); was not a candidate for renomination in 1906 to the Sixtieth Congress; resumed former business pursuits; died in Bradford, McKean County, Pa., January 21, 1911; interment in Oak Hill Cemetery.

**DREW, Ira Walton,** a Representative from Pennsylvania; born in Hardwick, Caledonia County, Vt., August 31, 1878; attended the public schools and Hardwick Academy; apprenticed as a printer, becoming a journeyman in 1899; newspaper reporter in Burlington, Vt., 1899-1906; reporter and news editor in Boston, Mass., 1906-1908; was graduated from Philadelphia (Pa.) College of Osteopathy in 1911 and began the practice of osteopathy in Philadelphia the same year; member of the faculty of the Philadelphia College of Osteopathy 1912-1933; elected as a Democrat to the Seventy-fifth Congress (January 3, 1937-January 3, 1939); unsuccessful candidate for reelection in 1938 to the Seventy-sixth Congress; member of the board of trustees, Philadelphia College of Osteopathy; resumed the practice of osteopathy in Philadelphia where he died February 12, 1972; interment in Whitemarsh Memorial Park, Prospectville, Pa.

**DREW, Irving Webster,** a Senator from New Hampshire; born in Colebrook, Coos County, N.H., January 8, 1845; attended Kimball Union Academy and was graduated from Dartmouth College, Hanover, N.H., in 1870; moved to Lancaster, N.H., where he studied law; was admitted to the bar in 1871 and commenced practice in Lancaster; appointed major of the New Hampshire National Guard in 1876 and served three years; member, State senate 1883-1884; left the Democratic Party in 1896 and became a member of the Republican Party; delegate to the State constitutional conventions in 1902 and 1912; engaged in banking and the railroad business; appointed as a Republican to the United States Senate to fill the vacancy caused by the death of Jacob H. Gallinger and served from September 2, to November 5, 1918, when a successor was elected; was not a candidate for election; retired from active business pursuits; died in Montclair, Essex County, N.J., April 10, 1922; interment in Summer Street Cemetery, Lancaster, Coos County, N.H.

**DREWRY, Patrick Henry,** a Representative from Virginia; born in Petersburg, Dinwiddie County, Va., May 24, 1875; attended the public schools, Petersburg High School, and McCabe's University School; was graduated from Randolph-Macon College, Ashland, Va., in 1896; studied law at the University of Virginia at Charlottesville; was admitted to the bar in 1901 and commenced practice in Petersburg; director of the Petersburg Savings & American Trust Co.; member of the Virginia senate 1912-1920; delegate to the Virginia Democratic conventions in 1912, 1916, 1920, and 1924; delegate to the Democratic National Convention in 1916; chairman of the Economy and Efficiency Commission of Virginia 1916-1918; chairman of the Virginia auditing committee 1916-1920; chairman of the Virginia advisory board in 1919; member of the Democratic National Congressional Committee 1923-1927; member of the Board of Visitors to the United States Naval Academy at Annapolis in 1925; elected as a Democrat to the Sixty-sixth Congress to fill the vacancy caused by the death of Walter A. Watson; reelected to the Sixty-seventh and to the thirteen succeeding Congresses and served from April 27, 1920, until his death in Petersburg, Va., December 21, 1947; interment in Blandford Cemetery.

**DRIGGS, Edmund Hope,** a Representative from New York; born in Brooklyn, N.Y., May 2, 1865; attended the public schools and Adelphi Academy in Brooklyn; became engaged in the casualty-insurance business; elected as a Democrat to the Fifty-fifth Congress to fill the vacancy caused by the resignation of Francis H. Wilson; reelected to the Fifty-sixth Congress and served from December 6, 1897, to March 3, 1901; unsuccessful candidate for reelection in 1900 to the Fifty-seventh Congress; resumed the casualty-insurance business and also engaged in safety engineering; died in Brooklyn, N.Y., September 27, 1946; interment in Cypress Hills Cemetery.

**DRIGGS, John Fletcher,** a Representative from Michigan; born in Kinderhook, N.Y., March 8, 1813; completed preparatory studies; moved with his parents to Tarrytown, N.Y., in 1825; moved to New York City in 1827; apprentice, journeyman, and master mechanic in the trade of sash, door, and blind manufacturing 1829-1856; superintendent of the New York penitentiary and public institutions on Blackwells Island in 1844; moved to Michigan in 1856; engaged in the real-estate business and salt manufacturing; president of the common council of East Saginaw, Mich., in 1858; member of the State house of representatives in 1859 and 1860; was tendered an appointment as colonel during the Civil War; organized the Twenty-ninth Michigan Infantry July 29, 1864; elected as a Republican to the Thirty-eighth, Thirty-ninth, and Fortieth Congresses (March 4, 1863-March 3, 1869); unsuccessful candidate for election in 1870 to the Forty-second Congress; one of the committee appointed to accompany the body of President Lincoln to Springfield, Ill., for interment; injured by a fall on the ice in the winter of 1875-1876, as a result of which he died in East Saginaw, Mich., December 17, 1877; interment in Brady Hill Cemetery, Saginaw, Mich.; reinterment in Forest Lawn Cemetery.

**DRINAN, Robert Frederick,** a Representative from Massachusetts; born in Boston, Mass., November 15, 1920; attended the public schools of Hyde Park, Mass.; A.B., M.A., Boston College, 1942; entered the Jesuit Order, 1942, and was ordained a Catholic priest, 1953; LL.B., LL.M., Georgetown University Law Center, Washington, D.C., 1950; S.T.L. (licentiate in sacred theology), Gregorian University, Rome, Italy, 1954; studied in Florence, Italy, 1954-1955; admitted to the Massachusetts bar in 1956 and commenced practice in Boston; dean, Boston College Law School, 1956-1970; professor of family law and church-state relations; visiting professor, University

of Texas Law School, 1966-1967; vice president, Massachusetts Bar Association, 1961-1964; author and editor; lecturer on church-state relations, Andover Newton Theological Seminary, Newton, Mass., 1966, 1968; chairman, Advisory Committee for Massachusetts to United States Commission on Civil Rights, 1962-1971; member, Governor's commission to study conflict of interests, 1962; Griswold commission to study judicial salaries, 1962; and Massachusetts Attorney General's Committee on Civil Rights and Civil Liberties; delegate to Massachusetts Democratic convention, 1972; delegate to Democratic National Convention, 1972; elected as a Democrat to the Ninety-second and to the four succeeding Congresses (January 3, 1971-January 3, 1981); was not a candidate for reelection in 1980 to the Ninety-seventh Congress; member, board of directors, Civil Liberties Public Education Fund; is a resident of Washington, D.C.

**Bibliography:** Lapomarda, Vincent A. "A Jesuit Runs for Congress: The Rev. Robert F. Drinan, S.J. and His 1970 Campaign." *Journal of Church and State* 15 (Spring 1973): 205-22.

**DRISCOLL, Daniel Angelus,** a Representative from New York; born in Buffalo, Erie County, N.Y., March 6, 1875; attended the public schools and Central High School; engaged in the undertaking business with his father, and also in other business enterprises; elected as a Democrat to the Sixty-first and to the three succeeding Congresses (March 4, 1909-March 3, 1917); was an unsuccessful candidate for reelection in 1916 to the Sixty-fifth Congress; resumed undertaking business in Buffalo, N.Y.; served as postmaster of Buffalo from February 15, 1934, until February 28, 1947; president of the Phoenix Brewery Corp. of Buffalo, N.Y.; died in Buffalo, N.Y., June 5, 1955; interment in Holy Cross Cemetery, Lackawanna, N.Y.

**DRISCOLL, Denis Joseph,** a Representative from Pennsylvania; born in North Lawrence, St. Lawrence County, N.Y., March 27, 1871; attended the public schools, Lawrenceville (N.Y.) Academy, and State Teachers' College, Potsdam, N.Y.; taught school in Potsdam, N.Y., 1888-1889, and in St. Marys, Elk County, Pa., 1890-1891; principal of public schools, St. Marys, 1892-1897; studied law; was admitted to the bar on April 22, 1898, and on the same day enlisted as a private in the Sixteenth Regiment, Pennsylvania National Guard, which on that day had been called for service in the Spanish-American War; after the war commenced the practice of law in St. Marys; member of the Pennsylvania Democratic committee from 1899 to 1922, serving as chairman in 1905; chief burgess of St. Marys, 1903-1906; president of the St. Marys School Board, 1911-1936; delegate to the Democratic National Conventions of 1916 and 1920; United States attorney for the western district of Pennsylvania, 1920-1921; elected as a Democrat to the Seventy-fourth Congress (January 3, 1935-January 3, 1937); unsuccessful candidate for reelection in 1936 to the Seventy-fifth Congress; appointed chairman of the Pennsylvania Public Utility Commission for a ten-year term on April 1, 1937, from which position he resigned to accept an appointment on March 2, 1940, by the United States Court for the Southern District of New York, as one of two trustees in the reorganization of the bankrupt Associated Gas and Electric Corporation, and served until August 1946; died in St. Marys, Pa., January 18, 1958; interment in St. Marys Catholic Cemetery.

**DRISCOLL, Michael Edward,** a Representative from New York; born in Syracuse, N.Y., February 9, 1851; moved with his parents to the town of Camillus, Onondaga County, in 1852; attended the district schools, Monro Collegiate Institute, in Elbridge, Onondaga County, and was graduated from Williams College, Williamstown, Mass., in 1877; studied law; was admitted to the bar in 1879 and commenced practice in Syracuse, N.Y., the same year; appointed one of five commissioners to draft a uniform charter for second-class cities in the State; appointed attorney for the State superintendent of insurance in 1905; member of the Taft party that visited the Philippine Islands and Asian countries in 1905; chairman of the Republican State Convention in 1906; elected as a Republican to the Fifty-sixth and to the six succeeding Congresses (March 4, 1899-March 3, 1913); chairman, Committee on Elections No. 3 (Fifty-eighth through Sixty-first Congresses); unsuccessful candidate for reelection in 1912 to the Sixty-third Congress; engaged in the practice of law, traveling, and lecturing on his travels; died in Syracuse, N.Y., January 19, 1929; interment in Oakwood Cemetery.

**DRIVER, William Joshua,** a Representative from Arkansas; born near Osceola, Mississippi County, Ark., March 2, 1873; attended the public schools; studied law; was admitted to the bar in 1894 and commenced practice in Osceola, Ark.; member of the State house of representatives 1897-1899; judge of the second judicial circuit of Arkansas 1911-1918; member of the State constitutional convention in 1918; delegate to the Democratic National Convention in 1932; elected as a Democrat to the Sixty-seventh and to the eight succeeding Congresses (March 4, 1921-January 3, 1939); unsuccessful candidate for renomination in 1938; resumed the practice of law and also engaged in the banking business in Osceola, Ark., until his death there on October 1, 1948; interment in Violet Cemetery.

**DROMGOOLE, George Coke** (uncle of Alexander Dromgoole Sims), a Representative from Virginia; born in Lawrenceville, Brunswick County, Va., May 15, 1797; completed preparatory studies; studied law; was admitted to the bar and practiced; member of the Virginia house of representatives, 1823-1826; member of the Virginia senate, 1826-1835; delegate to the Virginia constitutional convention in 1829; elected as a Jacksonian to the Twenty-fourth Congress and reelected as a Democrat to the Twenty-fifth and Twenty-sixth Congresses (March 4, 1835-March 3, 1841); declined to be a candidate for reelection in 1840 to the Twenty-seventh Congress; elected to the Twenty-eighth and to the two succeeding Congresses, and served from March 4, 1843 until his death on his estate in Brunswick County, Va., April 27, 1847; interment in the family burying ground south of the Meherrin River.

**Bibliography:** Lewis, Henry W. "The Dugger-Dromgoole Duel." *North Carolina Historical Review* 34 (July 1957): 327-345.

**DRUKKER, Dow Henry,** a Representative from New Jersey; born in Sneek, Netherlands, February 7, 1872; immigrated to the United States with his parents, who settled in Grand Rapids, Mich., the same year; attended the public schools of Grand Rapids, Mich.; moved to New Jersey in 1897 and settled in Passaic; businessman and banker; member of the Passaic County Board of Chosen Freeholders 1906-1913, serving as director 1908-1912; elected as a Republican to the Sixty-third Congress to fill the vacancy caused by the death of Robert Gunn Bremner; reelected to the Sixty-fourth and Sixty-fifth Congresses and served from April 7, 1914, to March 3, 1919; was not a candidate for renomination in 1918 to the Sixty-sixth Congress; publisher of the Herald-News of Passaic-Clifton from 1916 until 1963; became president of the Union Building and Investment Co., in 1909; knighted as an Officer of the Order of Orange-Nassau by Queen Juliana for services rendered in the great flood of February 1953; resided in Clifton, N.J., and Lake Wales, Fla., until his death in Lake Wales on January 11, 1963; interment in Cedar Lawn Cemetery, Paterson, N.J.

**DRUM, Augustus,** a Representative from Pennsylvania; born in Greensburg, Pa., November 26, 1815; received private instruction and attended Greensburg Academy; was graduated from Jefferson College (now Washington and Jefferson), Canonsburg, Pa.; studied law; was admitted to the bar in 1836 and commenced practice in Greensburg; member of the Pennsylvania senate in 1852 and 1853; held several local offices; elected as a Democrat to the Thirty-third Congress (March 4, 1853-March 3, 1855); unsuccessful candidate for reelection in 1854 to the Thirty-fourth Congress; resumed the practice of law in Greensburg, Westmoreland County, Pa., and died there September 15, 1858; interment in St. Clair Cemetery.

**DRYDEN, John Fairfield,** a Senator from New Jersey; born in Temple, Franklin County, Maine, August 7, 1839; moved to Massachusetts in 1846 with his parents, who settled in Worcester; attended Yale College; founded the Prudential Insurance Co. of America in Newark, N.J., in 1875, becoming its first secretary and in 1881 its president, and served in the latter position until 1911; one of the founders of the Fidelity Trust Co.; involved in the establishment and management of various street railways, banks, and other financial enterprises in New Jersey, New York, and Pennsylvania; elected as a Republican to the United States Senate to fill the vacancy caused by the death of William J. Sewell and served from January 29, 1902, to March 3, 1907; was a candidate for reelection, but withdrew because of a deadlock in the legislature; chairman, Committee on Relations with Canada (Fifty-seventh Congress), Committee on Enrolled Bills (Fifty-eighth and Fifty-ninth Congresses); resumed his former business pursuits; died in Newark, N.J., November 24, 1911; interment in Mount Pleasant Cemetery.

**Bibliography:** *DAB*; Reynolds, Robert D., Jr. "The 1906 Campaign to Sway Muckraking Periodicals." *Journalism Quarterly* 56 (Autumn 1979): 513-20, 589.

**DUANE, James,** a Delegate from New York; born in New York City February 6, 1733; completed preparatory studies; studied law; was admitted to the bar August 3, 1754; clerk of the chancery court in 1762; attorney general of New York in 1767; boundary commissioner in 1768 and 1784; State Indian commissioner in 1774; delegate to the provincial convention in 1775; member of the Revolutionary Committee of One Hundred in 1775; Member of the Continental Congress 1774-1783; member of the Provincial Congress in 1776 and 1777; served in the State senate 1782-1785 and 1788-1790; chosen a member of the Annapolis Commercial Convention in 1786, but did not attend; first mayor of New York City 1784-1789; delegate to the State convention which ratified the Federal Constitution in 1788; United States district judge for the district of New York 1789-1794; believed to have died in either New York City or in Duanesburg, Schenectady County, N.Y., February 1, 1797; interment under Christ Church in Duanesburg.

**Bibliography:** *DAB*.

**DUBOIS, Fred Thomas,** a Delegate and a Senator from Idaho; born in Palestine, Crawford County, Ill., May 29, 1851; attended the public schools, and was graduated from Yale College in 1872; secretary of the Board of Railway and Warehouse Commissioners of Illinois, 1875-1876; moved to Idaho Territory in 1880 and engaged in business; United States marshal of Idaho, 1882-1886; elected as a Republican Delegate from the Territory of Idaho to the Fiftieth and Fifty-first Congresses, and served from March 4, 1887 to July 3, 1890; elected as a Republican to the United States Senate, and served from March 4, 1891 to March 3, 1897; unsuccessful Silver Republican candidate for reelection to the United States Senate in 1896; chairman, Committee on Public Lands (Fifty-fourth Congress); elected as a Silver Republican to the United States Senate, and served from March 4, 1901 to March 3, 1907; shortly after his election to the Senate as a Silver Republican he became a Democrat; took up his residence in Washington, D.C.; appointed civilian member of the Board of Ordnance and Fortifications, 1918-1920; appointed by President Calvin Coolidge to International Joint Commission created to prevent disputes regarding the use of the boundary waters between the United States and Canada, 1924-1930; died in Washington, D.C., February 14, 1930; interment in Grove City Cemetery, Blackfoot, Idaho.

**Bibliography:** Cook, Rufus G. "The Political Suicide of Senator Fred T. Dubois of Idaho." *Pacific Northwest Quarterly* 60 (October 1969): 193-98; Graff, Leo W., Jr. *The Senatorial Career of Fred T. Dubois of Idaho, 1890-1907.* New York: Garland Publishing, 1988.

**DU BOSE, Dudley McIver,** a Representative from Georgia; born in Shelby County, Tenn., October 28, 1834; attended the University of Mississippi at Oxford, and was graduated from the Lebanon (Tenn.) Law School in 1856; was admitted to the bar in 1857 and commenced the practice of law in Memphis, Tenn.; moved to Augusta, Ga., in 1860; served in the Confederate Army during the Civil War as colonel of the Fifteenth Regiment, Georgia Volunteer Infantry, and subsequently became brigadier general in the Western Army; moved to Washington, Wilkes County, Ga.; elected as a Democrat to the Forty-second Congress (March 4, 1871-March 3, 1873); resumed the practice of law; died in Washington, Ga., March 2, 1883; interment in Rest Haven Cemetery.

**DUDLEY, Charles Edward,** a Senator from New York; born in Johnston Hall, Staffordshire, England, May 23, 1780; immigrated to the United States with his mother, who settled in Newport, R.I., in 1794; entered a counting room as clerk; moved to Albany, N.Y., where he engaged in the mercantile business; member of the State senate 1820-1825; mayor of Albany 1821-1824, 1828-1829; elected to the United States Senate to fill the vacancy caused by the resignation of Martin Van Buren and served from January 15, 1829, to March 3, 1833; became interested in astronomical science; died in Albany, N.Y., January 23, 1841; interment in the Rural Cemetery.

Bibliography: *DAB.*

**DUDLEY, Edward Bishop,** a Representative from North Carolina; born near Jacksonville, Onslow County, N.C., December 15, 1789; attended the local academy; member of the North Carolina State house of commons 1811 and 1813; served in the North Carolina State senate in 1814; during the War of 1812, served as lieutenant colonel of the Onslow Regiment of Volunteers; member of the State house of commons from Wilmington in 1816 and 1817; elected to the Twenty-first Congress to fill the vacancy caused by the death of Gabriel Holmes and served from November 10, 1829, to March 3, 1831; declined to be a candidate for reelection in 1830 to the Twenty-second Congress; again a member of the State house of commons in 1834 and 1835; organized the Wilmington & Weldon Railroad Co. and was its first president; elected Governor of North Carolina in 1836, being the first Governor elected by popular vote instead of by the legislature; reelected in 1838, and served from December 31, 1836 until January 1, 1841; resumed his former railroad pursuits; died in Wilmington, N.C., October 30, 1855; interment in Oak Dale Cemetery.

Bibliography: *DAB.*

**DUELL, Rodolphus Holland,** a Representative from New York; born in Warren, Herkimer County, N.Y., December 20, 1824; completed preparatory studies; studied law; was admitted to the bar in 1845 and commenced practice in Fabius, N.Y.; moved to Cortland, N.Y., in 1847; district attorney of Cortland County 1850-1855; judge of Cortland County 1855-1859; assessor of internal revenue for the twenty-third district of New York from 1869 to 1871; elected as a Republican to the Thirty-sixth and Thirty-seventh Congresses (March 4, 1859-March 3, 1863); chairman, Committee on Revolutionary Claims (Thirty-seventh Congress); resumed the practice of law in Cortland; elected to the Forty-second and Forty-third Congresses (March 4, 1871-March 3, 1875); chairman, Committee on Expenditures on Public Buildings (Forty-third Congress); appointed by President Grant United States Commissioner of Patents on October 1, 1875, and served until January 30, 1877; resumed the practice of law in Cortland, N.Y., where he died February 11, 1891; interment in Cortland Rural Cemetery.

**DUER, William** (grandfather of William Duer [1805-1879]), a Delegate from New York; born in Devonshire, England, March 18, 1747; completed preparatory studies and attended Eton College, England; in 1765 became aide-de-camp to Robert Clive (Baron Clive of Plassey), Governor General of India; immigrated to America in 1768 and settled in Fort Miller, N.Y.; appointed justice of the peace on July 1, 1773; first judge of Charlotte (now Washington) County; built the first saw and grist mills at Fort Miller, and later erected a snuff mill and a powder mill; was prominent in the Revolutionary movement; member of the Provincial Congress in 1776 and 1777; served in the State senate in 1777; appointed judge of the court of common pleas in 1777 and reappointed in 1778; moved to Fishkill, N.Y., and later to what is now Paterson, N.J., where he erected the first cotton mill; Member of the Continental Congress in 1777 and 1778; moved to New York City in 1783; served as a member of the State assembly in 1786; assistant secretary of the treasury department 1789-1790; died in New York City on April 18, 1799; interment in the family vault under the old church of St. Thomas; reinterment in Jamaica, Long Island, N.Y.

Bibliography: Jones, Robert F. "The Public Career of William Duer: Rebel, Federalist Politician, Entrepreneur and Speculator 1775-1792." Ph.D. dissertation, University of Notre Dame, 1967.

**DUER, William** (grandson of William Duer [1747-1799]), a Representative from New York; born in New York City May 25, 1805; completed preparatory studies and was graduated from Columbia College, New York City, in 1824; studied law; was admitted to the bar in 1824 and commenced practice in New York City; unsuccessful candidate for the State assembly in 1832; moved to New Orleans, La., in 1832, where he continued the practice of law; moved to Oswego, N.Y., in 1836 and continued the practice of law; member of the New York State assembly in 1840 and 1841; unsuccessful candidate in 1842 for election to the Twenty-eighth Congress; delegate to the Whig National Convention in 1844; district attorney of Oswego County 1845-1847; elected as a Whig to the Thirtieth and Thirty-first Congresses (March 4, 1847-March 3, 1851); appointed by President Fillmore as consul to Valparaiso, Chile, on March 18, 1851, and served until May 23, 1853; settled in San Francisco, Calif., in 1854 and practiced his profession; served as clerk of San Francisco County in 1858 and 1859; returned to Staten Island, N.Y., in 1859 and lived in retirement until his death in New Brighton, Richmond County, N.Y., August 25, 1879; interment in Silver Mount Cemetery, Thompkinsville, Staten Island, N.Y.

**DUFF, James Henderson,** a Senator from Pennsylvania; born in Mansfield (now Carnegie), Allegheny County, Pa., January 21, 1883; was graduated from Princeton University in 1904; student at the University of Pennsylvania 1904-1906; graduated from the law school of the University of Pittsburgh in 1907; was admitted to the bar the same year and commenced the practice of law in Pittsburgh, Pa.; attorney general of Pennsylvania 1943-1947; elected Governor of Pennsylvania in 1946 and served from January 21, 1947 to January 16, 1951; member of the Pennsylvania Pardon Board; elected as a Republican to the United States Senate in 1950 for the term commencing January 3, 1951, and served until January 3, 1957; unsuccessful candidate for reelection in 1956; engaged in the practice of law in Washington, D.C., until his death there on December 20, 1969; interment in Chartiers Cemetery, Carnegie, Pa.

**DUFFEY, Warren Joseph,** a Representative from Ohio; born in Toledo, Ohio, January 24, 1886; attended the public schools; was graduated from St. John's University, Toledo, Ohio, in 1908 and from the law department of the University of Michigan at Ann Arbor in 1911; was admitted to the bar the same year and commenced the practice of law in Toledo, Ohio; served in the State house of representatives in 1913 and 1914; member of the Toledo City Council in 1917 and 1918; served as chairman of the Lucas County Democratic central committee 1919-1932; delegate to the Democratic National Convention in 1932; elected as a Democrat to the Seventy-third and Seventy-fourth Congresses and served from March 4, 1933, until his death; unsuccessful candidate for renomination in 1936; died in Toledo, Ohio, July 7, 1936; interment in Calvary Cemetery.

**DUFFY, Francis Ryan,** a Senator from Wisconsin; born in Fond du Lac, Fond du Lac County, Wis., June 23, 1888; attended the public schools; was graduated from the University of Wisconsin at Madison, in 1910 and from its law department in 1912; was admitted to the bar in 1912 and commenced practice in Fond du Lac, Wis.; during the First World War served in the United States Army 1917-1919, attaining the rank of major; resumed the practice of law in Fond du Lac, Wis.; elected as a Democrat to the United States Senate and served from March 4, 1933, to January 3, 1939; unsuccessful candidate for reelection in 1938; again resumed the practice of law before becoming United States district judge for the eastern district of Wisconsin, serving from 1939 to 1949, when he qualified as a United States circuit judge of the court of appeals for the seventh circuit, becoming chief judge in 1954 and served until 1959; retired as a full-time member of the court in 1966 and assumed the status of senior judge and continued to hear cases for several more years; died in Milwaukee, Wis., August 16, 1979; interment in Calvary Cemetery, Fond du Lac, Wis.

**DUFFY, James Patrick Bernard,** a Representative from New York; born in Rochester, N.Y., November 25, 1878; attended private schools; was graduated from Georgetown University, Washington, D.C., in 1901 and from the law department of Harvard University in 1904; was admitted to the bar in 1904 and commenced practice in Rochester, N.Y.; member of the Rochester (N.Y.) School Board 1905-1932; member of the New York State Alcoholic Beverage Control Board in 1933 and 1934; elected as a Democrat to the Seventy-fourth Congress (January 3, 1935-January 3, 1937); unsuccessful candidate for renomination in 1936 to the Seventy-fifth Congress; appointed by Governor Herbert H. Lehman justice of the supreme court of the State of New York, seventh judicial district, for term expiring December 31, 1937; member of the State Probation Commission 1938-1944; resumed the practice of law; died in Rochester, N.Y., January 8, 1969; interment in Holy Sepulchre Cemetery.

**DUGRO, Philip Henry,** a Representative from New York; born in New York City October 3, 1855; attended the public schools and was graduated from the school of arts of Columbia College, New York City, in 1876 and from the law department of the same institution in 1878; was admitted to the bar in the latter year and commenced practice in New York City; member of the State assembly in 1879; elected as a Democrat to the Forty-seventh Congress (March 4, 1881-March 3, 1883); was not a candidate for reelection; resumed the practice of law in New York City and also interested in the real-estate business; declined the office of State commissioner of immigration in 1885; judge of the superior court of New York County from 1887 to 1896, when the superior court was merged into the supreme court; associate justice of the New York Supreme Court from 1896 until his death in New York City March 1, 1920; interment in Woodlawn Cemetery.

**DUKE, Richard Thomas Walker,** a Representative from Virginia; born near Charlottesville, Albemarle County, Va., June 6, 1822; attended private schools; was graduated from the Virginia Military Institute, Lexington, Va., in 1844; was graduated from the law department of the University of Virginia, Charlottesville, Va., in 1850; elected Commonwealth attorney for the county of Albemarle in 1858 and continued in that office until 1869; during the Civil War entered the Confederate Army; became colonel of the Forty-sixth Regiment, Virginia Infantry; elected as a Conservative to the Forty-first Congress to fill the vacancy caused by the death of Robert Ridgway; reelected to the Forty-second Congress and served from November 8, 1870, to March 3, 1873; member of the Virginia house of delegates in 1879 and 1880; died at his country estate, "Sunny Side," near Charlottesville, Albemarle County, Va., on July 2, 1898; interment in Maplewood Cemetery, Charlottesville, Va.

**DULLES, John Foster,** a Senator from New York; born in Washington, D.C., February 25, 1888; attended the public schools of Watertown, N.Y.; was graduated from Princeton University in 1908; attended the Sorbonne, Paris, in 1908 and 1909; graduated from the law school of George Washington University, Washington, D.C., in 1911; was admitted to the bar and commenced the practice of law in New York City in 1911; special agent for the Department of State in Central America in 1917; during the First World War served as a captain and a major in the United States Army Intelligence Service, 1917-1918; assistant to the chairman of the War Trade Board in 1918; counsel to the American Commission to Negotiate Peace during 1918 and 1919; member of Reparations Commission and Supreme Economic Council in 1919; legal adviser, Polish Plan of Financial Stabilization, 1927; American representative to the Berlin Debt Conferences of 1933; member of the United States delegation to the San Francisco Conference on World Organization in 1945; adviser to the Secretary of State at the Council of Foreign Ministers meetings in London (1945), Moscow and London (1947), and Paris (1949); representative to the General Assembly of the United Nations, 1946-1949, and chairman of the United States delegation in Paris, 1948; chairman of the board, Carnegie Endowment for International Peace; member of the New York State Banking Board, 1946-1949; appointed as a Republican to the United States Senate to fill the vacancy caused by the resignation of Robert F. Wagner, and served from July 7, 1949 to November 8, 1949, when a duly elected successor qualified; unsuccessful candidate for election to the vacancy; United States representative to the Fifth General Assembly of the United Nations in 1950; consultant to Secretary of State Dean G. Acheson during 1951 and 1952; appointed Secretary of State by President Dwight D. Eisenhower, and served from January 21, 1953 until his resignation on April 22, 1959; died in Washington, D.C., May 24, 1959; interment in Arlington National Cemetery, Va.

**Bibliography:** *DAB*; Hoopes, Townsend. *The Devil and John Foster Dulles.* Boston: Little Brown, 1973; Pruessen, Ronald W. *John Foster Dulles: The Road to Power.* New York: Free Press, 1982.

**DULSKI, Thaddeus Joseph,** a Representative from New York; born in Buffalo, Erie County, N.Y., September 27, 1915; attended parochial school, Buffalo Technical High School, Canisius College, Buffalo, N.Y. and the University of Buffalo; with the Bureau of Internal Revenue, Treasury Department, 1940-1947; veteran of the Second World War; accountant and tax consultant; special agent in the Price Stabilization Administration 1951-1953; in 1953 was elected Walden district councilman for two terms and in 1957 was elected councilman-at-large of the city of Buffalo for a four-year term; elected as a Democrat to the Eighty-sixth Congress; reelected to the seven succeeding Congresses and served from January 3, 1959, until his resignation December 31, 1974; chairman, Committee on Post Office and Civil Service (Ninetieth through Ninety-third Congresses); was not a candidate for reelection in 1974 to the Ninety-fourth Congress; was a resident of Buffalo, N.Y.; died October 11, 1988.

**DUMONT, Ebenezer,** a Representative from Indiana; born in Vevay, Ind., November 23, 1814; pursued classical studies; studied law; was admitted to the bar and commenced practice in Vevay; member of the State house of representatives in 1838; treasurer of Vevay 1839-1845; lieutenant colonel of Volunteers in the Mexican War; member of the State house of representatives in 1850 and 1853; colonel of the Seventh Regiment, Indiana Volunteer Infantry, during the Civil War; promoted to brigadier general of Volunteers September 3, 1861, and served until February 28, 1863, when he resigned; elected as a Unionist to the Thirty-eighth Congress and reelected as a Republican to the Thirty-ninth Congress (March 4, 1863-March 3, 1867); chairman, Committee on District of Columbia (Thirty-eighth Congress), Committee on Expenditures in the Department of the Interior (Thirty-ninth Congress); was not a candidate for renomination in 1866 to the Fortieth Congress; appointed Governor of Idaho Territory by President Ulysses S. Grant, but died in Indianapolis, Ind., April 16, 1871, before taking the oath of office; interment in Crown Hill Cemetery.

**DUNBAR, James Whitson**, a Representative from Indiana; born in New Albany, Floyd County, Ind., October 17, 1860; attended the public schools and was graduated from New Albany High School in 1878; engaged in mercantile pursuits; manager of public utilities in New Albany and Jeffersonville; secretary-treasurer of the Western Gas Association 1894-1906; secretary of the American Gas Institute 1906-1909; president of the Indiana Gas Association 1908-1910 and secretary 1914-1919; elected as a Republican to the Sixty-sixth and Sixty-seventh Congresses (March 4, 1919-March 3, 1923); was not a candidate for reelection in 1922; elected to the Seventy-first Congress (March 4, 1929-March 3, 1931); unsuccessful candidate for reelection in 1930 to the Seventy-second Congress; resumed his former business pursuits; died in New Albany, Ind., May 19, 1943; interment in Fairview Cemetery.

**DUNBAR, William**, a Representative from Louisiana; born in Virginia in 1805; completed preparatory studies; moved to Alexandria, Va., and engaged in the practice of law in the early thirties; moved to Louisiana in 1852; appointed associate justice of the supreme court of Louisiana to fill the vacancy caused by the death of Judge Preston and served from September 1, 1852, to May 4, 1853; elected as a Democrat to the Thirty-third Congress (March 4, 1853-March 3, 1855); retired to his sugar plantation in the parish of St. Bernard and resided there until his death on March 18, 1861.

**DUNCAN, Alexander**, a Representative from Ohio; born in Bottle Hill (now Madison), Morris County, N.J., in 1788; studied and practiced medicine; moved to Ohio and settled in Cincinnati; member of the Ohio State house of representatives in 1828, 1829, 1831, and 1832; served in the State senate from 1832 until 1834; elected as a Democrat to the Twenty-fifth and Twenty-sixth Congresses (March 4, 1837-March 3, 1841); unsuccessful candidate for reelection in 1840 to the Twenty-seventh Congress; elected to the Twenty-eighth Congress (March 4, 1843-March 3, 1845); was not a candidate for reelection in 1844 to the Twenty-ninth Congress; resumed the practice of his profession; died in Madisonville (now a part of Cincinnati), Hamilton County, Ohio, March 23, 1853; interment in Laurel Cemetery.

**DUNCAN, Daniel**, a Representative from Ohio; born in Shippensburg, Cumberland County, Pa., July 22, 1806; completed preparatory studies; attended Jefferson College, Canonsburg, Pa., in 1825; moved to Newark, Ohio, in 1828; engaged in mercantile pursuits; member of the Ohio State house of representatives in 1843; unsuccessful Whig candidate for election to the State senate in 1844; elected as a Whig to the Thirtieth Congress (March 4, 1847-March 3, 1849); was an unsuccessful candidate for reelection in 1848 to the Thirty-first Congress; died in Washington, D.C., May 18, 1849; interment in the Newark Graveyard, Newark, Ohio.

**DUNCAN, Garnett**, a Representative from Kentucky. *(See DUNCAN, William Garnett.)*

**DUNCAN, James**, a Representative from Pennsylvania; born in Philadelphia, Pa., in 1756; attended the common schools and Princeton College; first prothonotary of Adams County; during the Revolutionary War was appointed on November 3, 1776, a lieutenant in Colonel Hazen's regiment, and on March 25, 1778, was promoted to captain; elected to the Seventeenth Congress, but resigned before Congress assembled; died in Mercer County, Pa., June 24, 1844.

**DUNCAN, James Henry**, a Representative from Massachusetts; born in Haverhill, Mass., December 5, 1793; attended Phillips Exeter Academy, Exeter, N.H., and was graduated from Harvard University in 1812; studied law; was admitted to the bar in 1815 and commenced practice in Haverhill; an active militia officer, and attained the rank of colonel; president of the Essex Agricultural Society; member of the Massachusetts house of representatives in 1827, 1837, 1838, and again in 1857; served in the Massachusetts senate from 1828 until 1831; delegate to the Whig National Convention at Harrisburg, Pa., in 1839; appointed commissioner in bankruptcy in 1841; elected as a Whig to the Thirty-first and Thirty-second Congresses (March 4, 1849-March 3, 1853); engaged in the real-estate business; died in Haverhill, Essex County, Mass., February 8, 1869; interment in Linwood Cemetery.

**DUNCAN, John James** (father of John James Duncan, Jr.), a Representative from Tennessee; born in Huntsville, Scott County, Tenn., March 24, 1919; attended the public schools in Huntsville, Tenn.; B.S., University of Tennessee, Knoxville, 1942; served in the United States Army from May 1942 to December 1945; LL.B., Cumberland University, Lebanon, Tenn., 1947; was admitted to the bar in 1947 and commenced the practice of law in Knoxville, Tenn.; assistant attorney general, Knoxville, 1947-1956, and city law director, 1956-1959; managed the 1954 campaign of Representative Howard H. Baker, Sr., and the 1955 campaign of Mayor Jack Dance of Knoxville; elected mayor of Knoxville, May 1959, by special election to fill an unexpired term; reelected to full terms in 1959 and 1963, and served as mayor until his election to Congress; State commander of the American Legion, 1954; delegate to the Republican National Conventions of 1960, 1968, and 1984; elected as a Republican to the Eighty-ninth and to the eleven succeeding Congresses and served from January 3, 1965, until his death in Knoxville, Tenn., June 21, 1988; had announced on May 27, 1988 that he would not be a candidate for reelection to the One Hundred First Congress; interment in the Duncan Family Cemetery, Scott County, Tenn.

**DUNCAN, John James, Jr.** (son of John James Duncan), a Representative from Tennessee; born in Lebanon, Wilson County, Tenn., July 21, 1947; attended public schools in Knoxville; B.S., University of Tennessee, 1969; J.D., National Law Center, George Washington University, Washington, D.C., 1973; United States Army National Guard and United States Army Reserve service, 1970-1987; admitted to Tennessee bar, 1973; practicing attorney in Knoxville, Tenn., 1973-1981; judge, Knox County Criminal Court, 1981-1988; elected as a Republican to the One Hundredth Congress, November 8, 1988, by special election to fill the vacancy caused by the death of his father, John J. Duncan, but was not sworn in because Congress had adjourned; elected at the same time to the One Hundred First Congress; reelected to the One Hundred Second and to the two succeeding Congresses, and served from November 8, 1988 to January 3, 1997; is a resident of Knoxville, Tenn.

**DUNCAN, Joseph**, a Representative from Illinois; born in Paris, Bourbon County, Ky., February 22, 1794; pursued classical studies; during the War of 1812 was commissioned ensign in the Seventeenth Infantry; promoted to first lieutenant in the Forty-sixth Infantry on July 16, 1814, and returned to the Seventeenth Infantry on July 16, 1814; received, by resolution of Congress, February 13, 1835, the testimonial of a sword for his part in the defense of Fort Stephenson, Ohio; moved to Illinois in 1818 and settled in Kaskaskia, later in Jackson County; engaged in agricultural pursuits; justice of the peace in Jackson County from 1821 until 1823; appointed major general of State militia in 1822 and commanded Illinois troops in the Black Hawk War in 1831; member of the Illinois State senate, 1824-1826; moved to Jacksonville, Ill., in 1829; elected as a Jacksonian to the Twentieth and to the three succeeding Congresses and served from March 4, 1827, until September 21, 1834, when he resigned, having been elected Governor; elected Governor of Illinois in 1834, and served from December 3, 1834 to December 7, 1838; unsuccessful candidate in 1842 for election for Governor; lived in retirement until his death in Jacksonville, Morgan County, Ill., January 15, 1844; interment in Diamond Grove Cemetery.

**Bibliography:** *DAB*.

**DUNCAN, Richard Meloan,** a Representative from Missouri; born near Edgerton, Platte County, Mo., November 10, 1889; attended the public schools; was graduated from Christian Brothers College, St. Joseph, Mo., in 1909; deputy circuit clerk of Buchanan County, Mo., from 1911 until 1917; studied law; was admitted to the bar in 1916 and commenced practice in St. Joseph, Mo.; city counselor of St. Joseph, 1926-1930; delegate to the Democratic National Convention of 1932; elected as a Democrat to the Seventy-third and to the four succeeding Congresses (March 4, 1933-January 3, 1943); chairman of Democratic Caucus for the Seventy-seventh Congress; unsuccessful candidate for reelection in 1942 to the Seventy-eighth Congress; appointed judge of the United States District Court for the Eastern and Western Districts of Missouri on July 8, 1943, and served until June 30, 1965; continued to serve actively under senior (retired) status; resided in Kansas City, Mo., where he died on August 1, 1974; interment in Memorial Park Cemetery, St. Joseph, Mo.

**DUNCAN, Robert Blackford,** a Representative from Oregon; born in Normal, McLean County, Ill., December 4, 1920; was raised in Bloomington, Ill., and attended public schools there; served in the Merchant Marine; worked in the placer gold fields of Alaska, with a seed corn company in Illinois, and with a bank in Chicago; student at University of Alaska at College, Alaska, in 1939 and 1940; B.A., Illinois Wesleyan University, Bloomington, 1942; took University of California correspondence courses in 1940; LL.B., University of Michigan Law School, Ann Arbor, 1948; served in the United States Naval Air Force, 1942-1945, and retired as a commander in the Naval Reserve; was admitted to the bar in October 1948 and commenced the practice of law in Medford, Oreg.; nominated in 1954 as a write-in candidate for the Oregon State legislature, but declined for business reasons; elected to the State house of representatives in 1956; was reelected in 1958 and 1960 and served as speaker from 1959 until 1962; elected as a Democrat to the Eighty-eighth and to the Eighty-ninth Congresses (January 3, 1963-January 3, 1967); was not a candidate for reelection in 1966 to the Ninetieth Congress; unsuccessful candidate for election to the United States Senate in 1968 and 1972; resumed the practice of law; elected as a Democrat to the Ninety-fourth and to the two succeeding Congresses (January 3, 1975-January 3, 1981); unsuccessful candidate for renomination in 1980 to the Ninety-seventh Congress; resumed the practice of law in Washington, D.C., 1981-1985; member, Northwest Power Planning Council, 1986 to 1988, and served as chairman in 1987; is a resident of Yachats, Oreg.

**DUNCAN, William Addison,** a Representative from Pennsylvania; born in Cashtown, Franklin Township, Adams County, Pa., February 2, 1836; attended the public schools; was graduated from Franklin and Marshall College, at Lancaster, in 1857; studied law; was admitted to the bar in 1859 and commenced practice in Gettysburg, Pa.; elected district attorney in 1862 and 1868; elected as a Democrat to the Forty-eighth Congress and served from March 4, 1883, until his death; had been reelected to the Forty-ninth Congress; died in Gettysburg, Pa., November 14, 1884; interment in Evergreen Cemetery.

**DUNCAN, William Garnett,** a Representative from Kentucky; born in Louisville, Ky., March 2, 1800; completed preparatory studies and was graduated from Yale College in 1821; studied law; was admitted to the bar in 1822 and commenced practice in Louisville; elected as a Whig to the Thirtieth Congress (March 4, 1847-March 3, 1849); declined to be a candidate for renomination in 1848 to the Thirty-first Congress; moved to Louisiana and settled in New Orleans in 1850, where he continued the practice of law; retired from active law practice in 1860 and traveled in Europe; resided for a while in Paris, France; returned to the United States in 1875 and resided in Louisville, Ky., until his death there on May 25, 1875; interment in Cave Hill Cemetery.

**DUNGAN, James Irvine,** a Representative from Ohio; born in Canonsburg, Washington County, Pa., May 29, 1844; attended the common schools; received an academic education at the local academy at Denmark, Iowa, and at the college at Washington, Iowa; studied law; was admitted to the bar in 1868 and commenced practice in Jackson, Jackson County, Ohio; during the Civil War served as color sergeant in the Nineteenth Regiment, Iowa Volunteer Infantry; superintendent of schools of Jackson, Ohio, and city and county school examiner in 1867 and 1868; mayor of Jackson in 1869; member of the State senate 1877-1879; delegate to the Democratic National Convention in 1880; elected as a Democrat to the Fifty-second Congress (March 4, 1891-March 3, 1893); unsuccessful candidate for reelection in 1892 to the Fifty-third Congress; attorney in the Interior Department 1893-1895; returned to Jackson, Ohio, and resumed the practice of law; city solicitor in 1913; engaged in the practice of his profession until his death in Jackson, Ohio, on Dec. 28, 1931; interment in Fairmont Cemetery.

**DUNHAM, Cyrus Livingston,** a Representative from Indiana; born in Dryden, Tompkins County, N.Y., January 16, 1817; attended the common schools; taught school; studied law and was admitted to the bar; moved to Salem, Washington County, Ind., in 1841 and commenced practice; elected prosecuting attorney of Washington County in 1845; member of the State house of representatives in 1846 and 1847; elected as a Democrat to the Thirty-first, Thirty-second, and Thirty-third Congresses (March 4, 1849-March 3, 1855); chairman, Committee on Roads and Canals (Thirty-third Congress); unsuccessful candidate for reelection in 1854 to the Thirty-fourth Congress; appointed secretary of state by Governor Ashbel P. Willard and served in 1859 and 1860; served in the Union Army as colonel of the Fiftieth Regiment, Indiana Volunteer Infantry, 1861-1863; resumed the practice of law in New Albany, Floyd County, Ind.; elected a member of the State house of representatives in 1864 and 1865; moved to Jeffersonville, Ind., in 1871; judge of Clark County Criminal Court 1871-1874; resumed the practice of law; died in Jeffersonville, Clark County, Ind., November 21, 1877; interment in Walnut Ridge Cemetery.

**DUNHAM, Ransom Williams,** a Representative from Illinois; born in Savoy, Berkshire County, Mass., March 21, 1838; attended the common schools and the high school in Springfield, Mass., engaged as a clerk for a life insurance company 1855-1857; moved to Chicago in 1857; became a grain and provision commission merchant; president of the Board of Trade of Chicago in 1882; elected as a Republican to the Forty-eighth, Forty-ninth, and Fiftieth Congresses (March 4, 1883-March 3, 1889); retired from active business pursuits; died in Springfield, Hampden County, Mass., on August 19, 1896, while en route to attend the centennial celebration of his native town, Savoy; interment in Mount Hope Cemetery, Chicago, Ill.

**DUNLAP, George Washington,** a Representative from Kentucky; born at Walnut Hills, near Lexington, Fayette County, Ky., February 22, 1813; pursued preparatory studies; was graduated from Transylvania University, Lexington, Ky., in 1834; studied law; was admitted to the bar and commenced practice in Lancaster, Ky.; commissioner of the circuit court 1843-1874; member of the Kentucky house of representatives in 1853; elected as a Unionist to the Thirty-seventh Congress (March 4, 1861-March 3, 1863); chairman, Committee on Expenditures in the Department of the Navy (Thirty-seventh Congress); member of the Border State convention in 1861; one of the managers appointed by the House of Representatives in 1862 to conduct the impeachment proceedings against West H. Humphreys, United States judge for the several districts of Tennessee; resumed the practice of law; died in Lancaster, Garrard County, Ky., on June 6, 1880; interment in Lancaster Cemetery.

**DUNLAP, Robert Pinckney,** a Representative from Maine; born in Brunswick, Maine, August 17, 1794; educated by private tutors; was graduated from Bowdoin College, Brunswick, Maine, in 1815; studied law; was admitted to the bar in 1818 and commenced practice in Brunswick; member of the Maine State house of representatives, 1821-1823; president of the board of overseers of Bowdoin College from 1821 until his death; member of the State militia, and was delegated to receive General Lafayette when he visited in Maine in 1824; served in the State senate, 1824-1828, and 1831-1833; president of the State senate for four years; executive councilor, 1829-1833; elected Governor of Maine in 1833, reelected in 1834, 1835 and 1836, and served from January 1, 1834 to January 3, 1838; elected as a Democrat to the Twenty-eighth and Twenty-ninth Congresses (March 4, 1843-March 3, 1847); chairman, Committee on Public Expenditures (Twenty-ninth Congress); collector of customs in Portland, Maine, in 1848 and 1849; postmaster of Brunswick, 1853-1857; died in Brunswick, Maine, October 20, 1859; interment in Pine Grove Cemetery.

**Bibliography:** *DAB.*

**DUNLAP, William Claiborne,** a Representative from Tennessee; born in Knoxville, Tenn., February 25, 1798; attended the Ebenezer Academy and Maryville College, Maryville, Tenn., 1813-1817; studied law; was admitted to the bar and commenced practice in Knoxville in 1819; served in the Indian campaign in 1818 and 1819; moved to Bolivar, Hardeman County, Tenn., in 1828; held a commission in the United States Volunteers in 1830; elected as a Jacksonian to the Twenty-third and Twenty-fourth Congresses (March 4, 1833-March 3, 1837); unsuccessful candidate for reelection in 1836 to the Twenty-fifth Congress; judge of the Eleventh Circuit Court of Tennessee from 1840 to 1849, when he resigned and resumed the practice of law; member of the State senate in 1851, 1853, and 1857; served in the State house of representatives 1857-1859; died near Memphis, Shelby County, Tenn., November 16, 1872; interment in Elmwood Cemetery, Memphis, Tenn.

**DUNN, Aubert Culberson,** a Representative from Mississippi; born in Meridian, Lauderdale County, Miss., November 20, 1896; attended the public schools, the University of Mississippi at Oxford, and the University of Alabama at Tuscaloosa; reporter on the Cincinnati Enquirer in 1917; served in the United States Navy from December 7, 1917, to June 16, 1919; studied law; was admitted to the bar in 1924 and commenced practice in Meridian, Miss.; district attorney for the tenth judicial district of Mississippi 1931-1934; elected as a Democrat to the Seventy-fourth Congress (January 3, 1935-January 3, 1937); was not a candidate for renomination in 1936; served as expert to the United States Senate Committee on Finance in 1938 and as attorney for the Social Security Board in 1939; resumed the practice of law; special trial attorney, United States Attorney General's office, 1952-1953; circuit judge, Tenth Judicial District, Mississippi, 1966; was a resident of Mobile, Ala. until his death there on January 4, 1987; interment in Magnolia Cemetery.

**DUNN, George Grundy,** a Representative from Indiana; born in Washington County, Ky., December 20, 1812; moved to Monroe County, Ind.; completed preparatory studies and attended the Indiana University at Bloomington; moved to Bedford, Lawrence County, Ind., in 1833, where he taught school; studied law; was admitted to the bar in 1835 and commenced practice in Bedford, Ind.; prosecuting attorney of Lawrence County in 1842; elected as a Whig to the Thirtieth Congress (March 4, 1847-March 3, 1849);

unsuccessful candidate for reelection in 1848; served in the State senate from 1850 until 1852, when he resigned; elected as a Republican to the Thirty-fourth Congress (March 4, 1855-March 3, 1857); was not a candidate for renomination in 1856; died in Bedford, Ind., September 4, 1857; interment in Green Hill Cemetery.

**DUNN, George Hedford,** a Representative from Indiana; born in New York City, November 15, 1794; moved to Lawrenceburg, Dearborn County, Ind., in 1817; studied law; was admitted to the bar in 1822 and commenced practice in Lawrenceburg; member of the State house of representatives in 1828, 1832, and 1833; promoter of the first railway in Indiana; unsuccessful candidate for election to the Twenty-fourth Congress; elected as a Whig to the Twenty-fifth Congress (March 4, 1837-March 3, 1839); unsuccessful candidate for reelection; resumed the practice of law; State treasurer 1841-1844; judge of Dearborn County, Ind.; president of the Cincinnati & Indianapolis Railroad at the time of his death in Lawrenceburg, Ind., January 12, 1854; interment in New Town Cemetery.

**DUNN, James Whitney,** a Representative from Michigan; born in Detroit, Wayne County, Mich., July 21, 1943; attended the public schools; B.A., Michigan State University, East Lansing, 1967; president, Dunn Development Group, builder and developer; delegate, Michigan State Republican convention, 1982; elected as a Republican to the Ninety-seventh Congress (January 3, 1981-January 3, 1983); unsuccessful candidate for reelection in 1982 to the Ninety-eighth Congress; is a resident of East Lansing, Mich.

**DUNN, Jennifer Blackburn,** a Representative from Washington; born in Seattle, Wash., July 29, 1941; attended the University of Washington, 1960-1962; B.A., Stanford University, Calif., 1963; systems engineer, IBM, Seattle, 1964-1969; section supervisor, King County Department of Assessments, 1978-1980; chairman, Washington State Republican Party, 1981-1992; King County coordinator, President Ford Committee, 1976; member at large, Republican State finance committee, 1977-1978; member, Board of Overlake Associated Republican Women, 1977-1979; founder and first coordinator, Sun Mountain Conference, 1978; various positions with State Republican committees and councils and Republican National Conventions, 1984, 1988, 1992; member, Republican National Committee delegation to Conservative Party conference, Blackpool, England, 1985; member, delegation of Republican State chairmen and members to Taiwan, 1982 and 1992; leader of 1988 delegation of Republican National Committee members to Thirteenth Kuomintang Congress, Taipei, Taiwan; Seventh Congressional District chair, Reagan-Bush campaign, 1980; elected as a Republican to the One Hundred Third and One Hundred Fourth Congresses (January 3, 1993-January 3, 1997); is a resident of Bellevue, Wash.

**DUNN, John Thomas,** a Representative from New Jersey; born in Tipperary, Ireland, June 4, 1838; immigrated to the United States with his father, who settled in New Jersey in 1845; completed elementary studies at home; engaged in business in 1862; elected a member of the board of aldermen of Elizabeth in 1878; member of the State house of assembly 1879-1882 and speaker of the house in 1882; studied law; was admitted to the bar in 1882 and commenced practice in Elizabeth, N.J.; again elected a member of the city council; elected as a Democrat to the Fifty-third Congress (March 4, 1893-March 3, 1895); unsuccessful candidate for reelection in 1894 to the Fifty-fourth Congress; resumed the practice of law; died in Elizabeth, N.J., February 22, 1907; interment in Mount Olivet Cemetery, Newark, N.J.

**DUNN, Matthew Anthony,** a Representative from Pennsylvania; born in Braddock, Allegheny County, Pa., August 15, 1886; attended the public schools in Pittsburgh and Meyersdale; by accidents, lost the sight of his left eye at the age of twelve and that of his right eye at the age of twenty; attended the school for the blind in Pittsburgh and was graduated from Overbrook (Philadelphia) School for the Blind in 1909; engaged in the sale of periodicals and newspapers, 1907-1908, and in the insurance brokerage business, 1920-1924; member of the Pennsylvania house of representatives, 1926-1932; elected as a Democrat to the Seventy-third and to the three succeeding Congresses (March 4, 1933-January 3, 1941); chairman, Committee on the Census (Seventy-sixth Congress); was not a candidate for renomination in 1940 to the Seventy-seventh Congress due to ill health; retired from active business pursuits; died in Pittsburgh, Pa., February 13, 1942; interment in Homewood Cemetery.

**DUNN, Poindexter,** a Representative from Arkansas; born near Raleigh, Wake County, N.C., November 3, 1834; moved with his father to Limestone County, Ala., in 1837; attended the country schools, and was graduated from Jackson College, Columbia, Tenn., in 1854; studied law; moved to St. Francis County, Ark., in 1856; elected to the State house of representatives in 1858; engaged in cotton growing until 1861; served as a captain in the Confederate Army during the Civil War; was admitted to the bar in 1867 and commenced the practice of law in Forrest City, Ark.; elected as a Democrat to the Forty-sixth and to the four succeeding Congresses (March 4, 1879-March 3, 1889); chairman, Committee on Merchant Marine and Fisheries (Fiftieth Congress); was not a candidate for renomination in 1888; moved to Los Angeles, Calif., in 1888 and continued the practice of law; appointed a special commissioner for the prevention of frauds on the customs revenue, New York City, in 1893; moved to Baton Rouge, La., in 1895 and engaged in the construction of railroads; settled in Texarkana, Bowie County, Tex., in 1905, and died there on October 12, 1914; interment in Rose Hill Cemetery.

**DUNN, Thomas Byrne,** a Representative from New York; born in Providence, R.I., March 16, 1853; moved with his parents to Rochester, N.Y., in 1858; attended the public schools and the De Graff Military Institute of Rochester; engaged in the manufacture of perfumes and extracts; president of the chamber of commerce in 1905 and 1906; member of the State senate in 1907; chief commissioner for New York to the Jamestown Tercentennial Exposition, Jamestown, Va., in 1907; State treasurer in 1908; elected as a Republican to the Sixty-third and to the four succeeding Congresses (March 4, 1913-March 3, 1923); chairman, Committee on Roads (Sixty-sixth and Sixty-seventh Congresses); was not a candidate for reelection in 1922 to the Sixty-eighth Congress; retired to private life; died in Rochester, N.Y., July 2, 1924; interment in Mount Hope Cemetery.

**DUNN, William McKee,** a Representative from Indiana; born in Hanover, Jefferson County, Territory of Indiana, December 12, 1814; attended school in the first schoolhouse in Hanover; was graduated from Indiana State College in 1832 and from Yale College in 1835; studied law; was admitted to the bar in 1837 and practiced; member of the State house of representatives in 1848; delegate to the State constitutional convention in 1850; elected as a Republican to the Thirty-sixth and Thirty-seventh Congresses (March 4, 1859-March 3, 1863); chairman, Committee on Patents (Thirty-seventh Congress); unsuccessful candidate for reelection in 1862 to the Thirty-eighth Congress; served in the Union Army as a volunteer aide-de-camp to General George B. McClellan from June 19, 1861, to August 1861, in the campaign in western Virginia; major and judge advocate of Volunteers, Department of the Missouri, from March 13, 1863, to July 6, 1864; appointed lieutenant colonel and Assistant Judge Advocate General of the United States Army June 22, 1864, and brigadier general and Judge Advocate General December 1, 1875; brevetted brigadier general March 13, 1865; retired January 22, 1881; died at his summer residence, "Maplewood," Dunn Loring, Fairfax County, Va., July 24, 1887; interment in Oak Hill Cemetery, Washington, D.C.

Bibliography: *DAB*.

**DUNNELL, Mark Hill,** a Representative from Minnesota; born in Buxton, York County, Maine, July 2, 1823; completed preparatory studies, and was graduated from Waterville College (now Colby University), Waterville, Maine, in 1849; for five years was principal of Norway and Hebron Academies; member of the Maine house of representatives in 1854; served in the State senate in 1855; State superintendent of common schools in 1855 and 1857-1859; delegate to the Republican National Convention in 1856; studied law; was admitted to the bar in 1856 and commenced practice in Portland, Maine, in 1860; entered the Union Army as colonel of the Fifth Regiment, Maine Volunteer Infantry, May 6, 1861; mustered out August 31, 1861; United States consul at Vera Cruz, Mexico, in 1861 and 1862; moved to Minnesota and settled in Winona in 1865, and in 1867, in Owatonna; member of the Minnesota house of representatives in 1867; State superintendent of public instruction from April 2, 1867, to August 1870, when he resigned; elected as a Republican to the Forty-second and to the five succeeding Congresses (March 4, 1871-March 3, 1883); unsuccessful candidate for Speaker of the Forty-seventh Congress; was not a candidate for renomination in 1882; unsuccessful candidate for election to the United States Senate in 1883; elected to the Fifty-first Congress (March 4, 1889-March 3, 1891); unsuccessful candidate for reelection in 1890 to the Fifty-second Congress; delegate to the Republican National Convention in 1892; one of the founders and a member of the board of trustees of Pillsbury Academy; died in Owatonna, Steele County, Minn., August 9, 1904; interment in Forest Hill Cemetery.

**DUNPHY, Edward John,** a Representative from New York; born in New York City May 12, 1856; attended the public schools and St. Francis Xavier College, New York City; was graduated from Mount St. Mary's College, Emmitsburg, Md., in 1876; studied law; was admitted to the bar in 1878 and commenced practice in New York City; connected with the law department of the New York Central & Hudson River Railroad Co.; elected as a Democrat to the Fifty-first, Fifty-second, and Fifty-third Congresses (March 4, 1889-March 3, 1895); chairman, Committee on Expenditures in the Department of Justice (Fifty-third Congress); was not a candidate for reelection in 1894; continued the practice of law in New York City until his death there on July 29, 1926; interment in Calvary Cemetery.

**DUNWELL, Charles Tappan,** a Representative from New York; born in Newark, Wayne County, N.Y., February 13, 1852; moved with his parents to Lyons, Wayne County, N.Y., in 1854; attended the Lyons Union School; entered Cornell University, Ithaca, N.Y., in the class of 1873; at the close of his junior year entered Columbia College Law School in the city of New York, and was graduated in 1874; was admitted to the bar in 1874 and commenced practice in New York City; general agent for the New York Life Insurance Co., in 1889; unsuccessful candidate for comptroller of the city of Brooklyn in 1890; member of the New York Republican State committee in 1891 and 1892; elected as a Republican to the Fifty-eighth, Fifty-ninth, and Sixtieth Congresses and served from March 4, 1903, until his death in Brooklyn, N.Y., June 12, 1908; interment in Evergreen Cemetery.

**du PONT, Henry Algernon** (cousin of Thomas Coleman du Pont), a Senator from Delaware; born at Eleutherean Mills, New Castle County, Del., July 30, 1838; attended private schools; attended the University of Pennsylvania in Philadelphia in 1855; was graduated from the United States Military Academy, West Point, N.Y., in 1861; served in the United States Army until 1875; during the Civil War served in the Union Army, attaining the rank of lieutenant colonel; awarded a Congressional Medal of Honor for his handling of the retreat at the battle of Cedar Creek, Va., on October 19, 1864; was president and general manager of the Wilmington & Northern Railroad Co. 1879-1899; retired from active business and engaged in agricultural pursuits; elected on June 13, 1906, as a Republican to the United States Senate to fill the vacancy in the term beginning March 4, 1905, caused by the failure of the legislature to elect; reelected in 1911 and served until March 3, 1917; unsuccessful candidate for reelection in 1916; chairman, Committee on Expenditures in the War Department (Sixty-first and Sixty-fourth Congresses), Committee on Military Affairs (Sixty-second Congress), Committee on Transportation and Sale of Meat Products (Sixty-third Congress); retired from public life and engaged in literary pursuits; died at Winterthur, near Wilmington, Del., December 31, 1926; interment in the du Pont Cemetery, Christiana Hundred, New Castle County, Del.

**du PONT, Pierre Samuel, IV (Pete),** a Representative from Delaware; born in Wilmington, New Castle County, Del., January 22, 1935; educated at Phillips Exeter Academy, Exeter, N.H., 1948-1952; B.S.E., Princeton University, 1952-1956; LL.B., Harvard University Law School, 1963; active duty as United States Naval Reserve Officer, construction battalions (Seabees), 1957-1960; admitted to the Delaware bar in 1964 and commenced practice in Wilmington; employed by E.I. du Pont Co., Wilmington, Del., 1963-1970; member, Delaware and National Republican Finance Committees; Delaware State representative, District 12, 1968-1971; delegate to Delaware State Republican convention, 1966; elected as a Republican to the Ninety-second and to the two succeeding Congresses (January 3, 1971-January 3, 1977); was not a candidate for reelection in 1976 to the Ninety-fifth Congress, but was elected Governor of Delaware; reelected in 1980, and served from January 18, 1977 to January 15, 1985; unsuccessful candidate for the Republican presidential nomination in 1988; member, National Commission on Economic Growth and Tax Reform, 1995-1996; is a resident of Rockland, Del.

**du PONT, Thomas Coleman** (cousin of Henry Algernon du Pont), a Senator from Delaware; born in Louisville, Ky., December 11, 1863; attended the public schools, Urbana University, Urbana, Ohio, Chauncy Hall School, Boston Mass., and Massachusetts Institute of Technology, Boston, Mass.; engaged in engineering, later being interested in coal mining, street railways, steel manufacturing, explosives, hotels, office buildings, and road building; moved to Central City, Ky., in 1883 and was engaged as a mining engineer; moved to Johnstown, Pa., in 1893 and engaged in steel manufacturing; moved to Wilmington, Del., in 1900; retired from business activities in 1915; member of the Republican National Committee 1908-1930; appointed as a Republican to the United States Senate to fill the vacancy caused by the resignation of Josiah O. Wolcott and served from July 7, 1921, to November 7, 1922; unsuccessful candidate for election to this vacancy and also for election to the full term; elected as a Republican to the United States Senate in 1924 and served from March 4, 1925, until his resignation on December 9, 1928; died in Wilmington, Del., November 11, 1930; was cremated and committed to a grave in the family burial ground near Christ Church in Christiana Hundred.
**Bibliography:** *DAB*; Rae, John B. "Coleman du Pont and his Road." *Delaware History* 16 (Spring-Summer 1975): 171-83.

**DUPRE, Henry Garland,** a Representative from Louisiana; born in Opelousas, St. Landry Parish, La., July 28, 1873; attended the public schools, and was graduated from Tulane University, New Orleans, La., in 1892; was subsequently graduated from the law school of the same university; was admitted to the bar and commenced practice in New Orleans in 1895; assistant city attorney of New Orleans 1900-1910; member of the State house of representatives 1900-1910 and served as speaker 1908-1910; chairman of the Democratic State convention in 1908; elected as a Democrat to the Sixty-first Congress to fill the vacancy caused by the death of Samuel L. Gillmore; reelected to the Sixty-second and to the six succeeding Congresses and served from November 8, 1910,

until his death in Washington, D.C., February 21, 1924; interment in the Catholic Cemetery, Opelousas, La.

**DURAND, George Harman,** a Representative from Michigan; born in Cobleskill, Schoharie County, N.Y., February 21, 1838; attended the common schools and Genesee Wesleyan Seminary at Lima, N.Y.; moved to Oxford, Oakland County, Mich., in 1856; taught school; studied law; was admitted to the bar and commenced practice at Flint, Genesee County, Mich., in 1858; member of the board of education; member of the board of aldermen 1862-1867; mayor of Flint in 1873 and 1874; elected as a Democrat to the Forty-fourth Congress (March 4, 1875-March 3, 1877); unsuccessful candidate for reelection in 1876 to the Forty-fifth Congress; resumed the practice of his profession; appointed temporarily justice of the Michigan Supreme Court in 1892; president of the State board of law examiners for many years; appointed special assistant United States attorney in Chinese and opium smuggling cases in Oregon and served from 1893 to 1896; died in Flint, Mich., June 8, 1903; interment in Glenwood Cemetery.

**DURBIN, Richard Joseph,** a Representative from Illinois; born in East St. Louis, St. Clair County, Ill., November 21, 1944; graduated from Assumption High School, East St. Louis, 1962; B.S.F.S., Georgetown University School of Foreign Service, Washington, D.C., 1966; J.D., Georgetown University Law Center, 1969; admitted to the Illinois bar, 1969 and commenced practice in Springfield; aide to Lieutenant Governor Paul Simon, 1969-1972; legal counsel, Illinois State senate judiciary committee, 1972-1982; parliamentarian, Illinois State senate, 1969-1972; unsuccessful Democratic candidate for election to the Illinois State senate in 1976, and for election for Lieutenant Governor in 1978; associate professor, Southern Illinois University School of Medicine, Springfield, 1978-1983; delegate, Illinois State Democratic convention, 1978; delegate, Democratic Mid-Term Meeting, 1978; elected as a Democrat to the Ninety-eighth and to the six succeeding Congresses (January 3, 1983-January 3, 1997); was not a candidate for reelection in 1996 to the House of Representatives, but was a candidate for election to the United States Senate; is a resident of Springfield, Ill.

**DURBOROW, Allan Cathcart, Jr.,** a Representative from Illinois; born in Philadelphia, Pa., November 10, 1857; moved to Indiana in 1862 with his parents, who settled in Williamsport, Warren County; attended the public schools; entered Wabash College, Crawfordsville, Ind., in the fall of 1872; was graduated from Indiana University at Bloomington in 1877; after residing in Indianapolis moved to Chicago in 1880 and in 1887 became business manager of the Western Electrician, a trade magazine; elected as a Democrat to the Fifty-second and Fifty-third Congresses (March 4, 1891-March 3, 1895); was not a candidate for renomination in 1894 to the Fifty-fourth Congress; engaged in the insurance business; unsuccessful candidate for election in 1902 to the Fifty-eighth Congress; died in Chicago, Ill., March 10, 1908; interment in Graceland Cemetery.

**DURELL, Daniel Meserve,** a Representative from New Hampshire; born in Lee, N.H., July 20, 1769; was graduated from Dartmouth College, Hanover, N.H., in 1794; studied law; was admitted to the bar in 1797 and commenced practice in Dover, N.H.; elected as a Republican to the Tenth Congress (March 4, 1807-March 3, 1809); member of the State house of representatives in 1816; chief justice of the district court of common pleas 1816-1821; United States attorney for the district of New Hampshire 1830-1834; resumed the practice of law; died in Dover, Strafford County, N.H., April 29, 1841; interment in Pine Hill Cemetery.

**DURENBERGER, David Ferdinand,** a Senator from Minnesota; born in St. Cloud, Stearns County, Minn., August 19, 1934; attended the public schools in Collegeville, Minn.; graduated, St. John's Prep School, Collegeville, 1951; B.A., St. John's University, 1955; J.D., University of Minnesota Law School, 1959; admitted to the Minnesota bar in 1959 and commenced practice in St. Paul; served in the United States Army, 1956-1963; executive secretary to Governor Harold LeVander of Minnesota, 1967-1971; counsel, corporate secretary, and manager of the international licensing division of H.B. Fuller Co., 1971-1978; chairman, Hennepin County board of commissioners, Hennepin County Park Reserve District, 1973-1978; elected as a Republican to the United States Senate, November 7, 1978, to complete the unexpired term of Hubert H. Humphrey for the term ending January 3, 1983; reelected in 1982 and again in 1988, and served from November 8, 1978 to January 3, 1995; was not a candidate for reelection in 1994; chairman, Select Committee on Intelligence (Ninety-ninth Congress); is a resident of Minneapolis, Minn.

**DUREY, Cyrus,** a Representative from New York; born in Caroga, Fulton County, N.Y. May 16, 1864; attended the common schools and Johnstown Academy; was supervisor's clerk; supervisor of Caroga in 1889 and 1890; engaged in the lumber and real-estate business; appointed postmaster of Johnstown on August 19, 1898, and served until February 28, 1907; member of the Republican State committee 1904-1906; elected as a Republican to the Sixtieth and Sixty-first Congresses (March 4, 1907-March 3, 1911); unsuccessful candidate for reelection in 1910 to the Sixty-second Congress; appointed on March 20, 1911, collector of internal revenue, fourteenth district of New York, and served until September 30, 1914; delegate to the Republican National Conventions in 1912 and 1920; again appointed collector of internal revenue on September 30, 1921, and served until his death at Albany, N.Y., January 4, 1933; interment in North Bush Cemetery, near Johnstown, N.Y.

**DURFEE, Job,** a Representative from Rhode Island; born in Tiverton, R.I., September 20, 1790; attended the common schools and was graduated from Brown University, Providence, R.I., in 1813; studied law; was admitted to the bar at Newport, R.I., in 1817 and commenced practice in Tiverton; member of the State house of representatives 1816-1820; elected to the Seventeenth and Eighteenth Congresses (March 4, 1821-March 3, 1825); unsuccessful candidate for reelection in 1824 to the Nineteenth Congress and for election in 1828 to the Twenty-first Congress; again a member of the State house of representatives 1826-1829 and served as speaker 1827-1829; declined to be a candidate for reelection; resumed the practice of law; elected associate justice of the State supreme court in 1833; chief justice of the State supreme court from June 1835 until his death in Tiverton, Newport County, R.I., July 26, 1847; interment in the family burying ground at Quaket Neck, near Tiverton, R.I.

Bibliography: *DAB.*

**DURFEE, Nathaniel Briggs,** a Representative from Rhode Island; born in Tiverton, R.I., September 29, 1812; completed preparatory studies; engaged in agricultural pursuits and conducted a fruit orchard; member of the Rhode Island house of representatives for eleven years; elected as a candidate of the American Party to the Thirty-fourth Congress and as a Republican to the Thirty-fifth Congress (March 4, 1855-March 3, 1859); resumed his former pursuits; was serving as county clerk at the time of his death in Tiverton, Newport County, R.I., on November 9, 1872; interment in the family burial ground near Tiverton, R.I.

**DURGAN, George Richard,** a Representative from Indiana; born in Westpoint, Tippecanoe County, Ind., January 20, 1872; attended the village school in Westpoint; moved to La Fayette, Ind., in 1892 and was employed as a clerk and later as a traveling salesman; engaged in mercantile pursuits; mayor of La Fayette

1904-1913 and 1917-1925; delegate to the Democratic National Convention in 1912; elected as a Democrat to the Seventy-third Congress (March 4, 1933-January 3, 1935); unsuccessful candidate for reelection in 1934 to the Seventy-fourth Congress; resumed mercantile pursuits; appointed to the Indiana Public Service Commission in 1941 and moved to Indianapolis, Ind.; died in Indianapolis January 13, 1942; interment in Springvale Cemetery, La Fayette, Ind.

**DURHAM, Carl Thomas,** a Representative from North Carolina; born in Bingham Township, Orange County, at White Cross, N.C., August 28, 1892; attended the public schools of Orange County, Mandale Private School, Saxapahaw, N.C., and the University of North Carolina at Chapel Hill; pharmacist at Chapel Hill 1912-1938; served as a pharmacist's mate in the United States Navy, 1917-1918; member of the city council of Chapel Hill, N.C., 1924-1932, and of the Orange County Board of Commissioners 1932-1938; member of the school board of Chapel Hill, N.C., 1924-1938; trustee of the University of North Carolina; elected as a Democrat to the Seventy-sixth and to the ten succeeding Congresses (January 3, 1939-January 3, 1961); chairman, Joint Committee on Atomic Energy (Eighty-second and Eighty-fifth Congresses); was not a candidate for renomination in 1960 to the Eighty-seventh Congress; in 1964 retired and resided in Chapel Hill, N.C.; died in Durham, N.C., April 29, 1974; interment in Antioch Baptist Church Cemetery, Chapel Hill, N.C.

**DURHAM, Milton Jameson,** a Representative from Kentucky; born near Perryville, Mercer County (now Boyle County), Ky., May 16, 1824; attended the common schools; was graduated from Indiana Asbury (now De Pauw) University, Greencastle, Ind., in 1844; taught school for several years; was graduated from the Louisville (Ky.) Law School in 1850; was admitted to the bar in the same year and commenced practice in Danville, Boyle County, Ky.; circuit judge of the eighth judicial district in 1861 and 1862; elected as a Democrat to the Forty-third and to the two succeeding Congresses (March 4, 1873-March 3, 1879); chairman, Committee on Revision of the Laws (Forty-fourth Congress); unsuccessful candidate for renomination in 1878 to the Forty-sixth Congress; resumed the practice of law in Danville, Ky.; appointed First Comptroller of the Treasury of the United States on March 20, 1885, and served until the office was discontinued on April 22, 1889; moved to Lexington, Ky., in 1890 and engaged in banking; appointed deputy clerk, Internal Revenue Service, at Lexington, Ky., in 1901 and served until his death in that city on February 12, 1911; interment in Belleview Cemetery, Danville, Ky.

**DURKEE, Charles,** a Representative and a Senator from Wisconsin; born in Royalton, Windsor County, Vt., December 10, 1805; attended the common schools and the Burlington (Vt.) Academy; engaged in mercantile pursuits; moved to Wisconsin in 1836 and was one of the founders of Southport, now Kenosha; engaged in agricultural pursuits and lumbering; member of the Territorial legislature, 1836-1838, 1847-1848; elected as a Free-Soiler to the Thirty-first and Thirty-second Congresses (March 4, 1849-March 3, 1853); delegate to the World's Peace Convention in Paris; elected as a Republican to the United States Senate and served from March 4, 1855, to March 3, 1861; Governor of Utah Territory from July 15, 1865 until failing health compelled him to resign in December 1869; died in Omaha, Nebr., January 14, 1870; interment in Green Ridge Cemetery, Kenosha, Wis.

**DURKIN, John Anthony,** a Senator from New Hampshire; born in Brookfield, Worcester County, Mass., March 29, 1936; attended public schools; B.A., Holy Cross College, Worcester, Mass., 1959; J.D., Georgetown University Law Center, Washington, D.C., 1965; served in the United States Navy, 1959-1961; admitted to the New Hampshire and Massachusetts bars in 1966 and commenced practice in Concord, N.H.; served in office of New Hampshire attorney general, 1966-1968; New Hampshire assistant attorney general, 1967-1968; New Hampshire insurance commissioner, 1968-1973; was a candidate for election in 1974 to the United States Senate for the six-year term commencing January 3, 1975; due to the contested election, the Senate declared the seat vacant as of August 8, 1975; elected as a Democrat, by special election, September 16, 1975, to fill the vacancy, and served from September 18, 1975 until his resignation on December 29, 1980; unsuccessful candidate for reelection in 1980; resumed the practice of law in New Hampshire; is a resident of Manchester, N.H.

**Bibliography:** Tibbetts, Don. *The Closest U.S. Senate Race in History: Durkin v. Wyman.* Manchester, N.H.: J.W. Cummings Enterprises, 1976.

**DURNO, Edwin Russell,** a Representative from Oregon; born on a farm in Linn County, near Albany, Oreg., January 26, 1899; attended public schools in Silverton, Oreg.; University of Oregon at Eugene, B.S., 1921; Harvard University Medical School, M.D., 1927; entered practice of medicine in Boston, Mass.; taught school and was high school athletic coach 1921-1923; during the First World War served in the United States Army as a sergeant of Infantry; served in the Second World War as a major in the Medical Corps, First Auxiliary Surgical Group, 1942-1945; awarded Purple Heart Medal; served on Oregon Board of Medical Examiners, 1947-1958; practiced medicine in Medford, Oreg.; member of the State senate in 1958-1960; delegate to Republican National Conventions in 1960 and 1964; elected as a Republican to the Eighty-seventh Congress (January 3, 1961-January 3, 1963); was not a candidate in 1962 for reelection but was an unsuccessful candidate for nomination to the United States Senate; resided in Medford, Oreg., until his death there November 20, 1976; entombment in the International Order of Oddfellows Mausoleum.

**DUVAL, Isaac Harding,** a Representative from West Virginia; born in Wellsburg, Brooke County, Va. (now West Virginia), September 1, 1824; attended the common schools; as a youth he went to Fort Smith, Ark., and joined an elder brother, who was conducting a trading post; became a scout on the Western Plains; crossed the Plains in 1849 for the gold fields of California; was a member of the Lopez expedition to Cuba in an attempt to aid the Cubans in gaining national independence; returned to Virginia in 1853 and engaged in mercantile pursuits at Wellsburg; during the Civil War was commissioned major of the First Regiment, West Virginia Volunteer Infantry, June 1, 1861; successively promoted to colonel of the Ninth Regiment, brigadier general, and brevet major general; member of the State senate 1867-1869; adjutant general of West Virginia, 1867-1869; elected as a Republican to the Forty-first Congress (March 4, 1869-March 3, 1871); declined to be candidate for renomination in 1870; United States assessor of internal revenue in 1871 and 1872; collector of internal revenue for the first district of West Virginia 1872-1884; member of the State house of delegates 1887-1889; died in Wellsburg, W.Va., July 10, 1902; interment in Brooke Cemetery.

**DUVAL, William Pope,** a Representative from Kentucky; born in Mount Comfort, near Richmond, Va., in 1784; completed preparatory studies; moved to Kentucky; studied law; was admitted to the bar about 1804 and practiced law in Bardstown, Ky.; during the Indian hostilities of 1812 commanded a company of mounted Volunteers; elected as a Republican to the Thirteenth Congress (March 4, 1813-March 3, 1815); resumed the practice of law in Bardstown, Ky.; appointed on May 18, 1821, by President James Monroe as United States judge for the east Florida district; appointed Governor of the Territory of Florida by President James Monroe on April 17, 1822, and served until 1834; appointed law agent in Florida on November 4, 1841; moved to Texas in 1848; was the original of "Ralph Ringwood" of Washington Irving and "Nimrod Wildfire" of James K. Paulding; died in Washington, D.C., March 19, 1854; interment in the Congressional Cemetery.

**Bibliography:** *DAB.*

**DUVALL, Gabriel,** a Representative from Maryland; born in Prince Georges County, Md., December 6, 1752; completed preparatory studies; studied law; was admitted to the bar and practiced; member of the Governor's council in 1783 and 1784; elected to the Third Congress to fill the vacancy caused by the resignation of John F. Mercer; reelected as a Republican to the Fourth Congress and served from November 11, 1794, to March 28, 1796, when he resigned; appointed chief justice of the general court of Maryland on April 2, 1796, and resigned in 1802; appointed First Comptroller of the Treasury December 15, 1802, and served until his resignation November 18, 1811; elected judge of the court of appeals of Maryland on January 16, 1806, but declined to serve; appointed by President James Madison on November 15, 1811, an Associate Justice of the Supreme Court of the United States and served until his resignation on January 15, 1835, because of deafness; died near Glenn Dale, in Prince Georges County, Md., on March 6, 1844; interment in the Marcus Duvall estate "Wigwam" family burial ground near Glenn Dale, Md.

**DWIGHT, Henry Williams,** a Representative from Massachusetts; born in Stockbridge, Mass., February 26, 1788; attended Williams College, Williamstown, Mass.; studied law; was admitted to the Massachusetts bar in 1809 and commenced practice in Stockbridge; during the War of 1812 served as aide-de-camp with the rank of colonel on the staff of General Whiton; member of the Massachusetts house of representatives in 1818; elected to the Seventeenth and to the four succeeding Congresses (March 4, 1821-March 3, 1831); was not a candidate for renomination in 1830 to the Twenty-second Congress; again a member of the Massachusetts house of representatives in 1834; interested in the breeding of purebred sheep and cattle; died in New York City February 21, 1845; interment in Stockbridge Cemetery, Stockbridge, Berskshire County, Mass.

**DWIGHT, Jeremiah Wilbur** (father of John Wilbur Dwight), a Representative from New York; born in Cincinnatus, Cortland County, N.Y., April 17, 1819; moved with his parents in 1830 to Caroline, and in 1836 to Dryden, Tompkins County, N.Y.; attended the district schools and the Burhan's School in Dryden; engaged in mercantile pursuits, farming, real-estate business, and in the manufacture and sale of lumber; chairman of the board of supervisors of the town of Dryden in 1857 and 1858; member of the State assembly in 1860 and 1861; appointed by Governor Edwin D. Morgan a member of the senatorial district war committee in 1861; delegate to the Republican National Conventions of 1868, 1872, 1876, 1880, and 1884; director, member of the executive committee, and vice president of the Southern Central Railroad for many years; elected as a Republican to the Forty-fifth, Forty-sixth, and Forty-seventh Congresses (March 4, 1877-March 3, 1883); declined to be a candidate for renomination in 1882 to the Forty-eighth Congress; resumed former business activities; died in Dryden, Tompkins County, N.Y., November 26, 1885; interment in Green Hills Cemetery.

**DWIGHT, John Wilbur** (son of Jeremiah Wilbur Dwight), a Representative from New York; born in Dryden, Tompkins County, N.Y., May 24, 1859; attended the public schools; pursued further studies at New Haven, Conn., in preparation for entering Yale College, but abandoned this plan to engage in the lumber business at Clinton, Iowa, in 1879; shortly thereafter moved to northern Wisconsin, where he continued in the lumber business and also engaged in farming; returned to Dryden, N.Y., in 1884; upon the death of his father in 1885 became president of the Dwight Farm & Land Co.; delegate to the Republican National Conventions in 1888, 1892, 1900, 1904, and 1920; elected as a Republican to the Fifty-seventh Congress to fill the vacancy caused by the resignation of George W. Ray; reelected to the Fifty-eighth and to the four succeeding Congresses and served from November 2, 1902, to March 3, 1913; majority whip (Sixty-first Congress), minority whip (Sixty-second Congress); retired and resided in Washington, D.C.; became president of the Virginia Blue Ridge Railway Co. in 1913, in which capacity he served until his death in Washington, D.C., January 19, 1928; interment in Rock Creek Cemetery.

**DWIGHT, Theodore** (cousin of Aaron Burr), a Representative from Connecticut; born in Northampton, Mass., December 15, 1764; completed preparatory studies; studied law; was admitted to the bar in 1787 and began practice in Haddam, Conn.; moved to Hartford, Conn., in 1791 and continued the practice of law; editor of the Hartford Courant and of the Connecticut Mirror; member of the State council 1909-1815; elected as a Federalist to the Ninth Congress to fill the vacancy caused by the resignation of John Cotton Smith and served from December 1, 1806, to March 3, 1807; declined to be a candidate for renomination in 1806; secretary of the Hartford Convention in 1814; moved to Albany, N.Y., in 1815; published the Albany Daily Advertiser 1815-1817; moved to New York City in 1817 and established the New York Daily Advertiser, with which he was connected until the great fire of 1835; returned to Hartford, Conn., and resided there until about three years before his death, when he returned to New York City; died in New York City, June 12, 1846; interment in Greenwood Cemetery, Brooklyn, N.Y.

Bibliography: *DAB*.

**DWIGHT, Thomas,** a Representative from Massachusetts; born in Springfield, Mass., October 29, 1758; pursued preparatory studies; was graduated from Harvard College in 1778; studied law; was admitted to the bar and commenced practice in Springfield, Mass.; member of the Massachusetts house of representatives in 1794 and 1795; served in the Massachusetts senate 1796-1803; elected as a Federalist to the Eighth Congress (March 4, 1803-March 3, 1805); selectman of the town of Springfield 1806-1809 and in 1811; member of the Governor's council in 1808 and 1809; retired from political life and engaged in the practice of his profession in Springfield, Hampden County, until his death January 2, 1819; interment in Peabody Cemetery.

**DWINELL, Justin,** a Representative from New York; born in Shaftsbury, Vt., October 28, 1785; attended a local private school and Williams College, Williamstown, Mass.; was graduated from Yale College in 1808; studied law; was admitted to the bar in 1811 and commenced practice in Cazenovia, N.Y., the same year; member of the State assembly in 1821 and 1822; elected to the Eighteenth Congress (March 4, 1823-March 3, 1825); was not a candidate for renomination; resumed the practice of law; judge of the common pleas court of Madison County, N.Y., 1828-1833; district attorney of Madison County 1837-1845; died in Cazenovia, Madison County, N.Y., September 17, 1850; interment in Evergreen Cemetery.

**DWORSHAK, Henry Clarence,** a Representative and a Senator from Idaho; born in Duluth, Minn., August 29, 1894; attended the public schools; worked at the printing trade 1909-1918; during the First World War served overseas as a sergeant in the Fourth Antiaircraft Machine Gun Battalion 1918-1919; manager of printers' supply business in Duluth, Minn., 1920-1924; editor and publisher of the Burley Bulletin in Burley, Idaho, 1924-1944; elected as a Republican to the Seventy-sixth and to the three succeeding Congresses and served from January 3, 1939, to November 5, 1946, when he resigned; elected as a Republican to the United States Senate on November 5, 1946, to fill the vacancy caused by the death of John Thomas and served from November 6, 1946, to January 3, 1949; unsuccessful candidate for reelection in 1948; appointed to the United States Senate and subsequently elected as a Republican to fill the vacancy caused by the death of Bert H. Miller; reelected in 1954 and again in 1960 and served from October 14, 1949, until his death in Washington, D.C., on July 23, 1962; interment in Arlington National Cemetery, Va.

**DWYER, Bernard James,** a Representative from New Jersey; born in Perth Amboy, Middlesex County, N.J., January 24, 1921; attended the public schools; attended Rutgers University, Newark, N.J.; served in the United States Navy, 1940-1945; owner of Fraser Brothers Insurance Brokerage, 1946 to present; member, Edison (N.J.) Township Council, 1958-1969; mayor, Township of Edison, 1969-1973; served in the New Jersey State senate, 1974-1980; elected as a Democrat to the Ninety-seventh and to the five succeeding Congresses (January 3, 1981-January 3, 1993); was not a candidate for reelection in 1992 to the One Hundred Third Congress; is a resident of Edison, N.J.

**DWYER, Florence Price,** a Representative from New Jersey; born July 4, 1902, in Reading, Berks County, Pa.; attended the public schools in Reading, Pa., and Toledo, Ohio; special courses at Rutgers Law School; State legislation chairman of New Jersey Business and Professional Women; moved to Elizabeth, Union County, N.J.; delegate to the Republican National Convention in 1944; member of the State house of assembly 1950-1956; United States Advisory Commission on Intergovernmental Relations, 1959-1973; elected as a Republican to the Eighty-fifth and to the seven succeeding Congresses (January 3, 1957-January 3, 1973); was not a candidate for reelection in 1972 to the Ninety-third Congress; retired and resided in Elizabeth, N.J., where she died February 29, 1976; interment in St. Gertrude's Cemetery, Colonia, N.J.

**DYAL, Kenneth Warren,** a Representative from California; born in Bisbee, Cochise County, Ariz., July 9, 1910; attended the public schools of San Bernardino and Colton, Calif.; moved to San Bernardino, Calif., in 1917; secretary to the San Bernardino County Board of Supervisors, 1941-1943; served as a lieutenant commander in the United States Naval Reserve, 1943-1946; postmaster of San Bernardino, 1947-1954; insurance company executive, 1954-1961; member of board of directors of Los Angeles Airways, Inc., 1956-1964; elected as a Democrat to the Eighty-ninth Congress (January 3, 1965-January 3, 1967); unsuccessful candidate for reelection in 1966 to the Ninetieth Congress; regional director, San Francisco, Calif., Post Office Department, 1966-1969; Regional Programs Coordinator, United States Post Office Department, 1969-1971; resided in Oakland, Calif., until his death there May 12, 1978; interment in Montecito Cemetery, Colton, Calif.

**DYER, David Patterson** (uncle of Leonidas Carstarphen Dyer), a Representative from Missouri; born in Henry County, Va., February 12, 1838; moved with his parents to Lincoln County, Mo., in 1841; completed preparatory studies; studied law in Bowling Green, Pike County, Mo., and was admitted to the bar in March 1859; elected prosecuting attorney for the third judicial circuit in 1860; during the Civil War served as a private in Captain Hardin's company, Pike County Regiment, Missouri Home Guard, and as lieutenant colonel and colonel in the Forty-ninth Regiment, Missouri Volunteer Infantry; member of the Virginia house of representatives 1862-1865; secretary of the Virginia senate in 1866; delegate to the Republican National Convention of 1868; elected as a Republican to the Forty-first Congress (March 4, 1869-March 3, 1871); unsuccessful candidate for reelection in 1870 to the Forty-second Congress; resumed the practice of his profession in St. Louis, Mo.; unsuccessful Republican candidate for election as Governor in 1880; appointed by President Theodore Roosevelt United States attorney for the eastern district of Missouri and served from March 9, 1902, to March 31, 1907; appointed on April 1, 1907, by President Roosevelt as United States judge for the eastern district of Missouri, and served until November 3, 1919, when he retired; died in St. Louis, Mo., April 29, 1924; interment in Bellefontaine Cemetery.

**DYER, Eliphalet,** a Delegate from Connecticut; born in Windham, Conn., September 14, 1721; pursued preparatory studies, and was graduated from Yale College in 1740; served as town clerk; appointed captain in the militia in 1745; studied law; was admitted to the bar in 1746 and commenced practice in Windham; justice of the peace in 1746; elected a deputy to the general assembly in 1747, 1749, 1752, and 1753; was active in the project of establishing a Connecticut colony in the Susquehanna Valley, and served as agent of the Susquehanna Co. in London in 1763; in 1755, during the French and Indian War, was appointed a lieutenant colonel in the Connecticut Regiment; again a member of the general assembly 1756-1784, serving as deputy from 1756 to 1762 and as assistant from 1762 to 1784; appointed comptroller of the port of New London in 1764; delegate to the Stamp-Act Congress in 1765; judge of the superior court 1766-1793, and served as chief judge from 1789 until 1793; Member of the Continental Congress 1774-1779 and 1782-1783; member of the committee of safety in 1775; retired from public life in 1793; died in Windham, Conn., May 13, 1807; interment in Windham Cemetery.

Bibliography: *DAB*; Willingham, William F. *Connecticut Revolutionary: Eliphalet Dyer.* Hartford: American Revolutionary Bicentennial Commission of Connecticut, 1977.

**DYER, Leonidas Carstarphen** (nephew of David Patterson Dyer), a Representative from Missouri; born near Warrenton, Warren County, Mo., June 11, 1871; attended the common schools, Central Wesleyan College, Warrenton, Mo., and Washington University, St. Louis, Mo.; studied law; was admitted to the bar in 1893 and commenced practice in St. Louis, Mo.; served in the Spanish-American War; was a member of the staff of Governor Hadley of Missouri, with the rank of colonel; commander in chief of the Spanish War Veterans in 1915 and 1916; elected as a Republican to the Sixty-second Congress (March 4, 1911-March 3, 1913); presented credentials as a Member-elect to the Sixty-third Congress and served from March 4, 1913, to June 19, 1914, when he was succeeded by Michael J. Gill, who contested his election; elected to the Sixty-fourth and to the eight succeeding Congresses (March 4, 1915-March 3, 1933); unsuccessful candidate for reelection in 1932 to the Seventy-third Congress and for election in 1934 to the Seventy-fourth Congress and in 1936 to the Seventy-fifth Congress; resumed the practice of law; died in St. Louis, Mo., December 15, 1957; interment in Oak Grove Cemetery.

**DYMALLY, Mervyn Malcolm,** a Representative from California; born in Cedros, Trinidad, British West Indies, May 12, 1926; attended Cedros Government School, Trinidad; graduated from St. Benedict and Naparima Secondary, San Fernando, Trinidad, 1944; studied at Lincoln University, Jefferson City, Mo.; B.A., California State University, Los Angeles, 1954; M.A., California State University, Sacramento, 1969; Ph.D., United States International University, San Diego, 1978; president, Mervyn M. Dymally Co., Inc., 1979-1981; teacher; lecturer; member, California State assembly, 1963-1966; California State senator, 1967-1975; lieutenant governor of California, 1975-1979; chaired the California State Commission for Economic Development, and the Commission of the Californias; elected as a Democrat to the Ninety-seventh and to the five succeeding Congresses (January 3, 1981-January 3, 1993); was not a candidate for reelection in 1992 to the One Hundred Third Congress; president, Dymally International Group, Inglewood, Calif.; is a resident of Los Angeles, Calif.

**DYSON, Royden Patrick,** a Representative from Maryland; born in Great Mills, St. Mary's County, Md., November 15, 1948; attended private schools; graduated from Great Mills High School, 1966; attended the University of Maryland, College Park, and the University of Baltimore, 1968, 1969, and 1970; legislative assistant, United States House of Representatives, 1973-1974; elected to the Maryland house of delegates, 1975-1980; delegate, 1978 Democratic National Issues Conference; unsuccessful candidate for election in 1976 to the Ninety-fifth Congress; elected as a Democrat to the Ninety-seventh and to the four succeeding Congresses (January 3, 1981-January 3, 1991); unsuccessful candidate for reelection in 1990 to the One Hundred Second Congress; elected in 1994 to the Maryland State senate, District 29, for a four-year term beginning January 11, 1995; is a resident of Great Mills, Md.

# E

**EAGAN, John Joseph,** a Representative from New Jersey; born in Hoboken, N.J., January 22, 1872; was graduated from public, parochial, and private schools; in 1894 founded and was president of the Eagan Schools of Business in Hoboken, Union Hill, and Hackensack, N.J., and Brooklyn, N.Y.; first vice president of the Merchants & Manufacturers' Trust Co.; collector of taxes of Union, N.J., 1896-1899; elected as a Democrat to the Sixty-third and to the three succeeding Congresses (March 4, 1913-March 3, 1921); delegate to the Democratic National Convention of 1920; unsuccessful candidate for reelection in 1920 to the Sixty-seventh Congress; elected to the Sixty-eighth Congress (March 4, 1923-March 3, 1925); unsuccessful candidate for renomination in 1924 to the Sixty-ninth Congress; resumed his former business pursuits; member and president of the Board of Education, Weehawken, N.J., 1932-1940; appointed collector of taxes and custodian of school moneys of Weehawken in 1940; collector of taxes, 1941-1955; resided in Weehawken, N.J., until his death in Paramus, N.J., June 13, 1956; interment in Rosendale Cemetery, Tillson, N.Y.

**EAGER, Samuel Watkins,** a Representative from New York; born in Neelytown, Orange County, N.Y., on April 8, 1789; attended Montgomery Academy, Montgomery, N.Y., and was graduated from Princeton College in 1809; studied law; was admitted to the bar in 1811 and commenced practice in Newburgh, N.Y.; moved to Montgomery, N.Y., in 1826, and continued the practice of his profession; elected to the Twenty-first Congress to fill the vacancy caused by the resignation of Hector Craig and served from November 2, 1830, to March 3, 1831; was not a candidate at the election held the same day for the Twenty-second Congress; returned to Newburgh in 1836 and engaged in literary pursuits; died in Newburgh, N.Y., December 23, 1860; interment in St. George Cemetery.

**EAGLE, Joe Henry,** a Representative from Texas; born in Tompkinsville, Monroe County, Ky., January 23, 1870; was graduated from the local high school in 1883 and obtained a teacher's certificate in 1884; was also graduated from Burritt College, Spencer, Tenn., in 1887; moved to Texas; taught school 1887-1893 and served as superintendent of the city schools of Vernon, Tex., 1889-1891; studied law; was admitted to the bar in 1893 and commenced practice in Wichita Falls, Tex.; city attorney of Wichita Falls in 1894 and 1895; moved to Houston in 1895 and continued the practice of law; elected as a Democrat to the Sixty-third and to the three succeeding Congresses (March 4, 1913-March 3, 1921); was not a candidate for renomination in 1920; elected on January 28, 1933, to both the Seventy-second and Seventy-third Congresses to fill the vacancies caused by the death of Daniel E. Garrett, who had been reelected in 1932; reelected to the Seventy-fourth Congress and served from January 28, 1933, to January 3, 1937; was not a candidate for renomination in 1936, but was an unsuccessful candidate for the Democratic nomination for United States Senator; resumed the practice of his profession; was a resident of Houston, Tex., until his death January 10, 1963; interment in Forest Park (Lawndale) Cemetery.

**EAGLETON, Thomas Francis,** a Senator from Missouri; born in St. Louis, Mo., September 4, 1929; enlisted in the United States Navy and served from 1948 to 1949; B.A., Amherst (Mass.) College, 1950; LL.B., Harvard University Law School, 1953; elected circuit attorney of St. Louis, Mo., 1956; elected attorney general of Missouri in 1960; Lieutenant Governor of Missouri, 1964-1968; elected as a Democrat to the United States Senate in 1968 for the six-year term commencing January 3, 1969; subsequently appointed December 28, 1968, to fill the vacancy caused by the resignation of Edward V. Long for the term ending January 3, 1969; reelected in 1974 and 1980, and served from December 28, 1968, to January 3, 1987; was not a candidate for reelection in 1986; unsuccessful Democratic candidate for Vice President of the United States in 1972; resumed the practice of law; is a resident of St. Louis, Mo.

Bibliography: Eagleton, Thomas. *Our Constitution and What It Means.* New York: McGraw-Hill, 1987; Eagleton, Thomas. *War and Presidential Power.* New York: Liveright, 1974.

**EAMES, Benjamin Tucker,** a Representative from Rhode Island; born in Dedham, Norfolk County, Mass., June 4, 1818; attended the common schools of Providence, R.I., and academies in Massachusetts and Connecticut; employed as a bookkeeper for several years; was graduated from Yale College in 1843; engaged as a teacher in the academy at North Attleboro, studying law at the same time; was admitted to the bar in 1845 and commenced practice in Providence, R.I.; recording and reading clerk of the State house of representatives 1845-1850; member of the State senate 1854-1857, 1863, and again in 1864; one of the commissioners on the revision of the public laws of the State of Rhode Island in 1857; served in the State house of representatives in 1859, 1860, 1868, and 1869; elected as a Republican to the Forty-second and to the three succeeding Congresses (March 4, 1871-March 3, 1879); chairman, Committee on Private Land Claims (Forty-third Congress); was not a candidate for renomination; again a member of the State house of representatives 1879-1881; again served in the State senate in 1884 and 1885; died in East Greenwich, R.I., October 6, 1901; interment in Swan Point Cemetery, Providence, R.I.

**EARHART, Daniel Scofield,** a Representative from Ohio; born in Columbus, Franklin County, Ohio, May, 28 1907; attended the public schools, and the College of Engineering of Ohio State University at Columbus; was graduated from the College of Law of Ohio State University in 1928; was admitted to the bar the same year and commenced practice in Columbus, Ohio; elected as a Democrat to the Seventy-fourth Congress to fill the vacancy caused by the death of Charles V. Truax and served from November 3, 1936, to January 3, 1937; was not a candidate for election in 1936 to the Seventy-fifth Congress; resumed the practice of law; member of the Officers' Reserve Corps 1928-1941; ordered to active service in the Infantry with rank of captain on May 26, 1941; transferred to the Army Air Forces with rank of major; promoted to lieutenant colonel and was relieved of active duty on February 24, 1946; commissioned lieutenant colonel in the Ohio Air National Guard in 1948; recalled to active Federal military service September 2, 1951, and served until September 7, 1953, as commanding officer, deputy commander, and operations officer of the One Hundred and Fifty-fifth Tactical Control Group, United States Air Force, building up NATO tactical air control facilities in western Europe; resumed the practice of law; resided in Columbus, Ohio, where he died January 2, 1976; cremated; ashes interred in Green Lawn Cemetery.

**EARLE, Elias** (uncle of Samuel Earle and John Baylis Earle and great-grandfather of John Laurens Manning Irby and Joseph Haynsworth Earle), a Representative from South Carolina; born in Frederick County, Va., June 19, 1762; attended private school; moved to Greenville County, S.C., in September 1787; was one of the earliest ironmasters of the South, and prospected and negotiated in the iron region of Georgia; member of South Carolina house of representatives, 1794-1797; member of the State senate in 1800; elected as a Republican to the Ninth Congress (March 4, 1805-March 3, 1807); elected to the Twelfth and Thirteenth Congresses (March 4, 1811-March 3, 1815); again elected to the Fifteenth and Sixteenth Congresses (March 4, 1817-March 3, 1821); died in Centerville, S.C., May 19, 1823; interment in Old Earle Cemetery, Buncombe Road, Greenville, S.C.

**EARLE, John Baylis** (nephew of Elias Earle and cousin of Samuel Earle), a Representative from South Carolina; born on the North Carolina side of the North Pacolet River, near Landrum, Spartanburg County, S.C., October 23, 1766; moved to South Carolina; completed preparatory studies; served as a drummer boy and soldier during the Revolutionary War; engaged in agricultural pursuits; elected as a Republican to the Eighth Congress (March 4, 1803-March 3, 1805); declined to be a candidate for reelection in 1804 to the Ninth Congress; resumed agricultural pursuits; adjutant and inspector general of South Carolina for sixteen years; served throughout the War of 1812; member of the nullification convention of 1832 and 1833; died in Anderson County, S.C., February 3, 1863; interment in the cemetery on his plantation, "Silver Glade," in Anderson County, S.C.

**EARLE, Joseph Haynsworth** (great-grandson of Elias Earle, cousin of John Laurens Manning Irby, and nephew of William Lowndes Yancey), a Senator from South Carolina; born in Greenville, Greenville County, S.C., April 30, 1847; attended private schools in Sumter, S.C.; at the outbreak of the Civil War enlisted in the Confederate Army; graduated from Furman University, Greenville, S.C., in 1867; taught school for two years; studied law; was admitted to the bar in 1870 and commenced practice in Anderson, S.C.; returned to Sumter, S.C., in 1875 and continued the practice of law; also interested in the logging business and in agricultural pursuits; member, State house of representatives 1878-1882; member, State senate 1882-1886; attorney general of South Carolina 1886-1890; declined the nomination for Governor in 1888; unsuccessful candidate for nomination for Governor in 1890; returned to Greenville in 1892; elected circuit judge in 1894; elected as a Democrat to the United States Senate and served from March 4, 1897, until his death in Greenville, S.C., May 20, 1897; interment in Christ Churchyard.

**EARLE, Samuel** (nephew of Elias Earle and cousin of John Baylis Earle), a Representative from South Carolina; born in Frederick County, Va., November 28, 1760; moved to South Carolina in 1774; participated in the Revolutionary War, entering the service as an ensign in 1777 and leaving as captain of a company of rangers in 1782; member of the State house of representatives 1784-1788; delegate to the State convention that ratified the Federal Constitution May 12, 1788; delegate to the State constitutional convention in 1790; elected as a Republican to the Fourth Congress (March 4, 1795-March 3, 1797); died in Pendleton District, S.C., November 24, 1833; interment in Beaverdam Cemetery, Oconee County, S.C.

**EARLL, Jonas, Jr.** (cousin of Nehemiah Hezekiah Earll), a Representative from New York; born in 1786; resided in Onondaga County, N.Y., and attended the common schools; sheriff of Onondaga County 1815-1819; member of the State assembly in 1820 and 1821; served in the State senate from January 1823 to January 1827; elected to the Twentieth Congress and reelected as a Jacksonian to the Twenty-first Congress (March 4, 1827-March 3, 1831); chairman, Committee on Expenditures in the Department of State (Twenty-first Congress); elected a canal commissioner and served from January 1832 to February 1840; postmaster of Syracuse, N.Y., from June 26, 1840, until March 10, 1842; again elected a canal commissioner and served from February 8, 1842, until his death in Syracuse, N.Y., October 28, 1846; interment in Walnut Grove Cemetery, Onondaga Hill, Onondaga County, N.Y.

**EARLL, Nehemiah Hezekiah** (cousin of Jonas Earll, Jr.), a Representative from New York; born in Whitehall, Washington County, N.Y., October 5, 1787; moved with his parents to Onondaga Valley in 1793; nine months later moved to Onondaga County and resided in Skaneateles until 1804; attended the public schools and Fairfield Academy for two years; studied law; was admitted to the bar in 1809 and commenced practice in Salina (which in 1848 became a part of Syracuse), Onondaga County; adjutant in the Army during the War of 1812 at Oswego; resumed the practice of law at Onondaga Hill, N.Y., in 1814; postmaster of Onondaga Hill in 1816; justice of the peace 1816-1820; master in chancery for six years; appointed first judge of Onondaga County and served from 1823 until his resignation in 1831; superintendent of the Onondaga Salt Springs 1831-1836, with residence in Syracuse, N.Y.; resigned, and engaged in the milling business in Jordan; returned to Syracuse, N.Y., in 1838; elected as a Democrat to the Twenty-sixth Congress (March 4, 1839-March 3, 1841); unsuccessful candidate for reelection in 1840 to the Twenty-seventh Congress; retired to private life, being blind for many years; died in Mottville, Onondaga County, N.Y., August 26, 1872; interment in Oakwood Cemetery, Syracuse, N.Y.

**EARLY, Joseph Daniel,** a Representative from Massachusetts; born in Worcester, Mass., Worcester County, January 31, 1933; attended parochial schools in Worcester; B.S., College of the Holy Cross, Worcester, 1955; served in United States Navy, 1955-1957; taught high school in Shrewsbury and Spencer, Mass., 1959-1963; member, Massachusetts house of representatives, 1963-1974; delegate to Massachusetts Democratic conventions, 1964-1970; elected as a Democrat to the Ninety-fourth and to the eight succeeding Congresses (January 3, 1975-January 3, 1993); unsuccessful candidate for reelection in 1992 to the One Hundred Third Congress; is a resident of Worcester, Mass.

**EARLY, Peter,** a Representative from Georgia; born near Madison, Madison County, Va., June 20, 1773; attended the Lexington Academy (later Washington College) in Rockbridge County; was graduated from Princeton College in 1792; studied law in Philadelphia, Pa.; was admitted to the bar and commenced practice in Wilkes County, Ga., in 1795; moved to Greene County in 1801 and continued the practice of law; elected as a Republican to the Seventh Congress to fill the vacancy caused by the resignation of John Milledge; reelected to the Eighth and Ninth Congresses, and served from January 10, 1803 to March 3, 1807; one of the managers appointed by the House of Representatives in January 1804 to conduct the impeachment proceedings against John Pickering, judge of the United States District Court for New Hampshire, and in December of the same year against Samuel Chase, Associate Justice of the United States Supreme Court; declined to be a candidate for reelection in 1806 to the Tenth Congress; first judge of the superior court of the Ocmulgee (Western) circuit of Georgia from December 1807 to November 1813; elected Governor of Georgia by the Legislature, and served from November 5, 1813 to November 10, 1815; elected to the State senate in 1815 and served until his death near Scull Shoals, Greene County, Ga., August 15, 1817; interment on the west bank of the Oconee River near his home, "Fontenoy"; reinterment in City Cemetery, Greensboro, Ga.

Bibliography: *DAB*; Thomason, Hugh M. "Governor Peter Early and The Creek Indian Frontier, 1813-1815." *Georgia Historical Quarterly* 45 (September 1961): 223-237.

**EARNSHAW, Manuel,** a Resident Commissioner from the Philippine Islands; born in Cavite, Philippine Islands, November 19, 1862; attended the Ateneo de Manila and the Nauti School, Manila, Philippine Islands; became engaged in engineering and in the drydocking business in 1884; founder, president, and general manager of the Earnshaw Slipways and Engineering Co.; elected as an Independent candidate a Resident Commissioner to the United States, and served from March 4, 1913 to March 3, 1917; was not a candidate for renomination in 1916; discontinued his former business pursuits in 1921 and lived in retirement with residence in Cavite; died in Manila, Philippine Islands, February 13, 1936; interment in Cementerio del Norte.

**EARTHMAN, Harold Henderson,** a Representative from Tennessee; born in Murfreesboro, Rutherford County, Tenn., April 13, 1900; attended the public schools, Webb School at Bell Buckle, Tenn., Southern Methodist University at Dallas, Tex., and the University of Texas at Austin; during the First World War served in the United States Army as a private and was assigned to the Student's Army Training Corps; moved to Nashville, Tenn., and engaged in the banking business, 1921-1925; was admitted to the bar in 1926 and commenced the practice of law in Murfreesboro, Tenn.; also engaged in agricultural pursuits; resumed the study of law and was graduated from the law department of Cumberland University, Lebanon, Tenn., in 1927; served in the Tennessee State house of representatives in 1931 and 1932; judge of Rutherford County, Tenn., 1942-1945; associate administrator of war bonds for the State of Tennessee, 1940-1946; elected as a Democrat to the Seventy-ninth Congress (January 3, 1945-January 3, 1947); unsuccessful candidate for renomination in 1946 to the Eightieth Congress; resumed the practice of law; owner of Earthman Enterprises; was a resident of Murfreesboro, Tenn., until his death there on February 26, 1987; interment in Evergreen Cemetery.

**EAST, John Porter,** a Senator from North Carolina; born in Springfield, Sangamon County, Ill., May 5, 1931; attended the public schools; B.S., Earlham College, Richmond, Ind., 1953; LL.B., University of Illinois Law School, Urbana, 1959; M.A., University of Florida, Gainesville, 1962, Ph.D., 1964; served in the United States Marine Corps, 1953-1955; admitted to the Florida bar in 1959 and commenced practice in Naples; professor, East Carolina University, Greenville, N.C., 1964-1980; elected as a Republican to the United States Senate in 1980 and served from January 3, 1981, until his death by suicide in Greenville, N.C., June 29, 1986; interment in Arlington National Cemetery, Va.

**EASTLAND, James Oliver,** a Senator from Mississippi; born in Doddsville, Sunflower County, Miss., November 28, 1904; moved with his parents to Forest, Miss., in 1905; attended the public schools, the University of Mississippi, Oxford, 1922-1924, Vanderbilt University, Nashville, Tenn., 1925-1926, and the University of Alabama, Tuscaloosa, 1926-1927; studied law; was admitted to the bar in 1927 and commenced practice in Forest, Miss.; also engaged in agricultural pursuits; member, Mississippi State house of representatives, 1928-1932; moved to Ruleville, Miss., in 1934; appointed as a Democrat to the United States Senate to fill the vacancy caused by the death of Byron Patton (Pat) Harrison and served from June 30, 1941, to September 28, 1941; was not a candidate for election to the vacancy; elected as a Democrat to the United States Senate in 1942; reelected in 1948, 1954, 1960, 1966, and again in 1972 and served from January 3, 1943, until his resignation December 27, 1978; was not a candidate for reelection in 1978; served as President pro tempore of the Senate during the Ninety-second through the Ninety-fifth Congresses; chairman, Committee on the Judiciary (Eighty-fourth through Ninety-fifth Congresses; was a resident of Doddsville, Miss., until his death February 19, 1986; interment in Forest Cemetery, Forest, Miss.

Bibliography: Schlauch, Wolfgang. "Representative William Colmer and Senator James O. Eastland and the Reconstruction of Germany, 1945." *Journal of Mississippi History* 34 (August 1972): 193-213.

**EASTMAN, Ben C.,** a Representative from Wisconsin; born in Strong, Maine, October 24, 1812; attended the public schools; studied law; was admitted to the bar in 1840 and practiced in Green Bay, Wis.; moved to Platteville, Wis., the same year and continued the practice of law; secretary of the legislative council of Wisconsin Territory 1843-1846; district attorney of Grant County; elected as a Democrat to the Thirty-second and Thirty-Third Congresses (March 4, 1851-March 3, 1855); declined to be a candidate for renomination in 1854; resumed the practice of law; died in Platteville, Grant County, Wis., February 2, 1856; interment in Forest Hill Cemetery, Madison, Wis.

**EASTMAN, Ira Allen** (nephew of Nehemiah Eastman), a Representative from New Hampshire; born in Gilmanton, N.H., January 1, 1809; attended the local schools; was graduated from Dartmouth College, Hanover, N.H., in 1829; studied law; was admitted to the bar in 1832 and commenced practice in Troy, N.H.; returned to Gilmanton in 1834 and continued the practice of law; clerk of the State house of representatives in 1835; member of the State house of representatives 1836-1838, and served as speaker in 1837 and 1838; register of probate from 1836 to 1839; elected as a Democrat to the Twenty-sixth and Twenty-seventh Congresses (March 4, 1839-March 3, 1843); chairman, Committee on Revisal and Unfinished Business (Twenty-seventh Congress); was not a candidate for renomination in 1842 to the Twenty-eighth Congress; judge of the court of common pleas 1844-1849; associate judge of the supreme court 1849-1855; judge of the superior judicial court from 1855 to 1859; chosen trustee of Dartmouth College in 1859; unsuccessful Democratic candidate for Governor in 1863 and for United States Senator in 1866; resumed the practice of law; died in Manchester, N.H., March 21, 1881; interment in Valley Cemetery.

**EASTMAN, Nehemiah** (uncle of Ira Allen Eastman), a Representative from New Hampshire; born in Gilmanton, Belknap County, N.H., June 16, 1782; attended the local academy in Gilmanton; studied law; was admitted to the bar in 1807 and practiced in Farmington, N.H.; member of the State house of representatives in 1813; served in the State senate 1820-1825; elected to the Nineteenth Congress (March 4, 1825-March 3, 1827); resumed the practice of law; died in Farmington, N.H., January 11, 1856; interment in Farmington Cemetery.

**EASTON, Rufus,** a Delegate from the Territory of Missouri; born in Litchfield, Conn., May 4, 1774; completed an academic course; studied law; was admitted to the bar and commenced practice in Rome, N.Y.; started west and settled in Vincennes, Indiana Territory, in 1804; moved to St. Louis, Mo. (then the District of Louisiana), and was appointed judge of the District of Louisiana in 1805; appointed the first postmaster of St. Louis and served from January 1, 1805, to January 1, 1815; elected a Delegate from the Territory of Missouri on September 17, 1814, and served until August 5, 1816; unsuccessfully contested the election of John Scott for the succeeding term; upon the organization of the State government in 1821 was appointed attorney general and served until 1826; engaged in the practice of law and in the real estate business; died in St. Charles, Mo., July 5, 1834; interment in Lindenwood College, Cemetery.

**EATON, Charles Aubrey** (uncle of William Robb Eaton), a Representative from New Jersey; born in Nova Scotia March 29, 1868; attended the public schools; was graduated from Acadia University, Nova Scotia, in 1890 and from Newton Theological Institution, Newton Center, Mass., in 1893; pastor in Natick, Mass., 1892-1895, Toronto, Canada, 1895-1901, and Cleveland, Ohio, 1901-1909; moved to Watchung, Somerset County, N.J., in 1909; pastor of the Madison Avenue Church, New York City, 1909-1919; sociological editor of the Toronto Globe, Toronto, Canada, 1896-1901; associate editor, Westminster, Toronto, Canada, 1899-1901; head of the national service section of the United States Shipping Board Emergency Fleet Corporation from November 1917 to January 1919; editor of Leslie's Weekly in 1919 and 1920; elected as a Republican to the Sixty-ninth and to the thirteen succeeding Congresses (March 4, 1925-January 3, 1953); chairman, Committee on Foreign Affairs (Eightieth Congress), Select Committee on Foreign Aid (Eightieth Congress); was not a candidate for renomination in 1952; died in Washington, D.C., January 23, 1953; interment in Hillside Cemetery, Plainfield, N.J.

**Bibliography:** *DAB.*

**EATON, John Henry,** a Senator from Tennessee; born near Scotland Neck, Halifax County, N.C., June 18, 1790; attended the common schools and the University of North Carolina at Chapel Hill in 1803 and 1804; studied law; was admitted to the bar and commenced practice in Franklin, Tenn.; member, Tennessee State house of representatives, 1815-1816; appointed in 1818 and subsequently elected as a Republican to the United States Senate to fill the vacancy caused by the resignation of George W. Campbell, and served from September 5, 1818 to March 3, 1821; elected to the Senate in September 1821, and again in 1826, and served from September 27, 1821 until March 9, 1829, when he resigned to accept a Cabinet portfolio; chairman, Committee on District of Columbia (Twentieth Congress); appointed Secretary of War by President Andrew Jackson and served from March 9, 1829 to June 18, 1831, when he resigned; appointed Governor of Florida Territory by President Jackson and served from April 24, 1834 until April 1836; appointed Envoy Extraordinary and Minister Plenipotentiary to Spain on March 16, 1836 and served until May 1840; died in Washington, D.C., November 17, 1856; interment in Oak Hill Cemetery.

**Bibliography:** *DAB*; Eaton, John Henry. *The Life of Andrew Jackson.* 1824. Reprint. New York: Arno Press, 1971; Lawrence, Frank, ed. *The Life of Andrew Jackson, John Reid, and John Eaton.* University: University of Alabama Press, 1974.

**EATON, Lewis,** a Representative from New York; born in that State; sheriff of Schenectady County in 1821 and 1822; resided in Duanesburg; elected to the Eighteenth Congress (March 4, 1823-March 3, 1825); member of the State senate 1829-1832.

**EATON, Thomas Marion,** a Representative from California; born on a farm near Edwardsville, Madison County, Ill., August 3, 1896; attended the public schools; was graduated from the State Normal School, Normal, Ill., in 1917; served as principal of a grade school, Clinton, Ill., in 1917 and 1918; during the First World War served in the United States Navy as an ensign; moved to Long Beach, Calif., in 1921 and engaged in the automobile sales business; elected to the city council in 1934; reelected in 1936, and was unanimously chosen mayor by the council; elected as a Republican to the Seventy-sixth Congress and served from January 3, 1939, until his death in Long Beach, Calif., September 16, 1939; interment in Sunnyside Mausoleum.

**EATON, William Robb** (nephew of Charles Aubrey Eaton), a Representative from Colorado; born in Pugwash, Nova Scotia, Canada, December 17, 1877; immigrated to the United States with his parents who settled in Boston, Mass., in 1878, and in Denver, Colo., in 1881; attended public and private schools; employed as a bank clerk from 1889 until 1901; engaged as a jobber and wholesaler and in the warehouse business, 1901-1909; served in Troop B, First Squadron Cavalry, National Guard of Colorado, 1898-1904; was graduated from the law department of the University of Denver at Denver in 1909; was admitted to the bar the same year and commenced practice in Denver, Colo.; served as deputy district attorney of the second judicial district, 1909-1913; member of the Colorado State senate, 1915-1918, and 1923-1926; elected as a Republican to the Seventy-first and Seventy-second Congresses (March 4, 1929-March 3, 1933); unsuccessful candidate for reelection in 1932 to the Seventy-third Congress, and for election in 1934 to the Seventy-fourth Congress; resumed the practice of law in Denver, Colo., until his death there on December 16, 1942; interment in Fairmount Cemetery.

**EATON, William Wallace,** a Senator and a Representative from Connecticut; born in Tolland, Conn., October 11, 1816; educated in the common schools and by private instruction; moved to Columbia, S.C., and engaged in mercantile pursuits; returned to Tolland, Conn.; studied law; was admitted to the bar in 1837 and commenced practice; clerk of courts of Tolland County 1846-1847; member, State house of representatives 1847-1848, 1853, 1863, 1868, 1870-1871, 1873-1874; served as speaker in 1853 and 1873; member, State senate 1859; moved to Hartford, Conn., in 1851; clerk of courts of Hartford County 1851 and 1854; city attorney 1857-1858; unsuccessful Democratic candidate for United States Senator in 1860; chief judge of the city court of Hartford 1863-1864, 1867-1872; appointed as a Democrat to the United States Senate to fill the vacancy caused by the death of William A. Buckingham and served from February 5, 1875, to March 3, 1875; elected for the full term beginning March 4, 1875, and served until March 3, 1881; chairman, Committee on Foreign Relations (Forty-sixth Congress); elected as a Democrat to the Forty-eighth Congress (March 4, 1883-March 3, 1885); unsuccessful candidate for reelection in 1884; resumed the practice of law; died in Hartford, Conn., September 21, 1898; interment in Spring Grove Cemetery.

**EBERHARTER, Herman Peter,** a Representative from Pennsylvania; born in Pittsburgh, Pa., April 29, 1892; attended Holy Trinity parish school, Morehead School and Fifth Avenue High School; during the First World War served in the United States Army as a private in the Twentieth Infantry and was commissioned as a second lieutenant; was graduated from Duquesne University Law School, Pittsburgh, Pa., in 1925; was admitted to the bar the same year and commenced practice in Pittsburgh, Pa.; was a member of the Officers' Reserve Corps with rank of captain; member of the Pennsylvania house of representatives, 1935-1936; elected as a Democrat to the Seventy-fifth and to the ten succeeding Congresses, and served from January 3, 1937 until his death in Arlington, Va., September 9, 1958; had been renominated to the Eighty-sixth Congress; interment in Mount Carmel Cemetery, Pittsburgh, Pa.

**ECHOLS, Leonard Sidney,** a Representative from West Virginia; born in Madison, Boone County, W.Va., October 30, 1871; attended the public schools; was graduated from the commercial department of the University of Kentucky at Lexington in 1894, from the Concord State Normal School, Athens, W.Va., in 1898, and from the law department of the Southern Normal University, Huntingdon, Tenn., in 1900; was admitted to the bar in 1900 and commenced practice in Point Pleasant, W.Va., in 1903; prosecuting attorney of Mason County 1904-1909; assistant State tax commissioner for West Virginia 1909-1919; elected as a Republican to the Sixty-sixth and Sixty-seventh Congresses (March 4, 1919-March 3, 1923); chairman, Committee on Expenditures in the Department of Navy (Sixty-sixth and Sixty-seventh Congresses); unsuccessful candidate for reelection in 1922 to the Sixty-eighth Congress and for election in 1924 to the Sixty-ninth Congress; member of the committee on appeals and review of the United States Treasury Department from May 1, 1923, to September 15, 1924; delegate to the Republican State convention in 1924; postmaster at Charleston, W.Va., 1925-1928; resumed the practice of law; served as referee in bankruptcy and as special master in the United States District Court, Charleston, W.Va.; died in Charleston, W.Va., May 9, 1946; interment in Sunset Memorial Park, South Charleston, W.Va.

**ECKART, Dennis Edward,** a Representative from Ohio; born in Cleveland, Cuyahoga County, Ohio, April 6, 1950; attended private schools in Euclid, Ohio; B.A., Xavier University, Cincinnati, 1971; LL.B., Cleveland State University, Cleveland Marshall College of Law, 1974; admitted to the Ohio bar in 1974 and commenced practice in Cleveland; member, Ohio State house of representatives, 1975-1980; elected as a Democrat to the Ninety-seventh and to the five succeeding Congresses (January 3, 1981-January 3, 1993); was not a candidate for reelection in 1992 to the One Hundred Third Congress; is a resident of Mentor, Ohio.

**ECKERT, Charles Richard,** a Representative from Pennsylvania; born in Pittsburgh, Pa., January 20, 1868; attended the public schools, Piersol's Academy at West Bridgewater, Pa., and Geneva College at Beaver Falls, Pa.; studied law; was admitted to the bar in 1894 and commenced practice in Beaver, Pa., the same year; delegate to the Democratic National Convention in 1928; elected as a Democrat to the Seventy-fourth and Seventy-fifth Congresses (January 3, 1935-January 3, 1939); unsuccessful candidate for reelection in 1938 to the Seventy-sixth Congress; member of board of directors of Beaver Trust Co.; resumed the practice of law until his death as the result of an automobile accident in Rochester, Pa., October 26, 1959; interment in Beaver Cemetery, Beaver, Pa.

**ECKERT, Fred J.,** a Representative from New York; born in Rochester, Monroe County, N.Y., May 6, 1941; was graduated from North Texas State University, Denton, Tex., in 1964 and took postgraduate courses at New York University, New York City, and at the New School for Social Research, New York City, 1965-1966; supervisor of the town of Greece, N.Y., 1970-1972; member of the State senate 1972-1982; president of the advertising agency Eckert-Hogan-Newell, Inc., Rochester, N.Y., 1973-1984; appointed United States Ambassador to Fiji, Tonga, Tuvalu and Kiribati on February 11, 1982 and served until May 1984; elected as a Republican to the Ninety-ninth Congress (January 3, 1985-January 3, 1987); unsuccessful candidate for reelection in 1986 to the One Hundredth Congress; United States ambassador to the United Nations Agencies for Food and Agriculture, 1987-1988; president of Eckert Associates; is a resident of Arlington, Va.

**ECKERT, George Nicholas,** a Representative from Pennsylvania; born in Womelsdorf, Berks County, Pa., July 4, 1802; was graduated from the medical department of the University of Pennsylvania at Philadelphia in 1824 and commenced practice in Reading, Pa.; one of the organizers of Berks County Medical Society in 1824; moved to Pine Grove, Schuylkill County, Pa., and engaged in the coal and iron trade; elected as a Whig to the Thirtieth Congress (March 4, 1847-March 3, 1849); appointed Director of the United States Mint at Philadelphia by President Millard Fillmore and served from June 1851 to June 6, 1853; died in Philadelphia, Pa., on June 28, 1865; interment in Laurel Hill Cemetery.

**ECKHARDT, Robert Christian** (grandnephew of Rudolph Kleberg, nephew of Harry McLeary Wurzbach, cousin of Richard Mifflin Kleberg, Sr.), a Representative from Texas; born in Austin, Tex., July 16, 1913; B.A., University of Texas, 1935; editor, Texas Ranger, University of Texas magazine, 1937-1938; LL.B., University of Texas, 1939; served in the United States Army Air Corps, 1942-1944; Southwestern Director of the Office of Coordinator of Inter-American Affairs, 1944-1945; was a practicing attorney until he entered Congress in 1967; served in the Texas State house of representatives from 1958 until 1966; elected as a Democrat to the Ninetieth and to the six succeeding Congresses (January 3, 1967-January 3, 1981); unsuccessful candidate for reelection in 1980 to the Ninety-seventh Congress; is a resident of Houston, Tex.

**ECKLEY, Ephraim Ralph,** a Representative from Ohio; born near Mt. Pleasant, Jefferson County, Ohio, December 9, 1811; moved with his parents to Hayesville, Ohio, in 1816; attended the common schools and was graduated from Vermillion Institute, Hayesville, Ohio; moved to Carrollton, Carroll County, Ohio, in 1833 and taught school; studied law; was admitted to the bar in 1836 and commenced practice in Carrollton; member of the State senate 1843-1846, 1849, and 1850; unsuccessful candidate for lieutenant governor of Ohio in 1851; served in the State house of representatives 1853-1857; unsuccessful candidate for election in 1853 to the United States

Senate; delegate to the first Republican National Convention at Philadelphia in 1856; during the Civil War served in the Union Army as colonel of the Twenty-sixth Regiment, Ohio Volunteer Infantry, and also of the Eighteenth Regiment, Ohio Volunteer Infantry; brevetted brigadier general; elected as a Republican to the Thirty-eighth and to the two succeeding Congresses (March 4, 1863-March 3, 1869); was not a candidate for renomination in 1868 to the Forty-first Congress; resumed the practice of law in Carrollton, Carroll County, Ohio, where he died March 27, 1908; interment in Grand View Cemetery.

**ECTON, Zales Nelson,** a Senator from Montana; born in Weldon, McCone County, Iowa, April 1, 1898; moved to Gallatin County, Mont., in 1907; attended the public schools of Gallatin County, Montana State College at Bozeman, and the University of Chicago Law School; rancher with interests in grain and livestock 1921-1946; member, State house of representatives 1933-1937; member, State senate 1937-1946; elected as a Republican to the United States Senate in 1946, and served from January 3, 1947, to January 3, 1953; unsuccessful candidate for reelection in 1952; resumed ranching activities; died at Bozeman, Mont., March 3, 1961; interment in Sunset Hills Cemetery.

**EDDY, Frank Marion,** a Representative from Minnesota; born in Pleasant Grove, Olmsted County, Minn., April 1, 1856; with his parents moved to Iowa in 1860, returned in 1863 to Olmsted County, Minn., and settled near Elmira, and in 1867 moved to Sauk Centre, Stearns County, Minn.; attended the common schools; taught school in a rural district; employed by the Northern Pacific Railroad Co. as a land examiner in 1881 and 1882; moved to Glenwood, Minn., and served as clerk of the district court of Pope County 1884-1893; was the first Representative from Minnesota who was a native of that State; elected as a Republican to the Fifty-fourth and to the three succeeding Congresses (March 4, 1895-March 3, 1903); chairman, Committee on Mines and Mining (Fifty-seventh Congress); declined to be a candidate for renomination in 1902; editor and owner of the Sauk Centre Herald 1901-1907; engaged in writing and lecturing 1907-1915; member of the Minnesota Immigration Bureau in 1916; became engaged in journalism in St. Paul; employed as a clerk in the automobile department in the office of the secretary of state of Minnesota in 1918, in which capacity he served until his death in St. Paul, Minn., January 13, 1929; interment in Greenwood Cemetery, Sauk Centre, Minn.

**EDDY, Norman,** a Representative from Indiana; born in Scipio, N.Y., December 10, 1810; attended the common schools, and was graduated from the medical department of the University of Pennsylvania at Philadelphia in 1835; moved to Indiana, settled in Mishawaka, and practiced medicine until 1847; studied law; was admitted to the bar in 1847 and commenced practice in South Bend, Ind.; member of the State senate in 1850; held several local offices; elected as a Democrat to the Thirty-third Congress (March 4, 1853-March 3, 1855); unsuccessful candidate for reelection in 1854 to the Thirty-fourth Congress; appointed by President Franklin Pierce attorney general of the Territory of Minnesota in 1855; colonel of the Forty-eighth Indiana Volunteer Infantry during the Civil War; collector of internal revenue 1865-1870; secretary of state of Indiana 1870-1872; died in Indianapolis, Ind., January 28, 1872; interment in the City Cemetery, South Bend, Ind.

**EDDY, Samuel,** a Representative from Rhode Island; born in Johnston, near Providence, R.I., March 31, 1769; completed preparatory studies; was graduated from Brown University, Providence, R.I., in 1787; studied law; was admitted to the bar in 1790 and practiced a short time in Providence; clerk of the Rhode Island Supreme Court 1790-1793; secretary of state 1798-1819; elected to the Sixteenth, Seventeenth, and Eighteenth Congresses (March 4, 1819-March 3, 1825); unsuccessful candidate for reelection in 1824 to the Nineteenth Congress and for election in 1828 to the

Twenty-first Congress; associate justice of the State supreme court in 1826 and 1827, and served as chief justice 1827-1835; died in Providence, R.I., February 3, 1839; interment in North End Cemetery.

**EDELSTEIN, Morris Michael,** a Representative from New York; born in Meseritz, Poland, February 5, 1888; at three years of age immigrated to the United States with his parents, who settled in New York City; attended the public schools and Cooper Union College in New York City; was graduated from the Brooklyn Law School of St. Lawrence University, New York City, in 1909; was admitted to the bar in 1910 and commenced the practice of law in New York City; elected as a Democrat to the Seventy-sixth Congress to fill the vacancy caused by the death of William I. Sirovich; reelected to the Seventy-seventh Congress and served from February 6, 1940, until his death on June 4, 1941, in the cloakroom of the House of Representatives, Washington, D.C., after completing the delivery of a speech on the floor of the House; interment in Mount Zion Cemetery, Maspeth, Long Island, N.Y.

**EDEN, John Rice,** a Representative from Illinois; born in Bath County, Ky., February 1, 1826; moved with his parents to Indiana; attended the public schools; studied law; was admitted to the bar in 1853 and commenced practice in Sullivan, Ill.; prosecuting attorney for the seventeenth judicial district of Illinois, 1856-1860; elected as a Democrat to the Thirty-eighth Congress (March 4, 1863-March 3, 1865); unsuccessful candidate for reelection in 1864 to the Thirty-ninth Congress; unsuccessful Democratic candidate for election for Governor of Illinois in 1868; elected to the Forty-third and to the two succeeding Congresses (March 4, 1873-March 3, 1879); chairman, Committee on War Claims (Forty-fourth and Forty-fifth Congresses); unsuccessful candidate for renomination in 1878 to the Forty-sixth Congress; resumed the practice of law in Sullivan, Ill.; elected to the Forty-ninth Congress (March 4, 1885-March 3, 1887); unsuccessful candidate for renomination in 1886 to the Fiftieth Congress; again engaged in the practice of law; died in Sullivan, Moultrie County, Ill., June 9, 1909; interment in Greenhill Cemetery.

**EDGAR, Robert William,** a Representative from Pennsylvania; born in Philadelphia, Pa., May 29, 1943; attended public schools in Springfield, Pa.; B.A., Lycoming College, Williamsport, Pa., 1965; M.Div., Drew University Theological School, Madison, N.J., 1968; certificate in pastoral psychiatry, Hahnemann Medical College and Hospital, Philadelphia, Pa., 1969; ordained a United Methodist minister in 1968; served as United Protestant Chaplain of Drexel University in Philadelphia, 1971-1974; elected as a Democrat to the Ninety-fourth and to the five succeeding Congresses (January 3, 1975-January 3, 1987); was not a candidate in 1986 for reelection to the House of Representatives, but was an unsuccessful candidate for election to the United States Senate; special assistant to Representative William H. Gray III of Pennsylvania, 1988; president, School of Theology at Claremont (Calif.), July 1, 1990 to present; is a resident of Claremont, Calif.

**EDGE, Walter Evans,** a Senator from New Jersey; born in Philadelphia, Pa., November 20, 1873; moved with his parents to Pleasantville, N.J., in 1877; attended the public schools; employed in a printing office in Atlantic City, N.J., 1890-1894; newspaper owner and publisher; journal clerk of the New Jersey State senate, 1897-1899; during the Spanish-American War served as a second lieutenant; secretary of the State senate, 1901-1904; member of the State house of assembly in 1910; member, State senate, 1911-1916, serving as president in 1915; elected Governor of New Jersey in 1916, and served from January 15, 1917 until May 16, 1919, when he resigned, having been elected Senator; elected as a Republican to the United States Senate in 1918; reelected in 1924 and served from March 4, 1919, until his resignation on November 21, 1929, to accept a diplomatic post; chairman, Committee on Coast and Insular

Survey (Sixty-sixth Congress), Committee on Interoceanic Canals (Sixty-seventh through Seventy-first Congresses), Committee on Post Office and Post Roads (Sixty-eighth Congress); appointed Ambassador to France by President Herbert Hoover on November 21, 1929 and served until April 1933; elected Governor of New Jersey in 1943, and served from January 18, 1944 to January 21, 1947; died in New York City, October 29, 1956; interment in Northbrook Cemetery, Downingtown, Pa.

**Bibliography:** Edge, Walter E. *A Jerseyman's Journal: Fifty Years of American Business and Politics.* 1948. Reprint. New York: Johnson Reprint Corp., 1972.

**EDGERTON, Alfred Peck** (brother of Joseph Ketchum Edgerton), a Representative from Ohio; born in Plattsburgh, N.Y., January 11, 1813; was graduated from Plattsburgh Academy; engaged in newspaper work for a brief period, and later in commercial pursuits in New York City; moved to Hicksville, Ohio, in 1837; manager of the American Land Co., and engaged in opening new land for settlement in northwestern Ohio, near Hicksville, 1837-1852; member of the Ohio State senate in 1845 and 1846; elected as a Democrat to the Thirty-second and Thirty-third Congresses (March 4, 1851-March 3, 1855); chairman, Committee on Claims (Thirty-third Congress); financial agent of the Board of State Fund Commissioners of Ohio in 1853, with residence in New York City; moved to Fort Wayne, Ind., in 1857; general manager of the Wabash & Erie Canal, 1859-1868; unsuccessful candidate for lieutenant governor of Ohio in 1868; chairman of the United States Civil Service Commission in 1885; died in Hicksville, Defiance County, Ohio, May 14, 1897; interment in Lindenwood Cemetery, Fort Wayne, Ind.

**Bibliography:** *DAB.*

**EDGERTON, Alonzo Jay,** a Senator from Minnesota; born in Rome, Oneida County, N.Y., June 7, 1827; pursued preparatory studies; was graduated from Wesleyan University, Middletown, Conn., in 1850; settled in Mantorville, Minn., in 1855; studied law; was admitted to the bar in 1855 and commenced practice in Mantorville; prosecuting attorney of Dodge County; member, Minnesota State senate, 1858-1859; during the Civil War served in the Tenth Minnesota Volunteer Regiment, August 1862-February 1864, attaining the rank of colonel; transferred to the Sixty-fifth United States Colored Infantry August 15, 1865, and was brevetted brigadier general; railroad commissioner, 1871-1875; member, State senate, 1877-1879; moved to Kasson, Minn., in 1878; appointed as a Republican to the United States Senate to fill the vacancy caused by the resignation of William Windom, and served from March 12 to October 30, 1881, when a successor was elected; appointed on December 21, 1881, by President Chester A. Arthur as chief justice of the Territorial Supreme Court of Dakota; upon the admission of South Dakota as a State into the Union was made United States judge of that district; served as president of the constitutional convention of South Dakota; died at Sioux Falls, S.Dak., on August 9, 1896; interment in Evergreen Cemetery, Mantorville, Minn.

**EDGERTON, Joseph Ketchum** (brother of Alfred Peck Edgerton), a Representative from Indiana; born in Vergennes, Addison County, Vt., February 16, 1818; attended the public schools of Clinton County, N.Y.; studied law in Plattsburgh (N.Y.) Academy; was admitted to the bar and commenced practice in New York City in 1839; moved to Fort Wayne, Ind., in 1844 and continued the practice of law; director of the Fort Wayne & Chicago Railroad Co. in 1854, and later its president; president of the Grand Rapids & Indiana Railroad Co. in 1855; director of the Ohio & Indiana Railroad Co. in 1856; elected as a Democrat to the Thirty-eighth Congress (March 4, 1863-March 3, 1865); unsuccessful candidate for reelection in 1864 to the Thirty-ninth Congress; died in Boston, Mass., August 25, 1893; interment in Lindenwood Cemetery, Fort Wayne, Ind.

**EDGERTON, Sidney,** a Representative from Ohio; born in Cazenovia, Madison County, N.Y., August 17, 1818; attended the country schools and the academy at Lima, N.Y., where he was later an instructor; moved to Ohio in 1844; taught in the academy at Tallmadge, Ohio, in 1844; studied law; was graduated from the Cincinnati Law School in 1845; was admitted to the bar and commenced practice in Akron, Ohio, in 1846; delegate to the convention that formed the Free-Soil Party in 1848; prosecuting attorney of Summit County, 1852-1856; delegate to the first Republican National Convention in 1856; elected as a Republican to the Thirty-sixth and Thirty-seventh Congresses (March 4, 1859-March 3, 1863); was not a candidate for renomination in 1862 to the Thirty-eighth Congress; served as colonel of the Squirrel Hunters during the Civil War; appointed March 6, 1863, by President Lincoln as United States judge for the Territory of Idaho; appointed Governor of Montana Territory by President Lincoln on May 26, 1864, and served until September 1865; resumed the practice of law in Akron, Ohio, where he died July 19, 1900; interment in Tallmadge Cemetery, Tallmadge, Ohio.

**Bibliography:** *DAB.*

**EDIE, John Rufus,** a Representative from Pennsylvania; born in Gettysburg, Adams County, Pa., January 14, 1814; attended the public schools, Emmitsburg (Md.) College, and the United States Military Academy at West Point, N.Y.; principal of the Gettysburg schools for several years; studied law; was admitted to the bar in 1840 and commenced practice in Somerset, Pa.; member of the Pennsylvania senate in 1845 and 1846; appointed deputy attorney general in 1847 and served until 1850; district attorney 1850-1854; elected as a Whig to the Thirty-fourth and Thirty-fifth Congresses (March 4, 1855-March 3, 1859); was not a candidate for renomination in 1858; commissioned a major of the Fifteenth Regiment, United States Infantry, May 14, 1861; promoted to the rank of lieutenant colonel in 1863 and served with the Fifteenth and Eighth Regiments, United States Infantry, until January 1871, when he was honorably discharged; brevetted colonel September 1, 1864; resumed the practice of law in Somerset, Pa., and died there August 27, 1888; interment in Union Cemetery.

**EDMANDS, John Wiley,** a Representative from Massachusetts; born in Boston, Mass., March 1, 1809; completed preparatory studies, and was graduated from the English High School at Boston; interested in woolen mills in Dedham, Mass., and the Pacific Mills Co. in Lawrence, Mass.; elected as a Whig to the Thirty-third Congress (March 4, 1853-March 3, 1855); declined to be a candidate for renomination in 1854; treasurer of the Pacific Mills at Lawrence in 1855; presidential elector on the Republican ticket in 1868; died in Newton, Mass., on January 31, 1877; interment in Mount Auburn Cemetery, Cambridge, Mass.

**EDMISTON, Andrew,** a Representative from West Virginia; born in Weston, Lewis County, W.Va., November 13, 1892; attended the Friends' Select School, Washington, D.C., Kentucky Military Institute at Lyndon, and the University of West Virginia at Morgantown; engaged in agricultural pursuits from 1915 to 1917, and in the manufacture of glass at Weston, W.Va., beginning in 1925; served overseas as a second lieutenant with the Thirty-ninth Infantry, Fourth Division, 1917-1919; awarded the Distinguished Service Cross, the Purple Heart with Oak Leaf Cluster, and the Distinguished Service Medal of West Virginia; editor of the Weston (W.Va.) Democrat 1920-1935; mayor of Weston, W.Va., 1924-1926; delegate to the Democratic National Conventions of 1928 and 1952; State chairman of the Democratic executive committee, 1928-1932; elected as a Democrat to the Seventy-third Congress to fill the vacancy caused by the death of Lynn S. Horner; reelected to the Seventy-fourth and to the three succeeding Congresses, and served from November 28, 1933 to January 3, 1943; unsuccessful candidate for reelection in 1942 to the Seventy-eighth Congress; resumed his former business pursuits; appointed State director of War Manpower for West Virginia on June 28, 1943, and served until his resignation on June 30, 1945, to return to private business; died in Weston, W.Va., August 28, 1966; interment in Machpelah Cemetery.

**EDMOND, William,** a Representative from Connecticut; born in Woodbury, Conn., September 28, 1755; attended the common schools and was graduated from Yale College in 1778; served in the Revolutionary Army; studied law; was admitted to the bar in 1780 and commenced practice in Newtown, Conn.; member of the State house of representatives 1791-1797, 1801, and 1802; served in the State senate 1797-1799; elected as a Federalist to the Fifth Congress to fill the vacancy caused by the death of James Davenport; reelected to the Sixth Congress and served from November 13, 1797, to March 3, 1801; declined to be a candidate for renomination in 1800; resumed the practice of law in Newtown; associate judge of the State supreme court 1805-1819; retired to private life and continued the practice of law; died in Newtown, Fairfield County, Conn., on August 1, 1838; interment in Newtown Cemetery.

**EDMONDS, George Washington,** a Representative from Pennsylvania; born in Pottsville, Schuylkill County, Pa., February 22, 1864; attended the public schools and Central High School; was graduated from the Philadelphia College of Pharmacy in 1887 and practiced pharmacy for several years; engaged in the coal business; member of the common council of Philadelphia 1896-1902; elected as a Republican to the Sixty-third and to the five succeeding Congresses (March 4, 1913-March 3, 1925); chairman, Committee on Claims (Sixty-sixth through Sixty-eighth Congresses); unsuccessful candidate for renomination in 1924; engaged in the wholesale coal and lumber business; elected manager of the Port of Philadelphia Ocean Traffic Bureau in September 1927 and served until 1933; again elected to the Seventy-third Congress (March 4, 1933-January 3, 1935); unsuccessful candidate for reelection in 1934 to the Seventy-fourth Congress; resumed the wholesale coal business in Philadelphia, Pa.; died in Philadelphia on September 28, 1939; interment in West Laurel Hill Cemetery.

**EDMONDSON, Edmond Augustus** (brother of James H. Edmondson), a Representative from Oklahoma; born in Muskogee, Okla., April 7, 1919; attended the public schools; graduated from Muskogee Junior College in 1938 and from the University of Oklahoma in 1940; special agent with the Federal Bureau of Investigation, Washington, D.C., 1940-1943; attended Georgetown University Law School; interrupted studies there and served in the United States Navy 1943-1946 with service in the South Pacific and discharged as a lieutenant; United States Naval Reserve, 1946-1970; returned to Georgetown University and graduated in 1947; was admitted to the bar in Washington, D.C., and Oklahoma the same year and commenced practice in Muskogee, Okla.; county attorney of Muskogee County, Okla.; delegate to the Democratic National Convention of 1968; elected as a Democrat to the Eighty-third and to the nine succeeding Congresses (January 3, 1953-January 3, 1973); was not a candidate in 1972 for reelection to the House of Representatives, but was an unsuccessful candidate for election to the United States Senate; unsuccessful candidate for nomination to the United States Senate in 1978; was a resident of Muskogee, Okla.; died December 8, 1990.

**EDMONDSON, James Howard** (brother of Edmond A. Edmondson), a Senator from Oklahoma; born in Muskogee, Okla., September 27, 1925; attended the public schools; during the Second World War enlisted in the United States Army Air Corps 1943-1945; graduated from the law department of the University of Oklahoma at Norman 1948; was admitted to the bar and began the practice of law in Muskogee the same year; moved to Tulsa in 1953 and was chief prosecutor in the Tulsa County attorney's office; elected Tulsa County attorney in 1954 and reelected in 1956; elected Governor of Oklahoma in 1958 and served from January 12, 1959 until January 6, 1963, when he resigned; appointed as a Democrat to the United States Senate to fill the vacancy caused by the death of Robert S. Kerr and served from January 7, 1963, to November 3, 1964; unsuccessful candidate for nomination to fill the vacancy in 1964; returned to Oklahoma City and resumed the practice of law; died in Edmond, Okla., November 17, 1971; interment in Memorial Park Cemetery, Oklahoma City, Okla.

**Bibliography:** Davis, Billy J. "J. Howard Edmondson: A Political Biography." Ph.D. dissertation, Texas Tech University, 1980.

**EDMUNDS, George Franklin,** a Senator from Vermont; born in Richmond, Chittenden County, Vt., February 1, 1828; attended the common schools and was privately tutored; studied law; was admitted to the bar in 1849 and commenced practice in Burlington, Vt.; member, Vermont State house of representatives, 1854-1859, serving three years as speaker; member of the State senate, serving as its presiding officer in 1861 and 1862; appointed on April 3, 1866, and elected on October 24, 1866, as a Republican to the United States Senate to fill the vacancy caused by the death of Solomon Foote; reelected in 1868, 1874, 1880, and 1886, and served from April 3, 1866 until his resignation, effective November 1, 1891; served as President pro tempore of the Senate during the Forty-seventh and Forty-eighth Congresses; chairman, Committee on Pensions (Forty-first and Forty-second Congresses), Committee on the Judiciary (Forty-second through Fifty-second Congresses, except the Forty-sixth), Committee on Private Land Claims (Forty-sixth Congress), Committee on Foreign Relations (Forty-seventh Congress); appointed a member of the Electoral Commission to decide the contests in various States in the presidential election of 1876; resumed the practice of law in Philadelphia, Pa.; subsequently moved to Pasadena, Calif., where he died on February 27, 1919; interment in Green Mount Cemetery, Burlington, Vt.

**Bibliography:** *DAB*; Adler, Selig. "The Senatorial Career of George Franklin Edmunds, 1866-1891." Ph.D. dissertation, University of Illinois, 1934; Welch, Richard E., Jr. "George Edmunds of Vermont: Republican Half-Breed." *Vermont History* 36 (Spring 1968): 64-73.

**EDMUNDS, Paul Carrington,** a Representative from Virginia; born at "Springwood," the country estate, near Halifax Court House, Halifax County, Va., November 1, 1836; studied under a private teacher; was graduated from the University of Virginia at Charlottesville in 1855, and from the law department of the College of William and Mary, Williamsburg, Va., in 1857; was admitted to the bar the same year and commenced practice in Jefferson City, Mo.; returned to Virginia in 1859 and engaged in agricultural pursuits on his farm in Halifax County; served as first lieutenant, Company A, Montague's battalion, in the Confederate Army during the Civil War; member of the Virginia senate, 1881-1888; delegate to the Democratic National Convention of 1884; elected as a Democrat to the Fifty-first and to the two succeeding Congresses (March 4, 1889-March 3, 1895); chairman, Committee on Expenditures in the Department of Agriculture (Fifty-second and Fifty-third Congresses); declined to be a candidate for renomination in 1894 to the Fifty-fourth Congress; died in Houston, Halifax County, Va., March 12, 1899; interment in St. John's Churchyard, Halifax, Va.

**EDMUNDSON, Henry Alonzo,** a Representative from Virginia; born in Blacksburg, Montgomery County, Va., June 14, 1814; attended private schools, and was graduated from Georgetown University, Washington, D.C.; studied law; was admitted to the bar in 1838 and commenced practice in Salem, Va.; elected as a Democrat to the Thirty-first and to the five succeeding Congresses (March 4, 1849-March 3, 1861); chairman, Committee on Expenditures on Public Buildings (Thirty-third Congress); served in the Confederate Army as lieutenant colonel of the Fifty-fourth Virginia Regiment until 1862, when he was assigned to the command of the

Twenty-seventh Virginia Cavalry; at the close of hostilities he resumed the practice of law, and subsequently, in 1880, engaged in agricultural pursuits; died at his home, "Falling Waters," Shawsville, Montgomery County, Va., December 16, 1890; interment in Fotheringay Cemetery, Montgomery County, Va.

**EDSALL, Joseph E.**, a Representative from New Jersey; born in Rudeville, near Hamburg, Sussex County, N.J., in 1789; attended the common schools; engaged in mercantile pursuits; operated a distillery and a tannery; served as county clerk; member of the New Jersey house of assembly; served as judge of the court of common pleas; elected as a Democrat to the Twenty-ninth and Thirtieth Congresses (March 4, 1845-March 3, 1849); died in Hamburg, N.J., in 1865; interment in the Baptist Burying Ground.

**EDWARDS, Benjamin** (father of Ninian Edwards), a Representative from Maryland; born in Stafford County, Va., August 12, 1753; attended the common schools; engaged in agricultural and mercantile pursuits in Montgomery County, Md.; member of the State house of delegates for several years; delegate to the State convention which ratified the Federal Constitution in 1788; elected to the Third Congress to fill the vacancy caused by the resignation of Uriah Forrest and served from January 2 to March 3, 1795; moved to Todd County, Ky.; died in Eklton, Ky., November 13, 1829; interment on his estate at Elkton, Ky.

**EDWARDS, Caldwell**, a Representative from Montana; born in Sag Harbor, Suffolk County, N.Y., January 8, 1841; was educated in the district schools; salesman and bookkeeper in dry-goods stores for several years; moved to Bozeman, Territory of Montana, in 1864 and became engaged in agricultural pursuits; member of the State house of representatives 1901-1905; elected as a Populist to the Fifty-seventh Congress (March 4, 1901-March 3, 1903); was not a candidate for renomination in 1902; at the expiration of his term returned to his ranch in Montana; died in Sag Harbor, N.Y., July 23, 1922; interment in Oakland Cemetery.

**EDWARDS, Charles Gordon**, a Representative from Georgia; born in Daisy, Tattnall (now Evans) County, Ga., July 2, 1878; attended the public schools, Gordon Institute, Barnesville, Ga., and Florida State College at Lake City; was graduated from the law department of the University of Georgia at Athens in 1898; was admitted to the bar the same year and commenced practice in Reidsville; moved to Savannah in 1900 and continued the practice of law; also interested in agricultural pursuits; served as a sergeant in the Savannah Volunteer Guards, Company B, Coast Artillery, in 1902 and 1903 and as a second lieutenant in the Oglethorpe Light Infantry of the First Georgia Regiment of Infantry in 1903 and 1904; elected as a Democrat to the Sixtieth and to the four succeeding Congresses (March 4, 1907-March 3, 1917); did not seek reelection in 1916; resumed the practice of law in Savannah, Ga.; president of the Savannah Board of Trade in 1919 and 1920; trustee of the Southern Methodist College, McRae, Ga.; member of the Harbor Commission of Savannah, Ga., 1920-1924; elected to the Sixty-ninth and to the three succeeding Congresses and served from March 4, 1925, until his death in Atlanta, Ga., July 13, 1931; interment in Bonaventure Cemetery, Savannah, Ga.

**EDWARDS, Don**, a Representative from California. (See EDWARDS, William Donlon.)

**EDWARDS, Don Calvin**, a Representative from Kentucky; born in Moulton, Appanoose County, Iowa, on July 13, 1861; moved to Erie, Neosho County, Kans., with his parents in 1869; attended the common schools of Iowa and Kansas, and Campbell University, Holton, Kans.; engaged in banking and in the insurance business in Erie, Kans., in 1883; moved to London, Laurel County, Ky., in 1892 and engaged in the manufacture of staves and in the wholesale lumber business; president of the National Bank of London, Ky.; clerk and master commissioner of the Laurel circuit court from 1898

to 1904; chairman of the Kentucky Republican convention in 1908; elected as a Republican to the Fifty-ninth and to the two succeeding Congresses (March 4, 1905-March 3, 1911); chairman, Committee on Expenditures in the Department of State (Sixty-first Congress); unsuccessful candidate for reelection in 1910 to the Sixty-second Congress; resumed the lumber and banking business in London, Ky.; delegate to the Republican National Convention of 1912; unsuccessful candidate for nomination in 1918 to the Sixty-sixth Congress; died in London, Ky., September 19, 1938; interment in Pine Grove Cemetery.

**EDWARDS, Edward Irving**, a Senator from New Jersey; born in Jersey City, N.J., December 1, 1863; attended the Jersey City public schools and New York University, New York City; studied law; engaged in banking and in the general contracting business; president and chairman of the board of directors of the First National Bank of Jersey City; comptroller of the treasury of New Jersey, 1911-1917; member, New Jersey State senate, 1918-1920; elected Governor of New Jersey in 1919, and served from January 20, 1920 to January 15, 1923; elected as a Democrat to the United States Senate in 1922, and served from March 4, 1923 to March 3, 1929; unsuccessful candidate for reelection in 1928; died in Jersey City, N.J., January 26, 1931; interment in New York Bay Cemetery.

**Bibliography:** Stickle, Warren E. "Edward I. Edwards and the Urban Coalition of 1919." *New Jersey History* 90 (Summer 1972): 83-96.

**EDWARDS, Edwin Washington** (husband of Elaine Schwartzenburg Edwards), a Representative from Louisiana; born in Avoyelles Parish near Marksville, La., August 7, 1927; attended the public schools; volunteered in the Naval Air Corps at age seventeen and served from May 1945 to April 1946; Louisiana State University, LL.B., January 1949, converted to J.D., 1969; was admitted to the bar in 1949 and began the practice of law in Crowley, Acadia Parish, La.; elected to the Crowley city council in 1954 and was reelected in 1958; elected to the Louisiana State senate in December 1964 and resigned October 1, 1965, having been elected to Congress; elected as a Democrat to the Eighty-ninth Congress, by special election, October 2, 1965, to fill the vacancy caused by the death of T. Ashton Thompson; reelected to the three succeeding Congresses and served from October 18, 1965, until his resignation May 9, 1972, to become Governor of Louisiana; reelected in 1975 and served until March 10, 1980; again elected Governor in 1983, and served from March 12, 1984 to March 14, 1988; was a candidate for reelection in 1987, but withdrew from the race after the open primary; again elected Governor in 1991, and served from January 8, 1992 to January 8, 1996; declined to be a candidate for reelection in 1995; is a resident of Crowley, La.

**EDWARDS, Elaine Schwartzenburg** (wife of Edwin Washington Edwards), a Senator from Louisiana; born in Marksville, Avoyelles Parish, La., March 8, 1929; attended the public schools; appointed to the United States Senate by her husband, Governor Edwin W. Edwards, August 1, 1972, as a Democrat to fill the vacancy caused by the death of Allen J. Ellender, and served from August 1, 1972, until her resignation on November 13, 1972; is a resident of Baton Rouge, La.

**EDWARDS, Francis Smith**, a Representative from New York; born in Windsor, Broome County, N.Y., May 28, 1817; completed preparatory studies; attended Hamilton (N.Y.) College (now Colgate University), but did not graduate; studied law; was admitted to the bar in New York City May 20, 1840, and practiced in Sherburne and Albany; moved to Fredonia in 1851 and continued the practice of law; appointed master and examiner in chancery for Chenango County in 1842; appointed special county surrogate of Chautauqua County in 1853, and served until November 1, 1855; elected as the candidate of the American Party to the Thirty-fourth Congress and served from March 4, 1855, to February 28, 1857, when he resigned;

unsuccessful candidate for reelection in 1856 to the Thirty-fifth Congress; settled in Dunkirk, N.Y., in 1859, and resumed the practice of his profession; city attorney for nine years; retired from the practice of law in 1892; elected police justice in 1895 and served until ten days before his death; died in Dunkirk, N.Y., on May 20, 1899; interment in Forest Hill Cemetery, Fredonia, N.Y.

**EDWARDS, Henry Waggaman** (son of Pierpont Edwards), a Representative and a Senator from Connecticut; born in New Haven, Conn., in October 1779; was graduated from the College of New Jersey (now Princeton University) in 1797; studied law at the Litchfield Law School; was admitted to the bar and commenced practice in New Haven, Conn.; elected to the Sixteenth and Seventeenth Congresses (March 4, 1819-March 3, 1823); appointed in 1823 to the United States Senate to fill the vacancy caused by the death of Elijah Boardman; subsequently elected and served from October 8, 1823, to March 3, 1827; member, Connecticut State senate, 1827-1829; member of the State house of representatives in 1830, and served as speaker; elected Governor of Connecticut in 1833, and served from May 4, 1833 to May 7, 1834; unsuccessful candidate for reelection in 1834; again elected Governor in 1835, reelected in 1836 and 1837, and served from May 6, 1835 to May 2, 1838; resumed the practice of law; died in New Haven, Conn., July 22, 1847; interment in Grove Street Cemetery.
**Bibliography:** *DAB.*

**EDWARDS, Jack,** a Representative from Alabama. (*See* EDWARDS, William Jackson.)

**EDWARDS, John** (granduncle of John Edwards Leonard), a Representative from Pennsylvania; born in Ivy Mills, Delaware County, Pa., in 1786; studied law; was admitted to the bar in 1807 and commenced practice in Chester, Delaware County, Pa.; deputy attorney general for Delaware County in 1811; moved to West Chester in 1825 and shortly thereafter engaged in the manufacture of iron and later of nails near Glen Mills, Delaware County; elected as an Anti-Masonic candidate to the Twenty-sixth Congress and reelected as a Whig to the Twenty-seventh Congress (March 4, 1839-March 3, 1843); resumed his former manufacturing pursuits; died on his estate near Glen Mills June 26, 1843; interment in the Friends' (Hicksite) Cemetery of the Middletown Meeting House, Middletown Township, Delaware County, Pa.

**EDWARDS, John,** a Representative from New York; born in Beekmans precinct, Dutchess County, near Poughkeepsie, N.Y., on August 6, 1781; attended the common schools; sheriff of Montgomery County and keeper of Johnstown Jail 1806-1812; moved to Fulton County and settled in the village of Ephratah; elected as a Democrat to the Twenty-fifth Congress (March 4, 1837-March 3, 1839); engaged in the mercantile business and also interested in manufacturing pursuits; died in Johnstown, Fulton County, N.Y., December 28, 1850; interment in Johnstown Cemetery.

**EDWARDS, John,** a Senator from Kentucky; born in Stafford County, Va., in 1748; attended the common schools; moved to Fayette County, Ky. (then a part of Virginia), in 1780; member, Virginia house of delegates 1781-1783, 1785, 1786; delegate to the convention called to define the limits of the proposed State of Kentucky 1785-1788; member of the convention of 1792 that framed the constitution of Kentucky; upon the admission of Kentucky Kentucky into the Union was elected to the United States Senate and served from June 18, 1792, to March 3, 1795; member, Kentucky house of representatives 1795; member, Kentucky senate 1796-1800; died on his plantation near Paris, Bourbon County, Ky., in 1837; interment in the family cemetery near Paris, Ky.
**Bibliography:** *DAB.*

**EDWARDS, John,** a Representative from Arkansas; born in Louisville, Jefferson County, Ky., October 24, 1805; received a limited schooling; studied law and was admitted to the bar; moved to Indiana, where he served in the State house of representatives in 1845 and 1846; moved to California, and in 1849 was elected an alcalde; returned to Indiana in 1852; member of the State senate in 1853; moved to Chariton, Iowa, in 1855; member of the Iowa constitutional convention; served in the State house of representatives 1856-1860, the last two years as speaker of the house; founder in 1857 of the Patriot, a newspaper; appointed lieutenant colonel May 21, 1861, on the staff of Governor Samuel J. Kirkwood of Iowa; colonel of the Eighteenth Regiment, Iowa Volunteer Infantry, August 8, 1862; brigadier general of Volunteers September 26, 1864; at the close of the war settled in Fort Smith, Ark.; appointed by President Andrew Johnson as United States assessor of internal revenue and served from August 15, 1866, to May 31, 1869; presented credentials of election as a Liberal Republican to the Forty-second Congress and served from March 4, 1871, to February 9, 1872, when he was succeeded by Thomas Boles, who contested the election; was not a candidate for renomination in 1872 to the Forty-third Congress; settled in Washington, D.C., and died there on April 8, 1894; interment in Arlington National Cemetery, Va.

**EDWARDS, John Cummins,** a Representative from Missouri; born in Frankfort, Franklin County, Ky., June 24, 1804; completed preparatory studies and was graduated from Black's College, Kentucky; studied law; was admitted to the bar in 1825 and practiced in Murfreesboro, Tenn., and later in Jefferson City, Mo.; secretary of state of Missouri 1830-1835 and in 1837; district judge of Cole County, Mo., 1832-1837; member of the State house of representatives in 1836; judge of the State supreme court 1837-1839; elected as a Democrat to the Twenty-seventh Congress (March 4, 1841-March 3, 1843); did not seek renomination in 1842 to the Twenty-eighth Congress, having become a candidate for the gubernatorial office; elected Governor of Missouri in 1844, and served from November 20, 1844 to December 27, 1848; moved to Stockton, Calif., in 1849 and continued the practice of his profession; mayor of Stockton in 1851; engaged in cattle raising, mercantile pursuits, and the real-estate business; died in Stockton, Calif., October 14, 1888; interment in the Rural Cemetery.

**EDWARDS, Marvin Henry (Mickey),** a Representative from Oklahoma; born in Cleveland, Ohio, July 12, 1937; attended the public schools; B.A., University of Oklahoma, 1958; J.D., Oklahoma City University Law School, 1969; admitted to the Oklahoma bar in 1970; newspaper reporter and editor, 1958-1963; engaged in advertising and public relations, 1963-1968; magazine editor, 1968-1973; author; special legislative consultant, Republican Steering Committee, Washington, D.C., 1973-1974; instructor of law and journalism, Oklahoma City University, 1976; elected as a Republican to the Ninety-fifth and to the seven succeeding Congresses (January 3, 1977-January 3, 1993); unsuccessful candidate for renomination in 1992 to the One Hundred Third Congress; lecturer in public policy, John F. Kennedy School of Government, Harvard University; is a resident of Belmont, Mass.

**EDWARDS, Ninian** (son of Benjamin Edwards), a Senator from Illinois; born at "Mount Pleasant," Montgomery County, Md., March 17, 1775; attended private schools; was graduated from Dickinson College, Carlisle, Pa., in 1792; studied law; moved to Bardstown, Ky., in 1795; member, Kentucky house of representatives, 1796-1797; was admitted to the bar in 1798 and commenced practice in Russellville, Ky.; judge of the general court of Kentucky, 1803; judge of the circuit court, 1804; judge of the court of appeals, 1806; chief justice of Kentucky in 1808; appointed Governor of the Territory of Illinois by President James Madison on April 24, 1809, and served until 1818; upon the admission of Illinois as a State into the Union was elected as a Republican to the United States Senate and served from December 3, 1818, to March 4, 1824, when he resigned, having been appointed Minister to Mexico; while en route to Mexico, he was recalled to testify before a select committee of the House of Representatives appointed to investigate charges made by him against William H. Crawford, Secretary of the Treasury, and never proceeded to his post; resumed the practice of law; interested in saw and grist mills and engaged in mercantile pursuits; elected Governor of Illinois in 1826 and served from December 6, 1826 to December 6, 1830; died in Belleville, Ill., on July 20, 1833; interment in that city; reinterment in 1855 in Oak Ridge Cemetery, Springfield, Ill.

Bibliography: *DAB*; Bakalis, Michael John. "Ninian Edwards and Territorial Politics in Illinois: 1775-1818." Ph.D. dissertation, Northwestern University, 1966; Wixon, Richard L. "Ninian Edwards: A Founding Father of Illinois." Ph.D. dissertation, Southern Illinois University, 1983.

EDWARDS, Pierpont (father of Henry Waggaman Edwards), a Delegate from Connecticut; born in Northampton, Mass., April 8, 1750; was graduated from Princeton College in 1768; studied law; was admitted to the bar and began practice in New Haven, Conn., in 1771; served in the Revolutionary Army; Member of the Continental Congress in 1788; member of the State house of representatives in 1789 and 1790 and served as speaker; appointed United States district judge for the district of Connecticut in 1806; member of the ratification convention in 1788 and of the constitutional convention which framed the constitution of Connecticut in 1818; died in Bridgeport, Conn., April 5, 1826; interment in Grove Street Cemetery, New Haven, Conn.

Bibliography: *DAB*.

EDWARDS, Samuel, a Representative from Pennsylvania; born in Chester Township, Delaware County, Pa., March 12, 1785; attended the common schools; studied law; was admitted to the bar in 1806 and commenced practice in Chester; served in the War of 1812; member of the Pennsylvania house of representatives 1814-1816; elected to the Sixteenth and to the three succeeding Congresses (March 4, 1819-March 3, 1827); chairman, Committee on Expenditures in the Department of Navy (Seventeenth and Eighteenth Congresses); resumed the practice of his profession in Chester; inspector of customs 1838-1842; died in Chester, Pa., November 21, 1850; interment in Chester Rural Cemetery.

EDWARDS, Thomas Chester (Chet), a Representative from Texas; born in Corpus Christi, Nueces County, Tex., November 24, 1951; graduated Memorial High School, Houston, Tex., 1970; B.A., Texas A&M University, 1974; M.B.A., Harvard University Business School, 1981; legislative and district administrative assistant to Representative Olin Teague of Texas, 1975-1977; sales director, Booz, Allen and Hamilton, 1978-1979; marketing representative, Trammell Crow Co., Dallas, Tex., 1981-1984; real estate, 1984; member, Texas State senate, 1983-1990; elected as a Democrat to the One Hundred Second and to the two succeeding Congresses (January 3, 1991-January 3, 1997); is a resident of Waco, Tex.

EDWARDS, Thomas McKey, a Representative from New Hampshire; born in Keene, Cheshire County, N.H., December 16, 1795; tutored privately; was graduated from Dartmouth College, Hanover, N.H., in 1813; studied law; was admitted to the bar in 1817 and commenced practice in Keene, N.H.; postmaster of Keene from June 30, 1818, to July 23, 1829; served in the State house of representatives in 1834, 1836, 1838, and 1839; abandoned his law practice in 1845 and superintended the construction of the Cheshire Railroad, serving as its first president; also served as president of a bank and a fire-insurance company; elected as a Republican to the Thirty-sixth and Thirty-seventh Congresses (March 4, 1859-March 3, 1863); was not a candidate for renomination in 1862 to the Thirty-eighth Congress; resumed his former business pursuits; died in Keene, N.H., May 1, 1875; interment in Woodlawn Cemetery.

EDWARDS, Thomas Owen, a Representative from Ohio; born in Williamsburg, Ind., March 29, 1810; completed preparatory studies; studied medicine at the University of Maryland, Baltimore, Md.; moved to Lancaster, Ohio, in 1836 and engaged in the practice of medicine; elected as a Whig to the Thirtieth Congress (March 4, 1847-March 3, 1849); unsuccessful candidate for reelection in 1848 to the Thirty-first Congress; attended former President John Quincy Adams, who was then a Representative, when he suffered a fatal stroke in the Hall of the House of Representatives on February 21, 1848; served as inspector of marine hospitals; moved to Cincinnati, Ohio, and engaged in the drug business; member and president of the city council; professor in the Ohio Medical College, Cincinnati, Ohio; moved to Madison, Wis., and thence to Dubuque, Iowa; during the Civil War served as surgeon in the Third Regiment, Iowa Volunteer Infantry; returned to Lancaster, Ohio, about 1870 and resumed the practice of medicine; moved to Wheeling, W.Va., in 1875 and continued the practice of his profession; died in Wheeling, W.Va., February 5, 1876; interment in Mount Wood Cemetery.

EDWARDS, Weldon Nathaniel, a Representative from North Carolina; born in Gaston, Northampton County, N.C., January 25, 1788; attended Warrenton Academy; studied law; was admitted to the bar in 1810 and commenced practice in Warrenton, N.C.; member of the State house of representatives in 1814 and 1815; elected as a Republican to the Fourteenth Congress to fill the vacancy caused by the resignation of Nathaniel Macon; reelected to the Fifteenth and to the four succeeding Congresses and served from February 7, 1816, to March 3, 1827; chairman, Committee on Expenditures in the Department of the Treasury (Eighteenth Congress), Committee on Public Expenditures (Nineteenth Congress); declined to be a candidate for reelection in 1826; returned to his plantation; member of the State senate 1833-1844; member of the State constitutional convention in 1835; again elected to the State senate in 1850 and chosen its president; president of the State secession convention in 1861; died in Warren County, N.C., December 18, 1873; interment in a private cemetery at his home, "Poplar Mount," about twelve miles from Warrenton, Warren County, N.C.

Bibliography: *DAB*.

EDWARDS, William Donlon (Don), a Representative from California; born in San Jose, Santa Clara County, Calif., January 6, 1915; attended the public schools of San Jose; B.A., Stanford University, 1936; attended Stanford University Law School and was admitted to the bar in 1940; special agent, Federal Bureau of Investigation, 1940 and 1941; served in the United States Navy as a naval intelligence and gunnery officer, 1942-1945; president, Valley Title Co., of Santa Clara County, 1951-1975; delegate to the Democratic National Conventions of 1964 and 1968; elected as a Democrat to the Eighty-eighth and to the fifteen succeeding Congresses (January 3, 1963-January 3, 1995); was not a candidate for reelection in 1994 to the One Hundred Fourth Congress; is a resident of San Jose, Calif.

EDWARDS, William Jackson (Jack), a Representative from Alabama; born in Birmingham, Jefferson County, Ala., September 20, 1928; attended the public schools of Homewood, Ala.; served in the United States Marine Corps (corporal) July 1946 to July 1948 and (sergeant) September 1950 to September 1951; attended the United States Naval School (academy and college preparatory) in 1947 and 1948; B.S., University of Alabama, 1952; LL.B., University of Alabama School of Law, 1954; was admitted to the bar the same year and began practice in Mobile, Ala.; instructor in business law in 1954; member of Transportation Advisory Committee to Mobile City Planning Commission, 1960-1963; delegate, Alabama Republican State convention, 1970; elected as a Republican to the Eighty-ninth and to the nine succeeding Congresses (January 3, 1965-January 3, 1985); was not a candidate for reelection in 1984 to the Ninety-ninth Congress; resumed the practice of law; nominated by President Ronald Reagan to the Metropolitan Washington Airports Authority, 1987; is a resident of Point Clear, Ala.

**EDWARDS, William Posey,** a Representative from Georgia; born near Talbotton, Talbot County, Ga., November 9, 1835; attended the common schools, and was graduated from Collinsworth Institute, Talbotton, Ga., in 1856; studied law; was admitted to the bar in 1857 and commenced practice in Butler, Ga.; member of the State constitutional convention in 1857 and 1858; served during the Civil War in the Confederate Army as captain of Company F, Twenty-seventh Georgia Volunteer Infantry; subsequently promoted to colonel of the regiment; upon the readmission of Georgia to representation was elected as a Republican to the Fortieth Congress and served from July 25, 1868, to March 3, 1869; presented credentials as a Member-elect to the Forty-first Congress, but was not permitted to qualify; resumed the practice of his profession at Butler, Ga., and died there June 28, 1900; interment in the Methodist Cemetery.

**EFNER, Valentine,** a Representative from New York; born in Blenheim Hill, near Blenheim, Schoharie County, N.Y., May 5, 1776; completed preparatory studies; engaged in agricultural pursuits; commissioned as major in the War of 1812; member of the State assembly in 1829; elected as a Jacksonian to the Twenty-fourth Congress (March 4, 1835-March 3, 1837); resumed agricultural pursuits; died in Blenheim Hill, N.Y., November 20, 1865; interment in Blenheim Hill Cemetery.

**EGBERT, Albert Gallatin,** a Representative from Pennsylvania; born near Sandy Lake, Mercer County, Pa., on April 13, 1828; attended the public schools and Austinburg Academy, Ohio; was graduated from the medical department of the Western Reserve University, Cleveland, Ohio, in 1856 and commenced the practice of medicine in Clintonville, Pa.; moved to Cherrytree, Pa., and practiced his profession until 1861, when he retired in order to devote his entire time to the production of oil and to agricultural pursuits; served during the Civil War as a volunteer surgeon; elected as a Democrat to the Forty-fourth Congress (March 4, 1875-March 3, 1877); chairman, Committee on Mileage (Forty-fourth Congress); declined to be a candidate for renomination in 1876; resumed his former business pursuits; died in Franklin, Venango County, Pa., March 28, 1896; interment in Franklin Cemetery.

**EGBERT, Joseph,** a Representative from New York; born near Bull Head, Staten Island, N.Y., April 10, 1807; attended the common schools; engaged in agricultural pursuits; elected as a Democrat to the Twenty-seventh Congress (March 4, 1841-March 3, 1843); was not a candidate for renomination in 1842; resumed agricultural pursuits; supervisor of Southfield, Richmond County, in 1855 and 1856; county clerk of Richmond County in 1869; died at his home near New Dorp, N.Y., July 7, 1888; interment in the Moravian Cemetery, New Dorp, Staten Island, N.Y.

**EGE, George,** a Representative from Pennsylvania; born near Womelsdorf, Berks County, Pa., March 9, 1748; attended the common schools; engaged in land and iron interests; member of the State house of representatives in 1783; appointed one of the first associate judges of Berks County under the constitution in 1790, and served from 1791 until 1818, when he resigned; resumed his extensive business interests; elected as a Federalist to the Fourth Congress to fill the vacancy caused by the resignation of Daniel Hiester; reelected to the Fifth Congress and served from December 8, 1796, until October 1797, when he resigned; resumed business interests; built and operated Schuylkill County Forge, near Port Clinton, Pa., in 1804; died at his residence, "Charming Forge," Marion Township, Berks County, Pa., December 14, 1829; interment in Zion's Church Cemetery, Womelsdorf, Pa.

**EGGLESTON, Benjamin,** a Representative from Ohio; born in Corinth, Saratoga County, N.Y., January 3, 1816; completed preparatory studies; moved with his parents to Hocking County, Ohio, in 1831; moved to Cleveland and worked on a canal boat, later becoming an owner of boats and interested in several companies; settled in Cincinnati in 1845 and engaged in mercantile pursuits; presiding officer of the city council of Cincinnati; delegate to the Republican National Convention in 1860; member of the State senate 1862-1865; elected as a Republican to the Thirty-ninth and Fortieth Congresses (March 4, 1865-March 3, 1869); unsuccessful candidate for reelection in 1868 to the Forty-first Congress; again served in the State senate in 1880 and 1881; resumed mercantile pursuits; died in Cincinnati, Ohio, February 9, 1888; interment in Spring Grove Cemetery.

**EGGLESTON, Joseph** (uncle of William Segar Archer), a Representative from Virginia; born in Middlesex County, Va., November 24, 1754; when four years old was taken to his father's plantation "Egglestetton," near Amelia Court House, Va.; studied under private teachers; was graduated from the College of William and Mary, Williamsburg, Va., in 1776; captain and major in Lee's Lighthorse Cavalry in the Revolutionary Army; member of the Virginia house of delegates 1785-1788 and 1791-1799; elected a member of the Virginia Privy Council on November 7, 1787; elected as a Republican to the Fifth Congress to fill the vacancy caused by the resignation of William B. Giles; reelected to the Sixth Congress and served from December 3, 1798, to March 3, 1801; was not a candidate for renomination in 1800; engaged in agricultural pursuits; justice of the peace from 1801 until his death in Amelia County, Va., February 13, 1811; interment in the Old Grubhill Church Cemetery, near Amelia Court House, Amelia County, Va.

**EHLERS, Vernon James,** a Representative from Michigan; born in Pipestone, Minn., February 6, 1934; educated at home by his parents; attended Calvin College, Grand Rapids, Mich., 1952-1956; A.B., University of California, Berkeley, 1956, and Ph.D., physics, 1960; teaching assistant, 1956-1957, research assistant, 1957-1960, physics department lecturer, then research physicist, 1960-1966, Lawrence Berkeley Laboratory, University of California at Berkeley; professor of physics, Calvin College, 1966-1983; science adviser to Representative Gerald R. Ford of Michigan; Kent County, Mich., commissioner, 1975-1983; member, Michigan State house of representatives, 1983-1985; member, Michigan State senate, 1985-1993; elected as a Republican to the One Hundred Third Congress, December 7, 1993, by special election to fill the vacancy caused by the death of Paul B. Henry; reelected to the One Hundred Fourth Congress, and served from January 25, 1994 to January 3, 1997; is a resident of Grand Rapids, Mich.

**EHRLICH, Robert L., Jr.,** a Representative from Maryland; born in Baltimore, Baltimore County, Md., November 25, 1957; B.A., Princeton University, 1979; J.D., Wake Forest University School of Law, 1982; practicing attorney in Baltimore, Md.; member, Maryland State general assembly, 1987-1994; elected as a Republican to the One Hundred Fourth Congress (January 3, 1995-January 3, 1997); is a resident of Timonium, Md.

**EICHER, Edward Clayton,** a Representative from Iowa; born on a farm near Noble, Washington County, Iowa, December 16, 1878; attended the public schools, Washington (Iowa) Academy, and Morgan Park (Ill.) Academy; was graduated from the University of Chicago, in 1904; studied law; was admitted to the bar in 1906 and commenced practice in Washington, Iowa; served as assistant registrar of the University of Chicago 1907-1909; moved to Burlington, Iowa, in 1909 and served as assistant attorney for a railroad company 1909-1918; returned to Washington, Iowa, in 1918 and continued the practice of law; delegate to the Democratic National Convention of 1932; elected as a Democrat to the Seventy-third and to the two succeeding Congresses and served from March 4, 1933, to December 2, 1938, when he resigned to accept a Presidential appointment; was renominated in 1938 to the Seventy-sixth Congress, but later withdrew and was not a candidate for reelection; appointed by President Franklin D. Roosevelt on December 2, 1938, as a commissioner of the Securities and Exchange Commission in Washington, D.C., and served until February 2, 1942, being chairman of the Commission at the time; appointed chief justice of the District Court of the United States for the District of Columbia on February 2, 1942, in which capacity he served until his death in Alexandria, Va., on November 29, 1944; interment in Woodlawn Cemetery, Washington, Iowa.

**EICKHOFF, Anthony,** a Representative from New York; born in Westphalia, Prussia, September 11, 1827; taught school in Prussia; immigrated to the United States in 1847; settled in St. Louis, Mo. where he studied law; became an editor; edited papers in St. Louis, Dubuque, Louisville, and finally in New York in 1852; appointed commissary general of subsistence for the State of New York in 1863; member of the State assembly in 1864; city coroner in 1874; elected as a Democrat to the Forty-fifth Congress (March 4, 1877-March 3, 1879); unsuccessful candidate for reelection in 1878 to the Forty-sixth Congress; Fifth Auditor in the United States Treasury Department from August 1, 1885, to May 17, 1889; appointed fire commissioner in New York City in 1889; reappointed in 1891; at the time of his death he was auditor of the fire department; died in New York City November 5, 1901; interment in Greenwood Cemetery.

**EILBERG, Joshua,** a Representative from Pennsylvania; born in Philadelphia, Pa., February 12, 1921; B.S., Wharton School, University of Pennsylvania, 1941; J.D., Temple University School of Law, 1948; during the Second World War served in the United States Naval Reserve; practicing attorney in Philadelphia since 1948; assistant district attorney, city of Philadelphia, 1952-1954; member of the general assembly of Pennsylvania, 1954-1966, serving as majority leader, 1965-1966; delegate to the Democratic National Conventions of 1960, 1964, and 1968; Democratic ward leader, fifty-fourth ward, city of Philadelphia; elected as a Democrat to the Ninetieth and to the five succeeding Congresses (January 3, 1967-January 3, 1979); unsuccessful candidate for reelection in 1978 to the Ninety-sixth Congress; resumed the practice of law; is a resident of Jenkintown, Pa.

**EINSTEIN, Edwin,** a Representative from New York; born in Cincinnati, Ohio, November 18, 1842; moved with his parents to New York City in 1846; worked as clerk in a store; received a collegiate training in the College of the City of New York, and entered Union College, but did not graduate; engaged in mercantile pursuits; elected as a Republican to the Forty-sixth Congress (March 4, 1879-March 3, 1881); was not a candidate for renomination in 1880 to the Forty-seventh Congress; unsuccessful Republican candidate for mayor of New York City in 1892; dock commissioner of New York City in 1895; was prominently identified with a number of investment companies and woolen factories; died in New York City January 24, 1905; interment in Shearith Israel Cemetery, Brooklyn, N.Y.

**EKWALL, William Alexander,** a Representative from Oregon; born in Ludington, Mason County, Mich., June 14, 1887; moved to Klamathon, Calif., with his parents in 1893, and to Portland, Oreg., in 1906; attended the public schools; was graduated in 1912 from the Oregon Law School at Portland; was admitted to the bar the same year and commenced practice in Portland, Oreg.; during the First World War served in the United States Army as a private in the Infantry, Central Officers Training School, in 1918; municipal judge of Portland 1922-1927; judge of the circuit court, fourth judicial

district (Multnomah County), department 8, from 1927 until elected to Congress; elected as a Republican to the Seventy-fourth Congress (January 3, 1935-January 3, 1937); unsuccessful candidate for reelection in 1936 to the Seventy-fifth Congress; resumed the practice of law at Portland, Oreg., 1937-1942; delegate to the Republican National Convention in 1940; appointed judge of the United States Customs Court, New York City on February 13, 1942, and served until his death in Portland, Oreg., October 16, 1956; interment in Portland Memorial Cemetery.

**ELA, Jacob Hart,** a Representative from New Hampshire; born in Rochester, N.H., July 18, 1820; attended the village school in Rochester; at fourteen years of age was apprenticed in a woolen manufactory and subsequently learned the printer's trade; member of the State house of representatives in 1857 and 1858; United States marshal from July 1861 to October 1866; elected as a Republican to the Fortieth and Forty-first Congresses (March 4, 1867-March 3, 1871); chairman, Committee on Expenditures in the Department of the Interior (Forty-first Congress); appointed by President Ulysses S. Grant as Fifth Auditor of the Treasury on January 1, 1872, and served until June 2, 1881; on June 3, 1881, was appointed Auditor of the Treasury for the Post Office Department and served in that position until his death in Washington, D.C., on August 21, 1884; interment in North Side Cemetery, Rochester, N.H.

**ELAM, Joseph Barton,** a Representative from Louisiana; born near Hope, Hempstead County, Ark., June 12, 1821; moved with his father to Natchitoches, La., in 1826; studied law; was admitted to the bar in 1843 and commenced practice in Alexandria, La.; moved to the parish of De Soto in 1851; member and speaker of the State house of representatives 1851-1861; elected a delegate to the State constitutional convention in 1861 and signed the ordinance of secession; elected as a Democrat to the Forty-fifth and Forty-sixth Congresses (March 4, 1877-March 3, 1881); unsuccessful candidate for reelection in 1880 to the Forty-seventh Congress; resumed the practice of law in Mansfield, De Soto Parish, La., where he died July 4, 1885; interment in Mansfield Cemetery.

**ELBERT, Samuel,** a Delegate from Georgia; born in Prince William Parish, S.C., in 1740; engaged in mercantile business in Savannah, Ga.; captain of a grenadier company in 1774; member of the council on safety in 1775; lieutenant colonel in 1776; placed in command of Georgia Continental troops in October 1777; commanded a brigade under General John Ashe at the Battle of Briar Creek, Ga., March 3, 1779; taken prisoner but was exchanged in June 1781 and took part in the battle of Yorktown; promoted to brigadier general in 1783; elected as a Delegate to the Continental Congress January 9, 1784, but declined to serve; Governor of Georgia in 1785 and appointed major general of militia; died in Savannah, Ga., November 1, 1788.

**Bibliography:** DAB; Jones, Charles Colcock, Jr. *The Life and Services of the Honorable Maj. Gen.* 1887. Reprint. New York: W. Abbatt, 1911.

**ELDER, James Walter,** a Representative from Louisiana; born in Grand Prairie, Dallas County, Tex., October 5, 1882; attended the public schools, and Baylor University, Waco, Tex., 1895-1901; studied law; was admitted to the bar in 1903 and commenced practice in Farmerville, Union Parish, La.; mayor of Farmerville, La.; moved to Monroe, Ouachita Parish, and continued the practice of his profession; member of the State senate 1908-1912; elected as a Democrat to the Sixty-third Congress (March 4, 1913-March 3, 1915); unsuccessful candidate for renomination in 1914 to the Sixty-fourth Congress; returned to the practice of law in Farmerville, La., until January 1, 1925; moved to Ruston, La., and continued the practice of law until his death on December 16, 1941; interment in Greenwood Cemetery.

**ELDREDGE, Charles Augustus,** a Representative from Wisconsin; born in Bridport, Vt., February 27, 1820; moved with his parents to Canton, St. Lawrence County, N.Y., in 1825; attended the common schools; studied law; was admitted to the bar in 1846 and commenced practice in Canton, N.Y.; moved to Fond du Lac, Wis., in 1848 and continued the practice of his profession; member of the State senate 1854-1856; elected as a Democrat to the Thirty-eighth and to the five succeeding Congresses (March 4, 1863-March 3, 1875); unsuccessful candidate for renomination in 1874 to the Forty-fourth Congress; resumed the practice of law; died in Fond du Lac, Wis., October 26, 1896; interment in Rienzi Cemetery.

**ELDREDGE, Nathaniel Buel,** a Representative from Michigan; born in Auburn, N.Y., March 28, 1813; attended the common schools; attended Fairfield Medical College; engaged in the practice of medicine in Commerce, Oakland County, Mich.; clerk of the Michigan senate in 1845; member of the State house of representatives in 1848; judge of probate 1852-1856; studied law; was admitted to the bar and commenced practice in 1854; held several minor offices; enrolled as captain of Company G, Seventh Regiment, Michigan Volunteers, June 19, 1861; was honorably discharged as a lieutenant colonel January 7, 1863; elected sheriff of Lenawee County in 1874; elected as a Democrat to the Forty-eighth and Forty-ninth Congresses (March 4, 1883-March 3, 1887); chairman, Committee on Pensions (Forty-ninth Congress); died in Adrian, Mich., on November 27, 1893; interment in Oakwood Cemetery.

**ELIOT, Samuel Atkins** (great-grandfather of Thomas Hopkinson Eliot), a Representative from Massachusetts; born in Boston, Mass., March 5, 1798; attended the Boston Latin School; was graduated from Harvard University in 1817 and from the divinity school in 1820; member of the Massachusetts house of representatives 1834-1837; mayor of Boston 1837-1839; served in the Massachusetts senate in 1843-1844; elected as a Whig to the Thirty-first Congress to fill the vacancy caused by the resignation of Robert C. Winthrop and served from August 22, 1850, to March 3, 1851; declined to be a candidate for renomination in 1850 to the Thirty-second Congress; treasurer of Harvard University 1842-1853; died in Cambridge, Mass., January 29, 1862; interment in Mount Auburn Cemetery.

Bibliography: *DAB.*

**ELIOT, Thomas Dawes,** a Representative from Massachusetts; born in Boston, Mass., March 20, 1808; attended the public schools of Washington, D.C., and was graduated from Columbian College (now George Washington University), in that city, in 1825; was admitted to the bar in 1831 and commenced practice in New Bedford, Mass.; member of the Massachusetts house of representatives in 1839; served in the Massachusetts senate in 1846; elected as a Whig to the Thirty-third Congress to fill the vacancy caused by the resignation of Zeno Scudder and served from April 17, 1854, to March 3, 1855; declined to be a candidate for renomination in 1854 to the Thirty-fourth Congress; delegate to the Free-Soil Convention in Worcester, Mass., in 1855; declined to be a candidate for nomination by the Republican Party for attorney general of Massachusetts in 1857; elected as a Republican to the Thirty-sixth and to the four succeeding Congresses (March 4, 1859-March 3, 1869); chairman, Committee on the Freedmen's Bureau (Thirty-ninth and Fortieth Congresses), Committee on Commerce (Fortieth Congress); declined to be a candidate for renomination in 1868; resumed the practice of law in New Bedford, Mass., where he died on June 14, 1870; interment in Oak Grove Cemetery.

**ELIOT, Thomas Hopkinson** (great-grandson of Samuel Atkins Eliot), a Representative from Massachusetts; born in Cambridge, Mass., June 14, 1907; attended Browne and Nichols School; was graduated from Harvard University in 1928; student at Emmanuel College, Cambridge University, in 1928 and 1929; was graduated from the law school of Harvard University in 1932; was admitted to the bar in 1933 and commenced practice in Buffalo, N.Y.; served as assistant solicitor in the United States Department of Labor 1933-1935; general counsel for the Social Security Board 1935-1938; lecturer on government at Harvard University in 1937 and 1938; regional director of the Wage and Hour Division in the Department of Labor in 1939 and 1940; unsuccessful candidate for election in 1938 to the Seventy-sixth Congress; elected as a Democrat to the Seventy-seventh Congress (January 3, 1941-January 3, 1943); unsuccessful candidate for renomination in 1942 to the Seventy-eighth Congress, and for nomination in 1944 to the Seventy-ninth Congress; director of the British Division, Office of War Information, London, England, and special assistant to the United States Ambassador, 1943; chairman of the appeals committee, National War Labor Board, 1943-1944; served with the Office of Strategic Services in 1944; served as chief counsel, Division of Power, Department of the Interior, from November 1944 to November 1945; engaged in the practice of law in Boston, Mass., 1945-1950; professor of political science, Washington University, St. Louis, Mo., 1952, and of constitutional law 1958; dean of Washington University College of Liberal Arts, 1961-1962, and chancellor, 1962-1971; vice chairman, United States Commission on Intergovernmental Relations, 1963-1967; president, Salzburg Seminar in American Studies, 1971-1977; teacher, Buckingham, Browne and Nichols School, 1977-1985; was a resident of Cambridge, Mass.; died October 14, 1991.

**ELIZALDE, Joaquin Miguel,** a Resident Commissioner from the Commonwealth of the Philippines; born in Manila, Philippine Islands, August 2, 1896; attended St. Joseph's College at London, England, and Dr. Schmidt's Institute at St. Gallen, Switzerland; industrialist and financier; economic adviser to President Manuel L. Quezon in 1937 and 1938; member of the National Economic Council from 1937 until 1941, and in 1952 and 1953; member of the Joint Preparatory Committee on Philippine Affairs in 1936 and 1937; member of the Council of State, 1936-1941, and 1952 and 1953; served as major, Cavalry reserve, Philippine Army; appointed as a Resident Commissioner to the United States on September 29, 1938, to fill the vacancy caused by the resignation of Quintin Paredes and served until his resignation on August 9, 1944; member of the war cabinet of President Manuel L. Quezon, 1941-1944; member of the board of governors of the International Monetary Fund and of the International Bank for Reconstruction and Development, 1946-1950; appointed Ambassador Extraordinary and Plenipotentiary of the Republic of the Philippines to the United States on July 6, 1946, in which capacity he served until January 1952; Minister of Foreign Affairs of the Republic of the Philippines in 1952 and 1953; economic adviser to the Philippine Mission at the United Nations, with the rank of Ambassador, 1956-1965; was a resident of Moreland Farms, Adamstown, Md.; died in Washington, D.C., February 9, 1965; interment in St. Joseph's Cemetery, Carrollton Manor, Md.

**ELKINS, Davis** (son of Stephen Benton Elkins and grandson of Henry Gassaway Davis), a Senator from West Virginia; born in Washington, D.C., January 24, 1876; attended the Lawrenceville (N.J.) School, Phillips Academy, Andover, Mass., and Harvard University; during the war with Spain enlisted as a private in the First West Virginia Volunteer Infantry, becoming assistant adjutant general in 1898; industrialist with interests in railroads, banking, utilities, and coal mining; appointed as a Republican to the United States Senate to fill the vacancy caused by the death of his father, Stephen B. Elkins, and served from January 9 to January 31, 1911, when a successor was elected; during the First World War served in the United States Army in France, 1917-1918; elected as a Republican to the United States Senate, and served from March 4, 1919 to March 3, 1925; was not a candidate for renomination in 1924; chairman, Committee on Expenditures in the Department of Commerce (Sixty-sixth Congress); owner of the Washington and Old

Dominion Railroad Company from 1936 to 1956; died in Richmond, Va., on January 5, 1959; interment in Maplewood Cemetery, Elkins, W.Va.

**ELKINS, Stephen Benton** (father of Davis Elkins), a Delegate from the Territory of New Mexico and a Senator from West Virginia; born in Perry County, Ohio, September 26, 1841; moved with his parents to Westport, Mo.; attended the public schools and was graduated from the law department of the University of Missouri at Columbia in 1860; during the Civil War enlisted in the Union Army as a captain in the Kansas Militia; moved to the Territory of New Mexico in 1864; was admitted to the bar in 1864 and commenced practice in Messila, N.Mex.; member, Territorial house of representatives 1864-1865; district attorney for the Territory of New Mexico 1866-1867; attorney general of the Territory 1867; United States district attorney for the Territory 1867-1870; elected as a Republican Delegate to the Forty-third and Forty-fourth Congresses (March 4, 1873-March 3, 1877); was not a candidate for renomination in 1876 to the Forty-fifth Congress; moved to Elkins, W.Va., which he founded, around 1890; extensively interested in developing natural resources and industry in West Virginia; appointed Secretary of War by President Benjamin Harrison on December 17, 1891 and served until March 5, 1893; elected as a Republican to the United States Senate in February 1895; reelected in 1901 and 1907 and served from March 4, 1895, until his death in Washington, D.C., January 4, 1911; chairman, Committee on the Geological Survey (Fifty-sixth and Fifty-ninth Congresses), Committee on Interstate Commerce (Fifty-seventh through Sixty-first Congresses); interment in Maplewood Cemetery, Elkins, W.Va.

**Bibliography:** *DAB*; Lambert, Oscar. *Stephen Benton Elkins.* Pittsburgh: University of Pittsburgh Press, 1955; Williams, John Alexander. "New York's First Senator From West Virginia: How Stephen B. Elkins Found a New Political Home." *West Virginia History* 31 (January 1970): 73-87.

**ELLENBOGEN, Henry,** a Representative from Pennsylvania; born in Vienna, Austria, April 3, 1900; attended the Vienna public schools and the University of Vienna Law School, Austria; immigrated to the United States and settled in Pittsburgh, Pa.; A.B., Duquesne University, Pittsburgh, Pa., 1921, and J.D., 1924; was admitted to the bar in 1926 and commenced practice in Pittsburgh, Pa.; appointed as arbitrator and public panel chairman by the National War Labor Board and the Third Regional War Labor Board in cases involving labor disputes; writer of articles on economic, social and legal problems; elected as a Democrat to the Seventy-third and to the two succeeding Congresses, and served from March 4, 1933 to January 3, 1938, when he resigned, having been elected judge of the common pleas court of Allegheny County, Pa.; reelected in November 1947 and again in 1957, and served as presiding judge, 1963-1966; was a resident of Miami, Fla., until his death there on July 4, 1985; interment in West View Cemetery of Rodef Shalom Congregation, Squirrel Hill, Pa.

**ELLENDER, Allen Joseph,** a Senator from Louisiana; born near Montegut, Terrebonne Parish, La., September 24, 1890; attended the public and private schools; graduated from St. Aloysius High School, New Orleans, La., in 1909; LL.B., Tulane University Law School, New Orleans, 1913; was admitted to the bar in 1913 and commenced practice in Houma, La.; city attorney of Houma, 1913-1915; appointed district attorney of Lafourche and Terrebonne Parishes, 1915-1916; unsuccessful candidate for reelection as district attorney in 1916; during the First World War was appointed to the Student Army Training Corps at Tulane University, 1918; delegate to the constitutional convention of Louisiana, March-June 1921; Democratic national committeeman from Louisiana 1939-1940; member, Louisiana State house of representatives, 1924-1936, serving as floor leader 1928-1932, and as speaker 1932-1936; elected as a Democrat to the United States Senate in 1936; reelected in

1942, 1948, 1954, 1960, and again in 1966, and served from January 5, 1937 until his death in the naval hospital at Bethesda, Md., on July 27, 1972; served as President pro tempore of the Senate during the Ninety-second Congress; chairman, Committee on Claims (Seventy-eighth and Seventy-ninth Congresses), Committee on Agriculture and Forestry (Eighty-second and Eighty-fourth through Ninety-first Congresses), Committee on Appropriations (Ninety-second Congress); interment in Magnolia Cemetery, Houma, La.

**Bibliography:** Becnel, Thomas A. *Senator Allen Ellender of Louisiana: A Biography.* Baton Rouge: Louisiana State University Press, 1995.

**ELLERBE, James Edwin,** a Representative from South Carolina; born in Sellers, Marion County, S.C., January 12, 1867; attended Pine Hill Academy and the University of South Carolina at Columbia; was graduated from Wofford College, Spartanburg, S.C., in 1887; engaged in agricultural pursuits; member of the South Carolina State house of representatives from 1894 until 1896; delegate to the State constitutional convention in 1895; elected as a Democrat to the Fifty-ninth and to the three succeeding Congresses (March 4, 1905-March 3, 1913); unsuccessful candidate for renomination in 1912 to the Sixty-third Congress; resumed his agricultural pursuits; died in Asheville, N.C., October 24, 1917; interment in the family burial ground near Sellers, S.C.

**ELLERY, Christopher** (nephew of William Ellery), a Senator from Rhode Island; born in Newport, R.I., November 1, 1768; was graduated from Yale College in 1787; studied law; was admitted to the bar and commenced practice in Newport; clerk of the superior court of Newport County 1794-1798; elected as a Republican to the United States Senate to fill the vacancy caused by the resignation of Ray Greene and served from May 6, 1801, to March 3, 1805; unsuccessful candidate for reelection in 1804; appointed by President Thomas Jefferson as United States commissioner of loans at Providence, R.I., in 1806; appointed collector of customs at Newport 1820-1834; died in Middletown, R.I., on December 2, 1840; interment in Island Cemetery, Newport, R.I.

**ELLERY, William** (uncle of Christopher Ellery), a Delegate from Rhode Island; born in Newport, R.I., on December 22, 1727; taught by private teachers; was graduated from Harvard College in 1747; naval officer of Rhode Island in 1754; clerk of the court of common pleas of Newport County in 1768 and 1769; studied law; was admitted to the bar in 1770 and commenced practice in Newport, R.I.; elected a Member of the Continental Congress to fill the vacancy caused by the death of Samuel Ward and served from May 14, 1776, to 1785; one of the signers of the Declaration of Independence; chosen to the newly constituted board of admiralty in 1779; appointed chief justice of Rhode Island in 1785; appointed by the Continental Congress commissioner of the Continental Loan Office in 1786; collector of the port of Newport from 1790 until his death in Newport, R.I., February 15, 1820; interment in the Common Cemetery.

**Bibliography:** *DAB*.

**ELLETT, Henry Thomas,** a Representative from Mississippi; born in Salem, N.J., March 8, 1812; attended the Latin School in Salem and Princeton College; studied law; was admitted to the bar in 1833 and commenced practice in Bridgeton, Cumberland County, N.J.; moved to Port Gibson, Claiborne County, Miss., in 1837 and continued the practice of law; elected as a Democrat to the Twenty-ninth Congress to fill the vacancy caused by the resignation of Jefferson Davis and served from January 26 to March 3, 1847; declined to be a candidate for reelection in 1846; resumed the practice of law; member of the State senate 1853-1865; member of the State secession convention in 1861, and member of the committee that framed and reported the ordinance of secession of Mississippi; appointed Postmaster General of the Confederacy in

February 1861 but declined; elected judge of the State supreme court on October 2, 1865, and served until January 1868, when he resigned; moved to Memphis, Tenn., in 1868 and resumed the practice of law; elected chancellor of the twelfth division of Tennessee in 1886; died while delivering an address of welcome to President Grover Cleveland in Memphis, Tenn., October 15, 1887; interment in Elmwood Cemetery.

**ELLETT, Tazewell,** a Representative from Virginia; born in Richmond, Va., January 1, 1856; attended private schools in Richmond; graduated from the Virginia Military Institute at Lexington in 1876; studied law; was graduated from the University of Virginia at Charlottsville in 1878 and immediately commenced practice in Richmond; member of the board of visitors of the Virginia Military Institute; elected as a Democrat to the Fifty-fourth Congress (March 4, 1895-March 3, 1897); was an unsuccessful candidate for reelection in 1896 to the Fifty-fifth Congress; resumed the practice of law in Richmond, Va., and New York City; died in Summerville, S.C., May 19, 1914; interment in Hollywood Cemetery, Richmond, Va.

**ELLICOTT, Benjamin,** a Representative from New York; born at Ellicotts Mills, Md., April 17, 1765; accompanied his brothers in 1789 to upper Canada on the survey to determine the western boundary of the State of New York; employed as a surveyor and draftsman for the Holland Land Co. in New York and Pennsylvania; one of the first judges of the court of common pleas of Genesee County, N.Y., in 1803, with residence in Batavia; elected as a Republican to the Fifteenth Congress (March 4, 1817-March 3, 1819); unsuccessful candidate for election in 1820 to the Seventeenth Congress; retired from active life, and in 1826 moved to Williamsville, Erie County, N.Y., where he died December 10, 1827; interment in the graveyard at Williamsville; reinterment in Batavia Cemetery, Batavia, N.Y., in 1849.

**ELLIOTT, Alfred James,** a Representative from California; born in Guinda, Yolo County, Calif., June 1, 1895; moved with his parents to Winters, Calif., in 1901 and to Tulare, Calif., in 1910; attended the public schools; engaged in farming and livestock raising; owned and published a newspaper; chairman of the board of supervisors of Tulare County 1933-1937; served on the California State Safety Council in 1936; member of the California Supervisor Association of the State welfare board in 1935 and 1936; elected as a Democrat to the Seventy-fifth Congress, by special election May 4, 1937, to fill the vacancy caused by the death of Henry E. Stubbs; reelected to the five succeeding Congresses and served from May 4, 1937, to January 3, 1949; was not a candidate for renomination in 1948 to the Eighty-first Congress; was president of Tulare Daily News; farmer and livestock breeder; retired in 1965 and resided in Tulare, Calif., until his death there on January 17, 1973; interment in Tulare Cemetery.

**ELLIOTT, Carl Atwood,** a Representative from Alabama; born in Vina, Franklin County, Ala., December 20, 1913; attended the public schools of Franklin County; was graduated from the University of Alabama at Tuscaloosa in 1933, and from its law school in 1936; was admitted to the bar the same year and commenced the practice of law in Russellville, Ala.; in December 1936 moved to Jasper, Ala., and continued the practice of law; served as judge of Recorders Court, Jasper, Ala., in 1942 and 1946; city attorney at various times for Dora, Parrish, Cordova, Carbon Hill, and Oakman, Ala.; served with the Seventy-ninth Division, Three Hundred and Thirteenth Infantry, United States Army, 1942-1944; member of the Alabama State Democratic Executive Committee, 1942-1950; elected as a Democrat to the Eighty-first and to the seven succeeding Congresses (January 3, 1949-January 3, 1965); chairman, Select Committee on Government Research (Eighty-eighth Congress); unsuccessful candidate for renomination in 1964 to the Eighty-ninth Congress; member of the bar of the District of

Columbia since 1965; unsuccessful candidate for nomination in 1966 for Governor of Alabama; served on President's Library Commission, 1967-1968; chairman, Public Evaluation Committee, Office of State Technical Services, United States Department of Commerce, 1967-1968; member, Commerce Technical Advisory Board, United States Department of Commerce, 1968-1970; resumed the practice of law until his retirement in 1986; owns and operates an editing and publishing business; is a resident of Jasper, Ala.

**Bibliography:** Elliott, Carl, Sr., and Michael D'Orso. *The Cost of Courage: The Journey of an American Congressman*. New York: Doubleday, 1992.

**ELLIOTT, Douglas Hemphill,** a Representative from Pennsylvania; born in Philadelphia, Pa., June 3, 1921; attended the schools of Philadelphia, Pa., and graduated from Haverford School in 1938; attended the University of Virginia at Charlottesville, 1938-1940; served in the United States Navy from 1941 until discharged as a chief petty officer in 1945; worked for insurance companies, 1945-1952; director of public relations of the Franklin Institute, Philadelphia, Pa., 1950-1952; vice president of Wilson College, Chambersburg, Pa., 1952-1960; elected in November 1956 to the State senate and served until elected to Congress; elected as a Republican to the Eighty-sixth Congress to fill the vacancy caused by the death of Richard M. Simpson, and served from April 26, 1960 until his death in Horse Valley, Franklin County, Pa., June 19, 1960; interment in Falling Spring Presbyterian Church Cemetery, Chambersburg, Pa.

**ELLIOTT, James,** a Representative from Vermont; born in Gloucester, Mass., August 18, 1775; during his early years worked on a farm and clerked in a store; moved to Guilford, Vt., in 1790; served as a sergeant in the Indian war of 1793 in Ohio; published several works of poems and essays in 1798; clerk of the State house of representatives 1801-1803; studied law; was admitted to the bar in 1803 and commenced practice in Brattleboro, Vt.; elected as a Federalist to the Eighth, Ninth, and Tenth Congresses (March 4, 1803-March 3, 1809); published a newspaper in Philadelphia, Pa., on his retirement from Congress; served in the War of 1812 for a short time as captain; resumed the practice of law in Brattleboro, Vt.; clerk of the Windham County Court 1817-1835; member of the State house of representatives in 1818 and 1819; moved to Newfane, Vt.; register of the probate court 1822-1834; again served in the State house of representatives in 1837 and 1838; State's attorney of Windham County 1837-1839; died in Newfane, Vt., November 10, 1839; interment in Prospect Hill Cemetery, Brattleboro, Vt.

**Bibliography:** Huddleston, Eugene L. "Indians and Literature of the Federalist Era: The Case of James Elliott." *New England Quarterly* 44 (June 1971): 221-37.

**ELLIOTT, James Thomas,** a Representative from Arkansas; born in Columbus, Monroe County, Ga., April 22, 1823; attended the common schools; studied law; was admitted to the bar in 1854 and commenced practice in Camden, Ark.; chosen president of the Mississippi, Ouachita and Red River Railroad in 1858; circuit judge of the sixth judicial district of Arkansas from October 2, 1865 to September 15, 1866; established and edited the South Arkansas Journal in 1867; elected as a Republican to the Fortieth Congress to fill the vacancy caused by the death of James Hinds, and served from January 13, 1869 to March 3, 1869; unsuccessful candidate for reelection in 1868 to the Forty-first Congress; elected to the Arkansas State senate in 1870; appointed judge of the ninth judicial district in 1872, and served until the adoption of the State constitution in 1874; died in Camden, Ouachita County Ark., on July 28, 1875; interment in Oakland Cemetery.

**ELLIOTT, John,** a Senator from Georgia; born in St. Johns Parish, now Liberty County, Ga., October 24, 1773; completed preparatory studies; was graduated from Yale College in 1794;

studied law; was admitted to the bar and commenced practice in Sunbury, Liberty County, Ga., in 1797; held several local offices; elected to the United States Senate, and served from March 4, 1819 to March 3, 1825; died in Sunbury, Ga., August 9, 1827; interment in Old Midway Cemetery in Liberty County.

**ELLIOTT, John Milton,** a Representative from Kentucky; born on the banks of Clinch River in Scott County, Va., May 20, 1820; moved to Morgan County (now Elliott County), Ky., and attended the common schools; was graduated from Emory and Henry College, Emory, Va., in 1841; studied law; was admitted to the bar in 1843 and commenced practice in Prestonsburg, Floyd County, Ky.; member of the Kentucky house of representatives in 1847; elected as a Democrat to the Thirty-third, Thirty-fourth, and Thirty-fifth Congresses (March 4, 1853-March 3, 1859); chairman, Committee on Public Expenditures (Thirty-fifth Congress); was not a candidate for renomination in 1858; resumed the practice of law; again a member of the Kentucky house of representatives in 1861; elected a Representative from Kentucky to the First and Second Confederate Congresses; circuit judge 1868-1874; judge of the court of appeals 1876-1879; assassinated at Frankfort, Ky., March 26, 1879; interment in the State Cemetery at Frankfort.

**ELLIOTT, Mortimer Fitzland,** a Representative from Pennsylvania; born in Cherry Flats, near Wellsboro, Tioga County, Pa., September 24, 1839; attended the common schools, Wellsboro Academy, and Alfred University, Allegheny County, Pa.; studied law; was admitted to the bar in 1860 and commenced practice in Wellsboro; member of the convention to revise the constitution of Pennsylvania in 1873; elected as a Democrat to the Forty-eighth Congress (March 4, 1883-March 3, 1885); unsuccessful candidate for reelection in 1884 to the Forty-ninth Congress; resumed the practice of law; general solicitor for the Standard Oil Co. in New York City; died in Mansfield, Tioga County, Pa., August 5, 1920; interment in Wellsboro Cemetery, Wellsboro, Pa.

**ELLIOTT, Richard Nash,** a Representative from Indiana; born near Connersville, Fayette County, Ind., April 25, 1873; attended the common schools; taught school three years; studied law; was admitted to the bar in 1896 and commenced practice in Connersville, Ind.; county attorney of Fayette County from 1897 until 1906; member of the Indiana State house of representatives, 1905-1909; city attorney of Connersville, 1905-1909; delegate to the Republican National Convention of 1916; chairman of the Republican State convention in 1930; elected as a Republican to the Sixty-fifth Congress to fill the vacancy caused by the death of Daniel W. Comstock; reelected to the Sixty-sixth and to the five succeeding Congresses and served from June 26, 1917, to March 3, 1931; chairman, Committee on Expenditures in the Department of State (Sixty-sixth and Sixty-seventh Congresses), Committee on Elections No. 3 (Sixty-eighth Congress), Committee on Public Buildings and Grounds (Sixty-ninth through Seventy-first Congresses); unsuccessful candidate for reelection in 1930 to the Seventy-second Congress; served as assistant comptroller general of the United States from March 6, 1931, to April 30, 1943, when he retired; resided in Washington, D.C., until his death on March 21, 1948; interment in Dale Cemetery, Connersville, Ind.

**ELLIOTT, Robert Brown,** a Representative from South Carolina; probably born in Liverpool, England, in 1842; received an education there and learned the typesetter's trade; served in the British Navy; arrived in Boston, Mass., about 1867, and later that same year moved to Charleston, S.C.; associate editor of the South Carolina Leader; member of the State constitutional convention in 1868; studied law and was admitted to the South Carolina bar in September 1868; member of the South Carolina State house of representatives from July 6, 1868, to October 23, 1870; appointed assistant adjutant general of South Carolina by Governor Robert K. Scott on March 25, 1869, and served until his resignation in December 1870; elected as a Republican to the Forty-second and Forty-third Congresses and served from March 4, 1871, until his resignation, effective November 1, 1874; again a member of the South Carolina State house of representatives, 1874-1876, and served as speaker; attorney general of South Carolina, 1876-1877; resumed the practice of law; special customs inspector of the Department of the Treasury in Charleston, 1879-1881, and in New Orleans, La., 1881-1882; practiced law in New Orleans until his death there on August 9, 1884; interment in St. Louis Cemetery No. 2.

**Bibliography:** Lamson, Peggy. *The Glorious Failure: Black Congressman Robert Brown Elliott and the Reconstruction in South Carolina.* New York: W.W. Norton, 1973.

**ELLIOTT, William,** a Representative from South Carolina; born in Beaufort, Beaufort County, S.C., September 3, 1838; attended Beaufort College and Harvard University; studied law at the University of Virginia at Charlottesville, and was admitted to the bar in Charleston, S.C., in 1861; upon the outbreak of the Civil War entered the Confederate Army as a lieutenant and served throughout the war, attaining the rank of lieutenant colonel; at the close of the war commenced the practice of law in Beaufort, S.C.; member of the South Carolina State house of representatives in 1866; intendant (administrative official) of Beaufort in 1866; delegate to the Democratic National Convention of 1876; unsuccessful Democratic candidate for election in 1884 to the Forty-ninth Congress; elected as a Democrat to the Fiftieth Congress (March 4, 1887-March 3, 1889); presented credentials as a Member-elect to the Fifty-first Congress, and served from March 4, 1889 until September 23, 1890, when he was succeeded by Thomas E. Miller, who contested the election; elected to the Fifty-second Congress (March 4, 1891-March 3, 1893); was not a candidate for renomination in 1892 to the Fifty-third Congress; presented credentials as a Member-elect to the Fifty-fourth Congress, and served from March 4, 1895 until June 4, 1896, when he was succeeded by George W. Murray, who contested the election; elected to the Fifty-fifth and to the two succeeding Congresses (March 4, 1897-March 3, 1903); was not a candidate in 1902 for renomination to the House of Representatives, but was an unsuccessful candidate for election to the United States Senate; appointed by President Theodore Roosevelt in 1906 as commissioner of the United States to mark the graves of Confederate dead in the North, and served in this capacity until his death in Beaufort, S.C., on December 7, 1907; interment in St. Helena Churchyard.

**ELLIS, Caleb,** a Representative from New Hampshire; born in Walpole, Mass., April 16, 1767; was graduated from Harvard University in 1793; studied law and was admitted to the bar; moved to Newport, N.H., and then to Claremont; member of the New Hampshire house of representatives in 1803; elected as a Federalist to the Ninth Congress (March 4, 1805-March 3, 1807); member of the Governor's council 1809 and 1810; served in the State senate in 1811; presidential elector on the DeWitt Clinton and Jared Ingersoll ticket in 1812; appointed judge of the superior court of New Hampshire in 1813, which office he held until his death in Claremont, N.H., May 6, 1816; interment in Broad Street Cemetery.

**ELLIS, Chesselden,** a Representative from New York; born in New Windsor, Vt., in 1808; completed preparatory studies and was graduated from Union College, Schenectady, N.Y., in 1823; studied law; was admitted to the bar in 1829 and commenced practice in Waterford, N.Y.; elected prosecuting attorney of Saratoga County, N.Y., and served from April 25, 1837, until September 11, 1843; elected as a Democrat to the Twenty-eighth Congress (March 4, 1843-March 3, 1845); unsuccessful candidate for reelection in 1844 to the Twenty-ninth Congress; resumed the practice of law in Waterford; moved to New York City in 1845 and continued the practice of his profession until his death there on May 10, 1854; interment in Albany Cemetery, Albany, N.Y.

**ELLIS, Clyde Taylor,** a Representative from Arkansas; born on a farm near Garfield, Benton County, Ark., December 21, 1908; attended the public schools of Fayetteville, Ark.; University of Arkansas at Fayetteville, B.S., and attended the school of law at the same university; attended George Washington University Law School and American University in Washington, D.C.; teacher in the rural schools at Garfield, Ark., in 1927 and 1928; superintendent of schools at Garfield, Ark., 1929-1934; was admitted to the bar in 1933 and commenced practice at Bentonville, Ark.; served in the State house of representatives, 1933-1935; member of the State senate, 1935-1939; delegate to the Democratic National Convention of 1940; elected as a Democrat to the Seventy-sixth Congress; reelected to the Seventy-seventh Congress (January 3, 1939-January 3, 1943); was not a candidate in 1942 for reelection to the House of Representatives, but was an unsuccessful candidate for nomination to the United States Senate; served as combat officer in the United States Navy, 1943-1945; general manager of the National Rural Electric Cooperative Association, Washington, D.C., from January 1943 until his retirement in September 1967; appointed as special consultant to Secretary of Agriculture Orville L. Freeman, January 1968 to January 1969; special area development assistant to Senator John L. McClellan from February 1971 until 1977; returned to the staff of the Secretary of Agriculture and was employed there until his retirement in August 1979; resided in Chevy Chase, Md.; died in Washington, D.C., February 9, 1980; interment in Arlington National Cemetery, Va.

**Bibliography:** *DAB.*

**ELLIS, Edgar Clarence,** a Representative from Missouri; born in Vermontville, Eaton County, Mich., October 2, 1854; attended Olivet (Mich.) College, and was graduated from Carleton College, Northfield, Minn., in 1881; instructor in Latin at Carleton College in 1881 and 1882; superintendent of the public schools at Fergus Falls, Minn., 1882-1885; studied law; was admitted to the bar and commenced practice in Beloit, Kans., in 1885; moved to Kansas City, Mo., in 1888 and continued the practice of his profession; elected as a Republican to the Fifty-ninth and Sixtieth Congresses (March 4, 1905-March 3, 1909); unsuccessful candidate for reelection in 1908 to the Sixty-first Congress; resumed the practice of law in Kansas City, Mo.; appointed a member of the Missouri Waterway Commission and served in 1911 and 1912; elected to the Sixty-seventh Congress (March 4, 1921-March 3, 1923); unsuccessful candidate for reelection in 1922 to the Sixty-eighth Congress; elected to the Sixty-ninth Congress (March 4, 1925-March 3, 1927); unsuccessful candidate for reelection in 1926 to the Seventieth Congress; elected to the Seventy-first Congress (March 4, 1929-March 3, 1931); unsuccessful candidate for reelection in 1930 to the Seventy-second Congress; retired from law practice and political life; died in St. Petersburg, Fla., March 15, 1947; remains were cremated and the ashes interred in Kansas City, Mo.

**ELLIS, Ezekiel John,** a Representative from Louisiana; born in Covington, St. Tammany Parish, La., October 15, 1840; attended private schools in Covington and Clinton, La., and Centenary College, Jackson, La., 1855-1858; was graduated from the law department of the Louisiana State University at Pineville (now at Baton Rouge), La., in 1861; during the Civil War joined the Confederate Army and was commissioned a first lieutenant; was promoted to captain in the Sixteenth Regiment, Louisiana Infantry, and served two years, when he was captured and held as a prisoner of war on Johnsons Island in Lake Erie until the end of the war; was admitted to the bar of Louisiana in 1866 and commenced practice in Covington, La.; member of the State senate 1866-1870; elected as a Democrat to the Forty-fourth and to the four succeeding Congresses (March 4, 1875-March 3, 1885); chairman, Committee on Mississippi Levees (Forty-fourth Congress); declined to be a candidate for renomination in 1884; resumed the practice of his profession in Washington, D.C., where he died April 25, 1889; interment in the Ellis family cemetery at "Ingleside," near Amite, Tangipahoa Parish, La.

**ELLIS, Hubert Summers,** a Representative from West Virginia; born in Hurricane, Putnam County, W.Va., July 6, 1887; attended the public schools and Marshall College, Huntington, W.Va.; engaged in banking and as a salesman 1910-1917 and in the general insurance business in 1920; served overseas as a first lieutenant in the One Hundred and Fiftieth Field Artillery, Forty-second Division, 1917-1919; elected as a Republican to the Seventy-eighth, Seventy-ninth, and Eightieth Congresses (January 3, 1943-January 3, 1949); unsuccessful candidate for reelection in 1948 to the Eighty-first Congress, and for election in 1950 to the Eighty-second Congress; appointed West Virginia director for the Federal Housing Administration February 2, 1954, and resigned February 10, 1958; died in Huntington, W.Va., December 3, 1959; interment in Woodmere Cemetery.

**ELLIS, Powhatan,** a Senator from Mississippi; born at "Red Hill," Amherst County, Va., January 17, 1790; was graduated from Washington Academy (now Washington and Lee University), Lexington, Va., in 1809; attended Dickinson College, Carlisle, Pa., 1809-1810; studied law at William and Mary College, Williamsburg, Va., 1813-1814; was admitted to the bar and commenced practice in Lynchburg, Va.; moved to Natchez, Miss., in 1816 and continued the practice of law; judge of the Mississippi State supreme court, 1823-1825; appointed to the United States Senate to fill the vacancy caused by the resignation of David Holmes, and served from September 28, 1825 to January 28, 1826, when a successor was elected and qualified; unsuccessful candidate for election to fill the vacancy; elected to the United States Senate and served from March 4, 1827, to July 16, 1832, when he resigned to accept a judicial position; judge of the United States court for the district of Mississippi 1832-1836; appointed by President Andrew Jackson Chargé d'Affaires of the United States to Mexico on January 5, 1836 and served until December 1836, when he closed the legation; appointed Minister Plenipotentiary to Mexico by President Martin Van Buren on February 15, 1839, and served until April 1842; moved to Richmond, Va., where he died on March 18, 1863; interment in Shockoe Cemetery.

**Bibliography:** *DAB*; Cobb, Edwin L. "Powhatan Ellis of Mississippi: A Reappraisal." *Journal of Mississippi History* 30 (May 1968): 91-110.

**ELLIS, William Cox,** a Representative from Pennsylvania; born in Fort Muncy, Pa., May 5, 1787; attended the public schools, and was graduated from the Friends' School near Pennsdale, Lycoming County, Pa., in 1803; deputy surveyor general 1803-1810; cashier of the Union and Northumberland County Bank 1810-1818; studied law; was admitted to the bar in 1817 and commenced practice in Muncy, Pa.; elected in 1820 to the Seventeenth Congress, but resigned before the Congress assembled; unsuccessful candidate for reelection to fill the vacancy caused by his own resignation; elected to the Eighteenth Congress (March 4, 1823-March 3, 1825); member of the Pennsylvania house of representatives in 1825 and 1826; became affiliated with the Republican Party in 1856; resumed the practice of law in Muncy, Pa., and died there December 13, 1871; interment in Muncy Cemetery.

**ELLIS, William Russell,** a Representative from Oregon; born near Waveland, Montgomery County, Ind., April 23, 1850; moved with his parents to Guthrie County, Iowa, in 1855; attended the district schools and the Iowa State Agricultural College at Ames; was graduated from the law department of the University of Iowa at Iowa City in 1874; was admitted to the bar and commenced practice in Panora, Iowa; mayor of Panora for one term; moved to Hamburg,

Iowa, where he continued the practice of law, and also engaged in newspaper work; served two years as city attorney; mayor of Hamburg in 1880 and 1881; moved to Heppner, Oreg., in 1884; superintendent of schools of Morrow County in 1885 and 1886; district attorney of the seventh judicial district of Oregon 1886-1892; elected as a Republican to the Fifty-third, Fifty-fourth, and Fifty-fifth Congresses (March 4, 1893-March 3, 1899); chairman, Committee on Expenditures in the Department of Justice (Fifty-fourth Congress), Committee on Irrigation of Arid Lands (Fifty-fifth Congress); unsuccessful candidate for renomination in 1898; circuit judge of the sixth judicial district of Oregon from July 10, 1900, to July 1, 1906; moved to Pendleton in 1901 and practiced law; elected to the Sixtieth and Sixty-first Congresses (March 4, 1907-March 3, 1911); unsuccessful candidate for renomination in 1910; resumed the practice of law in Pendleton, Oreg.; in July 1914 moved to Portland, Oreg., where he died January 18, 1915; interment in a mausoleum in Portland Crematorium.

**ELLIS, William Thomas,** a Representative from Kentucky; born near Knottsville, Daviess County, Ky., on July 24, 1845; attended the common schools; enlisted in 1861, at the age of sixteen, in the First Kentucky Confederate Cavalry, which became a part of the celebrated Orphan Brigade, and served with his regiment continuously until April 21, 1865; attended Pleasant Valley Seminary, Daviess County; principal of Mount Etna Academy, Ohio County, in 1867 and 1868; studied law and was admitted to the bar in 1868; was graduated from the Harvard Law School in 1870 and commenced practice in Owensboro, Ky., the same year; elected county attorney in 1870 and 1874; unsuccessful candidate for election in 1886 to the Fiftieth Congress; elected as a Democrat to the Fifty-first, Fifty-second, and Fifty-third Congresses (March 4, 1889-March 3, 1895); chairman, Committee on Revision of the Laws (Fifty-second and Fifty-third Congresses); declined to be a candidate for renomination in 1894; delegate to the Democratic National Convention in 1896; resumed the practice of law; also engaged in literary pursuits; died in Owensboro, Ky., January 8, 1925; interment in Elmwood Cemetery.

**ELLISON, Andrew,** a Representative from Ohio; born in West Union, Adams County, Ohio, in 1812; attended the public schools; studied law; was admitted to the bar in Adams County, Ohio, in August 1835 and commenced practice in Georgetown, Brown County, Ohio, the same year; elected prosecuting attorney of Brown County and served from 1840 to 1843; member of the State house of representatives in 1846; elected as a Democrat to the Thirty-third Congress (March 4, 1853-March 3, 1855); unsuccessful candidate for reelection in 1854 to the Thirty-fourth Congress; resumed the practice of law; died about 1860.

**ELLISON, Daniel,** a Representative from Maryland; born in Russia, February 14, 1886; as an infant, was brought to the United States by his parents; attended the public schools of Baltimore, Md.; was graduated from Johns Hopkins University, Baltimore, Md., in 1907 and from the law department of the University of Maryland at Baltimore in 1909; was admitted to the bar the same year and commenced practice in Baltimore, Md.; served as a member of the Baltimore city council 1923-1942; elected as a Republican to the Seventy-eighth Congress (January 3, 1943-January 3, 1945); unsuccessful candidate for reelection in 1944 to the Seventy-ninth Congress; resumed the practice of law in Baltimore, Md.; member of the State senate 1946-1950; died in Baltimore, Md., August 20, 1960, interment in Hebrew Friendship Cemetery.

**ELLMAKER, Amos,** a Representative from Pennsylvania; born at "Walnut Bottom" farm, Leacock Township, Lancaster County, Pa., February 2, 1787; attended the common schools; was graduated from Princeton College; studied law in Lancaster, Pa., and Litchfield, Conn.; was admitted to the bar and commenced practice in Harrisburg, Pa.; deputy attorney general for Dauphin County,

1809-1815; member of the Pennsylvania house of representatives in 1813 and 1814; elected to the Fourteenth Congress, but did not qualify, having been appointed and commissioned president judge of the twelfth judicial district on July 3, 1815, and served until his resignation on December 21, 1816; attorney general of Pennsylvania, 1816-1819; moved to Lancaster, Pa., in 1821 and resumed the practice of law; again attorney general of Pennsylvania in 1828 and 1829; unsuccessful candidate for Vice President of the United States in 1832 on the Anti-Masonic ticket headed by William Wirt; unsuccessful candidate for the United States Senate in 1833; continued the practice of law until his death in Lancaster, Pa., November 28, 1851; interment in St. James' Episcopal Churchyard.

**ELLSBERRY, William Wallace,** a Representative from Ohio; born in New Hope, Brown County, Ohio, December 18, 1833; attended the public schools of Brown County and a private academy in Clermont County; taught school two years; began the study of medicine with his father; attended medical lectures and was graduated from the Cincinnati College of Medicine and Surgery, and later from the Ohio Medical College; engaged in the practice of his profession at Georgetown, Ohio, until his election to Congress; county auditor; delegate to the Democratic National Convention in 1880; elected as a Democrat to the Forty-ninth Congress (March 4, 1885-March 3, 1887); was not a candidate for renomination in 1886; resumed the practice of medicine until his death in Georgetown, Brown County, Ohio, September 7, 1894; interment in Confidence Cemetery.

**ELLSWORTH, Charles Clinton,** a Representative from Michigan; born in West Berkshire, Franklin County, Vt., January 29, 1824; attended the common schools of West Berkshire and the academy at Bakersfield, Vt.; taught school in Vermont one winter; moved to Howell, Livingston County, Mich.; taught school one term; studied law; was admitted to the bar in 1848 and commenced practice in Howell, Mich.; prosecuting attorney of Livingston County in 1849; moved to Montcalm County and settled in Greenville in 1851; served as the first president of the village; member of the State house of representatives 1852-1854; prosecuting attorney of Montcalm County in 1853; served in the Union Army as paymaster with the rank of major in 1862; elected as a Republican to the Forty-fifth Congress (March 4, 1877-March 3, 1879); was not a candidate for renomination in 1878; resumed the practice of law; died in Greenville, Mich., June 25, 1899; interment in Forest Home Cemetery.

**ELLSWORTH, Franklin Fowler,** a Representative from Minnesota; born in St. James, Watonwan County, Minn., July 10, 1879; attended the grade and high schools; enlisted as a private in Company H, Twelfth Regiment, Minnesota Volunteer Infantry, during the Spanish-American War; attended the law department of the University of Minnesota at Minneapolis; was admitted to the bar in 1901 and commenced practice in St. James, Minn.; city attorney of St. James in 1904 and 1905; prosecuting attorney of Watonwan County 1905-1909; elected as a Republican to the Sixty-fourth and to the two succeeding Congresses (March 4, 1915-March 3, 1921); was not a candidate for renomination in 1920 to the Sixty-seventh Congress, having become a gubernatorial candidate; unsuccessful candidate for nomination for Governor of Minnesota in 1920 and 1924; moved to Minneapolis in 1921 and resumed the practice of his profession; died in Minneapolis, Minn., December 23, 1942; interment in Lakewood Cemetery.

**ELLSWORTH, Mathew Harris,** a Representative from Oregon; born in Hoquiam, Grays Harbor County, Wash., September 17, 1899; moved with his parents to Eugene and later to Wendling, Oreg.; attended the public schools; served in the Student Army Training Corps during the First World War; was graduated in journalism from the University of Oregon at Eugene in 1922; advertising manager of a newspaper in Eugene, Oreg., in 1923;

engaged in the lumber business, 1923-1925; manager of a lumber-industry publication, 1926-1928; associate professor in journalism at the University of Oregon in 1928 and 1929; publisher and part owner of the Roseburg (Oreg.) News-Review beginning in 1929; served by appointment in the Oregon State senate in 1941; elected as a Republican to the Seventy-eighth and to the six succeeding Congresses (January 3, 1943-January 3, 1957); unsuccessful candidate for reelection in 1956 to the Eighty-fifth Congress; appointed by President Dwight D. Eisenhower as chairman of the Civil Service Commission for a two-year term and served from April 18, 1957, to February 28, 1959; resumed the newspaper business profession; real estate broker; moved to Albuquerque, N.Mex., in 1975 and lived there until his death on February 7, 1986; interment in Gate of Heaven Cemetery.

**ELLSWORTH, Oliver** (father of William Wolcott Ellsworth), a Delegate and a Senator from Connecticut; born in Windsor, Conn., April 29, 1745; pursued preparatory studies; attended Yale College and was graduated from the College of New Jersey (now Princeton University) in 1766; studied law; was admitted to the bar in 1771 and commenced practice in Windsor; moved to Hartford, Conn., in 1775; member, Connecticut State general assembly, 1773-1776; appointed State attorney in 1777; Member of the Continental Congress, 1778-1783; member of the Governor's council, 1780-1785; judge of the Connecticut Superior Court, 1785-1789; delegate to the convention that framed the federal Constitution in 1787; elected to the United States Senate, reelected and served from March 4, 1789 until March 8, 1796, when he resigned to accept a judicial appointment; nominated by President George Washington as Chief Justice of the United States on March 3, 1796, confirmed by the Senate the following day, and served until September 30, 1800, when he resigned; appointed Envoy Extraordinary and Minister Plenipotentiary to France to negotiate a treaty in 1799; returned to the United States in 1801; again a member of the Governor's council, 1801-1807; died in Windsor, Conn., November 26, 1807; interment in the Old Cemetery.

Bibliography: *DAB*; Brown, William. *The Life of Oliver Ellsworth.* 1905. Reprint. New York: Da Capo Press, 1970; Lettieri, Ronald John. *Connecticut's Young Man of the Revolution: Oliver Ellsworth.* Hartford: American Revolution Bicentennial Commission of Connecticut, 1978.

**ELLSWORTH, Robert Fred,** a Representative from Kansas; born in Lawrence, Douglas County, Kans., June 11, 1926; attended the Lawrence, Kans., schools; B.S., University of Kansas, 1945; J.D., University of Michigan School of Law, 1949; served as an officer in the United States Navy, 1944-1946, and again during the Korean War, 1950-1953; teacher at the University of Kansas School of Business, 1954-1955; admitted to the Kansas and Massachusetts bar in 1949 and commenced practice in Springfield, Mass.; assistant to vice chairman Robert W. Williams of the Federal Maritime Board in 1953 and 1954; private law practice in Lawrence, Kans., 1955-1960; elected as a Republican to the Eighty-seventh and to the two succeeding Congresses (January 3, 1961-January 3, 1967); was not a candidate in 1966 for reelection to the House of Representatives, but was an unsuccessful candidate for nomination to the United States Senate; National Political Director of the 1968 presidential campaign of Richard M. Nixon; special assistant to President Nixon, 1969; appointed Permanent Representative on the Council of the North Atlantic Treaty Organization, with rank of Ambassador, on May 13, 1969 and served until June 30, 1971; general partner in Lazard Freres and Co. of New York City; Assistant Secretary of Defense for International Security Affairs, 1974-1975; nominated by President Gerald R. Ford to be Deputy Secretary of Defense, and served in that capacity from December 1975 until January 1977; vice chairman of the council, International Institute for Strategic Studies, London, 1977 to present; president of a private investment and consulting firm in Washington, D.C.;

adviser to the presidential campaign of Robert J. Dole, 1996; is a resident of Comus, Md.

**ELLSWORTH, Samuel Stewart,** a Representative from New York; born in Pownal, Vt., October 13, 1790; attended the common schools; moved to Penn Yan, N.Y., in 1819 and engaged in mercantile pursuits; supervisor of Milo, Yates County, 1824-1828; judge of Yates County 1824-1829; served in the State assembly in 1840; elected as a Democrat to the Twenty-ninth Congress (March 4, 1845-March 3, 1847); died in Penn Yan, N.Y., June 4, 1863; interment in Lake View Cemetery.

**ELLSWORTH, William Wolcott** (son of Oliver Ellsworth), a Representative from Connecticut; born in Windsor, Conn., November 10, 1791; completed preparatory studies, and was graduated from Yale College in 1810; studied law in Litchfield, Conn.; was admitted to the bar in 1813 and practiced; appointed professor of law at Trinity College, Hartford, Conn., in 1827, which position he held until his death; elected to the Twenty-first and to the two succeeding Congresses and served from March 4, 1829, to July 8, 1834, when he resigned; unsuccessful candidate for election in 1837 for Governor; elected Governor of Connecticut in 1838; reelected in 1839, 1840 and 1841, and served from May 2, 1838 to May 4, 1842; unsuccessful candidate for reelection in 1842; judge of the State supreme court from 1847 to 1861, when, by the constitutional provision relative to age, he was retired; twice declined to accept the nomination to the United States Senate; retired from public life; died in Hartford, Conn., January 15, 1868; interment in the Old North Cemetery.

Bibliography: *DAB*.

**ELLWOOD, Reuben,** a Representative from Illinois; born in Minden, Montgomery County, N.Y., February 21, 1821; attended the public schools and Cherry Valley Seminary, New York; manufacturer of agricultural implements; member of the New York State assembly in 1851; moved to Sycamore, Ill., about 1854; resumed manufacturing interests and engaged in the hardware business; elected as a Republican to the Forty-eighth and Forty-ninth Congresses and served from March 4, 1883, until his death, before the assembling of the Forty-ninth Congress, in Sycamore, Ill., July 1, 1885; interment in Elmwood Cemetery.

**ELLZEY, Lawrence Russell,** a Representative from Mississippi; born on a farm near Wesson, Copiah County, Miss., March 20, 1891; attended the rural schools and was graduated from Mississippi College at Clinton, A.B., 1912; attended the University of Chicago in 1927; engaged as a teacher in the consolidated county schools of Mississippi 1912-1917; volunteered as a private in the Quartermaster Corps on December 13, 1917, and served overseas nine months before being discharged as a first lieutenant on February 20, 1919; served as superintendent of education of Lincoln County, Miss., 1920-1922; teacher in the agricultural high school Wesson, Miss., 1922-1928; served as president of Copiah-Lincoln Junior College, Wesson, Miss., 1928-1932; elected as a Democrat to the Seventy-second Congress, by special election, March 15, 1932, to fill the vacancy caused by the death of Percy E. Quin; reelected to the Seventy-third Congress and served from March 15, 1932, to January 3, 1935; unsuccessful candidate for renomination in 1934 to the Seventy-fourth Congress; engaged in the life insurance business; executive secretary for the Mississippi Salvage Campaign in 1942 and 1943; resided in Jackson, Miss., where he died December 7, 1977; interment in Wesson Cemetery, Wesson, Miss.

**ELMENDORF, Lucas Conrad,** a Representative from New York; born in Kingston, N.Y., in 1758; was graduated from Princeton College in 1782; studied law; was admitted to the bar in 1785 and practiced; unsuccessful candidate in 1794 for election to the Fourth Congress; elected as a Republican to the Fifth, Sixth, and Seventh Congresses (March 4, 1797-March 3, 1803); declined to be a candidate for renomination in 1802; member of the State assembly in 1804 and 1805; served in the State senate 1814-1817; first judge of the court of common pleas (now county court) of Ulster County and served from 1815 to 1821; surrogate of Ulster County 1835-1840; died in Kingston, N.Y., August 17, 1843; interment in the crypt of the First Dutch Church.

**ELMER, Ebenezer** (brother of Jonathan Elmer and father of Lucius Quintius Cincinnatus Elmer), a Representative from New Jersey; born in Cedarville, Cumberland County, N.J., August 23, 1752; pursued an academic course; studied medicine and practiced in Cedarville; served in the Revolutionary Army as ensign, lieutenant, surgeon's mate, and regimental surgeon; practiced medicine in Bridgeton, N.J., 1783-1789; member of the State general assembly 1789-1795, serving as speaker in 1791 and 1795; elected as a Republican to the Seventh, Eighth, and Ninth Congresses (March 4, 1801-March 3, 1807); was not a candidate for renomination in 1806; member of the State council in 1807, and was chosen vice president of that body; collector of customs of Bridgeton from 1808 until 1817, when he resigned; reappointed in 1822 and served until 1832, when he again resigned; served in the War of 1812; adjutant general of the New Jersey Militia and brigadier general of the Cumberland brigade; vice president of Burlington College 1808-1817 and 1822-1832; retired from public life; died in Bridgeton, N.J., on October 18, 1843; interment in the Presbyterian Cemetery.

**Bibliography:** *DAB.*

**ELMER, Jonathan** (brother of Ebenezer Elmer and uncle of Lucius Quintius Cincinnatus Elmer), a Delegate and a Senator from New Jersey; born in Cedarville, Cumberland County, N.J., November 29, 1745; completed preparatory studies; was graduated from the first medical class of the University of Pennsylvania at Philadelphia in 1769 and practiced in Bridgeton, N.J.; high sheriff of Cumberland County 1772; was chosen captain of a light infantry company 1775; Member of the Continental Congress 1777-1778, 1781-1783, and 1787-1788; member, State council 1780, 1784; trustee of the College of New Jersey (now Princeton University) 1782-1795; surrogate of Cumberland County 1784-1802; president of the State medical society 1787; elected to the United States Senate and served from March 4, 1789, to March 3, 1791; appointed presiding judge of the county court of common pleas in 1802 and served until his resignation in 1804; appointed to the same office in the winter of 1813, but, in February 1814, declined to serve further because of impaired health; died in Bridgeton, N.J., September 3, 1817; interment in the Old Presbyterian Cemetery.

**Bibliography:** *DAB.*

**ELMER, Lucius Quintius Cincinnatus** (son of Ebenezer Elmer and nephew of Jonathan Elmer), a Representative from New Jersey; born in Bridgeton, N.J., February 3, 1793; attended the private schools and was graduated from the University of Pennsylvania at Philadelphia; during the War of 1812 served in the militia as a lieutenant of artillery, and was promoted to the rank of brigade major and inspector; studied law; was admitted to the bar in 1815 and commenced practice in Bridgeton, N.J.; prosecuting attorney for the State in 1824; member of the State general assembly 1820-1823, serving the last year as speaker; prosecutor of the pleas for Cumberland County in 1824; United States district attorney for the district of New Jersey 1824-1829; elected as a Democrat to the Twenty-eighth Congress (March 4, 1843-March 3, 1845); chairman, Committee on Elections (Twenty-eighth Congress); unsuccessful for reelection in 1844 to the Twenty-ninth Congress; attorney general of New Jersey 1850-1852; justice of the State supreme court from 1852 until 1869 when he retired; died in Bridgeton, N.J., on March 11, 1883; interment in Bridgeton Cemetery.

**Bibliography:** *DAB.*

**ELMER, William Price,** a Representative from Missouri; born in Robertsville, Franklin County, Mo., March 2, 1871; attended the public schools and Wingo Law School, Salem, Mo.; was admitted to the bar in 1892 and commenced practice in Salem, Mo.; prosecuting attorney for Dent County, Mo., in 1895 and 1896 and again in 1905 and 1906; member of the State house of representatives in 1903, 1904, 1921, 1922, and 1929-1933, serving as temporary speaker and floor leader in 1929; city attorney of Salem, Mo., 1920-1930; delegate or alternate to the Republican National Conventions of 1904, 1908, 1912, and 1920; chairman of the Republican county committee 1908-1944; member of the 1929 commission to revise Missouri laws; unsuccessful candidate for lieutenant governor in 1940; elected as a Republican to the Seventy-eighth Congress (January 3, 1943-January 3, 1945); unsuccessful candidate for reelection in 1944 to the Seventy-ninth Congress; unsuccessful candidate for the Republican nomination for United States Senator in 1946; resumed the practice of law; director of First National Bank of Salem; member of board of curators of University of Missouri 1949-1955; died in Salem, Mo., May 11, 1956; interment in Cedar Grove Cemetery.

**ELMORE, Franklin Harper,** a Representative and a Senator from South Carolina; born in Laurens District, S.C., October 15, 1799; was graduated from the South Carolina College at Columbia in 1819; studied law; was admitted to the bar in 1821 and commenced practice in Walterboro, S.C.; solicitor for the southern circuit, 1822-1836; colonel on the staff of Governor Richard I. Manning, 1824-1826; elected as a State Rights Democrat to the Twenty-fourth Congress to fill the vacancy caused by the resignation of James H. Hammond; reelected to the Twenty-fifth Congress, and served from December 10, 1836 to March 3, 1839; president of the Bank of the State of South Carolina, 1839-1850; declined appointment by President James K. Polk as Minister to Great Britain; appointed as a Democrat to the United States Senate to fill the vacancy caused by the death of John C. Calhoun, and served from April 11, 1850 until his death in Washington, D.C., May 29, 1850; interment in First Presbyterian Churchyard, Columbia, S.C.

**Bibliography:** *DAB*; Birney, James. *Correspondence Between the Honorable F.H. Elmore and James G. Birney.* 1838. Reprint. New York: Arno Press, 1969.'5

**ELSAESSER, Edward Julius,** a Representative from New York; born in Buffalo, Erie County, N.Y., March 10, 1904; attended the public schools; was graduated from the law department of the University of Buffalo, Buffalo, N.Y., in 1926; was admitted to the bar in 1927 and commenced practice in Buffalo, N.Y.; Republican State committeeman 1937-1945; elected as a Republican to the Seventy-ninth and Eightieth Congresses (January 3, 1945-January 3, 1949); unsuccessful candidate for reelection in 1948 to the Eighty-first Congress; unsuccessful candidate for nomination to the Eighty-second Congress in 1950; resumed the practice of law; was a resident of Williamsville, N.Y., until his death there on January 7, 1983; interment in Williamsville Cemetery.

**ELSTON, Charles Henry,** a Representative from Ohio; born in Marietta, Washington County, Ohio, August 1, 1891; attended the public schools of Marietta and Cincinnati, Ohio; Y.M.C.A. Law School, Cincinnati, Ohio, LL.B., 1914; was admitted to the bar the same year and commenced practice in Cincinnati, Ohio; assistant prosecuting attorney of Hamilton County, Ohio, 1915-1922; member of the faculty of the Y.M.C.A. Law school 1916-1936; during the First World War served as an aviation cadet in the aviation service of the United States Army; member of the Hamilton County Charter Commission; elected as a Republican to the Seventy-sixth and to the six succeeding Congresses (January 3, 1939-January 3, 1953); was not a candidate for renomination in 1952; resumed the practice of law in Cincinnati, Ohio; was a resident of Fort Lauderdale, Fla., where he died September 25, 1980; interment in Lauderdale Memorial Gardens, Fort Lauderdale, Fla.

**ELSTON, John Arthur,** a Representative from California; born in Woodland, Yolo County, Calif., February 10, 1874; attended the public schools; was graduated from Hesperian College, Woodland, Calif., in 1892 and the University of California at Berkeley in 1897; engaged in educational work; studied law; was admitted to the bar in 1901 and commenced practice in Berkeley, Calif.; executive secretary to Governor George C. Pardee of California 1903-1907; member of the board of trustees of the State Institution for the Deaf and Blind 1911-1914; elected as a Progressive to the Sixty-fourth Congress and reelected as a Republican to the three succeeding Congresses and served from March 4, 1915, until his death in Washington, D.C., December 15, 1921; chairman, Committee on Mileage (Sixty-sixth Congress); remains were cremated and the ashes placed in the California Crematorium at Oakland.

**ELTSE, Ralph Roscoe,** a Representative from California; born in Oskaloosa, Mahaska County, Iowa, September 13, 1885; attended the public schools; was graduated from Penn College; Oskaloosa, Iowa, in 1909 and from Haverford (Pa.) College in 1910; moved to Berkeley, Alameda County, Calif., in 1912; attended the law department of the University of California at Berkeley; was admitted to the bar in 1915 and commenced practice in Berkeley, Calif.; member of the Republican State committee 1932-1935; delegate to the Republican State conventions in 1932, 1934, and 1940; elected as a Republican to the Seventy-third Congress (March 4, 1933-January 3, 1935); unsuccessful candidate for reelection in 1934 to the Seventy-fourth Congress and for election in 1940 to the Seventy-seventh Congress; resumed the practice of law; resided in Berkeley, Calif., where he died March 18, 1971; entombment in Sunset Mausoleum.

**ELVINS, Politte,** a Representative from Missouri; born in French Village, St. Francois County, Mo., March 16, 1878; attended the public schools; was graduated from Carleton College, Farmington, Mo., in 1897 and from the law department of the University of Missouri at Columbia in 1899; was admitted to the bar the same year and commenced practice in Elvins, Mo.; elected as a Republican to the Sixty-first Congress (March 4, 1909-March 3, 1911); unsuccessful candidate for reelection in 1910 to the Sixty-second Congress; resumed the practice of law in Elvins, Mo.; delegate to the Republican National Convention in 1912; chairman of the State Republican committee 1912-1914; moved to Bonne Terre, Mo., in 1917 and continued the practice of law; member and chairman of the committee on rules and order of business for the Missouri constitutional convention in 1922 and 1923; moved to Pharr, Hidalgo County, Tex., in 1936; unsuccessful candidate to the United States Senate in 1940; died at McAllen, Tex., January 14, 1943; remains cremated.

**ELY, Alfred,** a Representative from New York; born in Lyme, New London County, Conn., February 15, 1815; attended the common schools and Bacon Academy at Colchester, Conn.; moved to Rochester, N.Y., in 1835; studied law; was admitted to the bar in 1841 and commenced practice in Rochester; elected as a Republican to the Thirty-sixth and Thirty-seventh Congresses (March 4, 1859-March 3, 1863); chairman, Committee on Invalid Pensions (Thirty-seventh Congress); was not a candidate for renomination in 1862 to the Thirty-eighth Congress; while witnessing the First Battle of Bull Run, July 21, 1861, was taken prisoner by the Confederates, and imprisoned in Richmond for nearly six months; resumed the practice of law; died in Rochester, N.Y., May 18, 1892; interment in the Ely vault in Mount Hope Cemetery.

**ELY, Frederick David,** a Representative from Massachusetts; born in Wrentham, Norfolk County, Mass., September 24, 1838; attended Day's Academy, Wrentham, and was graduated from Brown University, Providence, R.I., in 1859; studied law; was admitted to the bar and commenced practice at Dedham, Mass., in 1862; trial justice 1867-1885; member of the Massachusetts house of representatives in 1873; served in the Massachusetts senate in 1878 and 1879; member of the school committee of Dedham 1882-1894; elected as a Republican to the Forty-ninth Congress (March 4, 1885-March 3, 1887); unsuccessful candidate for reelection in 1886 to the Fiftieth Congress; resumed the practice of law; justice of the municipal court of Boston 1888-1914; died in Dedham, Mass., August 6, 1921; interment in Old Parish Cemetery.

**ELY, John,** a Representative from New York; born in Saybrook, Conn., October 8, 1774; completed preparatory studies; studied medicine, and practiced in Coxsackie, N.Y.; member of the State assembly in 1806 and 1812; one of the organizers of the New York State and Greene County Medical Societies in 1807 and also of the Albany Female Academy; elected as a Democrat to the Twenty-sixth Congress (March 4, 1839-March 3, 1841); resumed the practice of medicine; died in Coxsackie, N.Y., August 20, 1849; interment in Old Coxsackie Cemetery.

**ELY, Smith, Jr.,** a Representative from New York; born in Hanover, Morris County, N.J., April 17, 1825; completed preparatory studies; was graduated from the New York University Law School, New York City, in 1846; was admitted to the bar the same year, but never practiced his profession; engaged in mercantile pursuits in New York City; served as school commissioner 1856-1860; served in the State senate in 1858 and 1859; county supervisor in 1860-1870; commissioner of public instruction in 1867; elected as a Democrat to the Forty-second Congress (March 4, 1871-March 3, 1873); was not a candidate for renomination in 1872; elected to the Forty-fourth Congress and served from March 4, 1875, to December 11, 1876, when he resigned; chairman, Committee on Expenditures in the Department of the Treasury (Forty-fourth Congress); mayor of New York City in 1877 and 1878; appointed commissioner of parks in 1895 and served until 1897, when he retired from public life; died in Livingston, Essex County, N.J., July 1, 1911; interment in a private cemetery on his farm at Livingston.

**ELY, William,** a Representative from Massachusetts; born in Longmeadow, Mass., August 14, 1765; completed preparatory studies; was graduated from Yale College in 1787; studied law; was admitted to the bar in 1791 and commenced practice in Springfield, Mass.; member of the Massachusetts house of representatives 1801-1803; elected as a Federalist to the Ninth and to the four succeeding Congresses (March 4, 1805-March 3, 1815); again a member of the State house of representatives in 1815 and 1816; died in Springfield, Mass., October 9, 1817, and was buried there.

**EMBREE, Elisha,** a Representative from Indiana; born in Lincoln County, Ky., September 28, 1801; moved to Indiana in 1811 with his father, who settled in Knox (now Gibson) County, near where Princeton was subsequently located; received limited schooling; engaged in agricultural pursuits; studied law; was admitted to the bar in 1836 and commenced practice in Princeton, Gibson County, Ind.; circuit judge for the fourth circuit of Indiana 1835-1845; was nominated as the Whig candidate for Governor of Indiana in 1849, but declined, preferring to run for Congress; elected as a Whig to the Thirtieth Congress (March 4, 1847-March 3, 1849); unsuccessful candidate for reelection in 1848 to the Thirty-first Congress; resumed the practice of law and also interested in farming; died in Princeton, Ind., February 28, 1863; interment in Warnock Cemetery.

**EMERICH, Martin,** a Representative from Illinois; born in Baltimore, Md., April 27, 1846; attended the public schools; engaged in the importing business; appointed ward commissioner of the poor of Baltimore in 1870; member of the Maryland State house of delegates 1881-1883; aide-de-camp to Governor William T. Hamilton 1880-1884, and to Governor Elihu E. Jackson 1884-1887; moved to Chicago, Ill., in 1887 and engaged in mercantile pursuits until 1896, when he engaged in the manufacture of bricks; member of the Board of Commissioners of Cook County 1892-1894; assessor of South Chicago 1897; elected as a Democrat to the Fifty-eighth Congress (March 4, 1903-March 3, 1905); was not a candidate for renomination in 1904 to the Fifty-ninth Congress; retired in 1907; died while on a visit in New York City, September 27, 1922; interment in Rosehill Cemetery, Chicago, Ill.

**EMERSON, Henry Ivory,** a Representative from Ohio; born in Litchfield, Kennebec County, Maine, March 15, 1871; moved with his parents to Lewiston, Maine, where he attended the public schools and studied law; moved to Cleveland, Ohio, in 1892 and was graduated from the Cincinnati Law School in 1893; was admitted to the bar the same year and commenced practice in Cleveland, Ohio; member of the Cleveland City Council in 1902 and 1903; elected as a Republican to the Sixty-fourth, Sixty-fifth, and Sixty-sixth Congresses (March 4, 1915-March 3, 1921); unsuccessful candidate for renomination in 1920; resumed the practice of law; died in East Cleveland, Ohio, October 28, 1953; interment in Lakeview Cemetery, Cleveland, Ohio.

**EMERSON, Louis Woodard,** a Representative from New York; born in Warrensburg, Warren County, N.Y., July 25, 1857; attended the district school and was graduated from Warrensburg Academy; engaged in the lumber, banking, and manufacturing business; delegate to the Republican National Conventions in 1888, 1892, and 1896; member of the State senate 1890-1893; elected as a Republican to the Fifty-sixth and Fifty-seventh Congresses (March 4, 1899-March 3, 1903); resumed former business activities in Warrensburg, N.Y., and died there June 10, 1924; interment in the City Cemetery.

**EMERSON, Norvell William,** a Representative from Missouri; born in St. Louis, Jefferson County, Mo., January 1, 1938; raised in Jefferson County and attended public schools in Hillsboro; served as a page in the United States House of Representatives, 1953-1955; graduated from the United States Capitol Page School, Washington, D.C., 1955; B.A., Westminster College, Fulton, Mo., 1959; attended University of Missouri Law School, Columbia, 1960; LL.B., University of Baltimore, Md., 1964; served in the United States Air Force Reserve as a captain; special assistant to Representative Robert F. Ellsworth, 1961-1965; administrative assistant to Representative and Senator Charles McC. Mathias, Jr., 1965-1970; director, government relations, Fairchild Industries, 1970-1973; director, public affairs, Interstate Natural Gas Association, 1974-1975; executive assistant to Chairman Thomas B. Curtis of the Federal Election Commission, 1975; director, federal relations, TRW, Inc., 1975-1979; president, N. William Emerson and Associates, government relations consultants, 1979-1980; elected as a Republican to the Ninety-seventh and to the seven succeeding Congresses, and served from January 3, 1981 until his death in the naval hospital at Bethesda, Md., June 22, 1996; interment in Hillsboro, Mo.

**EMERY, David Farnham,** a Representative from Maine; born in Rockland, Knox County, Maine, September 1, 1948; attended public schools; B.S., Worcester (Mass.) Polytechnic Institute, 1970; member, Maine State house of representatives, 1971-1974; chairman, Rockland Republican city committee, 1972; delegate to Maine State Republican convention, 1972; delegate to the Republican National Convention of 1972; elected as a Republican to the Ninety-fourth and to the three succeeding Congresses (January 3, 1975-January 3, 1983); was not a candidate in 1982 for reelection to the House of Representatives, but was an unsuccessful candidate for election to the United States Senate; deputy director, United States Arms Control and Disarmament Agency, 1983-1988; consultant; is a resident of Rockland, Maine.

**EMOTT, James,** a Representative from New York; born in Poughkeepsie, N.Y., March 9, 1771; completed preparatory studies; studied law; was admitted to the bar in 1790 and commenced practice in Ballson Center, N.Y.; land commissioner to settle disputes of titles to military reservations in Onondaga County in 1797; moved to Albany, N.Y., in 1800; member of the State assembly from Albany County in 1804, and served as speaker; elected as a Federalist to the Eleventh and Twelfth Congresses (March 4, 1809-March 3, 1813); member of the State assembly from Dutchess County 1814-1817, and served as speaker the first year; judge of the court of common pleas of Dutchess County from April 8, 1817, to February 3, 1823; appointed judge for the second judicial circuit February 21, 1827, and held that office until February 1831, when he retired; died in Poughkeepsie, Dutchess County, N.Y., April 7, 1850; interment in Poughkeepsie Rural Cemetery.

**Bibliography:** *DAB*.

**EMRIE, Jonas Reece,** a Representative from Ohio; born in Hillsboro, Highland County, Ohio, April 25, 1812; pursued preparatory studies; studied law; was admitted to the bar and commenced practice in Hillsboro, Ohio; editor and publisher of the Hillsboro Gazette 1839-1848 and 1854-1856; leader in organizing the Hillsboro Female College; appointed postmaster of Hillsboro April 8, 1839, and served until February 23, 1841; member of the State senate in 1847 and 1848; first probate judge of Highland County 1851-1854; elected as a Republican to the Thirty-fourth Congress (March 4, 1855-March 3, 1857); unsuccessful candidate for reelection in 1856 to the Thirty-fifth Congress; moved to Mound City, Pulaski County, Ill., in 1857; engaged in mercantile pursuits, conducted a newspaper, and practiced law; police magistrate of the city in 1858; township treasurer of schools; master in chancery of Pulaski County, Ill.; died in Mound City, Ill., June 5, 1869; interment in Beech Grove Cemetery.

**ENGEL, Albert Joseph,** a Representative from Michigan; born in New Washington, Crawford County, Ohio, January 1, 1888; attended the public schools in Grand Traverse County, Mich., and the Central Y.M.C.A., Chicago, Ill.; was graduated from the law department of Northwestern University, Evanston, Ill., in 1910; was admitted to the bar the same year and commenced practice in Lake City, Mich.; prosecuting attorney of Missaukee County, Mich., in 1916, 1917, 1919, and 1920; during the First World War served as a first lieutenant in the War Department, Washington, D.C., later being promoted to captain and served overseas for twenty-three months, 1917-1919; served in the Michigan State senate, 1921-1922 and 1927-1932; elected as a Republican to the Seventy-fourth and to the seven succeeding Congresses (January 3, 1935-January 3, 1951); was not a candidate for renomination in 1950 to the Eighty-second Congress, but was an unsuccessful candidate for nomination for Governor of Michigan; operated a 1,400-acre tree plantation near Lake City, Mich.; died in Grand Rapids, Mich., December 2, 1959; interment in Lake City Cemetery, Lake City, Mich.

**ENGEL, Eliot Lanze,** a Representative from New York; born in New York City, February 18, 1947; attended Bronx public schools; B.A., Hunter-Lehman College, 1969; M.S., Herbert H. Lehman College, City University of New York, 1973; J.D., New York University School of Law, 1987; teacher and counselor, New York City public school system, 1973-1975; member, New York State assembly, 1977-1988; elected as a Democrat to the One Hundred First and to the three succeeding Congresses (January 3, 1989-January 3, 1997); is a resident of Co-op City, Bronx County, N.Y.

**ENGLAND, Edward Theodore,** a Representative from West Virginia; born in Gay, Jackson County, W.Va., September 29, 1869; attended the public schools; was graduated from the Concord Normal School, Athens, W.Va., in 1892; taught school for several years; was graduated from the law department of Southern Normal University, Huntingdon, Tenn., in 1898; was admitted to the bar the same year and commenced practice in Oceana, W.Va.; moved to Logan, W.Va., in 1901 and continued the practice of law; elected mayor of Logan in 1903; member of the West Virginia State senate, 1908-1916; elected president of the State senate in 1915, and by virtue of this office was lieutenant governor in 1915 and 1916; presided over the first meeting of all lieutenant governors of the United States at Rhea Springs, Tenn., in 1915; elected attorney general of West Virginia, and served from 1917 to 1925; represented the State of West Virginia before the Supreme Court of the United States in the Virginia debt controversy; elected president of the Attorney Generals' Association of the United States at Minneapolis, Minn., in 1923; was an unsuccessful candidate for the Republican nomination for Governor in 1924; elected as a Republican to the Seventieth Congress (March 4, 1927-March 3, 1929); unsuccessful candidate for reelection in 1928 to the Seventy-first Congress; resumed the practice of law in Charleston, W.Va.; died in Cleveland, Ohio, September 9, 1934; interment in Sunset Memorial Park, Charleston, W.Va.

**ENGLE, Clair,** a Representative and a Senator from California; born in Bakersfield, Kern County, Calif., September 21, 1911; attended the public schools; was graduated from Chico (Calif.) State College in 1930 and from the University of California Hastings College of Law in 1933; was admitted to the bar in 1933 and commenced practice in Corning, Calif.; district attorney of Tehama County, Calif., 1934-1942; member, State senate 1943; elected as a Democrat to the Seventy-eighth Congress to fill the vacancy caused by the death of Harry L. Englebright; reelected to the Seventy-ninth and to the six succeeding Congresses (August 31, 1943-January 3, 1959); chairman, Committee on War Claims (Seventy-ninth Congress), Committee on Interior and Insular Affairs (Eighty-fourth and Eighty-fifth Congresses); was not a candidate for renomination in 1958, having become a candidate for United States Senator; elected as a Democrat to the United States Senate in 1958 and served from January 3, 1959, until his death in Washington, D.C., July 30, 1964; interment in Oak Hill Cemetery, Red Bluff, Calif.

Bibliography: *DAB*; Sayles, Stephen. "Clair Engle and the Politics of California Reclamation, 1943-1960." Ph.D. dissertation, University of New Mexico, 1978.

**ENGLEBRIGHT, Harry Lane** (son of William F. Englebright), a Representative from California; born in Nevada City, Nevada County, Calif., January 2, 1884; attended the public schools; attended the University of California at Berkeley; was graduated as a mining engineer, and followed his profession; mineral inspector for the field division of the General Land Office, and also engineer for the State Conservation Commission of California 1911-1914; actively connected with various mining enterprises in California; elected as a Republican to the Sixty-ninth Congress to fill the vacancy caused by the death of John E. Raker; reelected to the Seventieth and to the eight succeeding Congresses and served from August 31, 1926, until his death; minority whip (Seventy-third through Seventy-eighth Congresses); died in Bethesda, Md., May 13, 1943; interment in Pine Grove Cemetery, Nevada City, Calif.

**ENGLEBRIGHT, William Fellows** (father of Harry Lane Englebright), a Representative from California; born in New Bedford, Mass., November 23, 1855; moved with his parents to Vallejo, Calif.; attended private and public schools; entered the service of the United States at the navy yard, Mare Island, as joiner's apprentice and completed his studies in engineering; established himself in Nevada City, Calif., as a mining engineer; member of the Nevada City Board of Education; elected as a Republican to the Fifty-ninth Congress to fill the vacancy caused by the resignation of James N. Gillett; reelected to the Sixtieth and Sixty-first Congresses and served from November 6, 1906, to March 3, 1911; unsuccessful candidate for reelection in 1910 to the Sixty-second Congress; resumed his occupation as a mining engineer; died in Oakland, Calif., February 10, 1915; interment in Pine Grove Cemetery, Nevada City, Calif.

**ENGLISH, Glenn Lee, Jr.,** a Representative from Oklahoma; born in Cordell, Washita County, Okla., November 30, 1940; attended public schools; B.A., Southwestern State College, Weatherford, Okla., 1960-1964; served as staff sergeant in United States Army Reserves, 1965-1971; engaged in oil and gas leasing; served as chief assistant to the majority caucus of the California assembly in the United States House of Representatives, 1965-1968; executive director of the Oklahoma State Democratic Party, 1969-1973; elected as a Democrat to the Ninety-fourth and to the nine succeeding Congresses, and served from January 3, 1975 until his resignation on January 7, 1994; vice president and general manager, National Rural Electric Cooperative Association; is a resident of Cordell, Okla.

**ENGLISH, James Edward,** a Representative and a Senator from Connecticut; born in New Haven, Conn., March 13, 1812; attended the common schools; engaged in the lumber business, banking, and manufacturing; member of the New Haven board of selectmen from 1847 until 1861; member, common council, 1848-1849; member, Connecticut State house of representatives, 1855; member, State senate, 1856-1858; unsuccessful candidate in 1860 for lieutenant governor; elected as a Democrat to the Thirty-seventh and Thirty-eighth Congresses (March 4, 1861-March 3, 1865); was not a candidate for renomination in 1864 to the Thirty-ninth Congress; unsuccessful candidate for election in 1866 for Governor; elected Governor of Connecticut in 1867, reelected in 1868, and served from May 1, 1867 to May 5, 1869; unsuccessful candidate for reelection in 1869; again elected Governor in 1870, and served from May 4, 1870 to May 1871; unsuccessful candidate for reelection in 1871; member of the State house of representatives in 1872; unsuccessful candidate for election in 1872 to the Forty-third Congress; appointed as a Democrat to the United States Senate to fill the vacancy caused by the death of Orris S. Ferry and served from November 27, 1875, to May 17, 1876, when a successor was elected; unsuccessful candidate for election in 1876 to fill the vacancy; resumed his manufacturing and commercial activities; died in New Haven, Conn., March 2, 1890; interment in Evergreen Cemetery.

Bibliography: *DAB*.

**ENGLISH, Karan,** a Representative from Arizona; born in Berkeley, Calif., March 23, 1949; attended Shasta Junior College, Redding, Calif., and the University of California, Santa Barbara; B.A., University of Arizona, 1973; Coconino County, Ariz. supervisor, 1980-1986, chair, 1984-1986; member, Arizona State house of representatives, 1987-1990; member, Arizona State senate, 1991-1993; elected as a Democrat to the One Hundred Third Congress (January 3, 1993-January 3, 1995); unsuccessful candidate for reelection in 1994 to the One Hundred Fourth Congress; is a resident of Flagstaff, Ariz.

**ENGLISH, Philip Sheridan,** a Representative from Pennsylvania; born in Erie, Pa., June 20, 1956; B.A., University of Pennsylvania, 1978; senior policy analyst, executive director of Transportation Committee and research director of Labor and Industry Committee, Pennsylvania senate; voting designee, Pennsylvania Minority Business Development Authority; Erie City, Pa., Controller, 1985-1988; unsuccessful Republican candidate in 1988 for election for Pennsylvania treasurer; minority executive director, Pennsylvania senate finance committee and chief of staff to Pennsylvania senator Melissa Hart, 1990-1994; regional vice chair, Young Republican National Federation; vice chair, College Republican National Committee; chair, Pennsylvania College Republicans; delegate to 1984 Republican National Convention; elected as a Republican to the One Hundred Fourth Congress (January 3, 1995-January 3, 1997); is a resident of Erie, Pa.

**ENGLISH, Thomas Dunn,** a Representative from New Jersey; born in Philadelphia, Pa., June 29, 1819; attended the Friends' Academy, Burlington, N.J., and was graduated from the medical department of the University of Pennsylvania at Philadelphia in 1839; studied law; was admitted to the Philadelphia bar in 1842, but mainly pursued journalism; wrote the song Ben Bolt in 1843, and was the author of many poems, ballads, and lyrics; moved to Virginia in 1852; moved to New York City in 1857, and to Newark, N.J., a year later; member of the State house of assembly in 1863 and 1864; elected as a Democrat to the Fifty-second and Fifty-third Congresses (March 4, 1891-March 3, 1895); chairman, Committee on Alcoholic Liquor Traffic (Fifty-third Congress); unsuccessful candidate for reelection in 1894 to the Fifty-fourth Congress; resumed his former literary pursuits in Newark, N.J., until his death on April 1, 1902; interment in Fairmont Cemetery.

**Bibliography:** *DAB.*

**ENGLISH, Warren Barkley,** a Representative from California; born in Charles Town, Va. (now West Virginia), May 1, 1840; attended the public schools and Charles Town Academy until June 1861; served in the Confederate Army; moved to Oakland, Calif., and attended the California Military Academy; elected a member of the board of supervisors of Contra Costa County in 1877 and served four years; elected State senator in 1882; delegate to the Democratic National Convention in 1884; successfully contested as a Democrat the election of Samuel G. Hilborn to the Fifty-third Congress and took his seat April 4, 1894, serving until March 3, 1895; unsuccessful candidate for reelection in 1894 to the Fifty-fourth Congress; engaged in the real estate business in Oakland, Calif.; in 1905 moved to Sonoma County, Calif., where he engaged in viticulture; died in Santa Rosa, Calif., January 9, 1913; interment in Mountain View Cemetery, Oakland, Calif.

**ENGLISH, William Eastin** (son of William Hayden English), a Representative from Indiana; born at "Englishton Park," near Lexington, Scott County, Ind., November 3, 1850; moved to Indianapolis in 1865; attended public and private schools; was graduated from the law department of the Northwestern Christian (now Butler) University at Indianapolis in 1873; was admitted to the bar the same year and practiced in Indianapolis until 1882; member of the State house of representatives in 1880; successfully contested as a Democrat the election of Stanton J. Peelle to the Forty-eighth Congress and served from May 22, 1884, to March 3, 1885; declined to be a candidate for renomination in 1884 to the Forty-ninth Congress and resumed his former business pursuits at Indianapolis; delegate to the Democratic National Conventions of 1892 and 1896, and chairman of the committee on rules and order of business in the former; left the Democratic Party in 1900 and became active in the Republican Party; served as captain and aide-de-camp on the staff of General Joseph Wheeler in the Spanish-American War; delegate to the Republican National Convention of 1912; elected a member of the State senate in 1916; reelected in 1920 and again in 1924 and served until his death in Indianapolis, Ind., April 29, 1926; interment in Crown Hill Cemetery.

**ENGLISH, William Hayden** (father of William Eastin English), a Representative from Indiana; born in Lexington, Scott County, Ind., August 27, 1822; pursued classical studies at Hanover (Ind.) College; studied law; was admitted to the bar in 1846 and commenced practice at Lexington, Ind.; principal clerk of the Indiana State house of representatives in 1843; clerk in the United States Treasury Department at Washington, D.C., 1844-1848; secretary of the Indiana State constitutional convention in 1850; member of the Indiana State house of representatives in 1851 and 1852, and served as speaker; elected as a Democrat to the Thirty-third and to the three succeeding Congresses (March 4, 1853-March 3, 1861); chairman, Committee on Post Office and Post Roads (Thirty-fifth Congress); Regent of the Smithsonian Institution, 1853-1861; moved to Indianapolis, Ind., at the end of his congressional term; unsuccessful candidate for Vice President of the United States in 1880 on the Democratic ticket headed by Winfield Scott Hancock; author of several books; died at his home in Indianapolis, Ind., February 7, 1896; interment in Crown Hill Cemetery.

**Bibliography:** *DAB*; Schimmel, Elliott L. "William H. English and the Politics of Self-Deception, 1845-1861." Ph.D. dissertation, Florida State University, 1986.

**ENLOE, Benjamin Augustine,** a Representative from Tennessee; born near Clarksburg, Carroll County, Tenn., January 18, 1848; attended the public schools, Bethel College, McKenzie, Tenn., and the Cumberland University, Lebanon, Tenn.; while a student at the latter institution in 1869 was elected a member of the State house of representatives; reelected under the new constitution in 1870; was graduated from the law department of Cumberland University in 1872; was admitted to the bar in 1873 and commenced practice in Jackson, Tenn.; delegate to the Democratic National Convention of 1872; appointed a commissioner by Governor Albert S. Marks in 1878 to negotiate a settlement of the State debt; served on the State executive committee 1878-1880; delegate to the Democratic National Convention of 1880; edited the Jackson Tribune and Sun 1874-1886; elected as a Democrat to the Fiftieth and to the three succeeding Congresses (March 4, 1887-March 3, 1895); chairman, Committee on Education (Fifty-second and Fifty-third Congresses); unsuccessful candidate for reelection in 1894 to the Fifty-fourth Congress; edited the Daily Sun in Nashville, Tenn., for two years; moved to Louisville, Ky., and edited the Louisville Dispatch for two years; secretary of the State fair commission and director of exhibits from Tennessee at St. Louis World's Fair in 1903; elected railroad commissioner of Tennessee and served from 1904 until his death in Nashville, Tenn., on July 8, 1922; interment in Mount Olivet Cemetery.

**ENOCHS, William Henry,** a Representative from Ohio; born near Middleburg, Noble County, Ohio, March 29, 1842; attended the common schools and Ohio University at Athens; enlisted as a private in Company B, Second Regiment, Ohio Infantry, April 17, 1861; also served with West Virginia Infantry and promoted to colonel; brevetted brigadier general of Volunteers March 13, 1865; was graduated from the Cincinnati Law School in 1866; was admitted to the bar and commenced practice in Ironton, Ohio; member of the State house of representatives in 1870 and 1871; elected as a Republican to the Fifty-second and Fifty-third Congresses and served from March 4, 1891, until his death in Ironton, Lawrence County, Ohio, July 13, 1893; interment in Arlington National Cemetery, Va.

**ENSIGN, John Eric,** a Representative from Nevada; born in Roseville, Placer County, Calif., March 25, 1958; graduated E.W. Clark High School, Las Vegas, Nev., 1976; attended University of Nevada; B.S., Oregon State University, Corvallis, 1981; D.V.M., Colorado State University, Fort Collins, 1985; kitchen worker, veterinary assistant, 21 dealer, parking valet, warehouseman; intern, West Los Angeles Veterinary Medical Group; owner, West Flamingo Animal Hospital, Las Vegas, 1987; general manager, Gold Strike Hotel and Casino, 1991; general manager, Navada Landing Hotel and Casino; elected as a Republican to the One Hundred Fourth Congress (January 3, 1995-January 3, 1997); is a resident of Las Vegas, Nev.

**EPES, James Fletcher** (cousin of Sydney Parham Epes), a Representative from Virginia; born near Blackstone, Nottoway County, Va., May 23, 1842; attended private schools and the University of Virginia at Charlottesville; during the Civil War served in the Confederate Army in Company E, Third Virginia Cavalry; was graduated from the law department of Washington and Lee University, Lexington, Va., in 1867; was admitted to the bar the same year and commenced practice at Nottoway Court House, Va.; also engaged in agricultural pursuits; prosecuting attorney for Nottoway County, 1870-1883; elected as a Democrat to the Fifty-second and Fifty-third Congresses (March 4, 1891-March 3, 1895); was not a candidate for renomination in 1894 to the Fifty-fourth Congress; retired to his plantation, "The Old Place," near Blackstone, and engaged in agricultural pursuits until his death there on August 24, 1910; interment in Lake View Cemetery, Blackstone, Va.

**EPES, Sydney Parham** (cousin of James Fletcher Epes and William Bacon Oliver), a Representative from Virginia; born near Nottoway Court House, Nottoway County, Va., August 20, 1865; moved with his parents to Kentucky and settled near Franklin, Ky.; attended the public schools; returned to Virginia in 1884 and edited and published a Democratic newspaper at Blackstone, Va.; member of the Virginia house of delegates in 1891 and 1892; register of the Virginia land office, 1895-1897; presented credentials as a Member-elect to the Fifty-fifth Congress, and served from March 4, 1897 until March 23, 1898, when he was succeeded by Robert T. Thorp, who contested the election; elected as a Democrat to the Fifty-sixth Congress, and served from March 4, 1899 until his death in Washington, D.C., March 3, 1900; interment in Lake View Cemetery, Blackstone, Va.

**EPPES, John Wayles,** a Representative and a Senator from Virginia; born at Eppington, Chesterfield County, Va., April 19, 1773; attended the University of Pennsylvania at Philadelphia; was graduated from Hampden-Sydney College in Virginia in 1786; studied law; was admitted to the bar in 1794 and commenced practice in Richmond, Va.; member, Virginia house of delegates 1801-1803; elected as a Republican to the Eighth and to the three succeeding Congresses (March 4, 1803-March 3, 1811); unsuccessful candidate for reelection to the Twelfth Congress; chairman, Committee on Ways and Means (Eleventh Congress); engaged in agricultural pursuits; elected to the Thirteenth Congress (March 4, 1813-March 3, 1815); unsuccessful candidate for reelection to the Fourteenth Congress; chairman, Committee on Ways and Means (Thirteenth Congress); elected to the United States Senate and served from March 4, 1817, until December 4, 1819, when he resigned because of ill health; chairman, Committee on Finance (Fifteenth Congress); retired to his estate, "Millbrooke," in Buckingham County, Va., where he died September 13, 1823; interment in the private cemetery of the Eppes family at Millbrook, near Curdsville, Va.

Bibliography: *DAB.*

**ERDAHL, Arlen Ingolf,** a Representative from Minnesota; born in Blue Earth, Faribault County, Minn., February 27, 1931; attended the Faribault County public schools; B.A., St. Olaf College, Northfield, Minn., 1953; served in the United States Army, 1954-1956; M.P.A., Harvard University, 1966; farmer; served in the Minnesota State house of representatives, 1963-1970; Congressional Fellow, Washington, D.C., 1967-1968; Minnesota Secretary of State, 1970-1974; member of the Minnesota Public Service Commission, 1975-1978; delegate to Minnesota State Republican conventions, 1963-1964; elected as a Republican to the Ninety-sixth and Ninety-seventh Congresses (January 3, 1979-January 3, 1983); unsuccessful candidate for reelection in 1982 to the Ninety-eighth Congress; country director, United States Peace Corps, Jamaica, 1983-1985; associate director, United States Peace Corps, 1986-1989; principal deputy assistant secretary, United States Department of Energy, 1989-1993; executive director, Minnesota International Health Volunteers, 1995 to present; is a resident of Burnsville, Minn.

**ERDMAN, Constantine Jacob** (grandson of Jacob Erdman), a Representative from Pennsylvania; born in Upper Saucon Township, near Allentown, Lehigh County, Pa., September 4, 1846; attended the common schools of the district and a classical school in Quakerstown, Pa.; was graduated from Pennsylvania College, Gettysburg, Pa., in 1865; studied law; was admitted to the bar in 1867 and practiced in Allentown, Pa.; elected district attorney in 1874; adjutant of the Fourth Regiment, National Guard of Pennsylvania, during the riots at Reading in 1877; elected as a Democrat to the Fifty-third and Fifty-fourth Congresses (March 4, 1893-March 3, 1897); was not a candidate for reelection in 1896 to the Fifty-fifth Congress; resumed the practice of law in Allentown; trustee of Muhlenberg College at Allentown; president of the Coplay Cement Manufacturing Co., the Allentown & Coopersburg Turnpike Co., and the Allen Fire Insurance Co. for many years; died in Allentown, Pa., January 15, 1911; interment in Fairview Cemetery.

**ERDMAN, Jacob** (grandfather of Constantine Jacob Erdman), a Representative from Pennsylvania; born in Coopersburg, Lehigh County, Pa., February 22, 1801; attended the common schools; engaged in agricultural pursuits; member of the State house of representatives 1834-1836; elected as a Democrat to the Twenty-ninth Congress (March 4, 1845-March 3, 1847); unsuccessful candidate for reelection in 1846 to the Thirtieth Congress; elected associate judge of Lehigh County Court November 9, 1866, and served until his death in Coopersburg, Pa., July 20, 1867; interment in Blue Church Cemetery near Coopersburg, Pa.

**ERDREICH, Benjamin Leader,** a Representative from Alabama; born in Birmingham, Ala., December 9, 1938; attended Jefferson County public schools; B.A., Yale University, 1960; J.D., University of Alabama School of Law, 1963; editor-in-chief, Alabama Law Review; served in the United States on active duty as a first lieutenant, 1963-1965; admitted to Alabama bar in 1963 and practiced law in Birmingham for eight years; member, Alabama State house of representatives, 1970-1974; Jefferson County, Ala. commissioner, 1974-1982; elected as a Democrat to the Ninety-eighth and to the four succeeding Congresses (January 3, 1983-January 3, 1993); unsuccessful candidate for reelection in 1992 to the One Hundred Third Congress; nominated June 7, 1993 to be a member and the chairman of the United States Merit Systems Protection Board for the term of seven years expiring March 1, 2000; confirmed by the Senate on June 30, 1993; is a resident of Birmingham, Ala.

**ERICKSON, John Edward,** a Senator from Montana; born in Stoughton, Dane County, Wis., March 14, 1863; moved with his parents to Eureka, Greenwood County, Kans., where he attended the public schools; graduated from Washburn College, Topeka, Kans., in 1890; studied law; was admitted to the bar in 1891 at Eureka, Kans., and commenced practice in Choteau, Teton County, Mont., in 1893; county attorney of Teton County, 1897-1905; judge of the eleventh judicial district of Montana from 1905 until 1915; resumed the practice of law at Kalispell, Mont., in 1916; elected Governor of Montana in 1924, reelected in 1928 and 1932, and served from January 4, 1925 until March 13, 1933, when he resigned to become a United States Senator; appointed as a Democrat to the United States Senate to fill the vacancy caused by the death of Thomas J. Walsh and served from March 13, 1933, until November 6, 1934, when a successor was elected; unsuccessful candidate for nomination in 1934 to fill the vacancy; resumed the practice of law in Helena, Mont., where he died on May 25, 1946; interment in Conrad Memorial Cemetery, Kalispell, Mont.

**ERK, Edmund Frederick,** a Representative from Pennsylvania; born in Allegheny City (now North Side, Pittsburgh), Pa., April 17, 1872; attended the public schools; engaged extensively in newspaper work in Pittsburgh, Pa.; served as secretary to Representative Stephen G. Porter 1911-1919, and as clerk of the

Committee on Foreign Affairs of the House of Representatives from June 1, 1919, to November 3, 1930; secretary of the American delegation to the League of Nations Conference at Geneva in 1924 and 1925; elected as a Republican to the Seventy-first Congress to fill the vacancy caused by the death of Stephen G. Porter, at the same time being elected to the Seventy-second Congress, and served from November 4, 1930, to March 3, 1933; unsuccessful candidate for reelection in 1932 to the Seventy-third Congress, and for election in 1934 to the Seventy-fourth Congress; secretary to Representative Michael J. Muldowney from March 4, 1933, to January 2, 1935; also an author and compiler; clerk to Senator James J. Davis of Pennsylvania from 1939 to 1945; resided in Bethesda, Md., until his death there on December 14, 1953; interment in St. John's Cemetery, Pittsburgh, Pa.

**ERLENBORN, John Neal,** a Representative from Illinois; born in Chicago, Cook County, Ill., February 8, 1927; graduated from Immaculate Conception High School in Elmhurst in 1944; served in the United States Navy, 1944-1946; attended the University of Notre Dame, 1944, Indiana State Teachers College, 1944-1945, and the University of Illinois, 1945-1946; J.D., Loyola University of Chicago Law School, 1949; was admitted to the Illinois bar in 1950 and engaged in the practice of law in Elmhurst; assistant State's attorney, Du Page County, 1950-1952; member of the Illinois State house of representatives, 1957-1965; elected as a Republican to the Eighty-ninth and to the nine succeeding Congresses (January 3, 1965-January 3, 1985); was not a candidate for reelection in 1984 to the Ninety-ninth Congress; nominated to be a member of the board of directors of the Legal Services Corporation on October 10, 1995 for a term expiring July 13, 1998; confirmed by the Senate on June 11, 1996; is a resident of Fairfax, Va.

**ERMENTROUT, Daniel,** a Representative from Pennsylvania; born in Reading, Berks County, Pa., January 24, 1837; attended the public and classical schools, Franklin and Marshall College, Lancaster, Pa., and Elmwood Institute, Norristown, Pa.; studied law; was admitted to the bar in 1859 and commenced practice in Reading, Pa.; elected district attorney in 1862 for three years; solicitor for the city of Reading 1867-1870; member of the board of school control of Reading 1868-1876; delegate to the Democratic National Conventions of 1868 and 1880; chairman of the standing committee of Berks County in 1869, 1872, and 1873; member of the Pennsylvania senate 1873-1880; appointed in October 1877 by Governor John F. Hartranft as a member of the Pennsylvania Statuary Commission; elected as a Democrat to the Forty-seventh and to the three succeeding Congresses (March 4, 1881-March 3, 1889); unsuccessful candidate for renomination in 1888 to the Fifty-first Congress; delegate to the Democratic State conventions 1895-1899; elected to the Fifty-fifth and Fifty-sixth Congresses and served from March 4, 1897, until his death in Reading, Pa., on September 17, 1899; interment in Charles Evans Cemetery.

**ERNST, Richard Pretlow,** a Senator from Kentucky; born in Covington, Ky., February 28, 1858; attended the public schools; graduated from Chickerings Academy, Cincinnati, Ohio, in 1874, from Centre College, Danville, Ky., in 1878, and from the law school of the University of Cincinnati in 1880; was admitted to the bar in 1880 and practiced in Covington and Cincinnati; member of the Covington city council 1888-1892; unsuccessful candidate for election to the Fifty-fifth Congress; elected as a Republican to the United States Senate in 1920 and served from March 4, 1921, to March 3, 1927; unsuccessful candidate for reelection in 1926; chairman, Committee on Revision of the Laws (Sixty-seventh Congress), Committee on Patents (Sixty-eighth and Sixty-ninth Congresses), Committee on Privileges and Elections (Sixty-ninth Congress); resumed the practice of law in Cincinnati, Ohio; also engaged in banking in Covington, Ky.; died at Johns Hopkins Hospital, Baltimore, Md., on April 13, 1934; interment in Highland Cemetery, Covington, Ky.

**ERRETT, Russell,** a Representative from Pennsylvania; born in New York City, November 10, 1817; moved to Pittsburgh, Pa., in 1829; engaged in newspaper work; elected comptroller of Pittsburgh in 1860; served as clerk of the Pennsylvania senate in 1860, 1861, and 1872-1876; during the Civil War was appointed additional paymaster in the United States Army in 1861 and served until mustered out in 1866; member of the Pennsylvania senate in 1867; appointed assessor of internal revenue in 1869, and served until 1873; elected as a Republican to the Forty-fifth, Forty-sixth, and Forty-seventh Congresses (March 4, 1877-March 3, 1883); chairman, Committee on Expenditures on Public Buildings (Forty-seventh Congress); unsuccessful candidate for reelection in 1882 to the Forty-eighth Congress; appointed by President Chester A. Arthur as United States pension agent at Pittsburgh in 1883 and served in this capacity until May 1887; died in Carnegie, Pa., April 7, 1891; interment in Chartiers Cemetery.

**ERTEL, Allen Edward,** a Representative from Pennsylvania; born in Williamsport, Lycoming County, Pa., November 7, 1937; attended the public schools; B.A., Dartmouth College, Hanover, N.H., 1958; M.S., Thayer School of Engineering and Amos Tuck School of Business Administration, 1959; LL.B., Yale University School of Law, 1965; admitted to the Pennsylvania bar in 1965 and commenced practice in Williamsport; served in the United States Navy, 1959-1962; clerked for Chief Judge Caleb M. Wright, Federal District Court of Delaware, 1965-1966; Lycoming County district attorney, 1968-1976; delegate to the Democratic National Convention of 1972; elected as a Democrat to the Ninety-fifth and to the two succeeding Congresses (January 3, 1977-January 3, 1983); was not a candidate for reelection in 1982 to the Ninety-eighth Congress, but was an unsuccessful candidate for election for Governor of Pennsylvania; resumed the practice of law in Williamsport; unsuccessful candidate for attorney general of Pennsylvania in 1984; chief officer, Regulation Scanning Technology Corp.; chairman of the board, Alcat Development and Technology Corp.; is a resident of Montoursville, Pa.

**ERVIN, James,** a Representative from South Carolina; born in Williamsburg District, S.C., October 17, 1778; was graduated from Rhode Island College (now Brown University), Providence, R.I., in 1797; studied law; was admitted to the bar in 1800 and commenced practice in Peedee, S.C.; member of the State house of representatives 1800-1804; solicitor of the northern judicial circuit 1804-1816; trustee of South Carolina College 1809-1817; again a member of the State house of representatives in 1810 and 1811; elected as a Republican to the Fifteenth Congress and reelected to the Sixteenth Congress (March 4, 1817-March 3, 1821); declined to be a candidate for renomination in 1820; engaged in agricultural pursuits; member of the State senate 1826-1829; served as a delegate to the State convention in 1832; died in Darlington, S.C., July 7, 1841; interment at his home.

**ERVIN, Joseph Wilson** (brother of Samuel James Ervin, Jr.), a Representative from North Carolina; born in Morganton, Burke County, N.C., March 3, 1901; attended the public schools; was graduated from the University of North Carolina at Chapel Hill in 1921 and from its law school in 1923; was admitted to the bar in 1923 and commenced practice in Charlotte, N.C.; elected as a Democrat to the Seventy-ninth Congress and served from January 3, 1945, until his death in Washington, D.C., December 25, 1945; interment in Forest Hill Cemetery, Morganton, N.C.

**ERVIN, Samuel James, Jr.** (brother of Joseph Wilson Ervin), a Representative and a Senator from North Carolina; born in Morganton, Burke County, N.C., September 27, 1896; attended the public schools; graduated from the University of North Carolina at

Chapel Hill in 1917 and from the law school of Harvard University in 1922; during the First World War served in France with the First Division 1917-1919; admitted to the bar in 1919 and commenced practice in Morganton, N.C., in 1922; member, North Carolina general assembly 1923, 1925, 1931; judge of the Burke County criminal court 1935-1937; judge of the North Carolina superior court 1937-1943; elected as a Democrat to the Seventy-ninth Congress to fill the vacancy caused by the death of his brother, Joseph W. Ervin, and served from January 22, 1946, to January 3, 1947; was not a candidate for renomination in 1946 to the Eightieth Congress; resumed the practice of law; associate justice of the North Carolina State supreme court 1948-1954; appointed as a Democrat on June 5, 1954, and subsequently elected to the United States Senate to fill the vacancy caused by the death of Clyde R. Hoey for the term ending January 3, 1957; reelected in 1956, 1962, and again in 1968 and served from June 5, 1954, until his resignation December 31, 1974; was not a candidate for reelection in 1974; chairman, Committee on Government Operations (Ninety-second and Ninety-third Congresses), Select Committee on Presidential Campaign Activities (Ninety-third Congress); resumed the practice of law and engaged in literary pursuits in Morganton, N.C.; died in Winston-Salem, N.C., on April 23, 1985; interment in the Forest Hill Cemetery in Morganton, N.C.

**Bibliography:** Clancy, Paul. *Just A Country Lawyer: A Biography of Senator Sam Ervin.* Bloomington: Indiana University Press, 1974; Ervin, Sam. *Preserving the Constitution: An Autobiography of Senator Sam Ervin.* Charlottesville, Va.: Michie Co., 1984.

**ESCH, John Jacob,** a Representative from Wisconsin; born near Norwalk, Monroe County, Wis., March 20, 1861; moved with his parents to Milwaukee in 1865 and thence to Sparta, Wis., in 1871; attended the public schools; was graduated from the University of Wisconsin at Madison in 1882 and from its law department in 1887; was admitted to the bar in 1887 and commenced practice at La Crosse, Wis.; assistant principal of Sparta High School 1883-1886; city treasurer of Sparta in 1885; was commissioned acting judge advocate general with the rank of colonel by Governor William H. Upham in January 1894 and held the position for two years; delegate to the Republican State conventions in 1894 and 1896; elected as a Republican to the Fifty-sixth and to the ten succeeding Congresses (March 4, 1899-March 3, 1921); chairman, Committee on Interstate and Foreign Commerce (Sixty-sixth Congress); unsuccessful candidate for renomination in 1920 to the Sixty-seventh Congress; appointed by President Warren G. Harding as a member of the Interstate Commerce Commission on March 11, 1921; elected chairman on January 1, 1927, and served until May 31, 1928; resumed the practice of law in Washington, D.C., until he retired in 1938; returned to La Crosse, Wis., where he died on April 27, 1941; interment in Oak Grove Cemetery.

**Bibliography:** *DAB.*

**ESCH, Marvin Lionel,** a Representative from Michigan; born in Flinton, Cambria County, Pa., August 4, 1927; received primary and secondary education in Akron, Ohio, and Jackson, Mich.; A.B., University of Michigan, 1950, M.A., 1951, and Ph.D., speech and education, 1957; served in the Maritime Service and United States Army; served for fourteen years on the staff at Wayne State University as associate professor of speech, and as a lecturer in the University of Michigan-Wayne State University Institute of Labor and Industrial Relations; member of the Michigan Legislature, 1965-1966; elected as a Republican to the Ninetieth and to the four succeeding Congresses (January 3, 1967-January 3, 1977); was not a candidate in 1976 for reelection to the House of Representatives, but was an unsuccessful candidate for election to the United States Senate; director of public affairs, United States Steel Corporation, 1977-1980; director of programs and seminars, American Enterprise Institute, 1981 to present; is a resident of Ann Arbor, Mich.

**ESHLEMAN, Edwin Duing,** a Representative from Pennsylvania; born in Quarryville, Lancaster County, Pa., December 4, 1920; Franklin and Marshall College, B.S., 1942; engaged in graduate work in political science at Temple University; lieutenant, United States Coast Guard in the Second World War; public school teacher; member, Pennsylvania house of representatives, 1954-1966; elected as a Republican to the Ninetieth and to the four succeeding Congresses (January 3, 1967-January 3, 1977); was not a candidate for reelection in 1976 to the Ninety-fifth Congress; was a resident of Lancaster, Pa., until his death there January 10, 1985; interment in Millersville Mennonite Cemetery, Manor Township, Millersville, Pa.

**ESHOO, Anna Georges,** a Representative from California; born in New Britain, Hartford County, Conn., December 13, 1942; A.A., Cañada College, Redwood City, Calif., 1975; member, San Mateo County board of supervisors, 1982-1992; unsuccessful candidate for election in 1988 to the One Hundred First Congress; chair, San Mateo County Democratic Party; Democratic National Committee, 1980-present; Democratic National Party Commission on Presidential Nominations, 1982; elected as a Democrat to the One Hundred Third and One Hundred Fourth Congresses (January 3, 1993-January 3, 1997); is a resident of Atherton, Calif.

**ESLICK, Edward Everett** (husband of Willa McCord Eslick), a Representative from Tennessee; born near Pulaski, Giles County, Tenn., April 19, 1872; attended the public schools and Bethel College, Russellville, Ky.; studied law; was admitted to the bar in 1893 and commenced practice in Pulaski; also engaged in banking and agricultural pursuits; served as Government appeal agent for Giles County during the First World War; elected as a Democrat to the Sixty-ninth and to the three succeeding Congresses and served from March 4, 1925, until his death in the Capitol, at Washington, D.C., on June 14, 1932, while addressing the House of Representatives; interment in Maplewood Cemetery, Pulaski, Tenn.

**ESLICK, Willa McCord Blake** (wife of Edward Everett Eslick), a Representative from Tennessee; born in Fayetteville, Lincoln County, Tenn., September 8, 1878; attended private schools, Dick White College and Milton College, Fayetteville, Tenn., Winthrop Model School and Peabody College, Nashville, Tenn., and Metropolitan College of Music and Synthetic School of Music, New York City; member of the State Democratic committee; elected as a Democrat to the Seventy-second Congress to fill the vacancy caused by the death of her husband, Edward E. Eslick, and served from August 4, 1932, to March 3, 1933; was not eligible for reelection to the Seventy-third Congress, not having qualified for nomination as required by the State law; died in Pulaski, Tenn., February 18, 1961; interment in Maplewood Cemetery.

**ESPY, Albert Michael,** a Representative from Mississippi; born in Yazoo City, Miss., November 30, 1953; B.A., Howard University, Washington, D.C., 1975; J.D., University of Santa Clara Law School, California, 1978; attorney with Central Mississippi Legal Services, 1978-1980; assistant secretary of state, chief, Mississippi Legal Services, 1978-1980; assistant secretary of Public Lands Division, 1980-1984; assistant State attorney general, 1984-1985; elected as a Democrat to the One Hundredth and to the three succeeding Congresses and served from January 3, 1987, until his resignation January 22, 1993 to become Secretary of Agriculture in the Cabinet of President William J. Clinton, and served until his resignation on December 31, 1994; is a resident of Yazoo City, Miss.

**ESSEN, Frederick,** a Representative from Missouri; born near Pond, St. Louis County, Mo., April 22, 1863; attended the public schools; engaged in agricultural pursuits; recorder of deeds of St. Louis County 1894-1902; engaged in newspaper business at Clayton, Mo., becoming the owner of two papers which he combined under the name of the Watchman-Advocate; delegate to the Republican National Conventions in 1904, 1908, and 1912; member of the board of education of Clayton and served as president 1909-1919; elected as a Republican to the Sixty-fifth Congress to fill the vacancy caused by the death of Jacob E. Meeker and served from November 5, 1918, until March 3, 1919; was not a candidate for renomination in 1918; resumed newspaper activities; also interested in banking; died in Creve Coeur, Mo., August 18, 1946; interment in Bethel Cemetery, Pond, Mo.

**ESTABROOK, Experience,** a Delegate from the Territory of Nebraska; born in Lebanon, N.H., April 30, 1813; moved with his parents to Clarence, Erie County, N.Y., in 1822; attended the public schools and Dickinson College, Carlisle, Pa.; was graduated from the Chambersburg (Pa.) Law School; was admitted to the bar in Brooklyn, N.Y., in 1839; worked as a clerk at the navy yard in Brooklyn and later commenced the practice of law in Buffalo; moved to Geneva, Wis., in 1840 and continued the practice of law; delegate to the second State constitutional convention in 1848; member of the State house of representatives in 1851; attorney general of Wisconsin in 1852 and 1853; appointed by President Franklin Pierce attorney general of the Territory of Nebraska and served from 1855 to 1859; presented credentials as a Delegate-elect to the Thirty-sixth Congress, and served from March 4, 1859 to May 18, 1860, when he was succeeded by Samuel G. Daily, who contested his election; appointed by the Governor to codify the Nebraska State laws in 1866; prosecuting attorney for Douglas County in 1867 and 1868; member of the State constitutional convention in 1871; died in Omaha, Nebr., March 26, 1894; interment in Forest Lawn Cemetery.

**ESTEP, Harry Allison,** a Representative from Pennsylvania; born in Pittsburgh, Pa., February 1, 1884; attended the public schools in Marion, Ind., and Purdue University, Lafayette, Ind.; was graduated from the law department of the University of Pittsburgh, Pittsburgh, Pa., in 1913; was admitted to the bar in 1914 and commenced practice in Pittsburgh, Pa.; assistant district attorney of Allegheny County, Pa., 1917-1927; elected as a Republican to the Seventieth, Seventy-first, and Seventy-second Congresses (March 4, 1927-March 3, 1933); unsuccessful candidate for reelection in 1932 to the Seventy-third Congress; resumed the practice of law until his retirement in 1964; died in Oakland, Pittsburgh, Pa., February 28, 1968; interment in Allegheny Cemetery.

**ESTERLY, Charles Joseph,** a Representative from Pennsylvania; born in Reading, Berks County, Pa., February 8, 1888; attended the public schools; employed with an electric company until 1916 and later in the sales department of a knitting mill; also engaged in the breeding of Ayrshire cattle and Berkshire hogs; served as president and director of a water company, and as a director of a knitting mill and bottle-stopper company; member of the board of school directors of Wyomissing, Pa., 1914-1920; committeeman of Wyomissing Borough 1917-1921; delegate to the Republican National Convention of 1920; member of the Pennsylvania Republican committee 1922-1924; elected as a Republican to the Sixty-ninth Congress (March 4, 1925-March 3, 1927); declined to be a candidate for renomination in 1926 to the Seventieth Congress; elected to the Seventy-first Congress (March 4, 1929-March 3, 1931); was not a candidate for renomination in 1930 to the Seventy-second Congress; resumed former business interests; died in Wernersville, Pa., September 3, 1940; interment in Charles Evans Cemetery, Reading, Pa.

**ESTIL, Benjamin,** a Representative from Virginia; born in Hansonville (now Russell County), Va., March 13, 1780; received an academic education, and attended Washington Academy (now Washington and Lee University), Lexington, Va.; studied law; was admitted to the bar and commenced practice in Abingdon, Va.; prosecuting attorney for Washington County; member of the Virginia house of delegates 1814-1817; elected to the Nineteenth Congress (March 4, 1825-March 3, 1827); judge of the fifteenth

judicial circuit from 1831 until 1852, when he resigned; retired to a farm in Oldham County, Ky., where he died July 14, 1853.

**ESTOPINAL, Albert,** a Representative from Louisiana; born in St. Bernard Parish, La., January 30, 1845; attended the public and private schools; left school in January 1862 to enlist in the Confederate Army and served in Company G, Twenty-eighth Regiment, Louisiana Infantry; made sergeant of Company G, Twenty-second Louisiana Heavy Artillery, and served throughout the Civil War; engaged in the commission business at New Orleans for several years, but most of his life was spent at his home, "Kenilworth Plantation," near New Orleans; sheriff of St. Bernard Parish, 1872-1876; member of the Louisiana State house of representatives, 1876-1880; member of the constitutional conventions in 1879 and 1898; served in the State senate, 1880-1900; lieutenant governor, 1900-1904; chairman of the Democratic State central committee in 1908; elected as a Democrat to the Sixtieth Congress to fill the vacancy caused by the death of Adolph Meyers; reelected to the Sixty-first and to the five succeeding Congresses, and served from November 3, 1908 until his death in New Orleans, La., April 28, 1919; interment in St. Louis Cemetery No. 3, New Orleans, La.

**ESTY, Constantine Canaris,** a Representative from Massachusetts; born in Framingham, Middlesex County, Mass., December 26, 1824; attended the local academies of Framingham and Leicester; was graduated from Yale College in 1845; studied law; was admitted to the bar and commenced practice in Framingham, Mass., in 1847; served in the Massachusetts senate in 1857 and 1858; member of the Massachusetts house of representatives in 1867; appointed assessor of internal revenue by President Lincoln in 1862 and served until he was removed for political reasons by President Andrew Johnson in 1866; reappointed by him in 1867; resigned in 1872; elected as a Republican to the Forty-second Congress to fill the vacancy caused by the resignation of George M. Brooks and served from December 2, 1872, to March 3, 1873; was not a candidate for renomination in 1872 to the Forty-third Congress; continued the practice of his profession in Framingham, Mass., until his death there December 27, 1912; interment in Edgell Grove Cemetery.

**ETHERIDGE, Emerson,** a Representative from Tennessee; born in Currituck, N.C., September 28, 1819; moved with his parents to Tennessee in 1831; completed preparatory studies; studied law; was admitted to the bar in 1840 and commenced practice in Dresden, Tenn.; member of the State house of representatives 1845-1847; elected as a Whig to the Thirty-third Congress and reelected as a candidate of the American Party to the Thirty-fourth Congress (March 4, 1853-March 3, 1857); unsuccessful candidate for reelection in 1856 to the Thirty-fifth Congress; elected as an Opposition Party candidate to the Thirty-sixth Congress (March 4, 1859-March 3, 1861); chairman, Committee on Indian Affairs (Thirty-sixth Congress); Clerk of the House of Representatives 1861-1863; unsuccessful candidate in 1867 for election for Governor of Tennessee; member of the State senate in 1869 and 1870; surveyor of customs in Memphis 1891-1894; died in Dresden, Tenn., on October 21, 1902; interment in Mount Vernon Cemetery, near Sharon, Tenn.

Bibliography: Belz, Herman. "Etheridge Conspiracy of 1863: A Projected Conservative Coup." *Journal of Southern History* 36 (November 1970): 549-67.

**EUSTIS, George, Jr.** (brother of James Biddle Eustis), a Representative from Louisiana; born in New Orleans, La., September 28, 1828; was graduated from Jefferson College, Convent, La., and from the law department of Harvard University; was admitted to the bar and commenced practice in New Orleans; elected as the American Party candidate to the Thirty-fourth and Thirty-fifth Congresses (March 4, 1855-March 3, 1859); secretary to John Slidell, Confederate envoy to England and France, and was taken prisoner with him from the British mail steamer *Trent* on November 8, 1861; secretary of the Confederate mission at Paris; remained in Paris after the close of the war; commissioned by Elihu B. Washburne, United States Minister at Paris, to negotiate a postal treaty with the French Government; died in Cannes, France, March 15, 1872; interment in Oak Hill Cemetery, Washington, D.C.

**Bibliography:** *DAB;* Tregle, Joseph G. "George Eustis, Jr., Non-Mythic Southerner." *Louisiana History* 16 (Fall 1975): 383-90.

**EUSTIS, James Biddle** (brother of George Eustis, Jr.), a Senator from Louisiana; born in New Orleans, La., August 27, 1834; pursued classical studies; graduated from the Harvard Law School in 1854; was admitted to the bar in 1856 and commenced practice in New Orleans; served as judge advocate during the Civil War in the Confederate Army; resumed the practice of law in New Orleans; elected a member of the State house of representatives prior to the reconstruction acts; one of the committee sent to Washington to confer with President Andrew Johnson on Louisiana affairs; member, Louisiana State house of representatives, 1872; member, State senate, 1874-1878; elected as a Democrat to the United States Senate to fill the vacancy in the term commencing March 4, 1873, caused by the action of the Senate in declining to seat certain claimants, and served from January 12, 1876 to March 3, 1879; unsuccessful candidate for reelection; professor of civil law at the University of Louisiana, 1877-1884; again elected as a Democrat to the United States Senate, and served from March 4, 1885 to March 3, 1891; was not a candidate for reelection; practiced law in Washington, D.C., in 1891; appointed Ambassador to France on March 20, 1893 and served until May 1897; settled in New York City; died in Newport, R.I., on September 9, 1899; interment in Cave Hill Cemetery, Louisville, Ky.

**Bibliography:** *DAB.*

**EUSTIS, William,** a Representative from Massachusetts; born in Cambridge, Mass., June 10, 1753; attended the Boston public schools and was graduated from Harvard College in 1772; studied medicine and served in the Revolutionary Army as surgeon; resumed practice in Boston; was a surgeon in the expedition sent to suppress Shays' Rebellion in 1786 and 1787; member of the Massachusetts house of representatives, 1788-1794; elected as a Republican to the Seventh and Eighth Congresses (March 4, 1801-March 3, 1805); one of the managers appointed by the House of Representatives in 1804 to conduct the impeachment proceedings against John Pickering, judge of the United States District Court for New Hampshire; unsuccessful candidate for reelection in 1804 to the Ninth Congress; appointed Secretary of War in the Cabinet of President James Madison and served from March 7, 1809 until his resignation on January 13, 1813; appointed Envoy Extraordinary and Minister Plenipotentiary to the Netherlands and served from December 19, 1814, to May 5, 1818; elected to the Sixteenth Congress to fill the vacancy caused by the resignation of Edward Dowse; reelected to the Seventeenth Congress and served from August 21, 1820, to March 3, 1823; chairman, Committee on Military Affairs (Seventeenth Congress); unsuccessful candidate for election in 1820, 1821 and 1822 for Governor; did not seek renomination in 1822 to the Eighteenth Congress; elected Governor of Massachusetts in 1823, reelected in 1824, and served from May 31, 1823, until his death in Boston, Mass., February 6, 1825; interment in the Old Burying Ground, Lexington, Mass.

**Bibliography:** *DAB.*

**EVANS, Alexander,** a Representative from Maryland; born in Elkton, Cecil County, Md., September 13, 1818; attended the public schools; was a civil engineer's assistant; attended the local academy at Elkton; studied law; was admitted to the bar in 1845 and commenced practice in his native city; elected as a Whig to the Thirtieth, Thirty-first, and Thirty-second Congresses (March 4, 1847-March 3, 1853); engaged in the practice of his profession until

his death in Elkton, Md., December 5, 1888; interment in Elkton Presbyterian Cemetery.

**EVANS, Alvin,** a Representative from Pennsylvania; born in Ebensburg, Cambria County, Pa., October 4, 1845; attended the public schools and the Iron City Business College, Pittsburgh, Pa.; engaged in lumbering; during the Civil War served in a volunteer company organized to repel the expected invasion of Pennsylvania by Confederate forces under General Robert E. Lee; studied law; was admitted to the bar in 1873 and commenced practice in Ebensburg, Pa.; later practiced in the superior and supreme courts of Pennsylvania and in the Federal courts; served one term as burgess of Ebensburg Borough; solicitor for the Pennsylvania Railroad in Cambria County for several years; one of the incorporators and president of the board of directors of the First National Bank of Ebensburg; for a number of years served on the school board and in the common council of his native town; elected as a Republican to the Fifty-seventh and Fifty-eighth Congresses (March 4, 1901-March 3, 1905); declined to be a candidate for renomination in 1904 to the Fifty-ninth Congress; resumed the practice of his profession; died in Ebensburg, Pa., June 19, 1906; interment in Lloyd Cemetery.

**EVANS, Billy Lee,** a Representative from Georgia; born in Tifton, Tift County, Ga., November 10, 1941; attended the public schools; A.B., 1963, University of Georgia, and LL.B., 1965; admitted to the Georgia bar in 1965 and commenced practice in Macon; member, Georgia State house of representatives, 1969-1976; elected as a Democrat to the Ninety-fifth and to the two succeeding Congresses (January 3, 1977-January 3, 1983); unsuccessful candidate for renomination in 1982 to the Ninety-eighth Congress; vice president of a governmental relations consulting firm in Washington, D.C.; is a resident of Vienna, Va.

**EVANS, Charles Robley,** a Representative from Nevada; born in Breckenridge, Sangamon County, Ill., August 9, 1866; attended the common schools; engaged in mining in Manhattan, Nev., in 1905; moved to Goldfield, Esmeralda County, Nev., in 1908 and continued mining operations; delegate to the Democratic National Convention in 1908; elected as a Democrat to the Sixty-sixth Congress (March 4, 1919-March 3, 1921); unsuccessful candidate for reelection in 1920 to the Sixty-seventh Congress; guide at the United States Capitol from 1934 until his retirement in 1948; died in Kearney, Nebr., November 30, 1954; interment in Waco Cemetery, Waco, Nebr.

**EVANS, Cooper,** a Representative from Iowa. (*See* EVANS, Thomas Cooper.)

**EVANS, Daniel Jackson,** a Senator from Washington; born in Seattle, King County, Wash., October 16, 1925; B.S., University of Washington, Seattle, 1948; M.S., University of Washington, 1949; served in the United States Navy from 1943 until 1946, and returned to duty 1951-1953; civil and structural engineer; member, Washington State house of representatives, 1956-1965; elected Governor of Washington in 1964, reelected in 1968 and 1972, and served from January 13, 1965 to January 12, 1977; delivered keynote address at the Republican National Convention of 1968; president, The Evergreen State College, Olympia, Wash., 1977-1983; appointed by the Governor to the United States Senate, September 12, 1983, to fill the vacancy caused by the death of Henry M. Jackson, and subsequently elected by special election as a Republican on November 8, 1983, to complete the term ending January 3, 1989; was not a candidate for reelection in 1988; chairman, Daniel J. Evans Associates; is a resident of Seattle, Wash.

**EVANS, David Ellicott,** a Representative from New York; born in Ellicotts Upper Mills, Md., March 19, 1788; attended the common schools; moved to New York in 1803 and settled in Batavia; employed as a clerk and afterward as an accounting clerk with the Holland Land Co.; member of the State senate 1819-1822; member of the council of appointment in 1820 and 1821; elected to the Twentieth Congress and served from March 4, 1827, until his resignation May 2, 1827, before the assembling of Congress; appointed resident agent of the Holland Land Co., in 1827 and served until his resignation in 1837; also engaged in banking; delegate to the convention held at Albany, N.Y., in 1827 to advocate a protective tariff; retired from active business pursuits in 1837 to devote his attention to his extensive land interests; died in Batavia, Genesee County, N.Y., May 17, 1850; interment in Batavia Cemetery.

**EVANS, David Reid,** a Representative from South Carolina; born in Westminster, England, February 20, 1769; immigrated to the United States in 1784 with his father, who settled in South Carolina; attended Mount Zion College; studied law; was admitted to the bar in 1796 and commenced practice in Winnsboro; member of the State house of representatives 1802-1805; solicitor of the middle judicial circuit 1804-1811; elected as a Republican to the Thirteenth Congress (March 4, 1813-March 3, 1815); declined to be a candidate for reelection and returned to his plantation; member of the State senate 1818-1826; first president of the Fairfield Bible Society; died in Winnsboro, Fairfield County, S.C., March 8, 1843; interment at a private residence in Winnsboro.

**EVANS, David Walter,** a Representative from Indiana; born in Lafayette, Tippecanoe County, Ind., August 17, 1946; attended public schools in Shoals, Ind.; A.B., Indiana University, 1967; engaged in postgraduate work at Indiana University, 1967-1969, and Butler University, Indianapolis, 1969-1971; teacher of social studies and science and assistant principal, 1968-1974; delegate to the Democratic National Mid-term Convention, 1974; elected as a Democrat to the Ninety-fourth and to the three succeeding Congresses (January 3, 1975-January 3, 1983); unsuccessful candidate for renomination in 1982 to the Ninety-eighth Congress; legislative consultant in Washington, D.C.; is a resident of McLean, Va.

**EVANS, Frank Edward,** a Representative from Colorado; born in Pueblo, Colo., September 6, 1923; attended public schools in Colorado Springs; entered Pomona College, Claremont, Calif., in 1941; interrupted his education in 1943 to serve in the United States Navy as a patrol pilot, 1943-1946; B.A., University of Denver, 1948; LL.B., University of Denver School of Law, 1950; was admitted to the bar in 1950 and began the practice of law in Pueblo; member of the Colorado State house of representatives, 1961-1964; elected as a Democrat to the Eighty-ninth and to the six succeeding Congresses (January 3, 1965-January 3, 1979); was not a candidate for reelection in 1978 to the Ninety-sixth Congress; is a resident of Beulah, Colo.

**EVANS, George,** a Representative and a Senator from Maine; born in Hallowell, Maine, January 12, 1797; was graduated from Bowdoin College, Brunswick, Maine, in 1815; studied law; was admitted to the bar and practiced in Gardiner, Maine; member, State house of representatives and served as speaker in 1829; elected to the Twenty-first Congress to fill the vacancy caused by the resignation of Peleg Sprague; reelected to the Twenty-second and five succeeding Congresses and served from July 20, 1829, until his resignation, effective March 3, 1841; chairman, Committee on Expenditures in the Department of the Treasury (Twenty-sixth Congress); elected as a Whig to the United States Senate and served from March 4, 1841, until March 3, 1847; unsuccessful candidate for reelection in 1846; chairman, Committee on Manufactures (Twenty-seventh Congress), Committee on Finance (Twenty-seventh and

Twenty-eighth Congresses), Committee on Territories (Twenty-eighth Congress); resumed the practice of law in Portland, Maine; member of the commission to ascertain claims against Mexico in 1849 and 1850; elected attorney general of Maine in 1850, 1854, and 1856; died in Portland, Cumberland County, Maine, April 6, 1867; interment in Oak Grove Cemetery, Gardiner, Maine.

**Bibliography:** *DAB.*

**EVANS, Henry Clay,** a Representative from Tennessee; born in Juniata County, Pa., June 18, 1843; moved to Wisconsin in 1844, with his parents, who settled in Platteville, Grant County; attended the common schools and a business school in Madison; was graduated from a business training school at Chicago in 1861; enlisted on May 6, 1864, as a corporal in Company A, Forty-first Regiment, Wisconsin Volunteer Infantry and served until September 24, 1864; settled in Chattanooga, Tenn., in 1870 and engaged in the manufacture of freight cars; elected mayor in 1881, serving two terms; organized the public-school system of Chattanooga and served as first school commissioner; elected as a Republican to the Fifty-first Congress (March 4, 1889-March 3, 1891); unsuccessful candidate for reelection in 1890 to the Fifty-second Congress; First Assistant Postmaster General, 1891-1893; elected Governor of Tennessee in 1894 on the face of the returns, but a legislative recount rejected certain votes and declared his Democratic opponent, Peter Turney, elected; appointed Commissioner of Pensions on April 1, 1897, and served until May 13, 1902, when he resigned to enter the diplomatic service; appointed United States consul general to London, England, May 9, 1902, retiring in 1905; chosen commissioner of health and education of Chattanooga in 1911; died in Chattanooga, Tenn., December 12, 1921; interment in Forest Hill Cemetery, St. Elmo, Chattanooga, Tenn.

**Bibliography:** *DAB.*

**EVANS, Hiram Kinsman,** a Representative from Iowa; born in Walnut Township, Wayne County, Iowa, March 17, 1863; attended the country schools and Seymour and Allerton (Iowa) High Schools; was graduated from the law department of the University of Iowa at Iowa City in 1886; was admitted to the bar in 1886 and commenced practice in Holdrege, Nebr.; moved to Seymour, Iowa, in 1887, and to Corydon, Iowa, in 1889 and continued the practice of law; prosecuting attorney for Wayne County 1891-1895; member of the State house of representatives in 1896 and 1897; member of the board of regents of the University of Iowa 1897-1904; mayor of Corydon 1901-1903; judge of the third judicial district of Iowa from 1904 until 1923, when he resigned; elected as a Republican to the Sixty-eighth Congress to fill the vacancy caused by the resignation of Horace M. Towner and served from June 4, 1923, to March 3, 1925; declined to be a candidate for renomination in 1924 to the Sixty-ninth Congress; resumed the practice of law in Corydon, Iowa; appointed by Governor John Hammill as a member of the Iowa State board of parole on July 1, 1927, and served to July 1, 1933; died in Corydon, Iowa, July 9, 1941; interment in Corydon Cemetery.

**EVANS, Isaac Newton,** a Representative from Pennsylvania; born near Westchester, Chester County, Pa., July 29, 1827; attended the common schools; was graduated from the medical department of Bowdoin College, Brunswick, Maine, in 1851 and from Jefferson Medical College, Philadelphia, in 1852; commenced the practice of medicine in Johnsville, Bucks County, Pa., in 1852; moved to Hatboro, Montgomery County, Pa., in 1856 and continued the practice of medicine; president of the Hatboro National Bank; elected as a Republican to the Forty-fifth Congress (March 4, 1877-March 3, 1879); was not a candidate for renomination; elected to the Forty-eighth and Forty-ninth Congresses (March 4, 1883-March 3, 1887); declined to be a candidate for renomination; engaged in the practice of medicine, the real estate business, and banking; died in Hatboro, Pa., December 3, 1901; interment in Friends Cemetery, Horsham, Montgomery County, Pa.

**EVANS, James La Fayette,** a Representative from Indiana; born in Clayville, Harrison County, Ky., March 27, 1825; attended the public schools; moved to Indiana, with his parents, who settled in Hancock County in 1837; moved to Marion, Ind., in 1845 and engaged in mercantile pursuits; moved to Hamilton County, Ind.; settled in Noblesville in 1850 and continued mercantile pursuits; also engaged in the grain-elevator business and in the pork-packing business; elected as a Republican to the Forty-fourth and Forty-fifth Congresses (March 4, 1875-March 3, 1879); was not a candidate for renomination in 1878; resumed the grain-elevator business; died in Noblesville, Ind., May 28, 1903; interment in Crownland Cemetery.

**EVANS, John,** a Delegate from Delaware; member of the Delaware Assembly in 1774, 1775, and 1776; deputy to the convention to formulate the State constitution in 1776; elected as a Delegate to the Continental Congress on November 10, 1776, but declined to serve on account of ill health; his credentials were presented December 2, 1776, and he was permitted to withdraw April 4, 1777, without having been present; justice of the State supreme court in 1777.

**EVANS, John Morgan,** a Representative from Montana; born in Sedalia, Pettis County, Mo., January 7, 1863; attended the common schools, the United States Military Academy, West Point, N.Y., in 1884 and 1885, and was graduated from the University of Missouri at Columbia in 1887; studied law; was admitted to the bar in 1888 and commenced practice in Missoula, Mont.; judge of the police court 1889-1894; register of the United States land office 1894-1898; mayor of Missoula under the first city commission government established in the State in 1911 and 1912; elected as a Democrat to the Sixty-third and to the three succeeding Congresses (March 4, 1913-March 3, 1921); unsuccessful candidate for reelection in 1920 to the Sixty-seventh Congress; resumed the practice of law in Missoula, Mont.; elected to the Sixty-eighth and to the four succeeding Congresses (March 4, 1923-March 3, 1933); chairman, Committee on Public Lands (Seventy-second Congress); unsuccessful candidate for renomination in 1932; retired from active practice and resided in Washington, D.C., until his death March 12, 1946; interment in Missoula Cemetery, Missoula, Mont.

**EVANS, Joshua, Jr.,** a Representative from Pennsylvania; born in Paoli, Chester County, Pa., January 20, 1777; attended the common schools; hotel keeper and also engaged in agricultural pursuits; member of the Pennsylvania house of representatives in 1820; appointed the first postmaster of Paoli December 9, 1826, and served until February 13, 1830; president of the Tredyffrin Township school board 1836-1846; brigadier general of Pennsylvania militia; elected as a Jacksonian to the Twenty-first and Twenty-second Congresses (March 4, 1829-March 3, 1833); was not a candidate for renomination in 1832; resumed his former business pursuits; died in Paoli, Pa., October 2, 1846; interment in the cemetery of the Great Valley Baptist Church, New Centerville, Pa.

**EVANS, Josiah James,** a Senator from South Carolina; born in Marlboro District, S.C., November 27, 1786; graduated from South Carolina College at Columbia in 1808; studied law; was admitted to the bar and began practice in Marlboro District in 1811; member, State house of representatives 1812-1813; moved to Darlington District in 1816; member, State house of representatives; State solicitor for the northern district of South Carolina 1816-1829; judge of the circuit court 1829-1835; judge of the State supreme court 1829-1852; elected as a Democrat to the United States Senate and served from March 4, 1853, until his death in Washington, D.C., May 6, 1858; chairman, Committee to Audit and Control the Contingent Expense (Thirty-third through Thirty-fifth Congresses), Committee on Revolutionary Claims (Thirty-fourth and Thirty-fifth Congresses); interment in a private cemetery at his ancestral home at Society Hill, Darlington County, S.C.

**EVANS, Lane Allen,** a Representative from Illinois; born in Rock Island, Rock Island County, Ill., August 4, 1951; attended Sacred Heart School, Rock Island; graduated from Alleman High School, Rock Island, 1969; B.A., Augusta College, Rock Island, 1974; J.D., Georgetown University Law Center, Washington, D.C., 1977; served, United States Marine Corps, 1969-1971; admitted to the Illinois bar, 1978, and commenced practice in Rock Island; Kennedy for President, 1980; elected as a Democrat to the Ninety-eighth and to the six succeeding Congresses (January 3, 1983-January 3, 1997); is a resident of Rock Island, Ill.

**EVANS, Lemuel Dale,** a Representative from Texas; born in Tennessee January 8, 1810; studied law and was admitted to the bar; moved to Marshall, Tex., in 1843 and engaged in the practice of law; member of the State convention that annexed the State of Texas to the Union in 1845; elected as the candidate of the American Party to the Thirty-fourth Congress (March 4, 1855-March 3, 1857); unsuccessful candidate for reelection in 1856 to the Thirty-fifth Congress; collector of internal revenue in 1867; member of the reconstruction convention in 1868; chief justice of the supreme court in 1870 and 1871; associate justice and presiding judge from 1872 to 1873, when he resigned; United States marshal for the eastern judicial district of Texas in 1875; died in Washington, D.C., on July 1, 1877; interment in the Congressional Cemetery.

**EVANS, Lynden,** a Representative from Illinois; born in La Salle, La Salle County, Ill., June 28, 1858; attended the public schools and was graduated from Knox College, Galesburg, Ill., in 1882; taught in the schools of La Salle and Evanston, Ill.; studied law; was admitted to the bar in 1885 and commenced practice at Chicago, Ill.; lecturer on corporation law in the John Marshall Law School in 1907 and 1908; elected as a Democrat to the Sixty-second Congress (March 4, 1911-March 3, 1913); unsuccessful candidate for reelection in 1912 to the Sixty-third Congress; resumed the practice of law in Chicago, Ill., until his death there on May 6, 1926; interment in Graceland Cemetery.

**EVANS, Marcellus Hugh,** a Representative from New York; born in Brooklyn, N.Y., September 22, 1884; attended St. John the Baptist School and St. James Academy, Brooklyn, N.Y.; was graduated from the law department of Fordham University in 1910; was admitted to the bar in 1910 and commenced practice in Brooklyn; member of the State assembly 1922-1926; served in the State senate 1927-1934; elected as a Democrat to the Seventy-fourth, Seventy-fifth, and Seventy-sixth Congresses (January 3, 1935-January 3, 1941); unsuccessful candidate in 1940 for renomination as a Democrat and for election as a Republican to the Seventy-seventh Congress; resumed the practice of law; died in Brooklyn, N.Y., November 21, 1953; interment in Calvary Cemetery, Long Island City, N.Y.

**EVANS, Melvin Herbert,** a Delegate from the Virgin Islands; born in Christiansted, St. Croix, V.I., August 7, 1917; attended the public schools; B.S., Howard University, Washington, D.C., 1940; M.D., Howard University College of Medicine, 1944; M.P.H., University of California, Berkeley, Calif., 1967; Virgin Islands Health Commissioner, 1959-1967; resumed the private practice of medicine, 1967-1969; appointed Governor of the United States Virgin Islands, and served from 1969 until 1971; was the first elected Governor of the Virgin Islands in 1970, and served from 1971 until 1975; unsuccessful candidate in 1974 for reelection as Governor; Republican National Committeeman for the Virgin Islands, 1976-1980; delegate to the Republican National Conventions of 1972 and 1976; elected as a Republican to the Ninety-sixth Congress (January 3, 1979-January 3, 1981); unsuccessful candidate for reelection in 1980 to the Ninety-seventh Congress; appointed

United States ambassador to Trinidad and Tobago on December 1, 1981, and served until his death in Christiansted, St. Croix, V.I., on November 27, 1984; was a resident of Christiansted; interment in Christiansted Cemetery.

**EVANS, Nathan,** a Representative from Ohio; born in Belmont County, Ohio, June 24, 1804; county clerk of Belmont County in 1827 and 1828; taught school; studied law; was admitted to the bar in 1831 and commenced practice in Hillsboro, Ohio; moved to Cambridge, Ohio, in 1832; mayor of Cambridge in 1841; prosecuting attorney of Guernsey County 1842-1846; elected as a Whig to the Thirtieth and Thirty-first Congresses (March 4, 1847-March 3, 1851); was not a candidate for renomination in 1850; resumed the practice of law in Cambridge; again mayor of Cambridge 1855-1857; judge of the court of common pleas 1859-1864; resumed the practice of law; died in Cambridge, Ohio, September 27, 1879; interment in South Cemetery.

**EVANS, Robert Emory,** a Representative from Nebraska; born in Coalmont, Huntingdon County, Pa., July 15, 1856; attended the public schools, the State normal school at Millersville, Pa., and the Indiana (Pa.) Normal School; employed in Colorado as a machinist 1877-1883; was graduated from the law department of the University of Michigan at Ann Arbor in 1886; was admitted to the bar and practiced; moved to Dakota City, Nebr., in 1887; superintendent of Winnebago Industrial School 1889-1891; prosecuting attorney of Dakota County in 1895; resigned to become judge of the eighth judicial district, in which capacity he served from 1895 to 1899; delegate to the Republican National Convention in 1912; president of the Nebraska State Bar Association in 1919; elected as a Republican to the Sixty-sixth and Sixty-seventh Congresses (March 4, 1919-March 3, 1923); unsuccessful candidate for reelection in 1922 to the Sixty-eighth Congress; resumed the practice of law in Dakota City, Nebr.; elected judge of the supreme court from the third district of Nebraska in 1924; moved to Lincoln, Nebr., where he died July 8, 1925; interment in Graceland Park Cemetery, Sioux City, Iowa.

**EVANS, Thomas,** a Representative from Virginia; born in Accomac County, Va.; attended the public schools and William and Mary College at Williamsburg; studied law and was admitted to the bar; member of the Virginia house of delegates in 1780, 1781, and 1794-1796; elected as a Federalist to the Fifth and Sixth Congresses (March 4, 1797-March 3, 1801); one of the managers appointed by the House of Representatives in 1798 to conduct the impeachment proceedings against William Blount, a Senator from Tennessee; moved to Wheeling, Va. (now West Virginia), in 1802; member of the West Virginia State house of representatives in 1805 and 1806.

**EVANS, Thomas Beverley, Jr.,** a Representative from Delaware; born in Nashville, Davidson County, Tenn., November 5, 1931; attended the public schools of Old Hickory, Tenn., and Seaford, Del., 1936-1943; graduated from Woodberry Forest School, Orange, Va., 1947; B.A., University of Virginia, 1953; LL.B., University of Virginia School of Law, 1956; admitted to the Virginia bar in 1956; engaged in insurance and mortgage brokerage business, Wilmington, Del., 1957-1968; served in Delaware National Guard, 1956-1960; clerk to Chief Justice Clarence O. Southerland of the Delaware Supreme Court, 1955; director, Delaware State Development Department, 1969-1970; co-chairman and chief operating officer, Republican National Committee, 1971-1973; delegate to the Republican National Conventions of 1972, 1976, and 1980; elected as a Republican to the Ninety-fifth and to the two succeeding Congresses (January 3, 1977-January 3, 1983); unsuccessful candidate for reelection in 1982 to the Ninety-eighth Congress; member of law firm of Manatt, Phelps, Rothenberg & Evans in Washington, D.C.; is a resident of Wilmington, Del.

**EVANS, Thomas Cooper,** a Representative from Iowa; born in Cedar Rapids, Linn County, Iowa, May 26, 1924; attended the public schools; attended St. Andrews University, Scotland, 1948; B.S., Iowa State College, Ames, 1949, and M.S., 1955; graduated from Oak Ridge School of Reactor Technology, Oak Ridge, Tenn., 1956; served in the United States Army, Infantry, 1943-1946; Corps of Engineers, lieutenant colonel, 1949-1965; engineer and farmer; president, Evans Farms, Inc., 1965-1980; member, Grundy County Board of Property Tax Review, 1968-1974; served in the Iowa State house of representatives, 1975-1979; delegate, Iowa State Republican conventions, 1966-1978; elected as a Republican to the Ninety-seventh and to the two succeeding Congresses (January 3, 1981-January 3, 1987); was not a candidate for reelection in 1986 to the One Hundredth Congress; is a resident of Grundy Center, Iowa.

**EVANS, Walter** (nephew of Burwell Clark Ritter), a Representative from Kentucky; born near Glasgow, Barren County, Ky., September 18, 1842; attended the public schools near Harrodsburg, Ky.; moved to Hopkinsville, Christian County; deputy county clerk in 1859; served as a captain in the Union Army, 1861-1863; served as deputy and later as chief clerk of the circuit court; studied law; was admitted to the bar in 1864 and commenced practice in Hopkinsville; delegate to the Republican National Conventions of 1868, 1872, 1880, and 1884; elected to the Kentucky house of representatives in 1871, and to the Kentucky senate in 1873; moved to Louisville, Ky., in 1874 and continued the practice of law; unsuccessful candidate for election in 1876 to the Forty-fifth Congress; unsuccessful Republican candidate in 1879 for election for Governor of Kentucky; appointed by President Chester A. Arthur as Commissioner of Internal Revenue on May 21, 1883 and served until April 20, 1885, when he returned to Louisville and resumed the practice of law; elected as a Republican to the Fifty-fourth and Fifty-fifth Congresses (March 4, 1895-March 3, 1899); unsuccessful candidate for reelection in 1898 to the Fifty-sixth Congress; appointed by President William McKinley judge of the District Court of the United States for the District of Kentucky on March 4, 1899, and served until his death in Louisville, Ky., December 30, 1923; interment in Cave Hill Cemetery.

**Bibliography:** *DAB.*

**EVANS, William Elmer,** a Representative from California; born near London, Laurel County, Ky., December 14, 1877; attended the public schools and Sue Bennett Memorial College, London, Ky.; studied law; was admitted to the bar in 1902 and commenced practice in London, Ky.; moved to Glendale, Calif., in 1910 and engaged in the practice of law and in banking; city attorney of Glendale, Calif., 1911-1921; delegate to the Republican National Convention in 1924; elected as a Republican to the Seventieth and to the three succeeding Congresses (March 4, 1927-January 3, 1935); unsuccessful candidate for reelection in 1934 to the Seventy-fourth Congress; resumed the practice of law, real estate development, and ranching until his death in Los Angeles, Calif., November 12, 1959; interment in Forest Lawn Cemetery, Glendale, Calif.

**EVARTS, William Maxwell** (grandson of Roger Sherman), a Senator from New York; born in Boston, Mass., February 6, 1818; attended the Boston Latin School and graduated from Yale College in 1837; studied at Harvard Law School; was admitted to the bar in New York City in 1841 and practiced law; assistant United States district attorney, 1849-1853; unsuccessful Republican candidate for election to the United States Senate in 1861; member of the State constitutional convention, 1867-1868; appointed Attorney General by President Andrew Johnson, and served from July 15, 1868 until March 3, 1869; chief counsel for President Johnson in the impeachment proceedings in 1868; counsel for the United States before the tribunal of arbitration on the *Alabama* claims at Geneva, Switzerland, in 1872; counsel for President Rutherford B. Hayes, in behalf of the Republican Party, before the Electoral Commission in

1876; appointed Secretary of State in the Cabinet of President Hayes, and served from March 12, 1877 to March 7, 1881; delegate to the International Monetary Conference at Paris in 1881; elected as a Republican to the United States Senate, and served from March 4, 1885 to March 3, 1891; chairman, Committee on the Library (Fiftieth and Fifty-first Congresses); retired from public life due to ill health; died in New York City, February 28, 1901; interment in Ascutney Cemetery, Windsor, Vt.

Bibliography: *DAB*; Barrows, Chester. *William M. Evarts: Lawyer, Diplomat, Statesman.* Chapel Hill: University of North Carolina Press, 1941; Dyer, Brainerd. *The Public Career of William M. Evarts.* 1933. Reprint. New York: Da Capo Press, 1969.

EVELEIGH, Nicholas, a Delegate from South Carolina; born in Charleston, S.C., about 1748; moved with his parents to Bristol, England, about 1755; was educated in England; returned to Charleston, S.C., in 1774; during the Revolutionary War was appointed captain in the Second South Carolina Regiment (Continentals) June 17, 1775; engaged in the battle with the British fleet and forces at Fort Moultrie on June 28, 1776; was promoted to colonel and appointed deputy adjutant general for South Carolina and Georgia on April 3, 1778; resigned August 24, 1778; engaged in agricultural pursuits; member of the State house of representatives in 1781; Member of the Continental Congress in 1781 and 1782; member of the State legislative council in 1783; appointed First Comptroller of the United States Treasury on September 11, 1789, and served until his death in Philadelphia, Pa., April 16, 1791; interment probably in Philadelphia.

EVERETT, Edward (father of William Everett), a Representative and a Senator from Massachusetts; born in Dorchester, Mass., April 11, 1794; graduated from Harvard University in 1811; tutor in that university 1812-1814; studied theology and was ordained pastor of the Brattle Street Unitarian Church, Boston, in 1814; professor of Greek literature at Harvard University from 1815 until 1826; overseer of Harvard University, 1827-1847, 1849-1854, and 1862-1865; elected to the Nineteenth and to the four succeeding Congresses (March 4, 1825-March 3, 1835); declined to be a candidate for renomination in 1834 to the Twenty-fourth Congress; chairman, Committee on Foreign Affairs (Twentieth Congress); elected Governor of Massachusetts in 1835, reelected in 1836, 1837 and 1838, and served from January 13, 1836 to January 18, 1840; unsuccessful candidate for reelection in 1839; appointed United States Envoy Extraordinary and Minister Plenipotentiary to Great Britain in September 1841 and served until August 1845; declined a diplomatic commission to China in March 1843; president of Harvard University, 1846-1849; appointed Secretary of State by President Millard Fillmore and served from November 6, 1852, to March 3, 1853; elected as a Whig to the United States Senate and served from March 4, 1853, until his resignation, effective June 1, 1854; unsuccessful candidate for vice president of the United States in 1860 on the Constitutional Union ticket headed by John Bell; died in Boston, Mass., January 15, 1865; interment in Mount Auburn Cemetery, Cambridge, Mass.

Bibliography: *DAB*; Frothingham, Paul. *Edward Everett: Orator and Statesman.* 1925. Reprint. New York: Kennikat Press, 1971; Horn, Stuart J. "Edward Everett and American Nationalism." Ph.D. dissertation, City University of New York, 1973; Varg, Paul A. *Edward Everett: The Intellectual in the Turmoil of Politics.* Selinsgrove, Pa.: Susquehanna University Press, 1992.

EVERETT, Horace, a Representative from Vermont; born in Foxboro, Mass., July 17, 1779; was graduated from Brown University, Providence, R.I., in 1797; studied law; was admitted to the bar in 1801 and commenced practice in Windsor, Vt.; prosecuting attorney for Windsor County 1813-1818; member of the State house of representatives in 1819, 1820, 1822, 1824, and again in 1834; delegate to the State constitutional convention in 1828; elected to

the Twenty-first, Twenty-second and Twenty-third Congresses, and reelected as a Whig to the Twenty-fourth through Twenty-seventh Congresses (March 4, 1829-March 3, 1843); died in Windsor, Vt., January 30, 1851; interment in Old South Burying Ground.

EVERETT, Robert Ashton, a Representative from Tennessee; born on a farm near Union City, Obion County, Tenn., February 24, 1915; attended the public schools in Obion County; was graduated from Murray (Ky.) State College in 1936; elected a member of Obion County Court in 1936 and in 1938 was elected circuit court clerk of Obion County; served in the United States Army, 1942-1945; administrative assistant to Senator Tom Stewart, 1945-1949; administrative assistant to Governor Gordon W. Browning, 1950-1952; executive secretary of the Tennessee County Services Association, 1954-1958; elected as a Democrat to the Eighty-fifth Congress to fill the vacancy caused by the death of Jere Cooper; reelected to the Eighty-sixth and to the five succeeding Congresses, and served from February 1, 1958 until his death in Nashville, Tenn., January 26, 1969; interment in East View Cemetery, Union City, Tenn.

EVERETT, Robert Terry (Terry), a Representative from Alabama; born in Dothan, Houston County, Ala., February 15, 1937; attended Enterprise (Ala.) State Junior College, the University of Alabama, and the University of Maryland; entered active duty, United States Air Force in 1955; released in 1959; newspaper executive; construction company owner; farm owner; real estate developer; elected as a Republican to the One Hundred Third and One Hundred Fourth Congresses (January 3, 1993-January 3, 1997); is a resident of Enterprise, Ala.

EVERETT, Robert William, a Representative from Georgia; born near Hayneville, Houston County, Ga., March 3, 1839; attended the village schools and Hayneville Academy; was graduated from Mercer University, Macon, Ga., in 1859; taught school in Polk and Houston Counties for two years; entered the Confederate Army as a sergeant in Captain Gartrell's company, General Nathan Bedford Forrest's escort squadron, and served until the close of the Civil War; again engaged in teaching school in Houston County and also in Cedartown, Ga., until 1872, when he abandoned the profession for agricultural pursuits; commissioner of roads and revenue of Polk County, 1875-1880; member of the Board of Education of Polk County from 1880 until 1891, and served as president of the board, 1882-1891; member of the Georgia State house of representatives, 1882-1885; elected as a Democrat to the Fifty-second Congress (March 4, 1891-March 3, 1893); was not a candidate for renomination in 1892 to the Fifty-third Congress; resumed agricultural pursuits; again a member of the Georgia State house of representatives in 1898 and 1899; lived in retirement until his death in Rockmart, Polk County, Ga., on February 27, 1915; interment in Cedartown Cemetery, Cedartown, Ga.

EVERETT, William (son of Edward Everett), a Representative from Massachusetts; born in Watertown, Middlesex County, Mass., October 10, 1839; attended the public schools of Cambridge and Boston; was graduated from Harvard University in 1859, from Trinity College, Cambridge University, England, in 1863, and from the law department of Harvard University in 1865; was admitted to the bar in 1866; studied for the ministry, and was licensed to preach in 1872 by the Suffolk Association of Unitarian Ministers; tutor at Harvard University 1870-1873; assistant professor of Latin 1873-1877; master of Adams Academy, Quincy, Mass., 1878-1893; elected as a Democrat to the Fifty-third Congress to fill the vacancy caused by the resignation of Henry Cabot Lodge and served from April 25, 1893, to March 3, 1895; was not a candidate for renomination in 1894 to the Fifty-fourth Congress; unsuccessful candidate in 1897 for election for Governor of Massachusetts; master of school at Quincy, Mass., where he died February 16, 1910; interment in Mount Auburn Cemetery, Cambridge, Mass.

**EVERHART, James Bowen** (son of William Everhart), a Representative from Pennsylvania; born in the Boot, near West Chester, West Whiteland Township, Chester County, Pa., July 26, 1821; attended Bolmar's Academy, West Chester, Pa., and was graduated from Princeton College in 1842; studied law at Harvard University and in Philadelphia, Pa.; was admitted to the bar in 1845; went abroad and spent two years in study at the Universities of Berlin and Edinburgh; returned to West Chester, Pa., and engaged in the practice of law; during the Civil War served in Company B, Tenth Regiment, Pennsylvania Militia; member of the Pennsylvania senate from 1876 to 1882; elected as a Republican to the Forty-eighth and Forty-ninth Congresses (March 4, 1883-March 3, 1887); unsuccessful candidate for renomination in 1886; resumed the practice of law; died in West Chester, Pa., August 23, 1888; interment in Oakland Cemetery, near West Chester.

**EVERHART, William** (father of James Bowen Everhart), a Representative from Pennsylvania; born in Chester County, Pa., May 17, 1785; attended the common schools and became a civil engineer; served in the War of 1812 as captain of a company of riflemen; was the only passenger saved from the packet ship *Albion,* wrecked off the coast of Ireland in 1822; upon his return to Pennsylvania he platted a large addition to the city of West Chester; was elected as a Whig to the Thirty-third Congress (March 4, 1853-March 3, 1855); was not a candidate for renomination; engaged in mercantile pursuits; died in West Chester, Pa., October 30, 1868; interment in Oakland Cemetery.

**EVINS, John Hamilton,** a Representative from South Carolina; born in Spartanburg District, S.C., July 18, 1830; attended the common schools and was graduated from South Carolina College at Columbia in 1853; studied law; was admitted to the bar in 1856 and commenced practice in Spartanburg, S.C.; entered the Confederate Army as a lieutenant and served until the close of the Civil War, attaining the rank of lieutenant colonel; resumed the practice of law in Spartanburg; member of the South Carolina State house of representatives, 1862-1864; delegate to the Democratic National Convention of 1876; elected as a Democrat to the Forty-fifth and to the three succeeding Congresses, and served from March 4, 1877 until his death in Spartanburg, S.C., October 20, 1884; chairman, Committee on Territories (Forty-eighth Congress); interment in Magnolia Street Cemetery, Spartanburg, S.C.

**EVINS, Joseph Landon,** a Representative from Tennessee; born on a farm near Blend, DeKalb County, Tenn., October 24, 1910; attended the public schools; was graduated from Vanderbilt University, Nashville, Tenn., in 1933 and from Cumberland University School of Law, Lebanon, Tenn., in 1934; postgraduate student of law at George Washington University, Washington, D.C., 1938-1940; was admitted to the bar in 1934 and commenced practice in Smithville, Tenn.; attorney for Federal Trade Commission in Washington, D.C., 1935-1938; assistant secretary of the Federal Trade Commission, 1938-1940; served in the United States Army on the staff of the Judge Advocate General, War Department, from March 1942 until discharged as a major in March 1946; resumed the practice of law in Smithville, Tenn.; chairman of the DeKalb County Democratic Executive Committee in 1946; elected as a Democrat to the Eightieth and to the fourteen succeeding Congresses (January 3, 1947-January 3, 1977); chairman, Select Committee on Small Business (Eighty-eighth through Ninety-third Congresses), Committee on Small Business (Ninety-fourth Congress); was not a candidate for reelection in 1976 to the Ninety-fifth Congress; was a resident of Smithville, Tenn., until his death in Nashville, Tenn., March 31, 1984; interment in Smithville Town Cemetery, Smithville, Tenn.

**Bibliography:** Evins, Joe L. *Understanding Congress.* New York: Clarkson N. Potter, Inc., Publisher, 1963; Graves, Susan B. *Evins of Tennessee: Twenty-five Years in Congress.* New York: Popular Library, 1971.

**EWART, Hamilton Glover,** a Representative from North Carolina; born in Columbia, Richland County, S.C., October 23, 1849; attended private schools; moved to Hendersonville, Henderson County, N.C., with his parents in 1862; was graduated from the literary and law departments of the University of South Carolina at Columbia; was admitted to the bar in 1870 and commenced practice in Hendersonville, N.C.; delegate to the Republican National Convention in 1876; elected mayor of Hendersonville in 1877; member of the State house of representatives 1887-1889, 1895-1897, and 1911-1913; elected as a Republican to the Fifty-first Congress (March 4, 1889-March 3, 1891); unsuccessful candidate for reelection in 1890 to the Fifty-second Congress and for election in 1904; resumed the practice of law in Hendersonville, N.C.; judge of the criminal court in 1895; judge of the circuit court in 1897; served as judge of the United States District Court for the Western District of North Carolina from July 16, 1898, to March 4, 1899, and April 14, 1899, to June 7, 1900; moved to Chicago, Ill., in 1916 and continued the practice of law; died in Chicago, Ill., April 28, 1918; interment in Oakdale Cemetery, Hendersonville, N.C.

**EWING, Andrew** (brother of Edwin Hickman Ewing), a Representative from Tennessee; born in Nashville, Tenn., June 17, 1813; completed preparatory studies, and was graduated from the University of Nashville in 1832; studied law; was admitted to the bar in 1835 and commenced practice in Nashville, Tenn.; chosen trustee of the University of Nashville in 1833, and served in that office until his death; elected as a Democrat to the Thirty-first Congress (March 4, 1849-March 3, 1851); declined to be a candidate for renomination in 1850 to the Thirty-second Congress; resumed the practice of law in Nashville; delegate to the Democratic National Convention at Baltimore in 1860; during the Civil War served as judge of General Braxton Bragg's military court; died in Atlanta, Ga., June 16, 1864; interment in Nashville City Cemetery, Nashville, Tenn.

**EWING, Edwin Hickman** (brother of Andrew Ewing), a Representative from Tennessee; born in Nashville, Tenn., December 2, 1809; completed preparatory studies, and was graduated from the University of Nashville in 1827; studied law; was admitted to the bar in 1831 and commenced practice in Nashville; became a trustee of the University of Nashville in 1831, and served until his death; member of the State house of representatives in 1841 and 1842; elected as a Whig to the Twenty-ninth Congress (March 4, 1845-March 3, 1847); was not a candidate for renomination in 1846 to the Thirtieth Congress; resumed the practice of law in Nashville; after the Civil War was appointed president of the University of Nashville; died in Murfreesboro, Tenn., April 24, 1902; interment in Murfreesboro City Cemetery.

**EWING, John,** a Representative from Indiana; born in Cork, Ireland, May 19, 1789; immigrated to the United States with his parents, who settled in Baltimore, Md.; attended the public schools; moved to Vincennes, Ind., in 1813 and engaged in commercial pursuits; established the Wabash Telegraph; associate judge of the circuit court of Knox County from 1816 to 1820, when he resigned; unsuccessful candidate for the State senate in 1816 and 1821; appointed lieutenant colonel of the State militia in 1825; member of the State senate 1825-1833; elected to the Twenty-third Congress (March 4, 1833-March 3, 1835); elected as a Whig to the Twenty-fifth Congress (March 4, 1837-March 3, 1839); unsuccessful candidate for reelection in 1838 to the Twenty-sixth Congress; again a member of the State senate 1842-1844; retired from public life and active business pursuits; died in Vincennes, Ind., April 6, 1858; interment in the City Cemetery.

**EWING, John Hoge,** a Representative from Pennsylvania; born near Brownsville, Fayette County, Pa., October 5, 1796; attended the common schools and was graduated from Washington (now Washington and Jefferson) College, Washington, Pa., in 1814; studied law; was admitted to the bar in 1818 and commenced practice in Washington, Pa.; engaged in agricultural pursuits; trustee of Washington College 1834-1887 and of Washington Female Seminary 1846-1887; member of the Pennsylvania house of representatives in 1835 and 1836; served in the Pennsylvania senate 1838-1842; elected as a Whig to the Twenty-ninth Congress (March 4, 1845-March 3, 1847); resumed agricultural pursuits; delegate to the Republican National Convention in 1860; died in Washington, Pa., June 9, 1887; interment in Washington Cemetery.

**EWING, Presley Underwood,** a Representative from Kentucky; born in Russellville, Ky., September 1, 1822; attended the public schools; completed preparatory studies; was graduated from Centre College, Danville, Ky., in 1840 and from the law school of Transylvania University, Lexington, Ky., in 1843; studied theology at the Baptist Seminary at Newton, Mass., in 1845 and 1846; returned to Kentucky and practiced law in Russellville; member of the Kentucky house of representatives in 1848 and 1849; elected as a Whig to the Thirty-second and Thirty-third Congresses and served from March 4, 1851, until his death in the town of Mammoth Cave, Ky., September 27, 1854; interment in Maple Grove Cemetery, Russellville, Ky.

**EWING, Thomas** (father of Thomas Ewing [1829-1896]), a Senator from Ohio; born near West Liberty, Ohio County, Va. (now West Virginia), December 28, 1789; moved to Ohio with his parents in 1792; pursued preparatory studies; graduated from Ohio University at Athens in 1816; studied law; was admitted to the bar in 1816 and commenced practice in Lancaster, Ohio; elected as a Whig to the United States Senate and served from March 4, 1831, to March 3, 1837; unsuccessful candidate for reelection in 1836; chairman, Committee on Public Lands (Twenty-fourth Congress); appointed Secretary of the Treasury by President William Henry Harrison, and served from March 5 to September 13, 1841; appointed Secretary of the Interior by President Zachary Taylor, and served from March 8, 1849 to July 22, 1850; was the first person to hold that office; appointed to the United States Senate to fill the vacancy caused by the resignation of Thomas Corwin, and served from July 20, 1850 to March 3, 1851; unsuccessful candidate for election to the United States Senate in 1851; resumed the practice of law in Lancaster; delegate to the peace convention held in Washington, D.C., in 1861 in an effort to devise means to prevent the impending war; appointed Secretary of War by President Andrew Johnson in February 1868, but the Senate refused to confirm the appointment; died in Lancaster, Ohio, October 26, 1871; interment in St. Mary's Cemetery.

**Bibliography:** *DAB*; Miller, Paul. "Thomas Ewing, Last of the Whigs." Ph.D. Dissertation, Ohio State University, 1933; Zsoldos, Sylvia. "Thomas Ewing, Sr., A Political Biography." Ph.D. dissertation, University of Delaware, 1933.

**EWING, Thomas** (son of Thomas Ewing [1789-1871]), a Representative from Ohio; born in Lancaster, Fairfield County, Ohio, August 7, 1829; pursued preparatory studies; private secretary to President Zachary Taylor in 1849 and 1850; was graduated from Brown University, Providence, R.I., in 1854; studied law; was admitted to the bar in 1855 and commenced practice in Cincinnati, Ohio; moved to Leavenworth, Kans., in 1856; member of the Leavenworth constitutional convention of 1858; delegate to the peace convention held in Washington, D.C., in 1861 in an effort to devise means to prevent the impending war; chief justice of the supreme court of Kansas in 1861 and 1862, when he resigned; recruited the Eleventh Regiment, Kansas Volunteer Cavalry, and was commissioned its colonel on September 15, 1862; brigadier

general of Volunteers March 13, 1863; brevetted major general of Volunteers; resigned his commission March 6, 1865; practiced law in Washington, D.C., until 1871, when he returned to Lancaster, Ohio; member of the Ohio State constitutional convention in 1873 and 1874; elected as a Democrat to the Forty-fifth and Forty-sixth Congresses (March 4, 1877-March 3, 1881); declined to be a candidate for renomination in 1880 to the Forty-seventh Congress; unsuccessful candidate in 1879 for election for Governor of Ohio; moved to New York City in 1881, where he engaged in the practice of law until his death there on January 21, 1896; interment in Oakland Cemetery, Yonkers, N.Y.

**Bibliography:** *DAB*; Taylor, David G. "The Business and Political Career of Thomas Ewing, Jr.: A Study of Frustrated Ambition." Ph.D. dissertation, University of Kansas, 1970.

**EWING, Thomas W.,** a Representative from Illinois; born in Atlanta, Logan County, Ill., September 19, 1935; attended Atlanta public schools; B.S., Millikin University, Decatur, Ill., 1957; J.D., John Marshall School of Law, Chicago, 1968; entered active duty, United States Army in 1957; United States Army Reserve service, 1957-1963; attorney; farm owner and manager; assistant state's attorney, Livingston County, Ill., 1968-1973; member, Illinois State house of representatives, 1974-1990; elected as a Republican to the One Hundred Second Congress, July 2, 1991, by special election to fill the vacancy caused by the resignation of Edward R. Madigan; reelected to the two succeeding Congresses, and served from July 2, 1991 to January 3, 1997; is a resident of Pontiac, Ill.

**EWING, William Lee Davidson,** a Senator from Illinois; born in Paris, Ky., August 31, 1795; pursued academic studies; studied law; was admitted to the bar and commenced practice in Shawneetown, Ill.; appointed by President James Monroe receiver of the land office at Vandalia, Ill., in 1820; brigadier general of State militia; colonel of the "Spy Battalion" during the Black Hawk War; clerk of the State house of representatives 1826-1828; member, State house of representatives 1830, and served as speaker; member, State senate 1832-1834, and was chosen president pro tempore in 1832; as acting lieutenant governor of Illinois, he succeeded to office as Governor on November 17, 1834, following the resignation of Governor John Reynolds, and served until December 3, 1834; appointed to the United States Senate to fill the vacancy caused by the death of Elias K. Kane and served from December 30, 1835, to March 3, 1837; unsuccessful candidate for election in 1837; member, State house of representatives in 1838 and 1840 and at both sessions was chosen speaker; clerk of the State house of representatives in 1842; appointed auditor of public accounts in 1843; died in Springfield, Ill., on March 25, 1846; final interment probably in Oak Ridge Cemetery, Springfield, Ill.

**EXON, John James,** a Senator from Nebraska; born in Geddes, Charles Mix County, S.Dak., August 9, 1921; attended the public schools in Lake Andes, S.Dak.; attended University of Omaha, Omaha, Nebr., 1939-1941; served in the United States Army Signal Corps, 1942-1945, and in the United States Army Reserve, 1945-1949; branch manager of a financial corporation; founder and president of Exon's Office Equipment, 1953-1971; elected Governor of Nebraska in 1970, reelected in 1974, and served from January 7, 1971 to January 3, 1979; elected as a Democrat to the United States Senate in 1978; reelected in 1984 and 1990, and served from January 3, 1979 to January 3, 1997; was not a candidate for reelection in 1996; is a resident of Lincoln, Nebr.

# F

**FADDIS, Charles Isiah,** a Representative from Pennsylvania; born in Loudonville, Ashland County, Ohio, June 13, 1890; moved with his parents to Waynesburg, Green County, Pa., in 1891; attended the public schools and Waynesburg (Pa.) College; was graduated from the agricultural department of Pennsylvania State

College at State College in 1915; served as a sergeant in the Tenth Infantry, Pennsylvania National Guard, on the Mexican border in 1916; served during the First World War with the Forty-seventh Regiment, United States Infantry, and the Fourth Ammunition Train; rose to rank of lieutenant colonel of Infantry; served in the Army of Occupation in Germany; awarded the Purple Heart Medal; engaged in the general contracting business in Waynesburg, Pa., 1919-1926; attended United States Army Command and General Staff School, Fort Leavenworth, Kans., in 1930; broker of oil and gas properties 1926-1933; elected as a Democrat to the Seventy-third and to the four succeeding Congresses and served from March 4, 1933, until his resignation on December 4, 1942, to enter the United States Army; unsuccessful candidate for renomination in 1942 to the Seventy-eighth Congress; during the Second World War was a colonel in the United States Army; awarded the Purple Heart and Bronze Star; engaged in raising Hereford cattle, producing oil and gas, and operating coal mines; died in Matzatlan, Mexico, April 1, 1972; interment in Rosemont Cemetery, Rogersville, Pa.

**FAIR, James Graham,** a Senator from Nevada; born near Belfast, County Tyrone, Ireland, December 3, 1831; immigrated to the United States in 1843 with his parents, who settled in Illinois; received a thorough business training; moved to California in 1849 and engaged in gold mining until 1860, when he moved to Virginia City, Nev.; in partnership with associates engaged in lucrative gold and silver mining; also engaged in the real estate business in San Francisco and was interested in various manufactures on the Pacific coast; elected as a Democrat to the United States Senate and served from March 4, 1881, to March 3, 1887; unsuccessful candidate for reelection in 1886; resumed his business interests in San Francisco, Calif., where he died on December 28, 1894; interment in Laurel Hill Cemetery.

Bibliography: *DAB*; Baur, John E. "The Senator's Happy Thought: Senator James G. Fair and the Chiricahua Apaches." *American West* 10 (January 1973): 35-39, 62-63; Lewis, Oscar. *Silver Kings: The Lives and Times of Mackay, Fair, Flood, and O'Brien.* New York: Knopf, 1947.

**FAIRBANKS, Charles Warren,** a Senator from Indiana and a Vice President of the United States; born near Unionville Center, Union County, Ohio, May 11, 1852; attended the common schools and graduated from Ohio Wesleyan University, Delaware, Ohio, in 1872; agent of the Associated Press in Pittsburgh, Pa., and in Cleveland, Ohio; studied law; was admitted to the Ohio bar in 1874; moved to Indianapolis, Ind., the same year and commenced practice; unsuccessful candidate for election to the United States Senate in 1893; appointed a member of the United States and British Joint High Commission which met in Quebec in 1898 for the adjustment of Canadian questions; elected as a Republican to the United States Senate in 1896; reelected in 1902 and served from March 4, 1897, until his resignation March 3, 1905, having been elected Vice President of the United States; chairman, Committee on Immigration (Fifty-fifth Congress), Committee on Public Buildings and Grounds (Fifty-sixth through Fifty-eighth Congresses); elected Vice President of the United States in 1904 on the Republican ticket with President Theodore Roosevelt, and served from March 4, 1905 to March 3, 1909; unsuccessful candidate for Vice President of the United States in 1916 on the Republican ticket headed by Charles Evans Hughes; resumed the practice of law in Indianapolis, Ind., where he died on June 4, 1918; interment in Crown Hill Cemetery.

Bibliography: *DAB*; Gould, Lewis L., ed. "Charles Warren Fairbanks and the Republican National Convention of 1900: A Memoir." *Indiana Magazine of History* 77 (December 1981): 358-72; Rissler, Herbert J. "Charles Warren Fairbanks: Conservative Hoosier." Ph.D. dissertation, Indiana University, 1961.

**FAIRCHILD, Benjamin Lewis,** a Representative from New York; born in Sweden (near Rochester), Monroe County, N.Y., January 5, 1863; attended the public schools of Washington, D.C., and a business college; was graduated from the law department of Columbian (now George Washington) University at Washington, D.C., in 1885; was admitted to the bar in 1885 and commenced practice in New York City; employed in the draftsman division of the United States Patent Office 1877-1879; clerk in the Bureau of Engraving and Printing 1879-1885; elected as a Republican to the Fifty-fourth Congress (March 4, 1895-March 3, 1897); unsuccessfully contested the election of William L. Ward to the Fifty-fifth Congress; resumed the practice of law in New York City; elected to the Sixty-fifth Congress (March 4, 1917-March 3, 1919); unsuccessful candidate for reelection in 1918 to the Sixty-sixth Congress; again elected to the Sixty-seventh Congress (March 4, 1921-March 3, 1923); unsuccessful candidate for reelection in 1922 to the Sixty-eighth Congress, but was subsequently elected to that Congress to fill the vacancy caused by the death of James V. Ganly; reelected to the Sixty-ninth Congress and served from November 6, 1923, to March 3, 1927; unsuccessful candidate for reelection in 1926 to the Seventieth Congress; resumed the practice of law in New York City; died in Pelham Manor, N.Y., October 25, 1946; interment in Woodlawn Cemetery, New York City.

**FAIRCHILD, George Winthrop,** a Representative from New York; born in Oneonta, Otsego County, N.Y., May 6, 1854; completed preparatory studies; engaged in agricultural pursuits and apprenticed as a printer; owner of the Oneonta Herald Publishing Co. 1890-1912; also interested in banking and in the manufacture of time recorders; elected as a Republican to the Sixtieth and to the five succeeding Congresses (March 4, 1907-March 3, 1919); elected vice president of the International Peace Conference; appointed by President William Howard Taft on August 10, 1910, as special commissioner to the First Centenary of Mexico at Mexico City, with the rank of Minister; resumed his former business pursuits; president and director of the White Plains Development Co., White Plains, N.Y.; died in New York City December 31, 1924; interment in Glenwood Cemetery, Oneonta, N.Y.

**FAIRCLOTH, Duncan McLauchlin (Lauch),** a Senator from North Carolina; born in Sampson County, N.C., January 14, 1928; manager, family farm; owner, construction company; ready-mix concrete company, 1953; owner, automobile dealership, Clinton, N.C., 1956; chair, North Carolina State highway commission; North Carolina State secretary of commerce for six years; elected as a Republican to the United States Senate in 1992 for the term ending January 3, 1999; is a resident of Clinton, N.C.

**FAIRFIELD, John,** a Representative and a Senator from Maine; born in Saco, York County, Maine, January 30, 1797; attended the Saco schools, Thornton Academy, and Bowdoin College, Brunswick, Maine; engaged in trade; studied law; was admitted to the bar in 1826 and commenced practice in Biddleford and Saco, Maine; appointed a trustee of Thornton Academy in 1826 and served as president of the board of trustees, 1845-1847; appointed reporter of the State supreme court in 1832; elected as a Democrat to the Twenty-fourth and Twenty-fifth Congresses and served from March 4, 1835, to December 24, 1838, when he resigned, having been elected Governor; elected Governor of Maine in 1838, reelected in 1839, and served from January 2, 1839 to January 6, 1841; unsuccessful candidate for reelection in 1840; again elected Governor in 1841, reelected in 1842, and served from January 5, 1842 until March 7, 1843, when he resigned, having been elected Senator; elected as a Democrat to the United States Senate to fill the vacancy caused by the resignation of Reuel Williams; reelected, and served from March 3, 1843, until his death in Washington, D.C., on December 24, 1847; chairman, Committee on Naval Affairs

(Twenty-ninth and Thirtieth Congresses); interment in Laurel Hill Cemetery, Saco, Maine.

**Bibliography:** *DAB*; Fairfield, John. *The Letters of John Fairfield.* Edited by Arthur B. Staples. Lewiston, Maine: Lewiston Journal Company, 1922.

**FAIRFIELD, Louis William,** a Representative from Indiana; born in a log cabin near Wapakoneta, Auglaize County, Ohio, October 15, 1858; moved to Allen County, Ohio, in 1866 and resided on a farm near Lima; attended the public schools; moved to Middle Point, Van Wert County, Ohio, in 1872; taught school for six months, and then attended the Ohio Northern University at Ada in 1876; continued teaching and attending school until 1888; editor of the Hardin County Republican at Kenton, Ohio, in 1881 and 1882; taught school in Middle Point in 1883 and 1884; moved to Angola, Steuben County, Ind., in 1885, being selected to assist in the building of Tri-State College, Angola, Ind.; vice president of and teacher at Tri-State College 1885-1917; unsuccessful candidate for the State senate in 1912; elected as a Republican to the Sixty-fifth and to the three succeeding Congresses (March 4, 1917-March 3, 1925); chairman, Committee on Insular Affairs (Sixty-eighth Congress); unsuccessful candidate for renomination in 1924; occasionally engaged as a lecturer and resided in Angola, Ind.; died in Joilet, Ill., while on a visit, February 20, 1930; interment in Circle Hill Cemetery, Angola, Ind.

**FAISON, John Miller,** a Representative from North Carolina; born near Faison, Duplin County, N.C., April 17, 1862; attended Faison Male Academy, and was graduated from Davidson College, North Carolina, in 1883; studied medicine at the University of Virginia at Charlottesville; completed a postgraduate medical course at New York Polyclinic in 1885, and commenced practice at Faison, N.C., the same year; also engaged in agricultural pursuits; member of the State and county Democratic executive committee 1898-1906; member of the North Carolina Jamestown Exposition Commission; elected as a Democrat to the Sixty-second and Sixty-third Congresses (March 4, 1911-March 3, 1915); was not a candidate for reelection in 1914; died in Faison, N.C., April 21, 1915; interment in Faison Cemetery.

**FALCONER, Jacob Alexander,** a Representative from Washington; born in Ontario, Canada, January 26, 1869; moved with his parents to Saugatuck, Mich., in 1873; attended the public schools; moved to Washburn, Wis.; was graduated from Beloit (Wis.) Academy in 1890 and later took college work at Beloit College; moved to Everett, Wash., in 1894; engaged in the lumber business; mayor of Everett in 1897 and 1898; member of the State house of representatives 1904-1908, serving as speaker during the 1907 session; member of the State senate 1909-1912; elected as a Progressive to the Sixty-third Congress (March 4, 1913-March 3, 1915); unsuccessful candidate for the nomination for United States Senator on the Progressive ticket in 1914; engaged in the ship-brokerage business in New York City 1915-1919; moved to Fort Worth, Tex., in 1919 and engaged in road-construction contracting; moved to Farmington, N.Mex., in 1925 and engaged in the oil and gas industry; died in Wingdale, Dutchess County, N.Y., July 1, 1928; interment in Saugatuck Cemetery, Saugatuck, Mich.

**FALEOMAVAEGA, Eni F.H.,** a Delegate from American Samoa; born in Vailoatai, American Samoa, August 15, 1943; graduate of Kahuku High School, Hawaii, 1962; A.A., Brigham Young University, Provo, Utah, 1964, and B.A., 1966; attended Texas Southern University School of Law, Houston; J.D., University of Houston Law School, 1972; LL.M., University of California, Berkeley, 1973; entered active duty, United States Army in 1966; released as captain in 1969 after service in Judge Advocate General's Corps; administrative assistant, American Samoa delegate to Washington, D.C., 1973-1975; assistant counsel, House Committee on Interior and Insular Affairs, 1975-1981; deputy attorney general, American

Samoa, 1981-1984; Lieutenant Governor of American Samoa, 1985-1988; elected as a Democrat a Delegate to the One Hundred First and to the three succeeding Congresses (January 3, 1989-January 3, 1997); is a resident of Pago Pago, American Samoa.

**FALL, Albert Bacon,** a Senator from New Mexico; born in Frankfort, Franklin County, Ky., November 26, 1861; attended the country schools; taught school; studied law; was admitted to the bar in 1891 and commenced practice at Las Cruces, N.Mex.; made a specialty of Mexican law; became interested in mines, lumber, land, railroads, farming, and stock raising; member, New Mexico Territorial house of representatives, 1891-1892; appointed judge of the third judicial district in 1893; associate justice of the supreme court of New Mexico in 1893; Territorial attorney general in 1897, and again in 1907; member of the Territorial council in 1897; served as captain of Company H in the First Territorial Infantry during the Spanish-American War; upon the admission of New Mexico as a State into the Union was elected in 1912 as a Republican to the United States Senate for the term ending March 3, 1913; reelected in June 1912, but as Governor William C. McDonald did not sign the credentials, was again elected in January 1913; reelected in 1918, and served from March 27, 1912 until March 4, 1921, when he resigned to accept a Cabinet portfolio; chairman, Committee on Expenditures in the Department of Commerce and Labor (Sixty-second Congress), Committee on Geological Survey (Sixty-fifth Congress), Committee on Pacific Islands, Puerto Rico, and the Virgin Islands (Sixty-sixth Congress); appointed Secretary of the Interior by President Warren G. Harding, and served from March 4, 1921 until March 4, 1923, when he resigned; found guilty on October 25, 1929 in the Supreme Court of the District of Columbia of accepting a bribe in connection with the "Teapot Dome" scandal; released from the New Mexico State penitentiary on May 9, 1932 after serving nine months and nineteen days; on June 2, 1932, three remaining conspiracy indictments against him were dismissed at the request of Federal prosecutors; resumed his former business pursuits in Three Rivers, N.Mex.; died in El Paso, Tex., November 30, 1944; interment in Evergreen Cemetery.

**Bibliography:** *DAB*; Bethune, Martha Fall. *Race With The Wind: The Personal Life of Albert B. Fall.* El Paso, Tex.: Complete Print., 1989; Fall, Albert. *The Memoirs of Albert B. Fall.* Edited with annotations by David H. Stratton. El Paso: Texas Western Press, 1966.

**FALLON, George Hyde,** a Representative from Maryland; born in Baltimore, Md., July 24, 1902; attended the public schools, Calvert Business College, and Johns Hopkins University, Baltimore, Md.; engaged in the advertising sign business; chairman of the Democratic State central committee of Baltimore, Md., in 1938; member of the Baltimore city council 1939-1944; elected as a Democrat to the Seventy-ninth and to the twelve succeeding Congresses (January 3, 1945-January 3, 1971); chairman, Committee on Public Works (Eighty-ninth through Ninety-first Congresses); wounded March 1, 1954 when three Puerto Rican Nationalists fired about thirty shots into a crowd of Representatives on the floor of the House; unsuccessful candidate for renomination in 1970 to the Ninety-second Congress; resided in Baltimore, Md., where he died March 21, 1980; interment in Greenmount Cemetery.

**FANNIN, Paul Jones,** a Senator from Arizona; born in Ashland, Boyd County, Ky., January 29, 1907; moved to Phoenix, Ariz., in October 1907; attended the University of Arizona; B.A., Stanford (Calif.) University, 1930; businessman involved in petroleum and equipment distribution in the Southwest and Mexico; elected Governor of Arizona in 1958, reelected in 1960 and 1962, and served from January 5, 1959 to January 4, 1965; chairman, Western Governors Conference; member, Executive Committee of Council of State Governors, National Civil Defense Advisory Council; elected as a Republican to the United States Senate in 1964; reelected in

1970 and served from January 3, 1965, to January 3, 1977; was not a candidate for reelection in 1976; is a resident of Phoenix, Ariz.

**FARAN, James John,** a Representative from Ohio; born in Cincinnati, Ohio, on December 29, 1808; attended the common schools, and was graduated from Miami University, Oxford, Ohio, in 1831; studied law; was admitted to the bar in 1833 and commenced practice in Cincinnati; elected as a Democrat a member of the State house of representatives 1835-1839 and served as speaker in 1838 and 1839; served in the State senate 1839-1843, and was its presiding officer 1841-1843; associate editor and proprietor of the Cincinnati Enquirer 1844-1881; elected as a Democrat to the Twenty-ninth and Thirtieth Congresses (March 4, 1845-March 3, 1849); chairman, Committee on Public Buildings and Grounds (Twenty-ninth Congress); was not a candidate for renomination in 1848 to the Thirty-first Congress; appointed by Governor William Medill one of the commissioners to supervise the erection of the State capitol in 1854; mayor of Cincinnati 1855-1857; appointed by President James Buchanan postmaster of Cincinnati on June 4, 1855, and served until October 21, 1859; delegate to the Democratic National Convention at Baltimore in 1860; engaged in newspaper work until shortly before his death; died in Cincinnati, Ohio, December 12, 1892; interment in Spring Grove Cemetery.
  **Bibliography:** *DAB.*

**FARBSTEIN, Leonard,** a Representative from New York; born in New York City October 12, 1902; attended public schools and graduated from High School of Commerce; studied at City College of New York and Hebrew Union Teachers College; graduated from New York University Law School in 1924; was admitted to the bar in 1925 and commenced the practice of law in New York City; member of the State assembly 1932-1956; during the First World War served in the United States Coast Guard Reserve; vice chairman of East River Day Camp, a philanthropic organization; elected as a Democrat to the Eighty-fifth and to the six succeeding Congresses (January 3, 1957-January 3, 1971); unsuccessful candidate for renomination in 1970 to the Ninety-second Congress; is a resident of New York City.

**FARIS, George Washington,** a Representative from Indiana; born near Rensselaer, Jasper County, Ind., June 9, 1854; attended the public schools; was graduated from Asbury (now De Pauw) University, Greencastle, Ind., in 1877; studied law; was admitted to the bar in 1877 and commenced practice in Indianapolis, Ind.; moved to Terre Haute, Ind., in 1880 and continued the practice of law; unsuccessful Republican candidate for judge of the circuit court in 1884; elected as a Republican to the Fifty-fourth, Fifty-fifth, and Fifty-sixth Congresses (March 4, 1895-March 3, 1901); chairman, Committee on Manufactures (Fifty-fifth and Fifty-sixth Congresses); declined to be a candidate for renomination in 1900; resumed the practice of law in Terre Haute, Ind., and shortly thereafter moved to Washington, D.C., and continued the practice of law until his death in that city on April 17, 1914; interment in Highland Lawn Cemetery, Terre Haute, Ind.

**FARLEE, Isaac Gray,** a Representative from New Jersey; born at White House, Hunterdon County, N.J., May 18, 1787; attended the public schools; engaged in mercantile pursuits in Flemington; member of the State general assembly in 1819, 1821, 1828, and 1830; clerk of Hunterdon County 1830-1840; brigadier general of the State militia; elected to the Twenty-eighth Congress (March 4, 1843-March 3, 1845); unsuccessful candidate for reelection in 1844 to the Twenty-ninth Congress; member of the State senate 1847-1849; judge of the court of common pleas 1852-1855; died in Flemington, N.J., January 12, 1855; interment in Presbyterian Cemetery.

**FARLEY, Ephraim Wilder,** a Representative from Maine; born in Newcastle, Maine, August 29, 1817; attended the common schools and was graduated from Bowdoin College, Brunswick, Maine, in 1836; studied law; was admitted to the bar and commenced practice in Newcastle; member of the State house of representatives in 1843 and 1851-1853; elected as a Whig to the Thirty-third Congress (March 4, 1853-March 3, 1855); unsuccessful candidate for reelection in 1854 to the Thirty-fourth Congress; member of the State senate in 1856; died in Newcastle, Maine, April 3, 1880; interment in a tomb on the family estate.

**FARLEY, James Indus,** a Representative from Indiana; born on a farm near Hamilton, Steuben County, Ind., on February 24, 1871; attended the public schools and Tri-State College, Angola, Ind., and Simpson College, Indianola, Iowa; taught in the public schools of Steuben and De Kalb Counties, Ind., 1890-1894; worked for the Auburn Automobile Company as sales manager, vice president, and president of the company, 1906-1926; delegate to the Democratic National Convention of 1928; elected as a Democrat to the Seventy-third and to the two succeeding Congresses (March 4, 1933-January 3, 1939); unsuccessful candidate for reelection in 1938 to the Seventy-sixth Congress; engaged in agricultural pursuits; died in Bryn Mawr, Pa., on June 16, 1948; interment in Woodlawn Cemetery, Auburn, Ind.

**FARLEY, James Thompson,** a Senator from California; born in Albemarle County, Va., August 6, 1829; attended the common schools; moved when quite young to Missouri and then to California in 1850 and settled in Jackson; studied law; was admitted to the bar in 1854 and commenced practice in Amador County; member, State assembly 1855-1856 and served as speaker in the latter year; member, State senate 1869-1876, and served as president pro tempore 1871-1872; elected as a Democrat to the United States Senate and served from March 4, 1879, until March 3, 1885; was not a candidate for renomination in 1884; resumed the practice of law; died in Jackson, Amador County, Calif., on January 22, 1886; interment in the City Cemetery.

**FARLEY, Michael Francis,** a Representative from New York; born in Birr, Ireland, March 1, 1863; immigrated to the United States in 1881 and settled in Brooklyn, N.Y.; attended the public schools of New York City; engaged in the liquor business; elected as a Democrat to the Sixty-fourth Congress (March 4, 1915-March 3, 1917); unsuccessful candidate for reelection in 1916 to the Sixty-fifth Congress; engaged in his former business pursuits until his death in New York City October 8, 1921; interment in Calvary Cemetery.

**FARLIN, Dudley,** a Representative from New York; born in Norwich, New London County, Conn., September 2, 1777; moved to Dutchess County, N.Y., in early youth, and later to Warren County; engaged in the lumber and grain business; supervisor of the town of Warrensburg 1818-1820, 1827, and 1828; sheriff of Warren County in 1821, 1822, and again in 1828; member of the State assembly in 1824; elected as a Jacksonian to the Twenty-fourth Congress (March 4, 1835-March 3, 1837); resumed his former business pursuits; died in Warrensburg, Warren County, N.Y., on September 26, 1837; interment in Warrensburg Cemetery.

**FARNSLEY, Charles Rowland Peaslee,** a Representative from Kentucky; born in Louisville, Jefferson County, Ky., March 28, 1907; attended Male High School, Louisville; A.B., University of Louisville, 1930; LL.B., University of Louisville School of Law, 1942; was admitted to the bar in 1930 and began practice in Louisville; served in the Kentucky house of representatives, 1936-1940; mayor of Louisville, 1948-1953; delegate to the Democratic National Convention of 1952; elected as a Democrat to the Eighty-ninth Congress (January 3, 1965-January 3, 1967); was not a candidate for reelection in 1966 to the Ninetieth Congress; served as publisher and president of Lost Cause Press; was a resident of Glenview, Ky.; died June 19, 1990.

**FARNSWORTH, John Franklin,** a Representative from Illinois; born in Eaton, Canada, March 27, 1820; completed preparatory studies; settled in Ann Arbor, Mich.; studied law; was admitted to the bar in 1841 and commenced practice at St. Charles, Ill.; moved to Chicago, Ill.; elected as a Republican to the Thirty-fifth and Thirty-sixth Congresses (March 4, 1857-March 3, 1861); was not a candidate for renomination in 1860 to the Thirty-seventh Congress; served in the Union Army during the Civil War, and participated in the Peninsular campaign, March-July 1862, and in the Antietam campaign of September 1862; commissioned colonel of the Eighth Regiment, Illinois Volunteer Cavalry, September 18, 1861; brigadier general of Volunteers December 5, 1862; resigned March 4, 1863, to take up his duties as Representative; elected to the Thirty-eighth and to the four succeeding Congresses (March 4, 1863-March 3, 1873); chairman, Committee on Post Office and Post Roads (Fortieth through Forty-second Congresses); unsuccessful candidate for renomination in 1872 to the Forty-third Congress; resumed the practice of law in Chicago, Ill.; moved to Washington, D.C., in 1880 and continued the practice of law until his death on July 14, 1897; interment in North Cemetery, St. Charles, Ill.

Bibliography: *DAB.*

**FARNUM, Billie Sunday,** a Representative from Michigan; born in Saginaw, Mich., April 11, 1916; raised in a farm community at Watrousville, Mich.; graduated from Vassar (Mich.) High School in 1933; continued education in the Civilian Conservation Corps, 1933-1935 and took special educational courses; was employed in the motorcar industry in Pontiac, Mich., 1936-1952; engaged in union activities ranging from shop steward to international representative for United Auto Workers-Congress of Industrial Organizations, 1942-1952; administrative aide to Senator Blair Moody, 1952-1954; assistant secretary of State of Michigan, 1955-1957; deputy secretary of State of Michigan, 1957-1960; auditor general of Michigan, 1961-1965; delegate, Democratic National Conventions, 1956, 1960, and 1964; elected as a Democrat to the Eighty-ninth Congress (January 3, 1965-January 3, 1967); unsuccessful candidate for reelection in 1966 to the Ninetieth Congress; deputy chairman, Democratic National Committee, 1967-1968; member, Waterford Board of Education, 1969-1970; owned a financial and management consulting firm; elected secretary of the Michigan State senate in 1975 and served in that capacity until his death November 18, 1979, in Lansing, Mich.; entombment in Deepdale Memorial Park Mausoleum.

**FARQUHAR, John Hanson,** a Representative from Indiana; born in Union Bridge, Carroll County, Md., December 20, 1818; attended the public schools; moved to Indiana with his parents, who settled in Richmond in 1833; employed as an assistant engineer on the White River Canal until 1840; studied law; was admitted to the bar and commenced practice in Brookville, Ind.; secretary of the State senate in 1842 and 1843; chief clerk of the Indiana State house of representatives in 1844; unsuccessful candidate for election in 1852 to the Thirty-third Congress; served as captain in the Nineteenth Infantry of the Regular Army in the Civil War; elected as a Republican to the Thirty-ninth Congress (March 4, 1865-March 3, 1867); was not a candidate for renomination in 1866 to the Fortieth Congress; moved to Indianapolis in 1870 and engaged in banking; appointed Indiana secretary of state by Governor Conrad Baker; died in Indianapolis, Ind., October 1, 1873; interment in Crown Hill Cemetery.

**FARQUHAR, John McCreath,** a Representative from New York; born near Ayr, Scotland, April 17, 1832; attended Ayr Academy; immigrated to the United States when a boy and settled in Buffalo, N.Y.; was a printer, editor, and publisher for thirty-three years; president of the International Typographical Union, 1860-1862; enlisted in the Union Army on August 9, 1862, as a private in Company B, Eighty-ninth Regiment, Illinois Volunteer Infantry, and promoted to major; served as judge advocate and as inspector in the Fourth Army Corps; was awarded the Congressional Medal of Honor for action at the Battle of Stone's River, Tenn., December 30, 1862-January 2, 1863; returned to Buffalo, N.Y., and resumed business activities; elected as a Republican to the Forty-ninth, Fiftieth, and Fifty-first Congresses (March 4, 1885-March 3, 1891); chairman, Committee on Merchant Marine and Fisheries (Fifty-first Congress); was not a candidate for renomination in 1890 to the Fifty-second Congress; member of the United States Industrial Commission, 1898-1902; retired from public life and active business pursuits; died in Buffalo, N.Y., April 24, 1918; interment in Forest Lawn Cemetery.

**FARR, Evarts Worcester,** a Representative from New Hampshire; born in Littleton, Grafton County, N.H., October 10, 1840; attended the common schools and Dartmouth College, Hanover, N.H.; during the Civil War entered the Union Army as first lieutenant of Company G, Second Regiment, New Hampshire Volunteer Infantry and served as major in the Eleventh Regiment, New Hampshire Volunteer Infantry; assistant assessor of internal revenue, 1865-1869; studied law; was admitted to the bar in 1867 and commenced practice in Littleton; assessor of internal revenue, 1869-1873; solicitor for Grafton County, 1873-1879; member of the executive council of New Hampshire in 1876; elected as a Republican to the Forty-sixth and Forty-seventh Congresses and served from March 4, 1879, until his death in Littleton, N.H., November 30, 1880; interment in Glenwood Cemetery.

**FARR, John Richard,** a Representative from Pennsylvania; born in Scranton, Lackawanna County, Pa., July 18, 1857; attended the public schools, School of the Lackawanna, Scranton, Pa., and Phillips Academy, Andover, Mass.; was graduated from Lafayette College, Easton, Pa.; newsboy, printer, and publisher; active in the real estate business; served four years on the Scranton School Board; member of the Pennsylvania house of representatives in 1891, 1893, 1895, 1897, and 1899, serving as speaker of the 1899 session; unsuccessful candidate for election in 1908 to the Sixty-first Congress; elected as a Republican to the Sixty-second and to the three succeeding Congresses (March 4, 1911-March 3, 1919); successfully contested the election of Patrick McLane to the Sixty-sixth Congress and served from February 25 to March 3, 1921; unsuccessful candidate for renomination in 1920 to the Sixty-seventh Congress; resumed the real estate business in Scranton, Pa.; unsuccessful candidate for nomination in 1930 to the Seventy-second Congress, and in 1932 to the Seventy-third Congress; died in Scranton, Pa., on December 11, 1933; interment in Shady Lane Cemetery, Chinchilla (near Scranton), Lackawanna County, Pa.

**FARR, Sam,** a Representative from California; born in San Francisco, Calif., July 4, 1941; attended Carmel (Calif.) public schools; B.S., Willamette University, Salem, Oreg., 1963; attended Santa Clara University, and the Monterey Institute of Foreign Studies; Peace Corps volunteer in Colombia, 1963-1965; member, Monterey County Board of Supervsiors, 1975-1980, chair, 1979; Monterey County Democratic Central Committee, 1976; member, California State assembly, 1980-1993; elected as a Democrat to the One Hundred Third Congress, June 8, 1993, by special election to fill the vacancy caused by the resignation of Leon E. Panetta; reelected to the One Hundred Fourth Congress, and served from June 8, 1993 to January 3, 1997; is a resident of Carmel, Calif.

**FARRELLY, John Wilson** (son of Patrick Farrelly), a Representative from Pennsylvania; born in Meadville, Crawford County, Pa., July 7, 1809; received a limited schooling; was graduated from Allegheny College at Meadville in 1826; studied law; was admitted to the bar in 1828 and commenced practice in Meadville; member of the Pennsylvania senate in 1828; served in the Pennsylvania house of representatives in 1837; again a member of the Pennsylvania senate 1838-1842; elected as a Whig to the Thirtieth Congress (March 4, 1847-March 3, 1849); chairman, Committee on Patents (Thirtieth Congress); was not a candidate for renomination in 1848 to the Thirty-first Congress; appointed Sixth Auditor of the Treasury by President Zachary Taylor and served from November 5, 1849, until April 9, 1853, when he resigned; engaged in the practice of law in Meadville, Pa., until his death on December 20, 1860; interment in Greendale Cemetery.

**FARRELLY, Patrick** (father of John Wilson Farrelly), a Representative from Pennsylvania; born in Ireland in 1770, where he completed his education; immigrated to the United States in 1798; studied law; was admitted to the bar July 11, 1803, and commenced practice in Meadville, Pa.; member of the Pennsylvania house of representatives in 1811 and 1812; served in the War of 1812 as a major of militia; elected to the Seventeenth, Eighteenth, and Nineteenth Congresses and served from March 4, 1821, until his death in Meadville, Crawford County, Pa., January 12, 1826; interment in Greendale Cemetery.

**FARRINGTON, James,** a Representative from New Hampshire; born in Conway, Carroll County, N.H., October 1, 1791; attended the common schools; was graduated from Fryeburg Academy, Fryeburg, Maine, in 1814; studied medicine and engaged in practice in Rochester, N.H., in 1818; member of the State house of representatives 1828-1831; served in the State senate in 1836; elected as a Democrat to the Twenty-fifth Congress (March 4, 1837-March 3, 1839); appointed one of the trustees of the New Hampshire Insane Asylum in 1845; resumed the practice of medicine; was one of the organizers of the Rochester Bank, and served as president until his death in Rochester, N.H., October 29, 1859; interment in the Old Cemetery.

**FARRINGTON, Joseph Rider** (husband of Mary Elizabeth Pruett Farrington), a Delegate from the Territory of Hawaii; born in Washington, D.C., October 15, 1897, and while still an infant moved with his parents to Hawaii; attended Punahou Academy, Honolulu, and the University of Wisconsin at Madison; left college at the close of his junior year in June 1918 and enlisted in the United States Army; commissioned a second lieutenant of Field Artillery in September and was discharged in December 1918; returned to the University of Wisconsin and graduated in 1919; reporter on the staff of the Public Ledger in Philadelphia in 1919 and in Washington, D.C., 1920-1923; returned to Honolulu to become associated with the Honolulu Star-Bulletin, Ltd., and was president and general manager from 1939 until his death; secretary to the Hawaii Legislative Commission in 1933; member of the Territorial senate, 1934-1942; elected as a Republican a Delegate to the Seventy-eighth and to the five succeeding Congresses, and served from January 3, 1943 until his death in Washington, D.C., June 19, 1954; interment in Nuuanu Cemetery, Honolulu, Hawaii.

Bibliography: *DAB.*

**FARRINGTON, Mary Elizabeth Pruett** (wife of Joseph Rider Farrington), a Delegate from the Territory of Hawaii; born in Tokyo, Japan, May 30, 1898; attended Tokyo Foreign School and grammar schools of Nashville, Tenn., El Paso, Tex., Los Angeles, Calif., and Hollywood (Calif.) High School; graduated from Ward-Belmont Junior College, Nashville, Tenn., in 1916 and from the University of Wisconsin in Madison in 1918; engaged in graduate work at the University of Hawaii; newspaper correspondent from 1918 until 1957; president of League of Republican Women in Washington, D.C., 1946-1948; president of National Federation of Women's Republican Clubs, 1949-1953; delegate to the Republican National Convention of 1952; elected as a Republican a Delegate to the Eighty-third Congress to fill the vacancy caused by the death of her husband, Joseph Rider Farrington; reelected to the Eighty-fourth

Congress and served from July 31, 1954, to January 3, 1957; unsuccessful candidate for reelection in 1956 to the Eighty-fifth Congress; publisher, president and director, Honolulu Star Bulletin, 1946-1963; director and chairman, Honolulu Lithograph Company, Ltd., 1945-1963; president, Hawaiian Broadcasting System, Ltd., 1960-1963; director, Office of Territories, Department of the Interior, District of Columbia, 1969; was a resident of Honolulu, Hawaii until her death there on July 21, 1984; ashes interred at Oahu Cemetery, Honolulu, Hawaii.

**FARROW, Samuel,** a Representative from South Carolina; born in Virginia in 1759; moved to South Carolina with his father's family, who settled in Spartanburg District in 1765; served in the Revolutionary War; studied law; was admitted to the bar in 1793 and commenced practice in Spartanburg, S.C.; also engaged in agricultural pursuits near Cross Anchor; lieutenant governor of South Carolina 1810-1812; elected as a Republican to the Thirteenth Congress (March 4, 1813-March 3, 1815); was not a candidate for renomination in 1814 to the Fourteenth Congress; resumed the practice of law; also engaged in agricultural pursuits; member of the State house of representatives 1816-1819 and 1822-1823; died in Columbia, S.C., November 18, 1824; interment in the family burial ground on his plantation, near the battlefield of Musgrove Mill, Spartanburg County, S.C.

**FARWELL, Charles Benjamin,** a Representative and a Senator from Illinois; born in Painted Post, Steuben County, N.Y., July 1, 1823; attended Elmira Academy; moved to Illinois in 1838 and settled in Mount Morris; employed in government surveying and in farming until 1844, when he engaged in the real estate business and banking in Chicago; clerk of Cook County 1853-1861; engaged in the wholesale dry goods business; member of the State board of equalization in 1867; chairman of the Board of Supervisors of Cook County in 1868; national-bank examiner in 1869; elected as a Republican to the Forty-second and Forty-third Congresses (March 4, 1871-March 3, 1875); chairman, Committee on Manufactures (Forty-third Congress); presented credentials as a Representative-elect to the Forty-fourth Congress and served from March 4, 1875, until May 6, 1876, when he was succeeded by John V. Le Moyne, who contested his election; declined to be a candidate for renomination in 1876; resumed mercantile pursuits; elected to the Forty-seventh Congress (March 4, 1881-March 3, 1883); declined to be a candidate for renomination in 1882; elected as a Republican to the United States Senate to fill the vacancy caused by the death of John A. Logan and served from January 19, 1887, until March 3, 1891; was not a candidate for reelection in 1891; chairman, Committee on Expenditures of Public Money (Fiftieth Congress), Committee on Enrolled Bills (Fifty-first Congress); resumed mercantile pursuits; died in Lake Forest, Ill., September 23, 1903; interment in Rosehill Cemetery, Chicago, Ill.

Bibliography: *DAB.*

**FARWELL, Nathan Allen** (cousin of Owen Lovejoy), a Senator from Maine; born in Unity, Waldo County, Maine, on February 24, 1812; attended the common schools; taught school 1832-1833; moved to East Thomaston, Maine, in 1834 and engaged in the manufacture of lime and in ship building; subsequently became a master mariner and trader; studied law; moved to Rockland, Maine, where he founded the Rockland Marine Insurance Co., and served as president; member, State senate 1853-1854, 1861-1862, the last year as presiding officer; member, State house of representatives 1860, 1863-1864; appointed and subsequently elected as a Republican to the United States Senate to fill the vacancy caused by the resignation of William Pitt Fessenden and served from October 27, 1864, to March 3, 1865; was not a candidate for reelection in 1865; resumed his activities in the insurance business; delegate to the Southern Loyalists Convention at Philadelphia in 1866; died in Rockland, Maine, December 9, 1893; interment in Achorn Cemetery.

**FARWELL, Sewall Spaulding,** a Representative from Iowa; born in Keene, Coshocton County, Ohio, April 26, 1834; attended the common schools and an academy in Cleveland, Ohio; moved to Iowa in 1852 and engaged in agricultural pursuits; during the Civil War enlisted in the Union Army in 1862 as captain of Company H, Thirty-first Regiment, Iowa Volunteer Infantry; promoted to major in 1864, and served until the close of the war; member of the State senate 1865-1869; assessor of internal revenue 1869-1873; collector of internal revenue 1875-1881; elected as a Republican to the Forty-seventh Congress (March 4, 1881-March 3, 1883); unsuccessful candidate for reelection in 1882 to the Forty-eighth Congress; president of the Monticello State Bank; died in Monticello, Iowa, September 21, 1909; interment in Oakwood Cemetery.

**FARY, John G.,** a Representative from Illinois, born in Chicago, Ill., April 11, 1911; attended St. Peter and Paul Polish Roman Catholic School, Holy Trinity High School, Loyola University, Real Estate School of Illinois, and Midwest Institute; member of Illinois general assembly 1955-1975; elected as a Democrat to the Ninety-fourth Congress, by special election, July 8, 1975, to fill the vacancy caused by the death of John Kluczynski; reelected to the three succeeding Congresses and served from July 8, 1975, to January 3, 1983; was an unsuccessful candidate for renomination in 1982 to the Ninety-eighth Congress; returned to Chicago where he resided until his death June 7, 1984.

**FASCELL, Dante B.,** a Representative from Florida; born in Bridgehampton, Long Island, Suffolk County, N.Y., March 9, 1917; moved with his parents to Miami, Fla., in 1925; graduated from Ponce de Leon High School, Coral Gables, Fla., in 1933; J.D., University of Miami School of Law, 1938; was admitted to the bar in 1938 and commenced the practice of law in Miami; during the Second World War entered the Federal service with the Florida National Guard on January 6, 1941; commissioned a second lieutenant May 23, 1942; served in the African, Sicilian, and Italian campaigns, and separated from the service as a captain on January 20, 1946; legal attache to the State legislative delegation from Dade County, Fla., 1947-1950; member of the Florida State house of representatives, 1950-1954; appointed by the President to represent the United States at the Twenty-fourth General Assembly of the United Nations, 1969; elected as a Democrat to the Eighty-fourth and to the eighteen succeeding Congresses (January 3, 1955-January 3, 1993); chairman, Committee on Foreign Affairs (Ninety-eighth through One Hundred Second Congresses); was not a candidate for reelection in 1992 to the One Hundred Third Congress; is a resident of Miami, Fla.

**FASSETT, Jacob Sloat,** a Representative from New York; born in Elmira, Chemung County, N.Y., November 13, 1853; attended the public schools and was graduated from the University of Rochester in 1875; studied law; was admitted to the bar in 1878 and commenced practice in Elmira; district attorney of Chemung County in 1878 and 1879; proprietor of the Elmira Daily Advertiser, 1879-1896; was a student in Heidelberg University, Germany; returned to Elmira, N.Y., in 1882 and resumed the practice of law; member of the New York State senate, 1884-1891, and served as president pro tempore, 1889-1891; delegate to the Republican National Conventions of 1880, 1892 and 1916; secretary of the Republican National Committee, 1888-1892; unsuccessful Republican candidate for Governor of New York in 1891; appointed by President Benjamin Harrison collector of customs of the port of New York, and served from August 1 to September 15, 1891; delegate to the State constitutional convention in 1904; elected as a Republican to the Fifty-ninth and to the two succeeding Congresses (March 4, 1905-March 3, 1911); unsuccessful candidate for reelection in 1910 to the Sixty-second Congress; chairman of the Republican advisory convention in 1918; engaged in the banking and lumber business in Elmira, N.Y.; died in Vancouver, British Columbia, on April 21, 1924,

while returning from a business trip to Japan and the Philippine Islands; interment in Woodlawn Cemetery, Elmira, N.Y.

Bibliography: *DAB.*

**FATTAH, Chaka,** a Representative from Pennsylvania; born in Philadelphia, Pa., November 21, 1956; attended Overbrook High School, the Community College of Philadelphia, and the University of Pennsylvania, Wharton Community Education Program; M.A., Fels School for State and Local Government, University of Pennsylvania, 1986; attended John F. Kennedy School of Government, Harvard University; special assistant to Managing Director, special assistant to Director of Housing and Community Development, Philadelphia; policy assistant, Greater Philadelphia Partnership; assistant director to House of Umoja; member, Pennsylvania house of representatives, 1984-1988; member, Pennsylvania senate, 1988-1994; elected as a Democrat to the One Hundred Fourth Congress (January 3, 1995-January 3, 1997); is a resident of Philadelphia, Pa.

**FAULKNER, Charles James** (son of Charles James Faulkner [1806-1884]), a Senator from West Virginia; born on the family estate, "Boydville," near Martinsburg, Va. (now West Virginia), September 21, 1847; accompanied his father, who was United States Minister to France, to that country in 1859; attended school in Paris and Switzerland; returned to the United States in 1861; during the Civil War entered the Virginia Military Institute at Lexington in 1862; served with the cadets in the Battle of New Market, Va., May 15, 1864; graduated from the law department of the University of Virginia at Charlottesville in 1868; admitted to the bar in 1868 and commenced practice in Martinsburg, W.Va.; elected judge of the thirteenth judicial circuit in 1880; elected as a Democrat to the United States Senate in 1887; reelected in 1893, and served from March 4, 1887 to March 3, 1899; chairman, Committee on Territories (Fifty-third Congress); appointed a member of the International Joint High Commission of the United States and Great Britain in 1898; retired from public life and devoted his time to the practice of law in Martinsburg, W.Va., and Washington, D.C., and to the management of his agricultural interests; died at "Boydville," near Martinsburg, W.Va., January 13, 1929; interment in the Old Norbourne Cemetery, Martinsburg, W.Va.

Bibliography: *DAB.*

**FAULKNER, Charles James** (father of Charles James Faulkner [1847-1929]), a Representative from Virginia and from West Virginia; born in Martinsburg, Va. (now West Virginia), July 6, 1806; was graduated from Georgetown University, Washington, D.C., in 1822; studied law; was admitted to the bar in 1829 and practiced; member of the Virginia house of delegates 1829-1834, 1848, and 1849; commissioner of Virginia on the disputed boundaries between that State and Maryland; member of the Virginia senate from 1838 to 1842, when he resigned; member of the Virginia constitutional convention in 1850; elected from Virginia as a Whig to the Thirty-second and Thirty-third Congresses and as a Democrat to the Thirty-fourth and Thirty-fifth Congresses (March 4, 1851-March 3, 1859); chairman, Committee on Military Affairs (Thirty-fifth Congress); appointed United States Minister to France by President James Buchanan on January 16, 1860; returned to the United States in August 1861 and was detained as a prisoner of state on charges of negotiating arms sales for the Confederacy while in Paris; released in December 1861 and negotiated his own exchange for Representative Alfred Ely of New York, who had been taken prisoner by the Confederates at the First Battle of Bull Run, July 21, 1861; during the Civil War entered the Confederate Army and was assistant adjutant general on the staff of General Thomas J. "Stonewall" Jackson; engaged in railroad enterprises; member of the State constitutional convention of West Virginia in 1872; elected as a Democrat from West Virginia to the Forty-fourth Congress (March 4, 1875-March 3, 1877); resumed the practice of law; died on the family estate, "Boydville," near Martinsburg, W.Va., November 1, 1884; interment in the family lot on the estate.

**Bibliography:** *DAB*; McVeigh, Donald R. "Charles James Faulkner: Reluctant Rebel." Ph.D. dissertation, West Virginia University, 1955.

**FAUNTROY, Walter Edward,** a Delegate from the District of Columbia; born in Washington, D.C., February 6, 1933; attended Washington (D.C.) public schools; B.A., Virginia Union University, Richmond, Va., 1955; B.D., Yale University Divinity School, 1958; pastor, New Bethel Baptist Church, 1959 to present; founder and director, Model Inner City Community Organization, 1966-1972; director, Washington Bureau, Southern Christian Leadership Conference, 1960-1971; vice chairman, District of Columbia City Council, 1967-1969; vice chairman, White House Conference to Fulfill These Rights, 1966; national coordinator, Poor People's Campaign, 1969; chairman, board of directors, Martin Luther King, Jr., Center for Social Change, Atlanta, Ga., 1969 to present; member, Leadership Conference on Civil Rights, 1961-1971; delegate, Democratic National Convention, 1972; elected as a Democrat a Delegate to the Ninety-second Congress, March 23, 1971, by special election; reelected to the nine succeeding Congresses and served from March 23, 1971 to January 3, 1991; was not a candidate for reelection in 1990 to the One Hundred Second Congress, but was an unsuccessful candidate for nomination for mayor of Washington, D.C.; is a resident of Washington, D.C.

**FAUST, Charles Lee,** a Representative from Missouri; born near Bellefontaine, Logan County, Ohio, April 24, 1879; moved with his parents to a farm near Highland, Doniphan County, Kans.; attended the public schools and Highland University; engaged in teaching in a country school near Highland from 1898 until 1900; was graduated from the law department of the University of Kansas at Lawrence in 1903, was admitted to the bar the same year, and commenced the practice of his profession in St. Joseph, Mo.; city counselor of St. Joseph, 1915-1919; elected as a Republican to the Sixty-seventh and to the three succeeding Congresses, and served from March 4, 1921 until his death at the United States Naval Hospital, Washington, D.C., on December 17, 1928; chairman, Committee on the Census (Sixty-eighth Congress); had been reelected to the Seventy-first Congress; interment in Highland Cemetery, Highland, Kans.

**FAVROT, George Kent,** a Representative from Louisiana; born in Baton Rouge, East Baton Rouge Parish, La., November 26, 1868; attended the public schools and was graduated from Louisiana State University at Baton Rouge in 1888 and from the law department of Tulane University, New Orleans, La., in 1890; was admitted to the bar in 1890 and commenced practice in Baton Rouge, La.; served as district attorney of the twenty-second judicial district of Louisiana 1892-1896; unsuccessful candidate for reelection in 1896; delegate at large to the State constitutional convention in 1898; again served as district attorney 1900-1904; district judge 1904-1906; elected as a Democrat to the Sixtieth Congress (March 4, 1907-March 3, 1909); unsuccessful candidate for renomination in 1908; member of the State house of representatives 1912-1916; resumed the practice of law in Baton Rouge; elected to the Sixty-seventh and Sixty-eighth Congresses (March 4, 1921-March 3, 1925); unsuccessful candidate for reelection in 1924 to the Sixty-ninth Congress; returned to the practice of law in Baton Rouge; elected judge of division B of the nineteenth judicial district court in 1926 and served until his death in Baton Rouge December 26, 1934; interment in Roselawn Memorial Park.

**FAWELL, Harris W.,** a Representative from Illinois; born in West Chicago, Du Page County, Ill., March 25, 1929; B.A., public schools; attended North Central College, Naperville, Ill., 1947-1949; J.D., Chicago-Kent College of Law, Chicago, Ill., 1952; admitted to the Illinois bar in 1953 and practiced law 1954-1984; member of the Illinois senate 1963-1977 and of the Illinois Commission on Children 1967-1977; unsuccessful candidate for the Illinois Supreme Court in 1976; elected as a Republican to the Ninety-ninth and to the five succeeding Congresses (January 3, 1985-January 3, 1997); is a resident of Naperville, Ill.

**FAY, Francis Ball,** a Representative from Massachusetts; born in Southboro, Worcester County, Mass., June 12, 1793; received a limited education; engaged in mercantile pursuits; postmaster of Southboro from September 15, 1817 to March 29, 1832; deputy sheriff of Worcester County, 1824-1830; member of the Massachusetts General Court, 1830-1831; moved to Chelsea, which he represented in the Massachusetts General Court from 1834 to 1836 and in 1840; served in the Massachusetts senate, 1843-1845, and again in 1848; elected as a Whig to the Thirty-second Congress to fill the vacancy caused by the death of Robert Rantoul, Jr., and served from December 13, 1852 to March 3, 1853; was not a candidate for reelection in 1852 to the Thirty-third Congress; mayor of Chelsea in 1857; founded the public library in Southboro, Mass.; settled in Lancaster in 1858; founded the Massachusetts reform school in Lancaster; again a member of the Massachusetts senate in 1868; died in South Lancaster, Mass., October 6, 1876; interment in Woodlawn Cemetery, Everett, Mass.

**FAY, James Herbert,** a Representative from New York; born in New York City April 29, 1899; attended the public schools and De La Salle Institute; during the First World War served overseas as a private first class, with the Sixty-ninth Regiment, One Hundred and Sixty-fifth Infantry, and was discharged October 11, 1919; awarded the Purple Heart Medal; was graduated from Brooklyn (N.Y.) Law School in 1929; served as deputy and acting commissioner of hospitals of New York City 1929-1934; chief field deputy, United States Bureau of Internal Revenue, 1935-1938; elected as a Democrat to the Seventy-sixth Congress (January 3, 1939-January 3, 1941); unsuccessful candidate for reelection in 1940 to the Seventy-seventh Congress; elected to the Seventy-eighth Congress (January 3, 1943-January 3, 1945); was not a candidate for renomination in 1944; engaged in the advertising and insurance business in New York City until his death September 10, 1948; interment in Pinelawn National Cemetery, Farmingdale, N.Y.

**FAY, John,** a Representative from New York; born in Hardwick, Worcester County, Mass., February 10, 1773; attended the common schools for a period of only six months; moved to New York with his parents, who settled in Montgomery County, and later in Galway, Saratoga County; moved to Northampton, Fulton County, in 1804; became a land surveyor and later engaged in agricultural pursuits, milling, and manufacturing; held various local offices and was postmaster of Northampton several years; member of the State assembly in 1808, 1809, and 1812; elected to the Sixteenth Congress (March 4, 1819-March 3, 1821); resumed his former activities; served as sheriff of Jefferson County from 1828 to 1831; presidential elector on the Democratic ticket in 1844; died in Northampton, N.Y., June 21, 1855; interment in the Old Presbyterian Church Cemetery.

**FAZIO, Victor Herbert, Jr.,** a Representative from California; born in Winchester, Middlesex County, Mass., October 11, 1942; attended the public schools; graduated from Williston Academy, Easthampton, Mass., 1961; B.A., Union College, Schenectady, N.Y., 1965; engaged in graduate work at California State University, Sacramento, 1969-1972; congressional and legislative consultant, 1966-1975; co-founder, California Journal magazine, 1970; Sacramento County Charter Commission, 1972-1974; Sacramento County Planning Commission, 1975; served in the California State assembly, 1975-1978; delegate to California State Democratic conventions, 1976-1978; delegate to the Democratic National Conventions of 1980 and 1984; elected as a Democrat to the Ninety-sixth and to the eight succeeding Congresses (January 3, 1979-January 3, 1997); is a resident of Sacramento, Calif.

**FEARING, Paul,** a Delegate from the Territory Northwest of the River Ohio; born in Wareham, Plymouth County, Mass., February 28, 1762; prepared for college by tutors; was graduated from Harvard University in 1785; studied law in Windham, Conn., and was admitted to the bar in 1787; moved to the Northwest Territory in May 1788 and engaged in the practice of law at Fort Harmer, now a part of Marietta, Ohio; appointed United States counsel for Washington County in 1788; probate judge in 1797; member of the Territorial legislature 1799-1801; elected as a Federalist a Delegate to the Seventh Congress (March 4, 1801-March 3, 1803); was not a candidate for renomination in 1802 to the Eighth Congress; resumed the practice of law and engaged in fruit and stock raising; appointed associate judge of the court of common pleas in 1810 and served seven years; appointed master in chancery in 1814; died at his home near Marietta, Ohio, August 21, 1822; interment in Harmer Cemetery, Marietta, Ohio.

Bibliography: Bloom, Jo Tice. "The Congressional Delegates from the Northwest Territory, 1799-1803." *The Old Northwest* 3 (March 1977): 3-21.

**FEATHERSTON, Winfield Scott,** a Representative from Mississippi; born near Murfreesboro, Rutherford County, Tenn., August 8, 1820; completed preparatory studies; moved to Mississippi and settled in Houston; studied law; was admitted to the bar in 1840 and commenced practice in Houston, Miss.; elected as a Democrat to the Thirtieth and Thirty-first Congresses (March 4, 1847-March 3, 1851); unsuccessful candidate for reelection in 1850 to the Thirty-second Congress; resumed the practice of law at Houston, Miss.; moved to Holly Springs in 1856; served in the Confederate Army during the Civil War; commissioned brigadier general March 4, 1862; paroled in Greensboro, N.C., May 1, 1865; unsuccessful candidate for United States Senator in 1865; member of the State house of representatives in 1876 and 1880; delegate to the Democratic National Convention in 1880; member of the State constitutional convention in 1890; died in Holly Springs, Miss., May 28, 1891; interment in Hill Crest Cemetery.

Bibliography: *DAB.*

**FEATHERSTONE, Lewis Porter,** a Representative from Arkansas; born in Oxford, Lafayette County, Miss., July 28, 1851; attended the common schools and the law department of Cumberland University, Lebanon, Tenn.; engaged in planting in Shelby County, Tenn., 1872-1881; moved to St. Francis County, Ark., and continued as a planter; member of the State house of representatives in 1887 and 1888; elected president of the State Wheel (a farmers' organization) in 1887 and reelected in 1888; successfully contested as a Labor Party candidate the election of William H. Cate to the Fifty-first Congress and served from March 5, 1890, until March 3, 1891; unsuccessful candidate on the Union Labor ticket for reelection in 1890 to the Fifty-second Congress; engaged in railroad building and in development of iron resources of Texas; was commissioned captain in the First Regiment, United States Volunteers (Immune), in 1898; died in Longview, Tex., March 14, 1922; interment in Mission Cemetery, San Antonio, Tex.

**FEAZEL, William Crosson,** a Senator from Louisiana; born near Farmerville, Union Parish, La., June 10, 1895; attended the public schools; engaged as an independent oil and gas producer; member, Louisiana State house of representatives, 1932-1936; appointed as a Democrat to the United States Senate to fill the vacancy caused by the death of John H. Overton, and served from May 18, 1948 to December 30, 1948; was not a candidate for election to the vacancy in 1948; resumed the oil and gas business in Monroe and Shreveport, La.; was a resident of West Monroe, La.; died in Shreveport, La., March 16, 1965; interment in Hasley Cemetery, West Monroe, La.

**FEELY, John Joseph,** a Representative from Illinois; born on a farm near Wilmington, Will County, Ill., August 1, 1875; attended the public schools; was graduated from Niagara (N.Y.) University in 1895 and from the law department of Yale University in 1897; was admitted to the bar in Connecticut in 1897; moved to Chicago, Ill., in 1898 and engaged in the practice of law; elected as a Democrat to the Fifty-seventh Congress (March 4, 1901-March 3, 1903); was not a candidate for renomination in 1902; engaged in the practice of his profession until his death in Chicago, Ill., February 15, 1905; interment in Mount Olivet Cemetery, Joilet, Ill.

**FEIGHAN, Edward Farrell** (nephew of Michael A. Feighan), a Representative from Ohio; born in Lakewood, Cuyahoga County, Ohio, October 22, 1947; attended schools in Cleveland, Ohio and Notre Dame International High School, Rome, Italy; B.A., Loyola University, New Orleans, La., 1969; J.D., Cleveland Marshall College of Law at Cleveland State University, 1978; admitted to the Ohio bar in 1978 and commenced practice in Cleveland in 1979; member of the Ohio house of representatives, 1973-1979; Cuyahoga County commissioner, 1979-1982; delegate, Ohio State Democratic convention, 1978; delegate to the Democratic National Convention of 1980; elected as a Democrat to the Ninety-eighth and to the four succeeding Congresses (January 3, 1983-January 3, 1993); was not a candidate for reelection in 1992 to the One Hundred Third Congress; is a resident of Lakewood, Ohio.

**FEIGHAN, Michael Aloysius** (uncle of Edward Farrell Feighan), a Representative from Ohio; born in Lakewood, Cuyahoga County, Ohio, February 16, 1905; attended the public and parochial schools; was graduated from St. Ignatius High School and attended John Carroll University, Cleveland, Ohio, for two years; A.B., Princeton University, 1927 and LL.B., Harvard Law School, 1931; was admitted to the bar in 1931 and commenced practice in Cleveland, Ohio; member of the Ohio State house of representatives, 1937-1940, serving as Democratic floor leader in 1939 and 1940; delegate to the Democratic National Conventions of 1944, 1948, 1952, 1956 and 1968; elected as a Democrat to the Seventy-eighth and to the thirteen succeeding Congresses (January 3, 1943-January 3, 1971); chairman, Joint Committee on Immigration and Nationality Policy (Eighty-ninth and Ninetieth Congresses); unsuccessful candidate for renomination in 1970 to the Ninety-second Congress; was a resident of Washington, D.C.; died March 19, 1992.

**FEINGOLD, Russell Dana,** a Senator from Wisconsin; born in Janesville, Rock County, Wis., March 2, 1953; graduated from Craig High School, Janesville, in 1971; B.A., University of Wisconsin, Madison, 1975; Oxford University, Magdalen College, England, Rhodes scholar, 1977; J.D., Harvard University Law School, 1979; attorney, Madison, Wis., 1979-1985; visiting professor, Beliot (Wis.) College; member, Wisconsin State senate, 1983-1993; elected in 1992 as a Democrat to the United States Senate for the term ending January 3, 1999; is a resident of Middleton, Wis.

**FEINSTEIN, Dianne,** a Senator from California; born in San Francisco, Calif., June 22, 1933; B.A., Stanford University, Calif., 1955; member, San Francisco Board of Supervisors, 1970-1978, president, 1970-1971, 1974-1975, 1978; mayor of San Francisco, 1978-1988; vice chair, United States Conference of Mayors, 1983-1988; unsuccessful candidate in 1990 for election for Governor of California; elected as a Democrat to the United States Senate, November 3, 1992, to fill the vacancy caused by the resignation of Pete Wilson for the term ending January 3, 1995; reelected in 1994 for the term ending January 3, 2001; is a resident of San Francisco, Calif.

**FELCH, Alpheus,** a Senator from Michigan; born in Limerick, York County, Maine, September 28, 1804; prepared for college in Phillips Academy, Exeter, N.H., and was graduated from Bowdoin College, Brunswick, Maine, in 1827; studied law; was admitted to the bar and practiced in Houlton, Maine, from 1830 to 1833; moved to Monroe, Mich., in 1833 and continued the practice of law; member, State house of representatives 1835-1837; State bank commissioner 1838-1839; state auditor general 1842; appointed associate justice of the Michigan supreme court in 1842 and served until his resignation in 1845, having been elected Governor; elected Governor of Michigan in 1845 and served from January 5, 1846 until his resignation on March 3, 1847, having been elected Senator; elected as a Democrat to the United States Senate in February 1847 and served from March 4, 1847, to March 3, 1853; chairman, Committee to Audit and Control the Contingent Expense (Thirtieth Congress), Committee on Public Land (Thirty-first and Thirty-second Congresses); president of the commission to settle Spanish and Mexican war claims 1853-1856; died in Ann Arbor, Mich., June 13, 1896; interment in Forest Hill Cemetery.

Bibliography: *DAB*.

FELDER, John Myers, a Representative from South Carolina; born in Orangeburg District, S.C., July 7, 1782; was graduated from Yale College in 1804; studied law in the Litchfield (Conn.) Law School; was admitted to the bar in 1808 and commenced practice in Orangeburg, S.C.; major of drafted militia in the War of 1812; elected a trustee of South Carolina College in 1812; member of the State house of representatives 1812-1816 and 1822-1824; served in the State senate 1816-1820; elected as a Jacksonian to the Twenty-second Congress and as a Nullifier to the Twenty-third Congress (March 4, 1831-March 3, 1835); declined to be a candidate for renomination in 1834; engaged extensively in agricultural pursuits and in the lumber business; member of the State senate from 1840 until his death in Union Point, Ga., September 1, 1851; interment in the family burial ground on his former plantation, "Midway," near Orangeburg, S.C.

FELL, John, a Delegate from New Jersey; born in New York City, February 5, 1721; attended the public schools; engaged in overseas commerce and also in agricultural pursuits; moved to Bergen County, N.J.; appointed judge of the court of common pleas on September 30, 1766, and served until October 1, 1774; member of the Provincial Congress which met in Trenton in May, June, and August 1775; chairman of the committee of safety of Bergen County, N.J.; member of the provincial council in 1776; captured by the British and held as a political prisoner from April 23, 1777, until January 1778, when he was released; Member of the Continental Congress 1778-1780; member of the State council in 1782 and 1783; moved to New York City in 1793, and subsequently to Coldenham, N.Y., where he resided with his son John until his death on May 15, 1798; interment in Colden Cemetery.

Bibliography: *DAB*; Fell, John. *Delegate from New Jersey; The Journal of John Fell*. Edited by Donald W. Whisenhunt. Port Washington, N.Y.: Kennikat Press, 1973.

FELLOWS, Frank, a Representative from Maine; born in Bucksport, Hancock County, Maine, on November 7, 1889; attended the public schools, East Maine Conference Seminary, Bucksport, Maine, and the University of Maine at Orono; was graduated from the University of Maine Law School; was admitted to the bar in 1911 and commenced practice in Portland, Maine; clerk of the United States District Court of Maine 1917-1920; elected as a Republican to the Seventy-seventh and to the five succeeding Congresses and served from January 3, 1941, until his death in Bangor, Maine, August 27, 1951; interment in Silver Lake Cemetery, Bucksport, Maine.

FELLOWS, John R., a Representative from New York; born in Troy, N.Y., July 29, 1832; moved to Saratoga County, N.Y., with his parents, who settled on a farm near Mechanicville; attended the country schools; moved to Camden, Ark., in 1850; studied law; was admitted to the bar in 1855 and commenced practice in Camden;

presidential elector on the Constitutional Union ticket of John Bell and Edward Everett in 1860; delegate to the State secession convention in 1861; entered the Confederate Army in the First Arkansas Regiment; appointed colonel on the staff of General William N.R. Beall; after the Battle of Shiloh, Tenn., April 6-7, 1862, was assigned to staff duties as assistant adjutant and inspector general at Vicksburg, Miss.; captured at the surrender of Port Hudson, La., July 9, 1863, and released June 10, 1865; returned to Camden, Ark., and resumed the practice of law; member of the State senate in 1866 and 1867; moved to New York City in 1868 and continued the practice of law; delegate to the Democratic National Convention of 1868; assistant district attorney, 1869-1872, and 1885-1887; elected district attorney in 1887, and served 1888-1890; elected as a Democrat to the Fifty-second and Fifty-third Congresses, and served from March 4, 1891 until his resignation, effective December 31, 1893; district attorney of New York City from January 1, 1894 until his death in New York City on December 7, 1896; interment in Trinity Church Cemetery.

FELTON, Charles Norton, a Representative and a Senator from California; born in Buffalo, N.Y., January 1, 1832; attended Syracuse (N.Y.) Academy; studied law; was admitted to the bar but never practiced; moved to California in 1849; engaged in mercantile pursuits and afterward in banking; sheriff of Yuba County 1853; subsequently tax collector; appointed treasurer of the United States Mint at San Francisco and Assistant Treasurer of the United States 1868-1877; member, State assembly 1878-1882; elected as a Republican to the Forty-ninth and Fiftieth Congresses (March 4, 1885-March 3, 1889); was not a candidate for renomination; elected as a Republican to the United States Senate to fill the vacancy caused by the death of George Hearst and served from March 19, 1891, to March 3, 1893; was not a candidate for reelection; State prison director 1903-1907; died at his home in Menlo Park, Calif., September 13, 1914; interment in Cypress Lawn Cemetery, Lawndale, San Mateo County, Calif.

FELTON, Rebecca Latimer (wife of William Harrell Felton), a Senator from Georgia; born near Decatur, De Kalb County, Ga., June 10, 1835; attended the common schools and graduated from the Madison Female College in 1852; moved to Bartow County, Ga., in 1854; taught school; writer, lecturer, newspaper columnist, and reformer with special interest in agricultural and women's issues; served as secretary to her husband while he was a Member of Congress from 1875 to 1881; appointed by the Governor as a Democrat to the United States Senate on October 3, 1922, to fill the vacancy caused by the death of Thomas E. Watson and served just two days, November 21 and 22, 1922, a successor having been elected; was not a candidate for election to fill the vacancy; the first woman to occupy a seat in the United States Senate; the Senator who, having served one day, served the shortest term; and the oldest Senator, at age eighty-seven, at the time of first swearing-in; engaged as a writer and lecturer and resided in Cartersville, Ga., until her death in Atlanta, Ga., January 24, 1930; interment in Oak Hill Cemetery, Cartersville, Ga.

Bibliography: *DAB*; Felton, Rebecca L. *My Memories of Georgia Politics*. Atlanta: The Index Printing Co., 1911; Talmadge, John E. *Rebecca Latimer Felton: Nine Stormy Decades*. Athens: University of Georgia Press, 1960.

FELTON, William Harrell (husband of Rebecca Latimer Felton), a Representative from Georgia; born near Lexington, Oglethorpe County, Ga., June 19, 1823; attended the common and primary schools; was graduated from the University of Georgia at Athens in 1843, and from the Medical College of Georgia at Augusta in 1844; practiced medicine, taught school, and also engaged in agricultural pursuits near Cartersville, Ga.; member of the Georgia State house of representatives from Cass (now Bartow) County in 1851; ordained as a Methodist minister in 1857; served as a surgeon during the Civil War; elected as an Independent Democrat to the Forty-fourth and to the two succeeding Congresses (March 4, 1875-March 3, 1881); unsuccessful candidate for reelection in 1880 to the Forty-seventh Congress; resumed his activity as a minister and again followed agricultural pursuits; again served in the State house of representatives, 1884-1890; trustee from the State at large for the University of Georgia, 1886-1892; died in Cartersville, Ga., September 24, 1909; interment in Oak Hill Cemetery.

**Bibliography:** *DAB*; Jones, George L. "William H. Felton and the Independent Democratic Movement in Georgia, 1870-1890." Ph.D. dissertation, University of Georgia, 1971; Roberts, William P. "The Public Career of Dr. William Harrell Felton." Ph.D. dissertation, University of North Carolina, 1953.

**FENERTY, Clare Gerald,** a Representative from Pennsylvania; born in Philadelphia, Pa., July 25, 1895; attended the parochial schools; was graduated from St. Joseph's College, Philadelphia, Pa., in 1916 and from the law department of the University of Pennsylvania at Philadelphia in 1921; during the First World War served in the United States Navy in 1917 and 1918; reentered the naval service as a lieutenant, senior grade, in 1933; was admitted to the bar in 1921 and commenced practice in Philadelphia, Pa.; member of the law faculty at the Wharton School, University of Pennsylvania, 1924-1929; member of the Philadelphia Board of Law Examiners 1928-1940; assistant district attorney at Philadelphia, Pa., 1928-1935; elected as a Republican to the Seventy-fourth Congress (January 3, 1935-January 3, 1937); unsuccessful candidate for reelection in 1936 to the Seventy-fifth Congress; resumed the practice of law; appointed judge of Common Pleas Court No. 5 of Philadelphia in November 1939 and was elected for a ten-year term in November 1941; reelected in November 1951 and served until his death in Philadelphia, Pa., July 1, 1952; interment in Holy Sepulchre Cemetery, Wyndmoor, Montgomery County, Pa.

**FENN, Edward Hart,** a Representative from Connecticut; born in Hartford, Conn., September 12, 1856; attended private schools, Hartford High School, and Yale University; associated with the Hartford Post and the Hartford Courant as reporter, city editor, State editor, and special and editorial writer; reported sessions of the Connecticut legislature from 1878 to 1908; member of the State house of representatives in 1907 and 1915; served in the State senate in 1909 and 1911; fish and game commissioner 1912-1916; served five years in the First Regiment of the Connecticut National Guard; elected as a Republican to the Sixty-seventh and to the four succeeding Congresses (March 4, 1921-March 3, 1931); chairman, Committee on the Census (Sixty-ninth through Seventy-first Congresses); was not a candidate for renomination in 1930; retired from public life and lived in Washington, D.C., and Wethersfield, Conn.; died in Washington, D.C., February 23, 1939; interment in Spring Grove Cemetery, Hartford, Conn.

**FENN, Stephen Southmyd,** a Delegate from the Territory of Idaho; born in Watertown, Conn., March 28, 1820; moved with his parents to Niagara County, N.Y., in 1824; attended the public schools; moved in 1841 to Jackson County, Iowa, where he held several local offices; moved to California in 1850 and engaged in mining and ranching; studied law; was admitted to the bar in 1862 and commenced practice in that part of Washington Territory which became a part of the Territory of Idaho upon its organization in 1863; also engaged in mining; member of the Idaho Territorial council 1864-1867; district attorney for the first judicial district in 1869; member of the Territorial house of representatives in 1872 and served as speaker of the house; engaged in agricultural pursuits; successfully contested as a Democrat the election of Thomas W. Bennett to the Forty-fourth Congress; reelected to the Forty-fifth Congress and served from June 23, 1876, to March 3, 1879; was not a candidate for renomination in 1878 to the Forty-sixth Congress;

continued his former pursuits until July 1891; died in Blackfoot, Idaho, on April 13, 1892; interment in Asylum Cemetery.

**FENNER, James,** a Senator from Rhode Island; born in Providence, R.I., January 22, 1771; received a classical education and graduated from Brown University, Providence, R.I., in 1789; elected as a Republican to the United States Senate and served from March 4, 1805, to September 1807, when he resigned to become Governor; elected Governor of Rhode Island in 1807, reelected in 1808, 1809 and 1810, and served from May 6, 1807 to May 1, 1811; unsuccessful candidate for reelection in 1811, and for election in 1812; again elected Governor in 1824, reelected every year from 1825 through 1830, and served from May 5, 1824 to May 4, 1831; unsuccessful candidate for reelection in 1831, and for election in 1832; delegate to the State constitutional convention in 1842, and served as president; retired to his estate, "What Cheer," near Providence, R.I., and resided there until his death on April 17, 1846; interment in North Burial Ground, Providence, R.I.

**Bibliography:** *DAB*.

**FENTON, Ivor David,** a Representative from Pennsylvania; born in Mahanoy City (Buck Mountain), Schuylkill County, Pa., August 3, 1889; attended the public schools, and Bucknell University, Lewisburg, Pa.; was graduated from Jefferson Medical College, Philadelphia, Pa., in 1912; served an internship at Ashland (Pa.) State Hospital in 1912 and 1913; commenced the practice of medicine in Mahanoy City, Pa., in 1914; enlisted in the United States Army Medical Corps and was commissioned a lieutenant August 8, 1917, rising later to the rank of captain; served twenty months (eleven overseas) with the Three Hundred and Fifteenth Infantry, Seventy-ninth Division; returned to Mahanoy City to resume his medical practice; elected as a Republican to the Seventy-sixty and to the eleven succeeding Congresses (January 3, 1939-January 3, 1963); unsuccessful candidate for reelection in 1962 to the Eighty-eighth Congress; medical adviser to secretary of welfare, Commonwealth of Pennsylvania, and medical consultant to Commonwealth General Hospital, Commonwealth of Pennsylvania, from March 1964 to January 1968, when he retired; was a resident of Mahanoy City, Pa., until his death in Sunbury, Pa., October 23, 1986; interment in German Protestant Cemetery, Mahonoy Township.

**FENTON, Lucien Jerome,** a Representative from Ohio; born in Winchester, Ohio, May 7, 1844; attended the public schools, Lebanon Normal School, and Ohio University at Athens; enlisted as a private in Company I, Ninety-first Regiment, Ohio Volunteer Infantry, August 11, 1862; discharged because of wounds on May 29, 1865; taught school from 1865 to 1881; unsuccessful candidate for clerk of the courts of Adams County in 1880; clerk in the United States Treasury Department, Washington, D.C., 1881-1884; returned to Ohio and organized the Winchester Bank in 1884; appointed a trustee of the Ohio University at Athens by Governor William McKinley in 1892; delegate to the Republican National Convention of 1892; elected as a Republican to the Fifty-fourth and Fifty-fifth Congresses (March 4, 1895-March 3, 1899); unsuccessful candidate for renomination in 1898 to the Fifty-sixth Congress; resumed banking in Winchester, Ohio; president of the Winchester School Board 1912-1922; president of the Adams County School Board 1918-1922; died in Winchester, Ohio, June 28, 1922; interment in Winchester Cemetery.

**FENTON, Reuben Eaton,** a Representative and a Senator from New York; born in Carroll, Chautauqua County, N.Y., on July 4, 1819; completed preparatory studies; studied law; engaged in mercantile pursuits; supervisor of Carroll from 1846 until 1852; elected as a Democrat to the Thirty-third Congress (March 4, 1853-March 3, 1855); unsuccessful candidate for reelection in 1854 to the Thirty-fourth Congress; elected to the Thirty-fifth and to the three succeeding Congresses and served from March 4, 1857, until his resignation, effective December 20, 1864, having been elected Governor of New York; elected Governor of New York in 1864, reelected in 1866, and served from January 1, 1865 to January 1, 1869; elected as a Republican to the United States Senate and served from March 4, 1869, to March 3, 1875; chairman, Committee to Audit and Control the Contingent Expense (Forty-second Congress), Committee on Manufactures (Forty-second Congress), Committee on Territories (Forty-second Congress); appointed chairman of the United States commission to the International Monetary Conference held at Paris in 1878; engaged in banking; died in Jamestown, N.Y., on August 25, 1885; interment in Lakeview Cemetery.

**Bibliography:** *DAB*; McMahon, Helen. "Reuben Eaton Fenton." Ph.D. dissertation, Cornell University, 1939.

**FENWICK, Millicent Hammond,** a Representative from New Jersey; born in New York City, February 25, 1910; attended Foxcroft School, Middleburg, Va., 1923-1925; attended Columbia University and New School for Social Research in New York City, 1933, 1942; held position of associate editor in New York publications firm, 1938-1952; member, board of education, Bernardsville (N.J.), 1938-1947, and Borough Council, 1958-1964; member, New Jersey Committee of the United States Commission on Civil Rights, 1958-1974; member, New Jersey general assembly, 1970-1973; served as director, New Jersey Consumer Affairs, 1973-1974; elected as a Republican to the Ninety-fourth and to the three succeeding Congresses (January 3, 1975-January 3, 1983); was not a candidate for reelection in 1982 to the House of Representatives, but was an unsuccessful candidate for election to the United States Senate; United States representative, with rank of ambassador, to the United Nations Agencies for Food and Agriculture, June 13, 1983, to March 1987; was a resident of Bernardsville, N.J.; died September 16, 1992.

**Bibliography:** Fenwick, Millicent. *Speaking Up.* Foreword by Norman Cousins. New York: Harper and Row, 1982.

**FERDON, John William,** a Representative from New York; born in Piermont, Rockland County, N.Y., December 13, 1826; was graduated from Rutgers College, New Brunswick, N.J., in 1847; studied law; was admitted to the bar and practiced; member of the State assembly in 1855; served in the State senate in 1856 and 1857; delegate to the Republican National Convention in 1864 and 1876; elected as a Republican to the Forty-sixth Congress (March 4, 1879-March 3, 1881); died in Monmouth Beach, N.J., on August 5, 1884; interment in private cemetery on the Ferdon estate in Piermont, N.Y.

**FERGUSON, Fenner,** a Delegate from the Territory of Nebraska; born in Nassau, Rensselaer County, N.Y., April 25, 1814; attended the common schools; studied law; was admitted to the bar in 1840 and commenced practice in Albany, N.Y.; moved to Albion, Mich., in 1846 and continued the practice of law; served successively as master in chancery, district attorney, and member of the State house of representatives 1854-1859; appointed by President Franklin Pierce as chief justice of the Territory of Nebraska in 1854; moved to Bellevue, Nebr., in October 1854; organized the first district and supreme courts of Nebraska; assisted the first Territorial legislature in drafting the first code of laws enacted for the government of the Territory; resigned as chief justice, having been elected as a Democrat to the Thirty-fifth Congress (March 4, 1857-March 3, 1859); was not a candidate for renomination in 1858 to the Thirty-sixth Congress; died in Bellevue, Nebr., on October 11, 1859; interment in Bellevue Cemetery.

**FERGUSON, Homer,** a Senator from Michigan; born in Harrison City, Westmoreland County, Pa., February 25, 1889; attended the public schools and the University of Pittsburgh, Pittsburgh, Pa.; graduated from the University of Michigan at Ann

Arbor in 1913; was admitted to the bar the same year and commenced practice in Detroit, Mich.; circuit judge of the circuit court for Wayne County, Mich., 1929-1942; professor of law at Detroit (Mich.) College of Law, 1929-1939; elected as a Republican to the United States Senate in 1942; reelected in 1948, and served from January 3, 1943 to January 3, 1955; unsuccessful candidate for reelection in 1954; chairman, Republican Policy Committee (Eighty-third Congress); appointed Ambassador to the Philippines on March 22, 1955 and served until March 1956; judge of the United States Court of Military Appeals at Washington, D.C., 1956-1971; served as senior judge on the United States Court of Military Appeals, 1971-1976; resident of Grosse Point, Mich., until his death on December 17, 1982; interment in Woodlawn Cemetery, Detroit, Mich.

**FERGUSON, Phillip Colgan,** a Representative from Oklahoma; born in Wellington, Sumner County, Kans., August 15, 1903; attended the public schools; was graduated from the University of Kansas at Lawrence, A.B., 1926; moved to Oklahoma and settled on a ranch near Woodward in 1926; engaged in agricultural pursuits and cattle raising; elected as a Democrat to the Seventy-fourth and to the two succeeding Congresses (January 3, 1935-January 3, 1941); unsuccessful candidate for reelection in 1940 to the Seventy-seventh Congress, and for election in 1944 to the Seventy-ninth Congress; resumed his former pursuits; commissioned a major in the United States Marine Corps in the Second World War and served from March 2, 1942, until August 1, 1944; received the Silver Star Medal; unsuccessful Republican candidate in 1958 for election for Governor of Oklahoma; engaged in cattle ranching; was director of the Bank of Woodward and a cattleman; resided in Woodward, Okla., until his death in Tiajuana, Mex., on August 8, 1978; cremated; ashes scattered on the Pacific Ocean at San Diego, Calif.

**FERGUSSON, Harvey Butler,** a Delegate from the Territory of New Mexico and a Representative from New Mexico; born near Pickensville, Pickens County, Ala., September 9, 1848; attended the public schools of Alabama; was graduated from Washington and Lee University, Lexington, Va., in 1873 and from the law department of that university in 1874; taught in the Shenandoah Valley Academy, Winchester, Va.; was admitted to the bar in 1875 and commenced the practice of law in Wheeling, W.Va.; moved to White Oaks, Lincoln County, N.Mex., in 1882, and to Albuquerque, N.Mex., in 1883; engaged in the practice of law; special United States attorney in 1893 and 1894; member of the Democratic National Committee 1896-1904; elected as a Democrat a Delegate to the Fifty-fifth Congress (March 4, 1897-March 3, 1899); unsuccessful candidate for reelection in 1898 to the Fifty-sixth Congress and for election in 1902 to the Fifty-eighth Congress; upon the admission of New Mexico as a State into the Union was elected to the Sixty-second Congress; reelected to the Sixty-third Congress and served from January 8, 1912, to March 3, 1915; unsuccessful candidate for reelection in 1914 to the Sixty-fourth Congress; died in Albuquerque, N.Mex., June 10, 1915.

**Bibliography:** Roberts, Calvin A. "H.B. Fergusson, 1848-1915: New Mexico Spokesman for Political Reform." *New Mexico Historical Review* 57 (July 1982): 237-55.

**FERNALD, Bert Manfred,** a Senator from Maine; born in West Poland, Androscoggin County, Maine, April 3, 1858; attended the public schools, Hebron Academy, and a business and preparatory school in Boston; taught school; elected supervisor of schools in 1878; engaged in the canning, dairy, and telephone businesses; member, Maine State house of representatives, 1896-1898; member, State senate, 1898-1902; elected Governor of Maine in 1908, and served from January 6, 1909 to January 4, 1911; unsuccessful candidate for reelection in 1910; elected as a Republican to the United States Senate in 1916 to fill the vacancy caused by the death of Edwin C. Burleigh; reelected in 1918 and 1924 and served from September 12, 1916, until his death in West Poland, Maine, August 23, 1926; chairman, Committee on Public Buildings and Grounds (Sixty-sixth through Sixty-ninth Congresses); interment in Highland Cemetery.

**FERNANDEZ, Antonio Manuel,** a Representative from New Mexico; born in Springer, Colfax County, N.Mex., January 17, 1902; attended the public schools, and Highlands University, Las Vegas, N.Mex.; received law training at Cumberland University, Lebanon, Tenn.; court reporter for the eighth judicial district of New Mexico 1925-1930; was admitted to the bar in 1931 and commenced practice in Raton, Colfax County, N.Mex.; assistant district attorney of the eighth judicial district in 1933; practiced law in Santa Fe, N.Mex., in 1934; served in the State house of representatives in 1935; chief tax attorney for the State Tax Commission in 1935 and 1936; first assistant attorney general 1937-1941; member of the first New Mexico Public Service Commission in 1941 and 1942; elected as a Democrat to the Seventy-eighth and to the six succeeding Congresses and served from January 3, 1943, until his death; chairman, Committee on Memorials (Seventy-ninth Congress); had been reelected on November 6, 1956, to the Eighty-fifth Congress; died in Albuquerque, N.Mex., November 7, 1956; interment in Rosario Catholic Cemetery, Santa Fe.

**FERNANDEZ, Joachim Octave,** a Representative from Louisiana; born in New Orleans, La., August 14, 1896; attended the public schools and Cecil Barrois School in New Orleans, La.; demurrage and storage tariff expert from 1921; delegate to the State constitutional convention in 1921; member of the State house of representatives 1924-1928; served in the State senate 1928-1930; elected as a Democrat to the Seventy-second and to the four succeeding Congresses (March 4, 1931-January 3, 1941); unsuccessful candidate for renomination in 1940 to the Seventy-seventh Congress; called to active duty as a lieutenant commander in the United States Naval Reserve on January 8, 1941, and served until placed on the inactive duty list on September 30, 1943; appointed collector of internal revenue for the district of Louisiana in September 1943 and served until October 1946; engaged in the general tax business and as a tax consultant; in 1951 employed as revenue examiner for department of revenue, State of Louisiana, and head of income tax section; resided in New Orleans, La., where he died August 8, 1978; interment in Metairie Cemetery.

**FERNÓS-ISERN, Antonio,** a Resident Commissioner from Puerto Rico; born in San Lorenzo, P.R., May 10, 1895; attended elementary and high schools in Puerto Rico and Pennsylvania State Normal School at Bloomsburg; was graduated from the University of Maryland, College of Physicians and Surgeons and School of Medicine, in May 1915; engaged in the practice of medicine in Caguas, P.R., 1916-1918; health officer of the city of San Juan in 1919; assistant commissioner of health of Puerto Rico in 1920, 1921, and 1923-1931; commissioner of health of Puerto Rico, 1931-1933, and 1942-1946; professor at the Public Health School of Tropical Medicine of Puerto Rico, 1931-1935; resumed the private practice of medicine in San Juan, P.R., 1933-1942; unsuccessful candidate as a Popular Democrat for Resident Commissioner in 1940; director of civilian defense, metropolitan area of Puerto Rico, 1942; Acting Governor of Puerto Rico at various times from 1943 to 1946; appointed as a Popular Democrat Resident Commissioner of Puerto Rico to the United States House of Representatives to fill the vacancy in the term ending January 3, 1949, caused by the resignation of Jesus T. Pinero; elected in 1948 for a four-year term commencing January 3, 1949; reelected in 1952, 1956, and again in 1960, and served from September 11, 1946, to January 3, 1965; was not a candidate for reelection in 1964 to the United States House of Representatives; senator, Commonwealth of Puerto Rico, 1965-1969;

died in San Juan, P.R., January 19, 1974; interment in National Cemetery, Old San Juan, P.R.

**FERRARO, Geraldine Anne,** a Representative from New York; born in Newburgh, Orange County, N.Y., August 26, 1935; attended Mount St. Mary's School, Newburgh; graduated from Marymount School, Tarrytown, 1952; B.A., Marymount College, 1956; J.D., Fordham University School of Law, New York City, 1960; admitted to the New York bar in 1961 and commenced practice in New York City; assistant district attorney, Queens County, 1974-1978; elected as a Democrat to the Ninety-sixth and to the two succeeding Congresses (January 3, 1979-January 3, 1985); was not a candidate for reelection in 1984 to the Ninety-ninth Congress but was the unsuccessful Democratic nominee for Vice President of the United States; is a resident of Forest Hills, N.Y.

**Bibliography:** Ferraro, Geraldine A., with Linda Bird Francke. *Ferraro: My Story.* New York: Bantam Books, 1985.

**FERRELL, Thomas Merrill,** a Representative from New Jersey; born in Glassboro, Gloucester County, N.J., June 20, 1844; attended the common schools and completed an academic course; elected a member of the township committee in 1872 and 1873; president of Hollow Ware Glassworkers' Association 1878-1883; member of the school board 1885-1890, serving as its president in 1887; member of the State house of assembly in 1879 and 1880; member of the State senate in 1880 and 1881; elected as a Democrat to the Forty-eighth Congress (March 4, 1883-March 3, 1885); unsuccessful candidate for reelection in 1884 to the Forty-ninth Congress; employed as a glassware salesman; died in Glassboro, N.J., October 20, 1916; interment in Methodist Episcopal Cemetery.

**FERRIS, Charles Goadsby,** a Representative from New York; born at "The Homestead," Throgs Neck, the Bronx, N.Y., about 1796; received a limited education; studied law; was admitted to the bar and practiced in New York City; member of the board of aldermen in 1832 and 1833; elected as a Jacksonian to the Twenty-third Congress to fill the vacancy caused by the resignation of Dudley Selden and served from December 1, 1834, to March 3, 1835; elected as a Democrat to the Twenty-seventh Congress (March 4, 1841-March 3, 1843); was largely instrumental in securing an appropriation through Congress to build the first telegraph line; died in New York City June 4, 1848.

**FERRIS, Scott,** a Representative from Oklahoma; born in Neosho, Newton County, Mo., November 3, 1877; attended the public schools and was graduated from Newton County High School in 1897 and from the Kansas City School of Law in 1901; was admitted to the bar in 1901 and commenced practice in Lawton, Okla., the same year; member of the State house of representatives in 1904 and 1905; upon the admission of Oklahoma as a State into the Union was elected as a Democrat to the Sixtieth Congress; reelected to the Sixty-first and to the five succeeding Congresses and served from November 16, 1907, until March 3, 1921; chairman, Committee on Public Lands (Sixty-second through Sixty-fifth Congresses); did not seek renomination as a Representative, but was an unsuccessful candidate for Senator; delegate to the Democratic National Conventions in 1912 and 1916; moved to New York City and engaged in the oil business 1921-1924; returned to Oklahoma in 1925; Democratic national committeeman from Oklahoma 1924-1940; resumed the practice of law; engaged in the oil business and also in agricultural pursuits; died in Oklahoma City, Okla., June 8, 1945; interment in Rosehill Cemetery.

**FERRIS, Woodbridge Nathan,** a Senator from Michigan; born in Spencer, Tioga County, N.Y., January 6, 1853; attended the academies of Spencer, Candor, and Oswego, N.Y., the Oswego (N.Y.) Normal Training School, 1870-1873, and the medical department of the University of Michigan at Ann Arbor in 1873 and 1874; principal and superintendent of various schools in Illinois from 1874 to 1884;

settled in Big Rapids, Mich., where he established the Ferris Industrial School in 1884 and served as president until his death; president of the Big Rapids Savings Bank; unsuccessful Democratic candidate for election in 1892 to the Fifty-third Congress, and for Governor of Michigan in 1904; elected Governor of Michigan in 1912, reelected in 1914, and served from January 1, 1913 to January 1, 1917; unsuccessful candidate for election as Governor in 1920; elected as a Democrat to the United States Senate in 1922 and served from March 4, 1923, until his death in Washington, D.C., March 23, 1928; interment in Highland View Cemetery, Big Rapids, Mich.

Bibliography: *DAB*.

FERRISS, Orange, a Representative from New York; born at Glens Falls, Warren County, N.Y., November 26, 1814; completed preparatory studies; attended the University of Vermont at Burlington; studied law; was admitted to the bar in 1840 and commenced practice in Glens Falls, N.Y.; justice of the peace 1838-1841 and 1845-1848; inspector of public schools in 1839 and 1840; corporation clerk 1839-1842; county judge and surrogate of Warren County 1851-1863; elected as a Republican to the Fortieth and Forty-first Congresses (March 4, 1867-March 3, 1871); chairman, Committee on Mines and Mining (Forty-first Congress); was not a candidate for renomination in 1870 to the Forty-second Congress; appointed by President Ulysses S. Grant as commissioner of southern claims and served from 1871 to 1877; Second Auditor of the Treasury from May 12, 1880, until his resignation on June 19, 1885; retired to Glens Falls, N.Y., where he died April 11, 1894; interment in Glens Falls Cemetery.

FERRY, Orris Sanford, a Representative and a Senator from Connecticut; born in Bethel, Fairfield County, Conn., August 15, 1823; pursued preparatory studies and graduated from Yale College in 1844; studied law; was admitted to the bar in 1846 and practiced; appointed judge of probate in 1849; member, State senate 1855-1856; prosecuting attorney for Fairfield County 1856-1859; unsuccessful candidate for election in 1856 to the Thirty-fifth Congress; elected as a Republican to the Thirty-sixth Congress (March 4, 1859-March 3, 1861); unsuccessful candidate for reelection to the Thirty-seventh Congress; entered the Union Army in 1861 as colonel of the Fifth Regiment, Connecticut Volunteer Infantry; brigadier general of United States Volunteers 1862-1865; elected as a Republican to the United States Senate in 1866; reelected in 1873 by a combination of Liberal Republicans and Democrats and served from March 4, 1867, until his death in Norwalk, Conn., November 21, 1875; chairman, Committee to Audit and Control the Contingent Expense (Forty-first Congress), Committee on Patents (Forty-second through Forty-fourth Congresses), Committee on Pensions (Forty-second Congress), Committee on Education and Labor (Forty-fourth Congress); interment in Norwalk Cemetery.

Bibliography: *DAB*.

FERRY, Thomas White, a Representative and a Senator from Michigan; born in the old mission house of the Astor Fur Co. on Mackinac Island, Mich., June 10, 1827; moved with his parents to Grand Haven, Mich.; attended the public schools; engaged in mercantile pursuits; member, State house of representatives 1850-1852; member, State senate 1856; delegate to the Loyalist Convention at Philadelphia in 1866; elected as a Republican to the Thirty-ninth and to the two succeeding Congresses (March 4, 1865-March 3, 1871); reelected in 1870 to the Forty-second Congress, but resigned, having been elected Senator; elected to the United States Senate in 1871, reelected in 1877 and served from March 4, 1871, to March 3, 1883; unsuccessful candidate for reelection in 1882; served as President pro tempore of the Senate during the Forty-fourth and Forty-fifth Congresses; chairman, Committee on Rules (Forty-third through Forty-fifth Congresses),

Committee on Post Office and Post Roads (Forty-fifth and Forty-seventh Congresses); presided over the high court of impeachment of Secretary of War William W. Belknap in March 1876, and over the sixteen joint meetings of the Senate and House of Representatives during the Hayes-Tilden presidential electoral contest in 1877; died in Grand Haven, Mich., October 13, 1896; interment in Lake Forest Cemetery.

Bibliography: *DAB*.

FESS, Simeon Davison, a Representative and a Senator from Ohio; born on a farm near Harrod, Allen County, Ohio, December 11, 1861; attended the country schools; graduated from the Ohio Northern University at Ada in 1889; taught American history at Ohio Northern University 1889-1896, graduated from its law department in 1894, dean of the law department 1896-1900, and vice president of the university 1900-1902; graduate student and lecturer at the University of Chicago 1902-1907; president of Antioch College, Yellow Springs, Ohio, 1907-1917; editor and author; delegate to the State constitutional convention in 1912; elected as a Republican to the Sixty-third and to the four succeeding Congresses (March 4, 1913-March 3, 1923); chairman, Committee on Education (Sixty-sixth and Sixty-seventh Congresses); did not seek renomination, having become a candidate for Senator; chairman of the Republican National Congressional Committee 1918-1922; elected as a Republican to the United States Senate in 1922; reelected in 1928 and served from March 4, 1923, to January 3, 1935; unsuccessful candidate for reelection in 1934; Republican whip 1929-1933; chairman, Committee on the Library (Sixty-ninth through Seventy-second Congresses); chairman of the Republican National Committee 1930-1932; engaged in literary pursuits; died in Washington, D.C., December 23, 1936; interment in Glen Forest Cemetery, Yellow Springs, Ohio.

Bibliography: *DAB*; Nethers, John. *Simeon D. Fess: Educator and Politician*. Brooklyn: Pageant-Poseidon, 1973.

FESSENDEN, Samuel Clement (brother of Thomas Amory Deblois Fessenden and William Pitt Fessenden), a Representative from Maine; born in New Gloucester, Cumberland County, Maine, March 7, 1815; pursued classical studies and was graduated from Bowdoin College, Brunswick, Maine, in 1834 and from Bangor (Maine) Theological Seminary in 1837; was ordained and installed as pastor of the Second Congregational Church, Thomaston, Maine, 1837-1856; studied law; was admitted to the bar and commenced practice in 1858; judge of the Rockland municipal court; elected as a Republican to the Thirty-seventh Congress (March 4, 1861-March 3, 1863); was not a candidate for renomination in 1862 to the Thirty-eighth Congress; examiner in the United States Patent Office, 1865-1879; United States consul at St. John, New Brunswick, Canada, 1879-1881; died in Stamford, Conn., April 18, 1882; interment in Woodland Cemetery.

FESSENDEN, Thomas Amory Deblois (brother of Samuel Clement Fessenden and William Pitt Fessenden), a Representative from Maine; born in Portland, Maine, January 23, 1826; attended North Yarmouth Academy and Dartmouth College, Hanover, N.H.; was graduated from Bowdoin College, Brunswick, Maine, in 1845; studied law; was admitted to the bar in April 1848 and commenced practice in Mechanic Falls, Maine; moved to Auburn, Maine, in 1850 and continued the practice of law; delegate to the Republican National Conventions of 1856 and 1868; member of the Maine State house of representatives in 1860 and 1868; prosecuting attorney for Androscoggin County, 1861-1862; elected as a Republican to the Thirty-seventh Congress to fill the vacancy caused by the resignation of Charles W. Walton, and served from December 1, 1862 to March 3, 1863; was not a candidate for renomination in 1862 to the Thirty-eighth Congress; resumed the practice of law; died in Auburn, Maine, September 28, 1868; interment in Riverside Cemetery, Lewiston, Maine.

**FESSENDEN, William Pitt** (brother of Samuel Clement Fessenden and Thomas Amory Deblois Fessenden), a Representative and a Senator from Maine; born in Boscawen, Merrimack County, N.H., October 16, 1806; attended the common schools; graduated from Bowdoin College, Brunswick, Maine, in 1827; studied law; was admitted to the bar in 1827 and practiced in Bridgeton, Bangor, and Portland, Maine; member of the Maine State house of representatives in 1832 and 1840; elected as a Whig to the Twenty-seventh Congress (March 4, 1841-March 3, 1843); declined to be a candidate for reelection in 1842 to the Twenty-eighth Congress; member, Maine State house of representatives, 1845-1846; unsuccessful Whig candidate for election in 1850 to the Thirty-second Congress; member, Maine State house of representatives, 1853-1854; elected as a Whig to the United States Senate to fill the vacancy in the term beginning March 4, 1853, caused by the failure of the legislature to elect; reelected in 1859 as a Republican, and served from February 10, 1854 to July 1, 1864, when he resigned to accept a Cabinet portfolio; chairman, Committee on Finance (Thirty-seventh through Thirty-ninth Congresses); appointed Secretary of the Treasury by President Abraham Lincoln, and served from July 5, 1864 until March 3, 1865; member of the peace convention of 1861 held in Washington, D.C., in an effort to devise means to prevent the impending war; again elected to the United States Senate as a Republican, and served from March 4, 1865 until his death in Portland, Maine, September 8, 1869; chairman, Committee on Public Buildings and Grounds (Fortieth Congress), Committee on Appropriations (Forty-first Congress), Committee on the Library (Forty-first Congress); interment in Evergreen Cemetery.

Bibliography: *DAB*; Cook, Robert. "'The Grave of All My Comforts': William Pitt Fessenden as Secretary of the Treasury, 1864-65." *Civil War History* 41 (September 1995): 208-226; Fessenden, Francis. *Life and Public Services of William Pitt Fessenden.* 1907. Reprint. New York: Da Capo Press, 1970; Jellison, Charles. *Fessenden of Maine: Civil War Senator.* Syracuse: Syracuse University Press, 1962.

**FEW, William,** a Delegate and a Senator from Georgia; born near Baltimore, Md., June 8, 1748; moved with his parents to Orange County, N.C., in 1758; completed preparatory studies; studied law; was admitted to the bar and commenced practice in Augusta, Ga., in 1776; member, Georgia State house of representatives, 1777, 1779, 1783, 1793; member of the State executive council in 1777 and 1778; engaged in the expedition for the subjugation of east Florida in 1778; presiding judge of the Richmond County court and surveyor general in 1778; served as lieutenant colonel of the Richmond County Militia in 1779; Member of the Continental Congress, 1780-1782, and 1786-1788; original trustee for establishing the University of Georgia in 1785; delegate to the convention which framed the Federal Constitution in 1787; delegate to the Georgia convention that ratified the Federal Constitution in 1788; elected to the United States Senate, and served from March 4, 1789 to March 3, 1793; unsuccessful candidate for election to the United States Senate in 1795; judge of the circuit court of Georgia, 1794-1797; moved to New York City in 1799; member, New York State assembly, 1802-1805; State prison inspector, 1802-1810; United States Commissioner of Loans in 1804; director of the Manhattan Bank, 1804-1814, and president in 1814; served as alderman in 1813 and 1814; died in Fishkill, N.Y., July 16, 1828; interment in Reformed Dutch Church Cemetery, Beacon, Dutchess County, N.Y.

Bibliography: *DAB*; Few, William. "Autobiography of Colonel William Few of Georgia." *Magazine of American History* 7 (November 1881): 343-358; "Senator Few on the Second Session of the First Congress, 1790." *American Historical Review* 16 (July 1911): 789-790.

**FICKLIN, Orlando Bell,** a Representative from Illinois; born in Scott County, Ky., December 16, 1808; attended the common schools; was graduated from Transylvania Law School, Lexington, Ky., in 1830; was admitted to the bar in 1830 and commenced practice in Mount Carmel, Ill.; served in the Black Hawk War as quartermaster in 1832; colonel of the militia of Wabash County in 1833; State's attorney for the Wabash circuit in 1835; member of the Illinois State house of representatives in 1835, 1838, and 1842; moved to Charleston, Ill., in 1837; elected as a Democrat to the Twenty-eighth and to the two succeeding Congresses (March 4, 1843-March 3, 1849); chairman, Committee on Public Buildings and Grounds (Twenty-ninth Congress); elected to the Thirty-second Congress (March 4, 1851-March 3, 1853); chairman, Committee on District of Columbia (Thirty-second Congress); resumed the practice of law in Charleston; delegate to the Democratic National Conventions of 1856, 1860 (Charleston, S.C.), and 1864; delegate to the State constitutional convention in 1869 and 1870; again served in the State house of representatives in 1878; died in Charleston, Ill., May 5, 1886; interment in Mound Cemetery.

**FIEDLER, Bobbi,** a Representative from California; born in Santa Monica, Los Angeles County, Calif., April 22, 1937; attended the public schools; attended Santa Monica Technical School, 1955-1957; attended Santa Monica City College, 1955-1959; businesswoman; member, Los Angeles (City) Board of Education, 1977-1980; delegate, California State Republican conventions, 1977-1987; delegate to the Republican National Conventions of 1980 and 1984; elected as a Republican to the Ninety-seventh and to the two succeeding Congresses (January 3, 1981-January 3, 1987); was not a candidate for reelection in 1986 to the House of Representatives, but was an unsuccessful candidate for nomination to the United States Senate; is a resident of Northridge, Calif.

**FIEDLER, William Henry Frederick,** a Representative from New Jersey; born in New York City, August 25, 1847; moved to New Jersey with his parents, who settled in Newark; attended the public and high schools; apprenticed to the hat-finishing trade at the age of fifteen; employed as clerk and engaged in the retail hat and later in the men's clothing business; elected an alderman of Newark in 1876 and 1878; member of the State house of assembly in 1878 and 1879; mayor of Newark 1880-1882; unsuccessful candidate for reelection in 1881; again a member of the State house of assembly in 1882; elected as a Democrat to the Forty-eighth Congress (March 4, 1883-March 3, 1885); unsuccessful candidate for reelection in 1884 to the Forty-ninth Congress; appointed postmaster of Newark, N.J., on March 29, 1886, and served until October 1, 1889; resumed his former business pursuits until 1905, when he engaged in the real estate business and in banking; unsuccessful candidate for mayor in 1904; died in Newark, N.J., January 1, 1919; interment in Fairmount Cemetery.

**FIELD, David Dudley,** a Representative from New York; born in Haddam, Middlesex County, Conn., February 13, 1805; educated by private tutors; was graduated from Williams College, Williamstown, Mass., in 1825; studied law in Albany, N.Y., and New York City; was admitted to the bar in 1828 and commenced practice in New York City; author of many works on political, civil, and criminal procedure; unsuccessful candidate for election to the State assembly in 1841; member of the commission on legal practice and procedure 1847-1850; member of a State commission to prepare a political, penal, and civil code 1857-1865; member of the peace convention of 1861 held in Washington, D.C., in an effort to devise means to prevent the impending war; elected as a Democrat to the Forty-fourth Congress to fill the vacancy caused by the resignation of Smith Ely, Jr., and served from January 11 to March 3, 1877; resumed the practice of law; died in New York City April 13, 1894; interment in Stockbridge Cemetery, Stockbridge, Mass.

Bibliography: *DAB*; Field, Henry M. *The Life of David Dudley Field*. New York: Scribner's Sons, 1898.

**FIELD, Moses Whelock,** a Representative from Michigan; born in Watertown, Jefferson County, N.Y., February 10, 1828; moved with his parents to Cato, Cayuga County, N.Y.; attended the public schools, and was graduated from the academy in Victor, N.Y.; moved to Detroit, Mich., in 1844 and engaged in mercantile and agricultural pursuits; alderman of Detroit 1863-1865; elected as a Republican to the Forty-third Congress (March 4, 1873-March 3, 1875); unsuccessful for reelection in 1874 to the Forty-fourth Congress; instrumental in organizing the Independent Greenback Party, having called the national convention at Indianapolis, Ind., May 17, 1876; regent of the University of Michigan in 1888; lived on his farm, "Linden Lawn," in the township of Hamtramck, a suburb of Detroit, where he died March 14, 1889; interment in Woodmere Cemetery.

**FIELD, Richard Stockton** (grandson of Richard Stockton [1730-1781] and son of Richard Stockton [1764-1828]), a Senator from New Jersey; born at White Hall, Burlington County, N.J., December 31, 1803; moved to Princeton with his mother in 1810; pursued an academic course and graduated from the College of New Jersey (now Princeton University) in 1821; studied law; was admitted to the bar in 1825 and commenced practice in Salem, N.J.; moved to Princeton, N.J., in 1832; member of the New Jersey State house of assembly in 1837; attorney general of New Jersey, 1838-1841; member of the State constitutional convention in 1844; professor at the Princeton Law School in 1847; appointed as a Republican to the United States Senate to fill the vacancy caused by the death of John R. Thomson, and served from November 21, 1862 to January 14, 1863, when a successor was elected; was not a candidate for election in 1863; appointed by President Abraham Lincoln judge of the United States District Court for the District of New Jersey, 1863-1870; died in Princeton, N.J., May 25, 1870; interment in Princeton Cemetery.

**Bibliography:** *DAB.*

**FIELD, Scott,** a Representative from Texas; born in Canton, Madison County, Miss., January 26, 1847; attended the McKee School in Madison County; during the Civil War enlisted in the Confederate Army as a member of the Harvey Scouts; later served in Major General William H. Jackson's division, Forrest's cavalry corps, Army of the Tennessee; after the war resumed his studies, and was graduated from the University of Virginia at Charlottesville in 1868; taught school for two years; studied law; was admitted to the bar in 1872; moved to Calvert, Tex., in 1872 and practiced law; prosecuting attorney of Robertson County 1878-1882; served in the State senate 1887-1891; delegate to the Democratic National Convention in 1892; elected as a Democrat to the Fifty-eighth and Fifty-ninth Congresses (March 4, 1903-March 3, 1907); was not a candidate for reelection in 1906 to the Sixtieth Congress; resumed the practice of law until 1913, when he engaged in extensive agricultural pursuits; died in Calvert, Tex., December 20, 1931; interment in Calvert Cemetery.

**FIELD, Walbridge Abner,** a Representative from Massachusetts; born in North Springfield, Windsor County, Vt., April 26, 1833; was graduated from Dartmouth College, Hanover, N.H., in 1855; tutor at Dartmouth College in 1856, 1857, and 1859; studied law in Boston in 1858 and at the Harvard Law School in 1859; was admitted to the bar in 1860 and commenced practice in Boston, Mass.; member of the school committee of Boston in 1863 and 1864; served in the common council 1865-1867; appointed assistant attorney of the United States in 1865, serving in this capacity until April 1869, when he was appointed Assistant Attorney General of the United States, holding this office until August 1870, when he resigned; resumed the practice of law in Boston; presented credentials as a Member-elect to the Forty-fifth Congress and served from March 4, 1877, to March 28, 1878, when he was succeeded by Benjamin Dean, who contested his election; elected as a Republican to the Forty-sixth Congress (March 4, 1879-March 3, 1881); declined to be a candidate for renomination in 1880 to the Forty-seventh Congress; appointed by Governor John Davis Long to the bench of the supreme judicial court on February 21, 1881; promoted to the position of chief justice on September 4, 1890, and served until his death in Boston, July 15, 1899; interment in Forest Hills Cemetery, West Roxbury, Mass.

**Bibliography:** *DAB.*

**FIELDER, George Bragg,** a Representative from New Jersey; born in Jersey City, N.J., July 24, 1842; attended private and public schools in his native town, and was graduated from the Dickinson Lyceum in Jersey City and from Selleck's Academy, Norwalk, Conn.; engaged in banking, and, in company with his father, built the New Jersey Southern and New York, New Hampshire & Willimantic Railroads; enlisted as a private in the Union Army in 1862 and served throughout the Civil War, being promoted to sergeant major and lieutenant; elected register of Hudson County in 1884, and reelected in 1889; elected as a Democrat to the Fifty-third Congress (March 4, 1893-March 3, 1895); declined to be a candidate for renomination in 1894; elected county register for a third time in 1895; died in Windham, N.Y., August 14, 1906; interment in Bay View Cemetery, Jersey City, N.J.

**FIELDS, Cleo,** a Representative from Louisiana; born in Baton Rouge, La., November 22, 1962; B.A., Southern University, 1984; J.D., Southern University School of Law, 1987; chair, College Students Voter Registration-Education March; law clerk to East Baton Rouge Parish Clerk of Court Prosecutor's Office and Parish Attorney's Office; unsuccessful candidate for election in 1990 to the One Hundred Second Congress; member, Louisiana State senate, 1986-1993; founder and executive director, Young Adults for Positive Action, Inc.; elected as a Democrat to the One Hundred Third and One Hundred Fourth Congresses (January 3, 1993-January 3, 1997); unsuccessful candidate in 1995 for election for Governor of Louisiana; was not a candidate for reelection in 1996 to the One Hundred Fifth Congress; is a resident of Baton Rouge, La.

**FIELDS, Jack Milton, Jr.,** a Representative from Texas; born in Humble, Harris County, Tex., February 3, 1952; attended the public schools; graduated Humble High School, 1970; B.A., Baylor University, Waco, Tex., 1974, J.D., 1977; admitted to the bar in 1977 and commenced practice in Humble, Tex.; vice president, Rosewood Memorial Funeral Home and Cemetery, 1977-1980; elected as a Republican to the Ninety-seventh and to the seven succeeding Congresses (January 3, 1981-January 3, 1997); was not a candidate for reelection in 1996 to the One Hundred Fifth Congress; is a resident of Humble, Tex.

**FIELDS, William Craig,** a Representative from New York; born in New York City, February 13, 1804; attended the common schools; moved to Laurens, Otsego County, N.Y., in 1836 and engaged in mercantile pursuits and in 1847 engaged in the manufacture of cotton and linen goods; justice of the peace for sixteen years; clerk of Otsego County from 1852 until 1855; supervisor of Otsego County in 1865 and 1866; elected as a Republican to the Fortieth Congress (March 4, 1867-March 3, 1869); retired from public life; died in Laurens, Otsego County, N.Y., October 27, 1882; interment in Laurens Cemetery.

**FIELDS, William Jason,** a Representative from Kentucky; born in Willard, Carter County, Ky., December 29, 1874; attended the public schools, and the University of Kentucky at Lexington; studied law; engaged in agricultural pursuits and also in the real estate business at Olive Hill, Ky.; elected as a Democrat to the Sixty-second and to the six succeeding Congresses and served from March 4, 1911, to December 11, 1923, when he resigned, having been elected Governor; Governor of Kentucky from December 11,

1923 to December 13, 1927; returned to Olive Hill and was admitted to the bar in 1927; Commonwealth's attorney for the thirty-seventh judicial district of Kentucky from July 1, 1932 to January 1, 1935; appointed a member of the State Workmen's Compensation Board January 20, 1936, and served until his retirement on August 8, 1944; co-owner of an insurance agency, 1940-1945; died in Grayson, Ky., October 21, 1954; interment in Olive Hill Cemetery, Olive Hill, Ky.

**FIESINGER, William Louis,** a Representative from Ohio; born in Willard, Huron County, Ohio, October 25, 1877; educated in the public schools of Norwalk, Ohio; was graduated from the law department of Baldwin-Wallace University, Berea, Ohio, in 1901; was admitted to the bar the same year and commenced practice in Sandusky, Ohio; served as city solicitor of Sandusky 1903-1909; judge of the common pleas court of Erie County 1925-1931; elected as a Democrat to the Seventy-second, Seventy-third, and Seventy-fourth Congresses (March 4, 1931-January 3, 1937); unsuccessful candidate for renomination in 1936; resumed the practice of law in Sandusky, Ohio; died in Cleveland, Ohio, September 11, 1953; interment in Oakland Cemetery, Sandusky, Ohio.

**FILLMORE, Millard,** a Representative from New York, Vice President and 13th President of the United States; born in Locke Township (now Summerhill), Cayuga County, N.Y., January 7, 1800; reared on a farm; largely self-taught; apprenticed to a clothier; taught school in Buffalo while studying law; was admitted to the bar in 1823 and commenced practice in East Aurora, N.Y.; moved to Buffalo, N.Y., in 1830; member, New York State assembly, 1829-1831; elected as a Whig to the Twenty-third Congress (March 4, 1833-March 3, 1835); elected to the Twenty-fifth and to the two succeeding Congresses (March 4, 1837-March 3, 1843); declined to be a candidate for renomination in 1842 to the Twenty-eighth Congress; unsuccessful Whig candidate for Governor in 1844; State comptroller, 1847-1849; elected Vice President of the United States on the Whig ticket headed by Zachary Taylor in 1848, and was inaugurated March 4, 1849; became President upon the death of President Taylor, and served from July 9, 1850 to March 3, 1853; unsuccessful candidate for the Whig nomination for president in 1852; unsuccessful candidate for president on the American (Know-Nothing) ticket in 1856; commanded a corps of home guards during the Civil War; traveled extensively; died in Buffalo, N.Y., March 8, 1874; interment in Forest Lawn Cemetery.

**Bibliography:** *DAB*; Grayson, Benson Lee. *The Unknown President: The Administration of President Millard Fillmore.* Washington, D.C.: University Press of America, 1981; Rayback, Robert J. *Millard Fillmore: Biography of a President.* Buffalo: Buffalo Historical Society, 1959.

**FILNER, Robert,** a Representative from California; born in Pittsburgh, Pa., September 4, 1942; B.A., Cornell University, Ithaca, N.Y., 1963; M.A., University of Delaware, 1968; Ph.D., history, Cornell University, 1972; history professor, San Diego (Calif.) State University, 1970 to present; Congressional Fellowship Program, American Political Science Association and legislative assistant to Senator Hubert H. Humphrey 1975; legislative assistant to Representative Donald M. Fraser, 1976; member, San Diego School Board, 1979-1983, president, 1982; assistant to Representative Jim Bates, 1984; member, San Diego City Council, 1987-1993; deputy mayor, San Diego, 1990; elected as a Democrat to the One Hundred Third and One Hundred Fourth Congresses (January 3, 1993-January 3, 1997); is a resident of San Diego, Calif.

**FINCH, Isaac,** a Representative from New York; born in Stillwater, Saratoga County, N.Y., October 13, 1783; moved with his parents to Peru, Clinton County, N.Y., in 1787; attended the public schools; studied law, but did not engage in extensive practice; settled near Jay, Essex County, N.Y., and became interested in agricultural pursuits; served as major in the Twenty-sixth Regiment of Infantry during the War of 1812; member of the State assembly 1822-1824; elected to the Twenty-first Congress (March 4, 1829-March 3, 1831); was not a candidate for renomination in 1830; resumed agricultural pursuits; died in Jay, N.Y., June 23, 1845; interment in Central Cemetery.

**FINCK, William Edward,** a Representative from Ohio; born in Somerset, Perry County, Ohio, September 1, 1822; attended the public schools and St. Joseph's College; studied law; was admitted to the bar in 1843 and commenced practice in Somerset, Ohio; unsuccessful candidate for election in 1850 to the Thirty-second Congress; member of the State senate in 1851; delegate to the Whig National Convention in 1852; again a member of the State senate in 1861; elected as a Democrat to the Thirty-eighth and Thirty-ninth Congresses (March 4, 1863-March 3, 1867); unsuccessful Democratic candidate for judge of the supreme court of Ohio in 1868; elected as a Democrat to the Forty-third Congress to fill the vacancy caused by the resignation of Hugh J. Jewett and served from December 7, 1874, to March 3, 1875; resumed the practice of law; died in Somerset, Ohio, January 25, 1901; interment in Holy Trinity Cemetery.

**FINDLAY, James** (brother of John Findlay and William Findlay), a Representative from Ohio; born in Mercersburg, Franklin County, Pa., October 12, 1770; attended the public schools; moved to Cincinnati, Ohio, in 1793; studied law; was admitted to the bar and practiced; member of the Territorial legislative council in 1798; United States receiver of public moneys at Cincinnati in 1800; United States marshal of Ohio in 1802; member of the State house of representatives in 1803; mayor of Cincinnati in 1805 and 1806, and again in 1810 and 1811; served in the War of 1812 as colonel of the Second Ohio Volunteer Infantry; elected to the Nineteenth and Twentieth Congresses and elected as a Jacksonian to the Twenty-first and Twenty-second Congresses (March 4, 1825-March 3, 1833); was not a candidate for renomination in 1832 to the Twenty-third Congress; unsuccessful Democratic candidate for Governor of Ohio in 1834; died in Cincinnati, Ohio, December 28, 1835; interment in Spring Grove Cemetery.

**Bibliography:** *DAB*.

**FINDLAY, John** (brother of James Findlay and William Findlay), a Representative from Pennsylvania; born in Mercersburg, Franklin County, Pa., March 31, 1766; received a limited schooling; prothonotary 1809-1821; served as captain in the War of 1812; moved to Chambersburg, Pa.; register and recorder of deeds; clerk of the orphans' court; clerk of the court of quarter sessions 1809-1818; elected to the Seventeenth Congress to fill the vacancy caused by the resignation of James Duncan; reelected to the Eighteenth and Nineteenth Congresses and served from October 9, 1821, to March 3, 1827; was not a candidate for renomination in 1826; appointed postmaster of Chambersburg, Pa., March 20, 1829, and held the office until his death there November 5, 1838; interment in Falling Spring Presbyterian Church Cemetery at Chambersburg.

**FINDLAY, John Van Lear,** a Representative from Maryland; born at Mount Tammany, near Williamsport, Washington County, Md., December 21, 1839; was privately tutored and pursued classical studies; was graduated from Princeton College in 1858; member of the State house of delegates in 1861 and 1862; studied law; was admitted to the bar and commenced practice in Baltimore, Md., in 1869; collector of internal revenue for the third district of Maryland at Baltimore in 1865 and 1866; appointed city solicitor for Baltimore in 1876 and served two years; elected as a Democrat to the Forty-eighth and Forty-ninth Congresses (March 4, 1883-March 3, 1887); resumed the practice of law; appointed a member of the Venezuelan Claims Commission in 1889; nominated as arbitrator on the Chilean Claims Commission in 1893, but the Senate rejected the nomination; died in Baltimore, Md., April 19, 1907; interment in Greenmount Cemetery.

**FINDLAY, William** (brother of James Findlay and John Findlay), a Senator from Pennsylvania; born in Mercersburg, Franklin County, Pa., June 20, 1768; attended the public schools; engaged in agricultural pursuits; served as brigade inspector in the Pennsylvania militia; studied law; was admitted to the bar and commenced practice in Franklinton, Pa.; member, Pennsylvania house of representatives 1797, 1804-1807; Pennsylvania treasurer, 1807-1817; Governor of Pennsylvania from December 16, 1817 to December 19, 1820; unsuccessful candidate for reelection in 1820; elected as a Republican to the United States Senate to fill the vacancy in the term commencing March 4, 1821, caused by the failure of the legislature to elect and served from December 10, 1821, to March 3, 1827; was not a candidate for reelection in 1826; chairman, Committee on Agriculture (Nineteenth Congress); Director of the United States Mint from 1827 until 1841, when he resigned on account of illness; died in Harrisburg, Pa., November 12, 1846; interment in Harrisburg Cemetery.

**FINDLEY, Paul,** a Representative from Ilinois; born in Jacksonville, Morgan County, Ill., June 23, 1921; attended the public schools of Jacksonville, Ill.; B.A., Illinois College at Jacksonville, 1943; served in the United States Navy in the Pacific as a lieutenant (jg) from 1943 to 1946; president of the Pike Press, Inc., Pittsfield, Ill.; unsuccessful candidate for the Republican nomination for State senator in 1952; member, United States delegation, North Atlantic Assembly, 1965-1970; elected as a Republican to the Eighty-seventh and to the ten succeeding Congresses (January 3, 1961-January 3, 1983); unsuccessful candidate for reelection in 1982 to the Ninety-eighth Congress; appointed to the Board for International Food and Agricultural Development, 1983; is a resident of Jacksonville, Ill.

Bibliography: Findley, Paul. *The Federal Farm Fable.* New Rochelle, N.Y.: Arlington House, 1968; Findley, Paul. *They Dare to Speak Out: People and Institutions Confront Israel's Lobby.* Westport, Conn.: Lawrence Hill, 1985.

**FINDLEY, William,** a Representative from Pennsylvania; born in Ireland in 1741 or 1742; attended the parish schools; immigrated to the United States and settled in Philadelphia, Pa., in 1762; enlisted as a private, rose to the rank of captain, and served during the Revolution; moved to Westmoreland County, Pa.; tailor; member of the council of censors in 1783; member of the general assembly, 1785-1786; member of the Pennsylvania supreme executive council, 1789-1790; served in the Pennsylvania house of representatives, 1790-1791; delegate to the Pennsylvania constitutional convention in 1790; elected to the Second Congress; reelected to the Third Congress, and reelected as a Republican to the Fourth and Fifth Congresses (March 4, 1791-March 3, 1799); engaged in agricultural pursuits; was in opposition to the Government during the Whiskey Rebellion of 1794, and wrote a book defending his course; again a member of the Pennsylvania senate, 1799-1802; elected to the Eighth and to the six succeeding Congresses (March 4, 1803-March 3, 1817); chairman, Committee on Elections (Eighth through Twelfth Congresses); died near Greensburg, Pa., on April 4, 1821; interment in Unity Meeting House Cemetery, near Latrobe, Pa.

Bibliography: *DAB*; Findley, William. *History of the Insurrection in the Four Western Counties of Pennsylvania.* Philadelphia: Samuel Harrison Smith, 1796.

**FINE, John,** a Representative from New York; born in New York City August 26, 1794; received private instructions; was graduated from Columbia College at New York City in 1809; studied law in the Litchfield (Conn.) Law School; was admitted to the bar in 1815 and commenced practice in Ogdensburg, St. Lawrence County, N.Y.; treasurer of St. Lawrence County 1821-1833; judge of the court of common pleas for St. Lawrence County from 1824 until his resignation in March 1839; elected as a Democrat to the Twenty-sixth Congress (March 4, 1839-March 3, 1841); again judge

of the court of common pleas from February 16, 1843, until the court was abolished in 1847; unsuccessful candidate for judge of the State supreme court in 1847 and again in 1849; member of the State senate in 1848; resumed the practice of law; died in Ogdensburg, N.Y., January 4, 1867; interment in Ogdensburg Cemetery.

**FINE, Sidney Asher,** a Representative from New York; born in New York City, September 14, 1903; attended public schools; was graduated from College of the City of New York in 1923 and from the law school of Columbia University in 1926; was admitted to the bar in 1926 and commenced practice in New York City; member of the State assembly in 1945 and 1946 and the State senate 1947-1950; elected as a Democrat to the Eighty-second, Eighty-third, and Eighty-fourth Congresses and served from January 3, 1951, until his resignation January 2, 1956; New York State Supreme Court, 1956-1975; resided in New York City until his death there on April 23, 1982; interment at Old Montefiore Cemetery, Queens, N.Y.

**FINERTY, John Frederick,** a Representative from Illinois; born in Galway, Ireland, September 10, 1846; completed preparatory studies; immigrated to the United States in 1864; enlisted in the Union Army during the Civil War and served in the Ninety-ninth Regiment, New York State Militia; correspondent for the Chicago Times in the Sioux War of 1876, in the Northern Indian (Sioux) War of 1879, in the Ute campaign of 1879, and afterward in the Apache campaign of 1881; correspondent in Washington during the sessions of the Forty-sixth Congress, 1879-1881; established the Citizen, a weekly newspaper, in Chicago in 1882; elected as an Independent Democrat to the Forty-eighth Congress (March 4, 1883-March 3, 1885); unsuccessful Republican and Anti-Monopoly candidate for reelection in 1884 to the Forty-ninth Congress; member of the board of local improvements, 1906-1908; died in Chicago, Ill., June 10, 1908; interment in Calvary Cemetery.

**FINGERHUT, Eric David,** a Representative from Ohio; born in Cleveland, Ohio, May 6, 1959; B.A., Northwestern University, Evanston, Ill., 1981; J.D., Stanford University, Calif., 1984; staff attorney, Older Persons Law Office, Legal Aid Society of Cleveland, 1984-1985; associate director, Cleveland Works; member, Ohio State senate, 1991-1993; campaign manager for Michael R. White for Mayor of Cleveland; transition director and special assistant to the Mayor; chair, Common Cause-Ohio, 1986-1988; elected as a Democrat to the One Hundred Third Congress (January 3, 1993-January 3, 1995); unsuccessful candidate for reelection in 1994 to the One Hundred Fourth Congress; director, Cleveland Federation for Community Planning; is a resident of Mayfield Heights, Ohio.

**FINKELNBURG, Gustavus Adolphus,** a Representative from Missouri; born near Cologne, Germany, April 6, 1837; immigrated to the United States in 1848 with his parents, who settled in St. Charles, Mo.; attended St. Charles College, Missouri, and was graduated from the Cincinnati (Ohio) Law School in 1859; was admitted to the bar in 1860 and commenced practice in St. Louis, Mo.; served in the Union Army during the Civil War; member of the State house of representatives 1864-1868, and served as speaker pro tempore in 1868; elected as a Republican to the Forty-first Congress and as a Liberal Republican to the Forty-second Congress (March 4, 1869-March 3, 1873); appointed in 1905 by President Theodore Roosevelt as United States judge for the eastern district of Missouri, and served until March 31, 1907, when he resigned; died in Denver, Colo., May 18, 1908; interment in Bellefontaine Cemetery, St. Louis, Mo.

**FINLEY, Charles** (son of Hugh Franklin Finley), a Representative from Kentucky; born in Williamsburg, Whitley County, Ky., March 26, 1865; attended the common and subscription schools, and Milligan College, Milligan, Tenn.; engaged in business as a coal operator, banker, and publisher; member of the Kentucky house of representatives 1894-1896; delegate to the Kentucky Republican convention in 1895; served as secretary of state of Kentucky 1896-1900; chairman of the Republican executive committee of the Eleventh Kentucky Congressional District 1912-1928; elected as a Republican to the Seventy-first Congress to fill the vacancy caused by the resignation of John M. Robsion; reelected to the Seventy-second Congress and served from February 15, 1930, to March 3, 1933; was not a candidate for renomination in 1932; retired from business activities; died in Williamsburg, Ky., March 18, 1941; interment in Highland Cemetery, Williamsburg, Ky.

**FINLEY, David Edward,** a Representative from South Carolina; born in Trenton, Phillips County, Ark., February 28, 1861; attended the public schools of Rock Hill and Ebenezer, S.C., and was graduated from the law department of South Carolina College (now the University of South Carolina) at Columbia in 1885; was admitted to the bar in 1886 and commenced practice in York, S.C.; member of the State house of representatives 1890-1891; served in the State senate 1892-1896; trustee of the University of South Carolina 1890-1896; elected as a Democrat to the Fifty-sixth and to the eight succeeding Congresses and served from March 4, 1899, until his death; had been reelected to the Sixty-fifth Congress; died in Charlotte, N.C., on January 26, 1917; interment in Rose Hill Cemetery, York, S.C.

**FINLEY, Ebenezer Byron** (nephew of Stephen Ross Harris), a Representative from Ohio; born in Orrville, Wayne County, Ohio, July 31, 1833; attended the public schools; studied law at Bucyrus, Ohio, from 1859 until the outbreak of the Civil War; was active in recruiting Company K, Twenty-fourth Ohio Volunteer Infantry, in which he served as a first lieutenant; resumed the study of law in 1862; was admitted to the bar in 1862 and commenced practice in Bucyrus, Ohio; elected as a Democrat to the Forty-fifth and Forty-sixth Congresses (March 4, 1877-March 3, 1881); chairman, Committee on Public Expenditures (Forty-sixth Congress); was not a candidate for renomination in 1880; adjutant general of Ohio in 1884; served as circuit judge of the third circuit of Ohio; resumed the practice of law in Bucyrus, Ohio, where he died August 22, 1916; interment in Oakwood Cemetery.

**FINLEY, Hugh Franklin** (father of Charles Finley), a Representative from Kentucky; born at Tyes Ferry, Whitley County, Ky., January 18, 1833; attended the common schools; engaged in agricultural pursuits; studied law; was admitted to the bar in 1859 and commenced practice in Williamsburg, Ky.; member of the Kentucky house of representatives from 1861 to August 1862, when he resigned; elected Commonwealth attorney in 1862, and served until 1866, when he resigned; again elected in 1867, and reelected in 1868 for six years; unsuccessful candidate for election in 1870 to the Forty-second Congress; served in the Kentucky senate in 1875 and 1876, when he resigned; appointed in 1876 by President Ulysses S. Grant as United States district attorney for Kentucky, and served until 1877; resumed the practice of law; judge of the fifteenth judicial circuit 1880-1886; elected as a Republican to the Fiftieth and Fifty-first Congresses (March 4, 1887-March 3, 1891); unsuccessful candidate for renomination in 1890 to the Fifty-second Congress; resumed the practice of law and also engaged in the coal mining business; died in Williamsburg, Ky., October 16, 1909; interment in Woodlawn Cemetery.

**FINLEY, Jesse Johnson,** a Representative from Florida; born near Lebanon, Wilson County, Tenn., November 18, 1812; pursued an academic course; captain of mounted volunteers in the Seminole War in 1836; studied law and was admitted to the bar in 1838; moved to Mississippi County, Ark., in 1840 and practiced his profession; served in the State senate in 1841; moved to Memphis, Tenn. in 1842, and continued the practice of law; mayor of Memphis in 1845; moved to Mariana, Fla., in November 1846; elected to the State senate of Florida in 1850; presidential elector on the Whig ticket in 1852; judge of the western circuit of Florida 1853-1861; appointed judge of the Confederate States court for the district of Florida in 1861; resigned and volunteered as a private in the Confederate Army in March 1862, and was successively promoted to the rank of brigadier general November 16, 1863; settled in Lake City, Fla., in 1865, and continued the practice of law; moved to Jacksonville, Fla., in 1871; successfully contested as a Democrat the election of Josiah J. Walls to the Forty-fourth Congress and served from April 19, 1876, to March 3, 1877; successfully contested the election of Horatio Bisbee, Jr., to the Forty-fifth Congress and served from February 20 to March 3, 1879; presented credentials as a Member-elect to the Forty-Seventh Congress and served from March 4, 1881, to June 1, 1882, when he was succeeded by Horatio Bisbee, Jr., who contested his election; presented credentials on December 5, 1887, as a Senator-designate to the United States Senate for the term commencing March 4, 1887, but was not permitted to qualify for the reason that the appointment was made before the vacancy occurred; died in Lake City, Fla., November 6, 1904; interment in Evergreen Cemetery, Gainesville, Fla.

**FINNEGAN, Edward Rowan,** a Representative from Illinois; born in Chicago, Ill., June 5, 1905; attended the St. Ritas, Northwestern, and DePaulus schools, Loyola University, and Northwestern University School of Law; LL.B., DePaul University School of Law, 1930; commenced the practice of law in Chicago, Ill., in 1931; assistant State's attorney, Cook County; assistant corporation counsel, city of Chicago; unsuccessful candidate for the Democratic nomination for municipal court judge in Chicago in 1939; elected as a Democrat to the Eighty-seventh and Eighty-eighth Congresses and served from January 3, 1961, until his resignation December 6, 1964; had been renominated for the Eighty-ninth Congress but withdrew, having been appointed judge, Circuit Court of Cook County, Ill., December 7, 1964, and served in this position until his death, February 2, 1971, in Chicago, Ill.; interment in All Saints Cemetery, Des Plaines, Ill.

**FINNEY, Darwin Abel,** a Representative from Pennsylvania; born in Shrewsbury, Rutland County, Vt., August 11, 1814; attended the public schools and was graduated from the military academy at Rutland, Vt.; moved with his parents to Meadville, Pa.; clerk in a law office in Kingsbury, N.Y., in 1834 and 1835; was graduated from Allegheny College, Meadville, Pa., in 1840; studied law; was admitted to the bar in 1842 and commenced practice in Meadville, Pa.; member of the Pennsylvania senate 1856-1861; elected as a Republican to the Fortieth Congress and served from March 4, 1867, until his death at Brussels, Belgium, August 25, 1868; interment in Greendale Cemetery, Meadville, Pa.

**FINO, Paul Albert,** a Representative from New York; born in New York City December 15, 1913; attended the public schools; graduated from St. John's University School of Law, New York City, 1937; was admitted to the New York State bar in 1938 and began practice in New York City; served as an assistant attorney general in the State government from March 1943 to December 1944; member of the State senate from January 1945 to May 1950; member of the New York City Civil Service Commission from June 1, 1950, to December 31, 1952; elected as a Republican to the Eighty-third and to the seven succeeding Congresses and served from January 3, 1953, until his resignation December 31, 1968, to become a New York Supreme Court Justice having been elected November 5, 1968, and assumed duties January 1, 1969; delegate to the Republican State convention 1940-1966, and to the Republican National Conventions of 1960, 1964 and 1968; is a resident of Atlantic Beach, N.Y.

**Bibliography:** Fino, Paul A. *My Life in Politics and Public Service*. Great Neck, N.Y.: Todd and Honeywell, Inc., 1986.

**FISCHER, Israel Frederick,** a Representative from New York; born in New York City August 17, 1858; moved to Brooklyn in September 1887; attended the public schools and Cooper Institute, New York City; employed as a clerk in a law office; studied law; was admitted to the bar in 1879 and commenced practice in New York City; member of the executive committee of the Republican State committee 1888-1890; elected as a Republican to the Fifty-fourth and Fifty-fifth Congresses (March 4, 1895-March 3, 1899); unsuccessful candidate for reelection in 1898 to the Fifty-sixth Congress; appointed on May 2, 1899, by President McKinley as a member of the United States Board of General Appraisers (now the United States Customs Court); appointed chief justice of that court by President Coolidge on April 16, 1927, and served until his retirement on March 31, 1933; delegate to the International Customs Congress held in New York City in 1903; died in New York City March 16, 1940; interment in Maimonides Cemetery, Brooklyn, N.Y.

**FISH, Hamilton** (son of Hamilton Fish [1808-1893], father of Hamilton Fish [1888-1991], and grandfather of Hamilton Fish, Jr. [1926-1996]), a Representative from New York; born in Albany, N.Y., April 17, 1849; attended private schools in this country and in Switzerland, and was graduated from Columbia College, New York City, in 1869; private secretary to his father, who was Secretary of State in the Cabinet of President Ulysses S. Grant, 1869-1871; was graduated from Columbia Law School in 1873; was admitted to the bar the same year and commenced practice in New York City; member of the New York State assembly, 1874-1896, serving as speaker in 1895 and 1896; appointed by President Theodore Roosevelt in 1903 as assistant treasurer of the United States at New York City; reappointed in 1907 and served until October 1908, when he resigned; elected as a Republican to the Sixty-first Congress (March 4, 1909-March 3, 1911); unsuccessful candidate for reelection in 1910 to the Sixty-second Congress; retired from public life and active pursuits and resided in Garrison, N.Y.; died in Aiken, S.C., January 15, 1936, while on a visit; interment in the cemetery of St. Philip's Church-in-the-Highlands, Garrison, N.Y.

**FISH, Hamilton** (father of Hamilton Fish [1849-1936], grandfather of Hamilton Fish [1888-1991], and great-grandfather of Hamilton Fish, Jr. [1926-1996]), a Representative and a Senator from New York; born in New York City August 3, 1808; attended Doctor Bancel's French School, New York City; graduated from Columbia College, New York City, in 1827; studied law; was admitted to the bar in 1830 and practiced in New York City; commissioner of deeds for the city and county of New York, 1832-1833; elected as a Whig to the Twenty-eighth Congress (March 4, 1843-March 3, 1845); unsuccessful candidate for reelection in 1844 to the Twenty-ninth Congress; resumed the practice of law; Lieutenant Governor of New York, 1848-1849; elected Governor of New York in 1848, and served from January 1, 1849 to January 1, 1851; elected to the United States Senate, and served from March 4, 1851 to March 3, 1857; was not a candidate for reelection; president general of the Society of the Cincinnati from 1854 until his death; appointed by President Lincoln as one of the board of commissioners for the relief and exchange of Union prisoners of war in the South; president of the New-York Historical Society, 1867-1869; appointed by President Ulysses S. Grant as Secretary of State and served from March 11, 1869 to March 12, 1877; resumed the practice of law and managed his large real estate holdings in New York City; died in Garrison, N.Y., September 7, 1893; interment in the cemetery of St. Philip's Church-in-the-Highlands, Garrison, N.Y.

**Bibliography:** *DAB*; Nevins, Allan. *Hamilton Fish: The Inner History of the Grant Administration*. New York: F. Ungar Publishing Company, 1957.

**FISH, Hamilton** (son of Hamilton Fish [1849-1936], grandson of Hamilton Fish [1808-1893], and father of Hamilton Fish, Jr. [1926-1996]), a Representative from New York; born in Garrison, Putnam County, N.Y., December 7, 1888; attended St. Marks School; was graduated from Harvard University in 1910; elected as a Progressive to the New York State assembly, 1914-1916; commissioned on July 15, 1917, captain of Company K, Fifteenth New York National Guard, which subsequently became the Three Hundred and Sixty-ninth Infantry; was discharged as a major on May 14, 1919; decorated with the Croix de Guerre and the American Silver Star and also cited in War Department general orders; colonel in the Officers' Reserve Corps; delegate to the Republican National Convention of 1928; elected as a Republican to the Sixty-sixth Congress to fill the vacancy caused by the resignation of Edmund Platt; reelected to the Sixty-seventh and to the eleven succeeding Congresses and served from November 2, 1920, to January 3, 1945; unsuccessful candidate for reelection in 1944 to the Seventy-ninth Congress; author; was a resident of New York City; died January 18, 1991; interment in the cemetery of St. Philip's Church-in-the-Highlands, Garrison, N.Y.

**Bibliography:** Fish, Hamilton. *Memoir of an American Patriot*. Epilogue by Brian Mitchell. Washington: Regnery Gateway, 1991; Hanks, Richard K. "Hamilton Fish and American Isolationism, 1920-1944." Ph.D. dissertation, University of California, Riverside, 1971.

**FISH, Hamilton, Jr.** (son of Hamilton Fish [1888-1991], grandson of Hamilton Fish [1849-1936] and Alfred Clark Chapin, great-grandson of Hamilton Fish [1808-1893], and a descendant of Lewis Morris), a Representative from New York; born in Washington, D.C., June 3, 1926; graduate of Kent School, Kent, Conn.; A.B., Harvard University, 1949; LL.B., New York University School of Law, 1957; attended John F. Kennedy School of Public Administration; admitted to New York State bar; enlisted in the United States Naval Reserve, 1944-1946; served in Ireland as vice counsul, United States Foreign Service, 1951-1953; attorney for the New York State assembly judiciary committee, Albany, N.Y., 1961; delegate to the Republican National Convention of 1984; elected as a Republican to the Ninety-first and to the twelve succeeding Congresses (January 3, 1969-January 3, 1995); was not a candidate for reelection in 1994 to the One Hundred Fourth Congress; was a resident of Washington, D.C., and Millbrook, N.Y. until his death in Washington on July 23, 1996; interment in the cemetery of St. Philip's Church-in-the-Highlands, Garrison, N.Y.

**FISHBURNE, John Wood** (cousin of Maury Maverick), a Representative from Virginia; born near Charlottesville, Albemarle County, Va., March 8, 1868; attended Pantop's Academy, near Charlottesville, Va., and Washington and Lee University, Lexington, Va.; taught at Fishburne Military Academy, Waynesboro, Va., in 1886 and 1887; was graduated from the law department of the University of Virginia at Charlottesville in 1890; was admitted to the bar the same year and commenced practice in Charlottesville; also engaged in agricultural pursuits; served in the Virginia house of delegates, 1895-1897; member of the Virginia State Library Board, 1904-1913; appointed judge of the eighth judicial circuit in 1913; subsequently elected by the legislature and served from 1913 until his resignation in 1930; elected as a Democrat to the Seventy-second Congress (March 4, 1931-March 3, 1933); was not a candidate for renomination in 1932 to the Seventy-third Congress; resumed the practice of law; died in Ivy Depot, near Charlottesville, June 24, 1937; interment in Riverview Cemetery, Charlottesville, Va.

**FISHER, Charles,** a Representative from North Carolina; born near Salisbury, Rowan County, N.C., October 20, 1789; educated by private tutors in Raleigh, N.C.; studied law; was admitted to the bar but did not practice to any extent; member of the State senate in 1818; elected as a Republican to the Fifteenth Congress to fill the vacancy caused by the death of George Mumford; reelected to the Sixteenth Congress and served from February 11, 1819, to March 3, 1821; declined to be a candidate for renomination in 1820; member of the State house of commons 1821-1836 and served as speaker in 1831 and 1832; member of the State constitutional convention in 1835; elected to the Twenty-sixth Congress (March 4, 1839-March 3, 1841); was not a candidate for renomination in 1840; unsuccessful candidate for election in 1844 to the Twenty-ninth Congress; died in Hillsboro, Miss., while on a visit, May 7, 1849.

**FISHER, David,** a Representative from Ohio; born in Somerset County, Pa., December 3, 1794; moved with his parents to Point Pleasant, Clermont County, Ohio, in 1799; pursued preparatory studies; was a lay preacher and newspaper contributor; member of the State house of representatives in 1834; unsuccessful candidate for Governor in 1844; editor and proprietor of a newspaper in Wilmington, Ohio, in 1846; elected as a Whig to the Thirtieth Congress (March 4, 1847-March 3, 1849); was not a candidate for renomination in 1848 to the Thirty-first Congress; while in Congress he occupied a seat next to John Quincy Adams, who fell into his arms when stricken with paralysis on February 21, 1848; returned to Cincinnati, Ohio; city magistrate in 1849 and 1850; resumed newspaper activities; died near Mount Holly, Ohio, May 7, 1886; interment in Wesleyan Cemetery, Cincinnati, Ohio.

**FISHER, George,** a Representative from New York; born in Franklin, Mass., March 17, 1788; attended the common schools and Brown University, Providence, R.I.; studied law; was admitted to the bar in Oswego County, N.Y., in 1816 and commenced practice in Oswego, N.Y.; appointed inspector of schools in 1818; trustee of the village of Oswego in 1828 and 1833; presented credentials as a Member-elect to the Twenty-first Congress and served from March 4, 1829, to February 5, 1830, when the seat was awarded to Silas Wright, Jr., who contested the election; trustee of schools in 1830; continued the practice of law in Oswego, N.Y., until 1833; took his family to France, where he spent five years for the education of his children; returned to Oswego and engaged in real estate operations; served as president of the Northwestern Insurance Co. for several years; moved to New York City about 1856 and died there March 26, 1861.

**FISHER, George Purnell,** a Representative from Delaware; born in Milford, Sussex County, Del., October 13, 1817; attended the public schools of Kent County and Mount St. Mary's College, Emmitsburg, Md.; was graduated from Dickinson College, Carlisle, Pa., in 1838; studied law; was admitted to the bar in 1841 and commenced practice in Dover, Del.; member of the State house of representatives in 1843 and 1844; secretary of state in 1846; confidential clerk to Secretary John M. Clayton in the Department of State at Washington in 1849; appointed by President Zachary Taylor a commissioner to adjudicate claims against Brazil, and served from 1850 to 1852; attorney general of Delaware, 1857-1860; elected as a Unionist to the Thirty-seventh Congress (March 4, 1861-March 3, 1863); unsuccessful candidate for reelection in 1862 to the Thirty-eighth Congress; appointed by President Lincoln on March 11, 1863, a judge of the Supreme Court of the District of Columbia, which position he resigned when appointed district attorney for the District of Columbia, serving until 1875; returned to Dover; appointed by President Benjamin Harrison on May 31, 1889, First Auditor of the Treasury Department and served until March 23, 1893; died in Washington, D.C., February 10, 1899; interment in Oak Hill Cemetery; reinterment in the Methodist Cemetery, Dover, Del.

**Bibliography:** Lore, Charles B. *The Life and Character of George B. Fisher.* Wilmington: Historical Society of Delaware, 1902.

**FISHER, Horatio Gates,** a Representative from Pennsylvania; born in Huntingdon, Pa., April 21, 1838; attended public and private schools; was graduated from Lafayette College, Easton, Pa., in July 1855; engaged in mining, shipping, and the wholesale coal business; member of the borough council 1862-1865; auditor of Huntingdon County 1865-1868; burgess of the borough of Huntingdon 1874-1876; member of the Pennsylvania senate 1876-1879; elected as a Republican to the Forty-sixth and Forty-seventh Congresses (March 4, 1879-March 3, 1883); chairman, Committee on Coinage, Weights, and Measures (Forty-seventh Congress); declined to be a candidate for renomination in 1882 to the Forty-eighth Congress; resumed his former business pursuits; appointed by Governor James A. Beaver a member of the board of managers of Huntingdon Reformatory in 1888; died in Punxsutawney, Pa., May 8, 1890; interment in River View Cemetery, Huntingdon, Pa.

**FISHER, Hubert Frederick,** a Representative from Tennessee; born in Milton, Santa Rosa County, Fla., October 6, 1877; attended the common schools and was graduated from the University of Mississippi at Oxford in 1898; took a postgraduate course at Princeton University in 1900 and 1901; studied law; was admitted to the bar in 1904 and commenced practice in Memphis, Tenn.; delegate to the Democratic National Convention in 1912; member of the State senate in 1913 and 1914; United States attorney for the western district of Tennessee 1914-1917; elected as a Democrat to the Sixty-fifth and to the six succeeding Congresses (March 4, 1917-March 3, 1931); was not a candidate for renomination in 1930; due to deafness retired from active legal and political activities and moved to Germantown, Tenn., where he engaged in nursery pursuits; died June 16, 1941, while on a visit in New York City; interment in Old Gray Cemetery, Knoxville, Tenn.

**FISHER, John,** a Representative from New York; born in Londonderry, Rockingham County, N.H., March 13, 1806; attended the common schools; engaged in mercantile pursuits; managed an iron manufacturing establishment in Hamilton, Canada, 1836-1856; member of the city council of Hamilton 1848 and 1849 and served as mayor in 1850; returned to New York State and settled in Batavia in 1856; acted as State commissioner in the erection of the institution for the blind in Batavia 1866-1868; president of a fire insurance company; elected as a Republican to the Forty-first Congress (March 4, 1869-March 3, 1871); unsuccessful candidate for reelection in 1870 to the Forty-second Congress; engaged in the fire insurance business; died in Batavia, N.Y., on March 28, 1882; interment in Batavia Cemetery.

**FISHER, Joseph Lyman,** a Representative from Virginia; born in Pawtucket, Providence County, R.I., January 11, 1914; attended public schools; B.S., Bowdoin College, Brunswick, Maine, 1935; Ph.D., economics, Harvard University, 1947; M.A., education, George Washington University, Washington, D.C., 1951; planning technician, National Resource Planning Board, 1939-1942; economist, United States Department of State, 1942-1943; teacher and lecturer at various universities; served in the United States Army, 1943-1946; senior economist, Council of Economic Advisers, 1947-1953; president, Resources for the Future, Inc., 1953-1974; elected as a Democrat to the Ninety-fourth, Ninety-fifth and Ninety-sixth Congresses (January 3, 1975-January 3, 1981); unsuccessful candidate for reelection in 1980 to the Ninety-seventh Congress; Virginia secretary of human resources, 1982-1986; professor of political economy, George Mason University; was a resident of Arlington, Va.; died February 19, 1992.

**FISHER, Ovie Clark,** a Representative from Texas; born near Junction, Kimble County, Tex., November 22, 1903; attended the public schools at Junction, Tex., the University of Colorado at Boulder, and the University of Texas at Austin; LL.B, J.D., Baylor University Law School, Waco, Tex., 1929; was admitted to the bar the same year and commenced practice in San Angelo Tex.; engaged in the ranching business; author; county attorney of Tom Green County, Tex., 1931-1935; member of the Texas State house of representatives 1935-1937; district attorney, fifty-first judicial district, 1937-1943; elected as a Democrat to the Seventy-eighth and to the fifteen succeeding Congresses and served from January 3, 1943, until his resignation December 31, 1974; chairman, Committee on Elections No. 3 (Seventy-ninth Congress); was not a candidate for reelection in 1974 to the Ninety-fourth Congress; was a resident of San Angelo, Tex.; died December 9, 1994.

**FISHER, Spencer Oliver,** a Representative from Michigan; born in Camden, Hillsdale County, Mich., February 3, 1843; attended the public schools and Albion and Hillsdale Colleges in Michigan; engaged in lumbering and banking in West Bay City, Mich.; mayor of West Bay City 1881-1884; delegate to the Democratic National Convention in 1884; elected as a Democrat to the Forty-ninth and Fiftieth Congresses (March 4, 1885-March 3, 1889); unsuccessful candidate for reelection in 1888 to the Fifty-first Congress; resumed his former business pursuits in Bay City, Mich., where he died June 1, 1919; interment in Elmlawn Cemetery.

**FISK, James,** a Representative and a Senator from Vermont; born in Greenwich, Hampshire County, Mass., October 4, 1763; self-educated; served in the Revolutionary War 1779-1782; member, Massachusetts general assembly 1785; entered the Universalist ministry and preached occasionally; moved to Barre, Vt., in 1798; studied law; was admitted to the bar and commenced practice in Barre; member, Vermont house of representatives 1800-1805, 1809-1810, 1815; judge of the Orange County Court 1802-1809, 1816; selected as the member from Orange County to locate the capital in 1803; chairman of the committee that endeavored to get a settlement of the northern boundary with Canada in 1804; elected as a Republican to the Ninth and Tenth Congresses (March 4, 1805-March 3, 1809); unsuccessful candidate for reelection in 1808 to the Eleventh Congress; elected as a Republican to the Twelfth and Thirteenth Congresses (March 4, 1811-March 3, 1815); chairman, Committee on Elections (Thirteenth Congress); unsuccessful candidate for reelection in 1814 to the Fourteenth Congress; appointed by President James Madison as United States judge for the Territory of Indiana in 1812, but declined; judge of the supreme court of Vermont 1815-1816; elected as a Republican to the United States Senate to fill the vacancy caused by the resignation of Dudley Chase and served from November 4, 1817, to January 8, 1818, when he resigned; collector of customs for the district of Vermont 1818-1826; moved to Swanton, Vt., in 1819, and died there November 17, 1844; interment in Church Street Cemetery.

**Bibliography:** *DAB.*

**FISK, Jonathan,** a Representative from New York; born in Amherst, N.H., September 26, 1778; attended the public schools; taught school; moved to Newburgh, N.Y., in 1800; studied law; was admitted to the bar in 1802 and commenced practice in Newburgh; elected as a Republican to the Eleventh Congress (March 4, 1809-March 3, 1811); elected to the Thirteenth and Fourteenth Congresses and served from March 4, 1813, until March 1815, when he resigned to accept the position of United States attorney for the southern district of New York, to which he was appointed by President James Madison and which position he held until June 30, 1819; resumed the practice of law; died in Newburgh, N.Y., July 13, 1832; interment in Old Town Cemetery.

**FITCH, Asa,** a Representative from New York; born in Groton, Conn., November 10, 1765; received a limited schooling; during the Revolutionary War served as a sergeant in Captain Livingston's company; studied medicine and practiced in Duanesburg and Salem, N.Y.; justice of the peace 1799-1810; president of the Washington County Medical Society 1806-1826; county judge 1810-1821; elected as a Federalist to the Twelfth Congress (March 4, 1811-March 3, 1813); declined to be a candidate for renomination in 1812; resumed the practice of medicine; died in Salem, N.Y., August 24, 1843; interment in Evergreen Cemetery.

**Bibliography:** *DAB.*

**FITCH, Ashbel Parmelee,** a Representative from New York; born in Moores, Clinton County, N.Y., October 8, 1848; attended the public schools of New York, Williston Seminary, East Hampton, Mass., the Universities of Jena and Berlin, Germany, and Columbia College Law School in New York City; was admitted to the bar in November 1869 and commenced practice in New York City; elected as a Republican to the Fiftieth Congress and as a Democrat to the Fifty-first, Fifty-second, and Fifty-third Congresses and served from March 4, 1887, until December 26, 1893, when he resigned; chairman, Committee on Private Land Claims (Fifty-second Congress), Committee on Election of President, Vice President, and Representatives (Fifty-third Congress); comptroller of New York City 1893-1897; president of the Trust Company of America in 1899; died in New York City on May 4, 1904; interment in Woodlawn Cemetery.

**FITCH, Graham Newell** (grandfather of Edwin Denby), a Representative and a Senator from Indiana; born in LeRoy, Genesee County, N.Y., December 5, 1809; attended Middlebury Academy and Geneva (N.Y.) College; studied medicine and completed his medical course at the College of Physicians and Surgeons; commenced practice in Logansport, Ind., in 1834; member of the Indiana State house of representatives in 1836 and 1839; professor of anatomy at the Rush Medical College, Chicago, Ill., 1844-1848, and at the Indianapolis (Ind.) Medical College in 1878; elected as a Democrat to the Thirty-first and Thirty-second Congresses (March 4, 1849-March 3, 1853); was not a candidate for renomination in 1852 to the Thirty-third Congress; resumed the practice of medicine; elected to the United States Senate to fill a vacancy in the term beginning March 4, 1855, and served from February 4, 1857, to March 3, 1861; was not a candidate for reelection in 1860; chairman, Committee on Printing (Thirty-fifth and Thirty-sixth Congresses); raised the Forty-sixth Regiment, Indiana Volunteer Infantry, during the Civil War and served as its colonel from 1861 until 1862, when he resigned because of injuries received in action; resumed the practice of medicine in Logansport, Ind.; died in Logansport, Ind., November 29, 1892; interment in Mount Hope Cemetery.

**FITCH, Thomas,** a Representative from Nevada; born in New York City, January 27, 1838; attended the public schools; moved to Chicago, Ill., in 1855, and to Milwaukee, Wis., in 1856; employed as a clerk; local editor of the Milwaukee Free Democrat, 1859-1860; moved to California in 1860; editor of the San Francisco Times and Placerville Republican; studied law; was admitted to the bar and practiced; member, California State assembly, 1862-1863; moved to Nevada in June 1863; elected a member of the convention which framed the State constitution in 1864; Union candidate for election for Territorial Delegate to Congress in 1864; district attorney of Washoe County in 1865 and 1866; elected as a Republican to the Forty-first Congress (March 4, 1869-March 3, 1871); unsuccessful candidate for reelection in 1870 to the Forty-second Congress; continued the practice of law; moved to Los Angeles, Calif., in 1909 and was employed as a writer on the Los Angeles Times; died in Decoto, Calif., November 12, 1923; interment in Cypress Cemetery.

**Bibliography:** Fitch, Thomas. *Western Carpetbagger: The Extraordinary Memoirs of "Senator" Thomas Fitch.* Edited by Eric N. Moody. Reno: University of Nevada Press, 1978.

**FITE, Samuel McClary,** a Representative from Tennessee; born near Alexandria, Smith County, Tenn., June 12, 1816; attended the common and private schools and was graduated from Clinton College, Tennessee; studied law in Lebanon; was admitted to the bar and commenced practice in Carthage, Tenn.; member of the State senate in 1850; presidential elector on the Whig ticket in 1852; judge of the sixth judicial district 1858-1861; resumed the practice of law in Carthage, Tenn.; appointed on July 24, 1869, judge of the sixth judicial district to fill a vacancy; elected to the same office on

January 8, 1870, and served until 1874; elected as a Democrat to the Forty-fourth Congress to fill the vacancy caused by the death of John W. Head and served from March 4, 1875, until his death, at Hot Springs, Ark., October 23, 1875, before the assembling of Congress; interment in Carthage Cemetery, Carthage, Tenn.; reinterment in Mount Olivet Cemetery, Nashville, Tenn., in 1908.

**FITHIAN, Floyd James,** a Representative from Indiana; born in Vesta, Johnson County, Nebr., November 3, 1928; attended public schools; B.A., Peru (Nebr.) State College, 1951; M.A., University of Nebraska, 1955, Ph.D., American history, 1964; high school teacher; associate professor of American history, Purdue University, West Lafayette, Ind.; engaged in agricultural pursuits; lieutenant, United States Navy, 1951-1955; commander, United States Navy Reserve, 1955-1971; unsuccessful candidate for election in 1972 to the Ninety-third Congress; elected as a Democrat to the Ninety-fourth and to the three succeeding Congresses (January 3, 1975-January 3, 1983); was not a candidate in 1982 for reelection to the House of Representatives, but was an unsuccessful candidate for election to the United States Senate; chief of staff for Senator Paul Simon of Illinois; secretary to the board, Farm Credit Administration, 1995 to present; is a resident of Annandale, Va.

**FITHIAN, George Washington,** a Representative from Illinois; born near Willow Hill, Jasper County, Ill., July 4, 1854; attended the common schools; learned the printer's trade in Mount Carmel, Ill.; studied law; was admitted to the bar in 1875 and commenced practice in Newton, Jasper County, Ill.; prosecuting attorney of Jasper County from 1876 until 1884; elected as a Democrat to the Fifty-first and to the two succeeding Congresses (March 4, 1889-March 3, 1895); chairman, Committee on Merchant Marine and Fisheries (Fifty-third Congress); unsuccessful candidate for reelection in 1894 to the Fifty-fourth Congress; railroad and warehouse commissioner of Illinois, 1895-1897; resumed the practice of law and engaged in agricultural pursuits and stock raising in Newton, Ill.; was also the owner of an extensive cotton plantation near Falcon, Miss.; died in Memphis, Tenn., January 21, 1921; interment in Riverside Cemetery, Newton, Ill.

**FITZGERALD, Frank Thomas,** a Representative from New York; born in New York City May 4, 1857; was graduated from the College of St. Francis Xavier, New York City, from St. Mary's College, Niagara Falls, N.Y., in 1876, and from the Columbia Law School, New York City, in 1878; was admitted to the bar the same year and commenced practice in New York City in 1879; elected as a Democrat to the Fifty-first Congress; served from March 4, 1889, until November 4, 1889, when he resigned, having been elected register of New York County and held that office until 1892; delegate to the State constitutional convention in 1893; elected surrogate of New York County in 1892 for a term of fourteen years; reelected in 1906 and served in this capacity until his death in New York City November 25, 1907; interment Calvary Cemetery, Long Island City, N.Y.

**FITZGERALD, John Francis** (grandfather of John Fitzgerald Kennedy, Edward Moore Kennedy, and Robert Francis Kennedy and great-grandfather of Joseph Patrick Kennedy II and Patrick Joseph Kennedy), a Representative from Massachusetts; born in Boston, Mass., February 11, 1863; was graduated from the Eliot Grammar School and from the Boston Latin School; attended Harvard Medical School for one year; held a position in the Boston customhouse from 1886 to 1891; member of the Boston Common Council in 1892; member of the Massachusetts senate in 1893 and 1894; elected as a Democrat to the Fifty-fourth, Fifty-fifth, and Fifty-sixth Congresses (March 4, 1895-March 3, 1901); was not a candidate for renomination in 1900 to the Fifty-seventh Congress; mayor of Boston in 1906, 1907, and 1910-1914; engaged in the insurance and investment business; also owner of a weekly newspaper; chairman of the Massachusetts delegation to the Democratic National Convention of

1912; unsuccessful candidate in 1916 for election to the United States Senate; presented credentials as a Democratic Member-elect to the Sixty-sixth Congress and served from March 4, 1919, until October 23, 1919, when he was succeeded by Peter F. Tague, who contested his election; resumed his newspaper activities and also engaged as an investment banker; unsuccessful candidate for Governor in 1922; member of the Port of Boston Authority 1934-1948; died in Boston, Mass., October 2, 1950; interment in St. Joseph's Cemetery, West Roxbury, Boston, Mass.

**Bibliography:** *DAB*; Fraser, James W. "Mayor John F. Fitzgerald and Boston's Schools, 1905-1913." *Historical Journal of Massachusetts* 12 (June 1984): 117-30; Goodwin, Doris Kearns. *The Fitzgeralds and the Kennedys.* New York: Simon and Schuster, 1987.

**FITZGERALD, John Joseph,** a Representative from New York; born in Brooklyn, N.Y., March 10, 1872; attended the public schools, La Salle Military Academy (formerly Sacred Heart Academy), and was graduated from Manhattan College, New York City, in 1891; studied law in the New York Law School; was admitted to the bar in 1893 and commenced practice in New York City; delegate to the Democratic National Conventions from 1900 to 1928; trustee of Manhattan College in New York City; elected as a Democrat to the Fifty-sixth and to the nine succeeding Congresses and served from March 4, 1899, until December 31, 1917, when he resigned to resume the practice of law; chairman, Committee on Appropriations (Sixty-second through Sixty-fifth Congresses); appointed county judge of Kings County in March 1932, elected in November 1932, and served until his retirement on December 31, 1942; resumed the private practice of law; died in Brooklyn, N.Y., May 13, 1952; interment in St. John's Cemetery, Middle Village, N.Y.

**FITZGERALD, Roy Gerald,** a Representative from Ohio; born in Watertown, Jefferson County, N.Y., August 25, 1875; moved to Ohio in 1890 with his parents, who settled in Dayton; attended the public schools; studied law; was admitted to the bar in 1896 and commenced practice in Dayton, Ohio; during the First World War served as captain in the Three Hundred and Twenty-ninth Infantry, Headquarters Company, American Expeditionary Forces, 1917-1919; commissioned lieutenant colonel of Infantry, United States Army Reserve Corps, in 1928; delegate to conferences of the Interparliamentary Union at Paris, Berlin, Geneva, and London; elected as a Republican to the Sixty-seventh and to the four succeeding Congresses (March 4, 1921-March 3, 1931); chairman, Committee on Expenditures in the Department of Commerce (Sixty-eighth Congress), Committee on Revision of the Laws (Seventieth and Seventy-first Congresses); unsuccessful candidate for reelection in 1930 to the Seventy-second Congress; resumed the practice of law; was a resident of Dayton, Ohio, until his death there on November 16, 1962; interment in Woodland Cemetery.

**FITZGERALD, Thomas,** a Senator from Michigan; born in Germantown, Herkimer County, N.Y., April 10, 1796; pursued an academic course; served and was severely wounded in the War of 1812 in the Fifth Regiment, New York Militia; taught school in Marcellus, N.Y.; in 1819 moved to Boonville, Warrick County, Ind., where he taught school; studied law; was admitted to the bar in 1821 and commenced practice in Boonville; member, State house of representatives 1821; appointed keeper of the lighthouse at the mouth of the St. Joseph River 1832; moved to St. Joseph, Mich.; clerk of Berrien County 1834; regent of the University of Michigan in 1837; appointed bank commissioner in 1838; elected to the State house of representatives in 1839; unsuccessful candidate for lieutenant governor in 1839; appointed as a Democrat to the United States Senate to fill the vacancy caused by the resignation of Lewis Cass and served from June 8, 1848, until March 3, 1849; moved to Niles, Mich., in 1851; probate judge of Berrien County 1852-1855;

died in Niles, Mich., March 25, 1855; interment in Silverbrook Cemetery.

**Bibliography:** *DAB.*

**FITZGERALD, William,** a Representative from Tennessee; born at Port Tobacco, Charles County, Md., August 6, 1799; educated in England; studied law; was admitted to the bar at Dover, Stewart County, Tenn., in 1821; clerk of the circuit court of Stewart County 1822-1825; member of the Tennessee Legislature in 1825-1827; served as attorney general of the sixteenth judicial circuit of Tennessee in 1826; elected as a Jacksonian to the Twenty-second Congress (March 4, 1831-March 3, 1833); unsuccessful candidate for reelection in 1832 to the Twenty-third Congress; moved to Paris, Tenn.; served as judge of the ninth judicial circuit of Tennessee 1845-1861; died at Paris, Tenn., in March 1864; interment in Fitzgerald Cemetery, near Paris, Tenn.

**FITZGERALD, William Joseph,** a Representative from Connecticut; born in Norwich, New London County, Conn., March 2, 1887; attended St. Patrick's Parochial School in Norwich, Conn.; employed in a foundry as a molder and later served as superintendent 1904-1930; served on the State commission to investigate widows' aid in 1916; member of the State senate 1931-1935; deputy State commissioner of labor 1931-1936; elected as a Democrat to the Seventy-fifth Congress (January 3, 1937-January 3, 1939); unsuccessful candidate for reelection in 1938 to the Seventy-sixth Congress; mayor of Norwich, Conn., in 1940 and 1941; elected to the Seventy-seventh Congress (January 3, 1941-January 3, 1943); unsuccessful candidate for reelection in 1942 to the Seventy-eighth Congress; appointed on March 1, 1943, as area director and later as State director of the War Manpower Commission of Connecticut and served until October 1, 1945; appointed State director of the United States Employment Service and served until his resignation in January 1947; died at Norwich, Conn., May 6, 1947; interment in St. Joseph's Cemetery.

**FITZGERALD, William Thomas,** a Representative from Ohio; born in Greenville, Darke County, Ohio, October 13, 1858; attended the rural schools and the Greenville High School; member of the National Guard of Ohio 1875-1882, and saw service during the Newark riots in 1877; was graduated from the National Normal University, Lebanon, Ohio, in 1887; taught in the Greenville High School 1886-1889; was graduated from the medical department of the University of Wooster, Cleveland, Ohio, in 1891 and commenced practice in Greenville in 1891; member of the board of education 1906-1914; mayor of Greenville 1921-1925; elected as a Republican to the Sixty-ninth and Seventieth Congresses (March 4, 1925-March 3, 1929); chairman, Committee on Revision of the Laws (Sixty-ninth Congress), Committee on Invalid Pensions (Seventieth Congress); was not a candidate for renomination in 1928 to the Seventy-first Congress; resumed the practice of medicine in Greenville, Ohio, where he died on January 12, 1939; interment in Greenville Cemetery.

**FITZGIBBONS, John,** a Representative from New York; born in Glenmore, Oneida County, N.Y., July 10, 1868; moved to Oswego, Oswego County, N.Y., in 1870; attended the public schools; employed as a railway trainman in 1885; served as legislative representative of the Brotherhood of Railroad Trainmen of New York State 1896-1914 and again from February 1915 until January 1, 1933; served as referee for the New York State Labor Bureau in 1914 and 1915; alderman of Oswego in 1908 and 1909; mayor of Oswego in 1910, 1911, and 1918-1921; delegate to the Democratic National Conventions in 1920, 1924, and 1932; elected as a Democrat to the Seventy-third Congress (March 4, 1933-January 3, 1935); was not a candidate for renomination in 1934 to the Seventy-fourth Congress; engaged as legislative representative for the Railroad Brotherhoods in Albany, N.Y., until his death in Buffalo, N.Y., on August 4, 1941; interment in St. Peter's Cemetery, Oswego, N.Y.

**FITZHENRY, Louis,** a Representative from Illinois; born in Bloomington, McLean County, Ill., June 13, 1870; attended the public and high schools of Bloomington; engaged in journalism; was graduated from the law department of Illinois Wesleyan University at Bloomington in 1897; was admitted to the bar in 1897 and commenced practice in Bloomington, Ill.; city attorney of Bloomington 1907-1911; unsuccessful candidate for election in 1910 to the Sixty-second Congress; elected as a Democrat to the Sixty-third Congress (March 4, 1913-March 3, 1915); unsuccessful candidate for reelection in 1914 to the Sixty-fourth Congress; resumed the practice of law in Bloomington; unsuccessful candidate for election as a justice of the State supreme court in 1915; appointed United States district judge for the southern district of Illinois July 1, 1918, serving until October 3, 1933, when he was appointed a judge of the United States Circuit Court of Appeals for the Seventh District, in which capacity he served until his death in Normal, Ill., November 18, 1935; interment in Bloomington Cemetery, Bloomington, Ill.

**FITZHUGH, William,** a Delegate from Virginia; born in Eagles Nest, King George County, Va., August 24, 1741; pursued classical studies with private teachers; engaged in agricultural pursuits; member of the Virginia house of delegates in 1776 and 1777; Member of the Continental Congress in 1779; again a member of the Virginia house of delegates in 1780, 1781, 1787, and 1788; served in the State senate 1781-1785; died in Ravensworth, Fairfax County, Va., June 6, 1809; interment in the private cemetery on the Ravensworth estate.

**FITZPATRICK, Benjamin,** a Senator from Alabama; born in Greene County, Ga., June 30, 1802; left an orphan, he was taken by his brother to Alabama in 1815; attended the public schools; studied law; was admitted to the bar in 1821 and commenced practice in Montgomery, Ala.; solicitor of the Montgomery circuit, 1822-1823; moved to his plantation in Autauga County in 1829 and engaged in planting; elected Governor of Alabama in 1841, reelected in 1843, and served from November 22, 1841 to December 10, 1845; appointed as a Democrat to the United States Senate to fill the vacancy caused by the death of Dixon H. Lewis and served from November 25, 1848, to November 30, 1849, when a successor was elected; again appointed and subsequently elected as a Democrat to the United States Senate to fill the vacancy caused by the resignation of William R. King, and served from January 14, 1853 to March 3, 1855; chairman, Committee on Printing (Thirty-third Congress), Committee on Engrossed Bills (Thirty-third Congress); elected to the United States Senate as a Democrat to fill the vacancy in the term commencing March 4, 1855, caused by the failure of the legislature to elect, and served from November 26, 1855 until January 21, 1861, when he withdrew with other secessionist Senators; served as President pro tempore of the Senate during the Thirty-fifth and Thirty-sixth Congresses; nominated for Vice President of the United States on the Democratic ticket with Stephen A. Douglas in 1860, but declined; president of the constitutional convention of Alabama in 1865; died on his plantation near Wetumpka, Ala., November 21, 1869; interment in Oakwood Cemetery, Montgomery, Ala.

**Bibliography:** *DAB.*

**FITZPATRICK, James Martin,** a Representative from New York; born in West Stockbridge, Berkshire County, Mass., June 27, 1869; attended the public schools; worked in the iron-ore mines in West Stockbridge, Mass.; moved to New York City in 1891 and worked in the various departments of the Metropolitan Street Railway Company and the Interborough Rapid Transit Company until 1925, when he became engaged in the real estate business; served as a commissioner of street openings in New York City in 1919; member of the broad of aldermen of New York City 1919-1927; elected as a Democrat to the Seventieth and to the eight succeeding Congresses (March 4, 1927-January 3, 1945); was not a candidate for renomination in 1944; died in New York City April 10, 1949; interment in St. Raymond's Cemetery.

**FITZPATRICK, Morgan Cassius,** a Representative from Tennessee; born near Carthage, Smith County, Tenn., October 29, 1868; attended the common schools and Lebanon (Ohio) University in 1887; was graduated from the law department of Cumberland University, Lebanon, Tenn., in 1891; was admitted to the bar the same year and commenced practice in Hartsville, Tenn.; edited a newspaper at Hartsville; member of the State house of representatives 1895-1899, serving as speaker in 1897; State superintendent of public instruction 1899-1903; chairman of the Democratic State executive committee; elected as a Democrat to the Fifty-eighth Congress (March 4, 1903-March 3, 1905); was not a candidate for renomination in 1904; resumed the practice of law; died in Nashville, Tenn., June 25, 1908; interment in Gallatin Cemetery, Gallatin, Tenn.

Bibliography: *DAB*.

**FITZPATRICK, Thomas Young,** a Representative from Kentucky; born near Prestonsburg, Floyd County, Ky., September 20, 1850; attended the common schools; studied law; was admitted to the bar in 1877 and practiced; county judge in 1874 and 1875; member of the Kentucky house of representatives in 1876 and 1877; county attorney 1880-1884; elected as a Democrat to the Fifty-fifth and Fifty-sixth Congresses (March 4, 1897-March 3, 1901); died in Frankfort, Ky., January 21, 1906; interment in Frankfort Cemetery.

**FITZSIMONS, Thomas,** a Delegate and a Representative from Pennsylvania; born in Ireland in 1741; immigrated to the United States and entered a counting-house in Philadelphia, Pa., as clerk; commanded a company of volunteer home guards during the Revolutionary War; Member of the Continental Congress in 1782 and 1783; member of the Pennsylvania house of representatives in 1786 and 1787; delegate to the United States Constitutional Convention in 1787; elected to the First, Second, and Third Congresses (March 4, 1789-March 3, 1795); unsuccessful candidate for reelection in 1794 to the Fourth Congress; president of the Philadelphia Chamber of Commerce; trustee of the University of Pennsylvania; founder and director of the Bank of North America; died in Philadelphia, Pa., on August 26, 1811; interment in St. Mary's Roman Catholic Churchyard.

Bibliography: *DAB*.

**FJARE, Orvin Benonie,** a Representative from Montana; born on a ranch near Big Timber, Sweet Grass County, Mont., April 16, 1918; attended public schools; employed as a clerk in a clothing store at Big Timber, Mont., and later became part owner; enlisted as a private in the United States Army in 1940; commissioned a second lieutenant of Artillery in 1942; served as a pilot in the South Pacific and was discharged as a captain in 1946; member of the Montana Public Welfare Commission, 1952-1954; member of board of trustees, Big Timber Public Schools, 1951-1954; elected as a Republican to the Eighty-fourth Congress (January 3, 1955-January 3, 1957); unsuccessful candidate for reelection in 1956 to the Eighty-fifth Congress; member, Montana State house of representatives, 1959; engaged in the life insurance business; unsuccessful candidate for election to the United States Senate in 1960; advertising director, Montana State Highway Department, 1962-1969; director of the Montana Federal Housing Administration, 1970-1979; is a resident of Big Timber, Mont.

**FLACK, William Henry,** a Representative from New York; born in Franklin Falls, Franklin County, N.Y., March 22, 1861; attended the public schools; became interested in lumbering and tanning; supervisor of the town of Waverly for seven years and chairman of the board for two years; county clerk of Franklin County in 1897, and reelected in 1900; chairman of the Republican county committee 1898-1902; served as trustee of the village of Malone and elected president of said village in 1902; elected as a Republican to the Fifty-eighth and Fifty-ninth Congresses and served from March 4, 1903, until his death in Malone, N.Y., February 2, 1907; interment in Morningside Cemetery.

**FLAGLER, Thomas Thorn,** a Representative from New York; born in Pleasant Valley, Dutchess County, N.Y., October 12, 1811; attended the common schools; learned the printer's trade and became one of the owners and publishers of the Chenango Republican, Oxford, N.Y.; moved to Lockport in 1836 and published the Niagara Courier until 1842, when he engaged in the hardware business; member of the State assembly in 1842 and 1843; treasurer of Niagara County 1849-1852; elected as a Whig to the Thirty-third and Thirty-fourth Congresses (March 4, 1853-March 3, 1857); was not a candidate for renomination in 1856; resumed former business pursuits; again a member of the State assembly in 1860; member of the State constitutional convention in 1867 and 1868; organized and became president of the Holly Manufacturing Co. in 1859, and for many years was the head of eight such organizations; died in Lockport, N.Y., on September 6, 1897; interment in Glenwood Cemetery.

**FLAHERTY, Lawrence James,** a Representative from California; born in San Mateo, San Mateo County, Calif., July 4, 1878; moved with his parents to San Francisco in 1888; attended the public schools; learned the trade of cement mason; member of the board of police commissioners of San Francisco 1911-1915; served in the State senate 1915-1922; president of the San Francisco Building Trades 1921-1926; appointed United States surveyor of customs for the port of San Francisco on November 1, 1921, and served until March 3, 1925, when he resigned, having been elected to Congress; elected as a Republican to the Sixty-ninth Congress and served from March 4, 1925, until his death in New York City, June 13, 1926; interment in Holy Cross Cemetery, near San Mateo, Calif.

**FLAHERTY, Thomas Aloysius,** a Representative from Massachusetts; born in Boston, Mass., December 21, 1898; attended the public schools and Northeastern University Law School, Boston, Mass.; served as a private in the United States Army in 1918; employed with the United States Veterans' Administration at Boston, Mass., 1920-1934; member of the Massachusetts house of representatives 1935-1937; elected as a Democrat to the Seventy-fifth Congress to fill the vacancy caused by the resignation of John P. Higgins; reelected to the Seventy-sixth and Seventy-seventh Congresses and served from December 14, 1937, to January 3, 1943; was not a candidate for renomination in 1942; served as transit commissioner of the city of Boston 1943-1945; chairman of the Department of Public Utilities of Massachusetts 1946-1953, serving as commissioner 1953-1955; chairman, Board of Review, Assessing Department, city of Boston, 1956-1960; real estate broker and appraiser; was a resident of Charlestown, Mass., where he died April 27, 1965; interment in Holy Cross Cemetery, Malden, Mass.

**FLAKE, Floyd Harold,** a Representative from New York; born in Los Angeles, Calif., January 30, 1945; attended public schools in Houston, Tex.; graduated G.W. Carver High School, Houston, 1962; B.A., Wilberforce University, Wilberforce, Ohio, 1967; B.A., Payne Theological Seminary (Ohio), 1970; attended Northeastern University, Boston, Mass., 1974-1976, and St. John's University, Jamaica, N.Y., 1980-1984; D.Min., United Theological Seminary, 1995; dean of students, University Chapter and Director, Afro-American Center, Boston (Mass.) University, 1973-1976; chairman and chief executive officer, Allen Christian Schools; pastor of Allen A.M.E. Church, Jamaica, N.Y., 1976-1986; unsuccessful candidate in 1986 for election to the Ninety-ninth Congress to fill the vacancy caused by the death of Joseph P. Addabbo; elected as a Democrat to the One Hundredth and to the four succeeding Congresses (January 3, 1987-January 3, 1997); is a resident of Rosedale, N.Y.

**FLANAGAN, De Witt Clinton,** a Representative from New Jersey; born in New York City December 28, 1870; attended the Callison and Woodbridge private schools and Columbia College, New York City; pursued a commercial career, being interested in a number of industrial enterprises; elected as a Democrat to the Fifty-seventh Congress to fill the vacancy caused by the death of Joshua S. Salmon and served from June 18, 1902, to March 3, 1903; delegate to the Democratic National Convention of 1904; organized the Boston, Cape Cod & New York Canal Co., which built and operated the Cape Cod Canal; engaged in the agricultural and civic development of Baldwin County, Ala.; died in Utica, N.Y., January 15, 1946; interment in the family mausoleum, Woodlawn Cemetery, New York City.

**FLANAGAN, James Winright,** a Senator from Texas; born in Gordonsville, Orange County, Va., September 5, 1805; attended the common schools and received private instruction; moved to Cloverport, Ky., in 1816, and engaged in mercantile pursuits; justice of the peace from 1823 to 1833; studied law; was admitted to the bar in 1825 and practiced in the Breckenridge County circuit, 1833-1843; moved to Henderson, Rusk County, Tex., in 1843 and continued the practice of law; also engaged in mercantile and agricultural pursuits; member, Texas State house of representatives, 1851-1852; Texas State senator, 1855-1856; member of the State constitutional conventions in 1866 and 1868; elected lieutenant governor of Texas in 1869 and served until his resignation in 1870 to become Senator; upon the readmission of Texas to representation was elected as a Republican to the United States Senate, and served from March 30, 1870 to March 3, 1875; chairman, Committee on Education and Labor (Forty-third Congress); died in Longview, Gregg County, Tex., September 28, 1887; interment in the family burying ground in East Henderson, Tex.

**FLANAGAN, Michael Patrick,** a Representative from Illinois; born in Chicago, Ill., November 9, 1962; graduated, Lane Technical High School, Chicago; B.A., Loyola University; J.D., Loyola University School of Law, 1988; United States Army service, four years, as Combat Arms Officer; practicing attorney, Chicago; elected as a Republican to the One Hundred Fourth Congress (January 3, 1995-January 3, 1997); is a resident of Chicago, Ill.

**FLANDERS, Alvan,** a Delegate from the Territory of Washington; born in Hopkinton, Merrimack County, N.H., August 2, 1825; attended the public schools; learned the machinist trade in Boston; moved to Humboldt County, Calif., in 1851, and there engaged in the lumber business until 1858, when he moved to San Francisco; one of the founders and proprietors of the San Francisco Daily Times; member of the California State house of representatives in 1861; officer of the United States branch mint in 1861; moved to the Territory of Washington in 1863 and engaged in mercantile pursuits in Wallula; first postmaster of Wallula, 1865-1867; elected as a Republican to the Fortieth Congress (March 4, 1867-March 3, 1869); was not a candidate for renomination in 1868 to the Forty-first Congress; appointed by President Ulysses S. Grant as Governor of the Territory of Washington on April 5, 1869, and served until his removal on March 14, 1870; moved to San Francisco, Calif., and died there on March 14, 1884; interment in Laurel Hill Cemetery.

**FLANDERS, Benjamin Franklin,** a Representative from Louisiana; born in Bristol, Grafton County, N.H., January 26, 1816; attended New Hampton (N.H.) Academy, and was graduated from Dartmouth College, Hanover, N.H., in 1842; moved to New Orleans in 1843; studied law, but never practiced; edited the New Orleans Tropic in 1845; elected alderman of New Orleans in 1847; superintendent of public schools in 1850; reelected alderman in 1852; assisted in organizing the New Orleans, Opelousas & Great Western Railroad Co.; secretary and treasurer of the company 1852-1861; appointed city treasurer by General Butler on July 20, 1862, and served until December 10 of the same year; elected as a

Unionist to the Thirty-seventh Congress and served from December 3, 1862, to March 3, 1863; was not a candidate for renomination in 1862 to the Thirty-eighth Congress; mustered into the Federal military service July 13, 1863, at New Orleans as captain of Company C, Fifth Regiment of Louisiana Volunteer Infantry, and served until August 12, 1863; appointed in 1863 special agent of the Treasury Department for the southern district, comprising the States of Louisiana, Texas, Mississippi, Alabama, and western Florida; unsuccessful candidate for election for Governor of Louisiana in 1864; first president of the First National Bank of New Orleans in 1864; reappointed special Treasury agent in 1866; served as Governor of Louisiana, under military authority, from June 3, 1867 to January 8, 1868; mayor of New Orleans 1870-1872; Assistant Treasurer of the United States at New Orleans 1873-1882; unsuccessful Republican candidate for State treasurer in 1888; died on his estate, "Ben Alva," near Youngsville, Lafayette Parish, La., March 13, 1896; interment in Metairie Cemetery, New Orleans, La.

**FLANDERS, Ralph Edward,** a Senator from Vermont; born in Barnet, Caledonia County, Vt., September 28, 1880; moved with his parents to Pawtucket, R.I., in 1886; attended the public schools at Pawtucket, Lincoln, and Central Falls, R.I.; engaged as a machinist apprentice at Providence, R.I., in 1897 and remained in the machine tool industry until his death; moved to Springfield, Vt., in 1910; president of the Federal Reserve Board of Boston, 1944-1946; appointed as a Republican to the United States Senate to fill the vacancy in the term ending January 3, 1947, caused by the resignation of Warren R. Austin; elected in 1946 and again in 1952 and served from November 1, 1946, to January 3, 1959; was not a candidate for renomination in 1958; inventor of important developments in the machine tool industry; author of several books and articles on technical and sociological subjects; died in Springfield, Vt., February 19, 1970; cremated in Springfield, Mass., February 23, 1970; ashes deposited in Summer Hill Cemetery, Springfield, Vt.

**Bibliography:** Flanders, Ralph E. *Senator From Vermont.* Boston: Little, Brown, 1961; Griffith, Robert. "Ralph Flanders and the Censure of Senator Joseph McCarthy." *Vermont History* 39 (Winter 1971): 5-20.

**FLANNAGAN, John William, Jr.,** a Representative from Virginia; born on a farm near Trevilians, Louisa County, Va., February 20, 1885; attended the public schools and was graduated from the law department of Washington and Lee University, Lexington, Va., in 1907; was admitted to the bar the same year and commenced practice in Appalachia, Wise County, Va.; served as Commonwealth's attorney for Buchanan County, Va., in 1916 and 1917; moved to Clintwood, Va., in 1917, and to Bristol, Va., in 1925, and continued the practice of law; also engaged in banking 1917-1930; congressional adviser to the first session of the Food and Agriculture Organization of the United Nations at Quebec in 1945; elected as a Democrat to the Seventy-second and to the eight succeeding Congresses (March 4, 1931-January 3, 1949); chairman, Committee on Agriculture (Seventy-eighth and Seventy-ninth Congresses); was not a candidate for renomination in 1948; resumed the practice of law in Bristol, Va., until his death there April 27, 1955; interment in Mountain View Cemetery.

**FLANNERY, John Harold,** a Representative from Pennsylvania; born in Pittston, Luzerne County, Pa., April 19, 1898; attended the public schools; was graduated from Wyoming Seminary, Kingston, Pa., in 1917 and from Dickinson School of Law, Carlisle, Pa., in 1920; during the First World War served as a private in the United States Army and was honorably discharged on December 14, 1918; was admitted to the bar in 1921 and commenced practice in Pittston, Pa.; solicitor for Pittston City, Pa., 1926-1930; served as assistant district attorney of Luzerne County, Pa., 1932-1936; elected as a Democrat to the Seventy-fifth, Seventy-sixth, and Seventy-seventh Congresses and served from January 3, 1937, until his resignation on January 3, 1942, to become judge of the common pleas court of Luzerne County, Pa.; reelected in 1951 for a ten-year term and served until his death; delegate to the Democratic National Conventions of 1944 and 1960; died in Bethesda, Md., June 3, 1961; interment in Mount Olivet Catholic Cemetery, Pittston, Pa.

**FLEEGER, George Washington,** a Representative from Pennsylvania; born in Concord Township, Butler County, Pa., March 13, 1839; attended the common schools and West Sunbury Academy; enlisted in the Union Army on June 10, 1861, as a private in Company C, Eleventh Regiment, Pennsylvania Reserves, and was commissioned a first lieutenant in June 1862; brevetted captain, and served until March 13, 1865; studied law; was admitted to the bar in 1866 and commenced practice in Butler; member of the Pennsylvania house of representatives in 1871 and 1872; chairman of the Pennsylvania Republican central committee; delegate to the Republican Pennsylvania conventions in 1882 and 1890; elected as a Republican to the Forty-ninth Congress (March 4, 1885-March 3, 1887); resumed the practice of law in Butler, Pa., and died there June 25, 1894; interment in the North Cemetery.

**FLEETWOOD, Frederick Gleed,** a Representative from Vermont; born in St. Johnsbury, Caledonia County, Vt., September 27, 1868; attended the common schools of St. Johnsbury, and was graduated from St. Johnsbury Academy in 1886; also attended the University of Vermont at Burlington and was graduated from Harvard University in 1891; secretary of the commission on revision of Vermont statutes in 1893 and 1894; studied law; was admitted to the bar and commenced practice in Morrisville, Vt., in 1894; prosecuting attorney for Lamoille County 1896-1898; town clerk and treasurer of Morrisville, Vt., 1896-1900; member of the State house of representatives 1900-1902; secretary of state and insurance commissioner of Vermont 1902-1908; again secretary of state 1917-1919; elected as a Republican to the Sixty-eighth Congress (March 4, 1923-March 3, 1925); was not a candidate for renomination in 1924; resumed the practice of law; also engaged in banking; died in Morrisville, Vt., January 28, 1938; interment in Pleasant View Cemetery.

**FLEGER, Anthony Alfred,** a Representative from Ohio; born in Austria-Hungary October 21, 1900; in 1903 immigrated to the United States with his parents, who settled in Cleveland, Cuyahoga County, Ohio; attended the public schools and was graduated from John Marshall School of Law, Cleveland, Ohio, in 1926; was admitted to the bar the same year and commenced practice in Cleveland, Ohio; moved to Parma, Cuyahoga County, Ohio, and continued the practice of law; served as justice of the peace in Parma, Ohio, 1930-1932; elected a member of the State house of representatives in 1932 and served from January 1, 1933, to December 31, 1933, when he resigned, having been elected mayor of Parma; served as mayor from January 1, 1934, to December 31, 1935; elected as a Democrat to the Seventy-fifth Congress (January 3, 1937-January 3, 1939); unsuccessful candidate for reelection in 1938 to the Seventy-sixth Congress and for election in 1940 to the Seventy-seventh Congress; resumed the practice of law in Cleveland, Ohio; served as special assistant to the Attorney General, Washington, D.C., from March 3, 1941, to July 9, 1950, and as an attorney in the Department of Justice from July 10, 1950, to May 9, 1953; engaged in the practice of law in Washington, D.C., and resided in Oxon Hill, Md.; died in Alexandria, Va., July 16, 1963; interment in Holy Cross Cemetery, Brook Park, Ohio.

**FLEMING, William,** a Delegate from Virginia; born in Cumberland County, Va., July 6, 1736; was graduated from the College of William and Mary, Williamsburg, Va., in 1763; studied law; was admitted to the bar and practiced; member of the provincial house of burgesses 1772-1775; delegate to the Revolutionary conventions in 1775 and 1776; member of the Cumberland County committee in 1776; served in the Virginia house of delegates

1776-1778; Member of the Continental Congress in 1779; judge of the general court in 1788; elected a member of the first supreme court of appeals in 1789 and served in this capacity until his death; became president of the court in 1809; died at his country home, "Summerville," Chesterfield County, Va., February 15, 1824; interment in the family cemetery on his estate.

Bibliography: *DAB.*

**FLEMING, William Bennett,** a Representative from Georgia; born on a plantation near Flemington, Liberty County, Ga., October 29, 1803; attended the common schools and was graduated from Yale College in 1825; studied law; was admitted to the bar and practiced in Savannah, Ga.; judge of the superior court of Chatham County, Ga., 1847-1849 and 1853-1868; resumed the practice of law in Savannah; recorder of the city of Savannah from 1868 until the office was abolished; elected as a Democrat to the Forty-fifth Congress to fill the vacancy caused by the death of Julian Hartridge and served from February 10, 1879, to March 3, 1879; was not a candidate for renomination; again judge of the superior court from 1879 until 1881, when he resigned on account of ill health; retired to Walthourville, Liberty County, Ga., and died there August 19, 1886; interment in Laurel Grove Cemetery, Savannah, Ga.

**FLEMING, William Henry,** a Representative from Georgia; born in Augusta, Richmond County, Ga., October 18, 1856; attended Summerville Academy and Academy of Richmond County; was graduated from the University of Georgia at Athens in 1874; superintendent of the public schools of Augusta and Richmond County, Ga., from 1877 to 1880, when he resigned; studied law; was admitted to the bar in 1880 and commenced practice in Augusta, Ga.; member of the State house of representatives 1888-1896, and served as speaker of the house in 1894 and 1895; president of the State bar association in 1894 and 1895; elected as a Democrat to the Fifty-fifth, Fifty-sixth, and Fifty-seventh Congresses (March 4, 1897-March 3, 1903); unsuccessful candidate for renomination in 1902; resumed the practice of law and engaged in literary pursuits; died in Augusta, Ga., June 9, 1944; interment in Summerville Cemetery.

**FLETCHER, Charles Kimball,** a Representative from California; born in San Diego, Calif., December 15, 1902; attended the public schools; was graduated from Stanford University of California in 1924; also attended Pembroke College, Oxford University, England, in 1934; engaged in the savings and loan business; served as a lieutenant with the United States Naval Reserve from 1943 to 1945; elected as a Republican to the Eightieth Congress (January 3, 1947-January 3, 1949); unsuccessful candidate for reelection in 1948 to the Eighty-first Congress; president and manager of the Home Federal Savings & Loan Association from 1934 until 1959 when he became chairman of the board of directors; member of California Commission on Correctional Facilities and Services, 1955-1957; was a resident of San Diego, Calif., until his death there September 29, 1985; cremated and the ashes scattered off the coast of Del Mar, Calif.

**FLETCHER, Duncan Upshaw,** a Senator from Florida; born near Americus, Sumter County, Ga., January 6, 1859; moved with his parents to Monroe County in 1860; attended the common schools and Gordon Institute, Barnesville, Ga.; graduated from Vanderbilt University, Nashville, Tenn., in 1880; studied law at the same institution; admitted to the bar in 1881 and commenced practice in Jacksonville, Fla.; member, city council 1887; member, State house of representatives 1893; mayor of Jacksonville 1893-1895, 1901-1903; chairman of the board of public instruction of Duval County 1900-1907; president of the Gulf Coast Inland Waterways Association in 1908, and, later, of the Mississippi to Atlantic Waterway Association; appointed and subsequently elected as a Democrat to the United States Senate for the term commencing March 4, 1909; reelected in 1914, 1920, 1926, and 1932 and served from March 4,

1909, until his death on June 17, 1936; chairman, Committee on Printing (Sixty-third and Sixty-fourth Congresses), Committee on Commerce (Sixty-fourth and Sixty-fifth Congresses), Committee on Transportation Routes to the Seaboard (Sixty-sixth Congress), Committee on Banking and Currency (Seventy-third and Seventy-fourth Congresses); president of the Southern Commercial Congress 1912-1918; appointed by President Woodrow Wilson in 1913 as chairman of the United States commission to investigate European land-mortgage banks, cooperative rural credit unions, and the betterment of rural conditions in Europe; delegate to the International High Commission at Buenos Aires, Argentina, in 1916; died in Washington, D.C.; interment in Evergreen Cemetery, Jacksonville, Fla.

**Bibliography:** *DAB*; Flynt, Wayne. *Duncan Upshaw Fletcher, Dixie's Reluctant Progressive*. Tallahassee: Florida State University Press, 1971.

**FLETCHER, Isaac,** a Representative from Vermont; born in Dunstable, Middlesex County, Mass., November 22, 1784; pursued classical studies, and was graduated from Dartmouth College, Hanover, N.H., in 1808; taught in the academy at Chesterfield, N.H.; studied law; was admitted to the bar in December 1811 and commenced practice at Lyndon, Vt., in 1812; member of the State house of representatives 1819-1824, and served one term as speaker; prosecuting attorney of Caledonia County, Vt., 1820-1829; member of the State constitutional convention in 1822; was graduated from the University of Vermont at Burlington in 1825; elected as a Democrat to the Twenty-fifth and Twenty-sixth Congresses (March 4, 1837-March 3, 1841); chairman, Committee on Patents (Twenty-fifth and Twenty-sixth Congresses); unsuccessful candidate for reelection in 1840 to the Twenty-seventh Congress; adjutant general on the staff of Governor Cornelius P. Van Ness; died in Lyndon, Vt., October 19, 1842; interment in Lyndon Town Cemetery.

**FLETCHER, Loren,** a Representative from Minnesota; born in Mount Vernon, Kennebec County, Maine, April 10, 1833; attended the public schools and Maine Wesleyan Seminary, Kents Hill, Maine; moved to Bangor in 1853; was a stonecutter, clerk in a store, and an employee of a lumber company; moved to Minneapolis, Minn., in 1856 and engaged in manufacturing and mercantile pursuits, largely in the manufacture of lumber and flour; member of the board of directors of the First National Bank upon its establishment in 1864; member of the State house of representatives 1872-1886 and served as speaker from 1880 to 1886; elected as a Republican to the Fifty-third and to the four succeeding Congresses (March 4, 1893-March 3, 1903); chairman, Committee on Expenditures on Public Buildings (Fifty-seventh Congress); unsuccessful candidate for reelection in 1902 to the Fifty-eighth Congress; elected to the Fifty-ninth Congress (March 4, 1905-March 3, 1907); declined to be a candidate in 1906 for reelection to the Sixtieth Congress; retired from active business; died in Atlanta, Ga., April 15, 1919; interment in Lakewood Cemetery, Minneapolis, Minn.

**FLETCHER, Richard,** a Representative from Massachusetts; born in Cavendish, Windsor County, Vt., January 8, 1788; pursued classical studies and was graduated from Dartmouth College, Hanover, N.H., in 1806; taught school at Salisbury, N.H., 1806-1808; studied law; was admitted to the bar and commenced practice at Salisbury, N.H., in 1809; moved to Boston, Mass., in 1819; elected as a Whig to the Twenty-fifth Congress (March 4, 1837-March 3, 1839); was not a candidate for renomination in 1838 to the Twenty-sixth Congress; judge of the supreme court of Massachusetts 1848-1853; died in Boston, Mass., on June 21, 1869, interment Mount Auburn Cemetery, Cambridge, Mass.

**Bibliography:** *DAB*.

**FLETCHER, Thomas,** a Representative from Kentucky; born in Westmoreland County, Pa., October 21, 1779; settled in Montgomery County, Ky.; member of the Kentucky house of representatives in 1803, 1805, and 1806; served in the War of 1812 as a major of Kentucky Volunteers under General William Henry Harrison; elected as a Republican to the Fourteenth Congress to fill the vacancy caused by the resignation of James Clark, and served from December 2, 1816 to March 3, 1817; declined to be a candidate for renomination in 1816 to the Fifteenth Congress; again elected a member of the Kentucky house of representatives, and served in 1817, 1820, 1821, 1823, and 1825; died near Sharpsburg, Bath County, Ky.; interment in a private burial ground near Sharpsburg, Ky.

**FLETCHER, Thomas Brooks,** a Representative from Ohio; born in Mechanicstown, Carroll County, Ohio, October 10, 1879; attended the public schools, a private school at Augusta, Ohio, and the Richard School of Dramatic Art in Cleveland; was graduated from Mount Union College, Alliance, Ohio, in 1900; editor of the Daily Leader, Alliance, Ohio, 1903-1905; served on the staff of the Morning News, Canton, Ohio, from 1905 to 1906; became a Redpath lecturer in 1906; editor and publisher of the Daily Tribune at Marion, Ohio, 1910-1922; elected as a Democrat to the Sixty-ninth and Seventieth Congresses (March 4, 1925-March 3, 1929); unsuccessful candidate for reelection in 1928 to the Seventy-first Congress; elected to the Seventy-third, Seventy-fourth, and Seventy-fifth Congresses (March 4, 1933-January 3, 1939); chairman, Committee on Election of President, Vice President, and Representatives (Seventy-fourth and Seventy-fifth Congresses), Committee on the Census (Seventy-fifth Congress); unsuccessful candidate for reelection in 1938 to the Seventy-sixth Congress and for election in 1942 to the Seventy-eighth Congress; resumed lecturing and chautauqua work; died in Washington, D.C., July 1, 1945; interment in Mechanicstown Cemetery, Mechanicstown, Ohio.

**FLICK, James Patton,** a Representative from Iowa; born in Bakerstown, Allegheny County, Pa., August 28, 1845; moved with his parents to Wapello County, Iowa, in 1852 and to Taylor County in 1857; attended the common schools; enlisted in Company K, Fourth Regiment, Iowa Volunteer Infantry, as a private soldier and served from April 3, 1862, to September 4, 1864; recorder of Taylor County in 1869 and 1870; studied law; was admitted to the bar in 1870 and commenced practice in Bedford, Iowa; member of the State house of representatives in 1878 and 1879; district attorney of the third judicial district of Iowa 1880-1886; elected as a Republican to the Fifty-first and Fifty-second Congresses (March 4, 1889-March 3, 1893); was not a candidate for renomination in 1892 to the Fifty-third Congress; resumed the practice of his profession in Bedford, Iowa, until his death there on February 25, 1929; interment in Bedford Cemetery.

**FLINT, Frank Putnam,** a Senator from California; born in North Reading, Middlesex County, Mass., July 15, 1862; moved with his parents to San Francisco, Calif., in 1869; attended the public schools; moved to Los Angeles in 1887; deputy United States marshal, 1888-1892; appointed clerk in the district attorney's office in 1892; studied law, was admitted to the bar in 1892, and commenced practice in Los Angeles; assistant United States attorney, 1892-1893; judge of the superior court of Los Angeles County, 1895-1897; United States district attorney for the southern district of California, 1897-1901; elected as a Republican to the United States Senate, and served from March 4, 1905 to March 3, 1911; was not a candidate for reelection; chairman, Committee on Geological Survey (Fifty-ninth and Sixtieth Congresses), Committee on Interoceanic Canals (Sixty-first Congress); resumed the practice of law in Los Angeles, Calif.; also engaged in banking; appointed a member of the California State land settlement board in 1917, and reappointed in 1926; died February 11, 1929, on board a steamer while on a world tour; interment in Forest Lawn Mausoleum, Glendale, Calif.

**FLIPPO, Ronnie Gene,** a Representative from Alabama; born in Florence, Lauderdale County, Ala., August 15, 1937; attended the public schools of Florence; B.S., Florence State University (later known as University of North Alabama), 1965; M.A., University of Alabama, Tuscaloosa, 1966; certified public accountant and partner, Flippo & Robbins, Florence, Ala., 1972-1976; member, Alabama State house of representatives, 1971-1975; State senate, 1975-1976; delegate to the Democratic National Convention of 1984; elected as a Democrat to the Ninety-fifth and to the six succeeding Congresses (January 3, 1977-January 3, 1991); was not a candidate for reelection in 1990 to the One Hundred Second Congress, but was an unsuccessful candidate for nomination for Governor of Alabama; is a resident of Florence, Ala.

**FLOOD, Daniel John,** a Representative from Pennsylvania; born in Hazleton, Luzerne County, Pa., November 26, 1903; attended the public schools of Wilkes-Barre, Pa., and St. Augustine, Fla.; A.B., M.A., Syracuse (N.Y.) University, 1924; attended Harvard University Law School; LL.B., Dickinson School of Law, Carlisle, Pa., 1929; was admitted to the bar in 1930 and commenced practice in Wilkes-Barre, Pa.; attorney for the Home Owners' Loan Corporation in 1934 and 1935; deputy attorney general for the Commonwealth of Pennsylvania and counsel for the Pennsylvania Liquor Control Board 1935-1939; director of the Pennsylvania Bureau of Public Assistance Disbursements and executive assistant to the Pennsylvania treasurer 1941-1944; elected as a Democrat to the Seventy-ninth Congress (January 3, 1945-January 3, 1947); unsuccessful candidate for reelection in 1946 to the Eightieth Congress; resumed the practice of law; elected to the Eighty-first and Eighty-second Congresses (January 3, 1949-January 3, 1953); unsuccessful candidate for reelection in 1952 to the Eighty-third Congress; again resumed the practice of law; elected to the Eighty-fourth and to the twelve succeeding Congresses and served from January 3, 1955, until his resignation January 31, 1980; was a resident of Wilkes-Barre, Pa.; died May 28, 1994.

**Bibliography:** Kashatus, William C., III. "'Dapper Dan' Flood, Pennsylvania's Legendary Congressman." *Pennsylvania Heritage* 21 (Summer 1995): 4-11.

**FLOOD, Henry De La Warr** (brother of Joel West Flood and uncle of Harry Flood Byrd), a Representative from Virginia; born in "Eldon," Appomattox County, Va., September 2, 1865; attended the public schools of Appomattox and Richmond, Washington and Lee University, Lexington, Va., and the University of Virginia at Charlottesville; studied law; was admitted to the bar in 1886 and commenced practice in Appomattox, Va.; member of the Virginia house of delegates 1887-1891; served in the Virginia senate 1891-1903; elected prosecuting attorney for Appomattox County in 1891, 1895, and 1899; unsuccessful candidate for election to the Fifty-fifth Congress; elected as a Democrat to the Fifty-seventh and to the nine succeeding Congresses and served from March 4, 1901, until his death; chairman, Committee on Foreign Affairs (Sixty-second through Sixty-fifth Congresses), Committee on Territories (Sixty-second Congress); author of the resolution declaring a state of war to exist between the United States and the Imperial German Government and with the Imperial Austro-Hungarian Government; died in Washington, D.C., December 8, 1921; interment in a mausoleum on the courthouse green at Appomattox, Va.

**Bibliography:** Kaufman, Burton Ira. "Henry De La Warr Flood: A Case Study of Organization Politics in An Era of Reform." Ph.D. dissertation, Rice University, 1966.

**FLOOD, Joel West** (brother of Henry De La Warr Flood and uncle of Harry Flood Byrd), a Representative from Virginia; born near Appomattox, Appomattox County, Va., August 2, 1894; attended the public schools, Washington and Lee University, Lexington, Va., the University of Virginia at Charlottesville, and Oxford University; studied law; was admitted to the bar in 1917 and commenced practice in Appomattox, Va.; also engaged in agricultural pursuits; served from March 29, 1918, until his discharge July 18, 1919, as a private in Company A, Three Hundred and Fifth Engineers, Eightieth Division; served as colonel on the staff of Governor E. Lee Trinkle of Virginia 1922-1926; elected Commonwealth attorney of Appomattox County in 1919 and served until November 8, 1932, having been elected to Congress; special assistant to the attorney general of Virginia from April 1, 1928, to July 1, 1932; elected as a Democrat to the Seventy-second Congress to fill the vacancy caused by the death of Henry St. George Tucker and served from November 8, 1932, to March 3, 1933; was not a candidate for election in 1932 to the Seventy-third Congress; resumed the practice of law and agricultural pursuits; delegate to the Democratic National Convention of 1936; appointed assistant United States attorney for the western district of Virginia and served from June 1, 1939, to January 28, 1940; elected as a judge of the fifth judicial circuit of Virginia in January 1940, in which capacity he served until his death in Richmond, Va., April 27, 1964; interment in the Flood Mausoleum, Appomattox Courthouse Square.

**FLOOD, Thomas Schmeck,** a Representative from New York; born in Lodi, Seneca County, N.Y., April 12, 1844; attended the common schools and Elmira Free Academy; studied medicine, but did not practice; engaged in the drug business; moved to Pennsylvania and founded the town of Dubois; first postmaster of Dubois; returned to Elmira, N.Y.; member of the Board of Aldermen of Elmira in 1882 and 1883; president of the Chemung County Agricultural Society in 1884 and 1885; engaged in agricultural pursuits and lumbering; elected as a Republican to the Fiftieth and Fifty-first Congresses (March 4, 1887-March 3, 1891); chairman, Committee on Expenditures on Public Buildings (Fifty-first Congress); was not a candidate for renomination in 1890; engaged in the real estate business; died, while on a visit, in Pittsburgh, Pa., on October 28, 1908; interment in Woodlawn Cemetery, Elmira, N.Y.

**FLORENCE, Elias,** a Representative from Ohio; born in Fauquier County, Va., February 15, 1797; attended the public schools; engaged in agricultural pursuits; moved to Ohio and settled in Circleville, Pickaway County; member of the State house of representatives in 1829, 1830, 1834, and 1840; served in the State senate in 1835; elected as a Whig to the Twenty-eighth Congress (March 4, 1843-March 3, 1845); member of the State constitutional convention in 1850; resumed agricultural pursuits; died in Muhlenberg Township, Pickaway County, Ohio, November 21, 1880; interment in Forest Cemetery, Circleville, Ohio.

**FLORENCE, Thomas Birch,** a Representative from Pennsylvania; born in Philadelphia, Pa., January 26, 1812; attended the public schools; learned the hatter's trade and engaged in that business in 1833; engaged in the newspaper business; unsuccessful Democratic candidate for election in 1846 to the Thirtieth Congress and in 1848 to the Thirty-first Congress; elected as a Democrat to the Thirty-second and to the four succeeding Congresses (March 4, 1851-March 3, 1861); after leaving Congress edited and published the Constitutional Union in Washington, D.C., and subsequently became the proprietor of the Sunday Gazette; unsuccessful candidate in his old district for election in 1868 to the Forty-first Congress and in 1874 to the Forty-fourth Congress; died in Washington, D.C., July 3, 1875; interment in Monument Cemetery, Philadelphia, Pa.

**Bibliography:** *DAB.*

**FLORIO, James Joseph,** a Representative from New Jersey; born in Brooklyn, N.Y., August 29, 1937; attended the public elementary schools in Brooklyn; received high school equivalency diploma from State of New Jersey; B.A., Trenton (N.J.) State College, 1962; engaged in graduate work, Columbia University, New York City, 1962-1963; J.D., Rutgers University Law School, 1967; admitted to the New Jersey bar in 1967 and commenced practice in Camden; served in United States Navy, 1955-1958, ensign; lieutenant commander, United States Navy Reserve, 1958-1975; assistant city attorney for Camden City Legal Department, 1967-1971; solicitor for the New Jersey towns of Runnemede, Wood-Lynne, and Somerdale, 1969-1974; assemblyman, New Jersey State Legislature, 1970-1974; unsuccessful candidate for the nomination for Governor of New Jersey in 1977 and unsuccessful candidate for Governor in 1981; elected as a Democrat to the Ninety-fourth and to the seven succeeding Congresses and served from January 3, 1975, until his resignation on January 16, 1990; elected Governor of New Jersey in 1989 and served from January 16, 1990 to January 18, 1994; unsuccessful candidate for reelection in 1993; is a resident of Pine Hill, N.J.

**Bibliography:** Aron, Michael. *Governor's Race: A TV Reporter's Chronicle of the 1993 Whitman/Florio Campaign*. New Brunswick, N.J.: Rutgers University Press, 1994.

**FLOURNOY, Thomas Stanhope,** a Representative from Virginia; born in Prince Edward County, Va., December 15, 1811; was educated at Hampden-Sidney (Va.) College; engaged as a private teacher; studied law; was admitted to the bar and commenced practice in Halifax, Va., in 1834; elected as a Whig to the Thirtieth Congress (March 4, 1847-March 3, 1849); unsuccessful candidate for reelection in 1848 to the Thirty-first Congress and for election in 1850 to the Thirty-second Congress; unsuccessful candidate of the American Party for Governor in 1855; member of the secession convention in 1861 at Richmond; entered the Confederate Army, raised a company of Cavalry, and served as captain; promoted to colonel of the Sixth Virginia Cavalry; again an unsuccessful candidate for Governor in 1863; after the war settled in Danville, Va., and practiced law; delegate to the Democratic National Convention of 1876; died at his home in Halifax County, Va., March 12, 1883; interment in the family plot on his estate.

**FLOWER, Roswell Pettibone,** a Representative from New York; born in Theresa, Jefferson County, N.Y., August 7, 1835; attended the public schools, and was graduated from the Theresa High School in 1851; engaged in mercantile and manufacturing pursuits in 1851; assistant postmaster of Watertown, N.Y., 1854-1860; moved to New York City in 1869 and engaged in banking; elected as a Democrat to the Forty-seventh Congress to fill the vacancy caused by the resignation of Levi P. Morton, and served from November 8, 1881 to March 3, 1883; elected to the Fifty-first and Fifty-second Congresses, and served from March 4, 1889 to September 16, 1891, when he resigned; elected Governor of New York in 1891, and served from January 1, 1892 to January 1, 1895; died in Eastport, N.Y., May 12, 1899; interment in Brookside Cemetery, Watertown, N.Y.

**Bibliography:** *DAB*; Taylor, Emma (Flower). *The Life of Roswell Pettibone Flower*. Watertown, N.Y.: The Hungerford-Holbrook Co., 1930.

**FLOWERS, Walter,** a Representative from Alabama; born in Greenville, Butler County, Ala., April 12, 1933; educated in the public schools of Tuscaloosa; University of Alabama, A.B., 1955, and LL.B., 1957; Rotary Foundation Fellow at University of London, England, 1957-1958 (graduate student in international law); commissioned as a Reserve officer, Military Intelligence, Army, 1955; served on active duty as lieutenant, 1958-1959; was admitted to the bar in 1957 and commenced practice in Alabama; elected as a Democrat to the Ninety-first and to the four succeeding Congresses (January 3, 1969-January 3, 1979); was not a candidate in 1978 for reelection to the House of Representatives, but was an unsuccessful candidate for nomination to the United States Senate; businessman;

was a resident of McLean, Va., until his death there on April 12, 1984; interment in Arlington National Cemetery, Va.

**FLOYD, Charles Albert,** a Representative from New York; born in Smithtown, Suffolk County, N.Y., in 1791; attended the common schools; engaged in agricultural pursuits; county clerk in 1820 and 1821; studied law; was admitted to the bar and practiced; district attorney in 1830; member of the State assembly in 1836 and 1838; president of the board of trustees of Huntington 1837-1840; elected as a Democrat to the Twenty-seventh Congress (March 4, 1841-March 3, 1843); county judge of Suffolk County 1843-1865; supervisor of the town of Huntington 1843-1865; resumed agricultural pursuits; died in Commack, Long Island, N.Y., February 20, 1873; interment in the Methodist Church Cemetery.

**FLOYD, John,** a Representative from Georgia; born in Beaufort, Beaufort County, S.C., October 3, 1769; learned the carpenter's trade; moved in 1791 with his father to Camden County, Ga., and engaged in boat building; served in the War of 1812 as brigadier general in the First (Floyd's) Brigade of Georgia Militia from August 30, 1813 to March 8, 1814, and from October 17, 1814 to March 10, 1815, having participated in expeditions against the Creek Indians; member of the Georgia State house of representatives, 1820-1827; elected to the Twentieth Congress (March 4, 1827-March 3, 1829); died near Jefferson, Ga., on June 24, 1839.

**FLOYD, John,** a Representative from Virginia; born at Floyds Station, near the present city of Louisville, Jefferson County, Ky. (then a part of Virginia), April 24, 1783; pursued an academic course; attended Dickinson College, Carlisle, Pa., and was graduated from the medical department of the University of Pennsylvania at Philadelphia in 1806; settled in Lexington, Va., the same year, and soon thereafter moved to Christiansburg, Montgomery County, Va., where he practiced his profession; justice of the peace in 1807; major of Virginia Militia 1807-1812; served as surgeon with rank of major in the War of 1812; subsequently became brigadier general of militia; member of the Virginia house of delegates in 1814 and 1815; elected as a Republican to the Fifteenth Congress and reelected to the five succeeding Congresses (March 4, 1817-March 3, 1829); was not a candidate for renomination in 1828 to the Twenty-first Congress; elected Governor of Virginia by the General Assembly, and served from March 4, 1830 to March 31, 1834; received the electoral vote of South Carolina for President in 1833; died near Sweetsprings, Monroe County, Va. (now West Virginia), August 17, 1837; interment in an unmarked grave in the cemetery at Sweetsprings.

**Bibliography:** *DAB*; Ambler, Charles Henry. *The Life and Diary of John Floyd, Governor of Virginia, An Apostle of Secession, and the Father of the Oregon Country*. Richmond: Richmond Press, 1918.

**FLOYD, John Charles,** a Representative from Arkansas; born in Sparta, White County, Tenn., April 14, 1858; moved to Benton County, Ark., in 1869 with his parents, who settled near Bentonville; attended the common and high schools, and was graduated from the Arkansas Industrial University (later the University of Arkansas) at Fayetteville in 1879; taught school at Springdale, Ark., in 1880 and 1881; studied law; was admitted to the bar in 1882 and commenced practice in Yellville, Ark.; served in the State house of representatives 1889-1891; prosecuting attorney of the fourteenth judicial circuit 1890-1894; elected as a Democrat to the Fifty-ninth and to the four succeeding Congresses (March 4, 1905-March 3, 1915); one of the managers appointed by the House of Representatives in 1912 to conduct the impeachment proceedings against Robert W. Archbald, judge of the United States Commerce Court; was not a candidate for renomination in 1914 to the Sixty-fourth Congress; resumed the practice of law in Yellville, Ark.; unsuccessful candidate for nomination for Governor of Arkansas in 1920; died in Yellville, Ark., November 4, 1930; interment in Layton Cemetery.

**FLOYD, John Gelston** (grandson of William Floyd), a Representative from New York; born in Mastic, near Moriches, Long Island, N.Y., February 5, 1806; attended the common schools, and was graduated from Hamilton College, Clinton, N.Y., in 1824; studied law; was admitted to the bar in 1825 and commenced practice in Utica, N.Y.; clerk and prosecuting attorney of Utica, N.Y., 1829-1833; founded the Utica Democrat (later the Observer-Dispatch) in 1836; appointed judge of Suffolk County; member of the State assembly 1839-1843; elected as a Democrat to the Twenty-sixth and Twenty-seventh Congresses (March 4, 1839-March 3, 1843); returned to Mastic, Long Island, about 1842; member of the State senate in 1848 and 1849; elected to the Thirty-second Congress (March 4, 1851-March 3, 1853); chairman, Committee on Agriculture (Thirty-second Congress); joined the Republican Party upon its formation in 1856; retired from public life; died in Mastic, Long Island, N.Y., October 5, 1881; interment in the family cemetery.

**FLOYD, William** (grandfather of John Gelston Floyd), a Delegate and a Representative from New York; born in Brookhaven, Long Island, N.Y., December 17, 1734; pursued an academic course; served as major general in the State militia; Member of the Continental Congress 1774-1776 and 1779-1783; signed the Declaration of Independence; served in the State senate in 1777 and 1778; again served in the State senate 1784-1788; elected to the First Congress (March 4, 1789-March 3, 1791); unsuccessful candidate for reelection in 1790 to the Second Congress; moved in 1794 to Westernville, Oneida County; delegate to the State constitutional convention in 1801; again a member of the State senate in 1808; died in Westernville, N.Y., August 4, 1821; interment in Westernville Cemetery.

**Bibliography:** *DAB.*

**FLYE, Edwin,** a Representative from Maine; born in Newcastle, Lincoln County, Maine, March 4, 1817; attended the common schools and Lincoln Academy, Newcastle, Maine; engaged in mercantile pursuits and shipbuilding; member of the State house of representatives in 1858; served for many years as president of the First National Bank of Damariscotta, Maine; during the Civil War served as paymaster with the rank of major in the Union Army; delegate to the Republican National Convention at Cincinnati in 1876; elected as a Republican to the Forty-fourth Congress to fill the vacancy caused by the resignation of James G. Blaine and served from December 4, 1876, to March 3, 1877; was not a candidate for renomination in 1876; resumed shipbuilding and also engaged in banking; died while on a visit to the home of his daughter at Ashland, Ky., July 12, 1886; interment in Congregational Cemetery, Newcastle, Maine.

**FLYNN, Dennis Thomas,** a Delegate from the Territory of Oklahoma; born in Phoenixville, Chester County, Pa., February 13, 1861; moved with his mother to Buffalo, N.Y., in 1863; became an orphan when three years of age; was raised in a Catholic orphanage where he remained until 1880; attended the common schools and Canisius College, Buffalo, N.Y.; moved to Riverside, Iowa, where he established and edited the Riverside Leader; studied law; was admitted to the bar in 1882 and commenced practice in Kiowa, Barber County, Kans.; publisher of the Kiowa Herald; first postmaster of New Kiowa (later Kiowa), and served from December 5, 1884, to July 17, 1885; city attorney 1886-1889; moved to Oklahoma; postmaster of Guthrie from April 4, 1889, to December 20, 1892; unsuccessful candidate for election in 1890 to the Fifty-second Congress; elected as a Republican to the Fifty-third and Fifty-fourth Congresses (March 4, 1893-March 3, 1897); unsuccessful candidate for reelection in 1896 to the Fifty-fifth Congress; elected to the Fifty-sixth and Fifty-seventh Congresses (March 4, 1899-March 3, 1903); was nominated but declined to be a candidate for reelection in 1902 to the Fifty-eighth Congress; resumed the practice of law in Oklahoma City, Okla., in 1904; unsuccessful Republican candidate for election in 1908 to the United States Senate; delegate to the Republican National Convention of 1912; died in Oklahoma City, Okla., June 19, 1939; interment in Fairlawn Cemetery.

**Bibliography:** Murdock, Victor. "Dennis T. Flynn." *Chronicles of Oklahoma* 18 (June 1940): 107-113.

**FLYNN, Gerald Thomas,** a Representative from Wisconsin; born on a farm in Racine County near Racine, Wis., October 7, 1910; attended a rural grade school and Racine (Wis.) High School; graduated from Marquette Law School in 1933; was admitted to the bar in 1933 and commenced the practice of law in Racine, Wis.; delegate to the Democratic National Conventions of 1940, 1944, 1948, 1952, 1956 and 1960; member of the Wisconsin State senate, 1950-1954; elected as a Democrat to the Eighty-sixth Congress (January 3, 1959-January 3, 1961); unsuccessful candidate for reelection in 1960 to the Eighty-seventh Congress, and for election in 1962 to the Eighty-eighth Congress; resumed the practice of law; was a resident of Racine, Wis.; died May 14, 1990.

**FLYNN, Joseph Vincent,** a Representative from New York; born in Brooklyn, N.Y., September 2, 1883; attended the public schools and the Boys' High School of Brooklyn; was graduated from the College of the City of New York in 1904 and from the Brooklyn Law School of St. Lawrence University in 1906; was admitted to the bar in the latter year and commenced the practice of law in New York City; elected as a Democrat to the Sixty-fourth and Sixty-fifth Congresses (March 4, 1915-March 3, 1919); was not a candidate for renomination in 1918; resumed the practice of law in New York City; delegate to the Democratic State conventions in 1925 and 1927; resided in Brooklyn, N.Y., until his death there February 6, 1940; interment in Calvary Cemetery, Long Island City, N.Y.

**FLYNT, John James, Jr.,** a Representative from Georgia; born in Griffin, Spalding County, Ga., November 8, 1914; attended the public schools and the Georgia Military Academy (now the Woodward Academy); A.B., University of Georgia, Athens, 1936; served as a second lieutenant in the Sixth Cavalry, United States Army, 1936-1937; attended Emory University Law School in 1937 and 1938, and graduated from George Washington University Law School, Washington, D.C., 1940; was admitted to the bar in 1938 and commenced the practice of law in Griffin, Ga.; again served in the United States Army from March 22, 1941, until discharged as a lieutenant colonel on December 12, 1945; was awarded the Bronze Star Medal; colonel in the Army Reserve; assistant United States attorney for northern district of Georgia 1939-1941 and in 1945 and 1946; member of the Georgia State house of representatives in 1947 and 1948; solicitor general for the Griffin Judicial Circuit from January 1, 1949, to November 2, 1954; president, Georgia Bar Association, 1953-1954; delegate, Georgia State Democratic conventions, 1946, 1950, 1954, 1958, 1962, and 1966; delegate to the Democratic National Conventions of 1960 and 1968; elected as a Democrat to the Eighty-third Congress, November 2, 1954, by special election to fill the vacancy caused by the death of A. Sidney Camp and at the same time was elected to the Eighty-fourth Congress; reelected to the eleven succeeding Congresses and served from November 2, 1954, to January 3, 1979; chairman, Committee on Standards of Official Conduct (Ninety-fourth and Ninety-fifth Congresses); was not a candidate for reelection in 1978 to the Ninety-sixth Congress; resumed the practice of law and farming operations; engaged in banking and real estate; is a resident of Griffin, Ga.

**FOCHT, Benjamin Kurtz,** a Representative from Pennsylvania; born in New Bloomfield, Perry County, Pa., March 12, 1863; attended the public schools, Bucknell University, Lewisburg, Pa., Pennsylvania State College at State College, and Susquehanna University, Selinsgrove, Pa.; established the Lewisburg (Pa.)

Saturday News in 1881, serving as editor and publisher until his death; delegate to the Pennsylvania Republican convention in 1889; served as an officer of the National Guard of Pennsylvania; member of the Pennsylvania house of representatives 1893-1897; served in the Pennsylvania senate 1901-1905; water supply commissioner of Pennsylvania 1912-1914; elected as a Republican to the Sixtieth, Sixty-first, and Sixty-second Congresses (March 4, 1907-March 3, 1913); unsuccessful candidate for reelection in 1912 to the Sixty-third Congress; elected to the Sixty-fourth and to the three succeeding Congresses (March 4, 1915-March 3, 1923); chairman, Committee on War Claims (Sixty-sixth Congress), Committee on District of Columbia (Sixty-seventh Congress); unsuccessful candidate for renomination in 1922 to the Sixty-eighth Congress and for nomination in 1924, 1926, 1928, and 1930, and also in 1932 for the unexpired term of Edward M. Beers in the Seventy-second Congress; resumed business activities in Lewisburg, Pa.; served as deputy secretary of the Commonwealth in 1928 and 1929; elected to the Seventy-third, Seventy-fourth, and Seventy-fifth Congresses and served from March 4, 1933, until his death in Washington, D.C., March 27, 1937; interment in Lewisburg Cemetery, Lewisburg, Pa.

**Bibliography:** Baumgartner, Donald J. "Benjamin K. Focht: Union County Politician." D.Ed. dissertation, Pennsylvania State University, 1975.

**FOELKER, Otto Godfrey,** a Representative from New York; born in the city of Mainz, Germany, December 29, 1875; immigrated to the United States in 1888 with his parents, who settled in Troy, N.Y.; attended the public schools; moved to Brooklyn in December 1895; studied law in the New York Law School; was admitted to the bar in 1908 and commenced practice in Brooklyn; member of the State assembly in 1905 and 1906; served in the State senate in 1907 and 1908; elected as a Republican to the Sixtieth Congress to fill the vacancy caused by the death of Charles T. Dunwell; reelected to the Sixty-first Congress and served from November 3, 1908, to March 3, 1911; declined to be a candidate for renomination in 1910 to the Sixty-second Congress; moved to California and resumed the practice of law in Oakland, Calif., where he died on January 18, 1943; interment in Evergreen Cemetery.

**FOERDERER, Robert Hermann,** a Representative from Pennsylvania; born in Frankenhausen, Germany, May 16, 1860, while his parents were sojourning in Europe; attended public and private schools in Philadelphia, Pa.; engaged in the manufacture of leather and in various other business enterprises; elected as a Republican to the Fifty-seventh and Fifty-eighth Congresses and served from March 4, 1901, until his death in Torresdale, Pa., July 26, 1903; interment in South Laurel Hill Cemetery, Philadelphia, Pa.

**FOGARTY, John Edward,** a Representative from Rhode Island; born in Providence, R.I., March 23, 1913; attended school in Harmony, R.I., and graduated from La Salle Academy in Providence in 1931; studied public speaking at night at Providence College, 1939; apprenticed as a bricklayer in 1931, and became a master bricklayer in 1935; served as president of Bricklayers and Masons Union, Local No. 1 of Rhode Island, 1936-1941; elected as a Democrat to the Seventy-seventh and Seventy-eighth Congresses, and served from January 3, 1941 until his resignation on December 7, 1944, to enlist in the United States Navy construction battalion (Seabees); reelected to the Seventy-ninth and to the eleven succeeding Congresses, and served from February 7, 1945 until his death in Washington, D.C., on January 10, 1967; interment in St. Ann's Cemetery, Cranston, R.I.

**Bibliography:** Bair, Barbara. "'The Full Light of This Dawn': Congressman John Fogarty and the Historical Cycle of Community Mental Health Policy in Rhode Island." *Rhode Island History* 41 (November 1982): 127-138; Healey, James Stewart. *John E. Fogarty: Political Leadership for Library Development.* Metuchen, N.J.: The Scarecrow Press, 1974.

**FOGG, George Gilman,** a Senator from New Hampshire; born in Meredith Center, Belknap County, N.H., May 26, 1813; pursued classical studies and graduated from Dartmouth College, Hanover, N.H., in 1839; studied law at Meredith and at the Harvard Law School; was admitted to the bar in 1842 and commenced practice at Gilmanton Iron Works, N.H.; moved to Concord in 1846; member, State house of representatives 1846; secretary of State of New Hampshire 1846; newspaper publisher 1847-1861; reporter of the State supreme court 1856-1860; secretary of the Republican National Executive Committee in 1860; appointed by President Abraham Lincoln as Minister Resident to Switzerland on March 28, 1861 and served until October 1865; appointed as a Republican to the United States Senate to fill the vacancy caused by the resignation of Daniel Clark and served from August 31, 1866, to March 3, 1867; was not a candidate for election to the Senate in 1866; editor of the Concord Daily Monitor; died in Concord, N.H., October 5, 1881; interment in Blossom Hill Cemetery.

**Bibliography:** *DAB.*

**FOGLIETTA, Thomas Michael,** a Representative from Pennsylvania; born in Philadelphia, Pa., December 3, 1928; graduated from South Catholic High School, Philadelphia, 1945; B.A., St. Joseph's College, Philadelphia, 1949; J.D., Temple University School of Law, Philadelphia, 1952; admitted to the Pennsylvania bar in 1953 and commenced practice in Philadelphia; city councilman, Philadelphia, 1955-1975; regional director, United States Department of Labor, 1976; elected as an Independent to the Ninety-seventh Congress and as a Democrat to the seven succeeding Congresses (January 3, 1981-January 3, 1997); is a resident of Philadelphia, Pa.

**FOLEY, James Bradford,** a Representative from Indiana; born near Dover, Mason County, Ky., October 18, 1807; received a limited schooling; employed on a flatboat on the Mississippi River in 1823; moved to Greensburg, Ind., in 1834; engaged in mercantile pursuits, 1834-1837, and afterwards in farming; treasurer of Decatur County, 1841-1843; member of the State constitutional convention in 1850; appointed commander of the Fourth Brigade of State militia in 1852; elected as a Democrat to the Thirty-fifth Congress (March 4, 1857-March 3, 1859); resumed agricultural pursuits in Decatur County; died in Greensburg, Ind., December 5, 1886; interment in South Park Cemetery.

**FOLEY, John Robert,** a Representative from Maryland; born in Wabasha, Minn., October 16, 1917; graduated from St. Felix High School, Wabasha, in 1935 and from St. Thomas College, St. Paul, Minn., in 1940; entered the United States Army on July 15, 1941; served overseas in Australia, New Guinea, and the Philippine Islands with the Four Hundred and Seventy-third Quartermaster Group from November 1943 to November 1945; discharged in February 1946 with the rank of major; graduated from Georgetown University Law School, Washington, D.C., in 1947 and from Catholic University Law School, Washington, D.C., in 1950; was admitted to the District of Columbia bar in 1947 and commenced the practice of law; admitted to the Maryland bar in 1953; instructor of administrative law, Catholic University Law School, 1953-1957; elected judge of the Orphan's (Probate) Court, Montgomery County, Md., in November 1954 for a four-year term and served until December 1958; unsuccessful candidate in 1956 for election to the Eighty-fifth Congress; elected as a Democrat to the Eighty-sixth Congress (January 3, 1959-January 3, 1961); unsuccessful candidate for reelection in 1960 to the Eighty-seventh Congress, and for election in 1962 to the Eighty-eighth Congress; resumed the practice of law in Washington, D.C., and Maryland; is a resident of Kensington, Md.

**FOLEY, Mark A.,** a Representative from Florida; born in Newton, Middlesex County, Mass., September 8, 1954; graduated Lake Worth (Fla.) High School; attended Palm Beach Community College, Lake Worth, 1973-1975; commissioner then 1982, vice mayor, City of Lake Worth; member, Florida State house of representatives, 1990-1992; member, Florida State senate, 1993-1995; elected as a Republican to the One Hundred Fourth Congress (January 3, 1995-January 3, 1997); is a resident of Palm Beach, Fla.

**FOLEY, Thomas Stephen,** a Representative from Washington; born in Spokane, Wash., March 6, 1929; graduated from Gonzaga High School in 1946; B.A., University of Washington, 1951; LL.B., University of Washington Law School, 1957; was admitted to the bar in 1957 and began the practice of law in Spokane, Wash.; appointed deputy prosecuting attorney of Spokane County in 1958; instructor in constitutional law, Gonzaga University Law School, 1958-1959; appointed assistant attorney general, State of Washington, in 1960; assistant chief clerk and special counsel of the Committee on Interior and Insular Affairs, United States Senate, 1961-1963; elected as a Democrat to the Eighty-ninth and to the fourteen succeeding Congresses (January 3, 1965-January 3, 1995); unsuccessful candidate for reelection in 1994 to the One Hundred Fourth Congress; chairman, Committee on Agriculture (Ninety-fourth through Ninety-sixth Congresses); majority whip (Ninety-seventh through Ninety-ninth Congresses), majority leader (One Hundredth and One Hundred First Congresses); Speaker of the House of Representatives (One Hundred First through One Hundred Third Congresses); resumed the practice of law; appointed chairman of the President's Foreign Intelligence Advisory Board in 1995; is a resident of Spokane, Wash.

**FOLGER, Alonzo Dillard** (brother of John Hamlin Folger), a Representative from North Carolina; born in Dobson, Surry County, N.C., July 9, 1888; attended the public schools; was graduated from the University of North Carolina at Chapel Hill in 1912 and from its law department in 1914; was admitted to the bar in 1914 and commenced practice in Dobson, N.C.; moved to Mount Airy, N.C., and continued the practice of law; also interested in banking; trustee of the University of North Carolina 1932-1938; served as judge of the State superior court in 1937, resigning after two months' service to become a Democratic national committeeman; member of the Democratic National Committee 1936-1941; elected as a Democrat to the Seventy-sixth and Seventy-seventh Congresses and served from January 3, 1939, until his death in an automobile accident in Mount Airy, N.C., April 30, 1941; interment in Dobson Cemetery, Dobson, N.C.

**FOLGER, John Hamlin** (brother of Alonzo D. Folger), a Representative from North Carolina; born in Rockford, Surry County, N.C., December 18, 1880; attended the public schools, Guilford College, Greensboro, N.C., and studied law at the University of North Carolina at Chapel Hill; was admitted to the bar in 1901 and commenced practice in Dobson, Surry County, N.C.; mayor of Mount Airy, N.C., 1908-1912; member of the State house of representatives in 1927 and 1928; served in the State senate in 1931 and 1932; delegate to the Democratic State conventions 1924-1940; delegate to the Democratic National Conventions in 1932 and 1944; elected as a Democrat to the Seventy-seventh Congress in a special election to fill the vacancy caused by the death of his brother, Alonzo D. Folger; reelected to the Seventy-eighth, Seventy-ninth, and Eightieth Congresses and served from June 14, 1941, to January 3, 1949; was not a candidate for renomination in 1948; resumed the practice of law until his retirement in 1959; was a resident of Mount Airy, N.C.; died in Clemmons, N.C., July 19, 1963; interment in Oakdale Cemetery, Mount Airy, N.C.

**Bibliography:** Christian, Ralph J. "The Folger-Chatham Congressional Primary of 1946." *North Carolina Historical Review* 53 (January 1976): 25-54.

**FOLGER, Walter, Jr.,** a Representative from Massachusetts; born in Nantucket, Mass., June 12, 1765; attended the public schools; studied law; was admitted to the bar and practiced; member of the Massachusetts senate 1809-1815 and in 1822; elected as a Republican to the Fifteenth Congress and reelected to the Sixteenth Congress (March 4, 1817-March 3, 1821); resumed the practice of law; died in Nantucket, Mass., September 8, 1849; interment in Friends Burying Ground.

**Bibliography:** *DAB*.

**FOLLETT, John Fassett,** a Representative from Ohio; born near Enosburg, Franklin County, Vt., February 18, 1831; moved to Ohio in 1837 with his parents, who settled in Licking County; pursued classical studies, and was graduated from Marietta (Ohio) College in 1855; taught school two years; studied law; was admitted to the bar in 1858 and practiced; member of the State house of representatives 1866-1868; served as speaker in 1868; moved to Cincinnati in 1868 and engaged in the practice of law; elected as a Democrat to the Forty-eighth Congress (March 4, 1883-March 3, 1885); unsuccessful candidate for reelection in 1884 to the Forty-ninth Congress; resumed the practice of law; unsuccessful candidate for election in 1898 to the Fifty-sixth Congress; died in Cincinnati, Ohio, April 15, 1902; interment in Spring Grove Cemetery.

**FOLSOM, Nathaniel,** a Delegate from New Hampshire; born in Exeter, Rockingham County, N.H., September 18, 1726; attended the public schools; served in the French and Indian Wars as a captain in Colonel Blanchard's regiment; successively major, lieutenant colonel, and colonel of the Fourth Regiment of New Hampshire Militia, which he commanded at the beginning of the Revolutionary War; brigadier general of the New Hampshire troops sent to Massachusetts and served during the siege of Boston; appointed major general and planned the details of troops sent from New Hampshire to Ticonderoga; Member of the Continental Congress in 1774 and 1777-1780; executive councilor in 1778; a delegate to the State constitutional convention of 1783, serving as its president; chief justice of the court of common pleas; died in Exeter, N.H., on May 26, 1790; interment in Winter Street Cemetery.

**Bibliography:** *DAB*.

**FONG, Hiram Leong,** a Senator from Hawaii; born in Honolulu, Hawaii, October 15, 1906; attended public schools; A.B., University of Hawaii, 1930; LL.B., Harvard University Law School, 1935; was admitted to the bar in 1935 and commenced the practice of law in Honolulu; deputy attorney for city and county of Honolulu, 1935-1938; during the Second World War served as judge advocate of the Seventh Fighter Command of the Seventh Air Force with rank of major, 1942-1945; retired with the rank of colonel; member of the Hawaii Territorial legislature, 1938-1954, serving four years as vice speaker and six years as speaker; vice president of the Territorial Constitutional Convention in 1950; chairman of the board and president of several insurance and financial institutions; engaged in developing a 700-acre botanical garden in Honolulu; elected as a Republican to the United States Senate in 1959 upon the admission of Hawaii as a State; reelected in 1964 and again in 1970, and served from August 21, 1959 to January 3, 1977; was not a candidate for reelection in 1976; chairman of the board, Finance Enterprises, Ltd.; is a resident of Honolulu, Hawaii.

**Bibliography:** Chou, Michaelyn P. "The Education of a Senator: Hiram L. Fong 1906-1954." Ph.D. dissertation, University of Hawaii, 1980.

**FOOT, Samuel Augustus,** a Representative and a Senator from Connecticut; born in Cheshire, Conn., November 8, 1780; pursued an academic course; graduated from Yale College in 1797; attended the Litchfield Law School; discontinued law studies because of ill health and engaged in the shipping trade at New Haven; returned to Cheshire in 1813 and engaged in agricultural pursuits; member, Connecticut State house of representatives, 1817-1818; elected to the Sixteenth Congress (March 4, 1819-March 3, 1821); member, State house of representatives, 1821-1823, 1825-1826, and served as speaker, 1825-1826; elected to the Eighteenth Congress (March 4, 1823-March 3, 1825); elected to the United States Senate, and served from March 4, 1827 to March 3, 1833; unsuccessful candidate for reelection in 1832; chairman, Committee on Pensions (Twenty-first and Twenty-second Congresses); elected to the Twenty-third Congress, and served from March 4, 1833 to May 9, 1834, when he resigned to become Governor of Connecticut; elected Governor of Connecticut in 1834, and served from May 7, 1834 to May 6, 1835; unsuccessful candidate for reelection in 1835; died in Cheshire, Conn., September 15, 1846; interment in Hillside Cemetery.

**Bibliography:** *DAB*.

**FOOT, Solomon,** a Representative and a Senator from Vermont; born in Cornwall, Addison County, Vt., November 19, 1802; pursued classical studies, and graduated from Middlebury (Vt.) College in 1826; taught school 1826-1831; studied law; was admitted to the bar in 1831 and commenced practice in Rutland, Vt.; member, State house of representatives 1833, 1836-1838, serving as speaker the last two sessions; delegate to the State constitutional convention in 1836; prosecuting attorney 1836-1842; elected as a Whig to the Twenty-eighth and Twenty-ninth Congresses (March 4, 1843-March 3, 1847); elected as a Whig to the United States Senate in 1850; reelected as a Republican in 1856 and 1862, and served from March 4, 1851, until his death on March 28, 1866; served as President pro tempore of the Senate during the Thirty-sixth, Thirty-seventh and Thirty-eighth Congresses; chairman, Committee on Public Buildings and Grounds (Thirty-seventh through Thirty-ninth Congresses); died in Washington, D.C.; funeral services were held in the Chamber of the United States Senate; interment in Evergreen Cemetery, Rutland, Vt.

**Bibliography:** *DAB*.

**FOOTE, Charles Augustus,** a Representative from New York; born in Newburgh, Orange County, N.Y., April 15, 1785; attended private schools in Newburgh and Kingston, N.Y., and was graduated from Union College, Schenectady, N.Y., in 1805; studied law; was admitted to the bar in 1808 and practiced in New York City and later in Delhi, Delaware County, N.Y.; colonel in the New York State Militia, Sixth Division; trustee of Delaware Academy; president of the village of Delhi; elected to the Eighteenth Congress (March 4, 1823-March 3, 1825); resumed the practice of law in Delhi, N.Y., where he died August 1, 1828; interment in the private burying ground at "Arbor Hill," the estate of his father.

**FOOTE, Ellsworth Bishop,** a Representative from Connecticut; born in North Branford, New Haven County, Conn., January 12, 1898; attended the public schools; was graduated from Yale Business College in 1916 and from Georgetown University Law School, Washington, D.C., in 1923; was admitted to the bar in 1924 and commenced practice in New Haven, Conn.; corporation counsel of North Branford, 1924-1946; special assistant to the Attorney General, Department of Justice, Washington, D.C., February 1925 to July 1926; chairman of the board of finance of North Branford, 1934-1946; judge of probate, North Branford District, 1938-1946; acting judge of probate, New Haven Probate Court, November 1944 to July 1945; attorney for the county of New Haven 1942-1946; again from 1949 to 1960; elected as a Republican to the Eightieth Congress (January 3, 1947-January 3, 1949); unsuccessful candidate for reelection in 1948 to the Eighty-first Congress; corporation counsel for town of North Branford; resumed the practice of law; died in Guilford, Conn., January 18, 1977; interment in Bare Plain Cemetery, North Branford, Conn.

**FOOTE, Henry Stuart,** a Senator from Mississippi; born in Fauquier County, Va., February 28, 1804; pursued classical studies; graduated from Washington College (now Washington and Lee University), Lexington, Va., in 1819; studied law; was admitted to the bar in 1823 and commenced practice in Tuscumbia, Ala., in 1825; moved to Mississippi in 1826 and practiced law in Jackson, Natchez, Vicksburg, and Raymond; elected as a Democrat to the United States Senate and served from March 4, 1847, until January 8, 1852, when he resigned to become Governor; chairman, Committee on Foreign Relations (Thirty-first and Thirty-second Congresses); following heated debate on the Compromise of 1850 on April 17, 1850, was threatened by Senator Thomas Hart Benton of Missouri, Senator Foote drew his pistol, but other members intervened before he could fire; elected Governor of Mississippi in 1851 and served from January 10, 1852 until his resignation on January 5, 1854; moved to California in 1854; returned to Vicksburg, Miss., in 1858; member of the Southern convention held at Knoxville in 1859; moved to Tennessee and settled near Nashville; elected to the First and Second Confederate Congresses; afterwards moved to Washington, D.C., and practiced law; appointed by President Rutherford B. Hayes superintendent of the mint at New Orleans 1878-1880; author; died in Nashville, Tenn., on May 20, 1880; interment in Mount Olivet Cemetery.

**Bibliography:** *DAB*; Foote, Henry S. *Casket of Reminiscences.* 1874. Reprint. New York: Negro University Press, 1968; Gonzales, John E. "The Public Career of Henry Stuart Foote: 1804-1880." Ph.D. dissertation, University of North Carolina, 1957.

**FOOTE, Samuel Augustus,** a Representative and a Senator from Connecticut. (*See* FOOT, Samuel Augustus.)

**FOOTE, Wallace Turner, Jr.,** a Representative from New York; born in Port Henry, Essex County, N.Y., April 7, 1864; attended the Port Henry Union School and Williston Seminary, Easthampton, Mass., and was graduated as a civil engineer from Union College, Schenectady, N.Y., in 1885; assistant superintendent of the Cedar Point Furnace in Port Henry 1885-1887; attended Columbia Law School, New York City; was admitted to the bar in 1889 and commenced practice in Port Henry; elected as a Republican to the Fifty-fourth and Fifty-fifth Congresses (March 4, 1895-March 3, 1899); was not a candidate for renomination in 1898; resumed the practice of law and also engaged in mining; died in New York City December 17, 1910; interment in Union Cemetery, Port Henry, N.Y.

**FORAKER, Joseph Benson,** a Senator from Ohio; born near Rainsboro, Highland County, Ohio, on July 5, 1846; pursued preparatory studies; during the Civil War served in the Eighty-ninth Regiment, Ohio Volunteer Infantry, attaining the rank of brevet captain; graduated from Cornell University, Ithaca, N.Y., in 1869; studied law; was admitted to the bar in 1869 and commenced practice in Cincinnati, Ohio; judge of the superior court of Cincinnati, 1879-1882; unsuccessful Republican candidate for Governor of Ohio in 1883; elected Governor of Ohio in 1885, reelected in 1887, and served from January 11, 1886 to January 13, 1890; unsuccessful candidate for reelection in 1889; elected in 1896 as a Republican to the United States Senate; reelected in 1902 and served from March 4, 1897, to March 3, 1909; unsuccessful candidate for reelection in 1908; chairman, Committee to Examine Branches of the Civil Service (Fifty-fifth Congress), Committee on Pacific Islands and Puerto Rico (Fifty-sixth through Sixtieth Congresses); resumed the practice of law in Cincinnati, Ohio, where he died on May 10, 1917; interment in Spring Grove Cemetery.

**Bibliography:** *DAB*; Foraker, Joseph B. *Notes of a Busy Life.* 2 vols. Cincinnati: Stewart and Kidd Co., 1916; Walters, Everett. *Joseph Benson Foraker: An Uncompromising Republican.* Columbus: Ohio History Press, 1948.

**FORAN, Martin Ambrose,** a Representative from Ohio; born in Choconut, Susquehanna County, Pa., November 11, 1844; attended the public schools and St. Joseph's College; taught school three years; spent two years in Ireland; served as a private in the Fourth Regiment, Pennsylvania Volunteer Cavalry, from April 1864 to July 1865; member of the State constitutional convention of Ohio in 1873; studied law; was admitted to the bar in 1874 and commenced practice in Cleveland; prosecuting attorney for the city of Cleveland 1875-1877; elected as a Democrat to the Forty-eighth, Forty-ninth, and Fiftieth Congresses (March 4, 1883-March 3, 1889); was not a candidate for reelection in 1888 to the Fifty-first Congress; resumed the practice of law in Cleveland, Ohio; judge of the court of common pleas from January 1911 until his death in Cleveland, Ohio, June 28, 1921; interment in Lake View Cemetery.

**FORAND, Aime Joseph,** a Representative from Rhode Island; born in Fall River, Bristol County, Mass., May 23, 1895; attended the public and parochial schools, Magnus Commercial School, Providence, R.I., and Columbia University, New York City; served in France as sergeant, first class, from May 1918 to July 1919, in the Motor Transport Corps; newspaper reporter at Pawtucket and Woonsocket, R.I., 1924-1930; member of the State house of representatives 1923-1926; served as secretary to Representative Jeremiah E. O'Connell in 1929 and 1930 and to Representative Francis B. Condon 1930-1935; chief of the Rhode Island State division of soldiers' relief and commandant of the Rhode Island Soldiers' Home in 1935 and 1936; elected as a Democrat to the Seventy-fifth Congress (January 3, 1937-January 3, 1939); unsuccessful candidate for reelection in 1938 to the Seventy-sixth Congress; elected to the Seventy-seventh and to the nine succeeding Congresses (January 3, 1941-January 3, 1961); was not a candidate for renomination in 1960 to the Eighty-seventh Congress; founder and first president, National Council of Senior Citizens, 1961-1972; resided in Boca Raton, Fla., until his death there January 18, 1972; interment in Boca Raton Mausoleum.

**FORBES, James,** a Delegate from Maryland; born near Benedict, Charles County, Md., about 1731; appointed justice of the peace of Charles County, Md., on April 1, 1777; tax commissioner of Charles County, and also a member of the Maryland State general assembly in 1777; Member of the Continental Congress, 1778-1780; died in Philadelphia, Pa., March 25, 1780; interment in the yard surrounding Christ Church.

**FORBES, Michael Patrick,** a Representative from New York; born in Riverhead, Suffolk County, N.Y., July 16, 1952; graduated Westhampton Beach High School, Westhampton, N.Y., 1970; B.A., State University of New York, Albany, 1983; worked in family newspaper business, Riverhead, N.Y.; managed Suffolk County Legislature campaign, 1971; staff member for Senator Alphonse M. D'Amato of New York and Senator Connie Mack of Florida; staff member for Speaker Perry B. Duryea, Jr., New York State assemblyman John Behan and New York State senator Caesar Trunzo; owner, public relations and marketing business; positions in Small Business Administration; regional director, New York office then principal liaison with House of Representatives for Chamber of Commerce of the United States; elected as a Republican to the One Hundred Fourth Congress (January 3, 1995-January 3, 1997); is a resident of Quogue, Long Island, N.Y.

**FORD, Aaron Lane,** a Representative from Mississippi; born in Potts Camp, Marshall County, Miss., December 21, 1903; attended public schools in Mississippi and the law department of Cumberland University, Lebanon, Tenn.; was admitted to the bar in 1927 and commenced practice in Aberdeen, Miss.; moved to Ackerman, Miss., the same year and continued the practice of law; district attorney of the fifth circuit court district 1932-1934; elected as a Democrat to the Seventy-fourth and to the three succeeding Congresses (January 3, 1935-January 3, 1943); unsuccessful candidate for renomination

in 1942 to the Seventy-eighth Congress; delegate to the Interparliamentary Union Conference at The Hague, Netherlands, in 1938; resumed the practice of law in Washington, D.C., and Jackson, Miss.; was a resident of Jackson, Miss., until his death there July 8, 1983; interment in Rosedale Cemetery, Cuthbert, Ga.

**FORD, George,** a Representative from Indiana; born in South Bend, St. Joseph County, Ind., January 11, 1846; attended the common schools; engaged in the cooper's trade in early youth; entered the law department of the University of Michigan at Ann Arbor, and was graduated from that institution in 1869; was immediately admitted to the bar and commenced practice in South Bend, Ind.; prosecuting attorney of St. Joseph County in 1873 and 1875-1884; elected as a Democrat to the Forty-ninth Congress (March 4, 1885-March 3, 1887); declined to be a candidate for reelection in 1866 to the Fiftieth Congress; became the head of the legal department of an implement concern, but subsequently resumed the private practice of his profession in South Bend, Ind.; elected judge of the superior court of St. Joseph County in 1914; died in South Bend, Ind., on August 30, 1917; interment in Riverview Cemetery.

**FORD, Gerald Rudolph, Jr.,** a Representative from Michigan, Vice President, and 38th President of the United States; born in Omaha, Douglas County, Nebr., July 14, 1913; moved to Grand Rapids, Mich., in 1914 and attended the public schools; B.A., University of Michigan, Ann Arbor, 1935; LL.B., Yale University Law School, 1941; was admitted to the bar in 1941 and commenced practice in Grand Rapids, Mich.; during the Second World War served in the United States Navy from 1942 until discharged as a lieutenant commander in 1946; elected as a Republican to the Eighty-first Congress; reelected to the twelve succeeding Congresses and served from January 3, 1949, until his resignation from the United States House of Representatives on December 6, 1973, to become the fortieth Vice President of the United States; minority leader (Eighty-ninth through Ninety-third Congresses); first Vice President to be nominated by the President and confirmed by the Congress pursuant to the twenty-fifth amendment to the Constitution of the United States; sworn in as the thirty-eighth President of the United States, August 9, 1974, when President Richard M. Nixon resigned, and served until January 20, 1977; unsuccessful candidate for election in 1976; is a resident of Rancho Mirage, Calif.

**Bibliography:** Cannon, James. *Time and Chance: Gerald Ford's Appointment with History.* New York: HarperCollins Publishers, 1994; Ford, Gerald R. *A Time to Heal: The Autobiography of Gerald R. Ford.* New York: Harper and Row, 1979.

**FORD, Harold Eugene,** a Representative from Tennessee; born in Memphis, Shelby County, Tenn., May 20, 1945; attended the elementary and secondary schools of Memphis, Tenn.; B.S., Tennessee State University, Nashville, 1967; engaged in graduate work at Tennessee State University, 1968; A.A., mortuary science, John Gupton College, 1969; M.B.A., Howard University, Washington, D.C., 1982; worked as a mortician; member, Tennessee State house of representatives, 1971-1974; delegate to Tennessee State Democratic convention, 1972; delegate to the Democratic National Convention of 1972; elected as a Democrat to the Ninety-fourth and to the ten succeeding Congresses (January 3, 1975-January 3, 1997); chairman, Select Committee on Aging (One Hundred Second and One Hundred Third Congresses); was not a candidate for reelection in 1996 to the One Hundred Fifth Congress; is a resident of Memphis, Tenn.

**FORD, James,** a Representative from Pennsylvania; born in Perth Amboy, Middlesex County, N.J., May 4, 1783; attended the common schools; moved to New York City in 1797 and to Lindsley Town (later Lindley), Steuben County, N.Y., in 1803; moved to Tioga County, Pa.; member of the Pennsylvania house of representatives in 1824 and 1825; elected as a Jacksonian to the Twenty-first and

Twenty-second Congresses (March 4, 1829-March 3, 1833); operated a sawmill and a gristmill at Lawrenceville, Tioga County, Pa., until his death at that place on August 18, 1859; interment in the old Lindsley family cemetery at Lindley, N.Y.

**FORD, Leland Merritt,** a Representative from California; born in Eureka, Eureka County, Nev., March 8, 1893; attended the public schools; also took various courses at the University of Arizona at Tucson, Virginia Polytechnic Institute at Blackburg, Sheldon Science of Business, Chicago, Ill., and the University of Southern California at Los Angeles; surveyor for Southern Sierras Power Co., in 1909 and 1910; employee of the Southern Pacific Railroad in California in 1911 and in New York in 1912 and 1913; moved to Los Angeles, Calif., in 1915 and was employed by the Union Pacific Railroad; moved to Lynchburg, Va., and engaged in farming and livestock breeding 1915-1919; moved to Santa Monica, Calif., in 1919 and engaged in the real estate business; member of the planning commission, Santa Monica, Calif., 1923-1927; county supervisor of Los Angeles County, Calif., 1936-1939; elected as a Republican to the Seventy-sixth and Seventy-seventh Congresses (January 3, 1939-January 3, 1943); unsuccessful candidate for reelection in 1942 to the Seventy-eighth Congress; resumed the real estate business; was a resident of Pacific Palisades, Calif.; died in Santa Monica, Calif., November 27, 1965; interment in Woodlawn Cemetery.

**FORD, Melbourne Haddock,** a Representative from Michigan; born in Salem, Washtenaw County, Mich., June 30, 1849; moved to Lansing with his parents in 1859; attended the common schools and the Michigan State College of Agriculture at East Lansing; enlisted in the United States Navy in 1864, and in 1867 was appointed a midshipman at the United States Naval Academy, Annapolis, Md.; resigned the following year and returned to Lansing; moved to Grand Rapids in 1873 and was engaged as official stenographer of several municipal, State, and Federal courts; studied law and was admitted to the bar in 1878; member of the State house of representatives in 1885 and 1886; elected as a Democrat to the Fiftieth Congress (March 4, 1887-March 3, 1889); unsuccessful candidate for reelection in 1888 to the Fifty-first Congress; commenced the practice of law at Grand Rapids in 1889; chairman of the Democratic State convention in 1890; elected to the Fifty-second Congress and served from March 4, 1891, until his death in Grand Rapids, Mich., April 20, 1891; interment in Oak Hill Cemetery.

**FORD, Nicholas,** a Representative from Missouri; born in Wicklow, Ireland, June 21, 1833; attended the village school and Maynooth College, Dublin, Ireland; immigrated to the United States in 1848 with his parents, who settled in Chicago, Ill.; moved to St. Joseph, Mo., in 1859 and later to Colorado and Montana, in which States he engaged in mining; returned to Missouri and settled in Rochester, Andrew County, and engaged in mercantile pursuits; elected a member of the State house of representatives in 1875; elected as a Greenbacker (National Party) to the Forty-sixth and Forty-seventh Congresses (March 4, 1879-March 3, 1883); unsuccessful candidate for reelection in 1882 to the Forty-eighth Congress and for election in 1890 to the Fifty-second Congress; unsuccessful Republican candidate for Governor of Missouri in 1884; moved to Virginia City, Nev.; member of the first city council; retired from active business and moved to Miltonvale, Kans., where he died June 18, 1897; interment in the Catholic Cemetery, Aurora, Cloud County, Kans.

**FORD, Thomas Francis,** a Representative from California; born in St. Louis, Mo., February 18, 1873; attended public and private schools; served in the United States Postal Service 1896-1903; studied law at Toledo, Ohio; engaged in newspaper work in Washington, Idaho, California, and Washington, D.C., 1913-1929; magazine and literary editor in Los Angeles 1919-1929; lecturer on

international trade at the University of Southern California at Los Angeles in 1920 and 1921; publicity director of the Los Angeles water and power department 1920-1931; member of the Los Angeles City Council 1931-1933; elected as a Democrat to the Seventy-third and to the five succeeding Congresses (March 4, 1933-January 3, 1945); was not a candidate for renomination in 1944 to the Seventy-ninth Congress; assumed the management of his rental properties; died in South Pasadena, Calif., December 26, 1958; interment in Forest Lawn Memorial Park, Glendale, Calif.

**Bibliography:** Ford, L.C., and Thomas F. Ford. *The Foreign Trade of the United States.* New York: Charles Scribner's Sons, 1920.

**FORD, Wendell Hampton,** a Senator from Kentucky; born near Owensboro, Daviess County, Ky., September 8, 1924; attended the public schools of Daviess County; attended the University of Kentucky, 1942-1943; graduated, Maryland School of Insurance, 1947; engaged in the insurance business in Kentucky; served in the United States Army, 1944-1946 and in the Kentucky National Guard, 1942-1962; chief assistant to Governor Bert T. Combs of Kentucky, 1959-1961; member, Kentucky senate, 1965-1967; lieutenant governor, 1967-1971; elected Governor of Kentucky in 1971, and served from December 7, 1971 until his resignation December 28, 1974; elected as a Democrat to the United States Senate in 1974 for the term commencing January 3, 1975; subsequently appointed by the Governor, December 28, 1974, to fill the vacancy caused by the resignation of Marlow W. Cook for the term ending January 3, 1975; reelected in 1980, 1986 and again in 1992 for the term ending January 3, 1999; chairman, Committee on Aeronautical and Space Sciences (Ninety-fifth Congress), Democratic Senatorial Campaign Committee (Ninety-fifth through Ninety-seventh Congresses), Select Committee to Study the Committee System (Ninety-eighth Congress), Joint Committee on Printing (One Hundred Third Congress), Committee on Rules and Administration (One Hundredth through One Hundred Third Congresses); Majority Whip (One Hundred Second through One Hundred Third Congresses); Minority Whip (One Hundred Fourth Congress); is a resident of Owensboro, Ky.

**FORD, William Donnison,** a Representative from New York; born in Herkimer County, N.Y., in 1779; educated at Fairfield Seminary, Herkimer County, N.Y.; studied law; was admitted to the bar in 1809 and commenced practice in Fairfield, N.Y.; member of the State assembly in 1816 and 1817; appointed commissioner to perform duties of judge of the supreme court in 1817; moved to Watertown, Jefferson County, N.Y., in 1817 and continued the practice of law; elected to the Sixteenth Congress (March 4, 1819-March 3, 1821); was not a candidate for reelection in 1820 to the Seventeenth Congress; resumed the practice of his profession in Watertown, N.Y.; served as district attorney of Jefferson County and also as master of chancery; trustee of the village of Watertown in 1827; moved to Sackets Harbor, N.Y., about 1830, and died there October 1, 1833; interment in the Village Cemetery.

**FORD, William David,** a Representative from Michigan; born in Detroit, Wayne County, Mich., August 6, 1927; attended Henry Ford Trade School, Melvindale High School, Nebraska State Teachers College, and Wayne University; B.A., University of Denver, 1949; LL.D., University of Denver School of Law, 1951; served in the United States Navy, 1944-1946, and the United States Air Force Reserve, 1950-1958; was admitted to the bar in 1951 and practiced law in Taylor, Mich.; justice of the peace, Taylor Township, 1955-1957; city attorney, Melvindale, Mich., 1957-1959; attorney, Taylor Township, 1957-1964; delegate, Michigan constitutional convention, 1961-1962; member of the Michigan State senate, 1962-1964; member and officer of the Sixteenth District Democratic Organization, 1952-1964; delegate, Michigan Democratic conventions, 1952-1970, and to the Democratic National Convention of 1968; elected as a Democrat to the Eighty-ninth and to the fourteen succeeding Congresses (January 3, 1965-January 3, 1995); chairman, Committee on Post Office and Civil Service (Ninety-seventh through One Hundred First Congresses), Committee on Education and Labor (One Hundred Second and One Hundred Third Congresses); was not a candidate for reelection in 1994 to the One Hundred Fourth Congress; is a resident of Taylor, Mich.

**FORDNEY, Joseph Warren,** a Representative from Michigan; born on a farm near Hartford City, Blackford County, Ind., November 5, 1853; attended the common schools; moved to Saginaw, Saginaw County, Mich., in June 1869 and engaged in the lumber industry; afterward became the owner of extensive lumber enterprises; vice president of the Saginaw Board of Trade; member, Saginaw board of aldermen, 1896-1900; elected as a Republican to the Fifty-sixth and the eleven succeeding Congresses (March 4, 1899-March 3, 1923); chairman, Committee on Expenditures in the Department of the Navy (Fifty-ninth Congress), Committee on Ways and Means (Sixty-sixth and Sixty-seventh Congresses); co-sponsor of the Fordney-McCumber Tariff of 1922; declined to be a candidate for renomination in 1922 to the Sixty-eighth Congress; delegate to the Republican National Convention of 1908; returned to the lumber business in Saginaw, Mich.; also interested in banking and agricultural pursuits; died in Saginaw, Mich., on January 8, 1932; interment in St. Andrew's Cemetery.

Bibliography: *DAB*; Russell, John A. *Joseph Warren Fordney: An American Legislator.* Boston: The Stratford Co., 1928.

**FOREMAN, Edgar Franklin,** a Representative from Texas and New Mexico; born in Portales, Roosevelt County, N.Mex., December 22, 1933; attended the public schools of Portales and Eastern New Mexico University at Portales, 1952-1953; B.S., New Mexico State University, 1955; served in the United States Navy, 1956-1957, and also in the United States Naval Reserve and United States Air Force Reserve; president, Valley Transit Mix, Atlas Land Co., and Foreman Oil, Inc.; resident of Odessa, Tex.; delegate to the Republican National Conventions of 1964 and 1968; elected as a Republican from Texas to the Eighty-eighth Congress (January 3, 1963-January 3, 1965); unsuccessful candidate for reelection in 1964 to the Eighty-ninth Congress; moved to Las Cruces, N.Mex.; elected to the Ninety-first Congress from New Mexico (January 3, 1969-January 3, 1971); unsuccessful candidate for reelection in 1970 to the Ninety-second Congress; assistant secretary, United States Department of Interior, 1971; assistant secretary, United States Department of Transportation, 1972-1976; president, Executive Development Systems, Inc.; is a resident of Dallas, Tex.

**FORESTER, John B.,** a Representative from Tennessee; born in McMinnville, Warren County, Tenn.; received a limited schooling; studied law; was admitted to the bar and practiced; elected as a Jacksonian to the Twenty-third Congress and reelected as a White suppporter to the Twenty-fourth Congress (March 4, 1833-March 3, 1837); died August 31, 1845.

**FORKER, Samuel Carr,** a Representative from New Jersey; born in Mount Holly, Burlington County, N.J., March 16, 1821; completed preparatory studies; moved to Bordentown and engaged in banking; director and cashier of the Bordentown Banking Co.; elected as a Democrat to the Forty-second Congress (March 4, 1871-March 3, 1873); unsuccessful candidate for reelection in 1872 to the Forty-third Congress; again engaged in banking; moved to Delanco, Burlington County, N.J., in 1890; lived in retirement with his son until his death in Edgewater Park, Burlington County, N.J., February 10, 1900; interment in Mount Holly Cemetery, Mount Holly, N.J.

**FORMAN, William St. John,** a Representative from Illinois; born in Natchez, Adams County, Miss., January 20, 1847; moved with his father to Nashville, Washington County, Ill., in 1851; attended the public schools, and Washington Seminary, Richview,

Ill.; studied law; was admitted to the bar in 1870 and commenced practice in Nashville, Ill.; mayor 1878-1884; delegate to all State and National Democratic Conventions from 1876 to 1896; member of the State senate 1884-1888; elected as a Democrat to the Fifty-first and to the two succeeding Congresses (March 4, 1889-March 3, 1895); chairman, Committee on Militia (Fifty-third Congress); moved to East St. Louis, Ill., in 1895; unsuccessful candidate as a Gold Standard Democrat for election for Governor in 1896; resumed the practice of his profession; appointed by President Grover Cleveland as Commissioner of Internal Revenue and served from 1895 to 1899; died in Champaign, Ill., June 10, 1908; interment in Masonic Cemetery, Nashville, Ill.

**FORNANCE, Joseph,** a Representative from Pennsylvania; born in Lower Merion Township, Montgomery County, Pa., October 18, 1804; attended the public schools and the Old Academy at Lower Merion; studied law; was admitted to the bar in 1832 and commenced practice in Norristown, Pa.; president of the council of the borough of Norristown; member of the Pennsylvania house of representatives in 1834; elected as a Democrat to the Twenty-sixth and Twenty-seventh Congresses (March 4, 1839-March 3, 1843); was not a candidate for renomination in 1842; resumed the practice of his profession; died in Norristown, Montgomery County, Pa., on November 24, 1852; interment in Montgomery Cemetery.

**FORNES, Charles Vincent,** a Representative from New York; born on a farm near Williamsville, Erie County, N.Y., January 22, 1844; attended the public schools, and was graduated from Union Academy, Lockport, N.Y., in 1864; moved to Buffalo, N.Y., in 1866 and worked for S.K. Worthington and Co., a commercial house; taught in a district school, and then served as principal of a Buffalo public school for three years; employed as a clerk for Dahlman and Co., a wholesale woolen merchant in Buffalo, and later established a similar business for himself; founder and president of the Buffalo Catholic Institute, a literary organization; moved to New York City in 1877 and engaged in business as an importer and jobber of woolens; president of the Catholic Club of New York City, 1889-1894; president of the board of aldermen of New York City, 1902-1907; trustee and director of several banks and corporations; elected as a Democrat to the Sixtieth and to the two succeeding Congresses (March 4, 1907-March 3, 1913); declined to be a candidate for renomination in 1912 to the Sixty-third Congress; resumed his former business pursuits in New York City; retired from active business in 1926 and returned to Buffalo, N.Y., where he died on May 22, 1929; interment in United German and French Roman Catholic Cemetery, Pine Hill, Buffalo, N.Y.

**FORNEY, Daniel Munroe** (son of Peter Forney and uncle of William Henry Forney), a Representative from North Carolina; born near Lincolnton, Lincoln County, N.C., in May 1784; attended the public schools and the University of North Carolina at Chapel Hill; engaged in agricultural pursuits; served as a major in the War of 1812; held several local offices; elected as a Republican to the Fourteenth and Fifteenth Congresses and served from March 4, 1815, until his resignation in 1818; appointed by President James Monroe a commissioner to treat with the Creek Indians in 1820; served as a member of the State senate 1823-1826; moved to Alabama in 1834 and settled in Lowndes County; resumed agricultural pursuits and became interested in various business enterprises; died in Lowndes County, Ala., October 15, 1847; interment in family burying ground, Lowndes County, Ala.

**FORNEY, Peter** (father of Daniel Munroe Forney and grandfather of William Henry Forney), a Representative from North Carolina; born near Lincolnton, Lincoln County, N.C., April 21, 1756; attended the public schools; served as a captain during the Revolutionary War; engaged in the manufacture of iron; member of the State house of commons 1794-1796; served in the State senate in 1801 and 1802; elected as a Republican to the Thirteenth Congress

(March 4, 1813-March 3, 1815); declined to be a candidate in 1814 for reelection to the Fourteenth Congress; retired from public life; died at his country home, "Mount Welcome," in Lincoln County, N.C., on February 1, 1834; interment in the private burying ground on his estate.

**FORNEY, William Henry** (grandson of Peter Forney and nephew of Daniel Munroe Forney), a Representative from Alabama; born in Lincolnton, Lincoln County, N.C., November 9, 1823; pursued classical studies, and was graduated from the University of Alabama at Tuscaloosa in 1844; served in the war with Mexico as a first lieutenant in the First Regiment of Alabama Volunteers; studied law; was admitted to the bar in 1848 and commenced practice in Jacksonville, Calhoun County, Ala.; trustee of the University of Alabama 1851-1860; member of the State house of representatives in 1859 and 1860; during the Civil War entered the Confederate Army in 1861 as a captain, and was successively promoted to major, lieutenant colonel, colonel, and brigadier general; surrendered at Appomattox Court House; member of the State senate in 1865 and 1866; elected as a Democrat to the Forty-fourth and to the eight succeeding Congresses (March 4, 1875-March 3, 1893); chairman, Committee on Expenditures in the Department of the Treasury (Forty-sixth Congress); was not a candidate for renomination in 1892 to the Fifty-third Congress; appointed by President Grover Cleveland a member of the Gettysburg Battlefield Commission and served until his death in Jacksonville, Ala., January 16, 1894; interment in the City Cemetery.

Bibliography: *DAB.*

**FORREST, Thomas,** a Representative from Pennsylvania; born in Philadelphia, Pa., in 1747; attended the common schools; during the Revolutionary War was commissioned a captain in Col. Thomas Proctor's Pennsylvania Artillery October 5, 1776, promoted to major March 3, 1777, and lieutenant colonel December 2, 1778; resigned October 7, 1781; elected to the Sixteenth Congress (March 4, 1819-March 3, 1821); chairman, Committee on Agriculture (Sixteenth Congress); elected to the Seventeenth Congress to fill the vacancy caused by the resignation of William Milnor and served from October 8, 1822, to March 3, 1823; unsuccessful candidate for reelection in 1822 to the Eighteenth Congress; died in Germantown (now a part of Philadelphia), Pa., March 20, 1825.

**FORREST, Uriah,** a Delegate and a Representative from Maryland; born near Leonardtown, St. Marys County, Md., in 1756; received a limited schooling; served as a first lieutenant, captain, and major in Maryland forces in the Revolutionary War; wounded at the Battle of Germantown and lost a leg at the Battle of Brandywine; Member of the Continental Congress in 1787; elected to the Third Congress and served from March 4, 1793, to November 8, 1794, when he resigned; commissioned major general of Maryland Militia in 1795; clerk of the circuit court of the District of Columbia 1800-1805; died at his home, "Rosedale," near Georgetown, D.C., July 6, 1805; interment in Oak Hill Cemetery, Washington, D.C.

**FORRESTER, Elijah Lewis (Tic),** a Representative from Georgia; born on a farm near Leesburg, Lee County, Ga., August 16, 1896; attended the Leesburg public schools; studied law and passed the State bar examination in 1917; during the First World War served as a private in the United States Army; commenced the practice of law in 1919 in Leesburg, Ga.; solicitor of the City Court, Leesburg, Ga., 1920-1933; mayor of Leesburg, 1922-1931; Lee County attorney, 1928-1937; solicitor general, southwestern judicial circuit, 1937-1950; delegate to the Democratic National Conventions of 1948 and 1952; elected as a Democrat to the Eighty-second and to the six succeeding Congresses (January 3, 1951-January 3, 1965); was not a candidate for renomination in 1964 to the Eighty-ninth Congress; returned to Leesburg and resumed the practice of law;

died in Albany, Ga., March 19, 1970; interment in Leesburg Cemetery, Leesburg, Ga.

**FORSYTH, John,** a Representative and a Senator from Georgia; born in Fredericksburg, Va., October 22, 1780; graduated from the College of New Jersey (now Princeton University) in 1799; moved to Augusta, Ga.; studied law; was admitted to the bar in 1802 and commenced practice; elected attorney general of Georgia in 1808; elected as a Republican to the Thirteenth and to the two succeeding Congresses, and served from March 4, 1813 until his resignation, effective November 23, 1818; chairman, Committee on Expenditures in the Department of State (Fifteenth Congress); elected to the United States Senate as a Republican on November 7, 1818, to fill the vacancy caused by the resignation of George M. Troup, and served from November 23, 1818 to February 17, 1819, when he resigned to accept a diplomatic appointment; appointed Minister to Spain on February 16, 1819 and served until March 1823; elected to the Eighteenth and to the two succeeding Congresses and served from March 4, 1823, until his resignation, effective November 7, 1827; chairman, Committee on Foreign Affairs (Eighteenth and Nineteenth Congresses); elected Governor of Georgia in 1827, and served from November 7, 1827 to November 4, 1829; again elected to the United States Senate as a Jacksonian to fill the vacancy caused by the resignation of John Macpherson Berrien, and served from November 9, 1829 to June 27, 1834, when he resigned to accept a Cabinet portfolio; chairman, Committee on Commerce (Twenty-second Congress), Committee on Foreign Relations (Twenty-second Congress), Committee on Finance (Twenty-second Congress); appointed Secretary of State by President Andrew Jackson, reappointed by President Martin Van Buren, and served from June 27, 1834 to March 3, 1841; died in Washington, D.C., October 21, 1841; interment in Congressional Cemetery.

Bibliography: *DAB*; Duckett, Alvin L. *John Forsyth: Political Tactician.* Athens: University of Georgia Press, 1962.

**FORSYTHE, Albert Palaska,** a Representative from Illinois; born in New Richmond, Clermont County, Ohio, May 24, 1830; attended the common schools and Asbury University (now De Pauw University), Greencastle, Ind.; admitted into the Indiana conference of the Methodist Church as a traveling preacher in 1853 and served eight years; during the Civil War served in the Union Army as first lieutenant of Company I, Ninety-seventh Regiment, Indiana Volunteer Infantry; moved to Illinois in 1865 and settled on a farm west of Paris, Edgar County; took an active part in the Grange movement and served six years as master of the State Grange of Illinois; elected as a Greenbacker (National Party) to the Forty-sixth Congress (March 4, 1879-March 3, 1881); unsuccessful candidate for reelection in 1880 to the Forty-seventh Congress; moved to Kansas in 1882 and engaged in agricultural pursuits near Liberty, Independence County; regent of the Kansas State Agricultural College 1886-1892; moved to Independence, Kans., where he died September 2, 1906; interment in Liberty Cemetery, Liberty, Kans.

**FORSYTHE, Edwin Bell,** a Representative from New Jersey; born in Westtown, Chester County, Pa., January 17, 1916; attended the public schools; secretary, Moorestown, N.J., Board of Adjustment, 1948-1952; member, Moorestown Township Committee, 1953-1962; mayor of Moorestown, 1957-1962; member, executive board of New Jersey State League of Municipalities, 1958-1962; chairman of Moorestown Planning Board, 1962-1963; member, New Jersey State senate, 1964-1970; delegate, New Jersey Constitutional convention, 1966; delegate, Republican National Convention, 1968; elected as a Republican to the Ninety-first Congress, November 3, 1970, by special election, to fill the vacancy caused by the resignation of William Cahill and at the same time elected to the Ninety-second Congress; reelected to the seven succeeding Congresses, and served from November 3, 1970, until his death in

Moorestown, N.J., on March 29, 1984; cremated; ashes interred at Union Street Friends Cemetery, Medford, N.J.

**FORT, Franklin William,** a Representative from New Jersey; born in Newark, N.J., March 30, 1880; moved in 1888 with his parents to East Orange, N.J.; attended the public schools and Newark Academy; was graduated from Lawrenceville School in 1897 and from Princeton University in 1901; attended New York Law School 1901-1903; was admitted to the bar in 1903 and commenced practice in Newark; recorder of East Orange, N.J., in 1907 and 1908; during the First World War served as a volunteer on the staff of the United States Food Administrator, Herbert Hoover, in Washington, D.C., 1917-1919; engaged in the insurance business in 1919 at Newark, N.J., and was also interested in banking; elected as a Republican to the Sixty-ninth, Seventieth, and Seventy-first Congresses (March 4, 1925-March 3, 1931); was not a candidate in 1930 for reelection to the House of Representatives, but was an unsuccessful candidate for nomination to the United States Senate; served as secretary of the Republican National Committee 1928-1930; resumed the practice of law; served as chairman of the Federal Home Loan Bank Board from January 1932 to March 1933; died on June 20, 1937, in Rochester, Minn.; interment in Bloomfield Cemetery, Bloomfield, N.J.

**FORT, Greenbury Lafayette,** a Representative from Illinois; born in French Grant, Scioto County, Ohio, October 17, 1825; moved with his parents to Marshall County, Ill., in April 1834; completed preparatory studies and attended Rock River Seminary; studied law; was admitted to the bar in 1847 and commenced practice in Lacon, Ill.; elected sheriff in 1850; clerk of Marshall County in 1852; county judge in 1857; was appointed a second lieutenant in the Eleventh Regiment, Illinois Volunteer Infantry, on April 30, 1861; promoted through the ranks to lieutenant colonel and quartermaster; brevetted major and lieutenant colonel of Volunteers March 13, 1865; member of the State senate in 1866; elected as a Republican to the Forty-third and to the three succeeding Congresses (March 4, 1873-March 3, 1881); was not a candidate for renomination in 1880; retired from public life; died in Lacon, Ill., January 13, 1883; interment in Lacon Cemetery.

**FORT, Tomlinson,** a Representative from Georgia; born in Warrenton, Warren County, Ga., July 14, 1787; completed preparatory studies; studied medicine; was graduated from the Philadelphia Medical College, and commenced practice in 1810; captain of a volunteer company in the War of 1812; member of the State house of representatives 1818-1826; elected to the Twentieth Congress (March 4, 1827-March 3, 1829); resumed the practice of medicine in Milledgeville, Ga.; president of the State Bank of Georgia in 1832, which position he held until his death in Milledgeville, Ga., May 11, 1859; interment in the City Cemetery.

**FORWARD, Chauncey** (brother of Walter Forward), a Representative from Pennsylvania; born in Old Granby, Conn., February 4, 1793; moved with his father to Ohio in 1800, and a short time afterward to Greensburg, Pa.; pursued classical studies; studied law; was admitted to the bar in Pittsburgh, Pa., in 1817 and began practice in Somerset, Pa.; member of the Pennsylvania house of representatives 1820-1822; elected to the Nineteenth Congress to fill the vacancy caused by the resignation of Alexander Thomson; reelected to the Twentieth Congress and reelected as a Jacksonian to the Twenty-first Congress and served from December 4, 1826, to March 3, 1831; appointed prothonotary and recorder of Somerset County in 1831; died in Somerset, Somerset County, Pa., October 19, 1839; interment in Aukeny Square Cemetery.

**FORWARD, Walter** (brother of Chauncey Forward), a Representative from Pennsylvania; born in East Granby, Conn., January 24, 1786; attended the common schools; moved with his father to Aurora, Ohio; settled in Pittsburgh, Pa., in 1803; studied law; was admitted to the bar in 1806 and commenced practice in Pittsburgh; also served for several years as editor of the Tree of Liberty; elected to the Seventeenth Congress to fill the vacancy caused by the resignation of Henry Baldwin; reelected to the Eighteenth Congress, and served from October 8, 1822, to March 3, 1825; unsuccessful candidate for reelection in 1824 to the Nineteenth Congress; member of the Pennsylvania constitutional convention in 1837; appointed by President William Henry Harrison as First Comptroller of the Treasury on April 6, 1841, and served until September 13, 1841, when he was appointed Secretary of the Treasury in the Cabinet of President John Tyler, which position he held until March 1, 1843; resumed the practice of law in Pittsburgh; appointed by President Zachary Taylor Chargé d'Affaires to Denmark and served from November 8, 1849, to October 10, 1851; returned to the United States to serve as president judge of the district court of Allegheny County; died in Pittsburgh, Pa., November 24, 1852; interment in Allegheny Cemetery.

**Bibliography:** *DAB.*

**FOSDICK, Nicoll,** a Representative from New York; born in New London, Conn., November 9, 1785; completed preparatory studies; moved to Norway, N.Y.; presidential elector on the Monroe ticket in 1816; member of the State assembly in 1818 and 1819; elected to the Nineteenth Congress (March 4, 1825-March 3, 1827); returned to New London, Conn., in 1843; collector of customs 1849-1853; engaged in mercantile pursuits; died in New London, Conn., May 7, 1868; interment in Cedar Grove Cemetery.

**FOSS, Eugene Noble** (brother of George Edmund Foss), a Representative from Massachusetts; born in West Berkshire, near St. Albans, Franklin County, Vt., on September 24, 1858; attended the public schools, Franklin County Academy at St. Albans, Vt., and the University of Vermont; settled in Boston, Mass., in 1882; engaged in the manufacture of iron and steel products; elected as a Democrat to the Sixty-first Congress to fill the vacancy caused by the death of William C. Lovering and served from March 22, 1910, until his resignation, effective January 4, 1911, having been elected Governor; elected Governor of Massachusetts in 1910, reelected in 1911 and 1912, and served from January 5, 1911 to January 8, 1914; resumed his former manufacturing pursuits, and managed his large real estate holdings in Boston, Mass.; died in Jamaica Plain (Boston), Mass., September 13, 1939; interment in Forest Hill Cemetery.

**Bibliography:** Sherman, Richard B. "Foss of Massachusetts: Demagogue or Progressive?" *Mid-America* 43 (April 1961): 75-94.

**FOSS, Frank Herbert,** a Representative from Massachusetts; born in Augusta, Kennebec County, Maine, September 20, 1865; attended the public schools, and was graduated from Kent Hill (Maine) Seminary in 1886; moved to Fitchburg, Mass., in 1893; member of a firm engaged as general contractors in the construction of industrial plants, and also interested in banking; member of the Fitchburg city council 1906-1912; water commissioner 1913-1915; mayor of Fitchburg 1917-1920; member of the Massachusetts Republican committee 1915-1946, and served as chairman 1921-1924; delegate to the Massachusetts Republican conventions from 1915 to 1946; elected as a Republican to the Sixty-ninth and to the four succeeding Congresses (March 4, 1925-January 3, 1935); unsuccessful candidate for reelection in 1934 to the Seventy-fourth Congress; resumed management in the contracting business and resided in Fitchburg, Mass., until his death there on February 15, 1947; interment in Forest Hill Cemetery.

**FOSS, George Edmund** (brother of Eugene Noble Foss), a Representative from Illinois; born in West Berkshire, Franklin County, Vt., July 2, 1863; attended the common schools, and was graduated from Harvard University in 1885; attended Columbia Law School and the School of Political Science in New York City; was graduated from Union College of Law at Chicago, Ill., in 1889; was admitted to the bar the same year and commenced the practice of law in Chicago; elected as a Republican to the Fifty-fourth and to the eight succeeding Congresses (March 4, 1895-March 3, 1913); chairman, Committee on Naval Affairs (Fifty-sixth through Sixty-first Congresses); unsuccessful candidate for reelection in 1912; elected to the Sixty-fourth and Sixty-fifth Congresses (March 4, 1915-March 3, 1919); was not a candidate for renomination in 1918, but was an unsuccessful candidate for nomination to the United States Senate; resumed the practice of law; unsuccessful candidate for nomination in 1932 to the Seventy-third Congress; died in Chicago, Ill., March 15, 1936; interment in Graceland Cemetery.

**FOSTER, A. Lawrence,** a Representative from New York; attended the public schools; studied law in Vernon; was admitted to the bar and commenced practice in Morrisville about 1827; elected as a Whig to the Twenty-seventh Congress (March 4, 1841-March 3, 1843); chairman, Committee on Expenditures in the Department of the Treasury (Twenty-seventh Congress); settled permanently in Virginia.

**FOSTER, Abiel,** a Delegate and a Representative from New Hampshire; born in Andover, Mass., August 8, 1735; was graduated from Harvard College in 1756; studied theology; was ordained and installed as pastor in Canterbury, N.H., in 1761 and served until 1779; deputy to the Provincial Congress at Exeter in 1775; Member of the Continental Congress 1783-1785; judge of the court of common pleas of Rockingham County 1784-1788; elected to the First Congress (March 4, 1789-March 3, 1791); member of the State senate 1791-1794, and served as its president in 1793; elected as a Federalist to the Fourth and to the three succeeding Congresses (March 4, 1795-March 3, 1803); died in Canterbury, N.H., February 6, 1806; interment in Center Cemetery.

**Bibliography:** *DAB.*

**FOSTER, Addison Gardner,** a Senator from Washington; born in Belchertown, Hampshire County, Mass., January 28, 1837; moved to Oswego, Kendall County, Ill., and attended the common schools; moved to Wabasha County, Minn., and engaged in the grain and real estate business; auditor and surveyor of Wabasha County; moved to St. Paul, Minn., in 1873 and engaged in the lumber business; moved to Tacoma, Wash., in 1888 and continued in the lumber business; also engaged in coal mine operations and railroad construction; elected as a Republican to the United States Senate and served from March 4, 1899, to March 3, 1905; was not a candidate for reelection; chairman, Committee on Coast and Insular Survey (Fifty-sixth and Fifty-seventh Congresses), Committee on Geological Survey (Fifty-eighth Congress); resumed the lumber business at Tacoma, Wash.; retired from active business pursuits in 1914 and resided in Tacoma until his death January 16, 1917; interment in Tacoma Cemetery.

**FOSTER, Charles,** a Representative from Ohio; born near Tiffin, Seneca County, Ohio, April 12, 1828; moved with his father to Rome, now the city of Fostoria, Seneca County, Ohio; attended the common schools until he was twelve years old; engaged in the dry goods business and later banking; elected as a Republican to the Forty-second and to the three succeeding Congresses (March 4, 1871-March 3, 1879); unsuccessful candidate for reelection in 1878 to the Forty-sixth Congress; elected Governor of Ohio in 1879, reelected in 1881, and served from January 12, 1880 to January 14, 1884; unsuccessful candidate for election in 1890 to the Fifty-second Congress; Secretary of the Treasury in the Cabinet of President Benjamin Harrison from February 25, 1891 to March 3, 1893; resumed his former business pursuits; died in Springfield, Ohio, January 9, 1904; interment in Fountain Cemetery, Fostoria, Ohio.

**Bibliography:** *DAB.*

**FOSTER, David Johnson,** a Representative from Vermont; born in Barnet, Caledonia County, Vt., June 27, 1857; attended the public schools of his native city and was graduated from the St. Johnsbury (Vt.) Academy in 1876 and from Dartmouth College, Hanover, N.H., in 1880; studied law; was admitted to the bar in 1883 and commenced practice in Burlington, Vt.; prosecuting attorney of Chittenden County 1886-1890; member of the State senate 1892-1894; commissioner of State taxes 1894-1898; chairman of the board of railroad commissioners 1898-1900; chairman of the commission representing the United States at the first Centennial of the Independence of Mexico at Mexico City in 1910; chairman of the United States delegation to the general assembly of the International Institute of Agriculture at Rome in May 1911; elected as a Republican to the Fifty-seventh and to the five succeeding Congresses and served from March 4, 1901, until his death in Washington, D.C., March 21, 1912; chairman, Committee on Expenditures in the Department of Commerce and Labor (Fifty-ninth through Sixty-first Congresses), Committee on Foreign Affairs (Sixty-first Congress); interment in Lakeview Cemetery, Burlington, Vt.

**FOSTER, Dwight** (brother of Theodore Foster), a Representative and a Senator from Massachusetts; born in Brookfield, Worcester County, Mass., December 7, 1757; completed preparatory studies and graduated from Brown University, Providence, R.I., in 1774; studied law; was admitted to the bar in 1778 and commenced practice in Providence, R.I.; justice of the peace for Worcester County 1781-1823; special justice of the court of common pleas 1792; sheriff of Worcester County 1792; member, Massachusetts house of representatives 1791-1792; elected to the Third and to the three succeeding Congresses and served from March 4, 1793, to June 6, 1800, when he resigned; chairman, Committee on Claims (Fourth through Sixth Congresses); delegate to the Massachusetts constitutional convention in 1799; elected to the United States Senate as a Federalist to fill the vacancy caused by the resignation of Samuel Dexter and served from June 6, 1800, to March 2, 1803, when he resigned; chief justice of the court of common pleas 1801-1811; member, Massachusetts house of representatives 1808-1809; member of the Governor's council and held other state and local offices; died in Brookfield, Mass., April 29, 1823; interment in Brookfield Cemetery.

**FOSTER, Ephraim Hubbard,** a Senator from Tennessee; born near Bardstown, Nelson County, Ky., September 17, 1794; moved to Tennessee with his parents, who settled near Nashville, Davidson County, in 1797; completed preparatory studies and graduated from Cumberland College (later the University of Nashville) in 1813; studied law; was admitted to the bar in 1820 and commenced practice in Nashville, Tenn.; served in the Creek War and was private secretary to General Andrew Jackson, 1813-1815; member, Tennessee State house of representatives, 1829-1831, 1835-1837, and served as speaker during that time; appointed as a Whig to the United States Senate to fill the vacancy caused by the resignation of Felix Grundy and served from September 17, 1838, to March 3, 1839; was reelected for the term beginning March 4, 1839, but resigned, not wishing to obey instructions given him by the State legislature; chairman, Committee on Claims (Twenty-eighth Congress); elected to the United States Senate to fill the vacancy caused by the death of his successor, Felix Grundy, and served from October 17, 1843, to March 3, 1845; unsuccessful Whig candidate for Governor in 1845; resumed the practice of law; died in Nashville, Tenn., September 6, 1854; interment in the City Cemetery.

**Bibliography:** *DAB.*

**FOSTER, George Peter,** a Representative from Illinois; born in Dover, Morris County, N.J., April 3, 1858; moved to Chicago in 1867; attended the public schools and the University of Chicago; was graduated from Union College of Law at Chicago in 1882; was admitted to the bar the same year and commenced practice in Chicago, Ill.; justice of the peace for the town of South Chicago 1891-1899; acting police magistrate of the principal police court of the city 1893-1899; elected as a Democrat to the Fifty-sixth, Fifty-seventh, and Fifty-eighth Congresses (March 4, 1899-March 3, 1905); unsuccessful candidate for reelection in 1904; resumed the practice of law; assistant corporation counsel of Chicago, Ill., 1912-1922; retired from active pursuits in 1928 and moved to Wheaton, Ill., where he died November 11, 1928; interment in Calvary Cemetery, Chicago, Ill.

**FOSTER, Henry Allen,** a Representative and a Senator from New York; born in Hartford, Conn., May 7, 1800; moved to Cazenovia, N.Y., when a boy; attended the common schools; studied law; was admitted to the bar in 1822 and commenced practice in Oneida County, N.Y.; surrogate to Oneida County 1827-1831, 1835-1839; supervisor of the town of Rome N.Y., 1829-1830, 1833-1834; member, State senate 1831-1834; elected as a Democrat to the Twenty-fifth Congress (March 4, 1837-March 3, 1839); resumed the practice of law in Rome; appointed as a Democrat to the United States Senate to fill the vacancy caused by the resignation of Silas Wright, Jr., and served from November 30, 1844, to January 27, 1845, when a successor was elected and qualified; judge of the supreme court for the fifth district 1864-1872; president of the board of trustees of Hamilton College; vice president of the American Colonization Society; died in Rome, N.Y., May 11, 1889; interment in Rome Cemetery.

**FOSTER, Henry Donnel** (cousin of John Cabell Breckinridge), a Representative from Pennsylvania; born in Mercer, Pa., December 19, 1808; pursued classical studies; was graduated from the College of Meadville; studied law; was admitted to the bar in 1829 and commenced practice in Greensburg, Pa.; elected as a Democrat to the Twenty-eighth and Twenty-ninth Congresses (March 4, 1843-March 3, 1847); member of the Pennsylvania house of representatives in 1857 and 1858; unsuccessful candidate for election in 1858 to the Thirty-sixth Congress; unsuccessful candidate for Governor in 1860; unsuccessfully contested the election of John Covode to the Forty-first Congress; elected to the Forty-second Congress (March 4, 1871-March 3, 1873); unsuccessful candidate for reelection in 1872 to the Forty-third Congress; resumed the practice of law in Greensburg, Pa.; moved to Irwin, Westmoreland County, Pa., in 1879 and died there October 16, 1880; interment in St. Clair Cemetery, Greensburg, Pa.

**FOSTER, Israel Moore,** a Representative from Ohio; born in Athens, Athens County, Ohio, January 12, 1873; attended the public schools, and was graduated from the Ohio University at Athens in 1895; studied law at the Harvard Law School in 1895 and 1896; was graduated from the Ohio State Law School in 1898 and commenced practice the same year in Athens, Ohio; prosecuting attorney of Athens County 1902-1910; member and secretary of the board of trustees of the Ohio University twenty-four years; secretary of the Republican State central committee in 1912; elected as a Republican to the Sixty-sixth, Sixty-seventh, and Sixty-eighth Congresses (March 4, 1919-March 3, 1925); unsuccessful candidate for renomination in 1924; appointed a commissioner of the court of claims April 1, 1925, and served until April 1, 1942, when he retired; died in Washington, D.C., June 10, 1950; interment in Rock Creek Cemetery.

**FOSTER, John Hopkins,** a Representative from Indiana; born in Evansville, Vanderburg County, Ind., January 31, 1862; attended the common schools of his native city and was graduated from Indiana University at Bloomington in 1882 and from the law department of Columbian University (now George Washington University), Washington, D.C., in 1884; was admitted to the bar in 1885 and commenced the practice of his profession in Evansville, Ind.; member of the State house of representatives in 1893; judge of the superior court of Vanderburg County 1896-1905; elected as a Republican to the Fifty-ninth Congress to fill the vacancy caused by the resignation of James A. Hemenway; reelected to the Sixtieth Congress and served from May 16, 1905, to March 3, 1909; unsuccessful candidate for reelection in 1908 to the Sixty-first Congress; resumed the practice of law in Evansville, Ind., where he died September 5, 1917; interment in Oak Hill Cemetery.

**FOSTER, Lafayette Sabine,** a Senator from Connecticut; born in Franklin, New London County, Conn., November 22, 1806; attended the common schools; received preparatory instruction and graduated from Brown University, Providence, R.I., in 1828; taught school in Providence and commenced the study of law in Norwich; took charge of an academy at Centerville, Md., and while there was admitted to the Maryland bar in 1830; returned to Norwich, Conn., and completed his law studies; was admitted to the bar in 1831 and commenced the practice of law; editor of the Republican, a Whig newspaper; member, State house of representatives, 1839-1840, 1846-1848, 1854, and served three years as speaker of the house; unsuccessful Whig candidate for Governor of Connecticut in 1850, and again in 1851; mayor of Norwich, 1851-1852; elected in 1854 as a Republican to the United States Senate; reelected in 1860, and served from March 4, 1855 to March 3, 1867; unsuccessful candidate for reelection; served as President pro tempore of the Senate during the Thirty-ninth Congress; chairman, Committee on Pensions (Thirty-seventh through Thirty-ninth Congresses); professor of law in Yale College in 1869; member of the Connecticut State house of representatives in 1870, and was elected speaker, but resigned to accept a judicial position; associate justice of the Connecticut supreme court from 1870 to 1876, when he retired; unsuccessful Democratic candidate for election in 1874 to the Forty-fourth Congress; died in Norwich, Conn., September 19, 1880; interment in Yantic Cemetery.

**Bibliography:** *DAB*; Campbell, W.H.W. *Memorial Sketch of Lafayette S. Foster, Senator From Connecticut.* Boston: Franklin Press, 1881.

**FOSTER, Martin David,** a Representative from Illinois; born near West Salem, Edwards County, Ill., September 3, 1861; attended the public schools and Eureka (Ill.) College; was graduated from the Eclectic Medical Institute, Cincinnati, Ohio, in 1882 and from the Hahnemann Medical College, Chicago, Ill., in 1884; commenced the practice of medicine in Olney, Richland County, Ill., in 1884; served as a member of a board of United States examining surgeons in 1885-1889, and again from 1893 to 1897; mayor of Olney, Ill., in 1895 and 1902; elected as a Democrat to the Sixtieth and to the five succeeding Congresses (March 4, 1907-March 3, 1919); chairman, Committee on Mines and Mining (Sixty-second through Sixty-fifth Congresses); unsuccessful candidate for reelection in 1918; engaged in the practice of medicine until his death in Olney, Ill., October 20, 1919; interment in Haven Hill Cemetery.

**FOSTER, Murphy James,** a Senator from Louisiana; born in Franklin, St. Mary Parish, La., January 12, 1849; attended a preparatory school at Whites Creek, near Nashville, Tenn., and the Washington and Lee University, Lexington, Va., 1867-1868; graduated from Cumberland University, Lebanon, Tenn., in 1870, and from the law school of the University of Louisiana (now Tulane University) at New Orleans in 1871; was admitted to the bar in 1871 and commenced practice in Franklin, La.; elected in 1876 to the state legislature, but was prevented from taking his seat; member of the Louisiana State senate from 1879 until 1895, and served as president pro tempore 1888-1890; elected Governor of Louisiana in 1892, reelected in 1896, and served from May 10, 1892 to May 8, 1900; elected as a Democrat to the United States Senate in 1901; reelected in 1907 and served from March 4, 1901, to March 3, 1913; chairman, Committee on Transportation and Sale of Meat Products (Sixty-first and Sixty-second Congresses); appointed by President

Woodrow Wilson in 1914 as collector of the port of New Orleans, and served until 1921; died at Dixie plantation, near Franklin, La., on June 12, 1921; interment in Franklin Cemetery.

**Bibliography:** *DAB.*

**FOSTER, Nathaniel Greene,** a Representative from Georgia; born near Madison, Greene (now Morgan) County, Ga., on August 25, 1809; attended private schools, and was graduated from the University of Georgia at Athens in 1830; studied law; was admitted to the bar in 1831 and commenced practice in Madison, Ga.; captain of a company in the Seminole War; elected solicitor general of the Ocmulgee circuit and served from March 3, 1838, to October 3, 1840, when he resigned; member of the State house of representatives in 1840; served in the State senate 1841-1843 and again in 1851 and 1852; elected as a candidate of the American Party to the Thirty-fourth Congress (March 4, 1855-March 3, 1857); affiliated with the Democratic Party; pastor of the Baptist Church at Madison 1855-1869; elected judge of the Ocmulgee circuit and served from September 30, 1867, until his resignation in 1868 on account of ill health; died in Madison, Ga., October 19, 1869; interment in Madison Cemetery.

**FOSTER, Stephen Clark,** a Representative from Maine; born in Machias, Maine, December 24, 1799; attended the common schools; learned the blacksmith's trade and subsequently became a shipbuilder; member of the Maine State house of representatives, 1834-1837; member of the State senate in 1840, and served as president; again elected to the State house of representatives in 1847; elected as a Republican to the Thirty-fifth and Thirty-sixth Congresses (March 4, 1857-March 3, 1861); member of the peace convention of 1861 held in Washington, D.C., in an effort to devise means to prevent the impending war; died in Pembroke, Washington County, Maine, October 5, 1872; interment in Forest Hill Cemetery.

**FOSTER, Theodore** (brother of Dwight Foster), a Senator from Rhode Island; born in Brookfield, Worcester County, Mass., April 29, 1752; pursued classical studies and graduated from Rhode Island College (now Brown University), Providence, R.I., in 1770; studied law; was admitted to the bar about 1771 and commenced practice in Providence, R.I.; town clerk of Providence 1775-1787; member, State house of representatives 1776-1782; appointed judge of the court of admiralty in May 1785; appointed Naval Officer of Customs for the district of Providence, R.I., 1790; appointed to the United States Senate in 1790; elected in 1791 and again in 1797 as a Federalist and served from June 7, 1790, to March 3, 1803; was not a candidate for reelection in 1802; retired from public life and engaged in writing and historical research; member, State house of representatives 1812-1816; trustee of Brown University 1794-1822; died in Providence, R.I., January 13, 1828; interment in Swan Point Cemetery.

**Bibliography:** *DAB.*

**FOSTER, Thomas Flournoy,** a Representative from Georgia; born in Greensboro, Ga., November 23, 1790; pursued preparatory studies, and was graduated from Franklin College in 1812; studied law at the Litchfield (Ga.) Law School; was admitted to the bar in 1816 and commenced practice in Greensboro; member of the Georgia State house of representatives, 1822-1825; elected to the Twenty-first and to the two succeeding Congresses (March 4, 1829-March 3, 1835); chairman, Committee on the Judiciary (Twenty-third Congress); unsuccessful candidate for reelection in 1834 to the Twenty-fourth Congress; member of the State convention from Greene County in 1833 to reduce membership of the general assembly; moved to Columbus, Muscogee County, Ga., in 1835 and continued the practice of his profession; delegate to a convention at Tuscaloosa, Ala., in the interest of General William Henry Harrison's candidacy for President of the United States; elected as a Whig to the Twenty-seventh Congress (March 4, 1841-March 3,

1843); died in Columbus, Ga., September 14, 1848; interment in Linwood Cemetery.

**FOSTER, Wilder De Ayr,** a Representative from Michigan; born in Orange County, N.Y., January 8, 1819; attended the common schools of his native county; moved to Michigan in 1837, and engaged in the hardware business at Grand Rapids in 1845; city treasurer and member of the board of aldermen; mayor of Grand Rapids in 1854; member of the State senate in 1855 and 1856; again elected mayor of Grand Rapids and served in 1865 and 1866; elected as a Republican to the Forty-second Congress to fill the vacancy caused by the resignation of Thomas White Ferry; reelected to the Forty-third Congress and served from December 4, 1871, until his death in Grand Rapids, Mich., September 20, 1873; interment in Fulton Street Cemetery.

**FOUKE, Philip Bond,** a Representative from Illinois; born in Kaskaskia, Ill., January 23, 1818; attended the public schools and became a civil engineer; established and published the Belleville Advocate in 1841; studied law; was admitted to the bar in 1845 and commenced practice in Belleville; prosecuting attorney for the Kaskaskia district (second circuit) 1846-1850; member of the State house of representatives in 1851; unsuccessfully contested the election of Lyman Trumbull to the Thirty-fourth Congress; elected as a Democrat to the Thirty-sixth and Thirty-seventh Congresses (March 4, 1859-March 3, 1863); was not a candidate for renomination in 1862 to the Thirty-eighth Congress; during the Civil War served as colonel of the Thirtieth Regiment, Illinois Volunteer Infantry, and was wounded at the Battle of Belmont, Mo., November 7, 1861; engaged in the practice of law in Washington, D.C., and died there on October 3, 1876; interment in Congressional Cemetery.

**FOULKES, George Ernest,** a Representative from Michigan; born in Chicago, Ill., December 25, 1878; attended the public schools of Chicago; was graduated from the law department of Lake Forest University, Chicago, Ill., in 1900; was admitted to the bar the same year and commenced practice in the United States Treasury Department; special agent of the United States Treasury Department in charge of field service at New York City, El Paso, Tex., St. Paul, Minn., and Minneapolis, Minn., 1900-1919; moved to Hartford, Mich., in 1920 and engaged in agricultural pursuits; delegate to the Democratic State conventions in 1924, 1926, and 1928; elected as a Democrat to the Seventy-third Congress (March 4, 1933-January 3, 1935); nominated for Governor by the Farmer-Labor Party in 1934, but declined; unsuccessful candidate for reelection in 1934 to the Seventy-fourth Congress; resumed agricultural pursuits; also engaged as an author and in farm-organization work; died in Hartford, Mich., December 13, 1960; interment in Hartford Cemetery.

**FOULKROD, William Walker,** a Representative from Pennsylvania; born in the Frankford district of east Philadelphia, Pa., November 22, 1846; attended public and private schools in Philadelphia; engaged in the wholesale dry-goods business and the manufacture of hosiery; president of the Philadelphia Trades League; interested in plans for the improvement of the Delaware River and Channel; elected as a Republican to the Sixtieth and Sixty-first Congresses and served from March 4, 1907, until his death; unsuccessful candidate for reelection in 1910; died in Frankford, Philadelphia, Pa., November 13, 1910; interment in Cedar Hill Cemetery.

**FOUNTAIN, Lawrence H.,** a Representative from North Carolina; born in Leggett, Edgecombe County, N.C., April 23, 1913; attended the Edgecombe public schools; A.B., University of North Carolina at Chapel Hill, 1934 and from the law school of the same university, J.D., 1936; was admitted to the bar in 1936 and practiced law in Tarboro, N.C.; eastern organizer, Young Democratic Clubs of North Carolina; chairman, Second Congressional District Executive

Committee; reading clerk in the North Carolina State senate, 1936-1941; enlisted as a private in the United States Army on March 4, 1942; was promoted through the ranks and released from service as a major from the Judge Advocate General's Office on March 4, 1946; lieutenant colonel (ret.), United States Army Reserve; member of the North Carolina State senate, 1947-1952; member, Advisory Commission on Intergovernmental Relations, 1959-1982, and Presidential Advisory Committee on Federalism, 1981-1982; appointed by President Lyndon B. Johnson as a United States delegate to the Twenty-second session of the United Nations General Assembly, 1967; elected as a Democrat to the Eighty-third and to the fourteen succeeding Congresses (January 3, 1953-January 3, 1983); was not a candidate for reelection in 1982 to the Ninety-eighth Congress; is a resident of Tarboro, N.C.

**FOWLER, Charles Newell,** a Representative from New Jersey; born in Lena, Stephenson County, Ill., November 2, 1852; attended the public schools in Lena, Ill., and Beloit College, Beloit, Wis.; was graduated from Yale College in 1876 and from Chicago Law School in 1878; was admitted to the bar in 1878 and commenced the practice of law in Beloit, Kans.; moved to Cranford, N.J., in 1883 and to Elizabeth in 1891 and engaged in banking, serving as president of a mortgage company; elected as a Republican to the Fifty-fourth and to the seven succeeding Congresses (March 4, 1895-March 3, 1911); chairman, Committee on Banking and Currency (Fifty-seventh through Sixtieth Congresses); unsuccessful candidate for nomination for election to the United States Senate in 1910; member of the Republican State committee 1898-1907; resumed banking activities at Elizabeth, N.J.; also engaged in literary pursuits and operated a group of marble quarries in Vermont; in 1930 moved to Orange, N.J., where he died May 27, 1932; interment in Fairview Cemetery, Westfield, N.J.

**FOWLER, Hiram Robert,** a Representative from Illinois; born near Eddyville, Pope County, Ill., February 7, 1851; attended the public schools of his native city, and was graduated from the Illinois Normal University at Normal in 1880; studied law at the University of Michigan at Ann Arbor and was graduated in 1884; was admitted to the bar in 1884 and commenced the practice of his profession in Elizabethtown, Ill.; State's attorney of Hardin County 1888-1892; served in the State house of representatives 1893-1895; member of the State senate 1900-1904; elected as a Democrat to the Sixty-second and Sixty-third Congresses (March 4, 1911-March 3, 1915); unsuccessful candidate for reelection in 1914 to the Sixty-fourth Congress; resumed the practice of law in Elizabethtown, Ill.; moved to Harrisburg, Ill., in 1915 and continued practice until his death on January 5, 1926; interment in Sunset Hill Cemetery.

**FOWLER, John,** a Representative from Kentucky; born in Virginia in 1755; attended the common schools; served as a captain in the Revolutionary War; member of the convention held in Danville, Fayette County, Va. (now Kentucky), in 1787; served in the Virginia house of delegates in 1787; member of the Virginia convention which ratified the Constitution; moved to Lexington, Ky.; elected as a Republican to the Fifth and to the four succeeding Congresses (March 4, 1797-March 3, 1807); postmaster of Lexington from 1814 until 1822; died in Lexington, Fayette County, Ky., August 22, 1840; interment in the Old Episcopal Cemetery.

**Bibliography:** Fowler, Ila E. *Captain John Fowler of Virginia and Kentucky: Patriot, Soldier, Pioneer, Statesman, Land Baron and Civic Leader.* Cynthiana, Ky.: Hobson Press, 1942.

**FOWLER, John Edgar,** a Representative from North Carolina; born in Honeycutt's Township, near Clinton, Sampson County, N.C., September 8, 1866; attended the common schools and Wake Forest (N.C.) College; studied law at the University of North Carolina at Chapel Hill; was admitted to the bar in 1894 and commenced practice in Clinton, N.C.; trustee of State Normal College for Women, Greensboro, N.C., 1895-1903; member of the State senate in 1895 and 1896; elected as a Populist to the Fifty-fifth Congress (March 4, 1897-March 3, 1899); resumed the practice of law in Clinton, N.C.; also engaged in agricultural pursuits; member of the State house of representatives in 1905 and 1906; died in Clinton, N.C., July 4, 1930; interment in Clinton Cemetery.

**FOWLER, Joseph Smith,** a Senator from Tennessee; born in Steubenville, Jefferson County, Ohio, August 31, 1820; attended the common schools and Grove Academy, Steubenville, Ohio; graduated from Franklin College, New Athens, Ohio, in 1843; taught school in Shelby County, Ky., in 1844; professor of mathematics at Franklin College, Davidson County, Tenn., 1845-1849; studied law in Bowling Green, Ky.; was admitted to the bar and practiced in Tennessee until 1861; president of Howard Female College, Gallatin, Tenn., 1856-1861; comptroller of Tennessee 1862-1865; active in the reconstruction of the State government; upon the readmission of the State of Tennessee to representation was elected as a Unionist to the United States Senate and served from July 24, 1866, to March 3, 1871; was not a candidate for reelection; chairman, Committee on Engrossed Bills (Fortieth Congress); engaged in the practice of law in Washington, D.C., until his death there on April 1, 1902; interment in Lexington Cemetery, Lexington, Ky.

**Bibliography:** *DAB*; Durham, Walter. "How Say You, Senator Fowler?" *Tennessee History Quarterly* 42 (Spring 1983): 39-57.

**FOWLER, Orin,** a Representative from Massachusetts; born in Lebanon, Conn., July 29, 1791; pursued classical studies and attended Williams College, Williamstown, Mass.; was graduated from Yale College in 1814; studied theology and pursued extensive missionary work in the Valley of the Mississippi; finally settled as a minister in Plainfield, Conn., in 1820; moved to Fall River, Mass., in 1829, where he was installed as pastor of the Congregational Church in 1831; wrote a history of Fall River in 1841; served in the Massachusetts senate in 1848; elected as a Whig to the Thirty-first and Thirty-second Congresses, and served from March 4, 1849 until his death in Washington, D.C., September 3, 1852; interment in the North Burial Ground, Fall River, Mass.

**Bibliography:** *DAB*.

**FOWLER, Samuel** (grandfather of Samuel Fowler [1851-1919]), a Representative from New Jersey; born in Newburgh, Orange County, N.Y., October 30, 1779; attended the Montgomery Academy; studied medicine at the Pennsylvania Medical College, Philadelphia, Pa., and commenced practice in Hamburg, N.J., in 1800; moved to Franklin, N.J.; member of the State council in 1827; elected as a Jacksonian to the Twenty-third and Twenty-fourth Congresses (March 4, 1833-March 3, 1837); was the discoverer of fowlerite, a rare mineral named in his honor, and of franklinite, named by him; owned and developed the zinc mines at Franklin, Sussex County; owned and conducted the Franklin Furnace Iron Works; was a frequent contributor to numerous scientific publications; died in Franklin, N.J., February 20, 1844; interment in North Church Cemetery, Hardyston Township, near Hamburg, N.J.

**FOWLER, Samuel** (grandson of Samuel Fowler [1779-1844]), a Representative from New Jersey; born in Port Jervis, Orange County, N.Y., March 22, 1851; attended the Newton (N.J.) Academy, Princeton College, and Columbia College Law School in New York City; was admitted to the bar of New York in 1873 and of New Jersey in 1876 and practiced law in Newark and Newton, N.J.; elected as a Democrat to the Fifty-first and Fifty-second Congresses (March 4, 1889-March 3, 1893); chairman, Committee on Merchant Marine and Fisheries (Fifty-second Congress); was not a candidate for reelection to the Fifty-third Congress; resumed the practice of his profession in Ogdensburg, N.J.; died in Newark, N.J., March 17, 1919; interment in North Church Cemetery, Hardyston Township, near Hamburg, N.J.

**FOWLER, Tillie K.,** a Representative from Florida; born in Milledgeville, Baldwin County, Ga., December 23, 1942; A.B., Emory University, Atlanta, Ga., 1964; J.D., Emory University School of Law, 1967; admitted to Georgia bar, 1967; legislative assistant to Representative Robert G. Stephens, Jr. of Georgia, 1967-1970; associate director of legislative affairs, deputy counsel then general counsel, White House Office of Consumer Affairs, 1970-1971; Jacksonville City Council, 1985-1993, president, 1989-1990, finance committee chair, 1990-1991; chair, Florida Endowment for the Humanities, 1989-1991; elected as a Republican to the One Hundred Third and One Hundred Fourth Congresses (January 3, 1993-January 3, 1997); is a resident of Jacksonville, Fla.

**FOWLER, W. Wyche, Jr.,** a Representative and a Senator from Georgia; born in Atlanta, Ga., October 6, 1940; attended the public schools; B.A., Davidson (N.C.) College, 1962; LL.B., Emory University School of Law, 1969; served as a United States Army intelligence officer, 1963-1964; chief of staff for Representative Charles L. Weltner of Georgia, 1965-1966; practicing attorney, 1969-1977; member, Atlanta board of aldermen 1970-1973; president, Atlanta city council, 1974-1977; elected as a Democrat to the Ninety-fifth Congress on April 6, 1977, by special election, to fill the vacancy caused by the resignation of Andrew Young; reelected to the four succeeding Congresses and served from April 6, 1977 to January 3, 1987; was not a candidate in 1986 for reelection to the House of Representatives, but was elected to the United States Senate and served from January 3, 1987 to January 3, 1993; unsuccessful candidate for reelection, November 24, 1992, in a general election runoff; nominated by President William J. Clinton as Ambassador to Saudi Arabia, June 11, 1996, and took the oath of office on August 16, 1996; is a resident of Atlanta, Ga.

**FOX, Andrew Fuller,** a Representative from Mississippi; born in Reform, Pickens County, Ala., April 26, 1849; moved to Calhoun County, Miss., with his parents in 1853; attended private schools, and was graduated from Mansfield (Tex.) College in 1872; studied law in Grenada, Miss.; was admitted to the bar in 1877 and commenced practice in Calhoun and Webster Counties; moved to West Point, Miss., in 1883; delegate to the Democratic National Convention of 1888; member of the State senate from 1891 until 1893, when he resigned to accept the office of United States attorney for the northern district of Mississippi; resigned the latter office on September 1, 1896; elected as a Democrat to the Fifty-fifth and to the two succeeding Congresses (March 4, 1897-March 3, 1903); was not a candidate for renomination in 1902 to the Fifty-eighth Congress; president of the Mississippi State Bar Association in 1911; engaged in the practice of law in West Point, Miss., until 1914, when he retired; died in West Point, Miss., August 29, 1926; interment in West Point Cemetery.

**FOX, John,** a Representative from New York; born in Fredericton, New Brunswick, Canada, June 30, 1835; moved to New York City with his parents in 1840; attended the public schools; engaged in mechanical pursuits; employed as a master block maker in the Brooklyn Navy Yard in 1857; member of the board of aldermen and supervisor of New York City in 1863 and 1864; supervisor of New York County in 1864; elected as a Democrat to the Fortieth and Forty-first Congresses (March 4, 1867-March 3, 1871); declined to be a candidate for renomination in 1870 to the Forty-second Congress; member of the State senate 1874-1878; president of the National Democratic Club 1894-1910; engaged in business as an iron merchant, with residence in New York City, where he died January 17, 1914; interment in Calvary Cemetery.

**FOX, Jon D.,** a Representative from Pennsylvania; born in Abington, Pa., April 22, 1947; graduated Cheltenham High School, Wyncote, Pa., 1965; B.A., Pennsylvania State University, 1969; J.D., Delaware School of Law (now Widener University School of Law), 1975; admitted to Pennsylvania bar, 1976; positions with General

Services Administration; guest lecturer, Presidential Classroom for Young Americans; Assistant District Attorney for Montgomery County, Pa., 1976-1980; Abington Township Board of Commissioners, 1979-1984; member, Pennsylvania house of representatives, 1984-1990; Montgomery County (Pa.) Board of Commissioners, 1991-1994; unsuccessful candidate for election in 1992 to the One Hundred Third Congress; elected as a Republican to the One Hundred Fourth Congress (January 3, 1995-January 3, 1997); is a resident of Elkins Park, Pa.

**FRAHM, Sheila,** a Senator from Kansas; born in Colby, Thomas County, Kans., March 22, 1945; B.S., Fort Hays State University, Hays, Kans., 1967; attended the University of Texas at Austin; member, Kansas State Board of Education, 1985-1988, and was vice chair, 1987-1989; Kansas State senator, District 40, 1988-1995, and served as majority leader from 1992 to 1995; Lieutenant Governor of Kansas, 1995-1996; appointed as a Republican to the United States Senate, May 24, 1996, to fill the vacancy caused by the resignation of Robert J. Dole, and took the oath of office June 11, 1996; unsuccessful candidate for nomination to the United States Senate in an August 1996 special primary for the remainder of the term ending January 3, 1999; is a resident of Colby, Kans.

**FRANCE, Joseph Irvin,** a Senator from Maryland; born in Cameron, Clinton County, Mo., October 11, 1873; attended the common schools and Canandaigua Academy, Canandaigua, N.Y.; graduated from Hamilton College, Clinton, N.Y., in 1895; attended the University of Leipzig, Germany; was graduated from the medical department of Clark University, Worcester, Mass., in 1897; taught natural science, Jacob Tome Institute, Port Deposit, Md., in 1897; resigned to enter the College of Physicians and Surgeons, Baltimore, Md., from which he was graduated in 1903; commenced the practice of medicine in Baltimore in 1903; member, State senate 1906-1908; engaged in finance in 1908; secretary to the medical and chirurgical faculty of Maryland 1916-1917; elected as a Republican to the United States Senate in 1916 and served from March 4, 1917, until March 3, 1923; unsuccessful candidate for reelection in 1922; chairman, Committee on Public Health and National Quarantine (Sixty-fifth Congress); president of the Republic International Corporation; resumed the practice of medicine in Port Deposit, Cecil County, Md.; unsuccessful candidate for election in 1934 to the United States Senate; died in Port Deposit, Md., January 26, 1939; interment in Hopewell Cemetery, near Port Deposit.

**FRANCHOT, Richard,** a Representative from New York; born in Morris, Otsego County, N.Y., June 2, 1816; attended the public schools and the Hartwick and Cherry Valley Academies; studied civil engineering at the Polytechnic Institute, Troy, N.Y.; served for some years as president of the Albany & Susquehanna Railroad Co.; elected as a Republican to the Thirty-seventh Congress (March 4, 1861-March 3, 1863); was not a candidate for renomination in 1862 to the Thirty-eighth Congress; moved to Schenectady, N.Y.; raised the One Hundred and Twenty-first Regiment, New York Volunteer Infantry, and was commissioned colonel August 23, 1862; brevetted brigadier general United States Volunteers March 13, 1865; associated with the Central Pacific Railroad Co.; died in Schenectady, N.Y., November 23, 1875; interment in Vale Cemetery.

**FRANCIS, George Blinn,** a Representative from New York; born in Cranston (now a part of Providence), R.I., August 12, 1883; attended the University School in Providence, R.I.; was graduated from Brown University, Providence, R.I., in 1904 and from the law department of Harvard University in 1907; was admitted to the bar in 1907 and commenced practice in New York City; elected as a Republican to the Sixty-fifth Congress (March 4, 1917-March 3, 1919); was not a candidate for renomination in 1918 to the Sixty-sixth Congress; resumed the practice of law in New York City; was special assistant United States attorney in Minnesota in 1926 and 1927; elected a member of the board of water commissioners of

Tarrytown, N.Y., and served as its president; retired in October 1953 and resided at Delray Beach, Fla.; died May 20, 1967, in Boca Raton, Fla.; interment in Greenwood Cemetery, Brooklyn, N.Y.

**FRANCIS, John Brown** (grandson of John Brown of Rhode Island), a Senator from Rhode Island; born in Philadelphia, Pa., May 31, 1791; attended the common schools of Providence, R.I., and graduated from Brown University, Providence, R.I., in 1808; engaged in mercantile pursuits; attended the Litchfield (Conn.) Law School; was admitted to the bar but never practiced; member, State house of representatives 1821-1829; member of the board of trustees of Brown University 1828-1857; member, State senate 1831, 1842; elected Governor of Rhode Island in 1833, reelected every year from 1834 through 1837, and served from May 1, 1833 to May 2, 1838; unsuccessful candidate for reelection in 1838; chancellor of Brown University 1841-1854; elected as a Whig to the United States Senate to fill the vacancy caused by the resignation of William Sprague and served from January 25, 1844, to March 3, 1845; was not a candidate for reelection; chairman, Committee on Engrossed Bills (Twenty-eighth Congress); member, State senate 1845-1856; retired from public life and engaged in agricultural pursuits until his death at "Spring Green," Warwick, R.I., August 9, 1864; interment in North Burial Ground, Providence, R.I.

Bibliography: *DAB*.

**FRANCIS, William Bates,** a Representative from Ohio; born near Updegraff, Jefferson County, Ohio, October 25, 1860; attended the public schools; studied law; was admitted to the bar in 1889 and commenced practice in Martins Ferry, Belmont County, Ohio; city solicitor in 1897, 1898, and 1900; member of the board of school examiners of Martins Ferry 1903-1908; delegate to the Democratic National Convention in 1904; member of the board of education of Martins Ferry 1908-1914; elected as a Democrat to the Sixty-second and Sixty-third Congresses (March 4, 1911-March 3, 1915); unsuccessful candidate for reelection in 1914 to the Sixty-fourth Congress; resumed the practice of his profession; chairman of the Ohio State Civil Service 1931-1935; supervisor of properties for aid to aged, until his retirement; resided in Martins Ferry and later in St. Clairsville, Ohio, until his death in Wheeling, W.Va., December 5, 1954; interment in Mount Pleasant Cemetery, Mount Pleasant, Ohio.

**FRANK, Augustus** (nephew of William Patterson of New York and George Washington Patterson), a Representative from New York; born in Warsaw, Wyoming County, N.Y., July 17, 1826; attended the common schools; engaged in mercantile pursuits; director and vice president of the Buffalo & New York City Railroad Co.; delegate to the Republican National Convention of 1856; elected as a Republican to the Thirty-sixth and to the two succeeding Congresses (March 4, 1859-March 3, 1865); was not a candidate for renomination in 1864 to the Thirty-ninth Congress; director of the Wyoming County National Bank in 1865; member of the State constitutional convention in 1867 and 1868; one of the managers of the Buffalo State Hospital for the Insane at Buffalo, N.Y., 1870-1882; organized the Bank of Warsaw in 1871 and served as president until his death; director of the Rochester Trust and Safe Deposit Co.; State commissioner for the preservation of public parks; member of the board of directors of the Buffalo, Rochester and Pittsburgh Railroad; delegate at large to the State constitutional convention in 1894; died in New York City on April 29, 1895; interment in Warsaw Cemetery, Warsaw, N.Y.

**FRANK, Barney,** a Representative from Massachusetts; born in Bayonne, Hudson County, N.J., March 31, 1940; attended the public schools, and graduated from Bayonne High School in 1957; A.B., Harvard University, 1962; pursued graduate studies in political science and worked as a teaching fellow in government, Harvard University, 1962-1972; J.D., Harvard University Law School, 1977; admitted to the Massachusetts bar in 1979 but did not practice;

executive assistant to Mayor Kevin White of Boston, 1968-1971; administrative assistant to Representative Michael F. Harrington, 1971-1972; member, Massachusetts legislature, 1973-1980; elected as a Democrat to the Ninety-seventh and to the seven succeeding Congresses (January 3, 1981-January 3, 1997); is a resident of Newton, Mass.

**FRANK, Nathan,** a Representative from Missouri; born in Peoria, Ill., February 23, 1852; attended the public schools of Peoria and St. Louis and Washington University, St. Louis, Mo.; was graduated from Harvard Law School in 1871; was admitted to the bar and commenced practice in St. Louis in 1872; unsuccessfully contested the election of John M. Glover to the Fiftieth Congress in 1886; elected as a Republican to the Fifty-first Congress (March 4, 1889-March 3, 1891); declined to be a candidate for renomination in 1890 to the Fifty-second Congress; founder and owner of the St. Louis Star; delegate to the Republican National Convention of 1896; vice president of the Louisiana Purchase Exposition at St. Louis in 1904; unsuccessful candidate for nomination for United States Senator in 1910, 1916, and 1928; retired from the active practice of law; died at St. Louis, Mo., April 5, 1931; interment in Mount Sinai Cemetery.

**FRANKHAUSER, William Horace,** a Representative from Michigan; born in Wood County, Ohio, March 5, 1863; moved with his parents to Monroe, Mich., in 1875; attended the public schools, Michigan State Normal School at Ypsilanti, and Oberlin College, Ohio; taught school for several years; studied law; was admitted to the bar in 1891 and commenced practice in Hillsdale, Mich.; city attorney and prosecutor of Hillsdale County 1896-1903; elected as a Republican to the Sixty-seventh Congress and served from March 4, 1921, until his death in Battle Creek, Mich., on May 9, 1921; interment in Oak Grove Cemetery, Hillsdale, Mich.

**FRANKLIN, Benjamin** (uncle of Franklin Davenport), a Delegate from Pennsylvania; born in Boston, Mass., January 17, 1706; attended the Boston Grammar School for one year; was instructed in elementary branches by a private tutor; employed in a tallow chandlery for two years; learned the art of printing, and after working at his trade in Boston, Philadelphia, and London established himself in Philadelphia as a printer and publisher; founded the Pennsylvania Gazette in 1728, and in 1732 began the publication of Poor Richard's Almanac; State printer; clerk of the Pennsylvania general assembly, 1736-1750; postmaster of Philadelphia in 1737; a member of the provincial assembly, 1744-1754; a member of several Indian commissions; elected a member of the Royal Society on account of his scientific discoveries; deputy postmaster general of the British North American Colonies, 1753-1774; agent of Pennsylvania in London, 1757-1762, and 1764-1775; Member of the Continental Congress, 1775-1776; signed the Declaration of Independence; president of the Pennsylvania constitutional convention of 1776; sent as a diplomatic commissioner to France by the Continental Congress; appointed Minister to France on September 14, 1778, and served until May 1785; appointed Minister to Sweden, September 28, 1782, and negotiated a treaty with Sweden that was signed in Paris, April 3, 1783; one of the negotiators of the treaty of peace with Great Britain; president of the executive council of Pennsylvania, 1785-1788; president of the trustees of the University of Pennsylvania; delegate to the Federal Convention in 1787; died in Philadelphia, Pa., April 17, 1790; interment in Christ Church Burial Ground.

Bibliography: *DAB*; Franklin, Benjamin. *The Papers of Benjamin Franklin*. 25 vols. Edited by Leonard W. Labaree and William B. Willcox. New Haven: Yale University Press, 1959-; Wright, Esmond. *Franklin of Philadelphia*. Cambridge, Mass.: The Belknap Press of Harvard University Press, 1986.

**FRANKLIN, Benjamin Joseph,** a Representative from Missouri; born in Maysville, Mason County, Ky., in March 1839; attended private schools, and Bethany College, Bethany, Va. (now West Virginia), 1849-1851; taught school; studied law; was admitted to the bar in 1859 and commenced practice in Leavenworth, Kans.; elected to the State senate of Kansas in 1861, but due to the outbreak of the Civil War never served; entered the Confederate Army as a private; was promoted to the rank of captain and served throughout the Civil War; moved to Columbia, Mo., and engaged in agricultural pursuits; moved to Kansas City, Mo., in 1868 and resumed the practice of law; prosecuting attorney for Jackson County, Mo., 1871-1875; elected as a Democrat to the Forty-fourth and Forty-fifth Congresses (March 4, 1875-March 3, 1879); chairman, Committee on Territories (Forty-fifth Congress); was a candidate for renomination in 1878 to the Forty-sixth Congress, but withdrew; again engaged in the practice of law in Kansas City, Mo.; appointed United States consul at Hankow, China, in 1885; returned to the United States in 1890 and settled in Phoenix, Ariz., and engaged in the practice of law; appointed Governor of the Territory of Arizona and served from April 18, 1896, to July 29, 1897; died in Phoenix, Ariz., May 18, 1898; interment in Rosedale Cemetery.

**FRANKLIN, Jesse** (brother of Meshack Franklin), a Representative and a Senator from North Carolina; born in Orange County, Va., March 24, 1760; moved to North Carolina 1774; served as major during the Revolutionary War; member, State house of commons 1793-1794, 1797-1798; member, State senate 1805-1806; elected to the Fourth Congress (March 4, 1795-March 3, 1797); elected as a Republican to the United States Senate and served from March 4, 1799, until March 3, 1805; served as President pro tempore of the Senate during the Eighth Congress; again elected as a Republican to the United States Senate in 1806 and served from March 4, 1807, until March 3, 1813; was not a candidate for reelection; appointed a commissioner to treat with the Chickasaw Indians in 1817; Governor of North Carolina from December 7, 1820 until December 7, 1821; died in Surry County, N.C., August 31, 1823; interment in the old National Park at Guilford battleground, near Greensboro, N.C.

Bibliography: *DAB.*

**FRANKLIN, John Rankin,** a Representative from Maryland; born near Berlin, Worcester County, Md., May 6, 1820; pursued classical studies, and was graduated from Jefferson College in 1836; studied law; was admitted to the bar in 1841 and commenced practice in Snow Hill, Md.; member of the State house of delegates 1840-1843, and served as speaker one term; president of the State board of public works in 1851; elected as a Whig to the Thirty-third Congress (March 4, 1853-March 3, 1855); again a member of the State house of delegates in 1859; judge of the first judicial circuit of Maryland from 1867 until his death in Snow Hill, Worcester County, Md., January 11, 1878; interment in the churchyard of Makemie Memorial Presbyterian Church.

**FRANKLIN, Meshack** (brother of Jesse Franklin), a Representative from North Carolina; born in Surry County, N.C., in 1772; member of the State house of commons in 1800 and 1801; served in the State senate in 1828, 1829, and 1838; elected as a Republican to the Tenth and to the three succeeding Congresses (March 4, 1807-March 3, 1815); died in Surry County, N.C., December 18, 1839.

**FRANKLIN, William Webster,** a Representative from Mississippi; born in Greenwood, Leflore County, Miss., December 13, 1941; attended public schools; B.A., Mississippi State University, Starkville, 1963; J.D., University of Mississippi, Oxford, 1966; admitted to bar; served in the United States Army, Judge Advocate General's Corps, 1966-1970; Master Parachutist, Army Commendation Medal; engaged in the private practice of law, Greenwood, 1970-1972; assistant district attorney, Fourth District, Mississippi;

1972-1978; circuit judge, Fourth District, Mississippi, 1978-1982; elected as a Republican to the Ninety-eighth and Ninety-ninth Congresses (January 3, 1983-January 3, 1987); unsuccessful candidate for reelection in 1986 to the One Hundredth Congress; resumed the practice of law; is a resident of Greenwood, Miss.

**FRANKS, Gary Alvin,** a Representative from Connecticut; born in Waterbury, New Haven County, Conn., February 9, 1953; graduated, Sacred Heart High School, Waterbury; B.A., Yale University, 1975; real estate businessman; City of Waterbury alderman, 1986-1990; unsuccessful candidate in 1986 for Connecticut State comptroller; elected as a Republican to the One Hundred Second and to the two succeeding Congresses (January 3, 1991-January 3, 1997); is a resident of Waterbury, Conn.

**FRANKS, Robert Douglas,** a Representative from New Jersey; born in Hackensack, Bergen County, N.J., September 21, 1951; B.A., DePauw University, Greencastle, Ind., 1973; J.D., Southern Methodist University, Dallas, 1976; member, New Jersey general assembly, 1979-1993; Republican State chairman, 1988, 1989 and 1990; campaign manager, Representative James A. Courter; and Representative Dean A. Gallo; elected as a Republican to the One Hundred Third and One Hundred Fourth Congresses (January 3, 1993-January 3, 1997); is a resident of New Providence, N.J.

**FRASER, Donald MacKay,** a Representative from Minnesota; born in Minneapolis, Hennepin County, Minn., February 20, 1924; educated in the public schools; B.A., University of Minnesota, Minneapolis, 1944 while in the Naval Reserve Officer Training Corps; served in the Pacific Theater as a radar officer, 1944-1946; LL.B., University of Minnesota, 1948; was admitted to the bar in 1948 and began the practice of law in Minneapolis, Minn.; member of the Minnesota State senate, 1954-1962; elected as a Democratic Farmer-Labor candidate to the Eighty-eighth and to the seven succeeding Congresses (January 3, 1963-January 3, 1979); was not a candidate in 1978 for reelection to the House of Representatives, but was an unsuccessful candidate for nomination to the United States Senate; elected mayor of Minneapolis in 1979 for the two-year term commencing in January 1980; reelected to a four-year term in 1981, 1985 and 1989; adjunct professor of law and public affairs, University of Minnesota; is a resident of Minneapolis, Minn.

**FRAZER, Victor O.,** a Delegate from the Territory of the Virgin Islands; born in St. Thomas, V.I., May 24, 1943; graduated, Charlotte Amalie High School, St. Thomas, 1960; B.A., Fisk University, Nashville, Tenn., 1964; J.D., Howard University School of Law, Washington, D.C., 1971; banker, Manufacturers Hanover Trust Co., New York City, and Security Trust Co., Rochester, N.Y., 1964-1968; attorney, Neighborhood Legal Services Program, Washington, D.C., and Virgin Islands; attorney, Interstate Commerce Commission, Patent Office, Office of the City Attorney, all in Washington, D.C.; administrative assistant and counsel to Representative Mervyn M. Dymally of California, Subcommittee on Judiciary and Education, Committee on the District of Columbia, and to Representative John Conyers, Jr., of Michigan; unsuccessful candidate for election in 1992 to the One Hundred Third Congress; elected as an Independent a Delegate to the One Hundred Fourth Congress (January 3, 1995-January 3, 1997); is a resident of St. Thomas, V.I.

**FRAZIER, James Beriah** (father of James Beriah Frazier, Jr.), a Senator from Tennessee; born in Pikeville, Bledsoe County, Tenn., October 18, 1856; attended the common schools and Franklin College near Nashville, Tenn.; graduated from the University of Tennessee at Knoxville in 1878; read law in Nashville, Tenn., was admitted to the bar in 1881, and commenced practice in Chattanooga, Tenn.; elected Governor of Tennessee in 1902, reelected in 1904, and served from January 19, 1903 until his resignation March 21, 1905, having been elected Senator; elected as a Democrat to the

United States Senate to fill the vacancy caused by the death of William B. Bate and served from March 21, 1905, to March 3, 1911; unsuccessful candidate for reelection in 1910; resumed the practice of law; died in Chattanooga, Tenn., March 28, 1937; interment in Forest Hill Cemetery.

**FRAZIER, James Beriah, Jr.** (son of James Beriah Frazier), a Representative from Tennessee; born in Chattanooga, Hamilton County, Tenn., June 23, 1890; educated in the public schools and Baylor Preparatory School in Chattanooga, Tenn., and the University of Virginia at Charlottesville; was graduated from Chattanooga College of Law in 1914; was admitted to the bar in 1914 and commenced the practice of law in Chattanooga, Tenn.; during the First World War volunteered for service on April 21, 1917, and was discharged as a major in March 1919; appointed United States attorney for the eastern district of Tennessee on September 25, 1933, and served until his resignation on April 12, 1948; elected as a Democrat to the Eighty-first and to the six succeeding Congresses (January 3, 1949-January 3, 1963); unsuccessful candidate for renomination in 1962 to the Eighty-eighth Congress; resumed the practice of law in Chattanooga, Tenn., where he died October 30, 1978; interment in Forest Hills Cemetery.

**FRAZIER, Lynn Joseph,** a Senator from North Dakota; born near Medford, Steele County, Minn., December 21, 1874; moved to Dakota Territory (now North Dakota) in 1881 with his parents, who homesteaded in Pembina County; attended the country schools; graduated from Mayville State Normal School, North Dakota, in 1895, and from the University of North Dakota at Grand Forks in 1901; engaged in agricultural pursuits; elected Governor of North Dakota in 1916, reelected in 1918 and 1920, and served from January 3, 1917 until his removal on November 23, 1921, after having been defeated in a recall election held October 28, 1921; elected as a Republican to the United States Senate in 1922; reelected in 1928 and in 1934 and served from March 4, 1923, to January 3, 1941; unsuccessful candidate for renomination in 1940; chairman, Committee on Indian Affairs (Seventieth through Seventy-second Congresses); resumed his agricultural pursuits; died in Riverdale, Md., January 11, 1947; interment in Park Cemetery, Hoople, N.Dak.

Bibliography: *DAB*; Briley, Ronald. "Lynn J. Frazier and Progress Indian Reform: A Plodder in the Ranks of a Ragged Regiment." *South Dakota History* 7 (Fall 1977): 438-54; Erickson, Nels. *The Gentleman from North Dakota: Lynn J. Frazier*. Bismarck: State Historical Society of North Dakota, North Dakota Heritage Center, 1986.

**FREAR, James Archibald,** a Representative from Wisconsin; born in Hudson, St. Croix County, Wis., October 24, 1861; attended the public schools, and Laurence University, Appleton, Wis., in 1878; moved with his parents to Washington, D.C., in 1879; served in the Signal Service, United States Army, 1879-1884; was graduated from the National Law University, Washington, D.C., in 1884; was admitted to the bar the same year and commenced practice in Hudson, Wis.; city attorney of Hudson in 1894 and 1895; served eleven years with the Wisconsin National Guard, retiring with the rank of colonel and judge advocate; district attorney of St. Croix County, 1896-1901; member of the State assembly in 1903; served in the State senate in 1905; secretary of state of Wisconsin, 1907-1913; elected as a Republican to the Sixty-third and to the ten succeeding Congresses (March 4, 1913-January 3, 1935); was not a candidate for renomination in 1934 to the Seventy-fourth Congress; resumed the practice of law in Washington, D.C., where he died on May 28, 1939; interment in Arlington National Cemetery, Va.

**FREAR, Joseph Allen, Jr.,** a Senator from Delaware; born on a farm near Rising Sun, Kent County, Del., March 7, 1903; attended the public schools of Dover, Del., and graduated from Caesar Rodney High School; graduated from the University of Delaware in 1924; president and owner of a retail business in Dover, Del.; banker; commissioner of Delaware State College, 1936-1941, and the Delaware Old Age Welfare Commission, 1938-1948; director, Federal Land Bank Board, Baltimore, Md., 1938-1947, and served as chairman of the board the last two years; president of Kent General Hospital, Dover, Del., 1947-1951; during the Second World War served in the United States Army as a major, 1944-1946; elected as a Democrat to the United States Senate in 1948; reelected in 1954 and served from January 3, 1949, to January 3, 1961; unsuccessful candidate for reelection in 1960; appointed to the Securities and Exchange Commission, 1961-1963; resumed his former business and banking pursuits; was a resident of Dover, Del.; died January 15, 1993.

**FREDERICK, Benjamin Todd,** a Representative from Iowa; born in Fredericktown, Columbiana County, Ohio, October 5, 1834; attended the district schools; completed preparatory studies; engaged in the foundry and machine business Marshalltown, Iowa, 1865-1888; went to Marysville, Calif., in 1857 and engaged in placer mining; returned to Marshalltown, Iowa, in 1859; member of the city council of Marshalltown 1874-1877; member of the school board three terms; successfully contested as a Democrat the election of James Wilson to the Forty-eighth Congress and took his seat the last day of that Congress, March 3, 1885; reelected to the Forty-ninth Congress (March 4, 1885-March 3, 1887); was not a candidate for renomination in 1886; moved to San Diego, Calif., in 1887 and engaged in the real estate business; collector of internal revenue 1893-1902; died in San Diego, Calif., November 3, 1903; interment in Mount Hope Cemetery.

**FREDERICKS, John Donnan,** a Representative from California; born in Burgettstown, Washington County, Pa., September 10, 1869; attended the public schools and Washington and Jefferson College, Washington, Pa.; studied law; was admitted to the bar in 1896 and commenced practice in Los Angeles, Calif.; served as an adjutant in the Seventh Regiment, California Volunteer Infantry, during the Spanish-American War in 1898; district attorney of Los Angeles County from 1903 until 1915; unsuccessful Republican candidate in 1914 for election for Governor of California; elected as a Republican to the Sixty-eighth Congress to fill the vacancy caused by the death of Henry Z. Osborne; reelected to the Sixty-ninth Congress and served from May 1, 1923, to March 3, 1927; was not a candidate for renomination in 1926 to the Seventieth Congress; resumed the practice of law in Los Angeles, where he died on August 26, 1945; interment in Forest Lawn Memorial Park.

**FREE, Arthur Monroe,** a Representative from California; born in San Jose, Calif., January 15, 1879; attended the public schools of Santa Clara and the University of the Pacific, Stockton, Calif.; was graduated from Stanford University, Palo Alto, Calif., in 1901, and from its law department in 1903; was admitted to the bar in 1903 and commenced practice in San Jose; moved to Mountain View, Calif., and served as city attorney from 1904 until 1910; district attorney of Santa Clara County, 1907-1919; voluntarily retired and resumed the practice of law at San Jose; delegate to the Republican State conventions in 1914 and from 1920 to 1936; elected as a Republican to the Sixty-seventh and to the five succeeding Congresses (March 4, 1921-March 3, 1933); unsuccessful candidate for reelection in 1932 to the Seventy-third Congress; resumed the practice of law in San Jose, Calif., where he died on April 1, 1953; interment in Oak Hill Memorial Park.

**FREEDLEY, John,** a Representative from Pennsylvania; born in Norristown, Montgomery County, Pa., May 22, 1793; attended the public schools and Norristown Academy; assistant to his father, who operated a brickyard; studied law; was admitted to the bar in 1820 and commenced practice in Norristown; also became interested in marble and soapstone quarries; elected as a Whig to the Thirtieth and Thirty-first Congresses (March 4, 1847-March 3, 1851); died in Norristown, Montgomery County, Pa., December 8, 1851.

**FREEMAN, Chapman,** a Representative from Pennsylvania; born in Philadelphia, Pa., October 8, 1832; was educated at public and private schools and was graduated from the Philadelphia High School in 1850; commenced the study of law, but engaged in mercantile pursuits until he entered the United States Navy as acting assistant paymaster in 1863; on account of impaired health resigned in 1864 and resumed the study of law; was admitted to the bar in 1867 and commenced practice in Philadelphia; one of the commissioners on behalf of the Centennial from the city of Philadelphia to Vienna, Austria, in 1873; elected as a Republican to the Forty-fourth and Forty-fifth Congresses (March 4, 1875-March 3, 1879); declined to be a candidate for renomination in 1878; died in Strafford, Pa., March 22, 1904.

**FREEMAN, James Crawford,** a Representative from Georgia; born in Clinton (later Gray), Jones County, Ga., April 1, 1820; attended the common schools; engaged in agricultural pursuits; moved to Griffin, Ga., in 1865 and continued in farming operations; engaged in mercantile pursuits and in banking; elected as a Republican to the Forty-third Congress (March 4, 1873-March 3, 1875); moved to Atlanta, Ga., and again engaged in mercantile pursuits; died in Atlanta, Ga., September 3, 1885; interment in Oakland Cemetery.

**FREEMAN, John D.,** a Representative from Mississippi; born in Cooperstown, N.Y.; attended the common schools; moved to Mississippi and located in Grand Gulf; studied law; was admitted to the bar and practiced; district attorney; moved to Natchez, Miss.; attorney general of Mississippi 1841-1851; author of the first volume of reports of decisions of the Chancery Court of Mississippi published in 1844; elected as a Unionist to the Thirty-second Congress (March 4, 1851-March 3, 1853); served as attorney general; member of the Democratic State central committee and served as chairman; moved to Colorado and settled in Canon City in 1882; resumed the practice of his profession; died in Canon City, Colo., January 17, 1886; interment in Jackson, Miss.

**FREEMAN, Jonathan** (uncle of Nathaniel Freeman, Jr.), a Representative from New Hampshire; born in Mansfield, Conn., March 21, 1745; attended the public schools; moved to New Hampshire in 1769 and settled in Hanover; engaged in agricultural pursuits; was town clerk and also justice of the peace; executive councilor 1789-1797; member of the State house of representatives 1787-1789; served in the State senate 1789-1794; delegate to the Constitutional convention of 1791; member of the State council; overseer of Dartmouth College, Hanover, N.H., 1793-1808; treasurer of Dartmouth College for more than forty years; elected as a Federalist to the Fifth and Sixth Congresses (March 4, 1797-March 3, 1801); resumed agricultural pursuits; died in Hanover, N.H., August 20, 1808; interment in Hanover Center Cemetery.

**FREEMAN, Nathaniel, Jr**. (nephew of Jonathan Freeman), a Representative from Massachusetts; born in Sandwich, Barnstable County, Mass., on May 1, 1766; attended the common schools; was graduated from Harvard University in 1787; studied law; was admitted to the bar about 1791 and commenced practice in Sandwich and the Cape Cod district; served as brigade major in the Massachusetts Militia for sixteen years; justice of the peace in 1793; elected as a Federalist to the Fourth Congress and reelected as a Republican to the Fifth Congress (March 4, 1795-March 3, 1799); died in Sandwich, Mass., August 22, 1800; interment in the Old Burial Ground.

**FREEMAN, Richard Patrick,** a Representative from Connecticut; born in New London, New London County, Conn., April 24, 1869; attended the public schools; was graduated from Bulkeley High School at New London in 1887, from Noble and Greenough's Preparatory School, Boston, Mass., in 1888, from Harvard University in 1891, and from the law department of Yale University in 1894; was admitted to the bar in 1894 and commenced practice in New London, Conn.; special agent for the Department of the Interior in the States of Oregon and Washington 1896-1898; during the war with Spain served as regimental sergeant major in the Third Regiment, Connecticut Volunteer Infantry, and afterward became major and judge advocate of the Connecticut National Guard; prosecuting attorney of the city of New London 1898-1901; unsuccessful candidate for the Republican nomination to Congress in 1912; elected as a Republican to the Sixty-fourth and to the eight succeeding Congresses (March 4, 1915-March 3, 1933); unsuccessful candidate for renomination in 1932; resumed the practice of law in New London, Conn.; died in Newington, Conn., July 8, 1944; interment in Cedar Grove Cemetery, New London, Conn.

**FREER, Romeo Hoyt,** a Representative from West Virginia; born in Bazetta, Trumbull County, Ohio, November 9, 1846; attended the common schools of Ashtabula County, Ohio, where his parents had moved when he was three years old; during the Civil War served in the Union Army as a private; settled in Charleston, W.Va., in March 1866; taught school; studied law; was admitted to the bar in 1868 and practiced; assistant prosecuting attorney of Kanawha County, 1868-1871; Kanawha County prosecuting attorney, 1871-1873; appointed commercial agent to San Juan del Norte, Nicaragua, January 15, 1873, and served until January 1877; moved to Harrisville, Ritchie County, W.Va., in 1882; member of the West Virginia State house of delegates in 1891; prosecuting attorney of Ritchie County, 1892-1897; judge of the fourth circuit of West Virginia, 1896-1899; elected as a Republican to the Fifty-sixth Congress (March 4, 1899-March 3, 1901); unsuccessful candidate for reelection in 1900 to the Fifty-seventh Congress; attorney general of West Virginia, 1901-1905; appointed postmaster of Harrisville, W.Va., on October 4, 1907 and served until his death on May 9, 1913; interment in Harrisville Cemetery.

**FRELINGHUYSEN, Frederick** (father of Theodore Frelinghuysen, great-uncle of Frederick Theodore Frelinghuysen, great-great-great-grandfather of Peter Hood Ballantine Frelinghuysen, Jr., and great-great-great-great-grandfather of Rodney P. Frelinghuysen), a Delegate and a Senator from New Jersey; born near Somerville, Somerset County, N.J., April 13, 1753; graduated from the College of New Jersey (now Princeton University) in 1770; studied law; was admitted to the bar in 1774 and commenced practice in Somerset County, N.J.; member, provincial congress of New Jersey, 1775-1776; served in the Revolutionary War, attaining the rank of colonel; Member of the Continental Congress in 1779; clerk of the common pleas court of Somerset County from 1781 until 1789, when he resigned; member of the New Jersey State general assembly in 1784, and from 1800 until 1804; member of the New Jersey convention that ratified the Federal Constitution in 1787; member, New Jersey State council, 1790-1792; appointed by President George Washington brigadier general in 1790 in the campaign against the western Indians; elected to the United States Senate, and served from March 4, 1793 to November 12, 1796, when he resigned; commissioned major general in 1794 during the Whiskey Rebellion; died in Millstone, N.J., April 13, 1804; interment in the Old Cemetery, Weston, N.J.

**Bibliography:** *DAB.*

**FRELINGHUYSEN, Frederick Theodore** (nephew and adopted son of Theodore Frelinghuysen, great-nephew of Frederick Frelinghuysen, uncle of Joseph Sherman Frelinghuysen, great-grandfather of Peter Hood Ballantine Frelinghuysen, Jr., and great-great-grandfather of Rodney P. Frelinghuysen), a Senator from New Jersey; born in Millstone, N.J., August 4, 1817; graduated from Rutgers College, New Brunswick, N.J., in 1836; studied law; was admitted to the bar in 1839 and commenced practice in Newark, N.J.; city attorney of Newark in 1849; member of the city council 1850; trustee of Rutgers College, 1851-1885; member of the peace convention of 1861 held in Washington, D.C., in an effort to devise means to prevent the impending war; attorney general of New Jersey, 1861-1866; appointed and subsequently elected as a Republican to the United States Senate to fill the vacancy caused by the death of William Wright, and served from November 12, 1866 to March 3, 1869; unsuccessful candidate for reelection in 1868; appointed Minister to Great Britain by President Ulysses S. Grant on July 15, 1870 and confirmed, but declined the appointment; again elected to the United States Senate as a Republican, and served from March 4, 1871 to March 3, 1877; appointed a member of the Electoral Commission in 1877 to decide the contests in various States in the presidential election of 1876; unsuccessful candidate for reelection; chairman, Committee on Agriculture (Forty-second through Forty-fourth Congresses); resumed the practice of law in Newark, N.J.; appointed Secretary of State by President Chester A. Arthur on December 12, 1881 and served until March 6, 1885; died in Newark, N.J., May 20, 1885; interment in Mount Pleasant Cemetery.

**Bibliography:** *DAB*.

**FRELINGHUYSEN, Joseph Sherman** (nephew of Frederick Theodore Frelinghuysen and cousin of Peter Hood Ballantine Frelinghuysen, Jr.), a Senator from New Jersey; born in Raritan, Somerset County, N.J., March 12, 1869; attended the public schools; interested in insurance companies; served in the Spanish American War in 1898 as second lieutenant, first lieutenant, and ordnance officer; member, New Jersey State senate, 1906-1912, serving as president in 1909 and 1910; Acting Governor of New Jersey ad interim; president of the State board of agriculture, 1912-1925; president of the State board of education, 1915-1919; elected as a Republican to the United States Senate, and served from March 4, 1917 to March 3, 1923; unsuccessful candidate for reelection in 1922; chairman, Committee on Coast Defenses (Sixty-sixth Congress); resumed his insurance business until his death in Tucson, Ariz., February 8, 1948; interment in St. Bernard's Cemetery, Bernardsville, N.J.

**FRELINGHUYSEN, Peter Hood Ballantine, Jr**. (father of Rodney P. Frelinghuysen, cousin of Joseph Sherman Frelinghuysen, great-grandson of Frederick Theodore Frelinghuysen, great-great-nephew of Theodore Frelinghuysen, and great-great-great-grandson of Frederick Frelinghuysen), a Representative from New Jersey; born in New York City, January 17, 1916; attended St. Mark's School, Southboro, Mass.; graduated from Princeton University in 1938 and from Yale Law School in 1941; admitted to the bar the same year and practiced law in New York City from December 1941 to April 1942; served in Office of Naval Intelligence from September 1942 to December 1945 and was released to inactive duty with a commission as lieutenant; engaged in postgraduate work in history at Columbia University in 1946 and 1947; staff member, Foreign Affairs Task Force, Commission on Organization of the Executive Branch of the Government (Hoover Commission) from May to October 1948; engaged in investment business in New York City; director of Howard Savings Bank, Livingston, N.J.; elected as a Republican to the Eighty-third Congress and to the ten succeeding Congresses (January 3, 1953-January 3, 1975); was not a candidate in 1974 for reelection to the Ninety-fourth Congress; is a resident of Morristown, N.J.

**FRELINGHUYSEN, Rodney P**. (son of Peter Hood Ballantine Frelinghuysen, Jr., great-great grandson of Frederick Theodore Frelinghuysen, great-great-great-great-grandson of Frederick Frel-

inghuysen, and great-great-great nephew of Theodore Frelinghuysen), a Representative from New Jersey; born in New York City, April 29, 1946; B.A., Hobart College, Geneva, N.Y., 1969; graduate studies, Trinity College, Hartford, Conn.; entered active duty, United States Army in 1969; released in 1971 after service in Vietnam; state and federal aid coordinator and administrative assistant to Board of Chosen Freeholders, Morris County, N.J., 1972; member, Morris County Board of Chosen Freeholders, elected 1974, 1977 and 1980 for three-year terms, director, 1980; member, New Jersey Commission on Capitol Budgeting and Planning; member, New Jersey State general assembly, 1983-1994; Morris County Republican Committee; elected as a Republican to the One Hundred Fourth Congress (January 3, 1995-January 3, 1997); is a resident of Morristown, N.J.

**FRELINGHUYSEN, Theodore** (son of Frederick Frelinghuysen, uncle and adoptive father of Frederick Theodore Frelinghuysen, great-great-uncle of Peter Hood Ballantine Frelinghuysen, Jr., and great-great-great uncle of Rodney P. Frelinghuysen), a Senator from New Jersey; born in Millstone, N.J., March 28, 1787; pursued classical studies and graduated from the College of New Jersey (now Princeton University) in 1804; studied law; was admitted to the bar in 1808, and commenced practice in Newark, N.J.; served as captain of Volunteer Militia in the War of 1812; attorney general of New Jersey from 1817 until 1829, when he resigned; declined the office of justice of the State supreme court in 1826; unsuccessful candidate for election to the United States Senate in 1826; elected to the United States Senate in 1828, and served from March 4, 1829 to March 3, 1835; chairman, Committee on Manufactures (Twenty-eighth Congress); resumed the practice of law in Newark, N.J.; mayor of Newark, 1837-1838; chancellor of New York University, 1839-1850; very active in religious organizations throughout his life; vice president of the American Colonization Society; unsuccessful Whig candidate in 1844 for Vice President of the United States on the Whig ticket headed by Henry Clay; president of Rutgers College, New Brunswick, N.J., from 1850 until his death in New Brunswick, N.J., April 12, 1862; interment in First Reformed Church Cemetery.

**Bibliography:** *DAB*; Chambers, T.W. *Memoir of the Life and Character of Honorable Theodore Frelinghuysen*. New York: Harper and Brothers, 1863; Eells, Robert J. *Forgotten Saint: The Life of Theodore Frelinghuysen; A Case Study of Christian Leadership*. Lanham, Md.: University Press of America, 1987.

**FRÉMONT, John Charles** (son-in-law of Thomas Hart Benton), a Senator from California; born in Savannah, Ga., January 21, 1813; pursued classical studies and attended Charleston College, 1828-1830; instructor in mathematics in the United States Navy, 1833-1835; civil engineer assistant, 1838-1839, exploring the territory between the Missouri River and the northern boundary of the United States; appointed second lieutenant of Topographical Engineers of the United States Army in 1838; commenced in 1842 explorations and surveys for an overland route from the Mississippi to the Pacific Ocean; major of a battalion of California Volunteers in 1846; appointed lieutenant colonel of the United States Mounted Rifles in 1846 and ordered to act as Governor of California by Commodore Robert F. Stockton; General Stephen W. Kearny of the United States Army revoked this order and placed him under arrest for mutiny on August 22, 1847; tried by court martial, found guilty January 31, 1848, and pardoned by President James K. Polk, but resigned; settled in California on the Mariposa grant; commissioner to run the boundary line between United States and Mexico in 1849; upon the admission of California as a State into the Union was elected as a Democrat to the United States Senate and served from September 9, 1850, to March 3, 1851; nominated in Philadelphia on June 17, 1856 as the first candidate of the Republican Party for President of the United States, but was unsuccessful for election; appointed major general in the United States Army by President Lincoln on July 3, 1861, and placed in command of the western military district; relieved November 2, 1861; took command of the mountain department March 29, 1862 and was relieved on June 28, 1862; nominated for President of the United States by the Radical Democratic Party on May 31, 1864, but withdrew his candidacy on September 22; appointed Governor of Arizona Territory by President Rutherford B. Hayes on June 12, 1878, and served until his resignation October 11, 1881; appointed a major general in the United States Army on the retired list in 1890; died in New York City on July 13, 1890; interment in Trinity Church Cemetery; reinterment in Rockland Cemetery, Nyack, N.Y., March 17, 1891.

**Bibliography:** Bartlett, Ruhl J. *John C. Frémont and the Republican Party*. 1930. Reprint. New York: Da Capo Press, 1970; Frémont, John C. *Memoirs of My Life*. Chicago: Belford, Clarke and Co., 1887; Nevins, Allan. *Frémont, Pathmarker of the West*. 1928. Rev. and enlarged ed. Lincoln: University of Nebraska Press, 1992.

**FRENCH, Burton Lee,** a Representative from Idaho; born near Delphi, Carroll County, Ind., August 1, 1875; moved with his parents to Kearney, Nebr., in 1880, and thence to Idaho in 1882; attended the public schools; was graduated from the University of Idaho at Moscow in 1901; fellow at the University of Chicago 1901-1903; studied law; was admitted to the bar and commenced practice in Moscow, Idaho; member of the State house of representatives 1898-1902; elected as a Republican to the Fifty-eighth and to the two succeeding Congresses (March 4, 1903-March 3, 1909); unsuccessful candidate for reelection in 1908 to the Sixty-first Congress; elected to the Sixty-second and Sixty-third Congresses (March 4, 1911-March 3, 1915); was not a candidate for renomination in 1914 to the House of Representatives, but was an unsuccessful candidate for nomination to the United States Senate; elected to the Sixty-fifth and to the seven succeeding Congresses (March 4, 1917-March 3, 1933); chairman, Committee on Memorials (Seventieth and Seventy-first Congresses); unsuccessful candidate for reelection in 1932 to the Seventy-third Congress, and for election in 1934 to the Seventy-fourth Congress; delegate to the Interparliamentary Union Conventions in London in 1930, and in Bucharest in 1931; professor of government at Miami University, Oxford, Ohio, from 1935 until his retirement in 1947; appointed by President Harry S Truman in 1947 a member of the Federal Loyalty Review Board and served until 1953; died in Hamilton, Ohio, September 12, 1954; interment in Moscow Cemetery, Moscow, Idaho.

**FRENCH, Carlos,** a Representative from Connecticut; born in Humphreysville (later Seymour), Conn., August 6, 1835; attended the common schools of Seymour and General Russell's Military School, New Haven, Conn.; engaged in manufacturing; invented the spiral steel car spring and the corrugated volute spring; member of the State house of representatives in 1860 and again in 1868; president and treasurer of the Fowler Nail Co. from 1869 until his death; vice president of the H.A. Matthews Manufacturing Co.; director of the Union Horse Shoe Nail Co. of Chicago, of the Second National Bank of New Haven, of the Colonial Trust Co. of Waterbury, Conn., and of the New York, New Haven & Hartford Railroad Co.; member of the Democratic National Committee; elected as a Democrat to the Fiftieth Congress (March 4, 1887-March 3, 1889); was not a candidate for renomination in 1888; resumed his former manufacturing pursuits and corporate connections; died in Seymour, New Haven County, Conn., April 14, 1903; interment in Union Cemetery.

**FRENCH, Ezra Bartlett,** a Representative from Maine; born in Landaff, Grafton County, N.H., September 23, 1810; attended the common schools and pursued an academic course; studied law in Bath, N.H., and Plymouth, N.H.; was admitted to the bar in 1833 and commenced practice in Portland and Waldoboro, Maine; moved to Noblesboro (later Damariscotta), Maine, and continued practice; member of the State house of representatives 1838-1840; served in the State senate 1842-1845; secretary of state of Maine 1845-1850;

bank commissioner; newspaper editor in 1856; assisted in organizing the Republican Party in 1856; elected as a Republican to the Thirty-sixth Congress (March 4, 1859-March 3, 1861); was not a candidate for renomination in 1860; member of the peace convention of 1861 held in Washington, D.C., in an effort to devise means to prevent the impending war; appointed Second Auditor of the Treasury August 3, 1861, by President Lincoln, and continued in office during the administrations of Presidents Johnson, Grant, and Hayes, serving until his death in Washington, D.C., April 24, 1880; interment in Hillside Cemetery, Damariscotta, Maine.

**FRENCH, John Robert,** a Representative from North Carolina; born in Gilmanton, Belknap County, N.H., May 28, 1819; received an academic education in Gilmanton and Concord, N.H.; learned the printer's trade; publisher and associate editor of the New Hampshire Statesman at Concord for five years; editor of the Eastern Journal at Biddeford, Maine, two years; moved to Lake County, Ohio, in 1854; editor of the Telegraph, the Press, and, in 1856, of the Cleveland Morning Leader; member of the State house of representatives in 1858 and 1859; appointed by Secretary Salmon P. Chase to a position in the Treasury Department, Washington, D.C., in 1861; appointed by President Lincoln in 1864 a member of the board of direct-tax commissioners for the State of North Carolina; settled in Edenton, N.C., at the close of the Civil War; delegate to the State constitutional convention in 1867; upon the readmission of the State of North Carolina to representation was elected as a Republican to the Fortieth Congress and served from July 6, 1868, to March 3, 1869; was not a candidate for renomination in 1868 to the Forty-first Congress; elected Sergeant at Arms of the United States Senate on March 22, 1869, and served in that capacity until March 24, 1879; appointed secretary of the Ute Commission in July 1880; returned to Washington, D.C.; moved to Omaha, Nebr., and thence to Boise City, Idaho, where he was editor of the Boise City Sun until his death on October 2, 1890; interment in Boise City Cemetery.

**FRENCH, Richard,** a Representative from Kentucky; born near Boonesborough, Madison County, Ky., June 20, 1792; attended private schools; studied law; was admitted to the bar in 1820 and commenced practice in Winchester, Ky.; member of the Kentucky house of representatives, 1820-1826; judge of the circuit court in 1829; elected as a Jacksonian to the Twenty-fourth Congress (March 4, 1835-March 3, 1837); unsuccessful candidate for reelection to the Twenty-fifth Congress; unsuccessful Democratic candidate for Governor of Kentucky in 1840; elected as a Democrat to the Twenty-eighth Congress (March 4, 1843-March 3, 1845); unsuccessful candidate for reelection to the Twenty-ninth Congress; elected to the Thirtieth Congress (March 4, 1847-March 3, 1849); resumed the practice of law; died in Covington, Ky., on May 1, 1854; interment in the family burial ground near Mount Sterling, Montgomery County, Ky.

**FRENZEL, William Eldridge,** a Representative from Minnesota; born in St. Paul, Ramsey County, Minn., July 31, 1928; educated at the St. Paul (Minn.) Academy; B.A., Dartmouth College, Hanover, N.H., 1950, M.B.A., 1951; lieutenant, United States Naval Reserve, 1951-1954, Korean Theater; president, Minneapolis Terminal Warehouse Co., 1966-1970; executive committee, Hennepin County, 1966-1967; member of the advisory committee, National Rivers and Harbors Congress, 1967-1970; served in the Minnesota State house of representatives, 1962-1970; delegate to each Minnesota State Republican convention since 1963; elected as a Republican to the Ninety-second and to the nine succeeding Congresses (January 3, 1971-January 3, 1991); was not a candidate for reelection in 1990 to the One Hundred Second Congress; is a resident of Bloomington, Minn.

**FREY, Louis, Jr.,** a Representative from Florida; born in Rutherford, Bergen County, N.J., January 11, 1934; educated in New Jersey public schools; Colgate University, B.A., 1955; enlisted in United States Navy, 1955, served in naval aviation, honorable discharge, 1958, as lieutenant (jg); captain, United States Naval Reserve (retired); J.D., University of Michigan Law School, 1961; admitted to Florida bar, 1961; practiced law in Orlando, Fla., and served as assistant county solicitor until 1963; associate, and partner, law firm of Gurney, Skolfield and Frey, Winter Park, Fla., 1963-1967; acting general counsel, Florida State Turnpike Authority, 1966-1967; partner, law firm of Mateer, Frey, Young and Harbert, Orlando Fla., 1967; former member, Republican State executive committee; former State treasurer of Republican Party; former chairman, Florida Federation of Young Republicans; elected as a Republican to the Ninety-first and to the four succeeding Congresses (January 3, 1969-January 3, 1979); was not a candidate for reelection in 1978 to the Ninety-sixth Congress, but was an unsuccessful candidate for nomination for Governor of Florida; unsuccessful candidate for nomination to the United States Senate in 1980; resumed the practice of law in Washington, D.C., 1979-1987, and in Orlando, Fla., 1987 to present; president and director, Florida Council on Economic Education, 1990 to present; president, Center for Independence Training and Education; syndicated columnist; co-host of "Florida Round Table," a statewide radio news show; television commentator for ABC News, Orlando, Fla.; is a resident of Winter Park, Fla.

**FREY, Oliver Walter,** a Representative from Pennsylvania; born near Quakertown, Richland Township, Bucks County, Pa., September 7, 1887; moved to Ohio with his parents in 1891 and to Allentown, Pa., in 1893; attended the public schools of Allentown; was graduated from the College of William and Mary, Williamsburg, Va., in 1915; enlisted in the United States Army and served from April 1917 until honorably discharged in June 1919; was commissioned a first lieutenant in the Three Hundred and Fourteenth Infantry, serving overseas in the Seventy-ninth Division; resumed his studies at the University of Pennsylvania and graduated from its law department in 1920; was admitted to the bar the same year and commenced practice in Allentown, Pa.; elected as a Democrat to the Seventy-third Congress to fill the vacancy caused by the death of Henry W. Watson; reelected to the Seventy-fourth and Seventy-fifth Congresses, and served from November 7, 1933 to January 3, 1939; unsuccessful candidate for reelection in 1938 to the Seventy-sixth Congress; general counsel for the Farm Credit Administration in Baltimore, Md., from April 1939 until his death in Allentown, Pa., August 26, 1939; interment in Grandview Cemetery.

**FRICK, Henry,** a Representative from Pennsylvania; born in Northumberland, Pa., March 17, 1795; attended the public schools; apprenticed to a printer in Philadelphia; served in the War of 1812; settled in Milton, Pa., in 1816; established the Miltonian, a political journal, with which he was connected for over twenty years; member of the Pennsylvania house of representatives 1828-1831; elected as a Whig to the Twenty-eighth Congress and served from March 4, 1843, until his death in Washington, D.C., March 1, 1844; interment in the Congressional Cemetery.

**FRIEDEL, Samuel Nathaniel,** a Representative from Maryland; born in Washington, D.C., April 18, 1898; moved with his family to Baltimore, Md., when six months of age; attended the public schools and Strayer Business College; mailing clerk in a Baltimore store 1919-1923; founder and president of Industrial Loan Co., 1926-1956; member of the State house of delegates 1935-1939; member of the city council of Baltimore, 1939-1952, representing the first and later the fifth district; delegate, Democratic National Conventions, 1964 and 1968; elected as a Democrat to the Eighty-third and to the eight succeeding Congresses (January 3, 1953-January 3, 1971); chairman, Committee on

House Administration (Ninetieth and Ninety-first Congresses), Joint Committee on the Library (Ninety-first Congress), Joint Committee on Printing (Ninety-first Congress); unsuccessful candidate for renomination in 1970 to the Ninety-second Congress; died in Towson, Md., March 21, 1979; interment in the Hebrew Friendship Cemetery, Baltimore, Md.

**FRIES, Frank William,** a Representative from Illinois; born in Hornsby, Macoupin County, Ill., May 1, 1893; moved with his parents to Gillespie, Ill., in 1904; attended the public schools; coal miner 1915-1917; during the First World War served as a sergeant in the Thirty-seventh Company, One Hundred and Fifty-third Depot Brigade, United States Army, from April 1918 to December 1918; coal mine operator in 1920 and 1921; engaged in the insurance business 1922-1927; moved to Carlinville, Ill., in 1930 and engaged in the wholesale produce business; sheriff of Macoupin County 1930-1934; member of the State house of representatives 1934-1936; elected as a Democrat to the Seventy-fifth and Seventy-sixth Congresses (January 3, 1937-January 3, 1941); unsuccessful candidate for reelection in 1940 to the Seventy-seventh Congress; an arbitrator in the coal industry from 1941 to 1969; was a resident of Gillespie, Ill., until his death on July 17, 1980; interment in Holy Cross Cemetery.

**FRIES, George,** a Representative from Ohio; born in Pennsylvania in 1799; attended the common schools; studied medicine and commenced practice in Hanoverton, Ohio, in 1833; elected as a Democrat to the Twenty-ninth and Thirtieth Congresses (March 4, 1845-March 3, 1849); declined to be a candidate for renomination in 1848; moved to Cincinnati, Ohio, and resumed the practice of medicine; treasurer of Hamilton County 1860-1862; died in Cincinnati, Ohio, on November 13, 1866; interment in the Catholic Cemetery.

**FRISA, Daniel,** a Representative from New York; born in Westbury, Nassau County, N.Y., April 27, 1955; attended East Meadow, N.Y. public schools; B.S., St. John's University, Jamaica, N.Y., 1977; marketing representative, Johnson and Johnson Baby Products Co., 1977-1978; retail representative then senior store management position, Fortunoff, 1979-1982; vice president, Long Island Development Corp.; direct-mail consultant; member, New York State assembly, 1985-1993; elected as a Republican to the One Hundred Fourth Congress (January 3, 1995-January 3, 1997); is a resident of Westbury, N.Y.

**FRIST, William H.,** a Senator from Tennessee; born in Nashville, Tenn., February 22, 1952; graduated Montgomery Bell Academy, Nashville, 1970; B.S., Princeton University, 1974, M.D., Harvard University, 1978; heart and lung transplantation surgeon, Vanderbilt University; founder, Vanderbilt Transplant Center, 1988; chair, Tennessee Task Force on Medicaid; elected as a Republican to the United States Senate in 1994 for the term ending January 3, 2001; is a resident of Nashville, Tenn.

**FROEHLICH, Harold Vernon,** a Representative from Wisconsin; born in Appleton, Outagamie County, Wis., May 12, 1932; attended the public schools; B.B.A., University of Wisconsin School of Commerce, Madison, Wis., June 1959; LL.B., University of Wisconsin Law School, January 1962; served in the United States Navy, 1951-1955; admitted to the Wisconsin bar in 1962 and commenced practice in Appleton; certified public accountant; real estate broker; Wisconsin State representative, 1963-1973; assembly Republican caucus chairman, 1965-1967; assembly speaker, 1967-1971; assembly minority leader, 1971-1973; delegate, Wisconsin State Republican conventions, 1957-1981; delegate to the Republican National Conventions of 1972 and 1976; elected as a Republican to the Ninety-third Congress (January 3, 1973-January 3, 1975); unsuccessful candidate for reelection in 1974 to the Ninety-fourth Congress; resumed the practice of law; unsuccessful candidate for election in 1976 to the Ninety-fifth Congress; appointed as Judge of the Wisconsin Circuit Court for the Outagamie County Circuit by Governor Lee S. Dreyfus in September 1981; subsequently elected for a six-year term ending in 1988, and reelected for a six-year term ending July 31, 1994; chief judge, 1988-1994; president, Wisconsin Trial Judges Association, 1991-1997; is a resident of Appleton, Wis.

**FROMENTIN, Eligius,** a Senator from Louisiana; born in France; pursued classical studies; ordained a Catholic priest; exercised his ministry at Etampes, France; fled from France during the Reign of Terror and immigrated to the United States, settling in Pennsylvania; moved to Maryland, where he taught school; studied law; subsequently left the church and moved to Louisiana; was admitted to the bar and commenced practice in New Orleans; clerk to house of representatives of Orleans Territory 1807-1811; secretary of the State constitutional convention 1812; secretary of the State senate 1812-1813; elected to the United States Senate as a Republican and served from March 4, 1813, to March 3, 1819; appointed judge of the criminal court of New Orleans in 1821; appointed on May 18, 1821, by President James Monroe as United States judge for west Florida and east Florida westward of the cape, but soon resigned; resumed the practice of law in New Orleans and died there on October 6, 1822.

**FROST, George,** a Delegate from New Hampshire; born in Newcastle, N.H., April 26, 1720; entered business in Kittery Point, near Portsmouth; followed the sea as captain for twenty years; returned to Newcastle in 1760; moved to Durham, N.H., in 1770; judge of the court of common pleas of Strafford County 1773-1791; served as chief justice several years; Member of the Continental Congress 1777-1779; executive councilor 1781-1784; died in Durham, N.H., June 21, 1796; interment in Pine Hill Cemetery, Dover, N.H.

**FROST, Joel,** a Representative from New York; born in Westchester County, N.Y.; attended the public schools; member, Westchester County Board of Supervisors, 1803; member of the State assembly 1806-1808; first surrogate of Putnam County in 1812, and served in 1813, 1815-1819, 1821, and 1822; member of the State constitutional convention in 1821; judge, Court of Common Pleas; moved to Schenectady; elected to the Eighteenth Congress (March 4, 1823-March 3, 1825); died September 11, 1827; interment in Gilead Cemetery at Carmel, N.Y.

**FROST, Jonas Martin,** a Representative from Texas; born in Glendale, Los Angeles County, Calif., January 1, 1942; attended the Fort Worth, Tex., public schools; graduated R.L. Paschal High School, Fort Worth, 1960; B.A. and B.J., University of Missouri, Columbia, Mo., 1964; J.D., Georgetown University Law Center, Washington, D.C., 1970; served in United States Army Reserve, 1966-1972; admitted to the Texas bar in 1970 and commenced practice in Dallas; staff writer for the Congressional Quarterly Weekly, 1965-1967; law clerk for Federal Judge Sarah T. Hughes, 1970-1971; vice president and board member, Dallas Democratic Forum, 1976-1977; delegate, Democratic National Convention, 1976, 1984 and 1988; elected as a Democrat to the Ninety-sixth and to the eight succeeding Congresses (January 3, 1979-January 3, 1997); is a resident of Dallas, Tex.

**FROST, Richard Graham,** a Representative from Missouri; born in St. Louis, Mo., December 29, 1851; attended St. John's College, New York City, the University of London, and the St. Louis (Mo.) Law School; was admitted to the bar and practiced in St. Louis, Mo.; unsuccessfully contested as a Democrat the election in 1876 of Lyne S. Metcalfe to the Forty-fifth Congress; elected as a Democrat to the Forty-sixth Congress (March 4, 1879-March 3, 1881); presented credentials as a Member-elect to the Forty-seventh Congress and served from March 4, 1881, until March 2, 1883, when he was succeeded by Gustavus Sessinghaus, who contested his

election; resumed the practice of law; died in St. Louis, Mo., February 1, 1900; interment in Calvary Cemetery.

**FROST, Rufus Smith,** a Representative from Massachusetts; born in Marlboro, Cheshire County, N.H., July 18, 1826; moved to Boston, Mass., in 1833; attended the public schools; engaged in mercantile pursuits; mayor of Chelsea, Mass., in 1867 and 1868; member of the State senate in 1871 and 1872 and of the Governor's council in 1873 and 1874; presented credentials as a Republican Member-elect to the Forty-fourth Congress and served from March 4, 1875, until July 28, 1876, when he was succeeded by Josiah G. Abbott, who contested his election; unsuccessful candidate for election in 1876 to the Forty-fifth Congress; president of the National Association of Woolen Manufacturers 1877-1884; president of the Boston Board of Trade 1878-1880; president of the New England Conservatory of Music; one of the founders of the New England Law and Order League and of the Boston Art Club; delegate to the Republican National Convention in 1892; died in Chicago, Ill., March 6, 1894; interment in Woodlawn Cemetery, Chelsea, Mass.

**FROTHINGHAM, Louis Adams,** a Representative from Massachusetts; born in Jamaica Plain, Mass., July 13, 1871; attended the public schools and Adams Academy; was graduated from Harvard University in 1893 and from Harvard Law School in 1896; admitted to the bar in 1896 and commenced practice in Boston; second lieutenant, United States Marine Corps, in the Spanish-American War in 1898; member of the Massachusetts house of representatives, 1901-1905, and served as speaker in 1904 and 1905; Lieutenant Governor, 1909-1911; unsuccessful Republican candidate for election for Governor in 1911; lecturer at Harvard University, 1913-1916; moved to North Easton, Mass., in 1916 and continued the practice of law; delegate to the Republican National Convention of 1916; major in the United States Army during the First World War; member of the commission to visit the soldiers and sailors from Massachusetts in France in 1918; first vice commander of the Massachusetts branch of the American Legion in 1919; overseer of Harvard University for eighteen years; elected as a Republican to the Sixty-seventh and to the three succeeding Congresses, and served from March 4, 1921 until his death on board the yacht *Winsome*, at North Haven, Maine, August 23, 1928; interment in Village Cemetery, North Easton, Mass.

**FRY, Jacob, Jr.,** a Representative from Pennsylvania; born in Trappe, Montgomery County, Pa., June 10, 1802; attended the public schools; taught school in Trappe, Pa.; clerk of courts of Montgomery County 1830-1833; elected as a Jacksonian to the Twenty-fourth Congress and reelected as a Democrat to the Twenty-fifth Congress (March 4, 1835-March 3, 1839); was not a candidate for renomination in 1838; engaged in mercantile business in Trappe, Pa.; member of the Pennsylvania house of representatives in 1853 and 1854; auditor general of Pennsylvania 1857-1860; resumed mercantile pursuits; died in Trappe, Pa., November 28, 1866; interment in Lutheran Cemetery.

**FRY, Joseph, Jr.,** a Representative from Pennsylvania; born in Upper Saucon Township, Northampton (later Lehigh) County, Pa., August 4, 1781; attended the rural schools; engaged in mercantile pursuits in Fryburg (later Coopersburg), Lehigh County, Pa.; member of the Pennsylvania house of representatives in 1816 and 1817; served in the Pennsylvania senate 1817-1821; served in the Pennsylvania militia and attained the rank of colonel; elected to the Twentieth Congress and reelected as a Jacksonian to the Twenty-first Congress (March 4, 1827-March 3, 1831); was not a candidate for renomination in 1830; resumed business activities; member of the Pennsylvania constitutional convention in 1837 and 1838; died in Allentown, Pa., August 15, 1860; interment in Union Cemetery.

**FRYE, William Pierce** (grandfather of Wallace Humphrey White, Jr.), a Representative and a Senator from Maine; born in Lewiston, Androscoggin County, Maine, September 2, 1830; attended the public schools in Lewiston and graduated from Bowdoin College, Brunswick, Maine, in 1850; studied law; was admitted to the bar and commenced practice in Rockland, Maine, in 1853; returned to Lewiston, Maine, and practiced law; member, State house of representatives 1861-1862, 1867; mayor of Lewiston 1866-1867; attorney general of State of Maine 1867-1869; elected as a Republican to the Forty-second and to the five succeeding Congresses and served from March 4, 1871, to March 17, 1881, when he resigned, having been elected Senator; elected as a Republican to the United States Senate on March 15, 1881, to fill the vacancy caused by the resignation of James G. Blaine; reelected in 1883, 1889, 1895, 1901, and 1907 and served from March 18, 1881, until his death on August 8, 1911; served as President pro tempore of the Senate during the Fifty-fourth through the Sixty-second Congresses; chairman Committee on Rules (Forty-seventh through Forty-ninth Congresses), Committee on Commerce (Fiftieth through Sixty-second Congresses, except for the Fifty-third Congress); member of the commission which met in Paris in September 1898 to adjust terms of peace between the United States and Spain; died in Lewiston, Maine, August 8, 1911; interment in Riverside Cemetery.

Bibliography: *DAB*.

**FUGATE, Thomas Bacon,** a Representative from Virginia; born near Tazewell, Claiborne County, Tenn., April 10, 1899; attended the public schools of Tennessee; student at the University of Tennessee at Knoxville in 1917 and at the Lincoln Memorial University, Harrogate, Tenn., in 1918; moved to Rose Hill, Va., in 1921 and engaged in the mercantile business; engaged in the hardware business at Ewing, Va., 1936-1940; also engaged in agricultural pursuits; member of the Virginia house of delegates 1928-1930; became president of the Peoples Bank of Ewing in 1935, director, Virginia-Tennessee Farm Bureau, Inc., in 1936, and president of Ewing Live Stock Co., Inc., in 1938; member of Virginia Board of Public Welfare 1937-1947; delegate to the Democratic National Convention in 1944; member of Constitutional Convention of Virginia in 1945; elected as a Democrat to the Eighty-first and Eighty-second Congresses (January 3, 1949-January 3, 1953); was not a candidate for renomination in 1952; banker and farmer; was a resident of Ewing, Va., where he died September 22, 1980; interment in Richmond Cemetery, Ewing, Va.

**FULBRIGHT, James Franklin,** a Representative from Missouri; born near Millersville, Cape Girardeau County, Mo., January 24, 1877; attended the public schools and was graduated from the State Normal School, Cape Girardeau, Mo., in 1900; taught school in Cape Girardeau and Ripley Counties for several years; attended the Washington Law School, St. Louis, Mo., for a short time; was admitted to the bar in 1903 and commenced practice in Doniphan, Mo., in 1904; appointed and subsequently elected prosecuting attorney of Ripley County in 1906; reelected in 1908 and 1910; member of the State house of representatives 1913-1919, serving as speaker pro tempore 1915-1919; mayor of Donihan, Mo., 1919-1921; elected as a Democrat to the Sixty-eighth Congress (March 4, 1923-March 3, 1925); unsuccessful candidate for reelection in 1924 to the Sixty-ninth Congress; elected to the Seventieth Congress (March 4, 1927-March 3, 1929); unsuccessful candidate for reelection in 1928 to the Seventy-first Congress; elected to the Seventy-second Congress (March 4, 1931-March 3, 1933); unsuccessful candidate for renomination in 1932 to the Seventy-third Congress; resumed the practice of law; delegate to the Democratic National Convention of 1928; permanent chairman of the Democratic State convention in 1936; elected judge of the Springfield Court of Appeals in 1936 and served from January 1, 1937, until his death in Springfield, Mo., April 5, 1948; interment in Doniphan Cemetery, Doniphan, Mo.

**FULBRIGHT, James William,** a Representative and a Senator from Arkansas; born in Sumner, Chariton County, Mo., April 9, 1905; moved with his parents to Fayetteville, Ark., in 1906; attended the public schools; A.B., University of Arkansas, Fayetteville, 1925; B.A. in 1928, and M.A. in 1931 as a Rhodes scholar from Oxford University, England; LL.B., George Washington University School of Law, Washington, D.C., 1934; was admitted to the District of Columbia bar in 1934; attorney, United States Department of Justice, Antitrust Division, 1934-1935; instructor in law, George Washington University, 1935, and lecturer in law, University of Arkansas, 1936-1939; president of the University of Arkansas, 1939-1941; also engaged in the newspaper business, in the lumber business, in banking, and in farming; elected as a Democrat to the Seventy-eighth Congress (January 3, 1943-January 3, 1945); was not a candidate for renomination in 1944 to the House of Representatives, but was elected to the United States Senate; reelected in 1950, 1956, 1962, and again in 1968, and served from January 3, 1945 until his resignation on December 31, 1974; unsuccessful candidate for renomination in 1974; chairman, Committee on Banking and Currency (Eighty-fourth through Eighty-sixth Congresses), Committee on Foreign Relations (Eighty-sixth through Ninety-third Congresses); counsel to the law firm of Hogan and Hartson, Washington, D.C.; was a resident of Washington, D.C., until his death there on February 9, 1995; cremated; ashes interred in family plot near the University of Arkansas, Fayetteville.

Bibliography: Fulbright, J. William. *The Arrogance of Power.* New York: Random House, 1966; Powell, Lee Riley. *J. William Fulbright and His Time.* Foreword by President Bill Clinton. Memphis, Tenn.: Guild Bindery Press, 1996; Woods, Randall Bennett. *Fulbright: A Biography.* New York: Cambridge University Press, 1995.

**FULKERSON, Abram,** a Representative from Virginia; born in Washington County, Va., May 13, 1834; was graduated from the Virginia Military Institute at Lexington in 1857; taught school in Palmyra, Va., and Rogersville, Tenn., until the beginning of the Civil War; entered the Confederate service in June 1861 as captain; promoted to major in the Nineteenth Tennessee Regiment; lieutenant colonel and colonel of the Sixty-third Tennessee Regiment; at the close of the war studied law; was admitted to the bar and commenced practice in Goodson (later Bristol), Va., in 1866; member of the Virginia house of delegates 1871-1873; served in the Virginia senate 1877-1879; was a Democrat, but assisted in organizing the Readjuster Party, after which he returned to the Democratic Party; elected as a Readjuster Democrat to the Forty-seventh Congress (March 4, 1881-March 3, 1883); resumed the practice of law after leaving Congress; elected to the Virginia house of delegates in 1888; delegate to the Democratic National (Gold) Convention in 1896; died in Bristol, Va., on December 17, 1902; interment in East Hill Cemetery.

**FULKERSON, Frank Ballard,** a Representative from Missouri; born near Edinburg, Grundy County, Mo., March 5, 1866; moved with his parents to a farm near Higginsville, Lafayette County, Mo.; attended the common schools and was graduated from Westminster College, Fulton, Mo., in 1888; taught school for two years; attended the law department of the University of Michigan at Ann Arbor; was graduated from the law department of the University of Missouri at Columbia in 1892; was admitted to the bar the same year and commenced practice in Warrensburg, Mo.; city attorney of Warrensburg 1893-1895; prosecuting attorney of Johnson County in 1895 and 1896; moved to Holden, Mo., in 1897 and to St. Joseph, Mo., in 1900 and continued the practice of law; city attorney of Holden in 1899 and 1900; elected as a Republican to the Fifty-ninth Congress (March 4, 1905-March 3, 1907); unsuccessful candidate for reelection in 1906 to the Sixtieth Congress; unsuccessful Republican candidate for attorney general of Missouri in 1908; unsuccessful candidate for mayor of St. Joseph, Mo., in

1908; resumed the practice of law in St. Joseph, Mo.; delegate to several Republican State conventions; delegate to the Republican National Convention in 1908; president of the city police board in 1909; city counselor in 1913 and 1914; returned to Lafayette County, Mo., in 1918 and continued the practice of law; also engaged in agricultural pursuits near Higginsville; prosecuting attorney of Lafayette County 1921-1925; died near Higginsville, Mo., August 30, 1936; interment in Higginsville City Cemetery.

**FULLER, Alvan Tufts,** a Representative from Massachusetts; born in Boston, Mass., February 27, 1878; attended the public schools; engaged in the bicycle business in 1896; founder and owner of the Packard Motor Car Co. of Boston; member of the Massachusetts house of representatives in 1915; delegate to the Republican National Convention of 1916; elected as an Independent Republican to the Sixty-fifth Congress; reelected as a Republican to the Sixty-sixth Congress and served from March 4, 1917, to January 5, 1921; Lieutenant Governor of Massachusetts, 1921-1924; elected Governor of Massachusetts in 1924, reelected in 1926, and served from January 8, 1925 to January 3, 1929; chairman of the board of Cadillac-Oldsmobile Co., of Boston; did not accept compensation for services while in public office; died in Boston, Mass., April 30, 1958; remains were cremated and interred in East Cemetery, Rye Beach, N.H.

**FULLER, Benoni Stinson,** a Representative from Indiana; born near Boonville, Warrick County, Ind., November 13, 1825; attended the common schools; taught school in Warrick County; sheriff of Warrick County in 1856 and 1858; served in the State senate in 1862, 1870, and 1872; member of the State house of representatives 1866-1868; elected as a Democrat to the Forty-fourth and Forty-fifth Congresses (March 4, 1875-March 3, 1879); was not a candidate for renomination in 1878; engaged in agricultural pursuits in Warrick County; died in Boonville, Ind., April 14, 1903; interment in Old Boonville Cemetery.

**FULLER, Charles Eugene,** a Representative from Illinois; born near Belvidere, Boone County, Ill., March 31, 1849; attended the common schools; studied law; was admitted to the bar in 1870 and commenced practice in Belvidere, Ill.; city attorney of Belvidere in 1875 and 1876; prosecuting attorney for Boone County 1876-1878; served in the Illinois State senate, 1878-1882; member of the Illinois State house of representatives, 1882-1888; again a member of the State senate, 1888-1892; raised a provisional regiment for the war with Spain and was commissioned colonel of the Thirteenth Illinois Infantry by Governor John R. Tanner; judge of the seventeenth judicial circuit 1897-1903; vice president of the People's Bank of Belvidere for many years; elected as a Republican to the Fifty-eighth and to the four succeeding Congresses (March 4, 1903-March 3, 1913); unsuccessful candidate for reelection in 1912 to the Sixty-third Congress; elected to the Sixty-fourth and to the five succeeding Congresses and served from March 4, 1915, until his death at a hospital in Rochester, Minn., June 25, 1926; chairman, Committee on Invalid Pensions (Sixty-sixth through Sixty-ninth Congresses); interment in Belvidere Cemetery, Belvidere, Ill.

**FULLER, Claude Albert,** a Representative from Arkansas; born in Prophetstown, Whiteside County, Ill., January 20, 1876; in 1885 moved to Arkansas with his parents, who settled on a farm near Eureka Springs; attended the public schools in Eureka Springs, Ark., and Kent College of Law, Chicago, Ill.; was admitted to the bar in 1898 and commenced practice in Eureka Springs the same year; city clerk of Eureka Springs 1898-1902; member of the State house of representatives 1903-1905; mayor of Eureka Springs 1906-1910 and 1920-1928; prosecuting attorney of the fourth Arkansas judicial district 1910-1914; president of the Eureka Springs School Board 1916-1928; delegate to all Democratic State conventions 1903-1943; delegate to the Democratic National Conventions in 1908, 1912, and others 1924-1960; elected as a Democrat to the Seventy-first and to the four succeeding Congresses (March 4, 1929-January 3, 1939); unsuccessful candidate for renomination in 1938; resumed the practice of law, also engaged in banking and agricultural pursuits; died in Eureka Springs, Ark., January 8, 1968; interment in I.O.O.F. Cemetery.

**Bibliography:** Beals, Frank Lee. *Backwoods Baron; The Life of Claude Albert Fuller.* Wheaton, Ill.: Morton Publishing Co., 1951.

**FULLER, George,** a Representative from Pennsylvania; born in Norwich, Conn., November 7, 1802; attended the public schools; moved to Pennsylvania and resided in Montrose; engaged in mercantile pursuits; elected as a Democrat to the Twenty-eighth Congress to fill the vacancy caused by the death of Almon H. Read and served from December 2, 1844, to March 3, 1845; editor of the Montrose (Pa.) Democrat, the Montrose Gazette, and the Susquehanna Register; treasurer of Susquehanna County; member of the Republican Party during the last twenty-five years of his life; died in Scranton, Lackawanna County, Pa., on November 24, 1888; interment in Montrose, Pa.

**FULLER, Hadwen Carlton,** a Representative from New York; born in West Monroe, Oswego County, N.Y., August 28, 1895; attended the public schools and Central Square (N.Y.) High School; engaged as bank clerk and later as assistant cashier of the First National Bank of Central Square, N.Y., 1912-1918; during the First World War served in the United States Army; organized the State Bank of Parish, N.Y., in 1919 and served as a director; organizer of the Parish Oil Co., Inc., in 1926, serving as president beginning in 1937; chairman of the Oswego County Republican Committee in 1942; served in the State assembly in 1942 and 1943; elected as a Republican to the Seventy-eighth Congress to fill the vacancy caused by the death of Francis D. Culkin; reelected to the Seventy-ninth and Eightieth Congresses and served from November 2, 1943, to January 3, 1949; unsuccessful candidate for reelection in 1948 to the Eighty-first Congress; delegate to the Republican National Convention of 1948; resumed his former business pursuits; was a resident of Parish, N.Y.; died January 29, 1990.

**FULLER, Henry Mills,** a Representative from Pennsylvania; born in Bethany, Wayne County, Pa., January 3, 1820; pursued classical studies and was graduated from Princeton College in 1839; studied law; was admitted to the bar January 3, 1842, and commenced practice in Wilkes-Barre, Luzerne County, Pa.; member of the Pennsylvania house of representatives in 1848 and 1849; elected as a Whig to the Thirty-second Congress (March 4, 1851-March 3, 1853); unsuccessful candidate for reelection in 1852 to the Thirty-third Congress; elected to the Thirty-fourth Congress (March 4, 1855-March 3, 1857); was not a candidate for renomination in 1856; resumed the practice of law; died in Philadelphia, Pa., December 26, 1860; interment in Hollenback Cemetery, Wilkes-Barre, Pa.

**FULLER, Philo Case,** a Representative from New York; born near Marlboro, Mass., August 14, 1787; attended the common schools; studied law and was admitted to the bar in 1813; served in the War of 1812; private secretary to General Wadsworth at Geneseo, N.Y.; practiced law in Albany, N.Y.; member of the New York State assembly in 1829 and 1830; served in the New York State senate in 1831 and 1832; elected as an Anti-Masonic candidate to the Twenty-third Congress, reelected as a Whig to the Twenty-fourth Congress, and served from March 4, 1833, until September 2, 1836, when he resigned; moved to Adrian, Mich., in 1836; engaged in banking; president of the Erie & Kalamazoo Railroad Co.; member of the Michigan State assembly in 1841 and served as speaker; unsuccessful Whig candidate for Governor of Michigan in 1841; returned to Geneseo, N.Y.; appointed Second Assistant Postmaster General in 1841; appointed comptroller of the State of New York on December 18, 1850, and served until November 4, 1851; died near

Geneva, Ontario County, N.Y., August 16, 1855; interment in Temple Hill Cemetery, Geneseo, Livingston County, N.Y.

**FULLER, Thomas James Duncan,** a Representative from Maine; born in Hardwick, Caledonia County, Vt., March 17, 1808; attended the common schools; studied law; was admitted to the bar and commenced practice in Calais, Maine; elected as a Democrat to the Thirty-first and to the three succeeding Congresses (March 4, 1849-March 3, 1857); chairman, Committee on Commerce (Thirty-third Congress); was not a candidate for renomination in 1856; appointed by President James Buchanan as Second Auditor of the Treasury and served from April 15, 1857, to August 3, 1861; engaged in the practice of law before the United States Supreme Court and the Court of Claims in Washington, D.C.; died, while on a visit to his son, near Upperville, Fauquier County, Va., February 13, 1876; interment in Oak Hill Cemetery, Washington, D.C.

**FULLER, Timothy,** a Representative from Massachusetts; born in Chilmark, Dukes County, Mass., July 11, 1778; received a classical education and was graduated from Harvard University in 1801; taught at Leicester Academy; studied law; was admitted to the bar and commenced practice in Boston in 1804; served in the Massachusetts senate 1813-1817; elected as a Republican to the Fifteenth Congress and reelected to the three succeeding Congresses (March 4, 1817-March 3, 1825); chairman, Committee on Naval Affairs (Seventeenth Congress); member of the Massachusetts house of representatives 1825-1828; Massachusetts councilor in 1828; again elected to the Massachusetts house of representatives in 1831; died in Groton, Middlesex County, Mass., October 1, 1835; interment in Mount Auburn Cemetery, Cambridge, Mass.

**FULLER, William Elijah,** a Representative from Iowa; born in Howard, Centre County, Pa., March 30, 1846; moved with his parents to West Union, Fayette County, Iowa, in 1853; attended the common schools, the Upper Iowa University at Fayette, and the State University of Iowa at Iowa City; was graduated from the law department of the latter university in June 1870; was admitted to the bar the same year and commenced practice in West Union; held a position in the Office of Indian Affairs, Department of the Interior, in 1866 and 1867; member of the West Union Board of Education for six years; member, Iowa State house of representatives, 1876-1877; member of the Republican State and congressional committees; elected as a Republican to the Forty-ninth and Fiftieth Congresses (March 4, 1885-March 3, 1889); declined to be a candidate for renomination in 1888 to the Fifty-first Congress; Assistant Attorney General, Spanish Treaty Claims Commission, 1901-1907; resumed the practice of law in West Union; died in Washington, D.C., April 23, 1918; interment in West Union Cemetery, West Union, Iowa.

**FULLER, William Kendall,** a Representative from New York; born in Schenectady, N.Y., November 24, 1792; attended the common schools, and was graduated from Union College in 1810; studied law; was admitted to the bar in 1814 and commenced practice in Schenectady; adjutant general of New York in 1823; district attorney of Madison County 1821-1829; member of the State assembly in 1829 and 1830; elected as a Jacksonian to the Twenty-third and Twenty-fourth Congresses (March 4, 1833-March 3, 1837); resumed the practice of law; died in Schenectady, N.Y., on November 11, 1883; interment in Vale Cemetery.

**FULLERTON, David** (uncle of David Fullerton Robison), a Representative from Pennsylvania; born in the Cumberland Valley, near Greencastle, Franklin County, Pa., October 4, 1772; attended the public schools; served as major in the War of 1812; settled in Greencastle and engaged in mercantile pursuits and banking; elected to the Sixteenth Congress and served from March 4, 1819, until May 15, 1820, when he resigned; was not a candidate for renomination; resumed mercantile pursuits and banking; member of

the Pennsylvania senate 1827-1839; died in Greencastle, Pa., February 1, 1843; interment in Cedar Hill Cemetery.

**FULMER, Hampton Pitts** (husband of Willa L. Fulmer), a Representative from South Carolina; born near Springfield, Orangeburg County, S.C., June 23, 1875; attended the public schools and was graduated from Massey's Business College, Columbus, Ga., in 1897; engaged in agricultural and mercantile pursuits in Norway, S.C.; also engaged in banking; member of the State house of representatives 1917-1920; elected as a Democrat to the Sixty-seventh and to the eleven succeeding Congresses and served from March 4, 1921, until his death; chairman, Committee on Agriculture (Seventy-sixth through Seventy-eighth Congresses); had been nominated for reelection to the Seventy-ninth Congress; died in Washington, D.C., October 19, 1944; interment in Memorial Park Cemetery, Orangeburg, S.C.

**FULMER, Willa Lybrand** (wife of Hampton P. Fulmer), a Representative from South Carolina; born in Wagener, Aiken County, S.C., February 3, 1884; attended the Wagener, (S.C.) public schools and Greenville (S.C.) Female College; elected as a Democrat to the Seventy-eighth Congress to fill the vacancy caused by the death of her husband, Hampton P. Fulmer, and served from November 7, 1944, to January 3, 1945; was not a candidate for election to the Seventy-ninth Congress; engaged in agricultural pursuits until her retirement; died May 13, 1968, aboard a ship en route to Europe; interment in Memorial Park Cemetery, Orangeburg, S.C.

**FULTON, Andrew Steele** (brother of John H. Fulton), a Representative from Virginia; born near Waynesboro, Augusta County, Va., on September 29, 1800; attended the common schools and Hampden-Sidney College, Hampden-Sidney, Va.; studied law in Staunton, Va.; was admitted to the bar in 1825 and commenced practice in Abingdon, Va., in 1826; moved to Wytheville in 1828; elected a member of the Virginia house of delegates in 1840 and 1845; prosecuting attorney for Wythe County; elected as a Whig to the Thirtieth Congress (March 4, 1847-March 3, 1849); chairman, Committee on Invalid Pensions (Thirtieth Congress); was not a candidate for renomination in 1848; resumed the practice of law; judge of the fifteenth judicial circuit of Virginia 1852-1869; died near Austinville, Wythe County, Va., on November 22, 1884; interment in the family cemetery on New River, near Austinville, Va.

**FULTON, Charles William** (brother of Elmer Lincoln Fulton), a Senator from Oregon; born in Lima, Allen County, Ohio, August 24, 1853; moved to Iowa in 1855 with his parents, who settled in Magnolia; attended the common schools; moved to Pawnee City, Nebr., in 1870; studied law; was admitted to the bar in 1875 and practiced; moved to Oregon and settled in Astoria in 1875; member, State senate 1878; city attorney 1880-1882; elected to the State senate in 1890, 1898, and 1902, and was its president in 1893 and 1901; elected as a Republican to the United States Senate and served from March 4, 1903, to March 3, 1909; unsuccessful candidate for reelection; chairman, Committee on Canadian Relations (Fifty-eighth and Fifty-ninth Congresses), Committee on Claims (Fifty-ninth and Sixtieth Congresses); resumed the practice of law in Portland, Oreg., where he died January 27, 1918; interment in Ocean View Cemetery, Astoria, Oreg.

**FULTON, Elmer Lincoln** (brother of Charles William Fulton), a Representative from Oklahoma; born in Magnolia, Harrison County, Iowa, April 22, 1865; moved to Nebraska in 1870 with his parents, who settled in Pawnee City; attended the public schools and Tabor College, Tabor, Iowa; studied law; was admitted to the bar in 1895 and commenced practice at Pawnee City, Nebr.; moved to Stillwater, in the Territory of Oklahoma, in 1901 and continued the practice of law; elected as a Democrat to the Sixtieth Congress September 17, 1907, and served from November 16, 1907, when

Oklahoma was admitted as a State into the Union, until March 3, 1909; unsuccessful candidate for reelection in 1908 to the Sixty-first Congress; resumed the practice of law in Oklahoma City, Okla.; appointed assistant attorney general of Oklahoma in 1919 and served until 1922, when he resigned and again resumed the practice of his profession; died in Oklahoma City, Okla., October 4, 1939; interment in Valhalla Cemetery, St. Louis, Mo.

**FULTON, James Grove,** a Representative from Pennsylvania; born in Dormont Borough, Allegheny County, Pa., March 1, 1903; attended the public schools in South Hills and the Fine Arts Department of Carnegie Institute of Technology, Pittsburgh, Pa.; was graduated from Pennsylvania State College at State College in 1924 and from Harvard Law School, Doctor of Laws, 1927; was admitted to the bar in 1928 and commenced practice in Pittsburgh, Pa.; also engaged in agricultural pursuits; member of the Allegheny County Board of Law Examiners 1934-1942; served in the Pennsylvania senate in 1939 and 1940; solicitor for Dormont Borough in 1942; publisher of the Mount Lebanon (Pa.) News and several other newspapers; enlisted in the United States Naval Reserve in 1942 and served in the South Pacific as a lieutenant until discharged in 1945; in 1944 while still in the service was elected as a Republican to the Seventy-ninth Congress; reelected to the thirteen succeeding Congresses and served from January 3, 1945, until his death in Washington, D.C., October 6, 1971; delegated to the United Nations Conference on Trade and Employment at Havana in 1947 and 1948, and to the fourteenth General Assembly of United Nations in 1959; served as adviser on space to United States Mission at United Nations, 1960-1969; interment in Mt. Lebanon Cemetery, Pittsburgh, Pa.

**FULTON, John Hall** (brother of Andrew Steele Fulton), a Representative from Virginia; born in Augusta County, Va.; attended the common schools and was graduated from Hampden-Sidney College, Hampden-Sidney, Va.; studied law; was admitted to the bar and commenced practice in Abingdon, Va.; member of the Virginia house of delegates in 1823 and 1824; served in the Virginia senate 1829-1831; elected as a Jacksonian to the Twenty-third Congress (March 4, 1833-March 3, 1835); unsuccessful candidate for reelection in 1834 to the Twenty-fourth Congress; also was a candidate for election to the Twenty-fifth Congress at the time of his death in Abingdon, Washington County, Va., January 28, 1836; interment in Sinking Spring Cemetery.

**FULTON, Richard Harmon,** a Representative from Tennessee; born in Nashville, Davidson County, Tenn., January 27, 1927; graduated from the public schools of Nashville and attended the University of Tennessee at Knoxville; served in the United States Navy in 1945 and 1946; member, Tennessee State senate, 1958-1960; engaged in business and was a real estate broker; delegate to the Democratic National Convention of 1964; elected as a Democrat to the Eighty-eighth and reelected to the six succeeding Congresses and served from January 3, 1963, until his resignation August 14, 1975; mayor, Metropolitan Government of Nashville and Davidson County, Tenn., August 14, 1975, to October 5, 1987; unsuccessful candidate in 1978 and 1986 for nomination for Governor of Tennessee; established private firm in governmental relations; is a resident of Nashville, Tenn.

**FULTON, William Savin,** a Senator from Arkansas; born in Cecil County, Md., June 2, 1795; pursued classical studies and was graduated from Baltimore College in 1813; commenced the study of law but during the War of 1812 enlisted in a company of Volunteers at Fort McHenry; after the war moved to Tennessee and resumed the study of law; was admitted to the bar in 1817 and commenced practice in Gallatin, Tenn.; military secretary to General Andrew Jackson in his Florida campaign in 1818; moved to Alabama in 1820 and settled in Florence; elected judge of the county court in 1822; appointed by President Andrew Jackson secretary of the Territory of

Arkansas in 1829; appointed Governor of Arkansas Territory by President Jackson, and confirmed by the Senate on February 3, 1835; served as Territorial Governor until September 13, 1836, when he was succeeded by an elected chief executive of the State; upon the admission of Arkansas as a State was elected as a Democrat to the United States Senate; reelected in 1840 and served from September 18, 1836, until his death in Little Rock, Ark., August 15, 1844; chairman, Committee on Public Buildings (Twenty-fifth and Twenty-sixth Congresses); interment in Mount Holly Cemetery.

**Bibliography:** *DAB.*

**FUNDERBURK, David Britton,** a Representative from North Carolina; born at Langley Field Air Force Base, Hampton, Va., April 28, 1944; attended Aberdeen (N.C.) High School, 1958-1962; B.A., Wake Forest University, Winston-Salem, N.C., 1966, and M.A., 1967; Ph.D., modern history, University of South Carolina, 1974; instructor of history and government, Wingate (N.C.) College, 1967-1969; associate professor of history and president of graduate faculty, Hardin-Simmons University, Abilene, Tex., 1972-1978; professor of history and Title III coordinator, Campbell University, Buies Creek, N.C., 1978-1981; appointed by President Ronald Reagan as Ambassador to Romania on October 2, 1981 and served until May 1985; chair, Department of History and Graham Barden Professor of Government, Campbell University, 1985-1986; unsuccessful candidate in 1986 for Republican nomination to the United States Senate; consultant, Department of Education, 1987-1988; project director, National Research and Reporting Center, 1993 to present; elected as a Republican to the One Hundred Fourth Congress (January 3, 1995-January 3, 1997); is a resident of Buies Creek, N.C.

**FUNK, Benjamin Franklin** (father of Frank Hamilton Funk), a Representative from Illinois; born in Funks Grove Township, McLean County, Ill., October 17, 1838; attended the public schools and Wesleyan University in Bloomington; left school in 1862 to enlist in the Sixty-eighth Regiment, Illinois Volunteer Infantry, as a private, and served five months during the Civil War; returned to the university and finished the course; engaged in agricultural pursuits; moved to Bloomington, Ill., in 1869; mayor of Bloomington 1871-1876 and 1884-1886; trustee of the asylum for the blind at Jacksonville; president of the board of trustees of Wesleyan University for twenty years; delegate to the Republican National Convention in 1888; elected as a Republican to the Fifty-third Congress (March 4, 1893-March 3, 1895); unsuccessful candidate for renomination in 1894; resumed agricultural pursuits; died in Bloomington, Ill., February 14, 1909; interment in Bloomington Cemetery.

**FUNK, Frank Hamilton** (son of Benjamin Franklin Funk), a Representative from Illinois; born in Bloomington, McLean County, Ill., April 5, 1869; attended the public schools and the Illinois Normal School at Normal, Ill.; was graduated from the Lawrenceville School, Lawrenceville, N.J., in 1888 and from Yale University in 1891; engaged in agricultural pursuits and livestock production in Bloomington, Ill., member, Illinois Republican State central committee, 1906-1912; member of the State senate, 1909-1911; unsuccessful candidate of the Progressive Party for election for Governor of Illinois in 1912; chairman of the Illinois delegation to the Progressive National Conventions of 1912 and 1916; unsuccessful Progressive candidate for election for United States Senator in 1913; member, Illinois Public Utilities Commission, 1914-1921; delegate to the Republican National Convention of 1920; elected as a Republican to the Sixty-seventh and to the two succeeding Congresses (March 4, 1921-March 3, 1927); unsuccessful candidate for renomination in 1926 to the Seventieth Congress; retired from public life and active business pursuits; resided at Bloomington, Ill., until his death there on November 24, 1940; interment in Funk's Grove Cemetery, Funk's Grove, Ill.

**FUNSTON, Edward Hogue,** a Representative from Kansas; born near New Carlisle, Clark County, Ohio, September 16, 1836; attended the country schools, Lindle Hill Academy, New Carlisle, Ohio, and Marietta (Ohio) College; taught school; during the Civil War entered the Union Army in 1861 as lieutenant, Sixteenth Ohio Battery; participated in the principal engagements along the Mississippi River; mustered out in 1865; located on a prairie farm near Carlyle, Allen County, Kans., in 1867; member of the State house of representatives 1873-1876, and served as speaker in 1875; member of the State senate 1880-1884, and served as president pro tempore in 1880; elected as a Republican to the Forty-eighth Congress to fill the vacancy caused by the death of Dudley C. Haskell; reelected to the Forty-ninth and to the three succeeding Congresses and served from March 21, 1884, to March 3, 1893; chairman, Committee on Agriculture (Fifty-first Congress); presented credentials as a Member-elect to the Fifty-third Congress and served from March 4, 1893, until August 2, 1894, when he was succeeded by Horace L. Moore, who contested the election; resumed agricultural pursuits; died in Iola, Kans., on September 10, 1911; interment in Iola Cemetery.

**FUQUA, Don,** a Representative from Florida; born in Jacksonville, Duval County, Fla., August 20, 1933; when four years old moved with his family to a farm in Calhoun County, near Altha, Fla.; attended public schools; student at the University of Florida at Gainesville, 1951-1953; served in the United States Army Medical Corps during the Korean War, 1953-1955; B.S., University of Florida, 1957; engaged in operation of general farm and dairy; member of the Florida State house of representatives from Calhoun County, 1958-1962; delegate to the Democratic National Convention of 1968; elected as a Democrat to the Eighty-eighth and to the eleven succeeding Congresses (January 3, 1963-January 3, 1987); chairman, Committee on Science and Technology (Ninety-sixth through Ninety-ninth Congresses); was not a candidate for reelection in 1986 to the One Hundredth Congress; president, Aerospace Industries Association of America, 1987 to present; is a resident of Arlington, Va.

**FURCOLO, Foster,** a Representative from Massachusetts; born in New Haven, Conn., July 29, 1911; attended the public schools of New Haven, Conn., and Springfield, Mass.; was graduated from Yale University in 1933 and from its law school in 1936; was admitted to the Massachusetts bar in 1937 and commenced the practice of law in Springfield, Mass., the same year; unsuccessful candidate in 1942 for district attorney of Hampden County, Mass.; during the Second World War served in the United States Navy with service in the Pacific Theater; elected as a Democrat to the Eighty-first and Eighty-second Congresses and served from January 3, 1949, until his resignation September 30, 1952; appointed Massachusetts treasurer and receiver general on July 5, 1952, and served until 1955; unsuccessful candidate in 1954 for election to the United States Senate; elected Governor of Massachusetts in 1956, reelected in 1958, and served from January 3, 1957 to January 5, 1961; unsuccessful candidate in 1960 for nomination to the United States Senate; assistant district attorney in Middlesex County, Mass., 1967-1972; chairman, Attorney General's Advisory Committee on Narcotics, 1969; administrative law judge, United States Occupational Safety and Health Review Commission; was a resident of Cambridge, Mass., until his death there on July 5, 1995.

**FURLONG, Robert Grant,** a Representative from Pennsylvania; born in Roscoe, Washington County, Pa., January 4, 1886; attended the public schools at Roscoe, Pa.; was graduated from State Teachers College, California, Pa., in 1904 and from Jefferson Medical College, Philadelphia, Pa., in 1909; taught school at Roscoe, Pa., in 1904 and 1905; practiced medicine in Donora, Pa., 1910-1968; during the First World War served as a first lieutenant with the Two Hundred and Eightieth Ambulance Company, Twentieth Division;

burgess of Donora, Pa., 1922-1926 and in 1941 and 1942; postmaster of Donora, Pa., 1933-1938; elected as a Democrat to the Seventy-eighth Congress (January 3, 1943-January 3, 1945); unsuccessful candidate for renomination in 1944 to the Seventy-ninth Congress; resumed the practice of medicine; elected sheriff of Washington County, Pa., in 1945, 1949, 1953, 1957, and again in 1961 for a four-year term; retired and resided in Donora, Pa., where he died March 19, 1973; interment in Monongahela Cemetery, Monongahela, Pa.

**FURLOW, Allen John,** a Representative from Minnesota; born in Rochester, Olmsted County, Minn., November 9, 1890; attended the public schools; was graduated from Rochester High School in 1910; during the First World War served overseas as a pilot in the aviation branch of the Army; promoted to first lieutenant; was graduated from the law department of George Washington University, Washington, D.C., in 1920; was admitted to the bar in 1920 and commenced practice in Rochester, Minn.; member, Minnesota State senate, 1923-1925; elected as a Republican to the Sixty-ninth and Seventieth Congresses (March 4, 1925-March 3, 1929); unsuccessful candidate for renomination in 1928 to the Seventy-first Congress; employed in the legal department of the Curtiss-Wright Corporation, Washington, D.C., 1929-1930; in 1933 was appointed by the United States Attorney General as a special assistant in cases assigned under the petroleum code; was in the legal department of the Veterans Administration, Washington, D.C., 1934-1937; returned to Rochester, Minn., and practiced law until his death on January 29, 1954; interment in Oakwood Cemetery.

**FURSE, Elizabeth,** a Representative from Oregon; born in Nairobi, Kenya, October 13, 1936; B.A., Evergreen State College, Olympia, Wash., 1974; attended Northwestern School of Law, Portland, Oreg., 1978-1979; director of restoration program for Native American Tribes, Oregon Legal Services, 1980-1986; founder, Oregon Peace Institute; organized "Citizen's Train" to Washington, D.C., 1988; co-owner and co-operator of Helvetia Vineyards, Hillsboro, Oreg.; elected as a Democrat to the One Hundred Third and One Hundred Fourth Congresses (January 3, 1993-January 3, 1997); is a resident of Hillsboro, Oreg.

**FUSTER, Jaime B.,** a Resident Commissioner from Puerto Rico; born January 12, 1941, in Guayama, Puerto Rico; attended parochial schools; B.A., Notre Dame University, 1962; J.D., University of Puerto Rico Law School, 1965; LL.M., Columbia University Law School, 1966; Law and Humanities Fellow, Harvard University, 1973-1974; professor of law, 1966-1979, and dean of law, 1974-1978, University of Puerto Rico; United States Deputy Assistant Attorney General, 1980-1981; president, Catholic University of Puerto Rico, 1981-1984; elected as a Democrat to the United States House of Representatives in 1984 for a four-year term; reelected in 1988, and served from January 3, 1985 until his resignation on March 4, 1992; is a resident of San Juan, P.R.

**FYAN, Robert Washington,** a Representative from Missouri; born in Bedford Springs, Bedford County, Pa., March 11, 1835; attended the common schools; studied law; was admitted to the bar in 1858 and commenced practice in Marshfield, Webster County, Mo.; county attorney in 1859; entered the Union Army in June 1861, serving with Colonel Hampton's regiment, Webster County Home Guards, the Twenty-fourth Regiment, Missouri Volunteer Infantry, and the Forty-sixth Regiment, Missouri Volunteer Infantry; circuit attorney in 1865 and 1866; circuit judge of the fourteenth judicial circuit of Missouri from April 1866 to January 1883; member of the State constitutional convention in 1875; elected as a Democrat to the Forty-eighth Congress (March 4, 1883-March 3, 1885); elected to the Fifty-second and Fifty-third Congresses (March 4, 1891-March 3, 1895); resumed the practice of law; died in Marshfield, Mo., July 28, 1896; interment in Lebanon Cemetery, Lebanon, Mo.

# G

**GABALDON, Isauro,** a Resident Commissioner from the Philippine Islands; born in San Isidoro, Nueva Ecija, Philippine Islands, Spain, December 8, 1875; attended the public schools in Tebar, Spain, and the Colleges Quintanar del Rey and Villa Nueva de la Jara, Cuenca, Spain; studied law in the Universidad Central, Madrid, Spain, and was graduated from the Universidad Santo Tomas, Manila, Philippine Islands, in 1900; practiced law from 1903 to 1906; Governor of the Province of Nueva Ecija in 1906 and 1912-1916; member of the Philippine house of representatives 1907-1911; served in the Philippine senate 1916-1919; elected as a Nationalist a Resident Commissioner to the United States in 1920; reelected in 1923 and 1925, and served from March 4, 1920, until his resignation effective July 16, 1928, having been nominated for election to the Philippine house of representatives; had also been elected in 1925 as a member of the Philippine house of representatives, but did not qualify, preferring to continue as Commissioner; died in Manila, Philippine Islands, December 21, 1942; interment in North Cemetery in Manila.

**GADSDEN, Christopher,** a Delegate from South Carolina; born in Charleston, S.C., February 16, 1723; attended schools in England; employed in a commercial house in Philadelphia, Pa., 1742-1745; delegate to the Stamp Act Congress that met in New York in 1765; Member of the First Continental Congress in Philadelphia, Pa., 1774-1776; served as an officer in the Continental Army, 1776-1783, and participated in the defense of Charleston in 1780; entered the service as colonel and subsequently attained the rank of brigadier general; was a framer of the State constitution in 1778; Lieutenant Governor, 1778-1780; elected Governor of South Carolina in 1781, but declined; died in Charleston, S.C., September 15, 1805; interment in St. Philip's Churchyard.
**Bibliography:** *DAB*; Godbold, E. Stanly, Jr., and Robert H. Woody. *Christopher Gadsden and the American Revolution.* Knoxville: University of Tennessee Press, 1982.

**GAGE, Joshua,** a Representative from Massachusetts; born in Harwich, Mass., on August 7, 1763; completed preparatory studies; in 1795 moved to Augusta, Maine (until 1820 a district of Massachusetts); was a master mariner, and subsequently became engaged in mercantile pursuits; member of the Massachusetts house of representatives in 1805 and 1807; served in the Massachusetts senate in 1813 and 1815; treasurer of Kennebec County, Maine, 1810-1831; elected as a Republican to the Fifteenth Congress (March 4, 1817-March 3, 1819); member of the Maine executive council in 1822 and 1823; died in Augusta, Maine, January 24, 1831; interment in Augusta, Maine.

**GAHN, Harry Conrad,** a Representative from Ohio; born in Elmore, Ottawa County, Ohio, April 26, 1880; attended the public schools; taught school three years; was graduated from the law department of the University of Michigan at Ann Arbor in 1904; was admitted to the bar and commenced practice in Cleveland, Ohio; attorney for the Cleveland Legal Aid Society 1909-1911; member of the city council 1910-1921, serving as its president in 1918 and 1919; member of the Cleveland River and Harbor Commission 1911-1921; treasurer of the American Association of Port Authorities 1912-1919; was in charge of Liberty Loan campaigns in his district during the First World War; elected as a Republican to the Sixty-seventh Congress (March 4, 1921-March 3, 1923); unsuccessful candidate for reelection in 1922 to the Sixty-eighth Congress and for election in 1936 to the Seventy-fifth Congress; resumed the practice of his profession; solicitor for Independence, Ohio, 1936-1956; died in Cleveland, Ohio, November 2, 1962; interment in Elmore Community Cemetery, Elmore, Ohio.

**GAILLARD, John** (uncle of Theodore Gaillard Hunt), a Senator from South Carolina; born in St. Stephens District, S.C., September 5, 1765; educated for the legal profession in England; member, State house of representatives 1794-1796; member, State senate 1796-1804, serving as president 1803-1804; elected as a Republican to the United States Senate in 1804 to fill the vacancy caused by the resignation of Pierce Butler; reelected in 1806, 1812, 1818, and 1824 and served from December 6, 1804, until his death on February 26, 1826; served as President pro tempore of the Senate during the Eleventh and Thirteenth through Nineteenth Congresses; died in Washington, D.C.; interment in the Congressional Cemetery.
**Bibliography:** *DAB*.

**GAINES, John Pollard,** a Representative from Kentucky; born in Augusta, Va. (now West Virginia), September 22, 1795; moved to Boone County, Ky., in early youth; received a thorough English training; studied law; was admitted to the bar and commenced practice in Walton, Ky.; volunteered for service in the War of 1812; represented Boone County for several years in the Kentucky legislature; served in the Mexican War as major in General Thomas Marshall's Kentucky Cavalry Brigade, and also as aide-de-camp on the staff of General Winfield Scott; captured at Incarnacion in January 1847 and was confined for several months in the City of Mexico; while in captivity was elected as a Whig to the Thirtieth Congress (March 4, 1847-March 3, 1849); unsuccessful candidate for reelection in 1848 to the Thirty-first Congress; appointed Governor of Oregon Territory by President Zachary Taylor in 1850 and served until May 16, 1853; resumed agricultural pursuits; died near Salem, Marion County, Oreg., December 9, 1857; interment in Odd Fellows Cemetery, Salem, Oreg.
**Bibliography:** *DAB*.

**GAINES, John Wesley,** a Representative from Tennessee; born in Wrencoe, near Nashville, Davidson County, Tenn., August 24, 1860; attended private and public schools, in which he also taught; studied law at home; studied medicine, and was graduated from the University of Nashville and from Vanderbilt University, Nashville, Tenn., in 1882; never practiced medicine, but the day after graduation resumed the study of law; was admitted to the bar in 1884 and commenced practice in Nashville in 1885; elected as a Democrat to the Fifty-fifth and to the five succeeding Congresses (March 4, 1897-March 3, 1909); unsuccessful for reelection in 1908 to the Sixty-first Congress; practiced law in Nashville, Tenn., where he died July 4, 1926; interment in Mount Olivet Cemetery.

**GAINES, Joseph Holt,** a Representative from West Virginia; born in Washington, D.C., September 3, 1864; moved with his parents to Fayette County, W.Va., in 1867; attended the University of West Virginia at Morgantown and was graduated from Princeton College in 1886; was admitted to the bar in 1887 and commenced practice in Fayetteville, W.Va.; appointed United States district attorney for West Virginia by President McKinley in 1897; resigned in 1901; elected as a Republican to the Fifty-seventh and to the four succeeding Congresses (March 4, 1901-March 3, 1911); chairman, Committee on Election of President, Vice President, and Representatives (Fifty-eighth through Sixty-first Congresses); unsuccessful candidate for reelection in 1910; resumed the practice of law in Charleston, W.Va.; died in Montgomery, W.Va., April 12, 1951; interment in Spring Hill Cemetery, Charleston, W.Va.

**GAINES, William Embre,** a Representative from Virginia; born near Charlotte Court House, Charlotte County, Va., August 30, 1844; attended the common schools; during the Civil War enlisted as a private in Company K, Eighteenth Virginia Regiment (Pickett's division); reenlisted in the Army of the Cape Fear, and surrendered with Johnston, near Greensboro, N.C., in April 1865, having attained the rank of adjutant of Manly's artillery battalion; studied law; was admitted to the bar and practiced; engaged in the tobacco business and banking at Burkeville, Va.; member of the Virginia senate from 1883 to 1887, when he resigned; delegate to the Republican National Convention in 1884; mayor of Burkeville; delegate to several Virgrinia conventions; elected as a Republican to the Fiftieth Congress (March 4, 1887-March 3, 1889); was not a candidate for renomination in 1888; died in Washington, D.C., May 4, 1912; interment in Glenwood Cemetery.

**GAITHER, Nathan,** a Representative from Kentucky; born near Mocksville, Davie County, N.C., September 15, 1788; completed preparatory studies; attended Bardstown College; studied medicine; was graduated from Jefferson Medical College and began practice in Columbia, Ky.; served as assistant surgeon in the War of 1812; member of the Kentucky house of representatives 1815-1818; elected as a Jacksonian to the Twenty-first and Twenty-second Congresses (March 4, 1829-March 3, 1833); unsuccessful candidate for reelection 1832 to the Twenty-third Congress; delegate to the Kentucky constitutional convention in 1849; again a member of the Kentucky house of representatives 1855-1857; resumed the practice of medicine; died in Columbia, Ky., August 12, 1862; interment in Columbia Cemetery.

**GALBRAITH, John,** a Representative from Pennsylvania; born in Huntingdon, Pa., on August 2, 1794; moved with his parents in 1796 to Allegheny Township, Huntingdon County, Pa., and subsequently, in 1802, to Centre Township, Butler County; attended the common schools; served an apprenticeship at the printer's trade; taught school; studied law; was admitted to the bar in 1817 and commenced practice in Butler, Pa.; moved to Franklin, Venango County, Pa., in 1822 and continued the practice of his profession; member of the Pennsylvania house of representatives 1829-1832; elected as a Jacksonian to the Twenty-third and Twenty-fourth Congresses (March 4, 1833-March 3, 1837); unsuccessful candidate for renomination in 1836; moved to Erie, Pa., in 1837; resumed the practice of law; elected as a Democrat to the Twenty-sixth Congress (March 4, 1839-March 3, 1841); was not a candidate for renomination in 1840; again engaged in the practice of law; elected president judge of the sixth judicial district in 1851 and served until his death in Erie, Pa., and June 15, 1860; interment in Erie Cemetery.

**GALE, George** (father of Levin Gale), a Representative from Maryland; born in Somerset County, Md., June 3, 1756; attended the common schools; served during the Revolutionary War; member of the Maryland convention which ratified the Federal Constitution in 1788; elected to the First Congress (March 4, 1789-March 3, 1791); appointed by President Washington on March 4, 1791, supervisor of distilled liquors for the district of Maryland; died at "Brookland," Cecil County, Md., January 2, 1815; interment in the family burying ground on his estate.

**GALE, Levin** (son of George Gale), a Representative from Maryland; born in Elkton, Cecil County, Md., April 24, 1784; attended the common schools; studied law; was admitted to the bar and practiced in Elkton, Md.; member of the State senate in 1816; elected to the Twentieth Congress (March 4, 1827-March 3, 1829); declined to be a candidate for renomination in 1828; resumed the practice of law; died in Elkton, Md., December 18, 1834.

**GALE, Richard Pillsbury,** a Representative from Minnesota; born in Minneapolis, Hennepin County, Minn., October 30, 1900; attended the public schools of Minneapolis, Blake School at Hopkins, Minn., Minnesota Farm School, and University of Minnesota at Minneapolis; was graduated from Yale University in 1922; became engaged in agricultural pursuits and securities in 1923; member of the State house of representatives in 1939 and 1940; member of the Mound (Minn.) School Board for eight years; trustee of Blake School at Hopkins, Minn.; elected as a Republican to the Seventy-seventh and to the Seventy-eighth Congresses (January 3, 1941-January 3, 1945); unsuccessful candidate for

reelection in 1944 to the Seventy-ninth Congress; author of newspaper articles on social, economic, and political life of people in various foreign countries; returned to agricultural pursuits and resided at his Wickham Farm near Mound, Minn.; died in Minneapolis, Minn., December 4, 1973; interment in Lakewood Cemetery.

**GALIFIANAKIS, Nick,** a Representative from North Carolina; born in Durham, N.C., July 22, 1928; attended the public schools; A.B., Duke University, 1951; LL.B., Duke University School of Law, 1953; active duty in the United States Marine Corps Reserve, October 1953 to April 1956; admitted to the bar in 1956 and commenced practice in Durham, N.C.; commanding officer, Forty-first Rifle Company, Durham, N.C., 1960-1962; assistant professor of business law, Duke University, 1960-1967; member, North Carolina State assembly, 1961-1967; elected as a Democrat to the Ninetieth and to the two succeeding Congresses (January 3, 1967-January 3, 1973); was not a candidate in 1972 for reelection to the House of Representatives, but was an unsuccessful candidate for election to the United States Senate; resumed the practice of law; is a resident of Durham, N.C.

**GALLAGHER, Cornelius Edward,** a Representative from New Jersey; born in Bayonne, Hudson County, N.J., March 2, 1921; attended the local schools of Bayonne; was graduated from John Marshall College, Jersey City, N.J., in 1946; LL.B., John Marshall Law School, 1948; additional studies at New York University in 1948 and 1949; commanded an Infantry rifle company in General George S. Patton's Third Army in Europe, was wounded three times and received eight decorations, and served from September 1941 until discharged as a captain in November 1946; served one year during the Korean War; was admitted to the bar in 1949 and commenced the practice of law in Bayonne, N.J.; served on faculty of Rutgers University in 1945 and 1946; director of the Broadway National Bank; elected to the Hudson County Board of Freeholders in 1953 and resigned in 1956; appointed commissioner of New Jersey Turnpike Authority in 1956, and served as vice chairman, 1956-1958; delegate to the Democratic National Conventions of 1952, 1956, and 1960; elected as a Democrat to the Eighty-sixth and to the six succeeding Congresses (January 3, 1959-January 3, 1973); unsuccessful candidate for renomination in 1972 to the Ninety-third Congress; vice president of Baron/Canning International in New York City; is a resident of Columbia, N.J.

**GALLAGHER, James A.,** a Representative from Pennsylvania; born in Philadelphia, Pa., January 16, 1869; attended the public schools and Pierce Business College, Philadelphia, Pa., 1891-1893; engaged in merchandise warehousing and transportation, beginning in 1886; also engaged in banking; elected as a Republican to the Seventy-eighth Congress (January 3, 1943-January 3, 1945); unsuccessful candidate for reelection in 1944 to the Seventy-ninth Congress; elected in 1946 to the Eightieth Congress (January 3, 1947-January 3, 1949); unsuccessful candidate for renomination in 1948 to the Eighty-first Congress; returned to the merchandise warehousing and transportation business; died in Philadelphia, Pa., December 8, 1957; interment in Holy Cross Cemetery, Yeadon, Pa.

**GALLAGHER, Thomas,** a Representative from Illinois; born in Concord, Merrimack County, N.H., July 6, 1850; moved to Chicago in 1866; attended the public schools; learned the trade of iron molder; entered the hat business in Chicago in 1878; director of the Cook County State Savings Bank; member of the city council of Chicago 1893-1897; member of the board of education 1897-1903; chairman of the Democratic central committee of Cook County in 1902; president of the Democratic county committee in 1906 and 1907 and a member of the executive committee in 1909, 1911, and 1913; elected as a Democrat to the Sixty-first and to the five succeeding Congresses (March 4, 1909-March 3, 1921); unsuccessful candidate for reelection in 1920 to the Sixty-seventh Congress;

retired from active pursuits and resided in Chicago, Ill.; died February 24, 1930, in San Antonio, Tex., while on a visit; interment in St. Boniface Cemetery, Chicago, Ill.

**GALLAGHER, William James,** a Representative from Minnesota; born in Minneapolis, Hennepin County, Minn., May 13, 1875; attended the public schools, and was graduated from North High School in 1894; engaged as an editorial employee and proofreader in Minneapolis, Minn., in 1895 and 1896; moved to Spokane, Wash., in 1897 and continued his former pursuits with a labor journal until 1899; returned to Minneapolis, Minn., and engaged as a trucker and clerk in freight houses until 1919; employed as a street sweeper for Hennepin County 1919-1927 and for the city of Minneapolis, Minn., from 1927 until his retirement in 1942; was elected as a Democrat to the Seventy-ninth Congress and served from January 3, 1945, until his death; had been renominated to the Eightieth Congress in 1946; died in a hospital at Rochester, Minn., August 13, 1946; interment in Crystal Lake Cemetery, Minneapolis, Minn.

**GALLATIN, Albert,** a Senator and a Representative from Pennsylvania; born in Geneva, Switzerland, January 29, 1761; was graduated from the University of Geneva in 1779; immigrated to the United States and settled in Boston, Mass., in 1780; served in the Revolutionary Army; instructor of French in Harvard University in 1782; moved to Virginia in 1785 and settled in Fayette County (now in Pennsylvania); his estate becoming a portion of Pennsylvania, he was made a member of the Pennsylvania constitutional convention in 1789; member, Pennsylvania house of representatives, 1790-1792; elected to the United States Senate and presented credentials as a Senator-elect on February 28, 1793; no action was taken during the Second Congress, but when he took his seat, a petition was presented by nineteen Pennsylvania Federalists alleging Gallatin had not been a citizen of the United States the term of years required by Article I, Section 3 of the Constitution, and the Senate declared the election void; served from December 2, 1793 to February 28, 1794; elected to the Fourth and to the two succeeding Congresses (March 4, 1795-March 3, 1801); was not a candidate for renomination in 1800 to the Seventh Congress; appointed Secretary of the Treasury by President Thomas Jefferson, reappointed by President James Madison, and served from May 14, 1801 until February 9, 1814; appointed one of the commissioners to negotiate the Treaty of Ghent in 1814; one of the commissioners who negotiated a commercial convention with Great Britain in 1816; appointed Envoy Extraordinary and Minister Plenipotentiary to France by President Madison on February 28, 1815, and served until May 1823; appointed Minister Plenipotentiary to Great Britain on May 10, 1826, and served until October 1827; returned to New York City and became president of the National Bank of New York; died in Astoria, N.Y., August 12, 1849; interment in Nicholson Vault, Trinity Churchyard, New York City.

**Bibliography:** *DAB*; Gallatin, Albert. *Selected Writings of Albert Gallatin*. Edited by E. James Ferguson. Indianapolis: Bobbs-Merrill, 1967; Walters, Raymond, Jr. *Albert Gallatin: Jeffersonian Financier and Diplomat*. New York: Macmillan, 1957.

**GALLEGLY, Elton W.,** a Representative from California; born in Huntington Park, Calif., March 7, 1944; attended public schools in Cudahy and Huntington Park, Calif., and graduated from Huntington Park High School in 1962; attended Los Angeles State College, 1962-1963; real estate broker; member of the Simi Valley City Council, 1979; mayor of Simi Valley, 1980-1986; chairman, Ventura County Association of Governments, 1983; elected as a Republican to the One Hundredth and to the four succeeding Congresses (January 3, 1987-January 3, 1997); is a resident of Simi Valley, Calif.

**GALLEGOS, José Manuel,** a Delegate from the Territory of New Mexico; was born in what is now Rio Arriba County, N.Mex., October 30, 1815; attended parochial schools; studied theology at the

College of Durango, Republic of Mexico, and was graduated in 1840; member of the legislative assembly of what was then the Department of New Mexico, Republic of Mexico, 1843-1846; member of the first Territorial council of the Territory of New Mexico in 1851; elected as a Democrat to the Thirty-third Congress (March 4, 1853-March 3, 1855); presented credentials as a Delegate-elect to the Thirty-fourth Congress, and served from March 4, 1855 to July 23, 1856, when he was succeeded by Miguel A. Otero, who contested his election; member of the Territorial house of representatives, 1860-1862, and served as speaker; unsuccessful candidate for election in 1862 to the Thirty-eighth Congress; made a prisoner of war by the Texas Confederate troops in 1862; treasurer of the Territory in 1865 and 1866; superintendent of Indian affairs in New Mexico in 1868; elected as a Democrat to the Forty-second Congress (March 4, 1871-March 3, 1873); unsuccessful candidate for reelection in 1872 to the Forty-third Congress; died in Santa Fe, N.Mex., April 21, 1875; interment in the Catholic Cemetery.

**Bibliography:** Chavez, Angelico. *Tres Macho--He Said: Padre Gallegos of Albuquerque, New Mexico's First Congressman*. Santa Fe, N.Mex.: William Gannon, 1985.

**GALLINGER, Jacob Harold,** a Representative and a Senator from New Hampshire; born in Cornwall, Ontario, Canada, March 28, 1837; attended the common schools and completed an academic course; became a printer; studied medicine and was graduated from the Cincinnati (Ohio) Medical Institute in 1858; studied abroad for two years; returned to the United States and engaged in the practice of medicine and surgery in Concord, N.H.; member, New Hampshire State house of representatives, 1872-1873, 1891; member of the State constitutional convention in 1876; member, State senate, 1878-1880; was surgeon general of New Hampshire, with the rank of brigadier general, 1879-1880; elected as a Republican to the Forty-ninth and Fiftieth Congresses (March 4, 1885-March 3, 1889); declined to be a candidate for reelection in 1888 to the Fifty-first Congress; elected as a Republican to the United States Senate in 1891; reelected in 1897, 1903, 1909, and 1914, and served from March 4, 1891 until his death in Franklin, N.H., August 17, 1918; served as President pro tempore during the Sixty-second Congress; Republican caucus chairman 1913-1918; chairman, Committee on Transportation Routes to the Seaboard (Fifty-second Congress), Committee on Pensions (Fifty-fourth through Fifty-seventh Congresses), Committee on the District of Columbia (Fifty-seventh through Sixty-second Congresses), Republican Conference (Sixty-third through Sixty-fifth Congresses); chairman of the Merchant Marine Commission, 1904-1905; interment in Blossom Hill Cemetery, Concord, N.H.

**Bibliography:** *DAB*; Schlup, Leonard. "Consistent Conservative: Jacob Harold Gallinger and the Presidential Campaign of 1912 in New Hampshire." *International Review of History and Political Science* 21 (August 1984): 49-57.

**GALLIVAN, James Ambrose,** a Representative from Massachusetts; born in Boston, Mass., October 22, 1866; attended the public schools; was graduated from the Boston Latin School in 1884 and from Harvard University in 1888; engaged in newspaper work in 1888; member of the Massachusetts house of representatives in 1895 and 1896; served in the Massachusetts senate in 1897 and 1898; street commissioner of Boston 1900-1914; elected as a Democrat to the Sixty-third Congress to fill the vacancy caused by the resignation of James M. Curley; reelected to the Sixty-fourth and to the six succeeding Congresses and served from April 7, 1914, until his death in Arlington, Mass., April 3, 1928; interment in St. Joseph's Cemetery (West Roxbury), Boston, Mass.

**GALLO, Dean A.,** a Representative from New Jersey; born in Hackensack, Bergen County, N.J., November 23, 1935; attended public schools and graduated from Boonton (N.J.) High School in 1954; realtor; president, Parsippany-Troy Hills Township Council,

1970; director, Morris County Board of Chosen Freeholders, 1973-1975; member, New Jersey State general assembly, 1976-1984; elected as a Republican to the Ninety-ninth and to the four succeeding Congresses and served from January 3, 1985, until his death on November 6, 1994; had been renominated to the One Hundred Fourth Congress, but withdrew his name from consideration on August 23, 1994 because of ill health.

**GALLOWAY, Joseph,** a Delegate from Pennsylvania; born at West River, Anne Arundel County, Md., 1731; moved with his father to Pennsylvania in 1740; received a liberal schooling; studied law; was admitted to the bar and began practice in Philadelphia, Pa.; member of the Pennsylvania House of Representatives 1757-1775, and served as speaker 1766-1774; Member of the Continental Congress in 1774; signed the nonimportation agreement, but was opposed to independence of the Colonies and remained loyal to the King; in December 1776 joined the British Army of General Howe in New York; moved to England in 1778; the same year the General Assembly of Pennsylvania convicted him of high treason and confiscated his estates; died in Watford, Herts, England, August 29, 1803.

Bibliography: *DAB*; Boyd, Julian P. *Anglo-American Union; Joseph Galloway's Plans to Preserve the British Empire, 1774-1788.* Philadelphia: University of Pennsylvania Press, 1941.

**GALLOWAY, Samuel,** a Representative from Ohio; born in Gettysburg, Adams County, Pa., March 20, 1811; attended the public schools; moved to Ohio and settled in Highland County in 1830; graduated from Miami University, Oxford, Ohio, in 1833; attended Princeton Theological Seminary in 1835 and 1836; taught school in Hamilton, Ohio, 1836 and 1837, at Miami University in 1837 and 1838, and Hanover College, Indiana, in 1839 and 1840; studied law; was admitted to the bar in 1843 and commenced practice in Chillicothe, Ohio; secretary of state in 1844; moved to Columbus in 1844; delegate to the Whig National Convention of 1848; elected as a Republican to the Thirty-fourth Congress (March 4, 1855-March 3, 1857); unsuccessful candidate for reelection in 1856 to the Thirty-fifth Congress and for election in 1858 to the Thirty-sixth Congress; resumed the practice of law; during the Civil War appointed judge advocate of Camp Chase, Columbus, Ohio, by President Lincoln; appointed by President Andrew Johnson to investigate conditions in the South during the period of reconstruction; died in Columbus, Ohio, April 5, 1872; interment in Greenlawn Cemetery.

Bibliography: *DAB*.

**GALLUP, Albert,** a Representative from New York; born in East Berne, Albany County, N.Y., January 30, 1796; received a limited schooling; studied law; was admitted to the bar and practiced in Albany; sheriff of Albany County 1831-1834; elected as a Democrat to the Twenty-fifth Congress (March 4, 1837-March 3, 1839); unsuccessful candidate for reelection in 1838 to the Twenty-sixth Congress; appointed by President James K. Polk collector of customs at Albany, N.Y.; died in Providence, R.I., November 5, 1851; interment in Swan Point Cemetery.

**GAMBLE, James,** a Representative from Pennsylvania; born in Jersey Shore, Lycoming County, Pa., on January 28, 1809; attended the common schools and Jersey Shore (Pa.) Academy; studied law; was admitted to the bar in December 1833 and commenced practice in Jersey Shore, Pa.; county treasurer 1834-1836; resumed the practice of law in Jersey Shore; member of the Pennsylvania house of representatives in 1841 and 1842; elected as a Democrat to the Thirty-second and Thirty-third Congresses (March 4, 1851-March 3, 1855); president judge of Clearfield County in 1859 and 1860; president judge of the court of common pleas of Lycoming County 1868-1878; died in Williamsport, Lycoming County, Pa., February 22, 1883; interment in Wildwood Cemetery.

**GAMBLE, John Rankin** (brother of Robert Jackson Gamble and uncle of Ralph Abernethy Gamble), a Representative from South Dakota; born in Alabama, Genesee County, N.Y., January 15, 1848; attended the common schools; moved with his parents to Fox Lake, Wis., in 1862; was graduated from Lawrence University, Appleton, Wis., in 1872; studied law; was admitted to the bar in 1873 and commenced practice in Yankton, Territroy of Dakota (now South Dakota); district attorney for Yankton County 1876-1878; United States attorney for Dakota Territory in 1878; member of the Territorial house of representatives 1877-1879; served in the Territorial council 1881-1885; elected as a Republican to the Fifty-second Congress and served from March 4, 1891, until his death in Yankton, S.Dak., August 14, 1891, before the assembling of the Congress; interment in Yankton Cemetery.

**GAMBLE, Ralph Abernethy** (son of Robert Jackson Gamble and nephew of John Rankin Gamble), a Representative from New York; born in Yankton, S.Dak., May 6, 1885; attended the public schools of Yankton, S.Dak., and Washington, D.C.; was graduated from Tome Prep School, Port Deposit, Md., in 1905, from Princeton University, in 1909, from George Washington Law School, Washington, D.C., in 1911, and from Columbia University Law School, New York City, in 1912; was admitted to the bar in 1913 and commenced practice in New York City; counsel for the town of Mamaroneck, N.Y., 1918-1933, and for Larchmont, N.Y., 1926-1928; member of the State assembly 1931-1937; elected as a Republican to the Seventy-fifth Congress to fill the vacancy caused by the resignation of Charles D. Millard; reelected to the Seventy-sixth and to the eight succeeding Congresses and served from November 2, 1937, to January 3, 1957; chairman, Joint Committee on Housing (Eightieth Congress); was not a candidate for renomination in 1956; retired and resided in St. Michaels, Md., until his death there on March 4, 1959; interment in Hopewell Cemetery, Port Deposit, Md.

**GAMBLE, Robert Jackson** (brother of John Rankin Gamble and father of Ralph Abernethy Gamble), a Representative and a Senator from South Dakota; born in Genesee County, near Akron, Erie County, N.Y., February 7, 1851; moved with his parents to Fox Lake, Wis., in 1862; graduated from Lawrence University, Appleton, Wis., in 1874; studied law; was admitted to the bar in 1875 and commenced practice in Yankton, Territory of Dakota (now South Dakota); district attorney for the second judicial district of the Territory of Dakota 1880; city attorney of Yankton 1881-1882; member, Territorial council 1885; elected as a Republican to the Fifty-fourth Congress (March 4, 1895-March 3, 1897); unsuccessful candidate for reelection in 1896; elected to the Fifty-sixth Congress (March 4, 1899-March 3, 1901); chairman, Committee on Expenditures on Public Buildings (Fifty-sixth Congress); elected as a Republican to the United States Senate in 1901; reelected in 1906, and served from March 4, 1901, to March 3, 1913; unsuccessful candidate for renomination in 1912; chairman, Committee on Indian Depredations (Fifty-seventh Congress), Committee on Transportation Routes to the Seaboard (Fifty-eighth through Sixtieth Congresses), Committee on Enrolled Bills (Sixty-first Congress), Committee on Indian Affairs (Sixty-second Congress); moved to Sioux Falls, S.Dak., in 1915; resumed the practice of law; referee in bankruptcy, southern district of South Dakota 1916-1924; member of the National Executive Committee of the League to Enforce Peace; died in Sioux Falls, S.Dak., September 22, 1924; interment in Yankton Cemetery, Yankton, S.Dak.

**GAMBLE, Roger Lawson,** a Representative from Georgia; born near Louisville, Jefferson County, Ga., in 1787; completed preparatory studies; studied law; was admitted to the bar about 1815 and commenced practice in Louisville, Ga.; cotton planter; served in the War of 1812 as a commissioned officer; member of the State house of representatives in 1814 and 1815; elected as a Jacksonian to the Twenty-third Congress (March 4, 1833-March 3,

1835); unsuccessful candidate for reelection in 1834 to the Twenty-fourth Congress; elected as a Whig to the Twenty-seventh Congress (March 4, 1841-March 3, 1843); unsuccessful candidate for reelection in 1842 to the Twenty-eighth Congress; judge of the superior court of Georgia 1845-1847; died in Augusta, Ga., December 20, 1847; interment in Old Capitol Cemetery, Louisville, Ga.

**GAMBRELL, David Henry,** a Senator from Georgia; born in Atlanta, Fulton County, Ga., December 20, 1929; attended public schools; B.S., Davidson (N.C.) College, 1949; LL.B., Harvard University Law School, 1952; United States Army Reserve, First Lieutenant, 1949-1957; admitted to the Georgia bar in 1951 and commenced practice in Atlanta; director, National Legal Aid and Defenders Association, 1965-1971; president, State bar of Georgia, 1967-1968; chairman, state Democratic Party of Georgia, 1970-1971; appointed as a Democrat to the United States Senate, February 1, 1971, to fill the vacancy caused by the death of Richard B. Russell, and served from February 1, 1971, to November 7, 1972; unsuccessful candidate for nomination in the runoff primary of August 29, 1972 to complete the term ending January 3, 1973, and for the full six-year term; practices law in Atlanta, Ga.; is a resident of Atlanta, Ga.

**GAMBRILL, Stephen Warfield,** a Representative from Maryland; born near Savage, Howard County, Md., October 2, 1873; attended the common schools and Maryland Agricultural College (now the University of Maryland); was graduated from the law department of Columbian College (now George Washington University), Washington, D.C., in 1896; was admitted to the bar in 1897 and practiced in Baltimore, Md.; member of the State house of delegates 1920-1922; served in the State senate in 1924; elected as a Democrat to the Sixty-eighth Congress to fill the vacancy caused by the death of Sidney E. Mudd; reelected to the Sixty-ninth and to the six succeeding Congresses and served from November 4, 1924, until his death; had been reelected to the Seventy-sixth Congress; died in Washington, D.C., on December 19, 1938; interment in Cedar Hill Cemetery.

**GAMMAGE, Robert Alton,** a Representative from Texas; born in Houston, Harris County, Tex., March 13, 1938; attended the public schools of Houston; A.A., Del Mar College, Corpus Christi, Tex., 1958; B.S., University of Corpus Christi, 1963; M.A., Sam Houston State University, 1965; J.D., University of Texas School of Law, Austin, 1969; LL.M., University of Virginia School of Law, 1986; admitted to the Texas bar in 1969 and practiced in Houston, 1969-1979; served in United States Army, 1959-1960 and United States Navy Reserve, commander, 1965 to present; teaching fellow, Sam Houston State University, 1963-1965; dean of men, director of student activities, University of Corpus Christi, 1965-1966; instructor of government, San Jacinto College, Pasadena, Tex., 1969-1970; adjunct professor of law, South Texas College of Law, Houston, 1971-1973; member, Texas State house of representatives, 1971-1973; Texas State senator, 1973-1976; elected as a Democrat to the Ninety-fifth Congress (January 3, 1977-January 3, 1979); unsuccessful candidate for reelection in 1978 to the Ninety-sixth Congress; assistant attorney general of Texas, 1979-1980; special consultant, United States Department of Energy, 1980; resumed the practice of law in Austin, 1980-1982; justice, Texas State court of appeals, third supreme judicial district, 1982-1990; elected a justice of the Texas State supreme court for the term beginning January 1, 1991 and ending December 31, 1996; is a resident of Austin, Tex.

**GANDY, Harry Luther,** a Representative from South Dakota; born in Churubusco, Whitley County, Ind., August 13, 1881; attended the public schools; was graduated from Tri-State College, Angola, Ind., in 1901; moved to Rapid City, S.Dak., in 1907; publisher of the Wasta (S.Dak.) Gazette 1910-1918; United States commissioner at Wasta, S.Dak., 1910-1913; member of the State senate in 1911; appointed by President Woodrow Wilson as receiver of public moneys of the United States land office at Rapid City, and served from July 16, 1913, to March 3, 1915; elected as a Democrat to the Sixty-fourth and to the two succeeding Congresses (March 4, 1915-March 3, 1921); unsuccessful candidate for reelection in 1920 to the Sixty-seventh Congress; engaged in agricultural pursuits and in the raising of livestock near Wasta, S.Dak., 1910-1945; executive secretary of the National Coal Association, Washington, D.C., 1923-1930; connected with subsidiary companies of the Pittston Co., 1930-1937; chairman, Bituminous Coal Producers Board, Cincinnati, Ohio, 1937-1940; assistant to the president, Elk River Coal and Lumber Co. and Buffalo Creek and Gauley Railroad Co., Widen, W.Va., from 1944 until his retirement; died in Los Gatos, Calif., August 15, 1957; interment in Mountain View Cemetery, Rapid City, S.Dak.

**GANLY, James Vincent,** a Representative from New York; born in New York City September 13, 1878; attended the public schools and Packard Business College; engaged in the oil, real estate, and automobile businesses; member of the State assembly in 1907; was the first county clerk of Bronx County 1914-1918; elected as a Democrat to the Sixty-sixth Congress (March 4, 1919-March 3, 1921); unsuccessful candidate for reelection in 1920 to the Sixty-seventh Congress; elected to the Sixty-eighth Congress and served from March 4, 1923, until his death in an automobile accident in New York City September 7, 1923, before the convening of Congress; interment in St. Raymond's Cemetery, Borough of the Bronx, New York City.

**GANNETT, Barzillai,** a Representative from Massachusetts; born in Bridgewater, Mass., June 17, 1764; was graduated from Harvard University in 1785; studied theology, but did not enter the ministry; selectman of Pittston, Maine (then a district of Massachusetts), in 1793, 1794, 1796-1798, 1801, and 1802; town clerk in 1794; moderator 1797-1802; selectman and assessor, Gardiner, Maine, 1803-1808; appointed as the first postmaster of Gardiner and served from September 30, 1804, to October 1, 1809; moderator 1804-1806, 1808, 1809, and 1811; member of the Massachusetts house of representatives in 1805 and 1806; served in the Massachusetts senate in 1807 and 1808; elected as a Republican to the Eleventh and Twelfth Congresses and served from March 4, 1809, until his resignation in 1812; died in New York City in 1832.

**GANSEVOORT, Leonard,** a Delegate from New York; born in Albany, N.Y., July 14, 1751; studied law; was admitted to the bar in 1771 and commenced practice in Albany, N.Y.; colonel of Light Cavalry in the Revolutionary War; member of the Provincial Congress in 1775 and 1776; president of New York from April 18 to May 14, 1777; clerk of Albany County in 1777 and 1778; member of the State assembly in 1778, 1779, and 1788; member of the commercial convention in Annapolis, Md., in 1786; Member of the Continental Congress in 1788; served in the State senate 1791-1793; judge of Albany County 1794-1797; member of the council of appointment in 1797; judge of the probate court from 1799 until his death in Albany, N.Y., August 26, 1810; interment in Albany Rural Cemetery.

**Bibliography:** *DAB.*

**GANSKE, Greg,** a Representative from Iowa; born in New Hampton, Chickasaw County, Iowa, March 31, 1949; B.A., University of Iowa, 1972; M.D., University of Iowa Medical School, 1976; Harvard Medical School, surgical training under Joseph E. Murray, 1990 Nobel Laureate in medicine; United States Army reserve service as lieutenant colonel, Medical Corps, 1986 to present; plastic and reconstructive surgeon; elected as a Republican to the One Hundred Fourth Congress (January 3, 1995-January 3, 1997); is a resident of Des Moines, Iowa.

**GANSON, John,** a Representative from New York; born in Le Roy, Genesee County, N.Y., January 1, 1818; attended the public schools and Le Roy Academy; was graduated from Harvard University in 1839; studied law; was admitted to the bar in 1846 and commenced practice in Canandaigua, Ontario County, N.Y.; moved to Buffalo the same year; member of the State senate in 1862 and 1863; elected as a Democrat to the Thirty-eighth Congress (March 4, 1863-March 3, 1865); was not a candidate for renomination in 1864; resumed the practice of law at Buffalo, N.Y.; railroad director; delegate to the Democratic National Convention in 1864; died in Buffalo, N.Y., September 28, 1874; interment in Forest Lawn Cemetery.

**GANTZ, Martin Kissinger,** a Representative from Ohio; born in Bethel Township, Miami County, Ohio, January 28, 1862; attended the common schools and Lebanon (Ohio) College; was graduated from the Cincinnati Law College in 1883; was admitted to the bar in 1883 and commenced practice in Troy, Ohio; mayor of the city of Troy in 1889; elected as a Democrat to the Fifty-second Congress (March 4, 1891-March 3, 1893); unsuccessful candidate for reelection in 1892 to the Fifty-third Congress; resumed the practice of law in Troy; commissioner from the State of Ohio to the Louisiana Purchase Exposition in 1904; delegate to all Democratic State conventions from 1892 to 1906; delegate to the Democratic National Convention in 1908; represented the Department of State on the directorate of El Banco Nacional de Nicaragua y El Ferrocarril del Pacífico de Nicaragua in 1914 and 1915; died in Troy, Ohio, February 10, 1916; interment in Riverside Cemetery.

**GARBER, Harvey Cable,** a Representative from Ohio; born in Hill Grove, Darke County, Ohio, July 6, 1866; moved to Greenville, Ohio, with his parents in 1872; attended the public schools; manager of the Western Union Telegraph Co.; superintendent of the Central Union Telephone Co. for Ohio, and served four years as assistant general solicitor; member of the State house of representatives 1890-1893; chairman of the Democratic State committee in 1901 and chairman of the Democratic State executive committee 1902-1908; elected as a Democrat to the Fifty-eighth and Fifty-ninth Congresses (March 4, 1903-March 3, 1907); was not a candidate for renomination in 1906 to the Sixtieth Congress; moved to Columbus, Ohio, in 1910 and served as assistant to the president of the Bell Telephone Co. in Ohio, Indiana, and Illinois 1910-1915; also studied law; was admitted to the bar in 1921 and commenced practice in Columbus, Ohio; died at his winter home in Naples, Fla., March 23, 1938; interment in Greenville Cemetery, Greenville, Ohio.

**GARBER, Jacob Aaron,** a Representative from Virginia; born near Harrisonburg, Rockingham County, Va., January 25, 1879; attended the public schools of Rockingham County, and Bridgewater (Va.) College; principal of Brentsville Academy in 1904 and 1905; was graduated from Emerson College, Boston, Mass., in 1907; taught in Well's Memorial Institute, Boston, Mass., in 1906 and 1907; secretary of Emerson College in 1907 and 1908; moved to Timberville, Va., in 1908 and was employed as a bank cashier until 1924; served as treasurer of Rockingham County 1924-1929; member of the Virginia house of delegates 1920-1922; interested in various orchard and canning organizations; elected as a Republican to the Seventy-first Congress (March 4, 1929-March 3, 1931); unsuccessful candidate for reelection in 1930 to the Seventy-second Congress; served as chief of the field and processing-tax divisions, Internal Revenue Office, Richmond, Va., 1931-1935; delegate to the Republican National Convention in 1932; unsuccessful candidate for election in 1940 to the Seventy-seventh Congress; served in the Virginia senate 1945-1947; resumed operation of commercial orchards; died in Harrisonburg, Va., December 2, 1953; interment in Church of the Brethren Cemetery, Timberville, Va.

**GARBER, Milton Cline,** a Representative from Oklahoma; born in Humboldt, Calif., November 30, 1867; was reared on a farm in Iowa; attended the common schools, Upper Iowa University at Fayette 1887-1890, and the law department of the University of Iowa at Iowa City 1891-1893; settled in Oklahoma upon the opening of the Cherokee Strip; was admitted to the bar in 1893 and commenced the practice of law in Guthrie, Okla.; in company with his father and brother founded the town of Garber in 1893 and opened up the Garber oil fields; appointed probate judge of Garfield County in 1902 and subsequently elected in 1904; appointed associate justice of the supreme court of the Territory of Oklahoma and trial judge of the fifth judicial district in 1906, serving in these capacities until Oklahoma became a State; elected judge of the twentieth judicial district in 1908 and served until 1912, when he resigned; resumed the practice of law; mayor of Enid, Okla., 1919-1921; engaged in the newspaper business and in agricultural pursuits; elected as a Republican to the Sixty-eighth and to the four succeeding Congresses (March 4, 1923-March 3, 1933); unsuccessful candidate for reelection in 1932 to the Seventy-third Congress; died in Alexandria, Minn., September 12, 1948; interment in Memorial Park Cemetery, Enid, Okla.

**GARCIA, Robert,** a Representative from New York; born in New York, Bronx County, N.Y., January 9, 1933; attended the public schools; graduated from Haaren High School, New York City, in 1950; attended the City College of New York and the Community College of New York; graduated from the RCA Institute, 1957; served in the United States Army during the Korean War with the Third Infantry Division, 1950-1953; computer engineer, IBM, Control Data, 1957-1965; member, New York State assembly, 1965-1967; New York State senator, 1967-1978; deputy minority leader, 1975-1978; delegate to the Democratic National Conventions of 1976, 1980, 1984 and 1988; registered as a Democrat but elected as a Republican-Liberal to the Ninety-fifth Congress, February 14, 1978, by special election to fill the vacancy caused by the resignation of Herman Badillo; resumed prior party affiliation as a Democrat, effective February 21, 1978; reelected to the six succeeding Congresses, and served from February 14, 1978 until his resignation on January 7, 1990; consultant; is a resident of Florida and Washington, D.C.

**GARD, Warren,** a Representative from Ohio; born in Hamilton, Butler County, Ohio, July 2, 1873; attended the public schools and was graduated from the Cincinnati Law School in 1894; admitted to the bar in 1894 and commenced practice in Hamilton, Ohio; prosecuting attorney of Butler County, 1898-1903; judge of the court of common pleas, 1907-1912; elected as a Democrat to the Sixty-third and to the three succeeding Congresses (March 4, 1913-March 3, 1921); was not a candidate for renomination in 1920 to the Sixty-seventh Congress; resumed the practice of law in Hamilton, Ohio, where he died on November 1, 1929; interment in Greenwood Cemetery.

**GARDENIER, Barent,** a Representative from New York; born in Kingston, Ulster County, N.Y.; completed preparatory studies; studied law; was admitted to the bar and practiced; held several local offices; elected as a Federalist to the Tenth and Eleventh Congresses (March 4, 1807-March 3, 1811); declined to be a candidate for renomination in 1810 to the Twelfth Congress; engaged in the practice of law in Ulster and Columbia Counties; district attorney of the first district from March 1813 to April 1815; died in Kingston, N.Y., January 10, 1822; interment beneath the First Reformed Dutch Church of that city.

**GARDNER, Augustus Peabody** (uncle of Henry Cabot Lodge, Jr.), a Representative from Massachusetts; born in Boston, Mass., November 5, 1865; attended St. Paul's School, Concord, N.H., and was graduated from Harvard University in 1886; studied law in Harvard Law School, but never practiced, devoting himself to the management of his estate; captain and assistant adjutant general on the staff of General James H. Wilson during the Spanish-American War; member of the Massachusetts senate in 1900 and 1901; elected as a Republican to the Fifty-seventh Congress to fill the vacancy caused by the resignation of William H. Moody; reelected to the Fifty-eighth and to the seven succeeding Congresses, and served from November 3, 1902 until May 15, 1917, when he resigned to enter the Army; chairman, Committee on Industrial Arts and Expositions (Fifty-ninth and Sixtieth Congresses); during the First World War served at Governors Island and in Macon, Ga., as colonel in the Adjutant General's Department, and later was transferred at his own request to the One Hundred and Thirty-first Regiment, United States Infantry, with the rank of major; died at Camp Wheeler, Macon, Ga., January 14, 1918; interment in Arlington National Cemetery, Va.

Bibliography: Gardner, Augustus Peabody. *Some Letters of Augustus Peabody Gardner*. Edited by Constance Gardner. Boston: Houghton Mifflin Co., 1920; Gardner, Constance. *Augustus Peabody Gardner, Major, United States National Guard, 1865-1918*. Cambridge, Mass.: The Riverside Press, privately printed, 1919.

GARDNER, Edward Joseph, a Representative from Ohio; born in Hamilton, Butler County, Ohio, August 7, 1898; attended the parochial schools; was graduated from the College of Commerce and Finance of St. Xavier University, Cincinnati, Ohio, in 1920; engaged in graduate work at the Wharton School of Business of the University of Pennsylvania at Philadelphia, and at the University of Cincinnati, Ohio; during the First World War served as a private in the United States Army in 1918; district controller of a food distributing company at Philadelphia, Pa., 1920-1924; public accountant, Hamilton, Ohio, 1924-1950; president of Hamilton city council and vice mayor 1926-1928; member of the State house of representatives in 1937, 1938, 1941, and 1942; elected as a Democrat to the Seventy-ninth Congress (January 3, 1945-January 3, 1947); unsuccessful candidate for reelection in 1946 to the Eightieth Congress; continued his profession as an accountant; died in Hamilton, Ohio, December 7, 1950; interment in St. Mary's Cemetery.

GARDNER, Francis, a Representative from New Hampshire; born in Leominster, Mass., on December 27, 1771; was graduated from Harvard University in 1793; studied law; was admitted to the bar in Cheshire County, N.H., in 1796 and commenced practice at Walpole, N.H.; moved to Keene, N.H., in 1806; solicitor of Cheshire County 1807-1820; elected as a Republican to the Tenth Congress (March 4, 1807-March 3, 1809); was not a candidate for reelection in 1808 to the Eleventh Congress; died in Roxbury, Mass., June 25, 1835.

GARDNER, Frank, a Representative from Indiana; born on a farm in Finley Township, near Scottsburg, Scott County, Ind., May 8, 1872; attended the rural schools; was graduated from Borden Institute, Clark County, Ind., in 1896 and from the law department of the University of Indiana at Bloomington in 1900; was admitted to the bar in 1900 and commenced the practice of law in Scottsburg, Ind.; auditor of Scott County 1903-1911; county attorney 1911-1917; member of the Democratic county committee and served as chairman 1912-1922; served as field examiner for the State board of accounts 1911-1920; elected as a Democrat to the Sixty-eighth, Sixty-ninth, and Seventieth Congresses (March 4, 1923-March 3, 1929); unsuccessful candidate for reelection in 1928 to the Seventy-first Congress; resumed the practice of law in Scottsburg, Ind.; elected judge of the sixth judicial circuit of Indiana in 1930; reelected in 1936 and served until his death in Scottsburg, Ind., February 1, 1937; interment in Scottsburg Cemetery.

GARDNER, Gideon, a Representative from Massachusetts; born in Nantucket, Mass., May 30, 1759; received a limited schooling; was a successful shipmaster, and later became a shipowner; also engaged in mercantile pursuits; elected as a Republican to the Eleventh Congress (March 4, 1809-March 3, 1811); resumed his former business pursuits; was the bearer of a petition from the citizens of Nantucket to Congress for tax relief in 1813; died in Nantucket, Mass., March 22, 1832; interment in Friends Burying Ground.

GARDNER, James Carson, a Representative from North Carolina; born in Rocky Mount, Nash County, N.C., April 8, 1933; educated in the public schools of Rocky Mount, and North Carolina State University at Raleigh, N.C.; served in the United States Army, 1953-1955; co-founder and executive vice president of Hardee's Food Systems, Inc., Rocky Mount, N.C., 1962-1967; chairman, North Carolina Republican Party, 1965-1966; elected as a Republican to the Ninetieth Congress (January 3, 1967-January 3, 1969); was not a candidate for reelection in 1968 to the Ninety-first Congress, but was an unsuccessful candidate for election for Governor of North Carolina; president, Gardner Foods, Inc., Rocky Mount; is a resident of Rocky Mount, N.C.

GARDNER, John, a Delegate from Rhode Island; born in South Kingstown, R.I., in 1747; engaged in agricultural pursuits in Narragansett, R.I.; served in the Revolutionary War; captain of the "Kingstown Reds" in 1775 and 1776; representative to the general assembly by the Paper Money Party in 1786 and 1787; Member of the Continental Congress in 1789; justice of the peace for South Kingstown in 1791; died in South Kingstown, R.I., October 18, 1808.

Bibliography: *DAB*.

GARDNER, John James, a Representative from New Jersey; born in Atlantic County, N.J., October 17, 1845; attended the common schools and the law school of the University of Michigan at Ann Arbor in 1866 and 1867; served in the Sixth New Jersey Volunteers 1861-1865 and one year in the United States Veteran Volunteers; engaged in the real estate and insurance business; elected alderman of Atlantic City, N.J., in 1867; mayor of Atlantic City 1868-1872, 1874, and 1875; member of the common council and coroner of Atlantic County in 1876; member of the State senate 1878-1893, serving as its president in 1883; engaged in agricultural pursuits; delegate to the Republican National Convention in 1884; elected as a Republican to the Fifty-third and to the nine succeeding Congresses (March 4, 1893-March 3, 1913); chairman, Committee on Labor (Fiftieth through Sixty-first Congresses); unsuccessful candidate for reelection in 1912 to the Sixty-third Congress; resumed agricultural pursuits; died in Indian Mills, Burlington County, N.J., February 7, 1921; interment in Atlantic City Cemetery, Pleasantville, N.J.

GARDNER, Joseph, a Delegate from Pennsylvania; born in Honeybrook Township, Chester County, Pa., in 1752; studied medicine and practiced; raised a company of Volunteers in 1776 and commanded the Fourth Battalion of militia from Chester County; member of the committee of safety in 1776 and 1777; member of the Pennsylvania assembly 1776-1778 and of the supreme executive council in 1779; Member of the Continental Congress in 1784 and 1785; resumed the practice of medicine in Philadelphia, Pa., 1785-1792, and in Elkton, Md., 1792-1794; died in Elkton, Md., in 1794.

GARDNER, Mills, a Representative from Ohio; born in Russellville, Brown County, Ohio, January 30, 1830; attended the common schools of Highland County and Rankins Academy at Ripley, Ohio; moved to Fayette County in 1854; studied law; was admitted to the bar in 1855 and commenced practice at Washington Court House, Ohio; prosecuting attorney of Fayette County 1855-1859; member of the Ohio State senate in 1862 and 1863; member of the State house of representatives in 1866 and 1867; member of the State constitutional convention in 1872; elected as a Republican to the Forty-fifth Congress (March 4, 1877-March 3,

1879); was not a candidate for renomination in 1878 to the Forty-sixth Congress; resumed the practice of law until his death; died at Washington Court House, Ohio, February 20, 1910; interment in Washington Cemetery.

**GARDNER, Obadiah,** a Senator from Maine; born near Port Huron, Mich., September 13, 1852; moved to Union, Maine, with his parents in 1864; attended the common schools, Eastman's Business College, Poughkeepsie, N.Y., and Coburn Classical Institute, Waterville, Maine; engaged in the lumber, lime, and creamery business in Rockland, Maine, and also in agricultural pursuits and in cattle raising; member of the State board of agriculture; master of the Maine State Grange 1897-1907; unsuccessful candidate for election for Governor of Maine in 1908; appointed chairman of the board of State assessors in 1911, but resigned, having been appointed Senator; appointed and subsequently elected as a Democrat to the United States Senate to fill the vacancy caused by the death of William P. Frye and served from September 23, 1911, until March 3, 1913; unsuccessful candidate for reelection in 1913; appointed a member of the International Joint Commission created to prevent disputes regarding the use of the boundary waters between the United States and Canada in 1913, and served as chairman of the United States section from 1914 until 1923; returned to Rockland, Maine, and retired; moved to Augusta, Maine, where he died July 24, 1938; interment in Achorn Cemetery, Rockland, Maine.

**GARDNER, Sylvester,** a Delegate from Rhode Island; born in South Kingstown, R.I., about 1730; admitted a freeman from West Greenwich, Kent County, R.I., in 1757; commissioned major for Kings County in 1769 and again 1770; justice of the peace for North Kingstown in 1774; deputy from North Kingstown in 1775, 1776-1778, 1780, and 1781; appointed major in Kings County Militia in 1780; made sixth assistant in 1781 and again in 1782; justice of the court of common pleas for Washington County 1781-1788; again made assistant in 1783; elected a Delegate to the Continental Congress in 1787, but did not take his seat; deputy from North Kingstown in 1790; chief justice of the court of common pleas in 1792; died in North Kingstown, R.I., in 1803.

**GARDNER, Washington,** a Representative from Michigan; born in Morrow County, Ohio, February 16, 1845; entered the Union Army and served in Company D, Sixty-fifth Regiment, Ohio Volunteer Infantry, from October 1861 to December 1865; severely wounded in action at Resaca, Ga.; attended school at Berea, Ohio, the Hillsdale College, Hillsdale, Mich., and was graduated from the Ohio Wesleyan University, Delaware, Ohio, in 1870; studied in the school of theology, Boston University, 1870-1871; was graduated from the Albany Law School in 1876; was admitted to the bar and commenced practice in Grand Rapids, Mich.; entered the ministry of the Methodist Episcopal Church, in which he served twelve years; commander of the Department of Michigan, Grand Army of the Republic, in 1888; professor at Albion College, 1889-1894; appointed secretary of state of Michigan in March 1894, and served until 1899; elected as a Republican to the Fifty-sixth and to the five succeeding Congresses (March 4, 1899-March 3, 1911); chairman, Committee on Expenditures in the Department of Commerce and Labor (Sixty-first Congress); unsuccessful candidate for reelection in 1910 to the Sixty-second Congress; commander in chief of the Grand Army of the Republic, 1913-1914; Commissioner of Pensions from March 22, 1921 to March 4, 1925, when he resigned; retired from public life; died in Albion, Mich., March 31, 1928; interment in Riverside Cemetery.

**GARFIELD, James Abram,** a Representative from Ohio and 20th President of the United States; born in Orange, Cuyahoga County, Ohio, November 19, 1831; attended district school; at the age of seventeen worked as a driver and helmsman on the Ohio Canal; entered Geauga Seminary, Chester, Ohio, in March 1849, and at the close of the fall term taught a district school; attended the Eclectic Institute, Hiram, Ohio, 1851-1854; was graduated from Williams College, Williamstown, Mass., in 1858; professor of ancient languages and literature at Hiram (Ohio) College; president of Hiram College, 1857-1861; member of the Ohio State senate in 1859; studied law and was admitted to the bar in 1860; during the Civil War entered the Union Army; commissioned lieutenant colonel of the Forty-second Regiment, Ohio Volunteer Infantry, August 21, 1861, and promoted through the ranks to major general; resigned December 5, 1863; elected as a Republican to the Thirty-eighth and to the eight succeeding Congresses, and served from March 4, 1863 until November 8, 1880, when he resigned, having been elected President of the United States; appointed a member of the Electoral Commission created by act of Congress approved January 29, 1877, to decide the contests in various States in the presidential election of 1876; elected to the United States Senate on January 13, 1880, for the term beginning March 4, 1881, but on December 23, 1880, he declined to accept his election as Senator, having been elected President; nominated for President of the United States on the Republican ticket, June 8, 1880, and was elected November 4, 1880; was inaugurated March 4, 1881; on the morning of July 2, 1881, while passing through the Pennsylvania Railroad Depot in Washington, D.C., was shot by Charles J. Guiteau; died from the effects of the wound, in Elberon, N.J., September 19, 1881; interment in Lake View Cemetery, Cleveland, Ohio.

**Bibliography:** *DAB*; Garfield, James A. *The Diary of James Abram Garfield.* 2 vols. Edited by Harry James Brown and Frederick D. Williams. East Lansing, Mich.: Michigan State University, 1967; Peskin, Allan. *Garfield.* Kent, Ohio: Kent State University Press, 1978.

**GARFIELDE, Selucius,** a Delegate from the Territory of Washington; born in Shoreham, Addison County, Vt., December 8, 1822; moved to Gallipolis, Ohio, and later to Paris, Ky., where he engaged in newspaper work; pursued an academic course; member of the State constitutional convention in 1849; immigrated to California in 1851; member of the State house of representatives in 1852; elected by the legislature to codify the laws of the State in 1853; studied law; was admitted to the bar in 1854 and commenced practice in San Francisco, Calif.; returned to Kentucky in 1855; delegate to the Democratic National Convention of 1856; moved to the Territory of Washington in 1857; receiver of public moneys 1857-1860; unsuccessful Democratic candidate for election in 1860 to the Thirty-seventh Congress; surveyor general of the Territory of Washington 1866-1869; elected as a Republican to the Forty-first and Forty-second Congresses (March 4, 1869-March 3, 1873); unsuccessful candidate for reelection in 1872 to the Forty-third Congress; appointed collector of customs for the Puget Sound district in 1873; moved to Seattle, Wash., where he engaged in the practice of law; also practiced in Washington, D.C.; died in Washington, D.C., April 13, 1881; interment in Glenwood Cemetery.

**GARLAND, Augustus Hill,** a Senator from Arkansas; born in Tipton County, Tenn., June 11, 1832; moved with his parents to Hempstead County, Ark., in 1833; attended St. Mary's College and graduated from St. Joseph's College in Kentucky in 1849; studied law; was admitted to the bar in 1853 and commenced practice in Washington, Ark.; moved to Little Rock in 1856; Union delegate to the State convention that passed the ordinance of secession in 1861; member of the provisional congress that met in Montgomery, Ala., in May 1861, and subsequently of the Confederate Congress and served in both houses; elected to the United States Senate for the term beginning March 4, 1867, but was not permitted to take his seat, as Arkansas had not been readmitted to representation; elected Governor of Arkansas in 1874, and served from November 12, 1874 to January 11, 1877; elected as a Democrat to the United States Senate in 1876; reelected in 1883, and served from March 4, 1877 to March 6, 1885, when he resigned to accept a Cabinet portfolio; chairman, Committee on Territories (Forty-sixth Congress); appointed Attorney General by President Grover Cleveland, and served from March 6, 1885 until March 4, 1889; resumed the practice of law in Little Rock; died in Washington, D.C., January 26, 1899; interment in Mount Holly Cemetery, Little Rock, Ark.

**Bibliography:** *DAB*; Newberry, Farrar. *A Life of Mr. Garland of Arkansas*. Arkadelhia, Ark.: n.p., 1908; Schlup, Leonard. "Augustus Hill Garland: Gilded Age Democrat." *Arkansas Historical Quarterly* 40 (Winter 1981): 338-46.

**GARLAND, David Shepherd,** a Representative from Virginia; born near New Glasgow (now Clifford), Amherst County, Va., September 27, 1769; pursued an academic course; studied law; was admitted to the bar and commenced practice in Virginia; member of the Virginia house of delegates 1799-1802 and 1805-1809; served in the Virginia senate 1809-1811; elected as a Republican to the Eleventh Congress to fill the vacancy caused by the resignation of Wilson Cary Nicholas and served from January 17, 1810, to March 3, 1811; again a member of the Virginia house of delegates in 1814, 1815, 1819-1826, and 1832-1836; died in Clifford, Va., October 7, 1841; interment in the Meredith and Garland families' graveyard, Clifford, Va.

**GARLAND, James,** a Representative from Virginia; born at Ivy Depot, Albemarle County, Va., June 6, 1791; pursued preparatory studies; studied law; was admitted to the bar and commenced practice in Lovingston, Va.; served in the War of 1812; resumed the practice of law; served in the Virginia house of delegates 1829-1831; elected as a Jacksonian to the Twenty-fourth Congress; reelected as a Democrat to the Twenty-fifth Congress and as a Conservative to the Twenty-sixth Congress (March 4, 1835-March 3, 1841); unsuccessful candidate for reelection in 1840 to the Twenty-seventh Congress; resumed the practice of law; moved to Lynchburg, Va., in 1841; Commonwealth attorney for Lynchburg 1849-1872; elected judge of the corporation court in 1841, and served until December 31, 1882; lived in retirement until his death in Lynchburg, Va., August 8, 1885; interment in Spring Hill Cemetery.

**GARLAND, Mahlon Morris,** a Representative from Pennsylvania; born in Pittsburgh, Pa., May 4, 1856; moved with his parents to Alexandria, Huntingdon County, Pa.; attended the common schools; having learned the trade of puddling and heating, joined the Amalgamated Association of Iron, Steel and Tin Workers, of which he became president; member of the select council of Pittsburgh in 1886 and 1887; appointed by President William McKinley United States collector of customs (then called surveyor of customs) at Pittsburgh on April 7, 1898; reappointed by President Theodore Roosevelt in 1902 and 1906, and by President William Howard Taft in 1910, and served until March 3, 1915; served as vice president of the American Federation of Labor; member of the Pittsburgh School Board; member of the borough council of Edgewood, Pa.; elected as a Republican to the Sixty-fourth, Sixty-fifth, and Sixty-sixth Congresses and served from March 4, 1915, until his death; chairman, Committee on Mines and Mining (Sixty-sixth Congress); had been reelected to the Sixty-seventh Congress; died in Washington, D.C., November 19, 1920; interment in Woodlawn Cemetery, Pittsburgh, Pa.

**GARLAND, Peter Adams,** a Representative from Maine; born in Boston, Mass., June 16, 1923; attended the public schools of Saco, Maine, and the Hotchkiss School, Lakeville, Conn.; graduated from Bowdoin College, Brunswick, Maine, in 1945; officer and director of Garland Manufacturing Co., Saco, Maine, and Snocraft Co., Norway, Maine; served as an enlisted man in the United States Air Corps from 1943 to 1946; director of New England Council and Associated Industries of Maine, 1955-1957; member of the Saco Superintending School Committee, 1952-1954; mayor of Saco, 1956-1959; New England field adviser, Small Business Administration, 1958-1960; elected as a Republican to the Eighty-seventh Congress (January 3,

1961-January 3, 1963); unsuccessful candidate for renomination in 1962 to the Eighty-eighth Congress, and for election in 1966 to the Ninetieth Congress; municipal town manager, Gorham, Maine, 1967-1969; marketing director for an engineering firm, 1970-1972; city manager, Claremont, N.H., 1972-1973; community manager, Ocean Pines, Ocean City, Md., 1973-1974; town manager, Searsport, Maine, 1974-1981; city manager, Bath, Maine, 1981 to present; is a resident of Bath, Maine.

**GARLAND, Rice,** a Representative from Louisiana; born in Lynchburg, Va., about 1795; pursued an academic course; studied law; was admitted to the bar and commenced practice; moved to Opelousas, La., in 1820 and continued the practice of his profession; elected to the Twenty-third Congress to fill the vacancy caused by the resignation of Henry A. Bullard; reelected as an Anti-Jacksonian to the Twenty-fourth Congress and as a Whig to the Twenty-fifth and Twenty-sixth Congresses and served from April 28, 1834, to July 21, 1840, when he resigned to accept an appointment as judge of the supreme court of Louisiana, in which capacity he served, with residence in New Orleans, La., until 1846; chairman, Committee on Expenditures in the Department of War (Twenty-sixth Congress); moved to Brownsville, Tex., in 1846 and continued the practice of law until his death in that city in 1861; interment in a cemetery at Brownsville.

**GARMATZ, Edward Alexander,** a Representative from Maryland; born in Baltimore, Md., February 7, 1903; attended the public schools and Polytechnic Institute; engaged in the electrical business 1920-1942; associated with the Maryland State Racing Commission 1941-1944; served as police magistrate 1944-1947; elected as a Democrat to the Eightieth Congress, by special election, July 15, 1947, to fill the vacancy caused by the resignation of Thomas D'Alesandro; reelected to the twelve succeeding Congresses and served from July 15, 1947, to January 3, 1973; chairman, Committee on Merchant Marine and Fisheries (Eighty-ninth through Ninety-second Congresses); was not a candidate for reelection in 1972 to the Ninety-third Congress; employed by the International Organization of Masters, Mates, and Pilots Union; was a resident of Baltimore, Md., until his death there on July 22, 1986.

**GARN, Edwin Jacob (Jake),** a Senator from Utah; born in Richfield, Sanpete County, Utah, October 12, 1932; attended Salt Lake City public schools; B.S., University of Utah, 1955; engaged in graduate work at the University of Utah, 1955-1956; engaged in the insurance business, 1961-1968; served as an aviator in the United States Navy, 1956-1960; Salt Lake City commissioner, 1968-1972; mayor of Salt Lake City, 1971-1974; president, Utah League of Cities and Towns, 1972; first vice president, National League of Cities, 1974; elected as a Republican to the United States Senate in 1974 for the term commencing January 3, 1975; subsequently appointed by the Governor, December 21, 1974, to fill the vacancy caused by the resignation of Wallace F. Bennett for the term ending January 3, 1975; reelected in 1980 and again in 1986 and served from December 21, 1974 to January 3, 1993; was not a candidate for reelection in 1992; chairman, Committee on Banking, Housing and Urban Affairs (Ninety-seventh through Ninety-ninth Congresses); payload specialist aboard the space shuttle *Discovery*, 1985; is a resident of Salt Lake City, Utah.

**GARNER, Alfred Buckwalter,** a Representative from Pennsylvania; born in Ashland, Schuylkill County, Pa., March 4, 1873; attended the public schools; studied law; was admitted to the bar in 1897 and commenced practice in Ashland, Pa.; member of the Pennsylvania house of representatives 1901-1907; elected as a Republican to the Sixty-first Congress (March 4, 1909-March 3, 1911); again a member of the Pennsylvania house of representatives 1915-1917; resumed the practice of law in Ashland, Pa.; taxing officer, auditor general's department, Harrisburg, Pa., from May

1917, until his death in Harrisburg on July 30, 1930; interment in Fountain Spring Cemetery, Fountain Spring, Pa.

**GARNER, John Nance,** a Representative from Texas and a Vice President of the United States; born near Detroit, Red River County, Tex., November 22, 1868; had limited educational advantages; studied law, was admitted to the bar in 1890, and commenced practice in Uvalde, Uvalde County, Tex.; judge of Uvalde County, Tex., 1893-1896; member, Texas State house of representatives, 1898-1902; elected as a Democrat to the Fifty-eighth and to the fourteen succeeding Congresses (March 4, 1903-March 3, 1933); served as minority floor leader (Seventy-first Congress) and as Speaker of the House of Representatives (Seventy-second Congress); reelected to the Seventy-third Congress on November 8, 1932, and on the same day was elected Vice President of the United States on the ticket headed by Franklin D. Roosevelt; reelected Vice President on November 3, 1936, and served in that office from March 4, 1933 to January 20, 1941; retired to private life and resided in Uvalde, Tex., until his death there on November 7, 1967; interment in Uvalde Cemetery.

**Bibliography:** James, Marquis. *Mr. Garner of Texas.* Indianapolis: Bobbs-Merrill, 1939; Timmons, Bascom. *Garner of Texas: A Personal History.* New York: Harper, 1948.

**GARNETT, James Mercer** (brother of Robert Selden Garnett and grandfather of Muscoe Russell Hunter Garnett), a Representative from Virginia; born at "Mount Pleasant," near Loretto, Essex County, Va., June 8, 1770; studied under private teachers; engaged in planting; member of the Virginia house of delegates in 1800 and 1801; elected as a Republican to the Ninth and Tenth Congresses (March 4, 1805-March 3, 1809); member of the grand jury that indicted Aaron Burr, former Vice President, for treason in 1807; was not a candidate for renomination in 1808; again engaged in planting, and during the later years of his life conducted a school for boys on his plantation; president of the Fredericksburg Agricultural Society 1817-1837; again a member of the Virginia house of delegates in 1824 and 1825; member of the anti-tariff conventions of 1821 and 1831; one of the founders of the Virginia State Agricultural Society; vice president of the Virginia Colonization Society; delegate to the Virginia constitutional convention in 1829; died on his estate, "Elmwood," near Loretto, Va., April 23, 1843; interment in the family burying ground on his estate.

**Bibliography:** *DAB.*

**GARNETT, Muscoe Russell Hunter** (grandson of James Mercer Garnett), a Representative from Virginia; born at "Elmwood," near Loretto, Essex County, Va., July 25, 1821; tutored at home and was graduated from the University of Virginia at Charlottesville (literary department in 1839 and the law department in 1842); was admitted to the bar in 1842 and commenced the practice of his profession in Loretto, Va.; delegate to the Virginia constitutional convention in 1850 and 1851; delegate to the Democratic National Convention in 1852 and 1856; member of the Virginia house of delegates 1853-1856; member of the board of visitors of the University of Virginia 1855-1859; elected as a Democrat to the Thirty-fourth Congress to fill the vacancy caused by the death of Thomas H. Bayly; reelected to the Thirty-fifth and Thirty-sixth Congresses and served from December 1, 1856, to March 3, 1861; delegate to the Virginia secession convention and to the Virginia constitutional convention in 1861; member from Virginia of the First Confederate Congress 1862-1864; died at "Elmwood," near Loretto, Va., on February 14, 1864; interment in the family cemetery on his estate.

**Bibliography:** *DAB.*

**GARNETT, Robert Selden** (brother of James Mercer Garnett and cousin of Charles Fenton Mercer), a Representative from Virginia; born at "Mount Pleasant," near Loretto, Essex County, Va.,

April 26, 1789; attended the College of New Jersey (now Princeton University); studied law; was admitted to the bar and commenced practice in Lloyds, Va.; member of the Virginia house of delegates in 1816 and 1817; elected as a Republican to the Fifteenth Congress and reelected to the four succeeding Congresses (March 4, 1817-March 3, 1827); was not a candidate for renomination in 1826; resumed the practice of law in Lloyds; died on his estate, "Champlain," near Lloyds, Essex County, Va., August 15, 1840; interment in the family burying ground on his estate.

**GARNSEY, Daniel Greene,** a Representative from New York; born in Canaan, Columbia County, N.Y., June 17, 1779; attended private schools; member of the State militia in 1805; brigade inspector in Saratoga County, N.Y., in 1810 and 1811; studied law in Norwich, Chenango County, N.Y.; was admitted to the bar in 1811 and practiced in Rensselaer and Saratoga Counties; served in the War of 1812 as aide-de-camp to major general with rank of major; moved to Pomfret in 1816 and labored to promote the building up of the village of Dunkirk; commissioner to perform certain duties of a judge of the supreme court at chambers; surrogate of Chautauqua County 1813-1831; brigade inspector, Chautauqua County, N.Y., in 1817; district attorney of Chautauqua County from June 11, 1818, to March 4, 1826; elected to the Nineteenth and Twentieth Congresses (March 4, 1825-March 3, 1829); moved to Michigan in 1831 and settled in the vicinity of Battle Creek; appointed postmaster and Government superintendent of public works near Detroit and Ypsilanti; served with General Scott in the Black Hawk War in 1836; moved to Rock Island, Ill.; appointed on March 22, 1841, by President William Henry Harrison, receiver of public moneys at the land office in Dixon, Ill., and served until removed by President John Tyler on August 25, 1843; president of the Harrison celebration in Galena, Ill., July 4, 1840; died in Gowanda, N.Y., May 11, 1851; interment in Pine Hill Cemetery.

**GARRETT, Abraham Ellison,** a Representative from Tennessee; born near Livingston, Overton County, Tenn., March 6, 1830; attended the public schools and Poplar Springs College, Kentucky; studied law; was admitted to the bar and commenced practice in Livingston, Tenn.; also engaged in agricultural pursuits; served as lieutenant colonel of the First Regiment, Tennessee Mounted Infantry, in the Union Army during the Civil War; delegate to the State constitutional convention in 1865; member of the State house of representatives in 1865 and 1866; elected as a Democrat to the Forty-second Congress (March 4, 1871-March 3, 1873); unsuccessful candidate for reelection in 1872; resumed the practice of law in Carthage, Tenn., where he died February 14, 1907; interment in Carthage Cemetery.

**GARRETT, Clyde Leonard,** a Representative from Texas; born on a farm near Gorman, Eastland County, Tex., December 16, 1885; attended the public schools and Hankins' Normal College in his native city; raised on a farm; worked as a railroad section hand; taught school at Sweetwater, Nolan County, Tex., in 1906 and 1907; deputy in the office of the tax collector 1907-1912; county clerk of Eastland County, Tex., 1913-1919; engaged in the real estate, insurance, and banking businesses, 1920-1922; city manager of Eastland, Tex., 1922-1923; county judge, 1929-1936; elected as a Democrat to the Seventy-fifth and Seventy-sixth Congresses (January 3, 1937-January 3, 1941); unsuccessful candidate for renomination in 1940 to the Seventy-seventh Congress; administrative officer in the office of the Secretary of Commerce from January 15, 1941 to May 1, 1942, at which time he became staff specialist in the Office of War Information and served until October 15, 1943; unsuccessful candidate for nomination in 1944 to the Seventy-ninth Congress; technical assistant, Veterans Administration, Washington, D.C., and Dallas, Tex., 1949-1950; manager, Veterans Administration regional office, Waco, Tex., 1951-1956; was an unsuccessful candidate for Eastland County judgeship in 1958; died in Eastland, Tex., December 18, 1959; interment in Eastland Cemetery.

**GARRETT, Daniel Edward,** a Representative from Texas; born near Springfield, Robertson County, Tenn., April 28, 1869; attended the common schools of his native county; studied law; was admitted to the bar and commenced practice in Springfield, Tenn., in 1893; member of the State house of representatives 1892-1896; elected to the State senate in 1902 and again in 1904; moved to Houston, Tex., in 1905 and continued the practice of law; elected as a Democrat to the Sixty-third Congress (March 4, 1913-March 3, 1915); unsuccessful candidate for reelection in 1914 to the Sixty-fourth Congress; resumed the practice of law in Houston, Tex.; elected to the Sixty-fifth Congress (March 4, 1917-March 3, 1919); was not a candidate for renomination in 1918; elected to the Sixty-seventh and to the five succeeding Congresses and served from March 4, 1921, until his death; had been reelected to the Seventy-third Congress; died in Washington, D.C., on December 13, 1932; interment in Forest Park Cemetery, Houston, Tex.

**GARRETT, Finis James,** a Representative from Tennessee; born near Ore Springs, Weakley County, Tenn., August 26, 1875; attended the common schools and Clinton (Ky.) College; was graduated from Bethel College, McKenzie, Tenn., in 1897; editor of country newspapers at Dresden and McKenzie, Tenn., before completing his college course; engaged in teaching at Como and Milan, Tenn.; studied law; was admitted to the bar in 1899 and commenced practice in Dresden, Tenn.; appointed master in chancery September 14, 1900, and served until January 24, 1905; delegate to all Democratic State conventions from 1896 to 1925; delegate to the Democratic National Convention of 1924; elected as a Democrat to the Fifty-ninth and to the eleven succeeding Congresses (March 4, 1905-March 3, 1929); chairman, Committee on Flood Control (Sixty-fifth Congress); minority leader (Sixty-eighth through Seventieth Congresses); was not a candidate for renomination in 1928 to the House of Representatives, but was an unsuccessful candidate for nomination to the United States Senate; appointed judge of the United States Court of Customs and Patent Appeals by President Calvin Coolidge, taking office on March 5, 1929, and became presiding judge of the court on December 9, 1937, by appointment of President Franklin D. Roosevelt, and served until his retirement September 15, 1955; died in Washington, D.C., May 25, 1956; interment in Sunset Cemetery, Dresden, Tenn.

Bibliography: *DAB*.

**GARRISON, Daniel,** a Representative from New Jersey; born in Lower Penns Neck Township, near Salem, N.J., April 3, 1782; pursued an academic course; engaged in agricultural pursuits; member of the State general assembly 1806-1808; surrogate of Salem County 1809-1823; elected to the Eighteenth and Nineteenth Congresses (March 4, 1823-March 3, 1827); was not a candidate for renomination in 1826 to the Twentieth Congress; appointed by President Andrew Jackson inspector of the revenue and collector of the customs at the port of Bridgeton, N.J., in 1834 and served until 1838; died in Salem, N.J., February 13, 1851; interment in St. John's Episcopal Cemetery.

**GARRISON, George Tankard,** a Representative from Virginia; born in Accomack County, Va., January 14, 1835; was graduated from Dickinson College, Carlisle, Pa., in 1853 and from the law department of the University of Virginia, Charlottesville, Va., in 1857; was admitted to the bar and commenced practice in Accomac; served as a private in the Confederate Army during the Civil War; member of the Virginia house of delegates 1861-1863; served in the Virginia senate 1863-1865; resumed the practice of law and also engaged in agricultural pursuits; elected judge of the eighth Virginia circuit in 1870 and subsequently judge of the seventeenth circuit; elected as a Democrat to the Forty-seventh Congress (March 4, 1881-March 3, 1883); successfully contested the election of Robert M. Mayo to the Forty-eighth Congress and served from March 20, 1884, to March 3, 1885; resumed the practice of law; elected judge of the county court of Accomack County, Va.; died at Accomac, Va., November 14, 1889; interment in Edge Hill Cemetery.

**GARROW, Nathaniel,** a Representative from New York; born in Barnstable, Barnstable County, Mass., April 25, 1780; attended the public schools; followed the sea; moved to Auburn, N.Y., in 1796; appointed justice of the peace in 1809; sheriff of Cayuga County 1815-1819 and 1821-1825; elected to the Twentieth Congress (March 4, 1827-March 3, 1829); United States marshal of the northern district of New York from February 1837 to March 1841; died in Auburn, Cayuga County, N.Y., March 3, 1841; interment in the family burying ground on his estate; reinterment in Fort Hill Cemetery, Auburn, N.Y.

**GARTH, William Willis,** a Representative from Alabama; born in Morgan County, Ala., October 28, 1828; pursued classical studies in Lagrange, Va., and at Emory and Henry College, Emory, Va.; studied law at the University of Virginia at Charlottesville; was admitted to the Alabama bar and commenced the practice of law in Huntsville, Ala.; during the Civil War was lieutenant colonel on the staff of General James Longstreet in the Confederate Army; elected as a Democrat to the Forty-fifth Congress (March 4, 1877-March 3, 1879); was an unsuccessful candidate for reelection in 1878 to the Forty-sixth Congress; resumed the practice of law; died in Huntsville, Ala., on February 25, 1912; interment in Maple Hill Cemetery.

**GARTNER, Fred Christian,** a Representative from Pennsylvania; born in Philadelphia, Pa., March 14, 1896; attended the public schools and Brown Preparatory School in Philadelphia; served as a yeoman in the United States Naval Reserve in 1918 and 1919; was graduated from the law department of Temple University, Philadelphia in 1920; was admitted to the bar the same year and commenced practice in Philadelphia; member of the Pennsylvania civil service commission at Philadelphia 1928-1932; served in the Pennsylvania house of representatives in 1933 and 1934; elected as a Republican to the Seventy-sixth Congress (January 3, 1939-January 3, 1941); was an unsuccessful candidate for reelection in 1940; resumed the practice of law; chairman of the board, Hol-Gar Manufacturing Corporation of Pennsylvania; died in Somers Point, N.J., September 1, 1972; interment in Chelten Hills Cemetery, Philadelphia, Pa.

**GARTRELL, Lucius Jeremiah** (uncle of Choice Boswell Randell), a Representative from Georgia; born near Washington, Wilkes County, Ga., January 7, 1821; attended private schools, Randolph-Macon College, and Franklin College, Georgia; studied law; was admitted to the bar in 1842 and practiced in Washington, Ga.; moved to Atlanta, Ga.; elected solicitor general of the northern judicial circuit in 1843; resigned in 1847; member of the State house of representatives 1847-1850; elected as a Democrat to the Thirty-fifth and Thirty-sixth Congresses and served from March 4, 1857, to January 23, 1861, when he joined other secessionist members of the Georgia delegation in withdrawing from the Thirty-sixth Congress; organized the Seventh Regiment, Georgia Volunteer Infantry, of which he was elected colonel; resigned his commission January 3, 1862, having been elected to the Confederate Congress and served until 1864; commissioned brigadier general in the Confederate service on August 22, 1864; resumed the practice of law; member of the State constitutional convention in 1877; unsuccessful candidate for election for Governor in 1882; died in Atlanta, Ga., April 7, 1891; interment in Oakland Cemetery.

Bibliography: *DAB*.

**GARVIN, William Swan,** a Representative from Pennsylvania; born in Mercer, Mercer County, Pa., on July 25, 1806; pursued an academic course; editor of the Western Press, in Mercer, for fifty years; appointed postmaster of Mercer January 3, 1837, and served until June 12, 1841; elected as a Democrat to the Twenty-ninth Congress (March 4, 1845-March 3, 1847); chairman, Committee on Expenditures on Public Buildings (Twenty-ninth Congress); flour inspector in Pittsburgh, Pa.; again appointed postmaster of Mercer April 10, 1867, and served until June 23, 1869; engaged in journalism; died in Mercer, Pa., February 20, 1883; interment in the Citizens' Cemetery.

**GARY, Frank Boyd,** a Senator from South Carolina; born in Cokesbury, Abbeville County, S.C., March 9, 1860; attended the Cokesbury Conference School and Union College, Schenectady, N.Y.; studied law; was admitted to the bar and commenced practice in Abbeville, S.C., in 1881; member, State house of representatives 1890-1900, serving as speaker 1895-1900; delegate to the State constitutional convention in 1895; member, State house of representatives 1906; elected as a Democrat to the United States Senate to fill the vacancy caused by the death of Asbury C. Latimer and served from March 6, 1908, to March 3, 1909; was not a candidate for reelection in 1908; member, State house of representatives 1910; elected judge of the eighth judicial circuit in 1912 and served until his death in Charleston, S.C., December 7, 1922; interment in Long Cane Cemetery, Abbeville, S.C.

**GARY, Julian Vaughan,** a Representative from Virginia; born in Richmond, Va., February 25, 1892; attended the public schools; B.A., University of Richmond, 1912, and from its law department, B.L., 1915; taught at Blackstone Academy for Boys, 1912-1913; was admitted to the bar in 1915 and commenced practice in Richmond, Va.; during the First World War served in the United States Army; counsel and executive assistant of the Virginia tax board, 1919-1924; served in the Virginia house of delegates, 1926-1933; member of the board of trustees of the University of Richmond; elected as a Democrat to the Seventy-ninth Congress, March 6, 1945, by special election to fill the vacancy caused by the resignation of David E. Satterfield, Jr.; reelected to the nine succeeding Congresses, and served from March 6, 1945 to January 3, 1965; was not a candidate for renomination in 1964 to the Eighty-ninth Congress; resumed the practice of law; retired and resided in Richmond, Va., where he died on September 6, 1973; interment in Hollywood Cemetery.

**GASQUE, Allard Henry** (husband of Elizabeth Hawley Gasque), a Representative from South Carolina; born on Friendfield plantation, near Hyman, Marion (now Florence) County, S.C., March 8, 1873; attended the public schools; worked on a farm and taught in the country schools for several years; was graduated from the University of South Carolina at Columbia in 1901; principal of Waverly Graded School, Columbia, S.C., in 1901 and 1902; elected superintendent of education of Florence County in 1902 and served by reelection until 1923; president of the county superintendents' association of the State in 1911 and 1912 and of the State teachers' association in 1914 and 1915; member of the Democratic State executive committee 1912-1920; chairman of the Democratic county committee 1919-1923; elected as a Democrat to the Sixty-eighth and to the seven succeeding Congresses and served from March 4, 1923, until his death in Washington, D.C., on June 17, 1938; chairman, Committee on Pensions (Seventy-second through Seventy-fifth Congresses); interment in Mount Hope Cemetery, Florence, S.C.

**GASQUE, Elizabeth Hawley** (wife of Allard Henry Gasque), a Representative from South Carolina; born Elizabeth Mills Hawley on February 26, 1896, near Blythewood, on Rice Creek Plantation, Richland County, S.C.; attended private schools, South Carolina Coeducational Institute in Edgefield, and graduated from Greenville Female College in 1907; moved to Florence, S.C., in 1908; elected as a Democrat to the Seventy-fifth Congress to fill the vacancy caused by the death of her husband, Allard H. Gasque, and served from September 13, 1938, to January 3, 1939; was not a candidate for election in 1938 to the Seventy-sixth Congress; active in dramatics;

author and lecturer; was a resident of Cedar Tree Plantation, Ridgeway, S.C.; died November 2, 1989.

**GASSAWAY, Percy Lee,** a Representative from Oklahoma; born in Waco, McLennan County, Tex., August 30, 1885; moved to Fort Sill, Okla. (then Indian Territory), with his parents in 1899; attended the public schools in Fort Sill and Oklahoma City, Okla.; employed as a clerk in a law office; studied law; was admitted to the bar in 1918 and commenced practice in Coalgate, Okla.; also engaged in agricultural and ranching pursuits; appointed county judge of Coal County, Okla., in 1923, elected in 1924, and served until 1926; district judge of the twenty-sixth judicial district 1926-1934; elected as a Democrat to the Seventy-fourth Congress (January 3, 1935-January 3, 1937); unsuccessful candidate for renomination in 1936; resumed the practice of law and also engaged as a rancher near Coalgate, Coal County, Okla.; died in Coalgate, Okla., May 15, 1937; interment in Coalgate Cemetery.

**GASTON, Athelston,** a Representative from Pennsylvania; born in Castile, Wyoming County, N.Y., April 24, 1838; moved with his parents to Crawford County, Pa., in 1854; attended the common schools; engaged in agricultural pursuits until 1873, when he became a dealer in and manufacturer of lumber; mayor of Meadville, Pa., 1891-1895; elected as a Democrat to the Fifty-sixth Congress (March 4, 1899-March 3, 1901); unsuccessful candidate for reelection in 1900 to the Fifty-seventh Congress; resumed the lumber business; killed while on a hunting trip along Lake Edward in northern Quebec, Canada, September 23, 1907; interment in Greendale Cemetery, Meadville, Pa.

**GASTON, William,** a Representative from North Carolina born in New Bern, N.C., September 19, 1778; entered Georgetown College, Washington, D.C., at the age of thirteen; later returned to his native State and became a student in the Academy of New Bern; was graduated from Princeton College in 1796; studied law; was admitted to the bar in 1798 and commenced practice in New Bern; member of the State senate in 1800; served in the State house of representatives 1807-1809, and as speaker in 1808; again a member of the State senate in 1812, 1818, and 1819; elected as a Federalist to the Thirteenth and Fourteenth Congresses (March 4, 1813-March 3, 1817); was not a candidate for renomination in 1816; again served in the State house of representatives in 1824, 1827, 1828, 1829, and 1831; appointed judge of the supreme court of North Carolina in 1833, holding the position until his death; member of the State constitutional convention in 1835; declined a nomination for election to the United States Senate in 1840; died in Raleigh, N.C., January 23, 1844; interment in Cedar Grove Cemetery, New Bern, N.C.

**Bibliography:** *DAB*; Schauinger, Joseph Herman. *William Gaston, Carolinian*. Milwaukee: Bruce Publishing, 1949.

**GATES, Seth Merrill,** a Representative from New York; born in Winfield, Herkimer County, N.Y., October 10, 1800; moved with his parents to Sheldon, Genesee (now Wyoming) County, N.Y. in 1806; attended the common schools and Middleburg Academy, Wyoming, N.Y.; inspector of common schools and deputy sheriff of Le Roy about 1825; studied law; was admitted to the bar in 1827 and commenced practice in Le Roy, N.Y.; supervisor of Le Roy in 1830; member of the State assembly in 1832; declined to be a candidate for reelection; edited the Le Roy Gazette in 1838; elected as a Whig to the Twenty-sixth and Twenty-seventh Congresses (March 4, 1839-March 3, 1843); unsuccessful candidate for reelection in 1842 to the Twenty-eighth Congress; moved to Warsaw, Wyoming County, N.Y., in 1843 and continued the practice of law; also engaged in the lumber trade and as a hardware and dry-goods merchant; unsuccessful Free-Soil candidate for lieutenant governor of New York in 1848; secretary of the Wyoming County Insurance Co. 1851-1865; appointed postmaster of Warsaw on May 28, 1861, and served until July 9, 1870, when his successor was appointed; vice president of the Genesee County Pioneer Association in 1872; died in Warsaw, N.Y., August 24, 1877; interment in Warsaw Cemetery.

**GATHINGS, Ezekiel Candler,** a Representative from Arkansas; born in Prairie, Monroe County, Miss., November 10, 1903; attended the public schools and the University of Alabama at Tuscaloosa; was graduated from the law department of the University of Arkansas at Fayetteville in 1929; was admitted to the bar the same year and commenced practice in Helena, Ark.; moved to West Memphis, Ark., in 1932 and continued the practice of law; served in the State senate 1935-1939; elected as a Democrat to the Seventy-sixth and to the fourteen succeeding Congresses (January 3, 1939-January 3, 1969); was not a candidate for reelection in 1968 to the Ninety-first Congress; resumed the practice of law; served as a member of West Memphis, Ark., Port Authority; resided in West Memphis, Ark., where he died May 2, 1979; interment in Crittenden Memorial Park, Marion, Ark.

**GATLIN, Alfred Moore,** a Representative from North Carolina; born in Edenton, N.C., April 20, 1790; pursued classical studies at New Bern, N.C., and was graduated from the University of North Carolina at Chapel Hill in 1808; studied law; was admitted to the bar in 1823 and commenced practice in Camden, Camden County, N.C., in the same year; elected to the Eighteenth Congress (March 4, 1823-March 3, 1825); unsuccessful candidate for reelection in 1824 to the Nineteenth Congress; moved to the Territory of Florida.

**GAUSE, Lucien Coatsworth,** a Representative from Arkansas; born near Wilmington, Brunswick County, N.C., December 25, 1836; moved to Lauderdale County, Tenn.; studied under a private tutor; was graduated from the University of Virginia at Charlottesville; studied law and was graduated from Cumberland University, Lebanon, Tenn.; was admitted to the bar and commenced practice in Jacksonport, Ark., in 1859; during the Civil War entered the Confederate service as lieutenant, attaining the rank of colonel; resumed the practice of law in Jacksonport in 1865; member of the State house of representatives in 1866; commissioner to represent the State government at Washington; unsuccessfully contested the election of Asa Hodges to the Forty-third Congress; elected as a Democrat to the Forty-fourth and Forty-fifth Congresses (March 4, 1875-March 3, 1879); was not a candidate for renomination in 1878; resumed the practice of law; died in Jacksonport, Ark., November 5, 1880; interment in the private burying ground near Jacksonport.

**GAVAGAN, Joseph Andrew,** a Representative from New York; born in New York City August 20, 1892; attended the public and parochial schools; was graduated from the law department of Fordham University, New York City in 1920; during the First World War enlisted as a private and later was promoted to second lieutenant in the Quartermaster Corps and served from August 20, 1917, to October 13, 1919; first lieutenant in the Quartermaster Reserve Corps 1920-1925; was admitted to the bar in 1920 and commenced practice in New York City; member of the State assembly 1923-1929; elected as a Democrat to the Seventy-first Congress to fill the vacancy caused by the death of Royal H. Weller; reelected to the Seventy-second and to the six succeeding Congresses and served from November 5, 1929, until December 30, 1943, when he resigned, having been elected a justice of the New York Supreme Court in November 1943 for a fourteen-year term; chairman, Committee on Elections No. 2 (Seventy-second through Seventy-sixth Congresses), Committee on War Claims (Seventy-seventh and Seventy-eighth Congresses); reelected in 1957 for a second term as a justice; died in Bennington, Vt., October 18, 1968; interment in Gate of Heaven Cemetery, Hawthorne, N.Y.

**GAVIN, Leon Harry,** a Representative from Pennsylvania; born in Buffalo, Erie County, N.Y., February 25, 1893; moved to Oil City, Pa., in 1915; during the First World War served in the United States Army as a sergeant in the Fifty-first Infantry Regiment of the Sixth Division; served on the Defense Council of Venango County; member of the Pennsylvania Board of Appeals of the Selective Service System; executive secretary of the Oil City Chamber of Commerce; member of the National Migratory Bird Conservation Commission 1958-1963; elected as a Republican to the Seventy-eighth and to the ten succeeding Congresses and served from January 3, 1943, until his death in Washington, D.C., September 15, 1963; interment in Arlington National Cemetery, Va.

**GAY, Edward James** (grandson of Edward James Gay [1816-1889]), a Senator from Louisiana; born on Union Plantation, Iberville Parish, La., May 5, 1878; attended Pantops Academy, Charlottesville, Va., the Lawrenceville (N.J.) School, and Princeton University; engaged in sugar production and the cultivation of various agricultural products; member, State house of representatives 1904-1918; elected as a Democrat to the United States Senate to fill the vacancy caused by the death of Robert F. Broussard and served from November 6, 1918, to March 3, 1921; declined to be a candidate for reelection in 1920; chairman, Committee on Coast and Insular Survey (Sixty-fifth Congress); president of a manufacturing company and of the Lake Long Drainage District, Iberville Parish; died in New Orleans, La., December 1, 1952; interment in Metairie Cemetery.

**GAY, Edward James** (grandfather of Edward James Gay [1878-1952], and father-in-law of Andrew Price), a Representative from Louisiana; born in Liberty, Bedford County, Va., February 3, 1816; moved with his parents to Illinois in 1820, and thence to St. Louis, Mo., in 1824; spent several years under a private instructor in Belleville, Ill., and attended Augusta College, Kentucky, 1833-1834; engaged in commercial affairs in St. Louis from 1838 until 1860; moved to Louisiana and engaged in commercial manufacturing, and agricultural pursuits; first president of the Louisiana Sugar Exchange in New Orleans; elected as a Democrat to the Forty-ninth and to the two succeeding Congresses, and served from March 4, 1885 until his death on his St. Louis plantation, Iberville Parish, La., May 30, 1889; interment in Bellefontaine Cemetery, St. Louis, Mo.

**GAYDOS, Joseph Matthew,** a Representative from Pennsylvania; born in Braddock, Allegheny County, Pa., July 3, 1926; attended Duquesne University, 1945-1947; LL.B., University of Notre Dame Law School, 1951; admitted to the bar in 1952 and commenced practice in Pittsburgh, Pa.; served in the Pacific theater with the United States Navy Reserves, 1944-1946; member, Pennsylvania senate, 1967-1968; Pennsylvania deputy attorney general, 1955; assistant solicitor of Allegheny County; former general counsel to the United Mine Workers of America, District 5; elected as a Democrat to the Ninetieth Congress, November 5, 1968, by special election to fill the vacancy caused by the death of Elmer J. Holland, and at the same time elected to the Ninety-first Congress; reelected to the eleven succeeding Congresses, and served from November 5, 1968 to January 3, 1993; was not a candidate for reelection in 1992 to the One Hundred Third Congress; is a resident of McKeesport, Pa.

**GAYLE, John,** a Representative from Alabama; born in Sumter District, S.C., September 11, 1792; pursued classical studies and was graduated from South Carolina College at Columbia in 1813; studied law; was admitted to the bar and commenced practice in Mobile, Ala., in 1818; member of the Territorial council in 1817; solicitor of the first judicial district in 1819; member of the Alabama State house of representatives in 1822 and 1823; judge of the State supreme court from 1823 until 1828; member and speaker of the State house of representatives in 1829; elected Governor of Alabama in 1831, reelected in 1833, and served from November 26, 1831 to November 21, 1835; elected as a Whig to the Thirtieth Congress (March 4, 1847-March 3, 1849); chairman, Committee on Private Land Claims (Thirtieth Congress); appointed United States district judge of Alabama on March 13, 1849; died near Mobile, Ala., July 21, 1859; interment in Magnolia Cemetery, Mobile, Ala.

**Bibliography:** *DAB*.

**GAYLE, June Ward,** a Representative from Kentucky; born in New Liberty, Owen County, Ky., February 22, 1865; attended Concord College, New Liberty, Ky., and Georgetown College, Georgetown, Ky.; deputy sheriff; member of the Kentucky Democratic central committee and of the Kentucky executive committee; high sheriff of Owen County 1892-1896; unsuccessful candidate for Kentucky auditor in 1899; engaged in banking and in the tobacco business; elected as a Democrat to the Fifty-sixth Congress to fill the vacancy caused by the death of Evan E. Settle and served from January 15, 1900, to March 3, 1901; resumed his former business activities; died in Owenton, Ky., on August 5, 1942; interment in New Liberty Cemetery, New Liberty, Ky.

**GAYLORD, James Madison,** a Representative from Ohio; born in Zanesville, Ohio, May 29, 1811; moved to McConnelsville, Ohio, in 1818; attended the common schools and the University of Ohio at Athens; studied law; was admitted to the bar and practiced; appointed clerk of the court of common pleas in 1834; elected to the Thirty-second Congress (March 4, 1851-March 3, 1853); at the expiration of his term in Congress he was elected probate judge; appointed deputy United States marshal in 1860; elected justice of the peace in 1865, and by successive reelections was continued in that office until his death in McConnelsville, Ohio, June 14, 1874; interment in McConnelsville Cemetery.

**GAZLAY, James William,** a Representative from Ohio; born in New York City July 23, 1784; moved with his parents to Dutchess County, N.Y., in 1789; attended the common schools, after which he pursued an academic course; studied law in Poughkeepsie, N.Y.; was admitted to the bar in 1809 and practiced; moved to Cincinnati, Ohio, in 1813 and continued the practice of law; elected to the Eighteenth Congress (March 4, 1823-March 3, 1825); unsuccessful candidate for reelection in 1824 to the Nineteenth Congress; edited a weekly paper called the Western Tiller in 1826 and 1827; engaged in literary pursuits; died in Cincinnati, Ohio, June 8, 1874; interment in Spring Grove Cemetery.

**GEAR, John Henry,** a Representative and a Senator from Iowa; born in Ithaca, Tompkins County, N.Y., April 7, 1825; attended the common schools; moved to Galena, Ill., in 1836, to Fort Snelling, Iowa, in 1838, and to Burlington in 1843, where he engaged in mercantile pursuits; mayor of Burlington 1863; member, Iowa State house of representatives, 1871-1873, serving as speaker for two terms; elected Governor of Iowa in 1877, reelected in 1879, and served from January 17, 1878 to January 12, 1882; elected as a Republican to the Fiftieth and Fifty-first Congresses (March 4, 1887-March 3, 1891); unsuccessful candidate for reelection in 1890 to the Fifty-second Congress; appointed by President Benjamin Harrison as Assistant Secretary of the Treasury, and served from 1892 until 1893; elected to the Fifty-third Congress (March 4, 1893-March 3, 1895); elected as a Republican to the United States Senate in 1894; reelected in 1900 and served from March 4, 1895, until his death on July 14, 1900, before the start of his second term; chairman, Committee on Pacific Railroads (Fifty-fourth through Fifty-Sixth Congresses); died in Washington, D.C.; interment in Aspen Grove Cemetery, Burlington, Iowa.

**Bibliography:** *DAB*.

**GEARHART, Bertrand Wesley,** a Representative from California; born in Fresno, Calif., May 31, 1890; attended the public schools; was graduated from Boones University School, Berkeley, Calif., in 1910 and from the law department of the University of Southern California at Los Angeles in 1914; was admitted to the California bar in 1913 and commenced practice in Fresno, Calif., in 1914; served overseas as a second lieutenant in the Six Hundred and Ninth Aero Squadron 1917-1919; assistant district attorney and district attorney of Fresno County, Calif., 1917-1923; served as a member of the board of directors of the California Veterans' Home in 1932; delegate to the California Constitutional convention in 1933; elected as a Republican to the Seventy-fourth and to the six succeeding Congresses (January 3, 1935-January 3, 1949); was an unsuccessful candidate for reelection in 1948 to the Eighty-first Congress; resumed the practice of law in Fresno, Calif.; died in San Francisco, Calif., October 11, 1955; interment in Mountain View Cemetery, Fresno, Calif.

**GEARIN, John McDermeid,** a Senator from Oregon; born near Pendleton, Umatilla County, Oreg., August 15, 1851; attended the country schools, St. Mary's College, San Francisco, and graduated from Notre Dame University, Indiana, in 1871; studied law; was admitted to the bar in 1873 and commenced practice in Portland, Oreg.; member, State house of representatives 1874; city attorney of Portland in 1875; unsuccessful Democratic candidate for election in 1878 to the Forty-sixth Congress; district attorney for Multnomah County 1884-1886; when the celebrated opium frauds were unearthed in 1893 was appointed by President Grover Cleveland as special prosecutor for the government for these cases; appointed as a Democrat to the United States Senate to fill the vacancy caused by the death of John H. Mitchell and served from December 13, 1905, until January 23, 1907, when a successor was elected; was not a candidate for election in 1907 to fill the vacancy; resumed the practice of law in Portland, Oreg., until his death there November 12, 1930; interment in Mount Calvary Cemetery.

**GEARY, Thomas J.,** a Representative from California; born in Boston, Mass., January 18, 1854; moved with his parents to San Francisco, Calif., in April 1863; attended the public schools; studied law at St. Ignatius College; was admitted to the bar in 1877 and commenced practice in Petaluma, Calif., moving to Santa Rosa, Calif., in 1882; district attorney of Sonoma County, Calif., in 1883 and 1884; resumed the practice of law; elected as a Democrat to the Fifty-first Congress to fill the vacancy caused by the resignation of John J. De Haven; reelected to the Fifty-second and Fifty-third Congresses and served from December 9, 1890, to March 3, 1895; unsuccessful candidate for reelection in 1894 to the Fifty-fourth Congress; resumed the practice of law; moved to Nome, Alaska, in 1900, to San Francisco, Calif., in 1902, and returned to Santa Rosa, Calif., in 1903, continuing the practice of law; city attorney in 1906; retired from active pursuits in 1923; died in Santa Rosa, Calif., July 6, 1929; interment in Rural Cemetery.

**GEBHARD, John,** a Representative from New York; born in Claverack, Columbia County, N.Y., February 22, 1782; attended the public schools; studied law; was admitted to the bar and practiced; surrogate of Schoharie County 1811-1813, and again from 1815 to 1822; elected to the Seventeenth Congress (March 4, 1821-March 3, 1823); resumed the practice of law; died in Schoharie, N.Y., January 3, 1854; interment in St. Paul's Lutheran Cemetery.

**GEDDES, George Washington,** a Representative from Ohio; born in Mount Vernon, Knox County, Ohio, July 16, 1824; attended the common schools; studied law; was admitted to the bar in July 1845 and practiced; judge of the court of common pleas of the sixth judicial district in 1856; reelected in 1861; again elected in 1868, and served until 1873; resumed the practice of law; unsuccessful Democratic candidate for judge of the State supreme court in 1872; resumed the practice of law in Mansfield; elected as a Democrat to the Forty-sixth and to the three succeeding Congresses (March 4, 1879-March 3, 1887); chairman, Committee on War Claims (Forty-eighth and Forty-ninth Congresses); declined to be a candidate for reelection in 1886 to the Fiftieth Congress; resumed the practice of his profession; died in Mansfield, Richland County, Ohio, November 9, 1892; interment in Mansfield Cemetery.

**GEDDES, James,** a Representative from New York; born near Carlisle, Pa., July 22, 1763; attended the public schools; moved to Onondaga County, N.Y., in 1794, and began the manufacture of salt at Liverpool, N.Y.; justice of the peace in 1800; member of the State assembly in 1804; associate justice of the county court in 1809; judge of the court of common pleas in 1809; elected as a Federalist to the Thirteenth Congress (March 4, 1813-March 3, 1815); again a member of the State assembly in 1822; appointed chief engineer of the Ohio Canal in 1822; engineer on the Chesapeake & Ohio Canal in 1827; died in Geddes, N.Y., August 19, 1838; interment in Oakwood Cemetery, Syracuse, N.Y.

    **Bibliography:** *DAB.*

**GEELAN, James Patrick,** a Representative from Connecticut; born in New Haven, Conn., August 11, 1901; attended the public schools of New Haven, Conn., and was graduated from St. Anthony's College, San Antonio, Tex., in 1922; engaged in the retail cigar business from 1922 until 1941; member of the Connecticut State senate in 1939, 1941, and 1943; assistant clerk of the New Haven City Court, 1941-1943; vice president of the New Haven Central Labor Council in 1942; engaged in the insurance business, beginning in 1943; elected as a Democrat to the Seventy-ninth Congress (January 3, 1945-January 3, 1947); unsuccessful candidate for reelection in 1946 to the Eightieth Congress; resumed business pursuits until his retirement in 1972; was a resident of Branford, Conn., until his death in New Haven on August 10, 1982; interment at St. Lawrence Cemetery, West Haven, Conn.

**GEHRMANN, Bernard John,** a Representative from Wisconsin; born in Gnesen, near Koenigsberg, East Prussia, Germany, February 13, 1880; attended the common schools in Germany; in 1893 immigrated to the United States with his parents, who settled in Chicago, Ill.; employed in a packing plant in Chicago and later learned the printing trade on a German-language daily newspaper; attended night school; moved to Wisconsin and settled on a farm near Neillsville, Clark County, in 1896 and engaged in agricultural pursuits; moved to a farm near Mellen, Ashland County, in 1915; clerk of the school board from 1916 until 1934, town assessor, 1916-1921, and chairman of the town board from 1921 to 1932; conducted farmers' institutes throughout the State for the University of Wisconsin College of Agriculture, 1920-1933; served in the Wisconsin State assembly, 1927-1933; delegate to the Republican National Convention of 1932; member of the Wisconsin State senate in 1933 and 1934; elected as a Progressive to the Seventy-fourth and to the three succeeding Congresses (January 3, 1935-January 3, 1943); unsuccessful candidate for reelection in 1942 to the Seventy-eighth Congress; engaged in work for the United States Department of Agriculture from January 1943 until April 1945; elected to the Wisconsin State assembly in 1946, 1948, 1950, and 1952; elected to the Wisconsin State senate in 1954 for the term ending in January 1957; died in Mellen, Wis., July 12, 1958; interment in Mellen Union Cemetery.

**GEISSENHAINER, Jacob Augustus,** a Representative from New Jersey; born in New York City on August 28, 1839; attended private schools, and was graduated from Columbia College at New York City in 1858; studied law at Yale College, and at the New York University, where he was graduated; also a student in the University of Berlin; was admitted to the bar and commenced practice in New York City in 1862; elected as a Democrat to the Fifty-first, Fifty-second, and Fifty-third Congresses (March 4, 1889-March 3, 1895); chairman, Committee on Immigration and Naturalization (Fifty-third Congress), Committee on Naval Affairs (Fifty-third Congress); unsuccessful candidate for reelection in 1894 to the Fifty-fourth Congress; resumed the practice of law; died at Mount Pocono, Monroe County, Pa., on July 20, 1917; interment in West Laurel Hill Cemetery, Philadelphia, Pa.

**GEJDENSON, Samuel,** a Representative from Connecticut; born in Eschwege, Germany, in an American displaced persons camp, May 20, 1948; attended Fields Memorial School; graduated from Norwich Free Academy, Norwich, 1966; A.S., Mitchell Junior College, New London, 1968; B.A., University of Connecticut, Storrs, 1970; farmer; broker, FAI Trading Co.; chairman, Bozrah Town Committee, 1973; member, Connecticut State house of representatives, 1974-1978; president, Maria Montessori School of Norwich; elected as a Democrat to the Ninety-seventh and to the seven succeeding Congresses (January 3, 1981-January 3, 1997); is a resident of Bozrah, Conn.

**GEKAS, George William,** a Representative from Pennsylvania; born in Harrisburg, Dauphin County, Pa., April 14, 1930; attended public schools in Harrisburg; graduated William Penn High School, 1948; B.A., Dickinson College, Carlisle, Pa., 1952; LL.B. and J.D., Dickinson School of Law, 1958; admitted to the Pennsylvania bar, 1958, and commenced practice in Harrisburg; served, United States Army, corporal, 1953-1955; assistant district attorney, Dauphin County, 1960-1966; elected to the Pennsylvania house of representatives, 1966-1974; Pennsylvania senate, 1976-1982; elected as a Republican to the Ninety-eighth and to the six succeeding Congresses (January 3, 1983-January 3, 1997); is a resident of Harrisburg, Pa.

**GELSTON, David,** a Delegate from New York; born in Bridgehampton, Suffolk County, N.Y., July 4, 1744; signed the articles of association in 1775; delegate to the Second, Third, and Fourth Provincial Congresses of New York 1775-1777; member of the State constitutional convention in 1777; elected a member of the State assembly under the constitution of 1777, and served from 1777 to 1785; was speaker in 1784 and 1785; appointed one of the commissioners on specie in 1780; Member of the last Continental Congress in 1789; member of the council of appointment in 1792 and 1793; served in the State senate 1791-1794, 1798, and 1802; canal commissioner in 1792; surrogate of the county of New York 1787-1801; collector of the port of New York 1801-1820; engaged in mercantile pursuits in New York City, where he died August 21, 1828; interment in First Presbyterian Church Cemetery.

**GENSMAN, Lorraine Michael,** a Representative from Oklahoma; born near Wichita, Sedgwick County, Kans., August 26, 1878; attended the district schools, the Garden Plain Graded School, Wichita Commercial College, Lewis Academy, and the Kansas State Normal School at Emporia; principal of the Andale (Kans.) schools in 1896 and 1897; was graduated from the law department of the University of Kansas at Lawrence in 1901; was admitted to the bar the same year and commenced practice in Lawrence, Kans.; moved to Lawton, Okla., in 1901; served as referee in bankruptcy 1902-1907; prosecuting attorney of Comanche County in 1918 and 1919; elected as a Republican to the Sixty-seventh Congress (March 4, 1921-March 3, 1923); unsuccessful candidate for reelection in 1922 to the Sixty-eighth Congress and for election in 1936 to the Seventy-fifth Congress; delegate to the Republican National Convention in 1924; engaged in the oil business; resumed the practice of law until his retirement in 1953; died in Lawton, Okla., May 27, 1954; interment in Highland Cemetery.

**GENTRY, Brady Preston,** a Representative from Texas; born in Colfax, Van Zandt County, Tex., March 25, 1896; attended the public schools and East Texas State College, Commerce, Tex.; graduated from Cumberland University, Lebanon, Tenn.; studied law; was admitted to the bar and began practice in Tyler, Tex.; enlisted in the United States Army in 1918; served in Europe and rose to the rank of captain of Infantry; county attorney of Smith County 1921-1924; county judge of Smith County 1931-1939; chairman of the Texas State Highway Commission 1939-1945; elected as a Democrat to the Eighty-third and Eighty-fourth Congresses (January 3, 1953-January 3, 1957); was not a candidate for renomination in 1956 to the Eighty-fifth Congress; resumed the practice of law; died in Houston, Tex., November 9, 1966; interment in Rose Hill Cemetery, Tyler, Tex.

**GENTRY, Meredith Poindexter,** a Representative from Tennessee; born in Rockingham County, N.C., September 15, 1809; moved with his parents to Williamson County, Tenn., in 1813; completed preparatory studies; studied law; was admitted to the bar and commenced practice in Franklin, Tenn.; member of the State house of representatives 1835-1839; elected as a Whig to the Twenty-sixth and Twenty-seventh Congresses (March 4, 1839-March 3, 1843); on account of the death of his wife refused to be a candidate for renomination in 1842 to the Twenty-eighth Congress; elected to the Twenty-ninth and to the three succeeding Congresses (March 4, 1845-March 3, 1853); chairman, Committee on Indian Affairs (Thirtieth Congress); was not a candidate for renomination in 1852 to the Thirty-third Congress; unsuccessful candidate for Governor of Tennessee in 1855; retired to his plantation in Tennessee, where he remained until 1861; member of the First and Second Confederate Congresses 1862-1863; died in Nashville, Tenn., November 2, 1866; interment in Mount Olivet Cemetery.

**GEORGE, Henry, Jr.,** a Representative from New York; born in Sacramento, Calif., November 3, 1862; attended the common schools; at the age of sixteen entered a printing office where he was employed for one year; moved with his parents to Brooklyn, N.Y., in 1880; reporter on the Brooklyn Eagle in 1881; in 1884 accompanied his father as his secretary on a lecture tour of Great Britain, at the close of which he joined the staff of the London Truth; returned to this country and joined the staff of the North American Review; managing editor of the Standard, 1887-1891; served as correspondent in Washington, D.C., for a syndicate of Western newspapers in 1891; correspondent in England for the same syndicate in 1892; in 1893 became managing editor of the Florida Citizen at Jacksonville; returned to New York City in 1895; on the death of his father in 1897 was nominated to succeed him as the candidate of the Jefferson Party for mayor of New York City, but was unsuccessful; special correspondent in Japan in 1906; elected as a Democrat to the Sixty-second and Sixty-third Congresses (March 4, 1911-March 3, 1915); was not a candidate for reelection in 1914 to the Sixty-fourth Congress; engaged in literary pursuits until his death in Washington, D.C., on November 14, 1916; interment in Greenwood Cemetery, Brooklyn, N.Y.

**GEORGE, James Zachariah,** a Senator from Mississippi; born in Monroe County, Ga., October 20, 1826; moved to Mississippi as a child; attended the old field schools; joined the Mississippi Rifles in 1846 and served in Mexico until discharged on account of ill health; studied law; was admitted to the bar in 1847 and commenced practice in Carrollton, Miss.; reporter of the Mississippi Supreme Court in 1854; member of the Mississippi secession convention and signed the ordinance of secession; served in the Confederate Army during the Civil War, attaining the rank of brigadier general of State troops; resided in Jackson, Miss., 1872-1887, when he returned to Carrollton; appointed judge of the State supreme court in 1879 and was elected chief justice; elected as a Democrat to the United States Senate in 1880; reelected in 1886, and again in 1892, and served from March 4, 1881, until his death on August 14, 1897; chairman, Committee on Agriculture and Forestry (Fifty-third Congress); member of the constitutional convention of the State of Mississippi in 1890; died in Mississippi City, Miss.; interment in Evergreen Cemetery, Carrollton, Miss.

Bibliography: *DAB*; Peck, Lucy. "The Life and Times of James Z. George." Ph.D. dissertation, Mississippi State University, 1964.

**GEORGE, Melvin Clark,** a Representative from Oregon; born near Caldwell, Noble County, Ohio, May 13, 1849; moved with his parents over the Old Oregon Trail in 1851, and settled on a homestead near Lebanon, Linn County, Oreg.; attended the country schools, Santiam Academy, and Willamette University, Oregon; studied law; was admitted to the bar and commenced practice in Portland, Oreg., in 1875; member of the Oregon State senate from the Multnomah district, 1876-1880; elected as a Republican to the Forty-seventh and Forty-eighth Congresses (March 4, 1881-March 3, 1885); declined to be a candidate for renomination in 1884 to the Forty-ninth Congress; resumed the practice of law in Portland, Oreg.; judge of the Oregon State circuit court, 1897-1907; appointed by the circuit judges to superintend the construction of the Burnside Bridge over the Willamette River at Portland; director of the Portland public schools for five years; died in Portland, Oreg., February 22, 1933; interment in Lone Fir Cemetery.

**GEORGE, Myron Virgil,** a Representative from Kansas; born in Erie, Neosho County, Kans., January 6, 1900; attended the grade schools and graduated from Labette County High School at Altamont, Kans.; enlisted in the United States Army in April 1917, and served with the rank of corporal until discharged in May 1919; learned the printing trade on the Altamont Journal, published by his father; owner and publisher of the Edna Sun from 1924 until 1941; officer with Kansas State Highway Commission, 1939-1950; elected as a Republican to the Eighty-first Congress, November 7, 1950, by special election to fill the vacancy caused by the death of Herbert A. Meyer, and at the same time was elected to the Eighty-second Congress; reelected to the three succeeding Congresses, and served from November 7, 1950 to January 3, 1959; unsuccessful candidate for reelection in 1958 to the Eighty-sixth Congress; engaged in public relations in the transportation and construction fields; resided in Parsons, Kans., until his death there on April 11, 1972; interment in Memorial Lawn Cemetery.

**GEORGE, Newell Adolphus,** a Representative from Kansas; born in Kansas City, Mo., September 24, 1904; attended public schools, Kansas City, Kans., Wentworth Military Academy, Lexington, Mo., Park College, Parkville, Mo., and University of Kansas City School of Law; graduated from National University, Washington, D.C., in 1935; was admitted to the District of Columbia bar in 1935 and to the Kansas bar in 1941; commenced the practice of law in Kansas City, Kans.; member of the staff of Senator George McGill of Kansas, 1933-1934; regional attorney, Bureau of Employment Security, 1941-1945, and Federal Security Agency, 1947-1953; chief legal counsel of the Regional War Manpower Commission during the Second World War; first assistant Wyandotte County attorney, 1953-1958; delegate to the Democratic National Convention of 1960; elected as a Democrat to the Eighty-sixth Congress (January 3, 1959-January 3, 1961); unsuccessful candidate for reelection in 1960 to the Eighty-seventh Congress; appointed United States attorney for the district of Kansas on March 28, 1961, and served until June 20, 1968; was a resident of Kansas City, Kans., until his death there on October 22, 1992.

**GEORGE, Walter Franklin,** a Senator from Georgia; born on a farm near Preston, Webster County, Ga., January 29, 1878; attended the common schools; was graduated from Mercer University, Macon, Ga., in 1900 and from its law department in 1901; was admitted to the bar in 1901 and commenced practice in Vienna, Ga.; solicitor general of the Cordele judicial circuit, 1907-1912, and judge of the superior court, 1912-1917; judge of the State court of appeals from January to October 1917, when he resigned; associate justice of the State supreme court from 1917 until 1922, when he resigned; elected as a Democrat to the United States Senate in 1922 to fill the vacancy caused by the death of Thomas E. Watson; reelected in 1926, 1932, 1938, 1944, and again in 1950, and served from November 22, 1922 to January 2, 1957; was not a candidate for renomination in 1956; served as President pro tempore of the Senate during the Eighty-fourth Congress; chairman, Committee on Privileges and Elections (Seventy-third through Seventy-sixth Congresses), Committee on Foreign Relations (Seventy-sixth,

Seventy-seventh, and Eighty-fourth Congresses), Committee on Finance (Seventy-seventh through Seventy-ninth Congresses and Eighty-first and Eighty-second Congresses), Joint Committee on Internal Revenue Taxation (Eighty-first and Eighty-second Congresses), Select Committee on Case Influence (Eighty-fourth Congress), Special Committee on Foreign Assistance (Eighty-fourth Congress); appointed by President Dwight D. Eisenhower as special ambassador to the North Atlantic Treaty Organization, and served until his death in Vienna, Ga., August 4, 1957; interment in Vienna Cemetery.

Bibliography: *DAB*; Zeigler, Luther. "Senator Walter George's 1938 Campaign." *Georgia Historical Quarterly* 43 (December 1959): 333-52.

**GEPHARDT, Richard Andrew,** a Representative from Missouri; born in St. Louis, Mo., January 31, 1941; attended the public schools of St. Louis; graduated Southwest High School, 1958; B.S., Northwestern University, Evanston, Ill., 1962; J.D., University of Michigan Law School, 1965; admitted to the Missouri bar in 1965 and commenced practice in St. Louis; served in Missouri Air National Guard, 1965-1971; Democratic committeeman, Fourteenth Ward, St. Louis, 1968-1971; alderman, Fourth Ward, St. Louis, 1971-1976; elected as a Democrat to the Ninety-fifth and to the nine succeeding Congresses (January 3, 1977-January 3, 1997); unsuccessful candidate for the Democratic presidential nomination in 1988; majority leader (One Hundred First through One Hundred Third Congresses), minority leader (One Hundred Fourth Congress); is a resident of St. Louis, Mo.

**GERAN, Elmer Hendrickson,** a Representative from New Jersey; born in Matawan, Monmouth County, N.J., October 24, 1875; attended the public schools and Glenwood Military Academy; was graduated from Peddie Institute, Hightstown, N.J., in 1895, from Princeton University in 1899, and from New York Law School in 1901; was admitted to the New Jersey bar in 1901 and commenced practice in Jersey City, N.J.; member of the State house of assembly in 1911 and 1912; member of the New Jersey State Water Supply Commission 1912-1915; assistant prosecutor of the pleas of Monmouth County 1915-1917; again a member of the State house of assembly in 1916 and 1917 and served as minority leader; sheriff of Monmouth County 1917-1920; appointed United States district attorney for New Jersey by President Wilson in 1920; resigned in 1921 and resumed the practice of law in Asbury Park, N.J.; elected as a Democrat to the Sixty-eighth Congress (March 4, 1923-March 3, 1925); unsuccessful candidate for reelection in 1924 to the Sixty-ninth Congress; resumed the practice of his profession until September 22, 1927; in 1927 became associated with the New Jersey Gravel & Sand Co. at Farmington, and was serving as vice president and treasurer at time of death; died in Marlboro Township, Morganville, N.J., January 12, 1954; interment in Old Tennent Cemetery, Tennent, N.J.

**GEREN, Preston M. (Pete),** a Representative from Texas; born in Fort Worth, Tarrant County, Tex., Janury 29, 1952; graduated from Arlington Heights High School, Fort Worth, 1970; attended Georgia Institute of Technology, Atlanta, 1970-1973; B.A., University of Texas, 1974; J.D., University of Texas Law School, 1978; associate attorney, Houston, Tex., 1979, and Fort Worth, 1979-1981; practicing attorney, Fort Worth, 1981-1983; executive assistant to Senator Lloyd M. Bentsen, Jr., of Texas, 1983-1985; partner, Blum and Geren, 1985-1989; unsuccessful candidate for election in 1986 to the One Hundredth Congress; elected as a Democrat to the One Hundred First Congress, September 12, 1989, by special election to fill the vacancy caused by the resignation of James C. Wright, Jr.; reelected to the three succeeding Congresses, and served from September 12, 1989 to January 3, 1997; was not a candidate for reelection in 1996 to the One Hundred Fifth Congress; is a resident of Fort Worth, Tex.

**GERLACH, Charles Lewis,** a Representative from Pennsylvania; born in Bethlehem, Northampton County, Pa., September 14, 1895; attended the public schools of Bethlehem, Pa.; moved to Allentown, Pa., in 1914; organizer, and later president, of a fuel and heating supply company; Pennsylvania Republican committeeman in 1936 and 1937; elected as a Republican to the Seventy-sixth and to the four succeeding Congresses and served from January 3, 1939, until his death in Allentown, Pa., May 5, 1947; interment in Greenwood Cemetery.

**GERMAN, Obadiah,** a Senator from New York; born in Amenia, Dutchess County, N.Y., April 22, 1766; attended the district schools; studied law; was admitted to the bar in 1792 and commenced practice in Norwich, N.Y.; member, State assembly 1798, 1804-1805, 1807-1809; elected as a Republican to the United States Senate and served from March 4, 1809, to March 3, 1815; judge of Chenango County 1815-1819; appointed commissioner of public works in 1817; member, State assembly 1819, and served as speaker; affiliated with the Whig Party on its organization; died in Norwich, N.Y., September 24, 1842; interment in Riverside Cemetery, North Norwich, N.Y.

**GERNERD, Fred Benjamin,** a Representative from Pennsylvania; born in Allentown, Lehigh County, Pa., November 22, 1879; attended the public schools; was graduated from Franklin and Marshall College, Lancaster, Pa., in 1901, from the school of political science of Columbia University, New York City, in 1903, and from the law school of Columbia University in 1904; was admitted to the bar in 1904 and commenced practice in Buffalo, N.Y.; returned to Allentown, Pa., in 1905; district attorney of Lehigh County, 1908-1912; Pennsylvania Republican committeeman, 1912-1920; trustee of Franklin and Marshall College, and of Cedar Crest College, Allentown, Pa.; elected as a Republican to the Sixty-seventh Congress (March 4, 1921-March 3, 1923); unsuccessful candidate for reelection in 1922 to the Sixty-eighth Congress; resumed the practice of law in Allentown, Pa.; delegate to the Republican National Convention of 1928; died in Allentown, Pa., August 7, 1948; interred in Trexlertown Cemetery, Trexlertown, Pa.

**GERRY, Elbridge** (grandfather of Elbridge Gerry [1813-1886] and great-grandfather of Peter Goelet Gerry), a Delegate and a Representative from Massachusetts and a Vice President of the United States; born in Marblehead, Mass., July 17, 1744; pursued classical studies and graduated from Harvard College in 1762; engaged in commercial pursuits; member, colonial house of representatives, 1772-1775; Member of the Continental Congress, 1776-1780, and 1783-1785; a signer of the Declaration of Independence; delegate to the Constitutional Convention in Philadelphia in 1787; refused to sign the instrument, but subsequently gave it his support; elected to the First and Second Congresses (March 4, 1789-March 3, 1793); sent to France on a diplomatic mission in 1797; unsuccessful Republican candidate for election in 1800, 1801, 1802 and 1803 for Governor; elected Governor of Massachusetts in 1810, reelected in 1811, and served from June 1810 to June 1812; unsuccessful candidate for reelection in 1812; elected Vice President of the United States on the ticket with James Madison in 1812 and served from March 4, 1813, until his death in Washington, D.C., on November 23, 1814; interment in the Congressional Cemetery.

Bibliography: *DAB*; Billias, George. *Elbridge Gerry, Founding Father and Republican Statesman.* New York: McGraw-Hill, 1976; Kramer, Eugene. "The Public Career of Elbridge Gerry." Ph.D. dissertation, Ohio State University, 1955.

**GERRY, Elbridge** (grandson of Elbridge Gerry [1744-1814]), a Representative from Maine; born in Waterford, Oxford County, Maine, December 6, 1813; pursued an academic course and attended Bridgton Academy; studied law; was admitted to the bar in 1839 and commenced practice in Waterford; clerk of the State house of representatives in 1840; appointed United States commissioner in bankruptcy in 1841; prosecuting attorney for Oxford County 1842-1845; member of the State house of representatives in 1846; elected as a Democrat to the Thirty-first Congress (March 4, 1849-March 3, 1851); was not a candidate for renomination in 1850 to the Thirty-second Congress; moved to Portland, Maine, where he resumed the practice of law; died in Portland, Maine, April 10, 1886; interment in Evergreen Cemetery.

**GERRY, James,** a Representative from Pennsylvania; born near Rising Sun, Cecil County, Md., August 14, 1796; pursued an academic course and was graduated from West Nottingham Academy; studied medicine at the University of Maryland, Baltimore, Md., and commenced practice in Shrewsbury, Pa., in 1824; elected as a Democrat to the Twenty-sixth and Twenty-seventh Congresses (March 4, 1839-March 3, 1843); continued the practice of medicine until 1870, when he retired; died in Shrewsbury, York County, Pa., July 19, 1873; interment in Lutheran Cemetery.

**GERRY, Peter Goelet** (great-grandson of Elbridge Gerry [1744-1814]), a Representative and a Senator from Rhode Island; born in New York City September 18, 1879; attended the public schools; graduated from Harvard University in 1901; studied law; was admitted to the Rhode Island bar in 1906; member of the representative council of Newport in 1912; elected as a Democrat to the Sixty-third Congress (March 4, 1913-March 3, 1915); unsuccessful candidate for reelection in 1914; elected as a Democrat to the United States Senate in 1916; reelected in 1922 and served from March 4, 1917, to March 3, 1929; unsuccessful candidate for renomination in 1928; Democratic whip 1919-1929; chairman, Committee on Railroads (Sixty-fifth Congress); member of the Democratic National Committee 1932-1936; again elected as a Democrat to the United States Senate in 1934; reelected in 1940 and served from January 3, 1935, to January 3, 1947; was not a candidate for renomination in 1946; resumed the practice of law; died in Providence, R.I., October 31, 1957; interment in St. James Cemetery, Hyde Park, N.Y.

**GERVAIS, John Lewis,** a Delegate from South Carolina; born of Huguenot parents in Hanover, Germany, circa 1741; attended schools and colleges in Hanover; immigrated to England and later to the United States, arriving in Charleston, S.C., on June 27, 1764; merchant, planter, and landowner; delegate to the provincial convention and Provincial Congress in 1775 and 1776; member of the council of safety in 1775, 1776, and 1781; appointed by Congress deputy postmaster general for South Carolina in 1778; served in the Revolutionary War, in organizing the Army and in the defense of Charleston in 1780; member of the State senate in 1781 and 1782 and served as president; Member of the Continental Congress in 1782 and 1783; commissioner of public accounts for South Carolina in 1794 and 1795; died in Charleston, S.C., August 18, 1798; interment in St. Philip's Churchyard.

**GEST, William Harrison,** a Representative from Illinois; born in Jacksonville, Morgan County, Ill., January 7, 1838; moved with his parents to Rock Island in 1842; was graduated from Williams College, Williamstown, Mass., in 1860; studied law; was admitted to the bar in 1862 and commenced practice in Rock Island, Ill.; elected as a Republican to the Fiftieth and Fifty-first Congresses (March 4, 1887-March 3, 1891); unsuccessful candidate for reelection in 1890 to the Fifty-second Congress; circuit judge of the fourteenth judicial district of Illinois from June 1897 until his death in Rock Island, Ill., August 9, 1912; interment in Chippiannook Cemetery.

**GETTYS, Thomas Smithwick,** a Representative from South Carolina; born in Rock Hill, York County, S.C. June 19, 1912; educated in the Rock Hill public schools; attended Clemson (S.C.) College; A.B., Erskine College, Due West, S.C., 1933; engaged in graduate work at Duke University and Winthrop College, Rock Hill; served with the Navy in the Pacific Theater, 1942-1946; taught and

coached at Rock Hill High School, 1933-1935; principal at Central School, 1935-1941; secretary to Representative James P. Richards, 1942-1951; postmaster of Rock Hill, 1951-1954; studied law; was admitted to the South Carolina bar in 1953 and practiced law in State and Federal courts; past member and chairman of the board of trustees of Rock Hill School District Three, 1953-1960; elected as a Democrat to the Eighty-eighth Congress, November 3, 1964, by special election to fill the vacancy caused by the resignation of Robert W. Hemphill and at the same time elected to the Eighty-ninth Congress; reelected to the four succeeding Congresses, and served from November 3, 1964 until his resignation on December 31, 1974; was not a candidate for reelection in 1974 to the Ninety-fourth Congress; is a resident of Rock Hill, S.C.

**GETZ, James Lawrence,** a Representative from Pennsylvania; born in Reading, Berks County, Pa., September 14, 1821; pursued an academic course; one of the founders of the Reading Gazette in 1840; purchased the Jefferson Democrat and merged the two papers under the name of the Reading Gazette and Democrat, disposing of his interests in 1868; studied law; was admitted to the bar in 1846 but never practiced; member of the Pennsylvania house of representatives in 1856 and 1857 and served as speaker of the house during the latter year; elected as a Democrat to the Fortieth, Forty-first, and Forty-second Congresses (March 4, 1867-March 3, 1873); was not a candidate for renomination in 1872; again engaged in the newspaper business; city comptroller of Reading, Pa., from 1888 until his death in that city December 25, 1891; interment in Charles Evans Cemetery.

**GEYER, Henry Sheffie,** a Senator from Missouri; born in Frederick, Frederick County, Md., December 9, 1790; was instructed privately; studied law; was admitted to the bar in 1811 and practiced law in Frederick; during the War of 1812 served as a first lieutenant in the Thirty-sixth Regiment, Maryland Infantry 1813-1815; settled in St. Louis, Mo., in 1815 and resumed the practice of law; member, Territorial assembly 1818; delegate to the State constitutional convention in 1820; member, State house of representatives 1820-1824 and again in 1834-1835, serving as speaker on two occasions; elected as a Whig to the United States Senate and served from March 4, 1851, to March 3, 1857; was not a candidate for reelection; resumed the practice of law in St. Louis; attorney for the defendant slave-owner in the Dred Scott case; died in St. Louis, Mo., March 5, 1859; interment in Bellefontaine Cemetery.

**Bibliography:** *DAB.*

**GEYER, Lee Edward,** a Representative from California; born in Wetmore, Nemaha County, Kans., September 9, 1888; attended the public schools; was graduated from Baker University, Baldwin City, Kans., in 1922; engaged in postgraduate work at the University of Wisconsin at Madison and the University of Southern California at Los Angeles; teacher in the rural schools in Nemaha County, Kans., 1908-1912; principal of Hamlin (Kans.) High School, 1916-1918; during the First World War served as a private in the Third Company, First Battalion, Central Officers' Training School, Camp Grant, Ill.; teacher and administrator in high schools in Kansas, Arizona, and California, 1919-1938; member of the California State house of representatives, 1934-1936; unsuccessful candidate for election in 1936 to the Seventy-fifth Congress; delegate to the Democratic National Convention of 1940; elected as a Democrat to the Seventy-sixth and Seventy-seventh Congresses, and served from January 3, 1939 until his death in Washington, D.C., October 11, 1941; interment in Wetmore Cemetery, Wetmore, Kans.

**GHOLSON, James Herbert,** a Representative from Virginia; born in Gholsonville, Brunswick County, Va., in 1798; pursued an academic course and was graduated from Princeton College in 1820; studied law; was admitted to the bar and commenced practice in Percivals, Va.; member of the Virginia house of delegates 1824-1828 and 1830-1833; elected as an Anti-Jacksonian to the Twenty-third Congress (March 4, 1833-March 3, 1835); served as judge of the circuit court for the Brunswick circuit for many years; died in Brunswick County, Va., July 2, 1848.

**GHOLSON, Samuel Jameson,** a Representative from Mississippi; born near Richmond, Madison County, Ky., May 19, 1808; moved with his father to Franklin County, Ala., in 1817; attended the common schools; studied law; was admitted to the bar at Russellville, Ala., in 1829; moved to Athens, Monroe County, Miss., and commenced the practice of law; member of the State house of representatives in 1835, 1836, and 1839; elected as a Jacksonian to the Twenty-fourth Congress to fill the vacancy caused by the death of David Dickson and served from December 1, 1836, to March 3, 1837; presented credentials as a Democratic Member-elect to the Twenty-fifth Congress and served from July 18, 1837, until February 5, 1838, when the seat was declared vacant; appointed United States district judge in 1839 and served until 1861, when Mississippi seceded from the Union; member of the State secession convention in 1861; after service in the Confederate Army as a private, captain, and colonel he was commissioned brigadier general of Mississippi State troops in 1861; taken prisoner at Fort Donelson, Tenn., in February 1862 but was exchanged; appointed major general in 1863 and brigadier general on May 6, 1864; again a member of the State house of representatives in 1865, 1866, and 1878; continued the practice of law in Aberdeen, Miss., until his death there October 16, 1883; interment in Odd Fellows Cemetery.

Bibliography: *DAB.*

**GHOLSON, Thomas, Jr.,** a Representative from Virginia; born in Brunswick, Brunswick County, Va.; pursued an academic course; studied law; was admitted to the bar and commenced practice in Brunswick County, Va.; member of the Virginia house of delegates 1806-1809; elected as a Republican to the Tenth Congress to fill the vacancy caused by the death of John Claiborne; reelected to the Eleventh and to the three succeeding Congresses and served from November 7, 1808, until his death in Brunswick County, Va., July 4, 1816; chairman, Committee on Claims (Twelfth Congress).

**GIAIMO, Robert Nicholas,** a Representative from Connecticut; born in New Haven, Conn., October 15, 1919; attended North Haven public schools; A.B., Fordham College, New York City, 1941; LL.B., University of Connecticut, 1943; served in the United States Army from 1943 until separated from the service as a first lieutenant in 1946; captain, Judge Advocate General Corps, United States Army Reserve; was admitted to the bar in 1947 and commenced the practice of law in New Haven, Conn.; member of the North Haven Board of Education, 1949-1955; assistant clerk, Probate Court, New Haven, Conn., 1952-1954; chairman, Connecticut Personnel Appeals Board, 1955-1958; third selectman, North Haven, 1955-1957; unsuccessful Democratic candidate for election in 1956 to the Eighty-fifth Congress; elected as a Democrat to the Eighty-sixth and to the ten succeeding Congresses (January 3, 1959-January 3, 1981); chairman, Committee on the Budget (Ninety-fifth and Ninety-sixth Congresses); was not a candidate for reelection in 1980 to the Ninety-seventh Congress; is a resident of Arlington, Va.

**GIBBONS, Sam Melville,** a Representative from Florida; born in Tampa, Hillsborough County, Fla., January 20, 1920; attended the public schools of Tampa; attended the University of Florida; LL.B., University of Florida School of Law, 1947; was admitted to the bar in 1947 and began the practice of law in Tampa; served in the United States Army with the Five Hundred and First Parachute Infantry, One Hundred and First Airborne Division, 1941 to 1945, and was released from active duty as a major; member, Florida State house of representatives, 1953-1958; Florida State senator, 1959-1962; delegate to the Democratic National Conventions of 1964, 1968, and 1984; elected as a Democrat to the Eighty-eighth and to the sixteen succeeding Congresses (January 3, 1963-January 3,

1997); chairman, Committee on Ways and Means (One Hundred Third Congress); was not a candidate for reelection in 1996 to the One Hundred Fifth Congress; is a resident of Tampa, Fla.

**GIBBONS, William,** a Delegate from Georgia; born at Bear Bluff, S.C., April 8, 1726; studied law in Charleston, S.C.; was admitted to the bar and practiced in Savannah, Ga.; member of the colonial assembly 1760-1762; joined the Sons of Liberty in 1774, and on May 11, 1775, was one of the party that broke open the magazine in Savannah and removed 600 pounds of the King's powder; delegate to the Provincial Congress of July 1775, and was chosen a member of the committee of safety on December 11, 1775; member of the executive council 1777-1781; associate justice of Chatham County in 1781 and 1782; Member of the Continental Congress in 1784; member of the State house of representatives in 1783, 1785-1789, and 1791-1793, and served as speaker in 1783, 1786, and 1787; president of the State constitutional convention in 1789; justice of the inferior court of Chatham County 1790-1792; died in Savannah, Ga., September 27, 1800; interment probably in Colonial Park, formerly called the Old Cemetery, or Christ Church Cemetery.

Bibliography: *DAB.*

**GIBBS, Florence Reville** (wife of Willis Benjamin Gibbs), a Representative from Georgia; born in Thomson, McDuffie County, Ga., April 4, 1890; attended the public schools; was graduated from Brenau College, Gainesville, Ga.; elected as a Democrat to the Seventy-sixth Congress to fill the vacancy caused by the death of her husband, Willis Benjamin Gibbs, and served from October 1, 1940, to January 3, 1941; was not a candidate for reelection in 1940 to the Seventy-seventh Congress; retired from public life and resided in Jesup, Ga., until her death there August 19, 1964; interment in Jesup Cemetery.

**GIBBS, Willis Benjamin** (husband of Florence Reville Gibbs), a Representative from Georgia; born in Dupont, Clinch County, Ga., April 15, 1889; attended the public schools and Mercer University, Macon, Ga.; was graduated from the Atlanta (Ga.) Law School in 1911; admitted to the bar and commenced practice in Folkston, Ga., the same year; moved to Jesup, Ga., in 1912 and continued the practice of law; served as solicitor of the city court of Jesup 1913-1924, and solicitor general of the Brunswick judicial circuit 1925-1939; county attorney for Wayne County, Ga., 1922-1938; lieutenant colonel on the staff of Governor Clifford Walker in 1924 and 1925; served on the State Board of Control of Eleemosynary Institutions 1931-1937; elected as a Democrat to the Seventy-sixth Congress and served from January 3, 1939, until his death in Washington, D.C., on August 7, 1940; interment in Jesup Cemetery, Jesup, Ga.

**GIBSON, Charles Hopper** (cousin of Henry Richard Gibson), a Representative and a Senator from Maryland; born near Centerville, Queen Anne County, Md., January 19, 1842; attended Centerville Academy and the Archer School in Harford County; graduated from Washington College, Chestertown, Md.; studied law; was admitted to the bar in 1864 and commenced practice in Easton, Md.; appointed by President Andrew Johnson in 1867 collector of internal revenue for the Eastern Shore district, but was not confirmed; auditor and commissioner in chancery in 1869 and resigned in 1870 to accept the appointment of State's attorney for Talbot County 1871-1875; elected as a Democrat to the Forty-ninth, Fiftieth, and Fifty-first Congresses (March 4, 1885-March 3, 1891); was not a candidate for reelection in 1890; appointed and subsequently elected as a Democrat to the United States Senate to fill the vacancy caused by the death of Ephraim K. Wilson and served from November 19, 1891, to March 3, 1897; chairman, Committee on Manufactures (Fifty-third Congress); resumed the practice of law; died in Washington, D.C., March 31, 1900; interment in Chesterfield Cemetery, Centerville, Md.

**GIBSON, Ernest Willard** (father of Ernest William Gibson, Jr.), a Representative and a Senator from Vermont; born in Londonderry, Windham County, Vt., December 29, 1872; attended the common schools and Black River Academy, Ludlow, Vt.; graduated from Norwich University, Northfield, Vt., in 1894; high school principal, 1894-1898; attended the law department of the University of Michigan at Ann Arbor in 1899; was admitted to the bar the same year and commenced practice in Brattleboro, Vt.; register of probate and deputy clerk of the United States district court; member of the Vermont State house of representatives in 1906; member of the State senate, serving as president pro tempore in 1908; served in the Vermont National Guard, 1899-1908, retiring as a colonel; returned to service in 1915, served during the Mexican border disputes, two years during the First World War, and served until 1923; State's attorney, 1919-1921; secretary of civil and military affairs for Vermont, 1921-1922; chairman of the board of commissioners of Brattleboro, Vt., for eight years; vice president of Norwich University; elected as a Republican to the Sixty-eighth Congress to fill the vacancy caused by the resignation of Porter H. Dale; reelected to the Sixty-ninth and to the four succeeding Congresses, and served from November 6, 1923 to October 19, 1933, when he resigned; chairman, Committee on Expenditures in the Department of the Treasury (Sixty-ninth Congress), Committee on Territories (Seventy-first Congress); appointed as a Republican to the United States Senate and subsequently elected to fill the vacancy caused by the death of Porter H. Dale; reelected in 1938, and served from November 21, 1933 until his death in Washington, D.C., June 20, 1940; interment in Morningside Cemetery, Brattleboro, Vt.

**GIBSON, Ernest William, Jr.** (son of Ernest Willard Gibson), a Senator from Vermont; born in Brattleboro, Windham County, Vt., March 6, 1901; attended the public schools; graduated from Norwich University, Northfield, Vt., in 1923; active in the Reserves throughout his life; member of the faculty of New York Military Academy, Cornwall, N.Y., 1923-1924; computer in the Coast and Geodetic Survey from 1924 until 1927; attended George Washington University Law School, Washington, D.C.; was admitted to the bar in 1926 and commenced practice in Brattleboro, Vt., in 1927; State's attorney of Windham County, Vt., 1929-1933; assistant secretary of the Vermont State senate, 1931-1933, and secretary, 1933-1940; appointed as a Republican to the United States Senate to fill the vacancy caused by the death of his father, Ernest W. Gibson, and served from June 24, 1940, to January 3, 1941; was not a candidate for election to fill the vacancy; during the Second World War served in the South Pacific and was discharged as a colonel, 1941-1945; elected Governor of Vermont in 1946, reelected in 1948, and served from January 9, 1947 until his resignation on January 16, 1950 to accept a judicial position; appointed a United States district judge for the district of Vermont, 1950-1969; died in Brattleboro, Vt., November 4, 1969; interment in Morningside Cemetery.

**Bibliography:** Hand, Samuel B. *Friends, Neighbors and Political Allies: Reflections on the Gibson-Aiken Connection.* Occasional Paper No. 11, Center for Research on Vermont. Burlington: University of Vermont, 1986.

**GIBSON, Eustace,** a Representative from West Virginia; born in Culpeper County, Va., October 4, 1842; attended the common schools; studied law; was admitted to the bar and commenced practice in 1861; enlisted in the Confederate Army in June 1861 as first lieutenant; promoted to captain in 1863 and retired on account of wounds; member of the constitutional convention of Virginia in 1867 and 1868; settled in Huntington, W.Va., in 1871; member of the State house of delegates in 1877 and 1878, and served as speaker in 1877; elected as a Democrat to the Forty-eighth and Forty-ninth Congresses (March 4, 1883-March 3, 1887); chairman, Committee on Expenditures in the Department of Justice (Forty-ninth Congress); unsuccessful candidate for renomination in 1886 and for nomination in 1888; again resumed the practice of law; died in Clifton Forge, Va., on December 10, 1900; interment in Spring Hill Cemetery, Huntington, W.Va.

**GIBSON, Henry Richard** (cousin of Charles Hopper Gibson), a Representative from Tennessee; born on Kent Island, Queen Annes County, Md., December 24, 1837; attended the common schools on Kent Island and at Bladensburg, Md.; was graduated from Decker's Academy at Bladensburg in 1858 and from Hobart College, Geneva, N.Y., in 1862; served in the commissary department of the Union Army from March 1863 to July 1865; entered Albany (N.Y.) Law School in September 1865; was admitted to the bar in December 1865 and commenced practice in Knoxville, Tenn., in January 1866; moved to Jacksboro, Campbell County, Tenn., in October 1866; appointed commissioner of claims by Governor William G. Brownlow in 1868; delegate to the State constitutional convention in 1870; member of the Tennessee State senate, 1871-1875; member of the Tennessee State house of representatives, 1875-1877; returned to Knoxville in 1876; founded the Knoxville Republican in 1879 and became its editor; appointed post-office inspector in 1881; became editor of the Knoxville Daily Chronicle in 1882; appointed United States pension agent at Knoxville on June 22, 1883, and served until June 9, 1885; chancellor of the second chancery division of Tennessee 1886-1894; professor of medical jurisprudence in the Tennessee Medical College 1889-1906; author of "Gibson's Suits in Chancery" in 1891; elected as a Republican to the Fifty-fourth and to the four succeeding Congresses (March 4, 1895-March 3, 1905); declined to be a candidate for renomination in 1904 to the Fifty-ninth Congress; associate editor in 1896 and associate reviser in 1918 of the "Code of Tennessee"; retired from public life and resided in Washington, D.C., being engaged as a writer and author and as a consulting editor of the American and English Encyclopedia of Law and Practice; died in Washington, D.C., May 25, 1938; remains were cremated and the ashes deposited in the Old Gray Cemetery, Knoxville, Tenn.

**GIBSON, James King,** a Representative from Virginia; born in Abingdon, Washington County, Va., February 18, 1812; attended the common schools; moved to Huntsville, Limestone County, Ala., in 1833; returned to Abingdon, Va., the following year and engaged in mercantile pursuits; deputy sheriff of Washington County in 1834 and 1835; appointed postmaster of Abingdon on December 19, 1837, and served until July 26, 1849, when a successor was appointed; upon the readmission of Virginia to representation was elected as a Conservative to the Forty-first Congress and served from January 28, 1870, to March 3, 1871; declined to be a candidate for renomination in 1870; engaged in agricultural pursuits and banking; died in Abingdon, Va., March 30, 1879; interment in Sinking Spring Cemetery.

**GIBSON, John Strickland,** a Representative from Georgia; born near Folkston, Charlton County, Ga., January 3, 1893; attended the common schools; studied law by correspondence from La Salle Extension University, Chicago, Ill.; was admitted to the bar in 1922 and commenced practice in Douglas, Ga., in 1923; solicitor of the city court of Douglas, Ga., 1928-1934; solicitor general Waycross judicial circuit, 1934-1940; elected as a Democrat to the Seventy-seventh, Seventy-eighth, and Seventy-ninth Congresses (January 3, 1941-January 3, 1947); unsuccessful candidate for renomination in 1946; resumed the practice of law; died in Douglas, Ga., October 19, 1960; interment in City Cemetery.

**GIBSON, Paris,** a Senator from Montana; born in Brownfield, Oxford County, Maine, July 1, 1830; attended the common schools and the Fryeburg Academy, Fryeburg, Maine; graduated from Bowdoin College, Brunswick, Maine, in 1851; engaged in the real estate business; member, State house of representatives 1854; settled in Minneapolis, Minn., in 1858; built and operated flour and woolen mills; in 1879 moved to Fort Benton, Mont.; engaged in sheep raising, coal mining, railroads and water power; founded the city of Great Falls, Mont., in 1882 and became the first mayor; delegate to the State constitutional convention in 1889; elected to the State senate in 1890; elected as a Democrat to the United States Senate to fill the vacancy caused by the resignation of William A. Clark and served from March 7, 1901, to March 3, 1905; was not a candidate for reelection; resumed his business interests; died in Great Falls, Mont., December 16, 1920; interment in Highland Cemetery.

**Bibliography:** *DAB.*

**GIBSON, Randall Lee,** a Representative and a Senator from Louisiana; born September 10, 1832, at Spring Hill, near Versailles, Woodford County, Ky.; was educated by a private tutor at "Live Oak," his father's plantation in Terrebonne Parish, La.; graduated from Yale College in 1853 and from the law department of the University of Louisiana (later Tulane University), New Orleans, La., in 1855; traveled in Europe for several years; engaged in planting until the outbreak of the Civil War; enlisted in the Confederate Army in 1861 and served until 1864, when he was promoted to brigadier general; after the war was admitted to the bar and practiced in New Orleans, La.; resumed agricultural pursuits; served as administrator of the Howard Memorial Library, trustee of the Peabody Fund, Regent of the Smithsonian Institution, and as president of the board of administrators of Tulane University, New Orleans, La.; unsuccessful candidate for election in 1872 to the Forty-third Congress; elected as a Democrat to the Forty-fourth and to the three succeeding Congresses (March 4, 1875-March 3, 1883); elected as a Democrat to the United States Senate in 1882; reelected in 1889 and served from March 4, 1883, until his death at Hot Springs, Ark., December 15, 1892; interment Lexington Cemetery, Lexington, Ky.

**Bibliography:** *DAB*; McBride, Mary. "Senator Randall Lee Gibson and the Establishment of Tulane University." *Louisiana History* 28 (Summer 1987): 245-262.

**GIDDINGS, De Witt Clinton,** a Representative from Texas; born in Susquehanna County, Pa., July 18, 1827; pursued an academic course; studied law in Honesdale, Pa.; was admitted to the bar in Texas in 1852 and commenced practice in Brenham, Tex.; served in the Confederate Army throughout the Civil War; member of the State constitutional convention in 1866; successfully contested as a Democrat the election of William T. Clark to the Forty-second Congress; reelected to the Forty-third Congress and served from May 13, 1872, to March 3, 1875; elected to the Forty-fifth Congress (March 4, 1877-March 3, 1879); engaged in the banking business in Brenham, Tex.; delegate to the Democratic National Conventions of 1884, 1888 and 1892; died in Brenham, Tex., on August 19, 1903; interment in Prairie Lea Cemetery.

**GIDDINGS, Joshua Reed,** a Representative from Ohio; born in Tioga Point (later Athens), Bradford County, Pa., October 6, 1795; moved with his parents to Canandaigua, N.Y., in 1795; received a common-school education; again moved with his parents to Ashtabula County, Ohio, in 1806; completed preparatory studies; served in the War of 1812; taught school; studied law; was admitted to the bar in February 1821 and commenced practice in Jefferson, Ohio; member of the State house of representatives in 1826; elected as a Whig to the Twenty-fifth Congress to fill the vacancy caused by the resignation of Elisha Whittlesey; reelected to the Twenty-sixth and Twenty-seventh Congresses and served from December 3, 1838, until March 22, 1842, when he resigned, after a vote of censure had been passed upon him by the House in response to his motion in defense of the slave mutineers in the *Creole* case; subsequently elected to the Twenty-seventh Congress to fill the vacancy caused by his own resignation; reelected as a Whig to the Twenty-eighth through Thirtieth Congresses, as a Free-Soil candidate to the Thirty-first through Thirty-third Congresses and as a Republican to

the Thirty-fourth and Thirty-fifth Congresses and served from December 5, 1842, until March 3, 1859; chairman, Committee on Claims (Twenty-seventh and Thirty-fourth Congresses); declined to be a candidate for reelection; appointed consul general to the British North American Provinces by President Lincoln on March 25, 1861, and served until his death; died in Montreal, Canada, May 27, 1864; interment in Oakdale Cemetery, Jefferson, Ohio.

**Bibliography:** *DAB*; Solberg, Richard W. "Joshua Giddings, Politician and Idealist." Ph.D. dissertation, University of Chicago, 1952; Stewart, James Brewer. *Joshua R. Giddings and the Tactics of Radical Politics.* Cleveland: Press of Case Western Reserve University, 1970.

**GIDDINGS, Napoleon Bonaparte,** a Delegate from the Territory of Nebraska; born near Boonsborough, Clark County, Ky., January 2, 1816; moved with his parents to Fayette, Howard County, Mo., in 1828; attended the common schools; during the Texas war of independence enlisted in the army in 1836 and became sergeant major of his regiment; when Texas had gained her independence he was appointed chief clerk in the auditor's office of the Republic of Texas; served as acting auditor until his resignation in 1838; returned to Fayette, Mo., studied law; was admitted to the bar in 1841 and commenced practice in Fayette, Mo.; commissioned as captain of Company A, Second Regiment, Missouri Mounted Volunteers, in the Mexican War July 22, 1846, and served until March 3, 1847; edited the Union Flag in Franklin County, Mo.; went to California and engaged in gold mining; returned to Missouri, settled in Savannah, and practiced law; moved to Nebraska City, Nebr., and continued the practice of law; when the Territory of Nebraska was formed was elected as a Democrat to the Thirty-third Congress and served from January 5, to March 3, 1855; was not a candidate for renomination in 1854 to the Thirty-fourth Congress; resumed the practice of law in Savannah, Mo.; was commissioned lieutenant colonel of the Fifty-first Regiment, Missouri Volunteer Infantry and served from April 11, 1865, to August 31, 1865, when he was honorably discharged; died in Savannah, Mo., August 3, 1897; interment in the City Cemetery.

**GIFFORD, Charles Laceille,** a Representative from Massachusetts; born in Cotuit, Barnstable County, Mass., March 15, 1871; attended the common schools; taught school in Massachusetts and Connecticut from 1890 to 1900; engaged in the real estate business in 1900 on Cape Cod and later became interested in the propagation of oysters and the raising of cranberries; member of the Massachusetts house of representatives in 1912 and 1913; served in the Massachusetts senate 1914-1919; elected as a Republican to the Sixty-seventh Congress to fill the vacancy caused by the resignation of Joseph Walsh and on the same day was elected to the Sixty-eighth Congress; reelected to the Sixty-ninth and to the eleven succeeding Congresses and served from November 7, 1922, until his death at Cotuit, Mass., August 23, 1947; chairman, Committee on Elections No. 3 (Sixty-ninth and Seventieth Congresses), Committee on Election of President, Vice President, and Representatives (Seventy-first Congress); interment in Mosswood Cemetery.

**GIFFORD, Oscar Sherman,** a Delegate from the Territory of Dakota and a Representative from South Dakota; born in Watertown, Jefferson County, N.Y., October 20, 1842; moved with his parents to Wisconsin, who settled in Rock County, thence to Brown County, Ill., in 1853; attended the common schools and the local academy at Beloit, Wis.; served in the Union Army as a private in the Elgin (Ill.) Battery 1863-1865; studied law; was admitted to the bar in 1871 and commenced practice in Canton, Territory of Dakota (now South Dakota); district attorney for Lincoln County in 1874; mayor of Canton in 1881 and 1882; member of the State constitutional convention of South Dakota which convened at Sioux Falls September 7, 1883; elected as a Republican a Delegate to the Forty-ninth and Fiftieth Congresses (March 4, 1885-March 3, 1889);

upon the admission of South Dakota as a State into the Union was elected as a Representative to the Fifty-first Congress and served from November 2, 1889, to March 3, 1891; was not a candidate for renomination in 1890; resumed the practice of law in Canton, S.Dak., where he died on January 16, 1913; interment in Forest Hill Cemetery.

**GILBERT, Abijah,** a Senator from Florida; born in Gilbertsville, Otsego County, N.Y., June 18, 1806; attended Gilbertsville Academy, and graduated from Hamilton College, Clinton, N.Y., in 1822; engaged in mercantile pursuits in New York City 1822-1850; moved to St. Augustine, Fla., in 1865; elected as a Republican to the United States Senate and served from March 4, 1869, to March 3, 1875; retired from business and political life; died in Gilbertsville, N.Y., November 23, 1881; interment in Brookside Cemetery.

**GILBERT, Edward,** a Representative from California; born in Cherry Valley, Otsego County, N.Y., about 1819; attended the public schools; was a compositor on the Albany Argus in 1839, and later an associate editor; during the war with Mexico served as first lieutenant of Company H in Colonel J.D. Stevenson's New York Volunteer Regiment; arrived with his company in San Francisco in March 1847; was in command of the detachment and deputy collector of the port of San Francisco in 1847 and 1848, when the regiment was disbanded; became founder and editor of the Alta California in 1849; member of the California State constitutional convention in 1849; upon the admission of California as a State into the Union was elected as a Democrat to the Thirty-first Congress and served from September 11, 1850, to March 3, 1851; was not a candidate for renomination in 1850 to the Thirty-second Congress; killed in a duel with General James W. Denver, near Sacramento, Calif., August 2, 1852; interment in Lone Mountain (now Laurel Hill) Cemetery, San Francisco, Calif.

**GILBERT, Ezekiel,** a Representative from New York; born in Middletown, Middlesex County, Conn., March 25, 1756; pursued classical studies, and was graduated from Yale College in 1778; studied law; was admitted to the bar and commenced practice in Hudson, N.Y.; member of the State assembly in 1789 and 1790; elected to the Third Congress and reelected as a Federalist to the Fourth Congress (March 4, 1793-March 3, 1797); resumed the practice of law; again a member of the State assembly in 1800 and 1801; clerk of Columbia County 1813-1815; died in Hudson, N.Y., July 17, 1841.

**GILBERT, George Gilmore** (father of Ralph Waldo Emerson Gilbert), a Representative from Kentucky; born in Taylorsville, Spencer County, Ky., December 24, 1849; attended the common schools, Cecilian College in 1868 and 1869, and Lyndland Institute in Kentucky; taught school; was graduated from the law department of the University of Louisville, Kentucky, in 1873; was admitted to the bar and began practice in Taylorsville, Ky., in 1874; prosecuting attorney of Spencer County, 1876-1880; member of the Kentucky senate, 1885-1889; delegate to the Democratic National Convention of 1896; elected as a Democrat to the Fifty-sixth and to the three succeeding Congresses (March 4, 1899-March 3, 1907); was not a candidate for reelection in 1906 to the Sixtieth Congress; resumed the practice of law; died in Louisville, Ky., November 9, 1909; interment in Cave Hill Cemetery.

**GILBERT, Jacob H.,** a Representative from New York; born in New York City, June 17, 1920; attended the public schools; was graduated from St. John's College and from St. John's Law School; was admitted to the bar in 1944 and commenced the practice of law in New York City; appointed an assistant corporation counsel of the city of New York and served from January 1949 to December 1950; served in the New York State assembly, 1951-1954; member of the State senate from 1955 to March 1960; elected as a Democrat to the Eighty-sixth Congress, March 8, 1960, by special election to fill the vacancy caused by the resignation of Isidore Dollinger; reelected to the Eighty-seventh and to the four succeeding Congresses, and served from March 8, 1960 to January 3, 1971; unsuccessful candidate for renomination in 1970 to the Ninety-second Congress; resumed the practice of law; resided in the Bronx, N.Y., where he died on February 27, 1981; interment in Mount Hebron Cemetery, Flushing, N.Y.

**GILBERT, Newton Whiting,** a Representative from Indiana; born in Worthington, Franklin County, Ohio, May 24, 1862; moved with his parents to Steuben County, Ind., in 1875; attended the common schools of Ohio and Indiana and Ohio State University at Columbus; studied law; was admitted to the bar in 1885 and commenced practice in Angola, Ind.; appointed surveyor of Steuben County, Ind., in 1886 and elected to the office in 1888; member of the State senate 1896-1900; lieutenant governor of Indiana 1900-1904; captain of Company H, One Hundred and Fifty-seventh Indiana Volunteer Infantry, during the war with Spain; elected as a Republican to the Fifty-ninth Congress and served from March 4, 1905, to November 6, 1906, when he resigned; judge of the court of first instance at Manila, Philippine Islands, 1906-1908, by appointment of President Theodore Roosevelt; member of the Philippine Commission in 1908 and 1909; president of the board of regents, Philippine University, in 1908 and 1909; served as secretary of public instruction of the Philippine Islands in 1909; Vice Governor of the Philippine Islands 1909-1913; moved to New York City in 1916 and resumed the practice of law; delegate to the Republican National Convention of 1916; retired in 1937 and moved to Santa Ana, Calif. where he died on July 5, 1939; interment in Circle Hill Cemetery, Angola, Ind.

**GILBERT, Ralph Waldo Emerson** (son of George Gilmore Gilbert), a Representative from Kentucky; born in Taylorsville, Spencer County, Ky., January 17, 1882; attended the public schools and the University of Virginia at Charlottesville; was graduated from the law school of the University of Louisville in 1901; was admitted to the bar the same year and commenced practice in Shelbyville, Ky.; elected judge of the Shelby County Court in 1910; reelected in 1914 and served until his resignation in 1917; elected as a Democrat to the Sixty-seventh and to the three succeeding Congresses (March 4, 1921-March 3, 1929); unsuccessful candidate for reelection in 1928 to the Seventy-first Congress; member of the Kentucky house of representatives in 1929; elected to the Seventy-second Congress (March 4, 1931-March 4, 1933); was not a candidate for renomination in 1932 to the Seventy-third Congress; resumed the practice of law in Shelbyville, Ky.; again served in the Kentucky house of representatives in 1933; elected a member of the Kentucky senate in 1936, and served until his death in Louisville, Ky., July 30, 1939; interment in Grove Hill Cemetery, Shelbyville, Ky.

**GILBERT, Sylvester,** a Representative from Connecticut; born in Hebron, Tolland County, Conn., October 20, 1755; pursued classical studies, and was graduated from Dartmouth College, Hanover, N.H., in 1775; studied law; was admitted to the bar in November 1777 and commenced practice in Hebron; member of the State house of representatives 1780-1812; State's attorney for Tolland County 1786-1807; chief judge of the county court and judge of the probate court 1807-1818; principal of a law school 1810-1818; member of the State senate in 1815 and 1816; elected as a Republican to the Fifteenth Congress to fill the vacancy caused by the resignation of Uriel Holmes and served from November 16, 1818, to March 3, 1819; resumed the practice of law in Hebron; again judge of the county court 1820-1825; again a member of the State house of representatives in 1826; died in Hebron, Conn., January 2, 1846; interment in Old Cemetery.

**GILBERT, William Augustus,** a Representative from New York; born in Gilead, Conn., January 25, 1815; moved with his parents to Champion, N.Y.; attended the public schools; studied law; was admitted to the New York bar in 1843 and commenced the practice of law in Adams, N.Y.; member of the State assembly in 1851 and 1852; elected as a Whig to the Thirty-fourth Congress and served from March 4, 1855, until his resignation February 27, 1857; served as president of Adams village in 1859 and 1860; engaged in the banking business; died in Adams, Jefferson County, N.Y., on May 25, 1875; interment in the Rural Cemetery.

**GILCHREST, Wayne Thomas,** a Representative from Maryland; born in Rahway, Union County, N.J., April 15, 1946; graduated from Rahway High School, 1964; A.A., Wesley College, Dover, Del., 1971; B.A., Delaware State College, Dover, 1973; entered active duty, United States Marine Corps in 1964; released in 1966 after service in Vietnam; high school history and government teacher; unsuccessful candidate for election in 1988 to the One Hundred First Congress; elected as a Republican to the One Hundred Second and to the two succeeding Congresses (January 3, 1991-January 3, 1997); is a resident of Kennedyville, Md.

**GILCHRIST, Fred Cramer,** a Representative from Iowa; born in California, Washington County, Pa., June 2, 1868; moved with his parents to Cedar Falls, Iowa, in 1871; attended the public schools; was graduated from State Teachers' College, Cedar Falls, Iowa, in 1886; teacher and superintendent of schools in Laurens and Rolfe, Iowa, 1886-1890; superintendent of schools of Pocahontas County, Iowa, 1890-1892; was graduated from the law department of the State University of Iowa at Iowa City in 1893; was admitted to the bar in 1893 and commenced practice in Laurens, Iowa; member of the State house of representatives 1902-1904; president of the board of education of Laurens, Iowa, 1905-1928; served in the State senate 1923-1931; elected as a Republican to the Seventy-second and to the six succeeding Congresses (March 4, 1931-January 3, 1945); unsuccessful candidate for renomination in 1944; resumed the practice of law; died in Laurens, Iowa, March 10, 1950; interment in Laurens Cemetery.

**GILDEA, James Hilary,** a Representative from Pennsylvania; born in Coaldale, Schuylkill County, Pa., October 21, 1890; attended the public schools; apprenticed to the printing trade in 1905; engaged in the newspaper publishing business, beginning on September 10, 1910, when he founded the Coaldale (Pa.) Observer; chairman of the Coaldale Relief Society, 1930-1933, and of the Panther Valley Miners' Equalization Committee; elected as a Democrat to the Seventy-fourth and Seventy-fifth Congresses (January 3, 1935-January 3, 1939); unsuccessful candidate for reelection in 1938 to the Seventy-sixth Congress, for election in 1940 to the Seventy-seventh Congress, and for elelction in 1950 to the Eighty-second Congress; resumed newspaper publishing until his retirement in 1972; superintendent, Coaldale State Hospital, 1962-1965; resumed his career of editing, publishing, and printing; was a resident of Arlington, Va., until his death there on June 5, 1988; interment in St. Joseph's Cemetery, Summit Hill, Pa.

**GILES, William Branch,** a Representative and a Senator from Virginia; born near Amelia Court House, Amelia County, Va., August 12, 1762; pursued classical studies and graduated from the College of New Jersey (now Princeton University) in 1781; studied law; was admitted to the bar and practiced in Petersburg, Va., 1784-1789; elected to the First Congress to fill the vacancy caused by the death of Theodorick Bland; reelected to the Second and to the three succeeding Congresses, and served from December 7, 1790 to October 2, 1798, when he resigned; member, Virginia house of delegates, 1798-1800; elected as a Republican to the Seventh Congress (March 4, 1801-March 3, 1803); appointed to the United States Senate as a Republican to fill the vacancy in the term beginning March 4, 1803, caused by the resignation of Abraham B.

Venable; while holding the office of Senator-designate was elected on December 4, 1804, to fill the vacancy in the term beginning March 4, 1799, caused by the resignation of Wilson C. Nicholas; was reelected in 1804 and 1811, and served from August 11, 1804 to March 3, 1815, when he resigned; member, Virginia house of delegates, 1816-1817, 1826-1827; unsuccessful candidate for election to the United States Senate in 1825; elected Governor of Virginia by the General Assembly, and served from March 4, 1827 to March 4, 1830; was a member of the Virginia constitutional convention in 1829 and 1830; again elected Governor in 1830, but declined; died on his estate, "Wigwam," near Amelia Court House, Amelia County, Va., December 4, 1830; interment in a private cemetery on his estate.

Bibliography: *DAB*; Anderson, Dice. *William Branch Giles: A Study in the Politics of Virginia and the Nation from 1790 to 1831.* Gloucester, Mass.: P. Smith, 1965; Giunta, Mary A. "The Public Life of William Branch Giles, Republican, 1790-1815." Ph.D. dissertation, Catholic University, 1980.

**GILES, William Fell,** a Representative from Maryland; born in Harford County, Md., April 8, 1807; attended a private academy and the Bel Air Academy; studied law; was admitted to the bar in 1829 and commenced practice in Baltimore, Md.; member of the Maryland State house of delegates, 1838-1840; elected as a Democrat to the Twenty-ninth Congress (March 4, 1845-March 3, 1847); declined to be a candidate for renomination in 1846 to the Thirtieth Congress; officer of the American Colonization Society for more than thirty years, and for more than twenty years one of the commissioners of the State of Maryland supervising the emigration of free African-Americans to Liberia; United States district judge for the district of Maryland from July 18, 1853 until his death in Baltimore, Md., March 21, 1879; interment in Greenmount Cemetery.

**GILFILLAN, Calvin Willard,** a Representative from Pennsylvania; born near East Brook, Mercer (now Lawrence) County, Pa., February 20, 1832; attended the common schools and was graduated from Westminster College, New Wilmington, Pa.; superintendent of schools of Mercer County for two terms; clerk of the Pennsylvania house of representatives in 1859; studied law; was admitted to the bar in 1859 and commenced practice in Mercer, Pa.; appointed prosecuting attorney for Venango County in 1861 and elected in 1862 for three years; elected as a Republican to the Forty-first Congress (March 4, 1869-March 3, 1871); unsuccessful candidate for reelection in 1870 to the Forty-second Congress; resumed the practice of law, in which he continued until 1873; later engaged in banking; delegate to the Republican National Convention in 1872; died in Franklin, Pa., December 2, 1901; interment in the Franklin Cemetery.

**GILFILLAN, John Bachop,** a Representative from Minnesota; born in Barnet, Caledonia County, Vt., February 11, 1835; attended the common schools; was graduated from the Caledonia County Academy in 1855; moved to Minneapolis, Minn.; taught school; studied law; was admitted to the bar in July 1860 and commenced practice in Minneapolis, Minn.; member of the board of education 1860-1868; city prosecuting attorney 1861-1864; prosecuting attorney of Hennepin County 1863-1867 and 1869-1873; alderman of the city of Minneapolis 1865-1869; member of the State senate 1875-1885; regent of the University of Minnesota at Minneapolis 1880-1888; elected as a Republican to the Forty-ninth Congress (March 4, 1885-March 3, 1887); unsuccessful candidate for reelection in 1886 to the Fiftieth Congress; resumed the practice of law; died in Minneapolis, Minn., August 19, 1924; interment in Lakewood Cemetery.

**GILHAMS, Clarence Chauncey,** a Representative from Indiana; born in Brighton, Lagrange County, Ind., April 11, 1860; attended the common schools and the State normal school at Terre Haute, Ind.; taught school; was employed as a salesman; auditor of

Lagrange County 1894-1902; engaged in the life insurance business; elected as a Republican to the Fifty-ninth Congress to fill the vacancy caused by the resignation of Newton W. Gilbert; reelected to the Sixtieth Congress and served from November 6, 1906, to March 3, 1909; unsuccessful candidate for reelection in 1908 to the Sixty-first Congress; studied law; was admitted to the bar in 1910; resumed the life insurance business; died in Lagrange, Ind., June 5, 1912; interment in Greenwood Cemetery.

**GILL, John, Jr.,** a Representative from Maryland; born in Baltimore, Md., June 9, 1850; attended Hampden-Sidney (Va.) College; graduated from the University of Maryland at Baltimore in 1870; studied law; was admitted to the bar in 1871 and commenced practice in Baltimore, Md.; member of the Maryland State house of delegates, 1874-1877; examiner of titles in the Baltimore city legal department, 1879-1884; served in the Maryland State senate, 1882-1886, 1904, and 1905; delegate to the Democratic National Conventions of 1884, 1888, and 1892; police commissioner, 1888-1897; elected as a Democrat to the Fifty-ninth and to the two succeeding Congresses (March 4, 1905-March 3, 1911); was not a candidate for reelection in 1910 to the Sixty-second Congress; judge of the appeal tax court of the city of Baltimore, 1912-1918; died in Baltimore, Md., January 27, 1918.

**GILL, Joseph John,** a Representative from Ohio; born in Barnesville, Belmont County, Ohio, September 21, 1846; moved with his parents to Mount Pleasant, Jefferson County, in 1848; pursued an academic course and was graduated from the law department of the University of Michigan at Ann Arbor in 1868; was admitted to the bar and commenced practice in Jefferson County, Ohio; subsequently engaged in banking, and later in manufacturing and iron mining; elected as a Republican to the Fifty-sixth Congress to fill the vacancy caused by the death of Lorenzo Danford; reelected to the Fifty-seventh and Fifty-eighth Congresses, and served from December 4, 1899 until October 31, 1903, when he resigned; died in Steubenville, Ohio, May 22, 1920; interment in Union Cemetery.

**GILL, Michael Joseph,** a Representative from Missouri; born in Covington, Kenton County, Ky., December 5, 1864; attended the common schools and Oberlin (Ohio) College; engaged in the glass manufacturing business; executive member of the National Bottle Blowers' Association, 1892-1912; member of the Missouri State house of representatives, 1892-1896; delegate to the Democratic National Convention of 1912; successfully contested as a Democrat the election of Leonidas C. Dyer to the Sixty-third Congress, and served from June 19, 1914 to March 3, 1915; unsuccessful candidate for reelection in 1914 to the Sixty-fourth Congress; served as Government labor conciliator from March 31 to May 31, 1916, and from July 1 to October 2, 1916; died in St. Louis, Mo., November 1, 1918; interment in Calvary Cemetery.

**GILL, Patrick Francis,** a Representative from Missouri; born in Independence, Jackson County, Mo., August 16, 1868; moved with his widowed mother to St. Louis, Mo., in 1871; attended the parochial schools and St. Louis University in 1890; engaged in the grocery business; clerk of the circuit court, 1904-1908; unsuccessful candidate for sheriff in 1906; elected as a Democrat to the Sixty-first Congress (March 4, 1909-March 3, 1911); successfully contested the election of Theron E. Catlin to the Sixty-second Congress, and served from August 12, 1912 to March 3, 1913; unsuccessful candidate for renomination in 1912 to the Sixty-third Congress; served as mediator in the Bureau of Mediation and Conciliation, Department of Labor, from July 13, 1918 to September 11, 1922; died in St. Louis, Mo., May 21, 1923; interment in Calvary Cemetery.

**GILL, Thomas Ponce,** a Representative from Hawaii; born in Honolulu, Hawaii, April 21, 1922; attended the public schools and graduated from Roosevelt High School in 1940; attended the University of Hawaii in 1940 and 1941; served in the Hawaii Territorial Guard from December 1941 to October 1942; volunteered for service in the Twenty-fourth Infantry Division in November 1942, fought in New Guinea and in the Philippines and was discharged in November 1945; awarded the Bronze Star and the Purple Heart; graduated from the University of California in 1948 and from the University of California Law School in 1951; was admitted to the bar and commenced practice in Honolulu the same year; Democratic campaign chairman of Oahu County in 1952 and 1954; chairman of Oahu County Democratic Committee, 1954-1958; delegate to the Democratic National Convention of 1960; attorney for the Hawaiian senate in the 1955 regular session; administrative assistant to the speaker of the Hawaiian house of representatives in the 1957 regular and special sessions; member of the Thirtieth Territorial Session from the Fifteenth District; member of the first State legislature and served as majority floor leader, 1959-1962; elected as a Democrat to the Eighty-eighth Congress (January 3, 1963-January 3, 1965); was not a candidate in 1964 for renomination to the House of Representatives, but was an unsuccessful candidate for election to the United States Senate; director, Hawaii Office of Economic Opportunity, 1965-1966; lieutenant governor of Hawaii, 1966-1970; resumed the practice of law; is a resident of Honolulu, Hawaii.

**GILLEN, Courtland Craig,** a Representative from Indiana; born in Roachdale, Putnam County, Ind., July 3, 1880; attended the rural schools; was graduated from Fincastle High School in 1897; taught common and high schools for five years 1897-1904; attended De Pauw University at Greencastle, Ind., 1901-1903; was graduated from the law department of the University of Indianapolis (Indiana Law School) in 1905; was admitted to the bar in 1904 and commenced practice in Greencastle, Ind.; served as county attorney 1909-1914 and as prosecuting attorney of the sixty-fourth judicial circuit in 1917 and 1918; delegate to the Democratic State convention in 1924; elected as a Democrat to the Seventy-second Congress (March 4, 1931-March 3, 1933); unsuccessful candidate for renomination in 1932; elected judge of the sixty-fourth judicial circuit (Putnam Circuit Court) in 1934 and served from January 1, 1935, until his resignation on April 15, 1939; resumed the private practice of law; died in Greencastle, Ind., September 1, 1954; interment in Forest Hill Cemetery.

**GILLESPIE, Dean Milton,** a Representative from Colorado; born in Salina, Saline County, Kans., May 3, 1884; attended the public schools and Salina Normal University; engaged in agricultural pursuits and cattle raising in Clay County, Kans., 1900-1904; moved to Denver, Colo., in 1905 and worked as grocery clerk, sign painter, and salesman; engaged in the automobile and oil business, beginning in 1905; elected as a Republican to the Seventy-eighth Congress to fill the vacancy caused by the death of Lawrence Lewis, reelected to the Seventy-ninth Congress, and served from March 7, 1944 to January 3, 1947; unsuccessful candidate for reelection in 1946 to the Eightieth Congress; reengaged in his former business pursuits until his death, while on a business trip, in Baltimore, Md., February 2, 1949; interment in Fairmount Cemetery, Denver, Colo.

**GILLESPIE, Eugene Pierce,** a Representative from Pennsylvania; born in Greenville, Mercer County, Pa., September 24, 1852; attended the public schools, Allegheny College, Meadville, Pa., and St. Michael's College, Toronto, Canada; studied law; was admitted to the bar in August 1874 and commenced practice in Greenville, Pa.; elected as a Democrat to the Fifty-second Congress (March 4, 1891-March 3, 1893); unsuccessful candidate for reelection in 1892 to the Fifty-third Congress; returned to Greenville, Pa., and continued the practice of law until his death December 16, 1899; interment in Shenango Valley Cemetery.

**GILLESPIE, James,** a Representative from North Carolina; born in Kenansville, Duplin County, N.C.; pursued classical studies; member of the State constitutional convention in 1776; member of the State house of commons 1779-1783; served in the State senate 1784-1786; elected to the Third Congress and reelected as a Republican to the Fourth and Fifth Congresses (March 4, 1793-March 3, 1799); elected to the Eighth Congress and served from March 4, 1803, until his death in Washington, D.C., January 11, 1805; interment in Congressional Cemetery.

**GILLESPIE, James Frank,** a Representative from Illinois; born in White Sulphur Springs, Greenbrier County, W.Va., April 18, 1869; attended the graded schools and Concord (W.Va.) Normal School; taught in the public schools at White Sulphur Springs, W.Va., in 1891 and 1892; principal of White Sulphur Springs High School in 1891; studied law at Central College, Danville, Ind.; was admitted to the bar in 1892 and commenced practice in Charleston, W.Va.; moved to Bloomington, McLean County, Ill., in 1894 and continued the practice of law; also engaged in agricultural pursuits; served in the State house of representatives in 1913 and 1914; elected as a Democrat to the Seventy-third Congress (March 4, 1933-January 3, 1935); unsuccessful candidate for reelection in 1934 to the Seventy-fourth Congress and for election in 1936 to the Seventy-fifth Congress; resumed the practice of law in Bloomington, Ill., until his death there on November 26, 1954; interment in Park Hill Cemetery.

**GILLESPIE, Oscar William,** a Representative from Texas; born near Quitman, Clarke County, Miss., June 20, 1858; attended private schools, and was graduated from Mansfield College, Texas, in 1885; studied law; was admitted to the bar in 1886 and commenced practice in Fort Worth, Tex., assistant attorney of Tarrant County 1886-1888; prosecuting attorney of Tarrant County 1890-1894; elected as a Democrat to the Fifty-eighth and to the three succeeding Congresses (March 4, 1903-March 3, 1911); unsuccessful candidate for renomination in 1910; resumed the practice of law in Fort Worth, Tex., where he died August 23, 1927; interment in Mansfield Cemetery, Mansfield, Tex.

**GILLET, Charles William,** a Representative from New York; born in Addison, Steuben County, N.Y., November 26, 1840; attended the public schools and the Delaware Literary Institute, Franklin, N.Y.; was graduated from Union College, Schenectady, N.Y., in 1861; enlisted as a private in the Eighty-sixth Regiment, New York Volunteer Infantry, in August 1861; promoted to adjutant of the regiment in November 1861; was wounded and honorably discharged for physical disability in 1863; engaged in the manufacture of sash, doors, and blinds in Addison; appointed postmaster of Addison on June 15, 1878, and served until July 26, 1886; elected as a Republican to the Fifty-third and to the five succeeding Congresses (March 4, 1893-March 3, 1905); chairman, Committee on Expenditures in the Department of Agriculture (Fifty-fourth through Fifty-seventh Congresses), Committee on Public Buildings and Grounds (Fifty-eighth Congress); declined to be a candidate for renomination in 1904; died in New York City December 31, 1908; interment in the Rural Cemetery, Addison, N.Y.

**GILLET, Ransom Hooker,** a Representative from New York; born in New Lebanon, Columbia County, N.Y., January 27, 1800; pursued an academic course; studied law in Canton, N.Y.; was admitted to the bar and commenced practice in Ogdensburg; postmaster of Ogdensburg, N.Y., 1830-1833; delegate to the Democratic National Convention in 1832 and 1840; elected as a Democrat to the Twenty-third and Twenty-fourth Congresses (March 4, 1833-March 3, 1837); was not a candidate for renomination in 1836; commissioner to treat with the New York Indians in 1837-1839; appointed Register of the Treasury and served from April 1, 1845, to May 27, 1847, when he was appointed Solicitor of the Treasury, and continued in this office until October 31, 1849; appointed Assistant Attorney General and served from 1855 to 1858; appointed solicitor of the court of claims and served from 1858 to 1861; retired from public life in 1867 and engaged in literary pursuits; died in Washington, D.C., October 24, 1876; interment in Glenwood Cemetery.

**Bibliography:** *DAB.*

**GILLETT, Frederick Huntington,** a Representative and a Senator from Massachusetts; born in Westfield, Hampden County, Mass., October 16, 1851; attended the public schools; graduated from Amherst College, Amherst, Mass., in 1874 and from the law department of Harvard University in 1877; was admitted to the bar at Springfield, Mass., in 1877 and commenced practice in that city; assistant attorney general of Massachusetts 1879-1882; member, State house of representatives 1890-1891; elected as a Republican to the Fifty-third and to the fifteen succeeding Congresses; (March 4, 1893, to March 3, 1925); Speaker of the House of Representataives (Sixty-sixth, Sixty-seventh, and Sixty-eighth Congresses); chairman, Committee on Reform in the Civil Service (Fifty-sixth through Sixty-first Congresses); was not a candidate for renomination to the Sixty-ninth Congress; elected as a Republican to the United States Senate in 1924 and served from March 4, 1925 to March 3, 1931; was not a candidate for renomination in 1930; engaged in literary pursuits; died in Springfield, Mass., July 31, 1935; interment in Pine Hill Cemetery, Westfield, Mass.

**Bibliography:** *DAB.*

**GILLETT, James Norris,** a Representative from California; born in Viroqua, Vernon County, Wis., September 20, 1860; moved with his parents to Sparta, Wis., in 1865; attended the grammar and high schools; studied law; was admitted to the bar in 1881 and commenced practice in Sparta, Wis.; moved to Eureka, Humboldt County, Calif., in 1883 and continued the practice of law; city attorney 1889-1895; member of the State senate 1897-1899; elected as a Republican to the Fifty-eighth and Fifty-ninth Congresses and served from March 4, 1903, to November 4, 1906, when he resigned, having been elected Governor; elected Governor of California in 1906 and served from January 8, 1907 to January 3, 1911; resumed the practice of law in San Francisco, Calif., and resided in Berkeley, Calif., until his death there on April 20, 1937; interment in Oakland Columborium, Oakland, Calif.

**GILLETTE, Edward Hooker** (son of Francis Gillette), a Representative from Iowa; born in Bloomfield, Hartford County, Conn., October 1, 1840; attended the public schools at Hartford, Conn., and the New York State Agricultural College, Ovid, N.Y.; moved to Des Moines, Iowa, in 1863 and engaged in agricultural pursuits, building, and manufacturing; editor of the Iowa Tribune; chairman of the national committee of the Greenback Party; delegate to the Greenback National Convention at Indianapolis in 1876; elected as a Greenbacker (National Party) to the Forty-sixth Congress (March 4, 1879-March 3, 1881); unsuccessful candidate for reelection in 1880 to the Forty-seventh Congress; retired from public life and resided on his farm, "Clover Hills Place," near Valley Junction, Iowa, where he died August 14, 1918; interment in Glendale Cemetery.

**GILLETTE, Francis** (father of Edward Hooker Gillette), a Senator from Connecticut; born in that portion of Old Windsor now included in the town of Bloomfield, Hartford County, Conn., December 14, 1807; moved with his parents to Ashfield, Mass.; was graduated from Yale College in 1829; commenced the study of law, but his health becoming impaired he engaged in agricultural pursuits in Bloomfield; member, State house of representatives 1832, 1836, 1838; unsuccessful candidate for Governor in 1841 and several times subsequently; chairman of the board of education of Connecticut 1849-1865; moved to Hartford in 1852; elected as a Free-Soiler to the United States Senate to fill the vacancy caused by the resignation of Truman Smith and served from May 24, 1854, to March 3, 1855; was not a candidate for reelection in 1854; lecturer on agriculture and temperance; trustee of the State normal school and served as its president for many years; aided in the formation of the Republican Party in Connecticut and for several years was a silent partner in the Evening Press, the organ of that party; engaged in the real estate business in Hartford, Conn.; died in Hartford, Conn., on September 30, 1879; interment in Riverside Cemetery, Farmington, Conn.

**Bibliography:** *DAB.*

**GILLETTE, Guy Mark,** a Representative and a Senator from Iowa; born in Cherokee, Cherokee County, Iowa, February 3, 1879; attended the public schools; graduated from the law department of Drake University, Des Moines, Iowa, in 1900; was admitted to the bar in 1900 and commenced practice in Cherokee; during the Spanish-American War served as a sergeant in the Fifty-second Iowa Regiment, United States Army 1898; engaged in agricultural pursuits; city attorney of Cherokee 1906-1907; prosecuting attorney of Cherokee County 1907-1909; member, State senate 1912-1916; during the First World War served as a captain in the United States Army 1917-1919; elected as a Democrat to the Seventy-third Congress; reelected to the Seventy-fourth Congress and served from March 4, 1933, until his resignation on November 3, 1936, having been elected to the United States Senate; elected as a Democrat to the United States Senate to fill the vacancy caused by the death of Richard Louis Murphy during the term ending January 3, 1939; reelected in 1938 and served from November 4, 1936, to January 3, 1945; unsuccessful candidate for reelection in 1944; chairman of the Surplus Property Board 1945; president of the American League for a Free Palestine 1945-1948; again elected to the United States Senate and served from January 3, 1949, to January 3, 1955; unsuccessful candidate for reelection in 1954; counsel with the Senate Post Office and Civil Service Committee 1955-1956; counsel with the Senate Judiciary Committee 1956-1961; retired and resided in Cherokee, Iowa, until his death there March 3, 1973; interment in Oak Knoll Cemetery.

**Bibliography:** Harrington, Jerry. "Senator Guy Gillette Foils the Execution Committee." *Palimpsest* 62 (November/December 1981): 170-180.

**GILLETTE, Wilson Darwin,** a Representative from Pennsylvania; born on a farm near Sheshequin, Bradford County, Pa., July 1, 1880; attended the public schools, Ulster (Pa.) High School, and Susquehanna Collegiate Institute, Towanda, Pa.; engaged in agricultural pursuits, clerked in a general store and became a dealer of automobiles in 1913; member of the Pennsylvania house of representatives 1930-1941; elected as a Republican to the Seventy-seventh Congress to fill the vacancy caused by the death of Albert G. Rutherford; reelected to the Seventy-eighth and to the four succeeding Congresses and served from November 4, 1941, until his death in Towanda, Pa., August 7, 1951; interment in Oak Hill Cemetery.

**GILLIE, George W.,** a Representative from Indiana; born in Berwickshire, Scotland, August 15, 1880; moved to the United States with his parents, who settled in Kankakee, Ill., in 1882 and in Fort Wayne, Ind., in 1884; attended the public schools, International Business College, Fort Wayne, Ind., in 1898, and Purdue University, Lafayette, Ind., 1899-1901; was graduated from Ohio State University at Columbus in 1907 as doctor of veterinary surgery; meat and dairy inspector of Allen County, Ind., 1908-1914; began the practice of veterinary medicine in Fort Wayne, Ind., in 1914; sheriff of Allen County 1917-1920, 1929-1930, and 1935-1937; elected as a Republican to the Seventy-sixth and to the four

succeeding Congresses (January 3, 1939-January 3, 1949); unsuccessful candidate for reelection in 1948 to the Eighty-first Congress; engaged in agricultural pursuits; jury commissioner for the Federal courts for the northern district of Indiana; resident of Fort Wayne, Ind., until his death there on July 3, 1963; interment in Lindenwood Cemetery.

**GILLIGAN, John Joyce,** a Representative from Ohio; born in Cincinnati, Hamilton County, Ohio, March 22, 1921; graduated from St. Xavier High School in 1939, the University of Notre Dame in 1943, and the University of Cincinnati in 1947; served as a lieutenant (jg) in the United States Naval Reserve as a destroyer gunnery officer in the Atlantic, Pacific, and Mediterranean Theaters, 1942-1945; awarded the Silver Star for gallantry at Okinawa; instructor in literature at Xavier University, Cincinnati, Ohio, 1948-1953; member of the city council of Cincinnati, 1953-1963; elected as a Democrat to the Eighty-ninth Congress (January 3, 1965-January 3, 1967); unsuccessful candidate for reelection in 1966 to the Ninetieth Congress; unsuccessful candidate in 1968 for election to the United States Senate; elected Governor of Ohio in 1970, and served from January 11, 1971 to January 13, 1975; unsuccessful candidate for reelection in 1974; administrator, United States Agency for International Development, 1977-1979; director, Institute for Public Policy, 1979-1986, and Institute for International Peace Studies, University of Notre Dame; director, Civic Forum, University of Cincinnati School of Law; is a resident of Cincinnati, Ohio.

**Bibliography:** Larson, David Richard. "Ohio's Fighting Liberal: A Political Biography of John J. Gilligan." Ph.D. dissertation, Ohio State University, 1982.

**GILLIS, James Lisle,** a Representative from Pennsylvania; born in Hebron, Washington County, N.Y., October 2, 1792; attended the public schools; became a tanner; served in the War of 1812; moved to Ridgway, Pa., in 1822; appointed associate judge of Jefferson County by Governor David R. Porter; member of the Pennsylvania house of representatives in 1840 and 1851; one of the judges of Jefferson County in 1842; member of the Pennsylvania senate in 1845; served as a mail agent in San Francisco, Calif.; elected as a Democrat to the Thirty-fifth Congress (March 4, 1857-March 3, 1859); was an unsuccessful candidate for reelection in 1858 to the Thirty-sixth Congress; appointed agent for the Pawnee Tribe of Indians; died in Mount Pleasant, Henry County, Iowa, July 8, 1881; interment in Forest Home Cemetery.

**GILLMOR, Paul Eugene,** a Representative from Ohio; born in Tiffin, Seneca County, Ohio, Februry 1, 1939; graduated, Old Fort (Ohio) High School, 1957; B.A., Ohio Wesleyan University, Delaware, Ohio, 1961; J.D., University of Michigan Law School, 1964; entered active duty, United States Air Force in 1965; released as captain in 1966; admitted to Ohio bar, 1965; practicing attorney, Tiffin, Ohio, 1967-1988; member, Ohio State senate, 1967-1988, minority leader, 1978-1980, 1983-1984, president, 1981-1982, 1985-1988; unsuccessful candidate in 1986 for the Republican nomination for governor of Ohio; elected as a Republican to the One Hundred First and to the three succeeding Congresses (January 3, 1989-January 3, 1997); is a resident of Old Fort, Ohio.

**GILLON, Alexander,** a Representative from South Carolina; born in Rotterdam, Netherlands, in 1741; pursued an academic course; immigrated to London, England, and engaged in commerce; in 1766 settled in Charleston and established a large business; delegate to the Second Provincial Congress of South Carolina in 1775 and 1776; member of the first general assembly in 1776; was elected captain of the German Fusiliers of Charleston in May 1775; commodore of the South Carolina Navy in 1778 and was sent to France to procure vessels; joined the fleet of Spanish vessels in the capture of the Bahama Islands on May 8, 1782; elected to the Continental Congress in 1784, but did not attend; delegate to the

State convention which ratified the Federal Constitution in 1788; elected to the Third Congress and served from March 4, 1793, until his death at his plantation, "Gillon's Retreat," Orangeburg District, S.C., October 6, 1794; interment in the family burial ground at "Gillon's Retreat," Calhoun County, S.C.

**Bibliography:** *DAB*.

**GILMAN, Benjamin Arthur,** a Representative from New York; born in Poughkeepsie, Dutchess County, N.Y., December 6, 1922; educated in the public schools of Middletown, N.Y.; graduated Middletown High School, 1941; B.S., Wharton School of Business and Finance, University of Pennsylvania, 1946; LL.B., New York Law School, 1950; admitted to the New York bar in 1952 and commenced practice in Middletown, N.Y.; entered active duty, U.S. Army Air Corps in 1943, served with Twentieth Air Force, Nineteenth Bomb Group, released in 1945; awarded Distinguished Flying Cross and Air Medal for thirty-five missions over Japan; appointed assistant attorney general, New York State Department of Law, 1954; attorney, New York Commission on Courts, 1956-1957; counsel to assembly's Committee on Local Finance, 1956-1964; served in the New York State assembly, 1967-1972; member, New York State Southeastern Water Commission; elected as a Republican to the Ninety-third and to the eleven succeeding Congresses (January 3, 1973-January 3, 1997); chairman, Committee on International Relations (One Hundred Fourth Congress); is a resident of Middletown, N.Y.

**GILMAN, Charles Jervis** (grandnephew of John Taylor Gilman and Nicholas Gilman), a Representative from Maine; born in Exeter, Rockingham County, N.H., February 26, 1824; attended Phillips Exeter Academy, Exeter, N.H., and pursued classical studies; was graduated from Harvard Law School; was admitted to the bar in 1850 and commenced practice in Exeter, N.H.; member of the house of representatives of New Hampshire in 1851 and 1852; moved to Brunswick, Maine, and continued the practice of law; member of the house of representatives of Maine in 1854 and 1855; member of the State Whig committee; elected as a Republican to the Thirty-fifth Congress (March 4, 1857-March 3, 1859); declined to be a candidate for renomination in 1858 to the Thirty-sixth Congress; delegate to the Republican National Convention of 1860; interested in introducing waterworks and other public improvements; died in Brunswick, Maine, on February 5, 1901; interment in Pine Grove Cemetery.

**GILMAN, John Taylor** (brother of Nicholas Gilman and granduncle of Charles Jervis Gilman), a Delegate from New Hampshire; born in Exeter, Rockingham County, N.H., December 19, 1753; received a limited education; engaged in shipbuilding and also in agricultural pursuits; one of the Minutemen of 1775; selectman in 1777 and 1778; member of the New Hampshire State house of representatives in 1779 and 1781; delegate to the convention of the States in Hartford, Conn., in October 1780; Member of the Continental Congress in 1782 and 1783; State treasurer in 1791; moderator, 1791-1794, 1806, 1807, 1809-1811, 1817, 1818, and 1820-1825; unsuccessful candidate for election in 1793 for Governor; elected Governor of New Hampshire in 1794, reelected every year from 1795 through 1804, and served from June 5, 1794 to June 6, 1805; unsuccessful candidate for reelection in 1805, and for election in 1806; again a member of the State house of representatives in 1810 and 1811; again elected Governor in 1812, reelected in 1813, 1814, and 1815, and served from June 13, 1813 to June 6, 1816; declined to be a candidate for renomination in 1816; ex officio trustee of Dartmouth College, Hanover, N.H., 1794-1805, and 1813-1816, and trustee by election, 1817-1819; president of the board of trustees of Phillips Exeter Academy, Exeter, N.H., 1795-1827, and donor of the property upon which the older buildings stand; died in Exeter, N.H., August 31, 1828; interment in Exeter Cemetery.

**Bibliography:** *DAB*.

**GILMAN, Nicholas** (brother of John Taylor Gilman and granduncle of Charles Jervis Gilman), a Delegate, a Representative, and a Senator from New Hampshire; born in Exeter, Rockingham County, N.H., August 3, 1755; pursued an academic course; employed as a clerk in his father's countinghouse; served in the continental army during the Revolutionary War; Member of the Continental Congress 1787-1789; member of the Constitutional Convention, 1787-1789; elected to the First and to the three succeeding Congresses (March 4, 1789-March 3, 1797); declined to be a candidate for renomination in 1796; chairman, Committee on Revisal and Unfinished Business (Fourth Congress); elected in 1805 as a Republican to the United States Senate; reelected in 1811 and served from March 4, 1805, until his death in Philadelphia, Pa., May 2, 1814; interment in Exeter Cemetery, Exeter, N.H.

**Bibliography:** *DAB*.

**GILMER, George Rockingham,** a Representative from Georgia; born near Lexington, Wilkes (now Oglethorpe) County, Ga., April 11, 1790; attended a classical school and an academy at Abbeville, S.C.; taught a private school while studying law; served as first lieutenant in the Forty-third Regiment, United States Infantry, from 1813 to 1815 in the campaign against the Creek Indians and built a fort on the Chattahoochie River near the present city of Atlanta, Ga.; resumed the study of law and began practice in Lexington in 1818; member of the Georgia State house of representatives in 1818, 1819, and 1824; elected to the Seventeenth Congress (March 4, 1821-March 3, 1823); resumed the practice of law; trustee of the University of Georgia at Athens 1826-1857; elected to the Twentieth Congress to fill the vacancy caused by the resignation of Edward F. Tatnall and served from October 1, 1827, to March 3, 1829; reelected to the Twenty-first Congress, but failing to signify his acceptance, the Governor announced a vacancy and ordered a new election; elected Governor of Georgia in 1829, and served from November 4, 1829 to November 9, 1831; unsuccessful candidate for reelection in 1831; elected as a Jacksonian to the Twenty-third Congress (March 4, 1833-March 3, 1835); chairman, Committee on Indian Affairs (Twenty-third Congress); presidential elector in 1836 and voted for Hugh Lawson White and John Tyler; elected Governor in 1837, and served from November 8, 1837 to November 6, 1839; presidential elector on the Whig ticket in 1840; author and historian; died in Lexington, Ga., November 16, 1859; interment in Presbyterian Cemetery.

**Bibliography:** *DAB*; Coulter, E. Merton. "The Dispute over George R. Gilmer's Election to Congress in 1828." *Georgia Historical Quarterly* 52 (June 1968): 159-86.

**GILMER, John Adams,** a Representative from North Carolina; born near Greensboro, Guilford County, N.C., November 4, 1805; attended the public schools and an academy in Greensboro, N.C.; taught school; studied law; was admitted to the bar in 1832 and began practice in Greensboro, N.C.; county solicitor; member of the State senate 1846-1856; unsuccessful Whig candidate for Governor of North Carolina in 1856; elected as the candidate of the American Party to the Thirty-fifth Congress and reelected as a candidate of the Opposition Party to the Thirty-sixth Congress (March 4, 1857-March 3, 1861); chairman, Committee on Elections (Thirty-sixth Congress); member of the Second Confederate Congress in 1864; delegate to the Union National Convention of Conservatives at Philadelphia in 1866; died in Greensboro, N.C., May 14, 1868; interment in Presbyterian Church Cemetery.

**Bibliography:** *DAB*; Crofts, Daniel W. "A Reluctant Unionist; John A. Gilmer and Lincoln's Cabinet." *Civil War History* 24 (September 1978): 225-49.

**GILMER, Thomas Walker,** a Representative from Virginia; born in Gilmerton, Albemarle County, Va., April 6, 1802; attended the common schools; studied law; was admitted to the bar and commenced practice in Charlottesville, Va.; member of the Virginia house of delegates, 1829-1836, and again in 1839 and 1840, serving as speaker the last two years; elected Governor of Virginia by the General Assembly, and served from March 31, 1840 until his resignation on March 20, 1841; elected as a Whig to the Twenty-seventh Congress and as a Democrat to the Twenty-eighth Congress, and served from March 4, 1841, until February 16, 1844, when he resigned; appointed Secretary of the Navy in the Cabinet of President John Tyler on February 15, 1844, and served until he was killed by the bursting of a gun on board the U.S.S. *Princeton* on the Potomac River, near Washington, D.C., February 28, 1844; interment in Mount Air Cemetery, Albermarle County, Va.

**Bibliography:** *DAB.*

**GILMER, William Franklin (Dixie),** a Representative from Oklahoma; born in Mount Airy, Surry County, N.C., June 7, 1901; moved with his parents to Oklahoma; attended the public schools of Oklahoma City, Okla.; served as a page in the House of Representatives, 1911-1919; graduated from the law school of Oklahoma University at Norman in 1923; was admitted to the bar in 1923 and commenced the practice of law in Oklahoma; member of the Oklahoma State house of representatives; moved to Tulsa, Okla., in 1929; assistant county attorney of Tulsa County, 1931-1933; county attorney of Tulsa County, 1936-1946; unsuccessful candidate in 1946 for the Democratic nomination for Governor of Oklahoma; elected as a Democrat to the Eighty-first Congress (January 3, 1949-January 3, 1951); unsuccessful candidate for reelection in 1950 to the Eighty-second Congress; Oklahoma State safety commissioner until his death in Oklahoma City, Okla., June 9, 1954; interment in Memorial Park.

**GILMORE, Alfred** (son of John Gilmore), a Representative from Pennsylvania; born in Butler, Pa., June 9, 1812; attended the public schools, and was graduated from Washington College, Washington, Pa., in 1833; studied law; was admitted to the bar in 1836 and commenced practice in Butler, Pa.; elected as a Democrat to the Thirty-first and Thirty-second Congresses (March 4, 1849-March 3, 1853); was not a candidate for reelection in 1852 to the Thirty-third Congress; resumed the practice of law in Philadelphia, Pa.; moved to Lenox, Mass., in 1866, and continued the practice of his profession; died while on a visit in New York City, June 29, 1890; interment in Lenox Cemetery, Lenox, Mass.

**GILMORE, Edward,** a Representative from Massachusetts; born in Brockton, Plymouth County, Mass., January 4, 1867; attended the graded schools, the high school, and Massachusetts State University extension classes; engaged in mercantile pursuits; member of the Massachusetts Democratic committee, 1896-1903; delegate to the Democratic National Conventions of 1900 and 1904; president of the Brockton Board of Aldermen, 1901-1906; member of the Massachusetts house of representatives in 1907 and 1908; elected as a Democrat to the Sixty-third Congress (March 4, 1913-March 3, 1915); postmaster of Brockton, 1915-1923; city assessor in 1923 and 1924; died in Boston, Mass., April 10, 1924; interment in Calvary Cemetery, Brockton, Mass.

**GILMORE, John** (father of Alfred Gilmore), a Representative from Pennsylvania; born in Somerset County, Pa., February 18, 1780; moved with his parents to Washington, Pa., in 1780; attended the common schools; studied law; was admitted to the bar in 1801 and commenced practice in Washington; moved to Butler, Pa., in 1803; appointed deputy district attorney for Butler County in 1803; member of the Pennsylvania house of representatives, 1816-1821, and served as speaker in 1821; elected as a Jacksonian to the Twenty-first and Twenty-second Congresses (March 4, 1829-March 3, 1833); elected Pennsylvania treasurer by the legislature of in 1841; died in Butler, Pa., May 11, 1845; interment in North Cemetery.

**GILMORE, Samuel Louis,** a Representative from Louisiana; born in New Orleans, La., July 30, 1859; instructed by private tutors; was graduated from the Central High School of New Orleans in 1874, from Seton Hall College, South Orange, N.J., in 1877, and from the law department of the University of Louisiana (now Tulane University) at New Orleans in 1879; was admitted to the bar in 1880 and commenced practice in New Orleans, La.; assistant city attorney, 1888-1896; city attorney from 1896 until his resignation on March 15, 1909; delegate to the Democratic National Convention of 1908; elected as a Democrat to the Sixty-first Congress to fill the vacancy caused by the death of Robert C. Davey, and served from March 30, 1909 until his death in Abita Springs, La., July 18, 1910; interment in Metairie Cemetery, New Orleans, La.

**GINGERY, Don,** a Representative from Pennsylvania; born in Woodland, Clearfield County, Pa., February 19, 1884; moved to Clearfield, Pa., in 1892; attended the public schools of Clearfield, Pa., Mercersburg (Pa.) Academy, and Ohio Northern University at Ada; was engaged in the hardware and mine-supply business from 1902 to 1934; also engaged as a civil engineer in 1903; member of the Pennsylvania house of representatives in 1915 and 1916; served in the Pennsylvania National Guard, in grades from private to captain, 1902-1906; chairman of the Clearfield County Democratic committee in 1916 and 1917; member of the Pennsylvania Democratic committee in 1919 and 1920; member of the official delegation attending the inauguration of President Manuel Quezon of the Philippine Republic at Manila, in 1935; elected as a Democrat to the Seventy-fourth and Seventy-fifth Congresses (January 3, 1935-January 3, 1939); unsuccessful candidate for reelection in 1938 to the Seventy-sixth Congress; associated with the Bituminous Coal Division, the Coal Mines Administration, and the Solid Fuels Administration for War of the United States Department of the Interior, at Altoona, Pa., 1939-1946; died in Clearfield, Pa., October 15, 1961; interment in Hillcrest Cemetery.

**GINGRICH, Newton Leroy,** a Representative from Georgia; born in Harrisburg, Dauphin County, Pa., June 17, 1943; attended school at various military installations; graduated from Baker High School, Columbus, Ga., 1961; B.A., Emory University, Atlanta, Ga., 1965; M.A., Tulane University, New Orleans, La., 1968; Ph.D., European history, Tulane University, 1971; professor, West Georgia College, Carrollton, 1970-1978; elected as a Republican to the Ninety-sixth and to the eight succeeding Congresses (January 3, 1979-January 3, 1997); minority whip (One Hundred First through One Hundred Third Congresses), Speaker of the House of Representatives (One Hundred Fourth Congress); is a resident of Marietta, Ga.

**GINN, Ronald Bryan (Bo),** a Representative from Georgia; born in Morgan, Calhoun County, Ga., May 31, 1934; educated in the public schools of Morgan; attended Abraham Baldwin Agricultural College, Tifton, Ga., 1951-1953; B.S., Georgia Southern College, Statesboro, 1955; teacher; businessman; cattle farmer; former administrative assistant to Representative G. Elliott Hagan, 1961-1966, and Senator Herman E. Talmadge, 1967-1971; elected as a Democrat to the Ninety-third and to the four succeeding Congresses (January 3, 1973-January 3, 1983); was not a candidate in 1982 for reelection to the Ninety-eighth Congress, but was an unsuccessful candidate for nomination for Governor of Georgia; chairman of the board of a governmental relations firm in Alexandria, Va.; is a resident of Millen, Ga.

**GIST, Joseph,** a Representative from South Carolina; born near the mouth of Fair Forest Creek, Union District, S.C., January 12, 1775; moved to Charleston with his parents in 1788; attended the common schools; was graduated from the College of Charleston; studied law; was admitted to the bar in 1799 and began practice in Pinckneyville, S.C., in 1800; member of the State house of representatives, 1802-1817; member of the board of trustees of

South Carolina College at Columbia 1809-1821; elected to the Seventeenth, Eighteenth, and Nineteenth Congresses (March 4, 1821-March 3, 1827); was not a candidate for renomination; resumed the practice of law; died in Pinckneyville, S.C., on March 8, 1836; interment in the family burial ground.

**GITTINS, Robert Henry,** a Representative from New York; born in Oswego, Oswego County, N.Y., December 14, 1869; attended St. Paul's Academy, Oswego, N.Y.; engaged in the lumber, grain, and coal business; was graduated from the law department of the University of Michigan at Ann Arbor in 1900; was admitted to the bar in the States of Michigan and New York in 1900 and commenced the practice of law at Niagara Falls, N.Y., in 1901; member of the State senate 1911-1913; delegate to the Democratic National Convention in 1912; elected as a Democrat to the Sixty-third Congress (March 4, 1913-March 3, 1915); unsuccessful candidate for reelection in 1914 to the Sixty-fourth Congress; owner and publisher of the Niagara Falls Journal 1914-1918; postmaster of Niagara Falls, N.Y., from October 16, 1916, to January 21, 1920; resumed the practice of his profession; appointed commissioner of the State reservation at Niagara Falls in 1918 and served until 1940; moved to New York City in 1923 and continued the practice of law until 1956; resided in Sloatsburg, Rockland County, N.Y., until his death December 25, 1957.

**GLASCOCK, John Raglan,** a Representative from California; born in Panola County, Miss., August 25, 1845; in 1856 moved to California with his parents, who settled in San Francisco; attended the public schools and was graduated from the University of California at Berkeley in 1865; studied law at the University of Virginia at Charlottesville; was admitted to the bar by the supreme court of California in 1868 and commenced practice in Oakland, Calif.; admitted to practice before the Supreme Court of the United States in 1882; district attorney of Alameda County, Calif., 1875-1877; elected as a Democrat to the Forty-eighth Congress (March 4, 1883-March 3, 1885); unsuccessful candidate for reelection in 1884 to the Forty-ninth Congress; mayor of Oakland, Calif., 1887-1890; resumed the practice of law in Oakland; died at his country home in Woodside, Calif., November 10, 1913; interment in Mountain View Cemetery, Oakland, Calif.

**GLASCOCK, Thomas,** a Representative from Georgia; born in Augusta, Ga., October 21, 1790; attended the public schools; studied law; was admitted to the bar and commenced practice in Augusta; delegate to the constitutional convention in 1798; captain of Volunteers in the War of 1812; served with the rank of brigadier general in the Seminole War in 1817; member of the State house of representatives 1821, 1823, 1831, 1834, 1839, serving as speaker in 1833 and 1834; elected as a Jacksonian to the Twenty-fourth Congress to fill the vacancy caused by the resignation of John W.A. Sanford; reelected as a Democrat to the Twenty-fifth Congress and served from October 5, 1835, to March 3, 1839; chairman, Committee on Militia (Twenty-fourth and Twenty-fifth Congresses); retired from public life; lived in Decatur, Ga. until his death there May 19, 1841; interment in the City Cemetery, Augusta, Ga.

**GLASGOW, Hugh,** a Representative from Pennsylvania; born in Nottingham, Chester County, Pa., September 8, 1769; attended the public schools; engaged in agricultural pursuits; studied law; was admitted to the bar and practiced; judge of York County from July 1, 1800, to March 29, 1813; elected as a Republican to the Thirteenth and Fourteenth Congresses (March 4, 1813-March 3, 1817); died at Peach Bottom, York County, Pa., January 31, 1818; interment in Slate Ridge Burying Ground.

**GLASS, Carter,** a Representative and a Senator from Virginia; born in Lynchburg, Campbell County, Va., January 4, 1858; attended private and public schools; newspaper reporter, editor and owner; member of the Virginia senate from 1899 until 1903, when he resigned; delegate to the Virginia constitutional convention in 1901; elected as a Democrat to the Fifty-seventh Congress to fill the vacancy caused by the death of Peter J. Otey; reelected to the Fifty-eighth and to the eight succeeding Congresses, and served from November 4, 1902 until December 16, 1918, when he resigned to accept a cabinet portfolio; chairman, Committee on Banking and Currency (Sixty-third through Sixty-fifth Congresses); member of the Democratic National Committee, 1916-1928; appointed Secretary of the Treasury by President Woodrow Wilson, and served from December 16, 1918 until February 2, 1920, when he resigned, having been appointed a Senator; appointed as a Democrat to the United States Senate on November 18, 1919, and subsequently elected to fill the vacancy caused by the death of Thomas S. Martin in the term ending March 3, 1925, but did not qualify until February 2, 1920, preferring to retain his Cabinet post; reelected in 1924, 1930, 1936, and again in 1942, and served from February 2, 1920 until his death in Washington, D.C., May 28, 1946; served as President pro tempore during the Seventy-seventh and Seventy-eighth Congresses; chairman, Committee on Expenditures in the Interior Department (Sixty-sixth Congress), Committee on Appropriations (Seventy-third through Seventy-ninth Congresses); co-sponsor of the Glass-Steagall Act of 1933, which established the Federal Deposit Insurance Corporation to safeguard deposits and revive public confidence in the banking system; declined an appointment as Secretary of the Treasury in the Cabinet of President Franklin D. Roosevelt; interment in Spring Hill Cemetery, Lynchburg, Va.

**Bibliography:** *DAB*; Koeniger, Alfred C. "'Unreconstructed Rebel': The Political Thought and Senate Career of Carter Glass, 1929-1936." Ph.D. dissertation, Vanderbilt University, 1980; Lyle, John O. "The United States Senate Career of Carter Glass, 1920-1933." Ph.D. dissertation, University of South Carolina, 1974; Smith, Rixey, and Norman Beasley. *Carter Glass: A Biography.* 1939. Reprint. New York: Da Capo Press, 1972.

**GLASS, Presley Thornton,** a Representative from Tennessee; born in Houston, Halifax County, Va., October 18, 1824; in 1828 moved with his parents to Weakley County, Tenn., where he attended Dresden Academy; elected colonel of militia when eighteen years of age; studied law; attended one course at Lexington (Ky.) Law School; was admitted to the bar in 1847 and commenced practice in Ripley, Tenn.; member of the State house of representatives in 1848 and again in 1882; during the Civil War served as commissary with the rank of major in the Confederate service; elected as a Democrat to the Forty-ninth and Fiftieth Congresses (March 4, 1885-March 3, 1889); unsuccessful candidate for renomination in 1888 to the Fifty-first Congress; died in Ripley, Tenn., on October 9, 1902; interment in Maplewood Cemetery.

**GLATFELTER, Samuel Feiser,** a Representative from Pennsylvania; born near Loganville, Springfield Township, York County, Pa., April 7, 1858; attended the public schools, York County Academy, and Pennsylvania College at Gettysburg, Pa.; engaged in teaching for several years; later became a building contractor and also interested in banking; elected as a Democrat to the Sixty-eighth Congress (March 4, 1923-March 3, 1925); unsuccessful candidate for reelection in 1924 to the Sixty-ninth Congress; resumed his business as a building contractor; died in York, Pa., on April 23, 1927; interment in Prospect Hill Cemetery.

**GLEN, Henry,** a Representative from New York; born in Schenectady, N.Y., July 13, 1739; appointed clerk of Schenectady County February 27, 1767, and served until March 11, 1809; served as a deputy quartermaster general in the Revolutionary War; Member of the First, Second, and Third Provincial Congresses 1774-1776; served as a member of the State assembly in 1786 and 1787; elected to the Third Congress and reelected as a Federalist to the three succeeding Congresses (March 4, 1793-March 3, 1801);

member of the State assembly in 1810; died in Schenectady, N.Y., on January 6, 1814.

**GLENN, John Herschel, Jr.,** a Senator from Ohio; born in Cambridge, Guernsey County, Ohio, July 18, 1921; educated in the public schools of New Concord, Ohio; graduated New Concord High School, 1939; education having been interrupted in 1941 by World War II, attended additional courses at University of Maryland; B.S., Muskingum College, 1962; entered the United States Marine Corps as a second lieutenant in 1943, and retired as a colonel in 1965 following service during the Second World War and the Korean conflict; test pilot; joined the United States space program in 1959, having been selected as one of the original seven Mercury astronauts; on February 20, 1962, he became the first American to orbit the Earth, circling three times aboard a Mercury capsule; business executive; V.P. Royal Corwn Cola Co., 1966-1968; president, Royal Crown International, 1967-1969; unsuccessful candidate in 1970 for nomination to the United States Senate; elected as a Democrat to the United States Senate in 1974 for the term commencing January 3, 1975; subsequently appointed by the Governor, December 24, 1974, to fill the vacancy caused by the resignation of Howard M. Metzenbaum for the term ending January 3, 1975; reelected in 1980, 1986, and again in 1992 for the term ending January 3, 1999; chairman, Committee on Governmental Affairs (One Hundredth through One Hundred Third Congresses); is a resident of Columbus, Ohio.

**GLENN, Milton Willits,** a Representative from New Jersey; born in Atlantic City, N.J., June 18, 1903; attended the public schools in Atlantic City; attended Georgetown University, Washington, D.C., in 1921 and 1922 and graduated from Dickinson Law School, Carlisle, Pa., in 1924; was admitted to the bar in 1925 and commenced practice in Atlantic City, N.J.; during the Second World War was commissioned a lieutenant in the United States Navy and served from November 1943 to June 1946; municipal magistrate in Margate City, N.J., from January 1940 to November 1943; Atlantic County Freeholder from June 1946 to January 1951; lieutenant commander in the United States Naval Reserve; elected to the State house of assembly for an unexpired term in 1950; reelected in 1951, 1953, and 1955; elected as a Republican to the Eighty-fifth Congress to fill the vacancy caused by the death of T. Millet Hand; reelected to the Eighty-sixth, Eighty-seventh, and Eighty-eighth Congresses, and served from November 5, 1957, to January 3, 1965; unsuccessful candidate for reelection in 1964 to the Eighty-ninth Congress; resumed the practice of law; died in Margate City, N.J., December 14, 1967; interment in West Creek Cemetery, West Creek, N.J.

**GLENN, Otis Ferguson,** a Senator from Illinois; born in Mattoon, Coles County, Ill., August 27, 1879; attended the public schools; graduated from the law department of the University of Illinois at Urbana in 1900; was admitted to the bar in 1900 and commenced practice in Murphysboro, Ill.; State's attorney of Jackson County 1906-1908, 1916-1920; member, State senate 1920-1924; elected as a Republican to the United States Senate to fill the vacancy caused by the resignation of Frank L. Smith and served from December 3, 1928, to March 3, 1933; unsuccessful candidate for reelection in 1932 and for election in 1936; chairman, Committee on Privileges and Elections (Seventy-second Congress); resumed the practice of law in Chicago, Ill.; died in Portage Point, near Onekama, Mich., March 11, 1959; interment in Onekama Cemetery, Onekama, Mich.

**GLENN, Thomas Louis,** a Representative from Idaho; born near Bardwell, Ballard (now Carlisle) County, Ky., February 2, 1847; attended the public schools and the Commercial College, Evansville, Ind.; during the Civil War served in Company F, Second Regiment, Kentucky Cavalry (John H. Morgan's brigade), Confederate Army; was wounded in action at Mount Sterling, Ky., June 9, 1864; captured, and imprisoned in Transylvania University, Lexington,

Ky., until September 9, 1864, when he was paroled; clerk of Ballard County 1874-1882; member of the State senate 1887-1891; studied law; was admitted to the bar in 1890 and commenced practice in Montpelier, Idaho; elected as a Populist to the Fifty-seventh Congress (March 4, 1901-March 3, 1903); was not a candidate for renomination in 1902 to the Fifty-eighth Congress; mayor of Montpelier in 1904; served as prosecuting attorney; resumed the practice of law in Montpelier, Idaho, where he died on November 18, 1918; interment in the City Cemetery.

**GLICKMAN, Daniel Robert,** a Representative from Kansas; born in Wichita, Sedgwick County, Kans., November 24, 1944; attended the public schools of Wichita; B.A., University of Michigan, 1966; J.D., George Washington University, Washington, D.C., 1969; admitted to the District of Columbia bar in 1969; United States Securities and Exchange Commission, 1969-1970; in 1970 became officer in Glickman, Inc., a family concern specializing in recycling metals; practiced law, Wichita, 1971-1976; elected as a Democrat to the Ninety-fifth and to the eight succeeding Congresses (January 3, 1977-January 3, 1995); unsuccessful candidate for reelection in 1994 to the One Hundred Fourth Congress; chairman, Permanent Select Committee on Intelligence (One Hundred Third Congress); appointed Secretary of Agriculture in the Cabinet of President William J. Clinton, and served from March 30, 1995 to the present; is a resident of Wichita, Kans.

**GLONINGER, John,** a Representative from Pennsylvania; born in Lebanon Township, Lancaster County, Pa., September 19, 1758; attended the common schools; served as a subaltern officer in the Associaters during the Revolutionary War and later was in command of a battalion of militia; upon the organization of Dauphin County was appointed by the supreme executive council a lieutenant May 6, 1785; member of the Pennsylvania house of representatives in 1790; resigned and served in the Pennsylvania senate from 1790 until 1792; appointed by Governor Mifflin justice of the peace of Dauphin County on September 8, 1790; commissioned as associate judge August 17, 1791, and upon the formation of Lebanon County was commissioned on September 11, 1813, one of the associate judges for that county; elected as a Federalist to the Thirteenth Congress and served from March 4, 1813, until August 2, 1813, when he resigned; again appointed associate judge of Lebanon County; died in Lebanon, Pa., January 22, 1836; interment in First Reformed Churchyard.

**GLOSSBRENNER, Adam John,** a Representative from Pennsylvania; born in Hagerstown, Washington County, Md., August 31, 1810; learned the art of printing; publisher of the Western Telegraph in Hamilton, Ohio, in 1827 and 1828; moved to York, Pa., in 1829; established the York County Farmer in 1831; became a partner in the York Gazette in 1835, and continued his connection with that paper until 1860; clerk in the Pennsylvania house of representatives in 1836; clerk in the United States House of Representatives during the Twenty-eighth and Twenty-ninth Congresses, 1843-1847, and in the Department of State at Washington, D.C., in 1848 and 1849; Sergeant at Arms of the House of Representatives, 1850-1860; private secretary to President James Buchanan in 1860 and 1861; established the Philadelphia Age in 1862, although residing in York; elected as a Democrat to the Thirty-ninth and Fortieth Congresses (March 4, 1865-March 3, 1869); unsuccessful candidate for reelection in 1868 to the Forty-first Congress; engaged in banking in York, Pa., in 1872; moved to Philadelphia in 1880, and was in the employ of the Pennsylvania Railroad Co. until his death in that city on March 1, 1889; interment in Prospect Hill Cemetery, York, Pa.

**GLOVER, David Delano,** a Representative from Arkansas; born in Prattsville, Grant County, Ark., January 18, 1868; attended the public schools of Prattsville and Sheridan, Ark.; was graduated from Sheridan High School in 1886; engaged in agricultural pursuits and in the mercantile business; taught in the public schools of Hot Spring County, Ark., 1898-1908; studied law; was admitted to the bar in 1910 and commenced practice in Malvern, Ark.; member of the State house of representatives in 1909 and 1911; delegate to several State conventions; served as prosecuting attorney of the seventh judicial circuit of Arkansas 1913-1917; elected as a Democrat to the Seventy-first, Seventy-second, and Seventy-third Congresses (March 4, 1929-January 3, 1935); unsuccessful candidate for renomination in 1934; resumed the practice of law in Malvern, Ark., until his death April 5, 1952; interment in Shadowlawn Cemetery.

**GLOVER, John Milton** (nephew of John Montgomery Glover), a Representative from Missouri; born in St. Louis, Mo., June 23, 1852; attended the public schools of his native city and Washington University, St. Louis, Mo.; studied law; was admitted to the bar and commenced practice in St. Louis; elected as a Democrat to the Forty-ninth and Fiftieth Congresses (March 4, 1885-March 3, 1889); was not a candidate for renomination in 1888, having become a candidate for the Democratic gubernatorial nomination, in which he was unsuccessful; reengaged in the practice of law in St. Louis, Mo., until 1909, when he moved to Denver, Colo., and continued the practice of his profession until incapacitated by ill health in 1926; died in Pueblo, Colo., October 20, 1929; interment in Bellefontaine Cemetery, St. Louis, Mo.

**GLOVER, John Montgomery** (uncle of John Milton Glover), a Representative from Missouri; born in Harrodsburg, Mercer County, Ky., September 4, 1822; attended the public schools in Kentucky; moved to Missouri in 1836 with his parents, who settled in Knox County, near Newark, and continued his schooling; attended Marion and Masonic Colleges, Philadelphia, Mo.; studied law; was admitted to the bar and commenced practice in St. Louis, Mo.; moved to California in 1850 and continued the practice of his profession; returned to Knox County, Mo., in 1855 to take charge of his father's affairs; during the Civil War served as colonel of the Third Regiment, Missouri Volunteer Cavalry, from September 4, 1861, until February 23, 1864, when he resigned on account of impaired health; collector of internal revenue for the third district of Missouri from December 1, 1866, until March 3, 1867; elected as a Democrat to the Forty-third, Forty-fourth, and Forty-fifth Congresses (March 4, 1873-March 3, 1879); chairman, Committee on Expenditures in the Department of the Treasury (Forty-fifth Congress); unsuccessful candidate for renomination in 1878; engaged in agricultural pursuits; died near Newark, Knox County, Mo., November 15, 1891; interment on his farm near Newark, Mo.; reinterment in Woodland Cemetery, Quincy, Ill.

**GLYNN, James Peter,** a Representative from Connecticut; born in Winsted, Litchfield County, Conn., November 12, 1867; attended the public schools; studied law; was admitted to the bar in 1895 and commenced practice in Winsted, Conn.; town clerk 1892-1902; prosecuting attorney of the town court 1899-1902; postmaster of Winsted 1902-1914; elected as a Republican to the Sixty-fourth and to the three succeeding Congresses (March 4, 1915-March 3, 1923); chairman, Committee on Expenditures in the Post Office Department (Sixty-seventh Congress); unsuccessful candidate for reelection in 1922 to the Sixty-eighth Congress; elected to the Sixty-ninth, Seventieth, and Seventy-first Congresses and served from March 4, 1925, until his death on a train near Washington, D.C., March 6, 1930; interment in the new St. Joseph's Cemetery, Winsted, Conn.

**GLYNN, Martin Henry,** a Representative from New York; born in Kinderhook, Columbia County, N.Y., September 27, 1871; attended the public schools and was graduated from St. John's College, Fordham, N.Y., in 1894; studied law; was admitted to the bar in 1897 and commenced practice in Albany; engaged in journalistic work on several papers until he became managing editor and publisher of the Albany Times-Union; elected as a Democrat to the Fifty-sixth Congress (March 4, 1899-March 3, 1901); unsuccessful candidate for reelection in 1900 to the Fifty-seventh Congress; vice president of the National Commission of the Louisiana Purchase Exposition 1901-1905; comptroller of New York State 1906-1908; elected lieutenant governor of New York in 1912; became Governor upon the removal of William Sulzer from office on October 17, 1913, and served until December 31, 1914; unsuccessful candidate in 1914 for election for Governor; delegate to and temporary chairman of the Democratic State conventions of 1912 and 1916; temporary chairman of the Democratic National Convention of 1916; appointed a member of the Federal Industrial Commission in 1919; died in Albany, N.Y., December 14, 1924; interment in St. Agnes Cemetery.

Bibliography: *DAB.*

**GODDARD, Calvin,** a Representative from Connecticut; born in Shrewsbury, Worcester County, Mass., July 17, 1768; attended Plainfield (Conn.) Academy, where he pursued classical studies, and was graduated from Dartmouth College, Hanover, N.H., in 1786; studied law; was admitted to the bar in 1790 and commenced practice in Plainfield, Conn.; member of the State house of representatives 1795-1801; elected as a Federalist to the Seventh Congress to fill the vacancy caused by the resignation of Elizur Goodrich; reelected to the Eighth and Ninth Congresses and served from May 14, 1801, until his resignation in 1805 before the convening of the Ninth Congress; again elected to the State house of representatives in 1807 and served as a speaker; moved to Norwich, Conn., in 1807 and resumed the practice of his profession; member of the executive council 1808-1815; presidential elector on the ticket of Clinton and Ingersoll in 1812; delegate to the Hartford Convention in 1814; judge of the superior court in 1815 and 1818; mayor of Norwich 1814-1834; died in Norwich, Conn., May 2, 1842; interment in the City Cemetery.

**GODSHALK, William,** a Representative from Pennsylvania; born in East Nottingham, Chester County, Pa., October 25, 1817; moved with his parents to Bucks County in 1818; attended the common schools and Union Academy, Doylestown, Pa.; learned the miller's trade and in 1847 engaged in milling in Doylestown Township; served in the Union Army as a private in Company K, One Hundred and Fifty-third Regiment, Pennsylvania Volunteer Infantry, from October 11, 1862, to July 23, 1863; unsuccessful candidate for election to the Pennsylvania senate in 1864; elected associate judge of Bucks County in October 1871 and served five years; elected as a Republican to the Forty-sixth and Forty-seventh Congresses (March 4, 1879-March 3, 1883); engaged in milling; died in New Britain, Bucks County, Pa., February 6, 1891; interment in the Presbyterian Church Cemetery, Doylestown, Pa.

**GODWIN, Hannibal Lafayette,** a Representative from North Carolina; born on a farm near Dunn, Harrett County, N.C., November 3, 1873; attended the common schools and Trinity College (now Duke University), Durham, N.C.; studied law at the University of North Carolina at Chapel Hill; was admitted to the bar in 1896 and commenced practice in Dunn, N.C.; elected mayor of Dunn in 1897; member of the State senate in 1903; member of the Democratic State executive committee 1904-1906; elected as a Democrat to the Sixtieth and to the six succeeding Congresses (March 4, 1907-March 3, 1921); chairman, Committee on Reform in the Civil Service (Sixty-second through Sixty-fifth Congresses); unsuccessful candidate for renomination in 1920; engaged in the practice of his profession until his death in Dunn, N.C., June 9, 1929; interment in Greenwood Cemetery.

**GOEBEL, Herman Philip,** a Representative from Ohio; born in Cincinnati, Ohio, April 5, 1853; attended the public schools; employed as a messenger boy for a law firm; was graduated from the Cincinnati Law College in 1872; was admitted to the bar in 1874 and commenced practice in Cincinnati; member of the State house of representatives in 1875 and 1876; judge of the probate court of Hamilton County 1884-1890; elected as a Republican to the Fifty-eighth and to the three succeeding Congresses (March 4, 1903-March 3, 1911); unsuccessful candidate for reelection in 1910 to the Sixty-second Congress; engaged in the practice of his profession until his death in Cincinnati, Ohio, May 4, 1930; interment in Spring Grove Cemetery.

**GOEKE, John Henry,** a Representative from Ohio; born near Minster, Auglaize County, Ohio, October 28, 1869; attended the common schools and was graduated from Pio Nono College, St. Francis, Wis., in 1888; studied law at Cincinnati Law School and was graduated in 1891; was admitted to the bar in 1891 and commenced practice in St. Marys, Ohio; city solicitor of St. Marys 1892-1894; prosecuting attorney of Auglaize County 1894-1900; resumed the practice of law in Wapakoneta, Ohio, in 1900; also served as a director of several banks and manufacturing concerns; chairman of the Democratic State convention in 1903; elected as a Democrat to the Sixty-second and Sixty-third Congresses (March 4, 1911-March 3, 1915); unsuccessful candidate for renomination in 1914 to the Sixty-fourth Congress; delegate to the Democratic National Conventions in 1912, 1920, 1924, and 1928; resumed the practice of law in Wapakoneta, Ohio; moved to Lima, Ohio, in 1921 and continued the practice of law; died in Lima, Ohio, March 25, 1930; interment in Gethsemane Cemetery.

**GOFF, Abe McGregor,** a Representative from Idaho; born in Colfax, Whitman County, Wash., December 21, 1899; attended the public schools; during the First World War served as a private in the United States Army; was graduated from the College of Law of the University of Idaho in 1924; was admitted to the bar the same year and commenced practice in Moscow, Idaho; prosecuting attorney of Latah County, Idaho, 1926-1934; special lecturer at the University of Idaho Law School 1933-1941; president, Idaho State Bar Association, 1940; member of the State senate in 1941; called to active duty from the Reserves as a major in August 1941 and served until his discharge as a colonel in September 1946; was decorated with the Legion of Merit; elected as a Republican to the Eightieth Congress (January 3, 1947-January 3, 1949); unsuccessful candidate for reelection in 1948 to the Eighty-first Congress; solicitor and later general counsel, Post Office Department, 1954-1958; appointed a commissioner of the Interstate Commerce Commission on January 30, 1958; reappointed in 1959 for term ending December 31, 1966, and continued to serve until July 31, 1967, when he retired; engaged as a writer and lecturer; was a resident of Moscow, Idaho, until his death there on November 23, 1984; cremated and the ashes buried in Moscow Cemetery.

**GOFF, Guy Despard** (son of Nathan Goff and father of Louise Goff Reece), a Senator from West Virginia; born in Clarksburg, Harrison County, W.Va., September 13, 1866; attended the common schools and William and Mary College, Williamsburg, Va.; graduated from Kenyon College at Gambier, Ohio, in 1888 and from the law department of Harvard University in 1891; was admitted to the bar the same year and commenced practice in Boston, Mass.; moved to Milwaukee, Wis., in 1893 and continued the practice of law; elected prosecuting attorney of Milwaukee County, Wis., in 1895; appointed by President William Howard Taft as United States district attorney for the eastern district of Wisconsin 1911-1915; appointed special assistant to the Attorney General of the United States 1917; during the First World War was commissioned a colonel in the Judge Advocate General's Department, United States Army, and served in France and Germany in 1918 and 1919; appointed by President Woodrow Wilson as general counsel of the United States Shipping Board in 1920 and later became a member, serving until 1921; appointed an assistant to the Attorney General on several occasions between 1920-1923; returned to Clarksburg, W.Va., in 1923; elected as a Republican to the United States Senate and

served from March 4, 1925, to March 3, 1931; was not a candidate for renomination in 1930; chairman, Committee on Expenditures in Executive Departments (Seventy-first Congress); resided in Washington, D.C.; died at his winter home in Thomasville, Ga., January 7, 1933; interment in Arlington Cemetery.

**Bibliography:** Smith, Gerald Wayne. *Nathan Goff, Jr.; A Biography; with Some Account of Guy Despard Goff and Brazilla Carroll Reece.* Charleston, W. Va.: Education Foundation, 1959.

**GOFF, Nathan** (father of Guy Despard Goff and grandfather of Louise Goff Reece), a Representative and a Senator from West Virginia; born in Clarksburg, Harrison County, Va. (now West Virginia), February 9, 1843; attended the Northwestern Academy, Clarksburg, W.Va., and Georgetown University, Washington, D.C.; studied law and graduated from the University of the City of New York; during the Civil War enlisted in the Union Army in 1861 in the Third Regiment of Virginia Volunteer Infantry, later became a major in the Virginia Volunteer Cavalry; was admitted to the bar in 1865 and practiced law; member, West Virginia State house of delegates, 1867-1868; unsuccessful candidate in 1870 for election to the Forty-second Congress, and in 1874 for election to the Forty-fourth Congress; United States attorney for West Virginia from 1868 until 1881; appointed Secretary of the Navy by President Rutherford B. Hayes, and served from January 7 to March 6, 1881; reappointed United States attorney for West Virginia, and served 1881-1882; unsuccessful candidate for Governor of West Virginia in 1876 and 1888; elected as a Republican to the Forty-eighth and to the two succeeding Congresses (March 4, 1883-March 3, 1889); was not a candidate for renomination in 1888 to the Fifty-first Congress; United States circuit judge for the fourth judicial circuit from 1892 until 1913; elected as a Republican to the United States Senate for the term commencing March 4, 1913, but did not immediately take his seat, preferring to remain on the bench, and served from April 1, 1913, to March 3, 1919; chairman, Committee on Conservation of Natural Resources (Sixty-fifth Congress), Committee on Industrial Expositions (Sixty-fifth Congress); died in Clarksburg, W.Va., April 24, 1920; interment in Odd Fellows Cemetery.

**Bibliography:** Smith, Gerald W. "Nathan Goff, Jr.: A Biography." Ph.D. dissertation, West Virginia University, 1954.

**GOGGIN, William Leftwich,** a Representative from Virginia; born near Bunker Hill, Bedford County, Va., May 31, 1807; attended the country schools and was graduated from Tucker's Law School, Winchester, Va.; was admitted to the bar in 1828 and commenced practice in Liberty (now Bedford), Va.; also engaged in agricultural pursuits; member of the Virginia house of delegates in 1836 and 1837; elected as a Whig to the Twenty-sixth and Twenty-seventh Congresses (March 4, 1839-March 3, 1843); unsuccessfully contested the election of Thomas W. Gilmer to the Twenty-eighth Congress; subsequently elected to the Twenty-eighth Congress to fill the vacancy caused by the resignation of Thomas W. Gilmer and served from April 25, 1844, to March 4, 1845; was not a candidate for renomination in 1844 to the Twenty-ninth Congress; elected to the Thirtieth Congress (March 4, 1847-March 3, 1849); chairman, Committee on the Post Office and Post Roads (Thirtieth Congress); was not a candidate for renomination in 1848 to the Thirty-first Congress; unsuccessful Whig candidate for Governor in 1859; delegate to the Virginia constitutional convention in 1861; captain of the Home Guards, Confederate Army, during the Civil War; resumed the practice of law; died on his estate near Liberty, Bedford County, Va., January 3, 1870; interment in Goggin Cemetery on the family estate near Bunker Hill, Va.

**GOLD, Thomas Ruggles,** a Representative from New York; born in Cornwall, Conn., November 4, 1764; pursued classical studies, and was graduated from Yale College in 1786; studied law; was admitted to the bar and commenced practice in Goshen, Conn.; settled in Whitesboro, Oneida County, N.Y., in 1792; assistant attorney general of New York 1797-1801; member of the State senate 1796-1802; unsuccessful candidate for election in 1804 to the Ninth Congress; served in the State assembly in 1808; elected as a Federalist to the Eleventh and Twelfth Congresses (March 4, 1809-March 3, 1813); unsuccessful candidate for reelection in 1812 to the Thirteenth Congress; elected to the Fourteenth Congress (March 4, 1815-March 3, 1817); was not a candidate for renomination in 1816; resumed the practice of law in Whitesboro, N.Y., where he died October 24, 1827; interment in Grand View Cemetery.

**GOLDEN, James Stephen,** a Representative from Kentucky; born in Barbourville, Knox County, Ky., September 20, 1891; attended the grade schools in Barbourville and high school at Union College, Barbourville, Ky.; University of Kentucky at Lexington, A.B., 1912 and from the law school of the University of Michigan at Ann Arbor, LL.B., 1916; was admitted to the bar in 1916 and commenced the practice of law in Barbourville, Ky., the same year; elected county attorney of Knox County, Ky., in 1918 and served until 1922; delegate to Republican National Convention in 1952; elected as a Republican to the Eighty-first and to the two succeeding Congresses (January 3, 1949-January 3, 1955); was not a candidate for renomination in 1954 to the Eighty-fourth Congress; resumed the practice of law; died in Pineville, Ky., September 6, 1971; interment in Pineville Memorial Cemetery.

**GOLDER, Benjamin Martin,** a Representative from Pennsylvania; born in Alliance, near Vineland, Cumberland County, N.J., December 23, 1891; moved with his parents to Philadelphia, Pa., in 1893; attended the public schools and was graduated from the law department of the University of Pennsylvania at Philadelphia in 1913; was admitted to the bar in 1914 and commenced practice in Philadelphia; enlisted in the Naval Aviation Service during the First World War and was honorably discharged as ensign after the armistice; member of the Pennsylvania house of representatives 1916-1924; elected as a Republican to the Sixty-ninth and to the three succeeding Congresses (March 4, 1925-March 3, 1933); unsuccessful candidate for renomination in 1932 and for election in 1940 to the Seventy-seventh Congress; resumed the practice of law in Philadelphia, Pa.; commissioned a captain in the United States Army on February 5, 1943, and served until discharged as a lieutenant colonel July 1, 1945; resumed the practice of law and also engaged in the banking business; died December 30, 1946, at Philadelphia, Pa.; interment in Mount Sinai Cemetery.

**GOLDFOGLE, Henry Mayer,** a Representative from New York; born in New York City May 23, 1856; attended the public schools and Townsend College; studied law; was admitted to the bar in 1877 and commenced practice in New York City; justice of the fifth district court in New York in 1887 and 1893; judge of the municipal court of New York City 1888-1900; resumed the practice of law; delegate to the Democratic National Conventions in 1892 and 1896; elected as a Democrat to the Fifty-seventh and to the six succeeding Congresses (March 4, 1901-March 3, 1915); chairman, Committee on Elections No. 3 (Sixty-second and Sixty-third Congresses); unsuccessful candidate for reelection to the Sixty-fourth and Sixty-fifth Congresses; again elected to the Sixty-sixth Congress (March 4, 1919-March 3, 1921); unsuccessful candidate for reelection in 1920 to the Sixty-seventh Congress; resumed the practice of law; appointed president of the New York City Board of Taxes and Assessments in July 1921 and served until his death in New York City, June 1, 1929; interment in Union Hills Cemetery, Long Island, N.Y.

**GOLDSBOROUGH, Charles** (great-grandfather of Thomas Alan Goldsborough and Winder Laird Henry), a Representative from Maryland; born at "Hunting Creek," near Cambridge, Dorchester County, Md., July 15, 1765; pursued an academic course, and was graduated from the University of Pennsylvania at Philadelphia in 1784; studied law; was admitted to the bar in 1790; held several local offices; member of the State senate 1791-1795 and 1799-1801; elected as a Federalist to the Ninth and to the five succeeding Congresses (March 4, 1805-March 3, 1817); chosen Governor of Maryland by the general assembly of the State, and served from January 8 to December 20, 1819; retired from public life in 1820, and resided on his estate near Cambridge, Md.; died at "Shoal Creek," near Cambridge, Md., December 13, 1834; interment in Christ Episcopal Church Cemetery, Cambridge, Md.

**Bibliography:** *DAB.*

**GOLDSBOROUGH, Phillips Lee,** a Senator from Maryland; born in Princess Anne, Somerset County, Md., August 6, 1865; educated in public and private schools; studied law; admitted to the bar in 1886 and commenced practice in Cambridge, Md.; also interested in banking; State's attorney for Dorchester County 1892-1898; comptroller of the treasury of Maryland 1898-1899; collector of internal revenue, district of Maryland 1902-1911; elected Governor of Maryland in 1911 and served from January 10, 1912 to January 12, 1916; elected as a Republican to the United States Senate and served from March 4, 1929, to January 3, 1935; was not a candidate for reelection; unsuccessful candidate for nomination for Governor of Maryland in 1934; member of the Republican National Committee 1932-1936; resumed the practice of law; appointed a director of the Federal Deposit Insurance Corporation by President Franklin D. Roosevelt 1935-1946; died in Baltimore, Md., October 22, 1946; interment in the old churchyard of Christ Episcopal Church, Cambridge, Md.

**GOLDSBOROUGH, Robert** (great-great-great-grandfather of Thomas Alan Goldsborough), a Delegate from Maryland; born at "Horns Point," Dorchester County, Md., December 3, 1733; pursued an academic course; studied law at the Inner Temple, London, England; was admitted to the bar in 1754 and commenced practice in London; barrister of the Inner Temple, London, 1755-1759; returned to the colonies and was graduated from the Philadelphia College (now the University of Pennsylvania) in 1760; continued the practice of law at Cambridge, Md.; high sheriff of Dorchester County 1761-1765; burgess to the Maryland assembly in 1765; attorney general of Maryland in 1766; Member of the Continental Congress 1774-1776; member of the council of safety in 1775 and of the convention of the Province of Maryland, August 14, 1776, called to frame a constitution; member of the State senate in 1777; retired to his estate near Cambridge, Md. where he died on December 22, 1788; interment in Christ Episcopal Church Cemetery, Cambridge, Md.

**Bibliography:** *DAB.*

**GOLDSBOROUGH, Robert Henry** (great-grandfather of Winder Laird Henry), a Senator from Maryland; born at "Myrtle Grove," near Easton, Talbot County, Md., January 4, 1779; was educated by private tutors and graduated from St. John's College, Annapolis, in 1795; engaged in agricultural pursuits; member, State house of delegates 1804; commanded a troop of horsemen in the Maryland Militia during the War of 1812; elected as a Federalist to the United States Senate to fill the vacancy in the term commencing March 4, 1813, caused by the failure of the legislature to elect, and served from May 21, 1813, to March 3, 1819; chairman, Committee on Claims (Fifteenth Congress), Committee on District of Columbia (Fifteenth Congress); resumed agricultural pursuits; instrumental in establishing the Easton Gazette in 1817; member, State house of delegates 1825; again elected as a Whig to the United States Senate to fill the vacancy caused by the resignation of Ezekiel F. Chambers and served from January 13, 1835, until his death on October 5, 1836; chairman, Committee on Commerce (Twenty-fourth Congress); died at "Myrtle Grove" near Easton, Md.; interment at "Ashby," the family home in Talbot County, Md.

**GOLDSBOROUGH,** **Thomas Alan** (great-great-great-grandson of Robert Goldsborough and great-grandson of Charles Goldsborough), a Representative from Maryland; born in Greensboro, Caroline County, Md., September 16, 1877; attended the public schools and the local academy at Greensboro; was graduated from Washington College, Chestertown, Md., in 1899 and from the law department of the University of Maryland at Baltimore in 1901; was admitted to the bar in 1901 and commenced practice in Denton, Md.; prosecuting attorney for Caroline County 1904-1908; elected as a Democrat to the Sixty-seventh and to the nine succeeding Congresses and served from March 4, 1921, to April 5, 1939, when he resigned, having been appointed an associate justice of the District Court of the United States for the District of Columbia and served until his death; Regent of the Smithsonian Institution 1932-1939; died in Washington, D.C., June 16, 1951; interment in Denton Cemetery, Denton, Md.

**Bibliography:** *DAB.*

**GOLDTHWAITE,** **George,** a Senator from Alabama; born in Boston, Mass., December 10, 1809; attended the public schools; studied at the United States Military Academy, West Point, N.Y., 1823-1826; moved to Alabama in 1826; studied law; was admitted to the bar the same year and commenced practice in Monticello, Pike County, Ala.; judge of the circuit court 1843-1852; associate justice of the State supreme court 1852-1856; appointed chief justice in 1856, but resigned, and resumed the practice of law; served as adjutant general of Alabama during the Civil War; elected judge of the circuit court in 1868, but was disqualified from serving; elected as a Democrat to the United States Senate and served from March 4, 1871, to March 3, 1877; was not a candidate for reelection; retired from public life; died in Tuscaloosa, Ala., on March 16, 1879; interment in Oakwood Cemetery, Montgomery, Ala.

**Bibliography:** *DAB.*

**GOLDWATER,** **Barry Morris, Jr.** (son of Barry Morris Goldwater), a Representative from California, born in Los Angeles, Los Angeles County, Calif., July 15, 1938; attended grammar school in Phoenix, Ariz., and Staunton Military Academy in Virginia; attended the University of Colorado, 1957-1960; B.A., Arizona State University, 1962; stockbroker, 1962-1969; elected as a Republican to the Ninety-first Congress, April 29, 1969, by special election to fill the vacancy caused by the resignation of Edwin Reinecke; reelected to the six succeeding Congresses, and served from April 29, 1969 to January 3, 1983; was not a candidate in 1982 for reelection to the House of Representatives, but was an unsuccessful candidate for nomination to the United States Senate; involved in financial management, real estate development and public affairs; is a resident of Studio City, Calif., and Phoenix, Ariz.

**GOLDWATER,** **Barry Morris** (father of Barry Morris Goldwater, Jr.), a Senator from Arizona, born in Phoenix, Maricopa County, Ariz., January 1, 1909; attended the Phoenix public schools, Staunton Military Academy, and one year at the University of Arizona at Tuscon in 1928; began business career in 1929 in the family mercantile business; during the Second World War entered active service in August 1941 in the United States Army Air Corps, serving in the Asiatic Theater in India, and was discharged in November 1945 as a lieutenant colonel with rating as pilot; organized the Arizona National Guard, 1945-1952; commissioned brigadier general in the Air Force Reserve in 1959, and promoted to major general in 1962; retired in 1967 after thirty-seven years service; member of advisory committee, Indian Affairs, Department of the Interior, 1948-1950; member, Phoenix city council, 1949-1952; elected as a Republican to the United States Senate in 1952; reelected in 1958, and served from January 3, 1953 to January 3, 1965; did not seek reelection to the Senate in 1964; unsuccessful Republican candidate for election for President of the United States in 1964; elected to the United States Senate in 1968; reelected in

1974 and again in 1980, and served from January 3, 1969 to January 3, 1987; did not seek reelection in 1986; chairman, Select Committee on Intelligence (Ninety-seventh and Ninety-eighth Congresses), Committee on Armed Services (Ninety-ninth Congress); is a resident of Scottsdale, Ariz.

**Bibliography:** Goldberg, Robert Alan. *Barry Goldwater.* New Haven: Yale University Press, 1995; Goldwater, Barry M., with Jack Casserly. *Goldwater.* New York: Doubleday, 1988; Goldwater, Barry M. *With No Apologies: The Personal and Political Memoirs of United States Senator Barry Goldwater.* New York: William Morrow and Co., 1979.

**GOLDZIER,** **Julius,** a Representative from Illinois; born in Vienna, Austria, January 20, 1854; attended the public schools of Vienna; immigrated to the United States in 1866 and settled in New York; studied law and was admitted to the bar; moved to Chicago in 1872 and commenced the practice of law; member of the city council of Chicago 1890-1892; elected as a Democrat to the Fifty-third Congress (March 4, 1893-March 3, 1895); unsuccessful for reelection in 1894 to the Fifty-fourth Congress; practiced law in Chicago, Ill.; again a member of the Chicago city council in 1899; died in Chicago, January 20, 1925; interment in Graceland Cemetery.

**GOLLADAY,** **Edward Isaac** (brother of Jacob Shall Golladay), a Representative from Tennessee; born in Lebanon, Wilson County, Tenn., September 9, 1830; attended the common schools and was graduated from the literary department of Cumberland University, Lebanon, Tenn., in 1848 and from the law department of the same institution in 1849; was admitted to the bar in 1849 and commenced practice in Lebanon; member of the State house of representatives in 1857 and 1858; presidential elector on the Constitutional-Union ticket of Bell and Everett in 1860; served in the Confederate Army as a colonel during the entire Civil War; elected as a Democrat to the Forty-second Congress (March 4, 1871-March 3, 1873); unsuccessful candidate for reelection in 1872 to the Forty-third Congress; resumed the practice of law in Lebanon and Nashville; died in Columbia, S.C., while on a visit to his daughter, July 11, 1897; interment in Cedar Grove Cemetery, Lebanon, Tenn.

**GOLLADAY,** **Jacob Shall** (brother of Edward Isaac Golladay), a Representative from Kentucky; born in Lebanon, Wilson County, Tenn., January 19, 1819; attended the public schools; moved to Nashville, Tenn., in 1838 and thence to Kentucky in 1845; member of the Kentucky house of representatives 1851-1853; member of the Kentucky senate 1853-1855; elected as a Democrat to the Fortieth Congress to fill the vacancy caused by the death of Elijah Hise; reelected to the Forty-first Congress and served from December 5, 1867, until February 28, 1870, when he resigned; resumed the practice of his profession at Allensville, Ky.; died near Russellville, Logan County, Ky., May 20, 1887; interment in Maple Grove Cemetery, Russellville, Ky.

**GONZALEZ,** **Henry Barbosa,** a Representative from Texas; born in San Antonio, Bexar County, Tex., May 3, 1916, the son of Mexican immigrant parents; attended the public schools and the University of Texas at Austin; A.A., San Antonio College, 1937; LL.B., St. Mary's University School of Law, 1943; U.S. Navy service during the Second World War; operator of language and business consultant service in San Antonio, 1947-1951; chief probation officer of Bexar County Juvenile Court, 1946; deputy director, San Antonio Housing Authority, 1950-1951; member of San Antonio city council in 1953 through May 1956; serving as mayor pro tempore part of the first term; elected to the State senate in 1956 and reelected in 1960, serving until his resignation November 3, 1961; elected as a Democrat to the Eighty-seventh Congress, November 4, 1961, by special election to fill the vacancy caused by the resignation of Paul J. Kilday; reelected to the seventeen succeeding Congresses and served from November 4, 1961, to January 3, 1997; chairman, Select Committee on Assassinations (Ninety-fifth Congress), Committee on

Banking, Finance and Urban Affairs (One Hundred First through One Hundred Third Congresses); is a resident of San Antonio, Tex.

**GOOCH, Daniel Linn,** a Representative from Kentucky; born in Rumsey, McLean County, Ky., October 28, 1853; attended a private school; entered the drug business at the age of seventeen, and subsequently became president of a large wholesale drug and chemical company; elected as a Democrat to the Fifty-seventh and Fifty-eighth Congresses (March 4, 1901-March 3, 1905); unsuccessful candidate for renomination in 1904; retired from public life; died in Covington, Ky., April 12, 1913; interment in Woodlawn Cemetery, Dayton, Ohio.

**GOOCH, Daniel Wheelwright,** a Representative from Massachusetts; born in Wells, York County, Maine, January 8, 1820; attended the public schools and Phillips Academy, Andover, Mass., and was graduated from Dartmouth College, Hanover, N.H., in 1843; studied law; was admitted to the bar and commenced practice in Boston in 1846; member of the Massachusetts house of representatives in 1852; member of the Massachusetts constitutional convention in 1853; elected as a Republican to the Thirty-fifth Congress to fill the vacancy caused by the resignation of Nathaniel P. Banks; reelected to the four succeeding Congresses and served from January 31, 1858, to September 1, 1865 when he resigned; appointed Navy agent of the port of Boston in 1865; removed by President Andrew Johnson in 1866; again elected to the Forty-third Congress (March 4, 1873-March 3, 1875); unsuccessful candidate for reelection in 1874 to the Forty-fourth Congress; pension agent in Boston 1876-1886; resumed the practice of law and also engaged in literary pursuits; died in Melrose, Mass., November 11, 1891; interment in Wyoming Cemetery.

**GOOD, James William,** a Representative from Iowa; born near Cedar Rapids, Linn County, Iowa, September 24, 1866; attended the common schools, and was graduated from Coe College, Cedar Rapids, Iowa, in 1892 and from the law department of the University of Michigan at Ann Arbor in 1893; was admitted to the bar in 1893 and commenced practice in Indianapolis, Ind., the same year; moved to Cedar Rapids, Iowa, in 1896 and continued the practice of law; served as city attorney from 1906 until 1908; elected as a Republican to the Sixty-first and to the six succeeding Congresses and served from March 4, 1909, until his resignation on June 15, 1921; chairman, Committee on Appropriations (Sixty-sixth and Sixty-seventh Congresses); moved to Evanston, Ill., in 1921 and engaged in the practice of law in Chicago, Ill.; appointed Secretary of War in the Cabinet of President Herbert Hoover, and served from March 5, 1929 until his death in Washington, D.C., November 18, 1929; interment in Oak Hill Cemetery, Cedar Rapids, Iowa.

**GOODALL, Louis Bertrand,** a Representative from Maine; born in Winchester, Cheshire County, N.H., September 23, 1851; moved to Troy, N.H., with his parents in 1852; attended the common schools of Troy, N.H., a private school in Thompson, Conn., in 1862 and 1863, Vermont Episcopal Institute at Burlington 1863-1866, a private school in England in 1866 and 1867, and Kimball Union Academy at Meridian, N.H., in 1870; entered his father's mills at Sanford, Maine, in 1874 and afterward engaged extensively in the wool-manufacturing industry and in the railroad business; established the Goodall Worsted Co., which originated Palm Beach cloth; president of the Sanford National Bank from its organization in 1896; chairman of the Maine commission to the Louisiana Purchase Exposition, St. Louis, Mo., in 1904; lieutenant colonel on the staff of Governor Bert M. Fernald in 1909; elected as a Republican to the Sixty-fifth and Sixty-sixth Congresses (March 4, 1917-March 3, 1921); chairman, Committee on Elections No. 2 (Sixty-sixth Congress); was not a candidate for renomination in 1920 to the Sixty-seventh Congress; resumed manufacturing interests and banking in Sanford, Maine, until his death there June 26, 1935; interment in Oakdale Cemetery.

**GOODE, John, Jr.,** a Representative from Virginia; born near Liberty (now Bedford), Bedford County, Va., May 27, 1829; attended the New London Academy, and was graduated from Emory and Henry College, Emory, Va., in 1848; studied law; was admitted to the bar in April 1851 and commenced practice in Liberty, Va.; member of the Virginia house of delegates in 1852; member of the Virginia convention which passed the ordinance of secession in 1861; served as a colonel in the Confederate Army during the Civil War; twice elected a member of the Confederate Congress; moved to Norfolk, Va., in 1865 and continued the practice of his profession; again served in the Virginia house of delegates, 1866-1867; member of the Democratic National Executive Committee, 1868-1876; delegate to the Democratic National Conventions of 1868, 1872, 1884 and 1892; elected as a Democrat to the Forty-fourth and to the two succeeding Congresses (March 4, 1875-March 3, 1881); chairman, Committee on Education and Labor (Forty-fifth and Forty-sixth Congresses); unsuccessful candidate for reelection in 1880 to the Forty-seventh Congress; appointed Solicitor General of the United States by President Grover Cleveland in May 1885, and served until August 1886; member of the United States and Chilean Claims Commission in 1893; president of the Virginia Bar Association in 1898; member and president of the Virginia constitutional convention in 1901 and 1902; resumed the practice of law in Washington, D.C.; died in Norfolk, Va., July 14, 1909; interment in Longwood Cemetery, Bedford, Va.

**Bibliography:** *DAB;* Goode, John. *Recollections of a Lifetime.* New York: The Neale Publishing Co., 1906.

**GOODE, Patrick Gaines,** a Representative from Ohio; born in Cornwall parish, Charlotte County, Va., May 10, 1798; moved with his parents early in life to Wayne County, Ohio; attended Xenia (Ohio) Academy and the public schools in Philadelphia, Pa.; studied law; was admitted to the bar in 1821 and practiced in Madison, Ind., and then in Shelby County, Ohio; member of the Ohio house of representatives 1833-1835; elected as a Whig to the Twenty-fifth, Twenty-sixth, and Twenty-seventh Congresses (March 4, 1837-March 3, 1843); was not a candidate for renomination in 1842; was a local preacher nearly all his life and occupied a pulpit almost every Sunday while in Washington during his congressional career; subsequently joined the Methodist Episcopal clergy in the central Ohio conference and preached until near the close of his life; judge of the court of common pleas 1844-1851; died in Sidney, Ohio, on October 17, 1862; interment in Graceland Cemetery.

**GOODE, Samuel,** a Representative from Virginia; born in "Whitby," Chesterfield County, Va., March 21, 1756; completed preparatory studies; studied law; was admitted to the bar and practiced; during the Revolutionary War served as a lieutenant in the Chesterfield Troop of Horse and later as a colonel of militia; member of the Virginia house of delegates 1778-1785; elected to the Sixth Congress (March 4, 1799-March 3, 1801); died in Invermay, Mecklenburg County, Va., November 14, 1822; interment on his estate near Invermay, Mecklenburg County, Va.

**GOODE, William Osborne,** a Representative from Virginia; born in Inglewood, Mecklenburg County, Va., September 16, 1798; completed preparatory studies and was graduated from the College of William and Mary, Williamsburg, Va., in 1819; studied law; was admitted to the bar in 1821 and commenced practice in Boydton, Mecklenburg County, Va.; served in the Virginia house of delegates in 1822 and 1824-1832; member of the State constitutional convention in 1829 and 1830; unsuccessful candidate for election in 1832 to the Twenty-third Congress; again served in the Virginia house of delegates in 1839, 1840, 1845, 1846, and 1852; served as speaker three terms; elected as a Democrat to the Twenty-seventh Congress (March 4, 1841-March 3, 1843); was not a candidate for renomination; delegate to the Virginia constitutional convention in 1850; again elected to the Thirty-third and three succeeding

Congresses and served from March 4, 1853, until his death in Boydton, Va., July 3, 1859; chairman, Committee on District of Columbia (Thirty-fifth Congress); interment on his estate, "Wheatland," near Boydton, Va.

**GOODELL, Charles Ellsworth,** a Representative and a Senator from New York; born in Jamestown, Chautauqua County, N.Y., March 16, 1926; attended the public schools of Jamestown; graduated from Williams College, Williamstown, Mass., in 1948; during the Second World War served in the United States Navy as a seaman second class 1944-1946 and the United States Air Force as a first lieutenant during the Korean conflict 1952-1953; graduated from Yale University School of Law in 1951; received a graduate degree from Yale University Graduate School of Government in 1952; teacher at Quinnipiac College, New Haven, Conn. 1952; was admitted to the Connecticut bar in 1951, the New York bar in 1954, and commenced practice in Jamestown, N.Y.; congressional liaison assistant for the Department of Justice 1954-1955; elected as a Republican to the Eighty-sixth Congress to fill the vacancy caused by the death of Daniel A. Reed; reelected to the Eighty-seventh and to the three succeeding Congresses and served from May 26, 1959, until his resignation September 9, 1968; appointed as a Republican to the United States Senate to fill the unexpired term of the late Senator Robert F. Kennedy and served from September 10, 1968 to January 3, 1971; unsuccessful candidate for election to a full term in 1970; resumed the practice of law; was a resident of Washington, D.C., until his death there on January 21, 1987; interment in Lake View Cemetery, Jamestown, N.Y.

**GOODENOW, John Milton,** a Representative from Ohio; born in Westmoreland, Cheshire County, N.H., in 1782; attended the public schools; engaged in mercantile pursuits; studied law; was admitted to the bar and commenced practice in Steubenville, Ohio, in 1813; appointed collector of direct taxes and internal duties for the sixth collection district of Ohio in 1817; member of the State house of representatives in 1823; elected to the Twenty-first Congress and served from March 4, 1829, until April 9, 1830, when he resigned, having been chosen a judge of the supreme court of Ohio; resigned in the summer of 1830 on account of ill health; moved to Cincinnati in 1832; appointed presiding judge of the court of common pleas in 1833; died in New Orleans in July 1838; interment in Spring Grove Cemetery, Cincinnati.

**Bibliography:** *DAB*.

**GOODENOW, Robert** (brother of Rufus King Goodenow), a Representative from Maine; born in Henniker, Merrimack County, N.H., on April 19, 1800; moved with his parents to Brownfield, Maine, in 1802; attended the common schools at that place and at Sanford in 1815 and 1816; studied medicine; studied law; was admitted to the bar in 1822 and commenced practice in Wilton, Maine; county attorney 1828-1834; moved to Farmington, Maine, in 1832 and continued the practice of law; elected as a Whig to the Thirty-second Congress (March 4, 1851-March 3, 1853); unsuccessful candidate for renomination in 1852 to the Thirty-third Congress; appointed State bank commissioner in 1857; county treasurer of Franklin County 1866-1868; again county attorney in 1869 and 1870; treasurer of the Franklin County Savings Bank 1868-1874; died in Farmington, May 15, 1874; interment in Riverside Cemetery.

**GOODENOW, Rufus King** (brother of Robert Goodenow), a Representative from Maine; born in Henniker, Merrimack County, N.H., April 24, 1790; moved with his parents to Brownfield, Maine, in 1802; received a limited schooling; engaged in agricultural pursuits; also followed the sea, having made several voyages to European ports; served as a captain in the Thirty-third Regiment, United States Infantry, in the War of 1812; moved to Paris, Maine, in 1821; clerk of the Oxford County Courts 1821-1837; member of the State house of representatives in 1837 and 1838; delegate to the Whig National Convention at Harrisburg, Pa., in 1839; studied law;

was admitted to the bar and practiced in the courts of Maine; elected as a Whig to the Thirty-first Congress (March 4, 1849-March 3, 1851); died in Paris, Maine, March 24, 1863; interment in Riverside Cemetery, South Paris, Maine.

**GOODHUE, Benjamin,** a Representative and a Senator from Massachusetts; born in Salem, Mass., September 20, 1748; graduated from Harvard College in 1766; merchant; member, Massachusetts house of representatives 1780-1782; member, Massachusetts senate 1783, 1786-1788; member of the Massachusetts constitutional convention in 1779 and 1780; elected to the First and to the three succeeding Congresses and served from March 4, 1789, until his resignation in June 1796; chairman, Committee on Commerce and Manfactures (Fourth Congress); elected in 1796 as a Federalist to the United States Senate to fill the vacancy caused by the resignation of George Cabot; reelected and served from June 11, 1796, to November 8, 1800, when he resigned; died in Salem, Mass., on July 28, 1814; interment in Broad Street Cemetery.

**Bibliography:** *DAB*.

**GOODIN, John Randolph,** a Representative from Kansas; born in Tiffin, Seneca County, Ohio, December 14, 1836; moved with his father to Kenton, Ohio, in 1844; attended the Kenton High School and Geneva College; studied law; was admitted to the bar in 1857 and commenced practice in Kenton; moved to Humboldt, Kans., in 1859; elected to the State house of representatives in 1866; judge of the seventh judicial district of Kansas 1868-1876; elected as a Democrat to the Forty-fourth Congress (March 4, 1875-March 3, 1877); unsuccessful candidate for reelection; editor of the Inter State in Humboldt, Kans.; moved to Kansas City, Kans., in 1883, where he died December 18, 1885; interment in Oak Grove Cemetery.

**GOODING, Frank Robert,** a Senator from Idaho; born in Tiverton, England, September 16, 1859; immigrated in 1867 to the United States with his parents, who settled on a farm near Paw Paw, Mich.; attended the common schools; moved to Shasta, Calif., in 1877 and engaged in farming and mining; moved to Idaho in 1881 and settled in Ketchum, where he worked as a mail carrier, and subsequently engaged in the firewood and charcoal business; in 1888 settled near the present site of Gooding, which is named for him; engaged in farming and stock raising; member of the Idaho State senate from 1900 until 1904; elected Governor of Idaho in 1904, reelected in 1906, and served from January 2, 1905 to January 4, 1909; unsuccessful candidate for election in 1918 to the United States Senate; elected as a Republican in 1920 to the United States Senate for the term commencing March 4, 1921; was subsequently appointed to the Senate on January 8, 1921, to become effective January 15, 1921, to fill the vacancy in the term ending March 3, 1921, caused by the resignation of John F. Nugent; reelected in 1926, and served from January 15, 1921, until his death in Gooding, Idaho, June 24, 1928; interment in Elmwood Cemetery.

**GOODLATTE, Robert William,** a Representative from Virginia; born in Holyoke, Hampden County, Mass., September 22, 1952; B.A., Bates College, Lewiston, Maine, 1974; J.D., Washington and Lee University, Lexington, Va., 1975; district office manager to Representative M. Caldwell Butler of Virginia, 1977-1979; chairman, Roanoke City Republican Committee, 1980-1983; Sixth Congressional District coordinator of the gubernatorial campaigns of J. Marshall Coleman in 1981, and of Wyatt B. Durrette in 1985; chair, Sixth District Republican committee, 1983-1988; Sixth District chair of the campaigns of Vice President George Bush in 1988, Dalton for lieutenant governor, 1989, Senator John W. Warner in 1990, Brandon Bell for Senate, exploratory committee, 1991; elected as a Republican to the One Hundred Third and One Hundred Fourth Congresses (January 3, 1993-January 3, 1997); is a resident of Roanoke, Va.

**GOODLING, George Atlee** (father of William Franklin Goodling), a Representative from Pennsylvania; born in Loganville, York County, Pa., September 26, 1896; attended the public schools, York Collegiate Institute, and Bellefont Academy; Pennsylvania State University, B.S. 1921; served as a seaman, second class in the United States Navy from March 1918 to December 1918; operator of a fruit farm near Loganville, Pa.; director of a bank, motor club, and insurance company; served in the State house of representatives, 1943-1957; school director, 1933-1961; elected as a Republican to the Eighty-seventh and Eighty-eighth Congresses (January 3, 1961-January 3, 1965); unsuccessful candidate for reelection in 1964 to the Eighty-ninth Congress; elected to the Ninetieth and to the three succeeding Congresses (January 3, 1967-January 3, 1975); was not a candidate for reelection in 1974 to the Ninety-fourth Congress; resided in Loganville, Pa. until his death in York, Pa. on October 17, 1982; interment at Emmanuel United Methodist Church Cemetery, Loganville, Pa.

**GOODLING, William Franklin** (son of George Atlee Goodling), a Representative from Pennsylvania, born in Loganville, York County, Pa., December 5, 1927; graduated from William Penn High School, York, Pa., 1945; B.S., University of Maryland, 1953; M.Ed., Western Maryland College, 1957; doctoral studies at the Pennsylvania State University, 1958-1963; held various teaching and administrative positions throughout Pennsylvania; served in the United States Army, 1946-1948; President, Dallastown Area School Board; elected as a Republican to the Ninety-fourth and to the ten succeeding Congresses (January 3, 1975-January 3, 1997); chairman, Committee on Economic and Educational Opportunities (One Hundred Fourth Congress); is a resident of Jacobus, Pa.

**GOODNIGHT, Isaac Herschel,** a Representative from Kentucky; born near Scottsville, Allen County, Ky., January 31, 1849; attended the common schools; moved to Franklin, Ky., in 1870; was graduated from Cumberland University, Lebanon, Tenn., in 1872, and afterwards attended the law department of the same university; was admitted to the bar in 1873 and commenced practice in Franklin; member of the Kentucky house of representatives in 1877 and 1878; chairman of the Kentucky Democratic convention at Louisville, Ky., in 1891; elected as a Democrat to the Fifty-first, Fifty-second, and Fifty-third Congresses (March 4, 1889-March 3, 1895); was not a candidate for renomination in 1894; elected judge of the seventh Kentucky circuit in 1897 and served until his death in Franklin, Ky., July 24, 1901; interment in Green Lawn Cemetery.

**GOODRICH, Chauncey** (brother of Elizur Goodrich), a Representative and a Senator from Connecticut; born in Durham, Middlesex County, Conn., October 20, 1759; pursued preparatory studies; graduated from Yale College in 1776; taught in the Hopkins Grammar School, 1777-1778, and in Yale College, 1779-1781; studied law; was admitted to the bar in 1781 and began practice in Hartford, Conn.; member, Connecticut State house of representatives, 1793-1794; elected as a Federalist to the Fourth and to the two succeeding Congresses (March 4, 1795-March 3, 1801); resumed the practice of law in Hartford; member, State executive council, 1802-1807; elected as a Federalist to the United States Senate to fill the vacancy caused by the death of Uriah Tracy; reelected and served from October 25, 1807 until May 1813, when he resigned to become lieutenant governor; elected mayor of Hartford in 1812 and lieutenant governor of Connecticut in 1813, holding both offices at the time of his death; delegate to the Hartford Convention in 1814; died in Hartford, Conn., August 18, 1815; interment in the Old North Cemetery.

**Bibliography:** *DAB.*

**GOODRICH, Elizur** (brother of Chauncey Goodrich), a Representative from Connecticut; born in Durham, Middlesex County, Conn., March 24, 1761; pursued preparatory studies and was graduated from Yale College in 1779; studied law; was admitted to

the bar and commenced practice in New Haven in 1783; member of the State house of representatives 1795-1802, during which time he served as clerk of the house for six sessions and as speaker in two; Federalist presidential elector in 1796; elected as a Federalist to the Sixth Congress (March 4, 1799-March 3, 1801); had been reelected to the Seventh Congress, but resigned, effective March 3, 1801, having been appointed by President John Adams on February 19, 1801, collector of customs at New Haven; removed from that office by President Thomas Jefferson; elected in 1803 to the Governor's council, which office he held until the change in the State constitution in 1818; professor of law in Yale College 1801-1810; judge of the probate court 1802-1818; also chief judge of the county court 1805-1818; member of the city council and board of aldermen for several years; served as mayor of New Haven 1803-1822; member of the corporation of Yale College 1809-1818 and secretary of the same until 1846; died in New Haven, Conn., November 1, 1849; interment in Grove Street Cemetery.

**Bibliography:** *DAB.*

**GOODRICH, John Zacheus,** a Representative from Massachusetts; born in Sheffield, Berkshire County, Mass., September 27, 1804; attended the common schools and Lenox Academy, Lenox, Mass.; studied law; was admitted to the bar and practiced; engaged in manufacturing; served in the Massachusetts senate in 1848 and 1849; elected as a Whig to the Thirty-second and Thirty-third Congresses (March 4, 1851-March 3, 1855); member of the peace convention of 1861 held in Washington, D.C., in an effort to devise means to prevent the impending war; elected, as a Republican, lieutenant governor of Massachusetts in 1860 and served from January 1, 1861, until his resignation on March 29, 1861; appointed collector of customs at Boston on March 13, 1861, and served until March 11, 1865; retired from public life and died in Stockbridge, Mass., April 19, 1885; interment in Stockbridge Cemetery.

**GOODRICH, Milo,** a Representative from New York; born in East Homer, Cortland County, N.Y., January 3, 1814; moved with his parents to Cortlandville, N.Y., in 1816; attended the South Cortland district school, Cortland Academy, Homer, N.Y., and Oberlin College, Ohio; taught school in New York, Pennsylvania, and Ohio; studied law; was admitted to the bar in Worcester, Mass., in 1840, and practiced for two years in Beloit, Wis.; returned to New York and settled in Dryden in 1844; postmaster of Dryden from October 2, 1849, to June 25, 1853; member of the State constitutional convention in 1867 and 1868; elected as a Republican to the Forty-second Congress (March 4, 1871-March 3, 1873); unsuccessful candidate for reelection in 1872 to the Forty-third Congress; resumed the practice of law; moved to Auburn, N.Y., in 1875 and continued the practice of law; died in Auburn, N.Y., April 15, 1881; interment in Green Hills Cemetery, Dryden, N.Y.

**GOODWIN, Angier Louis,** a Representative from Massachusetts; born in Fairfield, Somerset County, Maine, January 30, 1881; attended the public schools; was graduated from Colby College, Waterville, Maine, in 1902; attended Harvard Law School in 1905; was admitted to the Maine bar in 1905, the Massachusetts bar in 1906, and commenced the practice of law in Boston, Mass.; member of the Melrose Board of Aldermen 1912-1914 and 1916-1920, serving as president in 1920; mayor of Melrose, Mass., 1921-1923; member of the Massachusetts Guard and legal adviser to aid draft registrants during the First World War; member of the Planning Board and chairman of the Board of Appeal, Melrose, Mass., 1923-1925; served in the Massachusetts house of representatives 1925-1928; member of the Massachusetts senate, 1929-1941, serving as president in 1941; chairman of the Massachusetts Commission on Participation in New York World's Fair, in 1939 and 1940; chairman of the Massachusetts Commission on Administration and Finance in 1942; elected as a Republican to the Seventy-eighth and to the five succeeding Congresses (January 3,

1943-January 3, 1955); unsuccessful candidate for reelection in 1954 to the Eighty-fourth Congress; member of the Massachusetts Massachusetts Board of Tax Appeals 1955-1960; retired and resided in Melrose, Mass., where he died June 20, 1975; interment in Wyoming Cemetery.

**GOODWIN, Forrest,** a Representative from Maine; born in Skowhegan, Somerset County, Maine, June 14, 1862; attended the common schools; was graduated from Skowhegan High School and Bloomfield Academy, and in 1887 from Colby College, Waterville, Maine, and Boston University Law School in 1890; was admitted to the bar in 1889 and commenced practice in Skowhegan, Maine, in 1891; member of the State house of representatives in 1889; clerk at the Speaker's table under Speaker Reed in the Fifty-first Congress 1889-1891; member of the State senate 1903-1905 and served as president in 1905; elected as a Republican to the Sixty-third Congress and served from March 4, 1913, until his death in Portland, Maine, May 28, 1913; interment in South Side Cemetery, Skowhegan, Maine.

**GOODWIN, Godfrey Gummer,** a Representative from Minnesota; born near St. Peter, Nicollet County, Minn., January 11, 1873; moved with his mother to St. Paul, Minn., in 1882; attended the public schools and was graduated from the University of Minnesota at Minneapolis in 1895 and from the law department of that university in 1896; was admitted to the bar in 1896 and commenced practice in Cambridge, Minn.; prosecuting attorney of Isanti County 1898-1907; again elected as prosecuting attorney of Isanti County in November 1913 and served until February 15, 1925, when he resigned, having been elected to Congress; president of the Cambridge (Minn.) Board of Education 1914-1917; elected as a Republican to the Sixty-ninth and to the three succeeding Congresses and served from March 4, 1925, until his death; unsuccessful candidate for renomination in 1932; died in Washington, D.C., on February 16, 1933; interment in Lakewood Cemetery, Minneapolis, Minn.

**GOODWIN, Henry Charles,** a Representative from New York; born in De Ruyter, Madison County, N.Y., June 25, 1824; completed preparatory studies; studied law; was admitted to the bar in 1846 and commenced practice in Hamilton, N.Y.; district attorney of Madison County 1847-1850; elected as a Whig to the Thirty-third Congress to fill the vacancy caused by the resignation of Gerrit Smith and served from November 7, 1854, to March 3, 1855; elected as a Republican to the Thirty-fifth Congress (March 4, 1857-March 3, 1859); resumed the practice of law; died in Hamilton, N.Y., November 12, 1860; interment in Madison Street Cemetery.

**GOODWIN, John Noble,** a Representative from Maine and a Delegate from the Territory of Arizona; born in South Berwick, York County, Maine, October 18, 1824; attended public schools and the local academy at Berwick, Maine; graduated from Dartmouth College in 1844; studied law; admitted to the bar in 1848, commencing practice in South Berwick; member of Maine State senate in 1854; elected as a Republican from Maine to the Thirty-seventh Congress (March 4, 1861-March 3, 1863); unsuccessful candidate for reelection in 1862 to the Thirty-eighth Congress; appointed March 6, 1863, by President Lincoln as chief justice of Arizona Territory and on August 21, 1863, as the first Governor of the Territory; entered the Territory and formally proclaimed its organization at Navajo Springs, December 29, 1863; resigned as Territorial Governor on April 10, 1866; elected as a Republican Delegate from Arizona Territory to the Thirty-ninth Congress (March 4, 1865-March 3, 1867); was not a candidate for reelection in 1866 to the Fortieth Congress, and did not return to Arizona; resumed the practice of law in New York City; died in Paraiso Springs, Calif., April 29, 1887; interment in Forest Grove Cemetery, Augusta, Maine.

**Bibliography:** *DAB.*

**GOODWIN, Philip Arnold,** a Representative from New York; born in Athens, Greene County, N.Y., January 20, 1882; attended the public schools; moved to Coxsackie, N.Y., with his parents in 1896; was graduated from the high school at Coxsackie, N.Y., in 1900, and from Albany (N.Y.) Business College in 1902; engaged in the steel bridge construction business at Albany, N.Y., 1902-1916; owner and operator of a lumber business at Coxsackie, N.Y., from 1916 until his death; also interested in banking, in a milling and supply company, and in a securities company; elected as a Republican to the Seventy-third, Seventy-fourth, and Seventy-fifth Congresses and served from March 4, 1933, until his death in Coxsackie, N.Y., June 6, 1937; interment in Riverside Cemetery.

**GOODWIN, Robert Kingman,** a Representative from Iowa; born in Des Moines, Iowa, May 23, 1905; attended the public schools; was graduated from Drake University, Des Moines, Iowa, in 1928 and later attended the law school of George Washington University, Washington, D.C.; moved to Redfield, Dallas County, Iowa, in 1929 and engaged in the brick and tile manufacturing business and farming 1934-1949; mayor of Redfield, Iowa, 1938-1940; delegate to the Republican State conventions in 1936 and 1938; vice president of the Dallas County Farm Bureau in 1939 and 1940; elected as a Republican to the Seventy-sixth Congress to fill the vacancy caused by the death of Cassius C. Dowell and served from March 5, 1940, to January 3, 1941; was not a candidate for renomination in 1940; director of the Central National Bank & Trust Co., 1941-1965; commissioned a lieutenant in the United States Naval Reserve in June 1942 and served until November 2, 1945; delegate to the Republican National Convention in 1952; member of the Republican National Committee 1952-1956; civilian aide to the Secretary of the Army 1952-1956; trustee and vice president of Herbert Hoover Foundation, Inc.; resumed his manufacturing business; was a resident of Des Moines, Iowa, until his death in Rochester, Minn., February 21, 1983; interment in Resthaven, Des Moines, Iowa.

**GOODWIN, William Shields,** a Representative from Arkansas; born in Warren, Bradley County, Ark., on May 2, 1866; attended the public schools, the Farmers' Academy near Duluth, Ga., Cooledge's Preparatory School, Moore's College, Atlanta, Ga., and the Universities of Arkansas and Mississippi; studied law; was admitted to the bar in 1894 and commenced practice in Warren, Ark.; member of the State house of representatives in 1895; served in the State senate 1905-1909; member of the board of trustees of the University of Arkansas at Fayetteville 1907-1911; elected as a Democrat to the Sixty-second and to the four succeeding Congresses (March 4, 1911-March 3, 1921); unsuccessful candidate for renomination in 1920; reengaged in the practice of law in Warren, Ark., until his death there August 9, 1937; interment in Oak Lawn Cemetery.

**GOODWYN, Albert Taylor,** a Representative from Alabama; born at Robinson Springs, Montgomery County, Ala., December 17, 1842; attended Robinson Springs Academy and South Carolina College at Columbia; during the Civil War enlisted in the Confederate Army and served until June 1865; mustered out at the close of the war as captain of a company of sharpshooters and was decorated with the Confederate Cross of Honor; was graduated from the University of Virginia at Charlottesville in 1867; engaged in agricultural pursuits near Robinson Springs; State inspector of convicts 1874-1880; member of the State house of representatives in 1886 and 1887; served in the State senate 1892-1896; successfully contested as a Populist the election of James E. Cobb to the Fifty-fourth Congress and served from April 22, 1896, until March 3, 1897; was an unsuccessful candidate for reelection in 1896 to the Fifty-fifth Congress; elected commander in chief of the United Confederate Veterans May 8, 1928; resumed agricultural pursuits near Robinson Springs, Ala.; died while on a visit in Birmingham, Ala., on July 2, 1931; interment in Oakwood Cemetery, Montgomery, Ala.

**GOODWYN, Peterson,** a Representative from Virginia; born at "Martins," near Petersburg, Dinwiddie County, Va., in 1745; received his education from private tutors; completed preparatory studies; engaged in planting; studied law; was admitted to the bar in 1776 and commenced practice in Petersburg, Va., and surrounding counties; during the Revolutionary War equipped his own company and rose from captain to major; was promoted to colonel for gallantry at the battles of Smithfield and of Great Bridge; member of the Virginia house of delegates 1789-1802; elected as a Republican to the Eighth and to the seven succeeding Congresses and served from March 4, 1803, until his death at his home, "Sweden," in Dinwiddie County, Va., February 21, 1818; interment in the family burying ground on his estate.

**GOODYEAR, Charles,** a Representative from New York; born in Cobleskill, Schoharie County, N.Y., April 26, 1804; attended the Hartwick Academy in Otsego County; was graduated from Union College, Schenectady, N.Y., in 1824; studied law; was admitted to the bar in 1826 and commenced practice in Schoharie, N.Y.; appointed first judge of Schoharie County in February 1838 and served until July 1847; member of the State assembly in 1840; elected as a Democrat to the Twenty-ninth Congress (March 4, 1845-March 3, 1847); continued the practice of law in Schoharie until 1852, when he established the Schoharie County Bank and served as its president; elected to the Thirty-ninth Congress (March 4, 1865-March 3, 1867); was not a candidate for renomination in 1866; resumed the practice of law; delegate to the Union National Convention of Conservatives at Philadelphia in 1866 and to the Democratic National Convention in 1868; retired in 1869 and moved to Charlottesville, Va.; served as judge of the Albemarle County Court; died in Charlottesville, Va., on April 9, 1876; interment in Maplewood Cemetery.

**GOODYKOONTZ, Wells,** a Representative from West Virginia; born near Newbern, Pulaski County, Va., June 3, 1872; educated under private tutors and attended Oxford Academy at Floyd, Va., and the law department of Washington and Lee University, Lexington, Va.; was admitted to the bar in 1893 and commenced practice at Williamson, W.Va., in 1894; also engaged in banking; member of the State house of delegates in 1911 and 1912; member of the State senate 1914-1918 and served as president of the senate and lieutenant governor ex officio of the State from 1917 to December 1, 1918; president of the West Virginia Bar Association in 1917 and 1918; chairman of the central legal advisory board for West Virginia during the First World War; elected as a Republican to the Sixty-sixth and Sixty-seventh Congresses (March 4, 1919-March 3, 1923); unsuccessful candidate for reelection in 1922 to the Sixty-eighth Congress; resumed the practice of law and banking interests in Williamson, W.Va.; also engaged in literary work; died in Cincinnati, Ohio, on March 2, 1944; interment in Fairview Cemetery, Williamson, W.Va.

**GORDON, Barton Jennings,** a Representative from Tennessee; born in Murfreesboro, Tenn., January 24, 1949; attended public schools; graduated Central High School, Murfreesboro, 1967; B.S., Middle Tennessee State University, Murfreesboro, 1971; J.D., University of Tennessee College of Law, Knoxville, 1973; admitted to the Tennessee State bar, 1974; private practice of law in Murfreesboro, 1974-1983; executive director, Tennessee Democratic Party, 1979; chairman, Tennessee Democratic Party, 1981-1983; elected as a Democrat to the Ninety-ninth and to the five succeeding Congresses (January 3, 1985-January 3, 1997); is a resident of Murfreesboro, Tenn.

**GORDON, George Washington,** a Representative from Tennessee; born in Pulaski, Giles County, Tenn., October 5, 1836; received a collegiate training and was graduated from the Western Military Institute, Nashville, Tenn., in 1859; practiced civil engineering until the beginning of the Civil War; enlisted in the military service of the Confederacy; was drillmaster of the Eleventh Regiment, Tennessee Infantry; was successively a captain, lieutenant colonel, colonel, and brigadier general, and served until the close of the war; studied law; was admitted to the bar and practiced in Memphis, Tenn., until 1883; appointed one of the railroad commissioners of Tennessee; received an appointment in the Department of the Interior, 1885, as special Indian agent in Arizona and Nevada and served until 1889; returned to Memphis, Tenn.; resumed the practice of law; superintendent of the Memphis city schools 1889-1907; elected as a Democrat to the Sixtieth, Sixty-first, and Sixty-second Congresses and served from March 4, 1907, until his death in Memphis, Tenn., on August 9, 1911; interment in Elmwood Cemetery.

Bibliography: *DAB.*

**GORDON, James,** a Representative from New York; born in the parish of Killead, County Antrim, Ireland, October 31, 1739; attended the local schools; immigrated to the United States in 1758; settled in Schenectady, N.Y., where he engaged in Indian trading; served as a lieutenant colonel in the Militia Regiment of Albany County, N.Y., during the Revolutionary War; captured and taken prisoner to Canada; returned to Albany, N.Y.; member of the State assembly 1777-1780, 1786, and 1790; moved to Ballston Spa, N.Y.; elected to the Second and Third Congresses (March 4, 1791-March 3, 1795); member of the board of trustees of Union College, Schenectady, N.Y., 1795-1809; served in the State senate 1797-1804; died in Ballston Spa, N.Y., January 17, 1810; interment in Briggs Cemetery.

**GORDON, James,** a Senator from Mississippi; born in Cotton Gin Port, Monroe County, Miss., December 6, 1833; moved with his parents to Pontotoc County in 1834; attended the public schools, St. Thomas Hall, Holly Springs, Miss., and La Grange College, Alabama; graduated from the University of Mississippi at Oxford in 1855; planter and newspaper and magazine writer; member, State house of representatives in 1857 and 1859; moved to Okolona, Miss., in 1859; during the Civil War served as colonel in the Confederate Army with Cavalry regiments he had raised and organized; special commissioner of the Confederacy to visit European countries in 1864; captured in the harbor of Wilmington, N.C., on his return in January 1865, but escaped in February 1865 and fled to Canada; received a passport to return to the United States and successfully defended himself against charges of conspiring with John Wilkes Booth to assassinate President Lincoln; member, State house of representatives in 1876 and 1886; member, State senate 1904-1906; appointed to the United States Senate to fill the vacancy caused by the death of Anselm J. McLaurin and served from December 27, 1909, to February 22, 1910; was not a candidate for election in 1910; resumed agricultural pursuits and literary activities; died in Okolona, Chickasaw County, Miss., November 28, 1912; interment in Odd Fellows Cemetery.

Bibliography: *DAB.*

**GORDON, John Brown,** a Senator from Georgia; born in Upson County, Ga., February 6, 1832; attended private schools and the University of Georgia at Athens; studied law; was admitted to the bar in 1853 and commenced practice in Atlanta, Ga.; superintendent of a coal mining operation in Alabama; upon the outbreak of the Civil War entered the Confederate Army as captain of Infantry and rose to be appointed major general on May 14, 1864; resumed the practice of law in Atlanta, Ga.; unsuccessful Democratic candidate for Governor in 1868; elected as a Democrat to the United States Senate in 1873; reelected in 1879, and served from

March 4, 1873 until May 26, 1880, when he resigned to promote the building of the Georgia Pacific Railroad; chairman, Committee on Commerce (Forty-sixth Congress); elected Governor of Georgia in 1886, reelected in 1888, and served from November 9, 1886 to November 8, 1890; again elected to the United States Senate, and served from March 4, 1891 to March 3, 1897; declined to be a candidate for reelection; chairman, Committee on Coastal Defenses (Fifty-third Congress); engaged in lecturing and literary work; died in Miami, Fla., January 9, 1904; interment in Oakland Cemetery, Atlanta, Ga.

Bibliography: *DAB*; Culpepper, Grady S. "The Political Career of John Brown Gordon, 1868 to 1897." Ph.D. dissertation, Emory University, 1981; Eckert, Ralph Lowell. *John Brown Gordon: Soldier, Southerner, American*. Baton Rouge: Louisiana State University Press, 1989.

GORDON, Robert Bryarly, a Representative from Ohio; born at St. Marys, Auglaize County, Ohio, August 6, 1855; attended the public schools; postmaster of St. Marys 1885-1889; auditor of Auglaize County 1890-1896; delegate to the Democratic National Convention in 1896; elected as a Democrat to the Fifty-sixth and Fifty-seventh Congresses (March 4, 1899-March 3, 1903); engaged in the flour and grain business at St. Marys, Ohio; superintendent of the document room of the House of Representatives 1911-1913; Sergeant at Arms of the House of Representatives 1913-1919; died in Washington, D.C., January 3, 1923; interment in Elm Grove Cemetery, St. Marys, Ohio.

GORDON, Samuel, a Representative from New York; born at Wattle's Ferry, Delaware County, N.Y., April 28, 1802; attended the public schools; engaged in agricultural pursuits until attaining the age of twenty-five; studied law in Delhi, N.Y.; was admitted to the bar in 1829 and commenced practice in Delhi; appointed postmaster of Delhi, N.Y., September 14, 1831, and served until August 16, 1841; member of the State assembly in 1834; district attorney of Delaware County 1841-1844; supervisor of the town of Delhi for several terms; elected as a Democrat to the Twenty-seventh Congress (March 4, 1841-March 3, 1843); owing to a realignment of the districts in the State was not a candidate for renomination; elected to the Twenty-ninth Congress (March 4, 1845-March 3, 1847); was not a candidate for renomination in 1846; resumed the practice of his legal profession; appointed provost marshal for the nineteenth district of New York 1863-1865; owing to ill health discontinued active business pursuits and lived in retirement until his death in Delhi, Delaware County, N.Y., October 28, 1873; interment in Woodland Cemetery.

GORDON, Thomas Sylvy, a Representative from Illinois; born in Chicago, Ill., December 17, 1893; attended the parochial schools and was graduated from St. Stanislaus College, Chicago, Ill., in 1912; engaged in the banking business 1916-1920; associated with a Polish-language daily newspaper 1921-1942, starting as a clerk and advancing to head cashier and office manager; commissioner of Chicago West Parks 1933-1936 and of public vehicle licenses 1936-1939; delegate to the Democratic National Convention in 1936; city treasurer of Chicago, Ill., 1939-1942; elected as a Democrat to the Seventy-eighth and to the seven succeeding Congresses (January 3, 1943-January 3, 1959); chairman, Committee on Foreign Affairs (Eighty-fifth Congress); was not a candidate for renomination in 1958; died in Chicago, Ill., January 22, 1959; interment in St. Adalbert Cemetery (Niles), Chicago, Ill.

GORDON, William, a Representative from New Hampshire; born near Boston, Mass., April 12, 1763; was graduated from Harvard College in 1779; studied law; was admitted to the bar in 1787 and commenced practice in Amherst, N.H.; appointed register of probate in 1793; member of the State senate in 1794 and 1795; solicitor of Hillsborough County 1794-1801; elected as a Federalist to the Fifth and Sixth Congresses and served from March 4, 1797,

until June 12, 1800, when he resigned to accept the office of attorney general of New Hampshire, which he held until his death; was one of the managers appointed by the House of Representatives in 1798 to conduct the impeachment proceedings against William Blount, a Senator from Tennessee; died in Boston, Mass., May 8, 1802; interment in Amherst Cemetery, Amherst, N.H.

GORDON, William, a Representative from Ohio; born on a farm near Oak Harbor, Ottawa County, Ohio, December 15, 1862; attended the public schools and Toledo (Ohio) Business College; taught school; deputy county treasurer 1887-1891; member of the board of school examiners of Ottawa County 1890-1896; was graduated from the law department of the University of Michigan at Ann Arbor in 1893; was admitted to the bar the same year and commenced practice in Oak Harbor, Ohio; prosecuting attorney for Ottawa County 1895-1901; delegate to the Democratic National Convention in 1896; member of the Democratic State committee in 1903 and 1904; founder of the Gordon Lumber Co.; moved to Cleveland, Ohio, in 1906; unsuccessful candidate for election in 1910 to the Sixty-second Congress; elected as a Democrat to the Sixty-third, Sixty-fourth, and Sixty-fifth Congresses (March 4, 1913-March 3, 1919); was an unsuccessful candidate for reelection in 1918 to the Sixty-sixth Congress; reengaged in the practice of law until his death in Cleveland, Ohio, January 16, 1942; interment in Oak Harbor Cemetery, Oak Harbor, Ohio.

GORDON, William Fitzhugh, a Representative from Virginia; born on Germanna plantation, near Fredericksburg, Spotsylvania County, Va., January 13, 1787; attended the country schools and Spring Hill Academy; studied law; was admitted to the bar in 1808 and commenced practice at Orange Court House, Va.; moved to Charlottesville, Va., in 1809 and continued the practice of law; Commonwealth attorney in 1812; served in the War of 1812; later attained the rank of major general in the Virginia Militia; member of the Virginia house of delegates 1818-1829; member of the Virginia constitutional convention in 1829 and 1830; elected as a Jacksonian to the Twenty-first Congress to fill the vacancy caused by the resignation of William Cabell Rives; reelected to the Twenty-second and Twenty-third Congresses and served from January 25, 1830, to March 3, 1835; unsuccessful candidate for reelection in 1834 to the Twenty-fourth Congress; engaged in agricultural pursuits; delegate to the Southern Convention at Nashville, Tenn., in 1850; died on his plantation, "Edgeworth," Albemarle County, Va., August 28, 1858; interment in the family burying ground at Springfield, near Gordonsville, Va.

Bibliography: *DAB*.

GORE, Albert Arnold (father of Albert Arnold Gore, Jr.), a Representative and a Senator from Tennessee; born in Granville, Jackson County, Tenn., December 26, 1907; attended the public schools; B.S., State Teachers' College, Murfreesboro, Tenn., 1932; LL.B., Nashville (Tenn.) Y.M.C.A. night law school, 1936; taught in the rural schools of Overton and Smith Counties, Tenn., 1926-1930; Smith County superintendent of education, 1932-1936; was admitted to the bar in 1936 and commenced practice in Carthage, Tenn.; Tennessee State commissioner of labor, 1936-1937; elected as a Democrat to the Seventy-sixth and to the two succeeding Congresses and served from January 3, 1939, until his resignation on December 4, 1944, to enter the United States Army; reelected to the Seventy-ninth and to the three succeeding Congresses (January 3, 1945-January 3, 1953); was not a candidate in 1952 for renomination to the House of Representatives, but was elected to the United States Senate; reelected in 1958 and again in 1964, and served from January 3, 1953 to January 3, 1971; unsuccessful candidate for reelection in 1970; chairman, Special Committee on Attempts to Influence Senators (Eighty-fourth Congress); resumed the practice of law with Occidental Petroleum Co. and became vice president and member of the Board of directors; taught law at Vanderbilt

University, 1970-1972; member of the board of petroleum and coal companies; is a resident of Carthage, Tenn.

**Bibliography:** Gardner, James B. "Political Leadership in a Period of Transition: Frank G. Clement, Albert Gore, Estes Kefauver, and Tennessee Politics, 1948-1956." Ph.D. dissertation, Vanderbilt University, 1978; Gore, Albert. *Let the Glory Out: My South and Its Politics.* New York: Viking Press, 1972.

**GORE, Albert Arnold, Jr.** (son of Albert Arnold Gore), a Representative and Senator from Tennessee; born in Washington, D.C., March 31, 1948; attended the public schools of Carthage, Tenn.; graduated, St. Albans High School, Washington, D.C., 1965; B.A., Harvard University, 1969; attended Vanderbilt University School of Religion, Nashville, Tenn., 1971-1972, and the School of Law, 1974-1976; engaged in real estate development in Carthage; served in United States Army in Vietnam, 1969-1971; investigative reporter for the Nashville Tennessean, 1971-1976; livestock and tobacco farmer; elected as a Democrat to the Ninety-fifth and to the three succeeding Congresses (January 3, 1977-January 3, 1985); was not a candidate in 1984 for reelection to the House of Representatives, but was elected to the United States Senate; reelected in 1990, and served from January 3, 1985 until his resignation on January 2, 1993; elected Vice President of the United States on the Democratic ticket headed by William J. Clinton in 1992 and took the oath of office on January 20, 1993; is a resident of Carthage, Tenn.

**GORE, Christopher,** a Senator from Massachusetts; born in Boston, Mass., September 21, 1758; graduated from Harvard College in 1776; studied law; was admitted to the bar and commenced practice in Boston; member of the Massachusetts constitutional convention in 1788; member, Massachusetts house of representatives, 1788-1789, 1808; United States attorney for the district of Massachusetts, 1789-1796; commissioner to England, 1796-1803; Chargé d'Affaires at London 1803-1804; member, Massachusetts senate, 1806-1807; unsuccessful candidate for election in 1808 for Governor; elected Governor of Massachusetts in 1809, and served from May 1809 to June 1810; unsuccessful candidate for reelection in 1810, and for election in 1811; appointed and subsequently elected to the United States Senate as a Federalist to fill the vacancy caused by the resignation of James Lloyd, and served from May 5, 1813 until May 30, 1816, when he resigned; overseer of Harvard University, 1810-1815, and a fellow, 1812-1820; died in Waltham, Mass., March 1, 1827; interment in Granary Burying Ground, Boston, Mass.

**Bibliography:** Pinkney, Helen. *Christopher Gore, Federalist of Massachusetts, 1758-1827.* Waltham, Mass.: Gore Place Society, 1969.

**GORE, Thomas Pryor,** a Senator from Oklahoma; born near Embry, Webster County, Miss., December 10, 1870; by accidents lost the sight of both eyes as a boy; attended the public schools; graduated from the normal school at Walthall, Miss., in 1890; taught school in 1890 and 1891; graduated from the law department of Cumberland University, Lebanon, Tenn., in 1892; was admitted to the bar in 1892 and commenced practice in Walthall, Miss.; moved to Corsicana, Tex., in 1895; unsuccessful Populist candidate for election in 1898 to the Fifty-sixth Congress; moved to Lawton, Okla., in 1901 and continued the practice of law; member, Oklahoma Territorial council, 1903-1905; upon the admission of Oklahoma as a State into the Union was elected as a Democrat to the United States Senate for the term ending March 3, 1909; reelected in 1908 and again in 1914, and served from December 11, 1907 to March 3, 1921; unsuccessful candidate for renomination in 1920; chairman, Committee on Railroads (Sixty-second Congress), Committee on Agriculture and Forestry (Sixty-third through Sixty-fifth Congresses), Committee on Expenditures in the Department of Justice (Sixty-sixth Congress); member of the Democratic National Committee, 1912-1916; appointed by President Woodrow Wilson in 1913 as a

member of the Commission to Investigate and Study Rural Credits and Agricultural Cooperative Organizations in European Countries; again elected to the United States Senate in 1930, and served from March 4, 1931 to January 3, 1937; unsuccessful candidate for renomination in 1936; chairman, Committee on Interoceanic Canals (Seventy-third and Seventy-fourth Congresses); practiced law in Washington, D.C., until his death on March 16, 1949; interment in Rose Hill Cemetery, Oklahoma City, Okla.

**Bibliography:** *DAB*; Billington, Monroe. *Thomas P. Gore: Blind Senator From Oklahoma.* Lawrence: University of Kansas Press, 1967.

**GORHAM, Benjamin** (son of Nathaniel Gorham), a Representative from Massachusetts; born in Charlestown, Mass., February 13, 1775; pursued preparatory studies; was graduated from Harvard University in 1795; studied law; was admitted to the bar and commenced practice in Boston, Mass.; member of the Massachusetts house of representatives 1814-1818; served in the Massachusetts senate from May 26, 1819, to January 10, 1821, when he resigned; elected to the Sixteenth Congress to fill the vacancy caused by the resignation of Jonathan Mason; reelected to the Seventeenth Congress and served from November 6, 1820, to March 3, 1823; again a member of the Massachusetts senate for one term beginning May 28, 1823; elected to the Twentieth Congress to fill the vacancy caused by the resignation of Daniel Webster; reelected to the Twenty-first Congress and served from July 23, 1827, to March 3, 1831; elected as an Anti-Jacksonian to the Twenty-third Congress (March 4, 1833-March 3, 1835); again a member of the Massachusetts house of representatives in 1841; resumed the practice of law; died in Boston, Mass., September 27, 1855; interment in the old burial ground of Phipps Street Cemetery, Charlestown, Mass.

**GORHAM, Nathaniel** (father of Benjamin Gorham), a Delegate from Massachusetts; born in Charlestown, Mass., May 27, 1738; attended the public schools; engaged in mercantile pursuits; member of the provincial legislature 1771-1775; delegate to the Provincial Congress in 1774 and 1775; member of the board of war 1778-1781; delegate to the Massachusetts constitutional convention in 1779; served in the Massachusetts senate in 1780 and 1781; member of the Continental Congress in 1782, 1783, 1786, 1787, and 1789, and was its president from June 6, 1786, to February 2, 1787; delegate to the Federal Convention at Philadelphia in 1787; delegate to the Massachusetts constitutional convention which ratified the Federal Constitution in 1788; judge of the court of common pleas from July 1, 1785, until his resignation on May 31, 1796; interested in the purchase and settlement of lands in the Genesee Valley, N.Y.; died in Charlestown, Mass., June 11, 1796; interment in Phipps Street Cemetery.

**Bibliography:** *DAB*.

**GORMAN, Arthur Pue,** a Senator from Maryland; born in Woodstock, Howard County, Md., March 11, 1839; attended the public schools; appointed a page in the House of Representatives in 1852; transferred to the Senate through the influence of Stephen A. Douglas, who made him his private secretary, and subsequently served the Senate as page, messenger, assistant doorkeeper, assistant postmaster, and finally postmaster; removed from his Senate office in September 1866; immediately appointed collector of internal revenue for the fifth district of Maryland, and served until 1869; director and later president of the Chesapeake and Ohio Canal Company; member, Maryland State house of delegates, 1869-1875, serving as speaker for one session; member, State senate, 1875-1881; elected as a Democrat to the United States Senate in 1880; reelected in 1886 and 1892, and served from March 4, 1881 to March 3, 1899; unsuccessful candidate for reelection; Democratic caucus chairman 1889-1893, 1895-1898; chairman, Committee on Printing (Fifty-third Congress), Committee on Private Land Claims (Fifty-fifth Congress); was again elected to the

United States Senate in 1902, and served from March 4, 1903 until his death in Washington, D.C., June 4, 1906; Democratic caucus chairman 1903-1906; interment in Oak Hill Cemetery.

**Bibliography:** *DAB*; Lambert, John. *Arthur Pue Gorman*. Baton Rouge: Louisiana State University Press, 1953; Sanderlin, Walter S. "Arthur P. Gorman and the Chesapeake and Ohio Canal: An Episode in the Rise of a Political Boss." *Journal of Southern History* 13 (August 1947): 323-337.

**GORMAN, George Edmund,** a Representative from Illinois; born in Chicago, Ill., April 13, 1873; attended the public schools of his native city; was graduated in law from Georgetown University at Washington, D.C., in 1895; was admitted to the bar in 1895 and commenced the practice of law in Chicago the following year; assistant prosecuting attorney of Chicago 1897-1900; elected as a Democrat to the Sixty-third Congress (March 4, 1913-March 3, 1915); declined to be a candidate for reelection in 1914; resumed the practice of law in Chicago; assistant State's attorney 1920-1928; served as master in chancery of the circuit court from 1930 until his death in Chicago January 13, 1935; interment in Holy Sepulchre Cemetery.

**GORMAN, James Sedgwick,** a Representative from Michigan; born in Lyndon Township, near Chelsea, Washtenaw County, Mich., December 28, 1850; attended the common schools and the Union School of Chelsea, and was graduated from the law department of the University of Michigan at Ann Arbor in 1876; was admitted to the bar and commenced practice in Jackson, Mich.; assistant prosecuting attorney of Jackson County for two years; moved to Dexter, Mich., in 1879; member of the Michigan State house of representatives in 1880; served in the State senate in 1886 and 1888; elected as a Democrat to the Fifty-second and Fifty-third Congresses (March 4, 1891-March 3, 1895); was not a candidate for renomination in 1894 to the Fifty-fourth Congress; engaged in farming near Chelsea, Mich., and resumed the practice of law; died in Detroit, Mich., May 27, 1923; interment in Mount Olivet Cemetery, Chelsea, Mich.

**GORMAN, John Jerome,** a Representative from Illinois; born in Minneapolis, Minn., June 2, 1883; attended the common schools and the Bryant and Stratton Business College at Chicago, Ill.; clerk and letter carrier in the Chicago city post office 1902-1918; studied law at Loyola University in Chicago and was graduated in 1914; was admitted to the bar in 1914 and commenced practice in Chicago; delegate to the State constitutional convention in 1920; elected as a Republican to the Sixty-seventh Congress (March 4, 1921-March 3, 1923); unsuccessful candidate for reelection; resumed the practice of law at Chicago; elected to the Sixty-ninth Congress (March 4, 1925-March 3, 1927); unsuccessful candidate for reelection; resumed the practice of law in Chicago, where he died February 24, 1949; interment in All Saints Cemetery.

**GORMAN, Willis Arnold,** a Representative from Indiana; born near Flemingsburg, Ky., January 12, 1816; pursued an academic course; moved to Bloomington, Ind., in 1835; was graduated from the law department of the Indiana University at Bloomington in 1845; was admitted to the bar the same year and commenced practice in Bloomington; clerk of the State senate in 1837 and 1838; member of Indiana house of representatives, 1841-1844; major and colonel of Indiana Volunteers in the Mexican War; elected as a Democrat to the Thirty-first and Thirty-second Congresses (March 4, 1849-March 3, 1853); was not a candidate for renomination in 1852 to the Thirty-third Congress; moved to Minnesota in 1853; Territorial Governor of Minnesota 1853-1857; delegate to the constitutional convention of Minnesota in 1857; practiced law in St. Paul, Minn., 1857-1861; member of the State house of representatives in 1858; entered the Union Army in 1861 and was colonel of the First Regiment, Minnesota Volunteer Infantry; was mustered out as a brigadier general in 1864; resumed the practice of law; prosecuting

attorney of St. Paul, 1869-1875; died in St. Paul, Minn., May 20, 1876; interment in Oakland Cemetery.

**Bibliography:** *DAB*.

**GORSKI, Chester Charles,** a Representative from New York; born in Buffalo, Erie County, N.Y., June 22, 1906; attended Sts. Peter and Paul Parochial School and Technical High School; member of the Erie County Board of Supervisors 1941-1945, serving as minority leader 1942-1945; member of the Buffalo Common Council 1946-1948, serving as minority leader 1946-1947 and majority leader in 1948; delegate to Democratic National Conventions in 1948, 1952, 1956, and 1968; elected as a Democrat to the Eighty-first Congress (January 3, 1949-January 3, 1951); unsuccessful candidate for reelection in 1950 to the Eighty-second Congress and for election in 1952 to the Eighty-third Congress; worked for United States Department of Commerce, 1951-1952; again elected to Buffalo Common Council and served from January 1, 1954, to February 1, 1956, and was majority leader; appointed to the New York State Building Code Commission on February 1, 1956, and served until April 1, 1959; elected president of the Buffalo Common Council January 1, 1960, and reelected to six succeeding terms, and served in that capacity until his resignation March 24, 1974; resided in Buffalo, N.Y., where he died April 25, 1975; interment in St. Stanislaus Cemetery, Cheektowaga, N.Y.

**GORSKI, Martin,** a Representative from Illinois; born in Poland, October 30, 1886; immigrated in 1889 to the United States with his parents, who settled in Chicago, Ill.; attended the public and high schools; was graduated from business college and from Chicago (Ill.) Law School in 1917; was admitted to the bar in 1917 and commenced practice in Chicago, Ill.; assistant State's attorney 1918-1920; master in chancery of the superior court of Cook County, Ill., 1929-1942; elected as a Democrat to the Seventy-eighth, Seventy-ninth, and Eightieth Congresses and served from January 3, 1943, until his death; had been reelected to the Eighty-first Congress; died in Chicago, Ill., December 4, 1949; interment in Resurrection Cemetery (Village of Justice).

**GORTON, Thomas Slade, III (Slade),** a Senator from Washington; born in Chicago, Ill., January 8, 1928; attended public schools in Evanston, Ill. graduated in 1945; A.B., Dartmouth College, Hanover, N.H., 1950; LL.B., Columbia University Law School, New York City, 1953; served in the United States Army, private, 1946-1947, United States Air Force, lieutenant, 1953-1956, United States Air Force Reserve, colonel, 1956-1980; admitted to the Washington State bar in 1953 and commenced practice in Seattle; served in the Washington State house of representatives, 1959-1969, majority leader 1967-1969; Washington State attorney general, 1969-1981; member, President's Consumer Advisory Council, 1975-1977; member, Washington State Law and Justice Commission, 1969-1980; member, State Criminal Justice Training Commission, 1969-1980; elected as a Republican to the United States Senate in 1980, and served from January 3, 1981, to January 3, 1987; unsuccessful candidate for reelection in 1986; resumed the practice of law; elected to the United States Senate in 1988 for the term commencing January 3, 1989; reelected in 1994 for the term ending January 3, 2001; is a resident of Seattle, Wash.

**GOSS, Edward Wheeler,** a Representative from Connecticut; born in Waterbury, Conn., April 27, 1893; attended the public schools and was graduated from Hill School, Pottstown, Pa.; entered the military service September 6, 1918, was assigned to the Fortieth Company, Tenth Battalion, One Hundred and Sixty-sixth Depot Brigade, and served until his discharge as a sergeant on December 4, 1918; engaged in the manufacture of brass 1912-1930; delegate to the Republican National Conventions in 1924, 1928, and 1932; served in the State senate 1926-1928; elected as a Republican to the Seventy-first Congress to fill the vacancy caused by the death of James P. Glynn and at the same time was elected to the

Seventy-second Congress; reelected to the Seventy-third Congress and served from November 4, 1930, to January 3, 1935; unsuccessful for reelection in 1934 to the Seventy-fourth Congress; statistical and research work in Washington, D.C., 1935-1939; enlisted in the United States Coast Guard Reserve, May 25, 1942, as chief bosun mate, promoted to lieutenant, and served until discharged February 15, 1948; distributor for Investors Diversified Services, Inc., of Minneapolis, Minn., 1948-1951; died in Miami, Fla., December 27, 1972; cremated; ashes interred in Riverside Cemetery, Waterbury, Conn.

**GOSS, James Hamilton,** a Representative from South Carolina; born in Union, Union County, S.C., August 9, 1820; attended the common schools and the Union Male Academy; engaged in mercantile pursuits; served with the South Carolina Militia during the Civil War; delegate to the State constitutional convention in 1867; upon the readmission of the State of South Carolina to representation was elected as a Republican to the Fortieth Congress and served from July 18, 1868, to March 3, 1869; was not a candidate for renomination in 1868; member of the board of commissioners of Union County 1871-1874; appointed postmaster of Union August 12, 1875, and served until September 23, 1884; died in Union, S.C., October 31, 1886; interment in the Presbyterian Cemetery.

**GOSS, Porter J.,** a Representative from Florida; born in Waterbury, New Haven County, Conn., November 26, 1938; attended Fessenden School, West Newton, Mass.; graduated, Hotchkiss School, Lakeville, Conn., 1956; B.A., Yale University, 1960; entered active duty, United States Army in 1960; released as a lieutenant in 1962; clandestine services officer, Central Intelligence Agency, 1962-1972; businessman; council, then mayor, Sanibel, Fla., 1974-1982; commissioner, Lee County, Fla., 1983-1988, and chair, 1985-1986; elected as a Republican to the One Hundred First and to the three succeeding Congresses (January 3, 1989-January 3, 1997); is a resident of Sanibel, Fla.

**GOSSETT, Charles Clinton,** a Senator from Idaho; born in Pricetown, Highland County, Ohio, September 2, 1888; attended the public schools; moved to Cunningham, Wash., in 1907, to Ontario, Oreg., in 1910, and to Nampa, Canyon County, Idaho, in 1922 and engaged in agriculture, livestock, feed, and shipping businesses; member, Idaho State house of representatives, 1933-1937; lieutenant governor, 1937-1939, and 1941-1943; elected Governor of Idaho in 1944, and served from January 1, 1945 until his resignation on November 17, 1945; appointed as a Democrat to the United States Senate to fill the vacancy caused by the death of John Thomas, and served from November 17, 1945 to January 3, 1947; unsuccessful candidate for nomination to fill the vacancy in 1946; resumed his former business pursuits; died in Boise, Idaho, on September 20, 1974; interment in Kohlerlawn Cemetery, Nampa, Idaho.

**GOSSETT, Ed Lee,** a Representative from Texas; born in a sawmill camp known as Yellow Pine, near Many, Sabine Parish, La., January 27, 1902; moved to Texas in 1908 with his parents, who settled on a farm near Henrietta, Clay County; attended the rural schools of Clay and Garza Counties, Tex.; University of Texas at Austin, A.B., 1924 and the law school of the same university, LL.B., 1927; was admitted to the bar the latter year and commenced practice in Vernon, Tex.; moved to Wichita Falls, Tex., in 1937 and continued the practice of law; served as district attorney of the forty-sixth judicial district 1933-1937; elected as a Democrat to the Seventy-sixth and to the six succeeding Congresses and served from January 3, 1939, until his resignation July 31, 1951; chairman, Committee on Elections No. 2 (Seventy-seventh through Seventy-ninth Congresses); resumed the practice of law and was general attorney for the Texas Southwestern Bell Telephone Co.; appointed judge of Criminal District Court, Dallas, Tex., by Governor John B. Connally in 1968; died November 9, 1990.

**GOTT, Daniel,** a Representative from New York; born in Hebron, near New London, Conn., July 10, 1794; attended the public schools; at the age of sixteen taught school; moved to Pompey, N.Y., in 1817; studied law; was admitted to the bar in 1819 and commenced practice in Pompey, N.Y.; elected as a Whig to the Thirtieth and Thirty-first Congresses (March 4, 1847-March 3, 1851); moved to Syracuse, N.Y., in 1853 and resumed the practice of his profession; died in Syracuse, N.Y., July 6, 1864; interment in Pompey Hill Cemetery, Pompey, N.Y.

**GOULD, Arthur Robinson,** a Senator from Maine; born in East Corinth, Penobscot County, Maine, March 16, 1857; attended the common schools and East Corinth Academy; moved to Presque Isle, Maine, in 1887; engaged in the lumber business and built power plants and an electric railroad; president of the Aroostook Valley Railroad Co. 1902-1946; member, State senate 1921-1922; elected on November 29, 1926, as a Republican to the United States Senate to fill the vacancy caused by the death of Bert M. Fernald and served from November 30, 1926, to March 3, 1931; was not a candidate for renomination in 1930; chairman, Committee on Immigration (Seventy-first Congress); engaged in the railroad and lumber businesses; died in Presque Isle, Maine, July 24, 1946; interment in Mount Hope Cemetery, Bangor, Maine.

**GOULD, Herman Day,** a Representative from New York; born in Sharon, Litchfield County, Conn., January 16, 1799; pursued an academic course; engaged in mercantile pursuits; president of the Delhi National Bank 1839-1849; unsuccessful candidate for election in 1840 to the Twenty-seventh Congress and in 1844 to the Twenty-ninth Congress; elected as a Whig to the Thirty-first Congress (March 4, 1849-March 3, 1851); was not a candidate for renomination in 1850; resumed business interests in Delhi, N.Y., and died there January 26, 1852; interment in Woodland Cemetery.

**GOULD, Norman Judd** (grandson of Norman Buel Judd), a Representative from New York; born at Seneca Falls, Seneca County, N.Y., March 15, 1877; attended school at Seneca Falls, N.Y., and at Lawrenceville, N.J.; was graduated from Cornell University in 1899; specialized in mechanical engineering; engaged in the manufacture of pumps; delegate to the Republican National Conventions in 1908 and 1916; chairman of the Seneca County Republican committee 1912-1923; member of the New York State committee 1914-1922; elected as a Republican to the Sixty-fourth Congress to fill the vacancy caused by the death of Sereno E. Payne; reelected to the Sixty-fifth, Sixty-sixth, and Sixty-seventh Congresses and served from November 2, 1915, to March 3, 1923; declined to be a candidate for renomination in 1922; resumed his former manufacturing pursuits; died in Geneva, N.Y., August 20, 1964; interment in Restvale Cemetery, Seneca Falls, N.Y.

**GOULD, Samuel Wadsworth,** a Representative from Maine; born in Porter, Oxford County, Maine, January 1, 1852; moved with his parents to Hiram, Maine; attended the public schools and North Parsonsfield Seminary; was graduated from the University of Maine at Orono in 1877; studied law; was admitted to the bar and commenced practice in Skowhegan, Maine in 1879; postmaster of Skowhegan 1896-1900; attended all Democratic State conventions for more than forty years; secretary of the Democratic State committee 1882-1890; delegate to the Democratic National Conventions of 1900, 1908, and 1912; unsuccessful candidate for Governor of Maine in 1902, and for election in 1908 to the Sixty-first Congress; elected as a Democrat to the Sixty-second Congress (March 4, 1911-March 3, 1913); unsuccessful candidate for reelection in 1912 to the Sixty-third Congress; resumed the practice of law in Skowhegan, Maine; interested in various business enterprises; president of the board of trustees of the University of Maine; died in Skowhegan, Maine, December 19, 1935; interment in Southside Cemetery.

**GOULDEN, Joseph Aloysius,** a Representative from New York; born in Littlestown, Adams County, Pa., August 1, 1844; attended the common schools; served in the Marine Corps in 1864 and 1865; member of the board of managers at the State reformatory, Morganza, Pa.; moved to New York City; commissioner and trustee of public schools for ten years; member of board of trustees of the soldiers' home, Bath, N.Y.; secretary and member of the New York City commission that erected the soldiers' and sailors' monument on Riverside Drive; elected as a Democrat to the Fifty-eighth and to the three succeeding Congresses (March 4, 1903-March 3, 1911); declined to be a candidate for reelection; engaged in the insurance business in New York City; elected to the Sixty-third and Sixty-fourth Congresses and served from March 4, 1913, until his death in Philadelphia, Pa., May 3, 1915; interment in St. Joseph's Cemetery, Taneytown, Md.

**GOURDIN, Theodore,** a Representative from South Carolina; born near Kingstree, Williamsburg County, S.C., March 20, 1764; was educated in Charleston, S.C., and in Europe; engaged in planting; elected as a Republican to the Thirteenth Congress (March 4, 1813-March 3, 1815); resumed agricultural pursuits; died in Pineville, S.C., January 17, 1826; interment in Episcopal Cemetery, St. Stephen, S.C.

**GOVAN, Andrew Robison,** a Representative from South Carolina; born in Orange Parish, Orangeburg District, S.C., January 13, 1794; pursued classical studies at a private school in Willington, S.C., and was graduated from South Carolina College at Columbia in 1813; member of the State house of representatives 1820-1821; elected to the Seventeenth Congress to fill the vacancy caused by the death of James Overstreet; reelected to the Eighteenth and Nineteenth Congresses and served from December 4, 1822, to March 3, 1827; moved to Mississippi in 1828 and devoted the remainder of his life to planting; died in Marshall County, Miss., June 27, 1841; interment in the family cemetery on the estate, "Snowdown" plantation, Marshall County, Miss.

**GOVE, Samuel Francis,** a Representative from Georgia; born in Weymouth, Norfolk County, Mass., March 9, 1822; attended the common schools; moved to Georgia in 1835 with his parents, who settled in Twiggs County; engaged in mercantile and agricultural pursuits; was also a missionary; upon the readmission of the State of Georgia to representation was elected as a Republican to the Fortieth Congress, and served from June 25, 1868 to March 3, 1869; presented credentials as a Member-elect to the Forty-first Congress, but was not permitted to qualify; ordained as a Baptist minister in 1877, and was a traveling missionary from 1879 until his death in St. Augustine, Fla., December 3, 1900; interment in Rose Hill Cemetery, Macon, Ga.

**GRABOWSKI, Bernard Francis,** a Representative from Connecticut; born in New Haven, Conn., June 11, 1923; attended St. Stanislaus Parochial School and Bristol High School; B.S., University of Connecticut, 1949; J.D., University of Connecticut School of Law, 1952; served three years in the Infantry, United States Army, 1943-1946; admitted to the bar in 1953 and began the practice of law in Bristol, Conn.; member of Bristol Town Committee eight years; city councilman, 1953-1955; judge of city court, 1955-1960; coordinator of redevelopment, city of Bristol, 1957-1959; chief prosecutor, circuit court, 1960-1962; elected as a Democrat to the Eighty-eighth and Eighty-ninth Congresses (January 3, 1963-January 3, 1967); unsuccessful candidate for reelection in 1966 to the Ninetieth Congress; resumed the practice of law; is a resident of Bristol, Conn.

**GRADISON, Willis David, Jr.,** a Representative from Ohio; born in Cincinnati, Hamilton County, Ohio, December 28, 1928; attended the elementary and secondary schools in Cincinnati; B.A., Yale University, 1949; M.B.A., Harvard Graduate School of Business Administration, 1951; D.C.S., Harvard University, 1954; investment broker; Assistant to the Under Secretary of the United States Treasury, 1953-1955; Assistant to the Secretary of Health, Education, and Welfare, 1955-1957; member, Cincinnati City Council, 1961-1974; mayor of Cincinnati, 1971; elected as a Republican to the Ninety-fourth and to the nine succeeding Congresses and served from January 3, 1975, until his resignation on January 31, 1993; president, Health Insurance Association of America; is a resident of McLean, Va.

**GRADY, Benjamin Franklin,** a Representative from North Carolina; born near Sarecta, Duplin County, N.C., October 10, 1831; attended private and public schools and was graduated from the University of North Carolina at Chapel Hill in 1857; professor of mathematics and natural sciences in Austin College, Huntsville, Tex., 1858-1862; enlisted during the Civil War in Company K, Twenty-fifth Regiment, Texas Cavalry; promoted to orderly sergeant in Granbury's brigade, Cleburne's division; became ill with typhoid fever and remained in Peace Institute Hospital at Raleigh until the end of the war; settled in Clinton, N.C., at the close of the war and engaged in teaching in Clinton and La Grange, N.C.; in 1877 returned to Duplin County, where he continued to teach and also engaged in agricultural pursuits; superintendent of public instruction for Duplin County, 1881-1890; justice of the peace 1878-1889; elected as a Democrat to the Fifty-second and Fifty-third Congresses (March 4, 1891-March 3, 1895); retired to a farm near Turkey, Sampson County, N.C., where he again taught school for several years; returned to Clinton, N.C., and died there March 6, 1914; interment in Clinton Cemetery.

**GRAFF, Joseph Verdi,** a Representative from Illinois; born in Terre Haute, Vigo County, Ind., July 1, 1854; was graduated from the Terre Haute High School, and attended Wabash College, Crawfordsville, Ind., one year; moved to Delavan, Ill., in 1873 and engaged in mercantile pursuits; studied law; was admitted to the bar in 1879 and commenced practice in Delavan, Ill.; moved to Pekin, Ill., and continued the practice of law; elected as an inspector of the Pekin public schools in 1891 and served as president of the board of education; delegate to the Republican National Convention in 1892; elected as a Republican to the Fifty-fourth and to the seven succeeding Congresses (March 4, 1895-March 3, 1911); chairman, Committee on Claims (Fifty-sixth through Fifty-eighth Congresses); unsuccessful candidate for reelection in 1910 to the Sixty-second Congress; continued the practice of law in Peoria, Ill., where he had moved in 1899; also engaged in banking; died in Peoria, Ill., November 10, 1921; interment in Glendale Cemetery, Washington, Tazewell County, Ill.

**GRAHAM, Daniel Robert (Bob),** a Senator from Florida; born in Coral Gables, Fla., November 9, 1936; attended the public schools of Dade County, Fla.; graduated Miami High School, 1955; B.A., University of Florida, Gainesville, 1959; LL.B., Harvard University Law School, 1962; admitted to the Florida bar in 1962; builder and cattleman; member, Florida State house of representatives, 1967-1971; Florida State senator, 1971-1978; elected Governor of Florida in 1978, reelected in 1982, and served from January 2, 1979 until his resignation January 3, 1987, having been elected Senator; elected to the United States Senate as a Democrat in 1986 for the term commencing January 3, 1987; reelected in 1992 for the term ending January 3, 1999; is a resident of Miami Lakes, Fla.

**GRAHAM, Frank Porter,** a Senator from North Carolina; born in Fayetteville, Cumberland County, N.C., October 14, 1886; attended the public schools of Charlotte and the preparatory academy at Warrenton, N.C.; graduated from the University of North Carolina in 1909; studied law at the University of North Carolina and received license to practice in 1913; received a graduate degree at Columbia University, New York City, in 1916; high school English instructor in Raleigh, N.C., 1910-1912; instructor, assistant professor, and professor of history at the

University of North Carolina from 1915 until 1930; during the First World War enlisted as a private in the United States Marine Corps in June 1917 and was discharged in July 1919 as a first lieutenant; returned to the University of North Carolina and served as its president from 1930 until 1949; served on the Consumers Board of National Recovery Administration, the National Advisory Council to the Cabinet Committee on Economic Security, the President's Committee on Education, the Industries Committee of American Railroads, the National Defense Mediation Board, the National War Labor Board, the Maritime War Emergency Board, and the Good Offices Committee of the Security Council of the United Nations on Indonesia; adviser to the Secretary of State on Indonesian Affairs in 1948; appointed as a Democrat on March 29, 1949, to the United States Senate to fill the vacancy caused by the death of J. Melville Broughton and served from March 29, 1949, to November 26, 1950; unsuccessful candidate for the nomination in 1950 to fill the vacancy; United Nations mediator and United Nations representative to India and Pakistan in the Kashmir dispute; chairman of the North Carolina Tercentenary Celebration Commission, 1963; retired from the United Nations in 1967 because of ill health and returned to Chapel Hill, N.C., where he died on February 16, 1972; interment in Old Chapel Hill Cemetery.

**Bibliography:** Ashby, Warren. *Frank Porter Graham: A Southern Liberal*. Winston-Salem, N.C.: J.F. Blair, 1980; Pleasants, Julian M., and Augustus M. Burns III. *Frank Porter Graham and the 1950 Senate Race in North Carolina*. Chapel Hill: University of North Carolina Press, 1990.

**GRAHAM, George Scott,** a Representative from Pennsylvania; born in Philadelphia, Pa., September 13, 1850; attended the public schools, and was privately tutored; was graduated from the law department of the University of Pennsylvania at Philadelphia in 1870; was admitted to the bar in 1871 and commenced practice in Philadelphia; member of the select council of Philadelphia 1877-1880; unsuccessful candidate for district attorney of Philadelphia County in 1877; district attorney of Philadelphia County 1880-1899; declined to be a candidate for further election and resumed the practice of law in Philadelphia and New York City; professor of criminal law and procedure in the University of Pennsylvania 1887-1898; delegate to the Republican National Conventions in 1892 and 1924; elected as a Republican to the Sixty-third and to the nine succeeding Congresses and served from March 4, 1913, until his death at his summer home in Islip, N.Y., July 4, 1931; chairman, Committee on the Judiciary (Sixty-eighth through Seventy-first Congresses); interment in Woodlawn Cemetery, New York City.

**GRAHAM, James** (brother of William Alexander Graham), a Representative from North Carolina; born in Lincoln County, N.C., January 7, 1793; pursued classical studies and was graduated from the University of North Carolina at Chapel Hill in 1814; studied law; was admitted to the bar in 1818 and commenced practice in Rutherford County; member of the State house of representatives in 1822, 1823, 1824, 1828, and 1829; elected to the Twenty-third Congress (March 4, 1833-March 3, 1835); presented credentials as a Whig Member-elect to the Twenty-fourth Congress and served from March 4, 1835, to March 29, 1836, when the seat was declared vacant; subsequently elected to the same Congress; elected as a Whig to the Twenty-fifth, Twenty-sixth, and Twenty-seventh Congresses and served from December 5, 1836, to March 3, 1843; chairman, Committee on Public Expenditures (Twenty-seventh Congress); unsuccessful candidate for reelection in 1842 to the Twenty-eighth Congress; elected as a Whig to the Twenty-ninth Congress (March 4, 1845-March 3, 1847); was not a candidate for renomination in 1846; engaged in agricultural pursuits near Rutherfordton, Rutherford County, N.C., where he died September 25, 1851.

**GRAHAM, James Harper,** a Representative from New York; born in Bovina, Delaware County, N.Y., September 18, 1812; attended the public schools; supervisor of the town of Delhi, N.Y.; chairman of the board of supervisors of Delaware County; engaged in agricultural pursuits; elected as a Republican to the Thirty-sixth Congress (March 4, 1859-March 3, 1861); was not a candidate for renomination in 1860; member of the State assembly in 1871; served in the State senate in 1872 and 1873; engaged in agricultural and mercantile pursuits; died in Delhi, N.Y., June 23, 1881; interment in Woodland Cemetery.

**GRAHAM, James McMahon,** a Representative from Illinois, born in Castleblayney, County Monaghan, Ireland, April 14 1852; immigrated with his family to the United States and settled in Sangamon County, Ill., in 1868; attended the common schools, the University of Illinois at Urbana, and Valparaiso University, Indiana; taught school for seven years; studied law; was admitted to the bar in 1885 and commenced practice in Springfield, Ill.; member of the State house of representatives in 1885 and 1886; prosecuting attorney for Sangamon County 1892-1896; member of the board of education of Springfield 1891-1894; elected as a Democrat to the Sixty-first, Sixty-second, and Sixty-third Congresses (March 4, 1909-March 3, 1915); chairman, Committee on Expenditures in the Department of the Interior (Sixty-second and Sixty-third Congresses); unsuccessful candidate for reelection in 1914 to the Sixty-fourth Congress; member of the National Conference of Commissioners on Uniform State Laws 1916-1928; member of the board of directors of Lincoln Library 1936-1945; resumed the practice of law in Springfield, Ill., where he died on October 23, 1945; interment in Calvary Cemetery.

**GRAHAM, John Hugh,** a Representative from New York; born in Belfast, Ireland, April 1, 1835; immigrated in 1836 to the United States with his parents, who settled in Brooklyn, N.Y.; attended the public schools of Brooklyn; during the Civil War recruited Company A, Fifth Regiment, Heavy Artillery, New York Volunteers, and served three years as its captain; for gallant and meritorious services at Harpers Ferry and in the Shenandoah Valley, Va., was commissioned major and brevetted lieutenant colonel; after the war engaged in the hardware business in Brooklyn, N.Y.; elected as a Democrat to the Fifty-third Congress (March 4, 1893-March 3, 1895); was not a candidate for renomination in 1894; died in Brooklyn, N.Y., on July 11, 1895; interment in Greenwood Cemetery.

**GRAHAM, Lindsey O.,** a Representative from South Carolina; born in Seneca, Oconee County, S.C., July 9, 1955; graduated, Daniel High School, Central, S.C.; B.A., University of South Carolina, 1977, and M.P.A., 1978; J.D., University of South Carolina School of Law, 1981; South Carolina Air National Guard service as major, 1989 to present; United States Air Force active duty assignments include Base Legal Officer and Area Defense Counsel, Shaw Air Force Base, Sumter, S.C., 1982-1984; chief prosecutor for United States Air Forces Europe, Rhein Main Air Force Base, Germany, 1984-1988; active duty during Operations Desert Shield and Desert Storm, 1990; practicing attorney, Oconee County, S.C., 1988 to present; assistant county attorney, Oconee County, 1988-1992; city attorney for Central, S.C., 1990-1994; member, South Carolina State house of representatives, 1992-1994; elected as a Republican to the One Hundred Fourth Congress (January 3, 1995-January 3, 1997); is a resident of Seneca, S.C.

**GRAHAM, Louis Edward,** a Representative from Pennsylvania; born in New Castle, Lawrence County, Pa., August 4, 1880; moved with his parents to Beaver, Pa., in 1893; attended preparatory school and Beaver (Pa.) High School; was graduated from Washington and Jefferson College, Washington, Pa., in 1901; served as deputy sheriff of Beaver County, Pa., 1903-1906; studied law; was admitted to the bar in 1906 and commenced practice in Beaver, Pa.; district attorney of Beaver County, 1912-1924; deputy attorney general of Pennsylvania, 1924-1927; chief legal adviser of the former sixth Federal prohibition district, 1927-1929; served as United States attorney for the western district of Pennsylvania from November 7, 1929, to September 1, 1933; special assistant to the Attorney General of the United States in the Pittsburgh, Pa., vote-fraud cases 1934-1936; elected as a Republican to the Seventy-sixth and to the seven succeeding Congresses (January 3, 1939-January 3, 1955); chairman, Joint Committee on Immigration and Nationality Policy (Eighty-third Congress); unsuccessful candidate for reelection in 1954 to the Eighty-fourth Congress; resumed the practice of law in Beaver, Pa.; died in Rochester, Pa., November 9, 1965; interment in Beaver Cemetery, Beaver, Pa.

**GRAHAM, William,** a Representative from Indiana; born at sea March 16, 1782; settled with his parents in Harrodsburg, Mercer County, Ky.; attended the public schools; moved to Vallonia, Ind., in 1811; engaged in agricultural pursuits; member of the Territorial house of representatives in 1812; delegate to the State constitutional convention in 1816; member of the State house of representatives 1816-1821 and served as speaker; served in the State senate 1821-1833; elected as a Whig to the Twenty-fifth Congress (March 4, 1837-March 3, 1839); unsuccessful candidate for reelection in 1838 to the Twenty-sixth Congress; resumed agricultural pursuits; died near Vallonia, Ind., August 17, 1858; interment in the White Church Cemetery, Vallonia, Ind.

**GRAHAM, William Alexander** (brother of James Graham), a Senator from North Carolina; born at Vesuvius Furnace, near Lincolnton, Lincoln County, N.C., September 5, 1804; pursued classical studies and graduated from the University of North Carolina at Chapel Hill in 1824; studied law; was admitted to the bar in 1825 and commenced practice in Hillsboro, N.C.; member, North Carolina State house of commons, 1833-1840, serving twice as speaker; elected as a Whig to the United States Senate to fill the vacancy caused by the resignation of Robert Strange and served from November 25, 1840, to March 3, 1843; chairman, Committee on Claims (Twenty-seventh Congress); elected Governor of North Carolina in 1844, reelected in 1846, and served from January 1, 1845 to January 1, 1849; declined the missions to Spain and Russia in 1849; appointed Secretary of the Navy in the Cabinet of President Millard Fillmore, and served from August 2, 1850 to July 25, 1852; unsuccessful Whig candidate for vice president in 1852 on the ticket with Winfield Scott; member, North Carolina State senate, 1854-1866, including service in the state Confederate Congress; elected to the United States Senate in 1866, but his credentials were not presented; member of the board of trustees of the Peabody Fund, 1867-1875; arbitrator in the boundary line dispute between Virginia and Maryland, 1873-1875; died at Saratoga Springs, N.Y., August 11, 1875; interment in the Presbyterian Church Cemetery, Hillsboro, N.C.

Bibliography: *DAB*; Graham, William. *The Papers of William Alexander Graham.* Edited by J.G. de Roulhac Hamilton, Max R. Williams, and Mary Reynolds Peacock. 8 vols. Raleigh: North Carolina Division of Archives and History, 1957-1992; Williams, Max. "William A. Graham, North Carolina Whig Party Leader." Ph.D. dissertation, University of North Carolina, 1965.

**GRAHAM, William Harrison,** a Representative from Pennsylvania; born in Allegheny (now part of Pittsburgh), Pa., August 3, 1844; attended the public schools; during the Civil War enlisted on April 5, 1861, in the Second Regiment, Virginia Infantry (Union Army), which, after a service of two years, was mounted and became the Fifth Regiment, West Virginia Cavalry; mustered out June 14, 1864; engaged in the leather business in Allegheny, Pa.; member of the Pennsylvania house of representatives 1875-1878; recorder of deeds of Allegheny County 1882-1891; engaged in banking; elected as a Republican to the Fifty-fifth Congress to fill the vacancy caused by the resignation of William A. Stone; reelected to the Fifty-sixth

and Fifty-seventh Congresses and served from November 29, 1898, to March 3, 1903; unsuccessful candidate for reelection in 1902 to the Fifty-eighth Congress; elected to the Fifty-ninth, Sixtieth, and Sixty-first Congresses (March 4, 1905-March 3, 1911); chairman, Committee on Ventilation and Acoustics (Sixtieth Congress), Committee on Expenditures in the Department of Agriculture (Sixty-first Congress); unsuccessful candidate in the Republican primaries for renomination; member of the Allegheny County Board of Viewers 1911-1923; died in Pittsburgh, Pa., March 2, 1923; interment in Highwood Cemetery.

**GRAHAM, William Johnson,** a Representative from Illinois; born near New Castle, Lawrence County, Pa., February 7, 1872; moved to Illinois with his parents, who settled near Aledo, Mercer County, in 1879; attended the public schools; was graduated from the law department of the University of Illinois at Urbana in 1893; was admitted to the bar in 1895 and commenced practice in Aledo, Ill.; prosecuting attorney of Mercer County 1901-1909; delegate to the Republican National Convention in 1912; member of the State house of representatives in 1915 and 1916; elected as a Republican to the Sixty-fifth and to the three succeeding Congresses and served from March 4, 1917, to June 7, 1924, when he resigned; chairman, Committee on Expenditures in the Department of War (Sixty-sixth Congress); appointed by President Calvin Coolidge on May 29, 1924, as presiding judge of the United States Court of Customs Appeals, Washington, D.C., and served from June 8, 1924, until his death in Washington, D.C., November 10, 1937; remains were cremated and the ashes interred in Aledo Cemetery, Aledo, Ill.

**GRAMM, William Philip (Phil),** a Representative and a Senator from Texas; born in Fort Benning, Muscogee County, Ga., July 8, 1942; attended the Muscogee County public schools; graduated, Georgia Military Academy, Atlanta, 1961; B.B.A., University of Georgia, Athens, 1964; Ph.D., economics, University of Georgia, 1967; professor of economics, Texas A&M University 1967-1978; president, Gramm and Associates, 1971-1987; author; elected in 1978 as a Democrat to the Ninety-sixth Congress; reelected as a Democrat to the two succeeding Congresses and served from January 3, 1979 until his resignation on January 5, 1983, to run for election to the Ninety-eighth Congress as a Republican; reelected as a Republican, by special election, and served from February 12, 1983 to January 3, 1985; was not a candidate in 1984 for renomination to the House of Representatives, but was elected as a Republican to the United States Senate for the term commencing January 3, 1985; reelected in 1990 for the term ending January 3, 1997; delivered keynote address at the Republican National Convention of 1992; unsuccessful candidate for the Republican presidential nomination in 1996; is a resident of College Station, Tex.

**GRAMMER, Elijah Sherman,** a Senator from Washington; born in Quincy, Hickory County, Mo., April 3, 1868; attended the common schools and Bentonville (Ark.) College; moved to Washington in 1887, where he was a logger and general manager in logging camps near Tacoma; returned to Bentonville (Ark.) College in 1892; went to Alaska in 1897 as general manager of logging camps; returned to Washington in 1901 and located in Seattle; engaged as owner-logger in many companies; served as president of the Employers' Association of Washington 1916-1917; during the First World War was appointed a major in the United States Army, assigned to the spruce-production division at Grays and Willapa Harbors 1918-1919; appointed as a Republican to the United States Senate to fill the vacancy caused by the death of Wesley L. Jones and served from November 22, 1932, to March 3, 1933; was not a candidate for election to the full term; resumed his interests in the logging business; also served as an officer of investment and railway companies; died in Seattle, Wash., on November 19, 1936; interment in Lakeview Cemetery.

**GRAMS, Rodney D.,** a Representative and a Senator from Minnesota; born in Princeton, Mille Lacs County, Minn., February 4, 1948; graduated, St. Francis High School in Anoka, Minn.; attended Brown Institute (Minneapolis, Minn.), Anoka-Ramsey Junior College (Coon Rapids, Minn.), and Carroll College (Helena, Mont.); engineering consultant, Orr-Schelen Mayeron and Associates, Minneapolis; television producer and anchor at KFBB-TV, Great Falls, Mont., WSAU-TV, Wausau, Wis., WIFR-TV, Rockford, Ill., and KMSP-TV, Minneapolis; president and chief executive officer, Sun Ridge Builders; elected as a Republican to the One Hundred Third Congress (January 3, 1993-January 3, 1995); was not a candidate for reelection in 1994 to the House of Representatives, but was elected to the United States Senate for the term ending January 3, 2001; is a resident of Anoka, Minn.

**GRANAHAN, Kathryn Elizabeth** (wife of William Thomas Granahan), a Representative from Pennsylvania; born Kathryn Elizabeth O'Hay in Easton, Northampton County, Pa., December 7, 1894; educated in Easton public schools; graduate of Easton High School and Mount St. Joseph Collegiate Institute (later Chestnut Hill College), Philadelphia, Pa.; supervisor of public assistance in the Pennsylvania Auditor General's Department, and liaison officer between that department and Department of Public Assistance, Commonwealth of Pennsylvania, 1940-1943; member of national board, Woman's Medical College of Pennsylvania; delegate to the Democratic National Convention in 1960; elected as a Democrat to the Eighty-fourth Congress, November 6, 1956, by special election to fill the vacancy caused by the death of her husband, William T. Granahan, and at the same time was elected to the Eighty-fifth Congress; reelected to the two succeeding Congresses and served from November 6, 1956, to January 3, 1963; was not a candidate for reelection in 1962 to the Eighty-eighth Congress; appointed Treasurer of the United States and served from January 9, 1963, to November 20, 1966; retired; died in Norristown, Pa., July 10, 1979; interment in Gethsemane Cemetery, Easton, Pa.

**GRANAHAN, William Thomas** (husband of Kathryn Elizabeth Granahan), a Representative from Pennsylvania; born in Philadelphia, Pa., July 26, 1895; attended parochial schools and La Salle Extension University at Chicago, Ill.; during the First World War served as a private in the Fourth Army Corps and served in the Army of Occupation in Germany in 1918 and 1919; engaged in the building business 1925-1929; member of the Pennsylvania Democratic committee 1938-1942; Pennsylvania supervisor of inheritance tax in 1940 and 1941; chief disbursing officer of the Pennsylvania treasury 1941-1944; elected as a Democrat to the Seventy-ninth Congress (January 3, 1945-January 3, 1947); unsuccessful candidate for reelection in 1946 to the Eightieth Congress; engaged in the building business; elected to the Eighty-first and to the three succeeding Congresses and served from January 3, 1949, until his death in Darby, Pa., May 25, 1956; had been renominated in the April 1956 primary election; interment in Saint Bernard Cemetery, Easton, Pa.

**GRANATA, Peter Charles,** a Representative from Illinois; born in Chicago, Ill., October 28, 1898; attended the public and high schools of his native city; was graduated from Bryant and Stratton Business College at Chicago in 1912; engaged in the coal business in 1917; chief clerk to the prosecutor of the city of Chicago 1926-1928 and chief deputy coroner 1928-1930; elected to the State house of representatives in 1930 to fill a vacancy; presented credentials as a Republican Member-elect to the Seventy-second Congress and served from March 3, 1931, to April 5, 1932, when he was succeeded by Stanley H. Kunz, who successfully contested the election; unsuccessful candidate for election in 1932 to the Seventy-third Congress; engaged in the coal and oil business in Chicago until May 1933; member of the State house of representatives 1933-1973; assistant director of finance of the State of Illinois 1941-1943; vice

president of a glass company in Chicago, Ill., 1948; was a resident of Chicago, Ill., until his death there on September 29, 1973; interment in Mount Carmel Cemetery.

**GRANDY, Frederick Lawrence,** a Representative from Iowa; born in Sioux City, Iowa, June 29, 1948; attended public schools; graduated from Phillips Exeter Academy, 1966; graduated from Harvard University, 1970; aide to Representative Wiley Mayne, 1970-1971; professional actor, 1971-1985; elected as a Republican to the One Hundredth and to the three succeeding Congresses (January 3, 1987-January 3, 1995); was not a candidate in 1994 for renomination to the One Hundred Fourth Congress, but was an unsuccessful candidate for nomination for Governor of Iowa; president and chief executive officer, Goodwill Industries International, Inc., July 1995 to present; is a resident of Bethesda, Md.

**GRANFIELD, William Joseph,** a Representative from Massachusetts; born in Springfield, Mass., December 18, 1889; attended the grammar and high schools; was graduated from Williston Academy, Easthampton, Mass., in 1910 and from the law school of the University of Notre Dame, South Bend, Ind., in 1913; member of the common council in 1915 and 1916; was admitted to the bar in 1916 and commenced practice in Springfield, Mass.; served in the Massachusetts house of representatives 1917-1919; delegate to the Massachusetts constitutional convention of 1918 and 1919; delegate to the Democratic National Convention in 1924 and 1928 and delegate at large in 1932, 1936, and 1940; elected as a Democrat to the Seventy-first Congress to fill the vacancy caused by the death of William K. Kaynor; reelected to the Seventy-second, Seventy-third, and Seventy-fourth Congresses and served from February 11, 1930, to January 3, 1937; was not a candidate for renomination in 1936; appointed for life as presiding justice of the district court, Springfield, Mass., in 1936, and served until his retirement July 27, 1949, due to illness; died in Springfield, Mass., May 28, 1959; interment in St. Michael's Cemetery.

**GRANGER, Amos Phelps** (cousin of Francis Granger), a Representative from New York; born in Suffield, Conn., June 3, 1789; attended the public schools; in 1811 moved to Manlius, N.Y., where he was president of the town for several years; served as captain in the War of 1812 at Sackets Harbor and on the Canadian border; moved to Syracuse, N.Y., in 1820 and engaged in numerous business enterprises; trustee of the city of Syracuse 1825-1830; delivered the address of welcome to General Lafayette when he visited Syracuse in 1825; delegate to the Whig National Convention in 1852; elected as a Whig to the Thirty-fourth Congress and reelected as a Republican to the Thirty-fifth Congress (March 4, 1855-March 3, 1859); was not a candidate for renomination in 1858; retired from active business pursuits; died in Syracuse, N.Y., on August 20, 1866; interment in Oakwood Cemetery.

**GRANGER, Bradley Francis,** a Representative from Michigan; born in Lowville, Lewis County, N.Y., March 12, 1825; attended the public schools; studied law; was admitted to the bar in 1847 and commenced practice in Tecumseh, Mich.; moved to Ann Arbor, Mich., and resumed practice; elected as a Republican to the Thirty-seventh Congress (March 4, 1861-March 3, 1863); engaged in the practice of law until his death in Ann Arbor, Mich., November 4, 1882; interment in Forest Hill Cemetery.

**GRANGER, Daniel Larned Davis,** a Representative from Rhode Island; born in Providence, R.I., May 30, 1852; attended the common schools; was graduated from Brown University, Providence, R.I., in 1874 and from the law department of Boston University in 1877; was admitted to the bar in 1877 and commenced practice in Providence, R.I.; reading clerk of the State house of representatives 1887-1890; treasurer of Providence from January 1890 to January 1901; mayor in 1901 and 1902; elected as a Democrat to the Fifty-eighth, Fifty-ninth, and Sixtieth Congresses and served from

March 4, 1903, until his death in Washington, D.C., February 14, 1909; interment in Swan Point Cemetery, Providence, R.I.

**GRANGER, Francis** (cousin of Amos Phelps Granger), a Representative from New York; born in Suffield, Conn., December 1, 1792; pursued classical studies and was graduated from Yale College in 1811; moved with his father to Canandaigua, N.Y. in 1814; studied law; was admitted to the bar in 1816 and commenced practice in Canandaigua, N.Y.; member of the New York State assembly, 1826-1828, and 1830-1832; unsuccessful candidate for lieutenant governor of New York in 1828; unsuccessful candidate of the National Republicans for Governor of New York in 1830 and 1832; delegate to the Anti-Masonic National Convention at Philadelphia on September 11, 1830; received seventy-seven electoral votes as the Whig and Anti-Masonic candidate for Vice President in 1836; elected as a Whig to the Twenty-fourth Congress (March 4, 1835-March 3, 1837); unsuccessful candidate for reelection in 1836 to the Twenty-fifth Congress; elected to the Twenty-sixth and Twenty-seventh Congresses, and served from March 4, 1839 to March 5, 1841, when he resigned; appointed Postmaster General in the Cabinet of President William Henry Harrison, and served from March 6 to September 18, 1841; again elected to the Twenty-seventh Congress to fill the vacancy caused by the resignation of John Greig, and served from November 27, 1841 to March 3, 1843; was not a candidate for reelection in 1842 to the Twenty-eighth Congress; member of the peace convention of 1861 held in Washington, D.C., in an effort to devise means to prevent the impending war; died in Canandaigua, N.Y., on August 31, 1868; interment in Woodlawn Cemetery.

**Bibliography:** *DAB*.

**GRANGER, Miles Tobey,** a Representative from Connecticut; born in New Marlboro, Berkshire County, Mass., August 12, 1817; moved with his parents to Canaan, Conn., in 1819; pursued common-school, academic, and collegiate studies, and was graduated from Wesleyan University, Middletown, Conn., in 1842; moved to Louisiana in 1843; studied law; was admitted to the bar of Wilkinson County, Miss., in April 1845; returned to Canaan, Conn.; was admitted to the bar in Litchfield County in October 1845 and practiced law in Canaan 1847-1867; member of the State house of representatives in 1857; served in the senate in 1866 and 1867; judge of probate court 1849-1867; judge of the superior court of Connecticut 1867-1876; elected judge of the supreme court in 1876 and served until March 1, 1887, when he resigned; elected as a Democrat to the Fiftieth Congress (March 4, 1887-March 3, 1889); was not a candidate for renomination in 1888; elected State referee in 1893 and served until his death in North Canaan, Litchfield County, Conn., October 21, 1895; interment in the Lower Cemetery.

**GRANGER, Walter Keil,** a Representative from Utah; born in St. George, Washington County, Utah, October 11, 1888; moved with his parents to Cedar City, Utah, in 1894; attended the public schools; was graduated from a branch of the University of Utah at Cedar City in 1909 and later attended the Branch Agricultural College at Cedar City, Utah; engaged in agricultural pursuits and livestock raising; member of the board of trustees of Utah State Agricultural College; Cedar City postmaster 1914-1922; served overseas as a sergeant in the Eleventh Regiment, United States Marines, in 1918 and 1919; mayor of Cedar City, Utah, 1923-1926 and 1930-1932; member of the State house of representatives 1932-1937, serving as speaker in 1935; member of the Public Service Commission of Utah 1937-1940; elected as a Democrat to the Seventy-seventh and to the five succeeding Congresses (January 3, 1941-January 3, 1953); was not a candidate for reelection in 1952 but was an unsuccessful candidate for election to the United States Senate; unsuccessful candidate for election in 1954 to the Eighty-fourth Congress; resumed his farming interests; member, Board of Appeals, United States Forest Service, Department of Agriculture 1967-1970; retired; resided in Cedar City, Utah, where he died April 21, 1978; interment in Cedar City Cemetery.

**GRANT, Abraham Phineas,** a Representative from New York; born in New Lebanon, Columbia County, N.Y., April 5, 1804; attended the public schools and was graduated from Hamilton College, Clinton, N.Y.; studied law; was admitted to the bar in 1828 and commenced practice in Oswego, N.Y.; district attorney of Oswego County in 1835; elected as a Democrat to the Twenty-fifth Congress (March 4, 1837-March 3, 1839); resumed the practice of law; died in Oswego, N.Y., December 11, 1871; interment in Riverside Cemetery.

**GRANT, George McInvale,** a Representative from Alabama; born in Louisville, Barbour County, Ala., July 11, 1897; attended the public schools; was graduated from the law department of the University of Alabama at Tuscaloosa in 1922; was admitted to the bar the same year and commenced practice at Troy, Ala.; served as a private and aviation cadet in the aviation section of the Signal Corps of the United States Army in 1918 and 1919; county solicitor of Pike County, Ala., 1927-1937; elected as a Democrat to the Seventy-fifth Congress to fill the vacancy caused by the resignation of Lister Hill; reelected to the Seventy-sixth and to the twelve succeeding Congresses and served from June 14, 1938, to January 3, 1965; unsuccessful candidate for reelection in 1964 to the Eighty-ninth Congress; resumed the practice of law; lobbyist; was a resident of Washington, D.C., until the time of his death on November 4, 1982, at sea, aboard the *Queen Elizabeth II*; interment at Arlington National Cemetery, Va.

**GRANT, James William,** a Representative from Florida; born in Lake City, Fla., February 21, 1943; attended public schools; B.A., Florida State University, 1963; engaged in graduate work at the University of Florida; served as organizing director and president of banks in north Florida; Florida State senator, 1982-1987; elected as a Democrat to the One Hundredth and One Hundred First Congresses (January 3, 1987-January 3, 1991); announced his affiliation with the Republican Party on February 21, 1989, and continued in office during the One Hundred First Congress as a Republican; unsuccessful candidate for reelection in 1990 to the One Hundred Second Congress; is a resident of Madison, Fla.

**GRANT, John Gaston,** a Representative from North Carolina; born in Edneyville Township, Henderson County, N.C., January 1, 1858; received a limited schooling; engaged in agricultural pursuits; member of the State house of representatives in 1889; declined a renomination; sheriff of Henderson County 1892-1896; refused a renomination in 1896; elected as a Republican to the Sixty-first Congress (March 4, 1909-March 3, 1911); unsuccessful candidate for reelection in 1910 to the Sixty-second Congress; resumed agricultural pursuits; died in Hendersonville, N.C., June 21, 1923; interment in Oak Dale Cemetery.

**GRANT, Robert Allen,** a Representative from Indiana; born near Bourbon, Marshall County, Ind., July 31, 1905; moved to Hamlet, Ind., in 1912 and to South Bend, Ind., in 1922; attended the public schools; A.B., University of Notre Dame, South Bend, Ind., 1928, and J.D. from its law department, 1930; was admitted to the bar in 1930 and commenced practice in South Bend; deputy prosecuting attorney of St. Joseph County, Ind., in 1935 and 1936; elected as a Republican to the Seventy-sixth and to the four succeeding Congresses (January 3, 1939-January 3, 1949); unsuccessful candidate for reelection in 1948 to the Eighty-first Congress; resumed the practice of law in South Bend, Ind.; United States district judge, northern district of Indiana, 1957 and chief judge 1961-1972, senior judge 1972 to present; served on United States Temporary Emergency Court of Appeals, 1976 to present; is a resident of Mishawaka, Ind.

**GRANTLAND, Seaton,** a Representative from Georgia; born in New Kent County, Va., on June 8, 1782; pursued an academic course; studied law; was admitted to the bar and commenced practice in Milledgeville, Ga.; elected as a Jacksonian to the Twenty-fourth Congress and reelected as a Democrat to the Twenty-fifth Congress (March 4, 1835-March 3, 1839); presidential elector on the Whig ticket in 1840; died at his home, "Woodville," near Milledgeville, Ga., October 18, 1864; interment in Milledgeville Cemetery.

**GRASSLEY, Charles Ernest,** a Representative and a Senator from Iowa; born in New Hartford, Butler County, Iowa, September 17, 1933; attended the public schools; graduated New Hartford Community High School, 1951; B.A., University of Northern Iowa, Cedar Falls, 1955; M.A., University of Northern Iowa, 1956; engaged in graduate work, University of Iowa, Iowa City, 1957-1958; engaged in agriculture; part-time university instructor; member, Iowa State house of representatives, 1959-1974; elected as a Republican to the Ninety-fourth and to the two succeeding Congresses (January 3, 1975-January 3, 1981); was not a candidate in 1980 for reelection to the House of Representatives, but was elected to the United States Senate for the term commencing January 3, 1981; reelected in 1986 and again in 1992 for the term ending January 3, 1999; is a resident of Cedar Falls, Iowa.

**GRASSO, Ella Tambussi,** a Representative from Connecticut; born in Windsor Locks, Hartford County, Conn., May 10, 1919; attended the St. Mary's School in Windsor Locks, and the Chaffee School in Windsor; B.A., Mount Holyoke College, South Hadley, Mass., 1940; M.A. Mount Holyoke College, 1942; during the Second World War served as assistant director of research for the War Manpower Commission of Connecticut; served in the Connecticut State house of representatives, 1953-1957, and became first woman to be elected floor leader, 1955; elected secretary of State of Connecticut in 1958, and reelected in 1962 and 1966; first woman chairman, Democratic State Platform Committee, 1956-1968; member of the Platform Drafting Committee at the Democratic National Convention of 1960; co-chair of the Resolutions Committee at the Democratic National Conventions of 1964 and 1968; elected as a Democrat to the Ninety-second and Ninety-third Congresses (January 3, 1971-January 3, 1975); was not a candidate for reelection in 1974 to the Ninety-fourth Congress, but was elected Governor of Connecticut; reelected in 1978, and served from January 8, 1975 until she resigned due to a physical disability, December 31, 1980; resided in Windsor Locks, Conn., until her death in Hartford, Conn., February 5, 1981; interment in St. Mary's Cemetery, Windsor Locks, Conn.

**Bibliography:** Purmont, Jon E. "Ella Grasso: As She Saw Herself." *Connecticut Review* 17 (Spring 1995): 23-29.

**GRAVEL, Maurice Robert (Mike),** a Senator from Alaska; born in Springfield, Hampden County, Mass., May 13, 1930; attended private schools; attended Assumption College, Worcester, Mass., 1949-1950, and American International College, Springfield, Mass., 1950-1951; B.S., Columbia University, 1956; served in the United States Army Counter Intelligence Corps during the Korean Conflict, 1951-1954; member, Alaska State house of representatives, 1962-1966, and was elected speaker in 1965; author; engaged in real estate development in Anchorage and Kenai; unsuccessful candidate for nomination in 1966 to the Ninetieth Congress; elected as a Democrat to the United States Senate in 1968; reelected in 1974, and served from January 3, 1969 to January 2, 1981; unsuccessful candidate for renomination in 1980; is a resident of Arlington, Va.

**GRAVELY, Joseph Jackson,** a Representative from Missouri; born near Leatherwood, Henry County, Va., September 25, 1828; attended the public schools; engaged in agricultural pursuits and taught school; studied law; was admitted to the bar and practiced; member of the State house of representatives in 1853 and 1854; moved to Missouri in 1854; delegate to the State constitutional convention in 1860; served in the State senate in 1862 and 1864; during the Civil War served in the Union Army as colonel of the Eighth Regiment, Missouri Volunteer Cavalry; elected as a Republican to the Fortieth Congress (March 4, 1867-March 3, 1869); lieutenant governor of Missouri in 1871 and 1872; died in Stockton, Cedar County, Mo., April 28, 1872; interment in Lindley Prairie Cemetery, near Bear Creek, Mo.

**GRAVES, Alexander,** a Representative from Missouri; born in Mount Carmel, Covington County, Miss., August 25, 1844; attended Centre College, Danville, Ky.; at the outbreak of the Civil War joined the Confederate Army and served under General Nathan Bedford Forrest; paroled with him at Gainesville, Ala., in May 1865; after being mustered out returned to college and was graduated from Oakland (later Alcorn) University, Mississippi, in July 1867; studied law; was graduated from the University of Virginia at Charlottesville in June 1869; was admitted to the bar and practiced law in Lexington, Mo.; city attorney in 1872; prosecuting attorney of Lafayette County, Mo., in 1874; elected as a Democrat to the Forty-eighth Congress (March 4, 1883-March 3, 1885); unsuccessful candidate for reelection in 1884 to the Forty-ninth Congress; continued the practice of law until his death in Lexington, Mo., on December 23, 1916; interment in Machpelah Cemetery.

**GRAVES, Dixie Bibb,** a Senator from Alabama; born on a plantation near Montgomery, Montgomery County, Ala., July 26, 1882; attended the public schools; civic leader; trustee of Alabama Boys' Industrial School, Birmingham, Ala.; president of the United Daughters of the Confederacy 1915-1917; active in the Women's Christian Temperance Union, the Alabama Federation of Women's Clubs, and the women's suffrage movement; appointed as a Democrat by Governor Bibb Graves, her husband, to the United States Senate to fill the vacancy caused by the resignation of Hugo L. Black and served from August 20, 1937, until her resignation January 10, 1938; was not a candidate for election to fill the vacancy; retired from public life; died in Montgomery, Ala., January 21, 1965; interment in Greenwood Cemetery.

**GRAVES, William Jordan,** a Representative from Kentucky; born in New Castle, Ky., in 1805; pursued an academic course; studied law; was admitted to the bar and practiced; member of the Kentucky house of representatives in 1834; elected as a Whig to the Twenty-fourth and to the two succeeding Congresses (March 4, 1835-March 3, 1841); engaged in a duel on the Marlboro Pike, Md., near Washington, D.C. with Representative Jonathan Cilley of Maine on February 24, 1838, in which the latter was killed; this duel prompted passage of a congressional act of February 20, 1839, prohibiting the giving or accepting, within the District of Columbia, of challenges to a duel; was not a candidate for renomination in 1840 to the Twenty-seventh Congress; again a member of the Kentucky house of representatives in 1843; died in Louisville, Ky., September 27, 1848; interment in the private burial grounds at his former residence in Henry County, Ky.

**GRAY, Edward Winthrop,** a Representative from New Jersey; born in Jersey City, N.J., August 18, 1870; attended the public schools; newspaper reporter in New York City, 1894-1896; owner and publisher of the Summit (N.J.) Herald in 1897 and 1898; city editor and managing editor of the Newark Daily Advertiser, 1898-1902; president and general manager of the Newark Daily Advertising Publishing Co., 1902-1904; secretary to Governor Edward C. Stokes, 1904-1907; appointed by Governor Franklin Murphy a commissioner to investigate tenement-house conditions in 1902; member of the board of tenement-house supervision, 1900-1908; secretary of the Republican State committee, 1908-1913; organized the Commercial Casualty Insurance Co., Newark, N.J., in 1909; elected as a Republican to the Sixty-fourth and Sixty-fifth Congresses (March 4, 1915-March 3, 1919); was not a candidate for renomination in 1918 to the House of Representatives, but was an unsuccessful candidate for election to the United States Senate; unsuccessful candidate for nomination in 1924 to the House of Representatives, and for nomination in 1928 to the United States Senate; writer, publisher, and lecturer; died in Newark, N.J., June 10, 1942; interment in Mount Pleasant Cemetery.

**GRAY, Edwin,** a Representative from Virginia; born in Southampton County, Va., July 18, 1743; educated at the College of William and Mary, Williamsburg, Va.; served in the colonial House of Burgesses from 1769 until 1775; member of the Virginia conventions in 1774, 1775, and 1776; member of the Virginia house of delegates in 1776, 1779, 1787, 1788, and 1791; served in the Virginia senate, 1777-1779; elected as a Federalist to the Sixth and to the six succeeding Congresses (March 4, 1799-March 3, 1813); died in Nansemond County, Va.

**GRAY, Finly Hutchinson,** a Representative from Indiana; born near Orange, Fayette County, Ind., July 21, 1863; attended the common schools; studied law; was admitted to the bar in 1892 and commenced practice in Connersville, Ind.; mayor of Connersville 1904-1910; elected as a Democrat to the Sixty-second, Sixty-third, and Sixty-fourth Congresses (March 4, 1911-March 3, 1917); unsuccessful candidate for reelection in 1916 to the Sixty-fifth Congress and for election in 1917 to fill the vacancy in the same Congress caused by the death of Daniel W. Comstock; resumed the practice of law and also engaged in lecturing; again elected to the Seventy-third, Seventy-fourth, and Seventy-fifth Congresses (March 4, 1933-January 3, 1939); unsuccessful candidate for reelection in 1938 to the Seventy-sixth Congress; reengaged in the practice of law in Connersville, Ind.; until his death there on May 8, 1947; interment in Dale Cemetery.

**GRAY, George,** a Senator from Delaware; born in New Castle, New Castle County, Del., May 4, 1840; attended the common schools and graduated from Princeton University in 1859; studied law with his father and attended Harvard Law School; was admitted to the bar in 1863 and commenced practice in New Castle; attorney general of Delaware 1879-1885, when he resigned, having been elected Senator; elected as a Democrat to the United States Senate to fill the vacancy caused by the resignation of Thomas F. Bayard; reelected in 1887 and 1893 and served from March 18, 1885, to March 3, 1899; unsuccessful candidate for reelection in 1899; chairman, Committee on Patents (Fifty-third Congress), Committee on Privileges and Elections (Fifty-third Congress), Committee on Revolutionary Claims (Fifty-fifth Congress); member of the Joint High Commission which met in Quebec in August 1898 to settle differences between the United States and Canada; member of the commission to arrange terms of peace between the United States and Spain 1898; appointed judge of the United States Circuit Court of Appeals for the third circuit by President William McKinley 1899-1914; chairman of the commission to investigate conditions of the 1902 coal strike in Pennsylvania; appointed by President McKinley to the Permanent Court of Arbitration at The Hague in 1900; reappointed in 1906 by President Theodore Roosevelt, in 1912 by President William Howard Taft, and in 1920 by President Woodrow Wilson; member of several commissions established to arbitrate various international disputes; member, Board of Regents of the Smithsonian Institution 1890-1925; vice president and trustee of the Carnegie Endowment for International Peace; died in Wilmington, Del., on August 7, 1925; interment in Presbyterian Cemetery, New Castle, Del.

Bibliography: *DAB*; Crosslin, Michael. "The Diplomacy of George Gray." Ph.D. dissertation, Oklahoma State University, 1980.

**GRAY, Hiram,** a Representative from New York; born in Salem, Washington County, N.Y., July 10, 1801; attended Salem Academy; was graduated from Union College in 1821; studied law; was admitted to the bar in 1823 and practiced in Elmira, N.Y.,

1825-1828; elected as a Democrat to the Twenty-fifth Congress (March 4, 1837-March 3, 1839); appointed by Governor Silas Wright circuit judge and vice chancellor of the sixth judicial district of New York in 1846; elected justice of the supreme court of New York in 1847; reelected in 1851 and served until 1860; commissioner of appeals 1870-1875; resumed the practice of law; died in Elmira, N.Y., May 6, 1890; interment in Woodlawn Cemetery.

**GRAY, John Cowper,** a Representative from Virginia; born in Southampton County, Va., in 1783; pursued an academic course; member of the Virginia house of delegates, 1804-1806, and 1821-1823; elected to the Sixteenth Congress to fill the vacancy caused by the resignation of James Johnson, and served from August 28, 1820 to March 3, 1821; unsuccessful candidate in 1820 for reelection to the Seventeenth Congress; died on May 18, 1823.

**GRAY, Joseph Anthony,** a Representative from Pennsylvania; born in Susquehanna Township (now Spangler Borough), Cambria County, Pa., February 25, 1884; attended the public schools and St. Benedict's School, Carrolltown, Pa.; was graduated from Eastman College at Poughkeepsie, N.Y., in 1905; served as a private in Company H, Fifth Infantry, United States Army, 1900-1902 and in the United States Signal Corps in 1902 and 1903; studied law; was admitted to the bar in 1910 and commenced practice in Ebensburg, Pa.; member of the Pennsylvania house of representatives in 1913 and 1914; served as president of the board of health 1916-1920; became a motion-picture exhibitor at Spangler, Pa., in 1920; school director of Spangler, Pa., 1930-1934 and councilman 1939-1943; elected as a Democrat to the Seventy-fourth and Seventy-fifth Congresses (January 3, 1935-January 3, 1939); unsuccessful candidate for reelection in 1938 to the Seventy-sixth Congress and for election in 1940 to the Seventy-seventh Congress; resumed the practice of law and also publisher of "The Conservative" a weekly newspaper; died in Spangler, Pa., May 8, 1966; interment in Holy Cross Cemetery.

**GRAY, Kenneth James,** a Representative from Illinois; born in West Frankfort, Franklin County, Ill., November 14, 1924; attended the West Frankfort and Pope County elementary schools and graduated from West Frankfort Community High School; owner of Gray Motors, West Frankfort, Ill., 1942-1954; also operated an air service at Benton, Ill., from 1948 to 1952; licensed auctioneer, airplane and helicopter pilot; during the Second World War served from January 1943 as a crew chief with the Twelfth Air Force in North Africa; served with the combat engineers of the Fifth Army in Italy; returned to the Twelfth Air Force and participated in combat over southern France and central Europe until discharged as a first sergeant in December 1945; one of the founders of the Walking Dog Foundation for the Blind; licensed auctioneer; elected as a Democrat to the Eighty-fourth and to the nine succeeding Congresses and served from January 3, 1955 until his resignation on December 31, 1974; was not a candidate for reelection in 1974 to the Ninety-fourth Congress; elected as a Democrat to the Ninety-ninth and One Hundredth Congresses (January 3, 1985-January 3, 1989); was not a candidate for reelection in 1988 to the One Hundred First Congress; is a resident of West Frankfort, Ill.

**GRAY, Oscar Lee,** a Representative from Alabama; born in Mississippi July 2, 1865; attended the common schools of Choctaw County, and was graduated from the University of Alabama at Tuscaloosa in 1885; taught school for several years; studied law; was admitted to the bar and commenced practice in March 1919 in Alabama; superintendent of education for Choctaw County; solicitor for the first judicial circuit 1904-1910; delegate to the Democratic National Convention in 1912; elected as a Democrat to the Sixty-fourth and Sixty-fifth Congresses (March 4, 1915-March 3, 1919); resumed the practice of law; elected judge of the first judicial circuit of Alabama in November 1934; died at Shreveport, La., January 2, 1936; interment in Forest Park Cemetery.

**GRAY, William Herbert, III,** a Representative from Pennsylvania; born in Baton Rouge, East Baton Rouge Parish, La., August 20, 1941; attended the public schools; graduated from Simon Gratz High School, Philadelphia, Pa., 1959; B.A., Franklin and Marshall College, Lancaster, Pa., 1963; M.Div., Drew Theological Seminary, Madison, N.J., 1966; Th.M., Princeton Theological Seminary, New Jersey, 1970; minister in Montclair, N.J., and Philadelphia, Pa., 1963 to present; taught at St. Peter's College, Jersey City, N.J., 1970-1974, Jersey City State College, 1968-1969, Rutgers University, 1971, and Montclair (N.J.) State College, 1970-1972; elected as a Democrat to the Ninety-sixth and to the six succeeding Congresses, and served from January 3, 1979 until his resignation on September 11, 1991; chairman, Committee on the Budget (Ninety-ninth and One Hundredth Congresses); majority whip (One Hundred First and One Hundred Second Congresses); president and chief executive officer, United Negro College Fund; appointed by President William J. Clinton as special adviser on Haitian affairs to the President and Secretary of State, May 8, 1994; is a resident of Philadelphia, Pa.

**GRAYSON, William** (uncle of Alexander Dalrymple Orr), a Delegate and a Senator from Virginia; born in Prince William County, Va., around 1740; attended the College of Philadelphia, now the University of Pennsylvania; pursued classical studies in England at the University of Oxford and studied law in London; returned to Virginia and practiced law in Dumfries; during the Revolutionary War was commissioned lieutenant colonel and aide-de-camp to General George Washington and promoted to colonel January 1777; commissioner of the Board of War 1780-1781; resumed the practice of law; member, Virginia house of delegates 1784-1785, 1788; member of the Continental Congress 1785-1787; delegate to the Virginia convention of 1788 for the adoption of the Federal Constitution, which he opposed; elected to the United States Senate and served from March 4, 1789, until his death in Dumfries, Va., March 12, 1790; interment on the old family estate at Belle Air, near Dumfries, Va.

**Bibliography:** *DAB*; Bristow, Weston. "William Grayson, A Study in Virginia Biography of the Eighteenth Century." *Richmond College Historical Papers* 2 (June 1917); Horrell, Joseph. "New Light on William Grayson." *Magazine of Virginia History and Biography* 92 (October 1984): 423-43.

**GRAYSON, William John,** a Representative from South Carolina; born in Beaufort, S.C., November 2, 1788; pursued classical studies, and was graduated from South Carolina College at Columbia in 1809; studied law; was admitted to the bar in 1822 and commenced practice in Beaufort, S.C.; member of the South Carolina State house of representatives, 1813-1815, and 1822-1825; served in the State senate, 1826-1831; elected commissioner in equity for Beaufort District in 1831, and resigned from the State senate; elected as a Nullifier to the Twenty-third and Twenty-fourth Congresses (March 4, 1833-March 3, 1837); collector of customs at Charleston from August 9, 1841 to March 19, 1853; retired to his plantation; was a frequent contributor to the Southern Quarterly Review; died in Newberry, S.C., October 4, 1863; interment in Magnolia Cemetery, Charleston, S.C.

**Bibliography:** Grayson, William J. *Witness to Sorrow: The Antebellum Autobiography of William J. Grayson.* Edited by Richard J. Calhoun. Columbia: University of South Carolina Press, 1990.

**GREELEY, Horace,** a Representative from New York; born in Amherst, Hillsborough County, N.H., February 3, 1811; attended the public schools; apprenticed to the art of printing in East Poultney, Vt., 1826-1830; worked as a journeyman printer in Erie, Pa., in 1831, and later in New York City; commenced the publication of the Morning Post on January 1, 1833, but it was soon discontinued; published the New Yorker from 1834 until 1841; edited the Log Cabin in 1840; founded the New York Tribune on April 10, 1841, and edited it until his death; elected as a Whig to the Thirtieth Congress to fill the vacancy caused by the unseating of David S. Jackson, and served from December 4, 1848 to March 3, 1849; was not a candidate for reelection in 1848 to the Thirty-first Congress; visited Europe during April-August 1851, and was chairman of one of the juries at the World's Fair in London; commissioner to the Paris Exposition in 1855; delegate to the Republican National Convention of 1860 from Oregon, being denied a place on the New York delegation; unsuccessful candidate in 1861 for election to the United States Senate; delegate to the New York State constitutional convention in 1867; at the close of the Civil War advocated universal amnesty, and in May 1867 offered bail for Jefferson Davis; unsuccessful Republican candidate for election in 1870 to the Forty-second Congress; nominated for President of the United States in Cincinnati on May 3, 1872 by the Liberal Republicans, and in Baltimore on July 9, 1872 by the Democrats; defeated by President Ulysses S. Grant in the election of November 5, 1872; died near Pleasantville, N.Y., on November 29, 1872; interment in Greenwood Cemetery, Brooklyn, N.Y.

**Bibliography:** *DAB*; Greeley, Horace. *Recollections of a Busy Life.* 1873. Reprint. Port Washington, N.Y.: Kennikat Press, 1971; Van Deusen, Glyndon G. *Horace Greeley, Nineteenth-Century Crusader.* Philadelphia: University of Pennsylvania Press, 1953.

**GREEN, Byram,** a Representative from New York; born in East Windsor, Berkshire County, Mass., April 15, 1786; attended the public schools and was graduated from Williams College, Williamstown, Mass., in 1808; professor in a college at Beaufort, S.C., in 1810; studied law; was admitted to the bar and practiced; judge of the circuit court of Wayne County in 1814; fought in the Battle of Sodus Point, N.Y., during the War of 1812; member of the State assembly 1816-1822; served in the State senate in 1823 and 1824; elected to the Twenty-eighth Congress (March 4, 1843-March 3, 1845); died in Sodus, N.Y., October 18, 1865; interment in the Rural Cemetery.

**GREEN, Edith Starrett,** a Representative from Oregon; born Edith Louise Starrett, January 17, 1910, in Trent, Moody County, S.Dak.; moved with her parents to Roseburg, Oreg. in 1916; attended schools in Salem, Oreg., and Willamette University, 1927-1929; received a teaching certificate from Oregon Normal School (now Western Oregon State College); was graduated from the University of Oregon, 1939; taught school in Salem, Oreg., 1930-1941; engaged in radio work, 1943-1947; state legislative chair, Oregon Congress of Parents and Teachers; director of public relations, Oregon Education Associations; Democratic candidate for secretary of State of Oregon in 1952; delegate, Democratic National Conventions, 1956, 1960, 1964, and 1968, and served as chairman of State delegation in 1960 and 1968; delegate to the Interparliamentary conference in Switzerland in 1958; delegate to the North Atlantic Treaty Organization conference in London in 1959; delegate, United Nations Educational, Scientific and Cultural Organization General Conference, 1964 and 1966; member, Presidential Commission on Status of Women; elected as a Democrat to the Eighty-fourth and to the nine succeeding Congresses, and served from January 3, 1955 until her resignation on December 31, 1975; was not a candidate for reelection in 1974 to the Ninety-fourth Congress; nominated by President Gerald R. Ford as a director of the Legal Services Corporation, but the nomination was withdrawn at her request on May 14, 1975; professor of government at Warner Pacific College; appointed to the Oregon Board of Higher Education in July 1979; was a resident of Portland, Oreg. until her death in Tualatin, Oreg. on April 21, 1987.

**Bibliography:** Rosenberg, Marie C. Barovic. "Women in Politics: A Comparative Study of Congresswomen Edith Green and Julia Butler Hansen." Ph.D. dissertation, University of Washington, 1973.

**GREEN, Frederick William,** a Representative from Ohio; born in Fredericktown (now Frederick), Md., February 18, 1816; settled in Tiffin, Ohio, in 1833; pursued an academic course; studied law; was admitted to the bar and commenced practice in Tiffin, Ohio; auditor of Seneca County for six years; elected as a Democrat to the Thirty-second and Thirty-third Congresses (March 4, 1851-March 3, 1855); was not a candidate for renomination in 1854 to the Thirty-fourth Congress; moved to Cleveland, Ohio, and served as clerk of the United States District Court for the Northern District of Ohio from 1855 until 1866; Ohio commissioner to the Philadelphia Centennial Exposition; editor of the Cleveland Plain Dealer, 1866-1874; State oil inspector in 1878 and 1879; died in Cleveland, Ohio, on June 18, 1879; interment in Woodland Cemetery.

**GREEN, Henry Dickinson,** a Representative from Pennsylvania; born in Reading, Berks County, Pa., May 3, 1857; attended the public schools, and was graduated from the Reading High School in 1872 and Yale College in 1877; studied law; was admitted to the bar in 1879 and commenced practice in Reading, Pa.; member of the Pennsylvania house of representatives 1883-1886; served in the Pennsylvania senate 1889-1896; captain of Company G, Ninth Regiment, Pennsylvania Volunteers, in the war with Spain in 1898; delegate to the Democratic National Convention of 1900; elected as a Democrat to the Fifty-sixth Congress to fill the vacancy caused by the death of Daniel Ermentrout; reelected to the Fifty-seventh Congress and served from November 7, 1899, to March 3, 1903; was not a candidate for renomination; editor of the Reading Telegram 1903-1912 and of the Reading Times 1911-1913; resumed the practice of law in Reading, Pa.; also admitted to the bar in Texas in 1920; engaged in oil operation in the midcontinent oil field; died in Reading, Pa., on December 29, 1929; interment in Arlington National Cemetery, Va.

**GREEN, Innis,** a Representative from Pennsylvania; born in Hanover Township, Pa., February 26, 1776; pursued an academic course; studied law; was admitted to the bar and practiced; appointed associate judge of Dauphin County by Governor William Findlay on August 10, 1818, and resigned October 23, 1827; elected to the Twentieth Congress and reelected as a Jacksonian to the Twenty-first Congress (March 4, 1827-March 3, 1831); reappointed associate judge of Dauphin County and served until his death in Dauphin, Pa., August 4, 1839; interment in Dauphin Cemetery.

**GREEN, Isaiah Lewis,** a Representative from Massachusetts; born in Barnstable, Barnstable County, Mass., December 28, 1761; pursued classical studies, and was graduated from Harvard University in 1781; studied law; was admitted to the bar and practiced; elected as a Republican to the Ninth and Tenth Congresses (March 4, 1805-March 3, 1809); elected to the Twelfth Congress (March 4, 1811-March 3, 1813); appointed by President James Madison collector of customs for the district of Barnstable, Mass., in 1814 and served until 1837; resumed the practice of law; died in Cambridge, Mass., on December 5, 1841; interment in the Old Cambridge Cemetery.

**GREEN, James Stephen,** a Representative and a Senator from Missouri; born near Rectortown, Fauquier County, Va., February 28, 1817; attended the common schools; moved to Alabama and then to Missouri about 1838; studied law; was admitted to the bar in 1840 and commenced practice in Monticello, Mo.; delegate to the State constitutional convention in 1845; elected as a Democrat to the Thirtieth and Thirty-first Congresses (March 4, 1847-March 3, 1851); was not a candidate for renomination in 1850 to the Thirty-second Congress; appointed Chargé d'Affaires to Colombia on May 24, 1853; appointed Minister Resident on June 29, 1854, but did not serve in this capacity; elected as a Democrat to the Thirty-fifth Congress, but did not take his seat, having been elected to the United States Senate to fill the vacancy in the term commencing March 4, 1855, and served from January 12, 1857 to March 3, 1861; chairman, Committee on Territories (Thirty-fifth and Thirty-sixth Congresses); died in St. Louis, Mo., January 19, 1870; interment in the Old Cemetery, Canton, Mo.

Bibliography: *DAB*.

**GREEN, Raymond Eugene (Gene),** a Representative from Texas; born in Houston, Tex., October 17, 1947; B.A., University of Houston, 1971; J.D., University of Houston, Bates College of Law, 1977; attorney; member, Texas State house of representatives, 1973-1985; member, Texas State senate, 1985-1993; elected as a Democrat to the One Hundred Third and One Hundred Fourth Congresses (January 3, 1993-January 3, 1997); is a resident of Houston, Tex.

**GREEN, Robert Alexis,** a Representative from Florida; born near Lake Butler, Bradford County (now Union County), Fla., February 10, 1892; attended the rural schools; commenced teaching in Liberty Public School at the age of sixteen; was graduated from the high school at Lake Butler in 1913; messenger in the State house of representatives 1913-1915; assistant chief clerk of the State house of representatives 1915-1917 and chief clerk in 1917 and 1918; University of Florida at Gainesville, B.S., 1916; studied accounting and business administration at Howard University; principal of Suwannee High School in 1916 and 1917; vice president of the Florida Educational Association in 1918; member of the State house of representatives 1918-1920, serving as speaker pro tempore in 1918; studied law at Yale University; was admitted to the bar in 1921 and commenced practice in Starke, Fla; elected judge of Bradford County, Fla., in 1921 and served until 1924, when he resigned, having been elected to Congress; elected as a Democrat to the Sixty-ninth Congress; reelected to the nine succeeding Congresses and served from March 4, 1925, until his resignation on November 25, 1944, to enter the United States Navy; chairman, Committee on Territories (Seventy-third through Seventy-eighth Congresses); was not a candidate for renomination in 1944 to the Seventy-ninth Congress, but was an unsuccessful candidate for the Florida gubernatorial nomination; served as a lieutenant commander in the United States Navy from November 25, 1944, to November 2, 1945; resumed the practice of law at Starke, Fla., and served as county prosecuting attorney and as city attorney for the city of Starke; member, Democratic Executive committee, Bradford County, and State Democratic Executive committee; died February 9, 1973, in Gainesville, Fla.; interment in New River Cemetery in Bradford County near the community of New River.

**GREEN, Robert Stockton,** a Representative from New Jersey; born in Princeton, N.J., March 25, 1831; attended the common schools, and was graduated from the College of New Jersey (now Princeton University) at Princeton in 1850; studied law; was admitted to the bar in 1853 and commenced practice in Elizabeth, N.J.; prosecutor of the borough courts in 1857; city attorney of Elizabeth, 1857-1868; delegate to the Democratic National Conventions of 1860, 1880, and 1888; surrogate of Union County, 1862-1867; member of the city council, 1863-1873; presiding judge of Union County Court of Common Pleas, 1868-1873; member of the commission to suggest amendments to the constitution of New Jersey in 1873; admitted to the bar of New York in 1874; elected as a Democrat to the Forty-ninth Congress and served from March 4, 1885, until his resignation on January 17, 1887; elected Governor of New Jersey in 1886, and served from January 18, 1887 until January 21, 1890; vice chancellor of the State 1890-1895; judge of the court of errors and appeals in 1894 and 1895; died in Elizabeth, N.J., May 7, 1895; interment in Greenwood Cemetery, Brooklyn, N.Y.

**GREEN, Sedgwick William,** a Representative from New York; born in New York City October 16, 1929; attended Hunter Model Elementary School, New York City; graduated from Horace Mann High School, Riverdale, N.Y., in 1946; A.B., Harvard College, 1950;

J.D., Harvard Law School, 1953; elected to the Harvard Law Review; admitted to the District of Columbia bar in 1953 and the New York bar in 1954 and commenced practice in New York City in 1956; served in the United States Army, 1953-1955; law secretary to Judge George T. Washington, United States Court of Appeals for the District of Columbia Circuit, 1955-1956; chief counsel, New York Joint Legislative Committee on Housing and Urban Development, 1961-1964; member of the New York State assembly, 1965-1968; regional administrator (N.Y.), United States Department of Housing and Urban Development, 1970-1977; elected as a Republican to the Ninety-fifth Congress, February 14, 1978, by special election to fill the vacancy caused by the resignation of Edward I. Koch; reelected to the seven succeeding Congresses and served from February 14, 1978, to January 3, 1993; unsuccessful candidate for reelection in 1992 to the One Hundred Third Congress; candidate in 1994 for nomination for Governor of New York until he withdrew from the race; member of the New York City Campaign finance board, and of the National Research Council; vice chair, New York City Housing Development Corporation; director, General American Investors Company; is a resident of New York City.

**GREEN, Theodore Francis** (grandnephew of Samuel Greene Arnold, great-grandnephew of Tristam Burges, great-grandson of James Burrill, Jr., great-great-grandson of Jonathan Arnold, and great-great-nephew of Lemuel Hastings Arnold), a Senator from Rhode Island; born in Providence, R.I., October 2, 1867; attended private and public schools; graduated from Brown University, Providence, R.I., in 1887; attended Harvard University Law School and the Universities of Bonn and Berlin in Germany; was admitted to the bar in 1892 and commenced practice in Providence, R.I.; instructor in Roman law at Brown University, Providence, R.I., 1894-1897; received a commission as lieutenant during the Spanish-American War; chairman of the city plan commission of Providence, 1917-1919; member, Rhode Island State house of representatives, 1907; unsuccessful candidate in 1912 and 1930 for election for Governor; unsuccessful candidate for election in 1920 to the Sixty-seventh Congress; elected Governor of Rhode Island in 1932, reelected in 1934, and served from January 3, 1933 to January 5, 1937; financially interested in numerous corporations and business enterprises and served as officer and director; elected as a Democrat to the United States Senate in 1936; reelected in 1942, 1948, and again in 1954, and served from January 3, 1937, to January 3, 1961; was not a candidate for renomination in 1960; chairman, Committee on Privileges and Elections (Seventy-seventh through Seventy-ninth Congresses), co-chairman, Joint Committee on the Library (Eighty-first and Eighty-second Congresses), chairman, Joint Committee on the Library (Eighty-fourth through Eighty-sixth Congresses), Committee on Rules and Administration (Eighty-fourth Congress), Committee on Foreign Relations (Eighty-fifth and Eighty-sixth Congresses); died in Providence, R.I., May 19, 1966; interment in Swan Point Cemetery.

Bibliography: Levine, Erwin. *Theodore Francis Green: The Rhode Island Years, 1906-1936.* Providence: Brown University Press, 1963; Levine, Erwin. *Theodore Francis Green: The Washington Years, 1937-1960.* Providence: Brown University Press, 1971.

**GREEN, Wharton Jackson** (grandson of Jesse Wharton and cousin of Matt Whitaker Ransom), a Representative from North Carolina; born in St. Marks, Wakula County, Fla., February 28, 1831; was instructed by private tutors; attended Georgetown College, Lovejoy's Academy, Raleigh, N.C., and the United States Military Academy, West Point, N.Y.; studied law at the University of Virginia at Charlottesville and at Cumberland University, Lebanon, Tenn.; was admitted to the bar in 1854 and commenced practice in Washington, D.C.; engaged in agricultural pursuits in Warren County, N.C., in 1859; during the Civil War enlisted in the Confederate service in 1861; commissioned as a lieutenant colonel, in the Second North Carolina Battalion; afterward served on

General Junius Daniel's staff; wounded and taken prisoner at the Battle of Gettysburg, July 1863; settled at "Tokay Vineyard," near Fayetteville, N.C., and became interested in viticulture; delegate to the Democratic National Conventions of 1868, 1872, 1876, and 1888; first president of the Society of Confederate Soldiers and Sailors in North Carolina; elected as a Democrat to the Forty-eighth and Forty-ninth Congresses (March 4, 1883-March 3, 1887); unsuccessful candidate for renomination in 1886 to the Fiftieth Congress; devoted his time to the cultivation of his vineyard and to literary pursuits; died at "Tokay," near Fayetteville, N.C., August 6, 1910; interment in Cross Creek Cemetery, Fayetteville, N.C.

**GREEN, William Joseph** (son of William Joseph Green, Jr.), a Representative from Pennsylvania; born in Philadelphia, Pa., June 24, 1938; attended St. Joseph's Prep School; B.A., St. Joseph's College, 1960; attended Villanova Law School; elected chairman of the Philadelphia County Executive Committee; elected as a Democrat to the Eighty-eighth Congress, April 28, 1964, by special election to fill the vacancy caused by the death of his father, William Joseph Green, Jr.; reelected to the six succeeding Congresses, and served from April 28, 1964 until January 3, 1977; was not a candidate in 1976 for reelection to the House of Representatives, but was an unsuccessful candidate for election to the United States Senate; elected mayor of Philadelphia in 1979, and served from January 7, 1980 to January 2, 1984; was not a candidate for reelection in 1983; resumed the practice of law; is a resident of Philadelphia, Pa.

Bibliography: Green, William J. *Congressman.* New York: McGraw-Hill, 1969.

**GREEN, William Joseph, Jr.** (father of William Joseph Green), a Representative from Pennsylvania; born in Philadelphia, Pa., March 5, 1910; attended the parochial schools and was graduated from St. Joseph's Preparatory School; attended St. Joseph's College, Philadelphia, Pa.; engaged in business as an insurance broker in Philadelphia, Pa., in 1937; served in the United States Army as a private in the Quartermaster Corps from March 22, 1944 to December 4, 1944; elected as a Democrat to the Seventy-ninth Congress (January 3, 1945-January 3, 1947); unsuccessful candidate for reelection in 1946 to the Eightieth Congress; elected to the Eighty-first and to the seven succeeding Congresses, and served from January 3, 1949 until his death in Philadelphia, Pa., December 21, 1963; interment in Holy Sepulchre Cemetery.

Bibliography: *DAB.*

**GREEN, William Raymond,** a Representative from Iowa; born in Colchester, New London County, Conn., November 7, 1856; attended the public schools in Malden, Ill. and Princeton (Ill.) High School; was graduated from Oberlin College at Oberlin, Ohio, in 1879; studied law; was admitted to the bar in 1882 and commenced practice in Dow City, Iowa; moved his office to Audubon, Iowa, in 1884; judge of the district court in the fifteenth judicial district of Iowa from 1894 until 1911, when he resigned; elected as a Republican to the Sixty-second Congress to fill the vacancy caused by the resignation of Walter I. Smith; reelected to the Sixty-third and to the seven succeeding Congresses, and served from June 5, 1911 until March 31, 1928, when he resigned; chairman, Committee on Ways and Means (Sixty-eighth through Seventieth Congresses); appointed a judge of the Court of Claims of the United States and served from April 1, 1928, until May 29, 1940, when he resigned, but was recalled and continued to serve until June 1942; retired from active pursuits and resided at Bellport, N.Y., until his death there on June 11, 1947; interment in Rock Creek Cemetery, Washington, D.C.

**GREEN, Willis,** a Representative from Kentucky; born in the Shenandoah Valley of Virginia; attended the public schools; settled in that part of Virginia which is now the Commonwealth of Kentucky; clerk of court of Lincoln County in 1783; served as a member of the Kentucky constitutional convention in 1792; surveyor for locating land warrants; member of the Kentucky house of representatives in 1836 and 1837; elected as a Whig to the Twenty-sixth, Twenty-seventh, and Twenty-eighth Congresses (March 4, 1839-March 3, 1845).

**GREENE, Albert Collins,** a Senator from Rhode Island; born in East Greenwich, R.I., April 15, 1792; graduated from Kent Academy; studied law; was admitted to the bar in 1812 and commenced practice in East Greenwich; member, house of representatives 1815-1825, serving as speaker 1821-1825; brigadier general and then major general of the Fourth Brigade of State Militia 1816-1823; attorney general of Rhode Island 1825-1843; member, State senate 1843-1844; elected as a Whig to the United States Senate and served from March 4, 1845, to March 3, 1851; was not a candidate for reelection; elected to the State senate in 1851 and 1852; member, State house of representatives 1857; retired from public life; died in Providence, R.I., January 8, 1863; interment in Grace Church Cemetery.

**GREENE, Enid,** a Representative from Utah. (*See* WALD-HOLTZ, Enid Greene.)

**GREENE, Frank Lester,** a Representative and a Senator from Vermont; born in St. Albans, Franklin County, Vt., February 10, 1870; attended the public schools; employed by the Central Vermont Railway Co. in various capacities from 1883 until 1891; served in the Vermont National Guard, 1888-1900, rising from private to captain; recruited an infantry company during the Spanish-American War, serving as captain; mustered out and commissioned colonel on the staff of Governor Edward C. Smith; reporter and later editor of the St. Albans Daily Messenger, 1891-1912; president of the Vermont Press Association, 1904-1905; member of the commission to prepare and propose amendments to the State constitution in 1908; elected as a Republican to the Sixty-second Congress to fill the vacancy caused by the death of David J. Foster; reelected to the Sixty-third and to the five succeeding Congresses, and served from July 30, 1912 until March 3, 1923; regent of the Smithsonian Institution, 1917-1923; elected in 1922 as a Republican to the United States Senate; reelected in 1928, and served from March 4, 1923 until his death in St. Albans, Vt., December 17, 1930; chairman, Committee on Enrolled Bills (Sixty-ninth through Seventy-first Congresses); interment in Greenwood Cemetery.

**GREENE, George Woodward,** a Representative from New York; born in Mount Hope, Orange County, N.Y., July 4, 1831; pursued classical studies and was graduated from the University of Pennsylvania at Philadelphia; taught school; studied law; was admitted to the bar in 1860 and commenced practice in Goshen, N.Y.; school commissioner for Orange County; judge of the Orange County Courts 1861-1864; presented credentials as a Democratic Member-elect to the Forty-first Congress and served from March 4, 1869, to February 17, 1870, when he was succeeded by Charles H. Van Wyck, who contested his election; member of the State assembly 1885-1888; died in New York City July 21, 1895; interment in "The Plains" Cemetery, Otisville, N.Y.

**GREENE, Ray,** a Senator from Rhode Island; born in Warwick, R.I., February 2, 1765; pursued classical studies and graduated from Yale College in 1784; studied law; was admitted to the bar and commenced practice in Providence, R.I.; attorney general of Rhode Island 1794-1797; elected as a Federalist to the United States Senate in 1797 to fill the vacancy caused by the resignation of William Bradford; reelected in 1799 and served from November 13, 1797, to March 5, 1801, when he resigned, having been nominated for a judicial position; designated a district judge of Rhode Island by President John Adams, but, through a technicality, was not appointed; died in Warwick, R.I., January 11, 1849; interment in the family burying ground on his estate at Warwick.

**GREENE, Thomas Marston,** a Delegate from Mississippi Territory; born in James City County, Va., February 26, 1758; moved with his parents to Natchez District, Mississippi Territory, in 1782; moved to Bruinsburg; engaged in planting; member of the first general assembly of the Territory in 1800; elected a Delegate to the Seventh Congress to fill the vacancy caused by the death of Narsworthy Hunter and served from December 6, 1802, to March 3, 1803; died February 7, 1813; interment on his Springfield plantation, west of Fayette, Miss.

**GREENE, William Laury,** a Representative from Nebraska; born near Ireland, Pike County, Ind., October 3, 1849; moved with his parents to Dubois County, in the same State; attended the common schools and was graduated from Ireland Academy, Indiana; taught school; studied law; was admitted to the bar in 1876 and commenced practice in Bloomington, Ind.; moved with his family to Kearney, Nebr., in 1883 and continued the practice of his profession; unsuccessful candidate for election to the United States Senate in 1893; judge of the twelfth judicial district of Nebraska 1895-1897; elected as a Populist to the Fifty-fifth and Fifty-sixth Congresses and served from March 4, 1897, until his death in Omaha, Nebr., March 11, 1899; interment in Kearney Cemetery, Kearney, Nebr.

**GREENE, William Stedman,** a Representative from Massachusetts; born in Tremont, Tazewell County, Ill., April 28, 1841; moved with his parents to Fall River, Mass., in 1844; attended the public schools; engaged in the real estate and insurance business; member of the common council 1876-1879, and served as president of that body 1877-1879; mayor of Fall River in 1880; reelected mayor in 1881, but resigned the same year; appointed postmaster of Fall River on March 22, 1881, and served until March 30, 1885; again served as mayor 1886 and 1895-1897; declined to be a candidate for reelection in 1898; general superintendent of Massachusetts prisons 1888-1893; appointed postmaster of Fall River and served from March 9, to July 1, 1898, when he resigned; elected as a Republican to the Fifty-fifth Congress to fill the vacancy caused by the death of John Simpkins; reelected to the Fifty-sixth and to the twelve succeeding Congresses and served from May 31, 1898, until his death at Fall River, Mass., September 22, 1924; chairman, Committee on Expenditures in the Department of the Navy (Fifty-eighth Congress), Committee on Merchant Marine and Fisheries (Sixtieth, Sixty-first, and Sixty-sixth through Sixty-eighth Congresses); interment in Oak Grove Cemetery.

**GREENHALGE, Frederic Thomas,** a Representative from Massachusetts; born in Clitheroe, England, July 19, 1842; immigrated with his parents to the United States in early childhood; attended the public schools of Lowell, Mass., and Harvard University, 1859-1862; taught school and studied law; during the Civil War was with the Union Army in New Bern, N.C., for five months; was admitted to the bar in Lowell, Mass., in 1865; served in the common council of Lowell in 1868 and 1869; member of the school committee, 1871-1873; mayor of Lowell in 1880 and 1881; unsuccessful candidate for election to the Massachusetts senate in 1881; delegate to the Republican National Convention of 1884; member of the Massachusetts house of representatives in 1885; unsuccessful candidate for reelection; city solicitor in 1888; practiced law in Middlesex and other counties; elected as a Republican to the Fifty-first Congress (March 4, 1889-March 3, 1891); unsuccessful candidate for reelection in 1890 to the Fifty-second Congress; elected Governor of Massachusetts in 1893, reelected in 1894 and 1895, and served from January 4, 1894 until his death in Lowell, Mass., on March 5, 1896; interment in Lowell Cemetery.

**Bibliography:** *DAB.*

**GREENLEAF, Halbert Stevens,** a Representative from New York; born in Guilford, Windham County, Vt., April 12, 1827; attended the common schools and completed an academic course; moved to Shelburne Falls, Mass., and engaged in the manufacture of locks; appointed justice of the peace in 1856; captain of Massachusetts Militia in 1857; organized the Yale & Greenleaf Lock Co.; enlisted as a private in the Union Army in August 1862; commissioned captain of Company E, Fifty-second Regiment, Massachusetts Volunteers, September 12, 1862; elected colonel of the regiment October 23, 1862; employed in a salt works near New Orleans, La., for several years; settled in Rochester, N.Y., in 1867 and resumed the manufacture of locks; elected as a Democrat to the Forty-eighth Congress (March 4, 1883-March 3, 1885); unsuccessful candidate for reelection in 1884 to the Forty-ninth Congress; elected to the Fifty-second Congress (March 4, 1891-March 3, 1893); was not a candidate for renomination in 1892; resumed his former business activities until retirement in 1896; died at his summer home in the town of Greece, near Charlotte, N.Y., on August 25, 1906; interment in Mount Hope Cemetery, Rochester, N.Y.

Bibliography: *DAB*.

**GREENMAN, Edward Whitford,** a Representative from New York; born in Berlin, Rensselaer County, N.Y., January 26, 1840; attended the common schools and De Ruyter Academy, Alfred, N.Y.; engaged in mercantile and manufacturing pursuits in Berlin, N.Y.; supervisor of Berlin 1866-1868; clerk of Rensselaer County 1868-1871; deputy county clerk for ten years; moved to Troy, N.Y., in 1874; elected as a Democrat to the Fiftieth Congress (March 4, 1887-March 3, 1889); was not a candidate for renomination in 1888; cashier of the Central National Bank of Troy, N.Y., 1888-1905; cashier of the National City Bank of Troy 1906-1908; died in Troy, N.Y., on August 3, 1908; interment in Oakwood Cemetery.

**GREENUP, Christopher,** a Representative from Kentucky; born in Westmoreland County, Va., in 1750; completed academic studies; studied law; was admitted to the bar in 1783 and commenced practice in Fayette County, Ky. (then a part of Virginia); clerk of the district court at Harrodsburg 1785-1792; served in the Revolutionary War and attained the rank of colonel; member of the Virginia house of delegates in 1785; member of the conventions at Danville, Ky., in 1785 and 1788 to consider separation from Virginia; moved to Frankfort, Ky., in 1792; upon the admission of Kentucky into the Union was elected to the Second Congress; reelected to the Third Congress and as a Republican to the Fourth Congress and served from November 9, 1792, to March 3, 1797; member of the Kentucky house of representatives in 1798; clerk of the Kentucky senate 1799-1802; appointed judge of the circuit court in 1802; Governor of Kentucky from June 1, 1804 to June 1, 1808; presidential elector on the Madison and Clinton ticket in 1808; justice of the peace in Franklin County in 1812; one of the original trustees of Transylvania University, Lexington, Ky.; died in Frankfort, Ky., April 27, 1818; interment in State Cemetery.

Bibliography: *DAB*.

**GREENWAY, Isabella Selmes** (later Mrs. Harry Orland King), a Representative from Arizona; born Isabella Selmes in Boone County, Ky., March 22, 1886; attended the public schools and Miss Chapin's School, in New York City; homesteaded near Tyrone, N.Mex., in 1910; served as chairman of the Women's Land Army of New Mexico in 1918; moved to Tucson, Ariz., in 1923; Democratic National committeewoman from Arizona; owner and operator of a cattle ranch; owner of Gilpin Air Lines, Los Angeles, Calif., 1929-1934; in 1929 established the Arizona Inn (a hotel resort) in Tucson; elected as a Democrat to the Seventy-third Congress to fill the vacancy caused by the resignation of Lewis W. Douglas; reelected to the Seventy-fourth Congress and served from October 3, 1933, to January 3, 1937; was not a candidate for renomination in 1936; member of the Mount Rushmore National Memorial Commission; retired from political activities; died in Tucson, Ariz., December 18, 1953; interment in the family cemetery on the Selmes farm in Boone County, Ky., twenty miles from Covington, Ky.

**GREENWOOD, Alfred Burton,** a Representative from Arkansas; born in Franklin County, Ga., July 11, 1811; pursued classical studies at Lawrenceville, Ga.; was graduated from the University of Georgia at Athens; studied law; was admitted to the bar in 1832 and commenced practice in Bentonville, Ark; member of the State house of representatives 1842-1845; State prosecuting attorney 1845-1851; circuit judge of Arkansas 1851-1853; elected as a Democrat to the Thirty-third, Thirty-fourth, and Thirty-fifth Congresses (March 4, 1853-March 3, 1859); chairman, Committee on Indian Affairs (Thirty-fifth Congress); Commissioner of Indian Affairs from May 13, 1859, to April 13, 1861; served in the Confederate House of Representatives 1862-1865; died in Bentonville, Ark., October 4, 1889; interment in Odd Fellows Cemetery.

**GREENWOOD, Arthur Herbert,** a Representative from Indiana; born near Plainville, Daviess County, Ind., January 31, 1880; attended the country schools of Daviess County; was graduated from the high school of Washington, Ind., from the law department of the University of Indiana at Bloomington, Ind., in 1905, and from George Washington University, Washington, D.C., in 1925; was admitted to the bar in 1905 and commenced practice in Washington, Ind.; member of the board of education 1910-1916; county attorney of Daviess County 1911-1915; prosecuting attorney for the forty-ninth judicial circuit 1916-1918; member of George Rogers Clark Memorial Commission, Vincennes, Ind.; member of the official delegation attending the inauguration of President Manuel Quezon of the Philippine Republic at Manila, P.I., in 1935; elected as a Democrat to the Sixty-eighth and to the seven succeeding Congresses (March 4, 1923-January 3, 1939); majority whip (Seventy-third Congress); unsuccessful candidate for reelection in 1938 to the Seventy-sixth Congress and for election in 1944 to the Seventy-ninth Congress; lawyer, farmer, and banker in Washington, Ind., until his retirement in 1946; resided in Bradenton, Fla., and Bethesda, Md.; died in Bethesda, Md., April 26, 1963; interment in Oak Grove Cemetery, Washington, Ind.

**GREENWOOD, Ernest,** a Representative from New York; born in Yorkshire, England, November 25, 1884; attended the public schools of Halifax, England, and the Evening Technical Institute and College; employed with engineering firms in Sheffield, England, in 1905 and 1906, and Halifax, England, 1907-1910; immigrated to the United States in 1910 and worked for the General Electric Co., Schenectady, N.Y., 1910-1914; attended City College of New York and Columbia University; teacher in the public schools of Schenectady, 1914-1916 and at Islip (N.Y.) High School, 1916-1920; member of committee on Census and Inventory of Military Resources during the First World War; supervisor, Federal Board of Vocational Education, 1920-1922; associate head master, Dwight School for Boys and New York Preparatory School for Adults, 1922-1927, headmaster, 1927-1946, and chairman of the board of trustees, 1946-1955; chairman of planning commission, Board of Education, Bay Shore, N.Y., in 1947 and 1948, and treasurer, 1947-1950; unsuccessful Republican candidate for the Suffolk County Board of Supervisors in 1949; elected as a Democrat to the Eighty-second Congress (January 3, 1951-January 3, 1953); unsuccessful candidate for reelection in 1952 to the Eighty-third Congress, and for election in 1954 to the Eighty-fourth Congress; died in Bay Shore, N.Y., June 15, 1955; interment in Oakwood Cemetery.

**GREENWOOD, James Charles,** a Representative from Pennsylvania; born in Philadelphia, Pa., May 4, 1951; B.A., Dickinson College, Carlisle, Pa., 1973; legislative assistant to Pennsylvania Representative John S. Renninger, 1972-1976; head house parent, The Woods Schools, 1974-1976; campaign coordinator, Renninger for Congress committee, 1976; caseworker, Bucks County Children and Youth Social Service Agency; member, Pennsylvania house of representatives, 1980-1986; member, Pennsylvania senate, 1986-

1993; elected as a Republican to the One Hundred Third and One Hundred Fourth Congresses (January 3, 1993–January 3, 1997); is a resident of Erwinna, Pa.

**GREEVER, Paul Ranous,** a Representative from Wyoming; born in Lansing, Leavenworth County, Kans., September 28, 1891; attended public and high schools, and was graduated from the law department of the University of Kansas at Lawrence in 1917; served as a first lieutenant in the Three Hundred and Fourteenth Trench Mortar Battery, Eighty-ninth Division, from April 1917 to March 1919; was admitted to the bar in 1917 and commenced practice in Pine Bluffs, Wyo., and in Cody, Park County, Wyo., in 1921; served as mayor of Cody 1930-1932; trustee of the University of Wyoming 1933-1934; also engaged in banking; elected as a Democrat to the Seventy-fourth and Seventy-fifth Congresses (January 3, 1935-January 3, 1939); unsuccessful candidate for reelection in 1938 to the Seventy-sixth Congress; resumed the practice of law; accidentally shot himself while cleaning a shotgun and died in Cody, Wyo., on February 16, 1943; interment in Riverside Cemetery.

**GREGG, Alexander White,** a Representative from Texas; born in Centerville, Leon County, Tex., January 31, 1855; attended the common schools of Texas, and was graduated from King College, Bristol, Tenn., in 1874; studied law at the University of Virginia at Charlottesville; was admitted to the bar in 1878 and commenced practice in Palestine, Tex.; member of the State senate 1886-1888; resumed the practice of law; elected as a Democrat to the Fifty-eighth and to the seven succeeding Congresses (March 4, 1903-March 3, 1919); chairman, Committee on War Claims (Sixty-third through Sixty-fifth Congresses); was not a candidate for renomination in 1918 to the Sixty-sixth Congress; died in Palestine, Anderson County, Tex., April 30, 1919; interment in East Hill Cemetery.

**GREGG, Andrew** (grandfather of James Xavier McLanahan), a Representative and a Senator from Pennsylvania; born in Carlisle, Cumberland County, Pa., June 10, 1755; attended the Reverend John Steel's Latin School in Carlisle and the Academy in Newark, Del.; served in the Delaware militia in the Revolution; tutor in the University of Pennsylvania at Philadelphia 1779-1783; moved to Middletown, Dauphin County, Pa., in 1783 and engaged in mercantile pursuits; moved to Penn's Valley (now in Bucks County), Pa., in 1789 and engaged in agricultural pursuits; elected to the Second and to the seven succeeding Congresses (March 4, 1791-March 3, 1807); chairman, Committee on Public Lands (Ninth Congress); elected as a Republican to the United States Senate and served from March 4, 1807, to March 3, 1813; served as President pro tempore of the Senate during the Eleventh Congress; moved to Bellefonte, Pa., in 1814 and engaged in banking; secretary of Commonwealth of Pennsylvania 1820-1823; unsuccessful candidate for Governor in 1823; died in Bellefonte, Pa., May 20, 1835; interment in Union Cemetery.

Bibliography: *DAB.*

**GREGG, Curtis Hussey,** a Representative from Pennsylvania; born in Adamsburg, Westmoreland County, Pa., August 9, 1865; attended the common schools and Greensburg (Pa.) Seminary; engaged in teaching; associate editor of the Greensburg (Pa.) Evening Press 1883-1887; studied law; was admitted to the bar in 1888, and commenced practice in Greensburg, Pa.; district attorney of Westmoreland County in 1891; member of the school board of Greensburg 1892-1896; delegate to the Pennsylvania Democratic conventions in 1892, 1894, and 1896; served as chairman of the Democratic county committee 1896-1913; unsuccessful candidate in 1900 for election to the Fifty-seventh Congress and in 1904 for election to the Pennsylvania senate; member of the council of the borough of Greensburg 1901-1905; delegate to the Democratic National Conventions of 1908, 1928, and 1932; elected as a Democrat to the Sixty-second Congress (March 4, 1911-March 3,

1913); unsuccessful candidate for renomination in 1912 to the Sixty-third Congress; reengaged in the practice of law at Greensburg, Pa., until his death there on January 18, 1933; interment in St. Clair Cemetery.

**GREGG, James Madison,** a Representative from Indiana; born in Patrick County, Va., June 26, 1806; attended the public schools; studied law; was admitted to the bar in 1830 and began practice in Danville, Ind.; county surveyor of Hendricks County 1834-1837; clerk of the circuit court 1837-1845; elected as a Democrat to the Thirty-fifth Congress (March 4, 1857-March 3, 1859); unsuccessful candidate for reelection in 1858 to the Thirty-sixth Congress; resumed the practice of law in Danville, Ind.; member of the State house of representatives in 1862; died in Danville, Ind., on June 16, 1869; interment in South Cemetery.

**GREGG, Judd Alan,** a Representative and a Senator from New Hampshire; born in Nashua, Hillsborough County, N.H., February 14, 1947; attended the public schools; graduated from Phillips Exeter Academy, Exeter, N.H., 1965; A.B., Columbia University, New York City, 1969; J.D., Boston University, Boston, Mass., 1972, and LL.M., 1975; admitted to the New Hampshire bar in 1972 and commenced practice in Nashua; delegate to the New Hampshire constitutional convention of 1974; member, Governor's executive council, 1978-1980; elected as a Republican to the Ninety-seventh and to the three succeeding Congresses and served from January 3, 1981 to January 3, 1989; was not a candidate in 1988 for renomination to the House of Representatives, but was elected Governor of New Hampshire; reelected in 1990, and served from January 4, 1989 to January 7, 1993; elected in 1992 to the United States Senate for the term ending January 2, 1999; is a resident of Greenfield, N.H.

**GREGORY, Dudley Sanford,** a Representative from New Jersey; born in Redding, Fairfield County, Conn., February 5, 1800; moved with his father to Albany, N.Y., in 1805; attended the public schools; was a member of the guard of honor to receive General Lafayette on his visit to the United States in 1824; moved to New York City in 1824, and to Jersey City in 1834; served three terms as a freeholder of Hudson County; elected the first mayor of Jersey City in 1838 and held the office for three terms; was at one time a director of sixteen different railroads; elected as a Whig to the Thirtieth Congress (March 4, 1847-March 3, 1849); declined to be a candidate for renomination in 1848 to the Thirty-first Congress; engaged in banking; died in Jersey City, N.J., December 8, 1874; interment in Greenwood Cemetery.

**GREGORY, Noble Jones,** (brother of William Voris Gregory), a Representative from Kentucky; born in Mayfield, Graves County, Ky., August 30, 1897; attended private and public schools and was graduated from Mayfield (Ky.) High School in 1915 and from Mayfield Business College; served as bookkeeper, cashier, and trust officer of the First National Bank of Mayfield, Ky., from 1917 until 1936; served as secretary-treasurer of the Mayfield Board of Education, 1923-1936; elected as a Democrat to the Seventy-fifth and to the ten succeeding Congresses (January 3, 1937-January 3, 1959); unsuccessful candidate for renomination in 1958 to the Eighty-sixth Congress; engaged in banking and general investments; died in Mayfield, Ky., September 26, 1971; interment in Maplewood Cemetery.

**GREGORY, William Voris** (brother of Noble J. Gregory), a Representative from Kentucky; born near Farmington, Graves County, Ky., October 21, 1877; attended private and public schools and was graduated from West Kentucky College, Mayfield, Ky., in 1896; taught school and served as superintendent of schools, Mayfield, 1898-1900; attended the law department of Cumberland University, Lebanon, Tenn.; was admitted to the bar in 1902 and commenced practice in Mayfield; county surveyor, 1902-1910; judge of the Graves County Court, 1913-1919; United States attorney for the western district of Kentucky, 1919-1923; member of the board of trustees of Presbyterian Theological Seminary, Louisville, Ky., 1920-1927, serving as president 1925-1927; served as vice president of the Jefferson Davis Memorial Commission; elected as a Democrat to the Seventieth and to the four succeeding Congresses, and served from March 4, 1927 until his death in Mayfield, Ky., October 10, 1936; had been renominated to the Seventy-fifth Congress, but died before the election; interment in Maplewood Cemetery.

**GREIG, John,** a Representative from New York; born in Moffat, Dumfriesshire, Scotland, August 6, 1779; attended the Edinburgh High School; immigrated to the United States in 1797; studied law; was admitted to the bar in 1804 and commenced practice in Canandaigua, N.Y.; president of the Ontario Bank 1820-1856; regent of the University of the State of New York from 1825 and vice chancellor of the same institution from 1845, serving in both capacities until his death; one of the founders of the Ontario Female Seminary; elected as a Whig to the Twenty-seventh Congress to fill the vacancy caused by the resignation of Francis Granger and served from May 21, 1841, to September 25, 1841, when he resigned; president of the Ontario Agricultural Society; died in Canandaigua, N.Y., April 9, 1858; interment in West Avenue Cemetery.

**GREIGG, Stanley Lloyd,** a Representative from Iowa; born in Ireton, Sioux County, Iowa, May 7, 1931; moved with his parents to Hawarden, Iowa, in 1938 and to Sioux City in 1941; attended the public schools; B.A., Morningside College, 1954, LL.D., 1984; M.A., Syracuse University, Maxwell Graduate School, 1982; served in the United States Navy, 1957-1959; returned to Morningside College in 1959 and served until 1964 as Dean of Men and professor of history and political science; elected to the city council of Sioux City in 1961 and was selected to be mayor by council members in January 1964; elected as a Democrat to the Eighty-ninth Congress (January 3, 1965-January 3, 1967); unsuccessful candidate for reelection in 1966 to the Ninetieth Congress; director, Post Office Department's Office of Regional Administration, 1967-1969; deputy chairman, Democratic National Committee, 1970-1972; director, Lawrence F. O'Brien Center for the Study of the Political Process, Dag Hammarskjold College, 1972; director, Office of Intergovernmental Relations, Congressional Budget Office, 1975 to present; is a resident of Bethesda, Md.

**GRENNELL, George, Jr.,** a Representative from Massachusetts; born in Greenfield, Mass., December 25, 1786; attended Deerfield Academy and was graduated from Dartmouth College, Hanover, N.H., in 1808; was admitted to the bar in 1811; prosecuting attorney for Franklin County 1820-1828; member of the Massachusetts senate 1825-1827; elected to the Twenty-first Congress; reelected as an Anti-Jacksonian to the Twenty-second and Twenty-third Congresses and as a Whig to the Twenty-fourth and Twenty-fifth Congresses (March 4, 1829-March 3, 1839); was not a candidate for renomination in 1838; trustee of Amherst College, Massachusetts, 1838-1859; judge of probate 1849-1853; clerk of Franklin County Courts 1853-1865; first president of the Troy & Greenfield Railroad; died in Greenfield, Mass., November 19, 1877; interment in Green River Cemetery.

**GRESHAM, Walter,** a Representative from Texas; born at "Woodlawn," near Newtown, King and Queen County, Va., July 22, 1841; attended Stevensville Academy and Edge Hill Academy, and was graduated from the University of Virginia at Charlottesville in 1863; served as a private in the Confederate Army during the Civil War; studied law; was admitted to the bar in 1867 and commenced practice in Galveston, Tex.; district attorney for the Galveston judicial district in 1872; member of the State house of representatives 1886-1891; elected as a Democrat to the Fifty-third Congress (March 4, 1893-March 3, 1895); unsuccessful candidate for reelection in 1894 to the Fifty-fourth Congress; resumed the practice of

law in Galveston, Tex.; died in Washington, D.C., November 6, 1920; interment in Lakeview Cemetery, Galveston, Tex.

**GREY, Benjamin Edwards** (grandson of Benjamin Edwards), a Representative from Kentucky; born at "Shiloh," near Bardstown, Nelson County, Ky.; pursued an academic course; studied law; was admitted to the bar and began practice in Hopkinsville, Ky.; member of the Kentucky house of representatives in 1838 and 1839; served in the Kentucky senate, 1847-1851; presiding officer of the senate and Acting Lieutenant Governor in 1850; elected as a Whig to the Thirty-second and Thirty-third Congresses (March 4, 1851-March 3, 1855); unsuccessful candidate for reelection in 1854 to the Thirty-fourth Congress; died in Selma, Ala.

**GRIDER, George William,** a Representative from Tennessee; born in Memphis, Shelby County, Tenn., October 1, 1912; attended the public schools; graduated from the United States Naval Academy in 1936 and served in the Navy from 1936 to 1947, when he retired as a captain because of a physical disability; during the Second World War served in the Pacific Theater, and commanded the United States submarine *Flasher*; awarded the Navy Cross, Silver Star, Bronze Star, and Presidential Unit Citation; graduated from the University of Virginia Law School in 1950; was admitted to the bar in 1950 and commenced the practice of law in Memphis; managed the mayoral campaign of Edmund Orgill in 1955; member of the city planning commission in 1956 and 1957; member of Shelby County Quarterly Court, 1959-1964; elected as a Democrat to the Eighty-ninth Congress (January 3, 1965-January 3, 1967); unsuccessful candidate for reelection in 1966 to the Ninetieth Congress; vice president and general counsel of the Carborundum Company of Niagara Falls, N.Y., 1967-1975; resumed the practice of law in Memphis; was a resident of Memphis until his death there on March 20, 1991; interment in National Cemetery.

**Bibliography:** Grider, George, and Lydel Sims. *War Fish.* Boston: Little, Brown, 1958.

**GRIDER, Henry,** a Representative from Kentucky; born in Garrard County, Ky., July 16, 1796; pursued an academic course; studied law; was admitted to the bar and commenced practice in Bowling Green, Ky.; served in the War of 1812; member of the Kentucky house of representatives in 1827 and 1831; served in the Kentucky senate, 1833-1837; elected as a Whig to the Twenty-eighth and Twenty-ninth Congresses (March 4, 1843-March 3, 1847); elected as a Unionist to the Thirty-seventh and Thirty-eighth Congresses and as a Democrat to the Thirty-ninth Congress and served from March 4, 1861, until his death in Bowling Green, Ky., September 7, 1866; interment in Old College Street Cemetery.

**GRIEST, William Walton,** a Representative from Pennsylvania; born in Christiana, Lancaster County, Pa., September 22, 1858; attended the common schools and was graduated from the Millersville State Normal School in 1876; engaged in teaching; member of the city school board of Lancaster, Pa., for twenty-four years; director and an incorporator of the Pennsylvania Public School Memorial Association; engaged in newspaper work; editor of the Inquirer, Lancaster, Pa., 1882-1888; chief clerk in the county commissioner's office, 1887-1899; member of the Pennsylvania Tax Commission; delegate to several Pennsylvania Republican conventions and to every Republican National Convention from 1896 to 1928; secretary of the Commonwealth of Pennsylvania, 1899-1903; member of the Pennsylvania sinking fund commission (to pay off the principal of the Commonwealth's debt) and of the board of pardons; president of lighting and street railway companies, 1903-1927; elected as a Republican to the Sixty-first and to the ten succeeding Congresses, and served from March 4, 1909 until his death at Mount Clemens, Mich., December 5, 1929; chairman, Committee on Post Office and Post Roads (Sixty-eighth through Seventieth Congresses); interment in Woodward Hill Cemetery, Lancaster, Pa.

**GRIFFIN, Anthony Jerome,** a Representative from New York; born in New York City April 1, 1866; attended the public schools and City College; B.S., Cooper Union, 1887; received a degree from the New York University Law School in 1892; was admitted to the bar in 1892 and commenced practice in New York City; organized and commanded Company F, Sixty-ninth Regiment, New York Volunteer Infantry, in the Spanish-American War, 1898-1899; founded and edited the Bronx Independent, 1905-1907; member of the New York State senate, 1911-1915; member of the New York State constitutional convention in 1915; elected as a Democrat to the Sixty-fifth Congress to fill the vacancy caused by the resignation of Henry Bruckner; reelected to the Sixty-sixth and to the eight succeeding Congresses, and served from March 5, 1918 until his death in New York City, January 13, 1935; interment in Arlington National Cemetery, Va.

**GRIFFIN, Charles Hudson** (great-great-grandson of Isaac Griffin), a Representative from Mississippi; born on a farm near Utica, Miss., May 9, 1926; educated at Utica High School, Hinds Junior College, and graduated from Mississippi State University in 1949; served in the United States Navy, 1944-1946, Pacific Theater, as an apprentice seaman and quartermaster, third class; assistant to Representative John Bell Williams from July 1, 1949, to January 15, 1968; elected as a Democrat to the Ninetieth Congress, by special election, March 12, 1968, to fill the vacancy caused by the resignation of John Bell Williams; reelected to the two succeeding Congresses and served from March 12, 1968, to January 3, 1973; was not a candidate for reelection in 1972 to the Ninety-third Congress; secretary of the Mississippi State senate; was a resident of Utica, Miss.; died September 10, 1989.

**GRIFFIN, Cyrus,** a Delegate from Virginia; born in Farnham, Richmond County, Va., July 16, 1748; sent to England to be educated; studied law at the University of Edinburgh and at the Temple in London; returned to Virginia; member of the Virginia house of delegates in 1777, 1778, 1786, and 1787; member of the Continental Congress 1778-1780, 1787-1788, and served as its president in 1788; president of the supreme court of admiralty; commissioner to the Creek Nation in 1789; judge of the United States District Court of Virginia from December 1789 until his death in Yorktown, Va., December 14, 1810; interment in Bruton Churchyard, Williamsburg, Va.
Bibliography: *DAB.*

**GRIFFIN, Daniel Joseph,** a Representative from New York; born in Brooklyn, N.Y., March 26, 1880; attended the parochial schools, St. Laurent College, near Montreal, Canada, and St. Peter's College, Jersey City; was graduated in law from the New York Law School; was admitted to the bar in 1902 and commenced practice in Brooklyn; commissioner of licenses for the Borough of Brooklyn, 1903-1906; head of the administration and guardianship departments of the surrogate's court of Kings County, 1906-1912; delegate to the Democratic National Convention of 1912; elected as a Democrat to the Sixty-third and to the two succeeding Congresses, and served from March 4, 1913 until his resignation on December 31, 1917; served as sheriff of Kings County in 1918 and 1919; resumed the practice of law; died in Brooklyn, N.Y., on December 11, 1926; interment in Holy Cross Cemetery.

**GRIFFIN, Isaac** (great-grandfather of Eugene McLanahan Wilson and great-great-grandfather of Charles Hudson Griffin), a Representative from Pennsylvania; born in Kent County, Del., February 27, 1756; attended the public schools; moved to Fayette County, Pa., and engaged in agricultural pursuits; commissioned a captain during the Revolutionary War; appointed justice of the peace in 1794; elected a member of the Pennsylvania house of representatives in 1807 and served four terms; elected as a Republican to the Thirteenth Congress to fill the vacancy caused by the death of John Smilie; reelected to the Fourteenth Congress and served from May 24, 1813, to March 3, 1817; unsuccessful candidate for reelection in 1816 to the Fifteenth Congress; died from the effects of a fall from a wagon, on his estate in Nicholson Township, Pa., October 12, 1827; interment on what was known as the old Woods farm, Nicholson Township, Pa.

**GRIFFIN, John King,** a Representative from South Carolina; born near Clinton, Laurens County, S.C., August 13, 1789; pursued an academic course; engaged as a planter; served in the State house of representatives 1816-1819; member of the State senate 1820-1824 and again in 1828; elected as a Nullifier to the Twenty-second through Twenty-fifth Congresses and as a Democrat to the Twenty-sixth Congress (March 4, 1831-March 3, 1841); died near Clinton, S.C., August 1, 1841; interment in Little River Church Cemetery.

**GRIFFIN, Levi Thomas,** a Representative from Michigan; born in Clinton, Oneida County, N.Y., May 23, 1837; moved with his parents to Rochester, Oakland County, Mich., in 1848; was graduated from the University of Michigan at Ann Arbor in 1857; studied law; was admitted to the bar in 1858 and commenced practice in Detroit, Mich.; entered the United States Army in August 1862 as second lieutenant, and served as first lieutenant, adjutant, captain, brigade inspector, acting assistant adjutant general of the Cavalry division, and acting assistant adjutant general of the Cavalry corps, Military Division of Mississippi, and brevetted major; at the close of the war resumed the practice of law in Detroit; Fletcher professor of law in the University of Michigan 1886-1897; unsuccessful candidate for judge of the State supreme court in 1887; elected as a Democrat to the Fifty-third Congress to fill the vacancy caused by the death of John Logan Chipman and served from December 4, 1893, to March 3, 1895; unsuccessful candidate for reelection in 1894 to the Fifty-fourth Congress; resumed the practice of his profession; pension agent in 1896 and 1897; died in Detroit, Mich., March 17, 1906; interment in Woodmere Cemetery.

**GRIFFIN, Michael,** a Representative from Wisconsin; born in County Clare, Ireland, September 9, 1842; immigrated with his parents to Canada in 1847 and to Ohio in 1851; moved to Wisconsin in 1856 and settled in Newport, Sauk County; attended the common schools of Ohio and Wisconsin; enlisted in the Union Army September 11, 1861, as a private in Company E, Twelfth Regiment, Wisconsin Volunteer Infantry, and served until the close of the war, attaining the rank of first lieutenant; moved to Kilbourn City, Wis., in 1865; studied law; was admitted to the bar in 1868 and commenced practice in Kilbourn City; cashier of the Bank of Kilbourn 1871-1876; member of the County Board of Columbia County, Wis., in 1874 and 1875; member of the State assembly in 1876; moved to Eau Claire, Wis., in 1876; city attorney of Eau Claire in 1878 and 1879; served in the State senate in 1880 and 1881; department commander of the Grand Army of the Republic in 1887 and 1888; elected as a Republican to the Fifty-third Congress to fill the vacancy caused by the death of George B. Shaw and at the same election to the Fifty-fourth Congress; reelected to the Fifty-fifth Congress and served from November 5, 1894, to March 3, 1899; was not a candidate for renomination in 1898 to the Fifty-sixth Congress; appointed chairman of the State tax commission by Governor Edward Schofield on May 28, 1899; died in Eau Claire, Wis., December 29, 1899; interment in Forest Hill Cemetery.

**GRIFFIN, Robert Paul,** a Representative and a Senator from Michigan; born in Detroit, Wayne County, Mich., November 6, 1923; attended public schools in Garden City and Dearborn, Mich.; during the Second World War enlisted in the United States Army in 1943 and spent fourteen months in Europe; A.B., B.S., Central Michigan College, Mount Pleasant, 1947; J.D., University of Michigan School of Law, 1950; was admitted to the bar in 1950 and commenced the practice of law in Traverse City, Mich.; elected as a Republican to the Eighty-fifth and to the four succeeding Congresses, and served from

January 3, 1957 until his resignation on May 10, 1966; co-sponsor of the Landrum-Griffin Act of 1959 (Labor-Management Relations Act), containing union democracy, financial reporting and anti-corruption provisions, and Taft-Hartley Act amendments closing secondary boycott "loopholes," curbing organizational and recognition picketing and giving states jurisdiction over "no man's land" labor disputes; appointed to the United States Senate, May 11, 1966, to fill vacancy caused by the death of Patrick V. McNamara; elected November 8, 1966, to a full six-year term commencing January 3, 1967; reelected in 1972, and served from May 11, 1966 to January 2, 1979; Republican whip 1969-1977; unsuccessful candidate for reelection in 1978; associate justice, Michigan State supreme court, 1987-1994; is a resident of Traverse City, Mich.

**Bibliography:** Griffin, Robert P. "The Landrum-Griffin Act: Twelve Years of Experience in Protecting Employee Rights." *Georgia Law Review* 5 (Summer 1971): 622-642.

**GRIFFIN, Samuel,** a Representative from Virginia; born in 1746 in Richmond County, Va.; pursued classical studies; studied law, was admitted to the bar and practiced; colonel in the Revolutionary War; was wounded at the Battle of Harlem Heights, N.Y., October 12, 1776; served on the Virginia board of war; member of the Virginia house of delegates, 1786-1788; elected to the First, Second, and Third Congresses (March 4, 1789-March 3, 1795); died on November 3, 1810.

**GRIFFIN, Thomas,** a Representative from Virginia; born in Yorktown, Va., in 1773; pursued classical studies; studied law; was admitted to the bar and practiced; also engaged in agricultural pursuits; member of the Virginia house of delegates, 1793-1800; appointed justice of the court of oyer and terminer on October 17, 1796, and served in this capacity until 1810; elected as a Federalist to the Eighth Congress (March 4, 1803-March 3, 1805); appointed chief justice of the court of quarter sessions on September 1, 1805, holding court at Yorktown, Va., and served until 1810; justice of the York County Court, 1810-1812; served in the War of 1812 as major of Infantry; again justice of the court of oyer and terminer (chairman of the court), 1814-1820; again a member of the Virginia house of delegates, 1819-1823, and 1827-1830; died at "The Mansion," near Yorktown, Va., October 7, 1837.

**GRIFFITH, Francis Marion,** a Representative from Indiana; born in Moorefield, Switzerland County, Ind., August 21, 1849; attended the country schools of the county, the high school in Vevay, Ind., and Franklin College, Franklin, Ind.; taught school; appointed school superintendent of Switzerland County in 1873; studied law; was admitted to the bar in 1875 and commenced practice in Vevay; Switzerland County treasurer, 1875-1877; delegate to the Democratic National Convention of 1880; member of the Indiana State senate, 1886-1894, and served as Acting Lieutenant Governor, 1891-1894; unsuccessful candidate for attorney general of Indiana in 1894; elected as a Democrat to the Fifty-fifth Congress to fill the vacancy caused by the death of William S. Holman; reelected to the Fifty-sixth and to the two succeeding Congresses, and served from December 6, 1897 to March 3, 1905; declined to be a candidate for renomination in 1904 to the Fifty-ninth Congress; resumed the practice of law in Vevay, Ind.; city attorney, 1912-1916; judge of the circuit court of the fifth judicial district, 1916-1922; again engaged in the practice of his profession; died in Vevay, Ind., February 8, 1927; interment in Vevay Cemetery.

**GRIFFITH, John Keller,** a Representative from Louisiana; born in Port Hudson, East Baton Rouge Parish, La., October 16, 1882; attended the public schools and Louisiana State University at Baton Rouge; was graduated from the medical department of Tulane University, New Orleans, La., in 1907; assistant superintendent, East Louisiana Hospital for the Insane, Jackson, La., in 1909 and 1910; practicing physician in Slidell, La., 1910-1937; also interested in banking; during the First World War served as a first lieutenant in the Medical Corps; elected as a Democrat to the Seventy-fifth and Seventy-sixth Congresses (January 3, 1937-January 3, 1941); unsuccessful candidate for renomination in 1940; served with the Milk Marketing Service of the Department of Agriculture at Slidell, La., until his death there on September 25, 1942; interment in Greenwood Cemetery.

**GRIFFITH, Samuel,** a Representative from Pennsylvania; born in Merthyr Tydfil, South Wales, Great Britain, February 14, 1816; instructed in elementary subjects by a private teacher; was graduated from Allegheny College, Meadville, Pa.; studied law; was admitted to the bar in 1846 and commenced practice in Mercer, Pa.; elected as a Democrat to the Forty-second Congress (March 4, 1871-March 3, 1873); unsuccessful candidate for reelection in 1872 to the Forty-third Congress; resumed the practice of law in Mercer, Pa.; died in Mercer, Pa., October 1, 1893; interment in Mercer Cemetery.

**GRIFFITHS, Martha Wright,** a Representative from Michigan; born January 29, 1912, in Pierce City, Lawrence County, Mo.; attended the public schools; B.A., University of Missouri, Columbia, 1934; J.D., University of Michigan School of Law, 1940; was admitted to the bar in 1941; member of the legal department of the American Automobile Insurance Co. in 1941 and 1942; joined the Detroit Ordnance District as a contract negotiator and served from 1942 to 1946; commenced the private practice of law in Detroit, Mich., in 1946; elected to the Michigan State house of representatives in 1948, reelected in 1950, and served until 1952; appointed in April 1953 as recorder and judge of Recorders Court in Detroit, and in November was elected as judge and served until 1954; delegate to the Democratic National Conventions of 1956 and 1968; unsuccessful candidate for election in 1952 to the Eighty-third Congress; elected as a Democrat to the Eighty-fourth and to the nine succeeding Congresses, and served from January 3, 1955 until her resignation on December 31, 1974; was not a candidate for reelection in 1974 to the Ninety-fourth Congress; elected lieutenant governor of Michigan in 1982, reelected in 1986 and served until 1991; resumed the practice of law; is a resident of Detroit, Mich.

**Bibliography:** George, Emily. *Martha W. Griffiths.* Washington, D.C.: University Press of America, 1982.

**GRIFFITHS, Percy Wilfred,** a Representative from Ohio; born in Taylor, Lackawanna County, Pa., March 30, 1893; attended the public schools and Bloomsburg (Pa.) Normal School, 1913-1916; was graduated from Pennsylvania State College at State College in 1921 and from Columbia University, New York City, in 1930; served in the United States Navy, 1910-1913, and during the First World War, 1917-1919; director of athletics at Marietta (Ohio) College, 1921-1927; football coach at various colleges, 1927-1936; in 1922 engaged as an automobile dealer in Marietta, Ohio; mayor of Marietta in 1938 and 1939; elected as a Republican to the Seventy-eighth and to the two succeeding Congresses (January 3, 1943-January 3, 1949); unsuccessful candidate for reelection in 1948 to the Eighty-first Congress; resumed the automobile business until his retirement in June 1961; was a resident of Clearwater, Fla., until his death there on June 12, 1983.

**GRIGGS, James Mathews,** a Representative from Georgia; born in Lagrange, Troup County, Ga., March 29, 1861; attended the common schools and was graduated from the Peabody Normal College, Nashville, Tenn., in 1881; taught school and studied law; was admitted to the bar in 1883 and commenced the practice of law in Alapaha, Berrien County, Ga.; engaged in the newspaper business; moved to Dawson, Ga., in 1885; elected by the legislature solicitor general of the Pataula judicial circuit in 1888; reelected in 1892 and served until his resignation in 1893 to accept appointment by Governor William J. Northen as judge of the Pataula judicial circuit; elected to the same office by the legislature; reelected and served until his resignation in 1896 to accept the Democratic nomination for Congress; delegate to the Democratic National Convention of 1892; chairman of the Democratic Congressional Campaign Committee 1904-1908; elected as a Democrat to the Fifty-fifth and to the six succeeding Congresses and served from March 4, 1897, until his death in Dawson, Ga., January 5, 1910; interment in Cedar Hill Cemetery.

**GRIGSBY, George Barnes,** a Delegate from the Territory of Alaska; born in Sioux Falls, Dak. (now South Dakota), December 2, 1874; attended the public schools, State University, Vermillion, S.Dak., and Sioux Falls (S.Dak.) University; studied law; was admitted to the bar in 1896 and commenced practice in Sioux Falls, S.Dak.; delegate to the State Democratic convention in 1896; during the Spanish-American War served as a lieutenant in the Third Regiment, United States Volunteer Cavalry; moved to Nome, Alaska, in 1902; assistant United States attorney 1902-1908; United States attorney 1908-1910; city attorney of Nome in 1911; mayor in 1914; member of the board of commissioners for the promotion of uniform legislation in 1915; elected the first attorney general in 1916 and resigned in 1919; presented credentials as a Democratic Delegate-elect to the Sixty-sixth Congress to fill the vacancy caused by the death of Charles A. Sulzer and served from June 3, 1920, until March 1, 1921, when he was succeeded by James Wickersham, who contested the election of Mr. Sulzer in the first instance and continued the contest against Mr. Grigsby; delegate to the Democratic National Conventions of 1920 and 1924; engaged in the practice of law in Ketchikan, Juneau, and Anchorage, Alaska; died in Santa Rosa, Calif., May 9, 1962; interment in Golden Gate National Cemetery, San Bruno, Calif.

**GRIMES, James Wilson,** a Senator from Iowa; born in Deering, N.H., October 20, 1816; graduated from Hampton Academy; attended Dartmouth College, Hanover, N.H.; studied law; moved west and commenced practice in the "Black Hawk Purchase," Wisconsin Territory, afterward the site of Burlington, Iowa; engaged in agriculture; member of the Iowa Territorial House of Representatives, 1838-1839, 1843-1844; elected Governor of Iowa in 1854, and served from December 9, 1854 to January 13, 1858; elected as a Republican to the United States Senate in 1859; reelected in 1865 and served from March 4, 1859, until December 6, 1869, when he resigned due to ill health; chairman, Committee on the District of Columbia (Thirty-seventh and Thirty-eighth Congresses), Committee on Naval Affairs (Thirty-ninth through Forty-first Congresses); member of the peace convention of 1861 held in Washington, D.C., in an effort to devise means to prevent the impending war; died in Burlington, Iowa, February 7, 1872; interment in Aspen Grove Cemetery.

**Bibliography:** *DAB*; Christoferson, Eli C. "The Life of James W. Grimes." Ph.D. dissertation, State University of Iowa, 1924; Salter, William. *The Life of James W. Grimes, Governor of Iowa.* New York: Appleton and Company, 1876.

**GRIMES, Thomas Wingfield,** a Representative from Georgia; born in Columbus, Muscogee County, Ga., December 18, 1844; attended private schools and was graduated from the University of Georgia at Athens in 1863; studied law; was admitted to the bar and commenced practice in Columbus, Ga.; served in the Confederate Army during the Civil War for eighteen months with Nelson's rangers, General Stephen D. Lee's escort company; member of the State house of representatives in 1868, 1869, 1875, and 1876; member of the State senate in 1878 and 1879; delegate to the Democratic National Convention of 1880; solicitor general of the Chattahoochee circuit from 1880 to 1888, when he resigned; elected as a Democrat to the Fiftieth and Fifty-first Congresses (March 4, 1887-March 3, 1891); unsuccessful candidate for reelection in 1890 to the Fifty-second Congress; resumed the practice of law in Columbus, Ga., and died there on October 28, 1905; interment in Linwood Cemetery.

**GRINNELL, Joseph** (brother of Moses Hicks Grinnell), a Representative from Massachusetts; born in New Bedford, Mass., November 17, 1788; completed preparatory studies; moved to New York City in 1809; engaged in mercantile pursuits; traveled in Europe, and returned to New Bedford; president of the First National Bank of New Bedford in 1832; president of the New Bedford & Taunton Railroad in 1839; member of the Governor's council 1839-1841; in 1840 he became a director of the Boston & Providence Railroad, the following year its president, resigning that position in 1846, but remaining a director until 1863; president of the Wamsutta Cotton Mills in 1847; elected as a Whig to the Twenty-eighth Congress to fill the vacancy caused by the death of Barker Burnell; reelected to the Twenty-ninth and to the two succeeding Congresses and served from December 7, 1843, to March 3, 1851; declined to be a candidate for renomination in 1850 to the Thirty-second Congress; resumed his former business activities; died in New Bedford, Mass., February 7, 1885; interment in Oak Grove Cemetery.

**Bibliography:** *DAB*.

**GRINNELL, Josiah Bushnell,** a Representative from Iowa; born in New Haven, Addison County, Vt., December 22, 1821; attended the common schools and Oneida Institute; pursued classical studies; was graduated from Auburn Theological Seminary in 1847; ordained a Presbyterian clergyman; held pastorates in Union Village, N.Y., Washington, D.C., and in the Congregational Church of New York City; moved to Iowa in 1854 and founded the town of Grinnell, Poweshiek County, and also Grinnell University; member of the State senate 1856-1860; studied law; was admitted to the bar in 1858 and practiced; delegate to the Republican National Convention in 1860; special agent for the Post Office Department for two years; elected as a Republican to the Thirty-eighth and Thirty-ninth Congresses (March 4, 1863-March 3, 1867); was not a candidate for renomination in 1866; resumed the practice of law; interested in building of railroads; director of the Rock Island Railroad; receiver of the Iowa Central Railroad (later the St. Louis & St. Paul Railroad); president of the State Horticultural Society and of the First National Bank in Grinnell; died in Grinnell, Iowa, March 31, 1891; interment in Hazelwood Cemetery.

**Bibliography:** *DAB*; Grinnell, Josiah B. *Men and Events of Forty Years.* Boston: Lothrop, 1891; Payne, Charles E. *Josiah Bushnell Grinnell.* Iowa City: State Historical Society of Iowa, 1938.

**GRINNELL, Moses Hicks** (brother of Joseph Grinnell), a Representative from New York; born in New Bedford, Mass., March 3, 1803; pursued an academic course; entered a countingroom in New York City in 1818; subsequently engaged in mercantile pursuits; elected as a Whig to the Twenty-sixth Congress (March 4, 1839-March 3, 1841); unsuccessful candidate for reelection in 1840 to the Twenty-seventh Congress; presidential elector on the Republican ticket in 1856; president of the chamber of commerce and of the Merchants Clerks' Savings Bank; commissioner of charities and corrections; Central Park commissioner; one of the Union defense committee; collector of the port of New York from March 1869 to July 1870; appointed naval officer of customs and served from July 1870 to April 1871; died in New York City November 24, 1877; interment in Sleepy Hollow Burying Ground, Tarrytown, N.Y.

**Bibliography:** *DAB*.

**GRISHAM, Wayne Richard,** a Representative from California; born in Lamar, Prowers County, Colo., January 10, 1923; attended the public schools of Long Beach, Calif.; A.A., Long Beach City College, 1947; B.A., Whittier (Calif.) College, 1949; engaged in graduate work at the University of Southern California, 1950-1951; served in the United States Army Air Corps as a fighter pilot in the European Theater, 1942-1946; shot down and was a prisoner of war; teacher and businessman; president, Wayne Grisham Realty,

1958-1978; chairman, board of directors, First Mutual Mortgage Co., 1974-1978; member of La Mirada City Council, 1970-1978; mayor of La Mirada, two terms, 1973-1974, 1977-1978; delegate, California League of Cities and National League of Cities, 1970-1978; elected as a Republican to the Ninety-sixth and Ninety-seventh Congresses (January 3, 1979-January 3, 1983); was an unsuccessful candidate for renomination in 1982 to the Ninety-eighth Congress; director of the Peace Corps in Nairobi, Kenya, 1983; member, California State assembly; is a resident of La Mirada, Calif.

**GRISWOLD, Dwight Palmer,** a Senator from Nebraska; born in Harrison, Sioux County, Nebr., November 27, 1893; graduated from Kearney (Nebr.) Military Academy in 1910; attended the Nebraska Wesleyan University, 1910-1912, and graduated from the University of Nebraska in 1914; served as a sergeant in the infantry on the Mexican border in 1916; during the First World War served as a first lieutenant and later as a captain of artillery, 1917-1918; banker; editor and publisher of the Gordon Journal from 1922 until 1940; member of the Nebraska State house of representatives in 1921; member, State senate, 1925-1929; unsuccessful Republican candidate for election for Governor in 1932, 1934, and 1936; elected Governor of Nebraska in 1940, reelected in 1942 and 1944, and served from January 9, 1941 to January 9, 1947; unsuccessful candidate for the Republican nomination for United States Senator in 1946; director, Division of Internal Affairs and Communications, Military Government of Germany, 1947; chief, American Mission for Aid to Greece, 1947-1948; member, Nebraska University Board of Regents, 1950-1954; elected as a Republican to the United States Senate for the term ending January 3, 1955, to fill the vacancy caused by the death of Kenneth S. Wherry, and served from November 5, 1952, until his death in the naval hospital at Bethesda, Md., April 12, 1954; interment in Fairview Cemetery, Scottsbluff, Nebr.

Bibliography: Paul, Justis F. "Butler, Griswold, Wherry: The Struggle for Dominance of Nebraska Republicanism, 1941-1946." *North Dakota Quarterly* 43 (Autumn 1975): 51-61.

**GRISWOLD, Gaylord,** a Representative from New York; born in Windsor, Hartford County, Conn., December 18, 1767; pursued classical studies and was graduated from Yale College in 1787; studied law; was admitted to the bar in 1790 and commenced practice in Windsor, Conn.; moved to Herkimer, N.Y., in 1792; member of the New York State assembly, 1796-1798; elected as a Federalist to the Eighth Congress (March 4, 1803-March 3, 1805); resumed the practice of law in Herkimer, N.Y., and died there on March 1, 1809; interment in Oak Hill Cemetery.

**GRISWOLD, Glenn Hasenfratz,** a Representative from Indiana; born in New Haven, Franklin County, Mo., January 20, 1890; attended the public schools; moved to Peru, Miami County, Ind., in 1911; attended Valparaiso (Ind.) Law School; was admitted to the bar in 1917 and commenced practice in Peru, Ind.; during the First World War served in the United States Army as a private in Company B, Fourth Regiment Casual Detachment; city attorney of Peru, Ind., 1921-1925; prosecuting attorney of Miami County, Ind., in 1925 and 1926; member of the Indiana Railroad Commission in 1930; elected as a Democrat to the Seventy-second and to the three succeeding Congresses (March 4, 1931-January 3, 1939); unsuccessful candidate for reelection in 1938 to the Seventy-sixth Congress; reengaged in the practice of law in Peru, Ind., until his death there on December 5, 1940; interment in Mount Hope Cemetery.

**GRISWOLD, Harry Wilbur,** a Representative from Wisconsin; born on a farm near West Salem, La Crosse County, Wis., May 19, 1886; attended the West Salem public and high schools and the college of agriculture of the University of Wisconsin at Madison; engaged in agricultural pursuits, specializing in the breeding of cattle; member of the West Salem School Board, 1912-1929, and of the Wisconsin Board of Vocational Education, 1930-1936; served in

the Wisconsin State senate, 1932-1936; elected as a Republican to the Seventy-sixth Congress, and served from January 3, 1939 until his death in Washington, D.C., July 4, 1939; interment in Hamilton Cemetery, West Salem, Wis.

**GRISWOLD, John Ashley,** a Representative from New York; born in Cairo, Greene County, N.Y., November 18, 1822; attended the common schools, and the academies in Prattsville and Catskill, N.Y.; studied law; was admitted to the bar in 1848 and commenced practice in Greene County; district attorney of Greene County, 1856-1859; Greene County judge, 1863-1867; elected as a Democrat to the Forty-first Congress (March 4, 1869-March 3, 1871); declined to be a candidate for renomination in 1870 to the Forty-second Congress; resumed the practice of his profession; elected supervisor of Catskill, N.Y., in 1871; member of the State constitutional convention in 1894; died in Catskill, Greene County, N.Y., February 22, 1902; interment in Catskill Village Cemetery.

**GRISWOLD, John Augustus,** a Representative from New York; born in Nassau, Rensselaer County, N.Y., November 11, 1822; received an academic training; engaged in mercantile pursuits and in steel manufacture; mayor of Troy in 1855; engaged in banking and also served as president of the Troy & Lansingburgh Railroad Co., of the Troy & Cohoes Railroad Co., and of the New Orleans, Mobile & Texas Railroad Co.; was an unsuccessful candidate for election in 1860 to the Thirty-seventh Congress; elected as a Democrat to the Thirty-eighth Congress (March 4, 1863-March 3, 1865); reelected as a Republican to the Thirty-ninth and Fortieth Congresses (March 4, 1865-March 3, 1869); was not a candidate for renomination in 1868 to the Forty-first Congress, but was an unsuccessful candidate for election for Governor of New York; elected regent of the University of the State of New York on April 29, 1869; died in Troy, N.Y., on October 31, 1872; interment in Oakwood Cemetery.

Bibliography: *DAB*.

**GRISWOLD, Matthew** (grandson of Roger Griswold), a Representative from Pennsylvania; born in Lyme, New London County, Conn., June 6, 1833; attended the common schools and pursued an academic course; engaged in teaching and in agricultural pursuits for a number of years; elected to various local offices; member of the Connecticut State house of representatives in 1862 and 1865; moved to Erie, Pa., in 1866; engaged in manufacturing; elected a trustee of Erie Academy for four successive terms; elected as a Republican to the Fifty-second Congress (March 4, 1891-March 3, 1893); was not a candidate for renomination in 1892 to the Fifty-third Congress; elected to the Fifty-fourth Congress (March 4, 1895-March 3, 1897); was not a candidate for renomination in 1896 to the Fifty-fifth Congress; resumed manufacturing pursuits; died in Erie, Pa., May 19, 1919; interment in Erie Cemetery.

**GRISWOLD, Roger** (grandfather of Matthew Griswold), a Representative from Connecticut; born in Lyme, New London County, Conn., May 21, 1762; pursued classical studies, and was graduated from Yale College in 1780; studied law; was admitted to the bar in 1783 and commenced practice in Norwich; returned to Lyme in 1794; elected as a Federalist to the Fourth and to the five succeeding Congresses and served from March 4, 1795, until his resignation in 1805 before the convening of the Ninth Congress; chairman, Committee on Revisal and Unfinished Business (Sixth Congress), Committee on Ways and Means (Sixth Congress); declined the portfolio of Secretary of War tendered by President John Adams in 1801; served as a judge of the supreme court of Connecticut in 1807; presidential elector on the Federalist ticket of Charles Cotesworth Pinckney and Rufus King in 1804; Lieutenant Governor of Connecticut, 1809-1811; unsuccessful candidate for election in 1810 for Governor; elected Governor of Connecticut in 1811, reelected in 1812, and served from May 9, 1811 until his death in Norwich, Conn., on October 25, 1812; interment in Griswold Cemetery at Black Hall, in the town of Lyme (now Old Lyme), Conn.

**Bibliography:** *DAB*; McBride, Rita M. "Roger Griswold: Connecticut Federalist." Ph.D. dissertation, Yale University, 1948.

**GRISWOLD, Stanley,** a Senator from Ohio; born in Torrington, Litchfield County, Conn., November 14, 1763; served in a militia company during the Revolution; pursued classical studies and was graduated from Yale College in 1786; studied theology; Congregational pastor in New Milford, Conn., 1790-1802, Greenfield, Mass., 1802-1803, and Walpole, N.H. 1803-1805; also edited a newspaper in Walpole, H.H. in 1804; secretary of Michigan Territory, 1805-1808; moved to Ohio; appointed to the United States Senate to fill the vacancy caused by the resignation of Edward Tiffin and served from May 18 to December 11, 1809, when a successor was elected; appointed March 16, 1810, by President James Madison as United States judge for Illinois Territory, and served until his death in Shawneetown, Ill., on August 21, 1815.

**Bibliography:** *DAB*.

**GROESBECK, William Slocum,** a Representative from Ohio; born in Kinderhook, Rensselaer County, N.Y., July 24, 1815; moved with his parents to Cincinnati, Ohio, in 1816; attended the common schools and Augusta (Ky.) College; was graduated from Miami University, Oxford, Ohio, in 1835; studied law; was admitted to the bar in 1836 and commenced practice in Cincinnati, Ohio; member of the State constitutional convention in 1851; commissioner to codify the laws of Ohio in 1852; elected as a Democrat to the Thirty-fifth Congress (March 4, 1857-March 3, 1859); unsuccessful candidate for reelection in 1858 to the Thirty-sixth Congress; member of the peace convention of 1861 held in Washington, D.C., in an effort to devise means to prevent the impending war; served in the State senate 1862-1864; delegate to the Union National Convention at Philadelphia in 1866; a counsel to President Andrew Johnson during his impeachment trial in 1868; Independent Liberal Republican candidate for President of the United States in 1872; delegate to the International Monetary Conference in Paris, France, in 1878; died in Cincinnati, Ohio, July 7, 1897; interment in Spring Grove Cemetery.

**Bibliography:** *DAB*.

**GRONNA, Asle Jorgenson,** a Representative and a Senator from North Dakota; born in Elkader, Clayton County, Iowa, December 10, 1858; moved with his parents to Houston County, Minn.; attended the public schools and the Caledonia Academy; taught school in Wilmington, Minn.; moved to Dakota Territory in 1879 and engaged in farming, teaching, and business; member, Territorial house of representatives 1889; president of the village board of trustees of Lakota and president of the board of education several terms; member, board of regents of the University of North Dakota 1902; elected as a Republican to the Fifty-ninth, Sixtieth, and Sixty-first Congresses and served from March 4, 1905, until February 2, 1911, when he resigned, having been elected Senator; elected as a Republican in 1911 to the United States Senate to fill the vacancy caused by the death of Martin N. Johnson; reelected in 1914 and served from February 2, 1911, to March 3, 1921; unsuccessful candidate for reelection in 1920; chairman, Committee on Expenditures in the Department of the Navy (Sixty-second and Sixty-fifth Congresses), Committee on Agriculture and Forestry (Sixty-sixth Congress); resumed agricultural pursuits; died in Lakota, N.Dak., May 4, 1922; interment in Lakota Cemetery.

**Bibliography:** Phillips, William W. "The Life of Asle J. Gronna." Ph.D. dissertation, University of Missouri, 1958.

**GROOME, James Black,** a Senator from Maryland; born in Elkton, Cecil County, Md., April 4, 1838; completed preparatory studies in the Tennent School, Hartsville, Pa.; studied law; was admitted to the bar in 1861 and commenced practice in Elkton, Md.;

member of the Maryland constitutional convention 1867; elected to the State house of delegates in 1871, 1872, and 1873; elected Governor of Maryland by the legislature to fill a vacancy caused by the resignation of Governor William P. Whyte, and served from March 4, 1874 to January 12, 1876; resumed the practice of law; elected as a Democrat to the United States Senate and served from March 4, 1879, to March 3, 1885; collector of customs for the port of Baltimore 1889-1893; died in Baltimore, Md., October 5, 1893; interment in Elkton Presbyterian Cemetery, Elkton, Md.

**GROSS, Chester Heilman,** a Representative from Pennsylvania; born on a farm in East Manchester Township, York County, Pa., October 13, 1888; attended the rural schools, a business college in York, Pa., and Pennsylvania State College at State College; engaged in agricultural pursuits; served as township supervisor 1918-1922; member of the Pennsylvania house of representatives in 1929 and 1930; school board director 1931-1940; president of the Pennsylvania School Directors Association in 1939 and 1940; elected as a Republican to the Seventy-sixth Congress (January 3, 1939-January 3, 1941); unsuccessful candidate for reelection in 1940 to the Seventy-seventh Congress; resumed agricultural pursuits near Manchester, Pa.; elected to the Seventy-eighth and to the two succeeding Congresses (January 3, 1943-January 3, 1949); unsuccessful candidate for reelection in 1948 to the Eighty-first Congress and for the Republican nomination in 1954 and 1956 to the Eighty-fifth Congress; real estate salesman until retirement, December 31, 1969; resided in York, Pa., until his death there January 9, 1973; interment in Manchester Lutheran Cemetery, Manchester, Pa.

**GROSS, Ezra Carter,** a Representative from New York; born in Hartford, Windsor County, Vt., July 11, 1787; pursued classical studies; was graduated from the University of Vermont at Burlington in 1806; studied law; was admitted to the bar in 1810 and practiced in Elizabethtown, N.Y., and later in Keeseville, N.Y.; was admitted as a master in chancery in 1812; served in the War of 1812 and took part in several engagements; held a commission in the New York Militia 1814-1821; surrogate of Essex County 1815-1819; supervisor of Elizabethtown in 1818 and again in 1823 and 1824; elected to the Sixteenth Congress (March 4, 1819-March 3, 1821); resumed the practice of law; member of the New York State assembly in 1828 and 1829; died in Albany, N.Y., April 9, 1829; interment in Evergreen Cemetery, Keeseville, N.Y.

**GROSS, Harold Royce,** a Representative from Iowa; born in Arispe, Union County, Iowa, June 30, 1899; educated in the rural schools; served with the First Iowa Field Artillery during the Mexican border campaign of 1916; during the First World War served in the United States Army, with overseas service, 1917-1919; attended Iowa State College and the University of Missouri School of Journalism at Columbia; newspaper reporter and editor for various newspapers, 1921-1935; radio news commentator, 1935-1948; delegate to the Republican National Convention of 1968; elected as a Republican to the Eighty-first and to the twelve succeeding Congresses (January 3, 1949-January 3, 1975); was not a candidate for reelection in 1974 to the Ninety-fourth Congress; was a resident of Arlington, Va., until his death in Washington, D.C., on September 22, 1987; interment in Arlington National Cemetery, Va.

**GROSS, Samuel,** a Representative from Pennsylvania; born in Upper Providence, Montgomery County, Pa., November 10, 1776; attended the public schools; engaged in agricultural pursuits; member of the Pennsylvania house of representatives 1803-1807; served in the Pennsylvania senate 1811-1815; elected to the Sixteenth and Seventeenth Congresses (March 4, 1819-March 3, 1823); retired from public life; died in Trappe, Pa., March 19, 1839; interment in Augustus Lutheran Cemetery.

**GROSVENOR, Charles Henry** (uncle of Charles Grosvenor Bond), a Representative from Ohio; born in Pomfret, Windham County, Conn., September 20, 1833; moved with his parents to Ohio in 1838; attended school in Athens County; taught school; studied law; was admitted to the bar in 1857 and practiced; during the Civil War served in the Eighteenth Regiment, Ohio Volunteer Infantry and was promoted through the ranks to colonel; brevetted colonel and brigadier general of Volunteers; held diverse township and village offices; member of the State house of representatives 1874-1878 and served as speaker two years; member of the board of trustees of the Ohio Soldiers and Sailors Orphans' Home in Xenia from April 1880 until 1888, and president of the board for five years; delegate to the Republican National Convention in 1896 and 1900; elected as a Republican to the Forty-ninth, Fiftieth, and Fifty-first Congresses (March 4, 1885-March 3, 1891); unsuccessful candidate for renomination in 1890; elected to the Fifty-third and to the six succeeding Congresses (March 4, 1893-March 3, 1907); chairman, Committee on Expenditures in the Department of the Treasury (Fifty-fourth Congress), Committee on Mines and Mining (Fifty-fifth Congress), Committee on Merchant Marine and Fisheries (Fifty-sixth through Fifty-ninth Congresses); unsuccessful candidate for renomination in 1906; resumed the practice of law in Athens, Ohio; appointed chairman of the Chickamauga and Chattanooga National Park Commission and served from 1910 until his death in Athens, Ohio, October 30, 1917; interment in Union Street Cemetery.

**Bibliography:** *DAB*.

**GROSVENOR, Thomas Peabody,** a Representative from New York; born in Pomfret, Windham County, Conn., December 20, 1778; pursued classical studies; was graduated from Yale College in 1800; studied law; was admitted to the bar in 1803 and commenced practice in Hudson, N.Y.; member of the State assembly 1810-1812; district attorney of Essex County in 1810 and 1811; elected as a Federalist to the Twelfth Congress to fill the vacancy caused by the resignation of Robert Le Roy Livingston; reelected to the Thirteenth and Fourteenth Congresses and served from January 29, 1813, to March 3, 1817; engaged in the practice of law in Baltimore, Md.; died in Waterloo, near Baltimore, Md., April 24, 1817; interment in Hudson, N.Y.

**GROTBERG, John,** a Representative from Illinois; born in Winnebago, Minn., March 23, 1925; graduated from Valley City (N.Dak.) High School; attended the University of Chicago; B.S., George Williams College, Chicago, 1961; corporate Director of Financial Development, YMCA of Metropolitan Chicago; Illinois State representative, 1973-1977; Illinois State senator, 1977-1985; elected as a Republican to the Ninety-ninth Congress, and served from January 3, 1985 until his death at his home in St. Charles, Ill., on November 15, 1986; was not a candidate for reelection in 1986 to the One Hundredth Congress; interment in Union Cemetery, St. Charles, Ill.

**GROUT, Jonathan,** a Representative from Massachusetts; born in Lunenburg, Worcester County, Mass., July 23, 1737; served in the expedition against Canada 1757-1760; studied law; was admitted to the bar and commenced practice in Petersham, Mass.; served in the Revolutionary War; member of the Massachusetts house of representatives in 1781, 1784, and 1787; served in the Massachusetts senate in 1788; member of the Massachusetts constitutional convention in 1788; elected to the First Congress (March 4, 1789-March 3, 1791); returned to Lunenburg, Mass. (now Vermont), in 1803; died in Dover, N.H., September 8, 1807; interment in Pine Hill Cemetery.

**GROUT, William Wallace,** a Representative from Vermont; born in Compton, Province of Quebec, May 24, 1836; pursued an academic course and graduated from the Poughkeepsie (N.Y.) Law School in 1857; was admitted to the bar in December of the same year and practiced in Barton, Vt.; served as lieutenant colonel of the

Fifteenth Regiment, Vermont Volunteer Infantry, in the Union Army during the Civil War; prosecuting attorney of Orleans County in 1865 and 1866; served in the State house of representatives 1868-1870 and in 1874; member of the State senate in 1876 and served as president pro tempore of that body; elected as a Republican to the Forty-seventh Congress (March 4, 1881-March 3, 1883); unsuccessful candidate for reelection in 1882 to the Forty-eighth Congress; elected to the Forty-ninth and to the seven succeeding Congresses (March 4, 1885-March 3, 1901); chairman, Committee on District of Columbia (Fifty-first Congress), Committee on Expenditures in the Department of War (Fifty-fourth through Fifty-sixth Congresses); engaged in agricultural pursuits; died in Kirby, Vt., October 7, 1902; interment in Pine Grove Cemetery.

**GROVE, William Barry,** a Representative from North Carolina; born in Fayetteville, Cumberland County, N.C., January 15, 1764; studied law; was admitted to the bar and practiced; member of the State house of commons in 1786, 1788, and 1789; delegate to the convention in 1788 called to consider the ratification of the Constitution of the United States and voted against postponement; delegate to the constitutional convention of 1789 when the Constitution was finally ratified; trustee of the University of North Carolina; president of the Fayetteville Branch of the Bank of the United States; elected to the Second Congress; reelected to the Third Congress and reelected as a Federalist to the Fourth through Seventh Congresses (March 4, 1791-March 3, 1803); unsuccessful candidate for reelection in 1802 to the Eighth Congress; died in Fayetteville, N.C., March 30, 1818; interment in Grove Creek Cemetery.

**GROVER, Asa Porter,** a Representative from Kentucky; born near Phelps, Ontario County, N.Y., February 18, 1819; attended the common schools; moved to Kentucky in 1837; attended Centre College, Danville, Ky.; taught school in Woodford and Franklin Counties; studied law; was admitted to the bar in 1843 and commenced practice in Owenton, Ky.; member of the Kentucky senate, 1857-1865; member of the Kentucky Democratic convention in 1863; elected as a Democrat to the Fortieth Congress (March 4, 1867-March 3, 1869); resumed the practice of law; moved to Georgetown, Scott County, Ky., in 1881, and continued the practice of law until his death in that city on July 20, 1887; interment in Georgetown Cemetery.

**GROVER, James Russell, Jr.,** a Representative from New York; born in Babylon, Suffolk County, N.Y., March 5, 1919; graduated from Babylon High School; A.B., Hofstra College, Hempstead, L.I., 1941; LL.B., Columbia University Law School, 1949; served in the Coast Artillery, 1942-1943 and in the Air Corps in the China Theater, 1943-1945, and was discharged with the rank of captain; was admitted to the bar in 1951 and began practice in Babylon; member, New York State assembly, 1957-1962; elected as a Republican to the Eighty-eighth and to the five succeeding Congresses (January 3, 1963-January 3, 1975); unsuccessful candidate for reelection in 1974 to the Ninety-fourth Congress; resumed the practice of law; is a resident of Babylon, N.Y.

**GROVER, La Fayette,** a Representative and a Senator from Oregon; born in Bethel, Oxford County, Maine, November 29, 1823; attended Gould's Academy in Bethel, and Bowdoin College, Brunswick, Maine 1844-1846; studied law in Philadelphia and was admitted to the bar in 1850; moved to Oregon in 1851 and entered upon the practice of law in Salem; elected by the Territorial legislature prosecuting attorney for the second judicial district and auditor of public accounts for the Territory; elected to the Territorial house of representatives in 1853 and 1855; appointed by the Department of the Interior as a commissioner to audit the spoliation claims growing out of the Rogue River Indian War in 1854; appointed by the Secretary of War a member of the board of commissioners to audit the Indian war expenses of Oregon and

Washington in 1856; delegate to the convention which framed the constitution of Oregon in 1857; upon the admission of Oregon as a State into the Union was elected as a Democrat to the Thirty-fifth Congress (February 15, 1859, to March 3, 1859); was not a candidate for renomination in 1858 to the Thirty-sixth Congress; resumed the practice of law and engaged in the manufacture of woolens; elected Governor of Oregon in 1870, reelected in 1874, and served from September 14, 1870 to February 1, 1877, when he resigned, having been elected as a Democrat to the United States Senate; elected to the United States Senate and served from March 4, 1877, to March 3, 1883; was not a candidate for reelection; chairman, Committee on Manufactures (Forty-sixth Congress); retired from public life and resumed the practice of law; died in Portland, Multnomah County, Oreg., May 10, 1911; interment in Riverview Cemetery.

**Bibliography:** *DAB.*

**GROVER, Martin,** a Representative from New York; born in Hartwick, Otsego County, N.Y., October 20, 1811; attended the common schools; studied law; was admitted to the bar and commenced practice in Angelica, N.Y.; elected as a Democrat to the Twenty-ninth Congress (March 4, 1845-March 3, 1847); elected justice of the supreme court of New York in November 1857, and reelected in 1859; elected judge of the court of appeals in 1867; after the reorganization of the court of appeals in 1869 was elected an associate judge in 1870 for a term of fourteen years, and served until his death in Angelica, Allegany County, N.Y., August 23, 1875; interment in Angelica Cemetery.

**GROW, Galusha Aaron,** a Representative from Pennsylvania; born in Ashford (now Eastford), Windham County, Conn., August 31, 1823; moved to Glenwood, Susquehanna County, Pa., in May 1834; attended the common schools and Franklin Academy, Susquehanna County; was graduated from Amherst College, Amherst, Mass., in 1844; studied law; was admitted to the bar of Susquehanna County in 1847 and practiced; elected as a Democrat to the Thirty-second and to the two succeeding Congresses, and as a Republican to the Thirty-fifth and to the two succeeding Congresses (March 4, 1851-March 3, 1863); chairman, Committee on Territories (Thirty-fourth and Thirty-sixth Congresses); unsuccessful Republican candidate for Speaker in 1857; Speaker of the House of Representatives (Thirty-seventh Congress); delegate to the Republican National Conventions of 1864, 1884 and 1892; president of the Houston and Great Northern Railroad Company of Texas, 1871-1876; returned to Pennsylvania and engaged in lumber, oil, and soft-coal pursuits; elected as a Republican to the Fifty-third Congress to fill the vacancy caused by the death of William Lilly; reelected to the Fifty-fourth and to the three succeeding Congresses, and served from February 26, 1894 to March 3, 1903; chairman, Committee on Education (Fifty-fourth through Fifty-seventh Congresses); declined to be a candidate for renomination in 1902 to the Fifty-eighth Congress; died in Glenwood, near Scranton, Pa., March 31, 1907; interment in Harford Cemetery, Harford, Pa.

**Bibliography:** *DAB*; Dubois, James T., and Gertrude S. Mathews. *Galusha A. Grow, Father of the Homestead Law.* Boston: Houghton Mifflin Company, 1917; Ilisevich, Robert D. *Galusha A. Grow: The People's Candidate.* Pittsburgh: University of Pittsburgh Press, 1988.

**GRUENING, Ernest,** a Senator from Alaska; born in New York City, February 6, 1887; attended Drisler School and Sachs School; graduated from Hotchkiss School in 1903, Harvard College in 1907, and Harvard Medical School in 1912; gave up the practice of medicine to enter journalism; reporter for the Boston American in 1912 and, after a variety of jobs with several newspapers, became managing editor of the New York Tribune in 1917; served in the Field Artillery Corps in 1918; editor of The Nation, 1920-1923; editor, New York Post, 1932-1933; adviser to the United States delegation to the Seventh Inter-American Conference, Montevideo,

Chile, in 1933; director of the Division of Territories and Island Possessions of the Department of the Interior, 1934-1939; administrator of the Puerto Rico Reconstruction Administration, 1935-1937; member of Alaska International Highway Commission, 1938-1942; appointed Governor of Alaska Territory by President Franklin D. Roosevelt, and served from December 6, 1939 until April 10, 1953; elected to the United States Senate on October 6, 1955, from the Territory of Alaska as an advocate of Alaska statehood, but did not take the oath of office and was not accorded senatorial privileges; known as "the father of Alaska statehood"; elected as a Democrat to the United States Senate on November 25, 1958, and upon admission of Alaska as a State into the Union on January 3, 1959, in the classification of Senators from that State, drew the four-year term beginning on that day and ending January 3, 1963; reelected in 1962 and served from January 3, 1959, to January 3, 1969; unsuccessful candidate for renomination in 1968; president of an investment firm; legislative consultant; died in Washington, D.C., June 26, 1974; cremated; ashes scattered over Mount Ernest Gruening, north of Juneau, Alaska.

**Bibliography:** Gruening, Ernest. *Many Battles.* New York: Liveright Publishers, 1973; Ross, Sherwood. *Gruening of Alaska.* New York: Best Books, 1968.

**GRUNDY, Felix,** a Representative and a Senator from Tennessee; born in Berkeley County, Va., on September 11, 1777; moved with his parents to Brownsville, Pa., and in 1780 to Kentucky; instructed at home and at the Bardstown Academy, Bardstown, Ky.; first studied medicine, then studied law; was admitted to the bar and commenced practice in Bardstown, Ky., in 1797; member of the Kentucky constitutional convention in 1799; member, Kentucky house of representatives, 1800-1805; chosen judge of the supreme court of Kentucky in 1806, and, in 1807, made chief justice, which office he soon resigned; moved to Nashville, Tenn., in 1807 and resumed the practice of law; elected as a Republican to the Twelfth and Thirteenth Congresses and served from March 4, 1811, until his resignation in 1814; member, Tennessee State House of Representatives, 1819-1825; in 1820 helped effect an amicable adjustment of the State line between Tennessee and Kentucky; elected as a Jacksonian in 1829 to the United States Senate to fill the vacancy in the term ending March 4, 1833, caused by the resignation of John H. Eaton; reelected in 1832, and served from October 19, 1829 to July 4, 1838, when he resigned to accept a Cabinet portfolio; chairman, Committee on Post Office and Post Roads (Twenty-first through Twenty-fourth Congresses), Committee on Judiciary (Twenty-fourth and Twenty-fifth Congresses); appointed Attorney General by President Martin Van Buren, and served from July 5, 1838 until he resigned on December 1, 1839, having been elected Senator; elected as a Democrat to the United States Senate on November 19, 1839, to fill the vacancy in the term commencing March 4, 1839, caused by the resignation of Ephraim Foster; the question of his eligibility to election as Senator while holding the office of Attorney General of the United States having been raised, he resigned from the Senate on December 14, 1839, and was reelected the same day, serving from December 14, 1839 until his death in Nashville, Tenn., December 19, 1840; chairman, Committee on Revolutionary Claims (Twenty-sixth Congress); interment in Mount Olivet Cemetery.

**Bibliography:** *DAB*; Ewing, Frances Howard. "The Senatorial Career of the Hon. Felix Grundy." *Tennessee Historical Magazine* 2 (October 1931): 3-27, 2 (January 1932): 111-35, 2 (April 1932): 220-24, 2 (July 1932): 270-91; Parks, Joseph. *Felix Grundy: Champion of Democracy.* Baton Rouge: Louisiana State University Press, 1940.

**GRUNDY, Joseph Ridgway,** a Senator from Pennsylvania; born in Camden, N.J., on January 13, 1863; attended private and public schools and Swarthmore College, Swarthmore, Pa.; engaged in the textile industry and in banking at Bristol, Pa., and became president of a large woolen manufacturing concern; served as president of and lobbyist for the Pennsylvania Manufacturers Association from 1909 until 1930; appointed as a Republican to the United States Senate to fill the vacancy caused by the refusal of the Senate to seat William S. Vare, and served from December 11, 1929 to December 1, 1930, when a duly elected successor qualified; was an unsuccessful candidate for nomination to fill this vacancy; engaged in the textile industry and banking in Bristol, Pa.; died in Nassau, Bahamas, March 3, 1961; interment in Beechwood Cemetery, Hulmeville, Pa.

**Bibliography:** *DAB*; Hutton, Ann. *The Pennsylvanian: Joseph R. Grundy*. Philadelphia: Dorrance, 1962.

**GUARINI, Frank Joseph, Jr.,** a Representative from New Jersey; born in Jersey City, Hudson County, N.J., August 20, 1924; graduated from Lincoln High School, 1942; commissioned a naval officer at Columbia University, 1944; served in the United States Navy aboard the U.S.S. *Mount McKinley*, 1944-1946; graduated from Dartmouth College, Hanover, N.H., 1947; J.D., New York University School of Law, 1950; engaged in graduate work at the Academy of International Law, The Hague, Netherlands; admitted to the New Jersey, New York and Washington, D.C. bars, and commenced practice in Jersey City in 1951; served in the New Jersey State senate, 1965-1972; elected as a Democrat to the Ninety-sixth and to the six succeeding Congresses (January 3, 1979-January 3, 1993); was not a candidate for reelection in 1992 to the One Hundred Third Congress; is a resident of Jersey City, N.J.

**GUBSER, Charles Samuel,** a Representative from California; born in Gilroy, Santa Clara County, Calif., February 1, 1916; attended the public schools; graduated from San Jose State Junior College in 1934; A.B., University of California, 1937; engaged in graduate work for two years; taught in Gilroy Union High School, 1939-1943; engaged in farming since 1940; member of the California State assembly in 1951 and 1952; elected as a Republican to the Eighty-third and to the ten succeeding Congresses, and served from January 3, 1953 until his resignation on December 31, 1974; was not a candidate for reelection in 1974 to the Ninety-fourth Congress; is a resident of Monument, Colo.

**Bibliography:** Duram, James C. "Ambivalence at the Top: California Congressman Charles Gubser and Federal Aid for Classroom Construction During the Eisenhower Presidency." *California History* 68 (Spring-Summer 1989): 26-35.

**GUDE, Gilbert,** a Representative from Maryland; born in Washington, D.C., March 9, 1923; educated in the public schools of Rockville, Md., and Washington, D.C.; attended the University of Maryland; B.S., Cornell University, Ithaca, N.Y., 1948; M.S., George Washington University, 1958; served in the United States Army Medical Department from 1943 to 1946, Pacific Theater; served in the Maryland State house of delegates, 1953-1958; elected to the Republican State central committee in 1958; Maryland State senator, 1962-1968; delegate, Republican State convention, 1952; delegate to the Republican National Convention of 1968; elected as a Republican to the Ninetieth and to the four succeeding Congresses (January 3, 1967-January 3, 1977); was not a candidate for reelection in 1976 to the Ninety-fifth Congress; congressional observer, United Nations Conference on Human Environment, Stockholm, 1972; director, Congressional Research Service, Library of Congress, 1977-1985; former member and chairman, Consultative Committee of Experts, International Centre for Parliamentary Documentation, Inter-Parliamentary Union, Geneva; is a resident of Bethesda, Md.

**GUDGER, James Madison, Jr.** (father of Katherine Gudger Langley), a Representative from North Carolina; born near Marshall, Madison County, N.C., October 22, 1855; attended the common schools at Sand Hill, N.C., and Emory and Henry College, Emory, Va.; studied law in Pearson's Law School, Asheville, N.C.;

was admitted to the bar and commenced practice in Marshall, N.C., in 1872; member of the State senate in 1900; State solicitor of the sixteenth district in 1901 and 1902; elected as a Democrat to the Fifty-eighth and Fifty-ninth Congresses (March 4, 1903-March 3, 1907); resumed the practice of law at Asheville, N.C.; elected to the Sixty-second and Sixty-third Congresses (March 4, 1911-March 3, 1915); chairman, Committee on Expenditures in the Post Office Department (Sixty-third Congress); unsuccessful candidate for reelection in 1914 to the Sixty-fourth Congress; again resumed the practice of his profession; died in Asheville, N.C., February 29, 1920; interment in Riverside Cemetery.

**GUDGER, Vonno Lamar, Jr.,** a Representative from North Carolina; born in Asheville, Buncombe County, N.C., April 30, 1919; attended the public schools of Asheville; B.A., University of North Carolina, 1940, and LL.B., 1942; admitted to the North Carolina bar in 1942 and commenced practice in Asheville; served in the United States Army Air Corps, 1942-1945; member, North Carolina house of representatives, 1951-1952; North Carolina State senator, 1971-1977; solicitor, Nineteenth Solicitorial District of North Carolina, 1952-1954; elected as a Democrat to the Ninety-fifth and Ninety-sixth Congresses (January 3, 1977-January 3, 1981); unsuccessful candidate for reelection in 1980 to the Ninety-seventh Congress; special superior court judge, Buncombe County, N.C., September 28, 1984 to present; is a resident of Asheville, N.C.

**GUENTHER, Richard William,** a Representative from Wisconsin; born in Potsdam, Prussia, on November 30, 1845; received a collegiate training and was graduated from the Royal Pharmacy in Potsdam; immigrated to the United States in July 1866 and settled in New York City; moved to Oshkosh, Wis., in 1867 and engaged in the drug business; State treasurer of Wisconsin 1878-1882; elected as a Republican to the Forty-seventh and to the three succeeding Congresses (March 4, 1881-March 3, 1889); appointed by President Benjamin Harrison consul general at Mexico City on January 28, 1890, and served until May 21, 1893, when he resigned; appointed by President William McKinley consul general at Frankfurt am Main, Germany, on November 11, 1898, and served until July 21, 1910; appointed by President William Howard Taft consul general at Cape Town, South Africa, May 4, 1910, and served until his death in Oshkosh, Wis., April 5, 1913; interment in Riverside Cemetery.

**GUERNSEY, Frank Edward,** a Representative from Maine; born in Dover, Piscataquis County, Maine, October 15, 1866; attended the common schools, Foxcroft Academy, Eastern Maine Conference Seminary, Bucksport, Maine, Wesleyan Seminary, Kents Hill, Maine, and Eastman's College, Poughkeepsie, N.Y.; studied law; was admitted to the bar in 1890 and commenced practice in Dover, Maine; treasurer of Piscataquis County 1890-1896; member of the State house of representatives 1897-1899; served in the State senate in 1903; delegate to the Republican National Convention in 1908; elected as a Republican to the Sixtieth Congress to fill the vacancy caused by the death of Llewellyn Powers; reelected to the Sixty-first and to the three succeeding Congresses and served from November 3, 1908, to March 3, 1917; did not run for reelection but was an unsuccessful candidate for the Republican nomination for Senator; president of the Piscataquis Savings Bank and trustee of the University of Maine at Orono; also engaged in the practice of law; died in Boston, Mass., January 1, 1927; interment in Dover Cemetery, Dover-Foxcroft, Maine.

**GUEVARA, Pedro,** a Resident Commissioner from the Philippine Islands; born in Santa Cruz, Laguna Province, Philippine Islands, February 23, 1879; attended the Ateneo Municipal, and was graduated from San Juan de Letran, Manila, in 1896; joined the forces fighting against Spain, and assisted in promoting the peace agreement of Biakna-bato in 1897; rejoined the Filipino forces and took part in the revolution, serving throughout the Spanish-American War and the Philippine Insurrection, and attaining the rank of lieutenant colonel; engaged in journalism as an editor and special correspondent; municipal councilor of San Felipe Neri in 1907; studied law at La Jurisprudencia, and was admitted to the bar in 1909; member of the Philippine house of representatives, 1909-1912; served in the Philippine senate, 1916-1922; chairman of the Philippine delegation to the Far Eastern Bar Conference at Peking, China, in 1921; elected as a Nationalist a Resident Commissioner to the United States in 1922; reelected in 1925, 1928, 1931, and again in 1934 and served from March 4, 1923, until February 14, 1936, when a successor qualified in accordance with the new form of government of the Commonwealth of the Philippine Islands; died in Manila, Philippine Islands, January 19, 1937; interment in Cematario del Norte.

**GUFFEY, Joseph F.,** a Senator from Pennsylvania; born at Guffey's Station, Westmoreland County, Pa., December 29, 1870; attended the public schools in Greensburg, Pa., Princeton Preparatory School in Princeton, N.J., and Princeton University; employed in the United States Postal Service at Pittsburgh, Pa., 1894-1899; secretary of a public utilities company from 1899 to 1901, and general manager from 1901 until 1918; also financially interested in the production of coal and oil; during the First World War served as a member of the War Industries Board, Petroleum Service Division, and as a director in the Bureau of Sales in the Alien Property Custodian's Office; member of the Democratic National Committee, 1920-1932; elected as a Democrat to the United States Senate in 1934; reelected in 1940, and served from January 3, 1935 to January 3, 1947; unsuccessful candidate for reelection in 1946; chairman, Committee on Mines and Mining (Seventy-sixth through Seventy-ninth Congresses); retired and resided in Washington, D.C., until his death there on March 6, 1959; interment in West Newton Cemetery, West Newton, Pa.

Bibliography: *DAB*; Guffey, Joseph. *Seventy Years on the Red-Fire Wagon: From Tilden to Truman, Through New Freedom and New Deal*. n.p., 1952; Halt, Charles. "Joseph F. Guffey, New Deal Politician From Pennsylvania," Ph.D. dissertation, Syracuse University, 1965.

**GUGGENHEIM, Simon,** a Senator from Colorado; born in Philadelphia, Pa., December 30, 1867; attended the public schools of Philadelphia and Pierce Business School, Philadelphia; studied languages in Europe for two years; engaged in the mining and smelting business in the United States and Mexico; moved to Pueblo, Colo., in 1888 as chief ore buyer for M. Guggenheim's Sons and became associated with his brothers in the management of the Philadelphia Smelting & Refining Co.; moved to Denver in 1892; elected as a Republican to the United States Senate and served from March 4, 1907, to March 3, 1913; was not a candidate for reelection; chairman, Committee on the University of the United States (Sixty-first Congress), Committee on the Philippines (Sixty-second Congress); philanthropist; moved to New York in 1913; member and later chairman of the board of the American Smelting & Refining Co. and elected president of that company in 1919; established in 1925, in memory of his son, the John Simon Guggenheim Memorial Foundation for scholarships for advanced study abroad; continued active in financial interests until his death in New York City, November 2, 1941; interment in Woodlawn Cemetery.

Bibliography: *DAB*; Davis, John. *The Guggenheims: An American Epic*. New York: William Morrow and Co., 1978; Hoyt, Edwin P., Jr. *The Guggenheims and the American Dream*. New York: Funk and Wagnalls, 1967.

**GUILL, Ben Hugh,** a Representative from Texas; born in Smyrna, Rutherford County, Tenn., September 8, 1909; moved to Hereford, Deaf Smith County, Tex., in 1918; attended the public schools of Hereford, El Paso, and Canyon, Tex.; was graduated from West Texas State College at Canyon in 1933; taught in the public schools of Amarillo, Pampa, Panhandle, and Hopkins, Tex.,

1929-1936; president of the Royal Crown Bottling Co., Amarillo, Tex., 1939-1942; served in the United States Navy as a lieutenant commander 1942-1945; awarded Bronze Star and Purple Heart Medal; returned to Pampa, Tex., in September 1945 and engaged in the real estate business; elected as a Republican to the Eighty-first Congress to fill the vacancy caused by the resignation of Eugene Worley, and served from May 6, 1950, to January 3, 1951; unsuccessful candidate for reelection in 1950 to the Eighty-second Congress; delegate to Republican National Convention of 1952; executive assistant to Postmaster General Arthur E. Summerfield, Washington, D.C., from February 1953 to January 1955; was appointed a member of the Federal Maritime Board in 1955; reappointed in 1957 and served as vice chairman until his resignation December 31, 1959; worked as a public relations consultant and as executive vice president of the National Automobile Dealers Association in Washington, D.C., until 1973; was a resident of Pampa, Tex., until his death in Amarillo, Tex., on January 15, 1994; interment in Fairview Cemetery, Pampa, Tex.

**GUION, Walter,** a Senator from Louisiana; born near Thibodaux, Lafourche Parish, La., April 3, 1849; tutored at home and then attended Jefferson College in St. James Parish; moved to Assumption Parish in 1866; deputy clerk of the court 1870-1871; studied law; was admitted to the bar in 1870 and commenced practice in the Parishes of Assumption, Lafourche, and Ascension; judge of the twentieth district 1888-1892 and of the twenty-seventh district 1892-1900; attorney general of the State 1900-1912; appointed by President Woodrow Wilson United States attorney for the eastern district of Louisiana in 1913-1917, when he resigned; resumed the practice of law in Napoleonville and Convent, La.; chairman of the district exemption board, division No. 2, eastern district of Louisiana, and a member of the State council of defense during the First World War; appointed as a Democrat to the United States Senate to fill the vacancy caused by the death of Robert F. Broussard and served from April 22, 1918, until November 5, 1918, when a successor was elected; chairman, Committee on Coast and Insular Survey (Sixty-fifth Congress); practiced law in New Orleans, La., until his death in that city on February 7, 1927; interment in Metairie Cemetery.

**GUNCKEL, Lewis B.,** a Representative from Ohio; born in Germantown, Montgomery County, Ohio, October 15, 1826; pursued preparatory studies; was graduated from Farmer's College in 1848 and from the law school of Cincinnati College in 1851; was admitted to the bar and commenced practice in Dayton, Ohio, in 1851; delegate to the Republican National Convention in 1856; member of the State senate 1862-1865; appointed by Congress a member of the Board of Managers of the National Homes for Disabled Volunteer Soldiers in 1864; reappointed in 1870 to serve six years; in 1871 appointed United States commissioner to investigate frauds practiced on the Cherokee, Chickasaw, and Creek Indians; elected as a Republican to the Forty-third Congress (March 4, 1873-March 3, 1875); unsuccessful candidate for reelection in 1874 to the Forty-fourth Congress; resumed the practice of his profession; died in Dayton, Montgomery County, Ohio, October 3, 1903; interment in Woodland Cemetery.

**GUNDERSON, Steven Craig,** a Representative from Wisconsin; born in Eau Claire, Eau Claire County, Wis.; May 10, 1951; attended the public schools in Pleasantville and Whitehall, Wis.; graduated Whitehall High School, 1969; B.A., University of Wisconsin, Madison, 1973; graduated, Brown School of Broadcasting, Minneapolis, Minn., 1974; served in the Wisconsin State house of representatives, 1975-1979; legislative director for Representative Toby Roth of Wisconsin, 1979-1980; delegate, Wisconsin State Republican conventions, 1974-1980; elected as a Republican to the Ninety-seventh and to the seven succeeding Congresses (January 3,

1981-January 3, 1997); was not a candidate for reelection in 1996 to the One Hundred Fifth Congress; is a resident of Osseo, Wis.

**GUNN, James,** a Representative from Idaho; born in County Fermanagh, Ireland, March 6, 1843; immigrated to the United States with his parents, who settled in Wisconsin; attended the common schools and Notre Dame Academy, Indiana; taught school; studied law, but did not practice; volunteered as a private in Company G, Twenty-seventh Regiment, Wisconsin Volunteer Infantry, in 1862 and served until October 1865; was mustered out with the rank of captain; in 1866 moved to Colorado, where he resided for nine years in the counties of Gilpin and Clear Creek; mayor of Georgetown, Colo., for three years; moved to Virginia City, Nev., in 1875, later to California, and to Hailey, Idaho, in Wood River Valley, in 1881, and was editor of the Sentinel; member of the State senate of the first State legislature in 1890; delegate to the Trans-Mississippi Congress in Denver, Colo.; editor of the Boise Sentinel 1892-1897; unsuccessful candidate for election in 1892 to the Fifty-third Congress, and in 1894 to the Fifty-fourth Congress; elected as a Populist and Democrat to the Fifty-fifth Congress (March 4, 1897-March 3, 1899); unsuccessful candidate for reelection in 1898 to the Fifty-sixth Congress; commandant of the Idaho Soldiers' Home 1901-1903; died in Boise, Idaho, November 5, 1911; interment in St. John's Cemetery.

**GUNN, James,** a Delegate and a Senator from Georgia; born in Virginia, March 13, 1753; attended the common schools; studied law; was admitted to the bar and commenced practice in Savannah, Ga.; served during the Revolutionary War and, as a captain of dragoons, participated in the relief of Savannah, Ga., in 1782; served in county and state militia, becoming brigadier general in the latter; elected to the Continental Congress in 1787 but did not serve; elected to the United States Senate in 1789; reelected in 1795 and served from March 4, 1789, to March 3, 1801; died in Louisville, Jefferson County, Ga., July 30, 1801; interment in Old Capitol Cemetery.

**GUNTER, Thomas Montague,** a Representative from Arkansas; born near McMinnville, Warren County, Tenn., September 18, 1826; pursued classical studies and was graduated from Irving College in 1850; studied law; was admitted to the bar in 1853 and commenced practice in Fayetteville, Washington County, Ark., in 1853; during the Civil War served in the Confederate Army as colonel of the Thirteenth Regiment, Arkansas Volunteers; prosecuting attorney for the fourth judicial circuit, 1866-1868; successfully contested as a Democrat the election of William W. Wilshire to the Forty-third Congress; reelected to the Forty-fourth and to the three succeeding Congresses and served from June 16, 1874, to March 3, 1883; chairman, Committee on Private Land Claims (Forty-fourth through Forty-sixth Congresses); was not a candidate for renomination in 1882 to the Forty-eighth Congress; resumed the practice of law in Fayetteville, Ark., and died there on January 12, 1904; interment in Evergreen Cemetery.

**GUNTER, William Dawson, Jr.,** a Representative from Florida; born in Jacksonville, Duval County, Fla., July 16, 1934; educated in the Live Oak, Fla., public schools; B.S.A., University of Florida, Gainesville, 1956; engaged in graduate work in government and history at the University of Georgia, 1957; served in the United States Army, 1957-1958; teacher in the public schools of Live Oak, Fla., 1956 and 1958; entered the insurance business in 1959; agriculturist; elected national president, Future Farmers of America, 1954; Florida State senator, 1966-1972; elected as a Democrat to the Ninety-third Congress (January 3, 1973-January 3, 1975); was not a candidate in 1974 for reelection to the House of Representatives, but was an unsuccessful candidate for nomination to the United States Senate; Florida State treasurer and insurance commissioner, 1976-1988; president, Rogers, Atkins, Gunter and Associates Insurance, Inc., 1989 to present; is a resident of Tallahassee, Fla.

**GURLEY, Henry Hosford,** a Representative from Louisiana; born in Lebanon, New London County, May 20, 1788; pursued classical studies; attended Williams College, Williamstown, Mass., 1805-1808; studied law; was admitted to the bar and commenced practice in Baton Rouge, La.; elected to the Eighteenth and to the three succeeding Congresses (March 4, 1823-March 3, 1831); chairman, Committee on Private Land Claims (Twenty-first Congress); served as judge of the district court at Baton Rouge until his death in that city March 16, 1833.

**GURLEY, John Addison,** a Representative from Ohio; born in East Hartford, Conn., on December 9, 1813; attended the district schools and received academic instruction; learned the hatter's trade; studied theology; pastor of the Universalist Church in Methuen, Mass., 1835-1838; moved to Cincinnati, Ohio, in 1838 and became owner and editor of the Star and Sentinel, later called the Star in the West, and also served as pastor in that city; retired from the ministry in 1850; sold his newspaper in 1854 and retired to his farm near Cincinnati; unsuccessful Republican candidate for election in 1856 to the Thirty-fifth Congress; elected as a Republican to the Thirty-sixth and Thirty-seventh Congresses (March 4, 1859-March 3, 1863); unsuccessful candidate for reelection in 1862 to the Thirty-eighth Congress; served as colonel and aide-de-camp on the staff of General John C. Frémont in 1861; appointed Governor of Arizona Territory by President Lincoln, but died in Green Township, near Cincinnati, Ohio, August 19, 1863, on the eve of his departure to assume his duties; interment in Spring Grove Cemetery, Cincinnati, Ohio.

**GURNEY, Edward John,** a Representative and a Senator from Florida; born in Portland, Cumberland County, Maine, January 12, 1914; attended the public schools of Skowhegan and Waterville, Maine; B.S., Colby College, Waterville, Maine, 1935; LL.B., Harvard University Law School, 1938; LL.M., Duke University Law School, Durham, N.C., 1948; was admitted to the New York bar in 1939; practiced law in New York City, 1938-1941; during the Second World War enlisted as a private in the United States Army in 1941, saw action in the European Theater, and was discharged as a lieutenant colonel in 1946; moved to Winter Park, Fla., in 1948 and practiced law; city commissioner of Winter Park, 1952-1958; city attorney of Maitland, Fla., 1957-1961; mayor of Winter Park, 1961-1962; elected as a Republican to the Eighty-eighth and to the two succeeding Congresses (January 3, 1963-January 3, 1969); was not a candidate in 1968 for reelection to the House of Representatives, but was elected to the United States Senate, and served from January 3, 1969, until his resignation December 31, 1974; was not a candidate for reelection in 1974; unsuccessful candidate for election in 1978 to the Ninety-sixth Congress; was a resident of Winter Park, Fla., until his death there on May 14, 1996.

**GURNEY, John Chandler (Chan),** a Senator from South Dakota; born in Yankton, S.Dak., May 21, 1896; attended the public schools; during the First World War served as a sergeant in Company A, Thirty-Fourth Engineers, United States Army, with service overseas, 1918-1919; engaged in the seed and nursery business from 1914 until 1926; operator of a radio station at Yankton, S.Dak., 1926-1932; moved to Sioux Falls, S.Dak., and engaged in the wholesale gasoline and oil business, 1932-1936; unsuccessful candidate for election to the United States Senate in 1936; elected as a Republican to the United States Senate in 1938; reelected in 1944, and served from January 3, 1939 to January 3, 1951; unsuccessful candidate for renomination in 1950; chairman, Committee on Armed Services (Eightieth Congress); appointed a member of the Civil Aeronautics Board in 1951, became chairman in 1954, reappointed in 1958, and served until 1964; retired to

Yankton, S.Dak., where he died on March 9, 1985; interment in Yankton Cemetery.

**GUSTINE, Amos,** a Representative from Pennsylvania; born in 1789; member of the board of managers of Mifflin Bridge Co., Mifflin County, in 1828; sheriff of Juniata County 1831-1834; awarded the contract for the first courthouse erected at Mifflintown in 1832; member of the first town council of Mifflintown in 1833; engaged in mercantile pursuits in that borough the same year; elected treasurer of Juniata County in 1837; elected as a Democrat to the Twenty-seventh Congress to fill the vacancy caused by the death of William S. Ramsey and served from May 4, 1841, to March 3, 1843; engaged in agricultural pursuits and milling; died in Jericho Mills, Juniata County, Pa., on March 3, 1844; interment in the Presbyterian Cemetery, Mifflintown, Pa.

**GUTHRIE, James,** a Senator from Kentucky; born near Bardstown, Nelson County, Ky., December 5, 1792; attended McAllister's Academy, Bardstown; engaged in transporting merchandise to New Orleans in 1812; studied law; was admitted to the bar in 1817 and commenced practice in Bardstown; appointed Commonwealth attorney in 1820 and moved to Louisville; member, Kentucky house of representatives, 1827-1831; member, Kentucky senate, 1831-1840; unsuccessful candidate for election to the United States Senate in 1835; delegate to and president of the Kentucky constitutional convention in 1849; road and railroad builder; founder and president of the University of Louisville; appointed Secretary of the Treasury by President Franklin Pierce, and served from March 7, 1853 until March 5, 1857; vice president and then president of the Louisville and Nashville Railroad Company and president of the Louisville and Portland Canal Company; member of the peace convention of 1861 held in Washington, D.C., to devise means to prevent the impending war; elected as a Democrat to the United States Senate, and served from March 4, 1865 to February 7, 1868, when he resigned because of failing health; died in Louisville, Ky., March 13, 1869; interment in Cave Hill Cemetery.

Bibliography: *DAB*; Cotterill, Robert S. "James Guthrie-Kentuckian, 1792-1869." *Register of the Kentucky State Historical Society* 20 (September 1922): 290-96.

**GUTIERREZ, Luis Vincente,** a Representative from Illinois; born in Chicago, Ill., December 10, 1953; B.A., Northeastern Illinois University, Chicago, 1976; teacher; social worker, Department of Children and Family Services; administrative assistant, Mayor's subcommittee on infrastructure, 1984 and 1985; co-founder, Westtown-26th Ward Independent Political Organization, 1985; member, Chicago City Council, 1986-1993; Democratic Committee, 1984; elected as a Democrat to the One Hundred Third and One Hundred Fourth Congresses (January 3, 1993-January 3, 1997); is a resident of Chicago, Ill.

**GUTKNECHT, Gilbert W.,** a Representative from Minnesota; born in Cedar Falls, Black Hawk County, Iowa, March 20, 1951; attended Cedar Falls High School; B.A., University of Northern Iowa, Cedar Falls, 1973; Worldwide College of Auctioneering (Iowa), 1978; salesman for school supply company, ten years; auctioneer and real estate broker; member, Minnesota State house of representatives, 1983-1994; elected as a Republican to the One Hundred Fourth Congress (January 3, 1995-January 3, 1997); is a resident of Rochester, Minn.

**GUYER, Tennyson,** a Representative from Ohio; born in Findlay, Hancock County, Ohio, November 29, 1913; educated in the public schools of Findlay; B.S., Findlay College, 1934; ordained minister; mayor of Celina, Ohio, 1940-1944; Ohio State central committeeman, 1954-1966; Ohio State senator, 1959-1972; public affairs director, Cooper Tire and Rubber Co., Findlay, Ohio, 1950-1972; delegate, Ohio State Republican conventions, 1950-1957; delegate to the Republican National Convention of 1956; elected as a

Republican to the Ninety-third and to the four succeeding Congresses, and served from January 3, 1973 until his death in Alexandria, Va., April 12, 1981; interment in Maple Grove Cemetery, Findlay, Ohio.

**GUYER, Ulysses Samuel,** a Representative from Kansas; born near Pawpaw, Lee County, Ill., December 13, 1868; attended the public schools, Lane University at Lecompton, Kans., and the University of Kansas School of Law at Lawrence; principal of St. John (Kans.) High School and superintendent of the city schools of St. John, 1896-1901; was admitted to the bar in 1902 and commenced practice in Kansas City, Kans.; judge of the first division city court of Kansas City, 1907-1909; mayor of Kansas City, 1909-1910; elected as a Republican to the Sixty-eighth Congress to fill the vacancy caused by the death of Edward C. Little, and served from November 4, 1924 to March 3, 1925; was not a candidate for election for the full term in 1924; resumed the practice of law in Kansas City; again elected to the Seventieth and to the eight succeeding Congresses, and served from March 4, 1927 until his death in Bethesda, Md., June 5, 1943; one of the managers appointed by the House of Representatives in 1933 to conduct the impeachment proceedings against Harold Louderback, judge of the United States District Court for the Northern District of California; interment in Fairview Cemetery, St. John, Kans.

**GUYON, James, Jr.,** a Representative from New York; born in Richmond, Richmond County, N.Y., December 24, 1778; pursued an academic course; appointed captain of the Second Squadron, First Division of Cavalry, in 1807; member of the State assembly 1812-1814; promoted to the rank of major in 1814, and in 1819 colonel of the First Regiment of Horse Artillery; successfully contested the election of Ebenezer Sage to the Sixteenth Congress and served from January 14, 1820, to March 3, 1821; was not a candidate for renomination; engaged in farming; died in Richmond, N.Y., March 9, 1846; interment in St. Andrew's Cemetery.

**GWIN, William McKendree,** a Representative from Mississippi and a Senator from California; born near Gallatin, Sumner County, Tenn., October 9, 1805; pursued classical studies; graduated from the medical department of Transylvania University, Lexington, Ky., in 1828; practiced medicine in Clinton, Miss., until 1833; United States marshal of Mississippi in 1833; elected as a Democrat from Mississippi to the Twenty-seventh Congress (March 4, 1841-March 3, 1843); declined to be a candidate for renomination in 1842 to the Twenty-eighth Congress; moved to California in 1849; member of the State constitutional convention in 1849; upon the admission of California as a State into the Union was elected as a Democrat to the United States Senate, and served from September 9, 1850 to March 3, 1855; reelected to the United States Senate to fill the vacancy occurring at the expiration of his term, caused by the failure of the legislature to elect, and served from January 13, 1857 to March 3, 1861; chairman, Committee on Naval Affairs (Thirty-second and Thirty-third Congresses); an outspoken proponent of slavery, was twice arrested for disloyalty during the Civil War; traveled to France in 1863 in an attempt to interest Napoleon III in a project to settle American slave-owners in Mexico; retired to California and engaged in agricultural pursuits; died in New York City on September 3, 1885; interment in Mountain View Cemetery, Oakland, Calif.

Bibliography: *DAB*; Quinn, Arthur. *The Rivals: William Gwin, David Broderick, and the Birth of California.* New York: Crown Publishers, 1994; Steele, Robert V. [Lately Thomas]. *Between Two Empires: The Life Story of California's First Senator.* Boston: Houghton Mifflin, 1969.

**GWINN, Ralph Waldo,** a Representative from New York; born in Noblesville, Hamilton County, Ind., March 29, 1884; attended the public schools and the preparatory school of Taylor University, Upland, Ind.; was graduated from DePauw University, Greencastle,

Ind., in 1905 and from the law school of Columbia University, New York City, in 1908; was admitted to the bar in 1908 and commenced practice in New York City; during the First World War served as special counsel for the War Shipping Board and as a special representative of the Secretary of War in the European Theater; engaged in agricultural pursuits at Pawling, N.Y., in 1928; member and president of the board of education, Bronxville, N.Y., 1920-1930; trustee of DePauw University, 1923-1962 and of Asheville (N.C.) School for Boys, 1930-1962; author of numerous articles on agriculture and religious education; elected as a Republican to the Seventy-ninth and to the six succeeding Congresses (January 3, 1945-January 3, 1959); was not a candidate for renomination in 1958 to the Eighty-sixth Congress; retired to his farm, Ravenwood, Pawling, N.Y.; died in Delray Beach, Fla., February 27, 1962; interment in Pawling Cemetery, Pawling, N.Y.

**GWINNETT, Button,** a Delegate from Georgia; born in Down Hatherly, Gloucestershire, England, and baptized in 1735; pursued an academic course; engaged in mercantile pursuits in Bristol, England; immigrated to the United States and settled in Charleston, S.C.; engaged in commercial pursuits; moved to Savannah, Ga., in 1765 and entered business as a general trader; elected to the Commons House of Assembly, 1769; moved to St. Catherines Island, Ga., in 1770 and engaged in planting; delegate to the Provincial Congress at Savannah in 1776; Member of the Continental Congress in 1776; a signer of the Declaration of Independence; member of the State constitutional convention in February 1777; Acting President and commander in chief of Georgia from February to March 1777; unsuccessful candidate for Governor of Georgia; engaged in a duel May 16, 1777, with General Lachlan McIntosh, which resulted in his death, near Savannah, Ga., May 19, 1777; interment probably in the Old Colonial Cemetery (later called Colonial Park), Savannah, Ga.

**Bibliography:** *DAB*; Jenkins, Charles F. *Button Gwinnett.* New York: Doubleday, Page, 1926.

**GWYNNE, John Williams,** a Representative from Iowa; born in Victor, Iowa County, Iowa, October 20, 1889; attended the public schools and was graduated from the law department of the State University of Iowa at Iowa City, LL.B., 1914; was admitted to the bar the same year and commenced practice in Waterloo, Black Hawk County, Iowa; also engaged in agricultural pursuits; during the First World War served as a second lieutenant in the Three Hundred and Thirteenth Trench Mortar Battery, Eighty-eighth Division, United States Army, 1917-1919; judge of the municipal court of Waterloo, Iowa, 1920-1926; county attorney of Black Hawk County, Iowa, 1929-1934; elected as a Republican to the Seventy-fourth and to the six succeeding Congresses (January 3, 1935-January 3, 1949); unsuccessful candidate for renomination in 1948 to the Eighty-first Congress; member of the Federal Trade Commission, 1953-1959, serving as chairman 1955-1959; retired to Waterloo, Iowa, where he died July 5, 1972; interment in Memorial Park Cemetery.

# H

**HABERSHAM, John** (brother of Joseph Habersham and uncle of Richard Wylly Habersham), a Delegate from Georgia; born at "Beverly," near Savannah, Ga., December 23, 1754; completed preparatory studies and later attended Princeton College; engaged in mercantile pursuits; served in the Revolutionary War as first lieutenant and brigade major of the First Georgia Continental Regiment; twice a prisoner of war; Member of the Continental Congress in 1785; appointed Indian agent by General Washington; appointed commissioner to the Beaufort convention to adjust the Georgia-South Carolina boundary; member of the first board of trustees to establish the University of Georgia; secretary of the Georgia branch of the Society of the Cincinnati upon its organization; collector of customs at Savannah from 1789 until his death near Savannah, Ga., December 17, 1799; interment in Colonial Park Cemetery.

**HABERSHAM, Joseph** (brother of John Habersham and uncle of Richard W. Habersham), a Delegate from Georgia; born in Savannah, Ga., July 28, 1751; attended preparatory schools and Princeton College; member of the council of safety and the Provincial Council in 1775; major of a battalion of Georgia militiamen and subsequently a colonel in the Continental Army; Delegate to the Continental Congress in 1785; member of the convention in 1788 which ratified the Federal Constitution; mayor of the city of Savannah in 1792; appointed Postmaster General of the United States by President Washington in 1795 and served until 1801; returned to Savannah and engaged in the mercantile business; president of the branch bank of the United States at Savannah, Ga., from 1802 until his death on November 17, 1815.

**Bibliography:** *DAB.*

**HABERSHAM, Richard Wylly** (nephew of John Habersham and Joseph Habersham), a Representative from Georgia; born in Savannah, Ga., in December 1786; attended private schools, and was graduated from Princeton College in 1810; studied law; was admitted to the bar and commenced practice in Savannah, Ga.; appointed United States attorney and served until 1825, when he resigned; attorney general of Georgia; moved to Clarksville, Habersham County, in 1835; elected as a Whig to the Twenty-sixth and Twenty-seventh Congresses and served from March 4, 1839, until his death; died in Clarksville, Ga., December 2, 1842; interment in the Old Cemetery.

**HACKETT, Richard Nathaniel,** a Representative from North Carolina; born in Wilkesboro, Wilkes County, N.C., December 4, 1866; attended the Wilkesboro High School, and was graduated from the University of North Carolina at Chapel Hill in 1887; studied law; was admitted to the bar in 1888 and commenced practice in Wilkesboro, N.C.; chairman of the Wilkes County Democratic executive committee 1890-1923; member of the Democratic State executive committee 1890-1923; mayor of Wilkesboro 1894-1896; represented North Carolina at the centennial of Washington's inauguration in New York in 1889; unsuccessful candidate for election in 1896 to the Fifty-fifth Congress; elected as a Democrat to the Sixtieth Congress (March 4, 1907-March 3, 1909); unsuccessful candidate for reelection in 1908 to the Sixty-first Congress; resumed the practice of law in North Wilkesboro, N.C.; died in Statesville, N.C., November 22, 1923; interment in the St. Paul's Episcopal Churchyard, Wilkesboro, N.C.

**HACKETT, Thomas C.,** a Representative from Georgia; born in that State; attended the common schools; solicitor general of the Cherokee circuit 1841-1843; served in the State senate in 1845; elected as a Democrat to the Thirty-first Congress (March 4, 1849-March 3, 1851); died in Marietta, Ga., October 8, 1851.

**HACKLEY, Aaron, Jr.,** a Representative from New York; born in Wallingford, New Haven County, Conn., May 6, 1783; attended the public schools, and was graduated from Williams College, Williamstown, Mass., in 1805; moved to Herkimer, N.Y.; elected county clerk in 1812 and again in 1815; judge advocate in the War of 1812; member of the State assembly 1814, 1815, and 1818; elected to the Sixteenth Congress (March 4, 1819-March 3, 1821); district attorney of Herkimer County 1828-1833; again a member of the State assembly in 1837; justice of the county court of St. Lawrence County, N.Y., in 1823 and 1824; master in chancery; recorder of Utica, N.Y.; died in New York City on December 28, 1868; interment in Trinity Church Cemetery.

**HACKNEY, Thomas,** a Representative from Missouri; born near Campbellsville, Giles County, Tenn., December 11, 1861; moved with his parents to Jackson County, Ill., in 1864; attended the common schools of Jackson County, the Southern Illinois Normal University at Carbondale, and the University of Missouri at Columbia; studied law; was admitted to the bar September 18, 1886, and commenced practice in Carthage, Mo.; also interested in zinc and lead mines in the Joplin district; member of the State house of representatives in 1901; elected as a Democrat to the Sixtieth Congress (March 4, 1907-March 3, 1909); unsuccessful candidate for reelection in 1908 to the Sixty-first Congress; resumed the practice of law in Carthage, Mo.; delegate to the Democratic National Convention in 1912; moved to Kansas City, Mo., in 1914 and continued the practice of law; general counsel for the Missouri Pacific Railroad 1914-1932; retired from public life and resided in Kansas City, Mo., until his death there on December 24, 1946; interment in Elmwood Cemetery.

**HADLEY, Lindley Hoag,** a Representative from Washington; born near Sylvania, Parke County, Ind., June 19, 1861; attended the common schools of his native city, Bloomingdale (Ind.) Academy, and Illinois Wesleyan University, Bloomington, Ill.; taught school in Rockville, Ind., 1884-1889; studied law; was admitted to the bar in 1889; moved to the State of Washington in 1890 and settled in Whatcom (now Bellingham), where he practiced law until elected to Congress; elected as a Republican to the Sixty-fourth and to the eight succeeding Congresses (March 4, 1915-March 3, 1933); unsuccessful candidate for reelection in 1932 to the Seventy-third Congress; reengaged in the practice of law in Washington, D.C., until 1940, when he retired from active life and moved to Wilton, Conn.; died in Wallingford, Conn., November 1, 1948; interment in St. Matthew's Cemetery, Wilton, Conn.

**HADLEY, William Flavius Lester,** a Representative from Illinois; born near Collinsville, Madison County, Ill., June 15, 1847; attended the common schools; was graduated from McKendree College, Lebanon, Ill., in June 1867, and from the law department of the University of Michigan at Ann Arbor in 1871; was admitted to the bar in 1871 and commenced practice at Edwardsville, Ill.; member of the State senate in 1886; delegate to the Republican National Convention in 1888; elected as a Republican to the Fifty-fourth Congress to fill the vacancy caused by the death of Frederick Remann and served from December 2, 1895, to March 3, 1897; unsuccessful candidate for reelection in 1896; engaged in banking; died in Riverside, Calif., April 25, 1901; interment in Woodlawn Cemetery, Edwardsville, Ill.

**HAGAN, George Elliott,** a Representative from Georgia; born in Sylvania, Screven County, Ga., May 24, 1916; attended the Screven County public schools and the University of Georgia; served five terms in the Georgia State house of representatives, and one term in the Georgia State senate; at the outbreak of the Second World War resigned from the State house of representatives and served two years in the Army Signal Corps; secretary-treasurer and deputy director of the State Board of Workmen's Compensation, 1946; member of National Council of State Governments for two terms; district director of Office of Price Stabilization for southern half of Georgia in 1951 and 1952 and deputy regional director, Atlanta Regional Office, in 1953; engaged in life insurance-estate planning, general farming and livestock raising; member of the board of trustees of Tift College, Forsyth, Ga.; elected as a Democrat to the Eighty-seventh and to the five succeeding Congresses (January 3, 1961-January 3, 1973); unsuccessful candidate for renomination in 1972 to the Ninety-third Congress; was a resident of Sylvania, Ga.; died December 26, 1990.

**HAGANS, John Marshall,** a Representative from West Virginia; born in Brandonville, Preston County, Va. (now West Virginia), August 13, 1838; attended the public schools; studied law at Harvard University; was admitted to the bar in 1859 and commenced practice in Morgantown; elected prosecuting attorney for Monongahela County in 1862, 1863, 1864, and 1870; law reporter for the supreme court of appeals from January 1864 to March 4, 1873; mayor of Morgantown 1866, 1867, and 1869; member of the State constitutional convention in 1871; elected as a Republican to the Forty-third Congress (March 4, 1873-March 3, 1875); unsuccessful candidate for renomination; member of the State house of delegates 1879-1883; elected judge of the second judicial district in 1888 and served until his death in Morgantown, W.Va., June 17, 1900; interment in Oak Grove Cemetery.

**HAGEDORN, Thomas Michael,** a Representative from Minnesota; born in Blue Earth, Faribault County, Minn., November 27, 1943; graduated from Blue Earth High School, 1961; served in United States Navy; engaged in grain and livestock farming, Watonwan County, Minn.; member, Minnesota State house of representatives, 1970-1974; delegate to Minnesota State and County Republican conventions, 1968, 1972; elected as a Republican to the Ninety-fourth and to the three succeeding Congresses (January 3, 1975-January 3, 1983); unsuccessful candidate for reelection in 1982 to the Ninety-eighth Congress; president of Tom Hagedorn Associates, a consulting and lobbying firm; is a resident of Arlington, Va.

**HAGEN, Harlan Francis,** a Representative from California; born in Lawton, Ramsey County, N.Dak., October 8, 1914; moved to Long Beach, Calif., at the age of fifteen; attended the public schools of Lawton, N.Dak., and Long Beach, Calif.; was graduated from Long Beach (Calif.) Junior College in 1933, the University of California at Berkeley in 1936, and from the law school of the same university in 1940; was admitted to the bar in 1940 and commenced the practice of law in Hanford, Calif.; served in the United States Army from February 1943 to April 1946 as a counterintelligence agent, and later as head of the Denver, Colo., office of the Security Intelligence Corps; later held a Reserve commission as a lieutenant colonel in Army Military Intelligence; member of the Hanford city council in 1948; member of the California State assembly 1949-1952; delegate to the Democratic National Conventions of 1960 and 1964; elected as a Democrat to the Eighty-third and to the six succeeding Congresses (January 3, 1953-January 3, 1967); unsuccessful candidate for reelection in 1966 to the Ninetieth Congress; resumed the practice of law; was a resident of Hanford, Calif.; died November 25, 1990.

**HAGEN, Harold Christian,** a Representative from Minnesota; born in Crookston, Polk County, Minn., November 10, 1901; attended the public and high schools; was graduated from St. Olaf College, Northfield, Minn., in 1917; engaged in railroading, in agricultural pursuits, and as reporter, editor, and publisher of a Norwegian-language newspaper 1920-1928; taught history and civics at Mandan (N.Dak.) High School in 1928; publisher and editor of the Polk County Leader, Crookston, Minn., 1928-1932; secretary to Hon. Richard T. Buckler 1934-1942; delegate to the National Rivers and Harbors Congress, Washington, D.C., in 1937; elected as a Farmer-Laborite to the Seventy-eighth Congress and as a Republican to the Seventy-ninth and to the four succeeding Congresses (January 3, 1943-January 3, 1955); unsuccessful candidate for reelection in 1954 to the Eighty-fourth Congress and for election in 1956 to the Eighty-fifth Congress; engaged in public relations work until his death in Washington, D.C., March 19, 1957; interment in Oakdale Cemetery, Crookston, Minn.

**HAGER, Alva Lysander,** a Representative from Iowa; born near Jamestown, Chautauqua County, N.Y., on October 29, 1850; moved in 1859 to Iowa with his parents, who settled near Cottonville, Jackson County; moved to Jones County in 1863; attended the public schools of Monticello and Anamosa; was graduated from the law department of the University of Iowa at Iowa City in 1875; was admitted to the bar in 1875 and commenced practice in Greenfield, Iowa; member of the State senate in 1891; chairman of the Iowa Republican State convention in 1892; elected as a Republican to the Fifty-third, Fifty-fourth, and Fifty-fifth Congresses (March 4, 1893-March 3, 1899); unsuccessful candidate for reelection; resumed the practice of law; moved to Des Moines in 1901 and continued the practice of his profession; engaged in banking 1911-1918; died in Des Moines, Iowa, January 29, 1923; interment in Harbach Funeral Home vault.

**HAGER, John Sharpenstein,** a Senator from California; born near Morristown, in German Valley, Morris County, N.J., March 12, 1818; completed preparatory studies and graduated from the College of New Jersey (later Princeton University) in 1836; studied law; was admitted to the bar in 1840 and practiced in Morristown, N.J.; moved to California in 1849 and engaged in mining; practiced law in San Francisco; member of the State constitutional convention in 1849; member, State senate 1852-1854, 1865-1871; elected State district judge for the district of San Francisco in 1855 and served until 1861; elected a regent of the University of California in 1871; elected as a Democrat to the United States Senate to fill the vacancy caused by the resignation of Eugene Casserly and served from December 23, 1873, to March 3, 1875; was not a candidate for renomination; member of the State constitutional convention in 1879; collector of customs of the port of San Francisco 1885-1889; died in San Francisco on March 19, 1890; interment in Bellefontaine Cemetery, St. Louis, Mo.

**Bibliography:** *DAB*.

**HAGGOTT, Warren Armstrong,** a Representative from Colorado; born near Sidney, Shelby County, Ohio, May 18, 1864; attended the common schools, Sidney Grammar School, and Xenia (Ohio) College; was graduated from Valparaiso (Ind.) College in 1886; taught school in Dallas County, Tex., in 1886 and 1887; moved to Idaho Springs, Colo., in 1887; taught school in Russell Gulch, Gilpin County, in 1887 and 1888; school principal in Black Hawk in 1888 and 1889; superintendent of public schools at Idaho Springs, Colo., 1890-1899; studied law; was admitted to the bar in 1892 and commenced practice in 1899 at Idaho Springs, Colo.; lieutenant governor of Colorado 1903-1905; chairman of the Republican State convention in 1904; elected as a Republican to the Sixtieth Congress (March 4, 1907-March 3, 1909); unsuccessful candidate in 1908 for reelection to the Sixty-first Congress; moved to Denver, Colo., in 1911; judge of the district court of the second judicial district of Colorado in 1921 and 1922; president of Vermillion Oil Co., 1925-1944; resumed the practice of law until his retirement in 1951; died in Denver, Colo., April 29, 1958; interment in Fairmount Cemetery.

**HAHN, John,** a Representative from Pennsylvania; born in New Hanover Township, Montgomery County, Pa., October 30, 1776; attended the common schools; studied medicine and practiced; elected as a Republican to the Fourteenth Congress (March 4, 1815-March 3, 1817); resumed the practice of medicine and also engaged in agricultural pursuits; died in New Hanover Township February 26, 1823; interment in Falkner Swamp Graveyard.

**HAHN, Michael,** a Representative from Louisiana; born in Bavaria, Germany, November 24, 1830; immigrated to the United States with his parents, who settled in New York City; moved to New Orleans, La., about 1840; attended the graded and high schools, and was graduated from the law department of the University of Louisiana in 1850; was admitted to the bar in 1851 and commenced practice in New Orleans, La.; elected as a Unionist to the Thirty-seventh Congress and served from December 3, 1862, to March 3, 1863; returned to New Orleans and engaged in newspaper work; appointed prize commissioner of New Orleans; served as Governor of Louisiana, within territory occupied by Union forces, from March 4, 1864 until March 4, 1865, when he resigned; manager and editor of the New Orleans Daily Republican 1867-1871; founded the village of Hahnville; member of the State house of representatives 1872-1876 and served as speaker in 1875; appointed State register of voters on August 15, 1876; superintendent of the United States Mint at New Orleans in 1878; district judge of the twenty-sixth district from 1879 until March 3, 1885, when he resigned; elected as a Republican to the Forty-ninth

Congress and served from March 4, 1885, until his death in Washington, D.C., March 15, 1886; interment in Metairie Cemetery, New Orleans, La.

**Bibliography:** *DAB*; Baker, Vaughn B., and Amos E. Simpson. "Michael Hahn: Steady Patriot." *Louisiana History* 13 (Summer 1972): 229-52.

**HAIGHT, Charles,** a Representative from New Jersey; born at Colts Neck, Monmouth County, N.J., January 4, 1838; attended private schools in Freehold, N.J., and was graduated from Princeton College in 1857; studied law; was admitted to the bar in 1861 and commenced practice in Freehold, N.J.; member of the State house of assembly 1860-1862 and served as speaker in 1861 and 1862; commissioned a brigadier general of militia on May 27, 1861; during the Civil War was in command of Camp Vredenburgh from August 22, 1862, until the close of the war; elected as a Democrat to the Fortieth and Forty-first Congresses (March 4, 1867-March 3, 1871); was not a candidate for renomination in 1870; resumed the practice of law; delegate to the Democratic National Convention in 1872, and served as chairman of the State delegation; appointed prosecutor of the pleas; appointed prosecuting attorney of Monmouth County in 1873 and served until his death in Freehold, N.J., August 1, 1891; interment in Maplewood Cemetery.

**HAIGHT, Edward,** a Representative from New York; born in New York City on March 26, 1817; attended the common schools; employed in a countinghouse early in life; later engaged in the wholesale dry-goods business and in banking; moved to Westchester, N.Y., in 1850; a director of the National Bank of New York; organized the Bank of the Commonwealth of New York City in 1856 and was its president until 1870; elected as a Democrat to the Thirty-seventh Congress (March 4, 1861-March 3, 1863); unsuccessful candidate of the Republican-Union Party for reelection to the Thirty-eighth Congress; member of the board of directors of several banks and insurance companies; died in Westchester, N.Y., September 15, 1885; interment in Trinity Church Cemetery, New York City.

**HAILE, William,** a Representative from Mississippi; born in 1797; moved to Mississippi and settled in Woodville, Wilkinson County; member of the State house of representatives in 1826; elected to the Nineteenth Congress to fill the vacancy caused by the death of Christopher Rankin; reelected to the Twentieth Congress and served from July 10, 1826, to September 12, 1828, when he resigned; unsuccessful candidate for reelection in 1828 to the Twenty-first Congress; delegate to the State constitutional convention in 1832; died near Woodville, Miss., March 7, 1837.

**HAILEY, John,** a Delegate from the Territory of Idaho; born in Smith County, Tenn., August 29, 1835; attended the common schools; moved in 1848 to Missouri with his parents, who settled in Dade County; crossed the plains to Oregon in 1853; enlisted as a private on the outbreak of the Rogue River Indian War in 1855 and subsequently promoted to lieutenant; moved to Idaho in 1862; engaged in agricultural pursuits, stock raising, and mining; elected as a Democrat to the Forty-third Congress (March 4, 1873-March 3, 1875); declined to be a candidate for renomination in 1874 to the Forty-fourth Congress; member of the Territorial council of Idaho in 1880 and served as its president; elected to the Forty-ninth Congress (March 4, 1885-March 3, 1887); unsuccessful candidate for reelection in 1886 to the Fiftieth Congress; appointed warden of the Idaho Penitentiary in 1899; died in Boise, Idaho, April 10, 1921; interment in the Masonic Cemetery.

**HAINER, Eugene Jerome,** a Representative from Nebraska; born in Funfkirchen, Hungary, August 16, 1851; immigrated to the United States with his parents, who settled in Columbia, Mo., in 1854, and in New Buda, Iowa, in 1861; spent his boyhood on a farm near Garden Grove, Iowa, until 1873; attended the public schools of

Decatur County, Garden Grove Seminary, and Iowa Agricultural College; was graduated from the law department of Simpson Centenary College, Indianola, Iowa, in 1876; was admitted to the bar the same year and commenced practice at Aurora, Nebr., in 1877; became interested in banking and in a group of creameries in southern Nebraska; elected as a Republican to the Fifty-third and Fifty-fourth Congresses (March 4, 1893-March 3, 1897); unsuccessful candidate for reelection in 1896 to the Fifty-fifth Congress; resumed the practice of law in Aurora and, after 1904, in Lincoln; retired in July 1928 and moved to Omaha, Nebr., where he resided until his death on March 17, 1929; interment in Wyuka Cemetery, Lincoln, Nebr.

**HAINES, Charles Delemere,** a Representative from New York; born in Medusa, Albany County, N.Y., June 9, 1856; moved with his parents to Coxsackie; attended the common schools; studied telegraphy and became a train dispatcher; was assistant superintendent and superintendent of a railroad; joined with his brothers in the building and operation of numerous railroad lines in the United States, Mexico, and Canada; settled in Kinderhook, N.Y., in 1888 and built the Kinderhook & Hudson Railroad; elected as a Democrat to the Fifty-third Congress (March 4, 1893-March 3, 1895); unsuccessful candidate for reelection in 1894 to the Fifty-fourth Congress; resumed his former business activities; resided at Altamonte Springs, Fla., until his death there April 11, 1929; interment in Hudson Falls Cemetery, Hudson Falls, N.Y.

**HAINES, Harry Luther,** a Representative from Pennsylvania; born in Red Lion, York County, Pa., February 1, 1880; attended the public schools, the Pennsylvania normal school at Lock Haven, Pa., and Patrick's Business College at York, Pa.; engaged in the manufacture and brokerage of cigars 1906-1934; burgess of Red Lion 1921-1930; delegate to the Pennsylvania Democratic convention in 1918; elected as a Democrat to the Seventy-second and to the three succeeding Congresses (March 4, 1931-January 3, 1939); unsuccessful candidate for reelection in 1938 to the Seventy-sixth Congress; served in the office of the Pennsylvania treasurer in 1939 and 1940; elected to the Seventy-seventh Congress (January 3, 1941-January 3, 1943); unsuccessful candidate for reelection in 1942 to the Seventy-eighth Congress; editor of the plant magazine of the York Safe & Lock Co. from 1943 to 1944, when he retired; died at Red Lion, Pa., March 29, 1947; interment in Red Lion Cemetery.

**HALDEMAN, Richard Jacobs,** a Representative from Pennsylvania; born in Harrisburg, Dauphin County, Pa., May 19, 1831; pursued an academic course, and was graduated from Yale College in 1851; attended Heidelberg and Berlin Universities; United States attaché of the legation at Paris in 1853 and later occupied similar positions at St. Petersburg and Vienna; returned to Harrisburg and purchased the Daily and Weekly Patriot and Union and was its editor until 1860; delegate to the Democratic National Conventions at Baltimore and Charleston in 1860; elected as a Democrat to the Forty-first and Forty-second Congresses (March 4, 1869-March 3, 1873); was not a candidate for renomination in 1872 to the Forty-third Congress; retired from active pursuits; died in Harrisburg, Pa., October 1, 1886; interment in Harrisburg Cemetery.

**HALE, Artemas,** a Representative from Massachusetts; born in Winchendon, Worcester County, Mass., October 20, 1783; received a limited education and worked on a farm; taught school in Hingham, Mass., 1804-1814; became interested in the manufacture of cotton gins in Bridgewater; member of the Massachusetts house of representatives 1824, 1825, 1827, and 1828; served in the Massachusetts senate 1833 and 1834; again a member of the Massachusetts house of representatives 1838-1842; delegate to the Massachusetts constitutional convention in 1853; elected as a Whig to the Twenty-ninth and Thirtieth Congresses (March 4, 1845-March 3, 1849); engaged in agricultural pursuits; presidential

elector on the Republican ticket in 1864; died in Bridgewater, Mass., August 3, 1882; interment in Mount Prospect Cemetery.

**HALE, Eugene** (father of Frederick Hale), a Representative and a Senator from Maine; born in Turner, Oxford County, Maine, June 9, 1836; educated in the common schools and at Hebron Academy; studied law in Portland, Maine; was admitted to the bar in 1857 and commenced practice in Ellsworth, Maine; prosecuting attorney for Hancock County from 1858 until 1866; member, Maine State house of representatives, 1867-1868, 1879-1880; elected as a Republican to the Forty-first and to the four succeeding Congresses (March 4, 1869-March 3, 1879); unsuccessful candidate for reelection in 1878 to the Forty-sixth Congress; declined appointments to the Cabinets of Presidents Ulysses S. Grant and Rutherford B. Hayes; elected as a Republican to the United States Senate in 1881; reelected in 1887, 1893, 1899, and 1905 and served from March 4, 1881, to March 3, 1911; was not a candidate for renomination; Republican caucus chairman, 1901-1902, 1903-1904, 1906-1907, 1909-1910; chairman, Committee on the Census (Fiftieth through Fifty-second Congresses, and Fifty-ninth Congress), Committee on Private Land Claims (Fifty-third Congress), Committee on Printing (Fifty-fourth Congress), Committee on Naval Affairs (Fifty-fifth through Sixtieth Congresses), Republican Conference (Fifty-seventh through Sixtieth Congresses), Committee on Appropriations (Sixtieth and Sixty-first Congresses), Committee on Public Expenditures (Sixty-first Congress); member of the National Monetary Commission; retired from public life and was a resident of Washington, D.C., until his death on October 27, 1918; interment in Woodbine Cemetery, Ellsworth, Hancock County, Maine.

**Bibliography:** *DAB.*

**HALE, Fletcher,** a Representative from New Hampshire; born in Portland, Maine, January 22, 1883; attended the public schools; was graduated from Dartmouth College, Hanover, N.H., in 1905; studied law; was admitted to the bar in 1908 and commenced practice in Littleton, N.H.; moved to Laconia, N.H., in 1912 and continued the practice of his profession; city solicitor of Laconia in 1915; solicitor for Belknap County, 1915-1920; member of the board of education, 1916-1925, serving as chairman from 1918 to 1925; delegate to the New Hampshire State constitutional convention in 1918; member of the State tax commission, 1920-1925; elected as a Republican to the Sixty-ninth and to the three succeeding Congresses, and served from March 4, 1925 until his death in the Brooklyn (N.Y.) Naval Hospital on October 22, 1931; interment in Union Cemetery, Laconia, N.H.

**HALE, Frederick** (son of Eugene Hale, grandson of Zachariah Chandler, and cousin of Robert Hale), a Senator from Maine; born in Detroit, Mich., October 7, 1874; attended preparatory schools in Lawrenceville, N.J., and Groton, Mass., and graduated from Harvard University in 1896; attended Columbia Law School, New York City, in 1896 and 1897; was admitted to the bar and commenced the practice of law in Portland, Maine, in 1899; member, State house of representatives 1905-1906; member of the Republican National Committee 1912-1918; elected as a Republican to the United States Senate in 1916; reelected in 1922, 1928, and again in 1934, and served from March 4, 1917, to January 3, 1941; was not a candidate for renomination in 1940; chairman, Committee on Canadian Relations (Sixty-sixth Congress), Committee on Naval Affairs (Sixty-eighth through Seventy-second Congresses), Committee on Appropriations (Seventy-second Congress); retired to private life; died in Portland, Maine, September 28, 1963; interment in Woodbine Cemetery, Ellsworth, Maine.

**Bibliography:** *DAB.*

**HALE, James Tracy,** a Representative from Pennsylvania; born in Towanda, Bradford County, Pa., October 14, 1810; attended the public schools; studied law; was admitted to the bar in 1832 and commenced practice in Bellefonte, Pa.; appointed president judge of the twentieth judicial district in 1851; elected as a Republican to the Thirty-sixth and Thirty-seventh Congresses and as an Independent Republican to the Thirty-eighth Congress (March 4, 1859-March 3, 1865); chairman, Committee on Claims (Thirty-eighth Congress); died in Bellefonte, Pa., April 6, 1865; interment in City Cemetery.

**HALE, John Blackwell,** a Representative from Missouri; born in Brooks (now Hancock) County, Va. (now West Virginia), February 27, 1831; attended the common schools; studied law; was admitted to the bar in 1849 and commenced practice in Brunswick, Mo.; member of the State house of representatives 1856-1858; presidential elector on the Democratic ticket of Douglas and Johnson in 1860; colonel of the Sixty-fifth Regiment, Missouri Militia, and of the Fourth Provisional Regiment, Missouri Militia, in the United States service during the Civil War; delegate to the Democratic National Conventions of 1864 and 1868; member of the Missouri constitutional convention in 1875; elected as a Democrat to the Forty-ninth Congress (March 4, 1885-March 3, 1887); unsuccessful candidate in 1886 for renomination on the Democratic ticket and for reelection as an Independent to the Fiftieth Congress; resumed the practice of law; died in Carrollton, Mo., on February 1, 1905; interment in Oak Hill Cemetery.

**HALE, John Parker,** a Representative and a Senator from New Hampshire; born in Rochester, Strafford County, N.H., March 31, 1806; received preparatory education at Phillips Exeter Academy, Exeter, N.H.; graduated from Bowdoin College, Brunswick, Maine, in 1827; studied law; was admitted to the bar in 1830 and commenced practice in Dover, N.H.; member, State house of representatives 1832; appointed by President Andrew Jackson United States attorney in 1834, and was removed by President John Tyler in 1841; elected as a Democrat to the Twenty-eighth Congress (March 4, 1843-March 3, 1845); refused to vote for the annexation of Texas, although instructed to do so by the State legislature, which then revoked his renomination to the Twenty-ninth Congress; elected as a Free Soil candidate to the United States Senate in 1846 and served from March 4, 1847, to March 3, 1853; unsuccessful candidate for President of the United States on the Free-Soil ticket in 1852; again elected to the Senate in 1855 to fill the vacancy caused by the death of Charles G. Atherton; reelected in 1859 and served from July 30, 1855, to March 3, 1865; chairman, Committee on Naval Affairs (Thirty-seventh and Thirty-eighth Congresses), Committee on the District of Columbia (Thirty-eighth Congress); appointed Minister to Spain on March 10, 1865 and served until July 1869; returned to Dover, N.H., and died there on November 19, 1873; interment in Pine Hill Cemetery.

**Bibliography:** *DAB*; Lowden, Lucy. "'Black as Ink–Bitter as Hell': John P. Hale's Mutiny in New Hampshire." *Historical New Hampshire* 27 (Spring 1972): 27-50; Sewell, Richard H. *John P. Hale and the Politics of Abolition.* Cambridge: Harvard University Press, 1965.

**HALE, Nathan Wesley,** a Representative from Tennessee; born near Gate City, Scott County, Va., February 11, 1860; attended the common schools of Nicholasville, Va., and Kingsley Academy near Kingsport, Tenn.; taught school at Hale's Mill, Va., in 1876; moved to Knoxville, Tenn., in 1878 and engaged in the nursery business; also engaged in the wholesale dry goods business, banking, and farming; member of the State house of representatives, 1891-1893; served in the State senate, 1893-1895; unsuccessful candidate for the Republican nomination in 1902 as a Representative to the Fifty-eighth Congress; elected as a Republican to the Fifty-ninth and Sixtieth Congresses (March 4, 1905-March 3, 1909); unsuccessful candidate for reelection in 1908 to the Sixty-first Congress; delegate to the Republican National Convention in 1908; member of the Republican National Committee 1908-1912; moved to Los Angeles, Calif., in 1909 and engaged in the oil and real estate

business until his death in Alhambra, Calif., September 16, 1941; interment in Rose Hills Memorial Park, Whittier, Calif.

**HALE, Robert** (cousin of Frederick Hale), a Representative from Maine; born in Portland, Cumberland County, Maine, November 29, 1889; attended the public schools; was graduated from Portland High School in 1906, from Bowdoin College, Brunswick, Maine, in 1910, and from Oxford University in England, in 1912; attended Harvard Law School in 1913 and 1914; was admitted to the Massachusetts bar in 1914, the Maine bar in 1917, and the District of Columbia bar in 1959; practiced in Portland, Maine, 1917-1942; during the First World War served in the United States Army in grades up to second lieutenant, with overseas service, 1917-1919; member of the State house of representatives 1923-1930, serving as speaker in 1929 and 1930; elected as a Republican to the Seventy-eighth and to the seven succeeding Congresses (January 3, 1943-January 3, 1959); unsuccessful candidate for reelection in 1958 to the Eighty-sixth Congress; resumed the practice of law in Washington, D.C., where he died November 30, 1976; interment in Evergreen Cemetery, Portland, Maine.

**HALE, Robert Safford,** a Representative from New York; born in Chelsea, Orange County, Vt., September 24, 1822; attended South Royalton (Vt.) Academy, and was graduated from the University of Vermont at Burlington in 1842; studied law; was admitted to the bar and commenced practice in Elizabethtown, N.Y., in 1847; judge of Essex County, 1856-1864; appointed a regent of the University of New York, New York City, in 1859; special counsel of the United States charged with the defense of the "abandoned and captured property claims," 1868-1870; agent and counsel for the United States before the American and British Mixed Commission under the Treaty of Washington, 1871-1873; elected as a Republican to the Thirty-ninth Congress to fill the vacancy caused by the death of Orlando Kellogg, and served from December 3, 1866 to March 3, 1867; elected to the Forty-third Congress (March 4, 1873-March 3, 1875); chairman, Committee on District of Columbia (Forty-third Congress); was not a candidate for reelection in 1874 to the Forty-fourth Congress; appointed a commissioner of the State survey on April 29, 1876, in which capacity he was serving when he died in Elizabethtown, N.Y., on December 14, 1881; interment in Riverside Cemetery.

**Bibliography:** *DAB*.

**HALE, Salma,** a Representative from New Hampshire; born in Alstead, Cheshire County, N.H., March 7, 1787; became a printer and in 1805 edited the Walpole Political Observatory; studied law; appointed clerk of the court of common pleas of Cheshire County; moved to Keene in 1813; elected as a Republican to the Fifteenth Congress (March 4, 1817-March 3, 1819); was not a candidate for renomination in 1818 to the Sixteenth Congress; clerk of the supreme court of New Hampshire, 1817-1834; member of the New Hampshire State house of representatives in 1823, 1828, and again in 1844; served in the State senate, 1824-1825, and 1845-1846; was admitted to the bar in October 1834; secretary to the commission appointed under the Treaty of Ghent for determining the northeastern boundary line of the United States; died in Somerville, Mass., November 19, 1866; interment in Woodland Cemetery, Keene, N.H.

**HALE, William,** a Representative from New Hampshire; born in Portsmouth, N.H., August 6, 1765; attended the public schools; was a merchant and shipowner; served in the State senate 1796-1800; member of the Governor's council 1803-1805; elected as a Federalist to the Eleventh Congress (March 4, 1809-March 3, 1811); elected to the Thirteenth and Fourteenth Congresses (March 4, 1813-March 3, 1817); died in Dover, N.H., November 8, 1848; interment in Pine Hill Cemetery.

**HALEY, Elisha,** a Representative from Connecticut; born in Groton, New London County, Conn., January 21, 1776; attended the common schools; engaged in agricultural pursuits; served in the Connecticut State house of representatives in 1820, 1824, 1826, 1829, 1833, and 1834; member of the State senate in 1830; captain in the State militia; elected as a Jacksonian to the Twenty-fourth Congress, and reelected as a Democrat to the Twenty-fifth Congress (March 4, 1835-March 3, 1839); chairman, Committee on Public Expenditures (Twenty-fifth Congress); engaged in civil engineering; died in Groton, Conn., January 22, 1860; interment in Crary Cemetery.

**HALEY, James Andrew,** a Representative from Florida; born in Jacksonville, Calhoun County, Ala., January 4, 1899; attended the public schools and the University of Alabama, 1919-1922; during the First World War enlisted in Troop A, Second Cavalry, in April 1917 and served overseas; accountant, Sarasota, Fla., from 1920 until 1933; general manager of the John Ringling estate, 1933-1943; first vice president of the Ringling Circus, 1943-1945; president and director of Ringling Brothers, Barnum & Bailey Circus, Sarasota, Fla., 1946-1948; engaged in newspaper publishing and later in general printing business; chairman of the Democratic executive committee of Sarasota County from 1935 to 1952; member of the Florida State house of representatives, 1949-1952; delegate to the Democratic National Conventions of 1952 and 1960; elected as a Democrat to the Eighty-third and to the eleven succeeding Congresses (January 3, 1953-January 3, 1977); chairman, Committee on Interior and Insular Affairs (Ninety-third and Ninety-fourth Congresses); was not a candidate for reelection in 1976 to the Ninety-fifth Congress; resided in Sarasota, Fla., where he died on August 6, 1981; interment in Boca Raton Cemetery, Boca Raton, Fla.

**HALL, Albert Richardson,** a Representative from Indiana; born near West Baden, Orange County, Ind., August 27, 1884; attended the district school and the Paoli (Ind.) High School; was graduated from Indiana Central Business College at Indianapolis in 1906 and from Earlham College, Richmond, Ind., in 1912; principal of the high school at French Lick 1909-1911; superintendent of schools of Fairmount 1913-1917, of Waterloo in 1917 and 1918, and of Grant County 1921-1925; elected as a Republican to the Sixty-ninth, Seventieth, and Seventy-first Congresses (March 4, 1925-March 3, 1931); unsuccessful candidate for reelection in 1930 to the Seventy-second Congress and for election in 1934 to the Seventy-fourth Congress; engaged in commercial printing 1932-1942; secretary and treasurer of Driveways Contractors, Inc.; engaged in the real estate business in Marion, Ind., editor of Fairmount, Ind., newspaper, and operator of Indiana Hotel in Marion, Ind., from 1961 until his death in Marion, Ind., November 29, 1969; interment in I.O.O.F. Cemetery.

**HALL, Augustus,** a Representative from Iowa; born in Batavia, Genesee County, N.Y., April 29, 1814; attended the common schools and Middleburg (N.Y.) Academy; studied law; was admitted to the bar in 1836 and commenced practice in Mount Vernon, Ohio; assistant United States marshal in 1839; prosecuting attorney of Union County 1840-1842; moved to Keosauqua, Iowa, in 1844; elected as a Democrat to the Thirty-fourth Congress (March 4, 1855-March 3, 1857); unsuccessful candidate for reelection in 1856 to the Thirty-fifth Congress; appointed by President James Buchanan as chief justice of Nebraska Territory in 1858 and served until his death in Bellevue, Nebr., February 1, 1861; interment in Prospect Hill Cemetery.

**HALL, Benton Jay,** a Representative from Iowa; born in Mount Vernon, Knox County, Ohio, January 13, 1835; moved with his parents to Iowa in December 1840; attended Knox College, Galesburg, Ill., and was graduated from Miami University, Oxford, Ohio, in 1855; studied law; was admitted to the bar in 1857 and practiced; member of the State house of representatives in 1872 and

1873; served in the State senate 1882-1886; elected as a Democrat to the Forty-ninth Congress (March 4, 1885-March 3, 1887); was an unsuccessful candidate for reelection in 1886 to the Fiftieth Congress; appointed Commissioner of Patents by President Cleveland and served from April 12, 1887, to March 31, 1889; resumed the practice of law; died in Burlington, Iowa, January 5, 1894; interment in Aspen Grove Cemetery.

**HALL, Bolling,** a Representative from Georgia; born in Dinwiddie County, Va., December 25, 1767; pursued classical studies; served in the Revolutionary War at the age of 16; moved to Hancock County, Ga., in 1792; held several local offices; member of the State house of representatives 1800-1802 and 1804-1806; elected as a Republican to the Twelfth, Thirteenth, and Fourteenth Congresses (March 4, 1811-March 3, 1817); retired to private life; moved to Alabama in 1808 and engaged in planting near Montgomery; chairman of the reception committee to welcome General Lafayette in 1824; died on his plantation, "Ellerslie," in Autauga (now Elmore) County, Ala., February 25, 1836; interment on his estate.

**HALL, Chapin,** a Representative from Pennsylvania; born in Busti, Chautauqua County, N.Y., July 12, 1816; attended the common schools and the Jamestown (N.Y.) Academy; moved to Pine Grove (now Russell), Warren County, Pa., about 1841 and engaged in the lumber business and mercantile pursuits; moved to Warren, Pa., in 1851 and engaged in banking; elected as a Republican to the Thirty-sixth Congress (March 4, 1859-March 3, 1861); was not a candidate for renomination in 1860; interested in the manufacture of lumber products at Louisville, Ky., Fond du Lac, Wis., and Newark, N.J., and in the manufacture of worsted goods at Jamestown, N.Y.; died in Jamestown, N.Y., September 12, 1879; interment in Lake View Cemetery.

**HALL, Darwin Scott,** a Representative from Minnesota; born in Mound Prairie, Wheatland Township, Kenosha County, Wis., January 23, 1844; moved with his parents to Waukaw, Winnebago County, in 1847, thence to Grand Rapids, Wis., in 1856; attended the common schools, the local academy at Elgin, Ill., and Markham's Academy, Milwaukee, Wis.; served as a private in Company K, Forty-second Regiment, Wisconsin Volunteer Infantry, during the Civil War; settled near Birch Cooley, Renville County, Minn., in 1866 and engaged in agricultural pursuits until 1868; auditor of Renville County 1869-1873; clerk of the district court 1873-1878; member of the State house of representatives in 1876; editor of the Renville Times, which he founded in 1876; register of the United States land office at Benson, Minn., 1878-1886; served in the State senate in 1886; elected as a Republican to the Fifty-first Congress (March 4, 1889-March 3, 1891); unsuccessful candidate for reelection in 1890 to the Fifty-second Congress; appointed chairman of the Chippewa Indian Commission by President Harrison in 1891 and served until 1893 and again in 1897; delegate to the Republican National Convention in 1892; member of the board of managers of the Minnesota State Agricultural Society 1905-1910; again a member of the State senate in 1906; engaged in agricultural pursuits near Olivia, Renville County, Minn., until his death there on February 23, 1919; interment in Olivia Cemetery.

**HALL, David McKee,** a Representative from North Carolina; born in Sylva, Jackson County, N.C., May 16, 1918; attended the public schools in Jackson County, N.C.; special student at the University of North Carolina, receiving a certificate of law in 1947 and a law degree in 1948; was admitted to the bar and in 1948 commenced practice in Sylva, N.C.; served as attorney for the towns of Sylva, Dillsboro, Webster, and Jackson County; in 1952 was appointed to the Twentieth Judicial District Committee; organized the Jackson County Savings & Loan Association and served as secretary; in 1953 organized Jackson County Industries, Inc., and served as president; member of the State senate in the 1955 session;

member of North Carolina Board of Water Commissioners 1955-1958; elected as a Democrat to the Eighty-sixth Congress and served from January 3, 1959, until his death in Sylva, N.C., January 29, 1960; interment in Webster Methodist Church Cemetery, Webster, N.C.

**HALL, Durward Gorham (Doc),** a Representative from Missouri; born in Cassville, Mo., September 14, 1910; graduated from Greenwood High School of Southwest Missouri State College in 1926; A.B., Drury College, Springfield, Mo., 1930; M.D., Rush Medical College, 1934; engaged in general practice and became chief surgeon with Smith-Glynn-Callaway Clinic, Springfield, Mo.; during the Second World War served in the United States Army, including chief of personnel service, Office of the Surgeon General, and was discharged as colonel with the Legion of Honor; member of the United States Army Reserve and retired in 1955 to honorary reserve; delegate to the Republican National Convention of 1964, and chairman of the Missouri delegation; elected as a Republican to the Eighty-seventh and to the five succeeding Congresses (January 3, 1961-January 3, 1973); was not a candidate for reelection in 1972 to the Ninety-third Congress; co-founder and member of the board of trustees, Uniformed Services, University of Health Sciences, Bethesda, Md., 1973-1981; member of the faculty, Eckerd College, St. Petersburg, Fla., and an elected member of the Academy of Senior Professionals; is a resident of St. Petersburg, Fla.

**HALL, Edwin Arthur** (great-grandson of John Allen Collier and grandnephew of Joseph Crocker Sibley), a Representative from New York; born in Binghamton, Broome County, N.Y., February 11, 1909; attended the public schools and Cornell University, Ithaca, N.Y.; engaged in the building and banking business and in agricultural pursuits; member of the Broome County Republican committee in 1935; elected a delegate to the New York State Republican convention in 1936; elected to the city council of Binghamton, N.Y., for a four-year term, and served from 1937 until his election to Congress; elected as a Republican to the Seventy-sixth Congress to fill the vacancy caused by the death of Bert Lord; reelected to the Seventy-seventh and to the five succeeding Congresses, and served from November 7, 1939 to January 3, 1953; unsuccessful candidate for renomination in 1952 to the Eighty-third Congress; administrative aide to Richard H. Knauf, member of the State legislature, in 1953 and 1954; employed by the New York State Civil Service Commission in Syracuse, N.Y., in 1955 and 1956, and with the New York State Soil Conservation Service in 1957 and 1958; member, Silver Lake School District Board, Susquehanna County, Pa., 1962-1965; member, Montrose Area School District Board, 1965-1971; resides on his estate, Indian Mountain, Brackney, Pa.

**HALL, George,** a Representative from New York; born in Cheshire, New Haven County, Conn., May 12, 1770; attended the common schools; studied law; was admitted to the bar and practiced in Onondaga County, N.Y.; moved to Onondaga, N.Y., in 1802 and continued the practice of law; postmaster of Onondaga Hollow in 1802; surrogate of Onondaga County 1800-1822; supervisor in 1811 and 1812; justice of the peace 1818-1822; member of the State assembly in 1816 and 1817; elected to the Sixteenth Congress (March 4, 1819-March 3, 1821); unsuccessful candidate in 1820 to the Seventeenth Congress; resumed the practice of law; died in Onondaga Valley, N.Y., March 20, 1840; interment in Onondaga Valley Cemetery.

**HALL, Hiland,** a Representative from Vermont; born in Bennington, Vt., July 20, 1795; attended the common schools; studied law; was admitted to the bar in 1819 and commenced practice in Bennington; member of the State house of representatives in 1827; clerk of Benton County in 1828 and 1829; State's attorney 1828-1831; elected to the Twenty-second Congress to fill the vacancy caused by the death of Jonathan Hunt; reelected as an

Anti-Jacksonian to the Twenty-third Congress, and as a Whig to the Twenty-fourth and to the three succeeding Congresses and served from January 1, 1833, to March 3, 1843; chairman, Committee on Revolutionary Claims (Twenty-seventh Congress); was not a candidate for renomination in 1842 to the Twenty-eighth Congress; State bank commissioner 1843-1846; judge of the State supreme court 1846-1850; Second Comptroller of the Treasury from November 27, 1850, to September 10, 1851; United States land commissioner for California 1851-1854; returned to Vermont; Governor of Vermont from October 10, 1858 to October 12, 1860; member of the peace convention of 1861 held in Washington, D.C., in an effort to devise means to prevent the impending war; died in Springfield, Mass., December 18, 1885; interment in Bennington Center Cemetery, Bennington, Vt.

**Bibliography:** *DAB.*

**HALL, Homer William,** a Representative from Illinois; born in Shelbyville, Shelby County, Ill., July 22, 1870; moved with his parents to Bloomington, Ill., in 1876; attended the public schools and Illinois Wesleyan University at Bloomington; studied law; was admitted to the bar in 1892 and commenced practice in Bloomington, Ill.; engaged in banking and was also interested in agricultural pursuits; county judge of McLean County 1909-1914, probate judge 1909-1914, and master in chancery 1916-1918; delegate to the Republican National Convention in 1916; elected as a Republican to the Seventieth, Seventy-first, and Seventy-second Congresses (March 4, 1927-March 3, 1933); unsuccessful candidate for reelection in 1932 to the Seventy-third Congress; resumed the practice of law and agricultural pursuits; again elected as county judge of McLean County, in 1934, and served until his retirement in 1942; died in Bloomington, Ill., September 22, 1954; interment in Park Hill Cemetery.

**HALL, James Knox Polk,** a Representative from Pennsylvania; born in Milesburg, Centre County, Pa., September 30, 1844; educated in Pittsburgh, Pa.; studied law; was admitted to the bar November 8, 1866; elected district attorney of Elk County in 1867; reelected in 1870 and 1873; retired from practice in 1883 to engage in the coal, lumber, and railroad business and also in banking; elected as a Democrat to the Fifty-sixth and Fifty-seventh Congresses and served from March 4, 1899, to November 29, 1902, when he resigned; member of the Pennsylvania senate in 1902-1914; died in Tampa, Fla., January 5, 1915; interment in Pine Grove Cemetery, Ridgway, Pa.

**HALL, John,** a Delegate from Maryland; born near Annapolis, Anne Arundel County, Md., November 27, 1729; completed preparatory studies; studied law; was admitted to the bar and commenced practice at Annapolis; member of the council of safety; delegate to the Maryland convention in 1775; Member of the Continental Congress in 1775; continued the practice of law; died on his plantation, "The Vineyard" (now known as "Iglehart"), near Annapolis, Md., March 8, 1797; interment in the family burial ground on his estate.

**HALL, Joseph,** a Representative from Maine; born in Methuen, Essex County, Mass., June 26, 1793; attended the common schools and Andover Academy, Andover, Mass.; moved to Camden, Maine, in 1809 and engaged in mercantile pursuits; during the War of 1812 served as ensign in 1814 in Colonel Forte's regiment, Massachusetts Militia, and was subsequently appointed colonel; deputy sheriff in 1821; sheriff in 1827; postmaster of Camden, 1830-1833; elected as a Jacksonian to the Twenty-third and Twenty-fourth Congresses (March 4, 1833-March 3, 1837); chairman, Committee on Expenditures in the Department of the Navy (Twenty-third and Twenty-fourth Congresses); again postmaster in 1837 and 1838; appointed measurer in the Boston custom house in 1838 and served until 1846; naval agent at Boston, 1846-1849; unsuccessful candidate for mayor of Boston in 1849; engaged in agricultural pursuits, 1850-1857; clerk in the Boston customhouse from 1857 until his death in that city on December 31, 1859; interment in Mountain Cemetery, Camden, Maine.

**HALL, Joshua Gilman,** a Representative from New Hampshire; born in Wakefield, Carroll County, N.H., November 5, 1828; attended Gilmanton Academy, and was graduated from Dartmouth College, Hanover, N.H., in 1851; studied law; was admitted to the bar in 1855 and practiced in Wakefield and Dover, N.H.; solicitor of the county of Strafford 1862-1874; mayor of Dover in 1866 and 1867; member of the State senate 1871 and 1872; served in the State house of representatives in 1874; attorney of the United States for the district of Hampshire from April 1874 to February 1879; elected as a Republican to the Forty-sixth and Forty-seventh Congresses (March 4, 1879-March 3, 1883); resumed the practice of his profession; died in Dover, Strafford County, N.H., on October 31, 1898; interment in Pine Hill Cemetery.

**HALL, Katie Beatrice,** a Representative from Indiana; born in Mound Bayou, Bolivar County, Miss., April 3, 1938; attended public schools of Mound Bayou, Miss.; B.S., Mississippi Valley State University, Itta Bena, Miss., 1960; M.S., Indiana University, Bloomington, Ind., 1968; teacher in the public schools of Gary, Ind., 1961-1975; served in the Indiana house of representatives, 1974-1976; Indiana State senator, 1976-1982; delegate to the Democratic Mini Convention, Memphis, Tenn., 1978; chair, Lake County Democratic Committee, 1978-1980; chair, Indiana State Democratic convention, 1980; elected as a Democrat to the Ninety-seventh Congress, November 2, 1982, by special election to fill the vacancy caused by the death of Adam Benjamin; also elected at the same time to the Ninety-eighth Congress (November 2, 1982-January 3, 1985); was an unsuccessful candidate for renomination in 1984 to the Ninety-ninth Congress; is a resident of Gary, Ind.

**Bibliography:** Catlin, Robert A. "Organizational Effectiveness and Black Political Participation: The Case of Katie Hall." *Phylon* 46 (September 1985): 179-192.

**HALL, Lawrence Washington,** a Representative from Ohio; born in Lake County, Ohio, in 1819; was graduated from Hudson College in 1839; studied law; was admitted to the bar in 1843 and commenced practice in Bucyrus, Ohio, in 1844; prosecuting attorney of Crawford County 1845-1851; judge of the court of common pleas 1852-1857; elected as a Democrat to the Thirty-fifth Congress (March 4, 1857-March 3, 1859); unsuccessful candidate for reelection in 1858 to the Thirty-sixth Congress; resumed the practice of his profession; imprisoned for alleged disloyalty to the Union in 1862; died in Bucyrus, Crawford County, Ohio, on January 18, 1863; interment in Oakwood Cemetery.

**HALL, Leonard Wood,** a Representative from New York; born in Oyster Bay, Nassau County, N.Y., October 2, 1900; attended the public schools; was graduated from the law department of Georgetown University, Washington, D.C., in 1920; was admitted to the bar in 1922 and commenced practice in New York City; member of the New York State assembly, 1927-1928, and 1934-1938; sheriff of Nassau County, N.Y., 1929-1931; delegate to Republican State conventions from 1930 until 1958, and to the Republican National Conventions of 1948, 1952, 1956, and 1968; elected as a Republican to the Seventy-sixth and to the six succeeding Congresses, and served from January 3, 1939 until December 31, 1952; did not seek reelection in 1952 to the Eighty-third Congress; elected surrogate of Nassau County, N.Y., in November 1952, resigning to become chairman of the Republican National Committee, serving from 1953 to 1957; unsuccessful candidate for nomination for Governor of New York in 1958; President Dwight D. Eisenhower's personal representative at opening of the Brussels World's Fair in April 1958; resumed the practice of law in Garden City, N.Y., and New York City; resided in Locust Valley, N.Y.; died in Glen Cove, N.Y., on June 2, 1979;

interment in Memorial Cemetery of St. John's Church, Laurel Hollow, Long Island, N.Y.

**Bibliography:** *DAB.*

**HALL, Lyman,** a Delegate from Georgia; born in Wallingford, New Haven County, Conn., April 12, 1724; was graduated from Yale College in 1747; studied theology for a short time and in 1749 began preaching; later studied medicine and commenced practice in Wallingford; moved to Dorchester, S.C., in 1752, and, a few years later, to the "Midway District," Liberty County, Ga., where he continued the practice of his profession and also engaged in the cultivation of rice; member of the conventions of 1774 and 1775 held in Savannah; Member of the Continental Congress 1775-1777; a signer of the Declaration of Independence; upon the fall of Savannah in 1778 and the capture of Sunbury, when his property was despoiled, went north with his family; resumed residence in Savannah in 1782 and again practiced medicine; Governor of Georgia in 1783; judge of the inferior court of Chatham County, which office he resigned upon moving to Burke County; died in Burke County, Ga., October 19, 1790; interment on his plantation near Shell Bluff, Burke County, Ga.; reinterment in 1848 beneath the monument in front of the courthouse on Greene Street, Augusta, Ga.

**Bibliography:** *DAB.*

**HALL, Nathan Kelsey,** a Representative from New York; born in Marcellus, Onondaga County, N.Y., March 28, 1810; moved to Erie County in early youth with his parents; attended the district school; became engaged as a shoemaker and also in agricultural pursuits; studied law in Buffalo with Millard Fillmore; was admitted to the bar in 1832 and practiced in Buffalo; from 1831 to 1837 held various local county and town offices in Erie County, including deputy clerk of the county, clerk of the board of supervisors, and city attorney; member of the board of aldermen; appointed master in chancery by Governor William H. Seward in 1839; judge of Erie County from January 1841 to January 1845; member of the State assembly in 1846; elected as a Whig to the Thirtieth Congress (March 4, 1847-March 3, 1849); was not a candidate for renomination in 1848 to the Thirty-first Congress; appointed Postmaster General in the Cabinet of President Millard Fillmore, and served from July 23, 1850 to August 31, 1852; appointed United States district judge for the western district of New York on August 31, 1852, and held the position until his death in Buffalo, N.Y., March 2, 1874; interment in Forest Lawn Cemetery.

**Bibliography:** *DAB.*

**HALL, Norman,** a Representative from Pennsylvania; born on the Muncy Farms, near Halls Station, Lycoming County, Pa., November 17, 1829; was graduated from Dickinson College, Carlisle, Pa., in 1847; engaged in the iron business; elected as a Democrat to the Fiftieth Congress (March 4, 1887-March 3, 1889); engaged in banking in Sharon, Pa.; retired from active business; died in Sharon, Pa., September 29, 1917; interment in Hall's Burying Ground, Halls Station, Pa.

**HALL, Obed,** a Representative from New Hampshire; born in Raynham, Bristol County, Mass., December 23, 1757; moved to Madbury, N.H., and thence to Upper Bartlett and engaged in agricultural pursuits; subsequently became an innkeeper; surveyor of highways in 1790; member of the board of selectmen 1791, 1798, 1800, 1802-1810, 1814-1819, and 1823; member of the New Hampshire State house of representatives in 1801 and 1802; appointed judge of the court of common pleas by Governor John Taylor Gilman; elected as a Republican to the Twelfth Congress (March 4, 1811-March 3, 1813); member of the New Hampshire State senate in 1819; died in Bartlett, Carroll County, N.H., April 1, 1828; interment in Garland Ridge Cemetery, about two miles south of Bartlett; reinterment in Evergreen Cemetery, Portland, Maine.

**HALL, Osee Matson,** a Representative from Minnesota; born in Conneaut, Ashtabula County, Ohio, September 10, 1847; attended the common schools; was graduated from Hiram (Ohio) College and Williams College, Williamstown, Mass., in 1868; studied law; was admitted to the bar and commenced practice in Red Wing, Minn.; member of the State senate 1885-1887; elected as a Democrat to the Fifty-second and Fifty-third Congresses (March 4, 1891-March 3, 1895); unsuccessful candidate for reelection in 1894 to the Fifty-fourth Congress; resumed the practice of law; member of the Minnesota State Tax Commission from 1907 until his death in St. Paul, Minn., November 26, 1914; interment in Oakwood Cemetery, Red Wing, Minn.

**HALL, Philo,** a Representative from South Dakota; born in Wilton, Waseca County, Minn., December 31, 1865; attended the common schools; studied law; was admitted to the bar in 1887 and commenced practice in Brookings, Dak. (now South Dakota); prosecuting attorney for Brookings County 1892-1898; member of the State senate 1901-1903; attorney general of South Dakota 1902-1906; elected as a Republican to the Sixtieth Congress (March 4, 1907-March 3, 1909); unsuccessful candidate for renomination in 1908 to the Sixty-first Congress; resumed the practice of law; delegate to the Republican State convention in 1923; died in Brookings, S.Dak., October 7, 1938; interment in Greenwood Cemetery.

**HALL, Ralph Moody,** a Representative from Texas; born in Fate, Rockwall County, Tex., May 3, 1923; attended the public schools; graduated Rockwall High School, 1941; attended Texas Christian University, Fort Worth, 1943; University of Texas, Austin, 1943 and 1947; LL.B., Southern Methodist University, Dallas, 1951; served as a carrier-based pilot in the United States Navy, lieutenant (senior grade), 1942-1945; admitted to the Texas bar in 1951 and commenced practice in Rockwall; president-chief executive officer, Texas Aluminum Corp.; general counsel, Texas Extrusion Co., Inc.; Rockwall County judge, 1950-1962; served in the Texas senate, 1962-1972; owner-president, North Texas Grain & Elevator Co., Inc., 1968-1980; elected as a Democrat to the Ninety-seventh and to the seven succeeding Congresses (January 3, 1981-January 3, 1997); is a resident of Rockwall, Tex.

**HALL, Robert Bernard,** a Representative from Massachusetts; born in Boston, Mass., January 28, 1812; entered the Boston Latin School in 1822; studied theology in New Haven in 1833 and 1834 and was ordained to the ministry, first as a Congregationalist and then as an Episcopalian; was one of the twelve original members of William Lloyd Garrison's Anti-Slavery Society in 1832; moved to Plymouth, Mass.; served in the Massachusetts senate in 1855; elected as the candidate of the American Party to the Thirty-fourth Congress and as a Republican to the Thirty-fifth Congress (March 4, 1855-March 3, 1859); delegate to the Union Convention at Philadelphia in 1866; died in Plymouth, Mass., April 15, 1868; interment in Oak Grove Cemetery.

**HALL, Robert Samuel,** a Representative from Mississippi; born in Williamsburg, Covington County, Miss., March 10, 1879; attended the common schools of Williamsburg and Hattiesburg, Miss.; taught school in Hancock County, Miss., in 1894; was graduated from Millsaps College, Jackson, Miss., in 1898; owned and edited the Hattiesburg Citizen 1895-1900 and 1920-1925; was graduated from the law department of Millsaps College in 1900; was admitted to the bar the same year and commenced practice in Hattiesburg; member of the State senate 1906-1908; delegate to the Democratic National Convention in 1908; prosecuting attorney of Forrest County 1910-1912; district attorney of the twelfth judicial district from 1912 to 1918 and circuit judge of that district from 1918 to 1929; elected as a Democrat to the Seventy-first and Seventy-second Congresses (March 4, 1929-March 3, 1933); chairman, Committee on Irrigation and Reclamation (Seventy-second

Congress); unsuccessful candidate for renomination in 1932; employed in the legal division of the Federal Trade Commission, Washington, D.C., from 1933 until his death in Arlington, Va., June 10, 1941; interment in the Old City Cemetery, Hattiesburg, Miss.

**HALL, Sam Blakeley, Jr.,** a Representative from Texas; born in Marshall, Harrison County, Tex., January 11, 1924; graduated from the public schools of Marshall in 1940; A.A., College of Marshall (now East Texas Baptist University), 1942; attended the University of Texas Law School, 1942-1943; served in the United States Air Force, 1943-1945; graduated from Baylor University, Waco, Tex., in 1946; LL.B., Baylor University Law School, 1948; admitted to the Texas bar in 1948 and commenced practice in Marshall; unsuccessful candidate for election in 1962 to the Eighty-eighth Congress; chairman, Marshall Board of Education, 1972-1976; elected as a Democrat to the Ninety-fourth Congress, June 19, 1976, by special election to fill the vacancy caused by the death of Wright Patman; reelected to the five succeeding Congresses and served from June 19, 1976, to May 27, 1985, when he resigned, having been appointed United States judge for the Eastern District of Texas; was a resident of Marshall, Tex.; died April 10, 1994.

**HALL, Thomas,** a Representative from North Dakota; born in Cliff Mine, Keweenaw County, Mich., June 6, 1869; moved with his parents to a homestead near Jamestown, Stutsman County, N.Dak., in 1883; attended the public schools and Concordia College, Moorehead, Minn.; construction worker for Aberdeen, Bismarck, and Northwestern Railroad, and clerk for Northern Pacific Railroad at Mandan and Fargo, N.Dak., 1887-1894; newspaper reporter at Fargo, N.Dak., 1896-1907; also engaged in agricultural pursuits; city assessor of Fargo, N.Dak., 1903-1907; member of Company B, North Dakota National Guard, 1893-1898 and 1903-1906; secretary of the Progressive Republican committee of North Dakota 1906-1912; secretary of the board of railroad commissioners 1910-1914; secretary of state of North Dakota 1912-1924; elected as a Republican to the Sixty-eighth Congress to fill the vacancy caused by the resignation of George M. Young; reelected to the Sixty-ninth and to the three succeeding Congresses and served from November 4, 1924, to March 3, 1933; unsuccessful candidate for renomination in 1932; engaged in ranching and farming in Oliver County, N.Dak.; secretary of state of North Dakota from 1942 until his retirement in 1954; died in Bismarck, N.Dak., December 4, 1958; interment in Fairview Cemetery.

**HALL, Thomas H.,** a Representative from North Carolina; born in Prince George County, Va., in June 1773; studied medicine and practiced in Tarboro, Edgecombe County, N.C.; elected as a Republican to the Fifteenth Congress and reelected to the three succeeding Congresses (March 4, 1817-March 3, 1825); unsuccessful candidate for reelection in 1824 to the Nineteenth Congress; elected to the Twentieth Congress and reelected as a Jacksonian to the three succeeding Congresses (March 4, 1827-March 3, 1835); chairman, Committee on Expenditures in the Department of the Treasury (Twentieth Congress), Committee on Public Expenditures (Twenty-first and Twenty-second Congresses); resumed the practice of medicine and also engaged in agricultural pursuits; member of the State senate in 1836; died in Tarboro, N.C., on June 30, 1853; interment in Macnail-Hall Cemetery, near Tarboro, N.C.

**HALL, Tim Lee,** a Representative from Illinois; born in West Frankfort, Franklin County, Ill., June 11, 1925; educated in West Frankfort public schools; B.A., Iowa Wesleyan College, Mt. Pleasant, Iowa, 1951; M.S., education, Southern Illinois University, 1956; engaged in graduate work at Southern Illinois University in 1961, and at Valparaiso (Ind.) University in 1965; taught school in Illinois public school system for fourteen years; served in United States Coast Guard Reserves, 1943-1946; elected as a Democrat to the Ninety-fourth Congress (January 3, 1975-January 3, 1977); unsuccessful candidate for reelection in 1976 to the Ninety-fifth Congress, and for election in 1978 to the Ninety-sixth Congress; administrative assistant to Illinois secretary of state, 1977-1983; teacher, 1983-1986; school superintendent, Dwight, Ill.; is a resident of Dwight, Ill.

**HALL, Tony Patrick,** a Representative from Ohio; born in Dayton, Montgomery County, Ohio, January 16, 1942; attended the public schools of Ohio; graduated from Fairmont High School, Kettering, 1960; A.B., Denison University, Granville, Ohio, 1964; United States Peace Corps, 1966-1967; realtor; served in the Ohio general assembly, 1969-1972; State senate, 1973-1978; elected as a Democrat to the Ninety-sixth and to the eight succeeding Congresses (January 3, 1979-January 3, 1997); chairman, Select Committee on Hunger (One Hundred First through One Hundred Third Congresses); is a resident of Dayton, Ohio.

**HALL, Uriel Sebree** (son of William Augustus Hall and nephew of Willard Preble Hall), a Representative from Missouri; born near Huntsville, Randolph County, Mo., April 12, 1852; was tutored privately and was graduated from Mount Pleasant College, Huntsville, Mo., in 1873; served as superintendent of schools at Moberly, Mo.; founded an academy at Prairie Hill, Mo., and served as its president; studied law; was admitted to the bar in 1879 and practiced in Moberly, Randolph County, Mo., until 1885, when he engaged in agricultural pursuits near Hubbard, Mo.; elected as a Democrat to the Fifty-third and Fifty-fourth Congresses (March 4, 1893-March 3, 1897); declined to be a candidate for renomination in 1896; president of Pritchett College, Glasgow, Mo., 1897-1901; moved to Columbia, Mo., in 1918 and founded the Hall West Point-Annapolis Coaching School, serving as its president and supervisor from 1918 to 1930, when he retired; died in Columbia, Mo., December 30, 1932; interment in Oakland Cemetery, Moberly, Mo.

**HALL, Willard,** a Representative from Delaware; born in Westford, Middlesex County, Mass., on December 24, 1780; attended the public schools and Westford Academy; was graduated from Harvard University in 1799; studied law; was admitted to the bar in 1803 and commenced practice in Dover, Del.; secretary of state of Delaware 1811-1814; elected as a Republican to the Fifteenth Congress; reelected to the Sixteenth Congress and served from March 4, 1817, until January 22, 1821, when he resigned; unsuccessful candidate in 1820 for reelection to the Seventeenth Congress; again secretary of state in 1821; member of the State senate in 1822; appointed United States district judge for Delaware and served from May 6, 1823, until December 6, 1871, when he resigned; moved to Wilmington, Del., in 1825; compiler of the Revised Code of Delaware in 1829; delegate to the State constitutional convention in 1821; president of the Wilmington School Board 1852-1870; died in Wilmington, Del., May 10, 1875; interment in Wilmington and Brandywine Cemetery.

**Bibliography:** *DAB*.

**HALL, Willard Preble** (brother of William Augustus Hall and uncle of Uriel Sebree Hall), a Representative from Missouri; born at Harpers Ferry, Jefferson County, Va. (now West Virginia), May 9, 1820; attended a private school in Baltimore, Md.; was graduated from Yale College in 1839; accompanied his father to Randolph County, Mo., in 1840; studied law; was admitted to the bar at Huntsville, Mo., in 1841 and commenced practice in Sparta, Mo., in 1842; appointed circuit attorney in 1843 and served several years; presidential elector on the Democratic ticket in 1844; during the Mexican War enlisted as a private in the First Missouri Cavalry and later promoted to lieutenant; was appointed by General Stephen W. Kearny, together with Colonel Alexander Doniphan, to construct the code of civil laws known as the "Kearny Code" in English and Spanish for the territory taken from Mexico; elected as a Democrat to the Thirtieth and to the two succeeding Congresses (March 4, 1847-March 3, 1853); chairman, Committee on Private Land Claims

(Thirty-first Congress), Committee on Public Lands (Thirty-second Congress); moved to St. Joseph, Mo., in 1854 and continued the practice of law; unsuccessful candidate for election to the United States Senate in 1856; member of the constitutional convention of Missouri in 1861 that determined the relations of Missouri to the Union and the other States and decided in favor of the Union; provisional lieutenant governor of Missouri 1861-1864; as brigadier general, Missouri Militia, commanded the northwestern Missouri district until 1863; Acting Governor of Missouri from January 31, 1864 until January 2, 1865; resumed the practice of law; died in St. Joseph, Mo., November 3, 1882; interment in Mount Moriah Cemetery.

**Bibliography:** *DAB*.

**HALL, William,** a Representative from Tennessee; born in Surry County, N.C., February 11, 1775; attended the country schools; moved with his parents to New River, N.C., in 1779 and to Sumner County, Tenn., in 1785 and engaged in agricultural pursuits; served in the Tennessee State house of representatives 1797-1805; brigadier general in the War of 1812; served under Andrew Jackson in the Creek War and against the British; member of the Tennessee State senate 1821-1829, and served as speaker 1827-1829; served as Governor of Tennessee from April 16, 1829 to October 1, 1829, succeeding Governor Sam Houston, who had resigned; major general of militia; elected as a Jacksonian to the Twenty-second Congress (March 4, 1831-March 3, 1833); resumed agricultural pursuits; died on his farm, "Locust Land," near Castalian Springs, Sumner County, Tenn., October 7, 1856; interment in the family cemetery on his farm.

**HALL, William Augustus** (father of Uriel Sebree Hall and brother of Willard Preble Hall), a Representative from Missouri; born in Portland, Maine, October 15, 1815; moved with his parents to Harpers Ferry, Va.; attended the public schools and Yale College; accompanied his father to Randolph County, Mo., in 1840; studied law; was admitted to the bar in 1841 and commenced practice in Huntsville, Mo.; moved to Fayette, Mo., and continued the practice of law; judge of the circuit court 1847-1861; during the Mexican War served as captain; delegate to the State constitutional convention in 1861; elected as a Democrat to the Thirty-seventh Congress to fill the vacancy caused by the expulsion of John B. Clark; reelected as a Unionist to the Thirty-eighth Congress and served from January 20, 1862, to March 3, 1865; was not a candidate for renomination in 1864; delegate to the Democratic National Convention in 1864; resumed the practice of law and also engaged in agricultural pursuits; died near Darkville, Randolph County, Mo., December 15, 1888; interment in the family private cemetery.

**HALL, Wilton Earle,** a Senator from South Carolina; born in Starr, Hall Township, Anderson County, S.C., March 11, 1901; attended the public schools and Furman University, Greenville, S.C.; founded a morning newspaper in Anderson, S.C., in 1924, and in 1929 acquired an evening newspaper; in 1935 established a radio station; chairman of the South Carolina Planning Board 1934-1938; appointed as a Democrat to the United States Senate to fill the vacancy caused by the death of Ellison D. Smith and served from November 20, 1944, to January 3, 1945; was not a candidate for election to the full term; resumed the newspaper publishing business as publisher of the Anderson Independent and Daily Mail of South Carolina; founder of a television station and owner of two radio stations; publisher of Quote Magazine; resided in Anderson, S.C., where he died on February 25, 1980; interment in a mausoleum, Forest Lawn Memorial Park.

**HALLECK, Charles Abraham,** a Representative from Indiana; born in Demotte, Jasper County, Ind., August 22, 1900; attended the public schools; during the First World War served in the Infantry of the United States Army; Indiana University at Bloomington, A.B., 1922 and from the law department of the same university, LL.B.,

1924; was admitted to the bar in 1924 and commenced practice in Rensselaer, Ind.; prosecuting attorney for the thirtieth judicial circuit 1924-1934; elected as a Republican to the Seventy-fourth Congress to fill the vacancy caused by the death of Representative-elect Frederick Landis; reelected to the Seventy-fifth and to the fifteen succeeding Congresses and served from January 29, 1935, to January 3, 1969; majority leader (Eightieth and Eighty-third Congresses); minority leader (Eighty-sixth, Eighty-seventh, and Eighty-eighth Congresses); was not a candidate for reelection in 1968 to the Ninety-first Congress; delegate to each Republican National Convention from 1936 to 1968, and permanent chairman in 1960; was a resident of Rensselaer, Ind. until his death in Lafayette, Ind., March 3, 1986; interment in Weston Cemetery, Rensselaer.

**Bibliography:** Peabody, Robert L. *The Ford-Halleck Minority Leadership Contest.* New York: McGraw-Hill, 1966; Womack, Steven Douglas. "Charles A. Halleck and the New Frontier: Political Opposition through the Madisonian Model." Ph.D. dissertation, Ball State University, 1980.

**HALLOCK, John, Jr.,** a Representative from New York; born in Oxford, Orange County, N.Y., in July 1783; member of the State assembly 1816-1821; member of the State constitutional convention in 1821; elected to the Nineteenth and Twentieth Congresses (March 4, 1825-March 3, 1829); died in Ridgebury, N.Y., December 6, 1840; interment in the Hallock family cemetery near Ridgebury, N.Y.

**HALLOWAY, Ransom,** a Representative from New York; born in Beekman, Dutchess County, N.Y., about 1793; engaged in agricultural pursuits; brigade paymaster of the New York Militia in 1818; elected as a Whig to the Thirty-first Congress (March 4, 1849-March 3, 1851); died in Mount Pleasant, N.Y., April 6, 1851.

**HALLOWELL, Edwin,** a Representative from Pennsylvania; born near Willow Grove, Abington Township, Montgomery County, Pa., April 2, 1844; attended the public schools; engaged in agricultural pursuits; member of the Pennsylvania house of representatives 1876-1879; chairman of the Democratic county committee of Montgomery County in 1886; delegate to the Democratic National Convention in 1888; elected as a Democrat to the Fifty-second Congress (March 4, 1891-March 3, 1893); unsuccessful candidate for reelection in 1892 to the Fifty-third Congress; resumed agricultural pursuits; died in Abington, Pa., September 13, 1916; interment in Abington Friends Burying Ground, Jenkintown, Pa.

**HALPERN, Seymour,** a Representative from New York; born in New York City November 19, 1913; graduate of Richmond Hill High School; attended Seth Low College of Columbia University, 1932-1934; newspaper reporter in New York and Chicago, 1931-1933; engaged in the insurance business; staff assistant to Mayor Fiorello H. LaGuardia of New York City, 1937; assistant to President A. Newbold Morris of the New York City Council, 1938-1940; member, New York State senate, 1941-1954; member, Temporary State Commission to Revise the Civil Service Laws, 1952-1954; member, Mayor's Committee on Courts, 1956-1958; vice president and later chairman of the board, The Insurist Corporation of America, 1948-1959; unsuccessful Republican candidate for election to the Eighty-fourth Congress in 1954; elected as a Republican to the Eighty-sixth and to the six succeeding Congresses (January 3, 1959-January 3, 1973); was not a candidate for reelection in 1972 to the Ninety-third Congress; is a resident of Forest Hills, N.Y.

**HALSELL, John Edward,** a Representative from Kentucky; born near Bowling Green, Warren County, Ky., September 11, 1826; attended the common schools at Rich Pond, Ky., and Cumberland University, Lebanon, Tenn.; studied law; was admitted to the bar in 1856 and commenced practice in Bowling Green; prosecuting attorney of Warren County for four years; elected circuit judge of the fourth judicial district of Kentucky in 1870; elected as a Democrat to the Forty-eighth and Forty-ninth Congresses (March 4, 1883-March 3, 1887); chairman, Committee on Private Land Claims (Forty-ninth Congress); unsuccessful candidate for renomination; resumed the practice of law; mayor of Bowling Green from December 5, 1888, to December 5, 1889; moved to Fort Worth, Tex., and continued the practice of law; died in Fort Worth, December 26, 1899; interment in Fair View Cemetery, Bowling Green, Ky.

**HALSEY, George Armstrong,** a Representative from New Jersey; born in Springfield, Union County, N.J., December 7, 1827; attended the local schools and Springfield Academy; engaged in the manufacture of leather at Newark in 1844 and later in the wholesale clothing business; resumed the leather business in 1866; member of the State house of assembly of New Jersey in 1861 and 1862; United States assessor of internal revenue 1862-1866; elected as a Republican to the Fortieth Congress (March 4, 1867-March 3, 1869); unsuccessful candidate for reelection in 1868 to the Forty-first Congress; elected to the Forty-second Congress (March 4, 1871-March 3, 1873); chairman, Committee on Public Buildings and Grounds (Forty-second Congress); was not a candidate for renomination in 1872; resumed his former manufacturing pursuits; president of an insurance company; died in Newark, N.J., April 1, 1894; interment in Mount Pleasant Cemetery.

**HALSEY, Jehiel Howell** (son of Silas Halsey and brother of Nicoll Halsey), a Representative from New York; born in Southampton, Suffolk County, Long Island, N.Y., October 7, 1788; moved to Herkimer County in 1793 with his parents, who settled in what is now the town of Lodi, Seneca County; attended the common schools; engaged in agricultural pursuits; county clerk of Seneca County 1819-1821; elected to the Twenty-first Congress (March 4, 1829-March 3, 1831); chairman, Committee on Accounts (Twenty-first Congress); resumed agricultural pursuits; member of the State senate 1832-1835; surrogate of Seneca County 1837-1843; supervisor of the town of Lodi 1845-1846; died in Lodi, Seneca County, N.Y., December 5, 1867; interment in West Lodi Cemetery.

**HALSEY, Nicoll** (son of Silas Halsey and brother of Jehiel Howell Halsey), a Representative from New York; born in Southampton, Suffolk County, Long Island, N.Y., March 8, 1782; moved to Herkimer County in 1793 with his parents, who settled in what is now the town of Lodi, Seneca County; attended the common schools; moved to Tompkins County and settled near Trumansburg in 1808; engaged in agricultural pursuits and milling; supervisor for Ulysses in 1812, 1814, 1815, 1818, 1821, and 1826; member of the State assembly in 1816 and again in 1824; sheriff of Tompkins County 1819-1821; elected as a Jacksonian to the Twenty-third Congress (March 4, 1833-March 3, 1835); was not a candidate for renomination in 1834; appointed judge of the Tompkins County Court on February 11, 1834; resumed the milling business; died while on a visit in Marshall, Calhoun County, Mich., March 3, 1865; interment in Grove Cemetery, Trumansburg, N.Y.

**HALSEY, Silas** (father of Jehiel Howell Halsey and Nicoll Halsey), a Representative from New York; born in Southampton, Long Island, N.Y., October 6, 1743 (old style); attended the public schools; studied medicine at Elizabethtown (later Elizabeth), N.J.; returned to Southampton and practiced medicine from 1764 to 1776; resided three years in Killingsworth, Conn., during the Revolutionary War, when he again returned to Southampton, N.Y.; undersheriff of Suffolk County 1784-1787; sheriff 1787-1792; moved to Herkimer County in 1793, settled in what is now the town of Lodi, Seneca County, and continued the practice of medicine; also erected and operated a grist mill; supervisor of the town of Ovid 1794-1804; member of the State assembly from Onondaga County in 1797 and 1798 and from Cayuga County in 1800, 1801, 1803, and 1804; member of the State constitutional convention in 1801; clerk of Seneca County 1804-1813 and 1815; elected as a Republican to the

Ninth Congress (March 4, 1805-March 3, 1807); served in the State senate in 1808 and 1809; engaged in farming; died at Lodi, Seneca County, N.Y., November 19, 1832; interment in Old Halsey Cemetery, South Lodi, N.Y.

**HALSEY, Thomas Jefferson,** a Representative from Missouri; born in Dover, Morris County, N.J., May 4, 1863; in 1878 moved to Missouri with his parents, who settled on a farm near Holden, Johnson County; attended public and private schools, Home Academy at Holden, Mo., Holden (Mo.) College, the State normal school at Warrensburg, Mo., and the University of Missouri at Columbia; taught school in 1880 and 1881; engaged in the mercantile business at Holden, Mo., in 1882; member of the State Republican committee 1896-1898; delegate to the Republican State conventions in 1896, 1908, and 1912; mayor of Holden 1902-1904; moved to Sedalia, Mo., in 1904 and engaged in the wholesale tea and coffee business; member of the executive committee of the Missouri State Roads commission 1906-1910; moved to Glendale, Calif., in 1910 and engaged in the mercantile business; returned to Holden, Mo., in 1911 and engaged in the milling and grain business; member of the Holden Board of Education in 1911 and 1912; member of the board of regents, Central Missouri Teachers College at Warrensburg, 1928-1932; elected as a Republican to the Seventy-first Congress (March 4, 1929-March 3, 1931); unsuccessful candidate for reelection in 1930 to the Seventy-second Congress; returned to former business activities in Holden, Mo.; died in Westfield, N.J., March 17, 1951; interment in Holden Cemetery, Holden, Mo.

**HALSTEAD, William,** a Representative from New Jersey; born in Elizabeth, N.J., June 4, 1794; was graduated from Princeton College in 1812; studied law; was admitted to the bar in 1816 and commenced practice in Trenton, N.J.; appointed State supreme court reporter on November 23, 1821, and served until 1832; published seven volumes of Halstead's Law Reports; prosecuting attorney of Hunterdon County 1824-1829 and 1833-1837; elected as a Whig to the Twenty-fifth Congress (March 4, 1837-March 3, 1839); presented credentials as a Member-elect to the Twenty-sixth Congress but the House declined to seat him; elected to the Twenty-seventh Congress (March 4, 1841-March 3, 1843); chairman, Committee on Elections (Twenty-seventh Congress); appointed by President Zachary Taylor United States district attorney for New Jersey and served from 1849 to 1853; raised the First Regiment of Volunteer Cavalry of New Jersey for the Civil War and served as colonel until February 18, 1862; retired from public life and died in Trenton, Mercer County, N.J., March 4, 1878; interment in Riverview Cemetery.

**HALTERMAN, Frederick,** a Representative from Pennsylvania; born in Vegesack on the Weser, part of the old Hanse town of Bremen, Germany, on October 22, 1831; attended high school; immigrated to the United States and settled in Philadelphia in September 1849; engaged in the grocery business, from which he retired in 1891; elected a member of the select council in 1880 for a term of three years; elected as a Republican to the Fifty-fourth Congress (March 4, 1895-March 3, 1897); was an unsuccessful candidate for reelection in 1896 to the Fifty-fifth Congress; elected president of the twelfth sectional school board of Philadelphia, Pa., in 1898 and served until his death; died in Philadelphia, Pa., March 22, 1907; interment in Laurel Hill Cemetery.

**HALVORSON, Kittel,** a Representative from Minnesota; born in Telemarken, Norway, December 15, 1846; in 1848 immigrated to the United States with his parents, who settled near White Water, Walworth County, Wis.; moved to Columbia County and then to Winnebago County; attended the public schools in Winchester, Wis.; enlisted in Company C, First Regiment, Wisconsin Heavy Artillery, in 1863, and served until the close of the Civil War; moved to Minnesota in November 1865 and settled near Belgrade, Stearns County; engaged in agricultural pursuits and stock raising; justice of the peace 1870-1875; chairman of the board of supervisors

1870-1880; township assessor in 1880; town clerk 1880-1891; member of the State house of representatives 1886-1888; elected as a Populist to the Fifty-second Congress (March 4, 1891-March 3, 1893); unsuccessful candidate for reelection in 1892 to the Fifty-third Congress; resumed agricultural pursuits near Brooten, Stearns County, Minn.; alternate delegate to the People's Party National Convention in 1896; moved to Tewaukon Township, Sargent County, N.Dak., in 1900 and engaged in agricultural pursuits; returned to Minnesota in 1910 and resumed farming in North Fork until 1924, when he retired; died in Havana, N.Dak., on July 12, 1936; interment in Big Grove Church Cemetery, North Fork Township, near Brooten, Minn.

**HAMBLETON, Samuel,** a Representative from Maryland; born at "Waterloo" farm, Talbot County, Md., January 8, 1812; educated by private tutors and attended Easton Academy; studied law; was admitted to the bar in 1833 and commenced practice in Easton, Talbot County, Md.; member of the State house of delegates in 1834 and 1835; State's attorney for Talbot County 1836-1844; served in the State senate 1844-1850; president of the Chesapeake & Ohio Canal in 1853 and 1854; again a member of the State house of delegates in 1853; elected as a Democrat to the Forty-first and Forty-second Congresses (March 4, 1869-March 3, 1873); died in Easton, Md., December 9, 1886; interment in Spring Hill Cemetery.

**HAMBURG, Daniel Eugene,** a Representative from California; born in St. Louis, Mo., October 6, 1948; graduated, Horton Watkins High School, St. Louis, 1966; B.A., Stanford University, Calif., 1970; M.A., California Institute of Integral Studies, San Francisco, 1992; founder, Mariposa School, 1970; appointed to Ukiah City planning commission, 1976, later elected chairman; Mendocino County supervisor, 1981-1985; elected as a Democrat to the One Hundred Third Congress (January 3, 1993-January 3, 1995); unsuccessful candidate for reelection in 1994 to the One Hundred Fourth Congress; field representative for parliamentary and political party development in South Africa for the National Democratic Institute for International Affairs; is a resident of Ukiah, Calif.

**HAMER, Thomas Lyon** (uncle of Thomas Ray Hamer), a Representative from Ohio; born in Northumberland County, Pa., in July 1800; attended the public schools; moved to Ohio in 1817 and taught school; studied law; was admitted to the bar in 1821 and commenced practice in Georgetown, Brown County, Ohio; member of the State house of representatives in 1825, 1828, and 1829, and served as speaker in 1829; elected as a Jacksonian to the Twenty-third Congress; reelected as a Jacksonian to the Twenty-fourth Congress and as a Democrat to the Twenty-fifth Congress (March 4, 1833-March 3, 1839); nominated Ulysses S. Grant to be a cadet at the United States Military Academy at West Point; volunteered as a private for the Mexican War and received the next day, July 1, 1846, the commission of brigadier general; had been elected to the Thirtieth Congress, but died in the service at Monterrey, Mexico, December 2, 1846; on March 2, 1847, Congress passed a resolution of sorrow and presented his nearest male relative with a sword; interment near Monterrey, Mexico; reinterment in Georgetown Cemetery, Georgetown, Ohio.

Bibliography: *DAB.*

**HAMER, Thomas Ray** (nephew of Thomas Lyon Hamer), a Representative from Idaho; born in Vermont, Fulton County, Ill., May 4, 1864; attended the public schools, Hedding College, and Bloomington Law School; was admitted to the bar and commenced practice in St. Anthony, Idaho, in 1893; engaged in agricultural pursuits in Fremont County, Idaho; member of the State house of representatives in 1896; enlisted in April 1898 as a private in the First Regiment, Idaho Volunteer Infantry and served as captain and lieutenant colonel in the Philippines; Military Governor of the island of Cebu; associate justice of the supreme court of the Philippine Islands; returned to St. Anthony, Idaho in 1901; delegate to the

Republican State conventions in 1908 and 1912; elected as a Republican to the Sixty-first Congress (March 4, 1909-March 3, 1911); unsuccessful candidate for renomination in 1910 to the Sixty-second Congress; resumed the practice of law in St. Anthony, Idaho; engaged in banking at St. Anthony and Boise, Idaho, 1912-1921; served as major and lieutenant colonel, Judge Advocate General's Department, during the First World War; reengaged in the practice of law at Portland, Oreg., until 1943, when he retired and moved to Los Angeles, Calif.; died in Phoenix, Ariz., December 22, 1950; interment in Greenwood Memorial Park.

**HAMILL, James Alphonsus,** a Representative from New Jersey; born in Jersey City, N.J., March 30, 1877; attended St. Bridget's Academy; was graduated from St. Peter's College, Jersey City, N.J., in 1897 and from the New York Law School in 1899; was admitted to the bar in 1900 and commenced practice in Jersey City, N.J.; member of the State house of assembly 1902-1905; delegate to the Democratic National Convention in 1908; elected as a Democrat to the Sixtieth and to the six succeeding Congresses (March 4, 1907-March 3, 1921); chairman, Committee on Elections No. 2 (Sixty-second through Sixty-fifth Congresses), Committee on Reform in the Civil Service (Sixty-fourth Congress); was not a candidate for renomination in 1920; resumed the practice of law in New Jersey and New York; represented the Ukrainian people of the United States at the Peace Conference in Paris in 1919; decorated Chevalier of the French Legion of Honor for work in French literature; corporation counsel of Jersey City 1932-1941; died in Jersey City, December 15, 1941; interment in Holy Name Cemetery.

**HAMILL, Patrick,** a Representative from Maryland; born in Allegany County, near Altamont, Md., April 28, 1817; attended the common schools in Westernport; engaged in the real estate business and mercantile pursuits; collector of taxes in 1841 and 1842; member of the State house of delegates in 1843 and 1844; judge of the orphans' court of Allegany County 1854-1869 and elected chief judge in 1867; elected as a Democrat to the Forty-first Congress (March 4, 1869-March 3, 1871); was not a candidate for renomination in 1870; engaged in the real estate business until his death in Oakland, Garrett County, Md., January 15, 1895; interment in Odd Fellows Cemetery.

**HAMILTON, Alexander,** a Delegate from New York; born on the island of Nevis, British West Indies, January 11, 1757; immigrated to the United States in 1772, where he received educational training in the schools of Elizabethtown, N.J., and King's College (now Columbia University), New York City; entered the Continental Army in New York in 1776 as captain of Artillery; appointed aide-de-camp to General Washington on March 1, 1777, and served in that capacity until February 16, 1781; Member of the Continental Congress in 1782, 1783, and 1788; member of the Annapolis Convention of 1786; served in the New York State assembly in 1787; member of the Philadelphia Constitutional Convention in 1787 which adopted the Constitution of the United States; member of the New York ratification convention in 1788; studied law; was admitted to the bar and practiced in New York City; served as Secretary of the Treasury in the Cabinet of President Washington from September 11, 1789 until his resignation on January 31, 1795; returned to New York and resumed the practice of law; mortally wounded in a duel with Aaron Burr at Weehawken, N.J., and died in New York City the following day, July 12, 1804; interment in Trinity Churchyard.

**Bibliography:** *DAB*; Hamilton, Alexander. *The Papers of Alexander Hamilton.* 26 vols. Edited by Harold C. Syrrett and Jacob E. Cooke. New York: Columbia University Press, 1961-1979; McDonald, Forrest. *Alexander Hamilton: A Biography.* New York: Norton, 1979; Miller, John C. *Alexander Hamilton: Portrait in Paradox.* 1959. Reprint. Westport, Conn.: Greenwood Press, 1979.

**HAMILTON, Andrew Holman,** a Representative from Indiana; born in Fort Wayne, Ind., June 7, 1834; attended the common schools and was graduated from Wabash College, Crawfordsville, Ind., in 1854; studied law at Harvard University; was admitted to the bar in 1859 and commenced practice in Fort Wayne, Ind.; elected as a Democrat to the Forty-fourth and Forty-fifth Congresses (March 4, 1875-March 3, 1879); resumed the practice of law; died in Fort Wayne, Ind., May 9, 1895; interment in Lindenwood Cemetery.

**HAMILTON, Andrew Jackson** (brother of Morgan Calvin Hamilton), a Representative from Texas; born in Huntsville, Madison County, Ala., January 28, 1815; attended the common schools; studied law; was admitted to the bar in Talladega, Ala., in 1841; moved to Texas and commenced the practice of law in Lagrange, Fayette County, in 1846; attorney general of the State in 1850; member of the State house of representatives 1851-1853; elected as an Independent Democrat to the Thirty-sixth Congress (March 4, 1859-March 3, 1861); was not a candidate for renomination in 1860 to the Thirty-seventh Congress; moved to New Orleans, La., in 1862; during the Civil War was commissioned brigadier general of Volunteers November 14, 1862; appointed Military Governor of Texas in 1862 by President Lincoln; appointed provisional Governor by President Andrew Johnson on June 17, 1865 and served until August 9, 1866; justice of the supreme court of Texas in 1866; delegate to the Loyalist convention at Philadelphia in 1866; unsuccessful candidate for Governor of Texas in 1869; died in Austin, Tex., April 11, 1875; interment in Oakwood Cemetery.

**Bibliography:** *DAB.*

**HAMILTON, Charles Mann,** a Representative from New York; born in Ripley, Chautauqua County, N.Y., January 23, 1874; attended the Ripley High School, the Fredonia (N.Y.) Normal School, and the Pennsylvania Military College at Chester; interested in agricultural pursuits and in oil production; member of the State assembly 1906-1908; served in the State senate 1908-1912; represented the senate in 1911 on the New York State Factory Commission; delegate to the Republican National Convention at Chicago in 1912; elected as a Republican to the Sixty-third, Sixty-fourth, and Sixty-fifth Congresses (March 4, 1913-March 3, 1919); minority whip (Sixty-fourth and Sixty-fifth Congresses); was not a candidate for renomination in 1918; engaged in agricultural pursuits in Ripley, N.Y., and in the production of oil and gas in Kansas; died in Miami Beach, Fla., on January 3, 1942; interment in Quincy Rural Cemetery, Ripley, N.Y.

**HAMILTON, Charles Memorial,** a Representative from Florida; born in Pine Creek Township, Clinton County, Pa., November 1, 1840; attended the public schools and was graduated from the Columbia Law School, Columbia, Pa.; entered the Union Army as a private in 1861 and served in Company A, Fifth Regiment, Pennsylvania Reserve Corps; appointed judge advocate of the general court-martial and general pass officer for the Army of the Potomac; served on the staff of the Military Governor of Washington, D.C., until transferred to Marianna, Fla., in 1865; was admitted to the bar in 1867 and commenced practice in Marianna, Fla.; upon the readmission of the State of Florida to representation was elected as a Republican to the Fortieth and Forty-first Congresses and served from July 1, 1868, to March 3, 1871; unsuccessful candidate for renomination in 1870 to the Forty-second Congress; appointed senior major general of the Florida Militia in February 1871; postmaster of Jacksonville, Fla., from July 27, 1871, to March 1, 1872; appointed collector of customs at Key West, Fla., in February 1873; resigned on account of ill health; died in Pine Creek Township, Clinton County, Pa., October 22, 1875; interment in Jersey Shore Cemetery.

**HAMILTON, Cornelius Springer,** a Representative from Ohio; born in Gratiot, Muskingum County, Ohio, January 2, 1821; attended the common schools and Granville (Ohio) College; moved with his parents to Union County in 1839; engaged in agricultural pursuits with his father; studied law; was admitted to the bar in 1845 and commenced practice in Marysville, Ohio; land appraiser and assessor in 1845; delegate to the State constitutional convention 1850-1851; editor and proprietor of the Marysville Tribune 1850-1853; member of the State senate in 1856 and 1857; appointed by President Lincoln assessor of the eighth congressional district of Ohio in 1862 and served until 1866; elected as a Republican to the Fortieth Congress and served from March 4, 1867, until killed by an insane son in Marysville, Union County, Ohio, December 22, 1867; interment in Oakdale Cemetery.

**HAMILTON, Daniel Webster,** a Representative from Iowa; born near Dixon, Ogle County, Ill., December 20, 1861; moved to Miami County, Kans., with his parents in 1868 and to Prairie Township, Keokuk County, Iowa, in 1874; attended the country schools and was graduated from the law department of the University of Iowa at Iowa City in June 1884; was admitted to the bar in 1884 and commenced practice in Sigourney, Iowa; postmaster of Sigourney 1894-1898; elected as a Democrat to the Sixtieth Congress (March 4, 1907-March 3, 1909); unsuccessful candidate for reelection in 1908 to the Sixty-first Congress; resumed the practice of law in Sigourney, Iowa; moved to Grinnell, Iowa, when elected judge of the district court of the sixth judicial district of Iowa in 1918, in which capacity he served until his death in Rochester, Minn., August 21, 1936; interment in No. 16 Cemetery, near Thornburg, in Keokuk County, Iowa.

**HAMILTON, Edward La Rue,** a Representative from Michigan; born in Niles Township, Berrien County, Mich., December 9, 1857; attended the graded schools and was graduated from the Niles High School in 1876; studied law; was admitted to the bar in 1884 and commenced practice in Niles, Mich.; elected as a Republican to the Fifty-fifth and to the eleven succeeding Congresses (March 4, 1897-March 3, 1921); chairman, Committee on Territories (Fifty-eighth through Sixty-first Congresses); was not a candidate for renomination in 1920; engaged in the practice of law until his death in St. Joseph, Berrien County, Mich., November 2, 1923; interment in Silverbrook Cemetery, Niles, Mich.

**HAMILTON, Finley,** a Representative from Kentucky; born in Vincent, Owsley County, Ky., June 19, 1886; attended the public schools and Berea (Ky.) College; studied law; was admitted to the bar in 1915 and commenced practice in London, Laurel County, Ky.; was with the Signal Corps, United States Army, with service in the Philippine Islands and Alaska, from 1907 to 1915; during the First World War enlisted on March 18, 1916, and served in Company D, Three Hundred and Fifteenth Field Signal Battalion, Ninetieth Division, with service in France; elected as a Democrat to the Seventy-third Congress (March 4, 1933-January 3, 1935); was not a candidate for renomination in 1934; resumed the practice of law; died in London, Ky., January 10, 1940; interment in Pine Grove Cemetery.

**HAMILTON, James, Jr.,** a Representative from South Carolina; born in Charleston, S.C., May 8, 1786; completed academic studies; studied law; was admitted to the bar and commenced practice in Charleston; served in the War of 1812 as major; mayor of Charleston; member of the State house of representatives, 1819-1823; elected to the Seventeenth Congress to fill the vacancy caused by the resignation of William Lowndes; reelected to the three succeeding Congresses and served from December 13, 1822, to March 3, 1829; chairman, Committee on Military Affairs (Eighteenth through Twentieth Congresses); chosen Governor of South Carolina by the legislature of the State and served from December 1830 to December 13, 1832; moved to Texas; appointed diplomatic agent of the Republic of Texas to France, Great Britain, Belgium and the Netherlands in 1839; was drowned on November 15, 1857, while on his way from New Orleans to Galveston.

**Bibliography:** *DAB*; Glenn, Virginia L. "James Hamilton, Jr., of South Carolina: A Biography." Ph.D. dissertation, University of North Carolina at Chapel Hill, 1964; Kell, Carl Lewis. "A Rhetorical History of James Hamilton, Jr.: The Nullification Era in South Carolina, 1816-1834." Ph.D. dissertation, University of Kansas, 1971.

**HAMILTON, John,** a Representative from Pennsylvania; born in York (now Adams) County, Pa., November 25, 1754; moved to Washington County, Pa., in 1783; commissioned lieutenant colonel of militia in 1786 and brigadier general in 1800; major general of the Fourteenth Division of Militia of Washington and Greene Counties in 1807; appointed high sheriff of Washington County by Governor Thomas Mifflin in 1793 and served until November 1, 1796; member of the Pennsylvania senate 1796-1805; associate judge of Washington County 1802-1805; member of the first board of trustees of Jefferson (now Washington and Jefferson) College, Washington, Pa., 1802-1831; elected as a Republican to the Ninth Congress (March 4, 1805-March 3, 1807); again appointed associate judge of Washington County on May 31, 1820, and served until his death at his home near Ginger Hill, Washington County, Pa., August 22, 1837; interment in Mingo Cemetery, near Monongahela, Pa.

**HAMILTON, John M.,** a Representative from West Virginia; born in Weston, Lewis County, Va. (now West Virginia), March 16, 1855; attended the public schools; recorder of the town of Weston in 1876; studied law; was admitted to the bar in 1877 and commenced practice in Grantsville, Calhoun County, W.Va.; committee clerk in the State senate 1881 and 1882; assistant clerk of the senate 1883-1887; resumed the practice of law in 1887; member of the State house of delegates 1887 and 1888; clerk of the house of delegates 1888-1890; also engaged in banking and served as president of the Calhoun County Bank 1901-1916; elected as a Democrat to the Sixty-second Congress (March 4, 1911-March 3, 1913); unsuccessful candidate for reelection in 1912 to the Sixty-third Congress and for election in 1914 to the Sixty-fourth Congress; resumed the practice of law; served as president of the Calhoun County High School Board; died in Grantsville, W.Va., on December 27, 1916; interment in Odd Fellows Cemetery, Old Bethlehem, W.Va.

**HAMILTON, John Taylor,** a Representative from Iowa; born near Geneseo, Henry County, Ill., October 16, 1843; attended the common schools and the Geneseo Academy; moved to Cedar Rapids, Iowa, in 1868 and engaged in the wholesale farm-implement and seed business; mayor of Cedar Rapids in 1878; member of the Linn County Board of Supervisors 1882-1884; president of Cedar Rapids Savings Bank and director of the electric light company; member of the State house of representatives 1885-1891 and served as speaker for one term; elected as a Democrat to the Fifty-second Congress (March 4, 1891-March 3, 1893); unsuccessful candidate for reelection in 1892 to the Fifty-third Congress; resumed his former business pursuits in Cedar Rapids; member of the board of control of State institutions; unsuccessful candidate for Governor of Iowa in 1914; died in Cedar Rapids, Iowa, January 25, 1925; interment in Oak Hill Cemetery.

**HAMILTON, Lee Herbert,** a Representative from Indiana; born in Daytona Beach, Volusia County, Fla., April 20, 1931; moved with parents to Evansville, Ind., in 1944; attended the public schools of Evansville, Ind.; graduated Central High School, Evansville, 1948; B.A., De Pauw University, 1952; studied at Goethe University, Frankfurt on Main, Germany, in 1952 and 1953; J.D., Indiana University School of Law, 1956; was admitted to the bar in 1957 and began the practice of law in 1958 in Columbus, Ind.; treasurer of Bartholomew County Young Democrats, 1960-1963, and served as president in 1963 and 1964; elected as a Democrat to the Eighty-ninth and to the fifteen succeeding Congresses (January 3, 1965-January 3, 1997); chairman, Select Committee on Intelligence (Ninety-ninth Congress), Select Committee to Investigate Covert

Arms Transactions with Iran (One Hundredth Congress), Joint Economic Committee (One Hundred First Congress); Committee on Foreign Affairs (One Hundred Third Congress); is a resident of Nashville, Ind.

**HAMILTON, Morgan Calvin** (brother of Andrew Jackson Hamilton), a Senator from Texas; born near Huntsville, Madison County, Ala., February 25, 1809; attended the public schools; engaged in mercantile pursuits in Elyton, Ala.; moved to the Republic of Texas in 1837 and owned a store in Austin; clerk in the War Department of the Republic of Texas from 1839 until 1845, and acted as Secretary of War and Marine ad interim of that Republic from December 1844 to March 1845; appointed comptroller of the treasury of Texas in 1867; delegate to the State constitutional convention in 1868; upon the readmission of the State of Texas to representation was elected on February 22, 1870, as a Republican to the United States Senate to fill the vacancy in the term ending March 3, 1871; subsequently elected for the term commencing March 4, 1871, and served from March 31, 1870, to March 3, 1877; retired from public life and traveled extensively; was a resident of Brooklyn, N.Y., until his death; died in San Diego, Calif., where he had been visiting, November 21, 1893; interment in Oakwood Cemetery, Austin, Travis County, Tex.

**HAMILTON, Norman Rond,** a Representative from Virginia; born in Portsmouth, Norfolk County, Va., November 13, 1877; attended the public and high schools; newspaper reporter in Norfolk 1895-1914; publisher of the Portsmouth (Va.) Star from 1917 until merged with Norfolk Ledger in 1955; collector of customs of Virginia 1914-1922; chairman of the Port War Board of Hampton Roads 1916-1918; served as neutrality enforcement officer prior to the entrance of the United States in the First World War; delegate to the Democratic National Conventions in 1924, 1928, 1932, 1952, and 1960; trustee of Virginia State Teachers' College 1922-1926; appointed in 1933 as receiver at Washington, D.C., of five District of Columbia insolvent banks, resigning in June 1936; elected as a Democrat to the Seventy-fifth Congress (January 3, 1937-January 3, 1939); unsuccessful candidate for renomination in 1938 and for election in 1941 to fill a vacancy in the Seventy-seventh Congress; executive of the Norfolk-Portsmouth Newspapers, Inc.; died in Norfolk, Va., March 26, 1964; interment in Oak Grove Cemetery, Portsmouth, Va.

**HAMILTON, Robert,** a Representative from New Jersey; born in Hamburg, Sussex County, N.J., December 9, 1809; attended the common schools; moved to Newton, N.J., in 1831; studied law; was admitted to the bar in 1836 and commenced practice in Newton; prosecutor of pleas of Sussex County 1848-1858, 1868, and 1869; delegate to the Democratic National Conventions at Charleston and Baltimore in 1860; member of the State house of assembly 1863 and 1864 and served as speaker; president of the Merchant's National Bank 1865-1878; elected as a Democrat to the Forty-third and Forty-fourth Congresses (March 4, 1873-March 3, 1877); resumed the practice of law; director of the Morris & Essex Railroad Co.; died in Newton, Sussex County, N.J., March 14, 1878; interment in Newton Cemetery.

**HAMILTON, William Thomas,** a Representative and a Senator from Maryland; born in Boonsboro, Washington County, Md., September 8, 1820; attended Brown's School, Boonsboro, Md., and Jefferson College, Canonsburg, Pa.; studied law; was admitted to the bar in 1845 and commenced practice in Hagerstown; member, State house of delegates in 1846 and 1848; elected as a Democrat to the Thirty-first and to the two succeeding Congresses (March 4, 1849-March 3, 1855); was not a candidate for renomination in 1854 to the Thirty-fourth Congress; chairman, Committee on the District of Columbia (Thirty-third Congress); resumed the practice of law and farming in Hagerstown, Md.; elected as a Democrat to the United States Senate and served from March 4, 1869, to March 3,

1875; was not a candidate for reelection in 1874; elected Governor of Maryland in 1879 and served from January 14, 1880 to January 9, 1884; continued the practice of law until his death in Hagerstown, Md., October 26, 1888; interment in Rose Hill Cemetery.

**Bibliography:** *DAB.*

**HAMLIN, Courtney Walker** (cousin of William Edward Barton), a Representative from Missouri; born in Brevard, Transylvania County, N.C., October 27, 1858; in 1869 moved to Missouri with his parents, who settled in Leasburg, Crawford County; attended the common schools and Salem (Mo.) Academy; studied law; was admitted to the bar in 1882 and commenced practice in Bolivar, Polk County, Mo.; elected as a Democrat to the Fifty-eighth Congress (March 4, 1903-March 3, 1905); unsuccessful candidate for reelection in 1904 to the Fifty-ninth Congress; elected to the Sixtieth and to the five succeeding Congresses (March 4, 1907-March 3, 1919); chairman, Committee on Expenditures in the Department of State (Sixty-second through Sixty-fifth Congresses); unsuccessful candidate for renomination in 1918 to the Sixty-sixth Congress; resumed the practice of law in Springfield, Greene County, Mo., until November 1935, when he retired and moved to Santa Monica, Calif., where he died February 16, 1950; interment in East Lawn Cemetery, Springfield, Mo.

**HAMLIN, Edward Stowe,** a Representative from Ohio; born in Hillsdale, Columbia County, N.Y., July 6, 1808; attended the district school of Hillsdale, N.Y., and a private school in Stockbridge, Mass.; pursued an academic course in Hudson, N.Y.; studied law; was admitted to the bar in 1831 and commenced practice in Elyria, Ohio; prosecuting attorney of Lorain County 1833-1835; elected as a Whig to the Twenty-eighth Congress to fill the vacancy caused by the death of Henry R. Brinkerhoff and served from October 8, 1844, to March 3, 1845; was not a candidate for renomination in 1844 to the Twenty-ninth Congress; moved to Cleveland, Ohio, in 1844; engaged in the newspaper business; established the True Democrat (now the Cleveland Plain Dealer) in 1846; member of the Free-Soil Convention at Buffalo in 1848; president of the board of public works 1849-1852; moved to Cincinnati in 1856; attorney for the Cincinnati, Indianapolis & Lafayette Railroad for many years; moved to Williamsburg, James City County, Va., in 1884 to supervise his extensive land holdings at Newport News; died in Washington, D.C., November 23, 1894; interment in Cedar Grove Cemetery, Williamsburg, Va.

**HAMLIN, Hannibal,** a Representative and a Senator from Maine and a Vice President of the United States; born at Paris Hill, Oxford County, Maine, August 27, 1809; attended the district schools and Hebron Academy; took charge of the family farm and worked as a surveyor, compositor in a printing office, and school teacher; studied law; was admitted to the bar in 1833 and practiced in Hampden, Penobscot County, until 1848; member, Maine State house of representatives, 1836-1841, 1847, and served as speaker in 1837, 1839, and 1840; unsuccessful Democratic candidate for election in 1840 to the Twenty-seventh Congress; elected as a Democrat to the Twenty-eighth and Twenty-ninth Congresses (March 4, 1843-March 3, 1847); chairman, Committee on Elections (Twenty-ninth Congress); unsuccessful Democratic candidate for election to the United States Senate in 1846; elected to the United States Senate in 1848 by the anti-slavery wing of the Democratic party to fill the vacancy caused by the death of John Fairfield; reelected in 1850 and served from June 8, 1848, to January 7, 1857, when he resigned to become Governor; chairman, Committee on Commerce (Thirty-first through Thirty-fourth Congresses); Committee on Printing (Thirty-second Congress); left the Democratic Party in 1856; elected Governor of Maine in 1856 and served from January 8 to February 25, 1857, when he resigned; elected to the United States Senate as a Republican and served from March 4, 1857, until his resignation, effective January 17, 1861, to become vice president;

elected Vice President of the United States, November 6, 1860, on the ticket headed by Abraham Lincoln; inaugurated March 4, 1861, and served until March 4, 1865; appointed collector of the port of Boston in 1865, but resigned in 1866; again elected to the United States Senate in 1869; reelected in 1875 and served from March 4, 1869, until March 3, 1881; was not a candidate for renomination; chairman, Committee on the District of Columbia (Forty-first Congress), Committee on Manufactures (Forty-second Congress), Committee on Mines and Mining (Forty-second and Forty-third Congresses), Committee on Post Office and Post Roads (Forty-fourth and Forty-fifth Congresses), Committee on Foreign Relations (Forty-fifth Congress); appointed United States Minister to Spain on June 30, 1881 and served until October 1882; devoted the remainder of his life to agricultural pursuits; died in Bangor, Maine, July 4, 1891; interment in Mount Hope Cemetery.

Bibliography: *DAB*; Hamlin, Charles Eugene. *The Life and Times of Hannibal Hamlin*. 2 vols. 1899. Reprint. Port Washington, N.Y.: Kennikat Press, 1971; Hunt, H. Draper. *Hannibal Hamlin: Lincoln's First Vice President*. Syracuse, N.Y.: Syracuse University Press, 1969; Scroggins, Mark. *Hannibal: The Life of Lincoln's First Vice President*. Lanham, Md.: University Press of America, 1994.

HAMLIN, Simon Moulton, a Representative from Maine; born in Standish (Richville), Cumberland County, Maine, August 10, 1866; attended the public schools, Gorham (Maine) Normal School, and Bridgton (Maine) Academy; taught school; was graduated from Bowdoin College, Brunswick, Maine, in 1900; superintendent of the South Portland and Cape Elizabeth schools 1901-1925; city clerk of South Portland, Maine, in 1913; engaged in the real estate business at South Portland in 1925; also interested in farming; member of the board of registration 1926-1932; served as mayor in 1933 and 1934; elected as a Democrat to the Seventy-fourth Congress (January 3, 1935-January 3, 1937); chairman, Committee on Memorials (Seventy-fourth Congress); unsuccessful candidate for reelection in 1936 to the Seventy-fifth Congress; resumed the real estate business and farming in South Portland, Maine, until his death there July 27, 1939; interment in Hamlin Cemetery, Standish (Richville), Maine.

HAMMER, William Cicero, a Representative from North Carolina; born near Asheboro, Randolph County, N.C., March 24, 1865; attended private and common schools; studied at Yadkin Institute and Western Maryland College, Westminster, Md.; taught school and was principal of two academies; was graduated in law from the University of North Carolina at Chapel Hill in 1891; was admitted to the bar in September 1891 and commenced practice in Asheboro, N.C.; mayor of Asheboro, member of the city council, and school commissioner 1895-1899; superintendent of public instruction 1891-1895 and again in 1899-1901; solicitor in the superior court 1901-1914; for more than forty years was owner and editor of the Asheboro Courier; appointed United States attorney on February 24, 1914, and served until September 20, 1920; elected as a Democrat to the Sixty-seventh and to the four succeeding Congresses and served from March 4, 1921, until his death in Asheboro, N.C., September 26, 1930; interment in City Cemetery.

HAMMERSCHMIDT, John Paul, a Representative from Arkansas; born in Harrison, Boone County, Ark., May 4, 1922; completed high school at Harrison, Ark.; attended The Citadel, 1938-1939, the University of Arkansas, 1940-1941, and Oklahoma A.&M. (now Oklahoma State University), 1945-1946; entered the United States Army Air Corps in 1942 and served with the Third Combat Cargo Group in China-Burma-India Theater; awarded the Air Medal with four oak leaf clusters, Distinguished Flying Cross with three oak leaf clusters and three battle stars; retired, United States Air Force Reserve; president, Hammerschmidt Lumber Co.; president, Construction Products Co.; served as president, Arkansas Lumber Dealers Association and Southwestern Lumberman's Association; State committeeman from Boone County for fourteen

years; served as State treasurer and member of Republican National Finance Committee; delegate to the Republican National Conventions of 1964, 1968, 1972, 1976, 1980 and 1984; chairman, Arkansas Republican State Central committee, 1964-1966; Republican National Committeeman from Arkansas, 1976-1980; elected as a Republican to the Ninetieth and to the twelve succeeding Congresses (January 3, 1967-January 3, 1993); was not a candidate for reelection in 1992 to the One Hundred Third Congress; chairman, Northwest Arkansas Council; is a resident of Harrison, Ark.

HAMMETT, William Henry, a Representative from Mississippi; born March 25, 1799, in Don Manway, County Cork, Ireland; studied theology; chaplain of the University of Virginia at Charlottesville 1832-1834 and of the State house of delegates; moved to Princeton, Miss.; elected as a Democrat to the Twenty-eighth Congress (March 4, 1843-March 3, 1845); died July 9, 1861, in Washington County, Mississippi.

HAMMOND, Edward, a Representative from Maryland; born at "Font Hill," near Ellicott City, Anne Arundel (now Howard) County, Md., March 17, 1812; attended the common schools, Rockhill Academy, and was graduated from Yale College in 1830; studied law in New Haven, Conn., and in Baltimore, Md.; was admitted to the bar in 1833 and commenced practice in Annapolis, Md.; served in the State house of delegates from Anne Arundel County in 1839, 1841, and 1842; member of the State senate in 1848; elected as a Democrat to the Thirty-first and Thirty-second Congresses (March 4, 1849-March 3, 1853); chairman, Committee on Engraving (Thirty-first and Thirty-second Congresses); was not a candidate for renomination in 1852; elected to the State house of delegates from Howard County in 1861 and 1867; elected associate judge of the fifth judicial district in 1867 and was serving in that position when he died at "Font Hill," near Ellicott City, Md., October 19, 1882; interment in St. John's Cemetery, near Ellicott City, Md.

HAMMOND, Jabez Delno, a Representative from New York; born in New Bedford, Mass., August 2, 1778; attended preparatory schools; studied medicine; commenced practice in Reading, Vt., in 1799; studied law; was admitted to the bar and commenced practice in Cherry Valley, N.Y., in 1805; elected a trustee of the village of Cherry Valley in 1812; member of the council of appointment; elected as a Republican to the Fourteenth Congress (March 4, 1815-March 3, 1817); resumed the practice of law in Cherry Valley; served in the State senate 1817-1821; moved to Albany, N.Y., in 1822 and continued the practice of law; returned to Cherry Valley in 1838 and practiced law; also engaged in literary pursuits; elected judge of Otsego County, N.Y., in 1838 and served five years; served as county superintendent of schools; appointed a member of the State board of regents May 10, 1845, and served until his death in Cherry Valley, Otsego County, N.Y., August 18, 1855; interment in Cherry Valley Cemetery.

Bibliography: *DAB*.

HAMMOND, James Henry, a Representative and a Senator from South Carolina; born in Newberry District, S.C., November 15, 1807; graduated from the South Carolina College (now the University of South Carolina) at Columbia in 1825; taught school and wrote for a newspaper; studied law, was admitted to the bar in 1828 and practiced in Columbia; established a newspaper to support nullification; planter; elected as a Nullifier to the Twenty-fourth Congress and served from March 4, 1835, until February 26, 1836, when he resigned because of ill health; spent two years in Europe; returned to South Carolina and engaged in agricultural pursuits; chosen Governor of South Carolina by the legislature of the State and served from December 1842 to December 1844; elected as a Democrat to the United States Senate in 1857 to fill the vacancy caused by the resignation of Andrew P. Butler and served from December 7, 1857 until November 11, 1860, when he withdrew with other secessionist Senators; died at "Redcliffe," Beach Island, S.C., November 13, 1864.

**Bibliography:** *DAB*; Bleser, Carol. K. *The Hammonds of Redcliffe*. New York: Oxford University Press, 1981; Faust, Drew Gilpin. *James Henry Hammond*. Baton Rouge: Louisiana State University Press, 1982.

**HAMMOND, John,** a Representative from New York; born at Crown Point, Essex County, N.Y., August 17, 1827; attended the public schools and St. Albans Academy, St. Albans, Vt.; was graduated from Rensselaer Polytechnic Institute in Troy, N.Y.; pioneer in California in 1849; volunteered as a private in the Civil War; promoted to captain of Cavalry and advanced to brigadier general; a manufacturer of iron for twenty-five years; president of the Crown Point Iron Co.; elected as a Republican to the Forty-sixth and Forty-seventh Congresses (March 4, 1879-March 3, 1883); was not a candidate for renomination; retired from business; died at Crown Point, N.Y., May 28, 1889; interment in Forest Dale Cemetery.

**HAMMOND, Nathaniel Job,** a Representative from Georgia; born in Elbert County, Ga., December 26, 1833; attended the common schools and was graduated from the University of Georgia at Athens in 1852; studied law, was admitted to the bar in 1853 and commenced practice in Atlanta, Ga.; solicitor general of the Atlanta circuit 1861-1865; reporter of the supreme court 1867-1872; attorney general 1872-1877; member of the State constitutional conventions in 1865 and 1877; elected a trustee of the University of Georgia in 1872; elected as a Democrat to the Forty-sixth and to the three succeeding Congresses (March 4, 1879-March 3, 1887); unsuccessful candidate for renomination in 1886; resumed the practice of law in Atlanta, Ga., and died there April 20, 1899; interment in Oakland Cemetery.

**Bibliography:** *DAB*.

**HAMMOND, Peter Francis,** a Representative from Ohio; born in Lancaster, Fairfield County, Ohio, June 30, 1887; attended the parochial schools and St. Mary's High School, Lancaster, Ohio; was graduated from Josephinum College, Columbus, Ohio, in 1910; became engaged in the men's clothing business at Lancaster, Ohio, in 1913; elected as a Democrat to the Seventy-fourth Congress by special election, November 3, 1936, to fill the vacancy caused by the resignation of Mell G. Underwood and served from November 3, 1936, to January 3, 1937; was not a candidate for election in 1936 to the Seventy-fifth Congress; resumed the retail clothing business until 1938; postmaster of Lancaster, Ohio, from December 17, 1938, to May 31, 1954; resided in Lancaster, Ohio, where he died April 2, 1971; interment in St. Mary's Cemetery.

**HAMMOND, Robert Hanna,** a Representative from Pennsylvania; born in Milton, Northumberland County, Pa., April 28, 1791; attended the academies at Milton; engaged in mercantile pursuits; member of the Pennsylvania militia, with the rank of brigadier general; enlisted in the United States Army as a lieutenant in 1817; resigned and returned to Milton, Pa.; was register and recorder of Northumberland County; postmaster of Milton 1833-1837; elected as a Democrat to the Twenty-fifth and Twenty-sixth Congresses (March 4, 1837-March 3, 1841); reentered the Army and was commissioned paymaster during the Mexican War; was wounded and ordered home on sick leave; died at sea before reaching port on June 2, 1847; interment in Milton Cemetery, Milton, Pa.

**HAMMOND, Samuel,** a Representative from Georgia; born in Farnham Parish, Richmond County, Va., September 21, 1757; attended the common schools; served as a volunteer under Governor Dunmore against the Indians; during the Revolutionary War served in the Continental Army; promoted to assistant quartermaster at the siege of Savannah; member of the "council of capitulation" at Charleston; shortly after the war settled in Savannah, Ga.; surveyor general of Georgia in 1796; served in the Creek War and commanded a corps of Georgia Volunteers in 1793; member of the Georgia State house of representatives, 1796-1798; member of the State senate, 1799-1800; elected as a Republican to the Eighth Congress, and served from March 4, 1803 until February 2, 1805, when he became Military Governor of Upper Louisiana Territory and served from 1805 to 1824; receiver of public moneys in Missouri; president of the Bank of St. Louis; moved to South Carolina in 1824; member of the house of representatives of South Carolina; surveyor general in 1825; secretary of state of South Carolina, 1831-1835; retired from public life and died at "Varello Farm," on the South Carolina side of the Savannah River, near Augusta, Ga., September 11, 1842; interment in Hammond Cemetery, New Richmond, S.C.

**Bibliography:** *DAB*.

**HAMMOND, Thomas,** a Representative from Indiana; born in Fitchburg, Worcester County, Mass., February 27, 1843; attended the common schools; engaged in carpentry and contracting work until twenty-one years of age; moved to Detroit, Mich., and engaged in the packing-house business; moved to Hammond, Lake County, Ind., in 1876 and assisted in the establishment of the dressed-beef industry; mayor of Hammond 1888-1893; president of the Commercial Bank of Hammond 1892-1907; elected as a Democrat to the Fifty-third Congress (March 4, 1893-March 3, 1895); was not a candidate for renomination in 1894 to the Fifty-fourth Congress; resumed his former business pursuits; also engaged in the real estate business and banking; member of the city council; appointed a member of the metropolitan police board by Governor J. Frank Hanly; died in Hammond, Ind., September 21, 1909; interment in Oak Hill Cemetery.

**HAMMOND, Winfield Scott,** a Representative from Minnesota; born in Southboro, Worcester County, Mass., November 17, 1863; attended the public schools and was graduated from Dartmouth College, Hanover, N.H., in 1884; moved to Minnesota and settled in Madelia, Watonwan County; principal in the public schools; studied law; was admitted to the bar in 1891 and commenced practice in St. James, Minn.; prosecuting attorney of Watonwan County in 1895 and 1896 and again from 1900 to 1905; member of the State board of normal school directors, 1896-1900; elected as a Democrat to the Sixtieth and to the three succeeding Congresses; was not a candidate for reelection in 1914 to the Sixty-fourth Congress; served from March 4, 1907 until he resigned on January 6, 1915, having been elected Governor; elected Governor of Minnesota in 1914, and served from January 5, 1915 until his death; died in Clinton, La., December 30, 1915; interment in Mount Hope Cemetery, St. James, Minn.

**HAMMONS, David,** a Representative from Maine; born in Cornish, Maine, May 12, 1808; attended the common schools; studied law; was admitted to the bar in 1836 and commenced practice in Lovell, Oxford County, Maine; member of the State senate in 1840 and 1841; elected as a Democrat to the Thirtieth Congress (March 4, 1847-March 3, 1849); continued the practice of law until his death in Bethel, Oxford County, Maine, on November 7, 1888; interment in Woodland Cemetery.

**HAMMONS, Joseph,** a Representative from New Hampshire; born in Cornish, York County, Maine, March 3, 1787; educated by private tutors and in the common schools; studied medicine in Ossipee, N.H., and commenced practice in Farmington, N.H., in 1817; elected as a Jacksonian to the Twenty-first and Twenty-second Congresses (March 4, 1829-March 3, 1833); postmaster at Dover, N.H., from June 1833 until his death in Farmington, N.H., March 29, 1836; interment in the old family cemetery.

**HAMPTON, James Giles,** a Representative from New Jersey; born in Bridgeton, Cumberland County, N.J., June 13, 1814; attended the common schools and was graduated from Princeton College in 1835; studied law; was admitted to the bar in 1839 and commenced practice in Bridgeton, N.J.; collector of the port of Bridgeton, N.J., 1841-1844; elected as a Whig to the Twenty-ninth and Thirtieth Congresses (March 4, 1845-March 3, 1849); was not a candidate for renomination in 1848 to the Thirty-first Congress; resumed the practice of law in Bridgeton, N.J.; solicitor of the board of chosen freeholders of Cumberland County in 1852; died in Bridgeton, N.J., on September 22, 1861; interment in Broad Street Presbyterian Cemetery.

**HAMPTON, Moses,** a Representative from Pennsylvania; born in Beaver, Pa., October 28, 1803; moved with his parents to Trumbull County, Ohio; pursued classical studies and was graduated from Washington College (now Washington and Jefferson University), Washington, Pa., in 1827; studied law in Uniontown; was admitted to the bar in 1829 and commenced practice in Somerset; moved to Pittsburgh in 1838 and continued the practice of law; elected as a Whig to the Thirtieth and Thirty-first Congresses (March 4, 1847-March 3, 1851); was not a candidate for renomination in 1850 to the Thirty-second Congress; president judge of the Allegheny County District Court 1853-1873; died at his home, "Hampton Place," adjoining the village of Wilkinsburg, Allegheny County, Pa., June 27, 1878; interment in Allegheny Cemetery, Pittsburgh, Pa.

**HAMPTON, Wade** (grandfather of Wade Hampton [1818-1902]), a Representative from South Carolina; born in Virginia in 1752; received a thorough education; engaged in agricultural pursuits; moved to South Carolina; served in the Revolutionary War as lieutenant colonel of the regiment of light dragoons in General Sumter's brigade of State troops; served in the state assembly, 1779-1786 and 1791; elected as a Republican to the Fourth Congress (March 4, 1795-March 3, 1797); unsuccessful candidate for reelection in 1796 to the Fifth Congress; elected to the Eighth Congress (March 4, 1803-March 3, 1805); unsuccessful candidate for reelection in 1804 to the Ninth Congress; colonel in the United States Army in 1808; appointed brigadier general in February 1809 and major general March 2, 1813; served in the War of 1812 until April 6, 1814, when he resigned; died in Columbia, S.C., on February 4, 1835; interment in Trinity Churchyard, Columbia, S.C.

**Bibliography:** *DAB*; Bridwell, Ronald Edward. "The South's Wealthiest Planter: Wade Hampton I of South Carolina, 1754-1835." Ph.D. dissertation, University of South Carolina, 1980; Cauthern, Charles Edward, ed. *Family Letters of the Three Wade Hamptons, 1782-1901.* South Carolina Sesquicentennial Series, No. 4. Columbia: University of South Carolina Press, 1953.

**HAMPTON, Wade** (grandson of Wade Hampton [1752-1835]), a Senator from South Carolina; born in Charleston, S.C., March 28, 1818; received private instruction, graduated from the South Carolina College (now the University of South Carolina) at Columbia in 1836; studied law but never practiced; planter; member, South Carolina State house of representatives, 1852-1856; member, State senate, 1858-1861; served in the Confederate Army during the Civil War, raising and commanding "Hampton's Legion"; wounded at the battles of First Bull Run, Seven Pines, and Gettysburg; appointed brigadier general on May 23, 1862, major general on September 3, 1863 and lieutenant general on February 15, 1865; elected Governor of South Carolina in 1876, reelected in 1878, and served from December 14, 1876 until his resignation February 26, 1879; elected in 1878 as a Democrat to the United States Senate; reelected in 1884 and served from March 4, 1879, until March 3, 1891; unsuccessful candidate for reelection; United States railroad commissioner, 1893-1897; died in Columbia, S.C., April 11, 1902; interment in Trinity Churchyard.

**Bibliography:** *DAB*; Jarrell, Hampton. *Wade Hampton and the Negro: The Road Not Taken.* Columbia: University of South Carolina Press, 1949; Wellman, Manly. *Giant in Gray: A Biography of Wade Hampton of South Carolina.* New York: Scribner's Sons, 1949.

**HANBACK, Lewis,** a Representative from Kansas; born in Winchester, Scott County, Ill., March 27, 1839; attended the common schools and Cherry Grove Seminary in Knox County, Ill., for three years; taught school in Morgan County, Ill., in 1860 and 1861; during the Civil War enlisted as a private in Illinois Volunteer Infantry and was promoted to brigade inspector; studied law in Albany, N.Y.; returned to Illinois and from there moved to Topeka, Kans.; was admitted to the bar in 1865 and practiced; elected justice of the peace in 1867; probate judge of Shawnee County 1868-1872; assistant chief clerk of the State house of representatives; assistant secretary of the State senate in 1877; assistant United States district attorney of Kansas 1877-1879; receiver of public moneys at Salina; elected as a Republican to the Forty-eighth and Forty-ninth Congresses (March 4, 1883-March 3, 1887); unsuccessful candidate for reelection to the Fiftieth Congress; resumed the practice of law; died in Kansas City, Kans., September 7, 1897; interment in Topeka Cemetery, Topeka, Kans.

**HANBURY, Harry Alfred,** a Representative from New York; born in Bristol, England, January 1, 1863; immigrated to the United States with his parents at an early age; attended the public schools and was graduated from the Boys' High School in New York City; entered mercantile life and established ironworks; delegate to State conventions in 1896, 1898, 1900, 1902, 1906, and 1914; elected as a Republican to the Fifty-seventh Congress (March 4, 1901-March 3, 1903); United States shipping commissioner, port of New York, from March 1903 to November 1909; established a foundry and machine works in Brooklyn, N.Y.; engaged in mechanical engineering and ship reconstruction in Brooklyn, N.Y.; died in Methuen, Mass., August 22, 1940; interment in Greenwood Cemetery, Brooklyn, N.Y.

**HANCE, Kent Ronald,** a Representative from Texas; born in Dimmitt, Castro County, Tex., November 14, 1942; attended the public schools of Dimmitt; B.B.A., Texas Tech University, 1965; LL.B., University of Texas School of Law, 1968; admitted to the Texas bar in 1968 and commenced practice in Lubbock; professor, Texas Tech University, 1968-1973; served in the Texas State senate, 1974-1978; elected as a Democrat to the Ninety-sixth and to the two succeeding Congresses (January 3, 1979-January 3, 1985); was not a candidate for reelection in 1984 to the House of Representatives, but was an unsuccessful candidate for nomination to the United States Senate; changed party affiliation to Republican in 1985; was an unsuccessful candidate for the Republican nomination for Governor of Texas in 1986; chairman, Texas State railroad commission, 1987-1990; resumed the practice of law with Hance, Scarborough, Woodward and Weisbart, Austin, Tex.; is a resident of Austin, Tex.

**HANCHETT, Luther,** a Representative from Wisconsin; born in Middlebury, Portage County, Ohio, October 25, 1825; attended the common schools; studied law; was admitted to the bar in 1846 and commenced practice in Fremont, Ohio; moved to Portage County, Wis., in 1849; engaged in lumber and mining enterprises; county attorney two years; member of the State senate 1856-1860; elected as a Republican to the Thirty-seventh Congress and served from March 4, 1861, until his death in Plover, Portage County, Wis., November 24, 1862; interment in Plover Cemetery.

**HANCOCK, Clarence Eugene,** a Representative from New York; born in Syracuse, N.Y., February 13, 1885; attended the public schools; was graduated from Wesleyan University, Middletown, Conn., in 1906 and from New York (N.Y.) Law School in 1908; was admitted to the bar in 1908 and commenced practice in Syracuse, N.Y.; served as a sergeant in the First New York Cavalry on the Mexican border in 1916; during the First World War served overseas as a captain with the One Hundred and Fourth Machine Gun Battalion, Twenty-seventh Division, 1917-1919; corporation counsel of Syracuse, N.Y., 1926-1927; trustee of Wesleyan University, Middletown, Conn.; elected as a Republican to the Seventieth Congress to fill the vacancy caused by the death of Walter W. Magee; reelected to the Seventy-first and to the eight succeeding Congresses and served from November 8, 1927, to January 3, 1947; was not a candidate for renomination in 1946 to the Eightieth Congress; resumed the practice of law in Syracuse, N.Y.; died January 3, 1948, in a hospital in Washington, D.C.; interment in Woodlawn Cemetery, Syracuse, N.Y.

**HANCOCK, Franklin Wills, Jr.,** a Representative from North Carolina; born in Oxford, Granville County, N.C., November 1, 1894; attended the public schools, Horner Military Academy, Oxford, N.C., and the University of North Carolina at Chapel Hill; studied law; was admitted to the bar in 1916 and commenced practice in Oxford, N.C.; also interested in insurance and real estate; during the First World War attended officers' training camp at Fort Oglethorpe, Ga.; chairman of the Granville County Democratic Executive committee in 1924; served in the North Carolina State senate, 1926-1928; member of the State house of representatives, 1928-1930; trustee of the Colored Orphanage of North Carolina at Oxford, 1920-1937; delegate to the Democratic National Convention of 1940; elected as a Democrat to the Seventy-first Congress to fill the vacancy caused by the death of Charles M. Stedman, and on the same day was elected to the Seventy-second Congress; reelected to the three succeeding Congresses, and served from November 4, 1930 to January 3, 1939; did not seek renomination in 1938 to the House of Representatives, but was an unsuccessful candidate for nomination to the United States Senate; member of the Federal Home Loan Bank Board from January 4, 1939, to April 24, 1942; appointed special representative of the Reconstruction Finance Corporation and served until June 1943; administrator of the Farm Security Administration from November 1943 to November 1945; president of the Commodity Credit Corporation from December 1944 to August 1945; resumed the general practice of law at Oxford, N.C.; elected judge of Granville County Recorder's Court, 1950 and 1952; died in Oxford, N.C., January 23, 1969; interment in Elmwood Cemetery.

**HANCOCK, George,** a Representative from Virginia; born in Chesterfield County, Va., on June 13, 1754; pursued classical studies; served in the Revolutionary War as colonel of Infantry, Virginia Line; studied law; was admitted to the bar in June 1774 and commenced practice in Chesterfield County; appointed ensign in Chesterfield County, Va., in 1776 and later promoted to captain; admitted to the practice of law in the courts of Powhatan County, Va., July 20, 1780, and later moved to Botetourt County, Va., where on April 12, 1782, he was admitted to the practice of law; appointed colonel of militia of Botetourt County, Va., on August 10, 1785; served as Commonwealth's attorney of Botetourt County from March 4, 1787, to October 11, 1789, and as deputy Commonwealth's attorney from 1789 to 1793; elected to the Third and Fourth Congresses (March 4, 1793-March 3, 1797); engaged in the management of his estate, "Fotheringay," Elliston Valley, Montgomery County, Va., where he died July 18, 1820; interment in a tomb on his estate.

**HANCOCK, John,** a Representative from Texas; born near Bellefonte, Jackson County, Ala., October 24, 1824; attended the public schools and the University of Tennessee at Knoxville; studied law; was admitted to the bar in 1846; settled in Austin, Tex., in 1847 and practiced his profession there until August 1851; served as judge of the second judicial district of Texas from 1851 to 1855, when he resigned; resumed the practice of law and engaged in planting and stock raising; member of the State house of representatives in 1860 and 1861; refused to take the oath of allegiance to the Confederate States and was expelled from the legislature; took up

his residence in the North until the conclusion of the war, when he returned to Texas; member of the State constitutional convention in 1866; elected as a Democrat to the Forty-second and to the two succeeding Congresses (March 4, 1871-March 3, 1877); unsuccessful candidate for renomination in 1876 to the Forty-fifth Congress; elected to the Forty-eighth Congress (March 4, 1883-March 3, 1885); was not a candidate for renomination in 1884 to the Forty-ninth Congress; resumed the practice of law; died in Austin, Tex., July 19, 1893; interment in Oakwood Cemetery.

**Bibliography:** *DAB.*

**HANCOCK, John,** a Delegate from Massachusetts; born in Quincy, Norfolk County, Mass., January 12, 1737; pursued classical studies; was graduated from Harvard College in 1754; a selectman of Boston several terms; member of the provincial legislature 1766-1772; president of the Provincial Congress in 1774; Member of the Continental Congress 1775-1778 and served as President of the Congress from May 24, 1775, to October 1777; first signer of the Declaration of Independence; served as senior major general of Massachusetts Militia during the Revolutionary War; member of the Massachusetts constitutional convention in 1780; Governor of Massachusetts 1780-1785; was again elected President of the Continental Congress on November 23, 1785, but resigned May 29, 1786, not having served on account of illness; again Governor of Massachusetts from May 30, 1787 until his death in Quincy, Mass., October 8, 1793; interment in Old Granary Burying Ground, Boston, Mass.

**Bibliography:** *DAB*; Allan, Herbert S. *John Hancock, Patriot in Purple.* New York: Macmillan Co., 1948; Baxter, William T. *The House of Hancock; Business in Boston, 1724-1775.* Cambridge, Mass.: Harvard University Press, 1945.

**HANCOCK, Melton D. (Mel),** a Representative from Missouri; born in Cape Fair, Stone County, Mo., September 14, 1929; graduated, Senior High School, Springfield, Mo., 1947; B.S., Southwest Missouri State University, Springfield, 1951; entered active duty, United States Air Force in 1951, released in 1952; United States Air Force Reserve, 1953-1965; businessman; walnut grower; owner of a small security business; unsuccessful candidate in 1982 for the Republican nomination to the United States Senate; unsuccessful candidate for lieutenant governor of Missouri in 1984; elected as a Republican to the One Hundred First and to the three succeeding Congresses (January 3, 1989-January 3, 1997); not a candidate for reelection in 1996 to the One Hundred Fifth Congress; is a resident of Springfield, Mo.

**HAND, Augustus Cincinnatus,** a Representative from New York; born in Shoreham, Addison County, Vt., September 4, 1803; pursued academic studies; studied law in Litchfield, Conn.; was admitted to the bar in 1828 and commenced practice at Crown Point, N.Y.; moved to Elizabethtown, N.Y., in 1831; surrogate of Essex County 1831-1839; elected as a Democrat to the Twenty-sixth Congress (March 4, 1839-March 3, 1841); elected a member of the State senate in 1844 and served several years; associate justice of the State supreme court 1847-1855; delegate to the Democratic National Convention in 1868; resumed the practice of his profession; died in Elizabethtown, Essex County, N.Y., March 8, 1878; interment in Riverside Cemetery.

**HAND, Edward,** a Delegate from Pennsylvania; born in Clyduff, County Kings, Ireland, December 31, 1744; accompanied the Eighteenth Royal Irish Regiment to the United States as surgeon's mate in 1774, but resigned; settled in Pennsylvania and practiced medicine; during the Revolution was commissioned lieutenant colonel on June 25, 1775; promoted colonel on March 7, 1776, and brigadier general on April 1, 1777; succeeded General John Stark in command at Albany in 1778 and served in the expedition against the Indians of the Six Nations; took command of a brigade of the Light Infantry Corps in August 1780; adjutant general of the Army from January 1781 to November 1783; brevetted major general on September 30, 1783; mustered out on November 3, 1783; Member of the Continental Congress in 1783 and 1784; commissioned major general in the United States Army on June 19, 1798; honorably discharged on June 15, 1800; died in Rockford, Lancaster County, Pa., September 3, 1802; interment in St. James's Episcopal Cemetery.

**Bibliography:** *DAB.*

**HAND, Thomas Millet,** a Representative from New Jersey; born in Cape May, N.J., July 7, 1902; attended the public schools; was graduated from Dickinson College School of Law, Carlisle, Pa., in 1922; was admitted to the bar in 1924 and commenced practice in Cape May City, N.J.; clerk of the Board of Chosen Freeholders of Cape May County, N.J., 1924-1928; prosecutor of the pleas of Cape May County 1928-1933; mayor of Cape May, N.J., 1937-1944; publisher of the Cape May Star and Wave from 1940 until his death; also a partner in the Mecray-Hand Co., a real estate and insurance business; elected as a Republican to the Seventy-ninth and to the five succeeding Congresses and served from January 3, 1945, until his death in Cold Spring, N.J., December 26, 1956; had been reelected to the Eighty-fifth Congress; remains were cremated at Ewing Cemetery, Trenton, N.J., and interred in Cold Spring Cemetery.

**HANDLEY, William Anderson,** a Representative from Alabama; born at Liberty Hill, near Franklin, Heard County, Ga., December 15, 1834; moved to Alabama; attended the public schools; moved to Roanoke, Randolph County, Ala.; during the Civil War served in the Confederate Army as captain of the Twenty-fifth Regiment; engaged in mercantile pursuits; elected as a Democrat to the Forty-second Congress (March 4, 1871-March 3, 1873); served in the State senate 1888-1892; delegate to the State constitutional convention in 1901; member of the State house of representatives 1903-1907; resumed his former mercantile activities; died in Roanoke, Ala., June 23, 1909; interment in the City Cemetery.

**HANDY, Levin Irving** (nephew of William Campbell Preston Breckenridge), a Representative from Delaware; born in Berlin, Worcester County, Md., December 24, 1861; attended the public schools in Maryland and New York; taught school at Damos Quarter, Somerset County, Md.; elected principal of the high school at Smyrna, Del., in 1881; superintendent of free schools in Kent County 1887-1890; principal of Old Newark Academy, Newark, Del., 1890-1892; chairman of the Democratic State central committee 1892-1896; editorial writer on the Wilmington Every Evening in 1894 and 1895; unsuccessful candidate for election in 1894 to the Fifty-fourth Congress; studied law; was admitted to the bar in 1899 and practiced in Wilmington, Del.; elected as a Democrat to the Fifty-fifth Congress (March 4, 1897-March 3, 1899); unsuccessful candidate for reelection to the Fifty-sixth Congress; unsuccessful candidate for attorney general in 1904; unsuccessful candidate for election to the Sixty-first Congress; delegate to the Democratic National Conventions in 1900, 1904, and 1908; resumed the practice of law in Wilmington, Del., and died there February 3, 1922; interment in Glenwood Cemetery, Smyrna, Del.

**HANKS, James Millander,** a Representative from Arkansas; born in Helena, Phillips County, Ark., February 12, 1833; attended the public schools, the college at New Albany, Ind., and Jackson College, Columbia, Tenn.; studied law; was graduated from the University of Louisville in 1855; was admitted to the bar and commenced practice in Helena; judge of the first judicial district of Arkansas 1864-1868; elected as a Democrat to the Forty-second Congress (March 4, 1871-March 3, 1873); was not a candidate for renomination in 1872; engaged in agricultural pursuits; died in Helena, Ark., May 24, 1909; interment in Maple Hill Cemetery.

**HANLEY, James Michael,** a Representative from New York; born in Syracuse, Onondaga County, N.Y., July 19, 1920; attended the Syracuse, N.Y., schools; graduated from St. Lucy's Academy in 1938; served in the United States Army from October 14, 1942 to January 31, 1946; owner and director, Callahan-Hanley-Mooney Funeral Home, 1953-1964; served on the advisory board of Maria Regina College, Syracuse, N.Y.; executive secretary to the Onondaga County Democratic committee, 1963-1964; elected as a Democrat to the Eighty-ninth and to the seven succeeding Congresses (January 3, 1965-January 3, 1981); chairman, Committee on Post Office and Civil Service (Ninety-sixth Congress); was not a candidate for reelection in 1980 to the Ninety-seventh Congress; vice chairman, Board of Trustees, College of Environmental Science and Forestry, State University of New York; is a resident of Syracuse, N.Y.

**HANLY, James Franklin,** a Representative from Indiana; born near St. Joseph, Champaign County, Ill., April 4, 1863; attended the common schools and the Eastern Illinois Normal School at Danville, Ill., 1879-1881; moved to Warren County, Ind., in 1879; taught in the public schools of the State 1881-1889; studied law; was admitted to the bar in 1889 and commenced practice in Williamsport, Warren County, Ind.; member of the State senate in 1890 and 1891; elected as a Republican to the Fifty-fourth Congress (March 4, 1895-March 3, 1897); unsuccessful candidate for renomination in 1896 to the Fifty-fifth Congress; moved to Lafayette, Ind., in 1896; elected Governor of Indiana in 1904 and served from January 9, 1905 to January 11, 1909; prohibition lecturer throughout the United States 1910-1920 and in France in 1919; organized and was editor of the Enquirer Publishing Co. and the Indianapolis Commercial in 1915; resumed the practice of law in Indianapolis; unsuccessful candidate of the Prohibition Party for President of the United States in 1916; died as the result of an automobile accident near Dennison, Tuscarawas County, Ohio, August 1, 1920; interment in Hillside Cemetery, near Williamsport, Ind.

**HANNA, John,** a Representative from Indiana; born near Indianapolis, Ind., September 3, 1827; pursued classical studies; was graduated from the Indiana Asbury (now De Pauw) University, Greencastle, Ind., in 1850; studied law; was admitted to the bar and commenced practice in Greencastle; mayor of Greencastle, 1851-1854; moved to Kansas; was a member of its Territorial legislature in 1857 and 1858; returned to Indiana; United States district attorney, 1861-1869; elected as a Republican to the Forty-fifth Congress (March 4, 1877-March 3, 1879); unsuccessful candidate for reelection in 1878 to the Forty-sixth Congress; died in Plainfield, Ind., October 24, 1882; interment in Forest Hill Cemetery, Greencastle, Ind.

**HANNA, John Andre** (grandfather of Archibald McAllister), a Representative from Pennsylvania; born in Flemington, Hunterdon County, N.J., in 1762; received a classical education; was graduated from Princeton College in 1782; studied law; was admitted to the bar of Lancaster County in 1783 and commenced practice in Lancaster, Pa.; moved to Harrisburg, and was admitted to the Dauphin County bar in 1785; delegate to the Pennsylvania convention to ratify the Federal Constitution in 1787; secretary of the anti-Federal conference in 1788; member of the Pennsylvania house of representatives in 1791; was elected lieutenant colonel of the Third Battalion of Dauphin County on December 29, 1792; appointed brigadier general of Dauphin County Brigade, April 19, 1793, and was in command during the Whiskey Rebellion of 1794; appointed major general of the Sixth Division of Dauphin and Berks Counties on April 23, 1800; elected as a Republican to the Fifth and to the four succeeding Congresses, and served from March 4, 1797 until his death in Harrisburg, Pa., July 23, 1805; interment in Mount Kalmia Cemetery.

**HANNA, Louis Benjamin,** a Representative from North Dakota; born in New Brighton, Beaver County, Pa., August 9, 1861; attended the common schools of Ohio, Massachusetts, and New York; moved to Dakota Territory in 1881 and settled near what is now Hope, N.Dak.; moved to Page, Cass County, in 1882 and engaged in the lumber business and in mercantile pursuits; member of the North Dakota State house of representatives, 1895-1897; moved to Fargo in 1899 to become vice president of the First National Bank of Fargo; served in the State senate, 1897-1901, and 1905-1909; chairman of the Republican State central committee from 1902 until 1908; trustee of Fargo College beginning in 1898; delegate to the Republican National Convention of 1904; elected as a Republican to the Sixty-first and Sixty-second Congresses and served from March 4, 1909, to January 7, 1913; elected Governor of North Dakota in 1912, reelected in 1914, and served from January 8, 1913 to January 3, 1917; unsuccessful candidate for the Republican nomination for United States Senator in 1916 and 1926; chairman of the State Liberty Loan Committee in 1917 and 1918; served as captain in the American Red Cross in France during the First World War, and was decorated with the Grand Cross of St. Olaf by King Haakon VII of Norway, and cited an officer of the French Legion of Honor by the French Government; chairman of the Republican State campaign committee in 1924; engaged in agricultural pursuits and banking until his retirement; died in Fargo, N.Dak., on April 23, 1948; interment in Riverside Cemetery.

**HANNA, Marcus Alonzo** (father of Ruth Hanna McCormick), a Senator from Ohio; born in New Lisbon (now Lisbon), Columbiana County, Ohio, September 24, 1837; moved with his parents to Cleveland in 1852; attended the common schools of that city and Western Reserve College, Hudson, Ohio; engaged in the wholesale grocery business and later in the iron and coal business, the lake carrying trade, and railroads; chairman of the Republican National Committee in 1896; appointed in 1897 and subsequently elected as a Republican to the United States Senate to fill the vacancy caused by the resignation of John Sherman; reelected in January 1898 and also was elected for the succeeding full term and served from March 5, 1897, until his death in Washington, D.C., February 15, 1904; chairman, Committee on Relations with Canada (Fifty-fifth through Fifty-seventh Congresses), Committee on Enrolled Bills (Fifty-seventh Congress), Committee on Interoceanic Canals (Fifty-eighth Congress); funeral services were held in the Chamber of the United States Senate; interment in Lake View Cemetery, Cleveland, Ohio.

Bibliography: *DAB*; Beer, Thomas. *Hanna.* New York: Octagon Books, 1973; Croly, Herbert. *Marcus Hanna: His Life and Works.* Hamden, Conn.: Archon Books, 1965.

**HANNA, Richard Thomas,** a Representative from California; born in Kemmerer, Lincoln County, Wyo., June 9, 1914; moved to Long Beach, Calif., with his parents in 1923; attended the Compton (Calif.) public schools; graduated from Pasadena (Calif.) Junior College; B.A., University of California at Los Angeles, 1937; LL.B., University of California at Los Angeles School of Law, 1952; admitted to the bar in 1952 and began practice in Westminister, Calif.; served in the Navy Air Corps, 1942-1945; practiced law in Fullerton, Calif.; member, California State assembly, 1957-1962; delegate to the Democratic National Convention of 1960; elected as a Democrat to the Eighty-eighth and to the five succeeding Congresses, and served from January 3, 1963 until his resignation on December 31, 1974; was not a candidate for reelection in 1974 to the Ninety-fourth Congress; is a resident of Tryon, N.C.

**HANNA, Robert,** a Senator from Indiana; born near Fountainius, Laurens District, S.C., April 6, 1786; settled in Brookville, Ind., in 1802; sheriff of the common pleas court from 1811 until 1820; member of the State constitutional convention in 1816; brigadier general of State militia; register of the land office, 1820-1830; moved to Indianapolis in 1825; appointed as a Whig to the United States Senate to fill the vacancy caused by the death of James Noble, and served from August 19, 1831 to January 3, 1832; member, Indiana State house of representatives, 1832-1833, 1836-1839; contractor for national roads in 1835; Indiana State senator, 1842-1846; killed by a train while walking upon the track in Indianapolis, Ind., November 16, 1858; interment in Crown Hill Cemetery.

**HANNAFORD, Mark Warren,** a Representative from California; born in Woodrow, Lincoln County, Colo., February 7, 1925; attended public schools in Anderson, Ind.; B.A., Ball State University, Muncie, Ind., 1950; M.A., same university, 1956; attended Yale University under John Hay Fellowship, 1961-1962; associate professor of political science, Long Beach (Calif.) City College, 1966-1975; served in the United States Army Air Corps, 1943-1946; Lakewood (Calif.) city councilman, 1966-1974; mayor of Lakewood, 1968-1970, 1972-1974; member, California State Democratic Central committee, 1966-1974; delegate to Democratic National Convention, 1968; elected as a Democrat to the Ninety-fourth and to the Ninety-fifth Congresses (January 3, 1975-January 3, 1979); unsuccessful candidate for reelection in 1978 to the Ninety-sixth Congress; unsuccessful candidate for nomination in 1980 to the Ninety-seventh Congress; was a resident of Lakewood, Calif, until his death there on June 2, 1985.

**HANNEGAN, Edward Allen,** a Representative and a Senator from Indiana; born in Hamilton County, Ohio, June 25, 1807; moved with his parents to Bourbon County, Ky., the same year; attended the public schools; studied law, taught school and worked as a farm hand; was admitted to the bar in 1827; moved to Indiana and settled in Covington, where he commenced the practice of law; member, Kentucky house of representatives, 1832-1833, and 1841-1842; elected as a Democrat to the Twenty-third and Twenty-fourth Congresses (March 4, 1833-March 3, 1837); was not a candidate for renomination in 1836 to the Twenty-fifth Congress; resumed the practice of law; elected as a Democrat to the United States Senate in 1842, and served from March 4, 1843 to March 3, 1849; unsuccessful candidate for renomination in 1848; chairman, Committee on Private Land Claims (Twenty-ninth Congress), Committee on Roads and Canals (Twenty-ninth and Thirtieth Congresses), Committee on Foreign Relations (Thirtieth Congress); appointed Minister to Prussia on March 22, 1849, and served until January 1850; resumed the practice of law in Covington; moved to St. Louis, Mo., in 1857, where he continued to practice law until his death there on February 25, 1859; interment in Woodlawn Cemetery, Terre Haute, Ind.

Bibliography: *DAB.*

**HANRAHAN, Robert Paul,** a Representative from Illinois; born in Chicago Heights, Cook County, Ill., February 25, 1934; educated in the public schools; Thornton Community College, Harvey, Ill., 1952-1954; B.S., Bowling Green State University, 1956; M.Ed., Bowling Green State University, 1959; teacher, administrator, and guidance counselor, 1960-1964; auditor of Bloom Township, Ill., 1965-1967; Cook County Superintendent of Schools, 1967-1971; appointed Midwest Regional Commissioner of Education, 1971; elected as a Republican to the Ninety-third Congress (January 3, 1973-January 3, 1975); unsuccessful candidate for reelection in 1974 to the Ninety-fourth Congress; deputy assistant secretary for education, Department of Health, Education and Welfare, 1975-1977; president, RPH & Associates, Lake Forest, Ill., 1977-1980; elected Lake County (Ill.) Commissioner, 1980-1982; vice president, Tobacco Institute, Washington, D.C., 1980-1984; executive director, American Security Council Foundation, Washington, D.C., 1984 to present; is a resident of McLean, Va., and Homewood, Ill.

**HANSBROUGH, Henry Clay,** a Representative and a Senator from North Dakota; born near Prairie du Rocher, Randolph County, Ill., January 30, 1848; attended the common schools; moved to San Jose, Calif., in 1867; learned the art of printing and worked at the trade in San Jose, Calif., and later at Baraboo, Wis.; moved to Dakota Territory and established the Grand Forks News in 1881 and the Inter-Ocean at Devils Lake in 1883; mayor of Devils Lake 1885-1888; member of the Republican National Committee 1888-1896; upon the admission of North Dakota as a State into the Union was elected as a Republican to the Fifty-first Congress and served from November 2, 1889, until March 3, 1891; did not seek renomination in 1891, having become a candidate for Senator; elected as a Republican to the United States Senate in 1891; reelected in 1897 and again in 1903 and served from March 4, 1891, to March 3, 1909; unsuccessful candidate for reelection in 1909; chairman, Committee on the Library (Fifty-fourth Congress), Committee on Public Lands (Fifty-fifth through Sixtieth Congresses), Committee on Agriculture and Forestry (Sixtieth Congress); resumed his former business pursuits in Devils Lake, N.Dak.; moved to Florida, New York, and finally to Washington, D.C., in 1927, where he died on November 16, 1933; cremated and the ashes scattered under an elm tree on the United States Capitol Grounds, Washington, D.C.

**Bibliography:** Schlup, Leonard. "Henry C. Hansbrough and the Fight Against the Tariff in 1894." *North Dakota History* 45 (Fall 1978): 32-39; Schlup, Leonard. "Quiet Imperialist: Henry C. Hansbrough and the Question of Expansion." *North Dakota History* 45 (Spring 1978): 26-31.

**HANSEN, Clifford Peter,** a Senator from Wyoming; born in Zenith, Teton (then Lincoln) County, Wyo., October 16, 1912; attended the public schools of Jackson, Wyo.; B.S., University of Wyoming, 1934; member of the University of Wyoming Board of Trustees from 1946 until 1966, serving as president, 1955-1962; engaged in cattle ranching; officer of the Wyoming Stock Growers Association, the American National Cattlemen's Association, and the Livestock Research and Marketing Advisory Committee; Columbia Interstate Compact commissioner; Snake River Compact commissioner; Teton County commissioner, 1943-1951; elected Governor of Wyoming in 1962, and served from January 7, 1963 to January 2, 1967; elected as a Republican to the United States Senate in 1966; reelected in 1972, and served from January 3, 1967, until his resignation December 31, 1978; serves on the board of several financial and civic organizations; is a resident of Jackson, Wyo.

**HANSEN, George Vernon,** a Representative from Idaho; born in Tetonia, Teton County, Idaho, September 14, 1930; attended public schools; B.A., Ricks College, Rexburg, Idaho, 1956; pursued graduate studies at Idaho State University, 1956-1957 and 1962-1963; graduated from Grimms Business College in 1958; served in the United States Air Force, 1951-1954, and was a graduate of the Army language school; officer in the United States Naval Reserve, 1964-1970; grain elevator manager, 1950-1951 and 1954; public school teacher, 1956-1958; engaged in the life insurance business, 1958-1965; mayor of Alameda, Idaho, 1961-1962; upon consolidation of Alameda and Pocatello served as city commissioner of Pocatello, 1962-1965; director of the Idaho Municipal League, 1961-1963; unsuccessful candidate for nomination to the United States Senate in 1962; delegate to the Republican National Convention of 1968; elected as a Republican to the Eighty-ninth and Ninetieth Congresses (January 3, 1965-January 3, 1969); was not a candidate for reelection in 1968 to the House of Representatives, but was an unsuccessful candidate for election to the United States Senate; deputy under secretary for congressional liaison, deputy administrator for Agriculture Stabilization and Conservation Service, and vice president of the Commodity Credit Corporation, United States Department of Agriculture, 1969-1971; returned to Pocatello and engaged in private business pursuits, 1971-1975; unsuccessful candidate for nomination to the United States Senate in 1972; elected as a Republican to the Ninety-fourth and to the four succeeding Congresses (January 3, 1975-January 3, 1985); was an unsuccessful candidate for reelection in 1984 to the Ninety-ninth Congress; chairman of a political consulting firm in Washington, D.C.; is a resident of Arlington, Va.

**Bibliography:** Kelly, Colleen E. "The 1984 Campaign Rhetoric of Representative George Hansen: A Pentadic Analysis." *Western Journal of Speech Communication* 51 (Spring 1987): 204-217.

**HANSEN, James Vear,** a Representative from Utah; born in Salt Lake City, Utah, August 14, 1932; attended the public schools; B.S., University of Utah, Salt Lake City, 1961; served in the United States Navy, 1951-1955; engaged in real estate and insurance; city councilman, Farmington, Utah, 1960-1972; member, Utah State house of representatives, 1973-1980, serving as speaker during last term; founder and president, James V. Hansen Insurance Agency, 1979-1980; president, Woodland Springs Development Co., 1977-1981; delegate, Utah State Republican conventions, 1978-1980; elected as a Republican to the Ninety-seventh and to the seven succeeding Congresses (January 3, 1981-January 3, 1997); is a resident of Farmington, Utah.

**HANSEN, John Robert,** a Representative from Iowa; born in Manning, Carroll County, Iowa, August 24, 1901; attended the Manning public schools; attended the State University of Iowa, 1919-1921; sales representative, general manager, and president of Dultmeier Manufacturing Co., Manning, Iowa, 1921-1962, and president of Dultmeier Sales, Omaha, Nebr., 1934-1957; member of the Carroll County Democratic Central committee, 1932-1944, and chairman, 1944-1952; delegate to the Democratic National Conventions of 1948 and 1964; district committeeman on the Democratic State central committee, 1952-1957; Sixth District Democratic chairman, 1953-1957; member of the Board of Control of State Institutions, 1957-1960; member of executive council of the Governor's Alcoholism Commission and the Commission on Interstate Cooperation, 1957-1960; Democratic candidate for election for Lieutenant Governor in 1960; elected as a Democrat to the Eighty-ninth Congress (January 3, 1965-January 3, 1967); unsuccessful candidate for reelection in 1966 to the Ninetieth Congress; served as a member of the Iowa State Highway Commission from February 1967 until his retirement on July 1, 1969; died in Des Moines, Iowa, September 23, 1974; interment in Manning Cemetery, Manning, Iowa.

**HANSEN, Julia Butler,** a Representative from Washington; born June 14, 1907, in Portland, Multnomah County, Oreg.; attended the public schools of Washington and Oregon State College, 1924-1926; graduated from the University of Washington at Seattle in 1930; member of the Cathlamet, Wash., city council 1938-1946; chairman of the Western Interstate Committee on Highway Policies, 1951-1961; manager of a title and casualty insurance business, 1958-1961; member of the State house of representatives from January 1939 until November 1960, serving as speaker pro tempore, 1955-1960; chairman and member of board of trustees of Century 21, State of Washington, beginning in 1958; elected as a Democrat to the Eighty-sixth Congress, November 8, 1960, by special election to fill the vacancy caused by the death of Russell V. Mack, and at the same time elected to the Eighty-seventh Congress; reelected to the six succeeding Congresses, and served from November 8, 1960 until her resignation on December 31, 1974; was not a candidate for renomination in 1974 to the Ninety-fourth Congress; appointed in 1975 to a six-year term on the Washington State Toll Bridge Authority and State Highway Commission; chairman, Washington State Transportation commission, 1979-1981; was a resident of Cathlamet, Wash., until her death there on May 3, 1988.

**Bibliography:** Rosenberg, Marie C. Barovic. "Women in Politics: A Comparative Study of Congresswomen Edith Green and Julia Butler Hansen." Ph.D. dissertation, University of Washington, 1973.

**HANSEN, Orval Howard,** a Representative from Idaho; born in Firth, Bingham County, Idaho, August 3, 1926; attended Idaho Falls public schools; during the Second World War served in the United States Navy, 1944-1946, and served in the Air Force Reserve until retirement as a lieutenant colonel; B.A., University of Idaho, 1950; J.D., George Washington University, 1954; Rotary Foundation Fellow, London School of Economics, University of London, 1954-1955; LL.M., in 1973 and Ph.D., George Washington University, 1986; private law practice, 1956-1968; member, Idaho State house of representatives, 1956-1962, and 1964-1966, serving as majority leader, 1961-1962; unsuccessful candidate for election in 1962 to the Eighty-eighth Congress; Idaho State senator, 1966-1968; elected as a Republican to the Ninety-first and to the two succeeding Congresses (January 3, 1969-January 3, 1975); unsuccessful candidate for renomination in 1974 to the Ninety-fourth Congress; resumed the practice of law; founder and president, Columbia Institute for Political Research, 1977 to present; is a resident of Arlington, Va.

**HANSON, Alexander Contee** (grandson of John Hanson), a Representative and a Senator from Maryland; born in Annapolis, Md., February 27, 1786; attended local private schools and graduated from St. John's College, Annapolis, in 1802; studied law; was admitted to the bar and commenced practice in Annapolis, Md.; member, State house of delegates 1811-1815; established and edited the Federal Republican, an extreme Federalist newspaper, in Baltimore, and on June 22, 1812, four days after war was declared, a mob, irritated by his articles denouncing the administration, destroyed the office; when he issued the paper from another building one week later, he was seriously injured by a mob; moved the paper to Georgetown, D.C., where he published it unmolested; moved to Rockville, Md.; elected as a Federalist to the Thirteenth and Fourteenth Congresses and served from March 4, 1813, until his resignation in 1816; unsuccessful candidate in 1816 for election to the State house of delegates; elected as a Federalist to the United States Senate to fill the vacancy caused by the resignation of Robert G. Harper and served from December 20, 1816, until his death on his estate, "Belmont," near Elkridge, Howard County, Md., April 23, 1819; interment in the family burial ground.

Bibliography: *DAB*.

**HANSON, John** (grandfather of Alexander Contee Hanson), a Delegate from Maryland; born at Mulberry Grove, near Port Tobacco, Charles County, Md., April 3, 1715; pursued an academic course; engaged in agricultural pursuits; member of the State house of delegates for nine terms; member of the State senate 1757-1773; moved to Frederick County in 1773; delegate to the General Congress at Annapolis in 1774; treasurer of Frederick County in 1775; member of the Maryland convention of 1775; Member of the Continental Congress 1780-1782; elected President of the Continental Congress on November 5, 1781; signer of the Articles of Confederation of the United States; died at the residence of his nephew at Oxon Hill, Prince Georges County, Md., November 22, 1783.

Bibliography: *DAB*; Levering, Ralph B. "John Hanson, Public Servant." *Maryland Historical Magazine* 71 (Summer 1976): 113-33; Smith, Seymour W. *John Hanson, Our First President.* New York: Brewer, Warren, and Putnam, 1932.

**HARALSON, Hugh Anderson,** a Representative from Georgia; born near Penfield, Greene County, Ga., November 13, 1805; attended the common schools and was also instructed by private tutors; was graduated from Franklin College (now the University of Georgia) in 1825; studied law; was admitted to the bar in 1825 and commenced practice in Monroe, Walton County, Ga.; moved to Lagrange, Troup County, Ga., in 1828, and continued the practice of law; also engaged in agricultural pursuits; member of the State house of representatives in 1831 and 1832; served in the State senate in 1837 and 1838; served in the State militia as a major general 1838-1850; elected as a Democrat to the Twenty-eighth, Twenty-ninth, Thirtieth, and Thirty-first Congresses (March 4, 1843-March 3, 1851); chairman, Committee on Military Affairs (Twenty-eighth and Twenty-ninth Congresses); was not a candidate for renomination in 1850; resumed the practice of law; died in Lagrange, Troup County, Ga., September 25, 1854; interment in Hill View Cemetery.

**HARALSON, Jeremiah,** a Representative from Alabama; born into slavery on a plantation near Columbus, Muscogee County, Ga., April 1, 1846; taken to Alabama in 1859 and remained in bondage until 1865; after attaining freedom he taught himself to read and write; engaged in agricultural pursuits; became a minister; member of the State house of representatives in 1870; served in the State senate in 1872; unsuccessful candidate for election in 1868 to the Forty-first Congress; elected as a Republican to the Forty-fourth Congress (March 4, 1875-March 3, 1877); unsuccessful candidate for reelection in 1876 to the Forty-fifth Congress, and for election in 1878 to the Forty-sixth Congress; appointed to a Federal position in the United States customhouse in Baltimore, Md.; later employed as a clerk in the Interior Department; appointed August 12, 1882, to the Pension Bureau in Washington, D.C., and resigned August 21, 1884; moved to Louisiana, where he engaged in agricultural pursuits, and thence to Arkansas in 1904; served as pension agent for a short time; returned to Alabama and settled in Selma in 1912; moved to Texas and later to Oklahoma and Colorado and engaged in coal mining in the latter State; killed by wild beasts near Denver, Colo., about 1916.

**HARD, Gideon,** a Representative from New York; born in Arlington, Bennington County, Vt., April 29, 1797; was graduated from Union College, Schenectady, N.Y., in 1822; taught school; studied law; was admitted to the bar in 1825 and commenced practice in Newport (now Albion), N.Y., in 1826; elected as an Anti-Masonic candidate to the Twenty-third Congress and reelected as a Whig to the Twenty-fourth Congress (March 4, 1833-March 3, 1837); commissioner of schools for Barre Township, Orleans County, N.Y., 1841-1848; served in the State senate 1841-1848; canal appraiser in 1849 and 1850; resumed the practice of law until 1850; county judge and surrogate for Orleans County 1856-1860; died in Albion, Orleans County, N.Y., April 27, 1885; interment in Mount Albion Cemetery.

**HARDEMAN, Thomas, Jr.,** a Representative from Georgia; born in Eatonton, Putnam County, Ga., January 12, 1825; was graduated from Emory College in 1845; studied law; was admitted to the bar in 1847; abandoned his profession and engaged in the warehouse and commission business; served in the State house of representatives in 1853, 1855, and 1857; elected as an Opposition candidate to the Thirty-sixth Congress and served from March 4, 1859, until January 23, 1861, when he joined other secessionist members of the Georgia delegation in withdrawing from Congress; captain of the Floyd Rifles; during the Civil War was major of the Second Georgia Battalion and, later, colonel of the Forty-fifth Georgia Infantry of the Confederate Army; again served in the State house of representatives, in 1863, 1864, and 1874, and was speaker during these sessions; delegate to the Democratic National Convention of 1872; president of the State convention and chairman of the Democratic State executive committee for four years; elected as a Democrat to the Forty-eighth Congress (March 4, 1883-March 3, 1885); chairman, Committee on Expenditures in the Department of State (Forty-eighth Congress); died in Macon, Ga., March 6, 1891; interment in Oak Hill Cemetery.

**HARDEN, Cecil Murray,** a Representative from Indiana; born in Covington, Fountain County, Ind., November 21, 1894; graduated from the public schools of Covington, Ind., in 1912, and attended the University of Indiana at Bloomington; taught all grades in Troy township schools, Fountain County, Ind., and Covington (Ind.) public schools 1912-1914; Republican National committeewoman from Indiana 1944-1959, and from 1964 to 1972; delegate at large to the Republican National Conventions of 1948, 1952, 1956, and 1968; elected as a Republican to the Eighty-first and to the four succeeding Congresses (January 3, 1949-January 3, 1959); unsuccessful candidate for reelection in 1958 to the Eighty-sixth Congress; special assistant for women's affairs to Postmaster General Arthur E. Summerfield, Washington, D.C., March 1959 to March 1961; appointed August 18, 1970, to the National Advisory Committee for the White House Conference on Aging; was a resident of Covington, Ind., until her death in Lafayette, Ind., December 5, 1984.

**HARDENBERGH, Augustus Albert,** a Representative from New Jersey; born in New Brunswick, Middlesex County, N.J., May 18, 1830; attended Rutgers College, New Brunswick, N.J., in 1844; took up residence in Jersey City in 1846 and was employed in a banking house in New York City; clerk in the Hudson County National Bank in 1852; member of the State house of assembly in 1853 and 1854; member of the board of education in 1855 and 1856; member of the common council of Jersey City 1857-1863, serving as president in 1860; moved to Bergen, N.J., in 1863; member of the city council of Bergen; elected State director of railroads in 1868; moved to Demarest, N.J., the same year; delegate to the Democratic National Convention of 1872; moved to Jersey City in 1873; elected president of the Northern Railroad of New Jersey in 1874; elected as a Democrat to the Forty-fourth and Forty-fifth Congresses (March 4, 1875-March 3, 1879); declined to be a candidate for renomination in 1878 to the Forty-sixth Congress; elected president of the Hudson County National Bank in 1878; elected to the Forty-seventh Congress (March 4, 1881-March 3, 1883); was not a candidate for renomination in 1882 to the Forty-eighth Congress; appointed a member of the Jersey City Board of Finance and Taxation in 1883-1889; appointed by Governor Leon Abbett as a trustee of the State reform school in 1884; died in Jersey City, N.J., on October 5, 1889; interment in Mount Pleasant Cemetery, Newark, N.J.

**HARDIN, Benjamin** (cousin of Martin Davis Hardin), a Representative from Kentucky; born at the Georges Creek settlement on the Monongahela River, Westmoreland County, Pa., February 29, 1784; moved with his parents to Washington County, Ky., in 1788; attended the schools of Nelson and Washington Counties, Ky.; studied law; was admitted to the bar in 1806 and commenced practice in Elizabethtown and Bardstown, Nelson County, Ky.; settled in Bardstown in 1808; member of the Kentucky house of representatives in 1810, 1811, 1824, and 1825; served in the Kentucky senate 1828-1832; elected as a Republican to the Fourteenth Congress (March 4, 1815-March 3, 1817); elected to the Sixteenth and Seventeenth Congresses (March 4, 1819-March 3, 1823); elected as an Anti-Jacksonian to the Twenty-third Congress and as a Whig to the Twenty-fourth Congress (March 4, 1833-March 3, 1837); secretary of Commonwealth of Kentucky 1844-1847; member of the Kentucky constitutional convention in 1849; died in Bardstown, Ky., September 24, 1852; interment in the family burying ground near Springfield, Ky.

**Bibliography:** *DAB.*

**HARDIN, John J.** (son of Martin Davis Hardin), a Representative from Illinois; born in Frankfort, Ky., January 6, 1810; pursued classical studies and was graduated from Transylvania University, Lexington, Ky.; studied law; was admitted to the bar in Kentucky in 1831 and commenced practice in Jacksonville, Morgan County, Ill.; served in the Illinois Militia during the Black Hawk War of 1831-1832; was brigadier general in command during the Mormon trouble in Hancock County in 1844, and later attained the rank of major general; appointed prosecuting attorney of Morgan County in 1832; member of the Illinois State house of representatives, 1836-1842; elected as a Whig to the Twenty-eighth Congress (March 4, 1843-March 3, 1845); was not a candidate for renomination in 1844 to the Twenty-ninth Congress; during the Mexican War recruited the First Regiment, Illinois Volunteer Infantry, of which he was commissioned colonel; was killed at the Battle of Buena Vista, near Monterrey, Mexico, February 23, 1847; interment in City Cemetery (East), Jacksonville, Ill.

**Bibliography:** *DAB.*

**HARDIN, Martin D.** (cousin of Benjamin Hardin and father of John J. Hardin), a Senator from Kentucky; born along the Monongahela River, western Pennsylvania, June 21, 1780; moved with his parents to Kentucky in 1786; pursued an academic course; attended Transylvania Seminary, Lexington, Ky.; studied law; was admitted to the bar and practiced in Richmond and Frankfort, Ky.; member, Kentucky house of representatives 1805-1806, 1812, 1818-1820, serving as speaker 1819-1820; secretary of Commonwealth of Kentucky 1812-1816; served as major in the War of 1812; appointed and subsequently elected as a Federalist to the United States Senate to fill the vacancy caused by the resignation of William T. Barry and served from November 13, 1816, to March 3, 1817; died in Frankfort, Ky., October 8, 1823; interment on his farm in Franklin County; reinterment in State Cemetery, Frankfort, Ky.

**Bibliography:** *DAB.*

**HARDING, Aaron,** a Representative from Kentucky; born near Campbellsville, Taylor County (now a part of Green County), Ky., February 20, 1805; attended the rural schools; became familiar with the classics; studied law; was admitted to the bar in 1833 and commenced practice in Greensburg, Ky.; elected prosecuting attorney of Green County in 1833; member of the Kentucky house of representatives in 1840; elected as a Unionist to the Thirty-seventh and Thirty-eighth Congresses and as a Democrat to the Thirty-ninth Congress (March 4, 1861-March 3, 1867); delegate to the Union National Convention in 1866; resumed the practice of law in Danville, Ky.; died in Georgetown, Scott County, Ky., December 24, 1875; interment in Georgetown Cemetery.

**HARDING, Abner Clark,** a Representative from Illinois; born in East Hampton, Middlesex County, Conn., February 10, 1807; attended Hamilton Academy, Clinton, N.Y.; studied law; was admitted to the bar and commenced practice in Oneida County, N.Y., about 1827; moved to Monmouth, Warren County, Ill., in 1838 and continued the practice of law; member of the State constitutional convention in 1848; member of the State house of representatives 1848-1850; during the Civil War enlisted as a private in the Union Army in the Eighty-third Regiment, Illinois Volunteer Infantry, and was commissioned colonel on August 21, 1862; promoted to brigadier general on March 13, 1863, and served until he resigned his commission June 3, 1863, due to failing eyesight; elected as a Republican to the Thirty-ninth and Fortieth Congresses (March 4, 1865-March 3, 1869); chairman, Committee on the Militia (Thirty-ninth Congress); was not a candidate for renomination in 1868 to the Forty-first Congress; engaged in banking and railroad building; died in Monmouth, Ill., July 19, 1874; interment in Monmouth Cemetery.

**Bibliography:** *DAB.*

**HARDING, Benjamin Franklin,** a Senator from Oregon; born near Tunkhannock, Wyoming County, Pa., on January 4, 1823; attended the public schools; studied law; was admitted to the bar in 1847 and commenced practice in Joliet, Ill., in 1849; moved to California and then to Oregon in 1850; clerk of the Territorial legislature in 1850 and 1851; member of that body and served as its speaker in 1852; United States district attorney in 1853; secretary of the Territory 1854-1859; member, State house of representatives 1858-1862, serving as speaker 1860-1861; elected as a Democrat to the United States Senate to fill the vacancy caused by the death of Edward D. Baker and served from September 12, 1862, to March 3,

1865; retired to his farm near Salem, Marion County, Oreg., and a few years later moved to Cottage Grove, Lane County, where he died June 16, 1899; interment in Cottage Grove Cemetery.

**HARDING, John Eugene,** a Representative from Ohio; born in Excello, Butler County, Ohio, June 27, 1877; attended the Amanda public schools and Pennsylvania Military Academy at Chester; was graduated from the University of Michigan at Ann Arbor in 1900; engaged in business in Middletown, Ohio, and in industrial enterprises; member of the State senate in 1902; elected as a Republican to the Sixtieth Congress (March 4, 1907-March 3, 1909); delegate to the Republican State convention in 1910; engaged in the paper business in Chicago, Ill., until he moved to New York City, where he was associated with the Pure Oil Co., 1921-1926; engaged in industrial enterprises until retirement in 1949; died in New Haven, Conn., July 26, 1959; interment in Woodside Cemetery, Middletown, Ohio.

**HARDING, Ralph R.,** a Representative from Idaho; born in Malad City, Oneida County, Idaho, September 9, 1929; attended the public schools of Malad City and St. Antony, Idaho; served two years as a missionary for the Church of Jesus Christ of Latter-Day Saints; graduated from Brigham Young University in 1956; enlisted as a private in the United States Army in December 1951, commissioned a lieutenant in December 1952, served in Korea, and was discharged in December 1953; member of the Idaho State house of representatives in 1955 and 1956; comptroller, American Potato Co., Blackfoot, Idaho, 1957-1960; elected as a Democrat to the Eighty-seventh and Eighty-eighth Congresses (January 3, 1961-January 3, 1965); unsuccessful candidate for reelection in 1964 to the Eighty-ninth Congress; served as Special Assistant to Secretary of the Air Force Harold Brown, 1965-1966; unsuccessful candidate in 1966 for election to the United States Senate; resumed business pursuits; elected Democratic National committeeman from Idaho, 1970; unsuccessful candidate for nomination in 1978 to the Ninety-sixth Congress; divisional vice president, E.F. Hutton Financial Services, 1979-1981; adviser and consultant to the Philippine sugar industry, 1982-1988; is a resident of Pocatello, Idaho.

**HARDING, Warren Gamaliel,** a Senator from Ohio and 29th President of the United States; born in Corsica (now Blooming Grove), Morrow County, Ohio, November 2, 1865; attended the public schools in and near Caledonia, Ohio; graduated from Ohio Central College at Iberia in 1882; moved to Marion, Ohio, in July 1882; studied law for a short time; taught school; engaged in the insurance business; became editor and publisher of the Marion Star in 1884; member, Ohio State senate, District 13, 1899-1903; lieutenant governor of Ohio, 1904-1905; unsuccessful Republican candidate for election for Governor in 1910; elected as a Republican to the United States Senate in 1914, and served from March 4, 1915 until his resignation, effective January 13, 1921, having been elected President; chairman, Committee on the Philippines (Sixty-sixth Congress); elected President of the United States on the Republican ticket, November 2, 1920, was inaugurated March 4, 1921, and served until his death in San Francisco, Calif., while on a tour of the Western States and Alaska, August 2, 1923; interment in Marion Cemetery, Marion, Ohio; reinterment in Harding Memorial Tomb.

**Bibliography:** *DAB*; Downes, Randolph C. *The Rise of Warren Gamaliel Harding, 1865-1920*. Columbus: Ohio State University Press, 1970; Murray, Robert K. *The Harding Era: Warren G. Harding and His Administration*. Minneapolis: University of Minnesota Press, 1969; Russell, Francis. *The Shadow of Blooming Grove: Warren G. Harding in His Times*. 1968. Reprint. Norwalk, Conn.: Easton Press, 1988.

**HARDWICK, Thomas William,** a Representative and a Senator from Georgia; born in Thomasville, Thomas County, Ga., on December 9, 1872; attended the common schools and Mercer University, Macon, Ga.; graduated from the law department of the University of Georgia at Athens in 1893; was admitted to the bar the same year and commenced practice in Sandersville, Ga.; prosecuting attorney for Washington County, 1895-1897; member, Georgia State house of representatives, 1898-1902; elected as a Democrat to the Fifty-eighth and to the five succeeding Congresses, and served from March 4, 1903 to November 2, 1914, when he resigned; chairman, Committee on Coinage, Weights, and Measures (Sixty-second and Sixty-third Congresses); elected as a Democrat to the United States Senate to fill the vacancy caused by the death of Augustus O. Bacon, and served from November 4, 1914 to March 3, 1919; unsuccessful candidate for renomination in 1918; chairman, Committee on Expenditures in the Post Office Department (Sixty-third and Sixty-fourth Congresses), Committee on Immigration (Sixty-fifth Congress), Committee on Industrial Expositions (Sixty-fifth Congress); elected Governor of Georgia in 1920, and served from June 25, 1921 to June 30, 1923; unsuccessful candidate in 1922 for renomination for Governor; unsuccessful candidate for nomination to the United States Senate in 1922 and 1924; resumed the practice of law, with offices in Washington, D.C., Atlanta, Ga., and Sandersville, Ga.; died in Sandersville, Ga., January 31, 1944; interment in the Old City Cemetery.

**Bibliography:** Grantham, Dewey W., Jr., ed. "Some Letters from Thomas W. Hardwick to Tom Watson Concerning the Georgia Gubernatorial Campaign of 1906." *Georgia Historical Quarterly* 34 (December 1950): 328-340.

**HARDY, Alexander Merrill,** a Representative from Indiana; born in Simcoe, Norfolk County, Ontario, Canada, December 16, 1847; pursued a college course and studied law; came to the United States in 1864, taking a commercial course at Eastman College, Poughkeepsie, N.Y.; went to New Orleans in 1869, where he engaged in newspaper work until 1873, when he moved to Natchez, Miss.; conducted a Republican newspaper until 1877; collector of the port of Natchez under appointment of President Ulysses S. Grant; moved to Washington, Daviess County, Ind., in 1884; was admitted to the bar in 1884 and commenced practice in Terre Haute, Ind.; elected as a Republican to the Fifty-fourth Congress (March 4, 1895-March 3, 1897); unsuccessful candidate for reelection in 1896 to the Fifty-fifth Congress; resumed the practice of law in Washington, Ind.; moved to Los Angeles, Calif., in 1904 and continued the practice of law; moved to Searchlight, Nev., thence to Salt Lake City, Utah, and finally settled in Tonopah, Nev., in 1914 and engaged in the practice of his profession; was also interested in mining; died in Tonopah, Nev., on August 31, 1927; interment in Tonopah Cemetery.

**HARDY, Guy Urban,** a Representative from Colorado; born in Abingdon, Knox County, Ill., April 4, 1872; attended the public schools, Albion (Ill.) Normal College, and Transylvania University, Lexington, Ky.; taught school in Illinois and Florida from 1890 until 1893; moved to Canon City, Colo., in 1894; editor and publisher of the Canon City Daily and Weekly Records, beginning in 1895; postmaster of Canon City from June 5, 1900 to July 30, 1904; president of the National Editorial Association in 1918 and 1919; elected as a Republican to the Sixty-sixth and to the six succeeding Congresses (March 4, 1919-March 3, 1933); unsuccessful candidate for reelection in 1932 to the Seventy-third Congress; resumed his former publishing pursuits in Canon City, Colo., and resided there until his death on January 26, 1947; interment in Greenwood Cemetery.

**HARDY, John,** a Representative from New York; born in Scotland September 19, 1835; immigrated to the United States in 1839 with his parents, who settled in New York City; attended the public schools and was graduated from the College of the City of New York in 1853; studied law; was admitted to the bar in 1861 and commenced practice in New York City; member of the State assembly in 1861; member of the board of aldermen of New York

City in 1863, 1864, and 1867-1869; clerk of the common council in 1870 and 1871; chief clerk in the office of the mayor in 1877 and 1878; elected as a Democrat to the Forty-seventh Congress to fill the vacancy caused by the death of Fernando Wood; reelected to the Forty-eighth Congress and served from December 5, 1881, until March 3, 1885; unsuccessful candidate for reelection in 1884 to the Forty-ninth Congress; resumed the practice of law in New York City and died there December 9, 1913; interment in Greenwood Cemetery, Brooklyn, N.Y.

**HARDY, Porter, Jr.,** a Representative from Virginia; born in Bon Air, Chesterfield County, Va., June 1, 1903; attended the public schools and Randolph-Macon Academy, Bedford, Va.; was graduated from Boykins (Va.) High School in 1918; B.A., Randolph-Macon College, Ashland, Va., 1922; attended the Graduate School of Business Administration at Harvard University in 1923 and 1924; accountant and warehouse manager at New York City and Norfolk, Va., 1924-1927; wholesaler of electrical equipment, Salisbury, Md., 1927-1932; moved to Churchland, Va., in 1932 and engaged in agricultural pursuits; elected as a Democrat to the Eightieth and to the ten succeeding Congresses (January 3, 1947-January 3, 1969); was not a candidate for reelection in 1968 to the Ninety-first Congress; formerly director of Dominion Bankshares Corp. and other Virginia financial institutions; was a resident of Virginia Beach, Va., until his death there on April 19, 1995.

**HARDY, Rufus,** a Representative from Texas; born near Aberdeen, Monroe County, Miss., December 16, 1855; attended private schools in Texas and Somerville Institute in Mississippi; was graduated from the law department of the University of Georgia at Athens in 1875; was admitted to the bar the same year and commenced practice in Navasota, Tex.; moved to Corsicana, Navarro County, Tex., in 1878; prosecuting attorney of Navarro County 1880-1884; district attorney for the thirteenth judicial district 1884-1888; district judge from 1888 to December 1896, when he retired; chairman of the Texas Sound Money Democracy in 1896; resumed the practice of law in Corsicana, Tex.; elected as a Democrat to the Sixtieth and to the seven succeeding Congresses (March 4, 1907-March 3, 1923); chairman, Committee on Expenditures in the Department of the Navy (Sixty-second through Sixty-fifth Congresses); was not a candidate for renomination in 1922; resumed the practice of his profession; died in Corsicana, Tex., March 13, 1943; interment in Oakwood Cemetery.

**HARDY, Samuel,** a Delegate from Virginia; born in Isle of Wight County, Va., about 1758; completed preparatory studies, and was graduated from the College of William and Mary, Williamsburg, Va., in 1781; studied law; was admitted to the bar and commenced the practice of law; member of the Virginia house of delegates in 1778 and 1780-1782; appointed a member of the executive council in June 1781; lieutenant governor of Virginia from May 29 to October 11, 1782; Member of the Continental Congress 1783-1785; died while attending Congress in Philadelphia, Pa., on October 17, 1785; interment in Christ Church Cemetery.

Bibliography: *DAB*.

**HARE, Butler Black** (father of James Butler Hare), a Representative from South Carolina; born on a farm in Edgefield (now Saluda) County, near Leesville, S.C., November 25, 1875; attended the public schools; was graduated from Newberry (S.C.) College in 1899; taught in the public schools 1900-1903; secretary to Representative George W. Croft in 1904 and to his successor, Representative Theodore G. Croft, in 1905; professor of history and economics in Leesville (S.C.) College, 1906-1908; special agent in the woman and child labor investigation conducted by the United States Bureau of Labor in 1908 and 1909; was graduated from George Washington University, Washington, D.C., in 1910, and from its law department in 1913; was admitted to the bar in 1913 Bind and commenced practice in Saluda, S.C., in 1915; worked for the United States Department of Agriculture, 1911-1924; engaged in agricultural pursuits; resumed the practice of law in Saluda, S.C., in 1924 and 1925; elected as a Democrat to the Sixty-ninth and to the three succeeding Congresses (March 4, 1925-March 3, 1933); chairman, Committee on Insular Affairs (Seventy-second Congress); was not a candidate for renomination in 1933; resumed his former pursuits; elected to the Seventy-sixth and to the three succeeding Congresses (January 3, 1939-January 3, 1947); unsuccessful candidate for renomination in 1946; resumed the practice of law and his agricultural pursuits; died in Saluda, S.C., December 30, 1967; interment in Travis Park Cemetery.

**HARE, Darius Dodge,** a Representative from Ohio; born near Adrian, Seneca County, Ohio, January 9, 1843; attended the common schools; entered the military service as a private in the Signal Corps, United States Army, in March 1864, and served during the remainder of the Civil War; attended the law department of the University of Michigan at Ann Arbor; was admitted to the bar in September 1867 and commenced practice in Carey, Ohio; moved to Upper Sandusky, Ohio, in May 1868; mayor of Upper Sandusky 1872-1882; elected as a Democrat to the Fifty-second and Fifty-third Congresses (March 4, 1891-March 3, 1895); declined to be a candidate for renomination in 1894; continued the practice of law until his death in Upper Sandusky, Ohio, February 10, 1897; interment in Oak Hill Cemetery.

**HARE, James Butler** (son of Butler Black Hare), a Representative from South Carolina; born in Saluda, S.C., September 4, 1918; attended the public schools; was graduated from Newberry College in 1939; engaged in postgraduate work at Erskine College, Due West, S.C., in 1941; enlisted in the United States Navy in August 1940 and released to inactive duty in the Naval Reserve as a lieutenant commander in January 1946 with thirty-two months in the Pacific Theater; was graduated from the law school of the University of South Carolina in 1947; was admitted to the bar the same year and commenced the practice of law in Saluda, S.C.; member of the board of trustees of the University of South Carolina; elected as a Democrat to the Eighty-first Congress (January 3, 1949-January 3, 1951); unsuccessful candidate for renomination in 1950; recalled to active duty in the United States Navy January 1, 1950, and served as law specialist until released to inactive duty as a commander in May 1952; resumed the practice of law in Saluda, S.C.; died in Columbia, S.C., July 16, 1966; interment in Travis Park Cemetery, Saluda, S.C.

**HARE, Silas,** a Representative from Texas; born in Ross County, Ohio, November 13, 1827; moved to Hamilton County, Ind., in 1840 with his parents, who settled near Noblesville; attended the common and private schools; served during the war with Mexico in the First Regiment, Indiana Volunteers, 1846 and 1847; studied law; was admitted to the bar in 1850 and commenced practice in Noblesville, Ind.; moved to Belton, Tex., in 1853 and continued the practice of law; chief justice of New Mexico in 1862 under the Confederate Government; during the Civil War served as a captain in the Confederate Army; settled in Sherman, Tex., in 1865 and resumed the practice of law; district judge of the criminal court 1873-1876; delegate to the Democratic National Convention in 1884; elected as a Democrat to the Fiftieth and Fifty-first Congresses (March 4, 1887-March 3, 1891); unsuccessful candidate for renomination in 1890; resumed the practice of law in Washington, D.C., where he died November 26, 1907; interment in West Hill Cemetery, Sherman, Grayson County, Tex.

**HARGIS, Denver David,** a Representative from Kansas; born in Key West, Fla., July 22, 1921; parents moved to Coffeyville, Montgomery County, Kans., in 1922; attended Coffeyville schools; enlisted in the United States Navy in January 1941 and served until October 1943; graduated from Washburn University, Topeka, Kans., B.A., 1946 and from the law department, LL.B., 1948; was admitted to the bar in 1948 and commenced the practice of law in Coffeyville, Kans.; in February 1949 was appointed district supervisor of the Census Bureau for the Third District of Kansas; promoted to administrative officer for Kansas, Missouri, and Nebraska, and later promoted to regional assistant and served until December 1950; mayor of Coffeyville, Kans., 1953-1958; appointed by Governor George Docking as a member of the Arkansas River Basin Committee 1956-1959; delegate at large to Democratic National Convention of 1960; unsuccessful candidate for election in 1956 to the Eighty-fifth Congress; elected as a Democrat to the Eighty-sixth Congress (January 3, 1959-January 3, 1961); unsuccessful candidate for reelection in 1960 to the Eighty-seventh Congress; consultant with the Department of Defense, 1961-1962, and the Department of Commerce, 1962-1966; manager and later owner of several title insurance companies in Florida until his retirement in 1985; is a resident of Sarasota, Fla.

**HARING, John,** a Delegate from New York; born in Tappan, Rockland County, N.Y., September 28, 1739; attended school in New York City; studied law; was admitted to the bar and practiced in New York City and Rockland County; Member of the Continental Congress in 1774 and 1785-1787; judge of Orange County in 1774, 1775, and 1778-1788; member of the provincial convention of April 1775 and of the four New York Provincial Congresses 1775-1777, serving as president pro tempore of the Second and Third Provincial Congresses; served in the State senate 1781-1789; member of the council of appointment in 1781 and 1782; member of the State board of regents in 1784; member of the State convention in 1788 to consider the Federal Constitution and voted to reject it; member of the State assembly in 1806; died in Blauveltville, Rockland County, N.Y., April 1, 1809; interment in Tappan Church Cemetery, Tappan, N.Y.

**HARKIN, Thomas Richard,** a Representative and Senator from Iowa; born in Cumming, Warren County, Iowa, November 19, 1939; attended the public schools; graduated, Dowling Catholic High School, Des Moines; B.S., Iowa State University, Ames, 1962; LL.B., Catholic University of America Law School, Washington, D.C., 1972; admitted to the Iowa bar in 1972 and commenced practice in Des Moines; served in United States Navy, 1962-1967; lieutenant commander, United States Naval Reserve; staff assistant to Representative Neal Smith of Iowa, 1969-1970; attorney for Polk County, Iowa, Legal Aid Society 1973-1974; member, board of directors, Iowa Consumers League; elected as a Democrat to the Ninety-fourth and to the four succeeding Congresses (January 3, 1975-January 3, 1985); was not a candidate for reelection in 1984 to the House of Representatives, but was elected to the United States Senate for the term commencing January 3, 1985; reelected in 1990 for the term ending January 3, 1997; unsuccessful candidate for the Democratic presidential nomination in 1992; is a resident of Cumming, Iowa.

**HARLAN, Aaron** (cousin of Andrew Jackson Harlan), a Representative from Ohio; was born in Warren County, Ohio, September 8, 1802; attended the public schools; studied law; was admitted to the bar and commenced practice in Xenia, Ohio, in 1825; member of the State house of representatives in 1832 and 1833; served in the State senate in 1838, 1839, and 1849; moved to a farm near Yellow Springs, Ohio, in 1841 and continued the practice of law; presidential elector on the Polk and Dallas ticket in 1844; delegate to the State constitutional convention in 1850; member of the board of trustees of Antioch College in 1852; elected as a Whig to the Thirty-third Congress and reelected as a Republican to the Thirty-fourth and Thirty-fifth Congresses (March 4, 1853-March 3, 1859); unsuccessful candidate for reelection in 1858 to the Thirty-sixth Congress and in 1861 to fill a vacancy in the Thirty-seventh Congress; resumed the practice of law and engaged in agricultural pursuits near Yellow Springs; lieutenant colonel of

the Ninety-fourth Regiment of Minutemen of Ohio in 1862; moved to San Francisco, Calif., in 1864 and resided there until his death on January 8, 1868; interment in Laurel Hill Cemetery.

**HARLAN, Andrew Jackson** (cousin of Aaron Harlan), a Representative from Indiana; born near Wilmington, Clinton County, Ohio, March 29, 1815; attended the public schools; studied law; was admitted to the bar in 1839 and commenced practice in Richmond, Ind.; moved to Marion, Ind., in 1839; clerk of the State house of representatives in 1842 and a member 1846-1848; elected as a Democrat to the Thirty-first Congress (March 4, 1849-March 3, 1851); elected to the Thirty-third Congress (March 4, 1853-March 3, 1855); chairman, Committee on Mileage (Thirty-third Congress); in a Democratic congressional convention at Marion, Ind., in 1854 he was publicly read out of the Democratic Party for voting against the repeal of the Missouri Compromise; declined the nomination from the People's Party in 1854 for the Thirty-fourth Congress; afterward allied himself with the Republican Party; moved to Dakota Territory in 1861; member of the Territorial house of representatives in 1861 and served as speaker; driven from the Territory by the Indians in September 1862 and settled in Savannah, Mo., where he resumed the practice of law; member of the State house of representatives 1864-1868, serving as speaker the last two years; moved to Wakeeney, Kans., in 1885 and practiced law; appointed by President Benjamin Harrison as postmaster of Wakeeney and served from 1890 to 1894; removed to Savannah, Andrew County, Mo., in 1894 and died there on May 19, 1907; interment in Savannah Cemetery.

**HARLAN, Byron Berry,** a Representative from Ohio; born in Greenville, Darke County, Ohio, October 22, 1886; moved with his parents to Dayton, Ohio, in 1894; attended the public schools; was graduated from the Law College of the University of Michigan at Ann Arbor in 1909 and from its College of Arts and Sciences in 1911; was admitted to the bar in 1909 and commenced practice in Dayton, Ohio, in 1911; assistant prosecuting attorney of Montgomery County, Ohio, 1912-1916; president of the Ohio Federated Humane Societies 1928-1943 and honorary vice president of the American Humane Association in 1938; elected as a Democrat to the Seventy-second and to the three succeeding Congresses (March 4, 1931-January 3, 1939); chairman, Committee on Revision of the Laws (Seventy-second and Seventy-third Congresses); unsuccessful candidate for reelection in 1938 to the Seventy-sixth Congress; resumed the practice of law; delegate to the Democratic National Convention in 1940; United States district attorney for the southern district of Ohio from May 1944 until March 1946; appointed judge of the Tax Court of the United States in 1946 and served until his death in Williamsport, Pa., November 11, 1949; interment in Woodland Cemetery, Dayton, Ohio.

**HARLAN, James,** a Representative from Kentucky; born in Mercer County, Ky., June 22, 1800; attended the public schools; engaged in mercantile pursuits from 1817 to 1821; studied law; was admitted to the bar in 1823 and commenced practice in Harrodsburg, Ky.; served as prosecuting attorney from 1829 until 1844; elected as a Whig to the Twenty-fourth and Twenty-fifth Congresses (March 4, 1835-March 3, 1839); Kentucky secretary from 1840 to 1844; member of the Kentucky house of representatives in 1845; attorney general of Kentucky from 1850 until his death in Frankfort, Franklin County, Ky., February 18, 1863.

**Bibliography:** *DAB*.

**HARLAN, James,** a Senator from Iowa; born in Clark County, Ill., August 26, 1820; when four years of age moved with his family to Indiana; attended the rural schools, assisted his father in farming, and taught school until 1841, when he entered college; graduated from Indiana Asbury (now DePauw) University, Greencastle, Ind., in 1845; moved to Iowa City, Iowa, in 1845; superintendent of public instruction in 1847; studied law; was admitted to the bar in 1850 and commenced practice in Iowa City;

declined the Whig nomination for Governor of Iowa in 1850; president of Iowa Wesleyan University, Mount Pleasant, Iowa, 1853-1855; elected as a Free Soiler to the United States Senate in 1855, presented his credentials, and took his seat on December 31, 1855; owing to irregularities in the legislative proceedings the Senate declared the seat vacant in January 1857; reelected as a Republican to fill the vacancy thus created; reelected in 1860, and served from January 29, 1857 until May 15, 1865, when he resigned to accept a Cabinet portfolio; chairman, Committee on Public Lands (Thirty-seventh through Thirty-ninth Congresses); Secretary of the Interior in the Cabinet of President Andrew Johnson from May 15, 1865 until his resignation on July 26, 1866; again elected to the United States Senate, and served from March 4, 1867 to March 3, 1873; chairman, Committee on the District of Columbia (Fortieth Congress), Committee on Education (Fortieth Congress), Committee on Indian Affairs (Forty-first and Forty-second Congresses); delegate to the peace convention held in Washington, D.C., in 1861, in an effort to devise means to prevent the impending war; presiding judge of the court of commissioners arbitrating claims for damages to United States shipping caused during the Civil War by the Confederate raider *Alabama*, 1882-1886; died in Mount Pleasant, Henry County, Iowa, on October 5, 1899; interment in Forest Home Cemetery.

Bibliography: *DAB*; Brigham, Johnson. *James Harlan*. Iowa City: The State Historical Society of Iowa, 1913; Davis, R.E. "James Harlan: A Case Study of Early Republicanism." *The Central States Speech Journal* 34 (Summer 1983): 104-13.

HARLESS, Richard Fielding, a Representative from Arizona; born in Kelsey, Upshur County, Tex., August 6, 1905; moved to Thatcher, Ariz., in 1917 and attended the grade and high schools; was graduated from the University of Arizona at Tucson in 1928; taught school at Marana, Ariz., 1928-1930; was graduated from the law school of the University of Arizona in 1933; was admitted to the bar the same year and commenced practice in Phoenix, Ariz.; assistant city attorney of Phoenix, Ariz., in 1935; assistant attorney general of Arizona in 1936; county attorney of Maricopa County, Ariz., 1938-1942; elected as a Democrat to the Seventy-eighth and to the two succeeding Congresses (January 3, 1943-January 3, 1949); was not a candidate in 1948 for renomination to the Eighty-first Congress, but was an unsuccessful candidate for nomination for Governor of Arizona; unsuccessful candidate for nomination in 1954 to the Eighty-fourth Congress; unsuccessful candidate for election in 1960 to the Eighty-seventh Congress; resumed the practice of law; died in Phoenix, Ariz., November 24, 1970; interment in Greenwood Memorial Park.

HARMAN, Jane F., a Representative from California; born in New York City, June 28, 1945; graduated, University High School, Los Angeles, 1962; B.A., Smith College, Northampton, Mass., 1966; J.D., Harvard University School of Law, 1969; general counsel and board member, Harman Industries, Calif.; attorney, Los Angeles, Calif.; special counsel to Department of Defense; Deputy Secretary to the Cabinet, The White House; chief counsel and staff director, Subcommittee on Constitutional Rights, United States Senate Committee on the Judiciary; adjunct professor, Georgetown University Law Center, Washington, D.C.; elected as a Democrat to the One Hundred Third and One Hundred Fourth Congresses (January 3, 1993-January 3, 1997); is a resident of Marina del Rey, Calif.

HARMANSON, John Henry, a Representative from Louisiana; born in Norfolk, Va., January 15, 1803; pursued classical studies and was graduated from Jefferson College, Washington, Miss.; moved to Avoyelles Parish, La., in 1830 and engaged in agricultural pursuits; studied law; was admitted to the bar and practiced; member of the State senate in 1844; elected as a Democrat to the Twenty-ninth, Thirtieth, and Thirty-first Congresses and served from March 4, 1845, until his death in New Orleans, La., October 24,

1850; chairman, Committee on Expenditures in the Post Office Department (Twenty-ninth Congress); interment in Moreau Plantation Cemetery, Pointe Coupee Parish, La.

HARMER, Alfred Crout, a Representative from Pennsylvania; born in Germantown (now part of Philadelphia), Pa., August 8, 1825; attended the public schools and Germantown Academy; commenced business as a shoe manufacturer; was a wholesale dealer until 1860; identified with railroad enterprises, shipping, and the wholesale coal business; member of the city council of Philadelphia 1856-1860; recorder of deeds for Philadelphia 1860-1863; elected as a Republican to the Forty-second and Forty-third Congresses (March 4, 1871-March 3, 1875); was an unsuccessful candidate for reelection in 1874 to the Forty-fourth Congress; elected to the Forty-fifth and to the eleven succeeding Congresses and served from March 4, 1877, until his death in Germantown, Philadelphia, Pa., on March 6, 1900; interment in West Laurel Hill Cemetery.

HARMON, Randall S., a Representative from Indiana; born in North Vernon, Jennings County, Ind., July 19, 1903; graduated from North Vernon High School; took extension courses in law and tool engineering; employed as a tool engineer with Delco Battery Operations in Muncie, Ind. from 1933 until 1959; elected as a Democrat to the Eighty-sixth Congress (January 3, 1959-January 3, 1961); unsuccessful candidate for reelection in 1960 to the Eighty-seventh Congress; unsuccessful candidate for nomination in 1962 to the Eighty-eighth Congress, in 1968 to the Ninety-first Congress, in 1970 to the Ninety-second Congress, in 1978 to the Ninety-sixth Congress, and in 1980 to the Ninety-seventh Congress; unsuccessful mayoral candidate in 1979 in Muncie, Ind.; was a resident of Muncie, Ind., until his death there on August 18, 1982; interment at Hillcrest Cemetery, North Vernon, Ind.

HARNESS, Forest Arthur, a Representative from Indiana; born in Kokomo, Howard County, Ind., June 24, 1895; attended the public schools and was graduated from the law department of Georgetown University, Washington, D.C., in 1917; served overseas as a first lieutenant, Three Hundred and Nineteenth Infantry, 1917-1919; awarded the Purple Heart; captain, Infantry Reserve, United States Army, 1920-1949; admitted to the District of Columbia bar in 1917, to the Indiana bar in 1919, and commenced practice in Kokomo, Ind.; prosecuting attorney of Howard County, Ind., 1920-1924; special assistant to the Attorney General of the United States from 1931 to 1935 when he resigned to resume private practice; elected as a Republican to the Seventy-sixth and to the four succeeding Congresses (January 3, 1939-January 3, 1949); chairman, Select Committee on the Federal Communications Commission (Eightieth Congress); unsuccessful candidate for reelection in 1948 to the Eighty-first Congress; resumed the practice of law; Sergeant at Arms of the United States Senate from January 3, 1953, to January 3, 1955; retired in 1960 and resided in Sarasota, Fla., where he died, July 29, 1974; entombment in the mausoleum at Crown Point Cemetery, Kokomo, Ind.

HARNETT, Cornelius, a Delegate from North Carolina; born near Edenton, Chowan County, N.C., April 20, 1723; moved with his parents to Brunswick in 1726 and later to Wilmington, N. C.; engaged in mercantile pursuits; appointed by Governor Johnston as justice of the peace for New Hanover County in April 1750; elected town commissioner in August 1750 and served at different times for eleven years; member of the colonial assembly 1754-1775; chairman of the Sons of Liberty of North Carolina and leader in the resistance to the Stamp Act in 1765 and 1766; member of the committee of correspondence in 1773 and 1774; chairman of the Wilmington Committee of Safety in 1774 and 1775; member of the Second, Third, Fourth and Fifth Provincial Congresses in 1775 and 1776, serving as president in the Fifth; delegate to the provincial council in 1775 and 1776, and served as president of the council, thus becoming chief executive of the new government; excepted by Sir Henry Clinton from his proclamation of general amnesty in 1776; councilor of state in 1777; Member of the Continental Congress 1777-1779; captured by the British upon their occupation of Wilmington, N.C., in January 1781, and died as a prisoner in Wilmington on April 28, 1781; interment in St. James' Churchyard.

**Bibliography:** *DAB*; Morgan, David T. "Cornelius Harnett: Revolutionary Leader and Delegate to the Continental Congress." *North Carolina Historical Review* 49 (July 1972): 229-41.

**HARPER, Alexander,** a Representative from Ohio; born near Belfast, Ireland, February 5, 1786; immigrated to the United States and settled in Zanesville, Muskingum County, Ohio; pursued preparatory studies; studied law; was admitted to the bar in 1813 and commenced practice in Zanesville, Ohio; member of the State house of representatives in 1820 and 1821; president judge of the court of common pleas 1822-1836; elected as a Whig to the Twenty-fifth Congress (March 4, 1837-March 3, 1839); elected to the Twenty-eighth and Twenty-ninth Congresses (March 4, 1843-March 3, 1847); chairman, Committee on Expenditures in the Post Office Department (Twenty-eighth Congress), Committee on Patents (Twenty-eighth Congress); again elected to the Thirty-second Congress (March 4, 1851-March 3, 1853); resumed the practice of law; died in Zanesville, Ohio, on December 1, 1860; interment in Greenwood Cemetery.

**HARPER, Francis Jacob,** a Representative from Pennsylvania; born in Frankford, Philadelphia County, Pa., March 5, 1800; member of the Pennsylvania house of representatives in 1832; served in the Pennsylvania senate in 1834 and 1835; elected as a Democrat to the Twenty-fifth Congress, but died in Frankford, Pa., March 18, 1837, before the assembling of Congress; interment in Frankford Cemetery; reinterment in December 1848 in the Congressional Cemetery, Washington, D.C.

**HARPER, James,** a Representative from Pennsylvania; born in Castlederg, County Tyrone, Ireland, March 28, 1780; immigrated to the United States and settled in Philadelphia, Pa.; attended the public schools; engaged in the manufacture of brick and from 1820 to 1830 in the wholesale grocery trade; elected to the Twenty-third Congress and reelected as a Whig to the Twenty-fourth Congress (March 4, 1833-March 3, 1837); was not a candidate for renomination in 1836; resumed the manufacture of brick until he retired in 1869; member of the board of guardians of the poor and the board of prison inspectors; died in Philadelphia, Pa., March 31, 1873; interment in Laurel Hill Cemetery.

**HARPER, James Clarence,** a Representative from North Carolina; born in Cumberland County, Pa., December 6, 1819; moved with his father to Darke County, Ohio, in 1831; attended the common schools; moved to Lenoir, Caldwell County, N.C., in 1840; land surveyor, civil engineer, and draftsman; laid out the town of Lenoir, N.C., in 1841; engaged in mercantile pursuits and subsequently became interested in the manufacture of cotton and woolen goods; held several local offices; colonel in the State militia; member of the State house of commons in 1865 and 1866; elected as a Democrat to the Forty-second Congress (March 4, 1871-March 3, 1873); was not a candidate for renomination in 1872; engaged in agricultural pursuits and in road building; died near Patterson, Caldwell County, N.C., January 8, 1890; interment in the Cemetery at Harpers Chapel, Patterson, N.C.

**HARPER, John Adams,** a Representative from New Hampshire; born in Derryfield, N.H., November 2, 1779; attended Phillips Exeter Academy, Exeter, N.H., in 1794; studied law; was admitted to the bar about 1802 and commenced practice in Sanbornton, N.H.; first postmaster of Sanbornton, N.H.; moved to Meredith Bridge (now Laconia, Belknap County) in 1806; clerk of the State senate 1805-1808; member of the State house of representatives in 1809 and 1810; served in the State militia 1809-1812; elected as a Republican to the Twelfth Congress (March 4, 1811-March 3, 1813); unsuccessful candidate for reelection in 1812 to the Thirteenth Congress; died at Meredith Bridge, N.H., June 18, 1816; interment in Union Cemetery.

**HARPER, Joseph Morrill,** a Representative from New Hampshire; born in Limerick, York County, Maine, June 21, 1787; attended the district school and the Fryeburg Academy; studied medicine; commenced practice in Sanbornton, N.H., in 1810; moved to Canterbury, N.H., in 1811 and continued the practice of medicine; served as assistant surgeon in the Fourth Infantry in the War of 1812; member of the State house of representatives in 1826 and 1827; justice of the peace in Canterbury 1826-1865; served in the State senate in 1829 and 1830, the last year as president of the senate and as ex officio Governor from February until June 1831; elected as a Jacksonian to the Twenty-second and Twenty-third Congresses (March 4, 1831-March 3, 1835); resumed the practice of medicine; justice of the peace and quorum in the State 1835-1865; president of Mechanics' Bank of Concord 1847-1856; died in Canterbury, N.H., January 15, 1865; interment in the Village Cemetery.

**HARPER, Robert Goodloe,** a Representative from South Carolina and a Senator from Maryland; born near Fredericksburg, Va., in January 1765; moved with his parents to Granville, N.C., about 1769; received his early education at home and later attended grammar school; joined a volunteer corps of Cavalry when only fifteen years of age and served in the Revolutionary Army; made a surveying tour through Kentucky and Tennessee in 1783; graduated from the College of New Jersey (now Princeton University) in 1785; studied law in Charleston, S.C., teaching school at the same time; was admitted to the bar in 1786 and commenced practice in Ninety-Sixth District, S.C.; moved to Charleston, S.C., in 1789; member, State house of representatives 1790-1795; elected from South Carolina to the Third Congress to fill the vacancy caused by the death of Alexander Gillon; reelected to the Fourth, Fifth, and Sixth Congresses and served from February 1795 to March 1801; unsuccessful candidate for reelection in 1800 to the Seventh Congress; chairman, Committee on Ways and Means (Fifth and Sixth Congresses); one of the managers appointed by the House of Representatives in 1798 to conduct the impeachment proceedings against William Blount, a Senator from Tennessee; moved to Baltimore, Md., and engaged in the practice of law; served in the War of 1812, attaining the rank of major general; assisted in organizing the Baltimore Exchange Co. in 1815 and was a member of the first board of directors; member, State senate of Maryland; elected from Maryland to the United States Senate for the term beginning March 4, 1815, and served from January 1816 until December 1816, when he resigned; unsuccessful Federalist candidate for vice president in 1816; traveled extensively in Europe in 1819 and 1820; took a prominent part in the ceremonies on the occasion of Lafayette's visit to Baltimore in 1824; died in Baltimore, Md., January 14, 1825; interment in the family burial ground on his estate, "Oakland"; reinterment in Greenmount Cemetery, Baltimore, Md.

**Bibliography:** *DAB*; Cox, Joseph. *Champion of Southern Federalism: Robert Goodloe Harper of South Carolina.* Port Washington, N.Y.: Kennikat Press, 1972; Sommerville, Charles W. "Robert Goodlow Harper." Ph.D. dissertation, Johns Hopkins University, 1899.

**HARPER, William,** a Senator from South Carolina; born on the island of Antigua, West Indies, January 17, 1790; immigrated to the United States with his parents, who settled in Charleston, and later in Columbia, S.C., in the 1790s; attended the common schools, Mount Bethel Academy, and Jefferson Monticello Seminary; graduated from South Carolina College (now the University of South

Carolina) at Columbia in 1808; studied medicine for a time in Charleston and later studied law; was admitted to the bar in 1813 and commenced the practice of law in Columbia; trustee of South Carolina College in 1813; member, State house of representatives 1816-1817; moved to Missouri in 1818; chancellor of the State of Missouri 1819-1823; member of the State constitutional convention in 1821; returned to Columbia, S.C., in 1823; reporter of the State supreme court 1823-1825; appointed as a Jacksonian to the United States Senate to fill the vacancy caused by the death of John Gaillard and served from March 8 to November 29, 1826, when a successor was elected; practiced law in Charleston; member, State house of representatives 1827-1828, serving as speaker; chancellor of the State of South Carolina 1828-1830; returned to Columbia, S.C.; appointed judge of the court of appeals 1830-1835; member of the State convention in 1832 and 1833 (known as the Nullification Convention); again chancellor of the State from 1835 until his death in Fairfield District, S.C., October 10, 1847; interment in Means Family Burial Ground, Fairfield County, S.C.

Bibliography: *DAB.*

**HARRELD, John William,** a Representative and a Senator from Oklahoma; born near Morgantown, Butler County, Ky., January 24, 1872; attended the public schools, the normal school at Lebanon, Ohio, and Bryant and Stratton Business College of Louisville, Ky., where he taught while studying law; was admitted to the bar in 1889 and commenced practice in Morgantown, Ky.; prosecuting attorney of Butler County, 1892-1896; moved to Ardmore, Okla., in 1906 and continued the practice of law; referee in bankruptcy from 1908 until 1915, when he resigned to become an executive with an oil corporation; moved to Oklahoma City, Okla., in 1917 and engaged in the production of oil and continued the practice of law; elected as a Republican to the Sixty-sixth Congress to fill the vacancy caused by the death of Joseph B. Thompson, and served from November 8, 1919 to March 3, 1921; was not a candidate in 1920 for renomination to the House of Representatives, but was elected to the United States Senate, and served from March 4, 1921 to March 3, 1927; unsuccessful candidate for reelection in 1926; chairman, Committee on Indian Affairs (Sixty-eighth and Sixty-ninth Congresses); unsuccessful candidate for election in 1940 to the Seventy-seventh Congress; returned to Oklahoma City and continued the practice of law and his interest in the oil business; died in Oklahoma City, Okla., December 26, 1950; interment in Fairlawn Cemetery.

Bibliography: Jones, Stephen. *Once Before: The Political and Senatorial Careers of Oklahoma's First Two Republican United States Senators, John W. Harreld and W.B. Pine.* Enid, Okla.: Dougherty Press, 1986.

**HARRIES, William Henry,** a Representative from Minnesota; born near Dayton, Montgomery County, Ohio, January 15, 1843; moved to La Crosse, Wis.; enlisted as a private in Company B, Second Regiment, Wisconsin Volunteer Infantry, April 18, 1861; commissioned captain of Company F, Third Regiment, United States Veteran Volunteers, General Hancock's corps, December 21, 1864; honorably discharged April 17, 1866; was graduated from the law school of the University of Michigan at Ann Arbor in 1868; was admitted to the bar in 1868, and commenced practice in Hokah, Minn.; afterwards practiced in Caledonia, Houston County, Minn.; prosecuting attorney of Houston County 1874-1878; elected as a Democrat to the Fifty-second Congress (March 4, 1891-March 3, 1893); unsuccessful candidate for reelection in 1892 to the Fifty-third Congress; appointed by President Grover Cleveland as collector of internal revenue for Minnesota and served from 1894 to 1898, residing in St. Paul, Minn.; resumed the practice of his profession in Caledonia in 1898; department commander of the Minnesota department of the Grand Army of the Republic in 1901; member of the board of trustees of the Minnesota Soldiers' Home in 1903, secretary of the board 1907-1911, and commandant of the

home 1911-1918; died in Seattle, Wash., July 23, 1921; interment in Evergreen Cemetery, Caledonia, Minn.

**HARRINGTON, Henry William,** a Representative from Indiana; born near Cooperstown, Otsego County, N.Y., September 12, 1825; attended the common schools and in 1845 entered Temple Hill Academy, Livingston County, N.Y., where he remained for three years; studied law in Geneseo; was admitted to the bar in 1848 and commenced practice in Nunda, N.Y.; moved to Madison, Ind., in 1856 and continued the practice of law; moved to St. Louis, Mo., in 1872; returned to Indiana in 1874, settled in Indianapolis, and resumed the practice of law; delegate to the Democratic National Conventions in 1860, 1868, and 1872; elected as a Democrat to the Thirty-eighth Congress (March 4, 1863-March 3, 1865); unsuccessful candidate for reelection in 1864 to the Thirty-ninth Congress; collector of internal revenue for the third district of Indiana from October 27, 1866, to March 3, 1867; again engaged in the practice of law; died in Indianapolis, Ind., March 20, 1882; interment in Evergreen Cemetery, Alpena, Mich.

**HARRINGTON, Michael Joseph,** a Representative from Massachusetts; born in Salem, Essex County, Mass., September 2, 1936; educated in parochial and public schools of Salem, Mass., and graduated from St. John's Preparatory School, Danvers, Mass., in 1954; B.A., Harvard University, 1958; J.D., Harvard University School of Law, 1961; Carnegie Institute internship in State government; Harvard Graduate School of Public Administration, 1962 and 1963; member of the Salem City Council, 1959-1961, city councilor, 1961-1962; Massachusetts Legislature, Sixth Essex District, 1964-1969; Democratic State committeeman, Second Essex District, 1968; began the practice of law in Salem, Mass., in 1962; elected as a Democrat to the Ninety-first Congress, September 30, 1969, by special election to fill the vacancy caused by the death of William H. Bates; reelected to the four succeeding Congresses, and served from September 30, 1969 to January 3, 1979; was not a candidate for reelection in 1978 to the Ninety-sixth Congress; real estate developer, 1979 to present; is a resident of Beverly, Mass.

**HARRINGTON, Vincent Francis,** a Representative from Iowa; born in Sioux City, Woodbury County, Iowa, May 16, 1903; attended the public schools and Trinity College of his native city; was graduated from the University of Notre Dame, South Bend, Ind., in 1925; instructor in history and economics and athletic director at the University of Portland, Portland, Oreg., 1926-1927; returned to Sioux City, Iowa, in 1927 and became vice president and general manager of a mortgage company; member of the State senate 1933-1937; was nominated as a candidate for lieutenant governor of Iowa in 1936 but withdrew to accept a nomination for the House of Representatives; elected as a Democrat to the Seventy-fifth and to the two succeeding Congresses and served from January 3, 1937, until his resignation on September 5, 1942, to accept a commission as major in the Air Corps, United States Army; died at Rutlandshire, England, on November 29, 1943, while on active duty in England; interment in the United States Military Cemetery at Brookwood, thirty miles southwest of London, England.

**HARRIS, Benjamin Gwinn,** a Representative from Maryland; born near Leonardtown, St. Marys County, Md., December 13, 1805; attended Yale College and Cambridge (Mass.) Law School; studied law; was admitted to the bar in 1840; member of the State house of delegates in 1833 and 1836; elected as a Democrat to the Thirty-eighth and Thirty-ninth Congresses (March 4, 1863-March 3, 1867); censured by the House of Representatives on April 9, 1864, for treasonable utterances; was tried by a military court in Washington, D.C., in May 1865 for harboring two paroled Confederate soldiers, and sentenced to three years imprisonment and forever disqualified from holding any office under the United States Government, but President Andrew Johnson subsequently remitted the sentence; died on his estate, "Ellenborough," near

Leonardtown, Md., April 4, 1895; interment in the family burying ground on his estate.

**HARRIS, Benjamin Winslow** (father of Robert Orr Harris), a Representative from Massachusetts; born in East Bridgewater, Mass., November 10, 1823; pursued an academic course and was graduated from Dane Law School, Harvard University, in 1849; was admitted to the bar in Boston in 1850 and commenced practice in East Bridgewater; served in the Massachusetts senate in 1857; member of the Massachusetts house of representatives in 1858; district attorney for the southeastern district of Massachusetts from July 1, 1858, to June 30, 1866; collector of internal revenue for the second district of Massachusetts from June 30, 1866, to March 1, 1873; elected as a Republican to the Forty-third and to the four succeeding Congresses (March 4, 1873-March 3, 1883); chairman, Committee on Naval Affairs (Forty-seventh Congress); was not a candidate for renomination in 1882; resumed the practice of law in East Bridgewater, Plymouth County; judge of probate for the county of Plymouth 1887-1906; died in East Bridgewater, Mass., on February 7, 1907; interment in Union Cemetery.

**HARRIS, Charles Murray,** a Representative from Illinois; born in Munfordsville, Hart County, Ky., April 10, 1821; attended the common schools; studied law; was admitted to the bar; moved to Illinois and located in Oquawka, where he commenced the practice of his profession; elected as a Democrat to the Thirty-eighth Congress (March 4, 1863-March 3, 1865); unsuccessful candidate for reelection in 1864 to the Thirty-ninth Congress; died in Chicago, Ill., September 20, 1896; interment in Oquawka, Ill.

**HARRIS, Christopher Columbus,** a Representative from Alabama; born near Mount Hope, Lawrence County, Ala., January 28, 1842; educated in the common schools and also by private tutors; enlisted in the Confederate Army in 1861 as a private in Company F, Sixteenth Alabama Infantry; was subsequently promoted to the rank of lieutenant; taken as a prisoner to Camp Chase, Ohio, where he remained until the close of the war; clerk of the circuit court of Lawrence County 1865-1867; studied law; was admitted to the bar and commenced practice in Moulton, Ala., in 1868; moved to Decatur, Ala., in 1872 and continued the practice of law; in 1887 assisted in organizing the First National Bank of Decatur, of which he served as president until January 1913; organized the Bank of Commerce in 1913 and became its president; chairman of the Democratic executive committee of the eighth congressional district; elected as a Democrat to the Sixty-third Congress to fill the vacancy caused by the death of William Richardson and served from May 11, 1914, to March 3, 1915; was not a candidate for renomination in 1914; became president of the City National Bank of Decatur, Ala.; elected chairman of the board of directors on January 10, 1928; died in Decatur, Ala., December 28, 1935; interment in Decatur Cemetery.

**HARRIS, Claude, Jr.,** a Representative from Alabama; born in Bessemer, Jefferson County, Ala., June 29, 1940; attended public schools; B.S., University of Alabama, 1962; LL.B., University of Alabama School of Law, 1965; admitted to the Alabama State bar in 1965 and was assistant district attorney, Tuscaloosa, Ala., 1965-1976; judge of the Alabama Circuit Court, 1977-1985; lieutenant colonel, Alabama Army National Guard; elected as a Democrat to the One Hundredth and to the two succeeding Congresses (January 3, 1987-January 3, 1993); nominated as United States Attorney for the Northern District of Alabama on September 7, 1993, and was confirmed by the Senate on September 30, 1993; died October 2, 1994.

**HARRIS, Fred Roy,** a Senator from Oklahoma; born in Walters, Cotton County, Okla., November 13, 1930; attended the public schools; B.A., University of Oklahoma, 1952; LL.B., University of Oklahoma School of Law, 1954; admitted to the bar in 1954 and

began to practice law in Lawton, Okla.; member, Oklahoma State senate, 1956-1964; unsuccessful gubernatorial candidate in 1962; elected as a Democrat to the United States Senate on November 3, 1964 to fill the vacancy caused by the death of Robert S. Kerr for the term ending January 3, 1967; reelected in 1966 and served from November 4, 1964, to January 2, 1973; was not a candidate for reelection in 1972; unsuccessful candidate for the Democratic presidential nomination in 1976; professor of political science, University of New Mexico; is a resident of Albuquerque, N.Mex.

**Bibliography:** Harris, Fred. *Potomac Fever.* New York: W.W. Norton, Inc., 1977.

**HARRIS, George Emrick,** a Representative from Mississippi; born in Orange County, N.C., January 6, 1827; moved to Tennessee and thence to Mississippi; attended the common schools; studied law; was admitted to the bar in 1854 and practiced; entered the Confederate Army and served as a lieutenant colonel until the close of the Civil War; elected district attorney in 1865 and reelected in 1866; upon the readmission of the State of Mississippi to representation was elected as a Republican to the Forty-first and Forty-second Congresses, and served from February 23, 1870 to March 3, 1873; attorney general of Mississippi, 1873-1877; lieutenant governor, 1877-1879; engaged as an author of books on legal subjects; died in Washington, D.C., March 19, 1911; interment in Oak Hill Cemetery.

**HARRIS, Henry Richard,** a Representative from Georgia; born in Sparta, Hancock County, Ga., February 2, 1828; moved to Greenville, Meriwether County, Ga., in 1833; attended an academy in Mount Zion, Hancock County, Ga., and was graduated from Emory College at Oxford, Ga., in 1847; member of the State constitutional convention in 1861; during the Civil War served in the Confederate Army as colonel; elected as a Democrat to the Forty-third, Forty-fourth, and Forty-fifth Congresses (March 4, 1873-March 3, 1879); unsuccessful candidate for reelection in 1878 to the Forty-sixth Congress; elected to the Forty-ninth Congress (March 4, 1885-March 3, 1887); was not a candidate for renomination in 1886 to the Fiftieth Congress; appointed by President Grover Cleveland as Third Assistant Postmaster General of the United States, and served from April 1, 1887 to March 18, 1889; engaged in agricultural pursuits; died in Odessadale, Meriwether County, Ga., October 15, 1909; interment in Greenville Cemetery, Greenville, Ga.

**HARRIS, Henry Schenck,** a Representative from New Jersey; born in Belvidere, Warren County, N.J., December 27, 1850; attended the common schools and was graduated from Princeton College in 1870; studied law; was admitted to the bar in 1873 and commenced practice in Belvidere, N.J.; appointed prosecutor of the pleas for Warren County in March 1877; elected as a Democrat to the Forty-seventh Congress (March 4, 1881-March 3, 1883); unsuccessful candidate for reelection in 1882 to the Forty-eighth Congress; resumed the practice of law; died in Belvidere, N.J., May 2, 1902; interment in Belvidere Cemetery.

**HARRIS, Herbert Eugene, II,** a Representative from Virginia; born in Kansas City, Mo., April 14, 1926; attended St. Francis Xavier Elementary School, Kansas City, 1930-1939; graduated from Rockhurst High School, Kansas City, 1943; attended Missouri Valley College, Marshall, 1944-1945, and the University of Notre Dame, 1945-1946; B.A., Rockhurst College, Kansas City, 1948; J.D., Georgetown University Law School, Washington, D.C., 1951; admitted to the Missouri and District of Columbia bars in 1951 and commenced practice in Kansas City; moved to the Washington, D.C., area in 1951; co-founder, vice president, and general counsel of the international trade consulting firm of Warner & Harris, Inc.; served on Fairfax County (Va.) Board of Supervisors, 1968-1974; member, Northern Virginia Transportation Authority, 1968-1974; vice chairman, Washington, D.C., Metropolitan Transit Authority, 1970-1974; elected as a Democrat to the Ninety-fourth and to the two succeeding Congresses (January 3, 1975-January 3, 1981); unsuccessful candidate for reelection in 1980 to the Ninety-seventh Congress; resumed the practice of law with the firm of Harris & Ellsworth in Washington, D.C.; is a resident of Mount Vernon, Va.

**HARRIS, Ira** (grandfather of Henry Riggs Rathbone), a Senator from New York; born in Charleston, Montgomery County, N.Y., May 31, 1802; attended the district school and Homer (N.Y.) Academy; graduated from Union College, Schenectady, N.Y., in 1824; studied law in Albany; was admitted to the bar in 1827 and commenced practice in Albany; member, New York State assembly, 1845-1846; delegate to the State constitutional convention in 1846; New York State senator in 1847; upon the organization of the Albany Law School in 1850 was engaged as lecturer on equity jurisprudence; justice of the State supreme court, 1847-1859; elected as a Republican to the United States Senate, and served from March 4, 1861 to March 3, 1867; unsuccessful candidate for reelection; chairman, Committee on Private Land Claims (Thirty-seventh through Thirty-ninth Congresses); delegate to the State constitutional convention in 1867; professor in the Albany Law School from 1867 until his death; died in Albany, N.Y., December 2, 1875; interment in Rural Cemetery, Colonie, near Watervliet, Albany County, N.Y.

Bibliography: *DAB*.

**HARRIS, Isham Green,** a Representative and a Senator from Tennessee; born near Tullahoma, Franklin County, Tenn., February 10, 1818; attended the common schools and Winchester Academy; moved to Paris, Tenn., to become a store clerk; studied law; was admitted to the bar and commenced practice in Paris, Henry County, Tenn., in 1841; member of the Tennessee State senate in 1847; elected as a Democrat to the Thirty-first and Thirty-second Congresses (March 4, 1849-March 3, 1853); declined to be a candidate for renomination in 1852 to the Thirty-third Congress; chairman, Committee on Invalid Pensions (Thirty-second Congress); moved to Memphis in 1853 and resumed the practice of law; elected Governor of Tennessee in 1857 and 1859, and served from November 3, 1857 until March 12, 1862; committed Tennessee to the Confederate cause; served in the Confederate Army during the Civil War as aide-de-camp to General Albert Sidney Johnston, and in the general headquarters of the Army of the West; after the Civil War, fled first to Mexico, then to England; returned to Tennessee and resumed the practice of law in Memphis; elected as a Democrat to the United States Senate in 1877; reelected in 1883, 1889, and 1895 and served from March 4, 1877, until his death in Washington, D.C., July 8, 1897; served as President pro tempore of the Senate during the Fifty-third Congress; chairman, Committee on District of Columbia (Forty-sixth and Fifty-third Congresses), Committee on Epidemic Diseases (Forty-ninth through Fifty-second Congresses), Committee on Private Land Claims (Fifty-fourth and Fifty-fifth Congresses); funeral services were held in the Chamber of the United States Senate; interment in Elmwood Cemetery, Memphis, Tenn.

Bibliography: *DAB*; Horn, Stanley F. "Isham G. Harris in the Pre-War Years." *Tennessee Historical Quarterly* 19 (September 1960): 195-207; Watters, George W. "Isham Green Harris, Civil War Governor and Senator from Tennessee, 1818-1897." Ph.D. dissertation, Florida State University, 1977.

**HARRIS, James Morrison,** a Representative from Maryland; born in Baltimore, Md., November 20, 1817; educated at private institutions in Baltimore; entered Lafayette College, Easton, Pa., in 1833; studied law; was admitted to the bar in 1843 and commenced practice in Baltimore; elected as a candidate of the American Party to the Thirty-fourth, Thirty-fifth, and Thirty-sixth Congresses (March 4, 1855-March 3, 1861); declined to be a candidate for renomination in 1860; resumed the practice of law and also engaged in educational and religious work; trustee of Lafayette College

1865-1872; died in Baltimore, Md., on July 16, 1898; interment in Westminster Presbyterian Burying Ground.

**HARRIS, John** (cousin of Robert Harris), a Representative from New York; born at Harris Ferry (now Harrisburg), Pa., September 26, 1760; moved to Aurelias (now in Cayuga County), Onondaga County, N.Y., in 1789; operated the first ferry across Cayuga Lake; acted as an Indian interpreter, and opened the first store and tavern in Cayuga County in 1789; appointed a colonel in the New York State Militia in 1806; elected as a Republican to the Tenth Congress (March 4, 1807-March 3, 1809); commanded the One Hundred and Fifty-eighth New York Regiment in the War of 1812; died in Bridgeport, near Seneca Falls, N.Y., in November 1824; interment in the local cemetery.

**HARRIS, John Spafford,** a Senator from Louisiana; born in Truxton, Cortland County, N.Y., on December 18, 1825; attended the common schools; moved to Du Page County, Ill., then on to Milwaukee, Wis., in 1846; employed as clerk in a mercantile establishment and pursued his education 1846-1849; engaged in mercantile pursuits 1849-1863; moved to Natchez, La., in 1863 and at the close of the Civil War was one of the largest cotton planters in the State; member of the State constitutional convention in 1868, being chosen one of a committee of seven to conduct the affairs of the State until the constitution could be adopted; member, State senate 1868; upon the readmission of Louisiana to representation was elected as a Republican to the United States Senate and served from July 8, 1868, to March 3, 1871; appointed surveyor general for Montana by President Chester Arthur on November 21, 1881; died in Butte, Mont., January 25, 1906; interment in Forestvale Cemetery, Helena, Mont.

**HARRIS, John Thomas** (cousin of John Hill of Virginia), a Representative from Virginia; born at Browns Gap, Albemarle County, Va., May 8, 1823; completed academic studies; studied law; was admitted to the bar in 1845 and commenced practice in Harrisonburg; Commonwealth attorney for Rockingham County, Va., 1852-1859; elected as an Independent Democrat to the Thirty-sixth Congress (March 4, 1859-March 3, 1861); was nominated for reelection in 1860 but no election was held, Virginia having seceded from the Union on April 17, 1861; member of the Virginia house of delegates 1863-1865; judge of the twelfth judicial circuit 1866-1869; on the readmission of Virginia to representation was an unsuccessful candidate for Congress at a special election held in July 1869; elected as a Democrat to the Forty-second and to the four succeeding Congresses (March 4, 1871-March 3, 1881); chairman, Committee on Elections (Forty-fourth and Forty-fifth Congresses), Committee on Revision of the Laws (Forty-sixth Congress); declined a unanimous renomination; chairman of the Virginia Democratic convention in 1884; commissioner to the World's Fair at Chicago; died in Harrisonburg, Va., October 14, 1899; interment in Woodbine Cemetery.

**HARRIS, Mark,** a Representative from Maine; born in Ipswich, Essex County, Mass., January 27, 1779; attended the common schools; moved to Portland, Maine (then a district of Massachusetts), in 1800; engaged in mercantile pursuits; member of the Massachusetts State senate in 1816; held several local offices; elected to the Seventeenth Congress to fill the vacancy caused by the resignation of Ezekiel Whitman and served from December 2, 1822, to March 3, 1823; resumed mercantile pursuits; member of the State house of representatives in 1830; treasurer of Cumberland County 1824-1832 and 1834-1840; State treasurer 1828 and 1832-1834; moved to New York City in 1842 and engaged in mercantile pursuits; died in New York City March 2, 1843; interment probably in Old Eastern Cemetery, Portland, Maine.

**HARRIS, Oren,** a Representative from Arkansas; born in Belton, Hempstead County, Ark., December 20, 1903; attended the public schools; B.A., Henderson State College (now Henderson State University), Arkadelphia, Ark., 1929; LL.B., Cumberland University Law School, Lebanon, Tenn., 1930; admitted to the bar in 1930 and commenced practice in El Dorado, Ark.; deputy prosecuting attorney of Union County, Ark., 1933-1936; prosecuting attorney of the thirteenth judicial circuit of Arkansas, 1937-1940; delegate to Democratic State conventions in 1936 and 1940; delegate to the Democratic National Conventions of 1944, 1952, 1956, and 1960; elected as a Democrat to the Seventy-seventh and to the twelve succeeding Congresses, and served from January 3, 1941 until his resignation on February 2, 1966; chairman, Committee on Interstate and Foreign Commerce (Eighty-fifth through Eighty-ninth Congresses), and chaired the Special Subcommittee on Legislative Oversight which conducted hearings on the television "quiz show" scandals of 1959; appointed United States district judge for the Eastern and Western Districts of Arkansas by President Lyndon B. Johnson, July 26, 1965, effective February 3, 1966; assumed senior status in 1976 and serves by assignment; is a resident of Little Rock, Ark.

**HARRIS, Robert** (cousin of John Harris), a Representative from Pennsylvania; born at Harris Ferry (now Harrisburg), Pa., September 5, 1768; was reared on a farm; attended the public schools; assisted in establishing various enterprises, including building of the bridge over the Susquehanna River, the organization of the Harrisburg Bank, and the construction of the Middletown Turnpike Road; surveyor to lay out the road from Chambersburg to Pittsburgh, and also for improving the Susquehanna River; appointed commissioner to choose the location of the capitol building in Harrisburg; paymaster in the Army during the War of 1812; elected to the Eighteenth and Nineteenth Congresses (March 4, 1823-March 3, 1827); prothonotary of Dauphin County; died in Harrisburg, Pa., September 3, 1851; interment in Harrisburg Cemetery.

**HARRIS, Robert Orr** (son of Benjamin Winslow Harris), a Representative from Massachusetts; born in Boston, Mass., November 8, 1854; attended the common schools and Phillips Exeter Academy, Exeter, N.H.; was graduated from Harvard University in 1877; studied law; was admitted to the bar in 1879 and practiced in Boston and Brockton, Mass., 1879-1902; member of the Massachusetts house of representatives in 1889; district attorney for the southeastern district of Massachusetts 1891-1901; associate judge of the superior court of Massachusetts from June 4, 1902, to March 1, 1911; elected as a Republican to the Sixty-second Congress (March 4, 1911-March 3, 1913); was not a candidate for renomination in 1912 to the Sixty-third Congress; resumed the practice of law; appointed United States district attorney for the Massachusetts district by President Warren G. Harding in 1921 and served until removed by President Calvin Coolidge in December 1924; died in Brockton, Mass., June 13, 1926; interment in Centeral Cemetery, East Bridgewater, Mass.

**HARRIS, Sampson Willis,** a Representative from Alabama; born in Elbert County, Ga., February 23, 1809; obtained his early education from his mother and was graduated from the University of Georgia at Athens in 1828; studied law; was admitted to the bar in 1830 and commenced practice in Athens, Ga.; member of the State house of representatives in 1834 and 1835; moved to Wetumpka, Ala., in 1838; elected solicitor of the eighth circuit in 1841; member of the State senate in 1844 and 1845; elected as a Democrat to the Thirtieth and to the four succeeding Congresses (March 4, 1847-March 3, 1857); declined to be a candidate for renomination in 1856; died in Washington, D.C., April 1, 1857; interment in Oconee Cemetery, Athens, Ga.

**HARRIS, Stephen Ross** (uncle of Ebenezer Byron Finley), a Representative from Ohio; born near Massillon, Stark County, Ohio, May 22, 1824; attended the common and select schools, Washington (Pa.) College, Norwalk (Ohio) Seminary, and Western Reserve College, then at Hudson, Ohio; studied law; was admitted to the bar in 1849 and commenced practice in Columbus, Ohio; moved to Bucyrus, Ohio, the same year and continued the practice of law; mayor of Bucyrus 1852, 1853, 1861, and 1862; deputy United States marshal in 1861; president of the State bar association in 1893 and 1894; elected as a Republican to the Fifty-fourth Congress (March 4, 1895-March 3, 1897); unsuccessful candidate for reelection in 1896 to the Fifty-fifth Congress; engaged in the practice of law in Bucyrus, Crawford County, Ohio, until his death there January 15, 1905; interment in Oakwood Cemetery.

**HARRIS, Thomas K.,** a Representative from Tennessee; studied law; was admitted to the bar and practiced in Sparta and McMinnville, Tenn.; trustee of Priestly Academy, Sparta, Tenn.; member of the State senate 1809-1811; elected as a Republican to the Thirteenth Congress (March 4, 1813-March 3, 1815); died from wounds received in an encounter with Col. John W. Simpson March 18, 1816, on the old Kentucky Road at Shells Ford of Collins River, between Sparta and McMinnville, Tenn.

**HARRIS, Thomas Langrell,** a Representative from Illinois; born in Norwich, Conn., October 29, 1816; pursued classical studies and was graduated from Washington (now Trinity) College, Hartford, Conn., in 1841; studied law; was admitted to the bar in 1842 and commenced practice in Petersburg, Menard County, Ill.; school commissioner for Menard County in 1845; during the Mexican War raised and commanded a company and joined the Fourth Regiment, Illinois Volunteer Infantry; subsequently elected major of the regiment; while absent and with the Army was elected a member of the State senate in 1846; was presented with a sword by the State of Illinois for gallantry at the Battle of Cerro Gordo, Mexico, on April 18, 1847; elected as a Democrat to the Thirty-first Congress (March 4, 1849-March 3, 1851); unsuccessful candidate for reelection in 1850 to the Thirty-second Congress; elected to the Thirty-fourth and Thirty-fifth Congresses and served from March 4, 1855, until his death; chairman, Committee on Expenditures in the Department of the Navy (Thirty-fourth Congress), Committee on Elections (Thirty-fifth Congress); had been reelected to the Thirty-sixth Congress; died in Springfield, Ill., November 24, 1858; interment in Rose Hill Cemetery, Petersburg, Ill.

**HARRIS, Wiley Pope,** a Representative from Mississippi; born near Holmesville, Pike County, Miss., November 9, 1818; attended the common schools and the University of Virginia at Charlottesville; was graduated from the law department of Transylvania College, Lexington, Ky., in 1840; was admitted to the bar in 1840 and commenced practice in Gallatin, Copiah County, Miss.; circuit judge of the second district, 1844-1850; member of the State constitutional conventions in 1850, 1861, and 1890; elected as a Democrat to the Thirty-third Congress (March 4, 1853-March 3, 1855); declined to be a candidate for renomination in 1854 to the Thirty-fourth Congress; resumed the practice of law in Jackson, Miss.; Member of the Provisional Congress of the Confederate States in 1861; continued the practice of law in Jackson, Miss., and died there on December 3, 1891; interment in Greenwood Cemetery.
Bibliography: *DAB.*

**HARRIS, William Alexander** (son of William Alexander Harris [1805-1864]), a Representative and a Senator from Kansas; born near Luray, Loudoun County, Va., October 29, 1841; attended the common schools, and graduated from Columbian College (later George Washington University), Washington, D.C., in 1859 and from the Virginia Military Institute at Lexington in 1861; during the Civil War served three years in the Confederate Army, becoming adjutant general, and later ordnance officer in the Army of Northern Virginia;

moved to Kansas in 1865 and was employed as a civil engineer in the construction of the Union Pacific Railroad until 1868; moved to Lawrence, Kans., in 1868; appointed agent for the railroad companies in the sale of the Delaware Reservation and other lands; moved to Linwood, Leavenworth County, in 1884 and engaged in agricultural pursuits and stock raising; elected as a Populist to the Fifty-third Congress (March 4, 1893-March 3, 1895); unsuccessful candidate for reelection in 1894 to the Fifty-fourth Congress; member, State senate 1895-1896; elected as a Populist to the United States Senate and served from March 4, 1897, to March 3, 1903; unsuccessful candidate for reelection; resumed his agricultural pursuits; unsuccessful candidate for Governor of Kansas in 1906; died in Chicago, Ill., where he had gone to work with the National Livestock Association, on December 20, 1909; interment in Oak Hill Cemetery, Lawrence, Kans.

**Bibliography:** *DAB.*

**HARRIS, William Alexander** (father of William Alexander Harris [1841-1909]), a Representative from Virginia; born near Warrenton, Fauquier County, Va., August 24, 1805; completed an academic course; studied law; was admitted to the bar and commenced practice in Luray; member of the Virginia house of delegates in 1830 and 1831; elected as a Democrat to the Twenty-seventh Congress (March 4, 1841-March 3, 1843); editor of the Spectator and the Constitution in Washington, D.C.; Chargé d'Affaires to the Argentine Republic 1846-1851; moved to Missouri and later returned to Washington, D.C., editor of the Washington Union and printer to the United States Senate 1857-1859; died in Pike County, Mo., March 28, 1864; interment in Riverview Cemetery, Louisiana, Mo.

**HARRIS, William Julius** (great-grandson of Charles Hooks), a Senator from Georgia; born in Cedartown, Polk County, Ga., February 3, 1868; attended the common schools and graduated from the University of Georgia at Athens in 1890; engaged in the general insurance business and banking at Cedartown; served as private secretary to Senator Alexander S. Clay of Georgia, 1904-1909; member, Georgia State senate, 1911-1912; Director of the United States Census Bureau from 1913 until 1915, when he resigned to become a member of the Federal Trade Commission; Acting Secretary of the Department of Commerce, 1913-1915; member of the Federal Trade Commission, 1915-1918, when he resigned to become a candidate for United States Senator; chairman of the commission, 1917-1918; member of the National Forest Reservation Commission, 1929-1932; elected as a Democrat to the United States Senate in 1918; reelected in 1924 and in 1930 and served from March 4, 1919, until his death in Washington, D.C., April 18, 1932; funeral services were held in the Chamber of the United States Senate; interment in Greenwood Cemetery, Cedartown, Ga.

**HARRIS, Winder Russell,** a Representative from Virginia; born in Wake County (now a part of Raleigh), N.C., December 3, 1888; attended the public schools and St. Mary's College (now Belmont Abbey College), Belmont, N.C.; served in various editorial positions on newspapers in North Carolina and Virginia 1908-1918; member of the staff of Universal Service in Washington, D.C., 1918-1925; assistant secretary to the American delegation to the International Narcotics Congress in Geneva, Switzerland, in 1924 and 1925; managing editor of the Virginian-Pilot, Norfolk, Va., 1925-1941; elected as a Democrat to the Seventy-seventh Congress, April 8, 1941, in a special election, to fill the vacancy caused by the resignation of Colgate W. Darden, Jr.; reelected to the Seventy-eighth Congress and served from April 8, 1941, until his resignation on September 15, 1944; engaged as vice president, Shipbuilders' Council of America, in Washington, D.C., until his retirement December 31, 1958; served as vice chairman of the Board of Commissioners of the Alexandria Redevelopment and Housing Authority from September 1955 until his resignation in November

1961; editor of the Alexandria Journal, the Arlington Journal, and the Fairfax County Journal-Standard until his retirement in March 1966; resided in Alexandria, Va., until his death there February 24, 1973; interment in Oakwood Cemetery, Raleigh, N.C.

**HARRISON, Albert Galliton,** a Representative from Missouri; born in Mount Sterling, Ky., June 26, 1800; completed preparatory studies and was graduated from Transylvania University, Lexington, Ky., in 1820; studied law; was admitted to the bar and commenced practice in Mount Sterling; moved to Fulton, Mo., in 1827 and continued the practice of law; member of the Board of Visitors to the United States Military Academy at West Point in 1828; member of the commission to adjust land titles growing out of Spanish grants 1829-1835; unsuccessful candidate for election in 1835 to the Twenty-fourth Congress; elected as a Democrat to the Twenty-fifth and Twenty-sixth Congresses and served from March 4, 1835 until his death in Fulton, Mo., on September 7, 1839, before the Twenty-sixth Congress had assembled; interment in Congressional Cemetery, Washington, D.C.

**HARRISON, Benjamin** (father of Carter Bassett Harrison and President William Henry Harrison [1773-1841], grandfather of John Scott Harrison, great-grandfather of President Benjamin Harrison [1833-1901] and great-great-great grandfather of William Henry Harrison [1896-1990]), a Delegate from Virginia; born on the plantation "Berkeley," Charles City County, Va., April 5, 1726; pursued classical studies and attended the College of William and Mary, Williamsburg, Va.; member of the Virginia house of burgesses 1749-1775; member of the Virginia revolutionary convention in March, July, and December, 1775; Member of the Continental Congress 1774-1777; as chairman of the Committee of the Whole House he reported the resolution on June 10, 1776, offered three days before by Richard Henry Lee, declaring the independence of the American Colonies, and reported the Declaration of Independence, of which he was one of the signers, on July 4, 1776; resigned in 1778; member of the Virginia house of delegates 1776-1782 and 1787-1791 and served as speaker 1778-1782, 1785, and 1786; Governor of Virginia 1782-1784; delegate to the Virginia convention for the ratification of the Federal Constitution in 1788; died at his home, "Berkeley," Charles City County, Va., April 24, 1791.

**Bibliography:** *DAB.*

**HARRISON, Benjamin** (great-grandson of Benjamin Harrison of Virginia [1726-1791], grandson of President William Henry Harrison [1773-1841], son of John Scott Harrison [1804-1878], and grandfather of William Henry Harrison [1896-1990]), a Senator from Indiana and 23rd President of the United States; born in North Bend, Hamilton County, Ohio, August 20, 1833; graduated from Miami University, Oxford, Ohio, in 1852; studied law in Cincinnati; moved to Indianapolis in 1854; was admitted to the bar and practiced; reporter of the decisions of the supreme court of the State; entered the Union Army as a second lieutenant of the seventieth Indiana in July 1862; brevetted brigadier general and mustered out in 1865; while in the field in October 1864 was reelected reporter of the State supreme court and served four years; unsuccessful Republican candidate for Governor of Indiana in 1876; appointed a member of the Mississippi River Commission in 1879; elected as a Republican to the United States Senate and served from March 4, 1881, to March 3, 1887; chairman, Committee on Transportation Routes to the Seaboard (Forty-seventh Congress), Committee on Territories (Forty-eighth and Forty-ninth Congresses); elected President of the United States on November 6, 1888; inaugurated on March 4, 1889, and served until March 3, 1893; unsuccessful candidate for reelection in 1892; attorney for the Republic of Venezuela in the boundary dispute between Venezuela and Great Britain in 1900; died in Indianapolis, Ind., March 13, 1901; interment in Crown Hill Cemetery.

**Bibliography:** *DAB;* Harrison, Benjamin. *This Country of Ours.*

New York: Scribners, 1897; Sievers, Harry J. *Benjamin Harrison*. 3 vols. New York: University Publishers, 1960-1966.

**HARRISON, Burr Powell** (son of Thomas Walter Harrison), a Representative from Virginia; born in Winchester, Frederick County, Va., July 2, 1904; attended the public schools, Woodberry Forest School, Virginia Military Institute, Hampden-Sydney College, and the University of Virginia; was graduated from Georgetown University Law School, Washington, D.C., in 1926; was admitted to the bar the same year and commenced practice in Winchester, Va.; attorney for Frederick County 1932-1940; served in Virginia senate 1940-1942; judge of the seventeenth judicial circuit and the corporation court of Winchester 1942-1946; elected on November 5, 1946, as a Democrat to the Seventy-ninth Congress, in a special election, to fill the vacancy caused by the resignation of A. Willis Robertson and at the same time was elected to the Eightieth Congress; reelected to the seven succeeding Congresses and served from November 6, 1946, to January 3, 1963; was not a candidate for renomination in 1962 to the Eighty-eighth Congress; resumed the practice of law; resided in Winchester, Va., until his death there December 29, 1973; interment in Mount Hebron Cemetery.

**HARRISON, Byron Patton (Pat),** a Representative and a Senator from Mississippi; born at Crystal Springs, Copiah County, Miss., August 29, 1881; attended the public schools; briefly attended the University of Mississippi and the University of Louisiana at Baton Rouge; taught school at Leakesville, Miss., and also studied law; was admitted to the bar in 1902 and commenced practice in Leakesville, Miss.; district attorney for the second district of Mississippi, 1906-1910, when he resigned; moved to Gulfport, Miss., in 1908; elected as a Democrat to the Sixty-second and to the three succeeding Congresses (March 4, 1911-March 3, 1919); was not a candidate in 1918 for renomination to the House of Representatives, having become a candidate for Senator; elected as a Democrat to the United States Senate in 1918; reelected in 1924, 1930, and again in 1936, and served from March 4, 1919 until his death in Washington, D.C., June 22, 1941; served as President pro tempore of the Senate during the Seventy-seventh Congress; chairman, Committee on Finance (Seventy-third through Seventy-seventh Congresses); services were held in the Chamber of the United States Senate; interment in Evergreen Cemetery, Gulfport, Miss.

**Bibliography:** Coker, William S. "Pat Harrison: The Formative Years." *Journal of Mississippi History* 25 (October 1963): 251-278; Swain, Martha H. *Pat Harrison: The New Deal Years*. Jackson: University Press of Mississippi, 1978.

**HARRISON, Carter Bassett** (son of Benjamin Harrison of Virginia [1726-1791] and brother of President William Henry Harrison [1773-1841]), a Representative from Virginia; born in Charles City County, Va.; pursued classical studies; attended the College of William and Mary, Williamsburg, Va.; member of the Virginia house of delegates 1784-1786; elected to the Third Congress and reelected as a Republican to the Fourth and Fifth Congresses (March 4, 1793-March 3, 1799); again a member of the Virginia house of delegates 1805-1808; died at the Maycock plantation, Prince George County, Va., April 18, 1808.

**HARRISON, Carter Henry,** a Representative from Illinois; born near Lexington, Fayette County, Ky., February 15, 1825; educated by private tutors; was graduated from Yale College in 1845; traveled and studied in Europe, 1851-1853; was graduated from the law department of Transylvania College, Lexington, Ky., in 1855; was admitted to the bar in 1855 and commenced practice in Chicago, Ill.; also engaged in the real estate business; unsuccessful candidate for election in 1872 to the Forty-third Congress; member of the board of commissioners of Cook County, 1874-1876; elected as a Democrat to the Forty-fourth and Forty-fifth Congresses (March 4, 1875-March 3, 1879); was not a candidate for renomination in 1878 to the Congress; mayor of Chicago from 1879 until 1887; declined a

renomination; unsuccessful candidate for Governor of Illinois in 1884; delegate to the Democratic National Conventions of 1880 and 1884; owner and editor of the Chicago Times, 1891-1893; again elected mayor of Chicago in 1893 and served until his death; died from the effects of an assassin's bullets at Chicago, Ill., October 28, 1893; interment in Graceland Cemetery.

**Bibliography:** *DAB*; Harrison, Carter Henry. *Stormy Years: The Autobiography of Carter H. Harrison, Five Times Mayor of Chicago*. Indianapolis: Bobbs-Merrill Co., 1935; Johnson, Claudius Osborne. *Carter Henry Harrison I, Political Leader*. Chicago: University of Chicago Press, 1928.

**HARRISON, Francis Burton,** a Representative from New York; born in New York City December 18, 1873; was graduated from Cutler School at New York City, from Yale University in 1895, and from the New York Law School in 1897; instructor in the New York Night Law School, 1897-1899; was admitted to the bar in 1898; served during the war with Spain in Troop A, New York Volunteer Cavalry, from May 19 to June 20, 1898, and was captain and assistant adjutant general, United States Volunteers, from June 20, 1898 to January 31, 1899; elected as a Democrat to the Fifty-eighth Congress (March 4, 1903-March 3, 1905); did not seek renomination in 1904 to the Fifty-ninth Congress, but was an unsuccessful candidate for Lieutenant Governor of New York; elected to the Sixtieth and to the three succeeding Congresses, and served from March 4, 1907 until his resignation, effective September 1, 1913; Governor General of the Philippine Islands from 1913 until 1921; resided in Scotland from 1921 to 1934; appointed adviser to the president of the Philippine Commonwealth in November 1935 and served for ten months; in May 1942 was again appointed to the same position; United States Commissioner of Claims in the civil service of the United States Army in Manila from November 1946 to February 1947; served as an adviser to the first four presidents of the Philippine Republic after their independence in 1946; resided in Spain for six years, returning to Califon, Hunterdon County, N.J., in August 1957; died in Flemington, N.J., November 21, 1957; interment in Manila Cemetery, Philippines.

**Bibliography:** *DAB*.

**HARRISON, Frank Girard,** a Representative from Pennsylvania; born in Washington, D.C., February 2, 1940; attended St. Mary's Grammar School, Wilkes-Barre, Pa.; graduated, St. Mary's High School, 1957; A.B., King's College, Wilkes-Barre, Pa., 1961; LL.B., Harvard Law School, 1964; admitted to the Pennsylvania bar, 1965, and commenced practice in Wilkes-Barre; served in the United States Air Force, captain, 1966-1969; college professor, 1969-1982; elected as a Democrat to the Ninety-eighth Congress (January 3, 1983-January 3, 1985); was an unsuccessful candidate for renomination in 1984 to the Ninety-ninth Congress; resumed the practice of law in Wilkes-Barre; visiting scholar in residence, King's College, Wilkes-Barre, 1988; director of forensics and associate professor of speech, Trinity University, San Antonio, Tex., 1988 to present; is a resident of San Antonio, Tex.

**HARRISON, George Paul,** a Representative from Alabama; born at "Monteith Plantation," near Savannah, Ga., March 19, 1841; attended Effingham Academy and the Georgia Military Institute at Marietta; during the Civil War entered the Confederate Army as second lieutenant of the First Georgia Regulars and was successively promoted to first lieutenant, major, colonel, and brigadier general; moved to Alabama in 1865; studied law; was admitted to the bar and commenced practice in Auburn, Ala.; member of the constitutional convention of Alabama in 1875; served in the State senate 1878-1884 and was its president 1882-1884; delegate to the Democratic National Convention in 1892; elected as a Democrat to the Fifty-third Congress to fill the vacancy caused by the resignation of William C. Oates; reelected to the Fifty-fourth Congress and served from November 6, 1894, to March 3, 1897; resumed the practice of law in Opelika, Lee County, Ala.; delegate to the State constitutional convention in 1901; general counsel for the Western Railway of Alabama; division counsel for the Central of Georgia Railway; died in Opelika, Ala., July 17, 1922; interment in Rosemere Cemetery.

**Bibliography:** *DAB.*

**HARRISON, Horace Harrison,** a Representative from Tennessee; born in Lebanon, Wilson County, Tenn., on August 7, 1829; attended Carroll Academy and completed the course in the ancient classics under a private instructor; moved with his parents to McMinnville in 1841; clerk of the county court; master of the chancery court; register of deeds; clerk of the State senate in 1851 and 1852; studied law; was admitted to the bar in 1857 and commenced practice in McMinnville; moved to Nashville in 1859 and continued the practice of law; United States district attorney 1863-1866; chancellor in the Nashville division in 1866; judge of the State supreme court in 1867 and 1868; again United States district attorney in 1872 and 1873; elected as a Republican to the Forty-third Congress (March 4, 1873-March 3, 1875); unsuccessful candidate for reelection; delegate to the Republican National Convention in 1880; member of the State legislature in 1880 and 1881; died in Nashville, Tenn., December 20, 1885; interment in Mount Olivet Cemetery.

**HARRISON, John Scott** (son of President William Henry Harrison [1773-1841], grandson of Benjamin Harrison [1726-1791], father of President Benjamin Harrison [1833-1901], and great-grandfather of William Henry Harrison [1896-1990]), a Representative from Ohio; born in Vincennes, Knox County, Ind., October 4, 1804; completed preparatory studies; studied medicine but abandoned the profession; engaged in agricultural pursuits; elected as a Whig to the Thirty-third Congress and reelected as a Republican to the Thirty-fourth Congress (March 4, 1853-March 3, 1857); unsuccessful candidate for reelection in 1856 to the Thirty-fifth Congress; retired to his estate "Point Farm," near North Bend, Ohio, and died there May 25, 1878; interment in the Harrison Tomb, North Bend, Ohio.

**HARRISON, Pat,** a Representative and a Senator from Mississippi. (*See* HARRISON, Byron Patton.)

**HARRISON, Richard Almgill,** a Representative from Ohio; born in Thirsk, Yorkshire, England, April 8, 1824; immigrated to the United States in 1832 with his parents, who settled in Ohio; attended the public schools and was graduated from the Cincinnati Law School in 1846; was admitted to the bar in 1846 and commenced practice in London, Madison County, Ohio; member of the State house of representatives 1858 and 1859; served in the State senate 1860 and 1861; elected as a Unionist to the Thirty-seventh Congress to fill the vacancy caused by the resignation of Thomas Corwin and served from July 4, 1861, to March 4, 1863; continued the practice of law in Columbus, Ohio, until his death there July 30, 1904; interment in Kirkwood Cemetery, London, Ohio.

**HARRISON, Robert Dinsmore,** a Representative from Nebraska; born on a farm near Panama, Lancaster County, Nebr., January 26, 1897; attended the public schools of Lancaster County; was graduated from Peru State Teachers College in 1926, University of California in 1928, and University of Nebraska in 1934; during the First World War served as a sergeant in the Twenty-second Engineers, 1918-1919; superintendent of schools in Bradshaw, Nebr., 1926-1929, and in De Witt, Nebr., 1929-1937; member of the Norfolk, Nebr., School Board 1942-1951, and the Governor's Highway Advisory Committee; owned and operated an oil business in Norfolk, Nebr.; also operated a farm in Cedar County, Nebr.; elected as a Republican to the Eighty-second Congress, December 4, 1951, by special election to fill the vacancy caused by the death of

Karl Stefan; reelected to the three succeeding Congresses, and served from December 4, 1951 to January 3, 1959; unsuccessful candidate for reelection in 1958 to the Eighty-sixth Congress; adviser to Board of Directors of the Commodity Credit Corporation, Department of Agriculture, from January 6, 1959 to April 1, 1960; appointed Nebraska State director, Federal Crop Insurance Corporation, April 1, 1960, and served until February 1, 1962; unsuccessful candidate for election in 1962 to the Eighty-eighth Congress; retired and resided in Norfolk, Nebr., where he died on June 11, 1977; interment in Panama Cemetery, Panama, Nebr.

**HARRISON, Samuel Smith,** a Representative from Pennsylvania; born in Virginia in 1780; completed preparatory studies; studied law; was admitted to the bar and practiced; moved to Kittanning, Armstrong County, Pa.; elected as a Jacksonian to the Twenty-third and Twenty-fourth Congresses (March 4, 1833-March 3, 1837); resumed the practice of law; died in Kittanning, Pa., April 1853; interment in Old Kittanning Cemetery.

**HARRISON, Thomas Walter** (father of Burr Powell Harrison), a Representative from Virginia; born in Leesburg, Loudoun County, Va., August 5, 1856; attended local academies at Leesburg, Middleburg, and Hanover; was graduated from the academic and law departments of the University of Virginia at Charlottesville in 1879; was admitted to the bar in 1879 and commenced practice in Winchester, Va.; member of the Virginia senate 1887-1894; judge of the circuit court for the seventeenth judicial district of Virginia from 1895 until September 1, 1916; editor of the Winchester Times; member of the Virginia constitutional convention in 1901 and 1902; elected as a Democrat to the Sixty-fourth Congress to fill the vacancy caused by the resignation of James Hay; reelected to the Sixty-fifth and Sixty-sixth Congresses and served from November 7, 1916, to March 3, 1921; presented credentials as a Member-elect to the Sixty-seventh Congress and served from March 4, 1921, to December 15, 1922, when he was succeeded by John Paul, who contested his election; elected to the Sixty-eighth, Sixty-ninth, and Seventieth Congresses (March 4, 1923-March 3, 1929); unsuccessful candidate for reelection in 1928 to the Seventy-first Congress; practiced law in Winchester, Va., until his death there on May 9, 1935; interment in Mount Hebron Cemetery.

**HARRISON, William, Jr.,** a Delegate from Maryland; born in that State; member of the Continental Congress in 1786; engaged in shipbuilding at St. Michaels, Talbot County, Md., in 1810; served as first lieutenant in Captain Robert H. Goldsborough's Troop of Horse, called the Independent Light Dragoons, Ninth Regiment of Cavalry, Maryland Militia, in 1812; later commanded this troop as captain; served as justice of the court at St. Michaels in 1813.

**HARRISON, William Henry,** (great-great-great-grandson of Benjamin Harrison [1726-1791], great-great-grandson of President William Henry Harrison [1773-1841], great-grandson of John Scott Harrison, and grandson of President Benjamin Harrison [1833-1901] and Alvin Saunders), a Representative from Wyoming; born in Terre Haute, Vigo County, Ind., August 10, 1896; attended the public schools of Omaha, Nebr., the Sidwell Friends School, Washington, D.C., and the College of Agriculture at the University of Nebraska in 1919 and 1920; during the First World War served in the United States Army as a private in the Signal Enlisted Air Corps; was admitted to the Indiana bar in 1925 and practiced in Indianapolis, 1925-1936; member of the Indiana State house of representatives, 1927-1929; was admitted to the Wyoming bar in 1937 and practiced in Sheridan, Wyo.; member of the Wyoming State house of representatives 1945-1950; secretary to the Wyoming Interim Committee 1947-1950; elected as a Republican to the Eighty-second and Eighty-third Congresses (January 3, 1951-January 3, 1955); was not a candidate in 1954 for renomination to the House of Representatives, but was an unsuccessful candidate for election to the United States Senate; regional administrator, Housing and

Home Finance Agency, from April 1955 to August 31, 1956; liaison officer, Housing and Home Finance Agency, Washington, D.C., from April 1, 1957, to November 15, 1958; elected to the Eighty-seventh and the Eighty-eighth Congresses (January 3, 1961-January 3, 1965); unsuccessful candidate for reelection in 1964 to the Eighty-ninth Congress; elected to the Ninetieth Congress (January 3, 1967-January 3, 1969); unsuccessful candidate for renomination in 1968 to the Ninety-first Congress; appointed by President Richard M. Nixon as a member to the Renegotiation Board of the United States, July 23, 1969, and served until October 4, 1971; was a resident of North Redington Beach, Fla.; died October 8, 1990.

**HARRISON, William Henry** (son of Benjamin Harrison [1726-1791], father of John Scott Harrison, brother of Carter Bassett Harrison, grandfather of President Benjamin Harrison [1833-1901], and great-great-grandfather of William Henry Harrison [1896-1990]), a Delegate from the Territory Northwest of the River Ohio, a Representative and a Senator from Ohio, and 9th President of the United States; born on "Berkeley Plantation," Charles City County, Va., February 9, 1773; pursued classical studies; attended Hampden-Sidney College, Virginia; studied medicine; entered the Army in 1798 as an ensign in the First Infantry, served in the Indian wars, and rose to the rank of lieutenant; resigning from the Army in 1798, was appointed secretary of the Northwest Territory, 1798-1799; elected as a Delegate from the Northwest Territory to the Sixth Congress and served from March 4, 1799, to May 14, 1800, when he resigned to become Territorial Governor; appointed Governor of the Territory of Indiana by President John Adams on May 13, 1800, and served until his resignation on December 28, 1812; defeated the Indians at Tippecanoe on November 7, 1811; major general in the United States Army during the War of 1812; resigned from the Army on May 11, 1814; head commissioner to treat with the Indians; elected to the Fourteenth Congress to fill the vacancy caused by the resignation of John McLean; reelected to the Fifteenth Congress and served from October 8, 1816, to March 3, 1819; member, State senate, 1819-1821; elected to the United States Senate and served from March 4, 1825, to May 20, 1828, when he resigned to become Minister to Colombia, serving until September 1829; chairman, Committee on Military Affairs (Nineteenth and Twentieth Congresses); unsuccessful Whig candidate for president in 1836; elected President of the United States and served from March 4, 1841, until his death in Washington, D.C., April 4, 1841; interment in William Henry Harrison Memorial State Park, opposite Congress Green Cemetery, North Bend, Ohio.

**Bibliography:** *DAB*; Cleaves, Freeman. *Old Tippecanoe: William Henry Harrison.* New York: Scribner's Sons, 1939; Goebel, Dorothy. *William Henry Harrison: A Political Biography.* Philadelphia: Porcupine Press, 1974.

**HARSHA, William Howard,** a Representative from Ohio; born in Portsmouth, Scioto County, Ohio, January 1, 1921; graduated from Portsmouth High School in 1939; A.B., Kenyon College, Gambier, Ohio, 1943; LL.B., Western Reserve University, 1947; studied law; was admitted to the bar in 1947 and commenced practice in Portsmouth, Ohio; served in the United States Marine Corps, 1942-1944; assistant city solicitor for Portsmouth, 1947-1951; Scioto County prosecutor, 1951-1955; elected as a Republican to the Eighty-seventh and to the nine succeeding Congresses (January 3, 1961-January 3, 1981); was not a candidate for reelection in 1980 to the Ninety-seventh Congress; consultant in Washington, D.C., 1981-1986; resumed the practice of law in Portsmouth, Ohio, in 1987; retired; is a resident of Portsmouth, Ohio.

**HART, Alphonso,** a Representative from Ohio; born in Vienna, Trumbull County, Ohio, July 4, 1830; attended the common schools and Grand River Institute, Austinburg, Ohio; studied law in Warren, Ohio; was admitted to the bar August 12, 1851, and commenced practice in Ravenna, Ohio; prosecuting attorney for Portage County 1861 to 1864, when he resigned; member of the State senate 1865, 1872, and 1873; lieutenant governor of Ohio 1873-1875; elected as a Republican to the Forty-eighth Congress (March 4, 1883-March 3, 1885); unsuccessful candidate for election in 1884 to the Forty-ninth Congress; served as Solicitor of Internal Revenue, Treasury Department, 1888-1892; resumed the practice of law in Washington, D.C., and died there December 23, 1910; interment in Maple Grove Cemetery, Ravenna, Portage County, Ohio.

**HART, Archibald Chapman,** a Representative from New Jersey; born in Lennoxville, Province of Quebec, Canada, February 27, 1873; moved with his parents to New York City in 1882 and to Hackensack, N.J., in 1884; attended the common schools; studied law; was admitted to the New Jersey bar in 1896 and commenced practice in Hackensack, N.J.; served in the Second Regiment, New Jersey Volunteer Infantry, during the Spanish-American War; served four years in the Twenty-third Regiment of the New York National Guard; banker, publisher, and real estate operator; delegate to the Democratic National Convention of 1908; elected as a Democrat to the Sixty-second Congress to fill the vacancy caused by the resignation of William Hughes and served from November 5, 1912, to March 3, 1913; unsuccessful candidate for nomination in 1912 to the Sixty-third Congress, but was later elected to this Congress to fill the vacancy caused by the death of Lewis J. Martin; reelected to the Sixty-fourth Congress and served from July 22, 1913, to March 3, 1917; declined to be a candidate for renomination in 1916 to the Sixty-fifth Congress; resumed the practice of law and his former business pursuits in Hackensack and resided in Teaneck, N.J.; prosecuting attorney for Bergen County 1920-1930; died in Teaneck, N.J., July 24, 1935; interment in Hackensack Cemetery, Hackensack, N.J.

**HART, Edward Joseph,** a Representative from New Jersey; born in Jersey City, N.J., March 25, 1893; attended the public and parochial schools; was graduated from St. Peter's College, Jersey City, N.J., in 1913 and from the law department of Georgetown University, Washington, D.C., in 1924; secretary to the Excise Commission, Washington, D.C., 1913-1917; chief field deputy, Internal Revenue Bureau, 1916-1921; admitted to the District of Columbia bar in 1924 and to the New Jersey bar in 1925; practiced law in Jersey City, beginning in 1927; assistant corporation counsel of Jersey City, 1930-1934; chairman of the Democratic State committee of New Jersey, 1944-1949; elected as a Democrat to the Seventy-fourth and to the nine succeeding Congresses (January 3, 1935-January 3, 1955); chairman, Committee on War Claims (Seventy-eighth Congress), Committee on Un-American Activities (Seventy-ninth Congress), Committee on Merchant Marine and Fisheries (Eighty-first and Eighty-second Congresses); was not a candidate for renomination in 1954 to the Eighty-fourth Congress; member of the State Board of Public Utility Commissioners, 1955-1960; died in West Allenhurst, Ocean Township, Monmouth County, N.J., April 20, 1961; interment in St. Catharine's Cemetery, Sea Girt, N.J.

**HART, Elizur Kirke,** a Representative from New York; born in Albion, Orleans County, N.Y., April 8, 1841; attended the Albion Academy; engaged in banking; member of the New York State assembly in 1872; director of the Niagara Falls International Bridge Company; elected as a Democrat to the Forty-fifth Congress (March 4, 1877-March 3, 1879); was not a candidate for renomination in 1878 to the Forty-sixth Congress; resumed his former business pursuits; founder and president of the Rochester (N.Y.) Post-Express in 1882; president of Orleans County National Bank, 1890-1893; died in Albion, N.Y., February 18, 1893; interment in Mount Albion Cemetery.

**HART, Emanuel Bernard,** a Representative from New York; born in New York City October 27, 1809; attended the public schools and prepared for college; engaged in mercantile pursuits; colonel in the militia; member of the board of aldermen in 1845; elected as a Democrat to the Thirty-second Congress (March 4, 1851-March 3, 1853); appointed by President James Buchanan surveyor of the port of New York, and served from 1857 to 1861; member of the city board of assessors; studied law; was admitted to the bar in 1868 and practiced; president of Mount Sinai Hospital 1870-1876; commissioner of immigration 1870-1873; excise commissioner in 1879; treasurer of the Society for the Relief of Poor Hebrews; died in New York City on August 29, 1897; interment in Cypress Hills Cemetery, Brooklyn, N.Y.

**HART, Gary Warren,** a Senator from Colorado; born in Ottawa, Franklin County, Kans., November 28, 1936; grew up in and attended the public schools of Ottawa, Kans.; B.A., Bethany (Okla.) Nazarene College, 1958; B.D., Yale University Divinity School, 1961, and J.D., Yale University Law School, 1964; admitted to the Colorado and District of Columbia bars in 1965; attorney for the United States Department of Justice 1964-1965; special assistant to the solicitor of the Interior Department 1965-1967; engaged in private law practice, Denver, Colo., 1967-1974; worked for the presidential campaigns of Senator John F. Kennedy in 1960 and Senator Robert F. Kennedy in 1968; managed the presidential campaign of Senator George S. McGovern in 1972; elected as a Democrat to the United States Senate in 1974; reelected in 1980 and served from January 3, 1975, to January 3, 1987; declined to be a candidate for reelection in 1986; unsuccessful candidate for the Democratic presidential nomination in 1984 and 1988; is a resident of Kittredge, Colo.

**Bibliography:** Hart, Gary. *Right From the Start: A Chronicle of the McGovern Campaign.* New York: Quadrangle, 1973; Hart, Gary. *The Good Fight: The Education of an American Reformer.* New York: Random House, 1993; Hart, Gary, with William S. Lind. *America Can Win: The Case for Military Reform.* Bethesda, Md.: Adler and Adler, 1986.

**HART, John,** a Delegate from New Jersey; born in Stonington, Conn., about 1713; moved with his parents to Hopewell Township, Hunterdon County, N.J.; attended private school; engaged in agricultural pursuits; member of the Provincial Assembly of New Jersey 1761-1771; judge of Hunterdon County courts 1768-1775; member of the New Jersey Provincial Congress from May 23, 1775, to June 22, 1776, and was elected vice president on June 16, 1776; member of the committee of safety from August 17 to October 4, 1775, and again from October 28, 1775, to January 31, 1776; Member of the Continental Congress from June 22 to August 30, 1776; a signer of the Declaration of Independence; elected to the first State general assembly under the State constitution in August 1776 and reelected in 1777 and 1778; served as speaker 1776-1778; chairman of the New Jersey Council of Safety in 1777 and 1778; died on his estate near Hopewell, Hunterdon County, N.J., on May 11, 1779; interment in the Old School Baptist Meeting House Burial Ground, Hopewell, N.J.

**Bibliography:** *DAB.*

**HART, Joseph Johnson,** a Representative from Pennsylvania; born in Nyack, Rockland County, N.Y., April 18, 1859; attended the schools of Nyack and was graduated from the Charlier Institute, New York City, in 1876; conducted and owned City and Country, a Democratic newspaper of Nyack, until 1883, when he moved to Pike County, Pa., where he engaged in the real estate, lumber, and insurance businesses; school director of Milford; conducted and owned the Milford Dispatch 1890-1900; elected as a Democrat to the Fifty-fourth Congress (March 4, 1895-March 3, 1897); was not a candidate for renomination in 1896; resumed his newspaper interests in Milford; moved to New York City in 1900 and engaged in

clerical work; deputy tax commissioner of the city of New York from 1907 until his death; died in Brooklyn, N.Y., July 13, 1926; interment in Oak Hill Cemetery, Nyack, N.Y.

**HART, Michael James,** a Representative from Michigan; born in Waterloo, Quebec Province, Canada, July 16, 1877; immigrated to the United States with his parents in 1880 and settled in James Township, Saginaw County, Mich.; attended the district schools of Jamestown and Saginaw, Mich., and a business college; teacher in the public schools of Saginaw County, Mich., 1896-1898; engaged in agricultural pursuits and in 1920 also engaged in the packing and shipping of farm products; unsuccessful candidate for election in 1930 to the Seventy-second Congress, but was later elected as a Democrat to the Seventy-second Congress to fill the vacancy caused by the death of Bird J. Vincent; reelected to the Seventy-third Congress and served from November 3, 1931, to January 3, 1935; unsuccessful candidate for reelection in 1934 to the Seventy-fourth Congress and in 1936 to the Seventy-fifth Congress and in 1942 to the Seventy-eighth Congress; was a delegate to the Democratic National Convention in 1932; returned to Saginaw, Mich., and former business activities; president of a brewing company, 1935-1937; died in Saginaw, Mich., February 14, 1951; interment in St. Andrews Cemetery.

**HART, Philip Aloysius,** a Senator from Michigan; born in Bryn Mawr, Montgomery County, Pa., December 10, 1912; attended Waldron Academy and parochial schools; graduated from Georgetown University, Washington, D.C., in 1934 and from the University of Michigan Law School at Ann Arbor in 1937; was admitted to the Michigan bar in 1938 and commenced the practice of law in Detroit, Mich.; during the Second World War served in the United States Army from 1941 until discharged in 1946 as a lieutenant colonel of Infantry; wounded during the D-Day assault on Utah Beach in Normandy; Michigan Corporation Securities Commissioner from 1949 until his resignation in 1951; State director of the Office of Price Stabilization, 1951-1952; United States district attorney of the Eastern Michigan District, 1952-1953; legal adviser to Governor G. Mennen Williams of Michigan, 1953-1954; lieutenant governor, 1955-1958; elected as a Democrat to the United States Senate in 1958; reelected in 1964 and again in 1970, and served from January 3, 1959 until his death in Washington, D.C., December 26, 1976; was not a candidate for reelection in 1976; in 1987 the third of the Senate Office Buildings was officially dedicated and named for him; interred in St. Anne's Catholic Cemetery, Mackinac Island, Mich.

**Bibliography:** *DAB*; O'Brien, Michael. *Philip Hart: The Conscience of the Senate.* East Lansing: Michigan State University Press, 1995.

**HART, Roswell,** a Representative from New York; born in Rochester, N.Y., August 4, 1824; completed preparatory studies and was graduated from Yale College in 1843; studied law; was admitted to the bar in 1847; engaged in commercial pursuits; elected as a Republican to the Thirty-ninth Congress (March 4, 1865-March 3, 1867); unsuccessful candidate for reelection in 1866 to the Fortieth Congress; superintendent of the Railway Mail Service for the States of New York and Pennsylvania 1869-1876; died in Rochester, N.Y., on April 20, 1883; interment in Mount Hope Cemetery.

**HART, Thomas Charles,** a Senator from Connecticut; born in Davidson, Genesee County, Mich., June 12, 1877; attended various public schools in Michigan; graduated from the United States Naval Academy, Annapolis, Md., in 1897; served in the Regular Navy from graduation until 1945, when he was placed on the inactive list as an admiral (retired); his naval career covered service afloat during the Spanish-American War and both World Wars; upon retirement, settled in Sharon, Conn.; appointed as a Republican to the United States Senate to fill the vacancy caused by the death of Francis T. Maloney, and served from February 15, 1945 to November 5, 1946; was not a candidate for election to the vacancy in 1946; resided in

Sharon, Conn., until his death there on July 4, 1971; interment in Arlington National Cemetery, Va.

**Bibliography:** Leutze, James. *A Different Kind of Victory: A Biography of Admiral Thomas C. Hart*. Annapolis: Naval Institute Press, 1981.

**HARTER, Dow Watters,** a Representative from Ohio; born in Akron, Summit County, Ohio, January 2, 1885; attended the Akron public schools; received preparatory education at the University of Mighigan at Ann Arbor and was graduated from the law department of the same university in 1907; was admitted to the Michigan and Ohio bars in 1907; commenced practice in Akron, Ohio, in 1911; first assistant prosecuting attorney of Summit County, Ohio, 1914-1916; member of the State house of representatives in 1919 and 1920; United States commissioner at Akron, Ohio, 1918-1926; elected as a Democrat to the Seventy-third and to the four succeeding Congresses (March 4, 1933-January 3, 1943); unsuccessful candidate for reelection in 1942 to the Seventy-eighth Congress; admitted to practice of law in the District of Columbia in 1943 and was a partner in a law firm there until his retirement in 1965; died in Washington, D.C., September 4, 1971; interment in Rock Creek Cemetery.

**HARTER, John Francis,** a Representative from New York; born in Perry, Wyoming County, N.Y., September 1, 1897; attended the public schools; during the First World War served in the United States Army at Officers' Training Camp, Camp Lee, Va.; was graduated from the law department of the University of Buffalo, Buffalo, N.Y., in 1919; was admitted to the bar in 1920 and commenced practice in Buffalo; elected as a Republican to the Seventy-sixth Congress (January 3, 1939-January 3, 1941); unsuccessful candidate for reelection in 1940 to the Seventy-seventh Congress; resumed the practice of law in Buffalo and resided in Eggertsville, N.Y., until his death there on December 20, 1947; interment in Forest Lawn Cemetery, Buffalo, N.Y.

**HARTER, Michael Daniel** (grandson of Robert Moore), a Representative from Ohio; born in Canton, Ohio, April 6, 1846; attended the public schools; engaged in mercantile pursuits and banking; moved to Mansfield, Ohio, in 1869; at the age of twenty-three became treasurer and manager of the Aultman & Taylor Co. upon its organization; elected as a Democrat to the Fifty-second and Fifty-third Congresses (March 4, 1891-March 3, 1895); declined to be a candidate for renomination in 1894; moved to Philadelphia, Pa., but spent his summers in Mansfield; died in Fostoria, Ohio, February 22, 1896; interment in Mansfield Cemetery, Mansfield, Ohio.

**HARTKE, Rupert Vance,** a Senator from Indiana; born in Stendal, Pike County, Ind., May 31, 1919; attended the public schools of Stendal; A.B., Evansville College, 1940; J.D., Indiana University School of Law, 1948; during the Second World War served in the United States Coast Guard and Navy as a seaman and through the ranks to lieutenant 1942-1946; admitted to the Indiana bar in 1948 and commenced the practice of law in Evansville, Ind.; deputy prosecuting attorney of Vandenburgh County, Ind., 1950-1951; mayor of Evansville, Ind., 1956-1958, when he resigned; elected as a Democrat to the United States Senate in 1958; reelected in 1964 and again in 1970, and served from January 3, 1959, to January 3, 1977; unsuccessful candidate for reelection in 1976; chairman, Committee on Veterans' Affairs (Ninety-second through Ninety-fourth Congresses); resumed the practice of law; is a resident of Falls Church, Va.

**Bibliography:** Hartke, Vance. *The American Crisis in Vietnam*. Indianapolis: Bobbs-Merrill, 1968; Hartke, Vance. *You and Your Senator*. New York: Coward-McCann, 1970.

**HARTLEY, Fred Allan, Jr.,** a Representative from New Jersey; born in Harrison, Hudson County, N.J., February 22, 1902; attended the public schools, Rutgers Prep, and Rutgers University, New Brunswick, N.J.; library commissioner of Kearny, N.J., in 1923 and 1924; police and fire commissioner 1924-1928; elected as a Republican to the Seventy-first and to the nine succeeding Congresses (March 4, 1929-January 3, 1949); chairman, Committee on Education and Labor (Eightieth Congress); co-sponsor of the Taft-Hartley Act of 1947, imposing certain restrictions on the internal affairs and political activities of labor unions, and on their application of economic pressure; was not a candidate for renomination in 1948 to the Eighty-first Congress; engaged as a business consultant; died in Linwood, N.J., May 11, 1969; interment in Fairmount Cemetery, Newark, N.J.

**Bibliography:** Hartley, Fred A. *Our New National Labor Policy; the Taft-Hartley Act and the Next Steps*. New York: Funk and Wagnalls, 1948.

**HARTLEY, Thomas,** a Representative from Pennsylvania; born in Reading, Pa., September 7, 1748; completed preparatory studies; studied law; was admitted to the bar and commenced practice in York, Pa., in 1789; member of the provincial convention at Philadelphia in 1775; served in the Revolutionary War as lieutenant colonel of Irvine's regiment and as colonel of the Sixth Pennsylvania Regiment in 1776; commanded an expedition against the Indians in 1778; member of the Pennsylvania house of representatives in 1778; member of the council of censors in 1783; member of the Pennsylvania convention which adopted the Constitution of the United States in 1787; elected to the First Congress; reelected to the Second and Third Congresses and reelected as a Federalist to the Fourth through Sixth Congresses and served from March 4, 1789, until his death in York, Pa., December 21, 1800; interment in St. John's Churchyard.

**Bibliography:** *DAB*.

**HARTMAN, Charles Sampson,** a Representative from Montana; born in Monticello, White County, Ind., March 1, 1861; attended the public schools and Wabash College, Crawfordsville, Ind.; moved to Bozeman, Mont., in January 1882; studied law; was admitted to the bar in 1884 and commenced practice in Bozeman, Mont.; probate judge of Gallatin County, 1884-1886; member of the State constitutional convention in 1889; elected as a Republican to the Fifty-third and Fifty-fourth Congresses; reelected as a Silver Republican to the Fifty-fifth Congress, and served from March 4, 1893 to March 3, 1899; declined to be a candidate for renomination in 1898 to the Fifty-sixth Congress; delegate to the Republican National Convention of 1896; resumed the practice of law; became affiliated with the Democratic Party in 1900; delegate to the Democratic National Convention of 1900; unsuccessful candidate for election as a Democrat in 1910 to the Sixty-second Congress; appointed Envoy Extraordinary and Minister Plenipotentiary to Ecuador on July 28, 1913 and served until March 1922; returned to Bozeman, Mont.; moved to Great Falls, Mont., in 1926 and resumed the practice of law; moved to Fort Benton, Mont., in 1927, having been appointed judge of the twelfth judicial district of Montana on March 3, 1927; elected to the same office in 1928, and served until his death in Great Falls, Mont., on August 3, 1929; interment in Riverside Cemetery, Fort Benton, Mont.

**HARTMAN, Jesse Lee,** a Representative from Pennsylvania; born at Cottage, Huntingdon County, Pa., June 18, 1853; attended public and private schools and Hollidaysburg (Pa.) Seminary; employed as a clerk in a general store in Hollidaysburg, Pa., 1872-1878; manager of a blast furnace at McKees Gap, Pa., 1878-1891; returned to Hollidaysburg, Pa., being elected prothonotary of Blair County, Pa., in 1891; reelected in 1894 and in 1897; extensively engaged in the quarrying and shipping of ganister; president of the Hollidaysburg Trust Co., 1898-1930; elected as a

Republican to the Sixty-second Congress (March 4, 1911-March 3, 1913); unsuccessful candidate for reelection in 1912 to the Sixty-third Congress and for election in 1914 to the Sixty-fourth Congress; resumed his former mining and banking pursuits at Hollidaysburg, Pa.; delegate to the Republican National Conventions in 1908, 1924, and 1928; died in Hollidaysburg, Pa., February 17, 1930; interment in Presbyterian Cemetery.

**HARTNETT, Thomas Forbes,** a Representative from South Carolina; born in Charleston, S.C., August 7, 1941; attended parochial schools; graduated from Bishop England High School, Charleston, 1960; attended the College of Charleston, 1960-1961; served in the United States Air Force Reserve, 1963-1969; member, South Carolina State house of representatives, 1965-1972; South Carolina State senator, 1972-1980; delegate, South Carolina State Republican conventions, 1972-1980; elected as a Republican to the Ninety-seventh and to the two succeeding Congresses (January 3, 1981-January 3, 1987); was not a candidate for reelection in 1986 to the One Hundredth Congress, but was an unsuccessful candidate for lieutenant governor of South Carolina; unsuccessful candidate in 1992 for election to the United States Senate; unsuccessful candidate in 1994 for nomination for Governor of South Carolina; president, Hartnett Realty Co., Inc., Charleston, since 1963; is a resident of Mount Pleasant, S.C.

**HARTRIDGE, Julian,** a Representative from Georgia; born in Savannah, Ga., September 9, 1829; attended Chatham Academy and Montpelier Institute; was graduated from Brown University, Providence, R.I., in 1848, and from Harvard Law School in 1850; was admitted to the bar in 1851 and commenced practice in Savannah, Ga.; solicitor general of the eastern judicial circuit of Georgia 1854-1858; member of the State house of representatives in 1858 and 1859; delegate to the Democratic National Convention at Charleston in 1860; during the Civil War served one year in the Confederate Army as a lieutenant in the Chatham Artillery; member of the First and Second Confederate Congresses 1862-1865; delegate to the Democratic National Conventions of 1872 and 1876; elected as a Democrat to the Forty-fourth and Forty-fifth Congresses and served from March 4, 1875, until his death in Washington, D.C., January 8, 1879; interment in Laurel Grove Cemetery, Savannah, Ga.

**HARTZELL, William,** a Representative from Illinois; born in Canton, Stark County, Ohio, February 20, 1837; moved with his parents to Danville, Ill, in 1840 and in 1844 to the Republic of Mexico, where he remained until 1853; returned to Randolph County, Ill.; was graduated from McKendree College, Lebanon, Ill., in 1859; settled in Chester, Randolph County, Ill.; studied law; was admitted to the bar in 1864 and commenced practice in Chester, Ill.; elected as a Democrat to the Forty-fourth and Forty-fifth Congresses (March 4, 1875-March 3, 1879); was not a candidate for renomination in 1878; resumed the practice of law in Chester; judge of the third judicial circuit of Illinois 1897-1903; died in Chester, Ill., August 14, 1903; interment in Evergreen Cemetery.

**HARVEY, David Archibald,** a Delegate from the Territory of Oklahoma; born in Stewiack, Province of Nova Scotia, Canada, March 20, 1845; moved with his parents to Clermont County, Ohio, in 1852; attended the public schools at Isabel, Ohio; enlisted in Company B, Fourth Regiment, Ohio Volunteer Cavalry, in September 1861 and served throughout the Civil War; attended Miami University, Oxford, Ohio; studied law; was admitted to the bar in 1868 and commenced practice in Topeka, Kans., in 1869; city attorney of Topeka 1871-1881; judge of the probate court 1881-1889; moved to Wyandotte, Okla., in 1889; elected as a Republican to the Fifty-first and Fifty-second Congresses and served from November 4, 1890, to March 3, 1893; unsuccessful candidate for reelection in 1892 to the Fifty-third Congress; resumed the practice of law, representing Indian tribes in northeast Oklahoma and the Cayugas

in New York, with residence in Wyandotte, Okla.; died in Hope, Eddy County, N.Mex., on May 24, 1916; interment in Seneca Cemetery, Seneca, Jasper County, Mo.

**HARVEY, James,** a Representative from Michigan; born in Iron Mountain, Dickinson County, Mich., July 4, 1922; enrolled in the University of Michigan in 1940, but interrupted his studies in 1942 to serve in the United States Army Air Corps for three years; LL.B., University of Michigan Law School, 1948; was admitted to the bar and commenced the practice of law in Saginaw, Mich., in 1949; assistant city attorney, 1949-1953; city councilman and member of the Saginaw County board of supervisors, 1955-1957; mayor of Saginaw, 1957-1959; elected as a Republican to the Eighty-seventh and to the six succeeding Congresses, and served from January 3, 1961 until his resignation on January 31, 1974; judge, United States District Court for the Eastern District, Michigan, 1974 to present; is a resident of Saginaw, Mich.

**HARVEY, James Madison,** a Senator from Kansas; born near Salt Sulphur Springs, Monroe County, Va., (now West Virginia), September 21, 1833; attended the common schools in Indiana, Illinois, and Iowa; became a civil engineer; moved to Kansas in 1859 and engaged in agricultural pursuits; served with the Union Army during the Civil War as captain in the Fourth and Tenth Regiments of Kansas Volunteer Infantry, 1861-1864; member, Kansas State house of representatives, 1865-1866; member, State senate, 1867-1868; elected Governor of Kansas in 1868, reelected in 1870, and served from January 11, 1869 to January 13, 1873; elected as a Republican to the United States Senate to fill the vacancy caused by the resignation of Alexander Caldwell and served from February 2, 1874, to March 3, 1877; government surveyor in New Mexico, Utah, Nevada, and Oklahoma; resumed agricultural pursuits; died near Junction City, Kans., April 15, 1894; interment in Highland Cemetery, Junction City, Kans.

**HARVEY, Jonathan** (brother of Matthew Harvey), a Representative from New Hampshire; born in Sutton, Merrimack County, N.H., February 25, 1780; attended the common schools; engaged in agricultural pursuits; member of the State house of representatives 1811-1816, 1831-1834, and 1838-1840; served in the State senate 1816-1823, and was president of that body 1817-1823; member of the executive council 1823-1825; elected to the Nineteenth, Twentieth, and Twenty-first Congresses (March 4, 1825-March 3, 1831); was not a candidate for renomination in 1830; retired to his farm at North Sutton, N.H., where he died on August 23, 1859; interment in North Sutton Cemetery.

**HARVEY, Matthew** (brother of Jonathan Harvey), a Representative from New Hampshire; born in Sutton, Merrimack County, N.H., June 21, 1781; studied under private tutors; graduated from Dartmouth College in 1806; studied law; was admitted to the bar and commenced practice in Hopkinton, N.H., in 1809; served in the State house of representatives 1814-1820 and as speaker three terms; elected to the Seventeenth and Eighteenth Congresses (March 4, 1821-March 3, 1825); member of the State senate 1825-1827 and served as its president; member of the executive council 1828 and 1829; elected Governor of New Hampshire in 1830 and served from June 3, 1830 until February 28, 1831, when he resigned; appointed by President Andrew Jackson judge of the United States District Court for New Hampshire in 1831 and served until his death in Concord, N.H., April 7, 1866; interment in Old North Cemetery.

**HARVEY, Ralph,** a Representative from Indiana; born on a farm near Mount Summit, Henry County, Ind., August 9, 1901; attended the public schools; was graduated from Purdue University, Lafayette, Ind., in 1923; engaged as an agricultural instructor 1923-1928; also engaged in agricultural pursuits; served as county councilman 1932-1942; member of the Indiana State house of representatives 1942-1947; elected as a Republican to the Eightieth Congress to fill the vacancy caused by the death of Raymond S. Springer; reelected to the Eighty-first and to the four succeeding Congresses and served from November 4, 1947, to January 3, 1959; unsuccessful candidate for reelection in 1958 to the Eighty-sixth Congress; elected to the Eighty-seventh and to the two succeeding Congresses (January 3, 1961-January 3, 1967); unsuccessful candidate for renomination in 1966 to the Ninetieth Congress; resumed agricultural pursuits; was a resident of New Castle, Ind.; died November 7, 1991.

**Bibliography:** Harvey, Ralph. *Autobiography of a Hoosier Congressman.* Greenfield, Indiana: Mitchell-Fleming, 1975.

**HARVIE, John,** a Delegate from Virginia; born in Albemarle County, Va., in 1742; studied law; was admitted to the bar and practiced; appointed commissioner to treat with the western Indians in 1774; member of the Virginia conventions of 1775 and 1776; Member of the Continental Congress 1777-1778 and one of the signers of the Articles of Confederation; purchasing agent for the State, with provisional rank of colonel; register of the land office 1780-1791; secretary of the Commonwealth 1788; engaged in building operations in Richmond, Va.; died as the result of an accident in Richmond, Va., on February 6, 1807; interment in Hollywood Cemetery.

**Bibliography:** *DAB.*

**HASBROUCK, Abraham Bruyn** (cousin of Abraham Joseph Hasbrouck), a Representative from New York; born in Kingston, Ulster County, N.Y., on November 29, 1791; graduated from Kingston Academy in 1806 and from Yale College, in 1810; studied law in Hudson, N.Y., and in Litchfield, Conn.; was admitted to the bar in 1813 and commenced law practice in Kingston, N.Y., in 1814; elected to the Nineteenth Congress (March 4, 1825-March 3, 1827); became president of Ulster County Bank in 1831; resided in New Brunswick, N.J., while president of Rutgers College, 1840-1850; moved to Kingston, N.Y., in 1850; president of the Kingston Bank; founded the Ulster County Historical Society; died in Kingston, N.Y., on February 24, 1879; interment in Pine Street Cemetery.

**Bibliography:** *DAB.*

**HASBROUCK, Abraham Joseph** (cousin of Abraham Bruyn Hasbrouck), a Representative from New York; born at "Guilford," Ulster County, N.Y., October 16, 1773; was privately tutored; moved to Kingston in 1795 and engaged in mercantile pursuits; one of the incorporators of the Delaware & Hudson Canal; appointed by Governor John Jay as first lieutenant of Cavalry; organizer and director of the Middle District Bank of Kingston; served in the State assembly in 1811; elected as a Republican to the Thirteenth Congress (March 4, 1813-March 3, 1815); was not a candidate for renomination in 1814 to the Fourteenth Congress; engaged in freighting goods to New York City by water; member of the State senate in 1822; died in Kingston, N.Y., January 12, 1845; interment in Albany Avenue Cemetery.

**HASBROUCK, Josiah,** a Representative from New York; born in New Paltz, Ulster County, N.Y., March 5, 1755; completed preparatory studies; conducted a general merchandising business; second lieutenant in the Third Regiment of Ulster County Militia in 1780; supervisor of New Paltz 1784-1786, 1793, 1794, and 1799-1805; member of the State assembly 1796, 1797, 1802, and 1806; elected as a Republican to the Eighth Congress to fill the vacancy caused by the resignation of John Cantine and served from April 28, 1803, to March 3, 1805; engaged in agricultural pursuits; elected to the Fifteenth Congress (March 4, 1817-March 3, 1819); chairman, Committee on Expenditures in the Department of State (Fifteenth Congress); died near Plattekill, Ulster County, N.Y., March 19, 1821; interment in the family burial ground; reinterment in New Paltz Rural Cemetery, New Paltz, N.Y.

**HASCALL, Augustus Porter,** a Representative from New York; born in Hinsdale, Berkshire County, Mass., June 24, 1800; moved to Le Roy, N.Y., in 1815; attended public and private schools; engaged in surveying; studied law; was admitted to the bar and commenced practice in Le Roy, N.Y.; justice of the peace and supervisor; judge of the court of common pleas; elected as a Whig to the Thirty-second Congress (March 4, 1851-March 3, 1853); resumed the practice of law; trustee of the village of Le Roy in 1858; died in Le Roy, Genesee County, N.Y., June 27, 1872; interment in Myrtle Street Cemetery.

**HASKELL, Dudley Chase** (grandfather of Otis Halbert Holmes), a Representative from Kansas; born in Springfield, Windsor County, Vt., March 23, 1842; moved with his parents to Lawrence, Kans., in 1855; attended school at Springfield, Vt., in 1857 and 1858; engaged in business as a shoe merchant; followed the gold rush to Pikes Peak, Colo., in 1859 and resided there until 1861; assistant to the quartermaster of the Union Army in Missouri, Arkansas, Kansas, and the Indian Territory in 1861 and 1862; left the service and entered Williston's Seminary, Easthampton, Mass., in 1863; was graduated from Yale College in 1865; returned to Lawrence, Kans., and engaged in the shoe business 1865-1867; member of the State house of representatives in 1872, 1875, and 1876, and served as speaker in 1876; elected as a Republican to the Forty-fifth and to the three succeeding Congresses and served from March 4, 1877, until his death in Washington, D.C., December 16, 1883; chairman, Committee on Indian Affairs (Forty-seventh Congress); interment in Oak Hill Cemetery, Lawrence, Douglas County, Kans.

**Bibliography:** *DAB.*

**HASKELL, Floyd Kirk,** a Senator from Colorado; born in Morristown, Morris County, N.J., February 7, 1916; B.A., Harvard University, 1937; LL.B., Harvard University Law School, 1941; admitted to the New York and Colorado bars in 1946 and commenced practice in Denver, Colo.; served in the United States Army, 1941-1945, attaining the rank of major; member, Colorado State house of representatives, 1965-1969, serving as assistant majority leader, 1967-1969; elected as a Democrat to the United States Senate in 1972, and served from January 3, 1973 to January 3, 1979; unsuccessful candidate for reelection in 1978; is a resident of Washington, D.C.

**HASKELL, Harry Garner, Jr.,** a Representative from Delaware; born in Wilmington, New Castle County, Del., May 27, 1921; educated at Tower Hill School, Wilmington, Del., and St. Mark's School, Southboro, Mass.; attended Princeton University 1940-1942; enlisted in the United States Coast Guard Reserve September 8, 1942, made an ensign in 1943, and was discharged as a lieutenant (jg) in 1946; personnel manager of Speakman Co., 1947-1948; president of Greenhill Dairies, Inc., 1948-1953; secretary of the Departmental Council of the Department of Health, Education, and Welfare 1953-1954; special assistant to President Dwight D. Eisenhower in 1955; owner and operator of Hill Girt Farm, Chadds Ford, Pa.; president of University of Delaware Research Foundation; delegate, Republican National Conventions, 1952-1984; elected as a Republican to the Eighty-fifth Congress (January 3, 1957-January 3, 1959); unsuccessful candidate for reelection in 1958 to the Eighty-sixth Congress; resumed former business interests; elected mayor of Wilmington, Del., for four-year term commencing January 7, 1969; member, Presidents National Reading Council, appointed September 1970; president, Abercrombie and Fitch; is a resident of Chadds Ford, Pa.

**HASKELL, Reuben Locke,** a Representative from New York; born in Brooklyn, N.Y., October 5, 1878; was graduated from Hempstead High School, Long Island, N.Y., in 1894; attended Ithaca High School in 1894 and 1895, New York City Law School in 1896, and 1897 and Cornell University, Ithaca, N.Y., LL.B., 1898; was admitted to the bar in 1899 and commenced practice in New York

City; served with the Twenty-second Regiment of New York Volunteers during the Spanish-American War; served in the Thirteenth Regiment of the National Guard, Company I and Company G, as private, corporal, and sergeant 1899-1902; delegate to the Republican National Conventions of 1908 and 1920; counsel to the county clerk of Kings County in 1908 and 1909; secretary for the Borough of Brooklyn 1910-1913; deputy commissioner of public works for the Borough of Brooklyn 1913-1915; member of the Republican State committee 1907-1913 and 1914-1919; unsuccessful candidate for election in 1912 to the Sixty-third Congress; elected as a Republican to the Sixty-fourth Congress; reelected to the two succeeding Congresses and served from March 4, 1915, to December 31, 1919, when he resigned; chairman, Committee on Expenditures in the Department of the Navy (Sixty-sixth Congress); judge of the Kings County Court 1920-1925; unsuccessful candidate for reelection; resumed the practice of law in New York City; transit commissioner for the State of New York, 1932-1942; died in Westwood, N.J., October 2, 1971; interment in Mt. Repose Cemetery, Haverstraw, N.Y.

**HASKELL, William T.** (nephew of Charles Ready), a Representative from Tennessee; born in Murfreesboro, Rutherford County, Tenn., July 21, 1818; privately tutored; also attended the public schools of Murfreesboro and the University of Nashville, Tennessee; fought in the Seminole War in 1836; studied law; was admitted to the bar in 1838 and commenced practice in Jackson, Tenn.; member of the State house of representatives in 1840 and 1841; served in the Mexican War; appointed on May 13, 1846, as colonel of the First Brigade, Second Regiment, Tennessee Volunteers; elected as a Whig to the Thirtieth Congress (March 4, 1847-March 3, 1849); resumed the practice of his profession; died in an asylum in Hopkinsville, Christian County, Ky., March 12, 1859; interment in Riverside Cemetery, Jackson, Tenn.

**HASKIN, John Bussing,** a Representative from New York; born in Fordham (now a part of New York City), N.Y., August 27, 1821; attended the public schools; studied law; was admitted to the bar in 1843 and commenced practice in New York City in 1845; civil justice of New York City 1847-1849; supervisor of Fordham 1850-1853; corporation attorney 1853-1856; elected as a Democrat to the Thirty-fifth Congress and reelected as an Anti-Lecompton Democrat to the Thirty-sixth Congress (March 4, 1857-March 3, 1861); chairman, Committee on Expenditures in the Department of the Navy (Thirty-fifth Congress), Committee on Public Expenditures (Thirty-sixth Congress); resumed the practice of law; supervisor of the town of West Farms, Westchester County, N.Y., in 1863; died at Friends Lake, N.Y., September 18, 1895; interment in Woodlawn Cemetery, New York City.

**HASKINS, Kittredge,** a Representative from Vermont; born in Dover, Vt., April 8, 1836; attended the public schools and received instruction from a private tutor; studied law; was admitted to the bar in 1858 and commenced practice in Wilmington, Vt.; moved to Williamsville in 1861 and continued the practice of law; enlisted as a private in Company I, Sixteenth Regiment, Vermont Volunteers, August 23, 1862; was commissioned first lieutenant September 20, 1862, and served until March 19, 1863, when he resigned on account of disabilities; returned to Vermont and settled in Brattleboro; entered the Government service as a civil employee in the office of the assistant quartermaster of Volunteers and served in that capacity until the close of the war; resumed the practice of law; appointed colonel and chief of staff to Governor Peter T. Washburn in 1869; member of the Republican State committee 1869-1872; State's attorney 1870-1872; member of the Vermont State house of representatives 1872-1874 and 1896-1900; speaker of the house 1898-1900; United States attorney for the district of Vermont from October 1880 to July 1887; served in the Vermont State senate 1892-1894; chairman of the Vermont board of commissioners to

establish the boundary line between that State and Massachusetts 1892-1900; elected as a Republican to the Fifty-seventh and to the three succeeding Congresses (March 4, 1901-March 3, 1909); chairman, Committee on War Claims (Sixtieth Congress); unsuccessful candidate for renomination in 1908 to the Sixty-first Congress; judge of the municipal court in Brattleboro, Vt., in 1910; postmaster of Brattleboro 1912-1915; died in Brattleboro, August 7, 1916; interment in Prospect Hill Cemetery.

**HASTERT, John Dennis,** a Representative from Illinois; born in Aurora, Ill., January 2, 1942; attended public schools; graduated Oswego High School, 1960; B.A., Wheaton College, Ill., 1964; M.S., Northern Illinois University, DeKalb, 1967; high school teacher and coach in Yorkville, Ill., 1964-1980; partner in the family restaurant business; member, Illinois house of representatives, 1980-1986; elected as a Republican to the One Hundredth and to the four succeeding Congresses (January 3, 1987-January 3, 1997); is a resident of Yorkville, Ill.

**HASTINGS, Alcee Lamar,** a Representative from Florida; born in Altamonte Springs, Seminole County, Fla., September 5, 1936; graduated, Crooms Academy, Sanford, Fla., 1953; B.A., Fisk University, Nashville, Tenn., 1958; Howard University School of Law, 1958-1960; J.D., Florida A&M University College of Law, Tallahassee, 1963; admitted to Florida bar, 1964; practicing attorney, 1964-1977; circuit court judge, Seventeenth Judicial Circuit, Florida, 1977-1979; judge, United States District Court for the Southern District of Florida, 1980-1989; elected as a Democrat to the One Hundred Third and One Hundred Fourth Congresses (January 3, 1993-January 3, 1997); is a resident of Miami, Fla.

**HASTINGS, Daniel Oren,** a Senator from Delaware; born near Princess Anne, Somerset County, Md., March 5, 1874; was educated under private tutorship; moved to Wilmington, Del., in 1894; attended the law department of Columbian (now George Washington) University, Washington, D.C.; was admitted to the bar in 1902 and commenced practice in Wilmington, Del.; served as deputy attorney general of Delaware, 1904-1909; appointed secretary of State of Delaware, January 1909 to June 1909, when he resigned, having been appointed an associate justice of the State supreme court, in which capacity he served until his resignation in January 1911; special counsel for the State legislature in 1911; city solicitor of Wilmington from 1911 until 1917; judge of the municipal court of Wilmington, 1920-1929; member of the Republican National Committee; appointed as a Republican on December 10, 1928, and elected on November 4, 1930, to the United States Senate to fill the vacancy in the term ending March 3, 1931, caused by the resignation of T. Coleman du Pont; on the same day was also elected for the term commencing March 4, 1931, and served from December 10, 1928, to January 2, 1937; unsuccessful candidate for reelection in 1936; resumed the practice of law in Wilmington, Del., where he died on May 9, 1966; interment in Lower Brandywine Cemetery.

**HASTINGS, George,** a Representative from New York; born in Clinton, Oneida County, N.Y., March 13, 1807; attended the public schools; was graduated from Hamilton College, Clinton, N.Y., in 1826; studied law; in 1830 was admitted to the bar and commenced practice in Mount Morris, Livingston County; district attorney from 1839 until 1848; elected as a Democrat to the Thirty-third Congress (March 4, 1853-March 3, 1855); elected judge of the county court of Livingston County and served from November 1855 until his death in Mount Morris, Livingston County, N.Y., August 29, 1866; interment in the City Cemetery.

**HASTINGS, James Fred,** a Representative from New York; born in Olean, Cattaraugus County, N.Y., April 10, 1926; served in the United States Navy, flight squadrons, 1943-1946; served for ten years on the Allegany (N.Y.) Town Board; five years as Allegany police justice; member, New York State assembly, 1963-1965; New

York State senator, 1965-1968; manager and vice president, radio station WHDL, 1952-1966; national advertising manager, The Times Herald, Olean, N.Y., 1964-1966; partner in real estate and insurance firm of Hastings & Jewell; delegate to the New York State convention, 1966; delegate to the Republican National Convention of 1968; elected as a Republican to the Ninety-first and to the three succeeding Congresses, and served from January 3, 1969, until his resignation on January 20, 1976, to become president of Associated Industries of New York State, Inc., Albany, N.Y.; is a resident of Belleair Beach, Fla.

**HASTINGS, John,** a Representative from Ohio; born in Ireland in 1778; engaged in agricultural pursuits; studied law in Lisbon, Ohio; was admitted to the bar and practiced in Mississippi; engaged in various business enterprises; returned to Ohio and settled in Hanover Township, Columbiana County; engaged in agricultural pursuits; elected as a Democrat to the Twenty-sixth and Twenty-seventh Congresses (March 4, 1839-March 3, 1843); resumed agricultural pursuits; died near Hanoverton, Ohio, December 8, 1854; interment in Grove Hill Cemetery, Hanoverton, Ohio.

**HASTINGS, Richard Norman (Doc),** a Representative from Washington; born in Spokane, Wash., February 7, 1941; graduated, Pasco (Wash.) High School, 1959; attended Columbia Basin College, Pasco, and Central Washington University, Ellensburg; president, Columbia Basin Paper and Supply, 1967 to present; member, Washington State house of representatives, 1979-1987; chairman, Franklin County Republican Central Committee, 1974-1978; delegate, Republican National Convention, 1976; member, 1984 National Platform Committee; unsuccessful candidate for election in 1992 to the One Hundred Third Congress; elected as a Republican to the One Hundred Fourth Congress (January 3, 1995-January 3, 1997); is a resident of Pasco, Wash.

**HASTINGS, Serranus Clinton,** a Representative from Iowa; born in Watertown, Jefferson County, N.Y., November 22, 1813; completed a preparatory course at Gouverneur Academy and was graduated from Hamilton College; principal of Norwich Academy in 1834; moved to Lawrenceburg, Ind., in 1835; edited the Indiana Signal in 1836; studied law; was admitted to the bar in 1837 and commenced practice in what is now Burlington, Iowa; when Iowa was made a separate Territory served as a member of the Territorial council from 1838 until 1846, and was president of the council during one session; upon the admission of Iowa as a State into the Union was elected as a Democrat to the Twenty-ninth Congress and served from December 28, 1846, to March 3, 1847; was not a candidate for renomination in 1846 to the Thirtieth Congress; chief justice of the supreme court of Iowa in 1848; resigned in 1849 and moved to Benicia, Calif.; chief justice of the supreme court of California, 1849-1851; attorney general of the State in 1851; at the end of his term of two years retired to private life; founded and endowed Hastings College of Law in the University of California in 1878; engaged in the real estate business; died in San Francisco, Calif., February 18, 1893; interment in St. Helena Cemetery, St. Helena, Calif.

Bibliography: *DAB*.

**HASTINGS, Seth** (father of William Soden Hastings), a Representative from Massachusetts; born in Cambridge, Mass., April 8, 1762; was graduated from Harvard University in 1782; studied law; was admitted to the bar in 1786 and commenced practice in Mendon, Mass.; town treasurer in 1794 and 1795; elected one of the first school commissioners in 1796; elected as a Federalist to the Seventh Congress to fill the vacancy caused by the resignation of Levi Lincoln; reelected to the two succeeding Congresses, and served from August 24, 1801 to March 3, 1807; declined to be a candidate for renomination in 1806 to the Tenth Congress; member of the Massachusetts senate in 1810 and 1814; chief justice of the

court of sessions for Worcester County from 1819 until 1828; died in Mendon, Mass., November 19, 1831; interment in the Old Cemetery.

**HASTINGS, William Soden** (son of Seth Hastings), a Representative from Massachusetts; born in Mendon, Worcester County, Mass., June 3, 1798; completed preparatory studies and was graduated from Harvard University in 1817; studied law; was admitted to the bar in 1820 and commenced practice in Mendon; member of the Massachusetts house of representatives in 1828; served in the Massachusetts senate, 1829-1833; elected as a Whig to the Twenty-fifth and to the two succeeding Congresses and served from March 4, 1837, until his death in Red Sulphur Springs, Monroe County, Va. (now West Virginia), June 17, 1842; interment in Old Cemetery, Mendon, Mass.

**HASTINGS, William Wirt,** a Representative from Oklahoma; born on a farm in Benton County, Ark., near the Indian Territory boundary, December 31, 1866; moved with his parents to a farm at Beatties Prairie, Delaware County (then part of the Cherokee Nation in Indian Territory), Okla., and attended the Cherokee tribal school; was graduated from Cherokee Male Seminary, at Tahlequah, in 1884; teacher in the Cherokee tribal schools, 1884-1886, and 1889-1891; was graduated from the law department of Vanderbilt University, Nashville, Tenn., in 1889; was admitted to the bar the same year and commenced practice in Tahlequah, Okla.; attorney general for the Cherokee Nation, 1891-1895; national attorney for the Cherokee tribe from 1907 until 1914; delegate to the Democratic State convention in 1912; delegate to the Democratic National Convention of 1912; elected as a Democrat to the Sixty-fourth and to the two succeeding Congresses (March 4, 1915-March 3, 1921); chairman, Committee on Expenditures in the Department of the Interior (Sixty-fifth Congress); unsuccessful candidate for reelection in 1920 to the Sixty-seventh Congress; elected to the Sixty-eighth and to the five succeeding Congresses (March 4, 1923-January 3, 1935); was not a candidate for renomination in 1934 to the Seventy-fourth Congress; resumed the practice of law in Tahlequah, Okla.; commissioned by President Franklin D. Roosevelt on January 22, 1936, as chief of the Cherokees for one day to sign certain papers; died in Muskogee, Okla., April 8, 1938; interment in City Cemetery, Tahlequah, Okla.

Bibliography: *DAB*.

**HATCH, Carl Atwood,** a Senator from New Mexico; born in Kirwin, Phillip County, Kans., November 27, 1889; attended the public schools of Kansas and Oklahoma; graduated from the law department of Cumberland University, Lebanon, Tenn., in 1912; was admitted to the bar the same year and began practice in Eldorado, Okla.; moved to Clovis, N.Mex., in 1916 and continued the practice of law; assistant attorney general of New Mexico, 1917-1918; collector of internal revenue, 1919-1922; district judge of the ninth judicial district of New Mexico, 1923-1929; member, New Mexico State board of bar examiners, 1930-1933; appointed as a Democrat to the United States Senate on October 10, 1933, and elected on November 6, 1934, to fill the vacancy caused by the resignation of Sam G. Bratton; reelected in 1936 and again in 1942, and served from October 10, 1933 to January 2, 1949; was not a candidate for renomination in 1948; sponsor of the Hatch Act of 1939 and 1940, prohibiting non-elected Federal employees from participating in the management of politicians or in political campaigns; chairman, Committee on Privileges and Elections (Seventy-seventh Congress), Committee on Public Lands and Surveys (Seventy-seventh through Seventy-ninth Congresses); appointed United States district judge for the district of New Mexico 1949-1963; retired; died in Albuquerque, N.Mex., September 15, 1963; interment in Fairview Park Cemetery.

Bibliography: Porter, David. "Senator Carl Hatch and the Hatch Act of 1939." *New Mexico Historical Review* 48 (April 1973): 151-61.

**HATCH, Herschel Harrison,** a Representative from Michigan; born in Morrisville, Madison County, N.Y., February 17, 1837; attended the common schools and was graduated from Hamilton College Law School, Clinton, N.Y., in 1857; was admitted to the bar and practiced in Morrisville, N.Y., 1858-1863; moved to Bay City, Mich.; elected alderman of Bay City at its first organization in 1865; judge of probate of Bay County 1868-1872; member of the constitutional commission of Michigan in 1873; member of the tax commission in 1881; elected as a Republican to the Forty-eighth Congress (March 4, 1883-March 3, 1885); declined to be a candidate for renomination in 1884; resumed the practice of law; moved to Detroit, Mich., in 1895 and practiced law until 1910, when he retired; died in Detroit, Mich., November 30, 1920; interment in Elm Lawn Cemetery, Bay City, Mich.

**HATCH, Israel Thompson,** a Representative from New York; born in Johnstown, Fulton County, N.Y., June 30, 1808; pursued preparatory studies; was graduated from Union College, Schenectady, N.Y., in 1829; studied law; was admitted to the bar in 1828; moved to Buffalo the same year and practiced law; assistant secretary of state 1829-1831; practiced law in Buffalo 1831-1840; member of the State assembly 1833, 1834, and 1851; surrogate of Erie County 1833-1836; president of the Commercial Bank of Buffalo 1840-1842; grain merchant; elected as a Democrat to the Thirty-fifth Congress (March 4, 1857-March 3, 1859); chairman, Committee on Militia (Thirty-fifth Congress); unsuccessful candidate for reelection in 1858 to the Thirty-sixth Congress; appointed by President James Buchanan as postmaster of Buffalo, N.Y., and served from November 11, 1859, to March 27, 1861; resumed the practice of law; also engaged in banking and was prominently connected with elevator and dock enterprises; member of the State constitutional convention 1867-1868; commissioner to negotiate a reciprocity treaty between the United States and the Dominion of Canada in 1869 and 1870; built the Marine and Empire elevators in Buffalo; died in Buffalo, N.Y., September 24, 1875; interment in Forest Lawn Cemetery.

**HATCH, Jethro Ayers,** a Representative from Indiana; born in Pitcher, Chenango County, N.Y., June 18, 1837; settled in Sugar Grove, Kane County, Ill.; attended the common schools and the institute in Batavia, Ill.; was graduated from Rush Medical College, Chicago, Ill., in February 1860 and commenced practice at Kentland, Ind., in July 1860; served as a local health officer; commissioned assistant surgeon of the Thirty-sixth Regiment, Illinois Volunteer Infantry, on December 11, 1862, and promoted to surgeon of the same regiment; mustered out of service February 8, 1865, and returned to Kentland, Ind.; secretary and later president of the pension examining board 1865-1907; member of the State house of representatives 1872 and 1873; elected as a Republican to the Fifty-fourth Congress (March 4, 1895-March 3, 1897); was not a candidate for renomination in 1896; returned to Kentland, Ind., and resumed the practice of medicine; member of board of the hospital for the insane at Logansport, Ind.; physician and surgeon for the Logansport division of the Pennsylvania Railroad for many years; physician and surgeon for the Chicago and Cairo division of the New York Central Railroad from the time it was built until 1907; moved to Victoria, Tex., in 1907 and engaged in the real estate business; died in Victoria, Tex., August 3, 1912; interment in Fair Lawn Cemetery, Kentland, Ind.

**HATCH, Orrin Grant,** a Senator from Utah; born in Homestead Park, Allegheny County, Pa., March 22, 1934; received early education in the public schools of Pittsburgh, Pa.; B.S., Brigham Young University, 1959; J.D., University of Pittsburgh Law School, 1962; admitted to the Pennsylvania bar in 1963 and commenced practice in Pittsburgh; moved to Utah in 1969 and continued practicing law; elected as a Republican to the United States Senate in 1976 for the term commencing January 3, 1977; reelected in 1982,

1988 and again in 1994 for the term ending January 3, 2001; chairman, Committee on Labor and Human Resources (Ninety-seventh through Ninety-ninth Congresses), Committee on the Judiciary (One Hundred Fourth Congress); is a resident of Salt Lake City, Utah.

**HATCH, William Henry,** a Representative from Missouri; born near Georgetown, Scott County, Ky., September 11, 1833; attended the schools of Lexington, Ky., studied law; was admitted to the bar in September 1854 and practiced; circuit attorney 1858 and 1860; during the Civil War served in the Confederate Army; commissioned captain and assistant adjutant general December 1862, and in March 1863 was assigned to duty as assistant commissioner of exchange of prisoners under the cartel, and continued in this position until the close of the war; elected as a Democrat to the Forty-sixth and to the seven succeeding Congresses (March 4, 1879-March 3, 1895); chairman, Committee on Agriculture (Forty-eighth through Fiftieth and Fifty-second and Fifty-third Congresses); unsuccessful candidate for reelection in 1894 to the Fifty-fourth Congress; engaged in agricultural pursuits; died near Hannibal, Marion County, Mo., December 23, 1896; interment in Riverside Cemetery.

**Bibliography:** *DAB.*

**HATCHER, Charles Floyd,** a Representative from Georgia; born in Doerun, Colquitt County, Ga., July 1, 1939; attended the public schools; B.S., Georgia Southern College, Statesboro, 1965; J.D., University of Georgia, Athens, 1969; served in the United States Air Force, 1958-1962; admitted to the Georgia bar in 1969 and commenced practice in Albany; member, Georgia State house of representatives, 1973-1980; elected as a Democrat to the Ninety-seventh and to the five succeeding Congresses (January 3, 1981-January 3, 1993); unsuccessful candidate for renomination in 1992 to the One Hundred Third Congress; director, Tobacco and Peanuts Division, Farm Service Agency, United States Department of Agriculture; is a resident of Alexandria, Va.

**HATCHER, Robert Anthony,** a Representative from Missouri; born in Buckingham County, Va., February 24, 1819; attended private schools in Lynchburg, Va.; studied law; was admitted to the bar in Kentucky and commenced practice at New Madrid, Mo., in 1847; circuit attorney for several years; member, Missouri State house of representatives, 1850-1851; during the Civil War enlisted in the Confederate Army and attained the rank of major; delegate to the State convention in 1862; member of the Confederate Congress, 1864-1865; elected as a Democrat to the Forty-third and to the two succeeding Congresses (March 4, 1873-March 3, 1879); chairman, Committee on Public Expenditures (Forty-fifth Congress); resumed the practice of law; died in Charleston, Mo., December 4, 1886; interment in Odd Fellows Cemetery.

**HATFIELD, Henry Drury,** a Senator from West Virginia; born in Logan County, W.Va., September 15, 1875; attended the local schools and Franklin College at New Athens, Ohio; graduated in medicine from the University of Louisville, Louisville, Ky., in 1895 and from New York University in 1904; pursued additional advanced medical training; commissioner of health of Mingo County, W.Va., 1895-1900; surgeon for the Norfolk and Western Railway from 1895 until 1913; surgeon in chief of West Virginia State Hospital No. 1 at Welsh, W.Va., 1899-1913; commissioner of district roads of McDonwell County, 1900-1905; member, county court of McDowell, 1906-1912; member, West Virginia State senate, 1908-1912, serving as president in 1911; elected Governor of West Virginia in 1912, and served from March 4, 1913 to March 4, 1917; during the First World War was a major in the Medical Corps of the United States Army, 1917-1919, and was chief of the Surgical Service at Base Hospital No. 36, at Detroit, Mich.; elected as a Republican to the United States Senate in 1928, and served from March 4, 1929 to January 3, 1935; unsuccessful candidate for reelection in 1934; chairman, Committee on Immigration (Seventy-second Congress); resumed the practice of medicine and also managed a hospital and several farms; was a resident of Huntington, W.Va., until his death there on October 23, 1962; interment in Woodmere Cemetery.

**Bibliography:** Karr, Carolyn. "A Political Biography of Henry Hatfield." *West Virginia History* 28 (October 1966): 35-64, 28 (January 1967): 137-170; Penn, Neil Shaw. "Henry D. Hatfield and Reform Politics: A Study of West Virginia Politics from 1908-1917." Ph.D. dissertation, Emory University, 1973.

**HATFIELD, Mark Odom,** a Senator from Oregon; born in Dallas, Polk County, Oreg., July 12, 1922; B.A., Willamette University, Salem, Oreg., 1943; A.M., Stanford (Calif.) University, 1948; served in the United States Navy in the Pacific theater during the Second World War, 1943-1946; associate professor of political science, 1949-1956, and dean of students, 1950-1956, Willamette University; member, Oregon State house of representatives, 1951-1955; Oregon State senator, 1955-1957; Oregon secretary of state, 1957-1959; elected Governor of Oregon in 1958, reelected in 1962, and served from January 12, 1959 to January 9, 1967; author; elected as a Republican to the United States Senate in 1966; reelected in 1972, 1978, 1984, and 1990, and served from January 3, 1967 to January 3, 1997; was not a candidate for reelection in 1996; delivered keynote address at the Republican National Convention of 1964; chairman, Committee on Appropriations (Ninety-seventh through Ninety-ninth Congresses, One Hundred Fourth Congress), Joint Committee on the Library of Congress (One Hundred Fourth Congress); is a resident of Portland, Oreg.

**HATFIELD, Paul Gerhart,** a Senator from Montana; born in Great Falls, Cascade County, Mont., April 29, 1928; educated in the public schools; B.A., College of Great Falls, 1950; entered the United States Army in September 1951, and was honorably discharged as a Signal Corpsman in September 1953 after service in Korea; LL.B., University of Montana Law School, Missoula, 1955; admitted to the Montana bar in 1955 and commenced practice in Great Falls; chief deputy county attorney, Cascade County, 1959-1960; judge of the Montana district court, eighth judicial district, 1961-1977; chief justice of the Montana State supreme court, 1977-1978; appointed as a Democrat to the United States Senate, January 22, 1978, to fill the vacancy caused by the death of Lee Metcalf for the term ending January 3, 1979, and served from January 22, 1978 until his resignation on December 14, 1978; unsuccessful candidate for nomination in the June 6, 1978 primary for the term ending January 3, 1985; United States federal judge for the District of Montana; Chief Judge until his resignation on February 9, 1996; is a resident of Great Falls, Mont.

**HATHAWAY, Samuel Gilbert,** a Representative from New York; born in Freetown, Bristol County, Mass., July 18, 1780; attended the public schools; worked at various occupations and made one sea voyage; moved to Chenango County, N.Y., in 1803 and two years later to Cincinnatus, Cortland County, and engaged in agricultural pursuits; justice of the peace from 1810 until 1858; member of the New York State assembly in 1814 and 1818; moved to Solon, N.Y., in 1819; served in the State senate in 1822; major general in the New York Militia, 1823-1858; elected as a Jacksonian to the Twenty-third Congress (March 4, 1833-March 3, 1835); presidential elector on the Democratic ticket in 1852; delegate to the Democratic National Convention at Charleston, S.C., in 1860; died in Solon, Cortland County, N.Y., May 2, 1867; interment in the family cemetery near Solon.

**HATHAWAY, William Dodd,** a Representative and a Senator from Maine; born in Cambridge, Middlesex County, Mass., February 21, 1924; attended Boston public schools; served in the United States Army Air Corps from 1942 until 1946, enlisted as a private and discharged as a captain; was shot down over Romania and held a prisoner of war for three months; A.B., Harvard University, 1949; LL.B., Harvard University Law School, 1953; was admitted to the bar in 1953 and began the practice of law in Lewiston, Maine; assistant county attorney, Androscoggin County, 1955-1957; hearing examiner for the Maine State Liquor Commission, 1957-1961; elected as a Democrat to the Eighty-ninth and to the three succeeding Congresses (January 3, 1965-January 3, 1973); was not a candidate in 1972 for reelection to the House of Representatives, but was elected to the United States Senate, and served from January 3, 1973 to January 3, 1979; unsuccessful candidate for reelection in 1978; resumed the practice of law; member, Federal Maritime Commission, 1990-1993, and chairman from 1993 until his retirement in February 1996; is a resident of McLean, Va.

**HATHORN, Henry Harrison,** a Representative from New York; born in Greenfield, Ulster County, N.Y., November 28, 1813; attended the common schools and was graduated from the public schools of Greenfield; discoverer of the "Hathorn Mineral Spring"; sheriff of Saratoga County 1853-1856 and 1862-1865; engaged in mercantile pursuits in Saratoga Springs 1839-1849; supervisor of Saratoga Springs 1858, 1860, 1866, and 1867; elected as a Republican to the Forty-third and Forty-fourth Congresses (March 4, 1873-March 3, 1877); again became engaged in the mineral-water business; died at Saratoga Springs, Saratoga County, N.Y., February 20, 1887; interment in Greenridge Cemetery.

**HATHORN, John,** a Representative from New York; born in Wilmington, Del., January 9, 1749; completed preparatory studies; surveyor by profession and a school teacher; captain of the Colonial Militia; colonel of the Fourth Orange County (N.Y.) Regiment February 7, 1776, and served throughout the Revolutionary War; brigadier general of the Orange County Militia September 26, 1786; major general of State militia October 8, 1793; member of the State assembly 1778, 1780, 1782-1785, 1795, and 1805, and served as speaker in 1783 and 1784; served in the State senate 1786-1790 and 1799-1803; member of the council of appointment in 1787 and 1789; elected to the Continental Congress in December 1788 but no further sessions were held; elected to the First Congress (March 4, 1789-March 3, 1791); unsuccessful candidate for reelection in 1790 to the Second Congress and for election in 1792 to the Third Congress; elected as a Republican to the Fourth Congress (March 4, 1795-March 3, 1797); unsuccessful candidate for reelection in 1796 to the Fifth Congress; engaged in mercantile pursuits; died in Warwick, Orange County, N.Y., February 19, 1825; interment in the cemetery on the family estate; reinterment in Warwick Cemetery.

**HATTON, Robert Hopkins,** a Representative from Tennessee; born in Steubenville, Jefferson County, Ohio, November 2, 1826; attended the common schools and was graduated from the Cumberland University, Lebanon, Tenn., in 1847; was a tutor in Cumberland University in 1847 and 1848; attended the law school of Cumberland University in 1848 and 1849; principal of Woodland Academy, Sumner County, Tenn., in 1849 and 1850; was admitted to the bar in 1850 and commenced practice in Lebanon, Tenn.; trustee of Cumberland University from 1854 until his death; member of the State house of representatives 1855-1857; unsuccessful candidate for Governor in 1857; elected as an Opposition Party candidate to the Thirty-sixth Congress (March 4, 1859-March 3, 1861); chairman, Committee on Expenditures in the Department of the Navy (Thirty-sixth Congress); colonel of the Seventh Regiment, Tennessee Volunteer Infantry, May 26, 1861; appointed brigadier general in the Confederate Army, May 23, 1862; assigned to the command of the Fifth Brigade, First Corps, Army of Virginia; killed in the Battle of Seven Pines, near Richmond, Va., on May 31, 1862, interment in Cedar Grove Cemetery, Lebanon, Tenn.

**Bibliography:** Cummings, Charles M. "Robert Hopkins Hatton: Reluctant Rebel." *Tennessee Historical Quarterly* 23 (June 1964): 169-81.

**HAUGEN, Gilbert Nelson,** a Representative from Iowa; born near Orfordville, Rock County, Wis., April 21, 1859; attended the rural schools; moved to Decorah, Winneshiek County, Iowa, in 1873 and engaged in agricultural pursuits; attended Breckenridge College, Decorah, Iowa, and Academic and Commercial College, Janesville, Wis.; engaged in various enterprises, principally real estate and banking; moved to Northwood, Iowa, in 1886 and engaged in banking; treasurer of Worth County, Iowa, 1887-1893; in 1890 organized the Northwood Banking Co. and became its president; member, Iowa State house of representatives, 1894-1898; elected as a Republican to the Fifty-sixth and to the sixteen succeeding Congresses (March 4, 1899-March 3, 1933); chairman, Committee on Expenditures in the Department of the Interior (Sixtieth Congress), Committee on Agriculture (Sixty-sixth through Seventy-first Congresses); co-sponsor of the McNary-Haugen farm bill of 1927, which would have required the government to support crop prices by buying up surplus commodities and either keeping them off the market or selling them abroad; unsuccessful candidate for reelection in 1932 to the Seventy-third Congress; died at Northwood, Iowa, July 18, 1933; interment in Sunset Rest Cemetery, Northwood, Iowa.

Bibliography: *DAB*; Harstad, Peter T., and Bonnie Lindemann. *Gilbert N. Haugen: Norwegian-American Farm Politician.* Iowa City: State Historical Society of Iowa, 1992; Michael, Bonnie. "Gilbert N. Haugen: Apprentice Congressman." *Palimpsest* 59 (July-August 1978): 118-129.

**HAUGEN, Nils Pederson,** a Representative from Wisconsin; born in Modum, Norway, March 9, 1849; immigrated to the United States in 1854 with his parents, who settled in Pierce County, Wis., in 1855; attended the common schools and Luther College, Decorah, Iowa; was graduated from the law department of the University of Michigan at Ann Arbor in 1874; was admitted to the bar the same year and commenced practice in River Falls, Wis.; member, Wisconsin State assembly, 1879-1880; State railroad commissioner, 1882-1887; elected as a Republican to the Fiftieth Congress to fill the vacancy caused by the death of William T. Price; reelected to the Fifty-first and to the two succeeding Congresses, and served from March 4, 1887 to March 3, 1895; was not a candidate for renomination in 1894 to the Fifty-fourth Congress, but was an unsuccessful candidate for nomination for Governor; member, Wisconsin State tax commission, 1901-1921; president of the National Tax Association in 1919 and 1920; adviser to the board of equalization of Montana, 1921-1923; moved to Madison, Wis., and engaged in literary pursuits; died in Madison, Wis., April 23, 1931; interment in Forest Hill Cemetery.

Bibliography: *DAB*; Haugen, Nils Pederson. *Pioneer and Political Reminiscences.* Evansville, Wis.: The Antes Press, 1930.

**HAUGHEY, Thomas,** a Representative from Alabama; born in Glasgow, Scotland, in 1826; received a limited education; immigrated to the United States with his father, who settled in New York City; moved to Jefferson County, Ala., in 1841; while teaching in St. Clair County, studied medicine; was granted a diploma by the New Orleans Medical College and engaged in practice at Elyton, Jefferson County; served as a surgeon in the Third Regiment, Tennessee Volunteer Infantry, in the Union Army 1862-1865; resumed the practice of his profession in Decatur, Ala.; delegate to the State constitutional convention in 1867; upon the readmission of the State of Alabama to representation was elected as a Republican to the Fortieth Congress and served from July 21, 1868, to March 3, 1869; was a candidate for renomination and while making a political speech was assassinated in Courtland, Ala., on July 31, 1869, and died on August 5, 1869; interment in Green Cemetery, near Pinson, Jefferson County, Ala.

**HAUN, Henry Peter,** a Senator from California; born near Newtown, Scott County, Ky., January 18, 1815; attended the common schools and Transylvania University, Lexington, Ky.; studied law; was admitted to the bar in 1839 and began practice in Lexington, Ky.; prosecuting attorney of Scott County in 1845; moved to Clinton County, Iowa, and settled in Hauntown in 1845; practiced law and owned a distillery, sawmill, and store; delegate to the Iowa constitutional convention in 1846; moved to Yuba County, Calif., in 1849 and settled in Marysville; continued the practice of law; also engaged in agricultural pursuits; judge of Yuba County, 1851-1854; appointed as a Democrat to the United States Senate to fill the vacancy caused by the death of David C. Broderick, and served from November 3, 1859 to March 4, 1860; unsuccessful candidate for election to complete the term ending March 4, 1863; chairman, Committee on Enrolled Bills (Thirty-sixth Congress); died in Marysville, Calif., June 6, 1860; interment in Marysville Cemetery.

**HAVEN, Nathaniel Appleton,** a Representative from New Hampshire; born in Portsmouth, N.H., July 19, 1762; pursued classical studies and was graduated in medicine from Harvard College in 1779; practiced his profession in Portsmouth, N.H., and also engaged in mercantile pursuits; served as a ship's surgeon in the latter part of the Revolutionary War; elected as a Federalist to the Eleventh Congress (March 4, 1809-March 3, 1811); died in Portsmouth, N.H., March 13, 1831; interment in Proprietors' Burying Ground.

**HAVEN, Solomon George,** a Representative from New York; born in Chenango County, N.Y., November 27, 1810; attended the common schools and was instructed by a private tutor in the classics; pursued a course in medicine; studied law; was admitted to the bar in 1835 and commenced practice in Buffalo, N.Y.; commissioner of deeds; district attorney of Erie County 1844-1846; mayor of Buffalo, N.Y., 1846 and 1847; elected as a Whig to the Thirty-second, Thirty-third, and Thirty-fourth Congresses (March 4, 1851-March 3, 1857); unsuccessful candidate for reelection in 1856 to the Thirty-fifth Congress and for election in 1860 to the Thirty-seventh Congress; engaged in the practice of his profession until his death in Buffalo, N.Y., December 24, 1861; interment in Forest Lawn Cemetery.

**HAVENNER, Franck Roberts,** a Representative from California; born in Sherwood, Baltimore County, Md., September 20, 1882; attended the public schools, Columbian College (now George Washington University), Washington, D.C., and Stanford University, California; newspaper writer in San Francisco, Calif., 1907-1917; member of the San Francisco board of supervisors, 1926-1936; elected as a Progressive to the Seventy-fifth Congress, and as a Democrat to the Seventy-sixth Congress (January 3, 1937-January 3, 1941); unsuccessful candidate for reelection in 1940 to the Seventy-seventh Congress; member of California Railroad Commission, 1941-1944; elected as a Democrat to the Seventy-ninth and to the three succeeding Congresses (January 3, 1945-January 3, 1953); unsuccessful candidate for reelection in 1952 to the Eighty-third Congress; director of the Union Labor Party, American Federation of Labor; died in San Francisco, Calif., July 24, 1967; internment in Cypress Lawn Memorial Park, Colma, Calif.

**HAVENS, Harrison Eugene,** a Representative from Missouri; born in Franklin County, Ohio, December 15, 1837; attended the common schools; studied law; was admitted to the bar and commenced practice in Ohio; served as captain of Company H, Forty-seventh Regiment, Iowa Volunteer Infantry, in the Union Army during the Civil War; moved to Illinois, thence to Iowa, and from there to Springfield, Mo., in 1867, becoming editor of the Springfield Patriot; elected as a Republican to the Forty-second and Forty-third Congresses (March 4, 1871-March 3, 1875); chairman, Committee on Public Expenditures (Forty-third Congress); unsuccessful candidate for reelection in 1874 to the Forty-fourth Congress and also to the State senate in 1878; superintendent of the Springfield & Western Missouri Railway Co. in 1881; resumed the practice of his profession in Springfield, Mo.; prosecuting attorney in 1893 and 1894; moved to Enid, Garfield County, Okla, and engaged in newspaper pursuits 1901-1906; moved to Herradura, Cuba, and engaged in planting; died in Havana, Cuba, where he had been taken on account of illness, August 16, 1916; interment in Colon Cemetery.

**HAVENS, James Smith,** a Representative from New York born in Weedsport, Cayuga County, N.Y., May 28, 1859; attended the public schools and Monroe Collegiate Institute, Elbridge, N.Y.; was graduated from Yale College in 1884; moved to Rochester, N.Y., the same year; studied law; was admitted to the bar in 1887 and commenced practice in Rochester, N.Y.; delegate to the Democratic National Convention in 1904; elected as a Democrat to the Sixty-first Congress to fill the vacancy caused by the death of James B. Perkins and served from April 19, 1910, to March 3, 1911; was not a candidate for renomination in 1910; resumed the practice of his profession in Rochester, N.Y.; declined the Democratic nomination for mayor of Rochester in 1913; vice president and secretary of the Eastman Kodak Co., and head of its legal department from 1919 until his death in Rochester, N.Y., February 27, 1927; interment in Mount Hope Cemetery.
**Bibliography:** *DAB*.

**HAVENS, Jonathan Nicoll,** a Representative from New York; born on Shelter Island, Suffolk County, N.Y., June 18, 1757; pursued classical studies and was graduated from Yale College in 1777; member of the State assembly 1786-1795; town clerk 1783-1787; elected to the State convention which ratified the Federal Constitution January 8, 1788; took a great interest in popular education and was chairman of the committee for establishing public schools in New York in 1795; justice of the peace of Suffolk County in 1795; elected as a Republican to the Fourth, Fifth, and Sixth Congresses and served from March 4, 1795, until his death on Shelter Island, N.Y., October 25, 1799; interment in the south burial ground of the Presbyterian Church.

**HAWES, Albert Gallatin** (brother of Richard Hawes, nephew of Aylett Hawes, granduncle of Harry Bartow Hawes, and cousin of Aylett Hawes Buckner), a Representative from Kentucky; born near Bowling Green, Caroline County, Va., April 1, 1804; moved to Kentucky in 1810 with his parents, who settled in Fayette County near Lexington; pursued classical studies at Transylvania University, Lexington, Ky.; moved to Hancock County and settled near Hawesville; engaged in agricultural pursuits; elected as a Jacksonian to the Twenty-second, Twenty-third, and Twenty-fourth Congresses (March 4, 1831-March 3, 1837); chairman, Committee on Expenditures in the Post Office Department (Twenty-second through Twenty-fourth Congresses); resumed agricultural pursuits; moved to Daviess County and settled near Yelvington and continued agricultural pursuits; died near Yelvington, Ky., March 14, 1849; interment in the Hawes family burial ground on the Owensboro and Yelvington Road.

**HAWES, Aylett** (uncle of Richard Hawes, Albert Gallatin Hawes, and Aylett Hawes Buckner), a Representative from Virginia; born in Culpeper County, Va., April 21, 1768; pursued classical studies; studied medicine and finished his education in Edinburgh, Scotland; returned to Virginia and practiced medicine; also engaged as a planter; member of the Virginia house of delegates, 1802-1806; elected as a Republican to the Twelfth and to the two succeeding Congresses (March 4, 1811-March 3, 1817); resumed the practice of medicine and was also an extensive landowner; died on his farm in Rappahannock County, Va., August 31, 1833; interment on a farm near Sperryville, Rappahannock County, Va.

**HAWES, Harry Bartow** (grandnephew of Albert Gallatin Hawes), a Representative and a Senator from Missouri; born in Covington, Kenton County, Ky., November 15, 1869; attended preparatory schools; moved to St. Louis, Mo., in 1887 and studied law; graduated from Washington University Law School at St. Louis in 1896, was admitted to the bar, and commenced practice in that city; represented the Republic of Hawaii during its annexation to the United States; president of the St. Louis police board 1898-1904; member, State house of representatives 1916-1917; served during the First World War with the Military Intelligence Department of the General Staff, and later was assigned to the United States Embassy in Madrid, Spain; chief organizer of the Lakes-to-the-Gulf Deep Waterways Association; president of the Missouri Good Roads Federation and of the Federated Roads Council of St. Louis 1917-1920; elected as a Democrat to the Sixty-seventh, Sixty-eighth, and Sixty-ninth Congresses and served from March 4, 1921, to October 15, 1926, when he resigned; elected on November 2, 1926, to the United States Senate as a Democrat to fill the vacancy caused by the death of Selden P. Spencer and on the same day was also elected for the full term commencing March 4, 1927; served from December 6, 1926, until his resignation effective February 3, 1933, to devote his time to the wildlife conservation movement and to the practice of law; served as counsel for the Philippine Commonwealth; engaged in the practice of law in Washington, D.C., until his death there on July 31, 1947; remains were cremated and the ashes scattered in the Current River near Doniphan, Mo.

**HAWES, Richard** (brother of Albert Gallatin Hawes, nephew of Aylett Hawes, and cousin of Aylett Hawes Buckner), a Representative from Kentucky; born near Bowling Green, Caroline County, Va., February 6, 1797; moved to Kentucky in 1810 with his parents, who settled in Fayette County, near Lexington; pursued classical studies at Transylvania University, Lexington, Ky.; studied law; was admitted to the bar in 1824 and commenced practice in Winchester; served in the Black Hawk War; member of the Kentucky house of representatives 1828, 1829, and 1834; unsuccessful candidate for election in 1834 to the Twenty-fourth Congress; elected as a Whig to the Twenty-fifth and Twenty-sixth Congresses (March 4, 1837-March 3, 1841); moved to Paris, Ky., in 1843 and continued the practice of law; was installed as Provisional Governor by Confederate sympathizers on October 4, 1862, and served until 1865; county judge in 1866, and later, in the same year, chosen master commissioner of the circuit and common pleas courts; served in this capacity until his death in Paris, Bourbon County, Ky., May 25, 1877; interment in Paris Cemetery.

**HAWK, Robert Moffett Allison,** a Representative from Illinois; born near Rushville, Hancock County, Ind., April 23, 1839; moved with his parents to Freedom Township, Carroll County, Ill., in 1844; attended the common and select schools of Carroll County, Ill., and Eureka (Ill.) College; studied law but never practiced; entered the Union Army during the Civil War as first lieutenant September 4, 1862; promoted to captain on January 1, 1863; brevetted major April 10, 1865; moved to Mount Carroll, Ill., in 1865 and engaged in agricultural pursuits; clerk of the court of Carroll County, Ill., from December 13, 1865, to February 27, 1879; elected as a Republican to the Forty-sixth and Forty-seventh Congresses and served from March 4, 1879, until his death in Washington, D.C., June 29, 1882; interment in Oak Hill Cemetery, Mount Carroll, Ill.

**HAWKES, Albert Wahl,** a Senator from New Jersey; born in Chicago, Ill., November 20, 1878; attended the public schools; graduated from Chicago College of Law in 1900 and was admitted to the bar the same year; studied chemistry at Lewis Institute (now the Illinois Institute of Technology), Chicago, Ill., for two years; engaged in the chemical business; during the First World War served as director of the Chemical Alliance, Washington, D.C., 1917-1918; president of Congoleum-Nairn, Inc., at Kearny, N.J., 1927-1942, becoming chairman of the board in 1937; president and director of the Chamber of Commerce of the United States 1941-1942; member of the Newark Labor Board and later appointed to the Board to Maintain Industrial Peace in New Jersey 1941-1942; member of the National War Labor Board, Washington, D.C., 1942; elected as a Republican to the United States Senate in 1942 and served from January 3, 1943, to January 3, 1949; was not a candidate for renomination in 1948; resumed former business activities in Montclair, N.J., until 1961 when he moved to Pasadena, Calif.; trustee of the Freedoms Foundation, where the Hawkes Library, Valley Forge, Pa., was named after him; died at Palm Desert, Calif., May 9, 1971; interment in Mt. Hebron Cemetery, Montclair, N.J.

**HAWKES, James,** a Representative from New York; born in Petersham, Worcester County, Mass., December 13, 1776; moved with his parents to Richfield, N.Y., in 1789; attended the common schools; taught school in Richfield and later in Burlington, N.Y.; returned to Richfield and served as sheriff of Otsego County 1815-1819; member of the State assembly in 1820; elected to the Seventeenth Congress (March 4, 1821-March 3, 1823); died in Rochester, N.Y., on October 2, 1865; interment in Mount Hope Cemetery.

**HAWKINS, Augustus Freeman (Gus),** a Representative from California; born in Shreveport, Caddo Parish, La., August 31, 1907; moved to Los Angeles, Calif., with his parents in 1918; attended local public schools and graduated from Jefferson High School in 1926; A.B., University of California at Los Angeles, 1931; graduated from the University of Southern California in 1932; engaged in the real estate business in 1941; member of the California State assembly, 1935-1963; elected as a Democrat to the Eighty-eighth and to the thirteen succeeding Congresses (January 3, 1963-January 3, 1991); was not a candidate for reelection in 1990 to the One Hundred Second Congress; chairman, Committee on House Administration (Ninety-seventh and Ninety-eighth Congresses), Committee on Education and Labor (Ninety-eighth through One Hundred First Congresses), Joint Committee on Printing (Ninety-sixth and Ninety-eighth Congresses), Joint Committee on the Library (Ninety-seventh Congress); is a resident of Los Angeles, Calif.

**HAWKINS, Benjamin** (uncle of Micajah Thomas Hawkins), a Delegate and a Senator from North Carolina; born in what was then Granville, later Bute, and now Warren County, N.C., August 15, 1754; attended the county schools; student at the College of New Jersey (now Princeton University) when the Revolutionary War began; acquired a knowledge of French, and, at the request of General George Washington, left school and was appointed to the General's staff as his interpreter; member, State house of commons 1778-1779, 1784; chosen by the North Carolina legislature in 1780 to procure arms and munitions of war to defend the State; Member of the Continental Congress 1781-1783 and 1787; appointed by Congress to negotiate treaties with the Creek and Cherokee Indians in 1785; delegate to the State constitutional convention which ratified the Federal Constitution in November 1789; elected to the United States Senate and served from November 27, 1789, to March 3, 1795; appointed Indian agent for all the tribes south of the Ohio River by President Washington in 1796 and held the office until his death in Crawford County, Ga., on June 6, 1818; interment on a plantation near Roberta, Crawford County, overlooking the Flint River.

Bibliography: *DAB*; Grant, C.L. "Senator Benjamin Hawkins: Federalist or Republican?" *Journal of the Early Republic* 1 (Fall 1981): 233-47; Hawkins, Benjamin. *Letters, Journals and Writings.* Edited by C.L. Grant. Savanah: Georgia Historical Society, 1980.

**HAWKINS, George Sydney,** a Representative from Florida; born in Kingston, Ulster County, N.Y., in 1808; attended the common schools and was graduated from Columbia University, New York City; studied law; was admitted to the bar and practiced; moved to Florida and settled in Pensacola; served as captain in the Indian war of 1837; member of the Legislative Council of the Territory of Florida; appointed district attorney in 1841; appointed United States district attorney for the Apalachicola district in Florida in 1842; associate justice of the State supreme court 1846-1850; elected judge of the circuit court in January 1851; member of the State house of representatives; served in the State senate; collector of customs for the port of Apalachicola; elected as a Democrat to the Thirty-fifth and Thirty-sixth Congresses and served from March 4, 1857, to January 21, 1861, when he joined other secessionist members of the Florida delegation in withdrawing from the Thirty-sixth Congress; judge of the district court under the Confederate Government 1862-1865; commissioned by the legislation of 1877 to prepare a digest of the State laws of Florida; died in Marianna, Fla., March 15, 1878; interment in St. Luke's Episcopal Cemetery.

**HAWKINS, Isaac Roberts,** a Representative from Tennessee; born near Columbia, Maury County, Tenn., May 16, 1818; moved with his parents to Carroll County in 1828; attended the common schools; engaged in agricultural pursuits; studied law; was admitted to the bar in 1843 and commenced practice in Huntingdon, Carroll County, Tenn.; served as a lieutenant in the Mexican War; resumed the practice of law; delegate from Tennessee to the peace conference held in Washington, D.C., in 1861 in an effort to devise means to prevent the impending war; elected to the convention for the consideration of Federal relations; judge of the circuit court in 1862; entered the Union Army as lieutenant colonel of the Seventh Regiment, Tennessee Volunteer Cavalry, in 1862; captured with his regiment at Union City, Tenn., in 1864 and imprisoned; exchanged in August 1864 and resumed active service, being in command of the Cavalry force in western Kentucky until the close of the Civil War; commissioned by Governor William G. Brownlow as one of the chancellors of Tennessee in July 1865 but declined to qualify; delegate to the Republican National Convention of 1868; upon the readmission of Tennessee to representation was elected as a Unionist to the Thirty-ninth Congress; reelected as a Republican to the Fortieth and Forty-first Congresses, and served from July 24, 1866 to March 3, 1871; chairman, Committee on Mileage (Forty-first Congress); died in Huntingdon, Tenn., August 12, 1880; interment in the Hawkins family burial ground near Huntingdon, Tenn.

**HAWKINS, Joseph,** a Representative from New York; born in that State on November 14, 1781; completed preparatory studies; studied law; was admitted to the bar and commenced practice in Henderson, N.Y., and also engaged in agricultural pursuits; elected as an Adams Democrat to the Twenty-first Congress (March 4, 1829-March 3, 1831); died in Henderson, Jefferson County, N.Y., April 20, 1832; interment in Clark Cemetery.

**HAWKINS, Joseph H.,** a Representative from Kentucky; born in Lexington, Ky.; pursued an academic course; studied law; was admitted to the bar and practiced; member of the Kentucky house of representatives, 1810-1813, and served two years as speaker; elected as a Republican to the Thirteenth Congress to fill the vacancy caused by the resignation of Henry Clay, and served from March 29, 1814 to March 3, 1815; was not a candidate for renomination in 1814 to the Fourteenth Congress; resumed the practice of law; also engaged in mercantile pursuits; moved to New Orleans, La., in 1819 and died in that city in 1823.

**HAWKINS, Micajah Thomas** (nephew of Benjamin Hawkins and Nathaniel Macon), a Representative from North Carolina; born near Warrenton, Warren County, N.C., May 20, 1790; attended the Warrenton (N.C.) Academy and the University of North Carolina at Chapel Hill; engaged in agricultural pursuits; member of the State house of commons in 1819 and 1820; served in the State senate 1823-1827; served in the State militia, attaining the rank of major general; elected as a Jacksonian to the Twenty-second Congress to fill the vacancy caused by the resignation of Robert Potter; reelected to the Twenty-third and Twenty-fourth Congresses and reelected as a Democrat to the Twenty-fifth and Twenty-sixth Congresses and served from December 15, 1831, to March 3, 1841; declined to be a candidate for renomination in 1840; resumed agricultural pursuits; again elected to the State senate in 1846; member of the council of state 1854 and 1855; died near Warrenton, Warren County, N.C., December 22, 1858; interment in the family burying ground near Warrenton.

**HAWKINS, Paula,** a Senator from Florida; born in Salt Lake City, Utah, January 24, 1927; attended the public schools of Salt Lake City and Richmond, Utah, and Atlanta, Ga.; attended Utah State University from 1944 until 1947; member, Florida Public Service Commission, 1972-1979; vice president, Air Florida, 1979-1980; director, Rural Telephone Bank Board, 1972-1978; member of the President's Commission on White House Fellowships in 1975; served on Federal Energy Administration Consumer Affairs/Special Impact Advisory Committee, 1974-1976; elected as a Republican to the United States Senate in 1980 for the six-year term commencing January 3, 1981; subsequently appointed January 1, 1981, to fill the vacancy caused by the resignation of Richard B. Stone for the term ending January 3, 1981, and served from January 1, 1981 to January 3, 1987; unsuccessful candidate for reelection in 1986; is a resident of Winter Park, Fla.

**HAWKS, Charles, Jr.,** a Representative from Wisconsin; born in Horicon, Dodge County, Wis., July 7, 1899; attended the public and high schools, and the commerce school of the University of Wisconsin at Madison; served as a yeoman, first class, in the United States Navy, 1917-1919; employed as a salesman, 1922-1925; engaged in the insurance business at Horicon, Wis., from 1925 until 1943; delegate to Republican State conventions, beginning in 1933; member of the Board of Supervisors of Dodge County, Wis., 1935-1939; elected as a Republican to the Seventy-sixth Congress (January 3, 1939-January 3, 1941); unsuccessful candidate for reelection in 1940 to the Seventy-seventh Congress, and for election in 1942 to the Seventy-eighth Congress; moved to Wynnewood, Pa., in 1943 and engaged in research on public relations work; vice president of General Grinding Wheel Corp., Philadelphia, Pa.; died in Bryn Mawr, Pa., January 6, 1960; interment in Oak Hill Cemetery, Horicon, Wis.

**HAWLEY, John Baldwin,** a Representative from Illinois; born in Hawleyville, Fairfield County, Conn., February 9, 1831; moved with his parents to Carthage, Hancock County, Ill., in 1833; attended the public schools and Jacksonville College, Jacksonville, Ill.; studied law; was admitted to the bar in 1854 and commenced practice at Rock Island, Ill.; elected State's attorney in 1856 and served four years; enlisted in the Union Army during the Civil War and served as captain of Company H, Forty-fifth Regiment, Illinois Volunteer Infantry; appointed postmaster of Rock Island, Ill., in 1865, and was removed the year following by President Andrew Johnson; elected as a Republican to the Forty-first, Forty-second, and Forty-third Congresses (March 4, 1869-March 3, 1875); chairman, Committee on Expenditures on Public Buildings (Forty-second Congress), Committee on Claims (Forty-third Congress); unsuccessful candidate for renomination in 1874 to the Forty-fourth Congress; Assistant Secretary of the Treasury from December 6, 1877, until April 1880, when he resigned; moved to Chicago, Ill., in 1880 and resumed the practice of law; moved to Omaha, Nebr., in 1886; general attorney for the western branches of the Northwestern Railroad Co.; died at Hot Springs, S.Dak., May 24, 1895; interment in Prospect Hill Cemetery, Omaha, Nebr.

**HAWLEY, Joseph Roswell,** a Representative and a Senator from Connecticut; born in Stewartsville, Richmond County, N.C., October 31, 1826; completed preparatory studies in Conn., and graduated from Hamilton College, Clinton, N.Y., in 1847; studied law; was admitted to the bar in 1850 and commenced practice in Hartford, Conn.; editor of the Hartford Evening Press in 1857, which in 1867 was consolidated with the Hartford Courant, of which he became editor; during the Civil War enlisted in the Union Army and was commissioned a captain on April 22, 1861; chief of staff to General Alfred H. Terry, and brevetted major general on September 28, 1865; mustered out in January 1866; elected Governor of Connecticut in 1866, and served from May 2, 1866 to May 1, 1867; unsuccessful candidate for reelection in 1867; president of the United States Centennial Commission to organize the Centennial Exposition, 1873-1876; elected as a Republican to the Forty-second Congress to fill the vacancy caused by the death of Julius L. Strong; reelected to the Forty-third Congress and served from December 2, 1872, to March 3, 1875; unsuccessful candidate for reelection in 1874 to the Forty-fourth Congress; elected to the Forty-sixth Congress (March 4, 1879-March 3, 1881); was not a candidate for reelection in 1880 to the Forty-seventh Congress; elected as a Republican to the United States Senate in 1881; reelected in 1887, 1893, and 1899 and served from March 4, 1881, to March 3, 1905; declined to be a candidate for renomination in 1904; chairman, Committee on Civil Service and Retrenchment (Forty-seventh through Forty-ninth Congresses), Committee on Military Affairs (Fiftieth through Fifty-second and Fifty-fourth through Fifty-eighth Congresses); appointed a brigadier general in the United States Army on the retired list in 1905; died in Washington, D.C., on March 17, 1905; interment in Cedar Hill Cemetery, Hartford, Conn.

**Bibliography:** *DAB.*

**HAWLEY, Robert Bradley,** a Representative from Texas; born in Memphis, Tenn., October 25, 1849; attended the public schools and the Christian Brothers' College, Memphis, Tenn.; moved to Galveston, Tex., in 1875; was a merchant, importer, and manufacturer in the city of Galveston for twenty years; president of the Galveston Board of Education 1889-1893; temporary chairman of the Republican State convention at San Antonio September 4, 1890; delegate to several Republican National Conventions; elected as a Republican to the Fifty-fifth and Fifty-sixth Congresses (March 4, 1897-March 3, 1901); was not a candidate for renomination in 1900; organized and became president of the Cuban-American Sugar Co. in 1900; died in New York City November 28, 1921; interment in Lake View Cemetery, Galveston, Tex.

**HAWLEY, Willis Chatman,** a Representative from Oregon; born on a farm in the old Belknap settlement near Monroe, Benton County, Oreg., May 5, 1864; attended the country schools and was graduated from the academic and law departments of Willamette University, Salem, Oreg., in 1888; principal of the Umpqua Academy, Wilbur, Oreg., 1884-1886; president of the Oregon State Normal School at Drain, 1888-1891; was admitted to the bar in Oregon in 1893; president of Willamette University, 1893-1902, and was professor of history and economics for sixteen years; engaged in numerous business and educational enterprises; member of the National Forest Reservation Commission; member of the Special Committee on Rural Credits created by Congress in 1915; member of the Commission for the Celebration of the Two Hundredth Anniversary of the Birth of George Washington; elected as a Republican to the Sixtieth and to the twelve succeeding Congresses (March 4, 1907-March 3, 1933); chairman, Committee on Ways and Means (Seventieth and Seventy-first Congresses); co-sponsor of the Smoot-Hawley Tariff of 1930; unsuccessful candidate for renomination in 1932 to the Seventy-third Congress; returned to Salem and resumed the practice of law; died in Salem, Oreg., July 24, 1941; interment in City View Cemetery.

**Bibliography:** *DAB.*

**HAWS, John Henry Hobart,** a Representative from New York; born in New York City in 1809; was graduated from Columbia College, New York City, in 1827; studied law; was admitted to the bar and commenced practice; elected as a Whig to the Thirty-seventh Congress (March 4, 1851-March 3, 1853); unsuccessful for reelection in 1852; died in New York City January 27, 1858; interment in St. Stephen's Cemetery; reinterment in Greenwood Cemetery, Brooklyn, N.Y., in 1866.

**HAY, Andrew Kessler,** a Representative from New Jersey; born near Lowell, Mass., January 19, 1809; completed preparatory studies; was employed in the manufacture of window glass; moved to Waterford Works, N.J., in 1829 and later to Winslow, N.J., and engaged in the manufacture of glass; was also largely interested in real estate and agriculture; elected as a Whig to the Thirty-first Congress (March 4, 1849-March 3, 1851); declined to be a candidate for renomination; resumed his business interests; presidential elector on the Republican ticket in 1872; president of the Camden & Atlantic Railroad Co. 1872-1876; died in Winslow, Camden County, N.J., February 7, 1881; interment in Colestown Cemetery, near Haddonfield, N.J.

**HAY, James,** a Representative from Virginia; born in Millwood, Clark County, Va., January 9, 1856; attended private schools and the University of Pennsylvania at Philadelphia; was graduated from the law department of Washington and Lee University, Lexington, Va., in 1877; was admitted to the bar and commenced practice in Harrisonburg, Va., in 1877; moved to Madison, Va., in June 1879 and continued the practice of law; Commonwealth attorney 1883-1896; member of the Virginia house of delegates 1885-1889; served in the Virginia senate 1893-1897; member of the Virginia Democratic committee in 1888; delegate to the Democratic National Convention in 1888; elected as a Democrat to the Fifty-fifth and to the nine succeeding Congresses and served from March 4, 1897, until his resignation on October 1, 1916; chairman, Committee on Military Affairs (Sixty-second through Sixty-fourth Congresses); appointed judge of the United States Court of Claims and served until December 1, 1927, when he resigned; died in Madison, Va., June 12, 1931; interment in Cedar Hill Cemetery.

**Bibliography:** Herring, George C., Jr. "James Hay and the Preparedness Controversy, 1915-1916." *Journal of Southern History* 30 (November 1964): 383-404.

**HAY, John Breese,** a Representative from Illinois; born in Belleville, St. Clair County, Ill., January 8, 1834; received a limited schooling; learned the art of printing; studied law; was admitted to the bar in 1851 and commenced practice in Belleville, Ill.; prosecuting attorney for the twenty-fourth judicial district of Illinois 1860-1868; delegate to the Republican State convention in 1860; served in the Union Army during the Civil War in the One Hundred and Thirtieth Regiment, Illinois Volunteer Infantry; elected as a Republican to the Forty-first and Forty-second Congress (March 4, 1869-March 3, 1873); unsuccessful candidate for reelection in 1872 to the Forty-third Congress and for election in 1880 to the Forty-seventh Congress; resumed the practice of law in Belleville; postmaster of Belleville, Ill., 1881-1885; judge of St. Clair County Court 1886-1900; served as mayor of Belleville from 1901 to 1905, when he resigned, having been again elected county judge, and served until 1914; died in Belleville, Ill., on June 16, 1916; interment in Green Mount Cemetery.

**HAYAKAWA, Samuel Ichiye,** a Senator from California; born in Vancouver, British Columbia, Canada, July 18, 1906; educated in the public schools of Calgary and Winnipeg, Canada; B.A., University of Manitoba, Winnipeg, Canada, 1927; M.A., McGill University, Montreal, Canada, 1928; Ph.D., English, University of Wisconsin, Madison, 1935; psychologist, semanticist, teacher, and writer; instructor at the University of Wisconsin 1936-1939, and at the Armour Institute of Technology 1939-1947; served as president of the International Society for General Semantics 1949-1950; United States director, Consumers Union, 1953-1955; lecturer, University of Chicago 1950-1955; professor, San Francisco State College 1955-1958; president, San Francisco State College 1968-1973, becoming president emeritus in 1973; columnist, Register & Tribune Syndicate 1970-1976; elected as a Republican to the United States Senate in 1976 and served from January 3, 1977, to January 3, 1983; was not a candidate for reelection in 1982; was a resident of Mill Valley, Calif.; died February 27, 1992.

**Bibliography:** Hayakawa, Samuel I. *Language in Thought and Action.* New York: Harcourt Brace Jovanovich, 1978.

**HAYDEN, Carl Trumbull,** a Representative and a Senator from Arizona; born in Hayden's Ferry (now Tempe), Maricopa County, Ariz., October 2, 1877; attended the public schools; graduated from the Normal School of Arizona at Tempe in 1896; attended Leland Stanford Junior University, California, 1896-1900; engaged in mercantile pursuits and in the flour-milling business at Tempe, 1900-1904; member, Tempe Town Council, 1902-1904; treasurer of Maricopa County, 1904-1906; sheriff of Maricopa County, 1907-1912; upon the admission of Arizona as a State into the Union was elected as a Democrat to the Sixty-second Congress; reelected to the seven succeeding Congresses and served from February 19, 1912, to March 3, 1927; did not seek renomination to the House of Representatives, having become a candidate for United States Senator; during the First World War was commissioned a major of Infantry in the United States Army; elected as a Democrat to the United States Senate in 1926 for the term commencing March 4, 1927; reelected in 1932, 1938, 1944, 1950, 1956, and again in 1962 for the term ending January 3, 1969; was not a candidate for reelection in 1968; served as President pro tempore of the Senate during the Eighty-fifth through the Ninetieth Congresses; chairman, Committee on Printing (Seventy-third through Seventy-ninth Congresses), Committee on Rules and Administration (Eighty-first and Eighty-second Congresses), co-chairman, Joint Committee on Printing (Eighty-first and Eighty-second, and Eighty-fourth through Ninetieth Congresses), co-chairman, Joint Committee on Inaugural Arrangements (Eightieth and Eighty-second Congresses), chairman, Committee on Appropriations (Eighty-fourth through Ninetieth Congresses); his record for fifty-six consecutive years of service in the Congress, including an unprecedented forty-two in the Senate, is unsurpassed; retired and resided in Tempe, Ariz.; died in Mesa, Ariz., on January 25, 1972; cremated; ashes interred in family plot at Tempe Butte Cemetery, Tempe, Ariz.

**Bibliography:** Rice, Ross R. *Carl Hayden: Builder of the American West.* Lanham, Md.: University Press of America, 1994.

**HAYDEN, Edward Daniel,** a Representative from Massachusetts; born in Cambridge, Mass., December 27, 1833; attended the Lawrence Academy, Groton, Mass., and was graduated from Harvard University in 1854; studied law; was admitted to the bar in 1857 and commenced practice in Woburn, Mass.; entered the United States Navy as assistant paymaster in 1861, and served in the Mississippi Squadron under Admiral David D. Porter in the Vicksburg and Red River campaigns; returned to Woburn, Mass., in 1866 and engaged in mercantile pursuits; president of the First National Bank, 1874-1900; member of the Massachusetts house of representatives, 1880-1882; elected as a Republican to the Forty-ninth and Fiftieth Congresses (March 4, 1885-March 3, 1889); was not a candidate for renomination in 1888 to the Fifty-first Congress; delegate to the Republican National Convention of 1888; served for more than thirty years on the directorate of the Boston and Albany Railroad, and at the time of his death was vice president; served as selectman and later as alderman; director of the Shawmut National Bank of Boston; died in Woburn, Mass., November 15, 1908; interment in Mount Auburn Cemetery, Cambridge, Mass.

**HAYDEN, Moses,** a Representative from New York; born near Westfield, Hampden County, Mass., in 1786; completed preparatory studies and was graduated from Williams College, Williamstown, Mass., in 1804; studied law; was admitted to the bar and commenced practice in York, Livingston County, N.Y.; was first judge of the court of common pleas of Livingston County 1821-1823; elected to the Eighteenth and Nineteenth Congresses (March 4, 1823-March 3, 1827); member of the State senate from January 6, 1829, until his death in Albany, N.Y., February 13, 1830; interment in Mount Pleasant Cemetery, York, near Fowlerville, N.Y.

**HAYES, Charles Arthur,** a Representative from Illinois; born in Cairo, Alexander County, Ill., February 17, 1918; graduated from Sumner High School, Cairo, Ill., 1935; worked as a machine operator and was one of the organizers of Local 1424, United Brotherhood of Carpenters and Joiners of America, and served as president 1940-1942; member, grievance committee, United Packinghouse Workers of America (U.P.W.A.) 1943; U.P.W.A. field representative 1949, and district director, 1954-1968; international vice president and director of Region 12, United Food and Commercial Workers International Union, 1968-1979, following merger of U.P.W.A. and Amalgamated Meatcutters; elected vice president and director of Meatcutters District 1; elected as a Democrat to the Ninety-eighth Congress, August 23, 1983, by special election to fill the vacancy caused by the resignation of Harold Washington; reelected to the Ninety-ninth and to the three succeeding Congresses and served from August 23, 1983, to January 3, 1993; unsuccessful candidate for renomination in 1992 to the One Hundred Third Congress; is a resident of Chicago, Ill.

**HAYES, Everis Anson,** a Representative from California; born in Waterloo, Jefferson County, Wis., March 10, 1855; attended the public schools; was graduated from the Waterloo High School in 1873 and from the literary and law departments of the University of Wisconsin at Madison in 1879; was admitted to the bar in 1879 and commenced practice in Madison, Wis.; moved to Ashland, Wis., in 1883 and in 1886 to Hurley, Wis., and continued the practice of his profession; moved to Ironwood, Mich., in 1886 and engaged in the mining of ore; moved to San Jose, Santa Clara County, Calif., in 1887 and engaged in fruit raising and mining; with his brother became publisher and proprietor of the San Jose Daily Mercury Herald in 1901; elected as a Republican to the Fifty-ninth and to the six succeeding Congresses (March 4, 1905-March 3, 1919); unsuccessful candidate for reelection in 1918 to the Sixty-sixth Congress; resumed his newspaper activities in San Jose, Calif., with mining interests in Ironwood, Mich., and Sierra City, Calif.; died in San Jose, Calif., June 3, 1942; interment in Oak Hill Memorial Park Cemetery.

**HAYES, James Allison,** a Representative from Louisiana; born in Lafayette, La., December 21, 1946; attended public schools; graduated Lafayette High School, 1964; B.S., University of Southwestern Louisiana, Lafayette, 1967; J.D., Tulane University Law School, New Orleans, 1970; sergeant, Louisiana Air National Guard, 1968-1974; admitted to the Louisiana State bar in 1970 and commenced practice in New Orleans; real estate developer; assistant district attorney, Lafayette Parish, 1974-1983; ; commissioner, Financial Institutions for the State of Louisiana, 1984-1985; elected as a Democrat to the One Hundredth and to the four succeeding Congresses (January 3, 1987-January 3, 1997); announced his affiliation with the Republican Party on December 1, 1995, and continued in office during the One Hundred Fourth Congress as a Republican; was not a candidate in 1996 for reelection to the House of Representatives, but was an unsuccessful candidate for nomination to the United States Senate; is a resident of Lafayette, La.

**HAYES, Philip Cornelius,** a Representative from Illinois; born in Granby, Hartford County, Conn., February 3, 1833; moved with his father's family to La Salle County, Ill.; attended the country schools; was graduated from Oberlin (Ohio) College in 1860 and from the Theological Seminary, Oberlin, Ohio, in 1863; served in the Union Army during the Civil War and commissioned captain in the One Hundred and Third Regiment, Ohio Volunteer Infantry, July 16, 1862; lieutenant colonel November 18, 1864; brevetted colonel and brigadier general March 13, 1865; superintendent of schools of Mount Vernon, Ohio, in 1866; moved to Circleville, Ohio, in 1867, to Bryan, Ohio, in 1869, and to Morris, Grundy County, Ill., in 1874; delegate to the Republican National Convention of 1872; elected as a Republican to the Forty-fifth and Forty-sixth Congresses (March 4, 1877-March 3, 1881); was not a candidate for renomination in 1880 to the Forty-seventh Congress; moved to Joliet, Ill., in 1892, where he resumed journalism; died in Joilet on July 13, 1916; interment in Elmhurst Cemetery.

**HAYES, Philip Harold,** a Representative from Indiana; born in Battle Creek, Calhoun County, Mich., September 1, 1940; attended Rensselaer (Ind.) Elementary School; graduated from Rensselaer High School, 1958; B.A., Indiana University, 1963; J.D., Indiana University Law School, 1967; admitted to the Indiana bar in 1967 and commenced practice in Evansville; served as deputy prosecuting attorney, Vanderburgh County, Ind., 1967-1968; member, Indiana State senate, 1971-1974; elected as a Democrat to the Ninety-fourth Congress (January 3, 1975-January 3, 1977); was not a candidate in 1976 for reelection to the House of Representatives, but was an unsuccessful candidate for nomination to the United States Senate; resumed the practice of law; is a resident of Evansville, Ind.

**HAYES, Rutherford Birchard,** a Representative from Ohio and 19th President of the United States; born in Delaware, Delaware County, Ohio, October 4, 1822; attended the common schools, the Methodist Academy in Norwalk, Ohio, and the Webb Preparatory School in Middletown, Conn.; was graduated from Kenyon College, Gambier, Ohio, in August 1842, and from the Harvard Law School in January 1845; was admitted to the bar on May 10, 1845, and commenced practice in Lower Sandusky (now Fremont); moved to Cincinnati in 1849 and resumed the practice of law; city solicitor, 1857-1859; commissioned major of the Twenty-third Regiment, Ohio Volunteer Infantry, on June 27, 1861; lieutenant colonel on October 24, 1861; colonel on October 24, 1862; brigadier general of Volunteers on October 9, 1864; brevetted major general of Volunteers on March 3, 1865; elected as a Republican to the Thirty-ninth and Fortieth Congresses and served from March 4, 1865, to July 20, 1867, when he resigned, having been nominated for Governor; elected Governor of Ohio in 1867, reelected in 1869, and served from January 13, 1868 to January 8, 1872; unsuccessful candidate for election in 1872 to the Forty-third Congress; elected Governor in 1875, and served from January 10, 1876 to March 2, 1877, when he resigned, having been elected President of the United States; was inaugurated March 5, 1877, and served until March 3, 1881; died in Fremont, Sandusky County, Ohio, January 17, 1893; interment in Oakwood Cemetery; following the gift of his home to the State of Ohio for the Spiegel Grove State Park was reinterred there in 1915.

**Bibliography:** *DAB*; Barnard, Harry. *Rutherford B. Hayes and His America.* Indianapolis: Bobbs-Merrill Co., 1954; Hayes, Rutherford B. *Diary and Letters of Rutherford Birchard Hayes.* 5 vols. Edited by Charles Richard Williams. Columbus, Ohio: The Ohio State Archeological and Historical Society, 1922-1926; Hoogenboom, Ari. *Rutherford B. Hayes: Warrior and President.* Lawrence: University Press of Kansas, 1995.

**HAYES, Walter Ingalls,** a Representative from Iowa; born in Marshall, Calhoun County, Mich., December 9, 1841; attended the common schools and was graduated from the law department of the

University of Michigan at Ann Arbor in 1863; was admitted to the bar in 1863 and commenced practice in Marshall, Mich.; city attorney of Marshall, 1864-1865; United States commissioner for the eastern district of Michigan, 1864-1865, and of Iowa, 1865-1875; city solicitor of Clinton, Iowa, in 1870; district judge of the seventh judicial district of Iowa, 1875-1887; delegate to the Democratic National Conventions of 1884 and 1892; elected as a Democrat to the Fiftieth and to the three succeeding Congresses (March 4, 1887-March 3, 1895); chairman, Committee on Education (Fifty-second Congress); unsuccessful candidate for reelection in 1894 to the Fifty-fourth Congress; resumed the practice of law in Clinton, Iowa; member of the State house of representatives in 1897 and 1898; died in Marshall, Mich., March 14, 1901; interment in Springdale Cemetery, Clinton, Iowa.

**HAYMOND, Thomas Sherwood,** a Representative from Virginia; born near Fairmont, Monongalia County, Va. (now West Virginia), January 15, 1794; attended private schools and the College of William and Mary, Williamsburg, Va.; served as a private in the War of 1812; studied law; was admitted to the bar in 1815 and commenced practice in Morgantown, Va. (now West Virginia); president of the county court of Marion County in 1842; elected as a Whig to the Thirty-first Congress to fill the vacancy caused by the death of Alexander Newman and served from November 8, 1849, to March 3, 1851; brigadier general of the Virginia militia prior to 1861; entered the Confederate Army as a colonel in 1861 and served throughout the Civil War; died in Richmond, Va., April 5, 1869; interment in Palatine Cemetery, near Fairmont, Marion County, W.Va.

**HAYMOND, William Summerville,** a Representative from Indiana; born near Clarksburg, Harrison County, Va. (now West Virginia), February 20, 1823; attended the common schools and was graduated from Bellevue Hospital Medical College, New York City; commenced the practice of his profession at Monticello, Ind., in 1852; during the Civil War entered the Union Army as a surgeon in 1862 and served one year; unsuccessful candidate for the State senate in 1866; president of the Indianapolis, Delphi & Chicago Railroad Co. 1872-1874; elected as a Democrat to the Forty-fourth Congress (March 4, 1875-March 3, 1877); unsuccessful candidate for reelection in 1876 to the Forty-fifth Congress; resumed his former professional and business activities; organized the Central Medical College in Indianapolis in 1877 and was dean until his death; published in 1879 a history of Indiana; died in Indianapolis, Ind., December 24, 1885; interment in Crown Hill Cemetery.

**HAYNE, Arthur Peronneau** (brother of Robert Young Hayne), a Senator from South Carolina; born in Charleston, S.C., March 12, 1788 or 1790; pursued classical studies; engaged in business; served in the War of 1812 as first lieutenant, major, and inspector general; brevetted lieutenant colonel for gallant conduct at New Orleans; studied law; was admitted to the bar and practiced; served in the Florida War as commander of the Tennessee Volunteers and retired in 1820; member, State house of representatives; United States naval agent in the Mediterranean for five years; declined the Belgian mission; appointed to the United States Senate to fill the vacancy caused by the death of Josiah J. Evans and served from May 11, 1858, to December 2, 1858; was not a candidate to succeed himself; died in Charleston, S.C., January 7, 1867; interment in St. Michael's Churchyard.

**HAYNE, Robert Young** (brother of Arthur Peronneau Hayne), a Senator from South Carolina; born on Pon Pon plantation, St. Paul's Parish, Colleton District, S.C., November 10, 1791; attended private schools in Charleston; studied law; was admitted to the bar in 1812 and commenced practice in Charleston, S.C.; served in the War of 1812, becoming captain of the Charleston Cadet Riflemen in 1814; appointed quartermaster general of the State in December 1814; member, State house of representatives 1814-1818, and served as

speaker in 1818; State attorney general 1818-1822; elected to the United States Senate in 1822; reelected in 1828 as a Jacksonian and served from March 4, 1823, to December 13, 1832, when he resigned to become Governor; participated in January and February 1830 in a notable exchange with Senator Daniel Webster of Massachusetts upon the principles of the Constitution, the authority of the general government, and the rights of the States; chairman, Committee on Naval Affairs (Nineteenth through Twenty-second Congresses); member of the South Carolina nullification convention in 1832; Governor of South Carolina from December 13, 1832 to December 11, 1834; mayor of Charleston 1835-1837; promoter and president of the Louisville, Cincinnati & Charleston Railroad 1836-1839; died in Asheville, N.C., September 24, 1839; interment in St. Michael's Churchyard, Charleston, S.C.

**Bibliography:** *DAB*; Jervy, Theodore. *Robert Y. Hayne and His Times* 1909. Reprint. New York: Da Capo Press, 1970; Patterson, Lane. "The Battle of the Giants: Webster and Hayne: Orators at Odds." *American History Illustrated* 17 (February 1983): 18-23.

**HAYNES, Charles Eaton,** a Representative from Georgia; born in Brunswick, Mecklenburg County, Va., April 15, 1784; moved to Sparta, Ga.; completed preparatory studies; was graduated in medicine from the University of Pennsylvania at Philadelphia and practiced; elected to the Nineteenth, Twentieth, and Twenty-first Congresses (March 4, 1825-March 3, 1831); chairman, Committee on Expenditures in the Department of War (Twentieth Congress); unsuccessful candidate for reelection in 1830 to the Twenty-second Congress and for election in 1832 to the Twenty-third Congress; elected to the Twenty-fourth and Twenty-fifth Congresses (March 4, 1835-March 3, 1839); died August 29, 1841; interment in Sparta, Ga.

**HAYNES, Martin Alonzo,** a Representative from New Hampshire; born in Springfield, Sullivan County, N.H., July 30, 1842; moved with his parents to Manchester, N.H., in 1846; attended the common schools; apprenticed to the printer's trade; enlisted in June 1861 in the Union Army as a private in the Second New Hampshire Regiment and served three years; moved to Lakeport, Belknap County, N.H., in 1868, where he established the Lake Village Times, which he conducted for twenty years; member of the State house of representatives in 1872 and 1873; clerk of the supreme court for Belknap County 1876-1883; president of the New Hampshire Veterans' Association in 1881 and 1882; department commander of the Grand Army of the Republic in 1881 and 1882; elected as a Republican to the Forty-eighth and Forty-ninth Congresses (March 4, 1883-March 3, 1887); unsuccessful candidate for reelection in 1886 to the Fiftieth Congress; internal-revenue agent of the Treasury 1890-1893 and 1898-1912; established internal-revenue service in the Philippine Islands; died in Lakeport, N.H., November 28, 1919; interment in Bayside Cemetery.

**HAYNES, William Elisha** (cousin of George William Palmer), a Representative from Ohio; born in Hoosick Falls, Rensselaer County, N.Y., October 19, 1829; moved to Ohio with his parents, who settled in Lower Sandusky (now Fremont) in 1839; attended the common schools; apprenticed as a printer; clerk on a steamer on Lake Superior in 1848 and 1849; engaged in mercantile pursuits at Fremont 1850-1856; auditor of Sandusky County, Ohio, 1856-1860; enlisted in the Union Army as a private April 16, 1861, in the Eighth Regiment, Ohio Volunteer Infantry; commissioned captain and served in western Virginia, the Shenandoah Valley, and in the Army of the Potomac until November 1862, when he was commissioned lieutenant colonel of the Tenth Regiment, Ohio Volunteer Cavalry, and served with it in the Army of the Cumberland until 1864, when he was honorably discharged; collector of internal revenue for the ninth district of Ohio in 1866 and 1867; again engaged in mercantile pursuits 1866-1873; engaged in banking 1873-1914; delegate to the Democratic National Convention in 1880 and 1884; elected as a Democrat to the Fifty-first and Fifty-second Congresses (March 4,

1889-March 3, 1893); declined to be a candidate for renomination in 1892; resumed banking in Fremont, Sandusky County, Ohio, in which he continued until his death there on December 5, 1914; interment in Oakwood Cemetery.

**HAYS, Charles,** a Representative from Alabama; born at "Hays Mount," near Boligee, Greene County, Ala., February 2, 1834; completed preparatory studies under private teachers; attended the University of Georgia at Athens and the University of Virginia at Charlottesville; was a cotton planter and also engaged in other agricultural pursuits; was a delegate to the Democratic National Convention at Baltimore in 1860; during the Civil War was a major in the Confederate Army; member of the constitutional convention of Alabama in 1867; served in the Alabama State senate in 1868; elected as a Republican to the Forty-first and to the three succeeding Congresses (March 4, 1869-March 3, 1877); chairman, Committee on Agriculture (Forty-third Congress); died at his home, "Myrtle Hall," in Greene County, Ala., June 24, 1879; interment in the family cemetery, "Hays Mount" plantation.

**Bibliography:** Rogers, William W. "'Politics is Mighty Uncertain': Charles Hays Goes to Congress." *Alabama Review* 30 (July 1977): 163-90; Rogers, William Warren, Jr. *Black Belt Scalawag: Charles Hays and the Southern Republicans in the Era of Reconstruction.* Athens: University of Georgia Press, 1993.

**HAYS, Edward Dixon,** a Representative from Missouri; born on a farm near Oak Ridge, Cape Girardeau County, Mo., April 28, 1872; attended the public schools; was graduated from the Oak Ridge High School in 1889 and from the Cape Girardeau State Normal School in 1893; taught school until 1895; moved to Jackson, Mo., in 1895; studied law; was admitted to the bar in 1896 and commenced practice in Jackson, Cape Girardeau County, Mo.; mayor of Jackson, 1903-1907; probate judge of Cape Girardeau County, 1907-1918; unsuccessful Republican candidate for election for circuit judge in 1916; moved to Cape Girardeau, Mo., in 1915 and continued the practice of law; elected as a Republican to the Sixty-sixth and Sixty-seventh Congresses (March 4, 1919-March 3, 1923); unsuccessful candidate for reelection in 1922 to the Sixty-eighth Congress; resumed the practice of his profession in Cape Girardeau; trial lawyer for the Department of Justice in the Court of Claims, 1923-1925; appointed valuation attorney for the Interstate Commerce Commission in 1925 and served until 1933; continued the practice of law in Washington, D.C., and resided in Bethesda, Md., where he died on July 25, 1941; interment in Cedar Hill Cemetery, Washington, D.C.

**HAYS, Edward Retilla,** a Representative from Iowa; born near Fostoria, Wood County, Ohio, May 26, 1847; attended rural schools near Fostoria and Heidelberg College, Tiffin, Ohio; served as a private in the First Regiment, Ohio Heavy Artillery, 1862-1865; studied law; was admitted to the bar in 1869 and commenced practice in Knoxville, Iowa; elected as a Republican to the Fifty-first Congress to fill the vacancy caused by the resignation of Edwin H. Conger and served from November 4, 1890, to March 3, 1891; was not a candidate for renomination in 1890; resumed the practice of law; died in Knoxville, Marion County, Iowa, February 28, 1896; interment in Graceland Cemetery.

**HAYS, Lawrence Brooks,** a Representative from Arkansas; born in London, Pope County, Ark., August 9, 1898; attended the public schools in Russellville, Ark.; A.B., University of Arkansas, Fayetteville, 1919; J.D., George Washington University School of Law, Washington, D.C., 1922; was admitted to the bar in 1922 and commenced practice in Russellville, Ark.; served in the United States Army in 1918; assistant attorney general of Arkansas, 1925-1927; Democratic National committeeman for Arkansas, 1932-1939; National Recovery Act labor compliance officer for Arkansas in 1934; assistant to the administrator of resettlement in 1935; held administrative and legal positions in the Farm Security

Administration, 1936-1942; elected as a Democrat to the Seventy-eighth and to the seven succeeding Congresses (January 3, 1943-January 3, 1959); unsuccessful candidate for reelection in 1958 to the Eighty-sixth Congress; president, Southern Baptist Convention, 1957-1958; member of the Board of Directors of the Tennessee Valley Authority 1959-1961; Assistant Secretary of State for congressional relations, 1961; Special Assistant to President John F. Kennedy and President Lyndon B. Johnson from December 1961 until February 1964, when he became professor of political science at the Eagleton Institute of Rutgers University; visiting professor of government at University of Massachusetts, 1966-1967; director of the Ecumenical Institute at Wake Forest University, 1968-1970; elected as co-chairman, Former Members of Congress, Inc., in 1970; chairman, Government Good Neighbor Council of North Carolina; unsuccessful candidate from North Carolina for election in 1972 to the Ninety-third Congress; resided in Chevy Chase, Md., until his death there on October 11, 1981; interment at Oakland Cemetery, Russellville, Ark.

**Bibliography:** Baker, James T. *Brooks Hays.* Macon, Ga.: Mercer University Press, 1989; Barnhill, John Herschel. "Politician, Social Reformer, and Religious Leader: The Public Career of Brooks Hays." Ph.D. dissertation, Oklahoma State University, 1981; Hays, Brooks. *Hotbed of Tranquility; My Life in Five Worlds.* New York: Macmillan, 1968.

**HAYS, Samuel,** a Representative from Pennsylvania; born in County Donegal, Ireland, September 10, 1783; immigrated to the United States with his mother, who settled in Franklin, Venango County, Pa., in 1792; treasurer of Venango County in 1808; elected sheriff of Venango County in 1808, 1820, 1829, and in 1833; member of the Pennsylvania house of representatives in 1813, 1816; 1823, and 1825; served in the Pennsylvania senate in 1822 and 1839; member of the board of trustees of Allegheny College, Meadville, Pa., 1837-1861; served as brigadier general, commanding the First Brigade, Seventeenth Division, Pennsylvania Militia, 1841-1843; elected as a Democrat to the Twenty-eighth Congress (March 4, 1843-March 3, 1845); was not a candidate for renomination in 1844; engaged in iron manufactures, operating furnaces on French Creek, near Franklin; appointed in 1847 marshal for the western district of Pennsylvania; associate judge of the district court in 1856; died in Franklin, Pa., July 1, 1868; interment in Old Town Cemetery, reinterment in New Franklin Cemetery.

**HAYS, Samuel Lewis,** a Representative from Virginia; born near Clarksburg, Harrison County, Va. (now West Virginia), October 20, 1794; moved to Stewarts Creek, Lewis County, Va. (now Glenville, Gilmer County, W.Va.), in 1833 and engaged in agricultural pursuits; member of the Virginia assembly; elected as a Democrat to the Twenty-seventh Congress (March 4, 1841-March 3, 1843); unsuccessful candidate for reelection to the Twenty-eighth Congress in 1842; delegate to the State constitutional convention in 1850; appointed receiver of public moneys at Sauk Rapids, Minn., April 28, 1857, by President Buchanan and served until June 10, 1860; resumed agricultural pursuits; died at Sauk Rapids, Benton County, Minn., March 17, 1871; interment in the original Old Benton County Cemetery.

**HAYS, Wayne Levere,** a Representative from Ohio; born in Bannock, Belmont County, Ohio, May 13, 1911; attended the public schools of Bannock and St. Clairsville, Ohio; B.S., Ohio State University, Columbus, 1933; student at Duke University, Durham, N.C., in 1935; teacher in Flushing, Ohio, 1934-1937 and Findlay, Ohio, in 1937 and 1938; also engaged in agricultural pursuits; mayor of Flushing, Ohio, 1939-1945; served in the State senate in 1941 and 1942; Commissioner, Belmont County, 1945-1949; member of the Officers' Reserve Corps, United States Army, from 1933 until called to active duty as a second lieutenant on December 8, 1941; was separated from service with medical discharge in August 1942;

chairman, board of directors, Citizens National Bank, Flushing, Ohio, beginning in December 1953; delegate to the Democratic National Conventions of 1960, 1964, and 1968; chairman, House of Representatives delegation to the North Atlantic Treaty Organization Parliamentarians Conference, and president of the conference in 1956 and 1967; president, North Atlantic Assembly, 1969-1970; elected as a Democrat to the Eighty-first and to the thirteen succeeding Congresses and served from January 3, 1949, until his resignation September 1, 1976; chairman, Committee on House Administration (Ninety-second through Ninety-fourth Congresses), Joint Committee on Printing (Ninety-second through Ninety-fourth Congresses), Joint Committee on the Library (Ninety-second Congress); resigned as chairman of Committee on House Administration on June 18, 1976; was renominated in June 1976 to the Ninety-fifth Congress, but withdrew before the general election; elected to the Ohio State house of representatives in 1978; was a resident of St. Clairsville, Ohio; died February 10, 1989.

**HAYWARD, Monroe Leland,** a Senator from Nebraska; born in Willsboro, Essex County, N.Y., December 22, 1840; served during the Civil War in the Twenty-second Regiment, New York Volunteer Infantry, and in the Fifth Regiment, New York Volunteer Cavalry; graduated from Fort Edward Collegiate Institute, New York, in 1865; studied law in Whitewater, Wis.; was admitted to the bar in 1867 and commenced practice in Nebraska City, Nebr.; member of the state constitutional convention in 1873; judge of the district court of Nebraska in 1886; elected as a Republican to the United States Senate March 8, 1899, to fill the vacancy in the term beginning March 4, 1899, caused by failure of the legislature to act; died before qualifying; died in Nebraska City, Otoe County, Nebr., December 5, 1899; interment in Wyuka Cemetery.

**HAYWARD, William, Jr.,** a Representative from Maryland; born at "Shipshead," near Easton, Talbot County, Md., in 1787; attended Easton Academy and was graduated from Princeton College in 1808; studied law; was admitted to the bar in 1809 and commenced practice in Easton; member of the State house of delegates 1818-1820; elected to the Eighteenth Congress (March 4, 1823-March 3, 1825); continued the practice of law in Easton, Md., until his death there October 19, 1836; interment in the family burial ground on his estate, "Shipshead," near Easton, Md.

**HAYWOOD, William Henry, Jr.,** a Senator from North Carolina; born in Raleigh, N.C., October 23, 1801; attended the Raleigh Male Academy and graduated from the University of North Carolina, at Chapel Hill, in 1819; studied law; was admitted to the bar in 1822 and commenced practice in Raleigh, N.C.; member, State house of commons 1831, 1834-1836, serving the last year as speaker; appointed Chargé d'Affaires to Belgium by President Martin Van Buren, but declined; elected as a Democrat to the United States Senate and served from March 4, 1843, until July 25, 1846, when he resigned, having refused to be instructed by the State legislature on a tariff question; chairman, Committee on Commerce (Twenty-ninth Congress), Committee on the District of Columbia (Twenty-ninth Congress); resumed the practice of law in Raleigh, N.C., and died there on October 7, 1852; interment in the Old City Cemetery, Raleigh, N.C.

**HAYWORTH, Donald,** a Representative from Michigan; born in Toledo, Tama County, Iowa, January 13, 1898; attended a country school in Mahaska County and high school in New Sharon, Iowa; was graduated from Grinnell (Iowa) College in 1918; during the First War World served as a private in the United States Army; M.A., University of Chicago, 1921; Ph.D., University of Wisconsin, 1929; teacher in Oskaloosa (Iowa) High School, 1921-1923; professor at Penn College, Oskaloosa, Iowa, 1923-1927, at the University of Akron, Akron, Ohio, 1928-1937, at Michigan State College, East Lansing, Mich., 1937-1963; in charge of speakers bureau, Office of Civil Defense, Washington, D.C., in 1942 and 1943; in charge of

relations with the States on fuel conservation for the Department of the Interior, 1944-1946; owner of Plastics Manufacturing Co., 1950-1963; unsuccessful candidate for election to the Eighty-third Congress in 1952; elected as a Democrat to the Eighty-fourth Congress (January 3, 1955-January 3, 1957); unsuccessful candidate for reelection in 1956 to the Eighty-fifth Congress, for election in 1958 to the Eighty-sixth Congress, and in 1962 to the Eighty-eighth Congress; consultant, Department of Agriculture, 1963-1964; consultant, Social Security Administration, 1965-1967; was a resident of Washington, D.C., until his death there on February 25, 1982.

**HAYWORTH, John D., Jr.,** a Representative from Arizona; born in High Point, Guilford County, N.C., July 12, 1958; graduated, High Point Central High School, 1976; B.A., North Carolina State University, 1980; sports anchor and reporter for television stations in Ohio, North Carolina, and South Carolina; sports director, Channel 10, Phoenix, Ariz.; news reporter, radio station KUKQ, Phoenix; Governor's Task Force on Domestic Violence; elected as a Republican to the One Hundred Fourth Congress (January 3, 1995-January 3, 1997); is a resident of Mesa, Ariz.

**HAZARD, Jonathan J.,** a Delegate from Rhode Island; born in Newport, R.I., in 1744; completed preparatory studies; member of the State house of representatives in 1776; paymaster in the Continental Battalion from Rhode Island in 1777 and joined General Washington's Army in New Jersey that year; again elected a member of the State house of representatives and a member of the council of war in 1778; Member of the Continental Congress 1788; again a member of the State house of representatives 1790-1805; moved to New York in 1805 and located upon an estate in the Friends' settlement at Verona, Oneida County, N.Y., where he died later than 1824.

**HAZARD, Nathaniel,** a Representative from Rhode Island; born in Newport, R.I., in 1776; was graduated from Brown University, Providence, R.I., in 1792; member of the State house of representatives in 1818 and 1819 and served as speaker; elected to the Sixteenth Congress and served from March 4, 1819, until his death in Washington, D.C., December 17, 1820; interment in the Congressional Cemetery.

**HAZELTINE, Abner,** a Representative from New York; born in Wardsboro, Windham County, Vt., June 10, 1793; attended the common schools; was graduated from Williams College, Williamstown, Mass., in 1815; moved to Jamestown, N.Y., November 2, 1815; taught school; studied law; was admitted to the bar in 1819 and commenced practice in Chautauqua County, N.Y.; moved to Warren, Pa., and was the first located lawyer in the county; moved to Jamestown, Chautauqua County, N.Y., and resumed the practice of law in 1823; editorial writer on the Jamestown Journal 1826-1829; member of the State assembly in 1829 and 1830; elected as an Anti-Masonic candidate to the Twenty-third Congress and reelected as a Whig to the Twenty-fourth Congress (March 4, 1833-March 3, 1837); was not a candidate for renomination in 1836; prosecuting attorney of Chautauqua County 1847-1850; judge of Chautauqua County 1859-1863; appointed special county judge of Chautauqua County in 1873 but did not qualify; United States commissioner for the northern district of New York until his death; died in Jamestown, N.Y., on December 20, 1879; interment in Lakeview Cemetery.

**HAZELTINE, Ira Sherwin,** a Representative from Missouri; born in Andover, Windsor County, Vt., July 13, 1821; attended the common schools and pursued an academic course; moved to Richland Center, Wis., in 1842; taught school in Natchez, Miss., for three years; studied law and was admitted to the bar; laid out and named the city of Richland Center, Wis., in 1851 and practiced law there; delegate to the Republican National Convention of 1860; member of the State house of representatives 1867-1869; engaged in farming near Springfield, Greene County, Mo., in 1870; elected as a Greenbacker to the Forty-seventh Congress (March 4, 1881-March 3, 1883); unsuccessful candidate for reelection in 1882 to the Forty-eighth Congress; died near Springfield, Mo., January 13, 1899; interment in Hazelwood Cemetery, Springfield, Mo.

**HAZELTON, George Cochrane** (brother of Gerry Whiting Hazelton and nephew of Clark Beaton Cochrane), a Representative from Wisconsin; born in Chester, Rockingham County, N.H., January 3, 1832; attended the district schools; prepared for college at Pinkerton Academy in New Hampshire and Dummer Academy in Massachusetts; was graduated from Union College, Schenectady, N.Y., in 1858; studied law; was admitted to the bar at Malone, N.Y., in 1858; settled in Boscobel, Wis., in 1863 and practiced his profession; prosecuting attorney of Grant County 1864-1868; member of the State senate 1867-1869; was reelected in 1869 and served as president pro tempore of the senate 1869-1871; elected as a Republican to the Forty-fifth, Forty-sixth, and Forty-seventh Congresses (March 4, 1877-March 3, 1883); chairman, Committee on Pacific Railroads (Forty-seventh Congress); unsuccessful candidate for renomination in 1882; settled in Washington, D.C., and practiced law; attorney for the District of Columbia during the Harrison administration; died in Chester, N.H., while on a visit, September 4, 1922; interment in Vale Cemetery, Schenectady, N.Y.

**HAZELTON, Gerry Whiting** (brother of George Cochrane Hazelton and nephew of Clark Beaton Cochrane), a Representative from Wisconsin; born in Chester, Rockingham County, N.H., on February 24, 1829; attended the common schools, Pinkerton Academy, Derry, N.H., and received instruction from a private tutor; taught school; studied law; was admitted to the bar in 1852 and commenced practice in Amsterdam, N.Y.; moved to Wisconsin in 1856 and settled in Columbus; served in the State senate in 1860 and was chosen president pro tempore; delegate to the Republican National Convention of 1860; district attorney for Columbia County in 1864; appointed collector of internal revenue for the second district of Wisconsin in 1866 and removed by President Andrew Johnson the same year; elected as a Republican to the Forty-second and Forty-third Congresses (March 4, 1871-March 3, 1875); was not a candidate for renomination in 1874 to the Forty-fourth Congress; moved to Milwaukee in 1876; United States attorney for the eastern district of Wisconsin 1876-1885; appointed special master in chancery in 1912; United States court commissioner and commissioner for Milwaukee County for many years; engaged in the practice of law at Milwaukee, Wis., until his death September 29, 1920; interment in Forest Home Cemetery.

**HAZELTON, John Wright,** a Representative from New Jersey; born in Mullica Hill, Gloucester County, N.J., December 10, 1814; attended the common schools; engaged in agricultural pursuits; delegate to the Republican National Convention in 1856 and 1868; elected as a Republican to the Forty-second and Forty-third Congresses (March 4, 1871-March 3, 1875); unsuccessful candidate for reelection in 1874 to the Forty-fourth Congress; resumed agricultural pursuits; died near Mullica Hill, N.J., December 20, 1878; interment in Friends Cemetery, Mullica Hill, N.J.

**HAZLETT, James Miller,** a Representative from Pennsylvania; born in Londonderry, Ireland, October 14, 1864; when two years of age immigrated to the United States with his parents who settled in South Philadelphia, Pa.; attended the public schools of Philadelphia; began working in his father's blacksmith shop in 1881, and, was engaged as a farrier (one specializing in the treatment of horses' feet) until 1915; nominated and elected to the Philadelphia Common Council in 1896 and served in councils for sixteen years, resigning as president of the select council in 1911; president of the Philadelphia Board of Road Viewers, 1911-1916; recorder of deeds of Philadelphia, 1915-1936; elected as a Republican to the Seventieth Congress, and served from March 4, 1927 until his resignation on

October 20, 1927, before the convening of Congress; elected chairman of the Republican Central Campaign Committee in May 1928 and served until 1934; delegate to the Republican National Conventions in 1928 and 1932; member of the Board of Road Viewers from November 7, 1935 until he retired on February 23, 1937; died at Philadelphia, Pa., November 8, 1941; interment in West Laurel Hill Cemetery.

**HEALD, William Henry,** a Representative from Delaware; born in Wilmington, Del., August 27, 1864; was graduated from the public schools of Wilmington, from the University of Delaware at Newark in 1883 and from the law department of George Washington University, Washington, D.C., in 1888; national bank examiner for the States of Montana, Idaho, Washington, and Oregon 1888-1892; was admitted to the bar and commenced practice in Wilmington, Del., in 1897; postmaster of Wilmington 1901-1905; elected as a Republican to the Sixty-first and Sixty-second Congresses (March 4, 1909-March 3, 1913); was not a candidate for renomination in 1912; resumed the practice of law in Wilmington, Del.; also engaged in banking; member of the board of trustees of the University of Delaware 1915-1939 and served as president from 1936 until his death; died in Wilmington, Del., June 3, 1939; interment in Wilmington and Brandywine Cemetery.

**HEALEY, Arthur Daniel,** a Representative from Massachusetts; born in Somerville, Middlesex County, Mass., on December 29, 1889; attended the public schools; was graduated from Somerville (Mass.) Latin School in 1908; attended Dartmouth College, Hanover, N.H., in 1909 and 1910 and was graduated from the law department of Boston (Mass.) University in 1913; was admitted to the bar in 1914 and commenced practice in Boston, Mass.; during the First World War enlisted on August 9, 1917, and served through the ranks to second lieutenant in the Quartermaster Corps, being discharged on March 6, 1919; elected as a Democrat to the Seventy-third and to the four succeeding Congresses and served from March 4, 1933, until his resignation on August 3, 1942, to accept an appointment as judge of the United States District Court for Massachusetts, in which capacity he served until his death in Somerville, Mass., September 16, 1948; interment in Oak Grove Cemetery, Medford, Mass.

**HEALEY, James Christopher,** a Representative from New York; born in the Bronx, New York City, December 24, 1909; attended the public schools of New York City; B.S., Wharton School of the University of Pennsylvania, Philadelphia, 1933; attended Fordham; LL.B., St. John's Law School, 1936; admitted to the New York bar in 1937; attorney, New York State Labor Relations Board, 1938-1940; assistant United States attorney for the southern district of New York, 1940-1943; served in the United States Navy, lieutenant, 1943-1946; assistant corporation counsel for the city of New York, 1946-1948; counsel to the borough president of the Bronx, 1948-1956; elected as a Democrat to the Eighty-fourth Congress, by special election, February 7, 1956, to fill the vacancy caused by the resignation of Sidney A. Fine; reelected to the Eighty-fifth and to the three succeeding Congresses and served from February 7, 1956, to January 3, 1965; unsuccessful candidate in 1964 to the Eighty-ninth Congress; delegate, Democratic National Conventions, 1956, 1960, and 1968; resided in Southampton, N.Y. until his death there on December 16, 1981; interment at Sacred Heart Cemetery.

**HEALY, Joseph,** a Representative from New Hampshire; born in Newton, Middlesex County, Mass., August 21, 1776; completed preparatory studies; was a hotel keeper and also engaged in agricultural pursuits; member of the State senate in 1824; elected to the Nineteenth and Twentieth Congresses (March 4, 1825-March 3, 1829); member of the State executive council 1829-1832; resumed agricultural pursuits and the hotel business; died in Washington, Sullivan County, N.H., October 10, 1861; interment in the Old Cemetery.

**HEALY, Ned Romeyn,** a Representative from California; born in Milwaukee, Wis., August 9, 1905; attended the public schools, Marquette University, Milwaukee, Wis., and the University of Wisconsin at Madison; stock and bond salesman at Milwaukee, Wis., 1929-1932; moved to Los Angeles, Calif., in 1932 and engaged in merchandising and office management; director of the Hollywood office of the California State Relief Administration in 1939 and 1940; member of the Los Angeles City Council in 1943 and 1944; delegate to the Democratic State conventions in 1944, 1946, and 1948; elected as a Democrat to the Seventy-ninth Congress (January 3, 1945-January 3, 1947); unsuccessful candidate for reelection in 1946 to the Eightieth Congress and for election in 1948 to the Eighty-first Congress; dealer in auto parts and accessories in Los Angeles, 1947-1969; died in Long Beach, Calif., September 10, 1977; cremated; ashes scattered at sea off the coast of Long Beach, Calif.

**HEARD, John Taddeus,** a Representative from Missouri; born in Georgetown, Pettis County, Mo., October 29, 1840; attended the public schools and was graduated from the University of Missouri at Columbia in 1860; studied law; was admitted to the bar in 1862 and practiced several years in Sedalia, Pettis County, Mo.; member of the State house of representatives 1872-1875; served in the State senate 1880-1884; employed in 1881 by the fund commissioners of the State to prosecute and adjust all claims of the State against the General Government; elected as a Democrat to the Forty-ninth and to the four succeeding Congresses (March 4, 1885-March 3, 1895); chairman, Committee on District of Columbia (Fifty-third Congress); unsuccessful candidate for reelection in 1894 to the Fifty-fourth Congress; delegate to the Democratic National Convention in 1904; engaged in banking; retired from active business in 1922; died while on a visit to Los Angeles, Calif., January 27, 1927; interment in Crown Hill Cemetery, Sedalia, Mo.

**HEARST, George** (father of William Randolph Hearst), a Senator from California; born near Sullivan, Franklin County, Mo., September 3, 1820; attended the public schools and graduated from the Franklin County Mining School in 1838; upon news of the discovery of gold, moved to California in 1850; highly successful prospector; engaged in mining, stock raising, and farming; moved to San Francisco in 1862; member of the California State assembly, 1865-1866; owner of the San Francisco Examiner; unsuccessful Democratic candidate for governor of California in 1882; appointed as a Democrat to the United States Senate to fill the vacancy caused by the death of John F. Miller, and served from March 23, 1886 to August 4, 1886, when a successor was elected; elected in 1887 to the United States Senate as a Democrat, and served from March 4, 1887 until his death in Washington, D.C., February 28, 1891; interment in Cypress Lawn Cemetery, Colma, Calif.

**Bibliography:** *DAB*; Older, Fremont. *George Hearst, California Pioneer*. Los Angeles: Westernlore, 1966.

**HEARST, William Randolph** (son of George Hearst), a Representative from New York; born in San Francisco, Calif., April 29, 1863; attended the public schools and Harvard University; became editor and proprietor of the San Francisco Examiner in 1887 and established a nationwide chain of newspapers; also owner and publisher of many magazines; elected as a Democrat to the Fifty-eighth and Fifty-ninth Congresses (March 4, 1903-March 3, 1907); was not a candidate for renomination in 1906 to the Sixtieth Congress, but was an unsuccessful candidate for election for Governor of New York; in 1904 was a prominent candidate for the Democratic presidential nomination, receiving 263 votes on the first ballot at the national convention in St. Louis; was the Municipal Ownership candidate for mayor of New York City in 1905 and 1909; organized the Independence League Party in 1908; resumed his publishing business; died in Beverly Hills, Calif., August 14, 1951; interment in Cypress Lawn Cemetery, Colma, Calif.

**Bibliography:** *DAB*; Myatt, James A. "William Randolph Hearst and the Progressive Era, 1900-1912." Ph.D. dissertation, University of Florida, 1960; Swanberg, W.A. *Citizen Hearst: A Biography of William Randolph Hearst*. New York: Scribner, 1961.

**HEATH, James P.,** a Representative from Maryland; born in Delaware, December 21, 1777; completed preparatory studies; served in the Regular Army as lieutenant of Engineers 1799-1802; register in chancery in Annapolis, Md.; served throughout the War of 1812 as aide-de-camp to General Winder; elected as a Jacksonian to the Twenty-third Congress (March 4, 1833-March 3, 1835); unsuccessful candidate for reelection in 1834 to the Twenty-fourth Congress; died in Georgetown, D.C., June 12, 1854; interment in Oak Hill Cemetery, Washington, D.C.

**HEATH, John,** a Representative from Virginia; born in Wicomico Parish, Northumberland County, Va., May 8, 1758; educated by tutors; attended the College of William and Mary, Williamsburg, Va.; one of the students who organized the Phi Beta Kappa on December 5, 1776, and was elected its president; served in the Revolutionary War; studied law; was admitted to the bar and practiced in Northumberland County; served as Commonwealth's attorney from September 10, 1781, to May 12, 1784, and from November 15, 1787, to May 13, 1793; member of the privy council for several years; served in the Virginia house of delegates in 1782 but declined reelection, having again been appointed Commonwealth's attorney; elected to the Third Congress and reelected as a Republican to the Fourth Congress (March 4, 1793-March 3, 1797); declined to be a candidate for renomination in 1796 to the Fifth Congress; resumed the practice of law in Heathsville, Northumberland County; moved to Richmond, Va., in 1803, having been appointed a member of the Virginia Privy Council on December 30, 1803, and served until his death; was also engaged in the practice of law; died in Richmond, Va., October 13, 1810.

**HEATON, David,** a Representative from North Carolina; born in Hamilton, Butler County, Ohio, March 10, 1823; completed preparatory studies; studied law; was admitted to the bar; elected to the State senate in 1855; moved to St. Anthony Falls, Minn., in 1857; member of the State senate of Minnesota 1858-1863; appointed special agent of the Treasury Department and the United States depository in New Bern, N.C., in 1863; appointed Third Auditor of the Treasury in 1864, but declined; served as a member of the constitutional convention of North Carolina in 1867; upon the readmission of North Carolina to representation was elected as a Republican to the Fortieth Congress; reelected to the Forty-first Congress and served from July 15, 1868, until his death; chairman, Committee on Coinage, Weights, and Measures (Forty-first Congress); had been nominated as a Republican candidate for reelection to the Forty-second Congress; died in Washington, D.C., on June 25, 1870; interment in the National Cemetery, New Bern, N.C.

**HEATON, Robert Douglas,** a Representative from Pennsylvania; born in Raven Run, Schuylkill County, Pa., July 1, 1873; moved to Ashland, Pa., with his parents in 1886; attended the common schools, the Canandaigua Academy, Canandaigua, N.Y., the New York Military Academy, at Cornwall on the Hudson, N.Y., and the University of Pennsylvania at Philadelphia; identified with many business enterprises of the Commonwealth and county; unsuccessful candidate for election in 1910 to the Sixty-second Congress; elected as a Republican to the Sixty-fourth and Sixty-fifth Congresses (March 4, 1915-March 3, 1919); did not seek renomination in 1918, having become a candidate for Pennsylvania senator; member of the Pennsylvania senate 1919-1932; resumed his former business activities; member of the board of trustees of the Ashland State Hospital; died at Ashland, Pa., June 11, 1933; interment in the family cemetery at Mauch Chunk, Pa.

**HEATWOLE, Joel Prescott,** a Representative from Minnesota; born at Waterford Mills, Elkhart County, Ind., August 22, 1856; attended the public schools; learned the printer's trade; taught school and later became superintendent of the Millersburg (Ind.) School; employed by the Millersburg newspaper in 1876 and afterward became editor and proprietor; moved to Minnesota in 1882 and settled in Glencoe; in 1884 moved to Northfield, Minn., and published the Northfield News; delegate to the Republican State conventions in 1886 and 1888; elected secretary of the Republican State central committee in 1886 and 1888 and served as chairman in 1890; delegate to the Republican National Convention of 1888; appointed a member of the board of regents of the State university in 1890; president of the State Editorial Association; unsuccessful candidate for election in 1892 to the Fifty-third Congress; elected mayor of Northfield in 1894; elected as a Republican to the Fifty-fourth and to the three succeeding Congresses (March 4, 1895-March 3, 1903); chairman, Committee on Ventilation and Acoustics (Fifty-fifth Congress); was not a candidate for renomination in 1902 to the Fifty-eighth Congress; resumed his former newspaper pursuits; unsuccessful candidate for nomination for Governor of Minnesota in 1908; died in Northfield, Minn., April 4, 1910; interment in Oaklawn Cemetery.

**HEBARD, William,** a Representative from Vermont; born in Windham, Conn., November 29, 1800; attended the common schools and the Orange County Grammar School in Randolph, Vt.; studied law; was admitted to the bar in 1827 and commenced practice in East Randolph, Vt.; prosecuting attorney of Orange County 1832-1836; member of the State house of representatives in 1835; served in the State senate in 1836 and 1838; judge of probate of Randolph district in 1838, 1840, and 1841; again a member of the State house of representatives 1840-1842, 1858, 1859, 1864, 1865, and 1872; elected associate judge of the State supreme court in 1842 and 1844; moved to Chelsea, Vt., in 1845; elected as a Whig to the Thirty-first and Thirty-second Congresses (March 4, 1849-March 3, 1853); delegate to the constitutional convention in 1857; again a member of the general assembly in 1858, 1859, 1864, 1865, and 1872; resumed the practice of law; delegate to the Republican National Convention in 1860; died in Chelsea, Orange County, Vt., October 20, 1875; interment in the Old Cemetery, Randolph Center, Vt.

**HÉBERT, Felix,** a Senator from Rhode Island; born near St. Hyacinthe, Province of Quebec, Canada, December 11, 1874; came to the United States when his parents returned in 1880 and resumed their residence in the town of Coventry, R.I.; attended the public schools, the parish school of St. Jean Baptiste, West Warwick, R.I., and La Salle Academy, Providence R.I.; employed as a railroad freight billing clerk from 1893 to 1896, and as a private secretary from 1896 to 1898; deputy insurance commissioner of Rhode Island, 1898-1906; studied law; was admitted to the bar in 1907 and commenced practice in Providence, R.I.; justice of the district court of the fourth judicial district of Rhode Island, 1908-1928; trustee of the Nathanael Green Homestead Association of Rhode Island, 1924-1934; member and secretary of the Providence County Courthouse Commission, 1925-1934; elected as a Republican to the United States Senate, and served from March 4, 1929 to January 3, 1935; unsuccessful candidate for reelection in 1934; Republican whip 1933-1935; chairman, Committee on Patents (Seventy-second Congress); resumed the practice of law; member of the Republican National Committee, 1944-1952; advisory counsel to the Associated Factory Mutual Fire Insurance Companies; died in Warwick, R.I., December 14, 1969; interment in St. Joseph's Cemetery, West Warwick, R.I.

**HÉBERT, Felix Edward,** a Representative from Louisiana; born in New Orleans, La., October 12, 1901; attended public and parochial schools, Jesuit High School, New Orleans, La., and Tulane University, New Orleans, La., 1920-1924; engaged in newspaper and editorial work in New Orleans, La., 1918-1940; colonel on the staff of the Governor of Louisiana in 1936; served as personal representative of the Governor in Washington, D.C., in 1940; elected as a Democrat to the Seventy-seventh and to the seventeen succeeding Congresses (January 3, 1941-January 3, 1977); chairman, Committee on Armed Services (Ninety-second and Ninety-third Congresses); was not a candidate for reelection in 1976 to the Ninety-fifth Congress; resided in New Orleans, La., where he died on December 29, 1979; entombment in Lake Lawn Park Mausoleum.

**Bibliography:** *DAB*; Conrad, Glenn R. *Creed of a Congressman: F. Edward Hébert of Louisiana.* Lafayette: University of Southwestern Louisiana, 1970; Hébert, Felix Edward, with John McMillan. *"Last of the Titans": The Life and Times of Congressman F. Edward Hébert of Louisiana.* Edited by Glenn R. Conrad. Lafayette: University of Southwestern Louisiana, 1976.

**HECHLER, Kenneth W.,** a Representative from West Virginia; born near Roslyn, Long Island, N.Y., September 20, 1914; attended the Roslyn public schools; A.B., Swarthmore (Pa.) College, 1935; A.M., Columbia University, 1936, Ph.D., 1940; taught political science at Columbia, Barnard, Princeton and Marshall Universities; research assistant to Judge Samuel I. Rosenman and President Franklin D. Roosevelt on Roosevelt's public papers; section chief, Bureau of the Census, 1940; personnel officer, Office for Emergency Management, 1941; administrative analyst, United States Bureau of the Budget, in 1942 and 1946; entered the United States Army in 1942 as a private in the Infantry; commissioned a second lieutenant, Armored Force, in 1943; assigned to European Theater of Operations as combat historian in 1944; discharged as a major in 1946; special assistant to President Harry S Truman, 1949-1953; associate director of American Political Science Association at Washington, D.C., 1953-1956; research director for the 1956 presidential campaign of Adlai E. Stevenson; administrative aide to Senator John A. Carroll of Colorado in 1957; moved to Huntington, W.Va., in 1957 to teach at Marshall University; delegate to the Democratic National Conventions of 1964, 1968, 1972, 1980 and 1984; elected as a Democrat to the Eighty-sixth and to the eight succeeding Congresses (January 3, 1959-January 3, 1977); was not a candidate for reelection in 1976 to the Ninety-fifth Congress, but was an unsuccessful candidate for nomination for Governor of West Virginia; subsequently was an unsuccessful write-in candidate in 1976 for reelection to the Ninety-fifth Congress; host of a daily talk show and a writer for a weekly newspaper column; unsuccessful Democratic candidate for nomination in 1978 to the Ninety-sixth Congress; science consultant, House Committee on Science and Technology, 1980-1982; taught at the University of Charleston and Marshall University, 1981-1984; elected secretary of state of West Virginia in 1984; is a resident of Huntington, W.Va.

**Bibliography:** Hechler, Ken. *Working with Truman. A Personal Memoir of the White House Years.* New York: G.P. Putnam's Sons, 1982; Moffat, Charles H. *Ken Hechler: Maverick Public Servant.* Charleston, W.Va.: Mountain State Press, 1987.

**HECHT, Jacob Chic,** a Senator from Nevada; born in Cape Girardeau, Mo., November 30, 1928; B.A., Washington University School of Business, St. Louis, Mo., 1949; served in the United States Army Intelligence Corps as a special agent 1951-1953; owner of clothing stores in Las Vegas, Nev.; president, Retail Merchants of Las Vegas; director, Las Vegas Chamber of Commerce; represented Clark County in the Nevada State senate 1967-1975; elected as a Republican to the United States Senate in 1982 for the term ending January 3, 1989; unsuccessful candidate for reelection in 1988; confirmed by the Senate as Ambassador to The Bahamas, July 11, 1989; is a resident of Las Vegas, Nev.

**HECKLER, Margaret M.,** a Representative from Massachusetts; born June 21, 1931, in Flushing, Queen's County, N.Y.; Albertus Magnus College, B.A., 1953; Boston College Law School, LL.B., 1956; attended the University of Leiden in the Netherlands, 1952; editor, Annual Survey of Massachusetts Law; admitted to Massachusetts bar in 1956; elected a Governor's councilor, Commonwealth of Massachusetts from 1962-1966; delegate to the Republican National Conventions of 1964 and 1968; elected as a Republican to the Ninetieth and to the seven succeeding Congresses (January 3, 1967-January 3, 1983); unsuccessful candidate for reelection in 1982 to the Ninety-eighth Congress; Secretary of Health and Human Services in the Cabinet of President Ronald Reagan, March 9, 1983 to December 13, 1985; appointed Ambassador to Ireland on December 17, 1985, and served until August 1989; is a resident of Wellesley, Mass.

**HEDGE, Thomas,** a Representative from Iowa; born in Burlington, Iowa, June 24, 1844; attended the common schools and Denmark (Iowa) Academy; was graduated from Phillips Academy, Andover, Mass., in 1861, Yale College in 1867, and Columbia College Law School, New York City, in 1869; was admitted to the bar in New York in 1869 and commenced practice in Burlington, Iowa; served as a private during the Civil War in Company E and as second lieutenant in Company G, One Hundred and Sixth Regiment, New York Volunteer Infantry, in 1864 and 1865; resumed the practice of law in Burlington, Iowa; elected as a Republican to the Fifty-sixth and to the three succeeding Congresses (March 4, 1899-March 3, 1907); was not a candidate for renomination in 1906; resumed the practice of law; died in Burlington, Iowa, November 28, 1920; interment in Aspen Grove Cemetery.

**HEDRICK, Erland Harold,** a Representative from West Virginia; born in Barn, Mercer County, W.Va., August 9, 1894; attended the public schools and Beckley (W.Va.) Institute; was graduated from the medical school of the University of Maryland at Baltimore in 1917; served in the United States Army Medical Corps as a first lieutenant 1917-1919; engaged in the practice of medicine in Beckley, W.Va., 1919-1944; medical examiner for the Veterans' Administration 1919-1944; city and county health officer 1927-1932; superintendent of Pinecrest Tuberculosis Sanitarium, Beckley, W.Va., 1943-1944; elected as a Democrat to the Seventy-ninth and to the three succeeding Congresses (January 3, 1945-January 3, 1953); was not a candidate for renomination in 1952 but was unsuccessful for the Democratic gubernatorial nomination; resumed business and professional interests; died in Beckley, W.Va., September 20, 1954; interment in Sunset Memorial Park.

**HEFFERNAN, James Joseph,** a Representative from New York; born in Brooklyn, Kings County, N.Y., November 8, 1888; attended private and public schools; was graduated from Bryant Stratton College, Brooklyn, N.Y., in 1906 and from Pratt Institute, Brooklyn, N.Y., in 1908; engaged in architectural pursuits in 1908; commissioner of highways, Brooklyn, N.Y., 1926-1933; delegate to the State constitutional convention in 1938; elected as a Democrat to the Seventy-seventh and to the five succeeding Congresses (January 3, 1941-January 3, 1953); was not a candidate for renomination in 1952; architect; died in Long Branch, N.J., January 27, 1967, interment in Holy Cross Cemetery, Brooklyn, N.Y.

**HEFLEY, Joel M.,** a Representative from Colorado; born in Ardmore, Okla., April 18, 1935; attended public schools; graduated Classen High School, Oklahoma City, Okla., 1953; B.A., Oklahoma Baptist University, Shawnee, 1957; M.S., Oklahoma State University, Stillwater, 1962; industrial relations, Western Electric Co., 1961-1962; executive director, Big Brothers, 1962-1965; executive director, Community Planning and Research Council, 1966-1986; executive director, Pikes Peak Health Planning, 1971-1973; member, Colorado State house of representatives, 1977-1978; Colorado State senate, 1979-1986; elected as a Republican to the One Hundredth and to the four succeeding Congresses (January 3, 1987-January 3, 1997); is a resident of Colorado Springs, Colo.

**HEFLIN, Howell Thomas** (nephew of James Thomas Heflin), a Senator from Alabama; born in Poulan, Worth County, Ga., June 19, 1921; attended the Alabama public schools; graduated Colbert County High School, Leighton, Ala.; B.A., Birmingham Southern College, 1942; J.D., University of Alabama School of Law, Tuscaloosa, 1948; admitted to the Alabama bar in 1948 and commenced practice in Tuscumbia, Ala.; served in the United States Marine Corps, 1942-1946; law professor; chief justice of the Alabama State supreme court from 1971 until 1977; elected as a Democrat to the United States Senate in 1978; reelected in 1984 and 1990, and served from January 3, 1979 to January 3, 1997; was not a candidate for reelection in 1996; chairman, Select Committee on Ethics (Ninety-sixth, One Hundredth through One Hundred Second Congresses); is a resident of Tuscumbia, Ala.

**HEFLIN, James Thomas** (nephew of Robert Stell Heflin and uncle of Howell Thomas Heflin), a Representative and a Senator from Alabama; born in Louina, Randolph County, Ala., April 9, 1869; attended the common schools of Randolph County, Southern University, Greensboro, Ala., and Alabama Agricultural and Mechanical College (later Auburn University), Auburn, Ala.; studied law, was admitted to the bar in 1893, and commenced practice in Lafayette, Ala.; mayor of Lafayette 1893-1894; register in chancery from 1894 to 1896, when he resigned; member, State house of representatives 1896-1900; member of the State constitutional convention in 1901; secretary of State 1902-1904, when he resigned; elected as a Democrat to the Fifty-eighth Congress to fill the vacancy caused by the death of Charles W. Thompson; reelected to the Fifty-ninth and to the seven succeeding Congresses and served from May 10, 1904, until November 1, 1920, when he resigned, having become a candidate for Senator; chairman, Committee on Industrial Arts and Expositions (Sixty-second Congress); elected to the United States Senate as a Democrat November 2, 1920, to fill the vacancy caused by the death of John H. Bankhead 1st, in the term ending March 3, 1925; reelected in 1924 and served from November 3, 1920, to March 3, 1931; unsuccessful candidate for reelection in 1930, and for election to the House and Senate on several other occasions; special assistant to the United States Attorney General in Alabama 1936-1937; appointed special representative of the Federal Housing Administration 1935-1936, 1939-1942; retired; died in Lafayette, Ala., April 22, 1951; interment in Lafayette Cemetery.

Bibliography: *DAB*; Tanner, Ralph M. "James Thomas Heflin: United States Senator, 1920-1931." Ph.D. dissertation, University of Alabama, 1967; Thornton, J. Mills. "Alabama Politics, J. Thomas Heflin, and the Expulsion Movement in 1929." *Alabama Review* 21 (April 1968): 83-ll2.

**HEFLIN, Robert Stell** (uncle of James Thomas Heflin), a Representative from Alabama; born near Madison, Morgan County, Ga., April 15, 1815; pursued academic studies; served in the Creek War in 1836; clerk of the superior court of Fayette County, Ga., 1836-1840; studied law; was admitted to the bar in 1840 and practiced in Fayetteville, Ga., and Wedowee, Ala.; served in the State senate of Georgia in 1840 and 1841; moved to Randolph County, Ala., in 1844; member of the Alabama house of representatives in 1849 and 1860; served in the State senate in 1860; judge of probate of Randolph County, Ala., in 1865 and 1866; elected as a Republican to the Forty-first Congress (March 4, 1869-March 3, 1871); died near Wedowee, Randolph County, Ala., January 24, 1901; interment in Masonic Cemetery.

**HEFNER, Willie Gathrel (Bill)** (father-in-law of Charles Grandison Rose III), a Representative from North Carolina; born in Elora, Lincoln County, Tenn., April 11, 1930; attended Elora (Tenn.) Elementary School, 1936-1941; graduated, Sardis (Ala.) High

School, 1948; attended University Center (a division of the University of Alabama), 1948; president and owner, radio station WRKB in Kannapolis, N.C.; member, Harvesters Quartet, a group of Gospel music singers based in North Carolina, 1954-1967; television performer on numerous North Carolina TV channels; elected as a Democrat to the Ninety-fourth and to the ten succeeding Congresses (January 3, 1975-January 3, 1997); is a resident of Concord, N.C.

**HEFTEL, Cecil Landau,** a Representative from Hawaii; born in Chicago, Cook County, Ill., September 30, 1924; attended the public schools of Chicago, Ill.; B.S. Arizona State University, Tempe, 1951; engaged in graduate work at the University of Utah and New York University; businessman; president, Heftel Broadcasting, Honolulu, Hawaii; served in United States Army, 1943-1946; delegate, Hawaii State Democratic convention, 1972; delegate to the Democratic National Convention of 1972; elected as a Democrat to the Ninety-fifth and to the four succeeding Congresses and served from January 3, 1977, until his resignation July 11, 1986; was an unsuccessful candidate for the Democratic nomination for Governor of Hawaii; resumed business interests; is a resident of Honolulu, Hawaii.

**Bibliography:** Rosen, Sidney M. "Cec Heftel: New Politics and the Media Man." Ph.D. dissertation, University of Hawaii, 1985.

**HEIDINGER, James Vandaveer,** a Representative from Illinois; born on a farm near Mount Erie, Wayne County, Ill., July 17, 1882; attended the rural schools, Northern Illinois Normal School, De Kalb, Ill., and Valparaiso (Ind.) University; taught in the rural schools of Wayne County, Ill.; was graduated from Northern Illinois College of Law, Dixon, Ill., in 1908; was admitted to the bar the same year and commenced practice in Fairfield, Ill.; county judge of Wayne County, Ill., 1914-1926; assistant attorney general of Illinois, 1927-1933; delegate to the Republican National Convention of 1928; unsuccessful candidate for election in 1930 to the Seventy-second Congress, and for election in 1934 to the Seventy-fourth Congress; elected as a Republican to the Seventy-seventh and to the two succeeding Congresses, and served from January 3, 1941 until his death in Phoenix, Ariz., on March 22, 1945; interment in Maple Hill Cemetery, Fairfield, Ill.

**HEILMAN, William** (great-grandfather of Charles Marion LaFollette), a Representative from Indiana; born in Albig, Duchy of Hesse-Darmstadt, Germany, October 11, 1824; immigrated to the United States in 1843 and settled on a farm in Vanderburg County, Ind.; moved to Evansville, Ind.; worked for a manufacturing company and subsequently became president of a cotton mill; founded a machine shop for the manufacture of drills in 1847; member of the city council 1852-1865; member of the State house of representatives 1870-1876; delegate to the Republican National Convention in 1876; served in the State senate from 1876 until March 3, 1879; elected as a Republican to the Forty-sixth and Forty-seventh Congresses (March 4, 1879-March 3, 1883); unsuccessful candidate for reelection in 1882 to the Forty-eighth Congress; resumed his former business activities; died in Evansville, Ind., September 22, 1890; interment in Oak Hill Cemetery.

**HEINEMAN, Frederick Kenneth (Fred),** a Representative from North Carolina; born in New York City, December 28, 1929; graduated Mount St. Michael High School, Bronx, N.Y., 1947; B.A., St. Francis College, Brooklyn, N.Y., 1970; M.A., City University of New York John Jay College of Criminal Justice, 1975; entered active duty, United States Marine Corps in 1951; released in 1954; various positions with New York City Police Department, retiring as deputy chief; chief of police, City of Raleigh, N.C., 1979-1995; elected as a Republican to the One Hundred Fourth Congress (January 3, 1995-January 3, 1997); is a resident of Raleigh, N.C.

**HEINER, Daniel Brodhead,** a Representative from Pennsylvania; born in Kittanning, Armstrong County, Pa., December 30, 1854; attended the public schools at Kittanning, Dayton (Pa.) Academy, and Dickinson Law School at Carlisle, Pa.; was graduated from Allegheny College, Meadville, Pa., in 1879; was admitted to the bar of Armstrong County, Pa., in 1882 and commenced practice in Kittanning; also engaged in banking; elected district attorney of Armstrong County, Pa., in 1885, reelected in 1888, and served until January 1, 1892; chairman of the Republican county executive committee 1884-1888; elected as a Republican to the Fifty-third and Fifty-fourth Congresses (March 4, 1893-March 3, 1897); was not a candidate for renomination in 1896; appointed by President McKinley as United States district attorney for the western district of Pennsylvania and served from 1897 to 1902; appointed on February 2, 1902, as internal-revenue collector for the twenty-third district of Pennsylvania by President Theodore Roosevelt and served until November 1, 1913; delegate to the Republican National Convention in 1920; again served as internal-revenue collector 1921-1933; died at Kittanning, Pa., on February 14, 1944; interment in Kittanning Cemetery.

**HEINKE, George Henry,** a Representative from Nebraska; born on a farm near Dunbar, Otoe County, Nebr., July 22, 1882; moved with his parents to Douglas, Nebr., in 1889, to San Angelo, Tex., in 1891, and to Talmage, Nebr., in 1894; attended the public schools; was graduated from the law department of the University of Nebraska at Lincoln in 1908; was admitted to the bar the same year and commenced practice in Nebraska City, Nebr.; prosecuting attorney of Otoe County, Nebr., 1919-1923 and 1927-1935; elected as a Republican to the Seventy-sixth Congress and served from January 3, 1939, until his death in Morrilton, Ark., January 2, 1940, as a result of injuries received in an automobile accident near there while en route to Washington, D.C., to attend a session of Congress; interment in Wyuka Cemetery, Nebraska City, Nebr.

**HEINTZ, Victor,** a Representative from Ohio; born on a farm near Grayville, White County, Ill., November 20, 1876; attended the public schools; was graduated from the University of Cincinnati in 1896 and from its law department in 1899; was admitted to the bar in 1898 and commenced practice in Cincinnati, Ohio; served six years in the Cavalry and Infantry of the Ohio National Guard; elected as a Republican to the Sixty-fifth Congress (March 4, 1917-March 3, 1919); was not a candidate for renomination in 1918; during the First World War absented himself from the House and was commissioned a captain in the One Hundred and Forty-seventh Regiment, United States Infantry, on August 4, 1917; went overseas June 22, 1918, and served until the end of the war; decorated with the Distinguished Service Cross with Oak Leaf Cluster, Silver Star Medal, Purple Heart, and the Croix de Guerre; vice president and secretary of Ohio Valley Real Estate Co.; resumed the practice of law until his retirement in 1961; died in Cincinnati, Ohio, December 27, 1968; interment in Armstrong Chapel Cemetery, Indian Hill, Cincinnati, Ohio.

**HEINZ, Henry John, III,** a Representative and a Senator from Pennsylvania; born in Pittsburgh, Pa., October 23, 1938; graduated, Phillips Exeter Academy, 1956; B.A., Yale University, 1960; M.A., Harvard Graduate School of Business Administration, 1963; served in the United States Air Force with the Nine Hundred and Eleventh Troop Carrier Group, 1963; United States Air Force Reserve, 1963-1969; special assistant to Senator Hugh D. Scott, 1964; faculty member and lecturer, Graduate School of Industrial Administration, Carnegie-Mellon University, Pittsburgh, Pa., 1970-1971; business career included positions as analyst, controller's division, and numerous positions in the marketing division of the H.J. Heinz Co., Pittsburgh, Pa., plus positions with other firms; elected as a Republican to the Ninety-second Congress, November 2, 1971, by special election to fill the vacancy caused by the death of Robert J.

Corbett; reelected to the Ninety-third and Ninety-fourth Congresses and served from November 2, 1971, to January 3, 1977; was not a candidate for reelection in 1976 to the House of Representatives, but was elected to the United States Senate; reelected in 1982 and again in 1988, and served from January 3, 1977 until his death in an airplane collision on April 4, 1991; chairman, Republican Senatorial Campaign Committee (Ninety-sixth and Ninety-ninth Congresses), Special Committe on Aging (Ninety-seventh through Ninety-ninth Congresses).

**HEISKELL, John Netherland,** a Senator from Arkansas; born in Rogersville, Hawkins County, Tenn., on November 2, 1872; attended the public and private schools of Memphis; graduated from the University of Tennessee at Knoxville in 1893; after leaving college engaged in newspaper work; became editor of the Arkansas Gazette and president of the Gazette Publishing Co. in 1902 at Little Rock, Ark.; appointed as a Democrat to the United States Senate, January 6, 1913, to fill the vacancy caused by the death of Jeff Davis and served from January 6 to January 29, 1913, when a successor was elected; was not a candidate for election in 1913; resumed his former newspaper career and took an active interest in the Arkansas Gazette, which won two Pulitzer prizes while under his editorship, until his death December 28, 1972, at the age of one hundred, in Little Rock, Ark.; interment in Mount Holly Cemetery.

**HEITFELD, Henry,** a Senator from Idaho; born in St. Louis, Mo., January 12, 1859; attended public and private schools; moved to Kansas, then Washington, and finally to Lewiston, Idaho, in 1883; engaged in agricultural pursuits and stock raising; member, State senate 1894-1897; elected as a Populist to the United States Senate on January 28, 1897, and served from March 4, 1897, to March 3, 1903; was not a candidate for reelection in 1902; unsuccessful candidate in 1904 for election for Governor of Idaho; mayor of Lewiston 1905-1909; register of the United States land office at Lewiston 1914-1922; engaged in fruit growing; member of the board of county commissioners 1930-1936, serving two terms as chairman; retired in 1938 and resided in Spokane, Wash., until his death in that city on October 21, 1938; interment in Norman Hill Cemetery, Lewiston, Idaho.

**HELGESEN, Henry Thomas,** a Representative from North Dakota; born near Decorah, Iowa, June 26, 1857; attended the public schools, the John Breckenridge Normal Institute, and the J.R. Slack Business College at Decorah; moved to Milton, Dakota Territory (now North Dakota), in 1887; engaged in the mercantile and lumber business and also in agricultural pursuits; State commissioner of agriculture and labor 1889-1892; member of the board of education of Milton, N.Dak., 1893-1896, and served as president in 1893 and 1894; member of the board of regents of the University of North Dakota 1897-1901 and 1907-1913; elected as a Republican to the Sixty-second and to the three succeeding Congresses and served from March 4, 1911, until his death in Washington, D.C., April 10, 1917; interment in Phelps Cemetery, Decorah, Iowa.

**HELLER, Louis Benjamin,** a Representative from New York; born in New York City on February 10, 1905; attended the public schools; LL.B., Fordham University School of Law, New York City, 1926; was admitted to the bar in 1927 and commenced the practice of law in Brooklyn, N.Y.; served as special deputy assistant attorney general in election fraud cases in New York 1936-1946; appeal agent, United States Selective Service, New York, 1941 and 1942; member of the New York State senate in 1943 and 1944; appointed by Governor Thomas E. Dewey as secretary of the New York State Temporary Commission Against Discrimination in 1944 and 1945; Democratic State committeeman and executive member (leader) of the sixth assembly district of Kings County, N.Y., 1944-1954; elected as a Democrat to the Eighty-first Congress to fill the vacancy caused by the death of John J. Delaney; reelected to the Eighty-second and

Eighty-third Congresses and served from February 15, 1949, until his resignation July 21, 1954; appointed a judge of the Court of Special Sessions of New York City and served from July 22, 1954, to December 1958, when elected a justice of the city court of the city of New York, in which position he served until August 6, 1966; judge of the Supreme Court of the State of New York, 1966-1977; was a resident of Brooklyn, N.Y.; died October 30, 1993.

**HELM, Harvey,** a Representative from Kentucky; born in Danville, Boyle County, Ky., December 2, 1865; attended the Stanford Male Academy and was graduated from the Central University of Kentucky in 1887; studied law; was admitted to the bar in 1890 and began practice in Stanford, Ky.; member of the Kentucky house of representatives in 1894; county attorney of Lincoln County 1897-1905; delegate to the Democratic National Convention in 1900; elected as a Democrat to the Sixtieth and to the six succeeding Congresses and served from March 4, 1907, until his death before the commencement of the Sixty-sixth Congress; chairman, Committee on Expenditures in the Department of War (Sixty-second Congress), Committee on the Census (Sixty-third through Sixty-fifth Congresses); died in Columbus, Miss., March 3, 1919; interment in Buffalo Spring Cemetery, Stanford, Ky.

**HELMICK, William,** a Representative from Ohio; born near Canton, Stark County, Ohio, September 6, 1817; attended the public schools; studied law; was admitted to the bar in 1845 and commenced practice in New Philadelphia, Tuscarawas County, Ohio; prosecuting attorney of Tuscarawas County in 1851; elected as a Republican to the Thirty-sixth Congress (March 4, 1859-March 3, 1861); unsuccessful candidate for reelection in 1860 to the Thirty-seventh Congress; appointed by President Lincoln chief clerk of the Pension Office on May 3, 1861, and served until January 31, 1865; resumed the practice of law in Washington, D.C.; appointed justice of the peace by President Rutherford B. Hayes in 1877; died in Washington, D.C., March 31, 1888; interment in the Congressional Cemetery.

**HELMS, Jesse A.,** a Senator from North Carolina; born in Monroe, Union County, N.C., October 18, 1921; educated in the public schools of Monroe, Wingate Junior College, and Wake Forest College; served in the United States Navy, 1942-1945; city editor, Raleigh Times, 1941-1942; news and program director, WRAL Radio, 1948-1951; administrative assistant to United States Senators Willis Smith, 1951-1953, and Alton Lennon, 1953; executive director, North Carolina Bankers Association, 1953-1960; television and radio executive, 1960-1972; member, Raleigh City Council, 1957-1961; elected as a Republican to the United States Senate in 1972 for the term commencing January 3, 1973; reelected in 1978, 1984, and again in 1990 for the term ending January 3, 1997; chairman, Committee on Agriculture, Nutrition, and Forestry (Ninety-seventh through Ninety-ninth Congresses), Committee on Foreign Relations (One Hundred Fourth Congress); is a resident of Raleigh, N.C.

**HELMS, William,** a Representative from New Jersey; born in Sussex County, N.J.; served during the Revolutionary War as second lieutenant, first lieutenant, and captain, and was brevetted major on September 30, 1783; member of the New Jersey State house of assembly in 1791 and 1792; elected as a Republican to the Seventh and to the four succeeding Congresses (March 4, 1801-March 3, 1811); moved to Hamilton County, Ohio; died in 1813.

**HELSTOSKI, Henry,** a Representative from New Jersey; born in Wallington, Bergen County, N.J., March 21, 1925; attended the Wallington and Rutherford schools; served in the United States Army Air Corps as instructor and radio technician, 1943-1945; attended Paterson State College and graduated from Montclair State Teachers College, B.A., 1947, and M.A., 1949; teacher, high school principal, and superintendent of schools in Bergen County,

N.J., 1949-1962; served as councilman of East Rutherford, N.J., in 1956, and as mayor 1957-1965; management consultant in advertising, 1962-1964; elected as a Democrat to the Eighty-ninth and to the five succeeding Congresses (January 3, 1965-January 3, 1977); unsuccessful candidate for reelection as an independent to the Ninety-fifth Congress; unsuccessful candidate for election as an independent in 1978 to the Ninety-sixth Congress and as a Democrat for nomination in 1980 to the Ninety-seventh Congress; superintendent, North Bergen schools, 1981-1985; currently engaged as a public relations consultant; is a resident of East Rutherford, N.J.

**HELVERING, Guy Tresillian,** a Representative from Kansas; born in Felicity, Clermont County, Ohio, January 10, 1878; moved to Kansas in 1887 with his parents, who settled in Beattie, Marshall County; attended the public schools; during the Spanish-American War enlisted as a corporal in Company M, Twenty-second Regiment, Kansas Infantry, and served from May 12 to November 3, 1898; attended the University of Kansas at Lawrence; was graduated from the law department of the University of Michigan at Ann Arbor in 1906; was admitted to the bar in the same year and commenced practice in Marysville, Kans.; prosecuting attorney of Marshall County 1907-1911; unsuccessful Democratic candidate for election in 1910 to the Sixty-second Congress; elected as a Democrat to the Sixty-third, Sixty-fourth, and Sixty-fifth Congresses (March 4, 1913-March 3, 1919); unsuccessful candidate for reelection in 1918 to the Sixty-sixth Congress; moved to Salina, Saline County, Kans., and became engaged in banking; Democratic State chairman 1930-1934; mayor of Salina, Kans., from February 15, 1926, until his resignation on December 8, 1930; State highway director in 1931 and 1932; appointed Commissioner of Internal Revenue by President Franklin D. Roosevelt in 1933 and served until his appointment as a Federal district judge for Kansas in 1943, in which capacity he was serving at the time of his death in Washington, D.C., on July 4, 1946; interment in Marysville Cemetery, Marysville, Kans.

**HEMENWAY, James Alexander,** a Representative and a Senator from Indiana; born in Boonville, Warrick County, Ind., March 8, 1860; attended the common schools; studied law; was admitted to the bar and commenced practice in Boonville in 1885; prosecuting attorney for the second judicial circuit of Indiana 1886-1890; elected as a Republican to the Fifty-fourth and to the five succeeding Congresses and served from March 4, 1895, until his resignation, effective March 3, 1905, at the close of the Fifty-eighth Congress, having been elected Senator; chairman, Committee on Appropriations (Fifty-eighth Congress); elected as a Republican to the United States Senate to fill the vacancy caused by the resignation of Charles W. Fairbanks and served from March 4, 1905, to March 3, 1909; unsuccessful candidate for reelection; chairman, Committee on University of the United States (Fifty-ninth and Sixtieth Congresses); resumed the practice of law in Boonville, Ind.; died in Miami, Dade County, Fla., February 10, 1923; interment in Maple Grove Cemetery, Boonville, Warrick County, Ind.

**HEMPHILL, John** (uncle of John James Hemphill and great-great-uncle of Robert Witherspoon Hemphill), a Senator from Texas; born in Chester District, S.C., December 18, 1803; attended the common schools; taught school; graduated from Jefferson College in 1825; studied law; was admitted to the bar in 1829 and commenced practice in Sumter, S.C.; edited a nullification newspaper in 1832 and 1833; second lieutenant in the war with the Seminole Indians in 1836; moved to Texas in 1838 and practiced law; elected judge of the fourth judicial district of Texas, 1840-1842; adjutant general on a military expedition to the Rio Grande in 1842; member of the state constitution convention in 1845; chief justice of the supreme court of Texas, 1846-1858; elected as a State Rights Democrat to the United States Senate and served from March 4,

1859, until expelled from the Senate by a resolution of July 11, 1861 for support of the Confederacy; representative of Texas in the Congress of the Confederate States of America until his death in Richmond, Va., January 4, 1862; interment in State Cemetery, Austin, Tex.

**Bibliography:** *DAB*; Curtis, Rosalee. *John Hemphill: First Chief Justice of the State of Texas.* Austin: Jenkins Publishing Co., 1971.

**HEMPHILL, John James** (cousin of William Huggins Brawley, nephew of John Hemphill and great-uncle of Robert Witherspoon Hemphill), a Representative from South Carolina; born in Chester, Chester County, S.C., August 25, 1849; attended the public schools and was graduated from the University of South Carolina at Columbia in 1869; studied law; was admitted to the bar in 1870 and practiced in Chester, S.C.; unsuccessful candidate for the State legislature in 1874; member of the State house of representatives 1876-1882; elected as a Democrat to the Forty-eighth and to the four succeeding Congresses (March 4, 1883-March 3, 1893); chairman, Committee on District of Columbia (Fiftieth and Fifty-second Congresses); unsuccessful candidate for reelection in 1892 to the Fifty-third Congress; resumed the practice of law in Washington, D.C., while retaining his residence in South Carolina; unsuccessful candidate for election as United States Senator from South Carolina in 1902; died in Washington, D.C., May 11, 1912; interment in Oak Hill Cemetery.

**HEMPHILL, Joseph,** a Representative from Pennsylvania; born in Thornburg Township, Chester County, Pa., January 7, 1770; completed a preparatory course; was graduated from the University of Pennsylvania at Philadelphia in 1791; studied law; was admitted to the bar in 1793 and commenced practice in West Chester, Pa.; member of the Pennsylvania house of representatives 1797-1800; elected as a Federalist to the Seventh Congress (March 4, 1801-March 3, 1803); moved to Philadelphia in 1803; again a member of the Pennsylvania house of representatives in 1805; appointed the first president judge of the district court of the city and county of Philadelphia; elected to the Sixteenth and to the three succeeding Congresses and served from March 4, 1819, until his resignation in 1826; elected as a Jacksonian to the Twenty-first Congress (March 4, 1829-March 3, 1831); member of the State house of representatives in 1831 and 1832; died in Philadelphia, Pa., May 29, 1842; interment in Laurel Hill Cemetery.

**Bibliography:** *DAB*.

**HEMPHILL, Robert Witherspoon** (great-great-nephew of John Hemphill, great-nephew of John J. Hemphill, great-nephew of William Huggins Brawley, and great-great-grandson of Robert Witherspoon), a Representative from South Carolina; born in Chester, S.C., May 10, 1915; attended the public schools; graduated from the University of South Carolina in 1936 and from the law school of the same university in 1938; was admitted to the bar in 1938 and commenced the practice of law in Chester; volunteered in 1941 as a flying cadet in the United States Air Force, and served as a bomber pilot until December 1945; chairman of Chester County Democratic conventions in 1946 and 1947; member of South Carolina State house of representatives, 1947-1948; solicitor of the Sixth South Carolina Judicial Circuit, 1951-1956; delegate to the North Atlantic Treaty Organization Congress in London in 1959; elected as a Democrat to the Eighty-fifth and to the three succeeding Congresses, and served from January 3, 1957 until his resignation on May 1, 1964, when he was sworn in as United States district judge of South Carolina; was a resident of Chester, S.C. until his death there on December 25, 1983; interment in Hopewell Associate Reformed Presbyterian Church Cemetery, Chester, S.C.

**HEMPSTEAD, Edward,** a Delegate from the Territory of Missouri; born in New London, Conn., June 3, 1780; pursued academic studies; studied law; was admitted to the bar in 1801 and commenced practice in Rhode Island; moved to St. Louis, Mo. (then District of Louisiana), in 1805; attorney general of the Territory of Upper Louisiana 1809-1811; served in several expeditions against the Indians north of the Missouri River; member of the third Territorial general assembly in 1812 and served as speaker; elected as a Delegate to the Thirteenth Congress on November 9, 1812, and served until September 17, 1814; declined to be a candidate for renomination; was thrown from a horse August 4, 1817, which resulted in his death August 10, 1817, at St. Louis, Mo.; interment on Hempstead Farm, now a part of Bellefontaine Cemetery.

**HEMSLEY, William,** a Delegate from Maryland; born at "Clover Fields Farm," near Queenstown, Queen Annes County, Md., in 1737; engaged in planting; provincial treasurer of Eastern Shore, Md., in 1773; surveyor of Talbot County, Md.; colonel of the Twentieth Battalion, Queen Annes County Militia, in 1777; justice of the peace of Queen Annes County in 1777; member of the State senate 1779-1781; Member of the Continental Congress 1782-1783; again served in the State senate in 1786, 1790, and 1800; resumed agricultural pursuits; died in Queen Annes County, June 5, 1812; interment in Clover Fields Farm Cemetery, Queen Annes County, Md.

**HENDEE, George Whitman,** a Representative from Vermont; born in Stowe, Lamoille County, Vt., November 30, 1832; attended the common schools of Morrisville, Vt., and People's Academy; studied law; was admitted to the bar in 1855 and commenced practice in Morrisville, Vt.; prosecuting attorney of Lamoille County in 1858 and 1859; member of the State house of representatives in 1861 and 1862; during the Civil War served as deputy provost marshal; served in the State senate 1866-1868; lieutenant governor of Vermont in 1869; assumed the office of Governor on February 7, 1870, after the death of Governor Peter T. Washburn, and served until October 6, 1870; elected as a Republican to the Forty-third and to the two succeeding Congresses (March 4, 1873-March 3, 1879); unsuccessful candidate for renomination in 1878 to the Forty-sixth Congress; resumed the practice of law; national-bank examiner 1879-1885; interested in the breeding of Morgan horses; died in Morrisville, Vt., on December 6, 1906; interment in Pleasant View Cemetery.

**HENDERSON, Archibald,** a Representative from North Carolina; born near Williamsborough, Granville County, N.C., August 7, 1768; attended the common schools and was graduated from Springer College; moved to Salisbury, N.C., about 1790; studied law; was admitted to the bar and commenced practice in Salisbury; clerk and master in equity 1795-1798; elected as a Federalist to the Sixth and Seventh Congresses (March 4, 1799-March 3, 1803); member of the State house of commons 1807-1809, 1814, 1819, and 1820; resumed the practice of law in Salisbury, N.C., and died there October 21, 1822; interment in the City Cemetery.

**Bibliography:** *DAB.*

**HENDERSON, Bennett H.,** a Representative from Tennessee; born in Bedford, Bedford County, Va., September 5, 1784; moved to Tennessee; elected as a Republican to the Fourteenth Congress (March 4, 1815-March 3, 1817); died in Summitville, Tenn.

**HENDERSON, Charles Belknap,** a Senator from Nevada; born in San Jose, Calif., June 8, 1873; moved with his parents to Nevada in 1876; attended the public schools of Elko, Nev.; attended the University of the Pacific in 1892, and Leland Stanford Junior University in California; received a law degree from the University of Michigan in 1895, and received a master's degree from the same institution in 1896; was admitted to the bar in 1896 and commenced practice in Elko, Nev.; served as a lieutenant in Torrey's Rough Riders during the Spanish-American War; district attorney of Elko County, 1901-1905; member, Nevada State house of representatives, 1905-1907; regent of the University of Nevada, 1907-1917; appointed and subsequently elected as a Democrat to the United States Senate to fill the vacancy caused by the death of Francis G. Newlands, and served from January 12, 1918 to March 3, 1921; unsuccessful candidate for reelection in 1920; chairman, Committee on Industrial Expositions (Sixty-fifth Congress), Committee on Mines and Mining (Sixty-fifth Congress); appointed a member of the board of directors of the Reconstruction Finance Corporation in 1934, elected chairman in 1941, and served until his resignation in 1947; retired from political activities; president and director of the Elko Telephone and Telegraph Co., and a director of the Western Pacific Railroad; died in San Francisco, Calif., November 8, 1954; interment in Elko Cemetery, Elko, Nev.

**HENDERSON, David Bremner,** a Representative from Iowa; born in Old Deer, Scotland, March 14, 1840; immigrated to the United States with his parents, who settled in Winnebago County, Ill., in 1846; moved to Fayette County, Iowa, in 1849; attended the common schools and the Upper Iowa University at Fayette; enlisted in the Union Army September 15, 1861, as a private in Company C, Twelfth Regiment, Iowa Volunteer Infantry; was elected and commissioned first lieutenant of that company and served with it until discharged, owing to the loss of a leg, February 26, 1863; commissioner of the board of enrollment of the third district of Iowa from May 1863 to June 1864; entered the Army as colonel of the Forty-sixth Regiment, Iowa Volunteer Infantry, and served until the close of the war; studied law; was admitted to the bar in 1865 and commenced practice in Dubuque, Iowa; collector of internal revenue for the third district of Iowa from November 1865 to June 1869 when he resigned; assistant United States district attorney for the northern district of Iowa 1869-1871; elected as a Republican to the Forty-eighth and to the nine succeeding Congresses (March 4, 1883-March 3, 1903); chairman, Committee on Militia (Fifty-first Congress), Committee on the Judiciary (Fifty-fourth and Fifty-fifth Congresses), Committee on Rules (Fifty-sixth and Fifty-seventh Congresses); Speaker of the House of Representatives (Fifty-sixth and Fifty-seventh Congresses); declined to be a candidate for renomination in 1902; died in Dubuque, Iowa, February 25, 1906; interment in Linwood Cemetery.

**Bibliography:** *DAB.*

**HENDERSON, David Newton,** a Representative from North Carolina; born on a farm near Hubert, Onslow County, N.C., April 16, 1921; graduated from Wallace (N.C.) High School in 1938; B.S., Davidson (N.C.) College, 1942; LL.B., University of North Carolina Law School, 1949; commissioned a second lieutenant in the United States Army Air Corps as a Reserve graduate of Davidson College in June 1942; served overseas in India, China, and on Okinawa, and was discharged as a major in 1946; began the practice of law in Wallace, N.C., in April 1949; assistant general counsel to the Committee on Education and Labor, United States House of Representatives, 1951-1952; solicitor of the Duplin County General Court, 1954-1958, and judge from December 1958 to December 1960; elected as a Democrat to the Eighty-seventh and to the seven succeeding Congresses (January 3, 1961-January 3, 1977); chairman, Committee on Post Office and Civil Service (Ninety-fourth Congress); was not a candidate for reelection in 1976 to the Ninety-fifth Congress; resumed the practice of law; is a resident of Wallace, N.C.

**HENDERSON, James Henry Dickey,** a Representative from Oregon; born near Salem, Ky., July 23, 1810; moved to Missouri Territory in 1817; attended the public schools; learned the art of printing; entered the ministry and was pastor of a church in Washington County, Pa., 1843-1851; returned to Missouri and published a literary magazine; moved to Oregon in 1852 and settled in Yamhill County; moved to Eugene, Lane County, and engaged in agricultural pursuits, specializing in the raising of fruits; superintendent of the public schools of Lane County in 1859; elected as a Union Republican to the Thirty-ninth Congress (March 4, 1865-March 3, 1867); unsuccessful candidate for renomination in 1866; returned to Eugene, Oreg., and engaged in agricultural pursuits; also preached, lectured, and wrote for periodicals; died in Eugene, Oreg., December 13, 1885; interment in Odd Fellows Cemetery.

**HENDERSON, James Pinckney,** a Senator from Texas; born in Lincolnton, Lincoln County, N.C., March 31, 1808; pursued academic studies in Lincolnton; attended the University of North Carolina at Chapel Hill; served in the Carolina Militia and subsequently was elected colonel; studied law; was admitted to the bar in 1828 and commenced practice in Lincolnton, N.C.; moved to Mississippi in 1835 and recruited a company for service in behalf of the Republic of Texas; preceded his company to Austin, Tex., in 1836 and was commissioned brigadier general; returned to the United States to recruit volunteers and raised a company at his own expense; appointed by President Sam Houston as Attorney General of the Republic of Texas in 1836, and as Secretary of State in 1837; visited Europe as the diplomatic representative of the Republic of Texas in 1838, and in 1844 visited the United States as special minister to negotiate annexation; member of the State constitutional convention in 1845; elected Governor of the State of Texas in 1846 and served from February 19, 1846 to December 21, 1847; commissioned major general in the United States Army and served in the Mexican War; appointed as a Democrat to the United States Senate to fill the vacancy caused by the death of Thomas J. Rusk and served from November 9, 1857, until his death in Washington, D.C., June 4, 1858; interment in Congressional Cemetery; reinterred in 1930 in the State Cemetery, Austin, Tex.

**Bibliography:** *DAB*; Winchester, Robert. *James Pickney Henderson, Texas' First Governor.* San Antonio: Naylor Company, 1971.

**HENDERSON, John,** a Senator from Mississippi; born in Cumberland County, N.J., February 28, 1797; a flatboat man on the Mississippi River; studied law; emigrated to Mississippi; was admitted to the bar and commenced practice in Woodville, Wilkinson County, Miss.; brigadier general of State militia; member, State senate 1835-1836; elected as a Whig to the United States Senate and served from March 4, 1839, to March 3, 1845; chairman, Committee on Engrossed Bills (Twenty-sixth Congress), Committee on the Post Office and Post Roads (Twenty-seventh Congress), Committee on Private Land Claims (Twenty-seventh and Twenty-eighth Congresses); resumed the practice of law in New Orleans, La.; in 1851 was tried in the United States district court in New Orleans for violation of the neutrality laws of 1818 for complicity in expeditions against Cuba, was acquitted, and retired from public life; died in Pass Christian, Miss., September 15, 1857; interment in Live Oak Cemetery.

**Bibliography:** *DAB.*

**HENDERSON, John Brooks,** a Senator from Missouri; born near Danville, Pittsylvania County, Va., November 16, 1826; moved with his parents to Lincoln County, Mo.; studied on his own while a farm hand; taught school; was admitted to the bar in 1844 and practiced; member, State house of representatives 1848-1850, 1856-1858; active in Democratic politics; commissioned a brigadier general in the State militia in 1861; appointed and subsequently elected to the United States Senate as a Unionist to fill the vacancy caused by the expulsion of Trusten Polk; reelected in 1863 and served from January 17, 1862, to March 3, 1869; was not a candidate for reelection; chairman, Committee to Audit and Control the Contingent Expense (Thirty-ninth Congress), Committee on Indian Affairs (Thirty-ninth and Fortieth Congresses); unsuccessful candidate in 1872 for election for Governor of Missouri; unsuccessful candidate for United States Senator; special United States attorney for prosecution of the Whiskey Ring at St. Louis in 1875; appointed a commissioner to treat with hostile tribes of Indians in 1877; moved to Washington, D.C., in 1888; writer; resided in the capital until his death, April 12, 1913; interment in Greenwood Cemetery, Brooklyn, N.Y.

**Bibliography:** *DAB*; Mattingly, Arthur H. "Senator John Brooks Henderson, United States Senator from Missouri." Ph.D. dissertation, Kansas State University, 1971.

**HENDERSON, John Earl,** a Representative from Ohio; born in Crafton, Allegheny County, Pa., January 4, 1917; moved to Cambridge, Ohio, in 1920 and to a dairy farm in Guernsey County, near Cambridge, Ohio, in 1922; attended the county schools of Guernsey County and high school at Cambridge; was graduated from Ohio Wesleyan University at Delaware in 1939 and from the University of Michigan Law School at Ann Arbor in 1942; was admitted to the Ohio bar in 1942; entered the United States Army as a private in 1942 and advanced to the rank of captain of infantry after combat service in Europe; following hostilities was assigned to the historical division of the European Theater and was discharged in 1946; commenced the practice of law in Cambridge, Ohio, in 1946; member of the Ohio State house of representatives 1951-1954; elected as a Republican to the Eighty-fourth and to the two succeeding Congresses (January 3, 1955-January 3, 1961); was not a candidate for renomination in 1960 to the Eighty-seventh Congress; resumed the practice of law; judge, Common Pleas Court, Guernsey County, Ohio; died December 3, 1994.

**HENDERSON, John Steele,** a Representative from North Carolina; born near Salisbury, Rowan County, N.C., January 6, 1846; attended a private school in Melville, N.C.; entered the University of North Carolina at Chapel Hill in January 1862 and left in November 1864 to enter the Confederate Army as a private in Company B, Tenth Regiment, North Carolina State Troops; served throughout the Civil War; was graduated from the University of North Carolina in 1865 without reentering; studied law; obtained a county court license in June 1866 and a superior court license in June 1867; appointed in June 1866 register of deeds for Rowan County and served until September 1868, when he resigned; delegate to the State constitutional covention in 1875; member of the State house of representatives in 1876; served in the State senate in 1878; elected by the general assembly in 1881 one of the three commissioners to codify the statute laws of the State; elected presiding justice of the inferior court of Rowan County in June 1884; elected as a Democrat to the Forty-ninth and to the four succeeding Congresses (March 4, 1885-March 3, 1895); chairman, Committee on the Post Office and Post Roads (Fifty-second and Fifty-third Congresses); resumed the practice of law in Salisbury, N.C.; elected to the State senate in 1900 and 1902; member of the board of aldermen in 1900; died in Salisbury, N.C., on October 9, 1916; interment in Chestnut Hill Cemetery.

**HENDERSON, Joseph,** a Representative from Pennsylvania; born in Shippensburg, Cumberland County, Pa., August 2, 1791; moved with his parents to Centre County, Pa., in 1802; attended the public schools and was graduated from the Jefferson Medical College at Philadelphia in 1813; during the War of 1812 was commissioned first lieutenant in the Twenty-second Regiment, Pennsylvania Volunteers, in the spring of 1813; promoted to captain in the fall of the same year; brevetted major and given command of a regiment in 1814; settled at Browns Mills, Pa., at the close of the war and engaged in the practice of medicine; elected as a Jacksonian to the Twenty-third and Twenty-fourth Congresses (March 4, 1833-March 3, 1837); was not a candidate for renomination in 1836; moved to Lewistown, Pa., in 1850 and continued the practice of medicine; died in Lewistown, Pa., December 25, 1863; interment in St. Mark's Cemetery.

**HENDERSON, Samuel,** a Representative from Pennsylvania; born in England on November 27, 1764; attended school in England; immigrated to the United States in 1782 and settled in Montgomery, Pa.; owned and operated the Henderson Marble Quarries in Montgomery County, Pa.; elected as a Federalist to the Thirteenth Congress to fill the vacancy caused by the resignation of Jonathan Roberts and served from October 11, 1814, to March 3, 1815; resumed former business pursuits; died on his estate at Upper Merion, Montgomery County, Pa., November 17, 1841; interment in the family burying ground, Montgomery County, Pa.

**HENDERSON, Thomas,** a Representative from New Jersey; born in Freehold, Monmouth County, N.J., August 15, 1743; attended the public schools and was graduated from Princeton College in 1761; studied medicine; practiced first in Freneau and afterwards in Freehold, N.J., about 1765; member of the committee of safety in 1774; served as a lieutenant in the New Jersey Militia in 1775; appointed second major in Colonel Charles Stewart's Battalion of Minutemen on February 15, 1776; brigade major, Monmouth County Militia, April 19, 1776; major of Colonel Nathaniel Heard's battalion June 14, 1776, and later lieutenant colonel and brigadier major at Monmouth; surrogate of Monmouth County in 1776; member of the provincial council in 1777; elected as a Delegate to the Continental Congress, November 17, 1779, but declined December 25, 1779; served in the State general assembly 1780-1784; master in chancery in 1790; member of the State council in 1793 and 1794, serving as vice president of that body; Acting Governor of New Jersey in 1794; elected as a Federalist to the Fourth Congress (March 4, 1795-March 3, 1797); judge of the court of common pleas 1783-1799; one of the commissioners appointed to settle the boundary line between New Jersey and Pennsylvania; again a member of the State council in 1812 and 1813; died in Freehold, N.J., December 15, 1824; interment in Old Tennent Cemetery, Tennent, N.J.

Bibliography: *DAB*.

**HENDERSON, Thomas Jefferson,** a Representative from Illinois; born in Brownsville, Haywood County, Tenn., November 29, 1824; moved with his parents to Illinois at the age of eleven; pursued academic studies; clerk of the Board of Commissioners of Stark County, Ill., 1847-1849; clerk of the court of Stark County 1849-1853; studied law; was admitted to the bar in 1852 and commenced practice in Toulon, Ill.; member of the State house of representatives in 1855 and 1856; served in the State senate 1857-1860; entered the Union Army in 1862 as colonel of the One Hundred and Twelfth Regiment, Illinois Volunteer Infantry; commanded Third Brigade, Third Division, Twenty-third Army Corps, from August 12, 1864, to the close of the war; was brevetted brigadier general in January 1865; resumed the practice of law; moved to Princeton, Ill., in 1867 and continued the practice of law; appointed collector of internal revenue for the fifth district of Illinois in 1871; elected as a Republican to the Forty-fourth and to the nine succeeding Congresses (March 4, 1875-March 3, 1895); chairman, Committee on Military Affairs (Forty-seventh Congress), Committee on Rivers and Harbors (Fifty-first Congress); unsuccessful candidate for renomination in 1894; appointed member of the board of managers for the National Home for Disabled Volunteer Soldiers in 1896; appointed civilian member on the Board of Ordnance and Fortifications in 1900 and served until his death in Washington, D.C., February 6, 1911; interment in Oakland Cemetery, Princeton, Ill.

**HENDON, William Martin,** a Representative from North Carolina; born in Asheville, Buncombe County, N.C., November 9, 1944; attended the public schools; graduated from Lee H. Edwards High School, 1962; B.S., University of Tennessee, Knoxville, 1966, and M.B.A., 1968; member of the faculty, University of Tennessee, 1968-1970, and Western Carolina University, Cullowhee, N.C., 1971-1972; general manager, Putsch and Co., 1974-1980; elected as a Republican to the Ninety-seventh Congress (January 3, 1981-January 3, 1983); unsuccessful candidate for reelection in 1982 to the Ninety-eighth Congress; elected to the Ninety-ninth Congress (January 3, 1985-January 3, 1987); unsuccessful candidate for reelection in 1986 to the One Hundredth Congress; fellow, American Defense Institute, Washington, D.C.; is a resident of McLean, Va.

**HENDRICK John Kerr,** a Representative from Kentucky; born in Caswell County, N.C., October 10, 1849; moved with his parents to Logan County and later to Todd County, Ky.; attended private schools and Bethel College, Russellville, Ky.; moved to Crittenden County, Ky., in 1869 and engaged in teaching school; studied law; was admitted to the bar in 1874 and commenced practice in Smithland, Ky.; prosecuting attorney of Livingston County 1878-1886; member of the Kentucky senate 1887-1891; delegate to the Democratic National Convention in 1888; elected as a Democrat to the Fifty-fourth Congress (March 4, 1895-March 3, 1897); unsuccessful candidate for renomination in 1896; resumed the practice of law in Paducah, Ky., where he died June 20, 1921; interment in Maplelawn Cemetery.

**HENDRICKS, Joseph Edward,** a Representative from Florida; born at Lake Butler, Union County, Fla., September 24, 1903; attended the rural schools and Montverde (Fla.) School; A.B., John B. Stetson University, De Land, Fla., 1930, and LL.B., 1934; was admitted to the bar in 1934 and commenced practice in De Land, Fla.; attorney for the legal tax survey of Florida in 1934; elected as a Democrat to the Seventy-fifth and to the five succeeding Congresses (January 3, 1937-January 3, 1949); was not a candidate for renomination in 1948 to the Eighty-first Congress; was president of Hendricks Homes, Inc.; chairman of Planning Board, Plant City, Fla.; member, County Planning Commission, Hillsborough County, Fla.; resided in Plant City, Fla., until his death in Lakeland, Fla., October 20, 1974; interment in Lakeland Memorial Cemetery.

Bibliography: Hendricks, Joseph Edward. *Little Joe: My Memories.* Kissimmee, Fla.: Cody Publications, Inc., 1966.

**HENDRICKS, Thomas Andrews** (nephew of William Hendricks), a Representative and a Senator from Indiana and a Vice President of the United States; born near Zanesville, Ohio, September 7, 1819; moved with his parents to Indiana in 1820; pursued classical studies and graduated from Hanover (Ind.) College in 1841; studied law in Chambersburg, Pa.; was admitted to the bar in 1843 and commenced practice in Shelbyville, Ind.; member of the Indiana State house of representatives in 1848; member of the State constitutional convention; elected as a Democrat to the Thirty-second and Thirty-third Congresses (March 4, 1851-March 3, 1855); unsuccessful candidate for reelection in 1854 to the Thirty-fourth Congress; chairman, Committee on Mileage (Thirty-second Congress), Committee on Invalid Pensions (Thirty-third Congress); Commissioner of the General Land Office, 1855-1859; unsuccessful candidate for election in 1860 and in 1868 for Governor of Indiana; moved to Indianapolis in 1860 and practiced law; elected as a Democrat to the United States Senate, and served from March 4, 1863 to March 3, 1869; elected Governor of Indiana in 1872, and served from January 13, 1873 to January 8, 1877; unsuccessful candidate for Vice President of the United States in 1876 on the Democratic ticket headed by Samuel J. Tilden; elected Vice President of the United States, November 4, 1884, on the Democratic ticket headed by Grover Cleveland, and served from March 4, 1885 until his death in Indianapolis, Ind., November 25, 1885; interment in Crown Hill Cemetery.

Bibliography: *DAB*; Holcombe, John W., and Hubert M. Skinner. *Life and Public Services of Thomas A. Hendricks.* Indianapolis: Carlon and Hollenbeck, 1886.

**HENDRICKS, William** (uncle of Thomas Andrews Hendricks), a Representative and a Senator from Indiana; born in Ligonier Valley, Westmoreland County, Pa., November 12, 1782; attended the common schools and graduated from Jefferson College (later Washington and Jefferson College), Washington, Pa., in 1810; taught school from 1810 to 1812; studied law in Cincinnati, Ohio; was admitted to the bar and practiced; moved to Madison, Indiana Territory, in 1813; became a printer and owner of the second printing press set up in the Territory; proprietor of the Western Eagle; elected to the territorial legislature in 1813 and 1814, and was chosen speaker of the Assembly in 1814; territorial printer; secretary of the first State constitutional convention in 1816; upon the admission of Indiana as a State into the Union was elected to the Fourteenth Congress; reelected to the three succeeding Congresses, and served from December 11, 1816 until his resignation on July 25, 1822, to become Governor; Governor of Indiana from December 5, 1822 until February 12, 1825, when he resigned to become a Senator; elected to the United States Senate in 1824; reelected in 1830, and served from March 4, 1825 to March 3, 1837; unsuccessful candidate for reelection in 1836; chairman, Committee on Roads and Canals (Twenty-first through Twenty-fourth Congresses); resumed the practice of law in Madison, Ind.; trustee of Indiana University at Bloomington 1829-1840; died in Madison, Ind., May 16, 1850; interment in Fairmount Cemetery.

**Bibliography:** *DAB*; Hill, Frederick Dinsmore. "William Hendricks: Indiana Politician and Western Advocate, 1812-1850." Ph.D. dissertation, Indiana University, 1972; Hill, Frederick D. "William Hendricks' Political Circulars to His Constituents: First Senatorial Term, 1826-1831." *Indiana Magazine of History* 71 (June 1975): 124-80; Hill, Frederick D. "William Hendricks' Political Circulars to His Constituents: Second Senatorial Term, 1831-1837. *Indiana Magazine of History* 71 (December 1975): 319-74.

**HENDRICKSON, Robert Clymer,** a Senator from New Jersey; born in Woodbury, Gloucester County, N.J., August 12, 1898; attended public schools; during the First World War enlisted in the United States Army in 1918 and served overseas; graduated from Temple University Law School, Philadelphia, Pa., in 1922, was admitted to the New Jersey bar, and commenced practice in Woodbury, N.J.; county supervisor 1929-1934; city solicitor of Woodbury 1931; State senator 1934-1940, serving as president of the senate in 1939; unsuccessful candidate in 1940 for election for Governor of New Jersey; State treasurer 1942-1948; member of board of managers, Council of State Governments, in 1940 and chairman in 1941; vice chairman of Commission on Delaware River Basin 1936-1951; during the Second World War enlisted in 1943, commissioned a major, served with the American Military Government in the Mediterranean Theater of Operations, promoted to lieutenant colonel in 1944, and separated from the service in 1946; elected as a Republican to the United States Senate in 1948, and served from January 3, 1949, to January 2, 1955; was not a candidate for renomination in 1954; appointed Ambassador to New Zealand by President Dwight D. Eisenhower on January 22, 1955 and served until November 1956; lawyer; was a resident of Woodbury, N.J., until his death December 7, 1964; interment in Eglington Cemetery, Clarksboro, N.J.

**HENDRIX, Joseph Clifford,** a Representative from New York; born in Fayette, Howard County, Mo., May 25, 1853; attended private schools and Central College at Fayette and Cornell University, Ithaca, N.Y., 1870-1873; moved to New York City in 1873 and worked for the New York Sun; appointed a member of the Board of Education of Brooklyn in 1882; unsuccessful Democratic candidate for mayor of Brooklyn in 1883; appointed trustee of the New York and Brooklyn Bridge in 1884; elected secretary of the board of bridge trustees in 1885; appointed postmaster of Brooklyn by President Cleveland in 1886 and served until July 1, 1890; elected president of the board of education of Brooklyn in 1887;

president of the Kings County Trust Co. 1889-1893; president of the National Union Bank of New York City 1893-1900; elected as a Democrat to the Fifty-third Congress (March 4, 1893-March 3, 1895); was not a candidate for renomination in 1894; president of the National Bank of Commerce in 1900; trustee of the Brooklyn Institute of Arts and Sciences; trustee of Cornell University; died in Brooklyn, N.Y., November 9, 1904; interment in Greenwood Cemetery.

**Bibliography:** *DAB*.

**HENKLE, Eli Jones,** a Representative from Maryland; born in Westminster, Carroll County, Md., November 24, 1828; completed an academic course; taught school in Anne Arundel County; studied medicine and was graduated from the University of Maryland at Baltimore in 1850; practiced his profession in Brooklyn, Md.; trustee and professor, Maryland Agricultural College at College Park; member of the State house of delegates in 1863; member of the State constitutional convention in 1864; served in the State senate in 1867, 1868, and 1870; again a member of the State house of delegates 1872-1875; delegate to the Democratic National Convention in 1872; elected as a Democrat to the Forty-fourth, Forty-fifth, and Forty-sixth Congresses (March 4, 1875-March 3, 1881); unsuccessful candidate for reelection in 1880 to the Forty-seventh Congress; moved to Chicago, Ill., in 1889, and later returned to Baltimore, Md., where he died November 1, 1893; interment in Druid Ridge Cemetery, Baltimore, Md.

**HENLEY, Barclay** (son of Thomas Jefferson Henley), a Representative from California; born in Charlestown, Clark County, Ind., March 17, 1843; moved with his parents to San Francisco, Calif., in 1853; returned to Indiana in 1858; attended the common schools and Hanover (Ind.) College; returned to San Francisco in 1861; studied law; was admitted to the bar in 1864 and commenced practice in Santa Rosa, Calif.; member of the State assembly in 1869 and 1870; district attorney of Sonoma County in 1875 and 1876; elected as a Democrat to the Forty-eighth and Forty-ninth Congresses (March 4, 1883-March 3, 1887); again settled in San Francisco and continued the practice of law until his death in that city on February 15, 1914; remains were cremated and the ashes interred in the Santa Rosa Cemetery, Santa Rosa, Calif.

**HENLEY, Thomas Jefferson,** (father of Barclay Henley), a Representative from Indiana; born in Richmond, Ind., April 2, 1810; attended Indiana University at Bloomington; studied law; was admitted to the bar in 1828 and commenced practice in Richmond, Ind.; engaged in banking; member of the State house of representatives 1832-1842 and served as speaker in 1840; elected as a Democrat to the Twenty-eighth, Twenty-ninth, and Thirtieth Congresses (March 4, 1843-March 3, 1849); chairman, Committee on Patents (Twenty-eighth and Twenty-ninth Congresses); moved to California in 1849 and engaged in banking in Sacramento; member of the first State house of representatives 1851-1853; superintendent of Indian affairs of California 1855-1858; postmaster of San Francisco 1860-1864; died in San Francisco, Calif., January 2, 1865; interment in Santa Rosa Cemetery, Santa Rosa, Calif.

**HENN, Bernhart,** a Representative from Iowa; born in Cherry Valley, N.Y., in 1817; attended the common schools; moved to Burlington, Iowa, in 1838; studied law; was admitted to the bar in Burlington, Iowa; moved to Fairfield, Iowa, when appointed register of the United States land office in 1845 by President Polk; elected as a Democrat to the Thirty-second and Thirty-third Congresses (March 4, 1851-March 3, 1855); engaged in banking and dealing in real estate; died in Fairfield, Iowa, August 30, 1865; interment in Evergreen Cemetery.

**HENNEY, Charles William Francis,** a Representative from Wisconsin; born on a farm near Dunlap, Harrison County, Iowa, February 2, 1884; attended the district school and Denison (Iowa) Normal School; taught in a district school in Crawford County, Iowa, 1902-1905; was graduated from the pharmacy department of Fremont (Nebr.) Normal School in 1906 and from the medical department of Northwestern University, Chicago, Ill., in 1910; moved to Portage, Columbia County, Wis., in 1912 and commenced the practice of medicine; delegate to all Democratic State conventions from 1920 to 1936; delegate to the Democratic National Conventions of 1936, 1940, 1944, and 1948; member of the Portage City Park Commission 1925-1933; chief of staff of St. Savior's Hospital, Portage City, Wis., in 1926 and 1927; elected as a Democrat to the Seventy-third Congress (March 4, 1933-January 3, 1935); unsuccessful candidate for reelection in 1934 to the Seventy-fourth Congress; resumed the practice of medicine and surgery; died in Portage, Wis., November 16, 1969; interment in St. Mary's Catholic Cemetery.

**HENNINGS, Thomas Carey, Jr.,** a Representative and a Senator from Missouri; born in St. Louis, Mo., June 25, 1903; attended the public schools; graduated from Cornell University, Ithaca, N.Y., in 1924 and from the law department of Washington University, St. Louis, Mo., in 1926; admitted to the bar in 1926 and commenced practice in St. Louis; served as assistant circuit attorney for St. Louis 1929-1934; served as a colonel on the staff of Governor Guy B. Park 1932-1936; lecturer on criminal jurisprudence at the Benton College of Law, St. Louis, Mo., 1934-1938; elected as a Democrat to the Seventy-fourth and to the two succeeding Congresses and served from January 3, 1935, until his resignation on December 31, 1940, to become a candidate for circuit attorney of St. Louis; circuit attorney for the city of St. Louis 1941-1944; served as a lieutenant commander in the United States Naval Reserve during Second World War 1941-1943; resumed the practice of law; elected as a Democrat to the United States Senate in 1950, reelected in 1956, and served from January 3, 1951, until his death in Washington, D.C., September 13, 1960; chairman, Committee on Rules and Administration (Eighty-fifth and Eighty-sixth Congresses); interment in Arlington National Cemetery, Va.

Bibliography: Kemper, Donald. *Decade of Fear: Senator Hennings and Civil Liberties.* Columbia: University of Missouri Press, 1965.

**HENRY, Charles Lewis,** a Representative from Indiana; born in Green Township, Hancock County, Ind., July 1, 1849; moved with his parents to Pendleton, Ind.; attended the common schools and Asbury (now De Pauw) University, Greencastle, Ind.; was graduated from the law department of Indiana University at Bloomington in 1872; was admitted to the bar and commenced practice in Pendleton; moved to Anderson, Ind., in 1875; member of the State senate in 1880, 1881, and 1883; elected as a Republican to the Fifty-fourth and Fifty-fifth Congresses (March 4, 1895-March 3, 1899); declined to be a candidate for renomination in 1898; interested in the development and operation of electric interurban railways; at the time of his death was president and receiver of the Indianapolis & Cincinnati Traction Co., which he had managed for twenty-three years; died in Indianapolis, Ind., May 2, 1927; interment in Maplewood Cemetery, Anderson, Ind.

**HENRY, Daniel Maynadier,** a Representative from Maryland; born near Cambridge, Dorchester County, Md., February 19, 1823; attended Cambridge Academy and St. John's College, Annapolis, Md.; studied law; was admitted to the bar in 1844 and practiced in Cambridge; member of the house of delegates in 1846 and 1849; served in the State senate in 1869; elected as a Democrat to the Forty-fifth and Forty-sixth Congresses (March 4, 1877-March 3, 1881); chairman, Committee on Accounts (Forty-sixth Congress);

resumed the practice of law; died in Cambridge, Md., August 31, 1899; interment in Christ Protestant Episcopal Church Cemetery.

**HENRY, Edward Stevens,** a Representative from Connecticut; born in the town of Gill, Franklin County, Mass., February 10, 1836; moved to Rockville, Conn.; attended the public schools; engaged in the dry-goods business; treasurer of the People's Saving Bank, Rockville, 1870-1921; member of the State house of representatives in 1883; served in the State senate in 1887 and 1888; delegate at large to the Republican National Convention in 1888; treasurer of the State of Connecticut 1889-1893; mayor of Rockville in 1894 and 1895; elected as a Republican to the Fifty-fourth and to the eight succeeding Congresses (March 4, 1895-March 3, 1913); chairman, Committee on Expenditures on Public Buildings (Sixtieth and Sixty-first Congresses); declined to be a candidate for renomination in 1912; resumed his former mercantile pursuits in Rockville, Tolland County, Conn., where he died October 10, 1921; interment in Grove Hill Cemetery.

**HENRY, James,** a Delegate from Virginia; born in Accomac County, Va., in 1731; pursued classical studies; studied law at the University of Edinburgh; was admitted to the bar and practiced; member of the house of burgesses 1772-1774; member of the Virginia house of delegates in 1776, 1777, and 1779; member of the Continental Congress in 1780; judge of the Virginia court of admiralty 1782-1788; judge of the general court from December 24, 1788, to January 1800, when he resigned; died at his home, "Fleet Bay," in Northumberland County, Va., December 9, 1804.

**HENRY, John,** a Representative from Illinois; born near Stanford, Lincoln County, Ky., November 1, 1800; attended the public schools; served as a private in Captain Arnett's company of Illinois volunteers in the Black Hawk War; member of the State house of representatives 1832-1840; was prominently identified with the construction of the first railway in Illinois in 1838; member of the State senate 1840-1847; elected as a Whig to the Twenty-ninth Congress to fill the vacancy caused by the resignation of Edward D. Baker and served from February 5, 1847, to March 3, 1847; was not a candidate for election in 1846 to the Thirtieth Congress; superintendent of the State insane asylum at Jacksonville, Ill., 1850-1855; during the Civil War was connected with the Quartermaster's Department at Jackson, Tenn., from August 25, 1862, to April 30, 1863; died in St. Louis, Mo., April 28, 1882; interment in Bellefontaine Cemetery.

**HENRY, John,** a Delegate and a Senator from Maryland; born at "Weston," on the Nanticoke River, near Vienna, Dorchester County, Md., in November 1750; attended West Nottingham Academy, Cecil County, Md., and graduated from the College of New Jersey (later Princeton University) in 1769; studied law at the Middle Temple in London; returned to the United States in 1775 and practiced law in Dorchester County, Md.; member, Maryland General Assembly; Member of the Continental Congress 1778-1780 and 1785-1786; was a member of the committee to prepare the ordinance for the government of the Northwest Territory; elected as one of Maryland's first two Members to the United States Senate in 1788; reelected in 1795 and served from March 4, 1789, until December 10, 1797, when he resigned, having been elected Governor; chosen Governor of Maryland by the general assembly of the State, and served from November 17, 1797 to November 14, 1798; died at his country estate, "Weston," Dorchester County, Md., December 16, 1798; interment in Christ Episcopal Church Cemetery, Cambridge, Md.

Bibliography: *DAB;* Henry, John. *Letters and Papers of Governor John Henry.* Baltimore: G.W. King Printing Company, 1904.

**HENRY, John Flournoy,** a Representative from Kentucky; born at Henrys Mill, Scott County, Ky., on January 17, 1793; attended Georgetown Academy, Kentucky, and Jefferson Medical College, Philadelphia, Pa.; was graduated from the College of Physicians and Surgeons in 1817; served at Fort Meigs in 1813 as surgeon's mate of Kentucky troops; engaged in agricultural pursuits and the practice of medicine; elected to the Nineteenth Congress to fill the vacancy caused by the death of Robert P. Henry and served from December 11, 1826, to March 3, 1827; unsuccessful candidate for reelection in 1827 to the Twentieth Congress; professor in the Medical College of Ohio at Cincinnati in 1831; moved to Bloomington, Ill., in 1834 and to Burlington, Iowa, in 1845 and resumed the practice of medicine; died in Burlington, Iowa, November 12, 1873; interment in Aspen Grove Cemetery.

**HENRY, Lewis,** a Representative from New York; born in Elmira, Chemung County, N.Y., June 8, 1885; attended the public schools; was graduated from Elmira (N.Y.) Academy in 1904, from Cornell University, Ithaca, N.Y., in 1909, and from the law department of Columbia University, New York City, in 1911; was admitted to the bar in 1912 and commenced practice in Elmira, N.Y.; supervisor of the first ward of that city 1914-1920; delegate to the Republican State convention in 1920; elected as a Republican to the Sixty-seventh Congress to fill the vacancy caused by the resignation of Alanson B. Houghton and served from April 11, 1922, to March 3, 1923; unsuccessful candidate for renomination; resumed the practice of law at Elmira, N.Y.; president of the Oriental Consolidated Mining Company until 1939; died at Boston, Mass., on July 23, 1941; interment in Woodlawn Cemetery, Elmira, N.Y.

**HENRY, Patrick** (grandfather of William Henry Roane, cousin of Isaac Coles, and great-great-great-grandfather of Robert Lee Henry), a Delegate from Virginia; born in Studley, Hanover County, Va., May 29, 1736; pursued classical studies; engaged in mercantile pursuits; studied law; was admitted to the bar in 1760; moved to Louisa County in 1764; served as a member of the colonial house of burgesses in 1765; Member of the Continental Congress, 1774-1775; elected Governor of Virginia by the legislature and served 1776-1779 and 1784-1786; member of the Virginia convention which ratified the Constitution in 1788; declined the appointment of United States Senator in 1794, the Cabinet portfolio of Secretary of State in 1795, the appointment of Chief Justice of the United States tendered by President Washington, and of Minister to France offered by President John Adams; elected to the Virginia senate in 1799, but did not take the seat; died in Red Hill, Va., June 6, 1799; interment on "Red Hill" estate near Brookneal, Va.

**Bibliography:** *DAB*; Beeman, Richard R. *Patrick Henry: A Biography.* New York: McGraw-Hill, 1974; Meade, Robert D. *Patrick Henry.* 2 vols. Philadelphia: Lippincott, 1957-1969.

**HENRY, Patrick** (nephew of Patrick Henry [1843-1930]), a Representative from Mississippi; born near Helena, Phillips County, Ark., February 15, 1861; moved with his parents to Vicksburg, Miss., in 1865; attended the public schools and was graduated from the University of Mississippi, Oxford, Miss.; attended the United States Military Academy; studied law; was admitted to the bar in 1882 and commenced practice in Vicksburg, Miss.; city attorney 1884-1888; member of the State senate from 1888 until he resigned to become district attorney in 1890; district attorney for the ninth judicial district 1890-1900; delegate to the Democratic National Convention in 1896; appointed circuit judge of the ninth judicial district in 1900 and served until 1901, when he resigned, having been elected as a Democrat to the Fifty-seventh Congress (March 4, 1901-March 3, 1903); unsuccessful candidate for renomination in 1902; resumed the practice of law in Vicksburg, Miss., until his death there on December 28, 1933; interment in Cedar Hill Cemetery.

**HENRY, Patrick** (uncle of Patrick Henry [1861-1933]), a Representative from Mississippi; born near Cynthia, Madison County, Miss., February 12, 1843; attended the common schools, Mississippi College, Clinton, Miss., Madison College, Sharon, Miss., and the Nashville (Tenn.) Military College; moved to Brandon, Miss., in 1858; enlisted in the Confederate service as a first lieutenant in Company B, Sixth Mississippi Infantry Regiment, in 1861; served throughout the Civil War and surrendered at Greensboro, N.C., April 26, 1865, as major of the Fourteenth (Consolidated) Mississippi Regiment; engaged in agricultural pursuits in Hinds and Rankin Counties until 1873; studied law; was admitted to the bar in 1873 and commenced practice in Brandon, Miss.; member of the State house of representatives 1878-1890; delegate to the State constitutional convention in 1890; assistant United States district attorney in 1896; elected as a Democrat to the Fifty-fifth and Fifty-sixth Congresses (March 4, 1897-March 3, 1901); unsuccessful candidate for renomination in 1900; resumed the practice of law in Brandon, Miss.; member of the State senate 1904-1908; served as mayor of Brandon from 1916 until his death in Brandon, Miss., May 18, 1930; interment in Brandon Cemetery.

**HENRY, Paul B.,** a Representative from Michigan; born in Chicago, Ill., July 9, 1942; graduated from Pasadena (Calif.) High School, 1959; B.A., Wheaton College, Ill., 1963; M.A., Duke University, Durham, N.C., 1968, Ph.D., political science, 1970; Peace Corps volunteer in Liberia and Ethiopia, 1963-1965; staff aide to Representative John B. Anderson of Illinois, 1962-1963, and 1968-1969; professor of political science, Calvin College, Grand Rapids, Mich.; chairman, Kent County Republican Committee; member, Michigan State Board of Education, 1975-1978; served in the Michigan State house of representatives, 1979-1982; Michigan State senator, 1983-1984; elected as a Republican to the Ninety-ninth and to the four succeeding Congresses, and served from January 3, 1985 until his death in Grand Rapids, Mich., on July 31, 1993; interment in Woodlawn Cemetery.

**HENRY, Robert Kirkland,** a Representative from Wisconsin; born in Jefferson, Jefferson County, Wis., February 9, 1890; attended the public schools of his native city and the University of Wisconsin at Madison; engaged in the banking business; served as State treasurer 1931-1935; member of the Jefferson Municipal Water and Light Commission from November 7, 1939, to December 1, 1944; member of the State Banking Commission 1940-1944; elected as a Republican to the Seventy-ninth Congress and served from January 3, 1945, until his death; had been reelected to the Eightieth Congress; died in Madison, Wis., November 20, 1946; interment in Greenwood Cemetery, Jefferson, Wis.

**HENRY, Robert Lee** (great-great-great-grandson of Patrick Henry [1736-1799]), a Representative from Texas; born in Linden, Cass County, Tex., May 12, 1864; attended the common schools; moved to Bowie County in 1878 and to McLennan County in 1895; was graduated from the Southwestern University of Texas at Georgetown in 1885; studied law; was admitted to the bar in 1886 and practiced for a short time in Texarkana, Tex.; was graduated from the University of Texas at Austin in 1887; elected mayor of Texarkana in 1890 but resigned in 1891; first office assistant to the attorney general of Texas 1891-1893; assistant attorney general 1893-1896; settled in Waco, McLennan County, Tex., in 1895 and practiced law; elected as a Democrat to the Fifty-fifth and to the nine succeeding Congresses (March 4, 1897-March 3, 1917); chairman, Committee on Rules (Sixty-second through Sixty-fourth Congresses); was not a candidate for renomination in 1916 to the House of Representatives, but was an unsuccessful candidate for nomination to the United States Senate; engaged in the practice of law in Waco, Tex.; again an unsuccessful candidate for nomination to the United States Senate in 1922 and 1928; moved to Houston, Tex., in 1923 and resumed the practice of his profession; died from a gunshot wound in Houston, Tex., July 9, 1931; interment in Rose Hill Cemetery, Texarkana, Tex.

**HENRY, Robert Pryor,** a Representative from Kentucky; born in Henrys Mills, Scott County, Ky. (then a part of Virginia), November 24, 1788; pursued classical studies and was graduated from Transylvania College, Lexington, Ky.; studied law; was admitted to the bar in 1809 and commenced practice in Georgetown, Ky.; prosecuting attorney in 1819; served in the War of 1812; moved to Hopkinsville in 1817; elected to the Eighteenth and Nineteenth Congresses and served from March 4, 1823, until his death in Hopkinsville, Ky., August 25, 1826; interment in Pioneer Cemetery.

**HENRY, Thomas,** a Representative from Pennsylvania; born in County Down, Ireland, in 1779; immigrated to America and settled in Beaver, Pa., in 1798; appointed justice of the peace by Governor Simon Snyder on December 24, 1808; elected county commissioner in 1810; captain of a company that went from Beaver to help defend the northern frontier from a threatened British invasion in 1814; elected a member of the Virginai house of representatives in 1815; prothonotary and clerk of courts 1816-1821; elected sheriff of the county in 1821; proprietor and editor of the Western Argus 1821-1831; county treasurer in 1828 and 1829; elected as an Anti-Masonic candidate to the Twenty-fifth and Twenty-sixth Congresses, and as a Whig to the Twenty-seventh Congress (March 4, 1837-March 3, 1843); died in Beaver, Pa., July 20, 1849; interment in Old Beaver Cemetery.

**HENRY, William,** a Delegate from Pennsylvania; born near Downington, Chester County, Pa., May 19, 1729; attended the common schools; worked as a gunsmith; justice of the court of common pleas of Lancaster County in 1770, 1773, and 1777; canal commissioner of Pennsylvania in 1771; member of the Pennsylvania assembly in 1776; assistant commissary general with the rank of colonel for the district of Lancaster, Pa., during the Revolutionary War; member of the council of safety 1777; treasurer of Lancaster County 1777-1785; president judge of the court of common pleas in 1780; inventor of the screw auger and the first to suggest steam as a motive power; Member of the Continental Congress 1784-1785; died in Lancaster, Pa., December 15, 1786; interment in the Moravian Cemetery; reinterment in Greenwood Cemetery.

Bibliography: *DAB*.

**HENRY, William,** a Representative from Vermont; born in Charlestown, N.H., March 22, 1788; attended the common schools; engaged in business in Chester, Vt., and later engaged in manufacturing in Vermont, New York, and Jaffery, N.H.; moved to Bellows Falls, Vt., in 1831; engaged in banking; member of the State house of representatives in 1834 and 1835; served in the State senate in 1836; a director of the Rutland & Burlington Railroad Co.; delegate to the Whig National Convention at Harrisburg, Pa., in 1839; elected as a Whig to the Thirtieth and Thirty-first Congresses (March 4, 1847-March 3, 1851); unsuccessful candidate for election in 1852 to the Thirty-third Congress; resumed banking; presidential elector on the Republican ticket in 1860; died in Bellows Falls, Vt., April 16, 1861; interment in South Street Cemetery, Chester, Vt.

**HENRY, Winder Laird** (great-grandson of Charles Goldsborough and Robert Henry Goldsborough), a Representative from Maryland; born near Cambridge, Dorchester County, Md., December 20, 1864; attended the public schools; engaged in mercantile pursuits; purchased an interest in and became editor of the Cambridge Chronicle; elected as a Democrat to the Fifty-third Congress to fill the vacancy caused by the death of Robert F. Bratton and served from November 6, 1894, to March 3, 1895; was not a candidate for renomination in 1894 to the Fifty-fourth Congress; resumed newspaper work until 1898; studied law; was admitted to the bar of Dorchester County in 1898 and engaged in practice in Cambridge; colonel on the staff of Governor John Walter Smith 1899-1903; commissioner of the land office of Maryland April 1 to May 1, 1908; appointed chief judge of the first judicial circuit in May 1908 and served until October 1, 1909; resumed the practice of law in Cambridge, Md., and also engaged in banking; member of the Public Service Commission of Maryland from August 1, 1914, to June 1, 1916; died in Cambridge, Md., July 5, 1940; interment in Christ Church Cemetery.

**HENSLEY, Walter Lewis,** a Representative from Missouri; born near Pevely, Jefferson County, Mo., September 3, 1871; attended the public schools and the law department of the University of Missouri at Columbia; was admitted to the bar in 1894 and commenced practice in Wayne County, Mo.; moved to Bonne Terre, St. Francois County, Mo., and continued the practice of law; prosecuting attorney of St. Francois County 1898-1902; moved to Farmington, Mo., and practiced law; elected as a Democrat to the Sixty-second and to the three succeeding Congresses (March 4, 1911-March 3, 1919); was not a candidate for renomination in 1918; United States district attorney from March 1919 until he resigned in May 1920; reengaged in the private practice of law in St. Louis, Mo., until 1936, when he retired and moved to near Pevely; died at his summer home in Ludington, Mich., July 18, 1946; interment in Sandy Baptist Cemetery, near Pevely, Mo.

**HEPBURN, William Peters** (great-grandson of Matthew Lyon), a Representative from Iowa; born in Wellsville, Columbiana County, Ohio, November 4, 1833; moved to Iowa with his parents, who settled near Iowa City in April 1841; attended the common schools of Iowa City and the academy conducted by James F. Harlan (later a Senator); served an apprenticeship in a printing office; studied law in Iowa City and Chicago; was admitted to the Illinois bar in 1854 and commenced practice in Iowa City, Iowa; settled in Marshalltown, Marshall County, in February 1856; prosecuting attorney of Marshall County in 1856; district attorney of the eleventh judicial district 1856-1861; clerk of the Iowa house of representatives in 1858; delegate to the Republican National Conventions of 1860, 1888 and 1896; during the Civil War served in the Second Iowa Cavalry as captain, major, and lieutenant colonel; resided in Memphis, Tenn., 1865-1867; moved to Clarinda, Iowa, in 1867; resumed the practice of law until 1881; elected as a Republican to the Forty-seventh and to the two succeeding Congresses (March 4, 1881-March 3, 1887); served as Solicitor of the Treasury during the administration of President Benjamin Harrison; unsuccessful candidate for reelection in 1886 to the Fiftieth Congress; elected to the Fifty-third and to the seven succeeding Congresses (March 4, 1893-March 3, 1909); chairman, Committee on Interstate and Foreign Commerce (Fifty-fourth through Sixtieth Congresses); sponsor of the Hepburn Act of 1906, defining and expanding the Interstate Commerce Commission's power to regulate the accounts, rates and routes of railroads and other carriers; unsuccessfully contested the election of William D. Jamieson to the Sixty-first Congress; engaged in the practice of law in Clarinda, Iowa, and Washington, D.C.; died in Clarinda, Iowa, February 7, 1916; interment in Clarinda Cemetery.

Bibliography: *DAB*; Briggs, John E. *William Peters Hepburn.* Iowa City: State Historical Society of Iowa, 1919.

**HERBERT, Hilary Abner,** a Representative from Alabama; born in Laurens, S.C., March 12, 1834; moved with his parents to Greenville, Butler County, Ala., in 1846; attended the University of Alabama at Tuscaloosa in 1853 and 1854 and the University of Virginia at Charlottesville in 1855 and 1856; studied law; was admitted to the bar in 1857 and commenced practice in Greenville, Ala.; entered the Confederate service as captain of the Greenville Guards; promoted to the rank of colonel of the Eighth Regiment, Alabama Infantry; disabled at the Battle of the Wilderness, May 6, 1864; resumed the practice of law in Greenville, Ala., until 1872, when he moved to Montgomery, Ala.; elected as a Democrat to the

Forty-fifth and to the seven succeeding Congresses (March 4, 1877-March 3, 1893); chairman, Committee on Naval Affairs (Forty-ninth, Fiftieth, and Fifty-second Congresses); appointed Secretary of the Navy in the Cabinet of President Grover Cleveland, and served from March 7, 1893 to March 5, 1897; located in Washington, D.C., and practiced law until his death; died in Tampa, Fla., March 6, 1919; interment in Oakwood Cemetery, Montgomery, Ala.

**Bibliography:** *DAB*; Hammett, Hugh B. *Hilary Abner Herbert: A Southerner Returns to the Union.* Philadelphia: American Philosophical Society, 1976; Herbert, Hilary Abner. *The Abolition Crusade and its Consequences; Four Periods of American History.* New York: Scribner's Sons, 1912.

**HERBERT, John Carlyle,** a Representative from Maryland; born in Alexandria, Va., August 16, 1775; received private instruction and was graduated from St. John's College, Annapolis, Md., in 1794; studied law; was admitted to the bar and commenced practice in Richmond, Va., about 1795; member of the Virginia house of delegates in 1798 and 1799; settled in Prince Georges County, Md., in 1805; member of the Maryland house of delegates 1808-1813 and served as speaker in 1812 and 1813; served as captain of the Bladensburg Troop of Horse in the War of 1812; elected as a Federalist to the Fourteenth and Fifteenth Congresses (March 4, 1815-March 3, 1819); chairman, Committee on District of Columbia (Fifteenth Congress); retired to his estate, "Walnut Grange," Beltsville, Md., in 1820 and resumed the practice of law; died in Buchanan, Botetourt County, Va., September 1, 1846; interment in Greenmount Cemetery, Baltimore, Md.

**HERBERT, Philemon Thomas,** a Representative from California; born in Pine Apple, Wilcox County, Ala., November 1, 1825; attended the common schools and the University of Alabama at Tuscaloosa; moved to Mariposa City, Calif., about 1850; member of the State assembly in 1853 and 1854; elected as a Democrat to the Thirty-fourth Congress (March 4, 1855-March 3, 1857); was not a candidate for renomination in 1856 to the Thirty-fifth Congress; moved to El Paso, Tex., about 1859 and practiced law; during the Civil War served with the Confederate Army as lieutenant colonel of the Seventh Texas Cavalry; was wounded at the Battle of Sabine Cross Roads, La., on April 8, 1864, and died in Kingston, La., July 23, 1864, from the effects of his wounds; interment in Evergreen Cemetery.

**HEREFORD, Frank,** a Representative and a Senator from West Virginia; born near Warrenton, Fauquier County, Va., July 4, 1825; completed preparatory studies and graduated from McKendree College, Lebanon, Ill., in 1845; studied law; was admitted to the bar and practiced; moved to California in 1849; district attorney of Sacramento County 1855-1857; moved to West Virginia; elected as a Democrat to the Forty-second, Forty-third, and Forty-fourth Congresses and served from March 4, 1871, until January 31, 1877, when he resigned; chairman, Committee on Commerce (Forty-fourth Congress); elected as a Democrat to the United States Senate on January 26, 1877, to fill the vacancy caused by the death of Allen Taylor Caperton and served from January 31, 1877, to March 3, 1881; chairman, Committee on Mines and Mining (Forty-sixth Congress); resumed the practice of law; died in Union, Monroe County, W.Va., December 21, 1891; interment in Green Hill Cemetery.

**HERGER, Walter William (Wally),** a Representative from California; born in Yuba City, Calif., May 20, 1945; attended public schools; graduated East Nicolaus High School; A.A., American River Community College, 1978; California State University, Sacramento, 1979-1980; cattle rancher; businessman; member, East Nicolaus High School Board of Trustees, 1977-1980; California State assemblyman, 1980-1986; elected as a Republican to the One

Hundredth and to the four succeeding Congresses (January 3, 1987-January 3, 1997); is a resident of Marysville, Calif.

**HERKIMER, John,** a Representative from New York; born in what is now Herkimer (then Tryon and later Montgomery) County, N.Y., in 1773; attended the public schools; member of the State assembly in 1800, 1804, and 1806; member of the State constitutional convention in 1801; moved to Danube, Herkimer County, N.Y.; major in the war of 1812 and commanded a battalion of New York Volunteers in the defense of Sackets Harbor May 29, 1813; judge of the circuit court for several years; elected as a Republican to the Fifteenth Congress (March 4, 1817-March 3, 1819); moved to Meriden, N.Y.; elected to the Eighteenth Congress (March 4, 1823-March 3, 1825); returned to Danube, where he died June 8, 1848; interment in General Herkimer Cemetery, Danube, N.Y.

**HERLONG, Albert Sydney, Jr.,** a Representative from Florida; born in Manistee, Monroe County, Ala., February 14, 1909; moved with his parents to Lake County, Fla., in 1911; attended the public schools of Sumter and Lake Counties and Leesburg High School; was graduated from the University of Florida at Gainesville in 1930; was admitted to the bar in 1930 and commenced the practice of law in Leesburg, Lake County, Fla.; served as postmaster of Leesburg in 1935; county judge of Lake County, 1937-1949; city attorney of Leesburg, 1946-1948; held Reserve commission as captain in the United States Army and was called to active duty in the Judge Advocate General's Department in August 1941; was discharged in 1942 due to physical disability; served two enlistments in the Florida State Guard; president of the Florida State Baseball League in 1947 and 1948; elected as a Democrat to the Eighty-first and to the nine succeeding Congresses (January 3, 1949-January 3, 1969); was not a candidate for reelection in 1968 to the Ninety-first Congress; resumed the practice of law; member of the Securities and Exchange Commission from 1969 until his resignation in 1973; affiliated with the Republican Party in 1985; was a resident of Leesburg, Fla., until his death there on December 27, 1995.

**HERMANN, Binger,** a Representative from Oregon; born in Lonaconing, Allegany County, Md., February 19, 1843; attended rural schools and was graduated from the Independent Academy, Manchester, Md., later known as Irving College; moved to Oregon in 1859, where he taught school; studied law; was admitted to the bar in 1866 and commenced practice in Oakland, Oreg.; member of the State house of representatives 1866-1868; served in the State senate 1868-1870; deputy collector of internal revenue for southern Oregon 1868-1871; receiver of public moneys at the United States land office in Roseburg, Oreg., 1871-1873; colonel Oregon State Militia 1882-1884; appointed by President William McKinley Commissioner of the General Land Office and served from March 27, 1897, until February 1, 1903, when he resigned; elected as a Republican to the Forty-ninth and to the five succeeding Congresses (March 4, 1885-March 3, 1897); chairman, Committee on Irrigation of Arid Lands (Fifty-fourth Congress); was not a candidate for renomination in 1896 to the Fifty-fifth Congress; elected to the Fifty-eighth Congress to fill the vacancy caused by the death of Thomas H. Tongue; reelected to the Fifty-ninth Congress and served from June 1, 1903, to March 3, 1907; was not a candidate for renomination in 1906 to the Sixtieth Congress; resumed the practice of law and engaged in literary pursuits in Roseburg, Oreg., where he died April 15, 1926; interment in the Masonic Cemetery.

**HERNANDEZ, Benigno Cardenas,** a Representative from New Mexico; born in Taos, N.Mex., February 13, 1862; attended common and private schools; clerk in a general merchandise establishment in Taos County from 1880 to 1889; engaged in general merchandising and stock raising; moved to Lumberton in 1896 and engaged in mercantile pursuits; probate clerk and ex officio recorder of deeds for Rio Arriba County 1900-1904; moved to Tierra Amarilla in 1901; sheriff of Rio Arriba County 1904-1906; county treasurer and ex officio collector of taxes from 1908 until 1912; delegate to numerous State Republican conventions; receiver of the land office at Sante Fe, N.Mex., in 1912 and 1913, when he resigned; again engaged in mercantile pursuits and stock raising; delegate to the Republican National Conventions of 1912 and 1916; member of the State exemption board during the First World War; elected as a Republican to the Sixty-fourth Congress (March 4, 1915-March 3, 1917); unsuccessful candidate for reelection in 1916 to the Sixty-fifth Congress; elected to the Sixty-sixth Congress (March 4, 1919-March 3, 1921); was not a candidate for renomination in 1920 to the Sixty-seventh Congress; appointed collector of internal revenue for the district of New Mexico by President Warren G. Harding on April 22, 1921, and served until 1933; member of the Selective Service Board 1940-1947; died in Los Angeles, Calif., on October 18, 1954; interment in Inglewood Park Cemetery, Inglewood, Calif.

**HERNANDEZ, Joseph Marion,** a Delegate from the Territory of Florida; born in St. Augustine, Fla. (then a Spanish colony), August 4, 1793; transferred his allegiance to the United States; upon the formation of Florida Territory was elected as a Delegate to the Seventeenth Congress and served from September 30, 1822, to March 3, 1823; member and presiding officer of the Territorial house of representatives; appointed brigadier general of Volunteers in the war against the Florida Indians; entered the United States service and served from 1835 to 1838; commanded the expedition in 1837 that captured the Indian chief Oceola; appointed brigadier general of Mounted Volunteers in July 1837; unsuccessful Whig candidate for the United States Senate in 1845; moved to Cuba and engaged as a planter in the District of Coliseo, near Matanzas; died at the family's sugar estate, "Audaz," in the District of Coliseo, Matanzas Province, Cuba, June 8, 1857; interment in the Junco family vault in San Carlos Cemetery, Matanzas, Cuba.

**HERNDON, Thomas Hord,** a Representative from Alabama; born in Erie, Greene (now Hale) County, Ala., July 1, 1828; attended a private school; was graduated from the University of Alabama at Tuscaloosa in 1847; attended the law school of Harvard University in 1848; was admitted to the bar in 1849 and commenced practice in Eutaw, Ala.; editor of the Eutaw Democrat in 1850; moved to Mobile, Ala., in 1853 and resumed the practice of law; member of the State house of representatives in 1857 and 1858; trustee of the University of Alabama in 1858 and 1859; returned to Greene County in 1859; member of the State secession convention in 1861; during the Civil War served as major, lieutenant colonel, and colonel of the Thirty-sixth Regiment, Alabama Infantry, in the Confederate Army and was wounded twice in battle; again moved to Mobile and resumed the practice of his profession; unsuccessful Democratic candidate for Governor of Alabama in 1872; member of the State constitutional convention which met September 6, 1875; member of the State house of representatives in 1876 and 1877; elected as a Democrat to the Forty-sixth and to the two succeeding Congresses and served from March 4, 1879, until his death in Mobile, Ala., March 28, 1883, before the convening of the Forty-eighth Congress; interment in Magnolia Cemetery.

**HERNDON, William Smith,** a Representative from Texas; born in Rome, Floyd County, Ga., November 27, 1835; moved to Wood County, Tex., in May 1852; attended the common schools and was graduated from McKenzie College in 1859; studied law; was admitted to the bar in 1860 and commenced practice in Tyler, Smith County, Tex.; served in the Confederate Army from 1861 to 1865 and attained the rank of captain; resumed the practice of law in Tyler; attorney, executive adviser, and general solicitor for numerous railroad companies 1868-1881; elected as a Democrat to the Forty-second and Forty-third Congresses (March 4, 1871-March 3, 1875); unsuccessful candidate for reelection in 1874 to the Forty-fourth Congress; again engaged in the practice of law in Tyler,

Tex., engaged in railroad construction; died in Albuquerque, N.Mex., October 11, 1903; interment in Oakwood Cemetery, Tyler, Tex.

**HEROD, William,** a Representative from Indiana; born in Bourbon County, Ky., March 31, 1801; completed preparatory studies; studied law and was admitted to the bar in Bracken County, Ky.; later moved to Columbus, Ind.; was admitted to the bar in Bartholomew County in 1825 and began practice in Columbus, Ind.; member of the State house of representatives in 1829, 1830, and 1844; served in the State senate 1831-1834, 1845, and 1846; elected prosecuting attorney of Bartholomew County and served from 1833 until 1837, when he resigned; elected as a Whig to the Twenty-fourth Congress to fill the vacancy caused by the death of George L. Kinnard; reelected to the Twenty-fifth Congress and served from January 25, 1837, to March 3, 1839; unsuccessful candidate for reelection in 1838 to the Twenty-sixth Congress; resumed the practice of his profession in Columbus, Ind.; clerk of the circuit court of Bartholomew County in 1853; became a Republican upon the formation of that party; engaged in the practice of law until his death at Columbus, Ind., October 20, 1871; interment in City Cemetery.

**HERRICK, Anson** (son of Ebenezer Herrick), a Representative from New York; born in Lewiston, Androscoggin County, Maine, January 21, 1812; attended the public schools; learned the art of printing; established the Citizen at Wiscasset, Maine, in 1833; moved to New York City in 1836; established the New York Atlas in 1838, which he continued until his death; member of the board of aldermen 1854-1856; naval storekeeper for the port of New York 1857-1861; elected as a Democrat to the Thirty-eighth Congress (March 4, 1863-March 3, 1865); unsuccessful candidate for reelection in 1864 to the Thirty-ninth Congress; resumed his journalistic pursuits; delegate to the Union National Convention at Philadelphia in 1866; died in New York City February 6, 1868; interment in Greenwood Cemetery, Brooklyn, N.Y.

**HERRICK, Ebenezer** (father of Anson Herrick), a Representative from Maine; born in Lewiston, Androscoggin County, Maine (then a district of Massachusetts), October 21, 1785; attended the common schools; studied law; was admitted to the bar and commenced practice in Bowdoinham, Lincoln County, Maine; engaged in mercantile pursuits 1814-1818; member of the Massachusetts house of representatives in 1819; member of the convention which formed the first constitution of the State of Maine in 1820; secretary of the Maine senate in 1821; elected to the Seventeenth, Eighteenth, and Nineteenth Congresses (March 4, 1821-March 3, 1827); declined to be a candidate for reelection in 1826; member of the Maine senate in 1828 and 1829; died in Lewiston, Maine, May 7, 1839; interment in the Old Herrick Burying Ground.

**HERRICK, Joshua,** a Representative from Maine; born in Beverly, Mass., March 18, 1793; attended the common schools; moved to the district of Maine in 1811 and engaged in the lumber business; served in the War of 1812; moved to Brunswick, Maine, and became connected with the first cotton factory of Maine; deputy sheriff of Cumberland County for many years; deputy collector and inspector of customs at Kennebunkport, Maine, 1829-1841; town clerk of Kennebunkport 1832-1842; also selectman, assessor, and overseer of the poor of Kennebunkport 1839-1842; county commissioner of York County in 1842 and 1843; elected as a Democrat to the Twenty-eighth Congress (March 4, 1843-March 3, 1845); unsuccessful candidate for renomination in 1844 to the Twenty-ninth Congress; again deputy collector at Kennebunkport 1847-1849; register of probate of York County 1849-1855; died in Alfred, Maine, August 30, 1874; interment in Village Cemetery, Kennebunkport, Maine.

**HERRICK, Manuel,** a Representative from Oklahoma; born in Perry, Tuscarawas County, Ohio, September 20, 1876; moved with his parents to Greenwood County, Kans., in 1877; was self-educated; engaged in agricultural pursuits; settled in the "Cherokee Strip," Oklahoma, in 1893; moved to Perry, Okla., and became interested in agriculture and stock raising; elected as a Republican to the Sixty-seventh Congress (March 4, 1921-March 3, 1923); unsuccessful candidate in 1922 for renomination to the Sixty-eighth Congress; became a resident of California in 1933 and of Plumas County, Calif., in 1937; disappeared during a Sierra blizzard on January 11, 1952, while on a trip to his mining claim eight miles northeast of Quincy, Calif., and was found dead in a snowbank two miles from his cabin on February 29, 1952; remains were cremated and the ashes interred in Quincy Cemetery, Quincy, Calif.

**Bibliography:** Aldrich, Gene. *Okie Jesus Congressman (The Life of Manuel Herrick)*. Oklahoma City: Times-Journal Publishing Co., 1974.

**HERRICK, Richard Platt,** a Representative from New York; born in Greenbush (now Rensselaer), Rensselaer County, N.Y., March 23, 1791; member of the New York State assembly in 1839; elected as a Whig to the Twenty-ninth Congress and served from March 4, 1845, until his death in Washington, D.C., June 20, 1846; interment in Greenbush Cemetery, Greenbush (now Rensselaer), N.Y.

**HERRICK, Samuel,** a Representative from Ohio; born in Amenia, Dutchess County, N.Y., April 14, 1779; pursued an academic course; studied law in Carlisle, Pa.; was admitted to the bar in 1805 and commenced practice in St. Clairsville, Ohio; moved to Zanesville, Ohio, in 1810; appointed prosecuting attorney of Guernsey County in 1810 and also United States district attorney; in 1814 appointed prosecuting attorney of Licking County and commissioned brigadier general of the Ohio Militia; elected as a Republican to the Fifteenth Congress and reelected to the Sixteenth Congress (March 4, 1817-March 3, 1821); chairman, Committee on Private Land Claims (Fifteenth Congress); was not a candidate for reelection in 1820; continued the practice of law; presidential elector on the Jackson and Calhoun ticket in 1828; appointed United States district attorney for Ohio in 1829 but resigned June 30, 1830; died in Zanesville, Ohio, June 4, 1852; interment in City (now Greenwood) Cemetery.

**HERRING, Clyde LaVerne,** a Senator from Iowa; born in Jackson, Jackson County, Mich., May 3, 1879; attended the public schools; moved to Detroit, Mich., in 1897; served as a private in Company D, Third Michigan Regiment, in the Spanish-American War; moved to Colorado Springs, Colo., and engaged in ranching from 1902 until 1906; moved to Massena, Iowa, and engaged in agricultural pursuits, 1906-1908; entered the automobile business in Atlantic, Iowa, 1908-1910; moved to Des Moines, Iowa, in 1910 and continued in the automobile business; during the First World War served with the Iowa National Guard on the Mexican border; unsuccessful candidate for election in 1920 for Governor of Iowa; unsuccessful candidate for election to the United States Senate in 1922; member of the Democratic National Committee of Iowa, 1924-1928; elected Governor of Iowa in 1932, reelected in 1934, and served from January 12, 1933 to January 14, 1937; elected as a Democrat to the United States Senate for the term beginning January 3, 1937, but did not qualify until the expiration of his term as Governor, and served from January 15, 1937, to January 3, 1943; unsuccessful candidate for reelection in 1942; senior assistant administrator in the Office of Price Administration 1943; resumed the automobile business in Des Moines, Iowa; died in Washington, D.C., September 15, 1945; interment in Glendale Cemetery, Des Moines, Iowa.

**HERSEY, Ira Greenlief,** a Representative from Maine; born in Hodgdon, Aroostook County, Maine, March 31, 1858; attended the public schools and Ricker Classical Institute, Houlton, Maine; studied law; was admitted to the bar in 1880 and commenced practice in Houlton, Maine; unsuccessful candidate for Governor of Maine in 1886; member of the State house of representatives 1909-1912; served in the State senate 1913-1916 and was president of that body in 1915 and 1916; elected as a Republican to the Sixty-fifth and to the five succeeding Congresses (March 4, 1917-March 3, 1929); chairman, Committee on Expenditures on Public Buildings (Sixty-sixth Congress); one of the managers appointed by the House of Representatives in 1926 to conduct the impeachment proceedings against George W. English, judge of the United States District Court for the Eastern District of Illinois; unsuccessful candidate for renomination in 1928 to the Seventy-first Congress; judge of probate for Aroostook County, Maine, 1934-1942, when he retired and moved to Washington, D.C., where he died on May 6, 1943; interment in Evergreen Cemetery, Houlton, Maine.

**HERSEY, Samuel Freeman,** a Representative from Maine; born in Sumner, Oxford County, Maine, April 12, 1812; attended the common schools of Sumner and Buckfield; taught school 1828-1831; was graduated from Hebron Academy in 1831; removed to Bangor the same year; engaged in the merchandise business in Lincoln in 1833 and in Milford in 1837; engaged in the lumber business in Stillwater, Maine, in 1842 and in Bangor in 1850; member of the State house of representatives in 1842, 1857, and 1865; member of the executive council 1852-1854; delegate to the Republican National Convention of 1860; member of the Republican National Committee 1864-1868; member of the State senate in 1868 and 1869; unsuccessful candidate for Governor of Maine in 1870; elected as a Republican to the Forty-third and Forty-fourth Congresses and served from March 4, 1873, until his death in Bangor, Maine, February 3, 1875, before the close of the Forty-third Congress; interment in Mount Hope Cemetery.

**HERSMAN, Hugh Steel,** a Representative from California; born in Port Deposit, Cecil County, Md., July 8, 1872; moved to California with his parents, who settled in Berkeley in 1881; attended the public schools in California; was graduated from the Southwestern Presbyterian University, Tennessee, in 1893; studied at the University of California at Berkeley in 1897 and 1898; president of the First National Bank, Gilroy, Calif., 1914-1918; officer and director of various corporations; elected as a Democrat to the Sixty-sixth Congress (March 4, 1919-March 3, 1921); unsuccessful for reelection in 1920 to the Sixty-seventh Congress; member of the board of directors of the American Trust Co., Gilroy, Calif.; died in San Francisco, Calif., March 7, 1954; interment in Nottingham Cemetery, Colora, Cecil County, Md.

**HERTEL, Dennis Mark,** a Representative from Michigan; born in Detroit, Wayne County, Mich., December 7, 1948; attended the public schools; graduated from Denby High School, Detroit, 1967; B.A., Eastern Michigan University, Ypsilanti, 1971; J.D., Wayne State University, Detroit, 1974; admitted to the Michigan bar in 1975 and commenced practice in Detroit; served in the Michigan house of representatives, 1975-1980; elected as a Democrat to the Ninety-seventh and to the five succeeding Congresses (January 3, 1981-January 3, 1993); was not a candidate for reelection in 1992 to the One Hundred Third Congress; is a resident of Detroit, Mich.

**HERTER, Christian Archibald,** a Representative from Massachusetts; born in Paris, France, March 28, 1895; attended school in Paris 1901-1904 and Browning School of New York City 1904-1911; was graduated from Harvard University in 1915; attaché of the American Embassy in Berlin, Germany, in 1916 and for two months was in charge of the American Legation in Brussels, Belgium; served in the State Department, Washington, D.C., 1917-1919; executive secretary of the European Relief Council in 1920; personal assistant to Secretary of Commerce Herbert Hoover, Washington, D.C., 1921-1924; engaged in the publishing business at Boston, Mass., 1924-1937; visiting lecturer on government at Harvard University in 1929 and 1930; overseer, Harvard University, 1940-1944 and 1946-1952; member of the Massachusetts house of representatives 1931-1943, serving as speaker 1939-1943; deputy director of the Office of Facts and Figures, Washington, D.C., in 1941 and 1942; delegate to the Republican National Convention of 1948; elected as a Republican to the Seventy-eighth and to the four succeeding Congresses (January 3, 1943-January 3, 1953); was not a candidate for renomination in 1952 to the Eighty-third Congress, but was elected Governor of Massachusetts, and served from January 8, 1953 to January 3, 1957; was not a candidate for reelection in 1956; Under Secretary of State from February 21, 1957, and Secretary of State from April 22, 1959 to January 20, 1961; chairman of the Honorary Council of the International Movement for Atlantic Union, 1961; co-chairman of United States Citizens Commission on NATO in 1961, and elected president of the resulting convention in Paris in January 1962; President's Special Representative for Trade Negotiations, February 27, 1963, until his death in Washington, D.C., on December 30, 1966; interment in Prospect Hill Cemetery, Millis, Mass.

**Bibliography:** Noble, George Bernard. *Christian A. Herter. American Secretaries of State and Their Diplomacy,* vol. 18. New York: Cooper Square Publishers, 1970.

**HESELTON, John Walter,** a Representative from Massachusetts; born in Gardiner, Kennebec County, Maine, March 17, 1900; attended the public schools of Gardiner, Maine, Amherst (Mass.) College, and Harvard Law School, Cambridge, Mass.; served in the United States Army from October 10, 1918, to December 12, 1918; was admitted to the bar in 1926 and commenced practice in Greenfield, Mass.; also interested in banking; secretary of the board of trustees of Deerfield Academy; selectman of Deerfield, Mass., 1932-1935; president of the Massachusetts Selectmen's Association 1935-1938; secretary of the Deerfield Republican Town committee 1928-1938; member of the Massachusetts Republican committee 1936-1938; district attorney of the northwestern district of Massachusetts 1939-1944; elected as a Republican to the Seventy-ninth and to the six succeeding Congresses (January 3, 1945-January 3, 1959); was not a candidate for renomination in 1958; engaged in the practice of law; was a resident of Vero Beach, Fla., at the time of his death, August 19, 1962; interment in Hope Cemetery, New Orleans, La.

**HESS, William Emil,** a Representative from Ohio; born in Cincinnati, Ohio, February 13, 1898; attended the public schools, the University of Cincinnati, Cincinnati, Ohio, and Cincinnati (Ohio) Law School; during the First World War served in the United States Army as a private; was admitted to the bar in 1919 and commenced the practice of law in Cincinnati, Ohio, the same year; member of the Cincinnati City Council 1922-1926; elected as a Republican to the Seventy-first and to the three succeeding Congresses (March 4, 1929-January 3, 1937); unsuccessful candidate for reelection in 1936 to the Seventy-fifth Congress; resumed the practice of law; elected to the Seventy-sixth and to the four succeeding Congresses (January 3, 1939-January 3, 1949); unsuccessful candidate for reelection in 1948 to the Eighty-first Congress; elected to the Eighty-second and to the four succeeding Congresses (January 3, 1951-January 3, 1961); was not a candidate for renomination in 1960; resumed the practice of law; was a resident of Cincinnati, Ohio, until his death there on July 14, 1986; interment in Spring Grove Cemetery.

**HEWES, Joseph,** a Delegate from North Carolina; born in Kingston, N.J., January 23, 1730; pursued classical studies and attended Princeton College; engaged in business in Philadelphia, Pa.; settled in Wilmington, N.C., and engaged in mercantile pursuits; moved to Edenton, N.C., in 1756; member of the State house of commons 1766-1775; member of the committee of correspondence in 1773; delegate to the Provincial congress; Member of the Continental Congress 1774-1776; again served in the State house of commons in 1778 and 1779; was a signer of the Declaration of Independence; again a Member of the Continental Congress in 1779 and served until his death in Philadelphia, Pa., on November 10, 1779; interment in Christ Church Burial Ground, 5th and Arch Streets.

**Bibliography:** *DAB.*

**HEWITT, Abram Stevens,** a Representative from New York; born in Haverstraw, N.Y., July 31, 1822; attended the public schools of New York City; A.B., Columbia College, 1842, and LL.D., 1857; taught at Columbia College and briefly served as an acting professor of mathematics; studied law; was admitted to practice in October 1845; his eyesight failing, he engaged in the iron business with Peter Cooper, forming the firm of Cooper and Hewitt; instrumental in introduction of the Martins-Siemens (open hearth) process of steel manufacture; traveled to Europe as a purchasing agent for the United States government during the Civil War; appointed one of the ten United States scientific commissioners to visit the French Exposition Universelle of 1867 and made a report on iron and steel, which was published by Congress; assisted in the organization and educational and financial management of the Cooper Union for the advancement of science and art, New York City; elected as a Democrat to the Forty-fourth and Forty-fifth Congresses (March 4, 1875-March 3, 1879); was not a candidate for renomination in 1878 to the Forth-sixth Congress; elected to the Forty-seventh and to the two succeeding Congresses, and served from March 4, 1881 until December 30, 1886, when he resigned, having been elected mayor; mayor of New York City in 1887 and 1888; appointed member of the Palisades Interstate Park Commission in 1900; served as a trustee of Barnard College, Columbia Institution and Columbia University; died in New York City on January 18, 1903; interment in Greenwood Cemetery.

**Bibliography:** *DAB*; Hewitt, Abram S. *Selected Writings of Abram S. Hewitt.* Edited by Allan Nevins. New York: Columbia University Press, 1937; Nevins, Allan. *Abram S. Hewitt; With Some Account of Peter Cooper.* New York: Harper and Brothers, 1935.

**HEWITT, Goldsmith Whitehouse,** a Representative from Alabama; born near Elyton (now Birmingham), Jefferson County, Ala., February 14, 1834; attended the country schools; entered the Confederate Army in June 1861 as a private in Company B, Tenth Regiment, Alabama Infantry; was promoted to captain of Company G, Twenty-eighth Regiment, Alabama Infantry, in 1862; was graduated from the law department of Cumberland University, Lebanon, Tenn., in 1866; was admitted to the bar the same year and commenced practice in Birmingham, Ala.; member of the Alabama State house of representatives, 1870-1871; served in the State senate from 1872 to 1874 and resigned in the latter year; elected as a Democrat to the Forty-fourth and Forty-fifth Congresses (March 4, 1875-March 3, 1879); elected to the Forty-seventh and Forty-eighth Congresses (March 4, 1881-March 3, 1885); chairman, Committee on Pensions (Forty-eighth Congress); was not a candidate for renomination in 1884 to the Forty-ninth Congress; resumed the practice of law; again a member of the State house of representatives, 1886-1888; died in Birmingham, Ala., on May 27, 1895; interment in Oak Hill Cemetery.

**HEYBURN, Weldon Brinton,** a Senator from Idaho; born near Chadds Ford, Delaware County, Pa., May 23, 1852; attended the public schools, Maplewood Institute, Concordville, Pa., and the University of Pennsylvania at Philadelphia; studied law; was admitted to the bar in 1876 and commenced practice in Media, Pa.; moved to Shoshone County, Idaho, in 1883 and continued the practice of law in Wallace; was a member of the convention that framed the constitution of the State of Idaho in 1889; unsuccessful Republican candidate for election in 1898 to the Fifty-sixth Congress; National Committeeman for Idaho 1904-1908; elected in 1903 as a Republican to the United States Senate; reelected in 1908 and served from March 4, 1903, until his death in Washington, D.C., October 17, 1912; chairman, Committee on Manufactures (Fifty-eighth through Sixty-second Congresses); interment in Lafayette Cemetery, near Chadds Ford, Pa.

Bibliography: Cook, R.G. "Pioneer Portraits: Weldon B. Heyburn." *Idaho Yesterdays* 10 (Spring 1966): 22-26; Simpson, John A. "Weldon Heyburn and the Image of the Bloody Shirt." *Idaho Yesterdays* 24 (Winter 1981): 20-28.

HEYWARD, Thomas, Jr., a Delegate from South Carolina; born on his father's plantation; settled in that part of St. Helena's Parish which later became St. Luke's Parish, South Carolina, July 28, 1746; pursued academic studies; studied law in the Middle Temple at London; returned to South Carolina in 1771; was admitted to the bar and established himself in the practice of law; member of the Commons House of Assembly of South Carolina in 1772; delegate to the provincial convention in 1774; member of the council of safety in 1775 and 1776; member of the general assembly 1776-1778; Member of the Continental Congress 1776-1778; signer of the Declaration of Independence; member of the State constitutional committee in 1776; served in the State house of representatives 1778-1780 and 1782-1790; served in the Revolutionary War as captain; taken prisoner at the capture of Charlestown May 12, 1780, and was a prisoner at St. Augustine one year; judge of the circuit court 1779-1789; founder and first president of the Agricultural Society of South Carolina in 1785; engaged in agricultural pursuits; member of the State constitutional convention in 1790; died on his plantation, "White Hall," in St. Luke's Parish, South Carolina, March 6, 1809; interment in the family burial ground on his father's plantation, "Old House," near Ridgeland, S.C.

Bibliography: *DAB.*

HIBBARD, Ellery Albee (cousin of Harry Hibbard), a Representative from New Hampshire; born in St. Johnsbury, Caledonia County, Vt., July 31, 1826; pursued academic studies; studied law in Haverhill and Exeter, N.H.; was admitted to the bar in 1849 and practiced in Plymouth, N.H., until 1853 and subsequently in Laconia; clerk of the State house of representatives 1852-1854; moderator of Laconia in 1862 and 1863; member of the State house of representatives in 1865 and 1866; elected as a Democrat to the Forty-second Congress (March 4, 1871-March 3, 1873); unsuccessful candidate for reelection in 1872 to the Forty-third Congress; appointed judge of the supreme court of New Hampshire in March 1873 and served until 1874, when he resigned and continued the practice of law; director of Laconia National Bank; member of board of education of Laconia; died in Laconia, N.H., July 24, 1903; interment in Union Cemetery.

HIBBARD, Harry (cousin of Ellery Albee Hibbard), a Representative from New Hampshire; born in Concord, Essex County, Vt., June 1, 1816; pursued classical studies and was graduated from Dartmouth College, Hanover, N.H., in 1835; studied law; was admitted to the bar in 1838 and commenced practice in Bath, Grafton County, N.H.; assistant clerk and clerk of the State house of representatives 1840-1842; member of the State house of representatives 1843-1845 and speaker in 1844 and 1845; served in the State senate in 1845, 1847, and 1848 and as president of that body in 1847 and 1848; delegate to the Democratic National Conventions in 1848 and 1856; elected as a Democrat to the Thirty-first, Thirty-second, and Thirty-third Congresses (March 4, 1849-March 3, 1855); was not a candidate for renomination in 1854; declined an appointment to the State supreme court; died in a sanatorium in Sommerville, Mass., on July 28, 1872; interment in the Village Cemetery, Bath, N.H.

HIBSHMAN, Jacob, a Representative from Pennsylvania; born on a farm near Ephrata, Lancaster County, Pa., January 31, 1772; attended the common schools and a private school in Harrisburg, Pa.; engaged in agricultural pursuits; associate judge of Lancaster County 1810-1819; elected to the Sixteenth Congress (March 4, 1819-March 3, 1821); unsuccessful candidate for reelection in 1820 to the Seventeenth Congress; deputy surveyor of Lancaster County for twenty years; justice of the peace; chairman of the board of canal appraisers; major general of Pennsylvania Militia for twelve years; organized the Northern Mutual Insurance Co., in 1844 and served as its first president; died at his residence near Ephrata, Pa., May 19, 1852; interment in the Hibshman Cemetery on the farm near Ephrata, Pa.

HICKENLOOPER, Bourke Blakemore, a Senator from Iowa; born in Blockton, Taylor County, Iowa, July 21, 1896; attended the public schools and Iowa State College at Ames until April 1917, when he enrolled in the officer's training camp at Fort Snelling, Minn.; commissioned a second lieutenant, embarked overseas in August 1918 and served in France as battalion orientation officer; returned to the United States in February 1919 and was honorably discharged; reentered Iowa State College and graduated in 1919; graduated from the College of Law of the State University of Iowa at Iowa City in 1922; admitted to the bar in 1922 and commenced practice in Cedar Rapids, Iowa; member, Iowa State house of representatives, 1934-1937; Lieutenant Governor of Iowa, 1939-1942; elected Governor of Iowa in 1942, and served from January 14, 1943 to January 11, 1945; elected as a Republican to the United States Senate in 1944 for the term commencing January 3, 1945; reelected in 1950, 1956, and 1962 for the term ending January 3, 1969; declined to be a candidate for reelection in 1968; co-chairman, Joint Committee on Atomic Energy (Eightieth Congress), chairman, Republican Policy Committee (Eighty-seventh through Ninetieth Congresses); died in Shelter Island, N.Y., September 4, 1971, while visiting; interment in Cedar Memorial Cemetery, Cedar Rapids, Iowa.

Bibliography: Schapsmeier, Edward, and Schapsmeier, Frederick. "A Strong Voice for Keeping America Strong: A Profile of Senator Bourke B. Hickenlooper." *Annals of Iowa* 47 (Spring 1984): 362-76.

HICKEY, Andrew James, a Representative from Indiana; born in Albion, Orleans County, N.Y., August 27, 1872; attended the public schools of his native city and Buffalo (N.Y.) Law School; was admitted to the New York bar in 1896 and commenced practice in La Porte, Ind., in 1897; elected as a Republican to the Sixty-sixth and to the five succeeding Congresses (March 4, 1919-March 3, 1931); unsuccessful candidate for reelection in 1930 to the Seventy-second Congress, for election in 1934 to the Seventy-fourth Congress, and in 1936 to the Seventy-fifth Congress; resumed the practice of law; died in Buffalo, Erie County, N.Y., August 20, 1942, while on a motor trip; interment in Pine Lake Cemetery, La Porte, Ind.

HICKEY, John Joseph, a Senator from Wyoming; born in Rawlins, Carbon County, Wyo., August 22, 1911; attended the public schools; graduated with a law degree from the University of Wyoming in 1934; practiced law in Rawlins in 1934; city treasurer of Rawlins 1935-1940; Carbon County Attorney 1939-1942, 1946-1949; in 1942 enlisted in Army and served for four years, two of which were in the European Theater of Operations; relieved from active duty as a captain in 1946; appointed United States district attorney for Wyoming by President Harry S Truman in 1949; elected Governor of Wyoming in 1958 and served from January 5, 1959 until January 2, 1961, when he resigned; appointed as a Democrat to the United States Senate on January 3, 1961, to fill the vacancy caused by the death of Senator-elect Keith Thomson, and served until November 6, 1962; unsuccessful candidate in 1962 for election to the vacancy; resumed the practice of law; was appointed a judge on the United States Tenth Circuit Court of Appeals in 1966 and served until his death in Cheyenne, Wyo., September 22, 1970; interment in Rawlins Cemetery, Rawlins, Wyo.

**HICKMAN, John,** a Representative from Pennsylvania; born in West Bradford Township, Chester County, Pa., September 11, 1810; pursued English and classical studies under private tutors; began the study of medicine but abandoned it for the study of law; was admitted to the bar in 1833 and commenced practice in West Chester; delegate to the Democratic National Convention of 1844; district attorney for Chester County in 1845 and 1846; elected as a Democrat to the Thirty-fourth and Thirty-fifth Congresses, as an Anti-Lecompton Democrat to the Thirty-sixth Congress, and as a Republican to the Thirty-seventh Congress (March 4, 1855-March 3, 1863); chairman, Committee on Revolutionary Pensions (Thirty-fifth Congress), Committee on the Judiciary (Thirty-sixth and Thirty-seventh Congresses); declined to be a candidate for renomination in 1862 to the Thirty-eighth Congress; one of the managers appointed by the House of Representatives in 1862 to conduct the impeachment proceedings against West H. Humphreys, United States judge for the several districts of Tennessee; resumed the practice of law; member of the Pennsylvania house of representatives in 1869; died in West Chester, Pa., March 23, 1875; interment in Oaklands Cemetery, near West Chester, Pa.

**HICKS, Floyd Verne,** a Representative from Washington; born in Prosser, Benton County, Wash., May 29, 1915; attended the public schools; served in the United States Army Air Corps, April 1942 to June 1946; entered the service as a private and was discharged as a captain; graduated from Central Washington State College, Ellensburg, Wash., in 1938; school teacher and coach, 1935-1942; took advanced work in education at Washington State University, 1940-1942; graduated from University of Washington Law School in 1948; was admitted to the bar in March 1949 and commenced the practice of law in Pierce County, Wash.; superior court judge of Pierce County in 1961 and 1962; elected as a Democrat to the Eighty-ninth and to the five succeeding Congresses (January 3, 1965-January 3, 1977); was not a candidate for reelection in 1976 to the Ninety-fifth Congress; is a resident of Tacoma, Wash.

**HICKS, Frederick Cocks** (original name, Frederick Hicks Cocks, brother of William Willets Cocks), a Representative from New York; born in Westbury, Long Island, N.Y., March 6, 1872; attended the public schools, Swarthmore (Pa.) College, and Harvard University; engaged in banking; unsuccessful candidate for election in 1912 to the Sixty-third Congress; elected as a Republican to the Sixty-fourth and to the three succeeding Congresses (March 4, 1915-March 3, 1923); was not a candidate for renomination in 1922 to the Sixty-eighth Congress; declined a diplomatic position to Uruguay, tendered by President Warren G. Harding; was eastern director of the Republican National Committee campaign in 1924; appointed by President Calvin Coolidge as a member of the commission to represent the United States at the celebration of the Centennial of the Battle of Aracucho, held at Lima, Peru, during December 1924; appointed Alien Property Custodian April 10, 1925, and served until his death in Washington, D.C., December 14, 1925; interment in Quaker Cemetery, Westbury, Long Island, N.Y.

**HICKS, Josiah Duane,** a Representative from Pennsylvania; born in Machen, Wales, August 1, 1844; immigrated to the United States with his parents, who settled in Chester County, Pa., in 1847, and in the same year moved to Duncansville, Pa.; attended the common schools of Blair and Huntingdon Counties; moved to Altoona, Pa., in 1861; during the Civil War enlisted in the One Hundred and Twenty-fifth Regiment, Pennsylvania Volunteer Infantry, as a private in 1862 and served nearly eighteen months; reentered civil life as a clerk on the Pennsylvania Railroad; studied law; was admitted to the bar in 1875 and commenced practice in Tyrone, Pa.; elected district attorney of Blair County in 1880; reelected in 1883; elected as a Republican to the Fifty-third,

Fifty-fourth, and Fifty-fifth Congresses (March 4, 1893-March 3, 1899); chairman, Committee on Patents (Fifty-fifth Congress); was not a candidate for renomination in 1898; resumed the practice of law; member of the Altoona Board of Education 1911-1919; Pennsylvania commander of the Grand Army of the Republic in 1921; died in Altoona, Pa., May 9, 1923; interment in Fairview Cemetery.

**HICKS, Louise Day,** a Representative from Massachusetts; born in South Boston, Mass., October 16, 1923; attended the public schools; graduated from Wheelock Teachers' College, 1938; B.S., Boston University School of Education, 1955; J.D., Boston University School of Law, 1958; admitted to the Massachusetts bar in 1959 and commenced practice in Boston; land court examiner, 1942; counsel for Boston Juvenile Court, 1960; treasurer, Boston School Committee, 1962-1967, and chairman, 1963-1965; candidate for mayor of Boston, Mass., 1967; elected member of the Boston City Council, 1969; president, Boston City Council, 1970-1971; past president, Massachusetts Association of Women Lawyers; elected as a Democrat to the Ninety-second Congress (January 3, 1971-January 3, 1973); unsuccessful candidate for reelection in 1972 to the Ninety-third Congress; resumed the practice of law; is a resident of Boston, Mass.

**HICKS, Thomas Holliday,** a Senator from Maryland; born near East New Market, Dorchester County, Md., September 2, 1798; attended the local subscription schools; sheriff of Dorchester County in 1824; member, State legislature 1830; member of the State electoral college in 1836 and while a member of the college was elected to the State house of delegates in 1836; member of the Governor's council in 1837; register of wills of Dorchester County 1838-1851, 1855-1861; member of the Maryland constitutional convention in 1851; elected Governor of Maryland in 1857 and served from January 13, 1858 to January 8, 1862; appointed and subsequently elected as a Unionist to the United States Senate to fill the vacancy caused by the death of James A. Pearce and served from December 29, 1862, until his death in Washington, D.C., February 14, 1865; interment in the Cambridge Cemetery, Cambridge, Md.

**Bibliography:** *DAB*; Radcliffe, George L.P. *Governor Thomas H. Hicks of Maryland and the Civil War.* Johns Hopkins University Studies in Historical and Political Science, ser. 19, nos. 11-12. Baltimore: The Johns Hopkins Press, 1901.

**HIESTAND, Edgar Willard,** a Representative from California; born in Chicago, Ill., December 3, 1888; attended the public schools; was graduated from Dartmouth College in 1910; during the First World War served as a civilian executive with Committee on Education and Special Training, War Plans Division, Army General Staff, in 1917 and 1918; member and president of board of education, San Marino, Calif.; engaged in merchandising business, 1912-1931; executive of a large mail-order house 1931-1949; elected as a Republican to the Eighty-third and to the four succeeding Congresses (January 3, 1953-January 3, 1963); unsuccessful candidate for reelection in 1962 to the Eighty-eighth Congress; remained active in the John Birch Society and Republican politics until his death in Pasadena, Calif., August 19, 1970; remains cremated; ashes inurned at San Gabriel Valley Cemetery, San Gabriel, Calif.

**HIESTAND, John Andrew,** a Representative from Pennsylvania; born in East Donegal Township, Lancaster County, Pa., October 2, 1824; attended the common schools, an academy in Marietta, Pa., and Pennsylvania College at Gettysburg; studied law; was admitted to the bar in 1849 and commenced practice in Lancaster, Pa.; elected as a Whig to the Pennsylvania house of representatives in 1852, 1853, and 1856; purchased an interest in the Lancaster Examiner in 1858 and relinquished the practice of law; served in the Pennsylvania senate in 1860; unsuccessful candidate for election to the

Fortieth Congress in a special election in 1868 to fill the vacancy caused by the death of Thaddeus Stevens; appointed naval officer at the port of Philadelphia by President Ulysses S. Grant in 1871, reappointed in 1875 and served until 1879; elected as a Republican to the Forty-ninth and Fiftieth Congresses (March 4, 1885-March 3, 1889); unsuccessful candidate for reelection in 1888 to the Fifty-first Congress; died in Lancaster, Pa., December 13, 1890; interment in Marietta Cemetery, Marietta, Pa.

**HIESTER, Daniel** (brother of John Hiester, cousin of Joseph Hiester, and uncle of William Hiester and Daniel Heister [1774-1834]), a Representative from Pennsylvania and from Maryland; born in Berks County, Pa., June 25, 1747; attended the public schools; engaged in business in Montgomery County; colonel and brigadier general of militia and served in the Revolutionary War; member of the supreme executive council of Pennsylvania 1784-1786; commissioner of the Connecticut land claims in 1787; elected from Pennsylvania to the First and to the three succeeding Congresses and served from March 4, 1789, to July 1, 1796, when he resigned and moved to Hagerstown, Md.; elected as a Republican from Maryland to the Seventh and Eighth Congresses and served from March 4, 1801, until his death in Washington, D.C., March 7, 1804; interment in Zion Reformed Graveyard, Hagerstown, Md.

Bibliography: *DAB.*

**HIESTER, Daniel** (son of John Hiester and nephew of Daniel Hiester [1747-1804]), a Representative from Pennsylvania; born in Chester County, Pa., in 1774; prothonotary and clerk of the courts of Chester County 1800-1809; elected to the Eleventh Congress (March 4, 1809-March 3, 1811); was instrumental in establishing the Bank of Chester County and was its first cashier 1814-1817; burgess of West Chester 1815-1817; appointed register of wills and recorder of deeds February 28, 1821; died in Hagerstown, Md., March 8, 1834; interment in Congressional Cemetery, Washington, D.C.

**HIESTER, Isaac Ellmaker** (son of William Hiester and cousin of Hiester Clymer), a Representative from Pennsylvania; born in New Holland, Earl Township, Lancaster County, Pa., May 29, 1824; pursued classical studies; was graduated from Yale College in 1842; studied law; was admitted to the bar in 1845 and commenced practice in Lancaster; district attorney for Lancaster County 1848-1851; elected as a Whig to the Thirty-third Congress (March 4, 1853-March 3, 1855); unsuccessful candidate for reelection in 1854 to the Thirty-fourth Congress and for election in 1856 to the Thirty-fifth Congress; resumed the practice of law; delegate to the Democratic National Convention of 1868; died in Lancaster, Pa., February 6, 1871; interment in Lancaster Cemetery.

**HIESTER, John** (father of Daniel Hiester [1774-1834], brother of Daniel Hiester [1747-1804], cousin of Joseph Hiester, and uncle of William Hiester), a Representative from Pennsylvania; born in Goshenhoppen, Montgomery County, Pa., April 9, 1745; attended the common schools; engaged with his father in the lumbering business in Berne Township, Berks County, Pa.; served in the Revolutionary War as captain in the Pennsylvania Militia; elected as a Republican to the Tenth Congress (March 4, 1807-March 3, 1809); died in Goshenhoppen, Pa., October 15, 1821; interment in Union Church Cemetery, Parker Ford, Pa.

**HIESTER, Joseph** (cousin of John Hiester and Daniel Hiester [1747-1804] and grandfather of Henry Augustus Muhlenberg), a Representative from Pennsylvania; born in Berne Township, Berks County, Pa., November 18, 1752; attended the common schools; engaged in mercantile pursuits; served in the Revolutionary Army as captain and colonel; member of the Pennsylvania conference in 1776 which assumed the government of the colony; member of the Pennsylvania constitutional convention which ratified the Federal Constitution on December 12, 1787, and of the Pennsylvania constitutional convention of 1790; member of the Pennsylvania

house of representatives, 1787-1790; served in the Pennsylvania senate, 1790-1794; elected as a Republican to the Fifth Congress to fill the vacancy caused by the resignation of George Ege; reelected to the three succeeding Congresses and served from December 1, 1797, to March 3, 1805; major general of the Pennsylvania Militia in 1807; elected to the Fourteenth and to the two succeeding Congresses and served from March 4, 1815, until his resignation in December 1820, having been elected chief executive of the Commonwealth; Governor of Pennsylvania from December 19, 1820 to December 16, 1823; died in Reading, Pa., June 10, 1832; interment in the burying ground of the Reformed Church; reinterment in Charles Evans Cemetery.

Bibliography: *DAB.*

**HIESTER, William** (father of Isaac Ellmaker Hiester, uncle of Hiester Clymer, and nephew of John Hiester and Daniel Hiester [1747-1804]), a Representative from Pennsylvania; born in Berne Township, near Reading, Berks County, Pa., October 10, 1790; attended the common schools; served as a lieutenant during the War of 1812; engaged in agricultural and mercantile pursuits in Lancaster County; justice of the peace 1823-1828; was an unsuccessful Anti-Masonic candidate for election in 1828 to the Twenty-first Congress; elected as an Anti-Masonic candidate to the Twenty-second, Twenty-third, and Twenty-fourth Congresses (March 4, 1831-March 3, 1837); delegate to the Pennsylvania constitutional convention in 1837; member of the Pennsylvania senate 1840-1842 and served as speaker in 1842; died in New Holland, Lancaster County, Pa., on October 13, 1853; interment in Lancaster Cemetery, Lancaster, Pa.

**HIGBY, William,** a Representative from California; born in Willsboro, N.Y., on August 18, 1813; attended a preparatory school in Westport, N.Y., and was graduated from the University of Vermont at Burlington in 1840; studied law; was admitted to the bar in 1847 and commenced practice in Elizabethtown, N.Y.; moved to California in 1850 and settled in Calaveras County; resumed the practice of law; district attorney 1853-1859; served in the State senate in 1862 and 1863; elected as a Republican to the Thirty-eighth, Thirty-ninth, and Fortieth Congresses (March 4, 1863-March 3, 1869); chairman, Committee on Mines and Mining (Thirty-ninth and Fortieth Congresses); unsuccessful candidate for renomination in 1868; editor of the Calaveras Chronicle for several years; was collector of internal revenue 1877-1881; devoted himself to horticulture until his death; died in Santa Rosa, Calif., November 27, 1887; interment in Mountain View Cemetery, Oakland, Calif.

**HIGGINS, Anthony,** a Senator from Delaware; born in Red Lion Hundred, New Castle County, Del., October 1, 1840; attended Newark Academy and Delaware College, and graduated from Yale College in 1861; studied law at the Harvard Law School; was admitted to the bar in 1864 and commenced practice in Wilmington, Del.; served in the Union Army in 1864; appointed deputy attorney general in 1864; United States attorney for Delaware, 1869-1876; unsuccessful Republican candidate for election in 1884 to the Forty-ninth Congress; elected as a Republican to the United States Senate, and served from March 4, 1889 to March 3, 1895; unsuccessful candidate for reelection in 1894; chairman, Committee to Examine Branches of the Civil Service (Fifty-first and Fifty-second Congresses), Committee on Manufactures (Fifty-second Congress); resumed the practice of his profession in Wilmington, Del.; served as one of the attorneys for the respondent in the impeachment proceedings of United States District Judge Charles Swayne of Florida, 1904-1905; died in New York City, June 26, 1912; interment in St. Georges Cemetery, near St. Georges, New Castle County, Del.

Bibliography: Higgins, John C. *The Life and Services of Hon. Anthony Higgins.* Wilmington: The Historical Society of Delaware, 1913.

**HIGGINS, Edwin Werter,** a Representative from Connecticut; born in Clinton, Middlesex County, Conn., July 2, 1874; attended Norwich Free Academy; was graduated from Yale Law School in 1897; was admitted to the bar in 1897 and commenced practice in Norwich, Conn.; member, Connecticut State house of representatives, 1899-1900; member of the Republican State central committee, 1900-1905; health officer of New London County, 1900-1905; corporation counsel of Norwich in 1901, 1902, and 1919-1922; prosecuting attorney of Norwich in 1905; delegate to the Republican National Conventions of 1904 and 1916; elected as a Republican to the Fifty-ninth Congress to fill the vacancy caused by the resignation of Frank B. Brandegee; reelected to the three succeeding Congresses, and served from October 2, 1905 to March 3, 1913; was not a candidate for renomination in 1912 to the Sixty-third Congress; resumed the practice of law; served in the Connecticut State National Guard during the First World War; prosecuting attorney, Court of Common Pleas, New London County, Conn., 1932-1946; resumed the general practice of law; died in Norwich, Conn., September 24, 1954; interment in Maplewood Cemetery.

**HIGGINS, John Patrick,** a Representative from Massachusetts; born in Boston, Mass., February 19, 1893; attended the public schools and was graduated from Harvard University in 1917; during the First World War served as an ensign in the United States Navy 1917-1919; employed as a chemist 1919-1922; student in Boston University Law School and Northeastern College of Law, Boston, Mass., in 1925 and 1926; was admitted to the bar in 1927 and commenced practice in Boston; member of the Massachusetts house of representatives 1929-1934; elected as a Democrat to the Seventy-fourth and Seventy-fifth Congresses and served from January 3, 1935, until his resignation on September 30, 1937, having been appointed by Governor Charles F. Hurley on October 1, 1937, as chief justice of the superior court of Massachusetts, in which capacity he served until his death; suspended by General Douglas MacArthur as a judge on the International Military Tribunal for the Far East at Tokyo, Japan, and resigned in June 1946; died in Boston, Mass., August 2, 1955; interment in St. Joseph Cemetery, West Roxbury, Mass.

**HIGGINS, William Lincoln,** a Representative from Connecticut; born in Chesterfield, Hampshire County, Mass., March 8, 1867; attended the public schools of Chesterfield and Northampton, Mass., and Deerfield (Mass.) Academy; was graduated from the medical department of the University of the City of New York in 1890 and commenced the practice of medicine in Willington, Conn., the same year; moved to South Coventry, Conn., in 1891; served in the State house of representatives 1905-1907, 1917, 1919-1921, 1925 and 1927; member of the State senate 1909-1911; first selectman of Coventry, Conn., 1917-1932; county commissioner of Tolland County, Conn., 1921-1932; secretary of state 1928-1932; delegate to the Republican National Conventions in 1928, 1932, and 1936; elected as a Republican to the Seventy-third and Seventy-fourth Congresses (March 4, 1933-January 3, 1937); unsuccessful candidate for reelection in 1936 to the Seventy-fifth Congress; resumed the practice of medicine in South Coventry, Conn.; died in Norwich, Conn., November 19, 1951; remains were cremated and interred in Chesterfield Center Cemetery, Chesterfield, Mass.

**HIGGINSON, Stephen,** a Delegate from Massachusetts; born in Salem, Mass., November 28, 1743; attended the common schools; engaged in mercantile pursuits and was an active and successful shipmaster 1765-1775; served in the Massachusetts legislature, 1782; Member of the Continental Congress in 1783; naval officer at the port of Boston 1797-1808; prominent in putting down Shays' Rebellion; served as lieutenant colonel of the Boston regiment; became a Federalist in politics; died in Boston, Mass., November 22, 1828; interment in Central Burying Ground.

**Bibliography:** *DAB.*

**HIGHTOWER, Jack English,** a Representative from Texas; born in Memphis, Hall County, Tex., September 6, 1926; attended public schools; B.A., Baylor University, 1949; LL.B., Baylor University School of Law, 1951; admitted to the Texas bar in 1951 and commenced practice in Vernon; served in the United States Navy, 1944-1946; served as district attorney, Forty-sixth Texas Judicial District, 1951-1961; member, Texas State house of representatives, 1953-1954; unsuccessful candidate for election to the United States House of Representatives in a special election in 1961; Texas State senator, 1965-1974; delegate to the Democratic National Convention of 1968; elected as a Democrat to the Ninety-fourth and to the four succeeding Congresses (January 3, 1975-January 3, 1985); unsuccessful candidate for reelection in 1984 to the Ninety-ninth Congress; first assistant attorney general of Texas, 1985-1987; is a resident of Vernon, Tex.

**HILBORN, Samuel Greeley,** a Representative from California; born in Minot, Androscoggin (then Cumberland) County, Maine, December 9, 1834; attended the common schools, Hebron Academy, and Gould's Academy, Bethel, Maine, and was graduated from Tufts College, Medford, Mass., in 1859; studied law and was admitted to the bar in 1861; moved to California; located in Vallejo, Solano County, and engaged in the practice of law; served in the State senate 1875-1879; member of the constitutional convention in 1879; moved to San Francisco, Calif., in 1883; appointed by President Chester A. Arthur United States district attorney for the district of California and served from 1883 to 1886; moved to Oakland in 1887 and continued the practice of his profession; elected as a Republican to the Fifty-second Congress to fill the vacancy caused by the resignation of Joseph McKenna; presented credentials as a Member-elect to the Fifty-third Congress and served from December 5, 1892, until April 4, 1894, when he was succeeded by Warren B. English, who contested his election; elected to the Fifty-fourth and Fifty-fifth Congresses (March 4, 1895-March 3, 1899); unsuccessful candidate for renomination in 1898 to the Fifty-sixth Congress; lived in retirement until his death in Washington, D.C., April 19, 1899; interment in Rock Creek Cemetery.

**HILDEBRANDT, Fred Herman,** a Representative from South Dakota; born in West Bend, Washington County, Wis., August 2, 1874; moved with his parents to Waupun, Wis., in 1888, where he attended the public and high schools; subsequently moved to Watertown, S.Dak., in 1900 and was employed as a railroad worker from 1903 to 1932; member of the South Dakota State house of representatives in 1922 and 1923; served as chairman of the South Dakota Game and Fish Commission, 1927-1931; elected as a Democrat to the Seventy-third and to the two succeeding Congresses (March 4, 1933-January 3, 1939); was not a candidate in 1938 for renomination to the House of Representatives, but was an unsuccessful candidate for nomination to the United States Senate; unsuccessful candidate for election in 1942 to the Seventy-eighth Congress; delegate to the Democratic National Convention of 1944; retired from active business life and resided in Watertown, S.Dak.; died in Bradenton, Fla., January 26, 1956; interment in Mount Hope Cemetery, Watertown, S.Dak.

**HILDEBRANT, Charles Quinn,** a Representative from Ohio; born in Wilmington, Clinton County, Ohio, October 17, 1864; attended the public schools and Ohio State University at Columbus; elected clerk of the court of Clinton County in 1890, and reelected in 1893 and 1896; elected as a Republican to the Fifty-seventh and Fifty-eighth Congresses (March 4, 1901-March 3, 1905); chairman, Committee on Accounts (Fifty-eighth Congress); unsuccessful candidate for reelection in 1904 to the Fifty-ninth Congress; resumed his business and agricultural pursuits; delegate to the Republican National Convention of 1908; secretary of state of Ohio, 1915-1917; mayor of Wilmington, Ohio, from November 1927 until his retirement on December 31, 1941; died in Wilmington, Ohio, March 31, 1953; interment in Sugar Grove Cemetery.

**HILER, John Patrick,** a Representative from Indiana; born in Chicago, Ill., April 24, 1953; attended public and Catholic schools in Walkerton and La Porte, Ind.; B.A., Williams College, Williamstown, Mass., 1975; M.B.A., University of Chicago School of Business, 1977; marketing director; delegate, White House Conference of Small Business, 1980; delegate, Indiana State Republican conventions, 1978-1980; elected as a Republican to the Ninety-seventh and to the four succeeding Congresses (January 3, 1981-January 3, 1991); unsuccessful candidate for reelection in 1990 to the One Hundred Second Congress; is a resident of La Porte, Ind.

**HILL, Benjamin Harvey** (cousin of Hugh Lawson White Hill), a Representative and a Senator from Georgia; born in Hillsborough, Jasper County, Ga., September 14, 1823; pursued classical studies and graduated from the University of Georgia at Athens in 1843; studied law; was admitted to the bar in 1844 and commenced practice in Lagrange, Troup County, Ga.; member, State house of representatives 1851; member, State senate 1859-1860; actively opposed disunion until the secession ordinance had been adopted; delegate to the Confederate Provisional Congress in 1861; senator in the Confederate Congress 1861-1865; arrested at the close of the Civil War and eventually paroled; resumed the practice of law; elected as a Democrat to the Forty-fourth Congress to fill the vacancy caused by the death of Representative-elect Garnett McMillan; reelected to the Forty-fifth Congress and served from May 5, 1875, until his resignation, effective March 3, 1877; elected as a Democrat to the United States Senate and served from March 4, 1877, until his death in Atlanta, Ga., August 16, 1882; chairman, Committee to Audit and Control the Contingent Expense (Forty-sixth Congress); interment in Oakland Cemetery.

**Bibliography:** *DAB*; Hill, Benjamin. *Senator Benjamin Hill of Georgia, His Life, Speeches and Writings*. Atlanta: H.C. Hudgkins and Co., 1891; Pearce, Haywood. *Benjamin H. Hill, Seccession and Reconstruction*. Chicago: The University of Chicago Press, 1928.

**HILL, Charles Augustus,** a Representative from Illinois; born in Truxton, Cortland County, N.Y., August 23, 1833; attended the common schools and a select school at Griffins Mills; taught school in Hamburg, Erie County, N.Y., and Will County, Ill.; attended Bell's Commercial College, Chicago, in 1856; studied law; was admitted to the bar in Indianapolis, Ind.; returned to Will County, Ill., in 1860 and practiced; during the Civil War enlisted in Company F, Eighth Regiment, Illinois Volunteer Cavalry, in August 1862; appointed first lieutenant in the First Regiment, United States Colored Troops; commissioned in 1865 captain of Company C of that regiment; returned to Will County, Ill., in 1865 and resumed the practice of law in Joliet; elected prosecuting attorney in 1868 for the counties of Will and Grundy and served four years; elected as a Republican to the Fifty-first Congress (March 4, 1889-March 3, 1891); unsuccessful candidate for reelection in 1890 to the Fifty-second Congress; resumed the practice of law in Joliet, Ill.; assistant attorney general of Illinois, 1897-1900; died in Joliet, Ill., May 29, 1902; interment in Oakwood Cemetery.

**HILL, Clement Sidney,** a Representative from Kentucky; born near Lebanon, Marion County, Ky., February 13, 1813; pursued academic studies; attended St. Mary's College, St. Mary, Ky.; studied law; was admitted to the bar in 1837 and commenced practice in Lebanon, Ky.; member of the Kentucky house of representatives in 1839; elected as a Whig to the Thirty-third Congress (March 4, 1853-March 3, 1855); resumed the practice of law in Lebanon, Ky., where he died January 5, 1892; interment in St. Augustine's Cemetery.

**HILL, David Bennett,** a Senator from New York; born in Havana (now Montour Falls), Chemung (now Schuyler) County, N.Y., August 29, 1843; attended the public schools; studied law; was admitted to the bar in 1864 and commenced practice in Elmira, N.Y.; city attorney the same year; member, State assembly 1871-1872, serving as speaker in 1872; mayor of Elmira 1882; president of the New York State Bar Association 1886-1887; elected lieutenant governor of New York in 1882, and assumed the office of governor to fill the vacancy caused by the resignation of Grover Cleveland; elected to a full term as Governor in 1885, reelected in 1888, and served from January 6, 1885 to January 1, 1892; elected as a Democrat to the United States Senate on January 1, 1891, for the term beginning March 4, 1891, but did not assume these duties until later, preferring to continue as Governor; served from January 7, 1892, to March 3, 1897; was not a candidate for reelection in 1896; chairman, Committee on Immigration (Fifty-third Congress); unsuccessful candidate in 1894 for election for Governor; resumed the practice of law; died in Albany, N.Y., October 20, 1910; interment in Montour Cemetery, Montour Falls, N.Y.

**Bibliography:** *DAB*; Bass, Herbert. *"I Am A Democrat:" The Political Career of David Bennett Hill*. Syracuse: Syracuse University Press, 1961.

**HILL, Ebenezer J.,** a Representative from Connecticut; born in Redding, Fairfield County, Conn., August 4, 1845; attended the public schools, Center Academy, and Yale College in 1865 and 1866; during the Civil War enlisted in the Union Army in 1863 and served until the close of the war; engaged in business and banking in Norwalk; burgess of Norwalk; chairman of the board of school visitors; delegate to the Republican National Convention in 1884; member of the State senate in 1886 and 1887; served one term on the Republican State central committee; elected as a Republican to the Fifty-fourth and to the eight succeeding Congresses (March 4, 1895-March 3, 1913); chairman, Committee on Expenditures in the Department of the Treasury (Sixty-first Congress); unsuccessful candidate in 1912 for reelection to the Sixty-third Congress; elected to the Sixty-fourth and Sixty-fifth Congresses and served from March 4, 1915, until his death in Norwalk, Conn., September 27, 1917; interment in Riverside Cemetery.

**HILL, Hugh Lawson White** (cousin of Benjamin Harvey Hill), a Representative from Tennessee; born near McMinnville, Warren County, Tenn., March 1, 1810; attended private schools and the Carroll Male Academy at McMinnville; was graduated from Cumberland College, Nashville, Tenn.; taught school for a short time; engaged in agricultural pursuits and fruit growing; member of the State house of representatives 1837-1839 and in 1841; elected as a Democrat to the Thirtieth Congress (March 4, 1847-March 3, 1849); was not a candidate for renomination in 1848; resumed agricultural pursuits; member of the State constitutional convention in 1870; died at Hills Creek, Warren County, Tenn., January 18, 1892; interment in Hill Graveyard, near McMinnville, Tenn.

**HILL, Isaac,** a Senator from New Hampshire; born in West Cambridge, near Arlington, Mass., on April 6, 1789; attended the common schools; moved with his parents to Ashburnham, Mass., in 1798; apprenticed to a printer in Amherst, N.H.; moved to Concord in 1809; purchased and for twenty years edited the New Hampshire Patriot; member, New Hampshire State senate, 1820-1823, 1827-1828; member of the New Hampshire State house of representatives in 1826; Second Comptroller of the United States Treasury, 1829-1830; elected as a Jacksonian to the United States Senate, and served from March 4, 1831 to May 30, 1836, when he resigned; elected Governor of New Hampshire in 1836, reelected in 1837 and 1838, and served from June 2, 1836 to June 5, 1839; United States subtreasurer at Boston, 1840-1841; returned to newspaper publishing, 1840-1847; died in Washington, D.C., March 22, 1851; interment in Blossom Hill Cemetery, Concord, N.H.

**Bibliography:** *DAB*; Bradley, Cyrus. *Biography of Isaac Hill.* Concord: J.F. Brown, 1935; Cole, Donald. *Jacksonian Democracy in New Hampshire, 1800-1851.* Cambridge: Harvard University Press, 1970.

**HILL, John,** a Representative from New Jersey; born in Catskill, Greene County, N.Y., June 10, 1821; attended private schools; employed as a bank clerk and learned bookkeeping in Catskill, N.Y.; moved to Boonton, N.J., in 1845; was employed as a bookkeeper and paymaster and later engaged in mercantile pursuits; served as postmaster from November 1849 to May 1853; member of the township committee 1852-1856 and 1863-1867; justice of the peace 1856-1861; member of the State house of assembly in 1861, 1862, and 1866, serving as speaker during the last year; unsuccessful candidate for election to the State senate in 1862; took an active part in raising troops during the Civil War; elected as a Republican to the Fortieth, Forty-first, and Forty-second Congresses (March 4, 1867-March 3, 1873); chairman, Committee on Expenditures in the Department of the Interior (Forty-second Congress); resumed mercantile pursuits until 1876, when he retired; delegate to the Republican National Convention in 1868; member of the State senate 1875-1877; elected as a Republican to the Forty-seventh Congress (March 4, 1881-March 3, 1883); was not a candidate for renomination in 1882; died in Boonton, N.J., July 24, 1884; interment in Boonton Cemetery.

**HILL, John,** a Representative from North Carolina; born near Germanton, Stokes County, N.C., April 9, 1797; completed preparatory studies and was graduated from the University of North Carolina at Chapel Hill in 1816; was a planter; clerk of court of Stokes County for thirty years; member of the State house of commons 1819-1823; served in the State senate 1823-1825, 1830, and 1831; elected as a Democrat to the Twenty-sixth Congress (March 4, 1839-March 3, 1841); reading clerk in the State senate in 1850; delegate to the State constitutional convention at Raleigh, N.C., in 1861; died in Raleigh, N.C., April 24, 1861; interment in Old Hill Burying Ground, near Germanton, N.C.

**HILL, John** (cousin of John Thomas Harris), a Representative from Virginia; born in New Canton, Buckingham County, Va., July 18, 1800; completed preparatory studies and was graduated from Washington Academy (now Washington and Lee University), Lexington, Va., in 1818; studied law; was admitted to the bar in 1821 and practiced; elected as a Whig to the Twenty-sixth Congress (March 4, 1839-March 3, 1841); unsuccessful candidate for reelection in 1840 to the Twenty-seventh Congress; resumed the practice of law; member of the Virginia constitutional convention 1850-1851; Commonwealth attorney for several years; county judge of Buckingham County 1870-1879; died at Buckingham Court House, Va., April 19, 1880; interment in the Presbyterian Cemetery.

**HILL, John Boynton Philip Clayton,** a Representative from Maryland; born in Annapolis, Anne Arundel County, Md., May 2, 1879; attended the common schools; was graduated from Johns Hopkins University in 1900 and from the law department of Harvard University in 1903; was admitted to the bar the same year and commenced practice in Boston, Mass.; returned to Baltimore, Md., in 1904 and continued the practice of law; unsuccessful candidate for election to the Sixty-first Congress in 1908; United States attorney for the district of Maryland 1910-1915; unsuccessful candidate for mayor of Baltimore in 1915; delegate to the Republican National Convention in 1916; judge advocate for the Fifteenth Division, and attached to the Fourteenth Cavalry, Mexican border service, from August 26 to December 15, 1916; during the First World War was major and lieutenant colonel in the United States Army in 1918 and 1919; elected as a Republican to the Sixty-seventh, Sixty-eighth, and Sixty-ninth Congresses (March 4, 1921-March 3, 1927); unsuccessful candidate for the Senate in 1926; unsuccessful candidate for election in 1928 to the Seventy-first

Congress and in 1936 to the Seventy-fifth Congress; moved to New York City in 1937 and continued the practice of law; returned in 1940 to Annapolis, Md.; died in Washington, D.C., May 23, 1941; interment in Arlington National Cemetery, Va.

**HILL, Joseph Lister,** a Representative and a Senator from Alabama; born in Montgomery, Ala., December 29, 1894; attended the public schools and the Starke University School at Montgomery, Ala.; graduated from the University of Alabama at Tuscaloosa in 1914 and from its law department in 1915; also studied law at the University of Michigan at Ann Arbor and Columbia University, New York City; was admitted to the Alabama bar in 1916 and commenced practice at Montgomery, Ala.; president, Montgomery Board of Education, 1917-1922; served in the Army with the Seventeenth and Seventy-first United States Infantry Regiments during the First World War, 1917-1919; elected as a Democrat to the Sixty-eighth Congress to fill the vacancy caused by the death of John R. Tyson; reelected to the Sixty-ninth and to the six succeeding Congresses, and served from August 14, 1923 to January 11, 1938, when he resigned, having been appointed to the United States Senate on January 10, 1938; chairman, Committee on Military Affairs (Seventy-fifth Congress); subsequently elected to the Senate as a Democrat on April 26, 1938, to fill the vacancy caused by the resignation of Dixie Bibb Graves for the term ending January 3, 1939; reelected in 1938, 1944, 1950, 1956, and again in 1962; served from January 11, 1938 to January 2, 1969; declined to be a candidate for reelection in 1968; Democratic whip 1941-1947; chairman, Committee on Expenditures in Executive Departments (Seventy-seventh through Seventy-ninth Congresses), Committee on Labor and Public Welfare (Eighty-fourth through Ninetieth Congresses); chairman, National Committee on Biological Research; the Lister Hill Center at the National Institutes of Health, Bethesda, Md., which he helped create, was named for him in 1968; died in Montgomery, Ala., December 21, 1984; interment in Greenwood Cemetery.

**Bibliography:** Hamilton, Virginia Van der Veer. *Lister Hill: Statesman From the South.* Chapel Hill: University of North Carolina Press, 1987.

**HILL, Joshua,** a Representative and a Senator from Georgia; born in Abbeville District, S.C., January 10, 1812; attended the common schools and was privately tutored; studied law; was admitted to the bar and commenced practice in Monticello, Jasper County, Ga.; elected by the American Party to the Thirty-fifth and Thirty-sixth Congresses, and served from March 4, 1857 to January 23, 1861, when he resigned; unsuccessful candidate for Governor in 1863; appointed collector of customs at Savannah in 1866 and register in bankruptcy in 1867 but declined both offices; upon the readmission of the State of Georgia to representation was elected as a Republican to the United States Senate on July 28, 1868, and served until March 3, 1873; was not a candidate for reelection; returned to Madison, Ga., and resumed the practice of law; member of the State constitutional convention in 1877; died in Madison, Ga., March 6, 1891; interment in Madison Cemetery.

**Bibliography:** Roberts, Lucien E. "The Political Career of Joshua Hill, Georgia Unionist." *Georgia Historical Quarterly* 21 (March 1937): 50-72.

**HILL, Knute,** a Representative from Washington; born on a farm near Creston, Ogle County, Ill., July 31, 1876; moved to De Forest, Wis., in 1877 and to Red Wing, Minn., in 1889; attended the public schools, Red Wing (Minn.) Seminary, and the University of Minnesota at Minneapolis; was graduated from the law department of the University of Wisconsin at Madison in 1906; was admitted to the bar the same year and practiced law in Milwaukee and Eau Claire, Wis., 1908-1910; moved to Prosser, Wash., in 1911 and taught in the public and high schools of Benton County, Wash., 1911-1922; lecturer, State Grange, 1922-1932; also engaged in agricultural pursuits; member of the State house of representatives 1927-1933; elected as a Democrat to the Seventy-third and to the four succeeding Congresses (March 4, 1933-January 3, 1943); unsuccessful candidate for reelection in 1942 to the Seventy-eighth Congress; superintendent of the Uintah-Ouray Indian agency at Fort Duchesne, Utah, from August 16, 1943, until his resignation on March 31, 1944; radio commentator in Spokane, Wash., 1944-1946; unsuccessful Independent Progressive candidate for election in 1946 to the Eightieth Congress; consulting appraiser and information clerk in the Bureau of Reclamation, Columbia Basin Project, Ephrata, Wash., from March 1949 until his retirement in 1951; died in Desert Hot Springs, Calif., December 3, 1963; interment in Yakima Calvary Cemetery, Yakima, Wash.

**HILL, Lister,** a Representative and a Senator from Alabama. (*See* HILL, Joseph Lister.)

**HILL, Mark Langdon,** a Representative from Massachusetts and from Maine; born in Biddeford, York County, Maine (then a district of Massachusetts), June 30, 1772; attended the public schools; merchant and shipbuilder at Phippsburg, Maine; overseer and trustee of Bowdoin College, Brunswick, Maine, 1796-1842; member of the Massachusetts house of representatives 1797-1808, 1810, 1813, and 1814; served in the Massachusetts senate in 1804 and 1815-1817; judge of the court of common pleas in 1810; served on the General Court of Massachusetts; elected from Massachusetts to the Sixteenth Congress (March 4, 1819-March 3, 1821); when Maine was separated from Massachusetts and admitted as a State into the Union was elected to the Seventeenth Congress from that State (March 4, 1821-March 3, 1823); postmaster of Phippsburg, Maine, 1819-1824; appointed as a collector of customs at Bath, Maine, in 1824; died in Phippsburg, Sagadahoc County, November 26, 1842; interment in the churchyard of the Congregational Church, Phippsburg Center, Maine.

**HILL, Nathaniel Peter,** a Senator from Colorado; born in Montgomery, Orange County, N.Y., February 18, 1832; attended Montgomery Academy and graduated from Brown University in Providence, R.I., in 1856; instructor and later professor of chemistry in Brown University 1856-1864; traveled to Colorado in the spring of 1865 to investigate mineral resources; spent a portion of 1865 and 1866 in Swansea, Wales, and Freiberg, Saxony, studying metallurgy; returned to the United States with a perfected method of smelting gold ore and took up a permanent residence in Black Hawk, Colo., in 1867 as manager of the Boston & Colorado Smelting Co.; mayor of Black Hawk 1871; member, Territorial council 1872-1873; moved to Denver, Colo., in 1873 and engaged in smelting and in the real estate business; elected as a Republican to the United States Senate and served from March 4, 1879, to March 3, 1885; chairman, Committee on Mines and Mining (Forty-seventh Congress), Committee on Post Office and Post Roads (Forty-eighth Congress); engaged in mining; owner and publisher of the Denver Republican; member of the United States delegation to the International Monetary Commmission in 1891; died in Denver, Colo., on May 22, 1900; interment in Fairmount Cemetery.
Bibliography: *DAB.*

**HILL, Ralph,** a Representative from Indiana; born in Trumbull County, Ohio, October 12, 1827; attended the district school, the Kinsman Academy and the Grand River Institute, Austinburg, Ohio; taught school in 1846, 1847, 1849, and 1850; studied law at the New York State and National Law School, Ballston, N.Y., and was admitted to the bar in Albany, N.Y., in 1851; returned to Jefferson, Ohio, in August 1851 and practiced; established a select school at Austinburg, Ohio, in November 1851; resumed the practice of law in Jefferson, Ohio, in March 1852; moved to Columbus, Ind., in August 1852 and continued the practice of law; elected as a Republican to the Thirty-ninth Congress (March 4, 1865-March 3, 1867); was not a candidate for renomination in 1866; collector of internal revenue for

the third district of Indiana 1869-1875; moved to Indianapolis, Ind., in 1879 and resumed the practice of law; died in Indianapolis, Ind., August 20, 1899; interment in Crown Hill Cemetery.

**HILL, Robert Potter,** a Representative from Illinois and from Oklahoma; born near Ewing, Franklin County, Ill., April 18, 1874; attended the public schools and Ewing College in 1889; taught school in Franklin County 1891-1893; graduated from Ewing College in 1896; moved to Marion, Williamson County, Ill., in 1896; justice of the peace in 1899; studied law; was admitted to the bar in 1902 and commenced practice in Marion; police magistrate of Marion in 1903; city attorney of Marion 1908-1910; member of the State house of representatives 1910-1912; elected as a Democrat from Illinois to the Sixty-third Congress (March 4, 1913-March 3, 1915); unsuccessful candidate for reelection in 1914 to the Sixty-fourth Congress; resumed the practice of law; moved to Oklahoma City, Okla., in 1918 and continued the practice of law; appointed assistant county attorney, Oklahoma County, in 1925 and served until 1929; served as district judge of the thirteenth judicial district from 1931 until his resignation on December 15, 1936, having been elected to Congress; elected as a Democrat from Oklahoma to the Seventy-fifth Congress and served from January 3, 1937, until his death in Oklahoma City, Okla., October 29, 1937; interment in Memorial Park Cemetery.

**HILL, Samuel Billingsley,** a Representative from Washington; born in Franklin, Izard County, Ark., April 2, 1875; attended the common schools, the University of Arkansas at Fayetteville, and was graduated from its law department in 1898; was admitted to the bar the same year and commenced practice in Danville, Ark.; moved to Waterville, Wash., in 1904 and continued the practice of law; prosecuting attorney of Douglas County 1907-1911; judge of the superior court for Douglas and Grant Counties 1917-1924; elected as a Democrat to the Sixty-eighth Congress to fill the vacancy caused by the resignation of J. Stanley Webster; reelected to the Sixty-ninth and to the five succeeding Congresses and served from September 25, 1923, until his resignation, effective June 25, 1936, having been confirmed as a member of the United States Board of Tax Appeals (now the Tax Court of the United States) on May 21, 1936, serving as a judge on the court until his retirement November 30, 1953; died in Bethesda, Md., March 16, 1958; interment in Rock Creek Cemetery, Washington, D.C.

**HILL, Whitmell,** a Delegate from North Carolina; born in Bertie County, N.C., February 12, 1743; attended the common schools and was graduated from the University of Pennsylvania at Philadelphia in 1760; served in the Revolutionary War, attaining the rank of colonel; engaged in agricultural pursuits; delegate to the assembly of freemen at Hillsboro in 1775; member of the State congress at Halifax in 1776; delegate to the State constitutional convention in 1776; member of the State house of commons in 1777; Member of the Continental Congress 1778-1780; served in the State senate 1778-1780, 1784, and 1785; died on his plantation at Hills Ferry, near Hamilton, Martin County, N.C., September 26, 1797; interment in the family cemetery on his estate; reinterment in 1887 in Trinity Cemetery, near Scotland Neck, N.C.

**HILL, William David,** a Representative from Ohio; born in Nelson County, Va., October 1, 1833; attended the country schools and Antioch College; moved to Springfield, Ohio, and published the Ohio Press in 1858; studied law; was admitted to the bar in 1859 and commenced practice in Springfield, Ohio; mayor of Springfield 1861-1863; member of the State house of representatives 1866-1870; member of the Board of Education of Defiance, Ohio; superintendent of insurance 1875-1878; delegate to the Democratic National Convention in 1880 and 1888; elected as a Democrat to the Forty-sixth Congress (March 4, 1879-March 3, 1881); elected to the Forty-eighth and Forty-ninth Congresses (March 4, 1883-March 3, 1887); chairman, Committee on Territories (Forty-ninth Congress);

unsuccessful candidate for reelection in 1886 to the Fiftieth Congress; resumed the practice of law in Defiance, Ohio; moved to Kalispell, Mont., in 1891; returned to Defiance in 1896 and continued the practice of law; city solicitor of Defiance 1903-1905; died near Litchfield, Ill., while en route to Los Angeles, Calif., December 26, 1906; interment in Riverside Cemetery, Defiance, Ohio.

**HILL, William Henry,** a Representative from North Carolina; born in Brunswick, Columbus County, N.C., on May 1, 1767; attended the public schools in Boston, Mass.; engaged in agricultural pursuits; studied law in Boston; was admitted to the bar and practiced; appointed United States district attorney for North Carolina by President Washington in 1790; member of the State senate in 1794; elected as a Federalist to the Sixth and Seventh Congresses (March 4, 1799-March 3, 1803); appointed judge of the United States District Court for the District of North Carolina by President John Adams at the close of his term but the designation was withdrawn by President Jefferson; returned to his estate near Wilmington, N.C., where he engaged in agricultural pursuits until his death there in 1809; interment in the family burial ground on his estate, "Hilton," near Wilmington, N.C.

**HILL, William Henry,** a Representative from New York; born in Plains, Luzerne County, Pa., March 23, 1877; attended the public schools; was graduated from the high school at Binghamton, N.Y.; mayor of Lestershire (now Johnson City), N.Y., 1898-1901; postmaster of Lestershire from 1902 until 1910; editor and publisher of the *Record* at Johnson City, 1898-1921; member of the New York State senate, 1914-1918; elected as a Republican to the Sixty-sixth Congress (March 4, 1919-March 3, 1921); was not a candidate for reelection in 1920 to the Sixty-seventh Congress; delegate to the Republican National Conventions of 1924, 1928, 1932, 1940, and 1944; appointed as a member of the New York State Parks Commission by Governor Alfred E. Smith in 1925, and elected chairman in 1933; chairman of the New York Hoover for President Committee in 1928; vice chairman of the Republican Campaign Committee in the East in 1932; trustee of Syracuse University; member of the Republican executive committee of the State of New York; newspaper publisher until 1960; resided in Binghamton, N.Y., where he died on July 24, 1972; interment in Riverhurst Cemetery, Endicott, N.Y.

**HILL, William Luther,** a Senator from Florida; born in Gainesville, Alachua County, Fla., October 17, 1873; attended private and public schools and the East Florida Seminary at Gainesville, Fla.; engaged in banking and insurance; was graduated from the law college of the University of Florida at Gainesville in 1914; was admitted to the bar the same year and commenced practice in Gainesville, Fla.; secretary to Senator Duncan U. Fletcher of Florida from 1917 until 1936; clerk to the Senate Committee on Commerce, 1917-1921, and to the Senate Committee on Banking and Currency, 1933-1936; appointed as a Democrat to the United States Senate to fill the vacancy caused by the death of Duncan U. Fletcher, and served from July 1 to November 3, 1936, when a successor was elected; was not a candidate for election to fill this vacancy; resumed the practice of law until his retirement in 1947; died in Gainesville, Fla., January 5, 1951; interment in Evergreen Cemetery.

**HILL, William Silas** a Representative from Colorado; born in Kelly, Nemaha County, Kans., January 20, 1886; attended the public schools, Kansas State Normal at Emporia, and Colorado State College of Agriculture at Fort Collins; homesteaded near Cheyenne Wells, Colo., 1907-1915; superintendent of Cache la Poudre Consolidated School of Larimer County, Colo., 1919-1922; secretary of the Colorado State Farm Bureau in 1923; served in the State house of representatives 1924-1926; engaged in the mercantile business at Fort Collins, Colo., 1927-1953; elected as a Republican to

the Seventy-seventh and to the eight succeeding Congresses (January 3, 1941-January 3, 1959); chairman, Select Committee on Small Business (Eighty-third Congress); was not a candidate for renomination in 1958 to the Eighty-sixth Congress; retired in 1958 and operated a farm southwest of Fort Collins until 1969; delegate to Republican National Convention in 1964; died in Fort Collins, Colo., August 28, 1972; interment in Grandview Cemetery.

**HILL, Wilson Shedric,** a Representative from Mississippi; born near Lodi, Choctaw County, Miss., January 19, 1863; attended the common schools and the University of Mississippi at Oxford; was graduated from the law department of Cumberland University, Lebanon, Tenn., in 1884; was admitted to the bar in 1884 and commenced practice in Winona, Miss.; member of the State house of representatives in 1885; district attorney for the fifth judicial district of Mississippi 1891-1903; member of the city council of Winona 1892-1894; elected as a Democrat to the Fifty-eighth, Fifty-ninth, and Sixtieth Congresses (March 4, 1903-March 3, 1909); unsuccessful candidate for renomination in 1908; resumed the practice of law in Greenwood, Miss.; delegate to the Democratic National Convention in 1912; district attorney for the northern judicial district 1914-1921; died in Greenwood, Miss., February 14, 1921; interment in Oakwood Cemetery, Winona, Miss.

**HILLEARY, Van,** a Representative from Tennessee; born in Dayton, Rhea County, Tenn., June 20, 1959; graduated, Rhea County High School, Dayton; B.S., University of Tennessee, 1981; J.D., Cumberland School of Law, Samford University, Birmingham, Ala., 1990; admitted to Tennessee bar; textile business executive; United States Air Force, 1982-1984, and United States Air Force Reserve service, 1984 to present, two tours of duty during Desert Shield and Desert Storm flying 24 combat and support missions; elected as a Republican to the One Hundred Fourth Congress (January 3, 1995-January 3, 1997); is a resident of Grandview, Tenn.

**HILLELSON, Jeffrey Paul,** a Representative from Missouri; born in Springfield, Clark County, Ohio, March 9, 1919; moved with his parents to St. Joseph, Mo., when two years of age; attended the public schools; moved to Kansas City, Mo., in 1940; enlisted in the United States Army as a private April 25, 1942; served in the Transportation Corps in the United States, Europe, and Alaska, and was discharged as a captain May 26, 1946, retaining his commission in the Reserve; returned to his studies and was graduated from the University of Missouri at Kansas City in 1947; engaged in the grocery business, 1947-1952; chairman of the Republican City Central Committee of Independence, Mo., in 1949; elected as a Republican to the Eighty-third Congress (January 3, 1953-January 3, 1955); unsuccessful candidate for reelection in 1954 to the Eighty-fourth Congress; executive assistant to Postmaster General Arthur E. Summerfield, Washington, D.C., from January 3, 1955 until his resignation on September 22, 1955; unsuccessful candidate for election in 1956 to the Eighty-fifth Congress; delegate to Republican State conventions in 1948, 1952, and 1956; delegate to the Republican National Convention of 1956; appointed acting postmaster of Kansas City, Mo., May 1, 1957, and served until January 1961; member of the Kansas City, Mo., city council from April 1963 until June 1969; regional administrator, General Services Administration, 1969-1974; served on the Johnson County, Kans., commission, September 1981 to December 1982; appointed honorary consul general for the Republic of Turkey for Kansas and Eastern Missouri on October 23, 1984, and continues to serve in that office; is a resident of Mission Hills, Kans.

**HILLEN, Solomon, Jr.,** a Representative from Maryland; born on the family estate, Hillen Road, near Baltimore, Md., July 10, 1810; was graduated from Georgetown College; studied law; was admitted to the bar and commenced practice in Baltimore; member of the State house of representatives 1834-1838; elected as a Democrat to the Twenty-sixth Congress (March 4, 1839-March 3,

1841); resumed the practice of law; mayor of Baltimore 1842-1845; died in New York City on June 26, 1873; interment in Greenmount Cemetery, Baltimore, Md.

**HILLHOUSE, James** (son of William Hillhouse), a Representative and a Senator from Connecticut; born in Montville, Conn., October 20, 1754; attended the Hopkins Grammar School, New Haven, Conn., and graduated from Yale College in 1773; studied law; was admitted to the bar in 1775 and commenced practice in New Haven, Conn.; served in the Revolutionary War and in 1779 was captain of the Governor's foot guards when New Haven was invaded by the British; member, State house of representatives 1780-1785; chosen as a delegate to the Continental Congress in 1786 and 1788 but did not attend; member, State council 1789-1790; elected to the Second, Third, and Fourth Congresses and served from March 4, 1791, until his resignation in the fall of 1796, having been elected to the United States Senate on May 12, 1796, to fill the vacancy caused by the resignation of Oliver Ellsworth; reelected in 1797, 1803, and 1809, and served from December 1796, until June 10, 1810, when he resigned; served as President pro tempore of the Senate during the Sixth Congress; member of the Hartford convention in 1814; treasurer of Yale College 1782-1832; died in New Haven, Conn., December 29, 1832; interment in Grove Street Cemetery.

Bibliography: *DAB*; Bacon, Leonard. *Sketch of the Life and Public Services of Hon. James Hillhouse of New Haven: With a Notice of His Son, Augustus Lucas Hillhouse.* New Haven: n.p., 1860.

**HILLHOUSE, William** (father of James Hillhouse), a Delegate from Connecticut; born in Montville, Conn., August 25, 1728; received a liberal schooling; studied law; was admitted to the bar and practiced; served in the State house of representatives 1756-1760 and 1763-1785; major in the Second Regiment of the Connecticut Cavalry in the Revolutionary War; elected to the Continental Congress in 1783 and 1785, but did not attend; judge of the court of common pleas 1784-1806; member of the State senate 1785-1808; judge of probate for New London district 1786-1807; died in Montville, Conn., January 12, 1816; interment in Raymond Hill Cemetery.

**HILLIARD, Benjamin Clark,** a Representative from Colorado; born near Osceola, Clarke County, Iowa, January 9, 1868; attended the public schools of Iowa and Kansas; taught school in Kansas; was graduated from the law department of the University of Iowa at Iowa City in 1891; was admitted to the bar the same year and commenced practice in Kansas City, Mo.; moved to Denver, Colo., in 1893; city attorney of Highlands, Colo., in 1896 and 1897; county attorney of Elbert County, Colo., 1897-1907; county attorney of Grand County 1909-1913; member of the State house of representatives in 1902; member of the Denver Board of Education 1900-1902, 1904-1909, and 1913-1917; elected as a Democrat to the Sixty-fourth and Sixty-fifth Congresses (March 4, 1915-March 3, 1919); was not a candidate for renomination in 1918 to the Sixty-sixth Congress; resumed the practice of law; elected justice of the supreme court of Colorado in 1930 and served as chief justice in 1939 and 1940; reelected in 1940 and again in 1950; again became chief justice in January 1949; died in Denver, Colo., August 7, 1951; interment in Crown Hill Cemetery.

**HILLIARD, Earl Frederick,** a Representative from Alabama; born in Birmingham, Ala., April 9, 1942; attended public schools of Birmingham; B.A., Morehouse College, Atlanta, Ga., 1964; J.D., Howard University, Washington, D.C., 1967; M.B.A., Atlanta University School of Business, 1970; attorney; insurance agent; member, Alabama State house of representatives, 1975-1981; member, Alabama State senate, 1981-1993; elected as a Democrat to

the One Hundred Third and One Hundred Fourth Congresses (January 3, 1993-January 3, 1997); is a resident of Birmingham, Ala.

**HILLIARD, Henry Washington,** a Representative from Alabama; born in Fayetteville, Cumberland County, N.C., on August 4, 1808; was graduated from South Carolina College (now the University of South Carolina) at Columbia in 1826; studied law; moved to Athens, Ga., where he was admitted to the bar in 1829; professor in the University of Alabama at Tuscaloosa from 1831 to 1834, when he resigned to practice law in Montgomery, Ala.; member of the State house of representatives 1836-1838; member of the Whig National Convention at Harrisburg, Pa., in 1839; Whig presidential elector in 1840; unsuccessful candidate for election to the Twenty-seventh Congress in 1840; Chargé d'Affaires to Belgium from May 12, 1842, to August 15, 1844; elected as a Whig to the Twenty-ninth, Thirtieth, and Thirty-first Congresses (March 4, 1845-March 3, 1851); was not a candidate for renomination in 1850; presidential elector on the National American ticket in 1856; during the Civil War served as brigadier general in the Confederate Army; moved to Augusta, Ga., in 1865 and resumed the practice of his profession; appointed by Jefferson Davis Confederate commissioner to Tennessee; unsuccessful Republican candidate for election in 1876 to the Forty-fifth Congress; resumed the practice of law in Augusta, Ga., moving later to Atlanta; appointed Minister to Brazil on July 31, 1877 and served until June 1881; died in Atlanta, Ga., December 17, 1892; interment in Oakwood Cemetery, Montgomery, Ala.

Bibliography: *DAB*; Jackson, Carlton. "Alabama's Hilliard: A Nationalistic Rebel of the Old South." *Alabama Historical Quarterly* 31 (Fall-Winter 1969): 183-205; Shields, Johanna N. "An Antebellum Alabama Maverick: Henry Washington Hilliard, 1845-1851." *Alabama Review* 30 (July 1977): 191-212.

**HILLINGS, Patrick Jerome,** a Representative from California; born in Hobart Mills, Nevada County, Calif., February 19, 1923; attended public schools; attended the University of Southern California until March 1943; served as a sergeant in the Signal Corps Intelligence Service from March 1943 to February 1946 with service in the South Pacific; returned to the University of Southern California and received a B.A. in 1947 and J.D. in 1949; was admitted to the bar in 1949 and commenced the practice of law in Arcadia, Calif.; delegate to the Republican National Conventions of 1952, 1956, 1960 and 1964; elected as a Republican to the Eighty-second and to the three succeeding Congresses (January 3, 1951-January 3, 1959); was not a candidate for renomination in 1958 to the Eighty-sixth Congress, but was an unsuccessful candidate for attorney general of California; resumed the practice of law in Los Angeles; chairman of the Republican central committee of Los Angeles County 1960-1961; was a resident of Los Angeles, Calif.; died July 20, 1994.

**HILLIS, Elwood Haynes,** a Representative from Indiana; born in Kokomo, Howard County, Ind., March 6, 1926; attended Kokomo public schools; graduated from Culver Military Academy, 1944; B.S., Indiana University, 1949; J.D., Indiana University School of Law, 1952; served in United States Army in the European Theater with rank of first lieutenant, 1944-1946; retired from the Reserves in 1954 with rank of captain in the infantry; admitted to the Indiana bar in 1952 and commenced practice in Kokomo; member, Indiana house of representatives, Ninety-fifth and Ninety-sixth General Assemblies; delegate, Indiana State Republican conventions, 1962-1970; elected as a Republican to the Ninety-second and to the seven succeeding Congresses (January 3, 1971-January 3, 1987); was not a candidate for reelection in 1986 to the One Hundredth Congress; is a resident of Culver, Ind.

**HILLYER, Junius,** a Representative from Georgia; born in Wilkes County, Ga., April 23, 1807; was graduated from the University of Georgia at Athens in 1828; studied law; was admitted to the bar and commenced practice in Athens; elected solicitor general for the western district of Georgia in 1834; circuit judge 1841-1845; elected as a Unionist to the Thirty-second Congress and reelected as a Democrat to the Thirty-third Congress (March 4, 1851-March 3, 1855); chairman, Committee on Private Land Claims (Thirty-third Congress); Solicitor of the United States Treasury from December 1, 1857, to February 13, 1861, when he resigned; died in Decatur, Ga., June 21, 1886; interment in Oakland Cemetery, Atlanta, Ga.

**Bibliography:** *DAB*; Vinson, Frank B. "Junius Hillyer's 1838 Union Party Letter." *Georgia Historical Quarterly* 64 (Summer 1980): 204-15.

**HIMES, Joseph Hendrix,** a Representative from Ohio; born in New Oxford, Adams County, Pa., August 15, 1885; attended the public schools, Gettysburg College, and Pennsylvania State College; employed in the steel industry; engaged as banker; elected as a Republican to the Sixty-seventh Congress (March 4, 1921-March 3, 1923); unsuccessful candidate in 1922 for reelection to the Sixty-eighth Congress; founder, president, and chairman of the board of directors of Group Hospitalization, Inc., Washington, D.C.; engaged in various business interests in Washington, D.C., New York City, and elsewhere; died in Washington, D.C., September 9, 1960; interment in Fort Lincoln Cemetery.

**HINCHEY, Maurice Dudley,** a Representative from New York; born in New York City, October 27, 1938; graduated, Saugerties (N.Y.) High School, 1956; B.A., State University of New York, New Paltz, 1968, and M.A., 1970; United States Navy Service with Seventh Fleet; member, New York State assembly, 1974-1993; elected as a Democrat to the One Hundred Third and One Hundred Fourth Congresses (January 3, 1993-January 3, 1997); is a resident of Saugerties, N.Y.

**HINDMAN, Thomas Carmichael,** a Representative from Arkansas; born in Knoxville, Tenn., January 28, 1828; moved with his parents to Jacksonville, Calhoun County, Ala., in 1832 and to Ripley, Tippah County, Miss., in 1841; attended public and private schools; was graduated from the Lawrenceville Classical Institute near Princeton, N.J., in 1846; raised a company in Tippah County in 1846 for the Second Mississippi Regiment under Colonel Clark in the war with Mexico; served throughout the war as lieutenant and later as captain of his company; returned to Ripley, Miss.; studied law; was admitted to the bar in 1851 and commenced practice in Ripley, Miss.; member of the State house of representatives in 1854-1856; moved to Helena, Ark., in 1853 and continued the practice of law; elected as a Democrat to the Thirty-sixth Congress (March 4, 1859-March 3, 1861); reelected to the Thirty-seventh Congress in 1860 but declined to take his seat and raised and commanded "Hindman's legion" in 1861 for the Confederate Army; commissioned brigadier general September 28, 1861, and major general April 18, 1862; moved to the city of Mexico after the war and engaged in literary pursuits; returned to Helena, Ark., in 1868 and resumed the practice of law; was assassinated in that city on September 27, 1868; interment in Maple Hill Cemetery.

**Bibliography:** *DAB*; Nash, Charles Edward. *Biographical Sketches of Gen. Pat Cleburne and Gen. T.C. Hindman, Together With Humorous Anecdotes and Reminiscences of the Late Civil War.* Dayton, Ohio: Press of Morningside Bookshop, 1977.

**HINDMAN, William,** a Delegate, a Representative, and a Senator from Maryland; born in Dorchester County, Md., April 1, 1743; pursued classical studies; attended the University of Pennsylvania; studied law at the Inns of Court, London, England; returned to the United States, was admitted to the bar, and commenced practice in Talbot County, Md.; was secretary of the Talbot (Md.) County committee of observation in 1775 and was designated to execute the resolves of the Continental Congress; sat in the State convention of 1775 and was named treasurer for the Eastern Shore 1775-1777; member, State senate 1777-1784, 1792; Member of the Continental Congress 1785 and 1786; member of the governor's executive council 1789-1792; elected to the Second Congress to fill the vacancy caused by the resignation of Joshua Seney; reelected to the Third, Fourth, and Fifth Congresses and served from January 30, 1793, to March 3, 1799; member, State house of delegates 1799-1800; elected in 1800 as a Federalist to the United States Senate to fill the vacancy caused by the resignation of James Lloyd; at expiration of the term was appointed to fill the vacancy caused by the failure of the legislature to elect his successor and served from December 12, 1800, to November 19, 1801; was not a candidate for reelection; engaged in agricultural pursuits on his estate near Wyes Landing; died in Baltimore, Md., January 19, 1822; interment in St. Paul's Burial Ground.

**Bibliography:** *DAB*.

**HINDS, Asher Crosby,** a Representative from Maine; born in Benton, Kennebec County, Maine, February 6, 1863; attended the public schools and Coburn Classical Institute; was graduated from Colby College, Waterville, Maine, in 1883; began newspaper work in Portland, Maine in 1884; clerk to Representative Thomas B. Reed, Speaker of the United States House of Representatives, 1889-1891; clerk at the Speaker's table, United States House of Representatives, 1895-1911; editor of the Rules, Manual, and Digest of the House of Representatives in 1899, and of Hinds' Precedents of the House of Representatives in 1908; elected as a Republican to the Sixty-second, Sixty-third, and Sixty-fourth Congresses (March 4, 1911-March 3, 1917); resided in Washington, D.C., until his death on May 1, 1919; interment in Evergreen Cemetery, Portland, Maine.

**Bibliography:** *DAB*.

**HINDS, James,** a Representative from Arkansas; born in the town of Hebron, near Salem, N.Y., December 5, 1833; attended the common schools and the State normal school at Albany, N.Y.; attended law school at St. Louis, Mo., and was graduated from the Cincinnati Law College in 1856; was admitted to the bar and commenced practice in St. Peter, Minn.; district attorney for three years and served for some time as United States district attorney for the State of Minnesota; joined an expedition under Governor Sibley against the Indians on the western frontier in 1862; although a member of the Democratic Party, was a supporter of President Lincoln; moved to Little Rock, Ark., in 1865 and continued the practice of law; delegate from Pulaski County to the State constitutional convention in 1867; served as a commissioner to codify the State laws; upon the readmission of Arkansas to representation was elected as a Republican to the Fortieth Congress and served from June 22, 1868, until assassinated near Indian Bay, Ark., October 22, 1868; interment in East Norwich, N.Y.

**HINDS, Thomas,** a Representative from Mississippi; born in Berkeley County, Va., January 9, 1780; moved to Greenville, Miss.; served in the War of 1812 as major of Cavalry; distinguished himself at the Battle of New Orleans, January 8, 1815, and was brevetted brigadier general for gallantry; unsuccessful candidate for Governor in 1820; elected as a Democrat to the Twentieth Congress to fill the vacancy caused by the resignation of William Haile; reelected to the Twenty-first Congress and served from October 21, 1828, to March 3, 1831; died in Greenville, Miss., August 23, 1840.

**HINEBAUGH, William Henry,** a Representative from Illinois; born near Marshall, Calhoun County, Mich., December 16, 1867; attended the common schools, Litchfield High School, the State normal school at Ypsilanti, Mich., and the University of Michigan at Ann Arbor; moved to Illinois and settled in Ottawa in 1891; studied law; was admitted to the bar in 1893 and commenced practice in Ottawa; appointed assistant prosecuting attorney of La Salle County in December 1900; judge of the La Salle County Court

1902-1912; president of the State Association of County Judges of Illinois 1908-1910; elected and reelected chairman of the Republican county central committee, but resigned in July 1912 to join the Progressive Party; elected as a Progressive to the Sixty-third Congress (March 4, 1913-March 3, 1915); unsuccessful candidate for reelection in 1914 to the Sixty-fourth Congress; resumed the practice of law in Ottawa, Ill.; assistant attorney general of Illinois 1916-1922; president and general counsel of the Central Life Insurance Co., of Illinois, and resided in Chicago; moved to Albion, Mich., in 1933 and continued the practice of law until his death there September 22, 1943; interment in Mount Hope Cemetery, Litchfield, Mich.

**HINES, Richard,** a Representative from North Carolina; born in Tarboro, Edgecombe County, N.C.; studied law; was admitted to the bar in 1816 and practiced in Raleigh, N.C.; member of the State house of commons in 1824; elected to the Nineteenth Congress (March 4, 1825-March 3, 1827); unsuccessful candidate for reelection in 1826 to the Twentieth Congress; resumed the practice of law in Raleigh, N.C., and died there November 20, 1851; interment in the Old City Cemetery, Raleigh, N.C.

**HINES, William Henry,** a Representative from Pennsylvania; born in Brooklyn, N.Y., March 15, 1856; moved to Pennsylvania in 1865 with his parents, who settled in Hanover Township, near Wilkes-Barre, Luzerne County, Pa.; attended the public schools in Brooklyn, N.Y., and Wyoming Seminary, Kingston, Pa.; studied law; was admitted to the bar in Luzerne County in 1881 and practiced; member of the Pennsylvania house of representatives in 1879, 1880, 1883, and 1884; served in the Pennsylvania senate 1888-1892; elected as a Democrat to the Fifty-third Congress (March 4, 1893-March 3, 1895); unsuccessful candidate for reelection in 1894 to the Fifty-fourth Congress; resumed the practice of law in Wilkes-Barre, Pa.; died there January 17, 1914; interment in St. Mary's Cemetery, Hanover Township, Luzerne County, Pa.

**HINRICHSEN, William Henry,** a Representative from Illinois; born in Franklin, Morgan County, Ill., May 27, 1850; attended the public schools and the Illinois Industrial University (now the University of Illinois) at Champaign; engaged in newspaper work; elected justice of the peace in 1871 and reelected in 1873; appointed deputy sheriff of Morgan County in 1874 and served three terms in that position, residing at Jacksonville; sheriff 1880-1882; editor of the Illinois Courier in 1882; moved to Quincy in 1887; editor of the Quincy Herald 1887-1890; returned to Jacksonville and elected clerk of the house of representatives of Illinois in 1891; secretary of state of Illinois 1892-1896; delegate to the Democratic National Convention in 1896; chairman of the Democratic State committee in 1895 and 1896; elected as a Democrat to the Fifty-fifth Congress (March 4, 1897-March 3, 1899); engaged in literary pursuits; died in Alexander, Ill., December 18, 1907; interment in Diamond Grove Cemetery, Jacksonville, Ill.

**HINSHAW, Andrew Jackson,** a Representative from California; born in Dexter, Stoddard County, Mo., August 4, 1923; educated in the public schools in Michigan and Los Angeles, Calif.; B.S., University of Southern California, Los Angeles, Calif., 1950; also attended University of Southern California School of Law; served in the United States Navy, 1942-1945; twice elected assessor, Orange County, Calif., 1965-1972; ten years with the California State Board of Equalization and five years with the Los Angeles, Calif., County Assessor's Office; delegate to California State Republican convention, 1972; elected as a Republican to the Ninety-third and the Ninety-fourth Congresses (January 3, 1973-January 3, 1977); unsuccessful candidate for renomination in 1976 to the Ninety-fifth Congress; resumed business interests in California; president of a business analysis firm, 1980-1983; conference director, World Computer Graphics Association, Washington, D.C., 1984-1985;

president, graphics firm, Rockville, Md., 1986 to present; is a resident of Mission Viejo, Calif.

**HINSHAW, Edmund Howard** (cousin of Edwin Bruce Brooks), a Representative from Nebraska; born in Greensboro, Henry County, Ind., December 8, 1860; attended the common schools and was graduated from Butler College, Indianapolis, in 1885; moved to Fairbury, Nebr., in 1887; superintendent of the public schools in 1887 and 1888; studied law; was admitted to the bar in 1888 and commenced practice in Fairbury; city clerk and attorney of Fairbury in 1889 and 1890; attorney of Jefferson County 1895-1899; unsuccessful candidate for election in 1898 to the Fifty-sixth Congress and in 1901 to the United States Senate; elected as a Republican to the Fifty-eighth and to the three succeeding Congresses (March 4, 1903-March 3, 1911); was not a candidate for renomination in 1910; resumed the practice of law in Fairbury, Nebr.; moved to Los Angeles, Calif., in 1912 and continued the practice of his profession; also engaged in the operation of a chain of motion-picture theaters; died in Los Angeles, Calif., on June 15, 1932; interment in Forest Lawn Cemetery, Glendale, Calif.

**HINSHAW, John Carl Williams,** a Representative from California; born in Chicago, Ill., July 28, 1894; attended the public schools and Valparaiso (Ind.) University; was graduated from Princeton University in 1916; pursued a postgraduate course in business administration at the University of Michigan at Ann Arbor; served overseas as a first lieutenant in the Sixteenth Railroad Engineers from May 1917 to September 1919, when he was discharged as a captain in the Corps of Engineers; served as laborer, salesman, and manager in automotive manufacturing in Chicago 1920-1926; engaged in investment banking in 1927 and 1928; moved to Pasadena, Calif., in 1929 and engaged in the real estate and insurance business; unsuccessful candidate for election in 1936 to the Seventy-fifth Congress; elected as a Republican to the Seventy-sixth and to the eight succeeding Congresses and served from January 3, 1939, until his death in Bethesda, Md., August 5, 1956; had been renominated in the June 1956 primary election; interment in Rock Creek Cemetery, Washington, D.C.

**HINSON, Jon Clifton,** a Representative from Mississippi; born in Tylertown, Walthall County, Miss., March 16, 1942; attended the Walthall County public schools; B.A., University of Mississippi, 1964; served in the United States Marine Corps Reserve, 1964-1970; administrative assistant to Representative Charles H. Griffin, 1968-1973; administrative assistant to Representative W. Thad Cochran, 1973-1977; elected as a Republican to the Ninety-sixth and to the Ninety-seventh Congresses, and served from January 3, 1979 until his resignation on April 13, 1981; was a resident of Silver Spring, Md., until his death there on July 21, 1995.

**HIRES, George,** a Representative from New Jersey; born in Elsinboro Township, Salem County, N.J., January 26, 1835; attended the common schools and the Friends' School and received a commercial training; engaged in mercantile and manufacturing pursuits; sheriff of Salem County 1867-1869; member of the State senate 1881-1884; elected as a Republican to the Forty-ninth and Fiftieth Congresses (March 4, 1885-March 3, 1889); was not a candidate for renomination in 1888; resumed mercantile pursuits; also engaged in banking; delegate to the State constitutional convention in 1894; delegate to the Republican National Convention in 1896; member of the Republican State committee for twelve years; died in Atlantic City, N.J., February 16, 1911; interment in the First Presbyterian Cemetery, Salem, N.J.

**HISCOCK, Frank,** a Representative and a Senator from New York; born in Pompey, Onondaga County, N.Y., September 6, 1834; graduated from Pompey Academy; studied law; was admitted to the bar in 1855 and commenced practice in Tully, Onondaga County; district attorney of Onondaga County 1860-1863; member of the

State constitutional convention in 1867; elected as a Republican to the Forty-fifth and to the five succeeding Congresses and served from March 4, 1877, until his resignation on March 3, 1887, at the close of the Forty-ninth Congress, having been elected Senator; chairman, Committee on Appropriations (Forty-seventh Congress); elected as a Republican to the United States Senate and served from March 4, 1887, to March 3, 1893; unsuccessful candidate for reelection; chairman, Committee on Organization, Conduct, and Expenditures of Executive Departments (Fifty-first and Fifty-second Congresses); resumed the practice of law in Syracuse, N.Y.; died in Syracuse, N.Y., June 18, 1914; interment in Oakwood Cemetery.

**HISE, Elijah,** a Representative from Kentucky; born in Allegheny County, Pa., July 4, 1802; moved with his parents to Russellville, Logan County, Ky., when young; completed preparatory studies; attended Transylvania University, Lexington, Ky.; studied law; was admitted to the bar and commenced practice; member of the Kentucky house of representatives in 1829; unsuccessful Democratic candidate for lieutenant governor in 1836; appointed Chargé d'Affaires to Guatemala on March 31, 1848, and served until June 21, 1849; chief justice of the court of appeals of Kentucky; elected as a Democrat to the Thirty-ninth Congress to fill the vacancy caused by the death of Henry Grider; reelected to the Fortieth Congress and served from December 3, 1866, until his death in Russellville, Ky., May 8, 1867; interment in Maple Grove Cemetery.

**Bibliography:** *DAB.*

**HITCHCOCK, Gilbert Monell** (son of Phineas Warren Hitchcock), a Representative and a Senator from Nebraska; born in Omaha, Nebr., September 18, 1859; attended the public schools of Omaha and the gymnasium at Baden-Baden, Germany; graduated from the law department of the University of Michigan at Ann Arbor in 1881; was admitted to the bar and commenced practice in Omaha, Nebr., in 1882; continued the practice of law until 1885, when he established and edited the Omaha Evening World; purchased the Nebraska Morning Herald in 1889 and consolidated the two into the Morning and Evening World Herald; unsuccessful Democratic candidate for election in 1898 to the Fifty-sixth Congress; elected as a Democrat to the Fifty-eighth Congress (March 4, 1903-March 3, 1905); unsuccessful candidate for reelection in 1904 to the Fifty-ninth Congress; elected as a Democrat to the Sixtieth and Sixty-first Congresses (March 4, 1907-March 3, 1911); did not seek renomination in 1910, having become a candidate for the United States Senate; elected as a Democrat to the United States Senate January 18, 1911; reelected in 1916 and served from March 4, 1911, to March 3, 1923; unsuccessful candidate for reelection in 1922 and for election in 1930; chairman, Committee on the Philippines (Sixty-third through Sixty-fifth Congresses), Committee on Foreign Relations (Sixty-fifth Congress), Committee on Forest Reservations and Game Protection (Sixty-sixth Congress); resumed newspaper work in Omaha, Nebr.; retired from active business in 1933 and moved to Washington, D.C., where he died on February 3, 1934; interment in Forest Lawn Cemetery, Omaha, Nebr.

**Bibliography:** Patterson, Robert. "Gilbert M. Hitchcock: A Story of Two Careers." Ph.D. dissertation, University of Colorado, 1940; Wimer, Kurt. "Senator Hitchcock and the League of Nations." *Nebraska History* 44 (September 1963): 189-204.

**HITCHCOCK, Herbert Emery,** a Senator from South Dakota; born in Maquoketa, Jackson County, Iowa, August 22, 1867; attended public schools in Iowa and San Jose, Calif., a business college at Davenport, Iowa, Iowa State College at Ames, and the University of Chicago Law School; moved to Mitchell, S.Dak, in 1884, attended school and worked as a stenographer; was admitted to the South Dakota bar in 1896 and commenced practice in Mitchell; also engaged in banking; clerk of the State senate 1896; elected as a State's attorney 1904 and 1906; elected to the State senate in 1909, 1911, and 1929; a trustee of Yankton (S.Dak.) College in 1936; president of Mitchell school board 1924-1934; appointed as a Democrat to the United States Senate to fill the vacancy caused by the death of Peter Norbeck and served from December 29, 1936, to November 8, 1938, when a successor was elected; unsuccessful candidate for the nomination to fill the vacancy in 1938; resumed the practice of law until his death in Mitchell, S.Dak., February 17, 1958; interment in Graceland Cemetery.

**HITCHCOCK, Peter,** a Representative from Ohio; born in Cheshire, Conn., October 19, 1781; pursued classical studies and was graduated from Yale College in 1801; studied law; was admitted to the bar in 1804 and commenced practice in Cheshire; moved to Geauga County, Ohio, in 1806; member of the State house of representatives in 1810; member of the State senate 1812-1815 and served as speaker in 1815; commissioned lieutenant colonel of the Fourth Regiment, Ohio State Militia, in 1814; commissioned major general, Fourth Division, Ohio State Militia, in 1816; elected to the Fifteenth Congress (March 4, 1817-March 3, 1819); was not a candidate for renomination in 1818; judge of the supreme court of Ohio 1819-1832 and served a portion of that time as chief justice; again a member of the State senate in 1833 and 1834; delegate to the State constitutional convention in 1850; died in Painesville, Lake County, Ohio, March 4, 1853; interment in Welton Cemetery, Burton, Ohio.

**Bibliography:** *DAB.*

**HITCHCOCK, Phineas Warren** (father of Gilbert Monell Hitchcock), a Delegate and a Senator from Nebraska; born in New Lebanon, Columbia County, N.Y., November 30, 1831; graduated from Williams College, Massachusetts, in 1855; studied law; moved to Omaha, Nebr., in 1857, was admitted to the bar, and commenced practice; appointed United States marshal 1861-1864; elected as a Republican Delegate to the Thirty-ninth Congress and served from March 4, 1865, to March 1, 1867, when the Territory was admitted as a State into the Union; appointed surveyor general of Nebraska and Iowa 1867-1869; elected as a Republican to the United States Senate and served from March 4, 1871, to March 3, 1877; unsuccessful candidate for reelection; chairman, Committee on Territories (Forty-fourth Congress); involved in newspaper publishing and various businesses; died in Omaha, Nebr., July 10, 1881; interment in Prospect Hill Cemetery.

**Bibliography:** *DAB.*

**HITT, Robert Roberts,** a Representative from Illinois; born in Urbana, Champaign County, Ohio, January 16, 1834; moved to Ogle County, Ill., in 1837 with his parents, who settled in Mount Morris; attended the Rock River Seminary (later Mount Morris College), and De Pauw University, Greencastle, Ind.; first secretary of legation and Chargé d'Affaires ad interim in Paris from December 1874 until March 1881; Assistant Secretary of State in 1881; elected as a Republican to the Forty-seventh Congress to fill the vacancy caused by the death of Robert M.A. Hawk; reelected to the Forty-eighth and to the eleven succeeding Congresses and served from November 7, 1882, until his death in Narragansett Pier, R.I., on September 20, 1906; chairman, Committee on Foreign Affairs (Fifty-first and Fifty-fourth through Fifty-ninth Congresses); Regent of the Smithsonian Institution from August 11, 1893, until his death; appointed by President William McKinley in July 1898 as a member of the commission to establish government in the Hawaiian Islands; interment in Oakwood Cemetery, Mount Morris, Ogle County, Ill.

**Bibliography:** *DAB.*

**HOAG, Truman Harrison,** a Representative from Ohio; born in Manlius, Onondaga County, N.Y., April 9, 1816; attended the public schools; moved to Syracuse, N.Y., in 1832 and was employed as a clerk in a store and later in the canal collector's office; moved to Oswego, N.Y., in 1839 and was employed for a commission merchants company, moving to Toledo, Ohio, in 1849 as agent of the same firm; later became engaged in transportation and in mercantile pursuits; also engaged in the manufacture of illuminating gas and of coke; unsuccessful candidate for mayor in 1867; elected as a Democrat to the Forty-first Congress and served from March 4, 1869, until his death in Washington, D.C., on February 5, 1870; interment in Forest Cemetery, Toledo, Ohio.

**HOAGLAND, Moses,** a Representative from Ohio; born near Baltimore, Md., June 19, 1812; attended the public schools; studied law; was admitted to the bar in 1842 and commenced practice in Millersburg, Ohio; served in the Mexican War and was promoted to the rank of major for bravery in action; elected as a Democrat to the Thirty-first Congress (March 4, 1849-March 3, 1851); unsuccessful candidate for reelection in 1850 to the Thirty-second Congress; resumed the practice of law; appointed associate justice for the Territory of Washington on June 21, 1853, but declined to accept; died in Millersburg, Ohio, April 16, 1865; interment in Oak Hill Cemetery.

**HOAGLAND, Peter J.,** a Representative from Nebraska; born in Omaha, Douglas County, Nebr., November 17, 1941; graduated, Omaha Central High School; A.B., Stanford University, Calif., 1963; LL.B., Yale University Law School, 1968; United States Army service, 1963-1965, lieutenant; law clerk, United States District Court for the District of Columbia, 1969-1970; staff attorney, Public Defender Service, Washington, D.C., 1970-1973; practicing attorney in Omaha, 1974-1988; member, Nebraska State senate, 1979-1987; elected as a Democrat to the One Hundred First and to the two succeeding Congresses (January 3, 1989-January 3, 1995); unsuccessful candidate in 1994 for reelection to the One Hundred Fourth Congress; resumed the practice of law at Arent Fox Kintner Plotkin and Kahn, Washington, D.C.; is a resident of Chevy Chase, Md.

**HOAR, Ebenezer Rockwood** (son of Samuel Hoar, brother of George Frisbie Hoar, father of Sherman Hoar, and uncle of Rockwood Hoar), a Representative from Massachusetts; born in Concord, Mass., February 21, 1816; pursued classical studies and was graduated from Harvard University in 1835; was admitted to the bar in 1840 and commenced practice in Concord and Boston, Mass.; served in the Massachusetts senate in 1846 as an anti-slavery Whig; judge of the court of common pleas, 1849-1855; judge of the Massachusetts supreme court, 1859-1869; Attorney General in the Cabinet of President Ulysses S. Grant from March 11, 1869 until his resignation on June 23, 1870; nominated on December 15, 1869 by President Grant as an Associate Justice of the United States Supreme Court, but the Senate, on February 3, 1870, refused to confirm the nomination; member of the joint high commission which framed the treaty of Washington in 1871 under which the tribunal was established to settle the *Alabama* claims; elected as a Republican to the Forty-third Congress (March 4, 1873-March 3, 1875); was not a candidate for renomination in 1874 to the Forty-fourth Congress; resumed the practice of his profession in Concord and Boston, Mass.; member of the board of overseers of Harvard University, 1868-1882; died in Concord, Mass., January 31, 1895; interment in Sleepy Hollow Cemetery.

Bibliography: *DAB*; Storey, Moorfield, and Edward W. Emerson. *Ebeneezer Rockwood Hoar; A Memoir.* Boston: Houghton Mifflin, 1911.

**HOAR, George Frisbie** (son of Samuel Hoar, brother of Ebenezer Rockwood Hoar, father of Rockwood Hoar, and uncle of Sherman Hoar), a Representative and a Senator from Massachusetts; born in Concord, Mass., August 29, 1826; attended Concord Academy; graduated from Harvard University in 1846 and from the Harvard Law School in 1849; was admitted to the bar in 1849 and commenced practice in Worcester, Mass.; elected to the Massachusetts house of representatives in 1852; elected to the Massachusetts senate in 1857; elected as a Republican to the Forty-first and to the three succeeding Congresses (March 4, 1869-March 3, 1877); was not a candidate for renomination in 1876 to the Forty-fifth Congress; one of the managers appointed by the House of Representatives in 1876 to conduct the impeachment proceedings against William W. Belknap, ex-Secretary of War; appointed a member of the Electoral Commission created by act of Congress to decide the contests in various States in the presidential election of 1876; elected as a Republican to the United States Senate in 1877; reelected in 1883, 1889, 1895, and 1901 and served from March 4, 1877, until his death in Worcester, Mass., September 30, 1904; Republican caucus chairman 1903; chairman, Committee on Privileges and Elections (Forty-seventh through Fifty-second Congresses), Committee on the Judiciary (Fifty-second Congress, Fifty-fourth through Fifty-eighth Congresses), Committee on the Library (Fifty-second Congress); overseer of Harvard University 1874-1880 and from 1896 until his death; Regent of the Smithsonian for many years; interment in Sleepy Hollow Cemetery, Concord, Mass.

Bibliography: *DAB*; Hoar, George F. *Autobiography of Seventy Years.* 2 vols., New York: Scribner's Sons, 1903; Welch, Richard E., Jr. *George F. Hoar and the Half-Breed Republicans.* Cambridge, Mass.: Harvard University Press, 1971.

**HOAR, Rockwood** (son of George Frisbie Hoar, grandson of Samael Hoar, nephew of Ebenezer Rockwood Hoar, and cousin of Sherman Hoar), a Representative from Massachusetts; born in Worcester, Mass., August 24, 1855; attended the Worcester public schools and was graduated from Harvard University in 1876; member of Company C, Fifth Massachusetts Infantry, 1875-1879; studied law; was admitted to the bar in 1879 and commenced practice in Worcester; assistant district attorney for the middle district of Massachusetts 1884-1887; member of the common council of Worcester 1887-1891; aide-de-camp with rank of colonel on the staff of Governor Oliver Ames 1887-1890; judge advocate general with rank of brigadier general on the staff of Governor Roger Wolcott 1897-1900; district attorney from January 1899 to January 1905; trustee of Clark University, Worcester, Mass., and trustee of the Worcester Insane Hospital; elected as a Republican to the Fifty-ninth Congress and served from March 1, 1905, until his death in Worcester, Mass., November 1, 1906; interment in the Rural Cemetery.

**HOAR, Samuel** (father of Ebenezer Rockwood Hoar and George Frisbie Hoar, grandfather of Rockwood Hoar and Sherman Hoar), a Representative from Massachusetts; born in Lincoln, Middlesex County, Mass., May 18, 1778; pursued classical studies and was graduated from Harvard University in 1802; studied law; was admitted to the bar in 1805 and commenced practice in Concord, Mass.; delegate to the Massachusetts constitutional convention in 1820; served in the Massachusetts senate in 1826, 1832, and 1833; elected as a Whig to the Twenty-fourth Congress (March 4, 1835-March 3, 1837); unsuccessful candidate for reelection in 1836 to the Twenty-fifth Congress; resumed the practice of law in Concord, Mass.; sent by the Massachusetts legislature to South Carolina to test the constitutionality of acts prohibiting free African-Americans from coming into South Carolina and on his arrival, December 5, 1844, the Legislature of South Carolina passed resolutions expelling him from the city of Charleston; member of the Massachusetts house of representatives in 1850; chairman of the Massachusetts convention in 1855 which formed the Republican Party in Massachusetts; died in Concord, Mass., November 2, 1856; interment in Sleepy Hollow Cemetery.

Bibliography: *DAB*.

**HOAR, Sherman** (son of Ebenezer Rockwood Hoar, grandson of Samuel Hoar, nephew of George Frisbie Hoar, and cousin of Rockwood Hoar), a Representative from Massachusetts; born in Concord, Mass., July 30, 1860; attended the public schools and Phillips Exeter Academy, Exeter, N.H.; was graduated from Harvard University in 1882 and from the law department of the university in 1884; president of the Young Men's Democratic Club of Massachusetts in 1884; was admitted to the bar of Middlesex County in 1885 and commenced practice in Concord; trustee of Phillips Exeter Academy and director of the American Unitarian Association; elected as a Democrat to the Fifty-second Congress (March 4, 1891-March 3, 1893); United States district attorney for Massachusetts 1893-1897; director of the Massachusetts Volunteer Aid Association in the war with Spain and served in Army hospitals in the South; died in Concord, Mass., October 7, 1898; interment in Sleepy Hollow Cemetery.

**HOARD, Charles Brooks,** a Representative from New York; born in Springfield, Windsor County, Vt., June 5, 1805; attended the public schools; moved to Antwerp, N.Y., where he was postmaster during the administrations of Jackson and Van Buren; member of the State assembly in 1837; moved to Watertown, N.Y., in January 1844; clerk of Jefferson County 1844-1846; elected as a Republican to the Thirty-fifth and Thirty-sixth Congresses (March 4, 1857-March 3, 1861); engaged in the manufacture of portable engines and, during the Civil War, the manufacture of arms for the Government; moved to West Virginia in 1870; died in Ceredo, W.Va., November 20, 1886; interment in Spring Hill Cemetery, Huntington, W.Va.

**HOBART, Aaron,** a Representative from Massachusetts; born in Abington, Mass., June 26, 1787; pursued classical studies and was graduated from Brown University, Providence, R.I., in 1805; studied law; was admitted to the bar in 1809 and commenced practice in Abington; moved to Hanover in 1811; member of the Massachusetts house of representatives in 1814 and served in the Massachusetts senate in 1819; moved to East Bridgewater in 1824; elected to the Sixteenth Congress to fill the vacancy caused by the resignation of Zabdiel Sampson; reelected to the Seventeenth, Eighteenth, and Nineteenth Congresses and served from November 24, 1820, to March 3, 1827; declined to be a candidate for renomination in 1826; executive councilor 1827-1831; judge of probate 1843-1858; died in East Bridgewater, Mass., September 19, 1858; interment in Central Cemetery.

**HOBART, Garret Augustus,** a Vice President of the United States; born near Long Branch, Monmouth County, N.J., June 3, 1844; attended the common schools and graduated from Rutgers College, New Brunswick, N.J., in 1863; taught school at Marlborough, N.J.; clerk for the grand jury of Passaic County, N.J., in 1865; studied law in the office of Socrates Tuttle; was admitted to the bar in 1866 and commenced practice at Paterson, N.J.; city counsel of Paterson in 1871 and 1872; elected counsel for the board of freeholders in 1872; member, New Jersey State house of assembly, 1872-1876, and served as speaker in 1874; member, New Jersey State senate, 1876-1882, and served as president, 1881-1882; chairman of the New Jersey State Republican committee, 1880-1890; delegate to every Republican National Convention from 1876 through 1892; president, general manager, or director of water and railway companies and banks; member of the Republican National Committee from 1884 until 1896, when he was nominated for vice president; elected Vice President of the United States, November 3, 1896, on the ticket headed by William McKinley, and served from March 4, 1897 until his death in Paterson, N.J., November 21, 1899; interment in Cedar Lawn Cemetery.

**Bibliography:** *DAB*; Hobart, Jennie Tuttle. *Memories*. Patterson, N.J.: n.p., 1930; Magie, David. *The Life of Garret Augustus Hobart*. New York: G.P. Putnam's Sons, 1910.

**HOBART, John Sloss,** a Delegate and a Senator from New York; born in Fairfield, Fairfield County, Conn., May 6, 1738; graduated from Yale College in 1757; studied law; was admitted to the bar and commenced practice in New York; member of the Committee of Correspondence 1774; deputy to the provincial convention in 1775 and delegate to the provincial congress 1775-1777; member of the council of safety in 1777; a puisne justice of the supreme court 1777-1798; member of the Hartford convention in 1780; member of the State convention in 1788 which ratified the Federal Constitution; elected to the United States Senate as a Federalist in 1798 to fill the vacancy caused by the resignation of Philip Schuyler and served from January 11 to April 16, 1798, when he resigned to accept the appointment as judge of the United States District Court of New York; died in New York City on February 4, 1805; interment in Trinity Churchyard.

**Bibliography:** *DAB*.

**HOBBIE, Selah Reeve,** a Representative from New York; born in Newburgh, Orange County, N.Y., March 10, 1797; studied law; was admitted to the bar and commenced practice in Delhi, N.Y.; district attorney of Delaware County 1823-1827; member of the State assembly 1827-1829; served in the militia as brigade major and inspector; elected as a Jacksonian to the Twentieth Congress (March 4, 1827-March 3, 1829); was appointed Assistant Postmaster General and served from 1829 until 1851, when he resigned on account of ill health; appointed First Assistant Postmaster General and served from March 22, 1853, until his death in Washington, D.C., March 23, 1854.

**HOBBS, Samuel Francis,** a Representative from Alabama; born in Selma, Dallas County, Ala., October 5, 1887; attended the public schools, Callaway's Preparatory School, Selma, Ala., Marion (Ala.) Military Institute, Vanderbilt University at Nashville, Tenn., and was graduated from the law department of the University of Alabama at Tuscaloosa in 1908; was admitted to the bar in 1908 and commenced practice in Selma, Ala.; appointed judge of the fourth judicial circuit of Alabama in 1921; elected to the same office in 1923 and served until his resignation in 1926; resumed the practice of law; chairman of the Muscle Shoals Commission in 1931 and of the Alabama National Recovery Administration Committee in 1933; elected as a Democrat to the Seventy-fourth and to the seven succeeding Congresses (January 3, 1935-January 3, 1951); one of the managers appointed by the House of Representatives in 1936 to conduct the impeachment proceedings against Halstead L. Ritter, judge of the United States District Court for the Southern District of Florida; did not seek renomination in 1950; returned to Selma, Ala., and reestablished his law practice; died in Selma, Ala., May 31, 1952; interment in Live Oak Cemetery.

**HOBLITZELL, Fetter Schrier,** a Representative from Maryland; born in Cumberland, Md., October 7, 1838; attended the primary schools and was graduated from the Allegany Academy, Cumberland, Md.; studied law; was admitted to the bar in 1859 and commenced practice in Baltimore, Md.; during the Civil War served as a private in the First Maryland Regiment of Infantry, Confederate Army; resumed the practice of law; member of the State house of delegates in 1870 and 1876; reelected in 1878 and served as speaker; elected as a Democrat to the Forty-seventh and Forty-eighth Congresses (March 4, 1881-March 3, 1885); city counselor of Baltimore in 1888 and 1889; resumed the practice of law; died in Baltimore, Md., May 2, 1900; interment in Loudon Park Cemetery.

**HOBLITZELL, John Dempsey, Jr.,** a Senator from West Virginia; born in Parkersburg, Wood County, W.Va., December 30, 1912; attended the public schools; graduated from the University of West Virginia in 1934; involved in the insurance, real estate, construction, and banking businesses; member, board of governors of West Virginia University, 1937-1944; served in the United States Naval Reserve, 1942-1946, retiring as a lieutenant; member, Wood

County School Board, 1950-1956; in 1954 served as a delegate to the White House Conference on Education, as chairman of the Governor's West Virginia Commission on State and Local Finance, and as president of the West Virginia School Board Association; member, National Citizens Committee on Higher Education, 1955; unsuccessful candidate for nomination in 1956 to the Eighty-fifth Congress; appointed as a Republican to the United States Senate to fill the vacancy caused by the death of Matthew M. Neely, and served from January 25, 1958 to November 4, 1958; unsuccessful candidate for election to the vacancy; resumed his business interests; died in Clarksburg, W.Va., January 6, 1962; interment in Mount Olivet Cemetery, Parkersburg, W.Va.

**HOBSON, David Lee,** a Representative from Ohio; born in Cincinnati, Ohio, October 17, 1936; graduated from Withrow High School, Cincinnati, 1954; B.A., Ohio Wesleyan University, Delaware, Ohio, 1958; J.D., Ohio State College of Law, 1963; Ohio Air National Guard service with One Hundred Twenty-first Tactical Fighter Wing; participated in Berlin Wall crisis of 1961; businessman; member, Ohio State senate, 1982-1990, majority whip, 1986, president pro tempore, 1988; elected as a Republican to the One Hundred Second and to the two succeeding Congresses (January 3, 1991-January 3, 1997); is a resident of Springfield, Ohio.

**HOBSON, Richmond Pearson,** a Representative from Alabama; born in Greensboro, Hale County, Ala., August 17, 1870; attended private schools and Southern University; was graduated from the United States Naval Academy in 1889 and from the French National School of Naval Design at Paris in 1893; served in the United States Navy from 1885 until 1903; awarded the Congressional Medal of Honor in 1933 for sinking the collier *Merrimac* in 1898; special representative of the Navy Department to the Buffalo Exposition in 1901 and to the Charleston Exposition in 1901 and 1902; naval architect, author, and lecturer; elected as a Democrat to the Sixtieth and to the three succeeding Congresses (March 4, 1907-March 3, 1915); unsuccessful candidate for renomination in 1916 to the Sixty-fifth Congress; moved to Los Angeles, Calif., and later to New York City; organized the American Alcohol Education Association in 1921 and served as general secretary; organized the International Narcotic Education Association in 1923 and served as president; organized the World Conference on Narcotic Education in 1926 and served as secretary general and as chairman of the board of governors; founder of the World Narcotic Defense Association in 1927, serving as president; was made a rear admiral by act of Congress in 1934; founder and president of the Constitutional Democracy Association in 1935; died in New York City on March 16, 1937; interment in Arlington National Cemetery, Va.

Bibliography: *DAB*; Pittman, Walter E. "Richmond P. Hobson, Crusader." Ph.D. dissertation, University of Georgia, 1969; Sheldon, Richard N. "Richmond Pearson Hobson as a Progressive Reformer." *Alabama Review* 25 (October 1972): 243-61.

**HOCH, Daniel Knabb,** a Representative from Pennsylvania; born on a farm near Reading, Pa., January 31, 1866; attended the public schools; served a printing apprenticeship on a Reading, Pa., newspaper; worked in various departments of a newspaper; member of the Pennsylvania house of representatives, 1899-1901; delegate to the Democratic National Convention of 1908; controller of Berks County, Pa., 1912-1916; trustee of St. Matthew's Lutheran Church, beginning in 1937; elected as a Democrat to the Seventy-eighth and Seventy-ninth Congresses (January 3, 1943-January 3, 1947); unsuccessful candidate for reelection in 1946 to the Eightieth Congress; engaged in historical research; died in Reading, Pa., October 11, 1960; interment in Charles Evans Cemetery.

**HOCH, Homer,** a Representative from Kansas; born in Marion, Marion County, Kans., July 4, 1879; attended the public schools and was graduated from Baker University, Baldwin, Kans., in 1902; attended George Washington Law School, Washington, D.C., and

Washburn Law School, Topeka, Kans., from which he was graduated in 1909; clerk and chief of the Appointment Division, Post Office Department, Washington, D.C., 1903-1905; private secretary to Governor Edward W. Hoch of Kansas in 1907 and 1908; engaged in the practice of law in Marion, Kans., 1909-1919; editor of the Marion (Kans.) Record; delegate to the Republican National Convention in 1928; elected as a Republican to the Sixty-sixth and to the six succeeding Congresses (March 4, 1919-March 3, 1933); unsuccessful candidate for reelection in 1932 to the Seventy-third Congress; member and chairman of the State Corporation Commission of Kansas 1933-1939; elected a member of the supreme court of Kansas in 1938; reelected in 1944 and served until his death in Topeka, Kans., January 30, 1949; interment in Marion Cemetery, Marion, Kans.

**HOCHBRUECKNER, George Joseph,** a Representative from New York; born in Queens, N.Y., September 20, 1938; attended State University of New York, Stony Brook; Hofstra University, Hempstead, N.Y.; Franklin Pierce College, Rindge, N.H.; and the University of California, Northridge; served in the United States Navy, 1956-1959; electronics engineer; member, New York State assembly, 1975-1984; unsuccessful candidate for election in 1984 to the Ninety-ninth Congress; elected as a Democrat to the One Hundredth and to the three succeeding Congresses (January 3, 1987-January 3, 1995); unsuccessful candidate for reelection in 1994 to the One Hundred Fourth Congress; is a resident of Coram, N.Y.

**HODGES, Asa,** a Representative from Arkansas; born near Moulton, Lawrence County, Ala., January 22, 1822; moved to Marion, Ark.; attended La Grange College; studied law; was admitted to the bar in 1848 and practiced until 1860; delegate to the State constitutional convention in 1867; served in the State house of representatives in 1868; member of the State senate 1870-1873; elected as a Republican to the Forty-third Congress (March 4, 1873-March 3, 1875); was not a candidate for reelection in 1874 to the Forty-fourth Congress; engaged in agricultural pursuits; died near Marion, Ark., June 6, 1900; interment in Elmwood Cemetery, Memphis, Tenn.

**HODGES, Charles Drury,** a Representative from Illinois; born in Queen Anne, Talbot County, Md., February 4, 1810; attended the public schools and was graduated from Trinity College, Hartford, Conn., in 1829; studied law in Annapolis, Md.; was admitted to the bar in 1831 and commenced practice in Annapolis; moved to Carrollton, Ill., in 1833 and resumed the practice of law; also engaged in the mercantile business for a short time; member of the State house of representatives 1851-1853; elected judge of Greene County in 1854; reelected for a four-year term in 1858 but resigned in 1859 having been elected to Congress; secretary and treasurer of the St. Louis, Jacksonville & Chicago Railroad in 1858; afterward director for many years; elected as a Democrat to the Thirty-fifth Congress to fill the vacancy caused by the death of Thomas L. Harris and served from January 4 to March 3, 1859; was not a candidate for election to fill the vacancy in the Thirty-sixth Congress, caused also by the death of Mr. Harris; resumed the practice of law in Carrollton, Ill.; circuit judge 1867-1873; member of the State senate 1873-1877; again practiced law in Carrollton, Ill., until his death April 1, 1884; interment in the City Cemetery.

**HODGES, George Tisdale,** a Representative from Vermont; born in Clarendon, Vt., July 4, 1789; attended the common schools; engaged in business in Rutland, Vt.; member of the State house of representatives 1827-1829, 1839, and 1840; served in the State senate 1845-1847 and was president pro tempore of that body in 1846 and 1847; presidential elector on the Whig ticket in 1848; president of the Bank of Rutland for over twenty-five years; elected as a Republican to the Thirty-fourth Congress to fill the vacancy caused by the death of James Meacham and served from December 1, 1856, to March 3, 1857; was not a candidate for renomination in

1856; died in Rutland, Vt., August 9, 1860; interment in Evergreen Cemetery.

**HODGES, James Leonard,** a Representative from Massachusetts; born in Taunton, Bristol County, Mass., April 24, 1790; attended the common schools; studied law; was admitted to the bar and practiced; bank cashier; postmaster of Taunton; member of the Massachusetts constitutional convention in 1820; served in the senate in 1823 and 1824; elected to the Twentieth, Twenty-first, and Twenty-second Congresses (March 4, 1827-March 3, 1833); declined to be a candidate for renomination; died in Taunton, Bristol County, Mass., March 8, 1846; interment in Plain Burying Ground.

**HODGES, Kaneaster, Jr.,** a Senator from Arkansas; born in Newport, Jackson County, Ark., August 20, 1938; attended the public schools; B.A., Princeton University, 1960; M.Th., Perkins School of Theology, Southern Methodist University, Dallas, Tex., 1963; LL.B., University of Arkansas School of Law, Fayetteville, 1967; admitted to the Arkansas bar in 1967 and commenced practice in Newport; lay minister, lawyer, and farmer; hospital and prison chaplain; city attorney and deputy prosecuting attorney, Newport, Ark., 1967-1974; legislative secretary to Governor David H. Pryor in 1975; chairman, Arkansas Natural Heritage Commission, 1974-1976; member, Arkansas Game and Fish Commission, 1976-1977; appointed by the Governor as a Democrat to the United States Senate, December 10, 1977, to fill the vacancy caused by the death of John J. McClellan for the term ending January 3, 1979, and served from December 10, 1977, to January 3, 1979; was not a candidate in the May 30, 1978 primary for the six-year term; is a resident of Newport, Ark.

**HOEKSTRA, Peter,** a Representative from Michigan; born in Groningen, The Netherlands, October 30, 1953; immigrated to the United States in 1957; graduated, Holland (Mich.) Christian High School; B.A., Hope College, Holland, Mich., 1975; M.B.A., University of Michigan, Ann Arbor, 1977; furniture executive with Herman Miller, Inc. as product manager, director of product management, director of dealer marketing, vice president for dealer marketing, 1988-1989, and vice president for product management, 1989-1993; elected as a Republican to the One Hundred Third and One Hundred Fourth Congresses (January 3, 1993-January 3, 1997); is a resident of Holland, Mich.

**HOEPPEL, John Henry,** a Representative from California; born near Tell City, Perry County, Ind., February 10, 1881; attended the grammar school in Evansville, Ind.; enlisted in the United States Army on July 27, 1898, and served successively as private, corporal, and sergeant until 1921, with service in France during the First World War; moved to Arcadia, Los Angeles County, Calif., in 1919; postmaster at Arcadia, Calif., 1923-1931; in 1928 became editor of National Defense magazine; elected as a Democrat to the Seventy-third and to the Seventy-fourth Congresses (March 4, 1933-January 3, 1937); chairman, Committee on War Claims (Seventy-fourth Congress); unsuccessful candidate for renomination in 1936 to the Seventy-fifth Congress; resumed his editorial interests; unsuccessful Prohibition candidate for election in 1946 to the Eightieth Congress; resided in Arcadia, Calif., where he died September 21, 1976; interment in Resurrection Cemetery, San Gabriel, Calif.

**HOEVEN, Charles Bernard,** a Representative from Iowa; born in Hospers, Sioux County, Iowa, March 30, 1895; attended the public schools and Alton (Iowa) High School; State University of Iowa at Iowa City, B.A., in 1920 and from its law department, LL.B., 1922; was admitted to the bar in 1922 and commenced practice in Alton, Iowa; during the First World War served as a sergeant, Company D, Three Hundred and Fiftieth Infantry, Eighty-eighth Division, and with the Intelligence Service, First Battalion, in England and France; county attorney of Sioux County, Iowa, 1925-1937; member

of the State senate 1937-1941, serving as president pro tempore 1939-1941; temporary and permanent chairman of Iowa Republican State Judicial convention in 1942; delegate to each Iowa State Republican convention from 1925 to 1970 and chairman in 1940; delegate to Republican National Convention, 1964; elected as a Republican to the Seventy-eighth and to the ten succeeding Congresses (January 3, 1943-January 3, 1965); chairman, Republican Conference (Eighty-ninth Congress); was not a candidate for renomination in 1964 to the Eighty-ninth Congress; vice president of savings bank; resided in Orange City, Iowa, where he died November 9, 1980; interment in Nassau Township Cemetery, Alton, Iowa.

**HOEY, Clyde Roark,** a Representative and a Senator from North Carolina; born in Shelby, Cleveland County, N.C., on December 11, 1877; attended the public schools; learned the printing trade and later became, at the age of sixteen, owner, editor and publisher of the Cleveland Star; graduated from the law department of the University of North Carolina at Chapel Hill; was admitted to the bar in 1899 and commenced the practice of law in Shelby, N.C.; member, North Carolina State house of commons, 1898-1902; member, State senate, 1902-1904; assistant United States attorney for the western district of North Carolina, 1913-1919; elected as a Democrat to the Sixty-sixth Congress to fill the vacancy caused by the resignation of Edwin Y. Webb and served from December 16, 1919, to March 3, 1921; declined to be a candidate for renomination in 1920 to the Sixty-seventh Congress; resumed the practice of law; elected Governor of North Carolina in 1936, and served from January 7, 1937 to January 9, 1941; elected as a Democrat to the United States Senate in 1944; reelected in 1950 and served from January 3, 1945, until his death in his Senate office in Washington, D.C., May 12, 1954; interment in Sunset Cemetery, Shelby, N.C.

**Bibliography:** *DAB*; Hatcher, Susan A. "The Senatorial Career of Clyde R. Hoey," Ph.D. dissertation, Duke University, 1983.

**HOFFECKER, John Henry,** (father of Walter Oakley Hoffecker), a Representative from Delaware; born at Mansion House, near Smyrna, Del., September 12, 1827; attended public and private schools; was graduated in civil engineering, and engaged in his profession in Smyrna in 1853; delegate to the Republican National Conventions of 1876 and 1884; member of the State house of representatives in 1888, and on January 1, 1889, was chosen speaker of the house; president of the town council in 1878 and served continuously by reelection until 1898; unsuccessful candidate for election in 1896 for Governor of Delaware; elected as a Republican to the Fifty-sixth Congress and served from March 4, 1899, until his death in Smyrna, Del., June 16, 1900; interment in Glenwood Cemetery.

**HOFFECKER, Walter Oakley** (son of John Henry Hoffecker) a Representative from Delaware; born near Smyrna, Kent County, Del., September 20, 1854; attended the public schools in Smyrna and was graduated from Smyrna Seminary in 1872; in September 1873 entered Lehigh University, Bethlehem, Pa.; studied civil engineering and followed that profession; president of the Philadelphia & Smyrna Transportation Co.; engaged in the general insurance business in 1884; also engaged in the canning industry and in banking; elected as a Republican to the Fifty-sixth Congress to fill the vacancy caused by the death of his father and served from November 6, 1900, until March 3, 1901; was not a candidate for renomination in 1900; resumed business activities in Smyrna, Del.; delegate to the Republican National Convention in 1908; member of the State highway commission; died in Smyrna, Del., January 23, 1934; interment in Glenwood Cemetery.

**HOFFMAN, Carl Henry,** a Representative from Pennsylvania; born in Bangor, Northampton County, Pa., August 12, 1896; attended the public schools and was graduated from Juniata College, Huntingdon, Pa., in 1922; served during the First World

War as a candidate in Officers' Training School for Infantry; taught school and was a coach of athletics at Juniata College in 1922; engaged in the lumber, oil, and banking businesses in Somerset, Pa., 1923-1946; elected as a Republican to the Seventy-ninth Congress to fill the vacancy caused by the death of J. Buell Snyder and served from May 21, 1946, to January 3, 1947; was not a candidate for renomination in 1946 to the Eightieth Congress; resumed his former business pursuits at Somerset, Pa., where he resided until his death November 30, 1980; interment in Husband Cemetery.

**HOFFMAN, Clare Eugene,** a Representative from Michigan; born in Vicksburg, Union County, Pa., September 10, 1875; attended the public schools and was graduated from the law department of Northwestern University, Evanston, Ill., in 1895; was admitted to the Michigan bar in 1896 and commenced practice in Allegan, Mich.; prosecuting attorney for Allegan County, Mich., 1904-1910; elected as a Republican to the Seventy-fourth and to the thirteen succeeding Congresses (January 3, 1935-January 3, 1963); chairman, Committee on Expenditures in the Executive Departments (Eightieth Congress), Committee on Government Operations (Eighty-third Congress); was not a candidate for renomination in 1962 to the Eighty-eighth Congress; retired to his home in Allegan, Mich., where he died November 3, 1967; interment in Oakwood Cemetery.

**Bibliography:** Walker, Donald Edwin. "The Congressional Career of Clare E. Hoffman, 1935-63." Ph.D. dissertation, Michigan State University, 1982.

**HOFFMAN, Elmer Joseph,** a Representative from Illinois; born on a farm in Du Page County, near Wheaton, Ill., July 7, 1899; attended the public schools of Wheaton; enlisted in the Artillery Corps during the First World War and served in France; helped operate his father's farm, as well as his own trucking firm, from 1919 to 1930; employed in Du Page County sheriff's office 1930-1938; sheriff of Du Page County 1939-1942; chief deputy sheriff 1943-1946; again sheriff 1947-1950; in 1951 was probation officer of Du Page County's circuit and county courts; elected State treasurer in 1952, reelected in 1956 and served until elected to Congress; elected as a Republican to the Eighty-sixth and to the two succeeding Congresses (January 3, 1959-January 3, 1965); was not a candidate for renomination in 1964 to the Eighty-ninth Congress; resided in Wheaton, Ill., where he died June 25, 1976; interment in St. Michael's Cemetery.

**HOFFMAN, Harold Giles,** a Representative from New Jersey; born in South Amboy, N.J., February 7, 1896; attended the public schools, and was graduated from the South Amboy High School in 1913; engaged in newspaper work; enlisted on July 25, 1917, as a private in Company H, Third Regiment, New Jersey Infantry, and served overseas as a captain; executive with the South Amboy Trust Co., 1919-1942; city treasurer of South Amboy 1920-1925; served in the New Jersey State house of assembly, 1923-1924; mayor of South Amboy, 1925-1926; delegate to the Republican State conventions in 1934, 1935, 1936, and 1937, and to the Republican National Convention of 1936; elected as a Republican to the Seventieth and Seventy-first Congresses (March 4, 1927-March 3, 1931); was not a candidate for renomination in 1930 to the Seventy-second Congress, having been appointed motor vehicle commissioner of New Jersey, and served until 1935; elected Governor of New Jersey in 1934, and served from January 15, 1935 to January 18, 1938; became executive director of the New Jersey Unemployment Compensation Commission in 1938, and served until granted military leave to reenter the United States Army on June 15, 1942, as a major in the Transportation Corps; was advanced to the rank of lieutenant colonel on December 15, 1942, and served until June 24, 1946, when he was discharged with the rank of colonel; resumed his former occupation as executive director of the New Jersey Unemployment Compensation Commission; died in New York City on June 4, 1954; interment in Christ Church Cemetery, South Amboy, N.J.

**HOFFMAN, Henry William,** a Representative from Maryland; born in Cumberland, Allegany County, Md., November 10, 1825; attended the public schools and Allegany County Academy; was graduated from Jefferson College, Pennsylvania, in 1846; studied law; was admitted to the bar in 1848; elected by the American Party to the Thirty-fourth Congress (March 4, 1855-March 3, 1857); unsuccessful candidate for reelection in 1856 to the Thirty-fifth Congress and for election in 1858 to the Thirty-sixth Congress; treasurer of the Chesapeake & Ohio Canal Co. 1858-1860; elected Sergeant at Arms of the House of Representatives in the Thirty-sixth Congress and served from February 3, 1860, to July 5, 1861; appointed by President Lincoln as collector of customs at Baltimore, Md., and served from 1861 to 1866; resumed the practice of law in Cumberland, Md.; elected associate judge of the sixth Maryland circuit court in 1883 and served until his death in Cumberland, Allegany County, Md., July 28, 1895; interment in Rose Hill Cemetery.

**HOFFMAN, Josiah Ogden,** a Representative from New York; born in New York City, May 3, 1793; pursued classical studies and was graduated from Columbia College in 1812; served for three years in the Navy and was warranted a midshipman in 1814; studied law; was admitted to the bar in 1818 and commenced practice in Goshen, Orange County; district attorney of that county 1823-1826; returned to New York City; member of the State assembly in 1825, 1826, and 1828; district attorney of the city and county of New York 1829-1835; elected as a Whig to the Twenty-fifth and Twenty-sixth Congresses (March 4, 1837-March 3, 1841); United States district attorney at New York 1841-1845; attorney general of the State November 8, 1853, to November 7, 1855; died in New York City May 1, 1856; interment in St. Mark's Church vault.

**Bibliography:** *DAB.*

**HOFFMAN, Michael,** a Representative from New York; born in Half Moon, Saratoga County, N.Y., October 11, 1787; completed academic studies; studied medicine and law; was admitted to the bar and commenced practice in Herkimer, Herkimer County, N.Y.; district attorney 1823-1825; elected to the Nineteenth Congress; reelected to the Twentieth Congress and reelected as a Jacksonian to the Twenty-first and Twenty-second Congresses (March 4, 1825-March 3, 1833); chairman, Committee on Naval Affairs (Twentieth through Twenty-second Congresses); judge of Herkimer County 1830-1833; canal commissioner of New York 1833-1835; register of the land office at Saginaw, Mich., in 1836; returned to Herkimer, N.Y.; member of the State assembly in 1841, 1842, and 1844; delegate to the State constitutional convention in 1846; naval officer of New York City from May 3, 1845, until his death in Brooklyn, N.Y., September 27, 1848.

**HOFFMAN, Richard William,** a Representative from Illinois; born in Chicago, Ill., December 23, 1893; veteran of the First World War; engaged in the printing and publishing business; owned and operated radio stations in Chicago, Ill.; president of the board of education of J. Sterling Morton High School and Junior College 1933-1936 and 1939-1948; elected as a Republican to the Eighty-first and to the three succeeding Congresses (January 3, 1949-January 3, 1957); was not a candidate for renomination in 1956 to the Eighty-fifth Congress; resumed former business activities; resided in Riverside, Ill.; died in Maywood, Ill., July 6, 1975; interment in Forest Home Cemetery, Forest Park, Ill.

**HOGAN, Earl Lee,** a Representative from Indiana; born in Hope, Bartholomew County, Ind., March 13, 1920; attended the public schools of Burney; also attended Indiana University and the University of Kentucky; served from 1940 to 1945 in the Air Force as a bombardier on a B-17; awarded the Distinguished Flying Cross, Purple Heart, and Air Medal with three oak leaf clusters; deputy sheriff of Bartholomew County, Ind., 1946-1950, and sheriff, 1950-1958; elected as a Democrat to the Eighty-sixth Congress

(January 3, 1959-January 3, 1961); unsuccessful candidate for reelection in 1960 to the Eighty-seventh Congress; assistant to Howard Bertsch, administrator of the Farmers Home Administration, 1961; assistant to Norman M. Clapp, administrator of the Rural Electric Administration, 1961-1962; midwest field representative, Office of Rural Areas Development, 1962-1966; rural development specialist, 1966-1970, special projects representative, 1971-1975, chief of business and industrial loan division, 1975-1980, all in the Farmers Home Administration; secretary, Indiana State Rural Development Committee, 1966-1980; chairman, State advisory board, Indiana Green Thumb, Inc., 1975-1982; owns and operates a farm; is a resident of Naples, Fla., and Columbus, Ind.

**HOGAN, John,** a Representative from Missouri; born in Mallow, County Cork, Ireland, January 2, 1805; immigrated to the United States in 1817 and settled in Baltimore, Md.; apprenticed to learn the shoemaker's trade; received a limited schooling; became a licensed Methodist preacher before twenty years of age; went West in 1826 and preached in the Illinois conference; entered general merchandise business in Madison, Ill., in 1831; president of the Illinois Board of Public Works, 1834-1837; member of the Illinois State house of representatives in 1836; unsuccessful Whig candidate for election in 1838 to the Twenty-sixth Congress; register of the land office at Dixon, Ill., 1841-1845; moved to St. Louis, Mo., and engaged in the wholesale grocery business; postmaster of St. Louis, 1857-1861; elected as a Democrat to the Thirty-ninth Congress (March 4, 1865-March 3, 1867); unsuccessful candidate for reelection in 1866 to the Fortieth Congress; died in St. Louis, Mo., February 5, 1892; interment in Bellefontaine Cemetery.

**Bibliography:** *DAB.*

**HOGAN, Lawrence Joseph,** a Representative from Maryland; born in Boston, Mass., September 30, 1928; graduated from Gonzaga High School, Washington, D.C., 1946; B.A., Georgetown University, 1949; J.D., Georgetown University School of Law, 1954; M.A., American University, 1965; engaged in graduate work at San Francisco State College, 1956-1957, and the University of Maryland, 1966-1967; admitted to the bar in 1954 and commenced practice in Washington, D.C.; taught at the University of Maryland, 1960-1968, and 1992-1994; served with Federal Bureau of Investigation, 1948-1958; member, Governor's Commission on Law Enforcement and the Administration of Justice (Md.), 1967-1968; delegate to the Republican National Conventions of 1964, 1968, 1972, 1976 and 1980; elected as a Republican to the Ninety-first and to the two succeeding Congresses (January 3, 1969-January 3, 1975); was not a candidate for reelection in 1974 to the Ninety-fourth Congress, but was an unsuccessful candidate for nomination for Governor of Maryland; executive vice president and general counsel of the Associated Builders and Contractors, Washington, D.C., January 1977 to March 1978; resumed the practice of law in Washington; elected county executive of Prince George's County, Md. in 1978, and served from December 4, 1978 until December 6, 1982; unsuccessful candidate for election in 1982 to the United States Senate; resumed the practice of law in Washington; operates a real estate business and legal seminar business; is a resident of Frederick, Md.

**HOGAN, Michael Joseph,** a Representative from New York; born in New York City, April 22, 1871; attended the parochial and public schools; member of the Thirteenth Regiment, New York National Guard, 1889-1898; served on the board of aldermen of New York City, 1914-1920; declined to be a candidate for renomination; elected as a Republican to the Sixty-seventh Congress (March 4, 1921-March 3, 1923); unsuccessful candidate for reelection in 1922 to the Sixty-eighth Congress; delegate to the Republican State conventions in 1914, 1918, 1920, 1922, 1924, and 1926; engaged in the management of transportation business in New York City; died in Rockville Centre, N.Y., May 7, 1940; interment in Greenwood Cemetery, Brooklyn, N.Y.

**HOGAN, William,** a Representative from New York; born in the parish of St. Paul's Covent Garden, London, England, July 17, 1792; as a young man went with his father to Cape Colony; immigrated to the United States in 1803 with his parents, who settled in New York City; pursued classical studies and was graduated from Columbia College, New York City, in 1811; served in the War of 1812 and fought in the Battle of Plattsburgh, N.Y., September 11, 1814, on Clinton's staff; studied law; was admitted to the bar but did not engage in practice; member of the New York State assembly in 1822 and 1823; county judge of Franklin County, 1829-1837; elected as a Jacksonian to the Twenty-second Congress (March 4, 1831-March 3, 1833); unsuccessful candidate for reelection in 1832 to the Twenty-third Congress; was appointed examiner of claims on March 30, 1855, and subsequently became a translator in the Department of State at Washington, D.C., serving until October 8, 1869; died in Washington, D.C., November 25, 1874; interment in Trinity Church Cemetery, New York City.

**HOGE, John** (brother of William Hoge), a Representative from Pennsylvania; born near Hogestown, Pa., September 10, 1760; pursued English studies; served in the Revolutionary War as ensign in the Ninth Pennsylvania Regiment; moved to what is now Washington, Pa., in 1782, which he and his brother William founded; delegate to the Pennsylvania constitutional convention in 1790; member of the Pennsylvania senate 1790-1795; elected as a Republican to the Eighth Congress to fill the vacancy caused by the resignation of his brother, William Hoge, and served from November 2, 1804, to March 3, 1805; died at Meadow Lands, near Washington, Pa., August 4, 1824; interment in the City Cemetery, Washington, Pa.

**HOGE, John Blair,** a Representative from West Virginia; born in Richmond, Va., on February 2, 1825; studied law; was admitted to the bar in April 1845 and commenced practice in Martinsburg; chosen president of the Bank of Berkeley, Virginia (now West Virginia), in 1853; served in the Virginia house of delegates 1855-1859; delegate to the Democratic National Conventions at Charleston and Baltimore in 1860; during the Civil War served in the Confederate Army in line and staff until paroled in 1865; engaged in journalism; resumed the practice of law in Martinsburg, W.Va., in 1870; delegate to the West Virginia State constitutional convention in 1872; member of the Democratic National Committee 1872-1876; judge of the third judicial circuit in 1872, which office he resigned in August 1880; elected as a Democrat to the Forty-seventh Congress (March 4, 1881-March 3, 1883); United States district attorney for the District of Columbia 1885-1889; died in Martinsburg, W.Va., March 1, 1896; interment in Norborne Cemetery.

**HOGE, Joseph Pendleton,** a Representative from Illinois; born in Steubenville, Ohio, December 15, 1810; attended the common schools and was graduated from Jefferson College; studied law; was admitted to the bar in 1836; moved to Illinois and located in Galena in 1836 and practiced law; held several local offices; elected as a Democrat to the Twenty-eighth and Twenty-ninth Congresses (March 4, 1843-March 3, 1847); was not a candidate for renomination in 1846; resumed the practice of law in Galena; moved to California in 1853 and continued the practice of his profession; unsuccessful candidate for election to the United States Senate in 1869; president of the State constitutional convention in 1878 and of the board of freeholders in 1880; judge of the superior court from January 1, 1889, until his death in San Francisco, Calif., August 14, 1891; interment in Laurel Hill Cemetery.

**HOGE, Solomon Lafayette,** a Representative from South Carolina; born in Pickreltown, Logan County, Ohio, July 11, 1836; attended Bellefontaine (Ohio) public schools and Northwood College, Northwood, Ohio (now Geneva College, Beaver Falls, Pa.); received a classical education and was graduated from the Cincinnati Law School in 1859; was admitted to the bar in 1859 and commenced practice in Bellefontaine, Ohio; entered the Union Army in 1861 as first lieutenant in the Ohio Volunteer Infantry and was subsequently promoted to the rank of captain; moved to Columbia, S.C. in 1868; associate justice of the State supreme court 1868-1870; successfully contested as a Republican the election of J.P. Reed to the Forty-first Congress and served from April 8, 1869, to March 3, 1871; comptroller general of South Carolina in 1874 and 1875; elected to the Forty-fourth Congress (March 4, 1875-March 3, 1877); was not a candidate for renomination in 1876 to the Forty-fifth Congress; moved to Kenton, Ohio, in September 1877 and practiced law until 1882; president of the First National Bank of Kenton; died in Battle Creek, Mich., February 23, 1909; interment in Grove Cemetery, Kenton, Ohio.

**HOGE, William** (brother of John Hoge), a Representative from Pennsylvania; born near Hogestown, Cumberland County, Pa., in 1762; received a limited schooling; moved to western Pennsylvania in 1782, where he and his brother John founded the town of Washington, Pa.; member of the Pennsylvania house of representatives in 1796 and 1797; elected as a Republican to the Seventh and Eighth Congresses and served from March 4, 1801, until his resignation on October 15, 1804; elected to the Tenth Congress (March 4, 1807-March 3, 1809); retired to his farm near Washington, Pa., where he died September 25, 1814; interment in the "Old Graveyard."

**HOGEBOOM, James Lawrence,** a Representative from New York; born in Ghent, Columbia County, N.Y., August 25, 1766; moved to Pittstown, Rensselaer County, N.Y., in 1794; moved to Castleton, N.Y., in April 1802; merchant; member of the State assembly in 1804, 1805, and 1808; judge of Rensselaer County 1805-1808; member of the State constitutional convention in 1821; elected to the Eighteenth Congress (March 4, 1823-March 3, 1825); engaged in the mercantile business; died in Castleton, N.Y., December 23, 1839; interment in Castleton Cemetery.

**HOGG, Charles Edgar** (father of Robert Lynn Hogg), a Representative from West Virginia; born on a farm near Point Pleasant, Mason County, Va. (now West Virginia), December 21, 1852; attended the common schools at Locust Grove, Carleton College, Racine, Ohio, and was graduated from Oldham & Hawe's Business College, Pomeroy, Ohio, in 1869; taught school and was employed as a bookkeeper 1870-1873; studied law; was admitted to the bar in 1875 and commenced practice in Point Pleasant, W.Va.; county superintendent of free schools of Mason County 1875-1879; elected as a Democrat to the Fiftieth Congress (March 4, 1887-March 3, 1889); unsuccessful candidate for renomination in 1888; resumed the practice of law in Point Pleasant, W.Va.; became affiliated with the Republican Party in 1900; dean of the College of Law of West Virginia University at Morgantown 1906-1913; author of several works on legal procedure; died in Point Pleasant, W.Va., June 14, 1935; interment in Lone Oak Cemetery.

**HOGG, David,** a Representative from Indiana; born near Crothersville, Jackson County, Ind., August 21, 1886; attended the common schools; was graduated from Indiana University College of Liberal Arts at Bloomington in 1909 and from the law department of Indiana University in 1912; was admitted to the bar in 1913 and commenced practice in Fort Wayne, Ind.; chairman of the Allen County Republican Committee 1922-1924; elected as a Republican to the Sixty-ninth and to the three succeeding Congresses (March 4, 1925-March 3, 1933); unsuccessful candidate for reelection in 1932 to the Seventy-third Congress and for election in 1934 to the Seventy-fourth Congress and in 1936 to the Seventy-fifth Congress; resumed the practice of law; organized a mutual life insurance company in 1939; president of Goodwill Industries of Fort Wayne 1940-1943; co-publisher of an interdenominational newspaper, 1941-1946; again resumed the practice of law; resided in Fort Wayne, Ind., until his death there October 23, 1973; interment in Lindenwood Cemetery.

**HOGG, Herschel Millard,** a Representative from Colorado; born in Youngstown, Mahoning County, Ohio, November 21, 1853; attended the common schools and was graduated from Monmouth College, Monmouth, Ill., in June 1876; studied law; was admitted to the bar in 1878 and commenced practice in Indianola, Iowa; moved to Gunnison, Colo., in 1881 and resumed the practice of law; city attorney of Gunnison in 1882 and 1883; district attorney of the seventh judicial district of Colorado 1885-1893; moved to Telluride, Colo., in 1888; city attorney 1890-1898; county attorney of San Miguel County, Colo., 1890-1902; elected as a Republican to the Fifty-eighth and Fifty-ninth Congresses (March 4, 1903-March 3, 1907); was not a candidate for renomination in 1906; resumed the practice of law in Cortez, Colo.; retired from political life in 1915; engaged in mining; resided in Denver, Colo., until his death there August 27, 1934; interment in Crown Hill Cemetery.

**HOGG, Robert Lynn** (son of Charles Edgar Hogg), a Representative from West Virginia; born in Point Pleasant, Mason County, W.Va., December 30, 1893; attended the public schools and West Virginia Preparatory School; was graduated from the University of West Virginia at Morgantown in 1914 and from its law department in 1916; was admitted to the bar in 1916 and commenced practice in Point Pleasant, W.Va.; during the First World War he served from 1917-1919 in the Coast Artillery Corps and the Air Sevice; resumed the practice of law in Point Pleasant, W.Va.; prosecuting attorney of Mason County 1921-1924; member of the State senate 1925-1929; elected as a Republican, in a special election, November 4, 1930, to the Seventy-first Congress to fill the vacancy caused by the death of James A. Hughes; reelected to the Seventy-second Congress and served from November 4, 1930, to March 3, 1933; unsuccessful candidate for reelection in 1932 to the Seventy-third Congress; resumed the practice of law in Point Pleasant, W.Va.; lawyer for the Association of Life Insurance Presidents, New York City, 1935-1944; executive and vice president of American Life Convention, Chicago, Ill., 1944-1954; senior vice president, advisory counsel, and vice chairman of the board, Equitable Life Assurance Society of United States, from 1954 until retirement in 1960, continuing to serve as a member of its board and executive committee; counsel to a law firm in Charleston, W.Va., 1960-1970; resided in Lewisburg, W.Va.; died in Charlottesville, Va., July 21, 1973; interment in Lone Oak Cemetery, Point Pleasant, W.Va.

**HOGG, Samuel,** a Representative from Tennessee; born in Halifax, N.C., April 18, 1783; attended the public schools in Caswell County; taught school for a short time; studied medicine in Gallatin, Sumner County, Tenn., about 1804; moved to Lebanon County, Tenn., after a short time; surgeon in the First Regiment of Tennessee Volunteer Infantry from November 21, 1812, to April 22, 1813; hospital surgeon on the staff of Major General Andrew Jackson in the expedition against the Creek Indians from February 22 to May 25, 1814; also hospital surgeon on the staff of Major General William Carroll from November 13, 1814, to May 13, 1815; member of the State house of representatives; elected as a Republican to the Fifteenth Congress (March 4, 1817-March 3, 1819); engaged in the practice of medicine in Lebanon, Tenn., until 1828, in Nashville 1828-1836 and 1838-1840, and in Natchez 1836-1838; president of the State Medical Society of Tennessee in 1840; died in Rutherford County, Tenn., May 28, 1842; interment in Nashville City Cemetery.

**HOIDALE, Einar,** a Representative from Minnesota; born in Tromso, Norway, August 17, 1870; immigrated in 1879 to the United States with his parents, who settled near Dawson, Lac qui Parle County, Minn.; attended the common schools; was graduated from the law department of the University of Minnesota at Minneapolis in 1898; was admitted to the bar the same year and commenced practice in New Ulm, Minn.; prosecuting attorney of Brown County, 1900-1906; also engaged as a newspaper publisher at Dawson and Madison, Minn., 1900-1904; judge advocate of the State militia, 1900-1908; moved to Minneapolis, Minn., in 1907 and continued the practice of law; delegate to the Democratic National Conventions of 1920, 1932 and 1936; unsuccessful Democratic candidate for election to the United States Senate in 1930; elected as a Democrat to the Seventy-third Congress (March 4, 1933-January 3, 1935); was not a candidate in 1934 for renomination to the House of Representatives, but was an unsuccessful candidate for election to the United States Senate; returned to Minneapolis, Minn., and practiced law; died in St. Petersburg, Fla., December 5, 1952; interment in Lakewood Cemetery, Minneapolis, Minn.

**HOKE, Martin Rossiter,** a Representative from Ohio; born in Lakewood, Cuyahoga County, Ohio, May 18, 1952; graduated, Western Reserve Academy, 1969; B.A., Amherst (Mass.) College, 1973; J.D., Case Western Reserve University Law School, Cleveland, Ohio, 1980; attorney; founder, Red Carpet Airport Car Care, 1980 and Red Carpet Cellular, 1985; elected as a Republican to the One Hundred Third and One Hundred Fourth Congresses (January 3, 1993-January 3, 1997); is a resident of Lakewood, Ohio.

**HOLADAY, William Perry,** a Representative from Illinois; born near Ridgefarm, Vermilion County, Ill., on December 14, 1882; attended the common schools, Vermilion Grove (Ill.) Academy, Penn College, Oskaloosa, Iowa, and the University of Missouri at Columbia; was graduated from the law department of the University of Illinois at Urbana in 1905; was admitted to the bar the same year and commenced practice in Danville, Vermilion County, Ill.; assistant prosecuting attorney of Vermilion County 1905-1907; member of the State house of representatives 1909-1923; elected as a Republican to the Sixty-eighth and to the four succeeding Congresses (March 4, 1923-March 3, 1933); unsuccessful candidate for reelection in 1932 to the Seventy-third Congress; resumed the practice of law in Danville, Ill.; died in Georgetown, Vermilion County, Ill., January 29, 1946; interment in Georgetown Cemetery.

**HOLBROCK, Greg John,** a Representative from Ohio; born in Hamilton, Butler County, Ohio, June 21, 1906; attended the parochial schools and Notre Dame University, South Bend, Ind.; Ph.D., Xavier University, Cincinnati, Ohio, 1928; J.D., University of Cincinnati School of Law, 1932; was admitted to the bar in 1932 and commenced practice in Hamilton, Ohio; elected as a Democrat to the Seventy-seventh Congress (January 3, 1941-January 3, 1943); unsuccessful candidate for reelection in 1942 to the Seventy-eighth Congress; served in the United States Navy from 1943 to January 18, 1946; resumed the practice of law; delegate to the Democratic National Conventions of 1948 and 1960; chairman, Butler County Democratic Executive Committee, 1950-1966; was a resident of Hamilton, Ohio until his death there on September 4, 1992; interment in St. Stephen's Cemetery.

**HOLBROOK, Edward Dexter,** a Delegate from Idaho; born in Elyria, Lorain County, Ohio, May 6, 1836; attended the common schools and Oberlin (Ohio) College; studied law; was admitted to the bar in 1859 and commenced practice in Elyria; moved to the Pacific coast in 1859 and practiced law for a short time at Weaverville, Calif.; moved to Placerville, Idaho, in 1863 and resumed the practice of law; elected as a Democrat to the Thirty-ninth and Fortieth Congresses (March 4, 1865-March 3, 1869); censured by the House of Representatives on February 14, 1869, for use of unparliamentary language; was not a candidate for reelection in 1868 to the Forty-first Congress; shot by Charles H. Douglas in Idaho City, Idaho, on June 17, 1870, and died from his wounds in that city the next day; interment in the Masonic Burial Ground.

**HOLCOMBE, George,** a Representative from New Jersey; born in West Amwell (now Lambertsville), Hunterdon County, N.J., in March 1786; completed preparatory studies and was graduated from Princeton College in 1805; attended the medical department of the University of Pennsylvania at Philadelphia; later studied medicine in Trenton, N.J., and was granted a license by the Medical Society of New Jersey; practiced medicine in Allentown, N.J., 1808-1815; held several local offices; member of the State general assembly in 1815 and 1816; elected to the Seventeenth and to the three succeeding Congresses and served from March 4, 1821, until his death in Allentown, N.J., January 14, 1828; interment in the Congressional Cemetery, Washington, D.C.

**HOLDEN, Thomas Timothy (Tim),** a Representative from Pennsylvania; born in St. Clair, Schuylkill County, Pa., March 5, 1957; attended St. Clair High School; Fork Union Military Academy; B.S., Bloomsburg (Pa.) State University, 1980; sheriff of Schuylkill County, 1985-1993; licensed insurance broker and real estate agent; probation officer; sergeant-at-arms, Pennsylvania House of Representatives, 1985-1993; elected as a Democrat to the One Hundred Third and One Hundred Fourth Congresses (January 3, 1993-January 3, 1997); is a resident of St. Clair, Pa.

**HOLIFIELD, Chester Earl,** a Representative from California; born in Mayfield, Graves County, Ky., December 3, 1903; moved with his family to Springdale, Ark., in 1912; attended the public schools; moved to Montebello, Calif., in 1920, and engaged in the manufacture and selling of men's apparel from 1920 until 1943; chairman of the Los Angeles County Democratic Central committee of the Fifty-first District, 1934-1938; chairman of the California State Central committee of the Twelfth Congressional District, 1938-1940; delegate to each Democratic National Convention from 1940 to 1964; elected as a Democrat to the Seventy-eighth and to the fifteen succeeding Congresses and served from January 3, 1943, until his resignation December 31, 1974; was not a candidate for reelection in 1974 to the Ninety-fourth Congress; chairman, Committee on Government Operations (Ninety-first through Ninety-third Congresses), Joint Committee on Atomic Energy (Eighty-seventh, Eighty-ninth, and Ninety-first Congresses); member, Commission on Organization of the Executive Branch of the Government (Hoover Commission); member, President's Special Evaluation Commission on Atomic Bomb Tests at Bikini Atoll, 1946; congressional adviser to international conferences on uses of atomic energy, nuclear weapons testing, water desalinization, and disarmament; resumed the manufacture and selling of men's apparel; was a resident of Montebello, Calif., until his death there on February 5, 1995.

**Bibliography:** Dyke, Richard Wayne, and Francis X. Gannon. *Chet Holifield: Master Legislator and Nuclear Statesman.* With a foreword by Gerald R. Ford and an afterword by Carl Albert. Lanham, Md.: University Press of America, 1995.

**HOLLADAY, Alexander Richmond,** a Representative from Virginia; born in Prospect Hill, Spotsylvania County, Va., September 18, 1811; attended the public schools, received special training under John Lewis of Spotsylvania County, and attended the University of Virginia at Charlottesville; studied law; was admitted to the bar and practiced in Spotsylvania, Orange, and Louisa Counties; member of the Virginia house of delegates 1845-1847; held several local offices; elected as a Democrat to the Thirty-first and Thirty-second Congresses (March 4, 1849-March 3, 1853); chairman, Committee on Expenditures in the Department of the Navy (Thirty-first Congress); declined to be a candidate for renomination; moved to Richmond, Va., in 1853 and practiced law; president of the Virginia Board of Public Works 1857-1861; died in Richmond, Va., January 29, 1877; interment in family burial ground called "Prospect Hill" in Spotsylvania County, Va.

**HOLLAND, Cornelius,** a Representative from Maine; born in Sutton, Mass., July 9, 1783; attended the common schools; studied medicine and commenced practice in Livermore, Maine, in 1814; moved to Canton, Maine, in 1815; also engaged in agricultural pursuits; delegate to the Maine constitutional convention in 1819; member, Maine State house of representatives, 1821-1822; served in the State senate in 1822, 1825, and 1826; justice of the peace from 1826 until 1855; elected as a Jacksonian to the Twenty-first Congress to fill the vacancy caused by the resignation of James W. Ripley; reelected to the Twenty-second Congress, and served from December 6, 1830 to March 3, 1833; resumed the practice of medicine and engaged in agricultural pursuits; died in Canton Point, Maine, June 2, 1870; interment in Hillside Cemetery.

**HOLLAND, Edward Everett,** a Representative from Virginia; born near Suffolk, Nansemond County, Va., February 26, 1861; attended private schools, Richmond (Va.) College, and was graduated from the University of Virginia at Charlottesville; studied law; was admitted to the bar in 1882 and commenced practice in Suffolk, Va.; mayor of Suffolk, 1885-1887; Commonwealth attorney for Nansemond County, 1887-1907; elected president of the Farmers Bank of Nansemond in 1892; member, Virginia senate, 1907-1911; elected as a Democrat to the Sixty-second and to the four succeeding Congresses (March 4, 1911-March 3, 1921); was not a candidate for renomination in 1920 to the Sixty-seventh Congress; resumed his banking pursuits; delegate to the Democratic National Conventions of 1920 and 1924; member, Virginia senate, 1930-1941; died in Suffolk, Va., on October 23, 1941; interment in Cedar Hill Cemetery, Suffolk, Va.

**HOLLAND, Elmer Joseph,** a Representative from Pennsylvania; born in Pittsburgh, Pa., January 8, 1894; attended the public schools, Duquesne University, Pittsburgh, Pa., and the University of Montpelier, France; was graduated from Samaur Cavalry School, France, in 1919; served with the American Expeditionary Forces during the First World War as a second lieutenant of Field Artillery; engaged as sales and advertising manager for a glass manufacturer, 1915-1933; member of the Pennsylvania house of representatives, 1934-1942; superintendent of highways and sewers, Pittsburgh, Pa., 1940-1942; elected as a Democrat to the Seventy-seventh Congress to fill the vacancy caused by the resignation of Joseph A. McArdle, and served from May 19, 1942 to January 3, 1943; was not a candidate for renomination in 1942 to the Seventy-eighth Congress; served as a major in the European Theater of Operations during the Second World War; member of the Pennsylvania senate, 1943-1956; elected to the Eighty-fourth Congress to fill the vacancy caused by the death of Vera Buchanan; reelected to the Eighty-fifth and the five succeeding Congresses, and served from January 24, 1956 until his death in Annapolis, Md., August 9, 1968; interment in Arlington National Cemetery, Va.

**HOLLAND, James,** a Representative from North Carolina; born in Anson County, near the present town of Rutherfordton, N.C., in 1754; received a very limited education; was a major in the State militia and also saw service in the Continental line, 1775-1783; sheriff of Tryon County from July 1777 to July 1778; justice of the peace of Rutherford County, 1780-1800; comptroller of Rutherford County from July 1782 to January 1785; member of the North Carolina State senate in 1783; served in the State house of commons in 1786, and again in 1789; delegate to the second State constitutional convention in 1789 that adopted the Federal Constitution; member of the first board of trustees of the University of North Carolina 1789-1795; studied law; was admitted to the bar on October 15, 1793, and commenced practice in Rutherfordton, N.C.; elected as a Republican to the Fourth Congress (March 4, 1795-March 3, 1797); declined to be a candidate for reelection in 1796 to the Fifth Congress, but was again a member of the State senate in 1797; resumed the practice of his profession and also

engaged in agricultural pursuits; elected to the Seventh and to the four succeeding Congresses (March 4, 1801-March 3, 1811); was not a candidate for renomination in 1810 to the Twelfth Congress; in 1811 moved to what is now Maury County, Tenn., engaging in agricultural pursuits near Columbia; justice of the peace, 1812-1818; died on his estate in Maury County, Tenn., May 19, 1823; interment in the Holland Family (now known as Watson) Cemetery, nine miles east of Columbia, Maury County, Tenn.

**HOLLAND, Kenneth Lamar,** a Representative from South Carolina; born in Hickory, Catawba County, N.C., November 24, 1934; attended the public schools of Gaffney, S.C.; A.B., University of South Carolina, Columbia, 1960; LL.B., University of South Carolina Law School, Columbia, 1963; admitted to the South Carolina bar in 1963 and commenced practice in Camden; served in the South Carolina National Guard, 1952-1959; chairman, South Carolina State Board of Municipal Canvassers, 1971-1973; delegate, South Carolina State Democratic conventions, 1968-1972; delegate to the Democratic National Convention of 1968; member, South Carolina Highway Commission, 1972-1975; elected as a Democrat to the Ninety-fourth and to the three succeeding Congresses (January 3, 1975-January 3, 1983); was not a candidate for reelection in 1982 to the Ninety-eighth Congress; is a resident of Gaffney, S.C.

**HOLLAND, Spessard Lindsey,** a Senator from Florida; born in Bartow, Polk County, Fla., July 10, 1892; attended the public schools; graduated from Emory College near Atlanta, Ga., in 1912 and from the University of Florida College of Law at Gainesville in 1916; taught in public schools of Warrenton, Ga., 1912-1914; was admitted to the bar in 1916 and commenced practice in Bartow, Fla.; during the First World War served in the Coast Artillery Corps and the Army Air Corps in France 1918; prosecuting attorney of Polk County, Fla., 1919-1920; county judge of Polk County from 1921 until 1929; member, Florida State senate, 1932-1940; elected Governor of Florida in 1940, and served from January 7, 1941 to January 2, 1945; trustee of Southern College, 1932-1935; trustee of Emory University, 1943-1946; appointed as a Democrat to the United States Senate on September 25, 1946, to fill the vacancy caused by the death of Charles O. Andrews for the term ending January 3, 1947; elected for the full term in 1946, reelected in 1952, 1958, and again in 1964 and served from September 25, 1946, to January 2, 1971; was not a candidate for reelection in 1970; sponsor of the Twenty-fourth Amendment to the Constitution, ratified January 23, 1964, outlawing the poll tax in federal elections; retired and resided in Bartow, Fla., where he died November 6, 1971; interment in Wildwood Cemetery.

**HOLLEMAN, Joel,** a Representative from Virginia; born near Smithfield, Isle of Wight County, Va., October 1, 1799; completed preparatory studies; was graduated from Wake Forest College, Wake Forest, N.C.; studied law; was admitted to the bar and commenced practice at Burwell Bay; member of the Virginia house of delegates 1832-1836; member of the Virginia senate 1836-1839; elected as a Democrat to the Twenty-sixth Congress and served from March 4, 1839, until 1840, when he resigned; again a member of the Virginia house of delegates 1841-1844, and served as speaker; resumed the practice of law; died in Smithfield, Va., August 5, 1844; interment in Ivy Hill Cemetery.

**HOLLENBECK, Harold Capistran,** a Representative from New Jersey; born in Passaic, N.J., December 29, 1938; attended the public schools of East Rutherford, N.J.; B.A., Fairleigh Dickinson University, Rutherford, 1961; LL.B., University of Virginia, 1964; admitted to the New Jersey bar in 1965 and commenced practice in Ridgewood; member, East Rutherford Borough Council, 1967-1969, New Jersey assembly, 1968-1971; New Jersey senate, 1972-1973; delegate to the Republican National Convention of 1968; elected as a Republican to the Ninety-fifth and to the two succeeding Congresses (January 3, 1977-January 3, 1983); unsuccessful candidate for reelection in 1982 to the Ninety-eighth Congress; appointed by Governor Thomas H. Kean judge of the Superior Court of New Jersey, Vicinage Two, and took the oath of office on July 1, 1987; is a resident of Ridgewood, N.J.

**HOLLEY, John Milton,** a Representative from New York; born in Salisbury, Conn., November 10, 1802; was graduated from Yale College in 1822; studied law; was admitted to the bar and commenced practice in Black Rock, N.Y., in 1825; moved to Lyons, N.Y., in 1826 and continued the practice of law; member of the State assembly 1838-1841; district attorney of Wayne County 1842-1845; unsuccessful candidate for election in 1844 to the Twenty-ninth Congress; elected as a Whig to the Thirtieth Congress and served from March 4, 1847, until his death in Jacksonville, Fla., March 8, 1848; interment in the Rural Cemetery, Lyons, N.Y.

**HOLLIDAY, Elias Selah,** a Representative from Indiana; born in Aurora, Dearborn County, Ind., March 5, 1842; spent the early part of his life on farms in Indiana, Missouri, and Iowa; attended the common schools and taught in the public schools in Iowa; during the Civil War enlisted in the Fifth Kansas Regiment and served until August 12, 1864, when he was mustered out with the rank of first sergeant; attended Hartsville College, Bartholomew County, Ind.; engaged in teaching in Jennings County, Ind.; studied law at Mount Vernon, Ind.; was admitted to the bar in 1873 and commenced practice in Carbon, Clay County, Ind.; moved to Brazil, Ind., in 1874; mayor of Brazil 1877-1880, 1887, and 1888; city attorney in 1884; member of the city council 1892-1896; elected as a Republican to the Fifty-seventh and to the three succeeding Congresses (March 4, 1901-March 3, 1909); was not a candidate for renomination in 1908; reengaged in the practice of law in Brazil until 1922; died in Brazil, Ind., March 13, 1936; interment in Cottage Hill Cemetery.

**HOLLINGS, Ernest Frederick,** a Senator from South Carolina; born in Charleston, Charleston County, S.C., January 1, 1922; attended the public schools of Charleston; B.A., The Citadel, 1942; LL.B., University of South Carolina Law School, 1947; admitted to the bar in 1947 and commenced practice in Charleston; served in the United States Army, 1942-1945; elected to the South Carolina State general assembly in 1948, 1950, and 1952; speaker pro tempore, South Carolina State house of representatives, 1951-1954; elected lieutenant governor of South Carolina in 1954; elected Governor of South Carolina in 1958, and served from January 20, 1959 to January 15, 1963; presidential appointee to several federal commissions; elected as a Democrat on November 8, 1966, to the United States Senate to complete the unexpired term of Olin D. Johnston; reelected in 1968 for the six-year term commencing January 3, 1969; reelected in 1974, 1980, 1986 and again in 1992 for the term ending January 3, 1999; chairman, Committee on the Budget (Ninety-sixth Congress), Committee on Commerce, Science and Transportation (One Hundredth through One Hundred Third Congresses); is a resident of Isle of Palms, S.C.

**HOLLINGSWORTH, David Adams,** a Representative from Ohio; born in Belmont, Belmont County, Ohio, November 21, 1844; moved with his parents to Flushing, Ohio; attended the public schools; served in the Union Army in Company B, Twenty-fifth Regiment, Ohio Volunteer Infantry, 1861-1863; studied law at Mount Union College, Alliance, Ohio; was admitted to the bar in St. Clairsville, Ohio, on September 17, 1867, and commenced practice in Flushing; mayor of Flushing in 1867; moved to Cadiz, Ohio, in 1869 and continued the practice of law; elected prosecuting attorney of Harrison County in 1873 and reelected in 1875; member of the State senate in 1879 and reelected in 1881; admitted to practice before the United States Supreme Court in 1880; chairman of the Republican State convention in 1882; attorney general of Ohio in 1883 and 1884; resumed the practice of law in Cadiz; one of the organizers of the Ohio State bar association, serving as chairman in 1908; elected as a Republican to the Sixty-first Congress (March 4, 1909-March 3,

1911); unsuccessful candidate for reelection in 1910 to the Sixty-second Congress; resumed the practice of law in Cadiz; elected to the Sixty-fourth and Sixty-fifth Congresses (March 4, 1915-March 3, 1919); declined to be a candidate for renomination in 1918; resumed the practice of law until his death in Cadiz, Ohio, December 3, 1929; interment in Cadiz Cemetery.

**HOLLIS, Henry French,** a Senator from New Hampshire; born in Concord, N.H., August 30, 1869; attended the public schools and studied under private tutors; engaged in civil engineering for the Chicago, Burlington & Quincy Railroad in 1886 and 1887; graduated from Harvard University in 1892; studied law; was admitted to the bar in 1893 and commenced practice in Concord; unsuccessful candidate for election in 1900 to the Fifty-seventh Congress; unsuccessful Democratic candidate for Governor in 1902 and 1904; elected as a Democrat to the United States Senate for the term beginning March 4, 1913, and served from March 13, 1913, until March 3, 1919; declined to be a candidate for renomination in 1918; chairman, Committee on Enrolled Bills (Sixty-third through Sixty-fifth Congresses); regent of the Smithsonian Institution 1914-1919; United States representative to the Inter-Allied War Finance Council 1918; member of the United States Liquidation Commission for France and England 1919; commenced the practice of international law in 1919; appointed to the International Bank of Bulgaria in 1922; died in Paris, France, July 7, 1949; interment in Blossom Hill Cemetery, Concord, N.H.

**HOLLISTER, John Baker,** a Representative from Ohio; born in Cincinnati, Ohio, November 7, 1890; attended the public schools and St. Paul's School, Concord, N.H.; was graduated from Yale University in 1911; attended the University of Munich, Germany, in 1911 and 1912, and was graduated from Harvard University Law School in 1915; was admitted to the bar the same year and commenced practice in Cincinnati, Ohio; appointed on August 15, 1917, a first lieutenant in the United States Army and served overseas as captain of Battery B, Forty-sixth Artillery Corps, later being in command of the Third Battalion of his regiment; on detached service with American Relief Administration under Herbert Hoover, 1919; resumed the practice of law in Cincinnati, Ohio; director of various financial and manufacturing corporations; member of the Cincinnati Board of Education 1921-1929; elected as a Republican to the Seventy-second Congress by special election, November 3, 1931, to fill the vacancy caused by the death of Nicholas Longworth; reelected to the two succeeding Congresses and served from November 3, 1931, to January 3, 1937; was an unsuccessful candidate for reelection in 1936 to the Seventy-fifth Congress; resumed the practice of his profession; delegate to the Republican National Conventions of 1940, 1944, 1948 and 1952; headed United Nations Relief Rehabilitation Association mission to the Netherlands, 1945; executive director, Commission on Organization of the Executive Branch of the Government (Hoover Commission), from October 1953 to July 1955; Director, International Cooperation Administration, from June 15, 1955, until his resignation September 13, 1957; resumed the practice of law in Cincinnati, Ohio, where he died January 4, 1979; cremated; ashes interred in Spring Grove Cemetery.

**HOLLOWAY, Clyde Cecil,** a Representative from Louisiana; born in Lecompte, La., November 28, 1943; attended public schools and the National Aeronautics School, Kansas City, Kans.; salesman for Pan American Airways; owned and operated a nursery; chairman of the board, Forest Hill Academy; elected as a Republican to the One Hundredth and to the two succeeding Congresses (January 3, 1987-January 3, 1993); unsuccessful candidate in 1991 for Governor of Louisiana; unsuccessful candidate for reelection in 1992 to the One Hundred Third Congress, and for nomination in 1996 to the One Hundred Fifth Congress; is a resident of Forest Hill, La.

**HOLLOWAY, David Pierson,** a Representative from Indiana; born in Waynesville, Warren County, Ohio, December 7, 1809; moved with his parents to Cincinnati in 1813; attended the common schools; learned the printing business and served four years in the office of the Cincinnati Gazette; moved to Richmond, Ind., in 1823; purchased the Richmond Palladium in 1832 and was its editor and proprietor until he died; member of the Indiana State house of representatives in 1843 and 1844; served in the Indiana State senate 1844-1850; appointed in 1849 examiner of land offices; elected as a Republican to the Thirty-fourth Congress (March 4, 1855-March 3, 1857); chairman, Committee on Agriculture (Thirty-fourth Congress); appointed Commissioner of Patents and served from 1861 to 1865; engaged as a patent attorney in Washington, D.C., until his death on September 9, 1883; interment in Maple Grove Cemetery, Richmond, Ind.; reinterment in Earlham Cemetery.

**HOLMAN, Rufus Cecil,** a Senator from Oregon; born in Portland, Oreg., October 14, 1877; attended the public schools; school teacher from 1896 until 1898; engaged in agricultural pursuits, steamboating, bookkeeping, accounting, and auditing, 1899-1910; in 1910 engaged in the manufacture of record books and paper boxes, and in the ice and cold storage business in Portland, Oreg.; member of a variety of civic commissions; Oregon State treasurer, 1931-1939; elected as a Republican to the United States Senate, and served from January 3, 1939 to January 3, 1945; unsuccessful candidate for renomination in 1944; resumed management of the Portland (Oreg.) Paper Box Company, and of a farm near Molalla, Oreg.; died in Portland, Oreg., November 27, 1959; interment in Riverview Cemetery.

**HOLMAN, William Steele,** a Representative from Indiana; born near Aurora, Dearborn County, Ind., September 6, 1822; attended the common schools and Franklin College, Franklin, Ind.; taught in the public schools; studied law; was admitted to the bar and practiced; judge of the probate court 1843-1846; prosecuting attorney 1847-1849; member of the State constitutional convention in 1850; member of the State house of representatives in 1851 and 1852; judge of the court of common pleas 1852-1856; elected as a Democrat to the Thirty-sixth, Thirty-seventh, and Thirty-eighth Congresses (March 4, 1859-March 3, 1865); not a candidate for reelection to the Thirty-ninth Congress; elected to the Fortieth and to the four succeeding Congresses (March 4, 1867-March 3, 1877); chairman, Committee on Appropriations (Forty-fourth Congress), Committee on Public Buildings and Grounds (Forty-fourth Congress); was not a candidate for election to the Forty-fifth Congress; elected to the Forty-seventh and to the six succeeding Congresses (March 4, 1881-March 3, 1895); chairman, Committee on Public Lands (Fiftieth Congress), Committee on Appropriations (Fifty-second Congress), Committee on Indian Affairs (Fifty-third Congress); unsuccessful candidate for reelection to the Fifty-fourth Congress; again elected to the Fifty-fifth Congress and served from March 4, 1897, until his death in Washington, D.C., April 22, 1897; interment in Veraestau Cemetery, Aurora, Ind.

**Bibliography:** *DAB.*

**HOLMES, Adoniram Judson,** a Representative from Iowa; born in Wooster, Wayne County, Ohio, March 2, 1842; moved with his parents to Palmyra, Wis., in 1853; attended the common schools; entered Milton College, Milton, Wis., but left in 1862 to enter the Union Army, where he served in the Twenty-fourth Regiment, Wisconsin Volunteer Infantry, until the close of the Civil War; completed his studies in Milton College and was graduated from the law department of the University of Michigan at Ann Arbor in 1867; was admitted to the bar and commenced practice in Boone, Iowa, in 1868; mayor in 1880 and 1881; member of the State house of representatives in 1882 and 1883; elected as a Republican to the Forty-eighth, Forty-ninth, and Fiftieth Congresses (March 4, 1883-March 3, 1889); unsuccessful candidate for renomination in

1888; Sergeant at Arms of the House of Representatives in the Fifty-first Congress; resumed the practice of law in Boone, Iowa; county attorney 1896-1899; died in Clarinda, Iowa, January 21, 1902; interment in Linwood Cemetery, Boone, Iowa.

**HOLMES, Charles Horace,** a Representative from New York; born in Albion, Orleans County, N.Y., October 24, 1827; attended the public schools, Albion (N.Y.) Academy and was graduated from the Albany Law School; was admitted to the bar in 1855 and commenced practice in Albion; elected as a Republican to the Forty-first Congress to fill the vacancy caused by the resignation of Noah Davis and served from December 6, 1870, to March 3, 1871; was not a candidate for renomination; resumed the practice of law in Albion, N.Y., where he died October 2, 1874; interment in Mount Albion Cemetery.

**HOLMES, David,** a Representative from Virginia and a Senator from Mississippi; born at Mary Ann Furnace, near Hanover, York County, Pa., March 10, 1770; moved to Virginia as a child; attended Winchester Academy, Winchester, Va.; studied law; was admitted to the bar in 1791 and commenced practice in Harrisonburg, Va.; held several local offices; elected to the Fifth and to the five succeeding Congresses (March 4, 1797-March 3, 1809); was not a candidate for renomination in 1808 to the Eleventh Congress; chairman, Committee on Claims (Ninth and Tenth Congresses); moved to the Mississippi Territory; appointed Governor of the Territory of Mississippi by President Thomas Jefferson and served from March 9, 1809 until 1817; Governor of the State of Mississippi from December 10, 1817 to January 5, 1820; appointed to the United States Senate from Mississippi as a Republican to fill the vacancy caused by the resignation of Walter Leake; subsequently elected and served from August 30, 1820, to September 25, 1825, when he resigned; chairman, Committee on Indian Affairs (Sixteenth Congress); elected Governor of Mississippi in 1825 and served from January 7, 1826 until he resigned due to ill health on July 25, 1826; returned to Winchester, Va., in 1827; died at Jordan's Sulphur Springs, near Winchester, Va., on August 20, 1832; interment in Mount Hebron Cemetery, Winchester, Va.

**Bibliography:** *DAB;* Conrad, D.H. "David Holmes: First Governor of Mississippi." *Publications of the Mississippi Historical Society.* Vol. 4. Jackson: Mississippi Historical Society, 1921; Horton, William B. "Life of David Holmes." Ph.D. dissertation, University of Colorado, 1935.

**HOLMES, Elias Bellows,** a Representative from New York; born in Fletcher, Vt., May 22, 1807; attended the district schools and St. Albans Academy; taught school; studied law at Pittsford, N.Y.; was admitted to the bar in 1830; moved to Brockport, N.Y., in 1831 and commenced the practice of law; engaged in agricultural pursuits and transportation; engaged in running canal packets between Rochester and Buffalo 1840-1855; one of the promoters and constructors of the Rochester & Niagara Falls Railroad and a director until it merged with the New York Central Railroad; elected as a Whig to the Twenty-ninth and Thirtieth Congresses (March 4, 1845-March 3, 1849); was not a candidate for renomination; resumed agricultural pursuits; died in Brockport, N.Y., July 31, 1866; interment in City Cemetery.

**HOLMES, Gabriel,** a Representative from North Carolina; born near Clinton, Sampson County, N.C., in 1769; attended Zion Parnassus Academy in Rowan County and Harvard University; studied law in Raleigh, N.C.; was admitted to the bar in 1790 and commenced practice in Clinton, N.C.; served in the State house of commons 1794 and 1795; member of the State senate 1797-1802, 1812, and 1813; Governor of North Carolina from December 7, 1821 to December 7, 1824; elected to the Nineteenth and to the two succeeding Congresses and served from March 4, 1825, until his death near Clinton, Sampson County, N.C., September 26, 1829;

chairman, Committee on Expenditures in the Post Office Department (Twentieth Congress); interment in the family burial plot on his estate.

**HOLMES, Isaac Edward,** a Representative from South Carolina; born in Charleston, S.C., April 6, 1796; attended the common schools, received private tuition, and was graduated from Yale College in 1815; studied law; was admitted to the bar in 1818 and commenced practice in Charleston; member of the city council; served in the State house of representatives 1826-1829 and 1832-1833; elected as a Democrat to the Twenty-sixth and to the five succeeding Congresses (March 4, 1839-March 3, 1851); chairman, Committee on Commerce (Twenty-eighth Congress), Committee on Naval Affairs (Twenty-ninth Congress); practiced law in San Francisco, Calif., 1851-1854, when he returned to Charleston, S.C.; again resided in San Francisco 1857-1861; returned to South Carolina in 1861 and was appointed a commissioner of the State to confer with the Federal Government; died in Charleston, S.C., February 24, 1867; interment in Circular Churchyard.

**Bibliography:** *DAB*.

**HOLMES, John,** a Representative from Massachusetts and a Senator from Maine; born in Kingston, Mass., March 14, 1773; attended the Kingston public schools; graduated from Rhode Island College (now Brown University), Providence, R.I., in 1796; studied law; was admitted to the bar in 1799 and commenced practice in Alfred, Maine (then a district of Massachusetts); also engaged in literary pursuits; elected to the Massachusetts General Court in 1802, 1803, and 1812; elected to the Massachusetts senate in 1813 and 1814; one of the commissioners under the Treaty of Ghent to divide the islands of Passamaquoddy Bay between the United States and Great Britain 1816; elected from Massachusetts to the Fifteenth and Sixteenth Congresses and served from March 4, 1817, to March 15, 1820, when he resigned; chairman, Committee on Expenditures in the Department of State (Sixteenth Congress); delegate to the Maine constitutional convention; upon separation from Massachusetts and the admission of the State of Maine into the Union was elected to the United States Senate from Maine and served from June 13, 1820, to March 3, 1827; again elected to the United States Senate to fill the vacancy caused by the resignation of Albion K. Parris and served from January 15, 1829, to March 3, 1833; chairman, Committee on Finance (Seventeenth Congress), Committee on Pensions (Twenty-first Congress); resumed law practice; member, Maine State house of representatives 1836-1837; appointed United States attorney for the Maine district in 1841 and served until his death in Portland, Maine, July 7, 1843; interment in private tomb of Cotton Brooks, Eastern Cemetery.

**Bibliography:** *DAB*.

**HOLMES, Otis Halbert** (grandson of Dudley Chase Haskell), a Representative from Washington; born in Cresco, Howard County, Iowa, February 22, 1902; moved in 1915 to Walla Walla, Wash., where he attended the public schools; was graduated from Whitman College, Walla Walla, Wash., in 1923 and from Columbia University, New York City, in 1927; teacher of economics at Ellensburg (Wash.) High School in 1924; member of the faculty of Central Washington College of Education at Ellensburg in 1925 and 1930-1942; taught at Columbia University, New York City, in 1928 and 1929; was livestock rancher and operator, 1934-1942; elected as a Republican to the Seventy-eighth and to the seven succeeding Congresses (January 3, 1943-January 3, 1959); was not a candidate for reelection in 1958 to the Eighty-sixth Congress; died in Yakima, Wash., July 27, 1977; interment in Terrace Heights Memorial Park.

**HOLMES, Pehr Gustaf,** a Representative from Massachusetts; born in Mölnbacka, Värmland, Sweden, April 9, 1881; in 1886 immigrated to the United States with his parents, who settled in Worcester, Mass.; attended the public schools; engaged in manufac-

turing; also engaged in the banking and insurance business; member of the common council of Worcester, Mass., 1908-1911; member of the board of aldermen 1913-1916, serving as president in 1915 and 1916; mayor of Worcester 1917-1919; member of the Governor's council, seventh Massachusetts district 1925-1928; elected as a Republican to the Seventy-second and to the seven succeeding Congresses (March 4, 1931-January 3, 1947); unsuccessful candidate for reelection in 1946 to the Eightieth Congress; returned to Worcester, Mass., and his electrotype business; died in Venice, Fla., December 19, 1952; interment in Old Swedish Cemetery, Worcester, Mass.

**HOLMES, Sidney Tracy,** a Representative from New York; born in Schaghticoke, Rensselaer County, N.Y., August 14, 1815; moved with his parents to Morrisville, Madison County, N.Y., in 1819; attended the public schools and was graduated from Morrisville (N.Y.) Academy; taught school; was engaged in civil engineering on the Chenango and Black River Canals for five years; studied law; was admitted to the bar in 1841 and commenced practice in Morrisville, N.Y.; loan commissioner for Madison County 1848-1851; judge and surrogate for Madison County 1851-1864; elected as a Republican to the Thirty-ninth Congress (March 4, 1865-March 3, 1867); was not a candidate for renomination in 1866; resumed the practice of law in Morrisville, N.Y., for a short time, and in Utica, N.Y., until 1872, when he moved to Bay City, Bay County, Mich., continuing the practice of law; died in Bay City, Mich., January 16, 1890; interment in Cedar Street Cemetery, Morrisville, N.Y.

**HOLMES, Uriel,** a Representative from Connecticut; born in East Haddam, Middlesex County, Conn., August 26, 1764; moved with his parents to Hartland, Conn.; attended the common schools and was graduated from Yale College in 1784; studied law; was admitted to the bar in 1798 and commenced practice in Litchfield, Conn.; member of the State house of representatives 1803-1805; prosecuting attorney of Litchfield County 1807-1814; judge of the Litchfield County court 1814-1817; elected as a Federalist to the Fifteenth Congress and served from March 4, 1817, until his resignation in 1818; died in Canton, Conn., May 18, 1827; interment in East Cemetery, Litchfield, Conn.

**HOLSEY, Hopkins,** a Representative from Georgia; born near Lynchburg, Campbell County, Va., August 25, 1779; received an English training and attended the University of Virginia at Charlottesville; was graduated from a law school in Litchfield, Conn.; was admitted to the bar and commenced practice in Hamilton, Ga.; held several local offices and represented Hancock County several years in the State house of representatives; moved to Harris County; elected as a Jacksonian to the Twenty-fourth Congress to fill the vacancy caused by the resignation of James C. Terrell; reelected as a Democrat to the Twenty-fifth Congress and served from October 5, 1835, to March 3, 1839; moved to Athens, Ga., and engaged in newspaper work as publisher of the Southern Banner; unsuccessful candidate for election in 1852 to the Thirty-third Congress; relinquished the newspaper business and resumed the practice of law, in Butler, Ga.; died at his home, "Brightwater," near Butler, Ga., March 31, 1859; interment on his estate.

**Bibliography:** Montgomery, Horace. "Hopkins Holsey." in *Georgians in Profile*, edited by Horace Montgomery. Athens, Ga.: University of Georgia Press, 1958.

**HOLT, Hines,** a Representative from Georgia; born near Milledgeville, Baldwin County, Ga., April 27, 1805; completed preparatory studies; was graduated from Franklin College (now the University of Georgia) at Athens in 1824; studied law; was admitted to the bar and commenced practice in Columbus, Ga.; elected as a Whig to the Twenty-sixth Congress to fill the vacancy caused by the resignation of Walter T. Colquitt and served from February 1 to

March 3, 1841; resumed the practice of law; member of the State senate in 1859; Member of the House of Representatives of the First Confederate Congress 1862-1864; died while attending as a delegate the State constitutional convention at Milledgeville, Ga., on November 4, 1865; interment in Linwood Cemetery, Columbus, Ga.

**HOLT, Joseph Franklin, III,** a Representative from California; born in Springfield, Hampden County, Mass., July 6, 1924; moved to Los Angeles, Calif., with his parents when one year of age; attended the public schools; enlisted as a private in the United States Marine Corps and was called to active duty in July 1943; discharged as a second lieutenant in October 1945; returned to the University of Southern California, B.S. in 1947; engaged in the insurance business and then entered the public relations field; State president of the Young Republicans of California; in January 1951 was recalled to active duty with the Marine Corps and volunteered for duty in Korea; awarded the Purple Heart; elected as a Republican to the Eighty-third and to the three succeeding Congresses (January 3, 1953-January 3, 1961); was not a candidate for renomination in 1960 to the Eighty-seventh Congress; unsuccessful candidate for election in 1968 to the Ninety-first Congress; business consultant; is a resident of Hollister, Calif.

**HOLT, Marjorie Sewell,** a Representative from Maryland; born in Birmingham, Jefferson County, Ala., September 17, 1920; attended Jacksonville Junior College, 1940-1941; LL.B., (J.D.), University of Florida College of Law, 1949; admitted to the Florida bar in 1949, and the Maryland bar in 1962 and commenced practice in Anne Arundel County, Md., 1962; clerk of the Circuit Court, Anne Arundel County, 1966-1972; supervisor of elections, Anne Arundel County, 1963-1965; counsel, Maryland State Federation of Republican Women, 1971-1972; member, Maryland Governor's Commission on Law Enforcement and the Administration of Justice, 1970-1972; member, Anne Arundel County Human Relations Commission, 1965-1966; delegate to the Republican National Conventions of 1968, 1976, 1980 and 1984; elected as a Republican to the Ninety-third and to the six succeeding Congresses (January 3, 1973-January 3, 1987); was not a candidate for reelection in 1986 to the One Hundredth Congress; resumed the practice of law in Baltimore; nominated by President Ronald Reagan as a member of the General Advisory Committee on Arms Control and Disarmament, July 1987; is a resident of Severna Park, Md.

**HOLT, Orrin,** a Representative from Connecticut; born in Willington, Conn., March 13, 1792; received a limited schooling; engaged in agricultural pursuits; member of the State house of representatives 1830-1832; served in the State senate in 1835 and 1836; elected as a Jacksonian to the Twenty-fourth Congress to fill the vacancy caused by the resignation of Andrew T. Judson; reelected as a Democrat to the Twenty-fifth Congress and served from December 5, 1836, to March 3, 1839; resumed agricultural pursuits; interested in military organizations of the State and held official ranks up to inspector general; died in East Willington, Conn., June 20, 1855; interment in Old Cemetery, Willington Hill, Tolland County, Conn.

**HOLT, Rush Dew,** a Senator from West Virginia; born in Weston, Lewis County, W.Va., June 19, 1905; attended the public schools and West Virginia University at Morgantown; graduated from Salem (W.Va.) College in 1924; became a high school teacher and athletic coach; instructor at Salem (W.Va.) College and Glenville (W.Va.) State Teachers' College; member, State house of delegates 1931-1935; member of the United States delegation to the Interparliamentary Conference, Oslo, Norway, in 1939; elected as a Democrat to the United States Senate on November 6, 1934, for the term beginning January 3, 1935, but not having reached the age qualification required by the Constitution did not take his seat until June 21, 1935, and served until January 3, 1941; unsuccessful candidate for renomination in 1940; elected to the State house of

delegates in 1942, 1944, 1946, and 1948; unsuccessful candidate in 1944 for nomination for Governor, and in 1948 for nomination to the United States Senate; engaged in research work; affiliated with the Republican Party in 1949, and was an unsuccessful Republican candidate for election in 1950 to the Eighty-second Congress, and for election for governor in 1952; elected to the State house of delegates in 1954 and served until his death; died in Bethesda, Md., February 8, 1955; interment in Macpelah Cemetery, Weston, W.Va.

**Bibliography:** Coffey, William. "Rush Dew Holt, The Boy Senator from West Virginia." Ph.D. dissertation, West Virginia University, 1970.

**HOLTEN, Samuel,** a Delegate and a Representative from Massachusetts; born in Danvers, Mass., June 9, 1738; completed preparatory studies; studied medicine and practiced in Gloucester, Mass., for a short time; returned to Danvers and continued the practice of medicine; member of the Massachusetts house of representatives in 1787; served in the Massachusetts senate 1780-1782, 1784, 1786, 1789, and 1790; member of the Governor's council 1780-1782, 1784, 1786, 1789-1792, 1795, and 1796; Member of the Provincial Congress 1774-1775; member of the committee of safety in 1775; Member of the Continental Congress 1778-1780, 1783-1785 and 1787; elected president pro tempore August 17, 1785; member of the Massachusetts constitutional convention in 1779; elected to the Third Congress (March 4, 1793-March 3, 1795); appointed judge of the probate court for Essex County in 1796 and served until his resignation in 1815; died in Danvers, Mass., on January 2, 1816; interment in the Holten Cemetery.

**Bibliography:** *DAB.*

**HOLTON, Hart Benton,** a Representative from Maryland; born near Elkton, Cecil County, Md., October 13, 1835; attended the common schools and Hopewell Academy, Chester, Pa.; moved to Baltimore, Md., in 1857; taught school in Alberton, Howard County, Md., 1857-1873; served in the State senate 1862-1867; moved to Woodlawn, Md., in 1873; engaged in the raising of blooded horses; elected as a Republican to the Forty-eighth Congress (March 4, 1883-March 3, 1885); unsuccessful candidate for reelection in 1884 to the Forty-ninth Congress; retired from public life and became interested in stock raising; died in Woodlawn, Md., January 4, 1907; interment in Loudon Park Cemetery, Baltimore, Md.

**HOLTZMAN, Elizabeth,** a Representative from New York; born in Brooklyn, N.Y., August 11, 1941; attended public and private schools; B.A., Radcliffe College, 1962; J.D., Harvard Law School, 1965; participated in civil rights work in Albany, Ga.; co-founder, Law Students Civil Rights Research Council; admitted to the New York bar in 1966 and commenced practice in New York City; Democratic State committeewoman and district leader, 1970-1972; assistant to Mayor John V. Lindsay, 1969-1970; founder, Brooklyn Women's Political Caucus; delegate to the Democratic National Conventions of 1972, 1976, and 1980; elected as a Democrat to the Ninety-third and to the three succeeding Congresses (January 3, 1973-January 3, 1981); was not a candidate for reelection in 1980 to the House of Representatives, but was an unsuccessful candidate for election to the United States Senate; district attorney of Kings County, Brooklyn, N.Y., 1981-1990; New York City comptroller, 1990-1994; resumed the practice of law; is a resident of Brooklyn, N.Y.

**Bibliography:** Holtzman, Elizabeth J., with Cynthia L. Cooper. *Who Said It Would Be Easy?: One Woman's Life in the Political Arena.* New York: Arcade, 1996.

**HOLTZMAN, Lester,** a Representative from New York; born in New York City, June 1, 1913; attended the public schools; graduated from St. John's Pre-Law School; LL.B., St. John's Law School, Brooklyn, N.Y., 1935; was admitted to the bar in 1935 and began practice in Middle Village, Queens County, N.Y.; elected as a

Democrat to the Eighty-third and to the four succeeding Congresses, and served from January 3, 1953 until his resignation on December 31, 1961; elected a justice of the New York State Supreme Court on November 7, 1961, and served from January 1, 1962 to 1973; president and chief executive officer of the Central Queens Savings and Loan Association; is a resident of Tamarac, Fla.

**HONEYMAN, Nan Wood,** a Representative from Oregon; born in West Point, Orange County, N.Y., July 15, 1881; moved with her parents to Portland, Oreg., in 1884; attended private schools, was graduated from St. Helens Hall, Portland, Oreg., in 1898, and later attended Finch School, New York City; delegate to the State constitutional convention in 1933 which ratified the Twenty-first amendment to the Constitution of the United States and served as president; member of the State house of representatives 1935-1937; delegate to the Democratic National Conventions in 1936 and 1940; elected as a Democrat to the Seventy-fifth Congress (January 3, 1937-January 3, 1939); unsuccessful candidate for reelection in 1938 to the Seventy-sixth Congress and for election in 1940 to the Seventy-seventh Congress; senior representative of the Pacific Coast Office of Price Administration from August 1941 to May 1942; appointed by the Multnomah County Commissioners to the State senate in 1941 to fill a vacancy and served until her resignation in 1942; collector of customs, twenty-ninth district, Portland, Oreg., from May 1, 1942, to July 13, 1953; died in Woodacre, Calif., December 10, 1970; cremated; interment in family plot in Riverview Cemetery, Portland, Oreg.

**HOOD, George Ezekial,** a Representative from North Carolina; born near Goldsboro, Wayne County, N.C., January 25, 1875; attended the public schools; became a telegraph operator; studied law; was admitted to the bar of the supreme court of North Carolina in 1896 and commenced practice in Goldsboro, N.C.; treasurer of Wayne County 1898-1900; served in the State house of representatives 1899-1901; mayor of Goldsboro 1901-1907; secretary of the Wayne County Democratic executive committee 1896-1900; captain in the Second Regiment of the North Carolina National Guard and subsequently promoted to colonel 1899-1909; name presented as a candidate for Congress in 1912, but lost out at the nominating convention; elected as a Democrat to the Sixty-fourth and Sixty-fifth Congresses (March 4, 1915-March 3, 1919); was not a candidate for renomination in 1918; practicing attorney in Goldsboro, N.C., until his death there March 8, 1960; interment in Willow Dale Cemetery.

**HOOK, Enos,** a Representative from Pennsylvania; born in Waynesburg, Greene County, Pa., December 3, 1804; received a limited schooling; studied law; was admitted to the bar in 1826 and commenced practice in Waynesburg, Pa.; member of the Pennsylvania house of representatives in 1837 and 1838; elected as a Democrat to the Twenty-sixth and Twenty-seventh Congresses and served from March 4, 1839, to April 18, 1841, when he resigned; died in Waynesburg, Pa., July 15, 1841; interment in Green Mount Cemetery.

**HOOK, Frank Eugene,** a Representative from Michigan; born in L'Anse, Baraga County, Mich., May 26, 1893; graduated from L'Anse High School in 1912; attended College of Law of the University of Detroit, Detroit, Mich.; was graduated from the law department of Valparaiso (Ind.) University in 1918; served in the Infantry, United States Army, from July 1918 until February 1919; employed in lumber woods and as an iron ore miner and also as a law clerk at Wakefield, Mich., 1919-1924; member of the board of supervisors of Gogebic County, Mich., 1921-1923; was admitted to the bar in 1924 and commenced practice in Wakefield, Mich.; admitted to practice before the United States Supreme Court in 1936; served as city commissioner of Wakefield 1921-1923; municipal judge of Wakefield in 1924 and 1925; moved to Ironwood, Mich., in 1925 and continued the practice of law; president of WJMS Radio Station in Ironwood 1930-1933; delegate to Democratic National

Conventions in 1936, 1940, 1944, and 1948; elected as a Democrat to the Seventy-fourth and to the three succeeding Congresses (January 3, 1935-January 3, 1943); unsuccessful candidate for reelection in 1942 to the Seventy-eighth Congress; elected to the Seventy-ninth Congress (January 3, 1945-January 3, 1947); unsuccessful candidate for reelection in 1946 to the Eightieth Congress and for election in 1948 to the United States Senate; member of President's Fair Employment Practices Committee in 1943 and 1944; appointed a member of Motor Carrier Claims Commission October 1, 1949, and served until his resignation August 22, 1950; unsuccessful candidate for election in 1954 to the Eighty-fourth Congress; resumed the practice of law in Detroit, Mich.; in 1953 moved to Ironwood, Mich., where he reestablished his law practice; admitted to Wisconsin bar in 1962; was a resident of Edina, Minn., until his death June 21, 1982; interment in Fort Snelling National Cemetery.

**HOOKER, Charles Edward,** a Representative from Mississippi; born in Union, Union County, S.C., in 1825; raised in Laurens District, S.C.; attended the common schools, and was graduated from the Harvard Law School in 1846; was admitted to the bar in 1848 and commenced practice in Jackson, Miss.; district attorney of the river district 1850-1854; member of the State house of representatives in 1859; resigned to enter the Confederate Army as a private during the Civil War; became lieutenant and later captain in the First Regiment of Mississippi Light Artillery; promoted to the rank of colonel of Cavalry; elected attorney general of Mississippi in 1865 and the same year was removed with the other officers of the State by the military authorities; again elected in 1868; resumed the practice of law in Jackson, Miss.; elected as a Democrat to the Forty-fourth and to the three succeeding Congresses (March 4, 1875-March 3, 1883); delegate to the Democratic National Convention in 1884; elected to the Fiftieth and to the three succeeding Congresses (March 4, 1887-March 3, 1895); again elected to the Fifty-seventh Congress (March 4, 1901-March 3, 1903); continued the practice of law in Jackson, Miss., where he died January 8, 1914; interment in Greenwood Cemetery.

**HOOKER, James Murray,** a Representative from Virginia; born in Buffalo Ridge, Patrick County, Va., October 29, 1873; attended the public schools; was graduated from the College of William and Mary, Williamsburg, Va., and from the law department of Washington and Lee University, Lexington, Va., in 1896; was admitted to the bar in 1896 and commenced practice in Stuart, Va.; Commonwealth attorney for Patrick County; delegate to the Virginia constitutional convention in 1901 and 1902; member of the board of visitors to the Virginia Military Institute at Lexington 1901-1906; member of the Virginia Fisheries Commission 1908-1914; elected as a Democrat to the Sixty-seventh Congress to fill the vacancy caused by the death of Rorer A. James; reelected to the Sixty-eighth Congress and served from November 8, 1921, to March 3, 1925; was not a candidate for renomination in 1924; delegate to the Democratic National Convention in 1924; chairman of the Virginia Democratic committee in 1925; resumed the practice of his profession at Stuart, Patrick County, Va., where he died August 6, 1940; interment in Stuart Cemetery.

**HOOKER, Warren Brewster,** a Representative from New York; born in Perrysburg, Cattaraugus County, N.Y., November 24, 1856; attended the public schools and Forestville Free Academy, Forestville, N.Y.; studied law; was admitted to the bar in 1879 and commenced practice in Forestville; special surrogate of Chautauqua County 1878-1881; moved to Tacoma, Wash., and practiced there 1882-1884; returned to Fredonia, Pomfret Township, N.Y., and resumed his profession 1884-1898; supervisor of the town of Pomfret in 1889 and 1890; elected as a Republican to the Fifty-second and to the four succeeding Congresses and served from March 4, 1891, until his resignation on November 10, 1898, before the close of the Fifty-fifth Congress, having been appointed a justice of the supreme court of New York on that date; chairman, Committee on Rivers and Harbors (Fifty-fourth and Fifty-fifth Congresses); elected to that office in 1899 for the term ending 1913; member of the appellate division 1902-1909; resumed the practice of law in Fredonia, Chautauqua County, N.Y., in 1914; appointed official referee of the State supreme court in 1919; died in Fredonia, N.Y., March 5, 1920; interment in Forest Hill Cemetery.

**HOOKS, Charles** (great-grandfather of William Julius Harris), a Representative from North Carolina; born in Bertie County, N.C., February 20, 1768; when he was two years old his parents moved to Duplin County and settled on a plantation near Kenansville; became a planter; member of the State house of commons 1801-1805; served in the State senate in 1810 and 1811; elected as a Republican to the Fourteenth Congress to fill the vacancy caused by the resignation of William R. King and served from December 2, 1816, to March 3, 1817; elected to the Sixteenth, Seventeenth, and Eighteenth Congresses (March 4, 1819-March 3, 1825); moved to Alabama in 1826, settled near Montgomery, and again engaged in planting; died near Montgomery, Ala., October 18, 1843; interment in the Molton family cemetery.

**HOOPER, Benjamin Stephen,** a Representative from Virginia; born near Buckingham, Buckingham County, Va., March 6, 1835; attended the common schools; engaged in mercantile pursuits and the manufacture of tobacco; served in the Confederate Army during the Civil War; elected as a Readjuster to the Forty-eighth Congress (March 4, 1883-March 3, 1885); resumed mercantile pursuits at Farmville, Va.; delegate to the Republican National Convention in 1888; died in Farmville, Prince Edward County, Va., on January 17, 1898; interment in the Farmville Cemetery.

**HOOPER, Joseph Lawrence,** a Representative from Michigan; born in Cleveland, Ohio, December 22, 1877; moved to Michigan with his parents, who settled in Battle Creek in 1891; attended the graded and high schools; studied law; was admitted to the bar in 1899 and commenced practice in Battle Creek; circuit court commissioner of Calhoun County 1901-1903; prosecuting attorney of Calhoun County 1903-1907; city attorney of Battle Creek 1916-1918; elected as a Republican to the Sixty-ninth Congress to fill the vacancy caused by the death of Arthur B. Williams; reelected to the Seventieth and to the three succeeding Congresses and served from August 18, 1925, until his death in Washington, D.C., February 22, 1934; interment in Oak Hill Cemetery, Battle Creek, Mich.

**HOOPER, Samuel,** a Representative from Massachusetts; born in Marblehead, Mass., February 3, 1808; attended the common schools; employed as agent for an importing firm and traveled extensively in foreign countries until 1832, when he engaged in the importing business in Boston, Mass., and later in the iron business; member of the Massachusetts house of representatives 1851-1853; served in the Massachusetts senate in 1858; elected as a Republican to the Thirty-seventh Congress to fill the vacancy caused by the resignation of William Appleton; reelected to the Thirty-eighth and to the five succeeding Congresses and served from December 2, 1861, until his death; chairman, Committee on Ways and Means (Forty-first Congress), Committee on Banking and Currency (Forty-second Congress), Committee on Coinage, Weights, and Measures (Forty-second and Forty-third Congresses); declined to be a candidate for renomination in 1874; died in Washington, D.C., February 14, 1875; interment in Oak Hill Cemetery.

**Bibliography:** *DAB.*

**HOOPER, William,** a Delegate from North Carolina; born in Boston, Mass., June 17, 1742; attended the Boston Latin School and was graduated from Harvard College in 1760; studied law; was admitted to the bar; moved to Wilmington, N.C., in 1767, where he began practice; member of the Colonial Assembly of North Carolina 1773-1776; published a series of articles against the Crown and was disbarred for one year; Member of the Continental Congress 1774-1777; a signer of the Declaration of Independence; mover for the first Provincial Congress in 1774; member of the State assembly in 1777 and 1778; member of the commission to settle a boundary dispute between Massachusetts and New York in 1786; died in Hillsboro, N.C., October 14, 1790; interment in Guilford Battle Ground, N.C.

**Bibliography:** *DAB*; Kneif, Robert Charles. "William Hooper, 1742-1790, Misunderstood Patriot." Ph.D. dissertation, Tulane University, 1980.

**HOOPER, William Henry,** a Delegate from the Territory of Utah; born in Cambridge, Dorchester County, Md., December 25, 1813; attended the common schools; engaged in mercantile pursuits; moved to Illinois in 1835 and settled in Galena; engaged in trade on the Mississippi River; moved to Utah in 1850 and settled in Salt Lake City; secretary of the Territory in 1857 and 1858; elected as a Democrat to the Thirty-sixth Congress (March 4, 1859-March 3, 1861); unsuccessful candidate for reelection in 1860 to the Thirty-seventh Congress; member of the State senate in 1862; elected to the Thirty-ninth and to the three succeeding Congresses (March 4, 1865-March 3, 1873); was not a candidate for renomination in 1872; engaged in mercantile pursuits and mining operations in Salt Lake City; superintendent of Zion's Cooperative Mercantile Institution 1873-1877, and its president 1877-1882; president of the Deseret National Bank, Salt Lake City, from 1872 until his death in Salt Lake City, Utah, December 30, 1882; interment in Salt Lake City Cemetery.

**HOPE, Clifford Ragsdale,** a Representative from Kansas; born in Birmingham, Van Buren County, Iowa, June 9, 1893; attended the public schools and Nebraska Wesleyan University, Lincoln, Nebr.; was graduated from Washburn Law School, Topeka, Kans., in 1917 and was admitted to the bar the same year; during the First World War served as a second lieutenant with the Thirty-fifth and Eighty-fifth Divisions in the United States and France, 1917-1919; commenced practice of law in Garden City, Kans., in 1919; member of the Kansas State house of representatives, 1921-1927, serving as speaker pro tempore in 1923 and as speaker in 1925; elected as a Republican to the Seventieth and to the fourteen succeeding Congresses (March 4, 1927-January 3, 1957); chairman, Committee on Agriculture (Eightieth and Eighty-third Congresses); was not a candidate for renomination in 1956 to the Eighty-fifth Congress; president, Great Plains Wheat, Inc., of Garden City, Kans., 1959-1963; died in Garden City, Kans., May 16, 1970; interment in Valley View Cemetery.

**Bibliography:** Duram, James C., and Eleanor A. Duram. "Congressman Clifford Hope's Correspondence with His Constituents: A Conservative View of the Court-Packing Plan of 1937." *Kansas Historical Quarterly* 37 (Spring 1971): 64-80; Forsythe, James L. "Clifford Hope of Kansas: Practical Congressman and Agrarian Idealist." *Agricultural History* 51 (April 1977): 406-420.

**HOPKINS, Albert Cole,** a Representative from Pennsylvania; born in Villanovia, near Jamestown, Chautauqua County, N.Y., September 15, 1837; attended the public schools; was graduated from Alfred University, Alfred, N.Y.; taught school; engaged in mercantile pursuits in Troy, Pa., where he remained until 1867; moved to Lock Haven, Clinton County, Pa., and engaged in the lumber business; elected as a Republican to the Fifty-second and Fifty-third Congresses (March 4, 1891-March 3, 1895); was not a candidate for renomination in 1894; resumed lumber manufacturing pursuits; Pennsylvania forestry commissioner 1899-1904; died in Lock Haven, Pa., June 9, 1911; interment in Highland Cemetery.

**HOPKINS, Albert Jarvis,** a Representative and a Senator from Illinois; born near Cortland, De Kalb County, Ill., August 15, 1846; attended the public schools and graduated from Hillsdale (Mich.)

College in 1870; studied law; was admitted to the bar in 1871 and commenced practice in Aurora, Ill.; prosecuting attorney of Kane County 1872-1876; presidential elector on the Republican ticket in 1884; elected as a Republican to the Forty-ninth Congress to fill the vacancy caused by the death of Reuben Ellwood; reelected to the Fiftieth and to the seven succeeding Congresses and served from December 7, 1885, to March 3, 1903; did not seek renomination, having become a candidate for Senator; elected as a Republican to the United States Senate and served from March 4, 1903, to March 3, 1909; unsuccessful candidate for reelection; chairman, Committee on Fisheries (Fifty-eighth and Fifty-ninth Congresses), Committee on Enrolled Bills (Sixtieth Congress); resumed the practice of law in Aurora and Chicago, Ill.; died in Aurora, Ill., August 23, 1922; interment in Spring Lake Cemetery.

**HOPKINS, Benjamin Franklin,** a Representative from Wisconsin; born in Hebron, N.Y., April 22, 1829; attended the common schools and became a telegraph operator; moved to Madison, Wis., in 1849; private secretary to Governor Coles Bashford in 1856 and 1857; served in the State senate in 1862 and 1863; member of the State assembly in 1866; elected as a Republican to the Fortieth and Forty-first Congresses and served from March 4, 1867, until his death in Madison, Dane County, Wis., January 1, 1870; chairman, Committee on Public Buildings and Grounds (Forty-first Congress); interment in Forest Hill Cemetery.

**HOPKINS, David William,** a Representative from Missouri; born in Troy, Doniphan County, Kans., on October 31, 1897; moved in 1899 to Missouri with his parents, who settled in St. Joseph; attended the public schools and was graduated from Graceland Academy, Lamoni, Iowa, in 1916; during the First World War served as a sergeant in Company F, Student Training Corps, from October 1918 until honorably discharged in December 1918; was graduated from Iowa State University at Iowa City in 1920 and from the University of Missouri at Columbia in 1926; taught in the high schools of St. Joseph from 1922 until elected to Congress; served as superintendent of schools of St. Joseph in 1928 and 1929; elected as a Republican to both the Seventieth and Seventy-first Congresses to fill the vacancies caused by the death of Charles L. Faust, who had been reelected in 1928; reelected to the Seventy-second Congress and served from February 5, 1929, to March 3, 1933; unsuccessful candidate for reelection in 1932 to the Seventy-third Congress; engaged in the insurance business; member of St. Joseph Board of Education, 1937-1967; died in St. Joseph, Mo., October 14, 1968; interment in Memorial Park Cemetery.

**HOPKINS, Francis Alexander,** a Representative from Kentucky; born in Jeffersonville, Tazewell County, Va., May 27, 1853; attended the public schools and the Tazewell High School; studied law; was admitted to the bar in November 1874 and commenced practice in Prestonsburg, Floyd County, Ky.; also engaged in agricultural pursuits; commissioner of common schools 1882-1884; member of the Kentucky constitutional convention in 1890; elected as a Democrat to the Fifty-eighth and Fifty-ninth Congresses (March 4, 1903-March 3, 1907); unsuccessful candidate for reelection in 1906 to the Sixtieth Congress; delegate to the Democratic National Convention in 1916; resumed agricultural pursuits and the practice of law in Prestonsburg, Ky., and died there on June 5, 1918; interment in Davidson Cemetery.

**HOPKINS, George Washington,** a Representative from Virginia; born near Goochland Court House, Goochland County, Va., February 22, 1804; attended the common schools; taught school; studied law; was admitted to the bar in 1834 and commenced practice in Lebanon, Va.; member of the Virginia house of delegates 1833-1835; elected as a Jacksonian to the Twenty-fourth Congress, as a Democrat to the Twenty-fifth Congress, as a Conservative to the Twenty-sixth Congress and as a Democrat to the Twenty-seventh through the Twenty-ninth Congresses (March 4, 1835-March 3,

1847); chairman, Committee on the Post Office and Post Roads (Twenty-eighth and Twenty-ninth Congresses); was not a candidate for reelection in 1846 to the Thirtieth Congress; appointed by President James K. Polk Chargé d'Affaires to Portugal and served from March 3, 1847, to October 18, 1849; again a member of the Virginia house of delegates in 1850 and 1851; member of the Virginia constitutional convention of 1850 and 1851; judge of the circuit court of Washington and other counties; elected as a Democrat to the Thirty-fifth Congress (March 4, 1857-March 3, 1859); chairman, Committee on Foreign Affairs (Thirty-fifth Congress); was not a candidate for renomination in 1858 to the Thirty-sixth Congress; resumed the practice of law in Abingdon, Va.; again elected to Virginia house of delegates and served from 1859 until his death in Richmond, Henrico County, Va., March 1, 1861; interment in Sinking Springs Cemetery, Abingdon, Va.

**HOPKINS, James Herron,** a Representative from Pennsylvania; born in Washington, Washington County, Pa., November 3, 1832; attended the common schools and was graduated from Washington College (now Washington and Jefferson University), Washington, Pa., in 1850; studied law; was admitted to the bar in 1852 and practiced in Pittsburgh, Pa., for twenty years; also engaged in banking, manufacturing, and mining; for several years vice president of the Pittsburgh chamber of commerce; unsuccessful candidate for election in 1872 to the Forty-third Congress; elected as a Democrat to the Forty-fourth Congress (March 4, 1875-March 3, 1877); unsuccessful candidate for reelection in 1876 to the Forty-fifth Congress; elected to the Forty-eighth Congress (March 4, 1883-March 3, 1885); chairman, Committee on Labor (Forty-eighth Congress); unsuccessful candidate for reelection in 1884 to the Forty-ninth Congress; engaged in the practice of law in Washington, D.C.; died at his summer home at North Hatley, Quebec, Canada, June 17, 1904; interment in Oak Hill Cemetery, Washington, D.C.

**HOPKINS, Larry Jones,** a Representative from Kentucky; born in Detroit, Wayne County, Mich., October 25, 1933; attended the public schools of Wingo, Ky.; attended Murray State University, 1951-1954; served in the United States Marine Corps, 1954-1956; stockbroker, Hilliard & Lyons, Inc.; county clerk, Fayette, Ky., 1969; served in the Kentucky house of representatives, 1972-1976; Kentucky senate, 1976-1978; elected as a Republican to the Ninety-sixth and to the six succeeding Congresses (January 3, 1979-January 3, 1993); was not a candidate for reelection in 1992 to the One Hundred Third Congress; is a resident of Lexington, Ky.

**HOPKINS, Nathan Thomas,** a Representative from Kentucky; born in Ashe County, N.C., October 27, 1852; moved to Pike County, Ky.; attended the common schools; engaged in agricultural pursuits; ordained to the ministry in the Baptist Church in 1876 and actively engaged in ministerial work for half a century; county tax assessor of Floyd County from 1878 until 1890; member of the Kentucky house of representatives in 1893 and 1894; successfully contested as a Republican the election of Joseph M. Kendall to the Fifty-fourth Congress, and served from February 18 to March 3, 1897; became a merchant, timberman, lumberman, and farmer in Pike County, Ky.; unsuccessful candidate for election in 1900 to the Fifty-seventh Congress; again a member of the Kentucky house of representatives in 1923 and 1924; engaged in agricultural pursuits near Yeager, Pike County, Ky.; died in Pikesville, Ky., February 11, 1927; interment in Potter Cemetery, Yeager, Ky.

**HOPKINS, Samuel,** a Representative from Kentucky; born in Albemarle County, Va., April 9, 1753; educated by private tutors; served in the Revolutionary War for a while on the staff of General Washington and later as lieutenant colonel and colonel of the Tenth Virginia Regiment; moved to Kentucky in 1796 and settled on the Ohio River in 1797 at a point then called Red Banks; studied law; was admitted to the bar and practiced; appointed chief justice of the first court of criminal common law and chancery jurisdiction in 1799 and served until his resignation in 1801; member of the Kentucky house of representatives in 1800, 1801, and 1803-1806; served in the Kentucky senate 1809-1813; appointed in 1812 commander in chief, with title of major general, of the western frontier (Illinois and Indiana Territory); elected as a Republican to the Thirteenth Congress (March 4, 1813-March 3, 1815); was not a candidate for renomination in 1814 to the Fourteenth Congress; retired to his country estate, "Spring Garden," near Henderson, Ky., and died there September 16, 1819; interment in the family burying ground at "Spring Garden."

**Bibliography:** *DAB*.

**HOPKINS, Samuel Isaac**, a Representative from Virginia; born near Owensville, Prince Georges County, Md., December 12, 1843; moved to Anne Arundel County with his parents, who settled near Annapolis; attended the common schools and was graduated from Owensville Academy; enlisted in Company A, Second Regiment, Maryland Confederate Infantry, during the Civil War and served until he was severely wounded at the Battle of Gettysburg, July 1863; after the war settled in Lynchburg, Va., and engaged in mercantile pursuits; elected as a candidate of the Labor Party to the Fiftieth Congress (March 4, 1887-March 3, 1889); declined to be a candidate for renomination in 1888 to the Fifty-first Congress; resumed mercantile pursuits in Lynchburg, Campbell County, Va., and died there January 15, 1914; interment in Spring Hill Cemetery.

**HOPKINS, Samuel Miles**, a Representative from New York; born in Salem, Conn., May 9, 1772; was graduated from Yale College in 1791; studied law; was admitted to the bar and commenced practice in Le Roy, Genesee County, N.Y., in 1793; moved to New York City in 1794 and continued the practice of law; elected as a Federalist to the Thirteenth Congress (March 4, 1813-March 3, 1815); member of the State assembly in 1820 and 1821; moved to Albany in 1821; served in the State senate in 1822; reporter of the New York Court of Chancery 1823-1826; member of the commission to superintend the construction of Sing Sing Prison 1825-1830; judge of the State circuit court 1832-1836; died in Geneva, Ontario County, N.Y., March 9, 1837; interment in Washington Street Cemetery.

**HOPKINS, Stephen**, a Delegate from Rhode Island; born in Providence, R.I., March 7, 1707; attended the public schools; was raised on a farm in the town of Scituate, Providence County; member of the general assembly 1732-1752 and 1770-1775; served as speaker 1738-1744 and 1749; chief justice of the court of common pleas in 1739; moved to Providence in 1742 and engaged in surveying and mercantile pursuits; chief justice of the superior court 1751-1754; delegate to the Colonial Congress which met in Albany in 1754; Colonial Governor of Rhode Island in 1755, 1756, 1758-1761, 1763, 1764, and 1767; again appointed chief justice of the superior court in 1773; Member of the Continental Congress 1774-1776; a signer of the Declaration of Independence; died in Providence, R.I., July 13, 1785; interment in the North Burial Ground.

**Bibliography:** *DAB*.

**HOPKINS, Stephen Tyng**, a Representative from New York; born in New York City March 25, 1849; attended the Anthon Grammar School in New York City; was an iron merchant and broker; moved to Catskill, N.Y.; member of the State assembly in 1885 and 1886; connected with several coal and iron syndicates in West Virginia and Tennessee; elected as a Republican to the Fiftieth Congress (March 4, 1887-March 3, 1889); watchman in the customhouse in New York City from April 9 to August 15, 1890, when he resigned; was found dead by a train crew alongside the railroad tracks near Pleasantville, adjacent to Atlantic City, N.J., March 3, 1892; interment in Greenwood Cemetery, Brooklyn, N.Y.

**HOPKINSON, Francis** (father of Joseph Hopkinson), a Delegate from New Jersey; born in Philadelphia, Pa., September 21, 1737 (O.S.); was graduated from the University of Pennsylvania at Philadelphia in 1757; the first native American composer of a secular song in 1759; studied law; was admitted to the bar in 1761 and commenced practice in Philadelphia; secretary of a commission of the Provincial Council of Pennsylvania which made a treaty between the Province and certain Indian tribes in 1761; appointed collector of customs at the port of Salem, N.J., in 1763, and at New Castle, Del., in 1772; settled in Bordentown, N.J., in 1774 and resumed the practice of law; member of the Provincial Council of New Jersey 1774-1776; member of the executive council from January 13 to November 15, 1775; was admitted to practice before the bar of the supreme court of New Jersey on May 8, 1775; elected an associate justice of that court in 1776 but declined the office; Member of the Continental Congress from June 22 to November 30, 1776; a signer of the Declaration of Independence; elected on November 18, 1776, to serve on the Navy Board at Philadelphia; returned to Philadelphia in 1777; treasurer of the Continental Loan Office in 1778; judge of the Admiralty Court of Pennsylvania in 1779 and reappointed in 1780 and 1787; member of the constitutional convention in 1787 which ratified the Constitution of the United States; judge of the United States District Court for the Eastern District of Pennsylvania 1789-1791; died in Philadelphia, Pa., May 9, 1791; interment in Christ Church Burial Ground.

**Bibliography:** *DAB*; Hastings, George E. *The Life and Works of Francis Hopkinson*. Chicago: University of Chicago Press, 1926.

**HOPKINSON, Joseph** (son of Francis Hopkinson), a Representative from Pennsylvania; born in Philadelphia, Pa., on November 12, 1770; was graduated from the University of Pennsylvania at Philadelphia in 1786; studied law; was admitted to the bar in Philadelphia in 1791 where he practiced his profession, except for the period of one year at Easton, Pa.; wrote the anthem "Hail Columbia!" in 1798; was associated with Daniel Webster in the Dartmouth College case; counsel for Justice Samuel Chase in his impeachment trial before the United States Senate in 1804 and 1805; elected as a Federalist to the Fourteenth Congress; reelected to the succeeding Congress (March 4, 1815-March 3, 1819); was not a candidate for reelection in 1818; moved to Bordentown, N.J., in 1820; member of the New Jersey house of assembly; returned to Philadelphia, Pa., in 1823; judge of the United States District Court for the Eastern District of Pennsylvania, 1828-1842; chairman of the Pennsylvania constitutional convention in 1837; secretary of the board of trustees of the University of Pennsylvania in 1790 and 1791; trustee, 1806-1819 and 1822-1842; died in Philadelphia, Pa., January 15, 1842; interment in the old Borden-Hopkinson Burial Ground, Bordentown, N.J.

**Bibliography:** *DAB*; Konkle, Burton Alva. *Joseph Hopkinson, 1770-1842, Jurist-Scholar-Inspirer of the Arts: Author of Hail Columbia*. Philadelphia: University of Pennsylvania Press, 1931.

**HOPWOOD, Robert Freeman**, a Representative from Pennsylvania; born in Uniontown, Fayette County, Pa., July 24, 1856; attended public schools; studied under private teachers; studied law; was admitted to the bar in 1879 and commenced practice in Uniontown; chairman of the Republican county committee; attorney for Uniontown Borough 1881-1891; solicitor of Fayette County 1894-1912; president of the Uniontown Hospital 1905-1920; elected as a Republican to the Sixty-fourth Congress (March 4, 1915-March 3, 1917); unsuccessful candidate for reelection in 1916 to the Sixty-fifth Congress; resumed the practice of law in Uniontown; died at his winter home in St. Petersburg, Fla., on March 1, 1940; interment in Oak Grove Cemetery, Uniontown, Pa.

**HORAN, Walter Franklin**, a Representative from Washington; born in Wenatchee, Chelan County, Wash., October 15, 1898; attended the public schools; was graduated from the high school at

Wenatchee, Wash., and from Washington State College at Pullman in 1925; during the First World War served as gunner's mate, third class, in the United States Navy from April 5, 1917, to November 24, 1919; in 1925 engaged in fruit growing, packing, storing, and shipping; elected as a Republican to the Seventy-eighth and to the ten succeeding Congresses (January 3, 1943-January 3, 1965); unsuccessful candidate for reelection in 1964 to the Eighty-ninth Congress; died in Manila, Philippines, December 19, 1966; interment in Wenatchee Cemetery, Wenatchee, Wash.

**HORN, Henry,** a Representative from Pennsylvania; born in Philadelphia, Pa., in 1786; completed preparatory studies; studied law; was admitted to the bar and practiced law in Philadelphia; elected as a Jacksonian to the Twenty-second Congress (March 4, 1831-March 3, 1833); unsuccessful candidate for reelection in 1832 to the Twenty-third Congress; resumed the practice of law in Philadelphia; collector of customs at Philadelphia from May 12, 1845 until August 4, 1846; died in Flourtown, Montgomery County, Pa., January 12, 1862; interment in Woodlands Cemetery, Philadelphia, Pa.

**HORN, Joan Kelly,** a Representative from Missouri; born in St. Louis, Mo., October 18, 1936; graduated from Academy of the Visitation High School, St. Louis, 1954; B.A., University of Missouri, 1973, and M.A., 1975; Montessori teacher; St. Louis Office of Community Development, 1977-1980; political consultant; campaign consultant to Representative Richard A. Gephardt of Missouri; Missouri Women's Political Caucus, 1982-1990; St. Louis County Democratic central committee, 1987-1990; Missouri Democratic State committee, 1988 to present; elected as a Democrat to the One Hundred Second Congress (January 3, 1991-January 3, 1993); unsuccessful candidate for reelection in 1992 to the One Hundred Third Congress; chaired Task Force on Defense Reinvestment, Department of Defense; special assistant to the Under Secretary for Technology Administration, Department of Commerce; candidate for election in 1996 to the One Hundred Fifth Congress; is a resident of St. Louis, Mo.

**HORN, John Stephen (Steve),** a Representative from California; born in San Juan Bautista, San Benito County, Calif., May 31, 1931; graduated, San Benito County High School, Hollister, Calif., 1949; A.B., Stanford University, Calif., 1953; M.P.A., Harvard University, 1955; Ph.D., political science, Stanford University, 1958; United States Army Reserve service, eight years; administrative assistant to Secretary of Labor James P. Mitchell, 1959-1960; principal legislative aide to Senator Thomas H. Kuchel of California, 1960-1966; senior fellow, The Brookings Institution, 1966-1969; dean of graduate studies and research, American University, Washington, D.C., 1969-1970; vice chair, 1969-1980 and member, 1969-1982, United States Commission on Civil Rights; founding member, 1970-1988 and chair, 1985-1987, National Institute of Corrections, Department of Justice; president, California State University, Long Beach, 1970-1988; trustee, professor of political science, California State University, 1988 to present; unsuccessful candidate for nomination in 1988 to the One Hundred First Congress; elected as a Republican to the One Hundred Third and One Hundred Fourth Congresses (January 3, 1993-January 3, 1997); is a resident of Long Beach, Calif.

**HORNBECK, John Westbrook,** a Representative from Pennsylvania; born in Montague, Sussex County, N.J., January 24, 1804; completed preparatory studies and was graduated from Union College, Schenectady, N.Y., in 1827; studied law; was admitted to the bar of Northampton County, Pa., in 1829 and commenced practice in Allentown, Pa., in 1830; commissioned deputy attorney general of the Commonwealth of Pennsylvania for the county of Lehigh in 1836 and served three years; elected as a Whig to the Thirtieth Congress and served from March 4, 1847, until his death in Allentown, Pa., January 16, 1848; chairman, Committee on Revisal and Unfinished Business (Thirtieth Congress); interment in Allentown Cemetery.

**HORNBLOWER, Josiah,** a Delegate from New Jersey; born in Staffordshire, England, February 23, 1729; completed preparatory studies and became a civil engineer; immigrated to the United States in 1753 and settled in Belleville, N.J.; captain of a company engaged in the defense of New Jersey during the French and Indian wars; member of the State general assembly in 1779 and 1780 and served as speaker in the latter year; Member of the Continental Congress in 1785 and 1786; judge of the Essex County court 1798-1809; died in Newark, N.J., January 21, 1809; interment in Dutch Reformed Churchyard, Belleville, N.J.

**Bibliography:** *DAB.*

**HORNOR, Lynn Sedwick,** a Representative from West Virginia; born in Clarksburg, Harrison County, W.Va., November 3, 1874; attended the public schools; was employed as a bank clerk in 1892 and served successively as cashier and director until his death; president and manager of a number of coal, oil and gas development, and land companies; president of the West Virginia Natural Gas Association in 1917 and 1918; during the First World War served as a member of the advisory State council of defense; elected as a Democrat to the Seventy-second and Seventy-third Congresses and served from March 4, 1931, until his death in Washington, D.C., September 23, 1933; interment in Odd Fellows Cemetery, Clarksburg, W.Va.

**HORR, Ralph Ashley,** a Representative from Washington; born in Saybrook, McLean County, Ill., August 12, 1884; attended the public schools and the University of Illinois at Urbana; moved to the State of Washington in 1908 and settled in Seattle; was graduated from the law department of the University of Washington at Seattle in 1911; was admitted to the bar the same year and commenced practice in Seattle; chief deputy county treasurer of King County in 1911 and 1912; served as chairman of the Republican county committee of King County; unsuccessful candidate for mayor of Seattle in 1918; served from August 31, 1918, as a lieutenant and battalion adjutant in the Twenty-sixth Infantry Regiment with overseas service and was discharged March 8, 1920; elected as a Republican to the Seventy-second Congress (March 4, 1931-March 3, 1933); unsuccessful candidate for renomination in 1932 to the Seventy-third Congress; unsuccessful candidate in 1934 for nomination to the United States Senate; unsuccessful candidate in 1936 for nomination for Governor; unsuccessful candidate for mayor of Seattle in 1948; practiced law until 1957; died in Seattle, Wash., January 26, 1960; remains were cremated and interred in Hillcrest Burial Park, Kent, Wash.

**HORR, Roswell Gilbert,** a Representative from Michigan; born in Waitsfield, Washington County, Vt., November 26, 1830; moved with his parents to Lorain County, Ohio, in 1834; attended the public schools; was graduated from Antioch College, Yellow Springs, Ohio, in 1857; clerk of the court of common pleas of Lorain County 1857-1862 and reelected in 1860; studied law; was admitted to the bar in 1862 and commenced practice in Elyria, Lorain County, Ohio; moved to southeastern Missouri in 1866 and engaged in mining for six years; moved to East Saginaw, Mich., in 1872; elected as a Republican to the Forty-sixth and to the two succeeding Congresses (March 4, 1879-March 3, 1885); unsuccessful candidate for reelection in 1884 to the Forty-ninth Congress; delegate to the Republican National Convention of 1884; unsuccessful candidate for election in 1886 to the Fiftieth Congress; moved to New York City in 1890; associate editor on the staff of the New York Tribune until his death in Plainfield, N.J., December 19, 1896; interment in Greenwood Cemetery, Wellington, Ohio.

**HORSEY, Outerbridge,** a Senator from Delaware; born near Laurel, Sussex County, Del., March 5, 1777; received a liberal education; studied law; was admitted to the bar in 1807 and commenced practice in Wilmington, Del.; member, State house of representatives 1800-1802; attorney general of Delaware 1806-1810; elected in 1810 as a Federalist to the United States Senate to fill the vacancy caused by the death of Samuel White; reelected in 1815 and served from January 12, 1810, to March 3, 1821; was not a candidate for reelection; chairman, Committee on the District of Columbia (Sixteenth Congress); retired to his wife's estate, "Needwood," near Petersville, Frederick County, Md., and died there June 9, 1842; interment in St. John's Cemetery, Frederick, Md.

**HORSFORD, Jerediah,** a Representative from New York; born in Charlotte, Chittenden County, Vt., March 8, 1791; attended the common schools; engaged in agricultural pursuits; served during the War of 1812; missionary to the Seneca Indians at Moscow, N.Y., in 1815; held several local offices; member of the State assembly in 1831; elected as a Whig to the Thirty-second Congress (March 4, 1851-March 3, 1853); served as colonel of light infantry in the State militia; moved to Livonia, N.Y., in 1863; resumed agricultural pursuits; died in Livonia, Livingston County, N.Y., January 14, 1875; interment in Moscow Cemetery, Moscow (now Leicester), N.Y.

**HORTON, Frank Jefferson,** a Representative from New York; born in Cuero, De Witt County, Tex., December 12, 1919; attended the public schools of Baton Rouge, La.; Louisiana State University, Baton Rouge, La., A.B., 1941 and from Cornell University Law School, Ithaca, N.Y., LL.B., 1947; served in the United States Army from June 1941 to August 1945, with service in North Africa and Italy; was admitted to the New York bar in 1947 and commenced the practice of law in Rochester, N.Y.; active in civil defense and Boy Scout work; president of Rochester Community Baseball, Inc., 1956-1962; executive vice president of the International Baseball League, 1959-1961, and also attorney for the league; member of the city council of Rochester, 1955-1961; elected as a Republican to the Eighty-eighth and to the fourteen succeeding Congresses (January 3, 1963-January 3, 1993); was not a candidate for reelection in 1992 to the One Hundred Third Congress; resumed the practice of law in Washington, D.C. in 1993 with the firm of Venable, Baetjer, Howard and Civiletti; is a resident of Annandale, Va.

**HORTON, Frank Ogilvie,** a Representative from Wyoming; born in Muscatine, Muscatine County, Iowa, October 18, 1882; attended the public schools; was graduated from Morgan Park (Ill.) Military Academy in 1899 and from the University of Chicago in 1903; during the Spanish-American War served as a private in Company C, Fiftieth Iowa Regiment, in 1898; moved to Saddlestring, Wyo., in 1905 and engaged in livestock raising; member of the State house of representatives 1921-1923; served in the State senate 1923-1931, being president in 1931; delegate to the Republican National Conventions in 1928 and 1936; Republican National committeeman 1937-1948; elected as a Republican to the Seventy-sixth Congress (January 3, 1939-January 3, 1941); unsuccessful candidate for reelection in 1940 to the Seventy-seventh Congress; resumed his former pursuits in Saddlestring, Wyo.; died in Sheridan, Wyo., August 17, 1948; interment in Willowgrove Cemetery, Buffalo, Wyo.

**HORTON, Thomas Raymond,** a Representative from New York; born in Fultonville, Montgomery County, N.Y., in April 1822; attended the public schools; studied law; was admitted to the bar and practiced; member of the board of trustees of Fultonville in 1848; clerk of the board of supervisors of Montgomery County for six years; justice of the peace eight years; editor and publisher of the Amsterdam (N.Y.) Recorder 1841-1857; elected as a Whig to the Thirty-fourth Congress (March 4, 1855-March 3, 1857); was not a candidate for renomination in 1856; delegate to the Republican National Convention in 1860; during the Civil War served as adjutant of the One Hundred and Fifteenth Regiment, New York Volunteer Infantry, 1862-1864; editor and publisher of the Montgomery County Republican; died in Fultonville, N.Y., July 26, 1894; interment in the Village Cemetery.

**HORTON, Valentine Baxter,** a Representative from Ohio; born in Windsor, Vt., January 29, 1802; attended the Partridge Military School and afterward became one of its tutors; studied law in Middletown, Conn.; was admitted to the bar in 1830; moved to Pittsburgh, Pa., where he practiced; moved to Cincinnati, Ohio, in 1833, and to Pomeroy, Ohio, in 1835; engaged in the sale and transportation of coal and the development of the salt industry; member of the State constitutional convention in 1860; elected as a Republican to the Thirty-fourth and Thirty-fifth Congresses (March 4, 1855-March 3, 1859); was not a candidate for renomination in 1858; elected as a Republican to the Thirty-seventh Congress (March 4, 1861-March 3, 1863); was not a candidate for renomination in 1862; member of the peace convention of 1861 held in Washington, D.C., in an effort to devise means to prevent the impending war; engaged in coal mining; died in Pomeroy, Ohio, January 14, 1888; interment in Beach Grove Cemetery.

Bibliography: *DAB.*

**HOSKINS, George Gilbert,** a Representative from New York; born in Bennington, N.Y., December 24, 1824; completed preparatory studies; engaged in mercantile pursuits; for a number of years town clerk of Bennington and justice of the peace; postmaster of Bennington, N.Y., 1849-1853 and 1861-1866; member of the State assembly in 1860, 1865, and 1866, and served as speaker in 1865; removed to Attica, N.Y., in 1867; commissioner of public accounts 1868-1870; appointed collector of internal revenue for the twenty-ninth district of New York May 1, 1871, and served until March 4, 1873; elected as a Republican to the Forty-third and Forty-fourth Congresses (March 4, 1873-March 3, 1877); unsuccessful candidate for reelection in 1876 to the Forty-fifth Congress; lieutenant governor of New York 1880-1883; delegate to the Republican National Convention of 1880; died in Attica, N.Y., June 12, 1893; interment in Forest Hill Cemetery.

**HOSMER, Craig,** a Representative from California; born in Brea, Orange County, Calif., May 6, 1915; attended the public schools; graduated from the University of California in 1937; attended the University of Michigan Law School in 1938 and was graduated from the University of Southern California Law School in 1940; was admitted to the bar in 1940 and began practice in Long Beach, Calif.; enlisted in the United States Navy in July 1940 and advanced to the rank of commander; rear admiral, Naval Reserve; attorney with the Atomic Energy Commission at Los Alamos, N.Mex., and special assistant United States district attorney for New Mexico in 1948; returned to Long Beach, Calif., to private practice; unsuccessful Republican candidate for election in 1950 to the Eighty-second Congress; elected as a Republican to the Eighty-third and to the ten succeeding Congresses and served from January 3, 1953, until his resignation December 31, 1974; was not a candidate for reelection in 1974 to the Ninety-fourth Congress; president of the American Nuclear Energy Council, Washington, D.C., 1975-1979; was a resident of Washington, D.C., until his death on October 11, 1982, aboard a cruise ship bound for Mexico; interment at Arlington National Cemetery, Arlington, Va.

**HOSMER, Hezekiah Lord,** a Representative from New York; born June 7, 1765; studied law; was admitted to practice in the mayor's court of Hudson, N.Y., in 1785; recorder of Hudson in 1793 and 1794; elected as a Federalist to the Fifth Congress (March 4, 1797-March 3, 1799); one of the managers appointed by the House of Representatives in 1798 to conduct the impeachment proceedings against William Blount, a Senator from Tennessee; again served as recorder of Hudson in 1810, 1811, 1813, and 1814; died in Hudson, N.Y., June 9, 1814.

Bibliography: *DAB.*

**HOSMER, Titus,** a Delegate from Connecticut; born in what is now West Hartford, Hartford County, Conn., in 1736; was graduated from Yale College in 1757; studied law; was admitted to the bar in 1760 and commenced practice in Middletown, Conn.; held several local offices; member of the State house of representatives 1773-1778, serving as speaker in 1776 and 1778; member of the council of safety in 1776 and 1777; served in the State senate from May 1778 until his death; Member of the Continental Congress in 1778; resumed the practice of law; judge of the United States Maritime Court of Appeals in 1780; died in Middletown, Conn., August 4, 1780; interment in Mortimer Cemetery.

**Bibliography:** *DAB.*

**HOSTETLER, Abraham Jonathan,** a Representative from Indiana; born in Washington County, Ind., November 22, 1818; attended the common schools; apprenticed to learn the blacksmith's trade; later engaged in agricultural pursuits; member of the Indiana State senate, 1854-1858; elected as a Democrat to the Forty-sixth Congress (March 4, 1879-March 3, 1881); unsuccessful candidate for reelection in 1880 to the Forty-seventh Congress; engaged in mercantile pursuits; delegate to the Democratic National Convention of 1880; died near Bedford, Ind., November 24, 1899; interment in the Leatherwood Church Cemetery, near Bedford, Ind.

**HOSTETTER, Jacob,** a Representative from Pennsylvania; born near York, Pa., May 9, 1754; attended the common schools; was a clockmaker; member of the general assembly of Pennsylvania 1797-1802; elected to the Fifteenth Congress to fill the vacancy caused by the resignation of Jacob Spangler; reelected to the Sixteenth Congress and served from November 16, 1818, until March 3, 1821; moved to Ohio and settled in Columbiana, where he died June 29, 1831.

**HOSTETTLER, John Nathan,** a Representative from Indiana; born in Evansville, Vanderburgh County, Ind., July 19, 1961; graduated from North Posey High School, Poseyville, Ind., 1979; B.S., Rose-Hulman Institute of Technology, Terre Haute, Ind., 1983; performance engineer, Warrick Power Plant, Southern Indiana Gas and Electric Co., 1985-1994; registered professional engineer in Indiana; elected as a Republican to the One Hundred Fourth Congress (January 3, 1995-January 3, 1997); is a resident of Wadesville, Ind.

**HOTCHKISS, Giles Waldo,** a Representative from New York; born in Windsor, Broome County, N.Y., October 25, 1815; attended the common schools, Windsor Academy, and Oxford Academy; studied law; was admitted to the bar in 1837 and began practice in Binghamton, N.Y.; delegate to the Republican National Convention in 1860; elected as a Republican to the Thirty-eighth and Thirty-ninth Congresses (March 4, 1863-March 3, 1867); unsuccessful candidate for renomination in 1866; elected to the Forty-first Congress (March 4, 1869-March 3, 1871); was not a candidate for renomination; resumed the practice of law in Binghamton, where he died July 5, 1878; interment in Spring Forest Cemetery.

**HOTCHKISS, Julius,** a Representative from Connecticut; born in Waterbury, Conn., July 11, 1810; attended the common schools; engaged in manufacturing pursuits; mayor of Waterbury in 1852; member of the State house of representatives in 1851 and 1858; elected as a Democrat to the Fortieth Congress (March 4, 1867-March 3, 1869); lieutenant governor of Connecticut in 1870; died in Middletown, Conn., December 23, 1878; interment in Pine Grove Cemetery.

**HOUCK, Jacob, Jr.,** a Representative from New York; born in Schoharie, N.Y., January 14, 1801; attended the common schools; was graduated from Union College, Schenectady, N.Y., in 1822; studied law; was admitted to the bar and practiced in Schoharie; district attorney of Schoharie County 1831-1836; elected as a Democrat to the Twenty-seventh Congress (March 4, 1841-March 3, 1843); resumed the practice of law; died in Schoharie, N.Y., October 2, 1857; interment in Lutheran Cemetery.

**HOUGH, David,** a Representative from New Hampshire; born in Norwich, Conn., March 13, 1753; attended the common schools; ship carpenter; moved to Lebanon, N.H., in 1778; member of the State house of representatives in 1788, 1789, and 1794; justice of the peace; colonel of militia; delegate to the State constitutional convention in 1783; commissioner of valuation in 1798; elected as a Federalist to the Eighth and Ninth Congresses (March 4, 1803-March 3, 1807); engaged in agricultural pursuits; died in Lebanon, N.H., April 18, 1831; interment in the cemetery in the southern vicinity of Lebanon.

**HOUGH, William Jervis,** a Representative from New York; born in Cazenovia, N.Y., March 20, 1795; completed preparatory studies; moved to Madison County; studied law; practiced in Syracuse, N.Y.; member of the State assembly in 1835 and 1836; general in the State militia; elected as a Democrat to the Twenty-ninth Congress (March 4, 1845-March 3, 1847); resumed the practice of law in Syracuse, N.Y., where he died October 4, 1869; interment in Oakwood Cemetery.

**HOUGHTON, Alanson Bigelow** (grandfather of Amory Houghton), a Representative from New York; born in Cambridge, Mass., October 10, 1863; moved to Corning, N.Y., with his parents in 1868; attended the public schools, Corning (N.Y.) Free Academy, and St. Paul's School, Concord, N.H.; was graduated from Harvard University in 1886; took postgraduate courses at Gottingen, Berlin, and Paris from 1886 to 1889; commenced the manufacture of glass at Corning, N.Y., in 1889; vice president of the Corning Glass Works from 1902 to 1910, when he was elected president of the company; president of the board of education of Corning; became trustee of Hobart College in 1917; elected as a Republican to the Sixty-sixth and Sixty-seventh Congresses and served from March 4, 1919, to February 28, 1922, when he resigned, having been appointed on February 10, 1922, by President Warren G. Harding, as Ambassador to Germany, in which capacity he served until April 6, 1925; appointed by President Calvin Coolidge as Ambassador to Great Britain on February 24, 1925, and served in that capacity until April 27, 1929; unsuccessful candidate for election to the United States Senate in 1928; resumed his interests in the glass manufacturing industry; died at his summer home in South Dartmouth, Mass., September 15, 1941; interment in Hope Cemetery Annex, Corning, N.Y.

**Bibliography:** *DAB.*

**HOUGHTON, Amory, Jr.,** (grandson of Alanson Bigelow Houghton), a Representative from New York; born in Corning, Steuben County, N.Y., August 7, 1926; graduated from St. Paul's School, Concord, N.H.; B.A., Harvard University, 1950; M.B.A., Harvard University Business School, 1952; served in the United States Marine Corps, 1945-1946; executive officer, Corning Glass Works, Corning, N.Y., 1964-1986; elected as a Republican to the One Hundredth and to the four succeeding Congresses (January 3, 1987-January 3, 1997); is resident of Corning, N.Y.

**HOUGHTON, Sherman Otis,** a Representative from California; born in New York City on April 10, 1828; completed preparatory studies and attended Collegiate Institute, New York; during the Mexican War enlisted in the First Regiment, New York Volunteers, in June 1846; honorably discharged at Monterey, Calif., in October 1848; proceeded to the gold mines and thence to San Jose; deputy clerk of the State supreme court in 1854; mayor of San Jose, Calif., in 1855 and 1856; studied law; was admitted to the bar in 1857 and commenced practice in San Jose; during the Civil War was commissioned captain and promoted to lieutenant colonel, and served successively as inspector and ordnance officer; elected as a

Republican to the Forty-second and Forty-third Congresses (March 4, 1871-March 3, 1875); chairman, Committee on Coinage, Weights, and Measures (Forty-third Congress); unsuccessful candidate for reelection in 1874 to the Forty-fourth Congress; appointed commissioner to investigate the affairs of the United States Mint at San Francisco in 1881; moved to Los Angeles in 1886 and continued the practice of law; died in Compton, Los Angeles County, Calif., August 31, 1914; interment in Rosedale Cemetery, Los Angeles, Calif.

**HOUK, George Washington,** a Representative from Ohio; born near Mount Holly Springs, Cumberland County, Pa., on September 25, 1825; moved to Ohio with his parents, who settled in Dayton in 1827; attended the common schools and the E. E. Barney Academy at Dayton; studied law; was admitted to the bar in 1847 and commenced practice in Dayton; member of the State house of representatives in 1852 and 1853; delegate to the Democratic National Conventions in 1860 and 1876; elected as a Democrat to the Fifty-second and Fifty-third Congresses and served from March 4, 1891, until his death in Washington, D.C., February 9, 1894; interment in Woodland Cemetery, Dayton, Ohio.

**HOUK, John Chiles** (son of Leonidas Campbell Houk), a Representative from Tennessee; born in Clinton, Anderson County, Tenn., February 26, 1860; attended the local schools; moved with his parents to Knoxville in 1871; was graduated from the University of Tennessee at Knoxville; employed as a clerk in the Pension Bureau at Washington, D.C., 1881-1883; studied law at Columbian (now George Washington) University, Washington, D.C.; was admitted to the bar in 1884 and commenced practice in Knoxville; secretary of the State Republican committee for four years; Assistant Doorkeeper of the House of Representatives in the Fifty-first Congress; elected as a Republican to the Fifty-second Congress to fill the vacancy caused by the death of his father, Leonidas C. Houk; reelected to the Fifty-third Congress and served from December 7, 1891, to March 3, 1895; unsuccessful candidate for reelection in 1894; served in the State senate, 1897-1899, 1911-1913, and 1917-1923; resumed the practice of law in Knoxville, Tenn.; died in Fountain City, Knox County, Tenn., June 3, 1923; interment in Greenwood Cemetery, Knoxville, Tenn.

**HOUK, Leonidas Campbell** (father of John Chiles Houk), a Representative from Tennessee; born near Boyds Creek, Sevier County, Tenn., June 8, 1836; attended the common schools less than three months; learned the trade of cabinet-making; studied law; was admitted to the bar on October 13, 1859, and practiced; enlisted in the Union Army as a private on August 9, 1861, and served with the Tennessee Volunteer Infantry until his resignation April 23, 1863, on account of ill health; presidential elector on the Republican ticket in 1864; member of the Tennessee State constitutional convention in 1865; judge of the circuit court of Tennessee from 1866 until 1870; moved to Knoxville and resumed the practice of law; delegate to the Republican National Conventions of 1868, 1880, 1884 and 1888; member of the Tennessee State house of representatives, 1873-1875; elected as a Republican to the Forty-sixth and to the six succeeding Congresses and served from March 4, 1879, until his death in Knoxville, Tenn., May 25, 1891; chairman, Committee on War Claims (Forty-seventh Congress); interment in the Old Gray Cemetery.

Bibliography: *DAB.*

**HOUSE, John Ford,** a Representative from Tennessee; was born near Franklin, Williamson County, Tenn., on January 9, 1827; attended the local academy and the Transylvania University, Lexington, Ky., and was graduated from the Lebanon Law School in 1850; was admitted to the bar and commenced practice in Franklin, Tenn.; moved to Montgomery County, Tenn.; member of the State house of representatives in 1853; presidential elector on the Constitutional Union ticket of Bell and Everett in 1860; member of the Provisional Congress of the Confederacy from Tennessee; during

the Civil War enlisted in the Confederate Army and served until paroled in Columbus, Miss., in June 1865; delegate to the Democratic National Convention in 1868; member of the State constitutional convention in 1870; elected as a Democrat to the Forty-fourth and to the three succeeding Congresses (March 4, 1875-March 3, 1883); was not a candidate for renomination in 1882; resumed the practice of law; died in Clarksville, Tenn., June 28, 1904; interment in Greenwood Cemetery.

**HOUSEMAN, Julius,** a Representative from Michigan; born in Zeckendorf, Bavaria, Germany, December 8, 1832; attended the common schools in Zeckendorf and the commercial school at Munich, Bavaria; immigrated to the United States in 1848 and settled in Battle Creek, Mich.; moved to Grand Rapids, Mich., in 1852; engaged in the mercantile and lumber business for forty years; member of the board of aldermen of Grand Rapids 1861-1870; served in the State house of representatives in 1871 and 1872; mayor of Grand Rapids 1873-1875; unsuccessful candidate for lieutenant governor in 1876; elected as a Democrat to the Forty-eighth Congress (March 4, 1883-March 3, 1885); was not a candidate for renomination in 1884 to the Forty-ninth Congress; resumed his former business pursuits; died in Grand Rapids, Mich., February 8, 1891; interment in Oak Hill Cemetery.

**HOUSTON, Andrew Jackson** (son of Samuel Houston), a Senator from Texas; born in Independence, Washington County, Tex., June 21, 1854; attended the common schools, Baylor University, Waco, Tex., Bastrop (Tex.) Military Academy, Texas Military Institute at Austin, Old Salado (Tex.) College, and the United States Military Academy at West Point, N.Y.; clerk in the State school department 1873-1875 and in the General Land Office, Washington, D.C., in 1875; one of the organizers of the Travis Rifles at Austin during the Reconstruction period in 1874; studied law; was admitted to the bar in 1876 and practiced in Tyler, and later in Dallas and Beaumont, Tex.; clerk of the United States district court at Dallas, Tex., 1879-1889; served in the Texas National Guard 1884-1893 with the rank of colonel; during the Spanish-American War formed a troop of Cavalry for the Rough Riders of Theodore Roosevelt but was not a member; appointed United States marshal for the eastern district of Texas 1902-1910; unsuccessful Prohibition Party candidate for Governor of Texas in 1910 and 1912; retired from active business pursuits in 1918, lived near La Porte, Tex., and studied and wrote history; appointed superintendent of the State park at the San Jacinto battleground 1924-1941; appointed as a Democrat to the United States Senate to fill the vacancy in the term ending January 3, 1943, caused by the death of Morris Sheppard and served from April 21, 1941, until his death; at the time of his swearing in, was the oldest man, at eighty-seven, ever to enter the Senate; died in a hospital in Baltimore, Md., June 26, 1941; interment in the State Cemetery, Austin, Tex.

Bibliography: Houston, Andrew Jackson. *Texas Independence.* Houston: The Anson Jones Press, 1938.

**HOUSTON, George Smith,** a Representative and a Senator from Alabama; born near Franklin, Williamson County, Tenn., January 17, 1811; moved with his parents to Lauderdale County, Ala., and attended an academy there; studied law in Florence, Ala., and Harrodsburg, Ky.; was admitted to the bar in 1831; commenced practice in Florence, Ala.; member of the Alabama State house of representatives in 1832; settled in Athens, Ala., in 1835; State's attorney for the Florence judicial district in 1836; elected as a Democrat to the Twenty-seventh and to the three succeeding Congresses (March 4, 1841-March 3, 1849); declined to be a candidate for renomination in 1848 to the Thirty-first Congress; elected to the Thirty-second and to the four succeeding Congresses and served from March 4, 1851, until January 21, 1861, when he joined other secessionist members of the Alabama delegation in withdrawing from the Thirty-sixth Congress; chairman, Committee on Ways and Means (Thirty-second and Thirty-third Congresses), Committee on Judiciary (Thirty-fifth Congress); presented credentials as a Senator-elect to the United States Senate on February 9, 1866, for the term ending March 3, 1867, but was not permitted to take his seat; elected Governor of Alabama in 1874, reelected in 1876, and served from November 24, 1874 to November 28, 1878; elected to the United States Senate and served from March 4, 1879, until his death in Athens, Ala., December 31, 1879; interment in Athens City Cemetery.

**Bibliography:** *DAB*; Draughon, Ralph. "George Smith Houston and Southern Unity, 1846-1849." *Alabama Review* 19 (July 1966): 186-207.

**HOUSTON, Henry Aydelotte,** a Representative from Delaware; born in Dagsboro Hundred, Sussex County, Del., July 10, 1847; attended the public schools and Newark Academy; engaged in agricultural pursuits; moved to Missouri in 1872; returned to Delaware and settled in Millsboro in 1875 and taught school for five years; engaged in mercantile pursuits; member of the Sussex County School Commission; elected as a Democrat to the Fifty-eighth Congress (March 4, 1903-March 3, 1905); was not a candidate for renomination in 1904 to the Fifty-ninth Congress; engaged in lumber manufacturing and banking in Millsboro, Del.; died in Milford, Del., April 5, 1925; interment in Brotherhood Cemetery, Millsboro, Del.

**HOUSTON, John Mills,** a Representative from Kansas; born on a farm near Formosa, Jewell County, Kans., September 15, 1890; attended the public schools of Wichita, Kans., St. John's Military School, Salina, Kans., and Fairmount University, Wichita, Kans.; engaged in the theatrical business 1912-1917; during the First World War served as a noncommissioned officer in the United States Marine Corps 1917-1919; engaged in the retail lumber business at Newton, Kans., 1919-1934; mayor of Newton 1927-1931; secretary of the Democratic State central committee in 1934 and 1935; elected as a Democrat to the Seventy-fourth and to the three succeeding Congresses (January 3, 1935-January 3, 1943); unsuccessful candidate for reelection in 1942 to the Seventy-eighth Congress; appointed a member of the National Labor Relations Board on March 15, 1943, and served until his retirement on August 27, 1953; resided in Laguna Beach, Calif., where he died April 29, 1975; interment in Melrose Abbey Cemetery, Anaheim, Calif.

**HOUSTON, John Wallace** (uncle of Robert Griffith Houston), a Representative from Delaware; born in Concord, Sussex County, Del., May 4, 1814; attended the country schools and Newark Academy, and was graduated from Yale College in 1834; studied law in Dover, Del.; was admitted to the bar in 1837; moved to Georgetown, Del., in 1839 and commenced the practice of law; secretary of state of Delaware 1841-1844; elected as a Whig to the Twenty-ninth and to the two succeeding Congresses (March 4, 1845-March 3, 1851); chairman, Committee on Public Buildings and Grounds (Thirtieth Congress); was not a candidate for renomination in 1850 to the Thirty-second Congress; appointed associate judge of the superior court of Delaware on May 4, 1855; member of the peace conference of 1861, held in Washington, D.C., in an effort to devise means to prevent the impending war; retired from the bench in 1893; died in Georgetown, Del., April 26, 1896; interment in Presbyterian Cemetery, Lewes, Del.

**HOUSTON, Robert Griffith** (nephew of John Wallace Houston), a Representative from Delaware; born in Milton, Sussex County, Del., October 13, 1867; attended the public schools at Lewes, Del., 1872-1882; engaged in agricultural pursuits; studied law; was admitted to the bar in 1888 and commenced practice in Georgetown, Sussex County, Del.; member of the Delaware National Guard 1890-1895; owner and publisher of the Sussex Republican 1893-1934; continued its publication under the name of the Sussex Countian 1934-1946; collector of customs for the district of Delaware 1900-1904; president of the First National Bank of Georgetown 1901-1903; member of the citizens' committee which drafted the Delaware school law enacted in 1921; assistant attorney general of the State 1920-1924 and 1933-1935; employed in the Bureau of Law, Office of the Alien Property; elected as a Republican to the Sixty-ninth and to the three succeeding Congresses (March 4, 1925-March 3, 1933); was not a candidate for renomination in 1932 to the Seventy-third Congress; resumed the publishing business and also the practice of law at Georgetown, Del.; died in Lewes, Del., January 29, 1946; interment in the Presbyterian Cemetery, Lewes, Del.

**HOUSTON, Samuel** (father of Andrew Jackson Houston and cousin of David Hubbard), a Representative from Tennessee and a Senator from Texas; born at Timber Ridge Church, near Lexington, Va., March 2, 1793; moved about 1808 with his widowed mother to Blount County, Tenn.; attended Maryville Academy (now Maryville College), Maryville, Tenn.; employed as a clerk in a store in Kingston, Tenn.; enlisted as a private in the United States Infantry in 1813; served under General Andrew Jackson in the Creek War, rose to lieutenant, and resigned from the Army in 1818; studied law, was admitted to the bar in 1818, and commenced practice in Lebanon, Tenn.; district attorney in 1819; adjutant general of Tennessee in 1820; major general, 1821; elected to the Eighteenth and Nineteenth Congresses (March 4, 1823-March 3, 1827); Governor of Tennessee from October 1, 1827 until April 16, 1829, when he resigned; moved to the territory of the Cherokee Nation, now a part of Oklahoma, was a trader, and was made a member of the Cherokee Nation by action of the National Council; moved to Texas around 1835 and was a member of the convention at San Felipe de Austin, the purpose of which was to establish separate statehood for Texas; member of the constitutional convention of March 1836; commander in chief of the Texas Army; successfully led the Texans against the Mexicans in the Battle of San Jacinto on April 21, 1836; took the oath of office as the first President of the Republic of Texas on October 22, 1836, and served until 1838; member, Texas Congress, 1838-1840; again President of the Republic from 1841 until 1844; upon the admission of Texas as a State into the Union was elected as a Democrat to the United States Senate; reelected in 1847 and 1853 and served from February 21, 1846, to March 3, 1859; chairman, Committee on Militia (Thirty-first through Thirty-fourth Congresses); unsuccessful candidate in 1857 for election for Governor of Texas; elected Governor of Texas in 1859, and served from December 21, 1859 until deposed on March 18, 1861, because he refused to take the oath of allegiance to the Confederate States; died in Huntsville, Tex., July 26, 1863; interment in Oakwood Cemetery.

**Bibliography:** *DAB*; Houston, Samuel. *The Autobiography of Sam Houston.* Edited by Donald Day and Harry Herbert Ullom. 1954. Reprint. Westport, Conn.: Greenwood Press, 1980; Houston, Samuel. *The Writings of Sam Houston, 1813-1863.* Edited by Amelia W. Williams and Eugene Campbell Barker. 8 vols. Austin: University of Texas Press, 1938-1943; James, Marquis. *The Raven: A Biography of Sam Houston.* 1929. Reprint. Norwalk, Conn.: The Easton Press, 1988.

**HOUSTON, Victor Stewart Kaleoaloha,** a Delegate from the Territory of Hawaii; born in San Francisco, Calif., July 22, 1876; received a preparatory education and attended Real Schule in Dresden, Saxony, Cantonal College, Lausanne, Switzerland, Force School, Washington, D.C., and Werntz Preparatory School, Annapolis, Md.; was graduated from the United States Naval Academy, Annapolis, Md., in 1897 and served in the United States Navy in various grades, retiring as commander in 1926; moved to Honolulu, T.H., in 1909; elected as a Republican a Delegate to the Seventieth and to the two succeeding Congresses (March 4, 1927-March 3, 1933); unsuccessful candidate for reelection in 1932 to the Seventy-third Congress; delegate to the Republican National

Conventions of 1928 and 1932; retired from active business and political life until recalled to active duty in the United States Navy on December 7, 1941, and served until March 1, 1945; promoted to the rank of captain on the retired list on June 9, 1943; died in Honolulu, Hawaii, July 31, 1959; interment in Oahu Cemetery.

**HOUSTON, William Cannon,** a Representative from Tennessee; born near Shelbyville, Bedford County, Tenn., March 17, 1852; moved with his mother to Woodbury, Cannon County, Tenn., in 1858; attended the schools of Woodbury and Sweetwater, Tenn.; engaged in agricultural pursuits and later in the publication of a newspaper; member of the State house of representatives 1877-1879 and 1881-1885; studied law; was admitted to the bar in 1878 and commenced practice in Woodbury, Tenn.; member of the Democratic State executive committee in 1888; chairman of the Democratic State convention in 1888; elected judge of the eighth judicial circuit in 1894, was reelected in 1902, and served until elected to Congress; elected as a Democrat to the Fifty-ninth and to the six succeeding Congresses (March 4, 1905-March 3, 1919); chairman, Committee on the Census (Sixty-second Congress), Committee on Territories (Sixty-third through Sixty-fifth Congresses); was not a candidate for renomination in 1918 to the Sixty-sixth Congress; delegate to the Democratic National Convention of 1920; died on his plantation, "Beaver Dam," near Woodbury, Tenn., August 30, 1931; interment in Riverside Cemetery, near Woodbury, Tenn.

**HOUSTON, William Churchill,** a Delegate from New Jersey; born in Sumter District, South Carolina, around 1746; pursued classical studies; was graduated from Princeton College in 1768; professor in the same college from 1769 to 1783, when he resigned; served as captain in the Second Regiment, Somerset Militia, during the Revolutionary War; deputy secretary of the Continental Congress in 1775 and 1776; member of the New Jersey Provincial Congress in 1776; member of the New Jersey house of assembly 1777-1779; member of the council of safety in 1778; Member of the Continental Congress 1779-1781; studied law; was admitted to the bar in 1781 and commenced practice in Trenton, N.J., in 1783; elected as the first Comptroller of the Treasury in 1781, but declined to serve; receiver of Continental taxes 1782-1785; clerk of the supreme court of New Jersey 1781-1788; again a Member of the Continental Congress in 1784 and 1785; member of the Annapolis Convention in 1786; delegate to the Philadelphia Constitutional Convention in 1787; died in Frankford, Pa., August 12, 1788; interment in the Second Presbyterian Churchyard, Philadelphia, Pa.

**Bibliography:** *DAB.*

**HOUSTOUN, John,** a Delegate from Georgia; born in Waynesboro, Ga., August 31, 1744; attended the common schools; studied law; was admitted to the bar and commenced practice in Savannah, Ga.; one of the four originators of the "Sons of Liberty"; delegate to the Provincial Congress of Georgia in 1775; Member of the Continental Congress in 1775; member of the executive council in 1777; Governor of Georgia in 1778 and 1784; member of the commission to establish the boundary line between Georgia and South Carolina; chief justice of Georgia in 1786; unsuccessful candidate for Governor in 1787; justice for Chatham County in 1787; mayor of Savannah in 1789 and 1790; judge of the State superior court in 1792; died at "White Bluff," near Savannah, Ga., July 20, 1796.

**HOUSTOUN, William,** a Delegate from Georgia; born in Savannah, Ga., in 1755; completed preparatory studies and attended higher schools in England; studied law; was admitted to the Inner Temple, London, in 1776; returned to Savannah at the beginning of the Revolution; Member of the Continental Congress 1784-1786; one of the agents on the part of Georgia to settle the boundary between that State and South Carolina in 1785; delegate

to the constitutional convention which framed the Federal Constitution in 1787, but declined to sign the instrument; was one of the original trustees for the establishment of the University of Georgia, at Athens; died in Savannah, Ga., March 17, 1813; interment in St. Paul's Chapel, New York City.

**HOVEY, Alvin Peterson,** a Representative from Indiana; born near Mount Vernon, Posey County, Ind., September 6, 1821; attended the common schools of Mount Vernon; studied law; was admitted to the bar September 25, 1842, and practiced; commissioned first lieutenant in June 1846 for service in the war with Mexico; delegate to the State constitutional convention in 1850; circuit judge 1851-1854; judge of the supreme court in 1854; district attorney of the United States in 1856; removed by President James Buchanan in 1858; commissioned colonel of the Twenty-fourth Regiment, Indiana Volunteers, July 31, 1861; brigadier general of Volunteers April 28, 1862; brevetted major general of Volunteers July 4, 1864; resigned his commission October 7, 1865; appointed United States Minister to Peru on August 12, 1865 and served until September 1870; elected as a Republican to the Fiftieth Congress and served from March 4, 1887, until January 17, 1889, when he resigned, having been elected Governor; elected Governor of Indiana in 1888 and served from January 14, 1889 until his death in Indianapolis, Ind., November 21, 1891; interment in Bellefontaine Cemetery.

**Bibliography:** *DAB.*

**HOWARD, Benjamin,** a Representative from Kentucky; born in Lexington, Ky. (then a part of Virginia), in 1760; completed preparatory studies; studied law; was admitted to the bar and commenced practice in Lexington; member of the Kentucky house of representatives from Fayette County in 1801 and 1802; elected as a Republican to the Tenth and Eleventh Congresses, and served from March 4, 1807 to April 10, 1810, when he resigned; appointed Governor of the Territory of Louisiana by President James Madison on April 18, 1810 and served until his resignation in 1813; appointed a brigadier general in the United States Army on March 12, 1813, and given command of the Eighth Military Department, embracing the territory west of the Mississippi River; died in St. Louis, Mo., September 18, 1814; interment in Old Grace Church Graveyard; reinterment in Bellefontaine Cemetery.

**Bibliography:** *DAB.*

**HOWARD, Benjamin Chew** (son of John Eager Howard), a Representative from Maryland; born at Belvedere, near Baltimore, Md., November 5, 1791; pursued classical studies, and was graduated from Princeton College in 1809; studied law; was admitted to the bar and commenced practice in Baltimore; served in the War of 1812; was promoted to command of the Fifth Regiment, subsequently becoming brigadier general, and continued for many years prominently identified with the State military organization; member of the city council of Baltimore in 1820; member of the Maryland State house of delegates in 1824; elected as a Jacksonian to the Twenty-first and Twenty-second Congresses (March 4, 1829-March 3, 1833); declined the mission to Russia tendered by President Martin Van Buren; commissioned by President Andrew Jackson in 1835, with Richard Rush, of Philadelphia, as peace emissary of the Federal Government in the controversy over the boundary line between Ohio and Michigan; elected as a Jacksonian to the Twenty-fourth Congress, and reelected as a Democrat to the Twenty-fifth Congress (March 4, 1835-March 3, 1839); chairman, Committee on Foreign Affairs (Twenty-fourth and Twenty-fifth Congresses); reporter of the decisions of the Supreme Court of the United States, 1843-1862; member of the peace conference of 1861, held in Washington, D.C., in an effort to devise means to prevent the impending war; unsuccessful Democratic candidate for Governor of Maryland in 1861; died in Baltimore, Md., March 6, 1872; interment in Greenmount Cemetery.

**Bibliography:** *DAB*.

**HOWARD, Edgar,** a Representative from Nebraska; born in Osceola, Clarke County, Iowa, September 16, 1858; attended the common schools, Western Collegiate Institute, and Iowa College of Law; reporter and city editor of various newspapers until 1884; editor of the Papillion (Nebr.) Times from 1884 until 1900; was admitted to the bar in 1886 and commenced practice in Papillion, Sarpy County, Nebr.; member of the Nebraska State house of representatives, 1894-1896; probate judge of Sarpy County, 1896-1900; delegate to the Democratic National Convention of 1896; purchased the Weekly Telegram of Columbus, Nebr., in 1900 and made it a daily publication in 1922; Lieutenant Governor of Nebraska, 1917-1919; elected as a Democrat to the Sixty-eighth and to the five succeeding Congresses (March 4, 1923-January 3, 1935); chairman, Committee on Indian Affairs (Seventy-second and Seventy-third Congresses); unsuccessful candidate for reelection in 1934 to the Seventy-fourth Congress, and for election in 1938 to the Seventy-sixth Congress; resumed the newspaper publishing business in Columbus, Nebr., where he died on July 19, 1951; interment in Columbus Cemetery.

**Bibliography:** *DAB*.

**HOWARD, Everette Burgess,** a Representative from Oklahoma; born in Morgantown, Butler County, Ky., September 19, 1873; attended the public schools; learned the art of printing and engaged in newspaper work in Kentucky, Oklahoma, and Missouri; moved to Tulsa, Okla., in 1905 and engaged in the manufacture of brick and in the production of oil and gas; member of the State board of public affairs 1911-1915; State auditor of Oklahoma 1915-1919; elected as a Democrat to the Sixty-sixth Congress (March 4, 1919-March 3, 1921); unsuccessful candidate for reelection in 1920 to the Sixty-seventh Congress; elected to the Sixty-eighth Congress (March 4, 1923-March 3, 1925); was not a candidate for renomination in 1924, but was an unsuccessful candidate for the Democratic nomination for United States Senator; elected to the Seventieth Congress (March 4, 1927-March 3, 1929); unsuccessful candidate for reelection in 1928 to the Seventy-first Congress; engaged in the production of oil and gas in Oklahoma and Texas in 1930; died in Midland, Tex., April 3, 1950; interment in Memorial Park, Oklahoma City, Okla.

**HOWARD, Guy Victor,** a Senator from Minnesota; born in Minneapolis, Minn., November 28, 1879; attended the public schools, Minneapolis (Minn.) School of Business, and Georgetown University, Washington, D.C.; served as a clerk in the post office in the United States House of Representatives 1897-1901; engaged in the insurance business at Minneapolis in 1901; deputy registrar of motor vehicles for Hennepin County, Minn., 1912-1934; presidential elector on the Republican ticket in 1916; elected as a Republican to the United States Senate to fill the vacancy caused by the death of Thomas D. Schall and served from November 4, 1936, to January 3, 1937; was not a candidate for election for the full term in 1936; resumed the insurance business; died in Minneapolis, Minn., August 20, 1954; interment in Lakewood Cemetery.

**HOWARD, Jacob Merritt,** a Representative and a Senator from Michigan; born in Shaftsbury, Bennington County, Vt., July 10, 1805; attended the district schools and the academies of Bennington and Brattleboro; graduated from Williams College, Williamstown, Mass., in 1830; studied law; moved to Detroit, Mich., in 1832; was admitted to the bar in 1833 and commenced practice in Detroit; city attorney of Detroit in 1834; member, State house of representatives 1838; elected as a Whig to the Twenty-seventh Congress (March 4, 1841-March 3, 1843); was not a candidate for renomination in 1842; helped draw up the platform of the first Republican convention in 1854; attorney general of Michigan 1855-1861; elected as a Republican to the United States Senate to fill the vacancy caused by the death of Kinsley S. Bingham; reelected in 1865 and served from

January 17, 1862, to March 3, 1871; chairman, Committee on Pacific Railroads (Thirty-eighth through Forty-first Congresses); died in Detroit, Mich., April 2, 1871; interment in Elmwood Cemetery.

**Bibliography:** *DAB*.

**HOWARD, James John,** a Representative from New Jersey; born in Irvington, Essex County, N.J., July 24, 1927; graduated from St. Rose School, Belmar, N.J., in 1941, Asbury Park (N.J.) High School in 1947, St. Bonaventure University, Olean, N.Y., in 1952; M.Ed., Rutgers University, New Brunswick, N.J., 1958; served in the United States Navy in the South Pacific from December 30, 1944 to July 19, 1946; teacher and acting principal in Wall Township school system from 1952 to 1964; elected as a Democrat to the Eighty-ninth and to the eleven succeeding Congresses, and served from January 3, 1965 until his death in Washington, D.C., on March 25, 1988; chairman, Committee on Public Works and Transportation (Ninety-seventh through One Hundredth Congresses); interment in St. Catharine's Cemetery, Sea Girt, N.J.

**HOWARD, John Eager** (father of Benjamin Chew Howard), a Delegate and a Senator from Maryland; born at "Belvedere," near Baltimore, Md., June 4, 1752; was instructed by private tutors; served throughout the Revolutionary War, beginning as a captain and holding the rank of colonel when peace was declared; was voted a medal and the thanks of Congress for gallantry at the Battle of Cowpens, January 17, 1781; Member of the Continental Congress 1788; Governor of Maryland from November 24, 1788 to November 14, 1791; member, State senate, 1791-1795; elected as a Federalist in 1796 to the United States Senate to fill the vacancy caused by the resignation of Richard Potts; reelected in 1797 and served from November 30, 1796, to March 3, 1803; served as President pro tempore of the Senate during the Sixth Congress; offered the position of Secretary of War by President George Washington, but declined; also declined a commission as brigadier general in the expected war with France in 1798; unsuccessful Federalist candidate for vice president in 1816; died at "Belvedere," near Baltimore, Md., October 12, 1827; interment in Old St. Paul's Cemetery, Baltimore, Md.; the county of Howard, Maryland, was named for him.

**HOWARD, Jonas George,** a Representative from Indiana; born on a farm near New Albany, Floyd County, Ind., May 22, 1825; attended private school, Indiana Asbury College (now De Pauw University), Greencastle, Ind., and Louisville (Ky.) Law School; was graduated from the law department of Indiana University at Bloomington in 1851; was admitted to the bar in 1852 and commenced the practice of law in Jeffersonville, Clark County, Ind.; city attorney of Jeffersonville in 1854, 1865, 1871-1873, and 1877-1879; member of the city council 1859-1863; member of the State house of representatives 1863-1866; elected as a Democrat to the Forty-ninth and Fiftieth Congresses (March 4, 1885-March 3, 1889); unsuccessful candidate for renomination in 1888; returned to Jeffersonville, Ind., where he resumed the practice of law; also engaged in agricultural pursuits; died in Jeffersonville, Ind., October 5, 1911; interment in Walnut Ridge Cemetery.

**HOWARD, Milford Wriarson,** a Representative from Alabama; born near Rome, Floyd County, Ga., December 18, 1862; attended the common schools; studied law in Cedartown, Ga.; moved to Fort Payne, De Kalb County, Ala., in 1880; was admitted to the bar in 1881 and commenced practice in Fort Payne; elected as a Populist to the Fifty-fourth and Fifty-fifth Congresses (March 4, 1895-March 3, 1899); was not a candidate for renomination in 1898; resumed the practice of law in Fort Payne in 1904; moved to Montrose, near Los Angeles, Calif., in 1918 and engaged in literary pursuits; returned to Fort Payne in 1923; established the Master Schools for underprivileged children; resumed literary pursuits and also engaged in educational work; died in Los Angeles, Calif. December 28, 1937;

interment in His Shrine Chapel, atop Lookout Mountain, near Mentone, Ala.

**Bibliography:** Harris, D. Alan. "Campaigning in the Bloody Seventh: The Election of 1894 in the Seventh Congressional District." *Alabama Review* 27 (April 1974): 127-38.

**HOWARD, Tilghman Ashurst,** a Representative from Indiana; born near Pickensville, S.C., November 14, 1797; attended the public schools; moved to Knoxville, Tenn., in 1816; studied law; was admitted to the bar in 1818 and commenced practice in Knoxville; member of the State senate in 1824; moved to Bloomington, Ind., in 1830 and resumed the practice of law; moved to Rockville, Ind., in 1833 and continued the practice of law; appointed by President Andrew Jackson district attorney for Indiana and served from 1833 to 1837; unsuccessful candidate for election to the United States Senate in 1838; elected as a Democrat to the Twenty-sixth Congress and served from August 5, 1839, until his resignation on July 1, 1840; unsuccessful candidate for election for Governor of Indiana in 1840, and for United States Senator in 1843; appointed Chargé d'Affaires to the Republic of Texas on June 11, 1844; died in Washington, Tex., August 16, 1844; interment in Rockville Cemetery, Rockville, Parke County, Ind.

**HOWARD, Volney Erskine,** a Representative from Texas; born in Norridgewock, Somerset County, Maine, October 22, 1809; completed preparatory studies; attended Bloomfield Academy and Waterville College; studied law; was admitted to the bar in 1832 and commenced practice in Brandon, Miss.; member of the State house of representatives in 1836; reporter of the supreme court of the State of Mississippi; unsuccessful Democratic candidate for election in 1840 to the Twenty-seventh Congress; editor of the Mississippian; moved to New Orleans, La., and was admitted to the bar there; moved to San Antonio, Tex., in 1847; member of the first State constitutional convention; elected as a Democrat to the Thirty-first and Thirty-second Congresses (March 4, 1849-March 3, 1853); unsuccessful candidate for reelection in 1852 to the Thirty-third Congress; engaged in the practice of law in San Francisco, Calif.; moved to Los Angeles in 1861 and continued the practice of law; district attorney 1861-1870; delegate to the State constitutional convention in 1878 and 1879; elected judge of the superior court of Los Angeles in 1879; retired at the end of one term on account of ill health; died in Santa Monica, Calif., May 14, 1889; interment in Fort Hill Cemetery, Los Angeles, Calif.

**Bibliography:** *DAB.*

**HOWARD, William,** a Representative from Ohio; born in Jefferson County, Va., December 31, 1817; attended the common schools; studied law; was admitted to the bar in 1840 and practiced; moved to Batavia, Ohio; prosecuting attorney 1845-1849; served in the war with Mexico and was made second lieutenant of Company C, Second Regiment, Ohio Volunteer Infantry; member of the State senate 1850-1852; elected as a Democrat to the Thirty-sixth Congress (March 4, 1859-March 3, 1861); commissioned major of the Fifty-ninth Regiment, Ohio Volunteer Infantry, on August 11, 1861, and served until February 24, 1863; resumed the practice of law; died in Batavia, Ohio, June 1, 1891; interment in Union Cemetery.

**HOWARD, William Alanson,** a Representative from Michigan; born in Hinesburg, Chittenden County, Vt., April 8, 1813; attended the public schools; moved to Albion, N.Y., in 1827 and was apprenticed as a cabinet maker until 1832; was graduated from Wyoming (N.Y.) Academy in 1835 and from Middlebury (Vt.) College in 1839; moved to Detroit, Mich., in 1840 and was a tutor in the branch of Michigan University; also studied law; was admitted to the bar in 1842 and commenced practice in Detroit; city treasurer 1848-1850; elected as a Republican to the Thirty-fourth and Thirty-fifth Congresses (March 4, 1855-March 3, 1859); successfully contested the election of George B. Cooper to the Thirty-sixth

Congress, and served from May 15, 1860 until March 3, 1861; was not a candidate for renomination in 1860 to the Thirty-seventh Congress; chairman of the Republican State central committee, 1860-1861; postmaster of Detroit, 1861-1866; delegate to the Republican National Conventions of 1868, 1872, and 1876; moved to Grand Rapids, Mich., to assume duties as land commissioner of the Grand Rapids and Indiana Railway, 1869-1871, and of the Northern Pacific Railway, 1872-1878; was an unsuccessful candidate for election to the United States Senate in 1871; member of the Republican National Committee, 1872-1876; appointed Territorial Governor of Dakota by President Rutherford B. Hayes in 1878 and served until his death in Washington, D.C., on April 10, 1880; interment in Elmwood Cemetery, Detroit, Mich.

**Bibliography:** *DAB.*

**HOWARD, William Marcellus,** a Representative from Georgia; born in Berwick City, St. Mary Parish, La., December 6, 1857; moved to Georgia with his parents at an early age; attended the common schools and Martin's Institute, Jefferson, Ga.; was graduated from the University of Georgia at Athens in 1877; studied law; was admitted to the bar in 1880 and commenced practice in Lexington, Ga.; solicitor general of the northern circuit of Georgia 1884-1896; elected as a Democrat to the Fifty-fifth and to the six succeeding Congresses (March 4, 1897-March 3, 1911); unsuccessful candidate for renomination in 1910 to the Sixty-second Congress; member of the Board of Regents of the Smithsonian Institution 1905-1912; one of the original trustees of the Carnegie Endowment for International Peace in 1910; appointed by President William Howard Taft as a member of the United States Tariff Board and served from 1911 to 1913; moved to Augusta, Ga., in 1913 and resumed the practice of law; died in Augusta, Ga., July 5, 1932; interment in Clarke Cemetery, Lexington, Ga.

**HOWARD, William Schley** (cousin of Augustus O. Bacon), a Representative from Georgia; born in Kirkwood, De Kalb County, Ga., June 29, 1875; attended Neel's Academy; was a page in the State house of representatives in 1888 and 1889; calendar clerk of the Georgia house of representatives in 1890 and 1891; private secretary to Senator Patrick Walsh of Georgia from August 8, 1894, to February 18, 1895; studied law; was admitted to the bar in 1897 and commenced practice in Wrightsville, Ga.; enlisted in the Third Regiment, Georgia Volunteer Infantry, on July 2, 1898, and served as sergeant during the Spanish-American War; returned to De Kalb County and resumed the practice of his profession; member of the State house of representatives in 1900 and 1901; solicitor general of the Stone Mountain judicial circuit 1905-1911; elected as a Democrat to the Sixty-second and to the three succeeding Congresses (March 4, 1911-March 3, 1919); was not a candidate in 1918 for reelection to the House of Representatives, but was an unsuccessful candidate for nomination to the United States Senate; resumed the practice of law in Atlanta, Ga., until his death there on August 1, 1953; interment in Decatur Cemetery, Decatur, Ga.

**HOWE, Albert Richards,** a Representative from Mississippi; born in Brookfield, Worcester County, Mass., January 1, 1840; pursued classical studies; enlisted in the Union Army in 1861 as a private in the Forty-seventh Regiment, Massachusetts Volunteer Infantry, and was promoted through the ranks to major until his discharge on November 30, 1865; settled in Como, Panola County, Miss., in 1865 and engaged in cotton planting; member of the Mississippi constitutional convention in 1868; delegate to the Republican National Convention in 1868; appointed treasurer of Panola County in 1869; member of the State house of representatives 1870-1872; elected as a Republican to the Forty-third Congress (March 4, 1873-March 3, 1875); unsuccessful candidate for reelection in 1874 to the Forty-fourth Congress; moved to Illinois in 1875 and engaged in the brokerage business in Chicago, where he died June 1, 1884; interment in Brookfield Cemetery, Brookfield, Mass.

**HOWE, Allan Turner,** a Representative from Utah; born in South Cottonwood, near the community of Murray, Salt Lake County, Utah, September 6, 1927; attended public schools; B.S., University of Utah, 1952, and J.D.L., 1954; admitted to the Utah bar in 1955 and commenced practice in Salt Lake City; served in the United States Coast Guard, 1946-1947; deputy Salt Lake County attorney, 1957-1959; city attorney, South Salt Lake, 1957-1960; administrative assistant and field representative to Senator Frank E. Moss, 1959-1964; assistant attorney general of Utah, 1965-1966; administrative assistant to Governor Calvin L. Rampton, 1966-1968; executive director, Four Corners Regional Development Commission, 1968-1972; again practiced law in Salt Lake City, 1972-1975; president, National Young Democrats, 1961-1963; delegate, Utah State Democratic conventions, 1954-1960; alternate delegate to the Democratic National Convention of 1960; elected as a Democrat to the Ninety-fourth Congress (January 3, 1975-January 3, 1977); unsuccessful candidate for reelection in 1976 to the Ninety-fifth Congress; resumed the practice of law in Washington, D.C.; Washington D.C. representative, National Park Hospitality Association; is a resident of Arlington, Va.

**HOWE, James Robinson,** a Representative from New York; born in New York City January 27, 1839; attended the common schools; employed as a clerk in a dry goods store; moved to Brooklyn in 1870 and engaged in the dry goods business; elected as a Republican to the Fifty-fourth and Fifty-fifth Congresses (March 4, 1895-March 3, 1899); declined to be a candidate for renomination in 1898 to the Fifty-sixth Congress; register of Kings County, 1900-1902; director of several banks; died in North Salem, N.Y., on September 21, 1914; interment in Greenwood Cemetery, Brooklyn, N.Y.

**HOWE, John W.,** a Representative from Pennsylvania; born in Maine in 1801; studied law; was admitted to the bar; moved to Smethport, Pa., and then to Franklin, Pa., in 1829 and commenced the practice of law; justice of the peace; elected as a Free-Soil candidate to the Thirty-first Congress and reelected as a Whig to the Thirty-second Congress (March 4, 1849-March 3, 1853); moved to Meadville, Pa., and later to Rochester, N.Y., where he died December 1, 1873; interment in Greendale Cemetery, Meadville, Crawford County, Pa.

**HOWE, Thomas Marshall** (father-in-law of James W. Brown), a Representative from Pennsylvania; born in Williamstown, Orange County, Vt., April 20, 1808; moved with his parents to Bloomfield, Ohio, in 1817; attended private schools and was graduated from Warren (Ohio) Academy; moved to Pittsburgh, Pa., in 1829; served as clerk in a wholesale dry-goods establishment; commenced business for himself in 1833; was cashier and president of the Exchange National Bank of Pittsburgh 1839-1859; engaged in copper mining, copper and steel manufacturing, commercial pursuits, and banking; elected as a Whig to the Thirty-second and Thirty-third Congresses (March 4, 1851-March 3, 1855); was not a candidate for renomination in 1854 to the Thirty-fourth Congress; resumed former business pursuits; delegate to the Republican National Convention of 1860; assistant adjutant general on the staff of Governor Andrew G. Curtin and chairman of the Allegheny County committee for recruiting Union soldiers during the Civil War; one of the organizers and first president of the Pittsburgh chamber of commerce; died in Pittsburgh, Pa., July 20, 1877; interment in Allegheny Cemetery.

**HOWE, Thomas Y., Jr.,** a Representative from New York; born in Auburn, N.Y., in 1801; completed preparatory studies; inspector of Auburn Prison 1834-1838; elected surrogate of Cayuga County and served from March 18, 1836, to April 14, 1840; elected as a Democrat to the Thirty-second Congress (March 4, 1851-March 3, 1853); mayor of Auburn, N.Y., from March 1853 to March 1854; died in Auburn, N.Y., July 15, 1860; interment in Fort Hill Cemetery.

**HOWE, Timothy Otis,** a Senator from Wisconsin; born in Livermore, Androscoggin County, Maine, February 24, 1816; attended the common schools and graduated from the Maine Wesleyan Seminary; studied law; was admitted to the bar in 1839 and commenced practice in Readfield, Maine; moved to Wisconsin in 1845 and settled in Green Bay; judge of the circuit court and supreme court justice of Wisconsin from 1850 until 1853, when he resigned; unsuccessful Republican candidate for the United States Senate in 1856; elected as a Republican to the United States Senate in 1860; reelected in 1866 and 1872, and served from March 4, 1861 to March 3, 1879; unsuccessful candidate for reelection; chairman, Committee on Enrolled Bills (Thirty-eighth and Thirty-ninth Congresses), Committee on Claims (Thirty-ninth through Forty-second Congresses), Committee on the Library (Thirty-ninth Congress, Forty-first Congress, Forty-third through Forty-fifth Congresses), Committee on Foreign Relations (Forty-second Congress); served as a commissioner for the purchase of the Black Hills territory from the Indians; delegate to the International Monetary Conference held at Paris in 1881; appointed Postmaster General in the Cabinet of President Chester A. Arthur, and served from January 5, 1882 until his death in Kenosha, Wis., on March 25, 1883; interment in Woodlawn Cemetery, Green Bay, Wis.

**Bibliography:** *DAB.*

**HOWELL, Benjamin Franklin,** a Representative from New Jersey; born in Cedarville, Cumberland County, N.J., January 27, 1844; attended the common schools; was graduated from Fort Edward Institute, New York; enlisted in the Twelfth Regiment, New Jersey Volunteers, in 1862 and served until the close of the war; engaged in mercantile pursuits in South Amboy, N.J., 1865; surrogate of Middlesex County 1882-1892; president of the People's National Bank of New Brunswick and vice president of the New Brunswick Savings Institution; elected as a Republican to the Fifty-fourth and to the seven succeeding Congresses (March 4, 1895-March 3, 1911); chairman, Committee on Immigration and Naturalization (Fifty-eighth through Sixty-first Congresses); unsuccessful candidate for reelection in 1910 to the Sixty-second Congress; delegate to the Republican National Convention in 1896; member of the United States Immigration Commission 1907-1910; died at New Brunswick, N.J., February 1, 1933; interment in Christ Cemetery, South Amboy, N.J.

**HOWELL, Charles Robert,** a Representative from New Jersey; born in Trenton, Mercer County, N.J., April 23, 1904; attended Trenton public schools and graduated from Hoosac School, Hoosick, N.Y.; student at Princeton University in 1923 and 1924 and took special courses at the University of Pennsylvania in 1936 and 1937; insurance broker in Trenton, N.J., 1928-1954; elected to the New Jersey house of assembly in 1944, reelected in 1945, and served until 1947; elected as a Democrat to the Eighty-first and to the two succeeding Congresses (January 3, 1949-January 3, 1955); was not a candidate for renomination in 1954 but was an unsuccessful candidate for election to the United States Senate; appointed New Jersey State Commissioner of Banking and Insurance in February 1955, serving until March 1, 1969; delegate at large to the Democratic National Convention in 1956; died in Trenton, N.J., July 5, 1973; cremated; ashes scattered at sea off Point Pleasant Beach, N.J.

**HOWELL, David** (father of Jeremiah Brown Howell), a Delegate from Rhode Island; born in Morristown, Morris County, N.J., January 1, 1747; attended Eaton's Academy, Hopewell, N.J., and was graduated from Princeton College in 1766; studied law; was admitted to the bar in 1768 and commenced practice in Providence, R.I.; tutor in Brown University, Providence, R.I., 1766-1769 and professor of natural philosophy 1769-1779; fellow of Brown University 1773-1824; justice of the peace in 1779; justice of the court of common pleas in 1780; Member of the Continental Congress

1782-1785; justice of the State supreme court in 1786 and 1787; attorney general of the State in 1789; secretary of Brown University 1780-1806, professor of law 1790-1824, and acting president of the university in 1791 and 1792; commissioner for settling the boundaries of the United States; district attorney of Rhode Island; judge of the United States District Court for Rhode Island from 1812 until his death in Providence, R.I., July 21, 1824; interment in North Burial Ground.

**Bibliography:** *DAB*.

**HOWELL, Edward,** a Representative from New York; was born in Newburgh, Orange County, N.Y., October 16, 1792; attended the public schools; moved to Sidney, N.Y., in 1808, and in the following year to Unadilla, N.Y., where he taught school; moved to Bath, N.Y., in 1811; appointed postmaster of Bath December 30, 1817, and served until August 13, 1821; county clerk of Steuben County 1818-1821; studied law; was admitted to the bar in 1823 and commenced practice in Bath; district attorney of Steuben County 1829-1834; member of the State assembly in 1832; elected as a Jacksonian to the Twenty-third Congress (March 4, 1833-March 3, 1835); was not a candidate for renomination in 1834; again district attorney of Steuben County 1836-1840; resumed the practice of law; died in Bath, N.Y., January 30, 1871; interment in Grove Cemetery.

**HOWELL, Elias** (father of James Bruen Howell), a Representative from Ohio; born in New Jersey in 1792; attended the public schools; moved to Newark, Ohio, in 1819; member of the State senate 1830-1832; elected as a Whig to the Twenty-fourth Congress (March 4, 1835-March 3, 1837); was not a candidate for renomination; died near Newark, Ohio, in May 1844.

**HOWELL, George,** a Representative from Pennsylvania; born in Scranton, Lackawanna County, Pa., June 28, 1859; attended the public schools, Pennington (N.J.) Seminary, Newton (Pa.) Collegiate Institute, and Lafayette College, Easton, Pa.; was graduated from the Illinois State Normal University at Normal, Ill.; taught school fourteen years in Illinois, New Jersey, and Pennsylvania, and served seven years as superintendent of the public schools of Scranton, Pa.; studied law; was admitted to the bar in 1904 and commenced practice in Scranton; presented credentials as a Democratic Member-elect to the Fifty-eighth Congress and served from March 4, 1903, to February 10, 1904, when he was succeeded by William Connell, who contested the election; assistant principal of the Scranton Technical High School 1906-1908; superintendent of schools from 1908 until his death in Scranton, Pa., November 19, 1913; interment in Forest Hill Cemetery.

**HOWELL, George Evan,** a Representative from Illinois; born in Marion, Williamson County, Ill., September 21, 1905; attended the public schools at Villa Grove, Douglas County, Ill.; graduated from the University of Illinois College of Commerce at Urbana in 1927 and from the College of Law in 1930; taught school in McHenry County, Ill., in 1927 and 1928; member of the faculty of the College of Commerce, University of Illinois, 1928-1930; was admitted to the bar in 1930 and commenced practice in Springfield, Ill.; became a member of the Officers' Reserve Corps in 1933; referee in bankruptcy, United States District Court, southern division of Illinois, 1937-1941; elected as a Republican to the Seventy-seventh and to the three succeeding Congresses and served from January 3, 1941, until his resignation on October 5, 1947; judge of the United States Court of Claims from October 6, 1947, until his resignation on September 30, 1953; chairman of the Illinois Toll Highway Commission 1953-1955; resumed the practice of law; resided in Largo, Fla., until his death in Clearwater, Fla., January 18, 1980; cremated; entombment in a niche in the Columbarium, Arlington National Cemetery, Arlington, Va.

**HOWELL, James Bruen** (son of Elias Howell), a Senator from Iowa; born near Morristown, Morris County, N.J., July 4, 1816; moved with his parents to Newark, Ohio, in 1819; attended the public schools; graduated from Miami University, Oxford, Ohio, in 1839; studied law; was admitted to the bar in 1839 and commenced practice in Newark; moved to Keosauqua, Iowa, in 1841, where he practiced law; owned a newspaper in Keosauqua and, in 1849, moved the newspaper to Keokuk, Iowa; postmaster of Keokuk 1861-1866; frequent, unsuccessful Republican candidate for state and national office; elected as a Republican to the United States Senate to fill the vacancy caused by the resignation of James W. Grimes and served from January 18, 1870, to March 3, 1871; was not a candidate for reelection; one of three commissioners of the court of Southern claims appointed by President Ulysses S. Grant in 1871 to adjust claims for stores and supplies and served until 1880; died in Keokuk, Iowa, June 17, 1880; interment in Oakland Cemetery.

**Bibliography:** *DAB*.

**HOWELL, Jeremiah Brown** (son of David Howell), a Senator from Rhode Island; born in Providence, R.I., August 28, 1771; attended private schools; pursued classical studies and graduated from Brown University, Providence, R.I., in 1789; studied law; was admitted to the bar in 1793 and commenced practice in Providence; brigadier general in the State militia; elected as a Republican to the United States Senate and served from March 4, 1811, to March 3, 1817; was not a candidate for reelection; chairman, Committee on Pensions (Fourteenth Congress); died in Providence, R.I., February 5, 1822; interment in North Burial Ground.

**HOWELL, Joseph,** a Representative from Utah; born in Brigham City, Boxelder County, Utah, February 17, 1857; moved with his parents to Wellsville, Utah, in 1863; attended the common schools and the University of Utah at Salt Lake City; taught school; engaged in mercantile pursuits; mayor of Wellsville 1882-1884; served in the Territorial house of representatives 1886-1892; regent of the University of Utah 1896-1900; member of the State senate 1896-1900; moved to Logan, Utah, in 1901; elected as a Republican to the Fifty-eighth and to the six succeeding Congresses (March 4, 1903-March 3, 1917); was not a candidate for renomination; engaged in banking and the real estate business; died in Logan, Utah, July 18, 1918; interment in the City Cemetery.

**HOWELL, Nathaniel Woodhull,** a Representative from New York; born in Blooming Grove, Orange County, N.Y., January 1, 1770; was graduated from Princeton College in 1788; taught school in Montgomery, N.Y., 1789-1792; studied law; was admitted to the bar and practiced in New York City and in Tioga County 1794-1796, and in Canandaigua, N.Y., 1796-1851; attorney general for western New York 1799-1802; member of the State assembly in 1804; elected as a Federalist to the Thirteenth Congress (March 4, 1813-March 3, 1815); appointed a member of the commission to appraise the Western Inland Lock Navigation Co. in 1817; was the first judge of Ontario County 1819-1832; died in Canandaigua, N.Y., October 15, 1851; interment in West Avenue Cemetery.

**HOWELL, Robert Beecher,** a Senator from Nebraska; born in Adrian, Lenawee County, Mich., January 21, 1864; attended the public schools; graduated from the United States Naval Academy, Annapolis, Md., in 1885; attended the Detroit School of Law; moved to Omaha, Nebr., for his health in 1888; State engineer of Nebraska, 1895-1896; city engineer of Omaha, 1896-1897; lieutenant in the United States Navy during the Spanish-American War; member, Nebraska State senate, 1902-1904; member of the Omaha Water Board and its successor, the Metropolitan Utilities District, 1904-1923; general manager of the Metropolitan Utilities District, 1912-1923; elected Republican national committeeman in 1912, 1916, and 1920; unsuccessful Republican candidate for Governor of Nebraska in 1914; lieutenant in the United States Naval Reserve

Force, 1917-1923; chairman of the radio commission, United States Post Office Department, 1921; elected as a Republican to the United States Senate in 1922; reelected in 1928, and served from March 4, 1923 until his death in Washington, D.C., March 11, 1933; chairman, Committee on Claims (Seventieth through Seventy-second Congresses); interment in Forest Lawn Cemetery, Omaha, Nebr.

**Bibliography:** O'Brien, Patrick G. "Senator Robert B. Howell: A Midwestern Progressive and Insurgent During 'Normalcy.'" *Emporia State Research Studies* 19 (December 1970): 1-28.

**HOWEY, Benjamin Franklin** (nephew of Charles Creighton Stratton), a Representative from New Jersey; born in Pleasant Meadows, near Swedesboro, Gloucester County, N.J., March 17, 1828; instructed by private tutors at Pleasant Meadows and the academies in Swedesboro and Bridgeton, N.J.; engaged in business in Philadelphia as a flour and grain commission merchant in 1847 and later in quarrying and manufacturing slate; served as captain of Company G, Thirty-first Regiment, New Jersey Volunteers, from September 3, 1862, to June 26, 1863; sheriff of Warren County, N.J., from November 13, 1878, to November 15, 1881; elected as a Republican to the Forty-eighth Congress (March 4, 1883-March 3, 1885); died in Columbia, N.J., February 6, 1895; interment in Trinity Church Cemetery, Swedesboro, N.J.

**HOWLAND, Benjamin,** a Senator from Rhode Island; born in Tiverton, R.I., July 27, 1755; attended the common schools; engaged in agricultural pursuits; collector of taxes 1801; town auditor 1802; town moderator 1805; member, State house of representatives 1810; general in the State militia during the War of 1812; elected as a Republican to the United States Senate to fill the vacancy caused by the death of Samuel J. Potter and served from October 29, 1804, until March 3, 1809; died in Tiverton, R.I., May 1, 1821; interment in the family lot on his estate.

**HOWLAND, Leonard Paul,** a Representative from Ohio; born in Jefferson, Ashtabula County, Ohio, December 5, 1865; completed preparatory studies; was graduated from Oberlin (Ohio) College in 1887 and from the law department of Harvard University in 1890; was admitted to the bar in 1890 and commenced practice in Jefferson, Ohio; moved to Cleveland in 1894 and continued the practice of law; served as second lieutenant, squadron adjutant, First Regiment, Ohio Volunteer Cavalry, during the Spanish-American War; elected as a Republican to the Sixtieth, Sixty-first, and Sixty-second Congresses (March 4, 1907-March 3, 1913); unsuccessful candidate for reelection in 1912 to the Sixty-third Congress; one of the managers appointed by the House of Representatives in 1912 to conduct the impeachment proceedings against Robert W. Archbald, judge of the United States Commerce Court; resumed the practice of law; delegate to the Republican National Conventions in 1916, 1920, and 1924; died in Cleveland, Ohio, December 23, 1942; interment in Lake View Cemetery.

**HOWLY, Richard,** a Delegate from Georgia; born in Liberty County, Ga., in 1740; pursued an academic course; studied law; was admitted to the bar and commenced practice in St. John's Parish, Georgia; also engaged in the planting of rice; moved to St. Paul's Parish in 1779; member of the State house of representatives 1779-1783; member of the executive council of Liberty County in 1779 and 1780; Governor of Georgia in 1780; Member of the Continental Congress in 1780 and 1781; practiced law in Sunbury, Ga.; chosen chief justice of Georgia and served from October 1, 1782, to January 3, 1783; moved to Savannah, Ga., and died there in December 1784.

**Bibliography:** *DAB.*

**HOXWORTH, Stephen Arnold,** a Representative from Illinois; born in Maquon Township, near Maquon, Knox County, Ill., May 1, 1860; attended the public schools; moved to Blue Springs, Gage County, Nebr., in 1880; engaged in banking and in the grain and implement business; member of the Nebraska State Militia; returned to Illinois in 1885 and engaged in agricultural pursuits near Rapatee, Knox County; served as supervisor of Maquon Township 1907-1912; elected as a Democrat to the Sixty-third Congress (March 4, 1913-March 3, 1915); was not a candidate for renomination in 1914; resumed agricultural pursuits; died in Rapatee, Ill., January 25, 1930; interment in Lyons Cemetery.

**HOYER, Steny Hamilton,** a Representative from Maryland; born in New York City June 14, 1939; graduated from Suitland High School, Suitland, Md., 1957; B.S., University of Maryland, College Park, 1963; J.D., Georgetown University Law Center, Washington, D.C., 1966; admitted to the Maryland bar in 1966 and commenced practice in Marlow Heights; Maryland State senator, 1966-1979; president, Maryland State senate, 1975-1979; member, State Board for Higher Education, 1978-1981; delegate to the Democratic National Conventions of 1968, 1974, 1976, and 1984; elected as a Democrat to the Ninety-seventh Congress, by special election, May 19, 1981, to fill the vacancy created by H. Res. 80, which declared Gladys Noon Spellman's seat vacant due to an incapacitating illness; reelected to the seven succeeding Congresses and served from May 19, 1981, to January 3, 1997; chairman, House Democratic Caucus (One Hundred First through One Hundred Third Congresses); is a resident of Mitchellville, Md.

**HRUSKA, Roman Lee,** a Representative and a Senator from Nebraska; born in David City, Butler County, Nebr., August 16, 1904; attended the public schools; attended the University of Omaha, 1923-1925, and the University of Chicago Law School, 1927-1928; J.D., Creighton University College of Law, Omaha, Nebr., 1929; was admitted to the bar in 1929 and commenced practice in Omaha, Nebr.; member of the Board of Douglas County Commissioners, 1944-1952, serving as chairman from 1945 until 1952; member of Advisory Committee to the Nebraska Board of Control, 1947-1952; president, Nebraska Association of County Officials, 1950-1951; vice president of the National Association of County Officials, 1951-1952; vice chairman of Nebraska Civil Defense, 1951-1952; member of the Board of Regents of the University of Omaha, 1950-1957; elected as a Republican to the Eighty-third Congress and served from January 3, 1953, until his resignation November 8, 1954, having been elected to the United States Senate, November 2, 1954, to fill the vacancy caused by the death of Hugh Butler; reelected in 1958, 1964, and again in 1970, and served from November 8, 1954 until his resignation December 27, 1976; was not a candidate for reelection in 1976; is a resident of Omaha, Nebr.

**HUBARD, Edmund Wilcox,** a Representative from Virginia; born near Farmville, Buckingham County, Va., February 20, 1806; attended private schools and the University of Virginia at Charlottesville; engaged in agricultural pursuits; justice of the peace; elected as a Democrat to the Twenty-seventh, Twenty-eighth, and Twenty-ninth Congresses (March 4, 1841-March 3, 1847); was not a candidate for renomination in 1846; resumed agricultural pursuits; colonel of a militia regiment in 1864; appraiser of the Confederate Government to regulate the value of the Confederate dollar; died at his home near Farmville, Buckingham County, Va., December 9, 1878; interment in the family cemetery near his home.

**HUBBARD, Asahel Wheeler** (father of Elbert Hamilton Hubbard), a Representative from Iowa; born in Haddam, Conn., January 19, 1819; attended the public schools; engaged as a stonecutter; subsequently pursued his studies at a select school in Middletown, Conn.; moved to Rushville, Ind., in 1838, where he was employed as a book agent and taught school; studied law; was admitted to the bar in 1841 and commenced practice in Rushville; member of the Indiana house of representatives 1847-1849; moved to Sioux City, Iowa, in 1857 and engaged in the real estate business; judge of the fourth judicial district 1859-1862; elected as a Republican to the Thirty-eighth and to the two succeeding Congresses (March 4, 1863-March 3, 1869); was not a candidate for renomination in 1868 to the Forty-first Congress; one of the organizers of the First National Bank of Sioux City in 1871 and served as its president until January 15, 1879; was also interested in railroad building in Iowa and in mining property in Leadville, Colo.; died in Sioux City, Iowa, September 22, 1879; interment in Floyd Cemetery.

**HUBBARD, Carroll, Jr.,** a Representative from Kentucky; born in Murray, Calloway County, Ky., July 7, 1937; attended public schools; graduated from Eastern High School, Middletown, Ky., 1955; B.A., Georgetown (Ky.) College, 1959; J.D., University of Louisville Law School, 1962; admitted to the Kentucky bar in 1962 and commenced practice in Mayfield; served in Kentucky Air National Guard, 1962-1967; Kentucky Army National Guard, 1968-1970; served in Kentucky senate, 1968-1975; unsuccessful candidate in 1979 for the Democratic nomination for Governor of Kentucky; elected as a Democrat to the Ninety-fourth and to the eight succeeding Congresses (January 3, 1975-January 3, 1993); unsuccessful candidate for renomination in 1992 to the One Hundred Third Congress; is a resident of Mayfield, Ky.

**HUBBARD, Chester Dorman** (father of William Pallister Hubbard), a Representative from West Virginia; born in Hamden, Middlesex County, Conn., November 25, 1814; moved with his parents in 1819 to Wheeling, Va. (now West Virginia); was graduated from the Wesleyan University, Middletown, Conn., in 1840; engaged in banking and in the manufacture of iron and lumber; member of the Virginia house of delegates in 1852 and 1853; delegate to the Virginia convention in Richmond in 1861 and opposed secession; delegate to the West Virginia convention in Wheeling the same year; served in the senate of West Virginia in 1863 and 1864; delegate to the Republican National Conventions of 1864 and 1880; elected as an Unconditional Unionist to the Thirty-ninth Congress and reelected as a Republican to the Fortieth Congress (March 4, 1865-March 3, 1869); chairman, Committee on Expenditures in the Department of the Interior (Fortieth Congress); resumed banking and manufacturing pursuits; died in Wheeling, W.Va., August 23, 1891; interment in Greenwood Cemetery.

**HUBBARD, David** (cousin of Samuel Houston), a Representative from Alabama; born near the town of Old Liberty (now Bedford), Bedford County, Va., in 1792; attended the county schools and an academy; during the War of 1812 entered the Army and served as major in the Quartermaster Corps; moved to Huntsville, Ala., where he worked as a carpenter; studied law; was admitted to the bar about 1820 and commenced practice in Huntsville; moved to Florence and served as solicitor 1823-1826; moved to Moulton in 1827 and entered the mercantile business; member of the State senate in 1827 and 1828; member of the board of trustees of the University of Alabama 1828-1835; moved to Courtland in 1829, where he engaged in buying and selling Chickasaw Indian land; member of the State house of representatives in 1831, 1842, 1843, 1845, and 1853; elected as a Democrat to the Twenty-sixth Congress (March 4, 1839-March 3, 1841); unsuccessful candidate for reelection in 1840 to the Twenty-seventh Congress; resumed the practice of law; elected to the Thirty-first Congress (March 4, 1849-March 3, 1851); unsuccessful candidate for reelection in 1850 to the Thirty-second Congress; delegate to the Southern Commercial Congress at Savannah, Ga., in 1859; presidential elector on the Breckinridge and Lane ticket in 1860; member of the Confederate States House of Representatives 1861-1863; first Confederate States Commissioner of Indian Affairs 1863-1865; moved to Spring Hill,

Tenn.; died at the home of his son in Pointe Coupee Parish, La., January 20, 1874; interment in Trinity Episcopal Churchyard, Rosedale, Iberville Parish, La.

**Bibliography:** *DAB*.

**HUBBARD, Demas, Jr.,** a Representative from New York; born in Winfield, Herkimer County, N.Y., January 17, 1806; attended the public schools and pursued an academic course; studied law; was admitted to the bar and commenced practice in Smyrna, N.Y., in 1835; member of the State assembly 1838-1840; supervisor of Smyrna 1859-1864; elected chairman of the board of supervisors of Chenango County, N.Y.; elected as a Republican to the Thirty-ninth Congress (March 4, 1865-March 3, 1867); was not a candidate for renomination in 1866 to the Fortieth Congress; resumed the practice of his profession; died in Smyrna, Chenango County, N.Y., September 2, 1873; interment in Smyrna East Cemetery.

**HUBBARD, Elbert Hamilton** (son of Asahel Wheeler Hubbard), a Representative from Iowa; born in Rushville, Rush County, Ind., August 19, 1849; attended the public schools and was instructed by a private tutor; was graduated from Yale College in 1872; studied law; was admitted to the bar in 1874 and commenced practice in Sioux City, Iowa; member of the State house of representatives in 1882; served in the State senate 1900-1902; elected as a Republican to the Fifty-ninth and to the three succeeding Congresses and served from March 4, 1905, until his death in Sioux City, Iowa, June 4, 1912; interment in Floyd Cemetery.

**HUBBARD, Henry,** a Representative and a Senator from New Hampshire; born in Charlestown, Sullivan County, N.H., May 3, 1784; pursued classical studies under private tutors and graduated from Dartmouth College, Hanover, N.H., in 1803; studied law in Portsmouth, N.H.; was admitted to the bar about 1806 and commenced practice in Charlestown; town moderator sixteen times, beginning in 1810; first selectman in 1819, 1820, and 1828; member, New Hampshire State house of representatives, 1812-1815, 1819-1820, 1823-1827, and served three years as speaker; State solicitor for Cheshire County, 1823-1828; probate judge of Sullivan County, 1827-1829; elected as a Jacksonian to the Twenty-first, Twenty-second, and Twenty-third Congresses (March 4, 1829-March 3, 1835); chairman, Committee on Revolutionary Pensions (Twenty-second Congress); elected as a Jacksonian to the United States Senate and served from March 4, 1835, to March 3, 1841; was not a candidate for reelection; chairman, Committee on Claims (Twenty-fourth through Twenty-sixth Congresses); elected Governor of New Hampshire in 1842, reelected in 1843, and served from June 2, 1842 to June 6, 1844; United States sub-treasurer at Boston, Mass., 1846-1849; died in Charlestown, N.H., June 5, 1857; interment in Forest Hill Cemetery.

**HUBBARD, Joel Douglas,** a Representative from Missouri; born near Marshall, Saline County, Mo., November 6, 1860; attended the public schools and Central College, Fayette, Mo.; was graduated from the Missouri Medical College at St. Louis in 1882; practiced medicine in Syracuse, Morgan County, Mo., until 1886; county clerk 1886-1894; elected as a Republican to the Fifty-fourth Congress (March 4, 1895-March 3, 1897); was an unsuccessful candidate for reelection in 1896 to the Fifty-fifth Congress; studied law; was admitted to the Missouri bar in 1899 and commenced practice in Versailles, Mo.; also engaged in the banking business; practiced medicine in Sedalia, Mo., in 1904 and 1905; returned to Versailles and resumed the practice of law and his banking interests; moved to El Paso, Tex., in 1917 and continued the practice of law; died in Tampa, Fla., on May 26, 1919; interment in Versailles Cemetery, Versailles, Mo.

**HUBBARD, John Henry,** a Representative from Connecticut; born in Salisbury, Litchfield County, Conn., March 24, 1804; attended the public schools; studied law; was admitted to the bar in 1828 and commenced practice in Lakeville; member of the State senate 1847-1849; prosecuting attorney 1849-1852; moved to Litchfield in 1855 and continued the practice of law; elected as a Republican to the Thirty-eighth and Thirty-ninth Congresses (March 4, 1863-March 3, 1867); unsuccessful candidate for renomination in 1866 to the Fortieth Congress; resumed the practice of law; died in Litchfield, Conn., on July 30, 1872; interment in the East Cemetery.

**HUBBARD, Jonathan Hatch,** a Representative from Vermont; born in Tolland, Tolland County, Conn., May 7, 1768; at the age of eleven moved with his parents to Claremont, N.H.; was instructed by a private tutor; studied law; was admitted to the bar in 1790 and commenced practice in Windsor, Vt.; elected as a Federalist to the Eleventh Congress (March 4, 1809-March 3, 1811); unsuccessful candidate in 1810 for reelection to the Twelfth Congress; judge of the State supreme court 1813-1815; resumed the practice of law; died in Windsor, Vt., September 20, 1849; interment in the Old South Cemetery.

**HUBBARD, Levi,** a Representative from Massachusetts; born in Worcester, Mass., December 19, 1762; attended the common schools; moved to Paris, Maine (then a district of Massachusetts), in 1785; engaged in agricultural pursuits; was prominent in Massachusetts military organizations; member of the Massachusetts house of representatives in 1804, 1805, and 1812; served in the Massachusetts senate 1806-1811; elected as a Republican to the Thirteenth Congress (March 4, 1813-March 3, 1815); again served in the Massachusetts senate in 1816; resumed agricultural pursuits; member of Maine Executive Council in 1829; died in Paris, Maine, February 18, 1836; interment in a tomb on his farm.

**HUBBARD, Richard Dudley,** a Representative from Connecticut; born in Berlin, Hartford County, Conn., September 7, 1818; pursued preparatory studies at East Hartford; was graduated from Yale College in 1839; studied law; was admitted to the bar in 1842 and commenced practice in Hartford, Conn.; member of the State house of representatives in 1842, 1855, and again in 1858; prosecuting attorney for Hartford County 1846-1868; elected as a Democrat to the Fortieth Congress (March 4, 1867-March 3, 1869); declined to be a candidate for renomination in 1868 to the Forty-first Congress; resumed the practice of law in Hartford; unsuccessful candidate for election in 1872 for Governor; elected Governor of Connecticut in 1876, and served from January 3, 1877 to January 9, 1879; unsuccessful candidate for reelection in 1878; engaged in the practice of law from 1877 until his death in Hartford, Conn., February 28, 1884; interment in Cedar Hill Cemetery.

**HUBBARD, Samuel Dickinson,** a Representative from Connecticut; born in Middletown, Conn., August 10, 1799; pursued classical studies; was graduated from Yale College in 1819; studied law; was admitted to the bar and practiced in Middletown, Conn., 1823-1837; also engaged in manufacturing; elected as a Whig to the Twenty-ninth and Thirtieth Congresses (March 4, 1845-March 3, 1849); served as Postmaster General in the Cabinet of President Millard Fillmore from August 31, 1852 to March 7, 1853; died in Middletown, Conn., October 8, 1855; interment in Indian Hill Cemetery.

**HUBBARD, Thomas Hill,** a Representative from New York; born in New Haven, Conn., December 5, 1781; pursued classical studies; was graduated from Yale College in 1799; studied law; was admitted to the bar in 1804 and commenced practice in Hamilton, N.Y.; surrogate of Madison County 1806-1816; presidential elector on the Clinton and Ingersoll ticket in 1812; district attorney of the sixth district 1816-1818 and of Madison County 1818-1821; elected as a Republican to the Fifteenth Congress (March 4, 1817-March 3, 1819); chairman, Committee on Expenditures in the Post Office Department (Fifteenth Congress); elected to the Seventeenth Congress (March 4, 1821-March 3, 1823); moved to Utica, N.Y., in 1823; appointed the first clerk of the court of chancery of Oneida County in 1823; clerk of the supreme court 1825-1835; one of the founders of Hamilton College, Clinton, N.Y., and Hamilton (N.Y.) Academy; served as a trustee of Utica (N.Y.) Academy; presidential elector on the Democratic ticket in 1844 and 1852; died in Utica, N.Y., May 21, 1857; interment in Forest Hill Cemetery.

**HUBBARD, William Pallister** (son of Chester Dorman Hubbard), a Representative from West Virginia; born in Wheeling, Va. (later West Virginia), December 24, 1843; attended the public schools and Linsly Institute of Wheeling; was graduated from Wesleyan University, Middletown, Conn., in 1863; studied law; was admitted to the bar in 1864; enlisted in the Union Army as a private in 1865 in the third West Virginia Cavalry, being a first lieutenant when honorably discharged; returned to Wheeling and commenced the practice of law in 1866; clerk of the West Virginia house of delegates 1866-1870; member of the house of delegates in 1881 and 1882; delegate to the Republican National Conventions of 1888 and 1912; unsuccessful Republican candidate for attorney general of West Virginia in 1888; unsuccessful candidate for election in 1890 to the Fifty-second Congress; chairman of the commission to revise the tax laws of West Virginia 1901-1903; elected as a Republican to the Sixtieth and Sixty-first Congresses (March 4, 1907-March 3, 1911); declined to be a candidate for renomination in 1910 to the Sixty-second Congress; resumed the practice of law in Wheeling, W.Va.; died in Wheeling, W.Va., December 5, 1921; interment in Greenwood Cemetery.

**HUBBELL, Edwin Nelson,** a Representative from New York; born in Coxsackie, Greene County, N.Y., August 13, 1815; pursued an academic course; several years supervisor of Greene County; elected as a Democrat to the Thirty-ninth Congress (March 4, 1865-March 3, 1867); moved to East Saginaw, Mich., and was employed as a clerk for a lumber company 1883-1887; served as assistant city treasurer 1887-1890 and as deputy city treasurer 1894-1896.

**HUBBELL, James Randolph,** a Representative from Ohio; born in Lincoln Township, Delaware County, Ohio, July 13, 1824; attended the common schools; taught school at Woodbury, Ohio; studied law; was admitted to the bar in 1845 and commenced practice at London, Ohio; moved to Delaware, Ohio, and continued the practice of law; member of the State house of representatives in 1849, 1858, 1859, 1862, and 1863 and served as speaker in 1863; elected as a Republican to the Thirty-ninth Congress (March 4, 1865-March 3, 1867); appointed by President Andrew Johnson as Minister to Ecuador, but his nomination was not confirmed; resumed the practice of law; served in the State senate in 1869; resigned for the purpose of accepting the Democratic nomination for Congress; unsuccessful Democratic candidate for election in 1870 to the Forty-second Congress; died at the home of his son in Bellville, Ohio, on November 26, 1890; interment in Oak Grove Cemetery, Delaware, Ohio.

**HUBBELL, Jay Abel,** a Representative from Michigan; born in Avon, Mich., September 15, 1829; attended the district schools; was graduated from the University of Michigan at Ann Arbor in 1853; studied law; was admitted to the bar in 1855; moved to Ontonagon, Mich., in November 1855 and engaged in the practice of law; elected district attorney of the Upper Peninsula in 1857 and 1859; moved to Houghton, Mich., in February 1860 and continued the practice of law until 1870; prosecuting attorney of Houghton County 1861-1867; identified with the development of the mineral interests of the Upper Peninsula; appointed by Governor John J. Bagley as Michigan State commissioner to the 1876 Centennial Exhibition in

Philadelphia, and collected and prepared the State exhibit of minerals; elected as a Republican to the Forty-third and to the four succeeding Congresses (March 4, 1873-March 3, 1883); chairman, Committee on Expenditures in the Department of the Interior (Forty-seventh Congress); member of the State senate 1885-1887; served as circuit judge of the twelfth judicial circuit from January 1, 1894, to December 31, 1899, when he resigned; died in Houghton, Mich., October 13, 1900; interment in Forest Hill Cemetery.

**HUBBELL, William Spring,** a Representative from New York; born in Painted Post, Steuben County, N.Y., January 17, 1801; attended the public schools; postmaster of Bath, N.Y., in 1829; town clerk in 1831; later engaged in banking; member of the State assembly in 1841; elected as a Democrat to the Twenty-eighth Congress (March 4, 1843-March 3, 1845); delegate to the Democratic National Convention at Charleston, S.C., in 1860; died in Bath, N.Y., November 16, 1873; interment in Grove Cemetery.

**HUBBS, Orlando,** a Representative from North Carolina; born in Commack, Suffolk County, N.Y., February 18, 1840; attended the district schools and the local academy at Commack; went to Northport in 1856 and learned the trade of a carriage and wagon builder and subsequently became employed as a ship's joiner at Hunters Point, N.Y.; moved to New Bern, N.C., in 1865 and became engaged in mercantile pursuits; took an active part in organizing the Republican Party in North Carolina; sheriff of Craven County 1871-1881; elected as a Republican to the Forty-seventh Congress (March 4, 1881-March 3, 1883); was not a candidate for renomination in 1882; returned to New York in 1890 and settled in Central Islip; engaged in agricultural pursuits; member of the New York assembly 1902-1908; served in the State senate in 1910 and 1911; resided in Smithtown Branch, Suffolk County, N.Y., until his death on December 5, 1930; interment in Commack Cemetery, Commack, N.Y.

**HUBER, Robert James,** a Representative from Michigan; born in Detroit, Wayne County, Mich., August 29, 1922; educated in the public schools of Detroit, Mich.; attended the University of Detroit, 1935-1937; graduated from Culver Military Academy, 1939; B.S., Sheffield Scientific School, Yale University, 1943; served in the United States Army, 1943-1946; banker; businessman; mayor, city of Troy, Mich., 1959-1964; board of supervisors, Oakland County, 1959-1963; State senator, 1965-1970; elected as a Republican to the Ninety-third Congress (January 3, 1973-January 3, 1975); unsuccessful candidate for reelection in 1974 to the Ninety-fourth Congress; unsuccessful candidate for nomination in 1976 to the United States Senate; chairman of the board, Michigan Chrome and Chemical Co., 1973 to present; is a resident of Troy, Mich.

**HUBER, Walter B.,** a Representative from Ohio; born in Akron, Summit County, Ohio, June 29, 1903; associated with the Summit County prosecuting attorney from 1936 until 1944; elected as a Democrat to the Seventy-ninth and to the two succeeding Congresses (January 3, 1945-January 3, 1951); unsuccessful candidate for reelection in 1950 to the Eighty-second Congress, and for election in 1952 to the Eighty-third Congress; investigator for the United States Senate Committee on the Judiciary, Subcommittee on Patents, Trademarks, and Copyrights, from October 20, 1955, to April 30, 1958; administrative assistant with House Subcommittee on Legislative Oversight from May 1, 1958, to January 3, 1959; consultant with the House Committee on Un-American Activities from 1959 until 1968; consultant with an environmental protection association; resided in Nanjemoy, Md. until his death in Lexington Park, Md., on August 8, 1982; interment at Christ Church, Ironsides, Md.

**HUBLEY, Edward Burd,** a Representative from Pennsylvania; born in Reading, Pa., in 1792; attended the public schools; studied law; was admitted to the bar in 1820 and commenced practice in Reading; afterwards moved to Orwigsburg, the county seat of Schuylkill County; elected as a Jacksonian to the Twenty-fourth Congress and reelected as a Democrat to the Twenty-fifth Congress (March 4, 1835-March 3, 1839); canal commissioner of Pennsylvania, 1839-1842; appointed on November 8, 1842, a commissioner to adjust and settle certain claims under the treaty with the Cherokee Indians of 1835; resumed the practice of law in Reading, Pa.; moved to Philadelphia, Pa., where he died on February 23, 1856; interment in Charles Evans Cemetery, Reading, Pa.

**HUCK, Winnifred Sprague Mason** (daughter of William Ernest Mason), a Representative from Illinois; born in Chicago, Ill., September 14, 1882; attended the public schools of Chicago and also at Washington, D.C., while her father was a Member of Congress; elected as a Republican to the Sixty-seventh Congress to fill the vacancy caused by the death of her father, William E. Mason, and served from November 7, 1922, to March 3, 1923; unsuccessful candidate for renomination in 1922; engaged in journalism and lecturing; died in Chicago, Ill., August 24, 1936; remains were cremated and the ashes deposited in Oakwood Cemetery, Waukegan, Ill.

**HUCKABY, Thomas Jerald (Jerry),** a Representative from Louisiana; born in Hodge, Jackson Parish, La., July 19, 1941; attended the public schools of Minden, La.; B.S., Louisiana State University, 1963; M.B.A., Georgia State University, Atlanta, 1968; businessman and dairy farmer, 1963-1976; owner-operator of Hallmark Farms in Ringgold, La.; management executive, Western Electric Co., Chicago, Ill., 1963-1973; elected as a Democrat to the Ninety-fifth and to the seven succeeding Congresses (January 3, 1977-January 3, 1993); unsuccessful candidate for reelection in 1992 to the One Hundred Third Congress; is a resident of Ringgold, La.

**HUDD, Thomas Richard,** a Representative from Wisconsin; born in Buffalo, N.Y., October 2, 1835; moved with his mother to Chicago, Ill., in 1842 and to Appleton, Wis., in 1853; attended the common schools and Lawrence University, Appleton, Wis.; studied law; was admitted to the bar in 1856 and commenced practice in Appleton, Wis.; district attorney of Outagamie County in 1856 and 1857; served in the State senate in 1862, 1863, 1876-1879, 1882, 1883, and 1885; moved to Green Bay in 1868 and continued the practice of law; member of the State assembly in 1868 and 1875; city attorney of Green Bay in 1873 and 1874; delegate to the Democratic National Convention in 1880; elected as a Democrat to the Forty-ninth Congress to fill the vacancy caused by the death of Joseph Rankin; reelected to the Fiftieth Congress and served from March 8, 1886, to March 3, 1889; chairman, Committee on Expenditures in the Department of the Interior (Fiftieth Congress); did not seek renomination in 1888; resumed the practice of law; died in Green Bay, Wis., on June 22, 1896; interment in Woodlawn Cemetery.

**HUDDLESTON, George** (father of George Huddleston, Jr.), a Representative from Alabama; born on a farm near Lebanon, Wilson County, Tenn., November 11, 1869; attended the common schools; studied law at Cumberland University, Lebanon, Tenn.; was admitted to the bar in 1891 and practiced in Birmingham, Ala., until 1911, when he retired from practice; during the Spanish-American War served as a private in the First Regiment, Alabama Volunteer Infantry; elected as a Democrat to the Sixty-fourth and to the ten succeeding Congresses (March 4, 1915-January 3, 1937); unsuccessful candidate for renomination in 1936 to the Seventy-fifth Congress; died in Birmingham, Ala., February 29, 1960; interment in Elmwood Cemetery.

**Bibliography:** Barnard, William D. "George Huddleston, Sr., and the Political Tradition of Birmingham." *Alabama Review* 36

(October 1983).

**HUDDLESTON, George Jr.** (son of George Huddleston), a Representative from Alabama; born in Birmingham, Jefferson County, Ala., March 19, 1920; attended the public schools; attended George Washington University, Washington, D.C., for one year; Birmingham (Ala.) Southern College, A.B., 1941; co-editor of an index to the official proceedings of the Alabama Constitutional Convention of 1901; served as a lieutenant in the United States Navy, 1942-1946, with thirty-two months overseas in the Pacific Theater; captain in the Naval Reserve; University of Alabama Law School, LL.B., 1948; was admitted to the bar in 1948; deputy circuit solicitor for the tenth judicial circuit of Alabama, 1948-1949; assistant United States attorney for the northern district of Alabama, 1949-1952; engaged in the practice of law in Birmingham, Ala., 1952-1954; elected as a Democrat to the Eighty-fourth and to the four succeeding Congresses (January 3, 1955-January 3, 1965); unsuccessful candidate for reelection in 1964 to the Eighty-ninth Congress; joined North American Rockwell Corp. in 1964, and was the firm's director of governmental affairs at the time of his death in Washington, D.C., September 14, 1971; was a resident of Middleburg, Va.; interment in Elmwood Cemetery, Birmingham, Ala.

**HUDDLESTON, Walter Darlington,** a Senator from Kentucky; born in Burkesville, Cumberland County, Ky., April 15, 1926; educated in the public schools; B.A., University of Kentucky, 1949; served in the United States Army as a tank gunner, Ninth Armored Division, European Theater of Operations, 1944-1946; program and sports director, radio station WKCT, Bowling Green, Ky., 1949-1952; general manager, radio station WIEL, Elizabethtown, Ky., 1952-1972; partner and director, radio station WLBN, Lebanon, Ky., 1957-1972; member, Elizabethtown (Ky.) Planning and Zoning Commission, 1960-1961; Kentucky senator, 1965-1972, serving as majority caucus chairman in 1968, and as majority floor leader, 1970-1972; elected as a Democrat to the United States Senate in 1972; reelected in 1978, and served from January 3, 1973 to January 3, 1985; unsuccessful candidate for reelection in 1984; is a resident of Elizabethtown, Ky.

**HUDNUT, William Herbert, III,** a Representative from Indiana; born in Cincinnati, Ohio, October 17, 1932; educated at Darrow School, New Lebanon, N.Y., 1946-1950; A.B., Princeton University, 1954; B.D., Union Theological Seminary, 1957; Presbyterian clergyman, ordained in Rochester, N.Y., 1957; member, Indianapolis, Ind. Board of Public Safety, 1970-1972; elected as a Republican to the Ninety-third Congress (January 3, 1973-January 3, 1975); unsuccessful candidate for reelection in 1974 to the Ninety-fourth Congress; elected mayor of Indianapolis in 1975; reelected in 1979, 1983, and 1987; is a resident of Indianapolis, Ind.

**HUDSON, Charles,** a Representative from Massachusetts; born in Marlboro, Middlesex County, Mass., November 14, 1795; attended the common schools and later an academy; taught school; served in the War of 1812; studied theology; was ordained as a Universalist minister in 1819 and located in Westminster in 1824; author of religous textbooks and sacred memoirs; member of the Massachusetts house of representatives, 1828-1833; served in the Massachusetts senate, 1833-1839; member of the Massachusetts Board of Education, 1837-1845; executive councilor, 1839-1841; elected as a Whig to the Twenty-seventh Congress to fill the vacancy caused by the resignation of Levi Lincoln; reelected to the three succeeding Congresses, and served from May 3, 1841 to March 3, 1849; unsuccessful candidate for reelection in 1848 to the Thirty-first Congress; moved to Lexington, Mass., in 1849; naval officer of the port of Boston, 1849-1853; edited the Boston Daily Atlas; assessor of internal revenue, 1864-1868; selectman of Lexington, Mass., 1868-1875; died in Lexington, Mass., May 4, 1881; interment in Munroe Cemetery.

Bibliography: *DAB.*

**HUDSON, Grant Martin,** a Representative from Michigan; born in Eaton Township, Lorain County, Ohio, July 23, 1868; attended the common schools; was graduated from Kalamazoo (Mich.) College and also attended the University of Chicago; minister at Dowagiac, Mich., 1894-1896; engaged in mercantile pursuits in Schoolcraft, Mich., in 1896; member of the Michigan State house of representatives, 1905-1909; president of the village of Schoolcraft, Mich., 1909-1911; member of the State industrial accident compensation commission in 1920 and 1921; elected as a Republican to the Sixty-eighth and to the three succeeding Congresses (March 4, 1923-March 3, 1931); chairman, Committee on Alcohol Liquor Traffic (Sixty-ninth Congress); unsuccessful candidate for renomination in 1930 to the Seventy-second Congress; engaged in the insurance business in Lansing, Mich.; State purchasing agent in 1939; State tax commissioner in 1940; died in Kalamazoo, Mich., October 26, 1955; interment in Mount Hope Cemetery, Lansing, Mich.

**HUDSON, Thomas Jefferson,** a Representative from Kansas; born near Jamestown, Boone County, Ind., October 30, 1839; attended Lebanon (Ind.) Academy and Wabash College, Crawfordsville, Ind.; moved to Nodaway, Mo., in 1854; moved to Coysville, Wilson County, Kans., in 1866 and taught in the first county school; studied law; was admitted to the bar in Iola, Kans., in June 1869; moved to Fredonia, Kans., in 1869 and commenced practice; aided in the adoption of the fifteenth amendment; treasurer and member of the first Fredonia school board in the early seventies; member of the State house of representatives in 1870; mayor of Fredonia in 1871; organized the Wilson County Bank in Fredonia in 1871; was graduated from the law department of the University of Cincinnati, Ohio, in 1874; prosecuting attorney for Wilson County 1884-1886; delegate to the Democratic National Conventions in 1884, 1888, 1896; elected as a Populist to the Fifty-third Congress (March 4, 1893-March 3, 1895); was not a candidate for renomination in 1894; resumed the practice of law in Fredonia; regent of the State college of agriculture in 1897 and 1898; died in Wichita, Kans., on January 4, 1923; interment in Fredonia Cemetery, Fredonia, Kans.

**HUDSPETH, Claude Benton,** a Representative from Texas; born in Medina, Bandera County, Tex., May 12, 1877; attended the country schools; learned the printing trade; moved to Ozona, Tex., in 1893 and published the Ozona Kicker for a few years; employed as a cowboy; engaged in the cattle trading business and later in ranching; member of the State house of representatives 1902-1906; served in the State senate 1906-1918 and was elected president of that body four times; studied law; was admitted to the bar in 1909 and commenced practice in El Paso, Tex.; director of the Texan Oil & Land Co.; elected as a Democrat to the Sixty-sixth and to the five succeeding Congresses (March 4, 1919-March 3, 1931); was not a candidate for renomination in 1930 to the Seventy-second Congress; resided in San Antonio, Tex., until his death there on March 19, 1941; interment in Mission Burial Park.

**HUFF, George Franklin,** a Representative from Pennsylvania; born in Norristown, Montgomery County, Pa., July 16, 1842; attended the public schools in Middletown and later in Altoona; at the age of eighteen worked for the Pennsylvania Railroad car shops in Altoona; moved to Westmoreland County in 1867 and engaged in banking in Greensburg, Pa., later becoming largely identified with the industrial and mining interests of western Pennsylvania; delegate to the Republican National Convention in 1880; member of the Pennsylvania senate 1884-1888; elected as a Republican to the Fifty-second Congress (March 4, 1891-March 3, 1893); elected to the Fifty-fourth Congress (March 4, 1895-March 3, 1897); was not a candidate for renomination in 1896; again elected to the Fifty-eighth and to the three succeeding Congresses (March 4, 1903-March 3, 1911); chairman, Committee on Mines and Mining (Sixtieth and Sixty-first Congresses); was not a candidate for renomination in

1910; died in Washington, D.C., on April 18, 1912; interment in St. Clair Cemetery, Greensburg, Pa.

**HUFFINGTON, Michael,** a Representative from California; born in Dallas, Tex., September 4, 1947; graduated from the Culver (Ind.) Military Academy; B.A., B.S., Stanford University, Calif., 1970; M.B.A., Harvard University, 1972; First National Bank of Chicago; Simmons and Huffington, 1974; vice chairman, Roy M. Huffington, Inc.; Deputy Assistant Secretary of Defense for Negotiations Policy, 1986; chairman, Crest Films, 1989 to present; elected as a Republican to the One Hundred Third Congress (January 3, 1993-January 3, 1995); was not a candidate in 1994 for renomination to the House of Representatives, but was an unsuccessful candidate for election to the United States Senate; is a resident of Santa Barbara, Calif.

**HUFFMAN, James Wylie,** a Senator from Ohio; born in Chandlersville, Muskingum County, Ohio, September 13, 1894; attended the public schools; also attended Ohio Wesleyan University and Ohio State University; taught high school; during the First World War served as a machine gun officer; graduated with a law degree from the University of Chicago in 1922; admitted to the bar in Ohio and Illinois in 1922 and commenced practice in Chicago, Ill.; assistant attorney general of Illinois in 1923; returned to Ohio in 1924 and was executive secretary to Governor A. Victor Donahey 1924-1926; member of the Public Utilities Commission of Ohio 1927-1929; engaged in the practice of law at Columbus, Ohio; served as director of commerce of Ohio 1945; appointed as a Democrat to the United States Senate to fill the vacancy caused by the resignation of Harold H. Burton and served from October 8, 1945, to November 5, 1946, when a successor was elected; was not a candidate for nomination to fill the vacancy in 1946, but was an unsuccessful candidate for election to the full term; vice president and director, Logan Clay Products Co., Logan, Ohio; director, later president and chairman of the board, Motorists Mutual Insurance Co. of Columbus, Ohio; member of board of trustees, Ohio State University 1951-1957; author; was a resident of Pickerington, Ohio, until his death on May 20, 1980.

**HUFTY, Jacob,** a Representative from New Jersey; born in New Jersey; was a blacksmith by trade; served as a private in the State militia; freeholder for Salem Township in 1792; elected overseer of the poor and collector of Salem Township in 1793; county justice of Salem County, N.J., in 1797, county judge in 1798, and county justice and judge in 1804; served as sheriff, 1801-1804; freeholder of Salem Township, 1800-1804; a director of the board of chosen freeholders in 1801; member of the State council in 1804, 1806, and 1807; county collector, 1805-1808; judge of Orphans Court, 1805-1808; surrogate in 1808; elected as a Republican to the Eleventh and Twelfth Congresses and as a Federalist to the Thirteenth Congress, and served from March 4, 1809 until his death in Salem, N.J., May 20, 1814; interment in St. John's Episcopal Churchyard.

**HUGER, Benjamin,** a Representative from South Carolina; born at or near Charleston, S.C., in 1768; pursued an academic course; engaged in the cultivation of rice on the Waccamaw River; member of the State house of representatives 1796-1798; elected as a Federalist to the Sixth, Seventh, and Eighth Congresses (March 4, 1799-March 3, 1805); again a member of the State house of representatives 1806-1813; elected to the Fourteenth Congress (March 4, 1815-March 3, 1817); member of the State senate 1818-1823 and served as president 1819-1822; died on his estate on Waccamaw River, near Georgetown, S.C., July 7, 1823; interment in All Saints' Churchyard.

**HUGER, Daniel** (father of Daniel Elliott Huger), a Delegate and a Representative from South Carolina; born on Limerick plantation in St. John's parish, Berkeley County, S.C., February 20, 1742; educated at home and in the schools of Charleston, S.C.; also studied in England; member of colonial assembly, 1773-1775; justice of the peace in 1775; member of the State house of representatives 1778-1780; member of the Governor's council in 1780; Member of the Continental Congress 1786-1788; elected to the First and Second Congresses (March 4, 1789-March 3, 1793); on retiring from Congress resided in Charleston and on his Wateree plantation; engaged in the management of his extensive estates; died in Charleston, S.C., July 6, 1799; interment in the western churchyard of St. Philip's Church, Charleston, S.C., with a memorial tablet in the Huguenot church there.

**HUGER, Daniel Elliott** (son of Daniel Huger), a Senator from South Carolina; born on Limerick plantation, near Charleston, S.C., June 28, 1779; pursued classical studies in Charleston; graduated from the College of New Jersey (later Princeton University) in 1798; studied law; was admitted to the bar in 1799 and began practice in Charleston, S.C.; member, State house of representatives 1804-1819; brigadier general of State troops in 1814; judge of the circuit court 1819-1830; member, State senate 1830-1832, 1838-1842; opposition member of the State nullification convention in 1832; elected as a State Rights Democrat to the United States Senate to fill the vacancy caused by the resignation of John C. Calhoun and served from March 4, 1843, to March 3, 1845, when he resigned; delegate to the state-rights convention in 1852, where he urged moderation; died on Sullivans Island, S.C., August 21, 1854; interment in Magnolia Cemetery, Charleston, S.C.

Bibliography: *DAB.*

**HUGHES, Charles,** a Representative from New York; born in New Orleans, La., February 27, 1822; completed preparatory studies; studied law; was admitted to the bar in 1846 and commenced practice in Sandy Hill, N.Y.; elected as a Democrat to the Thirty-third Congress (March 4, 1853-March 3, 1855); clerk of the court of appeals 1860-1862; provost marshal for the sixteenth district of New York in 1862; member of the Governor's staff and judge advocate general of State militia 1875-1879; member of the State senate in 1878 and 1879; resumed the practice of his profession; died in Sandy Hill, N.Y., August 10, 1887; interment in Union Cemetery, between Fort Edward and Sandy Hill (now Hudson Falls).

**HUGHES, Charles James, Jr.,** a Senator from Colorado; born in Kingston, Caldwell County, Mo., February 16, 1853; attended the common schools; graduated from Richmond (Mo.) College in 1871 and from the law department of the University of Missouri at Columbia in 1873; was admitted to the bar in 1877 and commenced practice at Richmond, Mo.; moved to Denver, Colo., in 1879; presidential elector on the Democratic ticket in 1900; professor of mining law in the law school of the University of Denver, Colorado, and Harvard University; elected as a Democrat to the United States Senate and served from March 4, 1909, until his death in Denver, Colo., January 11, 1911; interment in Fairmont Cemetery.

**HUGHES, Dudley Mays,** a Representative from Georgia; born in Jeffersonville, Twiggs County, Ga., October 10, 1848; attended the country schools; was graduated from the University of Georgia at Athens in 1870; engaged in agricultural pursuits in 1871; member of the State senate in 1882 and 1883; president of the Georgia State Agricultural Society 1904-1906; commissioner general of Georgia at the World's Fair, St. Louis, Mo., in 1904; trustee of the Danville School, the State Normal Institute, the University of Georgia, and the Georgia State Agricultural College; president of the Georgia Fruit Growers' Association; one of the original projectors and builders of the Macon, Dublin & Savannah Railroad and served as president and director; elected as a Democrat to the Sixty-first and to the three succeeding Congresses (March 4, 1909-March 3, 1917); chairman, Committee on Education (Sixty-third and Sixty-fourth Congresses); unsuccessful candidate for renomination in 1916 to the Sixty-fifth Congress; engaged in agricultural pursuits in Danville,

Ga.; died in Macon, Bibb County, Ga., January 20, 1927; interment in Evergreen Cemetery, Perry, Houston County, Ga.

**Bibliography:** *DAB*; Jones, Billy Walker. *Vocational Legacy: Biography of Dudley Mays Hughes*. Macon, Ga.: The Author, 1976.

**HUGHES, George Wurtz,** a Representative from Maryland; born in Elmira, N.Y., September 30, 1806; received a liberal schooling; was graduated from the United States Military Academy at West Point in 1827; became a civil engineer in New York City; reappointed to the Army July 7, 1838, as captain of topographical engineers; served in the Mexican War; lieutenant colonel of Maryland and District of Columbia Volunteers August 4, 1847; colonel October 1, 1847; honorably mustered out of the volunteer service July 24, 1848; commissioned lieutenant colonel on May 30, 1848; resigned August 4, 1851; became president of the Northern Central Railroad; elected as a Democrat to the Thirty-sixth Congress (March 4, 1859-March 3, 1861); consulting engineer and planter at West River, Md., until his death there on September 3, 1870; interment in the family burying ground of the Galloway family, "Tulip Hill," West River, Md.

**Bibliography:** *DAB*.

**HUGHES, Harold Everett,** a Senator from Iowa; born near Ida Grove, Ida County, Iowa, February 10, 1922; attended the public schools and the University of Iowa; Army combat rifleman in North Africa, Sicily, and Italy during the Second World War; engaged in the motor transportation business; elected to Iowa State Commerce Commission, 1959-1962; elected Governor of Iowa in 1962, reelected in 1964 and 1966, and served from January 17, 1963 to January 1, 1969; member of the executive committee, National Governors Conference, 1965-1967; chairman of the Democratic Governors Conference, 1966-1968; elected as a Democrat to the United States Senate in 1968 and served from January 3, 1969, to January 3, 1975; was not a candidate for reelection in 1974; briefly sought the Democratic presidential nomination in 1971; served on the Commission on the Operation of the Senate, 1975-1976; consultant to the Senate Judiciary Committee, 1975-1976; president, The Hughes Foundation; chairman of the board, Harold Hughes Centers for Alcoholism and Drug Treatment, Inc.; is a resident of Glendale, Ariz.

**Bibliography:** Hughes, Harold E., with Dick Schneider. *The Man From Ida Grove: A Senator's Personal Story*. Waco, Tex.: Word Books, 1979; Larew, James C. "A Party Reborn: Harold Hughes and the Iowa Democrats." *Palimpsest* 59 (September-October 1978): 148-161.

**HUGHES, James,** a Representative from Indiana; born in Baltimore County, Md., November 24, 1823; attended the common schools and Indiana University at Bloomington; studied law; was admitted to the bar in 1842 and commenced practice in Indiana; served in the Mexican War; served as judge of the sixth judicial circuit of Indiana from 1852 until 1856, when he resigned; professor of law in Indiana University 1853-1856; elected as a Democrat to the Thirty-fifth Congress (March 4, 1857-March 3, 1859); unsuccessful candidate for reelection in 1858 to the Thirty-sixth Congress; appointed judge of the Court of Claims and served from January 18, 1860, to December 1864, when he resigned; member, State house of representatives 1864-1866; cotton agent of Treasury Department 1866-1868; died in Wattsville, Md., on October 21, 1873; interment in Rose Hill Cemetery, Bloomington, Ind.

**Bibliography:** *DAB*.

**HUGHES, James Anthony,** a Representative from West Virginia; born near Corunna, Ontario, Canada, February 27, 1861; attended the public schools; moved with his parents to Ashland, Ky., in July 1873; completed preparatory studies; was graduated from Duff's Business College at Pittsburgh, Pa., in 1875; employed as a bank messenger 1879-1881 and as a traveling salesman in 1881 and

1882; moved to Louisa, Ky., in 1883 and engaged in the dry goods business; member of the Kentucky house of representatives 1888-1890; moved to Ceredo, W.Va., in 1891 and engaged in the timber business; moved to Huntington, W.Va., in 1892 and engaged in the real estate business; served in the State senate 1894-1898; delegate to the Republican State conventions in 1896 and 1898; delegate to all the Republican National Conventions from 1892 to 1924, inclusive; served as postmaster of Huntington 1896-1900; elected as a Republican to the Fifty-seventh and to the six succeeding Congresses (March 4, 1901-March 3, 1915); chairman, Committee on Expenditures on Public Buildings (Fifty-eighth and Fifty-ninth Congresses), Committee on Accounts (Sixtieth and Sixty-first Congresses); was not a candidate for renomination in 1914; resumed the real estate business in Huntington, W.Va.; elected to the Seventieth and Seventy-first Congresses and served from March 4, 1927, until his death in a sanitarium at Marion, Ohio, on March 2, 1930; interment in Spring Hill Cemetery, Huntington, W.Va.

**HUGHES, James Frederic,** a Representative from Wisconsin; born in Green Bay, Brown County, Wis., August 7, 1883; attended the public schools and was graduated from West Green Bay High School in 1901; moved to De Pere, Brown County, Wis., in 1901 and was employed as a salesman; member of the De Pere Board of Education 1914-1937; delegate to the Democratic National Conventions in 1920 and 1928; member of the Democratic State central committee 1920-1924; served as chairman of the eighth Wisconsin Democratic congressional committee 1928-1932; elected as a Democrat to the Seventy-third Congress (March 4, 1933-January 3, 1935); was not a candidate for renomination in 1934 to the Seventy-fourth Congress; resumed his former pursuits as sales manager in De Pere, Wis.; died in a hospital at Rochester, Minn., August 9, 1940; interment in Cady Cemetery, Lawrence, near De Pere, Wis.

**HUGHES, James Hurd,** a Senator from Delaware; born on a farm near Felton, Kent County, Del., January 14, 1867; attended the public schools and Collegiate Institute in Dover, Del., and also received instruction from private tutors; taught school in Kent County, Del., 1885-1889; studied law; was admitted to the bar in 1890 and commenced practice at Dover, Del.; also engaged in agricultural pursuits and banking; secretary of State of Delaware 1897-1901; Democratic presidential elector in 1912; unsuccessful candidate for election in 1916 for Governor of Delaware; elected as a Democrat in 1936 to the United States Senate and served from January 3, 1937, to January 2, 1943; unsuccessful candidate for renomination in 1942; returned to Dover, Del., and continued the practice of law; director of the Farmers Bank, Dover, Del., from 1905 until his death; died in Lewes, Del., August 29, 1953; interment in Lakeside Cemetery, Dover, Del.

**HUGHES, James Madison,** a Representative from Missouri; born in Bourbon County, Ky., April 7, 1809; received a liberal schooling; studied law; was admitted to the bar and practiced in Liberty, Clay County, Mo.; also engaged in mercantile pursuits in Liberty; member of the State house of representatives in 1839; elected as a Democrat to the Twenty-eighth Congress (March 4, 1843-March 3, 1845); moved to St. Louis, Mo., in 1855 and engaged in the banking business; died in Jefferson City, Mo., on February 26, 1861; interment in Bellefontaine Cemetery, St. Louis, Mo.

**HUGHES, Thomas Hurst,** a Representative from New Jersey; born in Cold Spring, Cape May County, N.J., January 10, 1769; attended the public schools; moved to Cape May City in 1800 and engaged in the mercantile business; in 1816 he built Congress Hall, a hotel which he conducted for many summer seasons; sheriff of Cape May County 1801-1804; member of the State general assembly 1805-1807, 1809, 1812, and 1813; member of the State council 1819-1823 and in 1824 and 1825; elected to the Twenty-first and

Twenty-second Congresses (March 4, 1829-March 3, 1833); was not a candidate for renomination in 1832 to the Twenty-third Congress; resumed the hotel business; died in Cold Spring, N.J., November 10, 1839; interment in Cold Spring Cemetery.

**HUGHES, William,** a Representative and a Senator from New Jersey; born in Drogheda, Ireland, April 3, 1872; immigrated to the United States in 1880 with his parents, who settled in Paterson, N.J.; attended the common schools; as a youth was employed in the silk mills of his home city; studied stenography at Columbia Business College at Paterson and was employed as a stenographer in New York City, and subsequently became a court reporter at Paterson; at the beginning of the Spanish-American War enlisted as a private in the United States Army and served throughout the war; studied law; was admitted to the bar in 1900 and commenced practice in Paterson, N.J.; elected as a Democrat to the Fifty-eighth Congress (March 4, 1903-March 3, 1905); unsuccessful candidate for reelection in 1904 to the Fifty-ninth Congress; elected to the Sixtieth and to the two succeeding Congresses and served from March 4, 1907, until September 27, 1912, when he resigned, having been appointed to a position on the judicial bench; judge of the court of common pleas of Passaic County from 1912 until 1913, when he resigned, having been elected Senator; elected as a Democrat to the United States Senate and served from March 4, 1913, until his death in Trenton, N.J., January 30, 1918; chairman, Committee on Expenditures in the Department of the Navy (Sixty-third and Sixty-fourth Congresses), Committee on Pensions (Sixty-fifth Congress); interment in Cedar Lawn Cemetery, Paterson, N.J.

**HUGHES, William John,** a Representative from New Jersey; born in Salem, Salem County, N.J., October 17, 1932; attended public schools and graduated from Penns Grove (N.J.) Regional High School in 1950; A.B., Men's College of Rutgers University, 1955; J.D., Rutgers Law School, 1958; admitted to the New Jersey bar in 1959 and commenced practice in Ocean City; served as township solicitor for Upper Township, N.J., 1959-1961; appointed assistant prosecutor for Cape May County, N.J., 1960; reappointed as first assistant prosecutor in 1961 and served until the spring of 1970; unsuccessful candidate for election in 1970 to the Ninety-second Congress; appointed by the Supreme Court of New Jersey to the Advisory Committee on Professional Ethics, 1972; elected as a Democrat to the Ninety-fourth and to the nine succeeding Congresses (January 3, 1975-January 3, 1995); was not a candidate for reelection in 1994 to the One Hundred Fourth Congress; nominated as Ambassador to Panama on June 5, 1995; and was confirmed by the Senate on September 29, 1995; is a resident of Ocean City, N.J.

**HUGHSTON, Jonas Abbott,** a Representative from New York; born in Sidney, Delaware County, N.Y., in 1808; completed preparatory studies; studied law; was admitted to the bar in 1839 and commenced practice at Delhi, N.Y.; district attorney of Delaware County 1842-1845; resumed the practice of law; elected as a Whig to the Thirty-fourth Congress (March 4, 1855-March 3, 1857); appointed by President Lincoln marshal of the consular court at Shanghai, China, on March 26, 1862, and served until his death in Shanghai, China, on November 10, 1862; interment in Poo-ting Cemetery.

**HUGUNIN, Daniel, Jr.,** a Representative from New York; born in Montgomery County, N.Y., February 6, 1790; pursued classical studies; served in the War of 1812; successfully contested the election of Egbert Ten Eyck to the Nineteenth Congress and served from December 15, 1825, until March 3, 1827; appointed on March 15, 1841, United States marshal for the Territory of Wisconsin; died in Kenosha, Wis., June 21, 1850; interment in Green Ridge Cemetery.

**HUKRIEDE, Theodore Waldemar,** a Representative from Missouri; born near New Truxton, Warren County, Mo., on November 9, 1878; attended the public schools, Central Wesleyan College, Warrenton, Warren County, Mo., and the University of Missouri at Columbia; studied law; was admitted to the bar in 1903 and commenced practice in Warrenton, Mo.; elected prosecuting attorney of Warren County in 1904, 1906, and 1908; probate judge of Warren County, 1910-1920; delegate to the Missouri State conventions in 1900, 1908, 1912, 1916, 1936, and 1940; delegate to the Republican National Conventions of 1916 and 1936; president of the Warrenton School Board, 1916-1920; chairman of the Republican State committee, 1916-1918; elected as a Republican to the Sixty-seventh Congress (March 4, 1921-March 3, 1923); unsuccessful candidate for reelection in 1922 to the Sixty-eighth Congress; appointed United States Marshal for the eastern district of Missouri on May 12, 1923, and served until March 1933; resumed the practice of law; elected to the Missouri State general assembly in 1942, reelected in 1944, and served until his death in Warrenton, Mo., April 14, 1945; interment in Warrenton Memorial Society Cemetery.

**HULBERT, George Murray,** a Representative from New York; born in Rochester, N.Y., May 14, 1881; moved to Waterloo, N.Y., where he attended the public schools; was graduated from the New York Law School; was admitted to the bar in 1902 and practiced law in New York City; elected as a Democrat to the Sixty-fourth and Sixty-fifth Congresses and served from March 4, 1915, to January 1, 1918, when he resigned to become commissioner of docks and director of the port of New York City; elected president of the Board of Aldermen of New York City in November 1921 and served as acting mayor during the long illness of Mayor Hylan; president of the Boston, Cape Cod & New York Canal Co.; resumed the practice of law until June 1934, when he was appointed by President Franklin D. Roosevelt as United States district judge of the southern district of New York, in which capacity he served until his death in Bayport, L. I., April 26, 1950; interment in Gate of Heaven Cemetery, Valhalla, N.Y.

**HULBERT, John Whitefield,** a Representative from Massachusetts; born in Alford, Mass., June 1, 1770; completed preparatory studies; was graduated from Harvard University in 1795; studied law; was admitted to the bar and commenced practice in Alford, Mass., in 1797; director of Berkshire Bank, Pittsfield, Mass.; elected as a Federalist to the Thirteenth Congress to fill the vacancy caused by the resignation of Daniel Dewey; reelected to the Fourteenth Congress and served from September 26, 1814, to March 3, 1817; was not a candidate for renomination in 1816; moved to Auburn, Cayuga County, N.Y., in 1817; member of the New York State house of representatives in 1825; resumed the practice of his profession; died in Auburn, N.Y., October 19, 1831; interment in North Street Cemetery.

**HULBURD, Calvin Tilden,** a Representative from New York; born in Stockholm, St. Lawrence County, N.Y., June 5, 1809; completed preparatory studies; was graduated from Middlebury College, Vermont; attended Yale College Law School; was admitted to the bar in 1833; member of the New York assembly 1842-1844 and in 1862; elected as a Republican to the Thirty-eighth, Thirty-ninth, and Fortieth Congresses (March 4, 1863-March 3, 1869); chairman, Committee on Public Expenditures (Thirty-eighth through Fortieth Congresses); superintendent of construction of the New York post office; died in Brasher Falls, N.Y., on October 25, 1897; interment in Fairview Cemetery.

**HULICK, George Washington,** a Representative from Ohio; born in Batavia, Clermont County, Ohio, June 29, 1833; attended the public schools; was graduated from Farmer's College, near Cincinnati; took charge of Pleasant Hill Academy and taught two years; studied law; was admitted to the bar in 1857 and commenced practice in Batavia; during the Civil War enlisted as a private in

Company E, Twenty-second Regiment, Ohio Volunteer Infantry, April 14, 1861; appointed orderly sergeant and afterward elected captain of the company; discharged August 16, 1861; probate judge of Clermont County 1864-1867; served nine years on the board of education; delegate to the Republican National Convention in 1868; elected as a Republican to the Fifty-third and Fifty-fourth Congresses (March 4, 1893-March 3, 1897); unsuccessful candidate for renomination in 1896; resumed the practice of law in Batavia, Ohio; died in Batavia, Ohio, August 13, 1907; interment in Union Cemetery.

**HULING, James Hall,** a Representative from West Virginia; born in Williamsport, Lycoming County, Pa., March 24, 1844; attended the public schools and Dickinson Seminary in Williamsport, Pa.; served in the Pennsylvania Cavalry in 1863; engaged in the lumber business; moved to West Virginia in 1870, where he continued in the lumber business until 1874; mayor of Charleston, W.Va., 1884-1888; declined a renomination; elected as a Republican to the Fifty-fourth Congress (March 4, 1895-March 3, 1897); resumed business in Charleston, W.Va., where he died April 23, 1918; interment in Pleasant View Cemetery.

**HULINGS, Willis James,** a Representative from Pennsylvania; born in Rimersburg, Clarion County, Pa., July 1, 1850; attended the public schools and Kittanning Academy; studied law; was admitted to practice in Pennsylvania, West Virginia, and Arizona; became a civil engineer and engaged in mining and the petroleum business; elected as a Republican to the Pennsylvania house of representatives and served from 1881 to 1887; member of the National Guard of Pennsylvania 1876-1912, serving in the various grades from private to brigadier general; served in the war with Spain; member of the Pennsylvania senate 1906-1910; elected as a Progressive to the Sixty-third Congress (March 4, 1913-March 3, 1915); unsuccessful candidate for reelection in 1914 to the Sixty-fourth Congress; elected as a Republican to the Sixty-sixth Congress (March 4, 1919-March 3, 1921); unsuccessful candidate for reelection in 1920 to the Sixty-seventh Congress; died in Oil City, Pa., August 8, 1924; interment in Grove Hill Cemetery.

**HULL, Cordell,** a Representative and a Senator from Tennessee; born in Olympus, Overton (now Pickett) County, Tenn., October 2, 1871; attended normal school and graduated from the law department of Cumberland University, Lebanon, Tenn., in 1891; was admitted to the bar the same year and commenced practice in Celina, Tenn.; member, Tennessee State house of representatives, 1893-1897; during the Spanish-American War served with the rank of captain; judge of the fifth judicial circuit of Tennessee, 1903-1906; elected as a Democrat to the Sixtieth and to the six succeeding Congresses (March 4, 1907-March 3, 1921); unsuccessful candidate for reelection in 1920 to the Sixty-seventh Congress; chairman of the Democratic National Executive Committee, 1921-1924; again elected to the Sixty-eighth and to the three succeeding Congresses (March 4, 1923-March 3, 1931); was not a candidate for renomination in 1930 to the House of Representatives, but was elected to the United States Senate, and served from March 4, 1931 to March 3, 1933, when he resigned to become Secretary of State; appointed Secretary of State in the Cabinet of President Franklin D. Roosevelt on March 4, 1933, and served until his resignation on December 1, 1944; known as "the Father of the United Nations"; awarded the Nobel Peace Prize in 1945; retired and resided in Washington, D.C., until his death there on July 23, 1955; interment in the Central Burial Vault of the Chapel of St. Joseph of Arimathea in the Washington Cathedral, Washington, D.C.

Bibliography: *DAB*; Hull, Cordell. *Memoirs of Cordell Hull.* New York: McMillan Company, 1948; Pratt, Julian. *Cordell Hull, 1933-1944.* 2 vols., New York: Cooper Square Publishers, 1964.

**HULL, Harry Edward,** a Representative from Iowa; born near Belvidere, Allegany County, N.Y., on March 12, 1864; moved with his parents to Cedar Rapids, Iowa, in 1873; attended the grammar and high schools; employed as a clerk and bookkeeper for a grain company; moved to Palo, Iowa, in 1883, and to Williamsburg, Iowa, in 1884 and engaged in the grain business; also engaged in the manufacture of brick and tile; president of the Williamsburg Telephone Co.; alderman of Williamsburg, 1887-1889; mayor of Williamsburg, 1889-1901; postmaster from 1901 to 1914; president of the Williamsburg Fair Association, 1900-1915; elected as a Republican to the Sixty-fourth and to the four succeeding Congresses (March 4, 1915-March 3, 1925); unsuccessful candidate for renomination in 1924 to the Sixty-ninth Congress; appointed by President Calvin Coolidge on May 15, 1925, as Commissioner General of Immigration and served until 1933, when he retired; continued to reside in Washington, D.C., until his death there on January 16, 1938; interment in Oak Hill Cemetery, Williamsburg, Iowa.

**HULL, John Albert Tiffin,** a Representative from Iowa; born in Sabina, Clinton County, Ohio, May 1, 1841; moved with his parents to Iowa in 1849; attended the public schools, Indiana Asbury (now De Pauw) University, Greencastle, Ind., and Iowa Wesleyan College at Mount Pleasant; was graduated from the Cincinnati (Ohio) Law School in the spring of 1862; was admitted to the bar the same year and commenced practice in Des Moines, Iowa; during the Civil War enlisted in the Twenty-third Regiment, Iowa Volunteer Infantry, in July 1862; first lieutenant and captain; resigned on account of wounds in October 1863; secretary of the Iowa senate in 1872 and reelected in 1874, 1876, and 1878; secretary of state in 1878 and reelected in 1880 and 1882; lieutenant governor in 1885 and reelected in 1887; engaged in agricultural pursuits and banking; elected as a Republican to the Fifty-second and to the nine succeeding Congresses (March 4, 1891-March 3, 1911); chairman, Committee on Military Affairs (Fifty-fourth through Sixty-first Congresses); unsuccessful candidate for renomination in 1910 to the Sixty-second Congress; resumed the practice of law in Washington, D.C.; retired in 1916, and died in Clarendon, Va., September 26, 1928; interment in Arlington National Cemetery, Va.

**HULL, Merlin,** a Representative from Wisconsin; born in Warsaw, Kosciusko County, Ind., December 18, 1870; attended Gale College, Galesville, Wis., and Columbian (now George Washington) University, Washington, D.C.; received a law degree from De Pauw University, Greencastle, Ind., in 1890; was admitted to the bar in 1894 and commenced practice in Black River Falls, Wis.; publisher of the Jackson County Journal, 1904-1926, and of the Banner-Journal, 1926-1953; also engaged in agricultural pursuits; district attorney of Jackson County, 1907-1909; member of the Wisconsin State assembly, 1909-1915, serving as speaker in 1913; secretary of state of Wisconsin, 1917-1921; elected as a Republican to the Seventy-first Congress (March 4, 1929-March 3, 1931); unsuccessful candidate for renomination, and unsuccessful Independent candidate for reelection in 1930 to the Seventy-second Congress; resumed former business pursuits; elected as a Progressive to the Seventy-fourth and to the five succeeding Congresses; affiliated with the Republican Party in March 1946; elected as a Republican to the Eightieth and to the three succeeding Congresses, and served from January 3, 1935 until his death in La Crosse, Wis., May 17, 1953; interment in Oak Grove Cemetery.

**HULL, Morton Denison,** a Representative from Illinois; born in Chicago, Ill., January 13, 1867; attended the public schools and Phillips Exeter Academy, Exeter, N.H., in 1885; was graduated from Harvard University in 1892; was admitted to the bar in 1892 and commenced the practice of law in Chicago, Ill.; also financially interested in various manufacturing concerns; member, Illinois State house of representatives, 1906-1914; Illinois State senator,

1915-1922; unsuccessful candidate for nomination in 1916 for Governor; delegate to the Republican National Convention of 1916; served as trustee of the Meadville (Pa.) Theological Seminary; delegate to the State constitutional convention in 1920; elected as a Republican to the Sixty-eighth Congress to fill the vacancy caused by the death of James R. Mann; reelected to the Sixty-ninth and to the three succeeding Congresses, and served from April 3, 1923 to March 3, 1933; was not a candidate for renomination in 1932 to the Seventy-third Congress; resumed his former pursuits; died at his summer home in Bennington, Vt., August 20, 1937; remains were cremated and the ashes placed in a crypt in the First Unitarian Church, Chicago, Ill.

**HULL, Noble Andrew,** a Representative from Florida; born in Little York, Camden County, Ga., March 11, 1827; attended the county schools and Chatham Academy, Savannah, Ga.; engaged in mercantile pursuits in Savannah in 1845; moved to Florida in 1851 and engaged in business in Columbia County; when Suwanee County was formed was elected sheriff; member of the Florida State house of representatives, 1860-1861; during the Civil War served as captain of Company H, First Florida Cavalry, in the Confederate Army; engaged in mercantile pursuits in Jacksonville and Sanford, Seminole County; Lieutenant Governor of Florida from 1877 until 1879, when he resigned to take his seat in Congress; presented credentials as a Democratic Member-elect to the Forty-sixth Congress, and served from March 4, 1879 to January 22, 1881, when he was succeeded by Horatio Bisbee, Jr., who contested his election; resumed business activities in Jacksonville; assistant postmaster of Jacksonville, 1884-1888; clerk of Duval County circuit court, 1888-1900; declined to be a candidate for reelection; died in Jacksonville, Fla., January 28, 1907; interment in Evergreen Cemetery.

**HULL, William Edgar,** a Representative from Illinois; born in Lewistown, Fulton County, Ill., January 13, 1866; attended the common schools, Lewistown High School, and Illinois College at Jacksonville, Ill.; president of the Manito Chemical Co.; postmaster of Peoria, Ill., 1898-1906; delegate to the Republican National Conventions of 1916 and 1920; member of the board of directors of the Illinois Highway Improvement Association; elected as a Republican to the Sixty-eighth and to the four succeeding Congresses (March 4, 1923-March 3, 1933); unsuccessful candidate for renomination in 1932 to the Seventy-third Congress; resumed his former pursuits in Peoria, Ill.; died in a hospital in Toronto, Canada, May 30, 1942, while on a visit; interment in Oak Hill Cemetery, Lewistown, Ill.

**HULL, William Raleigh, Jr.,** a Representative from Missouri; born in Weston, Platte County, Mo., April 17, 1906; attended the public schools and graduated from Weston High School; engaged in farming; co-owner of Hull's Tobacco Warehouse, Weston, Mo.; director of First National Bank, Leavenworth, Kans.; mayor of Weston, Mo., in 1939 and 1940; elected as a Democrat to the Eighty-fourth and to the eight succeeding Congresses (January 3, 1955-January 3, 1973); was not a candidate for reelection in 1972 to the Ninety-third Congress; died in Kansas City, Mo., August 15, 1977; interment in Graceland Cemetery, Weston, Mo.

**HUMPHREY, Augustin Reed,** a Representative from Nebraska; born near Madison, Jefferson County, Ind., February 18, 1859; moved with his parents to Drakesville, Davis County, Iowa, in 1864; attended the public schools; was graduated from the State normal school at Bloomfield in 1881 and from the law department of the University of Iowa at Iowa City in 1882; was admitted to the bar in 1882 and commenced practice at Broken Bow, Custer County, Nebr., in 1885; homesteaded in Custer County in 1886; delegate to every Republican State convention 1887-1936; engaged in agricultural and stock-raising pursuits; commissioner of public lands and buildings of Nebraska 1891-1895; president of the board of

education 1898-1914; judge of probate 1906-1910; mayor in 1916 and 1917; moved to his ranch on the South Loup River in 1920; elected as a Republican to the Sixty-seventh Congress to fill the vacancy caused by the death of Moses P. Kinkaid and served from November 7, 1922, to March 3, 1923; declined to be a candidate for renomination in 1922 to the Sixty-eighth Congress; resumed the practice of law in Broken Bow; died in Fort Collins, Colo., while on a visit, December 10, 1937; interment in Broken Bow Cemetery, Broken Bow, Nebr.

**HUMPHREY, Charles,** a Representative from New York; born in Little Britain, Orange County, N.Y., February 14, 1792; moved to Newburgh, N.Y., at an early age and attended the Newburgh Academy; commenced the study of law; entered the United States Army at the beginning of the War of 1812 as first sergeant of Newburgh Company Number Five; commissioned captain in the Forty-first Regiment, United States Infantry, on August 15, 1813; resumed the study of law; was admitted to the bar in Newburgh, N.Y., January 11, 1816; moved to Ithaca, N.Y., in 1818 and engaged in the practice of law; elected to the Nineteenth Congress (March 4, 1825-March 3, 1827); president of the village of Ithaca in 1828 and 1829; elected surrogate of Tompkins County and served from March 4, 1831, to January 8, 1834; member of the State assembly 1834-1836 and in 1842; speaker of the assembly in 1835 and 1836; appointed clerk of the New York Supreme Court in 1843 and held that position until 1847; died in Albany, N.Y., April 17, 1850; interment in City Cemetery, Ithaca, Tompkins County, N.Y.

**HUMPHREY, Gordon John,** a Senator from New Hampshire; born in Bristol, Hartford County, Conn., October 9, 1940; attended the public schools; attended George Washington University, Washington, D.C., 1962-1963, University of Maryland, College Park, 1961-1962, and Burnside-Ott Aviation Institute, 1962; served in the United States Air Force, 1958-1962; professional pilot, 1964-1978; elected as a Republican to the United States Senate in 1978, reelected in 1984, and served from January 3, 1979 to December 4, 1990, was not a candidate for reelection in 1990; member, New Hampshire State senate; is a resident of Chichester, N.H.

**HUMPHREY, Herman Leon,** a Representative from Wisconsin; born in Candor, Tioga County, N.Y., March 14, 1830; attended the common schools and also the Cortland Academy for one year; became a clerk in Ithaca, N.Y.; after several years in business he studied law; was admitted to the bar in July 1854 and in January 1855 moved to Hudson, Wis., where he commenced practice; appointed district attorney of St. Croix County; appointed county judge to fill a vacancy in the fall of 1860 and in the spring of 1861 was elected for the full term of four years, but resigned that office in February 1862; served in the State senate in 1862 and 1863; mayor of Hudson one year; elected in the spring of 1866 judge of the eighth judicial circuit of Wisconsin and reelected in 1872; elected as a Republican to the Forty-fifth, Forty-sixth, and Forty-seventh Congresses (March 4, 1877-March 3, 1883); unsuccessful candidate for renomination in 1882 to the Forty-eighth Congress; resumed the practice of law in Hudson, St. Croix County, Wis.; member of the State assembly in 1887; died in Hudson, Wis., June 10, 1902; interment in Willow River Cemetery.

**HUMPHREY, Hubert Horatio, Jr.** (husband of Muriel Buck Humphrey), a Senator from Minnesota and a Vice President of the United States; born in Wallace, Codington County, S.Dak., May 27, 1911; attended the public schools of Doland, S.Dak., where his family had moved; graduated from Denver (Colo.) College of Pharmacy in 1933 and worked in the family drugstore, Huron, S.Dak., 1933-1937; B.A., University of Minnesota, 1939; M.A., University of Louisiana, 1940; pharmacist with the Humphrey Drug Co., Huron, S.Dak., 1933-1937; assistant instructor of political science at the University of Louisiana, 1939-1940, and at the

University of Minnesota, 1940-1941; State director of war production training and reemployment, and State chief of Minnesota war service program, 1942; assistant director, War Manpower Commission, 1943; professor of political science at Macalester (Minn.) College, 1943-1944; radio news commentator, 1944-1945; State campaign manager, Roosevelt-Truman committee, 1944; mayor of Minneapolis from July 2, 1945 until his resignation on December 1, 1948, having been elected Senator; elected as a Democrat to the United States Senate in 1948; reelected in 1954, and 1960, and served from January 3, 1949 until December 29, 1964, when he resigned to become Vice President; unsuccessful candidate for the Democratic presidential nomination in 1960; Democratic whip 1961-1964; chairman, Select Committee on Disarmament (Eighty-fourth and Eighty-fifth Congresses); elected Vice President of the United States on the Democratic ticket with President Lyndon B. Johnson in 1964, and served from January 20, 1965 until January 20, 1969; unsuccessful Democratic candidate for election for President of the United States in 1968; resumed teaching at Macalester College and the University of Minnesota, 1969-1970; chairman, board of consultants, Encyclopedia Britannica Educational Corp.; unsuccessful candidate for the Democratic presidential nomination in 1972; elected in 1970 to the United States Senate; reelected in 1976, and served from January 3, 1971 until his death; the post of Deputy President pro tempore of the Senate was created for him, and he held it from January 5, 1977 until his death in Waverly, Minn., January 13, 1978; chairman, Joint Economic Committee (Ninety-fourth Congress); unprecedented sessions of the House and Senate were held in his honor in October 1977, when he was gravely ill; lay in state in the Rotunda of the Capitol; interment in Lakewood Cemetery, Minneapolis, Minn.

**Bibliography:** *DAB*; Humphrey, Hubert H. *The Education of a Public Man: My Life and Politics*. 1976. Reprint. Minneapolis: University of Minnesota Press, 1991; Solberg, Carl. *Hubert Humphrey: A Biography*. New York: W.W. Norton and Company, 1984.

**HUMPHREY, James,** a Representative from New York; born in Fairfield, Fairfield County, Conn., on October 9, 1811; pursued classical studies; was graduated from Amherst (Mass.) College in 1831; studied law; was admitted to the bar and practiced; moved to Louisville, Ky., in 1837 and one year later to Brooklyn, N.Y.; elected as a Republican to the Thirty-sixth Congress (March 4, 1859-March 3, 1861); unsuccessful candidate for reelection in 1860 to the Thirty-seventh Congress and for election in 1862 to the Thirty-eighth Congress; elected to the Thirty-ninth Congress and served from March 4, 1865, until his death in Brooklyn, N.Y., June 16, 1866; chairman, Committee on Expenditures in the Department of the Navy (Thirty-ninth Congress); interment in Greenwood Cemetery.

**HUMPHREY, James Morgan,** a Representative from New York; born in Holland, Erie County, N.Y., September 21, 1819; attended the common schools; studied law; was admitted to the bar in 1847 and commenced practice in East Aurora, Erie County, N.Y.; district attorney for Erie County 1857-1859; member of the State senate in 1863 and 1864; elected as a Democrat to the Thirty-ninth and Fortieth Congresses (March 4, 1865-March 3, 1869); was not a candidate in 1869 for renomination; appointed to the superior court of Buffalo, N.Y., in 1871 and served until January 1, 1873; practiced his profession in Buffalo from 1873 to 1894, when he retired; died in Buffalo, N.Y., February 9, 1899; interment in Forest Lawn Cemetery.

**HUMPHREY, Muriel Buck** (wife of Hubert Horatio Humphrey, Jr., now Muriel Humphrey Brown), a Senator from Minnesota; born Muriel Fay Buck in Huron, Beadle County, S.Dak., February 20, 1912; educated in the public schools; attended Huron College; appointed as a Democrat to the United States Senate by the Governor, January 25, 1978, to fill the vacancy caused by the death of her husband, Hubert Horatio Humphrey, Jr., and served from January 25, 1978, to November 7, 1978; was not a candidate for election to the unexpired term; is a resident of Excelsior, Minn.

**HUMPHREY, Reuben,** a Representative from New York, born in West Simsbury, Hartford County, Conn., September 2, 1757; completed preparatory studies; enlisted in the Revolutionary War as a private; mustered out as captain; held several local offices; keeper of Newgate State Prison in Simsbury, Conn., for five years; located near Marcellus, Onondaga County, N.Y., in 1801; first county judge 1804-1807; elected as a Republican to the Tenth Congress (March 4, 1807-March 3, 1809); was not a candidate for renomination in 1808 to the Eleventh Congress; member of the State senate 1811-1815; engaged in agricultural pursuits; died near Marcellus, August 12, 1831; interment in the Old Village Cemetery.

**HUMPHREY, William Ewart,** a Representative from Washington; born near Alamo, Montgomery County, Ind., March 31, 1862; attended the common schools; was graduated from Wabash College, Crawfordsville, Ind., in 1887; studied law; was admitted to the bar in 1887 and commenced practice in Crawfordsville; moved to Seattle, Wash., in 1893 and continued the practice of law; corporation counsel of the city of Seattle 1898-1902; elected as a Republican to the Fifty-eighth and to the six succeeding Congresses (March 4, 1903-March 3, 1917); did not seek renomination in 1916 to the House of Representatives, having become a Senatorial aspirant; resumed the practice of law in Seattle; appointed February 25, 1925, by President Calvin Coolidge as a member of the Federal Trade Commission and served until September 1933; died in Washington, D.C., February 14, 1934; interment in Oak Hill Cemetery, Crawfordsville, Ind.

**HUMPHREYS, Andrew,** a Representative from Indiana; born near Knoxville, Tenn., March 30, 1821; moved with his parents to Owen County, Ind., in 1829; afterwards moved to Putnam County and located near Manhattan; attended the common schools; moved to Greene County in 1842; member of the State house of representatives 1849-1852 and from January 8 to March 9, 1857; appointed Indian agent for Utah by President Buchanan in 1857; delegate to the Democratic National Convention in 1872 and 1888; served in the State senate 1874-1876, 1878-1882, and 1896-1900; elected as a Democrat to the Forty-fourth Congress to fill the vacancy caused by the resignation of James D. Williams and served from December 5, 1876, to March 3, 1877; resumed agricultural pursuits in Greene County, Ind.; attended almost every Democratic State convention during his political life; died in Linton, Ind., June 14, 1904; interment in Moss Cemetery.

**HUMPHREYS, Benjamin Grubb** (father of William Yerger Humphreys), a Representative from Mississippi; born in Claiborne County, Miss., August 17, 1865; attended the public schools at Lexington, Miss., and the University of Mississippi at Oxford; engaged in mercantile pursuits; studied law; was admitted to the bar in 1891 and commenced practice in Greenwood, Miss.; superintendent of education for Leflore County, 1892-1896; district attorney for the fourth district of Mississippi from 1895 until 1903; raised a company in April 1898 for service in the Spanish-American War and was its first lieutenant, serving under Major General Fitzhugh Lee in Florida during the entire war; delegate to the Democratic National Convention of 1920; elected as a Democrat to the Fifty-eighth and to the ten succeeding Congresses and served from March 4, 1903, until his death in Greenville, Miss., October 16, 1923; chairman, Committee on Territories (Sixty-second Congress), Committee on Flood Control (Sixty-fourth and Sixty-fifth Congresses); interment in Greenville Cemetery.

**HUMPHREYS, Charles,** a Delegate from Pennsylvania; born in Haverford, Delaware County, Pa., September 19, 1714; completed preparatory studies; engaged in milling; member of the Provincial Congress 1764-1774; Member of the Continental Congress 1774-1776; voted against the Declaration of Independence as he was a Quaker and opposed to war; died in Haverford, Pa., March 11, 1786; interment in Old Haverford Meeting House Cemetery.

**HUMPHREYS, Parry Wayne,** a Representative from Tennessee; born in Staunton, Va., in 1778; moved with his family to Kentucky in 1789 and later settled in Tennessee; completed preparatory studies; studied law; was admitted to the bar in 1801 and commenced practice in Nashville, Tenn.; judge of the superior court of Tennessee 1807-1809; judge of the State judicial circuit 1809-1813; elected as a Republican to the Thirteenth Congress (March 4, 1813-March 3, 1815); unsuccessful candidate for election to the United States Senate in 1817; again judge of the State judicial circuit 1818-1836; moved to Hernando, De Soto County, Miss., and engaged in banking until his death there February 12, 1839; interment in the Methodist Cemetery.

**HUMPHREYS, Robert,** a Senator from Kentucky; born in Fulgham, Hickman County, Ky., August 20, 1893; educated in public schools and graduated from Marvin College, Clinton, Ky., in 1914; attended the University of Wisconsin; during the First World War served overseas and was discharged as a first sergeant 1917-1919; registered pharmacist in the retail drug business in Mayfield, Ky., and later at Frankfort, Ky.; member, Kentucky house of representatives 1920; member, Kentucky senate 1932-1936; president pro tempore of Kentucky senate in 1934 and clerk of three senate sessions 1936-1942; Kentucky highway commissioner 1936-1940; served as a captain in the Medical Corps during the Second World War 1943-1945; Kentucky highway commissioner 1955-1956, when he resigned to accept appointment June 21, 1956, as a Democrat to the United States Senate to fill the vacancy caused by the death of Alben W. Barkley; served from June 21, 1956, to November 6, 1956; was not a candidate for election to the vacancy; resumed retail drug business; resided in Frankfort, Ky., where he died December 31, 1977; interment in Highland Park Cemetery, Mayfield, Ky.

**HUMPHREYS, William Yerger** (son of Benjamin Grubb Humphreys), a Representative from Mississippi; born in Greenville, Washington County, Miss., September 9, 1890; attended the public schools and Sewanee Grammar School, Sewanee, Tenn.; studied law at George Washington University, Washington, D.C., 1911-1914, while in the employ of the United States House of Representatives as assistant superintendent of the House document room; was admitted to the bar on June 1, 1914, and commenced practice in Greenville, Miss.; served as first lieutenant in the Chemical Warfare Service of the United States Army during the First World War; elected as a Democrat to the Sixty-eighth Congress to fill the vacancy caused by the death of his father, Benjamin G. Humphreys, and served from November 27, 1923, to March 3, 1925; was not a candidate for renomination in 1924; resumed the practice of law in Greenville, Miss.; elected prosecuting attorney of Washington County in 1928 and served until his death in Greenville, Miss., on February 26, 1933; interment in Greenville Cemetery.

**HUNGATE, William Leonard,** a Representative from Missouri; born in Benton, Franklin County, Ill., December 14, 1922; moved with his parents to Bowling Green, Mo., in 1929; attended the public schools, Central Methodist College, Fayette, Mo., and the University of Michigan at Ann Arbor; A.B., University of Missouri, Columbia, 1943; served in the United States Army from September 1943 to January 1946, serving overseas as a private first class, with the Ninety-fifth Infantry Division; received Combat Infantry Badge, three Battle Stars, and Bronze Star; LL.B., Harvard University Law School, 1948, and J.D., 1969; was admitted to the bar in 1948 and began the practice of law in Troy, Mo.; served three terms as

prosecuting attorney of Lincoln County, and as special assistant attorney general from 1958 until his election to Congress; elected as a Democrat to the Eighty-eighth Congress, November 3, 1964, by special election to fill the vacancy caused by the death of Clarence Cannon, and at the same time elected to the Eighty-ninth Congress; reelected to the five succeeding Congresses, and served from November 3, 1964 to January 3, 1977; was not a candidate for reelection in 1976 to the Ninety-fifth Congress; professor of politics, University of Missouri at St. Louis, 1977-1979; resumed the practice of law in St. Louis, 1977-1979; confirmed by the United States Senate, September 25, 1979, to be United States district judge for the eastern district of Missouri; president, American Bar Association's National Conference of Federal Trial Judges, 1985-1986; is a resident of St. Louis County, Mo.

**Bibliography:** Hungate, William L. *It Wasn't Funny At The Time.* St. Louis, Mo.: Full Court Press, 1994; Hungate, William L. *Glimpses of Politics.* St. Louis, Mo.: Full Court Press, 1996.

**HUNGERFORD, John Newton,** a Representative from New York; born in Vernon, Oneida County, N.Y., December 31, 1825; completed preparatory studies; was graduated from Hamilton College at Clinton, N.Y., in 1846; settled in Corning, N.Y., in 1848 and engaged in the banking business; delegate to the Republican National Convention in 1872; elected as a Republican to the Forty-fifth Congress (March 4, 1877-March 3, 1879); resumed banking business; died in Corning, N.Y., April 2, 1883; interment in Glenwood Cemetery, Watkins Glen, N.Y.

**HUNGERFORD, John Pratt,** a Representative from Virginia; born in Leeds, Westmoreland County, Va., January 2, 1761; received an elementary education under private teachers; studied law; was admitted to the bar and practiced; served in the Revolutionary War; member of the house of delegates 1797-1801; member of the Virginia senate 1801-1809; presented credentials as a Republican Member-elect to the Twelfth Congress and served from March 4 to November 29, 1811, when he was succeeded by John Taliaferro, who contested his election; elected to the Thirteenth and Fourteenth Congresses (March 4, 1813-March 3, 1817); served in the War of 1812 as brigadier general of militia; again a member of the Virginia house of delegates 1823-1830; died at "Twiford," Westmoreland County, Va., December 21, 1833; interment in Hungerford Cemetery, Leedstown, Va.

**HUNGERFORD, Orville,** a Representative from New York; born in Farmington, Hartford County, Conn., October 29, 1790; attended the public schools; moved with his father to Watertown, N.Y., in 1804; clerked in a store at Burrville, N.Y., and subsequently engaged in mercantile pursuits at Watertown; cashier of the Jefferson County National Bank at Watertown 1820-1833; served as its president 1834-1845, and was a director at the time of his death; elected as a Democrat to the Twenty-eighth and Twenty-ninth Congresses (March 4, 1843-March 3, 1847); unsuccessful candidate for reelection in 1846 to the Thirtieth Congress; unsuccessful Democratic candidate for State comptroller in 1847; elected president of the Watertown & Rome Railroad Co. in 1847, in which capacity he served until his death in Watertown, N.Y., April 6, 1851; interment in Brookside Cemetery.

**HUNT, Carleton** (nephew of Theodore Gaillard Hunt), a Representative from Louisiana; born in New Orleans, La., January 1, 1836; attended the University Grammar School at New Orleans; was graduated from Harvard University in 1856 and from the law department of the University of Louisiana (now Tulane University) at New Orleans in 1858; was admitted to the bar the same year and practiced in New Orleans, La.; member of the convention of the Constitutional Union Party which met in Baton Rouge, La., in 1860; appointed in April 1861 first lieutenant in the Louisiana Regiment of Artillery, Confederate Army; administrator of the University of

Louisiana in 1866; appointed professor of admiralty and international law in the University of Louisiana in 1869 and later professor of civil law; dean of the law school of the university for ten years; chairman of the committee formed for the purpose of organizing the American Bar Association in 1878; elected as a Democrat to the Forty-eighth Congress (March 4, 1883-March 3, 1885); resumed the practice of his profession in New Orleans, La.; city attorney 1888-1892; died in New Orleans, La., August 14, 1921; interment in St. Louis Cemetery No. 2.

Bibliography: *DAB.*

HUNT, Hiram Paine, a Representative from New York; born in Pittstown, Rensselaer County, N.Y., May 23, 1796; attended the public schools and was graduated from Union College, Schenectady, N.Y., in 1816; studied law at the Litchfield Law School; was admitted to the bar in May 1819 and commenced practice in Pittstown, N.Y.; served as town clerk of Pittstown in 1822; moved to Lansingburgh, N.Y., in 1825 and to Troy, N.Y., in 1831, where he continued the practice of law; elected as a Whig to the Twenty-fourth Congress (March 4, 1835-March 3, 1837); unsuccessful candidate for reelection in 1836 to the Twenty-fifth Congress; elected to the Twenty-sixth and Twenty-seventh Congresses (March 4, 1839-March 3, 1843); was not a candidate for renomination in 1842; resumed the practice of his profession in Troy, Rensselaer County, N.Y.; moved to New York City and continued the practice of law until his death on August 14, 1865.

HUNT, James Bennett, a Representative from Michigan; born in Demerara, British Guiana, South America, August 13, 1799; returned with his father to New York City in 1803; pursued an academic course; studied law; was admitted to the bar in 1824 and commenced practice in New York City; moved to Pontiac, Mich., in 1836; judge of the probate court in 1836; appointed commissioner of internal improvement by Governor Stevens T. Mason in March 1837; served as prosecuting attorney of Oakland County 1841-1843; elected as a Democrat to the Twenty-eighth and Twenty-ninth Congresses (March 4, 1843-March 3, 1847); appointed register of the land office at Sault Ste. Marie January 1848 and served until June 1849; returned to Pontiac and held the office of circuit court commissioner of Oakland County; moved to Washington, D.C., where he died on August 15, 1857; interment in Oak Hill Cemetery, Pontiac, Oakland County, Mich.

HUNT, John Edmund, a Representative from New Jersey; born in Lambertville, Hunterdon County, N.J., November 25, 1908; educated in the public schools of Hellertown and Bethlehem, Pa., Newark and Trenton, N.J.; attended Newark Business School for three years; graduate of the New Jersey State Police Academy, Trenton, N.J., the Federal Bureau of Investigation National Academy, Washington, D.C., the Harvard School of Police Science, Cambridge, Mass., and the United States Army Intelligence School, Harrisburg, Pa.; criminology consultant to the New Jersey State Police, 1930-1959; served in the United States Army, 1942-1946, commissioned a second lieutenant; served as Combat Intelligence Officer with Four Hundred and Fifty-sixth Bombardment Group; awarded Bronze Star Medal, Air Medal with two oak leaf clusters, Purple Heart, and Presidential Unit Citation with oak leaf cluster; discharged with rank of major; lieutenant colonel, Military Intelligence, United States Army Reserve, 1946-1963; elected sheriff of Gloucester County, N.J., in 1959 and reelected in 1962; elected to the New Jersey State senate in 1963 and reelected in 1965; elected as a Republican to the Ninetieth and to the three succeeding Congresses (January 3, 1967-January 3, 1975); unsuccessful candidate for reelection in 1974 to the Ninety-fourth Congress; was a resident of Pitman, N.J.; died September 22, 1989.

HUNT, John Thomas, a Representative from Missouri; born in St. Louis, Mo., February 2, 1860; attended the common schools; in his youth was a professional ball player and umpire; became a stonecutter and later a stone contractor; elected as a Democrat to the Fifty-eighth and Fifty-ninth Congresses (March 4, 1903-March 3, 1907); unsuccessful candidate for renomination in 1906 to the Sixtieth Congress, and for nomination in 1908 to the Sixty-first Congress; resumed the business of stone contractor; died in St. Louis, Mo., November 30, 1916; interment in Calvary Cemetery.

HUNT, Jonathan, a Representative from Vermont; born in Vernon, Windham County, Vt., August 12, 1787; was graduated from Dartmouth College, Hanover, N.H., in 1807; studied law; was admitted to the bar and commenced practice in Brattleboro, Vt., in 1812; first president of the Old Brattleboro Bank in 1821; member of the State house of representatives in 1811, 1816, 1817, and 1824; elected to the Twentieth, Twenty-first, and Twenty-second Congresses, and served from March 4, 1827, until his death in Washington, D.C., May 15, 1832; interment in Brattleboro, Vt.

HUNT, Lester Callaway, a Senator from Wyoming; born in Isabel, Edgar County, Ill., July 8, 1892; attended the public schools and Wesleyan University, Bloomington, Ill., 1912-1913; graduated from the St. Louis University College of Dentistry in 1917; moved to Wyoming in 1917 and commenced the practice of dentistry in Lander; during the First World War served in the United States Army Dental Corps, 1917-1919, rising to major; after postgraduate study at Northwestern University in 1920 resumed the practice of dentistry in Lander, Wyo.; president of the Wyoming State Board of Dental Examiners, 1924-1928; member, Wyoming State house of representatives, 1933-1934; secretary of State of Wyoming, 1935-1943; elected Governor of Wyoming in 1942, reelected in 1946, and served from January 4, 1943 until his resignation January 3, 1949, having been elected Senator; chairman of the Governors Conference in 1948; elected as a Democrat to the United States Senate in 1948; served from January 3, 1949, until his death in Washington, D.C., June 19, 1954; had announced that he could not be a candidate for reelection; committed suicide in his Senate office; interment in Beth El Cemetery, Cheyenne, Wyo.

Bibliography: *DAB*; Ewig, Rick. "McCarthy Era Politics: The Ordeal of Senator Lester Hunt." *Annals of Wyoming* 55 (Spring 1983): 9-21.

HUNT, Samuel, a Representative from New Hampshire; born in Charlestown, Sullivan County, N.H., July 8, 1765; completed preparatory studies; studied law; was admitted to the bar in 1790 and commenced practice in Alstead, N.H.; moved to Keene, N.H., the same year and in 1795 abandoned the practice of law; moved to Charlestown, N.H., and engaged in agricultural pursuits; member of the State house of representatives in 1802 and 1803; elected as a Federalist to the Seventh Congress to fill the vacancy caused by the resignation of Joseph Peirce; reelected to the Eighth Congress and served from December 6, 1802, to March 3, 1805; unsuccessful candidate for renomination in 1804 to the Ninth Congress; founded a colony in Ohio; died in Gallipolis, Ohio, July 7, 1807; interment in Mound Cemetery, Marietta, Ohio.

HUNT, Theodore Gaillard (nephew of John Gaillard and uncle of Carleton Hunt), a Representative from Louisiana; born in Charleston, S.C., October 23, 1805; completed preparatory studies; was graduated from the law department of Columbia College, New York City; was admitted to the bar and commenced practice in Charleston, S.C.; moved to New Orleans, La., about 1830; district attorney for New Orleans; member of the State house of representatives from 1837 until his election to Congress; elected as a Whig to the Thirty-third Congress (March 4, 1853-March 3, 1855); judge of the first Louisiana district (then the criminal court of New Orleans) in 1859; colonel of the Fifth Louisiana Regiment, Confederate Army, in 1861 and 1862; appointed by Governor Henry W. Allen adjutant general of Louisiana with the rank of brigadier general, and remained in active service until the close of the Civil

War; died in New Orleans, La., November 15, 1893; interment in Metairie Cemetery.

**HUNT, Washington,** a Representative from New York; born in Windham, Greene County, N.Y., August 5, 1811; moved with his parents to Portage, Livingston County, N.Y., in 1818; completed preparatory studies; studied law; was admitted to the bar in 1834 and commenced practice in Lockport, N.Y.; unsuccessful candidate for election in 1836 to the Twenty-fifth Congress; appointed judge of the court of common pleas of Niagara County and served from January 30, 1836, to February 4, 1841; elected as a Whig to the Twenty-eighth and to the two succeeding Congresses (March 4, 1843-March 3, 1849); chairman, Committee on Commerce (Thirtieth Congress); was not a candidate for renomination in 1848 to the Thirty-first Congress; comptroller of New York in 1849 and 1850; elected Governor of New York in 1850 and served from January 1, 1851 to January 1, 1853; unsuccessful candidate for reelection in 1852; retired to his farm near Lockport; temporary chairman of the Whig National Convention of 1856; was tendered the Democratic nomination for Vice President in 1860 but declined; delegate to the Democratic National Convention of 1864; died in New York City on February 2, 1867; interment in Glenwood Cemetery, Lockport, N.Y.
Bibliography: *DAB*.

**HUNTER, Allan Oakley,** a Representative from California; born in Los Angeles, Calif., June 15, 1916; attended the public schools of Fresno, Calif.; was graduated from Fresno State College in 1937, and from the law school of the University of California in 1940; was admitted to the bar in 1940; special agent for the Federal Bureau of Investigation, 1940-1944; served in the United States Naval Reserve, assigned to the Office of Strategic Services in England and Germany with a special counter-intelligence unit attached to the Sixth Army Group, 1944-1946; commenced the practice of law in Fresno, Calif., in 1946; elected as a Republican to the Eighty-second and Eighty-third Congresses (January 3, 1951-January 3, 1955); unsuccessful candidate for reelection in 1954 to the Eighty-fourth Congress; general counsel with the Housing and Home Finance Agency, Washington, D.C., from January 1955 to July 1957, when he resigned to return to the practice of law; delegate to the Republican National Conventions of 1952 and 1960; chairman, California State commission of housing and community development, 1966-1969; collaborated in the development and operation of Rossmor Leisure World Communities, 1960-1970; president and chairman, Federal National Mortgage Association, 1970-1981; housing and financial consultant; was a resident of Bethesda, Md., until his death there on May 2, 1995.

**HUNTER, Andrew Jackson,** a Representative from Illinois; born in Greencastle, Putnam County, Ind., December 17, 1831; moved with his parents to Paris, Edgar County, Ill., in 1832; attended the common schools and Edgar Academy; engaged as a civil engineer 1852-1856; studied law; was admitted to the bar in 1856 and commenced practice in Paris; member of the State senate 1864-1868; member of the board of investigation of State institutions; unsuccessful candidate in 1870 to the Forty-second Congress and again, in 1882, to the Forty-eighth Congress; judge of the Edgar County court 1886-1892; elected as a Democrat to the Fifty-third Congress (March 4, 1893-March 3, 1895); unsuccessful candidate for reelection in 1894 to the Fifty-fourth Congress; elected to the Fifty-fifth Congress (March 4, 1897-March 3, 1899); unsuccessful candidate for reelection in 1898 to the Fifty-sixth Congress; delegate to the Democratic National Convention in 1908; died in Paris, Ill., January 12, 1913; interment in Edgar Cemetery.

**HUNTER, Duncan Lee,** a Representative from California; born in Riverside, Riverside County, Calif., May 31, 1948; attended the public schools; graduated Rubidoux High School, 1966; B.S. Western State University, San Diego, 1968; J.D., Western State University School of Law, 1976; served in the United States Army Airborne,

first lieutenant, 1969-1971; admitted to the California bar in 1976 and commenced practice in San Diego; elected as a Republican to the Ninety-seventh and to the seven succeeding Congresses (January 3, 1981-January 3, 1997); is a resident of El Cajon, Calif.

**HUNTER, John,** a Representative and a Senator from South Carolina; born in South Carolina in either 1732 or 1760; completed preparatory studies; engaged in agricultural pursuits near Newberry, S.C.; member, State house of representatives 1786-1792; Federalist presidential elector in 1792; elected to the Third Congress (March 4, 1793-March 3, 1795); elected as a Republican to the United States Senate to fill the vacancy caused by the resignation of Pierce Butler and served from December 8, 1796, to November 26, 1798, when he resigned; resumed agricultural pursuits on his plantation; died in 1802; interment in the family plot in the Presbyterian Church Cemetery, at Little River, S.C.

**HUNTER, John Feeney,** a Representative from Ohio; born in Ford City, Armstrong County, Pa., October 19, 1896; moved with his parents in 1907 to Toledo, Ohio, where he attended the public schools; was graduated from the law department of St. John's University, Toledo, Ohio, in 1918; was admitted to the bar the same year and commenced practice in Toledo; during the First World War enlisted in the United States Army on March 6, 1918, and served until honorably discharged on November 26, 1918; delegate to the Democratic State conventions in 1932, 1934, 1936, and 1938; alternate to the Democratic National Conventions of 1932 and 1936; member of the State house of representatives in 1933 and 1934; served in the State senate in 1935 and 1936; elected as a Democrat to the Seventy-fifth, Seventy-sixth, and Seventy-seventh Congresses (January 3, 1937-January 3, 1943); unsuccessful candidate for reelection in 1942 to the Seventy-eighth Congress, and for election in 1944 to the Seventy-ninth Congress; resumed the practice of law in Toledo, Ohio, and Washington, D.C.; died in Alexandria, Va., December 19, 1957; interment in Calvary Cemetery, Toledo, Ohio.

**HUNTER, John Ward,** a Representative from New York; born in Bedford (now a part of Brooklyn), N.Y., October 15, 1807; received a liberal schooling; clerk in a wholesale grocery store in New York City in 1824; clerk in the United States customhouse at New York City 1831-1836; assistant auditor of the customhouse 1836-1865; engaged in banking as treasurer of the Dime Savings Bank in Brooklyn; elected to the Thirty-ninth Congress to fill the vacancy caused by the death of James Humphrey and served from December 4, 1866, to March 3, 1867; censured by the House of Representatives on January 26, 1867, for the use of unparliamentary language; was not a candidate for renomination in 1866 to the Fortieth Congress; mayor of Brooklyn in 1875 and 1876; resumed banking; died in Brooklyn, N.Y., April 16, 1900; interment in Greenwood Cemetery.

**HUNTER, Morton Craig,** a Representative from Indiana; born in Versailles, Ripley County, Ind., on February 5, 1825; completed a preparatory course; was graduated from the law department of Indiana University at Bloomington in 1849; was admitted to the bar and practiced; member of the State house of representatives in 1858; enlisted in the Union Army on August 27, 1862; commanded the First Brigade, Third Division, Fourteenth Army Corps; brevetted brigadier general of Volunteers; honorably discharged on June 24, 1865; elected as a Republican to the Fortieth Congress (March 4, 1867-March 3, 1869); elected to the Forty-third and to the two succeeding Congresses (March 4, 1873-March 3, 1879); unsuccessful candidate for reelection in 1878 to the Forty-sixth Congress; operated a quarry in the Indiana limestone district; died in Bloomington, Ind., October 25, 1896; interment in Rose Hill Cemetery.

**HUNTER, Narsworthy,** a Delegate from Mississippi Territory; born in Virginia; captain in the militia organization of the district formed in 1793; commissioned inspector of the military posts on the east side of the Mississippi River; elected to the Seventh Congress and served from March 4, 1801, until his death in Washington, D.C., March 11, 1802; interment in the Congressional Cemetery.

**HUNTER, Richard Charles,** a Senator from Nebraska, born on a farm near Westpoint, Cuming County, Nebr., December 3, 1884; moved with his parents to Omaha, Nebr., in 1885; attended the public schools of Omaha; graduated from the University of Nebraska at Lincoln in 1909; attended the law school of Harvard University 1909-1910; was graduated from the law department of Columbia University, New York City, in 1911; was admitted to the bar the same year and commenced practice in Lincoln, Nebr.; moved to Omaha, Nebr., in 1912 and continued the practice of law; member, State house of representatives 1915-1917; judge of the municipal court of Omaha 1915-1917; unsuccessful candidate for election as attorney general of Nebraska in 1920 and as State railway commissioner in 1928; elected as a Democrat to the United States Senate to fill the vacancy caused by the death of Robert B. Howell and served from November 7, 1934, to January 3, 1935; was not a candidate for election in 1934 to the full term; resumed the practice of law; attorney general of Nebraska 1937-1938; died in Tucson, Ariz., January 23, 1941; interment in West Lawn Memorial Park, Omaha, Nebr.

**HUNTER, Robert Mercer Taliaferro,** a Representative and a Senator from Virginia; was born at "Mount Pleasant," near Loretto, Essex County, Va., April 21, 1809; tutored at home; graduated from the University of Virginia at Charlottesville in 1828; studied law; was admitted to the bar in 1830 and commenced practice at Lloyds; member, Virginia general assembly 1834-1837; elected as a States-Rights Whig to the Twenty-fifth, Twenty-sixth, and Twenty-seventh Congresses (March 4, 1837-March 3, 1843); Speaker of the House of Representatives in the Twenty-sixth Congress; unsuccessful candidate for reelection in 1842 to the Twenty-eighth Congress; elected to the Twenty-ninth Congress (March 4, 1845-March 3, 1847); chairman, Committee on the District of Columbia (Twenty-ninth Congress); elected to the United States Senate in 1846; reelected in 1852 and 1858, and served from March 4, 1847 to March 28, 1861, when he withdrew with other secessionist Senators; expelled from the Senate by a resolution of July 11, 1861, for support of the Confederacy; chairman, Committee on Public Buildings (Thirtieth through Thirty-second Congresses), Committee on Finance (Thirty-first through Thirty-sixth Congresses); delegate from Virginia to the Confederate Provincial Congress at Richmond; Confederate Secretary of State from July 1861 to March 1862; served in the Confederate Senate from Virginia in the First and Second Congresses 1862-1865 and was President pro tempore on various occasions; was one of the peace commissioners who met with President Abraham Lincoln in Hampton Roads in February 1865; briefly imprisoned at the end of the Civil War; treasurer of Virginia, 1874-1880; collector for the port of Tappahannock, Va. 1885; died on his estate "Fonthill," near Lloyds, Va., on July 18, 1887; interment in "Elmwood," the family burial ground, near Loretto, Va.

Bibliography: *DAB*; Fisher, John E. "Statesman of a Lost Cause: The Career of R.M.T. Hunter, 1859-1887." Ph.D. dissertation, University of Virginia, 1966; Moore, Richard Randall. "In Search of a Safe Government: A Biography of R.M.T. Hunter of Virginia." Ph.D. dissertation, University of South Carolina, 1993; Scanlon, James. "A Life of Robert Hunter." Ph.D. dissertation, University of Virginia, 1969.

**HUNTER, Whiteside Godfrey,** a Representative from Kentucky; born near Belfast, Ireland, December 25, 1841; completed preparatory studies; immigrated to the United States in 1858 and settled in New Castle, Pa.; studied medicine in Philadelphia and was admitted to practice; surgeon in the Union Army during the Civil War; moved to Burkesville, Cumberland County, Ky., at the close of the war; member of the Kentucky house of representatives, 1874-1878; delegate to the Republican National Conventions of 1880 and 1892; appointed Minister to Guatemala and Honduras on November 8, 1897, and served until February 1903; elected as a Republican to the Fiftieth Congress (March 4, 1887-March 3, 1889); unsuccessful candidate for reelection in 1888 to the Fifty-first Congress, and for election in 1892 to the Fifty-third Congress; elected to the Fifty-fourth Congress (March 4, 1895-March 3, 1897); unsuccessful candidate for reelection in 1896 to the Fifty-fifth Congress; elected to the Fifty-eighth Congress to fill the vacancy caused by the death of Vincent S. Boreing, and served from November 10, 1903 to March 3, 1905; was not a candidate for renomination in 1904 to the Fifty-ninth Congress; interested in public utilities and the development of oil lands; resided in Louisville, Ky., until his death there on November 2, 1917; interment in Cave Hill Cemetery.

Bibliography: *DAB*.

**HUNTER, William,** a Senator from Rhode Island; born in Newport, R.I., November 26, 1774; attended Rogers School in Newport and graduated from Rhode Island College (later Brown University), Providence, R.I., in 1791; went abroad to study medicine, but preferred to study law at the Inner Temple, London; returned to Newport, R.I., in 1793; was admitted to the bar in 1795 and commenced practice in Newport; member of the State general assembly 1799-1812; elected as a Federalist to the United States Senate to fill the vacancy caused by the resignation of Christopher G. Champlin; reelected in 1814 and served from October 28, 1811, to March 3, 1821; chairman, Committee on Commerce and Manufactures (Fourteenth Congress); member, State house of representatives 1823-1825; resumed the practice of law in Newport; appointed by President Andrew Jackson Chargé d'Affaires to Brazil on June 28, 1834; elevated to Envoy Extraordinary and Minister Plenipotentiary in September 1841 and served until December 1843; died in Newport, R.I., December 3, 1849; interment in Trinity Church Graveyard.

Bibliography: *DAB*.

**HUNTER, William,** a Representative from Vermont; born in Sharon, Litchfield County, Conn., January 3, 1754; attended the common schools; resided near Fort Edward, N.Y., from 1763 until 1775, when he moved to Windsor, Vt.; served in the Revolutionary War as a sergeant and lieutenant under General Montgomery; member of the State house of representatives in 1795, 1807, and 1808; register of probate 1798-1801; judge of probate for the district of Windsor 1801-1816; assistant judge of the county court 1805-1816; member of the Vermont council of censors in 1806 and 1820; member of the executive council 1810-1813 and in 1815; elected as a Republican to the Fifteenth Congress (March 4, 1817-March 3, 1819); was not a candidate for reelection in 1818 to the Sixteenth Congress; died in Windsor, Windsor County, Vt., November 30, 1827; interment in Sheddsville Cemetery, West Windsor, Vt.

**HUNTER, William Forrest,** a Representative from Ohio; born in Alexandria, Va., December 10, 1808; received a common-school training; studied law; was admitted to the bar and commenced practice in Woodsfield, Ohio; elected as a Whig to the Thirty-first and Thirty-second Congresses (March 4, 1849-March 3, 1853); was not a candidate for renomination in 1852; died in Woodsfield Ohio, on March 30, 1874; interment in Woodsfield Cemetery.

**HUNTER, William H.,** a Representative from Ohio; born in Frankfort, Franklin County, Ky.; completed preparatory studies; studied law; was admitted to the bar and commenced practice in Tiffin, Ohio; moved to Norwalk, Huron County, Ohio, about 1825 and continued the practice of his profession for several years; moved to Sandusky, Ohio; appointed collector of customs at Sandusky in 1835; elected as a Democrat to the Twenty-fifth Congress (March 4, 1837-March 3, 1839); died under mysterious circumstances near Sandusky, Ohio, in 1842; interment in the Cholera Cemetery.

**HUNTINGTON, Abel,** a Representative from New York; born in Norwich, Conn., February 21, 1777; received a liberal schooling; moved to East Hampton, Long Island, N.Y., where he practiced medicine; member of the State senate in 1822; supervisor of East Hampton 1829-1832 and in 1844; elected as a Jacksonian to the Twenty-third and Twenty-fourth Congresses (March 4, 1833-March 3, 1837); chairman, Committee on Revisal and Unfinished Business (Twenty-fourth Congress); member of the State constitutional convention in 1846; collector of customs at Sag Harbor, N.Y., 1845-1849; died in East Hampton, Long Island, N.Y., May 18, 1858; interment in South End Cemetery.

**HUNTINGTON, Benjamin,** a Delegate and a Representative from Connecticut; born in Norwich, Conn., April 19, 1736; pursued academic studies; was graduated from Yale College in 1761; appointed surveyor of lands for Windham County in October 1764; studied law; was admitted to the bar in 1765 and commenced practice in Norwich; member of the State house of representatives 1771-1780 and served as speaker in 1778 and 1779; clerk of the State house of representatives in 1776 and 1777; delegate to the Provincial Congress at New Haven in January 1778; Member of the Continental Congress 1780, 1782, 1783, and 1788; member of the State senate 1781-1790 and 1791-1793; mayor of Norwich from 1784 to 1796, when he resigned; elected to the First Congress (March 4, 1789-March 3, 1791); judge of the superior court of the State 1793-1798; died in Rome, N.Y., October 16, 1800; interment in Old Colony Cemetery, Norwich, Conn.

**HUNTINGTON, Ebenezer,** a Representative from Connecticut; born in Norwich, Conn., December 26, 1754; pursued academic studies; was graduated from Yale College in 1775; served in the Revolutionary Army, first in the Lexington alarm in April 1775 and later with the Third and First Connecticut Regiments; commissioned a brigadier general, United States Army, July 19, 1798, when war with France was threatened; honorably discharged on June 15, 1800; elected as a Federalist to the Eleventh Congress to fill the vacancy caused by the resignation of Samuel W. Dana, and served from October 11, 1810 to March 3, 1811; elected to the Fifteenth Congress (March 4, 1817-March 3, 1819); died in Norwich, Conn., June 17, 1834; interment in Old Colony Cemetery.

**Bibliography:** Huntington, Ebenezer. *Letters Written by Ebenezer Huntington during the American Revolution.* New York: C.F. Heartman, 1915.

**HUNTINGTON, Jabez Williams,** a Representative and a Senator from Connecticut; born in Norwich, Conn., November 8, 1788; pursued classical studies; graduated from Yale College in 1806; taught in the Litchfield South Farms Academy one year; studied law; was admitted to the bar and commenced practice in Litchfield; member, State house of representatives 1829; elected to the Twenty-first, Twenty-second, and Twenty-third Congresses and served from March 4, 1829, to August 16, 1834, when he resigned to accept the appointment of judge of the State supreme court of errors; moved to Norwich in 1834; elected as a Whig to the United States Senate to fill the vacancy caused by the death of Thaddeus Betts; reelected, and served from May 4, 1840, until his death in Norwich, Conn., November 1, 1847; chairman, Committee on Commerce (Twenty-seventh and Twenty-eighth Congresses); interment in Old Colony Cemetery.

**HUNTINGTON, Samuel,** a Delegate from Connecticut; born in Windham (now Scotland), Conn., July 3, 1731; attended the common schools; learned the trade of cooper; studied law; was admitted to the bar in 1758 and commenced practice in Norwich, Conn., in 1758; executive councilor in 1763; member of the colonial assembly in 1764; appointed Crown attorney in 1765; judge of the superior court from 1774 to 1784 and served as chief justice in the last-named year; Member of the Continental Congress in 1776, 1778-1781 and 1783, and served as President from September 28, 1779, to July 6, 1781, when he retired, receiving the thanks of the Congress, but was returned again for a short period in 1783; a signer of the Declaration of Independence; lieutenant governor of the State in 1785, and Governor from May 11, 1786 until his death in Norwich, Conn., January 5, 1796; interment in Old Colony Cemetery.

**Bibliography:** *DAB*; Dreher, George Kelsey. *Samuel Huntington, President of Congress longer than expected: A Narrative Essay on the Letters of Samuel Huntington, 1779-1781.* Midland, Tex.: Iron Horse Free Press, 1995.

**HUNTON, Eppa,** a Representative and a Senator from Virginia; born near Warrenton, Fauquier County, Va., September 22, 1822; attended New Baltimore Academy; taught school three years; studied law; was admitted to the bar in 1843 and commenced practice in Brentsville, Va.; served as colonel, and later general, in the Virginia militia; Commonwealth attorney for Prince William County 1849-1861; member of the Virginia convention at Richmond in February 1861 and advocated secession; entered the Confederate Army as colonel of the Eighth Regiment, Virginia Infantry; promoted to brigadier general on August 9, 1863 and served through the remainder of the Civil War; resumed the practice of law; elected as a Democrat to the Forty-third and to the three succeeding Congresses (March 4, 1873-March 3, 1881); was not a candidate for renomination in 1880; chairman, Committee on Revolutionary Pensions (Forty-fourth Congress), Committee on the District of Columbia (Forty-sixth Congress); appointed a member of the Electoral Commission created by act of Congress in 1877 to decide the contests in various States in the presidential election of 1876; resumed the practice of law; appointed and subsequently elected as a Democrat to the United States Senate to fill the vacancy caused by the death of John S. Barbour and served from May 28, 1892, to March 3, 1895; was not a candidate for renomination in 1894; resumed the practice of law in Warrenton, Va.; died in Richmond, Va., October 11, 1908; interment in Hollywood Cemetery.

**Bibliography:** *DAB*; Hunton, Eppa. *The Autobiography of Eppa Hunton.* Richmond: William Byrd Press, 1933.

**HUNTSMAN, Adam,** a Representative from Tennessee; born in Charlotte County, Va., February 11, 1786; moved to Jackson, Tenn.; elected as a Jacksonian to the Twenty-fourth Congress (March 4, 1835-March 3, 1837); unsuccessful candidate for reelection in 1836 to the Twenty-fifth Congress; died August 23, 1849.

**Bibliography:** Mooney, Chase C. "The Political Career of Adam Huntsman." *Tennessee Historical Quarterly* 10 (June 1951): 99-126.

**HUOT, Joseph Oliva,** a Representative from New Hampshire; born in Laconia, Belknap County, N.H., August 11, 1917; educated at Sacred Heart Parochial School and Laconia High School; supervisor in tabulating department of a manufacturer of knitting machines 1935-1956; member of Laconia Board of Education 1953-1959; advertising manager of newspaper 1956-1964; general manager of a weekly newspaper 1959-1964; served as mayor of Laconia 1959-1963; Democratic candidate for Congress in 1962; delegate, Democratic National Convention, 1964; elected as a Democrat to the Eighty-ninth Congress (January 3, 1965-January 3, 1967); unsuccessful candidate for reelection in 1966 to the Ninetieth Congress; was a resident of Laconia, N.H., until his death there August 5, 1983; interment in Sacred Heart Cemetery, Laconia, N.H.

**HURD, Frank Hunt,** a Representative from Ohio; born in Mount Vernon, Knox County, Ohio, December 25, 1840; was graduated from Kenyon College, Gambier, Ohio, in 1858; studied law; was admitted to the bar in 1861 and practiced; prosecuting attorney of Knox County in 1863; member of the State senate in 1866; appointed to codify the criminal laws of Ohio in 1868; moved to Toledo, Ohio, in 1869; city solicitor of Toledo 1871-1873; unsuccessful Democratic candidate for election in 1872 to the Forty-third Congress; elected as a Democrat to the Forty-fourth Congress (March 4, 1875-March 3, 1877); unsuccessful candidate for reelection in 1876 to the Forty-fifth Congress; elected to the Forty-sixth Congress (March 4, 1879-March 3, 1881); unsuccessful candidate for reelection in 1880 to the Forty-seventh Congress; elected to the Forty-eighth Congress (March 4, 1883-March 3, 1885); unsuccessfully contested the election of Jacob Romeis to the Forty-ninth Congress; resumed the practice of law; unsuccessful Democratic candidate for election in 1886 to the Fiftieth Congress; continued the practice of law in Toledo, until his death on July 10, 1896; interment in Mound View Cemetery, Mount Vernon, Ohio.

Bibliography: Folk, Patrick A. "'Our Frank': The Congressional Career of Frank Hurd." *Northwest Ohio Quarterly* 41 (Spring 1969): 45-69; 42 (Summer 1970): 47-63; 47 (Fall 1975): 151-69; 48 (1975-1976): 24-34; 55-79, 143-52.

**HURLBUT, Stephen Augustus,** a Representative from Illinois; born in Charleston, S.C., November 29, 1815, completed preparatory studies; studied law; was admitted to the bar in 1837 and practiced; served as adjutant of a South Carolina regiment in the Florida War; moved to Belvidere, Ill., in 1845; Whig delegate to the State constitutional convention in 1847; presidential elector on the Whig ticket in 1848, and on the Republican ticket in 1868; member of the Illinois State house of representatives in 1859, 1861, and 1867; appointed brigadier general of Volunteers in the Union Army on May 17, 1861, and major general, September 17, 1862; mustered out on June 20, 1865; one of the founders of the Grand Army of the Republic, and served as commander in chief from 1866 to 1868; appointed Minister Resident to Colombia on April 22, 1869, and served until April 1872; elected as a Republican to the Forty-third and Forty-fourth Congresses (March 4, 1873-March 3, 1877); unsuccessful candidate for reelection as an independent Republican to the Forty-fifth Congress in 1876; appointed Minister to Peru on May 19, 1881, and served until his death in Lima, Peru, March 27, 1882; interment in Belvidere Cemetery, Belvidere, Ill.

Bibliography: *DAB*; Lash, Jeffrey Norman. "Stephen Augustus Hurlbut: A Military and Diplomatic Politician, 1815-1882." Ph.D. dissertation, Kent State University, 1980.

**HURLEY, Denis Michael,** a Representative from New York; born in the city of Limerick, Ireland, March 14, 1843; immigrated to the United States in 1850 with his parents, who settled in Brooklyn, N.Y.; moved to New York City in 1854; was educated in the public schools; returned to Brooklyn in 1866; learned the carpenter's trade; engaged in the building contractors' business; delegate to the Republican State conventions from 1879 to 1899; unsuccessful Republican candidate for member of the State assembly in 1880; elected as a Republican to the Fifty-fourth and Fifty-fifth Congresses and served from March 4, 1895, until his death; unsuccessful in 1898 for reelection to the Fifty-sixth Congress; died at Hot Springs, Va., February 26, 1899; interment in Holy Cross Cemetery, Brooklyn, N.Y.

**HUSTED, James William,** a Representative from New York; born in Peekskill, Westchester County, N.Y., March 16, 1870; attended private schools, the Peekskill Military Academy, and Cutler's School, New York City; was graduated from Phillips Academy, Andover, Mass., in 1888, from Yale University in 1892, and from the New York Law School in 1894; was admitted to the bar in 1894 and commenced practice in Peekskill, N.Y.; member of the

State assembly 1895-1897; moved to White Plains in 1897 and continued the practice of law; returned to Peekskill in 1902 and again practiced law; president of the village of Peekskill in 1903 and 1904; member and treasurer of the board of park commissioners from 1909 to 1920; unsuccessful candidate for election in 1912 to the Sixty-third Congress; elected as a Republican to the Sixty-fourth and to the three succeeding Congresses (March 4, 1915-March 3, 1923); was not a candidate for renomination in 1922 to the Sixty-eighth Congress; resumed the practice of law in Peekskill; also engaged in banking and served as president of the Peekskill Bank; died in New York City January 2, 1925; remains were cremated; interment of ashes in Hillside Cemetery, Peekskill, N.Y.

**HUSTING, Paul Oscar,** a Senator from Wisconsin; born in Fond du Lac, Fond du Lac County, Wis., April 25, 1866; moved with his parents to Mayville, Wis., in 1876; attended the public schools and the law school of the University of Wisconsin at Madison; was admitted to the bar in 1895 and commenced practice in Mayville, Wis.; district attorney of Dodge County 1902-1906; member, State senate 1907-1913; elected as a Democrat to the United States Senate in 1914 and served from March 4, 1915, until his accidental death while duck hunting on Rush Lake, near Picketts, Wis., on October 21, 1917; chairman, Committee to Investigate Trespassers Upon Indian Land (Sixty-fourth and Sixty-fifth Congresses), Committee on Fisheries (Sixty-fifth Congress); interment in Graceland Cemetery, Mayville, Wis.

**HUTCHESON, Joseph Chappell,** a Representative from Texas; born near Boydton, Mecklenburg County, Va., May 18, 1842; attended the common schools; was graduated from Randolph-Macon College, Ashland, Va., in 1861; enlisted as a private in the Twenty-first Virginia Regiment; served in the Valley of Virginia under Stonewall Jackson and surrendered at Appomattox, at which time he was in command of Company E, Fourteenth Virginia Regiment; was graduated from the law department of the University of Virginia at Charlottesville in 1866; was admitted to the bar in 1866 and commenced practice in Anderson, Grimes County, Tex.; moved to Houston, Tex., in 1874 and continued the practice of law; member of the State house of representatives in 1880; elected as a Democrat to the Fifty-third and Fifty-fourth Congresses (March 4, 1893-March 3, 1897); was not a candidate for renomination in 1896; resumed the practice of law in Houston, Tex.; died at his summer home on Signal Mountain, near Chattanooga, Tenn., May 25, 1924; interment in Glenwood Cemetery, Houston, Tex.

**HUTCHINS, John** (cousin of Wells Andrews Hutchins), a Representative from Ohio; born in Vienna, Trumbull County, Ohio, July 25, 1812; attended the district schools and Western Reserve College, Cleveland, Ohio; studied law; was admitted to the bar in 1837 and commenced practice in Warren, Trumbull County; clerk of the common pleas court for Trumbull County 1838-1843; member of the State house of representatives in 1849 and 1850; mayor of Warren two years; member of the Warren Board of Education six years; elected as a Republican to the Thirty-sixth and Thirty-seventh Congresses (March 4, 1859-March 3, 1863); chairman, Committee on Manufactures (Thirty-seventh Congress); unsuccessful candidate for renomination in 1862; resumed the practice of law in Warren; moved to Cleveland, Ohio, in 1868 and continued the practice of law; died in Cleveland, Ohio, November 20, 1891; interment in Lakeview Cemetery.

**HUTCHINS, Waldo,** a Representative from New York; born in Brooklyn, Windham County, Conn., September 30, 1822; was graduated from Amherst (Mass.) College in 1842; studied law; was admitted to the bar in 1845 and commenced practice in New York City; member of the State assembly in 1852; delegate to the State constitutional convention in 1867; park commissioner 1857-1869; elected as a Democrat to the Forty-sixth Congress to fill the vacancy caused by the death of Alexander Smith; reelected to the Forty-seventh and Forty-eighth Congresses and served from November 4, 1879, to March 3, 1885; was not a candidate for renomination in 1884; resumed the practice of law in New York City; appointed in 1887 member of the park commission and served until his death, February 8, 1891, in New York City; interment in Woodlawn Cemetery.

**HUTCHINS, Wells Andrews** (cousin of John Hutchins), a Representative from Ohio; born in Hartford, Trumbull County, Ohio, October 8, 1818; attended the public schools; taught school; studied law; was admitted to the bar in 1841 and commenced practice in Warren, Trumbull County, Ohio; moved to Portsmouth, Ohio, in 1842; member of the State house of representatives in 1852 and 1853; city solicitor of Portsmouth 1857-1861; United States provost marshal for Ohio in 1862; unsuccessful candidate in 1860 to the Thirty-seventh Congress; elected as a Democrat to the Thirty-eighth Congress (March 4, 1863-March 3, 1865); unsuccessful candidate in 1864 for reelection to the Thirty-ninth Congress and again in 1880 to the Forty-seventh Congress; resumed the practice of law in Portsmouth, Ohio, and died there January 25, 1895; interment in Greenlawn Cemetery.

**HUTCHINSON, Elijah Cubberley,** a Representative from New Jersey; born in Windsor, Mercer County, N.J., August 7, 1855; attended the public schools and Riders Business College, Trenton, N.J.; became a merchant miller in Hamilton Township; also interested in banking and in the manufacture of fertilizer; served as township clerk for three years; member of the New Jersey State house of assembly in 1895 and 1896; served in the State senate from 1899 to 1904, and was president of that body in 1903; State road commissioner, 1905-1908; elected as a Republican to the Sixty-fourth and to the three succeeding Congresses (March 4, 1915-March 3, 1923); unsuccessful candidate for reelection in 1922 to the Sixty-eighth Congress; resided in Trenton, N.J., until his death there on June 25, 1932; interment in Greenwood Cemetery.

**HUTCHINSON, J. Edward,** a Representative from Michigan; born in Fennville, Allegan County, Mich., October 13, 1914; graduated from Fennville High School in 1932, from the University of Michigan in Ann Arbor in 1936, and from the law school of the same university in 1938; was admitted to the bar in 1938 and began the practice of law in Allegan, Mich.; enlisted as a private in the United States Army in January 1941, served as a noncommissioned officer in the Fourteenth Coast Artillery, as a captain in the Transportation Corps, and was discharged in April 1946; elected to the Michigan State house of representatives in 1946 and 1948; served as State senator, 1951-1960; delegate to the Republican National Convention of 1948; chairman of the Republican State convention in April 1952; delegate and vice president, Michigan Constitutional convention, in 1961 and 1962; elected as a Republican to the Eighty-eighth and to the six succeeding Congresses (January 3, 1963-January 3, 1977); was not a candidate for reelection in 1976 to the Ninety-fifth Congress; was a resident of Fennville, Mich., until his death in Naples, Fla., on July 22, 1985.

**HUTCHINSON, John Guiher,** a Representative from West Virginia; born in Charleston, Kanawha County, W.Va., February 4, 1935; attended the public schools; B.S., West Virginia University, Morgantown, 1956; served in the United States Air Force, first lieutenant, 1956-1958; treasurer, city of Charleston, 1967-1971; mayor, city of Charleston, 1971-1980; elected as a Democrat to the Ninety-sixth Congress, by special election, June 3, 1980, to fill the vacancy caused by the death of Representative John M. Slack, Jr., and served from June 3, 1980, to January 3, 1981; was an unsuccessful candidate for reelection in 1980 to the Ninety-seventh Congress; vice president of an investment brokerage firm in Charleston, W.Va.; 1981 to present; is a resident of Charleston.

**HUTCHINSON, Young Timothy (Tim),** a Representative from Arkansas; born in Bentonville, Benton County, Ark., August 11, 1949; graduated from Springdale (Ark.) High School, 1967; B.A., Bob Jones University, Greenville, S.C., 1971; M.A., University of Arkansas, 1990; minister; co-owner and manager of radio station KBCV, 1982-1989; associate in Hendren Ford, Gravette, Ark.; adjunct instructor, John Brown University, Siloam Springs, Ark.; member, Arkansas State house of representatives, 1985-1993; elected as a Republican to the One Hundred Third and One Hundred Fourth Congresses (January 3, 1993-January 3, 1997); was not a candidate in 1996 for reelection to the House of Representatives, but was a candidate for election to the United States Senate; is a resident of Bentonville, Ark.

**HUTCHISON, Kathryn Ann Bailey (Kay),** a Senator from Texas; born in Galveston, Tex., July 22, 1943; attended the University of Texas, Austin, 1961-1964, B.A., 1992; J.D., University of Texas School of Law, 1967; political and legal correspondent, KPRC-TV, Houston, Tex.; member, Texas State house of representatives, 1973-1977; vice-chair, National Transportation Safety Board, and acting chair, 1976-1978; senior vice president and general counsel, Republic Bank Corp., 1979-1982; attorney, 1982-1990; former owner, McGraw Candies, Inc.; partner, Boyd-Levinson, Ltd.; co-founder, Fidelity National Bank, Dallas, Tex.; unsuccessful candidate for election in 1982 to the Ninety-eighth Congress; Texas State treasurer, 1991-1993; member, Texas Banking Board and Texas Bond Review Board, 1991-1993; elected as a Republican to the United States Senate, June 5, 1993, to fill the vacancy caused by the resignation of Lloyd M. Bentsen, Jr. for the term ending January 3, 1995; reelected in 1994 for the term ending January 3, 2001; is a resident of Dallas, Tex.

**HUTSON, Richard,** a Delegate from South Carolina; born in Prince William parish, South Carolina, July 9, 1748; pursued classical studies and was graduated from Princeton College in 1765; studied law; was admitted to the bar and practiced in Charleston, S.C.; member of the South Carolina State house of representatives, 1776-1779, 1781, 1782, 1785, and 1788; Member of the Continental Congress in 1778 and 1779, and signed the Articles of Confederation; captured at the fall of Charleston and was confined as a prisoner at St. Augustine, Fla., in 1780 and 1781; member of the Legislative Council of South Carolina, 1780-1782; Lieutenant Governor in 1782 and 1783; first intendant (administrative official) of Charleston in 1783 and 1784; chancellor of the court of chancery of South Carolina, 1784-1791; member of the State constitutional convention in 1788 which adopted the Federal Constitution; senior judge of the chancery court, 1791-1795; died in Charleston, S.C., on April 12, 1795; interment in the Perrineau family vault in Independent Congregational Church Cemetery.

**Bibliography:** *DAB.*

**HUTTO, Earl Dewitt,** a Representative from Florida; born in Midland City, Dale County, Ala., May 12, 1926; attended the public schools and graduated from Dale County High School, Ozark, Ala., in 1945; B.S., Troy State University, 1949; engaged in graduate work in broadcasting, Northwestern University, Evanston, Ill., 1951; served in United States Navy, 1944-1946; worked as sports director and president of radio stations, 1954-1974; owner of an advertising agency, 1973-1979; elected to the Florida State house of representatives, 1972, reelected in 1974 and 1976; elected as a Democrat to the Ninety-sixth and to the seven succeeding Congresses (January 3, 1979-January 3, 1995); was not a a candidate for reelection in 1994 to the One Hundred Fourth Congress; is a resident of Panama City, Fla.

**HUTTON, John Edward,** a Representative from Missouri; born in Polk County, Tenn., March 28, 1828; moved with his parents to Troy, Lincoln County, Mo., in 1831; attended the common schools; taught school and at the same time studied medicine; attended lectures at Pope's Medical College, St. Louis, Mo.; was graduated in medicine and began practice in Warrenton, Mo., in 1860; during the Civil War entered the Union Army and was commissioned colonel of the Fifty-ninth Regiment, Missouri Volunteer Infantry; studied law; was admitted to the bar in 1864 and commenced practice in Warrenton, Mo.; moved to Mexico, Mo., in 1865 and continued to practice law until 1873, when he became the owner and publisher of the Intelligencer, a Democratic newspaper; elected as a Democrat to the Forty-ninth and Fiftieth Congresses (March 4, 1885-March 3, 1889); was not a candidate for renomination in 1888; resumed his activities as a physician and also engaged in the practice of law; died in Mexico, Mo., December 28, 1893; interment in Elmwood Cemetery.

**HUYLER, John,** a Representative from New Jersey; born in New York City April 9, 1808; attended the common schools at Tenafly, N.J.; apprenticed as a mason and later engaged in contracting and building in New York City until 1846; moved to New Jersey and engaged in agricultural pursuits at Pollifly, Lodi Township; settled in the village of Hackensack, N.J., about 1855; engaged in the mercantile and lumber business; president of the board of freeholders of Bergen County; member of the State house of assembly 1849-1851, and served as speaker in 1851; judge of the court of appeals 1854-1857; elected as a Democrat to the Thirty-fifth Congress (March 4, 1857-March 3, 1859); unsuccessful candidate as a Lecompton Democrat for reelection in 1858 to the Thirty-sixth Congress; resumed the lumber business; assassinated in Hackensack, N.J., January 9, 1870; interment in New York Cemetery at Hackensack.

**HYDE, DeWitt Stephen,** a Representative from Maryland; born in Washington, D.C., March 21, 1909; attended the public schools; George Washington University, J.D., 1935; with the Farm Credit Administration for three years; admitted to the bar in 1935 and commenced the practice of law in Washington, D.C.; moved to Maryland in 1938 and continued law work; entered the United States Navy as a lieutenant (jg) in March 1943, served in the South Pacific, and was separated from the service as a lieutenant commander in May 1946; instructor of law, Benjamin Franklin University, Washington, D.C., 1946-1951; served in the State house of delegates 1947-1950; member of the State senate in 1951 and 1952; elected as a Republican to the Eighty-third, Eighty-fourth, and Eighty-fifth Congresses (January 3, 1953-January 3, 1959); unsuccessful candidate for reelection in 1958 to the Eighty-sixth Congress; engaged in the practice of law; in 1959 was appointed as associate judge of the District of Columbia Court of General Sessions; was a resident of Bethesda, Md., where he died on April 25, 1986.

**HYDE, Henry John,** a Representative from Illinois; born in Chicago, Cook County, Ill., April 18, 1924; graduated from St. George High School, Evanston, Ill., 1942; B.S.S., Georgetown University, Washington, D.C., 1947; J.D., Loyola University Law School, Chicago, 1949; admitted to the Illinois bar in 1950 and commenced practice in Chicago; served in United States Navy, 1944-1946; retired from Naval Reserve in 1968; member, Illinois house of representatives, 1967-1974, serving as majority leader, 1971-1972; delegate, Illinois State Republican conventions, 1958-1974; elected as a Republican to the Ninety-fourth and to the ten succeeding Congresses (January 3, 1975-January 3, 1997); chairman, Committee on the Judiciary (One Hundred Fourth Congress); is a resident of Bensenville, Ill.

**HYDE, Ira Barnes,** a Representative from Missouri; born near Guilford, Chenango County, N.Y., January 18, 1838; attended the public schools and the Norwich Academy; when fifteen years of age moved with his parents to East Cleveland, Cuyahoga County, Ohio, and later entered Oberlin (Ohio) College; studied law; was admitted to the bar by the Minnesota Supreme Court in 1861 and commenced

practice in St. Paul, Minn., in 1862; during the Civil War served in the Union Army; enlisted as a private in Company F, First Regiment of Minnesota Mounted Rangers, and served until the regiment was mustered out; also served in the campaigns against the Sioux Indians along the northwestern frontier; moved to Washington, D.C., in 1865 and resumed the practice of law; moved to Princeton, Mo., in 1866; appointed prosecuting attorney of Mercer County in 1872; delegate to many State conventions; elected as a Republican to the Forty-third Congress (March 4, 1873-March 3, 1875); unsuccessful candidate for reelection in 1874 to the Forty-fourth Congress; delegate to the Republican National Convention of 1884; resumed the practice of law in Princeton, Mo.; also engaged in banking; died in Princeton, Mo., December 6, 1926; interment in Princeton Cemetery.

**HYDE, Samuel Clarence,** a Representative from Washington; born in Fort Ticonderoga, Essex County, N.Y., April 22, 1842; moved to Wisconsin; attended the common schools; served in the Seventeenth Regiment, Wisconsin Volunteer Infantry, during the Civil War; spent several years as surveyor in northern Wisconsin and Michigan; studied law at the University of Iowa at Iowa City; was admitted to the bar in 1876 and commenced practice at Rock Rapids, Iowa; moved to the Territory of Washington in 1877 and practiced law at Puget Sound; moved to Spokane in 1880 and continued the practice of law; prosecuting attorney of Spokane County 1880-1886; elected as a Republican to the Fifty-fourth Congress (March 4, 1895-March 3, 1897); unsuccessful candidate for reelection in 1896 to the Fifty-fifth Congress; justice of the peace from 1904 until his death in Spokane, Wash., March 7, 1922; interment in Fairmount Cemetery.

**HYMAN, John Adams,** a Representative from North Carolina; born into slavery near Warrenton, Warren County, N.C., July 23, 1840; was sold and sent to Alabama; returned to North Carolina in March 1865 and engaged in agricultural pursuits; pursued elementary studies; delegate to the 1865 Freedmen's Convention of North Carolina, and to the 1867 Republican State convention; elected in November 1867 a delegate to the State constitutional convention of 1868; North Carolina State senator, 1868-1874; unsuccessful candidate in 1872 for nomination to the Forty-third Congress; elected as a Republican to the Forty-fourth Congress (March 4, 1875-March 3, 1877); unsuccessful candidate for renomination in 1876 to the Forty-fifth Congress; resumed agricultural pursuits and was engaged in the grocery business; special deputy collector of internal revenue for the fourth district of North Carolina from July 1, 1877, to June 30, 1878; moved to Maryland and worked as a mail clerks' assistant; moved to Washington, D.C. in 1889 and was employed in the seed dispensary of the Department of Agriculture; died in Washington, D.C., on September 14, 1891; interment in Harmony Cemetery.

**Bibliography:** Reid, George W. "Four in Black: North Carolina's Black Congressmen, 1874-1901." *Journal of Negro History* 64 (Summer 1979): 229-43.

**HYNEMAN, John M.,** a Representative from Pennsylvania; born in Reading, Berks County, Pa., about April 25, 1771; received a common-school education; member of the Pennsylvania house of representatives in 1809; clerk of the orphans' court 1810-1816; elected as a Republican to the Twelfth and Thirteenth Congresses and served from March 4, 1811, until his resignation August 2, 1813; was not a candidate for renomination in 1814; commissioned a brigadier general in the Pennsylvania Militia; surveyor of Berks County in 1816; died in Reading, Berks County, Pa., April 16, 1816; interment in the Trinity Lutheran Cemetery.

**HYNES, William Joseph,** a Representative from Arkansas; born in County Clare, Ireland, March 31, 1843; immigrated to the United States in 1854 and settled in New York; attended the public schools of Massachusetts; learned the art of printing; studied law;

was admitted to the bar in 1870 and commenced practice in Little Rock, Ark.; elected as a Liberal Republican to the Forty-third Congress (March 4, 1873-March 3, 1875); unsuccessful candidate for reelection in 1874 to the Forty-fourth Congress; moved to Chicago in 1876 and resumed the practice of his profession; retired from the practice of law in 1910 and moved to Los Angeles, Calif., where he remained until his death, April 2, 1915; interment in Calvary vault.

# I

**ICHORD, Richard Howard, II,** a Representative from Missouri; born in Licking, Texas County, Mo., June 27, 1926; attended the public schools; B.S., University of Missouri, 1949; J.D., University of Missouri School of Law, 1952; was admitted to the bar in 1952 and commenced the practice of law in Houston, Mo.; enlisted in the United States Navy Air Corps in 1944 and served in the Naval Air Transport Service until discharged in 1946; member of the Missouri State house of representatives, 1952-1960, serving as speaker pro tempore in 1957 and as speaker in 1959; elected as a Democrat to the Eighty-seventh and to the nine succeeding Congresses (January 3, 1961-January 3, 1981); chairman, Committee on Internal Security (Ninety-first through Ninety-third Congresses); was not a candidate for reelection in 1980 to the Ninety-seventh Congress; president, Washington Industrial Team, Inc., 1980-1984; president, Legislative Associates International; was a resident of Tantallon, Md.; died December 25, 1992.

**IGLESIAS, Santiago** (formerly Santiago Iglesias Pantin), a Resident Commissioner from Puerto Rico; born in La Coruña, Spain, February 22, 1872; attended the common schools; apprenticed as a cabinet maker; moved to Cuba and was secretary of the Workingmen Trades Circle in Habana from 1889 until 1896; moved to Puerto Rico and was the founder and editor of three labor newspapers: Porvenir Social (1898-1900), Union Obrera (1903-1906), Justicia (1914-1925); appointed general organizer of the American Federation of Labor for the districts of Puerto Rico and Cuba in 1901; member of the Puerto Rican senate from 1917 to 1933; served as secretary of the Pan American Federation of Labor, 1925-1933; elected as a Coalitionist a Resident Commissioner to the United States in 1932; reelected in 1936 for the term ending January 3, 1941, and served from March 4, 1933 until his death in Washington, D.C., December 5, 1939; interment in San Juan Cemetery, San Juan, P.R.

**Bibliography:** *DAB*.

**IGOE, James Thomas,** a Representative from Illinois; born in Chicago, Ill., October 23, 1883; attended the Holden School, Bryant and Stratton College, and St. Ignatius College, all in Chicago, Ill.; became engaged in the printing and publishing business in Chicago, Ill., in 1907; served as city clerk of Chicago 1917-1923; delegate to the Democratic National Conventions in 1920, 1928, and 1936; elected as a Democrat to the Seventieth and to the two succeeding Congresses (March 4, 1927-March 3, 1933); unsuccessful candidate for renomination in 1932 to the Seventy-third Congress; president of a building corporation in 1931; chairman of Illinois delegation to Golden Gate International Exposition in San Francisco in 1939 and 1940; entered the real estate business in 1942; director and later chairman of executive committee of Mercantile National Bank of Chicago 1955-1961; died in Evanston, Ill., December 2, 1971; interment in All Saints Cemetery, Des Plaines, Ill.

**IGOE, Michael Lambert,** a Representative from Illinois; born in St. Paul, Ramsey County, Minn., April 16, 1885; educated in the parochial schools and De La Salle Institute, Chicago, Ill.; was graduated from the law department of Georgetown University, Washington, D.C., in 1908; was admitted to the bar the same year and commenced practice in Chicago, Ill.; member of the State house of representatives 1913-1930; served as chief assistant in the United States attorney's office in Chicago 1915-1917; member of the board

of South Park Commissioners 1924-1934; delegate to the Democratic National Convention in 1928; member of the Democratic National Committee 1930-1932; elected as a Democrat to the Seventy-fourth Congress, serving from January 3, 1935, until his resignation effective June 2, 1935, having been appointed a United States attorney for the northern district of Illinois on May 16, 1935, and served until his appointment as United States district judge on March 4, 1939, in which capacity he served until 1965; died in Chicago, Ill., on August 21, 1967; interment in All Saints Cemetery, Park Ridge, Ill.

**IGOE, William Leo,** a Representative from Missouri; born in St. Louis, Mo., on October 19, 1879; attended the public and parochial schools of St. Louis and was graduated from the law department of Washington University at St. Louis in 1902; was admitted to the bar in the same year and commenced the practice of law in St. Louis; member of the municipal assembly of St. Louis from 1909 until March 3, 1913, when he resigned to enter Congress; elected as a Democrat to the Sixty-third and to the three succeeding Congresses (March 4, 1913-March 3, 1921); declined to become a candidate for renomination in 1920 to the Sixty-seventh Congress; resumed the practice of law; unsuccessful Democratic candidate for election for mayor of St. Louis in 1925; chairman of the St. Louis Board of Police Commissioners, 1933-1937; died in St. Louis, Mo., April 20, 1953; interment in Calvary Cemetery.

**Bibliography:** Thompson, Alice Anne. "The Life and Career of William L. Igoe, The Reluctant Boss, 1879-1953." Ph.D. dissertation, St. Louis University, 1980.

**IHRIE, Peter, Jr.,** a Representative from Pennsylvania; born in Easton, Pa., February 3, 1796; completed preparatory studies; was graduated from Dickinson College, Carlisle, Pa., in 1815; studied law; was admitted to the bar in 1818 and commenced practice in Easton, Pa.; charter member of the board of trustees of Lafayette College in 1826; member of the Pennsylvania house of representatives in 1826 and 1827; brigadier general of Pennsylvania militia in 1845; elected to the Twenty-first Congress to fill in part the vacancies caused by the resignation of George Wolf and Samuel D. Ingraham; reelected to the Twenty-second Congress and served from October 13, 1829, to March 3, 1833; member of the board of directors of the Easton Bank; died in Easton, Pa., on March 29, 1871; interment in Easton Cemetery.

**IKARD, Frank Neville,** a Representative from Texas; born in Henrietta, Clay County, Tex., January 30, 1913; attended the public schools and Schriener Institute, Kerrville, Tex.; A.B., University of Texas, 1936; LL.B., University of Texas School of Law, 1937; was admitted to the bar in 1937 and commenced the practice of law in Wichita Falls, Tex.; enlisted in the United States Army in January 1944 and served with Company K, One Hundred and Tenth Infantry, Twenty-eighth Division; prisoner of war in Germany in 1944 and 1945; awarded the Purple Heart Medal; judge of the Thirtieth Judicial District Court, Wichita Falls, Tex.; chairman of the Texas Veterans Affairs Commission in 1948 and 1949; appointed judge of the Thirtieth District Court by Governor Beauford Jester in November 1948, subsequently elected in 1950, and served until September 8, 1951; delegate to the Democratic National Conventions of 1956, 1960 and 1968; chairman, Texas State Democratic convention, 1960; elected as a Democrat to the Eighty-second Congress to fill the vacancy caused by the resignation of Ed Gossett; reelected to the Eighty-third and to the four succeeding Congresses and served from September 8, 1951, to December 15, 1961, when he resigned; executive vice president of American Petroleum Institute, 1962-1963, president, 1963-1980; resumed the practice of law in Washington, D.C.; was a resident of Washington, D.C.; died May 1, 1991.

**IKIRT, George Pierce,** a Representative from Ohio; born near West Beaver, Columbiana County, Ohio, November 3, 1852; attended the public schools of New Lisbon, Ohio; taught school and studied law, but on account of ill health was compelled to abandon both; attended the Columbus Medical College; moved to Cincinnati; was graduated from the Cincinnati College of Medicine and Surgery in 1877 and practiced five years; went to New York City in 1882 and was graduated from the Bellevue Hospital Medical College in 1883; again resumed practice in East Liverpool, Ohio; unsuccessful candidate for election in 1888 to the Fifty-first Congress; elected as a Democrat to the Fifty-third Congress (March 4, 1893-March 3, 1895); declined to be a candidate for renomination in 1894 to the Fifty-fourth Congress; resumed the practice of medicine in East Liverpool, Ohio, and died there February 12, 1927; interment in Riverview Cemetery.

**ILSLEY, Daniel,** a Representative from Massachusetts; born in Falmouth, Cumberland County, Maine (then a part of Massachusetts), May 30, 1740; received a liberal schooling; became a distiller and was also interested in shipping; member of the committee of correspondence and safety; major and mustering officer at Falmouth, Maine, during the Revolutionary War; delegate to the Massachusetts convention in 1788 that adopted the Federal Constitution; member of the Massachusetts house of representatives in 1793 and 1794; elected as a Republican to the Tenth Congress (March 4, 1807-March 3, 1809); unsuccessful candidate for reelection in 1808 to the Eleventh Congress; died in Portland, Maine, May 10, 1813; interment in the Eastern Cemetery.

**IMHOFF, Lawrence E.,** a Representative from Ohio; born at Round Bottom, Monroe County, Ohio, December 28, 1895; moved to St. Clairsville, Ohio, in 1907; attended the rural schools and St. Clairsville High School; during the First World War enlisted as a private in the Fifth Regiment, United States Marines, and served from August 9, 1917, until honorably discharged on April 1, 1919; received the Purple Heart Medal; after the war attended Ohio State University at Columbus; clerk of courts of Belmont County, Ohio, 1921-1925; studied law and was admitted to the bar in January 1930; served as probate judge of Belmont County 1925-1933; elected as a Democrat to the Seventy-third, Seventy-fourth, and Seventy-fifth Congresses (March 4, 1933-January 3, 1939); unsuccessful candidate for reelection in 1938 to the Seventy-sixth Congress; special assistant to the United States Attorney General in 1939 and 1940; again elected to the Seventy-seventh Congress (January 3, 1941-January 3, 1943); unsuccessful candidate for reelection in 1942 to the Seventy-eighth Congress; commissioned as a lieutenant commander in the United States Naval Reserve on January 21, 1943; promoted to rank of commander and released from active duty on November 8, 1945; appointed on November 9, 1945, a member of the Board of Veterans' Appeals, Washington, D.C., and retired December 31, 1964; was a resident of North Fort Myers, Fla., until his death there on April 18, 1988.

**IMLAY, James Henderson,** a Representative from New Jersey; was born in Imlaystown, Upper Freehold, Monmouth County, N.J., November 26, 1764; pursued classical studies; was graduated from Princeton College in 1786, where he was also a tutor; studied law; was admitted to the bar in 1791 and practiced; major in the Monmouth County Militia and served in the Revolutionary War; counselor in 1796; member of the State general assembly 1793-1796 and served as speaker in 1796; elected as a Federalist to the Fifth and Sixth Congresses (March 4, 1797-March 3, 1801); one of the managers appointed by the House of Representatives in 1798 to conduct the impeachment proceedings against William Blount, a Senator from Tennessee; postmaster of Allentown, N.J., 1804-1805; resumed the practice of law in Allentown, N.J., where he died March 6, 1823; interment in the Presbyterian Church Cemetery.

**INGALLS, John James,** a Senator from Kansas; born in Middleton, Essex County, Mass., December 29, 1833; attended the public schools in Haverhill, Mass., and was privately tutored; graduated from Williams College, Williamstown, Mass., in 1855; studied law; was admitted to the bar in 1857; moved to Kansas in 1858; member of the State constitutional convention 1859; secretary of the Territorial Council 1860; secretary of the State senate 1861; during the Civil War served as judge advocate of the Kansas Volunteers; member, State senate 1862; unsuccessful candidate for lieutenant governor of Kansas in 1862 and 1864; edited the Atchison Champion 1863-1865 and aided in founding the Kansas Magazine; elected as a Republican to the United States Senate in 1872; reelected in 1879 and again in 1885 and served from March 4, 1873, to March 3, 1891; served as President pro tempore of the Senate during the Forty-ninth, Fiftieth and Fifty-first Congresses; unsuccessful candidate for reelection in 1890; chairman, Committee on Pensions (Forty-fourth and Forty-fifth Congresses), Committee on the District of Columbia (Forty-seventh through Fifty-first Congresses); devoted his time to journalism, literature, and farming until his death in East Las Vegas, N.Mex., August 16, 1900; interment in Mount Vernon Cemetery, Atchison, Kans.

**Bibliography:** *DAB*; Ingalls, John. *A Collection of the Writings of John Ingalls.* Edited by William Connelley. Kansas City: Hudson-Kimberly Co., 1902; Williams, Burton. *Senator John James Ingalls, Kansas' Irridescent Republican.* Lawrence: University Press of Kansas, 1972.

**INGE, Samuel Williams** (nephew of William Marshall Inge), a Representative from Alabama; born in Warren County, N.C., on February 22, 1817; moved to Greene County, Ala.; attended the public schools; studied law; was admitted to the bar and commenced the practice of law in Livingston, Sumter County, Ala.; member of the Alabama house of representatives in 1844 and 1845; elected as a Democrat to the Thirtieth and Thirty-first Congresses (March 4, 1847-March 3, 1851); chairman, Committee on the District of Columbia (Thirty-first Congress); participated in a duel with Edward Stanly, a Representative from North Carolina, in Bladensburg, Md., near Washington, D.C., but neither was seriously injured; resumed the practice of law; was appointed by President Franklin Pierce a United States attorney for the northern district of California on April 1, 1853; died in San Francisco, Calif., on June 10, 1868; interment in Mount Calvary Cemetery.

**INGE, William Marshall** (uncle of Samuel Williams Inge), a Representative from Tennessee; born in Granville County, N.C., in 1802; attended the schools of North Carolina; moved to Tennessee and continued his school studies; studied law; was admitted to the bar and practiced; elected as a Jacksonian to the Twenty-third Congress (March 4, 1833-March 3, 1835); moved to Livingston, Sumter County, Ala., in 1836; resumed the practice of his profession; member of the State house of representatives in 1840, 1844, and 1845; died in Livingston, Sumter County, Ala., in 1846; interment in Livingston Cemetery.

**INGERSOLL, Charles Jared** (son of Jared Ingersoll and brother of Joseph Reed Ingersoll), a Representative from Pennsylvania; born in Philadelphia, Pa., October 3, 1782; received an academic training; studied law; was admitted to the bar in 1802 and commenced practice in Philadelphia, Pa.; elected as a Republican to the Thirteenth Congress (March 4, 1813-March 3, 1815); chairman, Committee on the Judiciary (Thirteenth Congress); was not a candidate for renomination in 1814 to the Fourteenth Congress, having been appointed United States district attorney for Pennsylvania, and served in that office from 1815 until 1829; member of the State improvement convention in 1825; member of the State house of representatives in 1830; member of the State constitutional convention in 1837; appointed secretary of the legation to Prussia on March 8, 1837; unsuccessful candidate in 1837 for election to fill the vacancy caused by the death of Francis J. Harper in the Twenty-fifth Congress; unsuccessful candidate for election in 1838 to the Twenty-sixth Congress; elected as a Democrat to the Twenty-seventh and to the three succeeding Congresses (March 4, 1841-March 3, 1849); chairman, Committee on Foreign Affairs (Twenty-eighth and Twenty-ninth Congresses); was not a candidate for renomination in 1848 to the Thirty-first Congress; appointed Minister to France in 1847, but was not confirmed by the Senate; died in Philadelphia, Pa., May 14, 1862; interment in the Woodlands Cemetery.

**Bibliography:** *DAB*; Ingersoll, Charles Jared. *Recollections, Historical, Political, Biographical, and Social, of Charles J. Ingersoll*. Philadelphia: Lippincott and Co., 1861; Meigs, William Montgomery. *The Life of Charles Jared Ingersoll*. 1897. Reprint. New York: Da Capo Press, 1970.

**INGERSOLL, Colin Macrae** (son of Ralph Isaacs Ingersoll), a Representative from Connecticut; born in New Haven, Conn., March 11, 1819; pursued academic studies and later attended Trinity College, Hartford, Conn.; was graduated from the law department of Yale College in 1839; was admitted to the bar in the same year and commenced practice in New Haven, Conn.; clerk of the State senate in 1843; secretary of the legation at St. Petersburg, by appointment of President James K. Polk, in 1847 and 1848 and was Acting Chargé d'Affaires in 1848; elected as a Democrat to the Thirty-second and Thirty-third Congresses (March 4, 1851-March 3, 1855); resumed the practice of law; adjutant general of Connecticut 1867-1871; died in New Haven, Conn., September 13, 1903; interment in the Grove Street Cemetery.

**INGERSOLL, Ebon Clark,** a Representative from Illinois; born in Dresden, Yates County, N.Y., on December 12, 1831; moved to Wisconsin Territory in 1843 and subsequently to Illinois; pursued classical studies in Peoria, Ill., and in Paducah, Ky.; studied law; was admitted to the bar in 1854 and commenced practice in Peoria, Ill.; member of the State house of representatives in 1856; elected as a Republican to the Thirty-eighth Congress to fill the vacancy caused by the death of Owen Lovejoy; reelected to the Thirty-ninth, Fortieth, and Forty-first Congresses and served from May 20, 1864, to March 3, 1871; chairman, Committee on District of Columbia (Thirty-ninth and Fortieth Congresses), Committee on Roads and Canals (Forty-first Congress), Committee on Railways and Canals (Forty-first Congress); unsuccessful candidate for reelection in 1870 to the Forty-second Congress; settled in Washington, D.C., and engaged in the practice of law until his death there on May 31, 1879; interment in Oak Hill Cemetery.

**INGERSOLL, Jared** (father of Charles Jared Ingersoll and Joseph Reed Ingersoll), a Delegate from Pennsylvania; born in New Haven, Conn., October 24, 1749; received a classical education; was graduated from Yale College in 1766; settled in Philadelphia, Pa., in 1771; studied law and was admitted to the bar in 1773; finished his legal education at the Middle Temple, London, England, in 1774, and then went to Paris in 1776; returned to Philadelphia in 1778 and commenced practice; Member of the Continental Congress in 1780; delegate to the convention that framed the Federal Constitution in 1787; was the first attorney general of Pennsylvania, 1790-1799, and served again from 1811 to 1817; United States district attorney for the eastern district of Pennsylvania; declined the appointment of judge of the Federal court in 1801; unsuccessful Federalist candidate for Vice President of the United States in 1812 on the ticket headed by De Witt Clinton; presiding judge of the district court of Philadelphia County until his death in Philadelphia, Pa., October 31, 1822; interment in the First Presbyterian Church Cemetery, Fourth and Pine Streets.

**Bibliography:** *DAB*; Gipson, Lawrence H. *American Loyalist, Jared Ingersoll*. New Haven, Conn.: Yale University Press, 1971; Ingersoll, Jared. *Jared Ingersoll Papers*. Edited by Franklin B. Dexter. New Haven, 1918.

**INGERSOLL, Joseph Reed** (son of Jared Ingersoll and brother of Charles Jared Ingersoll), a Representative from Pennsylvania; born in Philadelphia, Pa., June 14, 1786; pursued a classical course and was graduated from Princeton College in 1804; studied law; was admitted to the bar and commenced practice in Philadelphia, Pa.; elected as a Whig to the Twenty-fourth Congress (March 4, 1835-March 3, 1837); declined to be a candidate for renomination in 1836 to the Twenty-fifth Congress; resumed the practice of law; elected to the Twenty-seventh Congress to fill the vacancy caused by the resignation of John Sergeant; reelected to the Twenty-eighth, Twenty-ninth, and Thirtieth Congresses and served from October 12, 1841, to March 3, 1849; chairman, Committee on the Judiciary (Thirtieth Congress); declined to accept the nomination as a candidate for reelection in 1848 to the Thirty-first Congress; appointed Minister to Great Britain by President Millard Fillmore and served from August 21, 1852, to August 23, 1853; died in Philadelphia, Pa., February 20, 1868; interment in St. Peter's Protestant Episcopal Churchyard.

**INGERSOLL, Ralph Isaacs** (father of Colin Macrae Ingersoll), a Representative from Connecticut; born in New Haven, Conn., February 8, 1789; pursued classical studies, and was graduated from Yale College in 1808; studied law; was admitted to the bar in 1810 and commenced practice in New Haven; member of the State house of representatives 1820-1825 and served as speaker during the last two years; elected to the Nineteenth and to the three succeeding Congresses (March 4, 1825-March 3, 1833); was not a candidate for renomination in 1832 to the Twenty-third Congress; resumed the practice of law; appointed State's attorney for New Haven County in 1833; declined the appointment as United States Senator tendered by Governor Henry W. Edwards upon the death of Senator Nathan Smith in December 1835; appointed Minister to Russia by President James K. Polk and served from August 8, 1846, until July 1, 1848, when he resigned; again engaged in the practice of law; mayor of New Haven in 1851; died in New Haven, Conn., August 26, 1872; interment in Grove Street Cemetery.

**INGHAM, Samuel,** a Representative from Connecticut; born in Hebron, Conn., September 5, 1793; attended the common schools in Vermont; studied law; was admitted to the bar in 1815 and commenced practice in Canaan, Vt.; moved to Jewett City, Conn., and subsequently, in 1819, to Essex (then part of Saybrook), Conn., and continued the practice of his profession; State's attorney for Middlesex County 1827-1835 and again in 1843 and 1844; member of the State house of representatives in 1828, 1834, 1851, and 1852 and served as speaker in 1851 and 1852; judge of probate 1829-1833; judge of the Middlesex County Court 1849-1853; elected as a Jacksonian to the Twenty-fourth Congress and reelected as a Democrat to the Twenty-fifth Congress (March 4, 1835-March 3, 1839); chairman, Committee on Naval Affairs (Twenty-fifth Congress); unsuccessful candidate for reelection in 1838 to the Twenty-sixth Congress; served in the State senate 1843-1850; unsuccessful Democratic candidate for the United States Senate in 1854; United States commissioner of customs from December 5, 1857, to May 14, 1861; resumed the practice of law; died in Essex, Middlesex County, Conn., November 10, 1881; interment in River View Cemetery.

**INGHAM, Samuel Delucenna,** a Representative from Pennsylvania; born at Great Spring, near New Hope, Bucks County, Pa., September 16, 1779; pursued classical studies; engaged in the manufacture of paper; member of the Pennsylvania house of representatives, 1806-1808; elected as a Republican to the Thirteenth and to the two succeeding Congresses and served from March 4, 1813, until July 6, 1818, when he resigned; chairman, Committee on Pensions and Revolutionary Claims (Thirteenth Congress), Committee on the Post Office and Post Roads (Fourteenth and Fifteenth Congresses), Committee on Expenditures in the Post

Office Department (Fifteenth Congress); prothonotary of the courts of Bucks County in 1818 and 1819; served as secretary of the Commonwealth of Pennsylvania from October 1819 to December 1820; elected to the Seventeenth Congress to fill the vacancy caused by the resignation of Samuel Moore; reelected to the Eighteenth and to the three succeeding Congresses and served from October 8, 1822, until his resignation in 1829, before the convening of the Twenty-first Congress; chairman, Committee on the Post Office and Post Roads (Nineteenth and Twentieth Congresses); Secretary of the Treasury in the Cabinet of President Andrew Jackson from March 6, 1829 to June 21, 1831, when he resigned; resumed the manufacture of paper; also engaged in the development of anthracite coal fields; died in Trenton, N.J., on June 5, 1860; interment in the Solebury Presbyterian Churchyard, Solebury, Pa.

**Bibliography:** *DAB.*

**INGLIS, Robert Durden,** a Representative from South Carolina; born in Savannah, Chatham County, Ga., October 11, 1959; graduated, May River Academy, Bluffton, S.C., 1977; A.B., Duke University, 1981; J.D., University of Virginia School of Law, 1984; attorney, Greenville, S.C.; Greenville County Republican Party, executive committee; elected as a Republican to the One Hundred Third and One Hundred Fourth Congresses (January 3, 1993-January 3, 1997); is a resident of Greenville, S.C.

**INHOFE, James Mountain,** a Representative and a Senator from Oklahoma; born in Des Moines, Iowa, November 17, 1934; attended public schools in Tulsa, Okla.; graduated Central High School, Tulsa, 1953; B.A., University of Tulsa, 1959; served in the United States Army, 1955-1956; president, Quaker Life Insurance company; member, Oklahoma State house of representatives, 1967-1969; Oklahoma State senator, 1969-1977; Republican leader, 1975-1977; unsuccessful candidate for election in 1974 for Governor of Oklahoma; unsuccessful candidate for election in 1976 to the Ninety-fifth Congress; mayor of Tulsa, 1978-1984; unsuccessful candidate for reelection in 1984; elected as a Republican to the One Hundredth and to the three succeeding Congresses (January 3, 1987-November 17, 1994); was not a candidate in 1994 for reelection to the House of Representatives; elected to the United States Senate November 8, 1994, to fill the term ending January 3, 1997; vacancy caused by the resignation of David L. Boren; took the oath of office November 17, 1994; is a resident of Tulsa, Okla.

**INOUYE, Daniel Ken,** a Representative and a Senator from Hawaii; born in Honolulu, Hawaii, September 7, 1924; attended the public schools of Honolulu; during the Second World War volunteered as a private, U.S. Army in 1943, released as a captain in 1947; A.B., University of Hawaii, 1950; J.D., George Washington University Law School, Washington, D.C., 1952; admitted to the bar in 1953 and commenced practice in Honolulu; assistant public prosecutor in Honolulu, 1953-1954; majority leader in the Territorial house of representatives, 1954-1958; member of the Territorial senate, 1958-1959; upon the admission of Hawaii into the Union was elected as a Democrat to the Eighty-sixth Congress for the term commencing August 21, 1959; reelected to the Eighty-seventh Congress and served until January 3, 1963; was not a candidate for renomination to the House of Representatives in 1962, but was elected to the United States Senate for the term beginning January 3, 1963; reelected in 1968, 1974, 1980, 1986 and again in 1992 for the term ending January 3, 1999; delivered keynote address at the Democratic National Convention of 1968; chairman, Select Committee on Intelligence (Ninety-fourth and Ninety-fifth Congresses), Committee on Indian Affairs (One Hundredth through One Hundred Third Congresses), Select Committee on Secret Military Assistance to Iran and the Nicaraguan Opposition (One Hundredth Congress); is a resident of Honolulu, Hawaii.

**INSLEE, Jay Robert,** a Representative from Washington; born in Selah, Yakima County, Wash., February 9, 1951; graduated, Ingraham High School, Seattle, 1969; B.A., University of Washington, 1973; J.D., Willamette University College of Law, Salem, Oreg., 1976; member, Selah School Bond Committee, chair, 1980; New Valley Osteopathic Hospital, board member, 1978-1986; Washington State Trial Lawyer's Association, board of directors, 1984-1988; attorney, Selah, Wash., 1976 to present; City of Selah prosecutor, 1976-1982; member, Washington State house of representatives, 1988-1993; elected as a Democrat to the One Hundred Third Congress (January 3, 1993-January 3, 1995); unsuccessful candidate for reelection in 1994 to the One Hundred Fourth Congress; unsuccessful candidate in 1996 for nomination for Governor of Washington; is a resident of Selah, Wash.

**IRBY, John Laurens Manning** (great-grandson of Elias Earle and cousin of Joseph Haynsworth Earle), a Senator from South Carolina; born in Laurens, Laurens County, S.C., September 10, 1854; attended Laurensville Male Academy, Laurens, S.C., Princeton College, Princeton, N.J., in 1870-1871, and the University of Virginia at Charlottesville, 1871-1873; studied law; was admitted to the bar in 1875, commenced practice at Cheraw, Chesterfield County, S.C., returned to Laurens; appointed lieutenant colonel of the South Carolina Militia in 1877; served as intendant (administrative official) of Laurens in 1877; member, South Carolina State house of representatives, 1886-1892, serving as speaker in 1890; elected as a Democrat to the United States Senate, and served from March 4, 1891 to March 3, 1897; was not a candidate for reelection; chairman, Committee on Transportation Routes to the Seaboard (Fifty-third Congress); subsequently an unsuccessful candidate for election to the United States Senate in 1897 to fill the vacancy caused by the death of his cousin, Joseph H. Earle; delegate to the State constitutional convention in 1895; resumed the practice of law and also engaged in agricultural pursuits; died in Laurens, S.C., December 9, 1900; interment in the City Cemetery.

**IREDELL, James,** a Senator from North Carolina; born in Edenton, Chowan County, N.C., November 2, 1788; attended Edenton Academy and graduated from the College of New Jersey (now Princeton University) in 1806; studied law; was admitted to the bar in 1809 and commenced practice in Edenton; during the War of 1812 served as captain of a company of Volunteers; member, State house of commons 1813, 1816-1828, served as speaker 1817-1828; judge of the superior court of North Carolina 1819; Governor of North Carolina from December 8, 1827 to December 12, 1828; elected as a Jacksonian to the United States Senate to fill the vacancy caused by the resignation of Nathaniel Macon and served from December 15, 1828, to March 3, 1831; was not a candidate for reelection; chairman, Committee to Audit and Control the Contingent Expense (Twenty-first Congress); moved to Raleigh, N.C. in 1830 and resumed the practice of law; reporter of the supreme court of North Carolina 1840-1852; commissioner to revise the State laws 1836-1837; died in Edenton, N.C., April 13, 1853; interment in the Johnston Burial Ground on the Hayes plantation at Edenton.

**IRELAND, Andrew Poysell (Andy),** a Representative from Florida; born in Cincinnati, Hamilton County, Ohio, August 23, 1930; attended private schools in Cincinnati; graduated, Phillips Academy, Andover, Mass., 1948; B.S., Yale University, 1952; graduate studies, Columbia University, New York City, 1953-1954; graduated, Louisiana State University, School of Banking of the South, 1959; joined Barnett National Bank in Jacksonville, Fla., 1954; president of American National Bank of Winter Haven, 1962-1968; president, American National Bank at Cypress Gardens, 1964-1968; senior vice president, Barnett First National Bank of Jacksonville, 1968-1970; chairman of the board, chief executive officer of Barnett Bank of Winter Haven, Barnett Bank of Cypress Gardens, and Barnett Bank of Auburndale, 1970-1976; director,

Federal Reserve Bank of Atlanta, Jacksonville branch, 1966-1968; Winter Haven city commissioner, 1966-1968; elected as a Democrat to the Ninety-fifth and to the three succeeding Congresses; announced his affiliation with the Republican Party on July 5, 1984, and continued in office during the Ninety-eighth Congress as a Republican; reelected as a Republican to the Ninety-ninth and to the three succeeding Congresses (January 3, 1977-January 3, 1993); was not a candidate for reelection in 1992 to the One Hundred Third Congress; senior vice president, Ringling Bros. and Barnum & Bailey Circus; is a resident of Washington, D.C.

**IRELAND, Clifford Cady,** a Representative from Illinois; born in Washburn, Woodford County, Ill., February 14, 1878; attended the common schools, Cheltenham Military Academy, Ogontz, Pa., and Knox College, Galesburg, Ill.; was graduated from the University of Wisconsin at Madison in 1901, and from the Illinois College of Law at Chicago in 1908; was admitted to the bar in 1909 and commenced practice in Peoria; served as a private in the Illinois National Guard during the Spanish-American War; elected as a Republican to the Sixty-fifth and to the two succeeding Congresses (March 4, 1917-March 3, 1923); chairman, Committee on Accounts (Sixty-sixth and Sixty-seventh Congresses); unsuccessful candidate for renomination in 1922 to the Sixty-eighth Congress; resumed the practice of law at Peoria; appointed a director of the department of trade and commerce of Illinois in 1923, serving until his resignation in 1926; died in Chicago, Ill., May 24, 1930; interment in Linn-Mount Vernon Cemetery, Washburn, Ill.

**IRION, Alfred Briggs,** a Representative from Louisiana; born near Evergreen, Avoyelles Parish, La., February 18, 1833; attended the common schools, Franklin College, Opelousas, La., and was graduated from the University of North Carolina at Chapel Hill in 1855; studied law; was admitted to the bar in 1857 and commenced practice in Marksville, La.; delegate to the State secession convention in 1860 and was opposed to secession; during the Civil War served in the Confederate Army, being attached to General Walker's division under Colonel Randall; member of the State house of representatives in 1864 and 1865; resumed the practice of his profession; editor of a local newspaper in Marksville, La., 1866-1874; moved to Evergreen, La., in 1870 and engaged in planting; continued the practice of law and also engaged in literary pursuits; member of the State constitutional convention in 1879; judge of the third circuit court of appeals of Louisiana 1880-1884; elected as a Democrat to the Forty-ninth Congress (March 4, 1885-March 3, 1887); unsuccessful candidate for renomination in 1886 to the Fiftieth Congress; died in New Orleans, La., May 21, 1903; interment in the Baptist Cemetery, Evergreen, La.

**IRVIN, Alexander,** a Representative from Pennsylvania; born in Penns Valley, Centre County, Pa., January 18, 1800; attended the public schools; moved to Curwensville in 1820 and to Clearfield, Pa., in 1826; engaged in mercantile and lumbering pursuits; treasurer of Clearfield County 1828-1830; member of the Pennsylvania senate in 1837 and 1838; prothonotary of the court of common pleas in 1842; clerk of the several courts; recorder of deeds and register of wills of Clearfield County 1842-1844; elected as a Whig to the Thirtieth Congress (March 4, 1847-March 3, 1849); was not a candidate for renomination in 1848 to the Thirty-first Congress; United States marshal for the western district of Pennsylvania from January 17 to September 3, 1850, when he resigned, being succeeded by his brother, William Irvin; delegate to the Republican National Convention of 1872; engaged in mercantile pursuits at Clearfield, Clearfield County, Pa., until his death on March 20, 1874; interment in the Reed addition to the Old Graveyard.

**IRVIN, James,** a Representative from Pennsylvania; born in Linden Hall, Centre County, Pa., February 18, 1800; attended the common schools; became engaged in mercantile pursuits, milling, mining, and manufacturing in Oak Hill, Milesburg, and Bellefonte,

Pa.; elected as a Whig to the Twenty-seventh and Twenty-eighth Congresses (March 4, 1841-March 3, 1845); unsuccessful candidate for election in 1847 for Governor of Pennsylvania; United States naval storekeeper at Philadelphia in 1857; died in Hecla, Schuylkill County, Pa., on November 28, 1862; interment in the Union Cemetery, Bellefonte, Pa.

**IRVIN, William W.,** a Representative from Ohio; born near Charlottesville, Albemarle County, Va., about 1778; pursued an academic course; studied law; was admitted to the bar in 1800 and commenced practice in his native county; moved to Lancaster, Ohio, about 1801 and continued the practice of his profession; appointed an associate judge of the court of common pleas for Fairfield County by the first general assembly in 1803; was impeached in 1804 by the State house of representatives and subsequently removed from office by the decision of the senate; member of the State house of representatives in 1806 and 1807; justice of the State supreme court 1810-1815; again a member of the State house of representatives 1825-1827 and served as speaker in 1825 and 1826; elected as a Jacksonian to the Twenty-first and Twenty-second Congresses (March 4, 1829-March 3, 1833); was an unsuccessful candidate for reelection in 1832 to the Twenty-third Congress; returned to his farm near Lancaster, Ohio, and engaged in agricultural pursuits until his death March 28, 1842.

**IRVINE, William,** a Representative from New York; born in Whitneys Point, Broome County, N.Y., February 14, 1820; attended the common schools; moved to Greene County, N.Y., in 1841; studied law; was admitted to the bar in 1849 and commenced practice in Corning, Steuben County, N.Y.; elected as a Republican to the Thirty-sixth Congress (March 4, 1859-March 3, 1861); during the Civil War assisted in raising the Tenth Regiment, New York Volunteer Cavalry, of which he became lieutenant colonel November 25, 1861; brevetted colonel and brigadier general of Volunteers March 13, 1865; adjutant general on the staff of Governor Reuben E. Fenton in 1865 and 1866; moved to California and continued the practice of his profession until his death in San Francisco, Calif., November 12, 1882; interment in the Elmira Cemetery, Elmira, N.Y.

**IRVINE, William,** a Delegate and a Representative from Pennsylvania; born in County Fermanagh, Ulster, Ireland, on November 3, 1741; pursued classical studies and was graduated from the Dublin University; studied medicine and was admitted to practice; served as surgeon on a British man-of-war; immigrated to the United States and settled in Carlisle, Pa., in 1763; delegate to the Pennsylvania Revolutionary conventions 1764-1766; colonel of the Sixth Pennsylvania Regiment in the Revolutionary Army; captured in Canada June 16, 1776, and remained a prisoner of war until exchanged May 6, 1778; appointed brigadier general May 12, 1779, and served until the close of the war; Member of the Continental Congress 1787-1788; commanded the Pennsylvania troops during the Whiskey Rebellion in 1794; elected to the Third Congress (March 4, 1793-March 3, 1795); moved to Philadelphia, where he was superintendent of military stores 1801-1804; died in Philadelphia, Pa., July 29, 1804.

**Bibliography:** *DAB*.

**IRVING, Theodore Leonard,** a Representative from Missouri; born in St. Paul, Ramsey County, Minn., March 24, 1898; moved with his parents to a farm in North Dakota; attended the public schools of North Dakota; worked for a railroad as a boy and during the First World War; left the railroad to become manager of a theater in Montana; moved to California and was manager of a hotel; moved to Jackson County, Mo., in 1934 and was employed as a construction worker and later became a representative of the American Federation of Labor; elected as a Democrat to the Eighty-first and Eighty-second Congresses (January 3, 1949-January 3, 1953); unsuccessful candidate for reelection in 1952 to the Eighty-third Congress and for nomination in 1954 to the

Eighty-fourth Congress; labor organizer and later president of a labor union in Kansas City, Mo.; died in Washington, D.C., March 8, 1962, while on a business trip; interment in Mount Moriah Cemetery, Kansas City, Mo.

**IRVING, William,** a Representative from New York; born in New York City on August 15, 1766; completed preparatory studies; engaged in mercantile pursuits and also in fur trade with the Indians along the Mohawk River, residing at Johnstown and Caughnawaga, N.Y.; returned to New York City in 1793; elected as a Republican to the Thirteenth Congress to fill the vacancy caused by the resignation of Egbert Benson; reelected to the Fourteenth and Fifteenth Congresses and served from January 22, 1814, to March 3, 1819; contributed several essays and poems to Salmagundi, published by his brother, Washington Irving; died in New York City on November 9, 1821.
     **Bibliography:** *DAB.*

**IRWIN, Donald Jay,** a Representative from Connecticut; born of American parents in Argentina on September 7, 1926; came to the United States in 1945 to attend Yale University; entered the United States Army and served with the Joint Brazil-United States Military Commission in Rio de Janeiro; reentered Yale University and graduated in 1951 and also from Yale Law School in 1954; was admitted to the bar and commenced the practice of law in Connecticut; taught Spanish at Yale University while a student there; member of Norwalk Board of Education; elected as a Democrat to the Eighty-sixth Congress (January 3, 1959-January 3, 1961); unsuccessful candidate for reelection in 1960 to the Eighty-seventh Congress; appointed general counsel, United States Information Agency, 1961; appointed treasurer of the State of Connecticut by Governor John N. Dempsey in 1962; elected to the Eighty-ninth and the Ninetieth Congresses (January 3, 1965-January 3, 1969); unsuccessful candidate for reelection in 1968 to the Ninety-first Congress; resumed the practice of law; elected mayor of Norwalk, Conn., in November 1971; reelected in 1973, and was not a candidate for reelection in 1975; is a resident of Norwalk, Conn.

**IRWIN, Edward Michael,** a Representative from Illinois; born near Leasburg, Crawford County, Mo., on April 14, 1869; attended the public schools of his native city; taught school in Leasburg, Mo.; attended the University of Missouri at Columbia; was graduated from Missouri Medical College at St. Louis in 1892; moved to New Athens, St. Clair County, Ill., in the same year and commenced the practice of medicine; chairman of the Republican county central committee 1898-1924; moved to Belleville, St. Clair County, Ill., in 1903 and continued the practice of medicine; coroner of St. Clair County 1904-1908; elected president of the Belleville Bank & Trust Co. in 1910; delegate to the Republican National Convention of 1920; elected as a Republican to the Sixty-ninth, Seventieth, and Seventy-first Congresses (March 4, 1925-March 3, 1931); chairman, Committee on Claims (Seventy-first Congress); unsuccessful candidate for reelection in 1930 to the Seventy-second Congress; resumed the practice of his profession; died in Belleville, Ill., January 30, 1933; interment in Green Mount Cemetery.

**IRWIN, Harvey Samuel,** a Representative from Kentucky; born in Highland County, Ohio, December 10, 1844; attended the public schools; was graduated from the high school of Greenfield, Ohio; studied law, but abandoned the same to enlist in the Union Army during the Civil War; assisted in raising a regiment of Artillery and was commissioned a lieutenant; transferred to a special corps in the Regular Army, in which he served until the close of the war; settled in Louisville, Ky.; resumed the study of law; was admitted to the bar and practiced; appointed successively assistant internal revenue assessor, deputy clerk of the United States district court, and chief deputy collector of the fifth internal revenue district of Kentucky; railroad commissioner in 1895; elected as a Republican to the

Fifty-seventh Congress (March 4, 1901-March 3, 1903); unsuccessful candidate for reelection in 1902 to the Fifty-eighth Congress; resumed the practice of law in Washington, D.C.; was licensed as an evangelist in Washington, D.C., in 1913; had a charge in Idylwood and Vienna, Va.; died in Vienna, Va., September 3, 1916; interment in Cave Hill Cemetery, Louisville, Ky.

**IRWIN, Jared,** a Representative from Pennsylvania; born in Georgia on January 19, 1768; appointed commissioner for valuation of lands and dwellings and enumeration of slaves for the second division of Georgia on July 17, 1798; engaged in mercantile pursuits at Milton, Pa.; served as postmaster of Milton, Pa., from June 1, 1802, to June 29, 1803; sheriff of Northumberland County, Pa., 1808-1812; member of the Pennsylvania house of representatives in 1811; served as colonel of the Fifth Rifle Regiment in the War of 1812; elected as a Republican to the Thirteenth and Fourteenth Congresses (March 4, 1813-March 3, 1817); in 1817 assisted in the establishment of a short-lived revolutionary government on Amelia Island, Fla.; died in Fernandina, Fla., on September 20, 1818.

**IRWIN, Thomas,** a Representative from Pennsylvania; born in Philadelphia, Pa., February 22, 1785; attended the common schools and Franklin College, Lancaster, Pa.; became editor of the Philadelphia Repository in 1804; studied law; was admitted to the bar in 1808 and commenced practice in Uniontown, Pa.; appointed Indian agent at Natchitoches, La., where he also engaged in the practice of law for two years; returned to Uniontown, Pa., in 1811 and resumed the practice of law; deputy attorney general for Fayette County, Pa., 1812-1819; member of the Pennsylvania house of representatives 1824-1828; elected as a Jacksonian to the Twenty-first Congress (March 4, 1829-March 3, 1831); was not a candidate for renomination in 1830 to the Twenty-second Congress; appointed on April 14, 1831, by President Andrew Jackson as United States judge for the western district of Pennsylvania, and served until February 8, 1859, when a successor was appointed; lived in retirement until his death in Pittsburgh, Pa., May 14, 1870; interment in Allegheny Cemetery.

**IRWIN, William Wallace,** a Representative from Pennsylvania; born in Pittsburgh, Pa., in 1803; attended a private school in Pittsburgh and Allegheny College, Meadville, Pa.; studied law; was admitted to the bar in 1828 and commenced practice in Pittsburgh; mayor of Pittsburgh in 1840; elected as a Whig to the Twenty-seventh Congress (March 4, 1841-March 3, 1843); was not a candidate for reelection in 1842 to the Twenty-eighth Congress; appointed Chargé d'Affaires to Denmark by President John Tyler and served from March 3, 1843, to June 12, 1847; died in Pittsburgh, Pa., September 15, 1856; interment in Allegheny Cemetery.

**ISACKS, Jacob C.,** a Representative from Tennessee; born in Montgomery County, Pa.; moved to Winchester, Tenn.; elected to the Eighteenth Congress; reelected to the Nineteenth and Twentieth Congresses and reelected as a Jacksonian to the Twenty-first and Twenty-second Congresses (March 4, 1823-March 3, 1833); chairman, Committee on Public Lands (Twentieth and Twenty-first Congresses); unsuccessful candidate for reelection in 1832 to the Twenty-third Congress; died in Winchester, Tenn.

**ISACSON, Leo,** a Representative from New York; born in New York City, April 20, 1910; attended the public schools; was graduated from New York University in 1931, and from the law department of the same university in 1933; was admitted to the bar in 1934 and commenced practice in New York City; member of the New York State assembly in 1945 and 1946; elected as an American Laborite to the Eightieth Congress to fill the vacancy caused by the resignation of Benjamin J. Rabin, and served from February 17, 1948 to January 3, 1949; unsuccessful candidate for reelection in 1948 to the Eighty-first Congress; resumed the practice of law; delegate to Democratic National Convention of 1968; moved to

Florida in 1970; professor of political science, Nova University; was a resident of Fort Lauderdale, Fla., until his death there on September 28, 1996.

**ISTOOK, Ernest James, Jr.,** a Representative from Oklahoma; born in Fort Worth, Tex., February 11, 1950; graduated, Castleberry High School, Fort Worth, 1967; B.A., Baylor University, Waco, Tex., 1971; J.D., Oklahoma City University School of Law, 1977; attorney; State Capitol reporter, KOMA and WKY radio, 1972-1977; director, Oklahoma State alcoholic and beverage control board, 1977-1978; legal counsel to Governor David L. Boren of Oklahoma, 1978; member, Oklahoma City Council, Warr Acres, 1982-1986; board member, Oklahoma County Metropolitan Library System, 1982-1986, and chair, 1985-1986; member, Oklahoma State house of representatives, 1986-1993; elected as a Republican to the One Hundred Third and One Hundred Fourth Congresses (January 3, 1993-January 3, 1997); is a resident of Oklahoma City, Okla.

**ITTNER, Anthony Friday,** a Representative from Missouri; born in Lebanon, Warren County, Ohio, October 8, 1837; moved to St. Louis, Mo., with his parents in 1844; attended the common schools; learned the bricklaying trade; later engaged in the manufacture of brick; member of the Enrolled Missouri Militia; member of the city council of St. Louis, Mo., in 1867 and 1868; member of the State house of representatives 1868-1870; served in the State senate from 1870 until November 1876, when he resigned; elected as a Republican to the Forty-fifth Congress (March 4, 1877-March 3, 1879); declined to be a candidate for renomination in 1878 to the Forty-sixth Congress; resumed the manufacture of brick; president of the National Association of Builders and of the National Brick Manufacturers' Association; retired from active business in 1917 and resided in St. Louis, Mo., until his death there on February 22, 1931; interment in Bellefontaine Cemetery.

**IVERSON, Alfred, Sr.,** a Representative and a Senator from Georgia; born in Liberty County, Ga., December 3, 1798; attended private schools and graduated from The College of New Jersey (now Princeton University) in 1820; studied law; was admitted to the bar in 1822 and commenced practice in Clinton, Jones County, Ga.; member, State house of representatives 1827-1830; moved to Columbus, Muscogee County, Ga., in 1830 and continued the practice of law; judge of the State superior court 1835-1837; member, State senate 1843-1844; presidential elector on the Democratic ticket in 1844; elected as a Democrat to the Thirtieth Congress (March 4, 1847-March 3, 1849); again served as judge of the State superior court 1850-1854; elected to the United States Senate and served from March 4, 1855, to January 28, 1861, when he withdrew with other secessionist Senators; chairman, Committee on Claims (Thirty-fifth and Thirty-sixth Congresses); resumed the practice of law in Columbus, Ga., until 1868, when he purchased a plantation in East Macon, Ga., and engaged in agricultural pursuits until his death there on March 4, 1873; interment in Linwood Cemetery, Columbus, Ga.

**Bibliography:** *DAB.*

**IVES, Irving McNeil,** a Senator from New York; born in Bainbridge, Chenango County, N.Y., January 24, 1896; attended the public schools; during the First World War served overseas with the United States Army 1917-1919, discharged as first lieutenant, Infantry; graduated from Hamilton College, Clinton, N.Y., in 1920; engaged in the banking and insurance businesses in New York 1920-1930; member, New York State assembly 1930-1946, serving as minority leader in 1935, speaker in 1936, and majority leader 1937-1946; chairman of New York State Temporary Commission Against Discrimination 1944-1945; member, board of trustees of Hamilton College and Cornell University; dean of the New York State School of Industrial and Labor Relations 1945-1947; elected as a Republican to the United States Senate in 1946, reelected in 1952, and served from January 3, 1947, to January 3, 1959; was not a candidate for renomination in 1958; unsuccessful candidate for election in 1954 for Governor of New York; died in Norwich, N.Y., February 24, 1962; interment in Greenlawn Cemetery, Bainbridge, N.Y.

**Bibliography:** *DAB.*

**IVES, Willard,** a Representative from New York; born in Watertown, Jefferson County, N.Y., July 7, 1806; attended the common schools, also Belleville (N.Y.) Academy, and Lowville (N.Y.) Academy; engaged in agricultural pursuits and was also interested in banking; member of the State house of representatives in 1829 and 1830; delegate to the world convention of Methodists held in London, England, in 1846; unsuccessful candidate for election to the Thirtieth Congress in 1848; elected as a Democrat to the Thirty-second Congress (March 4, 1851-March 3, 1853); president of Ives Seminary, Antwerp, N.Y., which he endowed; one of the originators and organizers of Syracuse University and served on the board of trustees from 1870 to 1886; resumed agricultural pursuits; died in Watertown, N.Y., April 19, 1896; interment in Brookside Cemetery.

**IZAC, Edouard Victor Michel,** a Representative from California; born in Cresco, Howard County, Iowa, December 18, 1891; attended the School of the Assumption, Cresco, Iowa, the high school at South St. Paul, Minn., and Werntz Preparatory School, Annapolis, Md.; was graduated from the United States Naval Academy at Annapolis, Md., in 1915; served in the United States Navy as ensign, lieutenant (jg), and senior lieutenant until forced to retire in 1921 on account of wounds received while a prisoner of war in Germany; awarded Congressional Medal of Honor, the Croce di Guerra of Italy, and the Cross of Montenegro; located in San Diego, Calif., and engaged in newspaper work and writing, 1922-1928; unsuccessful candidate for election in 1934 to the Seventy-fourth Congress; delegate to the Democratic National Conventions of 1940 and 1944; elected as a Democrat to the Seventy-fifth and to the four succeeding Congresses (January 3, 1937-January 3, 1947); unsuccessful candidate for reelection in 1946 to the Eightieth Congress; interested in lumbering and the raising of thoroughbred cattle; was a resident of Washington, D.C.; died January 18, 1990.

**IZARD, Ralph,** a Delegate and a Senator from South Carolina; born at "The Elms," near Charleston, S.C., January 23, in 1741 or 1742; pursued classical studies in England; returned to America briefly in 1764, but went abroad to reside, taking up his residence in London in 1771; moved to Paris, France, in 1776; appointed commissioner to the Court of Tuscany by the Continental Congress in 1776, but was recalled in 1779; returned to America in 1780; pledged his large estate in South Carolina for the payment of war ships to be used in the Revolutionary War; Member of the Continental Congress in 1782 and 1783; elected to the United States Senate and served from March 4, 1789, to March 3, 1795; served as President pro tempore of the Senate during the Third Congress; one of the founders of the College of Charleston; retired from public life to the care of his estates; died near Charleston, May 30, 1804; interment in the churchyard of St. James Goose Creek Episcopal Church, near Charleston, S.C.

**Bibliography:** *DAB*; Izard, Ralph. *Correspondence of Mr. Ralph Izard of South Carolina, From the Year 1774 to 1804, with a Short Memoir.* Edited by Anne Deas. 1844. Reprint. New York: AMS Press, 1976.

**IZLAR, James Ferdinand,** a Representative from South Carolina; born near Orangeburg, Orangeburg County, S.C., November 25, 1832; attended the common schools; was graduated from Emory College, Oxford, Ga., in 1855; studied law; was admitted to the bar in 1858 and commenced practice in South Carolina; served as an officer in the Confederate Army during the Civil War; resumed the practice of law in Orangeburg, S.C.; member of the State senate 1880-1890; elected by the general assembly judge of the first judicial circuit in 1889; delegate to the Democratic National Convention in 1884; elected as a Democrat to the Fifty-third Congress to fill the vacancy caused by the resignation of William H. Brawley and served from April 12, 1894, to March 3, 1895; was not a candidate for renomination in 1894 to the Fifty-fourth Congress; again engaged in the practice of law in Orangeburg until 1907, when he retired; died in Orangeburg, S.C., May 26, 1912; interment in the Episcopal Cemetery.

# J

**JACK, Summers Melville,** a Representative from Pennsylvania; born in Summersville, Jefferson County, Pa., July 18, 1852; attended the public and private schools of Jefferson County and the Indiana Normal School (now State Teachers College) of Pennyslvania; taught school for six years; studied law; was admitted to the bar in 1879 and commenced practice in Indiana, Pa.; district attorney for Indiana County, 1884-1890; appointed member of the board of trustees of the Indiana Normal School in 1886, and by reappointment served more than forty years; chairman of the congressional conference for the twenty-first district in 1896; elected as a Republican to the Fifty-sixth and Fifty-seventh Congresses (March 4, 1899-March 3, 1903); was not a candidate for renomination in 1902 to the Fifty-eighth Congress; member of the congressional delegation sent to the Philippine Islands in 1901 to inquire into the advisability of establishing civil government; resumed the practice of law; delegate to the Republican National Convention of 1908; died in Indiana, Pa., September 16, 1945; interment in the Oakland Cemetery, Indiana, Pa.

**JACK, William,** a Representative from Pennsylvania; born in Greensburg, Westmoreland County, Pa., July 29, 1788; studied law; was admitted to the bar and practiced; moved to Brookville, Jefferson County, Pa., in 1831 and engaged in mercantile pursuits; division inspector of militia for Westmoreland and Fayette Counties, 1830-1835; sheriff of Brookville in 1833; was a contractor and builder in Mississippi, and assisted in the construction of a canal in that State; returned to Pennsylvania; served as judge of Jefferson County about 1840; elected as a Democrat to the Twenty-seventh Congress (March 4, 1841-March 3, 1843); engaged in agricultural pursuits; returned to Greensburg, Pa., in 1846, and died there on February 28, 1852; interment in the Old Cemetery of the St. Clair Cemetery Association.

**JACKSON, Alfred Metcalf,** a Representative from Kansas; born in South Carrollton, Muhlenburg County, Ky., July 14, 1860; attended the common schools and West Kentucky College; studied law; was admitted to the bar and practiced; moved to Howard, Elk County, Kans., in 1881 and engaged in the practice of law; prosecuting attorney of Elk County in 1890; judge of the thirteenth judicial district of Kansas in 1892; moved to Winfield, Kans., in 1898; elected as a Democrat to the Fifty-seventh Congress (March 4, 1901-March 3, 1903); unsuccessful candidate for reelection in 1902 to the Fifty-eighth Congress; resumed the practice of law in Winfield, Kans., and died there on June 11, 1924; interment in the Highland Mausoleum.

**JACKSON, Amos Henry,** a Representative from Ohio; born near Franklin, Delaware County, N.Y., May 10, 1846; moved with his parents to Gibson, Steuben County, N.Y., in 1854 and to a farm near Corning, Steuben County, N.Y., in 1862; attended the common schools; moved to Ohio in 1866; employed as a carpenter for several years and then engaged in selling notions from a wagon; settled in Fremont, Sandusky County, Ohio, in 1882 and engaged in the retail dry goods and shoe business and later engaged in manufactures; mayor of Fremont, 1897-1901; elected as a Republican to the Fifty-eighth Congress (March 4, 1903-March 3, 1905); was not a candidate for renomination in 1904 to the Fifty-ninth Congress; resumed manufacturing interests in Fremont, Ohio, until 1922, when he retired; died in Fremont, Ohio, August 30, 1924; interment in Oakwood Cemetery.

**JACKSON, Andrew,** a Representative and a Senator from Tennessee and 7th President of the United States; born on March 15, 1767, in the Waxhaw Settlement in South Carolina; attended an old-field school; though just a boy, participated in the battle of Hanging Rock, S.C., August 6, 1780, was captured by the British and imprisoned; worked for a time in a saddler's shop and afterward taught school; studied law in Salisbury, N.C.; was admitted to the bar in September 1787; moved to Jonesboro (now Tennessee) in 1788 and commenced practice; appointed solicitor of the western district of North Carolina, comprising what is now the State of Tennessee, in 1788; held the same position in the territorial government of Tennessee after 1791; delegate to the convention to frame a constitution for the new State in 1796; upon the admission of Tennessee as a State into the Union was elected to the Fourth and Fifth Congresses and served from December 5, 1796, until his resignation in September 1797; elected as a Republican in September 1797 to the United States Senate for the term that had commenced March 4, 1797, and served from September 26, 1797, until his resignation in April 1798; judge of the State supreme court of Tennessee 1798-1804; engaged in planting and in mercantile pursuits; served in the Creek War of 1813-1814 as commander of Tennessee forces; his victories in the Creek War brought him a commission as major general in the United States Army on May 22, 1814; led his army to victory over the British in the Battle of New Orleans on January 8, 1815; received the thanks of Congress and a gold medal by resolution of February 27, 1815; commanded an expedition which captured Florida in 1817; served as Governor of the new territory in 1821; again elected to the United States Senate and served from March 4, 1823, to October 14, 1825, when he resigned; chairman, Committee on Military Affairs (Eighteenth Congress); unsuccessful candidate for President in 1824; elected as a Democrat President of the United States in 1828; reelected in 1832 and served from March 4, 1829, to March 3, 1837; on January 30, 1835, Richard Lawrence fired two pistols at President Jackson as he stood in the Rotunda where he had come for the funeral of Representative Warren R. Davis of South Carolina; retired to his country home, the "Hermitage," near Nashville, Tenn., where he died June 8, 1845; interment in the garden on his estate.

**Bibliography:** *DAB*; Remini, Robert. *Andrew Jackson and the Course of American Empire, 1767-1821.* New York: Harper and Row, 1977; Jackson, Andrew. *The Papers of Andrew Jackson.* Edited by Sam B. Smith, Harriet Chappell Owsley, Harold D. Moser, Sharon Macpherson, David R. Hoth, John H. Reinbold, et al. 4 vols. to date. Knoxville: University of Tennessee Press, 1980- .

**JACKSON, David,** a Delegate from Pennsylvania; born in Newtown-Limavady, County Londonderry, Ireland, about 1730; immigrated to the United States and settled in Edenton, Chester County, Pa.; attended Nottingham Academy at West Nottingham Township; was graduated from the medical department of the University of Pennsylvania in 1768 and was an apothecary and physician in Philadelphia, Pa., 1768-1801; during the Revolutionary War was appointed paymaster of the Second Battalion of Philadelphia Militia December 3, 1776; quartermaster of militia in the field October 23, 1779; hospital physician and surgeon September 30, 1780; was present at the surrender of Lord Cornwallis, Yorktown, Va., October 19, 1781; Member of the Continental Congress in 1785; resumed the profession of apothecary, in addition to the practice of medicine; died in Oxford, Pa., September 17, 1801; interment in the Oxford Cemetery.

**Bibliography:** *DAB*.

**JACKSON, David Sherwood,** a Representative from New York; born in New York City in 1813; attended the public schools; alderman in the common council of New York City 1843-1846;

engaged in mercantile pursuits; presented credentials as a Democratic Member-elect to the Thirtieth Congress and served from March 4, 1847, until April 19, 1848, when the House declared the seat vacant, the election having been contested by James Monroe; resumed his former business pursuits; again an alderman in the common council in 1856 and 1857; died in New York City January 20, 1872; interment in the Marble Cemetery.

**JACKSON, Donald Lester,** a Representative from California; born in Ipswich, Edmunds County, S.Dak., January 23, 1910; attended the public schools of South Dakota and California; served as a private in the United States Marine Corps 1927-1931 and again from 1940 until discharged as a major in 1945 with two years' combat service overseas; engaged in public relations in Santa Monica, Calif.; reporter and editor, Santa Monica, 1938-1940; director of publicity, city of Santa Monica, Calif., in 1939 and 1940; congressional adviser at ninth conference of American States at Bogotá, Colombia, in 1948; elected as a Republican to the Eightieth and to the six succeeding Congresses (January 3, 1947-January 3, 1961); was not a candidate for renomination in 1960 to the Eighty-seventh Congress; radio and television commentator, 1960-1968; appointed by President Richard M. Nixon as a commissioner on the Interstate Commerce Commission in 1969; resided in Sosua, Puerta Plata, Dominican Republic, West Indies, until his death in Bethesda, Md., May 27, 1981; interment in Arlington National Cemetery, Va.

**JACKSON, Ebenezer, Jr.,** a Representative from Connecticut; born in Savannah, Ga., January 31, 1796; pursued academic studies; was graduated from St. Mary's College, near Baltimore, Md., in 1814; studied law at the Litchfield Law School, Connecticut; was admitted to the bar and commenced practice in Philadelphia, Pa., in 1821; moved to Middletown, Conn., in 1826; member of the State house of representatives 1829-1832; elected to the Twenty-third Congress to fill the vacancy caused by the resignation of Samuel A. Foote and served from December 1, 1834, to March 3, 1835; unsuccessful candidate for reelection in 1834 to the Twenty-fourth Congress; again a member of the State house of representatives in 1849; died in Middletown, Middlesex County, Conn., August 17, 1874; interment in Indian Hill Cemetery.

**JACKSON, Edward Brake** (son of George Jackson and brother of John George Jackson), a Representative from Virginia; born in Clarksburg, Harrison County, Va. (now West Virginia), January 25, 1793; attended Randolph Academy at Clarksburg; studied medicine and commenced practice in Clarksburg; during the War of 1812 was detailed surgeon's mate, Third Regular Virginia Militia, at Fort Meigs, Ohio; member of the Virginia house of delegates 1815-1818; clerk of the United States district court in 1819; elected to the Sixteenth Congress to fill the vacancy caused by the resignation of James Pindall; reelected to the Seventeenth Congress and served from October 23, 1820, to March 3, 1823; declined to be a candidate for renomination in 1822; died at Bedford Springs, near Bedford, Pa., September 8, 1826; interment near Bedford, Pa.

**JACKSON, Fred Schuyler,** a Representative from Kansas; born in Stanton, Miami County, Kans., April 19, 1868; moved to Greenwood County, Kans., with his parents in 1881; attended the public schools of Miami and Greenwood Counties; taught school in Kansas 1885-1890; was graduated in law from the University of Kansas at Lawrence in 1892; was admitted to the bar and commenced practice in Eureka, Kans.; prosecuting attorney of Greenwood County 1893-1897; assistant State attorney general in 1906 and 1907; attorney general 1907-1911; elected as a Republican to the Sixty-second Congress (March 4, 1911-March 3, 1913); unsuccessful candidate for reelection in 1912 to the Sixty-third Congress; resumed the practice of law in Eureka and Topeka, Kans.; moved to Topeka, Kans., in 1915, having been appointed attorney for the Public Utilities Commission of Kansas and served until 1924;

resumed the practice of law in Topeka, Kans.; also engaged in agricultural pursuits and stock raising in Greenwood, Wabaunsee, and Jefferson Counties; died in Topeka, Kans., November 21, 1931; interment in Greenwood Cemetery, Eureka, Kans.

**JACKSON, George** (father of John George Jackson and Edward Brake Jackson), a Representative from Virginia; born in Cecil County, Md., January 9, 1757; moved with his parents to Moorefield, Va. (now West Virginia), and in 1769 to Jacksons Fort, Va. (now Buckhannon, W.Va.); served in the Revolution, attaining the rank of colonel; studied law; was admitted to the bar in 1784 and commenced practice in Clarksburg, Va. (now West Virginia); justice of the peace in 1784; member of the Virginia house of delegates 1785-1791 and again in 1794; member of the Virginia convention which ratified the United States Constitution in 1788; elected as a Republican to the Fourth Congress (March 4, 1795-March 3, 1797); elected to the Sixth and Seventh Congresses (March 4, 1799-March 3, 1803); was not a candidate for reelection; moved to Zanesville, Ohio, about 1806 and engaged in agricultural pursuits; member of the Ohio State house of representatives 1809-1812; member of the Ohio State senate 1817-1819; died in Zanesville, Ohio, May 17, 1831; interment on an estate once owned by him in Falls Township, near Zanesville.

**JACKSON, Henry Martin,** a Representative and a Senator from Washington; born in Everett, Snohomish County, Wash., May 31, 1912; attended the public schools and Stanford University, Stanford, Calif.; graduated from the law school of the University of Washington at Seattle in 1935; was admitted to the bar the same year and commenced practice in Everett, Wash.; prosecuting attorney of Snohomish County, 1938-1940; attended the International Maritime Conference in Copenhagen, Denmark, in 1945 as adviser to the American delegation; elected president of the International Maritime Conference held in Seattle, Wash., in 1946; elected as a Democrat to the Seventy-seventh and to the five succeeding Congresses (January 3, 1941-January 3, 1953); chairman, Committee on Indian Affairs (Seventy-ninth Congress); was not a candidate for renomination in 1952 to the House of Representatives, but was elected to the United States Senate; reelected in 1958, 1964, 1970, 1976 and again in 1982, serving from January 3, 1953 until his death in Everett, Wash., on September 1, 1983; chairman, Committee on Interior and Insular Affairs (Eighty-eighth through Ninety-fifth Congresses), Committee on Energy and Natural Resources (Ninety-fifth and Ninety-sixty Congresses); chairman of the Democratic National Committee in 1960; unsuccessful candidate for the Democratic presidential nomination in 1972 and 1976; interment at Evergreen Cemetery, Everett, Wash.

**Bibliography:** Fosdick, Dorothy, ed. *Staying the Course: Henry M. Jackson and National Security*. Seattle: University of Washington Press, 1987; Ognibene, Peter J. *Scoop: The Life and Politics of Senator Henry M. Jackson*. New York: Stein and Day, 1975; Prochnau, William W., and Richard W. Larsen. *A Certain Democrat: Senator Henry M. Jackson, A Political Biography*. Englewood Cliffs, N.J.: Prentice-Hall, 1972.

**JACKSON, Howell Edmunds,** a Senator from Tennessee; born in Paris, Henry County, Tenn., April 8, 1832; moved with his parents to Jackson, Tenn., in 1840; pursued classical studies and graduated from West Tennessee College in 1849, from the University of Virginia at Charlottesville in 1854, and from the law department of Cumberland University, Lebanon, Tenn., in 1856; was admitted to the bar and commenced practice in Jackson; moved to Memphis, Tenn., in 1859 and engaged in the practice of law; served the Confederacy as receiver of sequestered property; returned to Jackson in 1874 and served on the court of arbitration for west Tennessee by appointment on two occasions; member, State house of representatives 1880; elected as a Democrat to the United States

Senate and served from March 4, 1881, until April 14, 1886, when he resigned to accept the appointment of United States circuit judge for the sixth Federal circuit, 1886-1893; nominated by President Benjamin Harrison as an Associate Justice of the United States Supreme Court on February 2, 1893; was confirmed by the Senate on February 18, 1893; took his seat on March 4, 1893 and served until his death in West Meade, Tenn., August 8, 1895; interment in Mount Olivet Cemetery, Nashville, Tenn.

**Bibliography:** *DAB*; Hardaway, Roger D. "Howell Edmunds Jackson: Tennessee Legislator and Jurist." *West Tennessee Historical Society Papers* 30 (1976): 104-119; Hudspeth, Harvey Gresham. "Forgotten Whig: The Life and Times of Howell Edmunds Jackson, 1832-1895." Ph.D. dissertation, University of Mississippi, 1994.

**JACKSON, Jabez Young** (son of James Jackson [1757-1806] and uncle of James Jackson [1819-1887]), a Representative from Georgia; born in Savannah, Ga., in July 1790; resided at Clarkesville; elected as a Jacksonian to the Twenty-fourth Congress to fill the vacancy caused by the resignation of James M. Wayne; reelected as a Democrat to the Twenty-fifth Congress and served from October 5, 1835, to March 3, 1839; died in Clarkesville, Habersham County, Ga.

**JACKSON, James** (grandson of James Jackson [1757-1806] and nephew of Jabez Y. Jackson), a Representative from Georgia; born in Jefferson County, Ga., on October 18, 1819; pursued classical studies and was graduated from the University of Georgia at Athens in 1837; studied law; was admitted to the bar in 1839 and commenced practice in Athens, Ga.; secretary of the State senate in 1842; served in the Georgia State house of representatives, 1845-1849; judge of the superior court from 1846 until his resignation in June 1859; elected as a Democrat to the Thirty-fifth and Thirty-sixth Congresses, and served from March 4, 1857 until January 23, 1861, when he joined other secessionist colleagues and withdrew; judge advocate on the staff of General Thomas J. "Stonewall" Jackson, 1861-1865; moved to Macon, Ga., and practiced law from 1865 until 1875, when he moved to Atlanta; appointed an associate justice of the State supreme court in 1875; elected to the position by the legislature in 1880 to fill an unexpired term; reelected in 1887; chief justice of Georgia from 1879 until his death in Atlanta, Ga., January 13, 1887; interment in Rose Hill Cemetery, Macon, Ga.

**Bibliography:** *DAB*.

**JACKSON, James** (father of Jabez Y. Jackson and grandfather of James Jackson [1819-1887]), a Representative and a Senator from Georgia; born in Moreton-Hampstead, Devonshire, England, September 21, 1757; emigrated to Georgia in 1772 and located in Savannah; served in the Revolution with the Georgia State forces; studied law and built a lucrative practice in Savannah; several times elected to the state legislature; elected governor of Georgia in 1788 but declined; planter; elected to the First Congress (March 4, 1789-March 3, 1791); contested the election of Anthony Wayne in the Second Congress and the seat was declared vacant by the House of Representatives March 21, 1792; elected to the United States Senate and served from March 4, 1793, until his resignation in 1795; again a member of the State legislature; Governor of Georgia from January 12, 1798 to March 3, 1801; was again elected as a Republican to the United States Senate and served from March 4, 1801, until his death in Washington, D.C., on March 19, 1806; interment in the Congressional Cemetery.

**Bibliography:** *DAB*; Charlton, Thomas. *The Life of Major General James Jackson.* Augusta: G.F. Randolph and Co., 1809; Foster, William. *James Jackson: Duelist and Militant Statesman.* Athens: University of Georgia Press, 1960.

**JACKSON, James Monroe** (cousin of William Thomas Bland), a Representative from West Virginia; born in Parkersburg, Wood County, Va. (now West Virginia), December 3, 1825; pursued an academic course and was graduated from Princeton College in 1845; studied law; was admitted to the bar in 1847 and commenced practice in Parkersburg, W.Va.; elected prosecuting attorney for Wood County in 1856 and 1860; member of the West Virginia State house of delegates in 1870 and 1871; member of the West Virginia State constitutional convention in 1872; elected judge of the fifth judicial circuit and served from 1873 to 1888, when he resigned; presented credentials as a Democratic Member-elect to the Fifty-first Congress and served from March 4, 1889, until February 3, 1890, when he was succeeded by Charles B. Smith, who contested the election; judge of the criminal court for Wood County, W.Va., from 1891 until his death in Parkersburg, W.Va., February 14, 1901; interment in Riverview Cemetery.

**JACKSON, James Streshly,** a Representative from Kentucky; born in Fayette County, Ky., September 27, 1823; pursued classical studies in Centre College, Danville, Ky.; was graduated from Jefferson College, Canonsburg, Pa., in 1844, and from the law department of Transylvania University, Lexington, Ky., in 1845; was admitted to the bar; commenced practice in Greenupsburg, Ky., in 1845; during the Mexican War enlisted as a private in the First Kentucky Cavalry on June 9, 1846; commissioned third lieutenant July 9, 1846; resigned October 10, 1846; moved to Hopkinsville in 1859; elected as a Unionist to the Thirty-seventh Congress and served from March 4 to December 13, 1861, when he resigned to enter the Union Army; raised a troop of cavalrymen and was commissioned colonel of the Third Regiment, Kentucky Volunteer Cavalry, December 13, 1861; commissioned brigadier general of Volunteers, July 16, 1862; killed in the Battle of Perryville, Ky., October 8, 1862; interment in Riverside Cemetery, Hopkinsville, Christian County, Ky.

**JACKSON, Jesse Louis, Jr.,** a Representative from Illinois; born in Greenville, S.C., March 11, 1965; graduated, St. Albans School, Washington, D.C.; B.S., North Carolina A&T State University, Greensboro, 1987; M.A., Chicago Theological Seminary, 1990; J.D., University of Illinois College of Law, 1993; president, Keep Hope Alive Political Action Committee; vice president at large, Operation PUSH; national field director, National Rainbow Coalition; member, Democratic National Committee; elected as a Democrat to the One Hundred Fourth Congress, December 12, 1995, by special election to fill the vacancy caused by the resignation of Mel Reynolds, and served from December 12, 1995 to January 3, 1997; is a resident of Chicago, Ill.

**JACKSON, John George** (son of George Jackson, brother of Edward Brake Jackson, and grandfather of William Thomas Bland), a Representative from Virginia; born in Buckhannon, Va. (now West Virginia), September 22, 1777; moved with his parents to Clarksburg in 1784; received an English training and became a civil engineer; appointed surveyor of public lands of what is now the State of Ohio in 1793; member of the Virginia house of delegates 1798-1801; elected as a Republican to the Eighth and to the three succeeding Congresses and served from March 4, 1803, to September 28, 1810, when he resigned; while in Congress fought a duel with Joseph Pearson, of North Carolina, and on the second fire was wounded in the hip; member of the Virginia house of delegates in 1811 and 1812; brigadier general of Virginia Militia in 1812; elected as a Republican to the Thirteenth and Fourteenth Congresses (March 4, 1813-March 3, 1817); declined to be a candidate for reelection in 1816 to the Fifteenth Congress; appointed United States district judge for the western district of Virginia in 1819 and served until his death in Clarksburg, Va. (now West Virginia), March 28, 1825; interment in the Old Jackson Cemetery.

**Bibliography:** *DAB*; Brown, Stephen W. *Voice of the New West: John G. Jackson: His Life and Times.* Macon, Ga.: Mercer University Press, 1985.

**JACKSON, Jonathan,** a Delegate from Massachusetts; born in Boston, Mass., June 4, 1743; pursued classical studies and was graduated from Harvard College in 1761; engaged in mercantile pursuits in Newburyport; member of the Provincial Congress in 1775; member of the Massachusetts house of representatives in 1777; Member of the Continental Congress in 1782; elected to the Massachusetts senate in 1789; United States marshal, district of Massachusetts, 1789-1791; treasurer of the Commonwealth 1802-1806; inspector and supervisor of internal revenue; president of the Massachusetts bank and of the Harvard corporation; died in Boston, Mass., March 5, 1810; interment in the Granary Burying Ground.

**JACKSON, Joseph Webber,** a Representative from Georgia; born at Cedar Hill, near Savannah, Ga., December 6, 1796; attended the common schools; studied law; was admitted to the bar and practiced; member of the municipal council of Savannah; mayor of Savannah; member of the State house of representatives; served in the State senate; elected as a Democrat to the Thirty-first Congress to fill the vacancy caused by the resignation of Thomas Butler King; reelected as a State Rights candidate to the Thirty-second Congress and served from March 4, 1850, to March 3, 1853; declined to be a candidate for renomination in 1852; captain of the Savannah Volunteer Guards and colonel of the First Georgia Regiment of Militia; judge of the superior court of Georgia; died in Savannah, Ga., September 29, 1854.

**JACKSON, Oscar Lawrence,** a Representative from Pennsylvania; born in Shenango Township, Lawrence County, Pa., September 2, 1840; attended the common schools, Tansy Hill Select School, and Darlington Academy; taught school in Hocking County, Ohio; served in the Union Army from 1861 to 1865; entered as captain of Company H, Sixty-third Regiment, Ohio Volunteer Infantry, and received promotions of major, lieutenant colonel, and colonel by brevet; studied law; was admitted to the bar in 1867 and commenced practice in New Castle, Pa.; district attorney 1868-1871; member of the commission to codify laws and devise a plan for the government of cities of Pennsylvania in 1877 and 1878; elected as a Republican to the Forty-ninth and Fiftieth Congresses (March 4, 1885-March 3, 1889); unsuccessful candidate for renomination in 1888 to the Fifty-first Congress; resumed the practice of law in New Castle, Pa.; delegate to the Republican National Convention in 1896; died in New Castle, Pa., on February 16, 1920; interment in Greenwood Cemetery.

**JACKSON, Richard, Jr.,** a Representative from Rhode Island; born in Providence, R.I., July 3, 1764; completed preparatory studies in the schools of Providence and Pomfret, Conn.; entered the mercantile and cotton manufacturing businesses; president of the Washington Insurance Co., Providence, R.I., 1800-1838; elected as a Federalist to the Tenth Congress to fill the vacancy caused by the death of Nehemiah Knight; reelected to the Eleventh, Twelfth, and Thirteenth Congresses and served from November 11, 1808, to March 3, 1815; was not a candidate for renomination in 1814; trustee of Brown University 1809-1838; died in Providence, R.I., on April 18, 1838.

**JACKSON, Samuel Dillon,** a Senator from Indiana; born near Zanesville, Allen County, Ind., May 28, 1895; attended the public schools of Fort Wayne, Ind.; graduated from the Indiana University Law School at Indianapolis in 1917, and was admitted to the bar the same year; during the First World War, served as a captain of Infantry 1917-1919; engaged in the practice of law at Fort Wayne, Ind., in 1919; prosecuting attorney of Allen County, Ind., 1924-1928; unsuccessful Democratic candidate for election in 1928 to the Seventy-first Congress; attorney general of Indiana 1940-1941; appointed as a Democrat to the United States Senate to fill the vacancy caused by the death of Frederick Van Nuys and served from January 28, 1944, to November 13, 1944, when a duly elected successor qualified; was not a candidate for election to fill the

vacancy; unsuccessful candidate for election in 1944 for Governor of Indiana; resumed the practice of law; died in Fort Wayne, Ind., March 8, 1951; interment in Lindenwood Cemetery.

**JACKSON, Thomas Birdsall,** a Representative from New York; born in Jerusalem, Long Island, N.Y., March 24, 1797; attended the public schools; engaged in agricultural pursuits; studied law; was admitted to the bar and practiced in Jerusalem, Hempstead, and Newtown, N.Y.; elected county judge in 1832; member of the State assembly 1833-1835; moved to Newtown, Long Island, N.Y., in 1835; justice of the peace; elected as a Democrat to the Twenty-fifth and Twenty-sixth Congresses (March 4, 1837-March 3, 1841); was not a candidate for renomination in 1840; resumed agricultural pursuits; died in Newtown (now Elmhurst Station), Flushing, Long Island, N.Y., April 23, 1881; interment in Flushing Cemetery.

**JACKSON, William,** a Representative from Massachusetts; born in Newton, Middlesex County, Mass., September 2, 1783; attended the district school; member of the board of selectmen; served on the school board committee of Newton; chief founder of Newton Temperance Society; engaged in the manufacture of soap and candles; became interested in railroads 1826-1836; member of the Massachusetts house of representatives 1829-1832; secretary of the Newton Female Academy in 1831; first president of the Newton Savings Bank 1831-1835; again president 1848-1855; elected as an Anti-Masonic candidate to the Twenty-third Congress and reelected as a Whig to the Twenty-fourth Congress (March 4, 1833-March 3, 1837); declined to be a candidate for renomination in 1836 to the Twenty-fifth Congress; resumed his manufacturing pursuits; one of the founders of the Liberty Party in 1846; president of the American Missionary Society 1846-1854; publisher of a newspaper; died in Newton, Mass., on February 27, 1855; interment in the Old Burial Ground.

**Bibliography:** *DAB.*

**JACKSON, William Humphreys** (father of William Purnell Jackson), a Representative from Maryland; born near Salisbury, Wicomico County, Md., October 15, 1839; received a common-school training; engaged in agricultural pursuits; moved to Salisbury, Md., in 1864 and engaged in the manufacture of lumber; elected as a Republican to the Fifty-seventh and Fifty-eighth Congresses (March 4, 1901-March 3, 1905); unsuccessful candidate for reelection in 1904 to the Fifty-ninth Congress; elected to the Sixtieth Congress (March 4, 1907-March 3, 1909); unsuccessful candidate for reelection in 1908 to the Sixty-first Congress; resumed lumber manufacturing in Salisbury, Md., and died there on April 3, 1915; interment in Parsons Cemetery.

**JACKSON, William Purnell** (son of William Humphreys Jackson), a Senator from Maryland; born in Salisbury, Wicomico County, Md., January 11, 1868; attended the public schools of Wicomico County and the Wilmington Conference Academy, Dover, Del.; engaged in the lumber business in 1887; member of the Republican National Committee 1908-1932; appointed as a Republican to the United States Senate to fill the vacancy caused by the death of Isidor Rayner and served from November 29, 1912, until January 28, 1914, when a duly elected successor qualified; was not a candidate for election to the vacancy in 1913; chairman, Committee on Expenditures in the Department of State (Sixty-second Congress); resumed his former business pursuits; Maryland State treasurer 1918-1920; president of the Salisbury National Bank and a director of the Baltimore, Chesapeake & Atlantic Railway Co.; died in Salisbury, Md., March 7, 1939; interment in Parsons Cemetery.

**JACKSON, William Terry,** a Representative from New York; born in Chester, Orange County, N.Y., December 29, 1794; attended the common schools and later studied surveying; taught school in Goshen 1813-1815; employed as a surveyor and later engaged in mercantile pursuits in Chester and Owego, N.Y., and Bermerville, Sussex County, N.J.; moved to Havana, Chemung County (now township of Montour, Schuyler County), N.Y., in 1825 and engaged in mercantile pursuits; justice of the peace 1836-1838; judge of the court of common pleas and general sessions of Chemung County 1839-1846; justice of the peace, town of Catherine, Chemung County; elected as a Whig to the Thirty-first Congress (March 4, 1849-March 3, 1851); resumed mercantile pursuits; died in Montour Falls, N.Y., September 15, 1882; interment in Montour Falls Cemetery.

**JACKSON LEE, Sheila,** a Representative from Texas; born in Jamaica, N.Y., January 12, 1950; graduated, Jamaica High School; B.A., Yale University, 1972; J.D., University of Virginia School of Law, 1975; practicing attorney; senior counsel, Select Committee on Assassinations, United States House of Representatives; associate judge, Municipal Court, Houston, Tex.; at-large council member, City of Houston, 1990-1994; elected as a Democrat to the One Hundred Fourth Congress (January 3, 1995-January 3, 1997); is a resident of Houston, Tex.

**JACOBS, Andrew** (father of Andrew Jacobs, Jr.), a Representative from Indiana; born near Gerald, Perry County, Ind., February 22, 1906; attended the public schools in Gerald, Ind., and St. Benedict's College, Atchison, Kans.; was graduated from Benjamin Harrison Law School, Indianapolis, Ind., in 1928; was admitted to the bar in June 1927 and commenced the practice of law in Indianapolis, Ind.; public defender in Marion County Felony Court, 1930-1933; elected as a Democrat to the Eighty-first Congress (January 3, 1949-January 3, 1951); was an unsuccessful candidate for reelection in 1950 to the Eighty-second Congress; delegate to the Democratic National Conventions of 1952 and 1956; resumed the practice of law; judge, criminal court of Marion County, 1975-1977; was a resident of Indianapolis, Ind.; died November 12, 1992.

**JACOBS, Andrew, Jr.** (son of Andrew Jacobs), a Representative from Indiana; born in Indianapolis, Marion County, Ind., February 24, 1932; graduated from Shortridge High School in 1949; entered the United States Marine Corps in 1950, and was released in 1952 after service in the Korean conflict; B.S., Indiana University, 1955; LL.B., Indiana University School of Law, 1958; was admitted to the bar in 1958 and commenced the practice of law in Indianapolis, Ind.; member of the Indiana State house of representatives in 1959 and 1960; elected as a Democrat to the Eighty-ninth and to the three succeeding Congresses (January 3, 1965-January 3, 1973); unsuccessful candidate for reelection in 1972 to the Ninety-third Congress; returned to Indianapolis and engaged in the private practice of law and teaching, 1973-1975; elected as a Democrat to the Ninety-fourth and to the ten succeeding Congresses (January 3, 1975-January 3, 1997); was not a candidate for reelection in 1996 to the One Hundred Fifth Congress; is a resident of Indianapolis, Ind.

**JACOBS, Ferris, Jr.,** a Representative from New York; born in Delhi, Delaware County, N.Y., March 20, 1836; attended Delaware Academy, Delhi, N.Y., and Delaware Literary Institute, Franklin, N.Y.; was graduated from Williams College, Williamstown, Mass., in 1856; studied law; was admitted to the bar in 1859 and commenced practice in Delhi; during the Civil War served in the Union Army; commissioned captain of the Third New York Cavalry August 26, 1861; lieutenant colonel of the Twenty-sixth New York Cavalry March 15, 1865; brevetted brigadier general of Volunteers March 13, 1865; resumed law practice in Delhi, N.Y.; elected district attorney in 1865 and 1866; delegate to the Republican National Convention of 1880; elected as a Republican to the Forty-seventh Congress (March 4, 1881-March 3, 1883); was not a candidate for renomination in 1882 to the Forty-eighth Congress; resumed the practice of law; died in White Plains, N.Y., August 30, 1886; interment in Woodland Cemetery, Delhi, N.Y.

**JACOBS, Israel,** a Representative from Pennsylvania; born near Perkiomen Creek, Providence Township, Montgomery County, Pa., June 9, 1726; attended the public schools; engaged in agricultural and mercantile pursuits; member of the colonial assembly 1770-1774; elected to the Second Congress (March 4, 1791-March 3, 1793); resumed agricultural pursuits; died in Providence Township about December 10, 1796; interment probably in graveyard of the Friends Meeting House.

**JACOBS, Orange,** a Delegate from the Territory of Washington; born near Geneseo, Livingston County, N.Y., May 2, 1827; moved with his parents to Michigan Territory in 1831; attended the common schools, Albion (Mich.) College, and the University of Michigan at Ann Arbor; studied law; was admitted to the Michigan bar in 1851 and commenced practice in Sturgis, Mich.; moved to the Territory of Oregon in 1852 and settled in Jacksonville, Jackson County, and continued the practice of law; edited and published the Jacksonville Sentinel until 1859, when he moved to the Territory of Washington; associate justice of the supreme court of the Territory of Washington in 1869; chief justice of the supreme court 1871-1875; elected as a Republican to the Forty-fourth and Forty-fifth Congresses (March 4, 1875-March 3, 1879); was not a candidate for renomination in 1878 to the Forty-sixth Congress; resumed the practice of law in Seattle; mayor of Seattle in 1880; member of the Territorial council 1885-1887; member of the Seattle charter revision commission in 1889; corporation counsel for the city of Seattle in 1890; judge of the superior court of King County 1896-1900; died in Seattle, Wash., May 21, 1914; interment in Mount Pleasant Cemetery.

**JACOBSEN, Bernhard Martin** (father of William Sebastian Jacobsen), a Representative from Iowa; born in Töendren, Schleswig-Holstein, Germany, March 26, 1862; attended the public schools; immigrated in 1876 to the United States with his parents, who settled in Clinton, Iowa; employed as a clerk in a dry goods store until 1886, when he engaged in the mercantile business; served as postmaster of Clinton 1914-1923; retired from the mercantile business in 1927 and engaged in the industrial finance business; elected as a Democrat to the Seventy-second, Seventy-third, and Seventy-fourth Congresses and served from March 4, 1931, until his death; had been renominated for reelection to the Seventy-fifth Congress at the time of his death; died in Rochester, Minn., June 30, 1936; interment in Springdale Cemetery, Clinton, Iowa.

**JACOBSEN, William Sebastian** (son of Bernhard Martin Jacobsen), a Representative from Iowa; born in Clinton, Clinton County, Iowa, January 15, 1887; attended the public schools and the Normal College of American Gymnastics Union, Indianapolis, Ind.; director of physical education of the Turner Society and Y.M.C.A., Clinton, Iowa, 1910-1915; manager and part owner of a mercantile store in Clinton, Iowa, 1915-1927; secretary, treasurer, manager, and organizer of Clinton Thrift Co., 1927-1937; also manager of business property and farm interests; delegate to Democratic State conventions 1932-1944; delegate to the Democratic National Conventions in 1936 and 1944; elected as a Democrat to the Seventy-fifth, Seventy-sixth, and Seventy-seventh Congresses (January 3, 1937-January 3, 1943); unsuccessful candidate for reelection in 1942 to the Seventy-eighth Congress; liaison officer, War Assets Administration, Washington, D.C., July 1945 to January 1947; acting postmaster, Clinton, Iowa, August 1, 1951, to January 1954; died in Dubuque, Iowa, April 10, 1955; interment in Springdale Cemetery, Clinton, Iowa.

**JACOBSTEIN, Meyer,** a Representative from New York; born in New York City, January 25, 1880; moved with his parents to Rochester, N.Y., in 1882; attended the public schools and the University of Rochester, Rochester, N.Y.; was graduated from Columbia University, New York City, in 1904; pursued postgraduate courses at the same university in economics and political science; special agent in the Bureau of Corporations, Department of Commerce, Washington, D.C., in 1907; assistant professor of economics, University of North Dakota at Grand Forks 1909-1913; professor of economics in the University of Rochester 1913-1918; was a director in emergency employment management at the University of Rochester under the auspices of the War Industry Board 1916-1918; elected as a Democrat to the Sixty-eighth and to the two succeeding Congresses (March 4, 1923-March 3, 1929); was not a candidate for renomination in 1928 to the Seventy-first Congress; delegate to the Democratic National Conventions of 1924 and 1932; declined the nomination of mayor of Rochester, N.Y., in 1925; engaged in banking in Rochester, N.Y., 1929-1936; in 1936 became chairman of the board of the Rochester Business Institute; member of the Brookings Institution staff 1939-1946; economic counsel in the legislative reference service of the Library of Congress from 1947 until his retirement May 31, 1952; resided in Rochester, N.Y., until his death there on April 18, 1963; interment in Mount Hope Cemetery.

**JACOWAY, Henderson Madison,** a Representative from Arkansas; born in Dardanelle, Yell County, Ark., November 7, 1870; attended the common schools; was graduated from the Dardanelle High School in 1887, from the Winchester Normal College, Winchester, Tenn., in 1892, and from the law department of Vanderbilt University, Nashville, Tenn., in 1898; was admitted to the bar in 1898 and commenced practice in Dardanelle; secretary of the so-called Dawes Commission, engaged in distributing the estates of the Five Civilized Tribes of Indians in the then Indian Territory; prosecuting attorney of the fifth judicial district 1904-1908; member of the State Democratic central committee 1910-1912; elected as a Democrat to the Sixty-second and to the five succeeding Congresses (March 4, 1911-March 3, 1923); was not a candidate for renomination in 1922 to the Sixty-eighth Congress; moved to Little Rock, Ark., in 1922 and served as vice president of the People's Savings Bank 1923-1929; resumed the practice of law; regional counsel of the Social Security Board for the States of Arkansas, Missouri, Oklahoma, and Kansas, 1936-1945; died in Little Rock, Ark., August 4, 1947; interment in Roselawn Cemetery.

**JADWIN, Cornelius Comegys,** a Representative from Pennsylvania; born in Carbondale, Lackawanna County, Pa., March 27, 1835; attended the common schools; taught school for four years; studied civil engineering and pharmacy; engaged as a civil and mining engineer 1857-1861; entered the drug business and located in Honesdale, Pa., in 1862; served on the board of education of his district for nine years and was president for three years; delegate to the Republican National Convention in 1880; elected as a Republican to the Forty-seventh Congress (March 4, 1881-March 3, 1883); was an unsuccessful Independent candidate for reelection in 1882 to the Forty-eighth Congress; continued the drug business in Honesdale, Pa., until his death there on August 17, 1913; interment in Glen Dyberry Cemetery.

**JAMES, Addison Davis** (grandfather of John Albert Whitaker), a Representative from Kentucky; born near Morgantown, Butler County, Ky., February 27, 1850; attended the public schools; began the study of medicine in 1870; was graduated from the University of Louisville, Louisville, Ky., in 1873; member of the Kentucky constitutional convention in 1890; member of the Kentucky house of representatives 1891-1893; commissioner to the World's Fair at Chicago representing the Commonwealth of Kentucky in 1892 and 1893; member of the Kentucky senate in 1895; appointed United States marshal for the district of Kentucky on July 6, 1897; reappointed on December 17, 1901, and served until December 31, 1905; elected as a Republican to the Sixtieth Congress (March 4, 1907-March 3, 1909); unsuccessful candidate for reelection; resumed

the practice of medicine; died in Penrod, Ky., June 10, 1947; interment in cemetery on the family estate.

**JAMES, Amaziah Bailey,** a Representative from New York; born in Stephentown, Rensselaer County, N.Y., July 1, 1812; moved with his father to Sweden, Monroe County, N.Y., in 1814; pursued an academic course; at the age of fourteen was apprenticed to the printer's trade in Batavia, N.Y.; moved to Ogdensburg, St. Lawrence County, N.Y., in 1831 and established the Northern Light, a weekly newspaper; later became part owner of the Times and Advertiser, the Whig paper of the county; captain of the Ogdensburg Artillery in 1836; afterward promoted to major general of militia; studied law; was admitted to the bar in 1838 and commenced practice in Ogdensburg; elected justice of the State supreme court in 1853; reelected in 1861 and again in 1869 and served until 1876; member of the peace convention of 1861 held in Washington, D.C., in an effort to devise means to prevent the impending war; elected as a Republican to the Forty-fifth and Forty-sixth Congresses (March 4, 1877-March 3, 1881); while serving his second term in Congress was stricken with paralysis, from which he partially recovered; died in Ogdensburg, N.Y., July 6, 1883; interment in the City Cemetery.

**JAMES, Benjamin Franklin,** a Representative from Pennsylvania; born in Philadelphia, Pa., August 1, 1885; attended the public schools of Philadelphia and continued education extensively in graphic arts; moved to Radnor Township, Delaware County, Pa., in 1910; during the First World War enlisted in the United States Army and was assigned to the Central Officers Training School; honorably discharged in November 1918 as second lieutenant, United States Army Reserves; former president and chairman of the board of directors of the Franklin Printing Co., Philadelphia, Pa. (founded in 1728 by Benjamin Franklin); member of the Radnor Township Board of Commissioners 1929-1936; served in the Pennsylvania house of representatives 1939-1947; elected as a Republican to the Eighty-first and to the four succeeding Congresses (January 3, 1949-January 3, 1959); was not a candidate for renomination in 1958; died in Bryn Mawr, Pa., January 26, 1961; interment in Arlington Cemetery, Drexel Park, Upper Darby Township, Pa.

**JAMES, Charles Tillinghast,** a Senator from Rhode Island; born in West Greenwich Center, Kent County, R.I., September 15, 1805; attended the common schools; in early youth moved to Providence, R.I., and learned the trade of a carpenter; subsequently became an expert textile machinist; erected cotton mills in Rhode Island, New York, Pennsylvania, Indiana, and Tennessee; served as major general of the Rhode Island Militia; elected as a Democrat to the United States Senate and served from March 4, 1851, to March 3, 1857; was not a candidate for reelection in 1856; chairman, Committee on Patents and the Patent Office (Thirty-second through Thirty-fourth Congresses) and Committee on Public Buildings (Thirty-second and Thirty-third Congresses); devoted his time to the improvement of firearms; died of wounds received from the explosion of a shell of his own manufacture with which he was experimenting at Sag Harbor, N.Y., on October 17, 1862; interment in Swan Point Cemetery, Providence, R.I.

**Bibliography:** *DAB.*

**JAMES, Craig T.,** a Representative from Florida; born in Augusta, Richmond County, Ga., May 5, 1941; graduated, DeLand (Fla.) High School, 1959; A.S., University of Florida, 1961; B.S., Stetson University at DeLand, 1963; J.D., Stetson University at St. Petersburg, 1967; Florida National Guard and United States Army Reserve service, 1963-1969; admitted to Florida bar, 1967; United States District Court for Middle District of Florida, 1968; practicing attorney, 1967-1968; commissioner, DeLand Housing Authority, 1971-1975; elected as a Republican to the One Hundred First and One Hundred Second Congresses (January 3, 1989-January 3,

1993); was not a candidate for reelection in 1992 to the One Hundred Third Congress; is a resident of DeLand, Fla.

**JAMES, Darwin Rush,** a Representative from New York; born in Williamsburg, Hampshire County, Mass., May 14, 1834; pursued an academic course in the Mount Pleasant Boarding School, Amherst, Mass.; moved with his parents to Williamsburg, N.Y., in 1847; entered the mercantile business in New York City in 1850; secretary of the New York Board of Trade and Transportation; park commissioner of Brooklyn 1876-1882; elected as a Republican to the Forty-eighth and Forty-ninth Congresses (March 4, 1883-March 3, 1887); declined to be a candidate for renomination in 1886 to the Fiftieth Congress; chairman of United States Board of Indian Commissioners in 1890; member of New York Canal Commission in 1898; resumed mercantile pursuits; died in Brooklyn, N.Y., November 19, 1908; interment in the City Cemetery, Williamsburg, Mass.

**JAMES, Francis,** a Representative from Pennsylvania; born in Thornbury Township, Chester County, Pa., April 4, 1799; attended the public schools and Gauses' Academy; studied law; was admitted to the bar of Chester County in 1825 and commenced practice in West Chester, Pa.; member of the Pennsylvania senate 1834-1836; elected as an Anti-Masonic candidate to the Twenty-sixth Congress and reelected as a Whig to the Twenty-seventh Congress (March 4, 1839-March 3, 1843); chairman, Committee on Revisal and Unfinished Business (Twenty-seventh Congress); resumed the practice of his profession in West Chester, Chester County, Pa.; chief burgess in 1850; died in West Chester, Pa., January 4, 1886; interment in Oakland Cemetery.

**JAMES, Hinton,** a Representative from North Carolina; born in Laurinburg, Richmond County (now Scotland County), N.C., April 24, 1884; attended public and private schools and Davidson College, Davidson, N.C.; engaged in agricultural pursuits and as a cotton merchant in Laurinburg, N.C.; also interested in banking; member of the city council 1917-1919; mayor of Laurinburg 1919-1921; elected as a Democrat to the Seventy-first Congress to fill the vacancy caused by the death of William C. Hammer and served from November 4, 1930, to March 3, 1931; was not a candidate for election in 1930 to the Seventy-second Congress; resumed his former business pursuits; member of the Laurinburg school board 1941-1944; State commissioner of game and inland fisheries 1941-1945; member of the county Democratic executive committee; engaged as a cotton and produce merchant; resident of Laurinburg, N.C., until his death November 3, 1948; interment in Hillside Cemetery.

**JAMES, Ollie Murray,** a Representative and a Senator from Kentucky; born near Marion, Crittenden County, Ky., July 27, 1871; attended the common schools; page in the Kentucky legislature in 1887; studied law; was admitted to the bar in 1891 and practiced; elected as a Democrat to the Fifty-eighth and to the four succeeding Congresses (March 4, 1903-March 3, 1913); did not seek renomination in 1912, having become a candidate for Senator; elected as a Democrat to the United States Senate and served from March 4, 1913, until his death in a hospital at Baltimore, Md., August 28, 1918; chairman, Committee on Patents (Sixty-third through Sixty-fifth Congresses); interment in Mapleview Cemetery, Marion, Ky.

**JAMES, Rorer Abraham,** a Representative from Virginia; born near Brosville, Pittsylvania County, Va., March 1, 1859; instructed by private tutors; attended Roanoke College; was graduated from the Virginia Military Institute at Lexington in 1882 and from the law department of the University of Virginia at Charlottesville in 1887; was admitted to the bar in 1887 and commenced practice in Danville, Va.; became owner and editor of the Danville Register in 1899 and later purchased the Danville Bee; member of the Virginia house of delegates 1889-1892; served in the Virginia senate

1893-1901; delegate to the Democratic National Convention of 1920; chairman of the fifth district Democratic committee; chairman of the Democratic State committee; elected as a Democrat to the Sixty-sixth Congress to fill the vacancy caused by the resignation of Edward W. Saunders; reelected to the Sixty-seventh Congress and served from June 15, 1920, until his death in Danville, Va., August 6, 1921; interment in Green Hill Cemetery.

**JAMES, William Francis,** a Representative from Michigan; born in Morristown, Morris County, N.J., May 23, 1873; moved with his parents to Hancock, Mich., in 1876; attended the public schools; student at local college in Albion, Mich., in 1890 and 1891; treasurer of Houghton County, Mich., 1900-1904; engaged in real estate and insurance business; served as a private in Company F of the Thirty-fourth Regiment, Michigan Volunteer Infantry, during the Spanish-American War; member of the board of aldermen of Hancock, 1906-1908; mayor of Hancock 1908 and 1909; member of the State senate, 1910-1914; elected as a Republican to the Sixty-fourth and to the nine succeeding Congresses (March 4, 1915-January 3, 1935); chairman, Committee on Military Affairs (Seventy-first Congress); unsuccessful candidate for reelection in 1934 to the Seventy-fourth Congress and for election in 1936 to the Seventy-fifth Congress; died in Arlington, Va., November 17, 1945; interment in Arlington National Cemetery.

**JAMESON, John,** a Representative from Missouri; born near Mount Sterling, Montgomery County, Ky., March 6, 1802; attended the common schools; moved to Callaway County, Mo., in 1825; studied law; was admitted to the bar in 1826 and commenced practice in Fulton, Mo.; held several local offices; member of the Missouri State house of representatives, 1830-1836, and served as speaker in 1834 and 1836; elected as a Democrat to the Twenty-sixth Congress to fill the vacancy caused by the death of Albert G. Harrison, and served from December 12, 1839 to March 3, 1841; was not a candidate for renomination in 1840 to the Twenty-seventh Congress; elected to the Twenty-eighth Congress (March 4, 1843-March 3, 1845); was not a candidate for renomination in 1844 to the Twenty-ninth Congress; elected to the Thirtieth Congress (March 4, 1847-March 3, 1849); was not a candidate for renomination in 1848 to the Thirty-first Congress; ordained as a minister in the Christian Church; also engaged in agricultural pursuits; served as a captain in the Black Hawk War; died in Fulton, Mo., January 24, 1857; interment in the Jameson family cemetery near Fulton, Mo.

**JAMIESON, William Darius** (great-grandson of James R. Gillis), a Representative from Iowa; born near Wapello, Louisa County, Iowa, November 9, 1873; attended the common schools and the University of Iowa at Iowa City; studied law at the National University Law School, Washington, D.C.; edited and published the Ida Grove Pioneer in 1893 and 1894, the Columbus Junction Gazette 1899-1901, the Shenandoah World 1901-1916, and was also editor of the Hamburg Democrat; member of the State senate from January 1, 1907, until March 3, 1909, when he resigned to enter Congress; elected as a Democrat to the Sixty-first Congress (March 4, 1909-March 3, 1911); declined to be a candidate for renomination in 1910; resumed newspaper activities in Shenandoah, Iowa; postmaster of Shenandoah from May 29, 1915, until September 1, 1916, when he resigned; assistant treasurer of the Democratic National Committee in 1916 and its director of finance 1917-1920; delegate at large to the Democratic National Convention in 1920; engaged in the practice of law in Washington, D.C.; editor of the Window Seat, a weekly syndicate letter for country newspapers, from 1925 until his death in Washington, D.C., November 18, 1949; interment in Fort Lincoln Cemetery.

**JANES, Henry Fisk,** a Representative from Vermont; born in Brimfield, Hampden County, Mass., October 10, 1792; moved with his parents to Calais, Vt.; pursued an academic course; served in the

War of 1812 and participated in the Battle of Plattsburgh, N.Y., September 11, 1814; studied law in Montpelier, Vt.; was admitted to the bar and commenced practice in Waterbury, Vt., in 1817; postmaster, 1820-1830; member of the Vermont State legislative council, 1830-1834; elected as an Anti-Masonic candidate to the Twenty-third Congress to fill the vacancy caused by the death of Benjamin F. Deming; reelected to the Twenty-fourth Congress and served from December 2, 1834, to March 3, 1837; unsuccessful Anti-Masonic candidate for reelection in 1836 to the Twenty-fifth Congress; Vermont State treasurer, 1838-1841; member of the Vermont State council of censors in 1848; town representative in 1854, 1861, and 1862; member of the Vermont State house of representatives in 1855; died in Waterbury, Vt., June 6, 1879; interment in the Village Cemetery.

**JARMAN, John,** a Representative from Oklahoma; born in Sallisaw, Sequoyah County, Okla., July 17, 1915; attended the public schools of Oklahoma City, Okla., and Westminster Presbyterian College, Fulton, Mo., 1932-1934; B.A., Yale University, 1937; LL.B., Harvard University Law School, 1941; was admitted to the bar in 1941 and commenced the practice of law in Oklahoma City, Okla.; enlisted as a private in the United States Army on January 12, 1942, and served in the Security Intelligence Corps, assigned to the United Nations Conference in California; was discharged as a master sergeant on December 11, 1945; member, Oklahoma State house of representatives, 1947-1948; served in the State senate in 1949 and 1950; elected as a Democrat to the Eighty-second and to the twelve succeeding Congresses (January 3, 1951-January 3, 1977); announced his affiliation with the Republican Party, effective January 24, 1975, and continued in office during the Ninety-fourth Congress as a Republican; was not a candidate for reelection in 1976 to the Ninety-fifth Congress; practiced law in Oklahoma City, Okla., where he resided until his death there on January 15, 1982; cremated and buried at Rose Hill Burial Park.

**JARMAN, Pete,** a Representative from Alabama; born in Greensboro, Hale County, Ala., on October 31, 1892; attended the public schools, the Normal College, Livingston, Ala., and Southern University, Greensboro, Ala.; was graduated from the University of Alabama at Tuscaloosa in 1913, and attended the University of Montpellier, France, in 1919; clerk in probate office in Sumter County, Ala., 1913-1917; during the First World War served overseas as second and first lieutenant in the Three Hundred and Twenty-seventh Infantry; served in the Alabama National Guard as inspector general with rank of major, 1922-1924, and as division inspector of the Thirty-first Infantry Division with rank of lieutenant colonel, 1924-1940; assistant State examiner of accounts, 1919-1930; secretary of state of Alabama, 1931-1934; assistant State comptroller in 1935 and 1936; member of the State Democratic executive committee of Alabama, 1927-1930; elected as a Democrat to the Seventy-fifth and to the five succeeding Congresses (January 3, 1937-January 3, 1949); chairman, Committee on Memorials (Seventy-fifth Congress); unsuccessful candidate for renomination in 1948 to the Eighty-first Congress; appointed by President Harry S Truman as Ambassador to Australia on June 8, 1949, and served until July 31, 1953; died in Washington, D.C., February 17, 1955; interment in Arlington National Cemetery, Va.

**JARNAGIN, Spencer,** a Senator from Tennessee; born in Grainger County, Tenn., in 1792; pursued classical studies and was graduated from Greenville College in 1813; studied law; was admitted to the bar in 1817 and commenced practice in Knoxville; member, Tennessee State senate, 1833-1835; trustee of East Tennessee College, 1836-1851; moved to Athens, Tenn., in 1837 and continued the practice of his profession; presidential elector on the Whig ticket in 1840; was nominated by the Whig Party to the United States Senate in 1841, but the general assembly adjourned without electing a Senator; elected as a Whig to the United States Senate,

and served from October 17, 1843 to March 3, 1847; chairman, Committee on Revolutionary Claims (Twenty-eighth Congress); unsuccessful candidate for reelection to the Senate and for election for the supreme court of Tennessee; moved to Memphis and continued the practice of law; died in Memphis, Tenn., June 25, 1853; interment in Elmwood Cemetery.

**JARRETT, Benjamin,** a Representative from Pennsylvania; born in Sharon, Mercer County, Pa., July 18, 1881; attended the public schools of Wheatland, Pa.; worked as a telegraph operator and later as foreman in a steel mill; studied law; was admitted to the bar in 1907 and commenced practice in Farrell, Mercer County, Pa.; city solicitor of Farrell, Pa., 1910-1930; served in the Pennsylvania senate 1911-1913; member of the Pennsylvania Workmen's Compensation Board 1919-1923; served as chairman of Mercer County Republican committee; elected as a Republican to the Seventy-fifth, Seventy-sixth, and Seventy-seventh Congresses (January 3, 1937-January 3, 1943); was not a candidate for renomination in 1942; resumed the practice of law; died, while on a visit, in Zanesville, Ohio, July 20, 1944; interment in Oakwood Cemetery, Sharon, Pa.

**JARRETT, William Paul,** a Delegate from the Territory of Hawaii; born in Honolulu, Hawaii, August 22, 1877; attended St. Louis College, Honolulu; deputy sheriff and sheriff of the city and county of Honolulu 1906-1914; high sheriff of the Territory of Hawaii and warden of Oahu Prison 1914-1922; member of the Board of Industrial Schools from May 1919 to January 1922; elected as a Democrat a Delegate to the Sixty-eighth and Sixty-ninth Congresses (March 4, 1923-March 3, 1927); unsuccessful candidate for reelection in 1926 to the Seventieth Congress; died at Honolulu, T.H., November 10, 1929; interment in Diamond Head Memorial Park.

**JARVIS, Leonard,** a Representative from Maine; born in Boston, Mass., October 19, 1781; attended the common schools; was graduated from Harvard University in 1800; moved to Surry, Maine; sheriff of Hancock County, Maine, 1821-1829; collector of customs for the Penobscot district 1829-1831; elected as a Jacksonian to the Twenty-first and to the three succeeding Congresses (March 4, 1829-March 3, 1837); chairman, Committee on Naval Affairs (Twenty-fourth Congress); Navy agent for the port of Boston 1838-1841; returned to Surry, Maine, where he died October 18, 1854; interment in Hillside Cemetery.

**JARVIS, Thomas Jordan,** a Senator from North Carolina; born in Jarvisburg, Currituck County, N.C., January 18, 1836; received his early schooling from his father; graduated from Randolph-Macon College, Virginia, in 1860; served in the Confederate Army during the Civil War as a captain and was permanently disabled in the right arm; member of the State constitutional convention in 1865; moved to Tyrrell County in 1866; opened a store and studied law; was admitted to the bar in 1867 and commenced practice; member, State house of representatives 1868, 1870, and served as speaker in 1870; moved to Greenville, N.C., in 1872; member of the State constitutional convention in 1875; elected lieutenant governor of North Carolina in 1876; became Governor on February 5, 1879, when Governor Zebulon B. Vance resigned; elected Governor for a full term in 1880 and served until January 21, 1885; appointed United States Minister to Brazil by President Grover Cleveland on April 2, 1885 and served until November 19, 1888; appointed as a Democrat to the United States Senate to fill the vacancy caused by the death of Zebulon B. Vance and served from April 19, 1894, until January 23, 1895, when a successor was qualified; chairman, Committee on Civil Service and Retrenchment (Fifty-third Congress); trustee of the University of North Carolina and East Carolina Teachers College at Greenville, N.C.; resumed the practice of law in Greenville, N.C., and died there June 17, 1915; interment in Cherry Hill Cemetery.

**Bibliography:** *DAB.*

**JAVITS, Jacob Koppel,** a Representative and a Senator from New York; born in New York City, May 18, 1904; attended the public schools; traveling salesman; attended night classes at Columbia University; graduated from the New York University Law School in 1926; was admitted to the bar in 1927 and commenced practice in New York City; lecturer and author of articles on political and economic problems; during the Second World War, served with the Chemical Warfare Service 1941-1944, with overseas service in the European and Pacific Theaters; discharged as a lieutenant colonel in 1945; resumed the practice of law; elected as a Republican to the Eightieth and to the three succeeding Congresses and served from January 3, 1947, until his resignation December 31, 1954; had been renominated in 1954 to the Eighty-fourth Congress but withdrew; attorney general of New York 1954-1957; elected as a Republican to the United States Senate in 1956 for the term commencing January 3, 1957, but did not assume his duties until January 9, 1957; reelected in 1962, 1968, and again in 1974, and served from January 9, 1957, to January 3, 1981; unsuccessful Republican candidate for renomination in 1980; unsuccessful Liberal candidate for election to the United States Senate in 1980; resumed the practice of law; adjunct professor of public affairs at Columbia University's School of International Affairs; author; died in West Palm Beach, Florida, on March 7, 1986; interment in Linden Hill Cemetery, Queens, New York City.

**Bibliography:** Javits, Jacob. "The Congressional Presence in Foreign Relations." *Foreign Affairs* 48 (January 1970): 221-34; Javits, Jacob, and Steinberg, Rafael. *Javits: The Autobiography of a Public Man.* Boston: Houghton Mifflin Company, 1981.

**JAY, John,** a Delegate from New York; born in New York City December 12, 1745; attended a boarding school in New Rochelle, N.Y., and was graduated from Kings College (now Columbia University) in 1764; studied law; was admitted to the bar in 1768; served on the New York committee of correspondence; Member of the Continental Congress, 1774-1776, and 1778-1779; recalled some months in 1777 to aid in forming the New York State constitution; appointed chief justice of the State of New York in May 1777 but resigned December 1778 to become President of the Continental Congress and served in that capacity from December 10, 1778, to September 28, 1779; appointed Minister Plenipotentiary to Spain on September 27, 1779; appointed one of the ministers to negotiate peace with Great Britain on June 14, 1781, and signed the Treaty of Paris; appointed one of the ministers to negotiate treaties with the European powers on May 1, 1783; returned to New York in 1784; appointed Secretary of Foreign Affairs in July 1784, which position he held until the establishment of the Federal Government in 1789; nominated the first Chief Justice of the United States by President Washington on September 24, 1789; was confirmed by the Senate on September 26, 1789, and served until June 29, 1795, when he resigned; unsuccessful Federal candidate for election in 1792 for Governor of New York; appointed Envoy Extraordinary and Minister Plenipotentiary to Great Britain on April 19, 1794, and served until April 8, 1795, still retaining his position as Chief Justice of the United States; elected Governor of New York in 1795, reelected in 1798, and served from July 1, 1795 to July 1, 1801; declined reelection and also a reappointment as Chief Justice of the United States; retired to his farm at Bedford, near New York City, where he died on May 17, 1829; interment in the family burying ground at Rye, N.Y.

**Bibliography:** *DAB*; Morris, Richard B. *John Jay: The Making of a Revolutionary: Unpublished Papers, 1745-1780.* New York: Harper and Row, 1980; Morris, Richard B. *John Jay: The Winning of the Peace: Unpublished Papers, 1780-1784.* New York: Harper and Row, 1980.

**JAYNE, William,** a Delegate from the Territory of Dakota; born in Springfield, Ill., October 8, 1826; completed preparatory studies at Illinois College, Jacksonville, Ill., and was graduated from the medical department of the University of Missouri at Columbia in 1849; commenced the practice of medicine in Springfield, Ill.; mayor of Springfield, 1859-1861; member of the Illinois State senate in 1860, but resigned in 1861 to accept the appointment of Governor of Dakota Territory from President Lincoln; served as Governor from March 27, 1861 until his resignation March 1, 1863, having been elected to Congress; presented credentials as a Delegate-elect to the Thirty-eighth Congress and served from March 4, 1863, to June 17, 1864, when he was succeeded by John B.S. Todd, who contested his election; returned to Springfield and continued the practice of medicine; served three terms as mayor of Springfield during the period 1865 to 1880; appointed by President Ulysses S. Grant pension agent at Springfield and served from 1869 to 1873; resumed the practice of medicine; died in Springfield, Ill., on March 20, 1916; interment in Oak Ridge Cemetery.

**JEFFERIS, Albert Webb,** a Representative from Nebraska; born near Embreeville, Chester County, Pa., December 7, 1868; attended the public schools in Romansville, Pa., and the State normal school at West Chester; taught school in West Bradford Township three years; was graduated from the law department of the University of Michigan, at Ann Arbor, in 1893; was admitted to the bar the same year and commenced practice in Omaha, Nebr.; member of various Republican State and county committees; assistant county attorney 1896-1898; unsuccessful candidate for election in 1908 to the Sixty-first Congress; chairman of the Republican State convention in 1910; elected as a Republican to the Sixty-sixth and Sixty-seventh Congresses (March 4, 1919-March 3, 1923); unsuccessful candidate for election to the United States Senate in 1922; resumed the practice of law; was elected delegate at large to the Republican National Convention in 1924; was manager of the Coolidge-Dawes automobile caravan from Plymouth, Vt., to Bellingham, Wash.; resumed the practice of law in Omaha, Nebr.; unsuccessful candidate for nomination as United States Senator in 1940; died at Omaha, Nebr., on September 14, 1942; interment in Forest Lawn Cemetery.

**JEFFERS, Lamar,** a Representative from Alabama; born in Anniston, Calhoun County, Ala., April 16, 1888; attended the public schools and the Alabama Presbyterian College at Anniston; served with the Alabama National Guard, 1904-1914; clerk of the circuit court of Calhoun County, taking office in January 1917; resigned that office in May 1917 and entered the United States Army, serving with the Eighty-second Division in France; was awarded the Distinguished Service Cross by the United States Government; promoted to rank of major of infantry; elected as a Democrat to the Sixty-seventh Congress to fill the vacancy caused by the death of Fred L. Blackmon; reelected to the Sixty-eighth and to the five succeeding Congresses, and served from June 7, 1921 to January 3, 1935; chairman, Committee on Civil Service (Seventy-second and Seventy-third Congresses); unsuccessful candidate for renomination in 1934 to the Seventy-fourth Congress; resided in Daytona Beach, Fla., until his death there on June 1, 1983; interment in Arlington National Cemetery, Va.

**JEFFERSON, Thomas** (father-in-law of Thomas Mann Randolph), a Delegate from Virginia and a Vice President and 3d President of the United States; born at "Shadwell," in present-day Albermarle County, Virginia, April 13, 1743; attended a preparatory school; graduated from the College of William and Mary, Williamsburg, Va., in 1762; studied law; was admitted to the bar and commenced practice in 1767; member, colonial House of Burgesses, 1769-1775; prominent in pre-Revolutionary movements; Member of the Continental Congress in 1775 and 1776; chairman of the committee that drew up the Declaration of Independence in the summer of 1776 and made the first draft; signer of the Declaration of Independence; resigned soon after and returned to his estate, "Monticello"; Governor of Virginia, 1779-1781; member of the

Virginia house of delegates in 1782; again a Member of the Continental Congress, 1783-1784; appointed Minister Plenipotentiary to France on March 10, 1785 and served until September 26, 1789; appointed Secretary of State in the Cabinet of President George Washington on September 26, 1789, and served until December 31, 1793; elected Vice President of the United States, and served under President John Adams, March 4, 1797 to March 4, 1801; elected President of the United States on February 17, 1801 by the House of Representatives on the thirty-sixth ballot; reelected in 1805, and served from March 4, 1801 to March 3, 1809; retired to his estate, "Monticello"; active in founding the University of Virginia at Charlottesville; died at "Monticello," Albemarle County, Va., July 4, 1826; interment in the grounds of "Monticello."

Bibliography: *DAB*; Malone, Dumas. *Jefferson and the Ordeal of Liberty*. Boston: Little, Brown, 1962; Jefferson, Thomas. *The Papers of Thomas Jefferson*. Edited by Julian Boyd, Charles Cullen, and Dickinson Adams. 26 vols. to date. Princeton: Princeton University Press, 1950- .

JEFFERSON, William J., a Representative from Louisiana; born in Lake Providence, East Carroll County, Louisiana, March 14, 1947; graduated, G.W. Griffin High School in Lake Providence, 1965; B.A., Southern University, 1969; J.D., Harvard University School of Law, 1972; LL.M. (taxation), Georgetown University School of Law, Washington, D.C., 1996; admitted to Louisiana bar, 1972; entered active duty, United States Army in 1969; released as captain in 1972 after service with Judge Advocate General's Corps; United States Army Reserve service, 1975; clerk, Judge Alvin B. Rubin, United States District Court, 1972-1973; legislative assistant to Senator J. Bennett Johnston of Louisiana, 1973-1975; practicing attorney, 1976-1990; member, Louisiana State senate, 1980-1990; elected as a Democrat to the One Hundred Second and to the two succeeding Congresses (January 3, 1991-January 3, 1997); was a candidate in 1995 for nomination for Governor of Louisiana until he withdrew from the race; is a resident of New Orleans, La.

JEFFORDS, Elza, a Representative from Mississippi; born in Ironton, Lawrence County, Ohio, May 23, 1826; attended the common schools in Portsmouth, Ohio; studied law; was admitted to the bar in 1847 and commenced practice in Portsmouth, Ohio; served in the Army of the Tennessee from June 1862 to December 1863 as clerk in the Quartermaster's Department; judge of the high court of errors and appeals in Mississippi 1868 and 1869; delegate to the Republican National Convention in 1872; elected as a Republican to the Forty-eighth Congress (March 4, 1883-March 3, 1885); unsuccessful candidate for reelection in 1884; died in Vicksburg, Miss., on March 19, 1885; interment in Cedar Hill Cemetery, near Vicksburg.

JEFFORDS, James Merrill, a Representative and a Senator from Vermont; born in Rutland, Vt., May 11, 1934; attended public schools; B.S., Yale University, 1956; LL.B., Harvard University School of Law, 1962; admitted to the Vermont bar in 1962 and commenced practice in Rutland; served in the United States Navy, 1956-1959, and later in the Naval Reserve, retiring as captain from the Naval Reserve; chair, Rutland County Board of Tax Appeals, 1964-1966; served in Vermont senate, 1967-1968; Vermont Attorney General, 1969-1973; delegate to Vermont State Republican conventions, 1964, 1968, 1972; elected as a Republican to the Ninety-fourth and to the six succeeding Congresses (January 3, 1975-January 3, 1989); was not a candidate in 1988 for reelection to the House of Representatives, but was elected to the United States Senate for the term commencing January 3, 1989; reelected in 1994 for the term ending January 3, 2001; is a resident of Shrewsbury, Vt.

JEFFREY, Harry Palmer, a Representative from Ohio; born in Dayton, Ohio, December 26, 1901; attended the public schools; was graduated from Ohio State University at Columbus in 1924, and from the College of Law of the same university in 1926; second

lieutenant, United States Army Reserve Corps, 1927-1930; was admitted to the bar in 1926 and commenced practice in Columbus, Ohio; moved to Dayton, Ohio, in 1927, and continued the practice of law; special assistant attorney general of Ohio, 1933-1936; elected as a Republican to the Seventy-eighth Congress (January 3, 1943-January 3, 1945); unsuccessful candidate for reelection in 1944 to the Seventy-ninth Congress; resumed the practice of law in Dayton, Ohio, where he resides.

JEFFRIES, James Edmund, a Representative from Kansas; born in Detroit, Wayne County, Mich., June 1, 1925; attended the public schools; graduated, Cranbrook Academy, Bloomfield Hills, 1943; attended Michigan State University, Lansing, 1947; served in United States Army Air Corps, 1943-1945; investment counselor, corporate director, 1956-1979; delegate to Kansas State Republican convention, 1978; elected as a Republican to the Ninety-sixth and Ninety-seventh Congresses (January 3, 1979-January 3, 1983); was not a candidate for reelection in 1982 to the Ninety-eighth Congress; is a resident of Atchison, Kans.

JEFFRIES, Walter Sooy, a Representative from New Jersey; born in Atlantic City, Atlantic County, N.J., October 16, 1893; attended the public schools and was graduated from the Atlantic City (N.J.) Business College in 1909; was also graduated in celestial navigation from Franklin Institute, Philadelphia, Pa., in 1943; engaged in the manufacture of paint, 1910-1934; mayor of Margate City, N.J., 1931-1935; served as sheriff of Atlantic County, N.J., 1935-1938; became engaged in the hotel business at Atlantic City in 1938; elected as a Republican to the Seventy-sixth Congress (January 3, 1939-January 3, 1941); unsuccessful candidate for reelection in 1940 to the Seventy-seventh Congress; treasurer of Atlantic County, 1941-1944; died in Margate City, N.J., October 11, 1954; interment in Laurel Memorial Cemetery, Egg Harbor Township, Atlantic County, N.J.

JENCKES, Thomas Allen, a Representative from Rhode Island; born in Cumberland, R.I., November 2, 1818; attended the public schools; was graduated from Brown University, Providence, R.I., in 1838; studied law; was admitted to the bar in 1840 and commenced practice in Providence, R.I.; clerk in the State legislature 1840-1844; secretary of the State constitutional convention in 1842; adjutant general 1845-1855; member of the State house of representatives 1854-1857; commissioner to revise the laws of the State in 1855; elected as a Republican to the Thirty-eighth and to the three succeeding Congresses (March 4, 1863-March 3, 1871); chairman, Committee on Patents (Thirty-eighth through Forty-first Congresses); unsuccessful candidate for reelection in 1870; resumed the practice of law; died in Cumberland, R.I., on November 4, 1875; interment in Swan Point Cemetery, Providence, R.I.

Bibliography: *DAB*; Hoogenboom, Ari. "Thomas A. Jenckes and Civil Service Reform." *Mississippi Valley Historical Review* 47 (March 1961): 636-58.

JENCKES, Virginia Ellis, a Representative from Indiana; born in Terre Haute, Vigo County, Ind., November 6, 1877; attended the public and high schools; engaged in agricultural pursuits in 1912; secretary of Wabash Maumee Valley Improvement Association, 1926-1932; elected as a Democrat to the Seventy-third and to the two succeeding Congresses (March 4, 1933-January 3, 1939); unsuccessful candidate for reelection in 1938 to the Seventy-sixth Congress; United States delegate to the Interparliamentary Union in Paris, France, in 1937; after leaving Congress, remained in Washington, D.C., for many years and worked for the American Red Cross; returned to her native Terre Haute, Ind., in the early 1970s; died in Terre Haute, Ind., January 9, 1975; interment in Highland Lawn Cemetery.

**JENIFER, Daniel** (nephew of Daniel of St. Thomas Jenifer), a Representative from Maryland; born in Charles County, Md., April 15, 1791; completed preparatory studies; studied law; served in the State house of delegates; elected as an Anti-Jacksonian to the Twenty-second Congress (March 4, 1831-March 3, 1833); unsuccessful candidate for reelection in 1832 to the Twenty-third Congress; elected to the Twenty-fourth Congress and reelected as a Whig to the Twenty-fifth and Twenty-sixth Congresses (March 4, 1835-March 3, 1841); appointed Minister to Austria on August 27, 1841, and served until July 1845; register of wills for Charles County, 1846-1851; died in Mulberry Grove, near Port Tobacco, Md., December 18, 1855; interment on a farm, "Charleston," in the southern part of Charles County, Md.

**JENIFER, Daniel of St. Thomas** (uncle of Daniel Jenifer), a Delegate from Maryland; born in Charles County, Md., in 1723; member of the provincial court in 1766; member of the Governor's council in 1773; member and president of the council of safety, 1775-1777; president of the Maryland State senate, 1777-1780; Member of the Continental Congress, 1779-1781, also of the convention that framed the Federal Constitution, and a signer of that instrument on September 17, 1787; unsuccessful candidate for Governor of Maryland in 1782 and 1785; died in Annapolis, Anne Arundel County, Md., November 16, 1790.

**JENISON, Edward Halsey,** a Representative from Illinois; born in Fond du Lac, Wis., July 27, 1907; attended the public schools and the University of Wisconsin at Madison; engaged in newspaper work with the Paris (Ill.) Daily Beacon from 1927 to 1937, and as a publisher, beginning in 1938, of the Paris Beacon-News; served as a lieutenant commander in the United States Navy, attached to the Deputy Chief of Naval Operations for Air, with service in the Pacific and Atlantic Forces, from April 1943 to September 1946; elected as a Republican to the Eightieth and to the two succeeding Congresses (January 3, 1947-January 3, 1953); unsuccessful candidate for reelection in 1952 to the Eighty-third Congress, for election in 1954 to the Eighty-fourth Congress, and for election in 1962 to the Eighty-eighth Congress; delegate to the Republican National Conventions of 1956 and 1968; member, Illinois State Board of Vocational Education, 1953-1960; director of the State department of finance from June 15, 1960 to January 20, 1961; member of the Legislature, 1965-1966, and was appointed to the Legislature in 1973 to complete an unexpired term; delegate to the Illinois Sixth Constitutional Convention, 1969-1970; resumed the publishing business; was a resident of Paris, Ill., until his death there on June 24, 1996; interment in Edgar Cemetery.

**JENKINS, Albert Gallatin,** a Representative from Virginia; born in Cabell County, Va. (now West Virginia), November 10, 1830; was graduated from Jefferson College, Canonsburg, Pa., in 1848 and from Harvard Law School in 1850; was admitted to the bar in 1850, but engaged in agricultural pursuits; delegate to the Democratic National Convention in 1856; elected as a Democrat to the Thirty-fifth and Thirty-sixth Congresses (March 4, 1857-March 3, 1861); delegate to the Confederate Provisional Congress in 1861; enlisted in the Confederate Army; appointed brigadier general August 5, 1862; wounded in the Battle of Cloyds Mountain, near Dublin, Va., May 9, 1864, and died May 21, 1864; interment in New Dublin Presbyterian Cemetery; reinterred after the close of the war at his home in Green Valley, near Huntington, W.Va.; again reinterred in the Confederate plot in Spring Hill Cemetery, Huntington, W.Va.

Bibliography: *DAB.*

**JENKINS, Edgar Lanier,** a Representative from Georgia; born in Young Harris, Towns County, Ga., January 4, 1933; attended the public schools; A.A., Young Harris (Ga.) College, 1951; LL.B., University of Georgia, Athens, 1959; admitted to the Georgia bar in 1958 and commenced practice in Jasper; employed by the Federal Bureau of Investigation, 1951; served in United States Coast Guard, 1952-1955; served as executive secretary to Representative Phillip M. Ladrum of Georgia, 1959-1962; Pickens County (Ga.) attorney, 1968-1972; assistant United States attorney, Northern District of Georgia, 1962-1964; resumed practice of law in Pickens County, 1965; elected as a Democrat to the Ninety-fifth and to the seven succeeding Congresses (January 3, 1977-January 3, 1993); was not a candidate for reelection in 1992 to the One Hundred Third Congress; is a resident of Jasper, Ga.

**JENKINS, John James,** a Representative from Wisconsin; born in Weymouth, England, August 24, 1843; attended the common schools; immigrated to the United States with his parents, who settled in Baraboo, Wis., in June 1852; served in the Civil War as a member of Company A, Sixth Regiment, Wisconsin Volunteer Infantry, 1861-1865; clerk of the circuit court of Sauk County, 1867-1870; moved to Chippewa Falls, Wis., in 1870; studied law; was admitted to the bar and practiced; city clerk and city attorney of Chippewa Falls; member of the Wisconsin State assembly in 1872; county judge of Chippewa County, 1872-1876; appointed United States attorney for the Territory of Wyoming in March 1876 and served until 1880, when he returned to Chippewa Falls, Wis., and resumed the practice of law; elected as a Republican to the Fifty-fourth and to the six succeeding Congresses (March 4, 1895-March 3, 1909); chairman, Committee on the Judiciary (Fifty-eighth through Sixtieth Congresses); unsuccessful candidate for renomination in 1908 to the Sixty-first Congress; appointed judge of Puerto Rico by President William Howard Taft in May 1910, and served until his death in Chippewa Falls, Wis., June 8, 1911; interment in Forest Hill Cemetery.

**JENKINS, Lemuel,** a Representative from New York; born in Bloomingburg, Sullivan County, N.Y., October 20, 1789; completed preparatory studies; studied law; was admitted to the Sullivan County bar in October 1815 and practiced in Bloomingburg, N.Y.; master in chancery; the first district attorney of Sullivan County and served from June 1818 to March 1819; elected to the Eighteenth Congress (March 4, 1823-March 3, 1825); moved to Albany, N.Y., and resumed the practice of law; died in Albany, N.Y., August 18, 1862; interment in Albany Rural Cemetery.

**JENKINS, Mitchell,** a Representative from Pennsylvania; born in Forty Fort, Luzerne County, Pa., January 24, 1896; attended the Kingston public schools and the Wyoming Seminary, Kingston, Pa.; was graduated from Wesleyan University, Middletown, Conn., in June 1919 and New York University Law School, New York City, in June 1923; was admitted to the New York bar in December 1923 and the Pennsylvania bar in January 1924 and commenced practice in Wilkes-Barre, Pa.; assistant district attorney of Luzerne County 1938-1946; enlisted as a private in the United States Army in April 1917, and was discharged as a first lieutenant January 2, 1919; enlisted in the Pennsylvania National Guard as a private in January 1926 and rose through the ranks to lieutenant colonel prior to induction into Federal service on February 17, 1941; served four and a half years during the Second World War, promoted to colonel and was placed on inactive status October 5, 1945; promoted to brigadier general (retired), Pennsylvania National Guard; elected as a Republican to the Eightieth Congress (January 3, 1947-January 3, 1949); was not a candidate for reelection in 1948 to the Eighty-first Congress; assistant district attorney of Luzerne County, Pa., in 1949 and in 1950; resumed the practice of law in Wilkes-Barre, Pa., where he died September 15, 1977; interment in Evergreen Cemetery, Shavertown, Pa.

**JENKINS, Robert,** a Representative from Pennsylvania; born in Windsor Forges, Lancaster County, Pa., July 10, 1769; attended the common schools and the select school of Dr. Robert Smith of Pequea; was an ironmaster in Caernarvon Township; member of the Pennsylvania house of representatives in 1804 and 1805; elected as a Republican to the Tenth and Eleventh Congresses (March 4, 1807-March 3, 1811); member of a Group of Horse, and took an active part in suppressing the Whiskey Rebellion in Pennsylvania; died in Windsor Forges, Pa., April 18, 1848; interment in the Caernarvon Presbyterian Churchyard, Churchtown, Lancaster County, Pa.

**JENKINS, Thomas Albert,** a Representative from Ohio; born at Oak Hill, Jackson County, Ohio, October 28, 1880; attended the grade and high schools; was graduated from Providence University, Oak Hill, Ohio, in 1901 and from the law department of the Ohio State University at Columbus in 1907; was admitted to the bar the same year and commenced practice in Ironton, Ohio; prosecuting attorney of Lawrence County, Ohio, 1916-1920; served in the State senate in 1923 and 1924; delegate to the Republican State conventions in 1920 and 1924; elected as a Republican to the Sixty-ninth and to the sixteen succeeding Congresses (March 4, 1925-January 3, 1959); was not a candidate for renomination in 1958; died in Worthington, Ohio, December 21, 1959; interment in Woodland Cemetery, Ironton, Ohio.

**JENKINS, Timothy,** a Representative from New York; born in Barre, Worcester County, Mass., January 29, 1799; located in Washington County, N.Y., in 1817; pursued an academic course; studied law; was admitted to the bar in 1825 and commenced practice in Oneida Castle, N.Y.; moved to Vernon, N.Y., in 1832; was attorney for the Oneida Indians in their dealings with the State of New York 1838-1845; district attorney for Oneida County 1840-1845; elected as a Democrat to the Twenty-ninth and Thirtieth Congresses (March 4, 1845-March 3, 1849); unsuccessful candidate for reelection in 1848 to the Thirty-first Congress; elected to the Thirty-second Congress (March 4, 1851-March 3, 1853); chairman, Committee on Private Land Claims (Thirty-second Congress); unsuccessful candidate for reelection in 1852 to the Thirty-third Congress; delegate to the Republican National Convention in 1856 and was thereafter a Republican; died in Martinsburg, N.Y., December 24, 1859; interment in the City Cemetery, Oneida Castle, N.Y.

**JENKS, Arthur Byron,** a Representative from New Hampshire; born in West Dennis, Barnstable County, Mass., October 15, 1866; attended the public schools; employed as a shoe worker in 1881; engaged in the shoe manufacturing business at Manchester, N.H., 1902-1930; also became engaged in the banking business in 1917 at Manchester, N.H.; unsuccessful candidate for election in 1934 to the Seventy-fourth Congress; delegate to the Republican National Conventions in 1936 and 1940; presented his credentials as a Republican Member-elect to the Seventy-fifth Congress and served from January 3, 1937, until June 9, 1938, when he was succeeded by Alphonse Roy, who contested his election; elected as a Republican to the Seventy-sixth and Seventy-seventh Congresses (January 3, 1939-January 3, 1943); unsuccessful candidate for renomination in 1942; resumed the banking business in Manchester, N.H., until his death there on December 14, 1947; interment in Pine Grove Cemetery.

**JENKS, George Augustus,** a Representative from Pennsylvania; born in Punxsutawney, Jefferson County, Pa., on March 26, 1836; attended the public school; learned the carpenter's trade; taught school; was graduated from Jefferson College, Canonsburg, Pa., in 1858; studied law; was admitted to the bar in 1859 and commenced practice in Brookville, Pa.; elected as a Democrat to the Forty-fourth Congress (March 4, 1875-March 3, 1877); unsuccessful candidate for reelection in 1876 to the Forty-fifth Congress; chairman, Committee on Invalid Pensions (Forty-fourth Congress); one of the managers appointed by the House of Representatives in 1876 to conduct the impeachment proceedings against William W. Belknap, ex-Secretary of War; unsuccessful candidate for the Pennsylvania supreme bench in 1880; Assistant Secretary of the

Department of the Interior in 1885 and 1886; Solicitor General of the United States from 1886 to 1889; unsuccessful candidate for election in 1898 for Governor of Pennsylvania; unsuccessful candidate for United States Senator in the joint legislative convention of 1899; resumed the practice of law; died in Brookville, Pa., February 10, 1908; interment in the Brookville Cemetery.

**JENKS, Michael Hutchinson,** a Representative from Pennsylvania; born at Bridgetown Mills, Bucks County, near Middletown, Pa., May 21, 1795; pursued an academic course; engaged in agricultural pursuits; commissioner of Bucks County 1830-1833; treasurer 1833-1835; moved to Newtown, Pa., in 1837; associate judge of the court of common pleas of Bucks County 1838-1843; elected as a Whig to the Twenty-eighth Congress (March 4, 1843-March 3, 1845); unsuccessful candidate for reelection in 1844 to the Twenty-ninth Congress; engaged in the real estate business and as general business agent 1845-1865; chief burgess of Newtown 1848-1853; died in Newtown, Bucks County, Pa., on October 16, 1867; interment in the Newtown Friends Meeting Cemetery.

**JENNER, William Ezra,** a Senator from Indiana; born in Marengo, Crawford County, Ind., July 21, 1908; attended public and preparatory schools; graduated from Indiana University at Bloomington in 1930 and from that university's law school in 1930; admitted to the bar in 1930 and commenced practice in Paoli, Ind., in 1932; member, State senate 1934-1942, serving as minority leader 1937-1939 and majority leader and president pro tempore 1939-1941; resigned his seat in 1942 to serve in the Second World War; served overseas and retired as a captain in the Army Air Corps in 1944; elected as a Republican to the United States Senate on November 7, 1944, to fill the vacancy caused by the death of Frederick Van Nuys and served from November 14, 1944, to January 3, 1945; was not a candidate for election to the full term; elected to the United States Senate in 1946 for the term commencing January 3, 1947; reelected in 1952, and served from January 3, 1947, until January 3, 1959; was not a candidate for renomination in 1958; co-chairman, Joint Committee on Printing (Eightieth and Eighty-third Congresses), chairman, Committee on Rules and Administration (Eighty-third Congress); resumed the practice of law; died in Bedford, Ind., March 9, 1985; interment at Crest Haven Memorial Gardens, Bedford, Ind.

**Bibliography:** Poder, Michael. "The Senatorial Career of William E. Jenner." Ph.D. dissertation, University of Notre Dame, 1976; Ross, Rodney. "Senator William E. Jenner: A Study in Cold War Isolation." Ed.D. dissertation, Pennsylvania State University, 1973.

**JENNESS, Benning Wentworth,** a Senator from New Hampshire; born in Deerfield, Rockingham County, N.H., July 14, 1806; attended Bradford Academy, Massachusetts; engaged in mercantile pursuits in Strafford, N.H., 1826-1856; held several local offices; member, State house of representatives; judge of probate of Strafford County 1841-1845; appointed to the United States Senate to fill the vacancy caused by the resignation of Levi Woodbury and served from December 1, 1845, to June 13, 1846; unsuccessful Democratic candidate for election in 1846 to the Thirtieth Congress; member of the State constitutional convention in 1850; nominated for Governor of New Hampshire in 1861 but withdrew; moved to Ohio and engaged in lumbering and banking; died in Cleveland, Ohio, November 16, 1879; interment in the family cemetery, Strafford, N.H.

**JENNINGS, David,** a Representative from Ohio; born in Readington Township, Hunterdon County, N.J., in 1787; attended the public schools; moved to St. Clairsville, Ohio, in 1812; studied law; was admitted to the bar in 1813 and commenced practice in St. Clairsville; prosecuting attorney of Belmont County 1815-1825; held several local offices; member of the State senate 1819-1824; elected to the Nineteenth Congress and served from March 4, 1825, until his resignation, May 25, 1826; died in Baltimore, Md., in 1834.

**JENNINGS, John, Jr.,** a Representative from Tennessee; born in Jacksboro, Campbell County, Tenn., June 6, 1880; attended the public schools and American Temperance University, Harriman, Tenn.; was graduated from U.S. Grant University, Athens, Tenn., in 1906; studied law; was admitted to the bar in 1903 and commenced practice in Jellico, Campbell County, Tenn.; superintendent of public instruction, Campbell County, Tenn., 1903-1904; Campbell County attorney, 1911-1918; delegate to the Republican National Conventions of 1912, 1936 and 1944; special assistant to the Attorney General of the United States in 1918 and 1919; served as judge of the second chancery division of Tennessee from September 1, 1918 until his resignation on July 1, 1923; moved to Knoxville, Tenn., in 1923 and continued the practice of law; elected as a Republican to the Seventy-sixth Congress to fill the vacancy caused by the death of J. Will Taylor; reelected to the Seventy-seventh and to the four succeeding Congresses, and served from December 30, 1939 to January 3, 1951; unsuccessful candidate for renomination in 1950 to the Eighty-second Congress; resumed the practice of law; died in Knoxville, Tenn., February 27, 1956; interment in Highland Memorial Cemetery.

**JENNINGS, Jonathan,** a Delegate from the Territory of Indiana and a Representative from Indiana; born in Hunterdon County, N.J., in 1784; moved about the year 1790 to Fayette County, Pa., with his parents, who settled near Dunlap's Creek; attended a grammar school conducted by Rev. John McMillin at Canonsburg, Pa.; moved to Indiana Territory in 1806 and settled at Jeffersonville; studied law and commenced the practice of law; moved to Vincennes in 1807; was admitted to the bar and continued his legal profession; clerk to the receiver of public money; became assistant to the clerk of the house of representatives of the Territorial government in 1807; engaged in newspaper work in 1808; moved to Clark County in 1809 and settled in Charlestown; elected a Delegate to the Eleventh and to the three succeeding Congresses and served from November 27, 1809, to December 11, 1816, when the Territory was admitted as a State into the Union; delegate to the State constitutional convention in 1816 and served as president; elected Governor of Indiana in 1816, reelected in 1819, and served from November 7, 1816 until September 12, 1822, when he resigned; member of the commission to negotiate a treaty with the Indians for lands in 1818; elected to the Seventeenth Congress to fill the vacancy caused by the resignation of William Hendricks; reelected to the Eighteenth and to the three succeeding Congresses and served from December 2, 1822, to March 3, 1831; unsuccessful candidate for reelection in 1830 to the Twenty-second Congress; retired to his farm and engaged in agricultural pursuits; in 1832 served as a commissioner to negotiate with the Indians for the purchase of lands in northern Indiana and southern Michigan; died near Charlestown, Ind., July 26, 1834; interment in Charlestown Cemetery.

Bibliography: *DAB*; Smith, Brent Edward. "Jonathan Jennings: Indiana's First State Governor." Ph.D. dissertation, Ball State University, 1987.

**JENNINGS, William Pat,** a Representative from Virginia; born on a farm in Camp, Smyth County, Va., August 20, 1919; attended the public schools; B.S., Virginia Polytechnic Institute, Blacksburg, 1941; entered the United States Army in July 1941; served in the United States for two years and in the European Theater of Operations for two and a half years with the Twenty-ninth Infantry as platoon leader, company commander, and operations officer; instructor in the Reserve Officer Training Corps at the University of Illinois; discharged as a major in May 1946; automobile and farm implement dealer in Marion, Va., from 1946 until his death; cattle farmer; delegate to the Democratic National Conventions of 1952, 1956, 1960 and 1968; elected sheriff of Smyth County, Va., in 1947,

reelected in 1951, and served until 1954; elected as a Democrat to the Eighty-fourth and to the five succeeding Congresses (January 3, 1955-January 3, 1967); unsuccessful candidate for reelection in 1966 to the Ninetieth Congress; elected Clerk of the House of Representatives for the Ninetieth Congress, and reelected to the four succeeding Congresses, and served from January 10, 1967, until his resignation November 15, 1975, to be president of Slurry Transport Association; was a resident of Marion, Va.; died August 2, 1994.

**JENRETTE, John Wilson, Jr.,** a Representative from South Carolina; born in Conway, Horry County, S.C., May 19, 1936; attended public schools; B.A., Wofford College, Spartanburg, S.C.; LL.B., University of South Carolina Law School, Columbia, 1962; admitted to the South Carolina bar in 1962 and commenced practice in North Myrtle Beach; served as North Myrtle Beach city judge, 1962-1965; city attorney, 1965-1969; served in the South Carolina house of representatives, 1964-1972; unsuccessful candidate for election in 1972 to the Ninety-third Congress; delegate to the Democratic Mid-Term Convention of 1974, and to the Democratic National Convention of 1976; elected as a Democrat to the Ninety-fourth, Ninety-fifth and Ninety-sixth Congresses and served from November 5, 1975, until his resignation, December 10, 1980; president of an advertising and public relations firm in Florence and Myrtle Beach, S.C.; is a resident of Myrtle Beach, S.C.

**JENSEN, Benton Franklin,** a Representative from Iowa; born in Marion, Linn County, Iowa, December 16, 1892; attended the rural and high schools; employed by a lumber company as yardman and assistant auditor 1914-1917; during the First World War served as a second lieutenant in 1918; manager of a lumber company 1919-1938; elected as a Republican to the Seventy-sixth and to the twelve succeeding Congresses (January 3, 1939-January 3, 1965); wounded March 1, 1954 when three Puerto Rican Nationalists fired about thirty shots into a crowd of Representatives on the floor of the House; unsuccessful candidate for reelection in 1964 to the Eighty-ninth Congress; returned to Exira, Iowa; died in Washington, D.C., February 5, 1970; interment in Exira Cemetery, Exira, Iowa.

**JEPSEN, Roger William,** a Senator from Iowa; born in Cedar Falls, Black Hawk County, Iowa, December 23, 1928; attended the public schools; attended the University of Northern Iowa, Cedar Falls, 1945-1946; B.S., Arizona State University, Tempe, 1950, and M.A., 1953; paratrooper in the United States Army, 1946-1947; captain, United States Army Reserve, 1948-1960; farming and insurance agent, 1954-1955; insurance executive, 1956-1972; business executive, 1973-1978; member, Scott County board of supervisors, 1962-1965; Iowa State senator, 1966-1968; lieutenant governor of Iowa, 1968-1972; elected as a Republican to the United States Senate in 1978, and served from January 3, 1979 to January 3, 1985; unsuccessful candidate for reelection in 1984; co-chairman, Joint Economic Committee (Ninety-eighth Congress); chairman, National Credit Union Administration; is a resident of Alexandria, Va.

**JETT, Thomas Marion,** a Representative from Illinois; born near Greenville, Bond County, Ill., May 1, 1862; attended the common schools and the Northern Indiana Normal School, Valparaiso, Ind., for two years; taught school in Bond and Montgomery Counties, Ill.; studied law; was admitted to the bar in 1887 and commenced practice in Nokomis, Ill.; moved to Hillsboro, Ill., and served as prosecuting attorney of Montgomery County 1889-1896; elected as a Democrat to the Fifty-fifth, Fifty-sixth, and Fifty-seventh Congresses (March 4, 1897-March 3, 1903); was not a candidate for renomination in 1902; resumed the practice of law in Hillsboro, Ill.; also interested in agricultural pursuits; delegate to the Democratic National Conventions in 1900 and 1908; was elected as a judge of the circuit court, fourth judicial district of Illinois, in 1909; reelected in 1915, 1921, 1927, and 1935 and served until his death; was a member of the appellate court of the second district of

Illinois 1922-1936; died in Litchfield, Ill., January 10, 1939; interment in Oak Grove Cemetery, Hillsboro, Ill.

**JEWETT, Daniel Tarbox,** a Senator from Missouri; born in Pittston, Kennebec County, Maine, September 14, 1807; completed preparatory studies; attended Colby College; graduated from Columbia College, New York City, in 1830 and from the Harvard Law School; was admitted to the bar and practiced in Bangor, Maine; city solicitor of Bangor 1834-1837; engaged with his brother in operating a steamboat line upon the Chagres River, Isthmus of Panama 1850-1853; moved to California and engaged in gold mining for two years; returned to Bangor, Maine, and practiced law; moved to St. Louis, Mo., in 1857 and continued the practice of law; member, State house of representatives 1866; appointed as a Republican to the United States Senate to fill the vacancy caused by the resignation of Charles D. Drake and served from December 19, 1870, to January 20, 1871, when a successor was elected; declined to be a candidate for election to the Senate to fill this vacancy; resumed the practice of law; died in St. Louis, Mo., October 7, 1906; interment in Bellefontaine Cemetery.

**JEWETT, Freeborn Garrettson,** a Representative from New York; born in Sharon, Litchfield County, Conn., August 4, 1791; pursued an academic course; moved to Skaneateles, N.Y., in 1815; justice of the peace in 1817; studied law; was admitted to the bar in 1818 and commenced practice in Skaneateles; surrogate of Onondaga County 1824-1831; member of the State assembly in 1826; elected as a Jacksonian to the Twenty-second Congress (March 4, 1831-March 3, 1833); was not a candidate for renomination in 1832; inspector of Auburn Prison in 1838 and 1839; district attorney for Onondaga County in 1839; appointed associate justice of the State supreme court March 5, 1845; elected a judge of the State court of appeals in 1847; reelected in 1849 and served until June 1853, when he resigned on account of ill health; served as chief justice of the court 1847-1850; died in Skaneateles, N.Y., January 27, 1858; interment in Lake View Cemetery.

**JEWETT, Hugh Judge** (brother of Joshua Husband Jewett), a Representative from Ohio; born at Deer Creek, near Darlington, Md., on July 1, 1817; completed preparatory studies and attended Hopewell Academy, Chester County, Pa.; studied law in Elkton, Cecil County, Md.; was admitted to the bar in 1838 and commenced practice in St. Clairsville, Ohio; moved to Columbus, Ohio, and thence to Zanesville, Ohio, in 1848; president of the branch State bank in 1852; United States attorney for the southern district of Ohio in 1854; member of the state senate in 1853; member of the State house of representatives in 1855; president of the Central Ohio Railroad Co. in 1857; organized the Pittsburgh, Cincinnati & St. Louis Railroad Co.; one of the organizers of the Pennsylvania Railroad; unsuccessful Democratic candidate for election in 1861 for Governor of Ohio, and for United States Senator in 1863; member of the State house of representatives in 1868 and 1869; general counsel of the Pennsylvania Railway system in 1871; elected as a Democrat to the Forty-third Congress and served from March 4, 1873, until June 23, 1874, when he resigned to become president of the Erie Railroad Co.; retired from public life and resided in New York City; died while on a visit to Augusta, Ga., March 6, 1898; interment in Woodlawn Cemetery, Zanesville, Ohio.

**Bibliography:** *DAB*.

**JEWETT, Joshua Husband** (brother of Hugh Judge Jewett), a Representative from Kentucky; born at Deer Creek, Harford County, Md., September 30, 1815; attended the common schools; studied law; was admitted to the bar in 1836 and commenced practice in Elizabethtown, Ky.; prosecuting attorney of Hardin County; elected as a Democrat to the Thirty-fourth and Thirty-fifth Congresses (March 4, 1855-March 3, 1859); chairman, Committee on Expenditures in the Department of War (Thirty-fourth Congress), Committee on Invalid Pensions (Thirty-fifth Congress); unsuccessful

candidate for reelection in 1858 to the Thirty-sixth Congress; resumed the practice of law; died in Elizabethtown, Hardin County, Ky., July 14, 1861; interment in the City Cemetery.

**JEWETT, Luther,** a Representative from Vermont; born in Canterbury, Windham County, Conn., December 24, 1772; was graduated from Dartmouth College, Hanover, N.H., in 1795; studied medicine and practiced in Putney, Vt.; member of the Vermont State house of representatives; elected as a Federalist to the Fourteenth Congress (March 4, 1815-March 3, 1817); moved to St. Johnsbury, Caledonia County, Vt.; studied theology; was ordained as a minister and officiated in Newbury, Vt., 1821-1828; returned to St. Johnsbury and published the Farmer's Herald, 1828-1832, and the Free Mason's Friend, 1830-1832; died in St. Johnsbury, Vt., March 8, 1860; interment in Mount Pleasant Cemetery.

**JOELSON, Charles Samuel,** a Representative from New Jersey; born in Paterson, Passaic County, N.J., January 27, 1916; attended the public schools, graduated from Montclair Academy; B.A., Cornell University, Ithaca, N.Y., 1937; LL.B., Cornell University School of Law, 1939; was admitted to the bar in 1940 and commenced the practice of law in Paterson, N.J.; enlisted in the United States Navy in 1942 and served in the Far Eastern Branch of the Division of Naval Intelligence; city counsel of Paterson, N.J., 1949-1952; deputy attorney general of the New Jersey criminal investigation division, 1954-1956, and the Passaic County Prosecutor's Office, 1956-1958; director of criminal investigation for the State of New Jersey, 1958-1960; elected as a Democrat to the Eighty-seventh and to the four succeeding Congresses, and served from January 3, 1961 until his resignation on September 4, 1969, to become a judge of the Superior Court of New Jersey; is a resident of Paramus, N.J.

**JOHANSEN, August Edgar,** a Representative from Michigan; born in Philadelphia, Pa., July 21, 1905; attended the public schools in Battle Creek, Mich.; attended Olivet (Mich.) College in 1922 and 1923, and Western Michigan College of Education in Kalamazoo in 1923 and 1924; graduated from the University of Chicago in 1926; reporter with the Battle Creek Moon-Journal during the summers 1922-1927; minister of the Seventh-day Baptist Church in Chicago, Ill., and the Congregational Church in Bedford, Mich., 1924-1934; manager of industrial relations of the Kellogg Co., Battle Creek, Mich., 1934-1944; editorial writer for the Battle Creek Enquirer-News, 1944-1948; editor of the Lakeview News and news editor on radio, 1944-1951; member of the Calhoun County Tax Allocation Board in 1949 and 1950; administrative assistant to Representative Paul W. Shafer 1951-1954; elected as a Republican to the Eighty-fourth and to the four succeeding Congresses (January 3, 1955-January 3, 1965); unsuccessful candidate for reelection in 1964 to the Eighty-ninth Congress; executive vice president, Robert A. Taft Institute of Government, 1966-1967; lecturer and writer; was a resident of Orlando, Fla., until his death there on April 16, 1995.

**JOHNS, Joshua Leroy,** a Representative from Wisconsin; born in the town of Eagle, Richland County, Wis., February 27, 1881; attended the public schools; engaged in banking in Richland Center, Wis., 1902-1905; was graduated from the law department of the University of Chattanooga, Chattanooga, Tenn., in 1906 and from Yale University in 1907; was admitted to the Tennessee bar in 1906 and commenced practice in Chattanooga, Tenn., in 1907; was admitted to the Wisconsin bar in 1910 and commenced practice in Richland Center, Wis.; moved to Appleton, Wis., in 1920 and continued the practice of law; also interested in various business enterprises; colonel in the Wisconsin National Guard 1928-1929; elected as a Republican to the Seventy-sixth and Seventy-seventh Congresses (January 3, 1939-January 3, 1943); unsuccessful candidate for reelection in 1942 to the Seventy-eighth Congress; resumed the practice of law in Green Bay, Wis., and also served as president of several lumber companies; died at Green Bay, Wis., March 16, 1947; interment in Fort Howard Cemetery.

**JOHNS, Kensey, Jr.,** a Representative from Delaware; born in New Castle, New Castle County, Del., December 10, 1791; pursued classical studies and was graduated from Princeton College in 1810; studied law; was admitted to the bar in 1813 and commenced practice in New Castle; elected to the Twentieth Congress to fill the vacancy caused by the resignation of Louis McLane; reelected to the Twenty-first Congress and served from October 2, 1827, to March 3, 1831; was not a candidate for renomination in 1830 to the Twenty-second Congress; appointed chancellor of Delaware in 1832 and served until his death in New Castle, Del., on March 28, 1857; interment in the Presbyterian Cemetery.

**Bibliography:** *DAB.*

**JOHNSON, Adna Romulus,** a Representative from Ohio; born in Sweet Springs, Saline County, Mo., December 14, 1860; moved with his mother to a farm in Lawrence County, Ohio, in 1864; attended the common schools; taught school seven years; studied law; was admitted to the bar in 1886; was graduated from the law department of the University of Michigan at Ann Arbor in 1887 and practiced his profession in Ironton, Ohio; prosecuting attorney of Lawrence County in 1889; elected as a Republican to the Sixty-first Congress (March 4, 1909-March 3, 1911); was renominated without opposition in 1910 but declined to accept; resumed the practice of law in Ironton, Ohio; also engaged in banking and was financially interested in various manufacturing concerns; served as president of the Ohio State Bar Association in 1933; died in Ironton, Ohio, June 11, 1938; interment in Woodland Cemetery.

**JOHNSON, Albert,** a Representative from Washington; born in Springfield, Sangamon County, Ill., March 5, 1869; attended the public and high schools at Atchison and Hiawatha, Kans.; reporter on the St. Joseph (Mo.) Herald and the St. Louis (Mo.) Globe-Democrat, 1888-1891; managing editor of the New Haven Register in 1896 and 1897; news editor of the Washington (D.C.) Post in 1898; moved to Tacoma, Wash., in 1898; editor of the Tacoma News, 1898-1906; became editor and publisher of Grays Harbor Washingtonian (Hoquiam, Wash.) in 1907; elected as a Republican to the Sixty-third and to the nine succeeding Congresses (March 4, 1913-March 3, 1933); chairman, Committee on Immigration and Naturalization (Sixty-sixth through Seventy-first Congresses); unsuccessful candidate for reelection in 1932 to the Seventy-third Congress; while a Member of Congress was commissioned a captain in the Chemical Warfare Service, during the First World War, receiving an honorable discharge on November 29, 1918; retired from the newspaper business in 1934; died in American Lake, Wash., January 17, 1957; interment in Sunset Memorial Park, Hoquiam, Wash.

**Bibliography:** *DAB.*

**JOHNSON, Albert Walter,** a Representative from Pennsylvania; born in Smethport, McKean County, Pa., April 17, 1906; graduated from Smethport High School in 1923; attended the Wharton School of the University of Pennsylvania, 1926-1929; member, Smethport Borough Council, 1933-1934; LL.B., John B. Stetson University Law School, De Land, Fla., 1938; was admitted to the bar in 1939 and began the practice of law in Smethport; member of the Pennsylvania house of representatives, 1947-1963, serving as majority whip in the 1951 session, minority whip in the 1955 session, majority leader in the 1953, 1957, and 1963 sessions, minority leader in the 1959 and 1961 sessions; elected as a Republican to the Eighty-eighth Congress, November 5, 1963, by special election to fill the vacancy caused by the death of Leon H. Gavin; reelected to the six succeeding Congresses, and served from November 5, 1963 to January 3, 1977; unsuccessful candidate for reelection in 1976 to the Ninety-fifth Congress; is a resident of Smethport, Pa.

**JOHNSON, Andrew,** a Representative and a Senator from Tennessee and a Vice President and 17th President of the United States; born in Raleigh, N.C., on December 29, 1808; self-educated; at the age of thirteen was apprenticed to a tailor; moved to Tennessee in 1826; employed as a tailor; alderman of Greeneville, Tenn., 1828-1830; mayor of Greeneville from 1830 until 1834; member, Tennessee State house of representatives, 1835-1837, 1839-1841; elected to the State senate in 1841; elected as a Democrat to the Twenty-eighth and to the four succeeding Congresses (March 4, 1843-March 3, 1853); chairman, Committee on Public Expenditures (Thirty-first and Thirty-second Congresses); did not seek renomination in 1852 to the Thirty-third Congress, having become a gubernatorial candidate; elected Governor of Tennessee in 1853, reelected in 1855, and served from October 17, 1853 to November 3, 1857; elected as a Democrat to the United States Senate and served from October 8, 1857, to March 4, 1862, when he resigned; chairman, Committee to Audit and Control the Contingent Expense (Thirty-sixth Congress); appointed military governor of Tennessee by President Lincoln, and served in that capacity from March 12, 1862 until his inauguration as Vice President; elected Vice President of the United States on the National Union (Republican) ticket headed by Abraham Lincoln, November 8, 1864 and was inaugurated March 4, 1865; became President of the United States April 15, 1865, upon the death of Abraham Lincoln; wide differences arising between the President and the Congress, a resolution for his impeachment passed the House of Representatives on February 24, 1868; eleven articles were set out in the resolution and the trial before the Senate lasted three months, at the conclusion of which he was acquitted (May 26, 1868) by a vote of thirty-five for conviction to nineteen for acquittal, the necessary two-thirds vote for impeachment not having been obtained; retired to his home in Tennessee upon the expiration of the presidential term, March 3, 1869; unsuccessful candidate for election to the United States Senate in 1869 and to the House of Representatives in 1872; elected to the United States Senate and served from March 4, 1875, until his death near Elizabethton, Carter County, Tenn., July 31, 1875; interment in the Andrew Johnson National Cemetery, Greeneville, Greene County, Tenn.

**Bibliography:** *DAB*; Benedict, Michael Les. *The Impeachment and Trial of Andrew Johnson.* New York: W.W. Norton and Company, Inc., 1973; Johnson, Andrew. *The Papers of Andrew Johnson.* Edited by LeRoy P. Graf, Ralph W. Haskins, and Paul H. Bergeron. 12 vols. to date. Knoxville: University of Tennessee Press, 1967- .; Trefousse, Hans L. *Andrew Johnson: A Biography.* New York: W.W. Norton and Company, 1989.

**JOHNSON, Anton Joseph,** a Representative from Illinois; born in Peoria, Ill., October 20, 1878; attended the public schools and the School of Agriculture of the University of Missouri at Columbia; served as first sergeant, Fifth Infantry, Company G, Illinois National Guard, 1898-1901; letter carrier, Peoria, Ill., 1900-1913; engaged in agricultural pursuits near Peoria, Ill., 1913-1921; engaged in dairy-products manufacturing in Macomb, Ill., 1926-1938; president of the Illinois Milk Dealers' Association 1931-1936; president of the Illinois Dairy Products Association in 1937; elected as a Republican to the Seventy-sixth and to the four succeeding Congresses (January 3, 1939-January 3, 1949); was not a candidate for renomination in 1948 to the Eighty-first Congress; elected mayor of Macomb, Ill., in 1949 for a four-year term but resigned after serving two years; died in Macomb, Ill., on April 16, 1958; interment in Springdale Cemetery, Peoria, Ill.

**JOHNSON, Ben,** a Representative from Kentucky; born near Bardstown, Nelson County, Ky., May 20, 1858; pursued preparatory studies; was graduated from St. Mary's College, Marion County, Ky., in June 1878 and from the Louisville Law University in 1882; was admitted to the bar in 1882 and commenced practice in Bardstown; member of the Kentucky house of representatives in 1885 and 1887, serving as speaker in the latter year; appointed by President Grover Cleveland collector of internal revenue for the fifth Kentucky district on July 10, 1893, and served until August 10, 1897; member of the Kentucky senate from 1905 until his resignation on November 5, 1906; elected as a Democrat to the Sixtieth and to the nine succeeding Congresses (March 4, 1907-March 3, 1927); chairman, Committee on District of Columbia (Sixty-second through Sixty-fifth Congresses); declined to be a candidate for renomination in 1926 to the Seventieth Congress; delegate at large to the Democratic National Conventions of 1912 and 1920; resumed the practice of law; died in Bardstown, Ky., June 4, 1950; interment in St. Joseph's Cemetery.

**Bibliography:** Klotter, James C., and John W. Muir. "Boss Ben Johnson, the Highway Commission, and Kentucky Politics, 1927-1937." *Register of the Kentucky Historical Society* 84 (Winter 1986): 18-50.

**JOHNSON, Byron Lindberg,** a Representative from Colorado; born in Chicago, Ill., October 12, 1917; moved to Oconomowoc, Wis., in 1927 and attended the public schools; B.A., University of Wisconsin, 1938, M.A., 1940, and Ph.D., economics, 1947; statistician and economist, State of Wisconsin, 1938-1942; Bureau of Budget, 1942-1944, and Social Security Administration, Washington, D.C., 1944-1947; professor of economics, University of Denver, 1947-1956; member of the Colorado State house of representatives in 1955 and 1956; unsuccessful candidate for election in 1956 to the Eighty-fifth Congress; assistant to Governor Stephen L.R. McNichols of Colorado in 1957 and 1958; elected as a Democrat to the Eighty-sixth Congress (January 3, 1959-January 3, 1961); unsuccessful candidate for reelection in 1960 to the Eighty-seventh Congress; delegate to the Democratic National Conventions of 1960 and 1968; appointed consultant for International Cooperation Administration (later the Agency for International Development) and served from February 1961 to January 1965; appointed professor of economics at University of Colorado in February 1965; elected a statewide member of the University of Colorado Board of Regents in 1970, reelected in 1976; unsuccessful candidate for election in 1972 to the Ninety-third Congress; member, board of directors, Denver Regional Transportation District, 1982-1984, serving as vice chairman, 1983, and chairman, 1984; professor emeritus, University of Colorado; is a resident of Denver, Colo.

**JOHNSON, Calvin Dean,** a Representative from Illinois; born in Fordsville, Ohio County, Ky., November 22, 1898; moved with his parents to St. Clair County, Ill., in 1904, and attended public schools; engaged in the general contracting business 1922-1944; member, St. Clair County School Board, 1926-1928; member of the St. Clair County, Ill., Board of Supervisors 1930-1934; served in the State house of representatives 1935-1941; elected as a Republican to the Seventy-eighth Congress (January 3, 1943-January 3, 1945); unsuccessful candidate for reelection in 1944 to the Seventy-ninth Congress, and for election in 1946 to the Eightieth Congress; executive assistant to the vice president of Remington-Rand, Inc., in Washington, D.C., 1952-1968; engaged in public relations; was a resident of Belleville, Ill., until his death there on October 13, 1985.

**JOHNSON, Cave,** a Representative from Tennessee; born in Robertson County, Tenn., January 11, 1793; pursued an academic course and attended Cumberland College, Nashville, Tenn.; studied law; was admitted to the bar in 1814 and commenced practice in Clarksville, Tenn.; prosecuting attorney of Montgomery County in 1817; elected as a Jacksonian to the Twenty-first and to the three succeeding Congresses (March 4, 1829-March 3, 1837); chairman, Committee on Private Land Claims (Twenty-second and Twenty-third Congresses); unsuccessful candidate for reelection in 1836 to the Twenty-fifth Congress; elected as a Democrat to the Twenty-sixth, Twenty-seventh, and Twenty-eighth Congresses (March 4, 1839-March 3, 1845); chairman, Committee on Military Affairs (Twenty-sixth Congress), Committee on Expenditures on Public Buildings (Twenty-seventh Congress), Committee on Indian Affairs (Twenty-eighth Congress); appointed Postmaster General in the Cabinet of President James K. Polk, and served from March 5, 1845 to March 5, 1849; judge of the seventh judicial circuit court in 1850 and 1851; president of the Bank of Tennessee, 1854-1860; United States commissioner in settling the affairs of the United States and Paraguay Navigation Company in 1860; during the Civil War was elected to the State senate but was not permitted to take his seat; died in Clarksville, Tenn., November 23, 1866; interment in Greenwood Cemetery.

**Bibliography:** *DAB*; Grant, Clement L. "The Public Career of Cave Johnson." Ph.D. dissertation, Vanderbilt University, 1951; Sioussat, St. George L., ed. "Letters of James K. Polk to Cave Johnson, 1833-1848." *Tennessee Historical Magazine* 1 (September 1915): 209-56.

**JOHNSON, Charles,** a Representative from North Carolina; born in Chowan County, N.C.; pursued an academic course; engaged as a planter; elected to the Continental Congress in 1781, 1784, and 1785, but did not attend; served in the State senate 1781-1784, 1788-1790, and 1792; elected as a Republican to the Seventh Congress and served from March 4, 1801, until his death in Bandon, near Edenton, Chowan County, N.C., July 23, 1802; interment in Edenton Cemetery.

**JOHNSON, Charles Fletcher,** a Senator from Maine; born in Winslow, Kennebec County, Maine, February 14, 1859; attended the common schools and the Waterville Classical Institute; graduated from Bowdoin College, Brunswick, Maine, in 1879; principal of the high school of Machias, Washington County, Maine, 1881-1886; studied law; was admitted to the bar in 1886 and commenced practice in Waterville, Maine; unsuccessful candidate for election in 1892 and 1894 for Governor of Maine; mayor of Waterville 1893; member, State house of representataives 1905, 1907; elected as a Democrat to the United States Senate in 1910 and served from March 4, 1911, until March 3, 1917; unsuccessful candidate for reelection 1916; chairman, Committee on National Banks (Sixty-third Congress), Committee on Fisheries (Sixty-fourth Congress), Committee on Pensions (Sixty-fourth Congress); judge of the United States Circuit Court of Appeals for the first circuit 1917-1929; died while on a visit in St. Petersburg, Fla., February 15, 1930; interment in Pine Grove Cemetery, Waterville, Maine.

**JOHNSON, Clete Donald (Don),** a Representative from Georgia; born in Royston, Ga., January 30, 1948; graduated, Franklin County High School; B.A., University of Georgia, 1970; J.D., University of Georgia School of Law, 1973; M.A., London School of Economics, 1978; staff attorney, United States House of Representatives Committee on Ways and Means; Continental Illinois National Bank, Chicago; practicing attorney, Atlanta then in Royston, Ga.; United States Air Force service; member, Georgia State senate, 1987-1993; elected as a Democrat to the One Hundred Third Congress (January 3, 1993-January 3, 1995); unsuccessful candidate for reelection in 1994 to the One Hundred Fourth Congress; adjunct professor of political science, University of Georgia; adviser to the University of Georgia School of Law and the Rusk Center for International and Comparative Law; president, Global Markets, Inc., an international trading company; is a resident of Royston, Ga.

**JOHNSON, Dewey William,** a Representative from Minnesota; born in Minneapolis, Minn., March 14, 1899; attended the public schools, the University of Minnesota at Minneapolis, and the Y.M.C.A. Law School; engaged in the insurance business; member of the State house of representatives 1929-1935; unsuccessful candidate for election in 1934 to the Seventy-fourth Congress; served as deputy commissioner of insurance and State fire marshal in 1935 and 1936; elected as a Farmer-Laborite to the Seventy-fifth Congress (January 3, 1937-January 3, 1939); unsuccessful candidate for reelection in 1938 to the Seventy-sixth Congress and for election in 1940 to the Seventy-seventh Congress; resumed insurance business in Minneapolis, Minn., and also engaged in retail radio sales business; died in Minneapolis, Minn., September 18, 1941; interment in Lakewood Cemetery.

**JOHNSON, Eddie Bernice,** a Representative from Texas; born in Waco, McLennan County, Tex., December 3, 1935; attended Holy Cross Central School of Nursing, St. Mary's College, University of Notre Dame, 1955, and North Texas State University (Denton), 1958-1966; B.S., Texas Christian University, Fort Worth, 1967; Texas Women's University (Denton), 1970-1971; M.P.A., Southern Methodist University, Dallas, 1976; registered nurse, St. Paul Catholic Hospital, Dallas, Tex., 1957-1958; chief psychiatric nurse-psychotherapist, Veterans Administration Hospital, Dallas, 1956-1972; executive assistant, personnel division, Neiman-Marcus, 1972-1975; consultant, Zale Corp., division of urban affairs, Dallas, 1976-1977; Texas State representative, 1972-1977; principal regional administrator, Region VI (Dallas), Department of Health, Education and Welfare, 1977-1979, and executive assistant to Administrator for Primary Health Care, Rockville, Md., 1979-1981; assistant to the president, Sammons Enterprises, Inc., Dallas, 1981; sole proprietor, Eddie Bernice Johnson and Associates, 1981-1993; vice president, governmental and community affairs, Visiting Nurse Association of Texas, Dallas, 1981-1987; member, Texas State senate, 1986-1993; elected as a Democrat to the One Hundred Third and One Hundred Fourth Congresses (January 3, 1993-January 3, 1997); is a resident of Dallas, Tex.

**JOHNSON, Edwin Carl,** a Senator from Colorado; born in Scandia, Republic County, Kans., January 1, 1884; moved with his parents to a cattle ranch near Elsie, Nebr., in 1884; attended the rural schools; employed as railroad laborer, telegrapher, and train dispatcher, 1901-1909; homesteaded on government land in Colorado in 1910; operated the Farmers' Cooperative Milling Elevator and also engaged in the produce business, 1920-1930; member, Colorado State house of representatives, 1923-1931; Lieutenant Governor of Colorado, 1931-1933; elected Governor of Colorado in 1932, reelected in 1934, and served from January 10, 1933 until his resignation January 3, 1937, having been elected Senator; elected as a Democrat to the United States Senate in 1936; reelected in 1942 and again in 1948 and served from January 3, 1937, to January 3, 1955; was not a candidate for reelection in 1954; chairman, Committee on Interstate and Foreign Commerce (Eighty-first and Eighty-second Congresses), Select Committee on the Joseph McCarthy Censure (Eighty-third Congress); elected Governor of Colorado in 1954, and served from January 11, 1955 to January 8, 1957; was not a candidate for renomination in 1956; retired but remained active as a volunteer on several State commissions and committees; died in Denver, Colo., May 30, 1970; interment in Fairmont Mausoleum.

**JOHNSON, Edwin Stockton,** a Senator from South Dakota; born near Spencer, Owen County, Ind., February 26, 1857; moved with his parents to Osceola, Iowa, in 1857; attended the public schools; engaged in the mercantile business; moved to Wheeler County, Nebr., in 1880; homesteaded and engaged in agricultural pursuits; returned to Osceola, Iowa, in 1881 and was employed as a bank cashier; moved to South Dakota and established the Citizens' Bank of Grand View, S.Dak., in 1884; also engaged in agricultural pursuits; later established a number of banks in South Dakota, Minnesota, and Iowa; studied law; was admitted to the bar in 1888 and practiced; prosecuting attorney of Douglas County 1892-1893; member, State senate 1894-1895; retired from the banking business

in 1902 and engaged in the real estate and loan business at Platte, S.Dak.; member of the Democratic National Committee 1904-1916; unsuccessful Democratic candidate for election in 1912 for Governor of South Dakota; elected as a Democrat to the United States Senate in 1914 and served from March 4, 1915, to March 3, 1921; declined to be a candidate for renomination in 1920; chairman, Committee on Revolutionary Claims (Sixty-fourth and Sixty-fifth Congresses); resumed his activities in the real estate and loan business; died in Platte, S.Dak., July 19, 1933, interment in Pleasant Ridge Cemetery, Armour, S.Dak.

**JOHNSON, Francis,** a Representative from Kentucky; born in Caroline County, Va., June 19, 1776; pursued preparatory studies; studied law; was admitted to the bar and practiced; moved to Woodford County, Ky., in 1796 and to Bowling Green in 1807; member of the Kentucky house of representatives in 1812, 1813, and 1815; elected to the Sixteenth Congress to fill the vacancy caused by the death of David Walker; reelected to the Seventeenth and to the two succeeding Congresses and served from November 13, 1820, to March 3, 1827; chairman, Committee on the Post Office and Post Roads (Seventeenth and Eighteenth Congresses); moved to Louisville, Ky., in 1829 and resumed the practice of law; served as Commonwealth attorney for the fifth district; unsuccessful Republican candidate for Governor; died in Louisville, Ky., May 16, 1842; interment in the old family burial ground, later a municipal playground.

**JOHNSON, Fred Gustus,** a Representative from Nebraska; born on a farm near Dorchester, Saline County, Nebr., October 16, 1876; attended the country schools; was graduated from Dorchester (Nebr.) High School in 1893 and from the law department of the University of Nebraska at Lincoln in 1903; was admitted to the bar in 1903 and commenced practice in Dorchester, Nebr.; also engaged in agricultural pursuits; moved to Oxford, Nebr., in 1909 and to Hastings, Nebr., in 1911, and continued the practice of law; served in the State house of representatives 1907-1909 and 1917-1919; member of the State senate in 1919 and 1920; lieutenant governor of Nebraska in 1923 and 1924; delegate to the Republican State conventions 1900-1938; elected as a Republican to the Seventy-first Congress (March 4, 1929-March 3, 1931); unsuccessful candidate for reelection in 1930 to the Seventy-second Congress and for election in 1932 to the Seventy-third Congress; engaged in the practice of law and the real estate business 1931-1933, and in an agricultural-industrial enterprise in Hastings, Nebr., 1934-1938, and Charleston, Miss., 1941-1943; elected judge of the county court of Adams County, Nebr., for the term commencing January 4, 1945; reelected in 1948 and served until his death in Hastings, Nebr., April 30, 1951; interment in Parkview Cemetery.

**JOHNSON, Frederick Avery,** a Representative from New York; born in Fort Edward, Warren County, N.Y., January 2, 1833; attended the common schools and was graduated from the Glens Falls Academy; engaged in banking and in the wool business in New York City and later in banking in Glens Falls; president of the village of Glens Falls; elected to the Forty-eighth and Forty-ninth Congresses (March 4, 1883-March 3, 1887); was not a candidate for renomination in 1886; died at Glens Falls, Warren County, N.Y., on July 17, 1893; interment in the Bay Street Cemetery.

**JOHNSON, George William,** a Representative from West Virginia; born near Charles Town, Jefferson County, W.Va., on November 10, 1869; attended the common schools and Shepherd College State Normal School, Shepherdstown, W.Va.; was graduated from the University of West Virginia at Morgantown in 1894 and from the law department of the same university in 1896; was admitted to the bar and commenced practice in Martinsburg, W.Va.; city attorney of Martinsburg; moved to Parkersburg, W.Va., in 1900 and continued the practice of law; member of the board of regents of the State Normal School 1897-1900; served as referee in bankruptcy for the United States District Court of West Virginia; general counsel to the West Virginia Public Service Commission; engaged in fruit growing and stock raising; elected as a Democrat to the Sixty-eighth Congress (March 4, 1923-March 3, 1925); unsuccessful candidate for reelection in 1924 to the Sixty-ninth Congress; elected to the Seventy-third and to the four succeeding Congresses (March 4, 1933-January 3, 1943); unsuccessful candidate for reelection in 1942 to the Seventy-eighth Congress; died in Martinsburg, W.Va., February 24, 1944; interment in Edgehill Cemetery, Charles Town, W.Va.

**JOHNSON, Glen Dale,** a Representative from Oklahoma; born in Melbourne, Izard County, Ark., September 11, 1911; moved to Paden, Okla., 1920; attended the public schools; graduated from the University of Oklahoma Law School at Norman in 1939; was admitted to the bar the same year and commenced practice at Okemah, Okla.; member of the State house of representatives 1940-1942; resigned his membership in the house in January 1942 and enlisted in the United States Army as a private and was discharged as a captain in May 1946; resumed the practice of law; elected as a Democrat to the Eightieth Congress (January 3, 1947-January 3, 1949); was not a candidate for renomination in 1948, but was an unsuccessful candidate for the Democratic nomination for United States Senator; neutral arbitrator for National Mediation Board in 1949 and 1950; served as attorney in the Office of the Solicitor, Department of the Interior, Washington, D.C., 1961-1967; chairman, Oil Import Appeals Board, representing the Department of the Interior, Washington, D.C., 1967-1969; attorney in Solicitor's Office, Department of the Interior, Muskogee, Okla., 1969-1972; was a resident of Okemah, Okla., until his death there on February 10, 1983.

**JOHNSON, Grove Lawrence,** (father of Hiram Warren Johnson), a Representative from California; born in Syracuse, N.Y., March 27, 1841; attended the common schools; studied law; was admitted to the bar April 2, 1862; school commissioner of Syracuse in 1862 and 1863; moved to California in October 1863; during the Civil War served as quartermaster clerk in the States of California, Arizona, and Washington; moved to Sacramento in May 1865; swamp-land clerk of Sacramento County 1866-1879; commenced the practice of law in Sacramento in 1873; member of the California Assembly 1878 and 1879; served in the State senate 1880-1882; delegate to the Republican State conventions in 1884, 1888, 1892, and 1908; delegate to the Republican National Convention in 1896; elected as a Republican to the Fifty-fourth Congress (March 4, 1895-March 3, 1897); unsuccessful candidate for reelection in 1896 to the Fifty-fifth Congress; resumed the practice of law in Sacramento, Calif.; again a member of the State assembly 1901-1903 and 1907-1909; appointed receiver of public moneys of the United States land office at Sacramento July 19, 1921, and served until the discontinuance of the office on June 30, 1925; died in Sacramento, Calif., February 1, 1926; interment in the City Cemetery.

**JOHNSON, Harold Terry,** a Representative from California; born in Broderick, Yolo County, Calif., December 2, 1907; attended the public schools of Roseville, Calif., and the University of Nevada; supervisor of Pacific Fruit Express Co.; district chairman of Brotherhood of Railway Clerks; served as school trustee, city councilman, and mayor of Roseville, 1941-1949; president of American River Development League 1945-1949; member of the California State senate from 1949 until elected to Congress; delegate, Democratic National Conventions, 1956, 1960, and 1964; elected as a Democrat to the Eighty-sixth and to the ten succeeding Congresses (January 3, 1959-January 3, 1981); chairman, Committee on Public Works and Transportation (Ninety-fifth and Ninety-sixth Congresses); unsuccessful candidate for reelection in 1980 to

the Ninety-seventh Congress; was a resident of Roseville, Calif., until his death there on March 16, 1988.

**JOHNSON, Harvey Hull,** a Representative from Ohio; born in West Rutland, Rutland County, Vt., September 7, 1808; attended the common schools and Middlebury Academy; studied law; was admitted to the bar in 1833 and commenced practice in Akron, Ohio; postmaster of Akron in 1837; moved to Ashland, Ohio, about 1848; elected as a Democrat to the Thirty-third Congress (March 4, 1853-March 3, 1855); unsuccessful candidate for reelection in 1854; moved to Minnesota in 1855 and settled in Winona; resumed the practice of law; president of the Winona & St. Peter Railroad during its construction to Rochester; moved to Owatonna, Steele County, Minn., in 1865 and engaged in the practice of law; mayor and city justice 1867-1870; died in Owatonna, Minn., February 4, 1896; interment in Forest Hill Cemetery.

**JOHNSON, Henry,** a Senator and a Representative from Louisiana; born in Virginia September 14, 1783; pursued an academic course; studied law; was admitted to the bar; moved to the Territory of Orleans in 1809 and became clerk of the second superior court of the Territory; district judge of the Parish Court 1811; delegate to the first State constitutional convention 1812; unsuccessful candidate for election in 1812 to the Thirteenth Congress; practiced law in Donaldsonville, La.; elected as a Republican to the United States Senate in 1818 to fill the vacancy caused by the death of William C.C. Claiborne; reelected in 1823 and served from January 12, 1818, to May 27, 1824, when he resigned to become a gubernatorial candidate; chairman, Committee on Indian Affairs (Seventeenth Congress); elected Governor of Louisiana in 1824 and served from December 13, 1824 to December 15, 1828; unsuccessful candidate for election in 1829 to the United States Senate; elected as a Whig to the Twenty-third Congress to fill the vacancy caused by the resignation of Edward D. White; reelected to the Twenty-fourth and Twenty-fifth Congresses and served from September 25, 1834, to March 3, 1839; unsuccessful Whig candidate for Governor in 1838 and 1842; again elected to the United States Senate to fill the vacancy caused by the death of Alexander Porter and served from February 12, 1844, to March 3, 1849; chairman, Committee on Pensions (Twenty-ninth and Thirtieth Congresses); unsuccessful candidate for election in 1850 to the Thirty-second Congress; moved to New River, La., and continued the practice of law; died in the Parish of Pointe Coupee, La., September 4, 1864; interment on his plantation.

**JOHNSON, Henry Underwood,** a Representative from Indiana; born in Cambridge City, Wayne County, Ind., October 28, 1850; attended the Centerville Collegiate Institute and Earlham College, Richmond, Ind.; studied law; was admitted to the bar in 1872 and commenced practice in Centerville, Wayne County, Ind.; moved to Richmond, Ind., in 1876 and continued the practice of his profession; prosecuting attorney of Wayne County 1876-1880; member of the State senate 1887-1889; elected as a Republican to the Fifty-second and to the three succeeding Congresses (March 4, 1891-March 3, 1899); chairman, Committee on Elections No. 2 (Fifty-fourth and Fifty-fifth Congresses); was not a candidate for renomination in 1898; affiliated with the Democratic Party upon the expiration of his congressional career; moved to St. Louis, Mo., in 1899 and continued the practice of law until 1900 when he returned to Richmond, Ind., to resume his former law practice; died in Richmond, Ind., June 4, 1939; interment in Earlham Cemetery.

**JOHNSON, Herschel Vespasian,** a Senator from Georgia; born near Farmer's Bridge, Burke County, Ga., September 18, 1812; attended private schools and Monaghan Academy near Warrenton; graduated from the University of Georgia at Athens in 1834; studied law; was admitted to the bar in 1834 and commenced practice; moved to a plantation, "Sandy Grove," in Jefferson County in 1839 and practiced law in Louisville; unsuccessful Democratic candidate in 1843 for election to fill the vacancy in the Twenty-eighth Congress caused by the resignation of Mark A. Cooper; presidential elector on the Democratic ticket in 1844; moved to Milledgeville, Ga., in 1844 and continued the practice of law; unsuccessful candidate for nomination for Governor in 1847; appointed as a Democrat to the United States Senate to fill the vacancy caused by the resignation of Walter T. Colquitt and served from February 4, 1848, to March 3, 1849; was not a candidate for election to fill this vacancy; chairman, Committee on the District of Columbia (Thirtieth Congress); judge of the superior court of the Ocmulgee circuit 1849-1853; presidential elector on the Democratic ticket in 1852; elected Governor of Georgia in 1853, reelected in 1855, and served from November 9, 1853 to November 6, 1857; returned to his plantation near Louisville, Jefferson County, in 1857; unsuccessful candidate for Vice President of the United States on the Democratic ticket with Stephen A. Douglas in 1860; delegate to the State secession convention at Milledgeville in 1861; a Senator from Georgia in the Second Confederate Congress, 1862-1865; president of the State constitutional convention in 1865; presented credentials in 1866 as a Senator-elect to the United States Senate but was not permitted to qualify; resumed the practice of law in Louisville; appointed judge of the middle circuit of Georgia in 1873 and served until his death on his plantation near Louisville, Ga., August 16, 1880; interment in the Old Louisville Cemetery.

**Bibliography:** *DAB*; Flippin, Percy. *Herschel V. Johnson of Georgia, State Rights Unionist.* Richmond: Press of Deitz Printing Co., 1931; Greeman, Elizabeth D. "Stephen A. Douglas and Herschel V. Johnson: Examples of National Men in the Sectional Crisis of 1860." Ph.D. dissertation, Duke University, 1974.

**JOHNSON, Hiram Warren** (son of Grove Lawrence Johnson), a Senator from California; born in Sacramento, Calif., September 2, 1866; attended the public schools; entered the University of California at Berkeley in 1884; studied law; was admitted to the bar in 1888 and commenced practice in Sacramento; moved to San Francisco in 1902; active in reform politics and the League of Lincoln-Roosevelt Clubs; served as assistant district attorney of San Francisco during the 1907 and 1908 graft trials of political and business leaders; candidate for Vice President of the United States in 1912 on the Progressive ticket headed by Theodore Roosevelt; elected Governor of California in 1910, reelected in 1914, and served from January 3, 1911 until March 15, 1917, when he resigned, having previously been elected Senator; elected as a Republican to the United States Senate in 1916 for the term beginning March 4, 1917, but, preferring to continue as Governor, did not assume his senatorial duties until March 16, 1917; reelected in 1922, 1928, 1934 and again in 1940, and served from March 16, 1917 until his death in the naval hospital at Bethesda, Md., August 6, 1945; chairman, Committee on Cuban Relations (Sixty-sixth Congress), Committee on Patents (Sixty-seventh Congress), Committee on Immigration (Sixty-eighth through Seventy-first Congresses), Committee on Territories and Insular Possessions (Sixty-eighth Congress), and Committee on Commerce (Seventy-first and Seventy-second Congresses); unsuccessful candidate for the Republican presidential nomination in 1920 and 1924; interment in Cyprus Lawn Cemetery, San Francisco, Calif.

**Bibliography:** *DAB*; Johnson, Hiram. *The Diary Letters of Hiram Johnson.* Edited by Robert Burke. 7 vols. New York: Garland Publishing, Inc., 1983; Lower, Richard Coke. *A Bloc of One: The Political Career of Hiram W. Johnson.* Stanford, Calif.: Stanford University Press, 1993; Weatherson, Michael A., and Hal W. Bochin. *Hiram Johnson: Political Revivalist.* Lanham, Md.: University Press of America, 1995.

**JOHNSON, Jacob,** a Representative from Utah; born in Aalborg, Denmark, November 1, 1847; immigrated to the United States in 1854 and was admitted to citizenship in California in 1868; attended common and private schools of California; studied law; was admitted to the bar in 1877 and commenced practice in Spring City, Utah; also engaged in agricultural pursuits; United States district attorney 1880-1888; United States commissioner for Utah 1881-1893; probate judge of Sanpete County 1888-1890; prosecuting attorney of Sanpete County 1892-1894; member of the Territorial house of representatives 1893-1895; judge of the seventh judicial district for the State of Utah 1896-1905; delegate to the Republican National Convention in 1912; elected as a Republican to the Sixty-third Congress (March 4, 1913-March 3, 1915); unsuccessful candidate for renomination in 1914; resumed the practice of law in Salt Lake City, Utah, and died there August 15, 1925; interment in Wasatch Lawn Cemetery.

**JOHNSON, James,** a Representative from Georgia; born in Robeson County, N.C., February 12, 1811; was graduated from the University of Georgia at Athens in 1832; taught school; studied law; was admitted to the bar in 1835 and commenced practice in Columbus, Ga., in 1836; prosecuting attorney of Muscogee County; elected as a Unionist to the Thirty-second Congress (March 4, 1851-March 3, 1853); unsuccessful candidate for reelection to the Thirty-third Congress; appointed Provisional Governor of Georgia in 1865 and served from June 17 to December 14 of that year; unsuccessful candidate for election to the United States Senate in 1866; collector of customs at Savannah 1866-1869; presidential elector on the Republican ticket in 1868; judge of the superior court of Georgia from July 1, 1869 until October 1, 1875, when he resigned and resumed the practice of law; died on his plantation in Chattahoochee County, November 20, 1891; interment in Linwood Cemetery, Columbus, Ga.

**JOHNSON, James,** a Representative from Virginia; born in Virginia; completed preparatory studies; was graduated from the College of William and Mary, Williamsburg, Va., about 1795; studied law; was admitted to the bar and practiced in Williamsburg; delegate to the Virginia constitutional convention in 1788; member of the Virginia house of delegates 1797-1804, 1806, 1807, and 1809-1813; moved to Isle of Wight County in 1807 and continued the practice of law; elected as a Republican to the Thirteenth and to the three succeeding Congresses and served from March 4, 1813, until February 1, 1820, when he resigned, having been appointed collector of customs at Norfolk, in which capacity he served until his death in that city on December 7, 1825.

**JOHNSON, James** (brother of Richard Mentor Johnson and John Telemachus Johnson and uncle of Robert Ward Johnson), a Representative from Kentucky; born in Orange County, Va., January 1, 1774; moved with his father to Kentucky in 1779; pursued preparatory studies; a member of the Kentucky senate in 1808; served as lieutenant colonel in the War of 1812; contractor for furnishing supplies to troops on the western frontier in 1819 and 1820; presidential elector on the ticket of Monroe and Tompkins in 1820; elected to the Nineteenth Congress and served from March 4, 1825, until his death in Washington, D.C., August 13, 1826; interment in the family cemetery, Great Crossings, Ky.

**Bibliography:** *DAB*.

**JOHNSON, James Augustus,** a Representative from California; born in Spartanburg, S.C., May 16, 1829; moved with his parents to Arkansas when quite young; attended the common schools; moved to California in 1853; studied medicine and was graduated from Jefferson Medical College, Philadelphia, Pa.; studied law; was admitted to the bar in 1859 and commenced the practice of law in Downieville, Calif.; member of the general assembly in 1859 and 1860; elected as a Democrat to the Fortieth and Forty-first Congresses (March 4, 1867-March 3, 1871); lieutenant governor of California 1875-1880; moved to San Francisco; registrar of voters in 1883 and 1884; engaged in the practice of his profession until his death in San Francisco, Calif., May 11, 1896; interment in the Masonic Cemetery.

**JOHNSON, James Hutchins,** a Representative from New Hampshire; born in Bath, Grafton County, N.H., June 3, 1802; attended the public schools; owned and operated a lumber mill; deputy sheriff of Grafton County in 1824 and 1825; served as paymaster of the Thirty-second Regiment Militia in 1826, later as adjutant and colonel; member of the State senate in 1839; State councilor in 1842 and 1845; elected as a Democrat to the Twenty-ninth and Thirtieth Congresses (March 4, 1845-March 3, 1849); died in Bath, N.H., September 2, 1887; interment in the Village Cemetery.

**JOHNSON, James Leeper,** a Representative from Kentucky; born near Smithland, Livingston County. Ky., October 30, 1818; attended private schools; moved to Owensboro, Ky., in 1836; studied law; was admitted to the bar in 1841 and commenced practice in Owensboro; member of the Kentucky house of representatives in 1844; elected as a Whig to the Thirty-first Congress (March 4, 1849-March 3, 1851); was nominated for reelection in 1850 but declined to accept; resumed the practice of law in Owensboro and also engaged in agricultural pursuits; appointed judge of the Daviess County circuit court May 4, 1867, and served until September 2 of that year; died in Owensboro, Ky., February 12, 1877; interment in Elmwood Cemetery.

**JOHNSON, James Paul,** a Representative from Colorado; born in Yankton, Yankton County, S.Dak., June 2, 1930; B.A., Northwestern University, Evanston, Ill., 1952; LL.B., University of Colorado, Boulder, 1959; served in the United States Marine Corps as a jet pilot in Korea, 1952-1956; admitted to the Colorado Bar in 1959 and commenced practice in Fort Collins; deputy district attorney, Eighth Judicial District, Colorado, 1959-1966; municipal judge, Ault, Colo., 1962-1965; assistant district attorney, 1964-1966; member, Poudre R-1 School Board, Fort Collins, 1969-1971; elected as a Republican to the Ninety-third and to the three succeeding Congresses (January 3, 1973-January 3, 1981); was not a candidate for reelection in 1980 to the Ninety-seventh Congress; resumed the practice of law in Fort Collins, Colo.; member, supreme court judicial nominating commission, State of Colorado, 1984-1986; member, Colorado water conservation board, 1985-1987; is a resident of Fort Collins, Colo.

**JOHNSON, Jed Joseph** (father of Jed Joseph Johnson, Jr.), a Representative from Oklahoma; born on a farm near Waxahachie, Ellis County, Tex., July 31, 1888; attended the public schools in Texas and Oklahoma; was graduated from the law department of the University of Oklahoma at Norman in 1915; engaged in postgraduate work at l'Universite de Clermont at Clermont-Ferrand, France; was admitted to the bar in 1918 and commenced practice at Walters, Okla.; served overseas as a private in Company L of the Thirty-sixth Division in 1918 and 1919; editor of a newspaper in Cotton County, Okla., 1920-1922; member of the State senate 1920-1927; delegate to the annual peace conference of the Interparliamentary Union at Paris, France, in 1927 and 1937, and at Geneva, Switzerland, in 1929; chairman of the speakers' bureau, Democratic National Congressional Committee; elected as a Democrat to the Seventieth and to the nine succeeding Congresses (March 4, 1927-January 3, 1947); was an unsuccessful candidate for renomination in 1946 to the Eightieth Congress; appointed by President Franklin D. Roosevelt to the United States Customs Court in 1945, which position he declined; was appointed by President Harry S Truman to the United States Customs Court in 1947, and served until his death in New York City on May 8, 1963; interment in Rose Hill Cemetery, Chickasha, Okla.

**JOHNSON, Jed Joseph, Jr.** (son of Jed Joseph Johnson), a Representative from Oklahoma; born in Washington, D.C., December 27, 1939; attended the public schools in Chickasha, Okla., and Friends Seminary in New York City; served as a congressional page and graduated from the Capitol Page School in Washington, D.C., in 1957; graduated from the University of Oklahoma in 1961; delegate

to International Student Movement for the United Nations Conference at Lund, Sweden, in 1961; president of the United States Youth Council, 1962-1964; led a United States Youth Council delegation to West Africa in 1963; member of the United States National Commission for the United Nations Educational, Scientific and Cultural Organization; served three years as nongovernmental observer at the United Nations; elected as a Democrat to the Eighty-ninth Congress (January 3, 1965-January 3, 1967); unsuccessful candidate for reelection in 1966 to the Ninetieth Congress; special assistant to the Director, Office of Economic Opportunity, 1967-1968; member, Equal Employment Opportunity Commission, 1968-1972; consultant, Select Committee on Presidential Campaign Activities, United States Senate, 1973; executive director, United States Association of Former Members of Congress; was a resident of Bethesda, Md.; died December 16, 1993.

**JOHNSON, Jeromus,** a Representative from New York; born in Wallabout, Kings County, N.Y., November 2, 1775; attended the public schools; moved to New York City; engaged in mercantile pursuits; member of the State assembly in 1822; elected to the Nineteenth and Twentieth Congresses (March 4, 1825-March 3, 1829); chairman, Committee on Public Expenditures (Twentieth Congress); appointed appraiser of merchandise for the port of New York May 26, 1830, and served until 1840, when he retired from active business and moved to Goshen, Orange County, N.Y.; died in Goshen, N.Y., September 7, 1846; interment in a private cemetery on his estate in Goshen.

**JOHNSON, John,** a Representative from Ohio; born near Dungannon, County Tyrone, Ireland, in 1805; immigrated with his mother to the United States in 1818; settled in Coshocton, Ohio, in 1819; received a limited schooling; learned the tanner's trade; later engaged in merchandising and banking; member of the Ohio State senate in 1843 and 1844; delegate to the State constitutional convention in 1849 and 1850; elected as an Independent Democrat to the Thirty-second Congress (March 4, 1851-March 3, 1853); was not a candidate for renomination in 1852 to the Thirty-third Congress; retired from political life and resided in Washington, D.C., for several years; returned to Coshocton, Ohio, and engaged in banking, and was also interested in agricultural pursuits until his death there on February 5, 1867; interment in Oakbridge Cemetery.

**JOHNSON, John Telemachus** (brother of James Johnson and Richard Mentor Johnson and uncle of Robert Ward Johnson), a Representative from Kentucky; born at Great Crossings, Scott County, Ky., October 5, 1788; pursued preparatory studies; attended Transylvania University, Lexington, Ky.; studied law; was admitted to the bar in 1809 and commenced practice in Georgetown, Ky.; served in the War of 1812 as an aide to General William Henry Harrison; member of the Kentucky house of representatives and served five terms; elected to the Seventeenth and Eighteenth Congresses (March 4, 1821-March 3, 1825); chairman, Committee on the Post Office and Post Roads (Eighteenth Congress); was not a candidate for renomination in 1824 to the Nineteenth Congress; appointed judge of the court of appeals on April 20, 1826, and served until December 30, 1826; minister of the Christian Church for a number of years; became editor of the Christian Messenger in 1832, the Gospel Advocate in 1835, and the Christian in 1837; was instrumental in establishing the old Bacon College at Georgetown, Ky., in 1836; died in Lexington, Mo., December 17, 1856; interment in Lexington Cemetery, Lexington, Ky.

**JOHNSON, Joseph** (uncle of Waldo Porter Johnson), a Representative from Virginia; born in Orange County, N.Y., December 19, 1785; moved with his mother to Belvidere, N.J., in 1791 and thence to Bridgeport, Va. (now West Virginia), in 1801; engaged in agricultural pursuits; served in the War of 1812 as captain of a company of Virginia riflemen; member of the Virginia house of delegates in 1815, 1816, and 1818-1822; elected to the

Eighteenth and Nineteenth Congresses (March 4, 1823-March 3, 1827); chairman, Committee on Expenditures on Public Buildings (Nineteenth Congress); unsuccessful candidate for reelection in 1826 to the Twentieth Congress; elected to the Twenty-second Congress to fill the vacancy caused by the death of Philip Doddridge, and served from January 21 to March 3, 1833; was not a candidate for renomination in 1832 to the Twenty-third Congress; elected as a Jacksonian to the Twenty-fourth Congress, and reelected as a Democrat to the Twenty-fifth and Twenty-sixth Congresses (March 4, 1835-March 3, 1841); chairman, Committee on Accounts (Twenty-fifth and Twenty-sixth Congresses); declined to be a candidate for renomination in 1840 to the Twenty-seventh Congress; delegate to the Democratic National Convention of 1844; elected to the Twenty-ninth Congress (March 4, 1845-March 3, 1847); chairman, Committee on Revolutionary Claims (Twenty-ninth Congress); declined to be a candidate for renomination in 1846 to the Thirtieth Congress; again a member of the Virginia house of delegates in 1847 and 1848; resumed agricultural pursuits; delegate to the Virginia constitutional convention of 1850 and 1851; elected Governor of Virginia in 1851, and served from January 16, 1852 to December 31, 1855; died in Bridgeport, Harrison County, W.Va., February 27, 1877; interment in the old Brick Church Cemetery.

**JOHNSON, Joseph Travis,** a Representative from South Carolina; born in Brewerton, Laurens County, S.C., February 28, 1858; attended the common schools and was graduated from Erskine College, Due West, S.C., in 1879; taught school for several years; studied law; was admitted to the bar in 1883; practiced law in Laurens and later in Spartanburg; elected as a Democrat to the Fifty-seventh and to the seven succeeding Congresses and served from March 4, 1901, until April 19, 1915, when he resigned; Federal judge of the western district of South Carolina from 1915 until his death in Spartanburg, S.C., May 8, 1919; interment in Oakwood Cemetery.

**JOHNSON, Justin Leroy,** a Representative from California; born in Wausau, Marathon County, Wis., April 8, 1888; attended the public schools and was graduated from the University of Wisconsin at Madison in 1911 and from the law department of the University of California at Berkeley in 1915; was admitted to the bar in 1915; served as a pilot in the One Hundred and Fourth Aero Squadron 1917-1919, participating in the St. Mihiel and Argonne drives; located in Stockton, Calif., in 1919 and commenced the practice of law; deputy district attorney of San Joaquin County, Calif., in 1920 and 1921; city attorney of Stockton, Calif., 1923-1933; member of the Planning Commission of Stockton 1934-1941; referee in bankruptcy in 1922 and 1923; delegate to the Republican National Conventions in 1936 and 1948; elected as a Republican to the Seventy-eighth and to the six succeeding Congresses (January 3, 1943-January 3, 1957); unsuccessful candidate for reelection in 1956 to the Eighty-fifth Congress; died in Stockton, Calif., March 26, 1961; interment in Casa Bonita Crematorium.

**JOHNSON, Lester Roland,** a Representative from Wisconsin; born in Brandon, Fond du Lac County, Wis., June 16, 1901; attended the public schools and Lawrence College, 1919-1921; graduated from the University of Wisconsin School of Commerce in 1924; was associated with his father in the lumber, feed, and coal business 1924-1938; entered the University of Wisconsin Law School in 1938 and graduated in February 1941; was admitted to the Wisconsin bar and commenced practice in Black River Falls, Wis., the same year; chief clerk of the Wisconsin assembly 1935-1939; with State banking commission in 1942; district attorney of Jackson County 1943-1946 and again in 1953; delegate to the Democratic National Conventions in 1952 and 1960; elected as a Democrat to the Eighty-third Congress, by special election, October 13, 1953, to fill the vacancy caused by the death of Merlin Hull; reelected to the six succeeding Congresses and served from October 13, 1953, to January 3, 1965;

was not a candidate for reelection in 1964 to the Eighty-ninth Congress; died in Augusta, Wis., July 24, 1975; interment in Brandon Cemetery, Brandon, Wis.

**JOHNSON, Luther Alexander,** a Representative from Texas; born in Corsicana, Navarro County, Tex., October 29, 1875; attended the public schools and was graduated from the law department of Cumberland University, Lebanon, Tenn., in 1896; was admitted to the bar the same year and commenced practice in Corsicana, Tex.; prosecuting attorney of Navarro County 1898-1902; district attorney of the thirteenth judicial district of Texas 1904-1910; delegate to the Democratic National Convention in 1916; chairman of the Democratic State convention in 1920; elected as a Democrat to the Sixty-eighth and to the eleven succeeding Congresses and served from March 4, 1923, until his resignation on July 17, 1946; judge of the Tax Court of the United States from July 1946 until his retirement in September 1956; was a resident of Corsicana, Tex., until his death there on June 6, 1965; interment in Oakwood Cemetery.

**JOHNSON, Lyndon Baines** (father-in-law of Charles Spittal Robb), a Representative and a Senator from Texas and a Vice President and 36th President of the United States; born on a farm near Stonewall, Gillespie County, Tex., on August 27, 1908; moved with his parents to Johnson City in 1913; attended the public schools of Blanco County, Tex.; taught school in Cotulla, Tex., September 1928 to May 1929; graduated from Southwest Texas State Teachers College at San Marcos in August 1930; taught high school speech and declamation classes in Houston, Tex., October 1930 to November 1931; served as secretary to Representative Richard M. Kleberg of Texas, 1931-1935; attended the Georgetown University Law School, Washington, D.C., 1934; appointed Texas State director of the National Youth Administration on July 26, 1935 and served until February 1937; elected as a Democrat to the Seventy-fifth Congress by special election, April 10, 1937, to fill the vacancy caused by the death of James P. Buchanan; reelected to the five succeeding Congresses and served from April 10, 1937, to January 3, 1949; served as lieutenant commander in the United States Navy, 1941-1942; was not a candidate for renomination in 1948 to the House of Representatives, but was elected to the United States Senate for the term commencing January 3, 1949; reelected in 1954 and again in 1960 for the term ending January 3, 1967; Democratic whip (Eighty-second Congress), minority leader (Eighty-third Congress), majority leader (Eighty-fourth through Eighty-sixth Congresses), chairman, Special Committee on the Senate Reception Room (Eighty-fourth Congress), Special Committee on Astronautics and Space (Eighty-fifth Congress), Committee on Aeronautical and Space Sciences (Eighty-fifth and Eighty-sixth Congresses); elected Vice President of the United States, November 8, 1960, on the Democratic ticket headed by John F. Kennedy, for the term beginning January 20, 1961; resigned from the United States Senate on January 3, 1961; on the death of President Kennedy was sworn in as President of the United States on November 22, 1963, elected President of the United States, November 3, 1964, for the term commencing January 20, 1965, and served until January 20, 1969; was not a candidate for reelection in 1968; retired to his ranch near Johnson City, Tex., where he died on January 22, 1973; interment in the family cemetery at the LBJ Ranch.

**Bibliography:** Caro, Robert A. *The Years of Lyndon Johnson: The Path To Power.* New York: Knopf, 1982; Caro, Robert A. *The Years of Lyndon Johnson: Means of Ascent.* New York: Knopf, 1990; Evans, Rowland, and Novak, Robert. *Lyndon B. Johnson: The Exercise of Power, A Political Biography.* New York: New American Library, 1966.

**JOHNSON, Magnus,** a Senator and a Representative from Minnesota; born near Karlstad in Ed Parish, Varmland, Sweden, September 19, 1871; attended the rural schools of his native country; apprenticed as a glass blower from 1888 to 1891; immigrated to the United States in 1891 and settled in La Crosse, Wis., where he was a lumberjack; moved to Meeker County, Minn., in 1893 and farmed; president of the Minnesota Union of the American Society of Equity, 1911-1914; vice president of the Equity Cooperative Exchange, 1912-1926; also served as school clerk and assessor of Kingston, Minn.; member, Minnesota State house of representatives, 1915-1919; member, Minnesota State senate, 1919-1923; unsuccessful candidate for election in 1922 and in 1926 for Governor of Minnesota on the Farmer-Labor ticket; elected on the Farmer-Labor ticket to the United States Senate to fill the vacancy caused by the death of Knute Nelson, and served from July 16, 1923 to March 3, 1925; unsuccessful candidate for reelection in 1924; resumed agricultural pursuits near Kimball, Minn.; elected as a Farmer-Laborite to the Seventy-third Congress (March 4, 1933-January 3, 1935); unsuccessful candidate for reelection in 1934 to the Seventy-fourth Congress; resumed agricultural pursuits; served as State supervisor of public stockyards, 1934-1936; unsuccessful candidate for the Farmer-Labor nomination for Governor of Minnesota in 1936; died in Litchfield, Minn., where he had gone for medical treatment, on September 13, 1936; interment in Dassel Cemetery, Dassel, Minn.

**Bibliography:** *DAB*.

**JOHNSON, Martin Nelson,** a Representative and a Senator from North Dakota; born in Racine County, Wis., March 3, 1850; moved with his parents to Decorah, Iowa, the same year; was taught at home and attended the country schools; was graduated from the law department of the University of Iowa at Iowa City in 1873; taught two years in the California Military Academy at Oakland, Calif.; returned to Iowa in 1875; was admitted to the bar in 1876 and commenced practice in Decorah; member, State house of representatives 1877; member, State senate 1878-1882; presidential elector on the Republican ticket 1876; moved to Dakota Territory in 1882; engaged in agricultural pursuits; prosecuting attorney of Nelson County 1886-1890; member of the constitutional convention of North Dakota in 1889; unsuccessful Republican candidate for election to the United States Senate in 1889; elected as a Republican to the Fifty-second and to the three succeeding Congresses (March 4, 1891-March 3, 1899); was not a candidate for renomination in 1898, having become a candidate for Senator; unsuccessful candidate for election to the United States Senate in 1899; elected as a Republican to the United States Senate and served from March 4, 1909, until his death in Fargo, N.Dak., October 21, 1909; chairman, Committee to Investigate Trespassers Upon Indian Lands (Sixty-first Congress); interment in the City Cemetery, Petersburg, N.Dak.

**JOHNSON, Nancy Lee,** a Representative from Connecticut; born in Chicago, Ill., January 5, 1935; attended elementary and secondary classes of the University of Chicago Laboratory School, Chicago, graduating, 1953; B.A., Radcliffe College, Cambridge, Mass., 1957; attended, University of London Courtauld Institute, 1957-1958; teacher; elected to the Connecticut senate, 1977-1982; delegate, Republican National Convention, 1980; elected as a Republican to the Ninety-eighth and to the six succeeding Congresses (January 3, 1983-January 3, 1997); chairman, Committee on Standards of Official Conduct (One Hundred Fourth Congress); is a resident of New Britain, Conn.

**JOHNSON, Noadiah,** a Representative from New York; born in Connecticut in 1795; completed preparatory studies; moved to Delaware County, N.Y., in 1817; studied law; was admitted to the bar and commenced practice in Delhi, N.Y.; district attorney for Delaware County from June 1825 to November 1833; one of the publishers of the Delaware Gazette; elected as a Jacksonian to the Twenty-third Congress (March 4, 1833-March 3, 1835); member of the State senate from 1837 until his death in Albany, N.Y., April 4, 1839; interment in the cemetery at Delhi, Delaware County, N.Y.

**JOHNSON, Noble Jacob,** a Representative from Indiana; born in Terre Haute, Vigo County, Ind., August 23, 1887; attended public schools; studied law; was admitted to the bar in 1911 and commenced practice in Terre Haute; deputy prosecuting attorney for the forty-third judicial circuit of Indiana in 1917 and 1918; prosecuting attorney for the same judicial circuit 1921-1924; elected as a Republican to the Sixty-ninth, Seventieth, and Seventy-first Congresses (March 4, 1925-March 3, 1931); unsuccessful candidate for reelection in 1930 to the Seventy-second Congress, and for election in 1936 to the Seventy-fifth Congress; elected to the Seventy-sixth and to the four succeeding Congresses and served from January 3, 1939, until his resignation on July 1, 1948; appointed a judge of the United States Court of Customs and Patent Appeals and served from July 2, 1948, to July 19, 1956, and as chief judge from July 20, 1956, until his retirement August 7, 1958; resided in Washington, D.C., until his death March 17, 1968; interment in Bethesda Cemetery, West Terre Haute, Ind.

**JOHNSON, Paul Burney,** a Representative from Mississippi; born in Hillsboro, Scott County, Miss., March 23, 1880; attended the public schools, Harpersville College, and Millsaps College, Jackson, Miss.; studied law; was admitted to the bar in 1903 and commenced practice in Hattiesburg, Forrest County, Miss.; judge of the city court in 1907 and 1908; circuit judge of the twelfth judicial district 1910-1919; elected as a Democrat to the Sixty-sixth and Sixty-seventh Congresses (March 4, 1919-March 3, 1923); declined to be a candidate for renomination in 1922 to the Sixty-eighth Congress; resumed the practice of his profession and also engaged in agricultural pursuits; elected Governor of Mississippi in 1939 and served from January 16, 1940 until his death in Hattiesburg, Miss., on December 26, 1943; interment in the City Cemetery.

**JOHNSON, Perley Brown,** a Representative from Ohio; born in the blockhouse in Marietta, Ohio, September 8, 1798; attended the public schools; studied medicine; commenced practice in Marietta in 1822; moved to McConnelsville, Morgan County, Ohio, in 1823 and continued practice; clerk of the court of common pleas in 1825; member of the State house of representatives 1833-1835; elected as a Whig to the Twenty-eighth Congress (March 4, 1843-March 3, 1845); unsuccessful candidate for reelection in 1844 to the Twenty-ninth Congress; resumed the practice of medicine in McConnelsville, Ohio; discontinued the practice of his profession in 1847 on account of ill health and lived in retirement until his death in McConnelsville, Ohio, February 9, 1870; interment in McConnelsville Cemetery.

**JOHNSON, Philip,** a Representative from Pennsylvania; born in Polkville, Knowlton Township, Warren County, N.J., January 17, 1818; moved to Mount Bethel, Pa., in 1839; attended the common schools and Lafayette College, Easton, Pa., 1842-1844; was a plantation tutor in Mississippi 1844-1846; returned to Pennsylvania; studied law; attended Union Law School in Easton, Pa.; was admitted to the bar in 1848 and commenced practice in Easton; county court clerk 1848-1853; member of the Pennsylvania house of representatives in 1853 and 1854; revenue commissioner of the third judicial district in 1859 and 1860; elected as a Democrat to the Thirty-seventh, Thirty-eighth, and Thirty-ninth Congresses and served from March 4, 1861, until his death in Washington, D.C., January 29, 1867; interment in Easton Cemetery, Easton, Pa.

**JOHNSON, Reverdy** (brother-in-law of Thomas Fielder Bowie), a Senator from Maryland; born in Annapolis, Md., May 21, 1796; graduated, St. John's College, Annapolis, Md., 1811; studied law; was admitted to the bar in 1815 and commenced practice in Upper Marlboro; deputy attorney general of Maryland, 1816-1817; moved to Baltimore in 1817; appointed chief commissioner of insolvent debtors of Maryland in 1817; member, Maryland State senate, 1821-1829; resumed the practice of law in Baltimore; elected to the United States Senate as a Whig, and served from March 4, 1845 to

March 7, 1849, when he resigned to become Attorney General; appointed Attorney General of the United States by President Zachary Taylor, and served from March 8, 1849 until July 22, 1850; member of the peace convention of 1861 held in Washington, D.C., in an effort to devise means to prevent the impending war; member, Maryland State house of representatives, 1860-1861; elected as a Democrat to the United States Senate, and served from March 4, 1863 to July 10, 1868, when he resigned; appointed Minister to Great Britain on June 12, 1868, and served until May 1869; returned to Baltimore, Md., where he resumed the practice of his profession; compiler of the reports of decisions of the Maryland Court of Appeals; died in Annapolis, Md., February 10, 1876; interment in Greenmount Cemetery, Baltimore, Md.

**Bibliography:** *DAB*; Steiner, Bernard. *Life of Reverdy Johnson.* 1914. Reprint. New York: Russell and Russell, 1970.

**JOHNSON, Richard Mentor** (brother of James Johnson [1774-1826] and John Telemachus Johnson, and uncle of Robert Ward Johnson), a Representative and a Senator from Kentucky and a Vice President of the United States; born at "Beargrass," Jefferson County, Ky., near the present site of Louisville, October 17, 1780; attended the common schools and Transylvania University, Lexington, Ky.; studied law; was admitted to the bar in 1802 and commenced practice in Great Crossings, Ky.; later moved his practice to Georgetown, Ky.; member, Kentucky house of representatives, 1804-1806, and again in 1819; elected as a Republican to the Tenth and to the five succeeding Congresses (March 4, 1807-March 3, 1819); chairman, Committee on Claims (Eleventh Congress), Committee on Expenditures in the Department of War (Fifteenth Congress); during the War of 1812 was commissioned colonel of Kentucky Volunteers; commanded a regiment of mounted riflemen in engagements against the British in lower Canada, and saw action at the Battle of the Thames, October 5, 1813; elected to the United States Senate to fill the vacancy caused by the resignation of John J. Crittenden; reelected and served from December 10, 1819 to March 3, 1829; unsuccessful candidate for reelection in 1828; chairman, Committee on Post Office and Post Roads (Nineteenth and Twentieth Congresses); elected to the Twenty-first and to the three succeeding Congresses (March 4, 1829-March 3, 1837); chairman, Committee on Post Office and Post Roads (Twenty-first and Twenty-second Congresses), Committee on Military Affairs (Twenty-second through Twenty-fourth Congresses); was chosen Vice President of the United States by the Senate on February 8, 1837, none of the four candidates having received a majority of the electoral vote, and served under President Martin Van Buren from March 4, 1837 to March 3, 1841; unsuccessful candidate for the Democratic presidential nomination in 1844; elected to the Kentucky house of representatives in August 1850, and served until his death in Frankfort, Ky., November 19, 1850; interment in the Frankfort Cemetery.

**Bibliography:** *DAB*; Meyer, Leland. *The Life and Times of Colonel Richard M. Johnson of Kentucky.* 1932. Reprint. New York: AMS Press, 1967; Padget, James A., ed. "The Letters of Colonel Richard M. Johnson of Kentucky." *Register of the Kentucky Historical Society* 38 (1940): 186-201, 323-39; 39 (1941): 22-46, 172-88, 260-74, 358-67; 40 (1942): 69-91.

**JOHNSON, Robert Davis,** a Representative from Missouri; born on a farm near Slater, Saline County, Mo., August 12, 1883; educated in the rural graded schools of his native county, and was graduated from the Portland (Ind.) High School in 1901; attended the Missouri Valley College, Marshall, Mo.; taught school in Saline Valley and Orearville, Mo., 1901-1907; served as clerk of the circuit court of Saline County, 1915-1923; while serving as clerk also studied law; was admitted to the bar in 1917 and commenced practice in Marshall, Mo., in 1923; served as prosecuting attorney of Saline County, 1925-1928; elected as a Democrat to the Seventy-second Congress to fill the vacancy caused by the death of Samuel C.

Major, and served from September 29, 1931 to March 3, 1933; unsuccessful candidate for renomination in 1932 to the Seventy-third Congress; resumed the practice of law in Marshall, Mo.; elected judge of the State circuit court of the fifteenth judicial circuit of Missouri on November 5, 1940, and served until January 1, 1947; again resumed the practice of law in Marshall, Mo., where he died on October 23, 1961; interment in Ridge Park Cemetery.

**JOHNSON, Robert Samuel (Sam),** a Representative from Texas; born in San Antonio, Bexar County, Tex., October 11, 1930; B.B.A., Southern Methodist University, Dallas, 1951; M.S.I.A., George Washington University, Washington, D.C., 1974; Armed Forces Staff College, Norfolk, Va., National War College, Fort McNair, Washington, D.C.; entered active duty, United States Air Force in 1951; released in 1979 after service as fighter pilot in Korean and Vietnam conflicts and as prisoner of war, Vietnam, 1966-1973; director of Air Force Fighter Weapons (Top Gun) School; flew with Air Force "Thunderbirds"; home builder; member, Texas State house of representatives, 1985-1991; elected as a Republican to the One Hundred Second Congress, May 18, 1991, by special election to fill the vacancy caused by the resignation of Steve Bartlett; reelected to the One Hundred Third and One Hundred Fourth Congresses, and served from May 18, 1991 to January 3, 1997; is a resident of Dallas, Tex.

**JOHNSON, Robert Ward** (nephew of James Johnson [1774-1826], John Telemachus Johnson and Richard Mentor Johnson, and brother-in-law of Ambrose Sevier), a Representative and a Senator from Arkansas; born in Scott County, Ky., July 22, 1814; moved with his father to Arkansas in 1821; attended the Choctaw Academy and St. Joseph's College, Bardstown, Ky.; studied law and commenced practice in Little Rock, Ark., in 1835; prosecuting attorney for the Little Rock circuit, 1840-1842, and State attorney general ex officio; elected as a Democrat to the Thirtieth and to the two succeeding Congresses (March 4, 1847-March 3, 1853); chairman, Committee on Indian Affairs (Thirty-first and Thirty-second Congresses); declined to be a candidate for renomination in 1852 to the Thirty-third Congress; appointed and subsequently elected to the United States Senate to fill the vacancy caused by the resignation of Solon Borland; reelected in 1855, and served from July 6, 1853 to March 3, 1861; was not a candidate for reelection in 1860; chairman, Committee on Printing (Thirty-fourth and Thirty-fifth Congresses), Committee on Public Lands (Thirty-sixth Congress); delegate to the Provisional Government of the Confederate States in 1862; member of the Confederate Senate, 1862-1865; engaged in the practice of law in Washington, D.C.; unsuccessful candidate for election to the United States Senate from Arkansas in 1878; died in Little Rock, Ark., July 26, 1879; interment in Mount Holly Cemetery.

**Bibliography:** Lewis, Elsie M. "Robert Ward Johnson: Militant Spokesman of the Old-South-West." *Arkansas Historical Quarterly* 13 (Spring 1954): 16-30.

**JOHNSON, Royal Cleaves,** a Representative from South Dakota; born in Cherokee, Cherokee County, Iowa, October 3, 1882; moved with his parents to Highmore, Hyde County, S.Dak., March 19, 1883; attended the public schools; was graduated from the law department of the University of South Dakota at Vermilion in 1906; was admitted to the bar in 1906 and commenced practice in Highmore, S.Dak.; assistant State's attorney of Hyde County in 1906 and 1907 and State's attorney of the same county in 1908 and 1909; moved to Aberdeen, S.Dak., in 1913 and resumed the practice of law; attorney general of South Dakota 1910-1914; elected as a Republican to the Sixty-fourth and to the eight succeeding Congresses (March 4, 1915-March 3, 1933); chairman, Committee on Expenditures in the Department of War (Sixty-seventh and Sixty-eighth Congresses), Committee on World War Veterans' Legislation (Sixty-ninth, Seventieth, and Seventy-first Congresses); was not a candidate for renomination in 1932; during the First

World War he absented himself from the House and on January 5, 1918, enlisted in the Army; served in the Three Hundred and Thirteenth Infantry as private, sergeant, second lieutenant, and first lieutenant; was awarded the Distinguished Service Cross by the United States Government and the Croix de Guerre with gold star by the Republic of France; continued to practice law in Washington, D.C., until his death there on August 2, 1939; interment in Arlington National Cemetery, Va.

**JOHNSON, Thomas,** a Delegate from Maryland; born near the mouth of St. Leonards Creek, Calvert County, Md., November 4, 1732; at an early age moved to Annapolis, Md.; studied law; was admitted to the bar; entered the provincial assembly as a delegate from Anne Arundel County in 1762; member of the committee of correspondence and of the council of safety; assisted in organizing the Potomac Co. for improving the navigation of the Potomac River; a member of the Annapolis Convention of June 1774; Member of the Continental Congress, 1774-1776; nominated George Washington as commander in chief of the American forces on June 15, 1775; delegate to the first constitutional convention of Maryland in 1776; served in the Revolutionary War as senior brigadier general of Maryland Militia; Governor of Maryland, 1777-1779; moved to Frederick County, Md.; member of the Maryland house of delegates in 1780, 1786, and 1787; member of the Maryland convention for ratification of the Federal Constitution in 1788; chief judge of the general court of Maryland, 1790-1791; appointed by President George Washington as the first United States judge for the district of Maryland in September 1789, but declined; nominated as an Associate Justice of the United States Supreme Court on November 1, 1791; was confirmed by the Senate on November 7, 1791, and served until March 4, 1793, when he resigned on account of ill health; declined a Cabinet portfolio of Secretary of State tendered by President Washington on August 24, 1795; appointed by President John Adams as chief judge of the Territory of Columbia on February 28, 1801; member of the Board of Commissioners of the Federal City; died at "Rose Hill," Frederick, Md., October 26, 1819; interment in All Saints' Episcopal Churchyard; reinterment in Mount Olivet Cemetery, Frederick, Md.

Bibliography: *DAB*; Delaplaine, Edward. *The Life of Thomas Johnson.* New York: F.H. Hitchcock, 1927.

**JOHNSON, Thomas Francis,** a Representative from Maryland; born in Worcester County, Md., June 26, 1909; attended the schools in Worcester County, Md.; graduated from Staunton (Va.) Military Academy in 1926, St. John's College, University of Virginia, and University of Maryland; was admitted to the bar and commenced the practice of law in Snow Hill, Md.; in 1932 was elected chairman of the board of Commercial National Bank of Snow Hill, Md.; elected State's attorney in 1934; elected to the State senate in 1938, reelected in 1942 and again 1946 and served until 1951; specialized in international law with practice in the Far East, Middle East, and continental Europe; elected as a Democrat to the Eighty-sixth and Eighty-seventh Congresses (January 3, 1959-January 3, 1963); unsuccessful candidate for reelection in 1962 to the Eighty-eighth Congress; resumed the practice of law; was a resident of Berlin, Md., until his death in Seaford, Del., on February 1, 1988.

**JOHNSON, Timothy Peter,** a Representative from South Dakota; born in Canton, Lincoln County, S.D., December 28, 1946; attended public schools; B.A., University of South Dakota, 1969, M.A., 1970; post-graduate studies, Mighigan State University, 1970-1971; J.D., University of South Dakota, 1975; budget adviser, Michigan State senate, 1971-1972; began the private practice of law in Vermillion, S.D., in 1975; treasurer, Clay County Democratic Party, 1976-1978; member, South Dakota house of representatives, 1979-1982; South Dakota senate, 1983-1986; Clay County deputy State's attorney, 1985; delegate, Democratic National Convention, 1988; elected as a Democrat to the One Hundredth and to the four succeeding Congresses (January 3, 1987-January 3, 1997); was not a candidate in 1996 for reelection to the House of Representatives, but was a candidate for election to the United States Senate; is a resident of Vermillion, S.D.

**JOHNSON, Tom Loftin,** a Representative from Ohio; born in Georgetown, Scott County, Ky., July 18, 1854; moved to Indiana in boyhood; attended the public schools; employed in a rolling mill; clerk in a street-railway office in Louisville, Ky., 1869-1875; later became secretary of the company; invented several street-railway devices; purchased a street railway in Indianapolis, Ind.; later acquired large street-railway interests in Cleveland, Detroit, and Brooklyn; settled in Cleveland, Ohio; became interested in rolling mills and iron manufacturing; unsuccessful Democratic candidate for election in 1888 to the Fifty-first Congress; elected as a Democrat to the Fifty-second and Fifty-third Congresses (March 4, 1891-March 3, 1895); unsuccessful candidate for reelection in 1894 to the Fifty-fourth Congress; mayor of Cleveland, Ohio, 1901-1909; unsuccessful candidate for reelection in 1909; unsuccessful candidate for election in 1903 for Governor of Ohio; died in Cleveland, Ohio, April 10, 1911; interment in Greenwood Cemetery.

Bibliography: *DAB*; Johnson, Tom L. *My Story.* Edited by Elizabeth J. Hauser. 1911. Reprint. Kent, Ohio: Kent State University Press, 1993; Murdock, Eugene C. *Tom Johnson of Cleveland.* Dayton, Ohio: Wright State University Press, 1993.

**JOHNSON, Waldo Porter** (nephew of Joseph Johnson), a Senator from Missouri; born in Bridgeport, Harrison County, Va., September 16, 1817; attended public and private schools; graduated from Rector College, Pruntytown, Taylor County, Va., in 1839; studied law; was admitted to the bar and commenced practice in Harrison County, Va., in 1841; moved to Osceola, St. Clair County, Mo., in 1842 and continued the practice of law; served in the war with Mexico as a member of the First Missouri Regiment of Mounted Volunteers; member of the Missouri State house of representatives in 1847; elected circuit attorney in 1848 and judge of the seventh judicial circuit in 1851; resigned in 1852 and resumed the practice of law; member of the peace convention of 1861 held in Washington, D.C., in an effort to devise means to prevent the impending war; elected as a Democrat to the United States Senate and served from March 17, 1861, to January 10, 1862, when he was expelled from the Senate for disloyalty to the Union; served in the Confederate Army during the Civil War; attained the rank of lieutenant colonel of the Fourth Missouri Infantry; appointed a member of the Senate of the Confederate States to fill a vacancy; resided in Hamilton, Canada, from August 1865 to April 1866; returned to Osceola, Mo., and resumed the practice of his profession; president of the State constitutional convention in 1875; died in Osceola, Mo., on August 14, 1885; interment in Forest Hill Cemetery, Kansas City, Mo.

**JOHNSON, William Cost,** a Representative from Maryland; born near Jefferson, Frederick County, Md., January 14, 1806; completed preparatory studies; studied law; was admitted to the bar in 1831 and commenced practice in Jefferson, Frederick County, Md.; member of the State house of representatives in 1831 and 1832; elected as an Anti-Jacksonian to the Twenty-third Congress (March 4, 1833-March 3, 1835); delegate to the State constitutional convention in 1836; elected as a Whig to the Twenty-fifth, Twenty-sixth, and Twenty-seventh Congresses (March 4, 1837-March 3, 1843); chairman, Committee on District of Columbia (Twenty-sixth Congress), Committee on Public Lands (Twenty-seventh Congress); continued the practice of his profession until his death in Washington, D.C., on April 14, 1860; interment in the Reformed Church Cemetery, Jefferson, Md.

**JOHNSON, William Richard,** a Representative from Illinois; born in Rock Island, Ill., May 15, 1875; moved with his parents to Freeport, Ill., in 1879; attended the public schools and the College of Commerce at Freeport; served from 1890 to 1894 as an apprentice, and from 1894 to 1899 as a locomotive blacksmith in the Illinois Central Railroad shops at Freeport; member of the United States Capitol police force, 1901-1919; appointed superintendent of the folding room of the House of Representatives on June 18, 1919, and served until March 3, 1925, when he resigned; elected as a Republican to the Sixty-ninth and to the three succeeding Congresses (March 4, 1925-March 3, 1933); unsuccessful candidate for renomination in 1932 to the Seventy-third Congress; returned to Freeport, Ill., where he died on January 2, 1938; interment in Oakland Cemetery.

**JOHNSON, William Samuel,** a Delegate and a Senator from Connecticut; born in Stratford, Conn., on October 7, 1727; was tutored privately by his father; graduated from Yale College in 1744 and from Harvard College in 1747; studied law; was admitted to the bar and practiced in Stratford; member of the colonial house of representatives, 1761, 1765, and of the upper house, 1766, 1771-1775; served as a delegate to the Stamp Act Congress held in New York City in October 1765; was Connecticut agent extraordinary to the court of England to determine the State title to Indian lands, 1767-1771; judge of Connecticut Supreme Court, 1772-1774; Member of the Continental Congress, 1785-1787; delegate to the constitutional convention in 1787; served as the first president of Columbia College of New York City, 1787-1800; elected to the United States Senate, and served from March 4, 1789 to March 4, 1791, when he resigned; died in Stratford, Conn., November 14, 1819; interment in the Episcopal Cemetery.

**Bibliography:** *DAB*; Groce, G.C. *William Samuel Johnson: A Maker of the Constitution.* New York: Columbia University Press, 1937; McCaughey, Elizabeth P. *From Loyalist to Founding Father: The Political Odyssey of William Samuel Johnson.* New York: Columbia University Press, 1980.

**JOHNSON, William Ward,** a Representative from California; born in Brighton, Washington County, Iowa, March 9, 1892; attended the public schools at Brighton, Iowa, and Twin Falls, Idaho, and the University of California at Berkeley in 1913 and 1914; was graduated from the law school of the University of Southern California at Los Angeles in 1925; member of the Idaho National Guard in 1910 and 1911; bookkeeper, stenographer, and manager of an automobile company at Montpelier, Idaho, and Price, Utah, 1912-1918; engaged in the mercantile business in Idaho and Utah, 1918-1922; also engaged in the banking and oil business at Twin Falls, Idaho, and Long Beach, Calif.; admitted to the bar in 1925 and commenced practice in Long Beach, Calif.; elected as a Republican to the Seventy-seventh and Seventy-eighth Congresses (January 3, 1941-January 3, 1945); unsuccessful candidate for reelection in 1944 to the Seventy-ninth Congress; resumed the practice of law in Long Beach, Calif., until his death there on June 8, 1963; interment in Sunnyside Mausoleum.

**JOHNSTON, Charles,** a Representative from New York; born in Salisbury, Conn., on February 14, 1793; attended the common schools; moved to Poughkeepsie, N.Y.; studied law; was admitted to the bar and practiced; elected as a Whig to the Twenty-sixth Congress (March 4, 1839-March 3, 1841); unsuccessful candidate for reelection in 1840 to the Twenty-seventh Congress; engaged in the practice of law until his death in Poughkeepsie, N.Y., September 1, 1845; interment in the burying ground of Christ Episcopal Church; reinterment in 1861 in the Rural Cemetery.

**JOHNSTON, Charles Clement** (brother of Joseph Eggleston Johnston and uncle of John Warfield Johnston), a Representative from Virginia; born in Longwood, near Farmville, Prince Edward County, Va., April 30, 1795; was educated at home; moved with his parents to Panicello, near Abingdon, Va., in 1811; studied law; was admitted to the bar in 1818 and commenced practice in Abingdon, Va.; elected as a Jacksonian to the Twenty-second Congress and served from March 4, 1831, until his death by drowning near one of the docks in Alexandria, Va., on June 17, 1832; interment in the Congressional Cemetery, Washington, D.C.

**JOHNSTON, David Emmons,** a Representative from West Virginia; born near Pearisburg, Giles County, Va., April 10, 1845; attended the common schools; enlisted in the Confederate Army in April 1861 and served four years in the Seventh Virginia Regiment of Infantry, Kemper's brigade of Pickett's division; studied law; was admitted to the bar in Giles County, Va., in 1867 and commenced practice in Pearisburg, Va.; moved to Mercer County, W.Va., in 1870; prosecuting attorney 1872-1876; member of the State senate in 1878; resigned; judge of the ninth judicial circuit 1880-1888; elected as a Democrat to the Fifty-sixth Congress (March 4, 1899-March 3, 1901); unsuccessful candidate for reelection in 1900 to the Fifty-seventh Congress; moved to Portland, Oreg., in 1908 and resumed the practice of law; died in that city July 7, 1917; interment in Mount Scott Park Cemetery.

**JOHNSTON, Harry Allison, II,** a Representative from Florida; born in West Palm Beach, Fla., December 2, 1931; graduated from Palm Beach High School, 1949; B.A., Virginia Military Institute, Lexington, 1953; J.D., University of Florida Law School, 1958; entered active duty, United States Army in 1953; released in 1955; admitted to Florida bar, 1958; practicing attorney, 1958-1988; member, Florida State senate, 1974-1986, president, 1984-1986; unsuccessful candidate in 1986 for nomination for Governor of Florida; elected as a Democrat to the One Hundred First and to the three succeeding Congresses (January 3, 1989-January 3, 1997); was not a candidate for reelection in 1996 to the One Hundred Fifth Congress; is a resident of West Palm Beach, Fla.

**JOHNSTON, James Thomas,** a Representative from Indiana; born near Greencastle, Putnam County, Ind., January 19, 1839; attended the common schools; studied law; during the Civil War enlisted as a private in Company C, Sixth Indiana Cavalry, in July 1862; transferred to Company A, Eighth Tennessee Cavalry, in September 1863 and commissioned as second lieutenant, serving until January 1864, when he resigned; afterwards served as commissary sergeant of the One Hundred and Thirty-third Regiment, Indiana Volunteer Infantry; commissioned lieutenant and assistant quartermaster of the One Hundred and Forty-ninth Regiment, Indiana Volunteer Infantry, and mustered out in September 1865; was admitted to the bar in March 1866 and commenced practice in Rockville, Parke County, Ind.; prosecuting attorney 1866-1868; member of the State house of representatives in 1868; served in the State senate 1874-1878; elected as a Republican to the Forty-ninth and Fiftieth Congresses (March 4, 1885-March 3, 1889); unsuccessful candidate for reelection in 1888 to the Fifty-first Congress; resumed the practice of law; commander of the Grand Army of the Republic, Department of Indiana, in 1893; died in Rockville, Ind., July 19, 1904; interment in the Rockville Cemetery.

**JOHNSTON, John Bennett, Jr.** (father-in-law of Tim Roemer), a Senator from Louisiana; born in Shreveport, Caddo Parrish, La., June 10, 1932; educated in the public schools of Shreveport, La.; attended Washington and Lee University and United States Military Academy; LL.B., Louisiana State University Law School, Baton Rouge, 1956; admitted to the Louisiana bar in 1956 and commenced practice in Shreveport; served in the United States Army, Judge Advocate General Corps, Germany, 1956-1959; member, Louisiana State house of representatives, 1964-1968, serving as floor leader; member, Louisiana State senate, 1968-1972; elected as a Democrat to the United States Senate, November 7, 1972, for the six-year term commencing January 3, 1973; subsequently appointed by the Governor to complete the unexpired term caused by the death of Allen J. Ellender, for the term ending January 3, 1973, left vacant by the resignation of Elaine S. Edwards; assumed office November 14, 1972; reelected in 1978, 1984, and again in 1990, and served from November 14, 1972 to January 3, 1997; was not a candidate for reelection in 1996; chairman, Democratic Senatorial Campaign Committee (Ninety-fourth Congress), Committee on Energy and Natural Resources (One Hundredth through One Hundred Third Congresses); is a resident of Shreveport, La.

**JOHNSTON, John Brown,** a Representative from New York; born in Glasgow, Scotland, July 10, 1882; immigrated to America in 1886 with his parents, who settled in Brooklyn, N.Y.; attended the public schools in Long Island City and Brooklyn and the New York Law School; was admitted to the bar and commenced the practice of law in Brooklyn; elected as a Democrat to the Sixty-sixth Congress (March 4, 1919-March 3, 1921); was not a candidate for renomination; resumed the practice of his profession in New York City; delegate to the Democratic National Conventions in 1920 and 1924; elected a justice of the supreme court for the second district of New York and assumed his duties on January 1, 1928, and on January 1, 1935, was designated an associate justice of the appellate division and served until his retirement December 31, 1952; on January 1, 1953, was appointed an official referee of the supreme court and continued until July 4, 1955, and then assumed the office of State Administrator of the Judicial Conference of the State of New York until his death; died in Brooklyn, N.Y., January 11, 1960; interment in Green Wood Cemetery.

**JOHNSTON, John Warfield** (uncle of Henry Bowen and nephew of Charles Clement Johnston and Joseph Eggleston Johnston), a Senator from Virginia; born in Panicello, near Abingdon, Va., September 9, 1818; attended Abingdon Academy, South Carolina College at Columbia, and the law department of the University of Virginia at Charlottesville; was admitted to the bar in 1839 and commenced practice in Tazewell, Tazewell County, Va.; Commonwealth attorney for Tazewell County 1844-1846; member, Virginia senate, 1846-1848; during the Civil War, held the position of Confederate States Receiver; judge of the circuit court of Virginia 1866-1870; upon the readmission of Virginia to representation was elected as a Democrat to the United States Senate and served from January 26, 1870, to March 3, 1871; reelected on March 15, 1871, for the term beginning March 4, 1871; reelected in 1877 and served from March 15, 1871, until March 3, 1883; unsuccessful candidate for reelection; chairman, Committee on Revolutionary Claims (Forty-fifth and Forty-seventh Congresses), Committee on Agriculture (Forty-sixth Congress); resumed the practice of his profession; died in Richmond, Va., February 27, 1889; interment in St. Mary's Cemetery, Wytheville, Va.

**JOHNSTON, Joseph Eggleston** (brother of Charles Clement Johnston and uncle of John Warfield Johnston), a Representative from Virginia; born in Longwood, Prince Edward County, Va., February 3, 1807; moved with his parents to Panicello, near Abingdon, Va., in 1811; attended the Abingdon Academy; was graduated from the United States Military Academy, West Point, N.Y., in 1829; pursued a career in the Army, serving in the Seminole and Mexican wars, on the western frontier and during the border conflict in Kansas; promoted through the ranks to brigadier general and quartermaster general; resigned April 22, 1861, to enter the Confederate service; during the Civil War was appointed major general of the Virginia forces on April 26, 1861; commissioned brigadier general, Confederate States Army, May 14, 1861, and general on August 31, 1861; appointed commander of the Department of the Potomac, but was relieved after being severely wounded at the Battle of Seven Pines; placed in command of the Army of Tennessee on December 27, 1863 and served until he was relieved July 17, 1864; again appointed commander of the Army of Tennessee on February 23, 1865, and served until April 26, 1865, when the

terms of surrender of his army were agreed upon; settled in Savannah, Ga.; was president of a railroad company in Arkansas; and engaged in the general insurance business in 1868 and 1869; returned to Virginia and settled in Richmond in 1877 and became president of an express company; elected as a Democrat to the Forty-sixth Congress (March 4, 1879-March 3, 1881); was not a candidate for renomination in 1880 to the Forty-seventh Congress; was appointed Commissioner of Railroads by President Grover Cleveland in 1887 and served until 1891; died in Washington, D.C., March 21, 1891; interment in Greenmount Cemetery, Baltimore, Md.

**Bibliography:** *DAB*; Govan, Gilbert E., and James W. Livingood. *A Different Valor: The Story of General Joseph E. Johnston, C.S.A.* New York: Bobbs-Merrill, 1956; Johnston, Joseph Eggleston. *Narrative of Military Operations.* Edited by Frank E. Vandiver. Bloomington: Indiana University Press, 1959.

**JOHNSTON, Joseph Forney,** a Senator from Alabama; born at "Mount Welcome," Lincoln County, N.C., March 23, 1843; attended the country schools in Lincoln County; while attending a military school in Alabama at the outbreak of the Civil War, enlisted as a private in the Confederate Army, rose to the rank of captain, and served from 1861 to 1865; studied law; was admitted to the bar in 1866 and practiced in Selma, Ala.; moved to Birmingham, Ala., in 1884 and became president of the Alabama National Bank, resigning in 1894; became president of the Sloss Iron & Steel Co. in 1887; elected Governor of Alabama in 1896, reelected in 1898, and served from December 1, 1896 to December 1, 1900; elected as a Democrat to the United States Senate in August 1909 to fill the vacancy in the term ending March 3, 1909, caused by the death of Edmund W. Pettus; simultaneously elected for the term commencing March 4, 1909, and served from August 6, 1907, until his death in Washington, D.C., August 8, 1913; chairman, Committee on University of the United States (Sixty-second Congress), Committee on Military Affairs (Sixty-third Congress); interment Elmwood Cemetery, Birmingham, Ala.

**Bibliography:** *DAB.*

**JOHNSTON, Josiah Stoddard,** a Representative and a Senator from Louisiana; born in Salisbury, Litchfield County, Conn., November 24, 1784; moved with his father to Kentucky in 1788; returned to Connecticut to attend primary school; graduated from Transylvania University, Lexington, Ky., in 1802; studied law; was admitted to the bar and commenced practice in Alexandria, La. (then the Territory of Orleans); member of the Territorial legislature, 1805-1812; during the War of 1812, raised and organized a regiment for the defense of New Orleans, but reached the city after the battle; engaged in agricultural pursuits; State district judge, 1812-1821; elected to the Seventeenth Congress (March 4, 1821-March 3, 1823); unsuccessful candidate for reelection in 1822 to the Eighteenth Congress; appointed to the United States Senate in 1824 to fill the vacancy caused by the resignation of James Brown; elected to the Senate in 1825, reelected in 1831, and served from January 15, 1824, until his death, caused by an explosion on the steamboat *Lioness,* on the Red River in Louisiana, May 19, 1833; chairman, Committee on Commerce (Nineteenth Congress); interment in Rapides Cemetery, Pineville, La.

**Bibliography:** *DAB.*

**JOHNSTON, Olin DeWitt Talmadge** (father of Elizabeth J. Patterson), a Senator from South Carolina; born near Honea Path, Anderson County, S.C., November 18, 1896; attended the public schools; graduated from Textile Industrial Institute, Spartanburg, S.C., in 1915; attended Wofford College, Spartanburg, S.C., until 1917 when he enlisted in the United States Army, serving eighteen months overseas, and becoming a sergeant; reentered Wofford College and was graduated in 1921; received a graduate degree from the University of South Carolina at Columbia in 1923 and graduated from that university's law department in 1924; was admitted to the bar the same year and commenced practice in Spartanburg, S.C.; member, State house of representatives 1923-1924, 1927-1930; unsuccessful Democratic candidate for the gubernatorial nomination in 1930; elected Governor of South Carolina in 1934 and served from January 15, 1935 to January 17, 1939; elected Governor in 1942 and served from January 19, 1943 until his resignation on January 2, 1945, having been elected Senator; unsuccessful Democratic candidate for the United States Senate in 1938 and 1941; elected as a Democrat to the United States Senate in 1944, 1950, 1956, and again in 1962, and served from January 3, 1945, until his death in Columbia, S.C., April 18, 1965; chairman, Committee on Post Office and Civil Service (Eighty-first and Eighty-second Congresses, and Eighty-fourth through Eighty-ninth Congresses), co-chairman, Joint Committee on Postal Service (Eighty-second Congress); interment in Barkers Creek Baptist Church Cemetery, Honea Path, S.C.

**Bibliography:** *DAB*; Huss, John. *Senator for the South: A Biography of Olin D. Johnston.* Garden City, N.Y.: Doubleday, 1961; Miller, Anthony. "Palmetto Politician: The Early Political Career of Olin D. Johnston, 1896-1945." Ph.D. dissertation, University of North Carolina, 1976.

**JOHNSTON, Rienzi Melville** (cousin of Benjamin Edward Russell), a Senator from Texas; born in Sandersville, Washington County, Ga., September 9, 1849; attended the public schools; during the Civil War served in the Confederate Army; moved to Austin, Tex., in 1878 and engaged in journalism; moved to Houston in 1883 and established the Houston Post; member of the Democratic National Committee 1900-1912; appointed as a Democrat to the United States Senate to fill the vacancy caused by the resignation of Joseph W. Bailey and served from January 4, to January 29, 1913, when a successor was elected and qualified; resumed his former activities as editor and president of the Houston Post; elected to the State senate in 1916; relinquished the active management of his newspaper business in 1919 and lived in retirement until his death in Houston, Tex., February 28, 1926; interment in Glenwood Cemetery.

**JOHNSTON, Rowland Louis,** a Representative from Missouri; born in Louisiana, Pike County, Mo., April 23, 1872; attended the public schools; studied law; was admitted to the bar in 1894 and commenced practice in St. Louis, Mo.; member of the State house of representatives 1892-1896; served as prosecuting attorney of St. Louis County 1904-1908; delegate to the Republican National Convention in 1908; assistant circuit attorney for the city of St. Louis 1920-1926; member of the State militia; during the Spanish-American War served as a recruiting officer; moved to Rolla, Mo., in 1926 and continued the practice of law; elected as a Republican to the Seventy-first Congress (March 4, 1929-March 3, 1931); unsuccessful candidate for reelection in 1930 to the Seventy-second Congress and for election in 1932 to the Seventy-third Congress; resumed the practice of law in Rolla, Mo., until his death there on September 22, 1939; remains were cremated and the ashes deposited in the mausoleum at Oak Grove Cemetery, St. Louis, Mo.

**JOHNSTON, Samuel,** a Delegate and a Senator from North Carolina; born in Dundee, Scotland, December 15, 1733; immigrated to the United States in 1736 with his parents, who settled in Chowan County, N.C.; attended school in New England; studied law in North Carolina, was admitted to the bar, and practiced in that State; member, State assembly 1760-1775; clerk of the courts for the Edenton District; deputy naval officer for the port of Edenton; member of the Committee of Correspondence in 1773; delegate to the first four provincial congresses and president of the third and fourth; colonial treasurer; member at large of the provincial Council of Safety, and district paymaster of troops 1775; member of the North Carolina State senate in 1779, 1783, and 1784; Member of the Continental Congress, 1780-1781, and elected first President after the Articles of Confederation were signed, but declined to serve; presided over the State conventions of 1788 and 1789; elected Governor of North Carolina and was twice reelected, but resigned in 1789 to become a United States Senator; elected to the United States Senate and served from November 27, 1789 to March 3, 1793; judge of the superior court of North Carolina, 1800-1803; died near Edenton, Chowan County, N.C., August 17, 1816; interment in the Johnston Burial Ground on the Hayes plantation, near Edenton, N.C.

**Bibliography:** *DAB*.

**JOHNSTON, Thomas Dillard,** a Representative from North Carolina; born in Waynesville, Haywood County, N.C., April 1, 1840; attended the common schools and Col. Stephen Lee's Preparatory School, Asheville, N.C.; entered the University of North Carolina at Chapel Hill in 1858, but left in the spring of 1859 on account of failing health; studied law; entered the Confederate Army in the spring of 1861; was admitted to the bar in 1867 and commenced practice in Asheville; mayor of Asheville in 1869; member of the North Carolina State house of representatives, 1870-1874; declined to be a candidate for reelection; served in the State senate in 1876; elected as a Democrat to the Forty-ninth and Fiftieth Congresses (March 4, 1885-March 3, 1889); was an unsuccessful candidate for reelection in 1888 to the Fifty-first Congress; resumed the practice of law; died in Asheville, N.C., on June 22, 1902; interment in Riverside Cemetery.

**JOHNSTON, Walter Eugene, III,** a Representative from North Carolina; born in Winston-Salem, Forsyth County, N.C., March 3, 1936; attended the public schools; graduated, Georgia Military Academy, College Park, Ga., 1953; attended Duke University, Durham, N.C., 1953-1954; served in the United States Army, specialist fifth class, 1954-1957; J.D., Wake Forest University, Winston-Salem, 1961, B.B.A., 1963; admitted to the North Carolina bar in 1961 and commenced practice in Greensboro; practiced tax law, 1967-1980; delegate, North Carolina State Republican conventions, 1976-1980; elected as a Republican to the Ninety-seventh Congress (January 3, 1981-January 3, 1983); unsuccessful candidate for reelection in 1982 to the Ninety-eighth Congress; chairman of the board of a commercial and industrial property company in Greensboro; is a resident of Greensboro, N.C.

**JOHNSTON, William,** a Representative from Ohio; born in Ireland in 1819; immigrated to the United States and settled in Ohio; attended the public schools; studied law; was admitted to the bar and practiced in Mansfield, Ohio, from 1859 to 1863; elected as a Democrat to the Thirty-eighth Congress (March 4, 1863-March 3, 1865); unsuccessful candidate for reelection in 1864 to the Thirty-ninth Congress; resumed the practice of law; died in Mansfield, Ohio, May 1, 1866; interment in Mansfield Cemetery.

**JOHNSTONE, George,** a Representative from South Carolina; born in Newberry, S.C., April 18, 1846; attended the common schools; entered the State Military Academy, from which he enlisted in the Confederate Army as a member of the battalion of State cadets and served until the close of the Civil War; attended the University of Edinburgh, Scotland, 1866-1869; returned to the United States; studied law; was admitted to the bar in 1871 and commenced practice in Newberry, S.C.; declined a nomination to the State house of representatives in 1874; member of the State house of representatives 1877-1884; declined to be a candidate for reelection; member of the commission that revised the tax laws and suggested amendments to the State constitution in 1881; member of the State executive committee of the Democratic Party 1880-1884; elected as a Democrat to the Fifty-second Congress (March 4, 1891-March 3, 1893); unsuccessful candidate for renomination in 1892; resumed the practice of law in Newberry, S.C.; member of the State constitutional convention in 1895; died in Newberry, S.C., March 8, 1921; interment in Johnstone Cemetery.

**JOLLEY, John Lawlor,** a Representative from South Dakota; born in Montreal, Quebec, Canada, July 14, 1840; attended the common schools; graduated from Eastman Business College; moved to Wisconsin in 1857; enlisted as a private in Company C, Twenty-third Regiment, Wisconsin Volunteer Infantry, August 22, 1862; was mustered out as second lieutenant July 4, 1865; studied law; was admitted to the bar in 1866 and commenced practice in Vermilion, Dakota Territory; member of the Territorial house of representatives in 1867 and 1868; president of the Territorial council in 1875 and 1881; mayor of Vermilion in 1877 and 1885; delegate to the Republican National Convention in 1884; member of the constitutional convention in 1889; member of the State senate in 1889 and 1890; elected as a Republican to the Fifty-second Congress to fill the vacancy caused by the death of John R. Gamble and served from December 7, 1891, to March 3, 1893; was not a candidate for renomination in 1892 to the Fifty-third Congress; resumed the practice of law; died in Vermilion, S.Dak., December 14, 1926; interment in Bluff View Cemetery.

**JONAS, Benjamin Franklin,** a Senator from Louisiana; born in Williamsport, Grant County, Ky., July 19, 1834; moved with his parents to Adams County, Ill.; attended the public schools; moved to New Orleans, La., in 1853; graduated from the law department of the University of Louisiana at Pineville in 1855; was admitted to the bar the same year and commenced practice in New Orleans; enlisted in the Confederate Army in 1862 and served throughout the Civil War; member of the Louisiana State house of representatives, 1865-1868; elected to the State senate in 1872, but declined to take the seat; city attorney of New Orleans, 1875-1879; member, State house of representatives, 1876-1877; elected as a Democrat to the United States Senate, and served from March 4, 1879 to March 3, 1885; unsuccessful candidate for reelection in 1884; chairman, Committee on Interior and Insular Affairs (Forty-sixth Congress); collector of the port of New Orleans, 1885-1889; resumed the practice of law; died in New Orleans, La., on December 21, 1911; interment in Dispersed of Judah Cemetery.

**JONAS, Charles Andrew** (father of Charles Raper Jonas), a Representative from North Carolina; born on a farm near Lincolnton, Lincoln County, N.C., August 14, 1876; attended the public schools, Ridge Academy, Henry, N.C., and Fallston (N.C.) Institute; was graduated from the University of North Carolina at Chapel Hill in 1902; taught school from 1902 until 1906; studied law; was admitted to the bar in 1906 and commenced practice in Lincolnton, N.C.; postmaster at Lincolnton, 1907-1910, and later editor of a newspaper which he helped to establish in 1906; city attorney of Lincolnton, 1908-1912; North Carolina State senator, 1915-1919; delegate to the Republican National Conventions of 1916, 1932, and 1936; member of the board of trustees of the University of North Carolina, 1917-1947; unsuccessful candidate for election in 1918 to the Sixty-sixth Congress; assistant United States attorney for the western district of North Carolina, 1921-1925; served in the State house of representatives, 1927-1929, and 1935-1937; member of the Republican National Committee; elected as a Republican to the Seventy-first Congress (March 4, 1929-March 3, 1931); unsuccessful candidate for reelection in 1930 to the Seventy-second Congress, and for election in 1932 to the Seventy-third Congress; served as United States attorney for the western district of North Carolina from April 1, 1931 to July 1, 1932; unsuccessful candidate for election in 1938 to the United States Senate; unsuccessful candidate for election in 1942 to the Seventy-eighth Congress; resumed the general practice of law at Lincolnton, N.C.; died in a nursing home near Charlotte, N.C., May 25, 1955; interment in Hollybrook Cemetery, Lincolnton, N.C.

**JONAS, Charles Raper** (son of Charles Andrew Jonas), a Representative from North Carolina; born near Lincolnton, Lincoln County, N.C., December 9, 1904; graduated from Lincolnton High School in 1921; A.B., University of North Carolina, Chapel Hill, 1925; J.D., University of North Carolina School of Law, 1928; was admitted to the bar in 1927 and commenced practice in Lincolnton, N.C., in 1928; assistant United States attorney for the western district of North Carolina, 1931-1933; member of the North Carolina National Guard; entered active duty in the United States Army as a captain, September 21, 1940, and was separated from the service April 20, 1946, as a lieutenant colonel in the Judge Advocate General's Corps; president, North Carolina Bar Association, 1946-1947; member, Board of Law Examiners, 1948-1950; resumed the practice of law; delegate to the Republican National Convention of 1952; elected as a Republican to the Eighty-third and to the nine succeeding Congresses (January 3, 1953-January 3, 1973); was not a candidate for reelection in 1972 to the Ninety-third Congress; was a resident of Lincolnton, N.C.; died September 28, 1988.

**JONAS, Edgar Allan,** a Representative from Illinois; born in Mishicot, Manitowoc County, Wis., October 14, 1885; attended the public schools and graduated from the Manitowoc County Normal School; taught in the rural schools of Manitowoc County from 1903 until 1907; was graduated from Chicago Law School in June 1910; was admitted to the bar in 1909 and commenced the practice of law in Chicago, Ill.; assistant corporation counsel of Chicago, Ill., in 1919 and 1920; first assistant State's attorney of Cook County, Ill., 1921-1923; judge of the Municipal Court of Chicago, 1923-1937; judge of the Superior Court of Cook County in 1941 and 1942; associate member of Board of Pardons and Paroles of Illinois, 1945-1947; delegate to the Republican National Convention of 1948; elected as a Republican to the Eighty-first and to the two succeeding Congresses (January 3, 1949-January 3, 1955); unsuccessful candidate for reelection in 1954 to the Eighty-fourth Congress, and for election in 1956 to the Eighty-fifth Congress; resumed the practice of law and was a resident of Chicago, Ill.; died in Evanston, Ill., November 14, 1965; interment in Rosehill Cemetery, Chicago, Ill.

**JONES, Alexander Hamilton,** a Representative from North Carolina; born in Buncombe County, N.C., July 21, 1822; completed preparatory studies; engaged in mercantile pursuits; enlisted in the Union Army in 1863; was captured in east Tennessee while raising a regiment of Union Volunteers and imprisoned; made his escape November 14, 1864; again joined the Union forces in Cumberland, Md.; after the war returned to North Carolina; member of the State convention in 1865; elected as a Republican to the Thirty-ninth Congress but was not permitted to qualify; upon the readmission of North Carolina to representation was elected to the Fortieth and Forty-first Congresses and served from July 6, 1868, to March 3, 1871; unsuccessful candidate for reelection in 1870 to the Forty-second Congress; resided in Washington, D.C., until 1876, in Maryland until 1884, in Asheville, N.C., until 1890, and in Oklahoma until 1897, when he moved to California; died in Long Beach, Calif., January 29, 1901; interment in Signal Hill Cemetery.

**JONES, Allen** (brother of Willie Jones), a Delegate from North Carolina; born in Edgecombe (now Halifax) County, N.C., December 24, 1739; attended Eton College, England; was a member of the colonial assembly 1773-1775; delegate to the five Provincial Congresses 1774-1776; served throughout the Revolutionary War, attaining the rank of brigadier general; served in the State senate 1777-1779, 1783, 1784, and 1787; Member of the Continental Congress in 1779 and 1780; member of the convention that rejected the proposed Constitution of the United States at Halifax, N.C., in 1788; died on his plantation, "Mount Gallant," near Roanoke Rapids, Northampton County, N.C., on November 10, 1798; interment in the private burial ground on his estate.

**Bibliography:** *DAB.*

**JONES, Andrieus Aristieus,** a Senator from New Mexico; born near Union City, Obion County, Tenn., May 16, 1862; attended the common schools and Bethel College, McKenzie, Tenn.; graduated from the Valparaiso University, Indiana, in 1885; taught school in Tennessee; moved to Las Vegas, N.Mex., where he was principal of the public schools 1885-1887; studied law while teaching school; was admitted to the bar in 1888 and commenced practice in Las Vegas; president of the New Mexico Bar Association in 1893; mayor of Las Vegas 1893-1894; special United States district attorney 1894-1898; member of the Democratic National Committee 1908-1922; unsuccessful candidate for election to the United States Senate in 1912; served as First Assistant Secretary of the Interior 1913-1916, when he resigned; elected as a Democrat to the United States Senate in 1916; reelected in 1922 and served from March 4, 1917, until his death in Washington, D.C., on December 20, 1927; chairman, Committee on Woman Suffrage (Sixty-fifth Congress); interment in the Masonic Cemetery, Las Vegas, N.Mex.

**JONES, Ben,** a Representative from Georgia; born in Tarboro, Edgecombe County, N.C., August 30, 1941; graduated, Woodrow Wilson High School, Portsmouth, Va.; attended the University of North Carolina, 1961-1965; actor; chairman, Georgia Film Board; past president, Georgia Screen Actor's Guild; unsuccessful candidate for election in 1986 to the One Hundredth Congress; elected as a Democrat to the One Hundred First and One Hundred Second Congresses (January 3, 1989-January 3, 1993); unsuccessful candidate for renomination in 1992 to the One Hundred Third Congress; is a resident of Covington, Ga.

**JONES, Benjamin,** a Representative from Ohio; born in Winchester, Frederick County, Va., on April 13, 1787; moved with his parents to Washington, Pa.; received a limited schooling; learned the trade of cabinet making; moved to Wooster, Ohio, in 1812 and engaged in mercantile pursuits; justice of the peace in 1815; commissioner for Wayne County in 1818; member of the Ohio State house of representatives in 1821 and 1822; member of the Ohio State senate, 1829-1832; elected as a Jacksonian to the Twenty-third and Twenty-fourth Congresses (March 4, 1833-March 3, 1837); chairman, Committee on Expenditures in the Department of War (Twenty-fourth Congress); was not a candidate for renomination in 1836 to the Twenty-fifth Congress; resumed business interests in Wooster, Ohio, and died there on April 24, 1861; interment in Oak Hill Cemetery.

**JONES, Burr W.,** a Representative from Wisconsin; born near Evansville, Rock County, Wis., March 9, 1846; attended the common schools and the Evansville (Wis.) Seminary; taught school for several years; was graduated from the literary department of the University of Wisconsin at Madison in 1870 and from the law department in 1871; was admitted to the bar in 1871 and commenced practice in Portage, Wis.; moved to Madison, Wis., in 1872 and continued the practice of law; prosecuting attorney of Dane County in 1872 and 1874; elected as a Democrat to the Forty-eighth Congress (March 4, 1883-March 3, 1885); unsuccessful candidate for reelection in 1884 to the Forty-ninth Congress; professor of law at the University of Wisconsin 1885-1915; served as city attorney in 1891; chairman of the Democratic State convention in 1892; delegate to the national convention (gold standard) at Indianapolis in 1896; member of the Wisconsin Tax Commission in 1897 and 1898 and served as chairman; appointed associate justice of the State supreme court September 6, 1920, to fill a vacancy; elected to the same office April 4, 1922, and served until his retirement on January 1, 1926; resumed the practice of law; died in Madison, Wis., January 7, 1935; interment in Forest Hill Cemetery.

Bibliography: Birge, Edward A. "Burr W. Jones." *Wisconsin Magazine of History* 21 (September 1937): 63-67; Jones, Burr W. "Reminiscences of Nine Decades." *Wisconsin Magazine of History* 20 (September 1936): 10-33; 20 (December 1936): 143-84; 20 (March 1937): 270-90; 20 (June 1937): 404-36; 21 (September 1937): 39-62.

**JONES, Charles William,** a Senator from Florida; born in Balbriggan, Ireland, on December 24, 1834; immigrated to the United States in 1844 with his mother and settled in New York City, where he attended the public schools; moved to Louisiana in 1848 and later to Mississippi; moved to Santa Rosa County, Fla., in 1854; worked as a carpenter and studied law at night; was admitted to the bar in 1857 and commenced practice in Pensacola, Fla.; unsuccessful Democratic candidate for election in 1872 to the Forty-third Congress; member, State house of representatives 1874; elected as a Democrat to the United States Senate in 1875; reelected in 1881 and served from March 4, 1875, to March 3, 1887; was not a candidate for reelection; chairman, Committee on Public Buildings and Grounds (Forty-sixth Congress), Committee on Revolutionary Claims (Forty-eighth and Forty-ninth Congresses); moved to Detroit, Mich., in 1885 and was absent from the Senate for nearly two years; died at St. Joseph's Retreat, an asylum for the insane, Dearborn, Mich., October 11, 1897; interment in St. Michael's Cemetery, Pensacola, Fla.

Bibliography: Etemadi, Judy. "A Love-Mad Man: Senator Charles W. Jones of Florida." *Florida Historical Quarterly* 56 (October 1977): 123-37.

**JONES, Daniel Terryll,** a Representative from New York; born in Hebron, Tolland County, Conn., August 17, 1800; received a liberal schooling; was graduated from the medical department of Yale College in 1826 and began the practice of his profession in Amboy, Oswego County, N.Y.; moved to Baldwinsville, N.Y., in 1841; elected as a Democrat to the Thirty-second and Thirty-third Congresses (March 4, 1851-March 3, 1855); was not a candidate for renomination in 1854; chairman of the Republican State convention at Syracuse, N.Y., in 1858; resumed the practice of medicine; died in Baldwinsville, Onondaga County, N.Y., March 29, 1861; interment in Riverside Cemetery.

**JONES, Ed,** a Representative from Tennessee; born in Yorkville, Gibson County, Tenn., April 20, 1912; B.S., University of Tennessee, 1934; employed by Tennessee Department of Agriculture as an inspector in the Division of Insect and Plant Diseases Control, November 1934; employed by Tennessee Dairy Products Association, 1941-1943; agricultural agent for the Illinois Central Railroad from 1944 until 1969, except for a four-year leave of absence to serve as Tennessee Commissioner of Agriculture, 1949-1953; chairman, United States Agriculture Stabilization and Conservation State Committee for Tennessee, 1961-1969; elected as a Democrat to the Ninety-first Congress, March 25, 1969, by special election to fill the vacancy caused by the death of Robert A. Everett; reelected to the nine succeeding Congresses, and served from March 25, 1969 to January 3, 1989; was not a candidate for reelection in 1988 to the One Hundred First Congress; is a resident of Yorkville, Tenn.

**JONES, Evan John,** a Representative from Pennsylvania; born in Shamokin, Northumberland County, Pa., October 23, 1872; attended the public schools; was graduated from Clarion Normal School, Clarion, Pa., in 1892; taught school; was graduated from the Dickinson Law School in 1896; was admitted to the bar in 1896 and commenced practice at St. Marys, Pa.; elected as a Republican to the Sixty-sixth and Sixty-seventh Congresses (March 4, 1919-March 3, 1923); unsuccessful candidate for renomination in 1922; resumed the practice of law at Bradford, McKean County, Pa.; vice president and general manager of the Emporium Forestry Co., director and general counsel of the Grasse River Railroad Corp.; died in Bradford, Pa., January 9, 1952; interment in Willow Dale Cemetery.

**JONES, Francis,** a Representative from Tennessee; received a limited schooling; studied law; was admitted to the bar and commenced practice in Winchester, Tenn.; solicitor general of the third Tennessee district in 1815; elected as a Republican to the Fifteenth, Sixteenth, and Seventeenth Congresses (March 4,

1817-March 3, 1823); resumed the practice of his profession in Winchester, Franklin County, Tenn., and died there.

**JONES, Frank,** a Representative from New Hampshire; born in Barrington, N.H., September 15, 1832; attended the public schools; moved to Portsmouth in 1849 and became a merchant and brewer; owned establishments in Portsmouth and South Boston, Mass.; mayor of Portsmouth in 1868 and 1869; elected as a Democrat to the Forty-fourth and Forty-fifth Congresses (March 4, 1875-March 3, 1879); was not a candidate for renomination in 1878 to the Forty-sixth Congress; unsuccessful candidate for election in 1880 for Governor of New Hampshire; affiliated with the Republican Party; interested in railroads; presidential elector on the Republican ticket in 1900; died in Portsmouth, N.H., October 2, 1902; interment in Harmony Grove Cemetery.

**Bibliography:** *DAB*; Brighton, Ray. *Frank Jones: King of the Alemakers*. Hampton, N.H.: Randall, 1976.

**JONES, George** (son of Noble Wymberley Jones), a Senator from Georgia; born in Savannah, Ga., February 25, 1766; received an academic training; studied medicine with his father and practiced for a number of years; participated in the Revolutionary War and during 1780 and 1781 was imprisoned upon an English ship; member, State house of representatives and senate; during the War of 1812 served as captain of a company of Savannah reserves; member of the Savannah board of aldermen in 1793-1794, 1802-1803, 1814-1815; mayor of Savannah 1812-1814; appointed judge of the eastern judicial circuit of Georgia in 1804, and served until appointed Senator; appointed to the United States Senate to fill the vacancy caused by the death of Abraham Baldwin and served from August 27 to November 7, 1807, when a successor was elected; died in Savannah, Chatham County, Ga., on November 13, 1838; interment in Bonaventure Cemetery.

**JONES, George Wallace,** a Delegate from the Territory of Michigan and the Territory of Wisconsin and a Senator from Iowa; born in Vincennes, Indiana Territory, April 12, 1804; served as a drummer boy in Captain William Linn's company in 1814; graduated from the Transylvania University, Lexington, Ky., on July 13, 1825; studied law; moved to Michigan Territory in 1827 and located in Sinsinawa Mound, where he was a lead smelter and storekeeper; served in the Black Hawk War of 1832; judge of the Iowa County court; elected as a Delegate from Michigan Territory to the Twenty-fourth Congress, and served from March 4, 1835 until the Territory of Wisconsin was formed from a portion of Michigan Territory; his residence being in the new Territory, he was elected and qualified as a Delegate from the Territory of Wisconsin, serving until March 3, 1837; presented credentials as a Delegate-elect from the Territory of Wisconsin to the Twenty-fifth Congress, and served from March 4, 1837 to January 14, 1839, when he was succeeded by James D. Doty, who contested his election; served as second to Representative Jonathan Cilley of Maine, who was killed by Representative William J. Graves of Kentucky in a duel on the Marlboro Pike, Md., near Washington, D.C., February 24, 1839; appointed surveyor of public lands for the Territories of Wisconsin and Iowa in January 1840 and served until 1848, when he resigned; elected in 1848 as a Democrat to the United States Senate as one of the first Senators from the State of Iowa; reelected in 1852, and served from December 7, 1848 to March 3, 1859; unsuccessful candidate for renomination in 1858; chairman, Committee on Engrossed Bills (Thirty-first and Thirty-second Congresses), Committee on Pensions (Thirty-first through Thirty-fifth Congresses), Committee on Enrolled Bills (Thirty-second through Thirty-fifth Congresses); appointed Minister Resident to New Granada (Colombia) on March 8, 1859 and served until November 1861; on his return to the United States was arrested in New York City by order of Secretary of State William H. Seward on the charge of disloyalty, based on correspondence with his friend Jefferson Davis; released on

February 22, 1862 by order of President Lincoln; retired from public life; returned to Dubuque, Iowa, and died there on July 22, 1896; interment in Mount Olivet Cemetery at Key West, Dubuque, Iowa.

**Bibliography:** *DAB*; Parish, John Carl. *George Wallace Jones*. Iowa City: The State Historical Society, 1912.

**JONES, George Washington,** a Representative from Texas; born in Marion County, Ala., September 5, 1828; moved with his parents to Tipton County, Tenn., and shortly afterward to Bastrop, Tex., in 1848; attended the common schools; studied law; was admitted to the bar in 1851 and commenced practice in Bastrop, Tex.; elected district attorney in 1856; during the Civil War enlisted in the Confederate Army as a private; commissioned lieutenant colonel and afterward promoted to the colonelcy of the Seventeenth Texas Infantry; returned to Bastrop County; member of the State constitutional convention in 1866; elected lieutenant governor of Texas in 1866; removed as "an impediment to reconstruction" in 1867 by General Philip H. Sheridan, military governor of Texas and Louisiana; elected on the Greenback Party ticket to the Forty-sixth and Forty-seventh Congresses (March 4, 1879-March 3, 1883); was not a candidate for reelection in 1882 to the Forty-eighth Congress; resumed the practice of his profession in Bastrop, Tex., and died there July 11, 1903; interment in Fairview Cemetery.

**JONES, George Washington,** a Representative from Tennessee; born in King and Queen County, Va., March 15, 1806; moved to Tennessee with his parents, who settled in Fayetteville; received a common-school and academical education; apprenticed to the saddler's trade; justice of the peace 1832-1835; member of the State house of representatives 1835-1839; served in the State senate 1839-1841; clerk of Lincoln County Court 1840-1843; elected as a Democrat to the Twenty-eighth and to the seven succeeding Congresses (March 4, 1843-March 3, 1859); chairman, Committee on Rules (Thirty-first and Thirty-second Congresses), Committee on Roads and Canals (Thirty-fifth Congress); delegate to the peace convention of 1861 held in Washington, D.C., in an effort to devise means to prevent the impending war, but did not attend; elected from Tennessee a Member of the House of Representatives in the First Confederate Congress and served from February 18, 1862, to February 18, 1864; was not a candidate for reelection; delegate to the State constitutional convention in 1870; died in Fayetteville, Lincoln County, Tenn., November 14, 1884; interment in Rose Hill Cemetery.

**JONES, Hamilton Chamberlain,** a Representative from North Carolina; born in Charlotte, Mecklenburg County, N.C., September 26, 1884; attended the schools of Charlotte, N.C., Central High School, Washington, D.C., and Horners Military School, Oxford, N.C.; was graduated from the University of North Carolina at Chapel Hill in 1906 and Columbia University, New York City, in 1907; studied law at both institutions; was admitted to the bar in 1906 and commenced practice in Charlotte, N.C., in 1910; also engaged in agricultural pursuits; judge of City Recorder's Court and Juvenile Court of Charlotte, N.C., 1913-1919; assistant United States district attorney for the western district of North Carolina 1919-1921; served in the State senate 1925-1927; trustee of the University of North Carolina; elected as a Democrat to the Eightieth, Eighty-first, and Eighty-second Congresses (January 3, 1947-January 3, 1953); unsuccessful candidate for reelection in 1952 to the Eighty-third Congress; resumed the practice of law; died in Charlotte, N.C., August 10, 1957; interment in Evergreen Cemetery.

**JONES, Homer Raymond,** a Representative from Washington; born in Martinsburg, Audrain County, Mo., September 3, 1893; moved to Bremerton, Wash., in 1901; attended the public schools and studied business administration at Seattle Business College; during the First World War served as an enlisted man in the United States Navy 1917-1919; engaged as a sheet-metal worker, Navy Yard, Bremerton, Wash., 1919-1921; city councilman of Charleston,

Wash., 1922-1924 and mayor 1924-1927; treasurer of Kitsap County, Wash., 1926-1929; assistant State treasurer of Washington 1929-1933; treasurer of Bremerton, Wash., 1933-1937; mayor of Bremerton, Wash., 1939-1941; served as an officer in the United States Naval Reserve from 1941 until his discharge as a captain in 1946; awarded Bronze Star Medal; elected as a Republican to the Eightieth Congress (January 3, 1947-January 3, 1949); unsuccessful candidate for reelection in 1948 to the Eighty-first Congress; superintendent of the Washington State Veterans' Home at Retsil 1949-1953; assistant State treasurer 1953-1957; real estate salesman; died in Bremerton, Wash., November 26, 1970; interment in Woodlawn Cemetery.

**JONES, Isaac Dashiell,** a Representative from Maryland; born on the family homestead, "Wetcpquin," Somerset County, Md., November 1, 1806; completed preparatory studies; was graduated from Washington Academy, Somerset County, where he became assistant tutor before his studies were completed; studied law; was admitted to the bar and commenced practice in Princess Anne, Somerset County, Md.; member of the Maryland State house of delegates in 1832, 1835, 1840, and 1866; elected as a Whig to the Twenty-seventh Congress (March 4, 1841-March 3, 1843); took an active part in the State constitutional conventions of 1864 and 1867; elected attorney general of Maryland in 1867; elected judge of the court of arbitration of Baltimore in 1877; director of the Maryland State School for the Deaf, Frederick, Md., 1867-1893, and of the Maryland School for the Colored Blind and Deaf at Baltimore, 1872-1893; died in Baltimore, Md., July 5, 1893; interment in Greenmount Cemetery.

**JONES, James,** a Representative from Georgia; born in Maryland; moved to Georgia with his uncle, Colonel Marbury, in 1740; attended the academy in Augusta; studied law; was admitted to the bar and practiced in Savannah; first lieutenant of East Company, Chatham County Regiment of Militia, in 1790; member of the State house of representatives 1796-1798; member of the State constitutional convention in May 1798; elected as a Federalist to the Sixth Congress and served from March 4, 1799, until his death in Washington, D.C., January 11, 1801; interment in the Congressional Cemetery.

**JONES, James,** a Representative from Virginia; born in Nottoway Parish, Amelia (now Nottoway) County, Va., on December 11, 1772; graduated from Hampden-Sidney College, Virginia, in 1791, and the Jefferson Medical College, Philadelphia, Pa.; was graduated in medicine from the University of Edinburgh, Scotland, in 1796; returned to Amelia County, where he practiced medicine and also engaged in agricultural pursuits; member of the Virginia house of delegates 1804-1809; privy councilor of Virginia from 1809 to 1811, when he resigned; served in the War of 1812 as director general of hospital and medical stores; member of the Virginia house of delegates in 1818; unsuccessful candidate for election to the Fifteenth Congress to fill the vacancy caused by the death of Peterson Goodwin; elected to the Sixteenth and Seventeenth Congresses (March 4, 1819-March 3, 1823); again a member of the Virginia house of delegates 1827-1829; resumed agricultural pursuits; died at his home, "Mountain Hall," near Nottoway, Nottoway County, Va., April 25, 1848; interment in the family burying ground on his estate.

**JONES, James Chamberlain,** a Senator from Tennessee; born near the line between Davidson and Wilson Counties, Tennessee, April 20, 1809; attended an old-field school; farmer; member of the Tennessee State house of representatives in 1839; elected Governor of Tennessee in 1841, reelected in 1843, and served from October 15, 1841 to October 14, 1845; presidential elector on the Whig ticket in 1848; elected as a Whig to the United States Senate and served from March 4, 1851, to March 3, 1857; was not a candidate for reelection;

retired to his farm near Memphis, Tenn., where he died on October 29, 1859; interment in Elmwood Cemetery, Memphis.

**Bibliography:** *DAB*; Osborne, Ray G. "Political Career of James Chamberlain Jones, 1840-1857." *Tennessee Historical Quarterly* 7 (1948): 195-228, 322-34.

**JONES, James Henry,** a Representative from Texas; born in Shelby County, Ala., September 13, 1830; moved with his parents to Talladega County, Ala., in early youth; pursued an academic course; studied law; was admitted to the bar in 1851 and commenced practice in Henderson, Tex.; during the Civil War enlisted in the Confederate Army and served as captain, lieutenant colonel, and colonel of the Eleventh Texas Infantry; elected as a Democrat to the Forty-eighth and Forty-ninth Congresses (March 4, 1883-March 3, 1887); resumed the practice of law in Henderson, Tex., and died there March 22, 1904; interment in the New Cemetery.

**JONES, James Kimbrough,** a Representative and a Senator from Arkansas; born in Marshall County, Miss., September 29, 1839; moved with his father to Dallas County, Ark., in 1848; pursued classical studies under a private tutor; served in the Confederate Army during the Civil War; returned to his plantation in Arkansas; studied law; was admitted to the bar in 1874 and commenced practice in Washington, Hempstead County, Ark.; member, Arkansas State senate 1873-1879, and served as president of that body 1877-1879; chairman of the Democratic National Committee in 1896 and 1900; elected as a Democrat to the Forty-seventh and Forty-eighth Congresses (March 4, 1881-March 3, 1885); had been reelected in 1884 to the Forty-ninth Congress, but tendered his resignation February 19, 1885, having been elected Senator; elected as a Democrat to the United States Senate in 1885; reelected in 1891 and 1897 and served from March 4, 1885, to March 3, 1903; unsuccessful candidate for reelection; Democratic caucus chairman 1902-1903; chairman, Committee on Indian Affairs (Fifty-third Congress), Committee on Corporations Organized in the District of Columbia (Fifty-fourth and Fifty-fifth Congresses), Committee on Private Land Claims (Fifty-fifth Congress); resumed the practice of law in Washington, D.C., and died there June 1, 1908; interment in Rock Creek Cemetery.

**Bibliography:** *DAB*; Newberry, Farrar. *James K. Jones, the Plumed Knight of Arkansas*. Arkadelphia: Siftings-Herald Printing Co., 1913.

**JONES, James Robert,** a Representative from Oklahoma; born in Muskogee, Muskogee County, Okla., May 5, 1939; attended Sacred Heart School, Muskogee, Okla.; graduated from Muskogee Central High School in 1957; A.B., University of Oklahoma, Norman, 1961; LL.B., Georgetown University Law Center, Washington, D.C., 1964; served in United States Army Counterintelligence Corps, captain, 1964-1965; United States Army Reserve, 1961-1968; admitted to the Oklahoma and District of Columbia bars in 1964 and commenced practice in Tulsa; legislative assistant to Representative Ed Edmondson of Oklahoma, 1961-1964; special assistant to President Lyndon B. Johnson, 1965-1969; resumed the practice of law in Tulsa, 1969-1972; elected as a Democrat to the Ninety-third and to the six succeeding Congresses (January 3, 1973-January 3, 1987); chairman, Committee on the Budget (Ninety-seventh and Ninety-eighth Congresses); was not a candidate for reelection in 1986 to the House of Representatives, but was an unsuccessful candidate for election to the United States Senate; chairman and chief executive officer, American Stock Exchange; nominated as Ambassador to Mexico on July 15, 1993, and was confirmed by the Senate on August 6, 1993; is a resident of Tulsa, Okla., New York City, and Washington, D.C.

**JONES, James Taylor,** a Representative from Alabama; born in Richmond, Va., July 20, 1832; moved with his father to Marengo County, Ala., in 1834; pursued classical studies; was graduated from

Princeton College in 1852 and from the law school of the University of Virginia at Charlottesville in 1855; was admitted to the bar in 1856 and commenced practice in Demopolis, Ala.; during the Civil War enlisted in the Confederate Army as a private in the Fourth Alabama Regiment; elected captain of Company D in this regiment in 1862; appointed judge advocate in the Confederate War Department in 1864 and served until the close of the war; delegate to the State constitutional convention in 1865; member of the State senate in 1872 and 1873; unsuccessful candidate for election in 1874 to the Forty-fourth Congress; elected as a Democrat to the Forty-fifth Congress (March 4, 1877-March 3, 1879); unsuccessful candidate for reelection in 1878 to the Forty-sixth Congress; elected to the Forty-eighth Congress to fill the vacancy caused by the death of Thomas H. Herndon; reelected to the Forty-ninth and Fiftieth Congresses and served from December 3, 1883, to March 3, 1889; was not a candidate for renomination in 1888; resumed the practice of law in Demopolis, Ala.; circuit judge of the first judicial circuit of Alabama from 1890 until his death in Demopolis, Marengo County, Ala., February 15, 1895; interment in Lyon Cemetery.

**JONES, Jehu Glancy,** a Representative from Pennsylvania; born in Caernarvon Township, Berks County, Pa., October 7, 1811; attended Kenyon College; studied theology; was ordained to the ministry of the Episcopal Church in 1835 and withdrew in 1841; studied law; was admitted to the bar in Georgia in 1841 and commenced practice at Easton, Pa.; district attorney for Berks County 1847-1849; delegate to the Pennsylvania Democratic conventions in 1848, 1849, and 1855, and served as president in 1855; delegate to the Democratic National Conventions of 1848 and 1856, and served as vice president in 1848; elected as a Democrat to the Thirty-second Congress (March 4, 1851-March 3, 1853); declined to be a candidate for renomination in 1852 to the Thirty-third Congress; elected to the Thirty-third Congress to fill the vacancy caused by the death of Henry A. Muhlenberg; reelected to the Thirty-fourth and Thirty-fifth Congresses and served from February 4, 1854, to October 30, 1858, when he resigned; chairman, Committee on Ways and Means (Thirty-fifth Congress); unsuccessful candidate for election in 1858 to the Thirty-sixth Congress; appointed Minister to Austria by President Buchanan December 7, 1858, and served from December 15, 1858, to November 14, 1861; resumed the practice of law; died in Reading, Pa., March 24, 1878; interment in the Charles Evans Cemetery.

**Bibliography:** *DAB*.

**JONES, John James,** a Representative from Georgia; born near Waynesboro, Burke County, Ga., on November 13, 1824; attended the Waynesboro Academy and was graduated from Emory College, Oxford, Ga., in 1845; studied law; was admitted to the bar in 1848 and practiced in Waynesboro, Ga.; elected as a Democrat to the Thirty-sixth Congress and served from March 4, 1859, to January 23, 1861, when he joined other secessionist members of the Georgia delegation in withdrawing from Congress; served as a lieutenant in the Confederate Army during the Civil War; resumed the practice of law in Burke County, Ga.; died in Waynesboro, Ga., on October 19, 1898; interment in the City Cemetery.

**JONES, John Marvin,** a Representative from Texas; born near Valley View, Cooke County, Tex., February 26, 1886; attended the common schools; John B. Denton College, A.B., 1902; B.S., Southwestern University, Georgetown, Tex., 1905; LL.B., University of Texas at Austin, 1907; was admitted to the bar the same year and commenced practice in Amarillo, Tex.; appointed a member of the board of legal examiners for the seventh supreme judicial district of Texas in 1913; member of the Democratic National Congressional Campaign Committee; served during the First World War as a private in Company A, Three Hundred and Eighth Battalion of the Tank Corps, in 1918; elected as a Democrat to the Sixty-fifth Congress; reelected to the eleven succeeding Congresses, and served

from March 4, 1917 until his resignation on November 20, 1940, to become a judge of the United States Court of Claims, having been appointed to that office by President Franklin D. Roosevelt; chairman, Committee on Agriculture (Seventy-second through Seventy-sixth Congresses); on leave from the Court of Claims beginning January 15, 1943, and served as adviser and assistant to the Director of Economic Stabilization until June 1943; appointed Administrator of the United States War Food Administration, June 29, 1943, and served until July 1, 1945, when he resumed his duties as judge of the United States Court of Claims; served as chief judge from July 10, 1947 until his retirement on July 14, 1964; special master, United States Supreme Court for Mississippi and Louisiana, 1965; accepted appointment as a senior judge after his retirement and remained active until his death in Amarillo, Tex., March 4, 1976; interment in Llano Cemetery.

**Bibliography:** *DAB*; Jones, Marvin. *Marvin Jones Memoirs 1917-1973: Fifty-six Years of Continuing Service in all Three Branches of the Federal Government.* Edited and annotated by Joseph M. Ray. El Paso: Texas Western Press, University of Texas at El Paso, 1973; May, Irvin M., Jr. *Marvin Jones: The Public Life of an Agrarian Advocate.* College Station: Texas A.&M. University Press, 1980.

**JONES, John Percival,** a Senator from Nevada; born at "The Hay," Herefordshire, England, January 27, 1829; immigrated the same year to the United States with his parents, who settled in the northern part of Ohio; attended the public schools in Cleveland, Ohio; moved to California and engaged in mining and farming in Trinity County; sheriff of the county; member, State senate 1863-1867; moved to Gold Hill, Nev., in 1868; engaged in mining; elected as a Republican to the United States Senate in 1873; reelected in 1879, 1885, 1891, and 1897 and served from March 4, 1873, to March 3, 1903; declined to be a candidate for reelection; chairman, Committee to Audit and Control the Contingent Expense (Forty-fourth and Forty-fifth Congresses, and Forty-seventh through Fifty-second Congresses), Committee on Epidemic Diseases (Fifty-third through Fifty-seventh Congresses); resumed his former business activities; retired to his home in Santa Monica, Calif.; died in Los Angeles, Calif., November 27, 1912; interment in Laurel Hill Cemetery, San Francisco, Calif.

**Bibliography:** *DAB*.

**JONES, John Sills,** a Representative from Ohio; born near St. Paris, Champaign County, Ohio, February 12, 1836; attended the public schools; was graduated from Ohio Wesleyan University, Delaware, Ohio, in 1855; studied law; was admitted to the bar in 1857 and commenced practice in Delaware, Ohio; prosecuting attorney for Delaware County in 1860 and 1861; served during the Civil War as first lieutenant and captain in the Union Army 1861-1864; reenlisted to command the One Hundred and Seventy-fourth Regiment, Ohio Volunteer Infantry, in September 1864; mustered out July 7, 1865; resumed the practice of law; mayor of Delaware, Ohio, in 1866; again prosecuting attorney for Delaware County 1866-1872; elected as a Republican to the Forty-fifth Congress (March 4, 1877-March 3, 1879); was not a candidate for renomination in 1878; member of the State house of representatives 1879-1884; again resumed the practice of law in Delaware, Ohio, and died there April 11, 1903; interment in Oak Grove Cemetery.

**JONES, John William,** a Representative from Georgia; born in Rockville, Montgomery County, Md., April 14, 1806; moved to Kentucky in 1810 with his parents, who settled in Nicholas (now Bourbon) County, near Carlisle; attended the common schools and Carlisle Seminary; studied medicine; commenced practice in Washington, Tenn., in 1826; moved to Monroe, Walton County, Ga., and thence to Campbellton, Ga., in 1829 and practiced his profession; attended the University of Pennsylvania at Philadelphia in 1830 and 1831; moved to Culloden, Ga., in 1833; was graduated from Jefferson Medical College and Therapeutic Institute at Philadelphia in 1836; member of the State house of representatives in 1837; moved to Griffin, Pike County, Ga., in 1841 and continued the practice of medicine; elected as a Whig to the Thirtieth Congress (March 4, 1847-March 3, 1849); declined to be a candidate for renomination in 1848; resumed the practice of medicine in Oak Bowery, Ala.; trustee of the Oak Bowery Female College in 1850; moved to Auburn, Ala., in 1851; one of the founders of the Auburn Masonic Female College (now Auburn College); moved to Atlanta, Ga., in 1856; professor in the Atlanta Medical College (now Emory University) 1856-1862; during the Civil War served as surgeon in the Confederate Army; again professor in the Atlanta Medical College 1865-1870; moved to Decatur, Ga., where he died April 27, 1871; interment in Oakland Cemetery, Atlanta, Ga.

**JONES, John Winston,** a Representative from Virginia; born near Amelia Court House, Amelia County, Va., November 22, 1791; attended private schools; was graduated from the law department of the College of William and Mary, Williamsburg, Va., in 1813; was admitted to the bar the same year and commenced practice in Chesterfield County, Va.; prosecuting attorney for the fifth Virginia circuit in 1818; member of the Virginia constitutional convention in 1829 and 1830; elected as a Jacksonian to the Twenty-fourth Congress and reelected as a Democrat to the four succeeding Congresses (March 4, 1835-March 3, 1845); chairman, Committee on Ways and Means (Twenty-sixth Congress); Speaker of the House of Representatives (Twenty-eighth Congress); declined to be a candidate for renomination in 1844; resumed the practice of law and also engaged in agricultural pursuits; member of the Virginia house of delegates in 1846 and served as speaker; reelected in 1847 but resigned on account of ill health; died at his residence, "Dellwood," in Chesterfield County, Virginia, January 29, 1848; interment in the family cemetery on his estate, "Dellwood," northwest of Petersburg, Va.

**Bibliography:** *DAB.*

**JONES, Joseph** (uncle of James Monroe), a Delegate from Virginia; born in King George County, Va., in 1727; member of the colonial House of Burgesses; served on the committee of safety in 1775; delegate to the Virginia constitutional convention of 1776; served in the Virginia house of delegates in 1776, 1777, 1780, 1781, and 1783-1785; Member of the Continental Congress in 1777 and 1780-1783; appointed judge of the Virginia General Court January 23, 1778, and resigned in October 1779; reappointed to the same court November 19, 1789; member of the Virginia convention in 1788 which ratified the Federal Constitution; major general of Virginia militia; died in Fredericksburg, Va., October 28, 1805.

**Bibliography:** *DAB.*

**JONES, Morgan,** a Representative from New York; born in London, England, February 26, 1830; immigrated in 1833 to the United States with his parents, who settled in New York City; attended the public schools; engaged in the plumbing business in 1850; member of the board of councilmen 1859-1863 and president of that body in 1860, 1861, and 1863; member of the board of aldermen in 1864 and 1865, serving as president of the board in 1865; elected as a Democrat to the Thirty-ninth Congress (March 4, 1865-March 3, 1867); resumed business interests in New York City until 1887, when he retired; died in that city July 13, 1894; interment in Greenwood Cemetery, Brooklyn, N.Y.

**JONES, Nathaniel,** a Representative from New York; born in Warwick, Orange County, N.Y., February 17, 1788; completed preparatory studies and later taught school; member of the State assembly in 1827 and 1828; engaged in banking in 1834; elected as a Democrat to the Twenty-fifth and Twenty-sixth Congresses (March 4, 1837-March 3, 1841); moved to Newburgh, N.Y., in 1841; surveyor general of New York from February 1842 to November 1844; State

canal commissioner 1844-1847; superintendent of schools and clerk of the Board of Education of Newburgh in 1851; member of the State senate in 1852 and 1853; died in Newburgh, Orange County, N.Y., July 20, 1866.

**JONES, Noble Wimberly** (father of George Jones), a Delegate from Georgia; born in Lambeth, near London, England, in 1723; immigrated to the United States with his parents, who settled in Savannah, Ga., in 1733; studied medicine and practiced in Savannah 1756-1774; member of the colonial assembly in 1755, 1756, 1760-1762, 1764, 1768, 1769, 1771, and 1772, and served as speaker in 1768 and 1769; member of the council of safety and the Provincial Congress in 1775; member of the State house of representatives in 1777 and 1778; moved to Charleston, S.C., in 1778; captured at the fall of Charleston in 1780 and imprisoned at St. Augustine, Fla.; exchanged in 1781; moved to Philadelphia, Pa., in 1781 and engaged in the practice of medicine; Member of the Continental Congress, accredited to Georgia, in 1781 and 1782; returned to Savannah, Ga., in 1782 and resumed his profession; again a member of the State house of representatives in 1783; president of State constitutional convention in 1795; died in Savannah, Ga., January 9, 1805; interment in Bonaventure Cemetery.

**Bibliography:** *DAB.*

**JONES, Owen,** a Representative from Pennsylvania; born near Ardmore, Montgomery County, Pa., December 29, 1819; attended the public schools and was graduated from the University of Pennsylvania at Philadelphia; studied law in Philadelphia; was admitted to the bar of Montgomery County May 19, 1842, and commenced practice in Ardmore, Pa.; elected as a Democrat to the Thirty-fifth Congress (March 4, 1857-March 3, 1859); chairman, Committee on Expenditures in the Department of State (Thirty-fifth Congress); unsuccessful candidate for reelection in 1858 to the Thirty-sixth Congress; during the Civil War raised a troop of Cavalry (Troop B, First Pennsylvania Cavalry); resumed the practice of law; died near Ardmore, Pa., December 25, 1878; interment in Laurel Hill Cemetery, Philadelphia, Pa.

**JONES, Paul Caruthers,** a Representative from Missouri; born in Kennett, Dunklin County, Mo., March 12, 1901; attended the Kennett, Mo., public schools; was graduated from the University of Missouri at Columbia with B.J. degree, 1923; member of the city council, 1931-1933, and mayor of Kennett, 1933-1935; member and president of board of education, 1934-1946; served in the State house of representatives 1935-1937; member of the State senate 1937-1944; copublisher of the Dunklin Democrat from 1923 until February 1953; general manager of a radio station from 1947 until October 1966; chairman of the Missouri Highway Commission from August 1945 to May 1948; appointed by Governor Lloyd C. Stark in December 1940 to organize the Sixth Missouri Infantry, Missouri State Guard and was commanding officer (colonel) of that voluntary regiment until June 1946; elected as a Democrat to the Eightieth Congress to fill the vacancy caused by death of Orville Zimmerman and at same time was elected to the Eighty-first Congress; reelected to the nine succeeding Congresses and served from November 2, 1948, to January 3, 1969; was not a candidate for reelection in 1968 to the Ninety-first Congress; resided in Kennett, Mo. where he died February 10, 1981, interment in Oak Ridge Cemetery.

**JONES, Phineas,** a Representative from New Jersey; born in Spencer, Worcester County, Mass., April 18, 1819; attended the common schools; moved to Elizabeth (then called Elizabethtown), N.J., in 1855; member of the city council of Elizabeth 1856-1860; moved to Newark in 1860; engaged in manufacturing and mercantile pursuits; vice president of the New Jersey State Agricultural Society; member of the State house of assembly in 1873 and 1874; elected as a Republican to the Forty-seventh Congress (March 4, 1881-March 3, 1883); declined to be a candidate for renomination in 1882; retired from active life and died in Newark, N.J., April 19, 1884; interment in Evergreen Cemetery, Elizabeth, N.J.

**JONES, Robert Emmett, Jr.,** a Representative from Alabama; born in Scottsboro, Jackson County, Ala., June 12, 1912; attended the public schools; received an LL.B. degree from the law department of the University of Alabama, Tuscaloosa, January 7, 1937; was admitted to the bar the same year and commenced practice in Scottsboro, Ala.; elected judge of the Jackson County Court in July 1940; reelected in absentia in May 1945 and served until October 1946; served in the United States Navy as a gunnery officer in both the Atlantic and Pacific theaters from December 1943 until February 1946; elected as a Democrat to the Eightieth Congress, January 28, 1947, by special election to fill the vacancy caused by the resignation of John J. Sparkman; reelected to the fourteen succeeding Congresses, and served from January 28, 1947 to January 3, 1977; chairman, Committee on Public Works and Transportation (Ninety-fourth Congress); was not a candidate for reelection in 1976 to the Ninety-fifth Congress; is a resident of Scottsboro, Ala.

**JONES, Robert Franklin,** a Representative from Ohio; born in Cairo, Allen County, Ohio, June 25, 1907; attended the village school in Cairo, Ohio; was graduated from the Lima Central High School, Lima, Ohio, in 1924 and from Ohio Northern University College of Law at Ada in 1929; was admitted to the bar the same year and commenced practice in Lima, Ohio; prosecuting attorney of Allen County, Ohio, 1935-1939; elected as a Republican to the Seventy-sixth and to the four succeeding Congresses and served from January 3, 1939, until his resignation on September 2, 1947; member of the Federal Communications Commission from September 1947 until his resignation on September 19, 1952; resumed the practice of law in Washington, D.C.; died in Olney, Md., June 22, 1968; interment in Lima Memorial Park Cemetery, Lima, Ohio.

**JONES, Roland,** a Representative from Louisiana; born in Salisbury, N.C., November 18, 1813; attended private schools; taught school in Wilkesboro, N.C., 1830-1835; was graduated from Cambridge (Mass.) Law School in 1838; was admitted to the bar and commenced practice in Brandon, Miss.; editor of the Brandon Republican 1838-1840; moved to Shreveport, La., in 1840 and continued the practice of law; member of the State house of representatives 1844-1848; district judge of Caddo Parish in 1851 and 1852; elected as a Democrat to the Thirty-third Congress (March 4, 1853-March 3, 1855); was not a candidate for renomination in 1854; resumed the practice of law; again elected district judge in 1860 and served until 1868; died in Shreveport, La., February 5, 1869; interment in Oakland Cemetery.

**JONES, Samuel,** a Delegate from New York; born in Oyster Bay, Long Island, N.Y., July 26, 1734; elected as a Delegate to the Continental Congress in 1788 but did not attend; died November 21, 1819.

**JONES, Seaborn,** a Representative from Georgia; born in Augusta, Ga., February 1, 1788; attended Princeton College; studied law; by a special act of the legislature was admitted to the bar in 1808; commenced practice in Milledgeville, Ga.; appointed solicitor general of the Ocmulgee circuit in September 1817; solicitor general of Georgia in 1823; one of the commissioners appointed to investigate the disturbances in the Creek Nation; moved to Columbus, Ga., in 1827; elected as a Jacksonian to the Twenty-third Congress (March 4, 1833-March 3, 1835); elected as a Democrat to the Twenty-ninth Congress (March 4, 1845-March 3, 1847); died in Columbus, Ga., March 18, 1864; interment in Linnwood Cemetery.

**JONES, Thomas Laurens,** a Representative from Kentucky; born in White Oak, Rutherford County, N.C., January 22, 1819; attended private schools; was graduated from Princeton College and from the law department of Harvard University; was admitted to the bar in Columbia, S.C., in 1846 and commenced practice in New York City in 1847; moved to Newport, Ky., in 1849 and continued the practice of law; member of the Kentucky house of representatives from Campbell County 1853-1855; elected as a Democrat to the Fortieth and Forty-first Congresses (March 4, 1867-March 3, 1871); was not a candidate for renomination in 1870; elected to the Forty-fourth Congress (March 4, 1875-March 3, 1877); chairman, Committee on Railways and Canals (Forty-fourth Congress); was not a candidate for renomination; resumed the practice of law; died in Newport, Ky., June 20, 1887; interment in Evergreen Cemetery.

**JONES, Walter,** a Representative from Virginia; born in Williamsburg, Va., December 18, 1745; was graduated from William and Mary College, Williamsburg, Va., in 1760; studied medicine in Edinburgh and received the degree of doctor of medicine in 1770; returned to Virginia and located in Northumberland County; physician general of the middle military department in 1777; member of the Virginia house of delegates 1785-1787; delegate to the Virginia constitutional convention in 1788; elected as a Republican to the Fifth Congress (March 4, 1797-March 3, 1799); again a member of the Virginia of delegates in 1802 and 1803; elected to the Eighth and to the three succeeding Congresses (March 4, 1803-March 3, 1811); died in Westmoreland County, Va., December 31, 1815; interment in the family burial ground at "Hayfield," a few miles from what is now Callo, Northumberland County, Va.

Bibliography: Mason, Thomas A. "The Luminary of the Northern Neck: Walter Jones, 1745-1815." *Northern Neck of Virginia Historical Magazine* 35 (1985): 3978-983.

**JONES, Walter Beaman** (father of Walter Beaman Jones, Jr.), a Representative from North Carolina; born in Fayetteville, N.C., August 19, 1913; attended Fayetteville public schools and Elise Academy, Hemp, N.C.; B.S., North Carolina State University, 1934; engaged in the office supply business, 1934-1949; mayor of Farmville, 1949-1953; representative in North Carolina State general assembly, 1955, 1957, and 1959; North Carolina State senator, 1965; trustee, Campbell University, Buies Creek, N.C., and the University of North Carolina; elected as a Democrat to the Eighty-ninth Congress, February 5, 1966, by special election to fill the vacancy caused by the death of Herbert C. Bonner; reelected to the thirteen succeeding Congresses and served from February 5, 1966, until his death on September 15, 1992; chairman, Committee on Merchant Marine and Fisheries (Ninety-seventh through One Hundred Second Congresses).

**JONES, Walter Beaman, Jr.** (son of Walter Beaman Jones), a Representative from North Carolina; born in Farmville, Pitt County, N.C., February 10, 1943; graduated Hargrave Military Academy, Chatham, Va., 1961; attended North Carolina State University; B.A., Atlantic Christian College, Wilson, N.C., 1967; president of Benefit Reserves, Inc. and Judson Co., Inc.; member, North Carolina State house of representatives, 1983-1992; unsuccessful candidate in 1992 for nomination to the One Hundred Third Congress; announced his affiliation with the Republican Party on April 15, 1993; elected as a Republican to the One Hundred Fourth Congress (January 3, 1995-January 3, 1997); is a resident of Farmville, N.C.

**JONES, Wesley Livsey,** a Representative and a Senator from Washington; born near Bethany, Moultrie County, Ill., October 9, 1863; attended the common schools; taught school; graduated from Southern Illinois College at Enfield in 1885; studied law; was admitted to the bar in 1886 and commenced practice in Decatur, Ill.; moved to North Yakima, Wash., in 1889, and continued the practice of his profession; elected as a Republican to the Fifty-sixth and to the four succeeding Congresses (March 4, 1899-March 3, 1909); did not seek renomination in 1908, having become a candidate for Senator; elected as a Republican to the United States Senate in 1909; reelected in 1914, 1920, and 1926, and served from March 4, 1909, until his death on November 19, 1932; was an unsuccessful candidate for reelection in 1932; Republican whip 1924-1929; chairman, Committee on Industrial Expositions (Sixty-first Congress), Committee on Fisheries (Sixty-second Congress), Committee on Disposition of Useless Executive Papers (Sixty-fourth and Sixty-fifth Congresses), Committee to Investigate Trespassers Upon Indian Land (Sixty-fifth Congress), Committee on Commerce (Sixty-sixth through Seventy-first Congresses), Committee on Appropriations (Seventy-first and Seventy-second Congresses); died in Seattle, Wash., November 19, 1932; remains were cremated and the ashes placed in the Bonney-Watson Mortuary, Seattle, Wash.

**Bibliography:** *DAB*; Forth, William S. "Wesley L. Jones: A Political Biography." Ph.D. dissertation, University of Washington, 1962.

**JONES, William,** a Representative from Pennsylvania; born in Philadelphia, Pa., in 1760; completed academic studies; served in the Revolutionary War, joining a company of volunteers at the age of sixteen; moved to Charleston, S.C.; returned to Pennsylvania; elected as a Republican to the Seventh Congress (March 4, 1801-March 3, 1803); appointed Secretary of the Navy in the Cabinet of President James Madison, and served from January 19, 1813 to December 1, 1814; president of the Second Bank of the United States from 1816 until 1819; collector of customs in Philadelphia, Pa., 1827-1829; died in Bethlehem, Pa., September 6, 1831; interment in St. Peter's Churchyard, Philadelphia, Pa.

**Bibliography:** *DAB*; Corrigan, M. Saint Pierre. "William Jones of the Second Bank of the United States: A Reappraisal." Ph.D. dissertation, St. Louis University, 1966.

**JONES, William Atkinson,** a Representative from Virginia; born in Warsaw, Richmond County, Va., on March 21, 1849; entered the Virginia Military Institute at Lexington in 1864 and served in the defense of Richmond, Va., until its evacuation; attended Coleman's School in Fredericksburg and was graduated from the law department of the University of Virginia at Charlottesville in 1870; was admitted to the bar in 1870 and commenced practice in Warsaw, Va.; Commonwealth attorney for several years; delegate to the Democratic National Conventions in 1880, 1896, and 1900; elected as a Democrat to the Fifty-second and to the thirteen succeeding Congresses and served from March 4, 1891, until his death in Warsaw, Richmond County, Va., on April 17, 1918; chairman, Committee on Insular Affairs (Sixty-second through Sixty-fifth Congresses); interment in St. John's Episcopal Church Cemetery.

**Bibliography:** Shelton, Charlotte Jean. "William Atkinson Jones 1849-1918: Independent Democracy in Gilded Age Virginia." Ph.D. dissertation, University of Virginia, 1980.

**JONES, William Carey,** a Representative from Washington; born in Remsen, Oneida County, N.Y., April 5, 1855; attended the public schools, the West Salem (Wis.) Seminary, and was graduated from the law department of the University of Wisconsin at Madison in 1876; was admitted to the bar the same year and practiced in Madelia, Minn., until 1883; city attorney of Madelia in 1882 and 1883; moved to the Territory of Washington in 1883 and settled in Cheney; city attorney of Cheney 1884-1889; moved to Spokane, Wash., in 1887; prosecuting attorney for the twelfth district of the Territory of Washington 1886-1889; upon the admission of Washington into the Union was elected attorney general of the State and served from 1889 to 1897; delegate to every Territorial and State Republican convention from 1884 to 1894; chairman of the State central committee of the Free Coinage Republican Party in 1896; elected as a Silver Republican to the Fifty-fifth Congress (March 4,

1897-March 3, 1899); unsuccessful candidate for reelection in 1898 to the Fifty-sixth Congress; affiliated with the Democratic Party; delegate to all Democratic State conventions from 1904 to 1924; resumed the practice of his profession; died in Spokane, Wash., June 14, 1927; remains were cremated and the ashes scattered over Liberty Lake, near Spokane, Wash.

**JONES, William Theopilus,** a Delegate from the Territory of Wyoming; born in Corydon, Harrison County, Ind., February 20, 1842; received a liberal schooling; studied law; was admitted to the bar in 1865 and commenced practice in Corydon, Ind.; during the Civil War served in the Union Army as major of the Seventeenth Regiment, Indiana Volunteer Infantry; appointed associate justice of the supreme court of the Territory of Wyoming in 1869; settled in Cheyenne, Wyo., in 1869; elected as a Republican a Delegate to the Forty-second Congress (March 4, 1871-March 3, 1873); unsuccessful candidate for reelection in 1872 to the Forty-third Congress; resumed the practice of law in Corydon, Ind., where he died October 9, 1882; interment in Cedar Hill Cemetery.

**JONES, Willie** (brother of Allen Jones), a Delegate from North Carolina; born in Northampton County, N.C., December 24, 1740; attended Eton College, England; engaged in agricultural pursuits; member of the Provincial Congress in 1774 and 1776; president of the North Carolina Committee of Safety in 1776 and first Governor ex officio of the new State; member of the first constitutional convention in 1776; member of the State house of commons 1776-1778; Member of the Continental Congress in 1780; elected to the United States Constitutional Convention in 1787, but declined to accept; member of the State constitutional convention called to ratify the Constitution of the United States July 21, 1788; resumed agricultural pursuits; died at his summer home in Raleigh, N.C., June 18, 1801; interment in the family burying ground on his plantation near Raleigh, N.C.

**JONES, Woodrow Wilson,** a Representative from North Carolina; born in Green Hill Township, Rutherford County, N.C., January 26, 1914; attended the public schools of Rutherford County; graduated from Mars Hill (N.C.) College in 1934 and from Wake Forest Law School in 1937, was admitted to the bar in 1937 and commenced the practice of law in Rutherfordton, N.C.; served in the United States Navy from November 1943 until discharged as a lieutenant (jg) in January 1946; city attorney of Rutherfordton, N.C., 1940-1943; served as prosecuting attorney of Rutherford County Recorder's Court, 1941-1943; member of the North Carolina State house of representatives, 1947-1949; elected as a Democrat to the Eighty-first Congress to fill the vacancy caused by the death of Alfred L. Bulwinkle; reelected to the three succeeding Congresses, and served from November 7, 1950 to January 3, 1957; was not a candidate for renomination in 1956 to the Eighty-fifth Congress; delegate to all Democratic State Conventions, 1940-1960, and delegate to the Democratic National Convention of 1960; resumed the practice of law; chairman of the North Carolina Democratic Executive Committee from 1958 to 1960; appointed by Governor Luther Hodges as a member of State constitution commission, serving from 1958 to 1960; appointed by President Lyndon B. Johnson as district judge of the United States Courts for the Western District of North Carolina, June 28, 1967, and served as chief district judge from 1968 to 1985; retired in 1993; is a resident of Rutherfordton, N.C.

**JONKMAN, Bartel John,** a Representative from Michigan; born in Grand Rapids, Mich., April 28, 1884; attended the public schools and was graduated from the law department of the University of Michigan at Ann Arbor in 1914; was admitted to the bar the same year and commenced practice in Grand Rapids, Mich.; assistant prosecutor of Kent County, Mich., 1915-1920 and prosecuting attorney 1929-1936; elected as a Republican to the Seventy-sixth Congress to fill the vacancy caused by the death of

Carl E. Mapes; reelected to the Seventy-seventh and to the three succeeding Congresses and served from February 19, 1940, to January 3, 1949; unsuccessful candidate for renomination in 1948; resumed the practice of law; died in Grand Rapids, Mich., June 13, 1955; interment in Woodlawn Cemetery.

**JONTZ, James Prather,** a Representative from Indiana; born in Indianapolis, Ind., December 18, 1951; attended public schools; A.B., Indiana University, Bloomington, 1973; pursued graduate studies at Purdue University, West Lafayette, Ind., and Butler University, Indianapolis; program director, Lake Michigan Federation and Indiana Conservation Council; public relations director, Sycamore Girl Scout Council; instructor, Butler University; chairman, Warren County Democratic Committee, 1978-1980; member, Indiana State house of representatives, District 25, 1974-1984; Indiana State senator, District 7, 1984-1986; elected as a Democrat to the One Hundredth and to the two succeeding Congresses (January 3, 1987-January 3, 1993); unsuccessful candidate for reelection in 1992 to the One Hundred Third Congress; is a resident of Brookston, Ind.

**JORDAN, Barbara Charline,** a Representative from Texas; born in Houston, Harris County, Tex., February 21, 1936; educated in the public schools of Houston, Tex.; graduated, Phillis Wheatley High School, 1952; B.A., Texas Southern University, Houston, Tex., 1956; LL.B., Boston University School of Law, Boston Mass., 1959; admitted to the Massachusetts and Texas bars in 1959 and commenced practice in Houston, Tex., 1960; unsuccessful candidate for the Texas State legislature in 1962 and 1964; elected to the Texas senate in 1967; reelected and served until 1972; administrative assistant to Judge Bill Elliott of Harris County, Tex., 1966; delegate to Texas State Democratic conventions, 1967, 1969; delegate to the Democratic National Convention of 1968; elected as a Democrat to the Ninety-third and to the two succeeding Congresses (January 3, 1973-January 3, 1979); delivered keynote address at the Democratic National Convention of 1976; was not a candidate for reelection in 1978 to the Ninety-sixth Congress; professor, Lyndon B. Johnson School of Public Affairs at the University of Texas in Austin; chair, Commission on Immigration Reform; was a resident of Austin, Tex., until her death there on January 17, 1996; interment in Texas State Cemetery.

**Bibliography:** Jordan, Barbara, and Shelby Hearon. *Barbara Jordan: A Self Portrait.* Garden City, N.Y.: Doubleday, 1979.

**JORDAN, Benjamin Everett,** a Senator from North Carolina; born in Ramseur, Randolph County, N.C., September 8, 1896; attended the public schools, Rutherford (N.C.) College Preparatory School in 1912 and 1913, and Trinity College (now Duke University), in 1914 and 1915; during the First World War served overseas with the United States Army Tank Corps, 1918-1919; organized Sellers Manufacturing Co., a textile firm, in 1927 and served as secretary-treasurer and general manager; Democratic national committeeman, 1954-1958; member, North Carolina Peace Officers Benefit and Retirement Commission, 1943-1958; member, North Carolina Medical Care Commission, 1945-1951; chairman, Board of Trustees, Alamance County General Hospital; appointed as a Democrat to the United States Senate, April 19, 1958, and elected November 4, 1958, to fill the vacancy caused by the death of W. Kerr Scott in the term ending January 3, 1961; reelected in 1960, and again in 1966, and served from April 19, 1958 to January 3, 1973; unsuccessful candidate for renomination in 1972; co-chairman, Joint Committee on Inaugural Arrangements (Eighty-eighth and Ninetieth Congresses), chairman, Joint Committee on the Library (Eighty-eighth through Ninety-second Congresses), Committee on Rules and Administration (Eighty-eighth through Ninety-second Congresses), Joint Committee on Printing (Ninety-first and Ninety-second Congresses); died in Saxapahaw, N.C., March 15, 1974; interment in Pine Hill Cemetery, Burlington, N.C.

**Bibliography:** Bulla, Ben F. *Textiles and Politics: The Life of B. Everett Jordan: From Saxapahaw to the United States Senate.* Durham, N.C.: Carolina Academic Press, 1992.

**JORDAN, Isaac M.,** a Representative from Ohio; born in Mifflinburg, Union County, Pa., May 5, 1835; moved with his parents to Springfield, Ohio, in 1837; attended Northwood (Ohio) Institute for two years and was graduated from Miami University, Oxford, Ohio, in 1857; studied law; was admitted to the bar in 1858 and commenced practice in Dayton, Ohio; moved to Cincinnati in 1859 and continued the practice of law; elected as a Democrat to the Forty-eighth Congress (March 4, 1883-March 3, 1885); declined to be a candidate for renomination in 1884 to the Forty-ninth Congress; engaged in the practice of law in Cincinnati; died from injuries received in an elevator accident in Cincinnati, Ohio, December 3, 1890; interment in the family vault in Spring Grove Cemetery.

**JORDAN, Leonard Beck,** a Senator from Idaho; born in Mount Pleasant, Sanpete County, Utah, May 15, 1899; educated in the public schools of Enterprise, Oreg.; enlisted in the United States Army during the First World War; A.B., University of Oregon, 1923; farmer, rancher, businessman, and economic adviser; director of Circle C Ranch and of the Jordan Motor Co.; resident of Grangeville, Idaho, 1941-1951; member, Idaho State legislature, 1947-1949; elected Governor of Idaho in 1950, and served from January 1, 1951 to January 3, 1955; chairman of the International Joint Commission, 1955-1957; member, International Development Advisory Board, 1958-1959; appointed as a Republican to the United States Senate on August 6, 1962, to fill the vacancy caused by the death of Henry C. Dworshak; elected November 6, 1962, for remainder of term, ending January 3, 1967; reelected in 1966 and served from August 6, 1962, to January 2, 1973; was not a candidate for reelection in 1972; was a resident of Boise, Idaho, until his death there on June 30, 1983; interment in Cloverdale Cemetery.

**Bibliography:** Jordan, Grace. *The Unintentional Senator.* Boise: Syms-York Co., 1972.

**JORDEN, Edwin James,** a Representative from Pennsylvania; born in Spring Hill, near Towanda, Bradford County, Pa., August 30, 1863; attended the common schools and Keystone Academy; was graduated from the Pennsylvania Normal School at Mansfield, Pa.; studied law; was admitted to the bar in 1888 and commenced practice in Tunkhannock, Pa.; elected as a Republican to the Fifty-third Congress to fill the vacancy caused by the death of Myron B. Wright and served from February 23 until March 4, 1895; was not a candidate for renomination in 1894; resumed the practice of his profession; died in Tunkhannock, Wyoming County, Pa., September 7, 1903; interment in Sunnyside Cemetery.

**JORGENSEN, Joseph,** a Representative from Virginia; born in Philadelphia, Pa., February 11, 1844; was graduated from the medical department of the University of Pennsylvania at Philadelphia; cadet surgeon, United States Army, March 17, 1864, to March 23, 1865; acting assistant surgeon April 10 to September 10, 1865, and June 5, 1867, to February 21, 1870; member of the Virginia house of delegates from Prince Edward County 1871-1873; moved to Petersburg, Va.; appointed postmaster of Petersburg, Va., May 21, 1874, and served until June 8, 1877, when he resigned, having been elected to Congress; elected as a Republican to the Forty-fifth, Forty-sixth, and Forty-seventh Congresses (March 4, 1877-March 3, 1883); chairman, Committee on Mileage (Forty-seventh Congress); delegate to the Republican National Convention in 1880; appointed register of the land office at Walla Walla, Wash., by President Chester A. Arthur February 27, 1883, and served until removed by President Cleveland in 1886; died in Portland, Oreg., January 21, 1888; interment in Mountain View Cemetery, Walla Walla, Wash.

**JOSEPH, Antonio,** a Delegate from the Territory of New Mexico; born in Taos, N.Mex., August 25, 1846; attended Lux's Academy in Taos, Bishop Lammy's School in Santa Fe, N.Mex., Webster College in St. Louis County, Mo., and Bryant and Stratton's Commercial College, St. Louis, Mo.; engaged in mercantile pursuits; county judge of Taos County, N.Mex., 1878-1880; moved to Ojo Caliente, N.Mex., in 1880; member of the Territorial house of representatives in 1882; elected as a Democrat to the Forty-ninth and to the four succeeding Congresses (March 4, 1885-March 3, 1895); unsuccessful candidate for reelection in 1894 to the Fifty-fourth Congress; served in the Territorial senate 1896-1898, serving as president of that body in 1898; again engaged in the mercantile business; owner of hotels and extensive lands; died in Ojo Caliente, N.Mex., April 19, 1910; interment in Fairmount Cemetery, Santa Fe, N.Mex.

**JOST, Henry Lee,** a Representative from Missouri; born in New York City December 6, 1873; moved to Hopkins, Nodaway County, Mo., in 1881; attended the common schools; studied law; was admitted to the bar in 1898; afterward attended the Kansas City Law School in 1898 and 1899 and commenced the practice of law in Kansas City, Mo., in 1899; associate city counselor in 1909; first assistant prosecuting attorney 1910-1912; mayor of Kansas City 1912-1916; lecturer on criminal law at Kansas City School of Law 1917-1936; elected as a Democrat to the Sixty-eighth Congress (March 4, 1923-March 3, 1925); was not a candidate for renomination in 1924; resumed law practice in Kansas City, Mo., where he died July 13, 1950; interment in Mount Moriali Cemetery, near Kansas City, Mo.

**JOY, Charles Frederick,** a Representative from Missouri; born in Jacksonville, Morgan County, Ill., December 11, 1849; attended the public schools; was graduated from Yale College in 1874; studied law; was admitted to the bar and commenced practice in St. Louis, Mo., in 1876; presented credentials as a Republican Member-elect to the Fifty-third Congress and served until April 3, 1894, when he was succeeded by John J. O'Neill, who contested the election; elected to the Fifty-fourth and to the three succeeding Congresses (March 4, 1895-March 3, 1903); unsuccessful candidate for renomination in 1902; resumed the practice of his profession in St. Louis; served as recorder of deeds from 1907 until March 22, 1921, when he resigned; died in St. Louis, Mo., on April 13, 1921; the remains were cremated and placed in Elks Rest in Bellefontaine Cemetery.

**JOYCE, Charles Herbert,** a Representative from Vermont; born near Andover, England, January 30, 1830; immigrated to the United States in 1836 with his parents, who settled in Waitsfield, Vt.; attended Northfield Academy and Newbury Seminary; studied law; was admitted to the bar in 1852 and commenced practice in Northfield, Vt.; State librarian for two years; district attorney for Washington County in 1857 and 1858; during the Civil War served in the Union Army as major and lieutenant colonel of the Second Vermont Volunteers; resumed the practice of law in Rutland, Vt.; member of the State house of representatives 1869-1871 and served as speaker in 1870 and 1871; elected as a Republican to the Forty-fourth and to the three succeeding Congresses (March 4, 1875-March 3, 1883); was not a candidate for renomination in 1882; resumed the practice of his profession in Rutland, Vt.; later retired and resided in Pittsfield, Vt., until his death, November 22, 1916; interment in Greenwood Cemetery, Rutland, Vt.

**JOYCE, James,** a Representative from Ohio; born in Cumberland, Guernsey County, Ohio, July 2, 1870; attended the common schools; taught school in Cumberland and Pleasant City, Ohio, and also studied law; entered the Cincinnati Law School in 1891 and was graduated in 1892; was admitted to the bar at Columbus, Ohio, on March 3, 1892; superintendent of the Senecaville (Ohio) High School 1893-1895; began the active practice of law in Cambridge, Ohio, in 1895; member of the State house of representatives

1896-1900; delegate to the Republican National Convention in 1904; elected as a Republican to the Sixty-first Congress (March 4, 1909-March 3, 1911); unsuccessful candidate for reelection in 1910 to the Sixty-second Congress; resumed the practice of law in Cambridge, Ohio; unsuccessful candidate for election as associate justice of the supreme court of Ohio in 1916; died in Cambridge, Ohio, March 25, 1931; interment in the mausoleum in Northwood Cemetery.

**JUDD, Norman Buel** (grandfather of Norman Judd Gould), a Representative from Illinois; born in Rome, Oneida County, N.Y., January 10, 1815; received a liberal schooling; studied law; was admitted to the bar in 1836 and commenced practice in Rome, N.Y.; moved to Chicago, Ill., in 1836 and continued the practice of his profession; city attorney 1837-1839; member of the State senate 1844-1860; delegate to the Republican National Convention of 1860; appointed Minister Plenipotentiary to Berlin by President Lincoln on March 6, 1861, and served until 1865; elected as a Republican to the Fortieth and Forty-first Congresses (March 4, 1867-March 3, 1871); declined to be a candidate for reelection in 1870 to the Forty-second Congress; appointed collector at the port of Chicago by President Ulysses S. Grant on December 5, 1872, and served until his death in Chicago, Ill., November 11, 1878; interment in Graceland Cemetery.

**Bibliography:** *DAB.*

**JUDD, Walter Henry,** a Representative from Minnesota; born in Rising City, Butler County, Nebr., on September 25, 1898; attended the public schools; was graduated from the University of Nebraska at Lincoln in 1920 and from the medical department of the same university in 1923; enlisted in the United States Army in 1918 as a private and was discharged as a second lieutenant, Field Artillery, in 1919; second lieutenant, Field Artillery, Officers Reserve Corps, 1919-1924; instructor of zoology, University of Omaha, 1920-1924; traveling secretary, Student Volunteer Movement in Colleges and Universities in 1924 and 1925; fellowship in surgery, Mayo Foundation, Rochester, Minn., 1932-1934; medical missionary and hospital superintendent in China, under auspices of American Board of Commissioners for Foreign Missions, 1925-1931, and 1934-1938; engaged in private medical practice in Minneapolis, Minn., in 1941 and 1942; elected as a Republican to the Seventy-eighth and to the nine succeeding Congresses (January 3, 1943-January 3, 1963); delivered keynote address at the Republican National Convention of 1960; unsuccessful candidate in 1962 for election to the Eighty-eighth Congress; contributing editor, Reader's Digest, 1963-1976; daily radio commentator and lecturer on international relations and government, 1964-1969; was a resident of Washington, D.C.; died February 13, 1994.

**Bibliography:** Edwards, Lee. *Missionary for Freedom: The Life and Times of Walter Judd.* New York: Paragon House, 1990; Goodno, Floyd Russell. "Walter H. Judd: Spokesman for China in the United States House of Representatives." Ed.D. dissertation, Oklahoma State University, 1970; Judd, Walter H. *Walter H. Judd: Chronicles of a Statesman.* Edited and with a Preface by Edward J. Rozek. Denver: Grier and Company, 1980.

**JUDSON, Andrew Thompson,** a Representative from Connecticut; born in Eastford, Windham County, Conn., November 29, 1784; received a limited schooling; studied law; was admitted to the bar in 1806; moved to Montpelier, Vt., where he began the practice of law; returned to Connecticut and settled in Canterbury in 1809; State's attorney for Windham County 1819-1833; member of the State house of representatives 1822-1825; elected as a Jacksonian to the Twenty-fourth Congress and served from March 4, 1835, until July 4, 1836, when he resigned; appointed on June 28, 1836, by President Andrew Jackson as United States judge for the district of Connecticut, and served until his death in Canterbury, Conn., March 17, 1853; interment in Hyde Cemetery.

**JULIAN, George Washington,** a Representative from Indiana; born near Centerville, Wayne County, Ind., on May 5, 1817; attended the common schools; studied law; was admitted to the bar in 1840 and commenced practice in Greenfield, Ind.; member of the State house of representatives in 1845; delegate to the Buffalo Free-Soil Convention in 1848; elected as a Free-Soiler to the Thirty-first Congress (March 4, 1849-March 3, 1851); unsuccessful candidate for election in 1850 to the Thirty-second Congress; unsuccessful candidate for Vice President of the United States in 1852 on the Free Soil ticket headed by John P. Hale; delegate to the Republican National Convention of 1856; elected as a Republican to the Thirty-seventh and to the four succeeding Congresses (March 4, 1861-March 3, 1871); chairman, Committee on Public Lands (Thirty-eighth through Forty-first Congresses), Committee on Expenditures in the Department of the Navy (Thirty-ninth Congress); appointed by President Grover Cleveland surveyor general of New Mexico and served from July 1885 until September 1889; returned to Indiana and settled in Irvington; engaged in literary pursuits; died in Irvington, a suburb of Indianapolis, Ind., July 7, 1899; interment in Crown Hill Cemetery, Indianapolis, Ind.

**Bibliography:** *DAB*; Julian, George Washington. *Political Recollections, 1840 to 1872.* 1884. Reprint. New York: Negro Universities Press, 1970; Riddleberger, Patrick W. *George Washington Julian, Radical Republican.* Indianapolis: Indiana Historical Bureau, 1966.

**JUNKIN, Benjamin Franklin,** a Representative from Pennsylvania; born near Carlisle, Cumberland County, Pa., November 12, 1822; attended private schools and was graduated from Lafayette College, Easton, Pa.; studied law; was admitted to the bar in 1844 and commenced practice in New Bloomfield, Pa.; district attorney for Perry County 1850-1853; elected as a Republican to the Thirty-sixth Congress (March 4, 1859-March 3, 1861); unsuccessful candidate for reelection in 1860 to the Thirty-seventh Congress; resumed the practice of his profession in New Bloomfield; president judge of the ninth judicial district 1871-1881; solicitor of the Pennsylvania Railroad Co. from 1886 until his death in New Bloomfield, Perry County, Pa., October 9, 1908; interment in New Bloomfield Cemetery.

**JUUL, Niels,** a Representative from Illinois; born in Randers, Denmark, April 27, 1859; attended the Real (Royal) School, Randers, Denmark; immigrated to the United States and settled in Chicago, Ill., in 1880; engaged in the publishing business; studied law; was graduated from the law department of Lake Forest University in 1898; was admitted to the bar in 1899 and commenced practice in Chicago, Ill.; member of the State senate 1898-1914; assistant attorney of the Sanitary District of Chicago 1907-1911; elected as a Republican to the Sixty-fifth and Sixty-sixth Congresses (March 4, 1917-March 3, 1921); unsuccessful candidate for renomination in 1920 to the Sixty-seventh Congress; appointed by President Warren G. Harding United States collector of customs for the port of Chicago January 1, 1921, and served until December 31, 1922, when he resigned; resumed the practice of law until his death in Chicago, Ill., on December 4, 1929; interment in Mount Olive Cemetery.

# K

**KADING, Charles August,** a Representative from Wisconsin; born in Lowell, Dodge County, Wis., January 14, 1874; attended the country schools, Lowell graded school, Horicon High School, and the University of Wisconsin at Madison; was graduated from the law department of Valparaiso University, Valparaiso, Ind., in 1900; was admitted to the bar the same year and commenced practice in Watertown, Wis.; also interested in agricultural pursuits; city attorney of Watertown 1905-1912; district attorney for Dodge County, Wis., 1906-1912; mayor of Watertown 1914-1916; elected as a Republican to the Seventieth, Seventy-first, and Seventy-second Congresses (March 4, 1927-March 3, 1933); unsuccessful candidate

for renomination in 1932; resumed the practice of law; died in Watertown, Wis., June 19, 1956; interment in Oak Hill Cemetery.

**KAHN, Florence Prag** (wife of Julius Kahn), a Representative from California; born in Salt Lake City, Utah, November 9, 1866; moved to California in 1869 with her parents, who settled in San Francisco; attended the public schools of San Francisco; was graduated from the University of California at Berkeley in 1887; elected as a Republican to the Sixty-ninth Congress on February 17, 1925, to fill the vacancy caused by the death of her husband, Representative-elect Julius Kahn; reelected to the Seventieth and to the four succeeding Congresses and served from March 4, 1925, to January 3, 1937; unsuccessful candidate for reelection in 1936 to the Seventy-fifth Congress; retired to private life and resided in San Francisco, Calif., until her death on November 16, 1948; interment in Home of Peace Cemetery, Colma, Calif.

**Bibliography:** *DAB*.

**KAHN, Julius** (husband of Florence Prag Kahn), a Representative from California; born in Kuppenheim, Grand Duchy of Baden, Germany, February 28, 1861; immigrated to the United States at age seven with his mother, and they joined his father, who had settled in Calaveras County, Calif. in 1865; attended the public schools of San Francisco; began work as a clerk in a commission house in 1877; followed the theatrical profession from 1879 to 1889; returned to San Francisco in 1890; studied law; member of the California State assembly in 1892; was admitted to the bar in January 1894 and commenced practice in San Francisco; elected as a Republican to the Fifty-sixth and Fifty-seventh Congresses (March 4, 1899-March 3, 1903); unsuccessfully contested the election of Edward J. Livernash to the Fifty-eighth Congress; elected to the Fifty-ninth and to the nine succeeding Congresses, and served from March 4, 1905 until his death in San Francisco, Calif., December 18, 1924; chairman, Committee on Military Affairs (Sixty-sixth through Sixty-eighth Congresses); had been reelected to the Sixty-ninth Congress; interment in the Home of Peace Cemetery, Colma, Calif.

**Bibliography:** *DAB*; Boxerman, Alan. "Kahn of California." *California Historical Quarterly* 55 (Winter 1976): 340-351.

**KALANIANAOLE, Jonah Kuhio,** a Delegate from the Territory of Hawaii; born in Koloa, island of Kauai, Hawaii, March 26, 1871; attended the Royal School and Punahou College, Honolulu; studied four years in St. Matthew's College, California; was a student at the Royal Agricultural College in England and was graduated from a business college in England; created a prince by royal proclamation in 1884; occupied a position in the Department of the Interior of the Hawaiian Government; took part in the revolution of the Hawaiians in 1895 and was sentenced to one year's imprisonment; visited Africa during the years 1899-1902 and fought in the British Army in the Boer War; elected as a Republican to the Fifty-eighth and to the nine succeeding Congresses and served from March 4, 1903, until his death in Waikiki, near Honolulu, Hawaii, on January 7, 1922; interment in Royal Mausoleum, Nuuanu.

**Bibliography:** *DAB*.

**KALBFLEISCH, Martin,** a Representative from New York; born in Flushing, Holland, on February 8, 1804; attended the public schools; studied chemistry; immigrated to the United States and settled in New York City in 1826; engaged in the manufacture and sale of paints; health warden in 1832; school trustee in 1836; established a chemical factory at Greenpoint, N.Y., in 1844; supervisor of Bushwick 1852-1854; unsuccessful candidate for mayor of Brooklyn in 1854; alderman in Brooklyn 1855-1861; mayor 1862-1864; elected as a Democrat to the Thirty-eighth Congress (March 4, 1863-March 3, 1865); delegate to the Union National Convention at Philadelphia in 1866; again mayor of Brooklyn 1867-1871; unsuccessful independent candidate for reelection;

retired from active pursuits; died in Brooklyn, N.Y., February 12, 1873; interment in Greenwood Cemetery.

**KANE, Elias Kent,** a Senator from Illinois; born in New York City on June 7, 1794; attended the public schools; was graduated from Yale College in 1813; studied law; was admitted to the bar and commenced practice in Nashville, Tenn.; moved to Kaskaskia, Ill., in 1814; appointed judge of the Territory of Illinois; delegate to the first State constitutional convention in 1818; unsuccessful candidate for election in 1820 to the Seventeenth Congress; first secretary of State of Illinois, 1820-1824; member of the Illinois State house of representatives in 1824; elected to the United States Senate in 1824; reelected in 1831, and served from March 4, 1825 until his death in Washington, D.C., December 12, 1835; chairman, Committee to Audit and Control the Contingent Expense (Nineteenth through Twenty-first Congresses), Committee on Private Land Claims (Twenty-first through Twenty-third Congresses), Committee on Public Lands (Twenty-second Congress); interment in the family cemetery on the old Kane farm, near Fort Gage, Ill.

**KANE, Nicholas Thomas,** a Representative from New York; born in County Waterford, Ireland, September 12, 1846; immigrated to the United States when a boy and settled near Albany, N.Y.; attended the common schools; enlisted in the Union Army in 1863 and served until 1865; engaged in mercantile pursuits; represented Watervliet on the Albany County Board of Supervisors 1883-1885; elected as a Democrat to the Fiftieth Congress and served from March 4, 1887, until his death in Albany, N.Y., September 14, 1887, before the assembling of the Congress; interment in St. Agnes Cemetery, Colonie, Albany County, N.Y.

**KANJORSKI, Paul Edmund,** a Representative from Pennsylvania; born in Nanticoke, Pa., April 2, 1937; attended the public schools of Nanticoke and the United States Capitol Page School, Washington, D.C., 1954; attended Wyoming Seminary, Kingston, Pa.; B.A., Temple University, Philadelphia, Pa., 1961; J.D., Dickinson School of Law, Carlisle, Pa., 1965; served as a private in the United States Army, 1960-1961; admitted to the Pennsylvania bar in 1966 and practiced law in Wilkes-Barre, 1966-1984; administrative law judge for workman's compensation, 1971-1980; elected as a Democrat to the Ninety-ninth and to the five succeeding Congresses (January 3, 1985-January 3, 1997); is a resident of Nanticoke, Pa.

**KAPTUR, Marcia Carolyn (Marcy),** a Representative from Ohio; born in Toledo on June 17, 1946; attended Little Flower School, Toledo; graduated from St. Ursula Academy, Toledo, 1964; B.A., University of Wisconsin, Madison, 1968; M.A., University of Michigan, Ann Arbor, 1974; attended the University of Manchester, England, 1974; post-graduate studies, Massachusetts Institute of Technology, 1981; urban planner, Toledo-Lucas County Plan Commissions, 1969-1975; director of planning, National Center for Urban Ethnic Affairs, 1975-1977; assistant director for urban affairs, domestic policy staff, White House, 1977-1979; elected as a Democrat to the Ninety-eighth and to the six succeeding Congresses; (January 3, 1983-January 3, 1997); is a resident of Toledo, Ohio.

**KARCH, Charles Adam,** a Representative from Illinois; born on a farm in Engleman Township, St. Clair County, Ill., March 17, 1875; attended the public schools; was graduated from Northern Illinois Normal University (now the Illinois State Normal University), at Normal, Ill., in 1894; taught school 1895-1900; was graduated from the law department of Wesleyan College, Bloomington, Ill., in 1898; was admitted to the bar in 1898 and commenced practice in Belleville, Ill.; served as secretary to Representative Fred J. Kern 1901-1903; member of the Illinois house of representatives 1904-1906 and 1910-1914; moved to East St. Louis in 1914 and continued the practice of law; served as United States attorney for

the eastern judicial district of Illinois 1914-1918; elected as a Democrat to the Seventy-second Congress and served from March 4, 1931, until his death; had been nominated for reelection to the Seventy-third Congress; died in St. Louis, Mo., on November 6, 1932; interment in Mount Hope Cemetery, Belleville, Ill.

**KARNES, David Kemp,** a Senator from Nebraska; born in Omaha, Nebr., December 12, 1948; attended the public schools; B.A., University of Nebraska, Lincoln, 1971; J.D., University of Nebraska School of Law, 1974; graduate studies at the University of Wisconsin School of Law; White House fellow 1981; executive assistant to the Under Secretary of Housing and Urban Development, 1982; special counsel, Federal Home Loan Bank Board, 1983; chairman of the regional office of the Federal Home Loan Bank Board, Topeka, Kans., 1983-1987; general counsel and senior vice president, Scoular Company, 1983-1987; appointed as a Republican to the United States Senate on March 11, 1987 to fill the vacancy caused by the death of Edward Zorinsky; unsuccessful candidate for reelection in 1988; is a resident of Omaha, Nebr.

**KARST, Raymond Willard,** a Representative from Missouri; born in South St. Louis, Mo., December 31, 1902; attended Wyman grade school and St. Louis Academy; was graduated from the law school of St. Louis University in 1927; was admitted to the bar in 1926 and commenced the practice of law in St. Louis, Mo.; member of the State house of representatives in 1935 and 1936; provisional city judge and judge of Court of Criminal Correction 1936-1940; served as a captain, Ordnance Department, United States Army, 1942-1945; elected as a Democrat to the Eighty-first Congress (January 3, 1949-January 3, 1951); was an unsuccessful candidate for reelection in 1950 to the Eighty-second Congress; appointed general counsel with Economic Stabilization Agency and later acting administrator; in 1955 resumed the practice of law in Clayton, Mo.; chairman of the board, Karst Enterprises; was a resident of Kirkwood, Mo., until his death there October 4, 1987.

**KARSTEN, Frank Melvin,** a Representative from Missouri; born in San Antonio, Bexar County, Tex., January 7, 1913; moved to St. Louis, Mo., with his family in 1925; attended public schools; served as secretary to Representative John Joseph Cochran, 1934-1946 and also served as staff director for two congressional committees; LL.B., National University (now George Washington University), Washington, D.C., 1940; LL.D., Parsons College, Fairfield, Iowa, 1969; was admitted to the bar in 1946 and commenced practice in Washington, D.C.; delegate, General Agreement on Trade and Tariffs, Geneva, 1957; delegate, British-American Parliamentary Conference, 1964-1965; elected as a Democrat to the Eightieth and to the ten succeeding Congresses (January 3, 1947-January 3, 1969); assistant Democratic whip, 1947-1969; was not a candidate for reelection in 1968 to the Ninety-first Congress; engaged in the practice of law in Washington, D.C.; was a resident of San Antonio, Tex.; died May 14, 1992.

**KARTH, Joseph Edward,** a Representative from Minnesota; born in New Brighton, Ramsey County, Minn., August 26, 1922; attended public schools and the University of Nebraska School of Engineering; interrupted his education during the Second World War to serve in the United States Army, with service in the European Theater of Operations; employed by the Minnesota Mining and Manufacturing Company; international representative of OCAW-AFL-CIO 1947-1958; member, Minnesota State house of representatives, 1950-1958; elected as a Democrat to the Eighty-sixth and to the eight succeeding Congresses (January 3, 1959-January 3, 1977); was not a candidate for reelection in 1976 to the Ninety-fifth Congress; established a consulting firm; is a resident of Phoenix, Ariz.

**KASEM, George Albert,** a Representative from California; born in Drumright, Creek County, Okla., April 6, 1919; attended the public schools; graduated from John H. Francis Polytechnic High School, Los Angeles, Calif., in 1938; entered the Army Air Force in 1941 and served overseas before his discharge in 1945; B.S., University of Southern California, 1949; J.D., University of Southern California School of Law, 1951; was admitted to the bar in 1951 and practiced law in Los Angeles; moved to Baldwin Park, Calif., in 1953 and continued the practice of law; elected as a Democrat to the Eighty-sixth Congress (January 3, 1959-January 3, 1961); unsuccessful candidate for reelection in 1960 to the Eighty-seventh Congress; resumed the practice of law; commissioner, Citrus Municipal Court, 1978-1984; is a resident of West Covina, Calif.

**KASICH, John Richard,** a Representative from Ohio; born in McKees Rocks, Allegheny County, Pa., May 13, 1952; attended the public schools in McKees Rocks; graduated Sto-Rox High School, 1970; B.A., Ohio State University, Columbus, 1974; administrative assistant to State senator Donald Lukens, 1975-1977; elected to the Ohio legislature, 1979-1982; elected as a Republican to the Ninety-eighth and to the six succeeding Congresses (January 3, 1983-January 3, 1997); chairman, Committee on the Budget (One Hundred Fourth Congress); is a resident of Westerville, Ohio.

**KASSEBAUM, Nancy Landon,** a Senator from Kansas; born in Topeka, Shawnee County, Kans., July 29, 1932; attended the public schools of Topeka, Kans.; B.A., University of Kansas, 1954; M.A., University of Michigan, 1956; radio station executive, Wichita, Kans.; member, Kansas governmental ethics commission, 1975-1976; member, Kansas committee for the humanities, 1975-1979; elected as a Republican to the United States Senate in 1978 for the term commencing January 3, 1979; subsequently appointed by the Governor, December 23, 1978, to fill the vacancy caused by the resignation of James B. Pearson for the term ending January 3, 1979; reelected in 1984 and again in 1990, and served from December 23, 1978 to January 3, 1997; was not a candidate for reelection in 1996; chairman, Committee on Labor and Human Resources (One Hundred Fourth Congress); is a resident of Burdick, Kans.

**KASSON, John Adam,** a Representative from Iowa; born in Charlotte, Chittenden County, Vt., January 11, 1822; attended the local school; was graduated from the University of Vermont at Burlington in 1842; studied law; was admitted to the bar and practiced in St. Louis, Mo., until 1857; moved to Des Moines, Iowa, and resumed the practice of law; delegate to the Republican National Convention of 1860; First Assistant Postmaster General in President Lincoln's administration in 1861 and resigned in 1862; United States commissioner to the International Postal Congress at Paris in 1863; elected as a Republican to the Thirty-eighth and Thirty-ninth Congresses (March 4, 1863-March 3, 1867); chairman, Committee on Coinage, Weights and Measures (Thirty-eighth and Thirty-ninth Congresses); unsuccessful candidate for renomination in 1866 to the Fortieth Congress; commissioner from the United States in 1867 to negotiate postal conventions with Great Britain, France, Belgium, Germany, Switzerland, Italy, and the Netherlands; member of the State house of representatives 1868-1872; elected to the Forty-third and Forty-fourth Congresses (March 4, 1873-March 3, 1877); was not a candidate for renomination in 1876 to the Forty-fifth Congress; appointed Minister to Austria-Hungary on June 11, 1877, and served until March 1881; elected to the Forty-seventh and Forty-eighth Congresses and served from March 4, 1881, until his resignation on July 13, 1884; appointed Minister to Germany on July 4, 1884, and served until June 1885; special envoy to the Congo International Conference at Berlin in 1885, and to the Samoan International Conference in 1889; United States special commissioner plenipotentiary to negotiate reciprocity treaties in 1897; member of the United States and British Joint High Commission in 1898 to adjust differences with Canada; died in Washington, D.C., May 18, 1910; interment in Woodland Cemetery, Des Moines, Iowa.

**Bibliography:** *DAB*; Schoonover, Thomas. "John A. Kasson's Opposition to the Lincoln Administration's Mexican Policy." *Annals of Iowa* 40 (1971): 584-93; Younger, Edward. *John A. Kasson; Politics and Diplomacy from Lincoln to McKinley.* Iowa City: State Historical Society of Iowa, 1955.

**KASTEN, Robert Walter, Jr.,** a Representative and a Senator from Wisconsin; born in Milwaukee, Wis., June 19, 1942; graduated, The Choate High School, Wallingford, Conn., 1960; B.A., University of Arizona, 1964; M.B.A., Columbia University Graduate School of Business, New York City, 1966; served in the Wisconsin Air National Guard, 1967-1972; vice president of marketing and sales manager for a Wisconsin shoe manufacturing company; member, Wisconsin State senate, 1972-1974; elected as a Republican to the Ninety-fourth and Ninety-fifth Congresses (January 3, 1975-January 3, 1979); was not a candidate for reelection in 1978 to the House of Representatives, but was an unsuccessful candidate for nomination for Governor of Wisconsin; elected as a Republican to the United States Senate in 1980; reelected in 1986, and served from January 3, 1981 to January 3, 1993; unsuccessful candidate for reelection in 1992; is a resident of Milwaukee, Wis.

**KASTENMEIER, Robert William,** a Representative from Wisconsin; born in Beaver Dam, Dodge County, Wis., January 24, 1924; attended the public schools of Beaver Dam, and Carleton College, Northfield, Minn.; LL.B., University of Wisconsin, 1952; was admitted to the bar the same year and commenced the practice of law in Watertown, Wis.; entered the United States Army as a private in February 1943; served in the Philippines and was discharged as a first lieutenant on August 15, 1946; War Department branch office director, claims service, in the Philippines, 1946-1948; elected justice of the peace for Jefferson and Dodge Counties in 1955 and served until 1959; elected as a Democrat to the Eighty-sixth and to the fifteen succeeding Congresses (January 3, 1959-January 3, 1991); unsuccessful candidate for reelection in 1990 to the One Hundred Second Congress; chairman, National Commission on Judicial Discipline and Removal, 1991-1993; is a resident of Arlington, Va.

**KAUFMAN, David Spangler,** a Representative from Texas; born in Boiling Springs, Cumberland County, Pa., December 18, 1813; pursued classical studies and was graduated from Princeton College in 1833; studied law; was admitted to the bar in Natchez, Miss., and commenced practice in Natchitoches, La.; moved to Nacogdoches, Republic of Texas, in 1837; served against the Indians; member of the Texas house of representatives 1839-1843; served in the Texas senate 1843-1845; appointed Chargé d'Affaires of Texas to the United States in 1845; moved to Lowes Ferry, Tex.; upon the admission of Texas as a State into the Union was elected as a Democrat to the Twenty-ninth Congress; reelected to the Thirtieth and Thirty-first Congresses and served from March 30, 1846, until his death in Washington, D.C., on January 31, 1851; chairman, Committee on Rules (Thirty-first Congress); interment in the Congressional Cemetery; reinterment in the State Cemetery at Austin, Tex., in 1932.

**KAVANAGH, Edward,** a Representative from Maine; born in Newcastle, Lincoln County, Maine, April 27, 1795; attended Montreal Seminary, Montreal, Canada, and Georgetown College, Georgetown, D.C.; was graduated from St. Mary's College, Baltimore, Md., in 1813; studied law; was admitted to the bar and commenced practice in Damariscotta, Maine; member of the State house of representatives 1826-1828; secretary of the State senate in 1830; elected as a Jacksonian to the Twenty-second and Twenty-third Congresses (March 4, 1831-March 3, 1835); unsuccessful candidate for reelection in 1834 to the Twenty-fourth Congress; appointed Chargé d'Affaires to Portugal on March 3, 1835, and served until his resignation in June 1841; one of the joint commission on the northeastern boundary in 1842; member of the State senate in 1842 and 1843 and served as president of that body; became Governor of Maine upon the resignation of Governor John Fairfield on March 7, 1843, and served until January 1, 1844; died in Newcastle, Maine, January 22, 1844; interment in St. Patrick's Catholic Cemetery, Damariscotta Mills, Maine.

**Bibliography:** *DAB*; Lucey, William Leo. *Edward Kavanagh, Catholic, Statesman, Diplomat, from Maine, 1795-1844.* Francestown, N.H.: Marshall Jones, 1947.

**KAVANAUGH, William Marmaduke,** a Senator from Arkansas; born near Eutaw, Green County, Ala., March 3, 1866; attended the common schools in Kentucky; graduated from the Kentucky Military Institute at Farmdale, Ky., in 1885; moved to Arkansas and settled in Little Rock; engaged in newspaper work, first as a reporter and subsequently became editor and manager of the Arkansas Gazette; sheriff and tax collector of Pulaski County 1896-1900; county and probate judge 1900-1904; engaged in banking, street railway, and gas supply interests; member, Democratic National Committee 1912-1915; elected as a Democrat to the United States Senate to fill the vacancy caused by the death of Jeff Davis and served from January 29 until March 3, 1913; director of the Lakes to Gulf Deep Waterways Association; died in Little Rock, Ark., February 21, 1915; interment in Oakland Cemetery.

**KAYNOR, William Kirk,** a Representative from Massachusetts; born in Sanborn, O'Brien County, Iowa, November 29, 1884; attended the common schools of Spencer and Clear Lake, Iowa; in his early youth was employed as a drug clerk in Clear Lake; moved to Gann Valley, Buffalo County, S.Dak., and herded cattle; was graduated from Hotchkiss School, Lakeville, Conn., in 1908 and from Yale University in 1912; moved to Springfield, Mass., in 1912 and engaged in the real estate and insurance business; during the First World War attended the officers' training school at Camp Lee, Va., from July to November 1918; member of the common council of Springfield 1920-1924; postmaster of Springfield 1923-1928; elected as a Republican to the Seventy-first Congress and served from March 4, 1929, until his death in an airplane accident near Washington, D.C., on December 20, 1929; interment in Oak Grove Cemetery, Springfield, Mass.

**KAZEN, Abraham, Jr.,** a Representative from Texas; born in Laredo, Webb County, Tex., January 17, 1919; graduated from Laredo High School in 1937; attended the University of Texas 1937-1940, Cumberland University Law School in Lebanon, Tenn., in 1941; admitted to the bar in 1942 and commenced practice in Laredo, Tex.; commissioned an Air Force pilot upon his graduation from Lubbock Air Force Base, 1942; during the Second World War served in North Africa, Sicily, and Italy as a pilot in Troop Carrier Command; discharged with the rank of captain in 1953; served in the Texas house of representatives, 1947-1952; elected to the Texas senate in 1952 and served continuously for fourteen years through 1966; elected president pro tempore of State senate in 1959; served as Acting Governor of Texas, August 4, 1959; member of Texas Legislative Council for sixteen years; delegate to the Democratic National Conventions of 1960 and 1964; elected as a Democrat to the Ninetieth and to the eight succeeding Congresses (January 3, 1967-January 3, 1985); unsuccessful candidate for renomination in 1984 to the Ninety-ninth Congress; was a resident of Laredo, Tex., until his death in Austin, Tex., on November 29, 1987; interment in Catholic Cemetery, Laredo, Tex.

**KEAN, Hamilton Fish** (father of Robert Winthrop Kean, brother of John Kean [1852-1914], and great-grandson of John Kean [1756-1795]), a Senator from New Jersey; born at "Ursino," his ancestral estate near Elizabeth, in Union Township, Union County,

N.J., February 27, 1862; attended the public schools of Elizabeth, N.J.; graduated from St. Paul's School, Concord, N.H.; engaged in banking and agricultural pursuits; member, Republican National Committee 1919-1928; unsuccessful candidate for the Republican nomination for United States Senator in 1924; elected as a Republican to the United States Senate in 1928 and served from March 4, 1929 to January 3, 1935; unsuccessful candidate for reelection in 1934; engaged in banking until his death in New York City, December 27, 1941; interment in Greenwood Cemetery, Brooklyn, N.Y.

**KEAN, John** (brother of Hamilton Fish Kean, great-grandson of John Kean [1756-1795], and uncle of Robert Winthrop Kean), a Representative and a Senator from New Jersey; born at "Ursino," near Elizabeth, N.J., December 4, 1852; studied in private schools and attended Yale College; graduated from the Columbia Law School, New York City, in 1875, and was admitted to the New Jersey bar in 1877, but did not engage in extensive practice; engaged in banking and interested in manufacturing; elected as a Republican to the Forty-eighth Congress (March 4, 1883-March 3, 1885); unsuccessful candidate for reelection in 1884 to the Forty-ninth Congress; elected to the Fiftieth Congress (March 4, 1887-March 3, 1889); unsuccessful candidate for reelection in 1888 to the Fifty-first Congress; unsuccessful candidate for election in 1892 for Governor of New Jersey; member of the committee to revise the judiciary system of New Jersey; elected to the United States Senate in 1899; reelected in 1905, and served from March 4, 1899, to March 3, 1911; chairman, Committee on the Geological Survey (Fifty-seventh Congress), Committee to Audit and Control the Contingent Expense (Fifty-eighth through Sixty-first Congresses); engaged in banking in Elizabeth, N.J.; died in Ursino, N.J., on November 4, 1914; interment in Evergreen Cemetery, Elizabeth, N.J.

**KEAN, John** (great-grandfather of Hamilton Fish Kean, and John Kean [1852-1914], and great-great-grandfather of Robert Winthrop Kean), a Delegate from South Carolina; born in Charleston, S.C., in 1756; engaged in mercantile pursuits; taken prisoner at the capture of Charleston in 1780 by General Clinton and was confined aboard a prison ship for several months; appointed by General Washington a member of the commission to audit accounts of the Revolutionary Army; Member of the Continental Congress 1785-1787; appointed by President Washington cashier of the Bank of the United States in Philadelphia and served from its organization until his death in Philadelphia, Pa., on May 4, 1795; interment in St. John's Churchyard.

**KEAN, Robert Winthrop** (son of Hamilton Fish Kean, nephew of John Kean [1852-1914], and great-great-grandson of John Kean [1756-1795]), a Representative from New Jersey; born in Elberon, Monmouth County, N.J., September 28, 1893; was graduated from St. Mark's School, Southboro, Mass., in 1911 and from Harvard University in 1915; bank clerk in Carteret, N.J., and New York City, 1915-1917; served with Squadron A in the New York National Guard on the Mexican border in 1916; during the First World War served overseas as a first lieutenant with the Fifteenth Field Artillery, Second Division, in 1917 and 1918; decorated with the Silver Star Medal and the Distinguished Service Cross; engaged in the investment and banking business in Livingston, N.J., Newark, N.J., and New York City, 1920-1969; delegate to the Republican National Convention in 1936, 1960 and 1964; elected as a Republican to the Seventy-sixth and to the nine succeeding Congresses (January 3, 1939-January 3, 1959); was not a candidate for renomination in 1958 but was unsuccessful as the Republican candidate for election to the United States Senate; resumed his investment and banking interests; chairman of the National Advisory Committee of the White House Conference on Aging May 1959-April 1961; chairman of Essex County Republican Committee 1959-1962; resided in

Livingston, N.J. where he died September 21, 1980; interment in Saint Bernards Cemetery, Bernardsville, N.J.

**KEARNEY, Bernard William,** a Representative from New York; born in Ithaca, N.Y., May 23, 1889; attended the public schools; was graduated from Schenectady (N.Y.) High School and from Union University Albany Law School in 1914; was admitted to the bar the same year and commenced practice in Albany, N.Y.; member of the New York National Guard 1909-1917, serving on the Mexican border in 1916 and 1917; served overseas in the First World War in various outfits; returned to the United States in 1919; continued active in the New York National Guard, retiring in 1940, with rank of major general; decorated with the French Legion of Honor, the Croix de Guerre, and the Philippine Legion of Honor (officer); city judge of Gloversville, N.Y., 1920-1924; assistant district attorney of Hamilton County, N.Y., 1924-1929, and of Fulton County, N.Y., 1929-1931; district attorney of Fulton County, N.Y., 1931-1942; elected as a Republican to the Seventy-eighth and to the seven succeeding Congresses (January 3, 1943-January 3, 1959); was not a candidate for renomination in 1958 to the Eighty-sixth Congress; resumed the practice of law; resided in Canandaigua, N.Y.; died in Venice, Fla., June 3, 1976; interment in Arlington National Cemetery, Va.

**KEARNEY, Dyre,** a Delegate from Delaware; born in Kent County, Del.; studied law; was admitted to the bar of New Castle County in 1784 and commenced practice in Dover, Del.; Member of the Continental Congress 1787-1788; resumed the practice of his profession in Dover, Del., where he died about November 1, 1791.

**KEARNS, Carroll Dudley,** a Representative from Pennsylvania; born in Youngstown, Mahoning County, Ohio, May 7, 1900; moved with his parents to New Castle, Lawrence County, Pa., in 1901; attended the public schools; student in the Army Training Corps at the University of Pittsburgh in 1918; B.M., Chicago (Ill.) Musical College, 1921, and D.M., 1948; B.S., Westminster College, New Wilmington, Pa., 1933; M.E., University of Pittsburgh, 1938, and took special studies at Pennsylvania State College at State College in 1932 and 1933; engaged in the construction business in Chicago, Ill., 1925-1929; taught school and engaged in educational work in supervisory and administrative positions in Illinois and Pennsylvania from 1924 until 1947; also pursued a musical career as a concert artist and conductor; elected as a Republican to the Eightieth and to the seven succeeding Congresses (January 3, 1947-January 3, 1963); unsuccessful candidate for renomination in 1962 to the Eighty-eighth Congress; engaged in manufacturing, 1963-1970; resided in Conneaut Lake, Pa.; died in Meadville, Pa., June 11, 1976; interment in Lakeview Cemetery, Conneaut Lake, Pa.

**KEARNS, Charles Cyrus,** a Representative from Ohio; born in Tonica, La Salle County, Ill., February 11, 1869; moved with his parents to Georgetown, Brown County, Ohio, in 1874; attended the public schools in Georgetown, Ohio, Northern College at Ada, and Lebanon (Ohio) College; taught school in Brown County; was graduated from the Cincinnati Law School in 1894; was admitted to the bar the same year and commenced practice in Batavia, Clermont County; managing editor of the Las Vegas (N.Mex.) Daily Record in 1900 and 1901 and of the Daily Record, Hot Springs, Ark., in 1901 and 1902; returned to Ohio in 1903 and practiced law in Batavia; prosecuting attorney of Clermont County, Ohio, 1906-1909; elected as a Republican to the Sixty-fourth and to the seven succeeding Congresses (March 4, 1915-March 3, 1931); unsuccessful candidate for reelection in 1930 to the Seventy-second Congress; engaged in the practice of law at Cincinnati, Ohio, in 1930; died in Amelia, Ohio, on December 17, 1931; interment in Mount Moriah Cemetery, Tobasco, Ohio.

**KEARNS, Thomas,** a Senator from Utah; born near Woodstock, Oxford County, Ontario, Canada, April 11, 1862; moved with his parents to Holt County, Nebr., and attended the public schools; worked on a farm; engaged in the freighting business; moved to Salt Lake City, and afterward to Park City, Utah; interested in mining and operated several mines; served in the City Council of Park City in 1895; member of the State constitutional convention in 1895; elected as a Republican to the United States Senate to fill the vacancy in the term commencing March 4, 1899, caused by the failure of the legislature to elect and served from January 23, 1901, to March 3, 1905; was not a candidate for reelection in 1904; resumed the mining business and resided in Salt Lake City, Utah, until his death on October 18, 1918; interment in Mount Calvary Cemetery.

**KEATING, Edward,** a Representative from Colorado; born on a small farm near Kansas City, Kans., on July 9, 1875; moved with his mother to Pueblo, Colo., in 1880; moved to Denver in 1889; attended the public schools; engaged in newspaper work as copyholder, reporter, city editor, and managing editor; city auditor of Denver, 1899-1901; member of the first convention elected to draft a charter for the city of Denver in 1903; editor of the Rocky Mountain News, 1906-1911; president of the International League of Press Clubs in 1906 and 1907; president of the Colorado State Board of Land Commissioners, 1911-1913; purchased the Pueblo Leader and moved to Pueblo in 1912; elected as a Democrat to the Sixty-third and to the two succeeding Congresses (March 4, 1913-March 3, 1919); chairman, Committee on Expenditures in the Post Office Department (Sixty-fifth Congress); unsuccessful candidate for reelection in 1918 to the Sixty-sixth Congress; editor and manager of Labor, official weekly newspaper of the associated railroad labor organizations, published in Washington, D.C., until his retirement in 1953; died in Washington, D.C. on March 18, 1965; interment in Cedar Hill Cemetery, Suitland, Md.

**Bibliography:** Keating, Edward. *The Gentleman from Colorado: A Memoir.* Denver: Sage Books, 1964.

**KEATING, Kenneth Barnard,** a Representative and a Senator from New York; born in Lima, Livingston County, N.Y., May 18, 1900; attended the public schools; graduated from Genesee Wesleyan Seminary, Lima, N.Y., in 1915, from the University of Rochester (N.Y.) in 1919, and from Harvard University Law School in 1923; was admitted to the bar in 1923 and commenced practice in Rochester, N.Y.; during the First World War served as a sergeant in the United States Army; during the Second World War served overseas and was promoted to brigadier general in 1948; resumed the practice of law; elected as a Republican to the Eightieth and to the five succeeding Congresses (January 3, 1947-January 3, 1959); was not a candidate in 1958 for renomination to the House of Representatives, but was elected to the United States Senate, and served from January 3, 1959 to January 3, 1965; unsuccessful candidate for reelection in 1964; elected to the New York State Court of Appeals in 1965 and served until his resignation in 1969; appointed United States Ambassador to India on May 1, 1969 and served until July 1972; appointed Ambassador to Israel on June 22, 1973, and served until his death in New York City, May 5, 1975; interment in Arlington National Cemetery, Va.

**Bibliography:** Keating, Kenneth. *Government of the People.* New York: The World Publishing Co., 1964; Paterson, Thomas G. "The Historian as Detective: Senator Kenneth Keating, the Missiles in Cuba, and His Mysterious Sources." *Diplomatic History* 11 (Winter 1987): 67-70.

**KEATING, William John,** a Representative from Ohio; born in Cincinnati, Hamilton County, Ohio, March 30, 1927; attended St. Xavier High School in Cincinnati; B.B.A., University of Cincinnati, 1950; J.D., University of Cincinnati School of Law, 1950; enlisted in the United States Navy during the Second World War, seaman, second class, 1945-1946; first lieutenant, United States Air Force Reserve (Judge Advocate General department); admitted to the Ohio bar in 1950 and commenced practice in Cincinnati; assistant attorney general, State of Ohio, 1957-1958; appointed judge of the Cincinnati Municipal Court in December 1958, and elected judge of same court, 1959-1964, serving as presiding judge, 1962-1963; judge of the Hamilton County Court of Common Pleas, 1964-1967; member, Cincinnati City Council, 1967-1970; delegate to the Republican National Convention of 1972; elected as a Republican to the Ninety-second and to the Ninety-third Congresses, and served from January 3, 1971 until his resignation on January 3, 1974; president and chief executive officer of the Cincinnati Enquirer, 1974-1984; president, Gannett Central Newspapers Group, 1979-1984; senior vice president, Gannett Co., Inc., and president, Gannett Newspaper Division, 1984-1985; chairman, Cincinnati Enquirer and executive vice president and general counsel, Gannett Co., Inc., 1986; chief executive officer, Detroit Newspaper Agency, May 1986 to April 1990; chairman and publisher, Cincinnati Enquirer, April 1, 1990 to April 1, 1992; chairman of the board, Associated Press, May 1, 1987 to May 1, 1992; is a resident of Cincinnati, Ohio.

**KEE, James** (son of John Kee and Maude Elizabeth Kee), a Representative from West Virginia; born in Bluefield, Mercer County, W.Va., April 15, 1917; educated in the public schools and Sacred Heart School in Bluefield, Greenbrier Military School, Southeastern University School of Law, and the School of Foreign Service at Georgetown University; assistant to the Clerk of the United States House of Representatives, 1936-1940; housing adviser to the United States Housing Authority, 1940-1942; served in the United States Army Air Force, 1944-1946; career foreign service staff officer of the United States Department of State, with domestic and foreign duties, 1949-1952; administrative assistant to Representative Elizabeth Kee, January 1953-January 1965; elected as a Democrat to the Eighty-ninth and to the three succeeding Congresses (January 3, 1965-January 3, 1973); unsuccessful candidate for renomination in 1972 to the Ninety-third Congress; was a resident of Fayetteville, W.Va.; died March 11, 1989.

**KEE, John** (husband of Maude Elizabeth Kee and father of James Kee), a Representative from West Virginia; born in Glenville, Gilmer County, W.Va., August 22, 1874; attended the public schools, Glenville (W.Va.) State Normal School, and West Virginia University at Morgantown; studied law; was admitted to the bar in 1897 and commenced practice in Glenville, W.Va.; associated with the South Penn Oil Company, 1900-1902; served as counsel for the Virginia Railway Company, 1902-1910; moved to Bluefield, Mercer County, W.Va., in 1910 and continued the practice of law; engaged in special legal work in Mexico, 1916-1918; returned to Bluefield, W.Va., in 1918 and resumed the practice of law; member of the West Virginia State senate, 1923-1927; elected as a Democrat to the Seventy-third and to the nine succeeding Congresses, and served from March 4, 1933 until his death in Washington, D.C., May 8, 1951; chairman, Committee on Foreign Affairs (Eighty-first and Eighty-second Congresses); interment in Monte Vista Cemetery, Bluefield, W.Va.

**Bibliography:** Hardin, William H. "John Kee and the Point Four Compromise." *West Virginia History* 41 (Fall 1979): 40-56.

**KEE, Maude Elizabeth** (wife of John Kee and mother of James Kee), a Representative from West Virginia; born in Radford, Montgomery County, Va., June 7, 1895; attended public and private schools of Montgomery County, Roanoke, Va., Washington, D.C., and Bluefield, W.Va.; graduated from Roanoke Business College, Roanoke, Va.; author of a weekly column in West Virginia newspapers; sponsor of a library for the physically handicapped at Woodrow Wilson Rehabilitation Center, Fishersville, Va.; served as executive secretary to her husband, John Kee, from November 1932 until his death; elected as a Democrat to the Eighty-second

Congress, July 17, 1951, by special election to fill the vacancy caused by the death of her husband, John Kee; reelected to the six succeeding Congresses, and served from July 17, 1951 to January 3, 1965; was not a candidate for reelection in 1964 to the Eighty-ninth Congress; resided in Bluefield, W.Va., where she died on February 15, 1975; interment in Monte Vista Park Cemetery.

**Bibliography:** Hardin, William H. "Elizabeth Kee: West Virginia's First Woman in Congress." *West Virginia History* 45 (1984): 109-124.

**KEEFE, Frank Bateman,** a Representative from Wisconsin, born in Winneconne, Winnebago County, Wis., September 23, 1887; attended the public schools; was graduated from Oshkosh (Wis.) State Normal School in 1906 and from the law department of the University of Michigan at Ann Arbor in 1910; teacher in the schools at Viroqua, Vernon County, Wis., in 1906 and 1907; was admitted to the bar in 1910 and commenced practice in Oshkosh, Wis.; prosecuting attorney of Winnebago County, Wis., 1922-1928; vice president and director of an Oshkosh bank; elected as a Republican to the Seventy-sixth and to the five succeeding Congresses (January 3, 1939-January 3, 1951); was not a candidate for renomination in 1950; resumed the practice of law; died in Neenah, Wis., February 5, 1952; interment in Lakeview Memorial Park, Oshkosh, Wis.

**KEENEY, Russell Watson,** a Representative from Illinois; born in Pittsfield, Pike County, Ill., December 29, 1897; attended grade and high schools in Naperville, Du Page County, Ill.; graduated from De Paul University, Chicago, Ill., in 1919 and in 1921; was admitted to the bar in 1919 and commenced the practice of law in Naperville, Ill.; in 1920 became justice of the peace of Lisle Township and in 1924 town clerk; assistant State's attorney until 1935; State's attorney of Du Page County, 1936-1939; county judge of Du Page County, 1940-1952; circuit judge of the sixteenth judicial district of Illinois, 1953-1956; elected as a Republican to the Eighty-fifth Congress and served from January 3, 1957, until his death in Bethesda, Md., January 11, 1958; interment in Naperville (Ill.) Protestant Cemetery.

**KEESE, Richard,** a Representative from New York; born in Peru (now Ausable) Township, Clinton County, N.Y., on November 23, 1794; attended the common schools and Keeseville Academy; engaged in agricultural pursuits; elected to the Twentieth Congress (March 4, 1827-March 3, 1829); engaged in auctioneering; judge of the Clinton County court of common pleas in 1835 and 1836; died in Keeseville, Ausable Township, Clinton County, N.Y., February 7, 1883; interment in Evergreen Cemetery.

**KEFAUVER, Carey Estes,** a Representative and a Senator from Tennessee; born on a farm near Madisonville, Monroe County, Tenn., July 26, 1903; attended the public schools; B.A., University of Tennessee, Knoxville, 1924; LL.B., Yale University School of Law, New Haven, Conn., 1927; was admitted to the Tennessee bar in 1926 and commenced practice in Chattanooga, Tenn., in 1927; unsuccessful candidate for the Tennessee State senate in 1938; Tennessee State commissioner of finance and taxation, January 1939 to April 1939; elected as a Democrat to the Seventy-sixth Congress to fill the vacancy caused by the death of Sam D. McReynolds; reelected to the Seventy-seventh and to the three succeeding Congresses and served from September 13, 1939, to January 3, 1949; did not seek renomination in 1948 to the House of Representatives, but was elected to the United States Senate; reelected in 1954 and again in 1960, and served from January 3, 1949, until his death in the naval hospital at Bethesda, Md., August 10, 1963; chairman, Special Committee on Organized Crime in Interstate Commerce (Eighty-first and Eighty-second Congresses), widely known as the "Kefauver Committee"; unsuccessful candidate for the Democratic presidential nomination in 1952 and 1956; unsuccessful Democratic nominee for Vice President of the United States in 1956 on the ticket with Adlai E. Stevenson; interment in the family cemetery, Madisonville, Tenn.

**Bibliography:** *DAB*; Fontenay, Charles L. *Estes Kefauver: A Biography*. Knoxville: University of Tennessee Press, 1980; Moore, William Howard. *The Kefauver Committee and the Politics of Crime, 1950-1952*. Columbia: University of Missouri Press, 1974.

**KEHOE, James Nicholas,** a Representative from Kentucky; born in Maysville, Mason County, Ky., July 15, 1862; attended public and private schools; engaged in the printing business until 1884; studied law in Louisville, Ky.; was admitted to the bar November 1, 1888, and engaged in practice in Maysville; served as precinct, county, and district chairman of the Democratic executive committee; city attorney of Maysville; master in chancery of the Mason County Circuit Court; elected as a Democrat to the Fifty-seventh and Fifty-eighth Congresses (March 4, 1901-March 3, 1905); unsuccessful candidate for reelection in 1904 to the Fifty-ninth Congress; delegate to the Democratic National Convention in 1912; engaged in banking; vice president of the Ohio Valley Improvement Association and of the Burley Tobacco Growers' Cooperation Association; president of the Kentucky Bankers' Association; died in Cincinnati, Ohio, June 16, 1945; interment in Maysville Cemetery, Maysville, Ky.

**KEHOE, James Walter,** a Representative from Florida; born in Eufaula, Barbour County, Ala., April 25, 1870; attended the common schools; moved to Florida in 1883; studied law; was admitted to the bar in 1889 and, being a minor, was authorized by a special act of the State legislature to commence practice in Milton, Fla.; member of the State house of representatives in 1900 but resigned before the legislature convened; member of the Democratic congressional executive committee; State's attorney for the first judicial circuit of Florida 1900-1909; elected as a Democrat to the Sixty-fifth Congress (March 4, 1917-March 3, 1919); unsuccessful candidate for reelection to the Sixty-sixth Congress in 1918; again State's attorney from June 1925 until March 1926, when he resigned; resumed the practice of law in Miami, Fla.; died in Coral Gables, Fla., on August 20, 1938; interment in Graceland Park Cemetery, Miami, Fla.

**KEHR, Edward Charles,** a Representative from Missouri; born in St. Louis, Mo., November 5, 1837; pursued an academic course; studied law; was admitted to the bar in 1858 and commenced practice in St. Louis; elected as a Democrat to the Forty-fourth Congress (March 4, 1875-March 3, 1877); unsuccessful candidate for reelection in 1878 to the Forty-fifth Congress; engaged in the practice of law in St. Louis, Mo., until his death in that city on April 20, 1918; the remains were cremated and the ashes deposited in the columbarium of the Missouri Crematory.

**KEIFER, Joseph Warren,** a Representative from Ohio; born near Springfield, Bethel Township, Clark County, Ohio, January 30, 1836; attended the common schools and Antioch College, Yellow Springs, Ohio; studied law; was admitted to the bar and began practice in Springfield, Ohio, January 12, 1858; enlisted in the Union Army on April 19, 1861; commissioned major in the Third Ohio Volunteer Infantry April 27, 1861; lieutenant colonel February 12, 1862; colonel of the One Hundred and Tenth Ohio Volunteer Infantry September 30, 1862; brevetted brigadier general of Volunteers October 19, 1864; promoted to major general April 9, 1865; mustered out June 27, 1865; resumed the practice of law in July 1865; member of the State senate in 1868 and 1869; commander of the Ohio Department of the Grand Army of the Republic in 1871 and 1872; trustee of Antioch College; delegate to the Republican National Convention in 1876; elected as a Republican to the Forty-fifth and to the three succeeding Congresses (March 4, 1877-March 3, 1885); Speaker of the House of Representatives (Forty-seventh Congress); chairman, Committee on Rules (Forty-seventh Congress); unsuccessful candidate for renomination in 1884; was a major general of Volunteers in the Spanish-American War from June 9, 1898, to May 12, 1899; first commander in chief of the Spanish War Veterans in 1900 and 1901; elected to the

Fifty-ninth, Sixtieth, and Sixty-first Congresses (March 4, 1905-March 3, 1911); unsuccessful candidate for reelection in 1910 to the Sixty-second Congress; resumed his law practice; president of the Lagonda National Bank of Springfield, Ohio, for more than fifty years; died in Springfield, Ohio, April 22, 1932; interment in Ferncliff Cemetery.

**Bibliography:** *DAB*.

**KEIGHTLEY, Edwin William,** a Representative from Michigan; born on a farm near Scott, Lagrange County, Ind., August 7, 1843; attended the common schools, Lagrange Academy, and Valparaiso Collegiate Institute; was graduated from the law department of the University of Michigan at Ann Arbor in 1865; was admitted to the bar in 1865 and commenced practice at White Pigeon, St. Joseph County, Mich.; prosecuting attorney of St. Joseph County in 1873 and 1874; appointed and subsequently elected judge of the fifteenth judicial circuit of Michigan in 1876 and served until 1877, having been elected to Congress; elected as a Republican to the Forty-fifth Congress (March 4, 1877-March 3, 1879); appointed by President Hayes Third Auditor of the United States Treasury Department and served from April 30, 1879, to April 30, 1885, when he resigned; resumed the practice of his profession in Chicago; moved to Constantine, Mich., in 1899 and engaged in agricultural pursuits; died there May 4, 1926; interment in Constantine Cemetery.

**KEIM, George May** (uncle of William High Keim), a Representative from Pennsylvania; born in Reading, Pa., March 23, 1805; pursued classical studies; attended Princeton College; studied law; was admitted to the bar in 1826 and commenced practice in Reading; major general of militia; delegate to the Pennsylvania constitutional convention of 1837 and 1838; elected as a Democrat to the Twenty-fifth Congress to fill the vacancy caused by the resignation of Henry A.P. Muhlenberg; reelected to the Twenty-sixth and Twenty-seventh Congresses and served from March 17, 1838, to March 3, 1843; chairman, Committee on Militia (Twenty-sixth and Twenty-seventh Congresses); appointed by President John Tyler United States marshal for the eastern district of Pennsylvania December 18, 1843; reappointed by President James K. Polk on January 3, 1848, and served until 1850; mayor of Reading in 1852; presidential elector on the Democratic ticket of Stephen A. Douglas and Herschel V. Johnson in 1860; died in Reading, Pa., June 10, 1861; interment in Charles Evans Cemetery.

**KEIM, William High** (nephew of George May Keim), a Representative from Pennsylvania; born near Reading, Pa., on June 13, 1813; attended Mount Airy Military School and attained the rank of major general of militia; mayor of Reading in 1848; elected as a Republican to the Thirty-fifth Congress to fill the vacancy caused by the resignation of J. Glancy Jones and served from December 7, 1858, to March 3, 1859; was not a candidate for renomination in 1858 to the Thirty-sixth Congress; surveyor general of Pennsylvania 1860-1862; during the Civil War enlisted in the Union Army and was commissioned a major general of Pennsylvania Volunteers on April 20, 1861; honorably mustered out on July 21, 1861; commissioned brigadier general of Volunteers December 20, 1861; died in the military service at Harrisburg, Pa., May 18, 1862; interment in Charles Evans Cemetery, Reading, Berks County, Pa.

**KEISTER, Abraham Lincoln,** a Representative from Pennsylvania; born in Upper Tyrone Township, Fayette County, Pa., near the present borough of Scottdale, Westmoreland County, Pa., September 10, 1852; attended the public schools; was graduated from Otterbein University, Westerville, Ohio, in 1874; studied law; was admitted to the bar by the supreme court of Ohio in 1878 and commenced practice in Columbus, Ohio; moved to Fayette County, Pa., in 1882; engaged in the manufacture of coke; organized the First National Bank of Scottdale, Pa., in 1889 and served continuously as its president for twenty-eight years; organized the

Scottdale Savings & Trust Co. in 1901, with which he was connected until the time of his death; member of the Scottdale Board of Education for more than twenty years; was elected as a Republican to the Sixty-third and Sixty-fourth Congresses (March 4, 1913-March 3, 1917); unsuccessful candidate for renomination in 1916; resumed his former business pursuits; died at his home in Scottdale, Westmoreland County, Pa., on May 26, 1917; interment in Scottdale Cemetery.

**KEITH, Hastings,** a Representative from Massachusetts; born in Brockton, Plymouth County, Mass., November 22, 1915; graduated from Brockton High School and the Deerfield Academy; B.S., University of Vermont, Burlington, 1938; engaged in graduate work at Harvard University in 1938; member of the faculty of the Boston University Evening College of Commerce in 1948 and 1949; in 1933 was a student in the Citizens Military Training Camps; served as battery officer in Massachusetts National Guard; during the Second World War served in the United States Army with eighteen months overseas service in Europe; graduate of the Command and General Staff School; colonel in the Army Reserve; salesman, and Chartered Life Underwriter (C.L.U.), District manger for the Equitable Life Insurance Company in Boston, Mass., 1946-1952; member of the Massachusetts senate, 1953-1956; partner in Roger Keith and Sons General Insurance, Brockton, Mass., 1946-1994; unsuccessful candidate for nomination in 1956 to the Eighty-fifth Congress; elected as a Republican to the Eighty-sixth and to the six succeeding Congresses (January 3, 1959-January 3, 1973); was not a candidate for reelection in 1972 to the Ninety-third Congress; is a resident of Falmouth, Mass., and Washington, D.C.

**KEITT, Laurence Massillon,** a Representative from South Carolina; born in Orangeburg District, S.C., October 4, 1824; pursued classical studies and was graduated from South Carolina College (now the University of South Carolina) at Columbia in 1843; studied law; was admitted to the bar in 1845 and commenced practice in Orangeburg; member of the state house of representatives, 1848-1853; elected as a Democrat to the Thirty-third and Thirty-fourth Congresses and served from March 4, 1853, to July 16, 1856, when he resigned after the Thirty-fourth Congress censured him on July 15, 1856, for his role in the assault made upon Senator Charles Sumner on May 22, 1856; again elected to the Thirty-fourth Congress to fill the vacancy caused by his own resignation; reelected to the Thirty-fifth and Thirty-sixth Congresses and served from August 6, 1856, until his retirement in December 1860; chairman, Committee on Public Buildings and Grounds (Thirty-fifth Congress); delegate to the secession convention of South Carolina; member of the Provisional Congress of the Confederacy in Montgomery, Ala., in February 1861 and in Richmond, Va., in July 1861; raised the Twentieth South Carolina Regiment of Volunteers and was commissioned its colonel on January 11, 1862; subsequently promoted to the rank of brigadier general; wounded in the Battle of Cold Harbor, near Richmond, Va., and died as a result of his wounds the following day, June 4, 1864; interment in the family cemetery, near St. Matthews, S.C.

Bibliography: *DAB*; Merchant, John H., Jr. "Laurence M. Keitt: South Carolina Fire Eater." Ph.D. dissertation, University of Virginia, 1976.

**KELIHER, John Austin,** a Representative from Massachusetts; born in Boston, Mass., November 6, 1866; attended the public schools; engaged in the real estate business in Boston, Mass.; member of the Massachusetts house of representatives in 1896 and 1897; served in the Massachusetts senate in 1899 and 1900; elected as a Democrat to the Fifty-eighth and to the three succeeding Congresses (March 4, 1903-March 3, 1911); unsuccessful candidate for reelection in 1910 to the Sixty-second Congress; chairman of the Massachusetts Statehouse Building Commission in 1915 and 1916; member of the Massachusetts constitutional convention 1917-1919;

elected sheriff of Suffolk County in 1917; reelected in 1920, 1926, and 1932, and served in that capacity until his death at Boston, Mass., on September 20, 1938; interment in Mount Calvary Cemetery, West Roxbury, Mass.

**KELLER, Kent Ellsworth,** a Representative from Illinois; born on a farm near Campbell Hill, Jackson County, Ill., June 4, 1867; attended the public schools in Ava, Ill.; was graduated from Southern Illinois Normal University at Carbondale in 1890; engaged as an editor and in the newspaper business in 1890 and 1891; taught school in Ava Township, Ill., in 1893 and 1894, and at Duckwater, Nye County, Nev., in 1884 and 1885; founded the Ava Community High School in 1889 and 1890; attended Heidelberg University, Germany, in 1891 and 1892; was graduated from St. Louis (Mo.) Law School in 1896; was admitted to the bar the same year and commenced practice in Ava, Ill.; went to Mexico in 1899, where he later engaged in mining; returned to Ava, Ill., in 1912 and engaged in literary work; served in the State senate 1913-1917; delegate to the Democratic National Convention of 1916; elected as a Democrat to the Seventy-second and to the four succeeding Congresses (March 4, 1931-January 3, 1941); unsuccessful candidate for reelection in 1940 to the Seventy-seventh Congress, for election in 1942 to the Seventy-eighth Congress, and for election in 1944 to the Seventy-ninth Congress; engaged in literary work and lecturing; served as special adviser to the United States Ambassador at Mexico City from June 1945 to August 1946; unsuccessful candidate for election in 1948 to the Eighty-first Congress and in 1950 to the Eighty-second Congress; died in Ava, Ill., September 3, 1954; interment in Ava Evergreen Cemetery.

Bibliography: Weiss, Stuart L. "Kent Keller, The Liberal Bloc, and the New Deal." *Journal of the Illinois State Historical Society* 68 (April 1975): 143-58.

**KELLER, Oscar Edward,** a Representative from Minnesota; born in Helenville, Jefferson County, Wis., July 30, 1878; attended the public schools and the University of Wisconsin at Madison; moved to Minnesota in 1901 and settled in St. Paul; employed as a billing clerk and later engaged in mercantile pursuits; member of the city council of St. Paul 1910-1914; city commissioner 1914-1919; commissioner of public utilities from 1914 until July 1, 1919; elected as an Independent Republican to the Sixty-sixth Congress to fill the vacancy caused by the death of Carl C. Van Dyke; reelected as a Republican to the Sixty-seventh, Sixty-eighth, and Sixty-ninth Congresses and served from July 1, 1919, to March 3, 1927; chairman, Committee on Railways and Canals (Sixty-eighth and Sixty-ninth Congresses); unsuccessful candidate for renomination in 1926; engaged in the real estate business; died in St. Paul, Minn., November 21, 1927; interment in Elmhurst Cemetery.

**KELLEY, Augustine Bernard,** a Representative from Pennsylvania; born in New Baltimore, Somerset County, Pa., July 9, 1883; attended a parochial school, Greensburg (Pa.) High School, and the United States Military Academy, West Point, N.Y., in 1904 and 1905; studied mining engineering with International Correspondence School 1907-1912; began business career in 1905 as clerk with the Pennsylvania Railroad Co., and later became superintendent of the H.C. Frick Coke Co., and was also associated with other coke and coal companies; member of the Greensburg (Pa.) Board of Education in 1935 and 1936; elected as a Democrat to the Seventy-seventh and to the eight succeeding Congresses and served from January 3, 1941, until his death in Bethesda, Md., November 20, 1957; chairman, Committee on Invalid Pensions (Seventy-ninth Congress); interment in Arlington National Cemetery, Va.

**KELLEY, Harrison,** a Representative from Kansas; born in Montgomery Township, Wood County, Ohio, May 12, 1836; attended the common schools; moved to Coffey County, Kans., in March 1858; during the Civil War enlisted in the Fifth Regiment, Kansas Volunteer Cavalry, and served through all grades to captain; captain of Company B, Fifth Cavalry, for over two years; returned to Burlington, Kans., in 1865; brigadier general of Kansas State Militia in 1865; member of the State house of representatives 1868-1870; director of the State penitentiary 1868-1873; receiver of the United States land office at Topeka in 1877 and 1878; served in the State senate 1880-1884; deputy collector of internal revenue; chairman of the livestock sanitary commission of the State; treasurer of the State board of charities in 1889; elected as a Republican to the Fifty-first Congress to fill the vacancy caused by the resignation of Thomas Ryan and served from December 2, 1889, to March 3, 1891; died in Burlington, Coffey County, Kans., July 24, 1897; interment in Bowman Cemetery, Ottumwa, near Burlington, Kans.

**KELLEY, John Edward,** a Representative from South Dakota; born near Portage City, Columbia County, Wis., March 27, 1853; attended the public schools; moved to Moody County, Dak. (now South Dakota), in 1878 and engaged in agricultural pursuits; engaged in the newspaper business at Flandreau; member of the State house of representatives in 1890 and 1891; unsuccessful Populist candidate for election to the Fifty-third and Fifty-fourth Congresses; elected as a Populist to the Fifty-fifth Congress (March 4, 1897-March 3, 1899); unsuccessful candidate for reelection in 1898; resumed agricultural pursuits near Coleman, S.Dak.; delegate to the Democratic National Convention in 1912; register of the United States land office at Pierre 1915-1918; moved to St. Paul, Minn., and became editor of the Cooperative Herald; died in Minneapolis, Minn., August 5, 1941; interment in St. Mary's Cemetery.

**KELLEY, Patrick Henry,** a Representative from Michigan; born near Dowagiac, Silver Creek Township, Cass County, Mich., October 7, 1867; moved to Berrien County with his parents, who settled in Watervliet in 1875; attended the district and village schools; was graduated from the Valparaiso (Ind.) Normal School in 1887; taught school at Fair Plain for several years; attended the Michigan Normal College at Ypsilanti and was graduated from the law department of the University of Michigan at Ann Arbor in 1900; was admitted to the bar the same year and commenced practice in Lansing, Mich.; member of the State board of education 1901-1905; State superintendent of public instruction 1905-1907; lieutenant governor of Michigan 1907-1911; elected as a Republican to the Sixty-third and to the four succeeding Congresses (March 4, 1913-March 3, 1923); did not seek renomination in 1922 to the House of Representatives, but was an unsuccessful candidate for nomination to the United States Senate; resumed the practice of law in Lansing, Mich.; died while on a visit to Washington, D.C., September 11, 1925; interment in Mount Hope Cemetery, Lansing, Mich.

**KELLEY, William Darrah,** a Representative from Pennsylvania; born in Philadelphia, Pa., April 12, 1814; pursued classical studies; apprentice in a jewelry establishment 1828-1835; moved to Boston, Mass, in 1835 and was engaged as a journeyman jeweler; returned to Philadelphia in 1840; studied law; was admitted to the bar in 1841 and practiced in Philadelphia, Pa.; deputy prosecuting attorney for the city and county of Philadelphia in 1845 and 1846; judge of the court of common pleas for Philadelphia 1846-1856; unsuccessful candidate for election in 1856 to the Thirty-fifth Congress; delegate to the Republican National Convention in 1860; elected as a Republican to the Thirty-seventh and to the fourteen succeeding Congresses and served from March 4, 1861, until his death in Washington, D.C., January 9, 1890; chairman, Committee on Coinage, Weights, and Measures (Fortieth, Forty-first, and Forty-second Congresses), Committee on Ways and Means (Forty-seventh Congress), Committee on Manufactures (Fifty-first Congress); interment in Laurel Hill Cemetery, Philadelphia, Pa.

**Bibliography:** *DAB*; Brown, Ira V. "William D. Kelley and Radical Reconstruction." *Pennsylvania Magazine of History and Biography* 85 (July 1961): 316-29; Nicklas, Floyd William. "William Kelley: The Congressional Years, 1861-1890." Ph.D. dissertation, Northern Illinois University, 1983.

**KELLOGG, Charles,** a Representative from New York; born in Sheffield, Berkshire County, Mass., October 3, 1773; attended the common schools; moved to Cayuga County, N.Y., in 1798 and founded Kelloggsville; engaged in mercantile pursuits; also operated a gristmill at New Hope; studied law; was admitted to the bar and practiced; county judge; member of the State assembly 1808-1810; justice of the peace for Sempronius Township; appointed postmaster of Kelloggsville on July 1, 1814, and served until September 6, 1825; again a member of the State assembly 1820-1822; elected to the Nineteenth Congress (March 4, 1825-March 3, 1827); engaged in agricultural pursuits; moved to Ann Arbor, Mich., in 1839; died in Ann Arbor, Mich., May 11, 1842; interment in Fairview Cemetery.

**KELLOGG, Francis William,** a Representative from Michigan and from Alabama; born in Worthington, Mass., May 30, 1810; attended the common schools; moved to Columbus, Ohio, in 1833; thence to Grand Rapids, Mich., in 1855 and engaged in the lumber business at Kelloggville, Kent County; member of the State house of representatives in 1857 and 1858; elected from Michigan as a Republican to the Thirty-sixth, Thirty-seventh, and Thirty-eighth Congresses (March 4, 1859-March 3, 1865); during the Civil War organized the Second, Third, and Sixth Regiments by authority of the War Department and was appointed colonel of the Third Regiment; appointed by President Andrew Johnson collector of internal revenue for the southern district of Alabama on April 30, 1866, and served until July 1868, residing in Mobile, Ala.; upon the readmission of Alabama to representation was elected as a Republican to the Fortieth Congress and served from July 22, 1868, to March 3, 1869; moved to New York City and later to Alliance, Stark County, Ohio, where he died January 13, 1879; interment in Fulton Street Cemetery, Grand Rapids, Mich.

**KELLOGG, Frank Billings,** a Senator from Minnesota; born in Potsdam, St. Lawrence County, N.Y., December 22, 1856; in 1865 moved with his parents to Minnesota; attended the public and rural schools; worked on the farm until 1875 and then studied law in Rochester, Minn.; admitted to the bar in 1877 and commenced practice in Rochester, Minn.; city attorney of Rochester, 1878-1881; Olmsted County attorney, 1882-1887; moved to St. Paul, Minn., in 1887 and resumed the practice of law; member of the Republican National Committee, 1904-1912; special counsel for the Government to prosecute antitrust suits; president of the American Bar Association, 1912-1913; elected as a Republican to the United States Senate, and served from March 4, 1917 to March 3, 1923; unsuccessful candidate for reelection in 1922; chairman, Committee on National Banks (Sixty-sixth Congress); delegate to the Fifth International Conference of American States, Santiago, Chile, 1923; appointed Ambassador to Great Britain on December 11, 1923 and served until February 1925, when he resigned; appointed Secretary of State in the Cabinet of President Calvin Coolidge on February 16, 1925 and served until March 28, 1929; co-author of the Kellogg-Briand Peace Pact signed in Paris by representatives of fifteen nations on August 27, 1928; resumed the practice of law in St. Paul, Minn.; associate judge of the Permanent Court for International Justice, 1930-1935; awarded the Nobel Peace Prize in 1930; died in St. Paul, Minn., December 21, 1937; interment in the Chapel of St. Joseph of Arimathea in Washington Cathedral, Washington, D.C.

**Bibliography:** *DAB*; Bryn-Jones, David. *Frank B. Kellogg, A Biography.* New York: G.P. Putnam's Sons, 1937; Ellis, Lewis Ethan. *Frank B. Kellogg and American Foreign Relations, 1925-1929.* New Brunswick, N.J.: Rutgers University Press, 1961.

**KELLOGG, Orlando,** a Representative from New York; born in Elizabethtown, Essex County, N.Y., June 18, 1809; pursued an academic course; engaged in the carpenter's trade in early youth; studied law; was admitted to the bar in 1838 and commenced practice in Elizabethtown; surrogate of Essex County 1840-1844; elected as a Whig to the Thirtieth Congress (March 4, 1847-March 3, 1849); was not a candidate for renomination in 1848 to the Thirty-first Congress; resumed the practice of his profession in Elizabethtown, N.Y.; delegate to the Republican National Convention of 1860; elected as a Republican to the Thirty-eighth and Thirty-ninth Congresses and served from March 4, 1863, until his death in Elizabethtown, N.Y., August 24, 1865; interment in Riverside Cemetery.

**KELLOGG, Stephen Wright,** a Representative from Connecticut; born in Shelburne, Mass., April 5, 1822; attended an academy at Shelburne Falls, Mass., and Amherst (Mass.) College; was graduated from Yale College in 1846; studied law; was admitted to the bar in 1848 and commenced practice in Naugatuck, Conn.; clerk in the State senate in 1851; member of the State senate in 1853; moved to Waterbury, Conn., in 1854; resumed the practice of law; judge of the New Haven County Court in 1854 and of the probate court 1854-1860; served in the State house of representatives in 1856; delegate to the Republican National Conventions of 1860, 1868 and 1876; served as colonel of the Second Regiment, Connecticut National Guard, 1863-1866; brigadier general of the regiment 1866-1870; city attorney of Waterbury, Conn., 1866-1869 and 1877-1883; elected as a Republican to the Forty-first, Forty-second, and Forty-third Congresses (March 4, 1869-March 3, 1875); chairman, Committee on Expenditures in the Department of the Navy (Forty-second Congress), Committee on Reform in the Civil Service (Forty-third Congress); unsuccessful candidate for election in 1874 to the Forty-fourth Congress and in 1876 to the Forty-fifth Congress; resumed the practice of his profession; died in Waterbury, New Haven County, Conn., on January 27, 1904; interment in Riverside Cemetery.

**KELLOGG, William,** a Representative from Illinois; born in Kelloggsville, Ashtabula County, Ohio, July 8, 1814; attended the public schools; studied law; was admitted to the bar and commenced practice in Canton, Fulton County, Ill.; member of the State house of representatives in 1849 and 1850; judge of the State circuit court 1850-1855; elected as a Republican to the Thirty-fifth, Thirty-sixth, and Thirty-seventh Congresses (March 4, 1857-March 3, 1863); moved to Peoria, Ill., in 1864; appointed by President Andrew Johnson chief justice of Nebraska Territory on December 20, 1865, and served until 1867; collector of internal revenue for the Peoria (Ill.) district 1867-1869; moved to Mississippi in 1869, having been appointed to a judgeship under the prevailing provisional government; upon the readmission of Mississippi to representation he was an unsuccessful candidate to the Forty-first Congress in 1869 and shortly afterward returned to Illinois; died in Peoria, Peoria County, Ill., on December 20, 1872; interment in Springdale Cemetery.

**KELLOGG, William Pitt,** a Senator and a Representative from Louisiana; born in Orwell, Addison County, Vt., December 8, 1830; attended Norwich University, Vermont; moved to Peoria, Ill., in 1848; taught school for several years, studying law in the meantime; was admitted to the bar in 1853 and commenced practice in Canton, Fulton County, Ill.; presidential elector on the Republican ticket in 1860; appointed by President Abraham Lincoln chief justice of the supreme court of the Territory of Nebraska in 1861; reappointed in 1865, but resigned upon the outbreak of the Civil War; returned to Illinois and joined the Illinois Volunteer Cavalry; resigned on account of ill health; appointed by President Lincoln collector of the port of New Orleans 1865-1868, when he resigned, having been elected Senator; upon the readmission of Louisiana to representation was elected as a Republican to the United States Senate and

served from July 9, 1868, until November 1, 1872, when he resigned, having been elected Governor; elected Governor of Louisiana in 1872 and served from January 13, 1873 to January 5, 1877; again elected to the United States Senate and served from March 4, 1877, to March 3, 1883; declined to be a candidate for reelection; chairman, Committee on Railroads (Forty-seventh Congress); elected to the Forty-eighth Congress (March 4, 1883-March 3, 1885); withdrew from active political life and lived in retirement in Washington, D.C., where he died on August 10, 1918; interment in Arlington National Cemetery, Va.

**Bibliography:** *DAB.*

**KELLY, Edna Flannery,** a Representative from New York; born , August 20, 1906, in East Hampton, Suffolk County, N.Y.; attended the public schools of East Hampton; B.A., Hunter College, New York City, 1928; elected a member of the executive committee of the Democratic Party of Kings County, N.Y., from the Eighteenth Assembly District in 1944; reelected in 1946 and again in 1948; appointed associate research director of the Democratic Party in the New York State Legislature in 1943; designated chief research director in 1944 and served in that capacity until elected to Congress; elected as a Democrat to the Eighty-first Congress to fill the vacancy caused by the death of Andrew L. Somers; reelected to the Eighty-second and to the eight succeeding Congresses, and served from November 8, 1949 to January 3, 1969; unsuccessful candidate for renomination in 1968 to the Ninety-first Congress; delegate to State conventions, 1944-1968; delegate to Democratic National Conventions from 1948 to 1968; Democratic national committeewoman, 1956-1968; is a resident of Alexandria, Va.

**KELLY, Edward Austin,** a Representative from Illinois; born in Chicago, Ill., April 3, 1892; attended Longfellow School and Lake High School; was graduated from Orr's Business College, Chicago, Ill., in 1911; played professional baseball 1912-1916; employed as an accountant with a steel corporation 1916-1920; served as a sergeant in Battery D of the Three Hundred and Thirty-second Field Artillery 1917-1919, with nine months' service overseas; engaged in the real estate and insurance brokerage business in 1920; elected as a Democrat to the Seventy-second and to the five succeeding Congresses (March 4, 1931-January 3, 1943); unsuccessful candidate for reelection in 1942 to the Seventy-eighth Congress; assistant to the chief justice of the municipal court of Chicago, Ill., 1943-1945; member of the Chicago Planning Committee 1944-1946; elected to the Seventy-ninth Congress (January 3, 1945-January 3, 1947); unsuccessful candidate for reelection in 1946 to the Eightieth Congress; returned to the real estate business; died in Chicago, Ill., August 30, 1969; interment in St. Mary's Cemetery.

**KELLY, George Bradshaw,** a Representative from New York; born in Waterloo, Seneca County, N.Y., December 12, 1900; attended parochial and high schools and the University of Rochester, Rochester, N.Y.; employed by a railway signal company 1915-1919; salesman for a candy company in 1920; production manager for a clothing manufacturer 1921-1933; member of the State assembly in 1933 and 1934; served in the State senate in 1935 and 1936; elected as a Democrat to the Seventy-fifth Congress (January 3, 1937-January 3, 1939); unsuccessful candidate for reelection in 1938 to the Seventy-sixth Congress and for election in 1940 to the Seventy-seventh Congress; regional director of the Wage-Hour Division of the United States Department of Labor for New York and Connecticut in 1939 and 1940; member of the State board of mediation in 1941 and 1942; manager of an industrial alcohol plant for war production during the Second World War; associated with a brewing company and also radio broadcasting companies; insurance broker; New York State assistant commissioner of labor; urban renewal consultant for Rochester, N.Y.; resided in Rochester, N.Y.; died in Lyon, France, June 26, 1971; interment in St. Mary's Cemetery, Waterloo, N.Y.

**KELLY, James,** a Representative from Pennsylvania; born in York County, Pa., July 17, 1760; pursued classical studies and was graduated from the University of Pennsylvania at Philadelphia in 1782; was a tutor at the University of Pennsylvania in 1782 and 1783; studied law; was admitted to the bar and practiced in Philadelphia 1785-1819; member of the Pennsylvania house of representatives in 1793, 1794, 1797, and 1798; elected as a Federalist to the Ninth and Tenth Congresses (March 4, 1805-March 3, 1809); resumed the practice of law in York, Pa., where he died on February 4, 1819.

**KELLY, James Kerr,** a Senator from Oregon; born in Centre County, Pa., February 16, 1819; attended the country schools and Milton and Lewisburg Academies; graduated from the College of New Jersey (now Princeton University) in 1839; studied law at Carlisle, Pa.; was admitted to the bar in 1842 and commenced practice in Lewistown, Mifflin County, Pa.; deputy attorney general for Mifflin County, Pa.; went to the California gold fields in 1849, and later, in 1851, to Oregon Territory and settled in Portland, where he engaged in the practice of law; one of three commissioners for the codification of the Territorial laws in 1852; member, Territorial legislature 1853-1857, and was twice its president; lieutenant colonel of the First Regiment, Oregon Mounted Volunteers, in the Yakima Indian War in 1855 and 1856; a member of the State constitutional convention in 1857; member, State senate 1860-1864; unsuccessful candidate for election in 1864 to the Thirty-ninth Congress; unsuccessful candidate for election in 1866 for Governor of Oregon; elected as a Democrat to the United States Senate and served from March 4, 1871, to March 3, 1877; was not a candidate for reelection; chief justice of the State supreme court 1878-1882; resumed the practice of law in Portland, Oreg.; moved to Washington, D.C., in 1890 and continued the practice of law until his death there on September 15, 1903; interment in Rock Creek Cemetery.

**KELLY, John,** a Representative from New York; born in New York City April 20, 1822; attended the common schools; apprenticed to the mason's trade and engaged in that business for himself in 1845; elected city alderman in 1854; elected as a Democrat to the Thirty-fourth and Thirty-fifth Congresses and served from March 4, 1855, to December 25, 1858, when he resigned; served as sheriff of the city and county of New York 1859-1862 and 1865-1867; was an unsuccessful candidate for mayor of New York City in 1868; appointed comptroller of New York in 1876 and served for three years; delegate to the Democratic National Conventions in 1864, 1868, 1872, 1876, 1880, and 1884; at the time of his death and for many years previous was head of Tammany Hall; died in New York City on June 1, 1886; interment in Old St. Patrick's Cathedral on Mott Street.

**KELLY, Melville Clyde,** a Representative from Pennsylvania; born in Bloomfield, Muskingum County, Ohio, August 4, 1883; attended the public schools, and Muskingum College, New Concord, Ohio; engaged in newspaper publishing at Braddock, Pa., in 1903 and established the Braddock Leader in 1904; in 1907 purchased the Daily News and the Evening Herald and consolidated them into the Daily News-Herald; member of the Pennsylvania house of representatives 1910-1913; elected as a Republican to the Sixty-third Congress (March 4, 1913-March 3, 1915); unsuccessful candidate in 1914 for reelection to the Sixty-fourth Congress; continued his newspaper work; elected as a Progressive to the Sixty-fifth and reelected as a Republican to the eight succeeding Congresses (March 4, 1917-January 3, 1935); unsuccessful candidate for reelection in 1934 to the Seventy-fourth Congress; resumed his former business pursuits; accidentally shot while cleaning a rifle and died in a hospital at Punxsutawney, Pa., on April 29, 1935; interment in Mahoning Union Cemetery, near Marchand, Pa.

**Bibliography:** Larner, John W., Jr. "Braddock's Congressman M. Clyde Kelly and Indian Policy Reform, 1919-1928." *Western Pennsylvania Historical Magazine* 66 (April 1983): 97-111.

**KELLY, Richard,** a Representative from Florida; born in Atlanta, Ga., July 31, 1924; attended the elementary schools of Crystal Springs, Fla.; graduated from Zephyrhills, Fla., high school in 1946; A.B., Colorado State College of Education, Greeley, 1949; attended the Vanderbilt College of Law, Nashville, Tenn., 1949; J.D., University of Florida College of Law, Gainesville, 1952; certificate of graduation, College of State Trial Judges, Reno, Nev., 1971; admitted to the Florida bar in 1952 and commenced practice in Zephyrhills; served in the United States Marine Corps, 1942-1946; city attorney, Zephyrhills, 1953; senior assistant United States Attorney, southern district of Florida, 1956-1959; circuit judge, sixth judicial circuit of Florida, 1960-1974; elected as a Republican to the Ninety-fourth and to the two succeeding Congresses (January 3, 1975-January 3, 1981); unsuccessful candidate for renomination in 1980 to the Ninety-seventh Congress; is a resident of Stevensville, Mont.

**KELLY, Sue W.,** a Representative from New York; born in Lima, Allen County, Ohio, September 26, 1936; attended Lima Central High School; B.A., Denison University, Granville, Ohio, 1958; M.A., Sarah Lawrence College, Bronxville, N.Y., 1988; biomedical researcher, Boston (Mass.) City Hospital, then at New England Institute for Medical Research; science and mathematics teacher, John Jay Junior High School, Cross River, N.Y., and Harvey School, Katonah, N.Y.; political assistant to Representative Hamilton Fish of New York; campaign manager, Jon Fossel for Assembly; businesswoman in Somers, N.Y.; intern, Ruth Taylor Home, Grasslands Complex, N.Y.; patient advocate, emergency room, St. Luke's Hospital, N.Y.; adjunct professor of patient advocacy, Graduate Program in Health Advocacy, Sarah Lawrence College; certified New York ombudsman for nursing homes; rape crisis counselor at St. Luke's Hospital, N.Y.; member, New York Republican family committee; elected as a Republican to the One Hundred Fourth Congress (January 3, 1995-January 3, 1997); is a resident of Katonah, N.Y.

**KELLY, William,** a Senator from Alabama; born September 22, 1786, probably in South Carolina; received a classical education; studied law; was admitted to the bar; moved to Tennessee where he practiced law and became a judge; moved to Alabama in 1818 and commenced practice in Huntsville; elected to the United States Senate to fill the vacancy caused by the resignation of John W. Walker and served from December 12, 1822, to March 3, 1825; member, State house of representatives 1825, 1827, serving as speaker in 1825; moved to New Orleans, La., in 1830 and died there on August 24, 1834.

**KELSEY, William Henry,** a Representative from New York; born in Smyrna, Chenango County, N.Y., October 2, 1812; attended the common schools; studied law; was admitted to the bar in 1843 and commenced practice in Geneseo, N.Y.; surrogate of Livingston County 1840-1844; district attorney of Livingston County 1850-1853; elected as a Whig to the Thirty-fourth Congress and reelected as a Republican to the Thirty-fifth Congress (March 4, 1855-March 3, 1859); chairman, Committee on Engraving (Thirty-fourth Congress); was not a candidate for renomination in 1858 to the Thirty-sixth Congress; resumed the practice of his profession; elected as a Republican to the Fortieth and Forty-first Congresses (March 4, 1867-March 3, 1871); voluntarily retired from political life and resumed the practice of law in Geneseo, N.Y., where he died on April 20, 1879; interment in Temple Hill Cemetery.

**KELSO, John Russell,** a Representative from Missouri; born near Columbus, Franklin County, Ohio, March 23, 1831; received a classical training and was graduated from Pleasant Ridge College, Missouri, in June 1859; during the Civil War served in the Union

Army as a member of the Twenty-fourth Missouri Infantry, the Fourteenth Missouri Cavalry, and the Eighth Missouri Cavalry, and was captain of Company M; elected as an Independent Radical to the Thirty-ninth Congress (March 4, 1865-March 3, 1867); was not a candidate for renomination in 1866 to the Fortieth Congress; principal of Kelso Academy, Springfield, Mo., 1867-1869; moved to Modesto, Calif., in 1872 and to Longmont, Boulder County, Colo., in July 1885; author and lecturer; died in Longmont, Colo., January 26, 1891; interment on his estate near Longmont; subsequently the remains were cremated and the ashes scattered.

**KEM, James Preston,** a Senator from Missouri; born in Macon, Mo., April 2, 1890; attended Blees Military Academy; graduated from the University of Missouri at Columbia in 1910, and from Harvard Law School in 1913; was admitted to the bar in 1913 and commenced practice in Kansas City, Mo.; during the First World War served in the infantry 1917-1919; resumed the general practice of law in Kansas City, Mo.; elected as a Republican to the United States Senate in 1946 and served from January 3, 1947, to January 3, 1953; was unsuccessful for reelection in 1952; resumed the practice of law in Washington, D.C., until retirement in 1961; resided at "Sherwood," The Plains, Va., and engaged in the breeding of Angus cattle; died in Charlottesville, Va., February 24, 1965; interment in Middleburg Memorial Cemetery, Middleburg, Va.

**Bibliography:** Atwell, Mary W. "A Conservative Response to the Cold War: James P. Kem and Foreign Aid." *Capitol Studies* 4 (Fall 1976): 53-66.

**KEM, Omer Madison,** a Representative from Nebraska; born in Hagerstown, Wayne County, Ind., on November 13, 1855; attended the public schools; moved to Custer County, Nebr., in 1882, thence to Broken Bow in 1890 and engaged in agricultural pursuits; deputy treasurer of Custer County in 1890 and 1891; elected as a Populist to the Fifty-second, Fifty-third, and Fifty-fourth Congresses (March 4, 1891-March 3, 1897); was not a candidate for renomination in 1896; engaged in fruit growing and cattle raising near Montrose, Colo.; member of the Colorado State house of representatives in 1907; moved to Cottage Grove, Oreg., in 1908 and became interested in electric light and power enterprises; retired in 1922; died in Cottage Grove, Oreg., February 13, 1942; remains were cremated and the ashes scattered.

**KEMBLE, Gouverneur,** a Representative from New York; born in New York City January 25, 1786; completed preparatory studies and was graduated from Columbia College, New York City, in 1803; engaged in mercantile pursuits; visited Spain in 1816 and while there studied the process of casting cannon; established a cannon foundry at Cold Spring, N.Y.; sent to the Mediterranean as a naval agent during the war with Tripoli; elected as a Democrat to the Twenty-fifth and Twenty-sixth Congresses (March 4, 1837-March 3, 1841); declined the nomination for reelection in 1840; delegate to the State constitutional convention in 1846; delegate to the Democratic National conventions in 1844 and 1860; interested in the promotion of the Hudson River and Panama Railroads; died at Cold Spring, Putnam County, N.Y., September 16, 1875; interment in Cold Spring Cemetery.

**Bibliography:** *DAB.*

**KEMP, Bolivar Edwards,** a Representative from Louisiana; born on the Kemp homestead near Amite, St. Helena Parish, La., December 28, 1871; was privately tutored and also attended the public schools of Amite, La., and the University of Louisiana at Baton Rouge; was graduated in law from Tulane University at New Orleans in 1897; was admitted to the bar the same year and commenced practice at Amite, La.; was active in the development of agricultural and trucking industries and also interested in banking; member of the board of supervisors, University of Louisiana, beginning in 1910; elected as a Democrat to the Sixty-ninth and to

the four succeeding Congresses, and served from March 4, 1925 until his death in Amite, La., on June 19, 1933; chairman, Committee on Territories (Seventy-third Congress); interment in Amite Cemetery.

**KEMP, Jack French,** a Representative from New York; born in Los Angeles, Los Angeles County, Calif., July 13, 1935; attended the public schools in Los Angeles; B.A., Occidental College, Los Angeles, 1957; graduate studies, political science and education; served in the United States Army Reserve, 1958-1962 (active duty, 1958); professional football player, National and American Football Leagues, 1957-1970; co-founder of the American Football League Players Association and president of the Association, 1956-1970; special assistant to Governor Ronald Reagan of California, 1967; special assistant to chairman Rogers C.B. Morton of the Republican National Committee, 1969; elected as a Republican to the Ninety-first and to the nine succeeding Congresses (January 3, 1969-January 3, 1989); was not a candidate for renomination in 1988 to the One Hundred First Congress, but was an unsuccessful candidate for the Republican presidential nomination; Secretary of Housing and Urban Development in the Cabinet of President George Bush, serving from February 13, 1989 to January 20, 1993; chair, National Commission on Economic Growth and Tax Reform, 1995-1996; Republican vice presidential nominee in 1996; is a resident of Bethesda, Md.

**Bibliography:** Kemp, Jack. *An American Renaissance: A Strategy for the 1980's.* New York: Harper and Row, 1979.

**KEMPSHALL, Thomas,** a Representative from New York; born in England about 1796; attended the common schools; immigrated to the United States with his father, who settled in Pittsford, N.Y., in 1806; moved to Rochester, N.Y., in 1813; employed as a carpenter; engaged in mercantile pursuits and later became engaged in milling; member of the board of aldermen in 1834 and again in 1844; mayor of Rochester, N.Y., in 1837; elected as a Whig to the Twenty-sixth Congress (March 4, 1839-March 3, 1841); resumed milling; unsuccessful candidate for mayor in 1852; died in Rochester, N.Y., January 14, 1865; interment in Mount Hope Cemetery.

**KEMPTHORNE, Dirk,** a Senator from Idaho; born in San Diego, Calif., October 29, 1951; B.A., University of Idaho, 1975; managed the campaign of Phil Batt for Governor of Idaho in 1982; executive director, Idaho State Home Builders Association, 1978-1981; mayor of Boise, Idaho, 1986-1992; elected as a Republican to the United States Senate in 1992 for the term ending January 3, 1999; is a resident of Boise, Idaho.

**KENAN, Thomas,** a Representative from North Carolina; born in Kenansville, Duplin County, N.C., February 26, 1771; educated by private tutors; member of the State house of commons 1799-1803; served in the State senate in 1804; elected as a Republican to the Ninth, Tenth, and Eleventh Congresses (March 4, 1805-March 3, 1811); was not a candidate for renomination; moved to Selma, Dallas County, Ala., in 1833 and engaged in planting; member of the Alabama house of representatives for several years; died near Selma, Ala., October 22, 1843; interment in Valley Creek Cemetery, near Selma.

**KENDALL, Charles West,** a Representative from Nevada; born in Searsmont, Waldo County, Maine, April 22, 1828; attended Phillips Academy, Andover, Mass., and Yale College; moved to California in 1849 and engaged in mining; editor and proprietor of the San Jose Tribune 1855-1859; studied law; was admitted to the bar in 1859 and commenced practice in Sacramento, Calif.; member of the State assembly in 1861 and 1862; moved to Hamilton, Nev., in 1862 and resumed the practice of law; elected as a Democrat to the Forty-second and Forty-third Congresses (March 4, 1871-March 3, 1875); declined to be a candidate for renomination in 1874; moved to Denver, Colo., and practiced law; assistant librarian in the

Interstate Commerce Commission, Washington, D.C., from 1892 until his death; died in Mount Rainier, Md., June 25, 1914; interment in Congressional Cemetery, Washington, D.C.

**KENDALL, Elva Roscoe,** a Representative from Kentucky; born near Carlisle, Nicholas County, Ky., February 14, 1893; attended the public schools, the Young Men's Christian Association School of Accountancy at New York City, and National University at Washington, D.C.; engaged as a public accountant and tax consultant; also interested in agricultural pursuits; during the First World War served in the personnel office of the Sixty-first Division; employed as a field auditor for the United States Treasury Department 1922-1927; elected as a Republican to the Seventy-first Congress (March 4, 1929-March 3, 1931); unsuccessful candidate for reelection in 1930 to the Seventy-second Congress; resumed agricultural pursuits and his profession as a public accountant; also engaged in the real estate business; was a resident of Carlisle, Ky., until his death on January 29, 1968.

**KENDALL, John Wilkerson** (father of Joseph Morgan Kendall), a Representative from Kentucky; born in Morgan County, Ky., June 26, 1834; attended the common schools and Owingsville Academy; studied law; was admitted to the bar in 1854 and commenced practice in West Liberty, Ky.; prosecuting attorney of Morgan County 1854-1858; during the Civil War served as first lieutenant and adjutant of the Tenth Kentucky Confederate Cavalry; member of the State house of representatives 1867-1871; Commonwealth attorney for the thirteenth judicial district 1872-1878; elected as a Democrat to the Fifty-second Congress and served from March 4, 1891, until his death in Washington, D.C., on March 7, 1892; interment in Barber Cemetery, West Liberty, Morgan County, Ky.

**KENDALL, Jonas** (father of Joseph Gowing Kendall), a Representative from Massachusetts; born in Leominster, Worcester County, Mass., October 27, 1757; pursued an academic course; engaged in the manufacture of paper in Leominster, Mass., in 1796; member of the Massachusetts house of representatives in 1800, 1801, 1803-1807, and 1821; served in the Massachusetts senate 1808-1811; member of the school board in 1803, 1811, and 1814; member of the executive council in 1822; presidential elector on the Federalist ticket in 1816; elected to the Sixteenth Congress (March 4, 1819-March 3, 1821); unsuccessful candidate for reelection in 1820 to the Seventeenth Congress; resumed the manufacture of paper; died in Leominster, Mass., October 22, 1844; interment in Evergreen Cemetery.

**KENDALL, Joseph Gowing** (son of Jonas Kendall), a Representative from Massachusetts; born in Leominster, Worcester County, Mass., October 27, 1788; pursued classical studies; was graduated from Harvard University in 1810 and taught there from 1812 to 1817; studied law; was admitted to the bar in 1818 and practiced in Leominster; elected to the Massachusetts senate in 1824 and served four years; elected to the Twenty-first and Twenty-second Congresses (March 4, 1829-March 3, 1833); was not a candidate for renomination in 1832; appointed clerk of the courts of Worcester County in 1833 and served until his death; moved to Worcester, Mass., in 1833 and died there October 2, 1847; interment in Evergreen Cemetery, Leominster, Mass.

**KENDALL, Joseph Morgan** (son of John Wilkerson Kendall), a Representative from Kentucky; born in West Liberty, Morgan County, Ky., May 12, 1863; received his early education from private tutors and in the public schools; attended the State College of Kentucky and the University of Michigan at Ann Arbor; was examined by the court of appeals of Kentucky and admitted to the practice of law before he was of age; settled in Prestonsburg, Ky.; Clerk of the House of Representatives in the Forty-ninth and Fiftieth Congresses; elected as a Democrat to the Fifty-second

Congress to fill the vacancy caused by the death of his father, John W. Kendall, and served from April 21, 1892, to March 3, 1893; declined to be a candidate for renomination in 1892 on account of ill health; presented credentials as a Member-elect to the Fifty-fourth Congress and served from March 4, 1895, to February 18, 1897, when he was succeeded by Nathan T. Hopkins, who contested his election; resumed the practice of law in West Liberty, Ky.; delegate to all Kentucky Democratic conventions 1884-1933; also engaged in agricultural pursuits near Boonsboro, Clark County, Ky.; died in West Liberty, Ky., November 5, 1933; interment in Barber Cemetery.

**KENDALL, Nathan Edward,** a Representative from Iowa; born on a farm near Greenville, Lucas County, Iowa, March 17, 1868; attended the rural schools; studied law; was admitted to the bar in 1887 and commenced practice in Albia, Monroe County, Iowa, in 1889; city attorney, 1890-1892; prosecuting attorney of Monroe County, Iowa, 1893-1897; member of the Iowa State house of representatives, 1899-1909, and served as speaker in 1909; elected as a Republican to the Sixty-first and Sixty-second Congresses (March 4, 1909-March 3, 1913); was not a candidate for renomination in 1912 to the Sixty-third Congress; resumed the practice of law in Albia, Iowa; moved to Des Moines, Iowa, in 1921; elected Governor of Iowa in 1920, reelected in 1922, and served from January 13, 1921 to January 15, 1925; resided in Des Moines, Iowa, until his death on November 5, 1936; remains were cremated and the ashes interred on the lawn of "Kendall Place," his former home in Albia, Iowa.

**KENDALL, Samuel Austin,** a Representative from Pennsylvania; born in Greenville Township, Somerset County, Pa., November 1, 1859; attended the public schools and was a student for some time at Valparaiso, Ind., and at Mount Union College, Alliance, Ohio; taught school from 1876 to 1890 and served five years as superintendent of the public schools of Jefferson, Iowa; returned to Somerset County, Pa., in 1890 and engaged in the lumber business and the mining of coal; vice president of the Kendall Lumber Co. of Pittsburgh and president of the Preston Railroad Co.; member of the State Pennsylvania of representatives 1899-1903; elected as a Republican to the Sixty-sixth and to the six succeeding Congresses and served from March 4, 1919, until his death; had been unsuccessful for reelection in 1932 to the Seventy-third Congress; died in the House Office Building, Washington, D.C., January 8, 1933; interment in Hochstetler Cemetery, Greenville Township, Somerset County, Pa.

**KENDRICK, John Benjamin,** a Senator from Wyoming; born near Jacksonville, Cherokee County, Tex., September 6, 1857; attended the public schools; moved to Wyoming in 1879 and settled on a ranch near Sheridan, where he engaged in the raising of cattle and sheep; member, Wyoming State senate, 1910-1914; unsuccessful candidate for election in 1913 to the United States Senate; elected Governor of Wyoming in 1914, and served from January 4, 1915 until February 26, 1917, when he resigned, having been elected Senator; elected as a Democrat to the United States Senate in 1916; reelected in 1922 and 1928, and served from March 4, 1917, until his death in Sheridan, Wyo., November 3, 1933; chairman, Committee on Canadian Relations (Sixty-fifth Congress), Committee on Public Lands and Surveys (Seventy-third Congress); interment in Mount Hope Cemetery.

**Bibliography:** *DAB*; Carroll, Eugene. "John B. Kendrick's Fight for Western Water Legislation, 1917-1933." *Annals of Wyoming* 50 (Fall 1978): 319-34; Carroll, Eugene. "John B. Kendrick, Cowpoke to Senator, 1879-1917." *Annals of Wyoming* 54 (Spring 1982): 51-57.

**KENNA, John Edward,** a Representative and a Senator from West Virginia; born near St. Albans, Kanawha County, Va. (now West Virginia), April 10, 1848; moved with his mother to Missouri in 1856; received a limited schooling; during the Civil War enlisted in the Confederate Army; attended St. Vincent's College, Wheeling,

W.Va.; studied law; was admitted to the bar in 1870 and commenced practice in Charleston, W.Va.; prosecuting attorney for Kanawha County 1872-1877; elected as a Democrat to the Forty-fifth, Forty-sixth, and Forty-seventh Congresses (March 4, 1877-March 3, 1883); had been reelected to the Forty-eighth Congress in 1882 but resigned as of March 4, 1883, having been elected Senator; elected as a Democrat to the United States Senate in 1883; reelected in 1889 and served from March 4, 1883, until his death in Washington, D.C., January 11, 1893; funeral services were held in the Chamber of the United States Senate; interment in Mount Olivet Cemetery, Charleston, W.Va.

**KENNEDY, Ambrose,** a Representative from Rhode Island; born in Blackstone, Worcester County, Mass., on December 1, 1875; attended the Blackstone public schools and St. Hyacinthe's College, Quebec, Canada; was graduated from Holy Cross College, Worcester, Mass., in 1897; principal of the Blackstone High School from 1898 to 1904, and superintendent of schools from 1906 until 1908; was graduated from the Boston University Law School in 1906; was admitted to the bar the same year and commenced practice in Woonsocket, R.I.; aide-de-camp on the personal staff of Governor Aram J. Pothier with the rank of colonel, 1909-1913; member of the Rhode Island State house of representatives, 1911-1913, serving as speaker in 1912; elected as a Republican to the Sixty-third and to the four succeeding Congresses (March 4, 1913-March 3, 1923); was not a candidate for renomination in 1922 to the Sixty-eighth Congress; resumed the practice of law; died in Woonsocket, R.I., March 10, 1967; interment in St. Paul's Cemetery, Blackstone, Mass.

**KENNEDY, Ambrose Jerome,** a Representative from Maryland; born in Baltimore Md., January 6, 1893; attended parochial schools, Calvert Hall College, and Polytechnic Institute in Baltimore, Md.; employed as a clerk for an insurance company 1909-1924; engaged in the brokerage and insurance business in 1924; unsuccessful candidate for election to the State house of representatives in 1918; member of the city council 1922-1926; served in the State senate in 1928 and 1929; delegate to the Democratic National Conventions in 1928 and 1932; appointed parole commissioner of Maryland in 1929 and served until elected to Congress; elected as a Democrat to the Seventy-second Congress to fill the vacancy caused by the death of J. Charles Linthicum and on the same day was elected to the Seventy-third Congress; reelected to the Seventy-fourth, Seventy-fifth, and Seventy-sixth Congresses and served from November 8, 1932, to January 3, 1941; chairman, Committee on Claims (Seventy-fourth, Seventy-fifth, and Seventy-sixth Congresses); unsuccessful candidate for renomination in 1940; resumed the brokerage and insurance business in Baltimore, Md.; member of the State Unemployment Compensation Board from June 1943 to September 1945; died in Baltimore, Md., August 29, 1950; interment in the New Cathedral Cemetery.

**KENNEDY, Andrew** (cousin of Case Broderick), a Representative from Indiana; born in Dayton, Ohio, July 24, 1810; moved with his parents to a farm on the Indian reserve near Lafayette, Ind.; soon afterward moved to Connersville, Ind.; became a blacksmith's apprentice; attended the common schools; studied law; was admitted to the bar in 1833 and commenced practice in Connersville; moved to Muncie (then Muncytown), Ind., in 1834 and continued the practice of law; member of the Indiana State house of representatives in 1835; served in the State senate in 1838; elected as a Democrat to the Twenty-seventh and to the two succeeding Congresses (March 4, 1841-March 3, 1847); nominated by the Democratic caucus to the United States Senate in 1847, but was stricken with smallpox on the eve of the legislative joint convention and died in Indianapolis, Ind., on December 31, 1847; interment in Greenlawn Cemetery; reinterment in Beech Grove Cemetery, Muncie, Ind.

**KENNEDY, Anthony** (brother of John Pendleton Kennedy), a Senator from Maryland; born in Baltimore, Md., December 21, 1810; was sent by his parents to Charles Town, Va. (now West Virginia), in 1821, where he attended the Jefferson Academy; studied law and also engaged in agricultural pursuits; member, Virginia house of delegates 1839-1843; magistrate on the bench of the Jefferson County Court in Virginia for ten years; unsuccessful Whig candidate for election in 1844 to the Twenty-ninth Congress; declined the offer of President Millard Fillmore as consul to Havana, Cuba, in 1850; returned to Baltimore, Md., in 1851; member, Maryland house of delegates 1856; elected by the American Party to the United States Senate and served from March 4, 1857, to March 3, 1863; delegate to the State constitutional convention in 1867; retired from active political life and resided on his farm near Ellicott City, Howard County, Md.; died in Annapolis, Md., July 31, 1892; interment in Greenmount Cemetery, Baltimore, Md.

**KENNEDY, Charles Augustus,** a Representative from Iowa; born in Montrose, Lee County, Iowa, March 24, 1869; completed preparatory studies; interested in horticultural pursuits and later engaged in business as a nurseryman; mayor of Montrose 1890-1895; member of the State house of representatives 1903-1905; elected as a Republican to the Sixtieth and to the six succeeding Congresses (March 4, 1907-March 3, 1921); chairman, Committee on Mileage (Sixtieth and Sixty-first Congresses), Committee on Rivers and Harbors (Sixty-sixth Congress); was not a candidate for renomination in 1920; engaged in banking until his retirement; died in Montrose, Iowa, January 10, 1951; interment in Montrose Cemetery.

**KENNEDY, Edward Moore** (father of Patrick Joseph Kennedy, brother of John Fitzgerald Kennedy and Robert Francis Kennedy, grandson of John Francis Fitzgerald, and uncle of Joseph Patrick Kennedy II), a Senator from Massachusetts; born in Boston, Suffolk County, Mass., February 22, 1932; graduated, Milton Academy, Milton, Mass., in 1950; A.B., Harvard University, 1956; attended the International Law School, The Hague, Netherlands, 1958; LL.B., University of Virginia Law School, 1959; served in the United States Army, 1951-1953; admitted to the Massachusetts bar in 1959; appointed assistant district attorney in Suffolk County in 1961; elected as a Democrat to the United States Senate, November 6, 1962, to fill the vacancy caused by the resignation of his brother, John Fitzgerald Kennedy, for the term ending January 3, 1965; reelected in 1964, 1970, 1976, 1982, 1988, and again in 1994 for the term ending January 3, 2001; Democratic whip (Ninety-first Congress), chairman, Committee on the Judiciary (Ninety-sixth Congress), Committee on Labor and Human Resources (One Hundredth through One Hundred Third Congresses); is a resident of Boston, Mass.

**KENNEDY, James,** a Representative from Ohio; born in Lowellville, Mahoning County, Ohio, September 3, 1853; prepared for college at Poland Union Seminary, Ohio, and was graduated from Westminster College, New Wilmington, Pa., in 1876; studied law; was admitted to the bar in March 1879 and commenced practice in Youngstown, Ohio; member of the city council April 1886 to November 1888; chairman of the Republican State convention at Steubenville, Ohio, in 1894; elected as a Republican to the Fifty-eighth and to the three succeeding Congresses (March 4, 1903-March 3, 1911); unsuccessful candidate for reelection in 1910 to the Sixty-second Congress; resumed the practice of his profession in Youngstown, Ohio; affiliated with the Democratic party in 1916; unsuccessful Democratic candidate for election in 1926 to the Seventieth Congress; died in Youngstown, Ohio, November 9, 1928; interment in Riverside Cemetery, Poland, Ohio.

**KENNEDY, John Fitzgerald** (brother of Edward Moore Kennedy and Robert Francis Kennedy, grandson of John Francis Fitzgerald, and uncle of Joseph Patrick Kennedy II and Patrick

Joseph Kennedy), a Representative and a Senator from Massachusetts and 35th President of the United States; born in Brookline, Norfolk County, Mass., May 29, 1917; attended the public and private schools of Brookline, Mass., Choate School, Wallingford, Conn., the London School of Economics at London, England, and Princeton University; graduated from Harvard University in 1940; attended Stanford University School of Business; during the Second World War served as a lieutenant in the United States Navy, 1941-1945; PT boat commander in the South Pacific; author and newspaper correspondent; elected as a Democrat to the Eightieth and to the two succeeding Congresses (January 3, 1947-January 3, 1953); was not a candidate for renomination in 1952 to the House of Representatives, but was elected to the United States Senate; reelected in 1958 and served from January 3, 1953 to December 22, 1960, when he resigned to become President of the United States; chairman, Special Committee on the Senate Reception Room (Eighty-fourth and Eighty-fifth Congresses); unsuccessfully sought the Democratic vice presidential nomination in 1956; elected thirty-fifth President of the United States on November 8, 1960, and was inaugurated on January 20, 1961; died in Dallas, Tex., November 22, 1963, from the effects of an assassin's bullets; remains returned to Washington, D.C., to lie in state in the Rotunda of the Nation's Capitol; interment in Arlington National Cemetery, Va.

**Bibliography:** *DAB*; Burns, James. *John Kennedy: A Political Profile*. New York: Harcourt, Brace and World, 1961. Sorenson, Theodore. *Kennedy*. New York: Harper and Row, 1965.

**KENNEDY, John Lauderdale,** a Representative from Nebraska; born in Ayrshire, Scotland, October 27, 1854; attended the public schools of Scotland; immigrated to the United States and settled in La Salle County, Ill., in 1874; engaged in agricultural pursuits; attended Knox College, Galesburg, Ill., in 1879 and was graduated from the law department of the University of Iowa at Iowa City in 1882; commenced the practice of law in Omaha, Nebr., in 1882; elected as a Republican to the Fifty-ninth Congress (March 4, 1905-March 3, 1907); unsuccessful candidate for reelection in 1906 to the Sixtieth Congress; resumed the practice of law in Omaha, Nebr.; member and chairman pro tempore of the board of fire and police commissioners for the city of Omaha, 1907-1908; chairman of the Republican State committee, 1911-1912; unsuccessful candidate for election to the United States Senate in 1916; Federal fuel administrator for Nebraska from October 1917 to March 1919; president of the United States National Bank, 1920-1925; president of the Omaha Chamber of Commerce, 1924-1925; retired from active pursuits in January 1933 and moved to Pacific Palisades, Calif., where he died on August 30, 1946; interment in Forest Lawn Cemetery, Glendale, Calif.

**KENNEDY, John Pendleton** (brother of Anthony Kennedy), a Representative from Maryland; born in Baltimore, Md., October 25, 1795; attended private schools and was graduated from Baltimore Academy in 1812; volunteered and served in the War of 1812; studied law; was admitted to the bar in 1816 and commenced practice in Baltimore, Md.; also engaged in literary pursuits and was a novelist; member of the Maryland State house of delegates, 1821-1823; appointed secretary of the legation in Chile on January 27, 1823, but did not proceed to his post, resigning June 23, 1823; unsuccessful candidate for election to the Twenty-fifth Congress; subsequently elected as a Whig to the same Congress to fill the vacancy caused by the death of Isaac McKim and served from April 25, 1838, to March 3, 1839; unsuccessful candidate for reelection in 1838 to the Twenty-sixth Congress; elected to the Twenty-seventh and Twenty-eighth Congresses (March 4, 1841-March 3, 1845); chairman, Committee on Commerce (Twenty-seventh Congress); unsuccessful candidate for reelection in 1844 to the Twenty-ninth Congress; again a member of the State house of delegates, in 1846, and served as speaker; appointed Secretary of the Navy in the Cabinet of President Millard Fillmore, and served from July 26,

1852 to March 7, 1853; resumed literary pursuits; died while on a visit to Newport, R.I., August 18, 1870; interment in Greenmount Cemetery, Baltimore, Md.

**Bibliography:** *DAB*; Bohner, Charles H. *John Pendleton Kennedy, Gentleman from Baltimore*. Baltimore: Johns Hopkins Press, 1961; Spelman, Georgia Peterman. "The Whig Rhetoric of John Pendleton Kennedy." Ph.D. dissertation, Indiana University, 1974.

**KENNEDY, Joseph Patrick, II** (son of Robert Francis Kennedy, nephew of Edward Moore Kennedy and John Fitzgerald Kennedy, cousin of Patrick Joseph Kennedy, and great-grandson of John Francis Fitzgerald), a Representative from Massachusetts; born in Brighton, Mass., September 24, 1952; B.A., University of Massachusetts at Boston, 1976; established and operated Citizens Energy Corporation and other public-interest energy companies; elected as a Democrat to the One Hundredth and to the four succeeding Congresses (January 3, 1987-January 3, 1997); is a resident of Boston, Mass.

**KENNEDY, Martin John,** a Representative from New York; born in New York City August 29, 1892; attended the public schools; was graduated from Columbia University in New York City in 1909 and from the College of the City of New York in 1914; engaged in the real estate and insurance business in 1916; chairman of the New York City School Board 1918-1924; member of the State senate 1924-1930; served in the United States Army Intelligence 1915-1918; elected as a Democrat to the Seventy-first Congress to fill the vacancy caused by the resignation of John F. Carew; reelected to the Seventy-second and to the six succeeding Congresses and served from March 11, 1930, to January 3, 1945; unsuccessful candidate for renomination in 1944 to the Seventy-ninth Congress; resumed the real estate and insurance business; died in New York City October 27, 1955; interment in Calvary Cemetery, Maspeth, Long Island, N.Y.

**KENNEDY, Michael Joseph,** a Representative from New York; born in New York City October 25, 1897; attended the Sacred Heart Parochial School, New York City; worked as a hotel clerk from 1914 until 1921; clerk of the New York City Board of Elections, 1921-1923; served as marshal of the city of New York, 1923-1938; became engaged in the insurance business in 1939; elected as a Democrat to the Seventy-sixth and Seventy-seventh Congresses (January 3, 1939-January 3, 1943); was not a candidate for renomination in 1942 to the Seventy-eighth Congress; resumed the insurance business in New York City; was killed in an airplane accident at the Washington (D.C.) National Airport on November 1, 1949; interment in Gate of Heaven Cemetery, Hawthorne, N.Y.

**KENNEDY, Patrick Joseph** (son of Edward Moore Kennedy, nephew of John Fitzgerald Kennedy and Robert Francis Kennedy, cousin of Joseph Patrick Kennedy II, and great-grandson of John Francis Fitzgerald), a Representative from Rhode Island; born in Brighton, Mass., July 14, 1967; graduated, Phillips Academy, Andover, Mass.; B.S., Providence (R.I.) College, 1991; delegate to the Democratic National Convention of 1988; member, Rhode Island State house of representatives, 1988-1994; elected as a Democrat to the One Hundred Fourth Congress (January 3, 1995-January 3, 1997); is a resident of Providence, R.I.

**KENNEDY, Robert Francis** (brother of John Fitzgerald Kennedy and Edward Moore Kennedy, grandson of John Francis Fitzgerald, father of Joseph Patrick Kennedy II, and uncle of Patrick Joseph Kennedy), a Senator from New York; born in Boston, Suffolk County, Mass., November 20, 1925; graduated from Milton (Mass.) Academy; served in the United States Navy Reserve, 1944-1946; graduated from Harvard University in 1948, and from the University of Virginia Law School in 1951; was admitted to the Massachusetts bar in 1951; attorney, Criminal Division, Department of Justice, 1951-1952; campaign manager for his brother,

Representative John F. Kennedy's election to the United States Senate in 1952; assistant counsel, Senate Permanent Subcommittee on Investigations, 1953; assistant counsel, Commission on Organization of the Executive Branch of the Government (Hoover Commission), 1953; chief counsel to the minority, Senate Permanent Subcommittee on Investigations, 1954, and chief counsel and staff director, 1955; chief counsel of Senate Select Committee on Improper Activities in the Labor or Management Field, 1957-1960; campaign manager for Senator John F. Kennedy's election to the Presidency in 1960; Attorney General of the United States from January 21, 1961 until his resignation on September 3, 1964, to be a candidate for the United States Senate; elected as a Democrat to the United States Senate, and served from January 3, 1965 until his death; died from the effects of an assassin's bullets in Los Angeles, Calif., June 6, 1968, while campaigning for the Democratic presidential nomination; interment in Arlington National Cemetery, Va.

**Bibliography:** Kennedy, Robert F. *The Enemy Within.* New York: Harper and Row, 1960. Schlesinger, Arthur, Jr. *Robert Kennedy and His Times.* Boston: Houghton Mifflin, 1978.

**KENNEDY, Robert Patterson,** a Representative from Ohio; born in Bellefontaine, Logan County, Ohio, January 23, 1840; attended the public schools; commissioned second lieutenant in the Twenty-third Regiment, Ohio Volunteer Infantry, June 11, 1861; captain and assistant adjutant general October 7, 1862; major and assistant adjutant general November 16, 1864; resigned April 8, 1865; recommissioned colonel of the One Hundred and Ninety-sixth Regiment, Ohio Volunteer Infantry, April 14, 1865; brevetted lieutenant colonel of Volunteers March 13, 1865, and brigadier general of Volunteers March 13, 1865; returned to Bellefontaine, Ohio; studied law; was admitted to the bar in 1866 and commenced practice in Bellefontaine; appointed by President Rutherford B. Hayes collector of internal revenue for the fourth district of Ohio and served from 1878 to 1883; lieutenant governor of Ohio 1885-1887; elected as a Republican to the Fiftieth and Fifty-first Congresses (March 4, 1887-March 3, 1891); was not a candidate for renomination in 1890 to the Fifty-second Congress; appointed by President William McKinley in 1899 a member of the Insular Commission, which was directed to investigate and report upon conditions existing in Cuba and Puerto Rico and served as its president; died in Columbus, Ohio, May 6, 1918; interment in Bellefontaine Cemetery.

**Bibliography:** *DAB.*

**KENNEDY, William,** a Representative from North Carolina; born near Washington, N.C., July 31, 1768; was graduated from the University of Pennsylvania at Philadelphia in 1782; studied law; was admitted to the bar; elected as a Republican to the Eighth Congress (March 4, 1803-March 3, 1805); elected to the Eleventh Congress (March 4, 1809-March 3, 1811); unsuccessful candidate for reelection to the Twelfth Congress but was subsequently elected to the same Congress to fill the vacancy caused by the death of Thomas Blount; reelected to the Thirteenth Congress and served from January 30, 1813, to March 3, 1815; died in Washington, Beaufort County, N.C., on October 11, 1834; interment in Kennedy Cemetery, near Washington, N.C.

**KENNEDY, William,** a Representative from Connecticut; born in Naugatuck, New Haven County, Conn., December 19, 1854; attended the public schools; studied law; was admitted to the bar in 1879 and commenced practice at Naugatuck, Conn.; member of the State senate 1899-1901; delegate to the Democratic National Conventions in 1896, 1900, 1908, and 1912; member of the Board of Education of Naugatuck 1901-1918; attorney for the town and borough of Naugatuck 1893-1918; elected as a Democrat to the Sixty-third Congress (March 4, 1913-March 3, 1915); was an unsuccessful candidate for reelection in 1914; resumed the practice

of his profession; died in Naugatuck, Conn., on June 19, 1918; interment in St. James' Cemetery.

**KENNELLY, Barbara Bailey,** a Representative from Connecticut; born , in Hartford, Conn., July 10, 1936; attended St. Joseph Cathedral School; graduated from Mount St. Joseph Academy, West Hartford, 1954; B.A., Trinity College, Washington, D.C., 1958; certificate in business administration, Harvard Business School, 1959; M.A., Trinity College, Hartford, Conn., 1971; member, Hartford Court of Common Council, 1975-1979; secretary of state of Connecticut, 1979-1982; elected as a Democrat to the Ninety-seventh Congress, January 12, 1982, by special election, to fill the vacancy caused by the death of William R. Cotter; reelected to the seven succeeding Congresses and served from January 12, 1982, to January 3, 1997; is a resident of Hartford, Conn.

**KENNETT, Luther Martin,** a Representative from Missouri; born in Falmouth, Pendleton County, Ky., March 15, 1807; attended private schools; deputy county clerk of Pendleton County in 1822 and 1823 and of Campbell County, Ky., in 1824; moved to St. Louis, Mo., in 1825; employed in a mercantile establishment; later engaged in lead mining and the manufacture of shot in Jefferson and St. Francis Counties, Mo.; returned to St. Louis in 1842; city alderman 1843-1846; declined to be a candidate for reelection; spent several years in Europe on account of ill health, returning to St. Louis in 1849; vice president of the Pacific Railroad Co.; mayor of St. Louis 1850-1853; president of the St. Louis & Iron Mountain Railroad in 1853; elected as a Whig to the Thirty-fourth Congress (March 4, 1855-March 3, 1857); unsuccessful candidate for reelection; retired to his home near St. Louis Mo.; went to Europe in 1867, where he remained until his death in Paris, France, April 12, 1873; interment in Bellefontaine Cemetery, St. Louis, Mo.

**KENNEY, Edward Aloysius,** a Representative from New Jersey; born in Clinton, Worcester County, Mass., August 11, 1884; attended the public schools; was graduated from Clinton High School in 1902, from Williams College, Williamstown, Mass., in 1906, and from the law department of New York University at New York City in 1908; was admitted to the New York State bar in 1908 and commenced practice in New York City; moved to Cliffside Park, Bergen County, N.J., in 1916 and continued the practice of law; during the First World War served as a member of the legal advisory draft board of New Jersey in 1917; judge of recorders court, Cliffside Park, 1919-1923; unsuccessful candidate for mayor of Cliffside Park as an Independent in 1921, as a Republican in 1923, and as a Democrat in 1927; chairman of the Cliffside Park Housing Commission in 1922 and 1923; member of the Republican county committee in 1925 and 1926; elected as a Democrat to the Seventy-third and to the two succeeding Congresses and served from March 4, 1933, until his accidental death from injuries received in a fall from the Carlton Hotel in Washington, D.C., on January 27, 1938; interment in St. John's Cemetery, Clinton, Mass.

**KENNEY, Richard Rolland,** a Senator from Delaware; born in Laurel, Sussex County, Del., September 9, 1856; attended the public schools and Laurel Academy, Delaware; attended Hobart College, Geneva, N.Y.; studied law; was admitted to the bar in 1881 and commenced practice in Dover, Del.; State librarian, 1879-1881; captain in the National Guard, 1880-1889; adjutant general of the State, 1887-1891; member of the Democratic National Committee, 1896-1908; elected as a Democrat to the United States Senate, January 19, 1897, for the term commencing March 4, 1895, to fill the vacancy caused by failure of the legislature to elect and served until March 3, 1901; unsuccessful candidate for reelection; resumed the practice of law in Dover, Del.; during the First World War, served in the Judge Advocate General's Department, 1917-1920; resumed the practice of law in Dover; elected counsel to the Delaware State house of representatives in 1921; elected prosecuting attorney by the levy court of Kent County in 1921, serving four years; appointed a member of the State board of supplies in 1921, serving two years; member and secretary of the State public lands commission from 1913 until 1929; died in Dover, Del., August 14, 1931; interment in Christ Churchyard.

**KENNON, William, Jr.** (cousin of William Kennon, Sr.), a Representative from Ohio; born in Carrickfergus, Ireland, June 12, 1802; immigrated to the United States in 1816 with his parents, who settled near Barnesville, Belmont County, Ohio; attended the common schools; was graduated from Franklin College, New Athens, Ohio, in 1826; studied law; was admitted to the bar in 1830 and commenced practice in St. Clairsville, Ohio; prosecuting attorney of Belmont County 1837-1841; elected as a Democrat to the Thirtieth Congress (March 4, 1847-March 3, 1849); was not a candidate for renomination; resumed the practice of law; judge of the court of common pleas of the fifteenth judicial district from 1865 to July 1, 1867, when he resigned; died in St. Clairsville, Ohio, October 19, 1867; interment in Union Cemetery.

**KENNON, William, Sr.** (cousin of William Kennon, Jr.), a Representative from Ohio; born in Uniontown, Fayette County, Pa., May 14, 1793; moved with his parents to Belmont County, Ohio, in 1804; attended the common schools and Franklin College, New Athens, Ohio; studied law; was admitted to the bar in 1824 and commenced practice in St. Clairsville, Ohio; elected as a Jacksonian to the Twenty-first and Twenty-second Congresses (March 4, 1829-March 3, 1833); unsuccessful candidate for reelection in 1832 to the Twenty-third Congress; elected to the Twenty-fourth Congress (March 4, 1835-March 3, 1837); unsuccessful candidate for reelection in 1836 to the Twenty-fifth Congress; president judge of the court of common pleas 1840-1847; delegate to the second State constitutional convention in 1850; appointed and subsequently elected to fill the unexpired term of William B. Caldwell as judge of the Ohio Supreme Court in 1854; resigned in 1856 and resumed the practice of law in St. Clairsville, Ohio; became affiliated with the Republican Party at the outbreak of the Civil War; died in St. Clairsville, Belmont County, Ohio, November 2, 1881; interment in Methodist Cemetery.

**KENT, Everett,** a Representative from Pennsylvania; born in East Bangor, Northampton County, Pa., November 15, 1888; attended the public schools in Lansford, East Bangor, Nazareth, and Bangor, Pa.; engaged as a machinist and as a newspaper reporter; taught school; principal of Roosevelt School, Bangor, Pa.; was graduated from the law department of the University of Pennsylvania at Philadelphia in 1911; was admitted to the bar the same year and commenced practice in Bangor; counsel for several municipalities; attorney for the board of prison inspectors of Northampton County 1912-1915; solicitor of Northampton County 1920-1923; elected as a Democrat to the Sixty-eighth Congress (March 4, 1923-March 3, 1925); unsuccessful candidate for reelection in 1924 to the Sixty-ninth Congress; elected to the Seventieth Congress (March 4, 1927-March 3, 1929); unsuccessful candidate for reelection in 1928 to the Seventy-first Congress; delegate to the Democratic National Conventions in 1936, 1940, 1944, 1948, 1952, and 1956; solicitor for the county controller of Northampton County, Pa., 1933-1943; resumed the practice of his profession in Bangor, Pa.; died in Bethlehem, Pa., October 13, 1963; interment in St. John's Cemetery, Bangor, Pa.

**KENT, Joseph,** a Representative and a Senator from Maryland; born in Calvert County, Md., January 14, 1779; received a liberal schooling; studied medicine; was admitted to medical practice in Lower Marlborough, Calvert County, in 1799; settled near Bladensburg, Md., about 1807; practiced medicine and also engaged in agricultural pursuits; served in the State militia as a surgeon; elected as a Republican to the Twelfth and Thirteenth Congresses (March 4, 1811-March 3, 1815); chairman, Committee on the District of Columbia (Thirteenth Congress); elected to the Sixteenth

and to the three succeeding Congresses and served from March 4, 1819, to January 6, 1826, when he resigned, having been elected Governor of the State; chairman, Committee on the District of Columbia (Sixteenth through Ninteenth Congresses); chosen Governor of Maryland by the general assembly of the State, and served from January 9, 1826 to January 15, 1829; elected to the United States Senate and served from March 4, 1833, until his death at his home, "Rose Mount," near Bladensburg, Md., November 24, 1837; chairman, Committee on the District of Columbia (Twenty-fourth and Twenty-fifth Congresses); interment at "Rose Mount," in Bladensburg, Md.

**Bibliography:** *DAB.*

**KENT, Moss,** a Representative from New York; born in Rensselaer County, N.Y., April 3, 1766; completed preparatory studies; studied law; was admitted to the bar and practiced; appointed first judge of Jefferson County about 1795; moved to Cooperstown, N.Y.; member of the New York State senate, 1799-1803; served in the New York State assembly in 1807 and 1810; appointed judge of Jefferson County, February 26, 1810; elected as a Federalist to the Thirteenth and Fourteenth Congresses (March 4, 1813-March 3, 1817); resumed the practice of law; died in Plattsburgh, N.Y., May 30, 1838; interment in Riverside Cemetery.

**KENT, William,** a Representative from California; born in Chicago, Ill., March 29, 1864; moved to California in 1871 with his parents, who settled in Marin County; attended private schools in California and Hopkins Grammar School, New Haven, Conn., 1881-1883; was graduated from Yale University in 1887; returned to Chicago, Ill., in 1887 and engaged in the real estate and livestock business; member of the city council 1895-1897; president of the Municipal Voters' League of Chicago in 1899 and 1900; returned to Marin County, Calif., in 1907; elected as a Progressive Republican to the Sixty-second Congress; reelected as an Independent to the Sixty-third and Sixty-fourth Congresses and served from March 4, 1911, to March 3, 1917; was not a candidate for renomination in 1916; appointed a member of the United States Tariff Commission March 21, 1917, and served until his resignation March 31, 1920; writer on political subjects and natural science; died in Kentfield, Calif., March 13, 1928; remains were cremated in Oakland, Calif., and the ashes returned to the family.

**Bibliography:** Nash, Roderick. "John Muir, William Kent, and the Conservative Schism." *Pacific Historical Review* 36 (November 1967): 423-33; Woodbury, Robert L. "William Kent: Progressive Gadfly, 1864-1928." Ph.D. dissertation, Yale University, 1967.

**KENYON, William Scheuneman,** a Representative from New York; born in Catskill, Greene County, N.Y., December 13, 1820; attended a private academy in Catskill, and the Kinderhook Academy; was graduated from Rutgers College, New Brunswick, N.J., in 1842; studied law in Kingston, N.Y.; was admitted to the bar in Albany, N.Y. in 1846 and commenced practice in Kingston; one of the incorporators of the Ulster County Savings Bank and served as trustee for forty-four years; elected as a Republican to the Thirty-sixth Congress (March 4, 1859-March 3, 1861); was not a candidate for renomination in 1860 to the Thirty-seventh Congress; resumed the practice of law; delegate to the Republican National Conventions of 1872 and 1876; judge of Ulster County, 1883-1889; chairman of the Republican county committee for many years; died in Kingston, Ulster County, N.Y., February 10, 1896; interment in Wiltwyck Rural Cemetery.

**KENYON, William Squire,** a Senator from Iowa; born in Elyria, Lorain County, Ohio, June 10, 1869; moved to Iowa in 1870 and attended the public schools; attended Grinnell (Iowa) College and completed a course of law at Iowa State University Law School at Iowa City in 1890; was admitted to the bar in 1891 and commenced practice in Fort Dodge, Iowa; prosecuting attorney for

Webster County, 1892-1896; district judge of the eleventh judicial district of Iowa, 1900-1902; general counsel for the Illinois Central Railroad, 1904-1907; assistant to the Attorney General of the United States from 1910 until 1911, when he resigned, having been elected Senator; elected in 1911 as a Republican to the United States Senate to fill the vacancy caused by the death of Jonathan P. Dolliver; reelected in 1912 and 1918, and served from April 12, 1911 to February 24, 1922, when he resigned; chairman, Committee on Expenditures in the Department of State (Sixty-second Congress), Committee on Expenditures in the War Department (Sixty-second Congress), Committee on Standards, Weights and Measures (Sixty-fifth Congress), Committee on Education and Labor (Sixty-sixth and Sixty-seventh Congresses), Committee on the Philippines (Sixty-sixth Congress); co-sponsor of the Webb-Kenyon Act of 1913, banning the transport of liquor into any state that prohibited its sale; judge of the United States Circuit Court of Appeals, Eighth Circuit, from 1922 until his death; twice declined Cabinet appointments offered by President Calvin Coolidge; appointed by President Herbert Hoover in 1929 as a member of the National Commission on Law Observance and Enforcement, better known as the "Wickersham Commission"; died at his summer home at Sebasco Estates, Maine, September 9, 1933; interment in Oakland Cemetery, Fort Dodge, Iowa.

**Bibliography:** *DAB*; Potts, E. Daniel. "William Squire Kenyon and the Iowa Senatorial Election of 1911." *Annals of Iowa* 38 (Fall 1966): 206-22.

**KEOGH, Eugene James,** a Representative from New York; born in Brooklyn, N.Y., August 30, 1907; attended the public schools and Commercial High School, Brooklyn, N.Y.; was graduated from the school of commerce of New York University at New York City in 1927 and from the school of law of Fordham University, New York City, in 1930; teacher in the New York City public schools in 1927 and 1928; clerk with New York City Board of Transportation, 1928-1930; law clerk in 1930 and 1931; was admitted to the bar in 1932 and commenced practice in New York City; member of the New York State assembly in 1936; elected as a Democrat to the Seventy-fifth and to the fourteen succeeding Congresses (January 3, 1937-January 3, 1967); chairman, Committee on Revision of the Laws (Seventy-sixth through Seventy-ninth Congresses); was not a candidate for reelection in 1966 to the Ninetieth Congress; resumed the practice of law; was a resident of New York City; died May 26, 1989.

**KERN, Frederick John,** a Representative from Illinois; born on a farm near Millstadt, St. Clair County, Ill., September 2, 1864; attended the public schools of Millstadt and Illinois State Normal University at Normal; employed as a coal miner; taught in the public schools for five years; editor of the East St. Louis Gazette, and in 1891 became owner of the Belleville News-Democrat; chief enrolling clerk of the Illinois State senate in 1892; unsuccessful candidate for election in 1898 to the Fifty-sixth Congress; elected as a Democrat to the Fifty-seventh Congress (March 4, 1901-March 3, 1903); unsuccessful candidate for reelection in 1902 to the Fifty-eighth Congress; resumed his newspaper pursuits in Belleville, Ill.; mayor of Belleville from 1902 until 1912; delegate to the Democratic National Conventions of 1904, 1908 and 1912; president of the State board of administration, 1913-1919; died in Belleville, Ill., November 9, 1931; interment in Walnut Hill Cemetery.

**KERN, John Worth,** a Senator from Indiana; born in Alto, Howard County, Ind., December 20, 1849; attended the common schools and the normal college at Kokomo, Ind.; taught school; graduated from the law department of the University of Michigan at Ann Arbor in 1869; was admitted to the bar the same year and commenced practice in Kokomo; unsuccessful candidate for election to the Indiana State house of representatives in 1870; city attorney

of Kokomo, 1871-1884; reporter of the Indiana Supreme Court, 1885-1889; member, Indiana State senate, 1893-1897; special assistant United States district attorney, 1893-1894; city solicitor of Indianapolis, 1897-1901; unsuccessful Democratic candidate for election in 1900 and 1904 for Governor of Indiana; unsuccessful candidate for Vice President of the United States in 1908 on the Democratic ticket headed by William Jennings Bryan; elected as a Democrat to the United States Senate, and served from March 4, 1911 to March 3, 1917; unsuccessful candidate for reelection in 1916; Democratic caucus chairman 1913-1917; chairman, Committee on Privileges and Elections (Sixty-third and Sixty-fourth Congresses); died in Asheville, N.C., August 17, 1917; interment on the Kern estate near Hollins, Va.; reinterment in Crown Hill Cemetery, Indianapolis, Ind., in 1929.

**Bibliography:** *DAB*; Bowers, Claude. *The Life of John Worth Kern*. Indianapolis: The Hollenbock Press, 1918; Haughton, Virginia. "John Worth Kern and Wilson's New Freedom." Ph.D. dissertation, University of Kentucky, 1973; Oleszek, Walter J. "John Worth Kern: Portrait of a Floor Leader." In *First Among Equals: Outstanding Senate Leaders of the Twentieth Century*, edited by Richard A. Baker and Roger H. Davidson, pp. 7-37. Washington: Congressional Quarterly, Inc., 1991.

**KERNAN, Francis,** a Representative and a Senator from New York; born in Wayne, Schuyler County, N.Y., January 14, 1816; attended public schools; graduated from Georgetown College, District of Columbia, in 1836; studied law in Watkins, N.Y.; was admitted to the bar in 1840 and practiced in Utica; reporter of the court of appeals of New York 1854-1857; member, State assembly 1861; elected as a Democrat to the Thirty-eighth Congress (March 4, 1863-March 3, 1865); unsuccessful candidate for reelection in 1864 to the Thirty-ninth Congress; member of the State constitutional conventions in 1867 and 1868; unsuccessful candidate for election in 1872 for Governor of New York; elected as a Democrat to the United States Senate and served from March 4, 1875, to March 3, 1881; unsuccessful candidate for reelection in 1880; chairman, Committee on Patents (Forty-sixth Congress); resumed the practice of law; member of the board of regents of the University of the State of New York 1870-1892; died in Utica, Oneida County, N.Y., September 7, 1892; interment in St. Agnes Cemetery.

**Bibliography:** *DAB*.

**KERR, Daniel,** a Representative from Iowa; born near Dalry, Ayrshire, Scotland, June 18, 1836; immigrated to the United States with his parents, who settled in Madison County, Ill., in 1841; attended the common schools; was graduated from McKendree College in 1858; studied law; was admitted to the bar in 1862 and commenced practice in Edwardsville, Madison County, Ill.; enlisted in the Union Army August 12, 1862; promoted to second lieutenant, Company G, One Hundred and Seventeenth Regiment, Illinois Volunteer Infantry, in 1863 and to first lieutenant in 1864; member of the house of representatives of Illinois in 1868; moved to Grundy Center, Iowa, in 1870 and continued the practice of law; school director in 1875; elected mayor of Grundy Center in 1877; member of the State house of representatives in 1883; elected as a Republican to the Fiftieth and Fifty-first Congresses (March 4, 1887-March 3, 1891); was not a candidate for renomination in 1890; delegate to the Republican National Convention in 1888 and 1896; resumed the practice of his profession; unsuccessful Democratic candidate for election in 1902 to the Fifty-eighth Congress; moved to Pasadena, Calif., in 1909 and resided there until 1916, when he returned to Grundy Center, Iowa, where he died October 8, 1916; interment in Rose Hill Cemetery.

**KERR, James,** a Representative from Pennsylvania; born in Reedsville, Mifflin County, Pa., October 2, 1851; resided in Blair County until 1864; moved to Clearfield in 1867; pursued an academic course; justice of the peace in 1878; prothonotary for

Clearfield County in 1880 and 1883; engaged in the coal and lumber business; elected as a Democrat to the Fifty-first Congress (March 4, 1889-March 3, 1891); unsuccessful candidate for renomination in 1890 to the Fifty-second Congress; during the Fifty-second and Fifty-third Congresses was appointed Clerk of the United States House of Representatives and served from March 4, 1891, to March 3, 1895; resumed business interests; died in New York City October 31, 1908; interment in Hillcrest Cemetery, Clearfield, Pa.

**KERR, John** (father of John Kerr, Jr., cousin of Bartlett Yancey, and granduncle of John Hosea Kerr), a Representative from Virginia; born near Yanceyville, Caswell County, N.C., August 4, 1782; attended the common schools; studied theology; was licensed as a Baptist minister in 1802; located in Halifax County, Va., in 1805; elected as a Republican to the Thirteenth Congress (March 4, 1813-March 3, 1815); unsuccessful candidate for reelection in 1814 to the Fourteenth Congress, but was subsequently elected to fill the vacancy in the Fourteenth Congress caused by the death of Matthew Clay and served from October 30, 1815, to March 3, 1817; was not a candidate for renomination in 1816 to the Fifteenth Congress; resumed the ministry and was pastor of the Baptist churches of Arbor and Mary Creek, Va.; moved to Richmond, Va., in March 1825 and was pastor of the First Baptist Church; resigned in 1832; settled upon a farm near Danville, Pittsylvania County, Va., in 1836 and died there September 29, 1842; interment in Baptist Cemetery, Yanceyville, Caswell County, N.C.

**KERR, John, Jr.** (son of John Kerr), a Representative from North Carolina; born near Danville, Pittsylvania County, Va., February 10, 1811; completed academic studies in Richmond, Va.; studied law; was admitted to the bar and commenced practice in Yanceyville, N.C.; trustee of Wake Forest College, North Carolina 1844-1856 and of the University of North Carolina at Chapel Hill 1846-1868; unsuccessful Whig candidate for election in 1852 for Governor of North Carolina; elected as a Whig to the Thirty-third Congress (March 4, 1853-March 3, 1855); unsuccessful candidate for reelection in 1854 to the Thirty-fourth Congress; member of the State house of representatives in 1858 and 1860; judge of the supreme court of North Carolina during the Civil War; judge of the superior court 1874-1879; died in Reidsville, N.C., September 5, 1879; interment in the City Cemetery, Yanceyville, N.C.

**KERR, John Bozman** (son of John Leeds Kerr), a Representative from Maryland; born in Easton, Talbot County, Md., March 5, 1809; attended the common schools and Easton (Md.) Academy; was graduated from Harvard University in 1830; studied law; was admitted to the bar and commenced practice in Easton, Md., in 1833; member of the State house of delegates 1836-1838; deputy attorney general for Talbot County 1845-1848; elected as a Whig to the Thirty-first Congress (March 4, 1849-March 3, 1851); was not a candidate for renomination in 1850 to the Thirty-second Congress; appointed by President Millard Fillmore Chargé d'Affaires to Nicaragua on March 7, 1851, and served until July 27, 1853; resumed the practice of law in Baltimore and St. Michaels, Md., in 1854; appointed one of the solicitors in the Court of Claims, Washington, D.C., and served from February 8, 1864, to June 25, 1868, when the position was abolished; solicitor in the office of the Sixth Auditor of the Treasury Department from November 6, 1869, until his death in Washington, D.C., January 27, 1878; interment in the family burial ground at "Bellville," near Oxford Neck, Talbot County, Md.

**KERR, John Hosea** (grandnephew of John Kerr), a Representative from North Carolina; born in Yanceyville, Caswell County, N.C., December 31, 1873; attended the local school and Bingham's Military School of North Carolina; was graduated from Wake Forest (N.C.) College in 1895; studied law; was admitted to the bar in 1895 and commenced practice in Warrenton, N.C.; mayor of Warrenton, N.C., in 1897 and 1898; solicitor for the third district of North Carolina 1906-1916; judge of the superior court 1916-1923; trustee of the University of North Carolina; delegate to the Democratic National Conventions of 1932 and 1940; chairman, United States delegation to the Inter-American Travel Congress in Mexico City in 1941; elected as a Democrat to the Sixty-eighth Congress to fill the vacancy caused by the death of Claude Kitchin; reelected to the Sixty-ninth and to the thirteen succeeding Congresses and served from November 6, 1923, to January 3, 1953; chairman, Committee on Elections No. 3 (Seventy-second through Seventy-fifth Congresses); unsuccessful candidate for renomination in 1952 to the Eighty-third Congress; died in Warrenton, N.C., June 21, 1958; interment in Fairview Cemetery.

**KERR, John Leeds** (father of John Bozman Kerr), a Representative and a Senator from Maryland; born at Greenbury Point, near Annapolis, Md., January 15, 1780; graduated from St. John's College, Annapolis, Md., in 1799; studied law; was admitted to the bar in 1801 and commenced practice in Easton, Md.; deputy State's attorney for Talbot County 1806-1810; commanded a company of militia in the War of 1812; appointed agent of the State of Maryland in 1817 to prosecute claims against the federal government growing out of the War of 1812; elected to the Nineteenth and Twentieth Congresses (March 4, 1825-March 3, 1829); unsuccessful candidate for reelection in 1828 to the Twenty-first Congress; elected to the Twenty-second Congress (March 4, 1831-March 3, 1833); chairman, Committee on Territories (Twenty-second Congress); presidential elector on the Whig ticket in 1840; elected to the United States Senate as a Whig to fill the vacancy caused by the death of John S. Spence and served from January 5, 1841, to March 3, 1843; chairman, Committee on Public Buildings (Twenty-seventh Congress), Committee on Patents and the Patent Office (Twenty-seventh Congress); died in Easton, Talbot County, Md., February 21, 1844; interment in the Bozman family cemetery at "Bellville," near Oxford Neck, Md.

**KERR, Joseph,** a Senator from Ohio; born in Kerrtown (now Chambersburg), Franklin County, Pa., in 1765; was privately tutored; moved to Ohio in 1792; employed by contractors furnishing supplies to troops in the Ohio Valley; surveyor; justice of the peace at Manchester, Adams County, Ohio, in 1797; appointed as a judge of the first quarter session court of Adams County, Northwest Territory, in 1797; elected clerk of the board of commissioners of Adams County; moved to Chillicothe in 1801, and farmed; deputy surveyor of the Virginia military lands in Ohio; became a leading industrialist, shipping produce by a fleet of boats to New Orleans for export; elected to the Ohio senate in 1804 and 1810, and to the Ohio house of representatives in 1808, 1816, 1818, and 1819; appointed by President Thomas Jefferson in 1806 as one of the commissioners to survey the road from Cumberland, Md., to the Ohio River; adjutant general of Ohio 1809-1810; appointed a brigadier general of Ohio Volunteers during the War of 1812; operated a hotel, slaughter house, salting establishment, cooperage, boat building works, and general merchandise business; supplied provisions to the Army of the Northwest during the War of 1812; elected to the United States Senate to fill the vacancy caused by the resignation of Thomas Worthington and served from December 10, 1814, to March 3, 1815; was not a candidate for reelection; returned to Chillicothe, Ohio, and was proprietor of an inn 1815-1826; lost his extensive farm and was forced into bankruptcy; in 1826 moved to Tennessee, where he engaged in agricultural pursuits near Memphis until 1828, when he moved to Louisiana and purchased a homestead near Lake Providence, Carroll (now East Carroll) Parish; also purchased a plantation near Bunches Bend, La., and was engaged as a planter until his death at his homestead near Providence, August 22, 1837; interment in the family burying ground.

**Bibliography:** Dickore, Marie Palla, ed. *General Joseph Kerr of Chillicothe, Ohio.* Oxford, Ohio: The Oxford Press, 1941.

**KERR, Josiah Leeds,** a Representative from Maryland; born in Vienna, Dorchester County, Md., January 10, 1861; attended the public schools in Vienna and Vienna Academy; taught school in Kennebec County; moved to Crisfield, Md., in 1880 and entered the employ of a lumber company as clerk; moved to Cambridge, Md., in 1885; elected school examiner in August 1898 and served two years; elected as a Republican to the Fifty-sixth Congress to fill the vacancy caused by the resignation of John Walter Smith and served from November 6, 1900, to March 3, 1901; was not a candidate for renomination in 1900 to the Fifty-seventh Congress; returned to Cambridge, Md., and became a traveling salesman; died in Cambridge, Md., September 27, 1920; interment in Christ Episcopal Church Cemetery.

**KERR, Michael Crawford,** a Representative from Indiana; born in Titusville, Crawford County, Pa., March 15, 1827; attended the common schools and Erie Academy; was graduated from the law department of Louisville (Ky.) University in 1851; was admitted to the bar and commenced practice in New Albany, Ind., in 1852; city attorney in 1854; prosecuting attorney of Floyd County in 1855; member of the State house of representatives in 1856 and 1857; reporter of the supreme court of Indiana 1862-1865; elected as a Democrat to the Thirty-ninth and to the three succeeding Congresses (March 4, 1865-March 3, 1873); unsuccessful candidate for reelection in 1872 to the Forty-third Congress; elected to the Forty-fourth Congress and served from March 4, 1875, until his death; Speaker of the House of Representatives (Forty-fourth Congress); died at Rockbridge Alum Springs, Rockbridge County, Va., on August 19, 1876; interment in Fairview Cemetery, New Albany, Ind.

**KERR, Robert Samuel,** a Senator from Oklahoma; born in the Chickasaw Indian Territory, Okla., near the present town of Ada, September 11, 1896; attended public schools; taught school; graduated from East Central Normal School, Ada, Okla., in 1911; studied law at the University of Oklahoma; during the First World War served as a second lieutenant with the First Field Artillery, United States Army, 1917-1919; captain and later major in Oklahoma National Guard, 1921-1929; was admitted to the Oklahoma bar in 1922 and commenced the practice of law in Ada, Okla.; drilling contractor and oil producer; chairman of the board of Kerr-McGee Oil Industries, Inc.; special justice, Oklahoma supreme court, 1931; president, Oklahoma County Juvenile Council, 1935-1936; member, Unofficial Pardon and Parole Board 1935-1938; elected Governor of Oklahoma in 1942, and served from January 11, 1943 to January 13, 1947; chairman, Southern Governors Conference, 1945-1946; delivered keynote address at the Democratic National Convention of 1944; Democratic national committeeman, 1940-1948; elected as a Democrat to the United States Senate in 1948; reelected in 1954, and again in 1960, and served from January 3, 1949, until his death in Washington, D.C., January 1, 1963; chairman, Select Committee on National Water Resources (Eighty-sixth Congress), Committee on Aeronautical and Space Sciences (Eighty-seventh Congress); interment in Rose Hill Cemetery, Oklahoma City, Okla., and subsequently at the Kerr family homestead near Ada, Okla.

Bibliography: *DAB*; Cox, Joseph. "Senator Robert S. Kerr and the Arkansas River Navigation Project: A Study in Legislative Leadership." Ph.D. dissertation, University of Oklahoma, 1972; Morgan, Anne Hodges. *Robert S. Kerr: The Senate Years.* Norman: University of Oklahoma Press, 1977.

**KERR, Winfield Scott,** a Representative from Ohio; born in Monroe, Richland County, Ohio, June 23, 1852; attended the common schools of his native city; was graduated from the law department of the University of Michigan at Ann Arbor in 1879; was admitted to the bar the same year and commenced practice in Mansfield, Ohio; member of the State senate 1888-1892; elected as a Republican to the Fifty-fourth, Fifty-fifth, and Fifty-sixth Congresses (March 4, 1895-March 3, 1901); chairman, Committee on Patents (Fifty-sixth Congress); unsuccessful candidate for renomination in 1900 to the Fifty-seventh Congress; resumed the practice of his profession in Mansfield, Richland County, Ohio, and died there September 11, 1917; interment in Mansfield Cemetery.

**KERREY, Joseph Robert,** a Senator from Nebraska; born in Lincoln, Lancaster County, Nebr., August 27, 1943; graduated, Northeast High School, Lincoln, 1961; B.S., University of Nebraska, 1965; entered active duty, United States Navy in 1966, released in 1969; awarded Congressional Medal of Honor; owner and developer, Grandmother's Restaurant, sport and fitness enterprises; elected Governor of Nebraska in 1982, and served from January 6, 1983 to January 9, 1987; declined to be a candidate for reelection in 1986; elected as a Democrat to the United States Senate in 1988 for the term commencing January 3, 1989; reelected in 1994 for the term ending January 3, 2001; unsuccessful candidate in 1992 for the Democratic presidential nomination; is a resident of Lincoln, Nebr.

**KERRIGAN, James,** a Representative from New York; born in New York City December 25, 1828; completed preparatory studies and attended Fordham College; served in Company D, First Regiment, New York Volunteer Infantry, during the Mexican War, after which he accompanied the Walker filibustering expedition to Nicaragua as a captain and served for a brief period as alcalde of the Nicaraguan capital; returned to New York City and was elected alderman of the sixth ward; also served as clerk of the Tombs police court; upon the outbreak of the Civil War organized and was commissioned colonel of the Twenty-fifth Regiment, New York Volunteer Infantry, in the Union Army and served from May 19, 1861, until February 21, 1862; elected as an Independent Democrat to the Thirty-seventh Congress (March 4, 1861-March 3, 1863); became an enthusiastic Irish Nationalist and when the invasion of Canada was planned in 1866 led a company across the border; in 1867 commanded the vessel *Erin's Hope,* which landed arms and ammunition on the Irish coast; accompanied an expedition to Alaska in 1899; returned in bad health and died in Brooklyn, N.Y., on November 1, 1899; interment in St. Raymond's Cemetery.

**KERRY, John Forbes,** a Senator from Massachusetts; born in Denver, Colo., December 11, 1943; graduated, St. Paul's School, Concord, N.H., 1962; B.A., Yale University, 1966; M.A., J.D., Boston College Law School, 1976; admitted to the Massachusetts bar in 1976 and commenced the practice of law; served in the United States Navy in Vietnam 1966-1969; unsuccessful candidate for election in 1972 to the Ninety-third Congress; district attorney of Middlesex County, Mass., 1977-1982; lieutenant governor of Massachusetts, 1983-1985; elected to the United States Senate in 1984 for the term commencing January 3, 1985; reelected in 1990 for the term ending January 3, 1997; is a resident of Boston, Mass.

**KERSHAW, John,** a Representative from South Carolina; born in Camden, Kershaw County, S.C., September 12, 1765; attended Rushworth School and Oxford College, England; studied law; was admitted to the bar and commenced practice in Camden, S.C.; engaged in planting and wheat milling; tobacco inspector in 1789; member of the constitutional convention in 1790; judge of the county court of Kershaw when first established in 1791; member of the State house of representatives in 1792-1794 and 1800-1801; mayor of Camden in 1798, 1801, 1811, and 1822; justice of quorum from Kershaw County in 1806; captain of the First South Carolina Light Dragoons; elected as a Republican to the Thirteenth Congress (March 4, 1813-March 3, 1815); chairman, Committee on Accounts (Thirteenth Congress); unsuccessful candidate for reelection in 1814 to the Fourteenth Congress; engaged in the settling of his father's estates and planting; died in Camden, S.C., August 4, 1829; interment in the Kershaw family burial ground.

**KERSTEN, Charles Joseph,** a Representative from Wisconsin; born in Chicago, Ill., May 26, 1902; was graduated from Marquette University College of Law, Milwaukee, Wis., in 1925 and was admitted to the bar the same year; commenced the practice of law in Milwaukee, Wis., in 1928; first assistant district attorney of Milwaukee County 1937-1943; elected as a Republican to the Eightieth Congress (January 3, 1947-January 3, 1949); unsuccessful candidate for reelection in 1948 to the Eighty-first Congress; elected to the Eighty-second and Eighty-third Congresses (January 3, 1951-January 3, 1955); chairman, Select Committee on Communist Aggression (Eighty-third Congress); unsuccessful candidate for reelection in 1954 to the Eighty-fourth Congress; White House consultant on psychological warfare, 1955-1956; unsuccessful candidate for nomination in 1956 to the Eighty-fifth Congress; resumed the practice of law until his death October 31, 1972, in Milwaukee, Wis.; interment in Holy Cross Cemetery.

**KETCHAM, John Clark,** a Representative from Michigan; born in Toledo, Ohio, January 1, 1873; moved with his parents to Maple Grove, near Nashville, Mich., the same year; attended the common schools of Barry County and high school at Nashville; taught in rural and high schools from 1890 to 1899; county commissioner of schools for Barry County 1899-1907; chairman of the Republican county committee 1902-1908; postmaster of Hastings 1907-1914; master of the Michigan State Grange 1912-1920; lecturer of the National Grange 1917-1921; elected as a Republican to the Sixty-seventh and to the five succeeding Congresses (March 4, 1921-March 3, 1933); unsuccessful candidate for reelection in 1932 to the Seventy-third Congress; president of the National Bank of Hastings 1933-1937; State commissioner of insurance 1935-1937; counsel for the Michigan Chain Store Bureau 1938-1941; died in Hastings, Mich., December 4, 1941; interment in Riverside Cemetery.

**KETCHAM, John Henry,** a Representative from New York; born in Dover Plains, Dutchess County, N.Y., December 21, 1832; pursued an academic course and was graduated from Suffield Academy at Suffield, Conn.; became interested in agricultural pursuits; supervisor in 1854 and 1855; member of the State assembly in 1856 and 1857; State senator in 1860 and 1861; entered the Union Army as colonel of the One Hundred and Fiftieth Regiment, New York Volunteer Infantry, October 11, 1862; brevetted brigadier general December 6, 1864; brigadier general April 1, 1865; brevetted major general of Volunteers March 13, 1865; elected as a Republican to the Thirty-ninth and to the three succeeding Congresses (March 4, 1865-March 3, 1873); chairman, Committee on Public Lands (Forty-second Congress); unsuccessful candidate for reelection in 1872 to the Forty-third Congress; delegate to the Republican National Convention in 1876 and 1896; Commissioner of the District of Columbia from July 3, 1874, until June 30, 1877, when he resigned; elected as a Republican to the Forty-fifth and to the seven succeeding Congresses (March 4, 1877-March 3, 1893); chairman, Committee on Expenditures in the Department of State (Fifty-seventh through Fifty-ninth Congresses); declined to be a candidate for renomination; elected as a Republican to the Fifty-fifth and to the four succeeding Congresses and served from March 4, 1897, until his death in New York City November 4, 1906; interment in Valley View Cemetery, Dover Plains, N.Y.

**KETCHUM, William Matthew,** a Representative from California; born in Los Angeles on September 2, 1921; attended schools in Los Angeles County and military school in North Hollywood, Calif.; attended Colorado School of Mines, 1939-1940, and the University of Southern California, 1940-1942; entered the United States Army in 1942 and served in the Pacific before discharge in 1946; recalled into service during the Korean War and served 1950-1953; owned and operated a hardware and auto-supply store, 1946-1950; salesman, 1953-1957; engaged in cattle ranching and farming; member,

Republican State Central committee, 1964-1966; member, California assembly, 1967-1972; delegate to the Republican National Convention, 1968; elected as a Republican to the Ninety-third and to the two succeeding Congresses and served from January 3, 1973, until his death in Bakersfield, Calif., on June 24, 1978.

**KETCHUM, Winthrop Welles,** a Representative from Pennsylvania; born in Wilkes-Barre, Pa., on June 29, 1820; pursued classical studies; instructor in Wyoming Seminary, Kingston, Pa., 1844-1847 and in Girard College, Philadelphia, in 1848 and 1849; studied law; was admitted to the bar January 8, 1850, and practiced; prothonotary of Luzerne County 1855-1857; member of the Pennsylvania house of representatives in 1858; served in the Pennsylvania senate 1859-1861; delegate to the Republican National Conventions in 1860 and 1864; unsuccessful candidate for election in 1864 to the Thirty-ninth Congress; solicitor of the United States Court of Claims 1864-1866; elected as a Republican to the Forty-fourth Congress and served from March 4, 1875, until July 19, 1876, when he resigned; judge of the United States Court for the Western District of Pennsylvania and served until his death in Pittsburgh, Pa., December 6, 1879; interment in Hollenback Cemetery, Wilkes-Barre, Pa.

**KETTNER, William,** a Representative from California; born in Ann Arbor, Mich., November 20, 1864; moved with his parents to Minnesota in 1873 and settled in St. Paul; attended the public schools; moved to California in 1884 and lived for several years at Julian, Santa Ana, and Visalia, where he engaged in mining, the hotel business, newspaper work, and the insurance business; member of the California National Guard in 1888; city councilman of Visalia, Calif., in 1900; moved to San Diego, Calif., in 1907 and engaged in insurance work, real estate business, and banking; elected as a Democrat to the Sixty-third and to the three succeeding Congresses (March 4, 1913-March 3, 1921); was not a candidate for reelection in 1920 to the Sixty-seventh Congress; delegate to the Democratic National Conventions in 1916 and 1924; resumed the real estate and insurance businesses; died in San Diego, Calif., November 11, 1930; interment in Greenwood Memorial Park Cemetery.

**Bibliography:** Duvall, Lucille Clark. "William Kettner: San Diego's Dynamic Congressman." *Journal of San Diego History* 25 (Summer 1979): 191-207; Jensen, Joan M. "The Politics and History of William Kettner." *Journal of San Diego History* 11 (June 1965): 26-36.

**KEY, David McKendree,** a Senator from Tennessee; born near Greeneville, Greene County, Tenn., January 27, 1824; attended the common schools; graduated from Hiawassee College in 1850; studied law; was admitted to the bar in 1850 and commenced practice in Kingston; moved to Chattanooga in 1853; presidential elector on the Democratic ticket in 1856 and 1860; during the Civil War enlisted in the Confederate Army and was promoted to lieutenant colonel of the Forty-third Tennessee Infantry; member of the Tennessee State constitutional convention in 1870; chancellor of the third chancery division, 1870-1875; unsuccessful Democratic candidate for election in 1872 to the Forty-third Congress; appointed as a Democrat to the United States Senate to fill the vacancy caused by the death of Andrew Johnson, and served from August 18, 1875 to January 19, 1877; unsuccessful candidate for election to fill the vacancy in 1876; appointed Postmaster General in the Cabinet of President Rutherford B. Hayes, and served from March 12, 1877 to August 24, 1880; appointed by President Hayes as United States judge for the eastern and middle districts of Tennessee, serving from 1880 until 1894; died in Chattanooga, Tenn., February 3, 1900; interment in Forest Hill Cemetery.

**Bibliography:** *DAB*; Abshire, David. *The South Rejects a Prophet: The Life of David Key*. New York: Praeger, 1967.

**KEY, John Alexander,** a Representative from Ohio; born in Marion, Marion County, Ohio, December 30, 1871; attended the public schools; learned the printer's trade; city letter carrier 1897-1903; recorder of Marion County 1903-1908; secretary to Representative Carl C. Anderson, of Ohio, 1908-1912; elected as a Democrat to the Sixty-third, Sixty-fourth, and Sixty-fifth Congresses (March 4, 1913-March 3, 1919); chairman, Committee on Pensions (Sixty-third through Sixty-fifth Congresses); unsuccessful candidate for reelection in 1918 to the Sixty-sixth Congress; engaged in the petroleum industry; inspector of Federal prisons from 1934 until his retirement in 1941; died in Marion, Ohio, March 4, 1954; interment in Marion Cemetery.

**KEY, Philip** (cousin of Philip Barton Key and great-grandfather of Barnes Compton), a Representative from Maryland; born probably on his father's estate near Leonardtown, St. Marys County, Md. in 1750; pursued an academic course in England; returned to Maryland and engaged in farming; studied law; was admitted to the bar and practiced; served in the Maryland house of delegates in 1773; member of the committee of correspondence, St. Marys County, in 1774; again a member of the house of delegates 1779-1790; elected to the Second Congress (March 4, 1791-March 3, 1793); member of the State house of delegates in 1795 and 1796 and served as speaker; died in St. Marys County, Md., January 4, 1820; interment probably in the churchyard at Chaptico, Md.

**KEY, Philip Barton** (cousin of Philip Key), a Representative from Maryland; born near Charlestown, Cecil County, Md., April 12, 1757; pursued an academic course; served in the British Army during the Revolutionary War; taken prisoner in Florida and went to England; released on parole; returned to Maryland in 1785; studied law; was admitted to the bar in 1787 and practiced law in Leonardtown, Md.; moved to Annapolis in 1790; member of the State house of delegates 1794-1799; nominated to the Fourth United States Circuit Court on February 25, 1801; in the fall of 1806 moved to Montgomery County and became interested in agricultural pursuits; elected as a Federalist to the Tenth, Eleventh, and Twelfth Congresses (March 4, 1807-March 3, 1813); chairman, Committee on District of Columbia (Tenth Congress); died in Georgetown, D.C., July 28, 1815; interment on his estate "Woodley," in Georgetown, D.C.; reinterment in Oak Hill Cemetery, Washington, D.C.

Bibliography: *DAB.*

**KEYES, Elias,** a Representative from Vermont; born in Ashford, Windham County, Conn., April 14, 1758; attended the common schools; studied law; moved to Stockbridge, Vt., in 1785; served in the State house of representatives 1793-1796, 1798-1802, 1818, 1820, and 1823-1825; member of the Governor's council 1803-1813 and 1815-1817; member of the State constitutional convention in 1814; assistant judge of the Windsor County Court 1803-1814 and judge 1815-1818; elected to the Seventeenth Congress (March 4, 1821-March 3, 1823); died in Stockbridge, Vt., July 9, 1844; interment in Maplewood Cemetery.

**KEYES, Henry Wilder,** a Senator from New Hampshire; born in Newbury, Orange County, Vt., May 23, 1863; attended public and private schools; attended New Hampshire College and Dartmouth College, Hanover, N.H.; graduated from Harvard University in 1887; engaged in agricultural pursuits; member, New Hampshire State house of representatives, 1891-1895, 1915-1917; member, State senate, 1903-1905; treasurer of the State license commission from 1903 until 1915; chairman of the State excise commission, 1915-1917; elected Governor of New Hampshire in 1916, and served from January 3, 1917 to January 2, 1919; president of the Woodsville (N.H.) National Bank; elected as a Republican to the United States Senate in 1918; reelected in 1924 and 1930 and served from March 4, 1919, to January 3, 1937; was not a candidate for renomination in 1936; chairman, Committee on Expenditures in the Post Office Department (Sixty-sixth Congress), Committee to Audit and Control the Contingent Expense (Sixty-eighth and Sixty-ninth Congresses), Committee on Public Buildings and Grounds (Seventieth through Seventy-second Congresses); died in North Haverhill, N.H., on June 19, 1938; interment in Oxbow Cemetery, Newbury, Vt.

**KEYS, Martha Elizabeth,** a Representative from Kansas; born in Hutchinson, Reno County, Kans., August 10, 1930; attended public schools in Kansas City, Mo.; graduated from Paseo High School, Kansas City, Mo., 1945; attended Olivet College, Kankakee, Ill., 1946-1947; B.A., University of Missouri, Kansas City, 1948-1949; elected as a Democrat to the Ninety-fourth and to the Ninety-fifth Congresses (January 3, 1975-January 3, 1979); unsuccessful candidate for reelection in 1978 to the Ninety-sixth Congress; special adviser to the Secretary of the Department of Health, Education, and Welfare, February 1979-May 1980; Assistant Secretary of Education, June 1980-January 1981; consultant in Washington, D.C., in governmental and educational fields, 1981-1984; director, Center for a New Democracy, 1985-1986; partner, Bracy, Williams and Co., a Washington consulting firm, 1987 to present; is a resident of Arlington, Va.

**KIDDER, David,** a Representative from Maine; born in Dresden, Lincoln County, Maine, December 8, 1787; pursued classical studies with private tutors; studied law; was admitted to the bar and commenced practice in Bloomfield; moved to Skowhegan, Maine, in 1817 and thence to Norridgewock in 1821; prosecuting attorney of Somerset County 1811-1823; elected to the Eighteenth and Nineteenth Congresses (March 4, 1823-March 3, 1827); was not a candidate for renomination in 1826; returned to Skowhegan in 1827 and resumed the practice of law; member of the State house of representatives in 1829; died in Skowhegan, Maine, November 1, 1860; interment in Bloomfield Cemetery.

**KIDDER, Jefferson Parish,** a Delegate from the Territory of Dakota; born in Braintree, Orange County, Vt., June 4, 1815; attended the common schools and was graduated from the Norwich Military Academy, Northfield, Vt.; engaged in agricultural pursuits and teaching; studied law at Montpelier, Vt.; was admitted to the bar in 1839 and practiced at Braintree and West Randolph; member of the State constitutional convention in 1843; State's attorney 1843-1847; member of the State senate in 1847 and 1848; lieutenant governor of Vermont in 1853 and 1854; delegate to the Democratic National Convention of 1856; moved to St. Paul, Minn., in 1857; affiliated with the Republican Party in 1860; member of the house of representatives of Minnesota in 1863 and 1864; moved to Vermillion, Dakota Territory, having been appointed by President Lincoln as associate justice of the supreme court of Dakota Territory on February 23, 1865; reappointed by President Ulysses S. Grant on April 6, 1869; again appointed March 18, 1873, and served until February 24, 1875, when he resigned, having been elected to Congress; elected as a Republican to the Forty-fourth and Forty-fifth Congresses (March 4, 1875-March 3, 1879); unsuccessful candidate for renomination in 1878 to the Forty-sixth Congress; appointed justice of the supreme court of Dakota Territory by President Rutherford B. Hayes on April 2, 1879; reappointed by President Chester A. Arthur on April 27, 1883, and served until his death in St. Paul, Minn., on October 2, 1883; interment in Oakland Cemetery.

**KIDWELL, Zedekiah,** a Representative from Virginia; born in Fairfax County, Va., January 4, 1814; received an English education; studied medicine; moved with his father to Clarksburg, Va. (now West Virginia), in 1834; taught school and also clerked in a store; resumed the study of medicine; was graduated from Jefferson Medical College, Philadelphia, Pa., in 1839, and practiced in Fairfax County, Va., 1839-1849; moved to Fairmont, Va. (now West Virginia); member of the Virginia house of delegates 1842-1845; studied law; was admitted to the bar in 1849; delegate to the Virginia constitutional convention in 1849; again a member of the Virginia house of delegates in 1849, 1850, and 1852; elected as a Democrat to the Thirty-third and Thirty-fourth Congresses (March 4, 1853-March 3, 1857); was not a candidate for reelection in 1856; resumed the practice of medicine; member of the West Virginia Board of Public Works 1857-1860; died in Fairmont, W.Va., April 27, 1872; interment in Fairmont Cemetery.

**KIEFER, Andrew Robert,** a Representative from Minnesota; born at Marienborn, Duchy of Hesse-Darmstadt, Germany, May 25, 1832; attended school in Mainz; immigrated to the United States in 1849 and settled in St. Paul, Minn., in 1855; inspector and collector of the wharf in 1857; engaged in mercantile pursuits; enrolling clerk of the State house of representatives in 1859 and 1860; entered the Union Army as captain of the Second Regiment, Minnesota Volunteer Infantry, on July 8, 1861, and served until July 18, 1863, when he was compelled to resign on account of ill health; commissioned by Governor Henry A. Swift colonel of the Thirty-first Regiment of State militia in 1863; member of the State house of representatives in 1864; was engaged in the wholesale mercantile business 1865-1878 and in 1880 became interested in real estate; clerk of the district courts of Ramsey County 1878-1883; unsuccessful Republican candidate for mayor of St. Paul in 1890; elected as a Republican to the Fifty-third and Fifty-fourth Congresses (March 4, 1893-March 3, 1897); was not a candidate for reelection in 1896 to the Fifty-fifth Congress; mayor of St. Paul, Minn., in 1898; at the time of his death was the Republican candidate for city controller; died in St. Paul, Ramsey County, Minn., May 1, 1904; interment in Oakland Cemetery.

**KIEFNER, Charles Edward,** a Representative from Missouri; born in Perryville, Perry County, Mo., November 25, 1869; attended the public schools; engaged in the retail lumber business and also in road construction; mayor of Perryville, 1900-1902; member of the Missouri State house of representatives, 1902-1908; delegate to the Republican National Convention of 1912; served on the staff of Governor Arthur M. Hyde of Missouri, 1920-1924; elected as a Republican to the Sixty-ninth Congress (March 4, 1925-March 3, 1927); unsuccessful candidate for reelection in 1926 to the Seventieth Congress; elected to the Seventy-first Congress (March 4, 1929-March 3, 1931); unsuccessful candidate for reelection in 1930 to the Seventy-second Congress; resumed the lumber and banking business in Perryville, Mo., until his death on December 13, 1942; interment in Home Cemetery.

**KIESS, Edgar Raymond,** a Representative from Pennsylvania; born in Warrensville, Lycoming County, Pa., August 26, 1875; attended the public schools; was graduated from Lycoming County Normal School, Muncy, Pa., in 1892; taught in the public schools of Lycoming County for two years; engaged in the newspaper publishing business in Hughesville in 1894; member of the Pennsylvania house of representatives 1904-1910; engaged in business in Williamsport in 1910; served as a trustee of Pennsylvania State College 1912-1930; elected as a Republican to the Sixty-third and to the eight succeeding Congresses and served from March 4, 1913, until his death at his summer home at Eagles Mere, Pa., July 20, 1930; chairman, Committee on Insular Affairs (Sixty-ninth through Seventy-first Congresses); interment Wildwood Cemetery, Williamsport, Pa.

**KILBOURNE, James,** a Representative from Ohio; born in New Britain, Conn., October 19, 1770; pursued classical studies; studied theology and entered the Episcopal ministry; one of the founders of the Scioto company to trade in Ohio and the Northwest in 1801; founded Worthington, Ohio, in 1803; appointed United States surveyor of public lands in 1805 and laid out the present city of Sandusky; appointed by President James Madison a member of the commission to ascertain the western boundary of the Virginia military reservation between the Little Miami and Scioto Rivers July 1, 1812; president of Worthington College; colonel of a frontier regiment during the War of 1812; elected as a Republican to the Thirteenth and Fourteenth Congresses (March 4, 1813-March 3, 1817); member of the State house of representatives in 1823, 1824, 1838, and 1839; president of the convention of 1839 to lay the cornerstone of the State capitol in Columbus and of the Whig State convention in 1840; died in Worthington, Ohio, April 9, 1850; interment in St. John's Episcopal Church Burying Ground.

**Bibliography:** *DAB.*

**KILBURN, Clarence Evans,** a Representative from New York; born in Malone, Franklin County, N.Y., April 13, 1893; attended the public schools and was graduated from Cornell University, Ithaca, N.Y., in 1916; during the First World War served as a captain in the Twenty-sixth Infantry, First Division, in 1917 and 1918; engaged in banking; became president of the People's Trust Co. of Malone in 1930; elected as a Republican to the Seventy-sixth Congress by special election, February 13, 1940, to fill the vacancy caused by the death of Wallace E. Pierce; reelected to the twelve succeeding Congresses and served from February 13, 1940, to January 3, 1965; was not a candidate for renomination in 1964 to the Eighty-ninth Congress; was a director of Marine Midland Trust Co. of Northern New York; resided in Malone, N.Y., where he died May 20, 1975; remains were cremated and ashes interred in Morningside Cemetery.

**KILDAY, Paul Joseph,** a Representative from Texas; born in Sabinal, Uvalde County, Tex., March 29, 1900; moved with his parents to San Antonio, Tex., in 1904; attended the public and parochial schools and St. Mary's College, San Antonio, Tex.; employed as a clerk, United States Air Force, Washington, D.C., 1918-1921 and as a law clerk, United States Shipping Board Emergency Fleet Corporation, in 1921 and 1922; was graduated from the law department of Georgetown University, Washington, D.C., in 1922; was admitted to the bar the same year and commenced practice in San Antonio, Tex.; served as first assistant district attorney of Bexar County, Tex., 1935-1938; elected as a Democrat to the Seventy-sixth and to the eleven succeeding Congresses and served from January 3, 1939, until his resignation September 24, 1961, having been appointed a judge of the Court of Military Appeals, and served in this capacity until his death in Washington, D.C., on October 12, 1968; interment in Arlington National Cemetery, Va.

**KILDEE, Dale Edward,** a Representative from Michigan; born in Flint, Genesee County, Mich., September 16, 1929; graduated from St. Mary's High School, Flint, 1947; B.A., Sacred Heart Seminary, Detroit, Mich., 1952; teacher's certificate, University of Detroit, 1955; engaged in graduate work at the University of Peshawar, Pakistan, 1958-1959; M.A., University of Michigan, Ann Arbor, 1962; high school teacher in Detroit and Flint, Mich., 1954-1964; served in the Michigan house of representatives, 1965-1974; Michigan senate, 1975-1976; delegate to Michigan State Democratic conventions, 1956-1977; delegate to Democratic National Conventions, 1968 and 1984; elected as a Democrat to the Ninety-fifth and to the nine succeeding Congresses (January 3, 1977-January 3, 1997); is a resident of Flint, Mich.

**KILGORE, Constantine Buckley,** a Representative from Texas; born in Newnan, Coweta County, Ga., February 20, 1835; moved with his parents to Rusk County, Tex., in 1846; received a common-school and academic training; studied law; during the Civil War entered the Confederate Army as a private and by 1862 had attained the rank of adjutant general of Brigadier General Matthew D. Ector's brigade, Army of the Tennessee; was admitted to the bar and practiced in Rusk County, Tex.; elected justice of the peace in 1869; member of the State constitutional convention in 1875; elected to the State senate in 1884 for a term of four years; was chosen president of that body in 1885 for two years; resigned from the State senate in 1886, having been elected to Congress; elected as a Democrat to the Fiftieth and to the three succeeding Congresses (March 4, 1887-March 3, 1895); appointed on March 20, 1895, by President Grover Cleveland as United States judge for the southern district of Indian Territory, and served until his death in Ardmore, Indian Territory (now Oklahoma), September 23, 1897; interment in White Rose Cemetery, Wills Point, Tex.

**KILGORE, Daniel,** a Representative from Ohio; born at Kings Creek, Va. (now West Virginia), in 1793; received a liberal schooling; moved to Cadiz, Ohio; member of the Ohio State senate, 1828-1832; elected as a Jacksonian to the Twenty-third Congress to fill the vacancy caused by the resignation of Humphrey H. Leavitt; reelected to the Twenty-fourth Congress and reelected as a Democrat to the Twenty-fifth Congress, and served from December 1, 1834 until July 4, 1838, when he resigned; died in New York City, December 12, 1851.

**KILGORE, David,** a Representative from Indiana; born in Harrison County, Ky., April 3, 1804; moved with his father to Franklin County, Ind., in 1819; attended the common schools; studied law; was admitted to the bar in 1830 and commenced practice in Yorktown, Ind.; member of the Indiana State house of representatives, 1833-1836, 1838, 1839, and 1855, and served as speaker in 1855; president judge of the Yorktown circuit, 1839-1846; delegate to the State constitutional convention in 1850; elected as a Republican to the Thirty-fifth and Thirty-sixth Congresses (March 4, 1857-March 3, 1861); delegate to the Union National Convention which met in Philadelphia on August 14, 1866; died near Yorktown, Delaware County, Ind., January 22, 1879; interment in Mount Pleasant Cemetery, near Yorktown, Ind.

**KILGORE, Harley Martin,** a Senator from West Virginia; born in Brown, Harrison County, W.Va., January 11, 1893; attended the public schools; graduated from the law department of West Virginia University at Morgantown in 1914 and was admitted to the bar the same year; taught school in Hancock, W.Va., in 1914 and 1915; organized the first high school in Raleigh County, W.Va., in 1915, serving as its principal for one year; commenced the practice of law in Beckley, W.Va., in 1916; during the First World War served in the Infantry from 1917, until discharged as a captain in 1920; organized the West Virginia National Guard in 1921 and retired as a colonel in 1953; judge of the criminal court of Raleigh County, W.Va., 1933-1940; elected as a Democrat to the United States Senate in 1940; reelected in 1946 and again in 1952, and served from January 3, 1941 until his death in the naval hospital at Bethesda, Md., February 28, 1956; chairman, Committee on the Judiciary (Eighty-fourth Congress); interment in Arlington National Cemetery, Va.

Bibliography: *DAB*; Maddox, Robert Franklin. *The Senatorial Career of Harley Martin Kilgore.* New York: Garland Publishing, 1981.

**KILGORE, Joe Madison,** a Representative from Texas; born in Brown County, near Brownwood, Tex., December 10, 1918; attended the public schools of Rising Star, Tex.; moved with his family to Mission, Hidalgo County, Tex., in 1929; attended the public schools; attended Westmoreland College (now Trinity University), San Antonio, Tex., in 1935 and 1936; entered the University of Texas in 1936; interrupted his law schooling at the University of Texas in July 1941 to enlist in the United States Army Air Corps, and served as a combat pilot in the Mediterranean Theater of Operations; separated from the service as a lieutenant colonel in 1945; retired from the Air Force Reserve as a major general; awarded the Silver Star, Distinguished Flying Cross, and Air Medal with two oak leaf clusters; returned to the University of Texas Law School; was admitted to the bar in 1946 and commenced the practice of law in Edinburg, Tex.; member of the Texas State house of representatives, 1947-1954; delegate to the Democratic National Conventions of 1956, 1960, and 1968; elected as a Democrat to the Eighty-fourth

and to the four succeeding Congresses (January 3, 1955-January 3, 1965); was not a candidate for renomination in 1964 to the Eighty-ninth Congress; resumed the practice of law; is a resident of Austin, Tex.

**KILLE, Joseph,** a Representative from New Jersey; born near Bridgeport, Gloucester County, N.J., April 12, 1790; pursued academic studies; located in Salem; sheriff of Salem County 1822-1829; clerk of Salem County 1829-1839; member of the State house of assembly in 1856; elected as a Democrat to the Twenty-sixth Congress (March 4, 1839-March 3, 1841); died in Salem, N.J., March 1, 1865; interment in St. John's Episcopal Cemetery.

**KILLINGER, John Weinland,** a Representative from Pennsylvania; born in Annville, Lebanon County, Pa., September 18, 1824; attended the public schools of Annville and the Lebanon Academy, Lebanon, Pa.; was graduated from the Mercersburg Preparatory School, Mercersburg, Pa., and from the Franklin and Marshall College, Lancaster, Pa., in 1843; studied law in Lancaster; was admitted to the bar in 1846 and practiced in Lebanon County 1846-1886; prosecuting attorney for Lebanon County in 1848 and 1849; member of the Pennsylvania house of representatives in 1850 and 1851; served in the Pennsylvania senate 1854-1857; delegate to the Republican National Convention in 1856; elected as a Republican to the Thirty-sixth and Thirty-seventh Congresses (March 4, 1859-March 3, 1863); chairman, Committee on Expenditures in the Post Office Department (Thirty-seventh Congress); was not a candidate for renomination in 1862; assessor of internal revenue 1864-1866; elected to the Forty-second and Forty-third Congresses (March 4, 1871-March 3, 1875); was not a candidate for renomination in 1874; resumed the practice of law; elected to the Forty-fifth and Forty-sixth Congresses (March 4, 1877-March 3, 1881); was not a candidate for renomination in 1880; solicitor for the Philadelphia & Reading Railroad Co.; died in Lebanon, Pa., June 30, 1896; interment in Mount Lebanon Cemetery.

**KIM, Jay C.,** a Representative from California; born in Seoul, Korea, March 27, 1939; B.S., University of Southern California, 1967, and M.S., 1973; M.P.A., California State University, Los Angeles, 1980; Diamond Bar (Calif.) City Council, 1990; mayor of Diamond Bar, 1991; founder and president, JayKim Engineers, Inc.; elected as a Republican to the One Hundred Third and One Hundred Fourth Congresses (January 3, 1993-January 3, 1997); is a resident of Diamond Bar, Calif.

**KIMBALL, Alanson Mellen,** a Representative from Wisconsin; born in Buxton, York County, Maine, March 12, 1827; pursued academic studies; moved to Wisconsin in 1852 and engaged in agricultural and mercantile pursuits; served in the State senate in 1863 and 1864; elected as a Republican to the Forty-fourth Congress (March 4, 1875-March 3, 1877); was an unsuccessful candidate for election in 1876 to the Forty-fifth Congress; engaged in the lumbering business; delegate to the Republican National Convention in 1884; died in Pine River, Waushara County, Wis., May 26, 1913; interment in Pine River Cemetery.

**KIMBALL, Henry Mahlon,** a Representative from Michigan; born in Orland, Steuben County, Ind., August 27, 1878; attended the common and high schools of Orland; was graduated from Hillsdale (Mich.) College; served as principal of Orland High School; attended the literary and law departments of the University of Michigan at Ann Arbor, graduating in law in 1904; commenced practice in Orland, Ind.; moved to Rosebud, Nev., in 1907 and continued the practice of law; employed as a traveling auditor in 1908 for a firm in San Francisco, Calif.; moved to Portland, Oreg., in 1909 and to Kalamazoo, Mich., in 1917, where he continued the practice of law; elected as a Republican to the Seventy-fourth Congress and served from January 3, 1935, until his death in Kalamazoo, Mich., October

19, 1935; remains were cremated and the ashes buried in Green Lawn Cemetery, Orland, Ind.

**KIMBALL, William Preston,** a Representative from Kentucky; born near East Hickman, Fayette County, Ky., November 4, 1857; attended public and private schools and Transylvania University in Lexington; member of the Kentucky house of representatives in 1883 and 1884; city clerk in 1889 and 1890; studied law; was admitted to the bar in 1891 and commenced practice in Lexington; city attorney of Lexington from October 1891 to January 1, 1901; prosecuting attorney of Fayette County from January 1, 1901, to March 4, 1907, when he resigned, having been elected to Congress; elected as a Democrat to the Sixtieth Congress (March 4, 1907-March 3, 1909); unsuccessful candidate for renomination in 1908; resumed the practice of law in Lexington; died in Lexington, Ky., February 24, 1926; interment in Lexington Cemetery.

**KIMMEL, William,** a Representative from Maryland; born in Baltimore, Md., August 15, 1812; attended St. Mary's and Baltimore Colleges; studied law; was admitted to the bar and commenced practice in Baltimore, Md.; interested in agricultural and business pursuits; State director of the Baltimore & Ohio Railroad Co.; director in the Union Railroad Co. and in the Western Maryland extension; member of the State Democratic committee 1862-1866; delegate to the Democratic National Convention in 1864; unsuccessful candidate for election in 1864 to the Thirty-ninth Congress; member of the State senate 1866-1871; a director of the Canton Co. of Baltimore 1869-1873; solicitor and land agent of the company in 1871 and 1872; elected as a Democrat to the Forty-fifth and Forty-sixth Congresses (March 4, 1877-March 3, 1881); resumed the practice of his profession in Baltimore, Md., and died there December 28, 1886; interment in Loudon Park Cemetery.

**KINCAID, John,** a Representative from Kentucky; born near Danville, Mercer County, Ky., February 15, 1791; attended the public schools; studied law; was admitted to the bar and commenced practice in Stanford, Ky.; Commonwealth attorney; member of the Kentucky house of representatives in 1819; elected as a Jacksonian to the Twenty-first Congress (March 4, 1829-March 3, 1831); again a member of the Kentucky house of representatives in 1836 and 1837; circuit judge in 1836 and 1837; resumed the practice of law and also engaged in agricultural pursuits; moved to Gallatin, Tenn., in 1870 and died there on February 7, 1873; interment in Bellview Cemetery, Danville, Ky.

**KINCHELOE, David Hayes,** a Representative from Kentucky; born near Sacramento, McLean County, Ky., April 9, 1877; attended the public schools and was graduated from Bowling Green College, Kentucky, in 1898; studied law; was admitted to the bar in 1899 and commenced practice in Calhoun, Ky.; prosecuting attorney of McLean County 1902-1906; moved to Madisonville in 1906 and continued the practice of law; elected as a Democrat to the Sixty-fourth and to the seven succeeding Congresses and served from March 4, 1915, until his resignation on October 5, 1930, having been appointed judge of the United States Customs Court, in which capacity he served until April 30, 1948, when he retired; died in Washington, D.C., April 16, 1950; interment in Odd Fellows Cemetery, Madisonville, Ky.

**KINDEL, George John,** a Representative from Colorado; born in Cincinnati, Ohio, March 2, 1855; attended the public schools and St. Augustine's School in Cincinnati; apprenticed as an upholsterer and mattress maker in 1871; moved to Denver, Colo., in 1877 and engaged in the upholstery and mattress business and later in the bedding and furniture business; member of the board of supervisors of the city and county of Denver, 1910-1914; elected as a Democrat to the Sixty-third Congress (March 4, 1913-March 3, 1915); was not a candidate in 1914 for renomination to the House of Representatives, but was an unsuccessful Independent candidate for election to the United States Senate; resumed his former business pursuits; was in an automobile accident near Hillrose, Colo., which resulted in his death in Brush, Colo., on February 28, 1930; interment in Fairmount Cemetery, Denver, Colo.

**KINDNESS, Thomas Norman,** a Representative from Ohio; born in Knoxville, Knox County, Tenn., August 26, 1929; attended Silver Spring (Md.) Intermediate School, 1944; graduated from Glendale (Calif.) High School, 1947; A.B., University of Maryland, College Park, 1951; LL.B., George Washington University, Washington, D.C., 1953; admitted to the Washington, D.C. bar in 1954 and commenced practice; assistant counsel, Champion International Corp., 1957-1973; mayor of Hamilton, Ohio, 1964-1967; member, Hamilton City Council, 1964-1969; served in the Ohio State house of representatives, 1971-1974; delegate, Ohio State Republican conventions, 1971-1974; elected as a Republican to the Ninety-fourth and to the five succeeding Congresses (January 3, 1975-January 3, 1987); was not a candidate in 1986 for reelection to the House of Representatives, but was an unsuccessful candidate for election to the United States Senate; resumed the practice of law in Washington, D.C.; is a resident of Alexandria, Va.

**KINDRED, John Joseph,** a Representative from New York; born near Courtland, Southampton County, Va., July 15, 1864; attended the local schools, Randolph-Macon College, Ashland, Va., and the University of Virginia at Charlottesville; taught school in Virginia in 1886 and 1887; was graduated from the Hospital College of Medicine, Louisville, Ky., in 1889 and commenced the practice of his profession in New York City the same year; was graduated in mental diseases from the University of Edinburgh, Scotland, in 1892; established several mental hospitals in Connecticut, New York, and New Jersey; was graduated in law in 1919 and admitted to the bar in 1926; elected as a Democrat to the Sixty-second Congress (March 4, 1911-March 3, 1913); was not a candidate for renomination in 1912; became interested in agricultural pursuits and in the construction of houses; elected to the Sixty-seventh and to the three succeeding Congresses (March 4, 1921-March 3, 1929); was not a candidate for renomination in 1928; resumed his medical profession in New York City 1930-1937 and also served as professor of medical jurisprudence at John B. Stetson University, De Land, Fla., 1933 to 1937; died October 23, 1937, at Astoria, N.Y.; interment in Poughkeepsie Rural Cemetery, Poughkeepsie, N.Y.

**KING, Adam,** a Representative from Pennsylvania; born in York, Pa., in 1790; pursued academic studies; studied medicine in the University of Pennsylvania at Philadelphia and commenced practice in York; edited and published the York Gazette 1818-1835; clerk of the courts of York County 1818-1826; elected to the Twentieth Congress and reelected as a Jacksonian to the Twenty-first and Twenty-second Congresses (March 4, 1827-March 3, 1833); unsuccessful candidate for reelection in 1832 to the Twenty-third Congress; resumed the practice of medicine; died in York, York County, Pa., May 6, 1835; interment in Prospect Hill Cemetery.

**KING, Andrew,** a Representative from Missouri; born in Greenbrier County, Va. (now West Virginia), March 20, 1812; attended the common schools; studied law; was admitted to the bar and commenced practice in St. Charles, Mo.; member of the State senate in 1846; served in the State house of delegates in 1858; judge of the circuit court for the nineteenth judicial district of Missouri 1859-1864; elected as a Democrat to the Forty-second Congress (March 4, 1871-March 3, 1873); was not a candidate for renomination in 1872; resumed the practice of law; died in Jefferson City, Mo., November 18, 1895; interment in Oak Grove Cemetery, St. Charles, Mo.

**KING, Austin Augustus,** a Representative from Missouri; born in Sullivan County, Tenn., September 21, 1802; attended the public schools; studied law; was admitted to the bar in 1822 and commenced practice in Jackson, Tenn.; moved to Columbia, Mo., in 1830 and continued the practice of law; served as a colonel in the Black Hawk War; member of the State house of representatives in 1834 and 1836; moved to Richmond, Mo., in 1837, having been appointed circuit judge of the fifth circuit, and served until 1848; elected Governor of Missouri in 1848 and served from December 27, 1848 to January 3, 1853; unsuccessful candidate in 1852 for election to the Thirty-third Congress; resumed the practice of law in Richmond, Mo.; delegate to the Democratic National Conventions at Charleston and Baltimore in 1860; again circuit judge from 1862 until 1863, when he resigned; elected as a Unionist to the Thirty-eighth Congress (March 4, 1863-March 3, 1865); unsuccessful candidate for reelection in 1864 to the Thirty-ninth Congress; resumed the practice of law; died in St. Louis, Mo., April 22, 1870; interment in Richmond Cemetery, Richmond, Ray County, Mo.

**Bibliography:** *DAB.*

**KING, Carleton James,** a Representative from New York; born in Saratoga Springs, N.Y., June 15, 1904; attended the public schools; graduated from Union University, Albany Law School 1926; was admitted to the bar and entered the practice of law in Saratoga Springs, N.Y., in 1926; acting city judge, Saratoga Springs, 1936-1941; assistant district attorney Saratoga County, 1942-1950, and district attorney, Saratoga County, 1950-1961; elected as a Republican to the Eighty-seventh Congress; reelected to the six succeeding Congresses and served from January 3, 1961, until his resignation December 31, 1974; unsuccessful candidate for reelection in 1974 to the Ninety-fourth Congress; resumed the practice of law in Saratoga Springs; died in Bradenton, Fla., November 19, 1977; cremated; ashes scattered in the Gulf of Mexico near Bradenton.

**KING, Cecil Rhodes,** a Representative from California; born in Fort Niagara, N.Y., January 13, 1898; moved to Los Angeles, Calif., in 1908 and attended the public schools; during the First World War served as a private in the United States Army in 1917 and 1918; engaged in business in southern California 1919-1942; member of the California assembly 1932-1942; elected as a Democrat to the Seventy-seventh Congress, by special election, August 25, 1942, to fill the vacancy caused by the death of Lee E. Geyer; reelected to the thirteen succeeding Congresses and served from August 25, 1942, to January 3, 1969; was not a candidate for reelection in 1968 to the Ninety-first Congress; resided in Inglewood, Calif., where he died March 17, 1974; interment in Inglewood Park Cemetery.

**KING, Cyrus** (half brother of Rufus King), a Representative from Massachusetts; born in Scarboro, Maine (then a district of Massachusetts), on September 6, 1772; attended Phillips Academy, Andover, Mass., and was graduated from Columbia College, New York City, in 1794; studied law; served as private secretary to Rufus King when he was United States Minister to England in 1796; completed law studies in Biddeford, Maine; was admitted to the bar in 1797 and commenced practice in Saco, Maine; served as major general of the Sixth Division, Massachusetts Militia; one of the founders of Thornton Academy, Saco, Maine; elected as a Federalist to the Thirteenth and Fourteenth Congresses (March 4, 1813-March 3, 1817); returned to Saco, York County, Maine, where he died on April 25, 1817; interment in Laurel Hill Cemetery.

**KING, Daniel Putnam,** a Representative from Massachusetts; born in Danvers, Mass., January 8, 1801; pursued classical studies and was graduated from Harvard University in 1823; studied law, but did not practice; engaged in agricultural pursuits; member of the Massachusetts house of representatives in 1836 and 1837; served in the Massachusetts senate 1838-1841, and was its president in 1840; again a member of the Massachusetts house of representatives in 1843 and 1844 and served as speaker in the latter year; elected as a Whig to the Twenty-eighth and to the three succeeding Congresses and served from March 4, 1843, until his death in South Danvers, Mass., July 25, 1850; chairman, Committee on Expenditures on Public Buildings (Twenty-eighth Congress), Committee on Accounts (Twenty-ninth through Thirty-first Congresses), Committee on Revolutionary Claims (Thirtieth Congress); interment in King Cemetery, Peabody, Mass.

**KING, David Sjodahl** (son of William Henry King), a Representative from Utah; born in Salt Lake City, Utah, June 20, 1917; attended the public schools in Washington, D.C.; graduated from the University of Utah at Salt Lake City in 1937; served as a missionary for the Church of Jesus Christ of Latter-day Saints in Great Britain, 1937-1939; graduated from Georgetown University School of Law, Washington, D.C., in 1942; was admitted to the bar in 1942; law clerk to Justice Harold M. Stephens of the United States Court of Appeals for the District of Columbia in 1943; returned to Salt Lake City in 1943; counsel for the Utah State Tax Commission, 1944-1946; engaged in the private practice of law in Salt Lake City since 1945; taught commercial law at Henager Business College, 1946-1958; elected as a Democrat to the Eighty-sixth and Eighty-seventh Congresses (January 3, 1959-January 3, 1963); was not a candidate for renomination in 1962 to the House of Representatives, but was an unsuccessful candidate for election to the United States Senate; elected to the Eighty-ninth Congress (January 3, 1965-January 3, 1967); unsuccessful candidate for reelection in 1966 to the Ninetieth Congress; appointed United States Ambassador to the Malagasy Republic and to Mauritius on January 26, 1967, and on June 24, 1968, respectively, and served in those two positions concurrently until August 1969; alternate executive director, International Bank for Reconstruction and Development (World Bank), 1979-1981; president, Haiti Port-au-Prince mission, Church of Jesus Christ of Latter-Day Saints, 1986-1989; president of the Washington Temple of the Church of Jesus Christ of Latter-Day Saints from 1990 to 1993; is a resident of Kensington, Md.

**KING, Edward John,** a Representative from Illinois; born in Springfield, Mass., July 1, 1867; moved to Illinois with his parents, who settled in Galesburg, Knox County, in 1880; attended the public schools, and Knox College at Galesburg, Ill.; studied law; was admitted to the bar in 1893 and commenced practice in Galesburg, Ill.; city attorney in 1893 and 1894; member of the State house of representatives 1907-1914; elected as a Republican to the Sixty-fourth and to the six succeeding Congresses and served from March 4, 1915, until his death; chairman, Committee on Expenditures in the Department of Agriculture (Sixty-seventh through Sixty-ninth Congresses); had been reelected to the Seventy-first Congress; died in Washington, D.C., February 17, 1929; interment in Hope Abbey Mausoleum, Hope Cemetery, Galesburg, Ill.

**KING, George Gordon,** a Representative from Rhode Island; born in Newport, R.I., June 9, 1807; pursued classical studies in Newport and in Phillips Academy, Andover, Mass.; was graduated from Brown University, Providence, R.I., in 1825; attended the Litchfield (Conn.) Law School; was admitted to the bar in 1827 and practiced in Providence and Newport; member and speaker of the State house of representatives in 1845 and 1846; elected as a Whig to the Thirty-first and Thirty-second Congresses (March 4, 1849-March 3, 1853); unsuccessful candidate for reelection; died in Newport, R.I., on July 17, 1870; interment in Island Cemetery.

**KING, Henry** (brother of Thomas Butler King and uncle of John Floyd King), a Representative from Pennsylvania; born in Palmer, Hampden County, Mass., July 6, 1790; pursued classical studies; studied law in New London, Conn., and Wilkes-Barre, Pa.; was admitted to the bar in 1815 and commenced practice in Allentown, Lehigh County, Pa.; member of the Pennsylvania senate 1826-1828 and 1830-1832; elected as a Jacksonian to the Twenty-second and Twenty-third Congresses (March 4, 1831-March 3, 1835); was not a candidate for renomination in 1834 to the Twenty-Fourth Congress; resumed the practice of law; died in Allentown, Pa., July 13, 1861; interment in Union Cemetery.

**KING, James Gore** (son of Rufus King and brother of John Alsop King), a Representative from New Jersey; born in New York City May 8, 1791; pursued classical studies in England and France; returned to United States; was graduated from Harvard University in 1810; studied law at the Litchfield Law School; served in the War of 1812 as assistant adjutant general of New York Militia; engaged in mercantile pursuits in New York City in 1815 and in banking in Liverpool, England, in 1818; returned to New York City in 1824 and engaged in banking, with residence in Weehawken, N.J.; president of the Erie Railroad in 1835; elected as a Whig to the Thirty-first Congress (March 4, 1849-March 3, 1851); declined to be a candidate for renomination in 1850; resumed the banking business; died at his country place, "Highwood," near Weehawken, N.J., October 3, 1853; interment in the churchyard of Grace Church, Jamaica, N.Y.

Bibliography: *DAB.*

**KING, John,** a Representative from New York; born in what is now Canaan, Columbia County, N.Y., in 1775; attended the common schools; supervisor of the town of Canaan 1806-1808; sheriff of Columbia County, N.Y., 1811-1813 and 1815-1819; supervisor of the town of New Lebanon 1819-1823, 1826, and 1829; member of the State assembly in 1824; elected as a Jacksonian to the Twenty-second Congress (March 4, 1831-March 3, 1833); died in New Lebanon, Columbia County, N.Y., September 1, 1836; interment in the Cemetery of Evergreens.

**KING, John Alsop** (son of Rufus King and brother of James Gore King), a Representative from New York; born in New York City, January 3, 1788; attended Harrow School, England, and also studied in Paris; returned to New York City; studied law; was admitted to the bar; served in the War of 1812 as lieutenant of Cavalry; engaged in farming near Jamaica, N.Y.; member of the New York State assembly, 1819-1821; served in the State senate from 1823 until his resignation in 1825; appointed secretary of the legation at London in 1825; served as Chargé d'Affaires from June 15 to August 5, 1826; again elected to the State assembly in 1832, 1838, and 1840; delegate to the Whig National Conventions of 1839 and 1852; elected as a Whig to the Thirty-first Congress (March 4, 1849-March 3, 1851); resumed the practice of law; elected Governor of New York in 1856, and served from January 1, 1857 to January 1, 1859; delegate to the Republican National Convention of 1856; member of the peace convention of 1861 held in Washington, D.C., in an effort to devise means to prevent the impending war; died in Jamaica, Long Island, N.Y., July 7, 1867; interment in Grace Church Cemetery.

Bibliography: *DAB.*

**KING, John Floyd** (son of Thomas Butler King and nephew of Henry King), a Representative from Louisiana; born on St. Simons Island, off the coast of Georgia, April 20, 1842; attended the Russell School, New Haven, Conn., Bartlett's College Hill School, Pough-keepsie, N.Y., the Military Institute of Georgia, and the University of Virginia at Charlottesville; enlisted in the Confederate Army and served in the Army of Virginia throughout the Civil War, attaining the rank of colonel of Artillery; moved to Louisiana and engaged in planting; studied law; was admitted to the bar in 1872 and commenced practice in Vidalia, La.; appointed brigadier general of State troops; elected inspector of levees and president of the board of school directors of his district and also a trustee of the University of the South; elected as a Democrat to the Forty-sixth and to the three succeeding Congresses (March 4, 1879-March 3, 1887); chairman, Committee on Levees and Improvements of the Mississippi River

(Forty-eighth and Forty-ninth Congresses); unsuccessful candidate for renomination in 1886; engaged in mining operations, with residence in Washington, D.C.; Assistant Register of the United States Treasury from May 19, 1914, until his death in Washington, D.C., May 8, 1915; interment in Arlington National Cemetery, Va.

**KING, John Pendleton,** a Senator from Georgia; born in Glasgow, Barren County, Ky., April 3, 1799; moved in infancy with his parents to Bedford County, Tenn., and then to Augusta, Ga., in 1815; graduated from Richmond Academy, Augusta, Ga.; studied law; was admitted to the bar in 1819 and practiced in Augusta; pursued studies in Europe 1822-1824; returned and continued the practice of law in Augusta, Ga., until 1829; member of the State constitutional conventions in 1830 and 1833; appointed judge of the court of common pleas in 1831; elected in 1833 as a Jacksonian to the United States Senate to fill the vacancy caused by the resignation of George M. Troup; reelected in 1834 and served from November 21, 1833, until November 1, 1837, when he resigned; president of the Georgia Railroad & Banking Co. 1841-1878; railroad promoter and cotton manufacturer; member of the State constitutional convention in 1865; died in Summerville, Chattooga County, Ga., March 19, 1888; interment in St. Paul's Churchyard, Augusta, Ga.

Bibliography: *DAB.*

**KING, Karl Clarence,** a Representative from Pennsylvania; born in Plevna, Reno County, Kans., January 26, 1897; attended high school in Bucklin, Kans., Kansas State Teachers College at Emporia, Columbia University, New York City, and Wharton School of Business at Philadelphia, Pa.; during the First World War served in the United States Navy; newspaper reporter in Kansas City, New York, and Philadelphia; engaged in farming and the farm supply business at Morrisville, Pa., in 1922; elected as a Republican to the Eighty-second Congress, by special election, November 6, 1951, to fill the vacancy caused by the death of Albert C. Vaughn; reelected to the two succeeding Congresses and served from November 6, 1951, to January 3, 1957; was not a candidate for renomination in 1956 to the Eighty-fifth Congress; resided on his farm near Morrisville, Pa.; died in Philadelphia, Pa., April 16, 1974; interment in Newtown Cemetery, Newtown, Pa.

**KING, Perkins,** a Representative from New York; born in New Marlboro, Mass., January 12, 1784; pursued an academic course; studied law; was admitted to the bar; moved to Greenville, N.Y., in 1802, where he commenced the practice of law; town clerk in 1815; member of the State assembly in 1827; elected as a Jacksonian to the Twenty-first Congress (March 4, 1829-March 3, 1831); county judge of Greene County 1838-1847; resumed the practice of law; died in Freehold, Greene County, N.Y., November 29, 1857; interment in Snyder Cemetery.

**KING, Peter Thomas,** a Representative from New York; born in New York City, April 5, 1944; B.A., St. Francis College, 1965; J.D., Notre Dame University, 1968; New York National Guard service; admitted to New York bar, 1968; attorney; Deputy Nassau County Attorney, 1972-1974; executive assistant to the Nassau County Executive, 1974-1976; general counsel, Nassau Off-Track Betting Corp., 1977; Hempstead Town Councilman, 1978-1981; Nassau County comptroller, 1981-1993; elected as a Republican to the One Hundred Third and One Hundred Fourth Congresses (January 3, 1993-January 3, 1997); is a resident of Seaford, N.Y.

**KING, Preston,** a Representative and a Senator from New York; born in Ogdensburg, N.Y., October 14, 1806; pursued classical studies and graduated from Union College in 1827; studied law; was admitted to the bar and commenced practice in St. Lawrence County, N.Y.; established the St. Lawrence Republican in 1830; postmaster of Ogdensburg 1831-1834; member, State assembly 1835-1838; elected as a Democrat to the Twenty-eighth and

Twenty-ninth Congresses (March 4, 1843-March 3, 1847); was not a candidate for reelection in 1846 to the Thirtieth Congress; chairman, Committee on Invalid Pensions (Twenty-ninth Congress); elected as a Free Soiler to the Thirty-first and Thirty-second Congresses (March 4, 1849-March 3, 1853); elected as a Republican to the United States Senate in 1856 and served from March 4, 1857, to March 3, 1863; did not seek reelection in 1862; chairman, Committee on Revolutionary Claims (Thirty-seventh Congress); resumed the practice of law; presidential elector on the Republican ticket in 1864; appointed collector of the port of New York 1865; committed suicide by leaping from a ferryboat in New York Harbor, N.Y., on November 12, 1865; interment in the City Cemetery, Ogdensburg, N.Y.

**Bibliography:** *DAB*; Muller, Ernest. "Preston King: A Political Biography." Ph.D. dissertation, Columbia University, 1957.

**KING, Rufus** (half brother of Cyrus King and father of John Alsop King and James Gore King), a Delegate from Massachusetts and a Senator from New York; born in Scarboro, Maine (then a district of Massachusetts), March 24, 1755; attended Dummer Academy, Byfield, Mass., and graduated from Harvard College in 1777; served in the Revolutionary War; studied law; was admitted to the bar and commenced practice in Newburyport in 1780; delegate to the Massachusetts General Court, 1783-1785; Member of the Continental Congress from Massachusetts, 1784-1787; delegate to the Federal constitutional convention at Philadelphia in 1787, and to the Massachusetts convention in 1788 which ratified the same; moved to New York City in 1788; member, New York assembly; elected to the United States Senate in 1789; reelected in 1795, and served from July 16, 1789 until May 1796, when he resigned to become United States Minister to Great Britain; appointed Minister to Great Britain on May 20, 1796 and served until May 1803; unsuccessful candidate in 1804 for Vice President of the United States on the Federalist ticket headed by Charles Cotesworth Pinckney; again elected as a Federalist to the United States Senate in 1813; reelected in 1819, and served from March 4, 1813 to March 3, 1825; chairman, Committee on Roads and Canals (Sixteenth Congress), Committee on Foreign Relations (Seventeenth Congress); unsuccessful candidate for Governor of New York in 1815; unsuccessful Federalist candidate for President of the United States in 1816; again appointed United States Minister to Great Britain on May 5, 1825, and served until June 1826; died in Jamaica, Long Island, N.Y., April 29, 1827; interment in the churchyard of Grace Church.

**Bibliography:** *DAB*; Ernst, Robert. *Rufus King: American Federalist*. Chapel Hill: University of North Carolina Press, 1968; King, Charles, ed. *The Life and Correspondence of Rufus King*. 6 vols. 1894-1900. Reprint. New York: Da Capo Press, 1971.

**KING, Rufus H.,** a Representative from New York; born in Rensselaerville, Albany County, N.Y., January 20, 1820; completed preparatory studies and was graduated from Wesleyan University, Lima, N.Y.; studied law; was admitted to the bar in 1843 and commenced practice in Catskill, N.Y.; elected as a Whig to the Thirty-fourth Congress (March 4, 1855-March 3, 1857); was not a candidate for renomination in 1856 to the Thirty-fifth Congress; resumed the practice of law; president of the Catskill National Bank, 1865-1867; on the consolidation of that bank with the Tanners' National Bank continued on the board of directors; presidential elector on the Republican ticket in 1860; delegate to the Republican National Conventions of 1868 and 1880; died in Catskill, Greene County, N.Y., September 13, 1890; interment in Village Cemetery.

**KING, Samuel Wilder,** a Delegate from the Territory of Hawaii; born in Honolulu, Island of Oahu, Hawaii, December 17, 1886; attended St. Louis School at Honolulu and Honolulu High School; was graduated from the United States Naval Academy, Annapolis,

Md., in 1910; served in the United States Navy from 1910 until December 31, 1924, when he resigned with the rank of lieutenant commander; engaged in the real estate and insurance business in Honolulu in 1925; member of the board of supervisors of the city and county of Honolulu, 1932-1934; elected as a Republican a Delegate to the Seventy-fourth and to the three succeeding Congresses (January 3, 1935-January 3, 1943); was renominated in 1942 to the Seventy-eighth Congress, but withdrew to accept a commission as lieutenant commander in the United States Naval Reserve; was promoted to commander and later to captain, and served in the central Pacific area from January 4, 1943 to February 21, 1946; delegate to the Republican National Conventions of 1936, 1940, 1948, and 1952; member of Governor's Emergency Housing Committee in 1946; member of Hawaii Statehood Commission in 1947 and chairman from 1949 to 1953; president of constitutional convention in 1950; appointed Governor of Hawaii by President Dwight D. Eisenhower and served from February 28, 1953 until his resignation on July 31, 1957; died in Honolulu, Hawaii, March 24, 1959; interment in National Memorial Cemetery of the Pacific at Punchbowl, Honolulu, Hawaii.

**KING, Thomas Butler** (brother of Henry King and father of John Floyd King), a Representative from Georgia; born in Palmer, Hampden County, Mass., August 27, 1800; received private instructions and also attended Westfield Academy; read law with his brother at Allentown, Pa.; was admitted to the bar in Philadelphia in 1822 and commenced practice in Waynesville, Ga., in 1823; settled on St. Simons Island, Ga., in 1826 and engaged in agricultural pursuits; also interested in canal and railroad projects; member of the State senate in 1832, 1834, 1835, and 1837; delegate to the State constitutional convention in 1833 and to the State Whig conventions in 1835 and 1843; unsuccessful candidate for election in 1836 to the Twenty-fifth Congress; elected as a Whig to the Twenty-sixth and Twenty-seventh Congresses (March 4, 1839-March 3, 1843); unsuccessful candidate for reelection in 1842 to the Twenty-eighth Congress; delegate to the Whig National Convention of 1844; elected to the Twenty-ninth and to the two succeeding Congresses and served from March 4, 1845, until his resignation in 1850; chairman, Committee on Naval Affairs (Thirtieth Congress); appointed by President Millard Fillmore as collector of the port of San Francisco, Calif., October 14, 1850, and served until October 1, 1852, when he resigned; returned to St. Simons Island, Ga.; again a member of the State senate in 1859; delegate to the Democratic National Convention at Baltimore in 1860; appointed a commissioner of Georgia in 1861 to visit Europe in the interest of trade, and was a commissioner of the Confederacy in Europe 1861-1863; died in Waresboro, Ware County, Ga., May 10, 1864; interment in the churchyard of Christ Church, Frederica, St. Simons Island, Ga.

**Bibliography:** *DAB*; Steel, Edward M., Jr. *T. Butler King of Georgia*. Athens: University of Georgia Press, 1964.

**KING, William Henry** (father of David S. King), a Representative and a Senator from Utah; born in Fillmore, Millard County, Utah, June 3, 1863; attended the public schools, Brigham Young University, Provo, Utah, and the University of Utah at Salt Lake City; church missionary for the Church of the Latter Day Saints in Great Britain 1880-1883; returned to his home in Utah and was elected to various offices in the city of Fillmore and in Millard County; member, Territorial legislature two terms; was graduated from the law department of the University of Michigan at Ann Arbor; was admitted to the bar in 1890 and commenced practice in Utah; member, Territorial council 1891 and served as president; associate justice of the Utah supreme court 1894-1896, when Utah was admitted as a State into the Union; elected as a Democrat to the Fifty-fifth Congress (March 4, 1897-March 3, 1899); was not a candidate for renomination in 1898; elected to the Fifty-sixth Congress to fill the vacancy caused by the unseating of Brigham H. Roberts and served from April 2, 1900, to March 3, 1901;

unsuccessful candidate for reelection in 1900 to the Fifty-seventh Congress and for election in 1902 to the Fifty-eighth Congress; elected as a Democrat to the United States Senate in 1916; reelected in 1922, 1928, and 1934 and served from March 4, 1917, to January 3, 1941; unsuccessful candidate for renomination in 1940; served as President pro tempore of the Senate during the Seventy-sixth Congress; chairman, Committee on Expenditures in the Post Office Department (Sixty-fifth Congress), Committee on the District of Columbia (Seventy-third through Seventy-sixth Congresses); engaged in the practice of law in Washington, D.C., until April 1947; returned to Salt Lake City, Utah, where he resided until his death on November 27, 1949; interment in Salt Lake City Cemetery.

**Bibliography:** Hauptman, Laurence M. "Utah Anti-Imperialist: Senator William H. King and Haiti, 1921-1934." *Utah Historical Quarterly* 41 (Spring 1973): 116-27.

**KING, William Rufus de Vane,** a Representative from North Carolina, a Senator from Alabama, and a Vice President of the United States; born in Sampson County, N.C., April 7, 1786; attended private schools; graduated from the University of North Carolina at Chapel Hill in 1803; studied law; was admitted to the bar in 1806 and commenced practice in Clinton, N.C.; member, North Carolina State house of commons, 1807-1809; city solicitor of Wilmington, N.C., 1810; elected to the Twelfth and to the two succeeding Congresses, and served from March 4, 1811 until November 4, 1816, when he resigned; secretary of the legation at Naples and later at St. Petersburg; returned to the United States in 1818 and located in Cahaba, Ala.; planter; delegate to the convention which organized the State government; upon the admission of Alabama as a State into the Union in 1819 was elected as a Republican to the United States Senate; reelected as a Republican and as a Jacksonian in 1822, 1828, 1834, and 1841, and served from December 14, 1819 until April 15, 1844, when he resigned; served as President pro tempore of the Senate during the Twenty-fourth through Twenty-seventh Congresses; chairman, Committee on Public Lands (Twenty-second Congress), Committee on Commerce (Twenty-second, Twenty-fifth and Twenty-sixth Congresses); appointed Minister to France on April 9, 1844 and served until September 1846; appointed and subsequently elected as a Democrat to the United States Senate to fill the vacancy caused by the resignation of Arthur P. Bagby, and served from July 1, 1848 until his resignation on December 20, 1852, due to poor health; served as President pro tempore of the Senate during the Thirty-first and Thirty-second Congresses; chairman, Committee on Foreign Relations (Thirty-first Congress), Committee on Pensions (Thirty-first Congress); elected Vice President of the United States in 1852 on the Democratic ticket headed by Franklin Pierce; took the oath of office March 4, 1853, in Havana, Cuba, where he had gone for his health, which was a privilege extended by a special act of Congress; returned to his plantation, "King's Bend," Alabama, and died there on April 18, 1853; interment in a vault on his plantation; reinterment in Live Oak Cemetery, Selma, Ala.

**Bibliography:** *DAB*; Martin, John M. "William Rufus King: Southern Moderate." Ph.D. dissertation, University of North Carolina, 1955.

**KING, William Smith,** a Representative from Minnesota; born in Malone, Franklin County, N.Y., December 16, 1828; attended the common schools; engaged in agricultural pursuits; moved to Otsego County, N.Y., in 1846 and engaged as a solicitor for mutual insurance companies; editor of the Free Democrat in Cooperstown, N.Y., in 1852; moved to Minneapolis, Minn., in 1858; engaged in journalism and agricultural pursuits; postmaster of the House of Representatives 1861-1865 and 1867-1873; surveyor general of logs and lumber in the Second Congressional District of Minnesota in 1874; elected as a Republican to the Forty-fourth Congress (March 4, 1875-March 3, 1877); was not a candidate for renomination in 1876 to the Forty-fifth Congress; engaged in cattle raising near Minneapolis; died in Minneapolis, Hennepin County, Minn., on February 24, 1900; interment in Lakewood Cemetery.

**KINGSBURY, William Wallace,** a Delegate from the Territory of Minnesota; born in Towanda, Bradford County, Pa., June 4, 1828; attended the academies at Towanda and Athens; clerked in a store; became a surveyor; moved to Endion, Minn., in 1852; member of the Territorial house of representatives in 1857; delegate to the State constitutional convention in 1857; elected as a Democrat to the Thirty-fifth Congress and served from March 4, 1857, to May 11, 1858, when a portion of the Territory was admitted as a State into the Union; was not a candidate for renomination in 1858 to the Thirty-sixth Congress; returned to Towanda, Pa., in 1865 and engaged in the real estate and insurance business; engaged as a commission merchant in Baltimore, Md., for three years; moved to Tarpon Springs, Pinellas County, Fla., in 1887; engaged in real estate and mercantile pursuits until his death there on April 17, 1892; interment in Cydia Cemetery.

**KINGSTON, John Heddens (Jack),** a Representative from Georgia; born in Bryan, Brazos County, Tex., April 24, 1955; B.A., Michigan State University, 1973-1974; attended University of Georgia, 1975-1977; insurance agent, Palmer, Cay and Carswell, Inc., 1979-1993; member, Georgia State general assembly, 1974-1993; elected as a Republican to the One Hundred Third and One Hundred Fourth Congresses (January 3, 1993-January 3, 1997); is a resident of Savannah, Ga.

**KINKAID, Moses Pierce,** a Representative from Nebraska; born near Morgantown, Monongalia County, W.Va., January 24, 1856; attended the public schools; was graduated from the law department of the University of Michigan at Ann Arbor in 1876; was admitted to the bar and practiced in Henry County, Ill., from 1876 until 1880 and in Pierre, S.Dak., in 1880 and 1881; moved to O'Neill, Nebr., and continued the practice of law; member of the State senate in 1883; district judge 1887-1900; unsuccessful candidate for election in 1902 to the Fifty-seventh Congress; elected as a Republican to the Fifty-eighth and to the nine succeeding Congresses and served from March 4, 1903, until his death in Washington, D.C., July 6, 1922; chairman, Committee on Irrigation of Arid Lands (Sixty-sixth and Sixty-seventh Congresses); interment in Prospect Hill Cemetery, O'Neill, Holt County, Nebr.

**KINKEAD, Eugene Francis,** a Representative from New Jersey; born while his parents were on a visit abroad, in Buttevant, County Cork, Ireland, March 27, 1876; attended parochial schools in Jersey City, N.J., and was graduated from Seton Hall, South Orange, N.J., in 1895; president of the Jersey Railway Advertising Co. and the Orange Publishing Co.; president of the board of aldermen of Jersey City, N.J., in 1898; elected as a Democrat to the Sixty-first, Sixty-second, and Sixty-third Congresses and served from March 4, 1909, until February 4, 1915, when he resigned; sheriff of Hudson County, N.J., 1915-1917; commissioned major of the military intelligence division of the American forces during the First World War and stationed at the War College, Washington, D.C.; chairman of the executive committee of Colonial Trust Co., New York City, 1929-1960; died in South Orange, N.J., September 6, 1960; interment in Gate of Heaven Cemetery, Hanover, N.J.

**KINLOCH, Francis,** a Delegate from South Carolina; born in Charleston, S.C., March 7, 1755; educated by private tutors; went to England in 1768 and entered Eton College, from which institution he graduated in 1774; studied law at Lincoln's Inn, London, which he entered in 1774 and was admitted to the bar in that city; studied in Paris and Geneva 1774-1777; returned to the United States and served as volunteer, lieutenant, and captain in the Revolutionary War 1778-1781; served in the State house of representatives in 1779 and 1786-1788; Member of the Continental Congress in 1780; was an extensive rice planter at "Kensington," Georgetown District, S.C.;

delegate to the State convention which ratified the Federal Constitution May 23, 1788; elected warden of the city of Charleston and justice of the peace and quorum in 1789; member of the State legislative council in 1789 and of the State constitutional convention in 1790; died in Charleston, S.C., February 8, 1826; interment in St. Michael's Church Cemetery.

**KINNARD, George L.,** a Representative from Indiana; born in Pennsylvania in 1803; moved with his widowed mother to Tennessee and completed preparatory studies; moved to Indianapolis, Ind., in 1823; studied law; was admitted to the bar and practiced in Marion County, Ind.; assessor for Marion County in 1826 and 1827; member of the State house of representatives 1827-1830; county surveyor 1831-1835; State auditor for several years; colonel of the State militia; elected as a Jacksonian to the Twenty-third and Twenty-fourth Congresses and served from March 4, 1833, until his death from injuries received in an explosion on the steamer *Flora* on the Ohio River November 26, 1836; interment probably in Presbyterian Burying Ground (now Washington Park), Cincinnati, Ohio.

**KINNEY, John Fitch,** a Delegate from the Territory of Utah; born in New Haven, Oswego County, N.Y., April 2, 1816; completed preparatory studies; studied law; was admitted to the bar in 1837 and commenced practice in Marysville, Ohio; moved to Mount Vernon, Ohio, in 1839 and thence to Lee County, Iowa, in 1844; secretary of the State council in 1845 and 1846; prosecuting attorney of Lee County in 1846 and 1847; judge of the supreme court of Iowa from 1847 until January 1854, when he resigned; appointed by President Franklin Pierce chief justice of the supreme court of the Territory of Utah and served from January 1854 to 1857; moved to Nebraska City, Nebr., in 1857 and practiced law until 1860; again appointed by President James Buchanan chief justice of the Territory of Utah on June 26, 1860, and served until March 1863; elected as a Democrat to the Thirty-eighth Congress (March 4, 1863-March 3, 1865); was not a candidate for renomination in 1864 to the Thirty-ninth Congress; returned to Nebraska City, Nebr., and resumed the practice of law; appointed by President Andrew Johnson as a commissioner in February 1867 to visit the Sioux Indians; appointed by President Chester A. Arthur as agent of the Yankton Sioux Indians and served from December 11, 1884, until January 1, 1889, when he resigned; resumed the practice of law in Nebraska City, Nebr.; moved to San Diego, Calif., in 1889; died in Salt Lake City, Utah, on August 16, 1902; interment in Mount Hope Cemetery, San Diego, Calif.

**KINSELLA, Thomas,** a Representative from New York; born in County Wexford, Ireland, December 31, 1832; immigrated to the United States and settled in New York City; attended the common schools; moved to Cambridge, N.Y., in 1851 and learned the printer's trade; worked for the Cambridge Post; moved to Brooklyn in 1858; became editor of the Brooklyn Daily Eagle September 7, 1861; postmaster of Brooklyn in 1866; member of the city water commission and board of education; elected as a Democrat to the Forty-second Congress (March 4, 1871-March 3, 1873); was not a candidate for renomination in 1872; established the Brooklyn Sunday Sun in 1874, afterward combined with the Daily Eagle, which he edited until his death in Brooklyn, N.Y., February 11, 1884; interment in Holy Cross Cemetery.
**Bibliography:** *DAB.*

**KINSEY, Charles,** a Representative from New Jersey; born in Baltimore, Md., in 1773; attended the common schools; in early life engaged in the manufacture of paper; moved to Bloomfield Township, Essex County, N.J., and continued the industry; moved to Paterson, N.J., in 1802 and later to New Prospect (now Waldwick), Bergen County, N.J., continuing in the paper industry; member of the State general assembly in 1812, 1813, 1819, and 1826; served in the State council in 1814; elected as a Republican to the Fifteenth Congress (March 4, 1817-March 3, 1819); elected to the Sixteenth

Congress to fill the vacancy caused by the resignation of John Condit and served from February 2, 1820, to March 3, 1821; moved to New Prospect, near Hohokus, Bergen County, N.J., and carried on the manufacture of paper; judge of the court of common pleas and of the orphans' court of Bergen County 1830-1845; died in New Prospect, N.J., June 25, 1849; interment in Union Cemetery, near New Prospect.

**KINSEY, James,** a Delegate from New Jersey; born in Philadelphia, Pa., March 22, 1731; attended the common schools; studied law; was admitted to the New Jersey bar in 1753 and practiced in the courts of Pennsylvania and New Jersey, with residence in Burlington County, N.J.; member of the State general assembly 1772-1775; member of the committee of correspondence for Burlington County in 1774 and 1775; Member of the Continental Congress from July 23, 1774, until his resignation effective November 22, 1775; appointed chief justice of the supreme court of New Jersey on November 20, 1789, and served until his death in Burlington, N.J., January 4, 1803; interment in St. Mary's Churchyard.

**KINSEY, William Medcalf,** a Representative from Missouri; born in Mount Pleasant, Jefferson County, Ohio, October 28, 1846; attended Hopedale Academy, Harrison County, Ohio, and Monmouth College, Illinois; became a resident of Muscatine County, Iowa, in 1863; studied law at the University of Iowa in Iowa City in 1871; was admitted to the bar in 1872 and commenced practice in Muscatine County, Iowa, the same year; moved to St. Louis, Mo., in 1875 and engaged in the practice of law; elected as a Republican to the Fifty-first Congress (March 4, 1889-March 3, 1891); unsuccessful candidate for reelection in 1890 to the Fifty-second Congress; resumed the practice of law in St. Louis, Mo.; judge of the circuit court of the city of St. Louis 1904-1917; during the First World War was chairman of the draft examining board in Carondelet; resumed the practice of his profession; died in St. Louis, Mo., June 20, 1931; interment in Sunset Hill Burial Park, St. Louis County, Mo.

**KINSLEY, Martin,** a Representative from Massachusetts; born in Bridgewater, Mass., June 2, 1754; was graduated from Harvard College in 1778; studied medicine; purveyor of supplies in the Revolutionary Army; member of the Massachusetts house of representatives in 1787, 1788, 1790-1792, 1794-1796, 1801-1804, and 1806; treasurer of Hardwick, Mass., 1787-1792; moved to Hampden in 1797; representative of Hampden in the general court 1801-1804 and 1806; member of the executive council in 1810 and 1811; judge of the court of common pleas in 1811; judge of the probate court; served in the State senate in 1814; elected to the Sixteenth Congress (March 4, 1819-March 3, 1821); unsuccessful candidate for reelection in 1820 to the Seventeenth Congress; died in Roxbury, Mass., June 20, 1835.

**KINZER, John Roland,** a Representative from Pennsylvania; born on a farm near Terre Hill in East Earl Township, Lancaster County, Pa., March 28, 1874; attended the public schools; was graduated from Franklin and Marshall College, Lancaster, Pa., in 1896; studied law; was admitted to the bar in 1900 and commenced practice in Lancaster, Pa.; served as county solicitor of Lancaster County 1912-1923; delegate to the Republican National Convention in 1928; elected as a Republican to the Seventy-first Congress to fill the vacancy caused by the death of William W. Griest; reelected to the Seventy-second and to the seven succeeding Congresses and served from January 28, 1930, to January 3, 1947; was not a candidate for renomination in 1946; resumed the practice of law; died in Lancaster, Pa., July 25, 1955; interment in Woodward Hill Cemetery.

**KIPP, George Washington,** a Representative from Pennsylvania; born in Green Township, Pike County, Pa., March 28, 1847; attended the public schools; engaged in the lumber business for thirty-five years; county commissioner of Wayne County, Pa., in 1880; elected as a Democrat to the Sixtieth Congress (March 4, 1907-March 3, 1909); was not a candidate for renomination in 1908 to the Sixty-first Congress, being an unsuccessful candidate for State treasurer; resumed his former business pursuits; elected to the Sixty-second Congress and served from March 4, 1911, until his death, before Congress assembled, on Vancouver Island, British Columbia, Canada, July 24, 1911; interment in Oak Hill Cemetery, Towanda, Bradford County, Pa.

**KIRBY, William Fosgate,** a Senator from Arkansas; born near Texarkana, Miller County, Ark., November 16, 1867; attended the common schools; studied law at Cumberland University, Lebanon, Tenn., and graduated in 1885; was admitted to the bar in 1885 and commenced practice in Texarkana, Ark.; member, State house of representatives 1893, 1897; member, State senate 1899-1901; author of "Kirby's Digest of the Statutes of Arkansas" in 1904; moved to Little Rock in 1907; attorney general of Arkansas 1907-1909; elected associate justice of the supreme court of Arkansas 1910-1916, when he resigned, having been elected as a Democrat to the United States Senate to fill the vacancy caused by the death of James P. Clarke; served from November 8, 1916, to March 3, 1921; unsuccessful candidate for renomination in 1920 and again in 1932; chairman, Committee on Expenditures in the Department of Agriculture (Sixty-fourth and Sixty-fifth Congresses), Committee on Patents (Sixty-fifth Congress); resumed the practice of law; an associate justice of the supreme court of Arkansas from 1926 until his death in Little Rock, Ark., July 26, 1934; interment in State Line Cemetery, Texarkana, Ark.

Bibliography: Niswonger, Richard L. "William F. Kirby, Arkansas's Maverick Senator." *Arkansas Historical Quarterly* 37 (Autumn 1978): 252-63.

**KIRK, Andrew Jackson,** a Representative from Kentucky; born near Warfield, Martin County, Ky., on March 19, 1866; attended the common schools; was graduated from the law department of Valparaiso (Ind.) University in 1890; was admitted to the bar the same year and commenced practice in Inez, Ky.; county attorney of Martin County 1894-1898; Commonwealth attorney for the twenty-fourth judicial district of Kentucky 1898-1904; circuit judge of the same district 1904-1916; resumed the practice of law in Jenkins, Letcher County, and in Paintsville, Johnson County, Ky., in 1918; elected as a Republican to the Sixty-ninth Congress to fill the vacancy caused by the resignation of John W. Langley and served from February 13, 1926, to March 3, 1927; unsuccessful candidate for renomination in 1926; resumed the practice of law in Paintsville, Ky.; Republican candidate for nomination as circuit judge at the time of his death in Paintsville, Ky., May 25, 1933; interment in Kirk Cemetery near Inez, Ky.

**KIRKLAND, Joseph,** a Representative from New York; born in Newent Society, in the present town of Lisbon (then part of Norwich), Conn., January 18, 1770; was graduated from Yale College in 1790; studied law; was admitted to the bar in 1794 and commenced practice in New Hartford, Oneida County, N.Y.; member of the State assembly in 1804 and 1805; moved to Utica, N.Y., in 1813; district attorney for the fifth district of New York 1813-1816; again served in the State assembly in 1818, 1820, 1821, and 1825; elected to the Seventeenth Congress (March 4, 1821-March 3, 1823); resumed the practice of law; mayor of Utica 1832-1836; died in Utica, Oneida County, N.Y., January 26, 1844; interment in Forest Hill Cemetery.

**KIRKPATRICK, Littleton,** a Representative from New Jersey; born in New Brunswick, N.J., October 19, 1797; was graduated from Princeton College in 1815; studied law in Washington, D.C.; was admitted to the bar in 1821 and commenced practice in New Brunswick, N.J.; master in court chancery in 1824; surrogate of Middlesex County 1831-1836; mayor of New Brunswick in 1841 and 1842; trustee of Rutgers College 1841-1859; elected as a Democrat to the Twenty-eighth Congress (March 4, 1843-March 3, 1845); chairman, Committee on Revisal and Unfinished Business (Twenty-eighth Congress); died in Saratoga Springs, N.Y., August 15, 1859; interment in Presbyterian Cemetery, New Brunswick, N.J.; reinterment in Van Liew Cemetery in 1921.

**KIRKPATRICK, Sanford,** a Representative from Iowa; born near London, Madison County, Ohio, February 11, 1842; moved to Iowa in 1849 with his parents, who settled on a farm in Highland Township, Wapello County; attended the common schools 1854-1858; during the Civil War entered the Union Army as a private in the Second Iowa Infantry and served four years and four months and was promoted to first lieutenant; engaged in agricultural pursuits; moved to Ottumwa, Iowa, in 1876 and engaged in mercantile pursuits until 1887; deputy recorder of Wapello County 1876-1880; member of the Ottumwa City Council 1884-1887; representative of the Internal Revenue Service 1887-1913; elected as a Democrat to the Sixty-third Congress (March 4, 1913-March 3, 1915); unsuccessful candidate for reelection in 1914 to the Sixty-fourth Congress; moved to Greensboro, N.C., in 1916 and engaged in agricultural pursuits; died in Greensboro, N.C., February 13, 1932; interment in Forest Lawn Cemetery.

**KIRKPATRICK, Snyder Solomon,** a Representative from Kansas; born near Mulkey, Franklin County, Ill., February 21, 1848; attended the common schools; during the Civil War served in the One Hundred and Thirty-sixth Regiment, Illinois Volunteer Cavalry, in 1864; engaged in mercantile pursuits in 1865; entered the law school at Ann Arbor, Mich., in 1867; returned to Illinois; admitted to the bar by the supreme court of Illinois June 30, 1868, and commenced practice at Cairo; moved to Kansas in 1873 and settled in Fredonia; engaged in the practice of law; elected prosecuting attorney of Wilson County in 1880; member of the State senate 1889-1893; unsuccessful candidate for election in 1892 to the Fifty-third Congress; elected as a Republican to the Fifty-fourth Congress (March 4, 1895-March 3, 1897); unsuccessful candidate for reelection to the Fifty-fifth Congress and for election to the Fifty-sixth and Fifty-seventh Congresses; member of the State house of representatives 1903-1905; died in Fredonia, Wilson County, Kans., April 5, 1909; interment in Fredonia Cemetery.

**KIRKPATRICK, William,** a Representative from New York; born in Amwell, Hunterdon County, near Zion, N.J., November 7, 1769; was graduated from Princeton College in 1788; studied medicine at the University of Pennsylvania and commenced practice in Whitestown, Oneida County, N.Y., in 1795; moved to Salina (now a part of Syracuse), Onondaga County, N.Y., in 1806 and continued the practice of medicine; subsequently became superintendent of the Onondaga Salt Springs; elected as a Republican to the Tenth Congress (March 4, 1807-March 3, 1809); again superintendent of the Onondaga Salt Springs 1810-1831; died in Salina, N.Y., September 2, 1832; interment in Oakwood Cemetery, Syracuse, N.Y.

**KIRKPATRICK, William Huntington** (son of William Sebring Kirkpatrick), a Representative from Pennsylvania; born in Easton, Northampton County, Pa., October 2, 1885; attended the public schools; was graduated from Lafayette College, Easton, Pa., in 1905 and attended the law department of the University of Pennsylvania in 1905 and 1906; was admitted to the bar and commenced the practice of law in Easton, Pa., in 1908; served in the First World War as major and lieutenant colonel, judge advocate, and was a member of the board of review of courts-martial, United States Army; elected as a Republican to the Sixty-seventh Congress (March 4, 1921-March 3, 1923); unsuccessful candidate for reelection to the Sixty-eighth Congress in 1922; resumed the practice of law;

appointed on March 3, 1927, judge of the United States District Court for the Eastern District of Pennsylvania, and became chief judge in 1933; became senior judge when he retired in 1958; died in Cumberstone, Md., November 28, 1970; interment in Christ Church Cemetery, Owensville, Md.

**KIRKPATRICK, William Sebring** (father of William Huntington Kirkpatrick), a Representative from Pennsylvania; born in Easton, Northampton County, Pa., April 21, 1844; attended the public schools and Lafayette College, Easton, Pa.; studied law; was admitted to the bar October 2, 1865, and commenced practice in Easton; solicitor of Easton 1866-1874; teacher in the Easton public schools in 1868 and 1869; appointed president judge of the third judicial district in 1874; member of the faculty of Lafayette College 1875-1877 and member of the board of trustees 1890-1932; presided temporarily over the Pennsylvania Republican convention in 1882; delegate to the Republican National Convention in 1884; attorney general of Pennsylvania 1887-1891; lecturer on municipal law at Lafayette College; unsuccessful candidate for election in 1894 to the Fifty-fourth Congress; elected as a Republican to the Fifty-fifth Congress (March 4, 1897-March 3, 1899); unsuccessful candidate for reelection in 1898 to the Fifty-sixth Congress; resumed the practice of law; died in Easton, Pa., November 3, 1932; interment in Easton Cemetery.

**KIRKWOOD, Samuel Jordan,** a Senator from Iowa; born in Harford County, Md., December 20, 1813; attended country schools and the academy of John McLoed in Washington, D.C.; clerked in a drug store and taught school; moved to Mansfield, Richmond County, Ohio, in 1835 and continued teaching until 1840; studied law; was admitted to the bar in 1843 and commenced practice in Mansfield; prosecuting attorney of Richland County from 1845 until 1849; member of the State constitutional convention in 1850 and 1851; moved to Coralville, Johnson County, Iowa, in 1855 and engaged in the milling business; member, Iowa State senate, 1856-1859; elected Governor of Iowa in 1859, reelected in 1861, and served from January 11, 1860 to January 14, 1864; appointed by President Abraham Lincoln as Minister to Denmark on March 11, 1863, but declined; elected as a Republican to the United States Senate to fill the vacancy caused by the resignation of James Harlan and served from January 13, 1866, to March 3, 1867; resumed the practice of law and also served as president of the Iowa & Southwestern Railroad Co.; elected Governor in 1875, and served from January 13, 1876 until February 1, 1877, when he resigned to become Senator; served in the United States Senate as a Republican from March 4, 1877 to March 7, 1881, when he resigned to accept a Cabinet portfolio; Secretary of the Interior in the Cabinet of President James A. Garfield from March 8, 1881 until his resignation on April 5, 1882; unsuccessful candidate for election in 1886 to the Fiftieth Congress; resumed the practice of law; president of the Iowa City National Bank; died in Iowa City, Johnson County, Iowa, on September 1, 1894; interment in Oakland Cemetery.

**Bibliography:** *DAB*; Clark, Dan E. *Samuel Jordan Kirkwood.* Iowa City: The State Historical Society of Iowa, 1917; Hake, Herbert. "The Political Firecracker: Samuel J. Kirkwood." *Palimpsest* 56 (January/February 1975): 2-14.

**KIRTLAND, Dorrance,** a Representative from New York; born in Coxsackie, Greene County, N.Y., July 28, 1770; was graduated from Yale College in 1789; studied law; was admitted to the bar and commenced practice in Coxsackie; surrogate of Greene County 1808-1838; elected as a Republican to the Fifteenth Congress (March 4, 1817-March 3, 1819); judge of the court of common pleas of Greene County 1828-1838; died in Coxsackie, N.Y., May 23, 1840; interment in Old Coxsackie Cemetery.

**KIRWAN, Michael Joseph,** a Representative from Ohio; born in Wilkes-Barre, Luzerne County, Pa., December 2, 1886; attended the public and high schools of his native city; moved to Youngstown,

Mahoning County, Ohio, in 1907; during the First World War served overseas as a sergeant in the Three Hundred and Forty-eighth Machine Gun Company with the Sixty-fourth Artillery, United States Army, 1917-1919; engaged in the mercantile business 1930-1936; member of the Youngstown City Council 1932-1936; elected as a Democrat to the Seventy-fifth and to the sixteen succeeding Congresses, serving from January 3, 1937, until his death in Bethesda, Md., July 27, 1970; interment in Calvary Cemetery, Youngstown, Ohio.

**KISSEL, John,** a Representative from New York; born in Brooklyn, N.Y., July 31, 1864; attended public and private schools; served as clerk in the Brooklyn Navy Yard; learned the printing trade and published the Kings County Republican 1889-1914; became a member of the Republican State committee in 1886; clerk to the board of supervisors in 1894 and 1895; engaged in the brewery business; member of State senate in 1909 and 1910; organized and for fifteen years conducted at his own expense the first free labor bureau in this country, which was subsequently merged into the National Employment Agency; elected as a Republican to the Sixty-seventh Congress (March 4, 1921-March 3, 1923); unsuccessful candidate for reelection in 1922 to the Sixty-eighth Congress; general tax consultant with offices in Brooklyn, N.Y.; employed as an attendant at the Empire State Building in 1932; died in Brooklyn, N.Y., October 3, 1938; interment in the Lutheran Cemetery, Queens, Long Island, N.Y.

**KITCHELL, Aaron** a Representative and a Senator from New Jersey; born in Hanover, N.J., July 10, 1744; attended the common schools; became a blacksmith; elected to the Second Congress (March 4, 1791-March 3, 1793); elected to the Third Congress to fill the vacancy caused by the death of Abraham Clark; reelected to the Fourth Congress, and served from January 29, 1795 to March 3, 1797; resumed his former business activities; again elected to the Sixth Congress (March 4, 1799-March 3, 1801); elected as a Republican to the United States Senate, and served from March 4, 1805 to March 12, 1809, when he resigned; member, New Jersey State general assembly, 1781-1782, 1784, 1786-1790, 1793-1794, 1797, 1801-1804, 1809; died in Hanover, Morris County, N.J., on June 25, 1820; interment in the churchyard of the Presbyterian Church.

**KITCHEN, Bethuel Middleton,** a Representative from West Virginia; born in Ganotown, Berkeley County, Va. (now West Virginia), March 21, 1812; attended the common schools; engaged in agricultural pursuits and stock raising; member of the Virginia house of delegates in 1861 and 1862; served in the West Virginia State senate in 1864 and 1865; presented credentials as a Member-elect to the Thirty-eighth Congress, but was not permitted to qualify because the votes cast included those from Berkeley County, which was not mentioned in the act of Congress admitting West Virginia, and hence the assent of Congress had not yet been given, and the county was still a part of Virginia; Lewis McKenzie contested the election, but inasmuch as the voting was confined to less than half the district neither claimant was admitted; elected as a Republican to the Fortieth Congress (March 4, 1867-March 3, 1869); was not a candidate for renomination in 1868 to the Forty-first Congress; resumed his former pursuits; president of the Agricultural and Mechanical Association of Berkeley, Jefferson, and Morgan Counties 1869-1875; master of West Virginia State Grange 1873-1879; again a member of the West Virginia State senate in 1878 and 1879; president of the county court of Berkeley County, W.Va., 1880-1895; died in Shanghai, Berkeley County, W.Va., December 15, 1895; interment in the Presbyterian Churchyard.

**KITCHENS, Wade Hampton,** a Representative from Arkansas; born on a farm near Falcon, Nevada County, Ark., December 26, 1878; attended the common schools, Southern Academy, and the University of Arkansas at Fayetteville; was graduated from the law department of Cumberland University at Lebanon, Tenn., in 1900; in 1898 served as a sergeant in Company I, First Arkansas Regiment, during the Spanish-American War; served as a private in Company E, Twentieth and Second United States Infantry, during the Philippine Insurrection, 1900-1902; was admitted to the bar in 1900 and practiced at Manila and at Lingayen, P.I., 1902-1909; returned to the United States in 1909, located in Magnolia, Ark., and continued the practice of law; delegate to the Democratic State conventions at Little Rock, Ark., in 1910 and 1912; during the First World War enlisted in the United States Army on May 18, 1917; commissioned captain of Infantry on August 5, 1917, and served overseas; member of the Arkansas State house of representatives, 1929-1933; elected as a Democrat to the Seventy-fifth and Seventy-sixth Congresses (January 3, 1937-January 3, 1941); unsuccessful candidate for renomination in 1940 to the Seventy-seventh Congress; resumed the practice of law; died in Magnolia, Ark., August 22, 1966; interment in Columbia Cemetery, Waldo, Ark.

**KITCHIN, Alvin Paul** (nephew of Claude Kitchin and William Walton Kitchin and grandson of William Hodges Kitchin), a Representative from North Carolina; born in Scotland Neck, Halifax County, N.C., September 13, 1908; educated in the public schools; attended the Oak Ridge Military Institute, 1923-1925; graduated from Wake Forest Law School in 1930; was admitted to the bar in 1930 and commenced the practice of law in Scotland Neck, N.C.; with Federal Bureau of Investigation, Washington, D.C., from January 1933 to August 1945; resumed the practice of law in Wadesboro, N.C.; elected as a Democrat to the Eighty-fifth and to the two succeeding Congresses (January 3, 1957-January 3, 1963); unsuccessful candidate for election in 1962 to the Eighty-eighth Congress; resumed the practice of law; was a resident of Wadesboro, N.C., until his death there on October 22, 1983.

**KITCHIN, Claude** (son of William Hodges Kitchin, brother of William Walton Kitchin, and uncle of Alvin Paul Kitchin), a Representative from North Carolina; born near Scotland Neck, Halifax County, N.C., March 24, 1869; attended the common schools and was graduated from Wake Forest College, North Carolina, in 1888; studied law; was admitted to the bar in 1890 and practiced in Scotland Neck; elected as a Democrat to the Fifty-seventh and to the eleven succeeding Congresses, and served from March 4, 1901 until his death in Wilson, N.C., May 31, 1923; chairman, Committee on Ways and Means (Sixty-fourth and Sixty-fifth Congresses); majority leader (Sixty-fourth and Sixty-fifth Congresses), minority leader (Sixty-seventh Congress); interment in the Baptist Cemetery, Scotland Neck, N.C.

**Bibliography:** *DAB*; Arnett, Alex M. *Claude Kitchin and the Wilson War Policies*. Boston: Little, Brown, 1937; Ingle, Homer L. "Pilgrimage to Reform: A Life of Claude Kitchin." Ph.D. dissertation, University of Wisconsin, 1967.

**KITCHIN, William Hodges** (father of Claude Kitchin and William Walton Kitchin, and grandfather of Alvin Paul Kitchin), a Representative from North Carolina; born in Lauderdale County, Ala., December 22, 1837; moved with his parents to North Carolina in 1841; attended Emory and Henry College, Emory, Va.; left college in April 1861 to enlist in the Confederate Army; was promoted to the rank of captain in 1863 and served throughout the Civil War; studied law; was admitted to the bar in 1869 and practiced in Scotland Neck, N.C.; elected as a Democrat to the Forty-sixth Congress (March 4, 1879-March 3, 1881); unsuccessful candidate for reelection in 1880 to the Forty-seventh Congress; died in Scotland Neck, Halifax County, N.C., February 2, 1901; interment in the Baptist Cemetery.

**Bibliography:** Ingle, H. Larry. "A Southern Democrat at Large: William Hodges Kitchin and the Populist Party." *North Carolina Historical Review* 45 (April 1968): 178-94.

**KITCHIN, William Walton** (son of William Hodges Kitchin, brother of Claude Kitchin, and uncle of Alvin Paul Kitchin), a Representative from North Carolina; born near Scotland Neck, Halifax County, N.C., October 9, 1866; attended private schools and Vine Hill Academy; was graduated from Wake Forest College, North Carolina, in 1884; edited the Scotland Neck Democrat in 1885; studied law in Scotland Neck and at the University of North Carolina at Chapel Hill; was admitted to the bar in 1887 and commenced practice in Roxboro, N.C., in 1889; chairman of the county executive committee in 1890; Democratic candidate for election to the North Carolina State senate in 1892; elected as a Democrat to the Fifty-fifth and to the five succeeding Congresses, and served from March 4, 1897 until January 11, 1909, when he resigned, having been elected Governor; elected Governor of North Carolina in 1908, and served from January 12, 1909 to January 15, 1913; resumed the practice of law in Raleigh, N.C.; died in Scotland Neck, N.C., November 9, 1924; interment in the Baptist Cemetery.

**Bibliography:** *DAB*.

**KITTERA, John Wilkes** (father of Thomas Kittera), a Representative from Pennsylvania; born near Blue Ball, East Earl Township, Lancaster County, Pa., in November 1752; was graduated from Princeton College in 1776; studied law; was admitted to the bar in 1782 and commenced practice in Lancaster, Pa.; elected to the Second Congress; reelected to the Third Congress and reelected as a Federalist to the Fourth through Sixth Congresses (March 4, 1791-March 3, 1801); appointed by President Jefferson as United States attorney for the eastern district of Pennsylvania March 4, 1801, and served until his death in Lancaster, Pa., on June 6, 1801; interment in the Presbyterian Cemetery.

**KITTERA, Thomas** (son of John Wilkes Kittera), a Representative from Pennsylvania; born in Lancaster, Pa., March 21, 1789; was graduated from the University of Pennsylvania at Philadelphia in 1805; studied law; was admitted to the bar in 1808 and commenced practice in Philadelphia; deputy attorney general of Pennsylvania in 1817 and 1818; deputy attorney general of Philadelphia 1824-1826; member of the select council and its president 1824-1825; elected to the Nineteenth Congress to fill the vacancy caused by the resignation of Joseph Hemphill and served from October 10, 1826, to March 3, 1827; at the same election was an unsuccessful candidate for election to the Twentieth Congress; died in Philadelphia, Pa., on June 16, 1839; interment in St. Paul's Protestant Episcopal Church Cemetery.

**KITTREDGE, Alfred Beard,** a Senator from South Dakota; born in Nelson, Cheshire County, N.H., March 28, 1861; attended the public schools; graduated from Yale College in 1882 and from the Yale Law School in 1885; was admitted to the bar in 1885 and commenced practice in Sioux Falls, S.Dak.; member, State senate 1889-1891; member of the Republican National Committee 1892-1896; appointed and subsequently elected as a Republican to the United States Senate to fill the vacancy caused by the death of James H. Kyle; reelected in 1903 and served from July 11, 1901, to March 3, 1909; unsuccessful candidate for renomination in 1908; chairman, Select Committee on Standards, Weights and Measures (Fifty-seventh Congress), Committee on Patents (Fifty-eighth and Fifty-ninth Congresses), Committee on Interoceanic Canals (Sixtieth Congress); engaged in the practice of law at Sioux Falls, S.Dak., until his death at Hot Springs, Ark., May 4, 1911; interment in Conant Cemetery, East Jaffrey, Cheshire County, N.H.

**Bibliography:** Coursey, Oscar. *Biography of Senator Alfred Beard Kittredge*. Mitchell, S.D.: The Educator Supply Company, 1915.

**KITTREDGE, George Washington,** a Representative from New Hampshire; born in Epping, N.H., January 31, 1805; received a liberal schooling; attended the medical department of Harvard

University and engaged in the practice of medicine in Newmarket, N.H., in 1835; member of the State house of representatives in 1835, 1847, 1848, and 1852, and served as speaker in the last-named year; a director of the Boston & Maine Railroad Co. 1836-1856; president of the Newmarket Savings Bank for forty years; elected as a Democrat to the Thirty-third Congress (March 4, 1853-March 3, 1855); chairman, Committee on Expenditures in the Department of War (Thirty-third Congress); unsuccessful candidate for reelection in 1854 to the Thirty-fourth Congress and for election in 1856 to the Thirty-fifth Congress; resumed the practice of medicine; died in Newmarket, N.H., March 6, 1881; interment in Forest Hills Cemetery near Boston, Mass.

**KLEBERG, Richard Mifflin, Sr.** (nephew of Rudolph Kleberg, cousin of Robert Christian Eckhardt), a Representative from Texas; born on a ranch near Kingsville, Kleberg County, Tex., November 18, 1887; attended the public schools; was graduated from Corpus Christi (Tex.) High School in 1905 and from the University of Texas at Austin in 1911; studied law; was admitted to the bar in 1909; employed as foreman of the King Ranch, Kingsville, Tex., in 1911, and was active in its management from 1913 to 1924; also engaged in banking; president of the board of Texas College of Arts and Industry, 1929-1931; elected as a Democrat to the Seventy-second Congress to fill the vacancy caused by the death of Harry M. Wurzbach; reelected to the Seventy-third and to the five succeeding Congresses and served from November 24, 1931, to January 3, 1945; unsuccessful candidate for renomination in 1944 to the Seventy-ninth Congress; resumed ranching activities; member of the Texas State Game and Fish Commission, 1951-1955; chairman of the board of the King Ranch Corp., Kingsville, Tex., at time of his death; died while on a visit in Hot Springs, Ark., May 8, 1955; interment in Chamberlain Burial Park, Kingsville, Tex.

**KLEBERG, Rudolph** (great uncle of Robert Christian Eckhardt, uncle of Richard Mifflin Kleberg, Sr.), a Representative from Texas; born in Cat Spring, Austin County, Tex., on June 26, 1847; instructed by private tutors; was graduated from Concrete College, De Witt County, in 1868; enlisted in Tom Green's brigade of Cavalry in the Confederate Army in the spring of 1864 and served until the close of the Civil War; studied law in San Antonio, Tex.; was admitted to the bar in 1872 and commenced practice in Cuero, Tex.; established the Cuero Star in 1873; prosecuting attorney of De Witt County from 1876 until 1890; member of the Texas State senate, 1882-1886; appointed United States attorney for the western district of Texas in 1885; elected as a Democrat to the Fifty-fourth Congress to fill the vacancy caused by the death of William H. Crain; reelected to the three succeeding Congresses and served from April 7, 1896, to March 3, 1903; was not a candidate for renomination in 1902 to the Fifty-eighth Congress; resumed the practice of law; moved to Austin, Tex., in 1905; appointed official reporter for the court of criminal appeals on February 24, 1905, and served until his death in Austin, December 28, 1924; interment in Oakwood Cemetery.

**KLECZKA, Gerald Daniel,** a Representative from Wisconsin; born in Milwaukee, Milwaukee County, Wis., November 26, 1943; attended St. Helen's grammar school; graduated from Don Bosco High School, 1961; attended University of Wisconsin, Milwaukee; accountant; served in the Wisconsin Air National Guard, 1963-1969; Milwaukee County Council representative, 1965-1968; served in the Wisconsin assembly, 1968-1974; Wisconsin senate, 1974-1984; delegate, Wisconsin State Democratic conventions, 1966-1984; delegate, Democratic National Convention, 1980 and 1984; elected as a Democrat to the Ninety-eighth Congress, by special election, April 3, 1984, to fill the vacancy caused by the death of Clement J. Zablocki; reelected to the six succeeding Congresses and served from April 3, 1984, to January 3, 1997; is a resident of Milwaukee, Wis.

**KLECZKA, John Casimir,** a Representative from Wisconsin; born in Milwaukee, Wis., on May 6, 1885; attended the parochial schools; was graduated from Marquette University, Milwaukee, Wis., in 1905; took postgraduate courses at Catholic University at Washington, D.C., and at the University of Wisconsin at Madison; studied law; was admitted to the bar in 1909 and commenced practice in Milwaukee; served in the State senate 1909-1911; delegate to the Republican National Convention in 1912; commissioner of the circuit court of Milwaukee County 1914-1918; major judge advocate in the United States Army Reserves after the First World War; elected as a Republican to the Sixty-sixth and Sixty-seventh Congresses (March 4, 1919-March 3, 1923); did not seek renomination in 1922 but returned to the practice of law; elected circuit court judge in 1930 and served until his retirement due to ill health in 1953; appointed a conciliation judge and court commissioner by the circuit judges in 1957 and served until his death; died in Milwaukee, Wis., April 21, 1959; interment in St. Adalbert's Cemetery.

**KLEIN, Arthur George,** a Representative from New York; born in New York City, August 8, 1904; attended the public schools and Washington Square College of New York University at New York City; was graduated from the law department of New York University in 1926; was admitted to the bar in 1927 and commenced practice in New York City; connected with the Securities and Exchange Commission in Washington, D.C., and New York City, 1935-1941; elected as a Democrat to the Seventy-seventh Congress to fill the vacancy caused by the death of M. Michael Edelstein; reelected to the Seventy-eighth Congress, and served from July 29, 1941 to January 3, 1945; was not a candidate for renomination in 1944 to the Seventy-ninth Congress; elected to the Seventy-ninth Congress to fill the vacancy caused by the resignation of Samuel Dickstein; reelected in 1946 to the Eightieth and to the four succeeding Congresses, and served from February 19, 1946 until his resignation on December 31, 1956; unsuccessful candidate in 1966 for election to the New York Surrogate's Court; elected to the New York State Supreme Court for the term commencing January 1, 1957, and served until his death in New York City on February 20, 1968; interment in Mount Moriah Cemetery, Fairview, N.J.

**KLEIN, Herbert Charles,** a Representative from New Jersey; born in Newark, N.J., June 24, 1930; B.A., Rutgers University, 1947; J.D., Harvard University School of Law, 1953; LL.M., New York University, 1958; United States Air Force service, two years; member, New Jersey State assembly, 1972-1976; attorney, Clifton, N.J.; elected as a Democrat to the One Hundred Third Congress (January 3, 1993-January 3, 1995); unsuccessful candidate for reelection in 1994 to the One Hundred Fourth Congress; resumed the practice of law with the firm of Hannoch Weisman in Roseland, N.J., and Washington, D.C.; is a resident of Clifton, N.J.

**KLEINER, John Jay,** a Representative from Indiana; born in West Hanover, Dauphin County, Pa., February 8, 1845; moved to Medina County, Ohio, in 1850 with his parents, who settled near Wadsworth; attended the public schools and assisted his father in agricultural pursuits; during the Civil War enlisted on June 20, 1863, in Company G, Eighty-sixth Regiment, Ohio Volunteer Infantry, and served until February 10, 1864; returned to Wadsworth, Ohio, where he resided until 1867; moved to Evansville, Ind., in 1867; taught in the Evansville Business College and edited the Saturday Argus of that city; member of the city council of Evansville in 1873; engaged in the manufacture and sale of lumber; mayor of Evansville 1874-1880; elected as a Democrat to the Forty-eighth and Forty-ninth Congresses (March 4, 1883-March 3, 1887); unsuccessful candidate for reelection in 1886 to the Fiftieth Congress; engaged in the real estate business and stock raising at Pierre, S.Dak., in 1887; moved to Washington, D.C., in 1890 and engaged in the real estate business until his death in Takoma Park, Md., April 8, 1911; interment in Rock Creek Cemetery, Washington, D.C.

**KLEPPE, Thomas Savig,** a Representative from North Dakota; born in Kintyre, Emmons County, N.Dak., July 1, 1919; graduated from Valley City High School; attended Valley City Teachers College; United States Army, warrant officer, 1942-1946; elected mayor of Bismarck in 1950 and 1954; served on the subcommittee of Federal Intergovernmental Relations Committee on Local Government (formerly the Hoover Commission); president and treasurer of Gold Seal Co.; vice president, J.M. Dain and Co., Minneapolis investment banking firm; unsuccessful Republican candidate in 1964 for election to the United States Senate; delegate, North Dakota Republican convention, 1966; former treasurer of the Republican Party of North Dakota; elected as a Republican to the Ninetieth and Ninety-first Congresses (January 3, 1967-January 3, 1971); was not a candidate in 1970 for reelection to the House of Representatives, but was an unsuccessful candidate for election to the United States Senate; Administrator of the Small Business Administration, 1971-1975; Secretary of the Interior in the Cabinet of President Gerald R. Ford, July 27, 1975 to January 20, 1977; member of the board, Lincoln Institute of Land Policy, for twelve years; worked with Alexander Proudfoot Co. consulting group, Chicago, Ill.; founding trustee, Government Investors Trust; chairman of the board, Presidential Savings Bank, Bethesda, Md.; is a resident of Bethesda, Md.

**KLEPPER, Frank B.,** a Representative from Missouri; born in St. John, Putnam County, Mo., June 22, 1864; moved with his parents to Mirabile, Caldwell County, Mo., where he remained for ten years; attended the common schools; moved to Clinton County, Mo., and engaged in agricultural pursuits; attended Baker University, Baldwin City, Kans.; engaged in teaching for two years; was graduated from the law department of the University of Missouri at Columbia in 1898; was admitted to the bar the same year and commenced practice in Polo, Caldwell County, Mo.; prosecuting attorney of Caldwell County 1900-1905; elected as a Republican to the Fifty-ninth Congress (March 4, 1905-March 3, 1907); unsuccessful candidate for reelection; moved to Cameron, Clinton County, Mo., in 1907 and continued the practice of law; also engaged in banking; prosecuting attorney of Clinton County 1916-1920; again engaged in the practice of law in Cameron, Mo., until his death in that city on August 4, 1933; interment in Evergreen Cemetery.

**KLINE, Ardolph Loges,** a Representative from New York; born near Newton, Sussex County, N.J., February 21, 1858; attended public schools in Newton, N.J., and Phillips Academy, Andover, Mass.; moved to New York City in 1873 and entered the employ of W.C. Peet & Co.; joined the New York National Guard as a private in 1876; served as lieutenant colonel of the Fourteenth Regiment, New York Volunteers, during the Spanish-American War; commissioned colonel of the Fourteenth Regiment, New York National Guard, January 24, 1901; served on the board of aldermen of New York City 1904-1907; appointed assistant appraiser of merchandise for the port of New York by President Theodore Roosevelt on January 1, 1908, and served until July 1, 1911, when he resigned; again a member of the board of aldermen in 1912 and 1913; vice chairman of the board of aldermen in 1912 and acting mayor of New York City that year; was president of the board of aldermen in 1913; upon the death of Mayor William J. Gaynor became mayor of New York City for the unexpired term and served from September 10, 1913, to January 1, 1914; again elected a member of the board of aldermen for the term 1914-1915, but resigned on January 6, 1914; commissioner of taxes and assessments 1914-1917; elected as a Republican to the Sixty-seventh Congress (March 4, 1921-March 3, 1923); unsuccessful candidate for reelection in 1922 to the Sixty-eighth Congress; served as New York manager of the sea

service bureau of the United States Shipping Board from May 4, 1923, until his death in Brooklyn, N.Y., October 13, 1930; interment in Holy Cross Cemetery.

**KLINE, Isaac Clinton,** a Representative from Pennsylvania; born in Mount Pleasant, Westmoreland County, Pa., August 18, 1858; attended the public schools, the State normal school, Bloomsburg, Pa., and Bucknell Academy, Lewisburg, Pa.; was graduated from Lafayette College, Easton, Pa., in 1893; taught school five years before entering college; studied law; was admitted to the bar in 1894 and commenced practice in Sunbury; unsuccessful candidate for election in 1912 to the Sixty-third Congress; elected as a Republican to the Sixty-seventh Congress (March 4, 1921-March 3, 1923); unsuccessful candidate for reelection in 1922 to the Sixty-eighth Congress; resumed the practice of his profession in Sunbury, Pa.; died in De Land, Fla., December 2, 1947; interment in Pomfret Manor, Sunbury, Pa.

**KLINE, Marcus Charles Lawrence,** a Representative from Pennsylvania; born in Emaus, Salisbury Township, Lehigh County, Pa., March 26, 1855; attended the common schools in the borough of Emaus, Pa., and was graduated from Muhlenberg College, Allentown, Pa., June 26, 1874; studied law; was admitted to the bar in 1876 and commenced practice in Allentown; city solicitor of Allentown in 1877; district attorney for Lehigh County 1887-1890; chairman of the Democratic county committee of Lehigh County 1895-1899; president Lehigh Valley Trust Co. 1899-1906; elected as a Democrat to the Fifty-eighth and Fifty-ninth Congresses (March 4, 1903-March 3, 1907); was not a candidate for renomination in 1906; resumed the practice of his profession and also engaged in banking; president Allentown Trust Co. 1907-1911; delegate to the Democratic National Convention in 1908; died in Allentown, Lehigh County, Pa., March 10, 1911; interment in Fairview Cemetery.

**KLINGENSMITH, John, Jr.,** a Representative from Pennsylvania; born in Westmoreland County, Pa., in 1785; was a resident of Stewartsville; elected sheriff of Westmoreland County in 1828; elected as a Jacksonian to the Twenty-fourth Congress and reelected as a Democrat to the Twenty-fifth Congress (March 4, 1835-March 3, 1839); secretary of the land office of Pennsylvania 1839-1842.

**KLINK, Ron,** a Representative from Pennsylvania; born in Canton, Stark County, Ohio, September 23, 1951; graduated Meyersdale High School, 1969; television news reporter, Altoona, Pa., and Pittsburgh, Pa. stations then with KDKA-TV, 1978-1993; member, Youngwood (Pa.) Volunteer Fire Department; serves on board of visitors, Forbes Road Vocational Technical School, Monroeville, Pa.; elected as a Democrat to the One Hundred Third and One Hundred Fourth Congresses (January 3, 1993-January 3, 1997); is a resident of Jeannette, Pa.

**KLOEB, Frank Le Blond** (grandson of Francis C. Le Blond), a Representative from Ohio; born in Celina, Mercer County, Ohio, June 16, 1890; attended the parochial and public schools, Ohio State University at Columbus, and the University of Wisconsin at Madison; during the First World War enlisted as a seaman in the United States Navy, advanced to quartermaster, third class, and then to ensign, and served from September 1917 to March 1919; was graduated from the College of Law of Ohio State University in 1917; was admitted to the bar the same year and commenced practice in Celina, Ohio, in April 1919; served as prosecuting attorney of Mercer County, Ohio, 1921-1925; elected as a Democrat to the Seventy-third Congress; reelected to the two succeeding Congresses and served from March 4, 1933, to August 19, 1937, when he resigned, having been appointed United States district judge by President Franklin D. Roosevelt for the northern district of Ohio, western division, in which capacity he served until September 30, 1964, when he retired to the status of senior United States district judge and continued to sit by assignment on criminal and civil matters until July 1974; died in Toledo, Ohio, March 11, 1976; interment in Calvary Cemetery.

**KLOTZ, Robert,** a Representative from Pennsylvania; born in Northampton (now Carbon) County, Pa., on October 27, 1819; attended the country schools; first register and recorder of Carbon County in 1843; during the war with Mexico served in the Second Pennsylvania Volunteers as a private, lieutenant, and adjutant in 1846 and 1847; member of the Pennsylvania house of representatives in 1848 and was reelected in 1849; moved to Pawnee, Kans., in 1855; member of the Topeka constitutional convention in 1855 and served as the first secretary of state under the constitution adopted; brigadier general under Governor Robinson; returned to Mauch Chunk, Pa., in 1857; treasurer of Carbon County in 1859; enlisted in the Union Army in 1861; was chosen colonel of the Nineteenth Pennsylvania Emergency Militia in 1862; trustee of Lehigh University, Bethlehem, Pa., 1874-1882; elected as a Democrat to the Forty-sixth and Forty-seventh Congresses (March 4, 1879-March 3, 1883); director and agent of the Laflin-Rand Powder Co., New York City; died in Mauch Chunk, Pa., on May 1, 1895; interment in City Cemetery.

**KLUCZYNSKI, John Carl,** a Representative from Illinois; born in Chicago, Ill., February 15, 1896; attended the public and parochial schools; during the First World War served overseas as a corporal with the Eighth Field Artillery in 1918 and 1919; engaged in the catering business in Chicago, Ill., beginning in 1920; member of the Illinois State house of representatives, 1933-1948; elected to the Illinois State senate in 1948 and served until December 1949, having become a candidate for Congress; elected as a Democrat to the Eighty-second and to the twelve succeeding Congresses, and served from January 3, 1951 until his death in Chicago, Ill., January 26, 1975; interment in Resurrection Mausoleum, Justice, Ill.

**KLUG, Scott Leo,** a Representative from Wisconsin; born in Milwaukee, Wis., January 16, 1953; attended grammar schools in West Allis, Wis.; graduated from Marquette University High School, 1971; B.S., Lawrence University, Appleton, Wis., 1975; M.S.J., Northwestern University, Evanston, Ill., 1976; M.B.A., University of Wisconsin, Madison, 1990; investment and development business; fourteen years broadcast journalist with WKOW-TV, Madison, Wis., WJLA-TV, Washington, D.C. and others; elected as a Republican to the One Hundred Second and to the two succeeding Congresses (January 3, 1991-January 3, 1997); is a resident of Madison, Wis.

**KLUTTZ, Theodore Franklin,** a Representative from North Carolina; born in Salisbury, Rowan County, N.C., October 4, 1848; attended the common schools; was a druggist; studied law; was admitted to the bar in 1881 and commenced practice in Salisbury, N.C.; was presiding justice of the inferior court of Rowan County from 1884 to 1886, when he resigned; delegate to the Democratic National Convention in 1896; elected as a Democrat to the Fifty-sixth, Fifty-seventh, and Fifty-eighth Congresses (March 4, 1899-March 3, 1905); declined to be a candidate for renomination in 1904 to the Fifty-ninth Congress; engaged in the practice of his profession in Salisbury, N.C., until his death on November 18, 1918; interment in Chestnut Hill Cemetery.

**KNAPP, Anthony Lausett** (brother of Robert McCarty Knapp), a Representative from Illinois; born in Middletown, Orange County, N.Y., June 14, 1828; moved with his parents to Illinois in 1839 and settled in Jerseyville; completed preparatory studies; studied law; was admitted to the bar and commenced practice in Jerseyville; member of the State senate 1859-1861; elected as a Democrat to the Thirty-seventh Congress to fill the vacancy caused by the resignation of John A. McClernand; reelected to the Thirty-eighth Congress and served from December 12, 1861, to March 3, 1865; was not a candidate for renomination in 1864; moved to Chicago in 1865 and to Springfield, Ill., in 1867 and continued the practice of law;

died in Springfield, Ill., May 24, 1881; interment in Springfield Cemetery; reinterment in Oak Ridge Cemetery.

**KNAPP, Charles** (father of Charles Junius Knapp), a Representative from New York; born in Colchester, Delaware County, N.Y., October 8, 1797; educated at home and later attended the common schools; engaged in agricultural pursuits; taught school in Delaware County; engaged in mercantile pursuits in 1825; member of the State assembly in 1841; moved to Deposit, Delaware County, N.Y., in 1848 and organized a bank in 1854 and subsequently became its president; elected as a Republican to the Forty-first Congress (March 4, 1869-March 3, 1871); was not a candidate for renomination in 1870; resumed banking; died in Deposit, N.Y., on May 14, 1880; interment in Laurel Bank Cemetery.

**KNAPP, Charles Junius** (son of Charles Knapp), a Representative from New York; born in Pepacton, Delaware County, N.Y., June 30, 1845; moved with his parents to Deposit, Delaware County, in 1848; was graduated from Hamilton College, Clinton, N.Y., in 1866; became engaged in banking with his father at Deposit, N.Y., in 1866; president of the board of education for many years; served on the board of supervisors of Delaware County in 1885 and 1886; member of the State assembly 1886-1888; elected as a Republican to the Fifty-first Congress (March 4, 1889-March 3, 1891); declined to be a candidate for renomination in 1890; moved to Binghamton, N.Y., and again engaged in banking; died in that city June 1, 1916; interment in Laurel Bank Cemetery, Deposit, N.Y.

**KNAPP, Charles Luman,** a Representative from New York; born on a farm near Harrisburg, Lewis County, N.Y., July 4, 1847; attended the rural schools, Lowville (N.Y.) Academy, and Irving Institute, Tarrytown, N.Y.; was graduated from Rutgers College, New Brunswick, N.J., in 1869; studied law; was admitted to the bar in 1873 and commenced practice in Lowville, N.Y.; served in the State senate 1886 and 1887; appointed by President Benjamin Harrison as consul general at Montreal in 1889 and served until September 1893, when he returned to Lowville and resumed the practice of law; also engaged in banking; elected as a Republican to the Fifty-seventh Congress to fill the vacancy caused by the death of Albert D. Shaw; reelected to the Fifty-eighth and to the three succeeding Congresses and served from November 5, 1901, to March 3, 1911; chairman, Committee on Elections No. 1 (Sixty-first Congress); declined to be a candidate for renomination in 1910 to the Sixty-second Congress; resumed the practice of law in Lowville, N.Y.; died in Lowville, N.Y., January 3, 1929; interment in the Rural Cemetery.

**KNAPP, Chauncey Langdon,** a Representative from Massachusetts; born in Berlin, Vt., February 26, 1809; completed preparatory studies; learned the art of printing and engaged in newspaper work in Montpelier; for a number of years was coproprietor and editor of the State Journal; secretary of state of Vermont 1836-1849; moved to Massachusetts and located in Lowell; editor of the Lowell News and other papers; secretary of the Massachusetts senate in 1851; elected as a candidate of the American Party to the Thirty-fourth Congress and as a Republican to the Thirty-fifth Congress (March 4, 1855-March 3, 1859); editor of the Lowell Daily Citizen 1859-1882; died in Lowell, Mass., May 31, 1898; interment in Lowell Cemetery.

**KNAPP, Robert McCarty** (brother of Anthony Lausett Knapp), a Representative from Illinois; born in New York City April 21, 1831; moved with his parents to Jerseyville, Ill., in 1839; attended the common schools and the Kentucky Military Institute in Frankfort, Ky.; studied law; was admitted to the bar in 1855 and commenced practice in Jerseyville; member of the State house of representatives in 1867; mayor of Jerseyville 1871-1876; elected as a Democrat to the Forty-third Congress (March 4, 1873-March 3, 1875); unsuccessful candidate for reelection in 1874; elected to the Forty-fifth

Congress (March 4, 1877-March 3, 1879); again an unsuccessful candidate for reelection in 1878; resumed the practice of law; died in Jerseyville, Jersey County, Ill., June 24, 1889; interment in Oak Grove Cemetery.

**KNICKERBOCKER, Herman,** a Representative from New York; born in Albany, N.Y., July 27, 1779; completed preparatory studies; studied law; was admitted to the bar in 1803 and commenced practice in Albany, N.Y.; moved to Schaghticoke, near Albany, and became known as "the Prince of Schaghticoke" on account of his hospitality and liberality; elected as a Federalist to the Eleventh Congress (March 4, 1809-March 3, 1811); was not a candidate for reelection in 1810; served in the State assembly in 1816; judge of Rensselaer County; died in Williamsburg (now a part of New York City), N.Y., January 30, 1855; interment in the Knickerbocker family cemetery, Schaghticoke, Rensselaer County, N.Y.

**Bibliography:** *DAB.*

**KNIFFIN, Frank Charles,** a Representative from Ohio; born on a farm near Stryker, Williams County, Ohio, April 26, 1894; attended the public schools; studied law at Stryker, Ohio; was admitted to the bar in 1919 and commenced practice in Napoleon, Ohio; unsuccessful candidate for election in 1922 to the Sixty-eighth Congress, in 1924 to the Sixty-ninth Congress, in 1926 to the Seventieth Congress, and in 1928 to the Seventy-first Congress; elected as a Democrat to the Seventy-second and to the three succeeding Congresses (March 4, 1931-January 3, 1939); unsuccessful candidate for reelection in 1938 to the Seventy-sixth Congress; resumed the practice of law; referee in bankruptcy, northern district of Ohio, western division, from 1939 until his death in Napoleon, Ohio, April 30, 1968; interment in Wauseon Cemetery, Wauseon, Ohio.

**KNIGHT, Charles Landon,** a Representative from Ohio; born near Milledgeville, Baldwin County, Ga., June 18, 1867; attended the public schools; graduated from Vanderbilt University, Nashville, Tenn., in 1889 and from Columbia University Law School, New York City, in 1890; was admitted to the bar in 1892 and commenced practice at Bluefield, W.Va.; studied in Europe 1891-1893; member of the staff of the Philadelphia Times 1896-1900; editor and publisher of the Beacon Journal, Akron, Ohio, 1900-1933; also engaged in stock farming; delegate to the Republican National Conventions of 1916 and 1924; elected as a Republican to the Sixty-seventh Congress (March 4, 1921-March 3, 1923); was not a candidate for reelection in 1922 to the Sixty-eighth Congress, but was an unsuccessful candidate for the nomination for Governor of Ohio; resumed his newspaper interests; died in Akron, Ohio, September 26, 1933; interment in Roselawn Cemetery.

**KNIGHT, Jonathan,** a Representative from Pennsylvania; born in Bucks County, Pa., November 22, 1787; moved with his parents to East Bethlehem, Washington County, Pa., in 1801; attended the common schools; became a civil engineer; appointed by the Commonwealth in 1816 to make and report on a map of Washington County; elected county commissioner and served three years; assisted in the preliminary surveys of the Chesapeake & Ohio Canal and the national road between Cumberland, Md., and Wheeling, Va. (now West Virginia); member of the Pennsylvania house of representatives 1822-1828; entered the service of the Baltimore & Ohio Railroad Co. and visited England to pursue further studies in engineering; upon his return in 1830 was appointed chief engineer of that company and served until 1842; engaged in agricultural pursuits; secretary of the first agricultural society organized in Washington County; elected as a Whig to the Thirty-fourth Congress (March 4, 1855-March 3, 1857); unsuccessful candidate for reelection in 1856 to the Thirty-fifth Congress and for election in 1858 to the Thirty-sixth Congress; resumed agricultural pursuits near East

Bethlehem, Pa.; died November 22, 1858; interment in West Land Cemetery, near West Brownsville, Washington County, Pa.

**Bibliography:** *DAB.*

**KNIGHT, Nehemiah** (father of Nehemiah Rice Knight), a Representative from Rhode Island; born in "Knightsville," Cranston (now a part of Providence), R.I., March 23, 1746; attended the common schools; engaged in agricultural pursuits; town clerk 1773-1800; elected to the general assembly of Rhode Island and Providence Plantations in 1783 and again in 1787; sheriff of Providence County in 1787; elected as a Republican to the Eighth, Ninth, and Tenth Congresses and served from March 4, 1803, until his death in Cranston, R.I., June 13, 1808; interment in a small cemetery on Cranston Street and Phoenix Avenue in a locality known as "Knightsville," Providence, R.I.

**KNIGHT, Nehemiah Rice** (son of Nehemiah Knight), a Senator from Rhode Island; born in Cranston, R.I., December 31, 1780; attended the common schools; member of the Rhode Island State house of representatives in 1802; moved to Providence, and was clerk of the court of common pleas from 1805 until 1811; clerk of the circuit court, 1812-1817; collector of customs for the same period; president of the Roger Williams Bank from 1817 until 1854; unsuccessful candidate for election in 1816 for Governor; elected Governor of Rhode Island in 1817, reelected in 1818, 1819, and 1820, and served from May 7, 1817 to January 9, 1821, when he resigned; elected in 1821 as a Republican to the United States Senate to fill the vacancy caused by the death of James Burrill, Jr.; reelected in 1823, 1829, and again in 1835, the last time as a Whig and served from January 9, 1821, to March 3, 1841; chairman, Committee to Audit and Control the Contingent Expense (Twenty-second, Twenty-third and Twenty-sixth Congresses), Committee on Manufactures (Twenty-fourth Congress); retired from public life; delegate to the State constitutional convention in 1843; died in Providence, R.I., April 18, 1854; interment in Grace Church Cemetery.

**KNOLLENBERG, Joseph Castl,** a Representative from Michigan; born in Mattoon, Coles County, Ill., November 28, 1933; B.S., Eastern Illinois University, Charleston, Ill., 1955; operates family insurance agency; past president, Bloomfield Glens Homeowner's Association; elected as a Republican to the One Hundred Third and One Hundred Fourth Congresses (January 3, 1993-January 3, 1997); is a resident of Bloomfield Hills, Mich.

**KNOPF, Philip,** a Representative from Illinois; born near Long Grove, Lake County, Ill., November 18, 1847; attended the public schools; during the Civil War enlisted in Company I, One Hundred and Forty-seventh Regiment, Illinois Volunteer Infantry, and served until the regiment was mustered out in Savannah, Ga.; moved to Chicago in 1866 and attended Bryant and Stratton's College for one year; engaged in the teaming business until 1884, when he was appointed chief deputy coroner and served eight years; member of the State senate 1886-1894; clerk of Cook County 1894-1902; delegate to the Republican National Convention in 1896; member of the State central committee; elected as a Republican to the Fifty-eighth, Fifty-ninth, and Sixtieth Congresses (March 4, 1903-March 3, 1909); chairman, Committee on Expenditures in the Department of the Treasury (Fifty-ninth and Sixtieth Congresses); died in Chicago, Ill., August 14, 1920; interment in Rosehill Cemetery.

**KNOTT, James Proctor,** a Representative from Kentucky; born in Raywick, near Lebanon, Marion County, Ky., on August 29, 1830; attended the public schools; studied law; moved to Memphis, Mo., in May 1850; was admitted to the bar in 1851 and commenced practice in Memphis, Mo.; member of the Missouri house of representatives in 1857 and resigned in August 1859; attorney general of Missouri in 1859 and 1860; returned to Kentucky and commenced the practice of law in Lebanon in 1863; elected as a Democrat to the Fortieth and

Forty-first Congresses (March 4, 1867-March 3, 1871); was not a candidate for renomination in 1870 to the Forty-second Congress; elected to the Forty-fourth and to the three succeeding Congresses (March 4, 1875-March 3, 1883); chairman, Committee on the Judiciary (Forty-fourth through Forty-sixth Congresses); declined to be a candidate for renomination in 1882 to the Forty-eighth Congress; one of the managers appointed by the House of Representatives in 1876 to conduct the impeachment proceedings against William W. Belknap, ex-Secretary of War; elected Governor of Kentucky in 1883 and served from September 1883 to September 1887; delegate to the Kentucky constitutional convention in 1891; professor of civics and economics, Centre College, Danville, Ky., 1892-1894, and dean of its law school 1894-1901; died in Lebanon, Ky., June 18, 1911; interment in Ryder Cemetery.

Bibliography: *DAB*; Crocker, Helen Bartter. "J. Proctor Knott's Education in Missouri Politics, 1850-1862." *Missouri Historical Society Bulletin* 30 (January 1974): 101-16; Mills, Edwin W. "The Career of James Proctor Knott in Missouri." *Missouri Historical Review* 31 (April 1937): 288-294.

KNOWLAND, Joseph Russell (father of William Fife Knowland), a Representative from California; born in Alameda, Calif., August 5, 1873; attended public and private schools and the University of the Pacific (later College of the Pacific), Stockton, Calif.; engaged in the wholesale lumber and shipping business; director of the American Trust Company; member of the California State assembly, 1898-1902; served in the State senate from 1902 until 1904, when he resigned, having been elected as a Republican to the Fifty-eighth Congress to fill the vacancy caused by the resignation of Victor H. Metcalf; reelected to the Fifty-ninth and to the four succeeding Congresses, and served from November 8, 1904 to March 3, 1915; was not a candidate in 1914 for reelection to the House of Representatives, but was an unsuccessful candidate for election to the United States Senate; president and publisher of the Oakland (Calif.) Tribune; chairman of the California State Park Commission from 1936 until 1960; chairman of California Centennial Commission in 1950; was a resident of Piedmont, Calif., at the time of his death there on February 1, 1966; remains cremated at Mountain View Cemetery, Oakland, Calif.

Bibliography: Gothberg, John A. "The Local Influence of J.R. Knowland's Oakland *Tribune*." *Journalism Quarterly* 45 (Autumn 1968): 487-495.

KNOWLAND, William Fife (son of Joseph Russell Knowland), a Senator from California; born in Alameda, Alameda County, Calif., June 26, 1908; attended the public schools and graduated from the University of California at Berkeley in 1929; engaged in the newspaper publishing business in Oakland, Calif., in 1933; member, California State assembly, 1933-1935; member, California State senate, 1935-1939; Republican National committeeman from California, 1938-1942, and chairman of the executive committee, 1940-1942; served in the Second World War as an enlisted man and officer; was serving overseas when appointed as a Republican to the United States Senate on August 14, 1945, to fill the vacancy caused by the death of Hiram W. Johnson; assumed office on August 26, 1945, and was subsequently elected November 5, 1946, to fill the unexpired term ending January 3, 1947, and at the same time elected for the six-year term ending January 3, 1953; reelected in 1952 and served from August 26, 1945 to January 2, 1959; was not a candidate for renomination in 1958, but was an unsuccessful candidate for election for Governor of California; majority leader (Eighty-third Congress), minority leader (Eighty-fourth and Eighty-fifth Congresses), chairman, Republican Policy Committee (Eighty-third Congress); resumed his newspaper career and took an active interest in civic affairs in the Oakland, Calif., area; died from a self-inflicted gunshot wound at his summer home near Guerneville, Calif., February 23, 1974; interment in Chapel of Memories Cemetery, Oakland, Calif.

KNOWLES, Freeman Tulley, a Representative from South Dakota; born in Harmony, Somerset County, Maine, October 10, 1846; attended Bloomfield Academy, Skowhegan, Maine; enlisted in the Sixteenth Maine Regiment June 16, 1862; served three years and nineteen days in the Army of the Potomac; moved to Denison, Iowa; studied law; was admitted to the bar in April 1869 and commenced practice in Denison; moved to Nebraska in 1886 and began the publication of the Ceresco Times; moved to the Black Hills in 1888 and began the publication of the Meade County Times at Tilfor; moved to Deadwood and began the publication of the Evening Independent; elected as a Populist to the Fifty-fifth Congress (March 4, 1897-March 3, 1899); continued the newspaper publishing business in Deadwood, Lawrence County, S.Dak., until his death there on June 1, 1910; interment in Mount Moriah Cemetery.

KNOWLTON, Ebenezer, a Representative from Maine; born in Pittsfield, N.H., December 6, 1815; moved with his parents to South Montville, Maine, in 1825; attended the common schools; studied theology and entered the ministry; member of the Maine State house of representatives, 1844-1850, and served as speaker in 1846; elected as a Republican to the Thirty-fourth Congress (March 4, 1855-March 3, 1857); resumed his ministerial duties; died in South Montville, Maine, September 10, 1874; interment in the City Cemetery.

KNOX, James, a Representative from Illinois; born in Canajoharie, N.Y., July 4, 1807; attended Hamilton College, Clinton, N.Y., and was graduated from Yale College in 1830; studied law; was admitted to the bar in 1833 and commenced practice in Utica, N.Y.; moved to Illinois in 1836 and settled in Knoxville, Knox County; continued the practice of law; also engaged in agricultural pursuits; delegate to the State constitutional convention in 1847; elected as a Whig to the Thirty-third Congress and reelected as a Republican to the Thirty-fourth Congress (March 4, 1853-March 3, 1857); chairman, Committee on Roads and Canals (Thirty-fourth Congress); continued the practice of law until his death in Knoxville, Ill., October 8, 1876; interment in City Cemetery.

KNOX, Philander Chase, a Senator from Pennsylvania; born in Brownsville, Fayette County, Pa., May 6, 1853; attended the University of West Virginia at Morgantown, and graduated from Mount Union College, Alliance, Ohio, in 1872; studied law; was admitted to the bar in 1875 and commenced practice in Pittsburgh, Pa.; assistant United States district attorney for the western district of Pennsylvania in 1876; president of the Pennsylvania Bar Association in 1897; appointed Attorney General of the United States in the Cabinet of President William McKinley on April 5, 1901; reappointed by President Theodore Roosevelt and served until June 30, 1904, when he resigned, having been appointed as a Republican to the United States Senate to fill the vacancy caused by the death of Matthew S. Quay; subsequently elected to fill the unexpired term and for the full term in 1905, and served from June 10, 1904 until March 4, 1909, when he resigned to enter the Cabinet; chairman, Committee on Coast Defenses (Fifty-eighth and Fifty-ninth Congresses, Committee on Rules (Sixtieth Congress); appointed Secretary of State by President William Howard Taft, and served from March 5, 1909 to March 5, 1913; again elected to the United States Senate, and served from March 4, 1917 until his death in Washington, D.C., October 12, 1921; chairman, Committee on Rules (Sixty-sixth and Sixty-seventh Congresses); interment in Washington Memorial Cemetery, Valley Forge, Pa.

Bibliography: *DAB*; Dodds, Archibald. "The Public Services of Philander Chase Knox." Ph.D. dissertation, University of Pittsburgh, 1950.

KNOX, Samuel, a Representative from Missouri; born in Blandford, Mass., on March 21, 1815; attended the common schools; was graduated from Williams College, Williamstown, Mass., in 1836 and from the law department of Harvard University in 1838; moved to St. Louis, Mo., in 1838; was admitted to the bar and practiced; city counselor in 1845; successfully contested as an Unconditional Unionist the election of Francis P. Blair, Jr., to the Thirty-eighth Congress and served from June 10, 1864, to March 3, 1865; unsuccessful candidate for reelection in 1864 to the Thirty-ninth Congress; resumed the practice of law in St. Louis, Mo.; returned to Blandford, Mass., where he died March 7, 1905; interment in Peabody Cemetery, Springfield, Mass.

**KNOX, Victor Alfred,** a Representative from Michigan; born on a farm in Chippewa County, Mich. (near Sault Ste. Marie), January 13, 1899; attended the public schools; engaged in farming until 1943; treasurer of Soo Township in 1923 and 1924; county supervisor 1925-1931; member of the State legislature 1937-1952, serving as speaker pro tempore and Republican floor leader 1943-1946 and as speaker 1947-1952; manager of the Chippewa County Farm Bureau 1943-1946; engaged in the retail plumbing and heating business in Sault Ste. Marie, Mich., in 1946; served on the Council of State Government, State Planning Commission, State Crime Commission, and Soo Locks Centennial Commission; elected as a Republican to the Eighty-third and to the five succeeding Congresses (January 3, 1953-January 3, 1965); unsuccessful candidate for reelection in 1964 to the Eighty-ninth Congress; died in Petoskey, Mich., December 13, 1976; interment in Oaklawn Chapel Gardens, fifteen miles south of Sault Ste. Marie, Mich.

**KNOX, William Shadrach,** a Representative from Massachusetts; born in Killingly, Conn., September 10, 1843; moved with his parents to Lawrence, Mass., in 1852; attended the public schools and Amherst (Mass.) College; studied law; was admitted to the bar in 1866 and commenced practice in Lawrence; member of the Massachusetts house of representatives in 1874 and 1875; city solicitor of Lawrence in 1875, 1876, and 1887-1890; elected as a Republican to the Fifty-fourth and to the three succeeding Congresses (March 4, 1895-March 3, 1903); chairman, Committee on Territories (Fifty-fifth through Fifty-seventh Congresses); was not a candidate for renomination in 1902 to the Fifty-eighth Congress; president of the Arlington National Bank of Lawrence; died in Lawrence, Mass., September 21, 1914; interment in Bellevue Cemetery.

**KNUTSON, Coya Gjesdal,** a Representative from Minnesota; born in Edmore, Ramsey County, N.Dak., August 22, 1912; attended the public schools of Edmore; B.S., Concordia College, Moorhead, Minn., 1934; engaged in postgraduate work at the State Teachers College in Moorhead and the Julliard School of Music, New York City; taught high school in Penn, N.Dak., and Plummer and Oklee, Minn., 1941-1943; member of Red Lake County Welfare Board, 1948-1950; delegate to the Democratic National Conventions of 1948, 1952 and 1956; served in the Minnesota State house of representatives, 1951-1954; member of the Youth Study Commission in 1953 and 1954; elected as a Democrat to the Eighty-fourth and Eighty-fifth Congresses (January 3, 1955-January 3, 1959); unsuccessful candidate for reelection in 1958 to the Eighty-sixth Congress, and for election in 1960 to the Eighty-seventh Congress; author of articles for farm magazines and interested in children's television programs; liaison officer, Department of Defense, Office of Civil Defense, 1961-1970; unsuccessful candidate for nomination to the Ninety-fifth Congress in a special election primary, February 8, 1977; is a resident of Bloomington, Minn.

**Bibliography:** Beito, Gretchen Urnes. *Coya Come Home: A Congresswoman's Journey.* Los Angeles: Pomegranate Press, Ltd., 1990.

**KNUTSON, Harold,** a Representative from Minnesota; born in Skien, Norway, October 20, 1880; immigrated to the United States in 1886 with his parents, who settled in Chicago, Ill., and later moved to a farm near Clear Lake, Sherburne County, Minn.; attended the common and agricultural schools; apprenticed as a

printer; published the Royalton (Minn.) Banner, the Foley (Minn.) Independent, and the Wadena (Minn.) Pioneer Journal; delegate to the Republican State conventions in 1902, 1904, and 1910, and to the Republican National Convention of 1940; associate editor of the St. Cloud Daily Journal-Press, 1910-1911; president of the Northern Minnesota Editorial Association, 1910-1911; elected as a Republican to the Sixty-fifth and to the fifteen succeeding Congresses (March 4, 1917-January 3, 1949); majority whip (Sixty-sixth and Sixty-seventh Congresses); chairman, Committee on Pensions (Sixty-seventh through Seventy-first Congresses), Committee on Indian Affairs (Sixty-eighth Congress), Committee on Insular Affairs (Seventy-first Congress), Committee on Ways and Means (Eightieth Congress), Joint Committee on Internal Revenue Taxation (Eightieth Congress); unsuccessful candidate for reelection in 1948 to the Eighty-first Congress; again became active in the publishing of the Wadena Pioneer Journal until his death in Wadena, Minn., on August 21, 1953; interment in North Star Cemetery, St. Cloud, Minn.

**Bibliography:** *DAB.*

**KOCH, Edward Irving,** a Representative from New York; born in the Bronx, N.Y., December 12, 1924; studied at City College of New York; LL.B., New York University Law School, 1948; served during the Second World War as a combat infantryman with the rank of sergeant, 1943-1946; admitted to the bar in 1949 and commenced practice in New York City; Democratic district leader of Greenwich Village from 1963 until 1965; delegate to the Democratic State convention, 1964; elected to New York City Council, 1966; elected as a Democrat-Liberal to the Ninety-first and to the four succeeding Congresses and served from January 3, 1969, until his resignation on December 31, 1977; elected mayor of New York City in 1977, reelected in 1981 and 1985; and served January 1, 1978 to December 31, 1989; unsuccessful candidate for renomination in 1989; resumed the practice of law and engaged in literary pursuits, radio and television commentary and film criticism; is a resident of New York City.

**KOCIALKOWSKI, Leo Paul,** a Representative from Illinois; born in Chicago, Ill., August 16, 1882; orphaned at an early age; educated in private schools, which he supplemented by a business course; worked in various capacities in several business houses in Chicago; engaged in tax appraisal and delinquent tax supervision in Cook County, Ill., 1916-1932; delegate to the Democratic National Convention in 1928; elected as a Democrat to the Seventy-third and to the four succeeding Congresses (March 4, 1933-January 3, 1943); chairman, Committee on Insular Affairs (Seventy-fourth through Seventy-seventh Congresses); unsuccessful candidate for renomination in 1942; member of the Civil Service Commission of Cook County, Ill., 1945-1949; died in Chicago, Ill., September 27, 1958; interment in St. Adelbert Cemetery.

**KOGOVSEK, Raymond Peter,** a Representative from Colorado; born in Pueblo, Colo., August 19, 1941; graduated from Pueblo Catholic High School, 1959; attended Pueblo (Colo.) Junior College, 1960-1962; B.S., Adams State College, Alamosa, Colo., 1964; engaged in graduate work at the University of Denver, 1965; clerk's office, Pueblo County, 1964-1973; paralegal aide, 1974-1978; served in the Colorado State house of representatives, 1968-1969, and the State senate, 1970-1978; delegate, Colorado State Democratic conventions, 1966-1979; elected as a Democrat to the Ninety-sixth and to the two succeeding Congresses (January 3, 1979-January 3, 1985); was not a candidate for reelection in 1984 to the Ninety-ninth Congress; is a resident of Pueblo, Colo.

**KOHL, Herbert,** a Senator from Wisconsin; born in Milwaukee, Wis., February 7, 1935; graduated, Washington High School, Milwaukee, 1952; B.A., University of Wisconsin, Madison, 1956; M.B.A., Harvard Graduate School of Business Administration, 1958; United States Army Reserve service, 1958-1964; businessman;

owner, Milwaukee Bucks professional basketball team; part owner, Milwaukee Brewers Baseball Club; chair, Wisconsin Democratic Party, 1975-1977; elected as a Democrat to the United States Senate in 1988 for the term commencing January 3, 1989; reelected in 1994 for the term ending January 3, 2001; is a resident of Milwaukee, Wis.

**KOLBE, James Thomas,** a Representative from Arizona; born in Evanston, Ill., June 28, 1942; attended public schools; graduated, United States Capitol Page School, Washington, D.C., 1960; International School of America study abroad program, 1962-1963; B.A., Northwestern University, Evanston, Ill., 1965; M.B.A., Stanford University, 1967; lieutenant, United States Navy, 1967-1969, with service in Vietnam; lieutenant commander, United States Naval Reserves; assistant to the architect, Illinois Building Authority, 197--1972; special assistant to Governor Richard B. Ogilvie of Illinois, 1972-1973; vice president, Wood Canyon Corp., Sonoita, Ariz.; Arizona State senator, 1977-1982; elected as a Republican to the Ninety-ninth and to the five succeeding Congresses (January 3, 1985-January 3, 1997); is a resident of Tucson, Ariz.

**KOLTER, Joseph Paul,** a Representative from Pennsylvania; born in McDonald, Ohio, September 3, 1926; graduated from New Brighton (Pa.) High School in 1944; B.S., Geneva College, Beaver Falls, Pa., 1950; served in the United States Army, 1944-1947; accountant and teacher; member, New Brighton city council, 1961-1965; member, Pennsylvania house of representatives, 1969-1982; elected as a Democrat to the Ninety-eighth and to the four succeeding Congresses (January 3, 1983-January 3, 1993); unsuccessful candidate for renomination in 1992 to the One Hundred Third Congress; is a resident of New Brighton, Pa.

**KONIG, George,** a Representative from Maryland; born near North Point, Baltimore County, Md., January 26, 1865; moved in infancy with his parents to Baltimore, Md.; was self-educated; worked as a ship calker for ten years; superintendent and general manager of the Baltimore Pulverizing Co. 1894-1913; member of the city council of Baltimore 1903-1911; elected as a Democrat to the Sixty-second and Sixty-third Congresses and served from March 4, 1911, until his death in Baltimore, Md., May 31, 1913; interment in Baltimore Cemetery.

**KONNYU, Ernest Leslie,** a Representative from California; born in Tamasi, Hungary, May 17, 1937; attended parochial schools in Jefferson City and St. Louis, Mo.; attended the University of Maryland, College Park; B.S., Ohio State University, 1965; served in the United States Air Force as a captain, 1959-1969, and as a major, Air Force Reserve, 1970-1981; director, internal audit, National Semiconductor, Santa Clara, Calif., 1974-1980; served in the California State assembly, 1980-1986; elected as a Republican to the One Hundredth Congress (January 3, 1987-January 3, 1989); unsuccessful candidate for renomination in 1988 to the One Hundred First Congress; owner, Premier Printing and Communication, 1990 to present; is a resident of Saratoga, Calif.

**KONOP, Thomas Frank,** a Representative from Wisconsin; born in Franklin, Wis., August 17, 1879; educated at Two Rivers High School, Oshkosh State Normal School, and Northern Illinois College of Law; was graduated from the law department of the University of Nebraska at Lincoln in 1904; was admitted to the bar in 1904 and commenced practice in Kewaunee, Wis.; district attorney of Kewaunee County 1905-1911; moved to Green Bay, Wis., and practiced law 1915-1917; elected as a Democrat to the Sixty-second, Sixty-third, and Sixty-fourth Congresses (March 4, 1911-March 3, 1917); chairman, Committee on Expenditures on Public Buildings (Sixty-third and Sixty-fourth Congresses); unsuccessful candidate for reelection; resumed the practice of law in

Madison, Wis.; member of the Wisconsin State Industrial Commission 1917-1922; member of State board of vocational education 1917-1922; moved to Milwaukee, Wis., and continued the practice of law in 1922 and 1923; dean of the College of Law of the University of Notre Dame 1923-1941, and dean emeritus and professor of law until his retirement in 1950; resided in South Bend, Ind., until 1962; died in San Pierre, Ind., October 17, 1964; interment in Highland Cemetery, South Bend, Ind.

**KOONTZ, William Henry,** a Representative from Pennsylvania; born in Somerset, Somerset County, Pa., July 15, 1830; completed preparatory studies; studied law; was admitted to the bar in 1851 and commenced practice in Somerset; district attorney for Somerset County 1853-1856; delegate to the Republican National Convention in 1860; prothonotary and clerk of the county court 1861-1868; successfully contested as a Republican the election of Alexander H. Coffroth to the Thirty-ninth Congress; reelected to the Fortieth Congress and served from July 18, 1866, to March 3, 1869; was not a candidate for renomination in 1868; resumed the practice of law at Somerset, Pa.; counsel for the Baltimore & Ohio Railroad Co.; member of the State house of representatives 1899-1902; died in Somerset, Pa., July 4, 1911; interment in Union Cemetery.

**KOPETSKI, Michael Joseph,** a Representative from Oregon; born in Pendleton, Umatilla County, Oreg., October 27, 1949; graduated, Pendleton High School, 1967; attended the University of Oregon, 1967-1968, and Blue Mountain Community College (Pendleton, Oreg.), 1968; B.A., American University, Washington, D.C., 1971; attended Northwestern University School of Law, Lewis and Clark College (Portland, Oreg.), J.D., 1978; county chairman, Robert F. Kennedy for President, 1968; Portland, Oreg,. coordinator of the campaign of Wayne L. Morse for the United States Senate in 1972; investigator, Senate Select Committee on Presidential Campaign Activities, 1973-1974; Frank Church for President campaign, 1976; administrative assistant, Oregon State house of representatives, 1977-1979; directed the campaign of Ted Kulogoski for the United States Senate, 1980; administrator, Oregon State house labor committee, 1981-1984; member, Oregon State house of representatives, 1984-1990; vice president, Currier-McCormick Communications, 1989-1990; elected as a Democrat to the One Hundred Second and One Hundred Third Congresses (January 3, 1991-January 3, 1995); was not a candidate for reelection in 1994 to the One Hundred Fourth Congress; is a resident of Keizer, Oreg.

**KOPP, Arthur William,** a Representative from Wisconsin; born in Big Patch, Grant County, Wis., February 28, 1874; attended the common schools of Grant County; was graduated from the State normal school at Platteville, Wis., in 1895; taught school for three years; was graduated from the law department of the University of Wisconsin at Madison in 1900; was admitted to the bar the same year and commenced practice in Platteville, Grant County; member of the board of aldermen of that city 1903-1904; city attorney in 1903 and 1904; district attorney of Grant County 1904-1908; elected as a Republican to the Sixty-first and Sixty-second Congresses (March 4, 1909-March 3, 1913); was not a candidate for reelection to the Sixty-third Congress; resumed the practice of law; elected circuit judge of the fifth judicial district of Wisconsin in 1942 and served until his retirement January 1, 1955; acted as reserve circuit judge after retirement, accepting occasional assignments; law consultant; died in Platteville, Wis., on June 2, 1967; interment in Greenwood Cemetery.

**KOPP, William Frederick,** a Representative from Iowa; born near Dodgeville, Des Moines County, Iowa, June 20, 1869; attended the common schools; was graduated from Iowa Wesleyan College at Mount Pleasant in 1892 and from the law department of the University of Iowa at Iowa City in 1894; was admitted to the bar in 1894 and commenced practice in Mount Pleasant, Iowa; prosecuting attorney of Henry County 1895-1899; postmaster of Mount Pleasant

1906-1914; member of the board of trustees of Iowa Wesleyan College 1908-1938; member of the State house of representatives 1915-1917; elected as a Republican to the Sixty-seventh and to the five succeeding Congresses (March 4, 1921-March 3, 1933); chairman, Committee on Expenditures in the Department of the Navy (Sixty-eighth Congress), Committee on Labor (Sixty-ninth through Seventy-first Congresses), Committee on Pensions (Seventy-first Congress); unsuccessful candidate for reelection in 1932 to the Seventy-third Congress; engaged in the practice of law at Mount Pleasant, Iowa, until his death there on August 24, 1938; interment in Forest Home Cemetery.

**KOPPLEMANN, Herman Paul,** a Representative from Connecticut; born in Odessa, Russia, May 1, 1880; immigrated to the United States in 1882 with his parents, who settled in Hartford, Conn.; attended the grade and high schools; engaged as publishers' agent for newspapers and magazines in 1894; member of the Hartford city council 1904-1912, serving as president in 1911; served in the State senate 1917-1920; elected as a Democrat to the Seventy-third, Seventy-fourth, and Seventy-fifth Congresses (March 4, 1933-January 3, 1939); unsuccessful candidate for reelection in 1938 to the Seventy-sixth Congress; elected to the Seventy-seventh Congress (January 3, 1941-January 3, 1943); unsuccessful candidate for reelection in 1942 to the Seventy-eighth Congress; elected to the Seventy-ninth Congress (January 3, 1945-January 3, 1947); unsuccessful candidate for reelection in 1946 to the Eightieth Congress; chairman of State Water Commission and Metropolitan District Commission; died in Hartford, Conn., August 11, 1957; interment in Emanuel Cemetery, Wethersfield, Conn.

**KORBLY, Charles Alexander,** a Representative from Indiana; born in Madison, Jefferson County, Ind., March 24, 1871; attended the parochial schools of Madison and St. Joseph's College, near Effingham, Ill.; reporter and editor of the Madison Herald; studied law; was admitted to the bar in 1892 and commenced practice in Madison, Ind.; moved to Indianapolis, Ind., in 1895 and continued the practice of law; elected as a Democrat to the Sixty-first, Sixty-second, and Sixty-third Congresses (March 4, 1909-March 3, 1915); chairman, Committee on Railways and Canals (Sixty-second Congress); unsuccessful candidate for reelection in 1914 to the Sixty-fourth Congress; served as receiver general of insolvent national banks in Washington, D.C., 1915-1917; member of the legal staff of the Alien Property Custodian in 1918; served with the War Labor Board until it dissolved in 1919 and with the Shipping Board until 1922; resumed the practice of law in Washington, D.C., in 1922; also engaged in literary pursuits; died in Washington, D.C., July 26, 1937; interment in Mount Olivet Cemetery.

**KORELL, Franklin Frederick,** a Representative from Oregon; born in Portland, Oreg., July 23, 1889; attended the public schools and Bishop Scott Academy, Portland, Oreg.; was graduated from the law department of the University of Oregon at Eugene in 1910; attended Yale Law School in 1911 and 1912; was admitted to the bar in 1910 and commenced practice in Portland, Oreg.; during the First World War served as a first lieutenant and captain in the Twelfth Regiment Infantry, Eighth Division, later being transferred to the Eighty-second Regiment Infantry, Sixteenth Division, and served from August 1917 until March 1919; resumed the practice of law in Portland, Oreg.; member of the Oregon State house of representatives, 1923-1925; elected as a Republican to the Seventieth Congress to fill the vacancy caused by the death of Maurice E. Crumpacker; reelected to the Seventy-first Congress, and served from October 18, 1927 to March 3, 1931; unsuccessful candidate for reelection in 1930 to the Seventy-second Congress; served as special assistant to the general counsel of the United States Treasury Department, 1931-1943, and in the chief counsel's office of the Bureau of Internal Revenue, 1943-1959; resided in Alexandria, Va., until his death there on June 7, 1965; interment in Arlington National Cemetery, Va.

**KORNEGAY, Horace Robinson,** a Representative from North Carolina; born in Asheville, Buncombe County, N.C., March 12, 1924; educated in the public schools of Greensboro, N.C. and attended the Georgia School of Technology; B.S., Wake Forest College (N.C.), 1947, LL.B., 1949; was admitted to the bar in 1949 and entered the practice of law in Greensboro, N.C.; served in the United States Army, One Hundredth Infantry, from December 14, 1942, to February 1, 1946, with service in the European Theater; assistant district solicitor, 1951-1953; elected district solicitor (prosecuting attorney), for the twelfth district of North Carolina in 1954 and again in 1958; delegate to the Democratic National Convention of 1964; elected as a Democrat to the Eighty-seventh and to the three succeeding Congresses (January 3, 1961-January 3, 1969); was not a candidate for reelection in 1968 to the Ninety-first Congress; vice president and counsel, January 1969-June 1970, president, June 1970-February 1981, and chairman, February 1982-December 1986, of the Tobacco Institute, Inc.; resumed the practice of law in Greensboro, N.C., in January 1987; is a resident of Greensboro, N.C.

**KOSTMAYER, Peter Houston,** a Representative from Pennsylvania; born in New York City September 27, 1946; attended elementary and intermediate schools in New York City and Solebury, Pa.; graduated from West Nottingham Academy, Colora, Md., 1965; B.A., Columbia University, New York City, 1971; reporter, 1971-1972; press secretary to the Pennsylvania attorney general, 1972-1973; deputy press secretary to Governor Milton J. Shapp, 1973-1976; elected as a Democrat to the Ninety-fifth and Ninety-sixth Congresses (January 3, 1977-January 3, 1981); unsuccessful candidate for reelection in 1980 to the Ninety-seventh Congress; elected as a Democrat to the Ninety-eighth and to the four succeeding Congresses (January 3, 1983-January 3, 1993); unsuccessful candidate for reelection in 1992 to the One Hundred Third Congress; is a resident of Solebury, Pa.

**KOWALSKI, Frank,** a Representative from Connecticut; born in Meriden, New Haven County, Conn., October 18, 1907; attended the grade and high schools in Meriden, Conn.; graduated from the United States Military Academy in 1930, the Massachusetts Institute of Technology in 1937, and studied international relations at Columbia University during 1945 and 1946; in 1925 joined the United States Army as an enlisted man, and served continuously until 1958, with service in the European Theater; director of program for the disarmament of Germany in 1944; helped the Japanese cabinet organize its defenses as acting chief of the American Advisory Group following the Second World War; in 1954 organized and was the first commandant of the United States Army Command Management School at Fort Belvoir, Va., and served until his retirement from the service as a colonel on July 31, 1958; writer and inventor; elected as a Democrat to the Eighty-sixth and Eighty-seventh Congresses (January 3, 1959-January 3, 1963); was not a candidate for renomination in 1962 to the House of Representatives, but was an unsuccessful candidate for nomination to the United States Senate; member of Subversive Activities Control Board, 1963-1966; died in Washington, D.C., October 11, 1974; interment in Arlington National Cemetery, Va.

**KRAMER, Charles,** a Representative from California; born in Paducah, McCracken County, Ky., April 18, 1879; moved to Chicago during his infancy; attended the public and parochial schools, Illinois College of Law, and De Paul University, Chicago, Ill.; was admitted to the bar in 1904 and began practice in Chicago, Ill.; director of a dress manufacturing concern; moved to Los Angeles, Calif., in 1920 and engaged in the practice of his chosen profession; elected as a Democrat to the Seventy-third and to the four succeeding Congresses (March 4, 1933-January 3, 1943); chairman, Committee on Patents (Seventy-sixth and Seventy-seventh Congresses); unsuccessful candidate for the Democratic nomination of mayor of Los Angeles, Calif., in 1941; unsuccessful candidate for reelection in 1942 to the Seventy-eighth Congress; died in Los Angeles, Calif., January 20, 1943; entombed in the mausoleum at Calvary Cemetery.

**KRAMER, Kenneth Bentley,** a Representative from Colorado; born in Chicago, Ill., February 19, 1942; attended the public schools of Illinois; B.A., University of Illinois, Champaign, 1963; J.D., Harvard University Law School, 1966; admitted to the Illinois bar in 1966 and to the Colorado bar in 1969, and commenced practice in Colorado Springs, Colo., in 1970; served in the United States Army, 1967-1970; deputy district attorney, Office of District Attorney, Fourth Judicial District, 1970-1972; practiced law, 1972-1978; State representative, Colorado general assembly, 1973-1978; delegate, Colorado State Republican conventions, 1974-1986; elected as a Republican to the Ninety-sixth and to the three succeeding Congresses (January 3, 1979-January 3, 1987); was not a candidate for reelection in 1986 to the House of Representatives, but was an unsuccessful candidate for election to the United States Senate; Assistant Secretary of the Army for Financial Management, 1988-1989; appointed by President George Bush to be an Associate Judge, United States Court of Veterans Appeals, and was confirmed by the Senate on September 14, 1989 for a fifteen-year term; is a resident of Arlington, Va.

**KRAUS, Milton,** a Representative from Indiana; born in Kokomo, Howard County, Ind., June 26, 1866; attended the common and high schools; was graduated from the law department of the University of Michigan at Ann Arbor in 1886; was admitted to the bar in 1887 and commenced practice in Peru, Ind.; organized a company of volunteers for the Spanish-American War; elected as a Republican to the Sixty-fifth, Sixty-sixth, and Sixty-seventh Congresses (March 4, 1917-March 3, 1923); unsuccessful candidate for reelection in 1922 to the Sixty-eighth Congress; resumed manufacturing activities; died in Wabash, Ind., November 18, 1942; interment in Mount Hope Cemetery, Peru, Ind.

**KREBS, Jacob,** a Representative from Pennsylvania; born in Orwigsburg, Schuylkill County, Pa., March 13, 1782; attended the public schools; engaged in agricultural pursuits; elected to the Nineteenth Congress to fill the vacancy caused by the death of Henry Wilson, and served from December 4, 1826 to March 3, 1827; resumed agricultural pursuits; died in Orwigsburg, Pa., September 26, 1847; interment in the Lutheran Cemetery.

**KREBS, John Hans,** a Representative from California; born in Berlin, Germany, December 17, 1926; moved to Israel in 1933 and attended Balfour School (elementary), 1937; passed matriculation examination, University of London, 1945; immigrated to America in 1946 and obtained United States citizenship in 1954; A.B., University of California at Berkeley, 1950; LL.B., University of California Hastings College of Law, San Francisco, 1957; admitted to the California bar in 1957 and commenced practice in Fresno in 1958; served in United States Army, 1952-1954; member, Fresno County Planning Commission, 1965-1969; served on Fresno County Board of Supervisors, 1970-1974; delegate, California State Democratic convention, 1966; elected as a Democrat to the Ninety-fourth and Ninety-fifth Congresses (January 3, 1975-January 3, 1979); unsuccessful candidate for reelection in 1978 to the Ninety-sixth Congress; is a resident of Fresno, Calif.

**KREBS, Paul Joseph,** a Representative from New Jersey; born in New York City, May 26, 1912; attended grade and high schools; served as shop steward, secretary, and as director of political action and education for the United Auto Workers, regional area nine, covering New Jersey, 1940-1954; president, New Jersey State Congress of Industrial Organizations, 1954-1961; president, New Jersey United Auto Workers Council, 1961-1965; member, executive committee, Essex County, N.J., Democratic Committee, 1958 to present; elected as a Democrat to the Eighty-ninth Congress (January 3, 1965-January 3, 1967); was not a candidate for reelection in 1966 to the Ninetieth Congress; director, New Jersey State Office of Consumer Protection, April 1967-June 1970; unsuccessful candidate for election to the United States Senate in 1972; is a resident of Livingston, N.J.

**KREIDER, Aaron Shenk,** a Representative from Pennsylvania; born on a farm in South Annville Township, Lebanon County, Pa., June 26, 1863; attended the public schools and Lebanon Valley College, Annville, Pa., and was graduated from Allentown Business College in 1880; moved to Fulton, Mo., in 1880 and engaged in agricultural pursuits and later was employed as a clerk in a store; returned to Pennsylvania and engaged in mercantile pursuits in Campbelltown in 1884 and in Roseland in 1885; established the town of Lawn in Lebanon County, Pa., in 1886; also engaged in agricultural pursuits and in the grain and coal business; moved to Palmyra, Pa., in 1893 and shortly thereafter to Annville, Pa., and became interested in shoe manufacturing and in banking; commissioner and chairman of the Board of Commissioners of Annville 1909-1912; delegate to the Pennsylvania Republican Convention in 1910; served as president of the National Association of Shoe Manufacturers of the United States 1913-1916; elected as a Republican to the Sixty-third and to the four succeeding Congresses (March 4, 1913-March 3, 1923); chairman, Committee on Expenditures in the Department of the Interior (Sixty-sixth and Sixty-seventh Congresses); unsuccessful candidate for reelection in 1922; president of the board of trustees of Lebanon Valley College, Annville, Pa.; resumed his former manufacturing pursuits in Annville, Pa., until his death there on May 19, 1929; interment in Mount Annville Cemetery.

**KREIDLER, Myron Bradford (Mike),** a Representative from Washington; born in Tacoma, Wash., September 28, 1943; M.P.H., University of California, Los Angeles, 1972; optometrist; member, Washington State house of representatives, 1977-1984; member, Washington State senate, 1985-1993; elected as a Democrat to the One Hundred Third Congress (January 3, 1993-January 3, 1995); unsuccessful candidate for reelection in 1994 to the One Hundred Fourth Congress; member, power committee, Northwest Power Planning Council, 1995 to present; is a resident of Olympia, Wash.

**KREMER, George,** a Representative from Pennsylvania; born in Middletown, Dauphin County, Pa., November 21, 1775; received a limited schooling; studied law; was admitted to the bar and commenced practice in Lewisburg, Pa.; member of the Pennsylvania house of representatives in 1812 and 1813; elected to the Eighteenth, Nineteenth, and Twentieth Congresses (March 4, 1823-March 3, 1829); died in Middleburg, Snyder County (then a part of Union County), Pa., September 11, 1854; interment in the private burial ground on the family estate near Middleburg, Pa.

**Bibliography:** Russ, William A., Jr. "The Political Ideas of George Kremer." *Pennsylvania History* 7 (October 1940): 201-12.

**KRIBBS, George Frederic,** a Representative from Pennsylvania; born on a farm in Clarion County, Pa., November 8, 1846; attended the common schools and the Emlenton Academy and was graduated from Muhlenberg College, Allentown, Pa., in 1873; studied law; was admitted to the bar in 1875 and commenced practice in Clarion, Pa.; mayor in 1876 and again in 1889; edited the Clarion Democrat 1877-1889; elected as a Democrat to the Fifty-second and Fifty-third Congresses (March 4, 1891-March 3, 1895); unsuccessful candidate for renomination in 1894; resumed the practice of law in Clarion; served as mayor; president of the board of directors of the Clarion State Normal School; moved to Osceola County, Fla., in 1896 and engaged in orange culture; located in Kissimmee, Fla., in 1907 and re-engaged in the practice of law; prosecuting attorney of Osceola County in 1908; judge of the county court in 1909 and 1910; resigned and resumed the practice of law in

Kissimmee, Fla., until 1926 when he retired; died in Kissimmee, Fla., September 8, 1938; interment in Rose Hill Cemetery.

**KRONMILLER, John,** a Representative from Maryland; born in Baltimore, Md., on December 6, 1858; attended private and public schools; engaged in the mercantile business and also became a manufacturer of ivory goods in Baltimore, Md.; served in the city council 1905-1907; elected as a Republican to the Sixty-first Congress (March 4, 1909-March 3, 1911); was not a candidate for renomination in 1910; served as a voluntary member of the board of visitors to the Baltimore city jail 1908-1912; director of the Maryland General Hospital in 1913 and 1914; resumed his former manufacturing pursuits; member of the board of supervisors of election for the city of Baltimore from December 29, 1914, to May 1, 1916; died in Baltimore, Md., June 19, 1928; interment in Loudon Park Cemetery.

**KRUEGER, Otto,** a Representative from North Dakota; born of German parents in the Volinia district of southwest Russia, September 7, 1890; attended grade and high school in Russian and German schools; immigrated to the United States in June 1910 and settled in Fessenden, N.Dak.; furthered his education through grade and high schools and two years of business school in Fargo, N.Dak., and Great Falls, Mont.; during the First World War served as a private in the Infantry from April 1918 to May 1919, with overseas service in the Ninety-first Division; county auditor of Wells County, N.Dak., 1920-1940; State treasurer in 1945; State insurance commissioner 1946-1951; budget director in 1951 and 1952; clerk of Fessenden school district 1922-1940; State treasurer of the Republican Party 1948-1952; elected as a Republican to the Eighty-third and to the two succeeding Congresses (January 3, 1953-January 3, 1959); was not a candidate for renomination in 1958 to the Eighty-sixth Congress; moved to Lodi, Calif., in 1959 and engaged in accounting and farming; died in Lodi, Calif., June 6, 1963; interment in Cherokee Memorial Park Cemetery.

**KRUEGER, Robert Charles,** a Representative and a Senator from Texas; born in New Braunfels, Comal County, Tex., September 19, 1935; attended New Braunfels public schools; B.A., Southern Methodist University, Dallas, Tex., 1957; M.A., Duke University, Durham, N.C., 1958; M.Litt., D.Phil., Oxford University (Merton College), England, 1961, 1964; associate professor of English, vice provost and dean of college of arts and sciences at Duke University until 1973; engaged in private business pursuits, chairman of board of Comal Hosiery Mills, New Braunfels, 1973-1975; elected as a Democrat to the Ninety-fourth and Ninety-fifth Congresses (January 3, 1975-January 3, 1979); was not a candidate in 1978 for reelection to the House of Representatives, but was an unsuccessful candidate for election to the United States Senate; Ambassador at Large and Coordinator for Mexican Affairs, October 23, 1979, to February 1, 1981; president, Krueger Associates, 1981-1993; professor of business and government relations, Lyndon B. Johnson School of Public Affairs, University of Texas, 1985-1986; professor of public affairs, Rice University, 1986-1988; Texas Railroad Commissioner, 1991-1993; appointed to the United States Senate, January 21, 1993, to fill the vacancy caused by the resignation of Lloyd M. Bentsen, Jr., and served until June 5, 1993; unsuccessful candidate in a special election to the remainder of the term ending January 3, 1995; nominated by President William J. Clinton as Ambassador to Burundi, April 13, 1994, and confirmed by the Senate on May 6, 1994; nominated as Ambassador to Botswana, March 6, 1996, and confirmed by the Senate on June 4, 1996; is a resident of New Braunfels, Tex.

**KRUSE, Edward H.,** a Representative from Indiana; born in Fort Wayne, Allen County, Ind., October 22, 1918; attended the public schools; graduated from Indiana University Law School in Indianapolis in January 1942; also attended Butler University at Indianapolis; admitted to the bar in 1942; commissioned as an ensign in October 1942 and served in the Pacific; commenced the

private practice of law in Fort Wayne, Ind.; elected as a Democrat to the Eighty-first Congress (January 3, 1949-January 3, 1951); unsuccessful candidate for reelection in 1950 to the Eighty-second Congress; judge of Allen County Superior Court No. 2, Fort Wayne, Ind., in 1952; trust officer of two national banks, 1953-1957; member of an actuarial and pension consulting firm, 1959-1965; president, consulting actuarial firm since January 1966; is a resident of Fort Lauderdale, Fla.

**KUCHEL, Thomas Henry,** a Senator from California; born in Anaheim, Orange County, Calif., August 15, 1910; attended the public schools; graduated from the University of Southern California in 1932 and from the law school of the same university in 1935; was admitted to the bar the same year and began practice in Anaheim, Calif.; member of the California State assembly, 1936-1939; California State senator, 1940-1945, and while serving as State senator volunteered and was called to active duty in the United States Naval Reserve as a lieutenant (jg), serving until 1945; appointed California State controller by Governor Earl Warren on February 11, 1946, elected State controller in November 1946, reelected in 1950, and served until 1953; appointed December 22, 1952 and subsequently elected as a Republican to the United States Senate to fill the vacancy caused by the resignation of Richard M. Nixon; reelected in 1956 and again in 1962 and served from January 2, 1953, to January 3, 1969; unsuccessful candidate for renomination in 1968; Republican whip (Eighty-sixth through Ninetieth Congresses); practiced law in Washington, D.C., and Los Angeles until his retirement in 1981; resided in Beverly Hills, Calif., and died at his home there on November 21, 1994.

**Bibliography:** Kuchel, Thomas. "The Role of the Senate Minority." In *The Senate Institution.* Edited by Nathaniel S. Preston. pp. 75-82. New York: Van Nostrand Reinhold, 1969.

**KUHNS, Joseph Henry,** a Representative from Pennnsylvania; born near Greensburg, Pa., in September 1800; attended the public schools and Greensburg Academy; was graduated from Washington (later Washington and Jefferson) College, Washington, Pa., in 1820; studied law; was admitted to the bar in 1823 and commenced practice in Greensburg; elected as a Whig to the Thirty-second Congress (March 4, 1851-March 3, 1853); unsuccessful candidate for reelection in 1852 to the Thirty-third Congress; resumed the practice of law in Greensburg, Pa.; died in Greensburg, Pa., November 16, 1883; interment in St. Clair Cemetery.

**KULP, Monroe Henry,** a Representative from Pennsylvania; born in Barto, Berks County, Pa., October 23, 1858; attended the public schools of Shamokin, the State Normal College, Lebanon, Ohio, and was graduated from Eastman Business College, Poughkeepsie, N.Y.; engaged in the lumber, brick, and ice business in Shamokin, Pa.; elected as a Republican to the Fifty-fourth and Fifty-fifth Congresses (March 4, 1895-March 3, 1899); unsuccessful candidate for renomination in 1898; delegate to the Republican National Convention in 1900; devoted himself to the lumber business and to many other interests; died in Shamokin, Northumberland County, Pa., on October 19, 1911; interment in the City Cemetery.

**KUNKEL, Jacob Michael,** a Representative from Maryland; born in Frederick, Frederick County, Md., July 13, 1822; attended the Frederick Academy for Boys and was graduated from the University of Virginia at Charlottesville in 1843; studied law; was admitted to the bar and commenced practice in Frederick in 1846; served in the State senate 1850-1856; elected as a Democrat to the Thirty-fifth and Thirty-sixth Congresses (March 4, 1857-March 3, 1861); resumed the practice of law in his native city; delegate to the Loyalist Convention in Philadelphia in 1866; died in Frederick, Md., April 7, 1870.

**KUNKEL, John Christian** (grandfather of John Crain Kunkel), a Representative from Pennsylvania; born in Harrisburg, Pa., September 18, 1816; attended the common schools of Gettysburg, Pa., and was graduated from Jefferson College, Canonsburg, Pa. (later Washington and Jefferson College, Washington, Pa.) in 1839; studied law at the Carlisle (Pa.) Law School; was admitted to the Dauphin County bar in 1842 and commenced practice in Harrisburg; served in the Pennsylvania house of representatives in 1844, 1845, and again in 1850; member of the Pennsylvania senate 1851-1853, and served as speaker in 1852 and 1853; elected as a Whig to the Thirty-fourth Congress and reelected as a Republican to the Thirty-fifth Congress (March 4, 1855-March 3, 1859); chairman, Committee on Militia (Thirty-fourth Congress); was not a candidate for renomination in 1858 to the Thirty-sixth Congress; resumed the practice of his profession; died in Harrisburg, Dauphin County, Pa., October 14, 1870; interment in Harrisburg Cemetery.

**KUNKEL, John Crain** (grandson of John Christian Kunkel, great-grandson of John Sergeant, and great-great-grandson of Jonathan Dickinson Sergeant and Robert Whitehill), a Representative from Pennsylvania; born in Harrisburg, July 21, 1898; attended Harrisburg (Pa.) Academy and Phillips Academy, Andover, Mass.; was graduated from Yale University in 1916 and from the law department of Harvard University in 1926; during the First World War served in the Students' Army Training Corps; was admitted to the bar in Oklahoma and Pennsylvania in 1926; engaged in banking and agricultural pursuits; elected as a Republican to the Seventy-sixth and to the five succeeding Congresses (January 3, 1939-January 3, 1951); was not a candidate for renomination in 1950 to the House of Representatives, but was an unsuccessful candidate for nomination to the United States Senate; county commissioner of Dauphin County, Pa., 1952-1956; elected to the Eighty-seventh Congress, May 16, 1961, by special election to fill the vacancy caused by the death of Walter M. Mumma; reelected to the Eighty-eighth and Eighty-ninth Congresses, and served from May 16, 1961, to January 3, 1967; was not a candidate for reelection in 1966 to the Ninetieth Congress; resided in Harrisburg, Pa., until his death there, July 27, 1970; interment in Harrisburg Cemetery.

**KUNZ, Stanley Henry,** a Representative from Illinois; born in Nanticoke, Luzerne County, Pa., September 26, 1864; attended the public schools, St. Ignatius College, and Metropolitan Business College, all in Chicago, Ill.; member of the State house of representatives 1888-1890; served in the State senate 1902-1906; member of the Chicago City council 1891-1921; member of the Democratic county central committee of Cook County 1891-1925; engaged in the breeding of thoroughbreds and racing horses in Palatine, Cook County, Ill., 1910-1933; delegate to the Democratic National Conventions in 1912, 1916, and 1924; elected as a Democrat to the Sixty-seventh and to the four succeeding Congresses (March 4, 1921-March 3, 1931); successfully contested the election of Peter C. Granata to the Seventy-second Congress and served from April 5, 1932, to March 3, 1933; unsuccessful candidate for renomination in 1932; lived in Chicago, Ill., until his death there on April 23, 1946; interment in St. Adalbert's Cemetery.

**KUPFERMAN, Theodore Roosevelt,** a Representative from New York; born in New York City on May 12, 1920; graduated from De Witt Clinton High School, New York City; B.S., City College of the City University of New York, 1940; LL.B., Columbia University Law School, 1943; admitted to the New York bar in 1943 and to the United States Supreme Court bar in 1948; law secretary, Appellate Division, New York State Supreme Court, 1948-1949; member, legal department, Warner Brothers Pictures, Inc., 1943-1948 and 1949-1951; member, legal department, National Broadcasting Co., Inc., 1951-1953; general counsel, Cinerama Productions Corp., 1953-1958; assistant and adjunct professor of law, New York Law School, 1959-1964; counsel and legislative assistant to minority leader, New York City Council, 1958-1962; councilman, city of New York, 1962-1966; elected as a Republican to the Eighty-ninth Congress on February 8, 1966, to fill the vacancy caused by the resignation of John V. Lindsay; reelected to the Ninetieth Congress and served from February 8, 1966, to January 3, 1969; was not a candidate for reelection in 1968 to the Ninety-first Congress; elected as a justice to the New York State Supreme Court, commencing in 1969; is a resident of New York City.

**KURTZ, Jacob Banks,** a Representative from Pennsylvania; born in Delaware Township, Juniata County, Pa., October 31, 1867; attended the public schools; was graduated from Dickinson College, Carlisle, Pa., and from Dickinson Law School in 1893; was admitted to the bar and commenced practice in Altoona, Pa.; district attorney of Blair County 1905-1912; chairman of the committee of public safety and council of national defense for Blair County during the First World War; elected as a Republican to the Sixty-eighth and to the five succeeding Congresses (March 4, 1923-January 3, 1935); unsuccessful candidate for reelection in 1934 to the Seventy-fourth Congress; resumed the practice of law; delegate to the Republican National Conventions in 1936, 1940, and 1948; city solicitor of Altoona, Pa., 1944-1946; died in Altoona, Pa., September 18, 1960; interment in Alto Reste Burial Park.

**KURTZ, William Henry,** a Representative from Pennsylvania; born in York, Pa., January 31, 1804; attended the common schools and the York County Academy at York, Pa.; studied law; was admitted to the bar on January 7, 1828, and commenced practice in York, Pa.; prosecuting attorney of York County; elected as a Democrat to the Thirty-second and Thirty-third Congresses (March 4, 1851-March 3, 1855); chairman, Committee on Public Expenditures (Thirty-third Congress); resumed the practice of law; died in York, Pa., June 24, 1868; interment in Prospect Hill Cemetery.

**KÜSTERMANN, Gustav,** a Representative from Wisconsin; born in Detmold, Germany, May 24, 1850; attended the academy of his native city (Gymnasium Leopoldinum) and was graduated in 1864; employed in a wholesale dry goods establishment in Hamburg, Germany, until 1868, when he immigrated to the United States and settled in Green Bay, Brown County, Wis.; engaged in mercantile pursuits and held various public offices; postmaster of Green Bay, 1892-1896; member of the Wisconsin State board of control, and served as its president, 1904-1907; elected as a Republican to the Sixtieth and Sixty-first Congresses (March 4, 1907-March 3, 1911); unsuccessful candidate for reelection in 1910 to the Sixty-second Congress; engaged in literary work in Green Bay, Wis., and died there on December 25, 1919; interment in Woodlawn Cemetery.

**KUYKENDALL, Andrew Jackson,** a Representative from Illinois; born in Gallatin County, Ill., March 3, 1815; completed preparatory studies; studied law; was admitted to the bar in 1840 and commenced practice in Vienna, Ill.; member of the State house of representatives 1842-1862; during the Civil War served one year in the Union Army as major in the Thirty-first Regiment, Illinois Volunteers; elected as a Republican to the Thirty-ninth Congress (March 4, 1865-March 3, 1867); resumed the practice of law in Vienna, Ill.; county and probate judge of Johnson County 1873-1881; member of the State senate 1878-1882; retired from public life and engaged in agricultural pursuits; died in Vienna, Johnson County, Ill., May 11, 1891; interment in the Fraternal Cemetery.

**KUYKENDALL, Dan Heflin,** a Representative from Tennessee; born in Cherokee, San Saba County, Tex., July 9, 1924; attended the public schools of Cherokee, Tex.; B.S., Texas A.&M. University, 1947; served as lieutenant, pilot in the United States Army Air Corps, 1942-1945; joined Procter & Gamble Co., in 1947 and worked in Corpus Christi and Houston, Tex., and Memphis, Tenn.; co-chairman, Shelby County (Tenn.) Republican Party, 1963-1964;

member of the board of directors of the charter group drafting a new charter for the city of Memphis in 1965-1966; unsuccessful candidate in 1964 for election to the United States Senate; elected as a Republican to the Ninetieth and to the three succeeding Congresses (January 3, 1967-January 3, 1975); unsuccessful candidate for reelection in 1974 to the Ninety-fourth Congress; is a resident of Bethesda, Md.

**KVALE, Ole Juulson** (father of Paul John Kvale), a Representative from Minnesota; born near Decorah, Winnesheik County, Iowa, February 6, 1869; attended the rural schools; was graduated from Luther College, Decorah, Iowa, in 1890, from Luther Theological Seminary, Minneapolis, Minn., in 1893, and from the University of Chicago in 1914; was ordained to the ministry in 1894 and served in Orfordville, Wis., from 1894 to 1917, and in Benson, Swift County, Minn., from 1917 until elected to Congress; unsuccessful candidate as an Independent Republican for election in 1920 to the Sixty-seventh Congress; elected as a Farmer-Labor candidate to the Sixty-eighth through Seventy-first Congresses and served from March 4, 1923, until his death near Otter Tail Lake, Minn., on September 11, 1929; interment in Benson Cemetery, Benson, Minn.

**KVALE, Paul John** (son of Ole Juulson Kvale), a Representative from Minnesota; born in Orfordville, Rock County, Wis., March 27, 1896; moved to Benson, Minn., with his parents in 1917; attended the Orfordville schools and the University of Illinois at Chicago; was graduated from Luther College, Decorah, Iowa, in 1917; served in the United States Army during the First World War as a sergeant in a machine-gun corps, from September 7, 1917, to August 4, 1919; student at the University of Minnesota at Minneapolis in 1919 and 1920; returned to Benson, Minn., and engaged as editor of the Swift County News in 1920 and 1921; staff editor of the Minneapolis Tribune in 1921; served as secretary to his father, Representative Ole J. Kvale, from 1922 to 1929; elected as a Farmer-Labor candidate to the Seventy-first Congress to fill the vacancy caused by the death of his father; reelected to the Seventy-second and to the three succeeding Congresses and served from October 16, 1929, to January 3, 1939; unsuccessful candidate for reelection in 1938 to the Seventy-sixth Congress; died in Minneapolis, Minn., June 14, 1960; interment in Protestant Cemetery, Benson, Minn.

**KYL, John Henry** (father of Jon Llewellyn Kyl), a Representative from Iowa; born in Wisner, Cumming, County, Nebr., May 9, 1919; graduated from Wayne (Nebr.) Prep High School in 1937; A.B., Nebraska State Teachers College, 1940; M.A., University of Nebraska, 1947; taught in the public schools of Nebraska and in Nebraska State Teachers College at Wayne, 1940-1950; manager, Wayne Chamber of Commerce, 1949-1953; engaged in business in Bloomfield, Iowa, 1953-1959; unsuccessful candidate for election in 1958 to the Eighty-sixth Congress; elected as a Republican to the Eighty-sixth Congress, December 15, 1959, by special election to fill the vacancy caused by the death of Steven V. Carter; reelected to the two succeeding Congresses, and served from December 15, 1959 to January 3, 1965; unsuccessful candidate for reelection in 1964 to the Eighty-ninth Congress; elected to the Ninetieth and to the two succeeding Congresses (January 3, 1967-January 3, 1973); unsuccessful candidate for reelection in 1972 to the Ninety-third Congress; assistant secretary, congressional and legislative affairs, Department of the Interior, 1973-1977; executive vice president, Occidental International Corporation, 1977-1985; is a resident of Phoenix, Ariz.

**KYL, Jon Llewellyn** (son of John Henry Kyl), a Representative and a Senator from Arizona; born in Oakland, Burt County, Nebr., April 25, 1942; graduated Bloomfield (Iowa) High School, 1960; B.A., University of Arizona, Tucson, 1964; LL.B., University of Arizona, 1966; admitted to the Arizona State bar in 1966 and practiced law as

a member of Jennings, Strouss and Salmon, in Phoenix, 1966-1986; chairman, Phoenix Metropolitan Chamber of Commerce, 1984-1985; elected as a Republican to the One Hundredth and to the three succeeding Congresses (January 3, 1987-January 3, 1995); was not a candidate in 1994 for reelection to the House of Representatives, but was elected to the United States Senate for the term ending January 3, 2001; is a resident of Phoenix, Ariz.

**KYLE, James Henderson,** a Senator from South Dakota; born near Xenia, Greene County, Ohio, on February 24, 1854; attended the public schools; completed a course of civil engineering at the University of Illinois at Urbana in 1871; graduated from Oberlin (Ohio) College in 1878; prepared for admission to the bar, but entered the Western Theological Seminary, Allegheny, Pa., and was graduated in 1882; pastor of Congregational churches in Echo and Salt Lake City, Utah, 1882-1885; moved to Ipswich and later to Aberdeen, Brown County, S.Dak.; pastor; financial secretary of Yankton (S.Dak.) College; elected to the South Dakota State senate in 1890; chairman of the United States Industrial Commission, 1898-1901; elected as an Independent to the United States Senate in 1891; reelected in 1897, and served from March 4, 1891 until his death in Aberdeen, S.Dak., on July 1, 1901; chairman, Committee on Education and Labor (Fifty-third, Fifty-fifth and Fifty-sixth Congresses), Committee to Establish the University of the United States (Fifty-fourth Congress); interment in Riverside Cemetery.

**Bibliography:** Quinion, Harold. "James H. Kyle, United States Senator from South Dakota, 1891-1901." *South Dakota Historical Collections* 13 (1926): 311-321.

**KYLE, John Curtis,** a Representative from Mississippi; born near Sardis, Panola County, Miss., July 17, 1851; attended Bethel College, Tennessee, and was graduated from the Cumberland University Law School in 1874; was admitted to the bar in 1874 and commenced practice in Sardis; mayor of Sardis 1879-1881; member of the State senate 1881-1885; member of the Mississippi Railroad Commission 1886-1890; chairman of the Democratic State executive committee in 1888; elected as a Democrat to the Fifty-second, Fifty-third, and Fifty-fourth Congresses (March 4, 1891-March 3, 1897); was not a candidate for renomination in 1896; resumed the practice of law and also engaged in banking in Sardis; retired from active business pursuits in 1912; died in Sardis, Miss., July 6, 1913; interment in Rosehill Cemetery.

**KYLE, Thomas Barton,** a Representative from Ohio; born in Troy, Miami County, Ohio, March 10, 1856; attended the public schools and Dartmouth College, Hanover, N.H.; studied law; was admitted to the bar in 1884 and commenced practice in Troy; elected prosecuting attorney of Miami County in 1890; president of the board of education of Troy; mayor of Troy; elected as a Republican to the Fifty-seventh and Fifty-eighth Congresses (March 4, 1901-March 3, 1905); unsuccessful candidate for renomination in 1904 to the Fifty-ninth Congress; resumed the practice of his profession in Troy, Ohio, where he died on August 13, 1915; interment in Riverside Cemetery.

**KYROS, Peter Nicholas,** a Representative from Maine; born in Portland, Maine, July 11, 1925; attended the public schools of Portland, Maine, and the Massachusetts Institute of Technology; graduated from the United States Naval Academy in 1947; graduated from Harvard Law School in 1957; served in the United States Navy, 1944-1953, discharged with rank of lieutenant; admitted to the bar in 1957 and commenced the practice of law in Portland, Maine; served from 1957 to 1959 as counsel to the Maine Public Utilities Commission, Augusta; elected as a Democrat to the Ninetieth and to the three succeeding Congresses (January 3, 1967-January 3, 1975); unsuccessful candidate for reelection in 1974 to the Ninety-fourth Congress; served in the United States Department of State, 1980-1982; resumed the practice of law in Washington, D.C.; is a resident of Portland, Maine.

# L

**LA BRANCHE, Alceé Louis,** a Representative from Louisiana; born near New Orleans, La., in 1806; attended the Université de Sorreze, France; engaged in planting; member of the Louisiana State house of representatives, 1831-1833, and was chosen speaker of the house on January 7, 1833; Chargé d'Affaires to Texas from 1837 to 1840, when he resigned; elected as a Democrat to the Twenty-eighth Congress (March 4, 1843-March 3, 1845); naval officer at the port of New Orleans in 1847; died at Hot Springs, Va., August 17, 1861; interment in Red Church Cemetery, St. Charles Parish; reinterment in Metairie Cemetery, New Orleans, La.

**LACEY, Edward Samuel,** a Representative from Michigan; born in Chili, Monroe County, N.Y., November 26, 1835; moved with his parents to Branch County, Mich., in October 1842, and to Eaton County in March 1843; attended the public schools and Olivet (Mich.) College; engaged in various business pursuits and in banking; a resident of Kalamazoo, Mich., 1853-1857; moved to Charlotte, Mich., and was register of deeds for Eaton County, 1860-1864; mayor of Charlotte in 1871; trustee of the Michigan Asylum for the Insane, 1874-1880; delegate to the Republican National Convention of 1876; elected as a Republican to the Forty-seventh and Forty-eighth Congresses (March 4, 1881-March 3, 1885); declined to be a candidate for reelection in 1884 to the Forty-ninth Congress; chairman of the Republican State central committee, 1882-1884; commissioned by President Benjamin Harrison to be Comptroller of the Currency on April 17, 1889; reappointed December 16, 1889, and served until 1892, when he resigned; moved to Chicago, Ill., and again engaged in banking; died in Evanston, Ill., October 2, 1916; interment in Maple Hill Cemetery, Charlotte, Mich.

**LACEY, John Fletcher,** a Representative from Iowa; born in New Martinsville, Va. (now West Virginia), May 30, 1841; moved to Iowa in 1855 with his parents, who settled in Oskaloosa; attended the common schools and pursued classical studies; engaged in agricultural pursuits; learned the trades of bricklaying and plastering; enlisted in Company H, Third Regiment, Iowa Volunteer Infantry, in May 1861 and afterward served in Company D, Thirty-third Regiment, Iowa Volunteer Infantry, as sergeant major, and as lieutenant in Company C of that regiment; promoted to assistant adjutant general; studied law; was admitted to the bar in 1865 and commenced practice in Oskaloosa, Iowa; member of the Iowa house of representatives in 1870; elected city councilman in 1880; served one term as city solicitor; temporary chairman of the Republican State convention in 1898; served on the city council 1880-1883; elected as a Republican to the Fifty-first Congress (March 4, 1889-March 3, 1891); unsuccessful candidate for reelection; elected to the Fifty-third and to the six succeeding Congresses (March 4, 1893-March 3, 1907); chairman, Committee on Public Lands (Fifty-fourth through Fifty-ninth Congresses); was an unsuccessful candidate for reelection; resumed the practice of law; died in Oskaloosa, Iowa, September 29, 1913; interment in Forest Cemetery.

**Bibliography:** *DAB*; Gallagher, Mary Annette. "John F. Lacey: A Study in Organizational Politics." Ph.D. dissertation, University of Arizona, 1970.

**LACOCK, Abner,** a Representative and a Senator from Pennsylvania; born near Alexandria, Va., July 9, 1770; moved with his parents to Washington County, Pa., as a youth; moved to Beaver (then in Allegheny County), Pa., in 1796; justice of the peace in 1796; innkeeper; member of the Pennsylvania legislature, 1801-1803, and 1804-1808; associate judge of the Beaver County Court, 1803-1804; member of the Pennsylvania Militia, and served as brigadier general in 1807; Pennsylvania senator, 1808-1810; elected as a Republican to the Twelfth Congress and served from March 4, 1811, until March 3, 1813; reelected to the Thirteenth Congress but resigned before it commenced, having been elected Senator; elected to the United States Senate as a Republican and served from March 4, 1813, to March 3, 1819; chairman, Committee on Pensions (Fifteenth Congress); appointed a commissioner to survey routes for canals and railways in Pennsylvania in 1825; member of the Pennsylvania legislature, 1832-1835; appointed to survey and construct the Pennsylvania & Ohio Canal in 1836; died near Freedom, Pa., April 12, 1837; interment in Lacock Cemetery, Rochester, Pa.

**Bibliography:** *DAB*; "Abner Lacock." *Pennsylvania Magazine of History and Biography* 4 (1880): 202-08.

**LADD, Edwin Freemont,** a Senator from North Dakota; born in Starks, Somerset County, Maine, December 13, 1859; attended the public schools and Somerset Academy, Athens, Maine, and graduated from the University of Maine at Orono in 1884; chemist of the New York State Experiment Station, Geneva, N.Y., 1884-1890; dean of the school of chemistry and pharmacy and professor of chemistry at the North Dakota Agricultural College, Fargo, N.Dak.; chief chemist of the North Dakota Agricultural Experiment Station, 1890-1916; editor of the North Dakota Farmer at Lisbon, 1899-1904; administrator of North Dakota's state pure-food laws, for which he actively crusaded from 1902 until 1921; president of the North Dakota Agricultural College, 1916-1921; elected as a Republican to the United States Senate in 1920 and served from March 4, 1921, until his death in Baltimore, Md., June 22, 1925; chairman, Committee on Public Roads and Surveys (Sixty-eighth Congress); interment in Glenwood Cemetery, Washington, D.C.

**Bibliography:** *DAB*.

**LADD, George Washington,** a Representative from Maine; born in Augusta, Kennebec County, Maine, September 28, 1818; attended the common schools and Kents Hill Seminary; engaged in the drug business in Bangor, Maine; later engaged in the lumber, commission, and wholesale grocery business in Bangor; was also interested in railroad development; elected as a Greenback candidate to the Forty-sixth and Forty-seventh Congresses (March 4, 1879-March 3, 1883); chairman, Committee on Expenditures in the Post Office Department (Forty-sixth Congress); unsuccessful candidate for reelection in 1882 to the Forty-eighth Congress; died in Bangor, Penobscot County, Maine, January 30, 1892; interment in Mount Hope Cemetery.

**LA DOW, George Augustus,** a Representative from Oregon; born near Syracuse, Cayuga County, N.Y., March 18, 1826; moved to McHenry County, Ill.; attended the common schools; studied law; was admitted to the bar in 1850 and commenced practice in Waupaca, Wis.; district attorney of Waupaca County, 1860-1862; moved to Minnesota in 1862 and settled in Wilton, Waseca (now Beltrami) County, and continued the practice of law; member of the Minnesota State house of representatives in 1868 and 1869; moved to Oregon in 1869, settled in Pendleton, and again engaged in the practice of law; member of the Oregon State house of representatives, 1872-1874; elected as a Democrat to the Forty-fourth Congress, and served from March 4, 1875 until his death in Pendleton, Oreg., May 1, 1875, prior to the convening of Congress; interment in Pioneer Park Cemetery.

**LaFALCE, John Joseph,** a Representative from New York; born in Buffalo, Erie County, N.Y., October 6, 1939; graduated from Canisius High School, Buffalo, 1957; B.S., Canisius College, 1961; J.D., Villanova Law School, Philadelphia, Pa., 1964; admitted to the New York bar in 1964 and commenced practice in Buffalo; served in the United States Army, 1965-1967; member, New York State senate, 1971-1972; member, New York State assembly, 1973-1974; elected as a Democrat to the Ninety-fourth and to the ten succeeding Congresses (January 3, 1975-January 3, 1997); chairman, Committee on Small Business (One Hundredth through One Hundred Third Congresses); is a resident of Kenmore, N.Y.

**LAFEAN, Daniel Franklin,** a Representative from Pennsylvania; born in York, York County, Pa., on February 7, 1861; attended the public schools; engaged in candy manufacturing and in banking in York; a director of the Gettysburg College and trustee of the Gettysburg Seminary, Gettysburg, Pa.; elected as a Republican to the Fifty-eighth and to the four succeeding Congresses (March 4, 1903-March 3, 1913); unsuccessful candidate for reelection in 1912 to the Sixty-third Congress; elected to the Sixty-fourth Congress (March 4, 1915-March 3, 1917); was not a candidate for renomination in 1916; appointed commissioner of banking of the Commonwealth of Pennsylvania in 1917; again engaged in manufacturing pursuits; died in Philadelphia, Pa., April 18, 1922; interment in Prospect Hill Cemetery, York, Pa.

**LAFFERTY, Abraham Walter,** a Representative from Oregon; born near Farber, Audrain County, Mo., June 10, 1875; attended the public schools; studied law at the University of Missouri at Columbia in 1895 and 1896; was admitted to the bar the latter year and commenced practice in Montgomery City, Mo.; prosecuting attorney of Montgomery County, Mo., 1902-1905; appointed special agent of the United States General Land Office, and moved to Portland, Oreg., March 1, 1905; resigned on October 1, 1906, and engaged in the practice of law in Portland; elected as a Republican to the Sixty-second and Sixty-third Congresses (March 4, 1911-March 3, 1915); unsuccessful candidate for reelection in 1914 to the Sixty-fourth Congress; resumed the practice of law in Portland; during the First World War served as major at the San Francisco training camp; moved to New York City in 1919 and continued the practice of law there until 1933, when he moved to Riverdale, Md.; returned to Portland, Oreg., in 1946; unsuccessful candidate for nomination as an Independent in 1950 to the Eighty-second Congress; unsuccessful Republican candidate for nomination in 1952 to the Eighty-third Congress, in 1954 to the Eighty-fourth Congress, and in 1956 to the Eighty-fifth Congress; unsuccessful Independent candidate for election to the United States Senate in 1962; was a resident of Portland, Oreg., until his death on January 15, 1964; interment in Fairmount Cemetery, Middletown, Mo.

**LAFFOON, Polk,** a Representative from Kentucky; born near Madisonville, Hopkins County, Ky., October 24, 1844; attended the common schools; during the Civil War entered the Confederate Army as a member of the Eighth Infantry; captured at Fort Donelson February 16, 1862, and exchanged at Vicksburg in September 1862; member of John Hunt Morgan's command during the remainder of his service; captured at Cheshire, Ohio; at the close of the war engaged in teaching for two years; studied law; was admitted to the bar in 1867 and practiced in Madisonville, Ky.; prosecuting attorney of Hopkins County; elected as a Democrat to the Forty-ninth and Fiftieth Congresses (March 4, 1885-March 3, 1889); chairman, Committee on Expenditures in the Department of War (Fiftieth Congress); was not a candidate for renomination in 1888; resumed the practice of law; died in Madisonville, Ky., October 22, 1906; interment in the Odd Fellows Cemetery.

**LAFLIN, Addison Henry,** a Representative from New York; born in Lee, Berkshire County, Mass., October 24, 1823; attended the common schools; was graduated from Williams College, Williamstown, Mass., in 1843; went to Herkimer County, N.Y., in 1849 and became interested in paper making; member of the New York State senate in 1858 and 1859; elected as a Republican to the Thirty-ninth and to the two succeeding Congresses (March 4, 1865-March 3, 1871); was not a candidate for renomination in 1870 to the Forty-second Congress; delegate to the Republican State convention in 1867; appointed by President Ulysses S. Grant to be naval officer at the port of New York on April 3, 1871, and served

until 1877, when he resigned; died in Pittsfield, Mass., September 24, 1878; interment in Oakwood Cemetery, Syracuse, N.Y.

**LA FOLLETTE, Charles Marion** (great-grandson of William Heilman), a Representative from Indiana; born in New Albany, Floyd County, Ind., February 27, 1898; moved with his parents to Evansville, Ind., in 1901; attended the public schools and entered Wabash College at Crawfordsville, Ind., in September 1916; during the First World War enlisted in the United States Army and served with the One Hundred and Fifty-first Infantry, Thirty-eighth Division, 1917-1919, with four months overseas; attended Wabash College until June 1921; studied law at Vanderbilt University, Nashville, Tenn., in 1921 and also in law offices in Dayton, Ohio, and Evansville, Ind.; was admitted to the bar in 1925 and commenced practice in Evansville, Ind.; member of the State house of representatives 1927-1929; elected as a Republican to the Seventy-eighth and to the Seventy-ninth Congresses (January 3, 1943-January 3, 1947); was not a candidate for reelection in 1946 but was an unsuccessful candidate for the Republican nomination for United States Senator; deputy chief of counsel for war crimes, Nuremberg, Germany, from January 4 to December 15, 1947; director of the Office of Military Government for Wurttemberg-Baden, Germany, from December 15, 1947 to January 16, 1949; appointed a director of Americans for Democratic Action on July 1, 1949, serving until May 1, 1950; member of first Subversive Activities Contol Board, 1950-1951; died in Trenton, N.J., June 27, 1974; cremated; ashes interred at Locust Hill Cemetery, Evansville, Ind.

**LA FOLLETTE, Robert Marion** (father of Robert Marion La Follette, Jr.), a Representative and a Senator from Wisconsin; born in Primrose, Dane County, Wis., June 14, 1855; graduated from the University of Wisconsin at Madison in 1879; studied law; admitted to the bar in 1880 and commenced practice in Madison, Wis.; district attorney of Dane County, 1880-1884; elected as a Republican to the Forty-ninth and to the two succeeding Congresses (March 4, 1885-March 3, 1891); unsuccessful candidate for reelection in 1890 to the Fifty-second Congress; chairman, Committee on Expenditures in the Department of Agriculture (Fifty-first Congress); resumed the practice of law in Madison, Wis.; elected Governor of Wisconsin in 1900, reelected in 1902 and 1904, and served from January 7, 1901 until his resignation on January 1, 1906, having previously been elected Senator; elected as a Republican to the United States Senate on January 25, 1905, for the term beginning March 4, 1905, but did not assume these duties until January 2, 1906, preferring to continue as Governor; reelected in 1911, 1917, and 1923, and served from January 2, 1906 until his death; chairman, Committee on the Census (Sixty-first and Sixty-second Congress), Committee on Corporations Organized in the District of Columbia (Sixty-third through Sixty-fifth Congresses), Committee on Manufactures (Sixty-sixth through Sixty-eighth Congresses); one of the founders of the National Progressive Republican League and several times unsuccessfully sought the Republican and Progressive Party presidential nominations; unsuccessful Progressive Party candidate for President of the United States in 1924; died in Washington, D.C., June 18, 1925; interment in Forest Hill Cemetery, Madison, Wis.

Bibliography: DAB; La Follette, Belle C., and La Follette, Fola. *Robert M. La Follette.* 2 vols. New York: Macmillan, 1953; Thelan, David. *Robert M. La Follette and the Insurgent Spirit.* Boston: Little, Brown, 1976.

**LA FOLLETTE, Robert Marion, Jr.** (son of Robert Marion La Follette), a Senator from Wisconsin; born in Madison, Wis., February 6, 1895; attended the public schools of Madison and Washington, D.C.; attended the University of Wisconsin at Madison, 1913-1917; private secretary to his father, 1919-1925; elected as a Republican to the United States Senate on September 29, 1925, to fill the vacancy caused by the death of his father, Robert M. La

Follette; reelected as a Republican in 1928, and as a Progressive in 1934 and 1940, and served from September 30, 1925, to January 3, 1947; announced his affiliation with the Republican Party on March 17, 1946; unsuccessful candidate for renomination as a Republican in 1946; chairman, Committee on Manufactures (Seventy-first and Seventy-second Congresses), Special Committee on the Organization of Congress (Seventy-ninth Congress); co-sponsor of the Legislative Reorganization Act of 1946, reducing the number of congressional committees and allowing the hire of committee staff, changing the method of dealing with the Federal budget, reducing the workload of Congress, and for the first time requiring lobbyists to register with and report their expenditures to the House clerk; author, economic-research consultant, and foreign aid adviser to President Harry S Truman's administration; died from a self-inflicted gunshot wound in Washington, D.C., February 24, 1953; interment in Forest Hill Cemetery, Madison, Wis.

**Bibliography:** *DAB*; Auerbach, Jerold. *Labor and Liberty: The La Follette Committee and the New Deal.* Indianapolis: Bobbs-Merrill, 1966; La Follette, Robert M., Jr. "Systematizing Congressional Control." *American Political Science Review* 41 (1947): 58-68; Maney, Patrick J. *"Young Bob" La Follette: A Biography of Robert M. La Follette, Jr., 1895-1953.* Columbia: University of Missouri Press, 1978.

**LA FOLLETTE, William Leroy,** a Representative from Washington; born in Thorntown, near Shammondale, Boone County, Ind., November 30, 1860; attended the graded schools in Thorntown, Ind., and at the same time clerked in a store and was employed at the jewelry trade; attended Indiana Central Normal College in Thorntown; moved to the Territory of Washington in 1876 and located in the Willamette Valley in Oregon; moved to the Palouse country in 1877; engaged in agricultural pursuits, stock raising, and fruit growing in Whitman County, and was also extensively engaged as an orchardist at Wawawai, Wash.; disposed of his fruit interests in 1908 and moved to Pullman, Wash.; member of the State house of representatives 1899-1901; member of the World's Fair Commission and had charge of the Washington State building at the Chicago Exposition in 1893; elected as a Republican to the Sixty-second and to the three succeeding Congresses (March 4, 1911-March 3, 1919); unsuccessful candidate for renomination in 1918; resided in Spokane, Wash., 1920-1923, and Princess Anne, Md., 1924 and 1925; moved to Colfax, Wash., in 1927; resumed his former business activities; died in Colfax, Wash., December 20, 1934; interment in Colfax Cemetery.

**LAFORE, John Armand, Jr.,** a Representative from Pennsylvania; born in Bala, Montgomery County, Pa., May 25, 1905; attended the Montgomery County schools; student at Swarthmore College in 1923 and 1925, and at the University of Pennsylvania in 1925 and 1926; automobile dealer in Philadelphia from 1932 until 1957; former comptroller of Montgomery County, Pa., and former chairman of the Lower Merion Township Committee; served as a lieutenant commander in the United States Navy, 1942-1945; member of the Pennsylvania house of representatives, 1950-1957; elected as a Republican to the Eighty-fifth Congress to fill the vacancy caused by the resignation of Samuel K. McConnell, Jr.; reelected to the Eighty-sixth Congress, and served from November 5, 1957 to January 3, 1961; unsuccessful candidate for renomination in 1960 to the Eighty-seventh Congress; president of an aircraft company in Willow Grove, Pa., 1961-1964; vice president, Day and Zimmerman of Philadelphia, Pa., 1965-1966; executive vice president, American Kennel Club, 1968-1971, and president, 1971-1979; is a resident of Villanova, Pa.

**LAGAN, Matthew Diamond,** a Representative from Louisiana; born in Maghera, Londonderry, Ireland, June 20, 1829; attended the common schools; immigrated to the United States and settled in New Orleans, La., December 28, 1843; engaged in manufacturing and mercantile pursuits; during the Civil War fitted out many vessels for the use of the Confederate States and later enlisted as a volunteer in the Confederate Navy; elected to the New Orleans Common Council in 1867; member of the State constitutional convention in 1879; again elected to the city council in 1882 and served as president and acting mayor during the term; elected as a Democrat to the Fiftieth Congress (March 4, 1887-March 3, 1889); declined a renomination for election to the Fifty-first Congress; elected to the Fifty-second Congress (March 4, 1891-March 3, 1893); died in New Orleans, La., April 8, 1901; interment in Metairie Cemetery.

**LAGOMARSINO, Robert John,** a Representative from California; born in Ventura, Calif., September 4, 1926; attended the public schools of Ventura; B.A., University of California, Santa Barbara, 1950; J.D., University of Santa Clara Law School, 1953; admitted to the California bar in 1954 and commenced practice in Ventura; served in the United States Navy, 1944-1946; elected to the Ojai City Council in 1958; mayor of Ojai, 1958-1961; elected to the California State senate, by special election, October 3, 1961, and served until 1974; delegate, California State Republican conventions, 1961-1974; delegate to the Republican National Conventions of 1968 and 1984; elected as a Republican to the Ninety-third Congress, March 5, 1974, by special election to fill the vacancy caused by the death of Charles M. Teague; reelected to the nine succeeding Congresses, and served from March 5, 1974 to January 3, 1993; unsuccessful candidate for renomination in 1992 to the One Hundred Third Congress; is a resident of Ventura, Calif.

**LA GUARDIA, Fiorello Henry,** a Representative from New York; born in New York City, December 11, 1882; moved to Arizona; attended the public schools and high school at Prescott, Ariz.; returned to New York; was graduated from the New York University Law School in 1910; was admitted to the bar the same year and commenced practice in New York City; served in the American Consular Service in Budapest, Hungary, and in Trieste, Austria, 1901-1904; American consular agent at Fiume, Hungary, 1904-1906; interpreter in the Immigration Service at Ellis Island, 1907-1910; deputy attorney general of the State of New York, 1915-1917; elected as a Republican to the Sixty-fifth and Sixty-sixth Congresses and served from March 4, 1917, until December 31, 1919, when he resigned; during the First World War absented himself from the House and on August 15, 1917, was commissioned a first lieutenant in the Army Air Service; promoted to the rank of captain and later to that of major; commanded the United States air forces on the Italian-Austrian front and was awarded the Italian War Cross; resigned his commission November 21, 1918; president of the board of aldermen of New York City in 1920 and 1921; elected as a Republican to the Sixty-eighth Congress, as an American Labor candidate to the Sixty-ninth Congress, and as a Republican to the Seventieth and to the two succeeding Congresses (March 4, 1923-March 3, 1933); unsuccessful candidate for reelection in 1932 to the Seventy-third Congress; co-sponsor of the Norris-LaGuardia Act of 1932, limiting judicial power to issue injunctions forbidding strikes and other labor union activities; elected mayor of New York City in 1933, reelected in 1937 and 1941, and served from January 1, 1934 to December 31, 1945; announced in May 1945 that he would not seek another term as mayor; president of the United States Conference of Mayors, 1936-1945; United States Director of Office of Civilian Defense from May 1941 to February 1942; chairman of the United States section of the Permanent Joint Board on Defense (United States and Canada), 1940-1946; special United States Ambassador to Brazil in 1946; director general of the United Nations Relief and Rehabilitation Administration in 1946; died in New York City, September 20, 1947; interment in Woodlawn Cemetery in the Bronx.

**Bibliography:** Kessner, Thomas. *Fiorello H. La Guardia and the Making of Modern New York.* New York: McGraw-Hill, 1989;

Zinn, Howard. *La Guardia in Congress*. 1959. Reprint. Westport, Conn.: Greenwood Press, 1972.

**LAHM, Samuel,** a Representative from Ohio; born in Leitersburg, Washington County, Md., April 22, 1812; completed preparatory studies; taught school; attended Washington College, Pennsylvania; studied law; was admitted to the bar in 1836 and commenced practice in Canton, Ohio; master of chancery 1837-1841; prosecuting attorney of Stark County 1841-1845; member of the State senate in 1842; delegate to the Democratic National Convention in 1844; brigadier general of militia; unsuccessful candidate for election in 1844 to the Twenty-ninth Congress; elected as a Democrat to the Thirtieth Congress (March 4, 1847-March 3, 1849); engaged in agricultural pursuits and sheep raising; died in Canton, Ohio, June 16, 1876; interment in West Lawn Cemetery.

**LaHOOD, Ray H.,** a Representative from Illinois; born in Peoria, Ill., December 6, 1945; graduated, Spalding High School; attended Spoon River Community College, Canton, Ill.; B.S., Bradley University, Peoria, Ill., 1971; school teacher, 1965-1971; director, Rock Island County Youth Services Bureau, 1972-1974; chief planner, Bi-State Metropolitan Planning Commission, 1974-1977; administrative assistant to Representative Thomas F. Railsback, 1977-1982; member, Illinois State house of representatives, 1982-1983; district assistant to Representative Robert H. Michel, 1983-1990, chief of staff, 1990-1994; elected as a Republican to the One Hundred Fourth Congress (January 3, 1995-January 3, 1997); is a resident of Peoria, Ill.

**LAIDLAW, William Grant,** a Representative from New York; born near Jedburgh, Roxburghshire, Scotland, January 1, 1840; immigrated to the United States in 1852 with his parents, who settled in Franklinville, Cattaraugus County, N.Y.; attended the common schools and Ten Broek Free Academy at Franklinville; studied law; was admitted to the bar in 1866 and practiced; served two years in the United States Navy during the Civil War; school commissioner of the first district of Cattaraugus County 1867-1870; moved to Ellicottville, N.Y., in 1870; assessor of internal revenue of the thirty-first collection district of New York 1871-1877; district attorney of Cattaraugus County 1877-1883; elected as a Republican to the Fiftieth and Fifty-first Congresses (March 4, 1887-March 3, 1891); chairman, Committee on Claims (Fifty-first Congress); resumed the practice of his profession in Ellicottville, Cattaraugus County, N.Y., and died there on August 19, 1908; interment in Sunset Hill Cemetery.

**LAIRD, James,** a Representative from Nebraska; born in Fowlerville, Livingston County, N.Y., June 20, 1849; in early childhood moved with his parents to Michigan, who settled in Hillsdale County; attended Adrian (Mich.) College; during the Civil War served with the Sixteenth Regiment, Michigan Volunteer Infantry, in the Army of the Potomac from 1862 until 1865, when he was honorably discharged; was graduated from the law department of the University of Michigan at Ann Arbor in 1871; was admitted to the bar and engaged in practice in Hastings, Nebr., in 1872; member of the Nebraska constitutional convention in 1875; elected as a Republican to the Forty-eighth and to the three succeeding Congresses and served from March 4, 1883 until his death in Hastings, Adams County, Nebr., August 17, 1889; interment in Parkview Cemetery.

**LAIRD, Melvin Robert,** a Representative from Wisconsin; born in Omaha, Douglas County, Nebr., September 1, 1922; attended the public schools; B.A., Carleton College, Northfield, Minn., 1942; secretary-treasurer of a lumber company; enlisted in the United States Navy in May 1942 and served in the Pacific; awarded the Purple Heart; member of the Wisconsin State senate from 1946 until 1952; delegate to the Republican National Conventions of 1948, 1952, 1956, and 1960; elected as a Republican to the Eighty-third and to the eight succeeding Congresses and served from January 3, 1953, until his resignation on January 21, 1969, to become Secretary of Defense in the Cabinet of President Richard M. Nixon, and served in that capacity until January 29, 1973; domestic adviser to President Nixon, 1973-1974; senior counsellor for national and international affairs, Reader's Digest Association, 1974 to present; is a resident of Marshfield, Wis.

**LAIRD, William Ramsey, III,** a Senator from West Virginia; born in Keswick, Shasta County, Calif., June 2, 1916; educated in the public schools; graduated from Greenbrier Military School, Kings College, Bristol, Tenn., and from West Virginia University in 1944; during the Second World War served in the United States Navy; was admitted to the bar in 1944 and commenced the practice of law in West Virginia; member of the West Virginia Board of Education in 1955; member of the board of directors of Merchants National Bank, Montgomery, W.Va., and the Upper Kanawha Valley Development Association; member of board of trustees of Laird Foundation, Montgomery, W.Va.; West Virginia State tax commissioner from 1955 until 1956, when he resigned, having been appointed to the Senate; appointed as a Democrat to the United States Senate to fill the vacancy caused by the death of Harley M. Kilgore, and served from March 13, 1956 to November 6, 1956; was not a candidate for election in 1956 to fill the vacancy; resumed the practice of law in Fayetteville and Montgomery, W.Va.; died in Montgomery, W.Va., January 7, 1974; interment in Huse Memorial Park, Fayetteville, W.Va.

**LAKE, William Augustus,** a Representative from Mississippi; born near Cambridge, Dorchester County, Md., January 6, 1808; pursued classical studies and was graduated from Jefferson College, Pennsylvania, in 1827; member of the Maryland house of delegates in 1831; moved to Vicksburg, Miss.; studied law; was admitted to the bar in 1834 and commenced practice in Vicksburg, Miss.; member of the State senate in 1848; elected as an American Party candidate to the Thirty-fourth Congress (March 4, 1855-March 3, 1857); unsuccessful candidate for reelection in 1856 to the Thirty-fifth Congress; served in the State house of representatives 1859-1861; resumed the practice of law; was a candidate for the Confederate Congress in 1861 and, during the canvass was killed in a duel by his opponent, Colonel Chambers, of Mississippi, October 15, 1861, at Hopefield, Ark., opposite Memphis, Tenn.; interment in the City Cemetery, Vicksburg, Miss.

**LAMAR, Henry Graybill,** a Representative from Georgia; born in Clinton, Jones County, Ga., July 10, 1798; pursued an academic course; studied law; was admitted to the bar and commenced practice in Macon, Ga.; judge of the State superior court; member of the State house of representatives; elected as a Jacksonian to the Twenty-first Congress to fill the vacancy caused by the resignation of George R. Gilmer; reelected to the Twenty-second Congress and served from December 7, 1829, to March 3, 1833; unsuccessful candidate for reelection in 1832 to the Twenty-third Congress; unsuccessful candidate for Governor in 1857; associate justice of the State supreme court; died in Macon, Ga., September 10, 1861; interment in Rose Hill Cemetery.

**LAMAR, James Robert,** a Representative from Missouri; born at Edgar Springs, Phelps County, Mo., March 28, 1866; attended the common schools and Licking (Mo.) Academy; taught school in Phelps and Texas Counties; was principal of Licking Academy in 1889; studied law; was admitted to the bar in Texas County in 1889 and practiced; prosecuting attorney of Texas County, 1890-1894; chairman of the Democratic congressional committee of the Thirteenth District of Missouri, 1894-1896; engaged in the practice of law in Houston, Texas County, Mo.; elected as a Democrat to the Fifty-eighth Congress (March 4, 1903-March 3, 1905); unsuccessful candidate for reelection in 1904 to the Fifty-ninth Congress; elected to the Sixtieth Congress (March 4, 1907-March 3, 1909); unsuccessful candidate for reelection in 1908 to the Sixty-first Congress; resumed the practice of law in Houston, Mo.; president of the Missouri Bar Association in 1920; died in St. Louis, Mo., August 11, 1923; interment in Houston Cemetery, Houston, Mo.

**LAMAR, John Basil,** a Representative from Georgia; born in Milledgeville, Baldwin County, Ga., on November 5, 1812; attended Dr. Beman's school at Mount Zion, Ga., and Franklin College (now University of Georgia) at Athens in 1827; moved to a plantation near Macon, Bibb County, Ga., in 1830 and engaged in agricultural pursuits; member of the Georgia State house of representatives in 1837 and 1838; elected as a Democrat to the Twenty-eighth Congress and served from March 4 until July 29, 1843, when he resigned; resumed the management of his plantations; trustee of the University of Georgia, 1855-1858; delegate to the Georgia convention which adopted the secession ordinance in 1861; during the Civil War served in the Confederate Army as an aide on the staff of General Howell Cobb; wounded in the battle at Cramptons Gap, Md., and died the following day, September 15, 1862; interment in Rose Hill Cemetery, Macon, Ga.

**LAMAR, Lucius Quintus Cincinnatus** (uncle of William Bailey Lamar and cousin of Absalom Harris Chappell), a Representative and a Senator from Mississippi; born near Eatonton, Putnam County, Ga., September 17, 1825; attended schools in Baldwin and Newton Counties; graduated from Emory College, Oxford, Ga., in 1845; studied law in Macon; admitted to the bar in 1847; moved to Oxford, Miss., in 1849, where he practiced law and served one year as professor of mathematics in the University of Mississippi at Oxford; moved to Covington, Ga., in 1852 and practiced law; member, Georgia State house of representatives, 1853; returned to Mississippi in 1855; elected as a Democrat to the Thirty-fifth and Thirty-sixth Congresses, and served from March 4, 1857 until December 1860, when he withdrew; member of the secession convention of Mississippi, and drafted the Mississippi ordinance of secession; during the Civil War served in the Confederate Army as lieutenant colonel until 1862; entered the diplomatic service of the Confederacy in 1862 and was sent on a special mission to Russia, France, and Great Britain; member of the Mississippi State constitutional conventions in 1865, 1868, 1875, 1877, and 1881; professor of metaphysics, social science, and law at the University of Mississippi; elected to the Forty-third and Forty-fourth Congresses (March 4, 1873-March 3, 1877); did not seek renomination in 1876 to the House of Representatives, having been elected Senator; chairman, Committee on Pacific Railroads (Forty-fourth Congress); elected as a Democrat to the United States Senate in 1876; reelected in 1883, and served from March 4, 1877 until March 6, 1885, when he resigned to accept a Cabinet portfolio; chairman, Committee on Interior and Insular Affairs (Forty-sixth Congress), Committee on Railroads (Forty-sixth Congress); Secretary of the Interior in the Cabinet of President Grover Cleveland, March 5, 1885 to January 16, 1888; nominated on December 6, 1887 by President Cleveland as an Associate Justice of the United States Supreme Court; was confirmed by the Senate on January 16, 1888, and served until his death in Vineville, Ga., January 23, 1893; interment in Riverside Cemetery, Macon, Ga.; reinterment in St. Peter's Cemetery, Oxford, Miss., in 1894.

Bibliography: *DAB*; Mayes, Edward. *Lucius Q.C. Lamar: His Life, Times, and Speeches, 1825-1893.* 1896. Reprint. New York: AMS Press, 1974; Murphy, James B. *L.Q.C. Lamar: Pragmatic Patriot.* Baton Rouge: Louisiana State University Press, 1973.

**LAMAR, William Bailey** (nephew of Lucius Quintus Cincinnatus Lamar), a Representative from Florida; born near Monticello, Jefferson County, Fla., June 12, 1853; attended Jefferson Academy at Monticello and the University of Georgia, Athens, Ga., where he resided from 1866 until 1873; returned to Florida in the latter year; was graduated from the Lebanon Law School, Lebanon, Tenn., in 1875; was admitted to the bar; commenced practice in Tupelo, Miss.; clerk of the circuit court of Jefferson County, Fla., January 1877 to January 1881; judge of the county court of Jefferson County 1883-1886; member of the State house of representatives in 1887 and was chosen speaker, but declined; attorney general of Florida 1889-1903; elected as a Democrat to the Fifty-eighth, Fifty-ninth, and Sixtieth Congresses (March 4, 1903-March 3, 1909); did not seek renomination; unsuccessful candidate for the nomination for United States Senator in 1908; national commissioner to the Panama-Pacific International Exposition at San Francisco in 1915; moved to Washington, D.C., in 1916; died at his winter home in Thomasville, Thomas County, Ga., September 26, 1928; interment in Oconee Hill Cemetery, Athens, Ga.

**LAMB, Alfred William,** a Representative from Missouri; born in Stamford, Delaware County, N.Y., March 18, 1824; moved with his parents to Ralls County, Mo., in 1836; attended Doctor Ely's school in Ely, Mo.; studied law; was admitted to the bar and commenced practice in Hannibal, Mo.; elected as a Democrat to the Thirty-third Congress (March 4, 1853-March 3, 1855); declined to be a candidate for renomination in 1854; resumed the practice of law; died in Hannibal, Marion County, Mo., April 29, 1888; interment in Riverside Cemetery.

**LAMB, John,** a Representative from Virginia; born in Sussex County, Va., June 12, 1840; attended a private school; during the Civil War enlisted in the Confederate Army in Company D, Third Virginia Cavalry; commanded his company three years; engaged in mercantile pursuits; served as sheriff, treasurer, and surveyor of Charles City County; elected as a Democrat to the Fifty-fifth and to the seven succeeding Congresses (March 4, 1897-March 3, 1913); chairman, Committee on Agriculture (Sixty-second Congress); unsuccessful candidate for reelection in 1912 to the Sixty-third Congress; superintendent of Battle Abbey, a Confederate memorial institute in Richmond, Va., where he died on November 21, 1924; interment in Hollywood Cemetery.

**LAMB, John Edward,** a Representative from Indiana; born in Terre Haute, Ind., December 26, 1852; attended the common schools and was graduated from the Terre Haute High School; studied law; was admitted to the bar in 1873 and commenced practice in Terre Haute; prosecuting attorney of the fourteenth judicial circuit 1875-1880; elected as a Democrat to the Forty-eighth Congress (March 4, 1883-March 3, 1885); resumed the practice of law in Terre Haute; appointed United States district attorney for Indiana July 10, 1885, and served until August 16, 1886; delegate to the Democratic National Conventions in 1892, 1896, 1904, 1908, and 1912; died in Terre Haute, Ind., August 23, 1914; interment in Calvary Cemetery.

**LAMBERT, Blanche M.,** a Representative from Arkansas. (*See* LINCOLN, Blanche Lambert.)

**LAMBERT, John,** a Representative and a Senator from New Jersey; born in Lambertville, N.J., February 24, 1746; pursued an academic course; engaged in agricultural pursuits; member, New Jersey State general assembly, 1780-1785, and in 1788; member, State council, 1790-1804, and served as vice president from 1801 to 1804; served as Acting Governor of New Jersey from November 15, 1802 to October 29, 1803; elected as a Republican to the Ninth and Tenth Congresses (March 4, 1805-March 3, 1809); elected to the United States Senate, and served from March 4, 1809 to March 3, 1815; owned and managed a plantation; died near Lambertville, N.J., February 4, 1823; interment in Barber's Burying Ground, Delaware Township, Hunterdon County, N.J.

**LAMBERTSON, William Purnell,** a Representative from Kansas; born in Fairview, Brown County, Kans., March 23, 1880; attended the public schools, Ottawa (Kans.) University, and the law school of the University of Chicago, Chicago, Ill.; engaged in agricultural pursuits; member of the State house of representatives 1909-1911 and 1919-1921, serving as speaker pro tempore in 1911 and as speaker in 1919; served in the State senate 1913-1915; chairman of Kansas State Efficiency and Economy Commission in 1917; member of Kansas State Board of Administration 1923-1925; unsuccessful candidate for nomination for Governor in 1922 and for Congress in 1924 and 1926; elected as a Republican to the Seventy-first and to the seven succeeding Congresses (March 4, 1929-January 3, 1945); unsuccessful candidate for renomination in 1944; returned to his farm near Fairview, Kans.; was defeated for the Republican nomination to Congress in 1946; mayor of Fairview from April 1949 until he resigned in December 1952; chairman, Board of County Commissioners of Brown County, Kans., 1953-1956; died in Fairview, Kans., October 26, 1957; interment in Sabetha Cemetery, Sabetha, Kans.

**LAMBETH, John Walter,** a Representative from North Carolina; born in Thomasville, Davidson County, N.C., January 10, 1896; attended the public schools; was graduated from Trinity College (now Duke University), Durham, N.C., in 1916, and later attended Harvard University; during the First World War entered the Army on January 15, 1918, serving overseas as a sergeant and was discharged July 26, 1919; engaged in the manufacture of furniture 1919-1930; also interested in banking; member of the State senate in 1921; mayor of Thomasville, N.C., 1925-1929; elected as a Democrat to the Seventy-second and to the three succeeding Congresses (March 4, 1931-January 3, 1939); was not a candidate for renomination in 1938; died in Washington, D.C., January 12, 1961; interment in City Cemetery, Thomasville, N.C.

**LAMISON, Charles Nelson,** a Representative from Ohio; born in Columbia County, Pa., in 1826; moved with his father to Dalton, Wayne County, Ohio, in 1836; privately instructed in elementary branches; studied law; was admitted to the bar in 1848 and commenced practice in Dalton, Wayne County, Ohio; moved to Lima, Ohio, in 1852 and resumed the practice of law; elected prosecuting attorney of Allen County in 1853; defeated in 1855; again elected in 1857; during the Civil War enlisted in the Union Army and was elected captain of Company F, Twentieth Regiment, Ohio Volunteer Infantry, and served in Virginia; assisted in raising the Eighty-first Regiment, Ohio Volunteer Infantry, of which he was commissioned major; resumed the practice of law in Lima, Ohio; unsuccessful candidate for election in 1866 to the Fortieth Congress; elected as a Democrat to the Forty-second and Forty-third Congresses (March 4, 1871-March 3, 1875); was not a candidate for renomination in 1874; appointed attorney for several railroad companies; was appointed United States land commissioner in 1892, with headquarters at Dodge City, Kans.; died in Topeka, Kans., on April 24, 1896; interment in Woodlawn Cemetery, Lima, Ohio.

**LAMNECK, Arthur Philip,** a Representative from Ohio; born in Port Washington, Tuscarawas County, Ohio, March 12, 1880; attended the public schools and was graduated from the Port Washington High School in 1897; engaged in sheet metal business at Columbus, Ohio, 1907 to 1929; delegate to the Democratic National Convention in 1924; member of the Columbus (Ohio) City Council 1913-1921; elected as a Democrat to the Seventy-second and to the three succeeding Congresses (March 4, 1931-January 3, 1939); unsuccessful candidate for reelection in 1938 to the Seventy-sixth Congress and for election in 1940 to the Seventy-seventh Congress; unsuccessful candidate for nomination for mayor of Columbus, Ohio, in 1943; engaged in the wholesale coal business from 1939 until his death at Columbus, Ohio, April 23, 1944; interment in Port Washington Cemetery, Port Washington, Ohio.

**LAMPERT, Florian,** a Representative from Wisconsin; born in West Bend, Washington County, Wis., July 8, 1863; attended the public schools; moved with his widowed mother to Oshkosh, Winnebago County, in 1875; engaged in the retail shoe business; city comptroller of Oshkosh from April 1893 to December 1896, when he resigned to take the position of sheriff of Winnebago County; sheriff in 1897 and 1898; resumed mercantile pursuits; commissioner of Oshkosh from May 1914 to November 1918, when he resigned, having been elected to Congress; elected as a Republican to the Sixty-fifth Congress to fill the vacancy caused by the death of James H. Davidson, and on the same day was elected to the Sixty-sixth Congress; reelected to the Sixty-seventh and to the four succeeding Congresses and served from November 5, 1918, until his death in Chicago Heights, Ill., July 18, 1930; chairman, Committee on Election of President, Vice President, and Representatives (Sixty-sixth Congress), Committee on Patents (Sixty-seventh and Sixty-eighth Congresses); interment in Riverside Cemetery, Oshkosh, Wis.

**LAMPORT, William Henry,** a Representative from New York; born in Brunswick, N.Y., May 27, 1811; moved with his parents to Gorham, Ontario County, in 1826; attended the public schools; engaged in agricultural pursuits; supervisor of Gorham in 1848 and 1849; sheriff of Ontario County 1850-1853; member of the State assembly in 1854; moved to Canandaigua in 1864; president of the village of Canandaigua in 1866 and 1867; elected as a Republican to the Forty-second and Forty-third Congresses (March 4, 1871-March 3, 1875); was not a candidate for renomination in 1874; retired to Canandaigua, N.Y., where he died July 21, 1891; interment in the West Avenue Cemetery.

**LANCASTER, Columbia,** a Delegate from the Territory of Washington; born in New Milford, Litchfield County, Conn., August 26, 1803; moved with his family to Canfield, Ohio, in 1817; attended the common schools; moved to Detroit, Mich., in 1824; studied law; was admitted to the bar in 1830 and commenced practice in Centerville, Mich.; appointed prosecuting attorney of Michigan Territory by Governor Cass; member of the Territorial legislature in 1837; settled in the Willamette Valley, Oreg., in 1847; associate justice of the supreme court under the provisional government; took up his residence near the mouth of the Lewis River, Oreg. (now Washington); unsuccessful candidate for Delegate to the Thirty-first Congress from Oregon before the separation of the Territories of Washington and Oregon; member of the Territorial council of Oregon, 1850-1852; when the Territory of Washington was admitted to representation was elected as a Democrat to the Thirty-third Congress and served from April 12, 1854, until March 3, 1855; unsuccessful candidate for renomination in 1854 to the Thirty-fourth Congress; regent of the University of Washington at Seattle in 1862; connected with the Puget Sound & Columbia River Railroad project in 1862; died in Vancouver, Wash., September 15, 1893; interment in the City Cemetery.

**LANCASTER, Harold Martin,** a Representative from North Carolina; born in Patetown Community, Wayne County, N.C., March 24, 1943; attended public schools and graduated from Pikeville (N.C.) High School in 1961; A.B., University of North Carolina, Chapel Hill, 1965; J.D., University of North Carolina Law School, 1967; served in the United States Navy, 1967-1970; commenced the practice of law in Goldsboro in 1970; member, North Carolina State house of representatives, 1978-1986; elected as a Democrat to the One Hundredth and to the three succeeding Congresses (January 3, 1987-January 3, 1995); unsuccessful candidate for reelection in 1994 to the One Hundred Fourth Congress; special adviser to the President and United States Arms Control and Disarmament Agency Director on the Chemical Weapons Convention, 1995; special assistant on federal issues for Governor James B. Hunt, Jr., of North Carolina; nominated as Assistant Secretary of the Army for Civil

Works, November 28, 1995, and confirmed by the Senate on January 26, 1996; is a resident of Falls Church, Va.

**LANDERS, Franklin,** a Representative from Indiana; born near the village of Landersdale, Morgan County, Ind., March 22, 1825; attended local schools; at the age of twenty-one engaged in teaching school; was associated with his brother in mercantile pursuits at Waverly, Ind.; laid out the town of Brooklyn, Ind., where he engaged in mercantile pursuits and stock raising; member of the State senate 1860-1864; moved to Indianapolis in 1865 and engaged in the dry-goods business; in 1873 became the head of a pork-packing house; elected as a Democrat to the Forty-fourth Congress (March 4, 1875-March 3, 1877); unsuccessful candidate for reelection in 1876 and for election as Governor of Indiana in 1880; engaged in the management of his farming lands; died in Indianapolis, Ind., September 10, 1901; interment in Crown Hill Cemetery.

**LANDERS, George Marcellus,** a Representative from Connecticut; born in Lenox, Mass., February 22, 1813; attended the public schools; moved to New Britain, Conn., in 1830 and engaged in the manufacture of hardware; member of the State house of representatives in 1851, 1867, and 1874; served in the State senate in 1853, 1869, and 1873; State bank commissioner in 1874; elected as a Democrat to the Forty-fourth and Forty-fifth Congresses (March 4, 1875-March 3, 1879); died in New Britain, Conn., March 27, 1895; interment in Fairview Cemetery.

**LANDES, Silas Zephaniah,** a Representative from Illinois; born in Augusta County, Va., May 15, 1842; attended the public schools; studied law; was admitted to the bar by the supreme court of Illinois in August 1863 and commenced practice in Mount Carmel, Ill.; prosecuting attorney of Wabash County 1872-1884; elected as a Democrat to the Forty-ninth and Fiftieth Congresses (March 4, 1885-March 3, 1889); declined to be a candidate for renomination in 1888; resumed the practice of law in Mount Carmel; elected circuit judge of the fourth judicial circuit of Illinois June 1, 1891, and served six years; resumed the practice of law; died in Mount Carmel, Ill., May 23, 1910; interment in Rose Hill Cemetery.

**LANDGREBE, Earl Fredrick,** a Representative from Indiana; born in Valparaiso, Porter County, Ind., January 21, 1916; attended Union Township Elementary and Wheeler High School; elected to the Indiana State senate, 1959-1968; owner and operator, Landgrebe Motor Transport, Inc.; elected as a Republican to the Ninety-first and to the two succeeding Congresses (January 3, 1969-January 3, 1975); unsuccessful candidate for reelection in 1974 to the Ninety-fourth Congress; was a resident of Valparaiso, Ind., until his death there on June 29, 1986; interment in Blachly Cemetery, Crown Point, Ind.

**LANDIS, Charles Beary** (brother of Frederick Landis), a Representative from Indiana; born in Millville, Butler County, Ohio, July 9, 1858; attended the public schools of Logansport, Ind., and was graduated from Wabash College, Crawfordsville, Ind., in 1883; editor of the Logansport Journal 1883-1887 and at the time of his nomination for Congress was editor of the Delphi (Ind.) Journal; president of the Indiana Republican Editorial Association in 1894 and 1895; elected as a Republican to the Fifty-fifth and to the five succeeding Congresses (March 4, 1897-March 3, 1909); unsuccessful candidate for reelection; resumed newspaper work in Delphi, Ind.; died in Asheville, N.C., where he had gone because of impaired health, April 24, 1922; interment in Mount Hope Cemetery, Logansport, Ind.

**LANDIS, Frederick** (brother of Charles Beary Landis), a Representative from Indiana; born at Sevenmile, Butler County, Ohio, August 18, 1872; moved with his parents to Logansport, Ind., in 1875; attended the public schools; was graduated from the law department of the University of Michigan at Ann Arbor in 1895; was

admitted to the bar the same year and commenced practice at Logansport, Ind.; elected as a Republican to the Fifty-eighth and Fifty-ninth Congresses (March 4, 1903-March 3, 1907); unsuccessful candidate for reelection in 1906 to the Sixtieth Congress; returned to Logansport and engaged in writing and lecturing; one of the organizers of the Progressive Party in 1912 and temporary chairman of its first State convention in Indiana; delegate to the National Progressive Convention at Chicago in 1912; unsuccessful candidate for Governor on the Progressive ticket in 1912; unsuccessful candidate for the nomination for Governor on the Republican ticket in 1928; author and lecturer; elected to the Seventy-fourth Congress on November 6, 1934, but died in a hospital in Logansport, Ind., November 15, 1934, before Congress had convened; interment in Mount Hope Cemetery.

**LANDIS, Gerald Wayne,** a Representative from Indiana; born in Bloomfield, Greene County, Ind., February 23, 1895; attended the public schools of Linton, Ind.; served as a lieutenant in the Infantry of the United States Army in 1918 and 1919; was graduated from Indiana University at Bloomington in 1923 and received master's degree in 1938; taught in the high schools at Linton, Ind., 1923-1938; elected as a Republican to the Seventy-sixth and to the four succeeding Congresses (January 3, 1939-January 3, 1949); unsuccessful candidate for reelection in 1948 to the Eighty-first Congress; delegate to the Republican National Convention in 1944 and Indiana State convention in 1964; assistant to the Administrator, Commodity Stabilization Service, Department of Agriculture, from April 1954 to January 1961; died in Linton, Ind., September 6, 1971; interment in Fairview Cemetery.

**LANDRUM, John Morgan,** a Representative from Louisiana; born in Edgefield District, S.C., July 3, 1815; pursued classical studies and was graduated from South Carolina College (now the University of South Carolina) at Columbia in 1842; taught school for several years; studied law; was admitted to the bar in 1844 and commenced the practice of law in Shreveport, La.; mayor of Shreveport in 1848 and 1849; elected as a Democrat to the Thirty-sixth Congress (March 4, 1859-March 3, 1861); was not a candidate for renomination in 1860 to the Thirty-seventh Congress; continued the practice of his profession until his death in Shreveport, Caddo Parish, La., October 18, 1861; interment in Oakland Cemetery.

**LANDRUM, Phillip Mitchell,** a Representative from Georgia; born in Martin, Stephens County, Ga., September 10, 1907; attended the public schools and Mercer University, Macon, Ga.; A.B., Piedmont College, Demorest, Ga., 1939; LL.B., Atlanta Law School, 1941; superintendent of Nelson (Ga.) High School, 1937-1941; was admitted to the bar in 1941 and commenced the practice of law in Canton, Ga.; was an unsuccessful candidate for nomination in 1942 to the Seventy-eighth Congress; during the Second World War enlisted as a private in the United States Army Air Corps on October 2, 1942; served in Europe and was discharged on June 1, 1945, as a first lieutenant; employed by Veterans' Administration after discharge; assistant attorney general of State of Georgia in 1946 and 1947; executive secretary to the Governor of Georgia in 1947 and 1948; practiced law in Jasper, Ga., until his election to Congress; elected as a Democrat to the Eighty-third and to the eleven succeeding Congresses (January 3, 1953-January 3, 1977); co-sponsor of the Landrum-Griffin Act of 1959 (Labor-Management Relations Act), containing union democracy, financial reporting and anti-corruption provisions, and Taft-Hartley Act amendments closing secondary boycott "loopholes," curbing organizational and recognition picketing and giving states jurisdiction over "no man's land" labor disputes; was not a candidate for reelection in 1976 to the Ninety-fifth Congress; was a resident of Jasper, Ga.; died November 19, 1990.

**LANDRY, Joseph Aristide,** a Representative from Louisiana; born near Donaldsonville, Ascension Parish, La., July 10, 1817; attended school in Cape Girardeau, Mo.; member of the State house of representatives in 1840; elected as a Whig to the Thirty-second Congress (March 4, 1851-March 3, 1853); president of police jury of Ascension Parish in 1861; before the Civil War was first sergeant in the Chasseurs de l'Ascension, and later attached to Company B of the Cannoneers of Donaldsonville; died near Donaldsonville, La., March 9, 1881; interment in Donaldsonville Catholic Cemetery.

**LANDY, James,** a Representative from Pennsylvania; born in Northern Liberties District, Philadelphia, Pa., October 13, 1813; attended the public schools; studied law, but abandoned the same and engaged in mercantile pursuits; member of the board of school commissioners in 1845; elected as a Democrat to the Thirty-fifth Congress (March 4, 1857-March 3, 1859); unsuccessful candidate for reelection; elected chief commissioner of highways in 1862; died in Philadelphia, Pa., July 25, 1875; interment in Monument Cemetery.

**LANE, Amos** (father of James Henry Lane), a Representative from Indiana; born near Aurora, N.Y., March 1, 1778; attended the public schools; studied law; was admitted to the bar and commenced practice at Lawrenceburg, Ind., in 1808; moved to Burlington, Boone County, Ky., and practiced law; returned to Lawrenceburg, Ind., in 1814 and continued the practice of his profession; elected a member of the first State house of representatives in 1816; reelected in 1817; elected as a Jacksonian to the Twenty-third and Twenty-fourth Congresses (March 4, 1833-March 3, 1837); unsuccessful candidate for reelection in 1836 to the Twenty-fifth Congress; resumed the practice of law; again a member of the State house of representatives in 1839 and served as speaker; died in Lawrenceburg, Ind., September 2, 1849; interment in the Lawrenceburg Cemetery; reinterment in Greendale Cemetery.

**LANE, Edward,** a Representative from Illinois; born in Cleveland, Ohio, March 27, 1842; moved to Illinois in May 1858 with his parents, who settled in Hillsboro, Montgomery County; attended the common schools and was graduated from Hillsboro Academy; taught school for several years; studied law; was admitted to the bar in February 1865 and commenced practice in Hillsboro, Ill.; city attorney of Hillsboro three years; elected judge of the Montgomery County Court in November 1869 and served until 1873; elected as a Democrat to the Fiftieth and to the three succeeding Congresses (March 4, 1887-March 3, 1895); chairman, Committee on Militia (Fifty-second Congress); unsuccessful candidate for reelection in 1894 to the Fifty-fourth Congress; resumed the practice of law in Hillsboro, Ill., where he died October 30, 1912; interment in Oak Grove Cemetery.

**LANE, Harry** (grandson of Joseph Lane and nephew of La Fayette Lane), a Senator from Oregon; born in Corvallis, Benton County, Oreg., August 28, 1855; attended the public schools and graduated from Willamette University, Salem, Oreg., in 1876; received a medical degree from the same university in 1878; engaged in postgraduate work in the College of Physicians and Surgeons of New York City; commenced the practice of medicine in San Francisco, Calif.; returned to Oregon and settled in Portland, where he practiced medicine; superintendent of the Oregon State Insane Asylum 1887-1891; mayor of Portland 1905-1909; elected as a Democrat to the United States Senate and served from March 4, 1913, until his death in San Francisco, Calif., May 23, 1917; chairman, committee on Forest Reservations and Game Protection (Sixty-third and Sixty-fourth Congresses), Committee on Fisheries (Sixty-fourth and Sixty-fifth Congresses); interment in Lone Fir Cemetery, Portland, Oreg.

**Bibliography:** Holbo, Paul S. "Senator Harry Lane: Independent Democrat in Peace and War." In *Experiences in a Promised Land.* Edited by Thomas Edwards and Carlos Schwantes. pp. 242-59. Seattle: University of Washington Press: 1986.

**LANE, Henry Smith,** a Representative and a Senator from Indiana; born near Sharpsburg, Bath County, Ky., February 24, 1811; received a classical education from private tutors; studied law; was admitted to the bar in Mount Sterling, Ky., in 1832 and commenced practice at Crawfordsville, Ind., in 1834; member of the Indiana State senate in 1837; member, Indiana State house of representatives, 1838-1839; elected as a Whig to the Twenty-sixth Congress to fill the vacancy caused by the resignation of Tilghman A. Howard; reelected to the Twenty-seventh Congress, and served from August 3, 1840 to March 3, 1843; served in the Mexican War at the head of a company he had raised; rose to lieutenant colonel of the First Indiana Regiment; abandoned the profession of law and engaged in the banking business at Crawfordsville, Ind., in 1854; elected Governor of Indiana in 1860; was inaugurated on January 14, 1861, and served just two days, when, by previous arrangement, he was elected to the Senate; elected as a Republican to the United States Senate, and served from March 4, 1861 to March 3, 1867; chairman, Committee on Engrossed Bills (Thirty-seventh through Thirty-ninth Congresses), Committee on Pensions (Thirty-ninth Congress); served as special Indian commissioner, 1869-1871; commissioner for improvement of the Mississippi River in 1872; died in Crawfordsville, Ind., June 18, 1881; interment in Oak Hill Cemetery.

**Bibliography:** *DAB*; Barringer, Graham. "The Life and Letters of Henry S. Lane." Ph.D. dissertation, University of Indiana, 1927; Sharp, Walter. "Henry S. Lane and the Formation of the Republican Party in Indiana." *Mississippi Valley Historical Review* 7 (September 1920): 93-112; Wernle, Robert F. *Henry Smith Lane: The Old War-Horse.* Crawfordsville, Ind.: Montgomery County Historical Society, 1938.

**LANE, James Henry** (son of Amos Lane), a Representative from Indiana and a Senator from Kansas; born in Lawrenceburg, Ind., June 22, 1814; attended the public schools; studied law; was admitted to the bar in 1840 and commenced practice in Lawrenceburg; member of the city council; served in the Mexican War; lieutenant governor of Indiana, 1849-1853; elected as a Democrat to the Thirty-third Congress (March 4, 1853-March 3, 1855); moved to the Territory of Kansas in 1855; member of the Topeka constitutional convention of 1855; elected to the United States Senate by the legislature that convened under the Topeka constitution in 1856, but the election was not recognized by the United States Senate; president of the Leavenworth constitutional convention in 1857; elected as a Republican to the United States Senate in 1861; reelected in 1865 and served from April 4, 1861, until his death; chairman, Committee on Agriculture (Thirty-eighth Congress); appointed by President Abraham Lincoln brigadier general of volunteers and saw battle during the Civil War; deranged and charged with financial irregularities, Lane shot himself on July 1, 1866, but lingered ten days, dying on July 11, near Fort Levenworth, Kans.; interment in the City Cemetery, Lawrence, Kans.

**Bibliography:** *DAB*; Bailes, Kendall. *Rider on the Wind: Jim Lane and Kansas.* Shawnee Mission, Kans.: Wagon Wheel Press, 1962; Stephenson, Wendell. *The Political Career of General James H. Lane.* Topeka: Kansas State Historical Society Publications, 1930.

**LANE, Joseph** (father of La Fayette Lane and grandfather of Harry Lane), a Delegate and a Senator from Oregon; born in Buncombe County, N.C., December 14, 1801; moved with his parents to Henderson, Ky., in 1810; attended the common schools; worked in a general store; moved to Vanderburg County, Ind., in 1821 and farmed; elected to the first of several terms in the Indiana State house of representatives in 1822; member, Indiana State senate, 1844-1846; during the Mexican War, led a brigade during operations in central Mexico; wounded in the shoulder during the Battle of Buena Vista, February 22-23, 1847; brevetted major general in 1847; appointed by President James K. Polk as Governor of the

Territory of Oregon on August 18, 1848, and arrived in Oregon City by boat on March 2, 1849; served as Governor until June 18, 1850, when he resigned; traveled to northern California and worked as a miner during 1850 and 1851; elected as a Delegate from the Oregon Territory to the Thirty-second and to the three succeeding Congresses, and served from June 21, 1851 until February 14, 1859, when the Territory became a State; upon the admission of Oregon as a State into the Union in 1859 was elected as a Democrat to the United States Senate, and served from February 14, 1859 to March 3, 1861; was not a candidate for reelection in 1860, having become a candidate for Vice President; chairman, Committee on Engrossed Bills (Thirty-sixth Congress), Committee on Revolutionary Claims (Thirty-sixth Congress); unsuccessful candidate for Vice President of the United States in 1860 on the Southern Democratic ticket headed by Vice President John C. Breckinridge; unsuccessful candidate for the Oregon State senate in 1880; died in Roseburg, Oreg., April 19, 1881; interment in the Masonic Cemetery.

**Bibliography:** *DAB*; Hendrickson, James E. *Joe Lane of Oregon: Machine Politics and the Sectional Crisis, 1849-1861*. New Haven: Yale University Press, 1967; Kelley, Margaret Jean. *The Career of Joseph Lane*. Washington: Catholic University of America Press, 1942.

**LANE, Joseph Reed,** a Representative from Iowa; born in Davenport, Scott County, Iowa, May 6, 1858; attended the public schools; was graduated from Knox College, Galesburg, Ill., in 1878 and from the law department of the State University of Iowa at Iowa City in 1880; was admitted to the bar in the latter year and commenced practice in Davenport, Iowa; served as regent of the State University of Iowa; member of the city council, 1884-1889; elected as a Republican to the Fifty-sixth Congress (March 4, 1899-March 3, 1901); was not a candidate for renomination in 1900 to the Fifty-seventh Congress; resumed the practice of law in Davenport, Iowa; delegate to the Republican National Convention of 1908; died in Davenport, Iowa, on May 1, 1931; interment in Oakdale Cemetery.

**LANE, La Fayette** (son of Joseph Lane and uncle of Harry Lane), a Representative from Oregon; born near Evansville, Vanderburg County, Ind., November 12, 1842; attended the public schools at Washington, D.C., and at Stamford, Conn.; studied law; was admitted to the bar and commenced practice in Roseburg, Oreg.; member of the State house of representatives in 1864; code commissioner in 1874; elected as a Democrat to the Forty-fourth Congress to fill the vacancy caused by the death of George A. La Dow and served from October 25, 1875, to March 3, 1877; unsuccessful candidate for reelection in 1876 to the Forty-fifth Congress; resumed practice of law; died in Roseburg, Oreg., November 23, 1896; interment in the Catholic Cemetery.

**LANE, Thomas Joseph,** a Representative from Massachusetts; born in Lawrence, Essex County, Mass., July 6, 1898; attended the public schools; during the First World War served as an enlisted man in the United States Army; was graduated from Suffolk Law School, Boston, Mass., in 1925; was admitted to the bar in 1926 and commenced practice in Lawrence, Mass.; member of the Massachusetts house of representatives 1927-1938; served in the Massachusetts senate from 1939 until his resignation in 1941; elected as a Democrat to the Seventy-seventh Congress to fill the vacancy caused by the death of Lawrence J. Connery; reelected to the Seventy-eighth and the nine succeeding Congresses and served from December 30, 1941, to January 3, 1963; unsuccessful candidate for reelection in 1962 to the Eighty-eighth Congress; resumed the practice of law; member, Governor's Council for the Commonwealth of Massachusetts, 1965-1970; was a resident of Lawrence, Mass.; died June 14, 1994.

**LANGDON, Chauncey,** a Representative from Vermont; born in Farmington, Conn., November 8, 1763; pursued classical studies and was graduated from Yale College in 1787; studied law at Litchfield, Conn.; was admitted to the bar in 1787 and commenced practice in Castleton, Vt.; settled in Winsdor, Vt., later returning to Castleton, Vt.; register of probate 1792-1797; judge of probate in 1798 and 1799; State councilor in 1808; member of the State house of representatives in 1813, 1814, 1817, 1819, 1820, and 1822; trustee of Middlebury (Vt.) College 1811-1830; elected as a Federalist to the Fourteenth Congress (March 4, 1815-March 3, 1817); was not a candidate for renomination to the Fifteenth Congress; again elected as State councilor and served from 1823 until his death in Castleton, Vt., July 23, 1830; interment in the Congregational Cemetery.

**LANGDON, John** (brother of Woodbury Langdon), a Delegate and a Senator from New Hampshire; born in Portsmouth, N.H., June 26, 1741; attended the local grammar school; served an apprenticeship as a clerk, went to sea, and engaged in mercantile pursuits; a prominent supporter of the revolutionary movement and active in the Revolutionary War; a representative in the general court; Member of the Continental Congress in 1775 and 1776; resigned in June 1776 to become agent for Continental prizes, and superintended the construction of several ships of war; served several terms as speaker of the New Hampshire State house of representatives, and during the session of 1777 staked his fortune to equip an expedition against the British; participated in the Battle of Bennington, N.Y., August 16, 1777, and commanded a company at Saratoga and in Rhode Island; member, New Hampshire State senate, 1784; President of New Hampshire in 1785 and 1788; again a Member of the Continental Congress in 1787; delegate to the Federal Constitutional Convention in 1787; member of the State ratifying convention; elected to the United States Senate and served from March 4, 1789, to March 3, 1801; elected the first President pro tempore of the Senate on April 6, 1789, in order that the Senate might organize to count the electoral vote for President and Vice President of the United States; as President pro tempore he administered the Presidential oath of office to George Washington on April 30, 1789; also served as President pro tempore of the Senate during the Second Congress; declined to accept the portfolio of Secretary of the Navy in the Cabinet of President Thomas Jefferson in 1801; member of the New Hampshire legislature from 1801 until 1805, the last two terms as speaker; unsuccessful candidate for Governor in 1802, 1803 and 1804; elected Governor of New Hampshire in 1805, reelected in 1806, 1807 and 1808, and served from June 6, 1805 to June 8, 1809; unsuccessful candidate for reelection in 1809; again elected Governor in 1810, reelected in 1811, and served from June 7, 1810 to June 5, 1812; declined the nomination as a candidate for Vice President of the United States in 1812; died in Portsmouth, N.H., September 18, 1819; interment in the Langdon tomb, North Cemetery.

**Bibliography:** *DAB*; Mayo, Lawrence. *John Langdon of New Hampshire*. 1932. Reprint. New York: Kennikat Press, l970.

**LANGDON, Woodbury** (brother of John Langdon), a Delegate from New Hampshire; born in Portsmouth, N.H., in 1739; attended the public schools; engaged in mercantile pursuits; prominent in pre-Revolutionary affairs and throughout the war; served in the State house of representatives in 1778 and 1779; Member of the Continental Congress in 1779; member of the State executive council 1781-1784; judge of the State superior court in 1782 and again from 1786 to January 1791, when he resigned; appointed in December 1790 by President George Washington a commissioner to settle Revolutionary War claims; died in Portsmouth, N.H., January 13, 1805; interment in the North Cemetery.

**Bibliography:** *DAB*.

**LANGEN, Odin Elsford Stanley,** a Representative from Minnesota; born in Minneapolis, Minn., January 5, 1913; attended the public schools; attended Dunwoody Institute, Minneapolis, Minn., in 1933 and 1934; engaged in farming in Kittson County, near Kennedy, Minn.; associated with Production Marketing Administration in Kittson County, Minn., 1935-1950; member of Kennedy (Minn.) School Board, serving as president, 1948-1950, South Red River Town Board 1947-1950, and the State house of representatives 1950-1958, serving as Republican leader in 1957 and 1958; elected as a Republican to the Eighty-sixth and to the five succeeding Congresses (January 3, 1959-January 3, 1971); unsuccessful candidate for reelection in 1970 to the Ninety-second Congress; Administrator of the Packers and Stockyards Administration of the United States Department of Agriculture from January 1971 to April 1972, when he resigned; resumed farming pursuits in Kennedy, Minn., where he died on July 6, 1976; interment in Red River Cemetery, Red River, Minn.

**LANGER, William,** a Senator from North Dakota; born on a farm in Everest Township, near Casselton, Cass County, N.Dak., September 30, 1886; attended the rural schools; graduated from the law department of the University of North Dakota at Grand Forks in 1906, and from Columbia University, New York City, in 1910; was admitted to the bar in 1911 and began practice in Mandan, N.Dak.; State's attorney of Morton County, N.Dak., 1914-1916; moved to Bismarck, N.Dak., in 1916 and continued the practice of law; attorney general of North Dakota, 1916-1920; legal adviser for Council of Defense during the First World War; unsuccessful candidate for Governor in 1920; elected Governor of North Dakota in 1932, and served from December 31, 1932 to July 17, 1934, when he was removed by the State supreme court; again elected Governor in 1936, and served from January 6, 1937 to January 5, 1939; unsuccessful candidate in 1938 for nomination to the United States Senate; elected as a Republican to the United States Senate in 1940; though there was an attempt to block his seating, Langer took his seat in the Senate in 1941; reelected in 1946, 1952, and again in 1958, and served from January 3, 1941 until his death in Washington, D.C., November 8, 1959; chairman, Committee on the Post Office and Civil Service (Eightieth Congress), Committee on the Judiciary (Eighty-third Congress); interment in St. Leo's Catholic Cemetery, Casselton, N.Dak.

Bibliography: *DAB*; Smith, Glenn H. *Langer of North Dakota: A Study in Isolationism, 1940-1959.* New York: Garland Publishing, 1979; Wilkins, Robert. "Senator William Langer and National Priorities: An Agrarian Radical's View of American Foreign Policy, 1945-1952." *North Dakota Quarterly* 42 (Autumn 1974): 42-59.

**LANGHAM, Jonathan Nicholas,** a Representative from Pennsylvania; born near Hillsdale, Indiana County, Pa., August 4, 1861; attended the common schools; taught school; was graduated from the State normal school at Indiana, Pa., in 1882; studied law; was admitted to the Indiana County bar in December 1888 and commenced practice in Indiana, Pa.; postmaster of Indiana, Pa., 1892-1893; assistant United States attorney for the western district of Pennsylvania 1898-1904; chief clerk and corporation deputy in the auditor general's department of Pennsylvania 1904-1909; elected as a Republican to the Sixty-first, Sixty-Second, and Sixty-third Congresses (March 4, 1909-March 3, 1915); was not a candidate for renomination in 1914; elected in 1915 judge of the court of common pleas for the fortieth judicial district of Pennsylvania for a term of ten years; reelected in 1925 and served until his retirement in January 1936; died in Indiana, Pa., May 21, 1945; interment in Oakland Cemetery.

**LANGLEY, John Wesley** (husband of Katherine Gudger Langley), a Representative from Kentucky; born in Floyd County, Ky., January 14, 1868; attended the common schools; taught school for three years; attended the law department of the National,

Georgetown, and Columbian (now George Washington) Universities in Washington, D.C., for an aggregate period of eight years; examiner in the Pension Office and a member of the Board of Pension Appeals; law clerk in the General Land Office; disbursing and appointment clerk of the Census Office 1899-1907; served in the Kentucky house of representatives 1886-1890; elected as a Republican to the Sixtieth and to the nine succeeding Congresses and served from March 4, 1907, until January 11, 1926, when he resigned; chairman, Committee on Public Buildings and Grounds (Sixty-sixth through Sixty-eighth Congresses); resumed the practice of law in Pikeville, Ky., where he died on January 17, 1932; interment in the Langley Cemetery at Middle Creek, Ky.

**LANGLEY, Katherine Gudger** (wife of John Wesley Langley and daughter of James Madison Gudger, Jr.), a Representative from Kentucky; born near Marshall in Madison County, N.C., February 14, 1888; attended the common schools; was graduated from the Woman's College, Richmond, Va.; attended Emerson College of Oratory, Boston, Mass.; taught expression at the Virginia Institute at Bristol, Tenn.; moved to Pikeville, Ky., in 1905; vice chairman of the Republican Central Committee of Kentucky 1920-1922; served as the first chairman of the Kentucky Woman's Republican Committee in 1920; alternate delegate to the Republican National Convention in 1920 and delegate in 1924; chairman of the Pike County Red Cross Society during the First World War; elected as a Republican to the Seventieth and Seventy-first Congresses (March 4, 1927-March 3, 1931); unsuccessful candidate for reelection in 1930 to the Seventy-second Congress; railroad commissioner, third Kentucky district, 1939-1942; died in Pikeville, Ky., on August 15, 1948; interment in Johnson Memorial Cemetery.

**LANGSTON, John Mercer,** a Representative from Virginia; born in Louisa, Va., December 14, 1829; attended the common schools in Ohio; was graduated from the literary department of Oberlin College in 1849 and from the theological department in 1852; studied law in Elyria, Ohio; was admitted to the bar in 1854 and commenced practice in Oberlin, Ohio; took an active part in recruiting black troops during the Civil War, especially for the Fifty-fourth and Fifty-fifth Massachusetts and Fifth Ohio Regiments; member of the council of Oberlin, 1865-1867; member of the city board of education in 1867 and 1868; appointed inspector general of the Bureau of Freedmen, Refugees, and Abandoned Lands in 1868; moved to Washington, D.C., and practiced law; dean of the law department of Howard University 1869-1876; appointed and commissioned by President Ulysses S. Grant as a member of the Board of Health of the District of Columbia in 1871; appointed by President Rutherford B. Hayes as Minister Resident and consul general to Haiti on September 28, 1877 and served until June 1885; appointed Chargé d'Affaires to Santo Domingo on November 12, 1883 and served until June 1885; elected vice president and acting president of Howard University in 1872; delegate to the Republican National Convention of 1876; returned to Virginia, having been elected president of the Virginia Normal and Collegiate Institute, Petersburg, Va., in 1885; delegate to the Virginia Republican convention in 1890; successfully contested as a Republican the election of Edward C. Venable to the Fifty-first Congress and served from September 23, 1890, to March 3, 1891; unsuccessful candidate for reelection in 1890 to the Fifty-second Congress; died in Washington, D.C., on November 15, 1897; interment in Woodlawn Cemetery.

Bibliography: *DAB*; Cheek, William F., and Aimee Lee Cheek. *John Mercer Langston and the Fight for Black Freedom, 1829-65.* Urbana: University of Illinois Press, 1989; Langston, John Mercer. *From Virginia Plantation to National Capitol.* 1894. Reprint. New York: Arno Press, 1969.

**LANGWORTHY, Edward,** a Delegate from Georgia; born in Savannah, Ga., in 1738; attended a school kept in connection with the Bethesda Orphan House, of which he was an inmate, and later became an instructor in the institution; assisted in organizing the Georgia Council of Safety and became secretary of the council December 11, 1775; Member of the Continental Congress 1777-1779; signer of the Articles of Confederation; moved to Baltimore, Md., in 1785; engaged in newspaper work until 1787; teacher of the classics in Baltimore Academy 1787-1791; moved to Elkton, Md., about 1791, where he was engaged in writing a history of Georgia; returned to Baltimore in 1795; clerk of customs from that time until his death in Baltimore, Md., November 2, 1802.

**Bibliography:** *DAB.*

**LANHAM, Fritz Garland** (son of Samuel Willis Tucker Lanham), a Representative from Texas; born in Weatherford, Tex., January 3, 1880; attended the public schools of Washington, D.C., and was graduated from Weatherford College, Weatherford, Tex., in 1897; attended Vanderbilt University in 1897 and 1898, and was graduated from the University of Texas at Austin in 1900, subsequently taking a law course in the same institution; was admitted to the bar in 1909 and commenced practice in Weatherford, Tex.; moved to Fort Worth, Tex., in 1917; elected as a Democrat to the Sixty-sixth Congress to fill the vacancy caused by the resignation of James C. Wilson; reelected to the Sixty-seventh and to the twelve succeeding Congresses and served from April 19, 1919, to January 3, 1947; chairman, Committee on Public Buildings and Grounds (Seventy-second through Seventy-ninth Congresses); was not a candidate for renomination in 1946; engaged as an adviser on legislation in Washington, D.C., until 1961; moved to Austin, Tex., where he died July 31, 1965; interment in City Greenwood Cemetery, Weatherford, Tex.

**LANHAM, Henderson Lovelace,** a Representative from Georgia; born in Rome, Floyd County, Ga., September 14, 1888; attended the public schools of Rome, Ga., and the Piedmont Institute at Rockmart, Ga.; was graduated from the University of Georgia at Athens in 1910, from the law department of the same university in 1911, and from the Harvard University Graduate School in 1912; was admitted to the bar in 1911 and commenced practice in Rome, Ga.; chairman of the board of education of Rome, Ga., in 1918 and 1919; member of the State house of representatives 1929-1933 and 1937-1940; solicitor general of Rome judicial circuit 1941-1946; elected as a Democrat to the Eightieth and to the five succeeding Congresses and served from January 3, 1947, until his death due to a train collision with his automobile at a crossing in Rome, Ga., November 10, 1957; interment in Myrtle Hill Cemetery.

**LANHAM, Samuel Willis Tucker** (father of Fritz Garland Lanham), a Representative from Texas; born in Spartanburg District, near Woodruff, S.C., on July 4, 1846; attended the common schools; entered the Confederate Army when a boy; moved to Texas in 1866 and settled at Boston, near Clarksville, Red River County; taught school for one year; moved to Weatherford in 1867 and continued teaching; studied law; was admitted to the bar in 1869 and engaged in practice in Weatherford, Tex.; district attorney, 1871-1876; elected as a Democrat to the Forty-eighth and to the four succeeding Congresses (March 4, 1883-March 3, 1893); chairman, Committee on Claims (Fiftieth Congress); was not a candidate for renomination in 1892 to the Fifty-third Congress; elected to the Fifty-Fifth and to the two succeeding Congresses, and served from March 4, 1897 until his resignation on January 15, 1903, having been elected Governor; elected Governor of Texas in 1902, reelected in 1904, and served from January 20, 1903 to January 15, 1907; died in Weatherford, Tex., on July 29, 1908; interment in Greenwood Cemetery.

**LANING, Jay Ford,** a Representative from Ohio; born in New London, Huron County, Ohio, May 15, 1853; attended the public schools, the Savannah (Ohio) Academy, and Baldwin University, Berea, Ohio; studied law; was admitted to the bar in May 1875 and commenced practice in New London; justice of the peace 1875-1881; member of the village council in 1876; moved to Norwalk, Ohio, in January 1882; practiced law until 1885 and then engaged in the publishing business; member of the city council 1887-1889; member of the State senate 1893-1897; delegate to the Republican National Conventions in 1904 and 1908; elected as a Republican to the Sixtieth Congress (March 4, 1907-March 3, 1909); renominated in 1908, but withdrew and resumed the publishing business in Norwalk, Ohio; devoted his time to the writing, editing, and publishing lawbooks and school textbooks; died in Norwalk, Ohio, on September 1, 1941; interment in Woodlawn Cemetery.

**LANKFORD, Menalcus,** a Representative from Virginia; born on the Bowers plantation near Franklin, Southampton County, Va., on March 14, 1883; attended public and private schools and the Norfolk High School; was graduated from the University of Richmond at Richmond in 1904, and from the law department of the University of Virginia at Charlottesville in 1906; was admitted to the bar the same year and commenced practice in Norfolk, Va.; during the First World War served as an ensign in the aviation service of the United States Navy; unsuccessful candidate for election in 1920 to the Sixty-seventh Congress, and in 1924 to the Sixty-ninth Congress; elected as a Republican to the Seventy-first and Seventy-second Congresses (March 4, 1929-March 3, 1933); unsuccessful candidate for reelection in 1932 to the Seventy-third Congress; delegate to the Republican National Conventions of 1932 and 1936; appointed referee in bankruptcy in 1933 of the Norfolk division, United States District Court, Eastern District of Virginia, and served until his death in Norfolk, Va., December 27, 1937; interment in Forest Lawn Cemetery.

**LANKFORD, Richard Estep,** a Representative from Maryland; born in Wilmington, New Castle County, Del., July 22, 1914; moved to Annapolis from Baltimore in 1940; attended private schools in Baltimore, Md., and Alexandria, Va.; B.S., University of Virginia, 1937; LL.B., University of Maryland School of Law, 1940; was admitted to the bar in 1940 and commenced the practice of law in Annapolis, Md.; engaged in active management of tobacco and cattle farms; commissioned an ensign in the United States Naval Reserve in July 1942; served two and one-half years in the European Theater of Operations and released to inactive duty as a lieutenant in February 1946; appointed in 1948 to fill an unexpired term in the Maryland State house of delegates; elected in 1950 and served until 1954; unsuccessful candidate for election in 1952 to the Eighty-third Congress; member of the Maryland Legislative Council in 1953; delegate to the Democratic National Convention of 1956; elected as a Democrat to the Eighty-fourth and to the four succeeding Congresses (January 3, 1955-January 3, 1965); was not a candidate for renomination in 1964 to the Eighty-ninth Congress; is a resident of Annapolis, Md.

**LANKFORD, William Chester,** a Representative from Georgia; born in Camp Creek Community, Clinch County, Ga., December 7, 1877; attended the public schools in Clinch County and Abbeville, Ga.; taught school for several years in his native county; was graduated from Jasper Normal Institute, Jasper, Fla., in 1897, from the Georgia Normal College and Business Institute, Abbeville, Ga., in 1900, and from the law department of the University of Georgia at Athens in 1901; moved to Douglas, Ga., in 1901 and commenced the practice of law; mayor of Douglas in 1906; member of the board of education of Douglas 1907-1918; judge of the city court from January 1, 1908, until May 1, 1916, when he resigned to seek the Democratic nomination for Congress, but was an unsuccessful candidate; elected as a Democrat to the Sixty-sixth and to the six succeeding Congresses (March 4, 1919-March 3, 1933); unsuccessful candidate for renomination in 1932; resumed the practice of law; with General Accounting Office in Washington, D.C., from January 1935 to October 1942; died in Twin Lakes, Ga., December 10, 1964; interment in Douglas Cemetery, Douglas, Ga.

**LANMAN, James,** a Senator from Connecticut; born in Norwich, Conn., June 14, 1767; pursued classical studies and graduated from Yale College in 1788; studied law; was admitted to the bar in 1791 and commenced practice in Norwich; State's attorney for New London County 1814-1819; member, State house of representatives 1817; delegate to the State constitutional convention in 1818; member, State senate 1819, 1832; elected as a Republican to the United States Senate and served from March 4, 1819, to March 3, 1825; chairman, Committee to Audit and Control the Contingent Expense (Seventeenth Congress), Committee on Engrossed Bills (Seventeenth and Eighteenth Congresses), Committee on Post Office and Post Roads (Eighteenth Congress); presented credentials as a Senator-designate to fill the vacancy in the term beginning March 4, 1825, but was not permitted to qualify; judge of the State superior and supreme courts 1826-1829; mayor of Norwich 1831-1834; member, State house of representatives 1833; died in Norwich, Conn., August 7, 1841; interment in the City Cemetery.

**LANNING, William Mershon,** a Representative from New Jersey; born in Ewingville, Mercer County, N.J., January 1, 1849; was graduated from the Lawrenceville School in 1866; employed as a teacher in the public schools of Mercer County and in the Trenton Academy 1866-1880; studied law; was admitted to the bar in 1880 and commenced practice in Trenton, N.J.; counselor in 1883; elected city solicitor for Trenton in 1884; appointed judge of the city district court in 1887 and served until 1891, when legislated out of office; member of a commission to frame township laws and of the constitutional commission of 1894; president of the Mechanics' National Bank of Trenton in 1899; elected as a Republican to the Fifty-eighth Congress and served from March 4, 1903, to June 6, 1904, when he resigned to accept an appointment as United States district judge for New Jersey; served in that capacity until May 18, 1909, when he was appointed United States circuit judge for the third circuit, which position he held until his death in Trenton, N.J., February 16, 1912; interment in the Presbyterian Cemetery, Ewing, N.J.

**LANSING, Frederick,** a Representative from New York; born in Manheim, Herkimer County, N.Y., February 16, 1838; attended the Little Falls Academy, New York; studied law; was admitted to the bar in 1859 and practiced in Watertown, N.Y.; served during the Civil War in the Eighth New York Cavalry; acting adjutant of that regiment from June 23 to October 11, 1863; member of the State senate 1881-1885; elected as a Republican to the Fifty-first Congress (March 4, 1889-March 3, 1891); died in Watertown, N.Y., January 31, 1894; interment in Brookside Cemetery.

**LANSING, Gerrit Yates** (nephew of John Lansing, Jr.), a Representative from New York; born in Albany, N.Y., August 4, 1783; pursued classical studies and was graduated from Union College in 1800; studied law; was admitted to the bar in 1804 and commenced practice in Albany; clerk of the State assembly in 1807; judge of the court of probates 1816-1823; elected regent of the University of the State of New York in 1829 and served until his death; was appointed chancellor of the board on October 31, 1842; elected as a Jacksonian to the Twenty-second, Twenty-third, and Twenty-fourth Congresses (March 4, 1831-March 3, 1837); was not a candidate for reelection in 1836; president of the Albany Savings Bank 1854-1862; president of the Albany Insurance Co. 1859-1862; died in Albany, N.Y., January 3, 1862; interment in the Albany Rural Cemetery.

**LANSING, John, Jr.** (uncle of Gerrit Yates Lansing), a Delegate from New York; born in Albany, N.Y., January 30, 1754; studied law in Albany and in New York City; was admitted to the bar in 1775; secretary to General Philip Schuyler during 1776 and 1777; engaged in the practice of law in Albany in 1778; member of the New York State assembly, 1781-1784, 1786, and 1789, and served as speaker in 1786 and 1789; Member of the Continental Congress in 1785; delegate to the Federal Constitutional Convention in 1787, but withdrew on July 10, 1787; delegate to the New York State convention in June 1788 to ratify the Federal Constitution; again a member and speaker of the State assembly in 1789; member of the commission to settle the New York-Vermont boundary line in 1790; justice of the supreme court of New York, 1790-1798, and chief justice, 1798-1801; chancellor, 1801-1814; commissioner to determine the claims of the city and county of New York to certain lands in Vermont in 1817; regent of the University of the State of New York, 1817-1829; mysteriously disappeared on December 12, 1829, after leaving his hotel to post a letter at one of the docks in New York City.

**Bibliography:** *DAB.*

**LANSING, William Esselstyne,** a Representative from New York; born in Perryville, Madison County, N.Y., December 29, 1821; attended the common schools; was graduated from Cazenovia Seminary in 1841; studied law in Utica, N.Y.; was admitted to the bar in 1845 and commenced practice in Chittenango; district attorney of Madison County, 1850-1853; president of the village of Chittenango, 1853-1855; Madison County clerk, 1855-1858; elected as a Republican to the Thirty-seventh Congress (March 4, 1861-March 3, 1863); was not a candidate for renomination in 1862 to the Thirty-eighth Congress; elected to the Forty-second and Forty-third Congresses (March 4, 1871-March 3, 1875); was not a candidate for renomination in 1874 to the Forty-fourth Congress; resumed the practice of law in Syracuse, N.Y., in 1876, and died there on July 29, 1883; interment in Oakwood Cemetery, Chittenango, N.Y.

**LANTAFF, William Courtland,** a Representative from Florida; born in Buffalo, Erie County, N.Y., July 31, 1913; moved to Jacksonville, Fla., in 1921 and to Miami, Fla., in 1929; graduated from the University of Florida in 1935 and from its law school in 1936; was admitted to the bar in 1936 and commenced the practice of law in Miami; Fla.; assistant city judge of Miami Beach in 1939 and 1940; inducted into the Federal service with Florida National Guard as a first lieutenant on January 6, 1941, serving as executive officer for the Military Intelligence Division, War Department General Staff; was discharged as a lieutenant colonel on November 15, 1945; again on active duty from September 15 to December 15, 1950; member of the State house of representatives 1947-1950; elected as a Democrat to the Eighty-second and Eighty-third Congresses (January 3, 1951-January 3, 1955); was not a candidate for renomination in 1954; delegate to Democratic National Conventions in 1956 and 1960; resumed the practice of law; other business interests included banking and advertising; died in Miami, Fla., January 28, 1970; interment in Woodlawn Park Cemetery.

**LANTOS, Thomas Peter** (father-in-law of Richard Swett), a Representative from California; born in Budapest, Hungary, February 1, 1928; came to the United States on an academic scholarship in 1947; B.A., University of Washington, Seattle, 1949, and M.A., 1950; Ph.D., economics, University of California, Berkeley, 1953; professor of economics, San Francisco State University; member of the Millbrae, Calif. board of education from 1950 until 1966; television news analyst and commentator; administrative assistant, economic and foreign policy adviser, United States Senate; delegate to the Democratic National Convention of 1976; elected as a Democrat to the Ninety-seventh and to the seven succeeding Congresses (January 3, 1981-January 3, 1997); is a resident of San Mateo, Calif.

**LANZETTA, James Joseph,** a Representative from New York; born in New York City December 21, 1894; attended the public schools; was graduated from Columbia University, School of Engineering, New York City, in 1917, and from the law school of Fordham University, New York City, in 1924; served in the United States Army during the First World War as a private in Company C., Three Hundred and Second Engineers, and as a sergeant first class, in the First Air Service Mechanics Regiment, serving overseas from February 1918 to July 1919; engineer and salesman in New York City 1919-1922; assistant supervisor, Department of Markets, 1922-1925; was admitted to the bar in 1925 and commenced the practice of law in New York City; member of the New York City Board of Aldermen from January 1932 to March 1933; elected as a Democrat to the Seventy-third Congress (March 4, 1933-January 3, 1935); unsuccessful candidate for reelection in 1934 to the Seventy-fourth Congress; elected to the Seventy-fifth Congress (January 3, 1937-January 3, 1939); unsuccessful candidate for reelection in 1938 to the Seventy-sixth Congress and for election in 1940 to the Seventy-seventh Congress; resumed the practice of law; appointed city magistrate of New York City July 2, 1947, and served until May 26, 1948, when he was appointed a justice of the Domestic Relations Court of New York City, in which capacity he served until his death in New York City October 27, 1956; interment in Woodlawn Cemetery, New York City (the Bronx), N.Y.

**LAPHAM, Elbridge Gerry,** a Representative and a Senator from New York; born in Farmington, N.Y., October 18, 1814; attended the public schools and the Canandaigua Academy; studied civil engineering and law; was admitted to the bar in 1844 and practiced in Canandaigua, N.Y.; member of the constitutional convention of New York in 1867; elected as a Republican to the Forty-fourth and to the three succeeding Congresses and served from March 4, 1875, until his resignation July 29, 1881, having been elected Senator; one of the managers appointed by the House of Representatives in 1876 to conduct the impeachment proceedings against ex-Secretary of War William W. Belknap; elected as a Republican to the United States Senate on July 22, 1881, to fill the vacancy caused by the resignation of Roscoe Conkling and served from August 2, 1881, to March 3, 1885; was not a candidate for reelection; chairman, Committee on Fish and Fisheries (Forty-eighth Congress); resumed the practice of law in Canandaigua, N.Y.; died at "Glen Gerry," on Canandaigua Lake, N.Y., January 8, 1890; interment in Woodlawn Cemetery, Canandaigua, N.Y.

**LAPHAM, Oscar,** a Representative from Rhode Island; born in Burrillville, Providence County, R.I., June 29, 1837; attended the seminary in Scituate, Mass., the academy in Pembroke, N.H., the University Grammar School, Providence, R.I., and was graduated from Brown University, Providence, R.I., in 1864; member of the board of trustees and of the advisory and executive committee of that university; studied law; was admitted to the bar in 1867 and practiced in Providence, R.I.; served in the Civil War as first lieutenant, adjutant, and captain in the Twelfth Rhode Island Volunteers; member of the State senate in 1887 and 1888; member and treasurer of the Democratic State central committee 1887-1891; unsuccessful candidate for election to the Forty-eighth, Fiftieth, and Fifty-first Congresses; elected as a Democrat to the Fifty-second and Fifty-third Congresses (March 4, 1891-March 3, 1895); unsuccessful candidate for reelection in 1894 to the Fifty-fourth Congress; resumed the practice of law in Providence, R.I., and died there March 29, 1926; interment in Swan Point Cemetery.

**LAPORTE, John,** a Representative from Pennsylvania; born in Asylum, Asylum Township, Bradford County, Pa., on November 4, 1798; attended the common schools; county auditor of Bradford County in 1827 and 1828; member of the Pennsylvania house of representatives 1828-1832 and served as speaker in 1831 and 1832; elected as a Jacksonian to the Twenty-third and Twenty-fourth Congresses (March 4, 1833-March 3, 1837); was not a candidate for renomination in 1836; associate judge of Bradford County 1837-1845; interested in the development of the North Branch Canal; surveyor general of Pennsylvania 1845-1851; engaged in banking at Towanda, Pa., 1850-1862; died in Philadelphia, Pa., August 22, 1862; interment in the family cemetery at Asylum, near Towanda, Pa.

**LARCADE, Henry Dominique, Jr.,** a Representative from Louisiana; born in Opelousas, St. Landry Parish, La., July 12, 1890; attended the public and parochial schools, Opelousas High School, Academy Immaculate Conception, and Opelousas Institute; during the First World War served as a private in the Three Hundred and Forty-eighth Infantry, Eighty-seventh Division, at Camp Pike, Ark., later obtaining a commission as second lieutenant, Quartermaster Corps, Officers' Reserve Corps; engaged in the banking business and the general insurance business; member of the St. Landry Parish School Board 1913-1928; member of the State senate 1928-1932; assistant clerk of the State senate 1932-1936; served in the State house of representatives 1936-1940; elected as a Democrat to the Seventy-eighth and to the four succeeding Congresses (January 3, 1943-January 3, 1953); was not a candidate for renomination in 1952; member of the State senate 1956-1960; engaged in banking business; was a resident of Opelousas, La., until his death there March 15, 1966; interment in St. Landry Cemetery.

**LARGENT, Steve,** a Representative from Oklahoma; born in Tulsa, Okla., September 28, 1955; B.S., University of Tulsa, 1976; played professional football with team in Seattle, Wash., 1976-1989; marketing consultant; elected as a Republican to the One Hundred Fourth Congress, November 8, 1994; elected to the One Hundred Third Congress pursuant to H.Res. 585, filling the vacancy caused by the resignation of James M. Inhofe, and served from November 29, 1994 to January 3, 1997; is a resident of Tulsa, Okla.

**LARNED, Simon,** a Representative from Massachusetts; born in Thompson, Conn., August 3, 1753; attended the common schools; sheriff of Berkshire County; served in the Revolutionary War with rank as captain in Colonel Shepherd's regiment; engaged in mercantile pursuits in Pittsfield, Mass., in 1784; was a representative in the general court in 1791; county treasurer 1792-1812; served as colonel of the Ninth United States Infantry in the War of 1812 and was engaged in action at Plattsburg, along the Mohawk River; elected as a Republican to the Eighth Congress to fill the vacancy caused by the resignation of Thomson J. Skinner and served from November 5, 1804, to March 3, 1805; president of the Berkshire Bank; died in Pittsfield, Mass., on November 16, 1817; interment in the Pittsfield Cemetery.

**LaROCCO, Larry,** a Representative from Idaho; born in Van Nuys, Los Angeles County, Calif., August 25, 1946; B.A., University of Portland, Oregon, 1967; Stanford University Institute of Television and Radio, 1967; John Hopkins School of Advanced International Studies, 1968-1969; M.S., Boston University, 1969; commissioned as second lieutenant, United States Army in 1969; released as captain in 1972 after service with Military Intelligence; account executive, Cline, Inc., 1973; assistant vice president, Twin Falls Bank and Trust Co., 1973-1974; north Idaho representative to Senator Frank Church, 1975-1981; coordinator, Church for President campaign, Oregon primary, 1976; vice president, E.F. Hutton and Shearson Lehman Hutton, 1983-1989; vice president, Piper, Jaffray and Hopwood, 1989-1990; elected as a Democrat to the One Hundred Second and One Hundred Third Congresses (January 3, 1991-January 3, 1995); unsuccessful candidate for reelection in 1994 to the One Hundred Fourth Congress; managing director, American Bankers Association Securities Association, Washington, D.C., 1995 to present.

**LARRABEE, Charles Hathaway,** a Representative from Wisconsin; born in Rome, N.Y., November 9, 1820; moved with his father to Ohio; attended Granville College; studied engineering and law; was admitted to the bar in 1841 and commenced practice in Pontotoc, Miss.; moved to Chicago, Ill., in 1844 and continued the practice of law; city attorney in 1846 and 1847; moved to Horicon, Wis., in 1847 and practiced law; delegate to the State constitutional convention in 1847; judge of the third judicial circuit and of the State supreme court, 1848-1858; resigned; elected as a Democrat to the Thirty-sixth Congress (March 4, 1859-March 3, 1861); unsuccessful candidate for reelection in 1860 to the Thirty-seventh Congress; during the Civil War served in the Union Army from April 17, 1861 until his resignation in September 1863, and was promoted from lieutenant to colonel; moved to California in 1864 and practiced law in San Bernardino and also in Salem, Oreg., and Seattle, Wash.; was seriously injured in a railroad accident at Tehachapi, Calif., which resulted in his death in Los Angeles, Calif., on January 20, 1883; interment in the Masonic Cemetery, San Francisco, Calif.

**Bibliography:** *DAB*; Marquette, Clare Leslie. "The Life and Letters of a Pontotoc Pioneer, Charles Hathaway Larrabee." *Journal of Mississippi History* 20 (April 1958): 77-98.

**LARRABEE, William Henry,** a Representative from Indiana; born on a farm near Crawfordsville, Montgomery County, Ind., February 21, 1870; attended the public schools, Indiana Central Normal School at Danville, and Indiana State Normal School at Terre Haute; taught in public schools at New Palestine, Ind., 1889-1895; was graduated from the Indiana School of Medicine at Indianapolis in 1898; commenced practice of medicine and surgery in New Palestine, Ind., in 1898; secretary of Hancock County Board of Health in 1917 and 1918; served on the city council of New Palestine, Ind., 1916-1920; member of the Indiana State house of representatives, 1923-1925; elected as a Democrat to the Seventy-second and to the five succeeding Congresses (March 4, 1931-January 3, 1943); chairman, Committee on the Census (Seventy-fourth and Seventy-fifth Congresses), Committee on Education (Seventy-fifth through Seventy-seventh Congresses); unsuccessful candidate for reelection in 1942 to the Seventy-eighth Congress; resumed the practice of medicine and surgery; died in New Palestine, Ind., November 16, 1960; interment in New Palestine Cemetery.

**LARRAZOLO, Octaviano Ambrosio,** a Senator from New Mexico; born in Allende, State of Chihuahua, Mexico, December 7, 1859; moved to Tucson, Ariz., in 1870 as a protege of the bishop of Arizona; attended St. Michael's College at Santa Fe, N.Mex., in 1875 and 1876; taught in the public schools in Tucson and in Texas; clerk of the district court at El Paso; clerk of the United States District and Circuit Courts for the Western District of Texas at El Paso, Tex.; studied law; was admitted to the bar in 1888; elected district attorney for the western district of Texas in 1890 and reelected in 1892; moved to Las Vegas, N.Mex., in 1895 and resumed the practice of law; unsuccessful Democratic candidate for election as a Delegate from New Mexico in 1890 to the Fifty-second Congress, in 1900 to the Fifty-seventh Congress, and in 1908 to the Sixty-first Congress; affiliated with the Republican Party in 1911; elected Governor of New Mexico in 1918 and served from January 1, 1919 to January 1, 1921; member, New Mexico State house of representatives in 1927 and 1928; elected as a Republican to the United States Senate to fill the vacancy caused by the death of Andrieus A. Jones and served from December 7, 1928, to March 3, 1929; was not a candidate for the full term; resumed the practice of law; died in Albuquerque, N.Mex., April 7, 1930; interment in Santa Barbara Cemetery.

**Bibliography:** *DAB*; Cordova, Alfred. *Octaviano Larrazolo: A Political Portrait.* Albuquerque: University of New Mexico, 1952.

**LARRINAGA, Tulio,** a Resident Commissioner from Puerto Rico; born in Trujillo Alto, P.R., January 15, 1847; attended the Seminario Consiliar of San Ildefonso at San Juan, P.R.; studied civil engineering in the Polytechnic Institute, Troy, N.Y., and was graduated from the University of Pennsylvania at Philadelphia in 1871; practiced his profession for some time in the United States; returned to Puerto Rico in 1872 and was appointed architect for the city of San Juan; built the first railroad in Puerto Rico in 1880 and introduced American rolling stock on the island; was for ten years chief engineer of the provincial works; in 1898 was appointed assistant secretary of the interior under the autonomic government and in 1900 was sent by his party as a delegate to Washington; member of the house of delegates for the district of Arecibo in 1902; elected as a Unionist Resident Commissioner to the United States in 1904; reelected in 1906 and 1908 and served from March 4, 1905, until March 3, 1911; delegate from the United States to the Third Pan American Congress at Rio de Janeiro in 1906; member of the executive council of Puerto Rico in 1911; resumed the practice of his profession as a civil engineer in San Juan, P.R., and died there on April 28, 1917; interment in the Municipal Cemetery at Santurce.

**Bibliography:** *DAB*.

**LARSEN, William Washington,** a Representative from Georgia; born in Hagan, Tattnall (now Evans) County, Ga., August 12, 1871; attended the common schools, Bryan Institute, Lanier, Ga., South Georgia Military Academy, Thomasville, Ga., and the literary department of the University of Georgia at Athens; left college and engaged in teaching in 1895; studied law; was admitted to the bar in 1897 and commenced practice in Swainsboro, Ga., the same year; served as a second lieutenant in the Swainsboro Guards, Company C, National Guard of Georgia, 1900-1904; prosecuting attorney for the city court of Swainsboro, with jurisdiction over Emanuel County and parts of what are now Jenkins, Toombs, Candler, and Treutlen Counties, 1899-1905; member of the council and mayor pro tempore of the city of Swainsboro 1905-1909; member of the board of trustees of the State normal school at Athens, Ga., 1912-1927; delegate to the Democratic State conventions in 1902, 1906, and 1912; secretary of the executive department of the State of Georgia 1910-1912; moved to Dublin, Ga., in January 1912; resumed the practice of law and also engaged in agricultural pursuits; judge of the superior courts of Dublin circuit in 1914 and 1915; elected as a Democrat to the Sixty-fifth and to the seven succeeding Congresses (March 4, 1917-March 3, 1933); was not a candidate for renomination in 1932; member of the board of trustees of the University of Georgia 1927-1938; appointed regional manager for the Farm Credit Administration with headquarters in Columbia, S.C., in 1933 and served until his resignation in 1936; appointed a member of the Georgia Unemployment Insurance Commission in 1937 and served until his death in Dublin, Ga., January 5, 1938; interment in Northview Cemetery.

**LARSON, Oscar John,** a Representative from Minnesota; born in Uleaborg, Finland, May 20, 1871; immigrated in 1876 to the United States with his parents, who settled in Calumet, Mich.; attended the public schools; was graduated from the Northern Indiana Normal School (now Valparaiso University) in 1891, and from the law department of the University of Michigan at Ann Arbor in 1894; was admitted to the bar and commenced practice in Calumet, Mich., in 1894; prosecuting attorney for Houghton County, 1899-1904; moved to Duluth, Minn., in 1907 and continued the practice of law; elected as a Republican to the Sixty-seventh and Sixty-eighth Congresses (March 4, 1921-March 3, 1925); was not a candidate for reelection in 1924 to the Sixty-ninth Congress; resumed the practice of law; died in Duluth, Minn., August 1, 1957; interment in Forest Hill Cemetery.

**LA SÉRE, Emile,** a Representative from Louisiana; born on the island of Santo Domingo in 1802; moved with his parents to New Orleans, La., about 1805; completed preparatory studies; employed as a clerk in a mercantile establishment at Jackson, La., and later in Mexico for several years; elected sheriff of the parish of New Orleans in 1840 and served several years; elected as a Democrat to the Twenty-ninth Congress to fill the vacancy caused by the resignation of John Slidell; reelected to the Thirtieth and Thirty-first Congresses, and served from January 29, 1846 to March 3, 1851; chairman, Committee on Expenditures in the Post Office Department (Twenty-ninth Congress); during the Civil War served in the Confederate Army as major in the Tenth Louisiana Regiment, and afterward as chief quartermaster of the Trans-Mississippi Department; chairman of the Democratic State central committee for more than fifteen years; president of the Tehuantepec Railroad Company in Mexico; died in New Orleans, La., August 14, 1882; interment in Metairie Cemetery.

**Bibliography:** Diket, A.L. "Slidell's Right Hand: Emile La Sére." *Louisiana History* 4 (Summer 1963): 177-205.

**LASH, Israel George,** a Representative from North Carolina; born in Bethania, Forsyth County, N.C., August 18, 1810; attended the common schools and the local academy in his native city; engaged in mercantile pursuits and subsequently became a cigar manufacturer; also engaged in banking in Salem, N.C.; delegate to the State constitutional convention in 1868; upon the readmission of the State of North Carolina to representation was elected as a Republican to the Fortieth Congress; reelected to the Forty-first Congress and served from July 20, 1868, to March 4, 1871; was not a candidate for renomination in 1870; again engaged in banking in Salem (now Winston-Salem) N.C., until his death there on April 1, 1878; interment in the Moravian Cemetery, Bethania, N.C.

**LASSITER, Francis Rives** (great-nephew of Francis Everod Rives), a Representative from Virginia; born in Petersburg, Dinwiddie County, Va., February 18, 1866; attended McCabe's University School at Petersburg and was graduated from the law department of the University of Virginia at Charlottesville in 1886; was admitted to the bar in 1887 and commenced practice in Boston, Mass.; returned to Petersburg, Va., in 1888 and continued the practice of law; city attorney of Petersburg from 1888 until 1893; appointed by President Grover Cleveland to be United States attorney for the eastern district of Virginia in 1893 and served until 1896, when he resigned; captain of Company G, Fourth Regiment, Virginia Militia; appointed supervisor of the Twelfth Census for the Fourth Congressional District of Virginia in 1899; elected as a Democrat to the Fifty-sixth Congress to fill the vacancy caused by the death of Sydney P. Epes; reelected to the Fifty-seventh Congress and served from April 19, 1900, to March 3, 1903; elected to the Sixtieth and Sixty-first Congresses and served from March 4, 1907, until his death in Petersburg, Va., October 31, 1909; interment in Blanford Cemetery.

**LATHAM, George Robert,** a Representative from West Virginia; born near Haymarket, Prince William County, Va.; March 9, 1832; attended the common schools; studied law; was admitted to the bar in 1859 and commenced practice in Grafton, Va. (now West Virginia); delegate to the convention at Wheeling for the formation of West Virginia; during the Civil War served in the Union Army as captain of Company B, Second Regiment, Virginia Volunteer Infantry, and later colonel of Volunteers; elected as an Unconditional Unionist to the Thirty-ninth Congress (March 4, 1865-March 3, 1867); was not a candidate for renomination in 1866; United States consul at Melbourne, Australia, 1867-1870; school superintendent of Upshur County, W.Va., 1875-1877; supervisor of census for the first census division of West Virginia; engaged in agricultural pursuits; died in Buckhannon, W.Va., December 16, 1917; interment in Heavner Cemetery.

**LATHAM, Henry Jepson,** a Representative from New York; born in Brooklyn, N.Y., on December 10, 1908; attended the public schools, Richmond Hill High School, St. John's College, Brooklyn, N.Y.; LL.B. and L.M., Brooklyn Law School of St. Lawrence University, 1931; was admitted to the bar in 1932 and commenced practice in Jamaica, N.Y.; unsuccessful Republican candidate for the State senate in 1938; elected to the New York house of assembly in 1941 and served until commissioned a lieutenant (junior grade) in the United States Navy in 1942; subsequently promoted to lieutenant and saw service in both the European and Pacific Theaters of war; was on active duty in the Pacific when elected as a Republican to the Seventy-ninth Congress; reelected to the Eightieth and to the five succeeding Congresses and served from January 3, 1945, until his resignation December 31, 1958; retired from the Navy Reserve as a captain; elected in 1958 a justice of the supreme court of the State of New York for the term ending December 31, 1972; appointed by Governor Nelson A. Rockefeller to the Appellate Division of the New York State Supreme Court, Second Judicial Department, on January 29, 1970, and served until his retirement December 31, 1978; is a resident of Southold, N.Y.

**LATHAM, Louis Charles,** a Representative from North Carolina; born in Plymouth, Washington County, N.C., September 11, 1840; attended private schools, and was graduated from the University of North Carolina at Chapel Hill in 1859; later attended the Harvard Law School; entered the Confederate Army in 1861; was commissioned captain and afterward major of the First Regiment of North Carolina State troops, and served throughout the Civil War; immediately after the war resumed the study of law; was admitted to the bar in 1868 and commenced practice in Plymouth, N.C.; member of the State house of commons in 1864; served in the State senate in 1870; elected as a Democrat to the Forty-seventh Congress (March 4, 1881-March 3, 1883); unsuccessful candidate for renomination in 1882; elected to the Fiftieth Congress (March 4, 1887-March 3, 1889); unsuccessful candidate for reelection in 1888 to the Fifty-first Congress; resumed the practice of law in Greenville, N.C.; died at Johns Hopkins University Hospital, Baltimore, Md., October 16, 1895; interment in the City Cemetery, Greenville, N.C.

**LATHAM, Milton Slocum,** a Representative and a Senator from California; born in Columbus, Ohio, May 23, 1827; pursued classical studies and graduated from Jefferson College, Pennsylvania, in 1845; moved to Russell County, Ala.; taught school; studied law; was admitted to the bar in 1848 and commenced practice; circuit court clerk for Russell County, 1848-1850; moved to San Francisco, Calif., in 1850; clerk of the recorder's court in 1850; district attorney for the Sacramento district in 1851; elected as a Democrat to the Thirty-third Congress (March 4, 1853-March 3, 1855); declined to be a candidate for renomination in 1854 to the Thirty-fourth Congress; collector of the port of San Francisco 1855-1857; elected Governor of California in 1859, and served from January 9 until January 14, 1860, when he resigned, having been elected Senator; elected as a Democrat on January 11, 1860, to the United States Senate to fill the vacancy caused by the death of David C. Broderick; took his seat March 5, 1860, and served until March 3, 1863; unsuccessful candidate for reelection; engaged in the practice of law in San Francisco, Calif.; manager at San Francisco of the London & San Francisco Bank (Ltd.) 1865-1878; moved to New York City in 1879, where he became president of the New York Mining and Stock Exchange; died in New York City on March 4, 1882; interment in Lone Mountain Cemetery, San Francisco, Calif.; reinterment in Cypress Lawn Cemetery, Colma, Calif.

**Bibliography:** *DAB*; Latham, Milton. "The Day Journal of Milton S. Latham, January 1 to May 6, 1860." Edited by Edgar Robinson. *Quarterly of the California Historical Society* 11 (March 1932): 3-28.

**LATHAM, Thomas Paul,** a Representative from Iowa; born in Hampton, Franklin County, Iowa, July 14, 1948; attended Alexander Community School; graduated, Cal (Latimer) Community College; attended Iowa State University, Ames, and Wartburg College, Waverly, Iowa; bank teller and bookkeeper in Brush, Colo., 1970-1972; insurance agent, Fort Lupton, Colo., 1972-1974; insurance company marketing representative in Des Moines, Iowa, 1974-1976; vice president and co-owner of a seed company since 1976; delegate and Iowa delegation Whip, Central Committee, to the Republican National Convention of 1992; secretary, Iowa Republican Party; co-chair, Franklin County Republican Central Committee; elected as a Republican to the One Hundred Fourth Congress (January 3, 1995-January 3, 1997); is a resident of Alexander, Iowa.

**LATHROP, Samuel,** a Representative from Massachusetts; born in West Springfield, Hampden County, Mass., on May 1, 1772; pursued classical studies and was graduated from Yale College in 1792; studied law; was admitted to the bar and commenced practice in West Springfield; clerk and treasurer 1796-1798; town moderator for eight years; elected to the Sixteenth and to the three succeeding Congresses (March 4, 1819-March 3, 1827); chairman, Committee on Revisal and Unfinished Business (Seventeenth and Eighteenth Congresses); resumed the practice of law and devoted considerable time to agricultural pursuits; member of the Massachusetts senate in 1829 and 1830 and served as its president; died in West Springfield, Mass., July 11, 1846; interment in the Park Street Cemetery.

**LATHROP, William** a Representative from Illinois; born near Le Roy, Genesee County, N.Y., April 17, 1825; attended the public schools and an academy at Brockport, N.Y.; studied law in Attica, N.Y.; moved to Knoxville, Ill., and was admitted to the bar in 1850; settled in Rockford, Ill., in 1851 and practiced his profession; city clerk and city attorney of Rockford in 1852; member of the State house of representatives in 1856 and 1857; elected as a Republican to the Forty-fifth Congress (March 4, 1877-March 3, 1879); resumed the practice of law in Rockford, Ill., where he died November 19, 1907; interment in Greenwood Cemetery.

**LATIMER, Asbury Churchwell,** a Representative and a Senator from South Carolina; born near Lowndesville, Abbeville County, S.C., July 31, 1851; attended the common schools; engaged in agricultural pursuits; moved to Belton, Anderson County, S.C., in 1880 and devoted his time to farming; elected as a Democrat to the Fifty-third and to the four succeeding Congresses (March 4, 1893-March 3, 1903); did not seek renomination in 1902, having become a candidate for Senator; elected as a Democrat to the United States Senate and served from March 4, 1903, until his death; during his service in the Senate was appointed in 1907 a member of the United States Immigration Commission; died in Washington, D.C., February 20, 1908; interment in Belton Cemetery, Belton, S.C.

**LATIMER, Henry,** a Representative and a Senator from Delaware; born in Newport, Del., on April 24, 1752; pursued classical studies; studied medicine in Philadelphia, Pa., graduated from the University of Pennsylvania at Philadelphia in 1773 and from the Edinburgh (Scotland) Medical College in 1775; returned to the United States and practiced his profession in Wilmington, Del.; served as a surgeon in the Revolutionary War; member, State house of representatives 1787-1788, 1790, serving as speaker in 1790; successfully contested the election of John Patton to the Third Congress and served from February 14, 1794, until February 7, 1795, when he resigned; elected in 1795 as a Federalist to the United States Senate to fill the vacancy caused by the resignation of George Read; reelected, and served from February 7, 1795, until February 28, 1801, when he resigned; died in Philadelphia, Pa., December 19, 1819; interment in the Presbyterian Cemetery, Wilmington, Del.

**LaTOURETTE, Steven C.,** a Representative from Ohio; born in Cleveland, Ohio, July 22, 1954; graduated Cleveland Heights High School, 1972; B.A., University of Michigan, 1976; J.D., Cleveland State University, 1979; admitted to the Ohio bar in 1980; Lake County, Ohio public defenders office, 1980-1983; elected prosecuting attorney of Lake County in 1988, reelected in 1992 and served 1989-1995; elected as a Republican to the One Hundred Fourth Congress (January 3, 1995-January 3, 1997); is a resident of Madison, Ohio.

**LATTA, Delbert Leroy,** a Representative from Ohio; born in Weston, Wood County, Ohio, March 5, 1920; attended the public schools in North Baltimore, Ohio; graduated from McComb (Ohio) High School in 1938; attended Findlay (Ohio) College, 1938-1940; LL.B., Ohio Northern University, Ada, 1943, and A.B., 1945; served in the Ohio National Guard and the United States Army, Thirty-seventh Division, 1938-1941, and in the United States Marine Corps Reserve in 1942 and 1943; was admitted to the bar and commenced the practice of law in Bowling Green, Ohio, in 1944; Ohio State senator, 1953-1958; delegate to the Republican National Convention of 1968; elected as a Republican to the Eighty-sixth and to the fourteen succeeding Congresses (January 3, 1959-January 3, 1989); was not a candidate for reelection in 1988 to the One Hundred First Congress; is a resident of Bowling Green, Ohio.

**LATTA, James Polk,** a Representative from Nebraska; born near Ashland, Ashland County, Ohio, October 31, 1844; moved with his parents to Jackson County, Iowa, in 1846; attended the district schools and worked on a farm; moved to the Territory of Nebraska in 1863; taught school in Tekamah, Nebr.; engaged in agricultural pursuits and stock raising in Burt County; became interested in banking at Tekamah in 1887; member of the State house of representatives in 1887; organized the First National Bank of Tekamah in 1890 and served as its president until his death; member of the State senate in 1907; elected as a Democrat to the Sixty-first and Sixty-second Congresses and served from March 4, 1909, until his death at Rochester, Minn., September 11, 1911; interment in Tekamah Cemetery, Tekamah, Nebr.

**LATTIMORE, William,** a Delegate from Mississippi Territory; born in Norfolk, Va., February 9, 1774; attended the common schools; studied medicine; moved to Natchez, Miss., and practiced his profession; on the formation of Mississippi Territory in 1798 took an active part in the organization of a government; elected as a Delegate to the Eighth and Ninth Congresses (March 4, 1803-March 3, 1807); elected to the Thirteenth and Fourteenth Congresses (March 4, 1813-March 3, 1817); delegate to the first State constitutional convention of Mississippi in 1817; appointed a censor of the medical profession under the constitution and code; one of the commissioners to select the site for the seat of the new State government; died in Natchez, Miss., April 3, 1843.

**Bibliography:** *DAB.*

**LAUGHLIN, Greg H.,** a Representative from Texas; born in Bay City, Matagorda County, Tex., January 21, 1942; graduated West Columbia (Tex.) High School, 1960; B.A., Texas A&M University, 1964; LL.B., University of Texas, 1967; entered active duty, United States Army, 1968; released in 1970; United States Army Reserve Service as lieutenant colonel, 1970-1988; admitted to Texas bar, 1967; attorney, West Columbia, Tex.; assistant district attorney for Harris County, Tex., 1970-1974; unsuccessful candidate for election in 1986 to the One Hundredth Congress; elected as a Democrat to the One Hundred First and to the three succeeding Congresses (January 3, 1989-January 3, 1997); announced his affiliation with the Republican Party on June 26, 1995, and continued in office during the One Hundred Fourth Congress as a Republican; unsuccessful candidate for nomination in 1996 to the One Hundred Fifth Congress; is a resident of West Columbia, Tex.

**LAURANCE, John,** a Delegate, a Representative, and a Senator from New York; born near Falmouth, England, in 1750; immigrated to the United States and settled in New York City in 1767; pursued academic studies; studied law; was admitted to the bar in 1772 and practiced in New York City; served in the Revolution as a commissioned officer; appointed judge advocate-general in 1777 and presided at the trial of Major John André; regent of the University of the State of New York 1784; trustee of Columbia College 1784-1810; Delegate to the Continental Congress 1785-1787; member, State senate 1789-1790; elected to the First and Second Congresses (March 4, 1789-March 3, 1793); appointed by President George Washington to be United States judge of the district of New York in May 1794, and served until November 8, 1796, when he resigned, having been elected Senator; elected to the United States Senate to fill the vacancy caused by the resignation of Rufus King and served from November 9, 1796, until August 1800, when he resigned; served as President pro tempore of the Senate during the Fifth Congress; died in New York City November 11, 1810; interment in the First Presbyterian Churchyard, Fifth Avenue and Twelfth Street.

**Bibliography:** *DAB.*

**LAURENS, Henry,** a Delegate from South Carolina; born in Charleston, S.C., March 6, 1724; received his early education in Charleston; went to Great Britain in 1744 to acquire a business education; upon his return to the United States in 1747 engaged in mercantile pursuits; served as lieutenant colonel in a campaign against the Cherokee Indians 1757-1761; member of the commons house of assembly in 1757 and reelected to every session, with one exception, until the Revolution; declined appointment to King's Council in Carolina in 1764 and 1768; member of the American Philosophical Society, Philadelphia, Pa., 1772-1792; was in Europe from 1771 until December 11, 1774, where he placed his sons in school; returned to Charleston, S.C., in the latter year; member of the First Provincial Congress January 9, 1775; President of the Provincial Congress in June 1775; also president of the general committee and of the first council of safety in 1775; member of the Second Provincial Congress from November 1775 to March 1776 and president of the second council of safety in 1775 and 1776; Vice President of South Carolina from March 1776 to June 27, 1777; elected as a Delegate to the Continental Congress January 10, 1777, and served until 1780; served as President of the Congress from November 1, 1777, to December 9, 1778; elected Minister to the Netherlands by the Continental Congress on October 21, 1779, and sailed for his post early in 1780; was captured on the voyage and held a prisoner in the Tower of London for fifteen months; released on December 31, 1781, in exchange for Lord Cornwallis; appointed one of the peace commissioners and signed the preliminary treaty of Paris on November 30, 1782; returned to the United States on August 3, 1784, and retired to his plantation, "Mepkin," on the Cooper River, near Charleston, S.C.; subsequently elected to the Continental Congress, to the State legislature, and in 1787 to the Federal Constitutional Convention, all of which offices he declined; continued as a planter until his death at "Mepkin," near Charleston, S.C., December 8, 1792; the remains were cremated and his ashes interred on his estate, "Mepkin," at the confluence east-west branches Cooper River, Berkeley County, S.C.

**Bibliography:** *DAB*; Laurens, Henry. *The Papers of Henry Laurens.* 14 vols. to date. Edited by Philip M. Hamer, George C. Rogers, Jr., and David R. Chesnutt. Columbia: University of South Carolina Press, 1968- ; Wallace, David Duncan. *The Life of Henry Laurens.* 1915. Reprint. New York: Russell and Russell, 1967.

**LAUSCHE, Frank John,** a Senator from Ohio, born in Cleveland, Cuyahoga County, Ohio, November 14, 1895; attended Central Institute Prep School in 1915 and 1916; during the First World War served as a second lieutenant in the United States Army; graduated from John Marshall School of Law in 1920; was admitted to the bar the same year and commenced the practice of law in Cleveland, Ohio; judge of Municipal Court, 1932-1937; judge of Common Pleas Court, 1937-1941; mayor of Cleveland, 1941-1944; elected Governor of Ohio in 1944, and served from January 8, 1945 to January 13, 1947; unsuccessful candidate for reelection in 1946; again elected Governor in 1948, reelected in 1950, 1952, and 1954, and served from January 10, 1949, until his resignation effective January 3, 1957, having been elected to the Senate; elected as a Democrat to the United States Senate in 1956, reelected in 1962, and served from January 3, 1957, until January 3, 1969; unsuccessful candidate for renomination in 1968; died April 21, 1990.

**Bibliography:** Bittner, William. *Frank J. Lausche: A Political Biography.* New York: Studia Slovenica, 1975.

**LAUTENBERG, Frank Raleigh,** a Senator from New Jersey; born in Paterson, Passaic County, N.J., January 23, 1924; graduated from Nutley High School, Nutley, N.J., 1941; B.S., Columbia University School of Business, New York City, 1949; served in the United States Army Signal Corps from 1942 until 1946; businessman; commissioner of the Port Authority of New York and New Jersey, 1978-1982; elected as a Democrat to the United States Senate in 1982 for the six-year term commencing January 3, 1983, and ending January 3, 1989; subsequently appointed by the Governor on December 27, 1982, to complete the unexpired term of Nicholas F. Brady, ending January 3, 1983; reelected in 1988 and again in 1994 for the term ending January 3, 2001; is a resident of Secaucus, N.J.

**LAW, Charles Blakeslee,** a Representative from New York; born in Hannibal, Oswego County, N.Y., February 5, 1872; attended the public schools; was graduated from Colgate Academy, Hamilton, N.Y., in 1891, and from Amherst College, Amherst, Mass., in 1895; studied law in Rome, N.Y., and at Cornell Law School, Ithaca, N.Y.; was admitted to the bar in Rochester, N.Y., in 1897; moved to Brooklyn, N.Y., in 1898 and commenced the practice of law; elected as a Republican to the Fifty-ninth, Sixtieth, and Sixty-first Congresses (March 4, 1905-March 3, 1911); chairman, Committee on War Claims (Sixty-first Congress); unsuccessful candidate for reelection in 1910; resumed the practice of law in the Borough of Brooklyn, New York City; sheriff of Kings County 1912 and 1913; justice of the municipal court of the city of New York from January 1, 1916, to January 1, 1926; again resumed the practice of law in Brooklyn, N.Y., and also engaged in banking; died while swimming at his summer home on Kattskill Bay, near Lake George, N.Y., on September 15, 1929; interment in Maple Grove Cemetery, Jordan Onondaga County, N.Y.

**LAW, John** (son of Lyman Law and grandson of Richard Law and Amasa Learned), a Representative from Indiana; born in New London, Conn., October 28, 1796; pursued classical studies and was graduated from Yale College in 1814; studied law; was admitted to the bar in 1817 and commenced practice in Vincennes, Ind.; prosecuting attorney, 1818-1820; member of the Indiana State house of representatives in 1824 and 1825; again prosecuting attorney from 1825 to 1828; judge of the seventh judicial circuit in 1830 and 1831; receiver of the land office at Vincennes, 1838-1842; again served as judge from 1844 to 1850, when he resigned; moved to Evansville, Ind., in 1851; invested in large tracts of land; was an author; appointed by President Franklin Pierce as judge of the court of land claims and served from 1855 to 1857; elected as a Democrat to the Thirty-seventh and Thirty-eighth Congresses (March 4, 1861-March 3, 1865); was not a candidate for renomination in 1864 to the Thirty-ninth Congress; resumed the practice of law; died in Evansville, Ind., on October 7, 1873; interment in Greenlawn Cemetery, Vincennes, Ind.

**Bibliography:** *DAB.*

**LAW, Lyman** (son of Richard Law and father of John Law), a Representative from Connecticut; born in New London, Conn., August 19, 1770; pursued classical studies and was graduated from Yale College in 1791; studied law; was admitted to the bar in 1793 and commenced practice in New London; member of the State house of representatives in 1801, 1802, 1806, 1809, 1810, 1819, and 1826, and served as speaker in 1806, 1809, and 1810; elected as a Federalist to the Twelfth, Thirteenth, and Fourteenth Congresses (March 4, 1811-March 3, 1817); resumed the practice of his profession; died in New London, Conn., February 3, 1842; interment in the "Second Burial Ground"; reinterment in Cedar Grove Cemetery in 1851.

**LAW, Richard** (father of Lyman Law and grandfather of John Law), a Delegate from Connecticut; born in Milford, Conn., March 7, 1733; pursued classical studies and was graduated from Yale College in 1751; studied law; was admitted to the bar in January 1755 and practiced in Milford, Conn., 1755-1757 and thereafter in New London; member of the general assembly in 1765; member of the Connecticut Council of Safety in May 1776; chief judge of the county court and of the superior court in 1784; member of the Governor's council, 1776-1786; Member of the Continental Congress in 1777 and 1781-1782; mayor of New London from 1784 until 1806; judge of the supreme court of Connecticut, 1784-1789, and was appointed chief justice of the superior court in May 1786; appointed by President Washington United States district judge for Connecticut on September 24, 1789, and served until his death in New London, New London County, Conn., January 26, 1806; interment in Cedar Grove Cemetery.

**Bibliography:** *DAB*.

**LAWLER, Frank,** a Representative from Illinois; born in Rochester, N.Y., June 25, 1842; attended the public schools; moved with his parents to Chicago, Ill., in 1854; news agent on a railroad for several years and also a brakeman; learned the trade of shipbuilder; was active in organizing trade and labor unions and served as president of the Ship Carpenters and Calkers' Association; employed in the Chicago post office as a letter carrier 1869-1877; member of the city council 1876-1885; engaged in business as a liquor merchant in 1878; elected as a Democrat to the Forty-ninth, Fiftieth, and Fifty-first Congresses (March 4, 1885-March 3, 1891); unsuccessful candidate for sheriff of Cook County in 1891; unsuccessful candidate for election in 1895 to the Fifty-fourth Congress; elected a member of the board of aldermen in 1896 and served until his death in Chicago, Ill., January 17, 1896; interment in Calvary Cemetery.

**LAWLER, Joab,** a Representative from Alabama; born in Union County, N.C., June 12, 1796; moved with his father to Tennessee and thence, in 1815, to Mississippi Territory; attended the public schools; studied theology and was licensed to preach; moved to Mardisville, Ala., in 1820 and pursued his ministerial duties; member of the Alabama State house of representatives, 1826-1831; served in the State senate, 1831-1832; receiver of public moneys for the Coosa land district, 1832-1835; treasurer of the University of Alabama at Tuscaloosa, 1833-1836; elected as a Jacksonian to the Twenty-fourth Congress; reelected as a Whig to the Twenty-fifth Congress, and served from March 4, 1835 until his death in Washington, D.C., on May 8, 1838; interment in the Congressional Cemetery.

**LAWRENCE, Abbott,** a Representative from Massachusetts; born in Groton, Mass., December 16, 1792; attended Groton Academy; became a merchant and importer in Boston; member of the Boston Common Council in 1831; elected as a Whig to the Twenty-fourth Congress (March 4, 1835-March 3, 1837); was not a candidate for renomination in 1836 to the Twenty-fifth Congress; elected to the Twenty-sixth Congress, and served from March 4, 1839 to September 18, 1840, when he resigned; in 1842 appointed as commissioner to settle the northeastern boundary dispute between Canada and the United States; delegate to the Whig National Convention of 1844; temporarily appointed by President Zachary Taylor to be Minister to Great Britain on August 20, 1849; reappointed on January 4, 1850; confirmed June 24, 1850, and served until October 1852, when he resigned and resumed his former business pursuits in Boston; founded the Lawrence Scientific School in Harvard University; died in Boston, Mass., August 18, 1855; interment in Mount Auburn Cemetery, Cambridge, Mass.

**Bibliography:** *DAB*; Brauer, Kinley J. "The Webster-Lawrence Feud; A Study in Politics and Ambitions." *Historian* 29 (November 1966): 34-59.

**LAWRENCE, Cornelius Van Wyck** (cousin of Effingham Lawrence), a Representative from New York; born in Flushing, N.Y., February 18, 1791; attended the common schools; moved to New York City in 1812 and engaged in mercantile pursuits; elected as a Jacksonian to the Twenty-third Congress and served from March 4, 1833 to May 14, 1834, when he resigned; first Mayor of New York City elected by popular vote, 1834-1837; director in several banks and trust companies; collector of customs at the port of New York, 1845-1849; died in Flushing, N.Y., on February 20, 1861; interment in the family burying ground at Bayside, N.Y.

**LAWRENCE, Effingham** (cousin of Cornelius Van Wyck Lawrence), a Representative from Louisiana; born in Bayside, near Flushing, Long Island, N.Y., March 2, 1820; attended schools in Bayside and Flushing; moved to Louisiana about 1843; engaged in planting and the refining of sugar; member of the State house of representatives; successfully contested as a Democrat the election of Jacob Hale Sypher to the Forty-third Congress and took his seat on March 3, 1875, the last day of the session; resumed agricultural pursuits; died on Magnolia plantation, Plaquemines Parish, La., December 9, 1878; interment in Greenwood Cemetery, New Orleans, La.

**LAWRENCE, George Pelton,** a Representative from Massachusetts; born in Adams, Berkshire County, Mass., May 19, 1859; graduated from Drury Academy in 1876 and from Amherst (Mass.) College in 1880; studied law at the Columbia Law School; admitted to the bar in 1883 and commenced practice in North Adams, Mass.; appointed judge of the district of northern Berkshire in 1885; resigned in 1894 upon being elected to the Massachusetts senate; served in the Massachusetts senate 1895-1897 and was its president in 1896 and 1897; elected as a Republican to the Fifty-fifth Congress to fill the vacancy caused by the death of Ashley B. Wright; reelected to the Fifty-sixth and to the six succeeding Congresses and served from November 2, 1897, to March 3, 1913; chairman, Committee on Expenditures in the Department of War (Fifty-ninth through Sixty-first Congresses); was not a candidate for renomination in 1912; member of the Massachusetts Public Service Commission from July 1 to September 17, 1913; died in New York City on November 21, 1917; interment in Hillside Cemetery, North Adams, Mass.

**LAWRENCE, George Van Eman** (son of Joseph Lawrence), a Representative from Pennsylvania; born in Washington County, Pa., November 13, 1818; attended the common schools and Washington College (now Washington and Jefferson College), Washington, Pa.; engaged in agricultural pursuits; member of the Pennsylvania house of representatives in 1844, 1847, 1858, and 1859; served in the Pennsylvania senate 1849-1851 and 1861-1863; presided over the senate in 1863; elected as a Republican to the Thirty-ninth and Fortieth Congresses (March 4, 1865-March 3, 1869); was not a candidate for renomination in 1868; delegate to the Pennsylvania constitutional convention in 1872; member of the Pennsylvania senate under the new constitution in 1875, 1876, and 1878; elected as a Republican to the Forty-eighth Congress (March 4, 1883-March 3, 1885); was not a candidate for renomination in 1884; again served in the Pennsylvania house of representatives 1893-1896; died in

Monongahela, Washington County, Pa., October 2, 1904; interment in the City Cemetery.

**LAWRENCE, Henry Franklin,** a Representative from Missouri; born near Greensburg, Decatur County, Ind., January 31, 1868; attended the public schools, the local high school, and Stanberry (Mo.) Normal School; moved to Cameron, Clinton County, Mo., and engaged in banking; clerk of Daviess County 1907-1911; mayor of Cameron 1914-1918; elected as a Republican to the Sixty-seventh Congress (March 4, 1921-March 3, 1923); unsuccessful candidate for reelection in 1922 to the Sixty-eighth Congress; delegate to the Republican National Convention in 1924; employed with the State finance department of Missouri; died in Cameron, Mo., January 12, 1950; interment in Graceland Cemetery.

**LAWRENCE, John Watson,** a Representative from New York; born in Flushing, N.Y., in August 1800; attended the local schools; engaged as a mercantile clerk; president of the village of Flushing, 1835-1845; member of the New York State assembly in 1840 and 1841; was extensively interested in banking; elected as a Democrat to the Twenty-ninth Congress (March 4, 1845-March 3, 1847); declined to be a candidate for renomination in 1846 and also declined the Democratic nomination for Lieutenant Governor of New York; resumed banking pursuits; trustee of the village of Flushing, 1860-1875; died in Flushing, N.Y., December 20, 1888; interment in Flushing Cemetery.

**LAWRENCE, Joseph** (father of George Van Eman Lawrence), a Representative from Pennsylvania; born near Hunterstown, Adams County, Pa., in 1786; moved with his widowed mother to a farm in Washington County in 1789; attended the common schools; engaged in agricultural pursuits; member of the Pennsylvania house of representatives 1818-1824 and served as speaker 1820-1822; elected to the Nineteenth and Twentieth Congresses (March 4, 1825-March 3, 1829); unsuccessful candidate for reelection in 1828 to the Twenty-first Congress; again a member of the Pennsylvania house of representatives 1834-1836; Pennsylvania treasurer in 1837; unsuccessful candidate for election in 1838 to the Twenty-sixth Congress; elected as a Whig to the Twenty-seventh Congress and served from March 4, 1841, until his death in Washington, D.C., April 17, 1842; chairman, Committee on Roads and Canals (Twenty-seventh Congress); interment in the Congressional Cemetery.

**LAWRENCE, Samuel** (brother of William Thomas Lawrence), a Representative from New York; born in Newtown, Queens County, N.Y., May 23, 1773; attended the common schools; studied law; was admitted to the bar in 1794 and commenced practice in New York City; clerk to the attorney general of the State of New York; appointed judge of marine court (later city court); member of the State assembly in 1808, 1817, and 1818; county clerk of New York County from February 19, 1811, to February 21, 1812; moved to Cayuta Lake, township of Cayuta, Chemung (now Schuyler) County, in 1814; again a member of the State assembly in 1820 and 1821; elected to the Eighteenth Congress (March 4, 1823-March 3, 1825); died at Cayuta Lake near Cayutaville, N.Y., October 20, 1837; interment in the family cemetery at that place.

**LAWRENCE, Sidney,** a Representative from New York; born in Weybridge, Addison County, Vt., December 31, 1801; moved with his parents to Moira, Franklin County, N.Y., in early childhood; attended the common schools; studied law; was admitted to the bar and commenced practice in Moira, N.Y.; was justice of the peace for more than half a century; served as supervisor and as assessor; surrogate of Franklin County 1837-1843; served in the State senate in 1843 and 1844; member of the State assembly in 1846; elected as a Democrat to the Thirtieth Congress (March 4, 1847-March 3, 1849); was not a candidate for renomination in 1848; resumed the practice of law; also engaged in the real estate business and in

banking; died in Moira, N.Y., May 9, 1892; interment in Moira Cemetery.

**LAWRENCE, William,** a Representative from Ohio; born in Washington (now Old Washington), Guernsey County, Ohio, September 2, 1814; pursued classical studies and was graduated from Jefferson College, Canonsburg, Pa., in 1835; engaged in agricultural pursuits; member of the State house of representatives in 1843; delegate to the State constitutional convention in 1851; served in the State senate in 1856 and 1857; elected as a Democrat to the Thirty-fifth Congress (March 4, 1857-March 3, 1859); chairman, Committee on Expenditures in the Department of the Treasury (Thirty-fifth Congress); declined to be a candidate for renomination in 1858; engaged in mercantile pursuits in Old Washington; again a member of the State senate in 1867, 1885, and 1886; member of the board of directors of the Ohio Penitentiary and served as president of the board; died in Old Washington, Guernsey County, Ohio, September 8, 1895; interment in the Washington Cemetery.

**LAWRENCE, William,** a Representative from Ohio; born in Mount Pleasant, Ohio, June 26, 1819; attended the common schools and Tidball's Academy, near Knoxville, Tenn.; taught school in Pennsville and McConnelsville, Ohio; was graduated from Franklin College, New Athens, Ohio, in 1838 and from the Cincinnati Law School in 1840; was admitted to the bar in 1840 and practiced in Zanesville, Ohio, and later in McConnelsville; moved to Bellefontaine in 1841 and continued the practice of law; studied medicine 1841-1843; commissioner of bankruptcy for Logan County in 1842; prosecuting attorney of Logan County in 1845; editor of the Logan Gazette 1845-1847; member of the State house of representatives in 1846 and 1847; served in the State senate 1849-1851 and 1854; supreme court reporter in 1851; judge of the court of common pleas and of the district court from 1857 to 1864, when he resigned; one of the editors of the Western Law Monthly 1859-1862; during the Civil War entered the Union Army in 1862 as colonel of the Eighty-fourth Regiment, Ohio Volunteer Infantry; appointed United States district judge of Florida in 1863 but declined to accept the office; elected as a Republican to the Thirty-ninth, Fortieth, and Forty-first Congresses (March 4, 1865-March 3, 1871); unsuccessful candidate for reelection in 1870 to the Forty-second Congress; organized the Bellefontaine National Bank in 1871, of which he was president; elected to the Forty-third and Forty-fourth Congresses (March 4, 1873-March 3, 1877); chairman, Committee on War Claims (Forty-third Congress); unsuccessful candidate for renomination in 1876; First Comptroller of the United States Treasury 1880-1885; elected president of the National Wool Growers' Association in 1891; died in Kenton, Ohio, May 8, 1899; interment in Bellefontaine Cemetery, Bellefontaine, Ohio.

**Bibliography:** *DAB*.

**LAWRENCE, William Thomas** (brother of Samuel Lawrence), a Representative from New York; born in New York City May 7, 1788; attended the common schools; engaged in mercantile pursuits; during the War of 1812 served in the Fourth Regiment, New York State Artillery; moved to Cayuga County in 1823 and engaged in farming; justice of the peace in 1838; elected to the Thirtieth Congress (March 4, 1847-March 3, 1849); died at his country home near Cayutaville, N.Y., October 25, 1859; interment in the family cemetery on the Shore Road, in the Borough of Queens, New York City.

**LAWS, Gilbert Lafayette,** a Representative from Nebraska; born near Olney, Richland County, Ill., March 11, 1838; moved with his parents to Iowa County, Wis., in 1845; attended the common schools, Haskell University, Mazomanie, Wis., and Milton College, Milton, Wis.; taught school; during the Civil War enlisted in the Fifth Regiment, Wisconsin Volunteer Infantry; returned to Wisconsin and settled in Richland County; county clerk in 1862 and twice reelected; engaged in the publication of a newspaper; member of the city council in 1868 and 1869; mayor of Richland Center in 1869; chairman of the county board of supervisors in 1869 and 1870; postmaster from 1866 to 1876, when he resigned and moved to Orleans, Nebr.; appointed register of the United States land office at McCook, Nebr., in 1883 and served until November 1, 1886; elected secretary of state of Nebraska in 1886 and 1888; elected as a Republican to the Fifty-first Congress to fill the vacancy caused by the death of James Laird and served from December 2, 1889, to March 3, 1891; was not a candidate for renomination in 1890; moved to Enid, Okla., and engaged in the real estate business; returned to Nebraska in 1895 and settled in Lincoln; secretary of the State board of transportation 1896-1900; died in Lincoln, Nebr., April 25, 1907; interment in Wyuka Cemetery.

**LAWSON, John Daniel,** a Representative from New York; born in Montgomery, Orange County, N.Y., February 18, 1816; attended the public schools; moved to New York City and was employed as a clerk in a dry-goods store; later, in 1843, engaged in mercantile pursuits; delegate to every Republican State, county, and district convention for thirty years; delegate to every Republican National Convention from 1868 to 1892; elected as a Republican to the Forty-third Congress (March 4, 1873-March 3, 1875); unsuccessful candidate for reelection; resumed his former business pursuits; died in New York City January 24, 1896; interment in Greenwood Cemetery.

**LAWSON, John William,** a Representative from Virginia; born in James City County, Va., September 13, 1837; attended the schools of Williamsburg, College of William and Mary at Williamsburg, and the University of Virginia at Charlottesville; studied medicine; graduated from the University of the City of New York March 4, 1861; returned to Virginia; during the Civil War enlisted in the Thirty-second Regiment of Virginia Infantry, Confederate Army; assistant surgeon in charge of Artillery battalion; promoted to surgeon March 10, 1864, and served until the surrender at Appomattox April 9, 1865; settled in Isle of Wight County, Va., December 1865; practiced medicine for ten years, when he engaged in agricultural pursuits; member of the Virginia house of delegates 1869-1873; served in the Virginia Senate, 1874-1877; again a member of the Virginia house of delegates in 1883 and 1884; elected as a Democrat to the Fifty-second Congress (March 4, 1891-March 3, 1893); was not a candidate for renomination in 1892; resumed farming; delegate to the Virginia constitutional convention in 1901 and 1902; died in Smithfield, Va., on February 21, 1905; interment in Ivy Hill Cemetery.

**LAWSON, Thomas Graves,** a Representative from Georgia; born near Eatonton, Putnam County, Ga., on May 2, 1835; attended private schools and was graduated from Mercer University, Macon, Ga., in 1855; studied law; was admitted to the bar in 1857 and commenced practice in Eatonton, Ga.; during the Civil War served two years in the Confederate Army; member of the State house of representatives 1861-1866, 1889, and 1890; delegate to the State constitutional convention in 1877; member of the board of trustees of Mercer University and the Eatonton Male and Female Academy; judge of the superior courts of Ocmulgee circuit 1879-1887; engaged in agricultural pursuits near Eatonton, Ga., 1888-1891; elected as a Democrat to the Fifty-second, Fifty-third, and Fifty-fourth Congresses (March 4, 1891-March 3, 1897); unsuccessful candidate for renomination in 1896; resumed agricultural pursuits in Putnam County, Ga.; died in Eatonton, Ga., April 16, 1912; interment in Pine Grove Cemetery.

**LAWYER, Thomas,** a Representative from New York; born in Schoharie, N.Y., October 14, 1785; studied law; was admitted to the bar and practiced in Schoharie County; member of the State house of representatives in 1816; brigadier general of State militia; elected as a Republican to the Fifteenth Congress (March 4, 1817-March 3, 1819); district attorney of Schoharie County 1822-1831; again a

member of the State house of representatives in 1846; died in Lawyersville, Schoharie County, N.Y., May 21, 1868.

**LAXALT, Paul Dominque,** a Senator from Nevada; born in Reno, Washoe County, Nev., August 2, 1922; attended the public schools of Carson City, Nev.; attended Santa Clara (Calif.) University 1940-1943; B.S., University of Denver, 1949; LL.B., University of Denver Law School, 1949; admitted to the Nevada bar in 1949 and commenced practice in Carson City; district attorney, Ormsby County, Nev., 1950-1954; city attorney, Carson City, 1951-1954; Lieutenant Governor of Nevada, 1963-1966; unsuccessful candidate in 1964 for election to the United States Senate; elected Governor of Nevada in 1966, and served from January 2, 1967 to January 4, 1971; elected as a Republican to the United States Senate on November 5, 1974, for the six-year term commencing January 3, 1975; subsequently appointed by the Governor, December 18, 1974, to fill the vacancy caused by the resignation of Alan Bible for the term ending January 3, 1975; reelected in 1980, and served from December 18, 1974, to January 3, 1987; did not seek reelection in 1986; lawyer, practicing in Washington, D.C.; is a resident of Carson City, Nev., and Falls Church, Va.

**LAY, Alfred Morrison,** a Representative from Missouri; born in Lewis County, Mo., May 20, 1836; moved with his parents to Benton County in 1842; attended private schools, and was graduated from Bethany College, Virginia (now in West Virginia), in 1856; studied law; was admitted to the bar in 1857 and commenced practice in Jefferson City, Mo.; appointed United States district attorney for the western district of Missouri by President James Buchanan and served until his resignation in 1861; enlisted as a private in the Missouri State Guard and was subsequently promoted to the rank of major; returned to Missouri when the command disbanded; served as captain of ordnance, Confederate Army; resumed the practice of law in Jefferson City, Mo.; member of the State constitutional convention in 1875; elected as a Democrat to the Forty-sixth Congress and served from March 4, 1879, until his death in Washington, D.C., on December 8, 1879; interment in Woodlawn Cemetery, Jefferson City, Mo.

**LAY, George Washington,** a Representative from New York; born in Catskill, N.Y., July 26, 1798; pursued classical studies and was graduated from Hamilton College at Clinton, N.Y., in 1817; studied law; was admitted to the bar and commenced practice in Batavia, N.Y., in 1820; treasurer of Genesee County, N.Y., 1825-1831; elected as an Anti-Masonic candidate to the Twenty-third Congress and reelected as a Whig to the Twenty-fourth Congress (March 4, 1833-March 3, 1837); member of the State assembly in 1840; Chargé d'Affaires to Sweden from May 12, 1842, to October 29, 1845; died in Batavia, Genesee County, N.Y., October 21, 1860; interment in Batavia Cemetery.

**LAYTON, Caleb Rodney,** a Representative from Delaware; born on the Long farm near Frankford, Sussex County, Del., September 8, 1851; attended the public schools and Georgetown Academy; was graduated from Amherst (Mass.) College in 1873 and from the medical department of the University of Pennsylvania at Philadelphia in 1876 and began the practice of medicine in Georgetown, Del.; secretary of the Republican county committee 1876-1888; chairman of the Union Republican county committee 1896-1901; delegate to the Republican National Conventions in 1896, 1900, and 1904; editor of the Union Republican 1897-1905; secretary of state of Delaware 1901-1905; appointed auditor for the State Department and other departments in Washington, D.C., and served from 1906 to 1910; member of the Progressive State committee 1912-1918; elected as a Republican to the Sixty-sixth and Sixty-seventh Congresses (March 4, 1919-March 3, 1923); unsuccessful candidate for reelection in 1922 to the Sixty-eighth Congress; resumed the practice of medicine in Georgetown, Sussex County,

Del., until his death there on November 11, 1930; interment in St. Paul's Churchyard.

**LAYTON, Fernando Coello,** a Representative from Ohio; born near St. Johns, Auglaize County, Ohio, April 11, 1847; attended the public schools and Wittenberg College, Springfield, Ohio; studied law; was admitted to the bar in 1869 and practiced in Wapakoneta, Ohio; county school examiner; prosecuting attorney of Auglaize County 1875-1878; served as captain of Company G, Ohio National Guard, 1878-1883; elected as a Democrat to the Fifty-second, Fifty-third, and Fifty-fourth Congresses (March 4, 1891-March 3, 1897); was not a candidate for renomination in 1896; resumed the practice of his profession in Wapakoneta, Ohio; elected judge of the court of common pleas in 1908; reelected in 1914 and in 1920, and served until his resignation on June 9, 1926; died in Wapakoneta, Auglaize County, Ohio, on June 22, 1926; interment in Greenlawn Cemetery.

**LAZARO, Ladislas,** a Representative from Louisiana; born near Ville Platte, Evangeline (then St. Landry) Parish, La., June 5, 1872; attended public and private schools and Holy Cross College, New Orleans, La.; was graduated from Louisville (Ky.) Medical College in 1894 and practiced his profession in Washington, La., until 1913; became interested in agricultural pursuits; president of the parish school board for four years; served in the State senate 1908-1912; elected as a Democrat to the Sixty-third and to the seven succeeding Congresses and served from March 4, 1913, until his death in Washington, D.C., March 30, 1927; interment in the Old City Cemetery, Ville Platte, La.

**LAZEAR, Jesse,** a Representative from Pennsylvania; born in Rich Hill Township, Greene County, Pa., December 12, 1804; received a limited schooling; taught school; engaged in mercantile pursuits; recorder for Greene County 1829-1832; bank cashier of the Farmers & Drovers' Bank, Waynesburg, Pa., 1835-1867; elected as a Democrat to the Thirty-seventh and Thirty-eighth Congresses (March 4, 1861-March 3, 1865); chairman, Committee on Expenditures on Public Buildings (Thirty-seventh Congress); was not a candidate for renomination in 1864; delegate to the Union National Convention at Philadelphia in 1866; retired to his country home, "Windsor Mill Farm," in Baltimore County, Md., in 1867; president of the Baltimore & Powhatan Railroad Co. 1871-1874; died at his country home September 2, 1877; interment in Green Mount Cemetery, Waynesburg, Pa.

**LAZIO, Enrico A. (Rick),** a Representative from New York; born in West Islip, Suffolk County, N.Y., March 13, 1958; B.A., Vassar College, 1980; J.D., American University, Washington College of Law; Suffolk County Executive Assistant District Attorney, 1983-1988; member, Suffolk County legislature, 1991-1993; elected as a Republican to the One Hundred Third and One Hundred Fourth Congresses (January 3, 1993-January 3, 1997); is a resident of Brightwaters, N.Y.

**LEA, Clarence Frederick,** a Representative from California; born near Highland Springs, Lake County, Calif., July 11, 1874; attended the common schools, Lakeport Academy, and Stanford University, California; was graduated from the law department of the University of Denver, Colo., in 1898; was admitted to the bar the same year and commenced practice in Santa Rosa, Calif.; district attorney of Sonoma County, 1907-1917; president of the District Attorney's Association of California in 1916 and 1917; elected as a Democrat to the Sixty-fifth and to the fifteen succeeding Congresses (March 4, 1917-January 3, 1949); chairman, Committee on Interstate and Foreign Commerce (Seventy-fifth through Seventy-ninth Congresses); was not a candidate for renomination in 1948 to the Eighty-first Congress; engaged in public relations work in Washington, D.C., 1949-1954; died in Santa Rosa, Calif., June 20, 1964; interment in Franklin Avenue Odd Fellows Cemetery.

**LEA, Luke** (great-grandfather of Luke Lea [1879-1945] and brother of Pryor Lea), a Representative from Tennessee; born in Surry County, N.C., January 21, 1783; moved to Tennessee in 1790 with his parents, who settled in Hawkins County; attended the common schools; clerk in the Tennessee State house of representatives, 1804-1806; commanded a regiment under General Andrew Jackson in the Creek and Seminole Wars in 1818; located at Campbells Station, Tenn., and held several minor offices; elected as a Jacksonian to the Twenty-third Congress and reelected as a Hugh L. White supporter to the Twenty-fourth Congress (March 4, 1833-March 3, 1837); secretary of state of Tennessee, 1837-1839; appointed by President Millard Fillmore as Indian agent at Fort Leavenworth, Kans., September 23, 1850, and served until his death near Fort Leavenworth, Kans., June 17, 1851; interment in Westport Cemetery (now abandoned), Kansas City, Mo.

**LEA, Luke** (great-grandson of Luke Lea [1783-1851]), a Senator from Tennessee; born in Nashville, Tenn., April 12, 1879; attended the public schools; graduated from the University of the South, Sewanee, Tenn., in 1899 and from the law department of Columbia University, New York City, in 1903; was admitted to the bar in 1903 and commenced practice at Nashville; founder, editor and publisher of the Nashville Tennessean; elected as a Democrat to the United States Senate in 1911, and served from March 4, 1911 to March 3, 1917; unsuccessful candidate for renomination in 1916; chairman, Committee on the Library (Sixty-third Congress), Committee to Audit and Control the Contingent Expense (Sixty-fourth Congress); during the First World War, fought in Europe with an artillery unit and rose to the rank of colonel; returned to Nashville and resumed newspaper interests; appointed to the United States Senate in 1929 to fill the vacancy caused by the death of Lawrence D. Tyson, but declined the appointment; entered into the banking and real estate businesses; died in Nashville, Tenn., on November 18, 1945; interment in Mount Olivet Cemetery, Nashville, Tenn.

**Bibliography:** *DAB*; Tidwell, Cromwell. "Luke Lea and the American Legion." *Tennessee Historical Quarterly* 28 (Spring/Winter 1968): 70-83; Tidwell, Mary Louise Lea. *Luke Lea of Tennessee.* Bowling Green, Ohio: Bowling Green State University Popular Press, 1993.

**LEA, Pryor** (brother of Luke Lea [1783-1851]), a Representative from Tennessee; born in Knox County, Tenn., August 31, 1794; completed preparatory studies; was graduated from Greeneville College; studied law; was admitted to the bar in 1817 and commenced the practice of his profession in Knoxville, Tenn.; served in the Creek War in 1813; United States attorney for Tennessee in 1824; elected as a Jacksonian to the Twentieth and Twenty-first Congresses (March 4, 1827-March 3, 1831); unsuccessful candidate for reelection in 1830 to the Twenty-second Congress; moved to Jackson, Miss., in 1836 and to Goliad, Goliad County, Tex., in 1846; engaged in railroad building and management; member of the State People's convention which met at Austin, Tex., in January 1861 and passed the ordinance of secession; died in Goliad, Tex., September 14, 1879; interment in Oak Hill Cemetery.

**LEACH, Anthony Claude, Jr.,** a Representative from Louisiana; born in Leesville, Vernon Parish, La., March 30, 1934; attended the public schools of Louisiana; B.S., Louisiana State University, Baton Rouge, 1955; served in the United States Army, 1956-1959; J.D., Louisiana State University Law School, Baton Rouge, 1963; admitted to the Louisiana bar in 1964 and commenced practice in Leesville; served in the Louisiana house of representatives, 1967-1978; elected as a Democrat to the Ninety-sixth Congress (January 3, 1979-January 3, 1981); unsuccessful candidate for reelection in 1980 to the Ninety-seventh Congress; member, Louisiana house of representatives, 1984 to present; is a resident of Leesville, La.

**LEACH, De Witt Clinton,** a Representative from Michigan; born in Clarence, Erie County, N.Y., November 23, 1822; moved with his parents to Genesee County, Mich., in early youth; attended the common schools; taught school; located in Lansing, Mich., in 1841; editor of the Michigan State Republican for several years; member of the Michigan State house of representatives in 1849 and 1850; delegate to the State constitutional convention in 1850; member of the convention that met under the oaks at Jackson, Mich., July 6, 1854, at the organization of the Republican Party in Michigan; State librarian from 1855 until 1857; elected as a Republican to the Thirty-fifth and Thirty-sixth Congresses (March 4, 1857-March 3, 1861); was not a candidate for renomination in 1860 to the Thirty-seventh Congress; Indian agent for Michigan, by appointment of President Lincoln, 1861-1865; moved to Traverse City, Mich., in 1865, and published the Grand Traverse Herald for nine years; delegate to the State constitutional convention in 1867; moved to Springfield, Mo., in 1875, where he published the Patriot Advertiser; returned to Traverse City, Mich., in 1882 and published the Northwest Farmer; retired in 1902 and returned to Springfield, Mo., where he died on December 21, 1909; interment in Maple Park Cemetery.

**LEACH, James Albert Smith,** a Representative from Iowa; born in Davenport, Scott County, Iowa, October 15, 1942; attended the public schools of Davenport; graduated, Davenport High School, 1960; B.A., Princeton University, 1964; M.A., School of Advanced International Studies of Johns Hopkins University, Washington, D.C., 1966; research student, London School of Economics, 1966-1968; member of the staff of Representative Donald Rumsfeld of Illinois, 1965-1966; served as a foreign service officer in United States Department of State, 1968-1969; special assistant to director, Office of Economic Opportunity, 1969-1970; again served in Department of State, as a member of the Delegation to the Geneva Disarmament Conference and the United Nations General Assembly, 1971-1972; in 1973 became president of Flamegas Co., Inc., Bettendorf, Iowa; appointed to the United Nations Conference on Natural Resources, 1975; served as a member of the United States Advisory Commission on International Education and Cultural Affairs, 1975; Director, Federal Home Loan Bank Board, 1975-1976; delegate, Iowa State Republican conventions 1974, 1976; elected as a Republican to the Ninety-fifth and to the nine succeeding Congresses (January 3, 1977-January 3, 1997); chairman, Committee on Banking and Financial Services (One Hundred Fourth Congress); is a resident of Davenport, Iowa.

**LEACH, James Madison,** a Representative from North Carolina; born at the family homestead, "Lansdowne," Randolph County, N.C., January 17, 1815; attended the common schools and Caldwell Institute, Greensboro, N.C.; was graduated from the United States Military Academy, West Point, N.Y., in 1838; studied law; was admitted to the bar in 1842 and commenced practice in Lexington, N.C.; member of the State house of commons 1848-1858; presidential elector on the American Party ticket in 1856; elected as an Opposition Party candidate to the Thirty-sixth Congress (March 4, 1859-March 3, 1861); captain and lieutenant colonel in the Confederate Army during the Civil War; member of the Confederate States Congress in 1864 and 1865; member of the State senate in 1865, 1866, and again in 1879; elected as a Democrat to the Forty-second and Forty-third Congresses (March 4, 1871-March 3, 1875); declined to be a candidate for renomination in 1874; died in Lexington, N.C., June 1, 1891; interment in Hopewell Cemetery, near Trinity, Randolph County, N.C.

**LEACH, Robert Milton,** a Representative from Massachusetts; born in Franklin, Merrimack County, N.H., April 2, 1879; attended the public schools, Phillips Academy, Andover, Mass., and Dartmouth College, Hanover, N.H.; moved to Taunton, Mass., in 1900 and engaged in the chain-store furniture business in New England; commissioned as captain in the Ordnance Division of the United States Army during the First World War; elected as a Republican to the Sixty-eighth Congress to fill the vacancy caused by the death of William S. Greene and served from November 4, 1924, to March 3, 1925; was not a candidate for renomination in 1924; resumed his former business activities in Taunton, Mass.; died in Eustis, Fla., February 18, 1952; interment in Franklin Cemetery, Franklin, N.H.

**LEADBETTER, Daniel Parkhurst,** a Representative from Ohio; born in Pittsfield, Berkshire County, Mass., September 10, 1797; attended the common schools; moved to Ohio in 1816 and settled in Steubenville, Jefferson County, where he studied law; was admitted to the bar in 1821 and commenced practice in Steubenville; commissioned captain of the Second Company, Third Regiment, Sixth Division, Ohio Militia, in 1821; moved to Millersburg, Holmes County, in 1828 and continued the practice of law; commissioned quartermaster of the Fourth Division of the Ohio Militia in 1831; county recorder 1831-1836; elected as a Democrat to the Twenty-fifth and Twenty-sixth Congresses (March 4, 1837-March 3, 1841); was not a candidate for renomination in 1840; resumed the practice of his profession; also engaged in agricultural pursuits and stock raising; member of the State constitutional convention in 1851; served as a captain in the Civil War in 1862; died in Millersburg, Ohio, on February 26, 1870; interment in Oak Hill Cemetery.

**LEAHY, Edward Laurence,** a Senator from Rhode Island; born in Bristol, R.I., February 9, 1886; attended the public schools; student at Brown University in 1904 and 1905; graduated from the law school of Georgetown University, Washington, D.C., in 1908; was admitted to the Rhode Island bar in 1908 and commenced the practice of law in Bristol, R.I.; judge of probate court, Bristol, R.I., 1910-1939; member, Rhode Island State house of representatives, 1911-1913; elected to the Bristol school committee in 1913; served as master of chancery in the superior court; during the First World War served as a first lieutenant, Judge Advocate General's Department, United States Army; administrator of State taxes, 1919-1948; director of State department of revenue and regulation in 1939; director of finance, member of the State sinking fund commission (instituted to pay off the principal of the State's debt), and the State retirement board, 1942-1946; adviser to the State department of finance, 1948-1949; appointed as a Democrat to the United States Senate to fill the vacancy caused by the resignation of J. Howard McGrath, and served from August 24, 1949 to December 18, 1950, a successor having been elected and qualified; was not a candidate for election to the vacancy; United States judge for the district of Rhode Island from January 1951 until his death in Bristol, R.I., July 22, 1953; interment in North Cemetery.

**LEAHY, Patrick Joseph,** a Senator from Vermont; born in Montpelier, Washington County Vt., March 31, 1940; graduated from St. Michael's High School, Montpelier, Vt., 1957; B.A., St. Michael's College, Winooski, Vt., 1961; J.D., Georgetown University Law Center, 1964; admitted to the Vermont bar in 1964 and commenced practice in Burlington; State's attorney, Chittenden County, Vt., 1966-1974; elected as a Democrat to the United States Senate in 1974 for the term commencing January 3, 1975; reelected in 1980, 1986, and again in 1992 for the term ending January 3, 1999; chairman, Committee on Agriculture, Nutrition and Forestry (One Hundredth through One Hundred Third Congresses); is a resident of Burlington, Vt.

**LEAKE, Eugene Walter,** a Representative from New Jersey; born in Jersey City, N.J., July 13, 1877; attended the public schools and Phillips Academy, Andover, Mass.; graduated from New York Law School in 1898; was admitted to the New Jersey bar in 1898 and commenced practice in Jersey City, N.J.; was admitted to the New York bar in 1908 and practiced in New York City; elected as a Democrat to the Sixtieth Congress (March 4, 1907-March 3, 1909);

was not a candidate for renomination in 1908; general counsel for the Adams Express Co., 1927-1932; in 1931 was elected chairman of the board of directors of the American Railway Express Co.; director of Loew's, Inc.; died in New York City on August 23, 1959; interment in Cedar Lawn Cemetery, Paterson, N.J.

**LEAKE, Shelton Farrar,** a Representative from Virginia; born near Hillsboro, Albemarle County, Va., November 30, 1812; completed preparatory studies; taught school; studied law; was admitted to the bar in 1835 and commenced practice in Charlottesville, Va.; member of the Virginia house of delegates in 1842 and 1843; elected as a Democrat to the Twenty-ninth Congress (March 4, 1845-March 3, 1847); resumed the practice of law; elected Lieutenant Governor of Virginia in 1851; elected as an Independent Democrat to the Thirty-sixth Congress (March 4, 1859-March 3, 1861); again resumed the practice of law; died in Charlottesville, Va., on March 4, 1884; interment in Maplewood Cemetery.

**LEAKE, Walter,** a Senator from Mississippi; born in Albemarle County, Va., May 25, 1762; served in the Revolutionary War; studied law; was admitted to the bar and practiced; appointed by President Thomas Jefferson as one of the United States judges for Mississippi Territory in 1807; moved to Hinds County, Miss., and engaged in the practice of law; upon the admission of Mississippi as a State into the Union was elected as a Republican to the United States Senate, and served from December 10, 1817 to May 15, 1820, when he resigned; chairman, Committee on Indian Affairs (Sixteenth Congress); appointed United States marshal for the district of Mississippi in 1820; elected Governor of Mississippi in 1821, reelected in 1823, and served from January 7, 1822 until his death in Mount Salus, Hinds County, Miss., November 17, 1825.

**Bibliography:** Fike, Claude. "The Administration of Walter Leake." *Journal of Mississippi History* 32 (May 1970): 103-15.

**LEARNED, Amasa** (grandfather of John Law), a Representative from Connecticut; born in Killingly, Conn., November 15, 1750; prepared for college by a private tutor; was graduated from Yale College in 1772; taught in the Union School, New London; studied theology; received a license from the Windham Association on October 10, 1773, and preached for a short time; commenced the study of law in 1778; member of the State house of representatives in 1779; moved to New London; member of the State house of representatives 1785-1791; member of the convention which ratified the Constitution of the United States in 1788; elected to the upper house of assistants in 1791; elected to the Second and Third Congresses (March 4, 1791-March 3, 1795); engaged in land speculations; delegate to the State constitutional convention in 1818; died in New London, New London County, Conn., May 4, 1825; interment in Cedar Grove Cemetery.

**LEARY, Cornelius Lawrence Ludlow,** a Representative from Maryland; born in Baltimore, Md., October 22, 1813; attended the public schools; was graduated from St. Mary's College, Baltimore, in 1833; moved to Louisville, Ky.; returned to Baltimore in 1837; Whig member of the State house of delegates in 1838 and 1839; studied law; was admitted to the bar in 1840 and commenced practice in Baltimore; presidential elector on the American Party ticket in 1856; elected as a Unionist to the Thirty-seventh Congress (March 4, 1861-March 3, 1863); resumed the practice of law in Baltimore, Md., and died there March 21, 1893; interment in Lorraine Cemetery.

**LEATH, James Marvin,** a Representative from Texas; born in Henderson, Rusk County, Tex., May 6, 1931; attended the Rusk County public schools; graduated from Henderson High School, 1949; attended Kilgore (Tex.) Junior College; B.B.A., University of Texas, Austin, 1954; served in the United States Army, 1954-1956; coached football and track, Henderson High School, 1957-1959; business salesman, 1959; banking, 1962; officer and director in five Texas banks, and two manufacturing companies; special assistant to

Representative W.R. Poage of Texas, 1972-1974; elected as a Democrat to the Ninety-sixth and to the five succeeding Congresses (January 3, 1979-January 3, 1991); was not a candidate for reelection in 1990 to the One Hundred Second Congress; is a resident of Waco, Tex.

**LEATHERWOOD, Elmer O.,** a Representative from Utah; born on a farm near Waverly, Pike County, Ohio, September 4, 1872; attended the public schools; moved to Emporia, Kans., in 1888; was graduated from the Kansas State Normal School at Emporia, Kans., in 1894; engaged in public school work from 1894 until 1898; studied law; was admitted to the bar at Hiawatha, Brown County, Kans., in 1898; was graduated from the law department of the University of Wisconsin at Madison in 1901 and was admitted to practice; moved to Salt Lake City, Utah, the same year and continued the practice of his profession; district attorney for the third judicial district of Utah, 1908-1916; delegate to the Republican National Convention of 1924; served as president of the Western Powder Co., Leary & Warren Stockyards, Hellgate Mining & Milling Co., and the Olympus Mining & Milling Co.; elected as a Republican to the Sixty-seventh and to the four succeeding Congresses and served from March 4, 1921, until his death in Washington, D.C., on December 24, 1929; chairman, Committee on Expenditures on Public Buildings (Sixty-eighth and Sixty-ninth Congresses); interment in Mount Olivet Cemetery, Salt Lake City, Utah.

**LEAVENWORTH, Elias Warner,** a Representative from New York; born in Canaan, N.Y., December 20, 1803; moved with his parents to Great Barrington, Mass., in 1806; attended the Hudson Academy and was graduated from Yale College in 1824; studied law in Great Barrington and in the Litchfield (Conn.) Law School, 1825-1827; was admitted to the bar in 1827 and practiced in Syracuse, N.Y., until 1850, when he abandoned the practice of law because of ill health; passed through the various grades and was appointed brigadier general of militia in 1836; president of Syracuse village, 1839-1841, 1846, and 1847; mayor of the town in 1849, 1850, 1859, and 1860; member of the New York State assembly in 1850 and 1857; secretary of state of New York in 1854 and 1855; president of the Republican State convention in 1860; commissioner for the United States under the convention with New Granada in Washington, D.C., in 1861 and 1862; appointed president of the board of commissioners to locate the State asylum for the blind, and a trustee of the State asylum for the insane in 1865; member of the New York and New Jersey Boundary Line Commission in 1875; elected as a Republican to the Forty-fourth Congress (March 4, 1875-March 3, 1877); declined to be a candidate for renomination in 1876 to the Forty-fifth Congress; resumed business activities in Syracuse, N.Y., and died there on November 25, 1887; interment in Oakwood Cemetery.

**LEAVITT, Humphrey Howe,** a Representative from Ohio; born in Suffield, Conn., June 18, 1796; moved to the Northwest Territory in 1800 with his parents, who settled in what became Trumbull County, Ohio; completed preparatory studies; attended an academy in western Pennsylvania; taught school; clerked in a store; studied law; was admitted to the bar in 1816 and commenced practice in Cadiz, Ohio; moved to Steubenville in 1819; prosecuting attorney of Jefferson County 1823-1829; member of the State house of representatives in 1825 and 1826; served in the State senate in 1827 and 1828; clerk of the common pleas and supreme court of Jefferson County in 1828; elected as a Jacksonian to the Twenty-first Congress to fill the vacancy caused by the resignation of John M. Goodenow; reelected to the Twenty-second and Twenty-third Congresses and served from December 6, 1830, until July 10, 1834, when he resigned to accept a judicial position; appointed by President Jackson to be United States judge of the district court for the district of Ohio on June 30, 1834, and served until March 31, 1871, when he resigned; moved to Cincinnati, Ohio, in 1855, when the State was divided into two Federal districts; returned to Springfield in 1871; engaged in literary pursuits; was a member of the World's Convention on Prison Reform in London in 1872; died in Springfield, Ohio, March 15, 1873; interment in Spring Grove Cemetery, Cincinnati, Ohio.

Bibliography: *DAB.*

**LEAVITT, Scott,** a Representative from Montana; born in Elk Rapids, Antrim County, Mich., June 16, 1879; moved with his father to Bellaire, Mich., in 1881; attended the public schools; while in high school enlisted in the Thirty-third Regiment, Michigan Volunteer Infantry, during the Spanish-American War, and served in the campaign at Santiago, Cuba; attended the University of Michigan at Ann Arbor; moved to Oregon in 1901 and took up a homestead in the Coast Range Mountains near Falls City; school principal in Falls City, North Yamhill, Dayton, and Lakeview, Oreg., 1901-1907; entered the Forest Service as a ranger at Fremont National Forest in Oregon in 1907 and served in Minnesota and Montana until 1917; elected as a Republican to the Sixty-eighth and to the four succeeding Congresses (March 4, 1923-March 3, 1933); chairman, Committee on Indian Affairs (Sixty-ninth through Seventy-first Congresses); unsuccessful candidate for reelection in 1932 to the Seventy-third Congress and for election in 1934 to the United States Senate; delegate to the Republican National Convention in 1932; again became connected with the Forest Service at Milwaukee, Wis., in 1935; commander-in-chief of the United Spanish War Veterans 1936-1937; retired from the Forest Service in 1941 and moved to Newberg, Oreg., where he died October 19, 1966; interment in Willamette National Cemetery, Portland, Oreg.

**LEAVY, Charles Henry,** a Representative from Washington; born on a farm near York, York County, Pa., February 16, 1884; moved to Kansas City, Mo., with his parents in 1887; attended the public schools of Missouri, the Warrensburg (Mo.) Normal School, the Bellingham (Wash.) Normal School, and the Kansas City (Mo.) School of Law; taught school near Independence, Mo., 1903-1906, and at Everson, Touchet, Kahlotus, and Connell, Wash., 1906-1913; studied law; was admitted to the bar in 1912 and commenced practice in Newport, Pend Oreille County, Wash.; prosecuting attorney of Pend Oreille County, Wash., 1915-1918; moved to Spokane, Wash., in 1918; special assistant United States district attorney for eastern Washington 1918-1921; prosecuting attorney of Spokane County, Wash., 1922-1926; served as judge of the superior court of the State of Washington 1926-1936; elected as a Democrat to the Seventy-fifth, Seventy-sixth, and Seventy-seventh Congresses and served from January 3, 1937, until his resignation on August 1, 1942, having been appointed United States district judge of the western district of Washington and served until his retirement September 1, 1952; died in Tacoma, Wash., September 25, 1952; interment in Mountain View Memorial Park, Tacoma, Wash.

**LE BLOND, Francis Celeste** (grandfather of Frank Le Blond Kloeb), a Representative from Ohio; born in Bellville, Ohio, February 14, 1821; pursued an academic course; studied law; was admitted to the bar in 1844 and commenced practice in Celina, Ohio; member of the State house of representatives 1851-1855; served as speaker of the house in 1854 and 1855; elected as a Democrat to the Thirty-eighth and Thirty-ninth Congresses (March 4, 1863-March 3, 1867); declined to be a candidate for renomination in 1866; resumed the practice of law and also engaged in business; died in Celina, Ohio, November 9, 1902; interment in North Grove Cemetery.

**LeBOUTILLIER, John,** a Representative from New York; born in Glen Cove, Nassau County, N.Y., May 26, 1953; attended grammar school in Greenvale, N.Y.; graduated from Brooks School, North Andover, Mass., 1971; A.B., Harvard University, 1976; M.B.A., Harvard University Business School, 1979; elected as a Republican to the Ninety-seventh Congress (January 3, 1981-January 3, 1983); unsuccessful candidate for reelection in 1982 to

the Ninety-eighth Congress; president of account, POW/MIA, Inc.; chairman of the board, Winston Churchill Foundation; is a resident of Westbury, N.Y.

**LECOMPTE, Joseph,** a Representative from Kentucky; born in Woodford County, near the town of Georgetown, Scott County, Ky., December 15, 1797; moved to Henry County with his parents, who settled in Lecomptes Bottom on the Kentucky River; attended the common schools; engaged in agricultural pursuits; during the War of 1812 served with the Kentucky Riflemen in the Battle of New Orleans, January 8, 1815; member of the Kentucky house of representatives in 1819, 1822, 1838, 1839, and 1844; served as a major in the Kentucky militia; elected to the Nineteenth Congress; reelected to the Twentieth and Twenty-first Congresses and reelected as a Jacksonian to the Twenty-second Congress (March 4, 1825-March 3, 1833); was not a candidate for renomination in 1832 to the Twenty-third Congress; resumed agricultural pursuits; member of the Kentucky constitutional convention in 1850; died in Henry County, Ky., April 25, 1851; interment in the private cemetery in Lecomptes Bottom, on the Kentucky River, Henry County, Ky.

**LE COMPTE, Karl Miles,** a Representative from Iowa; born in Corydon, Wayne County, Iowa, May 25, 1887; attended the public schools and was graduated from the State University of Iowa at Iowa City in 1909; became owner and publisher of the Corydon Times-Republican in 1910; during the First World War served as a private in the medical detachment of United States General Hospital No. 26 in 1918; member of the State senate 1917-1921; elected as a Republican to the Seventy-sixth and to the nine succeeding Congresses (January 3, 1939-January 3, 1959); chairman, Committee on House Administration (Eightieth and Eighty-third Congresses); was not a candidate for renomination in 1958 to the Eighty-sixth Congress; returned to newspaper publishing; retired but continued as a contributing editor; died in Centerville, Iowa, September 30, 1972; interment in Corydon Cemetery, Corydon, Iowa.

**LEDERER, Raymond Francis,** a Representative from Pennsylvania; born in Philadelphia, Pa., May 19, 1938; attended the Catholic schools of Philadelphia; graduated from Roman Catholic High School, 1956; attended St. Joseph's College of Philadelphia, 1960-1965, Community College of Philadelphia, 1967-1969, Pennsylvania State University, University Park, 1972; assistant engineer, Pennsylvania Department of Highways, 1957; probation officer, later director, Philadelphia Probation Department, 1967-1974; board member, Pennsylvania Committee on Probation; member, Pennsylvania house of representatives, 1974-1977; elected as a Democrat to the Ninety-fifth, Ninety-sixth and Ninety-seventh Congresses and served from January 3, 1977, until his resignation on April 29, 1981; is a resident of Philadelphia, Pa.

**LEE, Arthur** (brother of Francis Lightfoot Lee and Richard Henry Lee), a Delegate from Virginia; born at "Stratford," in Westmoreland County, Va., December 20, 1740; attended Eton College, England; studied medicine at the University of Edinburgh, Scotland, and was graduated in 1765; returned to London in 1766 and studied law at Temple Bar 1766-1770; was admitted to the bar and practiced in London 1770-1776; commissioned as agent of Massachusetts in England and France in 1770; appointed correspondent of Congress in London in 1775; commissioner to France in 1776 and to Spain in 1777; returned to Virginia in 1780; member of the Virginia house of delegates 1781-1783, 1785, and 1786; member of the Continental Congress 1782-1784; member of the Treasury board 1785-1789; died in Urbanna, Middlesex County, Va., on December 12, 1792; interment in Lansdowne Garden, in the rear of "Lansdowne," his home, at Urbanna, Va.

Bibliography: *DAB*; Potts, Louis W. *Arthur Lee, A Virtuous Revolutionary.* Baton Rouge: Louisiana State University Press,

1981; Riggs, A.R. *The Nine Lives of Arthur Lee, Virginia Patriot.* Williamsburg: Virginia Independence Bicentennial Commission, 1976.

**LEE, Blair** (great-grandson of Richard Henry Lee), a Senator from Maryland; born in Silver Spring, Montgomery County, Md., August 9, 1857; attended the common schools; graduated from Princeton College in 1880 and from the law department of Columbian (now George Washington) University, Washington, D.C., in 1882; was admitted to the bar of the District of Columbia and of Montgomery County, Md., in 1883 and commenced practice in Maryland; unsuccessful candidate for election to the Fifty-fifth Congress in 1896; member, Maryland State senate, 1905-1913; unsuccessful candidate for Governor of Maryland in 1911; elected as a Democrat to the United States Senate on November 4, 1913, to fill the vacancy caused by the death of Isidor Rayner; credentials were presented on December 5, 1913, but he did not qualify until January 28, 1914, and served until March 3, 1917; chairman, Committee on Expenditures in the Post Office Department (Sixty-third Congress), Committee on Coast Defenses (Sixty-third and Sixty-fourth Congresses); resumed the practice of law; died in Norwood, Md., on December 25, 1944; interment in Rock Creek Cemetery, Washington, D.C.

**LEE, Francis Lightfoot** (brother of Arthur Lee and Richard Henry Lee), a Delegate from Virginia; born at "Stratford," in Westmoreland County, Va., October 14, 1734; pursued classical studies under private teachers; member of the Virginia house of burgesses 1758-1775; signed the Westmoreland Association against the stamp act; Member of the Continental Congress 1775-1779; one of the signers of the Declaration of Independence; member of the Virginia house of delegates in 1780 and 1781; served in the Virginia senate 1778-1782; died at his home, "Menoken," in Richmond County, Va., January 11, 1797; interment in wife's family (Tayloe) burial ground, Mount Airy plantation, near Warsaw, Va.

**Bibliography:** *DAB*; Dill, Alonzo Thomas. *Francis Lightfoot Lee, The Improbable Signer.* Williamsburg: Virginia Independence Bicentennial Commission, 1977.

**LEE, Frank Hood,** a Representative from Missouri; born on a farm near De Soto, Johnson County, Kans., March 29, 1873; moved to Missouri with his parents, who settled near Virgil City, Vernon County, in 1876; attended the public schools of Virgil City, Mo.; studied law; served as justice of the peace in 1894; was admitted to the bar in 1904 and commenced practice in Joplin, Mo.; member of the State house of representatives 1915-1918; unsuccessful candidate for election in 1922 to the Sixty-eighth Congress and in 1930 to the Seventy-second Congress; elected as a Democrat to the Seventy-third Congress (March 4, 1933-January 3, 1935); unsuccessful candidate for reelection in 1934 to the Seventy-fourth Congress; resumed the practice of law until his retirement; owned and operated the Southwestern, a Jasper County newspaper, and the Jefferson Hotel; died in Joplin, Mo., November 20, 1952; interment in Ozark Memorial Park.

**LEE, Gary Alcide,** a Representative from New York; born in Buffalo, Erie County, N.Y., August 18, 1933; attended the public schools of Corning, N.Y.; graduated from Corning Northside High School, 1951; served in the United States Navy, 1952-1956; second class petty officer; B.A., Colgate University, Hamilton, N.Y., 1960; pursued graduate studies at Colgate University in 1960, and at Cornell University, Ithaca, N.Y., in 1963; educational administrator and consultant, Cornell University, 1963-1979; chairman, Tompkins County Republican Party, 1969-1974; alderman, Corning, N.Y., common council, 1962; councilman, Dryden, N.Y., town board, 1963-1967; supervisor, Dryden, N.Y., 1967-1969; member, Tompkins County Board of Supervisors and Board of Representatives, 1968-1974, and served as chairman in 1974; member of the New York State assembly, 1974-1978; delegate, New York State Republican conventions, 1966-1970; elected as a Republican to the Ninety-sixth and the Ninety-seventh Congresses (January 3, 1979-January 3, 1983); unsuccessful candidate for renomination in 1982 to the Ninety-eighth Congress; corporate vice president, IC Industries, Inc.; president and chief executive officer, Gary A. Lee Group, Inc.; is a resident of Sanibel Island, Fla.

**LEE, Gideon,** a Representative from New York; born in Amherst, Mass., April 27, 1778; attended the common schools; learned the trade of shoemaker and engaged in that business in Worthington, Mass.; moved to New York City and thence to Georgia, where he engaged in the mercantile business until 1807; returned to New York City in 1807 and engaged in the leather business; member of the State assembly in 1822; member of the board of aldermen 1828-1830; mayor of New York City in 1833; declined to be a candidate for reelection; elected as a Jacksonian to the Twenty-fourth Congress to fill the vacancy caused by the resignation of Campbell P. White and served from November 4, 1835, to March 3, 1837; was not a candidate for renomination in 1836; retired in 1836; moved to Geneva, N.Y.; died in Geneva, N.Y., August 21, 1841; interment in the Washington Street Cemetery.

**LEE, Gordon,** a Representative from Georgia; born near Ringgold, Catoosa County, Ga., May 29, 1859; attended the common schools; was graduated from Emory College, Oxford, Ga., in 1880; engaged in agricultural pursuits and in manufacturing at Chickamauga, Ga.; member of the Georgia State house of representatives in 1894 and 1895; served in the Georgia State senate, 1902-1904; appointed by Governor William Y. Atkinson a member of the State memorial board; elected as a Democrat to the Fifty-ninth and to the ten succeeding Congresses (March 4, 1905-March 3, 1927); was not a candidate for renomination in 1926 to the Seventieth Congress; member of the National Forest Reservation Commission created by the act of March 1, 1911; delegate to the Democratic National Convention of 1924; resumed agricultural pursuits; died at Chickamauga, Ga., November 7, 1927; interment in Chickamauga Cemetery.

**LEE, Henry** (brother of Richard Bland Lee and grandfather of William Henry Fitzhugh Lee), a Delegate and a Representative from Virginia; born at "Leesylvania," in Prince William County, Va., January 29, 1756; pursued classical studies and was graduated from Princeton College in 1773; served in the Revolutionary War; commissioned captain of a company of Virginia Dragoons on June 18, 1776, that became attached to and part of the First Continental Dragoons on March 31, 1777; commissioned lieutenant colonel on November 6, 1780, and served until the close of the war; commissioned major general, United States Army, July 19, 1798; honorably discharged on June 15, 1800; became universally known as "Light Horse Harry"; Member of the Continental Congress, 1786-1788; advocated the adoption of the Federal Constitution in the Virginia convention of 1788; elected Governor of Virginia by the General Assembly, and served from December 1, 1791 to December 1, 1794; commanded the United States forces in the Whiskey Rebellion of 1794; elected as a Federalist to the Sixth Congress (March 4, 1799-March 3, 1801); at the request of Congress pronounced the eulogy upon President George Washington before both branches of Congress, in which Washington was characterized as the man "first in war, first in peace, and first in the hearts of his countrymen"; died on Cumberland Island, Ga., March 25, 1818; interment at Dungeness, Ga.; reinterment in the crypt, Lee Memorial Chapel, Washington-Lee University, at Lexington, Va., May 30, 1913.

**Bibliography:** *DAB*; Royster, Charles. *Light-Horse Harry Lee and the Legacy of the American Revolution.* New York: Knopf, 1981.

**LEE, John** (son of Thomas Sim Lee), a Representative from Maryland; born at "Needwood," near Frederick, Frederick County, Md., January 30, 1788; was educated by private tutors and at Harvard University; in early life a member of the Federalist Party; studied law, but did not practice; engaged in the management of his estate "Needwood"; elected to the Eighteenth Congress (March 4, 1823-March 3, 1825); chairman of the committee of the House of Representatives appointed to escort the Marquis de Lafayette from Frederick City to Washington in 1825; member of the house of delegates; served in the State senate; one of the proponents of the Chesapeake & Ohio Canal and of the Baltimore & Ohio Railroad; resumed management of his estate; died while on a visit to his son in New York City May 17, 1871; interment in New Cathedral Cemetery, formerly called "Bonnie Brae," Baltimore, Md.

**LEE, Joshua,** a Representative from New York; born in Hudson, N.Y., in 1783; studied medicine and was licensed to practice in 1804; commissioned in 1811 by Governor Daniel D. Tompkins as surgeon of Colonel Avery Smith's regiment of Infantry, and served in that capacity during the War of 1812; supervisor of the town of Benton, Yates County, in 1815; member of the New York State assembly in 1817 and again in 1833; elected as a Jacksonian to the Twenty-fourth Congress (March 4, 1835-March 3, 1837); resumed the practice of his profession; unsuccessful candidate for election to the United States Senate in 1839; died in Penn Yan, N.Y., December 29, 1842; interment in Lake View Cemetery.

**LEE, Joshua Bryan,** a Representative and a Senator from Oklahoma; born in Childersburg, Talladega County, Ala., January 23, 1892; moved with his parents to Pauls Valley, Okla. (then Indian Territory), and then to Kiowa County, near Hobart in 1901; attended the public schools of Hobart and Rocky, Okla., and the Oklahoma Baptist University at Shawnee; teacher in the public schools of Rocky, Okla., 1911-1913; coach of athletics and teacher of public speaking at the Oklahoma Baptist University 1913-1915; graduated from the University of Oklahoma at Norman 1917; received a graduate degree in political science from Columbia University in 1924, and a law degree from Cumberland University, Lebanon, Tenn., in 1925; during the First World War served overseas as a private in the One Hundred and Thirty-fifth Infantry, Thirty-fourth Division 1917-1918; head of the public speaking department of the University of Oklahoma 1919-1934; author and lecturer; owned and operated a ranch in western Oklahoma and a farm near Norman, Okla.; elected as a Democrat to the Seventy-fourth Congress (January 3, 1935-January 3, 1937); was not a candidate for renomination in 1936; elected as a Democrat to the United States Senate and served from January 3, 1937, to January 3, 1943; unsuccessful candidate for reelection in 1942; member of the Civil Aeronautics Board 1943-1955; returned to Norman, Okla., and practiced law; died in Norman, Okla., August 10, 1967; interment in I. O. O. F. Cemetery.

**LEE, Moses Lindley,** a Representative from New York; born in Minisink, N.Y., May 29, 1805; pursued classical studies; was graduated from Union College in 1827 and from the College of Physicians and Surgeons of Western New York in 1830; practiced medicine in Fulton, Oswego County, N.Y.; postmaster at Fulton 1840-1844; member of the State assembly in 1847 and 1848; served in the State senate in 1855; elected as a Republican to the Thirty-sixth Congress (March 4, 1859-March 3, 1861); resumed the practice of medicine in Fulton, N.Y.; returning from a visit in the South became seriously ill at Petersburg, Va., and died there on May 19, 1876; interment in Mount Adnah Cemetery, Fulton, N.Y.

**LEE, Richard Bland** (brother of Henry Lee), a Representative from Virginia; born at "Leesylvania," in Prince William County, Va., January 20, 1761; pursued English and classical studies in private schools; attended the College of William and Mary, Williamsburg, Va.; member of the Virginia house of delegates, 1784-1788; elected to the First and to the two succeeding Congresses (March 4, 1789-March 3, 1795); unsuccessful candidate for reelection in 1794 to the Fourth Congress; again a member of the Virginia house of delegates in 1796, and from 1799 until 1806; moved to Washington, D.C., about 1815; appointed by President James Madison in 1816 commissioner to adjudicate claims arising out of the loss or destruction of property during the War of 1812; appointed by President James Monroe in 1819 judge of the Orphans' Court of the District of Columbia, and served until his death in Washington, D.C., March 12, 1827; interment in the Congressional Cemetery.

**Bibliography:** *DAB.*

**LEE, Richard Henry** (brother of Arthur Lee and Francis Lightfoot Lee, and great-grandfather of Blair Lee), a Delegate and a Senator from Virginia; born at "Stratford," in Westmoreland County, Va., January 20, 1732; after a course of private instruction attended Wakefield Academy, England; returned in 1751; justice of the peace for Westmoreland County in 1757; member of the Virginia house of burgesses, 1758-1775; member of the Continental Congress, 1774-1779; sponsor of the independence resolution; a signer of the Declaration of Independence; author of the first national Thanksgiving Day proclamation issued by Congress at York, Pa., October 31, 1777; member of the Virginia house of delegates in 1777, 1780, 1785; served as colonel of the Westmoreland Militia; again a member of the Continental Congress, 1784-1785 and 1787, and served as President of the Congress in 1784; member of the Virginia convention which ratified the Federal Constitution in 1788; elected to the United States Senate, and served from March 4, 1789 until his resignation on October 8, 1792; served as President pro tempore during the Second Congress; retired from public life; died at his home, "Chantilly," Westmoreland County, Va., June 19, 1794; interment in the old family burying ground at "Mount Pleasant," near Hague, Westmoreland County, Va.

**Bibliography:** *DAB*; Lee, Richard Henry. *The Letters of Richard Henry Lee.* Edited by James Ballagh. 1911-1914. Reprint. New York: Da Capo Press, 1970; Chitwood, Oliver. *Richard Henry Lee, Statesman of the Revolution.* Morgantown: University Library, 1967.

**LEE, Robert Emmett,** a Representative from Pennsylvania; born in Pottsville, Schuykill County, Pa., October 12, 1868; attended the common schools; apprenticed to the blacksmith's trade; engaged in mercantile pursuits in Pottsville; Schuykill county treasurer in 1905; unsuccessful candidate for election in 1908 to the Sixty-first Congress; elected as a Democrat to the Sixty-second and Sixty-third Congresses (March 4, 1911-March 3, 1915); chairman, Committee on Mileage (Sixty-second Congress); unsuccessful candidate for reelection in 1914 to the Sixty-fourth Congress; resumed his former business activities in Pottsville; unsuccessful candidate for election in 1916 to the Sixty-fifth Congress; died in Pottsville, Pa., November 19, 1916; interment in St. Patrick's Cemetery.

**LEE, Robert Quincy,** a Representative from Texas; born near Coldwater, Tate County, Miss., January 12, 1869; attended the public schools and the Fort Worth (Tex.) High School; moved with his father to Fort Worth, Tex., in 1886, and to Caddo, Stephens County, Tex., in 1891; engaged in the general merchandise business; moved to Cisco, Eastland County, Tex., in 1913 and engaged in ranching, agricultural pursuits, and banking; founder and builder in 1919 of the Cisco & Northeastern Railroad Co., and served as its president 1919-1927; president of the West Texas Chamber of Commerce in 1926 and 1927; elected as a Democrat to the Seventy-first Congress and served from March 4, 1929, until his death in Washington, D.C., April 18, 1930; interment in Oakwood Cemetery, Cisco, Tex.

**LEE, Silas,** a Representative from Massachusetts; born in Concord, Mass., July 3, 1760; pursued classical studies and graduated from Harvard University in 1784; studied law; admitted to the bar; member of the Massachusetts house of representatives in 1793, 1797, and 1798; elected as a Federalist to the Sixth and Seventh Congresses and served from March 4, 1799, until August 20, 1801, when he resigned; appointed by President Thomas Jefferson to be United States attorney for the district of Maine January 6, 1802, and served until his death; justice of the peace and of the quorum in 1803; probate judge from 1805 until 1814; chief judge of the common pleas court in 1810; died in Wiscasset, Maine, March 1, 1814; interment in Evergreen Cemetery.

**LEE, Thomas,** a Representative from New Jersey; born in Philadelphia, Pa., November 28, 1780; resided in Chester Valley, Pa., during his earlier years and attended the common schools; moved to Leesburg, Cumberland County, N.J., about 1798 and to Port Elizabeth in 1805; became a merchant, shipbuilder, and landowner; judge of the court of common pleas, 1813-1815; member of the New Jersey State general assembly in 1814 and 1815; postmaster of Port Elizabeth, 1818-1833, and 1846-1849; elected as a Jacksonian to the Twenty-third and Twenty-fourth Congresses (March 4, 1833-March 3, 1837); chairman, Committee on Accounts (Twenty-fourth Congress); founder of Port Elizabeth Library and Academy; died in Port Elizabeth, N.J., on November 2, 1856; interment in the Methodist Episcopal Churchyard.

**LEE, Thomas Sim** (father of John Lee), a Delegate from Maryland; born near Upper Marlboro, Prince Georges County, Md., October 29, 1745; completed preparatory studies; held several local offices; member of the provincial council in 1777; Governor of Maryland from 1779 until 1783; Member of the Continental Congress in 1783; member of the Maryland house of delegates in 1787; declined to serve in the convention which drafted the Constitution of the United States, but consented to serve in the State convention for the ratification of the Federal Constitution in 1788; elected Governor of Maryland by the General Assembly, and served from April 5, 1792 to November 14, 1794; effected the organization of the State militia while he was Governor, and took an active part in the suppression of the Whiskey Rebellion in western Pennsylvania and Maryland; appointed to the State senate in 1794, but declined to serve; again elected Governor, but declined in 1798; retired from public life and engaged in the management of his estate, "Needwood," in Frederick County, Md., until his death, November 9, 1819; interment in a private cemetery at Melwood, Prince Georges County, Md.; reinterment in the Roman Catholic Cemetery, near Upper Marlboro, Md., April 17, 1888.

**Bibliography:** *DAB.*

**LEE, Warren Isbell,** a Representative from New York; born in Bartlett, Oneida County, N.Y., February 5, 1876; attended the public schools; was graduated from Colgate Academy, Hamilton, N.Y., in 1894, from Hamilton College, Clinton, N.Y., in 1899, and from the New York Law School, New York City, in 1901; was admitted to the bar in 1901 and commenced practice in New York City; member of the State assembly 1906-1910 and in 1920; assistant district attorney of Brooklyn 1912-1914; first deputy comptroller of New York State 1914-1917; one of the counsel to the Public Service Commission of New York 1917-1919; delegate to the Republican State conventions in 1920, 1922, 1924, and 1927; trustee of Hamilton College 1917-1921; elected as a Republican to the Sixty-seventh Congress (March 4, 1921-March 3, 1923); unsuccessful candidate for reelection in 1922 to the Sixty-eighth Congress; resumed the practice of law; former director of Flatbush National Bank; died in Brooklyn, N.Y., December 25, 1955; interment in Green-Wood Cemetery.

**LEE, William Henry Fitzhugh** (grandson of Henry Lee), a Representative from Virginia; born at Arlington House, Arlington, Va., May 31, 1837; attended private school and Harvard University; appointed second lieutenant in the Sixth Regiment, United States Infantry, and accompanied his regiment in 1858 in the expedition to

Utah; resigned in 1859; returned to Virginia and took charge of his estates near White House, New Kent County, in 1859; during the Civil War he raised a company of Cavalry in 1861 and joined the Confederate service; was promoted successively from captain to major general of Cavalry; returned to his plantation; moved to Ravensworth, near Burke Station, Va., in 1874 and engaged in agricultural pursuits; member of the Virginia senate 1875-1878 and served as presiding officer; served as president of the Virginia agricultural society; elected as a Democrat to the Fiftieth, Fifty-first, and Fifty-second Congresses and served from March 4, 1887, until his death in Ravensworth, Va., on October 15, 1891; interment in the family burying ground at Ravensworth; reinterment in the crypt, Lee Memorial Chapel, Washington and Lee University, at Lexington, Va., in September 1922.

**Bibliography:** *DAB.*

**LEECH, James Russell,** a Representative from Pennsylvania; born in Ebensburg, Cambria County, Pa., November 19, 1888; educated in the public and high schools and the Mercersburg (Pa.) Academy; was graduated from Washington and Jefferson College, Washington, Pa., in 1911, and from the law department of the University of Pennsylvania at Philadelphia in 1915; was admitted to the bar in 1915 and commenced practice in Ebensburg, Pa.; during the First World War was appointed as a second lieutenant on November 27, 1917, and served with the Seventh Ammunition Train; was honorably discharged on January 20, 1919; elected as a Republican to the Seventieth and to the two succeeding Congresses, and served from March 4, 1927 until his resignation on January 29, 1932, having been appointed a member of the United States Board of Tax Appeals (now Tax Court of the United States) to fill a vacancy; was reappointed in 1934 and again in 1946, and served on this court until his death in Chevy Chase, Md., on February 5, 1952; interment in Lloyd Cemetery, Ebensburg, Pa.

**LEEDOM, John Peter,** a Representative from Ohio; born in Adams County, Ohio, December 20, 1847; attended the common schools; was graduated from Smith's Mercantile College, Portsmouth, Ohio, in 1863; taught in the public schools of Portsmouth; engaged in agricultural pursuits; elected clerk of the court of common pleas of Adams County in 1874 and reelected in 1877; member of the Democratic State central committee in 1879; elected as a Democrat to the Forty-seventh Congress (March 4, 1881-March 3, 1883); unsuccessful candidate for reelection in 1882 to the Forty-eighth Congress; Sergeant at Arms of the House of Representatives 1884-1890; died in Toledo, Ohio, March 18, 1895; interment in the Odd Fellows Cemetery, Manchester, Ohio.

**LEET, Isaac,** a Representative from Pennsylvania; born near Washington, Pa., in 1801; pursued preparatory studies and graduated from Washington College (now Washington and Jefferson College), Washington, Pa., in 1822; studied law; admitted to the bar in 1826 and commenced practice in Washington, Pa.; treasurer of Washington County 1826-1830; deputy attorney general of Washington County 1830-1834; member of the Pennsylvania senate 1834-1838; elected as a Democrat to the Twenty-sixth Congress (March 4, 1839-March 3, 1841); unsuccessful candidate for reelection in 1840 to the Twenty-seventh Congress; died in Washington, Pa., June 10, 1844; interment in the old Cooke private graveyard near Washington, Pa.

**LeFANTE, Joseph Anthony,** a Representative from New Jersey; born in Bayonne, Hudson County, N.J., September 8, 1928; educated in the public schools of Bayonne; attended St. Peter's Institute of Industrial Relations, 1953-1955, and the Real Estate Institute of New Jersey, 1957; real estate salesman and business executive; vice president and board director, New Jersey Furniture Association; served in the New Jersey National Guard, 1947-1952; member of the Bayonne Charter Commission, 1960-1961, the Bayonne City Council, 1962-1970, and the Bayonne Board of School

Estimate, 1964-1967; served in the New Jersey State general assembly, 1969-1976; delegate to New Jersey State Democratic convention, 1975; delegate to the Democratic National Convention of 1976; elected as a Democrat to the Ninety-fifth Congress, and served from January 3, 1977 until his resignation on December 14, 1978; was not a candidate for reelection in 1978 to the Ninety-sixth Congress; unsuccessful candidate in 1982 for nomination to the United States Senate; president of a furniture company; is a resident of Bayonne, N.J.

**LE FEVER, Jacob** (father of Frank Jacob Le Fevre), a Representative from New York; born in New Paltz, Ulster County, N.Y., April 20, 1830; attended New Paltz Academy and Amenia Seminary; supervisor of the town in 1861 and 1862; member of the State assembly 1863-1865 and again in 1867; delegate to many Republican State conventions; delegate to the Republican National Convention in 1888; elected as a Republican to the Fifty-third and Fifty-fourth Congresses (March 4, 1893-March 3, 1897); was not a candidate for renomination in 1896 to the Fifty-fifth Congress; president of the Huguenot National Bank until his death in New Paltz, N.Y., on February 4, 1905; interment in New Paltz Rural Cemetery.

**LEFEVER, Joseph,** a Representative from Pennsylvania; born in Strasburg Township, near Paradise, Lancaster County, Pa., April 3, 1760; attended the common schools; engaged in agricultural pursuits; elected as a Republican to the Twelfth Congress (March 4, 1811-March 3, 1813); resumed his agricultural pursuits; died in Paradise Township, Lancaster County, Pa., October 17, 1826; interment in Carpenter's Graveyard.

**LE FEVRE, Benjamin,** a Representative from Ohio; born near Maplewood, Shelby County, Ohio, on October 8, 1838; attended Miami University, Oxford, Ohio, in 1858 and 1859; studied law in Sidney, Ohio; during the Civil War enlisted in the Union Army in 1861 and served until the close of the war; mustered out as major of the Fiftieth Ohio Infantry and brevetted brigadier general; member of the State house of representatives in 1865; nominated in 1866 for secretary of state by the Democrats of Ohio; United States consul at Nuremberg, Bavaria, 1867-1869; elected as a Democrat to the Forty-sixth and to the three succeeding Congresses (March 4, 1879-March 3, 1887); was not a candidate for renomination in 1886 to the Fiftieth Congress; mail contract agent for Erie Railway Company; retired from political activities and engaged in agricultural pursuits in Salem Township, Shelby County, Ohio; died in Atlantic City, N.J., on March 7, 1922; interment in Glenn Cemetery, Salem Township, Shelby County, Ohio.

**LE FEVRE, Frank Jacob** (son of Jacob Le Fever), a Representative from New York; born in New Paltz, Ulster County, N.Y., November 30, 1874; attended the public schools and the New Paltz Normal School; became engaged in banking; member of the State senate in 1902; appointed superintendent of the New York State building at St. Louis, Mo., during the Louisiana Purchase Exposition; elected as a Republican to the Fifty-ninth Congress (March 4, 1905-March 3, 1907); unsuccessful candidate for renomination in 1906; became president of the Huguenot National Bank at New Paltz, N.Y., in 1905; engaged in banking and fruit growing; died in Atlantic City, N.J., April 29, 1941; interment in Moravian Cemetery, Richmond, Staten Island, N.Y.

**LE FEVRE, Jay,** a Representative from New York; born in New Paltz, Ulster County, N.Y., September 6, 1893; was graduated from the Lawrenceville (N.J.) Preparatory School and attended Dartmouth College at Hanover, N.H.; during the First World War served as a second lieutenant in the Reserve Officers Training Corps, Field Artillery, at Camp Taylor, Ark., in 1918; associated with his father in the coal, lumber, feed, and fuel-oil business in New Paltz, N.Y., 1916-1946; also engaged in the banking business; trustee of the

village of New Paltz; delegate to the Republican State conventions in 1942 and 1946; Republican committeeman of New Paltz 1930-1946; elected as a Republican to the Seventy-eighth and to the three succeeding Congresses (January 3, 1943-January 3, 1951); was not a candidate for renomination in 1950; resumed his merchandising interests; member of the New York State Bridge Authority 1951-1955; died in Kingston, N.Y., April 26, 1970; interment in Lloyd Cemetery, Highland, N.Y.

**LEFFERTS, John,** a Representative from New York; born in Brooklyn, N.Y., December 17, 1785; attended the public schools; elected as a Republican to the Thirteenth Congress (March 4, 1813-March 3, 1815); delegate to the State constitutional convention of 1821; member of the State senate 1820-1825; died in Brooklyn, N.Y., September 18, 1829; interment in Greenwood Cemetery.

**LEFFLER, Isaac** (brother of Shepherd Leffler), a Representative from Virginia; born on his grandfather's plantation, "Sylvia's Plain," Washington County, Pa., near Wheeling, Va. (now West Virginia), November 7, 1788; attended the public schools and graduated from Jefferson College, Canonsburg, Pa.; studied law; admitted to the bar and commenced practice in Wheeling, Va.; member of the Virginia house of delegates, 1817-1819, 1823-1827, 1832, and 1833; member of the Virginia board of public works in 1827; elected to the Twentieth Congress (March 4, 1827-March 3, 1829); unsuccessful candidate for reelection in 1828 to the Twenty-first Congress; moved to that portion of Michigan Territory that is now Des Moines County, Iowa, in 1835; admitted to the Des Moines County bar April 15, 1835, and practiced; chief justice of the first judicial tribunal of Des Moines County April 11, 1836; after the creation of Wisconsin Territory on April 20, 1836, served in the first legislature of the new Territory in 1836 and 1837 and served as speaker in 1837; unsuccessful Whig candidate for election in 1837 to the Twenty-fifth Congress; member of the of the Iowa Territorial house of representatives in 1841; appointed by President John Tyler as United States marshal for the district of Iowa December 18, 1843; confirmed January 16, 1844, and served until removed by President James K. Polk on December 29, 1845; resumed the practice of law in Burlington, Iowa; declined the appointment of register of the land office at Stillwater in 1849; appointed by President Millard Fillmore receiver of public moneys for the Chariton land district of Iowa on August 30, 1852, and served until removed by President Franklin Pierce on March 29, 1853; died in Chariton, Lucas County, Iowa, March 8, 1866; interment in Aspen Grove Cemetery, Burlington, Iowa.

**Bibliography:** *DAB*.

**LEFFLER, Shepherd** (brother of Isaac Leffler), a Representative from Iowa; born on his grandfather's plantation, "Sylvia's Plain," Washington County, Pa., near Wheeling, Va. (now West Virginia), April 24, 1811; attended private schools and graduated from Washington College, Washington, Pa., and from the law department of Jefferson College, Canonsburg, Pa., in 1833; admitted to the bar and commenced practice in Wheeling; moved to Burlington, Iowa (then a part of Michigan Territory), in 1835; member of the Territorial house of representatives in 1839 and 1841; served in the Territorial council, 1841-1843 and in 1845; member of the constitutional conventions in 1844 and 1846; permanent president during the first convention; upon the admission of Iowa as a State into the Union was elected as a Democrat to the Twenty-ninth Congress in 1846; reelected to the Thirtieth and Thirty-first Congresses, and served from December 28, 1846 to March 3, 1851; chairman, Committee on Invalid Pensions (Thirty-first Congress); engaged in the practice of his profession and in agricultural pursuits in Burlington; unsuccessful candidate for election in 1856 to the Thirty-fifth Congress; unsuccessful Democratic candidate for Governor of Iowa in 1875; died at his home,

"Flint Hills," near Burlington, Des Moines County, Iowa, September 7, 1879; interment in Aspen Grove Cemetery.

**LEFTWICH, Jabez,** a Representative from Virginia; born in Bedford County near Liberty (now Bedford), Va., September 22, 1765; attended the rural schools; member of the Virginia house of delegates from 1801 until 1809; inspector general with the rank of colonel on the staff of his brother, General Joel Leftwich, during the War of 1812; elected to the Seventeenth and Eighteenth Congresses (March 4, 1821-March 3, 1825); unsuccessful candidate for reelection in 1824 to the Nineteenth Congress; moved to Madison County, Ala., in 1825; engaged in agricultural and mercantile pursuits; member of the Alabama State house of representatives; died near Huntsville, Ala., June 22, 1855; interment in Maple Hill Cemetery.

**LEFTWICH, John William,** a Representative from Tennessee; born in Liberty (now Bedford), Bedford County, Va., September 7, 1826; attended the public schools; studied medicine and was graduated from the Philadelphia Medical College in 1850; moved to Memphis, Tenn., and engaged in mercantile pursuits; upon the readmission of the State of Tennessee to representation was elected as a Democrat to the Thirty-ninth Congress and served from July 24, 1866, to March 3, 1867; unsuccessful candidate for reelection; delegate to the Democratic National Convention in 1868; mayor of Memphis in 1869 and 1870; contested the election of William J. Smith to the Forty-first Congress, but, while on his way to Washington to prosecute the contest, died in Lynchburg, Va., March 6, 1870; interment in Elmwood Cemetery, Memphis, Tenn.

**LEGARDA Y TUASON, Benito,** a Resident Commissioner from the Philippine Islands; born in Manila, Philippine Islands, September 27, 1853; attended the Jesuits' College and St. Tomas University of Manila; member of Emilio Aguinaldo's cabinet at Malolos, and vice president of the Filipino Congress; resigned these positions to return to Manila in December 1898; appointed a member of the Philippine Commission on February 1, 1901, and served until elected a Resident Commissioner; elected as a Resident Commissioner to the United States in 1907; reelected in 1909 and served from November 22, 1907, to March 3, 1913; was not a candidate for renomination in 1912; went to France; died at Evian-les-Bains, France, August 27, 1915; interment in Cementerio del Norte, Manila, Philippine Islands.

**LEGARÉ, George Swinton,** a Representative from South Carolina; born in Rockville, Charleston County, S.C., November 11, 1869; moved to Charleston in boyhood; was graduated from Porter Academy, Charleston, S.C., in 1889 and attended the law department of the University of South Carolina at Columbia for two years; was graduated from Georgetown University Law School, Washington, D.C., in 1893; was admitted to the bar the same year and commenced practice in Charleston, S.C.; corporation counsel 1898-1903; elected as a Democrat to the Fifty-eighth and to the four succeeding Congresses and served from March 4, 1903, until his death, before the close of the Sixty-second Congress; had been reelected to the Sixty-third Congress; died in Charleston, S.C., January 31, 1913; interment in Magnolia Cemetery.

**LEGARÉ, Hugh Swinton,** a Representative from South Carolina; born in Charleston, S.C., January 2, 1797; attended Charleston College and the school of Reverend Moses Waddell at Abbeville; was graduated from the College of South Carolina (now University of South Carolina) at Columbia in 1814; studied law from 1814 until 1817; pursued further studies in Paris and Edinburgh in 1818 and 1819; admitted to the bar in 1822 and commenced practice in Charleston, S.C.; member of the South Carolina State house of representatives, 1820-1821, and 1824-1830; one of the founders and editor of the Southern Review, 1828-1832; attorney general of South Carolina, 1830-1832; appointed Chargé d'Affaires to Belgium on April 14, 1832 and served until June 1836; elected as a Democrat to the Twenty-fifth Congress (March 4, 1837-March 3, 1839); unsuccessful candidate for reelection in 1838 to the Twenty-sixth Congress; resumed the practice of law in Charleston; Attorney General in the Cabinet of President John Tyler from September 13, 1841, until his death; also filled the office of Secretary of State ad interim from May 8, 1843, up to the time of his death, in Boston, Mass., June 20, 1843; interment in Mount Auburn Cemetery, Cambridge, Mass.; reinterment in Magnolia Cemetery, Charleston, S.C.

Bibliography: *DAB*; O'Brien, Michael. *A Character of Hugh Legaré*. Knoxville: The University of Tennessee Press, 1985; Rhea, Linda. *Hugh Swinton Legaré; A Charleston Intellectual*. Chapel Hill: University of North Carolina Press, 1934.

**LEGGETT, Robert Louis,** a Representative from California; born in Richmond, Contra Costa County, Calif., July 26, 1926; attended the public schools of Richmond, Calif.; served as an enlisted man in the United States Navy Air Corps, 1944-1946; B.A., University of California, Berkeley, 1947; J.D., University of California Boalt Hall School of Jurisprudence, 1950; was admitted to the bar in 1951 and began the practice of law in Vallejo, Calif.; member of the California State assembly in 1960 and 1962; elected as a Democrat to the Eighty-eighth and to the seven succeeding Congresses (January 3, 1963-January 3, 1979); was not a candidate for reelection in 1978 to the Ninety-sixth Congress; is a resident of Orange, Calif.

**LEHLBACH, Frederick Reimold** (nephew of Herman Lehlbach), a Representative from New Jersey; born in New York City January 31, 1876; moved with his parents to Newark, N.J., in 1884; attended the public schools; was graduated from Yale University in 1897; attended the New York Law School; was admitted to the bar in February 1899 and commenced practice in Newark, N.J.; member of the Newark Board of Education, 1900-1903; member of the New Jersey State house of assembly, 1903-1905; clerk of the New Jersey State board of equalization of taxes from April 3, 1905, until his resignation on April 14, 1908; appointed assistant prosecutor of Essex County on April 15, 1908, and served until April 6, 1913, when he resigned to resume the practice of law; elected as a Republican to the Sixty-fourth and to the ten succeeding Congresses (March 4, 1915-January 3, 1937); chairman, Committee on Reform in the Civil Service (Sixty-sixth through Sixty-eighth Congresses), Committee on Civil Service (Sixty-ninth through Seventy-first Congresses); unsuccessful candidate for reelection in 1936 to the Seventy-fifth Congress; continued the practice of law in Washington, D.C., until his death there on August 4, 1937; interment in Fairmount Cemetery, Newark, N.J.

**LEHLBACH, Herman** (uncle of Frederick Reimold Lehlbach), a Representative from New Jersey; born in Heilig-Kreuz-Steinach, Baden, Germany, July 3, 1845; immigrated to the United States in 1851 with his parents, who settled in Newark, N.J.; attended the public schools and became a civil engineer; member of the New Jersey State house of assembly, 1884-1886; elected as a Republican to the Forty-ninth and to the two succeeding Congresses (March 4, 1885-March 3, 1891); was not a candidate for renomination in 1890 to the Fifty-second Congress; resumed the practice of his profession as a civil engineer in Newark; sheriff of Essex County, N.J., 1893-1896; died in Newark, N.J., on January 11, 1904; interment in Fairmount Cemetery.

**LEHMAN, Herbert Henry,** a Senator from New York; born in New York City, March 28, 1878; attended Sachs Collegiate Institute in New York City; graduated from Williams College, Williamstown, Mass., in 1899; employed by the J. Spencer Turner Co., textile manufacturers; in 1908 became a partner in Lehman Bros., investment bankers in New York City; during the First World War was commissioned a captain in the United States Army in August 1917, later attained the rank of colonel on the General Staff, and served until April 1919; Lieutenant Governor of New York, 1929-1932; elected Governor of New York in 1932, reelected in 1934, 1936, and 1938, and served from January 1, 1933, until his resignation on December 3, 1942; Director of Foreign Relief and Rehabilitation Operations in the State Department, Washington, D.C., 1943; Director General of the United Nations Relief and Rehabilitation Administration, 1943-1946; unsuccessful candidate for election to the United States Senate in 1946; member of Public Advisory Board of the Economic Cooperation Administration in 1948; elected as a Democrat to the United States Senate in 1949 to fill the vacancy caused by the resignation of Robert F. Wagner; reelected in 1950 and served from November 9, 1949, until January 3, 1957; was not a candidate for renomination in 1956; was a resident of New York City until his death there on December 5, 1963; interment in Kensico Cemetery, Valhalla, N.Y.

**Bibliography:** Ingalls, Robert. *Herbert H. Lehman and New York's Little New Deal.* New York: New York University Press, 1975; Nevins, Allan. *Herbert H. Lehman and His Era.* New York: Scribner, 1963.

**LEHMAN, Richard Henry,** a Representative from California; born in Sanger, Fresno County, Calif., July 20, 1948; attended public schools and graduated from Sanger High School in 1966; A.A., Fresno City College, 1968; attended California State University, Fresno, 1969; B.A., University of California, Santa Cruz, 1971; administrative assistant to State senator George Zenovich, 1970-1976; served in the California National Guard, 1970-1976; elected to the California State assembly, 1976-1982, assistant majority floor leader, 1978-1982; delegate to the Democratic National Convention of 1968; elected as a Democrat to the Ninety-eighth and to the five succeeding Congresses (January 3, 1983-January 3, 1995); unsuccessful candidate for reelection in 1994 to the One Hundred Fourth Congress; is a resident of Fresno, Calif.

**LEHMAN, William,** a Representative from Florida; born in Selma, Dallas County, Ala., October 4, 1913; educated at Dallas Academy and Selma (Ala.) High School; B.S., University of Alabama, 1934; studied at Barry College, Oxford University, King's College, Cambridge University, the University of Edinburgh, and at Harvard University; received a teaching certificate from the University of Miami, Fla., in 1963; served during the Second World War in the United States Army Air Corps, 1942-1946; owner of an automobile dealership, 1966-1972; teacher, Miami Norland Junior High School, 1963-1964; instructor, Miami Dade Junior College, 1965-1966; member, Dade County School Board, 1966-1972, chairman, 1971-1972; elected as a Democrat to the Ninety-third and to the nine succeeding Congresses (January 3, 1973-January 3, 1993); was not a candidate for renomination in 1992 to the One Hundred Third Congress; is a resident of Biscayne Park, Fla.

**LEHMAN, William Eckart,** a Representative from Pennsylvania; born in Philadelphia, Pa., August 21, 1821; pursued preparatory studies; graduated from the University of Pennsylvania at Philadelphia in 1841; studied law; admitted to the bar in 1844 and commenced practice in Philadelphia; appointed post office examiner for Pennsylvania and New York by President James K. Polk; elected as a Democrat to the Thirty-seventh Congress (March 4, 1861-March 3, 1863); unsuccessful candidate for renomination in 1862 to the Thirty-eighth Congress; United States provost marshal of the first district of Pennsylvania with the rank of captain from April 25, 1863, to June 15, 1865; having an ample income, he did not engage in any business or professional activities; died in Atlantic City, N.J., July 19, 1895; interment in St. Peter's Episcopal Church Cemetery, Philadelphia, Pa.

**LEHR, John Camillus,** a Representative from Michigan; born in Monroe, Monroe County, Mich., November 18, 1878; attended St. Mary's private school and Monroe High School, graduating from the latter in 1897; was graduated from the law department of the

University of Michigan at Ann Arbor in 1900; was admitted to the bar the same year and commenced practice in Monroe, Mich.; moved to Port Huron, Mich., in 1905 and continued the practice of law; returned to Monroe in 1916; served as city attorney 1918-1922 and 1928-1930; member of the board of education of Monroe 1926-1936, and served as vice president 1930-1936; elected as a Democrat to the Seventy-third Congress (March 4, 1933-January 3, 1935); unsuccessful candidate for reelection in 1934 to the Seventy-fourth Congress; member of Monroe Port Commission 1936-1942; delegate to the Democratic National Convention in 1936; appointed on July 2, 1936, by President Franklin D. Roosevelt, United States attorney for the eastern district of Michigan and served until September 2, 1947, when he resigned to devote his time as head of a fraternal beneficiary association in Detroit, Mich.; died in Monroe, Mich., February 17, 1958; interment in St. Joseph Cemetery.

**LEIB, Michael,** a Representative and a Senator from Pennsylvania; born in Philadelphia, Pa., January 8, 1760; attended the common schools; studied medicine and commenced practice in Philadelphia, Pa.; commissioned surgeon in the Philadelphia Militia in 1780, and served throughout the Revolutionary War; resumed the practice of medicine and served on the staff of several Philadelphia hospitals; member of the committee of correspondence in 1793; member of the Pennsylvania house of representatives, 1795-1798; elected to the Sixth and to the three succeeding Congresses, and served from March 4, 1799 until February 14, 1806, when he resigned; member, Pennsylvania house of representatives, 1806-1808; brigadier general of the Philadelphia Militia, 1807-1811; member of the committee of correspondence on the *Chesapeake* affair, June 1807; elected as a Republican to the United States Senate in 1808 for the term beginning March 4, 1809; subsequently elected to fill the vacancy in the term ending March 3, 1809, caused by the resignation of Samuel Maclay, and served from January 9, 1809 to February 14, 1814, when he resigned, having been appointed postmaster of Philadelphia; served as postmaster until 1815; member, the Pennsylvania house of representatives, 1817-1818, and the Pennsylvania senate, 1818-1821; appointed as a prothonotary of the United States district court at Philadelphia, and served from November 1822 until his death in Philadelphia, Pa., on December 8, 1822; interment in St. John's Lutheran Churchyard, Northern Liberties, Philadelphia, Pa.

**Bibliography:** *DAB.*

**LEIB, Owen D.,** a Representative from Pennsylvania; born in Pennsylvania; pursued classical studies; studied medicine and commenced practice in Catawissa, Pa.; elected as a Democrat to the Twenty-ninth Congress (March 4, 1845-March 3, 1847); chairman, Committee on Expenditures in the Department of War (Twenty-ninth Congress); died in Catawissa, Pa., June 17, 1848.

**LEIDY, Paul,** a Representative from Pennsylvania; born in Hemlock Township, Columbia County, Pa., November 13, 1813; attended the common schools; apprenticed as a tailor; taught school in Danville, Pa., for several years; studied law; admitted to the bar in 1837 and commenced practice in Danville; district attorney of Montour County 1852-1857; elected as a Democrat to the Thirty-fifth Congress to fill the vacancy caused by the death of John G. Montgomery and served from December 7, 1857, to March 3, 1859; unsuccessful candidate for reelection in 1858 to the Thirty-sixth Congress; died in Danville, Pa., September 11, 1877; interment in the Odd Fellows Cemetery.

**LEIGH, Benjamin Watkins,** a Senator from Virginia; born in Chesterfield County, Va., on June 18, 1781; studied under private tutors; graduated from the College of William and Mary, Williamsburg, Va., in 1802; studied law; admitted to the bar and commenced practice in Petersburg, Va.; served in the War of 1812; member, Virginia house of delegates 1811-1813; moved to Richmond, Va., in 1813; prepared the revised code of 1810; delegate to the Virginia constitutional convention of 1829 and 1830; member, Virginia house of delegates 1830-1831; official reporter of the Virginia court of appeals 1829-1841; elected as a Whig to the United States Senate to fill the vacancy in the term ending March 3, 1835, caused by the resignation of William C. Rives; reelected in 1835 and served from February 26, 1834, to July 4, 1836, when he resigned; resumed the practice of law; died in Richmond, Va., February 2, 1849; interment in Shockoe Cemetery.

**Bibliography:** *DAB*; Macfarland, William H. *An Address on the Life, Character, and Public Services of the Late Hon. Benjamin Watkins Leigh.* Richmond: Macfarlane and Fergusson, 1851.

**LEIGHTY, Jacob D.,** a Representative from Indiana; born near Greensburg, Westmoreland County, Pa., November 15, 1839; in 1844 moved with his parents to De Kalb County, Ind., where they settled on a farm at Spencerville; attended the public schools; taught in district schools; spent two years at a commercial school at Fort Wayne and then entered Wittenberg College, Springfield, Ohio; on July 1, 1861, after two years in college, he left to enlist in the Union Army and became a member of Company E, Eleventh Indiana Volunteer Zouave Infantry; engaged in farming and general merchandising with his father until 1875, when he established the town of St. Joe, Ind.; member of the State house of representatives 1886-1888; elected as a Republican to the Fifty-fourth Congress (March 4, 1895-March 3, 1897); unsuccessful candidate for reelection in 1896 to the Fifty-fifth Congress; United States pension agent at Indianapolis 1897-1901; died at St. Joe, De Kalb County, Ind., on October 18, 1912; interment in Riverview Cemetery.

**LEIPER, George Gray,** a Representative from Pennsylvania; born in Philadelphia, Pa., February 3, 1786; attended the common schools; was graduated from the University of Pennsylvania at Philadelphia in 1803; moved to "Lapidea," Delaware County, Pa., in 1810 and engaged in logging; also operated bark mills and stone quarries; served as first lieutenant of the Delaware County Fencibles in 1814 and was called into active service near Brandywine Creek; member of the Pennsylvania house of representatives in 1822 and 1823; elected as a Jacksonian to the Twenty-first Congress (March 4, 1829-March 3, 1831); chairman, Committee on Expenditures in the Department of the Treasury (Twenty-first Congress); was not a candidate for renomination in 1830; resumed the management of his quarry properties; appointed associate judge of the courts of Delaware County on February 25, 1843; reappointed on February 16, 1848, and served until December 1, 1851, when the office became elective; died at his home, "Lapidea," on Crum Creek, Delaware County, Pa., November 18, 1868; interment in the Ridley Presbyterian Church Cemetery, Ridley Township, Delaware County, Pa.

**LEISENRING, John,** a Representative from Pennsylvania; born in Ashton (now Lansford), Carbon County, Pa., June 3, 1853; attended the public schools, Schwartz's Academy, Bethlehem, Pa., and academies in Merchantville and Princeton, N.J.; became a civil and mining engineer and was identified with coal, iron, and lumber industries; also interested in banking; moved from Mauch Chunk, Pa., to Upper Lehigh, Pa., in 1885; member of the Pennsylvania house of representatives in 1894 and 1895; elected as a Republican to the Fifty-fourth Congress (March 4, 1895-March 3, 1897); declined to be a candidate for reelection in 1896 to the Fifty-fifth Congress; delegate to the Pennsylvania Republican convention in 1896; resumed his former business pursuits and served as president of the Upper Lehigh Coal Co.; died in Philadelphia, Pa., January 19, 1901; interment in the City Cemetery at Mauch Chunk, Pa.

**LEITER, Benjamin Franklin,** a Representative from Ohio; born in Leitersburg, Md., October 13, 1813; received a limited schooling; taught school in Maryland 1830-1834; moved to Ohio and taught school 1834-1842; studied law; was admitted to the bar in 1842 and commenced practice in Canton, Stark County, Ohio; justice

of the peace; mayor for ten years; member of the State house of representatives in 1848 and 1849 and served as speaker in the latter year; elected as a Republican to the Thirty-fourth and Thirty-fifth Congresses (March 4, 1855-March 3, 1859); died in Canton, Ohio, June 17, 1866; interment in West Lawn Cemetery.

**LELAND, George Thomas (Mickey),** a Representative from Texas; born in Lubbock, Lubbock County, Tex., November 27, 1944; attended the Harris County public schools; graduated from Phillis Wheatly Senior High School, Houston, 1963; B.S., Texas Southern University, Houston, 1970; senior vice president, King State Bank, 1977; director, special development projects, Hermann Hospital, 1977; Texas State representative, District 88, 1972-1979; delegate, Texas Constitutional convention, 1974; elected to the Democratic National Committee, 1976; delegate to the Democratic National Convention of 1972; elected as a Democrat to the Ninety-sixth and to the five succeeding Congresses, and served from January 3, 1979 until his death in an airplane crash near Gambela, Ethiopia, August 7, 1989, while traveling to a United Nations refugee camp near the border between Sudan and Ethiopia; chairman, Select Committee on Hunger (Ninety-eighth through One Hundred First Congresses).

**LEMKE, William,** a Representative from North Dakota; born in Albany, Stearns County, Minn., August 13, 1878; attended the public schools; graduated from the University of North Dakota at Grand Forks in 1902, and from Yale University in 1905; studied law at the University of North Dakota and Georgetown University, Washington, D.C.; admitted to the bar in 1905 and commenced practice at Fargo, N.Dak.; member of the national executive committee of the National Nonpartisan League, 1917-1921; chairman of the Republican State committee, 1916-1920; attorney general of North Dakota in 1921 and 1922; Union Party candidate for President of the United States in 1936; elected as a Nonpartisan on the Republican ticket to the Seventy-third and to the three succeeding Congresses (March 4, 1933-January 3, 1941); renominated as a Republican in 1940 to the Seventy-seventh Congress, but later withdrew and was an unsuccessful Independent candidate for election to the United States Senate; resumed the practice of law; elected as a Republican to the Seventy-eighth and to the three succeeding Congresses and served from January 3, 1943, until his death in Fargo, N.Dak., May 30, 1950; interment in Riverside Cemetery.

**Bibliography:** *DAB*; Blackorby, Edward C. *Prairie Rebel; The Public Life of William Lemke.* Lincoln: University of Nebraska Press, 1963.

**LE MOYNE, John Valcoulon,** a Representative from Illinois; born in Washington, Washington County, Pa., November 17, 1828; attended the common schools; was graduated from Washington and Jefferson College, Washington, Pa., in 1847; studied law; was admitted to the bar in Pittsburgh, Pa., in 1852; moved to Chicago the same year and commenced practice; unsuccessful candidate of the Liberal Party for election in 1872 to the Forty-third Congress; successfully contested as a Democrat the election of Charles B. Farwell to the Forty-fourth Congress and served from May 6, 1876, to March 3, 1877; unsuccessful candidate for reelection in 1876 to the Forty-fifth Congress; resumed the practice of law in Chicago, Ill.; retired in 1887 and moved to Baltimore, Md., where he resided until his death on July 27, 1918; interment in Washington Cemetery, Washington, Pa.

**LENAHAN, John Thomas,** a Representative from Pennsylvania; born in Jenkins Township, Luzerne County, Pa., November 15, 1852; attended private schools; was graduated from Villanova (Pa.) College in 1870; studied law at the University of Pennsylvania, Philadelphia, Pa.; was admitted to the bar in 1873 and commenced practice in Wilkes-Barre, Pa.; delegate to the Democratic National Conventions of 1892 and 1896; elected as a Democrat to the Sixtieth Congress (March 4, 1907-March 3, 1909); was not a candidate for renomination in 1908 to the Sixty-first Congress; resumed the practice of law; died in Wilkes-Barre, Pa., April 28, 1920; interment in St. Mary's Cemetery.

**L'ENGLE, Claude,** a Representative from Florida; born in Jacksonville, Fla., October 19, 1868; attended the public schools and the Duval High School; engaged in mercantile pursuits; became editor and publisher of Dixie, a weekly newspaper; elected as a Democrat to the Sixty-third Congress (March 4, 1913-March 3, 1915); unsuccessful candidate for renomination in 1914 to the Sixty-fourth Congress; again engaged in journalism; died in Jacksonville, Duval County, Fla., November 6, 1919; interment in Evergreen Cemetery.

**LENNON, Alton Asa,** a Senator and a Representative from North Carolina; born in Wilmington, New Hanover County, N.C., August 17, 1906; attended the public schools; graduated from Wake Forest College, Winston-Salem, N.C., in 1929; studied law; was admitted to the bar in 1929 and began practice in Wilmington, N.C.; served as judge of the New Hanover County Recorder's Court from 1934 until 1942; member, North Carolina State senate, 1947-1951; appointed as a Democrat to the United States Senate to fill the vacancy caused by the death of Willis Smith and served from July 10, 1953, to November 28, 1954; was an unsuccessful candidate for the nomination in 1954 to fill the vacancy; resumed law practice; elected as a Democrat to the Eighty-fifth and to the seven succeeding Congresses (January 3, 1957-January 3, 1973); was not a candidate for reelection in 1972 to the Ninety-third Congress; was a resident of Wilmington, N.C., until his death there on December 28, 1986; interment in Oakdale Cemetery.

**LENROOT, Irvine Luther,** a Representative and a Senator from Wisconsin; born in Superior, Wis., January 31, 1869; attended the common schools; worked as a logger and a court reporter; studied law; was admitted to the bar in 1898 and commenced practice in Superior, Wis.; member of the Wisconsin State assembly from 1901 until 1907, and served as speaker, 1903-1907; elected as a Republican to the Sixty-first and to the four succeeding Congresses and served from March 4, 1909, until April 17, 1918, when he resigned, having been elected Senator; elected as a Republican to the United States Senate on April 2, 1918, to fill the vacancy caused by the death of Paul O. Husting; reelected in 1920 and served from April 18, 1918, to March 3, 1927; unsuccessful candidate for renomination in 1926; chairman, Committee on Railroads (Sixty-sixth Congress), Committee on Public Lands and Surveys (Sixty-eighth Congress), Committee on Public Buildings and Grounds (Sixty-ninth Congress); resumed the practice of law in Washington, D.C.; appointed judge of the United States Court of Customs and Patent Appeals by President Herbert Hoover in 1929, and served until his retirement in 1944; died in Washington, D.C., January 26, 1949; interment in Greenwood Cemetery, Superior, Wis.

**Bibliography:** *DAB*; Griffith, Robert. "Prelude to Insurgency: Irvine L. Lenroot and the Republican Primary of 1908." *Wisconsin Magazine of History* 49 (Autumn 1965): 16-28; Margulies, Herbert. *Senator Irvine Lenroot of Wisconsin.* Columbia: University of Missouri Press, 1977.

**LENT, James,** a Representative from New York; born in Newtown, Long Island (now a part of the Borough of Queens), N.Y., in 1782; engaged in mercantile pursuits in New York City; judge of Queens County from February 5, 1823 to March 4, 1829; elected as a Jacksonian to the Twenty-first and Twenty-second Congresses, and served from March 4, 1829 until his death in Washington, D.C., February 22, 1833; chairman, Committee on Expenditures in the Department of State (Twenty-second Congress); interment in the Congressional Cemetery; reinterment in the Presbyterian Cemetery, Newtown, Long Island, N.Y.

**LENT, Norman Frederick,** a Representative from New York; born in Oceanside, Nassau County, N.Y., March 23, 1931; attended the public schools of East Rockaway, Lynbrook, and Malverne, N.Y.; B.A., Hofstra College, Hempstead, N.Y., 1952; LL.B., Cornell University Law School, Ithaca, N.Y., 1957; served in United States Naval Reserve during the Korean Conflict, with rank of lieutenant, 1952-1954; admitted to the New York bar in 1957 and commenced practice in Lynbrook; associate police justice, East Rockaway, N.Y., 1958-1960; confidential law secretary to New York Supreme Court Justice, 1960-1962; New York State senator, 1962-1970; delegate, New York State Republican convention, 1968; delegate to the Republican National Convention of 1972; elected as a Republican-Conservative to the Ninety-second and to the ten succeeding Congresses (January 3, 1971-January 3, 1993); was not a candidate for reelection in 1992 to the One Hundred Third Congress; is a resident of East Rockaway, N.Y.

**LENTZ, John Jacob,** a Representative from Ohio; born near St. Clairsville, Belmont County, Ohio, January 27, 1856; attended the common schools and the St. Clairsville High School; taught school for four years; was graduated from the National Normal University, Lebanon, Ohio, in 1877; attended the University of Wooster in 1877 and 1878; was graduated from the University of Michigan at Ann Arbor in 1882 and from the law department of Columbia University, New York City, in 1883; was admitted to the bar in Columbus, Ohio, in October 1883 and practiced; founder of the American Insurance Union in 1894 and its president continuously until his death; trustee of Ohio University at Athens; elected as a Democrat to the Fifty-fifth and Fifty-sixth Congresses (March 4, 1897-March 3, 1901); unsuccessful candidate for reelection in 1900 to the Fifty-seventh Congress; delegate to the Democratic National Convention in 1908; participated in campaigns in many States in support of the Eighteenth and Nineteenth amendments to the Constitution; retired from his law practice in 1915 and engaged in the insurance business; died in Columbus, Ohio, on July 27, 1931; interment in Greenlawn Cemetery.

**LEONARD, Fred Churchill,** a Representative from Pennsylvania; born in Elmer, Potter County, Pa., February 16, 1856; attended the public schools, the Pennsylvania normal school at Mansfield, Pa., and Williston Seminary, Easthampton, Mass.; graduated from Yale College in 1883; studied law in Wellsboro, Pa.; admitted to the bar in 1885; moved to Elmira, N.Y., and thence, in 1887, to Coudersport, Potter County, Pa., and practiced law; elected as a Republican to the Fifty-fourth Congress (March 4, 1895-March 3, 1897); unsuccessful candidate for renomination in 1896; resumed the practice of law in Coudersport, Pa.; served as United States marshal for the western district of Pennsylvania from January 15, 1898, until May 6, 1901, when he was transferred to the middle district and served until July 2, 1906; engaged in banking; died in Coudersport, Pa., December 5, 1921; interment in Eulalia Cemetery.

**LEONARD, George,** a Representative from Massachusetts; born in Norton, Mass., July 4, 1729; graduated from Harvard College in 1748; register of probate 1749-1783; studied law; admitted to the bar and commenced practice at Norton in 1750; member of the provincial assembly 1764-1766; executive councilor 1770-1775; judge of the probate court 1784-1790; judge of the common pleas court 1785-1798 and chief justice 1798-1804; elected to the First and Second Congresses (March 4, 1789-March 3, 1793); member of the Massachusetts senate in 1792 and 1793; elected as a Federalist to the Fourth Congress (March 4, 1795-March 3, 1797); served in the Massachusetts house of representatives in 1801 and 1802; died in Raynham, Mass., July 26, 1819; interment in the local cemetery at Norton, Mass.

**LEONARD, John Edwards** (grandnephew of John Edwards of Pennsylvania), a Representative from Louisiana; born in Fairville, Chester County, Pa., September 22, 1845; attended the public schools; was graduated from Phillips Exeter Academy, Exeter, N.H., in 1863 and from Harvard University in 1867; studied law in Germany; returned to the United States and was admitted to the bar in Louisiana in 1870 and commenced practice at Monroe, Ouachita Parish; district attorney of the thirteenth judicial district of Louisiana in 1871 and 1872; elected associate justice of the State supreme court in 1876; resumed the practice of his profession in Monroe, La.; elected as a Republican to the Forty-fifth Congress and served from March 4, 1877, until his death in Havana, Cuba, March 15, 1878; interment in the Friends' (Hicksite) Cemetery of the Middletown Meeting House, Middletown Township, Delaware County, Pa.

**LEONARD, Moses Gage,** a Representative from New York; born in Stafford, Conn., July 10, 1809; attended the public schools; moved to New York City; city alderman and judge of the city court 1840-1842; elected as a Democrat to the Twenty-eighth Congress (March 4, 1843-March 3, 1845); unsuccessful candidate for reelection in 1844 to the Twenty-ninth Congress; almshouse commissioner in 1846; proprietor and director of ice companies; commissioner of immigration at the port of New York; moved to San Francisco, Calif.; member of the city council of San Francisco in 1850; returned to New York and served as provost marshal in the Tenth Congressional District of New York during the Civil War; died in Brooklyn, N.Y., on March 20, 1899; interment in Oak Hill Cemetery, Nyack, N.Y.

**LEONARD, Stephen Banks,** a Representative from New York; born in New York City April 15, 1793; attended the public schools; moved with his parents to Owego, N.Y., and learned the printer's trade; engaged in newspaper work in Albany, N.Y.; moved to New York City and subsequently returned to Owego; publisher and editor of the Owego Gazette 1814-1835; trustee of the village of Owego; supervisor and commissioner of excise; trustee of Owego Academy for many years; established the first stage route from Owego to Bath in 1816; postmaster of Owego 1816-1820; elected as a Jacksonian to the Twenty-fourth Congress (March 4, 1835-March 3, 1837); elected as a Democrat to the Twenty-sixth Congress (March 4, 1839-March 3, 1841); chairman, Committee on Public Buildings and Grounds (Twenty-Sixth Congress); declined to be a candidate for reelection in 1840 to the Twenty-seventh Congress; engaged in mercantile and agricultural pursuits; supervisor of Owego 1854-1856; deputy United States marshal 1857-1861; died in Owego, Tioga County, N.Y., May 8, 1876; interment in the Presbyterian Church Burying Ground.

**LESHER, John Vandling,** a Representative from Pennsylvania; born on a farm on Blue Hill, Union Township, Union County, Pa., July 27, 1866; attended the rural schools in his native county and the Pennsylvania normal school at Bloomsburg; taught school for several years in Union and Snyder Counties; was graduated from Bucknell University, Lewisburg, Pa., in 1897; enlisted in Company K, National Guard of Pennsylvania, in 1898, and when it was transferred to the Twelfth Regiment served as a first lieutenant; promoted to quartermaster with rank of captain, serving until 1902; studied law; was admitted to the bar in 1900 and commenced practice in Sunbury, Northumberland County, Pa.; served as assistant district attorney of Northumberland County, Pa.; also engaged in banking and real estate development; elected as a Democrat to the Sixty-third and to the three succeeding Congresses (March 4, 1913-March 3, 1921); unsuccessful candidate for reelection in 1920 to the Sixty-seventh Congress; resumed the practice of law in Sunbury, Pa.; died in Danville, Pa., May 3, 1932; interment in Riverview Cemetery, Northumberland, Pa.

**LESINSKI, John** (father of John Lesinski, Jr.), a Representative from Michigan; born in Erie, Pa., January 3, 1885; and three months later moved with his parents to Detroit, Mich.; attended St. Albertus School, St. Cyril and Methodeusz Seminary, Orchard Lake, Mich., and Detroit Business University, Detroit, Mich.; engaged

extensively in the building and real estate business in Detroit; established lumber and supply companies in Hamtramck and Dearborn areas of Detroit; president of the Polish Citizens' Committee of Detroit from 1919 until 1932; State commissioner in charge of the sale of Polish bonds in 1920; awarded the Polonia Restituta by the Polish Government; delegate to the Democratic National Conventions of 1936, 1940, and 1944; delegate to the Democratic State conventions in 1936, 1940, and 1944; elected as a Democrat to the Seventy-third and to the eight succeeding Congresses, and served from March 4, 1933 until his death in Dearborn, Mich., May 27, 1950; chairman, Committee on Invalid Pensions (Seventy-fourth through Seventy-ninth Congresses), Committee on Immigration and Naturalization (Seventy-ninth Congress), Committee on Education and Labor (Eighty-first Congress); interment in Mount Olivet Cemetery, Detroit, Mich.

**LESINSKI, John, Jr.** (son of John Lesinski), a Representative from Michigan; born in Detroit, Wayne County, Mich., December 28, 1914; at the age of eleven years moved with his parents to Dearborn, Mich.; attended the parochial schools, St. Cyril and Methodeusz Seminary, Orchard Lake, Mich., and graduated from Fordson High School, Dearborn, Mich.; at the age of eighteen years enlisted in the United States Navy as an apprentice seaman and served from 1933 to 1937; was called to active duty again in February 1941 and served until October 1945; awarded the Purple Heart Medal and Navy and Marine Corps Medals; vice president, Hamtramck Lumber Co., 1939-1943, and 1951-1954; president, Dearborn Properties, 1955 to present; elected as a Democrat to the Eighty-second and to the six succeeding Congresses (January 3, 1951-January 3, 1965); was an unsuccessful candidate for renomination in 1964 to the Eighty-ninth Congress; member, board of commissioners, Wayne County, Mich., 1968-1973; is a resident of Dearborn, Mich.

**LESSLER, Montague,** a Representative from New York; born in New York City, January 1, 1869; attended the public schools; was graduated from the College of the City of New York in 1889 and later from the Columbia Law School; was admitted to the bar in 1891 and commenced the practice of his profession in New York City; elected as a Republican to the Fifty-seventh Congress to fill the vacancy caused by the resignation of Nicholas Muller and served from January 7, 1902, to March 3, 1903; unsuccessful candidate for reelection in 1902 to the Fifty-eighth Congress; resumed the practice of law in New York City until his death there on February 17, 1938; remains were cremated.

**LESTER, Posey Green,** a Representative from Virginia; born near the town of Floyd, Floyd County, Va., March 12, 1850; attended the common schools and the Jacksonville graded school at Floyd; engaged in teaching in Floyd County, Va.; ordained a minister in the primitive or old-school Baptist Church in 1876; became associate editor of Zion's Landmark, a church paper published at Wilson, N.C., in 1883, and editor in chief in 1920; elected as a Democrat to the Fifty-first and Fifty-second Congresses (March 4, 1889-March 3, 1893); was not a candidate for renomination in 1892 to the Fifty-third Congress; resumed his ministerial duties at Floyd, Va., until 1921, when he moved to Roanoke, Va., and served as pastor of the Primitive Baptist Church until his death in that city on February 9, 1929; interment in Evergreen Cemetery.

**LESTER, Rufus Ezekiel,** a Representative from Georgia; born near Waynesboro, Burke County, Ga., December 12, 1837; was graduated from Mercer University, Macon, Ga., in 1857; studied law; was admitted to the bar in Savannah, Ga., and commenced practice in 1859; entered the military service of the Confederate Army in 1861 and served throughout the Civil War; resumed the practice of law in Savannah; member of the State senate 1870-1879 and served as president of that body during the last three years; mayor of Savannah 1883-1889; elected as a Democrat to the Fifty-first and to the eight succeeding Congresses and served from

March 4, 1889, until his death in Washington, D.C., on June 16, 1906; chairman, Committee on Expenditures in the Department of State (Fifty-second and Fifty-third Congresses); interment in Bonaventure Cemetery, Savannah, Ga.

**LETCHER, John,** a Representative from Virginia; born in Lexington, Rockbridge County, Va., March 29, 1813; attended private rural schools and Randolph-Macon College; graduated from Washington Academy (now Washington and Lee University), Lexington, Va., in 1833; studied law; admitted to the bar and commenced practice in Lexington, Va., in 1839; editor of the Valley Star from 1840 to 1850; delegate to the Virginia constitutional convention in 1850; elected as a Democrat to the Thirty-second and to the three succeeding Congresses (March 4, 1851-March 3, 1859); was not a candidate for renomination in 1858 to the Thirty-sixth Congress, having become a candidate for Governor; elected Governor of Virginia in 1859, reelected in 1861, and served from January 1, 1860 to December 31, 1863; prominent in the organization of the peace convention that met in Washington, D.C., February 8, 1861, in an effort to devise means to prevent the impending war; discouraged secession, but was active in sustaining the ordinance passed by Virginia on April 17, 1861; after the expiration of his term as Governor resumed the practice of law in Lexington; member of the Virginia house of delegates, 1875-1877; member of the board of visitors of the Virginia Military Institute, 1866-1880, and served as president of the board for ten years; again resumed the practice of law in Lexington, Va., where he died on January 26, 1884; interment in the Presbyterian Cemetery.

**Bibliography:** *DAB*; Boney, F.N. *John Letcher of Virginia; The Story of Virginia's Civil War Governor.* University, Ala.: University of Alabama Press, 1966.

**LETCHER, Robert Perkins,** a Representative from Kentucky; born in Goochland County, Va., February 10, 1788; pursued an academic course; studied law; admitted to the bar and commenced practice in Lancaster, Ky.; member of the Kentucky house of representatives, 1813-1815, 1817, and 1836-1838, and served as speaker in the latter year; elected to the Eighteenth and the four succeeding Congresses (March 4, 1823-March 3, 1833); contested the election of Thomas P. Moore to the Twenty-third Congress, but the House did not seat either and declared a new election necessary; subsequently elected to fill the foregoing vacancy, and served from August 6, 1834 to March 3, 1835; was not a candidate for renomination in 1834 to the Twenty-fourth Congress; presidential elector on the Whig ticket in 1836; elected Governor of Kentucky in 1840, and served from June 1, 1840 to June 1, 1844; appointed Envoy Extraordinary and Minister Plenipotentiary to Mexico on August 9, 1849, and served until August 1852; unsuccessful candidate for election in 1852 to the Thirty-third Congress; resumed the practice of his profession; died in Frankfort, Ky., January 24, 1861; interment in the State Cemetery.

**Bibliography:** *DAB*; Gilliam, William D. "The Pubic Career of Robert Perkins Letcher." Ph.D. dissertation, Indiana University, 1942.

**LETTS, Fred Dickinson** (cousin of Lester Jesse Dickinson), a Representative from Iowa; born near Ainsworth, Washington County, Iowa, April 26, 1875; attended the common schools of Washington County; was graduated from Parsons College, Fairfield, Iowa, in 1897 and from the law department of the University of Iowa at Iowa City in 1899; was admitted to the bar in 1899 and commenced practice in Davenport, Iowa; appointed judge of the seventh judicial district of Iowa on March 25, 1911, and served until December 31, 1912; elected to the same position in 1914, and served until his resignation on February 28, 1925, having been elected to Congress; elected as a Republican to the Sixty-ninth and to the two succeeding Congresses (March 4, 1925-March 3, 1931); unsuccessful candidate for reelection in 1930 to the Seventy-second Congress;

appointed by President Herbert Hoover an associate justice of the Supreme Court of the District of Columbia (now the United States District Court for the District of Columbia) on May 5, 1931, and served until his retirement on May 31, 1961; died in Washington, D.C., January 19, 1965; interment in Ainsworth Cemetery, Ainsworth, Iowa.

**LEVER, Asbury Francis,** a Representative from South Carolina; born near Springhill, Lexington County, S.C., January 5, 1875; attended the country schools; was graduated from Newberry (S.C.) College in 1895; taught school for two years; private secretary to Representative J. William Stokes of South Carolina, 1897-1901; was graduated from the law department of Georgetown University, Washington, D.C., in 1899; was admitted to the bar in South Carolina the same year, but did not practice; delegate to the Democratic State conventions in 1896 and 1900; member of the South Carolina State house of representatives in 1901; elected as a Democrat to the Fifty-seventh Congress to fill the vacancy caused by the death of J. William Stokes; reelected to the Fifty-eighth and to the eight succeeding Congresses and served from November 5, 1901, until August 1, 1919, when he resigned to become a member of the Federal Farm Loan Board, in which capacity he served until 1922; chairman, Committee on Education (Sixty-second Congress), Committee on Agriculture (Sixty-third through Sixty-fifth Congresses); member of the boards of trustees of Clemson (S.C.) College and Newberry (S.C.) College; elected president of the First Carolinas Joint Stock Land Bank at Columbia, S.C., in 1922; field representative of Federal Farm Board; director of the public relations administration of the Farm Credit Administration until his death on April 28, 1940, at "Seven Oaks," near Charleston, S.C.; interment in College Hill Cemetery, on campus of Clemson Agricultural College, Clemson, S.C.

**Bibliography:** *DAB*.

**LEVERING, Robert Woodrow** (son-in-law of Usher L. Burdick and brother-in-law of Quentin N. Burdick), a Representative from Ohio; born near Fredericktown, Ohio, October 3, 1914; attended public schools; graduated from Denison University, Granville, Ohio, in 1936 and from George Washington University Law School, Washington, D.C., in 1940; assistant law librarian of Congress, Washington, D.C., 1937-1941; was admitted to the bar in 1941; with the United States War Department in the Philippines in defense program at the opening of the Second World War and served as a civilian volunteer in defense of Bataan; spent three and one-half years in Japanese prisoner of war camps; major in the Army Reserve; commenced the practice of law in Mount Vernon, Ohio, in 1946; assistant to Ohio attorney general in 1949 and 1950; unsuccessful Democratic candidate for election to Congress in 1948, 1950, 1954, and in 1956; elected as a Democrat to the Eighty-sixth Congress (January 3, 1959-January 3, 1961); unsuccessful candidate for reelection in 1960 to the Eighty-seventh Congress and for election in 1962 to the Eighty-eighth Congress; resumed the practice of law; is a resident of Fredericktown, Ohio.

**LEVIN, Carl** (brother of Sander Martin Levin), a Senator from Michigan; born in Detroit, Wayne County, Mich., June 28, 1934; attended Detroit public schools; graduated, Central High School, Detroit, Mich., 1952; B.A., Swarthmore College (Pa.), 1956; LL.B., Harvard University Law School, 1959; admitted to the Michigan bar in 1959 and commenced practice in Detroit; assistant attorney general and general counsel for the Michigan civil rights commission, 1964-1967; special assistant attorney general for the State of Michigan and chief appellate defender for the city of Detroit, 1968-1969; member of the Detroit city council, 1969-1973; president, Detroit city council, 1974-1977; elected as a Democrat to the United States Senate in 1978 for the term commencing January 3, 1979; reelected in 1984 and again in 1990 for the term ending January 3, 1997; is a resident of Detroit, Mich.

**LEVIN, Lewis Charles,** a Representative from Pennsylvania; born in Charleston, S.C., November 10, 1808; was graduated from South Carolina College (now the University of South Carolina) at Columbia; moved to Woodville, Miss., about 1828 and taught school; studied law; was admitted to the bar and practiced in several States; settled in Philadelphia, Pa., in 1838; one of the founders of the American Party in 1842; editor of the Philadelphia Daily Sun; elected as a candidate of the American Party to the Twenty-ninth and to the two succeeding Congresses (March 4, 1845-March 3, 1851); chairman, Committee on Engraving (Thirtieth Congress); unsuccessful candidate for reelection in 1850 to the Thirty-second Congress; resumed the practice of law; died in Philadelphia, Pa., March 14, 1860; interment in Laurel Hill Cemetery.

Bibliography: *DAB*.

**LEVIN, Sander Martin** (brother of Carl Levin), a Representative from Michigan; born in Detroit, Wayne County, Mich., September 6, 1931; attended public schools; graduated, Central High School, Detroit, 1949; B.A., University of Chicago, 1952; M.A., Columbia University, New York City, 1954; LL.B., Harvard University Law School, 1957; admitted to the Michigan bar in 1958 and commenced practice in Detroit; member, Michigan State senate, 1965-1970; unsuccessful candidate in 1970 and 1974 for election for Governor of Michigan; assistant administrator, United States Agency for International Development, 1977-1981; delegate to the Democratic National Conventions of 1964 and 1968; chair, Michigan Democratic Party, 1968-1969; elected as a Democrat to the Ninety-eighth and to the six succeeding Congresses (January 3, 1983-January 3, 1997); is a resident of Southfield, Mich.

**LEVINE, Meldon Edises,** a Representative from California; born in Los Angeles, Calif., June 7, 1943; graduated from Beverly Hills High School, Calif., 1960; B.A., University of California, Berkeley, 1964; M.P.A., Princeton University, 1966; J.D., Harvard University School of Law, 1969; admitted to the California bar in 1970 and commenced practice in Beverly Hills; member of the California State assembly, 1977-1982; delegate, California State Democratic convention, 1977-1983; delegate to the Democratic National Conventions of 1980 and 1984; elected as a Democrat to the Ninety-eighth and to the four succeeding Congresses (January 3, 1983-January 3, 1993); was not a candidate in 1992 for renomination to the House of Representatives, but was an unsuccessful candidate for nomination to the United States Senate; is a resident of Santa Monica, Calif.

**LEVITAS, Elliott Harris,** a Representative from Georgia; born in Atlanta, Fulton County, Ga., December 26, 1930; attended the public schools of Atlanta; B.A., Emory University, Atlanta, 1952; J.D., Emory University Law School, 1956; Rhodes scholar, receiving masters of law degree from Oxford University, England, 1958; additional study in law, University of Michigan, 1954-1955; admitted to the Georgia bar in 1955 and commenced practice in Atlanta; served in United States Air Force, 1955-1958; served in the Georgia State house of representatives, 1965-1974; delegate to the Democratic National Convention of 1964; elected as a Democrat to the Ninety-fourth and to the four succeeding Congresses (January 3, 1975-January 3, 1985); unsuccessful candidate for reelection in 1984 to the Ninety-ninth Congress; is a resident of Atlanta, Ga.

**LEVY, David,** a Delegate and a Senator from Florida. (*See* YULEE, David Levy.*)

**LEVY, David A.,** a Representative from New York; born in Franklin, Johnson County, Ind., December 18, 1953; B.A., Hofstra University, Hempstead, N.Y., 1974; J.D., Hofstra University School of Law, 1979; attorney; member, Hempstead, N.Y., town board, 1989-1993; elected as a Republican to the One Hundred Third Congress (January 3, 1993-January 3, 1995); unsuccessful Republican candidate for renomination and unsuccessful Conservative candidate for election in 1994 to the One Hundred Fourth Congress; is a resident of Baldwin, N.Y.

**LEVY, Jefferson Monroe,** a Representative from New York; born in New York City April 16, 1852; attended public and private schools; was graduated from the New York University Law School in 1873; was admitted to the bar and practiced in New York City; from his uncle, Commodore Uriah P. Levy, he inherited "Monticello" in Albemarle County, Va., formerly the estate of Thomas Jefferson; elected as a Democrat to the Fifty-sixth Congress (March 4, 1899-March 3, 1901); was not a candidate for renomination in 1900 to the Fifty-seventh Congress; resumed the practice of law in New York City; elected to the Sixty-second and Sixty-third Congresses (March 4, 1911-March 3, 1915); was not a candidate for renomination in 1914 to the Sixty-fourth Congress; resumed the practice of his profession in New York City, and died there on March 6, 1924; interment in Cypress Hills Cemetery.

**LEVY, William Mallory,** a Representative from Louisiana; born in Isle of Wight, Va., October 31, 1827; completed preparatory studies; was graduated from the College of William and Mary, Williamsburg, Va., in 1844; served in the Mexican War as second lieutenant in Company F, First Regiment, Virginia Volunteers; studied law; was admitted to the bar in 1851 and commenced practice in Norfolk, Va.; moved to Natchitoches, La., in 1852 and continued the practice of law; member of the Louisiana State house of representatives, 1859-1861; served in the Confederate Army during the Civil War; commissioned captain of Company A, Second Louisiana Infantry, May 11, 1861; subsequently served as a major in the Adjutant General's Department; elected as a Democrat to the Forty-fourth Congress (March 4, 1875-March 3, 1877); unsuccessful candidate for renomination in 1876 to the Forty-fifth Congress; member of the State constitutional convention in 1879; appointed associate justice of the Louisiana State supreme court in 1879, and served until his death in Saratoga, N.Y., August 14, 1882; interment in the American Cemetery, Natchitoches, La.

**LEWIS, Abner,** a Representative from New York; born in Panama, Chautauqua County, N.Y.; attended the public schools; member of the State assembly in 1838 and 1839; elected as a Whig to the Twenty-ninth Congress (March 4, 1845-March 3, 1847); county judge 1847-1852.

**LEWIS, Barbour,** a Representative from Tennessee; born in Alburg, Vt., January 5, 1818; attended the common schools; was graduated from Illinois College, Jacksonville, Ill., in 1846; taught school in Mobile, Ala.; was graduated from the law department of Harvard University; was admitted to the bar and practiced; delegate to the Republican National Convention in 1860; enlisted in the Union Army August 1, 1861, and served as captain of Company G, First Missouri Volunteers; appointed by the military authorities judge of the civil commission court at Memphis, Tenn., in 1863; discharged from the service November 15, 1864; president of the commissioners of Shelby County, Tenn., 1867-1869; elected as a Republican to the Forty-third Congress (March 4, 1873-March 3, 1875); unsuccessful candidate for reelection in 1874 to the Forty-fourth Congress; resumed the practice of law in Memphis, Tenn.; moved to St. Louis, Mo., in 1878; appointed to the United States land office at Salt Lake City, Utah; resigned this position in 1879 and moved to Whitman County, Territory of Washington, where he engaged in agricultural pursuits and stock raising; died in Colfax, Wash., July 15, 1893; interment in Colfax Cemetery.

**LEWIS, Burwell Boykin,** a Representative from Alabama; born in Montgomery, Ala., July 7, 1838; moved with his parents to Mobile, Ala.; after the death of his parents lived with an uncle in Montevallo, Shelby County, Ala.; attended a private school; was graduated from the University of Alabama at Tuscaloosa in 1857; studied law in Selma, Ala.; was admitted to the bar in 1859 and commenced practice in Montevallo; during the Civil War served in the Confederate Army and attained the rank of captain of the Second Alabama Cavalry; member of the State house of representatives 1870-1872; moved to Tuscaloosa, Ala., in 1872 and engaged in the iron and coal business; elected as a Democrat to the Forty-fourth Congress (March 4, 1875-March 3, 1877); unsuccessful candidate for reelection in 1876 to the Forty-fifth Congress; elected to the Forty-sixth Congress and served from March 4, 1879, to October 1, 1880, when he resigned to accept the presidency of the University of Alabama; served in this capacity until his death in Tuscaloosa, Ala., on October 11, 1885; interment in Evergreen Cemetery.

**LEWIS, Charles Jeremy (Jerry),** a Representative from California; born in Seattle, Wash., October 21, 1934; attended the public schools of San Bernardino, Calif.; graduated, San Bernardino High School, 1952; B.A., University of California, Los Angeles, 1956; Coro Foundation, 1956-1957; developed and operated a life insurance business since 1958; member, San Bernardino School Board, 1964-1968; field representative to Representative Jerry L. Pettis of California, 1966; member, California State assembly, 1969-1978; member, California Republican Central Committee, ten years; elected as a Republican to the Ninety-sixth and to the eight succeeding Congresses (January 3, 1979-January 3, 1997); chairman, House Republican Conference (One Hundred First and One Hundred Second Congresses); is a resident of Redlands, Calif.

**LEWIS, Charles Swearinger,** a Representative from Virginia; born in Clarksburg, Va. (now West Virginia), February 26, 1821; attended local schools and Ohio University at Athens; graduated from Augusta (Ky.) College in 1844; studied law; admitted to the bar in 1846 and commenced practice in Clarksburg, Va.; member of the Virginia house of delegates 1849-1852; elected as a Democrat to the Thirty-third Congress to fill the vacancy caused by the death of John F. Snodgrass and served from December 4, 1854, to March 3, 1855; unsuccessful candidate for reelection in 1854 to the Thirty-fourth Congress; resumed the practice of law in Clarksburg; delegate to the Virginia constitutional convention in 1861; served in the West Virginia State house of representatives in 1871; was West Virginia superintendent of free schools and adjutant general of the State of West Virginia from 1871 to 1873; resigned upon his election as judge of the second judicial circuit and served until his death in Clarksburg, W.Va., January 22, 1878; interment in Odd Fellows Cemetery.

**LEWIS, Clarke,** a Representative from Mississippi; born in Huntsville, Madison County, Ala., November 8, 1840; moved with his mother to Noxubee County, Miss., in 1844; attended the district schools and Somerville Institute; engaged in teaching for several years; entered the Confederate Army in February 1861 and served until the close of the Civil War; resumed teaching in 1865; employed as a clerk in a store in 1866 and 1867; engaged in mercantile and agricultural pursuits 1867-1879; member of the State house of representatives in 1878; elected as a Democrat to the Fifty-first and Fifty-second Congresses (March 4, 1889-March 3, 1893); resumed agricultural pursuits; died near Macon, Miss., March 13, 1896; interment in the Odd Fellows Cemetery, Macon, Miss.

**LEWIS, David John,** a Representative from Maryland; born in Nuttals Bank, Center County, near Osceola Mills, Clearfield County, Pa., May 1, 1869; worked in the coal mines 1878-1892; while so employed studied law and Latin; was admitted to the bar in 1892 and commenced practice in Cumberland, Md.; member of the State senate 1902-1906; unsuccessful Democratic candidate for election to the Sixty-first Congress in 1908; elected as a Democrat to the Sixty-second, Sixty-third, and Sixty-fourth Congresses (March 4, 1911-March 3, 1917); chairman, Committee on Labor (Sixty-third and Sixty-fourth Congresses); was not a candidate for renomination in 1916, but was an unsuccessful Democratic candidate for election to the United States Senate; member of the United States Tariff

Commission from April 1917 to March 1925; unsuccessful candidate for the Democratic nomination for United States Senator in 1922; resumed the practice of law in Cumberland, Md.; again elected to the Seventy-second and to the three succeeding Congresses (March 4, 1931-January 3, 1939); was not a candidate for renomination in 1938, but was an unsuccessful candidate for the Democratic nomination for United States Senator; member of the National Mediation Board 1939-1943; died in Cumberland, Md., August 12, 1952; interment in Hillcrest Cemetery.

**Bibliography:** Masterson, Thomas Donald. "David J. Lewis of Maryland: Formative and Progressive Years, 1869-1917." Ph.D. dissertation, Georgetown University, 1976.

**LEWIS, Dixon Hall,** a Representative and a Senator from Alabama; born on Bothwick plantation, Dinwiddie County, Va., August 10, 1802; moved to Hancock County, Ga., with his parents in 1806; graduated from Mount Zion Academy and from South Carolina College at Columbia in 1820; moved to Autauga County, Ala., the same year; studied law and was admitted to the bar in 1823, and commenced the practice of law in Montgomery, Ala.; member, State house of representatives 1826-1828; elected as a States Rights Democrat to the Twenty-first and to the seven succeeding Congresses and served from March 4, 1829, to April 22, 1844, when he resigned, having been appointed Senator; chairman, Committee on Indian Affairs (Twenty-second and Twenty-third Congresses); appointed and subsequently elected as a Democrat to the United States Senate to fill the vacancy caused by the resignation of William R. King; reelected in 1847 and served from April 22, 1844, until his death in New York City on October 25, 1848; chairman, Committee on Finance (Twenty-ninth Congress), Committee on Retrenchment (Twenty-ninth Congress); interment in Greenwood Cemetery, Brooklyn, N.Y.

**Bibliography:** *DAB.*

**LEWIS, Earl Ramage,** a Representative from Ohio; born in Lamira, Belmont County, Ohio, February 22, 1887; attended the public and high schools; was graduated from Muskingum College, New Concord, Ohio, in 1911, and from the law department of Western Reserve University, Cleveland, Ohio, in 1914; admitted to the bar the same year and commenced practice in St. Clairsville, Ohio; member of the State senate in 1927, 1928, and 1931-1934, serving as president pro tempore in 1931 and 1932 and as Republican floor leader 1931-1934; chairman of the Republican State campaign committee for Ohio in 1930; member of the Interstate Commission on Conflicting Taxation of the American Legislators Association 1931-1935; elected as a Republican to the Seventy-sixth Congress (January 3, 1939-January 3, 1941); unsuccessful candidate for reelection in 1940 to the Seventy-seventh Congress; resumed the practice of law; again elected to the Seventy-eighth, Seventy-ninth, and Eightieth Congresses (January 3, 1943-January 3, 1949); unsuccessful candidate for reelection in 1948 to the Eighty-first Congress; resumed the practice of law; trustee of Muskingum College; died in Wheeling, W.Va., February 1, 1956; interment in Union Cemetery, St. Clairsville, Ohio.

**LEWIS, Edward Taylor,** a Representative from Louisiana; born in Opelousas, St. Landry Parish, October 26, 1834; received his early education from private tutors; later attended Wesleyan University, Delaware, Ohio; studied law; was admitted to the bar in 1859 and commenced practice in Opelousas, La.; enlisted as a private in an Infantry regiment of the Confederate Army and served throughout the Civil War, attaining the rank of captain of Cavalry; member of the State house of representatives in 1865; elected as a Democrat to the Forty-eighth Congress on February 15, 1883, to fill the vacancy caused by the death of Representative-elect Andrew S. Herron and served from March 4, 1883, to March 3, 1885; unsuccessful candidate for renomination in 1884; served as judge for the fifth judicial district from 1887 to 1892; again a member of the

State house of representatives 1886-1888; served as judge of the court of appeals, third circuit of Louisiana, 1894-1896; judge of the sixteenth judicial district 1900-1908; resumed the practice of law; died in Opelousas, La., April 26, 1927; interment in Myrtle Grove Cemetery.

**LEWIS, Elijah Banks,** a Representative from Georgia; born in Coney, Dooly County, Ga., March 27, 1854; attended the common schools of Dooly and Macon Counties, Spalding Seminary, Spalding, Ga., and a business school in Macon, Ga.; moved to Montezuma, Macon County, Ga., in 1871 and engaged in banking and mercantile pursuits; member of the State senate in 1894 and 1895; elected as a Democrat to the Fifty-fifth and to the five succeeding Congresses (March 4, 1897-March 3, 1909); unsuccessful candidate for renomination in 1908 to the Sixty-first Congress; engaged in his former business activities until his death in Montezuma, Ga., on December 10, 1920; interment in Felton Cemetery.

**LEWIS, Francis,** a Delegate from New York; born in Llandaff, Wales, March 21, 1713; attended Westminster School, London; entered the countinghouse of a London merchant; immigrated to the United States in 1735 and established mercantile houses in New York and Philadelphia; secured a contract to clothe the British Army in America in 1753; participated in the French and Indian War as an aide to General Mercer; was captured in Oswego, N.Y., and taken as a prisoner to France; on his return the colonial government gave him 5,000 acres of land in recognition of his services; delegate in the Stamp Act Congress that met in New York City in 1765; retired from business in 1765 and located in Whitestone, Long Island, N.Y.; Member of the Continental Congress 1775-1779; was a signer of the Declaration of Independence; delegate to the provincial convention in 1775; member of the Committee of One Hundred in 1775; served in the Provincial Congress in 1776 and 1777; commissioner of the board of admiralty in 1779; died in New York City on December 30, 1803; interment in Trinity Churchyard.

**Bibliography:** *DAB.*

**LEWIS, Fred Ewing,** a Representative from Pennsylvania; born in Allentown, Lehigh County, Pa., February 8, 1865; attended the public schools, the Collegiate and Commercial Institute, New Haven, Conn., and Muhlenberg College, Allentown, Pa.; studied law; was admitted to the bar in 1888 and commenced practice of his profession in Allentown, Pa.; mayor of Allentown in 1896 and 1902; organized and was president of the Merchants' National Bank and was president of the Dime Savings & Trust Co. in Allentown; elected as a Republican to the Sixty-third Congress (March 4, 1913-March 3, 1915); resumed the practice of his profession and also engaged in banking; again mayor of Allentown, Pa. 1932-1936; died in Allentown, Pa., June 27, 1949; interment in Union-West End Cemetery.

**LEWIS, James Hamilton,** a Representative from Washington and a Senator from Illinois; born in Danville, Pittsylvania County, Va., May 18, 1863; moved with his parents to Augusta, Ga., in 1866; attended Houghton school in that city, and the University of Virginia at Charlottesville; studied law in Savannah, Ga., and was admitted to the bar in 1882; moved to the Territory of Washington in 1885 and commenced the practice of law in Seattle; member, Washington Territorial legislature, 1887-1888; elected as a Democrat to the Fifty-fifth Congress (March 4, 1897-March 3, 1899); unsuccessful candidate for reelection in 1898 to the Fifty-sixth Congress; served during the Spanish-American War as inspector general with rank of colonel in Puerto Rico; unsuccessful Democratic candidate for United States Senator in 1899; moved to Chicago, Ill. in 1903 and resumed the practice of law; corporation counsel for Chicago, 1905-1907; unsuccessful candidate for Governor in 1908; elected as a Democrat to the United States Senate, and served from March 26, 1913 to March 3, 1919; unsuccessful candidate for reelection in

1918; Democratic whip 1913-1919; chairman, Committee on Expenditures in the Department of State (Sixty-fourth and Sixty-fifth Congresses); unsuccessful Democratic candidate for Governor of Illinois in 1920; practiced international law; again elected as a Democrat to the United States Senate in 1930; reelected in 1936, and served from March 4, 1931 until his death in Washington, D.C., April 9, 1939; Democratic whip 1933-1939; chairman, Committee on Expenditures in Executive Departments (Seventy-third through Seventy-sixth Congresses); funeral services were held in the Chamber of the United States Senate; interment in the Abbey Mausoleum, adjoining Arlington National Cemetery.

**LEWIS, Jerry,** a Representative from California. (*See* LEWIS, Charles Jeremy.)

**LEWIS, John Francis,** a Senator from Virginia; born in Lynnwood, Rockingham County, Va., March 1, 1818; attended an old field school; engaged in agricultural pursuits; delegate to the Virginia secession convention in 1861 and refused to sign the ordinance of secession; elected lieutenant governor in 1869; upon the readmission of Virginia to representation was elected as a Republican to the United States Senate and served from January 26, 1870, to March 3, 1875; was not a candidate for reelection; chairman, Committee on the District of Columbia (Forty-third Congress); appointed by Presidents Ulysses S. Grant and Rutherford B. Hayes as United States marshal for the western district of Virginia from 1875 until 1882, when he resigned; again elected lieutenant governor in 1881; resumed agricultural pursuits; died at "Lynnwood," Rockingham County, Va., September 2, 1895; interment in the family burial ground.

**Bibliography:** *DAB.*

**LEWIS, John Henry,** a Representative from Illinois; born near Ithaca, Tompkins County, N.Y., July 21, 1830; moved to Illinois in 1836 with his parents, who settled on a farm in Fulton County, near Ellisville; attended the rural schools; moved to Knox County, Ill., in 1847 and engaged in agricultural pursuits near Knoxville; studied law; was admitted to the bar in 1860 and commenced practice in Knoxville, Ill.; clerk of the circuit court of Knox County 1860-1864; member of the State house of representatives in 1874 and 1875; elected as a Republican to the Forty-seventh Congress (March 4, 1881-March 3, 1883); unsuccessful candidate for reelection in 1882 to the Forty-eighth Congress; resumed the practice of law before retiring in 1900; died in Knoxville, Ill., on January 6, 1929; interment in Knoxville Cemetery.

**LEWIS, John R.,** a Representative from Georgia; born in Troy, Pike County, Ala., February 21, 1940; attended public schools; graduated, Pike County Training School, Brundidge, Ala., 1957; B.A., American Baptist Theological Seminary, Nashville, Tenn., 1961; B.A., Fisk University, Nashville, Tenn., 1963; chairman, Student Non-Violent Coordinating Committee, 1963-1966; staff member, Field Foundation; director of the Voter Education Project of the Southern Regional Council, 1970-1977; associate director of ACTION, 1977-1980; community affairs director, National Consumer Co-op Bank, Atlanta, 1980-1986; member, Atlanta City Council, 1982-1986; elected as a Democrat to the One Hundredth and to the four succeeding Congresses (January 3, 1987-January 3, 1997); is a resident of Atlanta, Ga.

**LEWIS, John William,** a Representative from Kentucky; born near Greensburg, Green County, Ky., October 14, 1841; attended the common schools; graduated from Centre College, Danville, Ky., in 1862; studied law; admitted to the bar in 1863 and practiced in Greensburg, Ky.; moved to Springfield, Ky., January 1, 1869; temporary chairman of the Republican convention April 10, 1880; delegate to the Republican National Conventions in 1880, 1884, 1888 and 1904; delegate to the constitutional convention of Kentucky in 1890 and was unseated upon a contest; member of the Republican central committee of Kentucky 1878-1891 and chairman in the Kentucky campaign of 1887; served as special judge in the circuit courts of Marion, Taylor, and other counties; elected as a Republican to the Fifty-fourth Congress (March 4, 1895-March 3, 1897); unsuccessful candidate for reelection in 1896 to the Fifty-fifth Congress; chairman of the congressional convention of his district in 1904 and 1908; resumed the practice of his profession in Springfield, Ky.; died in Fort Worth, Tex., December 20, 1913; interment in Lebanon Cemetery, Lebanon, Marion County, Ky.

**LEWIS, Joseph, Jr.,** a Representative from Virginia; born in Virginia in 1772; member of the Virginia house of delgates 1799-1803; elected as a Federalist to the Eighth and to the six succeeding Congresses (March 4, 1803-March 3, 1817); chairman, Committee on District of Columbia (Tenth and Twelfth Congresses); again a member of the Virginia house of delegates in 1817 and 1818; died in Clifton, Va., March 30, 1834.

**LEWIS, Joseph Horace,** a Representative from Kentucky; born near Glasgow, Barren County, Ky., October 29, 1824; attended the common schools; was graduated from Centre College, Danville, Ky., in 1843; studied law; was admitted to the bar in 1845 and commenced practice in Glasgow, Ky.; member of the Kentucky house of representatives, 1850-1855; unsuccessful candidate for election in 1857 to the Thirty-fifth Congress, and in 1861 to the Thirty-seventh Congress; during the Civil War commanded the Sixth Kentucky Regiment in the Confederate Army, the Second Brigade and the First Brigade in William B. Bate's division, and was commissioned brigadier general September 30, 1863; returned to Glasgow at the close of the Civil War and resumed the practice of law; again a member of the Kentucky house of representatives in 1869 and 1870; elected as a Democrat to the Forty-first Congress to fill the vacancy caused by the resignation of Jacob S. Golladay; reelected to the Forty-second Congress, and served from May 10, 1870 to March 3, 1873; was not a candidate for renomination in 1872 to the Forty-third Congress; resumed the practice of his profession; elected judge of the Kentucky Court of Appeals in 1874; reelected to subsequent terms and served until 1898; moved to a farm in Scott County, near Georgetown, where he died on July 6, 1904; interment in Glasgow Cemetery.

Bibliography: *DAB.*

**LEWIS, Lawrence,** a Representative from Colorado; born in St. Louis, Mo., June 22, 1879; attended the public schools in Evanston, Ill., Cambridge, Mass., and Pueblo, Colo., and the University of Colorado at Boulder; was graduated from Harvard University in 1901; engaged in newspaper and magazine work in Pueblo and Denver, Colo., 1901-1906; assistant instructor in English, Harvard University, 1906-1909; was graduated from the law department of Harvard University in 1909; was admitted to the bar the same year and commenced practice in Denver, Colo.; member of Colorado Civil Service Commission 1917-1918; private in the Seventeenth Observation Battery, Field Artillery, Central Officers' Training School, October to December 1918; unsuccessful candidate for election in 1930 to the Seventy-second Congress; elected as a Democrat to the Seventy-third and five succeeding Congresses and served from March 4, 1933, until his death; one of the managers appointed by the House of Representatives in 1933 to conduct the impeachment proceedings against Harold Louderback, judge of the United States District Court for the Northern District of California; died in Washington, D.C., on December 9, 1943; interment in Spring Grove Cemetery, Cincinnati, Ohio.

**LEWIS, Robert Jacob,** a Representative from Pennsylvania; born in Dover, Dover Township, York County, Pa., December 30, 1864; attended the public schools of York and was graduated from the high school in 1883; taught in the public schools until September 1889; was graduated from the law department of Yale University in 1891; was admitted to the New Haven (Conn.) bar June 1891 and to

the bar of York County, Pa., August 3, 1891, and commenced practice in York, Pa.; elected school controller of York in 1893 and reelected in 1897 and 1903; elected city solicitor in 1895; unsuccessful candidate for election in 1898 to the Fifty-sixth Congress; elected as a Republican to the Fifty-seventh Congress (March 4, 1901-March 3, 1903); declined to be a candidate for renomination in 1902; resumed the practice of his profession; died in Camden, Ark., July 24, 1933; remains were cremated and the ashes placed in the Iris Columbarium Mausoleum, St. Louis, Mo.

**LEWIS, Ron E.,** a Representative from Kentucky; born in Greenup County, Ky., September 14, 1946; graduated, McKell (Ky.) High School, 1964; attended Morehead State University, 1964-1967; B.A., University of Kentucky, 1969, and M.A., 1981; United States Navy service, Aviation Officer Candidate School; released in 1972; instructor, Watterson College, Louisville, Ky., 1980-1986; owner, Alpha Christian Bookstore; ordained clergy, Baptist Church, 1980; elected as a Republican to the One Hundred Third Congress, May 24, 1994, by special election to fill the vacancy caused by the death of William H. Natcher; reelected to the One Hundred Fourth Congress, and served from May 24, 1994 to January 3, 1997; is a resident of Cecilia, Ky.

**LEWIS, Thomas,** a Representative from Virginia; born in Augusta County, Va.; attended the common schools; presented credentials as a Federalist Representative-elect to the Eighth Congress and served from March 4, 1803, until March 5, 1804, when he was succeeded by Andrew Moore, who contested his election; by formal action of the House of Representatives counsel for the claimants in this case were heard at the bar of the House.

**LEWIS, Thomas F.,** a Representative from Florida; born in Philadelphia, Philadelphia County, Pa., October 26, 1924; attended St. Edwards School, Philadelphia; graduated from Central High School, Philadelphia, 1942; attended Palm Beach (Fla.) Junior College, 1957, and the University of Florida, Gainesville, 1959; served in the United States Air Force, master sergeant, 1943-1954; aircraft industry executive, 1957-1973; real estate and investments, 1972-1982; elected mayor/councilman of North Palm Beach, Fla., 1964-1971; member, Florida State house of representatives, 1972-1980; Florida State senator, 1980-1982; delegate, Florida State Republican convention, 1980 and 1982; delegate to the Republican National Convention of 1984; elected as a Republican to the Ninety-eighth and to the five succeeding Congresses (January 3, 1983-January 3, 1995); was not a candidate for reelection in 1994 to the One Hundred Fourth Congress; is a resident of North Palm Beach, Fla.

**LEWIS, William,** a Representative from Kentucky; born in Cutshin, Leslie County, Ky., September 22, 1868; raised on a farm and attended the common schools of Leslie and Perry Counties and the Laurel County Seminary, London, Ky.; studied law at the University of Kentucky at Lexington and at the University of Michigan at Ann Arbor; sheriff of Leslie County in 1891 and 1892; superintendent of schools of Leslie County 1894-1898; member of Kentucky house of representatives in 1900 and 1901; Commonwealth attorney 1904-1909; circuit judge of the twenty-seventh judicial district of Kentucky 1909-1922 and 1928-1934; entered the private practice of law; elected as a Republican to the Eightieth Congress to fill the vacancy caused by the death of John Marshall Robsion and served from April 24, 1948, to January 3, 1949; was not a candidate for renomination in 1948 to the Eighty-first Congress; died in London, Laurel County, Ky., August 8, 1959; interment in A.R. Dyche Memorial Park.

**LEWIS, William J.,** a Representative from Virginia; born in Augusta County, Va., July 4, 1766; attended the common schools; member of the Virginia house of delegates; elected as a Republican to the Fifteenth Congress (March 4, 1817-March 3, 1819); died at

"Mount Athos" plantation, near Lynchburg, Campbell County, Va., November 1, 1828; interment in a vault blasted out of a solid rock at the summit of "Mount Athos," Virginia.

**L'HOMMEDIEU, Ezra,** a Delegate from New York; born in Southold, Long Island, N.Y., August 30, 1734; was graduated from Yale College in 1754; studied law; was admitted to the bar and practiced in Southold, N.Y.; delegate to the Provincial Congress 1775-1777; member of the State assembly 1777-1783; Member of the Continental Congress 1779-1783 and 1788; served in the State senate 1784-1792 and 1794-1809; member of the State constitutional convention in 1801; clerk of Suffolk County from January 1784 to March 1810 and from March 1811 until his death; regent of the University of the State of New York 1787-1811; was a Federalist; died in Southold, N.Y., September 27, 1811; interment in the Presbyterian Cemetery.

**LIBBEY, Harry,** a Representative from Virginia; born in Wakefield, Carroll County, N.H., November 22, 1843; attended the common schools; moved to Virginia and settled in Hampton in 1863; engaged in mercantile pursuits; appointed one of the presiding justices of Elizabeth City County, Va., in 1869; elected as a Readjuster to the Forty-eighth Congress and reelected as a Republican to the Forty-ninth Congress (March 4, 1883-March 3, 1887); engaged in the oyster industry; served as chairman of the Republican county committee; appointed postmaster of Hampton, Va., January 18, 1907, and served until his death in Hampton, Elizabeth City County, Va., on September 30, 1913; interment in St. John's Cemetery.

**LIBONATI, Roland Victor,** a Representative from Illinois; born in Chicago, Cook County, Ill., December 29, 1900; A.A., Lewis Institute, 1918; during the First World War served as a lieutenant in the United States Army; graduated from the University of Michigan in 1921; J.D., University of Michigan and Northwestern University Law School, 1924; was admitted to the bar in 1924 and commenced law practice in Chicago, Ill.; member, Illinois State house of representatives, 1930-1934, 1940-1942, and State senate, 1942-1947; founder and owner of American Boys' Camp for indigent children at Coloma, Wis.; delegate to each State convention from 1942 to 1987; elected as a Democrat to the Eighty-fifth Congress to fill the vacancy caused by the death of James B. Bowler; reelected to the three succeeding Congresses, and served from December 31, 1957 to January 3, 1965; was not a candidate for renomination in 1964 to the Eighty-ninth Congress; resumed the practice of law; was a resident of Chicago, Ill.; died May 26, 1991.

**LICHTENWALNER, Norton Lewis,** a Representative from Pennsylvania; born in Allentown, Lehigh County, Pa., June 1, 1889; educated in the public schools, graduating from Allentown High School in 1905 and Bethlehem Preparatory School in 1906; attended Lehigh University, Bethlehem, Pa.; moved to New York City in 1908 and was employed in a banking institution; returned to Allentown, Pa., in 1915 and engaged in the retail furniture business until 1922, then in the retailing of automobiles until 1933; during the First World War enlisted as a seaman in the United States Naval Reserve; elected as a Democrat to the Seventy-second Congress (March 4, 1931-March 3, 1933); unsuccessful candidate for reelection in 1932 to the Seventy-third Congress; director for the Pennsylvania National Emergency Council, 1935-1941; director of Pennsylvania Office of Government Reports in 1941 and 1942; engaged in the investment securities business; in 1949 was elected to the Allentown City Council for one term, and in 1955 elected treasurer of Lehigh County for one term; died in Allentown, Pa., May 3, 1960; interment in Fairview Cemetery.

**LICHTENWALTER, Franklin Herbert,** a Representative from Pennsylvania; born in Palmerton, Carbon County, Pa., on March 28, 1910; attended the public schools of Palmerton and Upper Saucon Township; was graduated from Allentown High School in 1929; engaged in general insurance business from 1933 until 1973; member of the Pennsylvania house of representatives, 1938-1947, serving as majority leader, 1943-1946, and as speaker in 1947; elected as a Republican to the Eightieth Congress, September 9, 1947, by special election to fill the vacancy caused by the death of Charles L. Gerlach; reelected to the Eighty-first Congress, and served from September 9, 1947 to January 3, 1951; was not a candidate for renomination in 1950 to the Eighty-second Congress; resumed the insurance business; vice president and managing director of Pennsylvania Electric Association, Harrisburg, Pa.; died in Harrisburg, Pa., March 4, 1973; interment in St. Paul's Blue Church Cemetery, Coopersburg, Pa.

**LIEB, Charles,** a Representative from Indiana; born in Flehingen, Germany, May 20, 1852; immigrated to the United States in 1868 and settled in Rockport, Ind.; attended the public schools, the Rockport Collegiate Institute, and Bryant and Stratton's Business College, Louisville, Ky.; employed as a bookkeeper and accountant; member of the Rockport City Council 1879-1884; engaged in the lumber business and as a contractor in 1882; postmaster of Rockport 1893-1897; member of the State house of representatives 1907-1913; elected as a Democrat to the Sixty-third and Sixty-fourth Congresses (March 4, 1913-March 3, 1917); was not a candidate for renomination in 1916; delegate to the Democratic National Convention in 1916; served as president and director of the Farmers' Bank, Rockport, Ind.; also engaged in agricultural pursuits; died in Rockport, Ind., September 1, 1928; interment in Sun Set Hill Cemetery.

**LIEBEL, Michael, Jr.,** a Representative from Pennsylvania; born in Erie, Pa., December 12, 1870; attended the public schools of Erie; was graduated from Canisius College, Buffalo, N.Y.; accountant in the office of the New York, Chicago & St. Louis Railroad at Buffalo for five years; returned to Erie, Pa., and engaged in the hardware business, and later organized and was secretary-treasurer of a brewery company; in 1911 organized and became president of the Vulcan Rubber Co.; mayor of Erie, Pa., 1906-1911; delegate to the Democratic National Conventions in 1908, 1912, 1916, 1920, and 1924; elected as a Democrat to the Sixty-fourth Congress (March 4, 1915-March 3, 1917); was not a candidate for renomination in 1916; resumed his former business activities; died in Philadelphia, Pa., August 8, 1927; interment in Trinity Cemetery, Erie, Pa.

**LIEBERMAN, Joseph I.,** a Senator from Connecticut; born in Stamford, Fairfield County, Conn., February 24, 1942; attended Stamford public schools; B.A., Yale University, 1964; J.D., Yale University School of Law, 1967; admitted to the Connecticut bar in 1967; attorney; member, Connecticut State senate, 1971-1982, majority leader, 1975-1981; unsuccessful candidate for election in 1980 to the Ninety-seventh Congress; State attorney general of Connecticut, 1983-1988; elected as a Democrat to the United States Senate in 1988 for the term commencing January 3, 1989; reelected in 1994 for the term ending January 3, 2001; is a resident of New Haven, Conn.

**LIGHTFOOT, James Ross,** a Representative from Iowa; born in Sioux City, Iowa, September 27, 1938; raised on a farm near Farragut, Iowa; graduated from Farragut High School in 1956; served in the United States Army and the Army Reserve, 1956-1964; police officer in Tulsa, Okla., 1959-1961; managed a farm equipment plant in Corsicana, Tex., 1970-1976; member, Corsicana City Commission, 1974-1976; radio broadcaster and farm editor in Shenandoah, Iowa, 1961-1970 and 1976-1984; elected as a Republican to the Ninety-ninth and to the five succeeding Congresses (January 3, 1985-January 3, 1997); was not a candidate in 1996 for reelection to the House of Representatives, but was a candidate for election to the United States Senate; is a resident of Shenandoah, Iowa.

**LIGON, Robert Fulwood,** a Representative from Alabama; born in Watkinsville, Oconee County, Ga., December 16, 1823; attended the country schools of his native county, the academy near Watkinsville, and the University of Georgia at Athens; moved to Athens, Ga., and later, in 1844, to Tuskegee, Ala.; studied law; was admitted to the bar in 1845 and commenced practice in Tuskegee; served in the Mexican War as a captain in the First Alabama Battalion; member, Alabama State house of representatives, 1849-1850; served in the State senate, 1861-1864; during the Civil War served in the Confederate Army as captain of Company F, Twelfth Regiment, Alabama Infantry, Rhodes' division; resumed the practice of law; unsuccessful candidate for Governor in 1872; Lieutenant Governor of Alabama in 1874; elected as a Democrat to the Forty-fifth Congress (March 4, 1877-March 3, 1879); unsuccessful candidate for renomination in 1878 to the Forty-sixth Congress; continued the practice of law until 1884, when he retired from active practice and moved to Montgomery; engaged in banking and as a planter; served forty years as president of the board of trustees of the Alabama Female College; also a trustee of the Alabama Polytechnic Institute at Auburn for many years; died in Montgomery, Ala., October 11, 1901; interment in Oakwood Cemetery.

**LIGON, Thomas Watkins,** a Representative from Maryland; born near Farmville, Prince Edward County, Va., May 10, 1810; attended Hampden-Sidney College and the University of Virginia at Charlottesville in 1830 and 1831; studied law at Yale College; was admitted to the bar in 1833 and practiced in Baltimore from 1835 to 1853, and in other places in Maryland; member of the Maryland State house of delegates in 1843; elected as a Democrat to the Twenty-ninth and Thirtieth Congresses (March 4, 1845-March 3, 1849); resumed the practice of law; elected Governor of Maryland in 1853, and served from January 11, 1854 to January 13, 1858; retired from public life to "Chatham," his country place, near Ellicott City, Howard County, Md., where he died on January 12, 1881; interment in St. John's Cemetery, Ellicott City, Md.

**Bibliography:** *DAB.*

**LILLEY, George Leavens,** a Representative from Connecticut; born in Oxford, Worcester County, Mass., August 3, 1859; attended the common schools of Oxford, the Worcester High School, and Worcester Technical Institute, Worcester, Mass.; moved to Waterbury, Conn., in 1881 and engaged in mercantile pursuits and the real estate business; served in the Connecticut State house of representatives, 1901-1903; elected as a Republican to the Fifty-eighth and to the two succeeding Congresses, and served from March 4, 1903 to January 5, 1909; was not a candidate for renomination in 1908 to the Sixty-first Congress, but was elected Governor of Connecticut; by resolution of the House of January 20, 1909, his seat was declared to have been vacated on January 6, 1909, for the reason that he had entered upon his duties as Governor the preceding day; Governor of Connecticut from January 5, 1909 until his death in Hartford, Conn., April 21, 1909; interment in Riverside Cemetery, Waterbury, Conn.

**LILLEY, Mial Eben,** a Representative from Pennsylvania; born in Canton, Bradford County, Pa., May 30, 1850; attended public and private schools; worked as a blacksmith for several years; studied law in Canton; was admitted to the bar in 1880 and commenced practice in Towanda, Bradford County, Pa.; for several years was chairman of the Republican committee of Bradford County; elected prothonotary of Bradford County in 1893 and reelected in 1896; appointed assistant United States district attorney for the middle district of Pennsylvania in 1903; elected as a Republican to the Fifty-ninth Congress (March 4, 1905-March 3, 1907); unsuccessful candidate for reelection in 1906 to the Sixtieth Congress; engaged in

the practice of his profession until his death in Towanda, Pa., February 28, 1915; interment in Oak Hill Cemetery.

**LILLY, Samuel,** a Representative from New Jersey; born in Geneva, N.Y., October 28, 1815; moved to Lambertville, N.J., in 1829; attended Rev. P.O. Studdiford's classical school; was graduated from the medical department of the University of Pennsylvania on March 31, 1837, and commenced practice in Lambertville, N.J.; first mayor of Lambertville, 1849-1852; elected as a Democrat to the Thirty-third Congress (March 4, 1853-March 3, 1855); chairman, Committee on Expenditures in the Post Office Department (Thirty-third Congress); director of the Board of Freeholders of Hunterdon County for eight years; brigadier general of the State militia; appointed by President James Buchanan as consul general of the United States to British India, with residence in Calcutta, January 3, 1861, and served until July 4, 1862, when he resigned; judge of the court of common pleas of Hunterdon County, N.J., from 1868 until 1873; one of the members of the board of managers of the New Jersey Insane Asylum in 1871; judge of the court of errors and appeals and also a member of the State board of pardons from 1873 until his death in Lambertville, Hunterdon County, N.J., April 3, 1880; interment in Mount Hope Cemetery.

**LILLY, Thomas Jefferson,** a Representative from West Virginia; born in Dunns, Mercer County, W.Va., June 3, 1878; attended the rural schools of his county; taught school and also engaged in agricultural pursuits; justice of the peace 1902-1906; was graduated from the law department of McKinley University, Chicago, Ill., in 1911; was admitted to the bar the same year and commenced the practice of law in Hinton, Summers County, W.Va.; divorce commissioner of Summers County 1914-1922; State commissioner of accounts 1914-1927; elected as a Democrat to the Sixty-eighth Congress (March 4, 1923-March 3, 1925); unsuccessful candidate for reelection in 1924 to the Sixty-ninth Congress; resumed the practice of law and was also interested in agricultural pursuits; died in Sweet Springs, W.Va., April 2, 1956; interment in Restwood Memorial Cemetery, Hinton, W.Va.

**LILLY, William,** a Representative from Pennsylvania; born in Penn Yan, Yates County, N.Y., June 3, 1821; moved to Carbon County, Pa., in 1838; elected colonel of one of the militia regiments of the Lehigh Valley and subsequently brigadier general; member of the Pennsylvania house of representatives in 1850 and 1851; was a Democrat until 1862, when he affiliated with the Republican Party; delegate to six Republican National Conventions; delegate at large to the convention to revise the constitution of Pennsylvania in 1872 and 1873; engaged in the mining of anthracite coal; elected as a Republican to the Fifty-third Congress and served from March 4, 1893, until his death in Mauch Chunk, Pa., December 1, 1893; interment in the City Cemetery.

**LINCOLN, Abraham,** a Representative from Illinois and 16th President of the United States; born in Hardin County, Ky., February 12, 1809; moved with his parents to a tract on Little Pigeon Creek, Ind., in 1816; attended a log-cabin school at short intervals and was self-instructed in elementary branches; moved with his father to Macon County, Ill., in 1830 and later to Coles County, Ill.; read the principles of law and works on surveying; during the Black Hawk War he volunteered in a company of Sangamon County Rifles organized on April 21, 1832; was elected its captain, and served until May 27, 1832, when the company was mustered out of service; reenlisted as a private and served until mustered out on June 16, 1832; returned to New Salem, Ill., and was unsuccessful as a candidate for the Illinois State house of representatives; entered business as a general merchant in New Salem; postmaster of New Salem, 1833-1836; deputy county surveyor, 1834-1836; elected a member of the Illinois State house of representatives in 1834, 1836, 1838, and 1840; declined to be a candidate for renomination; admitted to the bar in 1836; moved to

Springfield, Ill., in 1837 and engaged in the practice of law; elected as a Whig to the Thirtieth Congress (March 4, 1847-March 3, 1849); was not a candidate for renomination in 1848 to the Thirty-first Congress; an unsuccessful applicant for Commissioner of the General Land Office in the summer of 1849; tendered the Governorship of Oregon Territory, but declined in September 1849; unsuccessful Whig candidate for election to the United States Senate before the legislature of 1855; unsuccessful Republican candidate for the United States Senate in 1858; elected President of the United States on the Republican ticket, November 6, 1860, for the term beginning March 4, 1861; reelected on November 8, 1864 for the term beginning March 4, 1865; served from March 4, 1861 until his assassination in Washington, D.C., April 14, 1865; died in Washington, D.C. the following day; interment in Oak Ridge Cemetery, Springfield, Ill.

**Bibliography:** *DAB*; Findley, Paul. *A. Lincoln: The Crucible of Congress*. New York: Crown Publishers, Inc., 1979; Lincoln, Abraham. *The Collected Works of Abraham Lincoln*. 8 Vols. Edited by Roy P. Basler. New Brunswick, N.J.: Rutgers University Press, 1953; Riddle, Donald W. *Congressman Abraham Lincoln*. Urbana: University of Illinois Press, 1957.

**LINCOLN, Blanche Lambert,** (served under the name of Blanche M. Lambert in the One Hundred Third Congress), a Representative from Arkansas; born in Helena, Phillips County, Ark., September 30, 1960; graduate of Helena Central High School; B.A., Randolph-Macon Woman's College, Lynchburg, Va., 1982; attended University of Arkansas; staff assistant to Representative William V. Alexander, Jr., of Arkansas, 1982; legislative researcher; associate, The Pagonis and Donnelly Group, Inc.; elected as a Democrat to the One Hundred Third and One Hundred Fourth Congresses (January 3, 1993-January 3, 1997); was not a candidate for reelection in 1996 to the One Hundred Fifth Congress; is a resident of Helena, Ark.

**LINCOLN, Enoch,** (son of Levi Lincoln [1749-1820] and brother of Levi Lincoln [1782-1868]), a Representative from Massachusetts and from Maine; born in Worcester, Mass., December 28, 1788; was graduated from Harvard University in 1807; studied law; was admitted to the bar and commenced the practice of his profession in Salem, Mass., in 1811; United States district attorney, 1815-1818; moved to Paris, Maine (then a district of Massachusetts), in 1819 and continued the practice of law; elected as a Republican to the Fifteenth Congress to fill the vacancy caused by the resignation of Albion K. Parris; reelected to the Sixteenth Congress, and served from November 4, 1818 to March 3, 1821; upon the admission of Maine as a State was elected to the Seventeenth and to the two succeeding Congresses, and served from March 4, 1821 until his resignation in 1826; elected Governor of Maine in 1826, reelected in 1827 and 1828, and served from January 3, 1827 until his death in Augusta, Kennebec County, Maine, on October 8, 1829; had declined to be a candidate for renomination; interment in a mausoleum in the State Park.

**Bibliography:** *DAB*.

**LINCOLN, Levi** (father of Enoch Lincoln and Levi Lincoln [1782-1868]), a Representative from Massachusetts; born in Hingham, Mass., May 15, 1749; attended the common schools; was graduated from Harvard College in 1772; studied law in Newburyport and Northampton, Mass.; joined the Minutemen in Cambridge at the outbreak of the Revolution; moved to Worcester, Mass.; was admitted to the bar and commenced practice in 1775; member of the committee of public safety; clerk of the court and judge of probate for Worcester County, 1775-1781; was specially designated to prosecute the claims of the Commonwealth to the numerous estates of loyalists in 1779; delegate to the Massachusetts constitutional convention in 1779; elected a Member of the Continental Congress in 1781, but declined to serve; member of the Massachusetts house

of representatives in 1796; served in the Massachusetts senate in 1797 and 1798; elected as a Republican to the Seventh Congress; subsequently elected to the Sixth Congress to fill the vacancy caused by the resignation of Dwight Foster and served from December 15, 1800, to March 5, 1801, when he resigned; appointed Attorney General in the Cabinet of President Thomas Jefferson, and served from March 5, 1801 to December 31, 1804, and as Acting Secretary of State from March 5 to May 2, 1801; member of the Governor's council of Massachusetts in 1806; Lieutenant Governor of Massachusetts in 1807 and 1808; became Governor upon the death of Governor James Sullivan and served in this capacity from December 10, 1808, to May 1, 1809; appointed an Associate Justice of the United States Supreme Court in 1810 by President James Madison, but declined to accept by reason of failing eyesight; again a member of the Governor's council in 1810 and 1811; died in Worcester, Worcester County, Mass., April 14, 1820; interment in the Rural Cemetery.

**Bibliography:** *DAB*; Petroelje, Marvin J. "Levi Lincoln, Sr.: Jeffersonian Republican of Massachusetts." Ph.D. dissertation, Michigan State University, 1969.

**LINCOLN, Levi** (son of Levi Lincoln [1749-1820] and brother of Enoch Lincoln), a Representative from Massachusetts; born in Worcester, Mass., October 25, 1782; attended Leicester Academy, Leicester, Mass., and was graduated from Harvard University in 1802; studied law; was admitted to the bar and commenced the practice of his profession at Worcester in 1805; served in the Massachusetts senate in 1812 and 1813; member of the Massachusetts house of representatives, 1814-1822, and served as speaker in 1822; delegate to the Massachusetts constitutional convention in 1820; elected Lieutenant Governor of Massachusetts in 1823; appointed associate justice of the Massachusetts supreme court in 1824; elected Governor of Massachusetts in 1825 and every year thereafter until 1833, and served from May 26, 1825 to January 9, 1834; declined to be a candidate for reelection in 1833; elected as an Anti-Jacksonian to the Twenty-third Congress to fill the vacancy caused by the resignation of John Davis; reelected as a Whig to the Twenty-fourth and to the three succeeding Congresses and served from February 17, 1834, to March 16, 1841, when he resigned; chairman, Committee on Public Buildings and Grounds (Twenty-fifth and Twenty-sixth Congresses); collector of the port of Boston, by appointment of President William Henry Harrison, 1841-1843; served in the Massachusetts senate in 1844 and 1845, and was president of that body in the latter year; first mayor of Worcester in 1848; presidential elector on the Republican ticket in 1864; died in Worcester, Worcester County, Mass., May 29, 1868; interment in the Rural Cemetery.

**Bibliography:** *DAB*.

**LINCOLN, William Slosson,** a Representative from New York; born in Berkshire (now Newark Valley), Tioga County, N.Y., August 13, 1813; attended the common schools; studied law; was admitted to the bar; engaged in mercantile pursuits and subsequently in the manufacture of leather; postmaster of Newark Valley from September 20, 1838, to February 24, 1841, and from December 19, 1844, to September 19, 1866; served as supervisor in 1841, 1844, 1865, and 1866; justice of the peace in 1852 and 1855; elected as a Republican to the Fortieth Congress (March 4, 1867-March 3, 1869); was not a candidate for reelection; engaged in the practice of law in Washington, D.C., until his death on April 21, 1893; interment in Oak Hill Cemetery.

**LIND, James Francis,** a Representative from Pennsylvania; born in York, Pa., October 17, 1900; attended the public schools in York, leaving high school to enlist in the United States Army in 1917; served overseas with the Third Infantry Division, and was discharged as a first sergeant in 1920; completed his formal education at the Penn State Extension School; cost accountant, York

Ice Machinery Corp., 1922-1941; active in Organized Reserve and Pennsylvania National Guard, 1934-1941; entered the service as a captain January 1941; served with the Twenty-eighth, Eighty-ninth, and Sixty-sixth Infantry Divisions; promoted to major in 1942 and lieutenant colonel in 1944; separated from the service in February 1946; in charge of the contact office of Veterans Administration of York County in 1946 and 1947; chief clerk to the York County Board of Commissioners in 1948; elected as a Democrat to the Eighty-first and Eighty-second Congresses (January 3, 1949-January 3, 1953); unsuccessful candidate for reelection in 1952 to the Eighty-third Congress; went on active duty with the United States Army in 1953 as special assistant to the controller in the office of Quartermaster General, Washington, D.C.; controller of York County, Pa., 1954-1974; is a resident of York, Pa.

**LIND, John,** a Representative from Minnesota; born in Kanna, Sweden, March 25, 1854; immigrated to the United States in 1867 with his parents, who settled in Goodhue County, Minn.; moved to Sibley County in 1872; attended the public schools and the University of Minnesota at Minneapolis; taught school; studied law; was admitted to the bar in 1877 and commenced practice in New Ulm, Minn.; receiver of the United States land office at Tracy from 1881 until 1885; elected as a Republican to the Fiftieth and to the two succeeding Congresses (March 4, 1887-March 3, 1893); chairman, Committee on Mileage (Fifty-first Congress); declined to be a candidate for renomination in 1892 to the Fifty-third Congress; unsuccessful candidate for Governor of Minnesota in 1896; during the Spanish-American War was mustered into the service on May 5, 1898, as first lieutenant and quartermaster in the Twelfth Regiment, Minnesota Volunteer Infantry; was honorably discharged with his regiment November 5, 1898; elected Governor of Minnesota in 1898, and served from January 2, 1899 to January 7, 1901; unsuccessful candidate for reelection in 1900; elected as a Democrat to the Fifty-eighth Congress (March 4, 1903-March 3, 1905); declined to be a candidate for renomination in 1904 to the Fifty-ninth Congress; resumed the practice of law in Minneapolis, Minn., president of the board of regents of the University of Minnesota; was appointed August 3, 1913 by President Woodrow Wilson as his personal representative to investigate the affairs of the United States Government in Mexico; practiced law in Minneapolis, Minn., until his death in that city on September 18, 1930; remains were cremated and the ashes interred in Lakewood Cemetery.

**Bibliography:** *DAB*; Stephenson, George Malcolm. *John Lind of Minnesota*. 1935. Reprint. Port Washington, N.Y.: Kennikat Press, 1971.

**LINDBERGH, Charles Augustus,** a Representative from Minnesota; born in Stockholm, Sweden, January 20, 1859; immigrated to the United States in 1860 with his parents, who settled on a farm near Melrose, Stearns County, Minn.; attended the common schools, Grove Lake (Minn.) Academy, and the St. Cloud (Minn.) Normal School; was graduated from the law department of the University of Michigan at Ann Arbor in 1883; was admitted to the bar the same year and commenced practice in Little Falls, Minn.; also engaged in agricultural pursuits; prosecuting attorney of Morrison County, 1891-1893; elected as a Republican to the Sixtieth and to the four succeeding Congresses (March 4, 1907-March 3, 1917); was not a candidate in 1916 for renomination to the House of Representatives, but was an unsuccessful candidate for election to the United States Senate on the Non-Partisan League ticket; resumed the practice of law; unsuccessful candidate for Governor of Minnesota as a Progressive Republican, with Non-Partisan League endorsement, in 1918; was a candidate for the nomination for Governor on the Farmer-Labor ticket in 1924, but his death occurred before the primary election was held; died in Crookston,

Minn., May 24, 1924; remains were cremated and the ashes deposited in the columbarium in Lakewood Cemetery, Minneapolis, Minn.

**Bibliography:** *DAB*; Larson, Bruce K. *Lindbergh of Minnesota; A Political Biography*. New York: Harcourt, Brace Jovanovich, 1973.

**LINDER, John Elmer,** a Representative from Georgia; born in Deer River, Itasca County, Minn., September 9, 1942; D.D.S., University of Minnesota; entered active duty, United States Air Force in 1967; released as a captain in 1969; dentist, 1969-1982; founder and president, Linder Financial Corp., 1977 to present; member, Georgia State house of representatives, 1983-1991; unsuccessful candidate for election in 1990 to the One Hundred Second Congress; elected as a Republican to the One Hundred Third and One Hundred Fourth Congresses (January 3, 1993-January 3, 1997); is a resident of Dunwoody, Ga.

**LINDLEY, James Johnson,** a Representative from Missouri; born in Mansfield, Richland County, Ohio, January 1, 1822; moved with his parents to Cynthiana, Ky., in 1836; attended Woodville College, Ohio; moved to St. Louis, Mo., in 1843; studied law; was admitted to the bar in 1846 and commenced practice in Monticello, Mo.; elected circuit attorney in 1848 and 1852; elected as a Whig to the Thirty-third and Thirty-fourth Congresses (March 4, 1853-March 3, 1857); was not a candidate for reelection in 1856; moved to Davenport, Iowa, in 1858 and continued the practice of law; commissioned to investigate the condition of Iowa troops serving in the Civil War; after the war practiced his profession in Chicago until 1868, when he moved to St. Louis, Mo.; judge of the circuit court of the eighth judicial district of Missouri 1871-1883; moved to Kansas City, Mo.; retired from business activities; died at the home of a son in Nevada, Mo., April 18, 1891; interment in Elmwood Cemetery, Kansas City, Mo.

**LINDQUIST, Francis Oscar,** a Representative from Michigan; born in Marinette, Marinette County, Wis., September 27, 1869; attended the common schools; moved to Greenville, Mich., in 1904 and engaged in the mail-order clothing and manufacturing business; moved to Grand Rapids, Mich., in 1915 and became president of the Canada Mills Co., of New York and Michigan; elected as a Republican to the Sixty-third Congress (March 4, 1913-March 3, 1915); was not a candidate for renomination in 1914; resumed the mail-order business in Grand Rapids; after the First World War returned to Greenville, Mich., and supervised a correspondence-school course for sales people; unsuccessful candidate for election in 1922 to the Sixty-eighth Congress; died in Grand Rapids, Mich., on September 25, 1924; interment in Forest Rose Cemetery, Greenville, Montcalm County, Mich.

**LINDSAY, George Henry** (father of George Washington Lindsay), a Representative from New York; born in New York City January 7, 1837; moved with his parents to Brooklyn, N.Y., in 1843; attended the public schools; engaged in the real estate and investment business; member of the State assembly 1882-1886; coroner of Kings County 1886-1892; appointed assistant tax commissioner in 1898; delegate to various national and State conventions; elected as a Democrat to the Fifty-seventh and to the five succeeding Congresses (March 4, 1901-March 3, 1913); declined to be a candidate for renomination in 1912; lived in retirement until his death in Brooklyn N.Y., May 25, 1916; interment in Evergreen Cemetery.

**LINDSAY, George Washington** (son of George Henry Lindsay), a Representative from New York; born in Brooklyn, N.Y., March 28, 1865; attended the public schools; deputy coroner of Kings County 1886-1892; engaged in the real estate business; member of the Democratic State committee and served as leader of the assembly district from 1919 to 1934; appointed as a confidential investigator in the State insurance department in 1914 and served until 1920;

elected to the State assembly in 1920; declined to be a candidate for renomination; deputy tenement-house commissioner for Brooklyn and Queens County 1921-1923; elected as a Democrat to the Sixty-eighth and to the five succeeding Congresses (March 4, 1923-January 3, 1935); unsuccessful candidate for renomination in 1934; resumed the real estate business; died in Brooklyn, N.Y., on March 15, 1938; interment in Evergreen Cemetery.

**LINDSAY, John Vliet,** a Representative from New York; born in New York City November 24, 1921; graduated from the Buckley School in New York City in 1935, St. Paul's School, Concord, N.H., in 1940; B.A., Yale University, 1944; LL.B., Yale University School of Law, 1948; joined the United States Navy in May 1943; discharged as a lieutenant in March 1946; was admitted to the bar in 1949 and began the practice of law in New York City; executive assistant to the United States Attorney General Herbert Brownell from January 1955 to January 1957; delegate to the Republican National Conventions of 1960, 1964 and 1968; elected as a Republican to the Eighty-sixth and to the three succeeding Congresses, and served from January 3, 1959, to December 31, 1965, when he resigned to become mayor of New York City; elected mayor of New York City in 1965, reelected in 1969, and served from January 1, 1966 to December 31, 1973; announced his affiliation with the Democratic Party on August 11, 1971; unsuccessful candidate in 1972 for the Democratic presidential nomination; resumed the practice of law in New York City; unsuccessful candidate for the Democratic nomination to the United States Senate in 1980; is a resident of New York City.

**Bibliography:** Lindsay, John V. *Journey into Politics.* New York: Dodd, Mead and Co., 1967.

**LINDSAY, William,** a Senator from Kentucky; born near Lexington, Rockbridge County, Va., September 4, 1835; attended the common schools; settled in Clinton, Hickman County, Ky., in 1854; taught school and studied law; admitted to the bar and commenced practice in Clinton in 1858; during the Civil War served in the infantry in the Confederate Army from July 1861 until May 1865; resumed the practice of law in Clinton, Ky.; member, Kentucky senate 1867-1870; judge of the Kentucky Court of Appeals 1870-1878; chief justice of the court 1876-1878; resumed the practice of his profession in Frankfort, Ky.; member, Kentucky senate 1889-1893; served as United States Commissioner to the World's Columbian Exposition, held at Chicago, Ill., 1893; elected as a Democrat to the United States Senate to fill the vacancy caused by the resignation of John G. Carlisle; reelected in January 1894 and served from February 15, 1893, until March 3, 1901; was not a candidate for renomination in 1900; chairman, Committee on Indian Depredations (Fifty-third Congress), Committee on Revolutionary Claims (Fifty-sixth Congress); moved to New York City and resumed the practice of his profession; appointed United States Commissioner to the Louisiana Purchase Exposition at St. Louis in 1901; died in Frankfort, Franklin County, Ky., October 15, 1909; interment in the State Cemetery.

**Bibliography:** *DAB*; Schlup, Leonard. "William Lindsay and the 1896 Party Crisis." *Register of the Kentucky Historical Society* 66 (January 1978): 22-23.

**LINDSEY, Stephen Decatur,** a Representative from Maine; born in Norridgewock, Somerset County, Maine, March 3, 1828; attended the common schools and Broomfield Academy; studied law; was admitted to the bar and commenced practice in Norridgewock in 1853; clerk of the judicial courts in Somerset County 1857-1860; member of the State house of representatives in 1856; served in the State senate 1868-1870 and was president of that body in 1869; delegate to the Republican National Conventions in 1860 and 1868; member of the executive council of Maine in 1874; elected as Republican to the Forty-fifth, Forty-sixth, and Forty-seventh Congresses (March 4, 1877-March 3, 1883); was not a candidate for renomination in 1882 to the Forty-eighth Congress; resumed the practice of his profession; died in Norridgewock, Somerset County, Maine, on April 26, 1884; interment in River View Cemetery.

**LINDSLEY, James Girard,** a Representative from New York; born in Orange, N.J., March 19, 1819; attended the public schools, Ransom's Military Academy, and Pierson's Orange Classical School; moved to New York and was a trustee of the village of Rondout, N.Y., 1859-1864; president of the village of Rondout in 1852 and 1867-1869; elected supervisor of Kingston, N.Y., in March 1872 and in April of the same year was elected the first mayor of Kingston, to which office he was reelected for six consecutive years; elected as a Republican to the Forty-ninth Congress (March 4, 1885-March 3, 1887); was not a candidate for reelection in 1886; general manager of the Newark Lime & Cement Manufacturing Co., Kingston, N.Y.; organizer and president of the Kingston Water Co.; died in Kingston, Ulster County, N.Y., on December 4, 1898; interment in Montrepose Cemetery, Rondout, N.Y.

**LINDSLEY, William Dell,** a Representative from Ohio; born in New Haven, Conn., December 25, 1812; attended the common schools; moved to Buffalo, N.Y., in 1832 and soon after to Erie County, Ohio, settling near Sandusky; engaged in agricultural pursuits; served as captain in the Ohio Militia from 1840 to 1843 and as brigadier general in 1843; elected as a Democrat to the Thirty-third Congress (March 4, 1853-March 3, 1855); unsuccessful candidate for reelection in 1854 to the Thirty-fourth Congress; resumed agricultural pursuits; died in Perkins Township, Erie County, Ohio, March 11, 1890; interment in Oakland Cemetery, Sandusky, Ohio.

**LINEBERGER, Walter Franklin,** a Representative from California; born near Whiteville, Hardeman County, Tenn., July 20, 1883; attended the public schools, the Agricultural and Mechanical College of Texas, and the Rensselaer Polytechnic Institute, Troy, N.Y.; engaged in mining and agriculture in Mexico; moved to Long Beach, Calif., in 1911 and engaged in banking and agriculture; president of the Guarantee Bond & Mortgage Co. (Inc.); served fifteen months in France with the engineering units of the First, Thirty-second, and Fortieth Combat Divisions during the First World War; elected as a Republican to the Sixty-seventh Congress to fill the vacancy caused by the death of Representative-elect Charles F. Van de Water; reelected to the Sixty-eighth and Sixty-ninth Congresses and served from March 4, 1921, to March 3, 1927; did not seek renomination, but was an unsuccessful candidate for the Republican nomination as United States Senator in 1926; died at Santa Barbara, Calif., October 9, 1943; interment in Santa Barbara Cemetery.

**LINEHAN, Neil Joseph,** a Representative from Illinois; born in Chicago, Ill., September 23, 1895; attended the public schools; was graduated from John L. Marsh School in 1913; engaged in the electrical business, beginning in 1919; during the First World War served in France with the Three Hundred and Fortieth Infantry, Eighty-fifth Division, United States Army; elected as a Democrat to the Eighty-first Congress (January 3, 1949-January 3, 1951); unsuccessful candidate for reelection in 1950 to the Eighty-second Congress, and for election in 1952 to the Eighty-third Congress; Director of Price Stabilization, Chicago district, 1951; resumed the electrical engineering business; died in Chicago, Ill., August 23, 1967; interment in St. Mary Cemetery.

**LINK, Arthur Albert,** a Representative from North Dakota; born in Alexander, McKenzie County, N.Dak., May 24, 1914; attended the McKenzie County schools, and North Dakota Agricultural College; member, North Dakota State house of representatives, 1946-1970, serving fourteen years as minority floor leader and speaker of the house, 1965; member of the Randolph Township Board, 1942-1972, the McKenzie County Welfare Board, 1948-1969, the Randolph School Board, 1945-1963, and the county and State Farm Security Administration committee, 1941-1946; delegate, North Dakota State conventions, 1964-1968; elected as a Democrat to the Ninety-second Congress (January 3, 1971-January 3, 1973); was not a candidate for reelection in 1972 to the Ninety-third Congress, but was elected Governor of North Dakota; reelected in 1976, and served from January 2, 1973 to January 7, 1981; is a resident of Alexander, N.Dak.

**LINK, William Walter,** a Representative from Illinois; born in Swiec, Poland, February 12, 1884; immigrated to the United States in 1897 with his parents, who settled in Chicago, Ill.; attended the parochial and public schools; attended the department of engineering of Lewis Institute, Chicago, Ill.; engaged in the enameling business at Chicago, Ill., 1912-1932; also interested in banking; president of the Board of Local Improvements, Chicago, Ill., 1933-1936; general secretary of the Polish-American Democratic Organization of Illinois, beginning in 1932; chief clerk of the superior court of Cook County, 1942-1943; vice president of the Board of Civil Service Commissioners of Cook County, Ill., 1943-1944; elected as a Democrat to the Seventy-ninth Congress (January 3, 1945-January 3, 1947); unsuccessful candidate for reelection in 1946 to the Eightieth Congress; resumed the banking business as a director of the Manufacturers' National Bank of Chicago; also interested in sociological work; died in Chicago, Ill., September 23, 1950; interment in St. Adelbert's Cemetery.

**LINN, Archibald Ladley,** a Representative from New York; born in New York City on October 15, 1802; was a member of the class of 1820 at Union College, Schenectady, N.Y.; studied law; was admitted to the bar and commenced practice in Schenectady; county judge of Schenectady County from January 17, 1840, to February 9, 1845; elected as a Whig to the Twenty-seventh Congress (March 4, 1841-March 3, 1843); chairman, Committee on Public Expenditures (Twenty-seventh Congress); member of the State assembly in 1844; died in Schenectady, N.Y., October 10, 1857.

**LINN, James,** a Representative from New Jersey; born in Bedminster Township, Somerset County, N.J., in 1749; pursued preparatory studies and was graduated from Princeton College in 1769; studied law; was admitted to the bar in 1772 and commenced practice in Trenton, N.J.; returned to Somerset County, N.J.; judge of the court of common pleas; member of the Provincial Congress of New Jersey in 1776; during the Revolutionary War served as captain in the Somerset County Militia in 1776; first major 1776-1781; member of the State council in 1777; returned to Trenton; served in the State general assembly in 1790 and 1791; again a member of the State council 1793-1797; elected as a Republican to the Sixth Congress (March 4, 1799-March 3, 1801); was not a candidate for renomination in 1800 to the Seventh Congress; was appointed by President Thomas Jefferson to be supervisor of the revenue and served from 1801 to 1809; served as secretary of state of New Jersey 1809-1820; died in Trenton, Mercer County, N.J., on January 5, 1821; interment in the Lamington Presbyterian Church Cemetery, Somerset County, N.J.

**LINN, John,** a Representative from New Jersey; born near Johnsonburg, Hardwick Township, Warren County, N.J., December 3, 1763; moved with his father to Sussex County, N.J.; attended the common schools; entered the Revolutionary Army as a private in the First Regiment, Captain Mannings's company; promoted to sergeant; member of the State general assembly 1801-1804; judge of the court of common pleas 1805-1821; sheriff of Sussex County in 1812; elected as a Republican to the Fifteenth and Sixteenth Congresses and served from March 4, 1817, until his death in Washington, D.C., January 5, 1821; interment in North Hardyston Cemetery, near Franklin Furnace, Sussex County, N.J.

**LINN, Lewis Fields,** a Senator from Missouri; born near Louisville, Ky., November 5, 1796; received a meager academic education; studied medicine in Louisville; served in the War of 1812 as a surgeon; completed his medical studies at Philadelphia, Pa., in 1816; was admitted to practice and located at Saint Genevieve, Territory of Missouri; member, State senate 1827; appointed to the French Land Claims Commission in Missouri in 1832; appointed and subsequently elected as a Jacksonian to the United States Senate to fill the vacancy caused by the death of Alexander Buckner; reelected in 1836 and again in 1842 and served from October 25, 1833, until his death in Saint Genevieve, Mo., on October 3, 1843; chairman, Committee on Private Land Claims (Twenty-fourth through Twenty-sixth Congresses), Committee on Agriculture (Twenty-seventh Congress); interment in the Protestant Cemetery.

**Bibliography:** *DAB*; Husband, Michael B. "Senator Lewis F. Linn and the Oregon Question." *Missouri Historical Review* 66 (October 1971): 1-19; Linn, Elizabeth and Nathan Sargent. *Life and Public Services of Dr. Lewis F. Linn.* New York: D. Appleton and Company, 1857.

**LINNEY, Romulus Zachariah,** a Representative from North Carolina; born in Rutherford County, N.C., December 26, 1841; attended the common schools, York's Collegiate Institute, and Doctor Millen's School in Taylorsville, N.C.; during the Civil War served in the Confederate Army until the Battle of Chancellorsville in May 1863, when he was severely wounded; returned to Taylorsville and joined a class in Doctor Millen's School; engaged in agricultural pursuits; studied law; was admitted to the bar by the supreme court in 1868 and commenced practice in Taylorsville; elected to the North Carolina State senate in 1870, 1873, and 1882; elected as a Republican to the Fifty-fourth and to the two succeeding Congresses (March 4, 1895-March 3, 1901); died in Taylorsville, Alexander County, N.C., April 15, 1910; interment in Taylorsville Cemetery.

**LINTHICUM, John Charles,** a Representative from Maryland; born near Baltimore, in the locality now known as Linthicum Heights, Anne Arundel County, Md., November 26, 1867; attended the public schools of that county and of Baltimore; was graduated from the Maryland State normal school in Baltimore in 1886; principal of Braddock School, Frederick County, in 1887, and taught in the schools of Anne Arundel County; studied history and political science at Johns Hopkins University in Baltimore; was graduated from the law department of the University of Maryland at Baltimore in 1890; was admitted to the bar and commenced practice in Baltimore in 1890; member of the Maryland State house of delegates in 1904 and 1905; served in the Maryland State senate, 1906-1909; unsuccessful candidate for mayor of Baltimore in 1907; judge advocate general on the staff of Governor Austin L. Crothers, 1908-1912; delegate to the Democratic National Convention of 1924; elected as a Democrat to the Sixty-second and to the ten succeeding Congresses and served from March 4, 1911, until his death in Baltimore, Md., October 5, 1932; chairman, Committee on Foreign Affairs (Seventy-second Congress); had been renominated to the Seventy-third Congress at the time of his death; interment in Druid Ridge Cemetery.

**LINTON, William Seelye,** a Representative from Michigan; born in St. Clair, St. Clair County, Mich., February 4, 1856; moved with his parents to Saginaw, Mich., in 1859; attended the public schools; engaged as clerk in a store at Farwell, Mich.; became engaged in various activities connected with the lumber industry at Wells (now Alger); member of the board of supervisors of Bay County two terms; returned to Saginaw in 1878 and engaged in the lumber business with his father and also was connected with other business enterprises; member of the East Saginaw common council in 1884 and 1885; member of the State house of representatives in 1887 and 1888; unsuccessful candidate for Lieutenant Governor on the

Republican ticket in 1890; president of the Saginaw Water Board; elected mayor of Saginaw in 1892; elected as a Republican to the Fifty-third and Fifty-fourth Congresses (March 4, 1893-March 3, 1897); chairman, Committee on Ventilation and Acoustics (Fifty-fourth Congress); appointed postmaster of Saginaw, Mich., by President McKinley on March 22, 1898, and recommissioned three times and served until 1914; president of the Saginaw Board of Trade 1905-1911 and 1913-1917; unsuccessful candidate for the Republican nomination for Governor of Michigan in 1913; appointed in 1919 a member of the Michigan State Board of Tax Commissioners and was named secretary a few weeks before his death in Lansing, Mich., on November 22, 1927; interment in Forest Lawn Cemetery, Saginaw, Mich.

**LIPINSKI, William Oliver,** a Representative from Illinois; born in Chicago, Ill., December 22, 1937; graduated from St. Patrick High School, Chicago, 1956; attended Loras College, Dubuque, Iowa, 1956-1957; served in the United States Army Reserve, active duty, sergeant first class, 1961-1967; served as an alderman on the Chicago City Council, 1975-1983; delegate to the Democratic National Midterm Convention, 1974; delegate to the Democratic National Conventions of 1976, 1984, 1988 and 1992; delegate to the Illinois State Democratic convention, 1977; elected as a Democrat to the Ninety-eighth and to the six succeeding Congresses (January 3, 1983-January 3, 1997); is a resident of Chicago, Ill.

**LIPPITT, Henry Frederick,** a Senator from Rhode Island; born in Providence, R.I., October 12, 1856; attended private schools; graduated from Brown University, Providence, R.I., in 1878; entered the cotton manufacturing business; director of a bank and of several mill insurance companies; vice president of the People's Savings Bank of Providence; served on the Governor's staff with the rank of colonel 1888-1889; served as president of the New England Cotton Manufacturers' Association in 1889; elected as a Republican to the United States Senate and served from March 4, 1911, to March 3, 1917; unsuccessful candidate for reelection in 1916; chairman, Committee on Expenditures in the Department of Agriculture (Sixty-second Congress); again became actively engaged in the textile industry; died in Providence, R.I., December 28, 1933; interment in Swan Point Cemetery.

**LIPSCOMB, Glenard Paul,** a Representative from California; born in Jackson, Mich., August 19, 1915, and moved to Los Angeles, Calif., with his parents in 1920; attended the Los Angeles public schools, the University of Southern California, and Woodbury College, Los Angeles; engaged in public accountancy after 1940; during the Second World War served in the Finance Corps, United States Army; elected a member of the California State assembly in 1947, and reelected in 1948, 1950, and 1952; delegate to the Republican National Convention of 1956; elected as a Republican to the Eighty-third Congress, November 10, 1953, by special election to fill the vacancy caused by the resignation of Norris Poulson; reelected to the Eighty-fourth and to the seven succeeding Congresses, and served from November 10, 1953 until his death in Bethesda, Md., February 1, 1970; interment in Forest Lawn Memorial Park, Hollywood Hills, Los Angeles, Calif.

**LISLE, Marcus Claiborne,** a Representative from Kentucky; born near Winchester, Clark County, Ky., September 23, 1862; attended the common schools of his native county and the University of Kentucky at Lexington; was graduated from the law department of Columbia College (now Columbia University), New York City; was admitted to the bar and commenced the practice of his profession in Winchester, Ky., in 1887; served as county judge of Clark County, Ky., in 1890; elected as a Democrat to the Fifty-third Congress and served from March 4, 1893, until his death in Winchester, Ky., July 7, 1894; interment in Winchester Cemetery.

**LITCHFIELD, Elisha,** a Representative from New York; born in Canterbury, Windham County, Conn., July 12, 1785; attended the common schools; learned the carpenter's trade; moved to Onondaga County, N.Y., and settled in Delphi (now Delphi Falls) in 1812; major in the War of 1812; served as justice of the peace and supervisor of Onondaga County; appointed postmaster of Delphi November 28, 1817, and served until June 25, 1821; engaged in mercantile pursuits; member of the State assembly in 1819, 1831-1833, 1844, and 1848, and served as speaker of that body in the latter year; elected to the Seventeenth and Eighteenth Congresses (March 4, 1821-March 3, 1825); was not a candidate for renomination in 1824 to the Nineteenth Congress and withdrew from public life and active business pursuits; moved to Cazenovia, Madison County, N.Y., in 1838 and died there August 4, 1859; interment in the City Cemetery, Delphi Falls, N.Y.

**LITTAUER, Lucius Nathan,** a Representative from New York; born in Gloversville, Fulton County, N.Y., January 20, 1859; moved with his parents to New York City in 1865; attended the Charlier Institute, New York City; was graduated from Harvard University in 1878; engaged in the manufacture of gloves in Gloversville; officer and director of many commercial and financial institutions; elected as a Republican to the Fifty-fifth and to the four succeeding Congresses (March 4, 1897-March 3, 1907); was not a candidate for reelection in 1906 to the Sixtieth Congress; delegate to all Republican State conventions from 1897 to 1912; resumed the glove-manufacturing business; delegate to the Republican National Conventions in 1900, 1904, 1908, and 1928; regent of the University of the State of New York 1912-1914; retired in 1927 and devoted his energies to education, medical research, and philanthropic work; died at his country home near New Rochelle, N.Y., on March 2, 1944; interment in the Jewish Cemetery, New Rochelle, N.Y.

**Bibliography:** *DAB.*

**LITTLE, Chauncey Bundy,** a Representative from Kansas; born in Olathe, Johnson County, Kans., February 10, 1877; attended the graded and high schools and the Kansas State College at Manhattan; was graduated from the law department of the University of Kansas at Lawrence in 1898; was admitted to the bar the same year and commenced practice in Olathe; city attorney of Olathe 1901-1906; county attorney of Johnson County, Kans., 1909-1913; elected as a Democrat to the Sixty-ninth Congress (March 4, 1925-March 3, 1927); unsuccessful candidate for reelection in 1926 to the Seventieth Congress; resumed the practice of law; unsuccessful candidate for Governor of Kansas in 1928; died in Olathe, Kans., September 29, 1952; interment in Olathe Cemetery.

**LITTLE, Edward Campbell,** a Representative from Kansas; born in Newark, Licking County, Ohio, December 14, 1858; moved to Kansas in 1866 with his parents, who settled in Olathe; attended the public schools of Abilene, Kans., and was graduated from the University of Kansas at Lawrence in 1883; connected with the Santa Fe Railroad for several years; studied law; was admitted to the bar in 1886 and commenced practice in Lawrence, Kans.; chairman of the Republican State convention in 1888; city attorney of Ness City in 1889; prosecuting attorney of Dickinson County, 1890-1892; delegate at large to the Republican National Convention of 1892; appointed United States diplomatic agent and consul general with rank of Minister Resident to Egypt on November 15, 1892 and served until August 1893; private secretary to Governor John W. Leedy in 1896 and 1897; unsuccessful candidate for election to the United States Senate in 1897; lieutenant colonel of the Twentieth Regiment, Kansas Volunteers, during the Spanish-American War in 1898 and 1899; received the Spanish War and Philippine Campaign Medals for services in the Philippines; settled in Kansas City, Kans., in 1908; elected as a Republican to the Sixty-fifth and to the three succeeding Congresses and served from March 4, 1917, until his death in Washington, D.C., June 27, 1924; chairman, Committee on

Revision of the Laws (Sixty-sixth through Sixty-eighth Congresses); interment in the City Cemetery, Abilene, Kans.

**LITTLE, Edward Preble,** a Representative from Massachusetts; born in Marshfield, Plymouth County, Mass., November 7, 1791; attended the public schools; at the age of nine he was on the United States frigate *Boston* with his father, Captain George Little, at the suggestion of President John Adams, who gave him a commission as midshipman; engaged in agricultural pursuits; member of the Massachusetts house of representatives, 1829-1834 and 1835-1838; elected as a Democrat to the Thirty-second Congress to fill the vacancy caused by the death of Orin Fowler, and served from December 13, 1852 to March 3, 1853; was not a candidate for renomination in 1852 to the Thirty-third Congress; served as collector of customs at the port of Plymouth, Mass., 1853-1857; resumed agricultural pursuits; died in Lynn, Mass., on February 6, 1875; interment in the Congregational Church Cemetery, Marshfield Hills, Mass.

**LITTLE, John,** a Representative from Ohio; born near Grape Grove, Ross Township, Greene County, Ohio, April 25, 1837; attended the common schools; was graduated from Antioch College, Yellow Springs, Ohio, in 1862; studied law; was admitted to the bar in 1865 and commenced practice in Xenia, Ohio; mayor of Xenia from 1864 to 1866; prosecuting attorney of Greene County, 1866-1870; member of the Ohio State house of representatives, 1869-1873; attorney general of Ohio, 1873-1877; elected as a Republican to the Forty-ninth Congress (March 4, 1885-March 3, 1887); resumed the practice of law; appointed by President Benjamin Harrison a member of the United States and Venezuela Claims Commission in 1889, and was its chairman; member of the Ohio State Board of Arbitration; trustee of Antioch College, 1880-1900; died in Xenia, Ohio, on October 18, 1900; interment in Woodland Cemetery.

**LITTLE, John Sebastian,** a Representative from Arkansas; born at Jenny Lind, Sebastian County, Ark., March 15, 1853; attended the common schools and Cane Hill College, Arkansas; studied law; was admitted to the bar in 1874 and commenced practice in Greenwood, Ark.; elected district attorney in 1877, and reelected for four successive terms; member of the Arkansas State house of representatives in 1884; elected circuit judge in 1886 for a term of four years; chosen chairman of the State judicial convention in 1893; elected as a Democrat to the Fifty-third Congress to fill the vacancy caused by the resignation of Clifton R. Breckinridge; reelected to the Fifty-fourth and to the five succeeding Congresses, and served from December 3, 1894 until January 14, 1907, when he resigned, having been elected Governor; after being sworn in as Governor of Arkansas on January 8, 1907, he suffered a physical and mental breakdown, from which he did not recover, and he resigned on February 11, 1907; died in Little Rock, Pulaski County, Ark., October 29, 1916; interment in City Cemetery, Greenwood, Ark.

**LITTLE, Joseph James,** a Representative from New York; born in Bristol, England, June 5, 1841; immigrated to the United States in 1846 with his parents, who settled in Morris, Otsego County, N.Y.; attended the common schools; apprenticed to the local printer and entered a New York book-printing office to complete his trade; served in the Union Army 1862-1864 as corporal, first sergeant, and first lieutenant; established a printing business in 1867 at New York City; elected as a Democrat to the Fifty-second Congress to fill the vacancy caused by the resignation of Roswell P. Flower and served from November 3, 1891, to March 3, 1893; was not a candidate for renomination in 1892 to the Fifty-third Congress; served as commissioner of education and president of the board of education of New York City; engaged in the printing and publishing business until his death in New York City on February 11, 1913; interment in Kensico Cemetery, Valhalla, N.Y.

**LITTLE, Peter,** a Representative from Maryland; born in Petersburg, Huntingdon County, Pa., December 11, 1775; attended the common schools; became a watchmaker; moved to Freedom, Baltimore County, Md., and engaged in agricultural pursuits; member of the State house of delegates in 1806 and 1807; elected as a Republican to the Twelfth Congress (March 4, 1811-March 3, 1813); was not a candidate for renomination in 1812; during the War of 1812 was commissioned colonel of the Thirty-eighth Maryland Infantry and served from May 19, 1813, to June 15, 1815; elected to the Fourteenth Congress to fill the vacancy caused by the resignation of William Pinkney; reelected to the six succeeding Congresses and served from September 2, 1816, to March 3, 1829; chairman, Committee on Accounts (Fourteenth and Fifteenth Congresses), Committee on Pensions and Revolutionary Claims (Eighteenth and Nineteenth Congresses), Committee on Revolutionary Claims (Nineteenth Congress), Committee on Expenditures in the Department of the Navy (Twentieth Congress); declined to be a candidate for renomination; judge of the orphans' court of Baltimore County; died in Freedom, Baltimore County, Md., February 5, 1830; interment in Freedom Methodist Episcopal Cemetery, near Eldersburg, Carroll County, Md.

**LITTLEFIELD, Charles Edgar,** a Representative from Maine; born in Lebanon, York County, Maine, June 21, 1851; attended the common schools and Foxcroft Academy; studied law; was admitted to the bar in 1876 and practiced in Rockland, Maine; member of the State house of representatives 1885-1887 and served as speaker the last year; attorney general of the State 1889-1893; delegate to the Republican National Conventions in 1892 and 1896; elected as a Republican to the Fifty-sixth Congress to fill the vacancy caused by the death of Nelson Dingley, Jr.; reelected to the four succeeding Congresses and served from June 19, 1899, until his resignation, effective September 30, 1908; chairman, Committee on Expenditures in the Department of Agriculture (Fifty-ninth and Sixtieth Congresses); moved to New York City and engaged in the practice of law until his death there on May 2, 1915; interment in Achorn Cemetery, Rockland, Knox County, Maine.

**LITTLEFIELD, Nathaniel Swett,** a Representative from Maine; born in Wells, York County, Maine, September 20, 1804; attended the common schools; studied law; was admitted to the bar in 1827 and commenced practice in Bridgton, Maine; postmaster of Bridgton, Maine, 1827-1841; filled important town offices, chiefly as selectman; secretary of the State senate in 1831 and 1832; member of the State senate 1837-1839 and president of the senate in 1838; elected as a Democrat to the Twenty-seventh Congress (March 4, 1841-March 3, 1843); elected to the Thirty-first Congress (March 4, 1849-March 3, 1851); chairman, Committee on Agriculture (Thirty-first Congress); was not a candidate for renomination in 1850 to the Thirty-second Congress; was a member of the State house of representatives in 1854; delegate to the Union convention at Philadelphia, Pa., in 1866; died in Bridgton, Cumberland County, Maine, August 15, 1882; interment in the High Street Cemetery.

**LITTLEJOHN, De Witt Clinton,** a Representative from New York; born in Bridgewater, Oneida County, N.Y., February 7, 1818; pursued an academic course; engaged in mercantile pursuits and in the manufacture of flour at Oswego, N.Y.; mayor of the city in 1849 and 1850; member of the State assembly 1853-1855, 1857, 1859-1861, 1866, 1867, 1870, and 1871, and served as speaker 1859-1861, 1866, 1867, 1870, and 1871; during the Civil War served as colonel of the One Hundred and Tenth New York Volunteer Infantry; resigned February 3, 1863; elected as a Republican to the Thirty-eighth Congress (March 4, 1863-March 3, 1865); chairman, Committee on Revolutionary Pensions (Thirty-eighth Congress); was not a candidate for renomination in 1864; brevetted brigadier general of Volunteers March 13, 1865; again a member of the State assembly in 1884; died in Oswego, Oswego County, N.Y., October 27, 1892; interment in Riverside Cemetery.

**LITTLEPAGE, Adam Brown,** a Representative from West Virginia; born near Charleston, Kanawha County, Va. (now West Virginia), April 14, 1859; attended the common schools; studied law; was admitted to the bar and commenced practice in Newport, Ind., in 1882; moved to Charleston, W.Va., in 1884 and continued the practice of law; general counsel in West Virginia for the United Mine Workers' Association; member of the State senate 1906-1910; elected as a Democrat to the Sixty-second Congress (March 4, 1911-March 3, 1913); unsuccessful candidate for reelection in 1912 to the Sixty-third Congress; elected to the Sixty-fourth and Sixty-fifth Congresses (March 4, 1915-March 3, 1919); unsuccessful candidate for reelection in 1918 to the Sixty-sixth Congress; resumed the practice of law; died in Charleston, W.Va., June 29, 1921; interment in Spring Hill Cemetery.

**LITTLETON, Martin Wiley,** a Representative from New York; born near Kingston, Roane County, Tenn., January 12, 1872; moved to Texas in 1881 with his parents, who settled in Dallas; attended the common schools; studied law; was admitted to the bar in 1891 and commenced practice in Dallas, Tex.; prosecuting attorney of Dallas County 1893-1896; moved to New York City in 1896 and continued the practice of his profession; district attorney of Kings County, N.Y., 1900-1904; delegate to the Democratic National Convention in 1904; president of the Borough of Brooklyn in 1904 and 1905; elected as a Democrat to the Sixty-second Congress (March 4, 1911-March 3, 1913); was not a candidate for reelection in 1912 to the Sixty-third Congress; resumed the practice of law and resided in New York City and Mineola, Nassau County, Long Island; died at Mineola, N.Y., on December 19, 1934; interment in the Littleton family mausoleum, Woodlawn Cemetery, New York City.

**Bibliography:** *DAB.*

**LITTON, Jerry Lon,** a Representative from Missouri; born on a farm near Lock Springs, Daviess County, Mo., May 12, 1937; educated in the public schools; B.S., University of Missouri, Columbia, Mo., 1961; served in the United States Army National Guard, 1955-1962; engaged in the scientific breeding of purebred cattle; vice president and co-owner, Litton Charolais Ranch, Inc.; State president, 1955-1956, and national secretary, 1956-1957, Future Farmers of America; elected as a Democrat to the Ninety-third Congress, November 7, 1972; reelected to the Ninety-fourth Congress, and served from January 3, 1973, until his death August 3, 1976, in a private aircraft crash at the Chillicothe Municipal Airport shortly after takeoff; was not a candidate in 1976 for reelection to the United States House of Representatives but was a successful candidate for nomination to the United States Senate; interment in Resthaven Memorial Gardens, Chillicothe, Mo.

**Bibliography:** Mitchell, Bonnie. *Jerry Litton, 1937-1976: A Biography.* Chillicothe, Mo.: Jerry Litton Family Memorial Foundation, 1978.

**LIVELY, Robert Maclin,** a Representative from Texas; born in Fayetteville, Washington County, Ark., on January 6, 1855; moved to Texas in 1864 with his parents, who settled in Smith County; attended private schools in eastern Texas; studied law; was admitted to the bar in 1876 and commenced practice in Kaufman, Kaufman County, Tex.; moved to Canton, Van Zandt County, and continued the practice of law; prosecuting attorney of Van Zandt County 1882-1884; elected as a Democrat to the Sixty-first Congress to fill the vacancy caused by the resignation of J. Gordon Russell and served from July 23, 1910, to March 3, 1911; declined to be a candidate for renomination in 1910; judge of Van Zandt County, Tex., 1916-1918; died in Canton, Tex., January 15, 1929; interment in Canton Cemetery.

**LIVERMORE, Arthur** (son of Samuel Livermore and brother of Edward St. Loe Livermore), a Representative from New Hampshire; born in Londonderry, Rockingham County, N.H., July 29, 1766; received classical instruction from his parents; studied law; was admitted to the bar and commenced practice in Concord in 1792; moved to Chester, N.H., the following year; member of the State house of representatives in 1794 and 1795; solicitor for Rockingham County 1796-1798; moved to Holderness, N.H., in 1798; associate justice of the superior court 1798-1809 and chief justice 1809-1813; presidential elector on the Federalist ticket in 1800; associate justice of the State supreme court 1813-1816; elected as a Republican to the Fifteenth and Sixteenth Congresses (March 4, 1817-March 3, 1821); chairman, Committee on the Post Office and Post Roads (Fifteenth and Sixteenth Congresses), Committee on Expenditures in the Post Office Department (Sixteenth Congress); unsuccessful candidate for reelection in 1822 to the Seventeenth Congress; served in the State senate in 1821 and 1822; judge of probate for Grafton County in 1822 and 1823; elected to the Eighteenth Congress (March 4, 1823-March 3, 1825); was not a candidate for renomination in 1824; chief justice of the court of common pleas 1825-1832; moved to Campton in 1827; trustee of Holmes Plymouth Academy 1808-1826; died in Campton, N.H., July 1, 1853; interment in Trinity Churchyard, Holderness, N.H.

**Bibliography:** *DAB.*

**LIVERMORE, Edward St. Loe** (son of Samuel Livermore and brother of Arthur Livermore), a Representative from Massachusetts; born in Portsmouth, N.H., April 5, 1762; pursued classical studies; studied law; was admitted to the bar and commenced practice in Concord, N.H., in 1783 and later practiced in Portsmouth, N.H.; United States district attorney 1789-1797; State solicitor for Rockingham County 1791-1793; associate justice of the State supreme court 1797-1799; naval officer for the port of Portsmouth 1799-1802; moved to Newburyport, Mass., in 1802; elected as a Federalist to the Tenth and Eleventh Congresses (March 4, 1807-March 3, 1811); was not a candidate for renomination in 1810; resumed the practice of law; moved to Boston, Mass., in 1811, thence to Zanesville, Ohio, in 1815; returned to Boston, and then moved to Tewksbury, Middlesex County, Mass., where he lived in retirement until his death there on September 15, 1832; interment in the Granary Burying Ground, Boston, Mass.

**Bibliography:** *DAB.*

**LIVERMORE, Samuel** (father of Arthur Livermore and Edward St. Loe Livermore), a Delegate, a Representative, and a Senator from New Hampshire; born in Waltham, Middlesex County, Mass., May 14, 1732; attended Waltham schools, and graduated from the College of New Jersey (now Princeton University) in 1752; studied law; was admitted to the bar in 1756 and commenced practice in Waltham, Mass.; moved to Portsmouth, N.H., in 1758 and later to Londonderry; member, State general assembly 1768-1769; judge-advocate in the Admiralty court and attorney general 1769-1774; moved to Holderness in 1775; State attorney for three years; Member of the Continental Congress 1780-1782 and 1785-1786; chief justice of the State supreme court 1782-1789; member of the State constitutional convention in 1788; elected to the First and Second Congresses (March 4, 1789-March 3, 1793); chairman, Committee on Elections (Second Congress); president of the State constitutional convention in 1791; elected as a Federalist to the United States Senate in 1792; reelected in 1798 and served from March 4, 1793, until his resignation effective June 12, 1801, due to ill health; served as President pro tempore of the Senate during the Fourth and Sixth Congresses; died in Holderness, Grafton County, N.H., May 18, 1803; interment in Trinity Churchyard.

**Bibliography:** *DAB.*

**LIVERNASH, Edward James** (subsequently Edward James de Nivernais), a Representative from California; born in Lower Calveritas, a California mining camp, near San Andreas, February 14, 1866; attended the common schools of California; became a printer at the age of fifteen, and a year later founded a country newspaper at Cloverdale, Calif.; studied law in preparation for journalism; was admitted to the bar in 1887; joined the staff of the San Francisco Examiner in 1891 and held various editorial posts; was sent by the Klondike miners in 1897 as commissioner to the Dominion of Canada to urge a modification of onerous laws; elected on a Democratic and Union Labor ticket to the Fifty-eighth Congress (March 4, 1903-March 3, 1905); became the editor of the Denver News in 1906; resided in France from 1909 to 1912, when he returned to the United States and settled near Belmont, Calif.; engaged in study and literary pursuits; after his congressional service he resumed the French form of the family name, de Nivernais, by decree of court; died in Agnew, Calif., June 1, 1938; remains were cremated at Cypress Lawn Cemetery, Colma, Calif.

**LIVINGSTON, Edward** (brother of Robert R. Livingston and cousin of Philip Livingston and William Livingston), a Representative from New York and a Representative and a Senator from Louisiana; born in Clermont, Livingston Manor, N.Y., May 28, 1764; attended private schools; graduated from the College of New Jersey (now Princeton University) in 1781; studied law in Albany, N.Y.; was admitted to the bar in 1785 and commenced practice in New York City; elected from New York to the Fourth and to the two succeeding Congresses (March 4, 1795-March 3, 1801); chairman, Committee on Commerce and Manufactures (Fifth Congress); United States district attorney, 1801-1803; mayor of New York City, 1801-1803; moved to New Orleans, La., in 1804; engaged in the practice of law and in the real estate business; author of a legal code for Louisiana; served at the Battle of New Orleans, January 8, 1815; member, Louisiana State house of representatives, 1820; elected from Louisiana to the Eighteenth and to the two succeeding Congresses (March 4, 1823-March 3, 1829); elected to the United States Senate and served from March 4, 1829, until May 24, 1831, when he resigned, having been appointed to the Cabinet; Secretary of State in the Cabinet of President Andrew Jackson from May 24, 1831 to May 29, 1833; appointed Minister Plenipotentiary to France on May 29, 1833 and served until April 1835; inherited from his sister "Montgomery Place," on the Hudson River, Barrytown, Dutchess County, N.Y., and died there May 23, 1836; interment in the family vault at "Clermont," Columbia County, N.Y.; remains later removed to Rhinebeck, N.Y.

**Bibliography:** *DAB*; Hatcher, William. *Edward Livingston: Jeffersonian Republican and Jacksonian Democrat.* 1940. Reprint. Gloucester, Mass.: P. Smith, 1970; Hunt, Charles H. *Life of Edward Livingston.* New York: Appleton and Company, 1864.

**LIVINGSTON, Henry Walter** (son of Walter Livingston), a Representative from New York; born in Linlithgo, Columbia County, N.Y., in 1768; was graduated from Yale College in 1786; studied law; was admitted to the bar and commenced practice in New York City; private secretary to Gouverneur Morris, American Minister Plenipotentiary to Paris, France, 1792-1794; judge of the court of common pleas of Columbia County, N.Y.; member of the State assembly in 1802 and again in 1810; elected as a Federalist to the Eighth and Ninth Congresses (March 4, 1803-March 3, 1807); died near Linlithgo, N.Y., December 22, 1810.

**LIVINGSTON, Leonidas Felix,** a Representative from Georgia; born near Covington, Newton County, Ga., April 3, 1832; attended the common schools; engaged in agricultural pursuits; entered the Confederate Army as a private in August 1861 and served throughout the Civil War; resumed agricultural pursuits in Newton County, Ga.; member of the State house of representatives in 1876, 1877, and 1879-1881; served in the State senate in 1882

and 1883; vice president of the Georgia State Agricultural Society for eleven years and president four years; president of the Georgia State Alliance for three years; elected as a Democrat to the Fifty-second and to the nine succeeding Congresses (March 4, 1891-March 3, 1911); unsuccessful candidate for renomination in 1910; again engaged in agricultural pursuits in Newton County; died in Washington, D.C., February 11, 1912; interment in Bethany Church Cemetery, near Covington, Ga.

**LIVINGSTON, Philip** (brother of William Livingston, cousin of Edward Livingston and Robert R. Livingston, and uncle of Walter Livingston), a Delegate from New York; born in Albany, N.Y., January 15, 1716; was graduated from Yale College in 1737; engaged in the mercantile business in New York City; member of the board of aldermen 1754-1762; member of the provincial house of representatives 1763-1769 and served as speaker in 1768; member of the New York Committee of Correspondence; delegate to the Stamp Act Congress in October 1765; register in chancery in 1768 and 1769; Member of the Continental Congress from 1775 until his death; a signer of the Declaration of Independence; president of the New York Provincial Convention in 1775; member of the State assembly in 1776; served in the State senate in 1777; prominent in commercial and educational societies; died while attending the sixth session of the Continental Congress in York, Pa., June 12, 1778; interment in a tomb in Prospect Hill Cemetery, York, York County, Pa.

**Bibliography:** *DAB*.

**LIVINGSTON, Robert Le Roy,** a Representative from New York; born in 1778 in Claverack, Columbia County, N.Y.; was graduated from Princeton College; was commissioned first lieutenant in the Twelfth United States Infantry on January 14, 1799, and honorably discharged on June 15, 1800; elected as a Federalist to the Eleventh and Twelfth Congresses and served from March 4, 1809, until May 6, 1812, when he resigned; participated in the War of 1812 and was commissioned lieutenant colonel of the Twenty-third Infantry on May 29, 1812, and served until February 1, 1813, when he resigned; died in 1836.

**LIVINGSTON, Robert Linligthgow, Jr.,** a Representative from Louisiana; born in Colorado Springs, El Paso County, Colo., April 30, 1943; graduated from St. Martin's High School, New Orleans, in 1960; B.A., Tulane University, New Orleans, 1967; J.D., Tulane University Law School, 1968; graduate, Loyola Institute of Politics, 1973; admitted to the Louisiana bar in 1968 and commenced practice in New Orleans; served in the United States Navy, 1961-1963; United States Naval Reserve, 1963-1967 (inactive); assistant United States Attorney, deputy chief, criminal division, 1970-1973; chief special prosecutor and chief, armed robbery division, Orleans Parish District Attorney's office, 1974-1975; chief prosecutor, organized crime unit, Louisiana State Attorney General's office, 1975-1976; delegate to the Republican National Convention of 1976; elected as a Republican to the Ninety-fifth Congress, August 27, 1977, by special election to fill the vacancy caused by the resignation of Richard A. Tonry; reelected to the nine succeeding Congresses, and served from August 27, 1977 to January 3, 1997; chairman, Committee on Appropriations (One Hundred Fourth Congress): is a resident of Metairie, La.

**LIVINGSTON, Robert R.** (brother of Edward Livingston and cousin of Philip Livingston and William Livingston), a Delegate from New York; born in New York City November 27, 1746; was graduated from King's College (now Columbia University), New York City, in 1765; studied law; was admitted to the bar in 1773 and commenced practice in New York City; city recorder, 1773-1775; member of the provincial convention of 1775; Member of the Continental Congress, 1775-1776, 1779-1780 and 1784; one of the committee of five appointed to draw up the Declaration of Independence, but returned to his duties in the provincial assembly before it was signed; delegate to the State constitutional convention in April 1777; Secretary of Foreign Affairs under the Continental Congress from October 20, 1781 to June 1783; chancellor of New York State from 1777 to 1801, and administered the oath of office to President Washington on April 30, 1789; unsuccessful candidate for Governor of New York in 1798; appointed Minister Plenipotentiary to France on October 2, 1801 and served until November 1804; assisted Robert Fulton and was his partner in constructing the first steamboat; died in Clermont, N.Y., February 26, 1813; interment on his estate, "Clermont," near Clermont, N.Y.; reinterment in St. Paul's Churchyard, Tivoli, N.Y.

**Bibliography:** *DAB*; Dangerfield, George. *Chancellor Robert R. Livingston of New York, 1746-1813.* New York: Harcourt, Brace and Co., 1960.

**LIVINGSTON, Walter** (nephew of Philip Livingston and father of Henry Walter Livingston), a Delegate from New York; born November 27, 1740; delegate to the provincial convention held in New York in April and May 1775; member of the First Provincial Congress from May to November 1775; judge of Albany County in 1774 and 1775; served as commissary of stores and provisions for the department of New York from July 17, 1775, until September 7, 1776, when he resigned; deputy commissary general of the northern department in 1775 and 1776; member of the State assembly 1777-1779 and served as speaker in 1778; member of the New York and Massachusetts Boundary Commission in 1784; a member of the board of regents of the University of the State of New York 1784-1787; Member of the Continental Congress in 1784 and 1785; appointed Commissioner of the United States Treasury in 1785; died in New York City on May 14, 1797; interment in Trinity Churchyard.

**LIVINGSTON, William** (brother of Philip Livingston and cousin of Edward Livingston and Robert R. Livingston), a Delegate from New Jersey; born in Albany, N.Y., November 30, 1723; was graduated from Yale College in 1741; studied law; was admitted to the bar in 1748 and commenced practice in New York; established and edited the Independent Reflector in 1752; a commissioner to adjust the boundary lines between New York and Massachusetts in 1754 and New York and New Jersey in 1764; member of the provincial assembly from Livingston Manor, 1759-1761; moved to Elizabethtown (now Elizabeth), N.J., in 1772; Member of the Continental Congress from July 23, 1774, to June 22, 1776; delegate to the Federal Constitutional Convention in Philadelphia in 1787 and one of the signers of the Constitution; commissioned a brigadier general of the New Jersey Militia on October 28, 1775, and served until August 31, 1776, having been elected Governor; served consecutively as Governor of New Jersey from August 31, 1776 until his death in Elizabeth, Union County, N.J., July 25, 1790; interment in the family vault in Trinity Churchyard, New York City; reinterred, 1846, in Brockholst Livingston vault, Greenwood Cemetery, Brooklyn, N.Y.

**Bibliography:** *DAB*.

**LLOYD, Edward** (father of Edward Lloyd [1779-1834]), a Delegate from Maryland; born at "Wye House," Talbot County, Md., December 15, 1744; completed preparatory studies; member of the lower house in the General Assembly of Maryland 1771-1774; member of the committee of safety for the Eastern Shore in 1775 and of the provincial convention in 1776; served on the executive council 1777-1779; member of the State house of delegates in 1780; served in the State senate in 1781, 1786, and 1791; Member of the Continental Congress 1783-1784; member of the State constitutional convention which ratified the Federal Constitution April 28, 1788; died at "Wye House," July 8, 1796; interment in the family burying ground at "Wye House" plantation, ten miles northwest of Easton, Md.

**Bibliography:** *DAB*.

**LLOYD, Edward** (son of Edward Lloyd [1744-1796]), a Representative and a Senator from Maryland; born at "Wye House," Talbot County, Md., July 22, 1779; educated by private tutors; member, Maryland State house of delegates, 1800-1805; elected to the Ninth Congress to fill the vacancy caused by the resignation of Joseph H. Nicholson; reelected to the Tenth Congress, and served from December 3, 1806 to March 3, 1809; elected Governor of Maryland by the General Assembly, and served from June 9, 1809 to November 16, 1811; commissioned lieutenant colonel of the Ninth Regiment of Maryland Militia; member, State senate, 1811-1815; elected as a Republican to the United States Senate in 1819; reelected in 1825, and served from March 4, 1819 until his resignation on January 14, 1826; chairman, Committee on the District of Columbia (Eighteenth and Nineteenth Congresses); member and president, State senate, 1826-1831; died in Annapolis, Md., June 2, 1834; interment in the family burying ground at "Wye House" plantation, near Easton, Md.

**Bibliography:** *DAB*.

**LLOYD, James,** a Senator from Maryland; born at "Farley," near Chestertown, Kent County, Md., in 1745; pursued classical studies; studied law; was admitted to the bar and practiced; commissioned second lieutenant in the Kent County Militia in 1776, and served during the Revolutionary War; general in the War of 1812; elected as a Federalist to the United States Senate to fill the vacancy caused by the resignation of John Henry and served from December 11, 1797, until December 1, 1800, when he resigned; engaged in the practice of law; died at "Ratclift Manor," near Easton, Talbot County, Md., in 1820; interment at "Clover," the estate of his daughter, in Queen Annes County, Md.

**LLOYD, James,** a Senator from Massachusetts; born in Boston, Mass., in December 1769; attended the Boston Latin School and graduated from Harvard University in 1787; became a merchant and was interested in foreign trade; member, Massachusetts house of representatives 1800-1801; member, Massachusetts senate 1804; elected as a Federalist to the United States Senate to fill the vacancy caused by the resignation of John Quincy Adams in 1808; reelected, and served from June 9, 1808, until May 1, 1813, when he resigned; again elected in 1822 to the United States Senate to fill the vacancy caused by the resignation of Harrison Gray Otis; reelected, and served from June 5, 1822, until May 23, 1826, when he resigned; chairman, Committee on Naval Affairs (Eighteenth Congress), Committee on Commerce (Nineteenth Congress); retired from public life and moved to Philadelphia, Pa., in 1826; died in New York City, April 5, 1831; interment in Kings' Chapel Burying Ground, Boston, Mass.

**LLOYD, James Fredrick,** a Representative from California; born in Helena, Lewis and Clark County, Mont., September 27, 1922; attended public schools in Washington, California, and Oregon; attended the University of Oregon, 1940-1942; B.A., Stanford University, Palo Alto, Calif., 1958; M.A., University of Southern California, 1966; pursued public relations and an advertising career; teacher and instructor of political science, Mount San Antonio College, Walnut, Calif., 1970-1973; served in the United States Navy, naval aviator, 1942-1963 (retired); member, Democratic State central committee, 1968-1972; served as city councilman of West Covina, Calif., 1968-1975; mayor of West Covina, 1973-1974; elected as a Democrat to the Ninety-fourth and to the two succeeding Congresses (January 3, 1975-January 3, 1981); unsuccessful candidate for reelection in 1980 to the Ninety-seventh Congress; is a resident of West Covina, Calif.

**LLOYD, James Tilghman,** a Representative from Missouri; born in Canton, Lewis County, Mo., August 28, 1857; attended the public schools; was graduated from Christian University (now Culver-Stockton College), Canton, Mo., in 1878; taught school; deputy sheriff of Lewis County 1879-1881; deputy circuit clerk and recorder 1880-1882; studied law; was admitted to the bar in 1882 and commenced practice in Monticello, Lewis County, Mo.; moved to Shelbyville, Mo., in 1885 and continued the practice of law; prosecuting attorney of Shelby County 1889-1893; elected as a Democrat to the Fifty-fifth Congress to fill the vacancy caused by the death of Richard P. Giles; reelected to the Fifty-sixth and to the eight succeeding Congresses and served from June 1, 1897, to March 3, 1917; chairman, Committee on Accounts (Sixty-second through Sixty-fourth Congresses); minority whip (Fifty-seventh through Sixtieth Congresses); was not a candidate for renomination in 1916; delegate to the Democratic National Convention in 1908; chairman of the Democratic Congressional Committee 1908-1912; settled in Washington, D.C., in 1917 and practiced law until 1925; president of the board of education in 1924 and 1925; president of the chamber of commerce in 1925; returned to Missouri in 1925 and engaged in the practice of his profession in Canton; member of the board of curators of Culver-Stockton College; died in Quincy, Ill., on April 3, 1944; interment in Forest Grove Cemetery, Canton, Mo.

**LLOYD, Marilyn Laird** (served under the name of Marilyn Lloyd Bouquard in the Ninety-sixth through Ninety-eighth Congresses), a Representative from Tennessee; born in Fort Smith, Sebastian County, Ark., January 3, 1929; attended Talco (Tex.) Elementary School, 1941; graduated from Western Kentucky College High School, Bowling Green, 1945; attended Shorter College, Rome, Ga., 1960; owned and operated radio station WTTI, in Dalton, Ga.; owned and operated Executive Aviation, Winchester, Tenn.; elected as a Democrat to the Ninety-fourth and to the nine succeeding Congresses (January 3, 1975-January 3, 1995); was not a candidate for reelection in 1994 to the One Hundred Fourth Congress; is a resident of Chattanooga, Tenn.

**LLOYD, Sherman Parkinson,** a Representative from Utah; born in St. Anthony, Fremont County, Idaho, January 11, 1914; attended St. Anthony and Rexburg public schools; B.S., Utah State University, Logan, 1935; LL.B., George Washington University Law School, Washington, D.C., 1939; was admitted to the bar in 1939 and began practice of law in Salt Lake City, Utah; general counsel for Utah Retail Grocers Association, 1940-1962; member of the Utah State senate, 1954-1962, serving as majority leader in 1957, president in 1959, and minority leader in 1961; member of the Utah Legislative Council, 1957-1961, chairman, 1959-1961; served as Utah representative on board of managers of Council of State Governments, 1959-1961; chairman, Council of State Governments Committee on State Taxation of Interstate Income, 1961-1962; director of Beehive State Bank, 1960-1966; delegate, State conventions 1960, 1962, 1964, and 1966; delegate to the Republican National Convention of 1960; unsuccessful candidate for election in 1960 to the Eighty-seventh Congress; elected as a Republican to the Eighty-eighth Congress (January 3, 1963-January 3, 1965); was not a candidate for reelection in 1964 to the House of Representatives, but was an unsuccessful candidate for nomination for the United States Senate; returned to Utah to become vice president of Prudential Federal Savings, in charge of public relations; lecturer at the University of Utah; elected to the Ninetieth and to the two succeeding Congresses (January 3, 1967-January 3, 1973); unsuccessful candidate for reelection in 1972 to the Ninety-third Congress; appointed assistant director of the United States Information Agency in 1973; again returned to Utah to teach at Utah State University, 1973-1974; trade specialist in charge of the Utah office of the Department of Commerce in 1974; unsuccessful candidate for nomination in 1976 to the United States Senate; became an editor and publisher; resided in Salt Lake City, Utah, where he died on December 15, 1979; interment in Salt Lake City Cemetery.

**LLOYD, Wesley,** a Representative from Washington; born at Arvonia, Osage County, Kans., on July 24, 1883, attended the public schools, Baker University, Baldwin, Kans., and Washburn College, Topeka, Kans.; engaged in newspaper work in Kansas City and Topeka; graduated from the Kansas City Law School in 1906; was admitted to the bar the same year; moved to Tacoma, Wash., in 1906, and engaged in newspaper work until 1908 when he commenced the practice of law in Tacoma; served as a corporal in the Washington National Guard 1918-1920; was elected as a Democrat to the Seventy-third and Seventy-fourth Congresses and served from March 4, 1933, until his death in Washington, D.C., January 10, 1936; interment in Tacoma Cemetery, Tacoma, Wash.

**LOAN, Benjamin Franklin,** a Representative from Missouri; born in Hardinsburg, Breckinridge County, Ky., October 4, 1819; pursued an academic course; studied law in Kentucky; moved to St. Joseph, Mo., in 1838; was admitted to the bar in 1840 and practiced in St. Joseph; served in the Union Army during the Civil War; commissioned brigadier general of Missouri State Militia in the service of the United States on November 27, 1861; honorably discharged on June 8, 1863; elected as an Unconditional Unionist to the Thirty-eighth Congress and reelected as a Republican to the Thirty-ninth and Fortieth Congresses (March 4, 1863-March 3, 1869); chairman, Committee on Revolutionary Pensions (Fortieth Congress); unsuccessful candidate for reelection in 1868 to the Forty-first Congress; appointed by President Ulysses S. Grant a visitor to the United States Military Academy in 1869; resumed the practice of law in St. Joseph, Mo.; delegate to the Republican National Convention of 1876; unsuccessful candidate for election in 1876 to the Forty-fifth Congress; died in St. Joseph, Mo., March 30, 1881; interment in Mount Mora Cemetery.

**LOBECK, Charles Otto,** a Representative from Nebraska; born in Andover, Henry County, Ill., April 6, 1852; attended the public schools in Geneseo, Ill., the German Wallace College, Berea, Ohio, and the Dyhrenfurth Commercial College, Chicago, Ill.; moved to Dayton, Iowa, in 1869 and was employed as a clerk in a general store; commercial traveler in Iowa and Nebraska 1875-1892; engaged in the hardware business in Omaha 1892-1895; elected as a Republican to the State senate in 1892; member of the city council of Omaha 1897-1903, during which time he was engaged in the real estate and insurance business; affiliated with the Democratic Party in 1896; served as city controller from 1903 until 1911; elected as a Democrat to the Sixty-second and to the three succeeding Congresses (March 4, 1911-March 3, 1919); chairman, Committee on Expenditures in the Department of the Treasury (Sixty-third through Sixty-fifth Congresses); unsuccessful candidate for reelection in 1918 to the Sixty-sixth Congress; again engaged in the real estate and insurance business; died in Omaha, Nebr., January 30, 1920; interment in Prospect Hill Cemetery.

**LoBIONDO, Frank A.,** a Representative from New Jersey; born in Bridgeton, Cumberland County, N.J., May 12, 1946; graduated, Georgetown Preparatory School, Rockville, Md., 1964; B.A., St. Joseph's University, Philadelphia, 1968; operations manager for a motor express company, 1968 to present; Cumberland County, N.J., freeholder, 1985-1988; member, New Jersey State assembly, 1988-1994; elected as a Republican to the One Hundred Fourth Congress (January 3, 1995-January 3, 1997); is a resident of Vineland, N.J.

**LOCHER, Cyrus,** a Senator from Ohio; born on a farm in Putnam County, Ohio, March 8, 1878; attended the country schools; graduated from Ohio Wesleyan University, Delaware, Ohio, in 1903; taught in the country schools and was superintendent of schools at Woodsfield, Ohio, 1904-1905; studied law at the University of Michigan at Ann Arbor and was graduated from the law school of Western Reserve University at Cleveland, Ohio, in 1906; was admitted to the bar in 1906 and commenced practice in Cleveland in 1907; assistant city solicitor of Cleveland 1908-1910; member of the faculty of Western Reserve University 1911-1912; prosecuting attorney of Cuyahoga County 1912-1916; State director of commerce 1923-1928; appointed as a Democrat to the United States Senate to fill the vacancy caused by the death of Frank B. Willis and served from April 5, 1928, to December 14, 1928; unsuccessful candidate for the nomination in 1928 to fill the vacancy; continued the practice of law in Cleveland, Ohio, until his death there on August 17, 1929; interment in Ebenezer Cemetery, Bluffton, Ohio.

**LOCKE, Francis** (nephew of Matthew Locke), a Senator from North Carolina; born in Rowan County, N.C., October 31, 1776; attended Zion-Parnassus Academy and the University of North Carolina at Chapel Hill; studied law; was admitted to the bar and practiced; elected judge of the superior court of North Carolina in 1803 and served until 1814, when he resigned; elected to the United States Senate in 1814 to fill the vacancy caused by the resignation of David Stone, but resigned December 5, 1815, without having qualified; died in Rowan County, N.C., on January 8, 1823; interment in the Thyatira Churchyard, near Salisbury, N.C.

**LOCKE, John,** a Representative from Massachusetts; born in Hopkinton, Middlesex County, Mass., February 14, 1764; attended Andover Academy and Dartmouth College, Hanover, N.H.; taught school; graduated from Harvard University in 1792; studied law; was admitted to the bar and commenced practice in Ashby in 1796; member of the Massachusetts house of representatives in 1804, 1805, 1813, and 1823; delegate to the Massachusetts constitutional convention in 1820; elected to the Eighteenth, Nineteenth, and Twentieth Congresses (March 4, 1823-March 3, 1829); declined to be a candidate for renomination in 1828; member of the Massachusetts senate in 1830 and of the Massachusetts executive council in 1831; resumed the practice of his profession; moved to Lowell, Mass., in 1837 and to Boston in 1849; died in Boston, Mass., March 29, 1855; interment in Lowell Cemetery, Lowell, Middlesex County, Mass.

**LOCKE, Matthew** (uncle of Francis Locke, and great-great-great-grandfather of Effiegene (Locke) Wingo), a Representative from North Carolina; born in the north of Ireland in 1730; immigrated to the United States and located in Rowan County, N.C.; engaged in transportation by wagon; treasury commissioner of the colony of North Carolina in 1771; elected a member of the safety committee of Rowan County on August 8, 1774, and of the committee of secrecy, intelligence, and observation of Rowan County on September 23, 1774; member of the Provincial Congress at Hillsboro, N.C., and Johnston Court House in 1775; served as paymaster of troops in the Salisbury District in 1775; member of the Colonial Congress at Halifax in 1776; delegate to the State constitutional convention in 1776; member of the State house of commons 1777-1781; brigadier general of North Carolina troops during the Revolutionary War; served in the State senate in 1781 and 1782; again a member of the State house of commons 1783-1792; delegate to the State constitutional convention in 1789 called to ratify the Federal Constitution and voted against ratification; elected to the Third Congress and reelected as a Republican to the Fourth and Fifth Congresses (March 4, 1793-March 3, 1799); unsuccessful candidate for reelection in 1798 to the Sixth Congress; engaged as a planter and was an extensive landowner; died in Salisbury, Rowan County, N.C., September 7, 1801; interment in the Thyatira Churchyard, near Salisbury, N.C.

**Bibliography:** *DAB.*

**LOCKHART, James,** a Representative from Indiana; born in Auburn, Cayuga County, N.Y., February 13, 1806; attended the public schools; moved to Ithaca, N.Y., about 1826 and operated a woolen mill; moved to Indiana in 1832; studied law; was admitted to the bar in 1832 and commenced practice in Evansville, Ind., in 1834; city clerk in 1836 and 1837; prosecuting attorney of Vanderburg County 1841-1845; judge of the fourth judicial district from 1846 until 1851, when he resigned; delegate to the State constitutional convention in 1850; elected as a Democrat to the Thirty-second Congress (March 4, 1851-March 3, 1853); was not a candidate for reelection in 1852 to the Thirty-third Congress; resumed the practice of his profession in Evansville; appointed by President Franklin Pierce superintendent of construction of the marine hospital at Evansville in 1853; elected to the Thirty-fifth Congress and served from March 4, 1857, until his death in Evansville, Ind., on September 7, 1857; interment in Oak Hill Cemetery.

**LOCKHART, James Alexander,** a Representative from North Carolina; born in Anson County, N.C., June 2, 1850; attended the common schools; was graduated from Trinity College, Durham, N.C., in June 1873; studied law in Charlotte, N.C.; was admitted to the bar in 1874; settled in Wadesboro, N.C., where he practiced his profession; mayor of Wadesboro in 1875; member of the State house of representatives in 1878; served in the State senate in 1880; presented credentials as a Democratic Member-elect to the Fifty-fourth Congress and served from March 4, 1895, to June 5, 1896, when he was succeeded by Charles H. Martin, who contested his election; resumed the practice of his profession in Wadesboro, N.C.; died in Charlotte, N.C., on December 24, 1905; interment in Eastview Cemetery, Wadesboro, N.C.

**LOCKWOOD, Daniel Newton,** a Representative from New York; born in Hamburg, Erie County, N.Y., June 1, 1844; attended common schools; was graduated from Union College, Schenectady, N.Y., in 1865; studied law; was admitted to the bar in 1866 and practiced in Buffalo, N.Y.; district attorney of Erie County, 1874-1877; elected as a Democrat to the Forty-fifth Congress (March 4, 1877-March 3, 1879); delegate to the Democratic National Conventions of 1880, 1884 and 1896; United States attorney for the northern district of New York from October 1886 until June 1889 when he resigned; elected to the Fifty-second and Fifty-third Congresses (March 4, 1891-March 3, 1895); was not a candidate for reelection in 1894 to the Fifty-fourth Congress, but was an unsuccessful candidate for Lieutenant Governor of New York; resumed the practice of his profession in Buffalo, N.Y.; general manager from New York at the Pan American Exposition in 1901; appointed in 1903 by Governor Benjamin B. Odell a member of the State lunacy commission, which office he held until his death in Buffalo, N.Y., June 1, 1906; interment in Forest Lawn Cemetery.

**LODGE, Henry Cabot** (great-grandson of George Cabot, grandfather of Henry Cabot Lodge, Jr., and John Davis Lodge), a Representative and a Senator from Massachusetts; born in Boston, Mass., May 12, 1850; attended a private school; graduated from Harvard University in 1871; editor of the North American Review from 1873 until 1876; was graduated from the Harvard Law School in 1874; admitted to the bar in 1875; earned the first Ph.D. degree in political science ever granted by Harvard University in 1876; lecturer on American history at Harvard University, 1876-1879; member, Massachusetts house of representatives, 1880-1881; author of many historical, biographical, and political works; appointed to the Alaskan Boundary Tribunal in 1903 by President Theodore Roosevelt; member of the United States Immigration Commission from 1907 until 1910; overseer of Harvard University from 1911 until his death; unsuccessful Republican candidate in 1882 for election to the Forty-eighth Congress and in 1884 to the Forty-ninth Congress; elected as a Republican to the Fiftieth and to the two succeeding Congresses, and served from March 4, 1887 until March 3, 1893, when he resigned; had been reelected to the Fifty-third Congress, but was later elected as a Republican to the United States Senate in 1893; reelected to the Senate in 1899, 1905, 1911, 1916, and 1922, and served from March 4, 1893 until his death in Cambridge, Mass., November 9, 1924; Republican caucus chairman, 1918-1924; served as President pro tempore of the Senate during the Sixty-second Congress; chairman, Committee on Immigration (Fifty-fourth and Sixty-second Congresses), Committee on Printing

(Fifty-fifth Congress), Committee on the Philippines (Fifty-sixth through Sixty-first Congresses), Committee on Private Land Claims (Sixty-third through Sixty-fifth Congresses), Committee on Foreign Relations (Sixty-sixth through Sixty-eighth Congresses), Republican Conference (Sixty-fifth through Sixty-eighth Congresses); represented the United States as a member of the Conference on Limitation of Armament in 1921; interment in Mount Auburn Cemetery, Cambridge, Mass.

**Bibliography:** *DAB*; Garraty, John A. *Henry Cabot Lodge: A Biography*. New York: Knopf, 1953; Widenor, William C. *Henry Cabot Lodge and the Search for an American Foreign Policy*. Berkeley: University of California Press, 1980; Widenor, William C. "Henry Cabot Lodge: The Astute Parliamentarian." In *First Among Equals: Outstanding Senate Leaders of the Twentieth Century*, edited by Richard A. Baker and Roger H. Davidson, pp. 38-62. Washington: Congressional Quarterly, Inc., 1991.

**LODGE, Henry Cabot, Jr.** (grandson of Henry Cabot Lodge, brother of John Davis Lodge, and nephew of Augustus P. Gardner), a Senator from Massachusetts; born in Nahant, Essex County, Mass., July 5, 1902; graduated from Middlesex School, Concord, Mass., in 1920 and from Harvard University in 1924; engaged in newspaper work, 1924-1931; member, Massachusetts legislature, 1933-1936; elected as a Republican to the United States Senate in 1936; reelected in 1942, and served from January 3, 1937, until his resignation on February 3, 1944, to go on active duty in the United States Army during the Second World War; the first United States Senator since the Civil War to leave the Senate in order to go to war; served in the Mediterranean and European Theaters, rising to the rank of lieutenant colonel; again elected to the United States Senate in 1946 and served from January 3, 1947, to January 3, 1953; unsuccessful candidate for reelection in 1952; appointed by President Dwight D. Eisenhower as Representative of the United States to the United Nations on January 23, 1953, and served until his resignation September 3, 1960; unsuccessful Republican candidate for Vice President of the United States in 1960 on the ticket headed by Vice President Richard M. Nixon; appointed by President John F. Kennedy as Ambassador to South Vietnam on August 1, 1963 and served until June 1964; again appointed Ambassador to South Vietnam in July 1965 and served until April 1967; appointed United States Ambassador at Large in April 1967 and served until May 1968; appointed Ambassador to the Federal Republic of Germany on April 22, 1968 and served until January 1969; appointed by President Richard M. Nixon to serve as head of the American delegation to the Vietnam peace negotiations in Paris, France, and served until December 1969; appointed by President Nixon to serve as personal representative to the Vatican in June 1970 and served until July 1977; died in Beverly, Mass., February 27, 1985; interment in Mt. Auburn Cemetery, Cambridge, Mass.

**Bibliography:** Lodge, Henry C., Jr. *The Storm Has Many Eyes, A Personal Narrative*. New York: Norton, 1973; Miller, William J. *Henry Cabot Lodge: A Biography*. New York: Heinman, 1967.

**LODGE, John Davis** (grandson of Henry Cabot Lodge, brother of Henry Cabot Lodge, Jr., and nephew of Augustus Peabody Gardner), a Representative from Connecticut; born in Washington, D.C., October 20, 1903; attended the Evans School, Mesa, Ariz., the Middlesex School, Concord, Mass., and Ecole de Droit, Paris, France; was graduated from Harvard University in 1925 and from the Harvard Law School in 1929; was admitted to the New York bar in 1932 and commenced practice in New York City; affiliated with the motion-picture industry and the theater, 1933-1942; served with the United States Navy as a lieutenant and lieutenant commander from August 1942 to January 1946, and was a liason officer between the French and American fleets; was decorated with the rank of Chevalier in the French Legion of Honor and with the Croix de Guerre with palm by General Charles de Gaulle; engaged in research work in economics; elected as a Republican to the Eightieth

and Eighty-first Congresses (January 3, 1947-January 3, 1951); was not a candidate for renomination in 1950 to the Eighty-second Congress, but was elected Governor of Connecticut, and served from January 3, 1951 to January 5, 1955; unsuccessful candidate for reelection in 1954; appointed by President Dwight D. Eisenhower as Ambassador to Spain on January 22, 1955 and served until April 1961; national president, Junior Achievement, Inc., 1963-1964; chairman, Committee Foreign Policy Research Institute, University of Pennsylvania, 1964-1969; delegate and assistant floor leader, Connecticut State constitutional convention, 1965; appointed by President Richard M. Nixon as Ambassador to Argentina on May 27, 1969 and served until November 1973; appointed by President Ronald Reagan as Ambassador to Switzerland on March 18, 1983 and served until April 1985; was a resident of Westport, Conn. until his death in New York City, October 29, 1985; interment in Arlington National Cemetery, Va.

**LOEFFLER, Thomas Gilbert,** a Representative from Texas; born in Fredericksburg, Gillespie County, Tex., August 1, 1946; attended the Mason County public schools and graduated from Mason High School in 1964; B.B.A., University of Texas, Austin, 1968; J.D., University of Texas Law School, 1971; admitted to the Texas bar in 1971; legal counsel, United States Department of Commerce, 1971-1972; chief legislative counsel to Senator John Tower, 1972-1974; deputy for congressional affairs, Federal Energy Administration, 1974-1975; special assistant for legislative affairs to President Gerald R. Ford, 1975-1977; private practice of law in Kerrville, 1977-1978; delegate to the Republican National Conventions of 1984, 1988 and 1992; elected as a Republican to the Ninety-sixth and to the three succeeding Congresses (January 3, 1979-January 3, 1987); was not a candidate for reelection in 1986 to the One Hundredth Congress, but was an unsuccessful candidate for nomination for Governor of Texas; resumed the practice of law in San Antonio, Tex., Austin, Tex., and Washington, D.C.; principal coordinator for Central America, Office of Legislative Affairs, The White House, 1987; Texas chairman of the 1988 presidential campaign of George Bush, and national adviser to the 1992 campaign of President George Bush and Vice President J. Danforth Quayle; Texas finance co-chairman of the 1994 gubernatorial campaign of George W. Bush; national finance chairman of the 1996 presidential campaign of Senator Phil Gramm; national deputy finance chairman of the presidential campaign of Senator Robert J. Dole in 1996; member, Board of Regents, University of Texas System; is a resident of San Antonio, Tex.

**LOFGREN, Zoe,** a Representative from California; born in San Mateo, Calif., December 21, 1947; graduated, Gunn High School, 1966; B.A., Stanford University, 1970; J.D., Santa Clara University School of Law, 1975; practicing attorney in San Jose, Calif.; member of the faculty, Santa Clara University School of Law, 1978-1980; served on the Washington, D.C. and San Jose staffs of Representative Don Edwards of California; executive director, Community Housing Developers; elected as a Democrat to the One Hundred Fourth Congress (January 3, 1995-January 3, 1997); is a resident of San Jose, Calif.

**LOFLAND, James Rush,** a Representative from Delaware; born in Milford, Del., November 2, 1823; received a classical education and was graduated from Delaware College (now the University of Delaware) at Newark in 1845; studied law; was admitted to the bar in 1848 and commenced practice in Milford; secretary of the State senate in 1849; member of the State constitutional convention in 1853; secretary of state of Delaware 1855-1859; paymaster in the United States Army 1863-1867; delegate to the Republican National Convention in 1872; elected as a Republican to the Forty-third Congress (March 4, 1873-March 3, 1875); unsuccessful candidate for reelection in 1874 to the Forty-fourth Congress; resumed the practice of law; died in Milford,

Kent County, Del., on February 10, 1894; interment in the Odd Fellows Cemetery.

**LOFT, George William,** a Representative from New York; born in New York City February 6, 1865; attended the public schools; engaged in the manufacture of candy from early boyhood; director in several corporations; elected as a Democrat to the Sixty-third Congress to fill the vacancy caused by the death of Timothy D. Sullivan; reelected in 1914 to the Sixty-fourth Congress and served from November 4, 1913, to March 3, 1917; was not a candidate for renomination in 1916; resumed the candy manufacturing business until 1929, when he founded the South Shore Trust Co. in Rockville Centre, Nassau County, N.Y., and served as president until his death; died in Baldwin, Nassau County, N.Y., November 6, 1943; interment in St. Raymond's Cemetery, Westchester, New York City.

**LOFTIN, Scott Marion,** a Senator from Florida; born in Montgomery, Montgomery County, Ala., September 14, 1878; moved to Pensacola, Fla., with his parents in 1887; attended the public schools and Washington and Lee University at Lexington, Va.; studied law; was admitted to the bar in 1899 and commenced practice in Pensacola, Fla.; member, State house of representatives 1903-1905; prosecuting attorney of Escambia County 1904-1917; moved to Jacksonville, Fla., in 1917 to continue the practice of law; member of the Attorney General's Advisory Committee on Crime 1934; president of the American Bar Association 1934; general counsel for the Florida East Coast Railway 1931-1941 and for a variety of other transportation-related businesses; businessman with interests in railroads, shipping, and newspapers; appointed as a Democrat to the United States Senate to fill the vacancy caused by the death of Park Trammell and served from May 26 to November 3, 1936, when a successor was elected; was not a candidate for election to fill the vacancy; resumed the practice of law in Jacksonville, Fla., until his death in Highlands, N.C., September 22, 1953; interment in Oaklawn Cemetery, Jacksonville, Fla.

**LOGAN, George,** a Senator from Pennsylvania; born at "Stenton," Philadelphia County, Pa., September 9, 1753; was sent to Great Britain for his schooling; returned to American and was apprenticed to a merchant; graduated in medicine from the University of Edinburgh, Scotland, in 1779; devoted himself to scientific farming; member, Pennsylvania house of representatives, 1785-1789, 1795-1796, and 1799; went to France in 1798 to treat unofficially for a better understanding between the two Governments, which action was subsequently responsible for the passage of the so-called Logan Act in 1799, prohibiting a private citizen from undertaking diplomatic negotiations; appointed and subsequently elected as a Republican to the United States Senate to fill the vacancy caused by the resignation of John Peter G. Muhlenberg and served from July 13, 1801, to March 3, 1807; declined to be a candidate for reelection; despite the Logan Act, went to Great Britain in 1810 on a private diplomatic mission as an emissary of peace, but was not successful; published several agricultural pamphlets; died at "Stenton," near Philadelphia, Pa., April 9, 1821; interment in the Logan Graveyard in Stenton Park, Philadelphia, Pa.

**Bibliography:** *DAB*; Logan, George. "Reminiscences of George B. Logan." Edited by Robert Christie. *Western Pennsylvania Historical Magazine* 51 (January 1968): 31-43, 51 (April 1968): 165-77, 51 (July 1968): 243-57, 51 (October 1968): 390-403; Tolles, Frederick. *George Logan of Philadelphia.* 1953. Reprint. New York: Arno Press, 1972.

**LOGAN, Henry,** a Representative from Pennsylvania; born near Dillsburg, Monaghan Township, York County, Pa., on April 14, 1784; attended the common schools; engaged in agricultural pursuits; volunteered for the defense of Baltimore in 1814; captain in the Nineteenth Regiment, Second Brigade, Fifth Division, Pennsylvania Militia, and was commissioned lieutenant colonel August 1, 1814;

member of the Pennsylvania house of representatives in 1818 and 1819; served in the Pennsylvania senate 1828-1831; elected as a Jacksonian to the Twenty-fourth Congress and reelected as a Democrat to the Twenty-fifth Congress (March 4, 1835-March 3, 1839); was not a candidate for renomination; resumed farming; member of the Board of Commissioners of York County in 1840; served as county auditor; died on the Logania plantation in Monaghan Township, near Dillsburg, Pa., December 26, 1866; interment in the Presbyterian Church Cemetery, Dillsburg, Pa.

**LOGAN, John Alexander,** a Representative and a Senator from Illinois; born in Murphysboro, Jackson County, Ill., on February 9, 1826; attended the common schools and studied law; served in the war with Mexico as a lieutenant; returned to Illinois; clerk of the Jackson County Court 1849; studied law, was admitted to the bar in 1852, and practiced; member, Illinois State house of representatives, 1852-1853, 1856-1857; prosecuting attorney for the third judicial district of Illinois, 1853-1857; presidential elector on the Democratic ticket in 1856; elected as a Democrat to the Thirty-sixth and Thirty-seventh Congresses, and served from March 4, 1859, until April 2, 1862 when he resigned and entered the Union Army; chairman, Committee on Revisal and Unfinished Business (Thirty-sixth and Thirty-seventh Congresses); during the Civil War was commissioned brigadier general, and then major general of Volunteers, and served until 1865; elected as a Republican to the Fortieth and Forty-first Congresses, and served from March 4, 1867 until his resignation on March 3, 1871, at the end of the Forty-first Congress, having been elected Senator; chairman, Committee on Military Affairs (Forty-first Congress); one of the managers appointed by the House of Representatives in 1868 to conduct the impeachment proceedings against President Andrew Johnson; conceived the idea of Memorial Day and inaugurated the observance in May 1868; elected as a Republican to the United States Senate, and served from March 4, 1871 to March 3, 1877; unsuccessful candidate for reelection; chairman, Committee on Military Affairs (Forty-third and Forty-fourth Congresses); resumed the practice of law in Chicago; again elected to the United States Senate in 1879; reelected in 1885, and served from March 4, 1879 until his death in Washington, D.C., December 26, 1886; chairman, Committee on Military Affairs (Forty-seventh and Forty-eighth Congresses); unsuccessful candidate in 1884 for Vice President of the United States on the ticket headed by James G. Blaine; died in Washington, D.C., December 26, 1886; interment in a tomb in the National Cemetery, Soldiers' Home, Washington, D.C.

**Bibliography:** *DAB*; Jones, James P. *John A. Logan: Stalwart Republican From Illinois.* Tallahassee: University of Florida Press, 1982; Logan, Mary S.C. *Reminiscences of a Soldier's Wife.* New York: Scribner's Sons, 1913.

**LOGAN, Marvel Mills,** a Senator from Kentucky; born on a farm near Brownsville, Edmonson County, Ky., January 7, 1874; educated in the public and private schools at Leitchfield and Brownsville, Ky.; taught school for two years and also conducted a training school for teachers; studied law; was admitted to the bar in 1896 and commenced practice in Brownsville, Ky.; chairman of the board of trustees of Brownsville; county attorney of Edmonson County, 1902-1903; assistant attorney general of Kentucky, 1912-1915; attorney general of Kentucky, 1915-1917; chairman of the Kentucky Tax Commission, 1917-1918; moved to Louisville, Ky., in 1918 and to Bowling Green, Ky., in 1922 and continued the practice of law; member of the Kentucky board of education, the Kentucky board of sinking fund commissioners (instituted to pay off the principal of the Commonwealth's debt), and the Kentucky board of printing commissioners; justice of the court of appeals of Kentucky, 1926-1930, and chief justice in 1931; elected as a Democrat to the United States Senate in 1930; reelected in 1936, and served from March 4, 1931 until his death in Washington, D.C., October 3, 1939; chairman, Committee on Mines and Mining (Seventy-third through

Seventy-fifth Congresses), Committee on Claims (Seventy-sixth Congress); interment in the Logan family cemetery near Brownsville, Ky.

**LOGAN, William,** a Senator from Kentucky; born within the fort at Harrodsburg, Mercer County, Ky., December 8, 1776; spent his early childhood in the fort at St. Asaphs, receiving private instruction from his parents and tutors; moved to Shelby County, Ky., about 1798; studied law; admitted to the bar and practiced; delegate to the Kentucky constitutional convention in 1799; served as a commissioner of the Kentucky River Co. in 1820; member, Kentucky house of representatives 1803-1806, 1808, and served as speaker two terms; judge of the court of appeals 1808-1812; presidential elector in 1808, 1812, and 1816; elected as a Republican to the United States Senate and served from March 4, 1819, to May 28, 1820, when he resigned to become a gubernatorial candidate; unsuccessful candidate for Governor in 1820; died at his residence in Shelby County on August 8, 1822; interment in the Logan family burial ground near Shelbyville, Ky.

**LOGAN, William Turner,** a Representative from South Carolina; born in Summerville, Dorchester County, S.C., June 21, 1874; attended the public schools, and was graduated from the College of Charleston, South Carolina, in 1895; studied law at the University of Virginia, Charlottesville, Va.; was admitted to the bar in 1895 and commenced practice in Charleston, S.C.; member of the State house of representatives 1901-1904; corporation counsel of Charleston 1914-1918; chairman of the Democratic executive committee of Charleston County 1916-1918; chairman of the city Democratic executive committee 1918-1922 and reelected in 1922; elected as a Democrat to the Sixty-seventh and Sixty-eighth Congresses (March 4, 1921-March 3, 1925); unsuccessful candidate for renomination in 1924; continued the practice of his profession in Charleston, S.C., until his death in that city on September 15, 1941; interment in Magnolia Cemetery.

**LOGUE, James Washington,** a Representative from Pennsylvania; born in Philadelphia, Pa., February 22, 1863; attended the public schools and was graduated from La Salle College, Philadelphia, Pa.; studied law; was admitted to the bar in 1888 and commenced the practice of his profession in Philadelphia; elected as a Democrat to the Sixty-third Congress (March 4, 1913-March 3, 1915); unsuccessful candidate for reelection in 1914 to the Sixty-fourth Congress; unsuccessful candidate for Lieutenant Governor of Pennsylvania in 1918; resumed the practice of law in Philadelphia; member of the speakers' bureau of the Council of National Defense during the First World War; secretary of the board of inspectors of the Eastern Penitentiary in 1923; died in Philadelphia, Pa., August 27, 1925; interment in Holy Sepulchre Cemetery.

**LONDON, Meyer,** a Representative from New York; born in Kalvaria, Russia, December 29, 1871; attended a primary school and also received private instruction, principally in languages; immigrated to the United States October 1, 1891, and settled in New York City; admitted to citizenship in the United States in 1896; studied law; was admitted to the bar in 1896 and practiced in New York City; active in the Socialist and labor movements for more than thirty years; leader of the garment workers' strike in New York City in 1910; elected as a Socialist to the Sixty-fourth and Sixty-fifth Congresses (March 4, 1915-March 3, 1919); unsuccessful candidate for reelection in 1918 to the Sixty-sixth Congress; elected to the Sixty-seventh Congress (March 4, 1921-March 3, 1923); unsuccessful candidate for reelection in 1922 to the Sixty-eighth Congress; engaged in the practice of law until his death in New York City on June 6, 1926, as the result of an automobile accident; interment in "Writers' Lane," a plot in Mount Carmel Cemetery, New York City.

**Bibliography:** DAB; Goldberg, Gordon J. "Meyer London: A Political Biography." Ph.D. dissertation, Lehigh University, 1971;

Rogoff, Harry. *An East Side Epic: The Life and Work of Meyer London.* New York: Vanguard Press, 1930.

**LONERGAN, Augustine,** a Representative and a Senator from Connecticut; born in Thompson, Windham County, Conn., May 20, 1874; attended the public schools of Rockville and Bridgeport; graduated from the law department of Yale University in 1902; was admitted to the bar in 1901 and commenced practice in Hartford, Conn.; member of the city planning commission 1910-1912; assistant corporation counsel of Hartford 1910-1912; elected as a Democrat to the Sixty-third Congress (March 4, 1913-March 3, 1915); unsuccessful candidate for reelection in 1914; elected to the Sixty-fifth and Sixty-sixth Congresses (March 4, 1917-March 3, 1921); was not a candidate for renomination in 1920, having become a candidate for United States Senator; unsuccessful candidate for election to the United States Senate in 1920 and again in 1928; resumed the practice of law in Hartford, Conn.; elected to the Seventy-second Congress (March 4, 1931-March 3, 1933); was not a candidate for renomination in 1932, having become a candidate for United States Senator; elected to the United States Senate as a Democrat in 1932 and served from March 4, 1933, to January 3, 1939; unsuccessful candidate for reelection in 1938; engaged in the practice of law in Washington, D.C., until his death there on October 18, 1947; interment in Mount St. Benedict's Cemetery, Hartford, Conn.

**LONG, Alexander,** a Representative from Ohio; born in Greenville, Mercer County, Pa., December 24, 1816; received an academic training; studied law; was admitted to the bar and commenced practice in Cincinnati, Ohio; member of the Ohio State house of representatives in 1848 and 1849; elected as a Democrat to the Thirty-eighth Congress (March 4, 1863-March 3, 1865); censured by the House of Representatives on April 9, 1864, for treasonable utterances; unsuccessful candidate for reelection in 1864 to the Thirty-ninth Congress; resumed the practice of law in Cincinnati, Ohio; delegate to the Democratic National Conventions of 1864, 1868, 1872, and 1876; died in Cincinnati, Ohio, November 28, 1886; interment in Spring Grove Cemetery.

**Bibliography:** Harlan, Louis R., ed. "The Autobiography of Alexander Long, 1858." *Bulletin of the Historical and Philosophical Society of Ohio* 19 (April 1961): 99-127.

**LONG, Catherine S.** (wife of Gillis W. Long), a Representative from Louisiana; born in Dayton, Ohio, February 7, 1924; attended high school in Camp Hill, Pa.; B.A., Louisiana State University, Baton Rouge, 1948; United States Navy, pharmacist's mate; staff assistant to Senator Wayne Morse of Oregon, and to Representative James G. Polk of Ohio; delegate to the Democratic National Conventions of 1980 and 1984; member, Louisiana State Democratic Finance Council and State central committee, and Democratic leadership council; elected to the Ninety-ninth Congress, March 30, 1985, by special election to fill the vacancy caused by the death of her husband, Gillis W. Long, and served from March 30, 1985 to January 3, 1987; was not a candidate for reelection in 1986 to the One Hundredth Congress; is a resident of Washington, D.C.

**LONG, Chester Isaiah,** a Representative and a Senator from Kansas; born in Greenwood Township, near Millerstown, Perry County, Pa., October 12, 1860; moved with his parents to Daviess County, Mo., in 1865 and to Paola, Kans., in 1879; attended the country schools and graduated from the normal school at Paola, Kans., in 1880; taught school for several years; studied law; was admitted to the bar in 1885 and commenced practice in Medicine Lodge, Kans.; member, Kansas State senate, 1889-1893; unsuccessful candidate for election in 1892 to the Fifty-third Congress; elected as a Republican to the Fifty-fourth Congress (March 4, 1895-March 3, 1897); unsuccessful candidate for reelection in 1896 to the Fifty-fifth Congress; elected to the Fifty-sixth and to the two succeeding Congresses and served from March 4, 1899, until his resignation, effective March 4, 1903, before the commencement of the Fifty-eighth Congress, to become Senator; elected as a Republican to the United States Senate and served from March 4, 1903, to March 3, 1909; unsuccessful candidate for renomination in 1908; chairman, Committee on the University of the United States (Fifty-eighth and Fifty-ninth Congresses), Committee on the Census (Fifty-ninth and Sixtieth Congresses); moved to Wichita in 1911 and continued the practice of law; chairman of the commission to revise the general statutes of Kansas, 1921-1923; moved to Washington, D.C., in 1925 and continued the practice of law; president of the American Bar Association, 1925-1926; died in Washington, D.C., July 1, 1934; interment in Old Mission Cemetery, Wichita, Kans.

**Bibliography:** Flory, Raymond L. "The Political Career of Chester I. Long." Ph.D. dissertation, University of Kansas, 1955.

**LONG, Clarence Dickinson,** a Representative from Maryland; born in South Bend, St. Joseph County, Ind., December 11, 1908; A.M., Washington and Jefferson College, Washington, Pa., 1932, and engaged in postgraduate work in 1933; A.M., Princeton University, 1935, Ph.D., economics, 1938; served as a lieutenant in the United States Navy, 1943-1946; professor of economics at Johns Hopkins University, Baltimore, Md., 1946-1962; associate task force director of the first Commission on Organization of the Executive Branch of the Government (Hoover Commission), 1948; senior staff member of the Council of Economic Advisers to the President in 1953-1954 and 1956-1957; acting chairman of the Democratic State Central Committee of Maryland in 1961-1962; author of numerous books and articles on unemployment, wages, labor force, and economic fluctuations; unsuccessful candidate in 1958 for nomination to the United States Senate; elected as a Democrat to the Eighty-eighth and to the ten succeeding Congresses (January 3, 1963-January 3, 1985); unsuccessful candidate for reelection in 1984 to the Ninety-ninth Congress; was a resident of Catonsville, Md.; died September 18, 1994.

**LONG, Edward Henry Carroll,** a Representative from Maryland; born in Princess Anne, Somerset County, Md., September 28, 1808; attended the common schools and was graduated from Yale College in 1828; studied law; was admitted to the bar in 1830 and commenced practice in Princess Anne, Somerset County; also engaged in agricultural pursuits; member of the Maryland State house of delegates, 1833-1835, 1839, 1844, and 1861; served in the Maryland State senate in 1860; elected as a Whig to the Twenty-ninth Congress (March 4, 1845-March 3, 1847); was not a candidate for renomination in 1846 to the Thirtieth Congress; resumed the practice of his profession and also engaged in agricultural pursuits; was an unsuccessful candidate for election to the United States Senate in 1860; died in Princess Anne, Somerset County, Md., on October 16, 1865; interment in the family burying ground on his farm, "Catalpa," near Princess Anne, Md.

**LONG, Edward Vaughn,** a Senator from Missouri; born in Lincoln County, near Whiteside, Mo., July 18, 1908; attended the public schools of Lincoln County, Culver-Stockton College, Canton, Mo., and the University of Missouri; was admitted to the bar in 1936 and commenced the practice of law in Bowling Green, Mo.; prosecuting attorney of Pike County from 1937 until 1941; city attorney of Bowling Green, Mo., 1941-1945; Missouri State senator, 1945-1955, serving as majority floor leader in 1952 and President pro tempore in 1955; Lieutenant Governor of Missouri, 1956-1960; appointed as a Democrat to the United States Senate on September 23, 1960, and elected November 8, 1960, to fill the vacancy caused by the death of Thomas C. Hennings, Jr., in the term ending January 3, 1963; reelected in 1962 and served from September 23, 1960, until his resignation on December 27, 1968; unsuccessful candidate for renomination in 1968; resumed the practice of law; farmer and banker; died on his estate, "Brookhill Farm," near Eolia,

Mo., November 6, 1972; interment in Grandview Burial Park, Hannibal, Mo.

**LONG, George Shannon** (brother of Huey Pierce Long, brother-in-law of Rose McConnell Long, and uncle of Russell Billiu Long), a Representative from Louisiana; born in Tunica, West Feliciana Parish, La., September 11, 1883; when five years of age moved with his parents to Winnfield, Winn Parish, La.; attended the public schools and Mount Lebanon College (now Louisiana College) 1897-1899; taught school in Winn and Grant Parishes; studied dentistry in Atlanta, Ga., Louisville, Ky., and New Orleans, La.; practiced dentistry in Oklahoma 1904-1935; studied law; was admitted to the Oklahoma bar in 1923; member of Oklahoma State house of representatives 1920-1922; practiced dentistry in Monroe, La., 1935-1940, and Pineville, La., 1948-1950; superintendent of Louisiana Colony and Training School 1948-1950; institutional inspector 1950-1952; delegate to the Democratic National Convention in 1948; unsuccessful for the Democratic nomination for Congress in 1948 and 1950; founder and director of the Dr. George S. Long Corp.; elected as a Democrat to the Eighty-third, Eighty-fourth, and Eighty-fifth Congresses and served from January 3, 1953 until his death in Bethesda, Md., March 22, 1958; interment in Greenwood Memorial Park, Pineville, La.

**LONG, Gillis William** (husband of Catherine Long, cousin of Huey Pierce Long, Rose McConnell Long, Russell Billiu Long, and George Shannon Long), a Representative from Louisiana; born in Winnfield, Winn Parish, La., May 4, 1923; attended the public schools of Winnfield and Alexandria, La.; B.A., Louisiana State University, Baton Rouge, 1949; J.D., Louisiana State University School of Law, 1951; was admitted to practice before the State supreme court in 1951 and before the Supreme Court of the United States in 1954; during the Second World War served in the Infantry as a private and rose through the ranks to captain; awarded the Purple Heart; was with the Internal Security Detachment at the Nuremberg war crimes trials, 1945-1946; served as legal counsel to the Senate Select Committee on Small Business, 1951-1952; chief counsel to the House of Representatives Special Committee on Campaign Expenditures, 1952-1954, and 1956; elected as a Democrat to the Eighty-eighth Congress (January 3, 1963-January 3, 1965); unsuccessful candidate for renomination in 1964 to the Eighty-ninth Congress; unsuccessful candidate for nomination for Governor of Louisiana in 1963; assistant director, Office of Economic Opportunity, 1965-1966; resumed the practice of law, 1970-1972; president, board of commissioners, Louisiana Deep Draft Harbor and Terminal Authority, 1972; investment banker; elected to the Ninety-third and to the six succeeding Congresses, and served from January 3, 1973 until his death in Washington, D.C., on January 20, 1985.

**Bibliography:** Fullerton, W.H., Jr. "Long Versus Long: The Congressional Race in the Eighth District of Louisiana, 1964." *North Louisiana Historical Association Journal* 16 (1985): 1-13.

**LONG, Huey Pierce** (husband of Rose McConnell Long, father of Russell Billiu Long, and brother of George Shannon Long), a Senator from Louisiana; born on a farm near Winnfield, Winn Parish, La., August 30, 1893; attended the public schools at Winnfield and briefly studied at high school in Shreveport, La.; attended the University of Oklahoma School of Law at Norman; was engaged as a book peddler, auctioneer, and salesman of cottonseed oil, wholesale groceries, and patent medicine in western Tennessee, and in northern Mississippi and Louisiana; studied law at Tulane University, New Orleans, La.; was admitted to the bar on May 15, 1915 and commenced practice in Winnfield; moved to Shreveport, La., in 1918; served as a member of the State railroad commission (renamed Public Service Commission in 1921), 1918-1928, and as commission chairman, 1924-1928; unsuccessful candidate for the

Democratic nomination for Governor of Louisiana in 1924; Democratic National committeeman, 1928-1935; elected Governor of Louisiana in 1928, and served from May 21, 1928 until his resignation effective January 25, 1932, having previously been elected Senator; elected as a Democrat to the United States Senate in 1930 for the term commencing March 4, 1931, but did not assume these duties until January 25, 1932, preferring to continue as Governor, and served until his death; known as "the Kingfish," Long espoused the redistribution of wealth in his "Share the Wealth" crusade; shot in the State Capitol Building in Baton Rouge on September 8, 1935, and died on September 10, 1935; interment on the Capitol Grounds at Baton Rouge, La.

**Bibliography:** *DAB*; Hair, William Ivy. *The Kingfish and His Realm: The Life and Times of Huey P. Long*. Baton Rouge: Louisiana State University Press, 1991; Long, Huey P. *Every Man A King: The Autobiography of Huey P. Long*. Introduction by T. Harry Williams. 1933. Reprint. New York: Da Capo Press, 1996; Williams, T. Harry. *Huey Long*. New York: Alfred A. Knopf, 1969.

**LONG, Jefferson Franklin,** a Representative from Georgia; born a slave near Knoxville, Crawford County, Ga., March 3, 1836; self-educated; became a merchant tailor in Macon, Ga.; active member of the Georgia Educational Association; member of the Georgia State Republican central committee; chairman of a convention held at Macon in October 1869 to address the problems of freedmen; elected as a Republican to the Forty-first Congress to fill the vacancy caused by the House declaring Samuel F. Gove not entitled to the seat, and served from December 22, 1870 to March 3, 1871; was not a candidate for renomination in 1870 to the Forty-second Congress; delegate to the Republican National Convention of 1880; resumed business activities in Macon, Ga., and died there on February 4, 1901; interment in Lynwood Cemetery.

**Bibliography:** Matthews, John M. "Jefferson Franklin Long: The Public Career of Georgia's First Black Congressman." *Phylon* 42 (June 1981): 145-56.

**LONG, Jill L.,** a Representative from Indiana; born in Warsaw, Kosciusko County, Ind., July 15, 1952; graduated from Columbia City Joint High School; B.S., Valparaiso (Ind.) University, 1974; M.B.A., Indiana University, 1978, and Ph.D., 1984; member, Valparaiso city council, 1984; management consultant, Campbell and Pryor, 1985-1986; assistant instructor and lecturer, Indiana Purdue University at Fort Wayne; assistant professor, College of Business Administration, Valparaiso University; owner of eighty-acre farm in northeastern Indiana; elected as a Democrat to the One Hundred First Congress, March 28, 1989, by special election to fill the vacancy caused by the resignation of Daniel R. Coats; reelected to the two succeeding Congresses, and served from March 28, 1989 to January 3, 1995; unsuccessful candidate for reelection in 1994 to the One Hundred Fourth Congress; fellow at the Institute of Politics, John F. Kennedy School of Government, Harvard University; member, board of directors, Commodity Credit Corporation; Under Secretary for Rural Economic and Community Development, Department of Agriculture, 1995 to present; is a resident of Larwill, Ind.

**LONG, John,** a Representative from North Carolina; born in Loudoun County, Va., February 26, 1785; moved with his parents to North Carolina, who settled at Longs Mill (now Liberty), Randolph County; attended private and public schools; engaged in agricultural pursuits in Randolph County, N.C.; served in the North Carolina State house of representatives in 1811 and 1812; member of the State senate in 1814 and 1815; elected to the Seventeenth and to the three succeeding Congresses (March 4, 1821-March 3, 1829); unsuccessful candidate for reelection in 1828 to the Twenty-first Congress; resumed his agricultural pursuits; died at Longs Mill (now Liberty), Randolph County, N.C., August 11, 1857; interment in Richland Graveyard.

**LONG, John Benjamin,** a Representative from Texas; born in Douglass, Nacogdoches County, Tex., September 8, 1843; moved with his parents to Rusk, Cherokee County, Tex., in 1846; educated in private schools; during the Civil War served in the Confederate Army in Company C, Third Texas Cavalry; studied law; was admitted to the bar but never practiced; became a planter; elected as a Democrat to the Fifty-second Congress (March 4, 1891-March 3, 1893); unsuccessful candidate for renomination in 1892 to the Fifty-third Congress; engaged in the newspaper business in Rusk, Tex., from 1886 until 1905; member of the Texas State house of representatives in 1913 and 1914; died in Rusk, Tex., April 27, 1924; interment in Cedar Hill Cemetery.

**LONG, John Davis,** a Representative from Massachusetts; born in Buckfield, Oxford County, Maine, October 27, 1838; attended the common schools at Buckfield and Hebron Academy, Maine; was graduated from the academic department of Harvard University in 1857; taught school in Westford Academy, Massachusetts; studied law at Harvard Law School and in private offices; was admitted to the bar in 1861 and commenced practice in Buckfield, Maine; moved to Boston, Mass., in 1863 and continued the practice of law, and in 1869 moved to Hingham, Mass.; member of the Massachusetts house of representatives, 1875-1878, and served the last three years as speaker of the house; Lieutenant Governor of Massachusetts in 1879; elected Governor of Massachusetts in 1879, reelected in 1880 and 1881, and served from January 8, 1880 to January 4, 1883; elected as a Republican to the Forty-eighth and to the two succeeding Congresses (March 4, 1883-March 3, 1889); declined to be a candidate for renomination in 1888 to the Fifty-first Congress; continued the practice of his profession in Boston; appointed Secretary of the Navy in the Cabinet of President William McKinley and served from March 6, 1897 until April 30, 1902, when he resigned; resumed the practice of law in Boston, with residence in Hingham, Mass.; president of overseers of Harvard University and of the Authors' Club of Boston; died in Hingham, Mass., August 28, 1915; interment in Hingham Cemetery.

**Bibliography:** *DAB*; Hess, James W. "John D. Long and Reform Issues in Massachusetts Politics, 1870-1889." *New England Quarterly* 33 (March 1960): 57-73; Long, John Davis. *Journal*. Edited by Margaret Long. Rindge, N.H.: R.R. Smith, 1956.

**LONG, Lewis Marshall,** a Representative from Illinois; born in Gardner, Grundy County, Ill., June 22, 1883; attended the public schools of Aurora, Ill., the Plano (Ill.) High School, and the University of Illinois at Urbana; was graduated from the John Marshall Law School, Chicago, Ill., in 1929; was employed as a telegraph operator and station agent at Plano, Ill., and Sandwich, Ill., 1904-1930; was admitted to the bar in 1930 and commenced practice in Sandwich, Ill.; member of the board of aldermen 1922-1926; served as mayor of Sandwich in 1935 and 1936; member of the board of education 1932-1936; elected as a Democrat to the Seventy-fifth Congress (January 3, 1937-January 3, 1939); unsuccessful candidate for renomination in 1938 and for election in 1940 to the Seventy-seventh Congress; resumed the practice of law; served as chief examiner of the Division of Motor Carriers of the State of Illinois from November 1, 1939, to July 1, 1941, when he resigned to engage in motor carrier practice in addition to law practice; died in Sandwich, Ill., September 9, 1957; interment in Oak Ridge Cemetery.

**LONG, Oren Ethelbirt,** a Senator from Hawaii; born in Altoona, Wilson County, Kans., March 4, 1889; attended the public schools; graduated from Johnson College, Kimberlin Heights, Tenn., in 1912, the University of Michigan in 1916, and Columbia University in 1922; teacher of history, Johnson Academy, Kimberlin Heights, Tenn., 1912-1914, and principal, 1914-1917; social settlement worker, Hilo, Hawaii, 1917-1918; educational director, Army Y.M.C.A., Fort Shafter, Hawaii, 1918-1919; vice principal of

McKinley High School, Honolulu, Hawaii, 1919-1920; personnel officer, Kohala Sugar Co., 1920-1921; principal, Church Farm School, Glen Loch, Pa., 1922-1924, and Kauai High School, Hawaii, 1924-1925; deputy superintendent of public instruction for Hawaii, 1925-1934, and superintendent of public instruction, Territory of Hawaii, 1934-1946; during the Second World War served as a lieutenant, Headquarters Staff, Hawaii Defense Volunteers; director, Hawaii Department of Public Welfare, 1946; chairman, Advisory Committee on Education for Trust Territories, 1946; secretary of the Territory of Hawaii, 1946-1951; appointed Governor of Territory of Hawaii in April 1951 and served until February 28, 1953; member and vice chairman, Hawaii Statehood Commission, 1954-1956; member of the Hawaii Territorial Senate, 1956-1959; elected as a Democrat to the United States Senate on July 28, 1959, and, upon the admission of Hawaii as a State into the Union on August 21, 1959, drew the four-year term beginning on that day and ending January 3, 1963; was not a candidate for renomination in 1962; member of the South Pacific Commission in 1964; died in Honolulu, Hawaii, May 6, 1965; interment in Oahu Cemetery.

**LONG, Pierse,** a Delegate from New Hampshire; born in Portsmouth, N.H., in 1739; completed preparatory studies; engaged in the shipping business; delegate to the Provincial Congress of New Hampshire in 1775; served in the Revolutionary War as colonel of the First New Hampshire Regiment; brevetted a brigadier general; Member of the Continental Congress 1785-1786; State councilor 1786-1789; delegate to the State constitutional convention which ratified the Federal Constitution June 21, 1788; appointed customs collector for the port of Portsmouth, N.H., in January 1789, by President George Washington but owing to ill health was unable to assume the duties of the office; died in Portsmouth, N.H., on April 13, 1789; interment in the Proprietors' Burying Ground.

**LONG, Rose McConnell** (wife of Huey Pierce Long, mother of Russell Billiu Long, and sister-in-law of George Shannon Long), a Senator from Louisiana; born in Greensburg, Decatur County, Ind., April 8, 1892; moved with her parents to Shreveport, La., in 1901; attended the public schools of Shreveport; appointed and subsequently elected in a special election as a Democrat to the United States Senate to fill the vacancy caused by the death of her husband, Huey P. Long, and served from January 31, 1936, to January 2, 1937; was not a candidate for reelection in 1936 for the full term; retired from public life to Shreveport, La.; died in in Boulder, Colo., May 27, 1970; interment in Forrest Park Cemetery, Shreveport, La.

**LONG, Russell Billiu** (son of Huey Pierce Long and Rose McConnell Long, and nephew of George Shannon Long), a Senator from Louisiana; born in Shreveport, Caddo Parish, La., November 3, 1918; attended the public schools of Shreveport, Baton Rouge, and New Orleans, La.; B.A., Louisiana State University, Baton Rouge, 1941; LL.B., Louisiana State University School of Law, 1942; was admitted to the bar in 1942 and commenced practice in Baton Rouge, La., in 1946; during the Second World War served in the United States Naval Reserve from June 1942 until discharged as a lieutenant in December 1945; elected as a Democrat to the United States Senate on November 2, 1948, to fill the vacancy in the term ending January 3, 1951, caused by the death of John H. Overton, and took his seat December 31, 1948; reelected in 1950, 1956, 1962, 1968, 1974, and again in 1980, and served from December 31, 1948 to January 3, 1987; was not a candidate for reelection in 1986; Democratic whip 1965-1969; chairman, Committee on Finance (Eighty-ninth through Ninety-sixth Congresses), co-chairman, Joint Committee on Internal Revenue Taxation (Eighty-ninth Congress), chairman, Joint Committee on Internal Revenue Taxation (Ninetieth through Ninety-fourth Congresses), Joint Committee on Taxation (Ninety-fifth and Ninety-sixth Congresses); practices law in Washington, D.C., and Baton Rouge, La.; is a resident of Baton Rouge, La.

**Bibliography:** Mann, Robert. *Legacy to Power: Senator Russell Long of Louisiana*. New York: Paragon House Publishers, 1992.

**LONG, Speedy Oteria,** a Representative from Louisiana; born in Tullos, La Salle Parish, La., June 16, 1928; attended the public schools of La Salle and Winn Parishes; graduated from Winnfield (La.) High School in 1945; served in the United States Navy from April 1946 to February 1948; graduated from Northeast Junior College, Monroe, La., in 1950; B.A., Northwestern State College, Natchitoches, La., 1951; was recalled to active duty in the Navy, September 1951 to December 1952; J.D., Louisiana State University Law School, Baton Rouge, February 1959; was admitted to the Louisiana bar in 1959 and commenced practice in Jena, La.; member of the Louisiana State senate from May 1956 to May 1964; elected as a Democrat to the Eighty-ninth and to the three succeeding Congresses (January 3, 1965-January 3, 1973); was not a candidate for reelection in 1972 to the Ninety-third Congress; district attorney, Twenty-eighth Judicial District, January 4, 1973 to January 3, 1985; served as temporary judge of the Twenty-eighth Judicial District Court in 1994; practices law; past president, Twenty-eighth District Bar Association; is a resident of Jena, La.

**Bibliography:** Fullerton, W.H., Jr. "Long Versus Long: The Congressional Race in the Eighth District of Louisiana, 1964." *North Louisiana Historical Association Journal* 16 (1985): 1-13.

**LONGFELLOW, Stephen,** a Representative from Maine; born in Gorham, Cumberland County, Maine (then a district of Massachusetts), June 23, 1775; was graduated from Harvard University in 1798; studied law; was admitted to the bar in 1801 and commenced practice in Portland, Maine; member of the general court of Massachusetts in 1814 and 1815; belonged to the Federalist Party and was a delegate to the Hartford convention in 1814 and 1815; Federalist presidential elector in 1816; elected to the Eighteenth Congress (March 4, 1823-March 3, 1825); was not a candidate for renomination in 1824; resumed the practice of his profession; member of the State house of representatives in 1826; overseer of Bowdoin College, Brunswick, Maine, 1811-1817; a trustee of Bowdoin College 1817-1836; president of the Maine Historical Society in 1834; died in Portland, Maine, August 2, 1849.

**Bibliography:** *DAB*.

**LONGLEY, James B., Jr.,** a Representative from Maine; born in Lewiston, Androscoggin County, Maine, July 7, 1951; graduated, Phillips Academy, Andover, Mass.; A.B., College of the Holy Cross, 1974; J.D., University of Maine School of Law, 1980; editorial assistant, Maine Management and Cost Survey, 1973; attorney and owner of an insurance company, 1980-present; United States Marine Corps, active duty 1976-1979; United States Marine Corps reserve service as lieutenant colonel, 1976 to present, including director of public affairs, Camp Lejeune, N.C., 1991; active duty in northern Iraq during the Kurdish relief effort of 1991; elected as a Republican to the One Hundred Fourth Congress (January 3, 1995-January 3, 1997); is a resident of Falmouth, Maine.

**LONGNECKER, Henry Clay,** a Representative from Pennsylvania; born in Allen Township, Cumberland County, Pa., April 17, 1820; was graduated from the Norwich Military Academy of Vermont and from Lafayette College, Easton, Pa.; studied law; was admitted to the bar and practiced in Easton, Pa.; served during the Mexican War as first lieutenant, captain, and adjutant in all principal engagements under General Winfield Scott; was wounded at the Battle of Chapultepec, September 13, 1847; returned to Pennsylvania; district attorney of Lehigh County, 1848-1850; elected as a Republican to the Thirty-sixth Congress (March 4, 1859-March 3, 1861); during the Civil War participated in organizing Pennsylvania troops and served in the Union Army as colonel of the Ninth Regiment, Pennsylvania Volunteers; resumed the practice of his profession in Allentown, Pa., in 1865; associate judge of Lehigh

County in 1867; died in Allentown, Lehigh County, Pa., September 16, 1871; interment in Fairview Cemetery.

**LONGWORTH, Nicholas** (son-in-law of Theodore Roosevelt, and nephew of Bellamy Storer), a Representative from Ohio; born in Cincinnati, Ohio, November 5, 1869; attended the Franklin School in Cincinnati; graduated from Harvard University in 1891; spent one year at Harvard Law School; graduated from the Cincinnati Law School in 1894; admitted to the bar in 1894 and commenced practice in Cincinnati, Ohio; member of the board of education of Cincinnati in 1898; member of the Ohio State house of representatives in 1899 and 1900; member, Ohio State senate, 1901-1903; elected as a Republican to the Fifty-eighth and to the four succeeding Congresses (March 4, 1903-March 3, 1913); unsuccessful candidate for reelection in 1912 to the Sixty-third Congress; elected to the Sixty-fourth and to the eight succeeding Congresses, and served from March 4, 1915 until his death in Aiken, S.C., while on a visit, April 9, 1931; majority leader (Sixty-eighth Congress), Speaker of the House of Representatives (Sixty-ninth through Seventy-first Congresses); interment in Spring Grove Cemetery, Cincinnati, Ohio.

Bibliography: *DAB*; De Chambrun, Clara Longworth. *The Making of Nicholas Longworth: Annals of an American Family.* 1933. Reprint. Freeport, N.Y.: Books for Libraries Press, 1971.

**LONGYEAR, John Wesley,** a Representative from Michigan; born in Shandaken, Ulster County, N.Y., October 22, 1820; pursued classical studies in the Lima (N.Y.) Academy; taught school for several years; moved to Mason, Ingham County, Mich., in 1844 and taught school; studied law; was admitted to the Ingham County bar in 1846; moved to Lansing, Mich., in 1847 and engaged in the practice of law; elected as a Republican to the Thirty-eighth and Thirty-ninth Congresses (March 4, 1863-March 3, 1867); chairman, Committee on Expenditures on Public Buildings (Thirty-eighth and Thirty-ninth Congresses); was not a candidate for renomination in 1866; delegate to the Loyalist Convention at Philadelphia, Pa., in 1866 and to the Michigan State constitutional convention in 1867; appointed by President Ulysses S. Grant judge of the United States District Court for the Eastern District of Michigan February 7, 1870; moved to Detroit in 1871, where he died March 11, 1875; interment in Mount Hope Cemetery, Lansing, Mich.

**LOOFBOUROW, Frederick Charles,** a Representative from Utah; born in Atlantic, Cass County, Iowa, February 8, 1874; was educated in the common schools of Iowa; moved with his parents to Utah in 1889; was graduated from the Ogden Military Academy, Ogden, Utah, in 1892, and from the law department of the University of California at Berkeley in 1896; was admitted to the bar the same year and commenced practice in Salt Lake City, Utah; district attorney of the third judicial district of Utah 1905-1911, and district judge 1911-1916; resumed the practice of law; elected as a Republican to the Seventy-first Congress to fill the vacancy caused by the death of Elmer O. Leatherwood and on the same day was elected to the Seventy-second Congress and served from November 4, 1930, to March 3, 1933; unsuccessful candidate for reelection in 1932 to the Seventy-third Congress and for election in 1934 to the Seventy-fourth Congress; resumed the practice of law in Salt Lake City, Utah, until his retirement; died in Salt Lake City, July 8, 1949; remains were cremated and the ashes scattered.

**LOOMIS, Andrew Williams,** a Representative from Ohio; born in Lebanon, Conn., June 27, 1797; was graduated in law from Union College, Schenectady, N.Y., in 1819; was admitted to the bar; moved to Canton, Ohio, and practiced; moved to New Lisbon (now Lisbon), Ohio; delegate to the National-Republican State convention in 1827 and 1828; elected as a Whig to the Twenty-fifth Congress and served from March 4, 1837, until October 20, 1837, when he resigned; moved to Pittsburgh, Pa., in 1839 and resumed the practice of his profession; member of the peace convention of 1861 held in Washington, D.C., in an effort to devise means to prevent the impending war; moved to Cleveland, Ohio, about 1868; died while on a visit to Cumberland, Md., August 24, 1873; interment in Allegheny Cemetery, Pittsburgh, Pa.

**LOOMIS, Arphaxed,** a Representative from New York; born in Winsted, Conn., April 9, 1798; moved to New York in 1801 with his parents, who settled upon a farm in the town of Salisbury, Herkimer County; attended the common schools and Fairfield Academy, Fairfield, N.Y.; studied law; was admitted to the bar at Albany in 1822 and commenced practice at Sackets Harbor, N.Y., the same year; returned to Salisbury in 1825; later in that year moved to Little Falls, N.Y., and continued the practice of his profession; surrogate of Herkimer County 1828-1836; commissioner to investigate the State prisons in 1834; county judge of Herkimer County 1835-1840; elected as a Democrat to the Twenty-Fifth Congress (March 4, 1837-March 3, 1839); chairman, Committee on Patents (Twenty-fifth Congress); was not a candidate for renomination in 1838; member of the State assembly in 1841 and 1842; member of the State constitutional convention in 1846; member of the commission to revise, abridge, and simplify pleadings and proceedings in civil actions in 1847; again a member of the State assembly in 1853 and 1854; delegate to the Democratic State conventions in 1861 and 1863; died at Little Falls, N.Y., September 15, 1885; interment in the Church Street Cemetery.

**LOOMIS, Dwight,** a Representative from Connecticut; born in Columbia, Tolland County, Conn., July 27, 1821; attended the common schools and academies in Monson and Amherst, Mass.; taught school; was graduated from the law department of Yale University in 1847; admitted to the bar the same year and commenced practice at Rockville, Conn.; member of the State house of representatives in 1851; delegate to the Republican National Convention in 1856; member of the State senate 1857-1859; elected as a Republican to the Thirty-sixth and Thirty-seventh Congresses (March 4, 1859-March 3, 1863); chairman, Committee on Expenditures in the Department of the Treasury (Thirty-sixth Congress); was not a candidate for renomination in 1862; judge of the superior court of the State 1864-1875; justice of the supreme court of the State 1875-1891; moved to Hartford, Conn., in 1892; State referee from 1892 until his death in a train accident near Waterbury, Conn., September 17, 1903; interment in Grove Hill Cemetery, Rockville, Conn.

Bibliography: *DAB.*

**LORD, Bert,** a Representative from New York; born in the town of Sanford, Broome County, N.Y., December 4, 1869; attended the public schools and the Afton (N.Y.) Union School and Academy; engaged in the mercantile business at Afton, N.Y., from 1893 to 1918, when he entered the lumber business and operated sawmills; served as supervisor of the town of Afton 1905-1915; member of the New York assembly 1915-1922 and 1924-1929; served as commissioner of motor vehicles of the State of New York 1921-1923; member of the State senate 1929-1935; elected as a Republican to the Seventy-fourth, Seventy-fifth, and Seventy-sixth Congresses and served from January 3, 1935, until his death in Washington, D.C., May 24, 1939; interment in Glenwood Cemetery, Afton, N.Y.

**LORD, Frederick William,** a Representative from New York; born in Lyme, New London County, Conn., December 11, 1800; attended Lyme Academy and was graduated from Yale College in 1821; professor of mathematics in Washington College, Chestertown, Md., for two years; in charge of an academy at Baltimore, Md., for three years; studied medicine in Baltimore and was graduated in medicine from Yale College in 1828; commenced the practice of medicine in Sag Harbor, N.Y., continuing in his profession there for fifteen years; delegate to the Whig National Convention at Harrisburg, Pa., in 1840; moved to Greenport, Long Island, N.Y., in 1846 and engaged in agricultural pursuits and the cultivation of fruit and ornamental trees; elected as a Democrat to the Thirtieth

Congress (March 4, 1847-March 3, 1849); resumed his former pursuits in Greenport; unsuccessful candidate for election in 1854 to the Thirty-fourth Congress and in 1856 to the Thirty-fifth Congress; elected a delegate to the Republican National Convention at Chicago in 1860, but on his way to attend the convention was taken ill on the steamer *Massachusetts,* and died in New York City May 24, 1860; interment in East Hampton Cemetery, East Hampton, Suffolk County, N.Y.

**LORD, Henry William,** a Representative from Michigan; born in Northampton, Mass., March 8, 1821; pursued an academic course; studied law, but did not practice; moved to Detroit, Mich., in 1839; four years later went to Pontiac, Mich., and engaged in agricultural and mercantile pursuits; returned to Detroit, Mich.; appointed by President Abraham Lincoln as United States consul to Manchester, England, in 1861 and served until his resignation in 1867; served on the State board of corrections and charities 1871-1882; elected as a Republican to the Forty-seventh Congress (March 4, 1881-March 3, 1883); unsuccessful candidate for reelection in 1882 to the Forty-eighth Congress; appointed by President Chester A. Arthur as register of the United States land office at Creelsburg, N.Dak., on August 1, 1883, continuing in that capacity after the office was transferred to Devils Lake, N.Dak., on January 17, 1884, and served until April 18, 1888; was killed in a railroad accident near Butte, Mont., January 25, 1891; interment in Elmwood Cemetery, Detroit, Mich.

**LORD, Scott,** a Representative from New York; born in Nelson, Madison County, N.Y., December 11, 1820; attended the common schools and the local academies at Morrisville and Geneseo; studied law; was admitted to the bar in 1842 and commenced practice in Mount Morris, Livingston County, N.Y.; moved to Geneseo, the county seat, in 1847; served as judge of Livingston County from 1847 until 1856; resumed the practice of law; moved to Utica, Oneida County, N.Y., in 1872 and continued the practice of his profession; elected as a Democrat to the Forty-fourth Congress (March 4, 1875-March 3, 1877); one of the managers appointed by the House of Representatives in 1876 to conduct the impeachment proceedings against William W. Belknap, ex-Secretary of War; unsuccessful candidate for reelection in 1876 to the Forty-fifth Congress; moved to New York City in 1877 and again engaged in the practice of law; died in Morris Plains, Morris County, N.J., September 10, 1885; interment in Temple Hill Cemetery, Geneseo, N.Y.

**LORE, Charles Brown,** a Representative from Delaware; born in Odessa, New Castle County, Del., March 16, 1831; attended the public schools and Middletown Academy, Delaware; was graduated from Dickinson College, Carlisle, Pa., in June 1852; studied law; was admitted to the bar of New Castle County, Del., in 1861 and practiced; clerk of the Delaware State house of representatives in 1857; during the Civil War served as commissioner of the draft for New Castle County, Del., in 1862; attorney general of Delaware, 1869-1874; elected as a Democrat to the Forty-eighth and Forty-ninth Congresses (March 4, 1883-March 3, 1887); was not a candidate for renomination in 1886 to the Fiftieth Congress; appointed chief justice of the supreme court of Delaware in 1893; reappointed in 1897 for a term of twelve years but retired in 1909; member of the code commission in 1909 and 1910; died in Wilmington, Del., March 6, 1911; remains were cremated and the ashes deposited in the Methodist Church Cemetery.

**Bibliography:** Pennewill, James. *The Life and Public Services of Hon. Charles B. Lore, of Delaware.* Wilmington: Historical Society of Delaware, 1913.

**LORIMER, William,** a Representative and a Senator from Illinois; born in Manchester, England, April 27, 1861; immigrated to the United States in 1866 with his parents, who settled in Michigan; moved to Chicago, Ill., in 1870; self-educated; apprenticed to the trade of sign painter at the age of ten; worked in the packing houses and for a street railroad company; ward boss and constable 1886; engaged in the real estate business and later as a builder and brick manufacturer; elected as a Republican to the Fifty-fourth, Fifty-fifth, and Fifty-sixth Congresses (March 4, 1895-March 3, 1901); unsuccessful candidate for reelection in 1900 to the Fifty-seventh Congress; elected to the Fifty-eighth and to the three succeeding Congresses and served from March 4, 1903, until his resignation, effective June 17, 1909, having been elected Senator; chairman, Committee on Expenditures in the Department of the Navy (Sixty-first Congress), Committee on Mines and Mining (Sixty-second Congress), Committee on Pacific Islands and Puerto Rico (Sixty-second Congress); presented credentials as a Senator-elect to the United States Senate for the term that had commenced March 4, 1909, and served from June 18, 1909, until July 13, 1912, when, after a Senate investigation and acrimonious debate, the Senate adopted a resolution declaring "that corrupt methods and practices were employed in his election, and that the election, therefore, was invalid"; resumed his former pursuits and was president of La Salle Street Trust & Savings Bank 1910-1915; subsequently engaged in the lumber business; unsuccessfully sought election to the House and Senate; died in Chicago, Ill., September 13, 1934; interment in Calvary Cemetery.

**Bibliography:** *DAB*; Tarr, Joel A. *A Study in Boss Politics: William Lorimer of Chicago.* Urbana: University of Illinois Press, 1971.

**LORING, George Bailey,** a Representative from Massachusetts; born in North Andover, Essex County, Mass., November 8, 1817; attended Franklin Academy at Andover; taught school; was graduated from Harvard University in 1838 and from the medical department in 1842; practiced medicine for a short time in North Andover; surgeon of the marine hospital at Chelsea, Mass., 1843-1850; surgeon of the Seventh Regiment, Massachusetts Volunteer Militia, 1842-1844; appointed commissioner to revise the United States marine hospital system in 1849; moved to Salem, Mass., in 1851; appointed postmaster of Salem on May 4, 1853, and served until his successor was appointed on February 16, 1858; member of the Massachusetts house of representatives, 1866-1867; chairman of the Massachusetts Republican committee, 1869-1876; served in the Massachusetts senate, 1873-1876, and was also president of that body; delegate to the Republican National Conventions of 1868, 1872, and 1876; appointed United States centennial commissioner for the Commonwealth of Massachusetts in 1872; elected as a Republican to the Forty-fifth and Forty-sixth Congresses (March 4, 1877-March 3, 1881); unsuccessful candidate for renomination in 1880 to the Forty-seventh Congress; United States Commissioner of Agriculture, 1881-1885; appointed Minister to Portugal on March 30, 1889 and served until May 1890; died in Salem, Mass., September 14, 1891; interment in Harmony Grove Cemetery.

**Bibliography:** *DAB*.

**LOSER, Joseph Carlton,** a Representative from Tennessee; born in Nashville, Davidson County, Tenn., October 1, 1892; educated in the public schools and the Y.M.C.A. Law School; member of Tennessee National Guard in 1910; secretary to the mayor of Nashville 1917-1920; Cumberland University, Lebanon, Tenn., LL.B., 1923; was admitted to the bar in 1922 and commenced the practice of law in Nashville, Tenn., in 1923; assistant city attorney of Nashville, 1923-1929; assistant district attorney general of the tenth judicial circuit 1929-1934 and district attorney 1934-1956; delegate to the Democratic National Conventions in 1944, 1952, and 1960; member of the United States Coast Guard Reserve in 1944; presidential elector in 1956; secretary of Democratic Executive Committee of Tennessee 1954-1958; elected as a Democrat to the Eighty-fifth, Eighty-sixth, and Eighty-seventh Congresses (January 3, 1957-January 3, 1963); unsuccessful candidate in 1962 for reelection to the Eighty-eighth Congress; resided in Nashville, Tenn., until his death July 31, 1984.

**LOTT, Chester Trent,** a Representative and a Senator from Mississippi; born in Grenada, Miss., October 9, 1941; graduated from the public schools of Pascagoula, Miss.; B.P.A., University of Mississippi, 1963; J.D., University of Mississippi School of Law, 1967; served as a field representative for the University of Mississippi, 1963-1965; admitted to the Mississippi bar in 1967 and commenced practice in Pascagoula; administrative assistant to Representative William M. Colmer of Mississippi, 1968-1972; elected as a Republican to the Ninety-third and to the seven succeeding Congresses (January 3, 1973-January 3, 1989); minority whip (Ninety-seventh through One Hundredth Congresses); was not a candidate in 1988 for reelection to the House of Representatives, but was elected to the United States Senate for the term commencing January 3, 1989; reelected in 1994 for the term ending January 3, 2001; secretary, Republican Conference, 1992-1995; majority whip (One Hundred Fourth Congress), majority leader (One Hundred Fourth Congress); is a resident of Pascagoula, Miss.

**LOUD, Eugene Francis,** a Representative from California; born in Abington, Plymouth County, Mass., March 12, 1847; went to sea and afterward settled in California; during the Civil War enlisted in a California Cavalry battalion in 1862, which formed a part of the Second Regiment, Massachusetts Volunteer Cavalry; returned to California; engaged in mining and as clerk for fifteen years; studied law; clerk in the customs service at San Francisco, Calif.; member of the State assembly in 1884; cashier of the city and county of San Francisco; elected as a Republican to the Fifty-second and to the five succeeding Congresses (March 4, 1891-March 3, 1903); chairman, Committee on the Post Office and Post Roads (Fifty-fourth and Fifty-seventh Congresses); unsuccessful candidate for reelection in 1902 to the Fifty-eighth Congress; died in San Francisco, Calif., December 19, 1908; remains were cremated and the ashes interred in the Odd Fellows Cemetery.

**LOUD, George Alvin,** a Representative from Michigan; born in Bracebridge, Ohio, June 18, 1852; moved with his parents to Massachusetts in 1856 and to Au Sable, Mich., in 1866; attended the English High School, Boston, Mass., and Professor Patterson's School at Detroit, Mich.; was graduated from the Ann Arbor High School in 1869; vice president and general manager of the Au Sable & Northwestern Railroad; for four years was a colonel on the staff of Governor Hazen S. Pingree; paymaster on the United States revenue cutter *McCulloch* when it participated in the Battle of Manila Bay during the Spanish-American War, May 1, 1898; elected as a Republican to the Fifty-eighth and to the four succeeding Congresses (March 4, 1903-March 3, 1913); unsuccessful candidate for reelection in 1912 to the Sixty-third Congress; elected to the Sixty-fourth Congress (March 4, 1915-March 3, 1917); unsuccessful candidate for renomination in 1916 to the Sixty-fifth Congress; engaged in the lumber business at Au Sable, Mich.; killed in an automobile accident at Myrtle Point, Mich., November 13, 1925; interment in Au Sable Cemetery, Oscoda, Mich.

**LOUDENSLAGER, Henry Clay,** a Representative from New Jersey; born in Mauricetown, Cumberland County, N.J., May 22, 1852; moved with his parents to Paulsboro, N.J., in 1856; attended the common schools; engaged in the produce commission business in Philadelphia, Pa., 1872-1882; county clerk of Gloucester County, N.J., 1882-1892; elected as a Republican to the Fifty-third and to the nine succeeding Congresses and served from March 4, 1893, until his death in Paulsboro, Gloucester County, N.J., August 12, 1911; chairman, Committee on Pensions (Fifty-fourth through Sixty-first Congresses); interment in Eglington Cemetery, Clarksboro, N.J.

**LOUGHRIDGE, William,** a Representative from Iowa; born in Youngstown, Mahoning County, Ohio, July 11, 1827; attended the common schools; studied law; was admitted to the bar in 1849 and commenced practice in Mansfield, Ohio; moved to Iowa in 1852 and settled in Oskaloosa, Mahaska County; member of the State senate 1857-1860; judge of the sixth judicial circuit of Iowa 1861-1867; elected as a Republican to the Fortieth and Forty-first Congresses (March 4, 1867-March 3, 1871); elected to the Forty-third Congress (March 4, 1873-March 3, 1875); died near Reading, Pa., September 26, 1889; interment in Forest Cemetery, Oskaloosa, Iowa.

**LOUNSBERY, William,** a Representative from New York; born at Stone Ridge, Ulster County, N.Y., December 25, 1831; was graduated from Rutgers College, New Brunswick, N.J., in 1851; attended the law department of the New York University in Albany, N.Y.; was admitted to the bar in 1853 and engaged in practice; during the Civil War was commissary of the Twentieth Regiment, New York Militia, with the rank of first lieutenant, during its three months' service; member of the State assembly in 1868; mayor of Kingston 1878-1880; elected as a Democrat to the Forty-sixth Congress (March 4, 1879-March 3, 1881); died in Kingston, N.Y., November 8, 1905; interment in the Wiltwyck Rural Cemetery.

**LOUTTIT, James Alexander,** a Representative from California; born in New Orleans, La., October 16, 1848; moved with his parents to California in 1849, who settled in Calaveras County; attended private and public schools and the State normal school at Sacramento; studied law; was admitted to the bar in 1869; settled in Stockton, Calif., in 1871 and practiced law; prosecuting attorney of Stockton 1871-1879; elected as a Republican to the Forty-ninth Congress (March 4, 1885-March 3, 1887); was not a candidate for renomination in 1886; resumed the practice of law in Stockton, Calif.; died in Pacific Grove, Monterey County, Calif., July 26, 1906; interment in the Stockton Rural Cemetery, Stockton, Calif.

**LOVE, Francis Johnson,** a Representative from West Virginia; born in Cadiz, Harrison County, Ohio, on January 23, 1901; attended the public schools; A.B., Bethany (W.Va.) College, 1924; principal of Warwood High School in Wheeling, W.Va., 1926-1929; J.D., West Virginia University Law School, Morgantown, 1932; was admitted to the bar the same year and commenced practice in Wheeling, W.Va.; elected as a Republican to the Eightieth Congress (January 3, 1947-January 3, 1949); unsuccessful candidate for reelection in 1948 to the Eighty-first Congress; resumed the general practice of law; delegate to the Republican National Conventions of 1956, 1960, 1964, and 1968; is a resident of Wheeling, W.Va.

**LOVE, James,** a Representative from Kentucky; born in Nelson County, Ky., May 12, 1795; attended the common schools in Bardstown, Ky.; volunteered at the age of eighteen and served during the War of 1812; studied law; was admitted to the bar and commenced practice in Barboursville, Knox County, Ky.; member of the Kentucky house of representatives, 1819-1831; elected as an Anti-Jacksonian to the Twenty-third Congress (March 4, 1833-March 3, 1835); declined to be a candidate for renomination in 1834 to the Twenty-fourth Congress; moved to Texas in 1837 and settled in Galveston; represented Galveston in the convention which framed the constitution of 1846, and was the first judge of the Galveston district; resigned to become clerk of the United States court and served until the opening of the Civil War; after war was declared he enlisted and served for two years with the Terry Rangers; after the war was elected first judge of the Galveston and Harris County Criminal Court, but was removed by the military commander; died in Galveston, Tex., June 12, 1874; interment in Trinity Church Cemetery.

**Bibliography:** Hicks, Jimmie, ed. "Some Letters of James Love." *Register of the Kentucky Historical Society* 63 (April 1965): 121-140.

**LOVE, John,** a Representative from Virginia; pursued an academic course; studied law; admitted to the bar in 1801 and commenced practice in Alexandria, Va.; member of the Virginia house of delegates 1805-1807; elected as a Republican to the Tenth and Eleventh Congresses (March 4, 1807-March 3, 1811); chairman, Committee on District of Columbia (Eleventh Congress); served in the Virginia senate 1816-1820; resumed the practice of law; died in Alexandria, Va., August 17, 1822.

**LOVE, Peter Early,** a Representative from Georgia; born near Dublin, Laurens County, Ga., July 7, 1818; was graduated from Franklin College (now a part of the University of Georgia), Athens, Ga., in 1829 and from the Philadelphia College of Medicine in 1838; practiced medicine while studying law; was admitted to the bar in 1839 and commenced practice in Thomasville, Thomas County, Ga.; solicitor general of the southern district of Georgia in 1843; member of the State senate in 1849; elected judge of the State superior court for the southern circuit in 1853; elected as a Democrat to the Thirty-sixth Congress and served from March 4, 1859, until his retirement on January 23, 1861; resumed the practice of law in Thomasville, Ga.; member of the State house of representatives in 1861; died in Thomasville, Ga., November 8, 1866; interment in the Old Cemetery.

**LOVE, Rodney Marvin,** a Representative from Ohio; born in Dayton, Montgomery County, Ohio, July 18, 1908; graduated from Steele High School in 1926; A.B., Ohio State University, Columbus, 1930; LL.B., University of Dayton Law School, 1933; was admitted to the bar in 1933 and commenced practice in Dayton, Ohio; chief deputy, Montgomery County Probate Court, 1941-1945; judge of the Montgomery County Probate Court, 1945-1959; resigned from the bench in 1960 to reenter private practice of law; elected as a Democrat to the Eighty-ninth Congress (January 3, 1965-January 3, 1967); unsuccessful candidate for reelection in 1966 to the Ninetieth Congress; judge, Ohio Court of Common Pleas, 1969-1981; retired; moved to Mesa, Ariz. in November 1995 and resided there until his death on May 5, 1996.

**LOVE, Thomas Cutting,** a Representative from New York; born in Cambridge, N.Y., November 30, 1789; attended the common schools; served as a Volunteer in the War of 1812; wounded and taken prisoner at the Battle of Fort Erie on September 17, 1814; taken to Quebec and kept imprisoned until the close of the war; studied law; was admitted to the bar and practiced; moved to Batavia, N.Y., and later to Buffalo; judge of Erie County in 1828 and 1829; district attorney, 1829-1835 and surrogate, 1841-1845; elected as a Whig to the Twenty-fourth Congress (March 4, 1835-March 3, 1837); declined to be a candidate for renomination in 1836 to the Twenty-fifth Congress; resumed the practice of law until 1847, when he retired from active practice; died in Buffalo, N.Y., September 17, 1853; interment in Forest Lawn Cemetery.

**LOVE, William Carter,** a Representative from North Carolina; born near Norfolk, Va., in 1784; moved to Chapel Hill, N.C.; was tutored at home; attended the University of North Carolina at Chapel Hill 1802-1804; studied law; was admitted to the bar and commenced practice in Salisbury, N.C., in 1806; elected as a Republican to the Fourteenth Congress (March 4, 1815-March 3, 1817); resumed the practice of law in Salisbury, Rowan County, N.C., where he died in 1835; interment in a private cemetery in Salisbury.

**LOVE, William Franklin,** a Representative from Mississippi; born near Liberty, Amite County, Miss., March 29, 1850; attended the common schools and the University of Mississippi at Oxford; engaged in agricultural pursuits; member of the State house of representatives 1878-1882 and 1884-1888; served in the State senate 1889-1896; delegate to the State constitutional convention in 1890; elected as a Democrat to the Fifty-fifth Congress and served from March 4, 1897, until his death in Gloster, Amite County, Miss., October 16, 1898; interment in Gloster Cemetery.

**LOVEJOY, Owen** (cousin of Nathan Allen Farwell), a Representative from Illinois; born in Albion, Maine, on January 6, 1811; attended the common schools and was graduated from Bowdoin College, Brunswick, Maine, in 1832; studied law but never practiced; studied theology; moved to Alton, Madison County, Ill., in 1836; ordained pastor of the Congregational Church in Princeton, Ill., 1839-1856; member of the State house of representatives in 1854; elected as a Republican to the Thirty-fifth and to the three succeeding Congresses and served from March 4, 1857, until his death in Brooklyn, N.Y., March 25, 1864; chairman, Committee on Agriculture (Thirty-seventh Congress), Committee on District of Columbia (Thirty-eighth Congress); interment in Oakland Cemetery, Princeton, Ill.

**Bibliography:** *DAB*; Magdol, Edward. *Owen Lovejoy: Abolitionist in Congress.* New Brunswick, N.J.: Rutgers University Press, 1967.

**LOVELL, James,** a Delegate from Massachusetts; born in Boston, Mass., October 31, 1737; attended the public schools; was graduated from the Boston Latin School in 1752 and from Harvard College in 1756; completed a postgraduate course at the latter institution in 1759; taught in the Boston Latin School 1757-1775 and was also master of the North Grammar (now the Eliot) School; imprisoned by General Howe during the Revolutionary War and conveyed to Halifax in 1775; Member of the Continental Congress 1777-1782; receiver of continental taxes 1784-1788; collector of customs at Boston, Mass., in 1788 and 1789; appointed naval officer of the port of Boston and Charlestown and served from August 3, 1789, until his death in Windham, Maine, July 14, 1814.

**Bibliography:** *DAB*; Jones, Helen F. "James Lovell in the Continental Congress 1777-1782." Ph.D. dissertation, Columbia University, 1968.

**LOVERING, Henry Bacon,** a Representative from Massachusetts; born in Portsmouth, N.H., April 8, 1841; attended the public schools of Lynn, Mass., and was graduated from Phillips Exeter Academy, Exeter, N.H.; during the Civil War enlisted in 1862 in the Eighth Regiment, Massachusetts Volunteer Infantry, and served out his term; reenlisted in the Third Massachusetts Cavalry; member of the Massachusetts house of representatives in 1872 and 1874; city assessor in 1879 and 1880; mayor of Lynn in 1881 and 1882; elected as a Democrat to the Forty-eighth and Forty-ninth Congresses (March 4, 1883-March 3, 1887); unsuccessful candidate for reelection in 1886 to the Fiftieth Congress; unsuccessful Democratic candidate for Governor in 1887; United States marshal for Massachusetts 1888-1891; warden of the State prison 1891-1893; United States pension agent at Boston 1894-1898; sealer of weights and measures for the city of Boston, Mass., 1902-1905; superintendent of the Chardon Street Soldiers' Home at Boston 1905-1907; moved to Wakefield, Mass., in 1907, where he died on April 5, 1911; interment in Pine Grove Cemetery, Lynn, Essex County, Mass.

**LOVERING, William Croad,** a Representative from Massachusetts; born in Woonsocket, R.I., February 25, 1835; moved with his parents to Taunton, Mass., in 1837; attended the Cambridge High School and the Hopkins Classical School, Cambridge, Mass.; left school in 1859 for employment in his father's mill; during the Civil War served as quartermaster of Engineers in the Second Massachusetts Brigade, consisting of the Second and Third Regiments; engaged in cotton manufacturing in Taunton; first president of the Taunton Street Railway; president of the American Liability Insurance Co.; interested in several other business enterprises; president of the New England Cotton Manufacturers' Association for two years; member of the Massachusetts senate in 1874 and 1875; delegate to the Republican National Convention in 1880; presided at the Massachusetts Republican convention in 1892; elected as a Republican to the Fifty-fifth and to the six succeeding Congresses and served from March 4, 1897, until his death in Washington, D.C., February 4, 1910; interment in Mount Pleasant Cemetery, Taunton, Mass.

**LOVETT, John,** a Representative from New York; born in Newent Society, in the present township of Lisbon, Conn., February 20, 1761; was graduated from Yale College in 1782; moved to Albany, N.Y., and thence to Fort Miller, N.Y., where he was employed as general agent and land steward; moved to Lansingburg, N.Y.; member of the New York State assembly in 1800 and 1801; returned to Albany and served as clerk of the common council until the outbreak of the War of 1812; military secretary to General Stephen Van Rensselaer at the northwestern frontier; was wounded at the Battle of Queenstown in October 1812; returned to Albany; county clerk of Albany County from March 3, 1813, to March 31, 1815; elected as a Federalist to the Thirteenth and Fourteenth Congresses (March 4, 1813-March 3, 1817); was not a candidate for renomination in 1816 to the Fifteenth Congress; began the settlement of Perrysburg, Ohio; died at Fort Meigs, Ohio, August 12, 1818.

**LOVETTE, Oscar Byrd,** a Representative from Tennessee; born in Greeneville, Greene County, Tenn., December 20, 1871; attended the common schools of Greene County and the Parrottsville (Tenn.) High School; was graduated from Tusculum (Tenn.) College in 1893; member of the State house of representatives 1895-1897; studied law at Vanderbilt University, Nashville, Tenn.; was admitted to the bar in 1896 and commenced practice in Greeneville, Tenn.; also engaged in banking, serving as president of a local bank 1912-1918; served as attorney general of the first judicial circuit of Tennessee 1918-1926; trustee of Tusculum College; elected as a Republican to the Seventy-second Congress (March 4, 1931-March 3, 1933); unsuccessful candidate for renomination and for reelection as an Independent candidate in 1932; continued the practice of law in Greeneville, Tenn., until his death there on July 6, 1934; interment in Oak Grove Cemetery.

**LOVRE, Harold Orrin,** a Representative from South Dakota; born in Toronto, Deuel County, S.Dak., January 30, 1904; attended the public schools of Toronto, S.Dak., and St. Olaf College, Northfield, Minn.; graduated from the University of South Dakota at Vermillion in 1927; was admitted to the bar in 1927 and practiced law in Hayti, Hamlin County, S.Dak., 1927-1944, and in Watertown, Codington County, S.Dak., 1944-1949; State's attorney for Hamlin County, S.Dak., 1929-1932, 1937-1940; president of the State Board of Agriculture in 1939 and 1940; chairman of the South Dakota Republican Committee in 1947 and 1948; member of the South Dakota State senate, 1941-1944; elected as a Republican to the Eighty-first and to the three succeeding Congresses (January 3, 1949-January 3, 1957); unsuccessful candidate for reelection in 1956 to the Eighty-fifth Congress; resumed the practice of law; died in Silver Spring, Md., January 17, 1972; interment in Parklawn Cemetery, Rockville, Md.

**LOW, Frederick Ferdinand,** a Representative from California; born in Frankfort (now Winterport), Waldo County, Maine, June 30, 1828; attended the common schools and Hampden Academy; moved to California, where he engaged in the shipping business in San Francisco in 1849; moved to Marysville, Calif. in 1854 and engaged in banking until 1861; presented credentials as a Republican Member-elect to the Thirty-seventh Congress but was not permitted to take his seat; subsequently qualified under authority of a special act of Congress and served from June 3, 1862, to March 3, 1863; was not a candidate for renomination in 1862 to the Thirty-eighth Congress; appointed collector of the port of San Francisco in 1863; elected Governor of California in 1863, and served from December 10, 1863 to December 5, 1867; appointed United States Minister to China on September 28, 1869 and served until July 1873; engaged in banking in San Francisco; died in San Francisco, Calif., July 21, 1894; interment in Laurel Hill Cemetery; reinterment in Cypress Lawn Cemetery, Colma, Calif.

**Bibliography:** *DAB.*

**LOW, Isaac,** a Delegate from New York; born at Raritan Landing, near New Brunswick, N.J., April 13, 1735; moved to New York City and engaged in mercantile pursuits; stamp-act commissioner for the Province of New York during the French and Indian War; Member of the Continental Congress in 1774; delegate to the Provincial Congress in 1775; was opposed to armed conflict with Great Britain and after the Declaration of Independence abandoned the patriot cause; returned to Raritan, N.J., in 1776 where he was accused of treason and imprisoned by the New Jersey Convention, but was released on the interposition of George Washington; returned to New York after the British occupation; one of the founders and president of the New York Chamber of Commerce 1775-1783; his property was confiscated in 1779 by the American authorities, and in 1783 he moved to England, where he died in Cowes, Isle of Wight, July 25, 1791.

**Bibliography:** *DAB.*

**LOW, Philip Burrill,** a Representative from New York; born in Chelsea, Suffolk County, Mass., May 6, 1836; attended the public schools and was graduated from high school; during the Civil War volunteered and was appointed acting ensign in the United States Navy and served in the North Atlantic Squadron during 1862 and 1863; resigned and engaged in commercial pursuits in Boston, Mass., until 1865, when he moved to New York City; identified with the shipping and maritime interests; elected as a Republican to the Fifty-fourth and Fifty-fifth Congresses (March 4, 1895-March 3, 1899); unsuccessful candidate for reelection in 1898 to the Fifty-sixth Congress; continued his activities in maritime pursuits in New York City until his death there on August 23, 1912; interment in Woodlawn Cemetery.

**LOWDEN, Frank Orren,** a Representative from Illinois; born in Sunrise, Chisago County, Minn., January 26, 1861; moved with his parents to Point Pleasant, Hardin County, Iowa, in 1868; attended the public schools of Iowa; was graduated from the Iowa State University at Iowa City in 1885 and the Union College of Law, Chicago, Ill., in 1887; was admitted to the bar in 1887 and commenced practice in Chicago; lieutenant colonel of the First Regiment Infantry, Illinois National Guard, 1898-1903; professor of law at Northwestern University, Chicago, Ill., in 1899; delegate to the Republican National Conventions of 1900 and 1904; moved to Oregon, Ill., in 1903; member of the Republican National Committee from Illinois, 1904-1912; elected as a Republican to the Fifty-ninth Congress to fill the vacancy caused by the death of Robert R. Hitt; reelected to the Sixtieth and Sixty-first Congresses, and served from November 6, 1906 to March 3, 1911; declined to be a candidate for renomination in 1910 to the Sixty-second Congress; elected Governor of Illinois in 1916, and served from January 8, 1917 to January 10, 1921; nominated as the Republican candidate for Vice President of the United States in 1924 but declined; died March 20, 1943, in Tucson, Ariz., where he had gone for his health; interment in Graceland Cemetery, Chicago, Ill.

**Bibliography:** *DAB*; Hutchinson, William Thomas. *Lowden of Illinois: The Life of Frank O. Lowden.* 2 vols. Chicago: University of Chicago Press, 1957.

**LOWE, David Perley,** a Representative from Kansas; born near Utica, Oneida County, N.Y., August 22, 1823; moved to Ohio; attended the common schools; was graduated from the Cincinnati Law College in 1851; was admitted to the bar and commenced practice in Cincinnati, Ohio; moved to Mound City, Kans., in 1861 and continued the practice of law; member of the State senate in 1863 and 1864; judge of the sixth judicial district 1867-1871; moved to Fort Scott in 1870; elected as a Republican to the Forty-second and Forty-third Congresses (March 4, 1871-March 3, 1875); chairman, Committee on Mines and Mining (Forty-third Congress); declined to be a candidate for renomination in 1874; appointed chief justice of Utah Territory by President Ulysses S. Grant in 1875; returned to Kansas and settled in Fort Scott, Bourbon County; again elected judge of the sixth judicial district of Kansas in 1879 and served until his death in Fort Scott, Kans., April 10, 1882; interment in Evergreen Cemetery.

**LOWE, William Manning,** a Representative from Alabama; born in Huntsville, Madison County, Ala., on June 12, 1842; attended the Wesleyan University, Florence, Ala., and the University of Virginia at Charlottesville; during the Civil War served in the Confederate Army as private, lieutenant, captain, and lieutenant colonel; studied law; was admitted to the bar and commenced practice in Huntsville, Ala.; solicitor of the fifth judicial circuit 1865-1867; member of the State house of representatives in 1870; delegate to the State constitutional convention in 1875; elected as a Greenback candidate to the Forty-sixth Congress (March 4, 1879-March 3, 1881); successfully contested the election of Joseph Wheeler to the Forty-seventh Congress and served from June 3, 1882, until his death in "The Grove," Huntsville, Ala., October 12, 1882; interment in Maple Hill Cemetery.

**LOWELL, John,** a Delegate from Massachusetts; born in Newburyport, Mass., June 17, 1743; was graduated from Harvard College in 1760; studied law; was admitted to the bar in 1762 and commenced practice in Newburyport, Mass.; an officer in the militia in 1776; moved to Boston, Mass., in 1777; member of the Massachusetts house of representatives 1778 and 1780-1782; delegate to the Massachusetts constitutional convention in 1780; Member of the Continental Congress in 1782; served in the Massachusetts senate in 1784 and 1785; commissioner on the New York and Massachusetts boundary line in 1784; judge of the court of appeals 1784-1789, of the United States district court 1789-1801, and of the United States Circuit Court for Massachusetts, Rhode Island, and Connecticut in 1801 and 1802; died in Roxbury, Mass., May 6, 1802.

**Bibliography:** *DAB.*

**LOWELL, Joshua Adams,** a Representative from Maine; born in Thomaston, Maine, March 20, 1801; attended the common schools; taught school; studied law; was admitted to the bar and commenced practice in East Machias, Maine, in 1826; member of the State house of representatives in 1832, 1833, 1835, and 1837; elected as a Democrat to the Twenty-sixth and Twenty-seventh Congresses (March 4, 1839-March 3, 1843); chairman, Committee on Expenditures in the Post Office Department (Twenty-seventh Congress); was not a candidate for renomination in 1842; resumed the practice of law; died in East Machias, Maine, March 13, 1874; interment in the Village Cemetery.

**LOWENSTEIN, Allard Kenneth,** a Representative from New York; born in Newark, Essex County, N.J., January 16, 1929; B.A., University of North Carolina, 1949; LL.B., Yale University School of Law, 1954; served in the United States Army, 1954-1956; taught at Stanford University, North Carolina State University, and City College of New York, 1967-1968; special assistant to Senator Frank Porter Graham in 1949; foreign policy assistant to Senator Hubert H. Humphrey in 1959; delegate to the Democratic National Conventions of 1960 and 1968; elected as a Democrat to the Ninety-first Congress (January 3, 1969-January 3, 1971); unsuccessful candidate for reelection in 1970 to the Ninety-second Congress; unsuccessful candidate for election in 1972 to the Ninety-third Congress, in 1974 to the Ninety-fourth Congress, and in 1976 to the Ninety-fifth Congress; appointed to head the United States delegation to the thirty-third regular annual session of the United Nations Commission on Human Rights in Geneva, Switzerland,

1977; alternate United States Representative for Special Political Affairs in the United Nations, with the rank of Ambassador, from August 1977 to June 1978; unsuccessful candidate for nomination in 1978 to the Ninety-sixth Congress; died from the effects of an assassin's bullets in New York City, March 14, 1980; interment in Arlington National Cemetery, Va.

**Bibliography:** *DAB*; Chafe, William H. *Never Stop Running: Allard Lowenstein and the Struggle to Save American Liberalism.* New York: BasicBooks, 1993; Cummings, Richard. *The Pied Piper: Allard K. Lowenstein and the Liberal Dream.* New York: Grove Press, 1985.

**LOWER, Christian,** a Representative from Pennsylvania; born in Tulpehocken Township, Berks County, Pa., January 7, 1740; attended school; worked as a blacksmith and was later proprietor of an iron foundry; colonel of associated battalions in 1775, and sub-lieutenant in 1780; county commissioner of Berks County, 1777-1779; member of the Pennsylvania house of representatives, 1783-1785, 1793, 1794, and 1796; served in the Pennsylvania senate, 1797-1804; elected as a Republican to the Ninth Congress, and served from March 4, 1805 until his death at his home in Tulpehocken Township, Pa., on December 19, 1806; interment in Tulpehocken Church Burial Ground.

**LOWERY, William David,** a Representative from California; born in San Diego, San Diego County, Calif., May 2, 1947; attended the public schools; graduated from Point Loma High School, 1965; attended San Diego State University, 1965-1969, and Western State University School of Law, 1972-1974; partner in an advertising and public relations firm; member, San Diego City Council, 1977-1980; deputy mayor, San Diego, 1979-1980; delegate to the Republican National Convention of 1980; elected as a Republican to the Ninety-seventh and to the five succeeding Congresses (January 3, 1981-January 3, 1993); was not a candidate for reelection in 1992 to the One Hundred Third Congress; is a resident of San Diego, Calif.

**LOWEY, Nita M.,** a Representative from New York; born in New York City, July 5, 1937; graduated, Bronx High School of Science, 1955; B.S., Mount Holyoke College, 1959; assistant to the New York Secretary of State for Economic Development and Neighborhood Preservation, and deputy director, Division of Economic Opportunity, 1975-1985; New York assistant secretary of state, 1985-1987; elected as a Democrat to the One Hundred First and to the three succeeding Congresses (January 3, 1989-January 3, 1997); is a resident of Rye, N.Y.

**LOWNDES, Lloyd, Jr.,** a Representative from Maryland; born in Clarksburg, Harrison County, Va. (now West Virginia), February 21, 1845; attended the common schools; was graduated from Allegheny College, Meadville, Pa., in 1865 and from the law department of the University of Pennsylvania at Philadelphia in 1867; was admitted to the bar and commenced practice in Cumberland, Md.; elected as a Republican to the Forty-third Congress (March 4, 1873-March 3, 1875); unsuccessful candidate for reelection in 1874 to the Forty-fourth Congress; engaged in banking; elected Governor of Maryland in 1895, and served from January 8, 1896 to January 10, 1900; unsuccessful candidate for reelection in 1899; died in Cumberland, Md., January 8, 1905; interment in Rose Hill Cemetery.

**Bibliography:** *DAB.*

**LOWNDES, Thomas** (brother of William Lowndes), a Representative from South Carolina; born in Charleston, S.C., January 22, 1766; educated at home and in grammar schools of Charleston; studied law; was admitted to the bar in 1789 and commenced practice in Charleston; member of the South Carolina State house of representatives, 1792-1799; elected as a Federalist to the Seventh and Eighth Congresses (March 4, 1801-March 3, 1805); unsuccessful candidate for reelection in 1804 to the Ninth Congress; unsuccessful candidate for election in 1808 to the Eleventh Congress; devoted himself to the management of his estate, with a residence on his Oaklands plantation, and also in Charleston, S.C.; died in Charleston, S.C., July 8, 1843; interment in St. Paul's Churchyard.

**LOWNDES, William** (brother of Thomas Lowndes), a Representative from South Carolina; born on "Horseshoe" plantation, near Jacksonborough, St. Bartholomew's parish, South Carolina, February 11, 1782; pursued classical studies in Great Britain and at home; studied law; was admitted to the bar in 1804 and commenced practice in Charleston, S.C.; also engaged in agricultural pursuits; member of the State house of representatives 1804-1808; captain of militia in 1807; elected as a Republican to the Twelfth and to the five succeeding Congresses and served from March 4, 1811, until May 8, 1822, when he resigned; chairman, Committee on Ways and Means (Fourteenth and Fifteenth Congresses), Committee on Expenditures in the Department of the Treasury (Fifteenth Congress); nominated by the general assembly of South Carolina for the office of President of the United States in 1821; died at sea, October 27, 1822, while en route to England; remains were buried at sea.

    **Bibliography:** *DAB*; Ravenel, Mrs. St. Julien. *Life and Times of William Lowndes* Boston: Houghton Mifflin, 1901; Vipperman, Carl J. *William Lowndes and the Transition of Southern Politics, 1782-1822*. Chapel Hill: University of North Carolina Press, 1989.

**LOWREY, Bill Green,** a Representative from Mississippi; born in Kossuth, Alcorn County, Miss., May 25, 1862; attended the public schools and Blue Mountain Academy, Blue Mountain, Miss.; was graduated from Mississippi College at Clinton in 1887; was a student at Tulane University, New Orleans, La., in 1888 and 1889; professor in Blue Mountain College, Blue Mountain, Miss., 1889-1898; president of the college 1898-1911; president of the Amarillo (Tex.) Military Academy 1911-1916; field secretary for Hillman College and Mississippi College at Clinton and Blue Mountain College at Blue Mountain, 1916-1920; vice president of Blue Mountain College in 1920 and 1921; elected as a Democrat to the Sixty-seventh and to the three succeeding Congresses (March 4, 1921-March 3, 1929); was an unsuccessful candidate for renomination in 1928 to the Seventy-first Congress; served as clerk of the United States Court for the Northern District of Mississippi 1929-1935; died in Olive Branch, De Soto County, Miss., September 2, 1947; interment in Blocker Cemetery.

**LOWRIE, Walter,** a Senator from Pennsylvania; born in Edinburgh, Scotland, December 10, 1784; immigrated to the United States in 1791 with his parents, who settled in Butler County, Pa.; pursued classical studies; taught school for several years and then became engaged in surveying and agricultural pursuits; member, Pennsylvania house of representatives 1811-1812; member, Pennsylvania senate 1813-1819; elected to the United States Senate and served from March 4, 1819, to March 3, 1825; was not a candidate for reelection in 1824; chairman, Committee on Finance (Seventeenth Congress); Secretary of the United States Senate from December 12, 1825, to December 11, 1836; secretary of the Presbyterian Board of Foreign Missions from 1836 until his death in New York City December 14, 1868; interment in the crypt of the First Presbyterian Church.

    **Bibliography:** *DAB*; Lowrie, Walter. *Memoirs of the Honorable Walter Lowrie.* Edited by John Lowrie. New York: The Baker and Taylor Company, 1896.

**LOWRY, Michael Edward,** a Representative from Washington; born in St. John, Whitman County, Wash., March 8, 1939; attended the public schools of Endicott, Wash.; B.A., Washington State University, Pullman, 1962; chief fiscal analyst and staff director, Washington State senate ways and means committee, 1969-1973; governmental affairs director, Puget Sound Group Health Cooperative, 1974-1975; member, King County Council, 1975-1978; elected

as a Democrat to the Ninety-sixth and to the four succeeding Congresses (January 3, 1979-January 3, 1989); unsuccessful candidate in 1983 for the United States Senate in a special election to fill the vacancy caused by the death of Henry M. Jackson; was not a candidate in 1988 for reelection to the House of Representatives, but was an unsuccessful candidate for election to the United States Senate; elected Governor of Washington in 1992; declined to be a candidate for reelection in 1996; is a resident of Seattle, Wash.

**LOWRY, Robert,** a Representative from Indiana; born in Killeleigh, County Down, Ireland, April 2, 1824; immigrated to the United States and settled in Rochester, N.Y.; educated in private schools and had partial academic course; librarian of Rochester Athenaeum and Young Men's Association; studied law; moved to Fort Wayne, Ind., in 1843; city recorder in 1844 and 1845; was admitted to the bar in 1846 and commenced practice in Goshen, Ind.; auditor of Elkhart County in 1852; circuit judge in 1852; president of the Democratic State convention; delegate to the Democratic National Conventions at Baltimore in 1860 and 1872; served as circuit judge from 1864 until January 1875, when he resigned; judge of the superior court in 1877 and 1878; elected the first president of the Indiana State Bar Association in July 1879; elected as a Democrat to the Forty-eighth and Forty-ninth Congresses (March 4, 1883-March 3, 1887); chairman, Committee on Expenditures in the Department of the Treasury (Forty-ninth Congress); unsuccessful candidate for reelection in 1886 to the Fiftieth Congress; resumed the practice of law; died in Fort Wayne, Allen County, Ind., January 27, 1904; interment in Linderwood Cemetery.

**LOYALL, George,** a Representative from Virginia; born in Norfolk, Va., May 29, 1789; was graduated from the College of William and Mary, Williamsburg, Va., in 1808; studied law but did not practice; visited Great Britain in 1815; member of the Virginia house of delegates 1818-1827; delegate to the Virginia constitutional convention in 1829; successfully contested the election of Thomas Newton to the Twenty-first Congress and served from March 9, 1830, to March 3, 1831; elected as a Jacksonian to the Twenty-third and Twenty-fourth Congresses (March 4, 1833-March 3, 1837); Navy agent at Norfolk, Va., 1837-1861, with the exception of two years; died in Norfolk, Va., February 24, 1868; interment in Elmwood Cemetery.

**LOZIER, Ralph Fulton,** a Representative from Missouri; born near Hardin, Ray County, Mo., January 28, 1866; attended the public schools; was graduated from the Carrollton (Mo.) High School in 1883; engaged in teaching for several years; studied law; was admitted to the bar in 1886 and commenced practice in Carrollton; also interested in agricultural pursuits and the raising of livestock; served as city attorney of Carrollton, Mo., 1915-1944; delegate to the Democratic National Convention in 1928; elected as a Democrat to the Sixty-eighth and to the five succeeding Congresses (March 4, 1923-January 3, 1935); chairman, Committee on the Census (Seventy-second and Seventy-third Congresses); unsuccessful candidate for renomination in 1934; judge of the circuit court, seventh judicial circuit of Missouri, in 1936; resumed the practice of law, with offices in Carrollton, Mo., and Washington, D.C., and also engaged in agricultural pursuits in Carroll County, Mo.; died in Kansas City, Mo., May 28, 1945; interment in Oak Hill Cemetery, Carrollton, Mo.

**LUCAS, Edward** (brother of William Lucas), a Representative from Virginia; born near Shepherdstown, Jefferson County, Va. (now West Virginia), October 20, 1780; attended the common schools; was graduated from Dickinson College, Carlisle, Pa., in 1809; served in the War of 1812 as first lieutenant and acting captain; studied law; was admitted to the bar and practiced in Shepherdstown until 1818; engaged in mercantile pursuits; member of the Virginia house of delegates 1819-1822, 1830, and 1831; elected as a Jacksonian to the

Twenty-third and Twenty-fourth Congresses (March 4, 1833-March 3, 1837); was not a candidate for renomination in 1836; resumed mercantile pursuits; served as military storekeeper of ordnance at the Harpers Ferry Armory from May 12, 1847, until his death at Harpers Ferry, Va. (now West Virginia), March 4, 1858; interment in the Harper Cemetery.

**LUCAS, Frank Dean,** a Representative from Oklahoma; born in Cheyenne, Roger Mills County, Okla., January 6, 1960; B.S., Oklahoma State University, 1982; past president, Oklahoma State University College Republicans; farmer and rancher; Republican chair, Roger Mills County and Sixth Congressional District; County coordinator for Senator Don Nickles of Oklahoma; member, Oklahoma State house of representatives, 1988-1994; elected as a Republican to the One Hundred Third Congress, May 10, 1994, by special election to fill the vacancy caused by the resignation of Glenn L. English, Jr.; reelected to the One Hundred Fourth Congress, and served from May 10, 1994 to January 3, 1997; is a resident of Roll, Okla.

**LUCAS, John Baptiste Charles,** a Representative from Pennsylvania; born in Pont-Audemer, Normandy, France, August 14, 1758; attended the Honfleur and Paris Law Schools, and was graduated from the law department of the University of Caen in 1782; practiced law in France until 1784; immigrated to the United States, settled near Pittsburgh, Pa., and engaged in agricultural pursuits; member of the Pennsylvania house of representatives, 1792-1798; judge of the common pleas court in 1794; elected as a Republican to the Eighth and Ninth Congresses, and served from March 4, 1803 until his resignation in 1805, before the assembling of the Ninth Congress; moved to St. Louis, La. (now Missouri), having been appointed district judge for the northern district of Louisiana (which became Missouri Territory in 1812), and served from 1805 until 1820, when he resigned; also served as commissioner of land claims of northern Louisiana, 1805-1812; resumed agricultural pursuits; died near St. Louis, Mo., August 17, 1842; interment in Calvary Cemetery.

**Bibliography:** *DAB*; Cleland, Hugh G. "John B.C. Lucas, Physiocrat on the Frontier." *Western Pennsylvania Historical Magazine* 36 (March 1953): 1-15; (June 1953): 87-100; (September-December 1953): 141-168.

**LUCAS, Scott Wike,** a Representative and a Senator from Illinois; born on a farm near Chandlerville, Cass County, Ill., February 19, 1892; attended the public schools and graduated from the law department of Illinois Wesleyan University at Bloomington in 1914; was admitted to the bar in 1915 and commenced practice in Havana, Mason County, Ill.; during the First World War served as an enlisted man and later as a lieutenant in the United States Army; State's attorney of Mason County 1920-1925; chairman of the Illinois State tax commission 1933-1935; elected as a Democrat to the Seventy-fourth and Seventy-fifth Congresses (January 3, 1935-January 3, 1939); did not seek renomination in 1938 to the House of Representatives, but was elected to the United States Senate; reelected in 1944 and served from January 3, 1939, to January 3, 1951; unsuccessful candidate for reelection in 1950; Democratic whip (Eightieth Congress), majority leader (Eighty-first Congress); chairman, Committee to Audit and Control the Contingent Expense (Seventy-seventh through Seventy-ninth Congresses); engaged in the practice of law in Springfield, Ill., and Washington, D.C.; died at Rocky Mount, N.C., February 22, 1968, while en route to Florida; interment in Laurel Hill Cemetery, Havana, Ill.

**Bibliography:** Schapsmeier, Edward, and Schapsmeier, Frederick. "Scott W. Lucas of Havana, His Rise and Fall as Majority Leader in the United States Senate." *Journal of the Illinois State Historical Society* 70 (November 1977): 302-20.

**LUCAS, William** (brother of Edward Lucas), a Representative from Virginia; born at "Cold Spring," near Shepherdstown, Jefferson County, Va. (now West Virginia), November 30, 1800; attended the village schools; was graduated from the Tucker Law School, Winchester, Va., in 1825; was admitted to the bar the same year and commenced practice in Shepherdstown; moved to Charles Town, Va. (now West Virginia), in 1830 and continued the practice of law; also engaged in horticultural pursuits; member of the Virginia house of delegates in 1838 and 1839; elected as a Democrat to the Twenty-sixth Congress (March 4, 1839-March 3, 1841); unsuccessful candidate for reelection in 1840 to the Twenty-seventh Congress; elected to the Twenty-eighth Congress (March 4, 1843-March 3, 1845); unsuccessful candidate for renomination in 1844; resumed the practice of law and horticultural pursuits; delegate to the Virginia constitutional convention in 1850 and 1851; died at his home, "Rion Hall," in Jefferson County, W.Va., August 29, 1877; interment in the Zion Episcopal Churchyard, Charles Town, W.Va.

**LUCAS, William Vincent,** a Representative from South Dakota; born near Delphi, Carroll County, Ind., July 3, 1835; attended the common schools; moved to Bremer County, Iowa, in 1856 and engaged in agricultural pursuits; during the Civil War enlisted in the Union Army in the Fourteenth Regiment, Iowa Volunteer Infantry; promoted to captain in 1863; treasurer of Bremer County 1866-1872; editor of the Waverly Republican 1872-1876; editor of the Cerro Gordo Republican, Mason City, Iowa, 1876-1883; chief clerk of the Iowa house of representatives 1878-1880; mayor of Mason City, Iowa, in 1879 and 1880; State auditor in 1881 and 1882; declined nomination for reelection; moved to Chamerlain, S.Dak., in 1883 and again engaged in agricultural pursuits; treasurer of Brule County 1888-1890; moved to Hot Springs, S.Dak., in 1890; elected as a Republican to the Fifty-third Congress (March 4, 1893-March 3, 1895); unsuccessful candidate for renomination in 1894; delegate to the Republican National Convention in 1896; returned to Chamberlain, S.Dak., in 1897; register of the United States land office 1897-1901; moved to Santa Cruz, Santa Cruz County, Calif., in 1904 and died there on November 10, 1921; interment in Oakwood Cemetery.

**LUCAS, Wingate Hezekiah,** a Representative from Texas; born in Grapevine, Tarrant County, Tex., May 1, 1908; attended the public schools, the North Texas Teachers College at Denton, the Oklahoma Agricultural and Mechanical College at Stillwater, and the Texas University at Austin; studied law; was admitted to the bar in 1938 and commenced practice in Grapevine, Tex.; served as an enlisted man in the United States Army from 1943 to 1945 with overseas service in the European Theater of Operations; resumed the practice of law; elected as a Democrat to the Eightieth and to the three succeeding Congresses (January 3, 1947-January 3, 1955); unsuccessful candidate for renomination in 1954 to the Eighty-fourth Congress; resumed the practice of law in Texas; government relations executive with General Electric in New York City, 1958-1966; executive director of the Mid-Appalachia College Council, 1966-1986; was a resident of Bristol, Tenn.; died May 26, 1989.

**LUCE, Clare Boothe** (stepdaughter of Albert Elmer Austin), a Representative from Connecticut; born in New York City, April 10, 1903; was graduated from St. Mary's School at Garden City, Long Island, N.Y., and from Miss Mason's School at Tarrytown, N.Y., in 1919, writer, associate editor, and managing editor of Vanity Fair, 1929-1934; administrative representative of the public to the National Recovery Administration Code Authority for the legitimate theater and motion pictures in 1934; author, playwright, journalist, foreign correspondent, and lecturer; elected as a Republican to the Seventy-eighth and Seventy-ninth Congresses (January 3, 1943-January 3, 1947); was not a candidate for renomination in 1946 to the Eightieth Congress; engaged in writing; declined appointment to the office of Secretary of Labor in the Cabinet of President Dwight D. Eisenhower; appointed by President Eisenhower as Ambassador to Italy on March 2, 1953, and served until December 1956; appointed as Ambassador to Brazil on April 28, 1959, but declined the appointment three days later; member, President's Foreign Intelligence Advisory Board, 1973-1977 and 1982-1987; was a resident of Washington, D.C., until her death there on October 9, 1987; interment at Mepkin Abbey, Moncks Corner, S.C.

**Bibliography:** Shadegg, Stephen C. *Clare Boothe Luce; A Biography*. New York: Simon and Schuster, 1970; Sheed, Wilfred. *Clare Boothe Luce*. New York: E.P. Dutton, 1982.

**LUCE, Robert,** a Representative from Massachusetts; born in Auburn, Androscoggin County, Maine, December 2, 1862; attended the public schools of Auburn and Lewiston, Maine, and Somerville, Mass., and was graduated from Harvard University in 1882; taught in the Waltham (Mass.) High School for a year; engaged in journalism, founding and serving as president of the Luce's Press Clipping Bureau in Boston and New York in 1888; Republican member of the Massachusetts house of representatives in 1899 and 1901-1908; studied law and was admitted to the bar in Boston in 1908, but did not engage in extensive practice; president of the Massachusetts Republican convention in 1910; Lieutenant Governor of Massachusetts in 1912; member of the Massachusetts Teachers Retirement Board 1914-1919; delegate to the Massachusetts constitutional convention 1917-1919; president of the Republican Club of Massachusetts in 1918; Regent of the Smithsonian Institution 1929-1931; author, notably on the subject of political science; elected as a Republican to the Sixty-sixth and the seven succeeding Congresses (March 4, 1919-January 3, 1935); chairman, Committee on Elections No. 2 (Sixty-seventh Congress), Committee on World War Veterans' Legislation (Sixty-eighth Congress); unsuccessful candidate for reelection in 1934 to the Seventy-fourth Congress; elected to the Seventy-fifth and Seventy-sixth Congresses (January 3, 1937-January 3, 1941); unsuccessful candidate for reelection in 1940 to the Seventy-seventh Congress; resumed his former business pursuits; died in Waltham, Mass., April 7, 1946; the remains were cremated and the ashes interred in Mount Auburn Cemetery, Cambridge, Mass.

**LUCKEY, Henry Carl,** a Representative from Nebraska; born near East St. Louis, St. Clair County, Ill., November 22, 1868; moved to Nebraska with his parents, who settled on a farm near Columbus in Platte County in 1873; attended the public schools and the Lutheran parochial school in Columbus, Nebr.; was graduated from the University of Nebraska at Lincoln in 1912; pursued a postgraduate course at Columbia University, New York City in 1914 and 1915; engaged in agricultural pursuits near Columbus, Nebr., 1894-1900; moved to Lincoln, Nebr., in 1900; was admitted to the bar in 1912 but did not practice; engaged in the real estate business and in the construction of homes 1917-1927; member of the board of trustees of Midland College, Fremont, Nebr., 1919-1925; elected as a Democrat to the Seventy-fourth and Seventy-fifth Congresses (January 3, 1935-January 3, 1939); unsuccessful candidate for reelection in 1938 to the Seventy-sixth Congress and for election in 1940 to the Seventy-seventh Congress; resumed the real estate business and also engaged in agricultural pursuits until 1946, when he retired and moved to Richmond, Calif.; died in El Cerrito, Calif., December 31, 1956; interment in Sunset View Cemetery.

**Bibliography:** Luckey, Henry Carl. *85 American Years; Memoirs of a Nebraska Congressman*. Hicksville, N.Y.: Exposition Press, 1955.

**LUCKING, Alfred,** a Representative from Michigan; born in Ingersoll, Ontario, Canada, December 18, 1856; moved with his parents to Ypsilanti, Mich., in 1858; attended the public schools, the Ypsilanti High School, and the Michigan State Normal College at Ypsilanti; was graduated from the law department of the University

of Michigan at Ann Arbor in 1878; was admitted to the bar the same year and practiced in Jackson, Mich.; moved to Detroit, Mich., in 1880 and continued the practice of law; temporary chairman of the Democratic State convention in 1900, and was both temporary and permanent chairman of the State conventions in 1902, 1908, and 1924; permanent chairman in 1928; elected as a Democrat to the Fifty-eighth Congress (March 4, 1903-March 3, 1905); unsuccessful candidate for reelection in 1904 to the Fifty-ninth Congress; resumed the practice of his profession in Detroit, Mich.; unsuccessful candidate for election to the United States Senate in 1912; general counsel for the Ford Motor Co. and the Henry Ford interests from 1914 to 1923; president of the Detroit-Vancouver Timber Co.; delegate to the Democratic National Convention of 1924; died in Detroit, Mich., on December 1, 1929; interment in Woodlawn Cemetery.

**LUDLOW, Louis Leon,** a Representative from Indiana; born on a farm near Connersville, Fayette County, Ind., June 24, 1873; attended the grade and high schools; moved to Indianapolis, Ind., in 1892 and became a reporter and later a political writer; Washington correspondent for Indiana and Ohio newspapers, and member of the Congressional Press Galleries from 1901 until 1929; elected as a Democrat to the Seventy-first and to the nine succeeding Congresses (March 4, 1929-January 3, 1949); election to the Seventy-first Congress was unsuccessfully contested by Ralph E. Updike; sponsor of the "Ludlow Resolution," a proposed amendment to the Constitution requiring that declarations of war be ratified by popular referendum; was not a candidate for renomination in 1948 to the Eighty-first Congress; resumed work as a newspaper correspondent until his death in Washington, D.C., November 28, 1950; interment in Rock Creek Cemetery.

**Bibliography:** Griffin, Walter R. "Louis Ludlow and the War Referendum Crusade, 1935-1941." *Indiana Magazine of History* 64 (December 1968): 267-288; Scherr, Arthur. "Louis Ludlow's War Referendum of 1938: A Reappraisal." *Mid-America* 76 (Spring/Summer 1994): 133-156.

**LUECKE, John Frederick,** a Representative from Michigan; born in Escanaba, Delta County, Mich., July 4, 1889; attended the public elementary schools; employed as a commercial and railroad telegrapher and station agent; served as a private in Company A, Signal Corps, United States Army, with the Punitive Expeditionary Force in Mexico in 1916 and 1917; during the First World War served as a sergeant first class, in Company B, Second Field Signal Battalion, American Expeditionary Forces, 1917-1919; commissioned a second lieutenant, Reserve Corps, while in Germany; engaged as a mill worker in a paper mill in Escanaba, Mich., 1923-1936; member of the Escanaba City Council 1934-1936; county supervisor of Delta County, Mich., 1934-1936; served in the State senate in 1935 and 1936; elected as a Democrat to the Seventy-fifth Congress (January 3, 1937-January 3, 1939); unsuccessful candidate for reelection in 1938 to the Seventy-sixth Congress; in 1939 was appointed commissioner of conciliation for the United States Department of Labor for upper Michigan and northern Wisconsin; died in Escanaba, Mich., March 21, 1952; interment in Lakeview Cemetery.

**LUFKIN, Willfred Weymouth,** a Representative from Massachusetts; born in Essex, Essex County, Mass., March 10, 1879; attended the public schools; newspaper correspondent; private secretary to Congressman Augustus P. Gardner of Massachusetts, 1902-1917; member and chairman of the Essex School Board, 1901-1906; member of the Massachusetts constitutional convention, 1917-1919; elected as a Republican to the Sixty-fifth Congress to fill the vacancy caused by the resignation of Augustus P. Gardner; reelected to the Sixty-sixth and Sixty-seventh Congresses and served from November 6, 1917, to June 30, 1921, when he resigned to accept a Treasury position; appointed by President Warren G.

Harding to be collector of customs at the port of Boston on July 1, 1921, and served until his retirement in 1933; again elected a member of the Essex School Board in 1922, 1925, and 1928; moderator of the town meeting in 1925; died in Essex, Mass., March 28, 1934; interment in Essex Cemetery.

**LUGAR, Richard Green,** a Senator from Indiana; born in Indianapolis, Marion County, Ind., April 4, 1932; attended the public schools of Indianapolis; graduated, Shortridge High School, 1950; B.A., Denison University, Granville, Ohio, 1954; B.A., M.A., Pembroke College, Oxford, England, as a Rhodes scholar, 1956; businessman, involved in the manufacturing of food production equipment, livestock and grain operations; served in the United States Navy from 1957 until 1960; member, Indianapolis Board of School Commissioners, 1964-1967; mayor of Indianapolis, 1968-1975; unsuccessful candidate in 1974 for election to the United States Senate; elected as a Republican to the United States Senate in 1976 for the term commencing January 3, 1977; reelected in 1982, 1988, and again in 1994 for the term ending January 3, 2001; delivered keynote address at the Republican National Convention of 1972; chairman, Republican Senatorial Campaign Committee (Ninety-eighth Congress), Committee on Foreign Relations (Ninety-ninth Congress), Committee on Agriculture, Nutrition, and Forestry (One Hundred Fourth Congress); unsuccessful candidate in 1996 for the Republican presidential nomination; is a resident of Indianapolis, Ind.

**LUHRING, Oscar Raymond,** a Representative from Indiana; born in Haubstadt, Gibson County, Ind., February 11, 1879; attended the public schools; was graduated in law from the University of Virginia at Charlottesville in 1900; was admitted to the bar the same year and commenced practice in Evansville, Vanderburg County, Ind.; member of the Indiana State house of representatives in 1903 and 1904; deputy prosecuting attorney of the same circuit, 1908-1912; elected as a Republican to the Sixty-sixth and Sixty-seventh Congresses (March 4, 1919-March 3, 1923); unsuccessful candidate for reelection in 1922 to the Sixty-eighth Congress; special assistant to Secretary of Labor James J. Davis, 1923-1925; appointed by President Calvin Coolidge to be Assistant Attorney General of the United States on September 9, 1925; appointed by President Herbert Hoover as an associate justice of the supreme court for the District of Columbia (now the United States District Court) on July 3, 1930, and served until his death in Washington, D.C., August 20, 1944; interment in the Abbey Mausoleum, adjoining Arlington National Cemetery.

**LUJAN, Manuel, Jr.,** a Representative from New Mexico; born on a small farm near the Indian Pueblo of San Ildefonso, N.Mex., May 12, 1928; attended grade school and junior high school of Our Lady of Guadalupe; graduated from St. Michael's High School, Sante Fe, N.Mex.; attended St. Mary's College, San Francisco, Calif., 1946-1947; B.A., College of Santa Fe (N.Mex.), 1950; former vice chairman, New Mexico Republican Party; engaged in his family's insurance business; member, New Mexico State corporation commission advisory board on insurance, 1965-1968; member, Bernalillo County crime commission, 1967-1968; president, New Mexico Independent Insurance Agents, 1968; elected as a Republican to the Ninety-first and to the nine succeeding Congresses (January 3, 1969-January 3, 1989); was not a candidate for reelection in 1988 to the One Hundred First Congress; Secretary of the Interior in the Cabinet of President George Bush from February 8, 1989 until January 20, 1993; is a resident of Albuquerque, N.Mex.

**LUKEN, Charles J.,** (son of Thomas Andrew Luken), a Representative from Ohio; born in Cincinnati, Ohio, July 18, 1951; B.A., University of Notre Dame, 1973; J.D., University of Cincinnati College of Law, 1976; admitted to Ohio bar in 1976; practicing attorney; mayor, City of Cincinnati, 1984-1990; elected as a Democrat to the One Hundred Second Congress (January 3,

1991-January 3, 1993); was not a candidate for reelection in 1992 to the One Hundred Third Congress; is a resident of Cincinnati, Ohio.

**LUKEN, Thomas Andrew,** (father of Charles J. Luken) a Representative from Ohio; born in Cincinnati, Hamilton County, July 9, 1925; graduated from Purcell High School, 1942; A.B., Xavier University, Cincinnati, 1947; attended Bowling Green State University, Toledo, Ohio, 1943-1944; LL.B., Salmon P. Chase Law School, Cincinnati, 1950; served in the United States Marine Corps, 1943-1945, with rank of first lieutenant; admitted to the Ohio bar in 1950 and commenced practice in Cincinnati; city solicitor of Deer Park, Ohio, 1955-1961; Federal district attorney, 1961-1964; member, Cincinnati City Council, 1964-1967, 1969-1971, 1973-1974; mayor of Cincinnati, 1971-1972; delegate to the Democratic National Conventions of 1964 and 1968; elected as a Democrat to the Ninety-third Congress, March 5, 1974, by special election to fill the vacancy caused by the resignation of William J. Keating, and served from March 5, 1974, to January 3, 1975; unsuccessful candidate for reelection in 1974 to the Ninety-fourth Congress; resumed the practice of law; elected to the Ninety-fifth and to the six succeeding Congresses (January 3, 1977-January 3, 1991); was not a candidate for reelection in 1990 to the One Hundred Second Congress; is a resident of Cincinnati, Ohio.

**LUKENS, Donald Edgar (Buz),** a Representative from Ohio; born in Harveysburg, Warren County, Ohio, February 11, 1931; attended grade school in Harveysburg and graduated from Waynesville (Ohio) High School; graduated from Ohio State University in 1954; joined the United States Air Force in 1954, attained rank of captain, and served six and one-half years on active duty; member of United States Air Force Reserve; minority counsel, House Rules Committee, 1961; elected as a Republican to the Ninetieth and Ninety-first Congresses (January 3, 1967-January 3, 1971); was not a candidate in 1970 for reelection to the House of Representatives, but was an unsuccessful candidate for nomination for Governor of Ohio; Ohio State senator, 1971-1986; elected to the One Hundredth and One Hundred First Congresses, and served from January 3, 1987 until his resignation October 24, 1990; is a resident of Middletown, Ohio.

**LUMPKIN, Alva Moore,** a Senator from South Carolina; born in Milledgeville, Baldwin County, Ga., on November 13, 1886; moved with his parents to Columbia, S.C., in 1898; attended the public schools of Milledgeville and Columbia; LL.B., University of South Carolina School of Law, Columbia, 1908; was admitted to the bar the same year and commenced the practice of law in Columbia; assistant clerk of the South Carolina State senate, 1906-1908; member of the State house of representatives from Richland County, 1911-1913; member of the Conciliation Commission for Advancement of Peace between the United States and Uruguay in 1914; acting assistant attorney general of South Carolina in 1918; member of the State board of pardons, 1922-1923; acting associate justice of the State supreme court, 1926-1934; Federal judge of the United States District Court for the Eastern and Western Districts of South Carolina, 1939-1941; appointed as a Democrat to the United States Senate, July 17, 1941, to fill the vacancy caused by the resignation of James F. Byrnes, and served from July 22, 1941 until his death in Washington, D.C., August 1, 1941; interment in Elmwood Cemetery, Columbia, S.C.

**LUMPKIN, John Henry** (nephew of Wilson Lumpkin), a Representative from Georgia; born in Lexington, Oglethorpe County, Ga., June 13, 1812; attended rural schools and Franklin College (now the University of Georgia) at Athens and Yale College in 1831 and 1832; appointed private secretary to his uncle, Wilson Lumpkin, Governor of Georgia from 1831 to 1835; studied law; was admitted to the bar in 1834 and commenced practice in Rome, Ga.; member of the Georgia State house of representatives in 1835; solicitor general of the Cherokee circuit in 1838; unsuccessful candidate for election in 1840 to the Twenty-seventh Congress; elected as a Democrat to the Twenty-eighth and to the two succeeding Congresses (March 4, 1843-March 3, 1849); judge of the superior court, Rome circuit, 1850-1853; elected to the Thirty-fourth Congress (March 4, 1855-March 3, 1857); was not a candidate for renomination in 1856 to the Thirty-fifth Congress; resumed the practice of law in Rome, Ga.; was an unsuccessful candidate for Governor of Georgia in 1857; served as a delegate to the Democratic National Convention at Charleston, S.C., in 1860; died in Rome, Ga., July 10, 1860; interment in Oak Hill Cemetery.

**LUMPKIN, Wilson** (uncle of John Henry Lumpkin and grandfather of Middleton Pope Barrow), a Representative and a Senator from Georgia; born near Dan River, Pittsylvania County, Va., January 14, 1783; moved in 1784 to Oglethorpe (then a part of Wilkes) County, Ga., with his parents, who settled near Point Peter, and subsequently at Lexington, Ga.; attended the common schools; taught school and farmed; studied law; was admitted to the bar and commenced practice in Athens, Ga.; member, Georgia State house of representatives, 1804-1812; elected to the Fourteenth Congress (March 4, 1815-March 3, 1817); unsuccessful candidate for reelection in 1816 to the Fifteenth Congress; State Indian Commissioner; elected to the Twentieth and to the two succeeding Congresses, and served from March 4, 1827 until his resignation in 1831 before the convening of the Twenty-second Congress to run for the governorship; commissioner on the Georgia-Florida boundary line commission; elected Governor of Georgia in 1831, reelected in 1833, and served from November 9, 1831 to November 4, 1835; appointed commissioner under the Cherokee treaty in 1835; elected to the United States Senate to fill the vacancy caused by the resignation of John P. King, and served from November 22, 1837 to March 3, 1841; chairman, Committee on Manufactures (Twenty-sixth Congress); member of the State board of public works; died in Athens, Ga., December 28, 1870; interment in Oconee Cemetery.

**Bibliography:** *DAB*; Lumpkin, Wilson. *The Removal of the Cherokee Indians from Georgia.* 2 vols. Edited by Wymberly Jones De Renne. 1907. Reprint (2 vols. in 1), with new introduction. New York: Arno Press, 1969; Vipperman, Carl J. "The 'Particular Mission' of Wilson Lumpkin." *Georgia Historical Quarterly* 66 (Fall 1982): 295-316.

**LUNA, Tranquilino,** a Delegate from the Territory of New Mexico; born in Los Lunas, Valencia County, N.Mex., February 25, 1849; attended the public schools and was graduated from the University of Missouri at Columbia; engaged extensively in stock raising; delegate to the Republican National Conventions in 1880 and 1888; elected as a Republican to the Forty-seventh Congress (March 4, 1881-March 3, 1883); presented credentials as a Delegate-elect to the Forty-eighth Congress and served from March 4, 1883, until March 5, 1884, when he was succeeded by Francisco A. Manzanares, who contested his election; sheriff of Valencia County 1888-1892; died in Peralta, Valencia County, N.Mex., November 20, 1892; interment in Los Lunas Cemetery, Los Lunas, N.Mex.

**LUNDEEN, Ernest,** a Representative and a Senator from Minnesota; born near Beresford, Union County, S.Dak., August 4, 1878; attended the common schools; served in Company B, Twelfth Minnesota Volunteers, during the Spanish-American War; was graduated from Carleton College, Northfield, Minn., in 1901; studied law at the University of Minnesota at Minneapolis; was admitted to the bar in 1906 and commenced practice at Minneapolis, Minn.; member, Minnesota State house of representatives, 1910-1914; elected as a Republican to the Sixty-fifth Congress (March 4, 1917-March 3, 1919); unsuccessful candidate for renomination in 1918 to the Sixty-sixth Congress; resumed the practice of law; unsuccessful Independent candidate for election in 1920 to the Sixty-seventh Congress; unsuccessful Farmer-Labor candidate for

election in 1926 to the Seventieth Congress; unsuccessful Farmer-Labor candidate for Governor of Minnesota in 1928; elected as a Farmer-Laborite to the Seventy-third and Seventy-fourth Congresses (March 4, 1933-January 3, 1937); elected on the Farmer-Labor ticket to the United States Senate in 1936, and served from January 3, 1937 until his death in an airplane crash near Lovettsville, Va., on August 31, 1940; interment in Little Arlington National Cemetery, Minneapolis, Minn.

**Bibliography:** *DAB*.

**LUNDIN, Frederick,** a Representative from Illinois; born in the parish of Vestra Tollstad, Hastholmen, Sweden, May 18, 1868; immigrated to the United States and settled in Chicago, Ill., in 1880; completed academic studies; president of Lundin & Co., manufacturing chemists; member of the State senate 1894-1898; elected as a Republican to the Sixty-first Congress (March 4, 1909-March 3, 1911); unsuccessful candidate for reelection in 1910 to the Sixty-second Congress; resumed manufacturing interests until retirement in 1916; died in Beverly Hills, Calif., August 20, 1947; interment in Forest Home Cemetery, Forest Park, Ill.

**LUNDINE, Stanley Nelson,** a Representative from New York; born in Jamestown, Chautauqua County, N.Y., February 4, 1939; attended public schools in Jamestown; A.B., Duke University, Durham, N.C., 1961; LL.B., New York University School of Law, 1964; admitted to the New York bar in 1965 and commenced practice in Jamestown; mayor, Jamestown, 1969-1976; elected as a Democrat to the Ninety-fourth Congress, by special election, March 2, 1976, to fill the vacancy caused by the resignation of James F. Hastings; reelected to the five succeeding Congresses, and served from March 2, 1976 to January 3, 1987; was not a candidate in 1986 for reelection to the One Hundredth Congress, but was elected Lieutenant Governor of New York; reelected in 1990, and served from January 1, 1987 to December 31, 1994; resumed the practice of law in Jamestown; is a resident of Jamestown, N.Y.

**LUNGREN, Daniel Edward,** a Representative from California; born in Long Beach, Los Angeles County, Calif., September 22, 1946; attended St. Barnabas School, Long Beach, 1960; graduated from St. Anthony High School, Long Beach, 1964; A.B., Notre Dame University, South Bend, Ind., 1968; attended University of Southern California Law Center, Los Angeles, 1968-1969; J.D., Georgetown University Law Center, Washington, D.C., 1971; served on staffs of Senators George L. Murphy of California and William E. Brock III of Tennessee; special assistant to the co-chairman of the Republican National Committee; admitted to the California bar in 1972 and commenced practice in Long Beach, 1973; delegate, California State Republican conventions, 1974 to present; co-chairman, National Congressional Council, 1977-1978; elected as a Republican to the Ninety-sixth and to the four succeeding Congresses (January 3, 1979-January 3, 1989); was not a candidate for reelection in 1988 to the One Hundred First Congress; California State attorney general, 1991 to present; is a resident of Long Beach, Calif.

**LUNN, George Richard,** a Representative from New York; born near Lenox, Taylor County, Iowa, June 23, 1873; attended the public schools at Lenox and Des Moines, Iowa; was graduated from Bellevue (Nebr.) College in 1897; during the Spanish-American War served as a corporal in Company I, Third Nebraska Regiment; engaged in postgraduate work at Princeton, New York, and Columbia Universities; was graduated from Union Theological Seminary, New York City, in 1901; pastor of churches in Brooklyn and Schenectady, N.Y., 1901-1914; served as mayor of Schenectady in 1912, 1913, 1916, and 1917; elected as a Democrat to the Sixty-fifth Congress (March 4, 1917-March 3, 1919); unsuccessful candidate for reelection in 1918 to the Sixty-sixth Congress; elected mayor of Schenectady in 1920 and served until January 1, 1923, when he resigned; delegate to the Democratic National Conventions of 1920, 1924, 1928, 1932, and 1936; Lieutenant Governor of New

York in 1923 and 1924; appointed public service commissioner of the State of New York in 1925 and served in that capacity until 1942, when he resigned due to ill health; died in Rancho Santa Fe, Calif., November 27, 1948; interment in Forest Lawn Cemetery, Los Angeles, Calif.

**Bibliography:** *DAB*; Hendrickson, Kenneth E., Jr. "George R. Lunn and the Socialist Era in Schenectady, New York, 1909-1916." *New York History* 47 (January 1966): 22-40.

**LUSK, Georgia Lee,** a Representative from New Mexico; born in Carlsbad, Eddy County, N.Mex., May 12, 1893; attended the public schools, Highlands University, Las Vegas, N.Mex., and the Colorado State Teachers College at Greeley; was graduated from New Mexico State Teachers College at Silver City in 1914; school teacher; manager of family ranch 1919-1943; county school superintendent of Lea County 1925-1929; State superintendent of public instruction 1931-1935 and 1943-1947; rural school supervisor in Guadalupe County in 1941 and 1942; delegate to the Democratic National Conventions in 1928 and 1948; elected as a Democrat to the Eightieth Congress (January 3, 1947-January 3, 1949); unsuccessful candidate for renomination in 1948; member of the War Claims Commission from September 1949 to December 1953; again State superintendent of public instruction for New Mexico 1955-1960; died in Albuquerque, N.Mex., January 5, 1971; interment in Sunset Gardens Memorial Park, Carlsbad, N.Mex.

**LUSK, Hall Stoner,** a Senator from Oregon; born in Washington, D.C., September 21, 1883; attended Georgetown Preparatory School, 1897-1900; graduated from Georgetown University in 1904, and from Georgetown University Law School in 1907; secretary to a Chief Justice of the Court of Appeals for the District of Columbia, 1906-1909; admitted to the District of Columbia bar in 1907 and to the Oregon bar in 1910, and commenced practice in Portland, Oreg.; assistant United States district attorney for Oregon, 1918-1920; unsuccessful candidate in 1922 for election to the Oregon legislature; circuit judge of Multnomah County, Oreg., 1930-1937; appointed, subsequently elected, and reelected to the Oregon supreme court and served from 1937, until his resignation on March 15, 1960; appointed as a Democrat to the United States Senate to fill the vacancy caused by the death of Richard L. Neuberger and served from March 16, 1960, to November 8, 1960; was not a candidate for election to a full term; returned to the Oregon supreme court as a justice pro tempore in 1961, serving until 1968; engaged in the revision of Oregon supreme court procedures as justice emeritus; resided in Beaverton, Oreg., until his death there on May 15, 1983; interment at Mt. Calvary Cemetery, Portland, Oreg.

**LUTHER, William Paul,** a Representative from Minnesota; born in Fergus Falls, Otter Tail County, Minn., June 27, 1945; graduated, Fergus Falls High School, 1963; B.S., University of Minnesota, 1967; J.D., University of Minnesota School of Law, 1970; prosecuting attorney, United States Court of Appeals, Eighth Circuit, 1970-1971; member, Minnesota State house of representatives, 1974-1976; member, Minnesota State senate, 1976-1994, served as majority leader, 1982-1994; elected as a Democrat to the One Hundred Fourth Congress (January 3, 1995-January 3, 1997); is a resident of Stillwater, Minn.

**LUTTRELL, John King,** a Representative from California; born near Knoxville, Knox County, Tenn., June 27, 1831; attended the common schools; moved with his parents to a farm in Alabama in 1844; moved to Missouri in 1845 with his parents, who settled on a farm near St. Joseph; moved to California in 1852 and engaged in mining; settled in Yolo County and engaged in agricultural pursuits; moved to Prairie City (later Folsom) in 1853, to El Dorado County in 1854 and thence to Watsonville, Santa Cruz County, and to Alameda County; studied law; was admitted to the bar and commenced practice in Oakland in 1856; justice of the peace in Brooklyn (now a part of Oakland) in 1856 and 1857; moved to Siskiyou County in 1858 and purchased a ranch near Fort Jones; engaged in agricultural pursuits, mining, and the practice of law; sergeant at arms of the State assembly in 1865 and 1866; member of the State house of representatives in 1871 and 1872; elected as a Democrat to the Forty-third, Forty-fourth, and Forty-fifth Congresses (March 4, 1873-March 3, 1879); declined to be a candidate for reelection; resumed the practice of law, farming, and mining; member of the board of State prison directors, 1887-1889; appointed United States Commissioner of Fisheries and special agent of the United States Treasury for Alaska in 1893; died in Sitka, Alaska, on October 4, 1893; interment in Fort Jones Cemetery, Fort Jones, Siskiyou County, Calif.

**LYBRAND, Archibald,** a Representative from Ohio; born in Tarlton, Pickaway County, Ohio, May 23, 1840; moved to Delaware, Ohio, in 1857; attended the common schools and the Ohio Wesleyan University at Delaware; during the Civil War enlisted in the Union Army April 26, 1861, and served in Company I, Fourth Regiment, Ohio Volunteer Infantry; transferred to Company E, Seventy-third Regiment, Ohio Volunteer Infantry, and promoted to first lieutenant; commissioned captain; remained in service three years; returned to Delaware, Ohio; mayor of Delaware in 1869; studied law; was admitted to the bar in 1871; landowner and engaged in agricultural and mercantile pursuits; postmaster of Delaware 1881-1885; elected as a Republican to the Fifty-fifth and Fifty-sixth Congresses (March 4, 1897-March 3, 1901); unsuccessful candidate for renomination in 1900; resumed business activities in Delaware, Ohio; died in Daytona, Fla., February 7, 1910; interment in Oak Grove Cemetery, Delaware, Ohio.

**LYLE, Aaron,** a Representative from Pennsylvania; born in Mount Bethel, Northampton County, Pa., November 17, 1759; attended the common schools; engaged in agricultural pursuits; served in the Revolutionary War; member of the Pennsylvania house of representatives 1797-1801; served in the Pennsylvania senate 1802-1804; commissioner of Washington County, Pa., 1806-1809; elected as a Republican to the Eleventh and to the three succeeding Congresses (March 4, 1809-March 3, 1817); resumed agricultural pursuits; trustee of Jefferson (later Washington and Jefferson) College, Washington, Pa., 1802-1822; died at Cross Creek, Washington County, Pa., September 24, 1825; interment in the Old Cemetery.

**LYLE, John Emmett, Jr.,** a Representative from Texas; born in Boyd, Wise County, Tex., September 4, 1910; attended the public schools, the Junior College at Wichita Falls, the University of Texas at Austin, and the Houston (Tex.) Law School; was admitted to the bar in 1934 and commenced practice in Corpus Christi, Tex.; served in the Texas State house of representatives from January 1941 until 1944; served in the United States Army as an operations officer in the Five Hundred and Thirty-sixth Antiaircraft Battalion, a separate battalion which also served as an infantry unit in Italy from 1942 until October 1944; elected as a Democrat to the Seventy-ninth and to the four succeeding Congresses (January 3, 1945-January 3, 1955); was not a candidate for renomination in 1954 to the Eighty-fourth Congress; resumed the practice of law; is a resident of Houston, Tex.

**LYMAN, Joseph,** a Representative from Iowa; born in Lyons, Ionia County, Mich., September 13, 1840; attended the common schools in Ohio; moved to Big Grove, Iowa, in 1857; attended Iowa College, Grinnell, Iowa; enlisted in the Union Army in 1861 and served in Company E, Fourth Regiment, Iowa Volunteer Cavalry; adjutant of the Twenty-ninth Regiment, Iowa Volunteer Infantry, from October 19, 1862, to February 21, 1865, and major of the same regiment from February 21, 1865, to August 10, 1865; studied law; was admitted to the bar in 1866 and commenced practice in Council Bluffs, Iowa; deputy collector of internal revenue of the fifth district of Iowa, 1867-1870; judge of the circuit court in 1884; elected as a

Republican to the Forty-ninth and Fiftieth Congresses (March 4, 1885-March 3, 1889); declined to be a candidate for renomination in 1888; resumed the practice of law; died in Council Bluffs, Iowa, July 9, 1890; interment in Fairview Cemetery.

**LYMAN, Joseph Stebbins,** a Representative from New York; born in Northfield, Franklin County, Mass., February 14, 1785; attended the common schools; was graduated from Dartmouth College, Hanover, N.H., in 1806; studied law; was admitted to the bar and commenced practice in Cooperstown, N.Y.; elected to the Sixteenth Congress (March 4, 1819-March 3, 1821); was not a candidate for renomination in 1821; died in Cooperstown, Otsego County, N.Y., March 21, 1821; interment in Greenfield, Franklin County, Mass.

**LYMAN, Samuel,** a Representative from Massachusetts; born in Goshen, Conn., January 25, 1749; attended Goshen Academy; was graduated from Yale College in 1770; taught school; studied law in Litchfield, Conn.; was admitted to the bar in 1773 and commenced practice in Hartford, Conn.; moved to Springfield, Mass., in 1784; member of the Massachusetts house of representatives 1786-1788; served in the Massachusetts senate 1790-1793; justice of the court of common pleas of Hampshire County 1791-1800; elected as a Federalist to the Fourth, Fifth, and Sixth Congresses and served from March 4, 1795, until November 6, 1800, when he resigned; died in Springfield, Mass., June 5, 1802; interment in Goshen, Conn.

**LYMAN, Theodore,** a Representative from Massachusetts; born in Waltham, Mass., August 23, 1833; was educated by private tutors; studied in Europe, 1847-1849; was graduated from Harvard University in 1855, and from the Lawrence Scientific School of Harvard University in 1858; served during the Civil War as lieutenant colonel and volunteer aide-de-camp on the staff of Major General George G. Meade from September 2, 1863, to April 20, 1865; member of the American Academy of Arts and Sciences and of the National Academy of Sciences; trustee of the Peabody Education Fund; one of the Massachusetts fishery commissioners, 1865-1882; overseer of Harvard University, 1868-1880; elected as an Independent Republican to the Forty-eighth Congress (March 4, 1883-March 3, 1885); was not a candidate for reelection in 1884 to the Forty-ninth Congress on account of ill health; died in Nahant, Mass., September 9, 1897; interment in Mount Auburn Cemetery, Cambridge, Mass.

Bibliography: *DAB*; Lyman, Theodore. *Meade's Headquarters, 1863-1865; Letters of Colonel Theodore Lyman from the Wilderness to Appomatox.* Selected and edited by George R. Agassiz. Freeport, N.Y.: Books for Librarians Press, 1970.

**LYMAN, William,** a Representative from Massachusetts; born in Northampton, Mass., December 7, 1755; was graduated from Yale College in 1776; served in the Revolutionary War; during Shays' Rebellion was aide to General Shepard, with rank of major; member of the Massachusetts house of representatives in 1787; served in the Massachusetts senate in 1789; elected to the Third Congress and reelected as a Republican to the Fourth Congress (March 4, 1793-March 3, 1797); brigadier general of Massachusetts militia 1796-1800; United States consul in London from 1805 until his death in Cheltenham, Gloucestershire, England, on September 22, 1811; interment in the cathedral at Gloucester, England, and later a monument was erected to his memory in the Old Cemetery, Northampton, Mass.

**LYNCH, John,** a Representative from Maine; born in Portland, Maine, February 18, 1825; attended the public schools; was graduated from the Portland High School in 1842; engaged in mercantile pursuits; manager of the Portland Daily Press in 1862; member of the State house of representatives 1862-1864; elected as a Republican to the Thirty-ninth and to the three succeeding Congresses (March 4, 1865-March 3, 1873); chairman, Committee on

Expenditures in the Department of the Navy (Forty-first Congress), Committee on Expenditures in the Department of the Treasury (Forty-second Congress); moved to Washington, D.C., and established the Washington Daily Union in 1877; engaged in the manufacture of bricks and drain pipes in Washington, D.C.; died while on a visit in Portland, Maine, on July 21, 1892; interment in Evergreen Cemetery.

**LYNCH, John,** a Representative from Pennsylvania; born in Providence, R.I., November 1, 1843; moved to Pennsylvania in 1856 with his parents, who settled in Wilkes-Barre; attended the public schools and Wyoming Seminary, Kingston, Pa.; worked on a farm and in the coal mines; taught school; studied law; was admitted to the bar November 1, 1868, and commenced practice in Wilkes-Barre, Pa.; elected as a Democrat to the Fiftieth Congress (March 4, 1887-March 3, 1889); unsuccessful candidate for reelection in 1888 to the Fifty-first Congress; resumed the practice of law in Wilkes-Barre; judge of the court of common pleas 1892-1910; died in Atlantic City, N.J., August 17, 1910; interment in St. Mary's Cemetery, Wilkes-Barre, Luzerne County, Pa.

**LYNCH, John Roy,** a Representative from Mississippi; born near Vidalia, Concordia Parish, La., September 10, 1847; after his father's death moved with his mother to Natchez, Miss., in 1863, where they were held as slaves; after emancipation engaged in photography and attended evening school; appointed by Governor Adelbert Ames as a justice of the peace in 1869; member of the Mississippi State house of representatives from 1869 to 1873, and served the last term as speaker; delegate to the Republican National Conventions of 1872, 1884, 1888, 1892 and 1900; elected as a Republican to the Forty-third and Forty-fourth Congresses (March 4, 1873-March 3, 1877); unsuccessful candidate for reelection in 1876 to the Forty-fifth Congress; successfully contested the election of James R. Chalmers to the Forty-seventh Congress and served from April 29, 1882, to March 3, 1883; unsuccessful candidate for reelection in 1882 to the Forty-eighth Congress; returned to his plantation in Adams County, Miss., and engaged in agricultural pursuits; chairman of the Republican State executive committee, 1881-1889; member of the Republican National Committee for the State of Mississippi, 1884-1889; temporary chairman of the Republican National Convention at Chicago in 1884; Fourth Auditor of the Treasury for the Navy Department under President Benjamin Harrison, 1889-1893; studied law; was admitted to the Mississippi bar in 1896; returned to Washington, D.C., in 1897, where he practiced his profession until 1898, when he was appointed a major and additional paymaster of Volunteers during the Spanish-American War by President William McKinley; was appointed by President McKinley as a paymaster in the Regular Army with the rank of captain in 1901; was promoted to major in 1906; retired from the Regular Army in 1911; moved to Chicago, Ill., in 1912 and continued the practice of his profession until his death in that city on November 2, 1939; interment in Arlington National Cemetery, Va.

Bibliography: *DAB*; Lynch, John Roy. *Reminiscences of an Active Life.* Edited by John Hope Franklin. Chicago: University of Chicago Press, 1970; McLaughlin, James Harold. "John R. Lynch, The Reconstruction Politician: A Historical Perspective." Ph.D. dissertation, Ball State University, 1981.

**LYNCH, Thomas** (father of Thomas Lynch, Jr.), a Delegate from South Carolina; born in St. James Parish, Berkeley County, S.C., in 1727; attended the common schools; engaged in planting, with extensive rice plantations on the Santee River and elsewhere; served in the commons house of assembly 1751-1757, 1761-1763, 1765, 1768, and 1772; delegate to the Colonial Congress in 1765; member of the general committee 1769-1774; delegate to the First and Second Provincial Congresses in 1775 and 1776; member of the first State general assembly in 1776; Member of the Continental

Congress in 1774-1776, but was unable to sign the Declaration of Independence because of illness; died in Annapolis, Anne Arundel County, Md., in December 1776 while en route to his home; interment in St. Anne's Churchyard, Annapolis, Md.

**Bibliography:** *DAB*.

**LYNCH, Thomas,** a Representative from Wisconsin; born in Granville, Milwaukee County, Wis., November 21, 1844; attended the common schools; moved to Chilton, Calumet County, in 1864; engaged in agricultural pursuits; taught school; held various local offices; member of the State assembly in 1873 and 1883; was graduated from the law department of the Wisconsin University at Madison in 1875; was admitted to the bar in the same year and commenced practice in Chilton, Wis.; district attorney 1878-1882; moved to Antigo, Langlade County, Wis., in 1883; mayor of Antigo in 1885 and 1888; elected as a Democrat to the Fifty-second and Fifty-third Congresses (March 4, 1891-March 3, 1895); chairman, Committee on Mileage (Fifty-third Congress); died in Antigo, Wis., May 4, 1898; interment in St. John's Cemetery.

**LYNCH, Thomas, Jr.** (son of Thomas Lynch [1727-1776]), a Delegate from South Carolina; born in Prince George's Parish, Winyah, S.C., August 5, 1749; educated at Eton and Cambridge, England, and studied law at the Middle Temple in London, 1764-1772; returned to America in 1772; became a planter on the North Santee River; member of the First and Second Provincial Congresses of South Carolina 1774-1776; member of the constitutional committee in 1776; member of the State general assembly in 1776; served as a captain in the First South Carolina Regiment, subsequently of the Continental Line, in the Revolutionary War from June 1775 until his election as a Delegate to the Continental Congress on February 1, 1776, and served in 1776; signer of the Declaration of Independence; did not seek reelection to the Continental Congress owing to ill health; embarked on an ocean voyage to France in 1779 and was lost at sea in that year.

**Bibliography:** *DAB*.

**LYNCH, Walter Aloysius,** a Representative from New York, born in New York City July 7, 1894; attended St. Jerome's Parochial School and Fordham Preparatory School; was graduated from Fordham University, New York, N.Y., in 1915 and from the law department of the same university in 1918; was admitted to the bar the same year and commenced practice in New York City; served as a magistrate of New York City in 1930; delegate to the New York State constitutional convention in 1938; elected as a Democrat to the Seventy-sixth Congress to fill the vacancy caused by the death of Edward W. Curley; reelected to the Seventy-seventh and to the four succeeding Congresses and served from February 20, 1940, to January 3, 1951; had been renominated in 1950 to the Eighty-second Congress but withdrew and was an unsuccessful candidate for election as Governor of New York; elected to the New York Supreme Court in 1954 and served from January 1955 until his death; died in Belle Harbor (Queens), Long Island, N.Y., September 10, 1957; interment in Gate of Heaven Cemetery, Hawthorne, N.Y.

**LYNDE, William Pitt,** a Representative from Wisconsin; born in Sherburne, Chenango County, N.Y., December 16, 1817; attended Hamilton Academy and Hamilton College, and was graduated from Yale College in 1838; attended the law department of the New York University for a year and was graduated from the Harvard Law School in 1841; was admitted to the bar in New York in 1841; moved to Wisconsin the same year and settled in Milwaukee; attorney general of Wisconsin in 1844; United States district attorney for Wisconsin in 1845; upon the admission of Wisconsin as a State into the Union was elected as a Democrat to the Thirtieth Congress and served from June 5, 1848, to March 3, 1849; unsuccessful candidate for reelection in 1848 to the Thirty-first Congress; unsuccessful candidate for election as associate justice of the Wisconsin State supreme court in 1849; elected mayor of Milwaukee in 1860; member of the Wisconsin State assembly in 1866; served in the Wisconsin State senate, 1869-1870; elected to the Forty-fourth and Forty-fifth Congresses (March 4, 1875-March 3, 1879); chairman, Committee on Expenditures on Public Buildings (Forty-fifth Congress); one of the managers appointed by the House of Representatives in 1876 to conduct the impeachment proceedings against William W. Belknap, Secretary of War in President Ulysses S. Grant's Cabinet; was not a candidate for renomination in 1878 to the Forty-sixth Congress; withdrew from political life; died in Milwaukee, Wis., December 18, 1885; interment in Forest Home Cemetery.

**LYON, Asa,** a Representative from Vermont; born in Pomfret, Conn., December 31, 1763; attended the common schools; was graduated from Dartmouth College, Hanover, N.H., in 1790; divinity student with the Rev. Charles Backus at Somers, Conn.; ordained pastor of the Congregational Church in Sunderland, Mass., in 1792; moved to South Hero, Vt., in 1794; studied law; member of the State house of representatives from South Hero 1799-1802, 1804-1806, and 1808, and was a member of the State executive council in 1808; pastor of South Hero 1802-1840; chief judge of Grand Isle County Courts 1805-1809, 1813, and 1814; member of the State house of representatives from Grand Isle 1810-1814; elected as a Federalist to the Fourteenth Congress (March 4, 1815-March 3, 1817); died in South Hero, Grand Isle County, Vt., April 4, 1841; interment in Grand Isle Cemetery, Grand Isle, Vt.

**LYON, Caleb,** a Representative from New York; born in Greig, N.Y., December 7, 1822; attended the common school in Lyondale and the schools in Montreal, Canada; was graduated from Norwich University, Northfield, Vt., in 1841; widely known as an extensive traveler and student of foreign countries and customs; became a noted lecturer, poet, author, and writer; appointed United States consul to Shanghai, China, in 1847, but intrusted the office to a deputy and moved to California, where he was chosen a secretary of the California constitutional convention; was the designer of the California State seal adopted in 1849; returned to Lyonsdale, N.Y., and was elected to the New York State assembly in 1850; resigned after opposing Erie Canal improvement; served in the New York State senate in 1851; active in State and local improvements and free schools; elected as an Independent to the Thirty-third Congress (March 4, 1853-March 3, 1855); moved to Staten Island, N.Y.; appointed Governor of the Territory of Idaho by President Abraham Lincoln on February 26, 1864, and served until June 1866; successfully negotiated the treaty for lands with the Shoshone Indians; returned to his home, "Lyonsmere," in Rossville, Staten Island, N.Y., where he died on September 8, 1875; interment in Greenwood Cemetery, New York City.

**Bibliography:** *DAB*.

**LYON, Chittenden** (son of Matthew Lyon), a Representative from Kentucky; born in Fair Haven, Vt., February 22, 1787; attended the common schools; in 1801 moved to Kentucky with his parents, who settled in Caldwell County; engaged in mercantile pursuits in Eddyville, Caldwell County, Ky., and had large agricultural interests; member of the Kentucky house of representatives 1822-1824; served in the Kentucky senate 1827-1835; elected to the Twentieth Congress and reelected as a Jacksonian to the three succeeding Congresses (March 4, 1827-March 3, 1835); was not a candidate for reelection in 1835 to the Twenty-fourth Congress; continued his business activities until his death; Lyon County, which was separated from Caldwell County in 1854, was named in his honor; died in Eddyville, Ky., November 23, 1842; interment in Eddyville Cemetery.

**LYON, Francis Strother,** a Representative from Alabama; born near Danbury, Stokes County, N.C., February 25, 1800; attended the common schools; moved to St. Stephens (an Indian agency), Ala., in

1817; employed in the bank at St. Stephens and in the office of the clerk of the county court; studied law; was admitted to the bar in 1821 and commenced practice in Demopolis; secretary of the State senate 1822-1830; member of the State senate in 1833; reelected to the State senate in 1834 and served as president of that body; elected as an Anti-Jacksonian to the Twenty-fourth Congress and reelected as a Whig to the Twenty-fifth Congress (March 4, 1835-March 3, 1839); was not a candidate for renomination; resumed the practice of law and also engaged in agriculture; in 1845, when the State banks were placed in liquidation, he was selected as one of three commissioners to adjust all claims and was afterward chosen sole commissioner until the final settlement in 1853; chairman of the Democratic State convention in 1860; delegate to the Democratic National Convention at Charleston in 1860, when the southern delegates withdrew, he among them; member of the State house of representatives in 1861; elected to the Provisional Confederate Congress but declined to serve; elected to the First and Second Confederate Congresses and served from 1862 until the close of the Civil War; delegate to the State constitutional convention in 1875 and made the draft of the constitution adopted by the convention; again elected to the State senate in 1876; died in Demopolis, Ala., December 31, 1882; interment in the Old Glover Vault.

Bibliography: *DAB*.

LYON, Homer Le Grand, a Representative from North Carolina; born in Elizabethtown, Bladen County, N.C., March 1, 1879; attended the public schools, the Davis Military School, Winston, N.C., and the law department of the University of North Carolina at Chapel Hill; was admitted to the bar in 1900 and commenced practice in Whiteville, Columbus County, N.C.; delegate to every Democratic State convention from 1901 to 1921; delegate to the Democratic National Conventions in 1904 and 1940; solicitor of the eighth judicial district of North Carolina 1913-1920; elected as a Democrat to the Sixty-seventh and to the three succeeding Congresses (March 4, 1921-March 3, 1929); was not a candidate for renomination in 1928; resumed the practice of law in Whiteville, N.C., until his retirement in 1950; died in Whiteville, N.C., May 31, 1956; interment in Memorial Cemetery.

LYON, Lucius, a Delegate, a Senator, and a Representative from Michigan; born in Shelburne, Chittenden County, Vt., February 26, 1800; attended the common schools; moved to Bronson, Mich., in 1821; became a land surveyor; elected as a Democrat Delegate to the Twenty-third Congress (March 4, 1833-March 3, 1835); served as a member of the convention which framed the State constitution in 1835; upon the admission of Michigan as a State into the Union was elected as a Democrat to the United States Senate and served from January 26, 1837, to March 3, 1839; was not a candidate for reelection; moved to Grand Rapids, Mich., in 1839; member of the board of regents of the University of Michigan 1837-1839; appointed Indian commissioner at La Pointe, Wis., in 1839; elected as a Democrat to the Twenty-eighth Congress (March 4, 1843-March 3, 1845); declined to be a candidate for renomination in 1844; appointed by President James K. Polk in 1845 surveyor general for Ohio, Indiana, and Michigan, moving the office from Cincinnati to Detroit for his convenience, and serving in this capacity until 1850; died in Detroit, Mich., September 24, 1851; interment in Elmwood Cemetery.

Bibliography: Shirigian, John. "Lucius Lyon: His Place in Michigan History." Ph.D. dissertation, University of Michigan, 1961.

LYON, Matthew (father of Chittenden Lyon and great-grandfather of William Peters Hepburn), a Representative from Vermont and from Kentucky; born near Dublin, County Wicklow, Ireland, July 14, 1749; attended school in Dublin; began to learn the trade of printer in 1763; immigrated to the United States in 1765; was landed as a redemptioner and worked on a farm in Woodbury,

Conn., where he continued his education; moved to Wallingford, Vt. (then known as the New Hampshire Grants), in 1774 and organized a company of militia; served as adjutant in Colonel Warner's regiment in Canada in 1775; commissioned second lieutenant in the regiment known as the Green Mountain Boys in July 1776; moved to Arlington, Vt., in 1777; resigned from the Army in 1778; member of the Vermont State house of representatives 1779-1783; founded the town of Fair Haven, Vt., in 1783; was a member of the Vermont house of representatives for ten years during the period 1783-1796; built and operated various kinds of mills, including one for the manufacture of paper; established a printing office in 1793 and published the Farmers' Library, afterward the Fair Haven Gazette; unsuccessful candidate for election to the Second and Third Congresses; unsuccessfully contested the election of Israel Smith to the Fourth Congress; elected as a Republican to the Fifth and Sixth Congresses (March 4, 1797-March 3, 1801); was not a candidate for renomination in 1800; moved to Kentucky in 1801 and settled in Caldwell (now Lyon) County; member of the Kentucky house of representatives in 1802; elected to the Eighth and to the three succeeding Congresses (March 4, 1803-March 3, 1811); unsuccessful candidate for reelection in 1810 to the Twelfth Congress; was appointed United States factor to the Cherokee Nation in Arkansas Territory in 1820; unsuccessfully contested the election of James W. Bates as a Delegate from Arkansas Territory to the Seventeenth Congress; died in Spadra Bluff, Ark., August 1, 1822; interment in Spadra Bluff Cemetery; reinterment in Eddyville Cemetery, Eddyville, Caldwell (now Lyon) County, Ky., in 1833.

Bibliography: *DAB*; Austin, Aleine. *Matthew Lyon: "New Man" of the Democratic Revolution, 1749-1822*. University Park: Pennsylvania State University Press, 1981; Montagno, George L. "Matthew Lyon, Radical Jeffersonian, 1796-1801: A Case Study in Partisan Politics." Ph.D. dissertation, University of California at Berkeley, 1954.

LYTLE, Robert Todd (nephew of John Rowan), a Representative from Ohio; born in Williamsburg, Clermont County, Ohio, May 19, 1804; attended the common schools and Cincinnati College; studied law in Louisville, Ky.; was admitted to the bar in that city in 1824 and commenced the practice of his profession in Cincinnati, Ohio; elected county prosecuting attorney; member of the State house of representatives in 1828 and 1829; elected as a Jacksonian to the Twenty-third Congress and served from March 4, 1833, until March 10, 1834, when he resigned; reelected to fill the vacancy caused by his own resignation and served from December 27, 1834, to March 3, 1835; unsuccessful candidate for reelection in 1834 to the Twenty-fourth Congress; resumed the practice of law; surveyor general of public lands in the Northwest Territory in 1836; major general of Ohio Militia in 1838; died in New Orleans, La., December 22, 1839; interment in Spring Grove Cemetery, Cincinnati, Ohio.

# M

MAAS, Melvin Joseph, a Representative from Minnesota; born in Duluth, St. Louis County, Minn., May 14, 1898; moved with his parents to St. Paul, Minn., in 1898; educated in the public schools; was graduated from St. Thomas College at St. Paul in 1919; attended the University of Minnesota at Minneapolis; engaged in the insurance business; during the First World War served in the aviation branch of the Marine Corps in 1918 and 1919; officer in the Marine Corps Reserve in 1925 and retired with rank of major general August 1, 1952; elected as a Republican to the Seventieth and to the two succeeding Congresses (March 4, 1927-March 3, 1933); unsuccessful candidate for renomination in 1932 to the Seventy-third Congress; received the Carnegie Silver Medal for disarming Marlin R.M. Kemmerer, who had entered the United States House of Representatives with a drawn pistol and demanded to address that body on December 13, 1932; elected to the Seventy-fourth and to the four succeeding Congresses (January 3,

1935-January 3, 1945); unsuccessful candidate for reelection in 1944 to the Seventy-ninth Congress; served in the South Pacific as a colonel in the United States Marine Corps, 1942-1945, while still a Member of Congress; special adviser to the House Naval Affairs Committee in 1946; assistant to the chairman of the board of the Sperry Corporation, New York City, 1947-1951; became a member of the President's Committee on Employment of the Physically Handicapped in 1949 and served as chairman 1954-1964; had been stricken with total blindness in August 1951; was a resident of Chevy Chase, Md., until his death in Bethesda, Md., April 13, 1964; interment in Arlington National Cemetery, Va.

**MacCRATE, John,** a Representative from New York; born in Dumbarton, Scotland, March 29, 1885; immigrated with his mother to the United States in 1893 and settled in Greenpoint, Brooklyn, N.Y., where his father had provided a home; attended the public schools and the Commercial High School in Brooklyn; was graduated from the law department of New York University in 1906; was admitted to the bar the same year and commenced practice in New York City; delegate to the Republican National Conventions in 1916 and 1920; was nominated in the primaries by both the Republican and Democratic Parties and was elected as a Republican to the Sixty-sixth Congress and served from March 4, 1919, to December 30, 1920, when he resigned; elected justice of the supreme court of the State of New York in 1920; reelected in 1934 and 1948 and served in the appellate division of the supreme court until December 31, 1955, when he reached age limit; official referee, New York State Supreme Court, in 1956, 1957, and to June 1958; died in Brooklyn, N.Y., June 9, 1976; interment in Mount Olivet Cemetery, Queens, N.Y.

**MacDONALD, John Lewis,** a Representative from Minnesota; born in Glasgow, Scotland, February 22, 1838; immigrated to Nova Scotia, Canada, with his parents, who later, in 1847, settled in Pittsburgh, Pa.; moved to Minnesota in 1855 and settled in Scott County; studied law; was admitted to the bar in 1859 and commenced practice at Belle Plain, Minn.; judge of the probate court of Scott County in 1860 and 1861; during the Civil War was commissioned to enlist and muster volunteers for the Union Army; prosecuting attorney of Scott County in 1863 and 1864; county superintendent of schools in 1865 and 1866; member of the State house of representatives in 1869 and 1870; served in the State senate in 1871 and 1873-1876; unsuccessful Democratic candidate for attorney general in 1872; mayor of Shakopee in 1876; elected judge of the eighth judicial district of Minnesota in 1876 for a term of seven years and reelected without opposition in 1883; resigned in the fall of 1886, having been elected to Congress; elected as a Democrat to the Fiftieth Congress (March 4, 1887-March 3, 1889); unsuccessful candidate for reelection in 1888 to the Fifty-first Congress; engaged in the practice of his profession in St. Paul, Minn.; moved to Kansas City, Mo., in 1898 and continued the practice of law until his death on July 13, 1903, from injuries received in a streetcar accident; interment in St. Mary's Cemetery, Kansas City, Mo.

**MACDONALD, Moses,** a Representative from Maine; born in Limerick, Maine, April 8, 1815; received an academic education; studied law; was admitted to the bar in 1837 and commenced practice in Biddeford, Maine, in 1837; member of the State house of representatives in 1841, 1842, and 1845; served as speaker in 1845; served in the State senate in 1847; State treasurer 1847-1850; elected as a Democrat to the Thirty-second and Thirty-third Congresses (March 4, 1851-March 3, 1855); chairman, Committee on Revolutionary Claims (Thirty-second Congress); appointed collector of customs at Portland, Maine, by President James Buchanan in 1857 and served until 1861; died in Saco, Maine, on October 18, 1869; interment in Laurel Hill Cemetery.

**MACDONALD, Torbert Hart,** a Representative from Massachusetts; born in Everett, Middlesex County, Mass., June 6, 1917; attended Malden public schools, Medford High School, and Phillips Academy, Andover, Mass.; was graduated from Harvard University, B.A., 1940 and from its law school, LL.B., 1946; served in the United States Navy as a PT boat commander in the Southwest Pacific 1942-1944; awarded Silver Star Combat Award and Presidential Citation; was admitted to the bar in 1946 and commenced the practice of law in Boston, Mass.; member of the National Labor Relations Board for the New England area 1948-1952; delegate to the Democratic National Conventions in 1960, 1964, and 1968; elected as a Democrat to the Eighty-fourth Congress; reelected to the ten succeeding Congresses and served from January 3, 1955, until his death, May 21, 1976, in Bethesda, Md.; interment in Holy Cross Cemetery, Malden, Mass.

**MacDONALD, William Josiah,** a Representative from Michigan; born in Potosi, Grant County, Wis., November 17, 1873; attended the common schools and was graduated from the high school at Fairmont, Minn.; attended the University of Minnesota at Minneapolis and Georgetown Law School, Washington, D.C.; was admitted to the bar and commenced practice at Calumet, Mich., in 1895; prosecuting attorney for Keweenaw County, Mich., 1898-1904; prosecuting attorney for Houghton County, Mich., 1906-1912; successfully contested as a Progressive the election of H. Olin Young to the Sixty-third Congress, and served from August 26, 1913 to March 3, 1915; unsuccessful candidate for reelection in 1914 to the Sixty-fourth Congress, and for election in 1916 to the Sixty-fifth Congress; resumed the practice of law in Springfield, Ill., in 1917; moved to East St. Louis, Ill., in 1922 and engaged in the practice of his profession; died in Chicago, Ill., March 29, 1946; interment in Graceland Cemetery, Chicago, Ill.

**Bibliography:** Boyer, Hugh E. "The Decline of the Progressive Party in Michigan's Upper Peninsula: The Case of Congressman William J. MacDonald in 1914." *Michigan Historical Review* 13 (Fall 1987): 75-94.

**MacDOUGALL, Clinton Dugald,** a Representative from New York; born near Glasgow, Scotland, June 14, 1839; immigrated to Canada in 1842 with his parents, who later settled in Auburn, N.Y.; pursued an academic course; studied law; engaged in banking 1856-1869; commissioned captain in the Seventy-fifth Regiment, New York Volunteer Infantry, September 16, 1861; lieutenant colonel of the One Hundred and Eleventh Regiment, New York Volunteer Infantry, August 20, 1862; colonel January 3, 1863; brevetted brigadier general of Volunteers February 25, 1865; honorably mustered out June 4, 1865; appointed postmaster of Auburn, N.Y., in 1869; elected as a Republican to the Forty-third and Forty-fourth Congresses (March 4, 1873-March 3, 1877); unsuccessful candidate for renomination in 1876; served as United States marshal of the northern judicial district of New York 1877-1885 and 1901-1910; died in Paris, France, May 24, 1914; interment in Arlington National Cemetery, Va.

**MACE, Daniel,** a Representative from Indiana; born in Pickaway County, Ohio, September 5, 1811; attended the public schools; studied law; was admitted to the bar in 1835 and practiced in LaFayette, Ind.; member of the State house of representatives in 1836; clerk of the State house of representatives in 1837; United States attorney for Indiana 1849-1853; elected as a Democrat to the Thirty-second and Thirty-third Congresses (March 4, 1851-March 3, 1855); reelected as a Republican to the Thirty-fourth Congress (March 4, 1855-March 3, 1857); chairman, Committee on the Post Office and Post Roads (Thirty-fourth Congress); resumed the practice of law; postmaster of LaFayette from September 22, 1866, until his death in LaFayette, July 26, 1867; interment in Greenbush Cemetery.

**MacGREGOR, Clarence,** a Representative from New York; born in Newark, Wayne County, N.Y., September 16, 1872; attended the public schools in Gloversville, Auburn, and Buffalo, N.Y., and was graduated from Hartwick Seminary, Otsego County, N.Y., in 1893; took a special course at the University of Rochester, Rochester, N.Y., in 1894 and 1895; was admitted to the bar in 1897 and commenced the practice of his profession in Buffalo, N.Y.; member of the State assembly 1908-1912; elected as a Republican to the Sixty-sixth and to the four succeeding Congresses and served from March 4, 1919, until his resignation on December 31, 1928, having been elected as a justice of the supreme court of the State of New York, and serving until his retirement on December 31, 1942; chairman, Committee on Accounts (Sixty-eighth through Seventieth Congresses); appointed official referee of the supreme court of the State of New York on January 7, 1943, and served until his death in Buffalo, N.Y., February 18, 1952; interment in Forest Lawn Cemetery.

**MacGREGOR, Clark,** a Representative from Minnesota; born in Minneapolis, Hennepin County, Minn., July 12, 1922; educated in the grade schools and Washburn High School; A.B., Dartmouth College, Hanover, N.H., 1946; LL.B., University of Minnesota Law School, 1948; was admitted to the bar in 1948 and commenced the practice of law in Minneapolis, Minn.; enlisted in the United States Army as a private and served with the Office of Strategic Services from 1942 to 1945; commissioned directly in the field as a second lieutenant while serving in Burma; delegate to the Republican National Conventions of 1964 and 1968; elected as a Republican to the Eighty-seventh and to the four succeeding Congresses (January 3, 1961-January 3, 1971); was not a candidate in 1970 for reelection to the House of Representatives, but was an unsuccessful candidate for election to the United States Senate; is a resident of Washington, D.C.

**MACHEN, Hervey Gilbert,** a Representative from Maryland; born in Washington, D.C., October 14, 1916; educated in the public schools of Prince Georges County, Md.; engaged in banking, 1935-1940; LL.B., Southeastern University, Washington, D.C., 1939, LL.M., 1941; was admitted to the bar in 1939 and commenced practice in 1940 at Hyattsville, Md.; served in the Coast Artillery Military Intelligence and Quartermaster Corps from April 1941 to February 1946 and was honorably discharged as a captain; elected to the Maryland State house of delegates in 1954 and reelected in 1958 and 1962; assistant State's attorney for Prince Georges County, 1947-1951; city attorney for Cheverly, Md., and Hyattsville, Md., 1949-1958; vice chairman of the Democratic State central committee, 1953-1957; elected as a Democrat to the Eighty-ninth and Ninetieth Congresses (January 3, 1965-January 3, 1969); unsuccessful candidate for reelection in 1968 to the Ninety-first Congress and in 1970 for nomination to the Ninety-second Congress; resumed the practice of law; was a resident of Hyattsville, Md.; died November 29, 1994.

**MACHEN, Willis Benson,** a Senator from Kentucky; born in Caldwell (now Lyon) County, Ky., April 10, 1810; attended the common schools and Cumberland College, Princeton, Ky.; engaged in agricultural pursuits near Eddyville; delegate to the Kentucky constitutional convention in 1849; member, Kentucky senate 1854; member, Kentucky house of representatives 1856, 1860; elected to the First and Second Confederate Congresses; appointed as a Democrat to the United States Senate to fill the vacancy caused by the death of Garrett Davis and served from September 27, 1872, to March 3, 1873; resumed agricultural interests; died in Hopkinsville, Ky., September 29, 1893; interment in Riverview Cemetery, Eddyville, Lyon County, Ky.

**MACHIR, James,** a Representative from Virginia; born in Virginia; member of the Virginia house of delegates, 1793-1796; elected as a Federalist to the Fifth Congress (March 4, 1797-March

3, 1799); again a member of the Virginia house of delegates, 1811-1813, and 1818-1821; died on June 25, 1827.

**MACHROWICZ, Thaddeus Michael,** a Representative from Michigan; born in Gostyn, Poland, August 21, 1899; immigrated to the United States with his parents in 1902 and settled in Chicago, Ill., later moving to Milwaukee, Wis.; naturalized in 1910; attended the parochial school in Milwaukee, Wis., Alliance College, Cambridge Springs, Pa., 1912-1916, and University of Chicago in 1917; during the First World War served as a lieutenant in the Polish Army of American Volunteers in Canada, France, and Poland, 1917-1920; served with the American Advisory Commission to Polish Government in 1920 and 1921; also acted as war correspondent with Floyd Gibbons in Poland 1919-1921; attended De Paul University in 1921 and graduated from the Detroit College of Law in 1924; was admitted to the Michigan bar in 1924 and commenced practice in Detroit; city attorney of Hamtramck, Mich., 1934-1936; legal director, Michigan Public Utilities Commission, in 1938 and 1939; municipal judge in Hamtramck, Mich., 1942-1950; elected as a Democrat to the Eighty-second and to the five succeeding Congresses and served from January 3, 1951, to September 18, 1961, when he resigned, having been appointed a judge of the United States District Court for the eastern district of Michigan and served until his death February 17, 1970, in Bloomfield Township, Mich.; interment in Mt. Olivet Cemetery, Detroit, Mich.

**MACHTLEY, Ronald K.,** a Representative from Rhode Island; born in Johnstown, Cambria County, Pa., July 13, 1948; graduated, Richland Junior and Senior High School, Johnstown, 1966; B.S., United States Naval Academy, 1970; J.D., Suffolk University Law School, Boston, Mass., 1978; United States Naval service, 1970-1975; commander, United States Naval Reserve (retired); admitted to Rhode Island bar, 1978; practicing attorney, 1978-1988; elected as a Republican to the One Hundred First and to the two succeeding Congresses (January 3, 1989-January 3, 1995); was not a candidate in 1994 for renomination to the One Hundred Fourth Congress, but was an unsuccessful candidate for nomination for Governor of Rhode Island; president, Bryant College, Smithfield, R.I., June 17, 1996 to present; is a resident of Smithfield and of Portsmouth, R.I.

**MACIEJEWSKI, Anton Frank,** a Representative from Illinois; born in Anderson, Grimes County, Tex., January 3, 1893; attended the public schools of Cicero, Ill., and Lewis Institute, Chicago, Ill.; became engaged in the wholesale and retail coal business in Cicero, Ill., in 1916; assistant agent in charge of relief of Cook County, Ill., 1925-1928; member of the Democratic State and National Committees; delegate to the Democratic National Convention of 1928; supervisor and treasurer of Cicero, Ill., 1932-1939; elected as a Democrat to the Seventy-sixth and Seventy-seventh Congresses and served from January 3, 1939, until his resignation on December 8, 1942; was not a candidate for renomination in 1942 to the Seventy-eighth Congress; resumed the wholesale and retail coal business; also engaged in the construction of defense housing; elected to the board of trustees of the sanitary district of Chicago in December 1942, and served until his death in Chicago, Ill., September 25, 1949; interment in Resurrection Cemetery, Justice, Ill.

**MacINTYRE, Archibald Thompson,** a Representative from Georgia; born near Marion, Twiggs County, Ga., October 27, 1822; moved with his parents to Thomas County, Ga., in 1826; attended the common schools and was graduated from Thomasville Academy; studied law in Monticello, Fla., and Macon, Ga.; was admitted to the bar in 1843 and commenced the practice of law at Thomasville; member of the State house of representatives in 1849; during the Civil War served as colonel of the Eleventh Infantry, Georgia Guards, in the Confederate Army; delegate to the State constitutional convention in 1865; elected as a Democrat to the Forty-second Congress (March 4, 1871-March 3, 1873); was not a candidate for renomination in 1872; resumed the practice of law in Thomasville, Ga.; member of the board of trustees of the University of Georgia and Georgia State Sanitarium; died in Thomasville on January 1, 1900; interment in Laurel Hill Cemetery.

**MACIORA, Lucien John,** a Representative from Connecticut; born in New Britain, Hartford County, Conn., August 17, 1902; attended the grade and high schools; engaged in the grocery business from 1920 until 1928; member of the New Britain Common Council, 1926-1934; engaged in the furniture and undertaking business, 1928-1939; one of the founders of the Peoples' Savings Bank, New Britain, Conn., and served as a director for over fifty years; member, Connecticut State house of representatives, 1932-1937; chairman of the New Britain Police Board, 1934-1940; engaged in the insurance business in 1939; past president of the Polish-American Congress; elected as a Democrat to the Seventy-seventh Congress (January 3, 1941-January 3, 1943); unsuccessful candidate for reelection in 1942 to the Seventy-eighth Congress; resumed the insurance business; collector of taxes for the city of New Britain, 1950-1969; was a resident of New Britain, Conn.; died October 19, 1993.

**MACK, Connie, III** (step-grandson of Tom Connally, grandson of Morris Sheppard and great-grandson of John Levi Sheppard), a Representative and a Senator from Florida; born Cornelius McGillicuddy, III, in Philadelphia, Pa., October 29, 1940; attended St. Francis Xavier School, Fort Myers, Fla.; graduated, Fort Myers High School, 1959; B.A., University of Florida, Gainesville, 1966; banker, 1966-1982; elected as a Republican to the Ninety-eighth and to the two succeeding Congresses (January 3, 1983-January 3, 1989); was not a candidate in 1988 for reelection to the House of Representatives, but was elected to the United States Senate for the term commencing January 3, 1989; reelected in 1994 for the term ending January 3, 2001; chairman, Joint Economic Committee (One Hundred Fourth Congress), secretary, Senate Republican Conference (One Hundred Fourth Congress); is a resident of Cape Coral, Fla.

**MACK, Peter Francis, Jr.,** a Representative from Illinois; born in Carlinville, Macoupin County, Ill., November 1, 1916; attended the public schools and Blackburn College in Carlinville, Ill., and St. Louis (Mo.) University; took special courses in aviation at Springfield (Ill.) Junior College and St. Louis (Mo.) University; engaged in the automotive sales and service business in Carlinville, Ill.; licensed commercial pilot; enlisted in the United States Navy in 1942 and served four years in naval air force; Naval Reserve officer with rank of commander; pilot of single-engine "Friendship Flame" airplane on a solo flight that traveled 33,000 miles and visited thirty nations, October 7, 1951 to January 27, 1952; elected as a Democrat to the Eighty-first and to the six succeeding Congresses (January 3, 1949-January 3, 1963); unsuccessful candidate for reelection in 1962 to the Eighty-eighth Congress; unsuccessful candidate for election in 1974 to the Ninety-fourth Congress, and for election in 1976 to the Ninety-fifth Congress; assistant to the president, Southern Railway, 1963-1975; owned and operated a real estate and investment firm; was a resident of Potomac, Md., until his death in Rockville, Md., July 4, 1986; interment in Arlington National Cemetery, Va.

**MACK, Russell Vernon,** a Representative from Washington; born in Hillman, Montmorency County, Mich., June 13, 1891; moved with his parents to Aberdeen, Grays Harbor County, Wash., in 1895; attended the public schools, Stanford University, Palo Alto, Calif., 1913-1914, and the University of Washington, Seattle, 1914-1915; joined the Aberdeen (Wash.) Daily World in 1913 as a cub reporter, and was business manager from 1920 until 1934; during the First World War served as a corporal in the Thirty-ninth Field Artillery, Thirteenth Division; owner and publisher of the Hoquiam Daily Washingtonian from 1934 to 1950; elected as a Republican to the Eightieth Congress to fill the vacancy caused by the death of Fred B. Norman; reelected to the Eighty-first and to the five succeeding Congresses, and served from June 7, 1947 until his death on the floor of the United States House of Representatives, Washington, D.C., March 28, 1960; interment in Fern Hill Cemetery, Aberdeen, Wash.

**MacKAY, James Armstrong,** a Representative from Georgia; born in Fairfield, Jefferson County, Ala., June 25, 1919; moved to Atlanta, Ga., with his parents in 1934; educated in the public schools; A.B., Emory University, Atlanta, Ga., 1940; attended Duke University, 1940-1941; LL.B., Emory University School of Law, 1947; admitted to the Georgia Bar in 1947 and commenced practice in Decatur; served in the United States Coast Guard Reserve, 1941-1945; awarded the Bronze Star Medal; trustee, Emory University; member, State legislature, 1951-1952, 1955-1964; elected as a Democrat to the Eighty-ninth Congress (January 3, 1965-January 3, 1967); unsuccessful candidate for reelection in 1966 to the Ninetieth Congress; resumed the practice of law; is a resident of Atlanta, Ga.

**MacKAY, Kenneth Hood, Jr. (Buddy),** a Representative from Florida; born in Ocala, Marion County, Fla., March 22, 1933; attended Ocala Elementary School; graduated, Ocala High School, 1950; B.S. and B.A., University of Florida, Gainsville, 1954; LL.B., University of Florida Law School, 1961; served in the United States Air Force as a captain, 1955-1958; admitted to the Florida bar in 1961, and commenced practice in Daytona Beach; member, Florida State house of representatives, 1968-1974; member, Florida State senate, 1974-1980; unsuccessful candidate for the United States Senate, 1980; elected as a Democrat to the Ninety-eighth and to the two succeeding Congresses (January 3, 1983-January 3, 1989); was not a candidate in 1988 for reelection to the House of Representatives, but was an unsuccessful candidate for election to the United States Senate; is a resident of Ocala, Fla.

**MACKEY, Edmund William McGregor,** a Representative from South Carolina; born in Charleston, S.C., March 8, 1846; pursued classical studies; appointed assistant assessor of internal revenue in South Carolina on September 8, 1865; delegate to the State constitutional convention in 1867; studied law; was admitted to the bar in 1868 and practiced; sheriff of Charleston County, 1868-1872; elected an alderman of the city of Charleston in 1868, 1873, and 1875; editor and proprietor of the Charleston Republican, 1871-1872; member of the South Carolina State house of representatives in 1873; presented credentials as an Independent Republican Member-elect to the Forty-fourth Congress, and served from March 4, 1875 to July 19, 1876, when the seat was declared vacant; again a member of the State house of representatives in 1877, and served as speaker; delegate to the Republican National Conventions of 1872 and 1880; assistant United States attorney for South Carolina, 1878-1881; unsuccessfully contested as a Republican the election of Michael P. O'Connor to the Forty-sixth Congress; successfully contested the election of Michael P. O'Connor to the Forty-seventh Congress, succeeding Samuel Dibble, who presented credentials as a Member-elect to fill the vacancy thought to exist upon the death of Mr. O'Connor, which occurred on April 26, 1881, while the contest was pending; reelected to the Forty-eighth Congress, and served from May 31, 1882 until his death in Washington, D.C., January 27, 1884; interment in Glenwood Cemetery.

**MACKEY, Levi Augustus,** a Representative from Pennsylvania; born in Whitedeer Township, Union County, Pa., November 25, 1819; moved with his parents in 1829 to Milton, Pa.; received an academic education and was graduated from Union College, Schenectady, N.Y., in 1837; studied law in Dickinson College, Carlisle, Pa.; was admitted to the bar in 1840 and practiced law in Lock Haven, Pa., from 1841 until 1855; engaged in banking and was elected president of the Lock Haven Bank in 1855; delegate to the Whig National Convention in 1852 and to the Democratic National

Convention in 1872; unsuccessful candidate for election in 1868 to the Forty-first Congress; mayor of Lock Haven, Pa., in 1870; served as president of the Bald Eagle Valley Railroad Co. and of several other corporations; member of the board of trustees of the normal school at Lock Haven Pa., from 1870 until the time of his death; elected as a Democrat to the Forty-fourth and Forty-fifth Congresses (March 4, 1875-March 3, 1879); chairman, Committee on Revolutionary Pensions (Forty-fifth Congress); resumed his former business pursuits; died in Lock Haven, Pa., February 8, 1889; interment in Highland Cemetery.

**MACKIE, John C.,** a Representative from Michigan; born in Toronto, Ontario, Canada, June 1, 1920; immigrated to the United States in 1924 with his parents, who settled in Detroit, Mich.; graduated from Detroit's Southeastern High School in 1938; attended Lawrence Institute of Technology, 1938-1939; B.S.C.E., Michigan State University, 1942, and LL.D., 1965; employed on airplane engine design in Detroit in 1942; enlisted in the United States Army Air Corps in September 1942, and served in the Pacific Theater until discharged as a first lieutenant in September 1946; employed by an engineering firm in the Flint, Mich., area, 1946-1952; in 1952 organized the Flint Surveying & Engineering Co.; elected Genesee County surveyor, 1952-1956; elected Michigan State highway commissioner in 1957, and reelected in 1961 to a new four-year term; elected as a Democrat to the Eighty-ninth Congress (January 3, 1965-January 3, 1967); unsuccessful candidate for reelection in 1966 to the Ninetieth Congress; presently engaged as owner of engineering company; is a resident of Warrenton, Va.

**MacKINNON, George Edward,** a Representative from Minnesota; born in St. Paul, Ramsey County, Minn., April 22, 1906; attended the public schools; the University of Colorado at Boulder, 1923-1924; was graduated from the law school of the University of Minnesota at Minneapolis in 1929; was admitted to the bar the same year and commenced practice in Minneapolis, Minn.; counsel for Investors Syndicate, 1929-1942; served in the State house of representatives 1935-1942; served in the United States Navy 1942-1946 and reached the rank of commander; elected as a Republican to the Eightieth Congress (January 3, 1947-January 3, 1949); unsuccessful candidate for reelection in 1948 to the Eighty-first Congress; resumed the general practice of law; appointed United States attorney for the district of Minnesota on March 23, 1953, reappointed June 26, 1957, and served until his resignation June 6, 1958; unsuccessful candidate in 1958 for election for Governor of Minnesota; in private practice of law from December 1958 to March 1960; special assistant to United States Attorney General William P. Rogers, January 1960 to February 1961; general counsel and vice president, Investors Mutual, Inc., Minneapolis, Minn., 1961-1969; judge, United States Court of Appeals, District of Columbia Circuit, by appointment of President Richard M. Nixon, and served from May 6, 1969, until his death; presiding judge, United States Foreign Intelligence Surveillance Court of Review, 1979-1982; member, United States Sentencing Commission, 1985-1991; presiding judge, division of the United States Court of Appeals, District of Columbia Circuit, for appointment of Independent Counsel, 1985-1992; was a resident of Potomac, Md., until his death there on May 1, 1995.

**MacLAFFERTY, James Henry,** a Representative from California; born in San Diego, Calif., February 27, 1871; moved with his parents to Oakland, Calif., in 1874, to Eugene, Oreg., in 1880, to Astoria, Oreg., in 1883, and to Tacoma, Wash., in 1884; attended the public schools; entered the lumber business in Tacoma and continued the same in Seattle until 1889; engaged in the wholesale paper business at Chicago in 1899; returned to the Pacific coast in 1900 and settled in Oakland, Calif.; worked as a traveling salesman and in the paper business; elected as a Republican to the Sixty-seventh Congress to fill the vacancy caused by the death of

John A. Elston; reelected to the Sixty-eighth Congress, and served from November 7, 1922 to March 3, 1925; unsuccessful candidate for reelection in 1924 to the Sixty-ninth Congress; assistant to Secretary of Commerce Herbert Hoover from March 24, 1925 until August 31, 1927; resumed his business activities in Oakland, Calif.; served as vice president of the Pacific American Steamship Association and of the Shipowners' Association of the Pacific Coast; died in Oakland, Calif., June 9, 1937; remains cremated.

**MACLAY, Samuel** (brother of William Maclay and father of William Plunkett Maclay), a Representative and a Senator from Pennsylvania; born in Lurgan Township, Franklin County, Pa., June 17, 1741; completed preparatory studies; engaged in agricultural pursuits and surveying; served in the Revolutionary War; member, lower house of the Pennsylvania legislature 1787-1791; associate judge of Franklin County 1792-1795; elected to the Fourth Congress (March 4, 1795-March 3, 1797); member, lower house of the Pennsylvania legislature 1797; member, Pennsylvania senate 1798-1802 and served as speaker 1801-1802; elected to the United States Senate as a Republican and served from March 4, 1803, until his resignation, January 4, 1809; retired and died in Buffalo Township, Union County, Pa., October 5, 1811; interment in Driesbach Church Cemetery.

**Bibliography:** *DAB.*

**MACLAY, William** (brother of Samuel Maclay and uncle of William Plunkett Maclay), a Senator from Pennsylvania; born in New Garden, Chester County, Pa., July 20, 1737; pursued classical studies; served as a lieutenant in an expedition to Fort Duquesne in 1758, and in other expeditions against the French and Indians; studied law; was admitted to the bar in 1760; became a surveyor in the employ of the Penn family; prothonotary and clerk of the courts of Northumberland County in the 1770s; served in the Continental Army as a commissary in the Revolutionary War; frequent member of the Pennsylvania legislature in the 1780s; Indian commissioner, judge of the court of common pleas, and member of the executive council; elected to the United States Senate and served from March 4, 1789, to March 3, 1791; retired to his farm in Dauphin, Pa.; member, Pennsylvania house of representatives 1795, and reelected in 1796 and 1797; presidential elector in 1796; county judge 1801-1803; member, Pennsylvania house of representatives 1803; died in Harrisburg, Dauphin County, Pa., April 16, 1804; interment in Old Paxtang Church Cemetery.

**Bibliography:** *DAB*; Maclay, William. *The Journal of William Maclay, United States Senator From Pennsylvania, 1789-1791.* New York: F. Ungar Publishing Co., 1965.

**MACLAY, William,** a Representative from Pennsylvania; born in Lurgan Township, Franklin County, Pa., March 22, 1765; attended the country schools; studied law; was admitted to the bar in 1800 and commenced the practice of his profession at Chambersburg, Franklin County, Pa.; county commissioner in 1805 and 1806; was a member of the Pennsylvania house of representatives in 1807 and 1808; associate judge for the Cumberland district in 1809; elected as a Republican to the Fourteenth and Fifteenth Congresses (March 4, 1815-March 3, 1819); died in Lurgan, Franklin County, Pa., January 4, 1825; interment in Middle Springs Cemetery.

**MACLAY, William Brown,** a Representative from New York; born in New York City March 20, 1812; received private instruction; was graduated from the College of the City of New York in 1836; associate editor of the New York Quarterly Review in 1836; taught Latin; studied law; was admitted to the bar in 1839 and commenced the practice of his profession in New York City; member of the State assembly 1840-1842; elected as a Democrat to the Twenty-eighth, Twenty-ninth, and Thirtieth Congresses (March 4, 1843-March 3, 1849); unsuccessful candidate for reelection in 1848 to the

Thirty-first Congress; elected to the Thirty-fifth and Thirty-sixth Congresses (March 4, 1857-March 3, 1861); was not a candidate for reelection in 1860 to the Thirty-seventh Congress; died in New York City February 19, 1882; interment in Greenwood Cemetery, Brooklyn, N.Y.

**Bibliography:** *DAB*.

**MACLAY, William Plunkett** (son of Samuel Maclay and nephew of William Maclay), a Representative from Pennsylvania; born in Northumberland County, Pa., August 23, 1774; attended the common schools; prothonotary of Mifflin County 1808-1814; member of the Pennsylvania house of representatives; elected as a Republican to the Fourteenth Congress to fill the vacancy caused by the resignation of Thomas Burnside; reelected to the Fifteenth and Sixteenth Congresses and served from October 8, 1816, until March 3, 1821; was not a candidate for renomination in 1820; member of the Pennsylvania convention to alter and amend the constitution at Harrisburg, Pa., in 1837; engaged as a surveyor and in agricultural pursuits; died in Milroy, Mifflin County, Pa., September 2, 1842; interment in Milroy Presbyterian Cemetery.

**MACON, Nathaniel** (uncle of Willis Alston and Micajah Thomas Hawkins, and great-grandfather of Charles Henry Martin), a Representative and a Senator from North Carolina; born near Warrenton, Warren County, N.C., December 17, 1757; pursued classical studies and attended the College of New Jersey (now Princeton University); served in the Revolutionary War; elected to the North Carolina State senate, 1781, 1782, and 1784; moved to a plantation on the Roanoke River; elected in 1785 to the Continental Congress but declined to serve; elected to the Second and to the twelve succeeding Congresses, and served from March 4, 1791 until December 13, 1815, when he resigned, having been elected Senator; Speaker of the House of Representatives (Seventh through Ninth Congresses); chairman, Committee on Revisal and Unfinished Business (Fifth Congress), Committee on Claims (Sixth Congress), Committee on Public Expenditures (Thirteenth Congress); elected as a Republican to the United States Senate on December 5, 1815, to fill the vacancy caused by the resignation of Francis Locke; reelected in 1819 and 1825, and served from December 13, 1815 until his resignation on November 14, 1828; served as President pro tempore of the Senate during the Nineteenth Congress; chairman, Committee on Foreign Relations (Fifteenth, Nineteenth and Twentieth Congresses), Committee to Audit and Control the Contingent Expense (Seventeenth Congress); unsuccessful candidate for Vice President of the United States in 1824; president of the State constitutional convention in 1835; presidential elector on the Democratic ticket in 1836; died at "Buck Spring," near Macon, Warren County, N.C., June 29, 1837; interment at "Buck Spring."

**Bibliography:** *DAB*; Dodd, William E. *The Life of Nathaniel Macon.* Raleigh, N.C.: Edwards and Broughton, 1903; Helmes, James M., Jr. "The Early Career of Nathaniel Macon." Ph.D. dissertation, University of Virginia, 1962.

**MACON, Robert Bruce,** a Representative from Arkansas; born near Trenton, Phillips County, Ark., July 6, 1859; was left an orphan at the age of nine; attended the public schools and studied at home; engaged in agricultural pursuits; studied law; was admitted to the bar in 1891 and commenced practice in Helena, Ark.; member of the State house of representatives 1883-1887; clerk of the circuit court 1892-1896; prosecuting attorney for the first judicial district 1898-1902; elected as a Democrat to the Fifty-eighth and to the four succeeding Congresses (March 4, 1903-March 3, 1913); unsuccessful candidate for renomination; continued the practice of law in Helena, Ark., until he retired in 1917; died in Marvell, Ark., October 9, 1925; interment in Elmwood Cemetery, Memphis, Tenn.

**MACY, John B.,** a Representative from Wisconsin; born in Nantucket, Mass., March 25, 1799; received a liberal education; moved to New York City in 1826 and later in that year to Buffalo, N.Y.; resided in Cincinnati, Ohio, 1842-1845; one of the founders of Toledo, Ohio, and one of the proprietors of the Rock River Valley Railroad; moved to Fond du Lac, Wis., in 1845 and engaged in the real estate business; moved with his family to the town of Empire, near de Nevew Lake, Wis., in 1850; elected as a Democrat to the Thirty-third Congress (March 4, 1853-March 3, 1855); unsuccessful for reelection in 1854 to the Thirty-fourth Congress; resumed his former business pursuits; lost his life in the burning of the steamer *Niagara* about one mile from Port Washington on Lake Michigan on September 24, 1856; his body was never recovered.

**MACY, William Kingsland,** a Representative from New York; born in New York City, November 21, 1889; was graduated from Groton (Mass.) School in 1908 and from Harvard University in 1912; engaged in wholesaling and importing, 1912-1915; served with the United States Food Administration and War Trade Board, 1917-1919; president of Union Pacific Tea Co., 1919-1922; member of a stock brokerage firm from 1922 until 1938; banker and publisher; chairman of the Suffolk County Republican Committee from 1926 until 1951; chairman of the New York State Republican Committee, 1930-1934; delegate to the Republican National Conventions of 1928, 1932, 1940, 1944, and 1948, and to Republican State Conventions from 1928 to 1946; was active in the investigation of the New York State Banking Department in 1929, and also in promoting Samuel Seabury's inquiry into the affairs of New York City in 1931 and 1932; Regent of the State of New York, 1941-1953; member of the New York State senate in 1946; elected as a Republican to the Eightieth and Eighty-first Congresses (January 3, 1947-January 3, 1951); unsuccessful candidate for reelection in 1950 to the Eighty-second Congress; chairman of the board of Suffolk Consolidated Press Co., Inc., and of Suffolk Broadcasting Corp.; died in Islip, N.Y., July 15, 1961; remains placed in a receiving vault at Oakwood Cemetery.

**MADDEN, Martin Barnaby,** a Representative from Illinois; born in Wolviston, England, March 21, 1855; immigrated to the United States with his parents, who settled in Chicago, Ill., in 1860; attended the public schools in Chicago and was graduated from Bryant and Stratton Business College in 1873; was also graduated from an engineering trade school; president of the Quarry Owners' Association of the United States 1885-1889; vice president and director of the Builders and Traders' Exchange of Chicago in 1886 and 1887; member of the Chicago City Council 1889-1897; served as presiding officer of that body 1891-1893 and chairman of the finance committee for seven years; chairman of the Republican committee of Chicago 1890-1896; president of the Western Stone Co. 1895-1915; director of the Metropolitan Trust & Savings Bank of Chicago 1895-1910; delegate to the Republican National Conventions in 1896, 1900, 1912, 1916 and 1924; unsuccessful candidate for election in 1902 to the Fifty-eighth Congress; elected as a Republican to the Fifty-ninth and to the eleven succeeding Congresses and served from March 4, 1905, until his death; chairman, Committee on Appropriations (Sixty-eighth through Seventieth Congresses); had been nominated for reelection to the Seventy-first Congress; died in the room of the Committee on Appropriations of the House of Representatives, Capitol Building, Washington, D.C., April 27, 1928; interment in Fairview Cemetery, near Hinsdale, Du Page County, Ill.

**Bibliography:** *DAB*; Bullard, Thomas Robert. "From Businessman to Congressman: The Careers of Martin B. Madden." Ph.D. dissertation, University of Illinois at Chicago Circle, 1973.

**MADDEN, Ray John,** a Representative from Indiana; born in Waseca, Minn., February 25, 1892; attended the public schools and Sacred Heart Academy in his native city; LL.B., Creighton

University School of Law, Omaha, Nebr., 1913; was admitted to the bar the same year and commenced practice in Omaha, Nebr.; elected municipal judge of Omaha, Nebr., in 1916, resigning during the First World War to serve in the United States Navy; engaged in the practice of law in Gary, Ind.; city comptroller of Gary, 1935-1938; treasurer of Lake County, Ind., 1938-1942; delegate to every State convention, beginning in 1936; delegate to every Democratic National Convention from 1940 through 1968; elected as a Democrat to the Seventy-eighth and to the sixteen succeeding Congresses (January 3, 1943-January 3, 1977); co-chairman, Joint Committee on Organization of Congress (Eighty-ninth and Ninetieth Congresses), chairman, Committee on Rules (Ninety-third and Ninety-fourth Congresses); unsuccessful candidate for renomination in 1976 to the Ninety-fifth Congress; was a resident of Washington, D.C., until his death there on September 28, 1987; interment in Arlington National Cemetery, Va.

**MADDOX, John W.,** a Representative from Georgia; born on a farm near Gore, Chattooga County, Ga., June 3, 1848; attended the common schools; during the Civil War enlisted in the Confederate Army in Company E, Sixth Georgia Cavalry, in 1863 and served until the end of the war; attended school in Summerville and Bethel Church; engaged in agricultural pursuits and in railroad construction work in 1871; deputy sheriff of Chattooga County; studied law; was admitted to the bar in 1877 and commenced practice in Summerville, Ga.; mayor of Summerville in 1877; county commissioner 1878-1880; member of the State house of representatives 1880-1884; served in the State senate 1884-1886; elected judge of the superior court, Rome circuit, in 1886, and was reelected in 1890, resigning the office September 1, 1892; moved to Rome, Ga., in 1890; elected as a Democrat to the Fifty-third and to the five succeeding Congresses (March 4, 1893-March 3, 1905); was not a candidate for renomination in 1904; resumed the practice of law; mayor of Rome in 1906 and 1907; appointed judge of the Superior Court of Georgia in 1908; elected in 1910 and served until his resignation on February 1, 1912, having become president of the State Mutual Life Insurance Co.; also engaged in the practice of law; died in Rome, Ga., September 27, 1922; interment in Myrtle Hill Cemetery.

**MADIGAN, Edward Rell,** a Representative from Illinois; born in Lincoln, Logan County, Ill., January 13, 1936; attended the local schools; A.A., Lincoln (Ill.) Junior College, 1955; manager and owner of a taxicab fleet and car leasing firm; served on the Lincoln Board of Zoning Appeals, 1965-1969; member, Illinois State house of representatives, 1967-1972; delegate, Illinois State Republican convention, 1966; delegate to the Republican National Convention of 1980; elected as a Republican to the Ninety-third and to the nine succeeding Congresses and served from January 3, 1973, until his resignation on March 8, 1991; appointed Secretary of Agriculture in the Cabinet of President George Bush, and served from March 12, 1991 until January 20, 1993; was a resident of Lincoln, Ill.; died December 7, 1994.

**MADISON, Edmond Haggard,** a Representative from Kansas; born in Plymouth, Hancock County, Ill., December 18, 1865; attended the common schools; taught school; moved to Wichita, Kans., in 1885; studied law; was admitted to the bar in 1888 and commenced the practice of his profession in Dodge City, Kans.; prosecuting attorney of Ford County, Kans., 1889-1893; appointed judge of the thirty-first judicial district of Kansas on January 1, 1900, and served until September 17, 1906, when he resigned to become a candidate for Congress; elected as a Republican to the Sixtieth, Sixty-first, and Sixty-second Congresses and served from March 4, 1907, until his death in Dodge City, Ford County, Kans., September 18, 1911; interment in Maple Grove Cemetery.

**MADISON, James,** a Delegate and a Representative from Virginia and 4th President of the United States; born in Port Conway, King George County, Va., March 16, 1751; studied under private tutors and was graduated from Princeton College in 1771; member of the committee of safety from Orange County in 1774; delegate in the Williamsburg (Va.) convention of May 1776; member of the First General Assembly of Virginia in 1776 and was unanimously elected a member of the executive council in 1778; Member of the Continental Congress, 1780-1783, and 1787-1788; delegate in the Federal Constitutional Convention at Philadelphia, Pa., in 1787; elected to the First Congress; reelected to the Second and Third Congresses and reelected as a Republican to the Fourth Congress (March 4, 1789-March 3, 1797); declined the mission to France, tendered by President George Washington in 1794 and also the position of Secretary of State, tendered the same year; again a member of the Virginia Assembly from Orange County in 1799; appointed by President Thomas Jefferson as Secretary of State on March 5, 1801; entered upon the duties of that office on May 2, 1801, and served until March 4, 1809; elected President of the United States in 1808; reelected in 1812, and served from March 4, 1809, to March 3, 1817; retired to his estate, "Montpelier," Orange County, Va.; delegate to the Virginia constitutional convention of 1829; rector of the University of Virginia at Charlottesville and visitor to the College of William and Mary, Williamsburg, Va.; died in the "Montpelier" mansion, Orange County, Va., June 28, 1836; interment in the private cemetery on the grounds at "Montpelier."

**Bibliography:** *DAB*; Brant, Irving. *James Madison*. 6 vols. Indianapolis: Bobbs-Merrill, 1948-1961; Madison, James. *The Papers of James Madison*. 17 vols. to date. Edited by William T. Hutchinson, William M.E. Rachal, and Robert Allen Rutland. Chicago: University of Chicago Press, 1962-1976; Charlottesville: University Press of Virginia, 1977-.

**MAFFETT, James Thompson,** a Representative from Pennsylvania; born in Clarion Township, Clarion County, Pa., February 2, 1837; attended the common schools, Rimersburg Academy, and Jefferson College, Canonsburg, Pa.; taught school in Missouri for one year, and then, in 1859, moved to California, where he taught school in Amador County and began the study of law; returned to Pennsylvania in 1870 and continued the study of law; was admitted to the bar in Brookville, Pa., in 1872 and commenced the practice of his profession in Clarion, Pa.; unsuccessful candidate for the Republican nomination for Congress in 1884; elected as a Republican to the Fiftieth Congress (March 4, 1887-March 3, 1889); was not a candidate for renomination in 1888; resumed the practice of his profession; died in Clarion, Pa., on December 19, 1912; interment in Clarion Cemetery.

**MAGEE, Clare,** a Representative from Missouri; born on a farm in Putnam County near Livonia, Mo., March 31, 1899; graduate of Unionville (Mo.) High School; student in Kirksville State Teachers College in 1916; during the First World War served in the United States Navy as a seaman first-class and small-arms instructor; homesteaded in Big Horn Basin, Wyo., and worked as a laborer for the United States Reclamation Service at Deaver, Wyo., in 1920 and 1921; was graduated from the University of Missouri at Columbia in 1922; admitted to the bar in 1922 and commenced the practice of law in Unionville, Putnam County, Mo.; owned and operated the farm where he was born, beginning in 1932; postmaster of Unionville, Mo., 1935-1941; served as a private in the Field Artillery, United States Army, in 1942 and as a captain in the Army Air Corps, 1942-1944; elected as a Democrat to the Eighty-first and Eighty-second Congresses (January 3, 1949-January 3, 1953); was not a candidate for renomination in 1952 to the Eighty-third Congress; resumed the practice of law; died in Unionville, Mo., August 7, 1969; interment in Unionville Cemetery.

**MAGEE, James McDevitt,** a Representative from Pennsylvania; born in Evergreen, near Pittsburgh, Pa., April 5, 1877; attended the common schools; was graduated from Yale University in 1899 and from the law department of the University of Pennsylvania at

Philadelphia in 1902; was admitted to the bar in 1903 and commenced practice at Pittsburgh, Pa.; was commissioned a first lieutenant in the Air Service during the First World War; promoted to captain and served until January 1919; later commissioned a lieutenant colonel in the Reserve; during his entire period of service was attached to the executive office of the Department of Military Aeronautics; elected as a Republican to the Sixty-eighth and Sixty-ninth Congresses (March 4, 1923-March 3, 1927); unsuccessful candidate for renomination in 1926; chairman, Pennsylvania Securities Commission, Harrisburg, Pa., 1931-1935; continued the practice of law in Pittsburgh, Pa., until his death there on April 16, 1949; interment in Calvary Cemetery.

**MAGEE, John,** a Representative from New York; born in Easton, Northumberland County, Pa., September 3, 1794; attended the common schools; served in the War of 1812; moved to Bath, Steuben County, N.Y., in 1812; elected constable in 1818 and served until 1820; appointed sheriff of Steuben County in 1821 and elected to that office in 1822; elected to the Twentieth Congress and reelected as a Jacksonian to the Twenty-first Congress (March 4, 1827-March 3, 1831); was not a candidate for renomination in 1830; delegate to the State constitutional convention in 1867; devoted the remaining years of his life to banking, railroading, and was also interested in mining; died at Watkins, Schuyler County, N.Y., April 5, 1868; interment in Glenwood Cemetery.

**MAGEE, John Alexander,** a Representative from Pennsylvania; born in Landisburg, Perry County, Pa., October 14, 1827; attended the common schools and was graduated from New Bloomfield Academy; engaged in the printing business and for a number of years published the Perry County Democrat; member of the Pennsylvania house of representatives in 1863; delegate to the Democratic National Convention in 1868, 1876, and 1896; elected as a Democrat to the Forty-third Congress (March 4, 1873-March 3, 1875); was an unsuccessful candidate for renomination in 1874 to the Forty-fourth Congress; resumed his former business pursuits; died in New Bloomfield, Perry County, Pa., November 18, 1903; interment in Bloomfield Cemetery.

**MAGEE, Walter Warren,** a Representative from New York; born in Groveland, Livingston County, N.Y., May 23, 1861; attended the common schools and Geneseo State Normal School; was graduated from Phillips Exeter Academy, Exeter, N.H., in 1885 and from Harvard University in 1889; studied law; was admitted to the bar in 1891 and commenced practice in Syracuse, N.Y.; served as a member of the board of supervisors of Onondaga County in 1892 and 1893; corporation counsel of Syracuse 1904-1914; elected as a Republican to the Sixty-fourth and to the six succeeding Congresses and served from March 4, 1915, until his death in Syracuse, N.Y., May 25, 1927; interment in Oakwood Cemetery.

**MAGINNIS, Martin,** a Delegate from the Territory of Montana; born near Pultneyville, Wayne County, N.Y., October 27, 1841; moved with his parents to Minnesota in 1852; pursued an academic course; attended Hamline University, but left to take charge of a Democratic newspaper; enlisted as a private in the First Regiment, Minnesota Volunteer Infantry, April 18, 1861; promoted to first lieutenant in September 1862 and to captain in July 1863; appointed major of the Eleventh Minnesota Volunteers in September 1864 and ordered to join the Army of the Cumberland, where he served under the command of General Thomas until mustered out with his regiment in July 1865; moved to Helena, Mont., in 1866; engaged in mining and subsequently in publishing and editing the Helena Daily Gazette; elected as a Democrat to the Forty-third and to the five succeeding Congresses (March 4, 1873-March 3, 1885); unsuccessful Democratic candidate for election in 1890 to the Fifty-first Congress; presented credentials on May 25, 1900, as a Senator-designate to fill the vacancy caused by the resignation of William A. Clark, but was not seated; State commissioner of mineral land 1890-1893; died in Los Angeles, Calif., March 27, 1919; interment in Resurrection Cemetery, Helena, Mont.

**Bibliography:** *DAB.*

**MAGNER, Thomas Francis** (uncle of John Francis Carew), a Representative from New York; born in Brooklyn, N.Y. March 8, 1860; attended the public schools; was graduated from St. Xavier College in 1880 and from Columbia University, New York City, in 1882; taught in a public school in Brooklyn; studied law; was admitted to the bar in 1883 and commenced practice in Brooklyn, N.Y., the same year; member of the State assembly in 1888; elected as a Democrat to the Fifty-first, Fifty-second, and Fifty-third Congresses (March 4, 1889-March 3, 1895); declined to be a candidate for renomination in 1894; resumed the practice of law; corporation counsel of the Borough of Brooklyn 1913-1917; continued the practice of his profession in Brooklyn, N.Y., until his death there on December 22, 1945; interment in Holy Cross Cemetery.

**MAGNUSON, Donald Hammer,** a Representative from Washington; born on a farm near Freeman, Spokane County, Wash., March 7, 1911; attended the public schools and Spokane University, 1926-1928; was graduated from the University of Washington at Seattle in 1931; after graduation worked as a harvester and then as a riveter in an aircraft factory; newspaper reporter for the Daily Olympian and Seattle Times, 1934-1952; elected as a Democrat to the Eighty-third and to the four succeeding Congresses (January 3, 1953-January 3, 1963); unsuccessful candidate for reelection in 1962 to the Eighty-eighth Congress; employed by the United States Department of the Interior, 1963-1969, and by the Department of Labor, 1969-1973; resided in Seattle, Wash., where he died on October 5, 1979; interment in Evergreen-Washelli Memorial Park.

**MAGNUSON, Warren Grant,** a Representative and a Senator from Washington; born in Moorhead, Clay County, Minn., April 12, 1905; attended the public schools; attended the University of North Dakota at Grand Forks, 1923, and North Dakota State College, 1923-1924; graduated from the University of Washington in 1926; LL.B., University of Washington School of Law, 1929; was admitted to the bar in 1929 and commenced practice in Seattle, Wash.; secretary of the Seattle Municipal League in 1930 and 1931; served as special prosecuting attorney of King County, Wash., in 1931; member, Washington State house of representatives, 1933-1934; delegate to the State constitutional convention in 1933; served in the United States Navy during the Second World War, attaining the rank of lieutenant commander; United States district attorney in 1934 and prosecuting attorney of King County, Wash., 1934-1936; elected as a Democrat to the Seventy-fifth and to the three succeeding Congresses and served from January 3, 1937, until his resignation on December 13, 1944; appointed to the United States Senate to fill the vacancy caused by the resignation of Homer T. Bone, and served from December 14, 1944, to January 3, 1945; elected in 1944 for the term commencing January 3, 1945; reelected in 1950, 1956, 1962, 1968, and again in 1974, and served from December 14, 1944, to January 3, 1981; served as President pro tempore of the Senate during the Ninety-sixth Congress; unsuccessful candidate for reelection in 1980; chairman, Committee on Interstate and Foreign Commerce (Eighty-fourth through Eighty-seventh Congresses), Committee on Commerce (Eighty-eighth through Ninety-fifth Congresses), Committee on Commerce, Science and Transportation (Ninety-fifth Congress), Committee on Appropriations (Ninety-fifth and Ninety-sixth Congresses); resumed the practice of law; died May 20, 1989.

**Bibliography:** Magnuson, Warren G. *How Much for Health?* Washington, D.C.: R.B. Luce, 1974; Magnuson, Warren G. *The Dark Side of the Marketplace: The Plight of the American Consumer.* Englewood Cliffs, N.J.: Prentice-Hall, 1968; McMannon, Timothy Joseph. "Warren G. Magnuson and Consumer Protection." Ph.D. dissertation, University of Washington, 1994.

**MAGOON, Henry Sterling,** a Representative from Wisconsin; born in Monticello, Lafayette County, Wis., January 31, 1832; attended the Rock River Seminary, Mount Morris, Ill., and was graduated from the Western Military College, Drennon, Ky., in 1853; studied law in the Montrose Law School, Frankfort, Ky.; was admitted to the bar in 1857 and commenced practice in Shullsburg, Wis.; professor of ancient languages in Nashville (Tenn.) University from 1855 until 1857; returned to Wisconsin and practiced law at Darlington, Lafayette County; elected district attorney in 1858; member of the Wisconsin State senate in 1871 and 1872; elected as a Republican to the Forty-fourth Congress (March 4, 1875-March 3, 1877); was not a candidate for renomination in 1876 to the Forty-fifth Congress; resumed the practice of law in Milwaukee, Wis.; regent of the University of Wisconsin at Madison for one term; first native of Wisconsin to serve in the State senate or in the House of Representatives; died while on a visit to his summer home in Darlington, Wis., March 3, 1889; interment in Union Grove Cemetery.

**MAGRADY, Frederick William,** a Representative from Pennsylvania; born near Pottsville, Schuylkill County, Pa., November 24, 1863; attended the public schools in Mount Carmel Township and was graduated from the Pennsylvania normal school (now Bloomsburg State Teachers' College) at Bloomsburg, Pa., in 1890; taught school thirteen years in Mount Carmel Borough; engaged in the coal business for a short time at Gauley, W.Va.; was graduated from Dickinson School of Law, Carlisle, Pa., in 1909; was admitted to the bar the same year and commenced practice in Mount Carmel, Pa.; director and solicitor of the First National Bank of Mount Carmel; president and solicitor of the Shamokin-Mount Carmel Transit Co., and of the Ashland & Shamokin Auto Bus Co., Inc.; director of the Mount Carmel Water Co.; elected as a Republican to the Sixty-ninth and to the three succeeding Congresses (March 4, 1925-March 3, 1933); unsuccessful candidate for renomination in 1932; resumed the practice of law; died in Danville, Pa., August 27, 1954; interment in Mount Carmel Cemetery, Mount Carmel, Pa.

**MAGRUDER, Allan Bowie,** a Senator from Louisiana; born in Kentucky in 1775; attended the common schools; pursued an academic course; studied law; was admitted to the bar in 1796 and practiced in Lexington, Ky.; moved to Louisiana and practiced his profession; member, State house of representatives; elected as a Republican to the United States Senate and served from September 3, 1812, to March 3, 1813; resumed the practice of law; died in Opelousas, St. Landry Parish, La., April 16, 1822.

**MAGRUDER, Patrick,** a Representative from Maryland; born at "Locust Grove," near Rockville, Montgomery County, Md., in 1768; attended Princeton College a short time; studied law; was admitted to the bar and practiced; elected as a Republican to the Ninth Congress (March 4, 1805-March 3, 1807); Clerk of the House of Representatives from March 4, 1807, until his resignation on January 18, 1815; Librarian of Congress from 1807 until January 18, 1815, when he resigned; died in Petersburg, Va., on December 24, 1819; interment in the family burying ground on the ancestral estate, "Sweden," near Petersburg, Dinwiddie County, Va.

Bibliography: Gordon, Martin K. "Patrick Magruder: Citizen, Congressman, Librarian of Congress." *Quarterly Journal of the Library of Congress* 32 (July 1975): 154-71.

**MAGUIRE, Gene Andrew,** a Representative from New Jersey; born in Columbus, Franklin County, Ohio, March 11, 1939; attended Budlong Elementary School, Los Angeles, Calif.; graduated, Ridgewood (N.J.) High School, 1956; B.A., Oberlin (Ohio) College, 1961; Ph.D., government, Harvard University, 1966; adviser on political and security affairs, United States Department of State, 1966-1969; member, United States Delegation to the United Nations General Assembly for five sessions while with the United States Department of State; director, urban development program for Jamaica, N.Y.,

1969-1972; consultant, National Affairs Division, Ford Foundation, 1972-1974; elected as a Democrat to the Ninety-fourth and to the two succeeding Congresses (January 3, 1975-January 3, 1981); unsuccessful candidate for reelection in 1980 to the Ninety-seventh Congress; industrial and labor consultant, 1981; unsuccessful candidate in 1982 for nomination to the United States Senate; fellow, Institute of Politics, John F. Kennedy School of Government, Harvard University, 1983; vice president for policy, World Resources Institute, 1984-1987; chief executive officer, North American Securities Administrators Association, 1987 to present; is a resident of Ringoes, N.J.

**MAGUIRE, James George,** a Representative from California; born in Boston, Mass., February 22, 1853; moved with his parents to California in April 1854; attended the public schools of Watsonville, Santa Cruz County, Calif., and the private academy of Joseph K. Fallon in Watsonville; member of the California State assembly, 1875-1877; studied law; was admitted to the bar by the supreme court of California in January 1878 and commenced practice in San Francisco, Calif.; judge of the superior court of the city and county of San Francisco, 1882-1888; elected as a Democrat to the Fifty-third and to the two succeeding Congresses (March 4, 1893-March 3, 1899); was not a candidate for renomination in 1898 to the Fifty-sixth Congress, but was an unsuccessful candidate for election for Governor of California; resumed the practice of law in San Francisco, Calif., and died in that city on June 20, 1920; interment in Greenlawn Cemetery.

**MAGUIRE, John Arthur,** a Representative from Nebraska; born near Elizabeth, Jo Daviess County, Ill., November 29, 1870; moved to Dakota Territory in 1882 with his parents, who settled near Plankinton, Aurora County (now in South Dakota); attended the district school, and was graduated from the Plankinton High School in 1889; taught in the district and city schools; attended the Agricultural College of South Dakota at Brookings, 1890-1893; was graduated from the Iowa State College of Agriculture at Ames in 1893, and from the law department of the University of Nebraska at Lincoln in 1899; deputy treasurer of Lancaster County, 1899-1901; was admitted to the bar in 1899 and commenced practice in Lincoln, Nebr., in 1902; delegate to the Democratic National Convention of 1904; secretary to the Democratic State committee in 1905; elected as a Democrat to the Sixty-first and to the two succeeding Congresses (March 4, 1909-March 3, 1915); unsuccessful candidate for reelection in 1914 to the Sixty-fourth Congress; resumed the practice of law in Lincoln, Nebr.; appointed a municipal judge on January 1, 1938, to fill an unexpired term; died in Lincoln, Nebr., July 1, 1939; interment in Calvary Cemetery.

**MAHAN, Bryan Francis,** a Representative from Connecticut; born in New London, New London County, Conn., May 1, 1856; attended the public schools and was graduated from the Robert Bartlett High School; learned the trade of plumber; studied law at the Albany (N.Y.) Law School, from which he graduated in 1880; was admitted to the bar in 1881 and commenced practice in New London; member of the State house of representatives in 1882 and 1883; member of the board of school visitors 1885-1887, and served as secretary; appointed prosecuting attorney in 1891, but resigned in 1892; one of the organizers of the City of Richmond Steamboat Co. in 1893 and served as president; postmaster of New London from October 30, 1894, to December 20, 1898; served as mayor 1904-1906 and 1910-1913; member of the State senate in 1910 and 1911; delegate to the Democratic National Conventions in 1904, 1908, 1912, and 1916; elected as a Democrat to the Sixty-third Congress (March 4, 1913-March 3, 1915); unsuccessful candidate for reelection in 1914 to the Sixty-fourth Congress; again appointed postmaster of New London, Conn., March 23, 1915, and served until his death there on November 16, 1923; interment in St. Mary's Cemetery.

**MAHANY, Rowland Blennerhassett,** a Representative from New York; born in Buffalo, N.Y., September 28, 1864; attended the public schools, Hobart College, Geneva, N.Y., and Union College, Schenectady, N.Y.; was graduated from Harvard University in 1888; studied law in Buffalo, N.Y.; associate editor of the Buffalo Express in 1888; instructor in Buffalo High School, 1889-1890; declined the appointment as secretary of the legation to Chile in 1890; appointed Envoy Extraordinary and Minister Plenipotentiary to Ecuador on February 24, 1892, and served until June 1893; unsuccessful candidate for election in 1892 to the Fifty-third Congress; returned to Ecuador in 1893 and concluded the Santos Convention; elected as a Republican to the Fifty-fourth and Fifty-fifth Congresses (March 4, 1895-March 3, 1899); unsuccessful candidate for reelection in 1898 to the Fifty-sixth Congress; was admitted to the bar in 1899 and engaged in the practice of law in Buffalo, N.Y.; harbor commissioner of Buffalo, 1899-1906; editor of the Buffalo Enquirer, 1910-1911; commissioner of conciliation, United States Department of Labor, 1914-1915; assistant to Secretary of Labor William B. Wilson, 1918-1919; member of the Foreign Trades Relation Committee of the State Department in 1919; appointed by President Woodrow Wilson as one of the ten Federal umpires for the War Labor Board in 1919; member of the United States Housing Corporation in 1919; appointed representative of the United States to the International Commission on Immigration and Emigration at Geneva, Switzerland, in 1920; solicitor and Acting Secretary of Labor, 1920-1921; resumed the practice of law in Washington, D.C., retaining his residence in Buffalo, N.Y.; delegate to the Democratic National Conventions of 1924 and 1928; died in Washington, D.C., May 2, 1937; interment in the Congressional Cemetery.

**MAHER, James Paul,** a Representative from New York; born in Brooklyn, N.Y., November 3, 1865; was graduated from St. Patrick's Academy, Brooklyn, N.Y.; apprenticed to the hatter's trade; moved to Danbury, Conn., in 1887 and was employed as a journeyman hatter; treasurer of the United Hatters of North America in 1897; returned to Brooklyn in 1902; unsuccessful candidate for election in 1908 to the Sixty-first Congress; elected as a Democrat to the Sixty-second and to the four succeeding Congresses (March 4, 1911-March 3, 1921); chairman, Committee on Expenditures in the Department of Labor (Sixty-third through Sixty-fifth Congresses); unsuccessful candidate for reelection in 1920 to the Sixty-seventh Congress; engaged in the real estate business in Brooklyn, N.Y.; moved to Keansburg, Monmouth County, N.J., and continued in the real estate business; elected mayor of Keansburg in 1926; died in Keansburg on July 31, 1946; interment in St. Joseph's Cemetery, Keyport, N.J.

**MAHON, Gabriel Heyward, Jr.,** a Representative from South Carolina; born in Williamston, Anderson County, S.C., November 11, 1889; moved with his parents to Greenville, S.C., in 1898; attended the public schools and the Citadel, Charleston, S.C.; employed as a clerk in a retail store 1900-1907 and as a traveling salesman 1907-1911; engaged in the retail clothing business in 1911; during the First World War served as a captain and later as a major of the First Battalion of the One Hundred and Eighteenth Infantry, Thirtieth Division, American Expeditionary Forces; awarded the Purple Heart and the Silver Star medal; trustee of Greenville Woman's College, Greenville, S.C., 1921-1936; elected as a Democrat to the Seventy-fourth Congress to fill the vacancy caused by the death of John J. McSwain and on the same day was elected to the Seventy-fifth Congress and served from November 3, 1936, to January 3, 1939; unsuccessful candidate for renomination in 1938; resumed former business pursuits in Greenville, S.C., until his death there June 11, 1962; interment in Woodlawn Memorial Park Mausoleum.

**MAHON, George Herman,** a Representative from Texas; born in the village of Mahon, near Haynesville, Claiborne Parish, La., September 22, 1900; moved to Texas in 1908 with his family, who settled on a farm near Loraine, Mitchell County; attended the public schools; was graduated from the high school at Loraine, Tex., in 1918; Simmons University, Abilene, Tex., B.A., 1924, and from the law department of the University of Texas at Austin, LL.B., 1925; also attended the University of Minnesota at Minneapolis; was admitted to the bar in 1925 and commenced practice in Colorado (now Colorado City), Tex.; elected county attorney of Mitchell County, Tex., in 1926; district attorney of the thirty-second judicial district of Texas, 1927-1933; delegate to each Democratic National Convention 1936-1964; regent of the Smithsonian Institution, 1964-1978; elected as a Democrat to the Seventy-fourth and to the twenty-one succeeding Congresses (January 3, 1935-January 3, 1979); chairman, Committee on Appropriations (Eighty-eighth through Ninety-fifth Congresses), Joint Committee on Reduction of Federal Expenditures (Ninetieth through Ninety-third Congresses); was not a candidate for reelection in 1978 to the Ninety-sixth Congress; was a resident of Colorado City, Tex., until his death on November 19, 1985, in San Angelo, Tex.; interment in Loraine City Cemetery, Loraine, Tex.

**MAHON, Thaddeus Maclay,** a Representative from Pennsylvania; born in Green Village, Franklin County, Pa., May 21, 1840; pursued an academic course; during the Civil War enlisted as a private in Company A, One Hundred and Twenty-sixth Regiment, Pennsylvania Volunteers, in August 1862; after a term of service in this regiment reenlisted as a veteran in January 1864 in the Twenty-first Regiment, Pennsylvania Volunteer Cavalry, and served until September 1865; studied law; admitted to the bar in 1871 and commenced practice in southern Pennsylvania; member of the Pennsylvania house of representatives 1870-1872; president of Baltimore & Cumberland Valley Railroad; member of the commission having charge of the soldiers' orphan schools of Pennsylvania; unsuccessful candidate for election in 1876 to the Forty-fourth Congress; elected as a Republican to the Fifty-third and to the six succeeding Congresses (March 4, 1893-March 3, 1907); chairman, Committee on War Claims (Fifty-fourth through Fifty-ninth Congresses); was not a candidate for renomination in 1906; engaged in business in Chambersburg, Franklin County, Pa.; died in Scotland, Franklin County, Pa., May 31, 1916; interment in Cedar Grove Cemetery, Chambersburg, Pa.

**MAHONE, William,** a Senator from Virginia; born in Southampton County, Va., December 1, 1826; was graduated from the Virginia Military Institute at Lexington in 1847; taught two years at the Rappahannock Military Academy; became a civil engineer with the Norfolk & Petersburg Railroad and rose to president, chief engineer, and superintendent; joined the Confederate Army and took part in the capture of Norfolk Navy Yard; was commissioned brigadier general and major general in 1864; at the close of the Civil War returned to railroad engineering, and became president of the Norfolk and Western; elected to the United States Senate as a Readjuster and served from March 4, 1881, until March 3, 1887; unsuccessful candidate for reelection in 1887; chairman, Committee on Agriculture (Forty-seventh Congress), Committee on Public Buildings and Grounds (Forty-eighth and Forty-ninth Congresses); died in Washington, D.C., October 8, 1895; interment in Blandford Cemetery, Petersburg, Dinwiddie County, Va.

**Bibliography:** *DAB*; Blake, Nelson. *William Mahone of Virginia: Soldier and Political Insurgent.* Richmond: Garrett and Massie, 1935.

**MAHONEY, Peter Paul,** a Representative from New York; born in New York City June 25, 1848; educated in the common schools of New York City; engaged in the dry-goods business for several years; moved to Brooklyn, N.Y., and engaged in the sale of liquor; elected as a Democrat to the Forty-ninth and Fiftieth Congresses (March 4, 1885-March 3, 1889); was not a candidate in 1888 for reelection to the Fifty-first Congress; became ill while attending the inauguration ceremonies of President Benjamin Harrison March 4, 1889, and died in Washington, D.C., March 27, 1889; interment in Calvary Cemetery, Long Island City, Queens County, N.Y.

**MAHONEY, William Frank,** a Representative from Illinois; born in Chicago, Ill., February 22, 1856; educated in the public schools of Chicago; engaged in mercantile pursuits in 1876; served as alderman in the Chicago City Council from 1884 to 1887 and again from 1890 to 1896; elected as a Democrat to the Fifty-seventh and Fifty-eighth Congresses and served from March 4, 1901, until his death in Chicago, Ill., December 27, 1904; interment in Calvary Cemetery, Evanston, Cook County, Ill.

**MAILLIARD, William Somers,** a Representative from California; born in Belvedere, Marin County, Calif., June 10, 1917; attended elementary and secondary schools in the San Francisco Bay area, and the Taft School, Watertown, Conn., 1933-1935; B.A., Yale University, 1939; engaged in the banking business with American Trust Co., San Francisco, Calif., in 1940 and 1941; served as assistant naval attache in the United States Embassy in London in 1939 and 1940; with Bureau of Naval Personnel, Washington, D.C., in 1941 and 1942; attended the Naval War College in 1942; was assigned to duty on staff of Seventh Amphibious Force as flag lieutenant and aide to Vice Admiral D.E. Barbey in 1943 and released to inactive duty in March 1946 as a lieutenant commander; promoted to commander in 1950 and to rear admiral in 1965 in the Naval Reserve; resumed his banking career in 1946 and 1947; assistant to the director of California Youth Authority in 1947 and 1948; unsuccessful Republican candidate for election in 1948 to the Eighty-first Congress; secretary to Governor Earl Warren, 1948-1951; executive assistant to the director of the California Academy of Sciences in 1951 and 1952; elected as a Republican to the Eighty-third and to the ten succeeding Congresses, and served from January 3, 1953, until his resignation March 5, 1974; Permanent Representative of the United States to the Organization of American States, with the rank of Ambassador, March 7, 1974, to February 1, 1977; nominated by President Gerald R. Ford and confirmed by the United States Senate on December 10, 1975, to be a member of the Board of Directors of the Inter-American Foundation; was a resident of San Francisco, Calif; died June 10, 1992.

**MAIN, Verner Wright,** a Representative from Michigan; born in Ashley, Delaware County, Ohio, December 16, 1885; attended the public schools; was graduated from Marion (Ohio) High School, from Hillsdale (Mich.) College in 1907, and from the law department of the University of Michigan at Ann Arbor in 1914; principal of the high schools at Hudson, Mich., in 1908 and 1909 and at Niles, Mich., 1909-1912; was admitted to the bar in 1914 and commenced the practice of law in Battle Creek, Mich.; during the First World War volunteered for military service with the Field Artillery and was in training at the officers' training camp at Louisville, Ky., when the armistice was signed; assistant prosecuting attorney of Calhoun County in 1926; served in the Michigan State house of representatives, 1927-1929; member of the Battle Creek School Board, 1929-1932; elected as a Republican to the Seventy-fourth Congress to fill the vacancy caused by the death of Henry M. Kimball and served from December 17, 1935, to January 3, 1937; unsuccessful candidate for renomination in 1936 to the Seventy-fifth Congress; resumed the practice of law; died in Battle Creek, Mich., July 6, 1965; interment in Oak Hill Cemetery.

**MAISH, Levi,** a Representative from Pennsylvania; born in Conewago Township, York County, Pa., November 22, 1837; attended the common schools and the York County Academy; taught school in Manchester Township and in York; during the Civil War recruited a company for the Union Army in 1862, and with it joined

the One Hundred and Thirtieth Regiment, Pennsylvania Volunteer Infantry; was promoted to lieutenant colonel; promoted to colonel after the Battle of Fredericksburg; mustered out with his regiment at the expiration of its term of service on May 21, 1863; attended lectures in the law department of the University of Pennsylvania at Philadelphia, and was admitted to the bar in 1864; member of the Pennsylvania house of representatives in 1867 and 1868; appointed by the legislature in 1872 to a commission to reexamine and reaudit the accounts of certain public officers of York County; elected as a Democrat to the Forty-fourth and Forty-fifth Congresses (March 4, 1875-March 3, 1879); was an unsuccessful candidate for reelection in 1878 to the Forty-sixth Congress; elected to the Fiftieth and Fifty-first Congresses (March 4, 1887-March 3, 1891); was an unsuccessful candidate for reelection in 1890 to the Fifty-second Congress; engaged in the practice of law in Washington, D.C., until his death there on February 26, 1899; interment in Arlington National Cemetery, Va.

**MAJOR, James Earl,** a Representative from Illinois; born in Donellson, Montgomery County, Ill., January 5, 1887; attended the common and high schools of his native city; was graduated from Brown's Business College in 1907 and from the Illinois College of Law at Chicago in 1909; was admitted to the bar in 1910 and commenced the practice of law in Hillsboro, Ill.; prosecuting attorney of Montgomery County, 1912-1920; elected as a Democrat to the Sixty-eighth Congress (March 4, 1923-March 3, 1925); unsuccessful candidate for reelection in 1924 to the Sixty-ninth Congress; resumed the practice of the legal profession in Hillsboro, Ill.; elected to the Seventieth Congress (March 4, 1927-March 3, 1929); unsuccessful candidate for reelection in 1928 to the Seventy-first Congress; elected to the Seventy-second Congress; reelected to the Seventy-third Congress and served from March 4, 1931, until his resignation October 6, 1933, having been appointed to the bench; one of the managers appointed by the House of Representatives in 1933 to conduct the impeachment proceedings against Harold Louderback, judge of the United States District Court for the Northern District of California; appointed as a judge of the United States District Court for the Southern District of Illinois and served until March 23, 1937, when he was appointed as a judge of the United States Circuit Court of Appeals for the Seventh Circuit, in which capacity he served until March 23, 1956, when he voluntarily retired; served as chief judge of the court from November 17, 1948, until September 1, 1954; after retirement on March 23, 1956, served part time as senior judge on the Court of Appeals and various United States district courts; resided in Hillsboro, Ill., until his death there January 4, 1972; interment in Oak Grove Cemetery.

**MAJOR, Samuel Collier,** a Representative from Missouri; born in Fayette, Howard County, Mo., July 2, 1869; attended the public schools and Central College at Fayette; was graduated from St. James Military Academy, Macon, Mo., in 1888; studied law; was admitted to the bar in 1890 and commenced practice in Fayette, Mo.; appointed prosecuting attorney of Howard County in 1892 and later was elected to the office for two terms; served in the State senate 1907-1911; unsuccessful candidate for election in 1916 to the Sixty-fifth Congress; elected as a Democrat to the Sixty-sixth Congress (March 4, 1919-March 3, 1921); unsuccessful candidate for reelection in 1920 to the Sixty-seventh Congress; resumed the practice of law in Fayette, Mo.; elected to the Sixty-eighth, Sixty-ninth, and Seventieth Congresses (March 4, 1923-March 3, 1929); unsuccessful candidate for reelection in 1928 to the Seventy-first Congress; elected to the Seventy-second Congress and served from March 4, 1931, until his death in Fayette, Mo., July 28, 1931; interment in Fayette City Cemetery.

**MAJORS, Thomas Jefferson,** a Representative from Nebraska; born in Libertyville, Jefferson County, Iowa, June 25, 1841; attended the common and select schools of Libertyville and the

Nebraska State Normal School; moved to Peru, Nebr., in 1860 and engaged in mercantile pursuits; entered the Union Army in June 1861 as first lieutenant of Company C, First Regiment, Nebraska Volunteer Infantry, and served successively as captain, major, and lieutenant colonel of that regiment; mustered out on June 15, 1866; member of the last Territorial council of Nebraska in 1866; member of the first State senate, 1867-1869; appointed assessor of internal revenue for the district of Nebraska in 1869, which office he held until the offices of collector and assessor were merged into one; elected as a Republican to the Forty-fifth Congress as a contingent (or additional) Member but did not present his credentials, subsequently elected to the Forty-fifth Congress to fill the vacancy caused by the death of Frank Welch, and served from November 5, 1878 until March 3, 1879; was reelected a contingent (or additional) Member to the Forty-sixth and Forty-seventh Congresses, but the House, on February 24, 1883, disallowed Nebraska's claim to an additional Member and refused to seat him; a director of the Citizens' State Bank of Peru; Lieutenant Governor of Nebraska, 1890-1894; unsuccessful candidate for Governor in 1894; member of the State board of education and served as its president; died in Peru, Nebr., July 11, 1932; interment in Mount Vernon Cemetery.

**MALBONE, Francis,** a Representative and a Senator from Rhode Island; born in Newport, R.I., March 20, 1759; received a limited schooling; engaged as a merchant in Newport; colonel of the Newport Artillery 1792-1809; elected to the Third and Fourth Congresses (March 4, 1793-March 3, 1797); was not a candidate for renomination; resumed his former pursuits; member, State house of representatives 1807-1808; elected as a Federalist to the United States Senate and served from March 4, 1809, until his death on the steps of the Capitol in Washington, D.C., June 4, 1809; interment in the Congressional Cemetery, Washington, D.C.

**MALBY, George Roland,** a Representative from New York; born in Canton, St. Lawrence County, N.Y., September 16, 1857; attended Canton Union School and St. Lawrence University, Canton, N.Y.; studied law; was admitted to the bar in 1881 and commenced the practice of law in Ogdensburg, St. Lawrence County, N.Y.; justice of the peace of Oswegatchie; member of the State assembly in 1890-1895; elected leader of his party in that body in 1893 and served as speaker in 1894; served in the State senate 1895-1907; elected as a Republican to the Sixtieth, Sixty-first, and Sixty-second Congresses and served from March 4, 1907, until his death in New York City July 5, 1912; interment in Ogdensburg Cemetery, Ogdensburg, N.Y.

**MALLARY, Richard Walker,** a Representative from Vermont; born in Springfield, Mass., February 21, 1929; educated at Bradford (Vt.) Academy; A.B., Dartmouth College, Hanover, N.H., 1949; operated a dairy farm in Fairlee, Vt., 1950-1970; elected chairman, Fairlee Board of Selectmen, 1951-1953; elected to the Vermont State house of representatives, 1961-1968, serving as speaker, 1966-1968; member, State senate, 1969-1970; chairman, Vermont Legislative Council, 1965-1967; delegate to the Republican National Convention of 1968; vice chairman, Governor's Committee on Administrative Coordination, 1969; trustee and treasurer, Vermont State Colleges, 1962-1965; Vermont secretary of administration, 1971; elected as a Republican to the Ninety-second Congress, January 7, 1972, by special election to fill the vacancy caused by the resignation of Robert T. Stafford; reelected to the Ninety-third Congress, and served from January 7, 1972 to January 3, 1975; was not a candidate in 1974 for reelection to the House of Representatives, but was an unsuccessful candidate for election to the United States Senate; bank vice president in Springfield, Mass., 1975-1977; secretary of administration, State of Vermont, 1977-1980; vice president, Central Vermont Public Service Corp., 1980-1983; chairman of the board of a heating company, 1984-1985; president,

Vermont Electric Power Company, 1986 to present; is a resident of Charlotte, Vt.

**MALLARY, Rollin Carolas,** a Representative from Vermont; born in Cheshire, New Haven County, Conn., May 27, 1784; was graduated from Middlebury (Vt.) College in 1805; moved to Poultney, Rutland County, Vt.; studied law; was admitted to the bar and commenced practice in Castleton, Vt., in 1807; elected trustee of the Rutland County Grammar School in 1807; secretary to the Governor and council in 1807, 1809-1812, and 1815-1819; State's attorney for Rutland County 1811-1813, 1815, and 1816; moved to Poultney in 1818; successfully contested the election of Orsamus C. Merrill to the Sixteenth Congress; reelected to the Seventeenth and to the five succeeding Congresses and served from January 13, 1820, until his death in Baltimore, Md., April 15, 1831; chairman, Committee on Manufactures (Nineteenth through Twenty-first Congresses); interment in East Poultney Cemetery, East Poultney, Vt.

**Bibliography:** *DAB*; Graffagnino, J. Kevin. "'I saw the ruin all around' and 'A comical spot you may depend': Orasmus C. Merrill, Rollin C. Mallary, and the Disputed Congressional Election of 1818." *Vermont History* 49 (Summer 1981): 159-68.

**MALLORY, Francis,** a Representative from Virginia; born at "Poplars," near Hampton, Elizabeth City County, Va., on December 12, 1807; attended the common schools and Hampton Academy; appointed midshipman in the United States Navy in 1822 and resigned in 1828; studied law but abandoned it for the study of medicine; was graduated from the medical department of the University of Pennsylvania at Philadelphia in 1831 and practiced in Norfolk, Va.; abandoned the practice of medicine and devoted himself to agricultural pursuits in Elizabeth City County, Va.; elected as a Whig to the Twenty-fifth Congress (March 4, 1837-March 3, 1839); unsuccessful candidate for reelection in 1838 to the Twenty-sixth Congress; subsequently elected to the Twenty-sixth Congress to fill the vacancy caused by the resignation of Joel Holleman; reelected to the Twenty-seventh Congress and served from December 28, 1840, to March 3, 1843; was not a candidate for renomination in 1842 to the Twenty-eighth Congress; resumed agricultural pursuits; delegate to the Southern Commercial Convention at Richmond, Va., in 1838; appointed by President Millard Fillmore as Navy agent at Norfolk on November 1, 1850, and served in this capacity until 1853, when he resigned; member of the Virginia house of delegates, 1853-1855, 1857, and 1858; member of the Common Council of Norfolk for several years; president of the Norfolk & Petersburg Railroad Co. from 1853 until 1859; died in Norfolk, Va., March 26, 1860; interment in Elmwood Cemetery.

**MALLORY, Meredith,** a Representative from New York; born in Connecticut; attended the common schools; served as supervisor of the town of Benton, Yates County, N.Y., in 1820; moved to Hammondsport, Steuben County, N.Y.; owned and operated a mill; held several local offices; member of the State assembly in 1835; served as justice of the peace in 1838; elected as a Democrat to the Twenty-sixth Congress (March 4, 1839-March 3, 1841).

**MALLORY, Robert,** a Representative from Kentucky; born at Madison Court House, Madison County, Va., November 15, 1815; attended private schools and was graduated from the University of Virginia at Charlottesville in 1827; engaged in agricultural pursuits in La Grange, Ky.; studied law; was admitted to the bar in 1837 and commenced practice in New Castle, Ky.; elected as an Opposition Party candidate to the Thirty-sixth Congress and reelected as a Unionist to the Thirty-seventh and Thirty-eighth Congresses (March 4, 1859-March 3, 1865); chairman, Committee on Roads and Canals (Thirty-sixth and Thirty-seventh Congresses); unsuccessful candidate for reelection in 1864 to the Thirty-ninth Congress; delegate to the Union National Convention at Philadelphia in 1866; one of the vice presidents of the Centennial Exhibition at

Philadelphia in 1876; resumed agricultural pursuits; died near La Grange, Ky., August 11, 1885; interment in the family cemetery at Spring Hill, Oldham County, Ky.

**MALLORY, Rufus,** a Representative from Oregon; born in Coventry, Chenango County, N.Y., January 10, 1831; attended the common schools and the Alfred (N.Y.) University; moved to New London, Iowa, and taught school 1855-1858; moved to Roseburg, Oreg., in 1858 and continued teaching; studied law; was admitted to the bar in 1860 and commenced practice in Salem, Oreg.; district attorney of the first judicial district in 1860 and of the third district 1862-1866; member of the State house of representatives in 1862; elected as a Republican to the Fortieth Congress (March 4, 1867-March 3, 1869); was not a candidate for renomination in 1868; delegate to the Republican National Conventions in 1868 and 1888; resumed the practice of law in Salem; member of the State house of representatives in 1872 and served as speaker; United States district attorney 1874-1882; commissioned as special agent of the United States Government at Singapore, British Malaysia; returned to Portland, Oreg., and resumed the practice of law in 1883; died in Portland, Multonomah County, Oreg., April 30, 1914; remains were cremated and the ashes deposited in the vaults of the Portland Cremation Association.

**MALLORY, Stephen Russell** (father of Stephen Russell Mallory [1848-1907]), a Senator from Florida; born in Trinidad, West Indies, about 1813; immigrated to the United States with his parents, who settled in Key West, Fla., in 1820; attended schools in Mobile Bay, and Nazareth, Pa.; appointed by President Andrew Jackson customs inspector at Key West in 1833; studied law; was admitted to the bar in 1840 and practiced in Key West; county judge of Monroe County, 1837-1845; appointed collector of the port of Key West in 1845; served in the Seminole War; elected as a Democrat to the United States Senate in 1851; reelected in 1857, and served from March 4, 1851 until his withdrawal on January 21, 1861, when Florida seceded; his seat was declared vacant and his name omitted from the roll by a resolution of March 14, 1861; chairman, Committee on Printing (Thirty-third Congress), Committee on Naval Affairs (Thirty-fourth through Thirty-sixth Congresses); Secretary of the Navy of the Confederacy; imprisoned at the close of the Civil War, 1865-1866; settled first in Lagrange, Troup County, Ga., then Pensacola, Fla.; engaged in the practice of law; died in Pensacola, Fla., November 9, 1873; interment in St. Michael's Cemetery.

**Bibliography:** *DAB*; Durkin, Joseph. *Confederate Navy Chief.* 1954. Reprint. Columbia: University of South Carolina Press, 1987.

**MALLORY, Stephen Russell** (son of Stephen Russell Mallory [1812-1873]), a Representative and a Senator from Florida; born in Columbia, Richland County, S.C., November 2, 1848; during the Civil War entered the Confederate Army in the fall of 1864; appointed midshipman in the Confederate Navy in the spring of 1865 and served until the end of the war; graduated from Georgetown College, Washington, D.C., in 1869, where he then served as instructor in Latin and Greek until 1871; studied law; was admitted to the bar in Louisiana in 1872 and commenced practice in New Orleans; moved to Pensacola, Fla., in 1874 and continued the practice of law; member, State house of representatives 1876; member, State senate 1880, and reelected in 1884; elected as a Democrat to the Fifty-second and Fifty-third Congresses (March 4, 1891-March 3, 1895); was not a candidate for renomination in 1894; elected as a Democrat to the United States Senate in 1897, subsequently appointed and then elected to the Senate in 1903, and served from May 15, 1897, until his death in Pensacola, Fla., December 23, 1907; chairman, Committee on Corporations Organized in the District of Columbia (Sixteenth Congress); interment in St. Michael's Cemetery.

**MALONE, George Wilson (Molly),** a Senator from Nevada; born in Fredonia, Wilson County, Kans., August 7, 1890; attended the public schools; graduated from the University of Nevada at Reno in 1917; engaged as a civil and hydraulic engineer at Reno, Nev., in 1914; during the First World War enlisted as a private in the Field Artillery; promoted to sergeant, and became a lieutenant and regimental intelligence officer, serving in Great Britain and France, 1917-1919; State engineer of Nevada from 1927 to 1935; special consultant to the United States Senate Military Affairs subcommittee on strategic and critical minerals and materials and for examination of military establishments during the Second World War; elected as a Republican to the United States Senate in 1946; reelected in 1952, and served from January 3, 1947 to January 3, 1959; unsuccessful candidate for reelection in 1958, and for election to the House of Representatives in 1960; consulting engineer in Washington, D.C., until his death there on May 19, 1961; interment in Arlington National Cemetery, Va.

**MALONEY, Carolyn Bosher,** a Representative from New York; born in Greensboro, N.C., February 19, 1948; A.B., Greensboro College, 1968; New School for Social Research, New York City and University of Dijon, Paris; member, Democratic State committee for Sixty-sixth Assembly District; director of special projects for New York State Senator Manfred Ohrenstein; executive director of Advisory Council to Democratic members of the State Senate; senior program analyst and legislative aide to State Assembly Cities Committee; member, New York City Council, 1982-1993; elected as a Democrat to the One Hundred Third and One Hundred Fourth Congresses (January 3, 1993-January 3, 1997); is a resident of Staten Island.

**MALONEY, Francis Thomas,** a Representative and a Senator from Connecticut; born in Meriden, New Haven County, Conn., March 31, 1894; attended the public and parochial schools of Meriden; newspaper reporter 1914-1921; during the First World War served in the United States Navy as a seaman first class 1917-1918; engaged in the real estate and insurance business; mayor of Meriden, Conn., 1929-1933; elected as a Democrat to the Seventy-third Congress (March 4, 1933-January 3, 1935); did not seek renomination, having become a candidate for Senator; elected to the United States Senate in 1934; reelected in 1940 and served from January 3, 1935, until his death in Meriden, Conn., on January 16, 1945; chairman, Committee on Public Buildings and Grounds (Seventy-seventh through Seventy-ninth Congresses); interment in Sacred Heart Cemetery.

**MALONEY, Franklin John,** a Representative from Pennsylvania; born in Philadelphia, Pa., March 29, 1899; attended the public schools and graduated from Temple University Law School in 1922; was admitted to the bar in 1923 and practiced in Philadelphia, Pa.; unsuccessful Republican candidate for election to the Seventy-ninth Congress in 1944; elected as a Republican to the Eightieth Congress (January 3, 1947-January 3, 1949); unsuccessful for reelection in 1948 to the Eighty-first Congress; resumed the practice of law; died in Philadelphia, Pa., September 15, 1958; interment in West Laurel Hill Cemetery.

**MALONEY, Paul Herbert,** a Representative from Louisiana; born in New Orleans, La., February 14, 1876; attended the public school and Mrs. Ashe's Private School, Pass Christian, Miss.; employed as an office boy in 1893 for a drayage company, advancing to president in 1916; also engaged in a linen supply company, a trucking and storage company, and an automobile distributing company; member of the Louisiana National Guard 1895-1898; served in the State house of representatives 1914-1916; member of the New Orleans Levee Board 1917-1920, serving as president in 1919 and 1920; member of the commission council of New Orleans; commissioner of public utilities 1920-1925; delegate to the Democratic National Conventions in 1924, 1928, 1932, and 1936; elected as a Democrat to the Seventy-second and to the four succeeding Congresses and served from March 4, 1931, until December 15, 1940, when he resigned; unsuccessful candidate for renomination in 1940; collector of internal revenue for the New Orleans district from December 16, 1940, to July 31, 1942; again elected to the Seventy-eighth and Seventy-ninth Congresses (January 3, 1943-January 3, 1947); was not a candidate for renomination in 1946; engaged in the trucking and storage business; died in New Orleans, La., March 26, 1967; interment in Metairie Cemetery.

**MALONEY, Robert Sarsfield,** a Representative from Massachusetts; born in Lawrence, Essex County, Mass., February 3, 1881; attended the public schools; learned the printer's trade; fraternal delegate of the American Federation of Labor to the Canadian Trades and Labor Congress, Winnipeg, Manitoba, in 1907; New England organizer for the International Typographical Union 1908-1912; member of the board of aldermen in 1909 and served as president; director of the Department of Public Health and Charities of Lawrence in 1912 and 1915-1920; engaged in commercial printing in 1913 and 1914; member of the city council 1916-1920 and served as president; elected as a Republican to the Sixty-seventh Congress (March 4, 1921-March 3, 1923); was not a candidate for renomination in 1922; again served as director of the Department of Public Health and Charities, from 1924 until 1928; published a weekly newspaper and, later, engaged in the restaurant business until his death in Lawrence, Mass., November 8, 1934; interment in Immaculate Conception Cemetery.

**MANAHAN, James,** a Representative from Minnesota; born near Chatfield, Fillmore County, Minn., on March 12, 1866; attended the country schools, and was graduated from Winona (Minn.) Normal School in 1886; taught school for two years at Graceville, Minn.; attended the law department of the University of Wisconsin at Madison and was graduated from the law department of the University of Minnesota at Minneapolis in 1889; was admitted to the bar the same year and commenced practice in St. Paul, Minn.; moved to Lincoln, Lancaster County, Nebr., in 1895 and continued the practice of his profession; moved to Minneapolis, Minn., in 1905 and practiced law until 1912; elected as a Republican to the Sixty-third Congress (March 4, 1913-March 3, 1915); was not a candidate for renomination in 1914 to the Sixty-fourth Congress; resumed the practice of law; died in St. Paul, Minn., January 8, 1932; interment in Calvary Cemetery.

**MANASCO, Carter,** a Representative from Alabama; born in Townley, Walker County, Ala., January 3, 1902; attended the public schools and Howard College, Birmingham, Ala.; graduated from the law department of the University of Alabama at Tuscaloosa, LL.B., 1927, and J.D., 1929; was admitted to the bar the same year and began practice in Jasper, Ala.; member of the Alabama State house of representatives, 1930-1934; served as secretary to Speaker William B. Bankhead, 1933-1940; elected as a Democrat to the Seventy-seventh Congress to fill the vacancy caused by the resignation of Walter W. Bankhead; reelected to the three succeeding Congresses, and served from June 24, 1941 to January 3, 1949; chairman, Committee on Expenditures in Executive Departments (Seventy-eighth and Seventy-ninth Congresses); unsuccessful candidate for renomination in 1948 to the Eighty-first Congress; resumed the practice of law and engaged in public relations work; member, first Commission on Organization of the Executive Branch of the Government (Hoover Commission), 1947-1949; legislative counsel, National Coal Association, 1949-1985; was a resident of McLean, Va.; died February 5, 1992.

**MANDERSON, Charles Frederick,** a Senator from Nebraska; born in Philadelphia, Pa., February 9, 1837; attended the schools and academies of his native city; moved to Canton, Ohio, in 1856; studied law; was admitted to the bar in 1859 and commenced practice in Canton; city solicitor of Canton 1860; during the Civil War entered the Army as a first lieutenant, rose through the grades of captain, major, lieutenant colonel, and colonel, and resigned in 1865; brevetted brigadier general of Volunteers, United States Army, in 1865; resumed the practice of law in Canton, Ohio; twice elected attorney of Stark County; moved to Omaha, Nebr., in 1869, and continued the practice of law; city attorney of Omaha for six years; member of the State constitutional conventions in 1871 and in 1875; elected as a Republican to the United States Senate in 1883; reelected in 1888 and served from March 4, 1883, to March 3, 1895; served as President pro tempore of the Senate during the Fifty-first, Fifty-second and Fifty-third Congresses; chairman, Committee on Printing (Forty-eighth through Fifty-second Congresses); appointed general solicitor of the Burlington system of railroads west of the Missouri River; vice president of the American Bar Association in 1899 and president in 1900; died on board the steamship *Cedric* in the harbor of Liverpool, England, September 28, 1911; interment in Forest Lawn Cemetery, Omaha, Nebr.

**Bibliography:** *DAB.*

**MANGUM, Willie Person,** a Representative and a Senator from North Carolina; born in Orange (now Durham) County, N.C., May 10, 1792; attended academies at Hillsboro, Fayetteville, and Raleigh; graduated from the University of North Carolina at Chapel Hill in 1815; studied law; was admitted to the bar in 1817 and commenced practice in Red Mountain, N.C.; member, State house of representatives 1818-1819; twice elected a superior court judge; elected to the Eighteenth and Nineteenth Congresses and served from March 4, 1823, until March 18, 1826, when he resigned; elected to the United States Senate in 1830 as a Jacksonian and served from March 4, 1831, until his resignation on November 26, 1836; chairman, Committee on Naval Affairs (Twenty-seventh Congress), Committee on Printing (Twenty-seventh Congress); received the eleven electoral votes of South Carolina for President of the United States in 1837; again elected, as a Whig, to the United States Senate to fill the vacancy caused by the resignation of Bedford Brown; reelected in 1841 and in 1847, and served from November 25, 1840, to March 3, 1853; served as President pro tempore of the Senate during the Twenty-seventh and Twenty-eighth Congresses; unsuccessful candidate for reelection in 1853; continued the practice of law until his death in Red Mountain, N.C., September 7, 1861; interment in the family burial ground at his home, "Walnut Hall," near Red Mountain, N.C.

**Bibliography:** *DAB*; Mangum, Willie. *Willie Mangum Papers.* Edited by Henry Shanks. 5 vols. Raleigh: North Carolina Department of Archives and History, 1950-1956.

**MANKIN, Helen Douglas,** a Representative from Georgia; born in Atlanta, Fulton County, Ga., on September 11, 1896; attended public and private schools; was graduated from Rockford (Ill.) College in 1917 and from Atlanta (Ga.) Law School in 1920; was admitted to the bar in 1920 and commenced practice in Atlanta, Ga.; during the First World War was an ambulance driver in a unit attached to the French Army in 1918 and 1919; member of the general assembly of Georgia 1937-1946; elected as a Democrat to the Seventy-ninth Congress to fill the vacancy caused by the resignation of Robert Ramspeck and served from February 12, 1946, to January 3, 1947; unsuccessful candidate for renomination in 1946; had her name written in by voters in the general election but was defeated; unsuccessfully contested election of James C. Davis to the Eightieth Congress; resumed the practice of law in Atlanta, Ga., and resided in Stonewall, Ga.; died as the result of an automobile accident near College Park, Ga., July 25, 1956; remains were cremated.

**Bibliography:** Spritzer, Lorraine N. *The Belle of Ashby Street: Helen Douglas Mankin and Georgia Politics.* Athens: University of Georgia Press, 1982.

**MANLOVE, Joe Jonathan,** a Representative from Missouri; born on a farm near Carthage, Jasper County, Mo., October 1, 1876; attended the public schools and was graduated from Presbyterian Academy at Mount Vernon, Mo.; studied law; was admitted to the bar in 1897 and commenced practice in Mount Vernon, Lawrence County, Mo.; also engaged in agricultural pursuits, in the livestock business, and in the general development of southwest Missouri; unsuccessful Republican candidate for election in 1914 to the Sixty-fourth Congress and in 1916 to the Sixty-fifth Congress; elected as a Republican to the Sixty-eighth and to the four succeeding Congresses (March 4, 1923-March 3, 1933); unsuccessful candidate for reelection in 1932 to the Seventy-third Congress; unsuccessful for the Republican nomination for Congress in 1934; resumed the practice of law and also engaged in the real estate business in Joplin, Mo.; in 1943 was elected one of the delegates to write a new constitution for the State of Missouri and served as a member of the constitutional convention; died in Joplin, Mo., January 31, 1956; interment in Mount Hope Cemetery near Joplin, Mo.

**MANN, Abijah, Jr.,** a Representative from New York; born in Fairfield, Herkimer County, N.Y., September 24, 1793; attended the common schools; engaged in mercantile pursuits; justice of the peace; appointed postmaster of Fairfield by President Andrew Jackson and served from May 28, 1830, to January 16, 1833; member of the State assembly 1828-1830 and in 1838; elected as a Jacksonian to the Twenty-third and Twenty-fourth Congresses (March 4, 1833-March 3, 1837); moved to New York City; unsuccessful candidate for attorney general of New York in 1855; delegate to the Republican State convention in 1856; unsuccessful candidate for State senator in 1857; died in Auburn, N.Y., September 6, 1868.

**MANN, David Scott,** a Representative from Ohio; born in Cincinnati, Ohio, September 25, 1939; A.B., Harvard University, 1961, LL.B., Harvard Law School, 1968; admitted to Ohio bar in 1968 and commenced practice in Cincinnati, 1968-1983; United States Navy service, 1961-1965; member, Cincinnati City Council, 1974-1992; mayor of Cincinnati, 1980-1982 and 1991; elected as a Democrat to the One Hundred Third Congress (January 3, 1993-January 3, 1995); unsuccessful candidate for reelection in 1994 to the One Hundred Fourth Congress; adjunct professor, University of Cincinnati School of Law; of counsel, Thompson, Hine and Flory; is a resident of Cincinnati, Ohio.

**MANN, Edward Coke,** a Representative from South Carolina; born in Lowndesville, Abbeville County, S.C., November 21, 1880; attended the common schools and was graduated from The Citadel, Charleston, S.C., in 1901; taught school one year and was connected with a tobacco company for four years; was graduated from the law department of the University of South Carolina at Columbia in 1906 and commenced practice in St. Matthews, Calhoun County, S.C.; solicitor of the first circuit of South Carolina, 1916-1919; elected as a Democrat to the Sixty-sixth Congress to fill the vacancy caused by the resignation of Asbury Francis Lever, and served from October 7, 1919 to March 3, 1921; unsuccessful candidate for renomination in 1920 to the Sixty-seventh Congress; practiced law in Orangeburg, S.C.; appointed master in equity for Orangeburg County in November 1923; reappointed in November 1927 and served until his death; was accidentally killed near Rowesville, S.C., November 11, 1931, while on a hunting trip; interment in Sunnyside Cemetery, Orangeburg, S.C.

**MANN, Horace,** a Representative from Massachusetts; born in Franklin, Norfolk County, Mass., May 4, 1796; attended the public schools and prepared for college under a private teacher; graduated from Brown University, Providence, R.I., in 1819, and tutored there from 1819 to 1821; studied law in Litchfield, Conn.; admitted to the bar and commenced practice in Dedham, Mass., in 1823; member,

Massachusetts house of representatives, 1827-1833; moved to Boston in 1833; commissioner for the revision of the Massachusetts statutes in 1835; member, Massachusetts senate, 1833-1837, and served as president, 1835-1837; secretary of the Massachusetts board of education from 1837 until 1848, and in this position reorganized the public school system; elected as a Whig to the Thirtieth Congress to fill the vacancy caused by the death of John Quincy Adams; reelected to the Thirty-first Congress and as a Free-Soiler to the Thirty-second Congress, and served from April 3, 1848 to March 3, 1853; declined to be a candidate for renomination in 1852 to the Thirty-third Congress; declined the nomination for Governor in 1852 to accept the position of president of Antioch College, Yellow Springs, Ohio, and served in that position from 1852 until his death at Yellow Springs, Ohio, August 2, 1859; interment in North Burial Ground, Providence, R.I.

**Bibliography:** *DAB*; Cassara, Ernest. "Reformer as Politician: Horace Mann and the Anti-Slavery Struggle in Congress, 1848-1853." *Journal of American Studies* 5 (December 1971): 247-64; Messerli, Jonathan. *Horace Mann: A Biography.* New York: Knopf, 1972.

**MANN, James,** a Representative from Louisiana; born in Gorham, Cumberland County, Maine, June 22, 1822; member of the Maine house of representatives in 1849 and 1850; served in the State senate 1851-1853; treasurer of Cumberland County in 1862 and 1863; customhouse officer in Portland, Maine; during the Civil War served in the Union Army as paymaster with rank of major; Treasury agent for Louisiana in 1867 and 1868 and resided in New Orleans; upon the readmission of the State of Louisiana to representation was elected as a Democrat to the Fortieth Congress and served from July 18, 1868, until his death in New Orleans, La., August 26, 1868; interment in Eastern Cemetery, Gorham, Maine.

**MANN, James Robert,** a Representative from Illinois; born near Bloomington, McLean County, Ill., on October 20, 1856; attended the public schools; was graduated from the University of Illinois at Urbana in 1876, and from the Union College of Law, Chicago, Ill., in 1881; was admitted to the bar in 1881 and commenced practice at Chicago, Ill.; member of the Oakland Board of Education in Chicago in 1887; attorney for Hyde Park and the South Park commissioners of Chicago; master in chancery of the superior court of Cook County; member of the Chicago city council, 1892-1896; chairman of the Illinois State Republican convention in 1894, and chairman of the Republican county conventions at Chicago in 1895 and 1902; elected as a Republican to the Fifty-fifth and to the thirteen succeeding Congresses, and served from March 4, 1897 until his death in Washington, D.C., on November 30, 1922; chairman, Committee on Elections No. 1 (Fifty-eighth through Sixtieth Congresses), Committee on Interstate and Foreign Commerce (Sixty-first Congress), Committee on Woman Suffrage (Sixty-sixth Congress); minority leader (Sixty-second through Sixty-fifth Congresses); sponsor of the Mann Act of 1910, prohibiting interstate or foreign travel or transportation of women and girls for illicit purposes; interment in Oakwood Cemetery, Chicago, Ill.

**Bibliography:** *DAB*; Ellis, L. Ethan. "James Robert Mann: Legislator Extraordinary." *Journal of the Illinois State Historical Society* 46 (Spring 1953): 28-44.

**MANN, James Robert,** a Representative from South Carolina; born in Greenville, S.C., April 27, 1920; attended the public schools of Greenville; B.A., The Citadel, Charleston, S.C., 1941; LL.B., University of South Carolina School of Law, 1947; entered the United States Army as a second lieutenant in July 1941, and was separated in March 1946 as a lieutenant colonel; colonel in the United States Army Reserve; was admitted to the bar in 1947 and commenced practice in Greenville, S.C.; commander, South Carolina Veterans of Foreign Wars, 1951-1952; member, South Carolina State house of representatives, 1949-1952; solicitor, Thirteenth Judicial

Circuit of South Carolina, 1953-1963; secretary, Greenville County Planning Commission, 1963-1967; trustee, Greenville Hospital System, 1966-1968; elected as a Democrat to the Ninety-first and to the four succeeding Congresses (January 3, 1969-January 3, 1979); was not a candidate for reelection in 1978 to the Ninety-sixth Congress; resumed the practice of law; is a resident of Greenville, S.C.

**MANN, Job,** a Representative from Pennsylvania; born in Bethel Township, Bedford (now Fulton) County, Pa., March 31, 1795; attended the common schools and the Bedford Academy; clerk to the board of county commissioners in 1816; was register, recorder, and clerk of Bedford County 1818-1835; elected as a Jacksonian to the Twenty-fourth Congress (March 4, 1835-March 3, 1837); unsuccessful candidate for reelection in 1836 to the Twenty-fifth Congress; studied law; was admitted to the bar in 1839 and commenced practice in Bedford, Pa.; Commonwealth treasurer of Pennsylvania 1842-1848; member of the Pennsylvania house of representatives; elected as a Democrat to the Thirtieth and Thirty-first Congresses (March 4, 1847-March 3, 1851); was not a candidate for renomination in 1850; resumed the practice of law; died in Bedford, Pa., October 8, 1873; interment in Bedford Cemetery.

**MANN, Joel Keith,** a Representative from Pennsylvania; born in Cheltenham Township, Montgomery County, Pa., August 1, 1780; attended the common schools; engaged in agricultural pursuits; member of the Pennsylvania house of representatives, 1817-1820; served in the Pennsylvania senate, 1824-1829; elected as a Jacksonian to the Twenty-second and Twenty-third Congresses (March 4, 1831-March 3, 1835); chairman, Committee on Accounts (Twenty-third Congress); resumed agricultural pursuits; died in Jenkintown, Montgomery County, Pa., August 28, 1857; interment in the Presbyterian Cemetery, Abington, Pa.

**MANNING, James,** a Delegate from Rhode Island; born in Elizabethtown (now Elizabeth), N.J., October 22, 1738; attended Hopewell Academy and was graduated from the College of New Jersey (now Princeton University) in 1762; studied theology and entered the Baptist ministry in 1763; moved to Warren, R.I., in 1764, and was one of the founders and first president of Rhode Island College (now Brown University); moved to Providence with the college in May 1770; served as pastor of the First Baptist Church of Providence from July 1771, until his resignation in April 1791; also resigned the college presidency the same year; Member of the Continental Congress in 1786; died in Providence, R.I., July 29, 1791; interment in North Burial Ground.
**Bibliography:** *DAB.*

**MANNING, John, Jr.,** a Representative from North Carolina; born in Edenton, Chowan County, N.C., July 30, 1830; attended Edenton Academy, the Norfolk Military Academy, and was graduated from the University of North Carolina at Chapel Hill in 1850; studied law; was admitted to the bar in 1853 and commenced practice in Pittsboro, Chatham County, N.C.; delegate to the constitutional convention in 1861; enlisted in the Chatham Rifles in 1861; was made first lieutenant, later becoming adjutant of the Fifteenth Regiment, North Carolina Volunteers, and served throughout the Civil War; elected as a Democrat to the Forty-first Congress to fill the vacancy caused by the resignation of John T. Deweese and served from December 7, 1870, to March 3, 1871; was not a candidate for reelection in 1870; member of the State constitutional convention in 1875; member of the State house of representatives in 1881; commissioner to codify the laws of the State in 1881; professor of law in the University of North Carolina and member of the board of trustees of that institution 1881-1899; died in Chapel Hill, N.C., February 12, 1899; interment in Episcopal Churchyard, Pittsboro, N.C.

**MANNING, Richard Irvine,** a Representative from South Carolina; born near Sumter, Sumter District, S.C., May 1, 1789; attended private schools and was graduated from South Carolina College at Columbia in 1811; served as captain of Volunteers in the War of 1812; engaged in agricultural pursuits; member of the South Carolina State house of representatives, 1820-1822; served in the State senate, 1822-1824; elected Governor of South Carolina by the Legislature, and served from December 1824 to December 1826; unsuccessful candidate for election in 1826 to the Twentieth Congress; elected as a Jacksonian to the Twenty-third Congress to fill the vacancy caused by the death of James Blair; reelected to the Twenty-fourth Congress, and served from December 8, 1834 until his death in Philadelphia, Pa., May 1, 1836; interment in Trinity Churchyard, Columbia, Richland County, S.C.
**Bibliography:** *DAB.*

**MANNING, Vannoy Hartrog,** a Representative from Mississippi; born near Raleigh, Wake County, N.C., July 26, 1839; moved with his parents to Mississippi in 1841; attended Horn Lake Male Academy, De Soto County, Miss., and the University of Nashville, Tennessee; moved to Arkansas in 1860; studied law; was admitted to the bar in 1861 and commenced practice in Hamburg, Ark.; during the Civil War served in the Confederate Army as a captain and subsequently as colonel of the Third Arkansas Infantry and Second Arkansas Battalion; after the war resumed the practice of law in Holly Springs, Miss.; elected as a Democrat to the Forty-fifth, Forty-sixth, and Forty-seventh Congresses (March 4, 1877-March 3, 1883); presented credentials as a Member-elect to the Forty-eighth Congress but did not qualify, and on June 25, 1884, the seat was awarded to James R. Chalmers, who contested his election; resumed the practice of law in Washington, D.C., in 1883; died in Branchville, Prince Georges County, Md., November 3, 1892; interment in Glenwood Cemetery, Washington, D.C.
**Bibliography:** *DAB.*

**MANSFIELD, Joseph Jefferson,** a Representative from Texas; born in Wayne, Wayne County, Va. (now West Virginia), February 9, 1861; attended the public schools; moved to Alleyton, Tex., in 1881; employed as a farm and nursery laborer and later as a baggage master and freight clerk with the Southern Pacific Railway; studied law; was admitted to the bar in 1886 and commenced practice at Eagle Lake, Colorado County, Tex.; also established the first newspaper in that city; organized two companies of the National Guard of Texas in 1886; received commissions successively as second lieutenant, first lieutenant, and captain, and was appointed adjutant of the Fourth Texas Regiment with the rank of captain; prosecuting attorney of Eagle Lake, Tex., in 1888; mayor of Eagle Lake in 1889; prosecuting attorney of Colorado County, 1892-1896; ex officio county superintendent of schools, 1896-1910; judge of Colorado County, 1896-1916; elected as a Democrat to the Sixty-fifth and to the fifteen succeeding Congresses, and served from March 4, 1917 until his death in Bethesda, Md., July 12, 1947; chairman, Committee on Rivers and Harbors (Seventy-second through Seventy ninth Congresses); interment in Masonic Cemetery, Eagle Lake, Tex.

**MANSFIELD, Michael Joseph (Mike),** a Representative and a Senator from Montana; born in New York City, March 16, 1903; moved with his family to Great Falls, Cascade County, Mont., in 1906; attended the public schools in Great Falls; served as a seaman when fourteen years old in the United States Navy during the First World War, as a private in the United States Army in 1919 and 1920, and as a private first class in the United States Marine Corps, 1920-1922; worked as a miner and mining engineer in Butte, Mont., 1922-1930; attended the Montana School of Mines at Butte in 1927 and 1928; A.B., Montana State University, Missoula, 1933; A.M., Montana State University, 1934; also attended the University of California at Los Angeles in 1936 and 1937; professor of history and political science at Montana State University from 1933 until 1942; elected as a Democrat to the Seventy-eighth and to the four succeeding Congresses (January 3, 1943-January 3, 1953); chairman, Special Committee on Campaign Expenditures (Eighty-first Congress); was not a candidate in 1952 for reelection to the House of Representatives, but was elected to the United States Senate; reelected in 1958, 1964, and again in 1970, and served from January 3, 1953 to January 3, 1977; Democratic whip 1957-1961; majority leader (Eighty-seventh through Ninety-fourth Congresses); chairman, Committee on Rules and Administration (Eighty-seventh Congress), Select Committee on Secret and Confidential Documents (Ninety-second Congress), Special Committee on Secret and Confidential Documents (Ninety-third Congress); was not a candidate for reelection in 1976; appointed Ambassador to Japan on April 22, 1977, and served until December 1988; is a resident of Washington, D.C.

**Bibliography:** Baker, Ross K. "Mike Mansfield and the Birth of the Modern Senate." In *First Among Equals: Outstanding Senate Leaders of the Twentieth Century*, edited by Richard A. Baker and Roger H. Davidson, pp. 264-296. Washington: Congressional Quarterly, Inc., 1991; Baldwin, Louis. *Honorable Politician: Mike Mansfield of Montana*. Missoula, Mont.: Mountain Press, 1979; Hood, Charles Eugene, Jr. "'China Mike' Mansfield: The Making of a Congressional Authority on the Far East." Ph.D. dissertation, Washington State University, 1980.

**MANSON, Mahlon Dickerson,** a Representative from Indiana; born in Piqua, Ohio, February 20, 1820; attended the common schools; moved to Montgomery County, Ind., and taught school for a year; studied medicine at the Ohio Medical College at Cincinnati; served as captain of Volunteers in the Mexican War October 8, 1847-July 28, 1848; member of the State house of representatives 1851 and 1852; engaged in the retail drug business at Crawfordsville; commissioned captain of the Tenth Regiment, Indiana Volunteer Infantry, April 17, 1861, and promoted through the ranks to brigadier general of Volunteers March 24, 1862; resigned December 21, 1864; unsuccessful Democratic candidate for Lieutenant Governor of Indiana in 1864; elected as a Democrat to the Forty-second Congress (March 4, 1871-March 3, 1873); unsuccessful candidate for reelection in 1872 to the Forty-third Congress; elected auditor of Indiana in 1878; elected Lieutenant Governor in 1884; appointed collector of internal revenue of the seventh district of Indiana August 11, 1886, and resigned November 5, 1889; died in Crawfordsville, Montgomery County, Ind., on February 4, 1895; interment in Oak Hill Cemetery.

**MANSUR, Charles Harley,** a Representative from Missouri; born in Philadelphia, Pa., March 6, 1835; attended Lawrence Academy, Groton, Mass.; studied law and was admitted to the bar in Richmond, Mo., August 30, 1856; moved to Chillicothe, Mo., in 1856 and practiced law; member of the board of education of Chillicothe for eight years; member of the Democratic State central committee, 1864-1868; delegate to the Democratic National Conventions of 1868 and 1884; prosecuting attorney of Livingston County, 1875-1879; unsuccessful Democratic and Liberal Republican candidate for election in 1872 to the Forty-third Congress; unsuccessful Democratic candidate for election in 1880 to the Forty-seventh Congress; elected as a Democrat to the Fiftieth and to the two succeeding Congresses (March 4, 1887-March 3, 1893); unsuccessful candidate for renomination in 1892 to the Fifty-third Congress; appointed by President Grover Cleveland as second Comptroller of the Treasury on May 29, 1893 and served until September 30, 1894; Assistant Comptroller from October 1, 1894 until his death in Washington, D.C., April 16, 1895; interment in Sunny Slope Cemetery, Richmond, Ray County, Mo.

**MANTLE, Lee,** a Senator from Montana; born in Birmingham, England, December 13, 1851; immigrated to the United States with his mother and settled at Salt Lake City, Utah, in 1864; attended a village school; moved to Idaho Territory in 1870; telegraph operator and stage agent; moved to Butte, Mont., in 1877 and became agent of the Wells-Fargo Express Co.; established the Inter Mountain, a daily Republican newspaper, in 1881; served as alderman the same year; member, Territorial house of representatives 1882, 1884, 1888, and served as speaker in 1888; mayor of Butte 1892; many times chairman of local and State conventions; appointed to the United States Senate to fill the vacancy in the term commencing March 4, 1893, caused by the failure of the legislature to elect, but was not seated; elected as a Republican to fill the vacancy and served from January 16, 1895, to March 3, 1899; unsuccessful candidate for renomination in 1899; organized and became chairman of the Silver Republican Party of Montana in 1896, but returned to the Republican Party in 1900; manager and part-time editor of the Inter Mountain until 1901; also engaged in the real estate and mining business; moved to Los Angeles, Calif., in 1921, and died there on November 18, 1934; interment in Mount Moriah Cemetery, Butte, Mont.

**MANTON, Thomas J.,** a Representative from New York; born in New York City, November 3, 1932; grduated St. Joseph's School, Astoria, N.Y., 1946, and St. John's Prep, Brooklyn, N.Y., 1950; B.B.A., St. John's University, 1958; LL.B., St. John's University School of Law, 1962; served in the United States Marine Corps, 1951-1953; member of New York City Police Department, 1955-1960; marketing representative, International Business Machine Corp., 1960-1964; admitted to the New York bar in 1963 and practiced, 1964-1984; member, New York City Council, 1970-1984; unsuccessful candidate in 1972 for nomination to the Ninety-third Congress, and in 1978 for nomination to the Ninety-sixth Congress; executive committee chair, Queens County Democratic Organization, 1986-present; elected as a Democrat to the Ninety-ninth and to the five succeeding Congresses (January 3, 1985-January 3, 1997); is a resident of Sunnyside Queens, N.Y.

**MANZANARES, Francisco Antonio,** a Delegate from the Territory of New Mexico; born in Abiquiu, N.Mex., January 25, 1843; early training was in Spanish; commenced the study of the English language and attended St. Louis (Mo.) University in 1863 and 1864; engaged in mercantile pursuits at Las Vegas in 1866; successfully contested as a Democrat the election of Tranquilino Luna to the Forty-eighth Congress and served from March 5, 1884, to March 3, 1885; was not a candidate for reelection in 1884; engaged in the wholesale grocery business; member of the board of county commissioners in 1896 and 1897; died in Las Vegas, N.Mex., September 17, 1904; interment in Calvary Cemetery.

**MANZULLO, Donald A.,** a Representative from Illinois; born in Rockford, Ill., March 24, 1944; B.A., American University, 1967; J.D., Marquette University School of Law, 1970; newspaper reporter in northern Illinois; staff, House of Representatives, 1964-1967; attorney, 1967 to present; unsuccessful candidate for nomination in 1990 to the One Hundred Second Congress; member, Republican National Committee, State of Illinois Republican Party, College Young Republicans, Winnebago County Young Republicans; elected as a Republican to the One Hundred Third and One Hundred Fourth Congresses (January 3, 1993-January 3, 1997); is a resident of Egan, Ill.

**MAPES, Carl Edgar,** a Representative from Michigan; born on a farm near Kalamo, Eaton County, Mich., December 26, 1874; attended the common schools; was graduated from Olivet (Mich.) College in 1896 and from the law department of the University of Michigan at Ann Arbor in 1899; was admitted to the bar and commenced the practice of law in Grand Rapids, Mich., in 1899; assistant prosecuting attorney of Kent County, Mich., 1900-1904;

member of the Michigan State house of representatives, 1905-1907; unsuccessful candidate for renomination in 1907; member of the Michigan State senate, 1909-1913; elected as a Republican to the Sixty-third and to the thirteen succeeding Congresses and served from March 4, 1913, until his death in New Orleans, La., on December 12, 1939; chairman, Committee on District of Columbia (Sixty-sixth Congress); interment in Oak Hill Cemetery, Grand Rapids, Mich.

**MARABLE, John Hartwell,** a Representative from Tennessee; born near Lawrenceville, Brunswick County, Va., November 18, 1786; pursued an academic course; studied medicine in Philadelphia, Pa., and practiced; moved to Yellow Creek, Tenn., and engaged in the practice of medicine; member of the Tennessee State senate in 1817 and 1818; elected to the Nineteenth and Twentieth Congresses (March 4, 1825-March 3, 1829); unsuccessful candidate for reelection in 1828 to the Twenty-first Congress; resumed the practice of medicine; died in Montgomery County, Tenn., April 11, 1844; interment in Marable Cemetery, near Clarksville, Tenn.

**MARAZITI, Joseph James,** a Representative from New Jersey; born in Boonton, Morris County, N.J., June 15, 1912; attended the public schools; attended Fordham University School of Law, and received LL.B., New Jersey Law School, 1937; served in Citizens Military Training Corps, Infantry and Judge Advocate, 1931; admitted to the New Jersey bar in 1938 and commenced practice in Boonton; legislative secretary, New Jersey State senate, 1931-1934 and 1938-1940; legislative secretary to New Jersey State assembly, 1936-1937; Boonton Municipal Court Judge, 1940-1947; first assistant prosecutor, Morris County, 1950-1953; member, New Jersey State assembly, 1958-1967; New Jersey State senator, 1968-1972, majority whip, 1972; delegate to New Jersey State Republican convention, 1966; alternate delegate to the Republican National Convention of 1968; elected as a Republican to the Ninety-third Congress (January 3, 1973-January 3, 1975); unsuccessful candidate for reelection in 1974 to the Ninety-fourth Congress; resumed the practice of law; was a resident of Boonton, N.J.; died May 20, 1991.

**MARCANTONIO, Vito Anthony,** a Representative from New York; born in New York City, December 10, 1902; attended the grade and high schools; was graduated from the law department of New York University at New York City in 1925; was admitted to the bar in June 1926 and commenced practice in New York City; served as assistant United States district attorney in 1930 and 1931; elected as a Republican to the Seventy-fourth Congress (January 3, 1935-January 3, 1937); unsuccessful candidate for reelection in 1936 to the Seventy-fifth Congress; resumed the practice of law; elected as an American Labor Party candidate to the Seventy-sixth and to the five succeeding Congresses (January 3, 1939-January 3, 1951); unsuccessful candidate for reelection in 1950 to the Eighty-second Congress; unsuccessful American Labor Party candidate for mayor of New York City in 1949; practiced law in Washington, D.C., and later in New York City, until his death in New York City on August 9, 1954; interment in Woodlawn Cemetery, Bronx, N.Y.

**Bibliography:** *DAB*; Marcantonio, Vito. *"I Vote My Conscience": Debates, Speeches and Writings of Vito Marcantonio.* Selected and edited by Annette T. Rubinstein and Associates. New York: The Vito Marcantonio Memorial, 1956; Meyer, Gerald. *Vito Marcantonio: Radical Politician, 1902-1954.* Albany: State University of New York Press, 1989; Schaffer, Alan L. *Vito Marcantonio: Radical in Congress.* Syracuse, N.Y.: Syracuse University Press, 1966.

**MARCHAND, Albert Gallatin** (son of David Marchand), a Representative from Pennsylvania; born near Greensburg, Westmoreland County, Pa., February 27, 1811; attended the common schools; studied law; admitted to the bar in 1833 and commenced practice in Greensburg; elected as a Democrat to the Twenty-sixth and Twenty-seventh Congresses (March 4, 1839-March 3, 1843);

chairman, Committee on Accounts (Twenty-seventh Congress); declined to be a candidate for renomination in 1842 to the Twenty-eighth Congress; resumed the practice of law; died in Greensburg, Pa., February 5, 1848; interment in Greensburg Cemetery.

**MARCHAND, David** (father of Albert Gallatin Marchand), a Representative from Pennsylvania; born near Irwin, Westmoreland County, Pa., December 10, 1776; attended private schools; studied medicine and practiced in Westmoreland County; major general of the Thirteenth Division of the Pennsylvania militia 1812-1814; elected as a Republican to the Fifteenth Congress and reelected to the Sixteenth Congress (March 4, 1817-March 3, 1821); elected prothonotary of Westmoreland County in 1821; resumed the practice of medicine; died in Greensburg, Westmoreland County, Pa., March 11, 1832; interment in Greensburg Cemetery.

**MARCHANT, Henry,** a Delegate from Rhode Island; born at Marthas Vineyard, Mass., April 9, 1741; attended school in Newport, R.I., where his father had moved, and was graduated from Philadelphia College (now the University of Pennsylvania) at Philadelphia in 1762; studied law; was admitted to the bar about 1767 and commenced practice in Newport, R.I.; attorney general of Rhode Island 1771-1777; Member of the Continental Congress 1777-1779 and was one of the signers of the Articles of Confederation; delegate to the Rhode Island State Convention in 1789 for the adoption of the Federal Constitution; served as United States district judge for the district of Rhode Island 1790-1796; died in Newport, R.I., on August 30, 1796; interment in the Common Burial Ground.

**Bibliography:** *DAB*; Lovejoy, David S. "Henry Marchant and the *Mistress of the World.*" *William and Mary Quarterly* 3d ser., 12 (July 1955): 375-98.

**MARCY, Daniel,** a Representative from New Hampshire; born in Portsmouth, N.H., November 7, 1809; attended the common schools; followed the sea and later engaged in shipbuilding; member of the State house of representatives 1854-1857; served in the State senate in 1857 and 1858; unsuccessful candidate for election to the Thirty-sixth Congress in 1858, and to the Thirty-seventh Congress in 1860; elected as a Democrat to the Thirty-eighth Congress (March 4, 1863-March 3, 1865); unsuccessful candidate for reelection in 1864 to the Thirty-ninth Congress; again served in the State senate in 1871 and 1872; died in Portsmouth, N.H., November 3, 1893; interment in Proprietors' Burying Ground.

**MARCY, William Learned,** a Senator from New York; born in Sturbridge (now Southbridge), Mass., December 12, 1786; attended the common schools and Leicester and Woodstock Academies; graduated from Brown University, Providence, R.I., in 1808; taught school in Newport, R.I.; studied law; was admitted to the bar in 1811 and commenced practice in Troy, N.Y.; served in the War of 1812; recorder of Troy, 1816-1818, 1821-1823; editor of the Troy Budget; New York State comptroller, 1823-1829; associate justice of the New York State supreme court, 1829-1831; elected as a Jacksonian to the United States Senate and served from March 4, 1831, until his resignation on January 1, 1833, to become Governor; chairman, Committee on the Judiciary (Twenty-second Congress); elected Governor of New York in 1832, reelected in 1834 and 1836, and served from January 1, 1833 to January 1, 1839; unsuccessful candidate for reelection in 1838; member, Mexican Claims Commission, 1839-1842; appointed Secretary of War in the Cabinet of President James K. Polk and served from March 6, 1845 to March 4, 1849; resumed the practice of law; appointed Secretary of State in the Cabinet of President Franklin Pierce on March 7, 1853, and served until March 6, 1857; died in Ballston Spa, N.Y., July 4, 1857; interment in the Rural Cemetery, Albany, N.Y.

**Bibliography:** *DAB*; Spencer, Ivor. *The Victor and the Spoils: The Life of William Marcy.* Providence: Brown University Press, 1955.

**MARDIS, Samuel Wright,** a Representative from Alabama; born in Fayetteville, Tenn., June 12, 1800; received an academic training; attended an "old field" school; studied law; was admitted to the bar and commenced practice in Montevallo, Ala., in 1823; member of the State house of representatives 1823-1825, 1828, and 1830; elected as a Jacksonian to the Twenty-second and Twenty-third Congresses (March 4, 1831-March 3, 1835); moved to Mardisville, Talladega County, Ala., in 1835 and continued the practice of his profession until his death in Talladega, Talladega County, Ala., November 14, 1836; interment in Oak Hill Cemetery.

**MARGOLIES-MEZVINSKY, Marjorie** (wife of Edward Maurice Mezvinsky), a Representative from Pennsylvania; born in Philadelphia, Pa., June 21, 1942; graduated from Forest Park High School, Baltimore, 1959; B.A., University of Pennsylvania, 1963; CBS News Foundation Fellow, Columbia University; television journalist, WCAU-TV, 1967-1971; member, Washington news team at NBC; elected as a Democrat to the One Hundred Third Congress (January 3, 1993-January 3, 1995); unsuccessful candidate for reelection in 1994 to the One Hundred Fourth Congress; chair, National Women's Business Council; director and deputy chair of the United States delegation to the United Nations Fourth World Conference on Women; is a resident of Narberth, Pa.

**MARION, Robert,** a Representative from South Carolina; born 1766 in Berkeley District, S.C.; pursued an academic course, and was graduated from the University of the State of Pennsylvania (now the University of Pennsylvania) at Philadelphia in 1784; owned and managed plantation at Belle Isle, S.C.; justice of quorum, St. Stephen's Parish; justice of the peace, Charleston, S.C.; served in the State house of representatives, 1790-1796, and in the State senate, 1802-1805; elected as a Republican to the Ninth, Tenth, and Eleventh Congresses and served from March 4, 1805, until his resignation on December 4, 1810; died on his plantation in St. Stephen's Parish, March 22, 1811.

**MARKELL, Henry** (son of Jacob Markell), a Representative from New York; born in Stone Arabia, Montgomery County, N.Y., February 7, 1792; attended the common schools; studied law; was admitted to the bar and practiced; elected to the Nineteenth and Twentieth Congresses (March 4, 1825-March 3, 1829); died in Palatine, N.Y., on August 30, 1831; interment in the cemetery at St. Johnsville, Montgomery County, N.Y.

**MARKELL, Jacob** (father of Henry Markell), a Representative from New York; born in Schenectady County, N.Y., May 8, 1770; attended the common schools; moved to Manheim in 1790 and engaged in agricultural pursuits; justice of the peace; supervisor of the town of Manheim 1797-1819 and 1824-1829; served as judge of the court of common pleas of Montgomery County; elected as a Federalist to the Thirteenth Congress (March 4, 1813-March 3, 1815); member of the State assembly from Herkimer County in 1820; died in Manheim, Herkimer County, N.Y., November 26, 1852; interment in Snells Bush Cemetery, Manheim, N.Y.

**MARKEY, Edward John,** a Representative from Massachusetts; born in Malden, Middlesex County, Mass., July 11, 1946; attended Immaculate Conception Grammar School in Malden; graduated, Malden Catholic High School, 1964; B.A., Boston (Mass.) College, 1968; J.D., Boston College Law School, 1972; admitted to the Massachusetts bar in 1974; served in United States Army Reserve, 1968-1973; member, Massachusetts house of representatives, 1973-1976; elected as a Democrat to the Ninety-fourth Congress, by special election, November 2, 1976, to fill the vacancy caused by the death of Torbert H. Macdonald, and at the same time elected to the Ninety-fifth Congress; reelected to the ten succeeding Congresses and served from November 2, 1976, to January 3, 1997; is a resident of Malden, Mass.

**MARKHAM, Henry Harrison,** a Representative from California; born in Wilmington, Essex County, N.Y., November 16, 1840; attended the common schools of his home town and Wheeler's Academy, Vermont; moved to Wisconsin in 1861; during the Civil War enlisted in the Union Army as a private in Company G, Thirty-second Regiment, Wisconsin Volunteer Infantry; promoted to second lieutenant; returned to Wisconsin and settled in Milwaukee; studied law; was admitted to the bar in 1867 and practiced in Milwaukee before the State and United States courts; moved to Pasadena, Los Angeles County, Calif., in 1879 and continued the practice of his profession; was also interested in gold and silver mining; elected as a Republican to the Forty-ninth Congress (March 4, 1885-March 3, 1887); declined to be a candidate for renomination in 1886 to the Fiftieth Congress; elected Governor of California in 1890 and served from January 8, 1891 to January 11, 1895; died in Pasadena, Calif., October 9, 1923; interment in Mountain View Cemetery.

**MARKLEY, Philip Swenk,** a Representative from Pennsylvania; born in Skippack, near Norristown, Montgomery County, Pa., July 2, 1789; pursued an academic course; located in Norristown; studied law; admitted to the bar in 1810 and commenced practice in Norristown, Pa.; deputy Commonwealth attorney for Pennsylvania 1819 and 1820; member of the Pennsylvania senate 1820-1823; elected to the Eighteenth and Nineteenth Congresses (March 4, 1823-March 3, 1827); unsuccessful candidate for reelection in 1826 to the Twentieth Congress; resumed the practice of law; appointed naval officer of Philadelphia by President Andrew Jackson; attorney general of Pennsylvania in 1829; died in Norristown, Pa., September 12, 1834; interment in St. John's Episcopal Church Cemetery.

**MARKS, Marc Lincoln,** a Representative from Pennsylvania; born in Farrell, Mercer County, Pa., February 12, 1927; attended the elementary schools of Farrell; graduated from Sharon (Pa.) High School, 1945; B.A., University of Alabama, 1951; LL.B., University of Virginia, Charlottesville, 1954; admitted to the Pennsylvania bar in 1955 and commenced practice in Farrell; served in United States Army Air Corps, 1945-1946; served as Mercer County Solicitor, 1960-1966; elected as a Republican to the Ninety-fifth and to the two succeeding Congresses (January 3, 1977-January 3, 1983); was not a candidate for reelection in 1982 to the Ninety-eighth Congress; nominated to be a member of the Federal Mine Safety and Health Review Commission on August 23, 1994 for a term ending August 30, 2000; confirmed by the Senate on September 30, 1994; is a resident of Chevy Chase, Md.

**MARKS, William,** a Senator from Pennsylvania; born near "Fogg's Manor," Chester County, Pa., October 13, 1778; moved with his father to Allegheny County in early childhood; received a limited schooling; learned the trade of tanner; studied law; was admitted to the bar and commenced practice in Pittsburgh, Pa.; held several local offices; coroner of Allegheny County; member, Pennsylvania house of representatives, 1810-1819, and served as speaker during the last six years; commanded the Pennsylvania Militia in 1814; member, Pennsylvania senate, 1820-1825; elected to the United States Senate, and served from March 4, 1825 to March 3, 1831; unsuccessful candidate for reelection; chairman, Committee on Engrossed Bills (Nineteenth through Twenty-first Congresses), Committee on Agriculture (Twenty-first Congress); resumed the practice of law in Pittsburgh; moved to Beaver, Pa., in 1850 and retired to private life; died in Beaver, Pa., April 10, 1858; interment in the McCreery lot in the old cemetery on Buffalo Street.

**MARLAND, Ernest Whitworth,** a Representative from Oklahoma; born in Pittsburgh, Pa., May 8, 1874; attended the grade and high schools, and a private school at Rugby, Tenn.; was graduated from the law department of the University of Michigan at Ann Arbor in 1893; was admitted to the bar in 1895 and commenced practice in Pittsburgh, Pa.; abandoned the practice of law and engaged in the oil business in Pennsylvania, Ohio, and West Virginia; elected as a Democrat to the Seventy-third Congress (March 4, 1933-January 3, 1935); was not a candidate for renomination in 1934 to the Seventy-fourth Congress, but was elected Governor of Oklahoma, and served from January 14, 1935 to January 9, 1939; unsuccessful candidate for the Democratic nomination for United States Senator in 1936; resumed his former business pursuits; unsuccessful candidate for nomination in 1940 to the Seventy-seventh Congress; died in Ponca City, Okla., October 3, 1941; interment in Odd Fellows Cemetery.

**Bibliography:** *DAB.*

**MARLENEE, Ronald Charles,** a Representative from Montana; born in Scobey, Daniels County, Mont., August 8, 1935; educated in the public schools of Daniels County; attended Montana State University, Bozeman, the University of Montana, Missoula, and the Reisch School of Auctioneering, Mason City, Iowa; farmer and rancher; committeeman, Second Congressional District of Montana, 1975-1976; elected as a Republican to the Ninety-fifth and to the seven succeeding Congresses (January 3, 1977-January 3, 1993); unsuccessful candidate for reelection in 1992 to the One Hundred Third Congress; is a resident of Montana with an office in Fairfax, Va.

**MARQUETTE, Turner Mastin,** a Representative from Nebraska; born near Springfield, Clark County, Ohio, July 19, 1831; attended the common schools, the Springfield High School, and Wittenberg College, Springfield, Ohio, and was graduated from Ohio University at Athens in 1855; moved to Plattsmouth, Nebr., in 1856; studied law; was admitted to the bar and commenced practice in Plattsmouth, Nebr., in 1859; member of the Territorial assembly 1857-1859; served in the Territorial council in 1860 and 1861; upon the admission of Nebraska as a State into the Union was elected as a Republican to the Thirty-ninth Congress and served two days only, March 2 and 3, 1867; had also been elected as a Delegate from the Territory of Nebraska to the Fortieth Congress, but the admission of the State voided the election; resumed the practice of law in Plattsmouth; moved to Lincoln, Nebr., in 1874; general attorney for the Chicago, Burlington & Quincy Railroad from 1869 until his death in Tampa, Hillsborough County, Fla., December 22, 1894; interment in Wyuka Cemetery, Lincoln, Nebr.

**MARR, Alem,** a Representative from Pennsylvania; born in Upper Mount Bethel, Northampton County, Pa., June 18, 1787; moved to Northumberland County in 1795 with his parents, who settled near Milton, Pa.; attended the common schools and was graduated from Princeton College in 1807; studied law; was admitted to the bar in 1813 and commenced practice in Danville, Montour County, Pa.; elected as a Jacksonian to the Twenty-first Congress (March 4, 1829-March 3, 1831); was not a candidate for renomination and retired to his farm near Milton, Northumberland County, where he died March 29, 1843; interment in Milton Cemetery.

**MARR, George Washington Lent,** a Representative from Tennessee; born near Marrs Hill, Henry County, Va., May 25, 1779; attended rural schools and the University of North Carolina at Chapel Hill; attorney general for west Tennessee, 1807-1809; attorney general of the fifth district, 1809-1813; served in the Creek War and was wounded; elected as a Republican to the Fifteenth Congress (March 4, 1817-March 3, 1819); unsuccessful candidate for renomination in 1818 to the Sixteenth Congress; engaged in planting; was one of the largest landowners in west Tennessee; moved from Clarksville to Obion County in 1821; member of the Tennessee State Constitutional convention in 1834; affiliated with the Whig Party after its formation; died at his residence on Island No. 10 (since washed away), in the Mississippi River, near New Madrid, Mo., on September 5, 1856; interment in Troy Cemetery, Troy, Tenn.

**MARRIOTT, David Daniel,** a Representative from Utah; born in Bingham, Tooele County, Utah, November 2, 1939; educated in the public schools of Sandy, Utah; graduated, Jordan High School, 1958; B.S., University of Utah, Salt Lake City, 1967; C.L.U., American College of Life Underwriters, 1968; life insurance agent; owner-president of a Utah-based firm specializing in business and pension consultation, 1968-1976; served in Utah Air National Guard, 1958-1963; elected as a Republican to the Ninety-fifth and to the three succeeding Congresses (January 3, 1977-January 3, 1985); was not a candidate in 1984 for reelection to the Ninety-ninth Congress, but was an unsuccessful candidate for nomination for Governor of Utah; is a resident of Salt Lake City, Utah.

**MARSALIS, John Henry,** a Representative from Colorado; born in McComb, Pike County, Miss., May 9, 1904; attended the public schools of McComb, Miss.; moved with his parents to Colorado Springs, Colo., in 1922; student at the University of Mississippi in 1925 and 1926; graduated from the University of Colorado Law School in 1934; was admitted to the bar March 14, 1935, and commenced the practice of law in Pueblo, Colo.; investigator in district attorney's office in Pueblo in 1935 and 1936; entered the United States Army May 11, 1942, assigned to the Weather Squadron, United States Air Force, and was discharged on June 16, 1945; elected district attorney, tenth judicial district of Colorado, in 1944 and took oath of office while on furlough January 9, 1945; assumed duties upon release from Army and served until December 1948; elected as a Democrat to the Eighty-first Congress (January 3, 1949-January 3, 1951); unsuccessful candidate for reelection in 1950 to the Eighty-second Congress and for election in 1952 to the Eighty-third Congress; appointed city attorney December 15, 1952, and served in that capacity until elected district judge, tenth judicial district of Colorado, November 1954; served in that office until his retirement February 28, 1962; resided in Pueblo, Colo., where he died June 26, 1971; interment in Roselawn Cemetery.

**MARSH, Benjamin Franklin,** a Representative from Illinois; born in Wythe Township, Hancock County, Ill., in 1839; attended private schools and Jubilee College; studied law; was admitted to the bar in 1860 and practiced in Warsaw, Hancock County, Ill.; during the Civil War enlisted as a private in the Sixteenth Regiment, Illinois Volunteer Infantry; later commissioned Colonel and served until January 1866; returned to Warsaw, Ill., and engaged in the practice of law until 1877; Republican candidate for member of the State constitutional convention in 1869; elected as a Republican to the Forty-fifth, Forty-sixth, and Forty-seventh Congresses (March 4, 1877-March 3, 1883); chairman, Committee on Pensions (Forty-seventh Congress); unsuccessful candidate for reelection in 1882 to the Forty-eighth Congress; engaged in agricultural pursuits and stock raising in Hancock County; appointed in 1889 State railroad and warehouse commissioner, and served four years; delegate to the Republican National Convention in 1888; elected to the Fifty-third and to the three succeeding Congresses (March 4, 1893-March 3, 1901); chairman, Committee on the Militia (Fifty-fourth through Fifty-sixth Congresses); unsuccessful candidate in 1900 for reelection to the Fifty-seventh Congress; elected to the Fifty-eighth and Fifty-ninth Congresses and served from March 4, 1903, until his death in Warsaw, Ill., June 2, 1905; interment in Oakland Cemetery.

**MARSH, Charles** (father of George Perkins Marsh), a Representative from Vermont; born in Lebanon, New London County, Conn., July 10, 1765; moved with his parents to Hartford, Conn., in 1773; educated under private tutors and was graduated from Dartmouth College, Hanover, N.H., in 1786; studied law in the law school of Judge Reeves at Litchfield, Conn.; was admitted to the bar in 1788 and commenced the practice of law in Woodstock, Windsor County, Vt., the same year; appointed by President George

Washington United States district attorney for Vermont and served from 1797 to 1801; elected as a Federalist to the Fourteenth Congress (March 4, 1815-March 3, 1817); founder of the American Colonization Society while in Washington; resumed the practice of law in Woodstock, Windsor County, Vt.; trustee of Dartmouth College 1809-1849; died in Woodstock, Vt., on January 11, 1849; interment in River Street Cemetery.

**MARSH, George Perkins** (son of Charles Marsh), a Representative from Vermont; born in Woodstock, Windsor County, Vt., March 15, 1801; was graduated from Dartmouth College, Hanover, N.H., in 1820; studied law; was admitted to the bar in 1825 and commenced practice in Burlington, Vt.; member of the Governor's council in 1835; elected as a Whig to the Twenty-eighth and to the three succeeding Congresses, and served from March 4, 1843 until his resignation in 1849; appointed by President Zachary Taylor as Minister Resident to Turkey on May 29, 1849, and served until December 1853; charged with a special mission to Greece in 1852; fish commissioner of Vermont in 1857, and railroad commissioner, 1857-1859; appointed by President Abraham Lincoln as Envoy Extraordinary and Minister Plenipotentiary to Italy on March 20, 1861, and served until his death in Vallombrosa, Italy, July 23, 1882; interment in English Cemetery, Rome, Italy.

Bibliography: *DAB*; Lowenthal, David. *George Perkins Marsh, Versatile Vermonter.* New York: Columbia University Press, 1958.

**MARSH, John Otho, Jr.,** a Representative from Virginia; born in Winchester, Frederick County, Va., August 7, 1926; attended the public schools of Harrisonburg, Va.; served in the United States Army, 1944-1947; commissioned a lieutenant at the age of nineteen, and was with occupation forces in Germany; officer, Virginia National Guard, 1951-1976; LL.B., Washington and Lee University, Lexington, Va., 1951; was admitted to the bar and began law practice in Strasburg, Va., in 1952; member, Shenandoah County (Va.) School Board, 1958-1960; attorney for the town of New Market, Va., 1954-1962; town judge of Strasburg, Va., 1954-1962; delegate, Virginia Democratic conventions, 1964 and 1968; served annual National Guard active duty tour in South Vietnam, 1966-1967; elected as a Democrat to the Eighty-eighth and to the three succeeding Congresses (January 3, 1963-January 3, 1971); was not a candidate for reelection in 1970 to the Ninety-second Congress; resumed the practice of law in Washington, D.C.; Assistant Secretary of Defense for Legislative Affairs, 1973-1974; Assistant to the Vice President for National Security Affairs, January 1974 to August 1974; Counsellor to President Gerald R. Ford, 1974-1977; returned to private practice of law, 1977-1981; served as Secretary of the Army, January 30, 1981 to August 1989; chairman of the Reserve Forces Policy Board, 1989-1994; chairman, Secretary of Defense Quality of Life Task Force, 1994-1995; is a resident of Strasburg, Va.

**MARSHALL, Alexander Keith,** a Representative from Kentucky; born at Buck Pond, near Versailles, Woodford County, Ky., on February 11, 1808; completed preparatory studies; settled in Nicholasville, Ky.; was graduated from the medical department of the University of Pennsylvania at Philadelphia in 1844; engaged in the practice of medicine at Nicholasville; member of the Kentucky constitutional convention held in Frankfort in 1849; elected as a candidate of the American Party to the Thirty-fourth Congress (March 4, 1855-March 3, 1857); moved to Missouri, but returned to Kentucky and settled in Fayette County; engaged in agricultural pursuits; died near East Hickman, Ky., April 28, 1884; interment in Lexington Cemetery, Lexington, Ky.

**MARSHALL, Alfred,** a Representative from Maine; born in New Hampshire about 1797; member of the State house of representatives in 1827, 1828, 1834, and 1835; served as a general in the State militia; elected as a Democrat to the Twenty-seventh Congress (March 4, 1841-March 3, 1843); collector at Belfast, Maine,

1846-1849; engaged in mercantile pursuits and the hotel business; died in China, Kennebec County, Maine, October 2, 1868; interment in Village Cemetery.

**MARSHALL, Edward Colston,** a Representative from California; born in Woodford County, Ky., June 29, 1821; attended Centre College, Danville, Ky., and was graduated from Transylvania University, Lexington, Ky.; attended Washington College (now Washington and Lee University); studied law and was admitted to the bar; moved to San Francisco and later to Sonora, Calif.; practiced law; served in the Mexican War; elected as a Democrat to the Thirty-second Congress (March 4, 1851-March 3, 1853); was renominated in 1852, but withdrew before the election; settled in Marysville, Calif., and again engaged in the practice of law; unsuccessful candidate for election to the United States Senate in 1856; moved to Kentucky and devoted himself to legal pursuits for twenty-one years; returned to San Francisco in 1877 and continued the practice of law; attorney general of California 1883-1886; died in San Francisco, Calif., July 9, 1893; interment in Mountain View Cemetery, Oakland, Calif.

**MARSHALL, Fred,** a Representative from Minnesota; born in Union Grove Township, near Grove City, Meeker County, Minn., March 13, 1906; graduated from Paynesville (Minn.) High School; engaged in farming; member of the Minnesota Agriculture Administration Committee, 1937-1941; State director of the Farm Security Administration (later the Farmers Home Administration) 1941-1948; delegate, Minnesota Democratic Farmer-Labor Party convention, 1966; elected as a Democrat to the Eighty-first and to the six succeeding Congresses (January 3, 1949-January 3, 1963); was not a candidate for reelection in 1962 to the Eighty-eighth Congress; resumed agriculture pursuits; member, National Commission on Food Marketing; member, United States Department of Agriculture Forest Appeals Board; was a resident of Grove City, Minn., until his death in Litchfield, Minn., on June 5, 1985; interment in Burr Oak Cemetery on the family farm in Union Grove Township, Meeker County.

**MARSHALL, George Alexander,** a Representative from Ohio; born near Sidney, Shelby County, Ohio, September 14, 1851; attended the public schools of Shelby County and Ohio Wesleyan University, Delaware, Ohio; studied law; was admitted to the bar in 1876 and commenced practice in Sidney, Ohio; prosecuting attorney of Shelby County for eight years, being elected in 1878, 1880, and 1883; elected as a Democrat to the Fifty-fifth Congress (March 4, 1897-March 3, 1899); was not a candidate for reelection in 1898; died in Sidney, Ohio, April 21, 1899; interment in Presbyterian Cemetery, Hardin, Shelby County, Ohio.

**MARSHALL, Humphrey** (father of Thomas Alexander Marshall and cousin of John Marshall, and grandfather of Humphrey Marshall [1812-1872]), a Senator from Kentucky; born in Orlean, Fauquier County, Va., in 1760; pursued classical studies; became a surveyor; served with the Virginia forces in the Revolutionary War; moved to Kentucky in 1782; studied law; was admitted to the bar and commenced practice in Fayette County; delegate to the Danville convention in 1787 to consider the separation of Kentucky from Virginia, which he opposed; delegate to the Virginia convention which ratified the Constitution of the United States; member, Kentucky house of representatives 1793-1794; elected as a Federalist to the United States Senate and served from March 4, 1795, to March 3, 1801; member, Kentucky legislature 1807-1809; engaged in literary pursuits and was the author of the first history of Kentucky, published in 1812; engaged in agricultural pursuits; died near Lexington, Ky., July 3, 1841; interment on his farm, "Glen Willis," Leestown, Ky.

Bibliography: *DAB*; Meredith, Howard. "The Historical Thought of Humphrey Marshall: A Note on Frontier Historicism."

*Filson Club History Quarterly* 47 (October 1973): 349-54; Quisenberry, Anderson C. *The Life and Times of Honorable Humphrey Marshall*. Winchester, Ky.: The Sun Publishing Co., 1892.

**MARSHALL, Humphrey** (grandson of Humphrey Marshall [1761-1841]), a Representative from Kentucky; born in Frankfort, Franklin County, Ky., January 13, 1812; pursued academic studies; graduated from the United States Military Academy at West Point in 1832; resigned from the United States Army on April 30, 1833; studied law; admitted to the bar in 1833 and practiced in Frankfort, 1833-1834, and in Louisville, 1834-1846; served in the Kentucky militia; colonel of Volunteers in the Mexican War; engaged in agricultural pursuits in Henry County, Ky.; elected as a Whig to the Thirty-first and Thirty-second Congresses and served from March 4, 1849, until his resignation on August 4, 1852; appointed Commissioner to China on August 4, 1852, and served until January 1854; elected on the American Party ticket to the Thirty-fourth and Thirty-fifth Congresses (March 4, 1855-March 3, 1859); renominated by acclamation to the Thirty-sixth Congress, but declined; during the Civil War served as a brigadier general in the Confederate Army from October 30, 1861 until June 17, 1863; moved to Richmond, Va., and continued the practice of law; elected to the Confederate Congress; after the war moved to New Orleans, La.; civil disabilities were removed by President Andrew Johnson on December 18, 1867; returned to Louisville and resumed the practice of law; died in Louisville, Ky., March 28, 1872; interment in the State Cemetery, Frankfort, Ky.

**Bibliography:** *DAB*; Rea, Kenneth W. "Humphrey Marshall's Commissionership to China, 1852-1854." Ph.D. dissertation, University of Colorado, 1970.

**MARSHALL, James William,** a Representative from Virginia; born near Staunton, Augusta County, Va., March 31, 1844; attended the country schools of his native county; during the Civil War served in the Confederate Army as a private for four years; was graduated from Roanoke College, Salem, Va., in 1870; studied law and was admitted to the bar; Commonwealth attorney for Craig County 1870-1875; served in the Virginia senate 1875-1878; member of the Virginia house of delegates in 1883 and 1884; elected Commonwealth attorney for Craig County in 1884 and served four years; again served in the Virginia senate in 1891 and 1892; elected as a Democrat to the Fifty-third Congress (March 4, 1893-March 3, 1895); unsuccessful candidate for renomination in 1894; resumed the practice of his profession in Newcastle; elected as delegate to the Virginia constitutional convention of 1901; died in Newcastle, Craig County, Va., November 27, 1911; interment in West View Cemetery.

**MARSHALL, John** (uncle of Thomas Francis Marshall and cousin of Humphrey Marshall [1760-1841]), a Representative from Virginia; born in Germantown, Fauquier County, Va., September 24, 1755; received instruction from a tutor and attended the classical academy of the Messrs. Campbell in Westmoreland County, Va.; at the outbreak of the Revolutionary War joined a company of Virginia militia that subsequently became part of the Eleventh Regiment of Virginia Troops; studied law at the College of William and Mary, Williamsburg, Va.; admitted to the bar on August 28, 1780; resigned his Army commission in 1781 and engaged in the practice of law in Fauquier County; member of the Virginia house of delegates in 1780; settled in Richmond, Va. and practiced law; member of the executive council, 1782-1795; again a member of the Virginia house of delegates, 1782-1788; delegate to the Virginia convention for the ratification of the Federal Constitution that met in Richmond, June 2, 1788; one of the special commissioners to France in 1797 and 1798 to demand redress and reparation for hostile actions of that country; resumed the practice of law in Virginia; declined the appointment of Associate Justice of the United States Supreme Court tendered by President John Adams on September 26, 1798; elected as a Federalist to the Sixth Congress, and served from March 4, 1799 to

June 7, 1800, when he resigned; was appointed Secretary of War by President Adams on May 7, 1800, but the appointment was not considered, and on May 12, 1800, was appointed Secretary of State; entered upon his new duties on June 6, 1800, and although appointed Chief Justice of the United States on January 20, 1801, and notwithstanding he took the oath of office as Chief Justice on February 4, 1801, and continued to serve in the Cabinet until March 4, 1801; member of the Virginia convention of 1829; continued as Chief Justice until his death in Philadelphia, Pa., July 6, 1835; interment in the Shockoe Hill Cemetery, Richmond, Va.

**Bibliography:** *DAB*; Beveridge, Albert J. *The Life of John Marshall*. 4 vols. Boston: Houghton Mifflin Co., 1916-1919; Marshall, John. *The Papers of John Marshall*. 8 vols. to date. Edited by Herbert A. Johnson, Charles T. Cullen, and Charles F. Hobson. Chapel Hill: University of North Carolina Press, 1974- ; Robarge, David Scott. "John Marshall and His Times: A Virginia Lawyer and Southern Federalist in the Early Republic." Ph.D. dissertation, Columbia University, 1995.

**MARSHALL, Leroy Tate,** a Representative from Ohio; born on a farm near Bellbrook, Greene County, Ohio, November 8, 1883; attended the public schools of Greene County; teacher in the public schools of Greene County, Ohio, 1903-1907; was graduated from Cedarville (Ohio) College in 1909; moved to Xenia, Ohio, and served as clerk of courts, Greene County, 1909-1913; studied law; was admitted to the Ohio bar in 1911 and commenced the practicing of law in Xenia, Ohio; served as chairman of the Greene County Republican county committee 1920-1932; member of the Ohio State Senate 1925-1928; elected as a Republican to the Seventy-third and Seventy-fourth Congresses (March 4, 1933-January 3, 1937); unsuccessful candidate for reelection in 1936 to the Seventy-fifth Congress; returned to Xenia, Ohio, and continued the practice of law until his death there on November 22, 1950; interment in Woodland Cemetery.

**MARSHALL, Lycurgus Luther,** a Representative from Ohio; born in Bucyrus, Crawford County, Ohio, July 9, 1888; attended the public schools; was graduated from Ohio Wesleyan University, Delaware, Ohio, in 1909 and from the law department of Western Reserve University, Cleveland, Ohio, in 1915; was admitted to the bar in 1915 and commenced practice in Cleveland, Ohio; member of the State house of representatives in 1921 and 1922; served in the State senate 1923-1935; member of the Euclid (Ohio) School Board for eight years; elected as a Republican to the Seventy-sixth Congress (January 3, 1939-January 3, 1941); unsuccessful candidate for reelection in 1940 to the Seventy-seventh Congress; resumed the practice of law; died in Aurora, Ohio, January 12, 1958; interment in Lake View Cemetery, Cleveland, Ohio.

**MARSHALL, Samuel Scott,** a Representative from Illinois; born near Shawneetown, Gallatin County, Ill., March 12, 1821; attended public and private schools in McLeansboro, Ill., and Cumberland College, Kentucky; studied law; was admitted to the bar in 1845 and commenced practice in McLeansboro, Ill.; member of the State house of representatives in 1846 and 1847; State's attorney for the third judicial circuit of Illinois in 1847 and 1848; circuit court judge 1851-1854 and 1861-1864; delegate to the Democratic National Conventions in 1860, 1864, and 1880; delegate to the Union National Convention at Philadelphia in 1866; elected as a Democrat to the Thirty-fourth and Thirty-fifth Congresses (March 4, 1855-March 3, 1859); chairman, Committee on Claims (Thirty-fifth Congress); was the candidate of his party for United States Senator in 1861; elected to the Thirty-ninth and to the four succeeding Congresses (March 4, 1865-March 3, 1875), and was the candidate of his party for Speaker of the House in 1867; unsuccessful candidate for reelection in 1874 to the Forty-fourth Congress; president of the board of managers of Hamilton College

1875-1880; died in McLeansboro, Hamilton County, Ill., July 26, 1890; interment in Odd Fellows Cemetery.

MARSHALL, Thomas Alexander (son of Humphrey Marshall [1760-1841]), a Representative from Kentucky; born near Versailles, Woodford County, Ky., January 15, 1794; pursued preparatory studies; was graduated from Yale College in 1815; studied law; was admitted to the bar and commenced practice in Frankfort in 1817; moved to Paris, Ky., in 1819; member of the Kentucky house of representatives in 1827 and 1828; elected as an Anti-Jacksonian to the Twenty-second and Twenty-third Congresses (March 4, 1831-March 3, 1835); unsuccessful candidate for reelection in 1834 to the Twenty-fourth Congress; judge of the Kentucky court of appeals 1835-1856; professor in the law department of Transylvania College, Lexington, Ky., 1836-1849; moved to Louisville in 1859; member of the Kentucky house of representatives in 1863; chief justice of the court of appeals in 1866 and 1867; died in Louisville, Ky., April 17, 1871; interment in Lexington Cemetery, Lexington, Ky.

Bibliography: *DAB*.

MARSHALL, Thomas Francis (nephew of John Marshall), a Representative from Kentucky; born in Frankfort, Franklin County, Ky., June 7, 1801; pursued classical studies in Virginia; studied law; was admitted to the bar and commenced practice in Versailles, Ky., in 1828; member of the Kentucky house of representatives 1832-1836, 1838, 1839, and 1854; moved to Louisville in 1833; unsuccessful candidate for election in 1836 to the Twenty-fifth Congress; elected as a Whig to the Twenty-seventh Congress (March 4, 1841-March 3, 1843); unsuccessful candidate for reelection in 1842 to the Twenty-eighth Congress; served in the Mexican War as captain of Volunteers; moved to Chicago, Ill., in 1856; returned to Kentucky and engaged in the practice of law until his death near Versailles, Ky., September 22, 1864; interment in State Cemetery, Frankfort, Ky.

MARSHALL, Thomas Frank, a Representative from North Dakota; born in Hannibal, Marion County, Mo., March 7, 1854; attended the common schools and the State normal school at Platteville, Grant County, Wis.; left school in 1873 two months before graduation, but received his diploma forty years later; became a surveyor; moved to Yankton, Dak. (now South Dakota), in 1873 and engaged in mercantile pursuits; moved to Columbia, Dak. (now North Dakota), in 1882 and engaged in banking; moved in 1886 to Oakes, Dak., where he engaged in banking and surveying; mayor 1888-1892; member of the State senate 1896-1900; delegate to the Republican National Convention in 1892; elected as a Republican to the Fifty-seventh and to the three succeeding Congresses (March 4, 1901-March 3, 1909); chairman, Committee on Private Land Claims (Sixtieth Congress); was not a candidate for renomination in 1908, but was an unsuccessful candidate for the United States Senate; again engaged in banking; died at his summer home in Detroit (now Detroit Lakes), Becker County, Minn., August 20, 1921; interment in Oakesview Cemetery, Oakes, Dickey County, N.Dak.

MARSHALL, Thomas Riley, a Vice President of the United States; born in North Manchester, Wabash County, Ind., March 14, 1854; attended the common schools and graduated from Wabash College, Crawfordsville, Ind., in 1873; studied law; was admitted to the bar in 1875 and commenced practice in Columbia City, Ind.; elected Governor of Indiana in 1908, and served from January 11, 1909 to January 13, 1913; elected Vice President of the United States on the Democratic ticket headed by Woodrow Wilson in 1912, and was inaugurated on March 4, 1913 for the term ending March 4, 1917; reelected in 1916 and served until March 4, 1921; resumed the practice of law and literary work in Indianapolis, Ind.; member of the Federal Coal Commission, 1922-1923; died in Washington, D.C., June 1, 1925; interment in Crown Hill Cemetery, Indianapolis, Ind.

Bibliography: *DAB*; Brown, John E. "Woodrow Wilson's Vice President: Thomas R. Marshall and the Wilson Administration 1913-1921." Ph.D. dissertation, Ball State University, 1970; Marshall, Thomas R. *Recollections of Thomas R. Marshall, Vice President and Hoosier Philosopher: A Hoosier Salad*. Indianapolis: Bobbs-Merrill, 1925.

MARSTON, Gilman, a Representative and a Senator from New Hampshire; born in Oxford, N.H., August 20, 1811; graduated from Dartmouth College, Hanover, N.H., in 1837 and from the law department of Harvard University in 1840; was admitted to the bar and commenced practice in Exeter, Rockingham County, N.H., in 1841; member, New Hampshire State house of representatives, 1845-1849; delegate to the State constitutional convention of 1850; elected as a Republican to the Thirty-sixth and Thirty-seventh Congresses (March 4, 1859-March 3, 1863); served in the Union Army during the Civil War, resigning his commission as brigadier general in 1865; elected to the Thirty-ninth Congress (March 4, 1865-March 3, 1867); declined the Governorship of Idaho Territory in 1870; member, New Hampshire State house of representatives, 1872, 1873, 1876-1878; unsuccessful candidate for election in 1876 to the Forty-fifth Congress; delegate to the State constitutional convention of 1876; appointed to the United States Senate on March 4, 1889, to fill the vacancy in the term commencing on that date and served until June 18, 1889, when a successor was elected; died in Exeter, N.H., July 3, 1890; interment in Exeter Cemetery.

MARTIN, Alexander, a Senator from North Carolina; born in Hunterdon County, N.J., in 1740; attended the common schools; graduated from the College of New Jersey (now Princeton University) in 1756; moved to Salisbury, N.C., and became a merchant, justice of the peace, and judge; represented Guilford County, to which he had moved, in the State house of commons, 1773-1774, and in the provincial congress, 1775; an officer during the Revolutionary War; member, North Carolina State senate, 1778-1782, 1785, 1787-1788, and served as speaker; Acting Governor, 1781-1782; elected Governor of North Carolina by the General Assembly and served 1782-1784, and from December 17, 1789 to December 14, 1792; elected to the Continental Congress in 1786 but resigned; delegate to the State convention for the adoption of the Federal Constitution in 1787; trustee of the University of North Carolina, 1790-1807, and served as president of the board, 1792-1793; elected to the United States Senate, and served from March 4, 1793 to March 3, 1799; unsuccessful candidate for reelection; member, State senate, 1804-1805; died on his plantation, "Danbury," on the Dan River, near Crawford (now Danbury), Stokes County, N.C., November 2, 1807; interment on his estate.

Bibliography: *DAB*.

MARTIN, Augustus Newton, a Representative from Indiana; born near Whitestown, Butler County, Pa., March 23, 1847; attended the common schools and Witherspoon Institute, Butler, Pa., and was graduated from Eastman College, Poughkeepsie, N.Y., in February 1867; enlisted July 3, 1863, in Company I, Fifty-eighth Regiment, Pennsylvania Volunteer Militia; enlisted again February 22, 1865, in Company E, Seventy-eighth Regiment, Pennsylvania Volunteer Infantry, and served until discharged for disability on August 30, 1865; taught school; studied law in Bluffton, Wells County, Ind., in 1869; was admitted to the bar in 1870 and practiced; member of the State house of representatives in 1875; elected reporter of the Supreme Court of Indiana in 1876 and served four years; unsuccessful candidate for reelection in 1880; resided in Austin, Tex., 1881-1883; returned to Bluffton, Ind., in 1883; elected as a Democrat to the Fifty-first and to the two succeeding Congresses (March 4, 1889-March 3, 1895); chairman, Committee on Invalid Pensions (Fifty-second and Fifty-third Congresses); unsuccessful candidate for reelection in 1894 to the Fifty-fourth Congress; engaged in the practice of law in Bluffton, Ind., until his death at the

Soldiers' Home Hospital, Marion, Ind., July 11, 1901; interment in Fairview Cemetery, Bluffton, Ind.

**MARTIN, Barclay** (uncle of Lewis Tillman), a Representative from Tennessee; born in Edgefield District, S.C., December 17, 1802; moved to Bourbon County, Ky., with his parents in 1804 and to Bedford County, Tenn., in 1806; pursued an academic course; moved to Columbia, Maury County, Tenn.; studied law; was admitted to the bar and practiced; member of the State house of representatives in 1839 and 1840; served in the State senate 1841-1843; elected as a Democrat to the Twenty-ninth Congress (March 4, 1845-March 3, 1847); resumed the practice of his profession; again served in the State house of representatives 1847-1849 and 1851-1853; member of the board of trustees of the Columbia Athenaeum from 1852 until his death; died in Columbia, Tenn., November 8, 1890; interment in Zion Cemetery.

**MARTIN, Benjamin Franklin,** a Representative from West Virginia; born near Farmington, Marion County, Va. (now West Virginia), October 2, 1828; was graduated from Allegheny College, Meadville, Pa., in June 1854; taught school in Fairmont, Marion County; studied law; was admitted to the bar and commenced practice in March 1856; moved to Pruntytown in 1856; member of the constitutional convention of West Virginia in 1872; delegate to the Democratic National Convention in 1872 and 1888; elected as a Democrat to the Forty-fifth and Forty-sixth Congresses (March 4, 1877-March 3, 1881); unsuccessful candidate for renomination in 1880; resumed the practice of law in Grafton, Taylor County, W.Va., and died there January 20, 1895; interment in Woodlawn Cemetery, Fairmont, W.Va.

**MARTIN, Charles,** a Representative from Illinois; born near Ogdensburg, St. Lawrence County, N.Y., May 20, 1856; moved with his parents to Chicago, Ill., in 1860; attended the public schools; engaged in business as a sewer contractor and later as a coal dealer; served as alderman in the city council 1894-1903, 1905-1907, and 1910-1913, and again elected in 1915; elected as a Democrat to the Sixty-fifth Congress and served from March 4, 1917, until his death in Chicago, Ill., October 28, 1917; interment in Mount Olivet Cemetery.

**MARTIN, Charles Drake,** a Representative from Ohio; born in Mount Vernon, Knox County, Ohio, August 5, 1829; attended the public schools and Kenyon College, Gambier, Ohio; studied law; was admitted to the bar in 1850 and commenced practice in Lancaster, Fairfield County, Ohio; elected as a Democrat to the Thirty-sixth Congress (March 4, 1859-March 3, 1861); unsuccessful candidate for reelection in 1860 to the Thirty-seventh Congress; resumed the practice of law; member of the supreme court commission 1883-1886; continued the practice of law in Lancaster, Ohio, until his death there August 27, 1911; interment in Forest Rose Cemetery.

**MARTIN, Charles Henry** (great-grandson of Nathaniel Macon), a Representative from North Carolina; born near Youngsville, Franklin County, N.C., August 28, 1848; attended the common schools and the preparatory department of Wake Forest (N.C.) College; was graduated from Wake Forest College in 1872 and from the University of Virginia at Charlottesville in 1875; studied in the Southern Baptist Theological Seminary, Louisville, Ky.; principal of the high schools at Badin and Lumberton, N.C.; professor of Latin in the female college at Murfreesboro, N.C., and later taught in Wake Forest College; studied law; was admitted to the bar in 1879 and commenced practice in Louisburg, Franklin County, N.C.; moved to Raleigh, N.C., and continued the practice of law; ordained as a Baptist minister in 1887; successfully contested as a Populist the election of James A. Lockhart to the Fifty-fourth Congress; reelected to the Fifty-fifth Congress, and served from June 5, 1896 to March 3, 1899; was not a candidate for renomination in 1898 to the Fifty-sixth Congress; resumed his ministerial duties at Polkton,

N.C., and died there on April 19, 1931; interment in Williams Cemetery.

**MARTIN, Charles Henry,** a Representative from Oregon; born on a farm near Albion, Edwards County, Ill., October 1, 1863; attended the public schools of Carmi, Ill., and Ewing (Ill.) College; was graduated from the United States Military Academy at West Point, N.Y., in 1887; served in the United States Army and saw active service in the Spanish-American War, Philippine Insurrection, Boxer campaign in China, and was a division commander in the First World War; awarded the Distinguished Service Medal and two citations for bravery in action; assistant chief of staff, United States Army, 1922-1924; commanded the Panama Canal Department from 1925 until 1927; retired from the Army as a major general on October 1, 1927, and established his residence in Portland, Oreg.; elected as a Democrat to the Seventy-second and Seventy-third Congresses (March 4, 1931-January 3, 1935); was not a candidate for renomination in 1934 to the Seventy-fourth Congress, but was elected Governor of Oregon, and served from January 14, 1935 to January 9, 1939; retired from public life and resided in Portland, Oreg., until his death there on September 22, 1946; interment in Riverview Cemetery.

**Bibliography:** Murrell, Gary. "Perfection of Means, Confusion of Goals: The Military Career of Charles Henry Martin." Ph.D. dissertation, University of Oregon, 1994.

**MARTIN, David O'Brien,** a Representative from New York; born in St. Lawrence County, N.Y., April 26, 1944; attended the public schools of Colton and Canton, N.Y.; graduated, Hugh C. Williams High School, Canton, N.Y., 1962; B.B.A., University of Notre Dame, 1966; J.D., Albany (N.Y.) Law School, 1973; served in the United States Marine Corps, captain, 1966-1970; admitted to the New York bar in 1974 and commenced practice in Canton; elected, St. Lawrence County Board of Legislators, 1973-1975; served in the New York State assembly, 1976-1980; delegate to the Republican National Conventions of 1988 and 1992; elected as a Republican to the Ninety-seventh and to the five succeeding Congresses (January 3, 1981-January 3, 1993); was not a candidate for reelection in 1992 to the One Hundred Third Congress; professor of national security decision making at the United States Naval War College, Newport, R.I., 1993-1994; vice president, state and local affairs, National Soft Drink Association, Washington, D.C., 1994 to present; is a resident of Rockville, Md.

**MARTIN, David Thomas,** a Representative from Nebraska; born in Kearney, Buffalo County, Nebr., July 9, 1907; attended the public schools; attended Dartmouth College, Hanover, N.H., 1925-1928; engaged in the retail lumber business; delegate to the Republican National Conventions of 1944 and 1948; chairman, Nebraska State Republican committee, 1949-1954; member, Republican National Committee, 1952-1954; unsuccessful candidate for the Republican nomination for United States Senator in 1952; elected as a Republican to the Eighty-seventh and to the six succeeding Congresses, and served from January 3, 1961 until his resignation on December 31, 1974; was not a candidate for reelection in 1974 to the Ninety-fourth Congress; is a resident of Kearney, Nebr.

**MARTIN, Eben Wever,** a Representative from South Dakota; born in Maquoketa, Jackson County, Iowa, April 12, 1855; attended the public schools and was graduated from Cornell College, Mount Vernon, Iowa, in 1879; attended the law department of the University of Michigan at Ann Arbor in 1879 and 1880; was admitted to the bar in 1880 and commenced the practice of law in Deadwood, Dak. (now South Dakota); member of the Territorial house of representatives of Dakota in 1884 and 1885; served as president of the board of education of the city of Deadwood 1886-1900; elected as a Republican to the Fifty-seventh, Fifty-eighth, and Fifty-ninth Congresses (March 4, 1901-March 3, 1907);

did not seek the renomination in 1906 but was an unsuccessful candidate for the United States Senate; elected to the Sixtieth Congress to fill the vacancy caused by the death of William H. Parker; reelected to the Sixty-first, Sixty-second, and Sixty-third Congresses and served from November 3, 1908, until March 3, 1915; was not a candidate for renomination in 1914 to the Sixty-fourth Congress; resumed the practice of law in Hot Springs, S.Dak., until his death in that city on May 22, 1932; interment in Evergreen Cemetery.

**MARTIN, Edward,** a Senator from Pennsylvania; born at Ten Mile, Greene County, Pa., September 18, 1879; attended the public schools; graduated from Waynesburg College, Waynesburg, Pa., in 1901; studied law; was admitted to the bar in 1905 and commenced practice in Waynesburg; served in the Spanish-American War on the Mexican Border, and in the First and Second World Wars; burgess of East Waynesburg, 1902-1905; solicitor of Greene County, 1908-1910, 1916-1920; auditor general of Pennsylvania, 1925-1929; Pennsylvania treasurer, 1929-1933; adjutant general of Pennsylvania, 1939-1943; president of the National Guard Association of the United States, 1940; elected Governor of Pennsylvania in 1942, and served from January 19, 1943 until his resignation January 2, 1947, having previously been elected Senator; had varied business interests, including fire insurance, oil and gas, and banking; author and editor; president of the Council of State Governments in 1946; elected as a Republican to the United States Senate in 1946; reelected in 1952, and served from January 3, 1947, to January 3, 1959; chairman, Committee on Public Works (Eighty-third Congress); was not a candidate for renomination in 1958; retired; died in Washington, Pa., March 19, 1967; interment in Greene Mount Cemetery, Waynesburg, Pa.

**Bibliography:** Martin, Edward. *Always Be On Time: An Autobiography.* Harrisburg: Telegraph Press, 1959.

**MARTIN, Edward Livingston,** a Representative from Delaware; born in Seaford, Sussex County, Del., March 29, 1837; attended private schools, Newark Academy, Bolmar's Academy, West Chester, Pa., and Delaware College, Newark, Del.; was graduated from the University of Virginia at Charlottesville in 1859; served as clerk of the State senate 1863-1865; delegate to the Democratic National Conventions in 1864, 1872, 1876, 1880, and 1884; studied law at the University of Virginia in 1866; was admitted to the bar the same year and practiced in Dover, Del., until 1867; returned to Seaford and engaged in agricultural and horticultural pursuits; served as director of the Delaware Board of Agriculture, president of the Peninsula Horticultural Society, and lecturer of the Delaware State Grange; commissioner to settle disputed boundary line between the States of Delaware and New Jersey 1873-1875; elected as a Democrat to the Forty-sixth and Forty-seventh Congresses (March 4, 1879-March 3, 1883); was not a candidate for renomination in 1882 to the Forty-eighth Congress; resumed horticultural and agricultural pursuits; twice an unsuccessful candidate for election to the United States Senate; died in Seaford, Del., January 22, 1897; interment in St. Luke's Episcopal Churchyard.

**MARTIN, Elbert Sevier** (brother of John Preston Martin), a Representative from Virginia; born near Jonesville, Lee County, Va., about 1829; attended the public schools and Emory and Henry College, Emory, Va., 1845-1848; engaged in mercantile pursuits in Jonesville, Va.; elected as an Independent Democrat to the Thirty-sixth Congress (March 4, 1859-March 3, 1861); unsuccessful candidate for reelection in 1860 to the Thirty-seventh Congress; served in the Confederate Army during the Civil War as captain of a company of volunteers formed in Jonesville, Va.; moved to Dallas, Tex., in 1870 and became interested in the newspaper publishing business; died in Dallas, Tex., September 3, 1876.

**MARTIN, Frederick Stanley,** a Representative from New York; born in Rutland County, Vt., April 25, 1794; went to New Hartford, N.Y., in 1804 and attended the local schools; moved to Whitehall, Vt., in 1810 and became employed in a mercantile establishment and later as a sailor; settled in Olean, Cattaraugus County, N.Y., in the spring of 1818, ran a hotel, and also carried on a lumber business, and in 1831 entered the mercantile business in which he engaged for twenty years; member of the board of supervisors of Olean in 1830, 1831, 1836, and 1838; appointed by President Andrew Jackson as postmaster at Olean, N.Y., December 23, 1830, and served until November 14, 1839; appointed judge of the county courts in January 1840 by Governor William H. Seward and served for five years; was actively interested in the construction of the Genesee Valley Canal; member of the New York State senate, 1847-1849; served in the New York State assembly in 1850 and 1851; elected as a Whig to the Thirty-second Congress (March 4, 1851-March 3, 1853); renewed his former business pursuits; died in Olean, N.Y., June 28, 1865; interment in Oak Lawn Cemetery; reinterment on April 29, 1896, in Mount View Cemetery.

**MARTIN, George Brown** (grandson of John Preston Martin), a Senator from Kentucky; born in Prestonsburg, Floyd County, Ky., August 18, 1876; moved with his parents to Catlettsburg, Boyd County, Ky., in 1877; attended the public schools and graduated from Centre University, Richmond (now at Danville), Ky., in 1895; studied law; was admitted to the bar in 1900 and commenced practice in Catlettsburg, Ky.; general counsel and director of the Big Sandy & Kentucky River Railway Co.; vice president, Ohio Valley Electric Railway Co.; director, Kentucky-Farmers Bank of Catlettsburg; county judge of Boyd County in 1904; member of the Council of National Defense for Kentucky in 1917; appointed major in the Judge Advocate General's Department of the United States Army, but did not serve, having been appointed Senator; appointed as a Democrat to the United States Senate to fill the vacancy caused by the death of Ollie M. James and served from September 7, 1918, to March 3, 1919; was not a candidate for election to the full term; chairman, Committee on Expenditures in the Department of Agriculture (Sixty-fifth Congress); resumed the practice of law in Catlettsburg, Ky., where he died November 12, 1945; interment in Catlettsburg Cemetery.

**MARTIN, James Douglas,** a Representative from Alabama; born in Tarrant, Jefferson County, Ala., September 1, 1918; educated in the public schools of Jefferson County and the Birmingham School of Law; employed in the petroleum industry in 1937; enlisted in the United States Army in July 1941, and commanded a battery of artillery in Europe; also served as an intelligence officer in the Army of Occupation and was discharged as a major in March 1946; returned to the oil industry; unsuccessful candidate in 1962 for election to the United States Senate; elected as a Republican to the Eighty-ninth Congress (January 3, 1965-January 3, 1967); was not a candidate in 1966 for reelection to the House of Representatives, but was an unsuccessful candidate for election for Governor of Alabama; unsuccessful candidate in 1972 for nomination to the United States Senate; unsuccessful candidate for election to the United States Senate in 1978 to complete the unexpired term of James B. Allen; resumed work in the petroleum industry; commissioner, Alabama Department of Conservation and Natural Resources, 1987 to present; is a resident of Gadsden, Ala.

**MARTIN, James Grubbs,** a Representative from North Carolina; born in Savannah, Chatham County, Ga., December 11, 1935; attended the public schools of Winnsboro, S.C.; B.S., Davidson (N.C.) College, 1957; Ph.D., chemistry, Princeton University, 1960; associate professor of chemistry at Davidson College, 1960-1972; Mecklenburg County (N.C.) Commissioner, 1966-1972, chairman, 1967-1968 and 1970-1971; founder and first chairman, Centralina Regional Council of governments, 1966-1969; delegate to the

Republican National Convention of 1968; elected as a Republican to the Ninety-third and to the five succeeding Congresses (January 3, 1973-January 3, 1985); was not a candidate for reelection in 1984 to the Ninety-ninth Congress, but was elected Governor of North Carolina; reelected in 1988, and served from January 5, 1985 to January 9, 1993; vice president for research, Carolinas Medical Center; is a resident of Charlotte, N.C.

**MARTIN, James Stewart,** a Representative from Illinois; born in Estillville (now Gate City), Scott County, Va., August 19, 1826; attended the common schools and Emory and Henry College, Emory, Va.; moved to Salem, Marion County, Ill., in 1846; served during the Mexican War in Company C, First Regiment of Illinois Volunteers; studied law; was admitted to the bar in 1861 and commenced practice in Salem, Ill.; clerk of the Marion County Court; during the Civil War served in the Union Army; commissioned colonel of the One Hundred and Eleventh Regiment, Illinois Volunteer Infantry, September 18, 1862; brevetted brigadier general of Volunteers on February 26, 1865; honorably mustered out on June 7, 1865; judge of Marion County Court; appointed by President Ulysses S. Grant as United States pension agent on April 13, 1869; elected as a Republican to the Forty-third Congress (March 4, 1873-March 3, 1875); unsuccessful candidate for reelection in 1874 to the Forty-fourth Congress; commissioner of the Southern Illinois Penitentiary at Menard in 1879; died in Salem, Ill., November 20, 1907; interment in East Lawn Cemetery.

**MARTIN, John,** a Senator from Kansas; born near Hartsville, Wilson County, Tenn., November 12, 1833; attended the common schools; clerked in stores and in the post office; moved to Tecumseh, Shawnee County, Kans., in 1855; elected assistant clerk of the first house of representatives in the Territory in 1855; county clerk and register of deeds 1855-1857; studied law; was admitted to the bar in 1856 and commenced practice in Tecumseh; justice of the peace 1857; county attorney of Shawnee County 1858-1860; postmaster of Tecumseh 1858-1859; deputy United States attorney 1859-1861; reporter of the State supreme court 1860; moved to Topeka and practiced law in 1861; member, State house of representatives 1871-1875; unsuccessful Democratic candidate for Governor in 1876 and for the United States Senate in 1877; district judge 1883-1885; unsuccessful candidate for election to the Fiftieth Congress; unsuccessful candidate for Governor in 1888; elected as a Democrat to the United States Senate on January 25, 1893, to fill the vacancy caused by the death of Preston B. Plumb and served from March 4, 1893, to March 3, 1895; chairman, Committee on Railroads (Fifty-third Congress); clerk of the Supreme Court of Kansas 1897-1899; died in Topeka, Kans., September 3, 1913; interment in Topeka Cemetery.

**MARTIN, John Andrew,** a Representative from Colorado; born in Cincinnati, Ohio, April 10, 1868; moved with his parents to Fulton, Mo., in 1872; attended the public schools of Mexico and Fulton, Mo.; moved with his parents to Kansas in 1884 and worked on a farm; moved to Colorado in 1887; employed on railroad construction work and as a locomotive fireman 1887-1894; member of the city council of La Junta in 1895 and 1896, and published the La Junta Times during the same period; studied law; was admitted to the bar in 1896 and commenced practice in Pueblo, Colo., in 1897; member of the State house of representatives in 1901 and 1902; city attorney in 1905 and 1906; elected as a Democrat to the Sixty-first and Sixty-second Congresses (March 4, 1909-March 3, 1913); declined to be a candidate for reelection in 1912; resumed the practice of law; again city attorney in 1916 and 1917; during the First World War recruited a volunteer battalion and was commissioned a major; resumed the practice of law in Pueblo, Colo.; elected to the Seventy-third and to the three succeeding Congresses and

served from March 4, 1933, until his death in Washington, D.C., December 23, 1939; interment in Mountain View Cemetery, Pueblo, Colo.

**MARTIN, John Cunningham,** a Representative from Illinois; born in Salem, Marion County, Ill., April 29, 1880; attended the public schools and Illinois College, Jacksonville, Ill.; became engaged in banking in 1907; director of the Federal Reserve Bank of St. Louis 1922-1932; president of the Salem National Bank 1933-1952; served as State treasurer of Illinois 1933-1935 and 1937-1939; member of the Illinois Tax Commission and served as chairman in 1935 and 1936; chairman of the Illinois Emergency Relief Commission 1935-1938; elected as a Democrat to the Seventy-sixth Congress (January 3, 1939-January 3, 1941); was not a candidate for renomination in 1940; resumed his banking interests; died in Long Beach, Calif., January 27, 1952; interment in East Lawn Cemetery, Salem, Ill.

**MARTIN, John Mason** (son of Joshua Lanier Martin), a Representative from Alabama; born in Athens, Limestone County, Ala., January 20, 1837; attended the common schools, the high school in Green Springs, Ala., and the University of Alabama at Tuscaloosa; was graduated from Centre College, Danville, Ky., in 1856; studied law; was admitted to the bar in 1858 and commenced practice in Tuscaloosa, Ala.; member of the State senate 1871-1876 and served as president pro tempore 1873-1876; professor of equity jurisprudence in the University of Alabama 1875-1886; elected as a Democrat to the Forty-ninth Congress (March 4, 1885-March 3, 1887); unsuccessful candidate for reelection in 1886 to the Fiftieth Congress; resumed the practice of law in Birmingham, Ala.; died in Bowling Green, Warren County, Ky., June 16, 1898; interment in Greenwood Cemetery, Tuscaloosa, Ala.

**MARTIN, John Preston** (brother of Elbert Sevier Martin and grandfather of George Brown Martin), a Representative from Kentucky; born near Jonesville, Lee County, Va., October 11, 1811; pursued an academic course; moved to Prestonsburg, Floyd County, Ky., in 1828; member of the Kentucky house of representatives 1841-1843; elected as a Democrat to the Twenty-ninth Congress (March 4, 1845-March 3, 1847); chairman, Committee on Mileage (Twenty-ninth Congress); was not a candidate for renomination in 1846; member of the Kentucky senate 1855-1859; delegate to the Democratic National Convention in 1856; died in Prestonburg, Ky., December 23, 1862; interment in May Cemetery.

**MARTIN, Joseph John,** a Representative from North Carolina; born in Williamston, Martin County, N.C., November 21, 1833; attended Williamston Academy; studied law; was admitted to the bar in 1859 and practiced; prosecuting attorney of Martin County, N.C.; elected solicitor for the second judicial district of North Carolina in 1868; reelected in 1874 and served in this capacity until his nomination for Congress in 1878, when he resigned; delegate to the Republican National Convention in 1876; presented credentials as a Republican Member-elect to the Forty-sixth Congress and served from March 4, 1879, until January 29, 1881, when he was succeeded by Jesse J. Yeates, who contested the election; resumed the practice of law in Tarboro, Edgecombe County, N.C.; postmaster of Tarboro from 1897 until his death in that city on December 18, 1900; interment in Williamston Cemetery, Williamston, N.C.

**MARTIN, Joseph William, Jr.,** a Representative from Massachusetts; born in North Attleboro, Bristol County, Mass., November 3, 1884; attended the public schools and graduated from North Attleboro High School in 1902; reporter on the Attleboro Sun and Providence Journal, 1902-1908; publisher of the Evening Chronicle at North Attleboro, beginning in 1908, and also publisher of the Franklin (Mass.) Sentinel; member of the Massachusetts house of representatives, 1912-1914; served in the Massachusetts senate,

1914-1917; chairman of the Massachusetts Street Railway Investigating Commission in 1917; chairman of the Massachusetts legislative campaign committee in 1917; executive secretary of the Massachusetts Republican committee, 1922-1925; delegate to the Republican National Conventions of 1916, 1936, 1940, 1948, 1952, and 1956; permanent chairman of the Republican National Conventions of 1940, 1944, 1948, 1952, and 1956; member of the Republican National Committee, serving as chairman from 1940 to 1942; elected as a Republican to the Sixty-ninth and to the twenty succeeding Congresses (March 4, 1925-January 3, 1967); minority leader (Seventy-sixth through Seventy-ninth Congresses, Eighty-first and Eighty-second Congresses, Eighty-fourth and Eighty-fifth Congresses); Speaker of the House of Representatives (Eightieth and Eighty-third Congresses); unsuccessful candidate for renomination in 1966 to the Ninetieth Congress; returned to North Attleboro, Mass.; died in Hollywood, Fla., March 6, 1968; interment in Mount Hope Cemetery, North Attleboro, Mass.

Bibliography: *DAB*; Hasenfus, William A. "Managing Partner: Joseph W. Martin, Jr., Republican Leader of the United States House of Representatives, 1939-1959." Ph.D. dissertation, Boston College, 1986; Martin, Joseph W., and Robert J. Donovan. *My First Fifty Years in Politics*. New York: McGraw-Hill, 1960.

MARTIN, Joshua Lanier (father of John Mason Martin), a Representative from Alabama; born in Blount County, Tenn., December 5, 1799; attended the country schools; taught school; studied law in Maryville, Tenn.; moved to Russellville, Franklin County, Ala., in 1819 and continued the study of law; was admitted to the bar and practiced in Athens, Limestone County, Ala.; member of the Alabama State house of representatives, 1822-1828; served as State solicitor, 1827-1831; judge of the circuit court in 1834; chancellor of middle Alabama in 1841; elected as a Jacksonian to the Twenty-fourth Congress and reelected as a Democrat to the Twenty-fifth Congress (March 4, 1835-March 3, 1839); was not a candidate for renomination in 1838 to the Twenty-sixth Congress; elected Governor of Alabama in 1845, and served from December 10, 1845 to December 16, 1847; resumed the practice of law in Tuscaloosa, Ala.; again a member of the State house of representatives in 1853; died in Tuscaloosa, Ala., on November 2, 1856; interment in Evergreen Cemetery.

Bibliography: *DAB*.

MARTIN, Lewis J., a Representative from New Jersey; born near Deckertown, Sussex County, N.J., on February 22, 1844; attended the common schools; studied law; was admitted to the bar in 1867 and commenced practice in Branchville, N.J.; chief clerk in the office of the county clerk of Sussex County in 1868 and 1869; county clerk of Sussex County in 1869; member of the New Jersey State house of assembly, 1879-1881; judge of the Sussex County Court, 1881-1896; served as attorney to the board of freeholders of Sussex County from 1896 to 1911, when he was appointed county judge by Governor Woodrow Wilson and served until his death; member of the town committee, 1896-1907; member of the New Jersey State senate, 1898-1903; elected as a Democrat to the Sixty-third Congress and served from March 4, 1913, until his death in Washington, D.C., on May 5, 1913; interment in Newton Cemetery, Newton, N.J.

MARTIN, Luther, a Delegate from Maryland; born in New Brunswick, Middlesex County, N.J., February 9, 1744; was graduated from Princeton College in 1766; taught school in Queenstown, Md., 1766-1771; studied law; was admitted to the bar in Williamsburg, Va., September 1, 1771, and commenced practice in Accomac County, Va.; member of the Annapolis convention of 1774; attorney general of Maryland from 1778 until 1805; elected to the Continental Congress in 1784, but did not attend; member of the Federal Constitutional Convention in 1787; counsel for Judge Samuel Chase in 1805 in the latter's impeachment, and for Aaron Burr in 1807 in his trial for treason; chief justice of the court of oyer and terminer in 1814; again attorney general of Maryland, 1818-1820; having suffered a stroke of paralysis, the Maryland Legislature passed an act requiring every lawyer in the State to pay an annual license tax of five dollars to be turned over to trustees for his use; passed his last years with Aaron Burr in New York City, where he died on July 10, 1826; interment in Trinity Cemetery.

Bibliography: *DAB*; Clarkson, Paul S. and Samuel Jett. *Luther Martin of Maryland*. Baltimore: Johns Hopkins University Press, 1970.

MARTIN, Lynn Morley, a Representative from Illinois; born in Chicago, Cook County, Ill., December 26, 1939; attended the public schools; B.A., University of Illinois, Urbana, 1960; teacher; member, Winnebago County Board, 1972-1976; member, Illinois State house of representatives, 1977-1979; Illinois State senator, 1979-1980; delegate, Illinois State Republican convention, 1980; elected as a Republican to the Ninety-seventh and to the four succeeding Congresses (January 3, 1981-January 3, 1991); was not a candidate in 1990 for reelection to the House of Representatives, but was an unsuccessful candidate for election to the United States Senate; appointed Secretary of Labor in the Cabinet of President George Bush, and served from February 22, 1991 until January 20, 1993; is a resident of Chicago, Ill.

MARTIN, Morgan Lewis (cousin of James Duane Doty), a Delegate from the Territory of Wisconsin; born in Martinsburg, Lewis County, N.Y., March 31, 1805; attended the common schools and was graduated from Hamilton College, Clinton, N.Y., in 1824; studied law; was admitted to the bar and commenced practice in Detroit, Mich.; moved to Green Bay, Wis., in 1827 (then a part of Michigan Territory); member of the Michigan Territorial legislature 1831-1835; member of the Wisconsin Territorial legislature 1838-1844 and served as president in 1842 and 1843; elected as a Democrat to the Twenty-ninth Congress (March 4, 1845-March 3, 1847); president of the second State constitutional convention in 1847 and 1848; again elected to the State assembly in 1855; member of the State senate in 1858 and 1859; served in the Union Army as paymaster with the rank of major 1861-1865; Indian agent 1866-1869; unsuccessful candidate for election in 1866 to the Fortieth Congress; resumed the practice of his profession; elected judge of Brown County in 1875, in which capacity he served until his death at Green Bay, Brown County, Wis., December 10, 1887; interment in Woodlawn Cemetery.

MARTIN, Patrick Minor, a Representative from California; born in Norfolk, Madison County, Nebr., November 25, 1924; attended the public schools; graduated from Riverside (Calif.) Junior College in 1947, the University of California at Berkeley in 1949, and the Hastings College of Law at San Francisco in 1953; passed the bar and began the practice of law in Riverside, Calif.; served in the United States Coast Guard, 1943-1945, as a radioman; elected as a Republican to the Eighty-eighth Congress (January 3, 1963-January 3, 1965); unsuccessful candidate for reelection in 1964 to the Eighty-ninth Congress; resumed the practice of law; died in Long Beach, Calif., July 18, 1968; interment in Arlington National Cemetery, Va.

MARTIN, Robert Nicols, a Representative from Maryland; born in Cambridge, Dorchester County, Md., January 14, 1798; attended the public schools; studied law; was admitted to the bar and practiced at Princess Anne, Md., from 1819 to 1827; elected to the Nineteenth Congress (March 4, 1825-March 3, 1827); settled in Baltimore and resumed the practice of law; appointed by Governor Thomas G. Pratt chief justice of the western judicial district in 1845, in which capacity he served until the office was vacated by the constitution of 1851; again engaged in the practice of his profession in Baltimore; judge of the superior court of Baltimore, 1859-1867; professor of international law in the University of Maryland at

Baltimore, 1867-1870; died at Saratoga Springs, N.Y., July 20, 1870; interment in Christ Protestant Episcopal Church Cemetery, Cambridge, Md.

**MARTIN, Thomas Ellsworth,** a Representative and a Senator from Iowa; born in Melrose, Monroe County, Iowa, January 18, 1893; attended the public schools; graduated from the State University of Iowa in 1916 and from its law college in 1927; graduated from Columbia University graduate school in 1928; sales analyst and accountant for a rubber company in Akron, Ohio, and Dallas, Tex., in 1916 and 1917; during the First World War served as a first lieutenant with the Thirty-fifth Infantry, United States Army 1917-1919; continued work in the rubber industry; assistant professor of military science and tactics, University of Iowa, 1921-1923; accountant; admitted to the Iowa bar in 1927 and commenced practice in Iowa City; city solicitor for Iowa City 1933-1935; mayor of Iowa City 1935-1937; elected as a Republican to the Seventy-sixth and to the seven succeeding Congresses (January 3, 1939-January 3, 1955); was not a candidate for renomination in 1954; elected as a Republican to the United States Senate in 1954, and served from January 3, 1955, to January 3, 1961; was not a candidate for renomination; retired and moved to Seattle, Wash., where he died June 27, 1971; interment in Willamette National Cemetery, Portland, Oreg.

**MARTIN, Thomas Staples,** a Senator from Virginia; born in Scottsville, Albemarle County, Va., July 29, 1847; attended the Virginia Military Institute at Lexington 1864-1865, and the University of Virginia at Charlottesville 1865-1867; served in the Confederate army; studied law; was admitted to the bar in 1869 and practiced in Albemarle County; member of the board of visitors of the Miller Manual Labor School of Albemarle County; member of the board of visitors of the University of Virginia; elected as a Democrat to the United States Senate in 1893; reelected in 1899, 1905, 1911, and 1918, and served from March 4, 1895, until his death in Charlottesville, Va., November 12, 1919; Democratic caucus chairman 1911-1913, 1917-1919; chairman, Committee on Corporations Organized in the District of Columbia (Fifty-seventh through Fifty-ninth Congresses), Committee on Public Health and National Quarantine (Sixty-first Congress), Committee on Appropriations (Sixty-third through Sixty-fifth Congresses); interment in the University of Virginia Cemetery.

Bibliography: *DAB*; Cox, Harold E. "The Jones-Martin Senatorial Campaign of 1911." In *Essays in History*, pp. 38-56. Charlottesville: University of Virginia, 1954; Holt, Wythe W., Jr. "The Senator from Virginia and the Democratic Floor Leadership: Thomas S. Martin and Conservatism in the Progressive Era." *Virginia Magazine of History and Biography* 83 (January 1975): 3-21; Reeves, Pascal. "Thomas S. Martin: Committee Statesman." *Virginia Magazine of History and Biography* 68 (July 1960): 344-64.

**MARTIN, Whitmell Pugh,** a Representative from Louisiana; born near Napoleonville, Assumption Parish, La., August 12, 1867; attended the public schools and was privately tutored; was graduated from the Louisiana State University, Baton Rouge, La., in 1888; professor of chemistry at the Kentucky Military Institute in 1889 and 1890; chemist for the Sugar Land Refinery, Texas, in 1890 and 1891; studied law at the University of Virginia, Charlottesville, Va., in 1891 and 1892; was admitted to the bar in 1892 and commenced practice in Napoleonville, La.; moved to Thibodaux, La., the same year and continued the practice of law; superintendent of schools for the parish of Lafourche, La., 1894-1900; district attorney of the twentieth district 1900-1906 and judge of the same district 1906-1914; elected as a Progressive to the Sixty-fourth and Sixty-fifth Congresses, and as a Democrat to the Sixty-sixth and to the five succeeding Congresses, and served from March 4, 1915, until his death in Washington, D.C., April 6, 1929; interment in St. John's Episcopal Cemetery, Thibodaux, La.

**MARTIN, William Dickinson,** a Representative from South Carolina; born in Martintown, Edgefield District, S.C., October 20, 1789; pursued an academic course; studied law at Edgefield and attended the Litchfield Law School; was admitted to the bar in 1811 and commenced practice in Edgefield, S.C., the same year; moved to Coosawhatchie, Beaufort County, in 1813; member of the State house of representatives for St. Luke's Parish 1816-1817; clerk of the State senate 1818-1826; elected as a Jacksonian to the Twentieth and Twenty-first Congresses (March 4, 1827-March 3, 1831); judge of the circuit courts of law and appeal 1831-1833; moved to Columbia, S.C., where he resided until his death in Charleston, S.C., November 17, 1833; interment in the churchyard cemetery of St. Michael's Church.

**MARTIN, William Harrison,** a Representative from Texas; born near Eufaula, Barbour County, Ala., May 23, 1823; attended the common schools; studied law in Troy, Ala., and was admitted to the bar; moved to Texas in 1850 and engaged in the practice of law; member of the Texas State senate, 1853-1857; during the Civil War raised a company for the Confederate Army in 1861 and was mustered into the Fourth Texas Regiment; assigned to the Army of Northern Virginia and participated in all the battles of that army until its surrender in April 1865; returned to Texas and engaged in the practice of law at Athens; elected district attorney in 1872; elected as a Democrat to the Fiftieth Congress to fill the vacancy caused by the resignation of John H. Reagan; reelected to the Fifty-first Congress and served from November 4, 1887, to March 3, 1891; resumed the practice of law in Athens, Tex.; died at his home near Hillsboro, Tex., February 3, 1898; interment in Hillsboro Cemetery.

**MARTINDALE, Henry Clinton,** a Representative from New York; born in Berkshire County, Mass., on May 6, 1780; was graduated from Williams College, Williamstown, Mass., in 1800; studied law; was admitted to the bar and practiced at Sandy Hill, Washington County, N.Y., 1801-1860; surrogate of Washington County, 1816-1819; district attorney, 1821-1828; elected to the Eighteenth and to the three succeeding Congresses (March 4, 1823-March 3, 1831); elected as an Anti-Masonic candidate to the Twenty-third Congress (March 4, 1833-March 3, 1835); appointed by Governor William H. Seward as canal appraiser, 1840-1843; died at Sandy Hill, N.Y., April 22, 1860; interment in Kingsbury Cemetery, Kingsbury, N.Y.

**MARTINE, James Edgar,** a Senator from New Jersey; born in New York City, August 25, 1850; moved with his parents to Plainfield, N.J., in 1857; attended the public schools; engaged in agricultural pursuits, the real estate business, and in building; member of the Plainfield common council; unsuccessful candidate for election as mayor of Plainfield; unsuccessful candidate in 1906 for election to the Sixtieth Congress; elected as a Democrat to the United States Senate and served from March 4, 1911, to March 3, 1917; chairman, Committee on Coast Defenses (Sixty-third Congress), Committee on Industrial Expositions (Sixty-third and Sixty-fourth Congresses); unsuccessful candidate for reelection in 1916; resumed agricultural pursuits; died in Miami, Fla., February 26, 1925; interment in Hillside Cemetery, Plainfield, N.J.

**MARTINEZ, Matthew Gilbert,** a Representative from California; born in Walsenberg, Huerfano County, Colo., February 14, 1929; attended public schools in Los Angeles, Calif.; received certificate of competence, Los Angeles Trade Technical School, 1949; served in the United States Marine Corps, private first class, 1947-1950; small businessman and building contractor; member of the Monterey Park, Calif., Planning Commission, 1971-1974; elected to the Monterey Park city council, 1974-1980; mayor of Monterey Park, 1974 and 1980; member, California State assembly, 1980-1982; elected as a Democrat to the Ninety-seventh Congress, July 13, 1982, by special election, to fill the vacancy caused by the resignation of George E. Danielson; reelected to the seven succeeding Congresses and served from July 13, 1982, to January 3, 1997; is a resident of Monterey Park, Calif.

**MARTINI, William J.,** a Representative from New Jersey; born in Passaic, Somerset County, N.J., February 10, 1947; graduated, Passaic High School; B.A., Villanova University, 1968; J.D., Rutgers University School of Law, 1972; admitted to the bar in 1972 and commenced practice in Cedar Grove, N.J.; served as a county and federal prosecutor; member, Clifton, N.J., city council, 1990-1994; president, Nicholas Martini Foundation, 1991 to present; member, Passaic County board of chosen freeholders, 1992-1994; elected as a Republican to the One Hundred Fourth Congress (January 3, 1995-January 3, 1997); is a resident of Clifton, N.J.

**MARVIN, Dudley,** a Representative from New York; born in Lyme, New London County, Conn., May 9, 1786; attended Colchester (Conn.) Academy; moved to Canandaigua, N.Y., in 1807 and studied law; was admitted to the bar in 1811 and commenced practice in Erie, Pa.; returned to Canandaigua, N.Y., the same year and continued the practice of law; lieutenant in the State militia in 1812; promoted successively to colonel, brigadier general, and major general; elected to the Eighteenth, Nineteenth, and Twentieth Congresses (March 4, 1823-March 3, 1829); devoted his time to developing various mechanical improvements, which he patented; moved to New York City in 1835 and to Ripley, Chautauqua County, N.Y. in 1843, and continued the practice of law; elected as a Whig to the Thirtieth Congress (March 4, 1847-March 3, 1849); resumed practice of law in Ripley, N.Y., where he died June 25, 1856; interment in East Ripley Cemetery.

**Bibliography:** *DAB.*

**MARVIN, Francis,** a Representative from New York; born in New York City March 8, 1828; attended the public schools in Port Jervis, Orange County; entered upon a commercial career and engaged in the promotion, construction, and operation of railroads, water-supply companies, bridges, manufacture of illuminating gas, and in banking; postmaster of Port Jervis in 1851; justice of the peace in the town of Deerpark in 1852; employed as bookkeeper in a bank in 1856; unsuccessful candidate of the Republican Party for member of the assembly in 1864 and for the State senate in 1881; was president of the village of Port Jervis in 1865; elected as a Republican to the Fifty-third Congress (March 4, 1893-March 3, 1895); declined to be a candidate for renomination in 1894 and devoted his time to the management of his several business enterprises; died in Port Jervis, N.Y., August 14, 1905; interment in Laurel Grove Cemetery.

**MARVIN, James Madison,** a Representative from New York; born in Ballston, Saratoga County, N.Y., February 27, 1809; attended the common schools; moved to Saratoga Springs, N.Y., and engaged in the hotel business in Saratoga Springs and Albany, N.Y.; Whig member of the State assembly in 1845; member of the board of supervisors of Saratoga County and served as chairman of the board in 1845, 1857, 1862, and 1874; elected as a Republican to the Thirty-eighth, Thirty-ninth, and Fortieth Congresses (March 4, 1863-March 3, 1869); chairman, Committee on Expenditures in the Department of the Treasury (Thirty-ninth and Fortieth Congresses); was not a candidate for renomination; president of the First National Bank of Saratoga Springs, N.Y.; director of the New York Central Railroad; died at Saratoga Springs, N.Y., April 25, 1901; interment in Greenridge Cemetery.

**MARVIN, Richard Pratt,** a Representative from New York; born in Fairfield, Herkimer County, N.Y., December 23, 1803; moved with his parents to Dryden, N.Y., in 1809; attended the public schools; studied law; was admitted to the bar in 1829 and commenced practice in Jamestown, Chautauqua County, N.Y.; member of the State assembly in 1836 and 1837; elected as a Whig

to the Twenty-fifth and Twenty-sixth Congresses (March 4, 1837-March 3, 1841); chairman, Committee on Expenditures in the Post Office Department (Twenty-sixth Congress); was not a candidate for renomination in 1840; delegate to the State constitutional convention in 1846; judge of the eighth judicial district 1847-1871; resumed the practice of law in Jamestown, N.Y., and died there January 11, 1892; interment in Lakeview Cemetery.

**MASCARA, Frank R.,** a Representative from Pennsylvania; born in Belle Vernon, Fayette County, Pa., January 19, 1930; graduated, Belle Vernon High School; B.S., California State University of Pennsylvania, 1972; entered active duty, United States Army, 1946, released in 1947; public accountant, 1954 to present; Washington County, Pa., controller, 1974-1980; chair, Washington County board of commissioners, 1980-1994; elected as a Democrat to the One Hundred Fourth Congress (January 3, 1995-January 3, 1997); is a resident of Charleroi, Pa.

**MASON, Armistead Thomson** (son of Stevens Thomson Mason), a Senator from Virginia; born at the "Armisteads," in Louisa County, Va., August 4, 1787; graduated from the College of William and Mary, Williamsburg, Va., in 1807; engaged in agricultural pursuits; colonel of Virginia Volunteers in the War of 1812 and subsequently brigadier general of Virginia Militia; elected as a Republican to the United States Senate to fill the vacancy caused by the resignation of William B. Giles and served from January 3, 1816, to March 3, 1817; chairman, Committee on the District of Columbia (Fourteenth Congress); moved to Loudoun County, Va.; unsuccessful candidate for election in 1816 to the Fifteenth Congress in a campaign of much bitterness, which gave rise to several duels, and later resulted in his being killed in a duel with his brother-in-law, John Mason McCarty, at Bladensburg, Md., near Washington, D.C., February 6, 1819; interment in the churchyard of the Episcopal Church at Leesburg, Loudoun County, Va.

**MASON, Harry Howland,** a Representative from Illinois; born on a farm in McLean County, near Farmer City, De Witt County, Ill., December 16, 1873; moved to Delavan, Tazewell County, with his parents and attended the public schools; engaged in newspaper work; moved to Pawnee, Sangamon County, Ill., in 1903 and engaged in the newspaper publishing business; secretary to Congressman J. Earl Major 1930-1933; treasurer of Sangamon County in 1933 and 1934; elected as a Democrat to the Seventy-fourth Congress (January 3, 1935-January 3, 1937); was not a candidate for renomination in 1936; resumed the newspaper publishing business in Pawnee, Ill.; died March 10, 1946, in Springfield, Ill.; interment in Prairie Rest Cemetery, Delavan, Ill.

**MASON, James Brown,** a Representative from Rhode Island; born in Thompson, Windham County, Conn., in January 1775; pursued classical studies; was graduated from Brown University, Providence, R.I., in 1791; studied medicine and was admitted to practice; moved to Charleston, S.C., and practiced 1795-1798; returned to Providence, R.I., and engaged in mercantile pursuits 1798-1819; member of the State house of representatives 1804-1814 and served as speaker from February 1812 to May 1814; elected as a Federalist to the Fourteenth and Fifteenth Congresses (March 4, 1815-March 3, 1819); was not a candidate for renomination in 1818 to the Sixteenth Congress; served as a trustee of Brown University 1804-1819; died in Providence, R.I., August 31, 1819; interment in North Burial Ground.

**MASON, James Murray,** a Representative and a Senator from Virginia; born on Analostan Island, Fairfax County, Va. (now Theodore Roosevelt Island, Washington, D.C.), November 3, 1798; studied under a private tutor and at an academy at Georgetown, D.C.; graduated from the University of Pennsylvania at Philadelphia in 1818 and from the law department of the College of William and Mary, Williamsburg in 1820; admitted to the bar and practiced in Winchester, Va., in 1820 and 1821; delegate to the Virginia constitutional convention in 1829; member, Virginia house of delegates, 1826-1832, with the exception of 1827-1828; presidential elector on the Democratic ticket in 1832; elected as a Jackson Democrat to the Twenty-fifth Congress (March 4, 1837-March 3, 1839); elected as a Democrat to the United States Senate in 1847 to fill the vacancy caused by the death of Isaac S. Pennybacker; reelected in 1850 and 1856, and served from January 21, 1847 until March 28, 1861, when he joined other secessionist Senators and withdrew; served as President pro tempore of the Senate during the Thirty-fourth and Thirty-fifth Congresses; expelled from the Senate by a resolution of July 11, 1861, for support of the Confederacy; chairman, Committee on Claims (Thirtieth Congress), Committee on the District of Columbia (Thirty-first Congress), Committee on Foreign Relations (Thirty-second through Thirty-sixth Congresses), Committee on Naval Affairs (Thirty-second Congress); delegate from Virginia to the Provisional Congress of the Confederacy; appointed commissioner of the Confederacy to Great Britain and France; on November 8, 1861, while on a diplomatic mission from the Confederate States to England and France, was taken from the British mail steamer *Trent*, sailing from Havana to England, and placed under arrest by Captain Charles Wilkes of the U.S.S. *San Jacinto*; confined in Fort Warren, Boston Harbor until his release in January 1862; proceeded to London and represented the Confederacy until its defeat in April 1865; resided in Canada after the close of the war until 1868, when he returned to Virginia; died near the city of Alexandria, Va., April 28, 1871; interment in St. Paul's Cemetery, Alexandria, Va.

**Bibliography:** *DAB*; Bugg, James L., Jr. "The Political Career of James Murray Mason: The Legislative Phase." Ph.D. dissertation, University of Virginia, 1950; Mason, James M. *The Public Life and Diplomatic Correspondence of James M. Mason.* Roanoke: Stone Printing Company, 1903; Young, Robert William. "James Murray Mason, 1798-1871: Virginia Statesman and Diplomat." Ph.D. dissertation, University of Maryland, 1993.

**MASON, Jeremiah,** a Senator from New Hampshire; born in Lebanon, New London County, Conn., April 27, 1768; graduated from Yale College in 1788; studied law; moved to Vermont and was admitted to the bar in 1791; moved to New Hampshire and practiced law; attorney general of New Hampshire 1802-1805; elected as a Federalist to the United States Senate to fill the vacancy in the term beginning March 4, 1813, and served from June 10, 1813, until June 16, 1817, when he resigned; member, State house of representatives 1820-1821, 1824; president of the Portsmouth branch of the United States Bank 1828-1829; moved to Boston, Mass., in 1832; retired from the practice of law in 1838, but continued as chamber counsel up to the time of his death in Boston, Mass., October 14, 1848; interment in Mount Auburn Cemetery, Cambridge, Mass.

**Bibliography:** *DAB*; Mason, Jeremiah. *Memoir and Correspondence of Jeremiah Mason.* Edited by George Hillard. Cambridge: Riverside Press, 1973.

**MASON, John Calvin,** a Representative from Kentucky; born near Mount Sterling, Montgomery County, Ky., August 4, 1802; attended country and city schools in Montgomery County and Mount Sterling Law School in Lexington, Ky.; graduated from Transylvania University, Lexington, Ky., in 1823; admitted to the bar and practiced in Mount Sterling; engaged extensively in the manufacture of iron; member of the Kentucky house of representatives in 1839, 1844, and 1848; served in the war with Mexico in 1846 and 1847 in Ben McCollough's company of Texas Rangers, Worth's division, under General Zachary Taylor; moved to Owingsville, Bath County, Ky., in 1847; elected as a Democrat to the Thirty-first and Thirty-second Congresses (March 4, 1849-March 3, 1853); chairman, Committee on Accounts (Thirty-first and Thirty-second Congresses); was not a candidate for renomination in 1852 to the Thirty-third Congress; elected to the Thirty-fifth Congress (March 4, 1857-March

3, 1859); chairman, Committee on Accounts (Thirty-fifth Congress); was not a candidate for renomination in 1858 to the Thirty-sixth Congress; delegate to the Democratic National Convention at Charleston, S.C., in 1860; presidential elector on the Democratic ticket of Stephen A. Douglas and Herschel V. Johnson in 1860; during the Civil War served with Texas State troops from Brenham, Tex. in 1863; died in August 1865 near New Orleans on board a steamer on the Mississippi River; interment in the State Cemetery, Frankfort, Ky.

**MASON, John Thomson,** a Representative from Maryland; born at "Montpelier," near Hagerstown, Washington County, Md., May 9, 1815; educated by a private tutor and was graduated from Princeton College in 1836; studied law; was admitted to the bar and commenced practice in Hagerstown, Md., in 1838; member of the State house of representatives in 1838 and 1839; elected as a Democrat to the Twenty-seventh Congress (March 4, 1841-March 3, 1843); judge of the court of appeals 1851-1857; collector of customs at Baltimore 1857-1861; moved to Annapolis, Md., where he died March 28, 1873; interment in Rose Hill Cemetery, Hagerstown, Md.

**MASON, John Young,** a Representative from Virginia; born near Hicksford (now Emporia), Greensville County, Va., April 18, 1799; was graduated from the University of North Carolina at Chapel Hill in 1816; studied law; was admitted to the bar in 1819 and commenced practice in Hicksford, Va.; member of the Virginia house of delegates, 1823-1827; served in the Virginia senate, 1827-1831; elected as a Jacksonian to the Twenty-second and to the two succeeding Congresses and served from March 4, 1831, until his resignation January 11, 1837; chairman, Committee on Foreign Affairs (Twenty-fourth Congress); appointed United States district judge for the eastern district of Virginia in 1837; delegate to the Virginia constitutional conventions of 1829 and 1850; appointed Secretary of the Navy in the Cabinet of President John Tyler, and served from March 26, 1844 to March 10, 1845, and again in the Cabinet of President James K. Polk from September 10, 1846 to March 7, 1849; Attorney General in the Cabinet of President Polk from March 11, 1845 to September 9, 1846; resumed the practice of law in Richmond, Va., 1849-1854; appointed United States Minister Plenipotentiary to France on January 22, 1854, and served until his death, in Paris, France, on October 3, 1859; his remains were conveyed to the United States and interred in Hollywood Cemetery, Richmond, Va.

**Bibliography:** *DAB*; Williams, Frances L. "The Heritage and Preparation of a Statesman, John Young Mason, 1799-1859." *Virginia Magazine of History and Biography* 75 (July 1967): 305-30.

**MASON, Jonathan,** a Senator and a Representative from Massachusetts; born in Boston, Mass., September 12, 1756; completed preparatory studies in the Boston Latin School and graduated from the College of New Jersey (now Princeton University) in 1774; studied law; admitted to the bar in 1779 and commenced practice in Boston; member, Massachusetts house of representatives 1786-1796; member, executive council 1797-1798; member, Massachusetts senate 1799-1800; elected as a Federalist to the United States Senate to fill the vacancy caused by the resignation of Benjamin Goodhue and served from November 14, 1800, to March 3, 1803; resumed the practice of law; member, Massachusetts senate 1803-1804; member, Massachusetts house of representatives 1805-1808; elected to the Fifteenth and Sixteenth Congresses and served from March 4, 1817, until his resignation on May 15, 1820; again engaged in the practice of his profession in Boston, Mass., where he died November 1, 1831; interment in Mount Auburn Cemetery, Cambridge, Mass.

**Bibliography:** *DAB*.

**MASON, Joseph,** a Representative from New York; born in Plattsburg, Clinton County, N.Y., March 30, 1828; moved with his parents to Hamilton, Madison County, N.Y., in 1840; attended Hamilton Academy and Madison College (later Colgate University), Hamilton, N.Y.; studied law; was admitted to the bar in 1849 and practiced in Hamilton, N.Y.; elected justice of the peace in 1849 and served in that capacity until 1904; elected county judge and surrogate of Madison County for the term commencing January 1, 1864, and served four years; collector of internal revenue 1871-1876; served as city attorney for many years; elected as a Republican to the Forty-sixth and Forty-seventh Congresses (March 4, 1879-March 3, 1883); was not a candidate for renomination in 1882; resumed the practice of law in Hamilton, N.Y., and died there May 31, 1914; interment in Woodlawn Cemetery.

**MASON, Moses, Jr.,** a Representative from Maine; born in Dublin, Cheshire County, N.H., June 2, 1789; moved with his parents to Bethel, Oxford County, Maine, in 1799; attended the common schools; studied medicine; and commenced practice in Bethel in 1813; appointed first postmaster of Bethel April 1, 1815, serving until December 27, 1833; justice of the peace 1821-1866; county commissioner 1831-1834; elected as a Jacksonian to the Twenty-third and Twenty-fourth Congresses (March 4, 1833-March 3, 1837); executive councilor 1843-1845; trustee of the State insane hospital in 1844; selectman of Bethel for fourteen years; president of Gould's Academy 1854-1856; died in Bethel, Maine, June 25, 1866; interment in Woodlawn Cemetery.

**MASON, Noah Morgan,** a Representative from Illinois; born in Glamorganshire, Wales, July 19, 1882; immigrated to the United States in 1888 with his parents, who settled in La Salle, Ill.; attended the public schools and Dixon (Ill.) College; was graduated from the Illinois State Normal University at Normal in 1925; teacher and principal of schools at Oglesby, Ill., 1902-1905, and was superintendent of schools from 1908 until 1936; city commissioner of Oglesby, 1918-1926; member of the Illinois State Normal School Board, 1926-1930; served in the Illinois State senate, 1930-1936; elected as a Republican to the Seventy-fifth and to the twelve succeeding Congresses (January 3, 1937-January 3, 1963); was not a candidate for renomination in 1962 for the Eighty-eighth Congress; retired and lived in Plainfield, Ill.; died in Joliet, Ill., March 29, 1965; interment in Plainfield Cemetery, Plainfield, Ill.

**Bibliography:** Samosky, Jack A. "Congressman Noah Morgan Mason: Illinois' Conservative Spokesman." *Journal of the Illinois State Historical Society* 76 (Spring 1983): 35-48.

**MASON, Samson,** a Representative from Ohio; born in Fort Ann, Washington County, N.Y., July 24, 1793; attended the common schools in Onondaga, N.Y.; studied law; was admitted to the bar and practiced in Springfield, Ohio; prosecuting attorney of Clark County in 1822; member of the State senate 1829-1831; president judge of the court of common pleas in 1834; elected as a Whig to the Twenty-fourth and to the three succeeding Congresses (March 4, 1835-March 3, 1843); chairman, Committee on Revisal and Unfinished Business (Twenty-fifth Congress); was not a candidate for renomination; member of the State house of representatives in 1845 and 1846; United States attorney for Ohio 1850-1853; delegate to the Ohio constitutional convention in 1850; served in the State senate 1862-1864; served from captain to major general in the State militia; died in Springfield, Ohio, February 1, 1869; interment in Ferncliff Cemetery.

**MASON, Stevens Thomson** (father of Armistead Thomson Mason), a Senator from Virginia; born in "Chappawamsic," Stafford County, Va., December 29, 1760; attended the College of William and Mary, Williamsburg, Va.; studied law; was admitted to the bar and commenced practice in Dumfries, Prince William County, Va.; served in the Revolutionary Army as an aide to General George Washington at Yorktown; brigadier general in the Virginia Militia; member,

Virginia house of delegates 1783, 1794; member, Virginia senate 1787-1790; delegate to the Virginia constitutional convention in 1788; elected to the United States Senate to fill the vacancy caused by the resignation of James Monroe; reelected in 1797 and again in 1803 as a Republican, and served from November 18, 1794, until his death in Philadelphia, Pa., May 10, 1803; interment in the family burying ground at "Raspberry Plain" in Loudoun County, Va.

**Bibliography:** *DAB.*

**MASON, William,** a Representative from New York; born in Lebanon, New London County, Conn., September 10, 1786; studied medicine in Vermont and practiced in Preston, N.Y.; surgeon of the Chenango County Company, New York Volunteers, in 1812; clerk of Chenango County in 1820-1821; member of the State assembly in 1821 and 1822; elected as a Jacksonian to the Twenty-fourth Congress (March 4, 1835-March 3, 1837); died in Norwich, N.Y., January 13, 1860; interment in Mount Hope Cemetery.

**MASON, William Ernest** (father of Winnifred Sprague Mason Huck), a Representative and a Senator from Illinois; born in Franklinville, Cattaraugus County, N.Y., July 7, 1850; moved with his parents to Bentonsport, Van Buren County, Iowa, in 1858; attended the Bentonsport Academy and Birmingham College, 1863-1865; taught school in Bentonsport, 1866-1868, and in Des Moines, Iowa, 1868-1870; studied law; moved to Chicago, Ill., in 1872; was admitted to the bar and commenced practice; member of the Illinois State house of representatives in 1879; member, State senate, 1882-1885; elected as a Republican to the Fiftieth and Fifty-first Congresses (March 4, 1887-March 3, 1891); unsuccessful candidate for reelection in 1890 to the Fifty-second Congress; resumed the practice of law in Chicago; elected to the United States Senate as a Republican, and served from March 4, 1897 to March 3, 1903; chairman, Committee on Manufactures (Fifty-fifth and Fifty-sixth Congresses), Committee on Post Office and Post Roads (Fifty-seventh Congress); again resumed the practice of law in Chicago; elected to the Sixty-fifth and to the two succeeding Congresses, and served from March 4, 1917 until his death in Washington, D.C., on June 16, 1921; interment in Oakwood Cemetery, Waukegan, Ill.

**Bibliography:** *DAB.*

**MASSEY, William Alexander,** a Senator from Nevada; born in Oakfield, Trumbull County, Ohio, October 7, 1856; moved with his parents to Edgar County, Ill., in 1865; attended the common schools, Union Christian College, Merom, Ind., and the Indiana Asbury (now De Pauw) University, Greencastle, Ind.; studied law; was admitted to the bar in 1877 and commenced practice in Sullivan, Ind.; moved to San Diego, Calif., in 1886; moved to Nevada in 1887, where he prospected and mined, subsequently taking up the practice of law in Elko, Nev.; member, State house of representatives 1892-1894; district attorney 1894-1896; justice of the State supreme court 1896-1902, when he resigned; moved to Reno, Nev., and resumed the practice of law; appointed as a Republican to the United States Senate to fill the vacancy caused by the death of George S. Nixon and served from July 1, 1912, to January 29, 1913, when a successor was elected; chairman, Committee on Mines and Mining (Sixty-second Congress); resumed the practice of law in Reno, Nev.; died on a train near Litchfield, Nev., March 5, 1914; interment in Mountain View Cemetery, Reno, Nev.

**MASSEY, Zachary David,** a Representative from Tennessee; born near Marshall, Madison County, N.C., November 14, 1864; attended the public schools; taught in the public schools of Marshall, 1882-1886; studied medicine in the Louisville (Ky.) Medical College, and commenced the practice of his profession in Wears Valley, Tenn., in 1889; moved to Sevierville, Sevier County, in 1890; during the Spanish-American War served as an assistant surgeon; postmaster of Sevierville, 1899-1904; member of the Tennessee State senate, 1904-1906; elected as a Republican to the Sixty-first Congress to fill the vacancy caused by the death of Walter P. Brownlow, and served from November 8, 1910 to March 3, 1911; was not a candidate for renomination in 1910 to the Sixty-second Congress; resumed the practice of medicine and also engaged in the real estate business; died in Sevierville, Tenn., July 13, 1923; interment in Shiloh Cemetery.

**MASSINGALE, Samuel Chapman,** a Representative from Oklahoma; born in Quitman, Clarke County, Miss., August 2, 1870; attended the public schools and the University of Mississippi at Oxford; moved to Fort Worth, Tex., in 1887 and was employed for a short time as a section hand; studied law; was admitted to the bar in 1895 and commenced practice in Cordell, Washita County, Okla., in 1900; during the Spanish-American War served as a private in Company D, Second Texas Infantry; member of the Oklahoma Territorial Council in 1902; unsuccessful candidate for election in 1906 to the Sixtieth Congress; elected as a Democrat to the Seventy-fourth and to the three succeeding Congresses and served from January 3, 1935, until his death in Washington, D.C., January 17, 1941; interment in Lawnview Cemetery, Cordell, Okla.

**MASTERS, Josiah,** a Representative from New York; born in Woodbury, Litchfield County, Conn., November 22, 1763; was graduated from Yale College in 1783; studied law; was admitted to the bar and commenced practice in Schaghticoke, Rensselaer County, N.Y.; member of the State assembly in 1792, 1800, and 1801; served as supervisor of Schaghticoke in 1796; justice of the peace in Rensselaer County 1801-1805; trustee of Lansingburgh Academy; school commissioner of Schaghticoke; elected as a Republican to the Ninth and Tenth Congresses (March 4, 1805-March 3, 1809); founder of the Schaghticoke Powder Co.; judge of the court of common pleas of Rensselaer County 1808-1822; died in Fairfield, Conn., June 30, 1822; interment in the Masters Cemetery, near Schaghticoke, N.Y.

**MATHEWS, Frank Asbury, Jr.,** a Representative from New Jersey; born in Philadelphia, Pa., August 3, 1890; attended the public schools of Palmyra, N.J.; during the First World War served in the Ordnance Department, United States Army, September 1917 to May 1919, with nineteen months' service overseas; was graduated from Temple University Law School, Philadelphia, Pa.; in 1920; was admitted to the bar in 1919 and commenced practice in Camden, N.J.; judge of the district court of the first judicial district of Burlington County, N.J., 1929-1933; assistant counsel for the State Highway Department of New Jersey, 1933-1944; deputy attorney general of New Jersey in 1944 and 1945; served as division judge advocate of the Forty-fourth Division from September 16, 1940, until relieved from active duty on October 15, 1940; elected as a Republican to the Seventy-ninth Congress to fill the vacancy caused by the resignation of D. Lane Powers; reelected in 1946 to the Eightieth Congress, and served from November 6, 1945 to January 3, 1949; was not a candidate for renomination in 1948 to the Eighty-first Congress; again appointed deputy attorney general of New Jersey, and served from 1949 to 1953; resumed the practice of law; was a resident of Riverton (Cinnaminson Township), N.J., until his death in Camden, N.J., February 5, 1964; interment in Morgan Cemetery, Palmyra, N.J.

**MATHEWS, George,** a Representative from Georgia; born in Augusta County, Va., August 30, 1739; commanded a volunteer company against the Indians in 1757, and in the Battle of Point Pleasant, October 10, 1774; colonel of the Ninth Virginia Regiment in the Revolutionary War; was exchanged in December 1781 and joined General Greene's army as colonel of the Third Virginia Regiment; engaged in farming in Oglethorpe County, Ga., in 1785; Governor of Georgia in 1787, and from November 7, 1793 until January 15, 1796; elected to the First Congress (March 4, 1789-March 3, 1791); brigadier general in the expedition for the capture of West Florida in 1811; died in Augusta, Ga., August 30, 1812; interment in St. Paul's Churchyard.

**Bibliography:** *DAB*; Kruse, Paul. "Secret Agent in East Florida: General George Mathews and the Patriot War." *Journal of Southern History* 18 (May 1952): 193-217.

**MATHEWS, George Arthur,** a Delegate from the Territory of Dakota; born in Potsdam, St. Lawrence County, N.Y., June 4, 1852; attended the common schools, Upper Iowa University, Fayette, Iowa, in 1874, and the law department of the University of Iowa at Iowa City in 1878; was admitted to the bar in 1878 and commenced practice in Corning, Iowa; moved to Brookings, Dakota Territory (now South Dakota), in 1879 and continued the practice of law; prosecuting attorney of the fifth judicial circuit for the Territory of Dakota in 1884; member of the Territorial council and served as its president in 1887; elected as a Republican a Delegate to the Fifty-first Congress, and served from March 4, 1889 to November 2, 1889, when the Territory was admitted into the Union; mayor of the city of Brookings, S.Dak., 1897-1903; resumed the practice of law at Brookings, S.Dak.; retired from active practice and moved to Los Angeles, Calif., in 1910, where he died on April 19, 1941; the remains were cremated and the ashes deposited in Greenwood Cemetery, Brookings, S.Dak.

**MATHEWS, Harlan,** a Senator from Tennessee; born in Sumiton, Walker County, Ala., January 17, 1927; B.A., Jacksonville (Ala.) State College, 1949; M.A., Vanderbilt University, 1950; J.D., Nashville School of Law, 1962; United States Navy service, Second World War; served on the staff of Governor Frank G. Clement, Tennessee, 1954-1961; commissioner, Tennessee Department of Finance, 1961-1971; senior vice president, Amcon International, Inc., 1971-1973; legislative assistant to Tennessee Comptroller William Snodgrass, 1973-1974; Tennessee State treasurer, 1974-1987; deputy to Governor Ned McWherter, 1987-1993; appointed as a Democrat to the United States Senate to fill the vacancy caused by the resignation of Albert Arnold Gore, Jr., and served from January 3, 1993 until his resignation on December 1, 1994; was not a candidate for election in 1994 to complete the term ending January 3, 1997; resumed the practice of government relations and administrative law; chair, Social Security Advisory Board; is a resident of Nashville, Tenn.

**MATHEWS, James,** a Representative from Ohio; born in Liberty, Trumbull County, Ohio, June 4, 1805; attended the common schools; studied law; was admitted to the bar in 1830 and commenced practice in Coshocton, Ohio; member of the Ohio State house of representatives, 1832-1837; served in the State senate in 1838 and 1839; elected as a Democrat to the Twenty-seventh and Twenty-eighth Congresses (March 4, 1841-March 3, 1845); was not a candidate for renomination in 1844 to the Twenty-ninth Congress; moved to Knoxville, Marion County, Iowa, in 1855; prosecuting attorney of Marion County, Iowa, 1857-1859; during the Civil War was appointed provost marshal of his district in 1861 and served until the close of the war; postmaster of Knoxville, 1869-1870; resigned to take the chair of pomology (science of fruit growing) at the Iowa State College at Ames and served four years; died in Knoxville, Iowa, March 30, 1887; interment in Graceland Cemetery.

**MATHEWS, John,** a Delegate from South Carolina; born in Charleston, S.C., in 1744; commissioned ensign on September 20, 1760, and lieutenant November 16, 1760, in the South Carolina Provincial Regiment in the Cherokee expedition; passed the Middle Temple, London, England, as a barrister in 1764; returned to South Carolina and was elected to the commons house of assembly in 1772; appointed by the convention of 1774 a member of the "general committee of ninety-nine"; member of the First and Second Provincial Congresses of South Carolina in 1775 and 1776; associate judge of the circuit court of the State in 1776; during the Revolutionary War served as a captain in the Colleton County regiment; member of the State house of representatives, 1776-1780, and served as speaker in 1777 and 1778; Member of the Continental Congress, 1778-1781; Governor of South Carolina in 1782 and 1783; elected judge of the court of chancery in March 1784; again elected to the State house of representatives in November 1784; elected judge of the court of equity in 1791 and served until 1797, when he resigned; died in Charleston, S.C., November 17, 1802.

**Bibliography:** *DAB*.

**MATHEWS, Vincent,** a Representative from New York; born at "Matthew's Field," near Newburgh, Orange County, N.Y., June 29, 1766; pursued an academic course in Noah Webster's School, Goshen, N.Y., and at the academy at Hackensack, N.J.; studied law in New York City; was admitted to the bar in 1790 and commenced practice in Elmira, N.Y.; member of the New York State assembly in 1794; served in the State senate in 1796, 1797, and 1809; bounty land claims commissioner in 1798; served as Cavalry commander and brigadier general in the State militia; elected as a Federalist to the Eleventh Congress (March 4, 1809-March 3, 1811); district attorney for the seventh district of New York, 1813-1815; moved to Bath and thence to Rochester in 1821; again a member of the State assembly in 1826; district attorney of Monroe County in 1831; resumed the practice of law in Rochester, N.Y., where he died August 23, 1846; interment in Mount Hope Cemetery.

**MATHEWSON, Elisha,** a Senator from Rhode Island; born in Scituate, R.I., April 18, 1767; pursued an academic course; justice of the peace of Scituate, R.I.; engaged in agricultural pursuits; member, State house of representatives 1821, and served as speaker during that period; member, State senate 1822; elected as a Republican to the United States Senate to fill the vacancy caused by the resignation of James Fenner and served from October 26, 1807, to March 3, 1811; resumed agricultural pursuits; died in Scituate, R.I., October 14, 1853; interment on his farm at the north end of Moswansicut Lake, Scituate, R.I.

**MATHIAS, Charles McCurdy, Jr.,** a Representative and a Senator from Maryland; born in Frederick, Md., July 24, 1922; attended the public schools; B.A., Haverford (Pa.) College, 1944; attended Yale University (Navy V-12 program), 1943-1944; LL.B., University of Maryland School of Law, 1949; was admitted to the bar and commenced the practice of law in Frederick, Md., in 1949; during the Second World War enlisted in the United States Navy as an apprentice seaman in 1942; commissioned an ensign in 1944, and was on sea duty in the Pacific Ocean area from 1944 until released from active duty in 1946; captain in the Naval Reserve; assistant attorney general of Maryland 1953-1954; city attorney of Frederick, Md., 1954-1959; member of the Maryland State house of delegates, 1959-1960; elected as a Republican to the Eighty-seventh and to the three succeeding Congresses (January 3, 1961-January 3, 1969); was not a candidate in 1968 for reelection to the House of Representatives, but was elected to the United States Senate; reelected in 1974 and 1980, and served from January 3, 1969 to January 3, 1987; was not a candidate for reelection in 1986; chairman, Special Committee on Termination of the National Emergency (Ninety-second through Ninety-fourth Congresses), co-chairman, Joint Committee on Printing (Ninety-seventh and Ninety-ninth Congresses), Joint Committee on the Library (Ninety-eighth and Ninety-ninth Congresses), chairman, Committee on Rules and Administration (Ninety-seventh through Ninety-ninth Congresses); practices law in Washington, D.C.; chairman and president, First American Bankshares, Inc.; is a resident of Chevy Chase, Maryland.

**Bibliography:** Mathias, Charles. "Executive Privilege and the Congress." In *Secrecy and Foreign Policy*, edited by Thomas M. Franck and Edward Weisband, pp. 69-86. New York: Oxford University Press, 1974.

**MATHIAS, Robert Bruce,** a Representative from California; born in Tulare, Calif., November 17, 1930; attended the public schools and is a graduate of Tulare High School; attended Kiski Preparatory School, Saltsburg, Pa., in 1949; B.A., Stanford University, Palo Alto, Calif., 1953; served in the United States Marine Corps, 1954-1956; served as a captain in the United States Marine Corps Reserve from 1956 until discharged in 1965; member of United States Olympic Team in 1948 and 1952, winning the decathlon event both years; served with the Department of State for international promotion of American youth programs in 1955; served, at the request of the Department of State, as goodwill ambassador, promoter, and participator in educational youth programs; elected as a Republican to the Ninetieth and to the three succeeding Congresses (January 3, 1967-January 3, 1975); unsuccessful candidate for reelection in 1974 to the Ninety-fourth Congress; Deputy Director of Selective Service from June 6, 1975, to August 11, 1975; worked with President Gerald R. Ford's campaign committee, 1975; director, United States Olympic Training Center, 1977-1983; president, Bob Mathias, Inc., 1984 to present; is a resident of Fresno, Calif.

**MATHIOT, Joshua,** a Representative from Ohio; born in Connellsville, Fayette County, Pa., April 4, 1800; moved to Newark, Licking County, Ohio, about 1830; studied law; was admitted to the bar and practiced in Newark; prosecuting attorney 1832-1836; mayor of Newark in 1834; elected as a Whig to the Twenty-seventh Congress (March 4, 1841-March 3, 1843); grand worthy patriarch of the Sons of Temperance in Ohio, and while attending a temperance convention at Sandusky contracted cholera, from which he died in Newark, Ohio, July 30, 1849; interment in Cedar Hill Cemetery.

**MATHIS, Marvin Dawson,** a Representative from Georgia; born in Nashville, Berrien County, Ga., November 30, 1940; attended the Nashville public schools; attended South Georgia College in Douglas, Ga.; news director, television station WALB, Albany, Ga., 1964-1970; elected as a Democrat to the Ninety-second and to the four succeeding Congresses (January 3, 1971-January 3, 1981); was not a candidate in 1980 for renomination to the House of Representatives, but was an unsuccessful candidate for nomination to the United States Senate; president of a political and legislative consulting firm in Washington, D.C., 1981 to present; is a resident of Upper Marlboro, Md.

**MATLACK, James,** a Representative from New Jersey; born in Woodbury, Gloucester County, N.J., January 11, 1775; attended the common schools; interested in various business enterprises; justice of the peace in 1803, 1808, 1813, 1816, and 1820; surrogate in 1815; chairman of the township committee; judge of the court of common pleas of Gloucester County 1806-1817; member of the board of freeholders 1812-1815, 1819-1821, and 1828; member of the State senate in 1817 and 1818; elected to the Seventeenth and Eighteenth Congresses (March 4, 1821-March 3, 1825); was not a candidate for renomination in 1824; affiliated with the Whig Party when it was formed; resumed business interests; died in Woodbury, N.J., January 16, 1840; interment in Eglington Cemetery, Clarksboro, N.J.

**MATLACK, Timothy,** a Delegate from Pennsylvania; born in Haddonfield, Camden County, N.J., in 1730; attended Quaker schools in Haddonfield and Philadelphia; engaged in mercantile pursuits in Philadelphia; was in command of a battalion of "Associators" during the Revolution; member of the provincial conference held in Carpenters' Hall, Philadelphia, June 18, 1775; delegate to the convention of July 15, 1776, and appointed secretary of state; member of the committee of safety in 1776; in 1777 was appointed keeper of the great seal; member of the board of trustees of the University of Pennsylvania in 1779; member of the Continental Congress in 1780; moved to Lancaster, Pa.; master of the rolls of Pennsylvania 1800-1809; moved to Philadelphia and was prothonotary of the district court for several years; member of the board of aldermen 1813-1818; died at Holmesburg, near Philadelphia, Pa., April 14, 1829; interment in the Free Quaker Burial Ground, Philadelphia, Pa.; reinterment in 1905 in Fatlands, on the Schuylkill River, opposite Valley Forge, Pa.

**Bibliography:** *DAB.*

**MATSON, Aaron,** a Representative from New Hampshire; born in Plymouth, Mass., in 1770; moved to Cheshire County, N.H.; judge of probate of Cheshire County; member of the State house of representatives 1806-1808, 1810-1814, 1817, and 1818; member of the executive council 1819-1821; elected to the Seventeenth and Eighteenth Congresses (March 4, 1821-March 3, 1825); again a member of the State house of representatives in 1827 and 1828; died in Newport, Orleans County, Vt., July 18, 1855.

**MATSON, Courtland Cushing,** a Representative from Indiana; born in Brookville, Franklin County, Ind., April 25, 1841; was graduated from Indiana Asbury (later De Pauw) University in 1862; during the Civil War enlisted as a private in the Sixteenth Regiment, Indiana Volunteers; after one year's service entered the Sixth Regiment, Indiana Volunteer Cavalry (Seventy-first Volunteers), and served until October 1865, and was subsequently promoted to the rank of colonel; studied law; was admitted to the bar and commenced practice in Greencastle, Putnam County, Ind.; was three times elected prosecuting attorney of the county; chairman of the Democratic State central committee in 1878; elected as a Democrat to the Forty-seventh and to the three succeeding Congresses (March 4, 1881-March 3, 1889); chairman, Committee on Invalid Pensions (Forty-eighth through Fiftieth Congresses); was not a candidate for renomination; unsuccessful Democratic candidate for Governor of Indiana in 1888; resumed the practice of law in Greencastle, Ind.; member of the board of tax commissioners 1909-1913; died in Chicago, Ill., September 4, 1915; interment in Forest Hill Cemetery, Greencastle, Ind.

**MATSUI, Robert Takeo,** a Representative from California; born in Sacramento, Sacramento County, Calif., September 17, 1941; attended the Sacramento County public schools; graduated C.K. McClatchy High School, 1959; A.B., University of California, Berkeley, 1963; J.D., Hastings College of Law, University of California, 1966; admitted to the California bar in 1967 and commenced practice in Sacramento; member, Sacramento City Council, District 8, 1971-1978; city representative on the Sacramento Regional Advisory Board of Justice Planning, the Sacramento Area Civil Defense and Disaster Council, and the Sacramento-Yolo Port District Board of Elections; member, California Democratic Central Committee, 1973-1978; vice mayor of Sacramento, 1977; elected as a Democrat to the Ninety-sixth and to the eight succeeding Congresses (January 3, 1979-January 3, 1997); is a resident of Sacramento, Calif.

**MATSUNAGA, Spark Masayuki,** a Representative and a Senator from Hawaii; born in Kukuiula, Kauai, Hawaii, October 8, 1916; Ed.B., University of Hawaii, Honolulu, 1941; J.D., Harvard University Law School, 1951; commissioned a second lieutenant in the United States Army Reserve, June 1941; volunteered for active service in July 1941; served with the First Battalion, Four Hundred Forty-second Regimental Combat Team, in the North African and Italian theaters; released from active service as a captain in December 1945; veterans counselor, United States Department of the Interior, 1945-1947; chief, Priority Claimants' Division, War Assets Administration, 1947-1948; admitted to the Hawaii bar in 1952; assistant public prosecutor, city and county of Honolulu 1952-1954; member of Hawaiian statehood delegation to Congress in 1950 and 1954; lawyer in private practice; member of the Hawaii Territorial legislature 1954-1959, serving as majority leader 1957-1959; author and poet; elected as a Democrat to the Eighty-eighth and to the six succeeding Congresses (January 3,

1963-January 3, 1977); was not a candidate for reelection in 1976 to the House of Representatives, but was elected to the United States Senate for the term commencing January 3, 1977; reelected in 1982 and 1988 and served until his death; died April 15, 1990.

**Bibliography:** Matsunaga, Spark M. *The Mars Project: Journeys Beyond the Cold War.* New York: Hill and Wang, 1986; Matsunaga, Spark M., and Ping Chen. *Rulemakers of the House.* Urbana: University of Illinois Press, 1976.

**MATTESON, Orsamus Benajah,** a Representative from New York; born in Verona, Oneida County, N.Y., August 28, 1805; attended the common schools; studied law in Utica, N.Y.; was admitted to the bar in 1830 and commenced practice in Utica; city attorney of Utica in 1834 and 1836; State supreme court commissioner; unsuccessful candidate for election in 1846 to the Thirtieth Congress; elected as a Whig to the Thirty-first Congress (March 4, 1849-March 3, 1851); unsuccessful candidate for reelection in 1850 to the Thirty-second Congress; elected to the Thirty-third and Thirty-fourth Congresses and served from March 4, 1853, until his resignation on February 27, 1857; chairman, Committee on District of Columbia (Thirty-fourth Congress); elected as a Republican to the Thirty-fifth Congress (March 4, 1857-March 3, 1859); interested in a scheme for the construction of the St. Mary's Ship Canal; engaged in lumbering and iron manufacturing and in the acquisition of large tracts of land; died in Utica, N.Y., December 22, 1889; interment in Forest Hill Cemetery.

**MATTHEWS, Charles,** a Representative from Pennsylvania; born in New Castle, Lawrence County, Pa., October 15, 1856; attended the public schools until fourteen years of age; later employed in rolling mills as a roll turner and attended night school; delegate to the Pennsylvania Republican convention in 1886; member of the city council 1887-1893; sheriff of Lawrence County 1897-1900; engaged in manufacturing and banking; elected as a Republican to the Sixty-second Congress (March 4, 1911-March 3, 1913); unsuccessful candidate for reelection in 1912 to the Sixty-third Congress; again engaged in banking; delegate to the Republican National Convention at Chicago in 1916; appointed county commissioner of Lawrence County, Pa., on November 26, 1924, and served until January 2, 1928; died in New Castle, Pa., December 12, 1932; interment in Graceland Cemetery.

**MATTHEWS, Donald Ray (Billy),** a Representative from Florida; born in Micanopy, Alachua County, Fla., October 3, 1907; attended the public schools of Hawthorne, Fla.; graduated from the University of Florida at Gainesville in 1929; taught school in Leesburg, Fla., and in Orlando, Fla., 1929-1935; high school principal in Newberry, Fla., in 1935 and 1936; member of the Florida State house of representatives in 1935; member of the administrative staff of the University of Florida, 1936-1952; served in the United States Army, 1942-1946, and was discharged as a captain of Infantry; assistant State 4-H agent in the summers from 1928 to 1938; elected as a Democrat to the Eighty-third and to the six succeeding Congresses (January 3, 1953-January 3, 1967); unsuccessful candidate for renomination in 1966 to the Ninetieth Congress; consultant and administrator, Rural Community Development Service, United States Department of Agriculture, 1967-1969; instructor of political science, Santa Fe Community College (Fla.) from 1969 until his retirement in 1977; is a resident of Gainesville, Fla.

**MATTHEWS, Nelson Edwin,** a Representative from Ohio; born in Ottawa, Putnam County, Ohio, April 14, 1852; attended the public schools; engaged in banking, mercantile, and manufacturing pursuits in Ottawa; delegate to the Republican National Convention in 1908; delegate to the fourth State constitutional convention in 1912; elected as a Republican to the Sixty-fourth Congress (March 4, 1915-March 3, 1917); unsuccessful candidate for reelection in 1916 to the Sixty-fifth Congress; died in Maumee, Lucas County, Ohio, on

October 13, 1917; interment in Fort Meigs Cemetery, Perrysburg, Wood County, Ohio.

**MATTHEWS, Stanley** (uncle of Henry Watterson), a Senator from Ohio; born in Cincinnati, Ohio, July 21, 1824; attended the public schools; graduated from Kenyon College, Gambier, Ohio, in 1840; studied law; was admitted to the bar in 1842 and commenced practice in Maury County, Tenn., the same year; returned to Cincinnati in 1844; appointed assistant prosecuting attorney of Hamilton County in 1845; editor of the Cincinnati Herald, 1846-1849; clerk of the Ohio State house of representatives, 1848-1850; judge of the court of common pleas of Hamilton County, 1850-1852; member, Ohio State senate, 1856-1857; appointed by President James Buchanan as United States district attorney for southern Ohio in 1858 and served until his resignation in March 1861; during the Civil War served as lieutenant colonel and then colonel with the Ohio Volunteers; resigned in the spring of 1863; resumed the practice of law in Cincinnati; judge of the Cincinnati superior court from 1863 until his resignation in July 1864; Republican presidential elector in 1864 and 1868; unsuccessful candidate for election in 1876 to the Forty-fifth Congress; was counsel before the electoral commission in 1877; elected as a Republican to the United States Senate to fill the vacancy caused by the resignation of John Sherman and served from March 21, 1877, to March 3, 1879; was not a candidate for renomination in 1878; nominated by President Rutherford B. Hayes as Associate Justice of the United States Supreme Court on January 26, 1881, but the nomination was not acted upon; was renominated by President James A. Garfield, confirmed by the Senate on May 12, 1881, and served until his death in Washington, D.C., March 22, 1889; interment in Spring Grove Cemetery, Cincinnati, Ohio.

Bibliography: *DAB*; Jager, Ronald. "Stanley Matthews for the Supreme Court." *Cincinnati Historical Society Bulletin* 38 (Fall 1980): 191-208; Wantland, William Robert. "Jurist and Advocate: The Political Career of Stanley Matthews." Ph.D. dissertation, Miami University, 1994.

**MATTHEWS, William,** a Representative from Maryland; born in Cecil County, Md., April 26, 1755; judge of Cecil County Court in 1778, 1780, and 1782-1786; member of the State general assembly 1786-1789; elected as a Federalist to the Fifth Congress (March 4, 1797-March 3, 1799).

**MATTINGLY, Mack Francis,** a Senator from Georgia; born in Anderson, Madison County, Ind., January 7, 1931; attended the public schools; B.S., Indiana University, Bloomington, 1957; served in the United States Air Force during the Korean War, staff sergeant, 1951-1955; production scheduler, Arvin Industries, Columbus, Ind., 1957-1959; marketing manager, IBM Corporation, 1959-1979; small business owner and chief executive officer, 1975-1980; member of the Georgia Republican Party, 1963 to present, serving as State chairman, 1975-1977; elected as a Republican to the United States Senate in 1980, and served from January 3, 1981 to January 3, 1987; unsuccessful candidate for reelection in 1986; Assistant Secretary General for Defense Support, North Atlantic Treaty Organization, Brussels, Belgium, 1987-1990; nominated as Ambassador to the Seychelles, July 2, 1992, confirmed by the Senate on August 12, 1992, and served until March 1993; self-employed entrepreneur and member of the board of directors of businesses and associations; is a resident of St. Simons Island, Ga.

**MATTOCKS, John,** a Representative from Vermont; born in Hartford, Conn., March 4, 1777; moved with his parents to Tinmouth, Vt., in 1778; pursued an academic course; studied law in Middlebury and Fairfield; was admitted to the bar in 1797 and commenced practice in Danville; moved to Peacham, Caledonia County, Vt.; member of the State house of representatives in 1807, 1815, 1816, 1823, and 1824; brigadier general of militia in the War of 1812; elected to the Seventeenth Congress (March 4, 1821-March

3, 1823); elected to the Nineteenth Congress (March 4, 1825-March 3, 1827); chairman, Committee on Expenditures in the Department of War (Nineteenth Congress); judge of the State supreme court in 1833 and 1834; declined to be a candidate for renomination; delegate to the State constitutional convention in 1836; elected as a Whig to the Twenty-seventh Congress (March 4, 1841-March 3, 1843); elected Governor of Vermont in 1843, and served from October 13, 1843 to October 11, 1844; died in Peacham, Vt., August 14, 1847; interment in Peacham Cemetery.

Bibliography: *DAB*.

**MATTOON, Ebenezer,** a Representative from Massachusetts; born in North Amherst, Hampshire County, Mass., on August 19, 1755; attended the common schools and received private instruction; graduated from Dartmouth College, Hanover, N.H., in 1776; served in the Revolutionary Army and attained the rank of major; taught school and also engaged in agricultural pursuits; member of the Massachusetts house of representatives in 1781 and 1794; justice of the peace 1782-1796; served in the Massachusetts senate in 1795 and 1796; served from the rank of captain to that of major general of the Fourth Division, Massachusetts militia; appointed sheriff of Hampshire County in 1796 and served twenty years; elected as a Federalist to the Sixth Congress to fill the vacancy caused by the resignation of Samuel Lyman; reelected to the Seventh Congress and served from February 2, 1801, to March 3, 1803; again a member of the Massachusetts house of representatives in 1812; major general of Massachusetts Militia 1799-1816; adjutant general of the Massachusetts militia 1816-1818; became totally blind in 1818 and retired from active public life; delegate to the Massachusetts constitutional convention in 1820; died in Amherst, Mass., September 11, 1843; interment in West Cemetery.

**MATTOX, James Albon,** a Representative from Texas; born in Dallas, Dallas County, Tex., August 29, 1943; educated in the public schools of Dallas; B.B.A., Baylor University, Waco, Tex., 1965; J.D., Southern Methodist University, Dallas, 1968; admitted to the Texas bar in 1968 and commenced practice in Dallas; intern, office of Representative Earle Cabell, 1967; assistant district attorney of Dallas County, 1968-1970; returned to general practice in Dallas, 1970; served in the Texas State house of representatives, 1973-1977; delegate, Texas State Democratic conventions, 1972, 1976; elected as a Democrat to the Ninety-fifth and to the two succeeding Congresses (January 3, 1977-January 3, 1983); was not a candidate for reelection in 1982 to the Ninety-eighth Congress; Texas State attorney general, 1983-1991; of counsel, Kreisner and Gladney, Austin, Tex.; is a resident of Austin, Tex.

**MAURICE, James,** a Representative from New York; born in New York City November 7, 1814; attended Broad Street Academy; became clerk in a law office at the age of twelve years; studied law; was admitted to the bar in 1835 and practiced in Maspeth, Queens County, N.Y.; appointed master in chancery by Governor William C. Bouck in 1843; member of the New York State assembly in 1850; delegate to the Democratic State conventions in 1851, 1853, and 1856; elected as a Democrat to the Thirty-third Congress (March 4, 1853-March 3, 1855); was not a candidate for renomination in 1854 to the Thirty-fourth Congress; resumed the practice of law; declined the nomination as justice of the New York State supreme court in 1865; elected as a Republican to the New York State assembly in 1866; died in Maspeth, N.Y., August 4, 1884; interment in Mount Olivet Cemetery.

**MAURY, Abram Poindexter** (cousin of Fontaine Maury Maverick), a Representative from Tennessee; born near Franklin, Williamson County, Tenn., December 26, 1801; completed preparatory studies and was editor of a newspaper in St. Louis, Mo., at the age of sixteen; entered the United States Military Academy, West Point, N.Y., in 1820, but left the following year to study law and edit a newspaper in Nashville, Tenn.; member of the Tennessee State house of representatives in 1831, 1832, 1843, and 1844; was admitted to the bar in 1839 and practiced in Williamson County; elected as a Hugh L. White supporter to the Twenty-fourth Congress and reelected as a Whig to the Twenty-fifth Congress (March 4, 1835-March 3, 1839); was not a candidate for renomination in 1838 to the Twenty-sixth Congress; resumed the practice of law in Williamson County; also engaged in literary pursuits and lecturing; served in the Tennessee State senate in 1845 and 1846; died near Franklin, Tenn., July 22, 1848; interment in the family cemetery at his home near Franklin, Tenn.

**MAVERICK, Fontaine Maury** (cousin of Abram P. Maury, nephew of James L. Slayden, and cousin of John W. Fishburne), a Representative from Texas; born in San Antonio, Tex., October 23, 1895; attended the common schools of Texas, Virginia Military Institute at Lexington, and the University of Texas at Austin; studied law; was admitted to the bar in 1916 and commenced practice in San Antonio, Tex.; during the First World War served as a first lieutenant in the One Hundred and Fifty-seventh Infantry, Fortieth Division, and was overseas with the Twenty-eighth Infantry, First Division; awarded the Silver Star and the Purple Heart; engaged in the lumber, building material, housing, and mortgage businesses, 1925-1930; collector of taxes of Bexar County, Tex., 1929-1931; delegate to several Democratic State conventions and to the Democratic National Conventions of 1928 and 1940; elected as a Democrat to the Seventy-fourth and Seventy-fifth Congresses (January 3, 1935-January 3, 1939); unsuccessful candidate for renomination in 1938 to the Seventy-sixth Congress; mayor of San Antonio, 1939-1941; divisional director and later vice chairman of the War Production Board and chairman of the Smaller War Plants Corporation, Washington, D.C., 1941-1946; resumed the practice of law; died in San Antonio, Tex., June 7, 1954; interment in San Jose Burial Park, San Antonio, Tex.

**Bibliography:** *DAB*; Doyle, Judith Kaaz. "Out of Step: Maury Maverick and the Politics of the Depression and the New Deal." Ph.D. dissertation, University of Texas, 1989; Henderson, Richard B. *Maury Maverick: A Political Biography*. Austin: University of Texas Press, 1970; Weiss, Stuart L. "Maury Maverick and the Liberal Bloc." *Journal of American History* 57 (March 1971): 880-95.

**MAVROULES, Nicholas James,** a Representative from Massachusetts; born in Peabody, Essex County, Mass., November 1, 1929; attended the public schools of Peabody; employed by GTE-Sylvania, 1949-1967, and served as supervisor of personnel; city councilor, Peabody, 1958-1965; Peabody mayor, 1967-1978; delegate, Massachusetts Democratic conventions, 1967-1978; delegate, Democratic National Convention, 1975; elected as a Democrat to the Ninety-sixth and to the six succeeding Congresses (January 3, 1979-January 3, 1993); unsuccessful candidate for reelection in 1992 to the One Hundred Third Congress; is a resident of Peabody, Mass.

**MAXEY, Samuel Bell,** a Senator from Texas; born in Tomkinsville, Monroe County, Ky., March 30, 1825; attended the common schools and graduated from the United States Military Academy, West Point, N.Y., in 1846; served in the Mexican War; returned to Kentucky; studied law; was admitted to the bar in 1850 and commenced practice in Albany, Ky.; clerk of the county and circuit courts and master in chancery 1852-1856; moved to Paris, Tex., in 1857 and practiced his profession; district attorney of Lamar County, Tex., 1858-1859; elected to the State senate in 1861, but declined; during the Civil War raised the Ninth Regiment, Texas Infantry, of which he was colonel, for the Confederate Army; was promoted to brigadier general and major general; commanded the Indian Territory military district 1863-1865 and was also superintendent of Indian affairs; remained in the service of the Confederacy until the surrender of the trans-Mississippi department in 1865; resumed the practice of law in Paris, Tex.; commissioned as judge of the eighth district of Texas in 1873, but declined the position; elected as a Democrat to the United States Senate in 1875; reelected in 1881 and served from March 4, 1875, to March 3, 1887; was an unsuccessful candidate for reelection; chairman, Committee on Post Office and Post Roads (Forty-sixth Congress); continued the practice of law in Paris, Tex., until his death at Eureka Springs, Ark., August 16, 1895; interment in Evergreen Cemetery, Paris, Tex.

**Bibliography:** *DAB*; Horton, Louise. *Samuel Bell Maxey: A Biography*. Austin: University of Texas Press, 1974.

**MAXWELL, Augustus Emmett** (grandfather of Emmett Wilson), a Representative from Florida; born in Elberton, Elbert County, Ga., September 21, 1820; attended private school; was graduated from the University of Virginia at Charlottesville in 1841; studied law; was admitted to the Alabama bar in 1843 and practiced in Eutaw, Ala., 1843-1845; moved to Tallahassee, Fla., in 1845; attorney general of Florida in 1846 and 1847; member of the State house of representatives in 1847; secretary of state in 1848; served in the State senate in 1849 and 1850; elected as a Democrat to the Thirty-third and Thirty-fourth Congresses (March 4, 1853-March 3, 1857); was not a candidate for renomination in 1856 to the Thirty-fifth Congress; United States Navy agent at Pensacola 1857-1861; served in the Senate of the Confederate States 1862-1865; judge of the State supreme court in 1865 and 1866; elected president of the Pensacola & Montgomery Railroad in 1866; judge of the circuit court of Florida 1877-1885; member of the State constitutional convention of 1885; chief justice and later associate justice of the State supreme court 1887-1891; died in Chipley, Washington County, Fla., on May 5, 1903; interment in St. John's Cemetery, Pensacola, Fla.

**Bibliography:** *DAB*.

**MAXWELL, George Clifford** (father of John Patterson Bryan Maxwell), a Representative from New Jersey; born in Sussex County, N.J., on May 31, 1771; was graduated from Princeton College in 1792; studied law; was admitted to the bar in 1797 and practiced in Hunterdon County, N.J.; elected as a Republican to the Twelfth Congress (March 4, 1811-March 3, 1813); resumed the practice of law in Flemington, N.J., where he died March 16, 1816; interment in Pleasant Ridge Cemetery Raritan Township, Hunterdon County, N.J.

**MAXWELL, John Patterson Bryan** (son of George Clifford Maxwell and uncle of George Maxwell Robeson), a Representative from New Jersey; born in Flemington, Hunterdon County, N.J., September 3, 1804; was graduated from Princeton College in 1823; studied law; was admitted to the bar in 1827 and commenced practice in Newark, N.J.; moved to Belvidere, Warren County, N.J.; for a while was editor of the Belvidere Apollo; elected as a Whig to the Twenty-fifth Congress (March 4, 1837-March 3, 1839); presented credentials as a Member-elect to the Twenty-sixth Congress, but the House declined to seat him; elected to the Twenty-seventh Congress (March 4, 1841-March 3, 1843); trustee of Princeton College 1842-1845; died in Belvidere, Warren County, N.J., November 14, 1845; interment in Belvidere Cemetery.

**MAXWELL, Lewis,** a Representative from Virginia; born in Chester County, Pa., April 17, 1790; moved with his mother to Virginia about 1800; completed a preparatory course; studied law; admitted to the bar and commenced practice in Weston, Va. (now West Virginia); member of the Virginia house of delegates 1821-1824; elected to the Twentieth Congress; reelected to the Twenty-first Congress and reelected as an Anti-Jacksonian to the Twenty-second Congress (March 4, 1827-March 3, 1833); chairman, Committee on Expenditures in the Department of War (Twenty-first Congress), Committee on Expenditures in the Department of the Navy (Twenty-second Congress); was not a candidate for renomination in 1832; resumed the practice of law and was also engaged as a surveyor and land patentee; died in West Union, Doddridge County,

Va. (now West Virginia), February 13, 1862; interment in Odd Fellows Cemetery.

**MAXWELL, Samuel,** a Representative from Nebraska; born in Lodi (then a suburb of Syracuse), N.Y., May 20, 1825; attended the common schools; moved with his family to Michigan in 1844; taught school and also engaged in agricultural pursuits; studied law; moved to Nebraska in 1856, settled in Cass County and engaged in agricultural pursuits; returned to Michigan, completed his law studies, and was admitted to the bar in 1859; returned to Nebraska the same year and commenced the practice of law at Plattsmouth; delegate to the first Republican Territorial convention; member of the Territorial house of representatives in 1859, 1860, 1864, and 1865; delegate to the Territorial constitutional conventions in 1864 and 1866, and to the State constitutional convention in 1875; member of the first State house of representatives in 1866; appointed by Governor David Butler as a member of the board of commissioners to select capitol building plans and university lands in 1867; elected associate justice of the State supreme court in 1872; reelected in 1875, 1881, and again in 1887; elected as a Populist to the Fifty-fifth Congress (March 4, 1897-March 3, 1899); was not a candidate for reelection in 1898 to the Fifty-sixth Congress; resumed the practice of law in Fremont, Dodge County, Nebr., where he died February 11, 1901; interment in Pleasant Hill Cemetery, Plattsmouth, Nebr.

Bibliography: *DAB.*

**MAXWELL, Thomas,** a Representative from New York; born at Tioga Point (now Athens), Bradford County, Pa., February 16, 1792; moved to Elmira (then Newtown Point), N.Y., in 1796; appointed quartermaster of a regiment of Cavalry attached to the brigade of General Vincent Matthews during the War of 1812; clerk of Tioga County, N.Y., from 1819 until 1829; elected as a Jacksonian to the Twenty-first Congress (March 4, 1829-March 3, 1831); chairman, Committee on Accounts (Twenty-first Congress); engaged in the prosecution of pension claims; studied law and was admitted to practice in the court of common pleas of old Tioga County, N.Y., in 1832; editor of the Elmira Gazette, 1834-1836; postmaster of Elmira from 1834 until 1839; deputy clerk of Chemung County in 1836; treasurer of Chemung County, 1836-1843; a vice president of the New York & Erie Railroad Co. in 1841; commissioner of loans of United States deposit and of New York State funds in 1843; moved to Geneva, N.Y., about 1845, upon his appointment as deputy clerk of the State supreme court; died in Elmira, Chemung County, N.Y., November 4, 1864; interment in Woodlawn Cemetery.

**MAY, Andrew Jackson,** a Representative from Kentucky; born on Beaver Creek, near Langley, Floyd County, Ky., June 24, 1875; attended the public schools; taught in the schools of Floyd and Magoffin Counties, Ky., for five years; was graduated from Southern Normal University Law School, Huntingdon, Tenn. (later Union College, Jackson, Tenn.), in 1898; was admitted to the bar the same year and commenced practice in Prestonsburg, Ky.; county attorney of Floyd County, 1901-1909; special judge of the circuit court of Johnson and Martin Counties, 1925-1926; also engaged in agricultural pursuits, coal mining, and banking; elected to the Seventy-second and to the seven succeeding Congresses (March 4, 1931-January 3, 1947); chairman, Committee on Military Affairs (Seventy-sixth through Seventy-ninth Congresses); unsuccessful candidate for reelection in 1946 to the Eightieth Congress; convicted on July 3, 1947, on charges of accepting bribes for his influence in the award of munitions contracts during the Second World War; served nine months in prison, and was released in September 1950; received a full pardon from President Harry S Truman on December 25, 1952; resumed the practice of law; died in Prestonsburg, Ky., September 6, 1959; interment in Mayo Cemetery.

Bibliography: *DAB.*

**MAY, Catherine Dean,** a Representative from Washington; born May 18, 1914, in Yakima, Wash.; attended the grade schools in Yakima; graduated from Yakima Valley Junior College in 1934; B.A., University of Washington, 1936, and with a five-year degree in education in 1937; studied speech at the University of Southern California in 1939; teacher of English in Chehalis (Wash.) High School 1937-1940; women's editor and news broadcaster, station KMO, Tacoma, Wash., 1940-1941, and station KOMO, Seattle, Wash., 1941-1942; head of radio department for Strang-Prosser, a Seattle advertising agency, 1942-1943, and for a Seattle insurance company, 1943-1944; writer and assistant commentator, National Broadcasting Co., New York City, 1944-1946; women's editor, station KIT, Yakima, Wash., 1948-1957; member of Washington State Legislature, 1952-1958; office manager and medical secretary, Yakima Medical Center, 1957-1958; elected as a Republican to the Eighty-sixth and to the five succeeding Congresses (January 3, 1959-January 3, 1971); unsuccessful candidate for reelection in 1970 to the Ninety-second Congress; appointed by President Richard M. Nixon to the United States International Trade Commission, and served from 1971 to 1981; appointed Special Consultant to the President on the 50 States Project, 1982; president, Bedell Associates; is a resident of Palm Desert, Calif.

Bibliography: Pidcock, Patricia Graham. "Catherine May: A Political Biography." Ph.D. dissertation, Washington State University, 1992.

**MAY, Edwin Hyland, Jr.,** a Representative from Connecticut; born in Hartford, Conn., May 28, 1924; educated in the public schools and graduated from Wethersfield (Conn.) High School in 1942; attended Wesleyan University, Middletown, Conn., but interrupted his education to enlist in November 1942 in the United States Army Air Corps, and served until October 1945 as a second lieutenant, instructor, and P-38 fighter pilot in the Fourth Air Force; returned to Wesleyan University and graduated in 1948; president of May, Potter & Murphy, Inc., an insurance firm in Hartford, Conn., 1956-1973; president, chairman of Alexander & Alexander of Connecticut, 1973-1984; elected as a Republican to the Eighty-fifth Congress (January 3, 1957-January 3, 1959); unsuccessful candidate for reelection in 1958 to the Eighty-sixth Congress; Republican State chairman, 1958-1962; unsuccessful candidate in 1962 for nomination for Governor of Connecticut; delegate, Connecticut Constitutional convention, 1965; unsuccessful candidate in 1968 for election to the United States Senate; sales executive, Mariner Sands Realty, Stuart, Fla., 1986 to present; is a resident of Wethersfield, Conn., and Stuart, Fla.

**MAY, Henry,** a Representative from Maryland; born in Washington, D.C., February 13, 1816; pursued an academic course; attended Columbian College (later George Washington University), Washington, D.C.; studied law; was admitted to the bar in 1840 and practiced; sent by President Franklin Pierce to Mexico to investigate claims under the Treaty of Guadalupe Hidalgo; moved to Baltimore, Md., in 1850; elected as a Democrat to the Thirty-third Congress (March 4, 1853-March 3, 1855); unsuccessful candidate for reelection in 1854 to the Thirty-fourth Congress; elected as a Unionist to the Thirty-seventh Congress (March 4, 1861-March 3, 1863); died in Baltimore, Md., September 25, 1866; interment in Cathedral Cemetery.

**MAY, Mitchell,** a Representative from New York; born in Brooklyn, N.Y., July 10, 1870; attended the public schools and Brooklyn Polytechnic Institute; was graduated from the law department of Columbia University, New York City, in 1892; was admitted to the bar in 1893 and commenced practice in Brooklyn; elected as a Democrat to the Fifty-sixth Congress (March 4, 1899-March 3, 1901); was not a candidate for renomination in 1900 to the Fifty-seventh Congress; member of the New York City Board of Education, 1906-1910; assistant district attorney of Kings County in 1910 and 1911; secretary of state of New York in 1913 and 1914; county judge of Kings County, 1916-1921; justice of the New York State supreme court from January 1, 1922 to December 31, 1940, when he retired because of age limitation; resumed the practice of law; died in Brooklyn, N.Y., March 24, 1961; interment in Valhalla Cemetery, Staten Island, N.Y.

**MAY, William L.,** a Representative from Illinois; born in Kentucky about 1793; attended the common schools; moved to Edwardsville, Madison County, Ill., and afterward to Jacksonville, Ill.; appointed justice of the peace in Madison County on December 10, 1817; captain of militia in 1822; elected justice of the peace in Morgan County on August 6, 1827, and resigned August 29, 1829; member of the Illinois State house of representatives in 1828; moved to Springfield, having been appointed by President Andrew Jackson as receiver of public moneys for the United States Land Office in that city; studied law; was admitted to the bar and practiced; also operated a ferry across the Illinois River at Peoria, and organized the Peoria Bridge Co.; elected as a Jacksonian to the Twenty-third Congress to fill the vacancy caused by the resignation of Joseph Duncan; reelected to the Twenty-fourth Congress, reelected as a Democrat to the Twenty-fifth Congress, and served from December 1, 1834 to March 3, 1839; chairman, Committee on Private Land Claims (Twenty-fifth Congress); was not a candidate for renomination in 1838 to the Twenty-sixth Congress; moved to Peoria, Ill., and continued the practice of law; mayor of Springfield, Ill., in May 1841; went to California during the gold rush; died in Sacramento, Calif., September 29, 1849.

**MAYALL, Samuel,** a Representative from Maine; born in North Gray, Cumberland County, Maine, June 21, 1816; attended the public schools and was tutored privately at home; moved to Gray, Maine; member of the State house of representatives in 1845, 1847, and 1848; served in the State senate in 1847 and 1848; declined the Democratic nomination as a candidate for Representative to the Thirty-second Congress; elected as a Democrat to the Thirty-third Congress (March 4, 1853-March 3, 1855); was not a candidate for renomination in 1854; delegate to the Republican National Convention in 1856; moved to St. Paul, Minn., in 1857; became a large landowner; commissioned as a captain at the beginning of the Civil War; devoted his time to looking after his large business interests; died in St. Paul, Minn., September 17, 1892; interment in Oakland Cemetery.

**MAYBANK, Burnet Rhett,** a Senator from South Carolina; born in Charleston, S.C., March 7, 1899; attended the public schools; graduated from Porter Military Academy, Charleston, S.C., and from the College of Charleston, South Carolina; served in the Navy during the First World War; engaged in the cotton export business, 1920-1938; alderman of Charleston, S.C., 1927-1931; mayor of Charleston, 1931-1938; member of the South Carolina State Advisory Board of the Federal Administration of Public Works, 1933-1934; chairman of the South Carolina Public Service Authority, 1934-1939; member of the Board of Bank Control, 1933-1934; elected Governor of South Carolina in 1938, and served from January 17, 1939 until his resignation November 4, 1941, having been elected Senator; was elected as a Democrat to the United States Senate in 1941 to fill the vacancy caused by the resignation of James F. Byrnes; reelected in 1942 and again in 1948, and served from November 5, 1941, until his death at his summer home in Flat Rock, N.C., September 1, 1954; had been renominated in the July 13, 1954 primary for the term ending January 3, 1961; chairman, Committee on Banking and Currency (Eighty-first and Eighty-second Congresses), co-chairman, Joint Committee on Defense Production (Eighty-first and Eighty-second Congresses); interment in Magnolia Cemetery, Charleston, S.C.

Bibliography: *DAB*; Cann, Marvin L. "Burnet Rhett Maybank and the New Deal in South Carolina, 1931-1941." Ph.D. dissertation, University of North Carolina, 1967.

**MAYBURY, William Cotter,** a Representative from Michigan; born in Detroit, Mich., November 20, 1848; attended the public schools; was graduated from the academic department of the University of Michigan at Ann Arbor in 1870 and from the law department in 1871; was admitted to the bar in the latter year and commenced practice in Detroit; city attorney of Detroit 1876-1880; lecturer on medical jurisprudence in the Michigan College of Medicine at Detroit in 1881 and 1882; elected as a Democrat to the Forty-eighth and Forty-ninth Congresses (March 4, 1883-March 3, 1887); was not a candidate for reelection in 1886; resumed the practice of law in Detroit; mayor of Detroit 1897-1905; unsuccessful candidate for Governor in 1900; died in Detroit, Wayne County, Mich., May 6, 1909; interment in Elmwood Cemetery.

**MAYFIELD, Earle Bradford,** a Senator from Texas; born in Overton, Rusk County, Tex., April 12, 1881; attended the public schools in eastern Texas; graduated from Southwestern University, Georgetown, Tex., in 1900; studied law at the University of Texas at Austin in 1900 and 1901; was admitted to the bar in 1907 and commenced practice in Meridian, Tex.; also engaged in agricultural pursuits and in the wholesale grocery business; member, State senate 1907-1913; member, State railroad commission 1913-1923; elected as a Democrat to the United States Senate and served from March 4, 1923, to March 3, 1929; unsuccessful candidate for renomination in 1928; resumed the practice of law in Tyler, Tex., until retiring in 1952; died in Tyler, Tex., June 23, 1964; interment in Oakwood Cemetery.

**MAYHAM, Stephen Lorenzo,** a Representative from New York; born in Blenheim, N.Y., October 8, 1826; pursued an academic course; studied law in Ithaca, N.Y.; was admitted to the bar and commenced practice in 1848; superintendent of schools in Schoharie County, N.Y., 1852-1857, and supervisor 1857-1860; district attorney of Schoharie County 1859-1862; member of the State assembly in 1863; elected as a Democrat to the Forty-first Congress (March 4, 1869-March 3, 1871); elected to the Forty-fifth Congress (March 4, 1877-March 3, 1879); judge of Schoharie County 1883-1887; delegate to the Democratic National Conventions in 1884 and 1892; judge of the supreme court of New York and afterward presiding justice 1886-1896; died in Schoharie, N.Y., March 3, 1908; interment in St. Paul's Lutheran Cemetery.

**MAYNARD, Harry Lee,** a Representative from Virginia; born in Portsmouth, Va., June 8, 1861; attended the common schools of Norfolk County; graduated from the Virginia Agricultural and Mechanical College at Blacksburg in 1880; engaged in the real estate business and the promotion of public utilities; member of the Virginia house of delegates, 1889-1890; served in the Virginia senate, 1893-1901; elected as a Democrat to the Fifty-seventh and to the four succeeding Congresses (March 4, 1901-March 3, 1911); unsuccessful candidate for renomination in 1910 to the Sixty-second Congress; moved to New York City and engaged in the insurance and real estate business; died in Fort Totten, N.Y., October 23, 1922; interment in Oak Grove Cemetery, Portsmouth, Va.

**MAYNARD, Horace,** a Representative from Tennessee; born in Westboro, Worcester County, Mass., August 30, 1814; attended the common schools of Westboro and the Millbury (Mass.) Academy, where he afterward taught, and was graduated from Amherst (Mass.) College in 1838; professor at the University of East Tennessee, 1839-1844; studied law; was admitted to the bar in 1844 and commenced practice in Knoxville, Tenn.; unsuccessful Whig candidate for election to the Thirty-third Congress in 1853; presidential elector on the Whig ticket in 1852, and on the Republican ticket in 1864; elected as an American Party candidate to the Thirty-fifth Congress, as an Opposition Party candidate to the Thirty-sixth Congress, and as a Unionist to the Thirty-seventh

Congress (March 4, 1857-March 3, 1863); attorney general of Tennessee, 1863-1865; delegate to the Southern Loyalist Convention at Philadelphia in 1866; upon the readmission of the State of Tennessee to representation was elected as an Unconditional Unionist to the Thirty-ninth Congress and reelected as a Republican to the four succeeding Congresses, and served from July 24, 1866, to March 3, 1875; chairman, Committee on Banking and Currency (Forty-third Congress); was not a candidate for renomination in 1874 to the Forty-fourth Congress; unsuccessful Republican candidate for Governor of Tennessee in 1874; Minister to Turkey from March 9, 1875 until May 1880; appointed Postmaster General in the Cabinet of President Rutherford B. Hayes, and served from June 2, 1880 to March 5, 1881; died in Knoxville, Tenn., May 3, 1882; interment in Old Gray Cemetery.

**Bibliography:** *DAB.*

**MAYNARD, John,** a Representative from New York; born in Whitestone, N.Y.; was graduated from Union College, Schenectady, N.Y., in 1810; studied law; was admitted to the bar and commenced practice at Seneca Falls, N.Y.; clerk of Seneca County in 1821 and 1822; member of the State assembly in 1822; elected to the Twentieth Congress (March 4, 1827-March 3, 1829); district attorney of Seneca County in 1836 and 1837; elected as a Whig to the Twenty-seventh Congress (March 4, 1841-March 3, 1843); member of the State senate 1838-1841; moved to Auburn, N.Y.; served as judge of the State supreme court, seventh district, from June 7, 1847, until his death in Auburn, N.Y., March 24, 1850.

**MAYNE, Wiley,** a Representative from Iowa; born in Sanborn, O'Brien County, Iowa, January 19, 1917; attended the public schools of Sanborn, Iowa; S.B., Harvard College, 1938, and attended the law school in 1938 and 1939; J.D., Iowa Law School, 1941; was a special agent to the Federal Bureau of Investigation, 1941-1943; served in the United States Naval Reserve as a lieutenant (junior grade) with destroyer escort duty in the Mediterranean, Atlantic, and Pacific, 1943-1946; admitted to the bar in 1941 and commenced practice in Sioux City, Iowa, in 1946; president, Iowa State Bar Association, 1963-1964; member, House of Delegates, American Bar Association, 1966-1968; chairman, Grievance Commission of Iowa Supreme Court, 1964-1966; commissioner of Uniform State Laws, 1956-1960; elected as a Republican to the Ninetieth and to the three succeeding Congresses (January 3, 1967-January 3, 1975); unsuccessful candidate for reelection in 1974 to the Ninety-fourth Congress; delegate to Food and Agricultural Organization, Rome, 1973; resumed the practice of law in Sioux City in 1975; is a resident of Sioux City, Iowa.

**MAYO, Robert Murphy,** a Representative from Virginia; born in Hague, Westmoreland County, Va., April 28, 1836; attended private schools and the College of William and Mary, Williamsburg, Va.; was graduated from Virginia Military Institute at Lexington in 1858; was instructor in mathematics at Mount Pleasant Military Academy, Sing Sing (now Ossining), N.Y., and later at Virginia Military Institute; studied law at Lexington Law School (now Washington and Lee University) in 1858 and 1859; served throughout the Civil War in the Confederate Army, first as major and later as colonel of the Forty-seventh Regiment of Virginia; admitted to the bar and commenced practice in Hague, Va., in 1865; member of the Virginia house of delegates in 1881, 1882, and 1885-1888; presented credentials as a Readjuster Member-elect to the Forty-eighth Congress and served from March 4, 1883, to March 20, 1884, when he was succeeded by George T. Garrison, who contested the election; unsuccessful candidate for reelection; resumed the practice of law; died in Hague, Va., March 29, 1896; interment in Yeocomico Cemetery, Tucker Hill, Westmoreland County, Va.

**MAYRANT, William,** a Representative from South Carolina; born in that State; elected as a Republican to the Fourteenth Congress and served from March 4, 1815, until October 21, 1816, when he resigned; unsuccessful candidate for reelection; member of South Carolina house of representatives, 1818-1821.

**MAYS, Dannite Hill,** a Representative from Florida; born near Madison, Madison County, Fla., April 28, 1852; attended the county schools, the public schools of Savannah, Ga., and Washington and Lee University, Lexington, Va.; moved to Monticello, Fla., and engaged in agricultural pursuits; delegate to the Democratic State convention in 1888; member of the State house of representatives in 1891, 1895, and 1897, serving as speaker in 1897; unsuccessful candidate for Governor in 1900 and 1904; elected as a Democrat to the Sixty-first and Sixty-second Congresses (March 4, 1909-March 3, 1913); unsuccessful candidate for renomination in 1912; returned to Monticello, Fla., and resumed agricultural pursuits; died in Monticello, Fla., May 9, 1930; interment in Roseland Cemetery.

**MAYS, James Henry,** a Representative from Utah; born in Morristown, Hamblen County, Tenn., June 29, 1868; attended the district schools; moved to Kansas in 1883 with his parents, who settled in Galena, Kans.; worked in the mines and as a lumberman; attended the Kansas State Normal School; from 1893 to 1902 engaged in the life insurance business at Chicago, Ill., Dubuque, Iowa, and Salt Lake City, Utah; was graduated from the law department of the University of Michigan at Ann Arbor in 1895; was admitted to the bar and commenced practice in Ann Arbor, Mich.; moved to Indianapolis, Ind., in 1896 and to Utah in 1902; organized several industrial organizations; elected as a Democrat to the Sixty-fourth, Sixty-fifth, and Sixty-sixth Congresses (March 4, 1915-March 3, 1921); was not a candidate for reelection in 1920; retired to his stock ranch near Wendell, Idaho, and died there on April 19, 1926; interment in Gooding Cemetery, Gooding, Idaho.

**MAZZOLI, Romano Louis,** a Representative from Kentucky; born in Louisville, Jefferson County, Ky., November 2, 1932; attended private schools in Louisville; B.S., University of Notre Dame, South Bend, Ind., 1954; J.D., University of Louisville Law School, 1960; United States Army, 1954-1956, discharged with rank of specialist third class; admitted to the Kentucky bar in 1960 and commenced practice in Louisville; lecturer in business law, Ballarmine College, Louisville, Ky., 1963-1967; elected to the Kentucky senate, 1968-1970; elected as a Democrat to the Ninety-second and to the eleven succeeding Congresses (January 3, 1971-January 3, 1995); was not a candidate for reelection in 1994 to the One Hundred Fourth Congress; visiting professor, University of Louisville School of Law; is a resident of Louisville, Ky.

**McADOO, William,** a Representative from New Jersey; born near Ramelton, County Donegal, Ireland, October 25, 1853; immigrated to the United States with his parents, who settled in Jersey City, N.J., in 1865; attended the common schools; studied law; was admitted to the bar in 1874 and commenced practice in Jersey City, N.J.; employed as a newspaper reporter 1870-1875; member of the State house of assembly in 1882; elected as a Democrat to the Forty-eighth and to the three succeeding Congresses (March 4, 1883-March 3, 1891); chairman, Committee on the Militia (Fiftieth Congress); unsuccessful candidate for renomination in 1890; moved to New York City in 1892 and resumed the practice of law; appointed by President Grover Cleveland as Assistant Secretary of the Navy and served from March 20, 1893, to April 18, 1897, when he resigned; police commissioner of New York City in 1904 and 1905; again resumed the practice of law and also engaged in literary pursuits; appointed by Mayor Gaynor as chief magistrate of the city magistrates' courts, first division, city of New York, July 1, 1910, in which capacity he served until his death in New York City, June 7, 1930; interment in Woodlawn Cemetery.

**McADOO, William Gibbs,** a Senator from California; born on a farm near Marietta, Cobb County, Ga., October 31, 1863; attended the rural schools and the University of Tennessee at Knoxville; appointed deputy clerk of the United States Circuit Court for the Southern Division, Eastern District of Tennessee, 1882; studied law; admitted to the bar in 1885 and commenced practice in Chattanooga, Tenn.; moved to New York City in 1892 and continued the practice of law; developed the system of rapid transit tunnels under the Hudson River between New York City and New Jersey and from 1902 to 1913 was president of the company which constructed and operated them; vice chairman of the Democratic National Committee in 1912; appointed Secretary of the Treasury in the Cabinet of President Woodrow Wilson, and served from March 6, 1913 to December 16, 1918; during the First World War served as director general of railways, chairman of the Federal Reserve Board, the Federal Farm Loan Board, and the War Finance Corporation; resumed the practice of law in New York City in 1919; moved to Los Angeles, Calif., in 1922 and continued to practice law; unsuccessful candidate for the Democratic nomination for President of the United States in 1920 and 1924; author; member of the Democratic National Committee, 1932-1940; elected in 1932 as a Democrat to the United States Senate, and served from March 4, 1933 to November 8, 1938, when he resigned; unsuccessful candidate for renomination in 1938; chairman, Committee on Patents (Seventy-third through Seventy-fifth Congresses); returned to Los Angeles, Calif., and served as chairman of the board of directors of a steamship line; died while on a visit to Washington, D.C., February 1, 1941; interment in Arlington National Cemetery, Va.

**Bibliography:** *DAB*; Broesamle, John J. *William Gibbs McAdoo: A Passion for Change, 1863-1917.* Port Washington, N.Y.: Kennikat, 1973; McAdoo, William G. *Crowded Years, the Reminiscences of William G. McAdoo.* 1931. Reprint. Port Washington, N.Y.: Kennikat Press, 1971.

**McALEER, William,** a Representative from Pennsylvania; born in County Tyrone, Ireland, January 6, 1838; immigrated to the United States with his parents, who settled in Philadelphia, Pa., in 1851; attended public and private schools; in 1861 became a partner with his father and brothers in the firm of John McAleer & Sons, flour merchants; member of the common council 1871-1873; president of the Friendly Sons of St. Patrick, organized for the relief of immigrants; member of the board of guardians of the poor 1873-1898, and served as vice president and later as president of the board; member of the commercial exchange and served successively as director, vice president, and president of the same; director of the chamber of commerce in 1880; member of the Pennsylvania senate 1886-1890; elected as a Democrat to the Fifty-second Congress and reelected as an Independent Democrat to the Fifty-third Congress (March 4, 1891-March 3, 1895); unsuccessful candidate for renomination in 1894; elected as a Democrat to the Fifty-fifth and Fifty-sixth Congresses (March 4, 1897-March 3, 1901); unsuccessful candidate for reelection in 1900 to the Fifty-seventh Congress; resumed business activities in Philadelphia, Pa.; died in Germantown, Philadelphia, Pa., April 19, 1912; interment in Holy Sepulchre Cemetery.

**McALLISTER, Archibald** (grandson of John Andre Hanna), a Representative from Pennsylvania; born at Fort Hunter, near Rockville, Dauphin County, Pa., October 12, 1813; attended the common schools and Dickinson College, Carlisle, Pa.; moved to Blair County, Pa., in 1842 and engaged in manufacturing charcoal iron at Springfield Furnace; elected as a Democrat to the Thirty-eighth Congress (March 4, 1863-March 3, 1865); was not a candidate for renomination in 1864; resumed the manufacture of iron; died in Royer, Blair County, Pa., July 18, 1883; interment in Mountain Cemetery.

**McANDREWS, James,** a Representative from Illinois; born in Woonsocket, Providence County, R.I., October 22, 1862; attended the common schools; moved to Chicago, Ill., and engaged in business; served as building commissioner of Chicago; elected as a Democrat to the Fifty-seventh and Fifty-eighth Congresses (March 4, 1901-March 3, 1905); elected to the Sixty-third and to the three succeeding Congresses (March 4, 1913-March 3, 1921); unsuccessful candidate for reelection in 1920 to the Sixty-seventh Congress; resumed his business activities; unsuccessful candidate for election in 1932 to the Seventy-third Congress; elected to the Seventy-fourth, Seventy-fifth, and Seventy-sixth Congresses (January 3, 1935-January 3, 1941); was an unsuccessful candidate for reelection in 1940 to the Seventy-seventh Congress; died in Chicago, Ill., August 31, 1942; interment in Calvary Cemetery, Evanston, Ill.

**McARDLE, Joseph A.,** a Representative from Pennsylvania; born in Muncie, Delaware County, Ind., June 29, 1903; moved to Pittsburgh, Pa., with his parents in 1905; attended the parochial schools; engaged in the insurance and bonding business; served in the Pennsylvania house of representatives 1936-1938; elected as a Democrat to the Seventy-sixth and Seventy-seventh Congresses and served from January 3, 1939, until his resignation on January 5, 1942, to become a member of the city council of Pittsburgh, Pa., in which capacity he served until 1949; announced his affiliation with the Republican Party in 1949; Pennsylvania Republican committeeman from Mt. Washington from early 1950 until 1966; died in Pittsburgh, Pa., December 27, 1967; interment in Calvary Cemetery.

**McARTHUR, Clifton Nesmith** (grandson of James Willis Nesmith), a Representative from Oregon; born in The Dalles, Wasco County, Oreg., June 10, 1879; attended the public schools at Rickreall, Oreg., and the Bishop Scott Academy, Portland, Oreg.; was graduated from the University of Oregon at Eugene in 1901; reporter on the Morning Oregonian, 1901-1903; engaged in agricultural pursuits near Rickreall, Oreg., 1903-1906; studied law; was admitted to the bar in 1906 and commenced practice in Portland; secretary of the Republican State central committee in 1908; secretary to Governor Frank W. Benson, 1908-1911; member of the Oregon State house of representatives, 1909-1913, and served as speaker two sessions; elected as a Republican to the Sixty-fourth and to the three succeeding Congresses (March 4, 1915-March 3, 1923); unsuccessful candidate for reelection in 1922 to the Sixty-eighth Congress; resumed the practice of his profession and his former business activities in Portland, Oreg., where he died on December 9, 1923; remains were cremated and the ashes deposited in the vaults of the Portland Cremation Association.

**McARTHUR, Duncan,** a Representative from Ohio; born in Dutchess County, N.Y., June 14, 1772; moved with his father to western Pennsylvania in 1780; received a limited education; served in the Indian campaign in 1790 under General Harmer; moved to Maysville, Ky., in 1793 and was employed in the salt works; settled in Ross County, Ohio, in 1796; acted as a spy among the Indians; member of the Ohio State house of representatives in 1804; helped to organize the Militia and was commissioned colonel in 1805 and major general in 1808; served in the Ohio State senate from 1805 until 1814, and was speaker in 1809 and 1810; raised a regiment of Volunteers during the War of 1812 and was commissioned colonel; elected to the Thirteenth Congress, but never qualified, resigning on April 5, 1813; commissioned brigadier general of Volunteers in March 1813; Indian treaty commissioner in 1816; member of the State house of representatives in 1817 and 1818 and served as speaker; served in the State senate, 1821-1823; elected to the Eighteenth Congress (March 4, 1823-March 3, 1825); chairman, Committee on Public Expenditures (Eighteenth Congress); declined to be a candidate for renomination in 1824 to the Nineteenth Congress; again a member of the State house of representatives in 1826; again served in the State senate in 1829 and 1830; elected

Governor of Ohio in 1830, and served from December 18, 1830 to December 7, 1832; unsuccessful candidate for election in 1832 to the Twenty-third Congress; died in Chillicothe, Ohio, on April 29, 1839; interment in Grandview Cemetery.

Bibliography: *DAB*.

**McBRIDE, George Wycliffe** (brother of John Rogers McBride), a Senator from Oregon; born near Lafayette, Yamhill County, Oreg., March 13, 1854; attended the public schools, the preparatory department of Willamette University, Salem, Oreg., and Christian College, Monmouth, Oreg.; studied law and was admitted to the bar, but never practiced; engaged in mercantile pursuits; member, State house of representatives 1882, and served as speaker; secretary of State of Oregon 1886, 1895; elected as a Republican to the United States Senate on February 23, 1895, and served from March 4, 1895, to March 3, 1901; unsuccessful candidate for renomination in 1900; chairman, Committee on Transportation Routes to the Seaboard (Fifty-fourth Congress), Committee on Coast Defenses (Fifty-fifth and Fifty-sixth Congresses); appointed a United States commissioner to the St. Louis Exposition in 1904; engaged as an agent of the Western Pacific Railroad in California; died in Portland, Oreg., June 18, 1911; remains were cremated and the ashes interred in Masonic Cemetery, St. Helens, Oreg.

**McBRIDE, John Rogers** (brother of George Wycliffe McBride), a Representative from Oregon; born near St. Louis, in Franklin County, Mo., August 22, 1832; attended the country schools in Missouri and Oregon; moved to Oregon in 1851 with his parents, who settled near Lafayette, in Yamhill County; superintendent of schools in 1854; studied law; was admitted to the bar in 1855 and commenced practice in Lafayette; delegate to the State constitutional convention in 1857; member of the State senate 1860-1862; elected as a Republican to the Thirty-eighth Congress (March 4, 1863-March 3, 1865); unsuccessful candidate for renomination in 1864; appointed by President Abraham Lincoln in 1865 to be chief justice of Idaho Territory; appointed by President Ulysses S. Grant in 1869 to be superintendent of the United States assay office at Boise, Idaho; practiced law in Boise, Idaho, and Salt Lake City, Utah; moved to Spokane, Wash., and continued the practice of his profession; member of the Republican National Committee 1880-1892; died in Spokane, Wash., July 20, 1904; interment in Germany Hill Cemetery, St. Helens, Oreg.

**McBRYDE, Archibald,** a Representative from North Carolina; born in Wigtownshire, Scotland, September 28, 1766; immigrated at an early age with his parents, who settled in Carbonton, Moore County, N.C.; studied under private teachers; studied law; was admitted to the bar and practiced; also engaged in agricultural pursuits; served as clerk of the superior court of Moore County 1792-1816; elected as a Federalist to the Eleventh and Twelfth Congresses (March 4, 1809-March 3, 1813); member of the State senate in 1813 and 1814; resumed the practice of his profession; died in Carbonton, N.C., February 15, 1816; interment in Farrar Cemetery.

**McCAIN, John Sidney, III,** a Representative and a Senator from Arizona; born in Panama Canal Zone, August 29, 1936; attended schools in Alexandria, Va.; graduated, Episcopal High School, Alexandria, Va., 1954; B.S., United States Naval Academy, Annapolis, Md., 1958, and the National War College, Washington, D.C., 1974; entered the United States Navy in 1958, retired as a captain in 1981 following service as a fighter pilot; shot down, captured and held prisoner in Vietnam from 1967 until 1973; elected as a Republican to the Ninety-eighth and Ninety-ninth Congresses (January 3, 1983-January 3, 1987); was not a candidate in 1986 for reelection to the House of Representatives, but was elected to the United States Senate for the term commencing January 2, 1987; reelected in 1992 for the term ending January 3, 1999; chairman,

Committee on Indian Affairs (One Hundred Fourth Congress); is a resident of Phoenix, Ariz.

**McCALL, John Ethridge,** a Representative from Tennessee; born in Clarksburg, Carroll County, Tenn., August 14, 1859; attended public and private schools and was graduated from the University of Tennessee at Knoxville in 1881; studied law in Huntingdon, Tenn.; was admitted to the bar in 1882 and commenced practice in Huntingdon; edited the Tennessee Republican in 1882; settled in Lexington, Tenn., in December 1883 and continued the practice of law; unsuccessful candidate for district attorney in 1886; member of the State house of representatives, 1887-1889; delegate to the Republican National Convention in 1888 and 1900; appointed assistant United States district attorney for western Tennessee in 1890, which office he resigned in 1891; unsuccessful candidate for nomination as Governor in 1892; elected as a Republican to the Fifty-fourth Congress (March 4, 1895-March 3, 1897); unsuccessful candidate for reelection in 1896 to the Fifty-fifth Congress; unsuccessful Republican candidate for Governor of Tennessee in 1900; collector of internal revenue for the fifth district of Tennessee 1902-1905; appointed United States district judge for the western district of Tennessee on January 17, 1905, and served until his death in Huntingdon, Tenn., August 8, 1920; interment in Forest Hill Cemetery, Memphis, Tenn.

**McCALL, Samuel Walker,** a Representative from Massachusetts; born in East Providence, Bedford County, Pa., February 28, 1851; spent his early life in Illinois; attended the Mount Carroll (Ill.) Seminary; was graduated from New Hampton (N.H.) Academy in 1870 and from Dartmouth College, Hanover, N.H., in 1874; studied law; was admitted to the bar in 1875 and practiced in Worcester, Mass., and later in Boston, Mass.; editor of the Boston Daily Advertiser; member of the Massachusetts house of representatives in 1888, 1889 and 1892; delegate to the Republican National Conventions of 1888, 1900 and 1916; elected as a Republican to the Fifty-third and to the nine succeeding Congresses (March 4, 1893-March 3, 1913); chairman, Committee on Elections No. 3 (Fifty-fourth Congress); was not a candidate for renomination in 1912 to the Sixty-third Congress; resumed the practice of law in Boston; unsuccessful candidate in 1914 for election for Governor; elected Governor of Massachusetts in 1915, reelected in 1916 and 1917, and served from January 6, 1916 to January 2, 1919; engaged in literary pursuits; died in Winchester, Mass., November 4, 1923; interment in Wildwood Cemetery.

Bibliography: *DAB*.

**McCANDLESS, Alfred A. (Al),** a Representative from California; born in Brawley, Imperial County, Calif., July 23, 1927; attended Los Angeles City schools; B.A., University of California at Los Angeles, 1951; served in the United States Marine Corps, 1945-1946 in the Pacific, China and with occupation forces in Japan, and 1950-1952 during the Korean conflict; attained the rank of captain; automobile and truck dealer in Indio, Calif., 1953-1975; member, Riverside County, Calif., Board of Supervisors, 1972-1982, and Riverside County Housing Authority, 1974-1982; founding member, South Coast Air Quality Management District, and chairman 1975-1982; member, California Air Resources Board, 1982; elected as a Republican to the Ninety-eighth and to the five succeeding Congresses (January 3, 1983-January 3, 1995); was not a candidate for reelection in 1994 to the One Hundred Fourth Congress; is a resident of La Quinta, Calif.

**McCANDLESS, Lincoln Loy,** a Delegate from the Territory of Hawaii; born in Indiana, Indiana County, Pa., September 18, 1859; moved to Volcano, Wood County, W.Va., with his parents in 1867; attended the public schools in Volcano, W.Va.; engaged in the oil and mining business in West Virginia and in Leadville, Colo.; moved to Hawaii in 1882, settled in Honolulu, and engaged in the drilling of artesian wells; also engaged in cattle ranching in 1887; served in the legislature of the Republic of Hawaii as a representative 1898-1900 and in the legislature of the Territory of Hawaii as a senator 1902-1906; unsuccessful candidate for election as a Delegate to the United States Congress on numerous occasions; elected as a Democrat a Delegate to the Seventy-third Congress (March 4, 1933-January 3, 1935); unsuccessful candidate for reelection in 1934 to the Seventy-fourth Congress; resumed his former business pursuits in Honolulu, Hawaii; also engaged in the building of roads and sewers and in the operation of his large plantations; died in Honolulu, Hawaii, October 5, 1940; the remains were cremated and interred in Nuuanu Cemetery.

**McCARRAN, Patrick Anthony (Pat),** a Senator from Nevada; born in Reno, Nev., August 8, 1876; attended the public schools and the University of Nevada at Reno; engaged in farming and in stock raising; member, Nevada State legislature, 1903; studied law; was admitted to the bar in 1905 and practiced in Tonopah and Goldfield, Nev.; district attorney of Nye County, Nev., 1907-1909; resumed the practice of law in Reno, Nev., in 1909; associate justice of the Nevada State supreme court, 1913-1917, and chief justice, 1917-1918; member of Nevada State Board of Pardons, 1913-1919; member of Nevada State Board of Parole Commissioners, 1913-1918; chairman of the Nevada State Board of Bar Examiners, 1919-1932; elected as a Democrat to the United States Senate in 1932; reelected in 1938, 1944, and again in 1950, and served from March 4, 1933 until his death in Hawthorne, Nev., September 28, 1954; chairman, Committee on the District of Columbia (Seventy-seventh and Seventy-eighth Congresses), Committee on the Judiciary (Seventy-eighth, Seventy-ninth, Eighty-first and Eighty-second Congresses), co-chairman, Joint Committee on Foreign Economic Cooperation (Eighty-first Congress); co-sponsor of the McCarran-Walter Act of 1952 (Immigration and Nationality Act), codifying the immigration and nationality laws, tightening the requirements for citizenship, and retaining the immigration quota system under which Great Britain, Germany and Ireland were allotted over two-thirds of the total quota; interment in Mountain View Cemetery, Reno, Nev.

**Bibliography:** *DAB*; Edwards, Jerome E. *Pat McCarran: Political Boss of Nevada.* Reno: University of Nevada Press, 1982; McCarran, Sister Margaret Patricia. "Patrick Anthony McCarran." *Nevada Historical Society Quarterly* 11 (Fall-Winter 1968): 5-66, 12 (Spring 1969): 5-75; Pittman, Von V., Jr. "Senator Patrick A. McCarran and the Politics of Containment." Ph.D. dissertation, University of Georgia, 1979.

**McCARTHY, Dennis,** a Representative from New York; born in Salina, N.Y., March 19, 1814; pursued an academic course; attended Valley Academy, Salina, N.Y.; engaged in the manufacture of salt; member of the State assembly in 1846; mayor of Syracuse, N.Y., in 1853; elected as a Republican to the Fortieth and Forty-first Congresses (March 4, 1867-March 3, 1871); unsuccessful candidate for reelection in 1870 to the Forty-second Congress; resumed his former business pursuits; served in the State senate 1876-1885, and was president pro tempore of that body in 1885; served as Lieutenant Governor of New York from January 6, 1885, to January 1, 1886; died in Syracuse, N.Y., February 14, 1886; interment in Oakwood Cemetery.

**McCARTHY, Eugene Joseph,** a Representative and a Senator from Minnesota; born in Watkins, Meeker County, Minn., March 29, 1916; attended public schools in Watkins, Minn.; A.B., St. John's University, Collegeville, Minn., 1935; M.A., University of Minnesota, Minneapolis, 1939; taught in the public high schools of Minnesota and North Dakota, 1935-1940; professor of economics and education at St. John's University, 1940-1943; civilian technical assistant in the Military Intelligence Division of the War Department in 1944; instructor in sociology and economics at St. Thomas College, St. Paul, Minn., 1946-1949; elected as a Democrat to the Eighty-first and to the four succeeding Congresses (January 3, 1949-January 3,

1959); was not a candidate in 1958 for renomination to the House of Representatives, but was elected to the United States Senate; reelected in 1964, and served from January 3, 1959 to January 3, 1971; was not a candidate for reelection in 1970; unsuccessful candidate for the Democratic nomination for President of the United States in 1968; Independent candidate for President of the United States in 1976; author of works of history, political science, poetry and children's literature; is a resident of Sperryville, Va.

**Bibliography:** McCarthy, Eugene J. *Gene McCarthy's Minnesota: Memories of a Native Son.* Minneapolis: Winston Press, 1982; McCarthy, Eugene J. *Up 'til Now: A Memoir.* San Diego: Harcourt Brace Jovanovich, 1987; McCarthy, Eugene J. *The Year of the People.* Garden City, N.Y.: Doubleday and Co., 1969.

**McCARTHY, John Henry,** a Representative from New York; born in New York City on November 16, 1850; attended De La Salle Institute, Christian Brothers, and St. Francis Xavier College; engaged in mercantile pursuits; studied law; was admitted to the bar in 1873 and commenced practice in New York City; member of the New York State assembly in 1880 and 1881; civil justice for the fifth judicial district, New York City, 1882-1888; elected as a Democrat to the Fifty-first Congress and served from March 4, 1889, until his resignation on January 14, 1891, to accept a judicial position; appointed on January 11, 1891, by Governor David B. Hill as justice of the city court of New York City to fill a vacancy; elected and reelected to the same office and served from 1891 until his death in New York City on February 5, 1908; interment in Calvary Cemetery, Long Island City, N.Y.

**McCARTHY, John Jay,** a Representative from Nebraska; born in Stoughton, Dane County, Wis., July 19, 1857; attended the common schools and Albion (Wis.) Academy; moved to David City, Nebr., in 1879 and thence to Dixon County in 1882; studied law; was admitted to the bar in 1884 and commenced practice in Emerson, Nebr.; elected prosecuting attorney of Dixon County in 1890, 1892, and 1894; elected as a member of the State house of representatives in 1898 and 1900; elected as a Republican to the Fifty-eighth and Fifty-ninth Congresses (March 4, 1903-March 3, 1907); unsuccessful candidate for renomination in 1906; delegate to the Republican National Convention in 1912; continued the practice of his profession in Ponca, Nebr., until his death there on March 30, 1943; interment in Ponca Cemetery.

**McCARTHY, Joseph Raymond,** a Senator from Wisconsin; born in Grand Chute, Outagamie County, Wis., November 15, 1908; attended a one-room country school; worked on a farm; moved to Manawa, Wis., in 1929 and enrolled in Little Wolf High School; while working in a grocery store and ushering at a theater in the evenings, completed a four-year course in one year; graduated from Marquette University, Milwaukee, Wis., with a law degree in 1935; was admitted to the bar the same year; commenced practice in Waupaca, Wis., and in February 1936 moved to Shawano, Wis., and continued to practice law; unsuccessful Democratic candidate for district attorney in 1936; elected judge of the tenth judicial circuit of Wisconsin in April 1939; while serving in this capacity enlisted on June 4, 1942 in the United States Marine Corps, and was commissioned a first lieutenant July 29, 1942; served as an intelligence officer for a dive-bomber squadron in the South Pacific; resigned his commission on December 11, 1944; unsuccessful candidate for the Republican nomination for United States Senator in 1944 while in military service; reelected judge of the tenth judicial circuit in 1945; elected as a Republican to the United States Senate in 1946; reelected in 1952, and served from January 3, 1947 until his death in the naval hospital at Bethesda, Md., May 2, 1957; co-chairman, Joint Committee on the Library (Eighty-third Congress), chairman, Committee on Government Operations (Eighty-third Congress), Special Committee on Unemployment Problems (Eighty-sixth Congress); used his position as chairman of the

Committee on Government Operations and its Permanent Subcommittee on Investigations to conduct investigations designed to document charges of Communists and Communist influence in government; censured by the Senate on December 2, 1954 for abuse of the Subcommittee on Privileges and Elections (in 1952) and of the Select Committee to Study Censure (in 1954); funeral services were held in the Chamber of the United States Senate; interment in St. Mary's Cemetery, Appleton, Wis.

**Bibliography:** *DAB*; Griffith, Robert. *The Politics of Fear: Joseph R. McCarthy and the Senate.* Lexington: University of Kentucky Press, 1970; Reeves, Thomas C. *The Life and Times of Joe McCarthy: A Biography.* New York: Stein and Day, 1982; Rovere, Richard H. *Senator Joe McCarthy.* Foreword by Arthur M. Schlesinger, Jr. 1959. Reprint. Berkeley: University of California Press, 1995.

**McCARTHY, Karen,** a Representative from Missouri; born in Haverhill, Essex County, Mass., March 18, 1947; graduated from Shawnee Mission East High School, Shawnee Mission, Kans., 1965; B.S., University of Kansas, Lawrence, 1969; M.A., University of Missouri, Kansas City, 1976; John F. Kennedy School of Government, Harvard University, 1982; M.B.A., University of Kansas, 1986; English teacher; investment and banking research analyst and consultant, 1984-1993; member Missouri State house of representatives, 1977-1995; elected as a Democrat to the One Hundred Fourth Congress (January 3, 1995-January 3, 1997): is a resident of Kansas City, Mo.

**McCARTHY, Kathryn O'Loughlin,** a Representative from Kansas. (*See* O'LOUGHLIN, Kathryn Ellen.)

**McCARTHY, Richard Dean,** a Representative from New York; born in Buffalo, Erie County, N.Y., September 24, 1927; graduated from Canisus High School in 1945, and from Canisus College, Buffalo, N.Y., 1950; engaged in graduate work at the University of Buffalo, Cornell University, and Harvard University; served in the United States Navy, November 1945 to August 1946 and in the United States Army, November 1950 to October 1952; engaged as a reporter for the Buffalo Evening News, October 1952 to September 1953 and in the public relations field, September 1953 to December 1956; director of public relations for the National Gypsum Co., 1956-1964; author; elected as a Democrat to the Eighty-ninth and to the two succeeding Congresses (January 3, 1965-January 3, 1971); was not a candidate for reelection in 1970 to the House of Representatives, but was an unsuccessful candidate for nomination to the United States Senate; press attaché, American Embassy, Tehran, 1975-1976; bureau chief 1978-1990, and columnist 1990-1995 for the Buffalo News, Washington, D.C.; was a resident of Arlington, Va., until his death there on May 5, 1995.

**Bibliography:** McCarthy, Richard Dean. *Elections For Sale.* Boston: Houghton Mifflin, 1972; McCarthy, Richard Dean. *The Ultimate Folly: War by Pestilence, Asphyxiation and Defoliation.* New York: Knopf, 1969.

**McCARTY, Andrew Zimmerman,** a Representative from New York; born in Rhinebeck, Dutchess County, N.Y., July 14, 1808; studied law; was admitted to the bar in 1831 and commenced practice in Pulaski, Oswego County, N.Y.; county clerk of Oswego County 1840-1843; member of the State assembly in 1846 and 1847; elected as a Whig to the Thirty-fourth Congress (March 4, 1855-March 3, 1857); resumed the practice of his profession in Pulaski; register of bankruptcy 1875-1879; died in Pulaski, Oswego County, N.Y., April 23, 1879; interment in Pulaski Cemetery.

**McCARTY, Johnathan,** a Representative from Indiana; born in Culpeper County, Va., August 3, 1795; attended the public schools; moved to Indiana in 1803 with his father, who settled in Franklin County; engaged in mercantile pursuits; member of the State house of representatives in 1818; moved to Connersville, Fayette County,

Ind.; clerk of the county court 1819-1827; elected as a Jacksonian to the Twenty-second Congress; reelected to the Twenty-third Congress and reelected as an Anti-Jacksonian to the Twenty-fourth Congress (March 4, 1831-March 3, 1837); unsuccessful candidate for reelection in 1836 to the Twenty-fifth Congress; presidential elector on the Whig ticket in 1840; moved to Keokuk, Iowa, where he died March 30, 1852; interment in Oakland Cemetery.

**McCARTY, Richard,** a Representative from New York; born in Coeymans, Albany County, N.Y., February 19, 1780; attended the common schools; county clerk of Greene County, 1811-1813; flour inspector of the State of New York; elected to the Seventeenth Congress (March 4, 1821-March 3, 1823); president of the Lafayette Bank in New York City; was one of the committee appointed to receive General Lafayette when he visited the United States in 1824 and 1825; died in New York City, May 18, 1844; interment in Adams Cemetery, Coxsackie, Greene County, N.Y.

**McCARTY, William Mason,** a Representative from Virginia; born at "Cedar Grove," Fairfax County, Va., about 1789; received his early education from private tutors; attended the College of William and Mary, Williamsburg, Va., in 1813 and 1814; studied law; was admitted to the bar and commenced practice in Virginia; member of the Virginia senate in 1823; moved to Florida and was prominently identified with the administration of the newly acquired territory; appointed by President John Quincy Adams as secretary of the Territory of Florida to fill the vacancy caused by the resignation of George Walton in 1826; returned to Virginia in 1830 and settled in Loudoun County; resumed the practice of his profession; again a member of the Virginia senate, 1830-1839; elected as a Whig to the Twenty-sixth Congress to fill the vacancy caused by the resignation of Charles F. Mercer, and served from January 25, 1840 to March 3, 1841; moved to Richmond, Va., in 1852 and died there on December 20, 1863; interment in Shockoe Hill Cemetery.

**McCAUSLEN, William Cochran,** a Representative from Ohio; born near Steubenville, Jefferson County, Ohio, in 1796; attended the public schools; studied law; was admitted to the bar and practiced in Steubenville; was a law partner of Secretary of War Edwin M. Stanton; member of the Ohio State house of representatives in 1829, 1830, 1832, and 1833; owned and edited a Democratic newspaper in Steubenville; elected as a Democrat to the Twenty-eighth Congress (March 4, 1843-March 3, 1845); commissioned August 31, 1846, during the Mexican War as a captain and commissary of subsistence of the Third Regiment, Ohio Infantry; honorably discharged June 24, 1847; died in Steubenville, Jefferson County, Ohio, March 13, 1863; interment in Union Cemetery.

**McCLAMMY, Charles Washington,** a Representative from North Carolina; born at Scotts Hill, Pender County, N.C., May 29, 1839; pursued an academic course and was graduated from the University of North Carolina at Chapel Hill in 1859; engaged in teaching 1859-1861; entered the Confederate Army in 1861; by successive promotions became major in the Third North Carolina Cavalry Regiment and served throughout the Civil War; engaged in agricultural pursuits at Scotts Hill; member of the State house of representatives in 1866; served in the State senate in 1871; elected as a Democrat to the Fiftieth and Fifty-first Congresses (March 4, 1887-March 3, 1891); resumed agricultural pursuits; unsuccessful candidate for reelection in 1890 to the Fifty-second Congress; died at Scotts Hill, N.C., February 26, 1896; interment in the family cemetery.

**McCLEAN, Moses,** a Representative from Pennsylvania; born in Gettysburg, Pa., June 17, 1804; pursued an academic course; studied law; admitted to the bar in 1825 and commenced practice in Gettysburg, Pa.; elected as a Democrat to the Twenty-ninth Congress (March 4, 1845-March 3, 1847); resumed the practice of law in Gettysburg, Pa.; member of the Pennsylvania house of representatives in 1855; continued the practice of law until his death in Gettysburg, Pa., September 30, 1870; interment in Evergreen Cemetery.

**McCLEARY, James Thompson,** a Representative from Minnesota; born in Ingersoll, Ontario, Canada, February 5, 1853; was educated at Ingersoll High School and McGill University, Montreal, Canada; engaged as superintendent of the Pierce County (Wis.) schools until 1881 when he resigned; moved to Minnesota and became State institute conductor of Minnesota and professor in the normal school in Mankato, Minn.; president of the Minnesota Educational Association in 1891; elected as a Republican to the Fifty-third and to the six succeeding Congresses (March 4, 1893-March 3, 1907); unsuccessful candidate for reelection in 1906 to the Sixtieth Congress; appointed Second Assistant Postmaster General, and served from March 29, 1907 until his resignation on September 15, 1908; secretary of the American Iron and Steel Institute in New York City, 1911-1920; moved to Maiden Rock, Pierce County, Wis., and engaged in farming; thence to Mill Valley, Calif., and engaged in literary pursuits; returned to Maiden Rock, Wis., in 1924; died in La Crosse, Wis., December 17, 1924; interment in Lakewood Cemetery, Maiden Rock, Wis.

**McCLEERY, James,** a Representative from Louisiana; born in Mecca Township, Trumbull County, Ohio, December 2, 1837; attended Oberlin (Ohio) College in 1859 and 1860; served in the Union Army during the Civil War; commissioned second lieutenant of Company A, Forty-first Regiment, Ohio Volunteer Infantry, in 1861, and promoted through the ranks to major in 1865; entered the Regular Army as captain in the Forty-fifth Infantry in 1866 and subsequently received the brevets of major and brigadier general of Volunteers; retired December 15, 1870, and settled in St. Marys Parish, La.; purchased a plantation; practiced law and was connected with the Freedmen's Bureau in North Carolina and Louisiana; moved to Shreveport, La.; appointed superintendent of public education for the fourth division; elected as a Republican to the Forty-second Congress and served from March 4, 1871, until his death while on a visit in New York City November 5, 1871; interment in the Christian Church Cemetery, Cortland, Ohio.

**McCLELLAN, Abraham,** a Representative from Tennessee; born at "White Top," on Beaver Creek, Sullivan County, Tenn., October 4, 1789; attended the common schools and was graduated from Washington (Tenn.) College; engaged in agricultural pursuits; member of the State house of representatives 1823-1825, 1827-1829; served in the State senate 1829-1833; member of the convention to revise the State constitution in 1834; member of the Second Regiment, Second Brigade, Tennessee Mounted Volunteer Militia, in 1836 and 1837 during the Seminole War; elected as a Democrat to the Twenty-fifth, Twenty-sixth, and Twenty-seventh Congresses (March 4, 1837-March 3, 1843); resumed agricultural pursuits; died at his home, "White Top," in Sullivan County, Tenn., May 3, 1866; interment in Weavers Cemetery, near Bristol, Tenn.

**McCLELLAN, Charles A.O.,** a Representative from Indiana; born in Ashland, Ashe County, Ohio, May 25, 1835; moved to Auburn, Ind., in 1856; attended the public schools; studied law in Auburn and Waterloo, Ind.; was admitted to the bar in 1863 and commenced practice in Waterloo; became engaged in banking in 1868; appointed judge of the fortieth judicial circuit of Indiana by Governor James D. Williams in 1879, and served for two years; elected as a Democrat to the Fifty-first and Fifty-second Congresses (March 4, 1889-March 3, 1893); chairman, Committee on Expenditures in the Department of the Navy (Fifty-second Congress); was not a candidate for renomination in 1892 to the Fifty-third Congress; again engaged in banking and the practice of law; died in Auburn, Ind., January 31, 1898; interment in Waterloo Cemetery, Waterloo, Ind.

**McCLELLAN, George,** a Representative from New York; born in Schodack, Rensselaer County, N.Y., October 10, 1856; attended the public schools and the local academies at Spencertown and Chatham, N.Y.; was graduated from the Albany Law School in 1880; was admitted to the bar and commenced practice in Chatham, N.Y.; police justice for two terms; president of the Columbia County Agriculture Society for ten years; served as postmaster of Chatham; surrogate of Columbia County 1907-1913; elected as a Democrat to the Sixty-third Congress (March 4, 1913-March 3, 1915); unsuccessful candidate for reelection in 1914 to the Sixty-fourth Congress; delegate to the Democratic National Convention in 1920; resumed the practice of his profession in Chatham, N.Y.; moved to Kinderhook, Columbia County, and died there February 20, 1927; interment in Nassau Cemetery at Nassau, Rensselaer County, N.Y.

**McCLELLAN, George Brinton,** a Representative from New York; born November 23, 1865, in Dresden, Saxony, where his parents were visiting; attended St. John's School, Sing Sing (now Ossining), N.Y.; was graduated from Princeton College in 1886; worked as a reporter and in editorial positions on several New York newspapers; studied law; was admitted to the bar in 1892 and commenced practice in New York City; treasurer of the New York and Brooklyn Bridge 1889-1893; president of the Board of Aldermen of New York City in 1893 and 1894; delegate to all Democratic National, State, and city conventions between 1890 and 1903; elected as a Democrat to the Fifty-fourth and to the four succeeding Congresses and served from March 4, 1895, to December 21, 1903, when he resigned, having been elected mayor of New York City; served as mayor from 1903 to 1910; university lecturer on public affairs 1908-1912; elected professor of economic history at Princeton University in 1912; an incorporator, trustee, and vice president of the American Academy in Rome; during the First World War entered the military service as major in the Ordnance Department in May 1917 and was honorably discharged in May 1919 as lieutenant colonel; commissioned colonel in the Ordnance Officers' Reserve Corps; resumed his position at Princeton University; resided in Washington, D.C., until his death on November 30, 1940; interment in Arlington National Cemetery, Va.

Bibliography: *DAB*; McClellan, George B. *The Gentleman and the Tiger.* Edited by Harold C. Syrett. Philadelphia: J.B. Lippincott Co., 1956.

**McCLELLAN, John Little,** a Representative and a Senator from Arkansas; born in Sheridan, Grant County, Ark., February 25, 1896; studied law and was admitted to the bar in 1913, when he was seventeen; commenced practice in Sheridan, Ark.; during the First World War served in the United States Army as a first lieutenant in the Aviation Section of the Signal Corps, 1917-1919; moved to Malvern, Ark., in 1919 and continued the practice of law; prosecuting attorney of the seventh judicial district of Arkansas, 1927-1930; elected as a Democrat to the Seventy-fourth Congress; reelected to the Seventy-fifth Congress (January 3, 1935-January 3, 1939); was not a candidate in 1938 for reelection to the House of Representatives, but was an unsuccessful candidate for election to the United States Senate; resumed the practice of law in Camden, Ark.; elected as a Democrat to the United States Senate in 1942; reelected in 1948, 1954, 1960, 1966, and again in 1972 and served from January 3, 1943, until his death; chairman, Committee on Expenditures in Executive Departments (Eighty-first and Eighty-second Congresses); Committee on Government Operations (Eighty-fourth through Ninety-second Congresses), Select Committee on Labor Management Relations (Eighty-fifth and Eighty-sixth Congresses), Committee on Appropriations (Ninety-second through Ninety-fifth Congresses); member, Commission on Organization of the Executive Branch of the Government (Hoover Commission); died in Little Rock, Ark., November 28, 1977; interment in Roselawn Memorial Park.

Bibliography: *DAB*; McClellan, John L. *Crime Without Punishment.* 1962. Reprint. Westport, Conn.: Greenwood Press, 1976.

**McCLELLAN, Robert,** a Representative from New York; born in Livingston, N.Y., October 2, 1806; was graduated from Williams College, Williamstown, Mass., in 1825; studied law; was admitted to the bar and practiced his profession in Middleburg, N.Y., 1828-1843; elected as a Democrat to the Twenty-fifth Congress (March 4, 1837-March 3, 1839); elected to the Twenty-seventh Congress (March 4, 1841-March 3, 1843); chairman, Committee on Patents (Twenty-seventh Congress); died in Greenpoint, Brooklyn, N.Y., June 28, 1860; interment in Greenwood Cemetery.

**McCLELLAND, Robert,** a Representative from Michigan; born in Greencastle, Franklin County, Pa., August 1, 1807; was graduated from Dickinson College, Carlisle, Pa., in 1829; engaged in teaching; studied law; was admitted to the bar in Chambersburg, Pa., in 1832; moved to Pittsburgh, Pa., and thence, in February 1833 to Monroe, Mich., and engaged in the practice of law; delegate to the convention called to frame a constitution for the proposed State of Michigan in 1835, and to the State constitutional conventions in 1850 and 1867; member of the board of regents of the University of Michigan at Ann Arbor in 1837 and 1850; member of the Michigan State house of representatives in 1837, 1839, and 1843, in the latter year being chosen speaker; mayor of Monroe in 1841; elected as a Democrat to the Twenty-eighth and to the two succeeding Congresses (March 4, 1843-March 3, 1849); chairman, Committee on Commerce (Twenty-ninth Congress); was not a candidate for renomination in 1848 to the Thirty-first Congress; delegate to the Democratic National Conventions of 1848, 1852, and 1868; delegate to the Democratic State convention in 1850; elected Governor of Michigan in 1851, reelected in 1852, and served from January 1, 1851 until his resignation on March 7, 1853 to accept a Cabinet portfolio; appointed Secretary of the Interior in the Cabinet of President Franklin Pierce on March 7, 1853 and served until March 6, 1857; resumed the practice of law in Detroit, Mich., where he died on August 30, 1880; interment in Elmwood Cemetery.

Bibliography: *DAB*.

**McCLELLAND, William,** a Representative from Pennsylvania; born in Mount Jackson, Lawrence County, Pa., March 2, 1842; attended Westminster College, New Wilmington, Pa.; served in the Civil War four years; attended Allegheny College; studied law; was admitted to the bar and commenced practice at Mount Jackson in 1870; elected as a Democrat to the Forty-second Congress (March 4, 1871-March 3, 1873); unsuccessful candidate for reelection in 1872 to the Forty-third Congress; resumed the practice of his profession; died in Harrisburg, Pa., February 7, 1892; interment in Allegheny Cemetery, Pittsburgh, Pa.

**McCLENACHAN, Blair,** a Representative from Pennsylvania; born in Ireland; immigrated to the United States at an early age and settled in Philadelphia, Pa.; engaged in mercantile pursuits and in banking and shipping; one of the founders of and served with the First Troop of Philadelphia Cavalry during the Revolutionary War; in 1780 he subscribed a large sum of money to help the American forces and aided the Continental Congress with money and credit; member of the Pennsylvania house of representatives 1790-1795; elected as a Republican to the Fifth Congress (March 4, 1797-March 3, 1799); died in Philadelphia, Pa., May 8, 1812; interment in a vault in St. Paul's Cemetery.

**McCLERNAND, John Alexander,** a Representative from Illinois; born in Breckinridge County, Ky., on May 30, 1812; moved with his parents to Shawneetown, Ill., in 1813; attended the village schools; engaged in agricultural pursuits; studied law; was admitted to the bar in 1832; served in the Black Hawk War; engaged as a trader on the Ohio and Mississippi Rivers, 1833-1834; established the Shawneetown Democrat in 1835 and in the same year commenced the practice of law; member of the Illinois State house of representatives in 1836, 1840, 1842, and 1843; elected as a Democrat to the Twenty-eighth and to the three succeeding Congresses (March 4, 1843-March 3, 1851); chairman, Committee on Public Lands (Twenty-ninth Congress), Committee on Foreign Affairs (Thirty-first Congress); declined to be a candidate for renomination in 1850 to the Thirty-second Congress; moved to Jacksonville, Ill., in 1851 and to Springfield in 1856; elected to the Thirty-sixth Congress to fill the vacancy caused by the death of Thomas L. Harris; reelected to the Thirty-seventh Congress, and served from November 8, 1859 until October 28, 1861, when he resigned to accept a commission as brigadier general of Volunteers for service in the Civil War; returned to Illinois to raise troops for the Union Army; was promoted to major general in 1862; resigned his commission on November 30, 1864 because of ill health; elected circuit judge of the Sangamon District of Illinois in 1870 and served until 1873; resumed the practice of law; presided over the Democratic National Convention of 1876; appointed by President Grover Cleveland as a member of the Utah Commission; died in Springfield, Ill., September 20, 1900; interment in Oak Ridge Cemetery.

Bibliography: *DAB*; Hicken, Victor. "From Vandalia to Vicksburg: The Political and Military Career of John A. McClernand." Ph.D. dissertation, University of Illinois, Urbana-Champaign, 1955; Hicken, Victor. "John A. McClernand and the House Speakership Struggle of 1859." *Journal of the Illinois State Historical Society* 53 (Summer 1960): 163-78.

**McCLINTIC, James Vernon,** a Representative from Oklahoma; born near Bremond, Robertson County, Tex., September 8, 1878; moved with his parents to Groesbeck, Limestone County, Tex., in 1880; attended the public schools, and Add-Ran University (now Texas Christian University), Fort Worth, Tex.; accepted a position with a wholesale dry-goods company at St. Louis, Mo., in 1901; traveling salesman in 1902; moved to Oklahoma Territory and engaged in mercantile pursuits at Snyder; homesteaded a farm in Texas County; city clerk of Snyder, Kiowa County, Okla., in 1908; clerk of Kiowa County in 1909; member of the Oklahoma State house of representatives in 1911; served in the State senate in 1913 and 1914; studied law at Georgetown University, Washington, D.C.; was admitted to the bar in 1928 and licensed to practice in all the courts of Oklahoma; elected as a Democrat to the Sixty-fourth and to the nine succeeding Congresses (March 4, 1915-January 3, 1935); chairman, Committee on Expenditures on Public Buildings (Sixty-fifth Congress); unsuccessful candidate for renomination in 1934 to the Seventy-fourth Congress; executive assistant to Governor Ernest W. Marland of Oklahoma, 1935-1940; unsuccessful candidate for nomination in 1941 to fill a vacancy in the Seventy-seventh Congress; administrative assistant in the District of Columbia Department of Vehicles and Traffic in 1940 and 1941; special assistant to Secretary of the Interior Harold L. Ickes, 1941-1944; member of the Readjustment Division of the War Department in 1944 and 1945; resumed the practice of law; died on a train in the vicinity of Chicago, Ill., April 22, 1948; interment in Rose Hill Cemetery, Oklahoma City, Okla.

**McCLINTOCK, Charles Blaine,** a Representative from Ohio; born in Paint Township, Wayne County, Ohio, near Beach City, Stark County, May 25, 1886; educated in the public schools; attended Wooster (Ohio) University, and was graduated from the law school of Western Reserve University, Cleveland, Ohio, in 1912; was admitted to the bar the same year and commenced law practice in Canton, Ohio; assistant prosecuting attorney of Stark County 1919-1923 and prosecuting attorney 1923-1927; elected as a Republican to the Seventy-first and Seventy-second Congresses (March 4, 1929-March 3, 1933); was an unsuccessful candidate for reelection in 1932 to the Seventy-third Congress and for election in 1934 to the Seventy-fourth Congress; resumed the practice of law; elected in 1946 as a judge of the court of appeals from the fifth appellate district of Ohio; reelected in 1952 and again in 1958; retired in March 1963; died in Canton, Ohio, February 1, 1965; interment in Greenlawn Cemetery, Wilmot, Ohio.

**McCLORY, Robert,** a Representative from Illinois; born in Riverside, Cook County, Ill. January 31, 1908; attended the public schools, L'Institut Sillig, Vevey, Switzerland, 1925-1926, and Dartmouth College, Hanover, N.H., 1926-1928; graduated from Chicago-Kent College of Law in 1932; admitted to the bar in 1932 and thereafter engaged in the practice of law in State and Federal courts in Cook and Lake Counties; served in the United States Marine Corps Reserve, 1933-1937; elected to the Illinois State house of representatives in 1950, and to the Illinois State senate in 1952, 1956 and 1960; elected as a Republican to the Eighty-eighth and to the nine succeeding Congresses (January 3, 1963-January 3, 1983); was not a candidate for reelection in 1982 to the Ninety-eighth Congress; resumed the practice of law in Washington, D.C.; United States delegate to the Interparliamentary Union Conference, 1963-1982, and honorary delegate, 1983 to 1988; was a resident of Washington, D.C., until his death there on July 24, 1988.

**McCLOSKEY, Augustus,** a Representative from Texas; born in San Antonio, Bexar County, Tex., September 23, 1878; attended Atascosa (Tex.) School, St. Joseph's Academy, San Antonio, Tex., and St. Mary's College, San Antonio, Tex.; employed as a stenographer 1903-1907; studied law; was admitted to the bar in 1907 and commenced practice in San Antonio, Tex.; judge of Bexar County 1920-1928; delegate to the Democratic National Convention at Houston, Tex., in 1928; presented credentials as a Democratic Member-elect to the Seventy-first Congress and served from March 4, 1929, to February 10, 1930, when he was succeeded by Harry M. Wurzbach, who successfully contested his election; was not a candidate for renomination in 1930; resumed the practice of law; judge of the corporation court of San Antonio, Tex., from January 1943 to July 1947; practiced law until his death in San Antonio, Tex., July 21, 1950; interment in San Fernando Cemetery.

**McCLOSKEY, Francis Xavier,** a Representative from Indiana; born in Philadelphia, Pa., June 12, 1939; graduated, Bishop Kendrick High School, Norristown, Pa., 1957; A.B., Indiana University, Bloomington, 1968; J.D., Indiana University School of Law, 1971; served in the United States Air Force, 1957-1961; newspaper reporter, 1961-1968; admitted to the Indiana bar in 1971 and commenced practice in Bloomington; mayor of Bloomington, 1972-1982; elected as a Democrat to the Ninety-eighth Congress (January 3, 1983-January 3, 1985); reelected to the Ninety-ninth Congress pursuant to H. Res. 146, taking his seat on May 1, 1985, and reelected to the four succeeding Congresses (May 1, 1985-January 3, 1995); unsuccessful candidate for reelection in 1994 to the One Hundred Fourth Congress; is a resident of Bloomington, Ind.

**McCLOSKEY, Paul Norton, Jr. (Pete),** a Representative from California; born in Loma Linda, San Bernardino County, Calif., September 29, 1927; attended public schools in South Pasadena-San Marino, Calif.; attended Occidental College and the California Institute of Technology under the Navy V-5 Pilot Program; B.A., Stanford University, 1950; LL.B., Stanford University Law School, 1953; served in the United States Navy, seaman, first class, 1945-1947; served in the United States Marine Corps during the Korean conflict, 1950-1952; second lieutenant, Fifth Marines; recipient of Navy Cross, Silver Star, and Purple Heart; Active Reserve, Seventh Infantry Battalion, United States Marine Corps Reserve, 1952-1960; Ready Reserve, 1960-1967; deputy district attorney, Alameda County, Calif., 1953-1954; practiced law in Palo Alto, Calif., from 1955 until 1967; lecturer on legal ethics, Santa Clara and Stanford Law Schools, 1964-1967; elected as a Republican to the Ninetieth Congress, December 12, 1967, by special election to fill the vacancy caused by the death of J. Arthur Younger; reelected

to the seven succeeding Congresses and served from December 12, 1967, to January 3, 1983; was not a candidate in 1982 for reelection to the House of Representatives, but was an unsuccessful candidate for nomination to the United States Senate; unsuccessful candidate for the Republican presidential nomination in 1972; returned to the practice of law in Palo Alto, Calif.; is a resident of Woodside, Calif.

**Bibliography:** Cannon, Lou. *The McCloskey Challenge.* New York: E.P. Dutton and Co., Inc., 1972; Paul N. McCloskey, Jr. *Truth and Untruth; Political Deceit in America.* New York: Simon and Schuster, 1972.

**McCLURE, Addison S.,** a Representative from Ohio; born in Wooster, Wayne County, Ohio, October 10, 1839; pursued an academic course in Jefferson College, Canonsburg, Pa.; studied law; was admitted to the bar in 1861 and commenced practice in Wooster; entered the Army as a private in April 1861; was elected captain of Company H, Sixteenth Regiment, Ohio Volunteer Infantry, in October of the same year; recorder of Wayne County in 1867; appointed postmaster of Wooster in 1867 and reappointed in 1872 and 1876; delegate to the Republican National Convention in 1868 and 1876; elected as a Republican to the Forty-seventh Congress (March 4, 1881-March 3, 1883); unsuccessful candidate for reelection in 1882 to the Forty-eighth Congress; elected to the Fifty-fourth Congress (March 4, 1895-March 3, 1897); was an unsuccessful candidate for reelection in 1896 to the Fifty-fifth Congress; resumed the practice of law; died in Wooster, Ohio, April 17, 1903; interment in Wooster Cemetery.

**McCLURE, Charles,** a Representative from Pennsylvania; born on Willow Grove farm, near Carlisle, Pa., in 1804; graduated from Dickinson College, Carlisle, Pa., in 1824; studied law; admitted to the bar in 1826 and practiced; member of the Pennsylvania house of representatives in 1835; elected as a Democrat to the Twenty-fifth Congress (March 4, 1837-March 3, 1839); elected to the Twenty-sixth Congress to fill the vacancy caused by the death of William S. Ramsey and served from December 7, 1840, to March 3, 1841; served as secretary of state of Pennsylvania 1843-1845, and was active in promoting the public-school system of Pennsylvania; died in Allegheny, Pa., on January 10, 1846; interment in Allegheny Cemetery, Pittsburgh, Pa.

**McCLURE, James Albertas,** a Representative and a Senator from Idaho; born in Payette, Idaho, December 27, 1924; attended the public schools of Payette; served in the United States Navy, 1942-1946; J.D., University of Idaho College of Law, 1950; admitted to the bar in 1950 and commenced practice in Payette, Idaho; prosecuting attorney of Payette County from 1950 until 1956; city attorney of Payette, 1953-1966; Idaho State senator from Payette County, 1961-1966; member of the Payette County Central Committee for fifteen years; elected as a Republican to the Ninetieth and to the two succeeding Congresses (January 3, 1967-January 3, 1973); was not a candidate in 1972 for reelection to the House of Representatives, but was elected to the United States Senate; reelected in 1978 and 1984, and served from January 3, 1973 to January 3, 1991; was not a candidate for reelection in 1990; chairman, Committee on Energy and Natural Resources (Ninety-seventh through Ninety-ninth Congresses), Republican Conference (Ninety-seventh and Ninety-eighth Congresses); is a resident of Payette, Idaho.

**McCLURG, Joseph Washington,** a Representative from Missouri; born near Lebanon, St. Louis County, Mo., February 22, 1818; attended Xenia (Ohio) Academy and Oxford (Ohio) College; taught school in Louisiana and Mississippi in 1835 and 1836; moved to Texas in 1839; studied law and was admitted to practice at Columbus, Tex.; clerk of the circuit court in 1840; returned to Missouri in 1841 and engaged in mercantile pursuits; served during the Civil War as colonel of Cavalry in the Union Army; member of the State convention, 1861-1863; elected as an Unconditional

Unionist to the Thirty-eighth Congress; reelected as a Republican to the Thirty-ninth and Fortieth Congresses, and served from March 4, 1865 until his resignation in 1868, having been elected Governor; elected Governor of Missouri in 1868, and served from January 12, 1869 to January 9, 1871; unsuccessful candidate for reelection in 1870; resumed mercantile pursuits at Linn Creek, Mo., and also engaged in steamboating and lead mining; register of the land office at Springfield, Mo., in 1889; died in London, Mo., on December 2, 1900; interment in Lebanon Cemetery.

**Bibliography:** *DAB*; Morrow, Lynn. "Joseph Washington McClurg: Entrepreneur, Politician, Citizen." *Missouri Historical Review* 78 (January 1984): 168-201.

**McCOID, Moses Ayers,** a Representative from Iowa; born near Bellefontaine, Logan County, Ohio, November 5, 1840; attended the public schools, Fairfield University, and Washington (now Washington and Jefferson) College, Washington, Pa.; studied law in Fairfield, Iowa; was admitted to the bar in 1861 and commenced practice in Fairfield; during the Civil War enlisted as a private in Company E, Second Regiment, Iowa Volunteer Infantry, May 6, 1861; was commissioned a second lieutenant; resumed the practice of law in Fairfield; district attorney of the sixth judicial district of Iowa in 1867 and 1871; member of the Iowa State senate, 1872-1879; elected as a Republican to the Forty-sixth and to the two succeeding Congresses (March 4, 1879-March 3, 1885); unsuccessful candidate for renomination in 1884 to the Forty-ninth Congress; again resumed the practice of law; died in Fairfield, Iowa, May 19, 1904; interment in Evergreen Cemetery.

**McCOLLISTER, John Yetter,** a Representative from Nebraska; born in Iowa City, Johnson County, Iowa, June 10, 1921; attended the public schools of Sioux Falls, S.Dak.; B.S., University of Iowa, Iowa City, 1943; lieutenant (junior grade), United States Naval Reserve, 1942-1946; president, McCollister and Co., Omaha, Nebr., 1960-1971, 1979-1986; served as Douglas County (Nebr.) Commissioner for two terms, 1965-1970; delegate, Nebraska State Republican conventions, 1960-1970; delegate to the Republican National Conventions of 1968 and 1988; elected as a Republican to the Ninety-second and to the two succeeding Congresses (January 3, 1971-January 3, 1977); was not a candidate in 1976 for reelection to the House of Representatives, but was an unsuccessful candidate for election to the United States Senate; is a resident of Omaha, Nebr.

**McCOLLUM, Ira William, Jr.,** a Representative from Florida; born in Brooksville, Hernando County, Fla., July 12, 1944; attended the public schools; graduated, Hernando High School, 1962; B.A., University of Florida, Gainesville, 1965; J.D., University of Florida School of Law, 1968; served in the United States Navy Judge Advocate General's Corps, commander, 1969-1972, with service in the United States Naval Reserve; admitted to the Florida bar in 1968 and commenced practice in Orlando, 1973; chairman, Republican Executive Committee of Seminole County, 1976-1980; county chairmen's representative, Florida State Executive Committee for Fifth District, 1976-1980; elected as a Republican to the Ninety-seventh and to the seven succeeding Congresses (January 3, 1981-January 3, 1997); is a resident of Longwood, Fla.

**McCOMAS, Louis Emory** (grandfather of Katharine Edgar Byron and great-grandfather of Goodloe Edgar Byron), a Representative and a Senator from Maryland; born near Hagerstown, Washington County, Md., October 28, 1846; attended St. James College, Maryland; graduated from Dickinson College, Carlisle, Pa., in 1866; studied law; was admitted to the bar in 1868 and practiced in Hagerstown, Md.; unsuccessful Republican candidate for election in 1876 to the Forty-fifth Congress; elected as a Republican to the Forty-eighth and to the three succeeding Congresses (March 4, 1883-March 3, 1891); unsuccessful candidate for reelection in 1890 to the Fifty-second Congress; secretary of the Republican National Committee 1892; on November 17, 1892, was appointed by President Benjamin Harrison an associate justice of the Supreme Court of the District of Columbia, which office he held until elected Senator; professor of international law, Georgetown University, Washington, D.C.; elected as a Republican to the United States Senate and served from March 4, 1899, until March 3, 1905; chairman, Committee on Organization, Conduct, and Expenditures of Executive Departments (Fifty-sixth Congress), Committee on Education and Labor (Fifty-seventh and Fifty-eighth Congresses); appointed by President Theodore Roosevelt as a justice of the Court of Appeals of the District of Columbia in 1905, and served until his death; died in Washington, D.C., November 10, 1907; interment in Rose Hill Cemetery, Hagerstown, Washington County, Md.

**Bibliography:** *DAB*.

**McCOMAS, William,** a Representative from Virginia; born near Pearisburg, Giles County, Va., in 1795; attended private schools and Emory and Henry College, Emory, Va.; engaged in agricultural pursuits and in the practice of law; also was a Methodist minister; member of the Virginia senate, 1830-1833; elected as a Jacksonian to the Twenty-third Congress and reelected as a Whig to the Twenty-fourth Congress (March 4, 1833-March 3, 1837); resumed his former activities; unsuccessful candidate for election in 1848 to the Thirty-first Congress; delegate to the Virginia secession convention in 1861 and voted against the ordinance; judge of the United States district court during the Civil War; died on his farm near Barboursville, Va. (now West Virginia), June 3, 1865; interment in the family cemetery.

**McCOMB, Eleazer,** a Delegate from Delaware; served in the Revolutionary War as captain of militia; appointed privy councilor in 1779; Member of the Continental Congress in 1783 and 1784; appointed as one of the commissioners to confer on the subject of the Chesapeake and Delaware Canal in 1786; auditor of accounts of the State of Delaware 1787-1793; moved from Dover to Wilmington about 1792; engaged in commercial pursuits and shipping in Wilmington; director of the Bank of Delaware in 1795; died at Wilmington, New Castle County, Del., in December 1798.

**McCONNELL, Addison Mitchell (Mitch),** a Senator from Kentucky; born in Tuscumbia, Colbert County, Ala., February 20, 1942; attended the Louisville, Ky., public schools; graduated Manual High School, Louisville, Ky., 1960; B.A., University of Louisville, 1964; J.D., University of Kentucky Law School, Lexington, 1967; admitted to the Kentucky bar in 1967; chief legislative assistant to Senator Marlow Cook of Kentucky, 1968-1970; deputy assistant United States Attorney General for legislative affairs, 1974-1975; judge-executive of Jefferson County, Ky., 1977-1984; elected as a Republican to the United States Senate in 1984 for the term commencing January 3, 1985; reelected in 1990 for the term ending January 3, 1997; chairman, Select Committee on Ethics (One Hundred Fourth Congress); is a resident of Louisville, Ky.

**McCONNELL, Felix Grundy,** a Representative from Alabama; born in Nashville, Tenn., April 1, 1809; moved with his parents to Fayetteville, Lincoln County, Tenn., in 1811; received a limited education and became a saddler; moved to Talladega, Talladega County, Ala., in 1834; studied law; was admitted to the bar in 1836 and commenced practice in Talladega, Ala.; member of the Alabama State house of representatives in 1838; served in the State senate, 1839-1843; elected as a Democrat to the Twenty-eighth and Twenty-ninth Congresses, and served from March 4, 1843 until his death in Washington, D.C., September 10, 1846; interment in the Congressional Cemetery.

**Bibliography:** Atkins, Leah R. "Felix Grundy McConnell: Old South Demagogue." *Alabama Review* 30 (April 1977): 83-100.

**McCONNELL, Samuel Kerns, Jr.,** a Representative from Pennsylvania; born in Eddystone, Delaware County, Pa., April 6, 1901; attended the grade schools in Philadelphia, Pa., and was graduated from the University of Pennsylvania at Philadelphia in 1923; engaged in the investment banking business in 1926; member of the board of trustees of the Norristown State Hospital, 1939-1944, serving as president, 1940-1944; served as township commissioner of Lower Merion Township, 1941-1944; elected as a Republican to the Seventy-eighth Congress to fill the vacancy caused by the death of J. William Ditter; reelected to the Seventy-ninth and to the six succeeding Congresses and served from January 18, 1944, until his resignation September 1, 1957, to become executive director of United Cerebral Palsy Associations, Inc., serving until June 1961; chairman, Committee on Education and Labor (Eighty-third Congress); served as vice president and president of Woodcock, Moyer, Fricke and French, Inc., 1961-1967; was a resident of Wynnewood, Pa., until his death in Bryn Mawr, Pa., on April 11, 1985; interment in West Laurel Hill Cemetery, Bala Cynwyd, Pa.

**McCONNELL, William John,** a Senator from Idaho; born in Commerce, Oakland County, Mich., September 18, 1839; pursued an academic course; moved to California in 1860 and engaged in mining, the cattle business, merchandising, and banking; resided in Oregon in 1862 and 1863 and taught school in Yamhill County; moved to Idaho in 1863; deputy United States marshal 1865-1867; returned to Oregon and was engaged in the cattle business; member, Oregon State senate 1882, and served as president; returned to Idaho in 1886; member of the constitutional convention of Idaho in 1890; upon the admission of Idaho as a State into the Union was elected as a Republican to the United States Senate and served from December 18, 1890, to March 3, 1891; was not a candidate for renomination; elected Governor of Idaho in 1892, reelected in 1894, and served from January 1893 to January 4, 1897; appointed Indian inspector by President William McKinley in 1897, and served until 1901; appointed by President William Howard Taft an inspector in the Immigration Service in 1909, and served until his death in Moscow, Idaho, on March 30, 1925; interment in Moscow Cemetery.

**McCOOK, Anson George,** a Representative from New York; born in Steubenville, Jefferson County, Ohio, October 10, 1835; attended the common schools of Lisbon (then New Lisbon), Ohio; employed as a drug clerk in Pittsburgh, Pa., 1850-1852; returned to Ohio and taught school near Lisbon; crossed the Plains to California in 1854 and engaged in mining in that State and also in Nevada; returned East in 1859 and at the outbreak of the Civil War was engaged in the study of law; entered the Union Army as captain of the Second Regiment, Ohio Volunteer Infantry, April 17, 1861, and served until October 21, 1865; returned to Steubenville and was admitted to the bar in 1866; appointed assessor of internal revenue for the seventeenth Ohio district in November 1865; moved to New York City in May 1873, and was admitted to the bar of that State in 1875; founded the Law Journal, and became president of the New York Law Publishing Co., which position he held until his death; elected as a Republican to the Forty-fifth, Forty-sixth, and Forty-seventh Congresses (March 4, 1877-March 3, 1883); unsuccessful candidate for renomination in 1882; Secretary of the United States Senate 1883-1893; appointed by Mayor William L. Strong city chamberlain of the city of New York and served from 1895 to 1898; died in New York City December 30, 1917; interment in Union Cemetery, Steubenville, Ohio.

Bibliography: *DAB.*

**McCORD, Andrew,** a Representative from New York; born at what is now Stony Ford, Wallkill Township, Orange County, N.Y., about 1754; attended the common schools and Newburgh Academy; delegate to the convention at New Paltz, N.Y., November 7, 1775, to choose deputies to the Second Provincial Congress; commissioned quartermaster in the Ulster County Militia, January 31, 1787; served as captain of Ulster County Militia, and resigned on April 10, 1798; member of the New York State assembly in 1795, 1796, 1798, 1800, 1802, and 1807, and served as speaker in 1807; elected as a Republican to the Eighth Congress (March 4, 1803-March 3, 1805); engaged in agricultural pursuits; died at Stony Ford, Orange County, N.Y., in 1808; interment in the family burying ground on his farm near Stony Ford.

**McCORD, Jim Nance,** a Representative from Tennessee; born on a farm near Unionville, Bedford County, Tenn., March 17, 1879; attended the public schools and also had private instructors; employed as a clerk in a hardware store in 1894; engaged in selling books and stationery at Lewisburg, Tenn., 1897-1900; traveling salesman, 1900-1910; editor and publisher of the Marshall Gazette, Lewisburg, Tenn., 1910; mayor of Lewisburg, Tenn., 1916-1942; auctioneer, 1920-1943; member of the Marshall County Court, 1915-1942; elected as a Democrat to the Seventy-eighth Congress (January 3, 1943-January 3, 1945); was not a candidate for renomination in 1944 to the Seventy-ninth Congress; elected Governor of Tennessee in 1944, reelected in 1946, and served from January 16, 1945 to January 17, 1949; unsuccessful candidate in 1948 for renomination for Governor; resumed the publishing business; member of the Tennessee State constitutional convention in 1953; delegate at large to the Democratic National Conventions of 1940 and 1956; unsuccessful independent candidate for election for Governor in 1958; maintained his interest in journalism; died in Nashville, Tenn., September 2, 1968; interment in Lone Oak Cemetery, Lewisburg, Tenn.

**McCORD, Myron Hawley,** a Representative from Wisconsin; born in Ceres, McKean County, Pa., November 26, 1840; attended Richburg Academy, New York; moved to Wisconsin in 1854 and settled in Shawano; moved to Merrill in 1875; became a publisher, lumberman, and farmer; published a newspaper, 1868-1883; served in the Wisconsin State senate in 1873 and 1874; member of the Wisconsin State assembly in 1881; delegate to the Republican National Convention of 1876; register of the United States land office at Wausau, Wis., from February 26, 1884, to June 24, 1885; elected as a Republican to the Fifty-first Congress (March 4, 1889-March 3, 1891); unsuccessful candidate for reelection in 1890 to the Fifty-second Congress, and for election in 1892 to the Fifty-third Congress; returned to Merrill, Wis., and engaged in agricultural pursuits and lumbering; appointed by President William McKinley as Governor of Arizona Territory on July 22, 1897; resigned effective August 1, 1898 and organized the Territorial Regiment for the Spanish-American War; appointed United States marshal for the district of Arizona on May 1, 1902, and served until July 1, 1905; later appointed collector of customs for the port of Nogales, Ariz.; died in Phoenix, Ariz., on April 27, 1908; interment in Merrill Cemetery, Merrill, Lincoln County, Wis.

**McCORKLE, Joseph Walker,** a Representative from California; born in Piqua, Ohio, June 24, 1819; attended the common schools and Kenyon College, Gambier, Ohio; studied law; was admitted to the bar about 1842 and commenced practice in Dayton, Ohio; postmaster of Dayton 1845-1849; moved to San Francisco, Calif., in 1849; unsuccessful candidate for judge of the eighth judicial district in 1850; member of the State assembly 1850-1852; elected as a Democrat to the Thirty-second Congress (March 4, 1851-March 3, 1853); unsuccessful candidate for renomination in 1852; moved to Marysville, Calif.; appointed judge of the ninth judicial district in 1853 and served in that capacity until 1857; unsuccessful candidate for election to the United States Senate in 1855; resumed the practice of his profession in San Francisco, Calif.; moved to Virginia City, Nev., in 1860 and continued the practice of law; moved to Washington, D.C., in 1870 and practiced before the Mexican Claims Commission; died in Branchville, Md., March 18, 1884; interment in Forest Hill Cemetery, Piqua, Ohio.

**McCORKLE, Paul Grier,** a Representative from South Carolina; born in Yorkville (now York), York County, S.C., December 19, 1863; attended the public schools of his native city and Kings Mountain Military School, York, S.C.; employed as a clerk in York, S.C.; cotton buyer and grader in Lancaster, S.C., and then in Chester, S.C.; returned to York, S.C., and engaged in business as a cotton broker and export classifier; elected as a Democrat to the Sixty-fourth Congress to fill the vacancy caused by the death of David E. Finley and served from February 24, 1917, to March 3, 1917; was not a candidate for renomination in 1916; engaged in the cotton brokerage business in York, S.C.; coroner of York County, S.C., from 1920 until his death in Knoxville, Tenn., on June 2, 1934; interment in Rose Hill Cemetery, York, S.C.

**McCORMACK, John William,** a Representative from Massachusetts; born in Boston, Suffolk County, Mass., December 21, 1891; attended the public schools; studied law in a private law office; admitted to the bar in 1913 and began practice in Boston, Mass.; member of the Massachusetts constitutional convention in 1917 and 1918; during the First World War served in the United States Army in 1917 and 1918; served in the Massachusetts house of representatives, 1920-1922; member of the Massachusetts senate, 1923-1926, serving as Democratic floor leader in 1925 and 1926; delegate to all Democratic State conventions, beginning in 1920; delegate to the Democratic National Conventions of 1932, 1940, 1944, and 1948; elected as a Democrat to the Seventieth Congress to fill the vacancy caused by the death of James A. Gallivan, and on the same day was elected to the Seventy-first Congress; reelected to the Seventy-second and to the nineteen succeeding Congresses, and served from November 6, 1928 to January 3, 1971; chairman, Committee on Territories (Seventieth Congress), Select Committee on Astronautics and Space Exploration (Eighty-fifth Congress); majority leader (Seventy-sixth through Seventy-ninth, Eighty-first, Eighty-second and Eighty-fourth through Eighty-seventh Congresses), minority whip (Eightieth and Eighty-third Congresses), elected Speaker of the House of Representatives on January 10, 1962 to fill the vacancy caused by the death of Sam Rayburn; reelected Speaker in the Eighty-eighth through Ninety-first Congresses; was not a candidate for renomination in 1970 to the Ninety-second Congress; resided in Boston, Mass., until his death in Dedham, Mass., November 22, 1980; interment in Saint Joseph Cemetery, West Roxbury, Mass.

Bibliography: *DAB*; Gordon, Lester I. "John McCormack and the Roosevelt Era." Ph.D. dissertation, Boston University, 1976.

**McCORMACK, Mike,** a Representative from Washington; born in Basil, Fairfield County, Ohio, December 14, 1921; attended the Toledo public schools and the University of Toledo; B.S., Washington State University, Pullman, 1948, and M.S., 1949; attended Gonzaga University Law School, Spokane, Wash.; entered military service in 1943; attended Officer Candidate School and was commissioned as second lieutenant, parachute infantry, United States Army, with occupation duty in Germany until 1946; discharged as first lieutenant; instructor, University of Puget Sound, Tacoma, Wash., 1949-1950; research scientist, Hanford Project, 1950-1970; elected to the Washington State house of representatives, 1956, reelected in 1958; elected to the Washington State senate in 1960, reelected in 1964 and 1968; delegate, Washington State Democratic conventions, 1952-1970; delegate to the Democratic National Conventions of 1972; elected as a Democrat to the Ninety-second and to the four succeeding Congresses (January 3, 1971-January 3, 1981); unsuccessful candidate for reelection in 1980 to the Ninety-seventh Congress; consultant in science, energy, and science policy, Washington, D.C., 1981; director, Institute for Science and Society, Ellensburg, Wash.; appointed in 1994 as a member of the Washington State Higher Education Coordinating Board; is a resident of Ellensburg, Wash.

**McCORMICK, Henry Clay,** a Representative from Pennsylvania; born in Washington Township, Lycoming County, Pa., June 30, 1844; attended the common schools and Dickinson Seminary, Williamsport, Pa.; studied law; was admitted to the bar in 1866 and practiced in Williamsport, Pa.; elected as a Republican to the Fiftieth and Fifty-first Congresses (March 4, 1887-March 3, 1891); chairman, Committee on Railways and Canals (Fifty-first Congress); delegate to the Republican National Convention in 1892; elected president of the Williamsport & North Branch Railroad January 1, 1892; attorney general of Pennsylvania 1895-1899; resumed the practice of law; died in Williamsport, Lycoming County, Pa., May 26, 1902; interment in Wildwood Cemetery.

**McCORMICK, James Robinson,** a Representative from Missouri; born near Irondale, Washington County, Mo., on August 1, 1824; attended the public schools in Washington County, Mo.; received private instruction and entered Transylvania University, Lexington, Ky., as a medical student; was graduated from the Memphis (Tenn.) Medical College in 1849 and commenced practice in Wayne County, Mo.; moved to Perry County in 1850 and continued the practice of his profession; delegate to the State constitutional convention in 1861; during the Civil War served as a surgeon in the Sixth Regiment, Missouri Volunteer Infantry, Union Army; served in the State senate in 1862, but resigned on account of duties in the Army; brigadier general of militia in 1863; after the war located in Arcadia, Mo., and resumed the practice of medicine; again served in the State senate in 1866, but resigned the following year; elected as a Democrat to the Fortieth Congress to fill the vacancy caused by the death of Thomas E. Noel; reelected to the Forty-first and Forty-second Congresses and served from December 17, 1867, to March 3, 1873; was not a candidate for reelection in 1872; moved to Farmington, Mo., in 1874; practiced medicine and engaged in the drug business; died in Farmington, St. Francois County, Mo., May 19, 1897; interment in Masonic Cemetery.

**McCORMICK, John Watts,** a Representative from Ohio; born near Gallipolis, Gallia County, Ohio, December 20, 1831; attended the common schools, the Ohio Wesleyan University at Delaware, and the Ohio University at Athens; engaged in agricultural pursuits and stock raising; taught school and later became a Methodist minister; delegate to the Ohio constitutional convention in 1873; elected as a Republican to the Forty-eighth Congress (March 4, 1883-March 3, 1885); unsuccessful candidate for reelection in 1884 to the Forty-ninth Congress; trustee of Rio Grande (Ohio) College, 1883-1885; resumed agricultural pursuits; died in Gallipolis, Ohio, June 25, 1917; interment in Mount Zion Cemetery near Gallipolis, Ohio.

**McCORMICK, Joseph Medill** (husband of Ruth Hanna McCormick), a Representative and a Senator from Illinois; born in Chicago, Ill., May 16, 1877; attended preparatory school at Groton, Mass.; graduated from Yale University in 1900; engaged in newspaper work as reporter, publisher, and owner of the Chicago Daily Tribune, and later purchased an interest in the Cleveland Leader and Cleveland News; war correspondent in the Philippine Islands in 1901; vice chairman of the national campaign committee of the Progressive Republican movement 1912-1914; elected to the State house of representatives in 1912 and 1914; elected as a Republican to the Sixty-fifth Congress (March 4, 1917-March 3, 1919); elected to the United States Senate in 1918 and served from March 4, 1919, until his death; unsuccessful candidate for renomination in 1924; chairman, Committee on Expenditures in the Department of Labor (Sixty-sixth Congress), Committee on Expenditures in Executive Departments (Sixty-seventh and Sixty-eighth Congresses); died in Washington, D.C., on February 25, 1925; interment in Middlecreek Cemetery, near Byron, Ogle County, Ill.

Bibliography: *DAB*.

**McCORMICK, Nelson B.,** a Representative from Kansas; born near Waynesburg, Greene County, Pa., November 20, 1847; attended the common schools; moved to Marion County, Iowa, in 1867, where he engaged in farming and stock raising until his removal to Phillips County, Kans., where he settled upon a homestead in 1877; studied law; was admitted to the bar in 1882 and commenced practice in Phillipsburg, Kans.; deputy prosecuting attorney of Phillips County 1886-1888; prosecuting attorney 1890-1894; declined to be a candidate for renomination; elected as a Populist to the Fifty-fifth Congress (March 4, 1897-March 3, 1899); unsuccessful candidate for reelection in 1898 to the Fifty-sixth Congress; resumed the practice of law in Phillipsburg; Kans.; delegate to the Democratic State conventions in 1904 and 1908; prosecuting attorney of Phillips County 1910-1914; died in Phillipsburg, Kans., April 10, 1914; interment in Fairview Cemetery.

**McCORMICK, Richard Cunningham,** a Delegate from the Territory of Arizona and a Representative from New York; born in New York City, May 23, 1832; attended the common schools; entered business in Wall Street in 1852; at Sevastopol as newspaper correspondent during the Crimean War, 1854-1855; editor, Young Men's Magazine, New York, 1857-1859; with the Army of the Potomac during the Civil War as correspondent of the New York Evening Post and New York Commercial Advertiser, 1861-1862; first chief clerk, Department of Agriculture, in 1862; appointed secretary of Arizona Territory by President Abraham Lincoln in 1863; appointed Governor of Arizona Territory by President Andrew Johnson on April 10, 1866, and served until his resignation in March 1869, having been elected to Congress; established the Prescott Arizona Miner in 1864, and the Tucson Arizona Citizen in 1870; elected as a Unionist as Delegate from the Territory of Arizona to the Forty-first and to the two succeeding Congresses (March 4, 1869-March 3, 1875); was not a candidate for renomination in 1874 to the Forty-fourth Congress; delegate to the Republican National Conventions of 1872, 1876, and 1880; returned to New York; United States commissioner to the Centennial Exposition at Philadelphia in 1876; First Assistant Secretary of the Treasury in 1877; commissioner general to the Paris Exposition of 1878; decorated Commander, Legion of Honor, by the President of France in 1878; declined appointments as Minister to Brazil in 1877, and as Minister to Mexico in 1879; elected as a Republican from New York to the Fifty-fourth Congress (March 4, 1895-March 3, 1897); was not a candidate for renomination in 1896 to the Fifty-fifth Congress; president, board of managers, State Normal School, Jamaica, N.Y.; died in Jamaica, Queens County, N.Y., June 2, 1901; interment in Grace Churchyard.

**Bibliography:** *DAB*.

**McCORMICK, Ruth Hanna** (daughter of Marcus Alonzo Hanna, wife of Joseph Medill McCormick and of Albert Gallatin Simms), a Representative from Illinois; born in Cleveland, Ohio, March 27, 1880; attended Hathaway Brown School in Cleveland, Dobbs Ferry (N.Y.) School, and Miss Porter's School in Farmington, Conn.; private secretary to her father, Senator Marcus A. Hanna of Ohio; owned and operated a dairy and breeding farm near Byron, Ill., which produced sanitary milk for invalids and children; publisher and president of the Rockford Consolidated Newspapers (Inc.), Rockford, Ill.; chairman of the first woman's executive committee of the Republican National Committee, and an associate member of the national committee, 1919-1924, in the latter year becoming the first elected national committeewoman from Illinois, and served until 1928; active worker for passage and ratification the Nineteenth Amendment from 1913 until August 1920, when the Constitution was amended; elected as a Republican to the Seventy-first Congress (March 4, 1929-March 3, 1931); was not a candidate in 1930 for renomination to the House of Representatives, but was an unsuccessful candidate for election to the United States Senate; resumed her newspaper interests; married Albert Gallatin

Simms, of New Mexico, who was also a Member of the Seventy-first Congress, and resided in Albuquerque, N.Mex.; owned and operated a cattle and sheep ranch, and a school for girls in Albuquerque; served as an adviser to the presidential campaigns of Thomas E. Dewey in 1940 and 1944; died in Chicago, Ill., December 31, 1944; interment in Fairview Cemetery, Albuquerque, N.Mex.

**Bibliography:** *DAB*; Miller, Kristie. *Ruth Hanna McCormick: A Life in Politics, 1880-1944*. Albuquerque: University of New Mexico Press, 1992; Strickland, Arvarh E. "'The lady candidate': Ruth Hanna McCormick and the Senatorial Election of 1930." *Illinois Historical Journal* 88 (Autumn 1995): 189-202.

**McCORMICK, Washington Jay,** a Representative from Montana; born in Missoula, Missoula County, Mont., January 4, 1884; attended the public schools, the State University of Montana at Missoula, and the University of Notre Dame, Indiana; was graduated from Harvard University in 1906 and from the law department of Columbia University, New York City, in 1910; was admitted to the New York bar the same year; returned to Missoula, Mont.; was admitted to the Montana bar in 1911 and engaged in the practice of law; member of the State house of representatives 1918-1920; elected as a Republican to the Sixty-seventh Congress (March 4, 1921-March 3, 1923); unsuccessful candidate for reelection in 1922 to the Sixty-eighth Congress; continued the practice of law until his retirement, when he devoted his time to writing; resided in Bitter Root Valley, near Stevensville, Mont., until his death in Missoula, Mont., March 7, 1949; interment in Missoula Cemetery.

**McCOWEN, Edward Oscar,** a Representative from Ohio; born in Bloom Township, Scioto County, Ohio, June 29, 1877; attended the public schools of South Webster, Ohio; was graduated from Ohio Northern University at Ada in 1908, Ohio State University at Columbus in 1917, and from the Graduate School of the University of Cincinnati, Cincinnati, Ohio, in 1939; was successively a high-school teacher, principal, and superintendent; superintendent of the Scioto County public schools 1914-1942; precinct committeeman and delegate to the Ohio Republican State conventions in 1935 and 1946; trustee of Rio Grande (Ohio) College; elected as a Republican to the Seventy-eighth, Seventy-ninth, and Eightieth Congresses (January 3, 1943-January 3, 1949); unsuccessful candidate for reelection in 1948 to the Eighty-first Congress; returned to Wheelersburg, Ohio, and continued his activity in politics until his death there November 4, 1953; interment in South Webster Cemetery, South Webster, Ohio.

**McCOY, Robert,** a Representative from Pennsylvania; born in Carlisle, Pa.; attended the common schools; prothonotary of Cumberland County; brigadier general of militia; Pennsylvania Canal commissioner; elected to the Twenty-second Congress to fill the vacancy caused by the death of William Ramsey and served from November 22, 1831, to March 3, 1833; died in Wheeling, Va. (now West Virginia), June 7, 1849.

**McCOY, Walter Irving,** a Representative from New Jersey; born in Troy, Rensselaer County, N.Y., December 8, 1859; attended the public schools, Troy Academy, Phillips Exeter Academy, Exeter, N.H., and Princeton College; was graduated from Harvard University in 1882 and from the law department of that institution in 1886; was admitted to the bar the same year and commenced practice in New York City; trustee of the village of South Orange, N.J., 1893-1895, 1901-1905, and in 1910; delegate to the Democratic National Conventions of 1904 and 1908; vice president of the Essex County (N.J.) Democratic committee; elected as a Democrat to the Sixty-second and Sixty-third Congresses and served from March 4, 1911, until October 3, 1914, when he resigned; appointed by President Woodrow Wilson on October 5, 1914, as an associate justice, and on May 31, 1918, as chief justice, of the supreme court of the District of Columbia and served until his retirement on

December 8, 1929; resided in Washington, D.C., until 1932, when he moved to Cambridge, Mass., where he died on July 17, 1933; interment in Troy Cemetery, Troy, N.Y.

**McCOY, William,** a Representative from Virginia; born near Warrenton, Fauquier County, Va.; member of the Virginia house of delegates 1798-1804; delegate to the Virginia constitutional convention in 1829 and 1830; elected as a Republican to the Twelfth Congress; reelected to the Thirteenth through Twentieth Congresses and reelected as a Jacksonian to the Twenty-first and Twenty-second Congresses (March 4, 1811-March 3, 1833); chairman, Committee on Claims (Twentieth Congress); died in Charlottesville, Va., in 1864; interment in the University of Virginia Cemetery.

**McCRACKEN, Robert McDowell,** a Representative from Idaho; born in Vincennes, Knox County, Ind., March 15, 1874; moved to Carmi, Ill., in 1880; attended the public schools; went West in 1891 and settled in Blackfoot, Bingham County, Idaho; taught school in Blackfoot until 1897; employed as a clerk in the United States Surveyor General's office in Boise, Idaho, 1897-1902; studied law; was admitted to the bar in 1902 and commenced practice in Blackfoot; chief clerk of the State house of representatives in 1903; prosecuting attorney of Bingham County 1904-1906; elected a member of the State house of representatives from Bingham County in 1906 for a two-year term; moved to Boise in 1907 and continued the practice of law; elected to the State house of representatives from Ada County in 1908 for a two-year term; elected as a Republican to the Sixty-fourth Congress (March 4, 1915-March 3, 1917); unsuccessful candidate for renomination; during the First World War was commissioned a captain in the Chemical Warfare Service; resumed the practice of his profession in Boise, Ada County, Idaho; was seeking the Republican nomination for election to Congress and while campaigning was in an automobile accident, which resulted in his death, in Emmett, Idaho, May 16, 1934; interment in Blackfoot Cemetery, Blackfoot, Idaho.

**McCRARY, George Washington,** a Representative from Iowa; born near Evansville, Vanderburg County, Ind., August 29, 1835; moved to the Territory of Iowa in 1836 with his parents, who settled in Van Buren County; attended the public schools; studied law; was admitted to the bar in 1856 and commenced practice in Keokuk, Iowa; member of the Iowa State house of representatives in 1857; served in the Iowa State senate, 1861-1865; elected as a Republican to the Forty-first and to the three succeeding Congresses (March 4, 1869-March 3, 1877); chairman, Committee on Elections (Forty-second Congress), Committee on Railways and Canals (Forty-third Congress); was not a candidate for renomination in 1876 to the Forty-fifth Congress; Secretary of War in the Cabinet of President Rutherford B. Hayes from March 12, 1877 until December 11, 1879, when he resigned; served as United States judge of the eighth judicial circuit, 1880-1884; moved to Kansas City, Mo.; became general counsel for the Atchison, Topeka & Santa Fe Railroad Co. in 1884; died in St. Joseph, Mo., June 23, 1890; interment in Oakland Cemetery, Keokuk, Iowa.

**Bibliography:** *DAB.*

**McCRATE, John Dennis,** a Representative from Maine; born in Wiscasset, Maine, October 1, 1802; was graduated from Bowdoin College, Brunswick, Maine, in 1819; studied law; was admitted to the bar and practiced in Damariscotta, Maine, 1823-1835 and in Wiscasset 1835-1850; member of the State house of representatives 1831-1835; customs collector 1836-1841; elected as a Democrat to the Twenty-ninth Congress (March 4, 1845-March 3, 1847); resumed the practice of law in Wiscasset, Maine; moved to Boston, Mass., and continued the practice of his profession until 1852 when he moved to Sutton, Mass., and engaged in agricultural pursuits; died in Sutton, Worcester County, Mass., on September 11, 1879; interment in Ancient Cemetery, Wiscasset, Lincoln County, Maine.

**McCREARY, George Deardorff,** a Representative from Pennsylvania; born at York Springs, Adams County, Pa., on September 28, 1846; moved with his parents to Philadelphia in 1864; attended public and private schools; entered the University of Pennsylvania at Philadelphia in 1864 and remained until 1867, when he left to take a position with a coal company of which his father was president; began an independent business career in 1870; elected treasurer of the city and county of Philadelphia in November 1891, and served until 1895; elected as a Republican to the Fifty-eighth and to the four succeeding Congresses and served from March 4, 1903, to March 3, 1913; chairman, Committee on Ventilation and Acoustics (Sixty-first Congress); was not a candidate for renomination in 1912; engaged in banking; died in Philadelphia, Pa., July 26, 1915; interment in Laurel Hill Cemetery.

**McCREARY, James Bennett,** a Representative and a Senator from Kentucky; born in Richmond, Madison County, Ky., July 8, 1838; attended the common schools; graduated from Centre College, Danville, Ky., in 1857 and from the law department of Cumberland University at Lebanon, Tenn., in 1859; was admitted to the bar in 1859 and commenced practice in Richmond, Ky.; entered the Confederate Army in 1862 and attained the rank of lieutenant colonel before the close of the Civil War; member, Kentucky house of representatives, 1869-1875, serving as speaker, 1871-1875; elected Governor of Kentucky in 1875, and served from September 1875 to September 1879; appointed by President Benjamin Harrison a delegate to the International Monetary Conference held in Brussels, Belgium, in 1892; elected as a Democrat to the Forty-ninth and to the five succeeding Congresses (March 4, 1885-March 3, 1897); unsuccessful candidate for renomination in 1896 to the Fifty-fifth Congress; resumed the practice of law; elected as a Democrat to the United States Senate in 1902, and served from March 4, 1903 to March 3, 1909; unsuccessful candidate for reelection in 1908; elected Governor of Kentucky in 1911, and served from December 12, 1911 to December 7, 1915; unsuccessful candidate for election to the United States Senate in 1914; resumed the practice of law; died in Richmond, Ky., October 8, 1918; interment in Richmond Cemetery.

**Bibliography:** *DAB.*

**McCREARY, John,** a Representative from South Carolina; born near Fishing Creek, about eighteen miles from Chester, S.C., in 1761; received his schooling from private tutors; became a surveyor; also engaged in agricultural pursuits; served in the Revolutionary War; member of the State house of representatives, 1794-1799 and 1802; sheriff of Chester District (now Chester County); elected to the Sixteenth Congress (March 4, 1819-March 3, 1821); resumed agricultural pursuits and surveying; died on his plantation in South Carolina November 4, 1833; interment in the Richardson Church Cemetery, Chester County, S.C.

**McCREDIE, William Wallace,** a Representative from Washington; born in Montrose, Susquehanna County, Pa., April 27, 1862; moved to Iowa with his parents, who settled on a farm near Manchester, Delaware County; attended the common schools; was graduated from Cornell College, Mount Vernon, Iowa, in 1885; taught school at Parkersburg, Iowa, 1885-1889; attended the law school of the University of Iowa at Iowa City in 1889 and 1890; moved to Portland, Oreg., in 1890 and completed the study of law; was admitted to the bar the same year and commenced practice in Vancouver, Wash.; prosecuting attorney of Clarke County, Wash., 1894-1896; judge of the superior court at Vancouver, Wash., 1904-1909; became part owner of the Portland baseball club in 1904; elected as a Republican to the Sixty-first Congress to fill the vacancy caused by the death of Francis W. Cushman and served from November 2, 1909, to March 3, 1911; unsuccessful candidate for renomination in 1910 to the Sixty-second Congress; resumed his interest in the Portland club of the Pacific Coast Baseball League, serving as president until 1921, when he retired; continued the practice of law in Portland, Oreg., until his death in that city on May 10, 1935; interment in Lincoln Memorial Cemetery.

**McCREERY, Thomas Clay,** a Senator from Kentucky; born near Owensboro, Daviess County, Ky., on December 12, 1816; attended the common schools, and graduated from Centre College, Danville, Ky., in 1837; studied law; was admitted to the bar and commenced practice in Frankfort, Franklin County, Ky.; returned to Owensboro and engaged in literary pursuits; unsuccessful candidate for election in 1842 to the Twenty-eighth Congress and again in 1844 to the Twenty-ninth Congress; presidential elector on the Democratic tickets in 1852, 1856, and 1860; elected as a Democrat to the United States Senate to fill the vacancy caused by the resignation of James Guthrie and served from February 19, 1868, to March 3, 1871; unsuccessful candidate for reelection; again elected to the United States Senate in 1872 and served from March 4, 1873, to March 3, 1879; declined to be a candidate for reelection; retired from public life and lived on his farm in Daviess County; moved to Owensboro, Ky., where he died July 10, 1890; interment in Elmwood Cemetery.

**McCREERY, William,** a Representative from Maryland; born in the Province of Ulster, Ireland, in 1750; received a limited education; immigrated to the United States in his youth and located in Maryland; engaged in agricultural pursuits; elected as a Republican to the Eighth, Ninth, and Tenth Congresses (March 4, 1803-March 3, 1809); resumed agricultural pursuits; member of the State senate from September 1811 until his death at his country home, "Clover Hill," near Reisterstown, Baltimore County, Md., March 8, 1814.

**McCREERY, William,** a Representative from Pennsylvania; born in Omagh, County Tyrone, Ireland, May 17, 1786; immigrated to the United States in 1791 with his parents, who settled near Fairfield, Westmoreland County, Pa.; attended private school; moved to Paris, Washington County, Pa., in 1812 and engaged in agricultural pursuits; member of the Pennsylvania house of representatives 1824-1827; constructor of the Pennsylvania State Canal and of the State highway 1826-1831; elected as a Jacksonian to the Twenty-first Congress (March 4, 1829-March 3, 1831); unsuccessful candidate for reelection in 1830 to the Twenty-second Congress; served as collector of internal revenue at Pittsburgh 1831-1833; again a member of the Pennsylvania house of representatives 1833-1836; superintendent of the Pennsylvania State Canal in 1835, residing in Allegheny City, Allegheny County, Pa.; acting president of the Pennsylvania Board of Canal Appraisers at the time of his death; died in Fairfield, Pa., on September 27, 1841; interment in Up-the-Valley United Presbyterian Church Cemetery.

**McCRERY, James O., III,** a Representative from Louisiana; born in Shreveport, Caddo Parish, La., September 18, 1949; graduated Leesville High School, 1967; B.A., Louisiana Tech University, 1971; J.D., Louisiana State University, 1975; admitted to the bar in 1975 and practiced law in Leesville, La., 1975-1978; district manager to Representative Anthony C. Leach, Jr., 1979; assistant city attorney, Shreveport, 1979-1980; district manager and legislative director to Representative Charles E. Roemer III of Louisiana, 1981-1984; regional manager for governmental affairs, Georgia-Pacific Corp., Baton Rouge, La., 1984-1988; elected as a Republican to the One Hundredth Congress, April 16, 1988, by special election to fill the vacancy caused by the resignation of Charles E. Roemer III; reelected to the four succeeding Congresses and served from April 16, 1988, to January 3, 1997; is a resident of Shreveport, La.

**McCULLOCH, George,** a Representative from Pennsylvania; born in Maysville, Mason County, Ky., February 22, 1792; upon the death of his parents was sent to Cumberland County, Pa., where he was reared by relatives; ironmaster, with extensive iron interests in Center County; member of the Pennsylvania senate in 1835 and 1836; one of the proprietors of Hannah Furnace 1836-1850; elected as a Democrat to the Twenty-sixth Congress to fill the vacancy caused by the death of William W. Potter and served from November 20, 1839, to March 3, 1841; unsuccessful candidate for election in 1842 to the Twenty-eighth Congress; retired from political life and active business pursuits with residence in Lewistown, Mifflin County, Pa.; died in Port Royal, Juniata County, Pa., April 6, 1861; interment in Church Hill Cemetery, southwest of Port Royal, Pa.

**McCULLOCH, John,** a Representative from Pennsylvania; born in McCulloch Mills, Pa., November 15, 1806; attended the common schools and was graduated from Jefferson College, Canonsburg, Pa., in 1825; studied medicine and graduated from the medical department of the University of Pennsylvania in 1829; commenced practice in Green Tree, Huntingdon County, Pa.; moved to Petersburg in 1830, where he engaged in the practice of his profession until 1852; elected as a Whig to the Thirty-third Congress (March 4, 1853-March 3, 1855); was not a candidate for renomination in 1854; resumed the practice of medicine in Huntingdon, Pa.; affiliated with the Republican Party upon its formation in 1856; member of the Pennsylvania constitutional convention in 1874; died in Huntingdon, Pa., May 15, 1879; interment in Riverside Cemetery.

**McCULLOCH, Philip Doddridge, Jr.,** a Representative from Arkansas; born in Murfreesboro, Rutherford County, Tenn., June 23, 1851; moved with his parents to Trenton, Gibson County, Tenn.; attended private schools and Andrew College in that city; studied law; was admitted to the bar in 1872 and commenced practice in Trenton; moved to Marianna, Ark., in February 1874 and continued the practice of law; elected prosecuting attorney for the first judicial district in 1878; reelected for three successive terms and served until 1884; chairman of the Democratic central committee of Lee County, Ark., 1875-1893; elected mayor of Marianna, Ark., in 1875, but declined to serve; member of the board of education; delegate to the Democratic State convention in 1890; elected as a Democrat to the Fifty-third and to the four succeeding Congresses (March 4, 1893-March 3, 1903); declined to be a candidate for renomination in 1902 to the Fifty-eighth Congress; resumed the practice of law in Marianna, Ark., where he died on November 26, 1928; interment in Cedar Heights Cemetery.

**McCULLOCH, Roscoe Conkling,** a Representative and a Senator from Ohio; born near Millersburg, Holmes County, Ohio, November 27, 1880; attended the public schools, the University of Wooster at Wooster, Ohio, Ohio State University Law School at Columbus, and Western Reserve University Law School, Cleveland, Ohio; was admitted to the bar in 1903 and commenced practice in Canton, Ohio; assistant prosecuting attorney of Stark County 1905-1907; unsuccessful Republican candidate for election in 1912 to the Sixty-third Congress; elected as a Republican to the Sixty-fourth, Sixty-fifth, and Sixty-sixth Congresses (March 4, 1915-March 3, 1921); was not a candidate for renomination in 1920; unsuccessful candidate for the Republican nomination for Governor of Ohio in 1920; special Assistant Attorney General of the United States 1922-1925; appointed as a Republican to the United States Senate to fill the vacancy caused by the death of Theodore E. Burton and served from November 5, 1929, until November 30, 1930, when a duly elected successor qualified; was unsuccessful for election to fill the vacancy; resumed the practice of law in Columbus, Ohio; died in West Palm Beach, Fla., March 17, 1958; interment in Hillcrest Cemetery.

**McCULLOCH, William Moore,** a Representative from Ohio; born near Holmesville, Holmes County, Ohio, November 24, 1901; attended the public schools; College of Wooster, Wooster, Ohio; was graduated from the college of law of Ohio State University at Columbus in 1925; was admitted to the bar the same year and commenced practice in Piqua, Ohio; member of the State house of representatives 1933-1944, serving as minority leader, 1936-1939 and as speaker, 1939-1944; served in the Military Government Forces from December 26, 1943, to October 12, 1945; elected as a Republican to the Eightieth Congress, by special election, November 4, 1947, to fill the vacancy caused by the resignation of Robert F. Jones; reelected to the twelve succeeding Congresses, and served from November 4, 1947 to January 3, 1973; was not a candidate for reelection in 1972 to the Ninety-third Congress; resumed the practice of law in Piqua, Ohio; died in Washington, D.C., February 22, 1980; interment in Arlington National Cemetery, Va.

**McCULLOGH, Welty,** a Representative from Pennsylvania; born in Greensburg, Westmoreland County, Pa., October 10, 1847; attended the common schools and Washington and Jefferson College, Washington, Pa.; served as second clerk under Capt. W.B. Coulter, provost marshal of twenty-first district of Pennsylvania, during the Civil War; graduated from Princeton College in June 1870; studied law; was admitted to the bar in 1872 and commenced practice in Greensburg; assistant solicitor for the Baltimore & Ohio Railroad; elected as a Republican to the Fiftieth Congress (March 4, 1887-March 3, 1889); unsuccessful candidate for renomination in 1888; continued the practice of law until his death in Greensburg, Pa., August 31, 1889; interment in the new St. Clair Cemetery.

**McCULLOUGH, Hiram,** a Representative from Maryland; born near Elkton, Cecil County, Md., September 26, 1813; pursued an academic course at Elkton Academy; studied law; was admitted to the bar in 1837 and practiced in Elkton; served in the State senate 1845-1851; unsuccessful candidate in 1850 for election to the Thirty-second Congress; in 1850 appointed one of the codifiers of the laws of Maryland; elected as a Democrat to the Thirty-ninth and Fortieth Congresses (March 4, 1865-March 3, 1869); resumed the practice of law and was for many years counsel for the Philadelphia, Wilmington & Baltimore Railroad; delegate to the Democratic National Convention in 1864 and 1868; member of the State house of delegates in 1880 and 1881 and served as speaker in 1880; died in Elkton, Md., March 4, 1885; interment in Presbyterian Cemetery.

**McCULLOUGH, Thomas Grubb,** a Representative from Pennsylvania; born in Greencastle, Franklin County, Pa., April 20, 1785; attended the common schools; studied law; admitted to the Franklin County bar April 8, 1806; served in the War of 1812 as a private and later as quartermaster; elected to the Sixteenth Congress to fill the vacancy caused by the resignation of David Fullerton and served from October 17, 1820, to March 4, 1821; served in the Pennsylvania house of representatives 1831-1835; first president of the Cumberland Valley Railroad Co.; managed and edited the Franklin Repository; was president of the Bank of Chambersburg at the time of his death; died in Chambersburg, Pa., September 10, 1848.

**McCUMBER, Porter James,** a Senator from North Dakota; born in Crete, Will County, Ill., February 3, 1858; moved with his parents to Rochester, Minn., the same year; attended the common schools; taught school for a few years; graduated from the law department of the University of Michigan at Ann Arbor in 1880; was admitted to the bar and commenced practice at Wahpeton, Dak. (now North Dakota), in 1881; member of the Territorial house of representatives in 1885, and of the Territorial senate in 1887; served as State's attorney of Richland County, 1889-1891; elected as a Republican to the United States Senate in 1899; reelected in 1905, 1911, and 1916, and served from March 4, 1899 to March 3, 1923; unsuccessful candidate for renomination in 1922; chairman, Committee on Manufactures (Fifty-seventh Congress), Committee on Pensions (Fifty-eighth through Sixty-second and Sixty-sixth and Sixty-seventh Congresses), Committee on Indian Affairs (Fifty-ninth Congress), Committee on Transportation Routes to the Seaboard (Sixty-third through Sixty-fifth Congresses), Committee on Finance (Sixty-seventh Congress); co-sponsor of the Fordney-McCumber

Tariff of 1922; resumed the practice of law in Washington, D.C.; appointed by President Calvin Coolidge in 1925 as a member of the International Joint Commission to pass upon all cases involving the use of the boundary waters between the United States and Canada, in which capacity he served until his death in Washington, D.C., May 18, 1933; interment in the Abbey Mausoleum, adjoining Arlington National Cemetery.

Bibliography: *DAB*; Schlup, Leonard. "Philosophical Conservative: Porter James McCumber and Political Reform." *North Dakota History* 45 (Summer 1978): 16-21; Wilkins, Robert P. "Tory Isolationist: Porter J. McCumber and World War I, 1914-1917." *North Dakota History* 34 (Summer 1967): 192-207.

**McCURDY, David Keith,** a Representative from Oklahoma; born in Canadian, Hemphill County, Tex., March 30, 1950; attended the public schools of Yukon, Okla., and graduated from Yukon High School in 1968; B.A., University of Oklahoma, Norman, 1972; J.D., University of Oklahoma College of Law, 1975; rotary graduate fellow, University of Edinburgh, Scotland, international economics, 1977-1978; served as an airman in the United States Air Force Reserve, 1969-1972; admitted to the Oklahoma bar in 1975; Oklahoma State assistant attorney general, 1975-1977; private practice, Norman, Okla., 1978-1980; elected as a Democrat to the Ninety-seventh and to the six succeeding Congresses (January 3, 1981-January 3, 1995); chairman, Permanent Select Committee on Intelligence (One Hundred Second Congress); was not a candidate in 1994 for reelection to the House of Representatives, but was an unsuccessful candidate for election to the United States Senate; is a resident of Norman, Okla.

**McDADE, Joseph Michael,** a Representative from Pennsylvania; born in Scranton, Lackawanna County, Pa., September 29, 1931; attended St. Paul's School and Scranton Preparatory School; B.A., University of Notre Dame, 1953; LL.B., University of Pennsylvania, 1956; admitted to the Pennsylvania bar in 1957; served clerkship in office of Chief Federal Judge John W. Murphy, Middle District of Pennsylvania; engaged in the general practice of law in 1957; solicitor of the city of Scranton in 1962; elected as a Republican to the Eighty-eighth and to the sixteen succeeding Congresses (January 3, 1963-January 3, 1997); is a resident of Clarks Summit, Pa.

**McDANIEL, William,** a Representative from Missouri; born in Grayson County, Ky., in 1801; moved to Missouri in the late 1820s; member of the State senate in 1838 and 1840; served in the Missouri Volunteers during the Seminole War; elected president of the bank in Palmyra, Marion County, Mo., on December 9, 1840; elected as a Democrat to the Twenty-ninth Congress to fill the vacancy caused by the resignation of Sterling Price and served from December 7, 1846, to March 3, 1847; was operating an agency for the location of land claims at Palmyra on June 10, 1847; moved to Solano County, Calif., and laid out the town of Vacaville; moved to Humboldt County, Calif., and established the land office at Humboldt Point in 1858; moved to the Idaho Territory in 1863 where he practiced law and was associated with the land office; died in Lewiston, Nez Perce County, Idaho, on December 14, 1866.

**McDANNOLD, John James,** a Representative from Illinois; born in Mount Sterling, Brown County, Ill., August 29, 1851; attended the common schools and a private school in Quincy; was graduated from the law department of the University of Iowa at Iowa City in June 1874; was admitted to the bar of Illinois in September 1874 and commenced practice in Mount Sterling; appointed master in chancery for Brown County in October 1885; elected county judge of Brown County in 1886; reelected in November 1890 and served until October 2, 1892, when he resigned, having been nominated for Congress; elected as a Democrat to the Fifty-third Congress (March 4, 1893-March 3, 1895); was not a candidate for renomination in 1894; moved to Chicago, Ill., in 1895 and resumed the practice of law; died in Chicago, Ill., February 3, 1904; interment in City Cemetery, Mount Sterling, Ill.

**McDEARMON, James Calvin,** a Representative from Tennessee; born in New Canton, Buckingham County, Va., June 13, 1844; moved with his parents to Gibson County, Tenn., in 1846; attended Andrew College, Trenton, Tenn., 1858-1861; entered the Confederate Army in April 1862 and served throughout the war in Cheatham's division, Army of the Tennessee; studied law; was admitted to the bar in 1867 and commenced practice in Trenton, Tenn.; elected as a Democrat to the Fifty-third and Fifty-fourth Congresses (March 4, 1893-March 3, 1897); unsuccessful candidate for renomination in 1896; resumed the practice of his profession; died in Trenton, Gibson County, Tenn., July 19, 1902; interment in Oakwood Cemetery.

**McDERMOTT, Allan Langdon,** a Representative from New Jersey; born in South Boston, Mass., March 30, 1854; attended the common schools; was graduated from the law department of New York University; was admitted to the bar in the November term in 1877 and commenced practice in Jersey City, N.J.; corporation attorney of Jersey City 1879-1883; member of the State house of assembly in 1880 and 1881; district court judge 1883-1886; president of the Jersey City Board of Finance and Taxation 1883-1886; member of the State board of taxation 1884-1886; chairman of the New Jersey State Democratic committee 1885-1895; member of the commission to revise the constitution of New Jersey in 1894; candidate of the Democratic legislative caucus for United States Senator in 1895 and 1902; delegate at large to the Democratic National Convention in 1896; member of the State senate in 1899 and 1900; elected as a Democrat to the Fifty-sixth Congress to fill the vacancy caused by the death of William B. Daly; reelected to the Fifty-seventh, Fifty-eighth, and Fifty-ninth Congresses and served from December 3, 1900, to March 3, 1907; was not a candidate for renomination in 1906; died in Jersey City, N.J., October 26, 1908; interment in Hoboken Cemetery, North Bergen, N.J.

**McDERMOTT, James,** a Representative from Washington; born in Chicago, Ill., December 28, 1936; attended public schools in Downers Grove, Ill.; B.S., Wheaton (Ill.) College, 1958; M.D., University of Illinois Medical School, 1963; residency in adult psychiatry, University of Illinois Hospitals; residency in child psychiatry, University of Washington Hospitals, 1964-1968; entered active duty, United States Navy Medical Corps in 1968; released as lieutenant commander in 1970; psychiatrist; member, Washington State house of representatives, 1971-1973; member, Washington State senate, 1975-1987; unsuccessful candidate in 1972, 1980 and 1984 for nomination for Governor of Washington; regional medical officer, United States Foreign Service, 1987-1988; psychiatrist and assistant clinical professor of psychiatry, University of Washington, 1970-1983; elected as a Democrat to the One Hundred First and to the three succeeding Congresses (January 3, 1989-January 3, 1997); chairman, Committee on Standards of Official Conduct (One Hundred Third Congress); is a resident of Seattle, Wash.

**McDERMOTT, James Thomas,** a Representative from Illinois; born in Grand Rapids, Mich., February 13, 1872; attended the graded schools and St. Andrew's Cathedral School at Grand Rapids; moved with his parents in 1884 to Detroit, Mich., where he was taught telegraphy; employed in this occupation until 1889, when he moved to Chicago, Ill.; engaged in the retail tobacco business; elected as a Democrat to the Sixtieth and to the three succeeding Congresses and served from March 4, 1907, until July 21, 1914, when he resigned; delegate to the Democratic National Convention in 1912; again elected to the Sixty-fourth Congress (March 4, 1915-March 3, 1917); declined to be a candidate for renomination in 1916; resumed his former business pursuits; died in Chicago, Ill., on February 7, 1938; interment in All Saints Cemetery.

**McDILL, Alexander Stuart,** a Representative from Wisconsin; born near Meadville, Crawford County, Pa., on March 18, 1822; attended Allegheny College; was graduated from Cleveland Medical College in 1848 and practiced medicine in Crawford County, Pa., 1848-1856; moved to Plover, Portage County, Wis., in 1856; member of the State assembly in 1862; member of the board of managers of the Wisconsin State Hospital for the Insane 1862-1868; served in the State senate in 1863 and 1864; medical superintendent of the Wisconsin State Hospital for the Insane 1868-1873 and in 1875; elected as a Republican to the Forty-third Congress (March 4, 1873-March 3, 1875); unsuccessful candidate for reelection to the Forty-fourth Congress; died near Madison, Wis., November 12, 1875; interment in Forest Hill Cemetery, Madison, Wis.

**McDILL, James Wilson,** a Representative and a Senator from Iowa; born in Monroe, Butler County, Ohio, March 4, 1834; attended the common schools, Hanover College, and Salem Academy; graduated from Miami University, Oxford, Ohio, in 1853; studied law in Columbus, Ohio, and was admitted to the bar in 1856; moved to Afton, Iowa, and commenced practice; elected superintendent of Union County, Iowa, in 1859; elected county judge of Union County in 1860; clerk in the office of the Third Auditor of the Treasury, Washington, D.C., 1862-1865, when he resigned and returned to Iowa; circuit judge and then district judge of the third judicial circuit of Iowa; elected as a Republican to the Forty-third and Forty-fourth Congresses (March 4, 1873-March 3, 1877); declined to be a candidate for renomination in 1876; resumed the practice of law in Afton, Iowa; member of the Board of Railroad Commissioners of the State of Iowa 1878-1881, 1883-1885; appointed and subsequently elected as a Republican to the United States Senate to fill the vacancy caused by the resignation of Samuel J. Kirkwood and served from March 8, 1881, until March 3, 1883; was not a candidate for reelection; appointed by President Benjamin Harrison a member of the Interstate Commerce Commission and served from 1892, until his death in Creston, Iowa, February 28, 1894; interment in Graceland Cemetery.

Bibliography: *DAB.*

**McDONALD, Alexander,** a Senator from Arkansas; born near Lock Haven, Clinton County, Pa., April 10, 1832; attended Dickinson Seminary, Williamsport, Pa., and Lewisburg University, Lewisburg, Pa.; moved to Kansas in 1857 and engaged in general business; served in the Union Army during the Civil War; became interested in banking in Arkansas in 1863 and finally settled in Little Rock; member of the State constitutional convention; upon the readmission of the State of Arkansas to representation was elected as a Republican to the United States Senate and served from June 22, 1868, to March 3, 1871; unsuccessful candidate for reelection in 1870; commissioned by President Chester Arthur to examine the conditions of two divisions of the Northern Pacific Railroad in 1885; engaged in development of railroads; moved to New York City in 1900; died in Norwood Park, St. Lawrence County, N.Y., December 13, 1903; interment in Highland Cemetery, Lock Haven, Pa.

**McDONALD, Edward Francis,** a Representative from New Jersey; born in Ireland September 21, 1844; immigrated to the United States when six years of age with his parents, who settled in Newark, N.J.; attended the public schools; during the Civil War enlisted in Company I, Seventh Regiment, New Jersey Volunteer Infantry, in 1861; was honorably discharged in 1862; learned the machinist trade and became a skilled mechanic; moved to Harrison, N.J., in 1874; member of the State house of assembly in 1874; director at large of the Board of Chosen Freeholders of Hudson County in 1877; reelected in 1879 and served four years; presented credentials as a member-elect to the State senate in 1890 and served throughout the session until the last day, when he was unseated, but was restored to the seat in the following session; interested in real estate business; treasurer of Harrison, Hudson County, N.J., in

1881; elected as a Democrat to the Fifty-second Congress and served from March 4, 1891, until his death in Harrison, N.J., November 5, 1892; interment in Holy Sepulchre Cemetery, Newark, N.J.

**McDONALD, Jack H.,** a Representative from Michigan; born in Detroit, Wayne County, Mich., June 28, 1932; educated in White Lake Township and Detroit; attended Wayne State University; served as supervisor of census for Wayne County, United States Department of Commerce, Bureau of Census, in 1960; elected supervisor of Redford Township in 1961 and 1963, reelected in 1964; elected chairman of the Wayne County Board of Supervisors in 1965; appointed to the Republican Task Force on Urban Affairs, 1967; elected as a Republican to the Ninetieth and to the two succeeding Congresses (January 3, 1967-January 3, 1973); unsuccessful candidate for renomination in 1972 to the Ninety-third Congress; consultant; is a resident of Great Falls, Va.

**McDONALD, John,** a Representative from Maryland; born in Dingle, County Kerry, Ireland, May 24, 1837; attended the schools of Ireland; immigrated to the United States and enlisted in the United States Army at Boston, Mass., in 1857; joined his regiment in Arizona; served in the Cavalry Corps of the Army of the Potomac throughout the Civil War; after the war was ordered to the West, where he again took part in several campaigns against hostile Indians; retired as a captain of Cavalry July 1, 1868, for disabilities incurred in the line of service; settled in Maryland; elected as a Republican to the Maryland house of delegates in 1881; elected as a Republican to the Fifty-fifth Congress (March 4, 1897-March 3, 1899); engaged in agricultural pursuits near Potomac, Montgomery County, Md.; died in Rockville, Md., January 30, 1917; interment in Union Cemetery.

**McDONALD, Joseph Ewing,** a Representative and a Senator from Indiana; born in Butler County, Ohio, August 29, 1819; moved with his mother to Montgomery County, Ind., in 1826; apprenticed to the saddler's trade when twelve years of age in La Fayette, Ind.; attended Wabash College, Crawfordsville, Ind., and graduated from Asbury (now De Pauw) University, Greencastle, Ind., in 1840; studied law in La Fayette, Ind., was admitted to the bar in 1843 and practiced; prosecuting attorney, 1843-1847; moved to Crawfordsville, Ind., in 1847, where he practiced law until 1859; elected as a Democrat to the Thirty-first Congress (March 4, 1849-March 3, 1851); was not a candidate for renomination in 1850 to the Thirty-second Congress; elected attorney general of Indiana in 1856 and was reelected in 1858; moved to Indianapolis in 1859; unsuccessful Democratic candidate for Governor of Indiana in 1864; elected as a Democrat to the United States Senate, and served from March 4, 1875 to March 3, 1881; unsuccessful candidate for reelection; chairman, Committee on Public Lands (Forty-sixth Congress); died in Indianapolis, Ind., June 21, 1891; interment in Crown Hill Cemetery.

**Bibliography:** *DAB*.

**McDONALD, Lawrence Patton,** a Representative from Georgia; born in Atlanta, Fulton County, Ga., April 1, 1935; educated in the public elementary schools of Georgia; graduated, Darlington High School, Rome, Ga., 1951; Davidson College, N.C., 1951-1953; M.D., Emory University School of Medicine, Atlanta, Ga., 1957; postgraduate training in urology, University of Michigan, Ann Arbor, 1963-1966; practiced medicine in Atlanta; served in the United States Navy, 1959-1961; chairman, vice chairman, Georgia State Medical Education Board, 1969-1974; elected as a Democrat to the Ninety-fourth and to the four succeeding Congresses and served from January 3, 1975, until his death, on September 1, 1983, caused by the mid-flight destruction of Korean Air Lines flight 007 by the Soviet military over the Sea of Japan.

**McDONOUGH, Gordon Leo,** a Representative from California; born in Buffalo, Erie County, N.Y., January 2, 1895; moved with his parents to Emporium, Cameron County, Pa., in 1898; attended the public schools; was graduated from the high school at Emporium, Pa.; engaged as an industrial chemist at Emporium, Pa., 1915-1918; moved to Los Angeles, Calif., and resumed his former occupation, 1918-1933; member of the Los Angeles County Board of Supervisors, 1933-1944, serving as chairman for one year; elected as a Republican to the Seventy-ninth and to the eight succeeding Congresses (January 3, 1945-January 3, 1963); unsuccessful candidate for reelection in 1962 to the Eighty-eighth Congress; died in Bethesda, Md., June 25, 1968; interment in Holy Cross Mausoleum, Los Angeles, Calif.

**Bibliography:** Mitchell, Franklin D. "An Act of Presidential Indiscretion: Harry S Truman, Congressman McDonough, and the Marine Corps Incident of 1950." *Presidential Studies Quarterly* 11 (Fall 1981): 565-75.

**McDOUGALL, Alexander,** a Delegate from New York; born in the Parish of Kildalton, on the island of Islay, Scotland, in 1731; immigrated to the United States in 1740, with his parents, who settled in New York; commanded two privateers during the war with France in 1756; at the conclusion of peace engaged in mercantile pursuits; was imprisoned as the author of Revolutionary pamphlets; member of the provincial convention in April 1775; served in the Revolutionary War; commissioned colonel of the First New York Infantry June 30, 1775; promoted to brigadier general, Continental Army, August 9, 1776; and major general October 20, 1777, and served until the close of the war; Member of the Continental Congress in 1781; member of the State senate from 1783 until his death; first president of the New York Society of the Cincinnati; first president of the Bank of New York; died in New York City June 9, 1786; interment in the family vault in the First Presbyterian Church, New York City.

**Bibliography:** *DAB*; Shannon, Sister Anna M. "General Alexander McDougall: Citizen and Soldier, 1732-1786." Ph.D. dissertation, Fordham University, 1957.

**McDOUGALL, James Alexander,** a Representative and a Senator from California; born in Bethlehem, N.Y., November 19, 1817; attended the Albany, N.Y., public schools; studied law; was admitted to the bar and commenced practice in Cook County, Ill., in 1837; attorney general of Illinois 1842-1846; made explorations of the southwestern part of the United States; finally settled in San Francisco; attorney general of California 1850-1851; elected as a Democrat to the Thirty-third Congress (March 4, 1853-March 3, 1855); was not a candidate for renomination in 1854; elected as a Democrat to the United States Senate and served from March 4, 1861, to March 3, 1867; was not a candidate for reelection; died in Albany, N.Y., September 3, 1867; interment in Lone Mountain (later Calvary) Cemetery, San Francisco, Calif.

**Bibliography:** Buchanan, Russell. "James A. McDougall, A Forgotten Senator." *California Historical Society Quarterly* 15 (September 1936): 199-212; Farr, James. "Not Exactly a Hero: James Alexander McDougall in the United States Senate." *California History* 65 (June 1986): 104-13, 152-53.

**McDOWELL, Alexander,** a Representative from Pennsylvania; born in Franklin, Venango County, Pa., March 4, 1845; attended the common schools; learned the printing trade; studied law but never practiced; during the Civil War served in the Union Army in the One Hundred and Twenty-first Regiment of Pennsylvania Volunteers; mustered out at the close of the war as brevet major; editor and publisher of the Venango Citizen until 1870, when he moved to Sharon and engaged in banking; treasurer and director of the School Board of Sharon 1880-1913; treasurer of the borough of Sharon 1880-1909; elected as a Republican to the Fifty-third Congress

(March 4, 1893-March 3, 1895); was not a candidate for renomination in 1894; elected Clerk of the House of Representatives on March 4, 1895, and served in that capacity until March 3, 1911; delegate to the Republican National Conventions in 1900, 1904, and 1908; resumed banking interests; died in Sharon, Mercer County, Pa., September 30, 1913; interment in Oakwood Cemetery.

**McDOWELL, Harris Brown, Jr.,** a Representative from Delaware; born on a farm near Middletown, New Castle County, Del., February 10, 1906; attended the public schools of Middletown, Wilmington (Del.) High School, and the Y.M.C.A. schools; graduated from Beacom Business College, Wilmington, Del.; engaged in farming, also in the insurance and real estate business; member of the Delaware State Board of Agriculture, 1937-1940; served in the State house of representatives, 1940-1942; director of Interstate Milk Producers Cooperative, and a member of Delaware Farm Bureau, 1941-1948; Delaware State senator, 1942-1946; Delaware secretary of state, 1949-1953; member of the New Castle County Zoning Commission, 1953-1954; delegate to the Democratic National Conventions of 1944, 1948, 1952, 1956, and 1960; elected as a Democrat to the Eighty-fourth Congress (January 3, 1955-January 3, 1957); unsuccessful candidate for reelection in 1956 to the Eighty-fifth Congress; elected to the Eighty-sixth and to the three succeeding Congresses (January 3, 1959-January 3, 1967); unsuccessful candidate for reelection in 1966 to the Ninetieth Congress; Federal State coordinator for Delaware, 1967-1968; retired; is a resident of Middletown, Del.

**McDOWELL, James,** a Representative from Virginia; born at "Cherry Grove," near Rockbridge County, Va., October 13, 1795; attended a classical school at Greenville, Va., a private school at Brownsburg, Washington College (now Washington and Lee University), Lexington, Va., and Yale College; was graduated from Princeton College in 1817; studied law; was admitted to the bar but did not practice; member of the Virginia house of delegates, 1831-1835, and again in 1838; elected Governor of Virginia by the General Assembly, and served from January 1, 1843 to January 1, 1846; elected as a Democrat to the Twenty-ninth Congress to fill the vacancy caused by the death of William Taylor; reelected to the Thirtieth and Thirty-first Congresses, and served from March 6, 1846, to March 3, 1851; died on his estate "Colalto" near Lexington, Va., August 24, 1851; interment in Presbyterian Cemetery.

**Bibliography:** *DAB*; Collier, James Glen. "The Political Career of James McDowell, 1830-1851." Ph.D. dissertation, University of North Carolina, 1963.

**McDOWELL, James Foster,** a Representative from Indiana; born in Mifflin County, Pa., December 3, 1825; moved with his parents to Ohio in 1835; attended the public schools; worked in a printing office; studied law; was admitted to the bar in 1846 and practiced; prosecuting attorney of Darke County, Ohio, in 1848; moved to Marion, Ind., in 1851 and engaged in the practice of law; established the Marion Journal in 1851; elected as a Democrat to the Thirty-eighth Congress (March 4, 1863-March 3, 1865); unsuccessful candidate for reelection in 1864 to the Thirty-ninth Congress; delegate to the Democratic National Convention in 1876; engaged in the practice of law in Marion, Ind., until his death in that city April 18, 1887; interment in Odd Fellows Cemetery.

**McDOWELL, John Anderson,** a Representative from Ohio; born in Killbuck, Holmes County, Ohio, September 25, 1853; attended the common schools, the Millersburg High School, and Lebanon (Ohio) Normal College; was graduated from the Mount Union College, Alliance, Ohio, in 1887; taught in rural schools 1870-1877; principal of Millersburg High School 1877-1879; superintendent of Millersburg schools 1879-1896; county school examiner for twenty years; instructor in the summer school of the College of Wooster, Ohio, 1896-1917 and in the summer school of Ashland (Ohio) College in 1918; elected as a Democrat to the Fifty-fifth and

Fifty-sixth Congresses (March 4, 1897-March 3, 1901); unsuccessful candidate for renomination in 1900; superintendent of public instruction of the Ashland city schools 1908-1927; trustee of the State normal college at Kent, Ohio, 1911-1922; president of Northeastern Ohio Teachers' Association in 1921 and of Ohio State Teachers' Association in 1926; also interested in agricultural pursuits; died in Cleveland, Ohio, October 2, 1927; interment in Oak Hill Cemetery, Millersburg, Ohio.

**McDOWELL, John Ralph,** a Representative from Pennsylvania; born in Pitcairn, Allegheny County, Pa., November 6, 1902; attended the public and high schools; was graduated from Randolph-Macon Military Academy, Front Royal, Va., in 1923; employed as a reporter on the Pitcairn Express in 1923 and worked on various newspapers until 1929; magistrate of Pitcairn 1925-1928; became editor of the Wilkinsburg Gazette in 1929 and president of the Wilkinsburg Gazette Publishing Co., in 1933; elected as a Republican to the Seventy-sixth Congress (January 3, 1939-January 3, 1941); unsuccessful candidate for reelection in 1940 to the Seventy-seventh Congress and for election in 1942 to the Seventy-eighth Congress; elected in 1946 to the Eightieth Congress (January 3, 1947-January 3, 1949); unsuccessful for reelection in 1948 to the Eighty-first Congress; resumed the publishing business; died in Wilkinsburg, Pa., December 11, 1957; interment in Woodlawn Cemetery.

**McDOWELL, Joseph** (father of Joseph Jefferson McDowell and cousin of Joseph McDowell [1758-1799]), a Representative from North Carolina; born in Winchester, Va., February 15, 1756; moved to North Carolina with his parents in 1758; attended the common schools and Washington College (now Washington and Lee University), Lexington, Va.; served against the Indians on the frontier and later took an active part in the Revolution, attaining the rank of colonel; engaged in planting; elected to the Continental Congress in 1787, but did not attend; delegate to the State constitutional convention which ratified the Constitution of the United States in 1789; member of the State house of commons in 1791 and 1792; unsuccessful candidate for election in 1794 to the Fourth Congress; elected as a Republican to the Fifth Congress (March 4, 1797-March 3, 1799); was not a candidate for renomination in 1798; moved to Kentucky in 1800, but returned to North Carolina in 1801; died at his brother's home at Quaker Meadows, near Morganton, Burke County, N.C., February 5, 1801; interment in Quaker Meadow Cemetery, on his father's plantation, near Morganton, N.C.

**Bibliography:** *DAB*.

**McDOWELL, Joseph** (cousin of Joseph McDowell [1756-1801]), a Representative from North Carolina; born at "Pleasant Gardens," near Morganton, Burke (now McDowell) County, N.C., February 25, 1758; attended schools at Winchester, Va.; served in the Revolutionary Army and was commissioned a major; was subsequently general of militia; studied law; was admitted to the bar in 1791 and practiced in Burke, Rowan, and Rutherford Counties, N.C.; member of the State house of commons 1785-1792; elected to the Third Congress (March 4, 1793-March 3, 1795); renominated but declined to be a candidate for reelection in 1794; resumed the practice of law and engaged in agricultural pursuits; member of the commission appointed to settle the boundary line between North Carolina and Tennessee in 1796; died on his estate, "Pleasant Gardens," near Morganton, N.C., March 7, 1799; interment at Round Hill on his estate.

**McDOWELL, Joseph Jefferson** (son of Joseph McDowell), a Representative from Ohio; born in Burke (now McDowell) County, N.C., November 13, 1800; moved to Kentucky with his mother in 1805 and to Augusta County, Va., in 1817; pursued preparatory studies; engaged in agricultural pursuits; moved to Highland County, Ohio, in 1824 and continued agricultural pursuits; moved to Hillsboro, Highland County, in 1829 and engaged in mercantile pursuits; member of the Ohio State house of representatives in 1832; served in the State senate in 1833; appointed brigadier general of the State militia in 1834; studied law; was admitted to the bar in 1835 and commenced the practice of his profession in Hillsboro, Ohio; unsuccessful candidate for election in 1840 to the Twenty-seventh Congress; elected as a Democrat to the Twenty-eighth and Twenty-ninth Congresses (March 4, 1843-March 3, 1847); chairman, Committee on Accounts (Twenty-eighth Congress); resumed the practice of law and also engaged in agricultural pursuits; died in Hillsboro, Ohio, on January 17, 1877; interment in Hillsboro Cemetery.

**McDUFFIE, George,** a Representative and a Senator from South Carolina; born in Columbia County, Ga., August 10, 1790; attended an old-field school and a private academy; graduated from South Carolina College (now the University of South Carolina) at Columbia in 1813; studied law; was admitted to the bar in 1814 and commenced practice in Pendleton, Anderson County, S.C.; member, South Carolina State house of representatives, 1818-1819; elected to the Seventeenth and to the six succeeding Congresses, and served from March 4, 1821 until his resignation in 1834; chairman, Committee on Ways and Means (Nineteenth through Twenty-second Congresses); one of the managers appointed by the House of Representatives in 1830 to conduct the impeachment proceedings against James H. Peck, United States judge for the district of Missouri; elected Governor of South Carolina by the Legislature, and served from December 11, 1834 to December 1836; president of the board of trustees of South Carolina College; elected as a Democrat to the United States Senate to fill the vacancy caused by the resignation of William C. Preston; reelected, and served from December 23, 1842 until August 17, 1846, when he resigned; chairman, Committee on Foreign Relations (Twenty-ninth Congress); died at "Cherry Hill," Sumter District, S.C., March 11, 1851.

Bibliography: *DAB*; Green, Edwin. *George McDuffie*. Columbia: The State Company, 1936.

**McDUFFIE, John,** a Representative from Alabama; born in River Ridge, Monroe County, Ala., September 25, 1883; educated by private tutors and attended Southern University, Greensboro, Ala.; was graduated from Alabama Polytechnic Institute at Auburn in 1904 and from the law department of the University of Alabama at Tuscaloosa in 1908; member of the State house of representatives 1907-1911; was admitted to the bar in 1908 and commenced practice in Monroeville, Ala.; prosecuting attorney for the first judicial circuit of Alabama 1911-1919; elected as a Democrat to the Sixty-sixth and to the eight succeeding Congresses and served from March 4, 1919, until his resignation, effective March 2, 1935, having been appointed a judge in the United States district court, and served until his death in Mobile, Ala., November 1, 1950; minority whip (Seventy-first Congress), majority whip (Seventy-second Congress); chairman, Committee on Insular Affairs (Seventy-third and Seventy-fourth Congresses); interment in Pine Crest Cemetery.

Bibliography: Brannen, Ralph Neal. "John McDuffie: State Legislator, Congressman, Federal Judge, 1883-1950." Ph.D. dissertation, Auburn University, 1975.

**McDUFFIE, John Van,** a Representative from Alabama; born in Addison, Steuben County, N.Y., May 16, 1841; attended the common schools; moved with his parents to Bureau County, Ill., in 1855; attended Luther College, Decorah, Iowa; enlisted in Company B, Second Regiment, Iowa Volunteer Cavalry, in July 1861 and served through the Civil War; settled in Lowndes County, Ala., and became a planter; studied law; was admitted to the bar and commenced practice in Hayneville, Ala.; elected judge of probate in 1868; reelected in 1874 and served until 1880; delegate to the Republican National Convention in 1872 and 1876; unsuccessful Republican candidate for election in 1886 to the Fiftieth Congress; successfully contested the election of Louis W. Turpin to the Fifty-first Congress and served from June 4, 1890, until March 3, 1891; unsuccessfully contested the election of Louis W. Turpin to the Fifty-second Congress; engaged in mercantile pursuits and continued as a planter; died in Hayneville, Lowndes County, Ala., November 18, 1896; interment in Pines Cemetery.

**McENERY, Samuel Douglas,** a Senator from Louisiana; born in Monroe, Ouachita Parish, La., May 28, 1837; attended the public schools, Spring Hill (Ala.) College, the United States Naval Academy at Annapolis, Md., and the University of Virginia at Charlottesville; graduated from the State and National Law School, Poughkeepsie, N.Y., in 1859; at the beginning of the Civil War entered the Confederate Army as a member of a volunteer company called the Pelican Greys, and in 1862 was commissioned a lieutenant; was admitted to the bar at Monroe, La., in 1866 and commenced the practice of his profession; elected Lieutenant Governor of Louisiana in 1879; upon the death of Governor Louis A. Wiltz on October 16, 1881, was his successor; elected Governor of Louisiana in 1884, and served from October 16, 1881 to May 20, 1888; unsuccessful candidate for reelection in 1888; appointed associate justice of the supreme court of Louisiana in 1888 and served until 1897, when he resigned, having been elected Senator; elected as a Democrat to the United States Senate in 1896; reelected in 1902 and again in 1908, and served from March 4, 1897, until his death in New Orleans, La., June 28, 1910; chairman, Committee on Corporations Organized in the District of Columbia (Fifty-ninth Congress), Committee on Transportation and Sale of Meat Products (Sixty-first Congress); interment in Metairie Cemetery.

Bibliography: *DAB*.

**McETTRICK, Michael Joseph,** a Representative from Massachusetts; born in Roxbury, Norfolk County, Mass., June 22, 1848; graduated from the Washington Grammar and the Roxbury Latin Schools; became a journalist; assistant assessor of Boston in 1884; member of the Massachusetts house of representatives 1885-1891 and chairman of the Democratic members of the house; served in the Massachusetts senate in 1892; elected as an Independent Democrat to the Fifty-third Congress (March 4, 1893-March 3, 1895); was an unsuccessful candidate for renomination in 1894 to the Fifty-fourth Congress; again a member of the Massachusetts house of representatives in 1906, 1907, and 1913; served in the Massachusetts senate in 1908; engaged in the real estate business in Boston, Mass., until his death there on December 31, 1921; interment in Calvary Cemetery.

**McEWAN, Thomas, Jr.,** a Representative from New Jersey; born in Paterson, N.J., February 26, 1854; attended the public schools; became a civil engineer; attended the law department of Columbia University; was admitted to the bar about 1885 and commenced practice in New York City and Jersey City, N.J.; assessor of the fourth district, Jersey City, in 1886 and 1887; secretary to Dr. Morgan Dix, rector of Trinity Church, New York City, 1886-1906; tax assessor of Jersey City in 1887 and 1888; United States commissioner and chief supervisor of elections for the district of New Jersey from August 1892 to October 1893; delegate to and secretary of every Republican convention of New Jersey and Hudson County 1877-1896; secretary of the Hudson County Republican general committee 1878-1893; delegate to the Republican National Convention in 1892 and 1896; member of the State house of assembly in 1893 and 1894 and served as Republican leader in 1894; elected as a Republican to the Fifty-fourth and Fifty-fifth Congresses (March 4, 1895-March 3, 1899); was not a candidate for renomination in 1898; resumed the practice of law and also engaged in banking in West Hoboken, N.J., from 1904 until July 1, 1924, when he retired; controller of Jersey City 1906 and 1907; died in Jersey City, N.J., September 11, 1926; interment in Flower Hill Cemetery, North Bergen, N.J.

**McEWEN, Robert,** a Representative from Ohio; born in Hillsboro, Highland County, Ohio, January 12, 1950; attended the public schools; B.B.A., University of Miami, Coral Gables, Fla., 1972; business executive; assistant to Representative William H. Harsha of Ohio; Ohio State representative, District 77, 1974-1980; delegate to Republican National Conventions; elected as a Republican to the Ninety-seventh and to the five succeeding Congresses (January 3, 1981-January 3, 1993); unsuccessful candidate for reelection in 1992 to the One Hundred Third Congress; is a resident of Hillsboro, Ohio.

**McEWEN, Robert Cameron,** a Representative from New York; born in Ogdensburg, St. Lawrence County, N.Y., January 5, 1920; attended the public schools and the Mount Hermon (Mass.) School; attended the University of Vermont, 1938-1939, and the Wharton School of Finance and Commerce of the University of Pennsylvania, 1939-1941; LL.B., Albany Law School, 1947; admitted to the bar in 1947 and commenced practice in Ogdensburg, N.Y.; served in the Army Air Corps from September 1942 to January 1946, and was discharged as a sergeant; member of the New York State senate, 1954-1964; elected as a Republican to the Eighty-ninth and to the seven succeeding Congresses (January 3, 1965-January 3, 1981); was not a candidate for reelection in 1980 to the Ninety-seventh Congress; appointed by President Ronald Reagan to the International Joint Commission, United States and Canada, 1981; is a resident of Ogdensburg, N.Y.

**McFADDEN, Louis Thomas,** a Representative from Pennsylvania; born in Granville Center, Troy Township, Bradford County, Pa., July 25, 1876; attended the public schools; graduated from Warner's Commercial College, Elmira, N.Y.; entered the employ of the First National Bank, Canton, Pa., in 1892; in 1899 was elected cashier, and became its president on January 11, 1916, serving until 1925; served as treasurer of the Pennsylvania Bankers' Association in 1906 and 1907 and as president in 1914 and 1915; appointed in 1914 by the agricultural societies of the Commonwealth of Pennsylvania as a trustee of Pennsylvania State College; elected as a Republican to the Sixty-fourth and to the nine succeeding Congresses (March 4, 1915-January 3, 1935); chairman, Committee on Banking and Currency (Sixty-sixth through Seventy-first Congresses); unsuccessful candidate for reelection in 1934 to the Seventy-fourth Congress and for nomination in 1936 to the Seventy-fifth Congress; died October 1, 1936, while on a visit in New York City; interment in East Canton Cemetery, Canton, Pa.

**Bibliography:** *DAB.*

**McFADDEN, Obadiah Benton,** a Delegate from the Territory of Washington; born in West Middletown, Washington County, Pa., November 18, 1815; attended the public schools and McKeever Academy, West Middletown, Pa.; studied law; was admitted to the bar in 1843 and commenced practice; member of the Pennsylvania house of representatives in 1843; elected prothonotary of Washington County; appointed associate justice of the supreme court of the Territory of Oregon in 1853, and of the Territory of Washington in 1854, and served as chief justice of the latter from 1858 to 1861; member of the legislative council, and was chosen its president in 1861; resumed the practice of law in Olympia, Wash., and also engaged in agricultural pursuits; elected as a Democrat to the Forty-third Congress (March 4, 1873-March 3, 1875); was not a candidate for renomination in 1874 to the Forty-fourth Congress; died in Olympia, Wash., June 25, 1875; interment in the Masonic Cemetery.

**Bibliography:** Teiser, Stanley. "Obadiah B. McFadden, Oregon and Washington Territorial Judge." *Oregon Historical Quarterly* 66 (March 1965): 25-37.

**McFALL, John Joseph,** a Representative from California; born in Buffalo, Erie County, N.Y., February 20, 1918; attended the public schools of Manteca, Calif.; A.A., Modesto (Calif.) Junior College, 1936; A.B., University of California, Berkeley, 1938; LL.B., University of California School of Law, 1941; admitted to the bar in 1941 and employed as an attorney in Oakland, Calif., 1941-1942; served as a staff sergeant in the United States Army, Security Intelligence Corps, 1942-1946; engaged in the practice of law in Manteca, Calif., in 1946; city councilman and mayor of Manteca, 1948-1951; member, California State assembly, 1951-1956; delegate to all State Democratic conventions, 1948-1958; elected as a Democrat to the Eighty-fifth and to the ten succeeding Congresses, and served from January 3, 1957 until his resignation December 31, 1978; majority whip (Ninety-third and Ninety-fourth Congresses); unsuccessful candidate for reelection in 1978 to the Ninety-sixth Congress; is a resident of Alexandria, Va.

**McFARLAN, Duncan,** a Representative from North Carolina; born at Laurel Hill, Scotland County, N.C.; attended the common schools; engaged in agricultural pursuits; member of the State house of commons in 1792; served in the State senate in 1793, 1795, 1800, and 1807-1809; unsuccessful candidate for election in 1802 to the Eighth Congress; elected as a Republican to the Ninth Congress (March 4, 1805-March 3, 1807); engaged in mercantile and agricultural pursuits; died at Laurel Hill, N.C., September 7, 1816; interment in Laurel Hill Cemetery.

**McFARLAND, Ernest William,** a Senator from Arizona; born on a farm near Earlsboro, Pottawatomie County, Okla., October 9, 1894; attended the rural schools; graduated from East Central State Teachers' College, Ada, Okla., in 1914, and from the University of Oklahoma at Norman in 1917; during the First World War served in the United States Navy; after the war moved to Phoenix, Ariz., and was employed as a clerk in a bank; was graduated from the law department of Stanford (Calif.) University in 1921; was admitted to the bar and commenced practice in Casa Grande, Pinal County, Ariz.; assistant attorney general of Arizona, 1923-1924, and county attorney of Pinal County, 1925-1930; moved to Florence, Ariz., in 1925; judge of the superior court of Pinal County, 1934-1940; elected as a Democrat to the United States Senate in 1940; reelected in 1946 and served from January 3, 1941, to January 3, 1953; unsuccessful candidate for reelection in 1952; majority leader (Eighty-second Congress); co-chairman, Joint Committee on Navaho-Hopi Indian Administration (Eighty-first and Eighty-second Congresses); elected Governor of Arizona in 1954, reelected in 1956, and served from January 3, 1955 to January 5, 1959; unsuccessful candidate in 1958 for election to the United States Senate; resumed the practice of law; elected an associate justice of the Arizona State supreme court in 1964, and served from January 4, 1965 until January 4, 1971, serving as chief justice in 1968; member, National Commission on the Causes and Prevention of Violence, 1968-1969; director, Federal Home Loan Bank of San Francisco; president of Arizona Television Company; died in Phoenix, Ariz., June 8, 1984; interment in Greenwood Memorial Park, Phoenix, Ariz.

**Bibliography:** McFarland, Ernest W. *Mac: The Autobiography of Ernest W. McFarland.* N.p., 1979; McMillan, James Elton, Jr. "Ernest W. McFarland: Southwestern Progressive. The United States Senate Years, 1940-1952." Ph.D. dissertation, Arizona State University, 1990.

**McFARLAND, William,** a Representative from Tennessee; born at Springvale Farm, near Morristown, Jefferson (now Hamblen) County, Tenn., September 15, 1821; attended the common schools and Tusculum College, Greene County, Tenn.; studied law; was admitted to the bar in 1861 and engaged in the practice of law in 1865 in Dandridge, Morristown, and Greeneville; held several local judicial offices; appointed judge of the county court in 1870; elected as a Democrat to the Forty-fourth Congress (March 4, 1875-March

3, 1877); unsuccessful candidate for reelection in 1876 to the Forty-fifth Congress; again resumed the practice of his profession; mayor of Morristown four years; member of the board of education; died in Morristown, Tenn., April 12, 1900; interment in City Cemetery.

**McFARLANE, William Doddridge,** a Representative from Texas; born in Greenwood, Sebastian County, Ark., July 17, 1894; attended the public schools and the University of Arkansas at Fayetteville, 1909-1914; engaged in the mercantile business in Greenwood, Ark., 1914-1918; during the First World War was commissioned a second lieutenant in August 1918, and served until honorably discharged on December 13, 1918; B.A., University of Arkansas, 1919; LL.B., Kent Law School, Chicago, Ill., 1921, and J.D., 1969; was admitted to the bar in 1921 and commenced practice in Graham, Young County, Tex.; member of the Texas State house of representatives, 1923-1927; served in the State senate, 1927-1931; elected as a Democrat to the Seventy-third and to the two succeeding Congresses (March 4, 1933-January 3, 1939); unsuccessful candidate for renomination in 1938 to the Seventy-sixth Congress; resumed the practice of law; special assistant to the attorney general at Texarkana, Tex., 1941-1944; director of the Surplus Property Smaller War Plants Corporation, Washington, D.C., from December 1944 to January 1946; special assistant to the Attorney General in Washington, D.C., January 1946 to July 1, 1951; unsuccessful candidate in 1951 to fill the vacancy in the Eighty-second Congress; served in the Lands Division, Department of Justice, from December 1, 1951 until his retirement on August 1, 1966; resumed the practice of law; resided in Graham, Tex., where he died on February 18, 1980; interment in Oak Grove Cemetery.

**McGANN, Lawrence Edward,** a Representative from Illinois; born in Galway, Ireland, February 2, 1852; immigrated to the United States in 1855 with his mother, who settled in Milford, Mass.; attended the public schools; moved to Chicago, Ill., with his mother in 1865 and worked at the boot and shoe trade until 1879; employed as a clerk in the service of the city until 1885; appointed superintendent of streets January 1, 1885, and served until his resignation in May 1891; elected as a Democrat to the Fifty-second and Fifty-third Congresses (March 4, 1891-March 3, 1895); chairman, Committee on Labor (Fifty-third Congress); presented credentials as a Member-elect to the Fifty-fourth Congress and served from March 4, 1895, until December 27, 1895, when he was succeeded by Hugh R. Belknap, who contested his election; served as president of the Chicago General Railways in 1896 and 1897; commissioner of public works of Chicago 1898-1901; city controller 1901-1907; again commissioner of public works 1911-1915; resided in Oak Park, Ill., until his death in that city on July 22, 1928; interment in Mount Olivet Cemetery, Chicago, Ill.

**McGARVEY, Robert Neill,** a Representative from Pennsylvania; born in Philadelphia, Pa., August 14, 1888; attended the public and parochial schools and the University of Pennsylvania Business College; engaged as a telegrapher and as manager of a news bureau; became an investment broker in 1922; elected as a Republican to the Eightieth Congress (January 3, 1947-January 3, 1949); unsuccessful candidate for reelection in 1948 to the Eighty-first Congress; returned to the investment brokerage business; died in Philadelphia, Pa., June 28, 1952; interment in Holy Cross Cemetery, Yeadon, Delaware County, Pa.

**McGAUGHEY, Edward Wilson,** a Representative from Indiana; born near Greencastle, Putnam County, Ind., January 16, 1817; attended the public schools; deputy clerk of Putnam County; studied law; was admitted to the bar in 1835 and commenced practice in Greencastle, Ind.; member of the Indiana State house of representatives, 1839-1840; served in the State senate for the session December 5, 1842, to February 13, 1843; resigned before the beginning of the next session; unsuccessful candidate for election in

1842 to the Twenty-eighth Congress; elected as a Whig to the Twenty-ninth Congress (March 4, 1845-March 3, 1847); unsuccessful candidate for reelection in 1846 to the Thirtieth Congress; moved to Rockville, Parke County, Ind., in 1846 and resumed the practice of law; elected to the Thirty-first Congress (March 4, 1849-March 3, 1851); unsuccessful candidate for reelection in 1850 to the Thirty-second Congress; nominated by President Zachary Taylor as Governor of Minnesota Territory in 1849, but the Senate failed to confirm the nomination; moved to California in 1852; died in San Francisco, Calif., August 6, 1852; interment in Yerba Buena Cemetery.

**McGAVIN, Charles,** a Representative from Illinois; born in Riverton, Sangamon County, Ill., January 10, 1874; attended the common schools in Springfield and the high school in Mount Olive, Ill.; studied law; was admitted to the bar in 1897 and practiced two years in Springfield; moved to Chicago in 1899 and resumed the practice of law; assistant city attorney of Chicago in 1903 and 1904; elected as a Republican to the Fifty-ninth and Sixtieth Congresses (March 4, 1905-March 3, 1909); was not a candidate for renomination in 1908; resumed the practice of law in Chicago; moved to Los Angeles in 1912 and practiced law until 1915, when he returned to Chicago; delegate to the Republican National Convention in 1920; died in Chicago, Ill., December 17, 1940; interment in Mount Auburn Cemetery, Berwyn, Ill.

**McGEE, Gale William,** a Senator from Wyoming; born in Lincoln, Lancaster County, Nebr., March 17, 1915; attended public schools; B.A., Nebraska State Teachers College, Wayne, 1936; M.A., University of Colorado, Boulder, 1939; Ph.D., history, University of Chicago, 1947; professor of American history at Crofton (Nebr.) High School, 1936-1937, Kearney (Nebr.) High School, 1937-1940, Nebraska Wesleyan University 1940-1943, Iowa State College of Agricultural and Mechanical Arts 1943-1944, University of Notre Dame, 1944-1945, University of Chicago, 1945-1946, and University of Wyoming 1946-1958; legislative assistant to Senator Joseph C. O'Mahoney in 1955 and 1956; elected as a Democrat to the United States Senate in 1958; reelected in 1964 and again in 1970, and served from January 3, 1959 to January 3, 1977; unsuccessful candidate for reelection in 1976; chairman, Committee on Post Office and Civil Service (Ninety-first through Ninety-fourth Congresses); Representative to the Organization of American States; served on several boards and commissions; president and founder of Gale W. McGee Associates, Washington, D.C.; senior consultant, Hill and Knowlton, Inc.; was a resident of Bethesda, Md.; died April 9, 1992.

**Bibliography:** McGee, Gale. *The Responsibilities of World Power*. Washington, D.C.: National Press, 1968.

**McGEHEE, Daniel Rayford,** a Representative from Mississippi; born in Little Springs, Miss., September 10, 1883; attended the public schools; was graduated from Mississippi College at Clinton in 1903 and from the law department of the University of Mississippi at Oxford in 1909; was admitted to the bar in 1909 and commenced practice at Meadville, Miss.; also engaged in agricultural pursuits and banking; member of the State senate 1924-1928; served in the State house of representatives 1928-1932; again a member of the State senate 1932-1934; elected as a Democrat to the Seventy-fourth and to the five succeeding Congresses (January 3, 1935-January 3, 1947); chairman, Committee on Claims (Seventy-seventh through Seventy-ninth Congresses); unsuccessful candidate for renomination in 1946 to the Eightieth Congress; resumed the practice of law, agricultural pursuits, and banking; died in Meadville, Miss., February 9, 1962; interment in Midway Cemetery.

**McGILL, George,** a Senator from Kansas; born on a farm near Russell, Lucas County, Iowa, February 12, 1879; moved to Kansas with his parents, who settled on a farm near Dundee, Barton County, in 1884; attended the common schools; graduated from

Central Normal College, Great Bend, Kans., in 1900; studied law; was admitted to the bar in 1902 and commenced practice in Hoisington, Kans.; moved to Wichita, Sedgwick County, Kans., in 1904 and continued the practice of law; deputy county attorney of Sedgwick County, 1907-1911, and county attorney, 1911-1915; elected as a Democrat to the United States Senate in 1930 to fill the vacancy caused by the resignation of Charles Curtis; reelected in 1932 and served from December 1, 1930, to January 3, 1939; unsuccessful candidate for reelection in 1938, and for election in 1942, 1948, and 1954; chairman, Committee on Pensions (Seventy-third through Seventy-fifth Congresses); member of the United States Tariff Commission from 1944 to 1954; resumed the practice of law in Wichita, Kans., until his death there on May 14, 1963; interment in Pawnee Rock Cemetery, Pawnee Rock, Kans.

**Bibliography:** McCoy, Donald. "George S. McGill of Kansas and the Agricultural Adjustment Act of 1938." *The Historian* 45 (February 1983): 186-205; Shockley, Dennis. "George McGill of Kansas: Depression Senator." Ph.D. dissertation, Kansas State University, 1986.

**McGILLICUDDY, Daniel John,** a Representative from Maine; born in Lewiston, Maine, August 27, 1859; attended the common schools and was graduated from Bowdoin College, Brunswick, Maine, in 1881; studied law; was admitted to the bar in 1883 and commenced practice in Lewiston, Maine; member of the State house of representatives in 1884 and 1885; mayor of Lewiston in 1887, 1890, and 1902; delegate at large from Maine to the Democratic National Conventions in 1892, 1904, 1912, and 1920; unsuccessful candidate for election in 1906 to the Sixtieth Congress and in 1908 to the Sixty-first Congress; elected as a Democrat to the Sixty-second, Sixty-third, and Sixty-fourth Congresses (March 4, 1911-March 3, 1917); unsuccessful candidate for reelection in 1916 to the Sixty-fifth Congress and for election in 1918 to the Sixty-sixth Congress; member of the Democratic National Committee 1917-1932; continued the practice of law in Lewiston, Maine, until his death in that city on July 30, 1936; interment in Mount Hope Cemetery.

**McGINLEY, Donald Francis,** a Representative from Nebraska; born on a ranch in Keith County, near Keystone, Nebr., June 30, 1920; attended the public schools in Keystone, Nebr.; graduated from Ogallala (Nebr.) High School in 1938 and from Notre Dame University in 1942; enlisted in the United States Army Air Corps in 1942 and served until discharged in 1945, with twenty months in Great Britain; reporter and copy reader on the Denver Register in 1945 and 1946; graduated from Georgetown University, Washington, D.C., in 1949; was admitted to the bar and commenced the practice of law in Ogallala, Nebr., in 1950; Arthur County attorney 1951-1955; member of the Nebraska legislature, 1955-1959; elected as a Democrat to the Eighty-sixth Congress (January 3, 1959-January 3, 1961); unsuccessful candidate for reelection in 1960 to the Eighty-seventh Congress; resumed the practice of law; delegate, Nebraska State legislature, 1963-1964; delegate, Democratic National Conventions, 1964 and 1968; judge, court of industrial relations, Lincoln, Nebr., 1976-1980; lieutenant governor of Nebraska, 1983-1987; is a resident of Ogallala, Nebr.

**McGLENNON, Cornelius Augustine,** a Representative from New Jersey; born in East Newark, N.J., December 10, 1878; attended Holy Cross School, Harrison, N.J., and St. Francis Xavier's High School in New York City; was graduated from Seton Hall College, South Orange, N.J., in 1899; public and high school principal 1901-1926; studied law at the New Jersey Law School, Newark, N.J.; was admitted to the bar in 1916 and commenced practice in East Newark, N.J.; member of the State senate in 1917 and 1918, serving as Democratic floor leader in 1918; mayor of East Newark 1907-1919; elected as a Democrat to the Sixty-sixth Congress (March 4, 1919-March 3, 1921); unsuccessful candidate for

reelection in 1920 to the Sixty-seventh Congress; resumed the practice of his profession in East Newark, N.J.; delegate to the Democratic National Convention in 1920; appointed judge of the court of errors and appeals in 1924 and served until his death; also supervising principal at Harrison, N.J., 1926-1931; died in Newark, N.J., June 13, 1931; interment in Holy Sepulchre Cemetery, East Orange, N.J.

**McGLINCHEY, Herbert Joseph,** a Representative from Pennsylvania; born in Philadelphia, Pa., November 7, 1904; attended the public and parochial schools; engaged as a manufacturers' agent in Philadelphia, Pa.; supervisor of labor and industry for the eastern district of Pennsylvania, 1935-1937; president of the Board of Mercantile Appraisers, Philadelphia, Pa., 1937-1944; member of the Philadelphia Democratic county committee since 1933; delegate to Democratic National Conventions since 1936; elected as a Democrat to the Seventy-ninth Congress (January 3, 1945-January 3, 1947); was an unsuccessful candidate for reelection in 1946 to the Eightieth Congress, for election in 1948 to the Eighty-first Congress, and for election in 1956 to the Eighty-fifth Congress; resumed his occupation as a manufacturers' agent; member of Tax Equalization Board, 1957-1963; member, Pennsylvania senate, 1964-1972; consultant; is a resident of Philadelphia and Longport, N.J.

**McGOVERN, George Stanley,** a Representative and a Senator from South Dakota; born in Avon, Bon Homme County, S.Dak., July 19, 1922; attended the public schools of Mitchell, S.Dak., and Dakota Wesleyan University, Mitchell, S.Dak., 1940-1942; B.A., Dakota Wesleyan University, 1946; enlisted in the United States Army Air Corps in June 1942, flew combat missions in the European Theater, and was discharged from the service in July 1945; held teaching assistantship and fellowship at Northwestern University, Evanston, Ill., 1948-1950, receiving his Ph.D. in history from that university in 1953; professor of history and government at Dakota Wesleyan University, 1950-1953; executive secretary of South Dakota Democratic Party, 1953-1956; member of the Democratic National Committee's Advisory Committee on Political Organization, 1954-1956; elected as a Democrat to the Eighty-fifth and Eighty-sixth Congresses (January 3, 1957-January 3, 1961); was not a candidate in 1960 for renomination to the House of Representatives, but was an unsuccessful candidate for election to the United States Senate; appointed special assistant to the President on January 20, 1961, as director of the Food for Peace Program, and served until his resignation July 18, 1962, to become a candidate for the United States Senate; elected to the United States Senate in 1962; reelected in 1968 and again in 1974, and served from January 3, 1963 to January 3, 1981; chairman, Select Committee on Unmet Basic Needs (Ninetieth Congress), Select Committee on Nutrition and Human Needs (Ninety-first through Ninety-fifth Congresses); unsuccessful candidate for Democratic presidential nomination in 1968; unsuccessful Democratic candidate for election for President of the United States in 1972; lecturer and teacher; unsuccessful candidate for reelection to the United States Senate in 1980; is a resident of Washington, D.C.

**Bibliography:** Anson, Robert Sam. *McGovern: A Biography.* New York: Holt, Rinehart and Winston, 1972; McGovern, George. *Grassroots: The Autobiography of George McGovern.* New York: Random House, 1977.

**McGOWAN, Jonas Hartzell,** a Representative from Michigan; born in the township of Smithtown, Columbiana (now Mahoning) County, Ohio, April 2, 1837; attended a seminary in Alliance, Ohio; moved with his parents to Orland, Steuben County, Ind., in 1854; was graduated from the University of Michigan at Ann Arbor in 1861; taught in the city schools of Coldwater, Mich., for one year; during the Civil War served in the Fifth and Ninth Regiments, Michigan Volunteer Cavalry; returned to Coldwater, Mich.; studied law; was admitted to the bar in 1867 and commenced practice; prosecuting attorney of Branch County 1868-1872; member of the State senate; served as regent of the University of Michigan for seven years; elected as a Republican to the Forty-fifth and Forty-sixth Congresses (March 4, 1877-March 3, 1881); declined to be a candidate for renomination in 1880 to the Forty-seventh Congress; resumed the practice of his profession in Washington, D.C., where he died on July 5, 1909; interment in Oak Grove Cemetery, Coldwater, Mich.

**McGRANERY, James Patrick,** a Representative from Pennsylvania; born in Philadelphia, Pa., July 8, 1895; attended the parochial schools and Maher Preparatory School, Philadelphia, Pa.; during the First World War served as observation pilot in the United States Air Force and as adjutant in the One Hundred and Eleventh Infantry, 1917-1919; graduated from the law department of Temple University, Philadelphia, Pa., in 1928; admitted to the bar the same year and commenced practice in Philadelphia, Pa.; admitted to practice before the United States Supreme Court in 1939; member of the Pennsylvania Democratic committee, 1928-1932; unsuccessful candidate for election as district attorney of Philadelphia in 1931, and for election to the Seventy-fourth Congress in 1934; served as chairman of the Philadelphia Registration Commission in 1935; elected as a Democrat to the Seventy-fifth and to the three succeeding Congresses, and served from January 3, 1937 until his resignation on November 17, 1943, to become the assistant to the Attorney General of the United States, and served until October 9, 1946, at which time he was sworn in as a United States district judge for the eastern district of Pennsylvania, in which capacity he served until May 26, 1952, when he resigned to accept a Cabinet portfolio; Attorney General in the Cabinet of President Harry S Truman from May 27, 1952 until January 20, 1953; returned to the general practice of law in Washington, D.C., in 1954; died in Palm Beach, Fla., December 23, 1962; interment in Arlington National Cemetery, Va.

Bibliography: *DAB.*

**McGRATH, Christopher Columbus,** a Representative from New York; born in New York City May 15, 1902; attended parochial schools, was graduated from Clason Military Academy, Bronx, N.Y., in 1921 and from Fordham University School of Law, New York City, in 1924; was admitted to the bar in 1927 and commenced the practice of law in New York City; member of the State assembly, 1928-1935; elected judge of the Municipal Court of New York City in 1935, reelected in 1945 for ten-year term, and served until his resignation on December 31, 1948; elected as a Democrat to the Eighty-first and Eighty-second Congresses (January 3, 1949-January 3, 1953); was not a candidate for renomination in 1952; elected judge of the Surrogate's Court of Bronx County in 1952 for a fourteen-year term; relected in 1966; former member of faculty of Fordham University School of Law; was a resident of New York City until his death there July 7, 1986.

**McGRATH, James Howard,** a Senator from Rhode Island; born in Woonsocket, Providence County, R.I., November 28, 1903; attended parochial schools; graduated from La Salle Academy, Providence, R.I., in 1922, from Providence (R.I.) College in 1926, and from the law department of Boston University, Boston, Mass., in 1929; was admitted to the bar the same year and commenced practice in Providence; city solicitor of Central Falls, R.I., 1930-1934; engaged in the real estate and insurance business and was also interested in banking; chairman of the Democratic National Committee, 1947-1949; United States district attorney for Rhode Island from 1934 until his resignation in 1940, having been elected Governor; elected Governor of Rhode Island in 1940, reelected in 1942 and 1944, and served from January 7, 1941 until his resignation on October 6, 1945, having been appointed solicitor general of the United States; solicitor general until his resignation

in October 1946 to become a candidate for United States Senator; elected as a Democrat in 1946 to the United States Senate for the term commencing January 3, 1947, and served until his resignation on August 23, 1949; chairman, Committee on the District of Columbia (Eighty-first Congress); appointed Attorney General in the Cabinet of President Harry S Truman, and served from August 24, 1949 until his resignation on April 3, 1952; resumed the practice of law in Washington, D.C., and Providence, R.I.; unsuccessful candidate in 1960 for nomination to the United States Senate; died in Narragansett, R.I., September 2, 1966; interment in St. Francis Cemetery, Pawtucket, R.I.

**McGRATH, John Joseph,** a Representative from California; born in Limerick, Ireland, July 23, 1872; attended the national schools and Christian Brothers College in Cork; immigrated to the United States when seventeen and located in Chicago, Ill.; studied law for two years; engaged as a salesman for two years and as a sales manager for eighteen years; naturalized July 25, 1896; postmaster of San Mateo, Calif., 1916-1925; justice of the peace of San Mateo County 1928-1932; president of Tri-City Chamber of Commerce for four years; elected as a Democrat to the Seventy-third, Seventy-fourth, and Seventy-fifth Congresses (March 4, 1933-January 3, 1939); unsuccessful candidate for reelection in 1938 to the Seventy-sixth Congress; commissioner of immigration and naturalization for San Francisco, Calif., in 1939 and 1940; died in San Mateo, Calif., August 25, 1951; interment in St. John's Cemetery.

**McGRATH, Raymond Joseph,** a Representative from New York; born in Valley Stream, Nassau County, N.Y., March 27, 1942; attended the private schools; graduated from Valley Stream High School in 1959; B.S., New York State University, Brockport, 1963; M.A., New York University, New York City, 1968; teacher; author; deputy commissioner, Hempstead Township Parks and Recreation, 1965-1971; served in the New York State assembly, 1976-1980; elected as a Republican to the Ninety-seventh and to the five succeeding Congresses (January 3, 1981-January 3, 1993); was not a candidate for reelection in 1992 to the One Hundred Third Congress; is a resident of Valley Stream, N.Y.

**McGRATH, Thomas Charles, Jr.,** a Representative from New Jersey; born in Philadelphia, Pa., April 22, 1927; graduated from St. Joseph's Preparatory School, Philadelphia, Pa., in 1944; attended University of Notre Dame in 1944-1945; served in the United States Navy as an enlisted man, June 1945 to November 1945; graduated from the United States Naval Academy, Annapolis, Md., in 1950; served in the Atlantic and Pacific Fleets, 1950-1954; graduated from the University of Pennsylvania Law School in 1957; was admitted to the bar in 1958 and practiced law in Philadelphia, Pa., until 1963; deputy attorney general of New Jersey, 1964; practiced law in Atlantic City, N.J., 1964-1965; elected as a Democrat to the Eighty-ninth Congress (January 3, 1965-January 3, 1967); unsuccessful candidate for reelection in 1966 to the Ninetieth Congress; general counsel, Department of Housing and Urban Development, 1967-1969; treasurer, New Jersey Democratic State committee, 1969-1973; consultant to the construction and finance industry; 1969-1992; was a resident of Margate City, N.J.; died January 15, 1994.

**McGREGOR, J. Harry,** a Representative from Ohio; born on a farm near Unionport, Jefferson County, Ohio, September 30, 1896; attended the public schools, West Lafayette (Ohio) College, and Oberlin (Ohio) College; during the First World War served as a sergeant with the One Hundred and Seventy-sixth Field Artillery, United States Army, in 1917 and 1918; engaged in the lumber and general contracting business at West Lafayette, Ohio, 1918-1945; member of the school board of West Lafayette, Ohio, for eight years; member of the State house of representatives 1935-1940, serving as minority whip 1937-1939 and as majority leader and speaker pro tempore in 1939 and 1940; elected as a Republican to the Seventy-sixth Congress to fill the vacancy caused by the death of William A. Ashbrook; reelected to the Seventy-seventh and to the eight succeeding Congresses and served from February 27, 1940, until his death; chairman, Special Committee on Chamber Improvements (Eightieth and Eighty-third Congresses); had been renominated to the Eighty-sixth Congress; died in Coshocton, Ohio, October 7, 1958; interment in Fairfield Cemetery, West Lafayette, Ohio.

**McGREW, James Clark,** a Representative from West Virginia; born near Brandonville, Monongalia County, Va. (now West Virginia), September 14, 1813; attended the common schools; engaged in mercantile pursuits and banking; delegate to the Virginia secession convention in 1861 and voted against secession; mayor of Kingwood, Preston County, Va. (now West Virginia), 1863-1865; member of the West Virginia house of delegates 1863-1865; managing director of the West Virginia Insane Hospital for four years; elected as a Republican to the Forty-first and Forty-second Congresses (March 4, 1869-March 3, 1873); chairman, Committee on Mileage (Forty-second Congress); declined to be a candidate for renomination in 1872; again mayor of Kingwood in 1879 and 1880; resumed banking in Kingwood, W.Va., from 1886 until his death in Kingwood, W.Va., September 18, 1910; interment in Maplewood Cemetery.

**McGROARTY, John Steven,** a Representative from California; born near Wilkes-Barre in Foster Township, Luzerne County, Pa., August 20, 1862; attended the public schools and Harry Hillman Academy, Wilkes-Barre, Pa.; treasurer of Luzerne County, Pa., 1890-1893; studied law; was admitted to the bar in 1894 and commenced practice in Wilkes-Barre; moved to Montana and was employed in an executive position with the Anaconda Copper Mining Co. at Butte and Anaconda 1896-1901; moved to Los Angeles, Calif., in 1901 and engaged in journalism; elected poet laureate of California by the State legislature in 1933; author of numerous books and dramas; elected as a Democrat to the Seventy-fourth and Seventy-fifth Congresses (January 3, 1935-January 3, 1939); was not a candidate for renomination in 1938; resumed the profession of journalism in Tujunga, Los Angeles County, Calif.; unsuccessful candidate for the Democratic nomination for secretary of state of California in 1938; died in Los Angeles, Calif., August 7, 1944; interment in Calvary Cemetery.

**McGUGIN, Harold Clement,** a Representative from Kansas; born on a farm near Liberty, Montgomery County, Kans., November 22, 1893; attended the public schools of Liberty, Kans.; moved to Coffeyville, Kans., in 1908; was graduated from the high school at Coffeyville in 1912, and from the law department of Washburn College, Topeka, Kans., in 1915, and took a postgraduate course at the Inns of Court, London, England, in 1919; was admitted to the bar in 1915 and commenced practice in Coffeyville, Kans.; during the First World War served as a second lieutenant, Adjutant General's Department, at Brest, France; member of the State house of representatives 1927-1929; city attorney of Coffeyville in 1929; elected as a Republican to the Seventy-second and Seventy-third Congresses (March 4, 1931-January 3, 1935); unsuccessful candidate for reelection in 1934 to the Seventy-fourth Congress and for election in 1936 to the Seventy-fifth Congress; resumed the practice of law; enlisted in the United States Army in 1942, advancing from captain to lieutenant colonel, and served in France, where he contracted an incurable disease; died in the Army and Navy General Hospital at Hot Springs, Ark., March 7, 1946; interment in Restlawn Cemetery, Coffeyville, Kans.

**McGUIRE, Bird Segle** (cousin of William Neville), a Delegate and a Representative from Oklahoma; born in Belleville, St. Clair County, Ill., October 13, 1865; moved to Randolph County, Mo., in 1867 with his parents; attended the common schools; moved to Chautauqua County, Kans., in the spring of 1881, and then to Indian Territory; engaged in the cattle business; attended the State normal school at Emporia, Kans.; taught school several terms; later attended the law department of the University of Kansas at Lawrence; was admitted to the bar in 1889 and commenced practice in Chautauqua, Kans.; prosecuting attorney of Chautauqua County, Kans., 1890-1894; moved to Pawnee County, Okla., in 1894 and practiced law in Pawnee; appointed assistant United States attorney for Oklahoma Territory in 1897, in which capacity he served until after his nomination for Congress; elected as a Republican a Delegate to the Fifty-eighth and Fifty-ninth Congresses and served from March 4, 1903, to March 3, 1907; elected as a Representative to the Sixtieth and to the three succeeding Congresses and served from November 16, 1907, when Oklahoma was admitted as a State into the Union, until March 3, 1915; chairman, Committee on Expenditures in the Department of the Interior (Sixty-first Congress); was not a candidate for renomination in 1914 to the Sixty-fourth Congress; resumed the practice of his profession in Tulsa, Okla.; also owned and operated a large ranch near Bartlesville, Okla.; died in Tulsa, Okla., November 9, 1930; interment in Memorial Park Cemetery.

**McGUIRE, John Andrew,** a Representative from Connecticut; born in Wallingford, New Haven County, Conn., February 28, 1906; attended the public schools; student at Lyman Hall, Wallingford, Conn., in 1924 and graduated from Dartmouth College, Hanover, N.H., in 1928; employed as a bank clerk, 1928-1934; town clerk of Wallingford from January 1, 1934, to December 31, 1949; Democratic State Chairman in 1946; engaged in general insurance business in Wallingford, Conn., in 1935; delegate, Democratic State conventions, 1936-1956, and Democratic National Convention in 1950; elected as a Democrat to the Eighty-first and to the Eighty-second Congresses (January 3, 1949-January 3, 1953); unsuccessful candidate for reelection in 1952 to the Eighty-third Congress; resumed insurance, real estate, and travel business; member of Connecticut State Legislature 1961-1962; appointed deputy sheriff, New Haven County, November 10, 1969; executive director of Wallingford Housing Authority at the time of his death; died in Wallingford, Conn., May 28, 1976; interment in St. John's Cemetery.

**McHALE, Paul,** a Representative from Pennsylvania; born in Bethlehem, Northampton County, Pa., July 26, 1950; B.A., Lehigh University, 1972; J.D., Georgetown University Law Center, 1977; entered active duty, United States Marine Corps in 1972; released in 1974; also served in Persian Gulf in 1990, and as Marine infantry officer in Saudi Arabia and Kuwait during Operations Desert Shield and Desert Storm in 1991; United States Marine Corps Reserve, operations officer, Second Battalion, Twenty-fifth Marines; attorney in Bethlehem, Pa., 1977-1982 and 1991-1993; unsuccessful candidate for nomination in 1980 to the Ninety-seventh Congress; member, Pennsylvania house of representatives, 1982-1991; elected as a Democrat to the One Hundred Third and One Hundred Fourth Congresses (January 3, 1993-January 3, 1997); is a resident of Bethlehem, Pa.

**McHATTON, Robert Lytle,** a Representative from Kentucky; born in Fayette County, Va. (now Kentucky), November 17, 1788; attended the common schools; engaged in agricultural pursuits; member of the Kentucky house of representatives 1814-1816; served as major of the Seventy-seventh Regiment of Kentucky militia in 1816; elected to the Nineteenth Congress to fill the vacancy caused by the death of James Johnson; reelected to the Twentieth Congress and served from December 7, 1826, to March 3, 1829; resumed agricultural pursuits; died in Marion County, Ind., May 20, 1835; interment in the Old Cemetery, Georgetown, Ky.

**McHENRY, Henry Davis** (son of John Hardin McHenry), a Representative from Kentucky; born in Hartford, Ohio County, Ky., February 27, 1826; attended the public schools at Hartford, and graduated from the law department of Transylvania University, Lexington, Ky., in 1845; admitted to the bar in 1845 and commenced practice in Hartford; member of the Kentucky house of representatives 1851-1853 and 1865-1867; served in the Kentucky senate 1861-1865; member of the Democratic National Committee from 1872 until his death; elected as a Democrat to the Forty-second Congress (March 4, 1871-March 3, 1873); resumed the practice of his profession in Hartford; delegate to the Kentucky constitutional convention in 1890; died in Hartford, Ky., December 17, 1890; interment in Oakwood Cemetery.

**McHENRY, James,** a Delegate from Maryland; born in Ballymena, County Antrim, Ireland, November 16, 1753; pursued classical studies; immigrated to the United States about 1771 and settled in Philadelphia, Pa.; attended Newark Academy in Delaware; studied medicine under Dr. Benjamin Rush, Philadelphia, Pa.; during the Revolution was appointed assistant surgeon in 1776 and later surgeon in the Fifth Pennsylvania Battalion; secretary to General George Washington, 1778-1780; appointed in 1780 on the staff of General Lafayette and served in that capacity until the end of the war; member of the Maryland State senate, 1781-1786; Member of the Continental Congress, 1783-1785; delegate to the Federal Constitutional Convention in Philadelphia in 1787; appointed Secretary of War in the Cabinet of Presidents George Washington and John Adams and served from January 29, 1796, to May 13, 1800; resided at "Fayetteville," his country estate, near Baltimore, Md., until his death on May 3, 1816; interment in Westminster (Presbyterian) Churchyard, Baltimore, Md.

Bibliography: *DAB*; Robbins, Karen Evelyn. "James McHenry: His American Experience." Ph.D. dissertation, Columbia University, 1994; Steiner, Bernard C. *The Life and Correspondence of James McHenry, Secretary of War under Washington and Adams.* Cleveland: Burrows Brothers Co., 1907.

**McHENRY, John Geiser,** a Representative from Pennsylvania; born in Benton Township, Columbia County, Pa., April 26, 1868; attended the public schools and Orangeville Academy; banker and manufacturer, and also engaged in agricultural pursuits; organizer of the Grange national banks throughout Pennsylvania; elected as a Democrat to the Sixtieth, Sixty-first, and Sixty-second Congresses and served from March 4, 1907, until his death in Benton, Pa., December 27, 1912; interment in Benton Cemetery.

**McHENRY, John Hardin** (father of Henry Davis McHenry), a Representative from Kentucky; born near Springfield, Washington County, Ky., October 13, 1797; was tutored privately; studied law; was admitted to the bar in 1818 and commenced practice in Leitchfield, Ky.; appointed postmaster of Leitchfield on October 8, 1819; major of the Eighty-seventh Regiment, Kentucky Militia, in 1821; appointed Commonwealth attorney by Governor John Adair in 1822; moved to Hartford, Ky., in 1823; appointed Commonwealth attorney by Governor Thomas Metcalfe in 1831, and again by Governor James Morehead in 1837; commissioned colonel in the Kentucky militia in 1837; member of the Kentucky house of representatives from Ohio County in 1840; unsuccessful Whig candidate for election in 1840 to the Twenty-seventh Congress; appointed to the board of Transylvania University, Lexington, Ky., in 1843; elected as a Whig to the Twenty-ninth Congress (March 4, 1845-March 3, 1847); was nominated for reelection in 1846 to the Thirtieth Congress, but withdrew his name on the eve of election; resumed the practice of law; member of the Kentucky constitutional convention in 1849 and served as chairman; moved to Owensboro, Ky., in 1854; judge of the circuit court of several counties in 1854; died in Owensboro, Ky., on November 1, 1871; interment in Elmwood Cemetery.

**McHUGH, John Michael,** a Representative from New York; born in Watertown, Jefferson County, N.Y., September 29, 1948; graduated from Watertown High School, 1966; B.A., Utica College, Syracuse University, 1970; M.P.A., State University of New York, Nelson A. Rockefeller Graduate School of Public Affairs, 1977; confidential assistant to city manager, Watertown; chief of research to New York State Senator H. Douglas Barclay, nine years; member, New York State senate, 1985-1993; elected as a Republican to the One Hundred Third and One Hundred Fourth Congresses (January 3, 1993-January 3, 1997); is a resident of Pierrepont Manor, N.Y.

**McHUGH, Matthew Francis,** a Representative from New York; born in Philadelphia, Pa., December 6, 1938; attended St. Thomas Aquinas Elementary School, Brooklyn, N.Y.; graduated from Brooklyn Technical High School in 1956; B.S., Mount St. Mary's College, Emmitsburg, Md., 1960; J.D., Villanova (Pa.) Law School, 1963; admitted to the New York bar in 1964 and commenced practice in New York City; Ithaca (N.Y.) city prosecutor, 1968; Tompkins County, N.Y., district attorney, 1969-1972; member, New York State Democratic Committee, 1972-1974; elected as a Democrat to the Ninety-fourth and to the eight succeeding Congresses (January 3, 1975-January 3, 1993); was not a candidate for renomination in 1992 to the One Hundred Third Congress; counselor to the president, International Bank for Reconstruction and Development (World Bank); is a resident of Falls Church, Va.

**McILVAINE, Abraham Robinson,** a Representative from Pennsylvania; born in Ridley, Delaware County, Pa., August 14, 1804; attended the common schools; engaged in agricultural pursuits in Chester County, Pa.; member of the Pennsylvania house of representatives in 1836 and 1837; elected as a Whig to the Twenty-eighth, Twenty-ninth, and Thirtieth Congresses (March 4, 1843-March 3, 1849); chairman, Committee on Expenditures in the Department of War (Twenty-eighth Congress); unsuccessful candidate for renomination in 1848; resumed agricultural interests and also engaged in the iron business; died on his estate, "Springton Manor Farm" in Chester County, Pa., August 22, 1863; interment in Caln Orthodox Quaker Meeting Burial Ground near Downingtown; reinterment in Northwood Cemetery, Downingtown, Pa.

**McILVAINE, Joseph,** a Senator from New Jersey; born in Bristol, Bucks County, Pa., October 2, 1769; pursued an academic course; studied law; was admitted to the bar of the supreme court of New Jersey in 1790 and commenced practice in Burlington, N.J., in 1791; clerk of Burlington County 1796-1800; clerk of the county court 1800-1823; United States attorney for New Jersey 1801-1820; appointed judge of the superior court of New Jersey in 1818, but declined; elected to the United States Senate to fill the vacancy caused by the resignation of Samuel L. Southard and served from November 12, 1823, until his death in Burlington, N.J., August 19, 1826; interment in St. Mary's Cemetery.

**McINDOE, Walter Duncan,** a Representative from Wisconsin; born in Dumbartonshire, Scotland, March 30, 1819; immigrated to the United States in 1834; engaged in business in New York, Charleston, and St. Louis; finally settled in Wisconsin in 1845 and engaged in the lumber business; member of the State assembly in 1850, 1854, and 1855; unsuccessful candidate for gubernatorial nomination in 1857; provost marshal of Wisconsin during the Civil War; elected as a Republican to the Thirty-seventh Congress to fill the vacancy caused by the death of Luther Hanchett; reelected to the Thirty-eighth and Thirty-ninth Congresses and served from January 26, 1863, to March 3, 1867; chairman, Committee on Revolutionary Pensions (Thirty-ninth Congress); declined to be a candidate for renomination in 1866; resumed his interests in the lumber business; died in Wausau, Marathon County, Wis., on August 22, 1872; interment in Pine Grove Cemetery.

**McINNIS, Scott Steve,** a Representative from Colorado; born in Glenwood Springs, Garfield County, Colo., May 9, 1953; graduated from Glenwood Springs High School; B.A., Fort Lewis College, 1975; J.D., St. Mary's University Law School, 1980; attorney; volunteer firefighter; member, Colorado State house of representatives, 1983-1993, majority leader, two years; elected as a Republican to the One Hundred Third and One Hundred Fourth Congresses (January 3, 1993-January 3, 1997); is a resident of Grand Junction, Colo.

**McINTIRE, Clifford Guy,** a Representative from Maine; born in Perham, Aroostock County, Maine, May 4, 1908; attended the public schools of Perham and Washburn (Maine) High School; was graduated from the University of Maine College of Agriculture at Orono in 1930; engaged in farming at Perham, 1930-1952; appraiser, supervisor, and regional manager for Farm Credit Administration, Springfield, Mass., 1933-1947; assistant general manager of Maine Potato Growers, Inc., at Presque Isle, 1947-1951; elected as a Republican to the Eighty-second Congress, October 22, 1951, by special election to fill the vacancy caused by the death of Frank Fellows; reelected to the six succeeding Congresses, and served from October 22, 1951 to January 3, 1965; was not a candidate in 1964 for reelection to the House of Representatives, but was an unsuccessful candidate for election to the United States Senate; director, American Farm Bureau Federation, Natural Resources Department; member of President Richard M. Nixon's Task Force on Rural Development, 1969-1970; member, Advisory Council, Public Land Law Review Commission, 1969-1970; appointed by President Gerald R. Ford in September 1974 to the newly created United States Railway Association; died in Bangor, Maine, October 1, 1974; interment in Fairview Cemetery, Perham, Maine.

**McINTIRE, Rufus,** a Representative from Maine; born in York, Maine, December 19, 1784; attended the common schools; was graduated from Dartmouth College, Hanover, N.H., in 1809; studied law; was admitted to the bar and commenced practice in Parsonfield, Maine, in 1812; served in the War of 1812; member of the Maine State house of representatives in 1820; prosecuting attorney of York County from 1820 until 1843; member of the boundary commission in 1820 to settle the northern and northeastern boundaries of Maine; elected to the Twentieth Congress to fill the vacancy caused by the death of William Burleigh; reelected as a Jacksonian to the Twenty-first and to the two succeeding Congresses and served from September 10, 1827, to March 3, 1835; State land agent in 1839 and 1840; appointed by President James K. Polk United States marshal for Maine in 1845, and served as surveyor of customs of the port of Portland, Maine, from April 13, 1853, to April 1, 1857; died in Parsonfield, Maine, April 28, 1866; interment in Middleroad Cemetery.

**McINTIRE, William Watson,** a Representative from Maryland; born in Chambersburg, Franklin County, Pa., June 30, 1850; moved with his parents to Washington County, Md.; attended public and private schools; learned the trade of machinist; moved in July 1872 to Baltimore; received an appointment in the United States Railway Mail Service in 1874; remained in this service until 1885, when he resigned; attended Hagerstown (Md.) Academy; was graduated from the law department of the University of Maryland at Baltimore and was admitted to the bar in Baltimore, Md.; elected as a Republican to the city council of Baltimore in 1887 and 1888; in the campaign of 1895 was treasurer of the Maryland Republican State and city committees; general agent of the United States Life Insurance Co. 1905-1912; elected as a Republican to the Fifty-fifth Congress (March 4, 1897-March 3, 1899); unsuccessful candidate for reelection in 1898 to the Fifty-sixth Congress; member of Baltimore Sewerage Commission in 1911 and 1912; died on a boat in the Middle River, in Baltimore County, Md., March 30, 1912; interment in Loudon Park Cemetery, Baltimore, Md.

**McINTOSH, David Martin,** a Representative from Indiana; born in Oakland, Calif., June 8, 1958; attended the public schools and graduated from East Noble High School; B.A., Yale University, 1980; J.D., University of Chicago School of Law, 1983; special assistant to Attorney General; special assistant to President Ronald Reagan for domestic affairs; liaison to the President's Commission on Privatization; special assistant and deputy counsel to Vice President Dan Quayle; executive director, President's Council on Competitiveness; fellow, Hudson Institute Competitiveness Center; senior fellow, Citizens For A Sound Economy; elected as a Republican to the One Hundred Fourth Congress (January 3, 1995-January 3, 1997); is a resident of Muncie, Ind.

**McINTOSH, Lachlan,** a Delegate from Georgia; born near Raits, in Badenoch, Scotland, March 17, 1725; immigrated with his parents to Georgia in 1736 and established the settlement of New Inverness; acquired an education and became a surveyor; delegate to the Provincial Congress at Savannah in 1775; entered the military service of Georgia and later served in the Continental Army and rose to the rank of brigadier general; fought a duel on May 16, 1777, with Button Gwinnett, fatally wounding his opponent; elected to the Continental Congress in 1784 but did not attend; died in Savannah, Ga., February 20, 1806.

Bibliography: *DAB*; Jackson, Harvey H. *Lachlan McIntosh and the Politics of Revolutionary Georgia.* Athens: University of Georgia Press, 1979.

**McINTOSH, Robert John,** a Representative from Michigan; born in Port Huron, Saint Clair County, Mich., September 16, 1922; attended public schools and Michigan State University, 1940-1942; graduated from University of Michigan Law School in 1948; was admitted to the bar in 1948 and commenced the practice of law in Port Huron, Mich.; served in the United States Air Force, 1942-1945 and was assigned to the Eighth Air Force in England as a fighter pilot; assistant prosecuting attorney, Saint Clair County, 1949-1951; postmaster at Port Huron, Mich., from October 1, 1953, to February 4, 1955; elected as a Republican to the Eighty-fifth Congress (January 3, 1957-January 3, 1959); unsuccessful candidate for reelection in 1958 to the Eighty-sixth Congress, and for election in 1960 to the Eighty-seventh Congress; chairman, Michigan State Public Service Commission, 1963; executive assistant to Governor George W. Romney of Michigan, 1964-1965; director, Michigan Department of Commerce, 1966; resumed the practice of law; is a resident of Port Huron, Mich., and Washington, D.C.

**McINTYRE, John Joseph,** a Representative from Wyoming; born on a farm in Dewey County, Okla., December 17, 1904; attended the grade schools at Ramona, Okla.; was graduated from high school at Tulsa, Okla., and from the law department of the University of Colorado at Boulder in 1928; was admitted to the bar in 1929 and commenced practice in Glenrock, Wyo.; moved to Douglas, Converse County, Wyo., in 1931 and continued the practice of law; served as county and prosecuting attorney of Converse County, 1933-1936; special attorney for the Department of Justice, Washington, D.C., 1936-1938; associate attorney in the solicitor's office, Department of Agriculture, Washington, D.C., in 1938; member of the Wyoming National Guard, with rank of captain, 1935-1941; elected as a Democrat to the Seventy-seventh Congress (January 3, 1941-January 3, 1943); unsuccessful candidate for reelection in 1942 to the Seventy-eighth Congress; deputy attorney general of Wyoming, 1943-1944; served as a staff sergeant, Headquarters Battery, Six Hundred and Sixtieth Field Artillery, from February 9, 1944 to August 22, 1945; decorated with the French Croix de Guerre; Wyoming State auditor in 1946; unsuccessful candidate for election in 1946 to the Eightieth Congress; unsuccessful candidate in 1950 for election for Governor of Wyoming; elected in 1960 as a justice of the Wyoming Supreme Court for a four-year term; reelected in 1964, and served until his death in Cheyenne, Wyo., November 30, 1974; interment in Memorial Gardens.

**McINTYRE, Thomas James,** a Senator from New Hampshire; born in Laconia, Belknap County, N.H., February 20, 1915; attended the public and parochial schools of Laconia; graduated from Manlius (N.Y.) Military School in 1933; graduated from Dartmouth College, Hanover, N.H., in 1937, and Boston (Mass.) University Law School in 1940; was admitted to practice law before the New Hampshire Supreme Court in 1940; served in the United States Army with the Three Hundred Seventy-sixth Infantry, Ninety-fourth Division, 1942-1946, and was discharged as a major; mayor of Laconia, N.H., 1949-1951; city solicitor in 1952 and 1953; unsuccessful candidate for election in 1954 to the Eighty-fourth Congress; elected as a Democrat to the United States Senate, November 6, 1962, to fill the unexpired term of Styles Bridges ending January 3, 1967; reelected in 1966, and again in 1972, and served from November 7, 1962, until January 3, 1979; unsuccessful candidate for reelection in 1978; was a resident of Laconia, N.H., and Tequesta, Fla., until his death in West Palm Beach, Fla., on August 8, 1992; interment in St. Lambert Cemetery, Laconia, N.H.

**Bibliography:** McIntyre, Thomas J., with John C. Obert. *The Fear Brokers.* New York: Pilgrim Press, 1979.

**McJUNKIN, Ebenezer,** a Representative from Pennsylvania; born at Center Top, Butler County, Pa., March 28, 1819; attended the common schools; was graduated from Jefferson College, Canonsburg, Pa., in 1841; studied law; was admitted to the bar in 1843, and commenced practice in Butler, Butler County, Pa.; deputy attorney general for Butler County in 1850; delegate to the Republican National Convention in 1860; served during the Civil War as first lieutenant of militia; elected as a Republican to the Forty-second and Forty-third Congresses and served from March 4, 1871, until he resigned January 1, 1875; chairman, Committee on Expenditures in the Department of the Navy (Forty-third Congress); president judge of the seventeenth judicial district of Pennsylvania 1875-1885; resumed the practice of his profession until 1900, when he retired; died in Butler, Pa., November 10, 1907; interment in North Cemetery.

**McKAIG, William McMahon,** a Representative from Maryland; born in Cumberland, Allegany County, Md., July 29, 1845; attended the Carroll School and the Allegany County Academy; studied law; was admitted to the Allegany bar in 1868; moved to Colorado Territory in 1873; returned to Maryland; appointed city attorney of Cumberland in 1876; member of the State house of delegates in 1877; served in the State senate in 1887; mayor of Cumberland in 1890; elected as a Democrat to the Fifty-second and Fifty-third Congresses (March 4, 1891-March 3, 1895); was not a candidate for renomination in 1894; resumed the practice of his profession; died in Cumberland, Md., June 6, 1907; interment in Rose Hill Cemetery.

**McKAY, James Iver,** a Representative from North Carolina; born near Elizabethtown, Bladen County, N.C., in 1793; pursued classical studies; studied law; was admitted to the bar and practiced; appointed United States attorney for the district of North Carolina on March 6, 1817; served in the State senate 1815-1819, 1822, 1826, and 1830; elected as a Jacksonian to the Twenty-second through Twenty-fourth Congresses and as a Democrat to the Twenty-fifth through Thirtieth Congresses (March 4, 1831-March 3, 1849); chairman, Committee on Military Affairs (Twenty-fifth Congress), Committee on the Post Office and Post Roads (Twenty-sixth Congress), Committee on Expenditures in the Department of War (Twenty-seventh Congress), Committee on Ways and Means (Twenty-eighth and Twenty-ninth Congresses); died in Goldsboro, Wayne County, N.C., September 4, 1853.

**Bibliography:** *DAB.*

**McKAY, Koln Gunn,** a Representative from Utah; born in Ogden, Weber County, Utah, February 23, 1925; attended the Weber County public schools and Weber State College, 1958-1960; B.S., Utah State University, Logan, 1962; entered the United States Coast Guard as an apprentice seaman in 1943, released in 1946 as a petty officer third class, following service in the Twelfth Naval District; businessman and teacher; member of the Utah State house of representatives, 1962-1966, and the Utah Legislative Council, 1963-1966; administrative assistant to Governor Calvin L. Rampton of Utah, 1967-1970; president of Ogden Stake, Church of Jesus Christ of Latter-Day Saints, 1967-1970; chairman, Utah Long Range Goals and Planning Committee, 1965-1967; member, legislative task force on Utah Government Reorganization Committee (Little Hoover Commission), 1965-1967; delegate, Utah State Democratic conventions, 1962-1970; elected as a Democrat to the Ninety-second and to the four succeeding Congresses (January 3, 1971-January 3, 1981); unsuccessful candidate for reelection in 1980 to the Ninety-seventh Congress; president, Scottish Mission, Church of Jesus Christ of Latter-Day Saints, 1981-1984; is a resident of Huntsville, Utah.

**McKEAN, James Bedell** (nephew of Samuel McKean), a Representative from New York; born in Bennington, Vt., August 5, 1821; moved to New York; pursued an academic course; taught in the district schools for several terms and was one of the professors in Jonesville Academy for some time; superintendent of the common schools in Half Moon in 1842; elected colonel of the One Hundred and Forty-fourth Regiment, New York Militia, in 1844; studied law; was admitted to the bar in 1849 and commenced practice in Ballston Spa, N.Y.; moved to Saratoga Springs in 1851; county judge of Saratoga County, 1854-1858; elected as a Republican to the Thirty-sixth and Thirty-seventh Congresses (March 4, 1859-March 3, 1863); chairman, Committee on Expenditures in the Department of State (Thirty-sixth and Thirty-seventh Congresses); during the Civil War organized the Seventy-seventh Regiment, New York Volunteers, in 1861 and served as colonel of the regiment until July 27, 1863, when he resigned his commission; appointed treaty commissioner to Honduras in 1865; appointed chief justice of the supreme court of Utah Territory by President Ulysses S. Grant in 1870 and served until 1875; died in Salt Lake City, Utah, January 5, 1879; interment in Mount Olivet Cemetery.

**McKEAN, Samuel** (uncle of James Bedell McKean), a Representative and a Senator from Pennsylvania; born in Kishocaquillas Valley in Huntington County, Pa., April 7, 1787; attended the common schools; engaged in mercantile pursuits in Burlington, Pa.; member of the board of commissioners for Bradford County in 1814; member, Pennsylvania house of representatives 1815-1819; served in the Pennsylvania militia as major general; elected to the Eighteenth, Nineteenth, and Twentieth Congresses (March 4, 1823-March 3, 1829); chairman, Committee on Post Office and Post Roads (Twentieth Congress); member, Pennsylvania senate 1829-1830; presidential elector on the Democratic ticket in 1832; elected as a Jacksonian to the United States Senate and served from March 4, 1833, to March 3, 1839; chairman, Committee to Audit and Control the Contingent Expense (Twenty-fourth and Twenty-fifth Congresses); died in West Burlington, Bradford County, Pa., December 14, 1841; interment in the Old Church Cemetery in the eastern part of West Burlington Township.

**Bibliography:** *DAB.*

**McKEAN, Thomas,** a Delegate from Delaware; born in New London, Chester County, Pa., March 19, 1734; was privately taught; engaged as clerk to the prothonotary of the court of common pleas for two years; deputy prothonotary and register for the probate of wills for New Castle County, studying law at the same time; was admitted to the bar in 1755 and commenced practice in New Castle, Del.; appointed deputy attorney general for Sussex County in 1756 and served until 1758, when he resigned; went to Great Britain and resumed the study of law at the Middle Temple in London; member of the Delaware House of Assembly, 1762-1775, and served as speaker in 1772; appointed one of the three trustees of the loan office for New Castle County in 1764 and served until 1776; member of the Stamp-Act Congress in 1765; appointed by the Governor sole notary for the lower counties of Delaware on July 10, 1765; in the same year received the commission of a justice of the peace, of the court of common pleas and quarter sessions, and of the orphans' court for New Castle County; appointed collector of the port of New Castle in 1771; Member of the Continental Congress, 1774-1776, 1778-1782 and served as President of Congress in 1781; a signer of the Declaration of Independence; member of the State house of representatives in 1776 and 1777, and served as speaker in the latter year; President of the State of Delaware in 1777; chief justice of Pennsylvania, 1777-1799; served in the Revolutionary War; member of the convention of Pennsylvania which ratified the Constitution of the United States on December 12, 1787; delegate to the State constitutional convention in 1789; Governor of Pennsylvania from December 17, 1799 until December 20, 1808; died in Philadelphia, Pa., June 24, 1817; interment in Laurel Hill Cemetery.

**Bibliography:** *DAB*; Coleman, John M. *Thomas McKean: Forgotten Leader of the Revolution.* Rockaway, N.J.: American Faculty Press, 1975; Rowe, G.S. *Thomas McKean: The Shaping of an American Republicanism.* Boulder: Colorado Associated University Press, 1978.

**McKEE, George Colin,** a Representative from Mississippi; born in Joliet, Ill., October 2, 1837; attended Knox College and Lombard College, both at Galesburg, Ill.; studied law; was admitted to the bar in 1858 and commenced practice in Centralia, Ill.; city attorney of Centralia 1858-1861; served throughout the Civil War with the Eleventh Regiment, Illinois Volunteer Infantry; resumed the practice of law in Vicksburg, Miss., and engaged in planting in Hinds County; appointed register in bankruptcy in 1867; member of the State constitutional convention in 1868; elected as a Republican to the Fortieth Congress, but his credentials were never presented to the House; elected as a Republican to the Forty-first, Forty-second, and Forty-third Congresses (March 4, 1869-March 3, 1875); chairman, Committee on Territories (Forty-third Congress); was appointed postmaster of Jackson, Miss., and served from June 28, 1881, to November 12, 1885; resumed the practice of his profession; receiver of public moneys from 1889 until his death in Jackson, Miss., on November 17, 1890; interment in Greenwood Cemetery.

**McKEE, John,** a Representative from Alabama; born in Augusta (now Rockbridge) County, Va., in 1771; attended Liberty Hall Academy (now Washington and Lee University), Lexington, Va.; United States agent for the Choctaw Indians in East Mississippi, 1802-1816; appointed an officer in the land office at Tuscaloosa on March 9, 1821, and was one of the first settlers of Tuscaloosa County; member of the commission to settle the boundary line between the States of Kentucky and Tennessee; elected to the Eighteenth and to the two succeeding Congresses (March 4, 1823-March 3, 1829); was not a candidate for renomination in 1828 to the Twenty-first Congress; was one of the commissioners in 1829 who negotiated the Treaty of Dancing Rabbit, by which a large tract of land west of the Tombigbee River was acquired from the Choctaw Indians; died at his home, "Hill of Howth," near Boligee, Green County, Ala., August 12, 1832; interment in Bethsalem Cemetery, Boligee, Ala.

**Bibliography:** *DAB*.

**McKEE, Samuel,** a Representative from Kentucky; born near Lexington, Augusta (now Rockbridge) County, Va., October 13, 1774; was graduated from Liberty Hall Academy (now Washington and Lee University), Lexington, Va., in 1794; studied law; was admitted to the bar in 1800 and commenced practice in Somerset, Pulaski County, Ky.; served as surveyor of Pulaski County; moved to Lancaster, Garrard County, Ky., in 1807 and continued the practice of law; member of the Kentucky house of representatives, 1802-1808; elected as a Republican to the Eleventh and to the three succeeding Congresses (March 4, 1809-March 3, 1817); chairman, Committee on Public Lands (Thirteenth Congress); served in the War of 1812 on the staff of General William Henry Harrison; after the war resumed the practice of his profession in Lancaster; appointed by President James Monroe a member of the commission to clear the Ohio and Mississippi Rivers of obstructions, and served until his death in Hickman County, Ky., on October 16, 1826; interment in Frankfort Cemetery, Frankfort, Ky.

**McKEE, Samuel,** a Representative from Kentucky; born near Mount Sterling, Montgomery County, Ky., November 5, 1833; attended the common schools; graduated from Miami University, Oxford, Ohio, in 1857, and the Cincinnati (Ohio) Law School in 1858; admitted to the bar and commenced practice in Mount Sterling, Ky., in 1858; served in the Union Army during the Civil War as a captain in the Fourteenth Regiment, Kentucky Volunteer Cavalry; elected as an Unconditional Unionist to the Thirty-ninth Congress (March 4, 1865-March 3, 1867); successfully contested as a Republican the election of John D. Young to the Fortieth Congress and served from June 22, 1868, to March 3, 1869; was not a candidate for renomination in 1868; delegate to the Southern Loyalist Convention at Philadelphia in 1866; pension agent in Louisville, Ky., 1869-1871; resumed the practice of law; died in Louisville, Ky., December 11, 1898; interment in Cave Hill Cemetery.

**McKEIGHAN, William Arthur,** a Representative from Nebraska; born in Millville, Cumberland County, N.J., January 19, 1842; moved with his parents to Fulton County, Ill., in 1848; attended the common schools; during the Civil War enlisted in the Eleventh Regiment, Illinois Volunteer Cavalry, in September 1861; at the close of the war located on a farm near Pontiac, Ill., and engaged in agricultural pursuits; moved to Nebraska in 1880 and resumed agricultural pursuits near Red Cloud; took an active interest in organizing the Farmers' Alliance; probate judge of Webster County 1885-1887; unsuccessful candidate in 1888 for election to the Fifty-first Congress; elected as a Populist to the Fifty-second and Fifty-third Congresses (March 4, 1891-March 3, 1895); unsuccessful candidate in 1894 for reelection to the Fifty-fourth Congress; died in Hastings, Adams County, Nebr., December 15, 1895; interment in Red Cloud Cemetery, Red Cloud, Webster County, Nebr.

**McKELLAR, Kenneth Douglas,** a Representative and a Senator from Tennessee; born in Richmond, Dallas County, Ala., January 29, 1869; received private instruction from his parents and his sister; graduated from the University of Alabama at Tuscaloosa in 1891 and from its law department in 1892; moved to Tennessee in 1892 and settled in Memphis; was admitted to the bar the same year and commenced the practice of law; presidential elector on the Democratic ticket in 1904; elected as a Democrat to the Sixty-second Congress to fill the vacancy caused by the death of George W. Gordon; reelected to the two succeeding Congresses, and served from November 9, 1911 to March 3, 1917; did not seek renomination in 1916 to the House of Representatives, having become a candidate for Senator; elected to the United States Senate in 1916; reelected in 1922, 1928, 1934, 1940, and 1946, and served from March 4, 1917 to January 3, 1953; unsuccessful candidate for renomination in 1952; served as President pro tempore of the Senate during the Seventy-ninth, Eighty-first and Eighty-second Congresses; chairman, Committee on Civil Service and Retrenchment (Sixty-fifth Congress), Committee on Post Office and Post Roads (Seventy-third through Seventy-ninth Congresses), Committee on Appropriations (Seventy-ninth through Eighty-second Congresses); retired from active pursuits; died in Memphis, Tenn., October 25, 1957; interment in Elmwood Cemetery.

**Bibliography:** *DAB*; McKellar, Kenneth. *Tennessee Senators as seen by one of their successors.* Kingsport, Tenn.: Southern Publishers, Inc., 1942; Pope, Robert Dean. "Senatorial Baron: The Long Political Career of Kenneth C. McKellar." Ph.D. dissertation, Yale University, 1975.

**McKENNA, Joseph,** a Representative from California; born in Philadelphia, Pa., August 10, 1843; moved with his parents to Benicia, Calif., in January 1855; attended the public schools and was graduated from the law department of Benicia Collegiate Institute in 1865; was admitted to the bar in 1865 and commenced practice in Benicia, Calif.; moved to Fairfield, Solano County, in 1866 and continued the practice of law for eight years; district attorney of Solano County, 1866-1868; member of the California State house of representatives in 1875 and 1876; unsuccessful candidate in 1876 for election to the Forty-fifth Congress, and in 1878 to the Forty-sixth Congress; elected as a Republican to the Forty-ninth and to the three succeeding Congresses and served from March 4, 1885, to March 28, 1892, when he resigned; appointed by President Benjamin Harrison as United States circuit judge for the ninth judicial circuit on February 11, 1892, and was confirmed on March 17, 1892; served five years and resigned; appointed Attorney General in the Cabinet of President William McKinley, and served from March 7, 1897 to January 25, 1898, when he resigned, having been nominated by President McKinley on December 16, 1897, as an Associate Justice of the United States Supreme Court; was confirmed by the Senate on January 21, 1898 and served until January 25, 1925, when he resigned; died in Washington, D.C., November 21, 1926; interment in Mount Olivet Cemetery.

**Bibliography:** *DAB*.

**McKENNAN, Thomas McKean Thompson,** a Representative from Pennsylvania; born in New Castle, New Castle County, Del., March 31, 1794; moved to Washington, Pa.; attended the public schools; was graduated from Washington (now Washington and Jefferson) College, Washington, Pa., in 1810; studied law; was admitted to the bar in 1814 and commenced practice in Washington, Pa.; deputy attorney general in 1815 and 1816; elected as an Anti-Masonic candidate to the Twenty-second and to the three succeeding Congresses (March 4, 1831-March 3, 1839); elected as a Whig to the Twenty-seventh Congress to fill the vacancy caused by the death of Joseph Lawrence, and served from May 30, 1842 to March 3, 1843; chairman, Committee on Roads and Canals (Twenty-seventh Congress); president of the Pennsylvania Electoral College in 1848; appointed Secretary of the Interior in the Cabinet of President Millard Fillmore, and served from August 15 to September 12, 1850; resigned and became president of the Hempfield Railroad (now the Baltimore and Ohio Railroad); died in Reading, Pa., July 9, 1852; interment in the Washington Cemetery, Washington, Pa.

**Bibliography:** *DAB*.

**McKENNEY, William Robertson,** a Representative from Virginia; born in Petersburg, Dinwiddie County, Va., December 2, 1851; attended McCabe's University School at Petersburg and the University of Virginia at Charlottesville; taught school; graduated from the law school of the University of Virginia in June 1876; admitted to the bar and practiced in Petersburg, Va.; elected president of the city council of Petersburg in 1888 and served six years; delegate to the Democratic National Convention in 1892; member of the Virginia Democratic executive committee; presented credentials as a Democratic Member-elect to the Fifty-fourth Congress and served from March 4, 1895, to May 2, 1896, when he was succeeded by Robert T. Thorp, who successfully contested his election; resumed the practice of law in Petersburg, Va., and died there January 3, 1916; interment in Blandford Cemetery.

**McKENTY, Jacob Kerlin,** a Representative from Pennsylvania; born in Douglassville, Amity Township, Berks County, Pa., January 19, 1827; was graduated from Yale College in 1848 and from the law department of that college in 1851; was admitted to the bar in 1851 and commenced practice in Reading, Pa.; prosecuting attorney of Berks County 1856-1858; elected as a Democrat to the Thirty-sixth Congress to fill the vacancy caused by the death of John Schwartz and served from December 3, 1860, to March 3, 1861; was not a candidate for reelection in 1860; unsuccessful candidate for nomination in 1862 and 1864; resumed the practice of his profession in Reading, Pa.; died in Douglassville, Berks County, Pa., January 3, 1866; interment in St. Gabriel's Episcopal Church Cemetery.

**McKENZIE, Charles Edgar,** a Representative from Louisiana; born in Pelican, De Soto Parish, La., October 3, 1896; attended the public schools of Monroe, La., and Louisiana State University at Baton Rouge; volunteered for service on the Mexican border in 1916 with the Louisiana National Guard; during the First World War was mustered into the Federal service on April 1, 1917, and commissioned a second lieutenant in the One Hundred and Fifty-sixth Infantry, serving overseas in the Thirty-ninth and Eighty-ninth Divisions from June 1918 to September 1919; engaged in oil drilling and as an oil operator at Wichita Falls and Burkburnett, Tex., 1919-1921; returned to Monroe, La., in 1921, and engaged in the oil, gas, finance-brokerage, trucking, and insurance businesses; also agricultural pursuits; served as executive assistant director in the Louisiana Department of Highways 1940-1942; director of planning, housing, and aeronautics in the Louisiana Department of Public Works in 1942 and 1943; elected as a Democrat to the Seventy-eighth and Seventy-ninth Congresses (January 3, 1943-January 3, 1947); unsuccessful candidate for renomination in 1946; resumed supervision of his business enterprises; died in Monroe, La., June 7, 1956; interment in Riverview Cemetery.

**McKENZIE, James Andrew** (uncle of John McKenzie Moss), a Representative from Kentucky; born in Bennettstown, Christian County, Ky., August 1, 1840; attended the common schools of Christian County and Centre College, Danville, Ky.; studied law; was admitted to the bar in 1861 and commenced practice in Hopkinsville, Ky.; also engaged in agricultural pursuits; during the Civil War served as a private in the Confederate Army; member of the Kentucky house of representatives, 1867-1871; elected as a Democrat to the Forty-fifth and to the two succeeding Congresses (March 4, 1877-March 3, 1883); unsuccessful candidate for renomination in 1882 to the Forty-eighth Congress; secretary of state of Kentucky under Governor J. Proctor Knott, 1884-1888; commissioner from Kentucky to the World's Columbian Exposition at Chicago, Ill., in 1893; appointed Envoy Extraordinary and Minister Plenipotentiary to Peru by President Grover Cleveland on April 4, 1893 and served until April 1897; settled on his farm near Long View, Ky.; died at Oak Grove, Christian County, Ky., on June 25, 1904; interment in Fairview Cemetery, Bowling Green, Ky.

**McKENZIE, John Charles,** a Representative from Illinois; born on a farm near Elizabeth, Woodbine Township, Jo Daviess County, Ill., February 18, 1860; attended the common schools, and the normal school at Valparaiso, Ind.; taught school in Jo Daviess County for six years; engaged in the grain, flour, and feed business; studied law; was admitted to the bar in 1890 and commenced the practice of his profession in Elizabeth, Ill.; director of the Elizabeth Exchange Bank; member of the State house of representatives 1892-1896; member of Illinois Claims Commission 1896-1900; served in the State senate from 1900 until his resignation on May 11, 1911, and was president pro tempore 1903-1905; elected as a Republican to the Sixty-second and to the six succeeding Congresses (March 4, 1911-March 3, 1925); chairman, Committee on Military Affairs (Sixty-eighth Congress); was not a candidate for renomination in 1924; appointed in 1925 a member of the commission to report the most practical method of utilizing the nitrate plant at Muscle Shoals, Ala.; resumed the practice of his profession in Elizabeth, Ill., until his death in that city on September 17, 1941; interment in Elizabeth Cemetery.

**McKENZIE, Lewis,** a Representative from Virginia; born in Alexandria, Va., October 7, 1810; pursued an academic course; prominently engaged in shipping and mercantile pursuits; member of the city council 1855-1859, 1863-1866, and 1868-1870; mayor of Alexandria 1861-1863; elected as a Unionist to the Thirty-seventh Congress to fill the vacancy caused by the unseating of Charles H. Upton and served from February 16, 1863, to March 3, 1863; upon the readmission of Virginia to representation was elected as a Conservative to the Forty-first Congress and served from January 31, 1870, to March 3, 1871; president of the Washington & Ohio Railroad Co.; appointed postmaster of Alexandria, Va., in 1878; again a member of the city council 1887-1891; died in Alexandria, Va., June 28, 1895; interment in Presbyterian Cemetery.

**McKEON, Howard Philip (Buck),** a Representative from California; born in Los Angeles, Calif., September 9, 1938; graduated, Verdugo Hills High School, Tujunga, Calif.; B.S., Brigham Young University, 1985; trustee and president, William S. Hart School District, 1979-1987; chairman and founding director, Valencia National Bank, 1987 to present; mayor and council member, Santa Clarita, Calif., 1987-1992; co-owner, Howard and Phil's Western Wear, Inc.; member, California Republican Central Committee, 1988-1992; elected as a Republican to the One Hundred Third and One Hundred Fourth Congresses (January 3, 1993-January 3, 1997); is a resident of Santa Clarita, Calif.

**McKEON, John,** a Representative from New York; born in Albany, N.Y., March 29, 1808; attended private schools and was graduated from the law department of Columbia College (later Columbia University), New York City, in 1828; was admitted to the bar the same year and practiced in New York City; a member of the State assembly 1832-1834; elected as a Jacksonian to the Twenty-fourth Congress (March 4, 1835-March 3, 1837); unsuccessful candidate for reelection in 1836 to the Twenty-fifth Congress; elected as a Democrat to the Twenty-seventh Congress (March 4, 1841-March 3, 1843); unsuccessful candidate for reelection in 1842 to the Twenty-eighth Congress; district attorney for New York County 1846-1850; appointed by President Pierce as United States district attorney for the southern district of New York and served from July 10, 1854, to January 7, 1858; again district attorney for New York County from November 1881 until his death in New York City November 22, 1883; interment in family vault under St. Patrick's Cathedral on Mott Street.

**McKEOUGH, Raymond Stephen,** a Representative from Illinois; born in Chicago, Ill., April 29, 1888; attended public and parochial schools; was graduated from De La Salle Institute, Chicago, Ill., in 1905; worked in the Union Stock Yards, Chicago, Ill., 1905-1909; employed in clerical work with a railroad from 1909 until 1925; engaged in the investment securities business, 1925-1929, and in the brokerage business, 1929-1934; delegate to the Democratic National Convention of 1940; elected as a Democrat to the Seventy-fourth and to the three succeeding Congresses (January 3, 1935-January 3, 1943); was not a candidate in 1942 for renomination to the House of Representatives, but was an unsuccessful candidate for election to the United States Senate; regional administrator of the Office of Price Administration, Chicago, Ill., from February 5, 1943, to January 15, 1944; appointed a member of the United States Maritime Commission on October 11, 1945, and served until 1950; Commissioner, International Claims Commission of the United States, 1951-1953; associated with Great American Oil Co., Chicago, in 1956; appointed administrative assistant to the State's attorney, criminal division, Chicago, Ill., December 3, 1956, and resigned December 3, 1960; engaged in general insurance

business; resided in Chicago, Ill., until his death on December 16, 1979; interment at St. Mary's Cemetery, Evergreen Park, Ill.

**McKEOWN, Thomas Deitz,** a Representative from Oklahoma; born in Blackstock, Chester County, S.C., June 4, 1878; attended the common schools, studied under a private tutor and attended lectures at Cornell University, Ithaca, N.Y., in 1898; was admitted to the bar in 1899 and began practice in Malvern, Ark.; moved to Ada, Indian Territory (now Oklahoma), in 1901 and resumed the practice of law; appointed a member of the first State bar commission, and elected president in 1909; judge of the seventh district of Oklahoma, 1910-1914; presiding judge of the fifth division of the supreme court commission in 1915 and 1916; elected as a Democrat to the Sixty-fifth and Sixty-sixth Congresses (March 4, 1917-March 3, 1921); unsuccessful candidate for reelection in 1920 to the Sixty-seventh Congress; elected to the Sixty-eighth and to the five succeeding Congresses (March 4, 1923-January 3, 1935); unsuccessful candidate for renomination in 1934 to the Seventy-fourth Congress; moved to Chicago, Ill., and resumed the practice of law in 1935 and 1936; returned to Ada, Okla., in 1937 and engaged in farming and oil production; delegate to the Democratic State convention in 1942; county attorney of Pontotoc County, Okla., from April 1, 1946 to January 1, 1947; appointed county judge in 1947; elected in 1948 and again in 1950, and served until his death in Ada, Okla., October 22, 1951; interment in Rosedale Cemetery.

**McKERNAN, John Rettie, Jr.,** (husband of Olympia Jean Snowe), a Representative from Maine; born in Bangor, Penobscot County, Maine, May 20, 1948; attended the public schools of Bangor; B.A., Dartmouth College, Hanover, N.H., 1970; J.D., University of Maine School of Law, Portland, 1974; served in the Maine Army National Guard, 1970-1973; member, Maine State house of representatives, 1972-1976; admitted to the Maine bar in 1974 and commenced practice in Bangor and Portland; delegate to the Republican National Conventions of 1976 and 1984; elected as a Republican to the Ninety-eighth and Ninety-ninth Congresses (January 3, 1983-January 3, 1987); was not a candidate for reelection in 1986 to the One Hundredth Congress, but was elected Governor of Maine; reelected in 1990, and served from January 7, 1987 to January 5, 1995; is a resident of Cumberland Foreside, Maine.

**McKEVITT, James Douglas (Mike),** a Representative from Colorado; born in Spokane, Wash., October 26, 1928; attended the Spokane public schools; graduated from Grant High School, Sacramento, Calif.; B.A., University of Idaho, Moscow, Idaho, 1951; LL.B., University of Denver School of Law, 1956; entered the United States Air Force in 1951 and served as combat intelligence officer in the Korean Theater of Operations, 1952-1953; admitted to the Colorado bar in 1956 and commenced practice in Boulder; assistant attorney general for State of Colorado, 1958-1967; Denver district attorney, 1967-1971; elected as a Republican to the Ninety-second Congress (January 3, 1971-January 3, 1973); unsuccessful candidate for reelection in 1972 to the Ninety-third Congress; assistant United States attorney general, Office of Legislation, 1973; counsel, Energy Policy Office, The White House, 1973-1974; director of federal legislation, National Federation of Independent Business, 1974-1986; partner in law firm of Webster, Chamberlain, Bean and McKevitt, 1986 to present; is a resident of Alexandria, Va.

**McKIBBIN, Joseph Chambers,** a Representative from California; born in Chambersburg, Franklin County, Pa., May 14, 1824; received a common-school education and attended Princeton College 1840-1842; moved to California and settled in Sierra County in 1849; studied law; was admitted to the bar in July 1852 and practiced in Downieville; member of the State senate in 1852 and 1853; elected as a Democrat to the Thirty-fifth Congress (March 4, 1857-March 3, 1859); unsuccessful candidate for reelection in 1858 to the Thirty-sixth Congress; during the Civil War enlisted in the

Union Army in 1861 and was one of the first six Cavalry officers appointed by President Abraham Lincoln; served as a colonel and aide-de-camp on the staffs of Major General Halleck and Major General Thomas; settled in Washington, D.C., after the Civil War, as a general contractor; purchased the property at Marshall Hall, Charles County, Md., in 1883; died at Marshall Hall, Md., near Washington, D.C., July 1, 1896; interment in Arlington National Cemetery, Va.

**McKIM, Alexander** (uncle of Isaac McKim), a Representative from Maryland; born in Brandywine, Del., January 10, 1748; pursued an academic course; moved to Baltimore, Md.; member of the house of delegates in 1778; served in the Revolutionary War as a member of the Baltimore Independent Cadets and of the First Baltimore Cavalry; fought under Lafayette in the Virginia campaign of 1781; member of the State senate 1806-1810; elected as a Republican to the Eleventh, Twelfth, and Thirteenth Congresses (March 4, 1809-March 3, 1815); engaged in mercantile pursuits; justice of court of quarter sessions; presiding judge of the Baltimore County Orphans' Court at the time of his death in Baltimore, Md., January 18, 1832; interment in Greenmount Cemetery.

**McKIM, Isaac** (nephew of Alexander McKim), a Representative from Maryland; born in Baltimore, Md., July 21, 1775; attended the public schools; engaged in mercantile pursuits; served in the War of 1812 as aide-de-camp to General Samuel Smith; member of the Maryland State senate from December 4, 1821, until January 8, 1823, when he resigned; elected to the Seventeenth Congress to fill the vacancy caused by the resignation of Samuel Smith; elected to the Eighteenth Congress to fill the vacancy caused by the resignation of Representative-elect Samuel Smith and served from January 4, 1823, to March 3, 1825; a director of the Baltimore & Ohio Railroad Co. from 1827 until 1831; elected as a Jacksonian to the Twenty-third and Twenty-fourth Congresses, and as a Democrat to the Twenty-fifth Congress, and served from March 4, 1833, until his death in Baltimore, Md., on April 1, 1838; interment in the burying ground of St. Paul's Church.
**Bibliography:** *DAB.*

**McKINIRY, Richard Francis,** a Representative from New York; born in New York City March 23, 1878; attended the public schools; was graduated from the College of St. Francis Xavier, New York City, and from the New York Law School; was admitted to the bar in 1899 and commenced the practice of his profession in New York City; assistant district attorney of Bronx County 1914-1917; secretary of the State supreme court, first district, 1917-1919; elected as a Democrat to the Sixty-sixth Congress (March 4, 1919-March 3, 1921); unsuccessful candidate for reelection in 1920 to the Sixty-seventh Congress; appointed a magistrate of New York City on January 1, 1923, and served until August 15, 1943, when he retired due to ill health; died in Yonkers, N.Y., May 30, 1950; interment in Calvary Cemetery, Long Island City, N.Y.

**McKINLAY, Duncan E.,** a Representative from California; born in Orillia, Ontario, Canada, October 6, 1862; attended the common schools; later learned the trade of carriage painting and worked in Flint, Mich., and San Francisco, Sacramento, and Santa Rosa, Calif.; studied law; was admitted to the bar by the supreme court of California in 1892 and commenced practice in Santa Rosa, Calif.; second assistant United States attorney at San Francisco, 1901-1904; first assistant United States attorney, 1904-1907; elected as a Republican to the Fifty-ninth and to the two succeeding Congresses (March 4, 1905-March 3, 1911); unsuccessful candidate for reelection in 1910 to the Sixty-second Congress; appointed by President William Howard Taft as United States surveyor of customs for the port of San Francisco, Calif., in 1910; died in Berkeley, Calif., December 30, 1914; interment in Sunset Cemetery.

**McKINLEY, John,** a Senator and a Representative from Alabama; born in Culpeper County, Va., May 1, 1780; moved to Kentucky; studied law; was admitted to the bar and commenced the practice of his profession in Louisville, Ky.; moved to Huntsville, Madison County, Ala.; member, Alabama State house of representatives, 1820-1822; elected to the United States Senate to fill the vacancy caused by the death of Henry Chambers and served from November 27, 1826, to March 3, 1831; unsuccessful candidate for reelection in 1830; member of the State house of representatives in 1831; moved to Florence, Lauderdale County, Ala.; elected as a Jacksonian to the Twenty-third Congress (March 4, 1833-March 3, 1835); was not a candidate for reelection in 1834 to the Twenty-fourth Congress; again a member of the State house of representatives in 1836; again elected to the United States Senate for the term beginning March 4, 1837, but resigned April 22, 1837, before qualifying; nominated on September 18, 1837 by President Martin Van Buren as an Associate Justice of the United States Supreme Court; was confirmed by the Senate on September 25, 1837, and served until his death in Louisville, Ky., July 19, 1852; interment in Cave Hill Cemetery.
**Bibliography:** *DAB;* Hicks, Jimmie. "Associate Justice John McKinley: A Sketch." *Alabama Review* 18 (1965): 227-33; Martin, John M. "John McKinley: Jacksonian Phase." *Alabama Historical Quarterly* 28 (Spring-Summer 1966): 7-31.

**McKINLEY, William,** a Representative from Virginia; born in Virginia; completed preparatory studies; member of the Virginia house of delegates from Ohio County, Va. (now West Virginia), 1798-1804, 1806, and 1807; elected as a Republican to the Eleventh Congress to fill the vacancy caused by the resignation of John G. Jackson and served from December 21, 1810, to March 3, 1811; again a member of the Virginia house of delegates in 1820, 1821, and 1824-1826.

**McKINLEY, William, Jr.,** a Representative from Ohio and 25th President of the United States; born in Niles, Ohio, January 29, 1843; attended the public schools, Poland Academy, and Allegheny College; taught school; enlisted in the Union Army on June 23, 1861, as a private in the Twenty-third Regiment, Ohio Volunteer Infantry, and was mustered out as captain and brevet major of the same regiment in September 1865; studied law; was admitted to the bar in 1867 and commenced practice in Canton, Ohio; prosecuting attorney of Stark County, Ohio, 1869-1871; elected as a Republican to the Forty-fifth and to the two succeeding Congresses (March 4, 1877-March 3, 1883); chairman, Committee on Revision of the Laws (Forty-seventh Congress); presented credentials as a Member-elect to the Forty-eighth Congress and served from March 4, 1883, until May 27, 1884, when he was succeeded by Jonathan H. Wallace, who successfully contested his election; again elected to the Forty-ninth and to the two succeeding Congresses (March 4, 1885-March 3, 1891); chairman, Committee on Ways and Means (Fifty-first Congress); unsuccessful candidate for reelection in 1890 to the Fifty-second Congress; delegate to the Republican National Conventions of 1884, 1888, and 1892; elected Governor of Ohio in 1891, reelected in 1893, and served from January 11, 1892 to January 13, 1896; elected President of the United States in 1896, and was inaugurated March 4, 1897; reelected in 1900, and inaugurated March 4, 1901; was shot on September 6, 1901, by an anarchist, Leon Czolgosz, while attending the Pan American Exposition in Buffalo, N.Y., and died in that city on September 14, 1901; interment in the McKinley Monument (adjacent to West Lawn Cemetery), Canton, Ohio.
**Bibliography:** *DAB;* Morgan, Howard W. "The Congressional Career of William McKinley." Ph.D. dissertation, U.C.L.A., 1960; Morgan, Howard W. *William McKinley and His America.* Syracuse, N.Y.: Syracuse University Press, 1963.

**McKINLEY, William Brown,** a Representative and a Senator from Illinois; born in Petersburg, Menard County, Ill., September 5, 1856; attended the common schools and the University of Illinois at Urbana; employed as a drug clerk in Springfield, Ill.; engaged in banking in Champaign, Ill., and also in the building and operation of public utilities and bridges; elected a trustee of the University of Illinois 1902-1905; philanthropist; elected as a Republican to the Fifty-ninth and to the three succeeding Congresses (March 4, 1905-March 3, 1913); was an unsuccessful candidate for reelection in 1912 to the Sixty-third Congress; chairman, Committee on Coinage, Weights and Measures (Sixtieth and Sixty-first Congresses); again elected to the Sixty-fourth, Sixty-fifth, and Sixty-sixth Congresses (March 4, 1915-March 3, 1921); was not a candidate for reelection, having become a candidate for Senator; elected as a Republican to the United States Senate in 1920 and served from March 4, 1921, until his death; unsuccessful candidate for renomination in 1926; chairman, Committee on Manufactures (Sixty-ninth Congress); died in Martinsville, Morgan County, Ind., on December 7, 1926; interment in Mount Hope Cemetery, Champaign, Ill.

Bibliography: *DAB.*

**McKINNEY, Cynthia Ann,** a Representative from Georgia; born in Atlanta, Ga., March 17, 1955; graduated St. Joseph High School, Atlanta; B.A., University of Southern California, 1978; Georgia State University; University of Wisconsin; Fletcher School of Law and Diplomacy; professor; unsuccessful candidate for Georgia State house of representatives, 1986; member, Georgia State house of representatives, 1989-1993; elected as a Democrat to the One Hundred Third and One Hundred Fourth Congresses (January 3, 1993-January 3, 1997); is a resident of Lithonia, Ga.

**McKINNEY, James,** a Representative from Illinois; born in Oquawka, Henderson County, Ill., April 14, 1852; attended the public schools and was graduated from Monmouth (Ill.) College in 1874; president of the Aledo (Ill.) Bank, 1892-1907; member of the Republican State central committee, 1894-1906; delegate to the Republican State convention in 1896 and 1900; appointed by Governor Richard Yates in 1901 a member of the Illinois State railroad and warehouse commission, but resigned in 1902; president of the Aledo Board of Education in 1902 and 1903; elected as a Republican to the Fifty-ninth Congress to fill the vacancy caused by the death of Benjamin F. Marsh; reelected to the Sixtieth and to the two succeeding Congresses and served from November 7, 1905, to March 3, 1913; declined to be a candidate for renomination in 1912 to the Sixty-third Congress; president of the Illinois State Bankers' Association in 1908 and 1909; engaged in the real estate loan business in Aledo, Ill., until his death in that city on September 29, 1934; interment in Aledo Cemetery.

**McKINNEY, John Franklin,** a Representative from Ohio; born near Piqua, Miami County, Ohio, April 12, 1827; attended the country and private schools, the Piqua Academy, and the Ohio Wesleyan College, Delaware, Ohio; studied law; was admitted to the bar in 1850 and commenced practice in Piqua; delegate to all the Democratic National Conventions from 1850 to 1888; elected as a Democrat to the Thirty-eighth Congress (March 4, 1863-March 3, 1865); unsuccessful candidate in 1864 for reelection to the Thirty-ninth Congress; again elected to the Forty-second Congress (March 4, 1871-March 3, 1873); was not a candidate for renomination in 1872; resumed the practice of law; chairman of the Democratic State executive committee in 1879 and 1880; died in Piqua, Ohio, June 13, 1903; interment in Forest Hill Cemetery.

**McKINNEY, Luther Franklin,** a Representative from New Hampshire; born in Newark, Licking County, Ohio, April 25, 1841; attended common and private schools; taught school; during the Civil War enlisted in Company D, First Regiment, Ohio Volunteer Cavalry, August 5, 1861, and served until February 1863; moved to Iowa in 1865, where he engaged in agricultural pursuits and also taught school until 1867; was graduated from St. Lawrence University, Canton, N.Y., June 30, 1870; moved to Bridgton, Maine, in 1871, where he was ordained a pastor of the Universalist Church; moved to Newfields, N.H., in 1873, and subsequently, in 1875, to Manchester, N.H., pursuing his ministerial duties in both places; unsuccessful candidate for election in 1884 to the Forty-ninth Congress; elected as a Democrat to the Fiftieth Congress (March 4, 1887-March 3, 1889); unsuccessful candidate for reelection in 1888 to the Fifty-first Congress; elected to the Fifty-second Congress (March 4, 1891-March 3, 1893); was not a candidate in 1892 for renomination to the Fifty-third Congress, but was an unsuccessful candidate for election for Governor of New Hampshire; appointed Minister to Colombia on April 24, 1893 and served until December 1896; returned to Bridgton, Maine, and engaged in the furniture business; member of the Maine State house of representatives, 1907-1908; again pastor of the Universalist Church at Bridgton, Cumberland County, Maine, and served until his death there on July 30, 1922; interment in Forest Hill Cemetery.

**McKINNEY, Stewart Brett,** a Representative from Connecticut; born in Pittsburgh, Allegheny County, Pa., January 30, 1931; graduated, Kent School, Kent, Conn., 1949; attended Princeton University, 1949-1951; B.A., Yale University, 1958; sergeant, United States Air Force, 1951-1955; elected State representative, Connecticut general assembly in 1966; reelected in 1968; serving as minority leader, 1969, 1970; director, Bridgeport Hospital, Bridgeport Child Guidance Clinic, Rehabilitation Center of Eastern Fairfield County, and Bridgeport Chamber of Commerce; delegate, Connecticut State Republican conventions, 1968-1970; delegate, Republican National Convention, 1972; elected as a Republican to the Ninety-second and to the eight succeeding Congresses and served from January 3, 1971, until his death in Washington, D.C., May 7, 1987.

**McKINNON, Clinton Dotson,** a Representative from California; born in Dallas, Tex., February 5, 1906; moved with his parents to Caldwell, Sumner County, Kans., in 1909, to San Diego, Calif., in 1918, and to Palo Alto, Calif., in 1920; attended Stanford University in 1924; graduated from the University of Redlands (Calif.) in 1930; engaged in postgraduate work at the University of Geneva, Switzerland in 1930; reporter, editor, and advertising manager for newspapers in California, 1931-1935; president and general manager of Valley News Corporation, North Hollywood, Calif., 1935-1943; purchased the San Diego Progress-Journal and in March 1944 converted it into the San Diego Daily Journal; established a radio station in San Diego, Calif., in 1946; elected as a Democrat to the Eighty-first and Eighty-second Congresses (January 3, 1949-January 3, 1953); was not a candidate in 1952 for renomination to the House of Representatives, but was an unsuccessful candidate for nomination to the United States Senate; delegate to the Democratic National Conventions of 1952 and 1956; vice chairman, California State Central Democratic committee; editor and publisher of several newspapers; president and general manager of broadcasting companies in Tucson, Ariz., Albuquerque, N.Mex., and Corpus Christi, Tex.; president of Sentinel Savings and Loan of San Diego and the San Diego Transit Corporation; president of San Diego Urban Coalition; is a resident of San Diego, Calif.

**McKISSOCK, Thomas,** a Representative from New York; born in Montgomery, Orange County, N.Y., April 17, 1790; studied medicine and law; was admitted to the bar and commenced practice in Newburgh, N.Y.; appointed a puisne justice of the State supreme court in 1847; elected as a Whig to the Thirty-first Congress (March 4, 1849-March 3, 1851); unsuccessful candidate for reelection in 1850 to the Thirty-second Congress; died in St. Andrews, Orange County, N.Y., June 26, 1866; interment in Oldtown Cemetery, Newburgh, N.Y.

**McKNEALLY, Martin Boswell,** a Representative from New York; born in Newburgh, Orange County, N.Y.; December 31, 1914; educated in the public schools of Newburgh; A.B., Holy Cross College, Worcester, Mass., 1936; LL.B., Fordham University Law School, New York City, 1940; enlisted in the United States Army, March 17, 1941, as a private, and was discharged as a major; practiced law in Newburgh and New York City; president, board of education, Newburgh School District; State commander, American Legion, 1956-1957, national commander, 1959-1960; appointed to New York State Defense Council by Governor Nelson A. Rockefeller; special counsel to Lieutenant Governor Malcolm Wilson of New York; elected as a Republican to the Ninety-first Congress (January 3, 1969-January 3, 1971); unsuccessful candidate for reelection in 1970 to the Ninety-second Congress; was a resident of Newburgh, N.Y.; died June 14, 1992.

**McKNIGHT, Robert,** a Representative from Pennsylvania; born in Pittsburgh, Pa., January 20, 1820; attended the common schools and a private school at Xenia, Ohio; was graduated from Princeton College in 1839; studied law; was admitted to the bar in 1842 and commenced practice in Pittsburgh; city councilman 1847-1849; elected as a Republican to the Thirty-sixth and Thirty-seventh Congresses (March 4, 1859-March 3, 1863); resumed the practice of his profession; died in Pittsburgh, Pa., October 25, 1885; interment in Allegheny Cemetery.

**McLACHLAN, James,** a Representative from California; born in Argyllshire, Scotland, August 1, 1852; immigrated to the United States in 1855 with his parents, who settled in Tompkins County, N.Y.; reared on a farm and attended the public schools; taught in the public schools; elected school commissioner of Tompkins County, N.Y., in 1877; was graduated from Hamilton College, Clinton, N.Y., in 1878; studied law; was admitted to practice before the supreme court of New York in 1880; practiced in Ithaca, N.Y., 1881-1888; moved to Pasadena, Calif., in 1888, and there continued the practice of law; district attorney of Los Angeles County 1890-1892; elected as a Republican to the Fifty-fourth Congress (March 4, 1895-March 3, 1897); unsuccessful candidate for reelection in 1896 to the Fifty-fifth Congress; elected to the Fifty-seventh and to the four succeeding Congresses (March 4, 1901-March 3, 1911); unsuccessful candidate for reelection in 1910 to the Sixty-second Congress; resumed the practice of his profession in Los Angeles, Calif., served as a member of the National Monetary Commission in 1911 and 1912; died in Los Angeles, Calif., November 21, 1940; interment in Forest Lawn Memorial Park, Glendale, Calif.

**McLAIN, Frank Alexander,** a Representative from Mississippi; born near Gloster, Amite County, Miss., January 29, 1852; attended the public schools, and was graduated from the University of Mississippi at Oxford in 1874; studied law; was admitted to the bar and commenced practice in Liberty, Miss., in 1880; member of the State house of representatives 1881-1883; district attorney for the judicial district from 1883 until January 1, 1896, when he resigned; resumed the practice of law in Gloster, Miss.; member of the State constitutional convention in 1890; elected as a Democrat to the Fifty-fifth Congress to fill the vacancy caused by the death of William F. Love; reelected to the Fifty-sixth and to the four succeeding Congresses and served from December 12, 1898, to March 3, 1909; State supreme court commissioner 1910-1912; died in Gloster, Miss., October 10, 1920; interment in the City Cemetery.

**McLANAHAN, James Xavier** (grandson of Andrew Gregg), a Representative from Pennsylvania; born near Greencastle, Franklin County, Pa., in 1809; graduated from Dickinson College, Carlisle, Pa., in 1827; studied law; admitted to the bar in 1837 and commenced practice in Chambersburg, Pa.; member of the Pennsylvania senate 1842-1844; elected as a Democrat to the Thirty-first and Thirty-second Congresses (March 4, 1849-March 3, 1853); chairman, Committee on the Judiciary (Thirty-second Congress);

was not a candidate for renomination in 1852; resumed the practice of law; died in New York City December 16, 1861; interment in First Presbyterian Church Cemetery.

**McLANE, Louis** (father of Robert Milligan McLane), a Representative and a Senator from Delaware; born in Smyrna, Del., May 28, 1786; attended private schools; entered the United States Navy in 1798 as a midshipman on the U.S.S. *Philadelphia* and served one year; attended Newark College; studied law; was admitted to the bar in 1807 and commenced practice in Smyrna; served in the War of 1812; elected to the Fifteenth and to the four succeeding Congresses (March 4, 1817-March 3, 1827); reelected to the Twentieth Congress, but resigned, having been elected a Senator; elected to the United States Senate and served from March 4, 1827, until April 16, 1829, when he resigned; appointed by President Andrew Jackson as Envoy Extraordinary and Minister Plenipotentiary to Great Britain on April 18, 1829 and served until June 1831; Secretary of the Treasury in the Cabinet of President Jackson, August 8, 1831 to May 28, 1833; appointed Secretary of State by President Jackson on May 29, 1833 and served until June 30, 1834; moved to Baltimore, Md.; president of the Baltimore and Ohio Railroad Company, 1837-1847; again appointed Minister to Great Britain on June 16, 1845 and served until August 1846; delegate to the Maryland constitutional convention in 1850; died in Baltimore, Md., October 7, 1857; interment in Greenmount Cemetery.

**Bibliography:** *DAB*; Munroe, John A. *Louis McLane: Federalist and Jacksonian.* New Brunswick, N.J.: Rutgers University Press, 1973.

**McLANE, Patrick,** a Representative from Pennsylvania; born in County Mayo, Ireland, March 14, 1875; immigrated to the United States in 1882 with his parents, who settled in Scranton, Pa.; attended the public schools; worked in the coal mines of Scranton, Pa., for thirteen years; during the Spanish-American War served in the Eleventh Regiment, United States Army, in 1898 and 1899; became a locomotive engineer; member of the Scranton School Board 1904-1911; delegate to the Democratic convention in 1905; member of the Pennsylvania Democratic committee in 1914; presented credentials as a Democratic Member-elect to the Sixty-sixth Congress and served from March 4, 1919, to February 25, 1921, when he was succeeded by John R. Farr, who contested the election; unsuccessful candidate for election in 1922 to the Sixty-seventh Congress and in 1924 to the Sixty-eighth Congress; employed as a locomotive engineer until his death in Scranton, Pa., November 13, 1946; interment in Cathedral Cemetery.

**McLANE, Robert Milligan** (son of Louis McLane), a Representative from Maryland; born in Wilmington, Del., June 23, 1815; attended private schools in Wilmington, St. Mary's College in Baltimore, and the College Bourbon in Paris; appointed a cadet in the United States Military Academy at West Point by President Andrew Jackson in 1833; was graduated in July 1837, and commissioned a second lieutenant of Artillery; served with his regiment during the Seminole War in 1837 and 1838; transferred to the Corps of Topographical Engineers in 1838, and served until he resigned in 1843; studied law; was admitted to the bar in 1843 and commenced practice in Baltimore, Md.; member of the Maryland State house of delegates in 1845; elected as a Democrat to the Thirtieth and Thirty-first Congresses (March 4, 1847-March 3, 1851); chairman, Committee on Commerce (Thirty-first Congress); was not a candidate for renomination in 1850 to the Thirty-second Congress; appointed commissioner to China on October 18, 1853, with the powers of a Minister Plenipotentiary, and at the same time accredited to Japan, Siam, Korea, and Cochin China, and served until December 1854; delegate to the Democratic National Conventions of 1856 and 1876; appointed Envoy Extraordinary and Minister Plenipotentiary to Mexico on March 7, 1859, and served until December 1860; delegate to the Democratic National Convention of 1876; member of the Maryland State senate in 1877; elected as a Democrat to the Forty-sixth and Forty-seventh Congresses (March 4, 1879-March 3, 1883); chairman, Committee on Pacific Railroads (Forty-sixth Congress); elected Governor of Maryland in 1883, and served from January 1884 until his resignation on March 27, 1885; appointed by President Grover Cleveland as Minister Plenipotentiary to France on March 23, 1885, and served until May 1889; died in Paris, France, April 16, 1898; interment in Greenmount Cemetery, Baltimore, Md.

**Bibliography:** *DAB*; McLane, Robert Milligan. *Reminiscences, 1827-1897, Governor Robert M. McLane.* Wilmington, Del.: Scholarly Resources, 1972.

**McLAUGHLIN, Charles Francis,** a Representative from Nebraska; born in Lincoln, Lancaster County, Nebr., June 19, 1887; attended the public schools; was graduated from the University of Nebraska at Lincoln in 1908 and from the law department of Columbia University, New York City in 1910; was admitted to the bar in 1910 and commenced practice in Omaha, Nebr.; special master in chancery in Federal Court, 1916-1918; during the First World War served as captain of the Three Hundred and Forty-seventh Field Artillery, Ninety-first Division, American Expeditionary Forces, until his discharge, April 30, 1919; major in the Officers' Reserve Corps, 1919-1921; delegate to the Nebraska State constitutional convention in 1920; elected as a Democrat to the Seventy-fourth and to the three succeeding Congresses (January 3, 1935-January 3, 1943); unsuccessful candidate for reelection in 1942 to the Seventy-eighth Congress; member of the American-Mexican Claims Commission, Washington, D.C., 1943-1947; member of the Indian Claims Commission from April 5, 1947, until November 14, 1949; took the oath of office November 15, 1949, as a United States district judge for the District of Columbia, became a senior United States district court judge for the District of Columbia on December 31, 1964, and continued to hear cases until June 1974; resided in Washington, D.C., where he died on February 5, 1976; interment in Gate of Heaven Cemetery, Silver Spring, Md.

**McLAUGHLIN, James Campbell,** a Representative from Michigan; born in Beardstown, Cass County, Ill., January 26, 1858; moved to Muskegon, Mich., in 1864; attended the public schools of Muskegon; was graduated from the literary department of the University of Michigan at Ann Arbor in 1879, and from its law department in 1883; was admitted to the bar and commenced practice at Muskegon, Mich., in 1883; prosecuting attorney of Muskegon County from 1887 until 1901; in 1901 was appointed by Governor Aaron T. Bliss as a member of the board of State tax commissioners and the State board of assessors, and served until 1906; elected as a Republican to the Sixtieth and to the twelve succeeding Congresses, and served from March 4, 1907 until his death; unsuccessful candidate for reelection in 1932 to the Seventy-third Congress; died in Marion, Va., November 29, 1932, while en route to Washington, D.C.; interment in Evergreen Cemetery, Muskegon, Mich.

**McLAUGHLIN, Joseph,** a Representative from Pennsylvania; born in Burt, County Donegal, Ireland, June 9, 1867; immigrated to the United States and settled in Philadelphia in 1889; employed as a mechanic in the Baldwin Locomotive Works and became shop superintendent of his department; interested in various business enterprises; elected as a Republican to the Sixty-fifth Congress (March 4, 1917-March 3, 1919); unsuccessful candidate for renomination in 1918; elected to the Sixty-seventh Congress (March 4, 1921-March 3, 1923); was not a candidate for renomination in 1922; retired from active business pursuits; died in Philadelphia, Pa., November 21, 1926; interment in Holy Cross Cemetery, Yeadon, Delaware County, Pa.

**McLAUGHLIN, Melvin Orlando,** a Representative from Nebraska; born in Osceola, Clarke County, Iowa, August 8, 1876; moved with his parents to Nebraska in 1884; attended the common schools and was graduated from the College View (Nebr.) High School; subsequently pursued his studies at the Lincoln (Nebr.) Normal University and the Nebraska State Normal School at Peru; taught school near Lincoln 1895-1900; was a student at the Iowa Christian College at Oskaloosa, Iowa, Omaha (Nebr.) University, and the Union Biblical Seminary, Dayton, Ohio; served in the ministry of the United Brethren Church, Omaha, Nebr., 1900-1913; moved to York, Nebr., in 1913; president of York College 1913-1918; was elected as a Republican to the Sixty-sixth and to the three succeeding Congresses (March 4, 1919-March 3, 1927); unsuccessful candidate for reelection in 1926 to the Seventieth Congress; engaged in mining and investments; died in York, York County, Nebr., on June 18, 1928; interment in Greenwood Cemetery.

**McLAURIN, Anselm Joseph,** a Senator from Mississippi; born in Brandon, Rankin County, Miss., March 26, 1848; moved with his parents to Smith County; attended the common schools and Summerville Institute; during the Civil War enlisted in the Confederate Army in 1864 and served as captain; again attended the Summerville Institute, 1865-1867; studied law; was admitted to the bar in 1868 and began practice in Raleigh, Miss.; district attorney, 1871-1875; member of the Mississippi State house of representatives in 1879; presidential elector on the Democratic ticket in 1888; delegate to the State constitutional convention in 1890; elected as a Democrat to the United States Senate to fill the vacancy caused by the resignation of Edward C. Walthall, and served from February 7, 1894 to March 3, 1895; elected Governor of Mississippi in 1895, and served from January 20, 1896 to January 16, 1900; again elected in 1900 to the United States Senate; reelected in 1906, and served from March 4, 1901 until his death in Brandon, Miss., December 22, 1909; interment in Brandon Cemetery.

**Bibliography:** *DAB*; Faries, Clyde J. "Redneck Rhetoric and the Last of the Redeemers: The 1899 McLaurin-Allen Campaign." *Journal of Missouri History* 33 (November 1971): 283-98.

**McLAURIN, John Lowndes,** a Representative and a Senator from South Carolina; born in Red Bluff, Marlboro County, S.C., May 9, 1860; attended schools at Bennettsville, S.C., and Englewood, N.J., Bethel Military Academy, near Warrenton, Va., and Swarthmore (Pa.) College; graduated from the Carolina Military Institute; studied law in the University of Virginia at Charlottesville; was admitted to the bar in 1883 and practiced in Bennettsville, Marlboro County, S.C.; member, South Carolina State house of representatives, 1890-1891; attorney general of the South Carolina, 1891-1897; elected as a Democrat to the Fifty-second Congress to fill the vacancy caused by the death of Eli T. Stackhouse; reelected to the three succeeding Congresses, and served from December 5, 1892 until May 31, 1897, when he resigned; appointed and subsequently elected as a Democrat to the United States Senate to fill the vacancy caused by the death of Joseph H. Earle, and served from June 1, 1897 to March 3, 1903; was not a candidate for reelection; censured by the Senate on February 28, 1902 for engaging in fisticuffs with his colleague from South Carolina, Benjamin R. Tillman, on the Senate floor; moved to New York City and resumed the practice of law; returned to Bennettsville, S.C., and engaged in agricultural pursuits; member, State senate, 1914-1915; author of the State warehouse system for storing and financing cotton; served as State warehouse commissioner from 1915 until his resignation in 1917; died at his estate near Bennettsville, S.C., on July 29, 1934; interment in McCall Cemetery.

**Bibliography:** Stroup, Rodger E. "John L. McLaurin: A Political Biography." Ph.D. dissertation, University of South Carolina, 1980.

**McLEAN, Alney,** a Representative from Kentucky; born in Burke County, N.C., June 10, 1779; pursued preparatory studies; moved to Kentucky; appointed surveyor of Muhlenberg County in 1799 and elected one of the trustees of Greenville on its formation; studied law; admitted to the bar and commenced practice in Greenville, Muhlenberg County, Ky., about 1805; member of the Kentucky house of representatives in 1812 and 1813; served as a captain in the War of 1812; elected as a Republican to the Fourteenth Congress (March 4, 1815-March 3, 1817); elected to the Sixteenth Congress (March 4, 1819-March 3, 1821); served as judge of the fourteenth district of Kentucky from 1821 until his death; presidential elector on the ticket headed by Henry Clay in 1824 and on the ticket of Henry Clay and Sergeant in 1832; died near Greenville, Muhlenberg County, Ky., December 30, 1841; interment in Old Caney Station Cemetery, near Greenville, Ky.

**McLEAN, Donald Holman,** a Representative from New Jersey; born in Paterson, Passaic County, N.J., March 18, 1884; attended the public schools; was graduated from the law department of George Washington University, Washington, D.C., in 1906; served as a page in the United States Senate, 1897-1902; secretary to Senator John Kean, 1902-1911; was admitted to the bar 1909 and commenced practice in Elizabeth, N.J.; special master in chancery of New Jersey; supreme court commissioner of New Jersey; assistant prosecutor of the pleas of Union County, N.J., 1918-1923; elected as a Republican to the Seventy-third and to the five succeeding Congresses (March 4, 1933-January 3, 1945); was not a candidate for reelection in 1944 to the Seventy-ninth Congress; served as prosecutor of the pleas of Union County, N.J., from June 24, 1945, to April 18, 1946, when he was appointed judge of the New Jersey Court of Errors and Appeals; became judge of New Jersey Superior Court under reorganization of New Jersey judiciary in September 1948; reappointed in April 1952; retired March 18, 1954, under age requirement and returned to law practice; retired in 1968; resided in Elizabeth, N.J.; died in Burlington, Vt., August 19, 1975; cremated; ashes interred in Vail Memorial Cemetery, Parsippany, N.J.

**McLEAN, Finis Ewing** (brother of John McLean and uncle of James David Walker), a Representative from Kentucky; born near Russellville, Logan County, Ky., February 19, 1806; attended the country schools and Lebanon Academy in Logan County; studied law; admitted to the bar and commenced practice in Elkton, Ky., in 1827; also engaged in agricultural pursuits; member of the Kentucky house of representatives in 1837; elected as a Whig to the Thirty-first Congress (March 4, 1849-March 3, 1851); resumed the practice of law and also engaged in agricultural pursuits; moved to Andrew County, Mo., in 1860 and engaged in farming until 1865; moved to Greencastle, Ind., in 1865, in which city he died April 12, 1881; interment in Forest Hill Cemetery.

**McLEAN, George Payne,** a Senator from Connecticut; born in Simsbury, Hartford County, Conn., October 7, 1857; attended the common schools; studied law; was admitted to the bar in 1881 and commenced practice in Hartford, Conn.; member, Connecticut State house of representatives, 1883-1884; member of the commission to revise the Connecticut statutes in 1885; member of the State senate in 1886; United States district attorney for Connecticut, 1892-1896; resumed the practice of law in Hartford; elected Governor of Connecticut in 1900, and served from January 9, 1901 to January 7, 1903; elected as a Republican to the United States Senate in 1911; reelected in 1916 and again in 1922, and served from March 4, 1911 to March 3, 1929; declined to be a candidate for reelection in 1928; chairman, Committee on Forest Reservations and Game Protection (Sixty-second and Sixty-fifth Congresses), Committee on Banking and Currency (Sixty-sixth through Sixty-ninth Congresses), Committee on Manufactures (Seventieth Congress); resumed the practice of law in Hartford, Conn.; died in Simsbury, Conn., June 6, 1932; interment in Simsbury Cemetery.

**McLEAN, James Henry,** a Representative from Missouri; born in Ayrshire, Scotland, August 13, 1829; reared in Nova Scotia, Canada; immigrated to the United States in 1842 and settled in Philadelphia, Pa.; employed as a clerk in a drug store; moved to St. Louis, Mo., in 1849, and in the following year to New Orleans, La., to take charge of the financial operations of Narciso Lopez' expedition to Cuba; returned to St. Louis in 1851; studied medicine and surgery; was graduated from the St. Louis (Mo.) Medical College in 1863 and practiced in St. Louis; elected as a Republican to the Forty-seventh Congress to fill the vacancy caused by the death of Thomas Allen, and served from December 15, 1882 to March 3, 1883; died in Dansville, Livingston County, N.Y., August 12, 1886; interment in Bellefontaine Cemetery, St. Louis, Mo.

**Bibliography:** "Doctor James Henry McLean and His 'Peacemakers.'" *Missouri Historical Society Bulletin* 5 (January 1949): 109-113.

**McLEAN, John** (brother of Finis Ewing McLean and uncle of James David Walker), a Representative and a Senator from Illinois; born near Guilford Court House (now Greensboro), Guilford County, N.C., February 4, 1791; moved with his parents to Logan County, Ky., in 1795; pursued an academic course; moved to Illinois Territory in 1815; studied law; was admitted to the bar and commenced practice in Shawneetown, Gallatin County, Ill.; upon the admission of Illinois as a State into the Union was elected to the Fifteenth Congress, and served from December 3, 1818 to March 3, 1819; unsuccessful candidate for reelection in 1818 to the Sixteenth Congress, and for election in 1820 and 1822 to the Seventeenth and Eighteenth Congresses, respectively; member, Illinois State house of representatives, 1820, 1826, 1828, and served as speaker; elected to the United States Senate to fill the vacancy caused by the resignation of Ninian Edwards, and served from November 23, 1824 to March 3, 1825; was not a candidate for reelection; resumed the practice of law; again elected to the United States Senate, and served from March 4, 1829 until his death in Shawneetown, Ill., October 14, 1830; interment in Westwood Cemetery, near Shawneetown, Ill.

**McLEAN, John** (brother of William McLean), a Representative from Ohio; born in Morris County, N.J., March 11, 1785; moved with his parents to Morgantown, Va., in 1789, to Nicholasville, Ky., in 1790, to Maysville, Ky., in 1793, and to Lebanon, Ohio, in 1797; attended the common schools and studied under private tutors; studied law; was admitted to the bar in 1807 and commenced practice in Lebanon, Ohio; founded the Western Star, a weekly newspaper; elected as a Republican to the Thirteenth and Fourteenth Congresses, and served from March 4, 1813 until his resignation in 1816; chairman, Committee on Accounts (Fourteenth Congress); associate judge of the Ohio State supreme court, 1816-1822; appointed by President James Monroe as Commissioner of the United States General Land Office in 1822; appointed Postmaster General in the administration of President Monroe; reappointed by President John Quincy Adams, and served from December 9, 1823 until March 7, 1829, when he resigned; declined Cabinet portfolios as Secretary of War and Secretary of the Navy in the administration of President Andrew Jackson; engaged in literary pursuits; nominated on March 6, 1829 by President Jackson as an Associate Justice of the United States Supreme Court; was confirmed by the Senate on March 7, 1829, and served until his death in Cincinnati, Ohio, April 4, 1861; interment in Spring Grove Cemetery.

**Bibliography:** *DAB.*

**McLEAN, Samuel,** a Delegate from the Territory of Montana; born at Summit Hill, Carbon County, Pa., August 7, 1826; attended the select schools of Wyoming Valley, Pa., and Lafayette College, Easton, Pa.; studied law; was admitted to the bar in 1849 and commenced practice in Mauch Chunk, Pa.; prosecuting attorney of

Carbon County, Pa., 1855-1860; attorney general of the provisional Territory of Jefferson (afterward Colorado) in 1860; moved to Bannock, Mont., in 1862; when the Territory of Montana was formed was elected as a Democrat to the Thirty-eighth and Thirty-ninth Congresses and served from January 6, 1865, to March 3, 1867; was not a candidate for renomination in 1866; president of McLean Silver Mining Co. in 1870; moved to Virginia and settled on a plantation near Burkeville in 1870; died in Burkeville, Nottoway County, Va., July 16, 1877; interment in the churchyard of the Presbyterian Church.

**McLEAN, William** (brother of John McLean), a Representative from Ohio; born in Mason County, Ky., August 10, 1794; moved with his parents to a farm in Warren County, Ohio, in 1799; attended the common schools; studied law; was admitted to the bar in 1814 and commenced practice in Cincinnati, Ohio; moved to Piqua, Miami County, Ohio, in 1820; receiver of public moneys in Piqua, Ohio; through his efforts a subsidy of 500,000 acres of land was procured for building the Ohio Canal from Cincinnati to Cleveland; elected to the Eighteenth, Nineteenth, and Twentieth Congresses (March 4, 1823-March 3, 1829); chairman, Committee on Indian Affairs (Twentieth Congress); returned to Cincinnati, Ohio; engaged in mercantile pursuits and the practice of his profession in Cincinnati; also interested in agricultural pursuits; died in Cincinnati October 12, 1839; interment in the Catharine Street Burying Ground; reinterment in Spring Grove Cemetery April 2, 1863.

**McLEAN, William Pinkney,** a Representative from Texas; born in Copiah County, Miss., August 9, 1836; moved with his mother to Marshall, Tex., in 1839; attended private schools and was graduated from the law department of the University of North Carolina at Chapel Hill in 1857; was admitted to the bar in 1857 and commenced the practice of his profession at Jefferson, Marion County, Tex.; member of the Texas State house of representatives in 1861; resigned to enter the Confederate Army as a private; was promoted to captain and then major, and served throughout the Civil War; again a member of the State house of representatives in 1869; elected as a Democrat to the Forty-third Congress (March 4, 1873-March 3, 1875); was not a candidate for renomination in 1874 to the Forty-fourth Congress; resumed the practice of law in Mount Pleasant, Titus County, Tex.; member of the Texas State constitutional convention in 1875; elected judge of the fifth judicial district in 1884; declined to be a candidate for reelection; appointed by Governor James S. Hogg a member of the first Texas State railroad commission in 1891; resigned and moved to Fort Worth, Tarrant County, Tex., in 1893; resumed the practice of his profession; died in Fort Worth on March 13, 1925; interment in Mount Olivet Cemetery.

**McLEMORE, Atkins Jefferson,** a Representative from Texas; born on a farm near Spring Hill, Maury County, Tenn., March 13, 1857; educated in the rural schools and by private tutors; moved to Texas in 1878; employed as a cowboy, printer, and newspaper reporter, and later as a miner in Colorado and Mexico; returned to Texas and settled in San Antonio and engaged principally in newspaper work; moved to Corpus Christi, Tex., in 1889, to Austin in 1895, and to Houston in 1911, where he engaged in the newspaper publishing business; member of the Texas house of representatives of 1892-1896; member of the board of aldermen of Austin, Tex., 1896-1898; secretary of the Democratic State executive committee 1900-1904; elected as a Democrat to the Sixty-fourth and Sixty-fifth Congresses (March 4, 1915-March 3, 1919); was an unsuccessful candidate for reelection in 1918 to the Sixty-sixth Congress; resumed the newspaper publishing business in Hebronville, Jim Hogg County, Tex., and resided in Laredo, Tex.; was an unsuccessful candidate for election to the United States Senate in 1928; died in Laredo, Tex., March 4, 1929; interment in Oakwood Cemetery, Austin, Tex.

**McLENE, James,** a Delegate from Pennsylvania; born in New London, Pa., October 11, 1730; moved to Antrim Township, Cumberland (now Franklin) County, in 1754; delegate to the Pennsylvania constitutional convention of 1776 to form a constitution for Pennsylvania; member of the Pennsylvania house of representatives in 1776 and 1777; member of the supreme executive council in 1778 and 1779; Member of the Continental Congress in 1779 and 1780; delegate to the Pennsylvania constitutional convention in 1789 and 1790; again a member of the Pennsylvania house of representatives in 1790, 1791, 1793, and 1794; died in Antrim Township, Pa., March 13, 1806.

**McLENE, Jeremiah,** a Representative from Ohio; born in Cumberland County, Pa., in 1767; attended the common schools; served in the Revolutionary War as major general of militia; moved to Ohio and settled in Chillicothe, Ross County; member of the State house of representatives in 1807 and 1808; secretary of state of Ohio 1808-1831; moved to Columbus, Ohio, in 1816; elected as a Jacksonian to the Twenty-third and Twenty-fourth Congresses (March 4, 1833-March 3, 1837); unsuccessful for reelection in 1836 to the Twenty-fifth Congress; died in Washington D.C., March 19, 1837; interment in Congressional Cemetery.

**McLEOD, Clarence John,** a Representative from Michigan; born in Detroit, Wayne County, Mich., July 3, 1895; attended the public schools; was graduated from the Detroit College of Law in 1918; during the First World War served as a private in the aviation section at the ground school, Cornell University, Ithaca, N.Y., and as sergeant in the Intelligence Division; accepted appointment May 12, 1919, as second lieutenant in the Officers' Reserve Corps, and successively as captain, major, and lieutenant colonel; was admitted to the bar in 1919 and commenced practice in Detroit, Mich.; elected as a Republican to the Sixty-sixth Congress to fill the vacancy caused by the death of Charles A. Nichols and served from November 2, 1920, to March 3, 1921; was not a candidate for election to the Sixty-seventh Congress; elected to the Sixty-eighth and to the six succeeding Congresses (March 4, 1923-January 3, 1937); unsuccessful candidate for reelection in 1936 to the Seventy-fifth Congress; defeated for the Republican nomination for Governor in 1934 and for mayor of Detroit in 1937; elected to the Seventy-sixth Congress (January 3, 1939-January 3, 1941); unsuccessful candidate for reelection in 1940 to the Seventy-seventh Congress, for election in 1942 to the Seventy-eighth Congress, and in 1944 to the Seventy-ninth Congress; unsuccessful candidate for the Republican nomination to the Eightieth Congress in 1946; unsuccessful candidate in 1950 to the Eighty-second Congress and in 1952 to the Eighty-third Congress; practiced law; consultant to Administrator of Federal Civil Defense Administration; died in Detroit, Mich., May 15, 1959; interment in Mount Olivet Cemetery.

**McLOSKEY, Robert Thaddeus,** a Representative from Illinois; born in Monmouth, Warren County, Ill., June 26, 1907; attended the public schools; graduated from Monmouth (Ill.) College in 1928, and Worsham College at Chicago, Ill., in 1932; associated with the Lugg Funeral Home, 1932-1935; county tax supervisor, 1935-1939; field supervisor, Bureau of Vital Statistics, Illinois Health Department, 1940-1950; member of the State house of representatives, 1951-1962 and served as Republican whip for three years; precinct committeeman for twenty years; chairman of Warren County Republican central committee for ten years; farm operator and manager; elected as a Republican to the Eighty-eighth Congress (January 3, 1963-January 3, 1965); unsuccessful candidate for reelection in 1964 to the Eighty-ninth Congress; chairman, Warren County, Ill., Planning Commission 1969-1972; was a resident of Monmouth, Ill.; died in 1992.

**McMAHON, Brien,** a Senator from Connecticut; born James O'Brien McMahon in Norwalk, Fairfield County, Conn., October 6, 1903; attended the public schools; graduated from Fordham

University, New York City, in 1924 and from the law school of Yale University, New Haven, Conn., in 1927; was admitted to the bar the same year, changed his name to Brien McMahon, and commenced practice in Norwalk, Conn.; city judge of Norwalk, Conn., in 1933, but resigned to become special assistant to Homer S. Cummings, Attorney General of the United States, 1933-1935; Assistant Attorney General of the United States in charge of the Department of Justice Criminal Division, 1935-1939; resumed the practice of his profession in Washington, D.C., and Norwalk, Conn.; elected as a Democrat to the United States Senate in 1944; reelected in 1950, and served from January 3, 1945 until his death in Washington, D.C., July 28, 1952; co-chairman, Joint Committee on Atomic Energy (Eighty-first and Eighty-second Congresses); interment in St. Mary's Cemetery, Norwalk, Conn.

**Bibliography:** *DAB*.

**McMAHON, Gregory,** a Representative from New York; born in New York City, March 19, 1915; attended a parochial school; was graduated from St. John's Prep School, Brooklyn, N.Y., in 1933 and from St. John's University, Brooklyn, N.Y., in 1938; also attended St. John's Law School, 1939-1941; certified public accountant since 1939; taught at St. John's College, 1939-1942; served in the United States Navy as an ensign from December 1941 to October 1945, serving in the Pacific; elected as a Republican to the Eightieth Congress (January 3, 1947-January 3, 1949); unsuccessful candidate for reelection in 1948 to the Eighty-first Congress; accountant and tax consultant; is a resident of Garden City, N.Y.

**McMAHON, John A.** (nephew of Clement Laird Vallandigham), a Representative from Ohio; born in Frederick County, Md., February 19, 1833; pursued academic studies; graduated from St. Xavier College, Cincinnati, in 1849; studied law; was admitted to the bar in 1854 and commenced practice in Dayton, Ohio; delegate to the Democratic National Conventions of 1872 and 1904; elected as a Democrat to the Forty-fourth and to the two succeeding Congresses (March 4, 1875-March 3, 1881); one of the managers appointed by the House of Representatives in 1876 to conduct the impeachment proceedings against William W. Belknap, Secretary of War; unsuccessful candidate for reelection in 1880 to the Forty-seventh Congress; resumed the practice of his profession in Dayton, Montgomery County, Ohio; served as president of the Ohio State Bar Association in 1886; unsuccessful candidate for election to the United States Senate in 1889; died in Dayton, Ohio, March 8, 1923; interment in Woodland Cemetery.

**McMANUS, William,** a Representative from New York; born in Brunswick, Rensselaer County, N.Y., in 1780; received an academic education; studied law; was admitted to the bar in 1817 and commenced practice in Troy, Rensselaer County, N.Y.; surrogate of Rensselaer County 1815-1818; district attorney 1818-1821; elected to the Nineteenth Congress (March 4, 1825-March 3, 1827); resumed the practice of law; moved to Texas in 1833; returned to Brunswick, N.Y., the following year, where he died January 18, 1835.

**McMASTER, William Henry,** a Senator from South Dakota; born in Ticonic, Monona County, Iowa, May 10, 1877; attended the public schools at Sioux City, Iowa; graduated from Beloit (Wis.) College in 1899; moved to Yankton, Yankton County, S.Dak., in 1901 and engaged in banking; member, South Dakota State house of representatives, 1911-1912; member, South Dakota State senate, 1913-1916; Lieutenant Governor of South Dakota, 1917-1920; elected Governor of South Dakota in 1920, reelected in 1922, and served from January 4, 1921 to January 6, 1925; elected as a Republican to the United States Senate and served from March 4, 1925, to March 3, 1931; unsuccessful candidate for reelection in 1930; moved to Dixon, Ill., in 1933 and engaged in banking until his death there on September 14, 1968; interment in Oakwood Cemetery.

**McMILLAN, Alexander,** a Representative from North Carolina; member of the North Carolina State senate, 1810-1812; elected to the Fifteenth Congress and served from March 4, 1817, until his death, which occurred before Congress assembled on December 1, 1817.

**McMILLAN, Clara Gooding** (wife of Thomas S. McMillan), a Representative from South Carolina; born in Brunson, Hampton County, S.C., August 17, 1894; attended the public schools, Confederate Home College, Charleston, S.C., and Flora MacDonald College, Red Springs, N.C.; elected as a Democrat to the Seventy-sixth Congress, November 7, 1939, by special election to fill the vacancy caused by the death of her husband, Thomas S. McMillan, and served from November 7, 1939 to January 3, 1941; was not a candidate for reelection in 1940 to the Seventy-seventh Congress; served in National Youth Administration, then the Office of Government Reports, Office of War Information, 1941; appointed information liaison officer for the Department of State, Washington, D.C., on January 1, 1946, and served until July 31, 1957; resided in Barnwell, S.C., where she died on November 8, 1976; interment in Magnolia Cemetery, Charleston, S.C.

**McMILLAN, James,** a Senator from Michigan; born in Hamilton, Ontario, Canada, May 12, 1838; educated in the public schools of Hamilton; moved to Detroit, Mich., in 1855, where he entered upon a business career; purchasing agent of the Detroit & Milwaukee Railroad; an organizer of the Michigan Car Co. in 1863; built the Duluth, South Shore & Atlantic Railroad and was its president; largely interested in shipbuilding and lake transportation companies; for three years was president of the Detroit Board of Park Commissioners, and for four years a member of the Detroit Board of Estimates; presidential elector on the Republican ticket in 1884; elected as a Republican to the United States Senate in 1889; reelected in 1895 and 1901, and served from March 3, 1889 until his death in Manchester, Essex County, Mass., August 10, 1902; chairman, Committtee on Manufactures (Fifty-first and Fifty-second Congresses), Committee on the District of Columbia (Fifty-fourth through Fifty-seventh Congresses); was instrumental in the formation of a panel of specialists to study and report on plans to develop and improve the public buildings and park systems of the District of Columbia; the panel's report is often referred to as the "McMillan Plan"; interment in Elmwood Cemetery, Detroit, Mich.

**Bibliography:** *DAB*; Heyda, Marie. "Senator James McMillan and the Flowering of the Spoils System." *Michigan History* 54 (Fall 1970): 183-200; Moore, Charles. "James McMillan, United States Senator From Michigan." *Michigan Historical Collections* 39 (1915): 173-87.

**McMILLAN, John Alexander, III (Alex),** a Representative from North Carolina; born in Charlotte, N.C., May 9, 1932; graduated from Woodberry Forest School, Va., 1950; B.A., University of North Carolina, Chapel Hill, 1954; M.B.A., University of Virginia, Charlottesville, 1958; served in United States Army as a special agent, intelligence, 1954-1956; president, Harris-Teeter Super Markets, 1977-1983; chairman, Charlotte-Mecklenburg Broadcasting Authority, 1978-1983; Mecklenburg County Board of Commissioners, 1972-1974; board member and chairman, Mecklenburg Board of Social Services, 1974-1977; elected as a Republican to the Ninety-ninth and to the four succeeding Congresses (January 3, 1985-January 3, 1995); was not a candidate for reelection in 1994 to the One Hundred Fourth Congress; founder of The McMillan Group, consulting and Merchant Banking company; is a resident of Charlotte, N.C.

**McMILLAN, John Lanneau,** a Representative from South Carolina; born on a farm near Mullins, Marion County, S.C., April 12, 1898; educated Mullins High School, University of North Carolina, and South Carolina, also University of South Carolina Law School and National Law School, Washington, D.C.; selected to represent United States Congress at the Interparliamentary Union in London in 1960, and in Tokyo in 1961; elected as a Democrat to the Seventy-sixth and to the sixteen succeeding Congresses (January 3, 1939-January 3, 1973); chairman, Committee on District of Columbia (Seventy-ninth, Eighty-first, Eighty-second and Eighty-fourth through Ninety-second Congresses); unsuccessful candidate for renomination in 1972 to the Ninety-third Congress; resided in Florence, S.C., where he died September 3, 1979; interment in the McMillan family cemetery, Mullins, S.C.

**McMILLAN, Samuel,** a Representative from New York; born in County Down, town of Drumore, Ireland, August 6, 1850; immigrated to the United States with his parents, who settled in New York City and later moved to Niles, Trumbull County, Ohio; attended the common schools; returned to New York City and took up the trade of carpenter; attended night school as a student of architecture; engaged in banking; vice president for a construction company that built Manhattan Bridge; served as a member of the board of examiners of the building department, city of New York, for twelve years, and park commissioner and president of the board for three years under Mayor Strong's administration; elected as a Republican to the Sixtieth Congress (March 4, 1907-March 3, 1909); was not a candidate for renomination in 1908 to the Sixty-first Congress; died in New York City on May 6, 1924; interment in Woodlawn Cemetery.

**McMILLAN, Samuel James Renwick,** a Senator from Minnesota; born in Brownsville, Fayette County, Pa., February 22, 1826; completed preparatory studies; graduated from Duquesne College, Pittsburgh, Pa., in 1846; studied law; was admitted to the bar in 1849 and commenced practice in Pittsburgh, Pa.; moved to St. Paul, Minn., in 1852, then to Stillwater, Minn., in 1854, and engaged in the practice of law in both cities; returned to St. Paul in 1856; judge of the first judicial district 1858-1864; served as second lieutenant of the Stillwater Frontier Guards during the Indian war of 1862; appointed and subsequently elected associate justice of the State supreme court in 1864; reelected in 1871 and served until his resignation in 1874; appointed in 1874 and subsequently elected chief justice of the State supreme court and served until 1875, when he resigned; elected as a Republican to the United States Senate in 1875; reelected in 1881 and served from March 4, 1875, to March 3, 1887; was not a candidate for renomination in 1886; chairman, Committee on Claims (Forty-fifth Congress), Committee on Commerce (Forty-seventh through Forty-ninth Congresses), Committee on Revision of the Laws of the United States (Forty-seventh Congress); engaged in the practice of law until his death in St. Paul, Minn., October 3, 1897; interment in Oakland Cemetery.

**McMILLAN, Thomas Sanders** (husband of Clara Gooding McMillan), a Representative from South Carolina; born near Ulmers, Allendale County, S.C., November 27, 1888; attended the common schools near Ulmers and was graduated from Orangeburg (S.C.) Collegiate Institute in 1907; taught school at Perry, Aiken County, S.C., in 1907 and 1908; graduated from the University of South Carolina at Columbia in 1912; completed the law course at the same university in 1913; was admitted to the bar in 1913 and commenced the practice of law in Charleston, S.C.; also interested in agricultural pursuits; member, South Carolina State house of representatives, 1917-1924, serving as speaker pro tempore in 1921 and 1922, and as speaker in 1923 and 1924; was not a candidate for renomination in 1924; member of the executive committee of the Interparliamentary Union, 1937-1939, serving as delegate to the convention held in Oslo, Norway, in 1939; elected as a Democrat to the Sixty-ninth and to the seven succeeding Congresses, and served from March 4, 1925 until his death in Charleston, S.C., September 29, 1939; interment in Magnolia Cemetery.

**McMILLAN, William,** a Delegate from the Territory Northwest of the River Ohio; born near Abingdon, Washington County, Va., March 2, 1764; was graduated from the College of William and Mary, Williamsburg, Va.; studied law; moved to Fort Washington (now Cincinnati, Ohio) in 1787; was admitted to the bar in 1788 and commenced practice in Cincinnati; first justice of the court of general quarter sessions in 1790; member of the Territorial house of representatives in 1799 and 1800; elected to the Sixth Congress to fill the vacancy caused by the resignation of William Henry Harrison, and served from November 24, 1800, to March 3, 1801; declined renomination in 1800; after admission of Ohio into the Union in 1803 was appointed United States district attorney for Ohio, but owing to declining health did not assume the duties; died in Cincinnati, Ohio, in May 1804; interment in Spring Grove Cemetery.

**Bibliography:** Bloom, Jo Tice. "The Congressional Delegates from the Northwest Territory." *Old Northwest* 3 (1977): 3-21.

**McMILLEN, Charles Thomas (Tom),** a Representative from Maryland; born in Elmira, Chemung County, N.Y., May 26, 1952; attended public schools in Mansfield, Pa., and graduated from Mansfield High School in 1970; B.S., University of Maryland, 1974; B.A., M.A., Oxford University (Rhodes Scholar), 1978; professional basketball player; founded an electronic equipment company and served as chairman of the board of an investment firm; elected as a Democrat to the One Hundredth and to the two succeeding Congresses (January 3, 1987-January 3, 1993); unsuccessful candidate for reelection in 1992 to the One Hundred Third Congress; appointed a co-chair of the President's Council on Physical Fitness and Sports, June 22, 1993; is a resident of Crofton, Md.

**McMILLEN, Rolla Coral,** a Representative from Illinois; born near Monticello, Piatt County, Ill., October 5, 1880; attended the public schools of Monticello, Ill., and the University of Illinois at Chicago; was graduated from the University of Michigan Law School at Ann Arbor in 1906; was admitted to the bar the same year and commenced practice in Decatur, Ill.; delegate to the Republican National Convention of 1940; member of the Illinois State housing board, 1940-1944; elected as a Republican to the Seventy-eighth Congress to fill the vacancy caused by the death of William H. Wheat; reelected to the Seventy-ninth and to the two succeeding Congresses, and served from June 13, 1944 to January 3, 1951; was not a candidate for renomination in 1950 to the Eighty-second Congress; died in Evanston, Ill., May 6, 1961; interment in Greenwood Cemetery, Decatur, Ill.

**McMILLIN, Benton,** a Representative from Tennessee; born in Monroe County, Ky., September 11, 1845; attended Philomath Academy, Tennessee, and the University of Kentucky at Lexington; studied law; was admitted to the bar and commenced practice in Celina, Clay County, Tenn., in 1871; member of the Tennessee State house of representatives in 1874; commissioned by Governor James D. Porter, Jr. to treat with the State of Kentucky for the purchase of territory in 1875; attended every Democratic National Convention between 1876 and 1932, except in 1920; member, Tennessee State house of representatives, 1875-1877; commissioned by Governor James D. Porter, Jr. as a special judge of the circuit court in 1877; elected as a Democrat to the Forty-sixth and to the nine succeeding Congresses, and served from March 4, 1879 until his resignation on January 6, 1899, to become Governor; chairman, Committee on Claims (Forty-eighth Congress), Committee on Expenditures in the Department of the Navy (Fifty-third Congress); elected Governor of Tennessee in 1898, reelected in 1900, and served from January 16, 1899 to January 19, 1903; engaged in the insurance business in Nashville, Tenn.; appointed Envoy Extraordinary and Minister Plenipotentiary to Peru on July 2, 1913, and served until September 22, 1919; represented the United States at Guatemala in the same capacity from September 23, 1919, to January 5, 1922; resumed the insurance business in Nashville, Tenn., where he died on January 8, 1933; interment in Mount Olivet Cemetery.

**Bibliography:** *DAB*; Braden, Kenneth S. "Ambition or Service: Benton McMillin's Political Races in Tennessee." *Tennessee Historical Quarterly* 49 (Spring 1990): 53-63.

**McMORRAN, Henry Gordon,** a Representative from Michigan; born in Port Huron, Mich., June 11, 1844; attended the Crawford Private School; engaged in the wholesale grocery business in 1865 and also in the milling, grain, and elevator business; member of the board of aldermen in 1867; city treasurer of Port Huron in 1875; general manager of the Port Huron & Northwestern Railway 1878-1889; member of the State canal commission; elected as a Republican to the Fifty-eighth and to the four succeeding Congresses (March 4, 1903-March 3, 1913); chairman, Committee on Manufactures (Sixtieth and Sixty-first Congresses); was not a candidate for renomination in 1912; engaged in numerous business enterprises at Port Huron, Mich.; organized the Great Lakes Foundry Co., serving as its president; died in Port Huron, Mich., July 19, 1929; interment in Lakeside Cemetery.

**McMULLEN, Chester Bartow,** a Representative from Florida; born in Largo, Pinellas County, Fla., December 6, 1902; attended the public schools of Largo, Fla.; was graduated from the college of law at the University of Florida in 1924; was admitted to the bar in 1924 and commenced the practice of law in Clearwater, Fla.; prosecuting attorney of Pinellas County, Fla., in 1927 and 1928; elected State attorney for the sixth judicial circuit of Florida in 1930 and served until elected to Congress in 1950; director of the First National Bank of Clearwater; elected as a Democrat to the Eighty-second Congress (January 3, 1951-January 3, 1953); was not a candidate for renomination in 1952; died in Clearwater, Fla., November 3, 1953; interment in Sylvan Abbey, Clearwater, Fla.

**McMULLEN, Fayette,** a Representative from Virginia; born in Estellville (now Gate City), Scott County, Va., May 18, 1805; attended private schools; Virginia Commonwealth driver and teamster; member of the Virginia senate, 1839-1849; elected as a Democrat to the Thirty-first and to the three succeeding Congresses (March 4, 1849-March 3, 1857); chairman, Committee on Expenditures in the Department of the Navy (Thirty-second and Thirty-third Congresses), Committee on Expenditures on Public Buildings (Thirty-fourth Congress); delegate to the Democratic National Conventions of 1852 and 1856; appointed Governor of Washington Territory by President James Buchanan on May 13, 1857, and served until July 1858; elected as a Representative from Virginia to the Second Confederate Congress and served to the end of the Confederacy; engaged in agricultural pursuits and banking; was killed by a train in Wytheville, Va., November 8, 1880; interment in Round Hill Cemetery, Marion, Va.

**McMURRAY, Howard Johnstone,** a Representative from Wisconsin; born in Harvey County, near Mount Hope, Kans., March 3, 1901; attended the public schools, Berea Academy at Berea, Ky., and high school at Madison, Wis.; was graduated from the University of Wisconsin at Madison in 1936; engaged in the life insurance business 1923-1928; executive with air transport companies 1928-1935; teacher of political science at the University of Wisconsin 1936-1942; elected as a Democrat to the Seventy-eighth Congress (January 3, 1943-January 3, 1945); was not a candidate for renomination in 1944, but was an unsuccessful Democratic candidate for election to the United States Senate in 1944 and again in 1946; lecturer in political science at the University of Wisconsin in 1945 and 1946; professor of political science at Occidental College, Los Angeles, Calif., 1947-1949; professor of government, University of New Mexico, from 1949 until his death in Albuquerque, N.Mex., August 14, 1961; interment in Fairview Park Cemetery.

**McNAGNY, William Forgy,** a Representative from Indiana; born in Talmadge, Summit County, Ohio, April 19, 1850; moved in early life to Whitley County, Ind.; attended the public schools and the Springfield Academy, South Whitley, Ind.; taught school; worked on his father's farm for six years; station agent for the Pennsylvania Railroad Co. at Larwill, Ind., 1868-1875; studied law; was admitted to the bar in 1875 and commenced practice in Columbia City, Whitley County, Ind.; elected as a Democrat to the Fifty-third Congress (March 4, 1893-March 3, 1895); unsuccessful candidate for reelection in 1894 to the Fifty-fourth Congress; resumed the practice of law in Columbia City, Ind., and died there August 24, 1923; interment in Masonic Cemetery.

**McNAIR, John,** a Representative from Pennsylvania; born in Bucks County, Pa., June 8, 1800; received an academic education; taught school; principal of Loller Academy, Hatboro, Pa., in 1825; established a school for boys in the village of Abington; clerk of the courts of Montgomery County 1845-1848; became a resident of Norristown, Pa.; elected as a Democrat to the Thirty-second and Thirty-third Congresses (March 4, 1851-March 3, 1855); chairman, Committee on Manufactures (Thirty-third Congress); settled on a plantation in Prince William County, near Gainesville, Va.; died at Evansport, near Aquia Creek, Va., August 12, 1861.

**McNAMARA, Patrick Vincent,** a Senator from Michigan; born in North Weymouth, Mass., October 4, 1894; attended the public schools in Weymouth and Fore River Apprentice School in Quincy, Mass.; moved to Detroit, Mich., in 1921, and became active in union and civic affairs; engaged in the construction industry 1921-1955; director, Detroit area of Office of Price Administration, Rent Division, 1942-1945; vice president of Stanley-Carter Co., Detroit, Mich., 1946-1954; member, Detroit City Council 1946-1947, and the Detroit Board of Education 1949-1955; elected as a Democrat to the United States Senate in 1954; reelected in 1960, and served from January 3, 1955, until his death in Bethesda, Md., April 30, 1966; chairman, Special Committee on Aging (Eighty-seventh Congress), Committee on Public Works (Eighty-eighth and Eighty-ninth Congresses); interment in Mt. Olivet Cemetery, Detroit, Mich.

**McNARY, Charles Linza,** a Senator from Oregon; born on a farm near Salem, Marion County, Oreg., June 12, 1874; attended the public schools and Leland Stanford Junior University, California; studied law at Willamette University, Salem, Oreg.; was admitted to the Oregon bar in 1898 and commenced practice in Salem; dean of the law school of Willamette University, 1908-1913; from 1906 to 1913 served as an assistant to his brother, John Hugh McNary, the district attorney of Marion County; appointed an associate justice of the Oregon State supreme court and served from 1913 to 1915; unsuccessful candidate for election to the State supreme court in 1914; chairman of the Republican State central committee, 1915-1916; appointed as a Republican to the United States Senate to fill the vacancy in the term ending March 3, 1919, caused by the death of Harry Lane, and served from May 29, 1917 until November 5, 1918, when Frederick W. Mulkey was elected to fill this vacancy; again appointed to the United States Senate, December 12, 1918, to become effective December 18, 1918, to fill the vacancy in the same term caused by the resignation of Frederick W. Mulkey, having been previously elected for the term beginning March 4, 1919; reelected in 1924, 1930, 1936, and again in 1942, and served from December 18, 1918 until his death in Fort Lauderdale, Fla., February 25, 1944; minority leader (Seventy-third through Seventy-eighth Congresses); chairman, Committee on Irrigation and Reclamation of Arid Lands (Sixty-sixth through Sixty-ninth Congresses), Committee on Agriculture and Forestry (Sixty-ninth through Seventy-second Congresses), Republican Conference (Seventy-third through Seventy-eighth Congresses); co-sponsor of the McNary-Haugen farm bill of 1927, which would have required the government to support crop prices by buying up surplus commodities and either keeping them off the market or selling them abroad; unsuccessful candidate for Vice President of the United States in 1940 on the Republican ticket headed by Wendell L. Willkie; interment in Odd Fellows Cemetery, Salem, Oreg.

**Bibliography:** *DAB*; Johnson, Roger T. "Charles L. McNary and the Republican Party During Prosperity and Depression." Ph.D. dissertation, University of Wisconsin, 1967; Neal, Steve. "Charles L. McNary: The Quiet Man." In *First Among Equals: Outstanding Senate Leaders of the Twentieth Century*, edited by Richard A. Baker and Roger H. Davidson, pp. 98-126. Washington: Congressional Quarterly, Inc., 1991; Neal, Steve. *McNary of Oregon: A Political Biography*. Portland: Western Imprints, 1985.

**McNARY, William Sarsfield,** a Representative from Massachusetts; born in Abington, Plymouth County, Mass., March 29, 1863; attended the public schools of Abington and graduated from the Boston English High School; engaged in newspaper work; reporter and managing editor of the Boston Commercial Bulletin from 1880 to 1892; also engaged in the retail and wholesale furniture business; member of the Boston City Council, 1887-1888; member of the Massachusetts house of representatives, 1889-1890, and of the Massachusetts senate, 1891-1892; water commissioner of Boston, 1893-1894; again a member of the State house of representatives, 1900-1902; engaged in the insurance business and a dealer in real estate; delegate to the Democratic National Conventions of 1900 and 1904; elected as a Democrat to the Fifty-eighth and Fifty-ninth Congresses (March 4, 1903-March 3, 1907); was not a candidate for renomination in 1906 to the Sixtieth Congress; continued his former business pursuits in Boston, Mass., until his death there on June 26, 1930; interment in St. Joseph's Cemetery, West Roxbury, Mass.

**McNEELY, Thompson Ware,** a Representative from Illinois; born in Jacksonville, Morgan County, Ill., October 5, 1835; attended the public schools and Jubilee College, Peoria, Ill.; was graduated from Lombard College, Galesburg, Ill., in 1856 and from the law department of the University of Louisville, Kentucky, in 1857; was admitted to the bar in 1857 and commenced practice in Petersburg, Menard County, Ill.; member of the Illinois constitutional convention in 1862; elected as a Democrat to the Forty-first and Forty-second Congresses (March 4, 1869-March 3, 1873); did not seek renomination in 1872; delegate to the Democratic National Conventions in 1872, 1892, and 1896; resumed the practice of law in Petersburg, Ill.; master in chancery for Menard County from 1910 until his death in Petersburg, Ill., July 23, 1921; interment in Rosehill Cemetery.

**McNEILL, Archibald,** a Representative from North Carolina; born in Moore County, N.C.; member of the State house of commons in 1808 and 1809; served in the State senate 1811-1813, 1820, and 1821; elected to the Seventeenth Congress (March 4, 1821-March 3, 1823); elected to the Nineteenth Congress (March 4, 1825-March 3, 1827); moved to Texas in 1836; in 1849 raised and was chosen captain of about one hundred men who started for California, where gold had been discovered; struck by a sandstorm while crossing a desert (in what is now part of Arizona), he and most of the men were killed; his remains were never recovered.

**McNULTA, John,** a Representative from Illinois; born in New York City November 9, 1837; pursued an academic course; visited the West Indies and Europe; moved to Attica, Fountain County, Ind., in 1853 and to Bloomington, Ill., in 1859; engaged in the manufacture of cigars; studied law; during the Civil War served in the Union Army with the First Regiment, Illinois Volunteer Cavalry and the Ninety-fourth Regiment, Illinois Volunteer Infantry; was admitted to the bar in 1865 and commenced the practice of law in Bloomington, Ill.; member of the State senate 1869-1873; elected as a Republican to the Forty-third Congress (March 4, 1873-March 3, 1875); unsuccessful candidate for reelection in 1874 to the Forty-fourth Congress; resumed the practice of law; died in

Washington, D.C., February 22, 1900; interment in Evergreen Cemetery, Bloomington, Ill.

**McNULTY, Frank Joseph,** a Representative from New Jersey; born in Londonderry, Ireland, August 10, 1872; immigrated to the United States in 1876 with his parents, who settled in New York City; attended the public schools of New York City; vice president of the International Brotherhood of Electrical Workers in 1901; elected president of the same organization in 1903, and served until 1918, when he resigned; president emeritus and chairman of the international board of directors of that organization; member of the commission to study municipal and public ownership of public utilities in Great Britain, Ireland, and Scotland by the National Civic Federation; during the First World War served as vice chairman of the Railway Board of Adjustment No. 2; deputy director of public safety of Newark 1917-1921; elected as a Democrat to the Sixty-eighth Congress (March 4, 1923-March 3, 1925); unsuccessful candidate for reelection in 1924 to the Sixty-ninth Congress; resumed his former business activities; died in Newark, N.J., May 26, 1926; interment in Holy Sepulchre Cemetery, East Orange, N.J.

**Bibliography:** *DAB*.

**McNULTY, James Francis, Jr.,** a Representative from Arizona; born in Boston, Suffolk County, Mass., October 18, 1925; attended Boston public schools; graduated, Boston Latin School, 1943; LL.B., University of Arizona, Tuscon, 1951; served, United States Army, 1944-1945; admitted to the Arizona bar, 1951 and commenced practice in Bisbee; city attorney: Bisbee, Tombstone, and Huachuca City, Ariz.; elected, Arizona senate, 1969-1975; delegate, Democratic National Convention, 1960; elected as a Democrat to the Ninety-eighth Congress (January 3, 1983-January 3, 1985); unsuccessful candidate for reelection in 1984 to the Ninety-ninth Congress; is a resident of Bisbee, Ariz.

**McNULTY, Michael Robert,** a Representative from New York; born in Troy, Rensselaer County, N.Y., September 16, 1947; graduated St. Joseph's Institute, Barrytown, N.Y., 1965; attended Loyola University Rome Center, Italy, 1967-1968; A.B., Holy Cross College, Worcester, Mass., 1969; staff, Committee on Education, New York State Constitutional Convention, 1967; executive assistant to the mayor of Green Island, N.Y., 1969-1970; president, Green Island Insurance Agency, 1970-1988; staff member, New York State general assembly, 1977-1982; supervisor, Town of Green Island, N.Y., 1970-1977, then mayor, Green Island, N.Y., 1977-1983; member, New York State general assembly, 1983-1988; member, New York State Democratic Committee; elected as a Democrat to the One Hundred First and to the three succeeding Congresses (January 3, 1989-January 3, 1997); is a resident of Green Island, N.Y.

**McPHERSON, Edward,** a Representative from Pennsylvania; born in Gettysburg, Pa., July 31, 1830; attended the common schools; was graduated from Pennsylvania College in 1848; studied law; edited the Harrisburg American in 1851, the Independent Whig, Lancaster, Pa., 1851-1854, and the Daily Times, Pittsburgh, Pa., in 1855; elected as a Republican to the Thirty-sixth and Thirty-seventh Congresses (March 4, 1859-March 3, 1863); unsuccessful candidate for reelection in 1862 to the Thirty-eighth Congress; appointed Deputy Commissioner of Internal Revenue in 1863; Clerk of the House of Representatives from December 8, 1863 to December 5, 1875; permanent president of the Republican National Convention of 1876; Director of the United States Bureau of Engraving and Printing, 1877-1878; editor of the Philadelphia Press, 1877-1880; again served as Clerk of the House of Representatives from December 1881 to December 1883, and from December 1889 to December 1891; editor and proprietor of a newspaper in Gettysburg, Pa., 1880-1895; editor of the New York Tribune Almanac, 1877-1895; American editor of the Almanach de Gotha;

died in Gettysburg, Pa., December 14, 1895; interment in Evergreen Cemetery.

**Bibliography:** *DAB.*

**McPHERSON, Isaac Vanbert,** a Representative from Missouri; born near Rome, Douglas County, Mo., March 8, 1868; moved to Bradleyville, Taney County, Mo., with his parents; attended the graded schools, Springfield (Mo.) High School, and Marionville (Mo.) College; studied law; was admitted to the bar in 1889 and commenced practice in Mount Vernon, Lawrence County, Mo.; prosecuting attorney of Lawrence County in 1901 and 1902; member of the State house of representatives in 1903 and 1904; appointed postmaster at Aurora, Lawrence County, Mo., in 1905 and served until 1912; continued the practice of law in Aurora, Mo.; elected as a Republican to the Sixty-sixth and Sixty-seventh Congresses (March 4, 1919-March 3, 1923); unsuccessful candidate for renomination in 1922; appointed as assistant counsel in the legal department of the United States Shipping Board Emergency Fleet Corporation in 1923 and served in that capacity until his death in Aurora, Mo., October 31, 1931; interment in Maple Park Cemetery.

**McPHERSON, John Rhoderic,** a Senator from New Jersey; born in York, Livingston County, N.Y., May 9, 1833; attended the common schools and pursued an academic course; moved to Jersey City, N.J., in 1859; engaged in agricultural pursuits and was also a dealer in livestock; member, board of aldermen of Jersey City 1864-1870, and served as president of the board for three years; member, State senate 1871-1873; presidential elector on the Democratic ticket in 1876; elected as a Democrat to the United States Senate in 1877; reelected in 1883 and 1889, and served from March 4, 1877, to March 3, 1895; chairman, Committee on Naval Affairs (Forty-sixth through Fifty-third Congresses); died in Jersey City, N.J., October 8, 1897; interment in Oak Hill Cemetery, Washington, D.C.

**McPHERSON, Smith,** a Representative from Iowa; born near Mooresville, Morgan County, Ind., February 14, 1848; attended the common schools and Mooresville Academy; was graduated from the law department of the University of Iowa at Iowa City in June 1870; was admitted to the bar the same year and commenced practice in Red Oak, Montgomery County, Iowa; State's attorney in 1872; attorney general of Iowa 1881-1885; resumed the practice of law; elected as a Republican to the Fifty-sixth Congress and served from March 4, 1899, until his resignation on June 6, 1900, to accept the appointment of United States district judge for the southern district of Iowa; served until his death in Red Oak, Iowa, January 17, 1915; interment in Evergreen Cemetery.

**Bibliography:** *DAB.*

**McQUEEN, John,** a Representative from South Carolina; born in Queensdale, near the town of Maxton, Robeson County, N.C., February 9, 1804; completed preparatory studies under private tutors and was graduated from the University of North Carolina at Chapel Hill; studied law; was admitted to the bar in 1828 and commenced practice in Bennettsville, S.C.; served in the State militia 1833-1837; unsuccessful candidate for election in 1844 to the Twenty-ninth Congress; elected as a Democrat to the Thirtieth and Thirty-first Congresses to fill the vacancies caused by the death of Alexander D. Sims; reelected to the Thirty-second and to the four succeeding Congresses, and served from February 12, 1849, until his retirement on December 21, 1860; Representative from South Carolina in the First Confederate Congress; died at Society Hill, S.C., August 30, 1867; interment in Episcopal Cemetery, Society Hill, S.C.

**McRAE, John Jones,** a Senator and a Representative from Mississippi; born in Sneedsboro (now McFarlan), N.C., January 10, 1815; moved with his parents to Winchester, Wayne County, Miss., in 1817; pursued an academic course; graduated from Miami University, Oxford, Ohio, in 1834; studied law in Pearlington, Miss.; was admitted to the bar and practiced; founded the Eastern Clarion at Paulding, Miss.; member, Mississippi State house of representatives, 1848-1850, serving as speaker in 1850; appointed as a Democrat to the United States Senate to fill the vacancy caused by the resignation of Jefferson Davis, and served from December 1, 1851 to March 17, 1852, when a successor was elected and qualified; elected Governor of Mississippi in 1853, reelected in 1855, and served from January 10, 1854 to November 16, 1857; elected as a Democrat to the Thirty-fifth Congress to fill the vacancy caused by the death of John A. Quitman; reelected to the Thirty-sixth Congress, and served from December 7, 1858 until January 12, 1861, when he withdrew; representative from Mississippi in the Confederate Congress, 1862-1864; went to British Honduras in May 1868, and died at Belize, May 31, 1868; interment at Belize, British Honduras.

**McRAE, Thomas Chipman** (cousin of Thomas Banks Cabaniss), a Representative from Arkansas; born in Mount Holly, Union County, Ark., December 21, 1851; attended private schools in Shady Grove, Columbia County, in Mount Holly, Union County, and in Falcon, Nevada County, Ark.; was graduated from Soule Business College, New Orleans, La., in 1869, and from the law school of Washington and Lee University, Lexington, Va., in 1872; was admitted to the bar in 1873 and commenced practice in Rosston, Nevada County, Ark.; appointed election commissioner in 1874; member of the Arkansas State house of representatives in 1877; chairman of the Democratic State conventions of 1884 and 1902; delegate to the Democratic National Convention of 1884; elected as a Democrat to the Forty-ninth Congress to fill the vacancy caused by the resignation of James K. Jones; reelected to the Fiftieth and to the seven succeeding Congresses, and served from December 7, 1885 to March 3, 1903; chairman, Committee on Public Lands (Fifty-second and Fifty-third Congresses); declined to be a candidate for reelection in 1902 to the Fifty-eighth Congress; resumed the practice of law and also engaged in banking in Prescott, Ark.; president of the Arkansas Bar Association, 1917-1918; member of the Arkansas constitutional convention in 1918; elected Governor of Arkansas in 1920, reelected in 1922, and served from January 11, 1921 to January 13, 1925; elected a life member of the Arkansas Democratic State convention in 1926; resumed the practice of law and engaged in banking until his death in Prescott, Ark., on June 2, 1929; interment in De Ann Cemetery.

**Bibliography:** *DAB.*

**McREYNOLDS, Samuel Davis,** a Representative from Tennessee; born on a farm near Pikeville, Bledsoe County, Tenn., April 16, 1872; attended the rural schools, People's College, Pikeville, Tenn., and Cumberland University, Lebanon, Tenn.; studied law; was admitted to the bar in 1893 and commenced practice at Pikeville; served as assistant district attorney of the sixth judicial circuit of Tennessee in 1894 and 1896; moved to Chattanooga in 1896 and continued the practice of law; appointed judge of the criminal court for the sixth circuit of Tennessee on April 16, 1903; subsequently elected and twice reelected to the same office and served until February 1, 1923, when he resigned, having been elected to Congress; elected as a Democrat to the Sixty-eighth and to the eight succeeding Congresses and served from March 4, 1923, until his death; chairman, Committee on Foreign Affairs (Seventy-second through Seventy-sixth Congresses); delegate to the International Monetary and Economic Conference at London in 1933; died in Washington, D.C., July 11, 1939; interment in Forest Hill Cemetery, Chattanooga, Tenn.

**Bibliography:** *DAB.*

**McROBERTS, Samuel,** a Senator from Illinois; born near Maeystown, Monroe County, Ill. (then a portion of the Territory Northwest of the River Ohio), April 12, 1799; educated by private tutors; graduated from the law department of Transylvania University, Lexington, Ky.; was admitted to the bar in 1821 and commenced practice in Monroe County, Ill.; clerk of the circuit court of Monroe County 1819-1821; State circuit judge 1824-1827; member, State senate 1828-1830; appointed United States district attorney by President Andrew Jackson in 1830 and served until 1832, when he resigned; appointed by President Martin Van Buren receiver of the land office at Danville in 1832; appointed Solicitor of the General Land Office at Washington in 1839 and served in that capacity until his resignation in 1841; elected as a Democrat to the United States Senate and served from March 4, 1841, until his death in Cincinnati, Ohio, March 27, 1843; chairman, Committee on Engrossed Bills (Twenty-seventh Congress); interment in the Moore Cemetery, Waterloo, Monroe County, Ill.

**McRUER, Donald Campbell,** a Representative from California; born in Bangor, Maine, March 10, 1826; pursued an academic course; moved to San Francisco, Calif., in 1851 and engaged in the business of a commission merchant in San Francisco; member of the board of education of San Francisco in 1859 and 1860; during the Civil War was a member of the United States Sanitary Commission; elected as a Republican to the Thirty-ninth Congress (March 4, 1865-March 3, 1867); was not a candidate for renomination in 1866; traveled in Europe for two years; returned to San Francisco and served as harbor commissioner for four years; served on the board of directors of the Security Savings Bank of San Francisco; died in St. Helena, Calif., January 29, 1898; interment in St. Helena Public Cemetery.

**McSHANE, John Albert,** a Representative from Nebraska; born in New Lexington, Perry County, Ohio, August 25, 1850; attended the common schools; moved to Wyoming Territory in 1871 and in 1874 to Omaha, Nebr., where he continued in the livestock business; director in the First National Bank of Omaha; member of the State house of representatives 1880-1882; served in the State senate 1882-1886; elected as a Democrat to the Fiftieth Congress (March 4, 1887-March 3, 1889); resumed former business activities; died in Omaha, Nebr., on November 10, 1923; interment in Holy Sepulchre Cemetery.

**McSHERRY, James,** a Representative from Pennsylvania; born in Littlestown, Adams County, Pa., July 29, 1776; attended the Lancaster (Pa.) Academy; engaged in mercantile pursuits; member of the Pennsylvania house of representatives 1807-1812; served in the Pennsylvania senate in 1813; during the War of 1812 served in the defense of the city of Baltimore; delegate to the Pennsylvania constitutional convention of 1837 and 1838; elected to the Seventeenth Congress (March 4, 1821-March 3, 1823); unsuccessful candidate for reelection in 1822 to the Eighteenth Congress; again a member of the Pennsylvania house of representatives 1824-1830, 1834, and 1835; resumed mercantile pursuits; died in Littlestown, Pa., February 3, 1849; interment in St. Aloysius' Catholic Cemetery.

**McSPADDEN, Clem Rogers,** a Representative from Oklahoma; born on a ranch near Bushyhead, Rogers County, Okla., November 9, 1925; educated in the public schools of Oologah, Okla; attended the University of Redlands, Calif., North Texas Agricultural College (now Arlington State), and the University of Texas; B.S., Oklahoma State University, Stillwater, Okla., 1948; served in the United States Navy, 1944-1946, lieutenant (junior grade); Oklahoma State senator, 1954-1972, and served as president pro tempore, 1965-1967; cattle rancher in northeastern Oklahoma; insurance executive; bank director; real estate and property developer; professional sportscaster and rodeo announcer; contract director, Professional Rodeo Cowboys Association, Colorado Springs, Colo., 1963; delegate to the Democratic National Convention of 1968; elected as a Democrat to the Ninety-third Congress (January 3, 1973-January 3, 1975); was not a candidate for reelection in 1974 to the Ninety-fourth Congress, but was an unsuccessful candidate

for nomination for Governor of Oklahoma; founded McSpadden and Associates governmental and public relations firm; is a resident of Chelsea, Okla.

**McSWAIN, John Jackson,** a Representative from South Carolina; born on a farm near Cross Hill, Laurens County, S.C., May 1, 1875; attended the public schools; was graduated from Wofford College Fitting School in 1893 and from the University of South Carolina at Columbia in 1897; taught school in Marlboro, Abbeville, and Anderson Counties; studied law; was admitted to the bar in 1901 and commenced practice in Greenville, S.C.; referee in bankruptcy 1912-1917; entered the officers' training camp at Fort Oglethorpe, Ga., May 12, 1917, and served in the First World War as captain of Company A, One Hundred and Fifty-fourth Infantry, until March 6, 1919, when he was honorably discharged; resumed the practice of law in Greenville, S.C.; elected as a Democrat to the Sixty-seventh and to the seven succeeding Congresses and served from March 4, 1921, until his death; chairman, Committee on Military Affairs (Seventy-second through Seventy-fourth Congresses); declined to be a candidate for renomination in 1936; died in Columbia, S.C., on August 6, 1936; interment in Springwood Cemetery, Greenville, S.C.

**McSWEEN, Harold Barnett,** a Representative from Louisiana; born in Alexandria, Rapides Parish, La., July 19, 1926; attended the public schools in Alexandria; during the Second World War served in the United States Merchant Marine, United States Naval Reserve, 1944-1946; J.D., Louisiana State University, 1950; was admitted to the bar in 1950 and commenced the practice of law in Alexandria, La.; member of the Rapides Parish School Board, 1955-1956, and of the Louisiana State Board of Education, 1957-1958; delegate to the Democratic National Convention of 1960; elected as a Democrat to the Eighty-sixth and Eighty-seventh Congresses (January 3, 1959-January 3, 1963); unsuccessful candidate for renomination in 1962 to the Eighty-eighth Congress; candidate on the slate of Democratic Party presidential electors from Louisiana, 1964; resumed the practice of law; president of a bank and of a savings and loan association, 1965-1975; published author of political and historical essays and an independent scholar in American studies; is a resident of Alexandria, La.

**McSWEENEY, John,** a Representative from Ohio; born in Wooster, Wayne County, Ohio, December 19, 1890; attended the public schools and was graduated from Wooster University in 1912; employed in the engineering corps of the Pennsylvania Railroad Co., 1912-1913; taught at Wooster High School, 1913-1917; served overseas during the First World War from May 10, 1917 to August 11, 1919, and was promoted to captain and aide-de-camp to General Charles S. Farnsworth on August 16, 1918; awarded the Purple Heart Medal and received the Croix de Guerre; studied law at the Inns of Court, London; returned to the United States in 1919 and resumed teaching; member of the Wooster City Council, 1919-1921 and served as president; unsuccessful candidate for election in 1920 to the Sixty-seventh Congress; was admitted to the bar in 1925 and commenced practice in Wooster; elected as a Democrat to the Sixty-eighth and to the two succeeding Congresses (March 4, 1923-March 3, 1929); unsuccessful candidate for reelection in 1928 to the Seventy-first Congress; resumed the practice of law in Wooster; State director of public welfare, 1931-1935; elected to the Seventy-fifth Congress (January 3, 1937-January 3, 1939); unsuccessful candidate for reelection in 1938 to the Seventy-sixth Congress; unsuccessful Democratic candidate for election to the United States Senate in 1940, and for election as Governor of Ohio in 1942; served as a lieutenant colonel with the Military Government in Italy, 1943-1946; resumed the practice of law; elected to the Eighty-first Congress (January 3, 1949-January 3, 1951); unsuccessful candidate for reelection in 1950 to the Eighty-second Congress, for election in 1952 to the Eighty-third Congress, and in

1956 to the Eighty-fifth Congress; resided in Wooster, Ohio, until his death there on December 13, 1969; interment in Wooster Cemetery.

**McVEAN, Charles,** a Representative from New York; born near Johnstown, N.Y., in 1802; pursued an academic course; studied law; was admitted to the bar and commenced practice in Johnstown; editor of a newspaper in Canajoharie 1827-1831; elected as a Jacksonian to the Twenty-third Congress (March 4, 1833-March 3, 1835); was not a candidate for renomination in 1834; district attorney of Montgomery County 1836-1839; moved to New York City in 1839; resumed the practice of his profession; appointed surrogate of New York County January 24, 1844, and served until 1848; appointed United States attorney for the southern district of New York September 1, 1848; died in New York City, December 22, 1848; interment in St. Andrew's Cemetery.

**McVEY, Walter Lewis, Jr.,** a Representative from Kansas; born in Independence, Montgomery County, Kans., February 19, 1922; educated in the public schools and graduated from high school in 1940; attended Independence Junior College for two years; A.B., University of Kansas, 1947, and J.D., 1948; admitted to the bar and commenced the practice of law in Independence, Kans.; during the Second World War served in the Army Air Corps, 1943-1946, and was discharged as a staff sergeant; member, Kansas State house of representatives, 1949-1952; judge of the city court, Independence, Kans., 1952-1956; Kansas State senator, 1957-1960; unsuccessful candidate for nomination in 1952 to the Eighty-third Congress; elected as a Republican to the Eighty-seventh Congress (January 3, 1961-January 3, 1963); unsuccessful candidate for renomination in 1962 to the Eighty-eighth Congress; management consultant, Washington, D.C., 1963-1964; executive director, Fulton County, Ga., Republican Committee, June 1964-September 1965; staff counsel, Georgia Municipal Association, November 1965-April 1966; admitted to the Georgia bar in 1965 and commenced the practice of law in Atlanta; professor of political science, Georgia State University, 1968-1980, Mercer University, 1971-1973, and DeKalb College, 1968 to present; is a resident of Atlanta, Ga.

**McVEY, William Estus,** a Representative from Illinois; born on a farm near Lee's Creek, Clinton County, Ohio, December 13, 1885; attended the public schools; was graduated from Ohio University in 1916 and from the University of Chicago in 1919; division superintendent in the Bureau of Education, Philippine Islands, 1908-1914; director of extension, University of Ohio, 1916-1919; superintendent of Thornton Township High School and Junior College, Harvey, Ill., 1919-1947; president of North Central Association of Colleges and Secondary Schools in 1943 and 1944; professor of education at De Paul University 1948-1950; author; elected assessor of Thornton Township in 1949; elected as a Republican to the Eighty-second and to the three succeeding Congresses and served from January 3, 1951, until his death; had been renominated to the Eighty-sixth Congress; died in Washington, D.C., August 10, 1958; interment in Linwood Cemetery, Galesburg, Ill.

**McVICKER, Roy Harrison,** a Representative from Colorado; born in Edgewater, Jefferson County, Colo., February 20, 1924; educated at South Denver High School, Denver University, Columbia College, and graduated from Columbia Law School in 1950; lay preacher in the Methodist Church at eighteen years of age; during the Second World War served in the United States Navy in the Southwest Pacific; assistant professor in psychology at Colorado State College in 1946 and 1947; worked under President Truman in establishment of the Admiral Nimitz Commission on Internal Security and Civil Rights in 1950 and 1951; was admitted to the bar in New York in 1950, and practiced law in Wheat Ridge, Colo., 1953-1964; member of the State senate 1956-1964; elected as a Democrat to the Eighty-ninth Congress (January 3, 1965-January 3, 1967); unsuccessful candidate for reelection in 1966 to the Ninetieth

Congress; contract consultant, Agency for International Development, Denver, Colo., 1967; resumed the practice of law; died in Westminster, Colo., September 15, 1973.

**McWILLIAMS, John Dacher,** a Representative from Connecticut; born in Norwich, New London County, Conn., July 23, 1891; attended the public schools and Norwich Free Academy; was graduated from Mercersburg (Pa.) Academy in 1910; associated with the building industry in Norwich, Conn.; during the First World War served as a private in the Twentieth Engineers, United States Army, with overseas service, from March 26, 1918, until discharged on July 1, 1919; resumed the building business; selectman of the town of Norwich, Conn., 1935-1942; elected as a Republican to the Seventy-eighth Congress (January 3, 1943-January 3, 1945); was an unsuccessful candidate for reelection in 1944 to the Seventy-ninth Congress; was employed at the electric boat division of General Dynamics Corporation, Groton, Conn., 1950-1960; was employed by the city of Norwich, where he resided until his death there, March 30, 1975; interment in Maplewood Cemetery, Norwich, Conn.

**McWILLIE, William,** a Representative from Mississippi; born in Kershaw District, S.C., November 17, 1795; served in the War of 1812 as adjutant in his father's regiment; was graduated from South Carolina College in 1817; studied law; was admitted to the bar in 1818 and commenced practice in Camden, S.C.; president of the Camden Bank in 1836; member of the Mississippi State senate, 1836-1840; moved to Madison County, Miss., in September 1845 and engaged in planting; elected as a Democrat to the Thirty-first Congress (March 4, 1849-March 3, 1851); chairman, Committee on Expenditures in the Post Office Department (Thirty-first Congress); unsuccessful candidate for reelection in 1850 to the Thirty-second Congress; elected Governor of Mississippi in 1857, and served from November 16, 1857 to November 21, 1859; active in support of the Confederacy; died on his estate "Kirkwood," Madison County, Miss., March 3, 1869; interment in St. Philip's Churchyard.

**MEACHAM, James,** a Representative from Vermont; born in Rutland, Rutland County, Vt., August 16, 1810; was graduated from Middlebury (Vt.) College in 1832; taught in the seminary at Castleton, Vt., and in the local academy at St. Albans, Vt.; attended Andover (Vt.) Theological Seminary, where he studied for the ministry and was ordained as a Congregational minister in 1838, assuming his duties as pastor in New Haven, Vt., and served from 1839 to 1846; tutor and professor at Middlebury College 1846-1850; elected as a Whig to the Thirty-first Congress to fill the vacancy caused by the resignation of George P. Marsh; reelected to the Thirty-second, Thirty-third, and Thirty-fourth Congresses and served from December 3, 1849, until his death in Rutland, Vt., August 23, 1856; chairman, Committee on District of Columbia (Thirty-fourth Congress); interment in West Cemetery, Middlebury, Vt.

**MEAD, Cowles,** a Representative from Georgia; born in Virginia October 18, 1776; moved to Georgia at an early age; received an English education; studied law; was admitted to the bar and practiced; presented credentials as a Member-elect to the Ninth Congress and served from March 4, 1805, to December 24, 1805, when he was succeeded by Thomas Spalding, who contested his election; appointed secretary of Mississippi Territory by President Thomas Jefferson in March 1806 and served until 1807; Acting Governor from June 1806 to January 1807 during the absence of Governor Robert Williams; resumed the practice of law; member of the Mississippi house of representatives in 1807; unsuccessful candidate for election in 1812 to the Thirteenth Congress; delegate to the first constitutional convention of Mississippi in 1817; unsuccessful candidate for election in 1818 to the Sixteenth Congress; served in the State senate in 1821; again a member of the State house of representatives in 1822 and 1823; unsuccessful candidate for election as Governor of Mississippi in 1825; died on his plantation, "Greenwood," near Clinton, Jefferson County, Miss., May 17, 1844; interment on his estate.

**MEAD, James Michael,** a Representative and a Senator from New York; born in Mount Morris, Livingston County, N.Y., December 27, 1885; moved to Buffalo, N.Y., with his parents in 1890; attended the grammar, technical, and evening schools of Buffalo, N.Y.; employed as a water boy, lamplighter, spike mauler, and switchman on various railroads; member of the Capitol police force in Washington, D.C., in 1911; served on the board of supervisors of Erie County in 1914; member, State assembly 1915-1918; elected as a Democrat to the Sixty-sixth and to the nine succeeding Congresses and served from March 4, 1919, until his resignation on December 2, 1938; was not a candidate for renomination in 1938, having become a candidate for Senator; elected as a Democrat to the United States Senate to fill the vacancy caused by the death of Royal S. Copeland; reelected in 1940 and served from December 3, 1938, to January 3, 1947; was not a candidate for renomination in 1946; unsuccessful for the gubernatorial nomination in 1942 and for election as Governor in 1946; member of the Federal Trade Commission 1949-1955; director of Washington office of the New York Department of Commerce 1955-1956; moved to Clermont, Fla., in 1954 and operated an orange grove until his death in Lakeland, Fla., on March 15, 1964; interment in Oakhill Cemetery, Clermont, Fla.

**Bibliography:** *DAB*; Mead, James M. *Tell the Folks Back Home.* New York: Appleton-Century, 1944.

**MEADE, Edwin Ruthven,** a Representative from New York; born in Norwich, Chenango County, N.Y., July 6, 1836; pursued an academic course; studied law; was admitted to the bar in 1858 and commenced practice in Norwich, N.Y.; moved to New York City in 1872 and continued the practice of law; elected as a Democrat to the Forty-fourth Congress (March 4, 1875-March 3, 1877); was not a candidate for reelection in 1876; resumed the practice of his profession; died in New York City November 28, 1889; interment in Greene Cemetery, Greene, Chenango County, N.Y.

**MEADE, Hugh Allen,** a Representative from Maryland; born in Netcong, Morris County, N.J., April 4, 1907; attended the public schools; moved to Baltimore, Md., in 1923; was graduated from Loyola High School in 1925, from Loyola College in 1929, and from the University of Maryland Law School in 1932; was admitted to the bar in 1933 and commenced practice in Baltimore, Md.; secretary to Governor Albert C. Ritchie in 1934; member of the Maryland State house of delegates, 1934-1936; supervisor of assessments of the city of Baltimore, 1936-1938; assistant attorney general of Maryland, 1938-1946; served in the United States Navy as a lieutenant in 1944 and 1945; resigned from the attorney general's office in 1946 to enter the private practice of law; elected as a Democrat to the Eightieth Congress (January 3, 1947-January 3, 1949); unsuccessful candidate for renomination in 1948 to the Eighty-first Congress; appointed general counsel of the Merchant Marine and Fisheries Committee of the United States House of Representatives in January 1949, and served until his death in Washington, D.C., July 8, 1949; interment in the New Cathedral Cemetery, Baltimore, Md.

**MEADE, Richard Kidder,** a Representative from Virginia; born near Lawrenceville, Brunswick County, Va., July 29, 1803; pursued an academic course; studied law; was admitted to the bar and commenced practice in Petersburg, Dinwiddie County, Va.; served in the Virginia senate 1835-1838; elected as a Democrat to the Thirtieth Congress to fill the vacancy caused by the death of George C. Dromgoole; reelected to the Thirty-first and Thirty-second Congresses, and served from August 5, 1847 to March 3, 1853; appointed by President James Buchanan as Minister to Brazil and served from July 27, 1857, to July 9, 1861; returned to Virginia and devoted himself to the cause of the Confederacy; died in Petersburg, Va., April 20, 1862; interment in Old Blandford Cemetery.

**MEADE, Wendell Howes,** a Representative from Kentucky; born in Paintsville, Johnson County, Ky., January 18, 1912; attended the grade schools; graduated from high school at Kentucky Military Institute at Lyndon, Ky., in 1929; attended Western State Teachers College, Bowling Green, Ky., 1930-1933; engaged in the banking business, 1933 to 1936; graduated from the University of Louisville Law School, Louisville, Ky., in 1939; was admitted to the bar the same year and commenced practice in Paintsville, Ky.; served as a lieutenant in the United States Navy from November 1943 until January 1946, with twenty months' service in the South Pacific; resumed the practice of law; elected as a Republican to the Eightieth Congress (January 3, 1947-January 3, 1949); was an unsuccessful candidate for reelection in 1948 to the Eighty-first Congress; was an unsuccessful candidate for the Republican gubernatorial nomination in 1951; zone operations commissioner, Federal Housing Administration, 1957-1961; employed with a building contractor in Phoenix, Ariz.; Commissioner of Personnel, Commonwealth of Kentucky, 1968 to February 1969; member, Kentucky Workman's Compensation Board, 1969-1970; was a resident of Richmond, Ky., until his death in Lexington, Ky, June 2, 1986.

**MEADER, George,** a Representative from Michigan; born in Benton Harbor, Berrien County, Mich., September 13, 1907; attended the public schools of various cities in Michigan; student at Ohio Wesleyan University, 1923-1925; A.B., University of Michigan, 1927; J.D., University of Michigan Law School, 1931; was admitted to the bar in 1932 and commenced the practice of law in Ann Arbor, Mich.; prosecuting attorney of Washtenaw County, Mich., 1941-1943; assistant counsel, United States Senate special committee investigating the national defense program, from July 1, 1943, to October 1, 1945, and chief counsel from October 1, 1945, to July 15, 1947, practiced law, 1948-1950; chief counsel, United States Senate Banking and Currency subcommittee investigating the Reconstruction Finance Corporation in 1950; elected as a Republican to the Eighty-second and to the six succeeding Congresses (January 3, 1951-January 3, 1965); unsuccessful candidate for reelection in 1964 to the Eighty-ninth Congress; associate counsel, Joint Committee on the Organization of the Congress, March 1965 to April 1967, and chief counsel to September 1968; resumed private practice of law; staff counsel, Joint Committee on Congressional Operations, 1971-1975; was a resident of Washington, D.C.; died October 15, 1994.

**MEANS, Rice William,** a Senator from Colorado; born in St. Joseph, Mo., November 16, 1877; moved with his parents to Yuma County, Colo., in 1887; settled in Denver in 1889; attended the public schools and Sacred Heart College, Denver, Colo.; served in the Spanish-American War and commanded a company of scouts in the Philippine campaign in 1899; graduated from the law department of the University of Michigan at Ann Arbor in 1901; was admitted to the bar in 1901 and commenced practice in Denver; county judge of Adams County 1902-1904; unsuccessful candidate for election in 1908 to the Sixty-first Congress; served during the First World War as lieutenant colonel and commandant of the Fortieth Division School of Arms; commander in chief of the Army of the Philippines in 1913 and of the Veterans of Foreign Wars in 1914; unsuccessful candidate for election to the United States Senate in 1920; attorney for the city and county of Denver 1923-1924; elected as a Republican to the United States Senate on November 4, 1924, to fill the vacancy caused by the death of Samuel D. Nicholson and served from December 1, 1924, to March 3, 1927; chairman, Committee on Claims (Sixty-ninth Congress); unsuccessful candidate for renomination in 1926; commander in chief of the United Spanish War Veterans 1926-1927; president of the National Tribune Corporation and publisher of the National Tribune and Stars and Stripes at Washington, D.C., 1927-1937, when he retired; died in Denver, Colo., January 30, 1949; interment in Fairmount Cemetery.

**MEBANE, Alexander,** a Representative from North Carolina; born in Hawfields, N.C., November 26, 1744; attended the common schools of Orange County; delegate to the Provincial Congress of North Carolina in 1776; justice of the peace in 1776 and sheriff of Orange County in 1777; auditor of the Hillsboro district in 1783 and 1784; member of the Hillsboro convention in 1788 and of the Fayetteville convention in 1789; member of the State house of commons 1787-1792; elected to the Third Congress (March 4, 1793-March 3, 1795); died at Hawfields, Orange County, N.C., July 5, 1795.

**MECHEM, Edwin Leard,** a Senator from New Mexico; born in Alamogordo, Otero County, N.Mex., July 2, 1912; attended the Alamogordo and Las Cruces, N.Mex., schools; student at New Mexico State University in 1930-1931 and 1935; land surveyor, United States Reclamation Service, Las Cruces, N.Mex., 1932-1935; LL.B., University of Arkansas Law School, 1939; admitted to the New Mexico bar in 1939 and practiced in Las Cruces, and Albuquerque, N.Mex.; agent, Federal Bureau of Investigation, 1942-1945; member, New Mexico State house of delegates, 1947-1948; member of the Committee on Government Security, 1956-1957, and the American Law Institute; elected Governor of New Mexico in 1950, reelected in 1952, and served from January 1, 1951 to January 1, 1955; again elected Governor in 1956, and served from January 1, 1957 to January 1, 1959; unsuccessful candidate in 1958 for reelection for Governor; again elected Governor in 1960, and served from January 1, 1961 until his resignation on November 30, 1962, to accept appointment to the United States Senate; had been an unsuccessful candidate for reelection in 1962; appointed as a Republican to the United States Senate, November 30, 1962, to fill the vacancy caused by the death of Dennis Chavez and served until November 3, 1964; was an unsuccessful candidate for election to the vacancy in 1964; resumed the practice of law in 1965; member of the New Mexico Commission on Reorganization of Executive Branch; member of the New Mexico State Police Commission; United States District Judge, 1970 to the present; is a resident of Albuquerque, N.Mex.

**MEDILL, William,** a Representative from Ohio; born in New Castle County, Del., in 1802; completed preparatory studies, and was graduated from Newark (Del.) Academy (later Delaware College) in 1825; studied law; was admitted to the bar and commenced practice in Lancaster, Fairfield County, Ohio, in 1830; member of the Ohio State house of representatives from 1835 until 1838, and served as speaker in 1836 and 1837; elected as a Democrat to the Twenty-sixth and Twenty-seventh Congresses (March 4, 1839-March 3, 1843); unsuccessful candidate for reelection in 1842 to the Twenty-eighth Congress; Second Assistant Postmaster General in 1845; Commissioner of Indian Affairs, 1845-1850; president of the Ohio constitutional convention in 1850; Lieutenant Governor of Ohio in 1852 and 1853, and became Acting Governor on July 13, 1853, when Governor Reuben Wood resigned; elected Governor in 1853 and served until January 14, 1856; unsuccessful candidate in 1855 for reelection as Governor; First Comptroller of the United States Treasury, 1857-1861; died in Lancaster, Ohio, on September 2, 1865; interment in Elmwood Cemetery.

**MEECH, Ezra,** a Representative from Vermont; born in New London, Conn., July 26, 1773; moved to Hinesburg, Vt., in 1785; attended the common schools; engaged in the fur trade in the Northwest and in ship-timber contracts in Canada; moved to Shelburne, Vt., and engaged in agricultural pursuits and stock raising; member of the State house of representatives 1805-1807; elected to the Sixteenth Congress (March 4, 1810-March 3, 1821); delegate to the State constitutional conventions in 1822 and 1826; chief justice of Chittenden County Court in 1822 and 1823; elected to the Nineteenth Congress (March 4, 1825-March 3, 1827); unsuccessful Democratic candidate for Governor of Vermont in 1830, 1831, 1832, and 1833; presidential elector on the Whig ticket in 1840; resumed agricultural pursuits; died in Shelburne, Chittenden County, Vt., on September 23, 1856; interment in Shelburne Cemetery.

**MEEDS, Lloyd,** a Representative from Washington; born in Dillon, Beaverhead County, Mont., December 11, 1927; moved with his parents to Monroe, Snohomish County, Wash., in 1944; graduated from Monroe High School in 1946; served in the United States Navy from January 1946 to November 1947; graduated from Everett Junior College in 1950; part owner-operator of a gasoline station, 1950-1954; LL.B., Gonzaga University School of Law, Spokane, Wash., 1958, and was admitted to the bar the same year; deputy prosecuting attorney in Spokane and Snohomish Counties, 1958-1960; practiced law in Everett, Wash., 1960-1962; prosecuting attorney, Snohomish County, 1962-1964; president of Snohomish County Young Democrats, 1960-1962; board member of Snohomish County Democratic Central Committee, 1961-1963; elected as a Democrat to the Eighty-ninth and to the six succeeding Congresses (January 3, 1965-January 3, 1979); was not a candidate for reelection in 1978 to the Ninety-sixth Congress; resumed the practice of law in Washington, D.C. and Everett, Wash.; is a resident of Everett, Wash.

**MEEHAN, Martin Thomas,** a Representative from Massachusetts; born in Lowell, Mass., December 30, 1956; graduated from Lowell High School, 1974; B.S., University of Massachusetts, 1978; M.P.A., Suffolk University, 1981; J.D., Suffolk University School of Law, 1986; Massachusetts Deputy Secretary of State for Securities and Corporations Divisions, 1986-1990; first assistant district attorney, Middlesex County, 1991-1992; Fifth Congressional District delegate to the Democratic National Conventions of 1980, 1984 and 1988; elected as a Democrat to the One Hundred Third and One Hundred Fourth Congresses (January 3, 1993-January 3, 1997); is a resident of Lowell, Mass.

**MEEK, Carrie P.,** a Representative from Florida; born in Tallahassee, Fla., April 29, 1926; graduated, Florida A&M High School, Tallahassee, 1943; B.S., Florida A&M University, 1946; M.S., University of Michigan, 1948; Florida Atlantic University, 1979, completed course requirements for Ed.D. in education administration; instructor, health and physical education, Florida A&M University, 1958-1961; professor, Miami-Dade Community College, 1961-1968; planner, Dade County Model City program, 1966-1969; special assistant to the vice president, Miami-Dade Community College, 1982 to present; member, Florida State house of representatives, 1979-1982; member, Florida State senate, 1982-1993; elected as a Democrat to the One Hundred Third and One Hundred Fourth Congresses (January 3, 1993-January 3, 1997); is a resident of Miami, Fla.

**MEEKER, Jacob Edwin,** a Representative from Missouri; born near Attica, Fountain County, Ind., October 7, 1878; attended the public schools; was graduated from Union Christian College, Merom, Ind., in 1900, and from Oberlin (Ohio) Theological Seminary in 1904; while a student at Union Christian College he became pastor of a rural church in Vermilion County, Ill.; was ordained as a minister in 1901 and assumed his duties in Vermilion County, Ill.; missionary at Eldon, Mo., for the Congregational Church in 1904; moved to St. Louis, Mo., in 1906 to take charge of the Compton Hill Congregational Church; resigned in 1912; studied law at Benton College of Law and was admitted to the bar in 1914; elected as a Republican to the Sixty-fourth and Sixty-fifth Congresses and served from March 4, 1915, until his death in St. Louis, Mo., October 16, 1918; interment in Union Cemetery, Attica, Ind.

**MEEKISON, David,** a Representative from Ohio; born in Dundee, Scotland, November 14, 1849; immigrated to the United States in 1855 with his parents, who settled in Napoleon, Ohio; attended the common schools; apprenticed to the printer's trade; served with the Artillery in the United States Army 1866-1869; returned to Napoleon and studied law; was appointed city clerk in 1872; was admitted to the bar in 1873 and commenced practice in Napoleon, Ohio; prosecuting attorney of Henry County 1873-1879; probate judge 1881-1888; delegate to the Democratic National Convention in 1884; engaged in banking; established the Meekison Bank at Napoleon, Ohio, in 1886; mayor of Napoleon 1890-1897; elected as a Democrat to the Fifty-fifth and Fifty-sixth Congresses (March 4, 1897-March 3, 1901); was not a candidate for renomination in 1900; resumed the practice of his profession; also engaged in banking; died in Napoleon, Henry County, Ohio, February 12, 1915; interment in Glenwood Cemetery.

**MEEKS, James Andrew,** a Representative from Illinois; born in New Matamoras, Washington County, Ohio, March 7, 1864; moved to Illinois with his parents, who settled on a farm near Danville, Vermilion County, in 1865; attended the public schools, Westfield (Ill.) College, and Illinois College at Jacksonville; studied law; was admitted to the bar in 1890 and commenced practice in Danville, Ill.; master in chancery of the circuit court 1903-1915; corporation counsel of Danville 1925-1931; delegate to the Democratic National Conventions in 1920, 1924, 1928, and 1932; elected as a Democrat to the Seventy-third, Seventy-fourth, and Seventy-fifth Congresses (March 4, 1933-January 3, 1939); unsuccessful candidate for reelection in 1938 to the Seventy-sixth Congress and for election in 1940 to the Seventy-seventh Congress; resumed the practice of law and also engaged in banking until his death in Danville, Ill., November 10, 1946; interment in Spring Hill Cemetery.

**MEIGS, Henry,** a Representative from New York; born in New Haven, Conn., October 28, 1782; attended the common schools; was graduated from Yale College in 1799; studied law; was admitted to the bar and commenced practice in New York City; served in the War of 1812 with the rank of adjutant; member of the State assembly in 1818; elected to the Sixteenth Congress (March 4, 1819-March 3, 1821); chairman, Committee on Expenditures on Public Buildings (Sixteenth Congress); served as president of the board of aldermen of New York City in 1832 and 1833; judge of one of the city courts and afterward clerk of the court of general sessions; elected recording secretary of the American Institute in 1845, and retained this position in connection with the secretaryship of the Farmers' Club until his death; died in New York City on May 20, 1861; interment in St. Ann's Churchyard, Perth Amboy, N.J.

**MEIGS, Return Jonathan, Jr.,** a Senator from Ohio; born in Middletown, Conn., November 17, 1764; graduated from Yale College in 1785; studied law; was admitted to the bar and commenced practice in Marietta, Washington County, Ohio (then known as the Northwest Territory), in 1788; participated in the Indian fighting of that period; appointed territorial judge 1798; member of the territorial legislature in 1799; chief justice of the Ohio supreme court, 1803-1804; brevetted colonel in the United States Army and commanded in the St. Charles district in Louisiana, 1804-1806; judge of the supreme court of Louisiana, 1805-1806; judge of the United States District Court for the Territory of Michigan, 1807-1808; returned to Ohio and was elected Governor in 1808, but his election was contested by his opponent, Nathanael Massie; the Legislature declared Meigs ineligible because of his prolonged absence from the State and provided for a new election; elected as a Republican to the United States Senate to fill the vacancy caused by the resignation of John Smith; reelected in 1809, and served from December 12, 1808 to May 1, 1810, when he resigned; elected Governor of Ohio in 1810, reelected in 1812, and served from December 8, 1810 until his resignation on March 24, 1814; Postmaster General in the administrations of Presidents James Madison and James Monroe, April 11, 1814 to June 30, 1823; died in Marietta, Ohio, March 29, 1825; interment in Mound Cemetery.

**Bibliography:** *DAB*; McKeown, James S. "Return J. Meigs: United States Agent in the Cherokee Nation, 1801-1823." Ph.D. dissertation, Pennsylvania State University, 1984.

**MEIKLEJOHN, George de Rue,** a Representative from Nebraska; born in Weyauwega, Waupaca County, Wis., on August 26, 1857; attended the State normal school in Oshkosh, Wis.; principal of the high schools in Weyauwega, Wis., and Liscomb, Iowa; was graduated from the law department of Michigan University at Ann Arbor in 1880; was admitted to the bar and commenced practice in Fullerton, Nance County, Nebr., the same year; prosecuting attorney for Nance County, 1881-1884; member of the Nebraska State senate, 1884-1888, and served as its president, 1886-1888; chairman of the Republican State convention of 1887; chairman of the Republican State central committee in 1887 and 1888; Lieutenant Governor of Nebraska, 1889-1891; elected as a Republican to the Fifty-third and Fifty-fourth Congresses (March 4, 1893-March 3, 1897); was not a candidate for renomination in 1896 to the Fifty-fifth Congress; appointed by President William McKinley as Assistant Secretary of War on April 14, 1897, and served until March 1901, when he resigned; unsuccessful candidate for election to the United States Senate in 1901; resumed the practice of law in Omaha, Nebr.; moved to Los Angeles, Calif., in 1918 and continued the practice of his profession; also interested in mining; died in Los Angeles, Calif., April 19, 1929; interment in Forest Lawn Cemetery, Glendale, Calif.

**MELCHER, John,** a Representative and a Senator from Montana; born in Sioux City, Woodbury County, Iowa, September 6, 1924; attended the University of Minnesota; served in the United States Army, 1943-1945; D.V.M., Iowa State University, 1950; moved to Forsyth, Mont., and established a veterinary clinic; alderman in Forsyth, Mont., 1953; elected mayor of Forsyth in 1955, reelected in 1957 and 1959; elected Montana State representative for Rosebud County, 1960; elected Montana State senator in 1962, and served in the 1963 and 1965 sessions; again served in 1969 as a Montana State representative; elected as a Democrat to the Ninety-first Congress, June 24, 1969, by special election to fill the vacancy caused by the resignation of James F. Battin; reelected to the three succeeding Congresses, and served from June 24, 1969 to January 3, 1977; was not a candidate for reelection in 1976 to the House of Representatives, but was elected to the United States Senate; reelected in 1982, and served from January 3, 1977 to January 3, 1989; unsuccessful candidate for reelection in 1988; chairman, Select Committee on Indian Affairs (Ninety-sixth Congress), Special Committee on Aging (One Hundredth Congress); is a resident of Forsyth, Mont.

**MELLEN, Prentiss,** a Senator from Massachusetts; born in Sterling, Worcester County, Mass., on October 11, 1764; graduated from Harvard University in 1784; studied law; was admitted to the bar in 1788 and commenced practice in Sterling and Bridgewater, Mass., and in Dover, N.H.; moved to Biddeford, Maine (until 1820 a district of Massachusetts), around 1791 and practiced law; settled in Portland, Maine, around 1806; member, Massachusetts executive council 1808-1809, 1817; presidential elector in 1817; trustee of Bowdoin College, Brunswick, Maine, 1817-1836; elected to the United States Senate to fill the vacancy caused by the resignation of Eli P. Ashmun and served from June 5, 1818, to May 15, 1820, when he resigned; upon the admission of the State of Maine into the Union in 1820 became chief justice of the supreme court of that State and served until his resignation in 1834; member and chairman of the commission to revise and codify the public statutes of Maine in 1838; died in Portland, Maine, December 31, 1840; interment in Western Cemetery.

**Bibliography:** *DAB*; Greenleaf, Simon. "Memoir of the Life and Character of the Late Chief Justice Mellen." *Maine Reports* 17 (1841): 467-76.

**MELLISH, David Batcheller,** a Representative from New York; born in Oxford, Worcester County, Mass., January 2, 1831; attended the public schools; became a printer in Worcester; taught school in Massachusetts, Maryland, and Pennsylvania; proofreader in New York City; reporter on the New York Tribune; stenographer to the police board of New York City for ten years; appointed assistant appraiser of merchandise for the port of New York in 1871; elected as a Republican to the Forty-third Congress and served from March 4, 1873, until his death in Washington, D.C., on May 23, 1874; interment in Hillside Cemetery, Auburn, Mass.

**MENEFEE, Richard Hickman,** a Representative from Kentucky; born in Owingsville, Bath County, Ky., December 4, 1809; attended the public schools and was graduated from Transylvania University, Lexington, Ky.; taught school for several years; studied law; was admitted to the bar in 1830 and commenced practice in Mount Sterling, Ky.; appointed as Commonwealth attorney in 1832; member of the Kentucky house of representatives in 1836 and 1837; elected as a Whig to the Twenty-fifth Congress (March 4, 1837-March 3, 1839); resumed the practice of law in Lexington; died in Frankfort, Franklin County, Ky., February 21, 1841; interment in a private cemetery in Fayette County, Ky.; reinterred in Cave Hill Cemetery, Louisville, Ky., October 28, 1893.

**Bibliography:** Townsend, John W. *Richard Hickman Menefee.* New York: Neale Publishing Co., 1907.

**MENENDEZ, Robert,** a Representative from New Jersey; born in New York City, January 1, 1954; graduated, Union Hill High School, Union City, 1972; B.A., Saint Peter's College, 1976; J.D., Rutgers University School of Law, 1979; attorney; school trustee, 1974-1978 and chief financial officer, 1978-1982, Union City (N.J.) Board of Education; mayor of Union City, 1986-1987; member, New Jersey State general assembly, 1987-1991, majority whip; member, New Jersey State senate, 1991-1993; treasurer, New Jersey State Democratic Party; elected as a Democrat to the One Hundred Third and One Hundred Fourth Congresses (January 3, 1993-January 3, 1997); is a resident of Union City, N.J.

**MENGES, Franklin,** a Representative from Pennsylvania; born at Menges Mills, York County, Pa., October 26, 1858; attended the public schools in North Codorus Township, York County, Pa., and Baugher Academy Preparatory School, Hanover, Pa.; graduated from Gettysburg (Pa.) College in 1886; instructor in chemistry and physics at that college from 1886 until 1896; head of the science department of York High School, 1897-1903; lecturer at farmers' institutes in Pennsylvania and other States, 1898-1918; represented the Pennsylvania Agriculture Department at the Louisiana Purchase Exposition at the World's Fair in 1904; made a soil survey of the Commonwealth of Pennsylvania; author of numerous articles on scientific agriculture; elected as a Republican to the Sixty-ninth and to the two succeeding Congresses (March 4, 1925-March 3, 1931); unsuccessful candidate for reelection in 1930 to the Seventy-second Congress; engaged in agricultural pursuits on his farm near York, Pa., until his retirement in 1947; moved to Arlington, Va., where he died on May 12, 1956; interment in Evergreen Cemetery, Gettysburg, Pa.

**MENZIES, John William,** a Representative from Kentucky; born in Bryants Station, Bourbon County, Ky., April 12, 1819; attended the common schools; graduated from the University of Virginia at Charlottesville in 1840; studied law; admitted to the bar and commenced practice in Covington, Ky., in 1841; member of the Kentucky house of representatives in 1848 and 1855; elected as a

Unionist to the Thirty-seventh Congress (March 4, 1861-March 3, 1863); resumed the practice of law in Covington; delegate to the Democratic National Convention in 1864; judge of the chancery court 1873-1893; again resumed the practice of law; died in Falmouth, Pendleton County, Ky., on October 3, 1897; interment in Linden Grove Cemetery, Covington, Ky.

**MERCER, Charles Fenton** (cousin of Robert Selden Garnett), a Representative from Virginia; born in Fredericksburg, Va., June 16, 1778; graduated from Princeton College in 1797; took a postgraduate course in the same college and received his degree in 1800; studied law; admitted to the bar in 1802 and commenced practice in Aldie, Loudoun County, Va.; member of the Virginia house of delegates 1810-1817; during the War of 1812 was appointed lieutenant colonel of a Virginia regiment and then major in command at Norfolk, Va.; inspector general in 1814; aide-de-camp to Governor Barbour and brigadier general in command of the Second Virginia Brigade; projector and first president of the Chesapeake & Ohio Canal Co. 1828-1833; delegate to the Virginia constitutional convention in 1829; elected as a Federalist to the Fifteenth Congress; reelected to the Sixteenth through Twenty-first Congresses, reelected as an Anti-Jacksonian to the Twenty-second and Twenty-third Congresses and reelected as a Whig to the Twenty-fourth through Twenty-sixth Congresses and served from March 4, 1817, to December 26, 1839, when he resigned; chairman, Committee on Roads and Canals (Twenty-second through Twenty-fifth Congresses); was one of the originators of the plan for establishing the Free State of Liberia; vice president of the Virginia Colonization Society in 1836; vice president of the National Society of Agriculture in 1842; died in Howard, near Alexandria, Va., May 4, 1858; interment in Union Cemetery, Leesburg, Loudoun County, Va.

**Bibliography:** *DAB;* Carter, Robert Allen. "Virginia Federalist in Dissent: A Life of Charles Fenton Mercer." Ph.D. dissertation, University of Virginia, 1988; Egerton, Douglas R. *Charles Fenton Mercer and the Trial of National Conservatism.* Jackson: University Press of Mississippi, 1989.

**MERCER, David Henry,** a Representative from Nebraska; born in Benton County, Iowa, July 9, 1857; moved with his parents to Adams County, Ill., in 1858; at the close of the Civil War moved with his parents to Brownville, Nebr., where he attended the public schools and was graduated from the University of Nebraska at Lincoln in 1880; was graduated from the law department of Michigan University at Ann Arbor in 1882; was admitted to the bar and commenced practice in Brownville, Nebr.; served one term as city clerk and police judge; moved to Omaha in 1885, and for several years was chairman of the Republican city and county committees; secretary of the Republican State central committee in 1896; elected secretary of the Republican National Congressional Committee in 1896; chairman of the Republican State Central committee of Nebraska in 1897 and 1898; elected as a Republican to the Fifty-third and to the four succeeding Congresses (March 4, 1893-March 3, 1903); chairman, Committee on Public Buildings and Grounds (Fifty-fifth, Fifty-sixth, and Fifty-seventh Congresses); unsuccessful candidate for reelection in 1902 to the Fifty-eighth Congress; settled in Washington, D.C., and resumed the practice of law; died in Omaha, Nebr., January 10, 1919; interment in Forest Lawn Cemetery.

**MERCER, James** (brother of John Francis Mercer), a Delegate from Virginia; born at "Marlborough," Stafford County, Va., February 26, 1736; received private schooling at home; graduated from the College of William and Mary, Williamsburg, Va.; served as a captain in the French and Indian War; commander of Fort Loudoun, Winchester, Va., in 1756; studied law; admitted to the bar; active in pre-Revolutionary affairs; member of the Virginia House of Burgesses 1762-1775; member of the Virginia conventions of 1774, 1775, and 1776; member of the committee of public safety in 1775 and 1776; member of the Virginia constitutional convention in May 1776; Member of the Continental Congress in 1779; served as a judge of the General Court of Virginia 1779-1789; trustee and president of the Fredericksburg Academy 1786-1790; judge of the first Virginia Court of Appeals from 1789 until his death in Richmond, Va., on October 31, 1793; interment in St. John's Church Cemetery.

**Bibliography:** *DAB.*

**MERCER, John Francis** (brother of James Mercer), a Delegate from Virginia and a Representative from Maryland; born at "Marlborough," Stafford County, Va., on May 17, 1759; after receiving his education at home from private teachers was graduated from the College of William and Mary, Williamsburg, Va., in 1775; studied law; was admitted to the bar and commenced practice in Williamsburg, Va., in 1781; during the Revolutionary War served as lieutenant in the Third Virginia Regiment; promoted to captain in 1777, and was aide-de-camp to General Charles Lee in 1778 and 1779; lieutenant colonel of Virginia Cavalry; Delegate from Virginia to the Continental Congress in 1783 and 1784; moved to West River, Anne Arundel County, Md.; delegate from Maryland to the Federal Convention in Philadelphia in 1787 but withdrew before signing the Constitution; delegate to the Maryland convention which ratified the Federal Constitution in 1788; member of the Maryland State house of delegates in 1788, 1789, 1791, and 1792; elected to the Second Congress to fill the vacancy caused by the resignation of William Pinkney; reelected to the Third Congress and served from February 5, 1792, until his resignation April 13, 1794; again a member of the State house of delegates in 1800, and from 1803 until 1806; elected Governor of Maryland by the General Assembly, and served from November 10, 1801 to November 15, 1803; retired to his estate "Cedar Park," West River, Md.; died in Philadelphia, Pa., August 30, 1821; remains deposited in a vault at St. Peter's Church, Philadelphia, Pa.; subsequently interred in a private cemetery at "Cedar Park," West River, Anne Arundel County, Md.

**Bibliography:** *DAB.*

**MERCUR, Ulysses,** a Representative from Pennsylvania; born in Towanda, Bradford County, Pa., August 12, 1818; pursued classical studies; was graduated from Jefferson College, Canonsburg, Pa., in 1842; studied law; was admitted to the bar and commenced practice in Towanda in 1843; delegate to the Republican National Convention in 1856; president judge of the thirteenth judicial district of Pennsylvania from 1861 until March 4, 1865, when he resigned; elected as a Republican to the Thirty-ninth and to the three succeeding Congresses and served from March 4, 1865, until December 2, 1872, when he resigned to accept a judicial position; chairman, Committee on Private Land Claims (Forty-second Congress); associate justice of the supreme court of Pennsylvania 1872-1883; appointed chief justice in 1883 and served until his death in Wallingford, Pa., June 6, 1887; interment in Oak Hill Cemetery, Towanda, Pa.

**Bibliography:** *DAB.*

**MEREDITH, Elisha Edward,** a Representative from Virginia; born in Sumter County, Ala., December 26, 1848; attended Hampden-Sidney College, Virginia; studied law; was admitted to the bar in 1869 and commenced practice in Prince William County; prosecuting attorney for Prince William County, 1876-1883; member of the Virginia senate, 1883-1887; elected as a Democrat to the Fifty-second Congress to fill the vacancy caused by the death of William Henry Fitzhugh Lee; reelected to the Fifty-third and Fifty-fourth Congresses, and served from December 9, 1891 to March 3, 1897; resumed the practice of his profession; died in Manassas, Prince William County, Va., on July 29, 1900; interment in Manassas Cemetery.

**MEREDITH, Samuel,** a Delegate from Pennsylvania; born in Philadelphia, Pa., in 1741; attended Doctor Allison's Academy in Philadelphia; engaged in mercantile pursuits; served in the Revolutionary War as major and lieutenant colonel of the Third Battalion of Associators in 1776; promoted to brigadier general of Pennsylvania Militia April 5, 1777; resigned in 1778; twice a member of the Pennsylvania Colonial Assembly; Member of the Continental Congress 1786-1788; appointed surveyor of the port of Philadelphia August 1, 1789; was the first United States Treasurer appointed under the Constitution, and served from September 11, 1789, until his resignation December 1, 1801; retired to his country home, "Belmont Manor," near Pleasant Mount, Wayne County, Pa., where he died February 10, 1817; interment in the family cemetery on his estate.

**Bibliography:** *DAB.*

**MERIWETHER, David** (father of James Meriwether), a Representative from Georgia; born at Clover Field, near Charlottesville, Va., April 10, 1755; completed preparatory studies; during the Revolutionary War was a lieutenant and served in New Jersey, and afterward with Virginia troops at the last siege of Savannah, Ga.; settled in Wilkes County, Ga., in 1785; commissioned brigadier general of Georgia State militia on September 21, 1797; member of the Georgia State house of representatives, and served as speaker, 1797-1800; elected as a Republican to the Seventh Congress to fill the vacancy caused by the resignation of Benjamin Taliaferro; reelected to the Eighth and Ninth Congresses and served from December 6, 1802, to March 3, 1807; was not a candidate for reelection and retired to his plantation near Athens, Ga.; appointed a commissioner to the Creek Indians in 1804 and repeatedly reappointed to treat with other tribes; died near Athens, Ga., November 16, 1822; interment in the private burial ground on his plantation.

**Bibliography:** Coulter, E. Merton. "David Meriwether of Virginia and Georgia." *Georgia Historical Quarterly* 54 (Fall 1970): 320-338.

**MERIWETHER, David,** a Senator from Kentucky; born in Louisa County, Va., October 30, 1800; moved with his parents to Jefferson County, Ky., in 1803; attended the common schools; engaged in fur trading in 1818 near what is now Council Bluffs, Iowa; later engaged in agricultural pursuits in Jefferson County, Ky.; studied law; was admitted to the bar and commenced practice; member, Kentucky house of representatives, 1832-1845; unsuccessful candidate for election in 1846 to the Thirtieth Congress; delegate to the Kentucky constitutional convention in 1849; secretary of state of Kentucky in 1851; appointed as a Democrat to the United States Senate to fill the vacancy caused by the death of Henry Clay, and served from July 6 to August 31, 1852, when a successor was elected; was not a candidate for renomination in 1852; appointed by President Franklin Pierce as Governor of the Territory of New Mexico on August 8, 1853, and served until May 1857; member, Kentucky house of representatives, 1858-1885, and served as speaker in 1859; retired to his plantation near Louisville, Ky., where he died April 4, 1893; interment in Cave Hill Cemetery.

**Bibliography:** Meriwether, David. *My Life in the Mountains and on the Plains: The Newly Discovered Autobiography.* Edited by Robert A. Griffen. Norman: University of Oklahoma Press, 1965.

**MERIWETHER, James** (son of David Meriwether and uncle of James A. Meriwether), a Representative from Georgia; born near Washington, Wilkes County, Ga., in 1789; attended the common schools; was graduated from the University of Georgia at Athens in 1807; instructor in the university for a year; studied law; was admitted to the bar and practiced for a short period, later engaging in agricultural pursuits; served under General Floyd in the war against the Creek Indians in 1813; United States commissioner to the Cherokee Indians; trustee of the University of Georgia

1816-1831; member of the State house of representatives 1821-1823; elected to the Nineteenth Congress (March 4, 1825-March 3, 1827); was not a candidate for renomination in 1826; resumed agricultural pursuits; died while on a trip to the West, near Memphis, Tenn., in 1854; interment in the family burying ground on the plantation in Clarke County, near Athens, Ga.

**MERIWETHER, James A.** (nephew of James Meriwether), a Representative from Georgia; born near Washington, Wilkes County, Ga., on September 20, 1806; completed preparatory studies; was graduated from the University of Georgia at Athens in 1826; studied law; was admitted to the bar and commenced practice in Eatonton, Putnam County, Ga.; engaged in agricultural pursuits; member of the State house of representatives 1831-1836 and 1838; delegate to the State internal improvement convention at Eatonton, Ga., in 1839; judge of the superior court for the Eatonton (Ocmulgee) district 1845-1849; elected as a Whig to the Twenty-seventh Congress (March 4, 1841-March 3, 1843); member of the State house of representatives in 1843, 1851, and 1852, serving as speaker; died in Eatonton, Ga., April 18, 1852; interment in the Union Cemetery.

**MERRIAM, Clinton Levi,** a Representative from New York; born in Leyden, N.Y., March 25, 1824; attended the common schools and Copenhagen Academy, Copenhagen, N.Y.; engaged in mercantile pursuits in Utica, N.Y.; moved to New York City in 1847 and became an importer; engaged in banking in 1860; returned to Leyden in 1864; elected as a Republican to the Forty-second and Forty-third Congresses (March 4, 1871-March 3, 1875); retired from active business pursuits and lived in retirement on his estate, "Homewood," Locust Grove, N.Y.; died while on a visit in Washington, D.C., February 18, 1900; interment in Leyden Hill Cemetery, Port Leyden, N.Y.

**MERRICK, William Duhurst** (father of William Matthew Merrick), a Senator from Maryland; born in Annapolis, Md., October 25, 1793; completed preparatory studies and graduated from Georgetown University, Washington, D.C.; held several local offices; served in the War of 1812; register of wills of Charles County, Md., 1825-1832; studied law; was admitted to the bar and commenced practice in Port Tobacco, Md.; member, State house of delegates 1832-1838; elected as a Whig to the United States Senate to fill the vacancy caused by the death of Joseph Kent; reelected in 1839 and served from January 4, 1838, to March 3, 1845; chairman, Committee on the District of Columbia (Twenty-sixth and Twenty-seventh Congresses), Committee on Post Office and Post Roads (Twenty-seventh and Twenty-eighth Congresses); member of the State constitutional convention in 1850; member, State house of delegates from January 1856 until his death in Washington, D.C., February 5, 1857; interment in Mount Olivet Cemetery.

**MERRICK, William Matthew** (son of William Duhurst Merrick), a Representative from Maryland; born near Faulkner, Charles County, Md., September 1, 1818; was graduated from Georgetown University, Washington, D.C., in 1831; studied law at the University of Virginia at Charlottesville; was admitted to the bar in Baltimore in 1839 and commenced practice in Frederick, Md., in 1844; deputy attorney general for Frederick County 1845-1850; moved to Washington, D.C., in 1854; associate justice of the United States Circuit Court for the District of Columbia 1854-1863; resumed the practice of law in Maryland; professor of law at Columbian College (now George Washington University), Washington, D.C., in 1866 and 1867; delegate to the State constitutional convention of 1867; member of the State house of delegates in 1870; elected as a Democrat to the Forty-second Congress (March 4, 1871-March 3, 1873); unsuccessful candidate for reelection in 1872 to the Forty-third Congress; resumed the practice of law; associate judge of the supreme court of the District of Columbia by appointment of President Cleveland 1885-1889; died in Washington, D.C., February 4, 1889; interment in Mount Olivet Cemetery.

**MERRILL, D. Bailey,** a Representative from Indiana; born in Hymera, Sullivan County, Ind., November 22, 1912; attended the public schools; was graduated from Indiana State Teachers College, Terre Haute, Ind., in 1933; taught high school in Hymera, Ind., 1933-1935; graduated from Indiana University Law School, Bloomington, Ind., 1937; was admitted to the bar in 1937 and began practice in Terre Haute, Ind.; moved to Evansville, Ind., in 1939 and continued law practice; in 1942 volunteered as a private in the field artillery and served overseas with the Two Hundred and Ninety-first Field Artillery Observation Battalion; was released from active duty as a captain in March 1946; resumed the practice of law; elected as a Republican to the Eighty-third Congress (January 3, 1953-January 3, 1955); was an unsuccessful candidate for reelection in 1954 to the Eighty-fourth Congress and for election in 1956 to the Eighty-fifth Congress; resumed law practice until his retirement in 1977; is a resident of Evansville, Ind.

**MERRILL, Orsamus Cook,** a Representative from Vermont; born in Farmington, Conn., June 18, 1775; completed preparatory studies; moved to Bennington, Vt., in 1791; studied law; was admitted to the bar in 1804; served in the War of 1812 as a major of the Eleventh Regiment, United States Infantry and a lieutenant colonel in the Twenty-sixth Infantry and the Eleventh Infantry; register of probate in 1815; clerk of the courts in 1816; elected as a Republican to the Fifteenth Congress (March 4, 1817-March 3, 1819); presented credentials as a Member-elect to the Sixteenth Congress and served from March 4, 1819, until January 12, 1820, when he was succeeded by Rollin C. Mallary, who contested his election; delegate to the State constitutional convention in 1822; served in the State house of representatives in 1822; judge of the probate court in 1822 and 1823; State's attorney 1823-1825; member of the State executive council 1824-1827; member of the State senate in 1836; again judge of probate court 1841-1847; postmaster of Bennington, Bennington County, Vt., several years; resumed the practice of law at Bennington, where he died April 12, 1865; interment in the Old Cemetery on Bennington Hill.

**Bibliography:** Graffagnino, J. Kevin. "'I saw the ruin all around' and 'A comical spot you may depend': Orsamus C. Merrill, Rollin C. Mallary, and the Disputed Congressional Election of 1818." *Vermont History* 49 (Summer 1981): 159-68.

**MERRIMAN, Truman Adams,** a Representative from New York; born in Auburn, N.Y., September 5, 1839; attended the Auburn Academy and was graduated from Hobart College, Geneva, N.Y., in 1861; entered the Union Army in September 1861 as captain of a company which he had raised and which was attached to the Ninety-second Regiment, New York Volunteer Infantry; was mustered out as a lieutenant colonel in December 1864; studied law and was admitted to the bar in 1867; moved to New York City and worked as a journalist in 1871; president of the New York Press Club in 1882, 1883, and 1884; elected as an Independent Democrat to the Forty-ninth Congress, and reelected as a Democrat to the Fiftieth Congress (March 4, 1885-March 3, 1889); was not a candidate for renomination in 1888 to the Fifty-first Congress; died in New York City, April 16, 1892; interment in Fort Hill Cemetery, Auburn, N.Y.

**MERRIMON, Augustus Summerfield,** a Senator from North Carolina; born at "Cherryfields," near Asheville, Buncombe County, N.C., September 15, 1830; received a limited education; studied law; was admitted to the bar in 1852 and commenced practice in Asheville, N.C.; prosecuting attorney of Buncombe and other counties in western North Carolina; member, State house of commons 1860-1861; entered the Confederate Army upon the outbreak of the Civil War as a captain; resigned in the fall of 1861 to become solicitor for the eighth judicial district of North Carolina 1861-1865; judge of the superior court 1866-1867; settled in Raleigh, N.C., in 1867 and resumed the practice of law; declined to be a candidate for Governor of North Carolina in 1868; unsuccessful candidate for associate justice of the State supreme court in 1868; unsuccessful candidate for Governor of North Carolina in 1872; elected as a Democrat to the United States Senate and served from March 4, 1873, to March 3, 1879; was not a candidate for renomination in 1878; resumed the practice of law at Raleigh, N.C.; associate judge of the supreme court of North Carolina 1883-1889; served as chief justice of the court from 1889 until his death in Raleigh, N.C., November 14, 1892; interment in Oakwood Cemetery.

**Bibliography:** *DAB*; Merrimon, Maud. *A Memoir of Augustus Summerfield Merrimon*. Raleigh: E.M. Uzzell and Co., 1894.

**MERRITT, Edwin Albert,** a Representative from New York; born in Pierrepont, St. Lawrence County, N.Y., July 25, 1860; attended the common schools; was graduated from Potsdam Normal School in 1879 and from Yale College in 1884; deputy consul general in London in 1885; connected with various business enterprises in Potsdam; member of the board of supervisors 1896-1903; studied law; was admitted to the bar in 1902 and commenced practice in Potsdam, N.Y.; member of the State assembly 1902-1912, minority leader from 1908, and served as speaker in 1912; elected as a Republican to the Sixty-second Congress to fill the vacancy caused by the death of George R. Malby; reelected to the Sixty-third and Sixty-fourth Congresses and served from November 5, 1912, until his death, before the close of the Sixty-third Congress; died in Potsdam, St. Lawrence County, N.Y., December 4, 1914; interment in the family cemetery plot, Pierrepont, N.Y.

**MERRITT, Matthew Joseph,** a Representative from New York; born in New York City April 2, 1895; attended the public and high schools; during the First World War served in 1918 as a sergeant in Company C, Three Hundred and Twenty-seventh Battalion, Tank Corps; engaged in the real estate and insurance business in New York City 1926-1933; served with the New York loan agency of the Reconstruction Finance Corporation in 1933 and 1934; elected as a Democrat to the Seventy-fourth and to the four succeeding Congresses (January 3, 1935-January 3, 1945); was not a candidate for renomination in 1944; engaged in the real estate and insurance business in New York City; died at Malba, Queens County, N.Y., September 29, 1946; interment in Mount St. Mary's Cemetery, Whitestone, N.Y.

**MERRITT, Samuel Augustus,** a Delegate from the Territory of Idaho; born in Staunton, Augusta County, Va., August 15, 1827; attended the Staunton Military Academy and was graduated from Washington College (now Washington and Lee University), Lexington, Va., in 1848; moved to Mariposa County, Calif., in 1849; county clerk and public administrator of Mariposa County in 1850; member of the State house of representatives in 1851 and 1852; studied law; was admitted to the bar in 1852 and commenced practice; served in the State senate 1857-1862; moved to the Territory of Idaho in 1862; elected as a Democrat to the Forty-second Congress (March 4, 1871-March 3, 1873); was an unsuccessful candidate for renomination in 1872; moved to Salt Lake City, Utah, in 1873 and engaged in mining operations and the practice of law; city attorney 1888-1890; member of the Democratic National Committee in 1892; chief justice of the supreme court of the Territory of Utah 1894-1896; died in Salt Lake City on September 8, 1910; interment in Salt Lake City Cemetery.

**MERRITT, Schuyler,** a Representative from Connecticut; born in New York City, December 16, 1853; moved with his parents to Stamford, Conn., in 1855; prepared for college at private schools in that city; was graduated from Yale College, New Haven, Conn., in 1873, and from Columbia Law School, New York City, in 1876; interested in the manufacture of locks and keys and also engaged in banking 1877-1917; member of the Connecticut constitutional convention in 1904; member of the State board of education 1910-1916; delegate to the Republican National Convention in 1916;

elected as a Republican to the Sixty-fifth Congress to fill the vacancy caused by the death of Ebenezer J. Hill; reelected to the Sixty-sixth and to the five succeeding Congresses and served from November 6, 1917, to March 3, 1931; unsuccessful candidate for reelection in 1930; again elected to the Seventy-third and Seventy-fourth Congresses (March 4, 1933-January 3, 1937); unsuccessful candidate for reelection in 1936 to the Seventy-fifth Congress; continued his interests in the Yale & Towne Manufacturing Co. and the First Stamford National Bank; died in Stamford, Conn., April 1, 1953; interment in Woodland Cemetery.

**MERROW, Chester Earl,** a Representative from New Hampshire; born in Center Ossipee, Carroll County, N.H., November 15, 1906; attended the public schools and Brewster Free Academy, 1921-1925; was graduated from Colby College, Waterville, Maine, in 1929 and from Teachers College (summers), Columbia University, New York City, in 1937; instructor of science at Kents Hill (Maine) School in 1929 and 1930 and at Montpelier (Vt.) Seminary, 1930-1937; assistant headmaster of Montpelier Seminary, 1935-1938; instructor of political science and history at Vermont Junior College, Montpelier, Vt., in 1937 and 1938; member of the New Hampshire house of representatives in 1939 and 1940; radio news commentator and lecturer; delegate to international conference on education and cultural relations of the United Nations held in London in 1945; congressional adviser to the first conference of the United Nations Educational, Scientific, and Cultural Organization held in Paris in 1946; member of the United States delegation to the United Nations Education, Scientific, and Cultural Organization 1946-1949; elected as a Republican to the Seventy-eighth and to the nine succeeding Congresses (January 3, 1943-January 3, 1963); was not a candidate for reelection in 1962 to the Eighty-eighth Congress, but was unsuccessful for nomination to the United States Senate; Special Adviser on Community Relations, Department of State, 1963-1968; unsuccessful candidate for election in 1970 to the Ninety-second Congress; unsuccessful candidate for election in 1972 to the Ninety-third Congress; resided in Center Ossipee, N.H., until his death there, February 10, 1974; interment in Chickville Cemetery.

**Bibliography:** Merrow, Chester Earl. *My Twenty Years in Congress*. Society for the Publication of New Hampshire Biographies, 1968.

**MERWIN, Orange,** a Representative from Connecticut; born in Merryall, near New Milford, Litchfield County, Conn., April 7, 1777; attended the common schools; engaged in agricultural pursuits; member of the Connecticut State house of representatives, 1815-1820; delegate to the State constitutional convention in 1818; served in the State senate, 1821-1825; member of the committee of twenty-four to draft the State constitution; elected to the Nineteenth and Twentieth Congresses (March 4, 1825-March 3, 1829); was not a candidate for renomination in 1828 to the Twenty-first Congress; resumed agricultural pursuits; was an unsuccessful candidate for Lieutenant Governor of Connecticut in 1831; died in New Milford, Conn., September 4, 1853; interment in Center Cemetery.

**MESICK, William Smith,** a Representative from Michigan; born in Newark, Wayne County, N.Y., August 26, 1856; attended the common schools, Kalamazoo (Mich.) Business College, and was graduated from the law department of the University of Michigan at Ann Arbor in 1881; was admitted to the bar in 1881 and commenced the practice of his profession in Mancelona, Mich.; prosecuting attorney of Antrim County, Mich., for one term; elected as a Republican to the Fifty-fifth and Fifty-sixth Congresses (March 4, 1897-March 3, 1901); chairman, Committee on Elections No. 3 (Fifty-sixth Congress); unsuccessful candidate for renomination in 1900; resumed the practice of his profession in Mancelona and subsequently moved to Petoskey, Emmet County, Mich., and continued practice; died in Petoskey, Mich., on December 1, 1942; interment in Greenwood Cemetery.

**MESKILL, Thomas Joseph,** a Representative from Connecticut; born in New Britain, Hartford County, Conn., January 30, 1928; attended the local schools and Saint Thomas Seminary in Bloomfield, Conn.; graduated from New Britain Senior High School, 1946; B.S., Trinity College, Hartford, Conn., 1950; enlisted in the United States Air Force in 1950 and served until discharged in 1953 with rank of first lieutenant; LL.B., University of Connecticut Law School, 1956; also studied at the New York University School of Law in 1955; admitted to the bar and commenced practice in New Britain, Conn., in 1956; assistant corporation counsel, New Britain, 1960-1962; mayor of New Britain, Conn., 1962-1964; corporation counsel of New Britain, Conn., 1965-1966; member of the State constitutional convention, 1965; elected as a Republican to the Ninetieth and Ninety-first Congresses (January 3, 1967-January 3, 1971); was not a candidate for reelection in 1970 to the Ninety-second Congress, but was elected Governor of Connecticut, and served from January 6, 1971 to January 8, 1975; appointed United States circuit judge for the Second Circuit on April 22, 1975; served as chief judge, July 1, 1992 to July 1, 1993; took senior status June 30, 1993; is a resident of Kensington, Conn.

**METCALF, Arunah,** a Representative from New York; was born August 15, 1771; attended the common schools; moved from Connecticut to New York and settled in Otsego (now Cooperstown), in 1802; elected as a Republican to the Twelfth Congress (March 4, 1811-March 3, 1813); member of the State assembly 1814-1816; president of the Otsego County Agricultural Society in 1818; unsuccessful candidate for election to the State senate in 1819; again a member of the New York State assembly in 1828; died in Cooperstown, Otsego County, N.Y., August 15, 1848.

**METCALF, Jack,** a Representative from Washington; born in Marysville, Snohomish County, Wash., November 30, 1927; B.A. and B.Ed., Pacific Lutheran University, Tacoma, Wash., 1951; M.A., University of Washington, 1966; served in the United States Army, 1946-1947; United States Marshal and patrol boat captain, United States Fish and Wildlife Service, Alaska, 1947-1948; school teacher, thirty years; unsuccessful candidate in 1968 and 1974 for election to the United States Senate; member, Washington State senate, 1966-1974 and 1980-1992; unsuccessful candidate in 1992 for election to the One Hundred Third Congress; co-owner, The Log Castle Bed and Breakfast near Langley, Wash.; elected as a Republican to the One Hundred Fourth Congress (January 3, 1995-January 3, 1997); is a resident of Langley, Wash.

**METCALF, Jesse Houghton,** a Senator from Rhode Island; born in Providence, R.I., November 16, 1860; educated in the private schools of Providence; studied textile manufacturing in Yorkshire, England; engaged in textile manufacturing; member, Rhode Island house of representatives, 1889-1891, 1907; member, Providence Common Council, 1888-1892; chairman, Metropolitan Park Commission of Rhode Island, 1909-1924; member, penal and charitable board, 1917-1923; president, Rhode Island Hospital; trustee, Rhode Island School of Design at Providence and of Brown University; Republican National committeeman, 1935-1940; elected as a Republican to the United States Senate on November 4, 1924, to fill the vacancy caused by the death of LeBaron B. Colt; on the same day was also elected for the term commencing March 4, 1925; reelected in 1930, and served from November 5, 1924 to January 3, 1937; unsuccessful candidate for reelection in 1936; chairman, Committee on Patents (Sixty-ninth and Seventieth Congresses), Committee on Education and Labor (Seventy-first and Seventy-second Congresses); died in Providence, R.I., October 9, 1942; interment in Swan Point Cemetery.

**METCALF, Lee Warren,** a Representative and a Senator from Montana; born in Stevensville, Ravalli County, Mont., January 28, 1911; attended the public schools; A.B., Stanford University, 1936; LL.B., Montana State University Law School, 1936; was admitted to the Montana bar in 1936 and commenced the practice of law; member, Montana State house of representatives, 1937; assistant attorney general of Montana, 1937-1941; in December 1942 enlisted in the Army, attended officers' training school, was commissioned, went overseas in 1944, and participated in the Normandy invasion and the Battle of the Bulge; after the close of the war in Europe was concerned with the care and repatriation of displaced; helped in drafting ordinances for the first free local elections in Germany and supervised the free elections in Bavaria; discharged from the Army as a first lieutenant in April 1946; associate justice of the Montana State supreme court, 1946-1952; elected as a Democrat to the Eighty-third and to the three succeeding Congresses (January 3, 1953-January 3, 1961); was not a candidate for reelection in 1960 to the House of Representatives, but was elected to the United States Senate; reelected in 1966 and again in 1972 and served from January 3, 1961, until his death in Helena, Mont., January 12, 1978; co-chairman, Joint Committee on Congressional Operations (Ninety-third and Ninety-fifth Congresses); cremated; ashes scattered in one of his favorite areas in the wilderness of the State of Montana.

**Bibliography:** *DAB*; Metcalf, Lee. *Overcharge*. New York: C. McKay Company, 1967; Warden, Richard D. *Metcalf of Montana: How a Senator Makes Government Work*. Washington, D.C.: Acropolis Books, 1965.

**METCALF, Victor Howard,** a Representative from California; born in Utica, Oneida County, N.Y., October 10, 1853; attended the public schools of Utica, and was graduated from the Utica Free Academy in 1871, from Russell's Military Academy, New Haven, Conn., in 1872, and from the law department of Yale College in 1876; was admitted to the Connecticut bar in June 1876 and to the New York bar in 1877, and commenced practice in Utica, N.Y., in 1877; moved to Oakland, Alameda County, Calif., in 1879 and continued the practice of law; elected as a Republican to the Fifty-sixth and to the two succeeding Congresses and served from March 4, 1899, until his resignation July 1, 1904; appointed Secretary of Commerce and Labor by President Theodore Roosevelt and served from July 1, 1904 to December 16, 1906, when he resigned; appointed by President Theodore Roosevelt as Secretary of the Navy, and served from December 17, 1906 until November 30, 1908, when he resigned; returned to Oakland, Calif., engaged in banking for several years, and then resumed the practice of law; died in Oakland, Calif., February 20, 1936; interment in Mountain View Cemetery.

**METCALFE, Henry Bleecker,** a Representative from New York; born in Albany, N.Y., January 20, 1805; moved to New York City in 1811 and to Richmond County in 1816; studied law; was admitted to the bar and commenced practice in New York City in 1826; prosecuting attorney of Richmond County, 1826-1832; elected county judge in 1840 and served until 1841, when he resigned; again county judge from 1847 to 1875; elected as a Democrat to the Forty-fourth Congress (March 4, 1875-March 3, 1877); chairman, Committee on Expenditures on Public Buildings (Forty-fourth Congress); died in Richmond, Staten Island, N.Y., February 7, 1881; interment in the Moravian Cemetery, New Dorp, Staten Island, N.Y.

**METCALFE, Lyne Shackelford,** a Representative from Missouri; born in Madisonville, Hopkins County, Ky., April 21, 1822; attended the common schools, Shurtleff College, Alton, Ill., and Illinois College, Jacksonville, Ill.; engaged in mercantile pursuits in Alton, Ill., in 1844; member of the board of aldermen of Alton; elected mayor of Alton; during the Civil War served in the Union Army as assistant quartermaster with rank of captain and later promoted to colonel; moved to St. Louis, Mo., in 1863; engaged in manufacturing; served in the city council of St. Louis; elected as a Republican to the Forty-fifth Congress (March 4, 1877-March 3, 1879); unsuccessful candidate for reelection in 1878 to the Forty-sixth Congress; died in Kirkwood, St. Louis County, Mo., January 31, 1906; interment in Alton Cemetery; Alton, Madison County, Ill.

**METCALFE, Ralph Harold,** a Representative from Illinois; born in Atlanta, Fulton County, Ga., May 29, 1910; attended the Chicago public schools; Ph.B., Marquette University, Milwaukee, Wis., 1936; M.A., University of Southern California, 1939; gold, silver, and bronze medal winner at the 1932 Olympics at Los Angeles, Calif., and the 1936 Olympics at Berlin, Germany; track coach and political science instructor, Xavier University, New Orleans, La., 1936-1942; served as first lieutenant in United States Army Transportation Corps, 1942-1945; received Legion of Merit for program planning as director of physcial training; director of the Chicago Commission on Human Relations Department of Civil Rights, 1945; Illinois State Athletic Commissioner, 1949-1952; elected Democratic committeeman (Third Ward), 1952, 1956, 1960, 1964, and 1968; elected alderman in 1955, 1959, 1963, and 1967; elected president pro tempore, Chicago City Council, 1969; appointed a member of the National Amateur Athletic Union and National Collegiate Athletic Association Sports Arbitration Board by Vice President Hubert H. Humphrey; member, Chicago Planning Commission, 1964; member of the committee chaired by United States District Judge Richard B. Austin to investigate the civil disturbance in Chicago following the assassination of the Rev. Dr. Martin Luther King, Jr.; delegate to Illinois State Democratic conventions, 1953-1972; delegate to Democratic National Conventions, 1952-1972; member of the President's Commission on Olympic Sports, 1975-1977; elected as a Democrat to the Ninety-second and to the three succeeding Congresses, and served from January 3, 1971 until his death in Chicago, Ill., October 10, 1978; had been a successful candidate in the primary to the Ninety-sixth Congress; interment in Holy Sepulchre Cemetery, Worth, Ill.

**Bibliography:** *DAB.*

**METCALFE, Thomas,** a Representative and a Senator from Kentucky; born in Fauquier County, Va., March 20, 1780; moved with his parents to Fayette County, Ky.; attended the common schools; learned the mason's trade; served as captain in the War of 1812; member, Kentucky house of representatives, 1812-1816; elected to the Sixteenth and the four succeeding Congresses and served from March 4, 1819, until his resignation June 1, 1828; chairman, Committee on Indian Affairs (Seventeenth Congress), Committee on Militia (Twentieth Congress); elected Governor of Kentucky in 1828 and served from June 1, 1828 to June 1, 1832; member, Kentucky senate, 1834-1838; president of the board of internal improvements in 1840; appointed and subsequently elected as a Whig to the United States Senate to fill the vacancy caused by the resignation of John J. Crittenden and served from June 23, 1848, to March 3, 1849; engaged in agricultural pursuits; died near Carlisle, Nicholas County, Ky., August 18, 1855; interment in the family burial ground at "Forest Retreat," in Nicholas County, Ky.

**Bibliography:** *DAB.*

**METZ, Herman August,** a Representative from New York; born in New York City October 19, 1867; attended private and public schools; manufacturer and importer of dyestuffs, chemicals, and pharmaceuticals; member of the board of education of Brooklyn and the city of New York; comptroller of the city of New York, 1906-1910; member of the commission appointed by Governor Charles Evans Hughes to draft the New York City charter in 1907 and 1908, and of the charter commission appointed by Governor Nathan L. Miller in 1922; commissioner of the New York State board of charities; was the candidate of Kings County for Governor at the Democratic State convention in 1912, but withdrew in favor of William Sulzer after

the second ballot; first lieutenant, captain, lieutenant colonel, and brigadier general of the Fourteenth Infantry, New York National Guard; elected as a Democrat to the Sixty-third Congress (March 4, 1913-March 3, 1915); was not a candidate for renomination in 1914 to the Sixty-fourth Congress; resumed former business activities; delegate to the Democratic National Conventions of 1904, 1908 and 1920; during the First World War was ordnance officer, with the rank of lieutenant colonel, in the Twenty-seventh Division; colonel in the ordnance department of the Officers' Reserve Corps; unsuccessful candidate for election in 1922 to the Sixty-eighth Congress; died in a hospital in New Rochelle, N.Y., May 17, 1934; interment in Kensico Cemetery, Westchester, N.Y.

**METZENBAUM, Howard Morton,** a Senator from Ohio; born in Cleveland, Cuyahoga County, Ohio, June 4, 1917; B.A., Ohio State University, Columbus, 1939; LL.B., Ohio State University School of Law, 1941; admitted to the Ohio bar in 1941 and commenced practice in Cleveland; member, Ohio State house of representatives, 1943-1947; member, Ohio State senate, 1947-1951; campaign manager for Senator Stephen M. Young of Ohio in 1958 and 1964; unsuccessful candidate in 1970 for election to the United States Senate; chairman of a group of suburban weeklies in the Cleveland area; appointed by the Governor, January 4, 1974, as a Democrat to the United States Senate to fill the vacancy caused by the resignation of William B. Saxbe and served from January 4, 1974, until his resignation December 23, 1974; unsuccessful candidate for renomination in 1974; resumed the practice of law; elected on November 2, 1976, to the United States Senate for the six-year term commencing January 3, 1977; subsequently appointed by the Governor, December 29, 1976, to fill the vacancy caused by the resignation of Robert Taft, Jr. for the term ending January 3, 1977; reelected in 1982 and 1988, and served from December 29, 1976 until January 3, 1995; was not a candidate for reelection in 1994; is a resident of Lyndhurst, Ohio.

**MEYER, Adolph,** a Representative from Louisiana, born in Natchez, Adams County, Miss., October 19, 1842; attended the common schools; matriculated at the University of Virginia at Charlottesville, but before graduation enlisted in the Confederate Army in 1862; served until the close of the Civil War on the staff of Brigadier General John S. Williams, of Kentucky, and attained the rank of assistant adjutant general; returned to Natchez and engaged extensively in the cultivation of cotton, sugar cane, and rice; also engaged in banking in the city of New Orleans; elected colonel of the First Regiment of the Louisiana State National Guard in 1879; appointed by Governor Louis A. Wiltz as brigadier general of the First Brigade, embracing all the uniformed militia in the State, in 1881; elected as a Democrat to the Fifty-second and to the eight succeeding Congresses and served from March 4, 1891, until his death in New Orleans, La., March 8, 1908; interment in Metairie Cemetery.

**MEYER, Herbert Alton,** a Representative from Kansas; born in Chillicothe, Ross County, Ohio, August 30, 1886; attended the grade schools, Washington, D.C., the Staunton Military Academy, Staunton, Va., 1900-1904, the George Washington University, Washington, D.C., 1905-1908, and was graduated from National University Law School, Washington, D.C., in 1910; was admitted to the bar in 1910; during the First World War served as a captain in the United States Army Air Corps; served as assistant to Secretary of the Interior, 1915-1917; executive of an oil marketing company from 1919 until 1937; in 1940 became publisher of the Independence (Kans.) Daily Reporter; elected as a Republican to the Eightieth and Eighty-first Congresses, and served from January 3, 1947 until his death in Bethesda, Md., October 2, 1950; had been nominated to the Eighty-second Congress; interment in Mount Hope Cemetery, Independence, Kans.

**MEYER, John Ambrose,** a Representative from Maryland; born in Baltimore, Md., May 15, 1899; attended the grade schools and Loyola High School; during the First World War enlisted as a private in the Students' Army Training Corps at Georgetown University, Washington, D.C., and served until honorably discharged from the United States Army; was graduated from Loyola College, Baltimore, Md., in 1921 and from the law department of the University of Maryland at Baltimore in 1922; was admitted to the bar in 1921 and commenced practice in Baltimore; associate judge of the traffic court of Baltimore 1929-1935; special assistant city solicitor in 1939 and 1940; elected as a Democrat to the Seventy-seventh Congress (January 3, 1941-January 3, 1943); was an unsuccessful candidate for renomination in 1942; served as district rent attorney for the Office of Price Administration during the Second World War; engaged in the general practice of law in Baltimore, Md., until his death there on October 2, 1969; interment in Holy Cross Cemetery.

**MEYER, William Henry,** a Representative from Vermont; born in Philadelphia, Pa., December 29, 1914; attended the public schools of Philadelphia; graduated from Pennsylvania State University in 1936; worked as a timber cruiser, State and Federal forester, Civilian Conservation Corps technician and supervisor in West Virginia, Maryland, Wisconsin, and New Jersey, 1936-1940; moved to a farm in Bennington County, Vt., in 1945; with Soil Conservation Service in Vermont, 1940-1950; in 1951 entered private practice as a consulting forester and became executive director of the Vermont Forest and Farmland Foundation; elected as a Democrat to the Eighty-sixth Congress (January 3, 1959-January 3, 1961); unsuccessful candidate for reelection in 1960 to the Eighty-seventh Congress; appointed as a consultant, Technical Review Staff, Department of the Interior, in May 1961, and served until December 1963; unsuccessful candidate for Democratic nomination as United States Senator in 1962, 1964, and 1970; delegate to Vermont State Democratic conventions, 1956, 1960, 1964, and 1968; unsuccessful candidate for election in 1972 to the Ninety-third Congress; was a resident of West Rupert, Vt. until his death there December 16, 1983; cremated; ashes interred at his home in West Rupert, Vt.

**MEYERS, Benjamin Franklin,** a Representative from Pennsylvania; born near New Centerville, Somerset County, Pa., July 6, 1833; attended Somerset Academy and Jefferson College, Canonsburg (now Washington and Jefferson College, Washington), Pa.; studied law; was admitted to the bar and commenced practice in 1855; member of the Pennsylvania house of representatives in 1864; delegate to the Democratic National Conventions of 1864, 1880, 1884, 1888, 1892, 1896, and 1900; editor of the Bedford Gazette and in 1868 of the Harrisburg Daily Patriot; elected as a Democrat to the Forty-second Congress (March 4, 1871-March 3, 1873); unsuccessful candidate for reelection in 1872 to the Forty-third Congress; postmaster of Harrisburg, Pa., by appointment of President Grover Cleveland, 1886-1891; publisher of the Daily Star Independent, Harrisburg, Pa.; engaged in public utilities; died in Harrisburg, Pa., August 11, 1918; interment in Harrisburg Cemetery.

**MEYERS, Jan,** a Representative from Kansas; born in Lincoln, Nebr., July 20, 1928; attended public schools in Superior, Nebr.; A.F.A., William Woods College, Fulton, Mo., 1948; B.A., University of Nebraska, Lincoln, 1951; advertising and public relations assistant for KFAB radio; member, Overland Park, Kans., city council, 1967-1972, president, 1970-1972; member, Kansas State senate, 1972-1984; elected as a Republican to the Ninety-ninth and to the five succeeding Congresses (January 3, 1985-January 3, 1997); was not a candidate for reelection in 1996 to the One Hundred Fifth Congress; chairman, Committee on Small Business (One Hundred Fourth Congress); is a resident of Overland Park, Kans.

**MEYNER, Helen Stevenson,** a Representative from New Jersey; born Helen Day Stevenson in New York City, Queens County, N.Y., March 5, 1929; attended Brearley Elementary School, New York City, 1934-1942; graduated, Rosemary Hall High School, Greenwich, Conn., 1946; B.A., Colorado College, Colorado Springs, Colo., 1950; served in Korea as an American Red Cross recreation worker, 1950-1952; guide at the United Nations, New York City, 1952-1953; travel adviser, Trans-World Airlines, 1953-1956; special assistant in the presidential campaign of Adlai E. Stevenson, 1956; newspaper columnist and television interviewer in New Jersey and New York; columnist, Newark (N.J.) Star-Ledger, 1962-1969; unsuccessful candidate for election in 1972 to the Ninety-third Congress; elected as a Democrat to the Ninety-fourth and to the Ninety-fifth Congresses (January 3, 1975-January 3, 1979); unsuccessful candidate for reelection in 1978 to the Ninety-sixth Congress; is a resident of Captiva, Fla.

**MEZVINSKY, Edward Maurice** (husband of Marjorie Margolies-Mezvinsky), a Representative from Iowa; born in Ames, Story County, Iowa, January 17, 1937; attended the public schools; B.A., University of Iowa, Iowa City, 1960; M.A., University of California, Berkeley, 1963, and J.D., 1965; admitted to the Iowa bar in 1965 and commenced practice in Iowa City; legislative assistant to Representative Neal Smith of Iowa, 1965-1967; member, Iowa State house of representatives, 1969-1970; elected as a Democrat to the Ninety-third and Ninety-fourth Congresses (January 3, 1973-January 3, 1977); unsuccessful candidate for reelection in 1976 to the Ninety-fifth Congress; appointed United States representative to the United Nations Commission on Human Rights, 1977-1979; elected Democratic Party State Chairman of Pennsylvania, 1981-1986; is a resident of Penn Valley, Pa.

**Bibliography:** Mezvinsky, Edward, with Kevin McCormally and John Greenya. *A Term to Remember.* New York: Coward, McCann and Geoghegan, 1977.

**MFUME, Kweisi,** a Representative from Maryland; born Frizzell Gray in Turners Corner, Baltimore County, Md., October 24, 1948; attended public schools; B.S., Morgan State University, 1976; M.A., Johns Hopkins University, Baltimore, 1984; assistant professor, Morgan State University, Baltimore; program director for radio station WEBB-AM, Baltimore; member, Baltimore City council, 1979-1986; elected as a Democrat to the One Hundredth and to the four succeeding Congresses, and served from January 3, 1987 until his resignation on February 18, 1996, to become president and chief executive officer of the National Association for the Advancement of Colored People; is a resident of Baltimore, Md.

**Bibliography:** Mfume, Kweisi, with Ron Stodghill II. *No Free Ride: From the Mean Streets to the Mainstream.* New York: One World/Ballantine Books, 1996.

**MICA, Daniel Andrew** (brother of John L. Mica), a Representative from Florida; born in Binghamton, Broome County, N.Y., February 4, 1944; attended Horace Mann School, Binghamton, N.Y., 1950; graduated, Miami Edison High School, Fla., 1961; attended the University of Florida, Gainesville, 1961; B.A., Florida Atlantic University, Boca Raton, 1966; teacher, Palm Beach, Fla., and Montgomery County, Md., 1966-1968; administrative assistant to Representative Paul G. Rogers, 1968-1978; elected as a Democrat to the Ninety-sixth and to the four succeeding Congresses (January 3, 1979-January 3, 1989); was not a candidate in 1988 for reelection to the House of Representatives, but was an unsuccessful candidate for nomination to the United States Senate; is a resident of West Palm Beach, Fla.

**MICA, John L.** (brother of Daniel Andrew Mica), a Representative from Florida; born in Binghamton, Broome County, N.Y., January 27, 1943; graduated, Miami-Edison High School, Miami, Fla.; A.A., Miami-Dade Community College, 1965; B.A., University of Florida, 1967; vice president, Winter Park (Fla.) Antique Mall; president, MK Development; John L. Mica and Associates; partner, Mica, Dudinsky and Associates; vice president, Moorehouse Cellular; member, Florida State house of representatives, 1976-1980; elected as a Republican to the One Hundred Third and One Hundred Fourth Congresses (January 3, 1993-January 3, 1997); is a resident of Winter Park, Fla.

**MICHAELSON, Magne Alfred,** a Representative from Illinois; born in Kristiansand, Norway, on September 7, 1878; immigrated to the United States with his parents, who settled in Chicago, Ill., in October 1885; attended the public schools and was graduated from Chicago Normal School in 1898; taught in the public schools of Chicago from 1898 until 1914; member of the common council of Chicago, 1915-1918; delegate to the State constitutional convention in 1920; chairman of the board of directors of the Madison and Kedzie State Bank of Chicago, 1924-1927; elected as a Republican to the Sixty-seventh and to the four succeeding Congresses (March 4, 1921-March 3, 1931); unsuccessful candidate for renomination in 1930 to the Seventy-second Congress; died in Chicago, Ill., October 26, 1949; interment in Mount Olivet Cemetery.

**MICHALEK, Anthony,** a Representative from Illinois; born in Radvanov, Bohemia, January 16, 1878; immigrated to the United States with his parents, who settled in Chicago, Ill., in 1878; attended the common schools; became engaged as a bookkeeper; elected as a Republican to the Fifty-ninth Congress (March 4, 1905-March 3, 1907); unsuccessful candidate for reelection in 1906 to the Sixtieth Congress, and for election in 1908 to the Sixty-first Congress; president and manager of the musical conservatory, Chicago, Ill.; died in Chicago, Ill., December 21, 1916; interment in St. Adalbert's Cemetery.

**MICHEL, Robert Henry,** a Representative from Illinois; born in Peoria, Ill., March 2, 1923; attended the public schools; served with the Thirty-ninth Infantry Regiment as a combat infantryman in Great Britain, France, Belgium, and Germany from February 10, 1943, to January 26, 1946; was wounded by machine gun fire; awarded two Bronze Stars, the Purple Heart, and four battle stars; B.S., Bradley University, Peoria, 1948; administrative assistant to Representative Harold H. Velde, 1949-1956; delegate to Republican National Conventions from 1964 to 1996, serving as permanent chairman of the 1984, 1988 and 1992 Conventions; elected as a Republican to the Eighty-fifth and to the eighteen succeeding Congresses (January 3, 1957-January 3, 1995); declined to be a candidate for renomination in 1994 to the One Hundred Fourth Congress; minority whip, (Ninety-fourth through Ninety-sixth Congresses), minority leader (Ninety-seventh through One Hundred Third Congresses); senior adviser for corporate and government affairs, Hogan and Hartson, Washington, D.C.; is a resident of Washington, D.C.

**MICHENER, Earl Cory,** a Representative from Michigan; born near Attica, Seneca County, Ohio, November 30, 1876; moved with his parents to Adrian, Mich., in 1889; attended the public schools of Adrian; during the Spanish-American War served as a private in Company B, Thirty-first Regiment, Michigan Volunteer Infantry, from April 26, 1898, to May 17, 1899; studied law at the University of Michigan at Ann Arbor in 1901 and 1902 and was graduated from the law department of Columbian University (now George Washington University) Washington, D.C., in 1903; was admitted to the bar the same year and commenced practice in Adrian, Mich.; assistant prosecuting attorney for Lenawee County, Mich., 1907-1910; prosecuting attorney 1911-1914; elected as a Republican to the Sixty-sixth and to the six succeeding Congresses (March 4, 1919-March 3, 1933); one of the managers appointed by the House of Representatives in 1926 to conduct the impeachment proceedings against George W. English, judge of the United States District Court for the Eastern District of Illinois; unsuccessful candidate for

reelection in 1932 to the Seventy-third Congress; elected to the Seventy-fourth and to the seven succeeding Congresses (January 3, 1935-January 3, 1951); chairman, Committee on Judiciary (Eightieth Congress); was not a candidate for renomination in 1950; maintained law offices in Adrian, Mich., until his death there July 4, 1957; interment in Oakwood Cemetery.

**MICKEY, J. Ross,** a Representative from Illinois; born on a farm in Eldorado Township, McDonough County, Ill., January 5, 1856; attended the public schools and Lincoln (Ill.) College; taught in the public schools of Macomb, McDonough County, Ill., for a number of years; studied law; was admitted to the bar in 1889 and practiced in Macomb, Ill., until 1898; elected judge of McDonough County in 1898 for a term of four years, but resigned February 22, 1901, having been elected to Congress; elected as a Democrat to the Fifty-seventh Congress (March 4, 1901-March 3, 1903); declined to be a candidate for renomination in 1902; resumed the practice of law in Macomb, Ill.; served as president of the Mystic Workers of the World 1908-1918 and as a director from 1918 until his death; died in Excelsior Springs, Mo., on March 20, 1928; interment in Oakwood Cemetery, Macomb, Ill.

**MIDDLESWARTH, Ner,** a Representative from Pennsylvania; born in Glasgow, Scotland, December 12, 1783; immigrated to the United States in 1792 with his parents, who settled in New Jersey; moved to Beavertown, Pa., the same year; had a very limited education; served as a captain in the War of 1812; member of the Pennsylvania house of representatives from 1815 until 1841, and served as speaker two terms; served in the Pennsylvania senate, 1853-1855; elected as a Whig to the Thirty-third Congress (March 4, 1853-March 3, 1855); was not a candidate for renomination in 1854 to the Thirty-fourth Congress; engaged in agricultural pursuits; president of the Beaver Furnace Co. in Snyder County; associate judge of Snyder County in 1858; died in Beavertown, Snyder County, Pa., June 2, 1865; interment in Union Cemetery.

**MIDDLETON, Arthur** (son of Henry Middleton [1717-1784] and father of Henry Middleton), a Delegate from South Carolina; born at "Middleton Place," his father's estate, on the Ashley River, near Charleston, Berkeley County, S.C., June 26, 1742; received his early education from private tutors and schools in Charleston; attended school at Hackney, Westminster School, and St. John's College, Cambridge University, in England; studied law at the Temple in London, but did not practice; returned to South Carolina in 1763 and engaged in planting; justice of the peace of Berkeley County in 1765; member of the provincial house of commons, 1765-1768 and from 1772 to 1775; delegate to the provincial convention in 1774 and 1775; again justice of the peace, 1776-1786; member of the council of safety in 1775 and 1776; delegate to the provincial congress which formed a State constitution in 1776; served in the Revolutionary War; held a prisoner by the British from May 1780 to July 1781, when he was exchanged and returned to South Carolina; Member of the Continental Congress, 1776-1777, and 1781-1782; a signer of the Declaration of Independence; elected Governor of South Carolina in 1778, but declined; member of the State house of representatives, 1778-1780, 1785, and 1786; served in the State senate in 1781 and 1782; member of the privy council in 1782; member of the board of trustees of Charleston College; died at "The Oaks," near Charleston, S.C., January 1, 1787; interment in the family mausoleum at "Middleton Place," near Charleston, S.C.

**Bibliography:** *DAB.*

**MIDDLETON, George,** a Representative from New Jersey; born in Philadelphia, Pa., October 14, 1800; moved to Burlington, N.J.; attended the public schools; became a tanner; moved to Allentown, Monmouth County, N.J.; held several local offices; member of the State general assembly in 1858 and 1859; elected as a Democrat to the Thirty-eighth Congress (March 4, 1863-March 3, 1865); unsuccessful candidate for reelection in 1864 to the

Thirty-ninth Congress; resumed the business of tanning; died in Allentown, N.J., December 31, 1888; interment in Crosswicks Community Cemetery, Crosswicks, Burlington County, N.J.

**MIDDLETON, Henry** (father of Arthur Middleton and grandfather of Henry Middleton [1770-1846]), a Delegate from South Carolina; born at "The Oaks," near Charleston, S.C., in 1717; educated at home and in Great Britain; justice of the peace and quorum 1742-1780; member of the provincial house of commons 1742-1755 and served as speaker 1745-1747, 1754, and 1755; commissioned officer of horse of the provincial forces in 1743; commissioner of Indian affairs in 1755; member of the King's Provincial Council from 1755 until his resignation in September 1770; member of the provincial convention in 1774; Member of the Continental Congress 1774-1775; served as president of that body from October 22, 1774, to May 10, 1775; member of the council of safety in 1775 and 1776; member of the Provincial Congress of South Carolina in 1775 and 1776; member of the committee to prepare a form of government in 1776; member of the legislative council under the transition government 1776-1778; member of the State senate 1778-1780; large landowner and planter in Berkeley, Colleton, and Granville Counties, residing at his estates, "The Oaks" and "Middleton Place"; died in Charleston, S.C., June 13, 1784; interment in Goosecreek Churchyard, St. James Parish, Berkeley County, S.C.

**Bibliography:** *DAB*.

**MIDDLETON, Henry** (son of Arthur Middleton and grandson of Henry Middleton [1717-1784]), a Representative from South Carolina; born in London, England, September 28, 1770; his parents, then traveling in Europe, returned a year later to South Carolina; pursued classical studies with tutors at his father's estate, "Middleton Place," near Charleston, S.C., with a year in England; returned to America after his father's death in 1787; later returned to England and resided at Clifton, Gloucestershire, until his return to Charleston in 1800; engaged in planting in South Carolina; member of the South Carolina State house of representatives, 1802-1810; elected to the State senate in 1810; elected Governor of South Carolina in December 1810 and served until December 1812; elected as a Republican to the Fourteenth and Fifteenth Congresses (March 4, 1815-March 3, 1819); unsuccessful candidate for renomination in 1818 to the Sixteenth Congress; appointed Minister to Russia on April 6, 1820 and served until August 1830; leader of the Union Party of South Carolina and vice president of the Union Convention in 1833; retired to private life; died in Charleston, S.C., June 14, 1846; interment in the family mausoleum at "Middleton Place," near Charleston, S.C.

**Bibliography:** *DAB*; Bergquist, Harold E., Jr. "Russo-American Economic Relations in the 1820's: Henry Middleton as a Protector of American Economic Interests in Russia and Turkey." *East European Quarterly* 11 (Spring 1977): 27-41.

**MIERS, Robert Walter,** a Representative from Indiana; born near Greensburg, Decatur County, Ind., January 27, 1848; attended the common schools; was graduated from the academic department of Indiana University at Bloomington in 1870 and from its law department in 1871; was admitted to the bar in April 1872 and commenced practice in Bloomington, Ind.; prosecuting attorney for the tenth judicial circuit of Indiana, 1875-1879; member of the State house of representatives in 1879; member of the board of trustees of Indiana University from 1879 until 1897; appointed judge of the tenth judicial circuit of Indiana in 1883, elected in 1884 and again in 1890, and served until September 1896, when he resigned to become a candidate for Congress; unsuccessful Democratic candidate for election for secretary of state in 1886 and 1888; elected as a Democrat to the Fifty-fifth and to the three succeeding Congresses (March 4, 1897-March 3, 1905); unsuccessful candidate for reelection in 1904 to the Fifty-ninth Congress; resumed the practice of

law; again elected judge of the tenth circuit of Indiana in 1914 and served until November 22, 1920; continued the practice of law in Bloomington, Ind. until 1928; died while on a visit in Martinsville, Ind., February 20, 1930; interment in Rosehill Cemetery, Bloomington, Ind.

**MIFFLIN, Thomas,** a Delegate from Pennsylvania; born in Philadelphia, Pa., January 10, 1744; graduated from the University of Pennsylvania at Philadelphia in 1760; member of the American Philosophical Society from 1765 to 1799; member of the colonial legislature, 1772-1774; member of the Continental Congress, 1774-1775 and 1782-1784, and was its President in 1783; commissioned major and chief aide-de-camp to General George Washington, July 4, 1775; appointed major and Quartermaster General of the Continental Army on August 14, 1775, and promoted through the ranks to major general on February 19, 1777; appointed a member of the board of war on November 7, 1777; resigned as major general, February 25, 1779; trustee of the University of Pennsylvania, 1778-1791; served as speaker of the Pennsylvania house of representatives, 1785-1788; delegate to the Federal Constitutional Convention in 1787; president of the supreme executive council of Pennsylvania, October 1788 to October 1790; president of the Pennsylvania constitutional convention in 1790; elected Governor of Pennsylvania in 1790, reelected in 1793 and 1796, and served from December 21, 1790 to December 17, 1799; again a member of the Pennsylvania house of representatives, 1799-1800; died in Lancaster, Pa., January 20, 1800; interment in the front yard of Trinity Lutheran Church.

**Bibliography:** *DAB*; Rossman, Kenneth R. *Thomas Mifflin and the Politics of the American Revolution.* Chapel Hill: University of North Carolina Press, 1952.

**MIKULSKI, Barbara Ann,** a Representative and a Senator from Maryland; born in Baltimore, Md., July 20, 1936; B.A., Mount St. Agnes College, 1958; M.S.W., University of Maryland School of Social Work, 1965; social worker and administrator, Baltimore Department of Social Services and Catholic Charities; adjunct professor, Loyola College, 1972-1976; member of the Baltimore City Council from 1971 until 1976; unsuccessful candidate in 1974 for election to the United States Senate; elected as a Democrat to the Ninety-fifth and to the four succeeding Congresses (January 3, 1977-January 3, 1987); was not a candidate for reelection to the House of Representatives in 1986, but was elected to the United States Senate for the term commencing January 3, 1987; reelected in 1992 for the term ending January 3, 1999; is a resident of Baltimore, Md.

**MIKVA, Abner Joseph,** a Representative from Illinois; born in Milwaukee, Wis., January 21, 1926; attended public schools in Milwaukee; J.D., University of Chicago Law School, 1951; editor in chief, University of Chicago Law Review, 1950-1951; admitted to the bar in 1951 and commenced practice in Chicago, Ill., in 1952; served two years as a navigator in United States Army Air Corps, 1944-1945; served as law clerk to United States Supreme Court Justice Sherman Minton, 1951-1952; practicing attorney, 1952-1968; elected to the Illinois State Legislature, 1956-1966; elected as a Democrat to the Ninety-first and to the Ninety-second Congresses (January 3, 1969-January 3, 1973); unsuccessful candidate for reelection in 1972 to the Ninety-third Congress, returned to Evanston, Ill.; served on the Illinois State Board of Ethics, 1973; practiced law in Chicago, 1973-1974; professor at Northwestern University School of Law, 1973-1975; elected as a Democrat to the Ninety-fourth and to the two succeeding Congresses, and served from January 3, 1975 until his resignation on September 26, 1979; judge in the United States Court of Appeals for the District of Columbia circuit, 1979-1991, chief judge, January 20, 1991 to October 1, 1994; Counsel to the President, October 1, 1994 to November 1, 1995; is a resident of Washington, D.C.

**Bibliography:** Mikva, Abner J., and Patti B. Saris. *The American Congress: The First Branch*. New York: Franklin Watts, 1983.

**MILES, Frederick,** a Representative from Connecticut; born in Goshen, Litchfield County, Conn., on December 19, 1815; attended the common schools and pursued an academic course; engaged in mercantile pursuits in Goshen until 1857; moved to Twinlakes and later, in 1858, to Salisbury and engaged in the manufacture of iron; member of the State senate from 1877 until February 1879, when he resigned; elected as a Republican to the Forty-sixth and Forty-seventh Congresses (March 4, 1879-March 3, 1883); declined a nomination for reelection; again elected to the Fifty-first Congress (March 4, 1889-March 3, 1891); unsuccessful candidate for reelection in 1890 to the Fifty-second Congress; resumed business activities; died near Salisbury, Litchfield County, Conn., November 20, 1896; interment in Salisbury Cemetery.

**MILES, John Esten,** a Representative from New Mexico; born in Murfreesboro, Rutherford County, Tenn., July 28, 1884; attended the grade schools of Rutherford County, Tenn.; in 1902 began farming in Fannin County, Tex., and in 1905 moved to Granite, Okla.; in 1906 moved to New Mexico and homesteaded on a farm near Endee, Quay County, N.Mex., in 1918; member of the school board, 1918-1921; postmaster of Endee, 1917-1920; moved to Tucumcari in 1920 and served as assessor of Quay County, 1920-1924; secretary of the State Tax Commission, 1925-1927; in 1927 was associate editor of the New Mexico Democrat and the Las Vegas Independent; again secretary of the State Tax Commission, 1931-1934; chief of the field division of the Bureau of Internal Revenue, Albuquerque, N.Mex., in 1934; delegate to all Democratic National Conventions, beginning in 1936; elected Governor of New Mexico in 1938, reelected in 1940, and served from January 1, 1939 to January 1, 1943; chairman, New Mexico Public Service Commission, 1943-1945; Commissioner of Public Lands, 1945-1948; elected as a Democrat to the Eighty-first Congress (January 3, 1949-January 3, 1951) was not a candidate in 1950 for reelection to the House of Representatives, but was an unsuccessful candidate for election for Governor; president of New Mexico School Book Depository; director of enforcement, Office of Price Stabilization, Denver, Colo., 1951-1952; appointed chairman of Public Service Commission, 1959-1960; chairman, Democratic Party of New Mexico, 1961-1964; died in Santa Fe, N.Mex., October 7, 1971; interment in Memorial Lawns Cemetery.

**MILES, Joshua Weldon,** a Representative from Maryland; born on his father's farm on the Great Annamessex River, near the village of Marion, Somerset County, Md., December 9, 1858; attended private schools and Marion (Md.) Academy; was graduated from Western Maryland College, Westminster, Md., in 1878; attended the law department of Maryland University; was admitted to the bar in July 1880 and commenced practice in Princess Anne, Md.; State's attorney of Somerset County 1883-1887; unsuccessful candidate for reelection; elected as a Democrat to the Fifty-fourth Congress (March 4, 1895-March 3, 1897); unsuccessful candidate for reelection in 1896 to the Fifty-fifth Congress; resumed the practice of law in Princess Anne, Md.; served as president of the Bank of Somerset from 1900 until his death; delegate at large to the Democratic National Conventions of 1900, 1912, 1920, and 1924; trustee of Western Maryland College for thirty years; collector of internal revenue for the district of Maryland 1914-1921; resumed the practice of law; died in Baltimore, Md., March 4, 1929; interment in Manokin Cemetery, Princess Anne, Md.

**MILES, William Porcher,** a Representative from South Carolina; born in Charleston, S.C., July 4, 1822; attended Wellington School in Charleston and was graduated from Charleston College in 1842; studied law; was admitted to the bar and commenced practice in Charleston; mayor of Charleston, 1855-1857;

elected as a Democrat to the Thirty-fifth and Thirty-sixth Congresses, with service beginning on March 4, 1857; did not occupy his seat after December 13, 1860; member of the Confederate Provisional Congress in Montgomery, Ala., in February 1861; Member of the Confederate Congress from February 1862 to March 1864; colonel on the staff of General Pierre G.T. Beauregard; president of the University of South Carolina at Columbia, 1880-1882; died in Burnside, La., on May 11, 1899; interment in Union Cemetery, Union, Monroe County, W.Va.

**Bibliography:** *DAB*.

**MILFORD, Dale,** a Representative from Texas; born in Bug Tussle, Fannin County, Tex., February 18, 1926; attended the public schools; attended Baylor University, Waco, Tex., 1953-1957; served in the United States Army Air Corps, 1944-1953, and attained the rank of captain; professional meteorologist; owned and operated a commercial flight service; television weathercaster; aerospace editor, television station WFAA, 1968-1971; consultant in aviation and meteorology, 1963-1971; delegate, Texas State Democratic convention, 1972; elected as a Democrat to the Ninety-third and to the two succeeding Congresses (January 3, 1973-January 3, 1979); unsuccessful candidate for renomination in 1978 to the Ninety-sixth Congress; is a resident of Howe, Tex.

**MILLARD, Charles Dunsmore,** a Representative from New York; born in Tarrytown, Westchester County, N.Y., December 1, 1873; attended the public schools, Phillips Academy, Andover, Mass., and Brown University, Providence, R.I., and was graduated from New York Law School, New York City, in 1897; was admitted to the bar in 1898 and commenced practice in Westchester County, N.Y.; member of the Westchester County Board of Supervisors 1907-1931, and chairman in 1916, 1917, 1927, and 1928; member of the Republican State committee 1920-1937; elected as a Republican to the Seventy-second and to the three succeeding Congresses and served from March 4, 1931, to September 29, 1937, when he resigned, having been elected surrogate of Westchester County, N.Y., in which capacity he served until his retirement in 1943; died in New York City, December 11, 1944; interment in Sleepy Hollow Cemetery, North Tarrytown, N.Y.

**MILLARD, Joseph Hopkins,** a Senator from Nebraska; born in Hamilton, Province of Ontario, Canada, April 20, 1836; moved to Iowa with his parents, who settled near Sabula, Jackson County; attended the district school; clerked in a store; moved to Omaha, Nebr., in 1856 and engaged in the land business; moved to Montana in 1864 and, through the assistance of an Iowa capitalist, opened a bank in Virginia City; returned to Omaha in 1866 and became director, president, and cashier of the Omaha National Bank; one of the incorporators of the Omaha & Northwestern Railroad Company in 1869; mayor of Omaha in 1871; for fifteen years was a director of the Union Pacific Railroad Company, six years of which he served in the capacity of a Government director; elected as a Republican to the United States Senate, March 28, 1901, to fill the vacancy in the term beginning March 4, 1901, caused by the failure of the legislature to act, and served from March 28, 1901, to March 3, 1907; was not a candidate for reelection in 1906; chairman, Committee on Inter-Oceanic Canals (Fifty-ninth Congress); resumed the banking business in Omaha, Nebr., and died there on January 13, 1922; interment in Prospect Hill Cemetery.

**MILLARD, Stephen Columbus,** a Representative from New York; born in Stamford, Bennington County, Vt., January 14, 1841; attended Powers Institute and was graduated from Williams College, Williamstown, Mass., in 1865; attended Harvard Law School; was admitted to the bar of the State of New York in May 1867 and commenced practice in Binghamton; chairman of the Republican county committee 1872-1879; elected as a Republican to the Forty-eighth and Forty-ninth Congresses (March 4, 1883-March 3, 1887); was not a candidate for renomination in 1886; resumed the practice of law in Binghamton, N.Y., where he died June 21, 1914; interment in Spring Forest Cemetery.

**MILLEDGE, John,** a Representative and a Senator from Georgia; born in Savannah, Ga., in 1757; was tutored privately; studied law; was admitted to the bar and commenced practice in Savannah, Ga.; served in the Revolutionary War and was one of the patriots who rifled the powder magazine in Savannah; narrowly missed being hanged as a spy; attorney general of Georgia in 1780; member of the Georgia State general assembly for several sessions; elected to the Second Congress to fill the vacancy caused by the House declaring the seat of Anthony Wayne vacant, and served from November 22, 1792 to March 3, 1793; subsequently elected to the Fourth and Fifth Congresses (March 4, 1795-March 3, 1799); again elected as a Republican to the Seventh Congress, and served from March 4, 1801 until his resignation in May 1802; chairman, Committee on Elections (Seventh Congress); elected Governor of Georgia by the Legislature, and served from November 4, 1802 to September 23, 1806; elected to the United States Senate to fill the vacancy caused by the death of James Jackson; reelected in 1806, and served from June 19, 1806 until his resignation on November 14, 1809; served as President pro tempore of the Senate during the Tenth Congress; one of the founders of the University of Georgia at Athens; died on his plantation near Augusta, Ga., on February 9, 1818; interment in Summerville Cemetery.

Bibliography: *DAB*; Milledge, John. *Correspondence of John Milledge.* Edited by Harriet (Milledge) Salley. Columbia, S.C.: State Commercial Printing Co., 1949.

**MILLEN, John,** a Representative from Georgia; born in Savannah, Ga., in 1804; completed preparatory studies; studied law; was admitted to the bar and practiced in Savannah many years; member of the State house of representatives in 1828, 1834, 1835, 1839, and 1840; elected as a Democrat to the Twenty-eighth Congress and served from March 4, 1843, until his death in Savannah, Ga., October 15, 1843; interment in Laurel Grove Cemetery.

**MILLENDER-McDONALD, Juanita,** a Representative from California; born in Birmingham, Jefferson County, Ala., September 7, 1938; moved to California in 1957; B.S., University of Redlands (Calif.), 1981; M.A., California State University-Los Angeles; member of the Carson, Calif., council, 1989-1992, and served as mayor pro tempore, 1990-1992; teacher, editor and writer, and director of gender equity programs, Los Angeles Unified School District; member of the board of directors, West Basin Municipal Water District, and Los Angeles County Sanitation District No. 8; delegate to the Democratic National Conventions of 1984 and 1992; member, California State assembly, District 55, 1993-1996; elected as a Democrat to the One Hundred Fourth Congress, March 26, 1996, by special election to fill the vacancy caused by the resignation of Walter R. Tucker III, and served from March 26, 1996 to January 3, 1997; is a resident of Carson, Calif.

**MILLER, Arthur Lewis,** a Representative from Nebraska; born on a farm near Plainview, Pierce County, Nebr., May 24, 1892; attended the public schools; was graduated from the high school at Plainview, Nebr., in 1911 and from Loyola Medical School, Chicago, Ill., in 1918; taught in a rural school at Plainview, Nebr., 1911-1913; member of the United States Medical Reserve Corps 1917-1919; practiced medicine and surgery in Kimball, Nebr., 1919-1942 and also engaged in agricultural pursuits; mayor of Kimball in 1933 and 1934; member of the Nebraska legislature 1937-1941; unsuccessful candidate for the Republican gubernatorial nomination in 1940; State health director in 1941 and 1942; elected as a Republican to the Seventy-eighth and to the seven succeeding Congresses (January 3, 1943-January 3, 1959); chairman, Committee on Interior and Insular Affairs (Eighty-third Congress); unsuccessful candidate for reelection in 1958 to the Eighty-sixth Congress;

director, Office of Saline Water, Department of the Interior, Washington, D.C., from February 1959 to January 1961; died in Chevy Chase, Md., March 16, 1967; interment in Parklawn Cemetery, Rockville, Md.

**MILLER, Bert Henry,** a Senator from Idaho; born in St. George, Washington County, Utah, December 15, 1879; graduated from Brigham Young University, Provo, Utah, in 1901 and from Cumberland University Law School, Lebanon, Tenn., in 1902; was admitted to the bar and commenced practice in St. Anthony, Idaho, in 1903; prosecuting attorney of Fremont County, Idaho, 1912-1914; was an unsuccessful Democratic candidate for Congress in 1914; elected attorney general of Idaho in 1932 and reelected in 1934; unsuccessful candidate for the Democratic gubernatorial nomination in 1936; served for two months in 1938 as Idaho's labor commissioner; unsuccessful Democratic candidate for election in 1938 to the Seventy-sixth Congress; attorney in the Wage and Hour Division, Department of Labor, at Seattle, Wash., 1939-1940; attorney general of Idaho 1940-1944; elected a justice of the State supreme court in 1944; elected as a Democrat to the United States Senate in 1948 for the term commencing January 3, 1949, and served until his death in Washington, D.C., October 8, 1949; interment in Morris Hill Cemetery, Boise, Idaho.

**MILLER, Clarence Benjamin,** a Representative from Minnesota; born in Pine Island, Goodhue County, Minn., March 13, 1872; attended the country school, high school, and the Minneapolis (Minn.) Academy; was graduated from the academic department of the University of Minnesota at Minneapolis in 1895 and from the law department of the same institution in 1900; superintendent of the public schools of Rushford, Minn., 1895-1898; was admitted to the bar in 1900 and commenced the practice of law in Duluth, Minn.; member of the State house of representatives in 1907; elected as a Republican to the Sixty-first and to the four succeeding Congresses (March 4, 1909-March 3, 1919); unsuccessful candidate for reelection in 1918; member of the congressional investigating committee to the Philippine Islands in 1915; special investigator for the War Department to the western front in France in 1917; elected assistant secretary of the Republican National Committee in 1919 and was chosen its secretary in 1920; engaged in the practice of law in Washington, D.C.; died in St. Paul, Minn., January 10, 1922; interment in Pine Island Cemetery, Pine Island, Minn.

**MILLER, Clarence E.,** a Representative from Ohio; born in Lancaster, Fairfield County, Ohio, November 1, 1917; graduate of Fairfield County public schools; utility company electrical engineer, received technical training as an electrical engineer from International Correspondence School, Scranton, Pa.; member, Lancaster City Council, 1957-1963; mayor of Lancaster, 1964-1966; while mayor, was a member of the legislative committee of the National League of Cities and the Ohio Municipal League, and a member of the executive committee of the Mayors Association of Ohio; elected as a Republican to the Ninetieth and to the twelve succeeding Congresses (January 3, 1967-January 3, 1993); unsuccessful candidate for renomination in 1992 to the One Hundred Third Congress; is a resident of Lancaster, Ohio.

**MILLER, Clement Woodnutt** (nephew of Thomas Woodnutt Miller), a Representative from California; born in Wilmington, Del., October 28, 1916; graduated from Lawrenceville (N.J.) School, from Williams College, Williamstown, Mass., in 1940, and the from Cornell University School of Industrial and Labor Relations in 1946; enlisted in the United States Army in 1940; served as a private in the Two Hundred and Fifty-eighth Field Artillery Regiment and was discharged in 1945 as a captain in the One Hundred and Fourth Infantry Division, with service in the Netherlands and Germany; veterans service officer in Nevada, 1946-1947; worked with the employment service, State of Nevada, in 1947; field examiner and hearing officer of the National Labor Relations Board for Northern

California, 1948-1953; became a landscape consultant in 1954; unsuccessful candidate for election in 1956 to the Eighty-fifth Congress; elected as a Democrat to the Eighty-sixth and Eighty-seventh Congresses, and served from January 3, 1959 until his death in an airplane accident near Eureka, Calif., October 7, 1962; elected posthumously to the Eighty-eighth Congress; interment in Point Reyes National Seashore Park, north of San Francisco, Calif.

Bibliography: Miller, Clem. *Member of the House: Letters of a Congressman.* Edited with additional text by John W. Baker. New York: Scribner, 1962.

MILLER, Daniel Fry, a Representative from Iowa; born in Cumberland, Allegany County, Md., October 4, 1814; moved with his parents to Wayne County, Ohio, in 1816; attended the public schools; taught for several years; engaged in newspaper work in Wooster, Ohio; moved to Pittsburgh, Pa., in 1830; employed as a clerk in stores; studied law; was admitted to the bar in 1839 and commenced practice in Fort Madison, Iowa; member of the Territorial house of representatives in 1840; contested the election of William H. Thompson to the Thirty-first Congress, but the House decided that neither was entitled to the seat; subsequently elected as a Whig to fill this vacancy and served from December 20, 1850, to March 3, 1851; resumed the practice of law; presidential elector on the Republican ticket in 1856; mayor of Fort Madison in 1859; moved to Keokuk, Iowa, and continued the practice of law; unsuccessful candidate for election as judge of the supreme court in 1860; elected mayor of Keokuk, Iowa, in 1873; member of the State house of representatives in 1894; retired from active practice in 1895 and moved to Omaha, Nebr., where he died December 9, 1895; interment in St. Peter's Cemetery, Keokuk, Lee County, Iowa.

Bibliography: Schmidt, Louis B. "The Miller-Thompson Election Contest." *Iowa Journal of History and Politics* 12 (January 1914): 34-127.

MILLER, Daniel H., a Representative from Pennsylvania; born in Philadelphia, Pa.; elected to the Eighteenth Congress; reelected to the Nineteenth Congress and reelected as a Jacksonian to the Twentieth and Twenty-first Congresses (March 4, 1823-March 3, 1831); died in Philadelphia, Pa., in 1846.

MILLER, Edward Edwin, a Representative from Illinois; born in Creston, Union County, Iowa, July 22, 1880; attended the common schools; moved to East St. Louis, St. Clair County, Ill., in 1892; engaged in the real estate and insurance business in 1900; served as private secretary to Representative William A. Rodenberg of Illinois; delegate to the Republican National Convention of 1912; State treasurer of Illinois, 1921-1923; elected as a Republican to the Sixty-eighth Congress (March 4, 1923-March 3, 1925); declined to be a candidate for renomination in 1924 to the Sixty-ninth Congress; engaged in the real estate and insurance business until 1942; director of transportation, American Red Cross, at St. Louis, Mo., from 1942 until his death; died at St. Louis, Mo., August 1, 1946; interment in St. Clair Memorial Park Cemetery, East St. Louis, Ill.

MILLER, Edward Tylor, a Representative from Maryland; born in Woodside, Montgomery County, Md., February 1, 1895; attended Sidwell Friends School, Washington, D.C.; was graduated from Yale University, New Haven, Conn., in 1916; during the First World War served in the United States Army as commanding officer of Company C, Three Hundred and Twentieth Infantry, Eightieth Division, from May 14, 1917, to August 8, 1919; studied law at George Washington University, Washington, D.C.; was admitted to the bar in 1920 and commenced practice in Easton, Md.; referee in bankruptcy 1923-1941; police and juvenile judge for Talbot County, Md., 1934-1938; served as a colonel in the Infantry, United States Army, 1942-1946, in North Africa, India, and China; elected as a Republican to the Eightieth and to the five succeeding Congresses (January 3, 1947-January 3, 1959); unsuccessful candidate for

reelection in 1958 to the Eighty-sixth Congress and for election in 1960 to the Eighty-seventh Congress; vice chairman, United States Delegation to Second United Nations Conference on the Law of the Sea at Geneva, Switzerland, in 1960; resumed the practice of law; unsuccessful candidate in 1962 for United States Senator; Republican national committeeman, 1960-1964; delegate, Republican National Convention, 1964; elected Talbot County delegate to State constitutional convention, 1967; died in Easton, Md., January 20, 1968; interment in Meeting House Cemetery.

MILLER, Frederick Daniel (Dan), a Representative from Florida; born in Highland Park, Wayne County, Mich., May 30, 1942; graduated Manatee High School, Bradenton, 1960; B.S.B.A., University of Florida, 1964; M.B.A., Emory University, Atlanta, Ga., 1965; Ph.D., economics, Louisiana State University, 1970; co-founder, Miller Enterprises; elected as a Republican to the One Hundred Third and One Hundred Fourth Congresses (January 3, 1993-January 3, 1997); is a resident of Bradenton, Fla.

MILLER, George, a Representative from California; born in Richmond, Contra Costa County, Calif., May 17, 1945; attended Montecito (Calif.) Elementary School, 1950-1957; graduated, Alhambra High School, Martinez, Calif., 1963; Diablo Valley College, Pleasant Hill, Calif.; B.A., San Francisco State University, 1968; J.D., University of California Law School, Davis, 1972; admitted to the California Bar in 1972 and commenced practice in Walnut Creek; legislative assistant to the majority leader of the California State senate, 1969-1974; elected as a Democrat to the Ninety-fourth and to the ten succeeding Congresses (January 3, 1975-January 3, 1997); chairman, Select Committee on Children, Youth, and Families (Ninety-eighth through One Hundred First Congresses); Committee on Natural Resources (One Hundred Second and One Hundred Third Congresses); is a resident of Martinez, Calif.

MILLER, George Funston, a Representative from Pennsylvania; born in Chillisquaque Township, Northumberland County, Pa., on September 5, 1809; attended Kirkpatrick's Academy in Milton, Pa.; taught school; studied law; was admitted to the bar of Union County May 15, 1833, and commenced practice in Lewisburg; member of the board of curators of the university at Lewisburg (now Bucknell University) 1846-1882; scribe of curators 1847-1851; secretary of the board of trustees of Bucknell University 1848-1864; elected as a Republican to the Thirty-ninth and Fortieth Congresses (March 4, 1865-March 3, 1869); resumed the practice of law; president of the Lewisburg, Centre & Spruce Creek Railroad; died in Lewisburg, Union County, Pa., October 21, 1885; interment in Lewisburg Cemetery.

MILLER, George Paul, a Representative from California; born in San Francisco, Calif., January 15, 1891; attended public and private schools; was graduated from St. Mary's (Calif.) College in 1912; engaged as a civil engineer 1912-1917; during the First World War served as a lieutenant in the Thirty-sixth and Three Hundred and Forty-sixth Field Artillery 1917-1919; member of the staff, United States Veterans' Bureau, 1921-1925; resumed activities as a civil engineer; also co-owner of a travel agency in San Francisco; member of the California State assembly 1937-1941; was executive secretary to the California Division of Fish and Game 1942-1944; elected as a Democrat to the Seventy-ninth and to the thirteen succeeding Congresses (January 3, 1945-January 3, 1973); chairman, Committee on Science and Astronautics (Eighty-seventh through Ninety-second Congresses); unsuccessful candidate for renomination in 1972 to the Ninety-third Congress; was a resident of Alameda, Calif., until his death there on December 29, 1982; interment in San Francisco National Cemetery, Presidio of San Francisco, San Francisco, Calif.

**MILLER, Homer Virgil Milton,** a Senator from Georgia; born in Pendleton District, S.C., April 29, 1814; moved with his parents to Rabun County, Ga., in 1820; attended the common schools and graduated from the Medical College of South Carolina in 1835; continued medical studies in Paris and commenced practice in Cassville, Ga., in 1838; unsuccessful Whig candidate for election to the Twenty-ninth Congress in 1844; served during the Civil War in the Confederate Army as a surgeon and as medical director, surgeon of posts, and inspector of hospitals in Georgia; resumed the practice of medicine in Rome, Ga.; member of the State reconstruction convention in 1867; member of the faculty of the Atlanta Medical College; upon the readmission of Georgia to representation was elected as a Democrat to the United States Senate on July 28, 1868; qualified on February 24, 1871, and served until March 3, 1871; trustee of the University of Georgia at Athens; died in Atlanta, Fulton County, Ga., May 31, 1896; interment in Myrtle Hill Cemetery, Rome, Ga.

**MILLER, Howard Shultz,** a Representative from Kansas; born in Somerset County, Pa., February 27, 1879; moved with his family in 1882 to Morrill, Kans.; attended the public schools of Brown County, and Sabetha (Kans.) High School; taught school 1894-1899; graduated from the University of Nebraska College of Law in 1900; was admitted to the bar in 1901 and began law practice in Kansas; engaged in agricultural pursuits and as a lawyer 1901-1952; elected as a Democrat to the Eighty-third Congress (January 3, 1953-January 3, 1955); unsuccessful candidate for reelection in 1954 to the Eighty-fourth Congress and for election in 1956 to the Eighty-fifth Congress; stockman and soil conservationist in Brown County; resumed farming activities; died January 2, 1970, in Hiawatha, Kans.; interment in Morrill Cemetery, Morrill, Kans.

**MILLER, Jack Richard,** a Senator from Iowa; born in Chicago, Cook County, Ill., June 6, 1916; moved to Sioux City, Iowa, with his parents in 1932; A.B., Creighton University, Omaha, Nebr., 1938; M.A., Catholic University, Washington, D.C., 1939; LL.B., Columbia University School of Law, 1946; postgraduate studies at State University of Iowa College of Law in 1946; during the Second World War served with the United States Army Air Corps, 1942-1946, attaining the rank of lieutenant colonel; service included Air Force Headquarters, Washington, D.C., the faculty of the United States Army Command and General Staff School, Fort Leavenworth, Kans., and the China-Burma-India Theater of Operations; brigadier general, Air Force Reserve; admitted to the Iowa and Nebraska bars in 1946; attorney, Office of Chief Counsel, Internal Revenue Service, Washington, D.C., 1947-1948; assistant professor of law, University of Notre Dame College of Law, 1948-1949; practiced tax and farm tax law in Sioux City, Iowa, 1949-1960; member, Iowa State house of representatives, 1955-1956; Iowa State senator, 1957-1960; elected as a Republican to the United States Senate in 1960; reelected in 1966, and served from January 3, 1961, to January 3, 1973; unsuccessful candidate for reelection in 1972; judge of the United States Court of Customs and Patent Appeals, 1973-1982; was a resident of Temple Terrace, Fla.; died August 29, 1994.

**MILLER, Jacob Welsh,** a Senator from New Jersey; born in German Valley, Morris County, N.J., August 29, 1800; attended the public schools; studied law; was admitted to the bar in 1823 and practiced in Morristown, N.J.; elected to the State general assembly in 1832; served in the State council 1838-1840; elected as a Whig to the United States Senate in 1840; reelected in 1846 and served from March 4, 1841, to March 3, 1853; chairman, Committee on the District of Columbia (Twenty-seventh and Twenty-eighth Congresses); died in Morristown, N.J., September 30, 1862; interment in St. Peter's Parish Churchyard.

**MILLER, James Francis,** a Representative from Texas; born in Winnsboro, Fairfield District, S.C., August 1, 1830; moved with his parents to Texas in 1842; attended the common schools and Reutersville College; studied law; was admitted to the bar in 1857 and commenced practice in Gonzales, Tex.; enlisted as a private in Company I, Eighth Texas Cavalry, better known as "Terry's Texas Rangers," and served throughout the Civil War; resumed the practice of law in Gonzales, Tex.; engaged in banking and stock raising; elected as a Democrat to the Forty-eighth and Forty-ninth Congresses (March 4, 1883-March 3, 1887); chairman, Committee on Banking and Currency (Forty-ninth Congress); declined renomination; resumed former pursuits; elected as first president of the Texas Bankers' Association in 1885; died in Gonzales, Tex., on July 3, 1902; interment in Masonic Cemetery.

**MILLER, James Monroe,** a Representative from Kansas; born at Three Springs, Huntingdon County, Pa., May 6, 1852; attended the district school and was graduated from Dickinson Seminary, Williamsport, Pa., in 1875; moved to Skiddy, Morris County, Kans., in 1875; superintendent of schools in Council Grove, Kans., for two terms, and while holding this position studied law; was admitted to the bar in 1879 and commenced practice in Council Grove, Kans.; elected prosecuting attorney of Morris County, Kans., in 1880 and again in 1884 and 1886; member of the State house of representatives in 1894 and 1895; elected as a Republican to the Fifty-sixth and to the five succeeding Congresses (March 4, 1899-March 3, 1911); chairman, Committee on Claims (Fifty-ninth and Sixtieth Congresses), Committee on Elections No. 2 (Sixty-first Congress); unsuccessful candidate for renomination in 1910; resumed the practice of law in Council Grove, Morris County, Kans., and died there January 20, 1926; interment in Greenwood Cemetery.

**MILLER, Jesse** (father of William Henry Miller), a Representative from Pennsylvania; born near Landisburg, Perry County, Pa., in 1800; attended the common schools; first clerk to county commissioner of Perry County 1820-1823; sheriff of Perry County 1823-1826; member of the Pennsylvania house of representatives from 1826 until February 7, 1828, when he resigned; served in the Pennsylvania senate 1828-1832; elected as a Jacksonian to the Twenty-third and Twenty-fourth Congresses and served from March 4, 1833, until his resignation on October 30, 1836; chairman, Committee on Invalid Pensions (Twenty-third and Twenty-fourth Congresses); First Auditor of the Treasury Department, by appointment of President Andrew Jackson, 1836-1842; canal commissioner of Pennsylvania in 1844 and 1845; secretary of state of Pennsylvania 1845-1848; died in Harrisburg, Pa., August 20, 1850; interment in Harrisburg Cemetery.

**MILLER, John,** a Representative from Missouri; born near Martinsburg, Berkeley County, Va. (now West Virginia), November 25, 1781; attended the common schools; moved to Steubenville, Ohio, about 1803 and published the Western Herald and Steubenville Gazette; served in the War of 1812 as lieutenant colonel of the Seventeenth United States Infantry and as colonel in command of the Nineteenth Infantry; resigned his Army commission on February 10, 1818; was appointed register of the land office at Franklin, Howard County, Mo., which position he held for eight years; elected Governor of Missouri in 1825 to fill the vacancy caused by the death of Governor Frederick Bates; reelected in 1828, and served from January 20, 1826 to November 14, 1832; elected as a Democrat to the Twenty-fifth and to the two succeeding Congresses (March 4, 1837-March 3, 1843); declined to be a candidate for renomination in 1842 to the Twenty-eighth Congress; retired to his residence near Florissant, Mo., where he died on March 18, 1846; interment in Colonel John O'Fallon's private vault on the O'Fallon farm; reinterment in Bellefontaine Cemetery, St. Louis, Mo.

Bibliography: *DAB.*

**MILLER, John,** a Representative from New York; born in Amenia, Dutchess County, N.Y., November 10, 1774; attended the district school one year and a private classical school in Kent, Conn., for a like period; studied medicine in the University of Pennsylvania at Philadelphia and commenced practice in Washington County, N.Y., in 1798; moved to Fabius, Onondaga County (now Truxton, Cortland County), N.Y., in 1801; coroner of Cortland County in 1802; postmaster of Truxton 1805-1825; organized the Cortland County Medical Society, and in 1808 was its first vice president; justice of the peace 1812-1821; member of the State assembly in 1817, 1820, and 1845; judge of the county court 1817-1820; elected to the Nineteenth Congress (March 4, 1825-March 3, 1827); delegate to the State constitutional convention in 1846; died in Truxton, Cortland County, N.Y., March 31, 1862; interment in the City Cemetery.

**MILLER, John Elvis,** a Representative and a Senator from Arkansas; born in Aid, Stoddard County, Mo., May 15, 1888; attended the public schools, Southeast Missouri State Teachers College at Cape Girardeau, and Valparaiso (Ind.) University; taught school in Sayre, Okla., and served as principal of a school in Aid, Mo.; teacher in Acron Ridge, Mo., 1909-1910; LL.B., University of Kentucky School of Law, Lexington, 1912; was admitted to the bar the same year and commenced practice in Searcy, White County, Ark.; also engaged in banking; delegate to the Arkansas State constitutional convention in 1918; served as prosecuting attorney, first judicial circuit of Arkansas, 1919-1922; elected as a Democrat to the Seventy-second and to the three succeeding Congresses and served from March 4, 1931, to November 14, 1937, when he resigned to become Senator; elected as a Democrat to the United States Senate to fill the vacancy caused by the death of Joseph T. Robinson for the term ending January 3, 1943, and served from November 15, 1937, until his resignation effective March 31, 1941, having been appointed United States district judge for the western district of Arkansas; retired as United States district judge in 1967 and became United States senior district judge; resided in Fort Smith, Sebastian County, Ark. until his death on January 30, 1981; interment at Forest Park Cemetery.

**MILLER, John Franklin** (uncle of John Franklin Miller [1862-1936]), a Senator from California; born in South Bend, St. Joseph County, Ind., November 21, 1831; pursued an academic course; studied law and graduated from the New York State Law School in 1852; was admitted to the bar and commenced practice in South Bend, Ind.; moved to California, where he practiced for a short time and then returned to South Bend; member, Indiana State senate, 1860-1861; entered the Union Army in August 1861 and was wounded in the Battle of Stone's River, Tenn., December 30, 1862-January 3, 1863; commissioned brigadier general January 5, 1864; brevetted major general in 1865, resigned in September 1865 and returned to California; collector of the port of San Francisco, 1865-1869, declining reappointment in 1869 to accept the presidency of the Alaska Commercial Company; delegate to the second California State constitutional convention, 1878-1879; elected as a Republican to the United States Senate, and served from March 4, 1881 until his death in Washington, D.C., March 8, 1886; chairman, Committee to Revise the Laws of the United States (Forty-seventh Congress), Committee on Foreign Relations (Forty-ninth Congress); interment in Laurel Hill Cemetery, San Francisco, Calif.; reinterment May 5, 1913 in Arlington National Cemetery.
**Bibliography:** *DAB.*

**MILLER, John Franklin** (nephew of John Franklin Miller [1831-1913]), a Representative from Washington; born on a farm near South Bend, St. Joseph County, Ind., June 9, 1862; attended the public schools; was graduated from the law department of Valparaiso (Ind.) University in 1887 and was admitted to the bar the same year; moved to Seattle, Wash., in 1888 and commenced the practice of law; prosecuting attorney of King County, 1890-1894; deputy prosecuting attorney, 1905-1908; mayor of Seattle, 1908-1910; elected as a Republican to the Sixty-fifth and to the six succeeding Congresses (March 4, 1917-March 3, 1931); unsuccessful

candidate for renomination in 1930 to the Seventy-second Congress; was a member of the congressional delegation which, with Secretary of War Newton D. Baker, visited the American forces in France and Germany in 1919; resumed the practice of law; died in Seattle, Wash., May 28, 1936; interment in Acacia Mausoleum.

**MILLER, John Gaines,** a Representative from Missouri; born in Danville, Ky., November 29, 1812; attended the common schools and was graduated from Centre College, Danville, Ky.; studied law and was admitted to the bar in 1834; moved to Boonville, Mo., in 1835; served as a member of the State house of representatives in 1840; elected as a Whig to the Thirty-second, Thirty-third, and Thirty-fourth Congresses and served from March 4, 1851, until his death near Marshall, Saline County, Mo., May 11, 1856; interment in Mount Olive Cemetery, near Marshall, Mo.

**MILLER, John Krepps,** a Representative from Ohio; born in Mount Vernon, Knox County, Ohio, May 25, 1819; attended the public schools; was graduated from Jefferson College, Canonsburg, Pa., in 1838; studied law; was admitted to the bar in 1841 and commenced practice in Mount Vernon, Ohio; delegate to the Democratic National Convention in 1844; elected as a Democrat to the Thirtieth and Thirty-first Congresses (March 4, 1847-March 3, 1851); died in Mount Vernon, Ohio, on August 11, 1863; interment in Mound View Cemetery.

**MILLER, John Ripin,** a Representative from Washington; born in New York City, May 23, 1938; attended public schools and Friends Seminary, New York City; B.A., Bucknell University, Lewisburg, Pa., 1959; M.A., Yale University, 1964; LL.B., Yale University Law School, 1964; served in the United States Army, 1960, and Reserves, 1961-1968; admitted to the bar in 1965 and began practice in Seattle, Wash.; adjunct professor, University of Puget Sound, Wash., 1981-1984; assistant attorney general of State of Washington, 1965-1968; member and president, Seattle City Council, 1972-1980; elected as a Republican to the Ninety-ninth and to the three succeeding Congresses (January 3, 1985-January 3, 1993); was not a candidate for renomination in 1992 to the One Hundred Third Congress; investment banker with Chanen, Painter and Co., Ltd., Seattle; board member, Advanced Technology Laboratories, Inc., and Discovery Institute, Seattle; is a resident of Seattle, Wash.

**MILLER, Joseph,** a Representative from Ohio; born in Virginia September 9, 1819; attended the common schools; moved to Ohio and settled in Chillicothe; was graduated from Miami University, Oxford, Ohio, in 1839; studied law; was admitted to the bar in 1841 and commenced practice in Chillicothe, Ohio; prosecuting attorney of Ross County, Ohio, 1844-1848; member of the State house of representatives in 1856; elected as a Democrat to the Thirty-fifth Congress (March 4, 1857-March 3, 1859); unsuccessful candidate for reelection in 1858 to the Thirty-sixth Congress; appointed United States judge for Nebraska Territory March 5, 1859; died in Cincinnati, Ohio, on May 27, 1862; interment in Grandview Cemetery, Chillicothe, Ohio.

**MILLER, Killian,** a Representative from New York; born in Claverack, Columbia County, N.Y., July 30, 1785; pursued an academic course; studied law; was admitted to the bar and commenced practice in Livingston, N.Y., in 1806; member of the State assembly in 1825 and 1828; moved to Hudson, N.Y., in 1833 and continued the practice of law; clerk of Columbia County 1837-1840; elected as a Whig to the Thirty-fourth Congress (March 4, 1855-March 3, 1857); resumed the practice of his profession; died in Hudson, Columbia County, N.Y., January 9, 1859; interment in Hudson City Cemetery.

**MILLER, Louis Ebenezer,** a Representative from Missouri; born in Willisburg, Washington County, Ky., April 30, 1899; attended the grade schools of Washington County, Ky., Springfield (Ky.) High School, and St. Mary's College, St. Marys, Kans.; during the First World War served as a private; was graduated from the law department of St. Louis University, St. Louis, Mo., in 1921; was admitted to the bar the same year and commenced practice in St. Louis, Mo.; member of the Republican city central committee of St. Louis 1936-1942; member of the advisory council of the Republican National Committee in 1943; delegate to the Republican National Convention in 1940; elected as a Republican to the Seventy-eighth Congress (January 3, 1943-January 3, 1945); unsuccessful candidate for reelection in 1944 to the Seventy-ninth Congress; continued the practice of law in St. Louis, Mo., until his death there November 1, 1952; interment in Calvary Cemetery.

**MILLER, Lucas Miltiades,** a Representative from Wisconsin; born in Livadia, Greece, September 15, 1824; was left an orphan at the age of four, when he was adopted by J.P. Miller, an American who served as a colonel in the Greek Army during the Greek revolution; accompanied his foster father upon his return to the United States and settled in Montpelier, Vt., in 1828; attended the common schools; studied law; was admitted to the bar in 1845 and commenced practice in Oshkosh, Winnebago County, Wis., in 1846; also engaged in agricultural pursuits; served as colonel of militia in the Mexican War; member of the State assembly in 1853; served as commissioner of the Wisconsin Board of Public Works; served ten years as chairman of the Winnebago County Board of Supervisors; elected as a Democrat to the Fifty-second Congress (March 4, 1891-March 3, 1893); unsuccessful candidate for renomination in 1892; died in Oshkosh, Winnebago County, Wis., December 4, 1902; interment in Riverside Cemetery.

**MILLER, Morris Smith** (father of Rutger Bleecker Miller), a Representative from New York; born in New York City, July 31, 1779; was graduated from Union College, Schenectady, N.Y., in 1798; studied law and was admitted to the bar; served as private secretary to Governor John Jay, and subsequently, in 1806, commenced the practice of his profession in Utica, N.Y.; president of the village of Utica in 1808; judge of the court of common pleas of Oneida County from 1810 until his death; elected as a Federalist to the Thirteenth Congress (March 4, 1813-March 3, 1815); represented the United States Government at the negotiation of a treaty between the Seneca Indians and the proprietors of the Seneca Reservation at Buffalo, N.Y., in July 1819; died in Utica, N.Y., November 16, 1824; interment in Rural Cemetery, Albany, N.Y.

**MILLER, Nathan,** a Delegate from Rhode Island; born in Warren, R.I., March 20, 1743; attended a private school; merchant and shipbuilder; deputy to the general assembly 1772-1774, 1780, 1782, 1783, and 1790; advanced through various grades until he was made brigadier general of the Rhode Island Militia for Newport and Bristol Counties and held this office from 1772 to 1778; deputy in the Rhode Island State Assembly for six years; Member of the Continental Congress and served from July 14 to November 3, 1786; reelected, but did not take his seat; member of the State constitutional convention in 1790; died in Warren, Bristol County, R.I., May 20, 1790; interment in Kickamuet Cemetery.

**MILLER, Orrin Larrabee,** a Representative from Kansas; born in Newburg, Penobscot County, Maine, January 11, 1856; attended the common schools and was graduated from the Maine Central Institute at Pittsfield; studied law; was admitted to the bar in 1880 and commenced practice in Bangor, Maine; moved to Kansas City, Kans., in 1880 and engaged in the practice of law; appointed and subsequently elected district judge for the twenty-ninth judicial district of Kansas in 1887, and served until 1891, when he resigned to resume the practice of law; counsel for many years for several large railroad corporations; elected as a Republican to the

Fifty-fourth Congress (March 4, 1895-March 3, 1897); declined to be a candidate for renomination in 1896; continued the practice of law in Kansas City, Kans., until his death there on September 11, 1926; interment in Woodlawn Cemetery.

**MILLER, Pleasant Moorman,** a Representative from Tennessee; born in Lynchburg, Campbell County, Va.; moved to Rogersville, Hawkins County, Tenn., in 1796, and thence to Knoxville, Knox County, Tenn., in 1800; one of the commissioners for the government of Knoxville in 1801 and 1802; elected as a Republican to the Eleventh Congress (March 4, 1809-March 3, 1811); moved to west Tennessee about 1824, and was chancellor of that division in 1836 and 1837; died in 1849; interment in Trenton, Gibson County, Tenn.

**MILLER, Rutger Bleecker** (son of Morris Smith Miller), a Representative from New York; born in Lowville, Lewis County, N.Y., July 28, 1805; attended the common schools in Utica, the Catholic College, Montreal, Canada, and Yale College; was graduated from the Litchfield Law School in 1824; was admitted to the bar and practiced in Utica, N.Y., 1829-1831; manager of the Utica Wilberforce Society 1829; interested in banking and railroads 1832-1833; trustee of the village of Utica 1829-1831; member of the first board of aldermen of the city of Utica; member of the State assembly in 1832; clerk of the United States district court in 1833 and 1834; elected as a Jacksonian to the Twenty-fourth Congress to fill the vacancy caused by the resignation of Samuel Beardsley and served from November 9, 1836, to March 3, 1837; engaged in the erection of buildings and in railroad construction, and subsequently in the management of his farm in Boonville, Oneida County; died in Utica, Oneida County, N.Y., November 12, 1877; interment in Forest Hill Cemetery.

**MILLER, Samuel Franklin,** a Representative from New York; born in Franklin, Delaware County, N.Y., May 27, 1827; was graduated from the Delaware Literary Institute and Hamilton College, Clinton, N.Y., in 1852; studied law and was admitted to the bar in 1853, but did not engage in extensive practice; engaged in farming and lumbering; member of the State assembly in 1854; served as a colonel in the State militia; elected as a Republican to the Thirty-eighth Congress (March 4, 1863-March 3, 1865); member of the State constitutional convention in 1867; district collector of internal revenue 1869-1873; member of the State board of charities 1869-1877; elected to the Forty-fourth Congress (March 4, 1875-March 3, 1877); continued agricultural pursuits and lumbering; died in Franklin, N.Y., on March 16, 1892; interment in Ouleout Valley Cemetery.

**MILLER, Samuel Henry,** a Representative from Pennsylvania; born at Coolspring, near Mercer, Mercer County, Pa., April 19, 1840; attended the common schools and was graduated from Westminster College, New Wilmington, Pa., in 1860; taught school during the Civil War served in the Fifty-fifth Regiment, Pennsylvania Militia; edited and published the Mercer (Pa.) Dispatch 1861-1870; studied law; was admitted to the bar and commenced practice in Mercer in 1871; elected as a Republican to the Forty-seventh and Forty-eighth Congresses (March 4, 1881-March 3, 1885); declined to be a candidate for renomination in 1884; resumed the practice of law in Mercer; president judge of the several courts of Mercer County, Pa., 1894-1904; resumed the practice of law; elected to the Sixty-fourth Congress (March 4, 1915-March 3, 1917); declined to be a candidate for renomination in 1916; resumed the practice of his profession; died in Mercer, Pa., September 4, 1918; interment in Mercer Cemetery.

**MILLER, Smith,** a Representative from Indiana; born near Charlotte, N.C., May 30, 1804; moved to Gibson County, Ind., with his parents who settled in Patoka in 1813; received a limited schooling; engaged in agricultural pursuits; member of the State house of representatives 1835-1839 and in 1846; served in the State senate 1841-1844 and 1847-1850; delegate to the State constitutional convention in 1850; elected as a Democrat to the Thirty-third and Thirty-fourth Congresses (March 4, 1853-March 3, 1857); resumed agricultural pursuits; delegate to the Democratic National Convention at Charleston, S.C., in 1860; died near Patoka, Ind., March 21, 1872; interment in Robb Cemetery.

**MILLER, Stephen Decatur,** a Representative and a Senator from South Carolina; born in Waxhaw settlement, Lancaster District, S.C., May 8, 1787; studied under a private tutor; graduated from South Carolina College at Columbia in 1808; studied law; was admitted to the bar and commenced practice in Sumterville in 1811; elected to the Fourteenth Congress to fill the vacancy caused by the resignation of William Mayrant; reelected to the Fifteenth Congress, and served from January 2, 1817 to March 3, 1819; resumed the practice of his profession; member, South Carolina State senate, 1822-1828; elected Governor of South Carolina by the Legislature, and served from December 1828 to December 1830; elected as a Nullifier to the United States Senate, and served from March 4, 1831 until March 2, 1833, when he resigned due to ill health; delegate to the South Carolina nullification conventions in 1832 and 1833; engaged in cotton planting in Mississippi in 1835; died in Raymond, Hinds County, Miss., March 8, 1838.

**Bibliography:** *DAB.*

**MILLER, Thomas Byron,** a Representative from Pennsylvania; born in Plymouth, Luzerne County, Pa., August 11, 1896; attended the public schools and Hillman Academy; M.A., Dickinson College Law School, Carlisle, Pa.; was admitted to the bar and commenced practice in Wilkes-Barre, Pa., in 1916; during the First World War served as a second lieutenant in the Sixteenth Field Artillery from February 25, 1918 until his discharge as a first lieutenant on September 23, 1919; elected as a Republican to the Seventy-seventh Congress, May 9, 1942, by special election to fill the vacancy caused by the resignation of J. Harold Flannery; reelected to the Seventy-eighth Congress, and served from May 9, 1942 to January 3, 1945; unsuccessful candidate for reelection in 1944 to the Seventy-ninth Congress; resumed the practice of law in Washington, D.C.; banker; died in Wilkes-Barre, Pa., March 20, 1976; cremated; ashes scattered on the grounds of his summer home in Orangeville, Pa.

**MILLER, Thomas Ezekiel,** a Representative from South Carolina; born in Ferrebeville, Beaufort County, S.C., June 17, 1849; moved with his parents to Charleston, S.C., in 1851; attended the public schools in Charleston, S.C., and in Hudson, N.Y.; employed as a newsboy on a railroad; was graduated from Lincoln University, Chester County, Pa., in 1872; moved to Grahamville, S.C., and served as school commissioner of Beaufort County in 1872; studied law, and was admitted to the bar in December 1875; member, South Carolina State house of representatives, 1874-1880, 1886-1887, and 1894-1896; member of the Republican State executive committee, 1878-1880, and served as State chairman in 1884; served in the State senate in 1880; successfully contested as a Republican the election of William Elliott to the Fifty-first Congress, and served from September 24, 1890 to March 3, 1891; unsuccessful candidate for reelection in 1890 to the Fifty-second Congress, and for nomination in 1892 to the Fifty-third Congress; again a member of the State house of representatives, 1894-1896; member of the State constitutional convention in 1895; president of the State college in Orangeburg, S.C. (now South Carolina State College), from 1896 until 1911, when he resigned; retired from active pursuits in 1911 and lived in Charleston, S.C., until 1923, when he moved to Philadelphia, Pa.; in 1934 returned to Charleston, S.C., where he resided until his death there on April 8, 1938; interment in Brotherhood Cemetery.

**MILLER, Thomas Woodnutt** (uncle of Clement Woodnutt Miller), a Representative from Delaware; born in Wilmington, Del., June 26, 1886; attended the Hotchkiss School; was graduated from Yale University in 1908; interested in mining in Nevada from early youth; employed as a steel roller by the Bethlehem Steel Co. in 1908 and 1909; secretary to Representative William H. Heald of Delaware, 1910-1912, and during this period studied law in Washington, D.C.; secretary of state of Delaware, 1913-1915; elected as a Republican to the Sixty-fourth Congress (March 4, 1915-March 3, 1917); unsuccessful candidate for reelection in 1916 to the Sixty-fifth Congress; during the First World War enlisted in July 1917 as a private in the Infantry of the United States Army; promoted to lieutenant colonel and served in France with the Seventy-ninth Division until discharged in September 1919; awarded the Purple Heart; a founder and incorporator of the American Legion and vice chairman of the Paris caucus in March 1919; Alien Property Custodian, 1921-1925; member of the American Battle Monuments Commission, 1923-1926; founder of the Nevada State park system, and chairman of the Nevada State Park Commission in 1935, 1936, 1953-1959, and 1967-1973; staff field representative of the United States Veterans' Employment Service, 1945-1957; died in Reno, Nev., May 5, 1973; cremated; ashes interred in Masonic Memorial Gardens.

**MILLER, Ward MacLaughlin,** a Representative from Ohio; born in Portsmouth, Ohio, November 29, 1902; graduate of Portsmouth High School; A.B., Ohio State University, 1923; A.M., Harvard University, 1931; assistant to Professor Irving Babbitt of Harvard University, 1929-1931; member of the editorial staff of Bookman Magazine, 1931-1933; engaged in the real estate business from 1935 until 1980; member of the Ohio Board of Education, 1955-1980; member of the Royal Institute of Philosophy, Great Britain; elected as a Republican to the Eighty-sixth Congress in 1960 to fill the vacancy caused by the death of James G. Polk, and served from November 8, 1960 to January 3, 1961; was not a candidate in 1960 to the Eighty-seventh Congress; was a resident of Portsmouth, Ohio, until his death there on March 11, 1984; interment in Greenlawn Cemetery.

**MILLER, Warner,** a Representative and a Senator from New York; born in Hannibal, Oswego County, N.Y., August 12, 1838; attended the common schools and Charlottesville Academy; graduated from Union College, Schenectady, N.Y., in 1860; professor of Latin and Greek in the Fort Edward Collegiate Institute; during the Civil War enlisted as a private in the Fifth Regiment, New York Volunteer Cavalry, in 1861; promoted to the rank of sergeant major and lieutenant; taken prisoner at the Battle of Winchester; exchanged and honorably discharged; engaged in agricultural pursuits; founder of a wood-pulp business, developed new techniques for paper production, and was president of the American Paper & Pulp Association; interested in various other business enterprises; member, New York State assembly, 1873-1876; elected as a Republican to the Forty-sixth and Forty-seventh Congresses and served from March 4, 1879, until his resignation July 26, 1881; elected as a Republican in 1881 to the United States Senate to fill the vacancy caused by the resignation of Thomas C. Platt and served from July 27, 1881, to March 3, 1887; unsuccessful candidate for reelection in 1887; chairman, Committee on Agriculture and Forestry (Forty-eighth and Forty-ninth Congresses); unsuccessful candidate for election for Governor of New York in 1888; chairman of the Special Tax Commission of the State of New York in 1906; retired and resided in Herkimer, N.Y.; died in New York City, March 21, 1918; interment in Oak Hill Cemetery, Herkimer, N.Y.

**Bibliography:** *DAB.*

**MILLER, Warren,** a Representative from West Virginia; born at Apple Grove, Meigs County, Ohio, April 2, 1847; moved about 1850 to that portion of Virginia which later became West Virginia and settled in Millwood, Jackson County; attended the common schools and was graduated from the Ohio University at Athens; taught school; studied law; was admitted to the bar and commenced practice in Ripley, Jackson County, W.Va., in 1871; mayor of Ripley in 1871; assistant prosecuting attorney of Jackson County 1878-1880; prosecuting attorney 1881-1890; delegate to the Republican National Convention in 1884; member of the State house of representatives in 1890 and 1891; unsuccessful candidate for judge of the State supreme court in 1892; elected as a Republican to the Fifty-fourth and Fifty-fifth Congresses (March 4, 1895-March 3, 1899); was not a candidate for renomination in 1898; resumed the practice of law and also engaged in agricultural pursuits; appointed judge of the fifth judicial circuit of West Virginia; elected in 1902 and served from 1900 until his resignation in 1903; judge of the State supreme court of appeals in 1903 and 1904; member of the State senate 1914-1918; died in Ripley, W.Va., on December 29, 1920; interment in Cottageville Cemetery, Cottageville, W.Va.

**MILLER, William Edward,** a Representative from New York; born in Lockport, Niagara County, N.Y., March 22, 1914; attended the parochial schools and Lockport High School; B.A., Notre Dame University, South Bend, Ind., 1935; LL.B., Albany Law School of Union University, 1938; was admitted to the bar in 1938 and commenced the practice of law in Lockport, N.Y.; appointed United States Commissioner for the Western District of New York in January 1940, and served until entering the United States Army on July 1, 1942; assigned to the Military Intelligence Branch; in May 1945 was commissioned a first lieutenant and assigned to the War Criminals Branch at Washington, D.C., until August 1945; assistant prosecutor of Nazi war criminals at Nuremberg, Germany, 1945-1946; was discharged in March 1946; appointed assistant district attorney of Niagara County in March 1946; appointed district attorney on January 1, 1948, and elected district attorney in November 1948; chairman of the National Republican Congressional Committee in 1960, and of the Republican National Committee in 1961; elected as a Republican to the Eighty-second and to the six succeeding Congresses (January 3, 1951-January 3, 1965); was not a candidate for reelection in 1964 to the Eighty-ninth Congress, but was the unsuccessful Republican candidate for Vice President of the United States on the ticket headed by Barry M. Goldwater; resumed the practice of law; resided in Lockport, N.Y. until his death in Buffalo, N.Y. on June 24, 1983; interment in Arlington National Cemetery, Va.

**MILLER, William Henry** (son of Jesse Miller), a Representative from Pennsylvania; born in Landisburg, Perry County, Pa., February 28, 1829; attended the public schools in Landisburg, Pa., and a private school in Harrisburg, Pa.; graduated from Franklin and Marshall College, Lancaster, Pa., in 1846; studied law; admitted to the bar the same year and practiced in Harrisburg, Pa., and later in New Bloomfield in 1849; returned to Harrisburg in 1854; clerk of the Pennsylvania supreme court 1854-1863; clerk of the Pennsylvania senate in 1858 and 1859; elected as a Democrat to the Thirty-eighth Congress (March 4, 1863-March 3, 1865); unsuccessful candidate for reelection in 1864 to the Thirty-ninth Congress; resumed the practice of law and also engaged in journalism; died in Harrisburg, Pa., September 12, 1870; interment in Harrisburg Cemetery.

**MILLER, William Jennings,** a Representative from Connecticut; born in North Andover, Essex County, Mass., March 12, 1899; attended the public schools; was graduated from Cannon's Commercial College, Lawrence, Mass., in 1917; during the First World War enlisted on August 5, 1917 as a private in the United States Army, and served in the Air Service in the Eightieth and One Thousand One Hundred and Fourth Aero Squadrons; later commissioned a second lieutenant; injured in an airplane crash in France in 1918, resulting in the loss of both legs; discharged on April 26, 1919; patient in United States veterans' hospitals from 1919 until 1931; moved to Wethersfield, Conn., in 1926; engaged in the insurance business in 1931; elected as a Republican to the Seventy-sixth Congress (January 3, 1939-January 3, 1941); unsuccessful candidate for reelection in 1940 to the Seventy-seventh Congress; elected to the Seventy-eighth Congress (January 3, 1943-January 3, 1945); unsuccessful candidate for reelection in 1944 to the Seventy-ninth Congress; elected to the Eightieth Congress (January 3, 1947-January 3, 1949); unsuccessful candidate for reelection in 1948 to the Eighty-first Congress; resumed the general insurance business; died in Wethersfield, Conn., November 22, 1950; interment in Jordan Cemetery, Waterford, Conn.

**MILLER, William Starr,** a Representative from New York; born in Wintonbury (now Bloomfield), Conn., August 22, 1793; completed preparatory studies; member of the Board of Aldermen of New York City in 1845; elected as an American Party candidate to the Twenty-ninth Congress (March 4, 1845-March 3, 1847); unsuccessful candidate for reelection in 1846 to the Thirtieth Congress; died in New York City November 9, 1854; interment in Greenwood Cemetery, Brooklyn, N.Y.

**MILLIGAN, Jacob Le Roy,** a Representative from Missouri; born in Richmond, Ray County, Mo., March 9, 1889; attended the public schools and the law department of the University of Missouri at Columbia 1910-1914; was admitted to the bar in 1913 and commenced practice in Richmond, Mo., in 1914; during the First World War enlisted in the Sixth Regiment, Missouri Infantry, on April 8, 1917; served as captain of Company G, One Hundred and Fortieth Infantry Regiment, Thirty-fifth Division, from August 4, 1917, to May 15, 1919; received the Purple Heart and Silver Star; returned April 28, 1919; elected as a Democrat to the Sixty-sixth Congress to fill the vacancy caused by the resignation of Joshua W. Alexander and served from February 14, 1920, to March 3, 1921; unsuccessful candidate for reelection in 1920 to the Sixty-seventh Congress; delegate to the Democratic National Convention in 1928; elected to the Sixty-eighth and to the five succeeding Congresses (March 4, 1923-January 3, 1935); was not a candidate for renomination in 1934, but was an unsuccessful candidate for nomination for United States Senator; resumed the practice of law; president of Kansas City Police Board 1949-1950; died in Kansas City, Mo., March 9, 1951; interment in Fairview Cemetery, Liberty, Clay County, Mo.

**MILLIGAN, John Jones,** a Representative from Delaware; born at Bohemia Manor, Cecil County, Md., December 10, 1795; attended Wilmington Academy and St. Mary's College, Baltimore, Md., and was graduated from Princeton College in 1814; studied law; was admitted to the bar and commenced practice in New Castle County, Del., in 1818; elected as an Anti-Jacksonian to the Twenty-second Congress; reelected to the Twenty-third Congress and as a Whig to the Twenty-fourth and Twenty-fifth Congresses (March 4, 1831-March 3, 1839); unsuccessful candidate for reelection in 1838 to the Twenty-sixth Congress; appointed judge of the State superior court on September 19, 1839, and served until September 16, 1864, when he resigned; died in Philadelphia, Pa., April 20, 1875; interment in Wilmington and Brandywine Cemetery, Wilmington, Del.

**MILLIKEN, Charles William,** a Representative from Kentucky; born near Murray, Calloway County, Ky., August 15, 1827; moved with his parents to Simpson County, Ky., in 1829 and settled near Franklin; pursued preparatory studies, and was graduated from Wirt College, Sumner County, Tenn., in 1849; studied law; was admitted to the bar in 1850 and commenced practice in Franklin, Ky.; prosecuting attorney of Simpson County 1857-1862; Commonwealth attorney of the fourth judicial district of Kentucky from 1867 until his resignation on February 24, 1872; elected as a Democrat to the Forty-third and Forty-fourth Congresses (March 4, 1873-March

3, 1877); chairman, Committee on Public Expenditures (Forty-fourth Congress); declined to be a candidate for reelection in 1876 to the Forty-fifth Congress; resumed the practice of law; referee in bankruptcy for the Bowling Green (Ky.) district and served from September 28, 1907, until his death in Franklin, Simpson County, Ky., October 16, 1915; interment in Greenlawn Cemetery.

**MILLIKEN, Seth Llewellyn,** a Representative from Maine; born in Montville, Waldo County, Maine, December 12, 1831; attended the common schools and Waterville College; was graduated from Union College, Schenectady, N.Y., in 1856; member of the State house of representatives in 1857 and 1858; moved to Belfast, Maine; clerk of the supreme judicial court 1859-1871; studied law; was admitted to the bar in 1871, but did not practice; delegate to the Republican National Convention in 1876 and 1884; elected as a Republican to the Forty-eighth and to the seven succeeding Congresses and served from March 4, 1883, until his death in Washington, D.C., April 18, 1897; chairman, Committee on Public Buildings and Grounds (Fifty-first and Fifty-fourth Congresses); interment in Grove Cemetery, Belfast, Waldo County, Maine.

**MILLIKEN, William H., Jr.,** a Representative from Pennsylvania; born in Philadelphia, Pa., August 19, 1897; moved to Sharon Hill, Delaware County, Pa., in 1906; attended Sharon Hill public schools; graduated from Drexel Institute, Philadelphia, Pa.; worked as a construction foreman; sales executive for the Whitehall Cement Manufacturing Co., Philadelphia, Pa.; member of the Pennsylvania house of representatives; clerk of courts of Delaware County, Pa.; appointed burgess of Sharon Hill, Pa., to fill unexpired term September 14, 1948, elected in 1949, reelected in 1953 and 1957 and served until elected to Congress; elected as a Republican to the Eighty-sixth, Eighty-seventh, and Eighty-eighth Congresses (January 3, 1959-January 3, 1965); was not a candidate for renomination in 1964 to the Eighty-ninth Congress; died in Ridley Park, Pa., July 4, 1969; interment in Arlington Cemetery, Lansdowne, Pa.

**MILLIKIN, Eugene Donald,** a Senator from Colorado; born in Hamilton, Butler County, Ohio, February 12, 1891; attended the public schools; graduated from the law school of the University of Colorado at Boulder in 1913; was admitted to the bar the same year and commenced practice in Salt Lake City, Utah; executive secretary to Governor George A. Carlson of Colorado, 1915-1917; during the First World War enlisted as a private in the Colorado National Guard in 1917; saw action in France and was mustered out as a lieutenant colonel; resumed the practice of law in Denver, Colo.; president of Kinney-Coastal Oil Co.; appointed and subsequently elected as a Republican to the United States Senate to fill the vacancy in the term ending January 3, 1945, caused by the death of Alva B. Adams; reelected in 1944 and again in 1950 and served from December 20, 1941, to January 3, 1957; was not a candidate for renomination in 1956; chairman, Committee on Finance (Eightieth and Eighty-third Congresses), Republican Conference (Eightieth through Eighty-fourth Congresses), Joint Committee on Internal Revenue Taxation (Eightieth and Eighty-third Congresses); died in Denver, Colo., July 26, 1958; interment in Fairmount Cemetery.

**Bibliography:** *DAB.*

**MILLINGTON, Charles Stephen,** a Representative from New York; born in Norway, Herkimer County, N.Y., March 13, 1855; attended the district schools of Poland, the Fairfield Academy, and Hungerford Collegiate Institute; entered the employ of the Hungerford National Bank, Adams, N.Y.; organized and became cashier of the Bank of Poland; moved to Herkimer, N.Y., in 1894 and continued in the banking business; delegate to the Republican National Convention of 1908; elected as a Republican to the Sixty-first Congress (March 4, 1909-March 3, 1911); unsuccessful candidate for reelection in 1910 to the Sixty-second Congress; resumed business activities in Herkimer, N.Y.; appointed by President William Howard Taft as assistant treasurer of the United States in charge of the subtreasury at New York on May 12, 1911, and served until his death in Herkimer, N.Y., October 25, 1913; interment in Pine Grove Cemetery, Poland, Herkimer County, N.Y.

**MILLS, Daniel Webster,** a Representative from Illinois; born near Waynesville, Warren County, Ohio, February 25, 1838; attended the common schools of Rayesville and the Waynesville High School; moved to Corwin, Ohio, in 1859 and engaged in the mercantile, grain-shipping, and pork-packing businesses; during the Civil War served in the Union Army as captain of Company D, One Hundred and Eightieth Regiment, Ohio Volunteers, until the close of the war; moved to Chicago, Ill.; engaged in lake shipping, 1866-1869, and later in the real estate business; served as warden of the Cook County Hospital, 1877-1881; member of the board of aldermen of Chicago, 1889-1893; elected as a Republican to the Fifty-fifth Congress (March 4, 1897-March 3, 1899); unsuccessful candidate for reelection in 1898 to the Fifty-sixth Congress; resumed the real estate business; died in Chicago, Ill., on December 16, 1904; interment in Graceland Cemetery.

**MILLS, Elijah Hunt,** a Representative and a Senator from Massachusetts; born in Chesterfield, Mass., December 1, 1776; educated by private tutors and graduated from Williams College, Williamstown, Mass., in 1797; studied law; was admitted to the bar and commenced practice in Northampton; district attorney for Hampshire County; opened a law school in Northampton in 1823; member, Massachusetts house of representatives, 1811-1814; elected as a Federalist to the Fourteenth and Fifteenth Congresses (March 4, 1815-March 3, 1819); elected to the Massachusetts house of representatives in 1819 and became speaker in 1820; elected to the United States Senate in 1820 to fill the vacancy caused by the resignation of Prentiss Mellen; reelected and served from June 12, 1820 to March 3, 1827; unsuccessful candidate for reelection; retired from public life due to ill health; died in Northampton, Hampshire County, Mass., on May 5, 1829; interment in Bridge Street Cemetery.

**Bibliography:** *DAB.*

**MILLS, Newt Virgus,** a Representative from Louisiana; born in Calhoun, Ouachita Parish, La., September 27, 1899; attended the public schools of his native city, Louisiana Polytechnic Institute at Ruston, Louisiana State University at Baton Rouge, Louisiana State Normal College at Natchitoches, and Spencer Business College, New Orleans, La.; also studied law; taught school at Mer Rouge, La., 1921-1932; supervisor of public accounts of Louisiana, 1933-1936; also engaged in agricultural pursuits, cattle raising, real estate, and oil; colonel on the staff of the Governor in 1936; elected as a Democrat to the Seventy-fifth and to the two succeeding Congresses (January 3, 1937-January 3, 1943); unsuccessful candidate for renomination in 1942 to the Seventy-eighth Congress; resumed interests in the oil and gas business, cotton planting, and the building supply business; was a resident of Monroe, La.; died May 7, 1996.

**Bibliography:** Mills, Newt V. *This Is The Last Message: The End Time—The Lord's Return.* Monroe, La.: Newt V. Mills Crusade, 1975.

**MILLS, Ogden Livingston,** a Representative from New York; born in Newport, R.I., August 23, 1884; attended the public schools; was graduated from the academic department of Harvard University in 1904 and from the law department of that institution in 1907; admitted to the New York bar in 1908 and commenced practice in New York City; unsuccessful Republican candidate for election in 1912 to the Sixty-third Congress; delegate to the Republican National Conventions of 1912, 1916 and 1920; member of the New York State senate from 1914 until 1917, when he resigned to enlist in the United States Army, and served with the rank of captain until the close of the First World War; president of the New York State

Tax Association; interested in various business enterprises; elected as a Republican to the Sixty-seventh and to the two succeeding Congresses (March 4, 1921-March 3, 1927); was not a candidate for renomination in 1926 to the Seventieth Congress, but was an unsuccessful candidate for election for Governor of New York; appointed by Undersecretary of the Treasury by President Calvin Coolidge, and served from March 4, 1927 until February 11, 1932; appointed by President Herbert Hoover as Secretary of the Treasury on February 12, 1932, and served until March 3, 1933; engaged as an author and lecturer; died in New York City, October 11, 1937; interment in St. James Churchyard, Hyde Park, N.Y.

Bibliography: *DAB*.

**MILLS, Roger Quarles,** a Representative and a Senator from Texas; born in Todd County, Ky., March 30, 1832; attended the common schools; moved to Texas in 1849; studied law; was admitted to the bar in 1852 and commenced practice in Corsicana, Tex.; member, Texas State house of representatives, 1859-1860; enlisted in the Confederate Army and served throughout the Civil War, attaining the rank of colonel of the Tenth Regiment, Texas Infantry; elected as a Democrat to the Forty-third and to the nine succeeding Congresses, and served from March 4, 1873 until his resignation on March 28, 1892, having been elected Senator; chairman, Committee on Ways and Means (Fiftieth Congress), Committee on Interstate and Foreign Commerce (Fifty-second Congress); elected to the United States Senate in 1892 to fill the vacancy caused by the resignation of John H. Reagan; reelected in 1893, and served from March 29, 1892 to March 3, 1899; was not a candidate for reelection; died in Corsicana, Tex., September 2, 1911; interment in Oakwood Cemetery.

Bibliography: *DAB*; Barr, C. Alwyn. "The Making of a Secessionist: The Antebellum Career of Roger Q. Mills." *South Western History Quarterly* 79 (October 1975): 129-44.

**MILLS, Wilbur Daigh,** a Representative from Arkansas; born in Kensett, White County, Ark., May 24, 1909; attended the public schools and graduated from Searcy (Ark.) High School; graduated from Hendrix College, Conway, Ark., in 1930; attended Harvard University School of Law for three years until 1933; was admitted to the bar in 1933 and commenced practice in Searcy, Ark.; served as county and probate judge of White County, Ark., 1934-1938; elected as a Democrat to the Seventy-sixth and to the eighteen succeeding Congresses (January 3, 1939-January 3, 1977); chairman, Committee on Ways and Means (Eighty-fifth through Ninety-third Congresses), Joint Committee on Internal Revenue Taxation (Eighty-sixth through Ninety-third Congresses); was not a candidate for reelection in 1976 to the Ninety-fifth Congress; tax consultant for the Washington office of Shea, Gould, Climenko & Casey, a New York law firm; was a resident of Kensett, Ark., until his death in Searcy, Ark., on May 2, 1992; interment in Kensett Cemetery, Kensett, Ark.

Bibliography: Goss, Kay C. "Congressman Wilbur D. Mills' Influence on Social Legislation." *Arkansas Historical Quarterly* 54 (Spring 1995): 1-12.

**MILLS, William Oswald,** a Representative from Maryland; born in Bethlehem, Caroline County, Md., August 12, 1924; attended the Caroline County public schools; entered the United States Army in 1942 and served with General George S. Patton's Third Army in Europe; awarded the Bronze Star; local manager, Chesapeake and Potomac Telephone Co., for Preston, Denton, and Bainbridge, Md., 1946-1950, and commerical manager for the Maryland counties of Caroline and Talbot, 1950-1962; administrative assistant to Representative Rogers C.B. Morton, 1962-1971; elected as a Republican to the Ninety-second Congress, May 27, 1971, by special election to fill the vacancy caused by the resignation of Rogers C.B. Morton; reelected to the Ninety-third Congress, and served from May 27, 1971, until his death from a self-inflicted gunshot wound near Easton, Md., May 24, 1973; interment in Hillcrest Cemetery, Federalsburg, Md.

**MILLSON, John Singleton,** a Representative from Virginia; born in Norfolk, Va., October 1, 1808; pursued an academic course; studied law; was admitted to the bar in 1829 and commenced practice in Norfolk; elected as a Democrat to the Thirty-first and to the five succeeding Congresses (March 4, 1849-March 3, 1861); chairman, Committee on Revolutionary Pensions (Thirty-second Congress); resumed the practice of law; died in Norfolk, Va., March 1, 1874; interment in Cedar Grove Cemetery.

**MILLSPAUGH, Frank Crenshaw,** a Representative from Missouri; born in Shawneetown, Gallatin County, Ill., January 14, 1872; attended the public schools; entered the grain commission business in New Orleans, La., in 1891; moved to Chicago in 1892, to St. Louis, Mo., in 1894 and to Canton, Mo., in 1896 and continued the grain-shipping business; engaged in banking 1900-1921; delegate to the Republican State convention in 1912; mayor of Canton, Mo., 1915-1919; elected as a Republican to the Sixty-seventh Congress and served from March 4, 1921, to December 5, 1922, when he resigned; unsuccessful candidate in 1922 for reelection to the Sixty-eighth Congress; State commissioner of finance in 1923 and 1924; moved to Jefferson City, Mo., in 1925 and engaged in the real estate business until 1929, when he entered the brokerage business; elected county judge of Jasper County, Mo., in 1942; reelected in 1944 and 1946 and served until his death in Joplin, Mo., July 8, 1947; interment in Forest Grove Cemetery, Canton, Mo.

**MILLWARD, William,** a Representative from Pennsylvania; born in the old district of Northern Liberties, Philadelphia, Pa., June 30, 1822; attended the public schools; engaged in the manufacture of leather; elected as a Whig to the Thirty-fourth Congress (March 4, 1855-March 3, 1857); unsuccessful as the Union Candidate for reelection in 1856; elected as a Republican to the Thirty-sixth Congress (March 4, 1859-March 3, 1861); chairman, Committee on Patents (Thirty-sixth Congress); United States marshal for the eastern district of Pennsylvania 1861-1865; appointed Director of the United States Mint in September 1866 but, as his appointment was not confirmed by the Senate, served for six months only; died in Kirkwood, New Castle County, Del., November 28, 1871; interment in Laurel Hill Cemetery, Philadelphia, Pa.

**MILNES, Alfred,** a Representative from Michigan; born in Bradford, Yorkshire, England, May 28, 1844; immigrated to the United States in 1854 with his parents, who settled in Newton, Jasper County, Iowa; moved to Coldwater, Branch County, Mich., in 1860; attended the common schools of Salt Lake City, Utah, and Newton, Iowa, and the high school of Coldwater, Mich.; enlisted as a private in Company C, Seventeenth Regiment, Michigan Volunteer Infantry, June 30, 1862, and served throughout the Civil War; engaged in mercantile pursuits; member of the board of aldermen of Coldwater in 1876 and 1877; mayor in 1885 and 1886; member of the State senate 1888-1890; Lieutenant Governor of Michigan in 1894, and presided over the State senate until his resignation June 1, 1895, when he became a candidate for Congress; elected as a Republican to the Fifty-fourth Congress to fill the vacancy caused by the resignation of Julius C. Burrows and served from December 2, 1895, to March 3, 1897; unsuccessful candidate for reelection in 1896 to the Fifty-fifth Congress; appointed postmaster of Coldwater in 1898 and served until 1902; delegate to the Michigan constitutional convention of 1907 and 1908; engaged in the real estate and insurance business in Coldwater, Mich., until his death there on January 15, 1916; interment in Oak Grove Cemetery.

**MILNES, William, Jr.,** a Representative from Virginia; born in Yorkshire, England, December 8, 1827; immigrated to the United States in 1829 with his parents, who settled in Pottsville, Pa.; attended the public schools; learned the machinist's trade; engaged in mining and shipping coal; moved to Virginia in 1865 and settled in Shenandoah; engaged in the iron business; member of the Virginia house of delegates in 1870 and 1871; upon the readmission of Virginia to representation was elected as a Conservative to the Forty-first Congress and served from January 27, 1870, to March 3, 1871; resumed the iron business; died in Shenandoah, Va., August 14, 1889; interment in the family plot in Old Cemetery.

**MILNOR, James,** a Representative from Pennsylvania; born in Philadelphia, Pa., June 20, 1773; attended the Philadelphia Grammar School and also the University of Pennsylvania at Philadelphia, but did not graduate; studied law; was admitted to the bar in 1794 and commenced practice in Norristown, Pa.; moved to Philadelphia in 1797 and continued the practice of his profession; member of the Philadelphia Common Council in 1800; member of the select council 1805-1810 and served as president in 1808 and 1809; elected as a Federalist to the Twelfth Congress (March 4, 1811-March 3, 1813); studied theology and was ordained as a minister of the Protestant Episcopal Church; in 1814 was appointed assistant minister of St. Peter's Church in Philadelphia and in 1816 rector of St. George's Church in New York City, in which capacity he served until his death in New York City April 8, 1844; interment in Greenwood Cemetery, Brooklyn, N.Y.

**MILNOR, William,** a Representative from Pennsylvania; born in Philadelphia, Pa., June 26, 1769; pursued an academic course; engaged in mercantile pursuits in Philadelphia; elected as a Federalist to the Tenth and Eleventh Congresses (March 4, 1807-March 3, 1811); chairman, Committee on Accounts (Eleventh Congress); elected to the Fourteenth Congress (March 4, 1815-March 3, 1817); again elected to the Seventeenth Congress and served from March 4, 1821, until his resignation on May 8, 1822; elected mayor of Philadelphia October 20, 1829, and served one year; died in Burlington, Burlington County, N.J., December 13, 1848; interment in St. Mary's Churchyard.

**MILTON, John Gerald,** a Senator from New Jersey; born in Jersey City, N.J., January 21, 1881; attended the public schools; studied law; was admitted to the bar in 1903 and commenced practice in Jersey City, N.J.; appointed as a Democrat to the United States Senate, January 18, 1938, to fill the vacancy caused by the resignation of A. Harry Moore and served from January 18, 1938, to November 8, 1938, when a successor was elected; was not a candidate to fill the vacancy; resumed the practice of law; resided in Jersey City, N.J., where he died on April 14, 1977; interment in Holy Cross Cemetery, North Arlington, N.J.

**MILTON, William Hall,** a Senator from Florida; born near Marianna, Jackson County, Fla., March 2, 1864; attended the public schools of Jackson County, Marianna Academy, and the Agricultural and Mechanical College, Auburn, Ala.; city clerk and treasurer of Marianna from 1885 until 1893; member, Florida State house of representatives, 1889-1891; studied law and was admitted to the bar in 1890; court commissioner, 1890-1894; engaged in banking at Marianna from 1890 to 1918; presidential elector on the Democratic ticket in 1892; United States surveyor general of Florida, 1894-1897; president of the board of managers of the State reform school at Marianna, 1897-1902; mayor of Marianna during 1898 and 1899; unsuccessful candidate for Governor of Florida in 1900 and 1912; appointed as a Democrat to the United States Senate, March 27, 1908, to fill the vacancy caused by the death of William James Bryan and served from March 27, 1908, to March 3, 1909; was not a candidate for reelection in 1908; resumed the practice of law and also engaged in the real estate and insurance business at Marianna, Fla.; member of the city council, 1916-1917; appointed United States commissioner for the northern district of Florida in 1923, reappointed in 1927, and served until his death; district member of the State board of social welfare, 1937-1942; died in Marianna, Fla., January 4, 1942; interment in St. Luke's Episcopal Cemetery.

**MINAHAN, Daniel Francis,** a Representative from New Jersey; born in Springfield, Ohio, August 8, 1877; attended Stevens Institute Preparatory School and Seton Hall College, South Orange, N.J.; superintendent of work for his father, who was a contractor; mayor of Orange, N.J., from May 1914 until August 1919, when he resigned; elected as a Democrat to the Sixty-sixth Congress (March 4, 1919-March 3, 1921); unsuccessful candidate for reelection in 1920 to the Sixty-seventh Congress; again elected to the Sixty-eighth Congress (March 4, 1923-March 3, 1925); unsuccessful candidate for reelection in 1924 to the Sixty-ninth Congress and for election in 1930 to the Seventy-second Congress; delegate to the Democratic National Convention in 1928; engaged in land development and resided in East Orange, N.J., until his death on April 29, 1947; interment in St. John's Cemetery, Orange, N.J.

**MINER, Ahiman Louis,** a Representative from Vermont; born in Middletown, Rutland County, Vt., September 23, 1804; attended the common schools and Castleton Academy; studied law in Poultney and Rutland, Vt.; was admitted to the bar in 1832 and practiced in Wallingford 1833-1836; moved to Manchester, Bennington County, Vt., in 1835 and continued the practice of law; clerk of the State house of representatives in 1836-1838; member of the State house of representatives in 1838, 1839, 1846, 1853, 1861 and 1865-1868; served in the State senate in 1840; State's attorney for Bennington County in 1843 and 1844; register of probate for seven years; judge of probate 1846-1849; justice of the peace 1846-1886; elected as a Whig to the Thirty-second Congress (March 4, 1851-March 3, 1853); declined to be a candidate for renomination in 1852; resumed the practice of law; died in Manchester, Vt., July 19, 1886; interment in Dellwood Cemetery.

**MINER, Charles,** a Representative from Pennsylvania; born in Norwich, Conn., February 1, 1780; attended the public schools of Norwich; moved in 1797 to his father's lands in Wyoming Valley, Pa., and to Wilkes-Barre, Pa., in 1802; became publisher of the Luzerne County Federalist; elected as a Federalist to the Pennsylvania house of representatives and served in 1807 and 1808; moved to West Chester, Pa., in 1816; elected to the Nineteenth and Twentieth Congresses (March 4, 1825-March 3, 1829); was not a candidate for renomination in 1828; editor and publisher of the Village Record 1829-1832; returned to Wilkes-Barre in 1834; involved in the mining of the large fields of anthracite coal in the Wyoming Valley; died in Wilkes-Barre, Pa., on October 26, 1865; interment in Hollenback Cemetery, Wilkes-Barre, Pa.

**Bibliography:** *DAB.*

**MINER, Henry Clay,** a Representative from New York; born in New York City March 23, 1842; attended the public schools and the American Institute of Physicians and Surgeons in New York City; engaged in the drug business; in 1864 became interested in the theatrical business and eventually owned five theaters in New York City and Newark, N.J.; president of a lithographing company and also publisher of the American Dramatic Directory; for many years president of the Actors' Fund Association; elected as a Democrat to the Fifty-fourth Congress (March 4, 1895-March 3, 1897); was not a candidate for renomination in 1896; resumed his theatrical and other business pursuits; died in New York City February 22, 1900; interment in Greenwood Cemetery, Brooklyn, N.Y.

**MINER, Phineas,** a Representative from Connecticut; born in Winchester, Litchfield County, Conn., November 27, 1777; completed preparatory studies; studied law; was admitted to the bar in 1797 and commenced practice in Winchester; elected justice of the peace in 1809; member of the State house of representatives in 1809, 1811,

1813, 1814, and 1816; moved to Litchfield, Conn., in 1816; again a member of the State house of representatives in 1823, 1827, and 1829; served in the State senate in 1830 and 1831; elected to the Twenty-third Congress to fill the vacancy caused by the resignation of Jabez W. Huntington and served from December 1, 1834, to March 3, 1835; resumed the practice of law; served in the State house of representatives in 1835; elected judge of the probate court for Litchfield district in 1838; died in Litchfield, Conn., September 15, 1839; interment in the East Burying Ground.

**MINETA, Norman Yoshio,** a Representative from California; born in San Jose, Santa Clara County, Calif., November 12, 1931; attended public schools in San Jose, Heart Mountain, Wyo., and Evanston, Ill.; graduated, San Jose High School, 1949; B.S., University of California, Berkeley, 1953; worked in the insurance business, 1956 to present; served in the United States Army, 1953-1956; member, San Jose Human Relations Commission, 1962-1964; member, board of directors, San Jose Housing Authority, 1966-1967; San Jose city councilman, 1967-1971; vice mayor of San Jose, 1968-1971; mayor, 1971-1974; delegate, California State Democratic conventions, 1971-1974; delegate to the Democratic National Conventions of 1972, 1976, 1980 and 1984; elected as a Democrat to the Ninety-fourth and to the ten succeeding Congresses and served from January 3, 1975, until his resignation on October 10, 1995, to become senior vice president, Transportation Systems and Services Division, Lockheed Martin Corp.; chairman, Committee on Public Works and Transportation (One Hundred Third Congress); is a resident of San Jose, Calif.

**MINGE, David,** a Representative from Minnesota; born in Clarkfield, Yellow Medicine County, Minn., March 19, 1942; B.A., St. Olaf College, 1964; J.D., University of Chicago, 1967; attorney, Minneapolis, Minn., 1967-1970; professor of law, University of Wyoming, 1970-1977; consultant, subcommittee on administrative law, House Committee on the Judiciary, 1975; attorney, 1977 to present; attorney, Minnesota Valley Cooperative Light and Power Association, 1984 to present; experience as factory worker, migrant farm worker, investigator of social services programs and director of legislator school, Fulbright lecturer and Assistant County Attorney; member and clerk, Montevideo school board; elected as a Democrat to the One Hundred Third and One Hundred Fourth Congresses (January 3, 1993-January 3, 1997); is a resident of Montevideo, Minn.

**MINISH, Joseph George,** a Representative from New Jersey; born in Throop, Lackawanna County, Pa., September 1, 1916; attended the public schools; graduated from Dunmore (Pa.) High School in 1935; served in the United States Army, 1945-1946; executive secretary of Essex-West Hudson Council, Congress of Industrial Organizations, 1954-1960, and executive director, Essex-West Industrial Union Council, AFL-CIO, 1960-1962; elected as a Democrat to the Eighty-eighth and to the ten succeeding Congresses (January 3, 1963-January 3, 1985); unsuccessful candidate for reelection in 1984 to the Ninety-ninth Congress; is a resident of West Orange, N.J.

**MINK, Patsy Takemoto,** a Representative from Hawaii, born December 6, 1927, in Paia, Maui, Hawaii; graduated from Maui High School in 1944; attended Wilson College, Chambersburg, Pa., in 1946, and the University of Nebraska, Lincoln, in 1947; A.B., University of Hawaii, 1948; LL.B., University of Chicago Law School, 1951; admitted to the bar in 1953 and began the practice of law in Hawaii; lecturer, University of Hawaii, 1952-1956, 1959-1962, and 1979-1981; attorney for the Hawaii Territorial house of representatives, 1955; member of the Hawaii Territorial house of representatives, 1956 and 1958; member of Hawaii Territorial senate, 1958-1959, and the Hawaii State senate, 1962-1964; delegate to the Democratic National Conventions of 1960, 1972, 1980 and 1984; vice president of the National Young Democrats of

America, 1957-1959; elected as a Democrat to the Eighty-ninth and to the five succeeding Congresses (January 3, 1965-January 3, 1977); was not a candidate in 1976 for reelection to the House of Representatives, but was an unsuccessful candidate for nomination to the United States Senate; Assistant Secretary of State for Oceans and International Environmental and Scientific Affairs, March 1977 to May 1978; president, Americans for Democratic Action, 1978-1981; member, Honolulu City Council, 1983-1987, and served as chair, 1983-1985; elected as a Democrat to the One Hundred First Congress, September 22, 1990, by special election, to fill the vacancy caused by the resignation of Daniel K. Akaka; reelected to the three succeeding Congresses and served from September 22, 1990, to January 3, 1997; is a resident of Honolulu, Hawaii.

**MINOR, Edward Sloman,** a Representative from Wisconsin; born at Point Peninsula, Jefferson County, N.Y., December 13, 1840; moved to Wisconsin in 1845 with his parents, who settled in Greenfield, Milwaukee County, and subsequently in the city of Milwaukee; attended the common schools; went with his parents to a farm in Sheboygan County in 1852 and engaged in agricultural pursuits; completed a common-school education; enlisted as a private in Company G, Second Regiment, Wisconsin Volunteer Cavalry, in 1861; mustered out as first lieutenant in November 1865; engaged in the hardware business in Sturgeon Bay, Wis., from 1865 until 1884; member of the Wisconsin State assembly in 1877, 1881, and 1882; served in the Wisconsin State senate, 1883-1886, and as president pro tempore of the senate during the last term; superintendent of the Sturgeon Bay and Lake Michigan Ship Canal, 1884-1891; member of the Wisconsin Fish Commission for four years; mayor of Sturgeon Bay in 1894; elected as a Republican to the Fifty-fourth and to the five succeeding Congresses (March 4, 1895-March 3, 1907); chairman, Committee on Expenditures in the Department of the Interior (Fifty-eighth and Fifty-ninth Congresses); unsuccessful candidate for renomination in 1906 to the Sixtieth Congress; engaged in horticulture; postmaster of Sturgeon Bay from 1911 to 1915; again mayor of Sturgeon Bay in 1918; died at Sturgeon Bay, Wis., July 26, 1924; interment in Bayside Cemetery.

**MINSHALL, William Edwin, Jr.,** a Representative from Ohio; born in East Cleveland, Cuyahoga County, Ohio, October 24, 1911; attended the public schools of East Cleveland, and the University School, Shaker Heights, Ohio; attended the University of Virginia, Charlottesville, 1932-1934; LL.B., Cleveland Law School, 1940; was admitted to the bar the same year and commenced the practice of law in Cleveland, Ohio; member of the Ohio State house of representatives in 1939 and 1940; enlisted in December 1940 as a private in the United States Army and served in the European Theater, G-2 section, Headquarters III Corps, and was discharged as a lieutenant colonel in March 1946; awarded Bronze Star; special assistant attorney general of Ohio, 1948-1952; general counsel, Maritime Administration, Washington, D.C., in 1953 and 1954; elected as a Republican to the Eighty-fourth and to the nine succeeding Congresses and served from January 3, 1955, until his resignation December 31, 1974; was not a candidate for reelection in 1974 to the Ninety-fourth Congress; was a resident of Delray Beach, Fla.; died October 15, 1990.

**MINTON, Sherman,** a Senator from Indiana; born in Georgetown, Floyd County, Ind., October 20, 1890; attended the public schools; graduated from the law department of Indiana University at Bloomington in 1915, and from Yale University in 1916; was admitted to the bar in 1915 and commenced practice in New Albany, Ind.; during the First World War served as a captain in the Motor Transport Corps, 1917-1919, serving overseas one year; captain in the Infantry section, Officers' Reserve Corps, 1919-1943; moved to Miami, Fla., in 1925 and continued the practice of law; returned to New Albany, Ind., in 1928 and resumed the practice of law; public counselor of Indiana, 1933-1934; elected as a Democrat to the

United States Senate and served from January 3, 1935, to January 3, 1941; Democratic whip (Seventy-sixth Congress); chairman, Committee on Pensions (Seventy-sixth Congress); unsuccessful candidate for reelection in 1940; served as administrative assistant in the Executive Office of the President, 1941; judge of the circuit court of appeals for the seventh circuit, 1941-1949; nominated on September 15, 1949 by President Harry S Truman as an Associate Justice of the United States Supreme Court; was confirmed by the Senate on October 4, 1949, and served from October 12, 1949 until October 15, 1956, when he resigned due to ill health; was a resident of New Albany, Ind., where he died on April 9, 1965; interment in Holy Trinity Catholic Cemetery.

**Bibliography:** *DAB*; Atkinson, David N. "From New Deal Liberal to Supreme Court Conservative." *Washington University Law Quarterly* 1975 (1975): 361-94; Corcoran, David H. "Sherman Minton: New Deal Senator." Ph.D. dissertation, University of Kentucky, 1977.

**MITCHEL, Charles Burton,** a Senator from Arkansas; born in Gallatin, Gallatin County, Tenn., September 19, 1815; attended the common schools; graduated from the University of Nashville, Tennessee, in 1833 and from the Jefferson Medical College, Philadelphia, Pa., in 1836; moved to Washington, Hempstead County, Ark., and practiced medicine for twenty-five years; member of the Arkansas State house of representatives in 1848; receiver of public moneys, 1853-1856; unsuccessful candidate for election in 1860 to the Thirty-seventh Congress; elected as a Democrat to the United States Senate, and served from March 4, 1861 until July 11, 1861, when he was expelled for support of the Confederacy; elected to the Confederate senate at the first session of the State legislature and served until his death in Little Rock, Ark., September 20, 1864; interment in Presbyterian Cemetery, Washington, Ark.

**MITCHELL, Alexander** (father of John Lendrum Mitchell), a Representative from Wisconsin; born in Ellon, Aberdeenshire, Scotland, October 18, 1817; attended the parish schools and completed a commercial course; studied law; became a banking-house clerk; immigrated to the United States in 1839 and settled in Milwaukee, Wis.; engaged in banking; president of the Chicago, Milwaukee & St. Paul Railroad Co. 1864-1887; unsuccessful candidate for election in 1868 to the Forty-first Congress; elected as a Democrat to the Forty-second and Forty-third Congresses (March 4, 1871-March 3, 1875); declined to be a candidate for renomination in 1874; nominated in 1877 for Governor, but declined to be a candidate; resumed banking interests; died while on a visit in New York City April 19, 1887; interment in Forest Home Cemetery, Milwaukee, Wis.

**Bibliography:** *DAB*.

**MITCHELL, Alexander Clark,** a Representative from Kansas; born in Cincinnati, Ohio, October 11, 1860; moved to Kansas in 1867 with his parents, who settled in Douglas County, near Lawrence; attended the public schools, and was graduated from the law department of the University of Kansas at Lawrence in 1889; was admitted to the bar the same year and commenced practice in Lawrence, Kans.; prosecuting attorney of Douglas County 1894-1898; member of the Kansas University board of regents 1904-1910; member of the State board of law examiners 1907-1910; member of the State house of representatives 1907-1911; elected as a Republican to the Sixty-second Congress and served from March 4, 1911, until his death in Lawrence, Kans., July 7, 1911; interment in Oak Hill Cemetery.

**MITCHELL, Anderson,** a Representative from North Carolina; born on a farm near Milton, Caswell County, N.C., June 13, 1800; attended Bingham's School, Orange County, N.C., and was graduated from the University of North Carolina at Chapel Hill in 1821; studied law; was admitted to the bar and commenced practice in Morganton, Burke County, N.C., in 1830; moved to Jefferson, Ashe County, N.C., in 1831; clerk of the superior court of Ashe County; moved to Wilkesboro, Wilkes County, N.C., in 1835, and resumed the practice of law; elected as a Whig to the Twenty-seventh Congress to fill the vacancy caused by the death of Lewis Williams and served from April 27, 1842, to March 3, 1843; unsuccessful candidate for reelection in 1842 to the Twenty-eighth Congress; member of the State house of commons 1852-1854; elected to the State senate in 1860; delegate to the State convention of May 20, 1861, that passed the ordinance of secession, and voted against secession; was appointed judge of the superior court by Provisional Governor Holden in September 1865, subsequently elected and reelected, and served until June 30, 1875, when he resigned; died in Statesville, N.C., December 24, 1876; interment in the Presbyterian Cemetery.

**MITCHELL, Arthur Wergs,** a Representative from Illinois; born on a farm near Lafayette, Chambers County, Ala., December 22, 1883; attended the public schools; entered the Tuskegee (Ala.) Institute in 1897; taught in the rural schools of Georgia and Alabama for many years; founder of the Armstrong Agricultural School, West Butler, Ala., and served as its president for ten years; studied law; was admitted to the bar in 1927 and commenced practice in Washington, D.C.; moved to Chicago in 1929 and continued the practice of law; also engaged in the real estate business; alternate delegate to the Democratic National Convention of 1936, and delegate at large in 1940; elected as a Democrat to the Seventy-fourth and to the three succeeding Congresses (Janaury 3, 1935-January 3, 1943); was not a candidate for renomination in 1942 to the Seventy-eighth Congress; resumed the practice of law; also engaged in civil rights work, public lecturing, and farming near Petersburg, Dinwiddie County, Va.; died at his home near Petersburg, Va., on May 9, 1968; interment on his estate, "Land of a Thousand Roses," in Dinwiddie County.

**MITCHELL, Charles F.,** a Representative from New York; born in New York City about 1808; attended the public schools; moved to Lockport, N.Y., in 1829; appointed one of the firemen of the village May 21, 1829; engaged in the milling business in 1835; elected as a Whig to the Twenty-fifth and Twenty-sixth Congresses (March 4, 1837-March 3, 1841); engaged in milling in the West.

**MITCHELL, Charles Le Moyne,** a Representative from Connecticut; born in New Haven, Conn., August 6, 1844; was graduated from Cheshire Academy in 1863; traveled in Europe, Asia, and Africa; returned to New Haven, Conn., and engaged in the manufacture of silver-plated ware and brass; member of the State house of representatives in 1877; elected as a Democrat to the Forty-eighth and Forty-ninth Congresses (March 4, 1883-March 3, 1887); chairman, Committee on Patents (Forty-ninth Congress); was not a candidate for renomination in 1886; moved to New York City in 1886; but retained his former business interests in Connecticut; died in New York City March 1, 1890; interment in Evergreen Cemetery, New Haven, Conn.

**MITCHELL, Donald Jerome,** a Representative from New York; born in Illion, Herkimer County, N.Y., May 8, 1923; attended Herkimer schools and Hobart College, Geneva, N.Y., 1946-1947; B.S., Columbia University, New York City, 1949; M.A., University's Teachers College, New York City, 1950; served during the Second World War as a naval aviator, 1942-1945, also served in the Korean Conflict as a flight instructor, 1951-1953; optometrist, 1950-1972; councilman, town of Herkimer, 1954-1956; mayor, village of Herkimer, 1956-1959; member, Herkimer Zoning Board of Appeals, 1963; member, New York State assembly, 1965-1972, and served as majority whip, 1969-1972; elected as a Republican to the Ninety-third and to the four succeeding Congresses (January 3, 1973-January 3, 1983); was not a candidate for reelection in 1982 to the

Ninety-eighth Congress; resumed the practice of optometry; retired; is a resident of Herkimer, N.Y., and Cedar Key, Fla.

**MITCHELL, Edward Archibald,** a Representative from Indiana; born in Binghamton, Broome County, N.Y., December 2, 1910; attended the grade and high schools and had three years of college training at the American Institute and Columbia University, New York City; moved to Evansville, Ind., in September 1937; engaged as a warehouseman and later as district manager for a large food distributor 1934-1937; in 1937 purchased a half interest in a food marketing and brokerage company and served as president; served in the United States Navy from November 1942 until his discharge as a lieutenant commander in January 1946, having been commanding officer of underwater demolition teams in the Pacific Theater for two years; awarded the Silver Star Medal at Okinawa; elected as a Republican to the Eightieth Congress (January 3, 1947-January 3, 1949); unsuccessful candidate for reelection in 1948 to the Eighty-first Congress; delegate in 1952 and 1956 to Republican National Conventions; resided in Evansville, Ind., where he died December 11, 1979; interment in Sunset Memorial Park.

**MITCHELL, George Edward,** a Representative from Maryland; born at Head of Elk (now Elkton), Cecil County, Md., March 3, 1781; completed preparatory studies and was graduated from the medical department of the University of Pennsylvania at Philadelphia on June 5, 1805; practiced medicine in Elkton, Md., 1806-1812; member of the Maryland State house of delegates in 1808; member of the executive council of Maryland, and served as president from 1809 until 1812; served in the War of 1812 with the Third Maryland Artillery; resigned June 1, 1821; elected to the Eighteenth and Nineteenth Congresses (March 4, 1823-March 3, 1827); was not a candidate for renomination in 1826 to the Twentieth Congress; unsuccessful candidate for the governorship of Maryland in 1829; elected as a Jacksonian to the Twenty-first and Twenty-second Congresses and served from December 7, 1829, until his death in Washington, D.C., June 28, 1832; interment in the Congressional Cemetery.

Bibliography: *DAB.*

**MITCHELL, George John,** a Senator from Maine; born in Waterville, Kennebec County, Maine, August 20, 1933; attended the public schools and graduated from Waterville High School in 1950; B.A., Bowdoin College, Brunswick, Maine, 1954; LL.B., Georgetown University Law Center, Washington, D.C., 1960; served in the United States Army Counterintelligence Corps, Berlin, Germany, 1954-1956; admitted to the District of Columbia and Maine bars in 1960 and commenced practice in Portland, Maine, 1965; trial attorney, Antitrust Division, Department of Justice, Washington, D.C., 1960-1962; executive assistant to Senator Edmund S. Muskie of Maine, 1962-1965; practiced law in Portland, Maine, 1965-1977; assistant county attorney for Cumberland County, Maine, 1971; unsuccessful candidate in 1974 for election for Governor of Maine; United States Attorney for Maine, 1977-1979; United States District Judge for Maine, 1979-1980; appointed as a Democrat to the United States Senate to fill the vacancy caused by the resignation of Edmund S. Muskie for the term ending January 3, 1983; reelected in 1982 and again in 1988, and served from May 17, 1980 to January 3, 1995; was not a candidate for reelection in 1994; chairman, Democratic Senatorial Campaign Committee (Ninety-ninth Congress); majority leader (One Hundred First through One Hundred Third Congresses); appointed by President William J. Clinton on December 1, 1994 as special adviser to the President and Secretary of State for economic initiatives in Ireland; chairman, International Body on decommissioning weapons in Northern Ireland; is a resident of Portland, Maine.

**MITCHELL, Harlan Erwin,** a Representative from Georgia; born in Dalton, Whitfield County, Ga., August 17, 1924; attended the public schools in Dalton, Ga., and The Citadel, Charleston, S.C.; served as a first lieutenant in the United States Army Air Corps, 1943-1946, and again in the United States Air Force in 1951 and 1952; graduated from the University of Georgia in 1948; was admitted to the bar on April 17, 1948, and commenced the practice of law in Dalton, Ga.; solicitor general, Cherokee Judicial Circuit, January 1, 1953 to December 31, 1956; judge, Superior Court, Cherokee Judicial Circuit, January 1, 1957 to January 8, 1958; elected as a Democrat to the Eighty-fifth Congress, by special election to fill the vacancy caused by the death of Henderson L. Lanham; reelected to the Eighty-sixth Congress, and served from January 8, 1958 to January 3, 1961; was not a candidate for renomination in 1960 to the Eighty-seventh Congress; Georgia State senator, 1960-1961; did not seek reelection; resumed the practice of law; is a resident of Dalton, Ga.

**MITCHELL, Henry,** a Representative from New York; born in Woodbury, Litchfield County, Conn., in 1784; pursued classical studies under private tutors and was graduated from the medical department of Yale College in 1804; engaged in the practice of medicine in Norwich, Chenango County, N.Y.; member of the State assembly in 1827; elected as a Jacksonian to the Twenty-third Congress (March 4, 1833-March 3, 1835); resumed the practice of medicine; died in Norwich, Chenango County, N.Y., January 12, 1856; interment in Mount Hope Cemetery.

**MITCHELL, Hugh Burnton,** a Senator and a Representative from Washington; born in Great Falls, Cascade County, Mont., March 22, 1907; attended the public schools of Great Falls, Mont., and Dartmouth College, Hanover, N.H.; engaged in editorial work on a newspaper in Everett, Wash., 1931-1933; elected Democratic precinct committeeman in Everett, Wash., 1931; served as executive assistant to Representative (later Senator) Monrad C. Wallgren of Washington, 1933-1945; appointed as a Democrat to the United States Senate to fill the vacancy caused by the resignation of Monrad C. Wallgren, and served from January 10, 1945 until his resignation on December 25, 1946; unsuccessful candidate for election to the United States Senate in 1946; engaged in economic research and public relations; elected to the Eighty-first and Eighty-second Congresses (January 3, 1949-January 3, 1953); was not a candidate in 1952 for renomination to the Eighty-third Congress, but was an unsuccessful candidate for election for Governor of Washington; unsuccessful candidate for election in 1954 to the Eighty-fourth Congress, and in 1958 to the Eighty-sixth Congress; engaged as owner and partner in transportation and manufacturing businesses from 1953; chairman, Committee for Washington Tax Reform; was a resident of Seattle, Wash., until his death there on June 10, 1996.

**MITCHELL, James Coffield,** a Representative from Tennessee; born in Staunton, Augusta County, Va., in March 1786; attended the common schools; studied law; was admitted to the bar and practiced; moved to Tennessee and settled in Rhea County; solicitor general of the second district of Tennessee, 1813-1817; moved to Athens, McMinn County, in 1817; elected to the Nineteenth and Twentieth Congresses (March 4, 1825-March 3, 1829); chairman, Committee on Military Pensions (Twentieth Congress); unsuccessful candidate for reelection in 1828 to the Twenty-first Congress; judge of the eleventh circuit, 1830-1836; moved to Hinds County, Miss., and settled near Jackson about 1837, engaging in agricultural pursuits; unsuccessful candidate on the Whig ticket for Governor of Mississippi and for the State house of representatives; author of *Mitchell's Justice;* died near Jackson, Miss., August 7, 1843.

**MITCHELL, James S.,** a Representative from Pennsylvania; born near Rossville, Warrington Township, York County, Pa., in 1784; attended the common schools; member of the Pennsylvania house of representatives 1812-1814; elected to the Seventeenth, Eighteenth, and Nineteenth Congresses (March 4, 1821-March 3, 1827); moved to Jefferson County, Ohio, in 1827, and later to Belleville, St. Clair County, Ill., where he died in 1844; interment at Dillsburg, Pa.

**MITCHELL, John,** a Representative from Pennsylvania; born near Newport, Perry County, Pa., March 8, 1781; attended the common schools; moved to Bellefonte, Centre County, in 1800 and was employed as a clerk in the ironworks; elected sheriff of Centre County in 1818; engineer and surveyor; laid out the Centre and Kishacoquillas Turnpike in 1821; constructed many of the turnpikes in middle and northern Pennsylvania; member of the Pennsylvania house of representatives in 1822 and 1823; elected to the Nineteenth and Twentieth Congresses (March 4, 1825-March 3, 1829); surveyed proposed canal routes between the Susquehanna and Potomac Rivers in 1826; engineer on the Erie extension in 1827; canal commissioner in 1829; moved to Bridgewater, Pa., in 1842; engaged in civil engineering and iron manufacturing; member of the canal survey commission from 1845 until his death in Bridgewater, Pa., August 3, 1849; interment in Old Beaver Cemetery.

**MITCHELL, John Hipple,** a Senator from Oregon; born John Mitchell Hipple in Washington County, Pa., June 22, 1835; moved with his parents to Butler County, Pa., in 1837; attended public and private schools and Witherspoon Institute; taught school; studied law; was admitted to the bar in 1857 and practiced; moved to California and then to Portland, Oreg., in 1860; practiced law in Portland under the name of John Hipple Mitchell; corporation attorney of Portland in 1861; member, Oregon State senate, 1862-1866, serving the last two years as president; unsuccessful candidate for election to the United States Senate in 1866; elected as a Republican in 1872 to the United States Senate, and served from March 4, 1873 to March 3, 1879; after his election, opponents tried to prevent his seating, charging him with bigamy, desertion, and living under an assumed name, but a Senate committee decided the charges did not merit investigation; chairman, Committee on Railroads (Forty-fifth Congress); unsuccessful candidate for election to the United States Senate in 1882; again elected as a Republican to the United States Senate on November 18, 1885, for the term beginning March 4, 1885; reelected in 1891 and served until March 3, 1897; unsuccessful candidate for reelection; chairman, Committee on Transportation Routes to the Seaboard (Fiftieth Congress), Committee on Railroads (Fifty-first and Fifty-second Congresses), Committee on Claims (Fifty-second Congress), Committee on Privileges and Elections (Fifty-fourth Congress); resumed the practice of law; again elected as a Republican to the United States Senate, and served from March 4, 1901 until his death in Portland, Oreg., December 8, 1905; chairman, Committee on Coast Defenses (Fifty-seventh and Fifty-eighth Congresses), Committee on Interoceanic Canals (Fifty-eighth Congress); at the time of his death, had been indicted and convicted of having received fees for expediting the land claims of clients before the United States Land Commissioner and an appeal was pending; interment in Riverview Cemetery.

Bibliography: *DAB*; O'Callaghan, Jerry A. "Senator John H. Mitchell and the Oregon Land Frauds, 1905." *Pacific Historical Review* 21 (August 1952): 255-61.

**MITCHELL, John Inscho,** a Representative and a Senator from Pennsylvania; born in Tioga Township, Tioga County, Pa., July 28, 1838; attended the common schools and received private instruction; attended the University of Lewisburg (later Bucknell University), Pa., 1857-1859; taught school from 1859 to 1861; during the Civil War served in the Union Army as a lieutenant and captain in the One Hundred and Thirty-sixth Regiment, Pennsylvania Volunteer Infantry; studied law; was admitted to the bar in 1864 and practiced in Tioga County; district attorney of Tioga County,

1868-1871; edited the Tioga County Agitator in 1870; member, Pennsylvania house of representatives, 1872-1876; elected as a Republican to the Forty-fifth and Forty-sixth Congresses (March 4, 1877-March 3, 1881); elected to the United States Senate, and served from March 4, 1881 to March 3, 1887; chairman, Committee on the Mississippi and Its Tributaries (Forty-seventh Congress), Commmittee on Pensions (Forty-seventh through Forty-ninth Congresses); judge of the court of common pleas of the fourth Pennsylvania district, 1888-1899; judge of the superior court of Pennsylvania and served one session; died in Wellsboro, Tioga County, Pa., August 20, 1907; interment in Wellsboro Cemetery.

**MITCHELL, John Joseph,** a Representative from Massachusetts; born in Marlboro, Middlesex County, Mass., May 9, 1873; attended the public schools, Boston College, and the Albany Law School; admitted to the bar in 1901 and commenced practice in Marlboro; member of the Massachusetts house of representatives 1903-1906; served in the Massachusetts senate in 1907 and 1908; elected as a Democrat to the Sixty-first Congress to fill the vacancy caused by the death of Charles Q. Tirrell and served from November 8, 1910, to March 3, 1911; unsuccessful candidate for reelection in 1910 to the Sixty-second Congress; elected to the Sixty-third Congress to fill the vacancy caused by the resignation of John W. Weeks and served from April 15, 1913, to March 3, 1915; unsuccessful candidate for reelection in 1914 to the Sixty-fourth Congress; served as United States marshal for Massachusetts during the First World War; collector of internal revenue for the district of Massachusetts 1919-1921; engaged in the practice of his profession in Boston, Suffolk County, Mass., until his death on September 13, 1925; interment in Immaculate Conception Cemetery, Marlboro, Mass.

**MITCHELL, John Lendrum** (son of Alexander Mitchell), a Representative and a Senator from Wisconsin; born in Milwaukee, Wis., October 19, 1842; attended the common schools at Milwaukee, and the military academy at Hampton, Conn.; studied in Dresden and Munich, Germany, and Geneva, Switzerland; returned to the United States in 1860; served in the Civil War, becoming first lieutenant and later chief of ordnance; resigned in 1864; engaged in agricultural pursuits near Milwaukee; member, Wisconsin State senate, 1872-1873, 1875-1876; president of the Milwaukee Public School Board, 1884-1885; member of the board of managers of the National Home for Disabled Volunteer Soldiers, 1886-1892; president of the Milwaukee Gas Company, 1890-1892; elected as a Democrat to the Fifty-second and Fifty-third Congresses, and served from March 4, 1891 until his resignation on March 3, 1893, before the beginning of the Congress, having been elected Senator; elected to the United States Senate, and served from March 4, 1893 to March 3, 1899; was not a candidate for renomination in 1898; went to Europe in 1899 and studied at Grenoble University, France; returned to the United States in 1902; president of the Wisconsin State Agricultural Society and of numerous banking institutions; trustee, director, and patron of numerous public institutions; died in Milwaukee, Wis., June 29, 1904; interment in Forest Home Cemetery.

**MITCHELL, John Murry,** a Representative from New York; born in New York City March 18, 1858; attended Leggett's School at New York City; was graduated from Columbia College, New York City, in 1877 and from the law department of that college in 1879; was admitted to the bar in 1879 and practiced in New York City; successfully contested as a Republican the election of James J. Walsh to the Fifty-fourth Congress; reelected to the Fifty-fifth Congress and served from June 2, 1896, to March 3, 1899; unsuccessful candidate for reelection in 1898 to the Fifty-sixth Congress; resumed the practice of law; died in Tuxedo Park, Orange County, N.Y., May 31, 1905; interment in Greenwood Cemetery, Brooklyn, N.Y.

**MITCHELL, John Ridley,** a Representative from Tennessee; born in Livingston, Overton County, Tenn., September 26, 1877; attended the public schools; was graduated from Peabody College of Teachers, Nashville, Tenn., in 1896; private secretary to Representative C.E. Snodgrass of Tennessee, 1899-1903; was graduated from the law department of Cumberland University, Lebanon, Tenn., in 1904; was admitted to the bar the same year and commenced practice in Crossville, Tenn.; member of the State Democratic executive committee, 1910-1914; assistant attorney general of the fifth circuit of Tennessee, 1908-1918 and attorney general of the same circuit, 1918-1925; served as judge of the fifth circuit, 1925-1931; moved to Cookeville, Tenn., in 1931; elected as a Democrat to the Seventy-second and to the three succeeding Congresses (March 4, 1931-January 3, 1939); was not a candidate for renomination in 1938 to the House of Representatives, but was an unsuccessful candidate for nomination to the United States Senate; resumed the practice of law; attorney in the office of Alien Property Custodian from January 1943 to September 1945; special assistant to Attorney General in the Antitrust Division, Department of Justice, Washington, D.C., 1945-1951; died in Crossville, Tenn., February 26, 1962; interment in Green Acres Memorial Gardens.

**MITCHELL, Nahum,** a Representative from Massachusetts; born in East Bridgewater, Plymouth County, Mass., February 12, 1769; attended the local school; was graduated from Harvard University in 1789; studied law in Plymouth, Mass.; was admitted to the bar and commenced practice in East Bridgewater, Mass.; member of the Massachusetts house of representatives 1798-1802; elected as a Federalist to the Eighth Congress (March 4, 1803-March 3, 1805); was not a candidate for renomination; again a member of the Massachusetts house of representatives in 1809 and 1812; judge of the common pleas court 1811-1821 and chief justice 1819-1821; served in the Massachusetts senate in 1813 and 1814; member of the Governor's council 1814-1820; treasurer of Massachusetts 1822-1827; librarian in 1835 and 1836 and treasurer 1839-1845 of the Massachusetts Historical Society; died in Plymouth, Mass., August 1, 1853; interment in Old Central Street Cemetery, East Bridgewater, Mass.

Bibliography: *DAB.*

**MITCHELL, Nathaniel,** a Delegate from Delaware; born near Laurel, Sussex County, Del., in 1753; engaged in agricultural pursuits; during the Revolutionary War became an adjutant in Colonel Dogworth's battalion of militia, afterward was with Colonel Patterson's battalion of the flying camp, and still later with Colonel Grayson's Continental regiment; in April 1779 he was transferred to Colonel Gist's regiment and subsequently was brigade major and inspector to General Peter Muhlenberg; Member of the Continental Congress in 1787 and 1788; prothonotary of Sussex County from 1788 until 1805; Governor of Delaware from January 1805 to January 1808; member of the Delaware State house of representatives in 1808; served in the Delaware State senate, 1810-1812; died in Laurel, Del., February 21, 1814; interment in Broad Creek Episcopal Graveyard, near Laurel, Del.

Bibliography: *DAB.*

**MITCHELL, Parren James,** a Representative from Maryland; born in Baltimore, Md., April 29, 1922; attended the public schools of Baltimore; A.B., Morgan State College, Baltimore, Md., 1950; M.A., University of Maryland, College Park, 1952; served in the United States Army, Ninety-second Infantry Division, commissioned officer and company commander, 1942-1945; received the Purple Heart; professor of sociology and assistant director, Urban Studies Institute, Morgan State College; executive secretary, Maryland Human Relations Commission, 1963-1965; director, Baltimore Community Action Agency, 1965-1968; supervisor, probation work, Supreme Bench of Baltimore City, 1954-1957; president, Baltimore Neighborhoods, Inc., 1969-1970; delegate, Maryland State Democratic convention, 1972; delegate to the Democratic National Convention of 1972; elected as a Democrat to the Ninety-second and to the seven succeeding Congresses (January 3, 1971-January 3, 1987); chairman, Committee on Small Business (Ninety-seventh, Ninety-eighth, and Ninety-ninth Congresses); was not a candidate for reelection in 1986 to the One Hundredth Congress; is a resident of Baltimore, Md.

**MITCHELL, Robert,** a Representative from Ohio; born in Westmoreland County, Pa., in 1778; attended the common schools; studied medicine; moved to Ohio in 1807 and practiced in Zanesville; clerk to the commissioners of Muskingum County in 1811 and 1812; county collector in 1812 and 1813; served in the War of 1812 as a member of Capt. John De Vault's company; member of the State house of representatives in 1815 and 1816; judge of the court of common pleas in 1818; brigadier general of the State militia in 1822; elected as a Jacksonian to the Twenty-third Congress (March 4, 1833-March 3, 1835); unsuccessful candidate for reelection in 1834 to the Twenty-fourth Congress; resumed the practice of medicine in Zanesville, Ohio, where he died November 13, 1848; interment in Greenwood Cemetery.

**MITCHELL, Stephen Mix,** a Delegate and a Senator from Connecticut; born in Wethersfield, Hartford County, Conn., December 9, 1743; pursued academic studies; was graduated from Yale College in 1763; served as tutor in Yale College, 1766-1769; studied law; was admitted to the bar in 1770 and commenced practice in Newton, Conn.; returned to Wethersfield in 1772 and continued the practice of law; member, Connecticut General Assembly, 1778-1784; member, State council, 1784-1793, with the exception of 1786; associate justice of the county court of Hartford County, 1779-1790, and presiding judge, 1790-1793; Member of the Continental Congress, 1785-1788; member of the State convention which ratified the Constitution of the United States in 1788; elected to the United States Senate to fill the vacancy caused by the death of Roger Sherman, and served from December 2, 1793 to March 3, 1795; was not a candidate for renomination in 1794; judge of the State supreme court, 1795-1807, and chief justice, 1807-1814; presidential elector on the Federalist ticket in 1800; member of the State constitutional convention in 1818; retired to Wethersfield, Conn., in 1814, where he died on September 30, 1835; interment in Wethersfield Cemetery.

Bibliography: *DAB.*

**MITCHELL, Thomas Rothmaler,** a Representative from South Carolina; born in Georgetown, Georgetown County, S.C., in May 1783; was graduated from Harvard University in 1802; studied law; was admitted to the bar in 1808 and commenced practice in Georgetown, S.C.; member of state house of representatives, 1809 and 1814-1819; elected to the Seventeenth Congress (March 4, 1821-March 3, 1823); unsuccessful candidate for reelection in 1822 to the Eighteenth Congress; elected to the Nineteenth and Twentieth Congresses (March 4, 1825-March 3, 1829); unsuccessful candidate for reelection in 1828 to the Twenty-first Congress; elected as a Jacksonian to the Twenty-second Congress (March 4, 1831-March 3, 1833); unsuccessful candidate for reelection in 1832 to the Twenty-third Congress; died in Georgetown, S.C., November 2, 1837.

**MITCHELL, William,** a Representative from Indiana; born in Root, Montgomery County, N.Y., January 19, 1807; attended the public schools; studied law; was admitted to the bar in 1836; moved to Kendallville, Noble County, Ind., and commenced the practice of law; appointed first postmaster of Kendallville December 7, 1836, and served until a successor was appointed March 7, 1846; member of the State house of representatives in 1841; justice of the peace; elected as a Republican to the Thirty-seventh Congress (March 4, 1861-March 3, 1863); unsuccessful candidate for reelection in 1862 to the Thirty-eighth Congress; engaged in the cotton business; died in Macon, Ga., September 11, 1865; interment in Lake View Cemetery, Kendallville, Ind.

**MITCHILL, Samuel Latham,** a Representative and a Senator from New York; born in Hempstead, Nassau County, N.Y., August 20, 1764; pursued classical studies; studied medicine and graduated from the University of Edinburgh, Scotland, in 1786; returned to the United States, studied law and was admitted to the bar; commissioner to purchase the lands of the Iroquois Indians in western New York in 1788; member, New York State assembly, 1791, 1798; professor of chemistry, botany, and natural history in Columbia College, 1792-1801; one of the founders of the State Society for the Promotion of Agriculture in 1793; editor of the New York Medical Repository, 1797-1813; elected as a Republican to the Seventh and to the two succeeding Congresses, and served from March 4, 1801 until his resignation on November 22, 1804, before the close of the Eighth Congress, having been elected Senator; one of the managers appointed by the House of Representatives in 1804 to conduct the impeachment proceedings against John Pickering, judge of the United States District Court of New Hampshire; chairman, Committee on Commerce and Manufacturers (Eighth Congress); elected to the United States Senate on November 9, 1804, to fill the vacancy caused by the resignation of John Armstrong, but did not qualify immediately, retaining his seat in the House; served in the Senate from November 23, 1804 to March 3, 1809; elected to the Eleventh Congress to fill the vacancy caused by the resignation of William Denning; reelected to the Twelfth Congress, and served from December 4, 1810 to March 3, 1813; surgeon general of the State militia in 1818; founder and president of the Lyceum of Natural History of New York City, 1817-1823; professor of chemistry and natural history in the New York College of Physicians and Surgeons, 1808-1820, and of botany and materia medica, 1820-1826; one of the founders and vice president of Rutgers Medical School, 1826-1830; died in New York City on September 7, 1831; interment in Greenwood Cemetery, Brooklyn, N.Y.

Bibliography: *DAB*; Aberbach, Alan David. *In Search of An American Identity: Samuel Latham Mitchill, Jeffersonian Nationalist.* New York: Peter Lang, 1988.

**MIZE, Chester Louis,** a Representative from Kansas; born in Atchison, Kans., December 25, 1917; attended the public schools; student at the University of Kansas School of Business Administration, 1935-1939; joined the United States Naval Reserve in 1940, served on active duty in the South Pacific Theater, 1941-1945, and was released to inactive service as a lieutenant commander; awarded the Bronze Star with Combat V; treasurer of a hardware company, 1945-1951; vice president of Locomotive Finished Materials Co., 1951-1958; vice president of Valley Co., Inc., 1958-1964; owned and operated a cattle ranch in New Mexico and a farm in Atchison County, Kans.; past member of the Atchison School Board; chairman, board of trustees of Mount St. Scholastica College, Atchison, Kans.; member of the School of Business Administration Advisory Board and the athletic board of the University of Kansas; elected as a Republican to the Eighty-ninth, Ninetieth, and Ninety-first Congresses (January 3, 1965-January 3, 1971), unsuccessful candidate for reelection in 1970 to the Ninety-second Congress; was a resident of La Jolla, Calif.; died January 11, 1994.

**MIZELL, Wilmer David,** a Representative from North Carolina; born in Vinegar Bend, Washington County, Ala., August 13, 1930; graduated from high school, Leakesville, Miss., 1949; served in the United States Army, 1953-1954; professional baseball pitcher with teams in St. Louis, Mo., Pittsburgh, Pa., and New York City, 1949-1963; employed by the Pepsi-Cola Co. in sales management and public relations, Winston-Salem, N.C., 1963-1967; elected Davidson County commissioner and later selected as chairman, Board of County Commissioners, 1966; elected as a Republican to

the Ninety-first and to the two succeeding Congresses (January 3, 1969-January 3, 1975); unsuccessful candidate for reelection in 1974 to the Ninety-fourth Congress; Assistant Secretary of Commerce for Economic Development, March 1975 to May 1976; unsuccessful candidate for election in 1976 to the Ninety-fifth Congress; Assistant Secretary of Agriculture for governmental and public affairs, 1982 to present; is a resident of Washington, D.C.

**MOAKLEY, John Joseph,** a Representative from Massachusetts; born in Boston, Suffolk County, Mass., April 27, 1927; B.A., University of Miami; LL.B., Suffolk University Law School, Boston, 1956; served in the United States Navy, 1943-1946; admitted to the Massachusetts bar in 1957 and commenced practice in Boston; elected to the Massachusetts house of representatives, 1953-1964, Democratic majority whip, 1957; member, Massachusetts senate, 1964-1971; member of the Boston City Council, 1971-1972; delegate to the Democratic National Convention of 1968; unsuccessful candidate for nomination in 1970 to the Ninety-second Congress; elected as an Independent Democrat to the Ninety-third Congress, November 7, 1972; changed party affiliation to Democrat, effective January 2, 1973; reelected as a Democrat to the eleven succeeding Congresses (January 3, 1973-January 3, 1997); chairman, Committee on Rules (One Hundred First through One Hundred Third Congresses); is a resident of Boston, Mass.

**MOBLEY, William Carlton,** a Representative from Georgia; born near Hillsboro, Jones County, Ga., December 7, 1906; attended the common schools; was graduated from the law department of Mercer University, Macon, Ga., in 1928; was admitted to the bar in 1928 and commenced practice in Forsyth, Ga.; served as secretary to Representative Samuel Rutherford of Georgia, 1929-1932; elected as a Democrat to the Seventy-second Congress to fill the vacancy caused by the death of Samuel Rutherford and served from March 2, 1932, to March 3, 1933; was not a candidate for renomination in 1932 to the Seventy-third Congress; secretary in the executive department of the State of Georgia, 1934-1937; assistant attorney general of Georgia, 1941-1943; served as a lieutenant commander in the United States Navy, 1943-1946; resumed the practice of law in Macon, Ga.; associate justice, supreme court of Georgia, from June 1, 1954, to December 1, 1960; reelected in 1960 and again in 1966 for the term ending December 31, 1972; elected presiding justice in August 1969; Chief Justice of Supreme Court of Georgia, 1969-1975; resided in Atlanta, Ga., until his death on October 14, 1981; interment in Forsyth, Ga.

**MOELLER, Walter Henry,** a Representative from Ohio; born on a farm, New Palestine, Hancock County, Ind., March 15, 1910; attended local schools; Concordia College and Seminary, Springfield, Ill., in 1935; A.B., Defiance (Ohio) College, 1951; M.S., Ed., Indiana University, 1953; Lutheran Church minister, Decatur, Ind., 1936-1942, and Van Wert and Lancaster, Ohio, 1942-1956; instructor at Giffen Junior College, Van Wert, Ohio, 1942-1952; delegate to North Atlantic Treaty Organization Congress in London in 1959; farm owner; elected as a Democrat to the Eighty-sixth and Eighty-seventh Congresses (January 3, 1959-January 3, 1963); unsuccessful candidate for reelection in 1962 to the Eighty-eighth Congress; assistant to the director, National Aeronautics and Space Administration's educational services division, 1963-1964; elected to the Eighty-ninth Congress (January 3, 1965-January 3, 1967); unsuccessful candidate for reelection in 1966 to the Ninetieth Congress; assistant to the Deputy Commissioner on Aging for the Department of Health, Education, and Welfare, 1967-1976; is a resident of Santa Barbara, Calif.

**MOFFATT, Seth Crittenden,** a Representative from Michigan; born in Battle Creek, Calhoun County, Mich., August 10, 1841; attended the common schools; was graduated from the law department of the University of Michigan at Ann Arbor in 1863; was admitted to the bar and commenced practice in Traverse City, Mich.;

prosecuting attorney for Grand Traverse and Leelanaw Counties for ten years; member of the Michigan State senate in 1871 and 1872; member of the constitutional commission in 1873; register of the United States Land Office at Traverse City, 1874-1878; member of the Michigan State house of representatives in 1881 and 1882, and served as speaker in both terms; delegate to the Republican National Convention of 1884; elected as a Republican to the Forty-ninth and Fiftieth Congresses and served from March 4, 1885, until his death in Washington, D.C., December 22, 1887; interment in Oakwood Cemetery, Traverse City, Grand Traverse County, Mich.

**MOFFET, John,** a Representative from Pennsylvania; born in County Antrim, Ireland, April 5, 1831; immigrated to the United States with his parents, who settled in Philadelphia, Pa.; attended the public schools in Philadelphia, Pa.; studied medicine in the University of Pennsylvania at Philadelphia and became an apothecary in 1853; also engaged in the practice of medicine; presented credentials as a Democratic Member-elect to the Forty-first Congress and served from March 4 to April 9, 1869, when he was succeeded by Leonard Myers, who contested his election; resumed the practice of pharmacy and medicine in Philadelphia, Pa., where he died June 19, 1884; interment in Laurel Hill Cemetery.

**MOFFETT, Anthony John, Jr. (Toby),** a Representative from Connecticut; born in Holyoke, Hampden County, Mass., August 18, 1944; attended Suffield (Conn.) Elementary School; graduated, Suffield High School; A.B., Syracuse (N.Y.) University, 1966; studied in Florence, Italy, 1963-1964; M.A., Boston College, 1968; served as Director, Office of Students and Youth, Office of United States Commissioner of Education, United States Department of Health, Education, and Welfare, 1969-1970; staff assistant to Senator Walter F. Mondale, 1970-1971; director, Connecticut (Hartford) Citizen Action Group, 1971-1974; elected as a Democrat to the Ninety-fourth and to the three succeeding Congresses (January 3, 1975-January 3, 1983); was not a candidate in 1982 for reelection to the House of Representatives, but was an unsuccessful candidate for election to the United States Senate; television news anchorman in West Hartford, Conn., 1986 to present; is a resident of Stony Creek, Conn.

**MOFFITT, Hosea,** a Representative from New York; born in Stephentown, Rensselaer County, N.Y., November 17, 1757; during the Revolutionary War served as ensign and later as lieutenant in the Fourth (Second Rensselaerwyck Battalion) Regiment, Albany County Militia; justice of the peace in 1791; town clerk in 1791 and 1797; member of the State assembly in 1794, 1795, and 1801; appointed brigadier general of militia March 22, 1806; supervisor of the town of Stephentown 1806-1809; sheriff of Rensselaer County 1810-1811; elected as a Federalist to the Thirteenth and Fourteenth Congresses (March 4, 1813-March 3, 1817); member of the board of managers of the Rensselaer County Bible Society in 1815; died in Stephentown, N.Y., August 31, 1825; interment in Old Presbyterian Cemetery on "Presbyterian Hill," at Garfield, in the town of Stephentown, N.Y.

**MOFFITT, John Henry,** a Representative from New York; born near Chazy, Clinton County, N.Y., January 8, 1843; attended the district school and Plattsburg (N.Y.) Academy; during the Civil War enlisted as a private in Company C, Sixteenth Regiment, New York Volunteers, April 27, 1861; mustered out of the service with his regiment on May 18, 1863; awarded the Congressional Medal of Honor; was graduated from Fort Edward (N.Y.) Collegiate Institute in 1864; deputy collector of customs at Rouses Point, N.Y., 1866-1872; engaged in the manufacture of charcoal bloom iron at Moffitsville, Clinton County, and at Belmont, Franklin (now Allegany) County, 1872-1891; elected supervisor of Saranac, Clinton County, in 1877; elected as a Republican to the Fiftieth and Fifty-first Congresses (March 4, 1887-March 3, 1891); was not a candidate for renomination in 1890 to the Fifty-second Congress; manager of the Syracuse Street Railway Company, 1891-1899; superintendent of the city water department, 1900-1902; cashier of the Plattsburg National Bank, 1902-1904, and from 1904 until his death was president of the Plattsburg National Bank and Trust Company; served as chairman of the Republican committee of Clinton County; delegate to the Republican National Convention of 1912; died in Plattsburg, Clinton County, N.Y., August 14, 1926; interment in Mount Carmel Cemetery.

**MOLINARI, Guy Victor** (father of Susan Molinari and father-in-law of Leon William (Bill) Paxon), a Representative from New York; born in New York City, November 23, 1928; attended private schools; graduated, New Dorp High School, Staten Island, 1945; B.A., Wagner College, Staten Island, 1949; LL.B., New York Law School, New York City, 1951; served in the United States Marine Corps as a sergeant, 1951-1953; admitted to the New York bar in 1953 and commenced practice in Staten Island; member, New York State assembly, 1974-1980; delegate, New York State Republican conventions, 1979-1980; delegate to the Republican National Conventions of 1980 and 1984; elected as a Republican to the Ninety-seventh and to the four succeeding Congresses and served from January 3, 1981, until his resignation January 1, 1990; Borough President of Staten Island, 1990 to present; unsuccessful candidate in 1995 for election for Staten Island district attorney; is a resident of Staten Island, N.Y.

**MOLINARI, Susan** (daughter of Guy Victor Molinari and wife of Leon William (Bill) Paxon), a Representative from New York; born in Staten Island, N.Y., March 27, 1958; graduated from St. Joseph Hill Academy, Staten Island, 1976; B.A., State University of New York, 1980, and M.A., 1982; intern, New York State Senator Christopher J. Mega; research analyst for New York State Senate Finance Committee; financial assistant, National Republican Governors' Association; ethnic community liaison for Republican National Committee; member, New York City Council, 1985-1990; elected as a Republican to the One Hundred First Congress, March 20, 1990, by special election to fill the vacancy caused by the resignation of her father, Guy V. Molinari; reelected to the three succeeding Congresses, and served from March 20, 1990 to January 3, 1997; delivered keynote address at the Republican National Convention of 1996; is a resident of Staten Island, N.Y.

**MOLLOHAN, Alan Bowlby** (son of Robert Homer Mollohan), a Representative from West Virginia; born in Fairmont, Marion County, W.Va., May 14, 1943; attended Butcher School, Fairmont, W.Va.; graduated from Greenbriar Military School, Lewisburg, W.Va., 1962; A.B., College of William and Mary, Williamsburg, Va., 1966; LL.D., West Virginia University, Morgantown, W.Va., 1970; admitted to the West Virginia bar in 1970 and commenced practice in Fairmont; admitted to the District of Columbia bar in 1975; served as a captain in the United States Army Reserve, 1970-1983; delegate to the Democratic National Conventions of 1968, 1972 and 1976; member, West Virginia Young Democrats; elected as a Democrat to the Ninety-eighth and to the six succeeding Congresses (January 3, 1983-January 3, 1997); is a resident of Fairmont, W.Va.

**MOLLOHAN, Robert Homer** (father of Alan Bowlby Mollohan), a Representative from West Virginia; born in Grantsville, Calhoun County, W.Va., September 18, 1909; attended the public schools; attended Glenville (W.Va.) State College, and Shepherd College, Shepherdstown, W.Va., 1929-1931; deputy collector of internal revenue at Parkersburg, W.Va., in 1933 and chief of the miscellaneous tax division and cashier, 1935-1938; district manager of the Works Progress Administration in 1939; West Virginia State director for the Census Bureau in 1940; superintendent of the West Virginia State Industrial School for Boys, 1941-1948; clerk of the Committee on the District of Columbia, United States Senate, in 1949 and 1950; United States marshal for the northern district of

West Virginia in 1950; again served as clerk of the Committee on the District of Columbia, United States Senate, 1950-1952; elected as a Democrat to the Eighty-third and Eighty-fourth Congresses (January 3, 1953-January 3, 1957); was not a candidate for renomination in 1956 to the Eighty-fifth Congress, but was an unsuccessful candidate for election for Governor of West Virginia; unsuccessful candidate in 1958 for election to the Eighty-sixth Congress; engaged in general insurance business; elected to the Ninety-first and to the six succeeding Congresses (January 3, 1969-January 3, 1983); was not a candidate for reelection in 1982 to the Ninety-eighth Congress; resumed insurance business; is a resident of Charles Town, W.Va.

**MOLONY, Richard Sheppard,** a Representative from Illinois; born in Northfield, N.H., June 28, 1811; studied medicine; was graduated from Dartmouth Medical School, Hanover, N.H., in 1838 and commenced the practice of his profession in Belvidere, Boone County, Ill.; delegate to the Democratic National Convention in 1852; elected as a Democrat to the Thirty-second Congress (March 4, 1851-March 3, 1853); was not a candidate for renomination in 1852; moved to Humboldt, Nebr., and engaged in agricultural pursuits 1866-1891; in 1882 declined the Democratic nomination for United States Senator from Nebraska on account of ill health; again a delegate to the Democratic National Convention at Chicago in 1884; died in Humboldt, Nebr., December 14, 1891; interment in Belvidere Cemetery, Belvidere, Ill.

**MONAGAN, John Stephen,** a Representative from Connecticut; born in Waterbury, New Haven County, Conn., December 23, 1911; attended Driggs, St. Mary's and Crosby high schools in Waterbury; A.B., Dartmouth College, Hanover, N.H., 1933; LL.B., Harvard University Law School, 1937; was admitted to the Connecticut bar in 1938 and commenced the practice of law in Waterbury, Conn., the same year; president of the Waterbury Board of Aldermen, 1940-1943; mayor of Waterbury, 1943-1948; member of the board of directors of Waterbury Savings Bank; delegate to the Democratic National Conventions of 1944, 1948, 1960, 1964, and 1968; elected as a Democrat to the Eighty-sixth and to the six succeeding Congresses (January 3, 1959-January 3, 1973); unsuccessful candidate for reelection in 1972 to the Ninety-third Congress; resumed the practice of law; president, United States Association of Former Members of Congress, 1981-1982; is a resident of Washington, D.C.

**MONAGHAN, Joseph Patrick,** a Representative from Montana; born in Butte, Mont., March 26, 1906; attended public and parochial schools; graduated from Mount St. Charles (Carroll College), Helena, Mont., in 1928; member of the State house of representatives 1929-1931; studied law at Montana State University at Missoula; was admitted to the bar in 1931 and commenced practice in Butte, Mont.; unsuccessful candidate for election in 1930 to the Seventy-second Congress; elected as a Democrat to the Seventy-third and Seventy-fourth Congresses (March 4, 1933-January 3, 1937); did not seek renomination in 1936, but was unsuccessful both as a candidate for the Democratic nomination for United States Senator and for election as an Independent candidate for the same office; resumed the practice of law; unsuccessful candidate for the Democratic nomination to the United States Senate in 1964; was a resident of Butte, Mont., until his death there on July 4, 1985; interment in Sunset Memorial Park.

**MONAHAN, James Gideon,** a Representative from Wisconsin; born at Willow Springs, near Darlington, Lafayette County, Wis., January 12, 1855; attended the common schools and was graduated from the Darlington High School in 1875; taught school; studied law; was admitted to the bar in 1878 and commenced practice in Mineral Point, Wis.; returned to Darlington in 1880; district attorney of Lafayette County 1880-1884; editor and owner of the Darlington Republican Journal 1883-1919; delegate to the Republican National Convention in 1888; collector of internal revenue for the second

Wisconsin district 1900-1908; elected as a Republican to the Sixty-sixth Congress (March 4, 1919-March 3, 1921); unsuccessful candidate for renomination in 1920 to the Sixty-seventh Congress; died in Dubuque, Iowa, December 5, 1923; interment in Union Grove Cemetery, Darlington, Wis.

**MONAST, Louis,** a Representative from Rhode Island; born in Marieville de Monior, Iberville, Province of Quebec, Canada, July 1, 1863; in the spring of 1865 immigrated to the United States with his father, who settled in Pawtucket, R.I.; attended parochial and night schools; employed in the textile mills from 1872 to 1882 and as a bricklayer, plasterer, and carpenter from 1882 to 1892; engaged in building construction and in the real estate business in 1892, and also operated several bakeries; member of the State house of representatives 1909-1911; delegate to the Republican National Convention in 1924; unsuccessful candidate for election in 1924 to the Sixty-ninth Congress; elected as a Republican to the Seventieth Congress (March 4, 1927-March 3, 1929); unsuccessful candidate for reelection in 1928 to the Seventy-first Congress; resumed the real estate business; died in Pawtucket, R.I., April 16, 1936; interment in Notre Dame Cemetery.

**MONDALE, Walter Frederick,** a Senator from Minnesota and a Vice President of the United States; born in Ceylon, Martin County, Minn., January 5, 1928; attended the Heron Lake and Elmore, Minn., public schools; attended Macalester College in St. Paul, Minn.; B.A., University of Minnesota, 1951; served in the United States Army, 1951-1953; LL.B., University of Minnesota School of Law, 1956; was admitted to the Minnesota bar in 1956 and commenced practice in Minneapolis; appointed and elected attorney general of Minnesota in 1960, and reelected in 1962; member of the President's Consumer Advisory Council, 1960-1964; appointed as a Democrat to the United States Senate, December 30, 1964, to fill the vacancy caused by the resignation of Hubert H. Humphrey for the term ending January 3, 1967; elected in 1966 for the term commencing January 3, 1967; reelected in 1972 and served from December 30, 1964, until his resignation December 30, 1976; chairman, Select Committee on Equal Education Opportunity (Ninety-first and Ninety-second Congresses); elected Vice President of the United States on the Democratic ticket headed by Jimmy Carter on November 2, 1976, was inaugurated on January 20, 1977 and served until January 20, 1981; unsuccessful candidate for reelection in 1980 for Vice President; unsuccessful Democratic candidate for election for President of the United States in 1984; nominated as Ambassador to Japan on July 23, 1993, and was confirmed by the Senate on July 30, 1993; is a resident of Washington, D.C.

**Bibliography:** Gillon, Steven M. *The Democrats' Dilemma: Walter F. Mondale and the Liberal Legacy.* New York: Columbia University Press, 1992; Lewis, Finlay. *Mondale: Portrait of An American Politician.* New York: Perennial Library, 1984; Mondale, Walter. *The Accountability of Power.* New York: David McKay Co., 1975.

**MONDELL, Franklin Wheeler,** a Representative from Wyoming; born in St. Louis, Mo., November 6, 1860; raised in Dickinson County, Iowa; attended the common schools; engaged in mercantile pursuits, mining, and railway construction in various western states and territories; settled in Wyoming in 1887 and engaged in the development of coal mines and oil property in the vicinity of Newcastle and Cambria; took an active part in the establishment and building of the town of Newcastle, Wyo.; elected mayor of Newcastle in 1888 and served until 1895; member of the first State senate in 1890 and served as president of the second senate in 1892; delegate to the Republican National Conventions in 1892, 1900, 1904, 1908, and 1912; elected as a Republican to the Fifty-fourth Congress (March 4, 1895-March 3, 1897); unsuccessful candidate for reelection in 1896 to the Fifty-fifth Congress; appointed assistant commissioner of the General Land Office on November 15, 1897, and served until March 3, 1899; elected to the Fifty-sixth and to the eleven succeeding Congresses (March 4, 1899-March 3, 1923); chairman, Committee on Irrigation of Arid Lands (Fifty-eighth and Fifty-ninth Congresses), Committee on Public Lands (Sixtieth and Sixty-first Congresses); majority leader (Sixty-sixth and Sixty-seventh Congresses); did not seek renomination in 1922, but was an unsuccessful candidate for United States Senator; appointed a director of the War Finance Corporation in 1923 and served until his resignation in July 1925; studied law; was admitted to the bar in 1924 and commenced practice in Washington, D.C.; delegate to the Republican National Convention in 1924, serving as chairman; died in Washington, D.C., August 6, 1939; interment in Cedar Hill Cemetery.

**Bibliography:** *DAB*.

**MONELL, Robert,** a Representative from New York; born in Columbia County, N.Y., in 1786; pursued classical studies; studied law; was admitted to the bar in 1809 and commenced practice at Binghamton, N.Y.; moved to Greene, Chenango County, in 1811 and continued the practice of his profession; member of the State assembly in 1814 and 1815; elected to the Sixteenth Congress (March 4, 1819-March 3, 1821); again a member of the State assembly in 1825, 1826, and 1828; district attorney of Chenango County in 1827; elected as a Jacksonian to the Twenty-first Congress, and served from March 4, 1829, until February 21, 1831, when he resigned; circuit judge of the sixth circuit 1831-1845; clerk of the State supreme court in 1846; resumed the practice of law; died in Greene, Chenango County, N.Y., November 29, 1860; interment in Hornby Cemetery.

**MONEY, Hernando De Soto,** a Representative and a Senator from Mississippi; born at Zeiglersville, Holmes County, Miss., August 26, 1839; moved in early childhood to Carrollton, Carroll County, Miss.; received his early education in the public schools and from a private tutor; graduated from the law department of the University of Mississippi at Oxford; was admitted to the bar and commenced practice in Carrollton about 1860; served in the Confederate Army throughout the Civil War; engaged in planting in Leflore County; returned to Carrollton and edited the Conservative; moved to Winona, Montgomery County, Miss., and edited the Winona Advance 1873-1875; mayor of Winona 1873-1874; elected as a Democrat to the Forty-fourth and to the four succeeding Congresses (March 4, 1875-March 3, 1885); declined to be a candidate for renomination in 1884; chairman, Committee on Post Office and Post Roads (Forty-sixth and Forty-eighth Congresses); engaged in the practice of law in Washington, D.C., until 1891, when he returned to Carrollton, Miss.; elected to the Fifty-third and Fifty-fourth Congresses (March 4, 1893-March 3, 1897); in January 1896, elected as a Democrat to the United States Senate for the term commencing March 4, 1899; during the interim was appointed and subsequently elected to the United States Senate to fill the vacancy caused by the death of James Z. George; reelected in 1906 and served from October 8, 1897, to March 3, 1911; declined to be a candidate for reelection; Democratic caucus chairman 1909-1911; chairman, Committee on Corporations Organized in the District of Columbia (Sixtieth Congress), Committee on Additional Accommodations for the Library (Sixtieth Congress); returned to his home near Biloxi, Harrison County, Miss., and died there September 18, 1912; interment in the family vault at Carrollton, Carroll County, Miss.

**Bibliography:** *DAB*.

**MONKIEWICZ, Boleslaus Joseph,** a Representative from Connecticut; born in Syracuse, N.Y., August 8, 1898; moved with his parents to New Britain, Conn., in 1899; attended the public schools and was graduated from New Britain (Conn.) High School in 1917; served as an apprentice seaman in the United States Navy

(Columbia University Naval Unit), October 3, 1918, to December 17, 1918; was graduated from the law department of Fordham University, New York City, in 1921; was admitted to the bar in 1933 and commenced practice in New York and Connecticut; also engaged in banking; clerk of the New Britain, Conn., city and police court from July 1932 to August 1933; prosecuting attorney, police court, 1937-1939; elected as a Republican to the Seventy-sixth Congress (January 3, 1939-January 3, 1941); unsuccessful candidate for reelection in 1940 to the Seventy-seventh Congress; elected to the Seventy-eighth Congress (January 3, 1943-January 3, 1945); unsuccessful candidate for reelection in 1944 to the Seventy-ninth Congress; resumed the practice of law and also was unemployment compensation commissioner of Connecticut; member of the United States Board of Parole at Washington, D.C., 1947-1953; resumed the practice of law in New Britain, Conn.; judge of circuit court of Connecticut, 1961-1968; resided in Kensington, Conn.; died in New Britain, Conn., July 2, 1971; interment in Sacred Heart Cemetery.

**MONROE, James** (nephew of James Monroe [1758-1831]), a Representative from New York; born in Albemarle County, Va., September 10, 1799; was graduated from the United States Military Academy, West Point, N.Y., in 1815 and assigned to the Artillery Corps; served in the war with Algiers; served as aide to General Winfield Scott from 1817 until 1822; commissioned a second lieutenant in the Fourth Artillery in 1821 and served on garrison and commissary duty until 1832, when he was again appointed General Scott's aide on the Black Hawk expedition, but did not reach the seat of war, owing to illness; resigned his commission on September 30, 1832; moved to New York City in 1832; assistant alderman of New York City in 1832; alderman from 1833 to 1835, and served as president of the board in 1834; elected as a Whig to the Twenty-sixth Congress (March 4, 1839-March 3, 1841); unsuccessful candidate for reelection in 1840 to the Twenty-seventh Congress; contested the election of David S. Jackson to the Thirtieth Congress in 1847, but the House decided that neither was entitled to the seat; declined a renomination for the vacancy thus created; member of the New York State senate in 1850 and 1852; retired from public life; moved to Orange, N.J., where he died on September 7, 1870; interment in Trinity Cemetery, One Hundred and Fifty-fifth Street and Broadway, New York City.

**MONROE, James,** a Representative from Ohio; born in Plainfield, Windham County, Conn., July 18, 1821; attended the common schools and Plainfield Academy; was graduated from Oberlin (Ohio) College in 1846; pursued a postgraduate course in theology; professor at Oberlin College, 1849-1862; member of the Ohio State house of representatives, 1856-1859; served in the State senate, 1860-1862, and was chosen president pro tempore in 1861 and 1862; resigned his seat in the senate in October 1862 to accept the position of United States consul to Rio de Janeiro, and served from 1863 to 1869; served for several months in 1869 as Chargé d'Affaires ad interim to Brazil; elected as a Republican to the Forty-second and to the four succeeding Congresses (March 4, 1871-March 3, 1881); chairman, Committee on Education and Labor (Forty-third Congress); was not a candidate for renomination in 1880 to the Forty-seventh Congress; professor at Oberlin College, 1883-1896; died in Oberlin, Ohio, July 6, 1898; interment in Westwood Cemetery.

**MONROE, James** (nephew of Joseph Jones and uncle of James Monroe [1799-1870]), a Delegate and a Senator from Virginia and 5th President of the United States; born in Westmoreland County, Va., April 28, 1758; pursued classical studies; attended the College of William and Mary , Va., in 1776 and left to enter the Continental Army in the Revolutionary War; appointed a lieutenant in the Third Virginia Regiment, participated in numerous engagements, and was severely wounded in the Battle of Trenton, N.J., December 26, 1776; rose to the rank of lieutenant colonel; member, Virginia assembly,

1782; member of the Continental Congress, 1783-1786; resumed the study of law; admitted to the bar and engaged in practice in Fredericksburg, Va.; member, Virginia assembly, 1786; delegate to the Virginia convention to consider the Federal Constitution in 1788; unsuccessful candidate for election to the First Congress; elected to the United States Senate to fill the vacancy caused by the death of William Grayson; reelected in 1791 and served from November 9, 1790, until his resignation May 27, 1794; appointed by President George Washington as Minister Plenipotentiary to France on May 28, 1794 and served until December 1796; elected Governor of Virginia by the General Assembly, and served from December 1, 1799 to December 1, 1802; appointed by President Thomas Jefferson as Minister Plenipotentiary to Great Britain on April 18, 1803 and served until October 1807, and during this period headed a diplomatic mission to Spain; returned home in 1808; member, Virginia assembly, 1810-1811; again elected Governor of Virginia and served from January 16, 1811 until his resignation on April 5, 1811 to accept a Cabinet portfolio; appointed Secretary of State in the Cabinet of President James Madison and served from April 2, 1811 to March 3, 1817; also served as Secretary of War from September 27, 1814 until March 2, 1815; elected President of the United States in 1816, reelected in 1820, and served from March 4, 1817, to March 4, 1825; retired to his farm in Loudoun County, Va.; member and president of the Virginia constitutional convention of 1829; moved to New York City in 1831, and died there July 4, 1831; interment in Marble Cemetery on Second Street, New York City; reinterred in Hollywood Cemetery, Richmond, Va., July 4, 1858.

**Bibliography:** *DAB*; Ammon, Harry. *James Monroe: The Quest for National Identity*. New York: McGraw-Hill, 1971; Monroe, James. *The Writings of James Monroe*. Edited by Stanislaus Hamilton. 7 vols. New York: G.P. Putnam's Sons. 1898-1903.

**MONRONEY, Almer Stillwell Mike,** a Representative and a Senator from Oklahoma; born in Oklahoma City, Okla., March 2, 1902; attended the public schools; B.A., University of Oklahoma, Norman, 1924; reporter and political writer for the Oklahoma News, 1924-1928; in 1928 became president of a retail furniture store; elected as a Democrat to the Seventy-sixth and to the five succeeding Congresses (January 3, 1939-January 3, 1951); co-sponsor of the Legislative Reorganization Act of 1946, reducing the number of congressional committees and allowing the hire of committee staff, changing the method of dealing with Federal budget, reducing the workload of Congress, and for the first time requiring lobbyists to register with and report their expenditures to the House clerk; was not a candidate in 1950 for reelection to the House of Representatives, but was elected to the United States Senate; reelected in 1956 and again in 1962, and served from January 3, 1951 to January 3, 1969; unsuccessful candidate for reelection in 1968; chairman, Committee on Post Office and Civil Service (Eighty-ninth and Nintieth Congresses), Special Committee on the Organization of Congress (Eighty-ninth and Ninetieth Congresses), co-chairman, Joint Committee on the Organization of Congress (Eighty-ninth and Ninetieth Congresses); was an aviation consultant and member of several boards of directors; resided in Washington, D.C.; died in Rockville, Md., February 13, 1980; cremated; part of the ashes placed in a niche in the Washington Cathedral, Washington, D.C., and the remaining ashes scattered on the grounds of the Mike Monroney Aeronautical Center, Oklahoma City, Okla.

**Bibliography:** *DAB*; Monroney, A.S. Mike, Thomas H. Kuchel, and David Truman, eds. "Reform of Congress: The Congress and America's Future—A Discussion." *Political Science Quarterly* 80 (December 1965): 606-20.

**MONSON, David Smith,** a Representative from Utah; born in Salt Lake City, Utah, June 20, 1945; attended public schools; B.S., University of Utah, 1970; served in the Utah Air National Guard as a sergeant, 1967-1973; certified public accountant; Utah State auditor, 1973-1976; lieutenant governor of Utah, 1977-1984; elected as a Republican to the Ninety-ninth Congress (January 3, 1985-January 3, 1987); was not a candidate for reelection in 1986 to the One Hundredth Congress; business executive involved in international trade and recycling paper; is a resident of Salt Lake City, Utah.

**MONTAGUE, Andrew Jackson,** a Representative from Virginia; born near Lynchburg, Campbell County, Va., October 3, 1862; attended public and private schools; was graduated from Richmond (Va.) College in 1882 and from the law department of the University of Virginia at Charlottesville in 1885; was admitted to the bar in 1885 and commenced practice in Danville, Va.; appointed by President Grover Cleveland as United States attorney for the western district of Virginia in 1893, and served until 1898; attorney general of Virginia, 1898-1902; elected Governor of Virginia in 1901, and served from January 1, 1902 to February 1, 1906; delegate at large to the Democratic National Convention of 1904; unsuccessful candidate for nomination to the United States Senate in 1905; American delegate to the Third Conference of American Republics at Rio de Janeiro in 1906; dean of Richmond College Law School, 1906-1909; resumed the practice of law in Richmond in 1909; delegate to the Third International Conference on Maritime Law at Brussels in 1909 and 1910; trustee of the Carnegie Institute, Washington, D.C., and the Carnegie Endowment for International Peace; president of the American Society for Judicial Settlement of International Disputes in 1917; president of the American Peace Society, 1920-1924; one of the managers appointed by the House of Representatives in 1926 to conduct the impeachment proceedings against George W. English, judge of the United States District Court for the Eastern District of Illinois; president of the American group of the Interparliamentary Union, 1930-1935; elected as a Democrat to the Sixty-third and to the twelve succeeding Congresses, and served from March 4, 1913 until his death at his country home in Urbanna, Middlesex County, Va., January 24, 1937; interment in Christ Church Episcopal Cemetery, near Urbanna, Va.

**Bibliography:** *DAB*; Larsen, William E. *Montague of Virginia: The Making of a Southern Progressive*. Baton Rouge: Louisiana State University Press, 1965.

**MONTET, Numa Francois,** a Representative from Louisiana; born in Thibodaux, La Fourche Parish, La., September 17, 1892; attended the common schools and Louisiana State Normal College at Natchitoches; was graduated from the law department of Tulane University, New Orleans, La., in 1913; was admitted to the bar the same year and commenced practice in Franklin, La.; served as secretary-treasurer of the city of Thibodaux in 1914 and as city attorney in 1915; member of the State house of representatives 1916-1920; unsuccessful candidate for attorney general of Louisiana in 1924; delegate to the Democratic National Conventions in 1924 and 1932; acting prosecuting attorney for the twentieth judicial district of Louisiana in 1925; general counsel for State highway commission in 1928 and 1929; elected as a Democrat to the Seventy-first Congress to fill the vacancy caused by the death of Whitmell P. Martin; reelected to the Seventy-second, Seventy-third, and Seventy-fourth Congresses and served from August 6, 1929, to January 3, 1937; unsuccessful candidate for renomination in 1936; resumed the practice of law in Thibodaux, La., where he resided until his death there October 12, 1985; interment in Assumption Catholic Cemetery, Plattenville, La.

**MONTGOMERY, Alexander Brooks,** a Representative from Kentucky; born near Tip Top, Hardin County, Ky., December 11, 1837; attended the common and private schools; graduated from Georgetown (Ky.) College in 1859 and from the Louisville Law School in 1861; engaged in agricultural pursuits in Hardin County, Ky., 1861-1870; admitted to the bar and commenced the practice of law in Elizabethtown, Hardin County, Ky., in 1870; county judge of

Hardin County, Ky., 1870-1874; member of the Kentucky senate 1877-1881; elected as a Democrat to the Fiftieth and to the three succeeding Congresses (March 4, 1887-March 3, 1895); chairman, Committee on Expenditures in the Department of War (Fifty-second and Fifty-third Congresses); unsuccessful candidate for reelection to the Fifty-fourth Congress; member of the Dawes Indian Commission, appointed under act of Congress to treat with the Five Civilized Tribes, 1895-1898; resumed the practice of law at Elizabethtown, Ky., where he died December 27, 1910; interment in City Cemetery.

**MONTGOMERY, Daniel, Jr.,** a Representative from Pennsylvania; born in Londonderry, Chester County, Pa., October 30, 1765; moved to Danville, Pa.; chief promoter of turnpike roads in the section around Danville; elected as a member of the Pennsylvania house of representatives in 1800; lieutenant colonel of the Eighty-first Pennsylvania Militia in 1805; appointed major general of the Ninth Division of Militia on July 27, 1809; elected as a Republican to the Tenth Congress (March 4, 1807-March 3, 1809); appointed canal commissioner in 1828; died in Danville, Montour County, Pa., December 30, 1831.

**MONTGOMERY, Gillespie V. (Sonny),** a Representative from Mississippi; born in Meridian, Lauderdale County, Miss., August 5, 1920; B.S., Mississippi State University, 1943; owner, Montgomery Insurance Agency, Meridian, Miss.; vice president of the Greater Mississippi Life Insurance Co., Meridian, Miss.; United States Army service beginning 1943 during the Second World War in the European Theater; received Bronze Star, European Theater Ribbon, Commendation Ribbon; recalled to active duty during the Korean conflict in 1951 with the Thirty-first (Dixie) Division; recipient of the Mississippi Magnolia Medal; retired major general in the Mississippi National Guard; past president of the Mississippi National Guard Association; former member of the Mississippi Agricultural and Industrial Board; served in the Mississippi State senate, representing Lauderdale County, 1956-1966; elected as a Democrat to the Ninetieth and to the fourteen succeeding Congresses (January 3, 1967-January 3, 1997); was not a candidate for reelection in 1996 to the One Hundred Fifth Congress; chairman, Select Committee on Military Involvement in Southeast Asia (Ninety-first Congress), Select Committee on Missing in Action in Southeast Asia (Ninety-fourth Congress), Committee on Veterans' Affairs (Ninety-seventh through One Hundred Third Congresses); is a resident of Meridian, Miss.

**MONTGOMERY, John,** a Representative from Maryland; born in Carlisle, Cumberland County, Pa., in 1764; pursued classical studies; studied law; was admitted to the bar in 1791 and commenced practice in Harford County, Md.; member of the Maryland State house of delegates, 1793-1798; State's attorney, 1793-1796; elected as a Republican to the Tenth and to the two succeeding Congresses and served from March 4, 1807, until April 29, 1811, when he resigned; moved to Baltimore, Md., in 1811; appointed attorney general of Maryland on April 29, 1811, and served until February 11, 1818; appointed captain of the Baltimore Union Artillery on March 25, 1814, and took part in the Battle of North Point; again a member of the State house of delegates in 1819; mayor of Baltimore, 1820-1826; died in Baltimore, Md., July 17, 1828; interment in the cemetery of the Methodist Episcopal Church (now abandoned) at Bel Air, Harford County, Md.

**MONTGOMERY, John,** a Delegate from Pennsylvania; born in Ireland in 1722; family migrated to Carlisle, Pa., about 1740; county justice; captain, Third Pennsylvania battalion and served in Forbes' expedition in 1758 and in the Indian wars; member, Pennsylvania's Committee of Safety, 1775-1776; colonel, Cumberland County regiment during Revolution, 1777; member, Pennsylvania Assembly, 1781-1782; member of the Continental Congress 1782-1784; burgess of Carlisle, Pa., in 1787; commissioned an associate judge of Cumberland County in 1794; a founder of Dickinson College of Pennsylvania; died in Carlisle, Pa., September 3, 1808.

**MONTGOMERY, John Gallagher,** a Representative from Pennsylvania; born in Northumberland, Northumberland County, Pa., June 27, 1805; studied under a private tutor; was graduated from Washington (now Washington and Jefferson) College, Washington, Pa., in 1824; studied law; was admitted to the bar in 1827 and commenced practice in Danville, Montour County, Pa.; member of the Pennsylvania house of representatives in 1855; elected as a Democrat to the Thirty-fifth Congress and served from March 4, 1857, until his death, in Danville, Pa., April 24, 1857, presumably from the effects of an illness contracted in Washington, D.C., during the inauguration of President James Buchanan; interment in Episcopal Cemetery.

**MONTGOMERY, Joseph,** a Delegate from Pennsylvania; born in Paxtang, Dauphin County, Pa., September 23, 1733; pursued classical studies and was graduated from Princeton College in 1755; studied for the ministry; licensed to preach by the presbytery of Philadelphia in 1759 and ordained as a minister in 1761; held several pastorates from 1761 until 1777; commissioned a chaplain in Colonel Smallwood's Maryland Regiment of the Continental Army and served from 1777 until 1780; delegate to the general assembly of Pennsylvania, 1780-1782; member of the Continental Congress, 1780-1782; recorder of deeds and register of wills for Dauphin County from 1785 to 1794; justice of the court of common pleas, 1786-1794; died in Harrisburg, Pa., on October 14, 1794; interment in the Lutheran Church Cemetery.

**MONTGOMERY, Samuel James,** a Representative from Oklahoma; born in Buffalo, Ky., December 1, 1896; moved to Oklahoma in 1902 with his parents, who settled in Bartlesville; attended the public schools; studied law at the University of Oklahoma at Norman; was admitted to the bar in 1919 and commenced practice in Bartlesville; during the First World War enlisted as a private in the Sixth Regiment, United States Marine Corps, on July 18, 1917, and served in the Second Division, American Expeditionary Forces, until May 19, 1919, when he was honorably discharged; received the Croix de Guerre from the Republic of France; elected as a Republican to the Sixty-ninth Congress (March 4, 1925-March 3, 1927); unsuccessful candidate for reelection in 1926 to the Seventieth Congress; practiced law in Tulsa and later in Oklahoma City; died in Oklahoma City, Okla., June 4, 1957; interment in Memorial Park Cemetery, Bartlesville, Okla.

**MONTGOMERY, Sonny,** a Representative from Mississippi. (*See* MONTGOMERY, Gillespie V.)

**MONTGOMERY, Thomas,** a Representative from Kentucky; born in what is now Nelson County, Va., in 1779; received a thorough English training; studied law; was admitted to the bar and commenced practice in Stanford, Lincoln County, Ky.; judge of the circuit court of Lincoln County; member of the Kentucky house of representatives in 1811; elected as a Republican to the Thirteenth Congress (March 4, 1813-March 3, 1815); unsuccessful candidate for reelection to the Fourteenth Congress; again elected to the Sixteenth Congress to fill the vacancy caused by the resignation of Tunstall Quarles; reelected to the Seventeenth Congress and served from August 1, 1820, to March 3, 1823; chairman, Committee on Public Expenditures (Seventeenth Congress); died in Stanford, Ky., April 2, 1828.

**MONTGOMERY, William,** a Representative from North Carolina; born in Guilford County, N.C., December 29, 1789; studied medicine and practiced his profession in Albrights, Orange County, N.C.; member of the State senate 1824-1827 and 1829-1834; elected as a Jacksonian to the Twenty-fourth Congress and reelected as a Democrat to the Twenty-fifth and Twenty-sixth Congresses (March 4, 1835-March 3, 1841); chairman, Committee on the Post Office and

Post Roads (Twenty-fifth Congress); declined to be a candidate for renomination in 1840; died in Albrights, N.C., November 27, 1844.

**MONTGOMERY, William,** a Delegate and a Representative from Pennsylvania; born in Londonderry Township, Chester County, Pa., August 3, 1736; served in the Revolutionary War as colonel of the Fourth Battalion of Chester County Militia; delegate to the provincial conventions of 1775 and 1776; moved to Northumberland County in 1776; elected in 1779 to the Pennsylvania assembly from Northumberland County and several times reelected; sent to Wyoming, Pa., in 1783 to settle boundary disputes; elected to the Continental Congress in 1784, but did not serve; appointed judge of Northumberland and Luzerne Counties in 1785; appointed deputy surveyor of Chester County on April 18, 1787; member of the first Pennsylvania senate in 1790; appointed justice of the peace for Northumberland County in 1791; elected to the Third Congress (March 4, 1793-March 3, 1795); commissioned major general of Pennsylvania Militia in 1793 and served for fourteen years; associate judge of Northumberland County 1801-1813; upon the establishment of a post office at Danville, he was made its first postmaster and served from April 1, 1801, to April 1, 1803; died in Danville, Montour County, Pa., May 1, 1816.

**MONTGOMERY, William,** a Representative from Pennsylvania; born in Canton Township, Washington County, Pa., April 11, 1818; pursued classical studies and was graduated from Washington (now Washington and Jefferson) College, Washington, Pa., in 1839; studied law; was admitted to the bar in 1841 and commenced practice in Washington, Pa.; district attorney in 1845; unsuccessful candidate for election in 1854 to the Thirty-fourth Congress; elected as a Democrat to the Thirty-fifth and Thirty-sixth Congresses (March 4, 1857-March 3, 1861); was not a candidate for renomination in 1860; resumed the practice of law; unsuccessful candidate for election in 1866 to the Fortieth Congress; died in Washington, Pa., April 28, 1870; interment in Washington Cemetery.

**MONTOYA, Joseph Manuel,** a Representative and a Senator from New Mexico; born in Penablanca, Sandoval County, N.Mex., September 24, 1915; attended Regis College, Denver, Colo., 1931, 1933-1934; LL.B., Georgetown University Law School, Washington, D.C., 1938; was admitted to the bar in 1939 and commenced the practice of law in Santa Fe, N.Mex.; elected to the New Mexico State house of representatives in 1936, reelected in 1938, and was majority leader in 1939 and 1940; New Mexico State senator, 1940-1946, and served as majority whip; lieutenant governor of New Mexico 1947-1951; unsuccessful candidate for election in 1950 to the Eighty-second Congress; New Mexico State senator, 1953-1954; lieutenant governor of New Mexico 1955-1957; elected as a Democrat to the Eighty-fifth Congress, April 9, 1957, by special election, to fill the vacancy caused by the death of Antonio M. Fernandez; reelected to the three succeeding Congresses and served from April 9, 1957, until his resignation November 3, 1964, having been elected as a Democrat to the United States Senate, November 3, 1964, to complete the unexpired term of Dennis Chavez for the term ending January 3, 1965, and at the same time elected for the six-year term ending January 3, 1971; reelected in 1970 and served from November 4, 1964, until January 3, 1977; unsuccessful candidate for reelection in 1976; died in Washington, D.C., June 5, 1978; interment in Rosario Cemetery, Santa Fe, N.Mex.

**Bibliography:** *DAB.*

**MONTOYA, Nestor,** a Representative from New Mexico; born in Old Albuquerque, Bernalillo County, N.Mex., April 14, 1862; attended the common schools, and was graduated from St. Michael's College, Santa Fe, N.Mex., in 1881; began newspaper work in 1889; owned and edited the Spanish paper called "La Bandera Americana"; member of the Territorial house of representatives 1892-1903 and served as speaker in the latter year; member of the Territorial senate in 1905 and 1906; president of the State press association 1908-1923; delegate to the convention that drafted and adopted the State constitution of New Mexico in 1910; regent of the University of New Mexico 1916-1919; member of the Council of National Defense 1917-1919; chairman of the Bernalillo County draft board during the First World War; clerk of Bernalillo County in 1919 and 1920; elected as a Republican to the Sixty-seventh Congress and served from March 4, 1921, until his death in Washington, D.C., January 13, 1923; interment in Santa Barbara Cemetery, Albuquerque, N.Mex.

**MOODY, Arthur Edson Blair,** a Senator from Michigan; born in New Haven, Conn., February 13, 1902; attended the public schools in Providence, R.I.; graduated from Brown University, Providence, R.I., in 1922; instructor in history, Moses Brown Preparatory School, Providence, R.I., 1922-1923; moved to Detroit, Mich.; worked as a reporter covering Washington, D.C., for the Detroit News from 1923 until 1951; correspondent for Barron's Financial Weekly, 1934-1948, and also wrote extensively for the North American Newspaper Alliance and the Bell Syndicate; combat war correspondent in 1944, covering the war in Italy, Africa, the British Isles, the Middle East, and Iran; moderated a radio and television program "Meet Your Congress," 1946-1952; foreign correspondent, 1947-1948; appointed as a Democrat to the United States Senate to fill the vacancy caused by the death of Arthur H. Vandenberg, and served from April 23, 1951 to November 4, 1952; unsuccessful candidate for election to fill the vacancy, and also for election to the full term; resumed his newspaper and radio career; died in Ann Arbor, Mich., while campaigning for the Democratic nomination for United States Senator, July 20, 1954; interment in Woodlawn Cemetery, Detroit, Mich.

**MOODY, Gideon Curtis,** a Senator from South Dakota; born in Cortland, Cortland County, N.Y., October 16, 1832; attended the common schools and pursued an academic course; studied law in Syracuse, N.Y.; moved to Indiana in 1852, and was admitted to the bar in 1853; appointed prosecuting attorney for Floyd County in 1854; member, Indiana State house of representatives, 1861; during the Civil War entered the Union Army as a captain in April 1861 and served as captain, lieutenant colonel, and colonel, until his resignation in March 1864; moved to the Territory of Dakota in 1864; member, Territorial house of representatives, 1867-1868, 1868-1869, 1874-1875, serving as speaker 1868-1869, 1874-1875; associate justice of the supreme court of the Territory of Dakota from 1878 to 1883; member of the constitutional conventions of South Dakota in 1883 and 1885; upon the admission of South Dakota as a State into the Union was elected as a Republican to the United States Senate, and served from November 2, 1889 to March 3, 1891; unsuccessful candidate for reelection; died in Los Angeles, Calif., March 17, 1904; interment in Rosedale Cemetery.

**MOODY, James Montraville,** a Representative from North Carolina; born near what is now Robbinsville, Graham (then Cherokee) County, N.C., February 12, 1858; moved with his parents to Haywood County; attended the common schools and Waynesville Academy, also Candler College, Buncombe County, N.C.; studied law; was admitted to the bar in 1881 and commenced practice in Waynesville, Haywood County, N.C.; delegate to the Republican State conventions in 1888, 1892, 1896, and 1900; prosecuting attorney of the twelfth judicial district of North Carolina from 1886 until 1900; member of the North Carolina State senate, 1894-1896; delegate to the Republican National Conventions of 1896 and 1900; during the Spanish-American War served as major and chief commissary of United States Volunteers on the staff of Major General J. Warren Keifer; elected as a Republican to the Fifty-seventh Congress and served from March 4, 1901, until his death in Waynesville, N.C., February 5, 1903; interment in Green Hill Cemetery.

**MOODY, Jim,** a Representative from Wisconsin; born James Powers Moody in Richlands, Tazewell County, Va., September 2, 1935; B.A., Haverford (Pa.) College, 1957; M.P.A., Harvard University, 1967; Ph.D., economics, University of California, Berkeley, 1973; Peace Corps and CARE assignments in Yugoslavia, Iran, and Pakistan, 1958-1965; economist for Federal Government, 1967-1969; member, Wisconsin State assembly, 1977-1978; Wisconsin State senator, 1979-1982; delegate, Wisconsin State Democratic conventions, 1977-1982; elected as a Democrat to the Ninety-eighth and to the four succeeeding Congresses (January 3, 1983-January 3, 1993); was not a candidate in 1992 for renomination to the House of Representatives, but was an unsuccessful candidate for nomination to the United States Senate; is a resident of Milwaukee, Wis.

**MOODY, Malcolm Adelbert,** a Representative from Oregon; born in Linn County, near the present town of Brownsville, Oreg., November 30, 1854; moved with his parents to Illinois the next year and to The Dalles, Wasco County, Oreg., in 1862; attended the public schools and the University of California at Berkeley; engaged in mercantile pursuits at The Dalles, Oreg.; cashier of The Dalles National Bank; member of the city council, 1885-1889; elected mayor of The Dalles in 1889 and served two terms; member of the Republican State central and congressional committees from 1888 to 1898; elected as a Republican to the Fifty-sixth and Fifty-seventh Congresses (March 4, 1899-March 3, 1903); was not a candidate for renomination in 1902 to the Fifty-eighth Congress; resumed the mercantile business at The Dalles, Oreg.; died in Portland, Oreg., on March 19, 1925; interment in Odd Fellows Cemetery, The Dalles, Oreg.

**MOODY, William Henry,** a Representative from Massachusetts; born in Newbury, Mass., December 23, 1853; was graduated from Phillips Academy, Andover, Mass., in 1872 and from Harvard University in 1876; studied law; was admitted to the bar in 1878 and practiced in Haverhill, Mass.; city solicitor, 1888-1890; district attorney for the eastern district of Massachusetts, 1890-1895; elected as a Republican to the Fifty-fourth Congress to fill the vacancy caused by the death of William Cogswell; reelected to the three succeeding Congresses and served from November 5, 1895, until his resignation on May 1, 1902; appointed Secretary of the Navy in the Cabinet of President Theodore Roosevelt, and served from May 1, 1902 until June 30, 1904; served as Attorney General from July 1, 1904 until December 12, 1906; nominated on December 3, 1906, by President Theodore Roosevelt as an Associate Justice of the United States Supreme Court; was confirmed by the Senate on December 12, 1906, and served from December 16, 1906, until his retirement by special act of Congress approved June 23, 1910, on account of ill health; died in Haverhill, Mass., July 2, 1917; interment in Byfield Cemetery, Georgetown, Mass.

**Bibliography:** *DAB*; McDonough, Judith Rene. "William Henry Moody." Ph.D. dissertation, Auburn University, 1983.

**MOON, John Austin,** a Representative from Tennessee; born near Charlottesville, Albemarle County, Va., April 22, 1855; moved with his parents to Bristol, Va., in 1857 and then to Chattanooga, Tenn., in 1870; attended private and public schools and King College, Bristol, Tenn.; studied law; was admitted to the bar in March 1874 and commenced practice in Chattanooga, Tenn.; city attorney of Chattanooga in 1881 and 1882; member of the State Democratic executive committee in 1888; was commissioned in May 1889 as special circuit judge, twice reappointed, and held the office until January 3, 1891; appointed regular judge for the fourth circuit and served until August 1892; elected circuit judge in 1892; reelected in 1894 for a term of eight years but resigned when elected to Congress; elected as a Democrat to the Fifty-fifth and to the eleven succeeding Congresses (March 4, 1897-March 3, 1921); chairman, Committee on the Post Office and Post Roads (Sixty-second through Sixty-fifth Congresses); delegate to the Democratic

National Convention in 1900; was renominated for Congress in 1921, but before election was taken ill and died in Chattanooga, Tenn., June 26, 1921; interment in Forest Hill Cemetery.

**MOON, John Wesley,** a Representative from Michigan; born near Ypsilanti, Wayne County, Mich., January 18, 1836; attended the common schools; moved to northern Michigan in 1854 and engaged in the lumber business; settled in Muskegon, Muskegon County, Mich., in 1856 and engaged in the manufacture of lumber and in banking; held the offices of supervisor, township treasurer, and president of the village; elected to the State senate in 1884 and reelected in 1886; elected president of the Muskegon Savings Bank in 1887; member of the board of education of Muskegon in 1891; elected as a Republican to the Fifty-third Congress (March 4, 1893-March 3, 1895); was not a candidate for renomination in 1894; resumed former business activities; died in Muskegon, Mich., April 5, 1898; interment in Evergreen Cemetery.

**MOON, Reuben Osborne,** a Representative from Pennsylvania; born in Jobstown, Burlington County, N.J., July 22, 1847; attended the common schools and was graduated from the National School of Oratory, in Philadelphia, in 1874; professor in the National School of Oratory; engaged in lecturing; studied law; was admitted to the bar in 1884 and commenced practice in Philadelphia; one of the founders and president of the Columbia Club; elected as a Republican to the Fifty-eighth Congress to fill the vacancy caused by the death of Robert H. Foerderer; reelected to the Fifty-ninth and to the three succeeding Congresses and served from November 2, 1903, to March 3, 1913; chairman, Committee on Revision of the Laws (Fifty-ninth through Sixty-first Congresses); unsuccessful candidate for renomination in 1912; continued the practice of law until his death in Philadelphia, Pa., on October 25, 1919; interment in West Laurel Hill Cemetery.

**MOONEY, Charles Anthony,** a Representative from Ohio; born in St. Marys, Auglaize County, Ohio, January 5, 1879; attended the public and Jesuit schools; was graduated from St. Marys High School in 1895; engaged in the life insurance business at St. Marys; moved to Cleveland, Ohio, in 1910 and continued the life insurance business; member of the State senate 1915-1919; elected as a Democrat to the Sixty-sixth Congress (March 4, 1919-March 3, 1921); unsuccessful candidate for reelection in 1920 to the Sixty-seventh Congress; delegate to the Democratic National Conventions in 1920, 1924, and 1928; elected to the Sixty-eighth and to the four succeeding Congresses and served from March 4, 1923, until his death in Cleveland, Ohio, on May 29, 1931; interment in Gethsemane Cemetery, St. Marys, Ohio.

**MOONEY, William Crittenden,** a Representative from Ohio; born in Beallsville, Monroe County, Ohio, June 15, 1855; attended the public schools and Ohio Wesleyan College at Delaware; engaged in banking and filled various positions, including that of president of the Monroe Bank of Woodsfield, Ohio; was a director of many manufacturing, insurance, and oil companies; elected as a Republican to the Sixty-fourth Congress (March 4, 1915-March 3, 1917); unsuccessful candidate for reelection in 1916 to the Sixty-fifth Congress; again engaged in banking; died in New York City, July 24, 1918; interment in Oaklawn Cemetery, Woodsfield, Monroe County, Ohio.

**MOOR, Wyman Bradbury Seavy,** a Senator from Maine; born in Waterville, Kennebec County, Maine, November 11, 1811; attended the town school; prepared for college at China Academy and graduated from Waterville College; taught school for one year in St. Stephen's, New Brunswick, and then returned to his native town to study law; attended Dane Law School, Cambridge, Mass.; was admitted to the bar in 1835 and commenced practice in Waterville, Maine; member, State house of representatives 1839; attorney general of Maine 1844-1848; moved to Bangor, Maine, in 1847 and continued the practice of his profession; appointed as a Democrat to the United States Senate to fill the vacancy caused by the death of John Fairfield and served from January 5, 1848, to June 7, 1848, when a successor was elected; resumed the practice of law in Bangor; returned to Waterville, Maine, in 1852 and continued his law practice; superintendent of the construction of a railroad from Waterville to Bangor; appointed by President James Buchanan as consul general to the British North American Provinces 1859-1861; returned to Waterville in 1861 and resumed the practice of law; purchased an estate near Lynchburg, Va., in 1868 and engaged in the operation of an iron furnace; died in Lynchburg, Va., March 10, 1869; interment in Pine Grove Cemetery, Waterville, Maine.

**MOORE, Allen Francis,** a Representative from Illinois; was born in St. Charles; Kane County, Ill., September 30, 1869; moved to Piatt County in 1870 with his parents, who settled in Monticello; attended the common schools; was graduated from the Monticello High School in 1886 and from Lombard College, Galesburg, Knox County, Ill., in 1889; engaged in the manufacture of proprietary medicines and later in banking; trustee of the University of Illinois 1908-1914; elected as a Republican to the Sixty-seventh and Sixty-eighth Congresses (March 4, 1921-March 3, 1925); declined to be a candidate for reelection in 1924 to the Sixty-ninth Congress; member of the Republican National Committee in 1925; resumed his former business pursuits in Monticello, Ill.; moved to San Antonio, Tex., in 1939 and engaged in oil development until his death there August 18, 1945; interment in Monticello Cemetery, Monticello, Ill.

**MOORE, Andrew** (father of Samuel McDowell Moore), a Representative and a Senator from Virginia; born at "Cannicello," near Fairfield, Rockbridge (formerly Augusta) County, Va., in 1752; attended Augusta Academy (now Washington and Lee University), Lexington, Va.; studied law; admitted to the bar in 1774 and practiced; served in the Revolutionary War as a captain until 1779; commissioned brigadier general, then major general of Virginia Militia; member, Virginia house of delegates 1780-1783, 1785-1788; delegate to the Virginia convention that ratified the Federal Constitution in 1788; elected to the First and to the three succeeding Congresses (March 4, 1789-March 3, 1797); member, Virginia house of delegates 1799-1800, and Virginia senate 1800-1801; successfully contested the election of Thomas Lewis to the Eighth Congress and served from March 5 to August 11, 1804, when he was appointed as a Republican to the United States Senate to fill the vacancy in the term beginning March 4, 1799, caused by the resignation of Wilson C. Nicholas; while holding the office of Senator-designate was elected on December 4, 1804, to fill the vacancy in the term beginning March 4, 1803, caused by the resignation of Abraham B. Venable and served successively in the two classes from August 11, 1804, until March 3, 1809; appointed United States marshal for the Commonwealth of Virginia in 1810 and served until his death in Lexington, Va., April 14, 1821; interment in Lexington Cemetery.

**Bibliography:** *DAB.*

**MOORE, Arch Alfred, Jr.,** a Representative from West Virginia; born in Moundsville, Marshall County, W.Va., April 16, 1923; educated in the public schools of Marshall County and studied at Lafayette College, Easton, Pa., in 1943; A.B., West Virginia University, 1948; LL.B., West Virginia University School of Law, 1951; admitted to the bar in 1951 and commenced the practice of law in Moundsville, W.Va.; served from May 15, 1943, to April 1, 1946, as a sergeant with the Three Hundred and Thirty-fourth Infantry Regiment with one year and a half in the European Theater; awarded the Bronze Star and Purple Heart Medal; member of the West Virginia State house of delegates, 1953-1955; elected as a Republican to the Eighty-fifth and to the five succeeding Congresses (January 3, 1957-January 3, 1969); was not a candidate for reelection in 1968 to the Ninety-first Congress, but was elected Governor of West Virginia; reelected in 1972, and served from

January 13, 1969 to January 17, 1977; unsuccessful candidate in 1978 for election to the United States Senate; elected Governor of West Virginia in 1984, and served from January 14, 1985 to January 16, 1989; unsuccessful candidate for reelection in 1988; is a resident of Glen Dale, W.Va.

**MOORE, Arthur Harry,** a Senator from New Jersey; born in Jersey City, N.J., July 3, 1879; attended the public schools and Cooper Union College, New York City; stenographer; graduated from the New Jersey Law School at Newark; was admitted to the bar in 1922 and commenced practice in Jersey City, N.J.; secretary to the mayor of Jersey City, 1908-1911; city collector, 1911-1913; commissioner of Jersey City, 1913-1925; elected Governor of New Jersey in 1925, and served from January 19, 1926 to January 15, 1929; again elected Governor in 1931, and served from January 19, 1932 until his resignation January 3, 1935, having been elected Senator; attained national prominence in 1932 when, as Governor, he took charge of the investigation into the kidnapping of Charles A. Lindbergh, Jr., son of the celebrated aviator; elected as a Democrat to the United States Senate, and served from January 3, 1935 to January 17, 1938, when he resigned, having been elected Governor; again elected Governor in 1937, and served from January 18, 1938 to January 21, 1941; resumed the practice of law in Jersey City, N.J.; died in Branchburg Township, Somerset County, N.J., November 18, 1952; interment in New York Bay Cemetery, Jersey City, N.J.

**MOORE, Charles Ellis,** a Representative from Ohio; born near Middlebourne, Guernsey County, Ohio, on January 3, 1884; attended the common schools and Mount Union College, Alliance, Ohio; taught school in Oxford Township, Ohio; was graduated from Muskingum College, New Concord, Ohio, in 1907 and from the law department of Ohio State University at Columbus in 1910; was admitted to the bar in 1910 and commenced practice in Cambridge, Guernsey County, Ohio; prosecuting attorney of Guernsey County 1914-1918; elected as a Republican to the Sixty-sixth and to the six succeeding Congresses (March 4, 1919-March 3, 1933); unsuccessful candidate for reelection in 1932 to the Seventy-third Congress; one of the managers appointed by the House of Representatives in 1926 to conduct the impeachment proceedings against George W. English, judge of the United States District Court for the Eastern District of Illinois; resumed the practice of law in Cambridge, Ohio; also engaged in the banking business; died in Cambridge, Guernsey County, Ohio, April 2, 1941; interment in Northwood Cemetery.

**MOORE, Edward Hall,** a Senator from Oklahoma; born on a farm near Maryville, Nodaway County, Mo., November 19, 1871; attended the public schools and Chillicothe (Mo.) Normal School; taught school in Nodaway, Atchinson, and Jackson Counties, Mo.; was graduated from the Kansas City School of Law in 1900; was admitted to the bar in 1901 and began practice in Maryville, Mo.; moved shortly thereafter to Okmulgee, Indian Territory, Okla., and practiced law until 1919; oil producer, farmer, and cattle raiser 1919-1942; elected as a Republican to the United States Senate in 1942 and served from January 3, 1943, to January 3, 1949; was not a candidate for renomination in 1948; retired from public life and political activities; died in Tulsa, Okla., September 2, 1950; interment in Okmulgee Cemetery, Okmulgee, Okla.

**MOORE, Eliakim Hastings,** a Representative from Ohio; born in Boylston, Worcester County, Mass., June 19, 1812; moved with his parents to Marietta and thence to Athens County, Ohio, in 1817; attended the common schools; educated himself at night as a civil engineer; county surveyor 1836-1846; auditor for Athens County 1846-1860; collector of internal revenue for the Marietta-Athens district of Ohio 1862-1866; organized the First National Bank of Athens in 1863 and was connected therewith as president and director until about 1895; elected as a Republican to the Forty-first Congress (March 4, 1869-March 3, 1871); was not a candidate for renomination in 1870; engaged in railroad enterprises in Athens, Athens County, Ohio; trustee of Ohio University at Athens; died in Athens April 4, 1900; interment in West Union Street Cemetery.

**Bibliography:** *DAB.*

**MOORE, Ely,** a Representative from New York; born near Belvidere, Warren County, N.J., July 4, 1798; attended the public schools; moved to New York City; studied medicine, but did not engage in extensive practice; became a printer and subsequently became editor of the National Trades Union, a labor paper in New York City; elected as a Jacksonian to the Twenty-fourth Congress and reelected as a Democrat to the Twenty-fifth Congress (March 4, 1835-March 3, 1839); political editor of the New York Evening Post in 1838 and 1839; president of the board of trade and surveyor of the port of New York City from 1839 until 1845; appointed by President James K. Polk United States marshal for the southern district of New York in 1845; became owner and editor of the Warren Journal of Belvidere, N.J.; appointed agent for the Miami and other tribes of Indians in Kansas in 1853; appointed register of the United States land office in Lecompton, Kans., in 1855 and served until 1860; died in Lecompton, Douglas County, Kans., January 27, 1860; interment on his farm near Lecompton.

**Bibliography:** *DAB*; Hugins, Walter Edward. "Ely Moore: The Case History of a Jacksonian Labor Leader." *Political Science Quarterly* 65 (March 1950): 105-25.

**MOORE, Gabriel,** a Representative and a Senator from Alabama; born in Stokes County, N.C., around 1785; pursued an academic course and graduated from the University of North Carolina at Chapel Hill in 1810; studied law; was admitted to the bar in 1810 and commenced practice in Huntsville, Mississippi Territory; member, Mississippi and then Alabama Territorial house of representatives, and served as speaker in 1817; delegate to the Alabama State constitutional convention in 1819; member, Alabama State senate, 1819-1820, and served as speaker in 1820; elected to the Seventeenth and to the three succeeding Congresses (March 4, 1821-March 3, 1829); was not a candidate for renomination in 1828 to the Twenty-first Congress; elected Governor of Alabama in 1829, and served from November 25, 1829 to March 3, 1831; elected to the United States Senate, and served from March 4, 1831 to March 3, 1837; chairman, Committee on Revolutionary Claims (Twenty-second through Twenty-fourth Congresses); unsuccessful candidate for election in 1836 to the Twenty-fifth Congress; moved to Caddo, Tex., in 1843, where he is thought to have died in 1845.

**Bibliography:** *DAB*; Martin, John. "The Senatorial Career of Gabriel Moore." *Alabama Historical Quarterly* 26 (Summer 1964): 249-81.

**MOORE, Heman Allen,** a Representative from Ohio; born in Plainfield, Washington County, Vt., August 27, 1809; pursued an academic course; studied law in Rochester, N.Y.; was admitted to the bar and commenced practice in Columbus, Ohio; elected as a Democrat to the Twenty-eighth Congress and served from March 4, 1843, until his death in Columbus, Ohio, April 3, 1844; interment in Greenlawn Cemetery.

**MOORE, Henry Dunning,** a Representative from Pennsylvania; born in Goshen, Orange County, N.Y., April 13, 1817; moved with his parents to New York City in 1828; attended the public schools; engaged in the tailoring business; moved to Philadelphia, Pa., in 1844 and engaged in the mahogany and marble business; elected as a Whig to the Thirty-first and Thirty-second Congresses (March 4, 1849-March 3, 1853); was not a candidate for reelection in 1852; unsuccessful candidate for mayor of Philadelphia in 1856; elected Pennsylvania treasurer during Governor Curtin's administration and served 1861-1863, 1864-1865; appointed collector of the port of Philadelphia, Pa., on March 30, 1869, and served until March 26, 1871, when he resigned; traveled in Europe and resided in St.

Petersburg, Russia, 1870-1877; became associated with and managed the silver mines known as "The Daisy" in Big Evens Gulch near Leadville, Colo., from 1885 until his death there on August 11, 1887; interment in Monument Cemetery, Philadelphia, Pa.

**MOORE, Horace Ladd,** a Representative from Kansas; born in Mantua, Portage County, Ohio, February 25, 1837; attended the common schools and the Western Reserve Eclectic Institute, Hiram, Ohio; moved to Lawrence, Douglas County, Kans., in 1858; studied law and one month after his admission to the bar enlisted in the Union Army in the Second Regiment, Kansas Volunteer Infantry, on May 14, 1861, and served continuously until June 30, 1865, when he was mustered out of the service as lieutenant colonel of the Fourth Regiment, Arkansas Volunteer Cavalry; as major of the Eighteenth and colonel of the Nineteenth Regiments of Kansas Cavalry served against the Indians on the Plains in 1867 and 1868; again engaged in the practice of law and later, from 1886 to 1892, engaged in the wholesale grocery business in Trinidad, Colo.; treasurer of Douglas County, Kans., in 1886 and 1887; successfully contested as a Democrat the election of Edward H. Funston to the Fifty-third Congress and served from August 2, 1894, until March 3, 1895; unsuccessful candidate for reelection in 1894 to the Fifty-fourth Congress; vice president of a national bank in Lawrence, Kans., until his death on May 1, 1914; interment in Oak Hill Cemetery.

**MOORE, Jesse Hale,** a Representative from Illinois; born near Lebanon, St. Clair County, Ill., April 22, 1817; was graduated from McKendree College, Lebanon, Ill., in 1842; taught school in Nashville, Ill., 1842-1844; and at Georgetown, Ill., 1844-1848; studied for the ministry and was ordained a Methodist minister in 1849; served in the Union Army as colonel of the One Hundred and Fifteenth Regiment, Illinois Volunteer Infantry, September 13, 1862; honorably mustered out June 11, 1865; presiding elder of the Decatur district of the Illinois conference in 1868 and resided in Decatur, Ill.; elected as a Republican to the Forty-first and Forty-second Congresses (March 4, 1869-March 3, 1873); chairman, Committee on Invalid Pensions (Forty-second Congress); unsuccessful candidate for renomination in 1872 to the Forty-third Congress; United States pension agent, Springfield, Ill., 1873-1877; served as pastor of Mechanicsburg (Ill.) Methodist Church; was appointed by President Chester A. Arthur as United States consul at Callao, Peru, October 27, 1881, and served until his death there on July 11, 1883; interment in Callao, Peru; reinterment in Greenwood Cemetery, Decatur, Ill.

**MOORE, John,** a Representative from Louisiana; born in Berkeley County, Va. (now West Virginia), in 1788; pursued an academic course; moved to Franklin, La.; member of the State house of representatives 1825-1834; elected as a Whig to the Twenty-sixth Congress to fill the vacancy caused by the resignation of Rice Garland; reelected to the Twenty-seventh Congress and served from December 17, 1840, to March 3, 1843; chairman, Committee on Private Land Claims (Twenty-seventh Congress); moved to New Iberia, La.; elected to the Thirty-second Congress (March 4, 1851-March 3, 1853); delegate to the State secession convention in 1861; died in Franklin, La., June 17, 1867; interment on his estate, "The Shadows," near New Iberia, Iberia Parish, La.

**MOORE, John Matthew,** a Representative from Texas; born on a farm near Richmond, Fort Bend County, Tex., November 18, 1862; attended the common schools and the Agricultural and Mechanical College, College Station, Tex.; engaged in mercantile pursuits, banking, stock raising, and farming; member of the State house of representatives 1896-1898; declined to be a candidate for renomination; delegate to the Democratic National Convention in 1900 and 1916; elected as a Democrat to the Fifty-ninth Congress to fill the vacancy caused by the death of John M. Pinckney; reelected to the Sixtieth, Sixty-first, and Sixty-second Congresses and served from June 6, 1905, to March 3, 1913; was was not a candidate for renomination in 1912; continued agricultural pursuits and stock raising near Richmond, Fort Bend County, Tex., until his death February 3, 1940; interment in Morton Cemetery.

**MOORE, John William,** a Representative from Kentucky; born in Morgantown, Butler County, Ky., June 9, 1877; attended the public schools and completed a commercial course at Bryant and Stratton College at Louisville in 1897; became a clerk with the Morgantown Deposit Bank in 1898; engaged in the timber business 1899-1919; cashier for the Morgantown Deposit Bank 1920-1925; elected as a Democrat to the Sixty-ninth Congress to fill the vacancy caused by the death of Robert Y. Thomas, Jr.; reelected to the Seventieth Congress and served from November 3, 1925, to March 3, 1929; was an unsuccessful candidate for reelection in 1928 to the Seventy-first Congress, but was subsequently elected to the Seventy-first Congress to fill the vacancy caused by the death of Charles W. Roark; reelected to the Seventy-second Congress and served from June 1, 1929, to March 3, 1933; was not a candidate for renomination in 1932; resumed his former business pursuits; employed in the Federal Housing Administration at Washington, D.C., as an assistant comptroller 1935-1941; died in Washington, D.C., December 11, 1941; interment in Morgantown Cemetery, Morgantown, Ky.

**MOORE, Joseph Hampton,** a Representative from Pennsylvania; born in Woodbury, Gloucester County, N.J., March 8, 1864; attended the common schools until the age of thirteen, and worked in an attorney's office for four years; studied law; reporter on the Philadelphia Public Ledger and the Court Combination, 1881-1894; chief clerk to the city treasurer of Philadelphia, 1894-1897; secretary to Mayor Samuel S. Ashbridge of Philadelphia in 1900; president of the Allied Republican Clubs of Philadelphia, of the Pennsylvania State League, and of the National League of Republican Clubs, 1900-1906; Philadelphia city treasurer, 1901-1903; appointed by President Theodore Roosevelt as the first Chief of the Bureau of Manufactures, Department of Commerce and Labor, in January 1905, but resigned after six months' service to become president of the City Trust, Safe Deposit and Surety Co. of Philadelphia; president of the Atlantic Deeper Waterways Association, 1907-1947; elected as a Republican to the Fifty-ninth Congress to fill the vacancy caused by the death of George A. Castor; reelected to the Sixtieth and to the six succeeding Congresses, and served from November 6, 1906 to January 4, 1920, when he resigned to become mayor of Philadelphia; delegate to the Republican National Convention of 1920; mayor of Philadelphia, Pa., 1920-1923; appointed by the State Department as a delegate to the International Navigation Congress at Cairo, Egypt, in 1926; again elected mayor of Philadelphia, 1932-1935; unsuccessful candidate for nomination for mayor in 1927 and 1939; died in Philadelphia, Pa., May 2, 1950; interment in West Laurel Hill Cemetery.

**Bibliography:** Drayer, Robert E. "J. Hampton Moore: An Old Fashioned Republican." Ph.D. dissertation, University of Pennsylvania, 1961; Moore, Joseph Hampton. *With Speaker Cannon Through the Tropics: A Descriptive Story of a Voyage to the West Indies, Venezuela and Panama.* Philadelphia: The Book Print, 1907.

**MOORE, Laban Theodore,** a Representative from Kentucky; born in Wayne County, Va. (now West Virginia), near Louisa, Ky., January 13, 1829; attended Marshall Academy in Virginia and was graduated from Marietta College in Ohio; attended Transylvania Law College at Lexington; was admitted to the bar in 1849 and commenced practice in Louisa, Ky.; unsuccessful candidate for election 1857 to the Kentucky house of representatives; elected as an Opposition Party candidate to the Thirty-sixth Congress (March 4, 1859-March 3, 1861); was not a candidate for renomination in 1860; during the Civil War raised and enlisted the Fourteenth Regiment, Kentucky Volunteer Infantry, of which he was elected colonel November 19, 1861, and resigned January 1, 1862; moved to

Catlettsburg, where he resumed the practice of law; became a Democrat after the war; member of the Kentucky senate in 1881; member of the Kentucky constitutional convention in 1890 and 1891; died in Catlettsburg, Boyd County, Ky., November 9, 1892; interment in Ashland Cemetery, Ashland, Ky.

**MOORE, Littleton Wilde,** a Representative from Texas; born in Marion County, Ala., March 25, 1835; moved with his parents to Mississippi in 1836; was graduated from the University of Mississippi at Oxford in 1855; studied law and was admitted to the bar in 1857; moved to Texas in 1857 and commenced practice in Bastrop; served as captain in the Confederate Army throughout the Civil War; elected to the State constitutional convention in 1875; district judge 1876-1885; elected as a Democrat to the Fiftieth, Fifty-first, and Fifty-second Congresses (March 4, 1887-March 3, 1893); resumed the practice of his profession; appointed judge of the twenty-second judicial district in 1901 and served until his death in Lagrange, Fayette County, Tex., October 29, 1911; interment in the City Cemetery.

**MOORE, Nicholas Ruxton,** a Representative from Maryland; born near Baltimore Town, Baltimore County, Md., July 21, 1756; attended the common schools; member of Gist's Baltimore Independent Cadets and served throughout the greater part of the Revolutionary War, attaining the rank of captain; took an active part in the suppression of the Whiskey Rebellion of 1794; member of the Maryland State house of delegates, 1801-1802; elected as a Republican to the Eighth and to the three succeeding Congresses (March 4, 1803-March 3, 1811); chairman, Committee on Accounts (Tenth and Eleventh Congresses); unsuccessful candidate for reelection in 1810 to the Twelfth Congress; appointed lieutenant colonel commandant of the sixth regimental cavalry district of Maryland on February 20, 1812; elected to the Thirteenth and Fourteenth Congresses, and served from March 4, 1813, until his resignation in 1815 before the convening of the Fourteenth Congress; chairman, Committee on Accounts (Thirteenth Congress); died in Baltimore, Md., October 7, 1816; interment in a private cemetery near Ruxton, Baltimore County, Md.

**MOORE, Orren Cheney,** a Representative from New Hampshire; born in New Hampton, Belknap County, N.H., August 10, 1839; attended the public schools; learned the trade of printer and became a journalist; member of the State house of representatives in 1863, 1864, 1875, 1876, and 1878; established the Nashua Daily Telegraph in 1869; member of the State tax commission in 1878; served in the State senate 1879-1881; again a member of the State house of representatives in 1887; chairman of the State railroad commission 1884-1888; elected as a Republican to the Fifty-first Congress (March 4, 1889-March 3, 1891); unsuccessful candidate for reelection in 1890 to the Fifty-second Congress; resumed former pursuits as editor and publisher; died in Nashua, Hillsborough County, N.H., on May 12, 1893; interment in the Woodlawn Cemetery.

**MOORE, Oscar Fitzallen,** a Representative from Ohio; born in Lagrange, Jefferson County, Ohio, January 27, 1817; attended the public schools and Wellsburg Academy, and was graduated from Washington (now Washington and Jefferson) College, Washington, Pa., in 1836; studied law; was admitted to the bar in 1838 and commenced practice in Portsmouth, Ohio, in 1839; member of the State house of representatives in 1850 and 1851; member of the State senate in 1852 and 1853; elected as a Republican to the Thirty-fourth Congress (March 4, 1855-March 3, 1857); unsuccessful candidate for reelection in 1856 to the Thirty-fifth Congress; served as lieutenant colonel and later as colonel of the Thirty-third Regiment, Ohio Volunteer Infantry, during the Civil War; resumed the practice of his profession in Portsmouth, Ohio; died at Waverly, Ohio, June 24, 1885; interment in Greenlawn Cemetery, Portsmouth, Ohio.

**MOORE, Paul John,** a Representative from New Jersey; born in Newark, N.J., August 5, 1868; attended the public and parochial schools and St. Benedict's College, at Newark, N.J.; entered the fire department November 1, 1892, and was promoted through the ranks to chief engineer, serving until his retirement on August 1, 1924, when he engaged as a fire-fighting-equipment salesman; elected as a Democrat to the Seventieth Congress (March 4, 1927-March 3, 1929); unsuccessful candidate for reelection in 1928 to the Seventy-first Congress and for election in 1930 to the Seventy-second Congress; served as chairman of the Essex County Democratic committee in 1928 and 1929; again engaged as a fire-fighting-equipment salesman in Newark, N.J., until 1931, when he moved to Maplewood, N.J., and retired; died in Newark, N.J., January 10, 1938; interment in Holy Sepulchre Cemetery, East Orange, N.J.

**MOORE, Robert** (grandfather of Michael Daniel Harter), a Representative from Pennsylvania; born on a farm near Washington, Washington County, Pa., March 30, 1778; pursued an academic course; attended Washington (now Washington and Jefferson) College, Washington, Pa.; studied law; admitted to the bar in 1802 and commenced practice in Beaver, Beaver County, Pa.; treasurer of Beaver County 1805-1811; served in the Pennsylvania Militia in the War of 1812; elected as a Republican to the Fifteenth and Sixteenth Congresses (March 4, 1817-March 3, 1821); was not a candidate for renomination; resumed the practice of law; member of the Pennsylvania house of representatives in 1830 and 1831; died in Beaver, Pa., January 14, 1831; interment in Beaver Cemetery.

**MOORE, Robert Lee,** a Representative from Georgia; born near Scarboro, Screven County, Ga., November 27, 1867; attended the common schools, Scarboro Academy, Georgia Military College, Milledgeville, Ga., and Moore's Business University, Atlanta, Ga.; was graduated from the law department of the University of Georgia at Athens in 1890; was admitted to the bar and commenced practice in Statesboro, Ga., the same year; mayor of Statesboro in 1906 and 1907; solicitor general of the middle judicial circuit 1913-1916; elected as a Democrat to the Sixty-eighth Congress (March 4, 1923-March 3, 1925); unsuccessful candidate for renomination in 1924; continued the practice of law in Statesboro, Ga., until his death there on January 14, 1940; interment in the City Cemetery.

**MOORE, Robert Walton,** a Representative from Virginia; born in Fairfax, Fairfax County, Va., February 6, 1859; attended the Episcopal High School near Alexandria, Va., and the University of Virginia at Charlottesville; studied law; admitted to the bar in 1880 and practiced in Virginia and Washington, D.C.; member of the Virginia senate 1887-1890; member of the Virginia constitutional convention in 1901 and 1902; president of the Virginia State Bar Association in 1911; member of the board of visitors to the College of William and Mary and the University of Virginia; from 1907 until the First World War was special counsel for carriers of the South in cases before the Interstate Commerce Commission, the Commerce Court, and the United States Supreme Court; assistant general counsel of the United States Railroad Administration in 1918 and 1919; elected as a Democrat to the Sixty-sixth Congress to fill the vacancy caused by the resignation of Charles C. Carlin; reelected to the Sixty-seventh and to the four succeeding Congresses and served from May 27, 1919, to March 3, 1931; was not a candidate for renomination in 1930; appointed a member of the Board of Regents of the Smithsonian Institution December 7, 1922; appointed as Assistant Secretary of State by President Franklin D. Roosevelt September 19, 1933, was made counselor in 1937, and served until his death in Fairfax, Va., February 8, 1941; interment in Fairfax Cemetery.

**MOORE, Samuel,** a Representative from Pennsylvania; born in Deerfield (now Deerfield Street), Cumberland County, N.J., February 8, 1774; pursued an academic course and graduated from the University of Pennsylvania at Philadelphia in 1791; instructor in the university 1792-1794; studied medicine and practiced in Dublin, Bucks County, Pa., and later at Greenwich, N.J.; spent several years in trading to the East Indies; returned to Bucks County, Pa., and in 1808 purchased and operated grist and oil mills at Bridge Point (now Edison) near Doylestown; later erected and operated a sawmill and woolen factory; elected as a Republican to the Fifteenth Congress to fill the vacancy caused by the resignation of Samuel D. Ingham; reelected to the Sixteenth and Seventeenth Congresses and served from October 13, 1818, until his resignation May 20, 1822; chairman, Committee on Indian Affairs (Seventeenth Congress); appointed by President James Monroe as Director of the United States Mint on July 15, 1824, and served until 1835; moved to Philadelphia, Pa.; became interested in the mining and marketing of coal and served as president of the Hazleton Coal Co. until his death in Philadelphia, Pa. February 18, 1861; interment in Woodland Cemetery.

**MOORE, Samuel McDowell** (son of Andrew Moore), a Representative from Virginia; born in Philadelphia, Pa., on February 9, 1796; attended the public schools and Washington College (now Washington and Lee University), Lexington, Va., where he settled after leaving college; member of the Virginia house of delegates 1825-1833; member of the Virginia constitutional convention of 1829; elected as an Anti-Jacksonian to the Twenty-third Congress (March 4, 1833-March 3, 1835); unsuccessful candidate for reelection in 1834 to the Twenty-fourth Congress; again a member of the house of delegates in 1836 and 1837; served in the Virginia senate 1845-1847; delegate to the secession convention in 1861; during the Civil War served in the Confederate Army; resumed the practice of his profession; died in Lexington, Rockbridge County, Va., on September 17, 1875; interment in Lexington Cemetery.

**MOORE, Sydenham,** a Representative from Alabama; born in Rutherford County, Tenn., May 25, 1817; pursued classical studies; attended the University of Alabama at Tuscaloosa, 1833-1836; studied law; was admitted to the bar and commenced practice in Greensboro, Ala.; judge of the Greene County court, 1840-1846, and 1848-1850; judge of the circuit court in 1857; served in the war with Mexico as captain in Colonel Coffey's regiment of Alabama Infantry from June 1846 to June 1847; elected brigadier general of Alabama Militia; elected as a Democrat to the Thirty-fifth and Thirty-sixth Congresses and served from March 4, 1857, until January 21, 1861, when he joined other secessionist members of the Alabama delegation in withdrawing from the Thirty-sixth Congress; during the Civil War served as colonel of the Eleventh Alabama Regiment in the Confederate Army; died in Richmond, Va., from wounds received in the Battle of Seven Pines, Virginia, May 31, 1862; interment in the City Cemetery, Greensboro, Hale County, Ala.

**MOORE, Thomas,** a Representative from South Carolina; born in Spartanburg District, S.C., in 1759; served in the Revolutionary War, taking part in the Battle of Cowpens at the age of sixteen; member of the South Carolina State house of representatives, 1794-1799; brigadier general in the War of 1812; engaged in planting; was one of the founders of the first high school in Spartanburg District; elected as a Republican to the Seventh and to the five succeeding Congresses (March 4, 1801-March 3, 1813); elected to the Fourteenth Congress (March 4, 1815-March 3, 1817); resumed his agricultural pursuits; died near Moores Station, Spartanburg County, S.C., on July 11, 1822; interment in Moore's Burying Ground.

**MOORE, Thomas Love,** a Representative from Virginia; born near Charles Town, Jefferson County, Va. (now West Virginia); pursued an academic course; studied law and practiced; elected to the Sixteenth Congress to fill the vacancy caused by the resignation of George F. Strother; reelected to the Seventeenth Congress and served from November 13, 1820, to March 3, 1823; resumed the practice of law at Warrenton, Va.; made the principal speech upon the visit of General Lafayette to Warrenton on August 23, 1825; died in Warrenton, Fauquier County, Va., in 1862; interment in Warrenton Cemetery.

**MOORE, Thomas Patrick,** a Representative from Kentucky; born in Charlotte County, Va., in 1797; attended the common schools; moved with his parents to Harrodsburg, Mercer County, Ky.; attended Transylvania University, Lexington, Ky.; served in the War of 1812; captain in the Twelfth Virginia Infantry March 12, 1812; major in the Eighteenth Infantry September 20, 1813; honorably discharged June 15, 1815; member of the Kentucky house of representatives in 1819 and 1820; elected to the Eighteenth, Nineteenth, and Twentieth Congresses (March 4, 1823-March 3, 1829); chairman, Committee on Revisal and Unfinished Business (Nineteenth Congress); appointed by President Andrew Jackson as Minister Plenipotentiary to Colombia on March 13, 1829, and served until April 16, 1833; returned to Kentucky; presented credentials as a Member-elect to the Twenty-third Congress, but the election was contested by Robert P. Letcher and the House declared a new election necessary; appointed lieutenant colonel of the Third United States Dragoons in the war with Mexico and served from March 3, 1847, to July 31, 1848; delegate to the Kentucky constitutional convention in 1849 and 1850; died in Harrodsburg, Ky., July 21, 1853.

**Bibliography:** *DAB.*

**MOORE, William,** a Representative from New Jersey; born in Norristown, Montgomery County, Pa., December 25, 1810; attended private schools for a short time; became engaged in mercantile pursuits and later in ironworks; moved to New Jersey in 1845 and settled in Weymouth; engaged in the iron business; also became interested in the building and sailing of vessels and in the development of banks and other financial institutions; judge of the court of common pleas for Atlantic County 1855-1865; was one of the founders of the Republican Party and a delegate to the Republican National Convention in 1856; moved to Mays Landing, N.J., in 1865 and engaged in the shipbuilding business, in banking, and in the iron industry; elected as a Republican to the Fortieth and Forty-first Congresses (March 4, 1867-March 3, 1871); chairman, Committee on Expenditures in the Post Office Department (Forty-first Congress); unsuccessful candidate for renomination in 1870; resumed his former business pursuits; served in the State senate 1872-1875; died at Mays Landing, N.J., April 26, 1878; interment in Union Cemetery.

**MOORE, William Henson, III,** a Representative from Louisiana; born in Lake Charles, Calcasieu Parish, La., October 4, 1939; graduated from Baton Rouge High School, 1958; B.A., Louisiana State University, Baton Rouge, 1961, and M.A., 1973; J.D., Louisiana State University School of Law, 1965; admitted to the Louisiana bar in 1966 and commenced practice in Baton Rouge, 1967; served in the United States Army, 1965-1967; elected a member of the Louisiana Republican State Central Committee, 1971-1975; delegate to the Republican National Convention of 1984; elected as a Republican to the Ninety-fourth Congress, November 5, 1974, but election was contested, and the result was vacated by the Louisiana Courts and a new election was ordered; elected by special election, January 7, 1975; reelected to the five succeeding Congresses and served from January 7, 1975, to January 3, 1987; was not a candidate for reelection in 1986 to the House of Representatives, but was an unsuccessful candidate for election to the United States Senate; resumed the practice of law with the firm of Sutherland, Asbill & Brennan in Washington, D.C.; appointed by President Ronald Reagan in 1987 a Commissioner to the Panama Canal Consultative Committee; resident of Baton Rouge, La., and Washington, D.C.

**MOORE, William Robert,** a Representative from Tennessee; born in Huntsville, Ala., March 28, 1830; moved to Beech Grove, Tenn., while an infant, and when six years old the family settled in Fosterville, Rutherford County; attended the district schools; at the age of fifteen became a clerk in a dry-goods store in Beech Grove and later in Nashville, Tenn.; engaged in the wholesale dry-goods business in New York City as a salesman from 1856 until 1859; moved to Memphis, Tenn., in 1859 and organized a wholesale dry-goods store; elected as a Republican to the Forty-seventh Congress (March 4, 1881-March 3, 1883); was not a candidate for renomination in 1882 to the Forty-eighth Congress; resumed his business activities; member, Tennessee State house of representatives, 1889-1891; died in Memphis, Tenn., June 12, 1909; interment in Forest Hill Cemetery.

**MOORE, William Sutton,** a Representative from Pennsylvania; born near Amity, Amwell Township, Washington County, Pa., November 18, 1822; attended the rural schools, and was graduated from Washington (now Washington and Jefferson) College, Washington, Pa., in 1847; studied law; was admitted to the bar in November 1848 and commenced practice in Washington, Pa.; prothonotary of Washington County, 1854-1857; delegate to the Republican National Convention of 1856; also engaged in the newspaper business as editor and part owner of the Reporter in 1857; treasurer of Washington County, 1863-1866; elected as a Republican to the Forty-third Congress (March 4, 1873-March 3, 1875); was not a candidate for renomination in 1874 to the Forty-fourth Congress; died in Washington, Pa., December 30, 1877; interment in Washington Cemetery.

**Bibliography:** Moore, Joseph William. "The Life of William Sutton Moore: A Washington County Editor." *Western Pennsylvania Historical Magazine* 44 (December 1961): 361-382.

**MOOREHEAD, Tom Van Horn,** a Representative from Ohio; born in Zanesville, Muskingum County, Ohio, April 12, 1898; attended the public schools, Ohio Wesleyan University at Delaware, and George Washington University at Washington, D.C.; during the First World War served in United States Naval Aviation Corps; engaged in the real estate and insurance business in Zanesville, Ohio; member of city council and mayor of Zanesville; member of the State senate (eight terms); elected as a Republican to the Eighty-seventh Congress (January 3, 1961-January 3, 1963); unsuccessful candidate for reelection in 1962 to the Eighty-eighth Congress; resided in Zanesville, Ohio, where he died October 21, 1979; interment in Greenwood Cemetery.

**MOORES, Merrill,** a Representative from Indiana; born in Indianapolis, Ind., April 21, 1856; attended the public schools, Butler University, Indianapolis, Ind., and Willamette University, Salem, Oreg.; was graduated from Yale University in 1878 and from the Central Law School of Indiana (now Indiana Law School) at Indianapolis in 1880; was admitted to the bar in 1880 and commenced practice in Indianapolis, Ind.; chairman of the Marion County Republican committee 1892-1896; assistant attorney general of Indiana 1894-1903; president of the Indiana State Bar Association and of the Indianapolis Bar Association in 1908; Indiana commissioner of the National Conference on Uniform State Laws 1909-1925; member of the executive council of the Interparliamentary Union in 1919; elected as a Republican to the Sixty-fourth and to the four succeeding Congresses (March 4, 1915-March 3, 1925); unsuccessful candidate for renomination in 1924 and for nomination in 1926; resumed the practice of law in Indianapolis, Ind.; served as vice president of the American Systems and Audit Co.; died October 21, 1929, in Indianapolis, Ind.; interment in Crown Hill Cemetery.

**MOORHEAD, Carlos John,** a Representative from California; born in Long Beach, Los Angeles County, Calif., May 6, 1922; attended the public schools of Glendale, Calif.; B.A., University of California, Los Angeles, 1943; J.D., University of Southern

California School of Law, Los Angeles, 1949; served in the United States Army, 1942-1945, presently holds rank of lieutenant colonel; admitted to the California bar in 1949 and commenced practice in Glendale; admitted to practice before the United States Supreme Court in 1973; member, California Law Revision Commission; member, California State assembly, 1967-1972; member, California Republican Central Committee, Los Angeles County Republican Central Committee, Forth-third District Republican Assembly; elected as a Republican to the Ninety-third and to the eleven succeeding Congresses (January 3, 1973-January 3, 1997); was not a candidate for reelection in 1996 to the One Hundred Fifth Congress; is a resident of Glendale, Calif.

**MOORHEAD, James Kennedy,** a Representative from Pennsylvania; born in Halifax, Dauphin County, Pa., September 7, 1806; attended the common schools; served an apprenticeship at the tanner's trade, after which he became a canal contractor; superintendent and supervisor on the Juniata Canal in 1828; projected and established the first passenger packet line on the Pennsylvania Canal in 1835; appointed adjutant general of Pennsylvania in 1838; constructed the Monongahela Navigation Canal and was president of the company twenty-one years; president of the Atlantic & Ohio Telegraph Co., which later became the Western Union Telegraph Co.; elected as a Republican to the Thirty-sixth and to the four succeeding Congresses (March 4, 1859-March 3, 1869); chairman, Committee on Manufactures (Thirty-eighth and Thirty-ninth Congresses); declined to be a candidate for renomination in 1868; resumed his former business activities; delegate to the Republican National Convention in 1868; was an unsuccessful candidate for election to the United States Senate in 1880; president of the chamber of commerce of Pittsburgh from 1877 until his death; died in Pittsburgh, Pa., March 6, 1884; interment in Allegheny Cemetery.

**Bibliography:** *DAB*.

**MOORHEAD, William Singer,** a Representative from Pennsylvania; born in Pittsburgh, Allegheny County, Pa., April 8, 1923; attended Shady Side Academy; graduated from Phillips Andover Academy in 1941 and from Yale University in 1944; served in the United States Navy from 1943 until discharged as a lieutenant (junior grade) in 1946 with service in the Pacific Theater; graduated from Harvard Law School in 1949; was admitted to the bar in 1949 and commenced the practice of law in Pittsburgh, Pa.; assistant city solicitor of Pittsburgh, 1954-1957; member of the Allegheny County Housing Authority, 1956-1958, and of the Pittsburgh Art Commission in 1958; elected as a Democrat to the Eighty-sixth and to the ten succeeding Congresses (January 3, 1959-January 3, 1981); was not a candidate for reelection in 1980 to the Ninety-seventh Congress; resumed the practice of law in Washington, D.C.; was a resident of The Plains, Va., until his death in Baltimore, Md., on August 3, 1987.

**MOORMAN, Henry DeHaven,** a Representative from Kentucky; born on a farm near Glen Dean, Breckinridge County, Ky., June 9, 1880; attended the public schools; studied law; was admitted to the bar in 1900 and commenced practice in Hardinsburg; also engaged in agricultural pursuits and in banking; county judge of Breckinridge County 1905-1909 and Commonwealth attorney of the ninth judicial district 1914-1927; served in the Spanish-American War as a private in Company C, First Regiment, Kentucky Volunteer Infantry, with service in Puerto Rico; during the First World War enlisted in the United States Army on January 14, 1918, and was assigned to Headquarters Company, Tenth Field Artillery; promoted to corporal and assigned to duty with the Judge Advocate General, Headquarters, Service of Supply, and was discharged April 1, 1919; elected as a Democrat to the Seventieth Congress (March 4, 1927-March 3, 1929); unsuccessful candidate for reelection in 1928 to the Seventy-first Congress; resumed his former professional and business pursuits in Hardinsburg, Ky.; died while on a visit in Hot

Springs, Ark., February 3, 1939; interment in Ivy Hill Cemetery, Hardinsburg, Ky.

**MORAN, Edward Carleton, Jr.,** a Representative from Maine; born in Rockland, Knox County, Maine, December 29, 1894; attended the public schools and was graduated from Bowdoin College, Brunswick, Maine, in 1917; during the First World War served from July 25, 1917, to March 14, 1919, in the Regular Army as a first lieutenant in Battery A, Seventy-third Artillery, Coast Artillery Corps, with service overseas; engaged in the insurance business in Rockland, Maine, in 1919; delegate to the Democratic State conventions 1922-1936 and to the Democratic National Conventions in 1924 and 1932; unsuccessful candidate for Governor of Maine in 1928 and 1930; elected as a Democrat to the Seventy-third and Seventy-fourth Congresses (March 4, 1933-January 3, 1937); was not a candidate for renomination in 1936; member of the United States Maritime Commission from April 17, 1937, to August 1, 1940; State director of the Office of Price Administration from April 12 to December 23, 1942; Second Assistant Secretary of Labor, Washington, D.C., from July 1 to November 22, 1945; chairman of the Rockland (Maine) City Council in 1946 and 1947; resumed the general insurance business; died in Rockland, Maine, on July 12, 1967; interment in Achorn Cemetery.

**MORAN, James P.,** a Representative from Virginia; born in Buffalo, N.Y., May 14, 1945; B.A., Holy Cross College, 1967; attended the Bernard Baruch School of Finance, City University of New York, 1967-1968; M.P.A., University of Pittsburgh, 1970; attended the University of Southern California in 1978; investment banker, J.P. Moran Investment Co., 1965-1968; staff, Department of Health, Education, and Welfare, 1968-1976; staff, Congressional Research Service, Library of Congress, 1974-1976; professional staff member, Subcommittee on Labor, Health, Education, and Welfare, United States Senate Appropriations Committee, 1976-1979; broker, A.G. Edwards and Sons, Inc.; assistant to the president, HumRRO (defense contractor); member, Alexandria (Va.) city council, 1979-1984; vice mayor, 1982-1984; mayor of Alexandria, 1985-1990; elected as a Democrat to the One Hundred Second and to the two succeeding Congresses (January 3, 1991-January 3, 1997); is a resident of Alexandria, Va.

**MORANO, Albert Paul,** a Representative from Connecticut; born in Paterson, Passaic County, N.J., January 18, 1908, moved to Greenwich, Conn., in 1912; attended the public schools of Greenwich, Conn.; member, Greenwich Board of Tax Review, 1933-1935; chairman of the Chickahominy Town Meeting District, 1935-1937; secretary to Representative Albert E. Austin, 1939-1940; engaged in the real estate and insurance business in Greenwich, Conn., in 1942; secretary to Representative Clare Booth Luce, 1943-1947; Connecticut State unemployment compensation commissioner, 1947-1950, serving as chairman of the commission in 1949 and 1950; elected as a Republican to the Eighty-second and to the three succeeding Congresses (January 3, 1951-January 3, 1959); unsuccessful candidate for reelection in 1958 to the Eighty-sixth Congress; special assistant to Senator Thomas J. Dodd, 1963-1969; was a resident of Greenwich, Conn., until his death there on December 16, 1987; interment in St. Mary's Cemetery.

**MOREHEAD, Charles Slaughter,** a Representative from Kentucky; born near Bardstown, Nelson County, Ky., July 7, 1802; attended the public schools and Transylvania University, Lexington, Ky.; studied law; was admitted to the bar and commenced practice in Christian County, Ky.; was also a planter, having plantations in Mississippi and Louisiana; member of the Kentucky house of representatives in 1828 and 1829; moved to Frankfort, Ky.; attorney general of Kentucky, 1830-1835; again a member of the Kentucky house of representatives, 1838-1842, and 1844, and served as speaker in 1841, 1842, and 1844; elected as a Whig to the Thirtieth and Thirty-first Congresses (March 4, 1847-March 3, 1851);

resumed the practice of law and the management of his plantations; again a member of the Kentucky house of representatives in 1853; elected Governor of Kentucky on the American Party ticket in 1855, and served from September 1855 to September 1859; moved to Louisville in 1859 and continued the practice of his profession; member of the peace convention of 1861 held in Washington, D.C., in an effort to devise means to prevent the impending war; arrested by the Federal authorities on the charge of disloyalty in September 1861 and confined in Fort Lafayette, New York Harbor, until January 1862; traveled in Europe until the close of the war, when he settled in Greenville, Miss.; died on one of his plantations near Greenville, Miss., December 21, 1868; interment in Frankfort Cemetery, Frankfort, Ky.

**Bibliography:** *DAB*.

**MOREHEAD, James Turner,** a Senator from Kentucky; born near Shepherdsville, Bullitt County, Ky., May 24, 1797; attended the public schools and Transylvania University, Lexington, Ky.; studied law; was admitted to the bar in 1818 and commenced practice in Bowling Green, Ky.; member, Kentucky house of representatives, 1828-1831; served as Lieutenant Governor in 1832; became Governor upon Governor John Breathitt's death on February 22, 1834, and served until June 1, 1836; member, Kentucky house of representatives, 1837-1838; president of the Kentucky board of internal improvements, 1838-1841; elected as a Whig to the United States Senate, and served from March 4, 1841 to March 3, 1847; chairman, Committee on Indian Affairs (Twenty-seventh Congress), Committee on Retrenchment (Twenty-seventh and Twenty-eighth Congresses); continued the practice of law in Covington, Kenton County, Ky., until his death in that city on December 28, 1854; interment in the State lot of Frankfort Cemetery, Frankfort, Ky.

**Bibliography:** *DAB*; Jillson, W.R., ed. "Early Political Papers of Governor James T. Morehead." *Register of the Kentucky State Historical Society* 22 (September 1924): 272-300, 23 (January 1925): 36-61.

**MOREHEAD, James Turner,** a Representative from North Carolina; born in Rockingham County, N.C., January 11, 1799; attended the common schools; was graduated from the University of North Carolina at Chapel Hill in 1819; studied law; was admitted to the bar and commenced practice in Greensboro, N.C.; commissioner of Greensboro in 1832, 1834, and 1835; served as a member of the North Carolina State senate in 1835, 1836, 1838, 1840, and 1842; trustee of the University of North Carolina 1836-1868; elected as a Whig to the Thirty-second Congress (March 4, 1851-March 3, 1853); declined to be a candidate for renomination in 1852 to the Thirty-third Congress; resumed the practice of his profession; also engaged in agricultural pursuits and operated an iron works; died in Greensboro, Guilford County, N.C., on May 5, 1875; interment in the Presbyterian Cemetery.

**MOREHEAD, John Henry,** a Representative from Nebraska; born on a farm near Columbia, Lucas County, Iowa, December 3, 1861; attended the public schools and a business college in Shenandoah, Iowa; moved to Nebraska in 1884 and settled in Richardson County; taught in a country school; engaged in agricultural pursuits and in the mercantile and banking business at Barada, Nebr.; moved to Falls City, Nebr., in 1895; treasurer of Richardson County, 1896-1899; mayor of Falls City in 1900; member of the Nebraska State senate, 1910-1912, serving as president pro tempore; upon the death of Lieutenant Governor M.R. Hopewell on May 2, 1911, Morehead succeeded to that office, as provided by the State constitution; elected Governor of Nebraska in 1912, reelected in 1914, and served from January 9, 1913 to January 4, 1917; unsuccessful candidate for election to the United States Senate in 1918, and for Governor of Nebraska in 1920; elected as a Democrat to the Sixty-eighth and to the five succeeding Congresses (March 4, 1923-January 3, 1935); chairman, Committee on Memorials

(Seventy-second and Seventy-third Congresses); was not a candidate for renomination in 1934 to the Seventy-fourth Congress; resumed agricultural pursuits and also engaged in the real estate business; delegate to the Democratic National Convention of 1940; died in St. Joseph, Mo., May 31, 1942; interment in Steele Cemetery, Falls City, Nebr.

**MOREHEAD, John Motley,** a Representative from North Carolina; born in Charlotte, Mecklenburg County, N.C., July 20, 1866; attended the public schools and the Bingham Military School of North Carolina at Mebane; was graduated from the University of North Carolina at Chapel Hill in 1886; also completed a business course in Bryant and Stratton College, Baltimore, Md.; collecting teller of the Charlotte National Bank, of Charlotte, N.C.; buyer and dealer in leaf tobacco at Durham, N.C.; interested in manufacturing and agricultural pursuits; elected as a Republican to the Sixty-first Congress (March 4, 1909-March 3, 1911); declined to be a candidate for renomination in 1910 to the Sixty-second Congress; chairman of the Republican State committee, 1910-1916; member of the Republican National Committee from 1916 until 1922, when he resigned; became extensively engaged in the manufacture of woolen goods and other commodities; died in Charlotte, N.C., December 13, 1923; interment in Elmwood Cemetery.

**Bibliography:** Steelman, Joseph F. "Republicanism in North Carolina: John Motley Morehead's Campaign to Revive a Moribund Party, 1908-1910." *North Carolina Historical Review* 42 (April 1965): 153-168; Steelman, Joseph F. "The Trials of a Republican State Chairman: John Motley Morehead and North Carolina Politics, 1910-1912." *North Carolina Historical Review* 43 (January 1966): 31-42.

**MORELLA, Constance A.,** a Representative from Maryland; born in Somerville, Mass., February 12, 1931; attended the public schools; graduated, Somerville High School, 1948; A.B., Boston University, 1954; M.A., American University, Washington, D.C., 1967; professor, Montgomery College, 1970-1986; member, Montgomery County Commission for Women, 1971-1975; delegate to the Maryland General Assembly, 1979-1986; elected as a Republican to the One Hundredth and to the four succeeding Congresses (January 3, 1987-January 3, 1997); is a resident of Bethesda, Md.

**MOREY, Frank,** a Representative from Louisiana; born in Boston, Mass., July 11, 1840; attended the public schools; moved to Illinois in 1857; studied law; entered the Union Army in 1861 in the Thirty-third Regiment, Illinois Volunteer Infantry, and served until the close of the Civil War; settled in Louisiana in 1866 and engaged in cotton planting and the insurance business; member of the State house of representatives in 1868 and 1869; appointed a commissioner to revise the statutes and codes of the State; commissioner to the Vienna Exposition in 1873; elected as a Republican to the Forty-first, Forty-second, and Forty-third Congresses; presented credentials as a Member-elect to the Forty-fourth Congress and served from March 4, 1869, to June 8, 1876, when he was succeeded by William B. Spencer, who contested the election; moved to Washington, D.C., and died there September 22, 1889; interment in the Congressional Cemetery.

**MOREY, Henry Lee,** a Representative from Ohio; born in Milford Township, near Collinsville, Butler County, Ohio, April 8, 1841; attended the common schools and Miami University, Oxford, Ohio; served in the Civil War and was successively promoted to second lieutenant, first lieutenant, and captain; was graduated from the Indianapolis Law School in 1867; was admitted to the bar and commenced practice in Hamilton, Ohio; city solicitor of Hamilton 1871-1875; prosecuting attorney of Butler County, Ohio, in 1873; unsuccessful candidate for election to the State senate in 1875; elected as a Republican to the Forty-seventh Congress (March 4, 1881-March 3, 1883); presented credentials as a Member-elect to the Forty-eighth Congress and served from March 4, 1883, to June 20,

1884, when he was succeeded by James E. Campbell, who contested the election; delegate to the Republican National Convention in 1884; elected to the Fifty-first Congress (March 4, 1889-March 3, 1891); unsuccessful candidate for reelection in 1890 to the Fifty-second Congress; resumed the practice of law; died in Hamilton, Butler County, Ohio, December 29, 1902; interment in Greenwood Cemetery.

**MORGAN, Charles Henry,** a Representative from Missouri; born in Cuba, Allegeny County, N.Y., July 5, 1842; moved to Wisconsin in 1845 with his parents, who settled in Pewaukee; attended the common schools and the Fond du Lac (Wis.) High School; during the Civil War served in the Union Army four years and three months as a private, noncommissioned officer, second and first lieutenant, and captain in the First Regiment and Twenty-first Regiment, Wisconsin Volunteer Infantry; was graduated from the Albany (N.Y.) Law School; was admitted to the bar and commenced practice in Lamar, Barton County, Mo., in 1868; prosecuting attorney of Barton County, Mo., four years; member of the Missouri house of representatives 1872-1874; elected as a Democrat to the Forty-fourth and Forty-fifth Congresses (March 4, 1875-March 3, 1879); unsuccessful candidate for reelection in 1878 to the Forty-sixth Congress; elected to the Forty-eighth Congress (March 4, 1883-March 3, 1885); chairman, Committee on Expenditures in the Post Office Department (Forty-eighth Congress); unsuccessful candidate for reelection in 1884 to the Forty-ninth Congress; delegate to the Democratic National Convention in 1880; elected to the Fifty-third Congress (March 4, 1893-March 3, 1895); unsuccessful candidate for renomination in 1894; served in the war with Spain as lieutenant colonel of the Fifth Missouri Volunteer Infantry; moved to Joplin, Mo., in 1907 and engaged in mining; elected as a Republican to the Sixty-first Congress (March 4, 1909-March 3, 1911); unsuccessful candidate for reelection in 1910 to the Sixty-second Congress; died in Joplin, Mo., January 4, 1912; interment in Mount Hope Cemetery.

**MORGAN, Christopher** (brother of Edwin Barber Morgan and nephew of Noyes Barber), a Representative from New York; born in Aurora, N.Y., June 4, 1808; pursued classical studies and was graduated from Yale College in 1830; studied law; was admitted to the bar and commenced practice in Aurora, Cayuga County, N.Y.; elected as a Whig to the Twenty-sixth and Twenty-seventh Congresses (March 4, 1839-March 3, 1843); unsuccessful candidate for reelection in 1842 to the Twenty-eighth Congress; moved to Auburn, N.Y., in 1843 and continued the practice of his profession; secretary of state of New York 1847-1851; superintendent of the New York public schools 1848-1852; served as mayor of Auburn in 1860 and 1862; trustee of the State lunatic asylum in Utica, N.Y.; died in Auburn, N.Y., April 3, 1877; interment in Fort Hill Cemetery.

**MORGAN, Daniel,** a Representative from Virginia; born near Junction, Hunterdon County, N.J., in 1736; moved to Charles Town, Va. (now West Virginia), in 1754; served with the Colonial forces during the French and Indian War; during the Revolution was commissioned captain of a company of Virginia riflemen in July 1775; was taken prisoner at Quebec on December 31, 1775; became colonel of the Eleventh Virginia Regiment on November 12, 1776 (designated the Seventh Virginia Regiment, September 14, 1778); commissioned brigadier general in the Continental Army on October 30, 1780; at the close of the war retired to his estate, known as "Saratoga," near Winchester, Va.; commanded the Virginia Militia ordered out by President George Washington in 1794 to suppress the Whiskey Rebellion in Pennsylvania; was an unsuccessful Federalist candidate for election to the Fourth Congress; elected as a Federalist to the Fifth Congress (March 4, 1797-March 3, 1799); declined to be a candidate for renomination in 1798 to the Sixth Congress on account of ill health; died in Winchester, Va., on July 6, 1802; interment in Mount Hebron Cemetery.

**Bibliography:** *DAB*; Higginbotham, Don. *Daniel Morgan: Revolutionary Rifleman.* Chapel Hill: University of North Carolina Press, 1961.

**MORGAN, Dick Thompson,** a Representative from Oklahoma; born at Prairie Creek, Vigo County, Ind., December 6, 1853; attended the country schools and the Prairie Creek High School; was graduated from Union Christian College, Merom, Ind., in 1876, and later was professor of mathematics in that college; was graduated from the Central Law School, Indianapolis, Ind., in 1880; was admitted to the bar the same year and commenced practice in Terre Haute, Ind.; member of the State house of representatives in 1880 and 1881; appointed register of the United States land office at Woodward, Okla., by President Theodore Roosevelt in 1904 and served until May 1, 1908; elected as a Republican to the Sixty-first and to the five succeeding Congresses and served from March 3, 1909, until his death in Danville, Ill., July 4, 1920; interment in Rose Hill Cemetery, Oklahoma City, Okla.

**MORGAN, Edwin Barber** (brother of Christopher Morgan and nephew of Noyes Barber), a Representative from New York; born in Aurora, Cayuga County, N.Y., May 2, 1806; attended the common schools; engaged in mercantile pursuits and banking in Aurora; elected as a Whig to the Thirty-third Congress and to the Thirty-fourth Congress and as a Republican to the Thirty-fifth Congress (March 4, 1853-March 3, 1859); chairman, Committee on Patents (Thirty-fourth Congress); was not a candidate for renomination in 1858; one of the founders and the first president of the Wells-Fargo Express Co. and a director of the American Express Co. up to the time of his death; trustee of Cornell University, Ithaca, N.Y., 1865-1874; charter trustee of Wells College, Aurora, N.Y., 1868-1881, and served as president of the board 1878-1881; member of the board of trustees of Auburn Theological Seminary 1870-1881; died in Aurora, N.Y., on October 13, 1881; interment in Oak Glen Cemetery.

**Bibliography:** *DAB*.

**MORGAN, Edwin Denison** (cousin of Morgan Gardner Bulkeley), a Senator from New York; born in Washington, Mass., February 8, 1811; moved with his parents to Windsor County, Conn., in 1822; attended the public schools and Bacon Academy, Colchester, Conn.; moved to Hartford, Conn., in 1828 and engaged in mercantile pursuits; member, city council of Hartford, 1832; moved to New York City in 1836 and engaged in the wholesale grocery business, banking and brokerage; alderman of New York City, 1849; member, New York State senate, 1850-1855; New York State commissioner of immigration, 1855-1858; chairman of the Republican National Committee, 1856-1864; elected Governor of New York in 1858, reelected in 1860, and served from January 1, 1859 to January 1, 1863; during the Civil War was commissioned on September 28, 1861 as major general of Volunteers in the Union Army; served as commander of the Department of New York from October 26, 1861 until his resignation January 3, 1863; elected as a Republican to the United States Senate and served from March 4, 1863, to March 3, 1869; unsuccessful candidate for reelection in 1868; chairman, Committee on the Library (Fortieth Congress); chairman of the Republican National Committee, 1872-1876; unsuccessful candidate in 1876 for election for Governor; declined the office of Secretary of the Treasury in the Cabinet of President Chester A. Arthur in 1881; died in New York City, February 14, 1883; interment in Cedar Hill Cemetery, Hartford, Conn.

**Bibliography:** *DAB*; Rawley, James A. *Edwin D. Morgan: Merchant in Politics.* New York: Columbia University Press, 1955.

**MORGAN, George Washington,** a Representative from Ohio; born in Washington, Pa., September 20, 1820; attended Washington (now Washington and Jefferson) College, Washington, Pa., until 1836; enlisted in a company commanded by his brother and assisted

Texas in gaining her independence; attained the rank of captain; returned to the United States; was a cadet in the United States Military Academy, West Point, N.Y., 1841-1843; studied law; was admitted to the bar and commenced practice in Mount Vernon, Ohio, in 1843; served in the Mexican War; commissioned colonel of the Second Regiment, Ohio Volunteer Infantry, June 23, 1846, and colonel of the Fifteenth Regiment, United States Infantry, April 9, 1847; brevetted brigadier general on August 20, 1847; appointed consul at Marseilles, France, in 1855; appointed Minister Resident at Lisbon, Portugal, on May 11, 1858 and served until July 1861; commissioned a brigadier general of Volunteers on November 12, 1861, and had command of the Seventh Division of the Army of the Ohio from March 26 to October 10, 1862; assigned to the Thirteenth Army Corps; resigned June 8, 1863, on account of ill health; unsuccessful candidate in 1865 for election for Governor of Ohio; presented credentials as a Democratic Member-elect to the Fortieth Congress and served from March 4, 1867, until June 3, 1868, when he was succeeded by Columbus Delano, who contested the election; elected to the Forty-first and Forty-second Congresses (March 4, 1869-March 3, 1873); unsuccessful candidate for reelection in 1872 to the Forty-third Congress; delegate to the Democratic National Convention of 1876; died at Fortress Monroe, Va., July 26, 1893; interment in Mound View Cemetery, Mount Vernon, Knox County, Ohio.

Bibliography: *DAB*.

**MORGAN, James,** a Representative from New Jersey; born in Amboy, N.J., on December 29, 1756; attended the public schools; served as an officer in the New Jersey Line during the Revolutionary War; representative in the general assembly in Philadelphia, Pa., 1794-1799; elected as a Republican to the Twelfth Congress (March 4, 1811-March 3, 1813); engaged in agricultural pursuits; became major general of militia; died in South Amboy, Middlesex County, N.J., November 11, 1822; interment in the Morgan private cemetery, Morgan, N.J.

**MORGAN, James Bright,** a Representative from Mississippi; born near Fayetteville, Lincoln County, Tenn., March 14, 1833; moved with his parents to De Soto County, Miss., in 1840 and settled in Hernando; received an academic education; studied law; was admitted to the bar in 1857 and commenced practice in Hernando, Miss.; elected probate judge of De Soto County and served from 1857 until 1861, when he resigned; during the Civil War enlisted in the Confederate Army as a private; was promoted to the rank of captain, and elected a major of the Twenty-ninth Mississippi Infantry; later became lieutenant colonel and colonel, and served until the close of the war; resumed the practice of law; again elected probate judge of De Soto County; member of the State senate 1876-1878; delegate to all State conventions 1876-1890; chancellor of the third chancery district 1878-1882; elected as a Democrat to the Forty-ninth, Fiftieth, and Fifty-first Congresses (March 4, 1885-March 3, 1891); resumed the practice of law; died near Horn Lake, Miss., June 18, 1892; interment in Baptist Cemetery, Hernando, Miss.

**MORGAN, John Jordan** (father-in-law of John Adams Dix), a Representative from New York; born in Queens County, N.Y., in 1770; attended the public schools; member of the State assembly in 1819; elected to the Seventeenth and Eighteenth Congresses (March 4, 1821-March 3, 1825); elected as a Jacksonian to the Twenty-third Congress to fill the vacancy caused by the resignation of Cornelius W. Lawrence and served from December 1, 1834, to March 3, 1835; again a member of the State assembly in 1836 and 1840; died in Port Chester, Westchester County, N.Y., on July 29, 1849; interment in Trinity Churchyard, New York City.

**MORGAN, John Tyler,** a Senator from Alabama; born in Athens, McMinn County, Tenn., June 20, 1824; moved with his parents to Alabama in 1833 and settled in Calhoun County; attended frontier schools; studied law; was admitted to the bar in 1845 and commenced practice in Talladega, Ala.; moved to Dallas County, Ala., in 1855 and resumed the practice of law in Selma and Cahaba; presidential elector on the Democratic ticket in 1860; delegate from Dallas County to the State convention of 1861 which passed the ordinance of secession; during the Civil War enlisted in the Confederate Army as a private in the "Cahaba Rifles" in 1861, and was commissioned brigadier general on June 6, 1863; after the war resumed the practice of law in Selma, Ala.; presidential elector on the Democratic ticket in 1876; elected as a Democrat to the United States Senate in 1876; reelected in 1882, 1888, 1894, 1900, and 1906, and served from March 4, 1877 until his death in Washington, D.C., June 11, 1907; Democratic caucus chairman 1901-1902; chairman, Committee on Rules (Forty-sixth Congress), Committee on Foreign Relations (Fifty-third Congress), Committee on Interoceanic Canals (Fifty-sixth and Fifty-seventh Congresses), Committee on Public Health and National Quarantine (Fifty-ninth Congress); interment in Live Oak Cemetery, Selma, Dallas County, Ala.

Bibliography: *DAB*; Anders, James M. "The Senatorial Career of John Tyler Morgan." Ph.D. dissertation, George Peabody College, 1956; Fry, Joseph A. *John Tyler Morgan and the Search for Southern Autonomy.* Knoxville: University of Tennessee Press, 1992; Radke, August C., Jr. "John Tyler Morgan, An Expansionist Senator, 1877-1907." Ph.D. dissertation, University of Washington, 1953.

**MORGAN, Lewis Lovering,** a Representative from Louisiana; born in Mandeville, St. Tammany Parish, La., March 2, 1876; attended the public schools and St. Eugene's College, St. Tammany Parish, La.; was graduated from the law department of Tulane University, New Orleans, La., in 1899; was admitted to the bar and commenced practice in Covington, La., in 1902; member of the State house of representatives in 1908; resigned to become district attorney and served from 1908 to 1912; delegate to the Democratic National Conventions in 1912, 1928, and 1936; delegate to the Democratic State conventions in 1912, 1916, 1920, and 1924; elected as a Democrat to the Sixty-second Congress to fill the vacancy caused by the death of Robert C. Wickliffe; reelected to the Sixty-third and Sixty-fourth Congresses and served from November 5, 1912, to March 4, 1917; chairman, Committee on Elections No. 3 (Sixty-fourth Congress); was not a candidate for renomination in 1916; resumed the practice of law in New Orleans and Covington; unsuccessful candidate for the Democratic gubernatorial nomination in 1944; died in New Orleans, La., June 10, 1950; interment in Covington Cemetery, Covington, La.

**MORGAN, Robert Burren,** a Senator from North Carolina; born in Lillington, Harnett County, N.C., October 5, 1925; attended the Lillington public schools; attended East Carolina College, Greenville, N.C., 1942-1944, and the University of North Carolina, 1945; B.S., East Carolina College, 1947; J.D., Wake Forest College School of Law, Winston-Salem, 1950; admitted to the North Carolina bar in 1950 and commenced practice in Lillington; following graduation from law school served four years as clerk of the superior court in Harnett County, N.C.; served in the North Carolina State senate, 1955-1957, 1959-1961, 1963-1968, named president pro tempore in 1965; served in United States Navy, 1944-1946, and was recalled during the Korean Conflict, 1952-1955; remained in the Navy Reserve through 1971, lieutenant commander; served in United States Air Force Reserve, 1971-1973, lieutenant colonel; attorney general of North Carolina, 1969-1974; elected as a Democrat to the United States Senate in 1974, and served from January 3, 1975 to January 3, 1981; unsuccessful candidate for reelection in 1980; resumed the practice of law; is a resident of Buies Creek, N.C.

**MORGAN, Stephen,** a Representative from Ohio; born in Jackson County, Ohio, January 25, 1854; attended the common schools, Central College, Worthington, Ohio, and the Normal

University, Lebanon, Ohio; taught in the public schools of Jackson County for a number of years; school examiner for nine years and principal of Oak Hill Academy for fifteen years; elected as a Republican to the Fifty-sixth, Fifty-seventh, and Fifty-eighth Congresses (March 4, 1899-March 3, 1905); unsuccessful candidate for reelection in 1904 to the Fifty-ninth Congress; moved to Columbus, Ohio, and retired from public life; died at Magnetic Springs, Union County, Ohio, February 9, 1928; interment in Horeb Cemetery, near Oak Hill, Jackson County, Ohio.

**MORGAN, Thomas Ellsworth,** a Representative from Pennsylvania; born in Ellsworth, Washington County, Pa., October 13, 1906; attended the public schools of Washington County and East Bethlehem Township High School, Fredericktown, Pa.; B.S., Waynesburg (Pa.) College, 1930; M.B., Detroit (Mich.) College of Medicine and Surgery, 1933; M.D., Wayne University, Detroit, Mich., 1934; began the practice of medicine and surgery in Fredericktown, Pa., in 1935; elected as a Democrat to the Seventy-ninth and to the fifteen succeeding Congresses (January 3, 1945-January 3, 1977); chairman, Committee on Foreign Affairs (Eighty-sixth through Ninety-third Congresses), Committee on International Relations (Ninety-fourth Congress); was not a candidate for reelection in 1976 to the Ninety-fifth Congress; resumed the practice of medicine in Fredericktown, Pa., until 1986; died in Waynesburg, Pa., on July 31, 1995.

**MORGAN, William Mitchell,** a Representative from Ohio; born in Brownsville, Licking County, Ohio, August 1, 1870; attended the public schools; pursued various occupations until 1898, when he moved to Newark, Ohio; employed as a laborer and later as a musician; studied literature and science; engaged in agriculture, merchandizing, and in the wool-buying business; also active in organized labor movements, serving as president of the Newark (Ohio) Musicians' Union; elected as a Republican to the Sixty-seventh and to the four succeeding Congresses (March 4, 1921-March 3, 1931); unsuccessful candidate for reelection in 1930 to the Seventy-second Congress and for election in 1932 to the Seventy-third Congress; resumed his former business pursuits; president of the Ohio State Federation of Labor in 1935, resigning the same year to become a member of the State industrial commission, in which he served until his death in Columbus, Ohio, on September 17, 1935; interment in Cedar Hill Cemetery, Newark, Ohio.

**MORGAN, William Stephen,** a Representative from Virginia; born in Monongalia County, Va. (now West Virginia), September 7, 1801; attended the public schools; engaged in agricultural pursuits at White Day, Va.; unsuccessful candidate for election in 1832 to the Twenty-third Congress; elected as a Jacksonian to the Twenty-fourth Congress and reelected as a Democrat to the Twenty-fifth Congress (March 4, 1835-March 3, 1839); chairman, Committee on Revolutionary Pensions (Twenty-fifth Congress); declined to be a candidate for renomination in 1838; employed as a clerk in the House of Representatives in 1840; transferred as a clerk to the legislature of Virginia; member of the Virginia house of delegates 1841-1844; appointed a clerk in the Treasury Department and served from August 3, 1845, until June 30, 1861; employed in the Smithsonian Institution 1861-1863; moved to Rivesville, W.Va.; died September 3, 1878, while on a visit to Washington, D.C.; interment in the Congressional Cemetery.

**MORIN, John Mary,** a Representative from Pennsylvania; born in Philadelphia, Pa., April 18, 1868; moved with his parents to Pittsburgh, Pa.; attended the common schools; began work in a glass factory in 1882; employed in steel mills until 1885; moved to Missoula, Mont., in 1889 and engaged in mercantile pursuits, during which time he took a night course at Haskins' Business College at Missoula and was graduated in 1892; returned to Pittsburgh, Allegheny County, Pa.; engaged in the hotel business; served as a director of the Washington Trust Co., beginning in 1910;

member of the Pittsburgh Common Council, 1904-1906; delegate to the Pennsylvania Republican conventions, 1905-1912; director of public safety in Pittsburgh, 1909-1913; elected as a Republican to the Sixty-third and to the seven succeeding Congresses (March 4, 1913-March 3, 1929); chairman, Committee on Military Affairs (Sixty-ninth and Seventieth Congresses); unsuccessful candidate for renomination in 1928 to the Seventy-first Congress; appointed a commissioner of United States Employees Compensation Commission in Washington, D.C., and served from 1928 until his death in Baltimore, Md., March 3, 1942; interment in Calvary Cemetery, Pittsburgh, Pa.

**MORITZ, Theodore Leo,** a Representative from Pennsylvania; born in Toledo, Lucas County, Ohio, February 10, 1892; attended the parochial schools; graduated from St. Mary's Institute, Dayton, Ohio, in 1913, and the University of Dayton, Ohio, in 1919; attended the law department of Duquesne University, Pittsburgh, Pa., 1920-1923; engaged as a teacher in parochial schools in Dayton, Ohio, 1910-1913, in Cleveland, Ohio, 1913-1916, and in Duquesne University Prep School, Pittsburgh, Pa., 1918-1923; was admitted to the bar in 1924 and commenced practice in Pittsburgh, Pa., in 1925; secretary to Mayor William N. McNair of Pittsburgh, 1933-1935; elected as a Democrat to the Seventy-fourth Congress (January 3, 1935-January 3, 1937); did not seek renomination as a Democrat, but was an unsuccessful candidate for nomination as a Republican, and for reelection as a Union (Royal Oak) candidate in 1936 to the Seventy-fifth Congress; resumed the practice of law; was a resident of Pittsburgh, Pa., until his death on March 13, 1982.

**MORPHIS, Joseph Lewis,** a Representative from Mississippi; born near Pocahontas, McNairy County, Tenn., April 17, 1831; pursued elementary studies; engaged in planting; member of the State house of representatives in 1859; entered the Confederate Army as captain in August 1861 and served until the close of the Civil War; moved with his family to Pontotoc, Miss., in 1863; member of the State constitutional convention in 1865; member of the State house of representatives 1866-1868; upon the readmission of the State of Mississippi to representation was elected as a Republican to the Forty-first and Forty-second Congresses and served from February 23, 1870, to March 3, 1873; unsuccessful candidate for renomination in 1872; appointed by President Rutherford B. Hayes as United States marshal of the northern district of Mississippi and served from 1877 to 1885; licensed as an Indian trader on the Osage Reservation in 1890 and engaged in that occupation until 1901; lived in retirement until his death in Cleveland, Pawnee County, Okla., July 29, 1913; interment in Woodland Cemetery.

**MORRELL, Daniel Johnson,** a Representative from Pennsylvania; born in North Berwick, York County, Maine, August 8, 1821; attended the public schools; moved to Philadelphia, Pa., in 1836; entered a counting room as clerk and afterward engaged in mercantile pursuits; moved to Johnstown, Pa., in 1855 and became general manager of the Cambria Iron Co.; also served as president of the local gas and water company 1860-1884 and president of the First National Bank of Johnstown 1863-1884; president of the city council many years; elected as a Republican to the Fortieth and Forty-first Congresses (March 4, 1867-March 3, 1871); chairman, Committee on Manufactures (Fortieth and Forty-first Congresses); unsuccessful candidate for reelection in 1870 to the Forty-second Congress; commissioner to the Paris Exposition of 1878; again engaged in banking; died in Johnstown, Cambria County, Pa., August 20, 1885; interment in Grandview Cemetery.

**MORRELL, Edward de Veaux,** a Representative from Pennsylvania; born in Newport, R.I., August 7, 1863; attended private schools and was graduated from the University of Pennsylvania at Philadelphia in 1885; studied law; was admitted to the bar in 1887 and commenced practice in Philadelphia; member of the select council of Philadelphia 1891-1894; active in the National Guard of Pennsylvania; colonel of the Third Regiment; afterward commissioned brigadier general and commanded the First Brigade; elected as a Republican to the Fifty-sixth Congress to fill the vacancy caused by the death of Alfred C. Harmer; reelected to the Fifty-seventh, Fifty-eighth, and Fifty-ninth Congresses and served from November 6, 1900, to March 3, 1907; chairman, Committee on Militia (Fifty-eighth and Fifty-ninth Congresses); was not a candidate for renomination in 1906; established the first telephone line north of Frankford, Pa., and built an electric-light plant in that section; member of the board of education of Philadelphia 1912-1916; a resident of Torresdale, Philadelphia, Pa.; went to Colorado Springs, Colo., for his health, and died there September 1, 1917; interment in the family crypt at Eden Hall, Torresdale, Philadelphia, Pa.

**MORRIL, David Lawrence,** a Senator from New Hampshire; born in Epping, N.H., June 10, 1772; taught by his grandfather and later attended Exeter Academy, Exeter, N.H.; studied medicine and engaged in practice in Epsom, N.H., 1793-1800; studied theology; was ordained; pastor of the Presbyterian Church of Goffstown, 1802-1811; resumed the practice of medicine; member, New Hampshire State house of representatives, 1808-1817, and served as speaker in 1816; elected as a Republican to the United States Senate, and served from March 4, 1817 to March 3, 1823; was not a candidate for renomination; member and president, State senate, 1823-1824; elected Governor of New Hampshire in 1824, reelected in 1825 and 1826, and served from June 3, 1824 to June 7, 1827; unsuccessful candidate for reelection in 1827; moved to Concord in 1831; edited the New Hampshire Observer, 1831-1833; died in Concord, N.H., January 28, 1849; interment in Old North Cemetery.

**Bibliography:** *DAB*; Brown, William. "David Lawrence Morrill." *Historical New Hampshire* 19 (Summer 1964): 3-26.

**MORRILL, Anson Peaslee** (brother of Lot Myrick Morrill), a Representative from Maine; born in Belgrade, Maine, June 10, 1803; attended the district schools; appointed postmaster at Dearborn, Kennebec County, Maine, and served from November 1, 1825, to June 3, 1841; engaged in mercantile pursuits in 1824; moved to Madison and thence to Readfield, Maine, in 1844, where he took charge of a wool mill, which he ultimately purchased; member of the Maine State house of representatives in 1833; sheriff of Somerset County in 1839; land agent, 1850-1853; unsuccessful Wildcat candidate for Governor of Maine in 1853; there being no choice in the popular election, he was appointed by the legislature the first Republican Governor of Maine, and served from January 3, 1855 to January 2, 1856; delegate to the Republican National Convention of 1856; elected as a Republican to the Thirty-seventh Congress (March 4, 1861-March 3, 1863); was not a candidate for renomination in 1862 to the Thirty-eighth Congress; resumed his manufacturing pursuits; moved to Augusta, Maine, in 1879; member of the State house of representatives in 1880; president of the Maine Central Railroad in 1866, and vice president, 1873-1887; died in Augusta, Maine, July 4, 1887; interment in Forest Grove Cemetery.

**Bibliography:** *DAB*.

**MORRILL, Edmund Needham,** a Representative from Kansas; born in Westbrook, Cumberland County, Maine, February 12, 1834; attended school in his native town and was graduated from Westbrook Seminary in 1855; superintendent of the Westbrook schools, 1856-1857; moved to Kansas in 1857 and settled in Brown County, where he erected a sawmill; member of the Territorial legislature in 1857 and 1858; enlisted on October 5, 1861, in the Union Army and served in the Seventh Regiment, Kansas Volunteer Cavalry; promoted to sergeant on October 10, 1861; appointed captain and commissary of subsistence in August 1862; mustered out as a major in October 1865; clerk of the district court of Brown County, Kans., 1866-1870; county clerk, 1866-1873; founded the first

bank in Brown County, in 1871, and was its president from 1887 until his death; president of the First National Bank of Leavenworth, Kans., for seven years; member of the Kansas State senate, 1872-1874, and 1876-1880, and served as president pro tempore in 1877; founded the Morrill Free Public Library at Hiawatha, Kans., in 1882; elected as a Republican to the Forty-eighth and to the three succeeding Congresses (March 4, 1883-March 3, 1891); chairman, Committee on Invalid Pensions (Fifty-first Congress); was not a candidate for renomination in 1890 to the Fifty-second Congress; resumed banking; founded the Hiawatha (Kans.) Academy in 1889; elected Governor of Kansas in 1894, and served from January 14, 1895 to January 11, 1897; unsuccessful candidate for reelection in 1896; died in San Antonio, Tex., March 14, 1909; interment in Mount Hope Cemetery, Hiawatha, Brown County, Kans.

**Bibliography:** *DAB*.

**MORRILL, Justin Smith,** a Representative and a Senator from Vermont; born in Strafford, Orange County, Vt., April 14, 1810; attended the common schools and Thetford and Randolph Academies; a merchant's clerk in Strafford from 1825 to 1828, and in Portland, Maine, from 1828 to 1831; merchant in Strafford, 1831-1848; engaged in agriculture and horticulture, 1848-1855; elected as a Whig to the Thirty-fourth Congress, and as a Republican to the five succeeding Congresses, and served from March 4, 1855, until March 3, 1867, when he became Senator; sponsor of the Morrill Land-Grant Act of 1862, which provided states with endowments of public land to establish institutions of higher learning for the agricultural and mechanical arts; chairman, Committee on Ways and Means (Thirty-ninth Congress); elected as a Union Republican to the United States Senate in 1866; reelected as a Republican in 1872, 1878, 1884, 1890, and again in 1896, and served from March 4, 1867, until his death in Washington, D.C., December 28, 1898; chairman, Committee on Public Buildings and Grounds (Forty-first through Forty-fourth Congresses), Committee on Finance (Forty-fifth, Forty-seventh through Fifty-second, Fifty-fourth and Fifty-fifth Congresses); regent of the Smithsonian Institution, 1883-1898; trustee of the University of Vermont, 1865-1898; interment in the City Cemetery, Strafford, Vt.

**Bibliography:** *DAB*; Hoyer, Randal L. "The Gentleman from Vermont: The Career of Justin S. Morrill in the United States House of Representatives." Ph.D. dissertation, Michigan State University, 1974; Parker, William. *The Life and Public Services of Justin Smith Morrill*. 1924. Reprint. New York: Da Capo Press, 1971.

**MORRILL, Lot Myrick** (brother of Anson Peaslee Morrill), a Senator from Maine; born in Belgrade, Maine, May 3, 1813; attended the district schools and Waterville (now Colby) College, Maine; studied law; was admitted to the bar in 1839 and commenced practice in Readfield; moved to Augusta in 1841; member of the Maine State house of representatives in 1854, and of the senate in 1856, and was elected president of the senate; elected Governor of Maine in 1857, reelected in 1858 and 1859, and served from January 8, 1858 to January 2, 1861; elected as a Republican to the United States Senate to fill the vacancy caused by the resignation of Hannibal Hamlin; reelected in 1863, and served from January 17, 1861 to March 3, 1869; member of the peace convention of 1861 held in Washington, D.C., in an effort to devise means to prevent the impending war; resumed the practice of law in Augusta; appointed in 1869 and subsequently elected to the United States Senate to fill the vacancy caused by the death of William Pitt Fessenden; reelected in 1871, and served from October 30, 1869 until his resignation on July 7, 1876 to accept a Cabinet portfolio; chairman, Committee to Audit and Control the Contingent Expense (Thirty-eighth and Thirty-ninth Congresses), Committee on the District of Columbia (Thirty-ninth Congress), Committee on Appropriations (Fortieth, Forty-first, Forty-third and Forty-fourth Congresses), Committee on the Library (Forty-first and Forty-second Congresses); appointed Secretary of the Treasury in the Cabinet of

President Ulysses S. Grant, and served from July 7, 1876 to March 9, 1877; appointed by President Rutherford B. Hayes collector of customs in Portland, and served from 1877 until his death; died in Augusta, Maine, on January 10, 1883; interment in Forest Grove Cemetery.

**Bibliography:** *DAB*; Talbot, George Foster. "Lot M. Morrill." *Collections and Proceedings of the Maine Historical Society* 5 (1894): 225-75.

**MORRILL, Samuel Plummer,** a Representative from Maine; born in Chesterville, Franklin County, Maine, February 11, 1816; attended the common schools and Farmington Academy, Farmington, Maine; studied theology; was ordained a minister and held pastorates in Farmington 1848-1853; elected in 1857 for a five-year term as register of deeds for Franklin County and was reelected to the same office in 1862; elected as a Republican to the Forty-first Congress (March 4, 1869-March 3, 1871); unsuccessful candidate for renomination in 1870; resumed his ministerial duties in East Dixfield 1877-1879; moved to Vienna in 1885; retired from the ministry in 1886; died in Chesterville, Franklin County, Maine, August 4, 1892; interment in Chesterville Hill Cemetery.

**MORRIS, Cadwalader,** a Delegate from Pennsylvania; born in Philadelphia, Pa., February 19, 1741; attended the rural school; engaged in commercial pursuits and in the management of his estate; resided for a time in the West Indies; during the Revolutionary War was a member of the Philadelphia Troop of Light Horse; assisted in the establishment and served as an inspector of the Bank of Pennsylvania in 1780; one of the founders and a director of the Bank of North America in 1781; member of the Continental Congress in 1783 and 1784; was elected for another term, but declined; after the war operated an iron furnace in Birdsborough, Pa., but subsequently engaged in mercantile pursuits in Philadelphia; member of the Democratic Society of Philadelphia; died in Philadelphia January 25, 1795.

**Bibliography:** *DAB*.

**MORRIS, Calvary,** a Representative from Ohio; born in Charleston, Kanawha County, Va. (now West Virginia), January 15, 1798; attended the common schools; moved to Ohio in 1819 and settled in Athens; sheriff of Athens County, 1823-1827; member of the Ohio State house of representatives, 1827-1829; member of the State senate, 1829-1835; again a member of the State house of representatives in 1835 and 1836; elected as a Whig to the Twenty-fifth and to the two succeeding Congresses (March 4, 1837-March 3, 1843); chairman, Committee on Invalid Pensions (Twenty-seventh Congress); was not a candidate for renomination in 1842 to the Twenty-eighth Congress; engaged in wool growing; moved to Cincinnati, Ohio, in 1847; engaged in mercantile pursuits; returned to Athens and in 1854 was elected probate judge of Athens County; died in Athens, Ohio, on October 13, 1871; interment in Athens Cemetery.

**MORRIS, Daniel,** a Representative from New York; born in Fayette, Seneca County, N.Y., January 4, 1812; attended the public schools and the Canandaigua Academy in Ontario County, N.Y.; studied law; was admitted to the bar in 1845 and commenced practice in Penn Yan, Yates County, N.Y.; district attorney of Yates County, N.Y., 1847-1850; member of the State assembly in 1859; elected as a Republican to the Thirty-eighth and Thirty-ninth Congresses (March 4, 1863-March 3, 1867); was not a candidate for reelection in 1866; resumed the practice of law; died in Penn Yan, N.Y., April 22, 1889; interment in Lake View Cemetery.

**MORRIS, Edward Joy,** a Representative from Pennsylvania; born in Philadelphia, Pa., July 16, 1815; attended the common schools and the University of Pennsylvania at Philadelphia; was graduated from Harvard University in 1836; studied law; was admitted to the bar in 1842 and practiced in Philadelphia; member

of the Pennsylvania house of representatives, 1841-1843; elected as a Whig to the Twenty-eighth Congress (March 4, 1843-March 3, 1845); unsuccessful candidate for reelection in 1844 to the Twenty-ninth Congress; appointed Chargé d'Affaires to the Two Sicilies on January 10, 1850, and served until August 1853; member of the board of directors of Girard College, Philadelphia; again a member of the Pennsylvania house of representatives in 1856; elected as a Republican to the Thirty-fifth and to the two succeeding Congresses, and served from March 4, 1857 until June 8, 1861, when he resigned to accept a diplomatic position; appointed Minister Resident to Turkey on June 8, 1861, and served until October 1870; died in Philadelphia, Pa., December 31, 1881; interment in Laurel Hill Cemetery.

**Bibliography:** *DAB*.

**MORRIS, Gouverneur** (half brother of Lewis Morris and uncle of Lewis Richard Morris), a Delegate and a Senator from New York; born in Morrisania (now a part of New York City), N.Y., January 31, 1752; instructed by private tutors; graduated from Kings College (now Columbia University), New York, in 1768; studied law; was admitted to the colonial bar in 1771 and commenced practice in New York City; member, New York provincial congress, 1775-1777; lieutenant colonel in the State militia in 1776; member of the committee to prepare a form of government for the State of New York in 1776; member of the first State council of safety in 1777; member, first New York State assembly, 1777-1778; Member of the Continental Congress in 1778 and 1779; signer of the Articles of Confederation in 1778; moved to Philadelphia in 1779; appointed assistant superintendent of finance, 1781-1785; Pennsylvania delegate to the convention that framed the Constitution of the United States in 1787; returned to live in New York in 1788; went to Europe on business in 1789; appointed Minister Plenipotentiary to France on January 12, 1792, and served until April 9, 1794, when his recall was requested by the French government; returned to the United States in 1798; elected in 1800 as a Federalist to the United States Senate to fill the vacancy caused by the resignation of James Watson, and served from April 3, 1800 to March 3, 1803; unsuccessful candidate for reelection in 1802; chairman of the Erie Canal Commission, 1810-1813; author on legal and political subjects; died in Morrisania, N.Y., November 6, 1816; interment in St. Anne's Episcopal Churchyard, Bronx, N.Y.

**Bibliography:** *DAB*; Kline, Mary-Jo. *Gouverneur Morris and the New Nation, 1775-1788*. New York: Arno Press, 1978; Mintz, Max M. *Gouverneur Morris and the American Revolution*. Norman: University of Oklahoma Press, 1970; Morris, Gouverneur. *The Diary and Letters of Gouverneur Morris*. Edited by Anne Cary Morris. 2 vols. 1888. Reprint. New York: Da Capo Press, 1970.

**MORRIS, Isaac Newton** (son of Thomas Morris and brother of Jonathan David Morris), a Representative from Illinois; born in Bethel, Ohio, January 22, 1812; attended Miami University, Oxford, Ohio; studied law; was admitted to the bar in 1835 and commenced practice in Warsaw, Ill., in 1836; moved to Quincy, Ill., in 1838 and continued the practice of law; appointed secretary of state of Illinois in 1840, but declined; president of the Illinois & Michigan Canal Co. in 1841; member of the State house of representatives 1846-1848; elected as a Democrat to the Thirty-fifth and Thirty-sixth Congresses (March 4, 1857-March 3, 1861); was not a candidate for renomination in 1860; appointed by President Ulysses S. Grant commissioner for the Union Pacific Railroad in 1869; died in Quincy, Adams County, Ill., October 29, 1879; interment in Woodland Cemetery.

**MORRIS, James Remley** (son of Joseph Morris), a Representative from Ohio; born in Rogersville, Greene County, Pa., January 10, 1819; attended the public schools; moved with his parents to Waynesburg, Ohio, in 1829; moved to Woodsfield the next year; served two years' apprenticeship at the printing trade in 1833 and

1834; studied under private tutor until 1839; studied law; was admitted to the bar in 1843 and commenced practice at Woodsfield; appointed county treasurer to fill the unexpired term of his father, who had been elected to Congress; editor and manager of the Spirit of Democracy 1844-1848; member of the State house of representatives in 1848; member of the Ohio State Board of Equalization in 1859; elected as a Democrat to the Thirty-seventh and Thirty-eighth Congresses (March 4, 1861-March 3, 1865); unsuccessful candidate for reelection in 1864 to the Thirty-ninth Congress; resumed the practice of his profession at Woodsfield; judge of the probate court 1872-1877; postmaster 1886-1889; died in Woodsfield, Monroe County, Ohio, December 24, 1899; interment in Morris Cemetery, near Woodsfield.

**MORRIS, Jonathan David** (son of Thomas Morris and brother of Isaac Newton Morris), a Representative from Ohio; born in Columbia, Hamilton County, Ohio, October 8, 1804; attended the public schools; studied law; was admitted to the bar and commenced practice in Batavia, Ohio; clerk of the courts of Clermont County; elected as a Democrat to the Thirtieth Congress to fill the vacancy caused by the death of Thomas L. Hamer; reelected to the Thirty-first Congress and served from March 4, 1847, to March 3, 1851; died in Connersville, Fayette County, Ind., May 16, 1875; interment in Citizens Cemetery, Batavia, Ohio.

**MORRIS, Joseph** (father of James Remley Morris), a Representative from Ohio; born in Greene County, Pa., October 16, 1795; attended the public schools; sheriff of Greene County in 1824; moved to Woodsfield, Monroe County, Ohio, in 1829 and engaged in mercantile pursuits; member of the State house of representatives in 1833 and 1834; treasurer of Monroe County; elected as a Democrat to the Twenty-eighth and Twenty-ninth Congresses (March 4, 1843-March 3, 1847); was not a candidate for renomination in 1846; resumed business interests; died in Woodsfield, Ohio, October 23, 1854; interment in Morris Cemetery, near Woodsfield.

**MORRIS, Joseph Watkins,** a Representative from Kentucky; born in Sulphur, Henry County, Ky., on February 26, 1879; moved to New Castle, Ky., with his father in 1889; attended the public schools and graduated from New Castle High School in 1899; engaged in mercantile pursuits at New Castle; secretary to Representative J. Campbell Cantrill from 1909 until 1923; delegate to every Kentucky Democratic convention, beginning in 1904; chairman of the Kentucky Democratic campaign committee in 1923; elected as a Democrat to the Sixty-eighth Congress to fill the vacancy caused by the death of J. Campbell Cantrill, and served from November 30, 1923 to March 3, 1925; was not a candidate for renomination in 1924 to the Sixty-ninth Congress; revenue agent for Kentucky, 1925-1927; manager of a bus terminal in Louisville, Ky., from 1929 until his death in Louisville, Ky., December 21, 1937; interment in Odd Fellows Cemetery, Carrollton, Ky.

**MORRIS, Lewis** (half brother of Gouverneur Morris and uncle of Lewis Richard Morris), a Delegate from New York; born in Morrisania (now a part of New York City), N.Y., April 8, 1726; instructed by private tutors and was graduated from Yale College in 1746; engaged in agricultural pursuits; appointed by the Crown a judge of the Court of Admiralty in 1760 and resigned in 1774; again appointed by the provincial congress in 1776, but declined; elected to the Colonial Assembly of New York in 1769, but was declared disqualified for nonresidence; delegate to the provincial convention of the colony in April 1775; Member of the Continental Congress 1775-1777, and was a signer of the Declaration of Independence; deputy to the State provincial congress in 1776 and 1777; county judge of Westchester County in 1777; member of the committee on detection of conspiracies in 1777; served in the State senate 1777-1781 and 1784-1788, and was a member of the council of appointment in 1786; member of the first board of regents of the University of New York and served from 1784 until his death;

delegate to the State convention which adopted the Federal Constitution in 1788; died in Morrisania, N.Y., January 22, 1798; interment in vault beneath St. Anne's of Morrisania Church, Bronx, N.Y.

**Bibliography:** *DAB.*

**MORRIS, Lewis Richard** (nephew of Gouverneur Morris and Lewis Morris), a Representative from Vermont; born in Scarsdale, N.Y., November 2, 1760; attended the common schools; moved to Springfield, Vt.; secretary of foreign affairs 1781-1783; member of the Springfield meeting-house committee in 1785; tax collector in 1786 and 1787; clerk of Windsor County Court 1789-1796 and judge of the same court until 1801; clerk of the State house of representatives in 1790 and 1791; member of the convention to ratify the Federal Constitution; secretary of the constitutional convention in Windsor in 1793; brigadier general in the State militia in 1793; major general of the First Division 1795-1817; member of the State house of representatives 1795-1797 and 1803-1808, and served as speaker; elected as a Federalist to the Fifth, Sixth, and Seventh Congresses (March 4, 1797-March 3, 1803); died in Springfield, Vt., December 29, 1825; interment in Forest Hill Cemetery, Charlestown, Sullivan County, N.H.

**MORRIS, Mathias,** a Representative from Pennsylvania; born in Hilltown, Bucks County, Pa., September 12, 1787; attended the common schools in Newtown and Doylestown, Pa.; studied law; admitted to the bar in 1809 and commenced practice in Newtown; deputy attorney general in 1819; member of the Pennsylvania senate 1828-1833; elected as a Whig to the Twenty-fourth and Twenty-fifth Congresses (March 4, 1835-March 3, 1839); chairman, Committee on Expenditures in the Department of State (Twenty-fifth Congress); unsuccessful candidate for reelection in 1838 to the Twenty-sixth Congress; died in Doylestown, Bucks County, Pa., November 9, 1839; interment in Hilltown Baptist Church Cemetery, near Fricks, Pa.

**MORRIS, Robert** (father of Thomas Morris [1771-1849]), a Delegate and a Senator from Pennsylvania; born in Liverpool, England, January 20, 1734; immigrated to the United States in 1747 and settled in Oxford, Md.; attended school in Philadelphia; became a merchant in Philadelphia in 1748; signed the non-importation agreement of 1765; member of the Pennsylvania Council of Safety in 1775; member of the Continental Congress, 1775-1778; signer of the Declaration of Independence; settled upon the Manheim estate; member, Pennsylvania assembly, 1778-1781; national superintendent of finance, 1781-1784; established the Bank of North America; member, Pennsylvania assembly, 1785-1787; delegate to the Constitutional Convention of 1787; elected to the United States Senate and served from March 4, 1789, to March 3, 1795; declined to be a candidate for renomination; declined the position of Secretary of the Treasury in the Cabinet of President George Washington; known as the "Financier of the American Revolution" and one of the richest men in America, Morris became involved in unsuccessful land speculations, and was confined in the "Prune Street" debtors' prison in Philadelphia from February 1798 until his release on August 26, 1801; died in Philadelphia, Pa., May 8, 1806; interment in the family vault of William White in the churchyard of Christ Church.

**Bibliography:** *DAB*; Morris, Robert. *Papers.* Edited by E. James Ferguson. 4 vols. Pittsburgh: University of Pittsburgh, 1973-78; VerSteeg, Clarence. *Robert Morris: Revolutionary Financier.* New York: Octagon Books, 1972.

**MORRIS, Robert Page Walter,** a Representative from Minnesota; born in Lynchburg, Campbell County, Va., June 30, 1853; attended a private school and the College of William and Mary, Williamsburg, Va.; was graduated from the Virginia Military Institute, Lexington, Va., in 1872; assistant professor of mathematics, Virginia Military Institute, 1872-1873; professor of mathematics in the Texas Military Institute in 1873; moved to Austin, Tex.; professor of applied mathematics in the Agricultural and Mechanical College of Texas in 1876; settled near Bryan, Tex.; studied law; was admitted to the bar and commenced practice in Lynchburg, Va., in 1880; unsuccessful candidate for election in 1884 to the Forty-ninth Congress; moved to Duluth, Minn., in 1886; elected municipal judge of Duluth in February 1889; elected city attorney of Duluth in March 1894; appointed district judge of the eleventh judicial district of Minnesota in August 1895; resigned in 1896; elected as a Republican to the Fifty-fifth, Fifty-sixth, and Fifty-seventh Congresses (March 4, 1897-March 3, 1903); declined to be a candidate for renomination in 1902 to the Fifty-eighth Congress; United States district judge for the district of Minnesota from 1903 until 1923; retired from public life in 1923 and moved to Pasadena, Los Angeles County, Calif.; died in Rochester, Olmsted County, Minn., December 16, 1924; interment in Forest Hill Cemetery, Duluth, Minn.

**MORRIS, Samuel Wells,** a Representative from Pennsylvania; born in Philadelphia, Pa., September 1, 1786; pursued an academic course at Princeton College; studied law; admitted to the bar and commenced practice in Wellsboro, Tioga County, Pa.; judge of the district court; first treasurer of Wellsboro County; postmaster of Wellsboro from July 1, 1808, to April 1, 1813; member of the Pennsylvania house of representatives; elected as a Democrat to the Twenty-fifth and Twenty-sixth Congresses (March 4, 1837-March 3, 1841); was not a candidate for reelection in 1840 to the Twenty-seventh Congress; died in Wellsboro, Tioga County, Pa., May 25, 1847.

**MORRIS, Thomas,** (son of Robert Morris), a Representative from New York; born in Philadelphia, Pa., February 26, 1771; attended school in Geneva, Switzerland, 1781-1786 and the University of Leipzig, Germany, 1786-1788; returned to Philadelphia; studied law; was admitted to the bar and commenced practice in Canandaigua, N.Y.; member of the New York State assembly, 1794-1796; elected as a Federalist to the Seventh Congress (March 4, 1801-March 3, 1803); was not a candidate for renomination in 1802 to the Eighth Congress; resumed the practice of law in New York City in 1803; appointed United States marshal for the southern district of New York in 1816, 1820, 1825, and 1829; died in New York City on March 12, 1849.

**MORRIS, Thomas** (father of Isaac Newton Morris and Jonathan David Morris), a Senator from Ohio; born in Berks County, Pa., January 3, 1776; settled with his parents near Clarksburg, now West Virginia; briefly attended the common schools; enlisted as a ranger and fought against the Indians in 1793; moved to Columbia, Ohio (now a part of Cincinnati), in 1795 and clerked in a store; moved to Bethel, Ohio, in 1800; studied law; was admitted to the bar in 1804 and commenced practice in Bethel, Ohio; member, Ohio State house of representatives, 1806-1808, 1810, 1820-1821; member, Ohio State senate, 1813-1815, 1821-1823, 1825-1829, and 1831-1833; elected as a Jacksonian to the United States Senate, and served from March 4, 1833 to March 3, 1839; was not a candidate for renomination; chairman, Committee on Engrossed Bills (Twenty-fourth Congress), Committee on Pensions (Twenty-fifth Congress); engaged in agricultural pursuits; unsuccessful candidate for Vice President of the United States in 1844 on the Liberty Party ticket headed by James G. Birney; died at his home near Bethel, Clermont County, Ohio, December 7, 1844; interment in First Bethel Cemetery.
Bibliography: DAB; Morris, Benjamin. *The Life of Thomas Morris: Pioneer and Long a Legislator of Ohio.* Cincinnati: Moore, Wilstach, Keys, and Overend, 1856; Neuenschwander, John. "Senator Thomas Morris: Antagonist of the South, 1836-1839." *Cincinnati Historical Society Bulletin* 32 (Fall 1974): 123-39.

**MORRIS, Thomas Gayle,** a Representative from New Mexico; born in Eastland County, Tex., August 20, 1919; moved to New Mexico; served as an enlisted man in the United States Navy from November 12, 1937 to March 22, 1944; engaged in farming and ranching in Quay County, N.Mex.; graduated from the University of New Mexico in 1948; member of the New Mexico State house of representatives, 1953-1958; elected as a Democrat to the Eighty-sixth and to the four succeeding Congresses (January 3, 1959-January 3, 1969); unsuccessful candidate for reelection in 1968 to the Ninety-first Congress; unsuccessful candidate in 1972 for nomination to the United States Senate; management consultant; resumed his activities as a rancher; is a resident of Tucumcari, N.Mex.

**MORRIS, Toby,** a Representative from Oklahoma; born in Granbury, Hood County, Tex., February 28, 1899; moved to what was then Comanche County, Okla., in 1906 and to Walters, Cotton County, Okla., in 1913; attended the public schools, leaving high school in his senior year, during the First World War, to enlist in the United States Army; served successively as private, corporal, and sergeant with the One Hundred and Tenth Combat Engineers, attached to the Thirty-fifth Division, from October 1917 to May 1919; studied law; was admitted to the bar in 1920; court clerk of Cotton County, Okla., 1921-1925 and prosecuting attorney 1925-1929; began the private practice of law in Walters, Okla., in 1929; district judge of the twenty-first judicial district of Oklahoma from 1937 to 1946; elected as a Democrat to the Eightieth and to the two succeeding Congresses (January 3, 1947-January 3, 1953); was an unsuccessful candidate for renomination in 1952 to the Eighty-third Congress; district judge of the fifth judicial district of Oklahoma from January 1955 to December 1956; elected to the Eighty-fifth and to the Eighty-sixth Congresses (January 3, 1957-January 3, 1961); unsuccessful candidate for renomination in 1960 to the Eighty-seventh Congress; judge, Oklahoma State Industrial Court, July 1, 1961, to July 17, 1963; district judge for the State of Oklahoma, retiring in January 1971; resided in Lawton, Okla., where he died September 1, 1973; interment in Sunset Memorial Gardens.

**MORRISON, Bruce Andrew,** a Representative from Connecticut; born in New York City, October 8, 1944; attended the public schools of Northport, N.Y., and graduated from Northport High School in 1962; S.B., Massachusetts Institute of Technology, Cambridge, 1965; M.S., University of Illinois, Urbana, 1970; J.D., Yale University Law School, 1973; admitted to the Connecticut bar, 1973 and commenced practice in New Haven; admitted to practice in the United States Supreme Court, 1976, to the Second Circuit Court of Appeals, 1979, and to the New York bar, 1981; elected as a Democrat to the Ninety-eighth and to the three succeeding Congresses (January 3, 1983-January 3, 1991); was not a candidate for reelection in 1990 to the One Hundred Second Congress, but was an unsuccessful candidate for election for Governor of Connecticut; member of the Commission on Immigration Reform, December 3, 1992 to present; nominated to be chairman of the Federal Housing Finance Board on January 5, 1995, and was confirmed by the Senate on May 25, 1995; is a resident of Hamden, Conn.

**MORRISON, Cameron A.,** a Senator and a Representative from North Carolina; born near Rockingham, Richmond County, N.C., October 5, 1869; attended private schools at Ellerbe Springs, N.C., and at Rockingham; studied law; was admitted to the bar in 1892 and commenced practice in Rockingham; mayor of Rockingham in 1893; presidential elector at large in 1916; moved to Charlotte, N.C., and continued the practice of law; elected Governor of North Carolina in 1920, and served from January 12, 1921 to January 14, 1925; member of the Democratic National Committee in 1928; appointed as a Democrat to the United States Senate to fill the vacancy caused by the death of Lee S. Overman, and served from

December 13, 1930 until December 4, 1932, when a duly elected successor qualified; was an unsuccessful candidate for election to fill the vacancy; resumed the practice of law; elected as a Democrat to the Seventy-eighth Congress (January 3, 1943-January 3, 1945); was not a candidate for reelection in 1944 to the Seventy-ninth Congress; again resumed the practice of his profession in Charlotte, N.C.; died in Quebec, Canada, August 20, 1953; interment in Elmwood Cemetery, Charlotte, N.C.

**MORRISON, George Washington,** a Representative from New Hampshire; born in Fairlee, Orange County, Vt., October 16, 1809; attended the common schools and Thetford (Vt.) Academy; engaged in teaching; studied law; was admitted to the bar in 1835 and commenced practice in Manchester in 1836; member of the New hampshire State house of representatives in 1840 and 1841; solicitor of Hillsborough County, 1845-1849; served in the State senate in 1849 and 1850; elected as a Democrat to the Thirty-first Congress to fill the vacancy caused by the resignation of James Wilson and served from October 8, 1850, to March 3, 1851; unsuccessful candidate for reelection in 1850 to the Thirty-second Congress; elected to the Thirty-third Congress (March 4, 1853-March 3, 1855); unsuccessful candidate for reelection in 1854 to the Thirty-fourth Congress; continued the practice of law until 1872, when he retired; died in Manchester, Hillsborough County, N.H., December 21, 1888; interment in Valley Cemetery.

**MORRISON, James Hobson,** a Representative from Louisiana; born in Hammond, Tangipahoa Parish, La., December 8, 1908; attended the public schools; was graduated from the law department of Tulane University at New Orleans, La., LL.B., and J.D., 1934; was admitted to the bar in 1934 and commenced practice in Hammond, La.; unsuccessful candidate in 1940, 1944, and 1948 for nomination for Governor of Louisiana; delegate to the Democratic National Conventions of 1956 and 1960; elected as a Democrat to the Seventy-eighth and to the eleven succeeding Congresses (January 3, 1943-January 3, 1967); unsuccessful candidate for renomination in 1966 to the Ninetieth Congress; resumed the practice of law; is a resident of Hammond, La.

**MORRISON, James Lowery Donaldson,** a Representative from Illinois; born in Kaskaskia, Ill., April 12, 1816; appointed midshipman in the Navy in 1832 and served until December 31, 1839, when he resigned; studied law; was admitted to the bar and commenced practice in Belleville, Ill.; member of the Illinois State house of representatives in 1844; raised a company and served in the Mexican War as lieutenant colonel of Bissell's regiment of Illinois Volunteers from July 1, 1846 to July 1, 1847; was presented a sword by the Illinois legislature for services at the Battle of Buena Vista, near Monterrey, Mexico, February 22-23, 1847; member of the Illinois State senate in 1848; unsuccessful Whig candidate for Lieutenant Governor in 1852; elected as a Democrat to the Thirty-fourth Congress to fill the vacancy caused by the resignation of Lyman Trumbull, and served from November 4, 1856 to March 3, 1857; was an unsuccessful candidate for nomination for Governor of Illinois in 1860; died in St. Louis, Mo., on August 14, 1888; interment in Calvary Cemetery.

**MORRISON, John Alexander,** a Representative from Pennsylvania; born in Colerain, Lancaster County, Pa., January 31, 1814; attended the public schools; studied medicine; was graduated from the Jefferson Medical College at Philadelphia, Pa., in 1837 and commenced practice in Cochranville, Pa.; elected as a Democrat to the Thirty-second Congress (March 4, 1851-March 3, 1853); inspector and appraiser of imports of drugs at the port of Philadelphia, Pa., from 1853 until 1861; resumed the practice of medicine in Cochranville, Pa., 1861-1865; engaged in agricultural and mercantile pursuits; again resumed the practice of medicine in Cochranville, Pa., and died there on July 25, 1904; interment in Fagg's Manor Presbyterian Church Cemetery, Londonderry Township, Chester County, Pa.

**MORRISON, Martin Andrew,** a Representative from Indiana; born in Frankfort, Clinton County, Ind., April 15, 1862; attended the public schools; was graduated from Butler College, Irvington, Ind., in June 1883, and from the law department of the University of Virginia at Charlottesville in 1886; was admitted to the bar the same year and commenced practice in Frankfort, Ind.; county attorney of Clinton County in 1905 and 1906; member of the board of education, 1907-1909; elected as a Democrat to the Sixty-first and to the three succeeding Congresses (March 4, 1909-March 3, 1917); chairman, Committee on Patents (Sixty-fourth Congress); was not a candidate for renomination in 1916 to the Sixty-fifth Congress; resumed the practice of law; president of the United States Civil Service Commission from March 1919 to July 1921; became a member of the legal staff of the chief counsel of the Federal Trade Commission at Washington, D.C., on December 10, 1925, and served until his retirement on April 30, 1942, maintaining his residence in Washington, D.C.; died in Abingdon, Va., July 9, 1944, while on a vacation; interment in Bunnell Cemetery, Frankfort, Ind.

**MORRISON, Sidney Wallace,** Representative from Washington; born in Yakima, Yakima County, Wash., May 13, 1933; attended Toppenish public schools, Toppenish, Wash.; attended Yakima Valley College, 1951; B.S., Washington State University, Pullman, 1954; served in the United States Army, 1954-1956; partner, Morrison Fruit Co., Inc.; member, Washington State house of representatives, 1966-1974; Washington State senator, 1974-1980; elected as a Republican to the Ninety-seventh and to the five succeeding Congresses (January 3, 1981-January 3, 1993); was not a candidate for renomination in 1992 to the One Hundred Third Congress, but was an unsuccessful candidate for nomination for Governor of Washington; Washington State secretary of transportation, 1993 to present; is a resident of Zillah, Wash., and Olympia, Wash.

**MORRISON, William Ralls,** a Representative from Illinois; born on a farm at Prairie du Long, near the present town of Waterloo, Monroe County, Ill., September 14, 1824; attended the common schools and McKendree College, Lebanon, Ill.; served in the war with Mexico; went to California with the gold seekers in 1849, but returned to Illinois in 1851; studied law; was admitted to the bar in 1855 and commenced practice in Waterloo, Ill.; clerk of the circuit court of Monroe County, Ill., 1852-1854; member of the Illinois State house of representatives, 1854-1860, 1870, and 1871, and served as speaker in 1859 and 1860; organized and was colonel of the Forty-ninth Regiment, Illinois Volunteer Infantry, during the Civil War; while in command of his regiment in the field was elected as a Democrat to the Thirty-eighth Congress (March 4, 1863-March 3, 1865); unsuccessful candidate in 1864 for reelection to the Thirty-ninth Congress; unsuccessful candidate for election in 1866 to the Fortieth Congress; continued the practice of law in Waterloo, Ill.; elected to the Forty-third and to the six succeeding Congresses (March 4, 1873-March 3, 1887); chairman, Committee on Ways and Means (Forty-fourth, Forty-eighth, and Forty-ninth Congresses), Committee on Public Lands (Forty-fifth Congress), Committee on Expenditures in the Department of the Treasury (Forty-sixth Congress); unsuccessful candidate for the United States Senate in 1885; unsuccessful candidate for reelection in 1886 to the Fiftieth Congress; delegate to the Democratic National Conventions of 1856, 1868 1884, and 1888; also a delegate to the Union National Convention at Philadelphia in 1866; appointed in 1887 by President Grover Cleveland a member of the Interstate Commerce Commission; reappointed by President Benjamin Harrison on January 5, 1892, and served from March 22, 1887, to December 31, 1897; was chairman of the commission from March 19, 1892, to the end of his term; resumed the practice of law in Waterloo, Monroe County, Ill., and died there September 29, 1909; interment in Waterloo Cemetery.

**Bibliography:** *DAB*; Robbins, David E. "The Congressional Career of William Ralls Morrison." Ph.D. dissertation, University of Illinois, 1963.

**MORRISSEY, John,** a Representative from New York; born in County Tipperary, Ireland, February 12, 1831; immigrated to the United States in 1833 with his parents, who settled in South Troy, N.Y.; attended the public schools; moved to New York City in 1848 and worked as a molder; moved to California in 1851; returned to New York and became a proprietor of gambling houses in New York and Saratoga; was the champion heavyweight boxer of the world in 1858; purchased the controlling interest in the Saratoga race course in 1863; elected as a Democrat to the Fortieth and Forty-first Congresses (March 4, 1867-March 3, 1871); was not a candidate for renomination in 1870; resumed his former business pursuits; elected to the State senate in 1875; reelected in 1877 and served until his death in Saratoga Springs, N.Y., May 1, 1878; interment in St. Peter's Cemetery, Troy, N.Y.

**Bibliography:** *DAB*; Kofoed, John C. *Brandy for Heroes: A Biography of the Honorable John Morrisey, Champion Heavyweight of America and State Senator*. New York: Dutton, 1938.

**MORROW, Dwight Whitney,** a Senator from New Jersey; born in Huntington, Cabell County, W.Va., January 11, 1873; moved with his parents to Allegheny (now a part of Pittsburgh), Pa., in 1875; attended the public schools; graduated from Amherst College in 1895; studied law at Columbia University; was admitted to the bar in 1899 and engaged in practice in New York City; moved to Englewood, N.J., in 1903; engaged in banking and served as director of many industrial and financial corporations; during the First World War was director of the National War Savings Committee for the State of New Jersey; served abroad as adviser to the Allied Maritime Transport Council, as a member of the Military Board of Allied Supply and as a civilian aid; chairman of the New Jersey Prison Inquiry Commission, 1917-1918 and of the New Jersey State Board of Institutions and Agencies, 1918-1920; chairman of the Aircraft Board created by President Calvin Coolidge in 1925; appointed Ambassador to Mexico by President Coolidge on September 21, 1927 and served until September 1930; delegate to the Sixth Pan American Conference held at Havana in 1928, and to the London Naval Conference in 1930; elected as a Republican to the United States Senate in 1930 to fill the vacancy in the term ending March 3, 1931, caused by the resignation of Walter E. Edge, and at the same time was elected for the term commencing March 4, 1931, and served from December 3, 1930, until his death in Englewood, N.J., on October 5, 1931; interment in Brookside Cemetery.

**Bibliography:** *DAB*; McBride, Mary. *The Story of Dwight W. Morrow*. New York: Farrar and Rinehart, 1930; Nicolson, Harold. *Dwight Morrow*. 1935. Reprint. New York: Arno Press, 1975.

**MORROW, Jeremiah,** a Representative and a Senator from Ohio; born near Gettysburg, Pa., October 6, 1771; attended the public schools; moved to that part of the Northwest Territory which is now the State of Ohio in 1795; surveyor; engaged in agricultural pursuits; member, Territorial house of representatives, 1801-1802; member of the Ohio State senate in 1803; upon the admission of Ohio as a State into the Union was elected as a Republican to the Eighth and to the four succeeding Congresses, and served from October 17, 1803 to March 3, 1813; did not seek renomination in 1812 to the House of Representatives, having become a candidate for Senator; chairman, Committee on Public Lands (Tenth through Twelfth Congresses); elected as a Republican to the United States Senate, and served from March 4, 1813 to March 3, 1819; was not a candidate for reelection; chairman, Committee on Public Lands (Fourteenth and Fifteenth Congresses); unsuccessful candidate for election for Governor in 1820; served as State canal commissioner in

1822; elected Governor of Ohio in 1822, reelected in 1824, and served from December 28, 1822 to December 19, 1826; member, State senate, 1827-1828; member of the State house of representatives in 1829 and 1835; elected as a Whig to the Twenty-sixth Congress to fill the vacancy caused by the resignation of Thomas Corwin, and on the same day was elected to the Twenty-seventh Congress, and served from October 13, 1840 to March 3, 1843; declined to be a candidate for renomination in 1842 to the Twenty-eighth Congress; chairman, Committee on Public Lands (Twenty-sixth and Twenty-seventh Congresses); resumed agricultural pursuits; died near Lebanon, Warren County, Ohio, March 22, 1852; interment in Union Cemetery, on the Montgomery Pike, near his home, in Warren County, Ohio.

**Bibliography:** *DAB*.

**MORROW, John,** a Representative from New Mexico; born near Darlington, Lafayette County, Wis., on April 19, 1865; attended the public schools and the normal university; taught school in Wisconsin, Iowa, Nebraska, and New Mexico; superintendent of public schools of Colfax County, N.Mex., 1892-1896; studied law; was admitted to the bar in 1895 and commenced practice in Raton, N.Mex.; member of the Territorial house of representatives in 1897 and 1898; city attorney of Raton in 1900 and 1901; president of the board of education 1903-1923; delegate to the Democratic National Convention in 1908; regent of New Mexico Normal University, Las Vegas, N.Mex., in 1921 and 1922; elected as a Democrat to the Sixty-eighth, Sixty-ninth, and Seventieth Congresses (March 4, 1923-March 3, 1929); unsuccessful candidate for reelection in 1928 to the Seventy-first Congress; engaged in banking, had extensive ranch and livestock holdings, and was a large owner of real estate in Raton; died in Santa Fe, N.Mex., on February 25, 1935; interment in the Fairmont Cemetery, Raton, N.Mex.

**MORROW, John,** a Representative from Virginia; elected as a Republican to the Ninth and Tenth Congresses (March 4, 1805-March 3, 1809).

**MORROW, William W.,** a Representative from California; born near Milton, Wayne County, Ind., July 15, 1843; moved with his parents to Adams County, Ill., in 1845; attended the common schools and received private instruction; moved to Santa Rosa, Calif., in 1859; taught school; explored mining regions; went East in 1862 to join the Union Army and served in the National Rifles of the District of Columbia; while in the Army of the Potomac was appointed special agent of the Treasury Department in January 1865 and was detailed to California; remained there and was employed during the next four years in confidential positions under the Secretary of the Treasury; studied law; was admitted to the bar in 1869 and commenced practice in San Francisco; assistant United States attorney for California 1870-1874; assisted in organizing the San Francisco Bar Association in 1872 and served as its president in 1892 and 1893; chairman of the Republican State central committee of California 1879-1882; attorney for the State board of harbor commissioners 1880-1883; also special United States attorney before the French and American Claims Commission 1881-1883, and before the Alabama Claims Commission 1882-1885; delegate to the Republican National Convention in 1884; elected as a Republican to the Forty-ninth, Fiftieth, and Fifty-first Congresses (March 4, 1885-March 3, 1891); was not a candidate for renomination in 1890; United States district judge for the northern district of California 1891-1897; United States circuit judge of the ninth judicial circuit 1897-1922; retired from the bench on January 1, 1923; was one of the incorporators of the American Red Cross; resided in San Francisco, San Francisco County, Calif., until his death in that city on July 24, 1929; interment in Cypress Lawn Cemetery, Colma, Calif.

**Bibliography:** *DAB*.

**MORSE, Elijah Adams,** a Representative from Massachusetts; born in South Bend, St. Joseph County, Ind., May 25, 1841; moved to Massachusetts with his parents, who settled in Boston in 1852; attended the public schools, the Boylston School in Boston, and Onondaga Academy, New York; enlisted in the Union Army in the Fourth Regiment, Massachusetts Volunteers, during the Civil War; served three months under General Benjamin Butler in Virginia and one year under General Banks in Louisiana; promoted to corporal; manufacturer of stove polish in Canton, Mass.; member of the Massachusetts house of representatives in 1876; unsuccessful Prohibition Party candidate for Lieutenant Governor in 1877; served in the Massachusetts senate in 1886 and 1887; member of the Governor's council in 1888; elected as a Republican to the Fifty-first and to the three succeeding Congresses (March 4, 1889-March 3, 1897); chairman, Committee on Alcohol Liquor Traffic (Fifty-fourth Congress); was not a candidate for renomination in 1896 to the Fifty-fifth Congress; resumed manufacturing activities; died in Canton, Norfolk County, Mass., June 5, 1898; interment in Canton Cemetery.

**MORSE, Elmer Addison,** a Representative from Wisconsin; born in Franksville, Racine County, Wis., on May 11, 1870; attended the common schools of Racine County; was graduated from Ripon College, Wisconsin, in 1893; elected county superintendent of schools of Racine County in 1893 and reelected in 1895; attended the law school of the University of Wisconsin at Madison; was admitted to the bar in 1900 and commenced practice in Antigo, Wis.; city attorney of Antigo 1900-1906; also engaged in the insurance and real estate business from 1900 until his death; elected as a Republican to the Sixtieth, Sixty-first, and Sixty-second Congresses (March 4, 1907-March 3, 1913); unsuccessful candidate for reelection in 1912 to the Sixty-third Congress; resumed the practice of law at Antigo, Wis.; delegate to the Republican State conventions in 1934 and 1940; died at Rochester, Minn., on October 4, 1945; interment in Elmwood Cemetery, Antigo, Wis.

**MORSE, Frank Bradford,** a Representative from Massachusetts; born in Lowell, Middlesex County, Mass., August 7, 1921; attended the public schools; B.S., Boston University, 1948; LL.B., Boston University School of Law, 1949; served in the United States Army, 1942-1946, with service in the Pacific Theater; was admitted to the bar in 1949 and commenced the practice of law in Lowell, Mass.; law clerk to the Chief Justice of the Supreme Judicial Court of Massachusetts in 1949; member of the faculty, Boston University School of Law, 1949-1953; member of the Lowell City Council in 1952 and 1953; served on United States Senate Armed Services Committee in 1953 and 1954; executive secretary and chief assistant to Senator Leverett Saltonstall, 1955-1958; deputy administrator of Veterans Administration, 1958-1960; elected as a Republican to the Eighty-seventh and reelected to the five succeeding Congresses and served from January 3, 1961, until his resignation May 1, 1972, to become Under Secretary General for Political and General Assembly Affairs at the United Nations, and served in that position until 1976; director, United Nations Development Program, 1976-1986; president, Salzburg Seminar; was a resident of New York City; died December 18, 1994.

**MORSE, Freeman Harlow,** a Representative from Maine; born in Bath, Maine, February 18, 1807; attended private schools and the academy in Bath; engaged in business as a carver of figureheads for ships; member of the State house of representatives 1840-1844; elected as a Whig to the Twenty-eighth Congress (March 4, 1843-March 3, 1845); mayor of Bath, Maine, in 1849, 1850, and again in 1855; again served in the State house of representatives in 1853 and 1856; elected as a Republican to the Thirty-fifth and Thirty-sixth Congresses (March 4, 1857-March 3, 1861); chairman, Committee on Naval Affairs (Thirty-sixth Congress); was not a candidate for renomination in 1860; delegate to the peace convention held in Washington, D.C., in 1861, in an effort to devise means to prevent the impending war; appointed by President Abraham Lincoln as United States consul at London March 22, 1861, and consul general April 16, 1869, and served until July 1870; resided in Great Britain after his retirement from office; died in Surbiton, Surrey, February 5, 1891; interment in the parish churchyard of St. Mary's, Long Ditton, Surrey County, England.

**Bibliography:** *DAB.*

**MORSE, Isaac Edward,** a Representative from Louisiana; born in Attakapas, La., May 22, 1809; attended school in Elizabethtown, N.J., and the Norwich (Vt.) Military Academy, and was graduated from Harvard University in 1829; studied law; was admitted to the bar and practiced in New Orleans, La., and St. Martinville, La., 1835-1842; member of the State senate 1842-1844; elected as a Democrat to the Twenty-eighth Congress to fill the vacancy caused by the death of Peter E. Bossier; reelected to the Twenty-ninth, Thirtieth, and Thirty-first Congresses and served from December 2, 1844, to March 3, 1851; chairman, Committee on Private Land Claims (Thirty-first Congress); was an unsuccessful candidate for reelection in 1850 to the Thirty-second Congress; delegate to the Democratic National Convention in 1848; attorney general of Louisiana 1853-1855; appointed by President Franklin Pierce on December 2, 1856, one of two special commissioners to New Granada to negotiate concerning the transit of citizens, officers, soldiers, and seamen of the United States across the Isthmus of Panama; died in New Orleans, La., February 11, 1866; interment in Washington Cemetery.

**MORSE, Leopold,** a Representative from Massachusetts; born in Wachenheim, Rhenish Palatinate, Bavaria, August 15, 1831; attended the common schools in Wachenheim; immigrated to the United States in 1849 and resided for about a year in Sandwich, N.H.; moved to Boston, Mass., and worked in a clothing store, which he later purchased and operated until his death; delegate to the Democratic National Convention in 1876 and 1880; unsuccessful Democratic candidate in 1870 and 1872 for election to the Forty-second and Forty-third Congresses; elected to the Forty-fifth and to the three succeeding Congresses (March 4, 1877-March 3, 1885); chairman, Committee on Expenditures in the Department of the Navy (Forty-eighth Congress); declined to accept a renomination in 1884; elected president of the Post Publishing Co. in 1884; elected to the Fiftieth Congress (March 4, 1887-March 3, 1889); chairman, Committee on Expenditures in the Department of State (Fiftieth Congress); was not a candidate for renomination in 1888; resumed business activities; died in Boston, Mass., December 15, 1892; interment in Mount Auburn Cemetery, Cambridge, Mass.

**MORSE, Oliver Andrew,** a Representative from New York; born in Cherry Valley, Otsego County, N.Y., March 26, 1815; pursued classical studies and was graduated from Hamilton College, Clinton, N.Y., in 1833; studied law; was admitted to the bar and commenced practice in Cherry Valley, N.Y.; elected as a Republican to the Thirty-fifth Congress (March 4, 1857-March 3, 1859); was not a candidate for renomination in 1858; writer and translator; died in New York City April 20, 1870; interment in Cherry Valley Cemetery, Cherry Valley, Otsego County, N.Y.

**MORSE, Wayne Lyman,** a Senator from Oregon; born near Madison, Dane County, Wis., October 20, 1900; attended the public schools; B.Ph., University of Wisconsin, Madison, 1923, and M.A., 1924; LL.B., University of Minnesota School of Law, Minneapolis, 1928; J.D., Columbia University School of Law, New York City, 1932; held a reserve commission as a second lieutenant in the Field Artillery, United States Army, 1923-1929; taught argumentation at the University of Wisconsin, 1924, and the University of Minnesota, 1924-1928; assistant professor of law at the University of Oregon at Eugene, 1929, associate professor, 1930, and dean and professor of law, 1931-1944; member of the Oregon Crime Commission;

administrative director, United States Attorney General's Survey of Release Procedures, 1936-1939; Pacific Coast arbitrator for the United States Department of Labor (maritime industry) 1938-1942, and also served in other capacities in the Labor Department; chairman of the Railway Emergency Board, 1941; alternate public member of the National Defense Mediation Board, 1941; public member of the National War Labor Board, 1942-1944; elected as a Republican to the United States Senate in 1944 and reelected in 1950; announced on October 24, 1952 that he was resigning from the Republican Party and would continue to serve in the Senate as an Independent; announced his affiliation with the Democratic Party on February 17, 1955; reelected as a Democrat in 1956 and again in 1962, and served from January 3, 1945 to January 3, 1969; unsuccessful candidate for reelection in 1968; lecturer and labor arbitrator; distinguished visiting scholar, State University of New York, 1969-1970; unsuccessful candidate in 1972 for election to the United States Senate; won the Democratic senatorial nomination, May 28, 1974, and was actively engaged in campaigning when he died in Portland, Oreg., on July 22, 1974; interment in Rest Haven Memorial Park, Eugene, Oreg.

**Bibliography:** Smith, Arthur. *Tiger in the Senate: The Biography of Wayne Morse*. Garden City, N.Y.: Doubleday, 1962; Wilkins, Lee. *Wayne Morse: A Bio-Bibliography*. Westport: Greenwood Press, 1985.

**MORTON, Jackson** (brother of Jeremiah Morton), a Senator from Florida; born near Fredericksburg, Spotsylvania County, Va., August 10, 1794; attended the common schools and graduated from Washington College (now Washington and Lee University), Lexington, Va., in 1814, and from the College of William and Mary, Williamsburg, Va., in 1815; moved to Pensacola, Fla., in 1820 and engaged in the lumber business; member of the Florida legislative council in 1836 and 1837, serving as president in 1837; delegate to the constitutional convention of Florida in 1838; Navy agent at Pensacola, 1841-1845; presidential elector on the Whig ticket in 1848; elected as a Whig to the United States Senate, and served from March 4, 1849 to March 3, 1855; was not a candidate for reelection; again engaged in the lumber business; deputy to the Provisional Congress of the Confederate States in Montgomery, Ala., in 1861; member of the Confederate congress, 1862-1865; died at his country home, "Mortonia," near Milton, Santa Rosa County, Fla., November 20, 1874; interment in the private cemetery at "Mortonia."

**Bibliography:** Rucker, Brian R. *Jackson Morton: West Florida's Soldier, Senator, and Secessionist*. Milton, Fla.: Patagonia Press, 1990.

**MORTON, Jeremiah** (brother of Jackson Morton), a Representative from Virginia; born in Fredericksburg, Spotsylvania County, Va., September 3, 1799; attended a private school and Washington College (now Washington and Lee University), Lexington, Va., in 1814 and 1815; graduated from the College of William and Mary, Williamsburg, Va., in 1819; studied law; admitted to the bar and practiced at Raccoon Ford, Va.; on account of illness abandoned the practice of law and engaged in agricultural pursuits; elected as a Whig to the Thirty-first Congress (March 4, 1849-March 3, 1851); unsuccessful candidate for reelection in 1850 to the Thirty-second Congress; resumed agricultural pursuits; member of the Virginia secession convention in 1861; trustee of the Theological Seminary of Virginia at Alexandria; died at "Lessland," Orange County, Va., November 28, 1878; interment in the private cemetery at his old home, "Morton Hall," Orange County, Va.

**MORTON, John,** a Delegate from Pennsylvania; born near the old Morris Ferry (now the Darby Creek Bridge), Ridley Township, Delaware County, Pa., in 1724; attended the common school for about three months and received some tutoring in surveying; a land surveyor for many years; became justice of the peace in 1757;

member of the colonial general assembly 1756-1766 and 1769-1775 and served as speaker 1771-1775; member of the Stamp Act Congress in 1765; high sheriff 1766-1770; appointed as a judge in 1770, serving as president judge of the court of general sessions and common pleas of the county, and in April 1774 was appointed an associate justice of the supreme court of appeals of Pennsylvania; member of the Continental Congress 1774-1776; was a signer of the Declaration of Independence; died in Ridley Park, Delaware County, Pa., in April 1777; interment in St. Paul's Burial Ground, Chester, Pa.

**Bibliography:** *DAB*; Springer, Ruth L. *John Morton in Contemporary Records*. Harrisburg, Pa.: Pennsylvania Historical and Museum Commission, 1967.

**MORTON, Levi Parsons,** a Representative from New York and a Vice President of the United States; born in Shoreham, Addison County, Vt., May 16, 1824; attended the public schools and Shoreham Academy; clerk in a general store in Enfield, Mass., 1838-1840; taught school in Boscawen, N.H., in 1840 and 1841; engaged in mercantile pursuits in Hanover, N.H., in 1845; moved to Boston in 1850; entered the dry-goods business in New York City in 1854; engaged in banking in New York City in 1863; unsuccessful candidate for election in 1876 to the Forty-fifth Congress; was appointed by President Rutherford B. Hayes as honorary commissioner to the Paris Exhibition of 1878; elected as a Republican to the Forty-sixth and Forty-seventh Congresses, and served from March 4, 1879 until his resignation, effective March 21, 1881, to accept a diplomatic position; appointed Minister to France on March 21, 1881 and served until May 1885; elected Vice President of the United States in 1888 on the Republican ticket headed by Benjamin Harrison in 1888, was inaugurated on March 4, 1889, and served until March 4, 1893; was not a candidate for reelection as Vice President in 1892; elected Governor of New York in 1894, and served from January 1, 1895 to January 1, 1897; was an investor in real estate; died in Rhinebeck, Dutchess County, N.Y., on May 16, 1920; interment in the Rhinebeck Cemetery.

**Bibliography:** *DAB*; McElroy, Robert. *Levi Parsons Morton: Banker, Diplomat, and Statesman*. 1930. Reprint. New York: Arno Press, 1975.

**MORTON, Marcus,** a Representative from Massachusetts; born in Freetown, Mass., December 19, 1784; pursued classical studies and graduated from Brown University, Providence, R.I., in 1804; studied law; admitted to the bar and commenced the practice of his profession in Taunton, Mass.; clerk of the Massachusetts senate in 1811; elected as a Republican to the Fifteenth and Sixteenth Congresses (March 4, 1817-March 3, 1821); chairman, Committee on Revisal and Unfinished Business (Sixteenth Congress); unsuccessful candidate for reelection in 1820 to the Seventeenth Congress; executive councilor in 1823; elected Lieutenant Governor in 1823; served as Acting Governor from February 6 to May 26, 1825; unsuccessful candidate for election for Governor in every year from 1828 to 1838; elected Governor of Massachusetts in 1839, and served from January 18, 1840 to January 7, 1841; unsuccessful candidate for reelection in 1840; unsuccessful candidate for election for Governor in 1841; again elected Governor in 1842, and served from January 17, 1843 to January 1844; unsuccessful candidate for reelection in 1843; judge of the supreme court, 1825-1840; appointed by President James K. Polk collector of customs in Boston, and served from 1845 to 1849; delegate to the Massachusetts constitutional convention in 1853; member of the Massachusetts house of representatives in 1858; died in Taunton, Bristol County, Mass., February 6, 1864; interment in Mount Pleasant Cemetery.

**Bibliography:** *DAB*.

**MORTON, Oliver Hazard Perry Throck,** a Senator from Indiana; born in Saulsbury, Wayne County, Ind., August 4, 1823; attended a private school in Springfield, Ohio; apprenticed to a hatter and worked at the trade for four years; attended Wayne County Seminary, Centerville, Ind., and Miami University, Oxford, Ohio; studied law; was admitted to the bar in 1847 and commenced practice in Centerville; elected judge of the sixth judicial circuit of Indiana in 1852; unsuccessful Republican candidate for Governor in 1856; elected lieutenant governor in 1860, and upon the election of Governor Henry S. Lane to the United States Senate became Governor of Indiana; elected Governor for a full term in 1864, and served from January 16, 1861 until his resignation on January 23, 1867; elected as a Republican to the United States Senate in 1867; reelected in 1873, and served from March 4, 1867 until his death; chairman, Committee on Manufactures (Forty-first Congress), Committee on Agriculture (Forty-second Congress), Committee on Privileges and Elections (Forty-second through Forty-fifth Congresses); appointed a member of the Electoral Commission of 1877, to decide the contests in various States in the presidential election of 1876; died in Indianapolis, Ind., on November 1, 1877; interment in Crown Hill Cemetery.

**Bibliography:** *DAB*; Foulke, William. *Life of Oliver H.P.T. Morton.* 2 vols. 1899. Reprint. New York: AMS Press, 1976; Walker, Charles Manning. *Sketch of the Life, Character and Public Services of Oliver P. Morton.* Indianapolis: Indianapolis Journal, 1878.

**MORTON, Rogers Clark Ballard** (brother of Thruston B. Morton), a Representative from Maryland; born in Louisville, Jefferson County, Ky., September 19, 1914; attended the public schools and Woodberry Forest School, Orange, Va.; A.B., Yale University, 1937; engaged in the food business from 1938 until 1951, with the exception of military service; served in Armored Field Artillery, United States Army, from private to captain, 1941-1945, and served in the European Theater; president of Ballard and Ballard Co., 1947-1951; farmer and beef cattle feeding operator, Talbot County, Md.; delegate and floor manager at the Republican National Convention of 1968; chairman, Republican National Committee, April 1969 to January 1971; elected as a Republican to the Eighty-eighth and to the three succeeding Congresses, and served from January 3, 1963, until his resignation on January 29, 1971 to accept a Cabinet portfolio; Secretary of the Interior in the Cabinets of Presidents Richard M. Nixon and Gerald R. Ford from January 29, 1971 until April 30, 1975; Secretary of Commerce in the Cabinet of President Ford from May 1, 1975 to February 2, 1976; Counsellor to President Ford, with cabinet rank for economic and domestic policy matters, from February 3, 1976 to March 30, 1976; chairman of President Ford's campaign committee from March 30, 1976 to November 2, 1976; retired from politics and engaged in boat building on his farm at Presquisle, near Easton, Md., where he died on April 19, 1979; interment in Old Wye Cemetery, Wye Mills, Md.

**Bibliography:** *DAB*.

**MORTON, Thruston Ballard** (brother of Rogers Clark Ballard Morton), a Representative and a Senator from Kentucky; born in Louisville, Jefferson County, Ky., August 19, 1907; attended the public schools and Woodberry Forest School, Orange, Va.; graduated from Yale University in 1929; engaged in the grain and milling business; during the Second World War served as a lieutenant commander in the United States Naval Reserve, 1941-1946; director of the Louisville Board of Trade, Louisville Goodwill Industries, Frontier Nursing Service, and Lincoln Institute; also interested in banking; elected as a Republican to the Eightieth and to the two succeeding Congresses (January 3, 1947-January 3, 1953); was not a candidate for renomination in 1952 to the Eighty-third Congress; was appointed Assistant Secretary of State for Congressional Relations by President Dwight D. Eisenhower on January 29, 1953, and served until February 1956; elected as a Republican to the United States Senate in 1956; reelected in 1962 and served from January 3, 1957, until his resignation on December 16, 1968; was not a candidate for reelection in 1968; served as chairman of the Republican National Committee from 1959 until 1961; vice

chairman of the board and director, Liberty National Bank, Louisville, Ky.; chairman of the board and director, Churchill Downs, Louisville, Ky.; president, American Horse Council; resided in Louisville, Ky. until his death there on August 14, 1982; interment at Cave Hill Cemetery, Louisville, Ky.

**Bibliography:** Smiley, Sara. "The Political Career of Thruston S. Morton: The Senate Years, 1956-1968." Ph.D. dissertation, University of Kentucky, 1975.

**MOSELEY, Jonathan Ogden,** a Representative from Connecticut; born in East Haddam, Conn., April 9, 1762; attended the common schools; was graduated from Yale College in 1780; studied law; was admitted to the bar and commenced practice in East Haddam, Conn.; member of the State house of representatives 1794-1804; justice of the peace of East Haddam, Conn., 1794-1817; State's attorney of Middlesex County 1801-1805; colonel of the Twenty-fourth Regiment, Connecticut Militia, in 1802; elected as a Federalist to the Ninth and to the seven succeeding Congresses (March 4, 1805-March 3, 1821); moved to Saginaw, Mich., and continued the practice of law until his death on September 9, 1838.

**MOSELEY, William Abbott,** a Representative from New York; born in Whitesboro, Oneida County, N.Y., October 20, 1798; was graduated from Yale College in 1816; studied medicine and practiced; studied law; was admitted to the bar and practiced in Buffalo, N.Y.; member of the State assembly in 1835; served in the State senate 1838-1841; elected as a Whig to the Twenty-eighth and Twenty-ninth Congresses (March 4, 1843-March 3, 1847); resumed the practice of law; died in New York City on November 19, 1873; interment in Forest Lawn Cemetery, Buffalo, N.Y.

**MOSELEY-BRAUN, Carol,** a Senator from Illinois; born in Chicago, Ill., August 16, 1947; J.D., University of Chicago School of Law, 1972; Cook County recorder of deeds, 1990-1993; elected as a Democrat to the United States Senate in 1992 for the term ending January 3, 1999; is a resident of Chicago, Ill.

**MOSER, Guy Louis,** a Representative from Pennsylvania; born on a farm in Amity Township, Berks County, Pa., January 23, 1886; attended the rural schools, and Keystone State Teachers' College, Kutztown, Pa.; engaged in painting and paperhanging 1898-1904; taught school in Amity Township, Berks County, Pa., in 1903 and 1904; railway postal clerk 1904-1914; post office inspector 1914-1926; engaged in investment banking in Philadelphia, Pa., 1926-1931 and later in agricultural pursuits; unsuccessful candidate for the Democratic nomination for Congress in 1932 and 1934; elected as a Democrat to the Seventy-fifth, Seventy-sixth, and Seventy-seventh Congresses (January 3, 1937-January 3, 1943); chairman, Committee on Census (Seventy-seventh Congress); unsuccessful candidate for renomination in 1942 and for the Democratic nomination in 1944, 1948, and in 1950; resumed agricultural pursuits and also engaged in public speaking; died in Reading, Pa., May 9, 1961; interment in Amityville Church Cemetery, Athol, Pa.

**MOSES, Charles Leavell,** a Representative from Georgia; born near Turin, Coweta County, Ga., May 2, 1856; attended the country schools and was graduated from Mercer University, Macon, Ga., in 1876; engaged in teaching and agricultural pursuits; for several years principal of the Newnan Academy for Boys; after 1886 devoted his time exclusively to agricultural interests; member of the Farmers' Alliance; elected as a Democrat to the Fifty-second, Fifty-third, and Fifty-fourth Congresses (March 4, 1891-March 3, 1897); chairman, Committee on Pensions (Fifty-third Congress); unsuccessful candidate for renomination in 1896; resumed agricultural pursuits in Turin, Ga.; delegate to several Democratic State and National conventions; returned to his farm near Turin, Ga., and resumed agricultural pursuits; member of the State house of representatives 1900-1904; retired and moved to Atlanta, Ga., where he died October 10, 1910; interment in Oak Hill Cemetery.

**MOSES, George Higgins,** a Senator from New Hampshire; born in Lubec, Washington County, Maine, February 9, 1869; attended the public schools of Eastport, Maine, and Franklin, N.H.; graduated from Phillips Exeter Academy, Exeter, N.H., in 1887 and from Dartmouth College, Hanover, N.H., in 1890; private secretary to Governor David H. Goodell, 1889-1891; reporter, news editor, and chief editor on the Concord Evening Monitor, 1892-1918; member and secretary of the New Hampshire Forestry Commission, 1893-1907; appointed United States Minister to Greece and Montenegro on April 5, 1909 and served until September 1912; elected as a Republican to the United States Senate on November 5, 1918, to fill the vacancy caused by the death of Jacob H. Gallinger; reelected in 1920, and again in 1926, and served from November 6, 1918, to March 3, 1933; served as President pro tempore of the Senate during the Sixty-ninth through the Seventy-second Congresses; chairman, Committee on Printing (Sixty-sixth through Sixty-eighth Congresses), Committee on Post Office and Post Roads (Sixty-ninth and Seventieth Congresses), Committee on Rules (Seventy-first and Seventy-second Congresses); unsuccessful candidate for reelection in 1932, and for nomination to the United States Senate in 1936; engaged in literary work in Concord, N.H., and Washington, D.C.; died in Concord, N.H., December 20, 1944; interment in Franklin Cemetery, Franklin, N.H.

Bibliography: *DAB*; Gallagher, Edward J. *George H. Moses: A Profile.* Laconia, N.H.: Citizen Publishing House, 1975; Symonds, Merrill A. "George Higgins Moses of New Hampshire–The Man and the Era." Ph.D. dissertation. Clark University, 1955.

**MOSES, John,** a Senator from North Dakota; born in Strand, Norway, June 12, 1885; attended the public schools and graduated from Junior College, Oslo, Norway; immigrated to the United States in 1905 and settled in Benson, Swift County, Minn.; worked as a laborer, farm hand, clerk, and freight-claim investigator; secretary of the State Teachers College, Valley City, N.Dak., from 1911 until 1913; graduated from the law school of the University of North Dakota at Grand Forks in 1915; was admitted to the bar in 1915 and practiced law in Hope and Hebron, N.Dak., before moving to Hazen, N.Dak., in 1917; also engaged in agricultural pursuits and banking; State's attorney of Mercer County, N.Dak., 1919-1923 and 1927-1933; unsuccessful candidate for Governor in 1936; elected Governor of North Dakota in 1938, reelected in 1940 and 1942, and served from January 5, 1939 to January 4, 1945; elected as a Democrat to the United States Senate in 1944 and served from January 3, 1945, until his death on March 3, 1945, at Rochester, Minn., where he had gone for an operation; interment in St. Mary's Cemetery, Bismarck, N.Dak.

**MOSGROVE, James,** a Representative from Pennsylvania; born in Kittanning, Armstrong County, Pa., June 14, 1821; attended the common schools; engaged in the iron business; unsuccessful candidate in 1878 on the Greenback ticket for election to the Forty-sixth Congress; elected as a Greenback candidate to the Forty-seventh Congress (March 4, 1881-March 3, 1883); declined to be a candidate for renomination in 1882; also declined to be a candidate for the Democratic nomination for Governor; engaged in banking and was president of the First National Bank from 1882 until his death in Kittanning, Armstrong County, Pa., on November 27, 1900; interment in Kittanning Cemetery.

**MOSHER, Charles Adams,** a Representative from Ohio; born in Sandwich, DeKalb County, Ill., May 7, 1906; graduated from Sandwich High School, and Oberlin College in 1928; employed on daily newspapers in Aurora, Ill., and Janesville, Wis., 1929-1940; president and manager of the Oberlin Printing Company and editor-publisher of the Oberlin News-Tribune, 1940-1961; vice chairman of Oberlin City Council, 1945-1951; member of the Ohio

State senate, 1951-1960; member of Ohio Legislative Service Commission, 1947-1959; vice chairman of Ohio School Survey Commission, 1954-1955; delegate to the White House Conference on Education, 1955; director, Oberlin Improvement and Development Corporation; member of Presidential Commission on Marine Science, Engineering and Resources, 1967-1969; elected as a Republican to the Eighty-seventh and to the seven succeeding Congresses (January 3, 1961-January 3, 1977); was not a candidate for reelection in 1976 to the Ninety-fifth Congress; executive director of the House Science and Technology Committee, Washington, D.C., September 1977-1979; fellow, Woodrow Wilson Center, Smithsonian Institution, 1980; M.A., Oberlin College, 1982; was a resident of Oberlin, Ohio, until his death there on November 16, 1984.

**MOSIER, Harold Gerard,** a Representative from Ohio; born in Cincinnati, Hamilton County, Ohio, July 24, 1889; attended the public and high schools of his native city; was graduated from Dartmouth College, Hanover, N.H., in 1912 and from the law department of Harvard University in 1915; was admitted to the bar in 1916 and commenced practice in Cleveland, Ohio; member of the State senate 1932-1934; Lieutenant Governor of Ohio 1934-1936; elected as a Democrat to the Seventy-fifth Congress (January 3, 1937-January 3, 1939); unsuccessful candidate for renomination in 1938; resumed the practice of law in Cleveland, Ohio, Baltimore, Md., and Washington, D.C.; counsel, Glenn L. Martin Co. and Aircraft Industries Association; retired in 1961; resided in Washington, D.C., until his death there August 7, 1971; interment in Fort Lincoln Cemetery.

**MOSS, Frank Edward,** a Senator from Utah; born in Salt Lake City, Utah, September 23, 1911; attended the public schools; B.A., University of Utah, 1933; J.D., George Washington University Law School, Washington, D.C., 1937; was admitted to the bar in 1937; attorney for the Securities and Exchange Commission, Washington, D.C., 1937-1939; during the Second World War served as judge advocate in the European Theater with the Air Corps, 1942-1945; colonel in the United States Air Force Reserve (Ret.); elected Salt Lake City judge in 1940, reelected in 1945, and served until 1950, when he resigned; elected Salt Lake County attorney in 1950, reelected in 1954 and served until 1959; elected as a Democrat to the United States Senate in 1958; reelected in 1964 and again in 1970, and served from January 3, 1959 to January 3, 1977; unsuccessful candidate for reelection in 1976; chairman, Committee on Aeronautical and Space Sciences (Ninety-third and Ninety-fourth Congresses); secretary, Democratic Conference, and served on the Steering and Policy Committees; resumed the practice of law in Washington, D.C.; is a resident of Salt Lake City, Utah.

Bibliography: Moss, Frank E. *The Water Crisis.* New York: Praeger, 1967.

**MOSS, Hunter Holmes, Jr.,** a Representative from West Virginia; born in Parkersburg, Wood County, W.Va., May 26, 1874; attended the public schools; in early youth was employed in a bank; was graduated from the law department of West Virginia University at Morgantown in 1896; was admitted to the bar and commenced practice in Parkersburg, W.Va., in 1896; prosecuting attorney of Wood County, W.Va., 1900-1904; judge of the fourth circuit court of West Virginia, 1904-1912; elected as a Republican to the Sixty-third and Sixty-fourth Congresses, and served from March 4, 1913 until his death in Atlantic City, N.J., July 15, 1916; interment in Odd Fellows Cemetery, Parkersburg, W.Va.

**MOSS, John Emerson,** a Representative from California; born in Hiawatha, Carbon County, Utah, April 13, 1915; moved to Sacramento, Calif., with his parents in 1923; attended the public schools; attended Sacramento Junior College, 1931-1933; engaged in the sales, credit executive, and retail business from 1938 to 1943; member of the California Democratic State Central committee,

1938-1980; national committeeman of California Young Democrats, 1942-1944; served in the United States Navy, 1943-1945; licensed real estate broker, 1945-1984; member of the California State assembly, 1948-1952, and served as assistant Democratic floor leader at the 1949-1952 sessions; elected as a Democrat to the Eighty-third and to the twelve succeeding Congresses, and served from January 3, 1953 until his resignation on December 31, 1978; was not a candidate for reelection in 1978 to the Ninety-sixth Congress; is a resident of Sacramento, Calif.

**MOSS, John McKenzie** (nephew of James Andrew McKenzie), a Representative from Kentucky; born on a farm near Bennettstown, Christian County, Ky., January 3, 1868; attended the common and private schools; employed in the Railway Mail Service, 1888-1891; studied law at Kent Law School in Chicago; was admitted to the bar in 1893 and practiced in Bowling Green, Warren County, Ky., and adjoining counties; successfully contested as a Republican the election of John S. Rhea to the Fifty-seventh Congress, and served from March 25, 1902 to March 3, 1903; unsuccessful candidate for reelection in 1902 to the Fifty-eighth Congress; resumed the practice of law in Bowling Green; elected judge of the eighth judicial district of Kentucky in 1909; reelected in 1915, and served until 1921; appointed assistant general counsel and general counsel for the Alien Property Custodian, 1921-1922; resigned on February 6, 1922, to become Deputy Commissioner of Internal Revenue in charge of estate and capital tax, in which capacity he served until his resignation on March 2, 1923; appointed Assistant Secretary of the Treasury on March 3, 1923 and served until July 13, 1926, when he resigned; assumed the duties of associate judge of the Court of Claims on July 14, 1926, and served until his death in Washington, D.C., June 11, 1929; interment in La Fayette Cemetery, Bennettstown, near Hopkinsville, Christian County, Ky.

**MOSS, Ralph Wilbur,** a Representative from Indiana; born in Center Point, Clay County, Ind., April 21, 1862; educated in the common schools of the township and attended Purdue University, West Lafayette, Ind., for two years; taught school in Sugar Ridge Township; principal of the graded schools in Harmony, Ind.; subsequently became engaged in agricultural pursuits; member of the Indiana State senate, 1905-1909; elected as a Democrat to the Sixty-first and to the three succeeding Congresses (March 4, 1909-March 3, 1917); chairman, Committee on Expenditures in the Department of Agriculture (Sixty-second Congress); unsuccessful candidate for reelection in 1916 to the Sixty-fifth Congress, and for election in 1918 to the Sixty-sixth Congress; retired to his farm near Ashboro, Clay County, Ind., where he died on April 26, 1919; interment in Moss Cemetery, near his home.

**MOTT, Gordon Newell,** a Delegate from the Territory of Nevada; born in Zanesville, Ohio, on October 21, 1812; completed preparatory studies; studied law; was admitted to the bar and commenced practice in Zanesville in 1836; moved to Texas during its struggle for independence and served nine months as a volunteer; returned to Ohio and resumed the practice of law; moved to California in 1849; judge of Sutter County in 1850; district judge 1851-1854; moved to Nevada in 1861; appointed by President Abraham Lincoln associate justice of the supreme court of Nevada Territory on March 27, 1861, and served until his resignation in 1863, having been elected to Congress; elected as a Republican to the Thirty-eighth Congress and served from March 4, 1863, to October 31, 1864, when the Territory of Nevada became a State; was not a candidate for Representative from the new State in 1864; died in San Francisco, Calif., April 27, 1887; interment in Laurel Hill Cemetery.

**MOTT, James,** a Representative from New Jersey; born near Middletown, Monmouth County, N.J., January 18, 1739; educated by private teachers; engaged in agricultural pursuits; captain in the Second Regiment of Monmouth County Militia in 1775; member of the State house of assembly 1776-1779; State treasurer 1783-1799; elected as a Republican to the Seventh and Eighth Congresses (March 4, 1801-March 3, 1805); died on his farm near Middletown, N.J., on October 18, 1823; interment in Middletown Baptist Churchyard.

**MOTT, James Wheaton,** a Representative from Oregon; born near New Washington, Clearfield County, Pa., November 12, 1883; moved with his parents to Salem, Oreg., in 1890; attended the public schools, the University of Oregon at Eugene, and Stanford University, Calif.; was graduated from Columbia University, New York City, in 1909; engaged as a newspaper reporter in New York City, San Francisco, Calif., and Salem, Oreg., 1909-1917; was graduated from the law department of Willamette University, Salem, Oreg., in 1917; was admitted to the bar in the same year and commenced practice in Astoria, Oreg.; during the First World War served as a seaman first class in the United States Navy; city attorney of Astoria, Oreg., 1920-1922; member of the State house of representatives 1922-1928 and 1930-1932; moved to Salem, Oreg., in 1929; corporation commissioner of Oregon 1931-1932; elected as a Republican to the Seventy-third and to the six succeeding Congresses and served from March 4, 1933, until his death in Bethesda, Md., on November 12, 1945; interment in Mount Crest Abbey Mausoleum, Salem, Oreg.

**MOTT, Luther Wright,** a Representative from New York; born in Oswego, Oswego County, N.Y., November 30, 1874; attended the public schools and was graduated from Harvard University in 1896; engaged in banking in Oswego; appointed State superintendent of banks in 1907, but resigned after five days' service; delegate to the Republican National Convention in 1908; president of the New York State Bankers' Association in 1910 and 1911; elected as a Republican to the Sixty-second and to the six succeeding Congresses and served from March 4, 1911, until his death in Oswego, N.Y., July 10, 1923; interment in Riverside Cemetery.

**MOTT, Richard,** a Representative from Ohio; born in Mamaroneck, Westchester County, N.Y., July 21, 1804; attended the Quaker Seminary in Dutchess County, N.Y.; engaged in banking in New York City; moved to Toledo, Ohio, in 1836 and engaged in the real estate business and other enterprises; mayor of Toledo in 1845 and 1846; elected as a Republican to the Thirty-fourth and Thirty-fifth Congresses (March 4, 1855-March 3, 1859); was not a candidate for renomination in 1858; returned to Toledo, Ohio, and engaged in banking and the real estate business; served as chairman of the citizens' military committee during the Civil War; died in Toledo, Ohio, January 22, 1888; interment in Mount Hope Cemetery, Rochester, Monroe County, N.Y.

**MOTTE, Isaac,** a Delegate from South Carolina; born in Charleston, S.C., December 8, 1738; appointed ensign in His Majesty's Sixtieth Royal American Regiment, December 19, 1756, and promoted to lieutenant April 15, 1759; served in Canada in the French and Indian War in 1756; resigned and returned to Charleston in 1766; member of the house of commons in 1772; delegate to the provincial congresses of 1774, 1775, and 1776; during the Revolution was commissioned lieutenant colonel of the Second South Carolina (Continental) Regiment June 17, 1775, and was promoted to the rank of colonel September 16, 1776; resigned on election to the privy council in 1779; elected to the assembly from Charleston in 1779; Member of the Continental Congress 1780-1782; delegate to the State convention that ratified the Federal Constitution on May 23, 1788; appointed naval officer for the port of Charleston by General George Washington; died in Charleston, S.C., May 8, 1795; interment in St. Philip's Churchyard.

**MOTTL, Ronald Milton,** a Representative from Ohio; born in Cleveland, Cuyahoga County, Ohio, February 6, 1934; attended Barkwill Elementary School in Cleveland; graduated, Parma (Ohio) Schaaf High School, 1952; B.S., University of Notre Dame, 1956; LL.B., University of Notre Dame School of Law, 1957; admitted to the Ohio bar in 1957 and commenced practice in Cleveland; served in the United States Army, 1957; served as city councilman and president of the council in Parma, Ohio, 1960-1966; member, Ohio State house of representatives, 1967-1969; served in the Ohio State senate, 1969-1975; elected as a Democrat to the Ninety-fourth and to the three succeeding Congresses (January 3, 1975-January 3, 1983); unsuccessful candidate for renomination in 1982 to the Ninety-eighth Congress; resumed the practice of law; unsuccessful candidate for election to the Ohio State senate in 1984; elected to the Parma school board in 1985 and served as president in 1986; member, Ohio State house of representatives, District 20, 1987 to present; is a resident of Parma, Ohio.

**MOULDER, Morgan Moore,** a Representative from Missouri; born in Linn Creek, Camden County, Mo., August 31, 1904; attended the public schools of Linn Creek and Lebanon, Mo., and the University of Missouri at Columbia; LL.B., Cumberland University, Lebanon, Tenn., 1927; was admitted to the bar in 1928 and commenced the practice of law in Linn Creek, Mo.; elected prosecuting attorney of Camden County, Mo., in 1928; reelected for three succeeding terms and served until 1938, when he returned to the private practice of law; special assistant to the United States attorney for the western district of Missouri 1943-1946; appointed by Governor Phil M. Donnelly in April 1947 to serve as a judge of the circuit court in the eighteenth judicial circuit, and served until December 31, 1948; elected as a Democrat to the Eighty-first and to the six succeeding Congresses (January 3, 1949-January 3, 1963); was not a candidate for reelection in 1962 to the Eighty-eighth Congress; resumed the practice of law in Camdenton, Mo., where he died on November 12, 1976; interment in Old Linn Creek Cemetery, near Camdenton, Mo.

**MOULTON, Mace,** a Representative from New Hampshire; born in Concord, N.H., May 2, 1796; attended the public schools; sheriff of Hillsborough County in 1845; elected as a Democrat to the Twenty-ninth Congress (March 4, 1845-March 3, 1847); State councilor in 1848 and 1849; engaged in banking; died in Manchester, Hillsborough County, N.H., May 5, 1867; interment in Valley Cemetery.

**MOULTON, Samuel Wheeler,** a Representative from Illinois; born in Wenham, Essex County, Mass., January 20, 1821; attended the public schools; moved to Kentucky, where he taught school for several years, thence to Mississippi where he continued to teach; moved to Illinois in 1845 and settled in Oakland, Coles County; studied law; was admitted to the bar in 1847 and commenced practice in Sullivan, Ill.; moved to Shelbyville in 1849 and continued the practice of law; member of the State house of representatives 1852-1859; presidential elector on the Democratic ticket in 1856; president of the board of education of the State of Illinois 1859-1876; unsuccessful candidate for election in 1862 to the Thirty-eighth Congress; elected as a Republican to the Thirty-ninth Congress (March 4, 1865-March 3, 1867); elected as a Democrat to the Forty-seventh and Forty-eighth Congresses (March 4, 1881-March 3, 1885); chairman, Committee on Mileage (Forty-eighth Congress); was not a candidate for renomination in 1884; resumed the practice of law in Shelbyville; affiliated with the Republican Party after 1896; died in Shelbyville, Shelby County, Ill., June 3, 1905; interment in Glenwood Cemetery.

**MOUSER, Grant Earl** (father of Grant Earl Mouser, Jr.), a Representative from Ohio; born in Larue, Marion County, Ohio, September 11, 1868; attended the Larue Union Schools and Ada University, Ada, Ohio; was graduated from the Cincinnati Law School in 1890; was admitted to the bar the same year and commenced practice in Marion, Ohio; prosecuting attorney of Marion County 1893-1896; delegate to many State conventions; elected as a Republican to the Fifty-ninth and Sixtieth Congresses (March 4, 1905-March 3, 1909); unsuccessful candidate for reelection in 1908 to the Sixty-first Congress; delegate to the Republican National Convention in 1908; resumed the practice of law in Marion; judge of the court of common pleas of Marion County 1916-1925; resumed the practice of law until 1935 when he retired; died in Marion, Ohio, May 6, 1949; interment in Marion Cemetery.

**MOUSER, Grant Earl, Jr.** (son of Grant Earl Mouser), a Representative from Ohio; born in Marion, Marion County, Ohio, February 20, 1895; attended the public schools and Ohio Wesleyan University at Delaware in 1913 and 1914; was graduated from the law college of Ohio State University at Columbus in 1917 and was admitted to the bar the same year; during the First World War was graduated from the Army Medical School at Washington, D.C., in 1918, and served in the United States Army as a second lieutenant in the Medical Corps with the Western Reserve University College Ambulance Unit; commenced the practice of law in Marion, Ohio, in 1920; city solicitor of Marion 1924-1927, resigning to become special counsel in the State attorney's office, and served in this capacity until 1929; also served as attorney for the State highway department in 1927 and 1928; elected as a Republican to the Seventy-first and Seventy-second Congresses (March 4, 1929-March 3, 1933); unsuccessful candidate for reelection in 1932 to the Seventy-third Congress and for election in 1936 to the Seventy-fifth Congress; continued the practice of law until his death in Marion, Ohio, December 21, 1943; interment in Marion Cemetery.

**MOUTON, Alexander,** a Senator from Louisiana; born in Attakapas district, now Lafayette Parish, La., November 19, 1804; pursued classical studies and graduated from Georgetown College, District of Columbia; studied law; was admitted to the bar in 1825 and commenced practice in Lafayette Parish; planter; member, Louisiana State house of representatives, 1827-1832, and served as speaker, 1831-1832; presidential elector on the Democratic ticket in 1828, 1832, and 1836; unsuccessful candidate for election in 1830 to the Twenty-second Congress; member of the State house of representatives in 1836; elected as a Democrat to the United States Senate to fill the vacancy caused by the resignation of Alexander Porter, was reelected to the full term, and served from January 12, 1837 until his resignation on March 1, 1842; chairman, Committee on Agriculture (Twenty-sixth Congress); elected Governor of Louisiana in 1842, and served from January 30, 1843 to February 11, 1846; actively involved in railroads; president of the State secession convention in 1861; died near Vermillionville (now Lafayette), La., on February 12, 1885; interment in St. John's Cemetery.

    **Bibliography:** *DAB.*

**MOUTON, Robert Louis,** a Representative from Louisiana; born in Duchamp, St. Martin Parish, La., October 20, 1892; moved with his parents to Lafayette, La., where he attended the public schools; was graduated from Southwestern Louisiana Institute, Lafayette, La.; employed as a clerk in a bank in 1911 and 1912; member of the faculty of St. Charles College, Grand Coteau, La., 1912-1914; engaged in the insurance business and also operated a night school at Lafayette, La., in 1915 and 1916; served as aide to the general receiver of customs on the island of Haiti, in 1916 and as collector of customs at Gonaives, Haiti, from March 1917 to April 1919; during the First World War enlisted in the United States Marine Corps; served as an interpreter and intelligence officer attached to the first squadron of the first marine aviation outfit overseas from May 1918 to January 1919; returned to Lafayette and engaged in horticultural pursuits; mayor of Lafayette 1919-1927 and 1931-1935; postmaster from May 1929 until his resignation in November 1930; member of the United States Marine Corps

Reserve, with rank of captain; delegate to the Democratic National Convention in 1936; elected as a Democrat to the Seventy-fifth and Seventy-sixth Congresses (January 3, 1937-January 3, 1941); unsuccessful candidate for renomination in 1940; resumed his horticultural and real estate interests; died in New Orleans, La., November 26, 1956; interment in St. John's Catholic Cemetery, Lafayette, La.

**MOWRY, Daniel, Jr.,** a Delegate from Rhode Island; born in Smithfield, Providence County, R.I., August 17, 1729; received a limited schooling and learned the cooper's trade; town clerk of Smithfield 1760-1780; member of the general assembly 1766-1776; judge of the court of common pleas 1776-1781; Member of the Continental Congress 1780-1782; declined to be a candidate for renomination; engaged in agricultural pursuits until his death in the town of Smithfield, Providence County, R.I., July 6, 1806; interment in the family cemetery in North Smithfield, R.I.

**MOXLEY, William James,** a Representative from Illinois; born in County Cork, Ireland, May 22, 1851; as an infant immigrated with his parents to the United States and settled in Chicago, Ill.; attended the common schools; engaged in the manufacture of oleomargarine in 1881 and, later, in banking; member of the Republican State central committee; member of the executive board of the Cook County central committee; colonel on the staff of Governor Richard Yates, 1900-1904; elected as a Republican to the Sixty-first Congress to fill the vacancy caused by the resignation of William Lorimer and served from November 23, 1909, to March 3, 1911; unsuccessful candidate for reelection in 1910 to the Sixty-second Congress; continued his former business activities in Chicago, Ill., until his retirement; died at his summer home on Delavan Lake, near Delavan, Wis., August 4, 1938; interment in Calvary Cemetery, Chicago, Ill.

**MOYNIHAN, Daniel Patrick,** a Senator from New York; born in Tulsa, Okla., March 16, 1927; attended the public and parochial schools of New York City; attended the City College of New York in 1943; B.N.S., Tufts University, Medford, Mass., 1946, B.A., 1948; M.A., Fletcher School of Law and Diplomacy, 1949, Ph.D., 1961, LL.D., 1968; studied as a Fulbright fellow at the London School of Economics and Political Science, 1950-1951; served as a gunnery officer in the United States Navy 1944-1947; assistant and secretary to New York Governor W. Averell Harriman 1955-1958; member, New York State Tenure Commission 1959-1960; director of Syracuse University's New York State Government Research Project 1959-1961; director, Joint Center for Urban Studies, Massachusetts Institute of Technology and Harvard University 1966-1969; author; delegate to the Democratic National Conventions of 1960 and 1976; Assistant Secretary for Policy Planning and Research, United States Department of Labor, 1963-1965; Assistant to the President for Urban Affairs, 1969-1970; appointed United States Ambassador to India on February 8, 1973 and served until January 1975; appointed United States Permanent Representative to the United Nations on June 10, 1975 and served until February 1976; elected as a Democrat to the United States Senate in 1976 for the term commencing January 3, 1977; reelected in 1982, 1988, and again in 1994 for the term ending January 3, 2001; chairman, Committee on the Environment and Public Works (One Hundred Second Congress); Committee on Finance (One Hundred Third Congress); is a resident of Pindars Corners, N.Y.

**MOYNIHAN, Patrick Henry,** a Representative from Illinois; born in Chicago, Ill., September 25, 1869; attended the public schools and St. Patrick's High School in Chicago, Ill.; engaged in the publishing and printing business and also in the coal business; member of the city council of Chicago 1901-1909; member of the Illinois State Commerce Commission 1921-1929, serving as chairman in 1928 and 1929; elected as a Republican to the Seventy-third Congress (March 4, 1933-January 3, 1935); unsuccessful candidate for reelection in 1934 to the Seventy-fourth Congress, for election in 1936 to the Seventy-fifth Congress, and in 1940 to the Seventy-seventh Congress; continued his former business activities in Chicago, Ill., until his death on May 20, 1946; interment in Mount Olivet Cemetery.

**MOZLEY, Norman Adolphus,** a Representative from Missouri; born on a farm in Johnson County, Ill., December 11, 1865; attended the common schools; moved to Stoddard County, Mo., in 1887 and taught school; studied law; was admitted to the bar in 1891 and practiced in Bloomfield, Stoddard County, Mo.; elected as a Republican to the Fifty-fourth Congress (March 4, 1895-March 3, 1897); was not a candidate for renomination in 1896; resumed the practice of law in Bloomfield, Mo.; commissioner of the State supreme court 1919-1921; moved to Poplar Bluff, Mo., and continued the practice of his profession; delegate to the State constitutional convention of 1921 and 1922; died in Bloomfield, Mo., May 9, 1922; interment in Bloomfield Cemetery.

**MRAZEK, Robert Jan,** a Representative from New York; born in Newport, Newport County, R.I., November 6, 1945; attended public schools in Huntington, N.Y.; A.B., Cornell University, Ithaca, N.Y., 1967; served in the United States Navy, 1967-1968, being honorably discharged as disabled-retired; aide to Senator Vance Hartke of Indiana, 1969-1971; small businessman, 1971-1975; member, Suffolk County, N.Y., legislature, 1975-1982; delegate to the Democratic National Conventions of 1980 and 1992; elected as a Democrat to the Ninety-eighth and to the four succeeding Congresses (January 3, 1983-January 3, 1993); was not a candidate for renomination to the House of Representatives, but was a candidate for nomination for the United States Senate until he withdrew from the race on April 8, 1992; is a resident of Centerport, N.Y.

**MRUK, Joseph,** a Representative from New York; born in Buffalo, N.Y., November 6, 1903; engaged in the jewelry business in Buffalo, N.Y., in 1928; unsuccessful candidate for election to the Buffalo Common Council in 1935; served as district councilman to the Buffalo Common Council 1937-1941; was elected councilman at large in 1941 and served until December 22, 1942, when he resigned; elected as a Republican to the Seventy-eighth Congress (January 3, 1943-January 3, 1945); unsuccessful candidate for renomination in 1944 to the Seventy-ninth Congress; resumed the retail jewelry business; unsuccessful candidate for election as mayor of Buffalo in 1945; elected to the Buffalo City Council in 1947; elected mayor of Buffalo in 1949 and served from January 1, 1950, to December 31, 1953; was a resident of Cheektowaga, N.Y.; died January 21, 1995.

**MUDD, Sydney Emanuel** (father of Sidney Emanuel Mudd [1885-1924]), a Representative from Maryland; born at "Gallant Green," Charles County, Md., February 12, 1858; attended Georgetown University, Washington, D.C., and was graduated from St. John's College, Annapolis, Md., in 1878; studied law privately and also attended the law department of the University of Virginia at Charlottesville; was admitted to the bar in 1880 and practiced; member of the State house of delegates in 1879 and 1881; successfully contested as a Republican the election of Barnes Compton to the Fifty-first Congress and served from March 20, 1890, to March 3, 1891; unsuccessful candidate for reelection in 1890 to the Fifty-second Congress; elected to the State house of delegates in 1895 and served as speaker; moved to La Plata in 1896; delegate to the Republican National Convention in 1896; elected to the Fifty-fifth and to the six succeeding Congresses (March 4, 1897-March 3, 1911); chairman, Committee on Expenditures in the Department of Justice (Sixtieth and Sixty-first Congresses); died in Philadelphia, Pa., October 21, 1911; interment in St. Ignatius' Catholic Church Cemetery, Chapel Point, near La Plata, Charles County, Md.

**MUDD, Sydney Emanuel** (son of Sydney Emanuel Mudd [1858-1911]), a Representative from Maryland; born at "Gallant Green," Charles County, Md., June 20, 1885; attended the public schools of Charles County and the District of Columbia; moved with his parents to La Plata, Md., in 1896; was graduated from the academic department of Georgetown University, Washington, D.C., in 1906 and from the law department in 1909; unsuccessful candidate for election to the Maryland house of delegates in 1909; was admitted to the bar in 1910; professor of criminal law at Georgetown University Law School in 1910; appointed assistant district attorney of the District of Columbia in February 1911 and resigned in March 1912; unsuccessful candidate for nomination in 1912 for election to the Sixty-third Congress; reappointed assistant district attorney in July 1912 and resigned in March 1914, to become a candidate for Congress; elected as a Republican to the Sixty-fourth and to the four succeeding Congresses and served from March 4, 1915, until his death in Baltimore, Md., October 11, 1924; interment in St. Ignatius' Catholic Church Cemetery, Chapel Point, near La Plata, Charles County, Md.

**MUHLENBERG, Francis Swaine** (son of John Peter Gabriel Muhlenberg and nephew of Frederick Augustus Conrad Muhlenberg), a Representative from Ohio; born in Philadelphia, Pa., April 22, 1795; attended the public schools of Philadelphia and Dickinson College, Carlisle, Pa.; studied law; was admitted to the bar in 1816 and commenced practice in Reading, Pa.; private secretary to Governor Joseph Hiester, 1820-1823; moved to Pickaway County, Ohio; member of the Ohio State house of representatives in 1827; elected to the Twentieth Congress to fill the vacancy caused by the resignation of William Creighton, Jr., and served from December 19, 1828, to March 3, 1829; engaged in the real estate business in Ohio and Kentucky; died in Pickaway County, Ohio, on December 17, 1831; interment in Protestant Cemetery, Circleville, Pickaway County, Ohio.

**MUHLENBERG, Frederick Augustus** (great-great-grandson of Frederick Augustus Conrad Muhlenberg and great-great-grandnephew of John Peter Gabriel Muhlenberg), a Representative from Pennsylvania; born in Reading, Berks County, Pa., September 25, 1887; attended the public schools; M.S., Gettysburg (Pa.) College, 1908; B.S., University of Pennsylvania at Philadelphia, 1912; during the First World War served as captain of the Three Hundred and Fourteenth Infantry from September 1917 to March 1919; awarded the Distinguished Service Cross, Purple Heart with Palm, Legion d'Honneur, and the Croix de Guerre; became engaged as an architect at Reading, Pa., in 1920; city councilman of Reading, Pa., 1934-1938; Republican county chairman in 1935 and 1936; served as a lieutenant colonel and later as a colonel in the Corps of Engineers, United States Army, from December 1940 to March 1946; awarded the Legion of Merit; elected as a Republican to the Eightieth Congress (January 3, 1947-January 3, 1949); unsuccessful candidate for reelection in 1948 to the Eighty-first Congress; resumed the practice of architecture in Reading, Pa.; chairman, Pennsylvania Art Commission 1952-1963 and the County Planning Commission, 1958-1972; resided in Wernersville, Pa., until his death in Reading, Pa., on January 19, 1980; interment in Arlington National Cemetery, Va.

**MUHLENBERG, Frederick Augustus Conrad** (brother of John Peter Gabriel Muhlenberg, uncle of Francis Swaine Muhlenberg and of Henry Augustus Philip Muhlenberg, and great-great-grandfather of Frederick Augustus Muhlenberg), a Delegate and a Representative from Pennsylvania; born in Trappe, Pa., January 1, 1750; pursued an academic course; attended the University of Halle, Germany; studied theology and was ordained by the ministerium of Pennsylvania as a minister of the Lutheran Church on October 25, 1770; preached in Stouchsburg and Lebanon, Pa., 1770-1774, and in New York City, 1774-1776; when the British entered New York in

September 1776 he felt obliged to leave, and returned to Trappe, Pa.; moved to New Hanover, Pa., and was pastor there and in Oley and New Goshenhoppen until August 1779; member of the Continental Congress in 1779 and 1780; served in the Pennsylvania house of representatives, 1780-1783, and was elected speaker on November 3, 1780; delegate to and president of the Pennsylvania constitutional convention in 1787 called to ratify the Federal Constitution; elected to the First and to the three succeeding Congresses (March 4, 1789-March 3, 1797); Speaker of the House of Representatives (First and Third Congresses); was not a candidate for renomination in 1796 to the Fifth Congress; president of the council of censors of Pennsylvania; appointed receiver general of the Pennsylvania Land Office on January 8, 1800, and served until his death in Lancaster, Pa., June 4, 1801; interment in Woodward Hill Cemetery.

**Bibliography:** *DAB*; Seidensticker, Oswald. "Frederick Augustus Conrad Muhlenberg: Speaker of the House of Representatives in the First Congress, 1789." *Pennsylvania Magazine of History and Biography* 13 (July 1889): 184-206; Wallace, Paul A.W. *The Muhlenbergs of Pennsylvania*. 1950. Reprint. Freeport, N.Y.: Books for Libraries Press, 1970.

**MUHLENBERG, Henry Augustus** (son of Henry Augustus Philip Muhlenberg and grandson of Joseph Hiester), a Representative from Pennsylvania; born in Reading, Pa., July 21, 1823; pursued classical studies; was graduated from Dickinson College, Carlisle, Pa., in 1841; studied law; was admitted to the bar in 1844 and commenced practice in Reading, Pa.; member of the Pennsylvania senate 1849-1852; elected as a Democrat to the Thirty-third Congress and served from March 4, 1853, until his death in Washington, D.C., January 9, 1854; interment in Charles Evans Cemetery, Reading, Pa.

**MUHLENBERG, Henry Augustus Philip** (father of Henry Augustus Muhlenberg and nephew of John Peter Gabriel Muhlenberg and of Frederick Augustus Conrad Muhlenberg), a Representative from Pennsylvania; born in Lancaster, Pa., May 13, 1782; pursued classical studies; studied theology and was ordained to the Lutheran ministry by the ministerium of Pennsylvania in 1802; pastor of Trinity Church, Reading, Pa., from April 1803 to June 1829; elected as a Jacksonian to the Twenty-first Congress; reelected as a Jacksonian to the Twenty-second through Twenty-fourth Congresses and reelected as a Democrat to the Twenty-fifth Congress, and served from March 4, 1829 until his resignation on February 9, 1838; chairman, Committee on Revolutionary Claims (Twenty-second through Twenty-fifth Congresses); unsuccessful Democratic candidate for Governor in 1835 and 1837; appointed Minister to Austria on February 8, 1838 and served until September 1840; was nominated as the Democratic candidate for Governor of Pennsylvania in 1844, but died in Reading, Pa., August 11, 1844, before the election; interment in Charles Evans Cemetery.

**Bibliography:** *DAB*.

**MUHLENBERG, John Peter Gabriel** (father of Francis Swaine Muhlenberg, brother of Frederick Augustus Conrad Muhlenberg, uncle of Henry Augustus Philip Muhlenberg, and great-great-granduncle of Frederick Augustus Muhlenberg), a Representative and a Senator from Pennsylvania; born in Trappe, Pa., October 1, 1746; pursued classical studies; attended the Academy of Philadelphia (later the University of Pennsylvania); studied in the University of Halle, Germany, 1763-1766; apprenticed to a grocer, absconded, and served in a German regiment of dragoons; returned to Philadelphia in 1766; studied theology and was ordained in 1768; pastor of Lutheran churches in New Germantown and Bedminster, N.J.; moved to Woodstock, Va.; on a visit to Great Britain in 1772 was ordained a priest in the Anglican Church; member, Virginia house of burgesses 1774; chairman of the committee of safety for Dunmore County, Va.; during the Revolutionary War, raised and commanded the Eighth Virginia (German) Regiment; commissioned brigadier general of the Continental Army in 1777, and brevetted major general in 1783; returned to Pennsylvania and settled in Montgomery County; elected a member of the supreme executive council of Pennsylvania in 1784 and served as vice president 1785-1788; elected to the First Congress (March 4, 1789-March 3, 1791), the Third Congress (March 4, 1793-March 3, 1795), and the Sixth Congress (March 4, 1799-March 3, 1801); presidential elector in 1796; elected to the United States Senate and served from March 4, 1801, until his resignation on June 30, 1801; appointed by President Thomas Jefferson supervisor of revenue for Pennsylvania in 1801 and collector of customs at Philadelphia in 1802, in which latter capacity he served until his death at Gray's Ferry, Montgomery County, Pa., October 1, 1807; interment in the Augustus Lutheran Church Cemetery, Trappe, Pa.

**Bibliography:** *DAB*; Hocker, E.W. *The Fighting Parson of the American Revolution: A Biography of General Peter Muhlenberg.* Philadelphia: published by author, 1936; Muhlenberg, Henry Augustus. *Life of Major General Peter Muhlenberg.* Philadelphia: Carey and Hart, 1849.

**MULDOWNEY, Michael Joseph,** a Representative from Pennsylvania; born in Philadelphia, Pa., on August 10, 1889; moved with his parents to Pittsburgh, Pa., in 1894; attended the public schools; was graduated from Duquesne University, Pittsburgh, Pa., in 1908; member of the Pennsylvania house of representatives 1925-1929; served in the city council of Pittsburgh 1930-1933; elected as a Republican to the Seventy-third Congress (March 4, 1933-January 3, 1935); unsuccessful candidate for reelection in 1934 to the Seventy-fourth Congress; member of the Pennsylvania board of mercantile appraisers 1935-1937; appointed Pennsylvania unemployment compensation referee in 1940 and served in that capacity until his death in Pittsburgh, Pa., on March 30, 1947; interment in Calvary Cemetery.

**MULDROW, Henry Lowndes,** a Representative from Mississippi; born near Tibbes Station, Clay County, Miss., February 8, 1837; was graduated from the University of Mississippi at Oxford in 1857, and from the law department of the same university in 1858; was admitted to the bar in 1859 and commenced practice in Starkville, Miss.; entered the Confederate Army as a private in 1861, and before the close of the Civil War attained the rank of colonel of cavalry; district attorney for the sixth judicial district of Mississippi, 1869-1871; member of the Mississippi State house of representatives in 1875; trustee of the University of Mississippi, 1876-1898; elected as a Democrat to the Forty-fifth and to the three succeeding Congresses (March 4, 1877-March 3, 1885); chairman, Committee on Territories (Forty-sixth Congress), Committee on Private Land Claims (Forty-eighth Congress); First Assistant Secretary of the Interior during the first administration of President Grover Cleveland; resigned in 1889 and resumed the practice of law in Starkville, Miss.; delegate to the State constitutional convention in 1890; appointed chancellor of the first district of Mississippi in September 1899 and served until 1905; died in Starkville, Oktibbeha County, Miss., March 1, 1905; interment in Odd Fellows Cemetery.

**MULKEY, Frederick William** (nephew of Joseph Norton Dolph), a Senator from Oregon; born in Portland, Oreg., January 6, 1874; attended the public schools; graduated from the University of Oregon at Eugene in 1896 and from the New York Law School of New York City in 1899; was admitted to the Oregon bar and commenced the practice of law at Portland; member, Portland City Council 1900-1902, and served as president 1901; chairman, the Oregon State Tax Commission 1905-1906; elected as a Republican to the United States Senate to fill the vacancy caused by the death of John H. Mitchell and served from January 23, 1907, until March 3, 1907; was not a candidate for reelection in 1907; resumed the practice of law in Portland, Oreg.; chairman of the Public Docks Commission, Portland, Oreg., 1911-1916; elected as a Republican to the United States Senate to fill the vacancy caused by the death of Harry Lane and served from November 6, 1918, until his resignation, effective December 17, 1918; resumed the practice of his profession in Portland; chairman of the Multnomah County Tax Supervising and Conservation Commission 1921-1924; died in Portland, Multnomah County, on May 5, 1924; interment in Riverview Cemetery.

**MULKEY, William Oscar,** a Representative from Alabama; born in Brundidge, Pike County, Ala., July 27, 1871; attended the public schools and was graduated from State Normal College, Troy, Ala., in 1892; studied law; was admitted to the bar in 1893 and commenced practice in Troy, Geneva County, Ala., in 1894; member of the State constitutional convention in 1901; served in the State house of representatives in 1911; elected as a Democrat to the Sixty-third Congress to fill the vacancy caused by the resignation of Henry D. Clayton and served from June 29, 1914, to March 3, 1915; was not a candidate for renomination in 1914; resumed the practice of law; died in Geneva, Ala., June 30, 1943; interment in Geneva Cemetery.

**MULLER, Nicholas,** a Representative from New York; born in the Grand Duchy of Luxemburg November 15, 1836; attended the common schools in the city of Metz and afterward the Luxemburg Athenaeum; immigrated to the United States with his parents, who settled in New York City; employed as a railroad ticket agent for over twenty years; one of the promoters and original directors of the Germania Bank, New York City; served in the State assembly in 1875 and 1876; member of the State central committee in 1875; elected as a Democrat to the Forty-fifth and Forty-sixth Congresses (March 4, 1877-March 3, 1881); chairman, Committee on Expenditures in the Department of the Interior (Forty-sixth Congress); unsuccessful candidate for reelection in 1880 to the Forty-seventh Congress; elected to the Forty-eighth and Forty-ninth Congresses (March 4, 1883-March 3, 1887); chairman, Committee on Militia (Forty-eighth and Forty-ninth Congresses); was not a candidate for renomination in 1886; appointed president of the city police board in 1888; subsequently served as president of the excise board and as quarantine commissioner; elected to the Fifty-sixth and Fifty-seventh Congresses and served from March 4, 1899, until his resignation on December 1, 1902; unsuccessful candidate for president of Richmond Borough in 1901; appointed as tax commissioner in 1904; died in New Brighton, Richmond Borough, New York City, December 12, 1917; interment in Greenwood Cemetery, Brooklyn, N.Y.

**MULLIN, Joseph,** a Representative from New York; born in Dromore, County Down, Ireland, August 6, 1811; immigrated to the United States in 1820 with his parents, who settled in Watertown, Jefferson County, N.Y.; attended the public schools; worked in a printing office; attended Union Academy, Belleville, N.Y., and was graduated from Union College, Schenectady, N.Y., in 1833; principal of Union Academy and subsequently taught in the Watertown Academy; studied law; was admitted to the bar in 1837; appointed examiner of chancery, supreme court commissioner, and commissioner in bankruptcy in 1841; prosecuting attorney of Jefferson County 1843-1849; elected as a Whig to the Thirtieth Congress (March 4, 1847-March 3, 1849); president of the village of Watertown in 1853 and 1854; associate justice of the supreme court 1857-1881 and also served as presiding justice; died at Saratoga Springs, N.Y., May 17, 1882; interment in Brookside Cemetery, Watertown, N.Y.

**MULLINS, James,** a Representative from Tennessee; born in Bedford County, Tenn., September 15, 1807; completed preparatory studies; apprenticed to the millwright's trade; colonel of the State militia in 1831; sheriff of Bedford County 1840-1846; compelled to flee from his home in 1862 on account of his loyalty to the Union;

during the Civil War served in the Union Army 1862-1864; member of the State house of representatives, 1865-1867; elected as a Republican to the Fortieth Congress (March 4, 1867-March 3, 1869); died in Shelbyville, Bedford County, Tenn., June 26, 1873; interment in the Arnold Graveyard, about nine miles northeast of Shelbyville.

**MULTER, Abraham Jacob,** a Representative from New York; born in New York City, December 24, 1900; attended the public schools of Coney Island, N.Y., Boys' High School, Brooklyn, N.Y., and evening classes at City College of New York; LL.B., Brooklyn Law School, 1921, and LL.M., 1922; LL.D., Yeshiva University, 1963; was admitted to the bar in 1923 and commenced practice in New York City; special assistant attorney general of New York State conventions, beginning in 1936, and of the Democratic National Conventions of 1960 and 1964; served in United States Coast Guard, 1943-1945; special counsel to Mayor William O'Dwyer of New York City in 1947; elected as a Democrat to the Eightieth Congress to fill the vacancy caused by the resignation of Leo F. Rayfiel; reelected to the Eighty-first and to the nine succeeding Congresses, and served from November 4, 1947 until he resigned on December 31, 1967; elected a New York State Supreme Court Justice on November 7, 1967, and served from January 1, 1968 to January 1, 1977; special referee, Brooklyn Appellate Division, 1979-1984; was a resident of Brooklyn; moved to West Hartford, Conn., and lived there until his death on November 4, 1986.

**MUMFORD, George,** a Representative from North Carolina; born in Rowan County, N.C.; attended the common schools; member of the State house of commons in 1810 and 1811; elected as a Republican to the Fifteenth Congress and served from March 4, 1817, until his death in Washington, D.C., December 31, 1818; interment in the Congressional Cemetery.

**MUMFORD, Gurdon Saltonstall,** a Representative from New York; born in New London, Conn., January 29, 1764; attended the common schools; private secretary to Benjamin Franklin during the latter part of his official residence in Paris; returned with Franklin to America in 1785 and settled in New York City; became associated with his brothers in the commission business in 1791; elected as a Republican to the Ninth Congress to fill the vacancy caused by the resignation of Representative-elect Daniel D. Tompkins; reelected to the Tenth and Eleventh Congresses and served from March 4, 1805, to March 3, 1811; chairman, Committee on Commerce and Manufactures (Ninth Congress); presidential elector in 1812 and voted for DeWitt Clinton and Jared Ingersoll; elected director of the Bank of New York the same year; opened a broker's office in Wall Street in 1813 and was one of the founders of the New York Exchange; died in New York City, April 30, 1831; interment in Old Collegiate Dutch Church Cemetery.

**MUMMA, Walter Mann,** a Representative from Pennsylvania; born in Steelton, Dauphin County, Pa., November 20, 1890; attended the public schools of Steelton; graduated from Pennsylvania State Forestry Academy, Mont Alto, Pa., in 1911; employed with the Pennsylvania Forestry Department 1911-1916; with sales department, Lehigh Portland Cement Co., Allentown, Pa., 1916-1921; organizer, president, and manager of the Pennsylvania Supply Co. of Harrisburg, Pa., 1921-1947, and vice president 1947-1951; register of wills, Dauphin County, Pa., 1940-1944; elected as a Republican to the Eighty-second and to the five succeeding Congresses and served from January 3, 1951, until his death in Bethesda, Md., February 25, 1961; interment in East Harrisburg Cemetery, Harrisburg, Pa.

**MUNDT, Karl Earl,** a Representative and a Senator from South Dakota; born in Humboldt, Minnehaha County, S.Dak., June 3, 1900; attended the public schools of Humboldt, Pierre, and Madison, S.Dak.; A.B., Carleton College, Northfield, Minn., 1923; A.M., Columbia University, New York City, 1927; high school teacher of speech and social science in Bryant, S.Dak., 1923-1924, and

superintendent of schools in Bryant, 1924-1927; speech and social science teacher in General Beadle State Teachers College, Madison, S.Dak., 1927-1936; also engaged in the real estate and insurance business and in agricultural pursuits; member of the State Game and Fish Commission, 1931-1937; also engaged in literary pursuits; elected as a Republican to the Seventy-sixth and to the four succeeding Congresses, and served from January 3, 1939 until his resignation on December 30, 1948, having been appointed to the United States Senate to fill the vacancy caused by the resignation of Vera C. Bushfield, and served from December 31, 1948 to January 3, 1949; elected as a Republican to the United States Senate in 1948; reelected in 1954, 1960, and again in 1966, and served from December 31, 1948 to January 3, 1973; was not a candidate for reelection in 1972; died in Washington, D.C., August 16, 1974; interment in Graceland Cemetery, Madison, S.Dak.

**Bibliography:** Heidepriem, Scott N. *A Fair Chance for A Free People: A Biography of Karl E. Mundt, United States Senator.* Madison, S.Dak.: Leader Printing Co., 1988; Lange, Gerald. "Mundt vs. McGovern: The 1960 Senate Election." *Heritage of the Great Plains* 15 (Fall 1982): 33-41; Lee, R. Alton. "New Dealers, Fair Dealers, Misdealers, and Hiss Dealers': Karl Mundt and the Internal Security Act of 1950." *South Dakota History* 10 (Fall 1980): 277-90.

**MUNGEN, William,** a Representative from Ohio; born in Baltimore, Md., May 12, 1821; moved with his parents to Ohio in 1830; attended the common schools; taught school; editor and publisher of the Findlay Democratic Courier; auditor of Hancock County, Ohio, 1846-1850; member of the State senate in 1851 and 1852; studied law; was admitted to the bar in 1853 and commenced practice in Findlay, Hancock County, Ohio; delegate to the Democratic National Convention in 1856; entered the Union Army on December 5, 1861, as lieutenant colonel of the Fifty-seventh Regiment, Ohio Volunteer Infantry; commissioned colonel December 16, 1861, and served until April 24, 1863, when he was honorably discharged; elected as a Democrat to the Fortieth and Forty-first Congresses (March 4, 1867-March 3, 1871); was not a candidate for renomination in 1870; resumed the practice of law; died in Findlay, Ohio, September 9, 1887; interment in Maple Grove Cemetery.

**MURCH, Thompson Henry,** a Representative from Maine; born in Hampden, Penobscot County, Maine, March 29, 1838; attended the common schools; passed his early life at sea; learned the stonecutter's trade and engaged in that occupation for eighteen years; became editor and publisher of the Granite Cutters' International Journal in 1877; secretary of the Granite Cutters' International Association of American in 1877 and 1878; elected as a Greenback candidate to the Forty-sixth and Forty-seventh Congresses (March 4, 1879-March 3, 1883); unsuccessful candidate for reelection in 1882 to the Forty-eighth Congress; engaged in mercantile pursuits; died in Danvers, Mass., December 15, 1886; interment in Hampden Cemetery, Hampden, Maine.

**MURDOCK, John Robert,** a Representative from Arizona; born in Homestead near Lewistown, Lewis County, Mo., April 20, 1885; attended the public schools; was graduated from State Teachers' College, Kirksville, Mo., in 1912 and from the State University of Iowa at Iowa City in 1925; engaged in graduate work at the University of Arizona at Tucson and at the University of California at Berkeley; taught elementary school in Missouri 1904-1908; served as principal of the high school at Lewistown, Mo., 1908-1910 and at Ridgeway, Mo., 1912-1914; instructor in the Normal School at Tempe, Ariz., 1914-1932; dean of the Arizona State Teachers' College at Tempe 1933-1937; author of textbooks on history and government; elected as a Democrat to the Seventy-fifth and to the seven succeeding Congresses (January 3, 1937-January 3, 1953); chairman, Committee on Memorials (Seventy-eighth Congress), Committee on Irrigation and Reclamation (Seventy-ninth

Congress), Committee on Interior and Insular Affairs (Eighty-second Congress); was an unsuccessful candidate for reelection in 1952 to the Eighty-third Congress; retired and resided in Scottsdale, Ariz.; died in Phoenix, Ariz., February 14, 1972; interment in Double Butte Cemetery, Tempe, Ariz.

**MURDOCK, Orrice Abram, Jr. (Abe),** a Representative and a Senator from Utah; born in Austin, Lander County, Nev., July 18, 1893; moved with his parents to Beaver, Beaver County, Utah, in 1898; attended the public schools and Murdock Academy in Beaver and the University of Utah at Salt Lake City; studied law; was admitted to the bar in 1922 and commenced practice in Beaver; member, Beaver city council 1920-1921; county attorney of Beaver County 1923-1924, 1927-1928, 1931-1932; city attorney of Beaver 1926-1933; unsuccessful Democratic candidate for district attorney for the fifth Utah district in 1928; elected as a Democrat to the Seventy-third Congress; reelected to the three succeeding Congresses (March 4, 1933-January 3, 1941); was not a candidate for reelection in 1940, having become a candidate for United States Senator; elected as a Democrat to the United States Senate in 1940 and served from January 3, 1941, to January 3, 1947; unsuccessful candidate for reelection in 1946; resumed the practice of law and engaged in agricultural pursuits and livestock raising; member, National Labor Relations Board 1947-1957; member, Atomic Energy Labor-Management Relations Panel 1960; died in Bethesda, Md., September 15, 1979; interment in Mountain View Cemetery, Beaver, Utah.

**MURDOCK, Victor,** a Representative from Kansas; born in Burlingame, Osage County, Kans. March 18, 1871; moved with his parents to Wichita in 1872; attended the common schools and Lewis Academy at Wichita; served as a reporter on the Wichita Eagle; moved to Chicago in 1891 and was employed as a newspaper reporter on the Chicago Inter-Ocean; returned to Wichita; managing editor of the Daily Eagle 1894-1903; clerk of the central division, southern department, Kansas Appellate Court 1895-1897; elected as a Republican to the Fifty-eighth Congress to fill the vacancy caused by the resignation of Chester I. Long; reelected to the Fifty-ninth and to the four succeeding Congresses and served from May 26, 1903, to March 3, 1915; was not a candidate for renomination in 1914 but was an unsuccessful candidate for nomination to the United States Senate; chairman of the National Committee of the Progressive Party in 1915 and 1916; war correspondent in 1916; member of the Federal Trade Commission from September 4, 1917, to January 31, 1924, when he resigned; chairman of the Commission in 1919, 1920, 1922, and 1923; editor of the Wichita Eagle until his death in Wichita, Kans., July 8, 1945; interment in Old Mission Mausoleum.
Bibliography: *DAB.*

**MURFREE, William Hardy** (uncle of David W. Dickinson), a Representative from North Carolina; born in Hertford County, N.C., October 2, 1781; was graduated from the University of North Carolina at Chapel Hill in 1801; studied law; was admitted to the bar and commenced practice in Edenton, N.C.; also interested in agricultural pursuits; member of the North Carolina State house of representatives in 1805 and 1812; elected as a Republican to the Thirteenth and Fourteenth Congresses (March 4, 1813-March 3, 1817); chairman, Committee on Public Expenditures (Fourteenth Congress); moved from Murfreesboro, N.C., to his estate in Williamson County, Tenn., in 1823 and died there on January 19, 1827; interment in Murfree Cemetery, northwest of Franklin, Williamson County, Tenn.

**MURKOWSKI, Frank Hughes,** a Senator from Alaska; born in Seattle, King County, Wash., March 28, 1933; attended the public schools of Ketchikan, Alaska; graduated, Ketchikan High School, 1951; attended the University of Santa Clara, Calif., 1951-1953; B.A., Seattle University (Wash.), 1953-1955; served in the United

States Coast Guard, 1955-1956; president, Alaska National Bank of the North, Fairbanks, 1971-1980; Alaska Commissioner of Economic Development, 1966-1970; unsuccessful candidate in 1970 for election to the Ninety-second Congress; president of the Alaska Chamber of Commerce in 1977; elected as a Republican to the United States Senate in 1980 for the term commencing January 3, 1981; reelected in 1986 and again in 1992 for the term ending January 3, 1999; chairman, Committee on Veterans' Affairs (Ninety-ninth Congress), Committee on Energy and Natural Resources (One Hundred Fourth Congress); is a resident of Fairbanks, Alaska.

**MURPHEY, Charles,** a Representative from Georgia; born near Anderson, Anderson County, S.C., May 9, 1799; attended the country schools; studied law; was admitted to the bar in 1825 and commenced practice in Decatur, Ga.; clerk of the superior court of De Kalb County, Ga., 1825-1827; member of the State house of representatives 1839-1841; served in the State senate in 1842, 1845, 1849-1850, 1855-1856; elected as a Unionist to the Thirty-second Congress (March 4, 1851-March 3, 1853); resumed the practice of law; delegate to the Democratic National Convention at Baltimore in 1860; died in Decatur, Ga., January 16, 1861; interment in Decatur City Cemetery.

**MURPHY, Arthur Phillips,** a Representative from Missouri; born in Hancock, Pulaski County, Mo., December 10, 1870; attended the public schools of Pulaski County and the School of Mines and Metallurgy at Rolla, Phelps County, Mo.; became a telegraph operator; studied law; was admitted to the bar March 4, 1894, and commenced practice in Rolla, Mo.; unsuccessful candidate for election as prosecuting attorney of Pulaski County in 1898; attorney for the Creek Nation of Indians 1902-1904; elected as a Republican to the Fifty-ninth Congress (March 4, 1905-March 3, 1907); unsuccessful candidate for reelection in 1906 to the Sixtieth Congress; elected to the Sixty-first Congress (March 4, 1909-March 3, 1911); unsuccessful candidate for reelection in 1910 to the Sixty-second Congress; resumed the practice of law; died in Rolla, Mo., February 1, 1914; interment in Rolla Cemetery.

**MURPHY, Austin John,** a Representative from Pennsylvania; born in North Charleroi, Washington County, Pa., June 17, 1927; attended the public elementary schools of New London, Conn.; graduated, Charleroi (Pa.) High School, 1944; B.A., Duquesne University, Pittsburgh, 1949; LL.B., University of Pittsburgh, 1952; admitted to the Pennsylvania bar in 1953 and commenced practice in Washington, Pa.; served in the United States Marine Corps, 1944-1946; served as assistant district attorney, Washington County, 1956-1957; served in the Pennsylvania house of representatives, 1958-1970; Pennsylvania senator, 1970-1976; elected as a Democrat to the Ninety-fifth and to the eight succeeding Congresses (January 3, 1977-January 3, 1995); was not a candidate for reelection in 1994 to the One Hundred Fourth Congress; is a resident of Monongahela, Pa.

**MURPHY, Benjamin Franklin,** a Representative from Ohio; born in Steubenville, Jefferson County, Ohio, December 24, 1867; attended the public schools; learned the glassworker's trade; later engaged in the retail shoe business, in banking, and in the real estate business; vice president of the Peoples National Bank; during the First World War served with the Young Men's Christian Association, stationed at Camp Sheridan, Montgomery, Ala., in 1917 and 1918; elected as a Republican to the Sixty-sixth and to the six succeeding Congresses (March 4, 1919-March 3, 1933); chairman, Committee on Expenditures in the Department of Commerce (Sixty-seventh Congress); unsuccessful candidate for reelection in 1932 to the Seventy-third Congress and for election in 1934 to the Seventy-fourth Congress; resided in Washington, D.C.; died in Takoma Park, Md., March 6, 1938; interment in Union Cemetery, Steubenville, Ohio.

**MURPHY, Edward, Jr.,** a Senator from New York; born in Troy, Rensselaer County, N.Y., December 15, 1836; attended the common schools; graduated from St. John's College, Fordham, N.Y., in 1857; engaged in the brewing business; city alderman 1864-1866; mayor of Troy 1875-1883; elected as a Democrat to the United States Senate and served from March 4, 1893, to March 3, 1899; unsuccessful candidate for reelection in 1898; chairman, Committee on Relations with Canada (Fifty-third Congress); resumed his former business activities and was also president of the Troy Gas Co. and vice president of the Manufacturers' National Bank of Troy; died in Elberon, Monmouth County, N.J., August 3, 1911; interment in St. Mary's Cemetery, Troy, N.Y.

**MURPHY, Everett Jerome,** a Representative from Illinois; born in Nashville, Washington County, Ill., July 24, 1852; moved with his parents to Sparta, Randolph County, Ill.; attended the public and high schools; city clerk of Sparta in 1877, but resigned in 1878 and moved to Chester, the county seat, to accept the appointment of deputy clerk of the circuit court; sheriff of Randolph County; member of the State house of representatives 1886-1888; warden of the Southern Illinois Penitentiary at Menard, Ill., in 1889; moved to East St. Louis in 1892; elected as a Republican to the Fifty-fourth Congress (March 4, 1895-March 3, 1897); unsuccessful candidate for reelection in 1896 to the Fifty-fifth Congress; member of the State board of pardons 1897-1899; warden of the State penitentiary at Joliet, Ill., 1899-1913; engaged in banking at Joliet, Ill., reappointed warden of the penitentiary on July 1, 1917, and served until his death in Joliet, Ill., April 10, 1922; interment in Elmherst Cemetery.

**MURPHY, George Lloyd,** a Senator from California; born in New Haven, Conn., July 4, 1902; educated at Peddie Institute in Hightstown, N.J., and the Pawling School of New York; attended Yale University; worked as a coal miner, and as a runner for a brokerage firm in New York City; engaged as an actor in New York in 1926 and appeared thereafter in four Broadway shows; moved to Hollywood, Calif., in 1935 and appeared in forty-five motion pictures; organized entertainment personnel for the Armed Forces during the Second World War; delegate to the Republican National Convention of 1948; member of the board of directors, Screen Actors Guild, 1937-1953, and served as president, 1944-1946; vice president, Desilu Studios, 1958-1961, Technicolor Corp., 1961-1964; director of entertainment for presidential inaugurations in 1953, 1957, and 1961; chairman of the Republican State Central Committee of California in 1953 and 1954; elected as a Republican to the United States Senate November 3, 1964, for the six year term commencing January 3, 1965; subsequently appointed January 1, 1965, to fill the vacancy caused by the resignation of Pierre Salinger for the term ending January 3, 1965, and served from January 1, 1965, to January 2, 1971; unsuccessful candidate for reelection in 1970; engaged in lobbying and public relations activities; was a resident of Palm Beach, Fla., until his death there on May 3, 1992.

**Bibliography:** Murphy, George. *Say...Didn't You Used to be George Murphy?* New York: Barthelomew House, 1970.

**MURPHY, Henry Cruse,** a Representative from New York; born in Brooklyn, N.Y., July 5, 1810; was graduated from Columbia College in New York City in 1830; studied law; was admitted to the bar in 1833 and commenced practice in Brooklyn, N.Y.; prosecuting attorney for Kings County in 1841 and 1842; edited the Brooklyn Daily Eagle; mayor of Brooklyn, N.Y., in 1842 and 1843; delegate to the State constitutional convention in 1846; elected as a Democrat to the Twenty-eighth Congress (March 4, 1843-March 3, 1845); unsuccessful candidate for reelection in 1844 to the Twenty-ninth Congress; elected to the Thirtieth Congress (March 4, 1847-March 3, 1849); unsuccessful candidate for renomination in 1848 to the Thirty-first Congress; appointed Minister Resident to the Netherlands on June 1, 1857, and served until June 1861; member of the New York State senate, 1861-1873; delegate to the State constitutional convention of 1867 and 1868; owner and editor of the Brooklyn Daily Eagle; died in Brooklyn, N.Y., December 1, 1882; interment in Greenwood Cemetery.

**Bibliography:** *DAB.*

**MURPHY, James Joseph,** a Representative from New York; born in Brooklyn, Kings County, N.Y., November 3, 1898; educated in the public schools of Staten Island, N.Y.; served as a noncommissioned officer with the First New York Cavalry on the Mexican border in 1916; during the First World War served as a sergeant with the One Hundred and Fourth Machine Gun Battalion, Twenty-seventh Division, with service in France and Belgium, 1918-1920; engaged in the import and export shipping business in New York City, beginning in 1920; elected as a Democrat to the Eighty-first and Eighty-second Congresses (January 3, 1949-January 3, 1953); unsuccessful candidate for reelection in 1952 to the Eighty-third Congress; New York city councilman for the Borough of Staten Island, 1954-1958; freight and shipping broker; resided at Grymes Hill, Staten Island, N.Y., until his death in Staten Island, October 19, 1962; interment in St. Peter's Cemetery.

**MURPHY, James William,** a Representative from Wisconsin; born in Platteville, Grant County, Wis., April 17, 1858; attended the public schools and was graduated from the State normal school at Platteville in 1873; taught school in Grant and Lafayette Counties for five years; studied law and was admitted to the bar in 1879; was graduated from the law department of the University of Michigan at Ann Arbor in 1880 and commenced the practice of his profession in Platteville, Wis., the same year; district attorney of Grant County 1887-1891; mayor of Platteville 1904-1906; elected as a Democrat to the Sixtieth Congress (March 4, 1907-March 3, 1909); unsuccessful candidate for reelection in 1908 to the Sixty-first Congress; resumed the practice of law; also engaged in lead and zinc mining; unsuccessful candidate for election in 1920 to the Sixty-seventh Congress; died in Rochester, Minn., July 11, 1927; interment in Calvary (Catholic) Cemetery, Platteville, Wis.

**MURPHY, Jeremiah Henry,** a Representative from Iowa; born in Lowell, Mass., February 19, 1835; moved with his parents to Fond du Lac County, Wis., in 1849, and to Iowa County, Iowa, in 1852; attended the Boston public schools and Appleton (Wis.) University; was graduated from the University of Iowa at Iowa City in 1857; studied law; was admitted to the bar in 1858 and commenced practice in Marengo, Iowa; elected alderman in 1860; delegate to the Democratic National Convention in 1864 and 1868; moved to Davenport in 1867 and continued the practice of law; elected mayor of Davenport in 1873 and again in 1878; member of the State senate 1874-1878; was an unsuccessful candidate for election in 1876 to the Forty-fifth Congress; elected as a Democrat to the Forty-eighth and Forty-ninth Congresses (March 4, 1883-March 3, 1887); was an unsuccessful candidate for renomination in 1886; lived in retirement in Washington, D.C., until his death in that city on December 11, 1893; interment in St. Marguerite's Cemetery, Davenport, Iowa.

**MURPHY, John,** a Representative from Alabama; born in Columbia, Robeson County, N.C., in 1786; was graduated from South Carolina College (now the University of South Carolina) at Columbia in 1808; served as clerk of the Alabama State senate, 1810-1817; moved to Alabama in 1818; delegate to the State constitutional convention in 1819; studied law and was admitted to the bar; member of the State senate in 1822; elected Governor of Alabama in 1825, reelected in 1827, and served from November 25, 1825 to November 25, 1829; unsuccessful candidate for election to the Twenty-second Congress; elected as a Jacksonian to the Twenty-third Congress (March 4, 1833-March 3, 1835); unsuccessful candidate for election in 1838 to the Twenty-sixth Congress; died near Gosport, Clarke County, Ala., September 21, 1841; interment on his plantation near Gosport, Ala.

**MURPHY, John Michael,** a Representative from New York; born in Staten Island, Richmond County, N.Y., August 3, 1926; educated in the public schools of New York City, La Salle Military Academy, Oakdale, L.I., and Amherst (Mass.) College; served in the United States Army from August 1944 until May 1945; appointed to the United States Military Academy, West Point, N.Y., in July 1946, and graduated in June 1950 with a B.S. degree in civil engineering; went to Korea and served with the Ninth Infantry Regiment; discharged as a captain in July 1956; awarded the Distinguished Service Cross and the Bronze Star with V Device and Oak Leaf Cluster; general manager, contract carrier of Staten Island, 1956-1962; president, Cleveland General Transport Co., Inc.; member of the board, Empire State Highway Transportation Association, 1960-1965; delegate to the Democratic National Conventions of 1964, 1968, and 1976; delegate, New York State Constitutional convention, 1967; elected as a Democrat to the Eighty-eighth and to the eight succeeding Congresses (January 3, 1963-January 3, 1981); chairman, Select Committee on the Outer Continental Shelf (Ad Hoc) (Ninety-fourth through Ninety-sixth Congresses), Committee on Merchant Marine and Fisheries (Ninety-fifth and Ninety-sixth Congresses); unsuccessful candidate for reelection in 1980 to the Ninety-seventh Congress; investor and developer of biotechnology and high technology companies; is a resident of Staten Island, N.Y.

**MURPHY, John William,** a Representative from Pennsylvania; born in Avoca, Luzerne County, Pa., April 26, 1902; attended the public schools; was graduated from the Wharton School of the University of Pennsylvania at Philadelphia in 1926 and from the law department of the same university in 1929; was admitted to the bar in 1929 and commenced practice in Scranton, Pa., assistant district attorney of Lackawanna County 1934-1941; elected as a Democrat to the Seventy-eighth and Seventy-ninth Congresses and served from January 3, 1943, until his resignation on July 17, 1946, to become judge of the United States District Court for the middle district of Pennsylvania; became chief judge in June 1955, in which capacity he served until his death in Scranton, Pa., March 28, 1962; interment in St. Catherine's Cemetery, Moscow, Pa.

**MURPHY, Maurice J., Jr.,** a Senator from New Hampshire; born in Dover, Strafford County, N.H., October 3, 1927; graduated from Holy Cross College, Worcester, Mass., in 1950, and from Boston College Law School in 1953; was admitted to the bar and commenced the practice of law in Portsmouth, N.H., in 1955; served as an enlisted man in the United States Army in 1946 and 1947 and again in 1953 and 1954; legal counsel to the New Hampshire State senate in 1957 and 1958; administrative assistant to Governor Wesley Powell, 1959-1961; deputy attorney general and attorney general of New Hampshire in 1961, until appointed as a Republican to the United States Senate on December 7, 1961, to fill the vacancy caused by the death of Styles Bridges and served until November 6, 1962; unsuccessful candidate for nomination in the 1962 special primary for election to the remainder of the term ending January 3, 1967; resumed the practice of law; chairman of the board and general counsel of the Portsmouth (N.H.) Savings Bank; is a resident of Greenland, N.H.

**MURPHY, Morgan Francis,** a Representative from Illinois; born in Chicago, Ill., April 16, 1932; attended Chicago parochial schools; B.S., Northwestern University, Evanston, Ill., 1955; J.D., DePaul University School of Law, Chicago, Ill., 1962; served in the United States Marine Corps, 1955-1957, including a one year tour of duty in the Far East; administrative assistant to Clerk of the Circuit Court of Chicago, 1958-1961; admitted to the Illinois bar in 1962 and commenced practice in Chicago; special attorney, Board of Election Commissioners, 1964 at-large elections; attorney for Chicago Dairymen's Association during the 1968 milk strikes; trustee-management representative, Milk Wagon Drivers Union;

hearing officer for Local Liquor Control Commission, 1969-1970; delegate to the Democratic National Conventions of 1968 and 1972; elected as a Democrat to the Ninety-second and to the four succeeding Congresses (January 3, 1971-January 3, 1981); was not a candidate for reelection in 1980 to the Ninety-seventh Congress; resumed the practice of law in Chicago; is a resident of Chicago, Ill.

**MURPHY, Nathan Oakes,** a Delegate from the Territory of Arizona; born in Jefferson, Lincoln County, Maine, October 14, 1849; attended the public schools; taught school in Wisconsin; went to the western frontier and finally settled in Prescott, Ariz., in April 1883 where he engaged in mining and the real estate business; secretary to the Governor of Arizona Territory in 1885; appointed secretary of Arizona Territory on March 21, 1889; delegate to the Republican National Convention of 1892; appointed Governor of Arizona Territory by President Benjamin Harrison on May 11, 1892, and served until his resignation on March 31, 1893; elected as a Republican to the Fifty-fourth Congress (March 4, 1895-March 3, 1897); was not a candidate for renomination in 1896 to the Fifty-fifth Congress; appointed Governor of Arizona Territory by President William McKinley on July 16, 1898, and served until May 7, 1902, when he resigned; unsuccessful candidate for election in 1900 to the Fifty-seventh Congress; died in Coronado, San Diego County, Calif., August 22, 1908; interment in the Masonic Cemetery, San Diego, Calif.

**MURPHY, Richard Louis,** a Senator from Iowa; born in Dubuque, Dubuque County, Iowa, November 6, 1875; attended the public schools of Dubuque; reporter for the Galena (Ill.) Gazette 1890-1892; returned to Dubuque, Iowa, in 1892 and was successively a reporter, city editor, and editor 1892-1914; member of the Dubuque County Library Board 1909-1914; served as collector of internal revenue for Iowa 1913-1920; income tax counselor 1920-1931, when he retired from active pursuits; elected as a Democrat to the United States Senate and served from March 4, 1933, until his death in an automobile accident near Chippewa Falls, Wis., July 16, 1936; interment in Mount Olivet Cemetery, Key West (a suburb of Dubuque), Iowa.

**MURPHY, William Thomas,** a Representative from Illinois; born in Chicago, Ill., August 7, 1899; attended Yale and Harvard elementary schools and Calumet High School in Chicago; graduated from Loyola University School of Law in 1926; was admitted to the bar in 1927 and commenced the practice of law in Chicago, Ill.; during the First World War served in the United States Army; alderman of the seventeenth ward, city of Chicago, 1935-1959; member of Chicago Planning Commission 1947-1959; licensed professional engineer; registered land surveyor; delegate to the Democratic National Conventions in 1944, 1948, 1952, and 1956; elected as a Democrat to the Eighty-sixth and to the five succeeding Congresses (January 3, 1959-January 3, 1971); was not a candidate for reelection in 1970 to the Ninety-second Congress; died in Oak Lawn, Ill., January 29, 1978; interment in Holy Sepulchre Cemetery, Worth, Ill.

**MURRAY, Ambrose Spencer** (brother of William Murray), a Representative from New York; born in Wallkill, Ulster County, N.Y., November 27, 1807; attended the common schools; employed as a clerk in a mercantile establishment in Middletown, N.Y., 1824-1831; moved to Goshen, Orange County, N.Y., and engaged in banking; treasurer of Orange County 1851-1854; elected as a Whig to the Thirty-fourth Congress and reelected as a Republican to the Thirty-fifth Congress (March 4, 1855-March 3, 1859); resumed banking in Goshen, N.Y.; delegate to the Republican National Convention in 1860; interested in various other business enterprises; died in Goshen, N.Y., November 8, 1885; interment in St. James' Cemetery.

**MURRAY, George Washington,** a Representative from South Carolina; born near Rembert, Sumter County, S.C., September 22, 1853; attended the public schools and the University of South Carolina at Columbia; taught school for fifteen years; inspector of customs at the port of Charleston, S.C., 1890-1892; elected as a Republican to the Fifty-third Congress (March 4, 1893-March 3, 1895); successfully contested the election of William Elliott to the Fifty-fourth Congress and served from June 4, 1896, to March 3, 1897; engaged in the real estate business; moved to Chicago, Ill., in 1905 and engaged in literary pursuits and lecturing; delegate to several Republican National Conventions; died in Chicago, Ill., April 21, 1926; interment in Lincoln Cemetery.

**Bibliography:** Gaboury, William J. "George Washington Murray and the Fight for Political Democracy in South Carolina." *Journal of Negro History* 62 (July 1977): 258-69.

**MURRAY, James Cunningham,** a Representative from Illinois; born in Chicago, Ill., May 16, 1917; attended the parochial schools, De Paul University College of Commerce, and Quigley Preparatory Seminary; LL.B., De Paul University Law School, Chicago, Ill., 1940; was admitted to the bar in 1940; employed in leases and contracts division of the Illinois Bell Telephone Co., 1940-1942; served in the United States Army Air Force from May 1942 until discharged as a sergeant in October 1945; assistant attorney general of Illinois, 1946-1950; regional enforcement director for the Office of Price Stabilization, 1950-1952; assistant State's attorney for Cook County, Ill., 1952-1954; elected as a Democrat to the Eighty-fourth Congress (January 3, 1955-January 3, 1957); unsuccessful candidate for reelection in 1956 to the Eighty-fifth Congress; delegate to the Democratic National Convention of 1964; alderman, eighteenth ward, city of Chicago, 1959-1967; president pro tempore, Chicago City Council, 1963-1967; first assistant State's attorney of Cook County, 1968-1970; circuit judge, Illinois Circuit Court of Cook County, December 1970 to present; assigned justice, Illinois Apellate Court, First Judicial District, from January 1986 until his retirement on December 5, 1995; appointed member, Chicago Police Board, March 1996 to present; is a resident of Chicago, Ill.

**MURRAY, James Edward,** a Senator from Montana; born on a farm near St. Thomas, Ontario, Canada, May 3, 1876; attended the public schools of Canada; graduated from St. Jerome's College, Berlin, Canada, in 1897; came to the United States in 1897, settled in Butte, Mont., and was naturalized in 1900; graduated from the law department of New York University in 1900; admitted to the bar in 1901 and commenced practice in Butte, Mont.; also engaged in banking; county attorney of Silver Bow County, Mont., 1906-1908; chairman of the Montana State advisory board of the Public Works Administration, 1933-1934; elected as a Democrat to the United States Senate to fill the vacancy caused by the death of Thomas J. Walsh; reelected in 1936, 1942, 1948, and again in 1954, and served from November 7, 1934 to January 3, 1961; was not a candidate for renomination in 1960; chairman, Committee on Education and Labor (Seventy-ninth Congress), co-chairman, Joint Committee on Labor-Management Relations (Eighty-first Congress), chairman, Committee on Labor and Public Welfare (Eighty-second Congress), Committee on Interior and Insular Affairs (Eighty-fourth through Eighty-sixth Congresses); died in Butte, Mont., March 23, 1961; interment in Holy Cross Cemetery.

**Bibliography:** *DAB*; Evans, William B. "Senator James E. Murray: A Voice of the People in Foreign Affairs." *Montana* 32 (Winter 1982): 24-35; Spritzer, Donald E. *Senator James E. Murray and the Limits of Post-War Liberalism.* New York: Garland Press, 1985.

**MURRAY, John** (cousin of Thomas Murray, Jr.), a Representative from Pennsylvania; born near Potts Grove, East Chillisquaque Township, Northumberland County, Pa., in 1768; attended private schools; engaged in agricultural pursuits; member of the Pennsylvania house of representatives 1807-1810; elected as a Republican to the Fifteenth Congress to fill the vacancy caused by the resignation of David Scott; reelected to the Sixteenth Congress and served from October 14, 1817, to March 3, 1821; resumed agricultural pursuits; died in East Chillisquaque Township, Northumberland County, Pa., March 7, 1834; interment in Chillisquaque Cemetery, near Potts Grove, Pa.

**MURRAY, John L.,** a Representative from Kentucky; born in Pennsylvania, January 25, 1806; studied law and was admitted to the bar; moved to Kentucky and held several local offices; served three terms in the Kentucky house of representatives 1830-1835; elected as a Democrat to the Twenty-fifth Congress (March 4, 1837-March 3, 1839); died in Wadesboro, Calloway County, Ky., January 31, 1842; interment in Irvin Cemetery.

**MURRAY, Patty L.,** a Senator from Washington; born in Seattle, King County, Wash., October 11, 1950; B.A., Washington State University, 1972; part-time secretary, Sacajawea State Park; certified parent educator, Shoreline Community College, Seattle; member, Shoreline School Board, president and legislative representative, 1985-1989; member, Washington State senate, 1988-1993, Democratic whip, 1990; elected as a Democrat to the United States Senate in 1992 for the term ending January 3, 1999; is a resident of Seattle, Wash.

**MURRAY, Reid Fred,** a Representative from Wisconsin; born in Ogdensburg, Waupaca County, Wis., October 16, 1887; attended the public schools and Manawa High School; was graduated from the College of Agriculture of the University of Wisconsin at Madison in 1916; served as agricultural agent for railroads in St. Paul, Minn., 1914-1917, for Winnebago County, Wis., 1917-1919, and for the First National Bank, Oshkosh, Wis., 1919-1922; professor of animal husbandry, at the College of Agriculture, University of Wisconsin, 1922-1927; engaged in agricultural pursuits and in the buying and selling of cattle and farms, Waupaca, Wis., 1927-1939; elected as a Republican to the Seventy-sixth and to the six succeeding Congresses and served from January 3, 1939, until his death in Bethesda, Md., April 29, 1952; interment in Park Cemetery, one mile north of Ogdensburg, Wis.

**MURRAY, Robert Maynard,** a Representative from Ohio; born in Concord, Lake County, Ohio, November 28, 1841; attended the common schools of Willoughby, Lake County, Ohio, and Oberlin, Ohio; studied law; was admitted to the bar but did not practice; cashier of the First National Bank in Painesville, Ohio; mayor of Painesville, Ohio, 1877-1879; moved to Piqua, Ohio, in 1879; engaged in the manufacture of handles for agricultural implements; elected as a Democrat to the Forty-eighth Congress (March 4, 1883-March 3, 1885); unsuccessful candidate for reelection in 1884 to the Forty-ninth Congress; resumed his former business pursuits; moved to Cleveland in 1892 and engaged in the storage business; died in Cleveland, Ohio, August 2, 1913; interment in Evergreen Cemetery, Painesville, Ohio.

**MURRAY, Thomas, Jr.** (cousin of John Murray), a Representative from Pennsylvania; born near Potts Grove, East Chillisquaque Township, Northumberland County, Pa., in 1770; attended private schools; engaged in agricultural pursuits; member of the Pennsylvania house of representatives in 1813; served in the Pennsylvania senate in 1814; elected to the Seventeenth Congress to fill the vacancy caused by the resignation of William Cox Ellis and served from October 9, 1821, to March 3, 1823; declined to be a candidate for renomination in 1822 to the Eighteenth Congress; died in East Chillisquaque Township, Northumberland County, Pa., August 26, 1823; interment in Chillisquaque Cemetery, near Potts Grove, Pa.

**MURRAY, Thomas Jefferson,** a Representative from Tennessee; born in Jackson, Madison County, Tenn., August 1, 1894; attended the public and high schools; was graduated from Union University at Jackson, Tenn., in 1914 and from the law department of Cumberland University at Lebanon, Tenn., in 1917; taught high school in Pinson and Alamo, Tenn., 1914-1916; during the First World War served overseas in the United States Army as a private in the Ordnance Department, Fifth Army Corps, in 1918 and 1919; was admitted to the bar in 1917 and commenced practice in Jackson, Tenn., in 1919; district attorney general for the twelfth judicial circuit of Tennessee from 1922 until his resignation in 1933 to become associated with the office of the Solicitor of the Post Office Department at Washington, D.C., and served from 1933 to 1942; chairman of the Democratic Executive Committee of Madison County, Tenn., 1924-1933; member of the State Democratic Executive Committee of Tennessee in 1923 and 1924; delegate to the Democratic National Conventions in 1928, 1932, and 1936; elected as a Democrat to the Seventy-eighth and to the eleven succeeding Congresses (January 3, 1943-January 3, 1967); chairman, Committee on the Post Office and Civil Service (Eighty-first, Eighty-second, and Eighty-fourth through Eighty-ninth Congresses); unsuccessful candidate for renomination in 1966 to the Ninetieth Congress; resided in Jackson, Tenn., until his death there November 28, 1971; interment in Hollywood Cemetery.

**MURRAY, William** (brother of Ambrose Spencer Murray), a Representative from New York; born near Middletown, Orange County, N.Y., October 1, 1803; attended the common schools; employed as a clerk in mercantile establishments in Middletown, N.Y., and later in New York City; subsequently engaged in mercantile pursuits; moved to Goshen, Orange County, N.Y., in 1841; elected as a Democrat to the Thirty-second and Thirty-third Congresses (March 4, 1851-March 3, 1855); engaged in agricultural pursuits; was instrumental in the organization of the Republican Party in 1856 and was afterward affiliated therewith; president of the Goshen Bank from 1857 until his death in Goshen, N.Y., August 25, 1875; interment in St. James' Cemetery.

**MURRAY, William Francis,** a Representative from Massachusetts; born in Boston, Mass., September 7, 1881; attended the public schools and the Boston Latin School; graduated from Harvard University in 1904 and from Harvard Law School in 1906; practiced law in Boston; served during the Spanish-American War as a corporal in the United States Volunteer Signal Corps; member of Boston Common Council in 1904 and 1905; member of the Massachusetts house of representatives in 1907 and 1908; member of the Governor's council in 1910; elected as a Democrat to the Sixty-second and Sixty-third Congresses; and served from March 4, 1911, until September 28, 1914, when he resigned, having been appointed postmaster; postmaster of Boston from October 1, 1914, until his death in that city on September 21, 1918; interment in Holyhood Cemetery, Chestnut Hill, Mass.

**MURRAY, William Henry David,** a Representative from Oklahoma; born near Collinsville, Grayson County, Tex., November 21, 1869; attended the public schools and was graduated from College Hill Institute, Springtown, Tex.; editor of newspapers in Dallas, Tex., in 1893 and in Corsicana, Tex., in 1894 and 1895; studied law; was admitted to the bar in 1895 and commenced practice in Fort Worth, Tex.; engaged in teaching in Limestone and Navarro Counties, Tex., 1886-1890; moved to Tishomingo, Johnston County, Indian Territory (now Oklahoma) in 1898; legal adviser to the Governor of the Chickasaw Nation from 1898 until 1901; engaged in ranching near Tishomingo, Okla.; member of the Choctaw-Chickasaw Coal Commission in 1903; chairman of the Oklahoma Code Commission in 1903; vice president of the Sequoyah constitutional convention in 1905; member of the Oklahoma constitutional convention in 1906, and served as president;

chairman of the first Democratic State convention held in Oklahoma in 1907; member of the Oklahoma State house of representatives, 1907-1909, and served as speaker in the first legislative session; delegate to the Democratic National Conventions of 1908, 1912, 1916 and 1932; elected as a Democrat to the Sixty-third and Sixty-fourth Congresses (March 4, 1913-March 3, 1917); unsuccessful candidate for renomination in 1916 to the Sixty-fifth Congress; unsuccessful candidate for the gubernatorial nomination in 1910 and in 1918; moved to South America and became engaged in setttling southeast Bolivia from 1924 until 1929; returned to Oklahoma in 1929; elected Governor of Oklahoma in 1930 and served from January 12, 1931 to January 14, 1935; unsuccessful candidate for the gubernatorial nomination in 1938; attempted by petition to enter the 1938 general election as an Independent candidate for the United States Senate, but the State supreme court ruled that the petition was filed too late; unsuccessful Democratic candidate for nomination to the United States Senate in 1942; retired to his farm near Tishomingo, Okla.; died in Oklahoma City, Okla., October 15, 1956; interment in Tishomingo Cemetery, Tishomingo, Okla.

**Bibliography:** *DAB*; Bryant, Keith L. *Alfalfa Bill Murray*. Norman: University of Oklahoma Press, 1968; Schruben, Francis W. "The Return of Alfalfa Bill Murray." *Chronicles of Oklahoma* 4 (Spring 1963): 38-65.

**MURRAY, William Vans,** a Representative from Maryland; born in Cambridge, Dorchester County, Md., February 9, 1760; completed preparatory studies; studied law at the Temple in London, which he entered April 28, 1784, and studied three years; returned to the United States; was admitted to the bar and commenced practice in Cambridge, Md., in 1791; member of the Maryland State house of delegates in 1791; elected to the Second and Third Congresses, and reelected as a Federalist to the Fourth Congress (March 4, 1791-March 3, 1797); Minister Resident to the Netherlands from March 2, 1797, to September 2, 1801; while holding this post was appointed by President John Adams in 1799 a member of a diplomatic mission to France; died on his estate in Dorchester County, near Cambridge, Md., December 11, 1803; interment in the Christ Protestant Episcopal Church Cemetery, Cambridge, Md.

**Bibliography:** *DAB*; DeConde, Alexander. "William Vans Murray and the Diplomacy of Peace: 1797-1800." *Maryland Historical Magazine* 48 (March 1953): 1-26; Hill, Peter P. *William Vans Murray, Federalist Diplomat; The Shaping of Peace with France,* 1797-1801. Syracuse, N.Y.: Syracuse University Press, 1971.

**MURTHA, John Patrick, Jr.,** a Representative from Pennsylvania; born in New Martinsville, Wetzel County, W.Va., June 17, 1932; graduated, Ramsey High School, Mount Pleasant, Pa., 1950; attended Kiskiminetas Spring School, 1951; B.A., University of Pittsburgh, 1962; engaged in postgraduate work, Indiana University of Pennsylvania, 1963; enlisted and served in the United States Marine Corps, 1952-1955, discharged with the rank of first lieutenant; maintained active reserve officer status; volunteered in 1966 for active duty in Vietnam as a major, and served as an intelligence officer with the First Marines, an infantry regiment, for one year in South Vietnam; awarded the Bronze Star, two Purple Hearts, and the Vietnamese Cross for Gallantry; elected to the Pennsylvania house of representatives in 1969 and served continuously until elected to the United States House of Representatives; businessman; elected as a Democrat to the Ninety-third Congress by special election, February 5, 1974, to fill the vacancy caused by the death of John P. Saylor; reelected to the eleven succeeding Congresses and served from February 5, 1974, to January 3, 1997; is a resident of Johnstown, Pa.

**MUSKIE, Edmund Sixtus,** a Senator from Maine; born in Rumford, Oxford County, Maine, March 28, 1914; attended the public schools; B.A., Bates College, Lewiston, Maine, 1936; LL.B., Cornell University Law School, Ithaca, N.Y., 1939; was admitted to the Massachusetts bar in 1939, and to the Maine bar in 1940; commenced the practice of law in Waterville, Maine, in 1940; during the Second World War enlisted in the United States Navy and served in the Atlantic and Asiatic-Pacific Theaters, 1942-1945; member and secretary of Waterville Board of Zoning Adjustment, 1948-1955; appointed district director for Maine Office of Price Stabilization, 1951-1952; city solicitor of Waterville in 1954; elected to the Maine State house of representatives in 1946, 1948, and 1950, and was Democratic floor leader 1949-1951; elected Governor of Maine in 1954, and served from January 5, 1955 until his resignation on January 3, 1959, having been elected Senator; elected as a Democrat to the United States Senate in 1958; reelected in 1964, 1970, and again in 1976, and served from January 3, 1959 until his resignation on May 7, 1980, to enter the Cabinet; chairman, Committee on the Budget (Ninety-third through Ninety-sixth Congresses); unsuccessful Democratic candidate for Vice President of the United States in 1968 on the ticket headed by Hubert H. Humphrey; unsuccessful candidate for the Democratic presidential nomination in 1972; appointed Secretary of State in the Cabinet of President Jimmy Carter, and served from May 8, 1980 to January 18, 1981; member of the President's Special Review Board ("Tower Commission") in 1987; resumed the practice of law; was a resident of Washington, D.C., until his death there on March 26, 1996; interment in Arlington National Cemetery, Va.

**Bibliography:** Lippman, Theo, Jr., and Donald J. Hansen. *Muskie.* New York: W.W. Norton and Co., 1971; Muskie, Edmund. *Journeys.* Garden City, N.Y.: Doubleday, 1972.

**MUSSELWHITE, Harry Webster,** a Representative from Michigan; born on a farm near Coldwater, Branch County, Mich., May 23, 1868; attended the district school and the high school in Coldwater, Mich.; apprenticed, and later employed, as a printer in Coldwater, Mich., 1886-1888; moved to Detroit, Mich., in 1888 and was employed as a newspaper reporter 1888-1905; served as city editor and sports writer of the Grand Rapids Herald 1905-1914; moved to Manistee, Mich., and became owner, editor, and publisher of the Manistee Daily News-Advocate 1915-1928; supervisor of census for the ninth Michigan district in 1920 and for the fourth Michigan district in 1930; member and vice chairman of the Michigan Hospital Commission 1927-1932; elected as a Democrat to the Seventy-third Congress (March 4, 1933-January 3, 1935); unsuccessful candidate for reelection in 1934 to the Seventy-fourth Congress; engaged in the management of newspaper properties until his retirement; died in San Lorenzo, Calif., December 14, 1955; interment in Cypress Lawn Cemetery, Colma, Calif.

**MUSTO, Raphael John,** a Representative from Pennsylvania; born in Pittston Township, Luzerne County, Pa., March 30, 1929; attended the public schools and graduated from Pittston Township High School in 1946; served in the United States Army, 1951-1953; B.S., Kings College, Wilkes-Barre, Pa., 1971; member of the Pennsylvania house of representatives from November 8, 1971 until April 15, 1980; elected as a Democrat to the Ninety-sixth Congress, April 9, 1980, by special election to fill the vacancy caused by the resignation of Daniel J. Flood, and served from April 9, 1980, to January 3, 1981; unsuccessful candidate for reelection in 1980 to the Ninety-seventh Congress; elected to the Pennsylvania senate, District 14, in 1982; reelected in 1986, 1990, and in 1994 for the term expiring November 30, 1998; is a resident of Pittston, Pa.

**MUTCHLER, Howard** (son of William Mutchler), a Representative from Pennsylvania; born in Easton, Northampton County, Pa., February 12, 1859; attended the public schools of his native city and Phillips Academy, Andover, Mass.; studied law with his father at Easton, but before qualifying for admission to the bar became editor and publisher of the Daily Express and the Northampton Democrat at Easton; elected as a Democrat to the Fifty-third Congress to fill the vacancy caused by the death of his father, William Mutchler, and served from August 7, 1893, to March 3, 1895; was not a candidate for renomination in 1894 to the Fifty-fourth Congress; elected to the Fifty-seventh Congress (March 4, 1901-March 3, 1903); was not a candidate for renomination to the Fifty-eighth Congress; resumed newspaper activities; died in Easton, Pa., on January 4, 1916; interment in Easton Cemetery.

**MUTCHLER, William** (father of Howard Mutchler), a Representative from Pennsylvania; born in Palmer Township, Northampton County, Pa., December 21, 1831; attended the public schools and Vandeveer's Academy, Easton, Pa.; studied law; admitted to the bar and commenced practice at Easton, Northampton County, Pa.; sheriff of Northampton County 1854-1860; prothonotary of Northampton County 1861-1867; adjutant of the Thirty-eighth Pennsylvania Volunteers in 1863; appointed assessor of internal revenue in March 1867 and served until May 1869; chairman of the Pennsylvania Democratic committee in 1869 and 1870; delegate to the Democratic National Conventions from 1876 until his death; elected as a Democrat to the Forty-fourth Congress (March 4, 1875-March 3, 1877); chairman, Committee on Expenditures in the Department of the Interior (Forty-fourth Congress); was not a candidate for renomination in 1876; elected to the Forty-seventh and Forty-eighth Congresses (March 4, 1881-March 3, 1885); was not a candidate for renomination in 1884; again elected to the Fifty-first, Fifty-second, and Fifty-third Congresses, and served from March 4, 1889, until his death in Easton, Northampton County, Pa., June 23, 1893; interment in Easton Cemetery.

**MYERS, Amos,** a Representative from Pennsylvania; born in Petersburg, Lancaster County, Pa., April 23, 1824; attended a private school near Clarion, Pa., and was graduated from Meadville College in 1843; studied law; was admitted to the bar in 1846 and commenced practice in Clarion, Clarion County, Pa.; held several local offices; was appointed district attorney of Clarion County in 1847; elected as a Republican to the Thirty-eighth Congress (March 4, 1863-March 3, 1865); chairman, Committee on Expenditures in the Department of the Treasury (Thirty-eighth Congress); resumed the practice of law in Clarion; moved to Kentucky, was ordained to the Baptist ministry, and preached in Kentucky, Pennsylvania, and New York; died in East Carleton (now Kent), Orleans County, N.Y., on October 18, 1893; interment in Crown Hill Cemetery, Indianapolis, Ind.

**MYERS, Francis John,** a Representative and a Senator from Pennsylvania; born in Philadelphia, Pa., December 18, 1901; attended the public schools; graduated from St. Joseph's College in 1923, and from the law department of Temple University, Philadelphia, Pa., in 1927; instructor in St. Joseph's High School, Philadelphia, Pa., 1923-1927; was admitted to the bar in 1927 and commenced practice in Philadelphia, Pa.; secretary to the district attorney of Philadelphia, 1929-1931; attorney for the Home Owners' Loan Corporation, 1934-1935; deputy attorney general of Pennsylvania in 1937; elected as a Democrat to the Seventy-sixth and to the two succeeding Congresses (January 3, 1939-January 3, 1945); was not a candidate in 1944 for renomination to the House of Representatives, but was elected to the United States Senate and served from January 3, 1945, to January 3, 1951; unsuccessful candidate for reelection in 1950; Democratic whip 1949-1951; resumed the practice of law; at time of death was chairman of Philadelphia Redevelopment Authority, and a member of the General State Authority and the Greater Philadelphia Movement; died in Philadelphia, Pa., July 5, 1956; interment in Holy Sepulchre Cemetery.

**MYERS, Gary Arthur,** a Representative from Pennsylvania; born in Toronto, Jefferson County, Ohio, August 16, 1937; attended Evans City (Pa.) Elementary School, 1943-1951; graduated, Evans City High School, 1955; B.S., University of Cincinnati, 1960; M.B.A., University of Pittsburgh, 1964; pursued professional career in mechanical and industrial engineering, steel mill turn foreman; served in the United States Air Force Reserve, 1961-1968; unsuccessful candidate for election in 1972 to the Ninety-third Congress; elected as a Republican to the Ninety-fourth and Ninety-fifth Congresses (January 3, 1975-January 3, 1979); was not a candidate for reelection in 1978 to the Ninety-sixth Congress; resumed work in the steel industry; consultant in technical services and project management for an engineering search firm; is a resident of Butler, Pa.

**MYERS, Henry Lee,** a Senator from Montana; born near Boonville, Cooper County, Mo., October 9, 1862; attended private schools, Cooper Institute, and Boonville Academy; studied law; was admitted to the bar in 1884 and commenced practice in Boonville; moved to Hamilton, Ravalli County, Mont., in 1893; prosecuting attorney of Ravalli County from 1895 until 1899; Montana State senator, 1899-1903; district judge of the fourth judicial district of Montana, 1907-1911; elected as a Democrat to the United States Senate in 1911; reelected in 1916 and served from March 4, 1911, until March 3, 1923; declined to be a candidate for renomination in 1922; chairman, Committee on Irrigation and Reclamation of Arid Lands (Sixty-third Congress), Committee on Public Lands (Sixty-third through Sixty-fifth Congresses), Committee on Indian Depredations (Sixty-sixth Congress); moved to Billings, Mont., in 1923 and continued the practice of his profession; appointed associate justice of the supreme court of Montana in 1927; resumed the practice of law in 1929; died in Billings, Mont., November 11, 1943; interment in Riverview Cemetery, Hamilton, Mont.

**Bibliography:** Myers, Henry L. *The United States Senate: What Kind of a Body?* Philadelphia: Dorrana and Co., 1939.

**MYERS, John Thomas,** a Representative from Indiana; born in Covington, Fountain County, Ind., February 8, 1927; attended the public schools of Covington; B.S., Indiana State University, 1951; served in the United States Army in the European Theater, 1945-1946; cashier and trust officer with The Fountain Trust Co. in Covington, Ind., 1952-1966; owns and operates a grain and livestock farm in Fountain County, Ind.; elected as a Republican to the Ninetieth and to the fourteen succeeding Congresses (January 3, 1967-January 3, 1997); was not a candidate for reelection in 1996 to the One Hundred Fifth Congress; is a resident of Covington, Ind.

**MYERS, Leonard,** a Representative from Pennsylvania; born in Attleboro (now Langhorne), Bucks County, Pa., on November 13, 1827; attended private academic schools and the University of Pennsylvania at Philadelphia; studied law; was admitted to the bar in 1848 and practiced in Philadelphia, Pa.; held local offices; major of the Ninth Regiment, Pennsylvania Militia, during the emergency service of September 1862; elected as a Republican to the Thirty-eighth and to the two succeeding Congresses (March 4, 1863-March 3, 1869); successfully contested the election of John Moffet to the Forty-first Congress; reelected to the Forty-second and Forty-third Congresses and served from April 9, 1869, to March 3, 1875; chairman, Committee on Foreign Affairs (Forty-second Congress), Committee on Patents (Forty-second Congress), Committee on Private Land Claims (Forty-third Congress); unsuccessful candidate for reelection in 1874 to the Forty-fourth Congress; resumed the practice of law; died in Philadelphia, Pa., February 11, 1905; interment in De Benneville family cemetery.

**MYERS, Michael Joseph (Ozzie),** a Representative from Pennsylvania; born in Philadelphia, Pa., May 4, 1943; attended the Catholic schools of Philadelphia; graduated, Philadelphia public school, 1961; longshoreman, Philadelphia, 1961-1970; served in the Pennsylvania house of representatives, 1970-1976; elected as a Democrat to the Ninety-fourth Congress, November 2, 1976, by special election to fill the vacancy caused by the death of William A. Barrett, and at the same time elected to the Ninety-fifth Congress; reelected to the Ninety-sixth Congress and served from November 2, 1976, until his expulsion from the House of Representatives pursuant to H. Res. 794, passed on October 2, 1980; employed in the family restaurant business; unsuccessful candidate for 39th ward leader in Philadelphia, May 1988; is a resident of Philadelphia, Pa.

**MYERS, William Ralph,** a Representative from Indiana; born near Wilmington, Clinton County, Ohio, June 12, 1836; moved with his parents to Anderson, Madison County, Ind., in October 1836; attended the common schools and later taught; surveyor of Madison County from 1858 until 1860; during the Civil War enlisted as a private in Company G, Forty-seventh Regiment, Indiana Volunteer Infantry; was promoted to orderly sergeant, second lieutenant, first lieutenant, and captain, and served four years and three months; after returning from the Army taught school; superintendent of the public schools of Anderson, Ind., in 1868 and 1869; member of the school board of Anderson, 1871-1879; studied law; was admitted to the bar in 1871 and commenced practice in Anderson; elected as a Democrat to the Forty-sixth Congress (March 4, 1879-March 3, 1881); unsuccessful candidate for reelection in 1880 to the Forty-seventh Congress; secretary of State of Indiana, 1882-1886; purchased the Anderson Democrat in 1886 and was its editor; unsuccessful Democratic candidate for Governor; again secretary of state of Indiana, 1892-1894; resumed the practice of law; died in Anderson, Ind., April 18, 1907; interment in East Maplewood Cemetery.

**MYRICK, Sue,** a Representative from North Carolina; born in Tiffin, Seneca County, Ohio, August 1, 1941; graduated, Port Clinton High School; attended Heidelberg College, 1959-1960; worked in television in Harrisonburg, Va.; former president and chief executive officer of an advertising agency; at-large member, Charlotte, N.C., city council, 1983-1985; mayor of Charlotte, 1987-1991; unsuccessful candidate in 1992 for nomination to the United States Senate; elected as a Republican to the One Hundred Fourth Congress (January 3, 1995-January 3, 1997); is a resident of Charlotte, N.C.

# N

**NABERS, Benjamin Duke,** a Representative from Mississippi; born in Franklin, Williamson County, Tenn., November 7, 1812; attended the common schools; moved to Hickory Flat, Miss.; engaged as a commission merchant; held several local offices; elected as a Unionist to the Thirty-second Congress (March 4, 1851-March 3, 1853); unsuccessful Unionist candidate for reelection in 1852 to the Thirty-third Congress; moved to Memphis, Tenn.; studied law; was admitted to the bar in 1860 and commenced practice in Memphis, Tenn.; presidential elector on the Constitutional-Union ticket of Bell and Everett in 1860; returned to Mississippi and settled at Holly Springs, Marshall County, in 1860; chancery clerk 1870-1874; member of the governing board of the State penitentiary at Jackson, Miss., for two years; died at Holly Springs, Miss., September 6, 1878; interment in Hill Crest Cemetery.

**NADLER, Jerrold Lewis,** a Representative from New York; born in Brooklyn, N.Y., June 13, 1947; graduated from Stuyvesant High School, 1965; A.B., Columbia University, 1969; J.D., Fordham University Law School, 1978; attorney; legislative assistant to New York State senator Jack Bronston, 1966-1968 and State assemblyman Richard Gottfried, 1972; member, New York State assembly, 1976-1993; Democratic district leader, 1969, 1973, 1975; elected as a Democrat to the One Hundred Second Congress, November 3, 1992, by special election to fill the vacancy caused by the death of Theodore S. Weiss, and at the same time elected to the One Hundred

Third Congress; reelected to the One Hundred Fourth Congress, and served from November 4, 1992 to January 3, 1997; is a resident of New York City.

**NAGLE, David Ray,** a Representative from Iowa; born in Grinnell, Poweshiek County, Iowa, April 15, 1943; attended public schools; attended the University of Northern Iowa, Cedar Falls, 1961-1965; LL.B., University of Iowa Law School, Iowa City, 1968; admitted to the Iowa State bar in 1968 and commenced practice in Waterloo; assistant Black Hawk county attorney, 1969-1970; city attorney, Evansdale, Iowa, 1972-1973; adjunct professor, University of Northern Iowa, 1978-1981; elected as a Democrat to the One Hundredth and to the two succeeding Congresses (January 3, 1987-January 3, 1993); unsuccessful candidate for reelection in 1992 to the One Hundred Third Congress; is a resident of Cedar Falls, Iowa.

**NAPHEN, Henry Francis,** a Representative from Massachusetts; born in Ireland August 14, 1852; immigrated to the United States with his parents, who settled in Lowell, Mass.; educated by private tutors and also attended the public schools; graduated from Harvard University in 1878; attended the Boston University Law School; admitted to the bar in 1880 and commenced practice in Boston; member of the school committee of Boston 1882-1885; member of the Massachusetts senate in 1885 and 1886; appointed bail commissioner by the justices of the superior court; elected as a Democrat to the Fifty-sixth and Fifty-seventh Congresses (March 4, 1899-March 3, 1903); was not a candidate for renomination in 1902; died in Boston, Mass., June 8, 1905; interment in Calvary Cemetery.

**NAPIER, John Light,** a Representative from South Carolina; born in Blenheim, Marlboro County, S.C., May 16, 1947; attended the public schools; A.B., Davidson (N.C.) College, 1969; J.D., University of South Carolina, Columbia, 1972; served in the United States Army Reserve, first lieutenant, 1969-1977; admitted to the South Carolina Bar in 1972; legislative assistant to United States Senator Strom Thurmond and minority counsel, United States Senate Subcommittee on Administrative Practice and Procedure, 1972-1973; minority counsel and professional staff member, United States Senate Committee on Veterans' Affairs, 1973-1976; chief legislative assistant and legal counsel to Senator Strom Thurmond, 1976-1978; chief minority counsel, United States Senate Committee on Official Conduct, 1977; engaged in the private practice of law in Bennettsville, S.C., 1978-1980; elected as a Republican to the Ninety-seventh Congress (January 3, 1981-January 3, 1983); unsuccessful candidate for reelection in 1982 to the Ninety-eighth Congress; returned to the private practice of law in Bennettsville, 1983-1986; nominated as a judge of the United States Court of Federal Claims on September 11, 1986; was confirmed by the Senate on October 8, 1986, and served until his resignation in July 1989 to enter the private practice of law; is a resident of Bennettsville, S.C., and Arlington, Va.

**NAREY, Harry Elsworth,** a Representative from Iowa; born in Spirit Lake, Dickinson County, Iowa, May 15, 1885; attended the public schools and Grinnell College, Grinnell, Iowa; was graduated from the State University of Iowa at Iowa City in 1907; was admitted to the bar the same year and commenced practice in Spirit Lake, Iowa; county attorney of Dickinson County, Iowa, 1914-1920 and 1943-1945; city attorney of Spirit Lake, Iowa, 1918-1943; delegate to the Republican State conventions 1916-1960; chairman of the Dickson County Republican Central Committee 1918-1943; elected as a Republican to the Seventy-seventh Congress to fill the vacancy caused by the resignation of Vincent F. Harrington and served from November 3, 1942, to January 3, 1943; was not a candidate for reelection in 1942 to the Seventy-eighth Congress; again practiced law; appointed judge of the fourteenth judicial district of Iowa in 1944 and served until his resignation in 1959;

resumed the private practice of law in Spirit Lake, Iowa, until his death August 18, 1962; interment in Lakeview Cemetery.

**NASH, Abner,** a Delegate from North Carolina; born at Templeton Manor, on the Appomattox River, near Farmville, Prince Edward County, Va., August 8, 1740; attended the rural schools in Virginia; member, Virginia House of Burgesses, 1761-1765; moved to Halifax, N.C., and subsequently to New Bern, N.C.; studied law; was admitted to the bar and commenced practice in Halifax, N.C.; town representative, North Carolina provincial congress, 1774-1776; member of the State house of commons in 1778, 1782, 1784, and 1785; member of the State senate in 1779 and 1780 and was president of that body in 1779; Governor of North Carolina in 1780 and 1781; Member of the Continental Congress 1782-1783; died in New York City on December 2, 1786; interment in St. Paul's Churchyard; reinterment in the family burial ground at "Pembroke," near New Bern, N.C.

**Bibliography:** *DAB.*

**NASH, Charles Edmund,** a Representative from Louisiana; born in Opelousas, St. Landry Parish, La., May 23, 1844; attended the common schools; was a bricklayer by trade; during the Civil War enlisted in 1863 as a private in the Eighty-second Regiment, United States Volunteers, and was promoted to the rank of sergeant major; appointed night inspector of customs in 1865; elected as a Republican to the Forty-fourth Congress (March 4, 1875-March 3, 1877); unsuccessful candidate for reelection in 1876 to the Forty-fifth Congress; postmaster at Washington, St. Landry Parish, La., from February 15, 1882, until May 1, 1882; died in New Orleans, La., June 21, 1913; interment in St. Louis Cemetery No. 3.

**NATCHER, William Huston,** a Representative from Kentucky; born in Bowling Green, Warren County, Ky., September 11, 1909; attended the public schools and received a high school education at Ogden Preparatory Department of Ogden College, Bowling Green, Ky.; B.A., Western Kentucky State College, Bowling Green, 1930; LL.B., Ohio State University, Columbus, 1933; was admitted to the bar in 1934 and commenced practice of law in Bowling Green, Ky.; Federal conciliation commissioner for the western district of Kentucky, 1936-1937; county attorney of Warren County, 1938-1950; president of the Young Democratic Clubs of Kentucky, 1941-1946; served in the United States Navy, 1942-1945; commonwealth attorney for the eighth judicial district of Kentucky, 1951-1953; delegate to the Democratic National Convention of 1940; elected as a Democrat to the Eighty-third Congress, August 1, 1953, by special election to fill the vacancy caused by the death of Garrett L. Withers; reelected to the twenty succeeding Congresses, and served from August 1, 1953 until his death in the naval hospital at Bethesda, Md., March 29, 1994; chairman, Committee on Appropriations (One Hundred Third Congress); interment in Fairview Cemetery, Bowling Green, Ky.

**NAUDAIN, Arnold,** a Senator from Delaware; born near Dover, Del., January 6, 1790; completed preparatory studies; graduated from the College of New Jersey (now Princeton University) in 1806 and from the medical department of the University of Pennsylvania at Philadelphia in 1810 and commenced the practice of medicine in Dover, Del.; surgeon general of the Delaware Militia in the War of 1812; member, State house of representatives 1823-1827, serving as speaker in 1826; unsuccessful candidate for Governor of Delaware in 1832; elected in 1829 to the United States Senate to fill the vacancy caused by the resignation of Louis McLane; reelected in 1832 and served from January 13, 1830, until his resignation on June 16, 1836; chairman, Committee on Claims (Twenty-fourth Congress); resumed the practice of medicine in Wilmington, Del.; member, State senate 1836-1839; collector of the port of Wilmington, Del., 1841-1845; moved to Philadelphia, Pa., in 1845 and practiced medicine; died in Odessa, New Castle County, Del., January 4, 1872; interment in the Old Drawyer's Presbyterian Churchyard.

**NAYLOR, Charles,** a Representative from Pennsylvania; born in Philadelphia County, Pa., October 6, 1806; completed preparatory studies; studied law; was admitted to the bar in 1828 and commenced practice in Philadelphia, Pa.; held several local offices; unsuccessful candidate for election in 1836 to the Twenty-fifth Congress; subsequently elected as a Whig to the Twenty-fifth Congress to fill the vacancy caused by the death of Francis J. Harper; reelected to the Twenty-sixth Congress and served from June 29, 1837, to March 3, 1841; declined to be a candidate for renomination in 1840; resumed the practice of law; during the Mexican War raised a company of volunteers known as the Philadelphia Rangers and served as captain; after the war settled in Pittsburgh, Pa., and continued the practice of law; returned to Philadelphia and practiced law until his death there on December 24, 1872; interment in South Laurel Hill Cemetery.

**NEAL, Henry Safford,** a Representative from Ohio; born in Gallipolis, Gallia County, Ohio, August 25, 1828; attended the common schools; was graduated from Marietta (Ohio) College in 1847; studied law; was admitted to the bar in 1851 and commenced practice in Ironton, Ohio; prosecuting attorney of Lawrence County about 1851; member of the Ohio State senate, 1861-1863; appointed consul to Lisbon, Portugal, in 1869; by the resignation of the Minister Resident became Chargé d'Affaires in December 1869 and served until July 1870, when he resigned and returned to Ohio; delegate to the Ohio constitutional convention in 1873; elected as a Republican to the Forty-fifth and to the two succeeding Congresses (March 4, 1877-March 3, 1883); chairman, Committee on District of Columbia (Forty-seventh Congress); was not a candidate for renomination in 1882 to the Forty-eighth Congress; resumed the practice of his profession at Ironton, Ohio; appointed Solicitor of the Treasury by President Chester A. Arthur, and served from July 3, 1884 to April 13, 1885, when a successor was appointed by President Grover Cleveland; again resumed the practice of law; died in Ironton, Ohio, July 13, 1906; interment in Woodland Cemetery.

**NEAL, John Randolph,** a Representative from Tennessee; born near Clinton, Anderson County, Tenn., November 26, 1836; attended the common schools and Hiwassee College, Monroe County, Tenn.; was graduated from Emory and Henry College, Emory, Va., in 1858; studied law; was admitted to the bar in 1859 and commenced practice in Athens, Tenn.; during the Civil War enlisted in the Confederate Army and was elected captain of a Cavalry troop, which afterward became a part of the Sixteenth Battalion, Tennessee Cavalry, and was subsequently promoted to lieutenant colonel of the battalion; taught school for several years; settled at Rhea Springs, Tenn., and continued the practice of law; member of the State house of representatives in 1874; served in the State senate in 1878 and 1879 and as presiding officer in 1879; elected as a Democrat to the Forty-ninth and Fiftieth Congresses (March 4, 1885-March 3, 1889); declined to be a candidate for renomination in 1888 on account of ill health; died at Rhea Springs, Rhea County, Tenn., March 26, 1889; interment in the W.F. Brown family cemetery, Post Oak Springs, Tenn.

**NEAL, Lawrence Talbot,** a Representative from Ohio; born in Parkersburg, Va. (now West Virginia), September 22, 1844; pursued classical studies; moved to Chillicothe, Ohio, in 1864; studied law; was admitted to the bar in 1866 and commenced practice in Chillicothe, Ross County, Ohio, in 1867; city solicitor in 1867 and 1868; declined to be a candidate for reelection; elected prosecuting attorney of Ross County, Ohio, in 1870 and resigned in October 1872 to become a candidate for Congress; elected as a Democrat to the Forty-third and Forty-fourth Congresses (March 4, 1873-March 3, 1877); unsuccessful candidate for reelection in 1876 to the Forty-fifth Congress, and for election in 1878 to the Forty-sixth Congress; unsuccessful candidate for election to the Ohio State senate in 1887; resumed the practice of law; delegate to the

Democratic National Conventions of 1888 and 1892; unsuccessful candidate in 1893 for election for Governor of Ohio; died in Chillicothe, Ohio, November 2, 1905; interment in Grandview Cemetery.

**NEAL, Richard Edmund,** a Representative from Massachusetts; born in Springfield, Hampden County, Mass., February 14, 1949; graduated, Springfield Technical High School, 1968; B.A., American International College, Springfield, 1972; M.P.A., University of Hartford, Barney School of Business and Public Administration, 1976; student, University of Massachusetts; lecturer in history and politics: Springfield Technical Community College, 1973-1983; Western New England College, 1979-1982; American International College, 1978; Springfield College, 1982; instructor, Cathedral High School, 1978-1980; assistant to the mayor of Springfield, 1973-1978; member, Springfield city council, 1978-1984, president, 1979; mayor of Springfield, 1984-1988; elected as a Democrat to the One Hundred First and to the three succeeding Congresses (January 3, 1989-January 3, 1997); is a resident of Springfield, Mass.

**NEAL, Stephen Lybrook,** a Representative from North Carolina; born in Winston-Salem, Forsyth County, N.C., November 7, 1934; attended schools in North Carolina and California; graduated from Narbonne High School, Lomita, Calif., in 1952; attended the University of California, Santa Barbara; B.A., University of Hawaii, Honolulu, 1959; president, Community Press, Inc., 1966-1974; delegate to the Democratic Mid-Term Convention, 1974; elected as a Democrat to the Ninety-fourth and to the nine succeeding Congresses (January 3, 1975-January 3, 1995); was not a candidate for renomination in 1994 to the One Hundred Fourth Congress; president, Z. Smith Reynolds Foundation; is a resident of Winston-Salem, N.C., and McLean, Va.

**NEAL, William Elmer,** a Representative from West Virginia; born on a farm near Proctorville, Lawrence County, Ohio, October 14, 1875; attended the public schools; graduated from Proctorville High School in 1894; taught school in Ohio and Kentucky for six years; graduated from National Normal University, Lebanon, Ohio, in 1900 and received a medical degree from the University of Cincinnati in 1906; commenced the general practice of medicine in Huntington, W.Va., in 1907; served as mayor of Huntington 1925-1928; member of Huntington Park Board 1931-1952, and West Virginia Public Health Council 1936-1940; member of West Virginia house of delegates in 1951 and 1952; elected as a Republican to the Eighty-third Congress (January 3, 1953-January 3, 1955); unsuccessful candidate for reelection in 1954 to the Eighty-fourth Congress; served as medical consultant to Foreign Operations Administration in Afghanistan from February 17, 1955, to June 20, 1955; elected to the Eighty-fifth Congress (January 3, 1957-January 3, 1959); unsuccessful candidate for reelection in 1958 to the Eighty-sixth Congress; died in Huntington, W.Va., November 12, 1959; interment in Spring Hill Cemetery.

**NEALE, Raphael,** a Representative from Maryland; born in St. Marys County, Md., and resided in Leonardtown; received a limited education; elected to the Sixteenth, Seventeenth, and Eighteenth Congresses (March 4, 1819-March 3, 1825); died in Leonardtown, Md., October 19, 1833.

**NEDZI, Lucien Norbert,** a Representative from Michigan; born in Hamtramck, Wayne County, Mich., May 28, 1925; graduated from Hamtramck High School in 1943; A.B., University of Michigan, 1948; attended University of Detroit Law School in 1949, and University of Michigan Law School in 1951; served as a combat infantryman in the Philippines and in the Corps of Engineers in Japan from July 12, 1944, to August 15, 1946; served in the Korean conflict from February 10, 1951, to October 16, 1951; member of the Army Reserve, August 15, 1946, to March 17, 1953; admitted to the Michigan bar in January 1952 and engaged in the practice of law in

Detroit; served as Wayne County public administrator, January 1, 1955 to November 7, 1961; delegate to the Democratic National Conventions of 1960 and 1968; elected as a Democrat to the Eighty-seventh Congress, November 7, 1961, by special election to fill the vacancy caused by the resignation of Thaddeus M. Machrowicz; reelected to the nine succeeding Congresses, and served from November 7, 1961 to January 3, 1981; was not a candidate for reelection in 1980 to the Ninety-seventh Congress; chairman, Select Committee on Intelligence (Ninety-fourth Congress), Joint Committee on the Library (Ninety-third through Ninety-fifth Congresses), Committee on House Administration (Ninety-sixth Congress); admitted to the District of Columbia bar in 1977; is a resident of McLean, Va.

**NEECE, William Henry,** a Representative from Illinois; born near Springfield, Sangamon County (later part of Logan County), Ill., February 26, 1831; moved with his parents to McDonough County; attended the common schools; taught school; studied law; was admitted to the bar in 1858 and commenced practice in Macomb, Ill.; member of the city council in 1861; member of the State house of representatives in 1864 and 1870; member of the State constitutional convention of 1869 and 1870; served in the State senate 1878-1882; elected as a Democrat to the Forty-eighth and Forty-ninth Congresses (March 4, 1883-March 3, 1887); unsuccessful candidate for reelection in 1886 to the Fiftieth Congress; resumed the practice of his profession and also interested in stock raising; died in Chicago, Ill., January 3, 1909; interment in Oakwood Cemetery, Macomb, Ill.

**NEEDHAM, James Carson,** a Representative from California; born in a covered wagon at Carson City, Nev., September 17, 1864; arrived with his parents at Mayfield, Santa Clara, Calif., October 1, 1864; attended the public schools; was graduated from the University of the Pacific at San Jose in 1886 and from the law department of the University of Michigan at Ann Arbor in 1889; clerk in The Adjutant General's Office of the War Department in Washington, D.C., from September 1, 1887, until September 1, 1888, when he resigned to complete his law course; was admitted to the bar in 1889 and commenced practice in Modesto, Stanislaus County, Calif.; unsuccessful candidate for election to the State senate in 1890; elected as a Republican to the Fifty-sixth and to the six succeeding Congresses (March 4, 1899-March 3, 1913); unsuccessful candidate in 1912 for reelection to the Sixty-third Congress; resumed the practice of law in San Diego, Calif., 1913-1916, when he returned to Modesto, Calif., and continued his profession; appointed judge of the superior court of California January 1, 1919; elected to the same office in 1920 to fill an unexpired term; reelected in 1922 and again in 1926, and served until January 1, 1935; died in Modesto, Calif., July 11, 1942; interment in the Masonic Cemetery.

**NEELEY, George Arthur,** a Representative from Kansas; born in Detroit, Pike County, Ill., August 1, 1879; attended the public schools; moved to Ingram, Indian Territory (now Wellston, Okla.), in 1893 and engaged in agricultural pursuits; taught school and worked his way through the high-school course; attended the Southwestern Baptist University, Jackson, Tenn., and was graduated in law from the University of Kansas at Lawrence in 1904; was admitted to the bar and commenced practice in Wellston, Okla.; continued the practice of law in Chandler 1905-1908 and in Hutchinson, Reno County, Kans., 1908-1919; unsuccessful candidate for election in 1910 to the Sixty-first Congress; elected as a Democrat to the Sixty-second Congress to fill the vacancy caused by the death of Edmond H. Madison; reelected to the Sixty-third Congress and served from November 11, 1912, to March 3, 1915; did not seek renomination in 1914, but was an unsuccessful candidate for election to the United States Senate; resumed the practice of his chosen profession in Hutchinson, Kans., where he died on January 1, 1919; interment in Oak Park Cemetery, Chandler, Okla.

**NEELY, Matthew Mansfield,** a Representative and a Senator from West Virginia; born near Groves, Doddridge County, W.Va., November 9, 1874; attended the public schools and Salem College at Salem, W.Va.; served as a private in the infantry during the Spanish-American War; graduated from the University of West Virginia at Morgantown in 1901, and from the law department of the same university in 1902; was admitted to the bar in 1902 and commenced practice in Fairmont, Marion County; mayor of Fairmont, 1908-1910; clerk of the West Virginia State house of delegates, 1911-1913; was elected as a Democrat to the Sixty-third Congress to fill the vacancy caused by the resignation of John W. Davis; reelected to the three succeeding Congresses, and served from October 14, 1913 to March 3, 1921; unsuccessful candidate for reelection in 1920 to the Sixty-seventh Congress; elected in 1922 as a Democrat to the United States Senate, and served from March 4, 1923 to March 3, 1929; unsuccessful candidate for reelection in 1928; elected to the United States Senate in 1930; reelected in 1936, and served from March 4, 1931 until his resignation on January 12, 1941, having been elected Governor; chairman, Committee on Rules (Seventy-fourth through Seventy-sixth Congresses), Committee on the Judiciary (Seventy-seventh Congress); elected Governor of West Virginia in 1940, and served from January 13, 1941 to January 15, 1945; elected as a Democrat to the Seventy-ninth Congress (January 3, 1945-January 3, 1947); unsuccessful candidate for reelection in 1946 to the Eightieth Congress; elected as a Democrat to the United States Senate in 1948; reelected in 1954, and served from January 3, 1949 until his death in the naval hospital at Bethesda, Md., January 18, 1958; chairman, Committee on the District of Columbia (Eighty-first, Eighty-second, Eighty-fourth and Eighty-fifth Congresses); interment in Woodlawn Cemetery, Fairmont, W.Va.

Bibliography: *DAB.*

**NEGLEY, James Scott,** a Representative from Pennsylvania; born in East Liberty, Allegheny County, Pa., December 22, 1826; attended the village schools and was graduated from the Western University of Pennsylvania at Allegheny in 1846; served in the Mexican War in the Duquesne Grays, First Regiment, Pennsylvania Volunteers; entered the Union Army as brigadier general April 19, 1861; commanded a division in Patterson's command for three months' service; organized and equipped a brigade of Infantry and Artillery for the West and joined General William T. Sherman in October 1861; promoted to major general; member of the board of managers of the National Home for Disabled Volunteer Soldiers 1874-1878 and 1882-1888; elected as a Republican to the Forty-first, Forty-second, and Forty-third Congresses (March 4, 1869-March 3, 1875); unsuccessful candidate for reelection in 1874 to the Forty-fourth Congress; elected to the Forty-ninth Congress (March 4, 1885-March 3, 1887); unsuccessful candidate for reelection in 1886 to the Fiftieth Congress; engaged in railroading; died in Plainfield, Union County, N.J. August 7, 1901; interment in Allegheny Cemetery, Pittsburgh, Pa.

Bibliography: *DAB.*

**NEILL, Robert,** a Representative from Arkansas; born near Desha, Independence County, Ark., on November 12, 1838; attended the common schools; took a course in land surveying under a tutor in Ohio in 1859; elected county surveyor of his native county in August 1860; entered the Confederate Army in May 1861 and served as a private in Company K, First Regiment, Arkansas Mounted Riflemen, General Benjamin McCulloch's Brigade, Army of the West; promoted to first lieutenant in 1862 and to captain in 1863; clerk of the circuit court of Independence County, 1866-1868; read law; was admitted to the bar in 1868 and commenced practice in Batesville in 1872; lieutenant colonel of the Arkansas State Guards, 1874-1877; brigadier general of the Arkansas State militia, 1877-1882; delegate to the Democratic National Convention of 1888, and vice president of the convention for Arkansas; elected as a Democrat to the Fifty-third and Fifty-fourth Congresses (March 4,

1893-March 3, 1897); unsuccessful candidate for renomination in 1896 to the Fifty-fifth Congress; resumed the practice of law; served one year as chairman of the Arkansas Railroad Commission, having been appointed in 1899 by Governor Daniel Webster Jones; died in Batesville, Independence County, Ark., February 16, 1907; interment in Oak Lawn Cemetery.

**NEILSON, John,** a Delegate from New Jersey; born at Raritan Landing, near New Brunswick, N.J., March 11, 1745; completed preparatory studies; attended the University of Pennsylvania at Philadelphia in 1758; engaged in mercantile pursuits in New Brunswick 1769-1775; member of the Revolutionary Army as captain of New Jersey Militia in 1775; appointed colonel of the Second Regiment, Middlesex County (N.J.) Militia, in 1776; brigadier general of militia in 1777; deputy quartermaster general for New Jersey 1780-1783; elected as a Member of the Continental Congress November 6, 1778, and declined December 12, 1778; trustee of Rutgers College at New Brunswick, N.J., from 1782 until his death; delegate to the State convention which ratified the Federal Constitution in 1787; member of the State general assembly in 1800 and 1801; engaged as a shipping merchant; General Lafayette presented him with a sword in 1824; died in New Brunswick, N.J., March 3, 1833; interment in Van Liew Cemetery, on the Cranberry Turnpike.

**NELLIGAN, James Leo,** a Representative from Pennsylvania; born in Wilkes-Barre, Luzerne County, Pa., February 14, 1929; attended parochial schools; graduated from Coughlin High School, 1947; B.S., Kings College, Wilkes-Barre, 1951; accountant; United States General Accounting Office, Washington, D.C., accountant and audit manager, 1951-1967; professional staff member, Subcommittee on Foreign Operations and Government Information, Committee on Government Operations, United States House of Representatives, 1967-1970; director, Finance and Grants Management Division, United States Office of Economic Opportunity, 1970-1973; director, Office of Property Management, Office of Federal Management Policy, United States General Services Administration, 1973-1975; operations director, Subcommittee on Oversight and Investigations, Committee on Interstate and Foreign Commerce, United States House of Representatives, 1975-1979; elected as a Republican to the Ninety-seventh Congress (January 3, 1981-January 3, 1983); unsuccessful candidate for reelection in 1982 to the Ninety-eighth Congress; deputy secretary of revenue, Commonwealth of Pennsylvania, 1983-1985; director, Governor of Pennsylvania, Washington, D.C., office, 1986-1987; is a resident of Harvey's Lake, Pa.

**NELSEN, Ancher,** a Representative from Minnesota; born on a farm in Renville County, near Buffalo Lake, Minn., October 11, 1904; attended grade school and graduated from high school in Brownton, Minn., in 1923; served on District No. 75 School Board, 1926-1935, and on the Lynn Township Board, 1929-1935; operated a farm in McLeod County, near Hutchinson, Minn.; member of the Minnesota State senate from McLeod County, 1935-1949; delegate to the Republican National Conventions of 1948 and 1952; Lieutenant Governor of Minnesota in 1953; National Administrator of the Rural Electrification Administration Program, 1953-1956; elected as a Republican to the Eighty-sixth and to the seven succeeding Congresses and served from January 3, 1959, until his resignation December 31, 1974; was not a candidate for reelection in 1974 to the Ninety-fourth Congress; was a resident of Hutchinson, Minn.; died November 30, 1992.

**NELSON, Adolphus Peter,** a Representative from Wisconsin; born in Holmes City, near Alexandria, Douglas County, Minn., March 28, 1872; attended the public schools and was graduated from Hamline University, St. Paul, Minn., in 1897; moved to Grantsburg, Burnett County, Wis., in 1897; engaged in banking; regent of the University of Wisconsin 1906-1919 and president of the board of regents 1916-1920; president of the local school board

1910-1916; mayor of Grantsburg 1914-1916; vice president of the board of trustees of Hamline University 1914-1918; elected as a Republican to the Sixty-fifth Congress to fill the vacancy caused by the resignation of Irvine L. Lenroot; reelected to the Sixty-sixth and Sixty-seventh Congresses and served from November 5, 1918, to March 3, 1923; unsuccessful candidate for renomination in 1922; again engaged in banking in Grantsburg, Wis., until his death in that city August 21, 1927; interment in Riverside Cemetery.

**NELSON, Arthur Emanuel,** a Senator from Minnesota; born in Browns Valley, Traverse County, Minn., May 10, 1892; attended the public schools, Macalester College, St. Paul, Minn., 1910-1912, and St. Paul College of Law 1912-1915; was admitted to the Minnesota bar in 1915 and the Illinois bar in 1939; commenced practice in St. Paul, Minn.; during the First World War enlisted as a private, Heavy Artillery, and served from August to November 1918; corporation counsel of St. Paul, Minn., 1920-1922; mayor of St. Paul 1922-1926; unsuccessful candidate for election to the United States Senate in 1928; elected as a Republican to the United States Senate on November 3, 1942, to fill the vacancy caused by the death of Ernest Lundeen and served from November 18, 1942, to January 3, 1943; was not a candidate for election to the full term; practiced law in St. Paul, Minn., and Chicago, Ill.; died in Chicago, Ill., April 11, 1955; interment in Oakland Cemetery, St. Paul, Minn.

**NELSON, Charles Pembroke** (son of John E. Nelson), a Representative from Maine; born in Waterville, Kennebec County, Maine, July 2, 1907; graduated from Cony High School, Augusta, Maine, in 1924, Colby College, Waterville, Maine, in 1928, and from Harvard Law School, in 1931; was admitted to the Maine bar in 1931; secretary to his father, Representative John E. Nelson, in 1931 and 1932; engaged in the general practice of law in Augusta, Maine, in 1932; city solicitor of Augusta 1934-1942; delegate to the Republican National Convention in 1936; chief, State Arson Division, in 1941 and 1942; entered the military service in 1942 as a second lieutenant in the United States Army Air Corps and served until discharged in 1946 as a lieutenant colonel with two years of service in the European Theater of Operations; member of the National Guard and Reserves; member of the State board of bar examiners 1946-1948; mayor of Augusta in 1947 and 1948; elected as a Republican to the Eighty-first and to the three succeeding Congresses (January 3, 1949-January 3, 1957); was not a candidate for renomination in 1956; teacher at University of Florida at Gainesville 1957-1959; chief trial attorney, State highway commission, 1959; moderator, town of West Bath, 1960; died in Augusta, Maine, June 8, 1962; remains were cremated and the ashes buried on family property at Georgetown, Maine.

**NELSON, Clarence William (Bill),** a Representative from Florida; born in Miami, Dade County, Fla., September 29, 1942; attended the Brevard County public schools; graduated from Melbourne High School, 1960; B.A., Yale University, 1965; J.D., University of Virginia School of Law, Charlottesville, 1968; admitted to the Florida bar in 1968 and commenced practice in Melbourne, 1970; served in United States Army Reserve, 1965-1971; active duty, 1968-1970; legislative assistant to Governor Reubin Askew of Florida, 1971; elected to Florida State house of representatives, 1972; reelected, 1974 and 1976; elected as a Democrat to the Ninety-sixth and to the five succeeding Congresses (January 3, 1979-January 3, 1991); was not a candidate for reelection in 1990 to the One Hundred Second Congress, but was an unsuccessful candidate for nomination for Governor of Florida; elected Florida State treasurer and insurance commissioner in November 1994, and served from January 1, 1995 to present; flew as one of the astronaut crew aboard the space shuttle *Columbia* during its seventh orbital mission in January 1986; is a resident of Melbourne, Fla.

**Bibliography:** Nelson, Bill, with Jamie Buckingham. *Mission: An American Congressman's Voyage to Space.* San Diego: Harcourt Brace Jovanovich, 1988.

**NELSON, Gaylord Anton,** a Senator from Wisconsin; born in Clear Lake, Polk County, Wis., June 4, 1916; attended the public schools of Clear Lake; B.A., San Jose (Calif.) State College, 1939; LL.B., University of Wisconsin Law School, 1942; was admitted to the Wisconsin bar the same year; during the Second World War served as a lieutenant in the United States Army for four years, serving overseas in the Okinawa campaign; engaged in the practice of law in Madison, Wis., in 1946; elected to the Wisconsin State senate in 1948, 1952, and 1956, and served as Democratic floor leader for eight years; elected Governor of Wisconsin in 1958, reelected in 1960, and served from January 5, 1959 to January 7, 1963; elected as a Democrat to the United States Senate in 1962 for the term commencing January 3, l963; subsequently served out his term as Governor, and commenced his term in the Senate on January 8, 1963; reelected in 1968, and again in 1974, serving from January 8, 1963, to January 3, 1981; unsuccessful candidate for reelection in 1980; chairman, Select Committee on Small Business (Ninety-third through Ninety-sixth Congresses), Special Committee on Official Conduct (Ninety-fifth Congress); founder of Earth Day, which was first observed on April 22, 1970; counselor, The Wilderness Society, Washington, D.C.; is a resident of Kensington, Md.

**Bibliography:** Nelson, Gaylord. *"What Are Me and You Gonna Do?" Letters to Senator Gaylord Nelson About the Environment.* New York: Ballantine Books, 1971; Nelson, Gaylord. *America's Last Chance.* Milwaukee: Country Beautiful, 1974.

**NELSON, Homer Augustus,** a Representative from New York; born in Poughkeepsie, Dutchess County, N.Y., August 31, 1829; completed preparatory studies; studied law; was admitted to the bar and commenced practice in Poughkeepsie, N.Y.; judge of Dutchess County 1855-1862; colonel of the One Hundred and Fifty-ninth Regiment, New York Volunteer Infantry, during the Civil War; resigned in 1863; elected as a Democrat to the Thirty-eighth Congress (March 4, 1863-March 3, 1865); unsuccessful candidate for reelection in 1864 to the Thirty-ninth Congress; delegate to the State constitutional convention in 1867; secretary of state of New York 1867-1870; member of the State senate in 1882 and 1883; appointed a member of the commission to report a revision of the judiciary article of the State constitution in 1890; died in Poughkeepsie, N.Y., April 25, 1891; interment in the Poughkeepsie Rural Cemetery.

**NELSON, Hugh** (son of Thomas Nelson, Jr.), a Representative from Virginia; born in Yorktown, York County, Va., September 30, 1768; completed preparatory studies; graduated from the College of William and Mary, Williamsburg, Va., in 1780; served in the Virginia senate, 1786-1791; member of the Virginia house of delegates, 1805-1809, 1828-1829; judge of the general court; elected as a Republican to the Twelfth and to the five succeeding Congresses, and served from March 4, 1811 until his resignation on January 14, 1823, having received an appointment in the diplomatic service; chairman, Committee on the Judiciary (Fourteenth, Fifteenth, and Seventeenth Congresses); appointed by President James Monroe as United States Minister to Spain on January 15, 1823, and served until July 1825; died at his home, "Belvoir," Albemarle County, Va., March 18, 1836; interment in "Belvoir" Cemetery, Cismont, Albemarle County, Va.

**Bibliography:** *DAB.*

**NELSON, Jeremiah,** a Representative from Massachusetts; born in Rowley, Essex County, Mass., September 14, 1769; completed preparatory studies; was graduated from Dartmouth College, Hanover, N.H., in 1790; engaged in the mercantile business in Newburyport, Essex County, Mass.; member of the general court of Massachusetts in 1803 and 1804; elected as a Federalist to the Ninth Congress (March 4, 1805-March 3, 1807); was not a candidate for renomination in 1806 to the Tenth Congress; chairman board of selectmen of Newburyport in 1811; elected to the Fourteenth and to the four succeeding Congresses (March 4, 1815-March 3, 1825); chairman, Committee on Expenditures on Public Buildings (Seventeenth and Eighteenth Congresses); was not a candidate for renomination in 1824 to the Nineteenth Congress; president of the Newburyport Mutual Fire Insurance Co. in 1829; elected as an Anti-Jacksonian to the Twenty-second Congress (March 4, 1831-March 3, 1833); declined to be a candidate for renomination in 1832; engaged in the shipping business; died in Newburyport, Mass., October 2, 1838; interment in Oak Hill Cemetery.

**NELSON, John** (son of Roger Nelson), a Representative from Maryland; born in Frederick, Frederick County, Md., June 1, 1794; was graduated from the College of William and Mary, Williamsburg, Va., in 1811; studied law; was admitted to the bar in 1813 and commenced practice in Frederick, Md.; held several local offices; elected to the Seventeenth Congress (March 4, 1821-March 3, 1823); was not a candidate for reelection in 1822 to the Eighteenth Congress; appointed by President Andrew Jackson as United States Chargé d'Affaires to the Two Sicilies on October 24, 1831 and served until October 15, 1832; served as Secretary of State ad interim from February 29 to March 31, 1844; Attorney General in the Cabinet of President John Tyler, July 1, 1843 to March 5, 1845; died in Baltimore, Md., January 18, 1860; interment in Greenmount Cemetery.

**NELSON, John Edward** (father of Charles Pembroke Nelson), a Representative from Maine; born in China, Kennebec County, Maine, July 12, 1874; attended the common and high schools of Waterville, Maine; was graduated from Friends School, Providence, R.I., in 1894, from Colby College, Waterville, Maine, in 1898, and from the law department of the University of Maine at Orono in 1904; was admitted to the bar in 1904 and commenced practice in Waterville, Maine; moved to Augusta, Maine, in 1913 and continued the practice of his chosen profession; elected as a Republican to the Sixty-seventh Congress to fill the vacancy caused by the resignation of John A. Peters; reelected to the Sixty-eighth and to the four succeeding Congresses and served from March 27, 1922, to March 3, 1933; unsuccessful candidate for reelection in 1932 to the Seventy-third Congress; trustee of Colby College 1926-1931; also served as trustee of Monmouth (Maine) Academy; practiced law until his retirement in 1946; died in Augusta, Maine, April 11, 1955; interment in Pine Grove Cemetery, Waterville, Maine.

**NELSON, John Mandt,** a Representative from Wisconsin; born in Burke, Dane County, Wis., October 10, 1870; attended the public schools and was graduated from the University of Wisconsin at Madison in 1892; superintendent of schools in Dane County in 1892 and 1894; bookkeeper in the office of the secretary of state 1894-1897; editor of The State, published in Madison, Wis., in 1897 and 1898; correspondent in the State treasury 1898-1902; was graduated from the law department of the University of Wisconsin in 1896, and pursued a postgraduate course 1901-1903; elected as a Republican to the Fifty-ninth Congress to fill the vacancy caused by the death of Henry C. Adams; reelected to the Sixtieth and to the five succeeding Congresses and served from September 4, 1906, to March 3, 1919; unsuccessful candidate for renomination in 1918; elected to the Sixty-seventh and to the five succeeding Congresses (March 4, 1921-March 3, 1933); chairman, Committee on Elections No. 2 (Sixty-eighth Congress); Committee on Invalid Pensions (Seventy-first Congress); was an unsuccessful candidate for renomination in 1932 to the Seventy-third Congress; retired from business and political activities; died in Madison, Wis., January 29, 1955; interment in Forest Hill Cemetery.

**NELSON, Knute,** a Representative and a Senator from Minnesota; born in Voss, Norway, February 2, 1843; immigrated to the United States in 1849 with his mother, settled in Chicago, Ill.; moved to Wisconsin in 1850; attended the common schools and

Albion Academy, Albion, Wis.; taught school; served as a private and noncommissioned officer with the Wisconsin Volunteer Infantry during the Civil War; wounded and taken prisoner at Port Hudson, La., 1863; at the close of the war he returned to Albion College and completed the course; studied law; was admitted to the bar in 1867 and commenced practice in Cambridge, Wis.; member, Wisconsin State assembly, 1868-1869; moved to Alexandria, Douglas County, Minn., in 1871; county attorney from 1872 until 1874; member, Minnesota State senate, 1874-1878; presidential elector on the Republican ticket in 1880; member of the board of regents of the University of Minnesota, 1882-1893; elected as a Republican to the Forty-eighth and to the two succeeding Congresses (March 4, 1883-March 3, 1889); was not a candidate for renomination in 1888 to the Fifty-first Congress; elected Governor of Minnesota in 1892; reelected in 1894, and served from January 4, 1893 to January 31, 1895, when he resigned, preparatory to becoming Senator; elected as a Republican to the United States Senate in 1895; reelected in 1901, 1907, 1913, and 1918, and served from March 4, 1895, until his death on a train near Timonium, Md., April 28, 1923, while en route to his home; chairman, Committee on the Improvement of the Mississippi River and Its Tributaries (Fifty-fourth through Sixtieth Congresses), Committee on Public Lands (Sixtieth through Sixty-second Congresses), Committee on Commerce (Sixty-second Congress), Committee on the Five Civilized Tribes of Indians (Sixty-third through Sixty-fifth Congresses), Committee on Private Land Claims (Sixty-fifth Congress), Committee on the Judiciary (Sixty-sixth and Sixty-seventh Congresses); interment in Kinkead Cemetery, Alexandria, Minn.

**Bibliography:** *DAB*; Odland, Martin. *The Life of Knute Nelson.* Minneapolis: The Lund Press, 1926; Preus, Jacob. "Knute Nelson." *Minnesota History Bulletin* 5 (February 1924): 329-47.

**NELSON, Roger** (father of John Nelson), a Representative from Maryland; born on "Point of Rocks" plantation, near Frederick, Md., in 1759; completed preparatory studies; attended the College of William and Mary, Williamsburg, Va.; served in the Revolutionary Army; wounded at the Battle of Camden, S.C., August 16, 1780, and attained the rank of brigadier general; studied law; was admitted to the bar about 1785 and practiced in Taneytown and Frederick; held several local offices; member of the Maryland State house of delegates in 1795, 1801, and 1802; served in the Maryland State senate from November 1803 to November 1804; elected as a Republican to the Eighth Congress to fill the vacancy caused by the death of Daniel Hiester; reelected to the Ninth and to the two succeeding Congresses and served from November 6, 1804, until his resignation May 14, 1810; one of the managers appointed by the House of Representatives in 1804 to conduct the impeachment proceedings against Samuel Chase, Associate Justice of the Supreme Court of the United States; elected associate justice of the fifth (later sixth) judicial circuit of Maryland in 1810; died in Frederick, Md., June 7, 1815; interment in Mount Olivet Cemetery.

**Bibliography:** *DAB*.

**NELSON, Thomas, Jr.** (father of Hugh Nelson), a Delegate from Virginia; born in Yorktown, Va., on December 26, 1738; attended private schools and graduated from Trinity College, Cambridge University in England, in 1761; member of the House of Burgesses of Virginia in 1774; member of the provincial convention in Williamsburg in 1774; Member of the Continental Congress 1775-1777; a signer of the Declaration of Independence; appointed commander of the Virginia forces in 1777 and served in this capacity until 1781 when he resigned on account of ill health as a result of his service in the field in the campaign against Cornwallis; again a member of the Continental Congress in 1779; Governor of Virginia in 1781; retired to his son's estate, "Mont Air," Hanover County, Va., and died there on January 4, 1789; interment in Grace Churchyard, Yorktown, Va.

**Bibliography:** *DAB*; Evans, Emory G. *Thomas Nelson of Yorktown: Revolutionary Virginian.* Williamsburg in America Series, vol. 10. Charlottesville: University Press of Virginia, 1978.

**NELSON, Thomas Amos Rogers,** a Representative from Tennessee; born in Kingston, Roane County, Tenn., March 19, 1812; completed preparatory studies and was graduated from East Tennessee College in 1828; studied law; was admitted to the bar in 1832 and commenced practice in Washington County, Tenn.; served two terms as attorney general of the first judicial circuit; appointed commissioner (diplomatic) to China on March 6, 1851, but did not proceed to his post, and resigned July 2, 1851; elected as a Opposition Party candidate to the Thirty-sixth Congress (March 4, 1859-March 3, 1861); reelected to the Thirty-seventh Congress, and while en route to Washington to take his seat, during the Civil War, was arrested by Confederate scouts, conveyed to Richmond as a prisoner, paroled, and allowed to return to his home; upon the advent of the Union Army into East Tennessee in 1863 he moved to Knoxville; delegate to the Union National Convention at Philadelphia in 1866, and to the Democratic National Convention of 1868; one of the counsel who defended President Andrew Johnson in his impeachment trial in 1868; elected judge of the State supreme court in 1870, and served until his resignation in 1871; died in Knoxville, Tenn., August 24, 1873; interment in Gray Cemetery.

**Bibliography:** Alexander, Thomas Benjamin. *Thomas A.R. Nelson of East Tennessee.* Nashville: Tennessee Historical Commission, 1956.

**NELSON, Thomas Maduit,** a Representative from Virginia; born in Oak Hill, Mecklenburg County, Va., September 27, 1782; attended the common schools; commissioned a captain in the Tenth Infantry Regiment and subsequently a major in the Thirtieth and Eighteenth Infantry Regiments in the War of 1812; after the war was reduced to the grade of captain, and resigned his commission May 15, 1815; elected as a Republican to the Fourteenth Congress to fill the vacancy caused by the death of Thomas Gholson, Jr.; reelected to the Fifteenth Congress and served from December 4, 1816, to March 3, 1819; was not a candidate for renomination in 1818; died near Columbus, Muscogee County, Ga., November 10, 1853; interment in Linwood Cemetery.

**NELSON, William,** a Representative from New York; born in Hyde Park, Dutchess County, N.Y., June 29, 1784; attended the common schools and was graduated from Poughkeepsie Academy; studied law; was admitted to the bar and commenced practice in Peekskill, Westchester County, N.Y., in 1807; for thirty years served as district attorney for Putnam, Rockland, and Westchester Counties; member of the State assembly in 1820 and 1821; served in the State senate 1824-1827; judge of the court for the correction of errors 1824-1827; elected as a Whig to the Thirtieth and Thirty-first Congresses (March 4, 1847-March 3, 1851); resumed the practice of his profession; died in Peekskill, N.Y., October 3, 1869; interment in Hillside Cemetery.

**NELSON, William Lester,** a Representative from Missouri; born on a farm near Bunceton, Cooper County, Mo., August 4, 1875; attended the country schools in his native county, Hooper Institute, William Jewell College at Liberty, Mo., and the Missouri College of Agriculture at Columbia; taught school for five years; subsequently entered the newspaper business at Bunceton, Mo.; member of the State house of representatives 1901-1903 and 1905-1907; moved to Columbia, Mo., to become assistant secretary of the State board of agriculture and served from 1908 to 1918; member of the editorial staff of the Iowa Homestead and other Pierce publications 1921-1924; also engaged in agricultural pursuits; author of various agricultural publications; elected as a Democrat to the Sixty-sixth Congress (March 4, 1919-March 3, 1921); unsuccessful candidate for reelection in 1920 to the Sixty-seventh Congress; resumed journalistic pursuits in Columbia, Mo.; elected to the Sixty-ninth and to the three succeeding Congresses (March 4, 1925-March 3, 1933); unsuccessful candidate for renomination in 1932; elected to the Seventy-fourth and to the three succeeding Congresses (January 3, 1935-January 3, 1943); unsuccessful candidate for reelection in 1942 to the Seventy-eighth Congress; served as assistant to War Food Administrator Marvin Jones in 1943; returned to Columbia, Mo.; died in Columbia, Mo., December 31, 1946; interment in Columbia Cemetery.

**NES, Henry,** a Representative from Pennsylvania; born in York, Pa., May 20, 1799; completed preparatory studies and was graduated from Princeton College; studied medicine and practiced in York, Pa.; elected as an Independent Democrat to the Twenty-eighth Congress (March 4, 1843-March 3, 1845); elected as a Whig to the Thirtieth and Thirty-first Congresses and served from March 4, 1847, until his death in York, Pa., September 10, 1850; chairman, Committee on Invalid Pensions (Thirtieth Congress), Committee on Revisal and Unfinished Business (Thirtieth Congress); interment in Prospect Hill Cemetery.

**NESBIT, Walter,** a Representative from Illinois; born in Belleville, St. Clair County, Ill., on May 1, 1878; attended the grade and night schools; employed as a coal miner 1892-1912; held various offices in the United Mine Workers of America, serving as subdistrict secretary 1912-1915, as traveling auditor 1915-1917, and as secretary-treasurer of district No. 12, 1917-1933; elected as a Democrat to the Seventy-third Congress (March 4, 1933-January 3, 1935); unsuccessful candidate for renomination in 1934; owned and operated the Club Congress in Belleville, Ill.; unsuccessful candidate for sheriff of St. Clair County, Ill., in 1938; died in Belleville, Ill., December 6, 1938; interment in Green Mount Cemetery.

**NESBITT, Wilson,** a Representative from South Carolina; resided in Spartanburg, Spartanburg County, S.C.; attended the common schools and was a student at South Carolina College (now the University of South Carolina) at Columbia in 1805 and 1806; engaged in agricultural pursuits and conducted an iron foundry; justice of quorum of Spartanburg County in 1810; member of the State house of representatives 1810-1814; elected as a Republican to the Fifteenth Congress (March 4, 1817-March 3, 1819); moved to Alabama; died in Montgomery, Ala., May 13, 1861; interment in Oakwood Cemetery.

**NESMITH, James Willis** (cousin of Joseph Gardner Wilson and grandfather of Clifton Nesmith McArthur), a Senator and a Representative from Oregon; born in New Brunswick, Canada, while his parents were on a visit from their home in Washington County, Maine, July 23, 1820; moved with his father to Claremont, N.H., about 1828; received a limited schooling; moved to Ohio in 1838, and to Oregon in 1843; studied law; was admitted to the bar but never practiced extensively; engaged in agricultural pursuits and stock raising; elected judge of the provisional government of Oregon in 1845; captain in 1848 and 1853 of expeditions against hostile Indians; United States marshal for Oregon, 1853-1855; superintendent of Indian affairs for Oregon and Washington Territories, 1857-1859; elected as a Democrat to the United States Senate, and served from March 4, 1861 to March 3, 1867; unsuccessful candidate for reelection; appointed Minister to Austria, but his nomination was not confirmed; served as road supervisor of Polk County in 1868; elected as a Democrat to the Forty-third Congress to fill the vacancy caused by the death of Joseph G. Wilson, and served from December 1, 1873 to March 3, 1875; was not a candidate for renomination in 1874 to the Forty-fourth Congress; died in Rickreall, Oreg., June 17, 1885; interment in Polk County, Oreg., on the south bank of Rickreall Creek.

**Bibliography:** *DAB*.

**NETHERCUTT, George R., Jr.,** a Representative from Washington; born in Spokane, Wash., October 7, 1944; attended the public schools and graduated from North Central High School; B.A., Washington State University, 1967; J.D., Gonzaga University School of Law, 1971; law clerk to United States District Court Judge Ralph Plummer; staff counsel and chief of staff to Senator Ted Stevens; commenced the private practice of law in Spokane; town attorney, Towns of Creston, Rearden, and Almira; fire district secretary, Hartline and Almira; co-founder, Vanessa Behan Crisis Nursery, Spokane; chairman, Spokane County Republican Party, 1990-1992; elected as a Republican to the One Hundred Fourth Congress (January 3, 1995-January 3, 1997); is a resident of Spokane, Wash.

**NEUBERGER, Maurine Brown** (wife of Richard Lewis Neuberger), a Senator from Oregon; born January 9, 1906 in Cloverdale, Tillamook County, Oreg.; attended the public schools, Oregon College of Education at Monmouth, 1922-1924, the University of Oregon, 1928-1929, and the University of California at Los Angeles, 1936-1937; teacher in Oregon public schools, 1932-1944; member, Oregon State house of representatives, 1951-1955; writer and photographer; member, board of directors, American Association for the United Nations; elected as a Democrat to the United States Senate to fill the vacancy caused by the death of her husband, Richard L. Neuberger, and served from November 9, 1960 to January 3, 1961; also elected in 1960 for the term commencing January 3, 1961, and ending January 3, 1967; was not a candidate for reelection in 1966; lecturer on consumer affairs and the status of women; teacher of American government at Boston University, Radcliffe Institute, and Reed College; is a resident of Portland, Oreg.

**Bibliography:** Neuberger, Richard, and Neuberger, Maurine. *Adventures in Politics: We Go to the Legislature*. 1954. Reprint. Port Washington, N.Y.: Kennikat Press, 1972.

**NEUBERGER, Richard Lewis** (husband of Maurine Brown Neuberger), a Senator from Oregon; born in Multnomah County, near Portland, Oreg., December 26, 1912; attended the public schools of Portland, Oreg.; attended the University of Oregon at Eugene in 1935; author and reporter, specializing in issues of concern to the Pacific Northwest; correspondent for the New York Times, 1939-1954; member, Oregon State house of representatives, 1941-1942; during the Second World War was commissioned a second lieutenant and later a captain in the United States Army, July 15, 1942 to August 12, 1945, serving as an aide to Brigadier General James A. O'Connor during construction of highways and air bases in Alaska; military aide to the United States delegation to the founding conference of the United Nations held at San Francisco, April-June 1945; Oregon State senator from Multnomah County, 1949-1954; elected as a Democrat to the United States Senate in 1954, and served from January 3, 1955 until his death in Portland, Oreg., March 9, 1960; interment in Beth Israel Cemetery.

**Bibliography:** *DAB*; Neuberger, Richard L., and Maurine B. Neuberger. *Adventures in Politics: We Go to the Legislature*. 1954. Reprint. Port Washington, N.Y.: Kennikat Press, 1972; Neuberger, Richard L. *They Never Go Back to Pocatello: The Selected Essays of Richard Neuberger*. Edited, with a biographical introduction, by Steve Neal. Portland: Oregon Historical Society Press, 1988.

**NEUMANN, Mark W.,** a Representative from Wisconsin; born in East Troy, Walworth County, Wis., February 27, 1954; attended the public schools; graduated, East Troy High School, 1972; B.S., University of Wisconsin, Whitewater, 1975; M.S., University of Wisconsin, River Falls, 1977; attended University of Wisconsin, Madison, 1979, 1983, 1993; mathematics teacher, football and basketball coach; real estate developer; builder; owner, Neumann Developments, Incorporated, Janesville, 1986-1993; Neumann Corporation, Incorporated, Janesville; unsuccessful candidate for the One Hundred Third Congress in a special election, May 4, 1993;

elected as a Republican to the One Hundred Fourth Congress (January 3, 1995-January 3, 1997); is a resident of Janesville, Wis.

**NEVILLE, Joseph,** a Representative from Virginia; born in 1730; burgess for Hampshire County 1773-1776; member of the conventions of December 1, 1775, and May 6, 1776; served in the Continental Army during the Revolutionary War; member of the Virginia house of delegates in 1777, 1780, and 1781; in 1782 was engaged with Colonel Alexander McLean, of Pennsylvania, in settling by survey the long-standing dispute over the boundary line between Pennsylvania and Maryland; elected to the Third Congress (March 4, 1793-March 3, 1795); was not a candidate for reelection in 1794 to the Fourth Congress; died in Hardy County, Va., March 4, 1819.

**NEVILLE, William** (cousin of Bird Segle McGuire), a Representative from Nebraska; born in Nashville, Washington County, Ill., December 29, 1843; moved with his parents to Chester, Randolph County, in 1851; attended the public schools and McKendree College, Lebanon, Ill.; during the Civil War served in the Union Army as second sergeant in Company H, One Hundred and Forty-second Regiment, Illinois Volunteer Infantry; studied law; was admitted to the bar in Chester, Ill., in 1874 and practiced; member of the Illinois house of representatives in 1872; moved to Nebraska in May 1874; moved to North Platte, Nebr., in April 1877 and continued the practice of law; unsuccessful candidate for election in 1884 to the Forty-ninth Congress; judge of the thirteenth judicial district 1891-1895; elected as a Populist to the Fifty-sixth Congress to fill the vacancy caused by the death of William L. Greene; reelected to the Fifty-seventh Congress and served from December 4, 1899, to March 3, 1903; was not a candidate for renomination in 1902; resumed the practice of law; moved to Douglas, Ariz., in 1903 and resumed the practice of his profession; member of the Arizona house of representatives in 1905; died in Douglas, Ariz., April 5, 1909; interment in North Platte Cemetery, North Platte, Nebr.

**NEVIN, Robert Murphy,** a Representative from Ohio; born in Danville, Highland County, Ohio, May 5, 1850; attended the public schools in Hillsboro, Ohio; was graduated from the Ohio Wesleyan University, Delaware, Ohio, in June 1868; moved to Dayton, Ohio, in 1868; studied law; was admitted to the bar in 1871 and commenced law practice in Dayton; counsel for the New York Central Railroad 1882-1912; prosecuting attorney of Montgomery County 1887-1890; delegate to the Republican National Convention in 1892; elected as a Republican to the Fifty-seventh, Fifty-eighth, and Fifty-ninth Congresses (March 4, 1901-March 3, 1907); declined renomination in 1906; resumed the practice of law; died in Dayton, Ohio, December 17, 1912; interment in Woodland Cemetery.

**NEW, Anthony,** a Representative from Virginia and from Kentucky; born in Gloucester County, Va., in 1747; completed preparatory studies; studied law; was admitted to the bar and practiced; colonel in the Revolutionary Army; elected from Virginia to the Third Congress and reelected as a Republican to the five succeeding Congresses (March 4, 1793-March 3, 1805); moved to Kentucky and settled in Elkton; elected as a Republican from Kentucky to the Twelfth Congress (March 4, 1811-March 3, 1813); elected to the Fifteenth Congress (March 4, 1817-March 3, 1819); elected to the Seventeenth Congress (March 4, 1821-March 3, 1823); engaged in agricultural pursuits; died on his estate, "Dunheath," near Elkton, Todd County, Ky., March 2, 1833; interment in the family burying ground on his estate.

**NEW, Harry Stewart,** a Senator from Indiana; born in Indianapolis, Ind., December 31, 1858; attended the public schools and Butler University, Indianapolis, Ind.; served with the Indianapolis Journal as reporter, editor, part owner, and publisher, 1878-1903; member, Indiana State senate, 1896-1900; member, Republican National Committee, 1900-1912, and chairman during 1907-1908; captain and assistant adjutant general in the Seventh Army Corps during the Spanish-American War; engaged in the stone quarrying and construction business; elected as a Republican to the United States Senate in 1916 and served from March 4, 1917, to March 3, 1923; unsuccessful candidate for renomination in 1922; chairman, Committee on Territories (Sixty-sixth Congress), Committee on Territories and Insular Possessions (Sixty-seventh Congress); Postmaster General in the Cabinets of Presidents Warren G. Harding and Calvin Coolidge from February 27, 1923 until March 4, 1929; retired from active business pursuits and resided in Washington, D.C.; United States Commissioner, Century of Progress Exposition, Chicago, Ill., 1933; died in Baltimore, Md., May 9, 1937; interment in the Crown Hill Cemetery, Indianapolis, Ind.

Bibliography: *DAB*.

**NEW, Jeptha Dudley,** a Representative from Indiana; born in Vernon, Jennings County, Ind., November 28, 1830; was graduated from Vernon (Ind.) Academy and Bethany (W.Va.) College; studied law; was admitted to the bar in 1851 and practiced in Vernon, Ind., until 1864; mayor of Vernon, 1852-1854; prosecuting attorney of Jennings County, Ind., 1860-1864; judge of the district court of common pleas, 1864-1868; resumed the practice of law in Vernon; elected as a Democrat to the Forty-fourth Congress (March 4, 1875-March 3, 1877); declined to be a candidate for reelection in 1876 to the Forty-fifth Congress; elected to the Forty-sixth Congress (March 4, 1879-March 3, 1881); was not a candidate for reelection in 1880 to the Forty-seventh Congress; judge of the sixth judicial circuit of Indiana, 1882-1888; appellate judge in 1891; was nominated by the Democratic Party as a candidate for judge of the supreme court of Indiana in 1892, but died before the election in Vernon, Ind., July 9, 1892; interment in Vernon Cemetery.

**NEWBERRY, John Stoughton** (father of Truman Handy Newberry), a Representative from Michigan; born in Waterville, Oneida County, N.Y., November 18, 1826; moved with his parents to Michigan when a child, residing successively in Detroit, Ann Arbor, and Romeo; completed preparatory studies in Romeo Academy; was graduated from Michigan University at Ann Arbor in 1847; spent two years in civil engineering on railroads; studied law in Detroit and was admitted to the bar in 1853; published the first volume of admiralty reports of decisions of cases arising on western lakes and rivers; established the Michigan Car Co. of Detroit in 1862; later established the Detroit Car Wheel Co.; appointed the first provost marshal for the State of Michigan by President Abraham Lincoln in 1862 with the rank of captain of Cavalry; resigned in 1864; engaged in several large manufacturing enterprises in 1864; elected as a Republican to the Forty-sixth Congress (March 4, 1879-March 3, 1881); declined to be a candidate for renomination in 1880; died in Detroit, Mich., January 2, 1887; interment in Elmwood Cemetery.

**NEWBERRY, Truman Handy** (son of John Stoughton Newberry), a Senator from Michigan; born in Detroit, Mich., November 5, 1864; attended public and private schools; graduated from Yale College in 1885; superintendent of construction, paymaster, general freight and passenger agent, and eventually manager of the Detroit, Bay City & Alpena Railway, 1885-1887; president and treasurer of the Detroit Steel & Spring Co., 1887-1901; engaged in various other manufacturing activities; organizer of the Michigan State Naval Brigade; served in the Navy during the Spanish-American War; Assistant Secretary of the Navy, 1905-1908; appointed Secretary of the Navy in the Cabinet of President Theodore Roosevelt, and served from December 1, 1908 to March 5, 1909; served as a lieutenant commander in the United States Navy Fleet Reserve in 1917, and as assistant to the commandant of the third naval district of New York until 1919; elected as a Republican to the United States Senate in 1918 and served from March 4, 1919, until his resignation on November 18, 1922; in March 1920, Newberry was convicted of election "irregularities"; the conviction was reversed in May 1921 by the Supreme Court, and, following an investigation, the Senate on January 12, 1922 declared Newberry entitled to his seat but expressed disapproval of the sum spent on his election; in the face of a new movement to unseat him, Newberry resigned; engaged in manufacturing; died in Grosse Pointe, Mich., October 3, 1945; interment in Elmwood Cemetery, Detroit, Mich.

**Bibliography:** *DAB*; Ervin, Spencer. *Henry Ford vs. Truman H. Newberry: The Famous Senate Election Contest.* 1935. Reprint. New York: Arno Press, 1974.

**NEWBERRY, Walter Cass,** a Representative from Illinois; born in Sangerfield, Oneida County, N.Y., December 23, 1835; pursued an academic course; engaged in mercantile pursuits in Chicago and Detroit; enlisted in the Union Army during the Civil War as a private in the Eighty-first Regiment, New York Volunteers; promoted to lieutenant in 1861, captain in 1862, major of the Twenty-fourth Regiment, New York Cavalry, in 1863, lieutenant colonel and colonel in 1864, and was brevetted brigadier general March 31, 1865; moved to Petersburg, Va., in 1865; mayor of Petersburg in 1869 and 1870, resigning in the latter year; moved to Richmond, Va., in 1870; superintendent of public property for the State for four years; moved to Chicago, Ill., in 1876; postmaster of Chicago in 1888 and 1889; elected as a Democrat to the Fifty-second Congress (March 4, 1891-March 3, 1893); was not a candidate for renomination in 1892; retired from active business pursuits; died in Chicago, Ill., July 20, 1912; interment in Graceland Cemetery.

**NEWBOLD, Thomas,** a Representative from New Jersey; born in Springfield Township, Burlington County, N.J., August 2, 1760; engaged in agricultural pursuits; member of the State general assembly in 1797; engaged in banking; elected as a Republican to the Tenth, Eleventh, and Twelfth Congresses (March 4, 1807-March 3, 1813); unsuccessful candidate for reelection in 1812 to the Thirteenth Congress; again a member of the State general assembly 1820-1822; died in Springfield Township, Burlington County, N.J., December 18, 1823; interment in the Old Upper Springfield Friends Burying Ground.

**NEWCOMB, Carman Adam,** a Representative from Missouri; born in Mercer, Mercer County, Pa., July 1, 1830; completed preparatory studies; moved to Kentucky, and later to Shreveport, La., where he studied law and was admitted to the bar; moved to West Union, Iowa, in 1854 and commenced the practice of law; judge of the circuit court of Fayette County, Iowa, 1855-1860; during the Civil War served as captain of Company F, Third Regiment, Iowa Volunteer Infantry, from June 18, 1861, until his discharge on account of illness April 8, 1862; moved to Vineland, Jefferson County, Mo., and resumed the practice of law; member of the State house of representatives in 1865 and 1866; elected as a Republican to the Fortieth Congress (March 4, 1867-March 3, 1869); was not a candidate for renomination in 1868; United States marshal for the eastern district of Missouri 1869-1875; census enumerator of St. Louis, Mo., in 1870; again resumed the practice of his profession; died in St. Louis, Mo., April 6, 1902; the remains were cremated at the Missouri Crematory in St. Louis, Mo., and the ashes deposited in the columbarium.

**NEWELL, William Augustus,** a Representative from New Jersey; born while his parents were on a visit in Franklin, Ohio, September 5, 1817; attended the common schools of New Brunswick, N.J.; was graduated from Rutgers College, New Brunswick, N.J., in 1836 and from the medical department of the University of Pennsylvania at Philadelphia in 1839; commenced practice in Allentown, N.J.; elected as a Whig to the Thirtieth and Thirty-first Congresses (March 4, 1847-March 3, 1851); was not a candidate for renomination in 1850 to the Thirty-second Congress; elected Governor of New Jersey in 1856, and served from January 20, 1857 to January 17, 1860; surgeon to superintend the drafting of

Monmouth County Militia in 1862; delegate to the Republican National Convention of 1864; elected as a Republican to the Thirty-ninth Congress (March 4, 1865-March 3, 1867); unsuccessful candidate for reelection in 1866 to the Fortieth Congress; resumed the practice of medicine in Allentown; unsuccessful candidate for election for Governor of New Jersey in 1877; Territorial Governor of Washington 1880-1884; United States Indian inspector from August 14, 1884, to June 26, 1885; died in Allentown, N.J., August 8, 1901; interment in the Presbyterian Cemetery.

**Bibliography:** *DAB*.

**NEWHALL, Judson Lincoln,** a Representative from Kentucky; born in Hunterstown (later changed to Louise), Province of Quebec, Canada, March 26, 1870; moved to Covington, Ky., with his parents in 1874; attended the public schools and was graduated from Martin's Academy, Covington, Ky., in 1886; attended the law department of Indiana University at Bloomington 1896-1898, and took special academic courses at the University of Cincinnati 1924-1926; employed in the United States Internal Revenue Service as a storekeeper-gauger from 1899 until his resignation in 1905 to engage in musical work; served as director of music in the Covington public schools 1913-1917; during the First World War served as a secretary in the Y.M.C.A. welfare service; after the war resumed his position with the Covington schools; elected as a Republican to the Seventy-first Congress (March 4, 1929-March 3, 1931); unsuccessful candidate for reelection in 1930 to the Seventy-second Congress and for election in 1934 to the Seventy-fourth Congress; engaged in the oil and gasoline business; died in Park Hills, Covington, Ky., July 23, 1952; interment in Forest Lawn Cemetery, Erlanger, Ky.

**NEWHARD, Peter,** a Representative from Pennsylvania; born in Allentown, Pa., July 26, 1783; completed preparatory studies and attended a private school in Allentown; opened the first hardware store in Allentown in 1812; street commissioner of the borough of Allentown in 1812; coroner of Lehigh County in 1816 and 1817; elected to the Pennsylvania house of representatives in 1817, 1818, 1819, 1824, 1825, and 1829, the term then being one year; chairman of the town council in 1824 and again in 1837; elected as a Democrat to the Twenty-sixth and Twenty-seventh Congresses (March 4, 1839-March 3, 1843); was not a candidate for renomination in 1842; burgess in 1843 and trustee of Allentown Academy in 1822, 1826, and 1843; died in Allentown, Lehigh County, Pa., February 19, 1860; interment in the City Cemetery.

**NEWLANDS, Francis Griffith,** a Representative and a Senator from Nevada; born in Natchez, Adams County, Miss., August 28, 1848; moved to Illinois in 1848 with his parents, who settled in Quincy; privately tutored; attended Yale College and the Columbian College Law School (now George Washington University), Washington, D.C.; was admitted to the bar in 1869; moved to San Francisco in 1870 and practiced law; moved to Nevada in 1888 and continued the practice of law; elected as a Democrat to the Fifty-third and to the four succeeding Congresses (March 4, 1893-March 3, 1903); did not seek renomination in 1902, having become a candidate for Senator; elected as a Democrat to the United States Senate in 1903; reelected in 1909 and again in 1915 and served from March 4, 1903, until his death in Washington, D.C., December 24, 1917; chairman, Committee on Corporations Organized in the District of Columbia (Sixty-second Congress), Committee on Revolutionary Claims (Sixty-second Congress), Committee on Interstate Commerce (Sixty-third through Sixty-fifth Congresses); interment in Oak Hill Cemetery.

**Bibliography:** *DAB*; Hudson, Millard, ed. *Senator Francis G. Newlands, His Work.* Washington, D.C.: The Carnahon Press, 1914; Lilley, William, III. "The Early Years of Francis G. Newlands, 1848-1897." Ph.D. dissertation, Yale University, 1965.

**NEWMAN, Alexander,** a Representative from Virginia; born near Orange, Va., on October 5, 1804; pursued an academic course; held several local offices; member of the Virginia house of delegates 1836-1838; served in the Virginia senate 1841-1846; postmaster of Wheeling, Va. (now West Virginia), from April 2, 1846, to March 2, 1849, when he resigned; elected as a Democrat to the Thirty-first Congress and served from March 4, 1849, until his death, before the assembling of Congress, while on a visit to Pittsburgh, Pa., September 8, 1849; interment in the Old First Street Cemetery, Moundsville, W.Va.

**NEWNAN, Daniel,** a Representative from Georgia; born in Salisbury, Rowan County, N.C., about 1780; completed preparatory studies; attended the University of North Carolina at Chapel Hill in 1796 and 1797; commissioned ensign and second lieutenant in the Fourth United States Infantry, March 3, 1799; promoted to first lieutenant the following November and resigned January 1, 1801; engaged in planting; commanded the Georgia Volunteers in the Creek War 1812-1814; major general of the third division of State militia in 1817; superintendent of the State penitentiary 1823-1825; secretary of State of Georgia 1825-1827; the city of Newnan, Ga., was named for him in 1828; elected to the Twenty-second Congress (March 4, 1831-March 3, 1833); unsuccessful for reelection in 1832 to the Twenty-third Congress; died near Rossville, Ga., January 16, 1851; interment in Newnan Springs (Ga.) Churchyard.

**NEWSHAM, Joseph Parkinson,** a Representative from Louisiana; born in Preston, Lancashire, England, on May 24, 1837; received an academic education; immigrated to the United States with his parents, who settled in Monroe County, Ill., in 1839; employed in a mercantile establishment for two years; studied law; was admitted to the bar in 1860 and commenced practice in Edwardsville, Ill.; served during the Civil War in the Union Army as adjutant of the Thirty-second Regiment, Missouri Volunteer Infantry; resigned on account of disabilities incurred in action July 4, 1864; moved to Donaldsonville, La., in 1864; clerk of the fourth judicial district court of the Parish of Ascension; was admitted to the Louisiana bar in 1865 and practiced law in Donaldsonville, La.; moved to St. Francisville, La., in 1867; member of the constitutional convention in 1867 and 1868; upon the readmission of the State of Louisiana to representation was elected as a Republican to the Fortieth Congress and served from July 18, 1868, to March 3, 1869; established the Feliciana Republican in 1869; successfully contested the election of Michael Ryan to the Forty-first Congress and served from May 23, 1870, until March 3, 1871; was not a candidate for renomination in 1870; planter and merchant in St. Francisville, La., until 1913, when he retired; died in St. Francisville, West Feliciana Parish, La., October 22, 1919; interment in Grace Church Cemetery.

**NEWSOME, John Parks,** a Representative from Alabama; born in Memphis, Shelby County, Tenn., February 13, 1893; attended the public schools of Thompsons Station, Tenn., and Battle Ground Academy, Franklin, Tenn.; stock clerk for wholesale hardware company in 1912; engaged as a salesman from 1913 until 1920; in 1920 became president and treasurer of an electrical company; during the First World War was commissioned a first lieutenant on November 27, 1917; later promoted to captain of Infantry, Fifth Division, and served until April 29, 1919, with overseas service; chairman of Appeals Board No. 2, State of Alabama, Selective Service System in 1942 and 1943; elected as a Democrat to the Seventy-eighth Congress (January 3, 1943-January 3, 1945); unsuccessful candidate for renomination in 1944 to the Seventy-ninth Congress; president of Associated Industries of Alabama, 1953-1955; was a director of the Exchange Security Bank and the Alabama Gas Corp.; died in Birmingham, Ala., November 10, 1961; interment in Elwood Cemetery.

**NEWTON, Cherubusco,** a Representative from Louisiana; born in Greensburg, St. Helena Parish, La., May 15, 1848; attended private schools in Bastrop, La., and the Louisiana State University, then at Alexandria, La.; taught school; studied law; was admitted to the bar in 1870 and commenced practice in Bastrop, La.; member of the State senate 1879-1883; declined a judgeship in 1885; elected as a Democrat to the Fiftieth Congress (March 4, 1887-March 3, 1889); unsuccessful candidate for renomination in 1888; delegate to the Democratic National Convention in 1888; resumed the practice of law in Bastrop, La., for several years, and then moved to Monroe, Ouachita Parish, La., where he continued the practice of law until his death on May 26, 1910; interment in the New Cemetery, Bastrop, La.

**NEWTON, Cleveland Alexander,** a Representative from Missouri; born in Wright County, Mo., September 3, 1873; attended the common schools and Drury College at Springfield, Mo.; was graduated from the law department of the University of Missouri at Columbia in 1902; was admitted to the bar and commenced practice in Hartville, Mo., the same year; member of the Missouri State house of representatives, 1902-1906; assistant United States attorney for the western district of Missouri from 1905 to 1907, when he resigned to become assistant attorney, United States circuit court at St. Louis; resigned this office in 1911 to become special assistant to George W. Wickersham, Attorney General of the United States, which office he resigned in 1912 to resume the practice of law in St. Louis, Mo.; elected as a Republican to the Sixty-sixth and to the three succeeding Congresses (March 4, 1919-March 3, 1927); was not a candidate for renomination in 1926 to the Seventieth Congress; unsuccessful candidate for election in 1934 to the Seventy-fourth Congress; again resumed the practice of law in St. Louis, Mo., and Washington, D.C.; served as general counsel of the Mississippi Valley Association from 1928 to 1943; died in Washington, D.C., on September 17, 1945; interment in Valhalla Mausoleum, St. Louis, Mo.

**NEWTON, Eben,** a Representative from Ohio; born in Goshen, Conn., October 16, 1795; attended the common schools; moved to Portage County, Ohio, in 1814 and engaged in agricultural pursuits; studied law; was admitted to the bar in 1823 and commenced practice in Canfield, Mahoning County, Ohio; member of the State senate 1842-1851; presiding judge of the court of common pleas 1844-1851; elected as a Whig to the Thirty-second Congress (March 4, 1851-March 3, 1853); was an unsuccessful candidate for reelection in 1852 to the Thirty-third Congress; served as president of the Ashtabula & New Lisbon Railroad 1856-1859; again served in the State senate 1862-1864; resumed the practice of law and also engaged in agricultural pursuits; died in Canfield, Ohio, on November 6, 1885; interment in Canfield Village Cemetery.

**NEWTON, Thomas, Jr.,** a Representative from Virginia; born in Norfolk, Va., November 21, 1768; completed preparatory studies; studied law; admitted to the Virginia bar and commenced practice in Norfolk; member of the Virginia house of delegates 1796-1799; elected as a Republican to the Seventh Congress and reelected to the thirteen succeeding Congresses (March 4, 1801-March 3, 1829); one of the managers appointed by the House of Representatives in 1804 to conduct the impeachment proceedings against John Pickering, judge of the United States District Court for New Hampshire; presented credentials as a Member-elect to the Twenty-first Congress and served from March 4, 1829, until March 9, 1830, when he was succeeded by George Loyall, who successfully contested the election; chairman, Committee on Commerce and Manufactures (Tenth through Fifteenth Congresses), Committee on Commerce (Sixteenth through Nineteenth Congresses); elected to the Twenty-second Congress (March 4, 1831-March 3, 1833); was not a candidate for reelection in 1832 to the Twenty-third Congress; died in Norfolk, Va., on August 5, 1847; interment in St. Paul's Churchyard.

**Bibliography:** *DAB*.

**NEWTON, Thomas Willoughby**, a Representative from Arkansas; born in Alexandria, Va., January 18, 1804; attended the local schools; moved to Arkansas in 1820 and settled in Little Rock; clerk of the court of Pulaski County 1825-1829; moved to Shelby County, Ky.; returned to Little Rock in 1837 and became cashier in a bank; member of the State senate 1844-1848; elected as a Whig to the Twenty-ninth Congress to fill the vacancy caused by the resignation of Archibald Yell and served from February 6 to March 3, 1847; was not a candidate for renomination in 1846 to the Thirtieth Congress; died in New York City on September 22, 1853; interment in Mount Holly Cemetery, Little Rock, Ark.

**NEWTON, Walter Hughes**, a Representative from Minnesota; born in Minneapolis, Hennepin County, Minn., October 10, 1880; attended the public schools and was graduated from the law department of the University of Minnesota at Minneapolis in 1905; was admitted to the bar the same year and commenced practice in Minneapolis, Minn.; first assistant prosecuting attorney of Hennepin County 1914-1918; elected as a Republican to the Sixty-sixth and to the five succeeding Congresses and served from March 4, 1919, until his resignation on June 30, 1929, having been appointed secretary to President Herbert Hoover, serving in that capacity until March 3, 1933; regent of the Smithsonian Institution; appointed a member of the Federal Home Loan Bank Board by President Franklin D. Roosevelt in 1933 and served until 1934 when he resumed the practice of law in Minneapolis, Minn.; also engaged as an author; unsuccessful candidate for election in 1936 to the Seventy-fifth Congress; appointed Federal referee in bankruptcy in 1938 and served until his death in Minneapolis, Minn., August 10, 1941; interment in Lakewood Cemetery.

**NEWTON, Willoughby**, a Representative from Virginia; born at "Lee Hall," near Hague, Westmoreland County, Va., December 2, 1802; received a liberal education from private tutors and attended the College of William and Mary, Williamsburg, Va.; studied law; admitted to the bar and commenced the practice of his profession in Westmoreland County, Va.; member of the Virginia house of delegates 1826-1832; elected as a Whig to the Twenty-eighth Congress (March 4, 1843-March 3, 1845); unsuccessful candidate for reelection in 1844 to the Twenty-ninth Congress; resumed the practice of his profession in Westmoreland County and also engaged in agricultural pursuits; president of the Virginia Agricultural Society in 1852; again a member of the Virginia house of delegates 1861-1863; died at "Linden," Westmoreland County, Va., on May 23, 1874; interment in a private cemetery on the family estate.

**NEY, Robert William**, a Representative from Ohio; born in Wheeling, Ohio County, W.Va., July 5, 1954; graduated, St. John's High School, Bellaire, Ohio; B.S., Ohio State University, 1976; public safety director of Bellaire, Ohio; program manager, health and education, Ohio Office of Appalachia; teacher; member, Ohio State house of representatives, 1981-1983; member, Ohio State senate, 1985-1995; elected as a Republican to the One Hundred Fourth Congress (January 3, 1995-January 3, 1997); is a resident of St. Clairsville, Ohio.

**NIBLACK, Silas Leslie** (cousin of William Ellis Niblack), a Representative from Florida; born in Camden County, Ga., March 17, 1825; attended the common schools; studied law; was admitted to the bar about 1851 and commenced practice in Lake City, Columbia County, Fla.; judge of the probate court of Columbia County; successfully contested as a Democrat the election of Josiah T. Walls to the Forty-second Congress and served from January 29 to March 3, 1873; unsuccessful candidate for reelection in 1872 to the Forty-third Congress; member of the State senate in 1879;

carried on extensive farming operations and engaged in the practice of law in Lake City, Columbia County, Fla., until his death on February 13, 1883; interment in the Old Cathey Cemetery.

**NIBLACK, William Ellis** (cousin of Silas Leslie Niblack), a Representative from Indiana; born in Dubois County, Ind., May 19, 1822; attended the country schools and the Indiana University at Bloomington; studied law; was admitted to the bar in 1843 and commenced practice in Vincennes, Ind.; surveyor of Dubois County; member of the State house of representatives in 1849 and 1850; served in the State senate 1850-1853; judge of the circuit court of the third judicial district from January 1854 until October 1859, when he resigned; moved to Vincennes, Ind., in 1855; elected as a Democrat to the Thirty-fifth Congress to fill the vacancy caused by the death of James Lockhart; reelected to the Thirty-sixth Congress and served from December 7, 1857, to March 3, 1861; was not a candidate for renomination in 1860; again a member of the State house of representatives in 1862 and 1863; delegate to the Democratic National Conventions in 1864, 1868, and 1876; elected to the Thirty-ninth and to the four succeeding Congresses (March 4, 1865-March 3, 1875); was not a candidate for renomination in 1874; resumed the practice of law; judge of the supreme court of Indiana 1877-1889; moved to Indianapolis in 1889 and retired from public life; died in Indianapolis, Ind., May 7, 1893; interment in Crown Hill Cemetery.

**Bibliography:** *DAB*.

**NICHOLAS, John** (brother of Wilson Cary Nicholas and uncle of Robert Carter Nicholas), a Representative from Virginia; born in Williamsburg, Va., about 1757; attended the common schools; was graduated from the College of William and Mary, Williamsburg, Va.; studied law; was admitted to the bar and practiced in his native county; elected to the Third Congress and reelected as a Republican to the three succeeding Congresses (March 4, 1793-March 3, 1801); moved to Geneva, Ontario County, N.Y.; member of the New York State senate 1806-1809; judge of the court of common pleas 1806-1819; engaged in agricultural pursuits; died in Geneva, Ontario County, N.Y., December 31, 1819; interment in Glenwood Cemetery.

**Bibliography:** *DAB*.

**NICHOLAS, Robert Carter** (nephew of John Nicholas and Wilson Cary Nicholas), a Senator from Louisiana; born in Hanover, Hanover County, Va., in 1793; served in the War of 1812 as captain and major; attended the College of William and Mary, Williamsburg, Va.; moved to Louisiana and became a sugar planter in Terrebonne Parish in 1820; elected as a Democrat to the United States Senate to fill the vacancy caused by the resignation of Senator-elect Charles E.A. Gayarre and served from January 13, 1836, to March 3, 1841; secretary of State of Louisiana 1843-1846, when he resigned; died in Terrebonne Parish, La., on December 24, 1857; interment in the Burthe vault, St. Louis Cemetery, New Orleans, La.

**NICHOLAS, Wilson Cary** (brother of John Nicholas and uncle of Robert Carter Nicholas), a Senator and a Representative from Virginia; born in Williamsburg, Va., January 31, 1761; attended the College of William and Mary, Williamsburg, Va.; served in the Revolutionary Army and commanded General George Washington's Life Guard until it disbanded in 1783; member, Virginia house of delegates, 1784-1789; delegate to the Virginia constitutional convention which ratified the Federal Constitution in 1788; again a member of the Virginia house of delegates, 1794-1800; elected as a Republican to the United States Senate to fill the vacancy caused by the death of Henry Tazewell, and served from December 5, 1799 until May 22, 1804, when he resigned to become collector of the port of Norfolk, in which capacity he served from 1804 to 1807; elected to the Tenth and Eleventh Congresses, and served from March 4, 1807 until his resignation on November 27, 1809; elected Governor of

Virginia by the General Assembly, and served from December 1, 1814 to December 1, 1817; died at "Tufton," near Charlottesville, Va., October 10, 1820; interment in the Jefferson burying ground at "Monticello," near Charlottesville.

**Bibliography:** *DAB.*

**NICHOLLS, John Calhoun,** a Representative from Georgia; born in Clinton, Jones County, Ga., April 25, 1834; attended private schools and was graduated from the College of William and Mary, Williamsburg, Va., in 1855; studied law; was admitted to the bar in 1855 and practiced in Clinch and Ware Counties, Ga.; also engaged as a planter; during the Civil War served in the Confederate Army as captain, Company I, Fourth Regiment, Georgia Cavalry; member of the State constitutional convention in 1865; delegate to the Democratic National Convention of 1876; served in the Georgia State senate, 1870-1875; elected as a Democrat to the Forty-sixth Congress (March 4, 1879-March 3, 1881); unsuccessful candidate for renomination in 1880 to the Forty-seventh Congress; elected to the Forty-eighth Congress (March 4, 1883-March 3, 1885); unsuccessful candidate for renomination in 1884 to the Forty-ninth Congress; resumed the practice of law in Blackshear, Pierce County, Ga., where he died on December 25, 1893; interment in Blackshear Cemetery.

**NICHOLLS, Samuel Jones,** a Representative from South Carolina; born in Spartanburg, Spartanburg County, S.C., May 7, 1885; attended Bingham Military Institute, Asheville, N.C., Wofford College, Spartanburg, S.C., Virginia Polytechnic Institute, Blacksburg, Va., and the law department of the University of Chicago; was admitted to the bar in 1906 and commenced practice in Spartanburg; city attorney of Spartanburg and prosecuting attorney of Spartanburg County; member of the South Carolina State house of representatives, 1907-1908; served by special appointment as circuit judge and as associate justice of the supreme court of South Carolina; organized and was captain for three years of Company I, First Regiment, South Carolina National Guard Infantry; elected as a Democrat to the Sixty-fourth Congress to fill the vacancy caused by the resignation of Joseph T. Johnson; reelected to the two succeeding Congresses and served from September 14, 1915, to March 3, 1921; declined to be a candidate for renomination in 1920 to the Sixty-seventh Congress; resumed the practice of law in Spartanburg, S.C., until his death there on November 23, 1937; interment in West Oakwood Cemetery.

**NICHOLLS, Thomas David,** a Representative from Pennsylvania; born in Wilkes-Barre, Luzerne County, Pa., September 16, 1870; moved to Nanticoke, Pa., with his parents; attended the public schools; worked in mines as a boy; studied mining by correspondence; passed a Pennsylvania examination in 1897, received a mine foreman's certificate of competency, and was appointed superintendent of mines; district president of District No. 1, United Mine Workers of America, from 1899 to 1909, resigning on account of ill health; elected as an Independent Democrat to the Sixtieth and Sixty-first Congresses (March 4, 1907-March 3, 1911); was not a candidate for renomination in 1910; moved to a farm in Somerset County, Md., near Princess Anne, in 1911 and engaged in the raising of poultry; died in Princess Anne, Md., January 19, 1931; interment in Antioch Methodist Episcopal Cemetery.

**NICHOLS, Charles Archibald,** a Representative from Michigan; born in Boyne City, Charlevoix County, Mich., August 25, 1876; attended the public schools; engaged in newspaper work as reporter and criminal investigator for the Detroit Journal and the Detroit News from 1898 to 1905; secretary of the Detroit city police department, 1905-1908; Detroit city clerk, 1908-1912; elected as a Republican to the Sixty-fourth and to the two succeeding Congresses, and served from March 4, 1915 until his death in Washington, D.C., April 25, 1920; chairman, Committee on the Census (Sixty-sixth Congress); interment in Grand Lawn Cemetery, Detroit, Mich.

**NICHOLS, John,** a Representative from North Carolina; born near Eagle Rock, Wake County, N.C., November 14, 1834; attended the common schools; learned the printing trade, serving six years; at the age of twenty-one attended Lovejoy Academy, Raleigh, N.C., for one year; engaged in the book and job printing business and newspaper publishing; principal of the North Carolina Institute for the Deaf and Dumb and the Blind, 1873-1877; revenue-stamp agent in Durham, N.C., 1879-1881; postmaster of Raleigh, N.C., 1881-1885; secretary and treasurer of the North Carolina State fair association; elected as an Independent to the Fiftieth Congress (March 4, 1887-March 3, 1889); unsuccessful candidate for reelection in 1888 to the Fifty-first Congress; appointed chief of the division of mail and files, Treasury Department, July 22, 1889; transferred as private secretary to the Assistant Secretary of the Treasury, April 1, 1893, and resigned June 30, 1893; returned to Raleigh, N.C., and served in the office of the collector of internal revenue from November 26 to December 17, 1893; appointed United States commissioner for the eastern district of North Carolina on July 1, 1897, and served until his death in Raleigh, N.C., September 22, 1917; interment in Oakwood Cemetery.

**NICHOLS, John Conover,** a Representative from Oklahoma; born in Joplin, Mo., August 31, 1896; attended the public schools in Joplin, Mo., and Colorado Springs, Colo., and the teachers college at Emporia, Kans.; studied law in the office of his brother in Eufaula, Okla.; was admitted to the bar in 1926 and commenced practice in Eufaula, Okla.; during the First World War served in the Nineteenth Infantry, United States Army, 1917-1919; elected as a Democrat to the Seventy-fourth and to the four succeeding Congresses, and served from January 3, 1935 until his resignation on July 3, 1943, to become vice president of Transcontinental & Western Air, Inc., in which capacity he served until his death in an airplane crash at Asmara, Eritrea, November 7, 1945; interment in the United States military cemetery in Asmara, Eritrea; reinterment in Greenwood Cemetery, Eufaula, Okla.

**NICHOLS, Matthias H.,** a Representative from Ohio; born in Sharptown, Salem County, N.J., October 3, 1824; attended the common schools; learned the trade of a printer; moved to Ohio in 1842 and settled in Lima; studied law; was admitted to the bar in 1849 and commenced practice in Lima, Ohio; elected prosecuting attorney for Allen County in 1851, but resigned the following year to campaign for Congress; elected as a Democrat to the Thirty-third Congress and as a Republican to the Thirty-fourth and Thirty-fifth Congresses (March 4, 1853-March 3, 1859); unsuccessful candidate for reelection in 1858 to the Thirty-sixth Congress; resumed the practice of his profession; died in Cincinnati, Ohio, September 15, 1862; interment in the Old Cemetery, Lima, Ohio; reinterment in Woodlawn Cemetery.

**NICHOLS, Richard Dale,** a Representative from Kansas; born in Fort Scott, Bourbon County, Kans., April 29, 1926; graduated, Fort Scott-Paola High School, Kans., 1943; attended the University of Kansas (Navy V-12 program), 1943-1944; Park College, Parkville, Mo., 1944-1945; Notre Dame University (V-12), 1945-1946; B.S., Kansas State University, 1951; United States Navy service, 1944-1947, United States Naval Reserve, 1947-1950, ensign; informational counsel, Kansas State Board of Agriculture, 1951-1954; associate farm director, WIBW and WIBW-TV, Topeka, Kans.; agricultural representative to vice president, Hutchinson (Kans.) National Bank and Trust Co., 1957-1969; president then chairman, Home State Bank and Trust, McPherson, Kans., 1969-1990; elected as a Republican to the One Hundred Second Congress (January 3, 1991-January 3, 1993); unsuccessful candidate for renomination in 1992 to the One Hundred Third Congress; resumed his activities in the banking business; is a resident of McPherson, Kans.

**NICHOLS, William Flynt,** a Representative from Alabama; born on a small farm in Monroe County, near Becker, Miss., October 16, 1918; graduated from Sylacauga (Ala.) High School in 1935; B.S., Auburn (Ala.) University, 1939, and M.A., 1941; entered military service in 1942, served five years in European Theater, wounded in the battle of Hurtgen Forest, Germany, November 30, 1944; retired in 1947 with rank of captain; awarded Bronze Star and Purple Heart; vice president, Parker Fertilizer Co., and president, Parker Gin Company, Sylacauga, Ala., 1947-1966; member, Alabama State house of representatives, 1959-1963; member, Alabama State senate, 1963-1966; elected as a Democrat to the Ninetieth and to the ten succeeding Congresses, and served from January 3, 1967 until his death on December 13, 1988; had been reelected to the One Hundred First Congress.

**NICHOLSON, Alfred Osborn Pope,** a Senator from Tennessee; born near Franklin, Williamson County, Tenn., August 31, 1808; attended the rural schools; graduated from the University of North Carolina at Chapel Hill in 1827; studied law; was admitted to the bar in 1831 and commenced practice in Columbia, Tenn.; edited the Western Mercury in Columbia, 1832-1835; member, Tennessee State house of representatives, 1833-1839; appointed as a Democrat to the United States Senate to fill the vacancy caused by the death of Felix Grundy, and served from December 25, 1840 to February 7, 1842; member, Tennessee State senate, 1843-1845; moved to Nashville, Tenn., and edited the Nashville Union, 1844-1846; a director and subsequently president of the Bank of Tennessee in 1846 and 1847; declined an appointment to the Cabinet of President Franklin Pierce in 1853; edited the Washington Union, 1853-1856; public printer of the United States House of Representatives; again elected to the United States Senate and served from March 4, 1859, until March 3, 1861, when he retired; subsequently expelled from the Senate by a resolution of July 11, 1861 for support of the Confederacy; chief justice of the supreme court of Tennessee, 1870-1876; died in Columbia, Maury County, Tenn., March 23, 1876; interment in Rose Hill Cemetery.

Bibliography: *DAB.*

**NICHOLSON, Donald William,** a Representative from Massachusetts; born in Wareham, Plymouth County, Mass., August 11, 1888; attended the public schools and took college extension courses; engaged as a salesman; during the First World War served in the United States Army 1917-1919, with overseas service; selectman, assessor, and overseer of the poor, Town of Wareham, Mass., 1920-1925; delegate to all Massachusetts Republican conventions 1924-1947; served in the Massachusetts house of representatives in 1925 and 1926; member of the Massachusetts senate 1926-1947, serving as president in 1946 and 1947; elected as a Republican to the Eightieth Congress to fill the vacancy caused by the death of Charles L. Gifford; reelected to the Eighty-first and to the four succeeding Congresses and served from November 18, 1947, to January 3, 1959; was not a candidate for renomination in 1958 to the Eighty-sixth Congress; retired and resided at Wareham, Mass., until his death February 16, 1968; interment in Center Cemetery.

**NICHOLSON, John,** a Representative from New York; born in Herkimer, N.Y., in 1765; received a limited education; studied law; was admitted to the bar and practiced; held various local offices; elected as a Republican to the Eleventh Congress (March 4, 1809-March 3, 1811); died in Herkimer, N.Y., January 20, 1820.

**NICHOLSON, John Anthony,** a Representative from Delaware; born in Laurel, Sussex County, Del., November 17, 1827; completed preparatory studies and was graduated from Dickinson College, Carlisle, Pa., in 1847; superintendent of free schools for Kent County in 1851; studied law in Dover, Del.; was admitted to the bar in 1850 and commenced practice in Dover; brigadier general of militia in Kent County in 1861; elected as a Democrat to the Thirty-ninth and Fortieth Congresses (March 4, 1865-March 3,

1869); was not a candidate for renomination in 1868; resumed the practice of his profession; died in Dover, Kent County, Del., November 4, 1906; interment in the Presbyterian Church Cemetery.

**NICHOLSON, Joseph Hopper,** a Representative from Maryland; born in Chestertown, Kent County, Md., May 15, 1770; completed preparatory studies; studied law; was admitted to the bar and practiced; member of the State house of delegates 1796-1798; elected as a Republican to the Sixth and to the three succeeding Congresses and served from March 4, 1799, until his resignation on March 1, 1806; one of the managers appointed by the House of Representatives in January 1804 to conduct the impeachment proceedings against John Pickering, judge of the United States District Court for New Hampshire, and in December of the same year against Samuel Chase, Associate Justice of the Supreme Court of the United States; participated in the defense of Fort McHenry during the War of 1812; served as chief justice of the sixth judicial district of Maryland and was associate justice of the court of appeals from March 26, 1806, until his death at his home in Baltimore County, Md., March 4, 1817; interment in the family cemetery on the Lloyd estate, known as "Wye House," near Easton, Talbot County, Md.

Bibliography: *DAB.*

**NICHOLSON, Samuel Danford,** a Senator from Colorado; born in Springfield, Prince Edward Island, Canada, February 22, 1859; attended the public schools; moved to Michigan, then to Nebraska, and later, in 1881, to Leadville, Colo.; became interested in mining, advancing from miner to foreman, superintendent, manager, and president of the Western Mining Company; discovered the zinc ore which bears his name, "Nicholsonite"; Populist mayor of Leadville, 1893-1897; moved to Denver in 1902; unsuccessful candidate for Governor in 1914 and 1916; during the First World War served as State chairman of the Liberty and Victory loan campaigns; member, United States Fuel Administration; elected as a Republican to the United States Senate, and served from March 4, 1921 until his death in Denver, Colo., March 24, 1923; interment in Fairmount Cemetery.

Bibliography: *DAB.*

**NICKLES, Donald Lee,** a Senator from Oklahoma; born in Ponca City, Kay County, Okla., December 6, 1948; attended the public schools; graduated, Ponca City High School, 1967; B.B.A., Oklahoma State University, Stillwater, Okla., 1971; served in the National Guard, 1970-1976; vice president and general manager, Nickles Machine Co., 1971-present; member, Oklahoma State senate, 1979-1980; elected as a Republican to the United States Senate in 1980 for the term commencing January 3, 1981; reelected in 1986, and again in 1992 for the term ending January 3, 1999; chairman, National Republican Senatorial Committee (One Hundred First Congress), Republican Policy Committee (One Hundred Second through One Hundred Fourth Congresses), majority whip (One Hundred Fourth Congress); is a resident of Ponca City, Okla.

**NICOLL, Henry,** a Representative from New York; born in New York City October 23, 1812; was graduated from Columbia College, New York City, in 1830; studied law; was admitted to the bar in 1835 and commenced practice in New York City; delegate to the State constitutional convention in 1847; elected as a Democrat to the Thirtieth Congress (March 4, 1847-March 3, 1849); resumed the practice of law; died in New York City on November 28, 1879; interment in the family burying ground, Mastic, Long Island, N.Y.

**NIEDRINGHAUS, Frederick Gottlieb** (uncle of Henry Frederick Niedringhaus), a Representative from Missouri; born in Luebbecke, Westphalia, North Germany, on October 21, 1837; attended the common schools; learned the glazing, painting, and tinning trades; immigrated to the United States in November 1855 and settled in St. Louis, Mo.; began the stamping of tinware in 1862;

invented what is called "granite ironware" in 1874 and established an extensive business; became interested in various other business enterprises in St. Louis; elected as a Republican to the Fifty-first Congress (March 4, 1889-March 3, 1891); was not a candidate for renomination in 1890; resumed his former business pursuits; died in St. Louis, Mo., November 25, 1922; interment in Bellefontaine Cemetery.

Bibliography: *DAB*.

**NIEDRINGHAUS, Henry Frederick** (nephew of Frederick Gottlieb Niedringhaus), a Representative from Missouri; born in St. Louis, Mo., December 15, 1864; attended the public schools, Central Wesleyan College, Warrenton, Mo., and Smith Academy, a branch of Washington University, St. Louis, Mo.; engaged in manufacturing pursuits, serving as general manager of the National Enameling & Stamping Co. in Granite City, Ill.; chairman of the board of governors of Shriners' Hospital for Crippled Children, St. Louis, Mo., 1924-1941; elected as a Republican to the Seventieth and to the two succeeding Congresses (March 4, 1927-March 3, 1933); unsuccessful candidate for reelection in 1932 to the Seventy-third Congress; retired from active business pursuits and resided in St. Louis, Mo., until his death in that city on August 3, 1941; interment in Bellefontaine Cemetery.

**NIELSON, Howard Curtis,** a Representative from Utah; born in Richfield, Sevier County, Utah, September 12, 1924; graduated from Richfield High School, 1942; B.S., University of Utah, Salt Lake City, 1947; M.S., University of Oregon, Eugene, 1949; M.B.A., Stanford University, Palo Alto, Calif., 1956, and Ph.D., 1958; served in the United States Army Air Forces as a sergeant, 1943-1946; statistician, C & H Sugar, 1949-1951; economist, Stanford Research Institute, 1951-1957; professor of statistics, economics and business management, Brigham Young University, 1957-1976, 1978-1982; member, Utah State house of representatives, 1967-1974, and served as majority leader, 1969-1970, and as speaker, 1973-1974; Utah State associate commissioner of higher education, 1976-1978; delegate, Utah State Republican conventions, 1960-1982; director of finance, Utah State system of higher education, 1976-1978; chairman, Utah County Republican Party, 1979-1981; elected as a Republican to the Ninety-eighth and to the three succeeding Congresses (January 3, 1983-January 3, 1991); was not a candidate for reelection in 1990 to the One Hundred Second Congress; is a resident of Provo, Utah.

**NILES, Jason,** a Representative from Mississippi; born in Burlington, Vt., December 19, 1814; attended the common schools and was graduated from the University of Vermont at Burlington in 1837; taught school in Ohio and Tennessee for a number of years; studied law; was admitted to the bar in 1851 and commenced practice in Kosciusko, Attala County, Miss.; delegate to the State constitutional conventions in 1851, 1865, and 1868; member of the State house of representatives in 1870; circuit judge for the thirteenth judicial district in 1871 and 1872; elected as a Republican to the Forty-third Congress (March 4, 1873-March 3, 1875); unsuccessful candidate for reelection in 1874 to the Forty-fourth Congress; editor of the Kosciusko Chronicle 1876-1880; resumed the practice of his profession; died in Kosciusko, Miss., July 7, 1894; interment in the City Cemetery.

**NILES, John Milton,** a Senator from Connecticut; born in Windsor, Hartford County, Conn., August 20, 1787; completed preparatory studies; studied law; was admitted to the bar in 1817 and commenced practice in Hartford, Conn.; established and edited the Hartford Weekly Times in 1817; associate judge of Hartford County Court, 1821-1826; member, Connecticut State house of representatives, 1826; unsuccessful candidate for the United States Senate in 1827; postmaster of Hartford, 1829-1836; appointed in 1835 as a Democrat to the United States Senate to fill the vacancy caused by the death of Nathan Smith; subsequently elected and served from December 21, 1835, to March 3, 1839; was not a candidate for renomination in 1838; chairman, Committee on Manufactures (Twenty-fourth and Twenty-fifth Congresses); unsuccessful candidate for Governor of Connecticut in 1839 and 1840; appointed Postmaster General in the Cabinet of President Martin Van Buren, and served from May 25, 1840 until March 3, 1841; again elected to the United States Senate, and served from March 4, 1843 to March 3, 1849; was not a candidate for reelection; chairman, Committee to Audit and Control the Contingent Expense (Twenty-ninth Congress), Committee on Post Office and Post Roads (Twenty-ninth and Thirtieth Congresses); author; died in Hartford, Conn., May 31, 1856; interment in Old North Cemetery.

Bibliography: *DAB*; Niles, John Milton. *The Life of Oliver Hazard Perry.* Hartford: O.D. Cooke, 1821; Niles, John Milton. *History of South America and Mexico.* Hartford: H. Huntington, 1838.

**NILES, Nathaniel,** a Representative from Vermont; born in South Kingston, R.I., April 3, 1741; attended Harvard College and was graduated from Princeton College in 1766; studied law and medicine; taught in New York City; studied theology and preached in Norwich and Torrington, Conn.; invented a process for making wire and erected mills in Norwich; after the Revolution moved to West Fairlee, Orange County, Vt.; member of the State house of representatives in 1784 and served as speaker; judge of the supreme court 1784-1788; member of the council in 1785 and 1787; delegate to the State constitutional convention of 1791; upon the admission of Vermont as a State into the Union was elected to the Second Congress; reelected to the Third Congress and served from October 17, 1791, to March 3, 1795; again a member of the State house of representatives 1800-1803 and 1812-1815; member of the Governor's council 1803-1809; presidential elector on the Jefferson ticket in 1804 and on the Madison ticket in 1813; delegate to the State constitutional convention of 1814; died in Fairlee, Vt., October 31, 1828; interment in West Fairlee Center Cemetery.

Bibliography: *DAB*.

**NIMTZ, F. Jay,** a Representative from Indiana; born in South Bend, St. Joseph County, Ind., December 1, 1915; graduated from Central High School in 1934; B.A., Indiana University, 1938; LL.B. (J.D.), Indiana University School of Law, 1940; admitted to the bar in 1940 and commenced the practice of law in South Bend, Ind.; inducted in the United States Army as a private on June 13, 1941, and served as legal adviser to purchasing officer, Fort Riley, Kans.; assigned to the Criminal Investigation Division, August 1942, and to the Prisoner of War Division, Office of the Theater Provost Marshal, London, 1943; served fourteen months as assistant executive officer on the staff of Robert H. Jackson, United States Chief of Counsel for Prosecution of Axis Criminality, Nuremberg, Germany; colonel, United States Army Reserve; unsuccessful candidate for South Bend city judge in 1947, and for St. Joseph County prosecutor in 1948; vice-chairman, Lincoln Sesquicentennial Commission, 1958; member of board of directors, Saint Joseph County Department of Public Welfare; elected as a Republican to the Eighty-fifth Congress (January 3, 1957-January 3, 1959); unsuccessful candidate for reelection in 1958 to the Eighty-sixth Congress, and for election in 1960 to the Eighty-seventh Congress; resumed the practice of law; graduate, United States Army Command and General Staff College, 1965; member, Indiana Air Pollution Control Board, 1979-1986, and Indiana Environmental Management Board, 1981-1986; president of the South Bend Redevelopment Commission from 1974 until his death in South Bend, Ind., December 6, 1990; interment in Riverview Cemetery.

**NISBET, Eugenius Aristides** (cousin of Mark Anthony Cooper), a Representative from Georgia; born near Union Point, Greene County, Ga., December 7, 1803; completed preparatory studies; attended the Powellton Academy, Hancock County, Ga., 1815-1817 and the University of South Carolina at Columbia 1817-1819; was graduated from the University of Georgia at Athens in 1821; was admitted to the bar by a special act of the legislature before he was twenty-one and commenced the practice of law in Madison, Morgan County, Ga., in 1824; member of the State house of representatives 1827-1830; served in the State senate 1830-1837; moved to Macon, Ga., in 1837 and resumed the practice of law; unsuccessful Whig candidate for election in 1836 to the Twenty-fifth Congress; elected as a Whig to the Twenty-sixth and Twenty-seventh Congresses and served from March 4, 1839, until October 12, 1841, when he resigned; associate judge of the supreme court of Georgia 1845-1853; member of the secession convention of Georgia in January 1861 and was the author of the ordinance of secession; unsuccessful candidate for governor in 1861; died in Macon, Bibb County, Ga., March 18, 1871; interment in Rose Hill Cemetery.

Bibliography: *DAB.*

**NIVEN, Archibald Campbell,** a Representative from New York; born in Newburgh, Orange County, N.Y., December 8, 1803; completed preparatory studies; surrogate of Sullivan County 1828-1840; adjutant general of New York in 1844; elected as a Democrat to the Twenty-ninth Congress (March 4, 1845-March 3, 1847); district attorney of Sullivan County 1847-1850; member of the State senate in 1864 and 1865; died in Monticello, Sullivan County, N.Y., February 21, 1882; interment in Rock Ridge Cemetery.

**NIX, Robert Nelson Cornelius, Sr.,** a Representative from Pennsylvania; born in Orangeburg, S.C., August 9, 1905; graduated from Townsend Harris Hall High School, New York City, Lincoln University, Chester County, Pa., and from University of Pennsylvania Law School at Philadelphia in 1924; was admitted to the bar in 1925 and commenced the practice of law in Philadelphia, Pa.; elected committeeman of the 44th ward in Philadelphia, 1932, and was elected chairman of the 44th ward executive committee in 1950; special deputy attorney general of the Pennsylvania department of revenue, and special assistant deputy attorney general of the Commonwealth of Pennsylvania, 1934-1938; delegate to the Democratic National Convention of 1956; elected as a Democrat to the Eighty-fifth Congress, by special election, May 20, 1958, to fill the vacancy caused by the resignation of Earl Chudoff; reelected to the Eighty-sixth and to the nine succeeding Congresses and served from May 20, 1958, to January 3, 1979; chairman, Committee on the Post Office and Civil Service (Ninety-fifth Congress); unsuccessful candidate for renomination in 1978 to the Ninety-sixth Congress; was a resident of Philadelphia, Pa., until his death there on June 22, 1987.

**NIXON, George Stuart,** a Senator from Nevada; born in Placer County, Calif., on April 2, 1860; attended the public schools; went to work for a railroad company and studied telegraphy; transferred in 1881 to Nevada; organized and became cashier of a bank at Winnemucca, Humboldt County, Nev.; built an opera house in Reno and a theater in Winnemucca; engaged in banking and agricultural pursuits; also interested in mining and stock raising; member, Nevada State house of representatives, 1891; elected in 1905 as a Republican to the United States Senate; reelected in 1911 and served from March 4, 1905, until his death in Washington, D.C., June 5, 1912; chairman, Committee on Coast Defenses (Sixtieth and Sixty-first Congresses), Committee on Irrigation and Reclamation of Arid Lands (Sixty-second Congress); interment in Masonic Cemetery, Reno, Nev.

**NIXON, John Thompson,** a Representative from New Jersey; born in Fairton, Cumberland County, N.J., on August 31, 1820; attended private schools and was graduated from Princeton College in 1841; studied law; was admitted to the bar in 1845 and commenced practice in Bridgeton, N.J.; member of the State house of assembly 1848-1850 and served as speaker in the latter year; elected as a Republican to the Thirty-sixth and Thirty-seventh

Congresses (March 4, 1859-March 3, 1863); was not a candidate for renomination in 1862; resumed the practice of law in Bridgeton, N.J., 1863-1870; appointed United States judge for the district of New Jersey on April 28, 1870, and served until his death at his summer home in Stockbridge, Berkshire County, Mass., September 28, 1889; interment in the City Cemetery, Bridgeton, N.J.

Bibliography: *DAB.*

**NIXON, Richard Milhous,** a Representative and a Senator from California and a Vice President and 37th President of the United States; born in Yorba Linda, Orange County, Calif., January 9, 1913; attended the public schools and graduated from Whittier (Calif.) High School; B.A., Whittier College, 1934; LL.B., Duke University Law School, Durham, N.C., 1937; was admitted to the bar the same year and commenced practice in Whittier, Calif.; attorney in the Office of Price Administration, Washington, D.C., January 1942 to June 1942; during the Second World War served in the United States Navy from August 1942 to January 1946 as an operations officer in support of air action in the South Pacific Combat Air Transport Command, and was discharged as a lieutenant commander; elected as a Republican to the Eightieth and Eighty-first Congresses, and served from January 3, 1947 until his resignation on November 30, 1950; appointed to the United States Senate to fill the vacancy caused by the resignation of Sheridan Downey, and served from December 1, 1950 to January 3, 1951; elected to the United States Senate in 1950 for the term commencing January 3, 1951, and served until his resignation January 1, 1953, to become Vice President; elected Vice President of the United States on the Republican ticket headed by Dwight D. Eisenhower, November 4, 1952, for the term beginning January 20, 1953; reelected on November 6, 1956, for the term beginning January 20, 1957, and served until January 20, 1961; unsuccessful Republican candidate for election for President of the United States in 1960; resumed the practice of law in Los Angeles, Calif.; unsuccessful candidate in 1962 for election for governor of California; resumed the practice of law in New York City; elected President of the United States on November 5, 1968, and inaugurated January 20, 1969; reelected on November 7, 1972, and inaugurated January 20, 1973; resigned August 9, 1974, during impeachment proceedings against him in the House Judiciary Committee arising from matters surrounding the "Watergate" affair; accepted a pardon from President Gerald R. Ford, September 8, 1974; author of autobiographical works and books on international politics and diplomacy; was a resident of Woodcliff Lake, N.J., until his death in New York City on April 22, 1994; interment on the grounds of the Nixon Library and Birthplace, Yorba Linda, Calif.

Bibliography: Ambrose, Stephen E. *Nixon: The Education of a Politician, 1913-1962.* New York: Simon and Schuster, 1987; Morris, Roger. *Richard Milhous Nixon: The Rise of an American Politician.* New York: Henry Holt and Co., 1990; Nixon, Richard. *RN: The Memoirs of Richard Nixon.* New York: Grosset and Dunlap, 1978.

**NOBLE, David Addison,** a Representative from Michigan; born in Williamstown, Berkshire County, Mass., November 9, 1802; attended a private school in Plainfield, Mass., and was graduated from Williams College, Williamstown, Mass., in 1825; studied law in Albany and New York City; was admitted to the bar in 1831 and commenced practice in New York City; moved to Monroe, Mich., in 1831 and continued the practice of law; city recorder of Monroe in 1838, 1839, and 1844-1850; mayor in 1852; served two terms as alderman; member of the State house of representatives in 1847 and 1848; prosecuting attorney and probate judge of Monroe County; elected as a Democrat to the Thirty-third Congress (March 4, 1853-March 3, 1855); unsuccessful candidate for reelection in 1854 to the Thirty-fourth Congress; appointed manager of the Louisville, New Albany & Chicago Railroad in 1858 and served four years; delegate to the Democratic National Convention in 1864; died in

Monroe, Monroe County, Mich., October 13, 1876; interment in Woodlawn Cemetery.

**NOBLE, James,** a Senator from Indiana; born near Berryville, Clarke County, Va., December 16, 1785; moved with his parents to Campbell County, Ky., in 1795; studied law; was admitted to the bar and practiced; moved to Indiana and settled in Brookville; ferryboat operator; judge; member of the convention to draft the constitution of the State in 1816; member, first State house of representatives 1816; elected as a Republican to the United States Senate in 1816; reelected in 1821 and again in 1827 and served from December 11, 1816, until his death in Washington, D.C., on February 26, 1831; chairman, Committee on Pensions (Fifteenth through Eighteenth and Twentieth Congresses), Committee on the Militia (Sixteenth and Seventeenth Congresses); interment in the Congressional Cemetery.

Bibliography: *DAB*.

**NOBLE, Warren Perry,** a Representative from Ohio; born near Berwick, Luzerne County, Pa., June 14, 1820; moved to Ohio; attended the common schools; taught school; was graduated from Wadsworth Academy, Wadsworth, Ohio, in 1840; studied law; was admitted to the bar in 1843 and commenced practice in Tiffin, Ohio; member of the State house of representatives 1846-1850; prosecuting attorney of Seneca County 1851-1854; elected as a Democrat to the Thirty-seventh and Thirty-eighth Congresses (March 4, 1861-March 3, 1865); unsuccessful candidate for reelection to the Thirty-ninth Congress; resumed the practice of law in Tiffin, Ohio, and died there July 9, 1903; interment in Green Lawn Cemetery.

**NOBLE, William Henry,** a Representative from New York; born in New Milford, Litchfield County, Conn., September 22, 1788; moved to Ballston Spa, then to Cato, N.Y., and later to Rochester, N.Y.; received a limited education; was a tanner by trade and later a farmer; member of the New York State assembly 1828-1830; elected as a Democrat to the Twenty-fifth Congress (March 4, 1837-March 3, 1839); unsuccessful candidate for reelection in 1838 to the Twenty-sixth Congress; inspector of Auburn Prison 1843-1845; died in Rochester, N.Y., February 5, 1850.

**NODAR, Robert Joseph, Jr.,** a Representative from New York; born in Brooklyn, N.Y., March 23, 1916; attended the public schools of New York City and was graduated from Newtown High School, Elmhurst, N.Y., in 1935; engaged as a clerk in the Manufacturers Trust Co., in New York City 1935-1939 and with the Crucible Steel Corp. of America 1940-1942; served in the United States Army Air Force, with service in the South Pacific, from March 18, 1942, until discharged as a master sergeant on January 6, 1946; elected as a Republican to the Eightieth Congress (January 3, 1947-January 3, 1949); unsuccessful candidate for reelection in 1948 to the Eighty-first Congress; engaged as a position clerk with Solomon Brothers & Hutzell, New York City; died in Flushing, N.Y., September 11, 1974; interment in Pinelawn Memorial Park, Farmingdale, N.Y.

**NOELL, John William** (father of Thomas Estes Noell), a Representative from Missouri; born in Bedford County, Va., February 22, 1816; attended the rural schools; at the age of seventeen moved to Missouri and settled near Perryville; engaged in milling and storekeeping; studied law; was admitted to the bar in 1843 and commenced practice in Perryville, Mo.; clerk of the circuit court for Perry County, 1841-1850; member of the Missouri State senate, 1851-1855; elected as a Democrat to the Thirty-sixth and Thirty-seventh Congresses; reelected as an Uncondiitional Unionist to the Thirty-eighth Congress, and served from March 4, 1859 until his death in Washington, D.C., March 14, 1863; interment in St. Mary's Cemetery, Perryville, Mo.

**NOELL, Thomas Estes** (son of John William Noell), a Representative from Missouri; born in Perryville, Perry County, Mo., April 3, 1839; attended the public schools; studied law; was admitted to the bar in 1858 and commenced practice in Perryville, Mo., the same year; during the Civil War was appointed a military commissioner in 1861; served as major in the State militia from July 1861 to April 1862; appointed captain unassigned in Company C, Nineteenth Infantry, United States Army, and served from April 1, 1862 until his resignation on February 20, 1865, to take his seat in Congress; elected as a Republican to the Thirty-ninth Congress; reelected as a Democrat to the Fortieth Congress, and served from March 4, 1865 until his death in St. Louis, Mo., on October 3, 1867; interment in St. Mary's Cemetery, Perryville, Mo.

**NOLAN, John Ignatius** (husband of Mae Ella Nolan), a Representative from California; born in San Francisco, Calif., January 14, 1874; attended the public schools; was an iron molder; member of the board of supervisors of the city and county of San Francisco in 1911; secretary of the San Francisco Labor Council in 1912; elected as a Republican to the Sixty-third and to the four succeeding Congresses and served from March 4, 1913, until his death; chairman, Committee on Patents (Sixty-sixth Congress), Committee on Labor (Sixty-seventh Congress); had been reelected in 1922 to the Sixty-eighth Congress; died in San Francisco, Calif., November 18, 1922; interment in Holy Cross Cemetery.

**NOLAN, Mae Ella** (wife of John Ignatius Nolan), a Representative from California; born in San Francisco, Calif., September 20, 1886; attended the public schools, St. Vincent's Convent and Ayres Business College of San Francisco; elected as a Republican to the Sixty-seventh and to the Sixty-eighth Congresses, January 23, 1923, by special election to fill the vacancies caused by the death of her husband, John Ignatius Nolan, who had been reelected in 1922, and she served from January 23, 1923, to March 3, 1925; chairman, Committee on Expenditures in the Post Office Department (Sixty-eighth Congress); was not a candidate for renomination in 1924 to the Sixty-ninth Congress; moved to Sacramento, Calif. in her later years, where she died on July 9, 1973; interment in Holy Cross Cemetery, Colma, Calif.

**NOLAN, Michael Nicholas,** a Representative from New York; born in County Carlow, Ireland, May 4, 1833; immigrated to the United States at the age of ten years; attended the public schools in Albany; studied law but did not complete the course; went to California during the gold rush; was employed on the street railway system of San Francisco and soon became manager; returned to Albany, N.Y., and engaged in business as a brewer; director of the National Savings Bank of Albany; fire commissioner of Albany 1869-1878; elected mayor of Albany and served from May 1878 to June 24, 1883, when he resigned; elected as a Democrat to the Forty-seventh Congress (March 4, 1881-March 3, 1883); did not seek renomination in 1882, having been reelected mayor; continued his business activities; died in Albany, N.Y., May 31, 1905; interment in St. Agnes' Cemetery.

**NOLAN, Richard Michael,** a Representative from Minnesota; born in Brainerd, Crow Wing County, Minn., December 17, 1943; graduated from Brainerd High School, 1962; attended St. John's University, Collegeville, Minn., 1962; B.A., University of Minnesota, 1966; engaged in postgraduate work in public administration and policy formation, University of Maryland, College Park, 1966; pursued a career in business and labor; teacher of social studies in the schools of Royalton, Minn., 1968-1972; served in the Minnesota State house of representatives, 1969-1973; elected as a Democrat to the Ninety-fourth and to the two succeeding Congresses (January 3, 1975-January 3, 1981); was not a candidate for reelection in 1980 to the Ninety-seventh Congress; president of a trading company, 1981-1986; president, Minnesota World Trade Center, St. Paul, Minn.; is a resident of St Paul, Minn.

**NOLAN, William Ignatius,** a Representative from Minnesota; born in St. Paul, Minn., May 14, 1874; moved with his parents to Minneapolis, Minn., in 1877; educated in the public schools of Minneapolis; member of the Minnesota National Guard, 1891-1896; engaged as a lecturer and humorist in 1894 and later as a Chautauqua lecturer; member, Minnesota State house of representatives, 1903-1907, 1911-1913, and 1917-1923, serving as speaker from 1919 until 1923; Lieutenant Governor of Minnesota, 1925-1929; chairman of the Minnesota Reforestation Commission in 1927; elected as a Republican to the Seventy-first Congress to fill the vacancy caused by the resignation of Walter H. Newton; reelected to the Seventy-second Congress, and served from June 17, 1929 to March 3, 1933; unsuccessful candidate for reelection in 1932 to the Seventy-third Congress; unsuccessful candidate for nomination in 1934 to the Seventy-fourth Congress, in 1936 to the Seventy-fifth Congress, and in 1938 to the Seventy-sixth Congress; resumed his profession as a lecturer; elected State railroad and warehouse commissioner in 1942 and served until his death in Winona, Minn., August 3, 1943, while on a visit; interment in Lakewood Cemetery, Minneapolis, Minn.

**NOLAND, James Ellsworth,** a Representative from Indiana; born in La Grange, Lewis County, Mo., April 22, 1920; with his parents moved to Indiana; attended the public schools of Spencer and Bloomington, Ind.; A.B., Indiana University, 1942; M.B.A., Harvard Graduate School of Business Administration, 1943; commissioned a second lieutenant in June 1943 in the Army Transportation Corps, assigned to the New Orleans Port of Embarkation, and served until discharged as a captain on May 26, 1946; unsuccessful candidate for election in 1946 to the Eightieth Congress; J.D., Indiana University Law School, 1948; was admitted to the bar and commenced the practice of law; elected as a Democrat to the Eighty-first Congress (January 3, 1949-January 3, 1951); unsuccessful candidate for reelection in 1950 to the Eighty-second Congress; resumed the practice of law; delegate to the Democratic National Convention of 1964; assistant state attorney general of Indiana, 1952; assistant city attorney, Indianapolis, 1956-1957; Democratic member of Indiana State Election Board, 1958-1966; secretary, Democratic State committee, 1959-1966; nominated by President Lyndon B. Johnson for appointment as judge of the United States District Court for the Southern District of Indiana in 1966; served as chief judge from June 9, 1984 until 1987, when he took senior status; died August 12, 1992.

**NOONAN, Edward Thomas,** a Representative from Illinois; born in Macomb, McDonough County, Ill., October 23, 1861; studied law in Chicago and was admitted to the bar in 1882; after admission to the bar was graduated from the University of Michigan at Ann Arbor in 1883 and commenced practice; member of the Illinois State senate, 1890-1894; colonel on the staff of Governor John P. Altgeld, 1893-1897; attorney for the Board of West Chicago Park Commissioners, 1893-1898; unsuccessful candidate for election in 1894 to the Fifty-fourth Congress, and in 1896 to the Fifty-fifth Congress; elected as a Democrat to the Fifty-sixth Congress (March 4, 1899-March 3, 1901); was not a candidate for renomination in 1900 to the Fifty-seventh Congress; resumed the practice of law in Chicago, Ill., until his death in that city on December 19, 1923; interment in St. Paul's Catholic Cemetery, Macomb, Ill.

**NOONAN, George Henry,** a Representative from Texas; born in Newark, N.J., August 20, 1828; received a liberal education; studied law; was admitted to the bar and practiced; moved to Texas in 1852 and settled in Castroville, Medina County; resumed the practice of law; elected judge of the eighteenth judicial district of Texas in 1862 and served until 1894 when he resigned; elected as a Republican to the Fifty-fourth Congress (March 4, 1895-March 3, 1897); unsuccessful candidate for reelection in 1896 to the Fifty-fifth

Congress; resumed the practice of law in San Antonio, Tex., and died there on August 17, 1907; interment in St. Mary's Cemetery.

**NORBECK, Peter,** a Senator from South Dakota; born near Vermillion, Clay County, Dakota Territory (now South Dakota), August 27, 1870; attended the public schools and the University of South Dakota at Vermillion; moved to Redfield, Spink County, S.Dak., in 1900; engaged in agricultural pursuits and in 1895 also engaged as a contractor and driller of deep water, oil, and gas wells; member, South Dakota State senate, 1909-1915; lieutenant governor, 1915-1916; elected Governor of South Dakota in 1916, reelected in 1918, and served from January 2, 1917 to January 4, 1921; was instrumental in the establishment of the Mount Rushmore National Monument; elected as a Republican to the United States Senate in 1920; reelected in 1926 and again in 1932 and served from March 4, 1921, until his death in Redfield, S.Dak., December 20, 1936; chairman, Committee on Pensions (Sixty-ninth Congress), Committee on Banking and Currency (Seventieth through Seventy-second Congresses); interment in Bloomington Church Cemetery, near Platte, S.Dak.

**Bibliography:** *DAB*; Fite, Gilbert. *Peter Norbeck: Prairie Statesman*. Columbia: University of Missouri Press, 1948; Norbeck, Lydia. "Recollections of the Years." Edited by Nancy Tystad Koupal. *South Dakota Historical Collections* 39 (1978): 1-147.

**NORBLAD, Albin Walter, Jr.,** a Representative from Oregon; born in Escanaba, Delta County, Mich., September 12, 1908, and moved with his parents to Astoria, Oreg., the same year; attended the public schools of Astoria and the New Mexico Military Academy at Roswell; was graduated from the University of Oregon at Eugene in 1932, and was also engaged in graduate work at Harvard University Law School; was admitted to the bar in 1932 and commenced practice in Astoria, Clatsop County, Oreg; member of the Oregon State house of representatives, 1935-1937; member of the board of trustees of Linfield College; delegate to the Republican National Convention of 1940; served as combat intelligence officer, Ninth Air Force, 1942-1945; elected as a Republican to the Seventy-ninth Congress to fill the vacancy caused by the death of James W. Mott; reelected to the Eightieth and to the eight succeeding Congresses, and served from January 11, 1946 until his death in Bethesda, Md., September 20, 1964; interment in Lone Oak Cemetery, Stayton, Oreg.

**NORCROSS, Amasa,** a Representative from Massachusetts; born in Rindge, Cheshire County, N.H., January 26, 1824; attended the common schools and Appleton Academy, New Ipswich, N.H.; studied law; admitted to the bar in 1847 and commenced practice in Worcester, Mass.; member of the Massachusetts house of representatives in 1858, 1859, and again in 1862; assessor of internal revenue from August 1862 until May 1873, when the office was abolished; mayor of the city of Fitchburg, Mass., in 1873 and 1874; served in the Massachusetts senate in 1874; elected as a Republican to the Forty-fifth, Forty-sixth, and Forty-seventh Congresses (March 4, 1877-March 3, 1883); was not a candidate for renomination in 1882; resumed the practice of law; died in Paris, France, April 2, 1898, while on a visit to his daughter; interment in Laurel Hill Cemetery, Fitchburg, Worcester County, Mass.

**NORMAN, Fred Barthold,** a Representative from Washington; born on a farm near Martinsville, Clark County, Ill., March 21, 1882; attended the public schools and was graduated from Martinsville (Ill.) High School; moved to Lebam, Pacific County, Wash., in 1901; worked on farms, in logging camps, sawmills, shingle mills, and shipyards from 1901 until 1922; engaged in the wholesale and retail tobacco and candy business, beginning in 1922; member of the city council of Raymond, Wash., 1916-1918; served in the Washington State house of representatives, 1919-1920; member of the State senate, 1925-1935; elected as a Republican to the Seventy-eighth Congress (January 3, 1943-January 3, 1945); unsuccessful candidate for reelection in 1944 to the Seventy-ninth Congress; elected in 1946 to the Eightieth Congress, and served from January 3, 1947 until his death in Washington, D.C., on April 18, 1947; interment in Fern Hill Cemetery, Menlo, Wash.

**NORRELL, Catherine Dorris** (wife of William Frank Norrell), a Representative from Arkansas; born in Camden, Ouachita County, Ark., March 30, 1901; attended high school in Monticello, Ouachita Baptist College in Arkadelphia, and the University of Arkansas in Fayetteville; taught in the public schools of Arkansas; director of music department at Arkansas A.&M. College; elected as a Democrat to the Eighty-seventh Congress, April 18, 1961, by special election to fill the vacancy caused by the death of her husband, William F. Norrell, and served until January 3, 1963; was not a candidate for renomination in 1962 to the Eighty-eighth Congress; Deputy Assistant Secretary of State, 1963-1965; Director, United States Department of State Reception Center, Honolulu, Hawaii, June 1, 1965 to January 5, 1969; resided in Monticello, Ark., until her death in Warren, Ark., August 26, 1981; interment in Oakland Cemetery, Monticello, Ark.

**NORRELL, William Frank** (husband of Catherine Dorris Norrell), a Representative from Arkansas; born in Milo, Ashley County, Ark., August 29, 1896; attended the public schools, the Arkansas Agricultural and Mechanical College of Monticello, the College of the Ozarks, Clarksville, Ark., and the University of Arkansas Law School at Little Rock; during the First World War served in the Quartermaster Corps of the United States Army; was admitted to the bar in 1920 and commenced practice in Monticello, Ark.; member of the State senate 1930-1938, serving as president for four years; elected as a Democrat to the Seventy-sixth and to the eleven succeeding Congresses and served from January 3, 1939, until his death in Washington, D.C., February 15, 1961; interment in Oakland Cemetery, Monticello, Ark.

**NORRIS, Benjamin White,** a Representative from Alabama; born in Monmouth, Maine, January 22, 1819; prepared for college at Monmouth Academy, and was graduated from Waterville (now Colby) College, Maine, in 1843; taught one term in Kents Hill Seminary; engaged in the grocery business in Skowhegan, Maine; delegate to the Free-Soil Convention at Buffalo in 1848; went to California in 1849, remaining one year, then returned to Skowhegan, and studied law; was admitted to the bar of Somerset County in January 1852 and commenced practice there; land agent for the State of Maine 1860-1863; delegate to the Republican National Convention in 1864; served as paymaster in the Union Army in 1864 and 1865; appointed major and additional paymaster in the Bureau of Freedmen and Abandoned Lands, serving from May 1 to August 2, 1865, at Mobile, Ala.; resided on a plantation in Elmore County and in Wetumpka, Ala., until 1872; member of the constitutional convention of Alabama in 1868; upon the readmission of Alabama to representation was elected as a Republican to the Fortieth Congress and served from July 21, 1868, to March 3, 1869; unsuccessful candidate for election in 1870 to the Forty-second Congress; died in Montgomery, Ala., January 26, 1873; interment in South Cemetery, Skowhegan, Somerset County, Maine.

**NORRIS, George William,** a Representative and a Senator from Nebraska; born on a farm near Clyde, Sandusky County, Ohio, on July 11, 1861; attended the district schools, Baldwin University, Berea, Ohio, and the Northern Indiana Normal School at Valparaiso; taught school while studying law; graduated from the law department of Valparaiso (Ind.) University in 1883 and was admitted to the bar the same year; continued teaching until he moved to Beaver City, Furnas County, Nebr., in 1885 and engaged in the practice of law; county attorney of Furnas County for three terms; district judge of the fourteenth district from 1895 until 1902; moved to McCook, Red Willow County, Nebr., in 1899; elected as a

Republican to the Fifty-eighth and to the four succeeding Congresses (March 4, 1903-March 3, 1913); did not seek renomination in 1912 to the House of Representatives, having become a candidate for Senator; one of the managers appointed by the House of Representatives in 1912 to conduct the impeachment proceedings against Robert W. Archbald, judge of the United States Commerce Court; elected as a Republican to the United States Senate in 1912; reelected in 1918, 1924, and 1930, and as an Independent Republican in 1936, and served from March 4, 1913 to January 3, 1943; unsuccessful candidate for reelection in 1942; chairman, Committee on the Five Civilized Tribes of Indians (Sixty-fifth Congress), Committee on Patents (Sixty-sixth Congress), Committee on Agriculture and Forestry (Sixty-seventh through Sixty-ninth Congresses), Committee on the Judiciary (Sixty-ninth through Seventy-second Congresses); known as the "father of the Tennessee Valley Authority," the first of that project's dams, on the Clinch River in northeastern Tennessee, was named Norris Dam; sponsor of the Twentieth Amendment to the Constitution, ratified January 23, 1933, which fixed the beginning and ending of terms for the President, Vice President, and Members of Congress; co-sponsor of the Norris-LaGuardia act of 1932, which limited judicial power to issue injunctions forbidding strikes and other labor union activities; retired from public life; died in McCook, Nebr., September 2, 1944; interment in Memorial Park Cemetery.

**Bibliography:** *DAB*; Lowitt, Richard. *George W. Norris: The Making of a Progressive, 1861-1912.* 1963. Reprint. Westport, Conn.: Greenwood Press, 1980; Lowitt, Richard. *George W. Norris: The Persistence of a Progressive, 1913-1933.* Urbana: University of Illinois Press, 1971; Lowitt, Richard. *George W. Norris: The Triumph of a Progressive, 1933-1944.* Urbana: University of Illinois Press, 1978; Norris, George. *Fighting Liberal: The Autobiography of George W. Norris.* Foreword by Arthur M. Schlesinger, Jr. 1945. Reprint. Lincoln: University of Nebraska Press, 1992.

**NORRIS, Moses, Jr.,** a Representative and a Senator from New Hampshire; born in Pittsfield, N.H., November 8, 1799; attended the public schools and the Pittsfield Academy, and graduated from Dartmouth College, Hanover, N.H., in 1828; studied law; was admitted to the bar in 1832 and commenced practice in Barnstead; returned to Pittsfield in 1834; member, State house of representatives 1837-1840, 1842; member, State council 1841-1842; elected as a Democrat to the Twenty-eighth and Twenty-ninth Congresses (March 4, 1843-March 3, 1847); member, State house of representatives 1847-1848, and served as speaker; elected to the United States Senate and served from March 4, 1849, until his death in Washington, D.C., January 11, 1855; chairman, Committee on Claims (Thirty-first Congress), Committee on Patents and the Patent Office (Thirty-second Congress), Committee on the District of Columbia (Thirty-third Congress); interment in Floral Park Cemetery, Pittsfield, N.H.

**NORTH, Solomon Taylor,** a Representative from Pennsylvania; born in Jefferson County, Pa., May 24, 1853; attended the public schools; taught school six years and served as a school director for twenty years; lumber merchant, farmer, and banker; member of the National Guard of Pennsylvania; delegate to the Pennsylvania Republican convention in 1898; director of the Punxsutawney National Bank; member of the board of education; member of the Pennsylvania house of representatives 1905-1907, 1911, and 1913; elected as a Republican to the Sixty-fourth Congress (March 4, 1915-March 3, 1917); unsuccessful candidate for renomination in 1916; died near Punxsutawney, Jefferson County, Pa., October 19, 1917; interment in Circle Hill Cemetery.

**NORTH, William,** a Senator from New York; born in Fort Frederick, Pemaquid, Maine, in 1755; attended the common schools; moved with his mother to Boston, Mass.; served in the Continental Army during the Revolutionary War; after the war settled in

Duanesburg, N.Y.; several times elected to the State assembly; appointed as a Federalist to the United States Senate to fill the vacancy caused by the resignation of John S. Hobart and served from May 5, 1798, to August 17, 1798, when a successor was elected and qualified; appointed adjutant general of the Army with the rank of brigadier general 1798-1800; member and speaker of the State assembly 1810; died in Duanesburg, Schenectady County, N.Y., on January 3, 1836; interment in the crypt under Christ Episcopal Church.

Bibliography: *DAB.*

**NORTHWAY, Stephen Asa,** a Representative from Ohio; born in Christian Hollow, Onondaga County, N.Y., June 19, 1833; moved with his parents in 1840 to the township of Orwell, Ashtabula County, Ohio; attended the district school, Kingsville Academy, and Orwell Academy; taught school; studied law; was admitted to the bar in 1859 and commenced practice in Jefferson, Ashtabula County, Ohio; prosecuting attorney of Ashtabula County 1861-1865; member of the State house of representatives in 1865 and 1866; resumed the practice of law; elected as a Republican to the Fifty-third, Fifty-fourth, and Fifty-fifth Congresses and served from March 4, 1893, until his death in Jefferson, Ashtabula County, Ohio, on September 8, 1898; interment in Oakdale Cemetery.

**NORTON, Daniel Sheldon,** a Senator from Minnesota; born in Mount Vernon, Knox County, Ohio, on April 12, 1829; pursued classical studies and graduated from Kenyon College, Gambier, Ohio; served in the Mexican War; after the war returned to Ohio; studied law; was admitted to the bar and commenced practice in Mount Vernon in 1852; moved to St. Paul, Minn., in 1855, and then to Winona, Minn., in 1856, where he continued the practice of law; member, State house of representatives 1857-1860; member, State senate 1861-1864; elected as a Unionist to the United States Senate and served from March 4, 1865, until his death in Washington, D.C., July 13, 1870; interment in Greenmount Cemetery, Baltimore, Md.

**NORTON, Ebenezer Foote,** a Representative from New York; born in Goshen, Litchfield County, Conn., November 7, 1774; completed preparatory studies; studied law; was admitted to the bar and practiced; moved to Buffalo, N.Y., in 1815; attorney for the Niagara Bank; held several local offices; was one of the founders of the original Buffalo Harbor Co. in 1819; elected as a Jacksonian to the Twenty-first Congress (March 4, 1829-March 3, 1831); unsuccessful for reelection in 1830 to the Twenty-second Congress; resumed his law practice; died in Buffalo, N.Y., May 11, 1851.

**NORTON, Eleanor Holmes,** a Delegate from the District of Columbia; born in Washington, D.C., June 13, 1937; graduated from Dunbar High School, 1955; B.A., Antioch College, Yellow Springs, Ohio, 1960; M.A., Yale University, 1963; LL.B., Yale University Law School, 1964; law clerk to Federal District Court Judge A. Leon Higginbotham, Third Circuit, 1964-1965; adjunct assistant professor of law, New York University Law School, 1970-1971; assistant legal director, American Civil Liberties Union, 1965-1970; executive assistant to the mayor, New York City, 1971-1974; chair, New York City Commission on Human Rights, 1970-1977; chair, Equal Employment Opportunity Commission, 1977-1981; senior fellow, The Urban Institute, 1981-1982; professor of law, Georgetown University Law Center, 1982-1990; elected as a Democrat a Delegate to the One Hundred Second and to the two succeeding Congresses (January 3, 1991-January 3, 1997); is a resident of Washington, D.C.

**NORTON, Elijah Hise,** a Representative from Missouri; was born in Russellville, Logan County, Ky., November 21, 1821; attended the public schools and Centre College, Danville, Ky.; was graduated from the law department of Transylvania University, Lexington, Ky., in 1842; was admitted to the bar and commenced practice in Platte City, Mo., in 1845; county attorney in 1850; judge

of the circuit court of Missouri 1852-1860; elected as a Democrat to the Thirty-seventh Congress (March 4, 1861-March 3, 1863); unsuccessful candidate for reelection in 1862 to the Thirty-eighth Congress; delegate to the State constitutional convention in 1875; appointed and subsequently elected as judge of the State supreme court, serving from 1876 to 1879; resumed the practice of law and the care of his estate; died in Platte City, Platte County, Mo., August 6, 1914; interment in Platte City Cemetery.

Bibliography: *DAB.*

**NORTON, James,** a Representative from South Carolina; born near Mullins, Marion County, S.C., October 8, 1843; pursued an academic course; left school in 1861 to enter the Confederate Army; served throughout the Civil War in the Army of Northern Virginia; after the war reentered school, but did not finish the regular course; teacher in the public schools 1866-1870; engaged in agricultural pursuits and merchandising; elected county school commissioner in 1870 and reelected in 1872; member of the State house of representatives in 1886, 1887, 1890, and 1891; assistant comptroller general of the State of South Carolina 1890-1894; comptroller general of the State from 1894 until 1897, when he resigned; elected as a Democrat to the Fifty-fifth Congress to fill the vacancy caused by the resignation of John L. McLaurin; reelected to the Fifty-sixth Congress and served from December 6, 1897, to March 3, 1901; was not a candidate for reelection in 1900 to the Fifty-seventh Congress; resumed agricultural pursuits and also engaged in the real estate business; again a member of the State house of representatives in 1907-1908; died in Mullins, S.C., October 14, 1920; interment in Miller's Churchyard.

**NORTON, James Albert,** a Representative from Ohio; born in Bettsville, Seneca County, Ohio, November 11, 1843; attended the district schools and was graduated from the Tiffin High School; during the Civil War enlisted in the Union Army in August 1862; sergeant of Company K, One Hundred and First Regiment, Ohio Volunteer Infantry; promoted to first lieutenant and adjutant of the One Hundred and Twenty-third Regiment, United States Colored Infantry, in 1864; mustered out of the service in 1865; studied medicine and commenced practice in Iowa in 1867; continued in that profession until 1879; studied law and was admitted to the bar in 1874; member of the State house of representatives, 1873-1879, serving as speaker in 1877 and 1878; chairman of the State Democratic committee, 1887-1892; county auditor, 1885-1892; commissioner of railroads and telegraphs from 1889 to 1895, when he resigned to accept a position in the legal department of the Baltimore and Ohio Railroad Co.; elected as a Democrat to the Fifty-fifth and to the two succeeding Congresses (March 4, 1897-March 3, 1903); unsuccessful candidate for reelection in 1902 to the Fifty-eighth Congress; resumed his legal service with the Baltimore and Ohio Railroad Co.; died in Tiffin, Ohio, July 24, 1912; interment in a mausoleum in Green Lawn Cemetery.

**NORTON, Jesse Olds,** a Representative from Illinois; born in Bennington, Bennington County, Vt., December 25, 1812; was graduated from Williams College, Williamstown, Mass., in 1835; moved to Illinois; studied law; was admitted to the bar in 1840 and began practice in Joliet, Ill.; member of the State constitutional convention in 1847; member of the State house of representatives in 1851 and 1852; elected as a Whig to the Thirty-third Congress and reelected as a Republican to the Thirty-fourth Congress (March 4, 1853-March 3, 1857); was not a candidate for renomination in 1856; judge of the eleventh judicial district of Illinois 1857-1862; elected to the Thirty-eighth Congress (March 4, 1863-March 3, 1865); was not a candidate for renomination in 1864; delegate to the Union National Convention at Philadelphia in 1866; resumed the practice of his profession; died in Chicago, Ill., August 3, 1875; interment in Oakwood Cemetery, Joliet, Ill.

**NORTON, John Nathaniel,** a Representative from Nebraska; born on a farm near Stromsburg, Polk County, Nebr., May 12, 1878; attended the public schools and Bryant Normal University, Stromsburg, Nebr.; was graduated from Nebraska Wesleyan University, Lincoln, in 1901, and from the University of Nebraska, Lincoln, in 1903; served as clerk and recorder of Polk County, 1906-1909; mayor of Osceola, Nebr., 1908-1909; moved to a farm near Polk, Nebr., and engaged in agricultural pursuits from 1910 until 1922; member of the Nebraska house of representatives, 1911-1918; member of the State constitutional convention in 1919 and 1920; unsuccessful Democratic candidate in 1924 for election for Governor of Nebraska; engaged as a Chautauqua and Lyceum lecturer, 1922-1927; elected as a Democrat to the Seventieth Congress (March 4, 1927-March 3, 1929); unsuccessful candidate for reelection in 1928 to the Seventy-first Congress; elected to the Seventy-second Congress (March 4, 1931-March 3, 1933); unsuccessful candidate for renomination in 1932 to the Seventy-third Congress; representative and adviser to the Agricultural Adjustment Administration from June 1933 to December 1936; member, Nebraska Legislature, 1937-1938; special adviser to the Federal Crop Insurance Corporation, Washington, D.C., 1939-1948; died in Washington, D.C., on October 5, 1960; interment in Swede Plain Cemetery, Polk County, Nebr.

**NORTON, Mary Teresa,** a Representative from New Jersey; born in Jersey City, N.J., March 7, 1875; attended parochial schools and the Jersey City High School; was graduated from Packard Business College, New York City, in 1896; president of the Queen's Daughters' Day Nursery Association of Jersey City, 1916-1927; appointed to represent Hudson County on the State Democratic committee in 1920; elected a member of that committee in 1921 and served as vice chairman, 1921-1931, and as chairman, 1932-1935; also served as vice chairman of the Hudson County Democratic Committee; elected county freeholder in 1922; delegate at large to the Democratic National Conventions of 1924, 1928, 1932, 1936, 1940, 1944, and 1948; delegate to International Labor Conference at Paris in 1945; elected as a Democrat to the Sixty-ninth and to the twelve succeeding Congresses (March 4, 1925-January 3, 1951); chairwoman, Committee on District of Columbia (Seventy-second through Seventy-fifth Congresses), Committee on Labor (Seventy-fifth through Seventy-ninth Congresses), Committee on Memorials (Seventy-seventh Congress), Committee on House Administration (Eighty-first Congress); was not a candidate for renomination in 1950 to the Eighty-second Congress; consultant, Women's Advisory Committee on Defense Manpower, Department of Labor, 1951-1952; died in Greenwich, Conn., August 2, 1959; interment in Holy Name Cemetery, Jersey City, N.J.

Bibliography: *DAB*; Mitchell, Gary. "Women Standing for Women: The Early Political Career of Mary T. Norton." *New Jersey History* 96 (Spring-Summer 1978): 27-42.

**NORTON, Miner Gibbs,** a Representative from Ohio; born in Andover, Ashtabula County, Ohio, May 11, 1857; attended the public schools, the National Normal University, Lebanon, Ohio, and Baldwin-Wallace College, Berea, Ohio; was graduated from Mount Union College, Alliance, Ohio, in 1878 and from the law department of Yale College in 1880; was admitted to the bar in the latter year and commenced practice in Cleveland, Ohio; director of law of Cleveland, Ohio 1895-1899; chairman of the Republican State executive committee in the early nineties; United States appraiser for the northern district of Ohio 1905-1909; elected as a Republican to the Sixty-seventh Congress (March 4, 1921-March 3, 1923); unsuccessful candidate for reelection in 1922 to the Sixty-eighth Congress; resumed the practice of law in Cleveland; appointed by President Coolidge collector of customs at Cleveland on February 7, 1925, and served until his death in Cleveland, Ohio, September 7, 1926; interment in Oakdale Cemetery, Jefferson, Ashtabula County, Ohio.

**NORTON, Nelson Ira,** a Representative from New York; born near Salamanca, in Great Valley, Cattaraugus County, N.Y., March 30, 1820; received a limited education; engaged in agricultural pursuits; county supervisor of Cattaraugus County 1860 and 1865-1867; justice of the peace 1852-1870; member of the State assembly in 1861 and 1862; elected as a Republican to the Forty-fourth Congress to fill the vacancy caused by the death of Augustus F. Allen and served from December 6, 1875, to March 3, 1877; resumed agricultural pursuits; died in Hinsdale, Cattaraugus County, N.Y., October 28, 1887; interment in Maplehurst Cemetery.

**NORTON, Patrick Daniel,** a Representative from North Dakota; born in Ishpeming, Marquette County, Mich., May 17, 1876; moved with his parents to Ramsey County, Dak., in 1883; attended the public schools; was graduated from the University of North Dakota at Grand Forks in 1897; studied law at the University of North Dakota; was admitted to the bar in 1903 and commenced practice at Devils Lake, N.Dak.; superintendent of the schools of Ramsey County 1905-1907; chief clerk of the State house of representatives in 1907 and 1908; moved to Hettinger, Adams County, in 1907; prosecuting attorney of Adams County 1907-1911; secretary of state of North Dakota 1911-1913; elected as a Republican to the Sixty-third, Sixty-fourth, and Sixty-fifth Congresses (March 4, 1913-March 3, 1919); unsuccessful candidate for renomination in 1918; moved to Mandan, N.Dak., in 1919 and engaged in farming, livestock raising, banking, and the practice of law; national bank receiver at Brookings, S.Dak., 1924-1927; moved to Minot, N.Dak., in 1927; delegate to the Republican National Convention in 1928; delegate to Republican State conventions 1920-1940; died in Minot, N.Dak., October 14, 1953; interment in Rosehill Cemetery.

**NORTON, Richard Henry,** a Representative from Missouri; born in Troy, Lincoln County, Mo., November 6, 1849; attended the common schools and the St. Louis (Mo.) University, where he took a classical course; was graduated from the law department of Washington University, St. Louis, Mo., in 1870; was admitted to the bar and commenced practice in Troy, Mo.; elected as a Democrat to the Fifty-first and Fifty-second Congresses (March 4, 1889-March 3, 1893); unsuccessful candidate for reelection in 1892 to the Fifty-third Congress; resumed the practice of law and also engaged in agricultural pursuits; died in St. Louis, Mo., March 15, 1918; interment in City Cemetery, Troy, Mo.

**NORVELL, John,** a Senator from Michigan; born in Danville, Va. (now Kentucky), December 21, 1789; attended the common schools; learned the trade of printer; edited a paper in Hagerstown, Md.; studied law; was admitted to the bar in 1814 and commenced practice in Baltimore, Md.; enlisted as a private in the War of 1812; edited an Anti-Federalist paper in Philadelphia 1816-1832; moved to Michigan Territory; postmaster of Detroit 1831-1836; delegate to the State constitutional convention at Detroit in 1837; upon the admission of Michigan as a State into the Union was elected as a Democrat to the United States Senate and served from January 26, 1837, to March 3, 1841; was not a candidate for reelection; chairman, Committee on Engrossed Bills (Twenty-fifth Congress); resumed the practice of law in Detroit; member, State senate 1841; member, State house of representatives 1842; United States district attorney of Michigan 1846-1849; died in Detroit, Mich., April 24, 1850; interment in Elmwood Cemetery.

**NORWOOD, Charles Whitlow, Jr.,** a Representative from Georgia; born in Valdosta, Lowndes County, Ga., July 27, 1941; attended the public schools and graduated, Baylor Military High School, Chattanooga, Tenn., 1959; B.A., Georgia Southern University, 1964; D.D.S., Georgetown University, 1967; served in the United States Army as a captain with the 173rd Airborne Brigade in Vietnam, 1967-1969; practiced dentistry in Augusta, Ga., 1969-1993; co-owner, Northwood Tree Nursery and Park Avenue Fabrics;

elected as a Republican to the One Hundred Fourth Congress (January 3, 1995-January 3, 1997); is a resident of Augusta, Ga.

**NORWOOD, Thomas Manson,** a Senator and a Representative from Georgia; born in Talbot County, Ga., April 26, 1830; pursued an academic course; graduated from Emory College, Oxford, Ga., in 1850; studied law; was admitted to the bar in 1852 and commenced practice in Savannah, Ga.; member, Georgia State house of representatives, 1861-1862; presidential elector on the Democratic ticket in 1868; elected as a Democrat to the United States Senate, and served from November 14, 1871 to March 3, 1877; resumed the practice of law in Savannah, Ga.; elected as a Democrat to the Forty-ninth and Fiftieth Congresses (March 4, 1885-March 3, 1889); again resumed the practice of law; appointed judge of the city court of Savannah in 1896 and served twelve years; retired to his country home, "Hancock Hall," near Savannah, Ga., and died there on June 19, 1913, interment in Laurel Grove Cemetery, Savannah, Ga.

**Bibliography:** Bragg, William Harris. "The Junius of Georgia Redemption: Thomas M. Norwood and the 'Nemesis' Letters." *Georgia Historical Quarterly* 77 (Spring 1993): 86-122; Norwood, Thomas Manson. *A True Vindication of the South, in a Review of American History*. Savannah, Ga.: Braid and Hutton, 1917.

**NOTT, Abraham,** a Representative from South Carolina; born in Saybrook, Middlesex County, Conn., February 5, 1768; educated in early life by a private teacher; was graduated from Yale College in 1787; moved in 1788 to McIntosh County, Ga., where he was employed as a private tutor for one year; moved to Camden, S.C., in 1789; studied law; was admitted to the bar in 1791 and commenced practice in Union, S.C.; member, South Carolina State house of representatives, 1796-1797; elected as a Federalist to the Sixth Congress (March 4, 1799-March 3, 1801); resumed the practice of his profession at Columbia, S.C., in 1804; elected a member of the board of trustees of South Carolina University in 1805; intendant (administrative official) of Columbia in 1807; president of the court of appeals in 1824; elected judge of the circuit court in 1810, and served until his death in Fairfield, S.C., on June 19, 1830; interment in the First Presbyterian Churchyard, Columbia, S.C.

**Bibliography:** *DAB*.

**NOURSE, Amos,** a Senator from Maine; born in Bolton, Worcester County, Mass., December 17, 1794; pursued a preparatory course and graduated from Harvard University in 1812; postmaster at Hallowell, Maine, 1822-1841; moved to Bath, Maine, in 1841; collector of customs at Bath 1845-1846; studied medicine and commenced practice in Bath; medical lecturer and professor of obstetrics at Bowdoin College, Brunswick, Maine, 1846-1854; elected to the United States Senate to fill the vacancy caused by the resignation of Hannibal Hamlin and served from January 16 to March 3, 1857; judge of probate of Sagadahoc County; died in Bath, Maine, April 7, 1877; interment in Hallowell Cemetery, Hallowell, Maine.

**NOWAK, Henry James,** a Representative from New York; born in Buffalo, Erie County, N.Y., February 21, 1935; attended public elementary schools in Buffalo; graduated from Riverside High School, Buffalo, 1953; B.A., Canisius College, Buffalo, 1957; J.D., University of Buffalo Law School, 1961; admitted to the New York bar in 1963 and commenced practice in Buffalo; served in the United States Army, 1957-1958, 1961-1962; served as assistant district attorney of Erie County, N.Y., 1964; served as Erie County comptroller, 1964-1974; delegate, New York State Democratic convention, 1970; delegate to the Democratic National Convention of 1972; elected as a Democrat to the Ninety-fourth and to the eight succeeding Congresses (January 3, 1975-January 3, 1993); was not a candidate for reelection in 1992 to the One Hundred Third Congress; is a resident of Buffalo, N.Y.

**NOYES, John,** a Representative from Vermont; born in Atkinson, Rockingham County, N.H., April 2, 1764; attended private schools and was graduated from Dartmouth College, Hanover, N.H., in 1795; tutor at Chesterfield (N.H.) Academy 1795-1797 and at Dartmouth College 1797-1799, having among his pupils Daniel Webster at the latter institution; studied theology; moved to Brattleboro, Vt., in 1800 and engaged in mercantile pursuits; member of the State house of representatives 1808-1810 and in 1812; moved to Dummesston in 1812 and resumed his mercantile pursuits; held several local offices in Vermont; elected as a Federalist to the Fourteenth Congress (March 4, 1815-March 3, 1817); resumed mercantile pursuits until 1819, when he retired on a farm near Putney, where he died October 26, 1841; interment in Maple Grove Cemetery, Putney, Vt.

**NOYES, Joseph Cobham,** a Representative from Maine; born in Portland, Maine, September 22, 1798; attended the common schools; moved to Eastport, Maine, in 1819; ship chandler and shipper of merchandise in Eastport; member of the State house of representatives in 1833; elected as a Whig to the Twenty-fifth Congress (March 4, 1837-March 3, 1839); unsuccessful candidate for reelection in 1838 to the Twenty-sixth Congress; collector of customs for the district of Passamaquoddy, Maine, 1841-1843; moved to Portland and engaged in the flour and commission business; treasurer of the Portland Co. (locomotive works) in 1859; one of the founders of the Portland Savings Bank in 1852 and served as treasurer from 1859 until his death in Portland, Cumberland County, Maine, July 28, 1868; interment in Evergreen Cemetery.

**NUCKOLLS, Stephen Friel,** a Delegate from the Territory of Wyoming; born in Grayson County, Va., August 16, 1825; completed preparatory studies; moved to Linden, Atchison County, Mo., in 1846; engaged in mercantile pursuits 1847-1853; moved to the Territory of Nebraska in 1854 and founded Nebraska City; held several local offices; established the Platte Valley Bank in 1855; served in the Nebraska Territorial legislature in 1859; moved to the Territory of Colorado in 1860 and engaged in banking and mining; moved to New York City in 1864; moved to the Territory of Dakota in 1867 and settled in Cheyenne; engaged in mercantile pursuits; upon the organization of the Territory of Wyoming was elected in 1869 as a Democrat to the Forty-first Congress and served from December 6, 1869, to March 3, 1871; was an unsuccessful candidate for reelection in 1870 to the Forty-second Congress; resumed his mercantile pursuits; served as a member of the second legislative council of Wyoming in 1871 and served as presiding officer; delegate to the Democratic National Conventions in 1872 and 1876; moved to Salt Lake City, Utah, in July 1872 and engaged in milling; died in Salt Lake City, February 14, 1879; interment in Mount Olivet Cemetery.

**NUCKOLLS, William Thompson,** a Representative from South Carolina; born near Hancockville, Union (now Cherokee) County, S.C., February 23, 1801; was graduated from South Carolina College (now the University of South Carolina) at Columbia in 1820; studied law; was admitted to the bar in 1823 and commenced practice in Spartanburg, S.C.; elected as a Jacksonian to the Twentieth, Twenty-first, and Twenty-second Congresses (March 4, 1827-March 3, 1833); died on his plantation near Hancockville, S.C., on September 27, 1855; interment in Whig Hill Cemetery.

**NUGEN, Robert Hunter,** a Representative from Ohio; born near Hallidays Cove, Washington County, Pa., on July 16, 1809; moved to Ohio in 1811 with his parents, who settled in Columbiana County; received a limited education; moved to Tuscarawas County in 1828; engaged in agricultural pursuits; contractor; held several local offices; delegate to the Democratic National Convention at Charleston in 1860; elected as a Democrat to the Thirty-seventh Congress (March 4, 1861-March 3, 1863); superintendent of the Ohio Canal until his death in Newcomerstown, Tuscarawas County, Ohio, February 28, 1872; interment in Newcomerstown Cemetery.

**NUGENT, John Frost,** a Senator from Idaho; born in La Grande, Union County, Oreg., June 28, 1868; attended the public schools; worked in the mines in Idaho and Australia; studied law; was admitted to the bar in 1898 and commenced practice in Silver City, Idaho; prosecuting attorney of Owyhee County, Idaho, from 1899 until 1906; appointed and subsequently elected as a Democrat to the United States Senate to fill the vacancy caused by the death of James H. Brady and served from January 22, 1918, until his resignation, effective January 14, 1921; unsuccessful candidate for reelection in 1920 to the United States Senate; chairman, Committee on Fisheries (Sixty-fifth Congress); appointed by President Woodrow Wilson a member of the Federal Trade Commission, 1921-1927; unsuccessful candidate for election in 1926 to the United States Senate; resumed the practice of law in Washington, D.C.; died in Silver Spring, Md., September 18, 1931; interment in Cedar Hill Cemetery, Washington, D.C.

Bibliography: *DAB*.

**NUNN, David Alexander,** a Representative from Tennessee; born near Brownsville, Haywood County, Tenn., July 26, 1833; attended private schools and the West Tennessee College at Jackson, Tenn.; studied law; graduated from Cumberland University, Lebanon, Tenn., in 1853; was admitted to the bar and commenced practice in Brownsville; presidential elector on the Constitutional Union ticket in 1860 and on the Republican ticket in 1864; member of the Tennessee State house of representatives, 1865-1867; elected as a Republican to the Fortieth Congress (March 4, 1867-March 3, 1869); unsuccessful Independent Republican candidate for reelection in 1868 to the Forty-first Congress; appointed by President Ulysses S. Grant as Minister Resident to Ecuador on April 21, 1869, and served until his resignation November 2, 1869; elected to the Forty-third Congress (March 4, 1873-March 3, 1875); unsuccessful candidate for reelection in 1874 to the Forty-fourth Congress; secretary of state of Tennessee, 1881-1885; appointed by President William McKinley as collector of internal revenue at Nashville, Tenn., July 20, 1897, and served until his resignation on January 17, 1902; retired to private life; died in Brownsville, Tenn., September 11, 1918; interment in Oakwood Cemetery.

**NUNN, Samuel Augustus** (grandnephew of Carl Vinson), a Senator from Georgia; born in Perry, Houston County, Ga., September 8, 1938; educated in the public schools of Perry; attended Georgia Institute of Technology, Atlanta, 1956-1959; A.B., Emory University, Atlanta, Ga., 1960, LL.B., 1962; served in the United States Coast Guard, 1959-1960, and in the United States Coast Guard Reserve from 1960 until 1968; admitted to the Georgia bar in 1962 and commenced practice in Perry; farmer; legal counsel, Committee on Armed Services, United States House of Representatives, 1963; member of the Georgia State house of representatives, 1968-1972; elected as a Democrat to the United States Senate, November 7, 1972, to fill the vacancy caused by the death of Richard B. Russell for the term ending January 3, 1973, and at the same time elected for the six-year term ending January 3, 1979; reelected in 1978, 1984, and again in 1990, and served from November 8, 1972 to January 3, 1997; was not a candidate for reelection in 1996; chairman, Committee on Armed Services (One Hundredth through One Hundred Third Congresses); is a resident of Perry, Ga.

Bibliography: Hammond, Ernest Lee. "Legislative Oversight and National Security: A Comparison of Senators Sam Nunn and Richard B. Russell." Ph.D. dissertation, University of Georgia, 1994.

**NUSSLE, James,** a Representative from Iowa; born in Des Moines, Polk County, Iowa, June 27, 1960; graduated, Carl Sandburg High School, 1978; B.A., Luther College, 1983; J.D., Drake University, 1985; admitted to the Iowa bar, 1985; practicing attorney; Delaware County (Iowa) attorney, 1987-1990; campaign aide, Representative Thomas Tauke of Iowa, 1988; elected as a Republican to the One Hundred Second and to the two succeeding Congresses (January 3, 1991-January 3, 1997); is a resident of Manchester, Iowa.

**NUTE, Alonzo,** a Representative from New Hampshire; born in Milton, Strafford County, N.H., February 12, 1826; attended the common schools; moved to Natick, Mass., in 1842; returned to New Hampshire in 1848 and engaged in the manufacture of boots and shoes in Farmington; entered the Union Army in the spring of 1861 in the Sixth Regiment, New Hampshire Volunteer Infantry; member of the New Hampshire State house of representatives in 1866; served in the New Hampshire State senate in 1867 and 1868; delegate to the Republican National Convention of 1876; elected as a Republican to the Fifty-first Congress (March 4, 1889-March 3, 1891); was not a candidate for renomination in 1890 to the Fifty-second Congress; died in Farmington, Strafford County, N.H., December 24, 1892; interment in Pine Grove Cemetery.

**NUTTING, Newton Wright,** a Representative from New York; born in West Monroe, Oswego County, N.Y., October 22, 1840; pursued an academic course; studied law; was admitted to the bar and practiced in Oswego, N.Y.; member of the school committee of Oswego County from January 1, 1864, to January 1, 1867; district attorney of Oswego County from January 1, 1869, to January 1, 1872; county judge of Oswego County from January 1, 1878, until March 4, 1883, when he resigned; elected as a Republican to the Forty-eighth Congress (March 4, 1883-March 3, 1885); resumed the practice of law in Oswego; elected to the Fiftieth and Fifty-first Congresses and served from March 4, 1887, until his death in Oswego, N.Y., October 15, 1889; interment in Riverside Cemetery.

**NYE, Frank Mellen,** a Representative from Minnesota; born in Shirley, Piscataquis County, Maine, March 7, 1852; moved to Wisconsin with his parents, who settled on a farm near River Falls, Pierce County, in 1855; attended the common schools and the local academy in River Falls, Wis.; taught school for several years and then studied law; was admitted to the bar in 1878 and commenced practice in Hudson, Wis.; district attorney of Polk County, Wis., 1879-1884; member of the Wisconsin State house of representatives in 1884 and 1885; moved to Minnesota in 1886, settled in Minneapolis, and continued the practice of law; assistant prosecuting attorney of Hennepin County; prosecuting attorney, 1893-1897; elected as a Republican to the Sixtieth and to the two succeeding Congresses (March 4, 1907-March 3, 1913); declined to be a candidate for renomination in 1912 to the Sixty-third Congress; resumed the practice of his profession in Minneapolis, Minn.; elected in 1920 judge of the district court of Hennepin County for a six-year term; reelected in 1926 and served until his retirement in 1932; died in Minneapolis, Minn., November 29, 1935; interment in Greenwood Cemetery, River Falls, Wis.

**NYE, Gerald Prentice,** a Senator from North Dakota; born in Hortonville, Outagamie County, Wis., December 19, 1892; attended the public schools; engaged in newspaper work in Wisconsin and Iowa; moved to North Dakota in 1915; publisher of the Billings County Pioneer, and later editor and publisher of the Griggs County Sentinel-Courier; unsuccessful candidate for election in 1924 to the Sixty-ninth Congress; appointed and subsequently elected as a Republican to the United States Senate to fill the vacancy caused by the death of Edwin F. Ladd; reelected in 1926, 1932, and again in 1938 and served from November 14, 1925, to January 3, 1945; unsuccessful candidate for reelection in 1944; chairman, Committee on Public Lands and Surveys (Seventieth through Seventy-second Congresses), Special Committee on Investigation of the Munitions Industry (Seventy-third through Seventy-fifth Congresses); president of Records Engineering, Inc., Washington, D.C., 1937-1959; special assistant for elderly housing, Federal Housing Administration, 1960-1964; staff member, Senate Committee on Aging, 1964-1968; practiced law in Washington, D.C., from 1964 to 1971;

was a resident of Chevy Chase, Md., until his death in Washington, D.C., July 17, 1971; interment in Fort Lincoln Cemetery.

**Bibliography:** Cole, Wayne S. *Senator Gerald P. Nye and Foreign Relations*. 1962. Reprint. Westport, Conn.: Greenwood Press, 1980; Larsen, Lawrence H. "Gerald Nye and the Isolationist Argument." *North Dakota History* 47 (Winter 1980): 25-28.

**NYE, James Warren,** a Senator from Nevada; born in De Ruyter, Madison County, N.Y., June 10, 1815; attended the common schools and Homer Academy, Homer, N.Y.; studied law in Troy, N.Y.; was admitted to the bar and practiced in Madison County, N.Y.; district attorney, 1839; served as judge of Madison County, 1840-1848; unsuccessful Free-Soiler candidate for election in 1846 to the Thirtieth Congress; first president of the Metropolitan Board of Police, New York City, 1857-1860; appointed by President Abraham Lincoln on March 22, 1861 as Governor of the newly created Nevada Territory, and served until December 1864; upon the admission of Nevada as a State into the Union in 1864 was elected as a Republican to the United States Senate; reelected in 1867 and served from December 16, 1864, to March 3, 1873; unsuccessful candidate for reelection; chairman, Committee on Enrolled Bills (Thirty-ninth Congress), Committee on Revolutionary Claims (Fortieth Congress), Committee on Territories (Forty-first Congress); died in White Plains, Westchester County, N.Y., December 25, 1876; interment in Woodlawn Cemetery, New York City.

**Bibliography:** Green, Michael. "Diehard or Swing Man: Senator James W. Nye and Andrew Johnson's Impeachment and Trial." *Nevada Historical Society Quarterly* 29 (Fall 1986): 175-191; Samon, Jud Burton. "Sagebrush Falstaff: A Biographical Sketch of James Warren Nye." Ph.D. dissertation, University of Maryland, 1979.

**NYGAARD, Hjalmar Carl,** a Representative from North Dakota; born on a farm near Sharon, Steele County, N.Dak., March 24, 1906; attended the public schools of Sharon, Mayville State Teachers College, and the University of North Dakota; taught in the rural schools of Emmons and Steele Counties, 1932-1935; engaged in the grocery business, 1936-1944, at Sharon, N.Dak., and in the hardware business, 1944-1960 at Enderlin, N.Dak.; served as mayor of Sharon and as a member of the school board; member of the State house of representatives, 1949-1960, serving as majority leader in 1955 and 1957 and as speaker in 1959; elected as a Republican to the Eighty-seventh and Eighty-eighth Congresses and served from January 3, 1961, until his death July 18, 1963; member, National Monument Commission, 1961-1963; died in the United States Capitol, Washington, D.C., July 18, 1963; interment in City Cemetery, Enderlin, N.Dak.

# O

**OAKAR, Mary Rose,** a Representative from Ohio; born in Cleveland, Cuyahoga County, Ohio, March 5, 1940; attended the Catholic schools of Cleveland; graduated from Lourdes Academy, 1958; B.A., Ursuline College, Cleveland, 1962; M.A., John Carroll University, Cleveland, 1966; further study at Westham Adult College, Warwickshire, England, 1968; worked as sales clerk, Cleveland, 1956-1958; instructor, English, drama, and speech, 1963-1970; assistant professor, English, drama, and speech, Cuyahoga Community College, 1968-1975; member, Cleveland City Council, 1973-1976; Democratic State central committeewoman, 1973-1975; alternate delegate to the Democratic National Convention of 1976; elected as a Democrat to the Ninety-fifth and to the seven succeeding Congresses (January 3, 1977-January 3, 1993); unsuccessful candidate for reelection in 1992 to the One Hundred Third Congress; president, Mary Rose Oakar and Associates, Inc., a public relations and consulting firm; is a resident of Cleveland, Ohio.

**OAKEY, Peter Davis,** a Representative from Connecticut; born in East Millstone, Somerset County, N.J., February 25, 1861; attended the public schools and the high school of Millstone, N.J.; moved to Hartford, Conn., in 1886 and engaged in mercantile pursuits; member of the city council 1891-1894; city alderman in 1894 and 1895; collector of city taxes of Hartford in 1894 and 1895; member of the Connecticut National Guard 1895-1901; city assessor 1900-1915; elected as a Republican to the Sixty-fourth Congress (March 4, 1915-March 3, 1917); unsuccessful candidate for reelection in 1916 to the Sixty-fifth Congress; died in New Haven, Conn., November 18, 1920; interment in Cedar Hill Cemetery, Hartford, Conn.

**OAKLEY, Thomas Jackson,** a Representative from New York; born near Poughkeepsie, Dutchess County, N.Y., November 10, 1783; was graduated from Yale College in 1801; studied law; was admitted to the bar in 1804 and commenced practice in Poughkeepsie, N.Y.; surrogate of Dutchess County in 1810 and 1811; elected as a Federalist to the Thirteenth Congress (March 4, 1813-March 3, 1815); member of the State assembly in 1816 and 1818-1820; attorney general of New York in 1819; elected to the Twentieth Congress and served from March 4, 1827, until May 9, 1828, when he resigned to go on the bench; judge of the superior court of New York City 1828-1847; appointed chief justice in October 1847 and served until his death in New York City May 11, 1857; interment in Trinity Churchyard.

**Bibliography:** *DAB*.

**OAKMAN, Charles Gibb,** a Representative from Michigan; born in Detroit, Wayne County, Mich., September 4, 1903; attended the public schools and Wayne State University; graduated from the University of Michigan at Ann Arbor in 1926; engaged in the real estate and transportation business 1927-1940; member of the Wayne County Board of Supervisors 1941-1952; served as executive secretary to the mayor of Detroit in 1941 and 1942; city controller 1942-1945; served four terms as city councilman 1947-1952; secretary of the Detroit-Wayne Joint Building Authority 1948-1954 and general manager 1955-1973; elected as a Republican to the Eighty-third Congress (January 3, 1953-January 3, 1955); was an unsuccessful candidate for reelection in 1954 to the Eighty-fourth Congress; died in Dearborn, Mich., October 28, 1973; interment in Roseland Park Cemetery, Berkley, Mich.

**OATES, William Calvin,** a Representative from Alabama; born at Oates Cross Roads, near Troy, Pike County, Ala., November 30, 1835; pursued elementary studies at home and attended an academy at Lawrenceville, Ala.; studied law; was admitted to the bar in 1858 and practiced in Abbeville, Ala., from 1859 to 1861; during the Civil War entered the Confederate Army as captain of Company G, Fifteenth Regiment, Alabama Infantry, in July 1861; appointed colonel in the Provisional Army of the Confederacy on May 1, 1863; resumed the practice of law in Abbeville in 1865; delegate to the Democratic National Convention of 1868; member, Alabama State house of representatives, 1870-1872; unsuccessful candidate for the nomination for Governor in 1872; member of the State constitutional convention in 1875; elected as a Democrat to the Forty-seventh and to the six succeeding Congresses, and served from March 4, 1881 until November 5, 1894, when he resigned, having been elected Governor; chairman, Committee on Revision of the Laws (Forty-eighth through Fiftieth Congresses), Committee on Expenditures in the Post Office Department (Fifty-second and Fifty-third Congresses); unsuccessful candidate for the United States Senate in 1897; elected Governor of Alabama in 1894, and served from December 1, 1894 to December 1, 1896; brigadier general of Volunteers in the Spanish-American War, and stationed at Camp Meade, Pa.; resumed the practice of law; died in Montgomery, Ala., September 9, 1910; interment in Oakwood Cemetery.

**Bibliography:** *DAB*.

**OBERSTAR, James Louis,** a Representative from Minnesota; born in Chisholm, St. Louis County, Minn., September 10, 1934; attended the public schools of Chisholm, Minn.; graduated, Chisholm High School, 1952; B.A., College of St. Thomas, St. Paul, Minn., 1956; M.A., College of Europe, Bruges, Belgium, 1957; served as administrative assistant to Representative John Anton Blatnik from 1963 until 1974; administrator, Committee on Public Works, United States House of Representatives, 1971-1974; elected as a Democrat to the Ninety-fourth and to the ten succeeding Congresses (January 3, 1975-January 3, 1997); is a resident of Chisholm, Minn.

**OBEY, David Ross,** a Representative from Wisconsin; born in Okmulgee, Okla., October 3, 1938; graduated from Wausau (Wis.) High School, 1956; B.A., University of Wisconsin, 1960, and M.A., 1962; member, Wisconsin State assembly, 1962-1969, serving as assistant minority leader, 1967-1969; licensed real estate broker; elected as a Democrat to the Ninety-first Congress, April 1, 1969, by special election to fill the vacancy caused by the resignation of Melvin R. Laird; reelected to the thirteen succeeding Congresses, and served from April 1, 1969 to January 3, 1997; chairman, Joint Economic Committee (Ninety-ninth Congress), Committee on Appropriations (One Hundred Third Congress); is a resident of Wausau, Wis.

**O'BRIEN, Charles Francis Xavier,** a Representative from New Jersey; born in Jersey City, N.J., March 7, 1879; attended the public schools, St. Aloysius Academy, and St. Peter's College, Jersey City, N.J.; was graduated from Fordham University, New York City; studied law at the New York Law School; was admitted to the bar and commenced practice in Jersey City, N.J.; judge of the second criminal court; director of public safety of Jersey City 1917-1921; delegate to the Democratic National Convention in 1920; elected as a Democrat to the Sixty-seventh and Sixty-eighth Congresses (March 4, 1921-March 3, 1925); voluntarily retired to accept the position of registrar of records of Hudson County, N.J., 1926-1936; was serving in the city law department at the time of his death in Jersey City, N.J., November 14, 1940; interment in Holy Name Cemetery.

**O'BRIEN, George Donoghue,** a Representative from Michigan; born in Detroit, Mich., January 1, 1900; attended the public and parochial schools; was graduated from the University of Detroit, Detroit, Mich., in 1921, and from the law school of the same university in 1924; was admitted to the bar in 1924 and commenced practice in Detroit, Mich.; during the First World War served as a private and was assigned to the Students' Training Corps; elected as a Democrat to the Seventy-fifth Congress (January 3, 1937-January 3, 1939); unsuccessful candidate for reelection in 1938 to the Seventy-sixth Congress; elected to the Seventy-seventh and to the two succeeding Congresses (January 3, 1941-January 3, 1947); chairman, Committee on the Post Office and Post Roads (Seventy-ninth Congress); unsuccessful candidate for reelection in 1946 to the Eightieth Congress; delegate to the Democratic National Convention of 1944; elected to the Eighty-first and to the two succeeding Congresses (January 3, 1949-January 3, 1955); unsuccessful candidate for renomination in 1954 to the Eighty-fourth Congress; assistant corporation counsel of the District of Columbia, assigned to the Civil Proceedings Division, from July 11, 1955 until his death in Washington, D.C., October 25, 1957; interment in Mount Olivet Cemetery, Detroit, Mich.

**O'BRIEN, George Miller,** a Representative from Illinois; born in Chicago, Ill., June 17, 1917; attended St. Ignatius Grammar School and Loyola Academy, Chicago, Ill.; A.B., Northwestern University, Evanston, Ill., 1939; J.D., Yale Law School, 1947; served with the Eighth and Twelfth Air Force, 1941-1945, attained the rank of lieutenant colonel; admitted to the Illinois bar in 1947 and commenced practice in Chicago; member, Will County Board of Supervisors, 1956-1964; Legislative Advisory Committee to Northeastern Illinois Planning Commission, 1970-1971; member, State house of representatives, 1970-1971; elected as a Republican to the Ninety-third and to the six succeeding Congresses and served from January 3, 1973, until his death; was a resident of Joliet, Ill., until his death in Bethesda, Md., July 17, 1986; interment in Resurrection Cemetery, Lockport, Ill.

**O'BRIEN, James,** a Representative from New York; born in County Kings, Ireland, March 13, 1841; attended the common schools; immigrated to the United States in 1861 and settled in New York City; alderman of the city of New York in 1864 and 1866; sheriff of the city and county of New York in 1867; served in the State senate in 1872 and 1873; unsuccessful candidate for mayor of the city of New York in 1873; unsuccessful candidate for election in 1874 to the Forty-fourth Congress; elected as an Independent Democrat to the Forty-sixth Congress (March 4, 1879-March 3, 1881); unsuccessful candidate for renomination in 1880; engaged as a broker until his death in New York City March 5, 1907; interment in Calvary Cemetery, Long Island, N.Y.

**O'BRIEN, James Henry,** a Representative from New York; born in Jamaica, Long Island, N.Y., July 15, 1860; attended the public schools and was graduated from Browne's Business College, Brooklyn, N.Y.; commenced work as a machinist and became an engineer; established a scale and overhead tramway business in New York City; member of the State senate in 1911 and 1912; delegate to the Democratic National Conventions in 1908, 1912, and 1916; elected as a Democrat to the Sixty-third Congress (March 4, 1913-March 3, 1915); unsuccessful candidate for reelection in 1914 to the Sixty-fourth Congress; resumed his former manufacturing pursuits; died in Brooklyn, N.Y., September 2, 1924; interment in Holy Cross Cemetery.

**O'BRIEN, Jeremiah,** a Representative from Maine; born in Machias, Washington County, Maine, on January 21, 1778; attended the common schools; engaged in lumber manufacturing and in shipping; member of the State senate 1821-1824; elected to the Eighteenth, Nineteenth, and Twentieth Congresses (March 4, 1823-March 3, 1829); chairman, Committee on Expenditures in the Department of the Navy (Nineteenth Congress); unsuccessful candidate for reelection in 1828 to the Twenty-first Congress; member of the State house of representatives 1832-1834; resumed his former lumber manufacturing and shipping business; died in Boston, Mass., May 30, 1858; interment in O'Brien Cemetery, Machias, Maine.

**O'BRIEN, Joseph John,** a Representative from New York; born in Rochester, Monroe County, N.Y., October 9, 1897; attended the public schools, SS. Peter and Paul's Catholic School, and the Cathedral High School, Rochester, N.Y., St. Jerome's College, Berlin (now Kitchener), Ontario, and McGill University, Montreal, Canada; during the First World War served as a master at arms in the United States Navy 1917-1919; chief construction inspector, New York Central Railroad, 1919-1938; professional football player 1919-1925; professional heavyweight wrestler 1919-1926; treasurer of East Rochester, N.Y., 1932-1935, and assessor 1935-1938; elected as a Republican to the Seventy-sixth, Seventy-seventh, and Seventy-eighth Congresses (January 3, 1939-January 3, 1945); unsuccessful candidate for reelection in 1944 to the Seventy-ninth Congress; district administrator for New York State Compensation Board from June 1, 1945, until his death; was also executive vice president of the General Sheet Signal Co., of Rochester, N.Y.; died in Rochester, N.Y., January 23, 1953; interment in Holy Sepulchre Cemetery.

**O'BRIEN, Leo William,** a Representative from New York; born in Buffalo, Erie County, N.Y., September 21, 1900; graduated from the Niagara (N.Y.) University in 1922; engaged in the newspaper field 1922-1952 as a reporter and also as radio and television commentator; member of the Albany Port District Commission 1935-1952; elected as a Democrat to the Eighty-second Congress to fill the vacancy caused by the death of William T. Byrne; reelected to the Eighty-third and to the six succeeding Congresses and served from April 1, 1952, to January 3, 1967; was not a candidate for reelection in 1966 to the Ninetieth Congress; chairman, Albany County Planning Board and Adirondack Study Commission; resided in Albany, N.Y., until his death there on May 4, 1982; interment at St. Agnes Cemetery, Albany, N.Y.

**O'BRIEN, Thomas Joseph,** a Representative from Illinois; born in Chicago, Ill., April 30, 1878; attended the grade and high schools and took advance courses in business law and accounting; engaged as a public accountant in 1918; member of the State house of representatives 1907-1910 and 1929-1932; served as State bank examiner 1913-1924; elected as a Democrat to the Seventy-third, Seventy-fourth, and Seventy-fifth Congresses (March 4, 1933-January 3, 1939); did not seek renomination in 1938, having become a candidate for sheriff of Cook County, Ill.; sheriff of Cook County, Ill., 1939-1942; elected to the Seventy-eighth and to the ten succeeding Congresses and served from January 3, 1943, until his death in Bethesda, Md., April 14, 1964; interment in the Queen of Heaven Cemetery, Hillside, Ill.

**O'BRIEN, William James,** a Representative from Maryland; born in Baltimore, Md., May 28, 1836; attended the common schools and pursued classical studies in the old St. Mary's College, Baltimore; studied law; was admitted to the bar in 1858 and commenced practice in Baltimore; elected as a Democrat to the Forty-third and Forty-fourth Congresses (March 4, 1873-March 3, 1877); was not a candidate for renomination in 1876; resumed the practice of law in Baltimore; appointed in 1901 and elected in 1903 judge of the orphans' court of Baltimore and served in that capacity until his death in Baltimore, Md., November 13, 1905; interment in Bonnie Brae Cemetery.

**O'BRIEN, William Smith,** a Representative from West Virginia; born in Audra, near Philippi, Barbour County, Va., (now West Virginia), January 8, 1862; attended the common schools, the Weston (W.Va.) Academy, and the University of West Virginia at Morgantown; worked on farms, in brick yards, and on public works; also taught school and was engaged as an editor; was graduated from the law school of the West Virginia University at Morgantown in 1891; was admitted to the bar the same year and commenced practice in Buckhannon, Upshur County, W.Va., in 1892; served as a captain in the West Virginia National Guard in 1894 and 1895; served as judge of the twelfth judicial circuit of West Virginia 1913-1919; elected as a Democrat to the Seventieth Congress (March 4, 1927-March 3, 1929); unsuccessful candidate for reelection in 1928 to the Seventy-first Congress; resumed the practice of law; elected secretary of state of West Virginia in 1932, 1936, 1940, and again in 1944, in which capacity he served until his death in Buckhannon, W.Va., on August 10, 1948; interment in Heavner Cemetery.

**O'BRYEN, William,** a Delegate from Georgia; treasurer of Georgia in 1778; nominated for commissioner of the Continental Loan Office by Georgia delegation in 1785; elected as a Delegate to the Continental Congress in 1789, but did not attend.

**OCAMPO, Pablo,** a Resident Commissioner from the Philippine Islands; born in Manila, Philippine Islands, January 25, 1853; attended San Juan de Letran College, and was graduated from Santo Tomas University in 1882; studied law; was admitted to the bar in 1882 and practiced in Manila; prosecuting attorney of the district of Tondo in 1883 and 1884; secretary of the Royal Court of Manila under the Spanish regime, 1885-1887; relator of the supreme court of the Philippine Islands in 1887 and 1888; counsel to the Economic Association of the Philippines, 1888-1890; was a representative of the Provinces of Principe, Infanta, Lepanto, and Bontoc in the Filipino Government in Malolos, and was elected secretary of the Filipino Parliament; professor of law in the University of Malolos in 1898; editor of La Patria at Manila, in 1899 and 1900; editor of the Faro Juridico y Consultor de los Jueces de Paz, the first law publication on the Philippine Islands, in 1907 and 1908; appointed by the Government of the Filipino Republic as its representative in Manila; elected as a Resident Commissioner to the United States and served from November 22, 1907, to November 22, 1909; one of the delegates of the American Congress to the Interparliamentary Congress of Nations held in the Reichstag at Berlin, Germany, in 1908; representative from Manila in the Second Philippine Legislature; member of the first independence mission to the United States; adviser and counsel to General Emilio Aguinaldo from the time of his connection with the revolutionary government until 1925; died in Manila, Philippine Islands, February 5, 1925; interment in La Loma Catholic Cemetery.

**OCHILTREE, Thomas Peck,** a Representative from Texas; born in Nacogdoches, Nacogdoches County, Tex., October 26, 1837; attended the public schools; volunteered in 1854 as a private in Captain John G. Walker's company of Texas Rangers in the campaign against the Apache and Comanche Indians in 1854 and 1855; admitted to the bar by special act of the Texas Legislature in 1857; clerk of the Texas State house of representatives, 1856-1859; secretary of the State Democratic convention in 1859; editor of the Jeffersonian in 1860 and 1861; delegate to the Democratic National Conventions at Charleston, S.C., and Baltimore, Md., in 1860; during the Civil War enlisted in the Confederate Army in the First Texas Regiment and was promoted successively to lieutenant, captain, and major; editor of the Houston Daily Telegraph 1866 and 1867; appointed commissioner of immigration for Texas in Europe, 1870-1873; appointed United States marshal for the eastern district of Texas by President Ulysses S. Grant on January 8, 1874; elected as an Independent to the Forty-eighth Congress (March 4, 1883-March 3, 1885); moved to New York City and retired; died at Hot Springs, Bath County, Va., November 25, 1902; interment in Greenwood Cemetery, Brooklyn, N.Y.; reinterment in Mount Hope Cemetery, Westchester County, N.Y., November 8, 1903.

**Bibliography:** Hall, Claude H. "The Fabulous Tom Ochiltree: Promoter, Politician, and Raconteur." *Southwestern Historical Quarterly* 71 (January 1968): 347-376.

**O'CONNELL, David Joseph,** a Representative from New York; born in New York City December 25, 1868; attended the public schools; employed in the publishing business in New York City, later becoming sales manager for Funk & Wagnalls; an organizer and first secretary of the Twenty-eighth Ward Board of Trade and the Allied Board of Trade, Brooklyn, N.Y.; president of the Booksellers' League of New York; delegate to the Democratic National Convention in 1920; elected as a Democrat to the Sixty-sixth Congress (March 4, 1919-March 3, 1921); unsuccessful candidate for reelection in 1920 to the Sixty-seventh Congress; elected to the Sixty-eighth and to the three succeeding Congresses and served from March 4, 1923, until his death; had been reelected in 1930 to the Seventy-second Congress; died in New York City, December 29, 1930; interment in St. John's Cemetery, Middle Village, Brooklyn, N.Y.

**O'CONNELL, Jeremiah Edward,** a Representative from Rhode Island; born in Wakefield, Middlesex County, Mass., July 8, 1883; attended the public schools; was graduated from Boston University in 1906 and from the law school of the same university in 1908; was admitted to the bar in 1907 and commenced practice in

Boston, Mass.; moved to Providence, R.I., in 1908 and continued the practice of law; member of the city council 1913-1919; member of the board of aldermen 1919-1921; elected as a Democrat to the Sixty-eighth and Sixty-ninth Congresses (March 4, 1923-March 3, 1927); unsuccessful candidate for reelection in 1926 to the Seventieth Congress; elected to the Seventy-first Congress and served from March 4, 1929, until his resignation on May 9, 1930, having been appointed an associate justice of the Rhode Island Superior Court, serving until January 10, 1935, when he was appointed presiding justice and served until his resignation in 1948; elected as an associate justice of the Rhode Island Supreme Court and served until his resignation on January 18, 1956; was a resident of Cranston, R.I., until his death September 18, 1964; interment in St. Francis Cemetery, Pawtucket, R.I.

**O'CONNELL, Jerry Joseph,** a Representative from Montana; born in Butte, Silver Bow County, Mont., June 14, 1909; attended the parochial schools and Butte Central High School; was graduated from Carroll College (formerly Mount St. Charles College), Helena, Mont., in 1931, and from Georgetown University, Washington, D.C., in 1934; studied law and was admitted to the bar in 1934; served in the Montana State house of representatives, 1931-1934; member of the Montana Public Service Commission, 1934-1936; delegate to Democratic State conventions, 1930-1940; elected as a Democrat to the Seventy-fifth Congress (January 3, 1937-January 3, 1939); unsuccessful candidate for reelection in 1938 to the Seventy-sixth Congress, and for election in 1940 to the Seventy-seventh Congress; newspaper editor and publisher in Hamilton, Mont., 1939-1941; commenced the practice of law in Butte, Mont., in 1940; delegate to the Democratic National Convention of 1944; moved to Seattle, Wash., in June 1944; executive secretary of the Washington State Democratic Central Committee from December 1944 to January 1947, for the Roosevelt Democrats in 1947, and for the Washington State Progressive Party in 1948 and 1949; returned to Montana in 1950, and practiced law in Great Falls until his death there on January 16, 1956; interment in Great Falls Mausoleum.

**Bibliography:** Ruetten, Richard T. "Showdown in Montana, 1938: Burton Wheeler's Role in the Defeat of Jerry O'Connell." *Pacific Northwest Quarterly* 54 (January 1963): 19-29.

**O'CONNELL, John Matthew,** a Representative from Rhode Island; born in Westerly, Washington County, R.I., August 10, 1872; attended the public schools; taught in the local schools 1892-1902; was graduated from the Philadelphia (Pa.) Dental College (now a branch of Temple University) in 1905 and commenced practice in Westerly, R.I., the same year; during the First World War served for sixteen months with Headquarters Sanitary Train, Twelfth Division, and later as major in the United States Dental Reserve; member of the State house of representatives 1929-1932; elected as a Democrat to the Seventy-third, Seventy-fourth, and Seventy-fifth Congresses (March 4, 1933-January 3, 1939); was not a candidate for renomination in 1938; died in Westerly, R.I., December 6, 1941; interment in St. Sebastian Cemetery.

**O'CONNELL, Joseph Francis,** a Representative from Massachusetts; born in Boston, Mass., December 7, 1872; attended the Mather School of Boston and prepared for college at St. Mary's Parochial School; was graduated from Boston College in 1893 and from the law department of Harvard University in 1896; was admitted to the Suffolk bar in 1897 and commenced practice in Boston; elected as a Democrat to the Sixtieth and Sixty-first Congresses (March 4, 1907-March 3, 1911); unsuccessful candidate for renomination in 1910 to the Sixty-second Congress; resumed the practice of law in Boston, Mass.; delegate to the Democratic National Conventions of 1912 and 1920; member of the Massachusetts constitutional convention, 1918-1920; appointed a member of the National Conference on Uniform State Laws by Governor David I. Walsh on September 2, 1914, and was reappointed by each

succeeding Governor until his death; member of the commission to revise the charter of the city of Boston in 1923; professor of law and vice president of the board of trustees of Suffolk Law School, Boston, Mass.; unsuccessful candidate for nomination to the United States Senate in 1930, and for mayor of Boston in 1933; died in Boston, Mass., December 10, 1942; interment in St. Joseph's Cemetery, West Roxbury, Mass.

**O'CONNOR, Charles,** a Representative from Oklahoma; born on a farm near Edina, Knox County, Mo., October 26, 1878; attended the rural schools; was graduated from the State Teachers' College, Greeley, Colo., in 1901 and from the law department of the University of Colorado at Boulder in 1904; was admitted to the bar the same year and commenced practice in Boulder, Colo.; served as first assistant attorney general of Colorado, 1911-1913; city attorney of Boulder, 1917-1918; moved to Tulsa, Okla., in 1919 and continued the practice of his profession; elected as a Republican to the Seventy-first Congress (March 4, 1929-March 3, 1931); unsuccessful candidate for reelection in 1930 to the Seventy-second Congress; resumed the practice of law in Tulsa, Okla.; moved to Boulder, Colo., in 1936 on account of failing health, and died in Denver, Colo., November 15, 1940; interment in Green Mountain Cemetery, Boulder, Colo.

**O'CONNOR, James,** a Representative from Louisiana; born in New Orleans, La., April 4, 1870; attended the public schools and was graduated from the law department of Tulane University, New Orleans, La., in 1900; member of the State constitutional conventions in 1898 and 1913; served in the State house of representatives 1900-1912; assistant city attorney of Orleans Parish from 1918 until his resignation in 1919, having been elected to the United States House of Representatives; elected as a Democrat to the Sixty-sixth Congress to fill the vacancy caused by the death of Albert Estopinal; reelected to the Sixty-seventh and to the four succeeding Congresses and served from June 5, 1919, to March 3, 1931; unsuccessful candidate for renomination in 1930; resumed the practice of law; served on the State attorney general's staff in New Orleans; died in Covington, La., January 7, 1941; interment in Metairie Cemetery, New Orleans.

**O'CONNOR, James Francis,** a Representative from Montana; born on a farm near California Junction, Iowa, May 7, 1878; attended the grade schools and normal school in Iowa; was graduated from the law department of the University of Nebraska at Lincoln in 1904; was admitted to the bar and commenced practice in Livingston, Mont., in 1905; also engaged in stock raising, ranching, and banking; judge of the sixth judicial district of Montana in 1912; member of the State house of representatives 1917-1918 and served as speaker; special counsel for the Federal Trade Commission in Washington, D.C., in 1918; member of Park County High School Board for a number of years; elected as a Democrat to the Seventy-fifth and to the four succeeding Congresses and served from January 3, 1937, until his death in Washington, D.C., on January 15, 1945; chairman, Committee on Indian Affairs (Seventy-eighth Congress); interment in Mount Calvary Cemetery, Livingston, Mont.

**O'CONNOR, John Joseph,** a Representative from New York; born in Raynham, near Taunton, Bristol County, Mass., on November 23, 1885; attended the public schools; was graduated from Brown University, Providence, R.I., in 1908, and from the law department of Harvard University in 1911; was admitted to the Massachusetts bar in 1910; moved to New York City in 1911; was admitted to the New York bar in 1912 and commenced the practice of law; secretary to the Democratic members of the State constitutional convention in 1915; member of the New York State assembly, 1920-1923; legislative secretary for the Child Welfare Commission in 1921 and 1922; vice chairman of the legislative committee on the exploitation of immigrants in 1922 and 1923; member of the legislative committee on the revision of the corporation laws of New York in 1922 and 1923; delegate to all New York State and county conventions from 1919 to 1938; delegate at large to the Democratic National Convention of 1936; elected as a Democrat to the Sixty-eighth Congress to fill the vacancy caused by the death of W. Bourke Cockran; reelected to the Sixty-ninth and to the six succeeding Congresses and served from November 6, 1923, to January 3, 1939; chairman, Committee on Rules (Seventy-fourth and Seventy-fifth Congresses); unsuccessful candidate for the Democratic nomination in 1938, but received the Republican nomination and was unsuccessful for reelection to the Seventy-sixth Congress; engaged in the practice of law in New York City and Washington, D.C., until his death in Washington, D.C., January 26, 1960; interment in Gate of Heaven Cemetery, Silver Spring, Md.

**Bibliography:** Polenberg, Richard. "Franklin Roosevelt and the Purge of John O'Connor: The Impact of Urban Change on Political Parties." *New York History* 49 (July 1968): 306-26.

**O'CONNOR, Michael Patrick,** a Representative from South Carolina; born in Beaufort, Beaufort County, S.C., September 29, 1831; attended the public schools and was graduated from St. John's College, Fordham, N.Y., in 1850; studied law; was admitted to the bar in 1854 and commenced practice in Charleston, S.C.; member of the South Carolina State house of representatives, 1858-1866; served in the Civil War as a lieutenant in the Lafayette Artillery; delegate to the Democratic National Conventions of 1872 and 1876; unsuccessful candidate for election in 1874 to the Forty-fourth Congress, and in 1876 to the Forty-fifth Congress; elected as a Democrat to the Forty-sixth Congress (March 4, 1879-March 3, 1881); received credentials as a Member-elect to the Forty-seventh Congress, but died, pending a contest by Edmund W.M. Mackey (which subsequently resulted successfully for the contestant), in Charleston, S.C., April 26, 1881; interment in St. Lawrence Cemetery.

**O'CONOR, Herbert Romulus,** a Senator from Maryland; born in Baltimore, Md., November 17, 1896; attended the parochial schools; graduated from Loyola College, Baltimore, Md., in 1917 and from the law department of the University of Maryland in 1920; during the First World War served in the United States Naval Reserve; was admitted to the bar in 1919 and commenced practice in Baltimore, Md.; member of the staff of the Baltimore Sun and Evening Sun in 1920; assistant State's attorney, 1920-1922; appointed people's counsel to the Public Service Commission in 1923; State's attorney from 1923 until 1934; State attorney general, 1935-1939; elected Governor of Maryland in 1938, reelected in 1942, and served from January 11, 1939 until his resignation on January 3, 1947, having been elected to the United States Senate; chairman of the Governors Conference in 1942; chairman of Interstate Commission on Potomac River Basin, 1943-1945; president and national chairman of Council of State Governments in 1943; national chairman, Interstate Committee on Postwar Reconstruction and Development, 1943-1946; director of the Fidelity-Baltimore National Bank & Trust Co., and of Arundel Corp.; member, senior advisory council of McCormick & Co.; elected as a Democrat to the United States Senate in 1946 and served from January 3, 1947 to January 3, 1953; was not a candidate for renomination in 1952; chairman, Special Committee on Organized Crime in Interstate Commerce (Eighty-first Congress); continued the practice of law in Baltimore, Md., and Washington, D.C., until his death in Baltimore, Md., March 4, 1960; interment in New Cathedral Cemetery.

**Bibliography:** Kirwin, Harry. *The Inevitable Success: Herbert R. O'Conor.* Westminster, Md.: Newman Press, 1962.

**O'DANIEL, Wilbert Lee (Pappy),** a Senator from Texas; born in Malta, Morgan County, Ohio, March 11, 1890; reared on a cattle ranch near Arlington, Kans.; attended the public schools and business college in Hutchinson, Kans.; engaged in the flour milling and merchandising business in Fort Worth, Tex., from 1909 until

1938; radio personality; elected Governor of Texas in 1938, reelected in 1940, and served from January 17, 1939 until August 4, 1941, when he resigned, having been elected to the Senate; elected as a Democrat to the United States Senate to fill the vacancy caused by the death of Morris Sheppard; reelected in 1942, and served from August 4, 1941 until January 3, 1949; was not a candidate for renomination in 1948; unsuccessful candidate for the gubernatorial nomination in 1956; owned and operated several life insurance companies in Texas; died in Dallas, Tex., May 11, 1969; interment in Hillcrest Memorial Park.

**Bibliography:** Douglas, Claude. *The Life Story of W. Lee O'Daniel.* Dallas: Regional Press, 1938.

**O'DAY, Caroline Love Goodwin,** a Representative from New York; born in Perry, Houston County, Ga., June 22, 1875; attended private schools and was graduated from Lucy Cobb Institute, Athens, Ga.; studied art in Paris, Munich, and the Netherlands; served as president of Rye (N.Y.) School Board; vice chairman of New York Democratic State committee 1916-1920; associate chairman 1923-1942; delegate to the Democratic National Conventions in 1924, 1928, 1932, and 1936; commissioner, State board of social welfare, 1923-1934; elected as a Democrat to the Seventy-fourth and to the three succeeding Congresses (January 3, 1935-January 3, 1943); chairwoman, Committee on Election of President, Vice President, and Representatives (Seventy-fifth through Seventy-seventh Congresses); was not a candidate for renomination in 1942; died in Rye, N.Y., January 4, 1943; interment in Kensico Cemetery, Valhalla, N.Y.

**ODDIE, Tasker Lowndes,** a Senator from Nevada; born in Brooklyn, Kings County, N.Y., October 20, 1870; reared in East Orange, N.J.; attended the public schools; while engaged in business in New York attended night law school, and graduated from the law department of New York University in 1895; was admitted to the bar the same year, but did not engage in extensive practice; moved to Nevada in 1898 and settled in Austin; became interested in mining, agricultural pursuits, and in livestock raising; developed the principal gold and silver mining properties in the Tonopah and Goldfield districts; district attorney for Nye County, 1901-1902; member, Nevada State senate, 1903-1906; resumed his former business pursuits; elected Governor of Nevada in 1910, and served from January 2, 1911 to January 4, 1915; unsuccessful candidate in 1914 for reelection, and in 1918 for election as Governor; elected as a Republican to the United States Senate in 1920; reelected in 1926 and served from March 4, 1921, to March 3, 1933; chairman, Committee on Mines and Mining (Sixty-eighth through Seventy-first Congresses), Committee on Post Office and Post Roads (Seventy-second Congress); unsuccessful candidate for reelection in 1932; engaged in mining; died in San Francisco, Calif., February 17, 1950; interment in Lone Mountain Cemetery, Carson City, Nev.

**Bibliography:** Chan, Loren. *Sagebrush Statesman: Tasker L. Oddie of Nevada.* Reno: University of Nevada Press, 1973.

**ODELL, Benjamin Baker, Jr.,** a Representative from New York; born in Newburgh, Orange County, N.Y., January 14, 1854; attended the public schools, Newburgh Academy, Bethany (W.Va.) College, and Columbia College, New York City; entered upon a commercial career; for ten years represented the seventeenth district on the Republican State committee, and was chairman of the executive committee; elected as a Republican to the Fifty-fourth and Fifty-fifth Congresses (March 4, 1895-March 3, 1899); chairman, Committee on Accounts (Fifty-fifth Congress); president of the Orange County Traction Co. and the Central Hudson Steamboat Co.; elected Governor of New York in 1900, reelected in 1902, and served from January 1, 1901 to January 1, 1905; president of the chamber of commerce of Newburgh, N.Y.; died in Newburgh, N.Y., May 9, 1926; interment in Woodlawn Cemetery, New Windsor, Orange County, N.Y.

**Bibliography:** *DAB.*

**ODELL, Moses Fowler,** a Representative from New York; born in Tarrytown, Westchester County, N.Y., February 24, 1818; completed preparatory studies; appointed entry clerk in the New York customhouse in 1845 and became public appraiser; elected as a Democrat to the Thirty-seventh and Thirty-eighth Congresses (March 4, 1861-March 3, 1865); chairman, Committee on Expenditures in the Department of the Treasury (Thirty-seventh Congress); appointed Navy agent at the city of New York in 1865, and served until his death in Brooklyn, N.Y., June 13, 1866; interment in Greenwood Cemetery.

**ODELL, Nathaniel Holmes,** a Representative from New York; born in Greenburgh, near Tarrytown, Westchester County, N.Y., October 10, 1828; attended private schools; engaged in the steamboat business on the North River; served in the New York State assembly, 1857-1861; established the First National Bank at Tarrytown and served as cashier from 1862 to 1864; elected county treasurer of Westchester County in 1866; reelected in 1869 and again in 1872; elected as a Democrat to the Forty-fourth Congress (March 4, 1875-March 3, 1877); was not a candidate for renomination in 1876 to the Forty-fifth Congress; engaged in the real estate business; postmaster of Tarrytown, 1887-1892, and 1894-1898; died in Tarrytown, N.Y., October 30, 1904; interment in Sleepy Hollow Cemetery.

**O'DONNELL, James,** a Representative from Michigan; born in Norwalk, Fairfield County, Conn., March 25, 1840; moved to Michigan with his parents, who settled in Jackson in 1848; pursued preparatory studies and learned the printing trade; during the Civil War enlisted as a private in the First Regiment, Michigan Volunteer Infantry, and served two years; recorder of the city of Jackson, 1863-1866; established the Jackson Daily Citizen in 1865; mayor of Jackson in 1876 and 1877; appointed in 1878 aide-de-camp on the staff of Governor Charles M. Crosswell, with the rank of colonel; elected as a Republican to the Forty-ninth and to the three succeeding Congresses (March 4, 1885-March 3, 1893); chairman, Committee on Education (Fifty-first Congress); unsuccessful candidate for reelection in 1892 to the Fifty-third Congress; returned to Jackson, Mich., and devoted his time to the publication of the Jackson Daily Citizen; retired in 1910; father of the beet-sugar industry of Michigan; died in Jackson, Mich., March 17, 1915; interment in Mount Evergreen Cemetery.

**O'FERRALL, Charles Triplett,** a Representative from Virginia; born in Brucetown, Frederick County, Va., October 21, 1840; attended the common schools; appointed clerk pro tempore of the circuit court of Morgan County, Va., in 1855; elected clerk in 1857; enlisted in the Confederate Cavalry as a private in May 1861; passed through all the grades from sergeant to colonel, and at the close of the Civil War was in command of the Confederate Cavalry in the Shenandoah Valley; graduated from the law department of Washington College, Lexington, Va., in 1869; admitted to the bar and commenced practice in Harrisonburg, Va.; member of the Virginia house of delegates, 1871-1873; unsuccessful candidate for election in 1872 to the Forty-third Congress; judge of the county court of Rockingham County, 1874-1880; Virginia Democratic canvasser, 1880-1883; successfully contested as a Democrat the election of John Paul to the Forty-eighth Congress; reelected to the Forty-ninth and to the four succeeding Congresses, and served from May 5, 1884 until December 28, 1893, when he resigned, having been elected Governor; chairman, Committee on Mines and Mining (Fiftieth Congress), Committee on Elections (Fifty-second and Fifty-third Congresses); elected Governor of Virginia in 1893, and served from January 1, 1894 to January 1, 1898; resumed the practice of law and also engaged in writing reminiscences of the Civil War; died in Richmond, Va., September 22, 1905; interment in Hollywood Cemetery.

**Bibliography:** *DAB*; Wynes, Charles E. "Charles T. O'Ferrall and the Virginia Gubernatorial Election of 1893." *Virginia Magazine of History and Biography* 64 (October 1956): 437-453.

**OGDEN, Aaron,** a Senator from New Jersey; born in Elizabeth (formerly Elizabethtown), N.J., December 3, 1756; graduated from the College of New Jersey (now Princeton University) in 1773; tutor in Barber's Grammar School, 1773-1775; served in the Revolutionary Army as a lieutenant, captain, and brigade major; studied law; was admitted to the bar in 1784 and commenced practice in Elizabeth, N.J.; presidential elector in 1796; clerk of Essex County from 1785 until 1803; elected as a Federalist to the United States Senate to fill the vacancy caused by the resignation of James Schureman, and served from February 28, 1801 to March 3, 1803; unsuccessful candidate for reelection in 1802; elected trustee of the College of New Jersey in 1803 and served until his death; elected Governor of New Jersey by the Legislature, and served from October 29, 1812 to October 29, 1813; nominated by President James Madison as major general of the Army in 1813, but declined the appointment; became engaged in steamboat navigation in 1813; moved to Jersey City in 1829 and continued the practice of law; appointed collector of customs in 1830, and served until his death in Jersey City, N.J., April 19, 1839; interment in the First Presbyterian Church Burial Ground, Elizabeth, N.J.

**Bibliography:** *DAB*.

**OGDEN, Charles Franklin,** a Representative from Kentucky; born in Charlestown, Clark County, Ind.; attended the public schools and the Jeffersonville (Ind.) High School; graduated from the University of Louisville Law School in 1896; admitted to the bar and commenced practice in Louisville, Ky., in 1897; member of the Kentucky house of representatives in 1898 and 1899; served in the Spanish-American War as captain of Company H, Eighth Regiment, United States Volunteer Infantry; unsuccessful candidate for county attorney in 1901 and for Kentucky senator in 1902; elected as a Republican to the Sixty-sixth and Sixty-seventh Congresses (March 4, 1919-March 3, 1923); was not a candidate for renomination in 1922; resumed the practice of law in Louisville, Ky., where he died on April 10, 1933; interment in Resthaven Cemetery.

**OGDEN, David A.,** a Representative from New York; born in Morristown, Morris County, N.J., January 10, 1770; attended King's College (now Columbia University), New York City; studied law; was admitted to the bar in November 1791 and began practice in Newark, N.J.; became counselor at law in New Jersey in 1796; moved to Hamilton (now Waddington), St. Lawrence County, N.Y., and continued the practice of law; associate judge of the court of common pleas of St. Lawrence County, N.Y., 1811-1815; member of the State assembly in 1814 and 1815; elected as a Federalist to the Fifteenth Congress (March 4, 1817-March 3, 1819); unsuccessful candidate for reelection in 1818 to the Sixteenth Congress; first judge of the court of common pleas 1820-1824 and 1825-1829; one of the commissioners to settle the boundary between Canada and the United States; died in Montreal, Canada, June 9, 1829; interment in Brookside Cemetery, Waddington, St. Lawrence County, N.Y.

**OGDEN, Henry Warren,** a Representative from Louisiana; born in Abingdon, Washington County, Va., October 21, 1842; moved with his parents to Warrensburg, Mo., in 1851; attended the common schools; entered the Confederate Army and served throughout the Civil War; first lieutenant of Company D, Sixteenth Regiment, Missouri Infantry, and afterward on the staff of Brigadier General Levin M. Lewis, Second Brigade, Parsons' division, Missouri Infantry; paroled at Shreveport, La., on June 8, 1865; remained in Louisiana and engaged in agricultural pursuits; member of the State constitutional convention in 1879; served in the State house of representatives, 1880-1888, and was speaker of the house from 1884 to 1888; elected as a Democrat to the Fifty-third Congress to fill the vacancy caused by the resignation of Newton C. Blanchard; reelected to the Fifty-fourth and Fifty-fifth Congresses, and served from May 12, 1894 to March 3, 1899; resumed agricultural pursuits; died in Benton, Bossier Parish, La., on July 23, 1905; interment in Cottage Grove Cemetery.

**OGLE, Alexander** (father of Charles Ogle and grandfather of Andrew Jackson Ogle), a Representative from Pennsylvania; born in Frederick, Frederick County, Md., August 10, 1766; completed preparatory studies; moved to Somerset, Pa., in 1795; member of the Pennsylvania house of representatives in 1803, 1804, 1807, 1808, and 1811; served as major general in the Pennsylvania militia; prothonotary, recorder of deeds, and clerk of courts 1812-1817; elected as a Republican to the Fifteenth Congress (March 4, 1817-March 3, 1819); was not a candidate for renomination in 1818; again a member of the Pennsylvania house of representatives 1819-1823; served in the Pennsylvania senate in 1827 and 1828; died in Somerset, Pa., October 14, 1832; interment in Union Cemetery.

**OGLE, Andrew Jackson** (grandson of Alexander Ogle and nephew of Charles Ogle), a Representative from Pennsylvania; born in Somerset, Somerset County, Pa., March 25, 1822; completed preparatory studies; attended Jefferson College, Canonsburg, Pa.; studied law; was admitted to the bar in 1843 and commenced practice in Somerset, Pa.; prothonotary of Somerset County in 1845; elected as a Whig to the Thirty-first Congress (March 4, 1849-March 3, 1851); unsuccessful candidate for reelection in 1850 to the Thirty-second Congress; appointed United States Chargé d'Affaires to Denmark January 22, 1852, but did not assume his duties at that post; died in Somerset, Pa., October 14, 1852; interment in Union Cemetery.

**OGLE, Charles** (son of Alexander Ogle and uncle of Andrew Jackson Ogle), a Representative from Pennsylvania; born in Somerset, Somerset County, Pa., in 1798; completed preparatory studies; studied law; was admitted to the bar in 1822 and commenced practice in Somerset; elected as an Anti-Masonic candidate to the Twenty-fifth and Twenty-sixth Congresses; reelected as a Whig to the Twenty-seventh Congress and served from March 4, 1837, until his death in Somerset, Pa., May 10, 1841; chairman, Committee on Roads and Canals (Twenty-sixth Congress); interment in Union Cemetery.

**OGLESBY, Richard James** (cousin of Woodson Ratcliffe Oglesby), a Senator from Illinois; born in Floydsburg, Oldham County, Ky., July 25, 1824; orphaned and raised by an uncle in Decatur, Ill.; received a limited schooling; worked as a farmer, rope-maker, and carpenter; studied law; was admitted to the bar in 1845 and commenced practice in Sullivan, Ill.; during the Mexican War served as first lieutenant of Company C, Fourth Illinois Regiment; spent two years mining in California; returned to Decatur, Ill., and resumed the practice of law; unsuccessful candidate for election in 1858 to the Thirty-sixth Congress; elected to the Illinois State senate in 1860 and served during one session, when he resigned to enter the Union Army during the Civil War; served as colonel, brigadier general, and major general of the Eighth Regiment, Illinois Volunteer Infantry; elected Governor of Illinois in 1864, and served from January 16, 1865 to January 11, 1869; again elected Governor in 1872, and served from January 13, 1873 until his resignation on January 23, 1873, having been elected Senator; elected as a Republican to the United States Senate, and served from March 4, 1873 to March 3, 1879; declined to be a candidate for reelection; chairman, Committee on Public Lands (Forty-fourth and Forty-fifth Congresses); elected Governor of Illinois in 1884, and served from January 30, 1885 to January 14, 1889; retired to his farm, "Oglehurst," Elkhart, Ill., where he died on April 24, 1899; interment in Elkhart Cemetery.

**Bibliography:** *DAB*; Wilkie, Franc B. *A Sketch of Richard Oglesby*. Chicago: W.A. Shanholtzer, 1984.

**OGLESBY, Woodson Ratcliffe** (cousin of Richard James Oglesby), a Representative from New York; born near Shelbyville, Shelby County, Ky., February 9, 1867; attended the public schools, Kentucky Wesleyan College (then at Millersburg), and the Illinois Wesleyan University at Bloomington; studied law; was admitted to the bar in 1890 and commenced practice in New York City; served during the Spanish-American War as a private in Company C, Seventy-first Regiment, New York National Guard; member of the State assembly in 1906; delegate to the Democratic National Convention in 1912; elected as a Democrat to the Sixty-third and Sixty-fourth Congresses (March 4, 1913-March 3, 1917); unsuccessful candidate for reelection in 1916 to the Sixty-fifth Congress; resumed the practice of law in New York City until his retirement in 1928 and resided in Yonkers, N.Y., and Quincy, Fla.; died in Quincy, Fla., April 30, 1955; interment in Eastern Cemetery, Quitman, Ga.

**O'GORMAN, James Aloysius,** a Senator from New York; born in New York City on May 5, 1860; attended the public schools and the College of the City of New York; graduated from the law department of New York University in 1882; was admitted to the bar the same year and commenced practice in New York City; justice of the New York District Court 1893-1900; justice of the New York State Supreme Court 1900-1911, when he resigned, having been elected Senator; elected as a Democrat to the United States Senate and served from March 4, 1911, to March 3, 1917; was not a candidate for renomination in 1916; chairman, Committee on Interoceanic Canals (Sixty-third and Sixty-fourth Congresses); president of the New York County Lawyers' Association; trustee of New York University 1920-1927 and of the College of New Rochelle; resumed the practice of law in New York City; official referee of the New York Supreme Court from 1934 until his death in New York City May 17, 1943; interment in Calvary Cemetery, Long Island City, N.Y.

**O'GRADY, James Mary Early,** a Representative from New York; born in Rochester, N.Y., March 31, 1863; attended the public schools; was graduated from the University of Rochester, New York, in 1885; studied law; was admitted to the bar in 1885 and commenced practice in Rochester, N.Y.; member of the board of education of Rochester 1887-1892, serving as president in 1891 and 1892; member of the State assembly from 1893 to 1898, serving as speaker in 1897 and 1898; elected as a Republican to the Fifty-sixth Congress (March 4, 1899-March 3, 1901); was not a candidate for renomination in 1900; continued the practice of his profession in Rochester, N.Y., until his death in that city on November 3, 1928; interment in Holy Sepulchre Cemetery.

**O'HAIR, Frank Trimble,** a Representative from Illinois; born near Paris, Edgar County, Ill., March 12, 1870; attended the common schools and was graduated from the law department of De Pauw University, Greencastle, Ind., in 1893; was admitted to the bar the same year and commenced practice in Paris, Ill.; elected as a Democrat to the Sixty-third Congress (March 4, 1913-March 3, 1915); unsuccessful candidate for reelection in 1914 to the Sixty-fourth Congress; resumed the practice of his profession in Paris, Ill., until his death there August 3, 1932; interment in Edgar Cemetery.

**O'HARA, Barratt,** a Representative from Illinois; born in Saint Joseph, Berrien County, Mich., April 28, 1882; attended the public schools of Berrien Springs and Benton Harbor, Mich.; went to Nicaragua with his father and attended school at San Juan del Norte; at the age of fifteen years enlisted during the Spanish-American War and served as a corporal in Company I, Thirty-third Michigan Volunteer Infantry, at the siege of Santiago; after two years returned to Benton Harbor, Mich., and graduated from high school; reporter for the Benton Harbor Evening News in 1900; attended Missouri University, 1901-1902, and Northwestern University, 1909-1910; graduated from Chicago-Kent College of Law in

1912; sports editor of the St. Louis, Mo., Chronicle in 1902, and of the Chicago American 1903-1905; editor with the Chicago Chronicle in 1906, the Chicago Examiner, 1907-1910, and the Chicago Magazine and Sunday Telegram, 1910-1912; Lieutenant Governor of Illinois, 1913-1917; chairman of Illinois State senate vice and wage investigations, 1913-1915; was admitted to the bar in 1912 and commenced the practice of law in Chicago, Ill.; unsuccessful Democratic candidate for the United States Senate in 1915; during the First World War served as a major with the Eightieth and Twelfth Infantry Divisions and later as divisional judge advocate of the Fifteenth Division; president of the Arizona Film Company in 1916 and 1917; unsuccessful candidate for Governor in 1920, and for Congressman-at-large in 1936 to the Seventy-fifth Congress; radio commentator in Chicago, 1933-1935; elected as a Democrat to the Eighty-first Congress (January 3, 1949-January 3, 1951); unsuccessful candidate for reelection in 1950 to the Eighty-second Congress; elected to the Eighty-third and to the seven succeeding Congresses (January 3, 1953-January 3, 1969); unsuccessful candidate for renomination in 1968 to the Ninety-first Congress; died in Washington, D.C., August 11, 1969; interment in Oak Woods Cemetery, Chicago, Ill.

**O'HARA, James Edward,** a Representative from North Carolina; born in New York City, February 26, 1844; pursued an academic course; moved to North Carolina in 1862 and studied law; attended law classes at Howard University, Washington, D.C.; delegate to and engrossing clerk in the constitutional convention of North Carolina in 1868; member, North Carolina State house of representatives, 1868-1869; chairman of the board of commissioners for Halifax County, 1873-1876; was admitted to the North Carolina bar in June 1871 and commenced practice in Enfield, Halifax County; member of the State constitutional convention held at Raleigh in 1875; unsuccessful candidate for nomination in 1874 to the Forty-fourth Congress, and in 1880 to the Forty-seventh Congress; unsuccessfully contested the election of William H. Kitchin in 1878 to the Forty-sixth Congress; elected as a Republican to the Forty-eighth and Forty-ninth Congresses (March 4, 1883-March 3, 1887); unsuccessful candidate for reelection in 1886 to the Fiftieth Congress; resumed the practice of law in New Bern, Craven County, N.C., and died there on September 15, 1905; interment in Greenwood Cemetery.

**Bibliography:** Reid, George W. "Four in Black: North Carolina's Black Congressmen, 1874-1901." *Journal of Negro History* 64 (Summer 1979): 229-43.

**O'HARA, James Grant,** a Representative from Michigan; born in Washington, D.C., November 8, 1925; moved with his parents to Michigan in 1939; graduated from University of Detroit High School in 1943; during the Second World War served as an enlisted man in the United States Army with Company B, Five Hundred and Eleventh Parachute Infantry Regiment, Eleventh Airborne Division, seeing action in the Pacific Theater of Operations; A.B., University of Michigan, 1954; LL.B., University of Michigan School of Law, 1955; was admitted to the bar in 1955 and commenced the practice of law in Detroit and Macomb County, Mich.; delegate to the Democratic National Conventions of 1960 and 1968; elected as a Democrat to the Eighty-sixth and to the eight succeeding Congresses (January 3, 1959-January 3, 1977); was not a candidate in 1976 for reelection to the House of Representatives, but was an unsuccessful candidate for nomination to the United States Senate; resumed the practice of law in Washington, D.C.; member, and later chairman, Federal Minimum Wage Study Commission, 1978-1981; was a resident of Alexandria, Va.; died March 13, 1989.

**O'HARA, Joseph Patrick,** a Representative from Minnesota; born in Tipton, Cedar County, Iowa, January 23, 1895; attended the public schools and graduated from Spirit Lake, Iowa, High School; during the First World War was commissioned a second lieutenant of Infantry in the Officers' Reserve Corps and later promoted to captain in the Quartermaster Corps, and served from May 13, 1917, to August 15, 1919, with overseas service; commissioned a major of Infantry in the Reserve Corps; attended Inns of Court, London, England, and was graduated from the law department of Notre Dame University, South Bend, Ind., in 1920; was admitted to the bar in 1921 and commenced practice in Glencoe, Minn.; served as attorney for various villages, cities, towns, and school districts, and as county attorney of McLeod County 1934-1938; elected as a Republican to the Seventy-seventh and to the eight succeeding Congresses (January 3, 1941-January 3, 1959); was not a candidate for reelection in 1958 to the Eighty-sixth Congress; resumed the practice of law in Washington, D.C., where he resided; died in Bethesda, Md., March 4, 1975; interment in Gate of Heaven Cemetery, Washington, D.C.

**OHLIGER, Lewis Philip,** a Representative from Ohio; born in Rheinpfalz, Bavaria, Germany, January 3, 1843; immigrated to the United States in October 1854 with his parents; settled in Canton, Ohio, in 1857; attended the public schools; moved to Wooster, Ohio, and engaged in the wholesale drug and grocery business; county treasurer 1875-1879; postmaster of Wooster from February 1885 until February 1890; trustee of the Wooster & Lodi Railway; delegate to the Democratic National Convention in 1892; elected as a Democrat to the Fifty-second Congress to fill the vacancy caused by the death of John G. Warwick and served from December 5, 1892, to March 3, 1893; unsuccessful for renomination in 1892; internal-revenue collector of the Cleveland district by appointment of President Grover Cleveland 1893-1898; resumed his former business pursuits; died in San Diego, Calif., January 9, 1923; interment in Wooster Cemetery, Wooster, Ohio.

**O'KONSKI, Alvin Edward,** a Representative from Wisconsin; born on a farm near Kewaunee, Kewaunee County, Wis., May 26, 1904; attended the public schools and the University of Iowa at Iowa City; was graduated from State Teachers College, Oshkosh, Wis., in 1927, and from the University of Wisconsin at Madison in 1932; instructor in high schools at Omro and Oconto, Wis., 1926-1929; member of the faculty of Oregon State College at Corvallis 1929-1931, and at the University of Detroit, Detroit, Mich., 1936-1938; superintendent of schools, Pulaski, Wis., 1932-1935; instructor at a junior college, Coleraine, Minn., in 1936; educator, journalist, and lecturer; editor and publisher, Hurley, Wis., 1940-1942; elected as a Republican to the Seventy-eighth and to the fourteen succeeding Congresses (January 3, 1943-January 3, 1973); unsuccessful candidate for nomination in 1957 to the United States Senate to fill a vacancy; unsuccessful candidate for reelection in 1972 to the Ninety-third Congress; was a resident of Rhinelander, Wis., until his death in Kewaunee, Wis., on July 8, 1987; interment in St. Hedwig's Cemetery.

**OLCOTT, Jacob Van Vechten,** a Representative from New York; born in New York City May 17, 1856; attended the public schools and the College of the City of New York; was graduated from the Columbia College Law School at New York City in May 1877; was admitted to the bar May 17, 1877, and commenced the practice of law in New York City in 1881; member of the Civil Service Commission of New York City 1895-1897; trustee and vice president of St. Luke's Hospital, New York City; elected as a Republican to the Fifty-ninth, Sixtieth, and Sixty-first Congresses (March 4, 1905-March 3, 1911); was not a candidate for renomination in 1910; continued the practice of law in New York City until his death June 1, 1940; interment in Greenwood Cemetery, Brooklyn, N.Y.

**OLCOTT, Simeon,** a Senator from New Hampshire; born in Bolton, Tolland County, Conn., October 1, 1735; graduated from Yale College in 1761; studied law; was admitted to the bar and commenced practice in Charlestown, N.H.; selectman 1769-1771; judge of probate for Cheshire County 1773; representative in the general assembly of the Province 1772-1773; appointed chief justice of the court of common pleas 1784, judge of the superior court 1790, and chief judge of the court 1795; elected as a Federalist to the United States Senate to fill the vacancy caused by the resignation of Samuel Livermore and served from June 17, 1801, to March 3, 1805; died in Charlestown, N.H., February 22, 1815; interment in Forest Hill Cemetery.

**OLDFIELD, Pearl Peden** (wife of William Allan Oldfield), a Representative from Arkansas; born in Cotton Plant, Woodruff County, Ark., on December 2, 1876; educated in the public schools and at Arkansas College, Batesville, Ark.; elected January 9, 1929, as a Democrat to fill the vacancy in both the Seventieth and Seventy-first Congresses caused by the death of her husband William A. Oldfield, who had been reelected in 1928, and served from January 9, 1929, to March 3, 1931; was not a candidate for renomination in 1930; died in Washington, D.C., April 12, 1962; interment in Oaklawn Cemetery, Batesville, Ark.

**OLDFIELD, William Allan** (husband of Pearl Peden Oldfield), a Representative from Arkansas; born in Franklin, Izard County, Ark., February 4, 1874; attended the public schools and was graduated from Arkansas College at Batesville in 1896; taught school; enlisted in 1898 as a private in Company M, Second Regiment, Arkansas Infantry, during the war with Spain; was promoted to first sergeant of the same company and later to first lieutenant, and was mustered out with that rank in March 1899; studied law; was admitted to the bar in 1900 and commenced practice in Batesville, Ark.; prosecuting attorney of Independence County 1902-1906; unsuccessful candidate for election in 1906 to the Sixtieth Congress; elected as a Democrat to the Sixty-first and to the nine succeeding Congresses and served from March 4, 1909, until his death; chairman, Committee on Patents (Sixty-second and Sixty-third Congresses); minority whip (Sixty-seventh through Seventieth Congress); had been reelected to the Seventy-first Congress; died in Washington, D.C., November 19, 1928; interment in Oak Lawn Cemetery, Batesville, Ark.

**OLDS, Edson Baldwin,** a Representative from Ohio; born in Marlboro, Windham County, Vt., June 3, 1802; completed preparatory studies; moved to Ohio about 1820; taught school; was graduated from the medical department of the University of Pennsylvania in 1824; commenced the practice of medicine in Kingston in 1824; moved to Circleville, Ohio, in 1828 and continued practice until 1837, when he engaged in the general produce business and mercantile pursuits; member of the State house of representatives in 1842, 1843, 1845, and 1846; served in the State senate 1846-1848 and was its presiding officer in 1846 and 1847; elected as a Democrat to the Thirty-first, Thirty-second, and Thirty-third Congresses (March 4, 1849-March 3, 1855); chairman, Committee on the Post Office and Post Roads (Thirty-second and Thirty-third Congresses); unsuccessful candidate for reelection in 1854 to the Thirty-fourth Congress; moved to Lancaster, Ohio, in 1857; was arrested for disloyalty and imprisoned in Fort Lafayette in 1862; while in prison was again elected a member of the State house of representatives; after his release from prison served in the above capacity from 1862 to 1866; resumed mercantile pursuits; died in Lancaster, Ohio, January 24, 1869; interment in Forest Cemetery at Circleville, Ohio.

**O'LEARY, Denis,** a Representative from New York; born in Manhasset, Queens County, N.Y., January 22, 1863; attended the public schools; taught in the public schools; was graduated from the law school of the University of the City of New York (now New York University) in 1890; was admitted to the bar the same year and commenced practice in New York City; assistant corporation counsel of New York City in 1905 and 1906; commissioner of public works of Queens Borough in 1911 and 1912; elected as a Democrat to the Sixty-third Congress and served from March 4, 1913, until

December 31, 1914, when he resigned; district attorney of Queens County 1915-1921; resumed the practice of law until 1929 when he retired; died in Douglaston, Queens County, N.Y., September 27, 1943; interment in Mount St. Mary's Cemetery, Flushing, N.Y.

**O'LEARY, James Aloysius,** a Representative from New York; born in New Brighton, Staten Island, N.Y., April 23, 1889; attended St. Peter's Academy, Augustinian Academy, and Westerleigh Collegiate Institute, all Staten Island institutions; studied law while engaged in the real estate and insurance business; became associated with the North Shore Ice Co. in 1917 and served as general manager and vice president 1920-1934; also an official in numerous other Staten Island enterprises; unsuccessful candidate for the nomination of State senator in 1930; elected as a Democrat to the Seventy-fourth and to the four succeeding Congresses and served from January 3, 1935, until his death at West Brighton, Staten Island, N.Y., March 16, 1944; chairman, Committee on Expenditures in the Executive Departments (Seventy-sixth, Seventy-seventh, and Seventy-eighth Congresses); interment in St. Peter's Cemetery.

**OLIN, Abram Baldwin** (son of Gideon Olin), a Representative from New York; born in Shaftsbury, Bennington County, Vt., September 21, 1808; attended the common schools, and was graduated from Williams College, Williamstown, Mass., in 1835; studied law; was admitted to the bar in 1838 and commenced practice in Troy, N.Y.; recorder of the city of Troy, 1844-1852; elected as a Republican to the Thirty-fifth and to the two succeeding Congresses (March 4, 1857-March 3, 1863); appointed by President Abraham Lincoln an associate justice of the supreme court of the District of Columbia, and served from March 11, 1863 until he voluntarily retired on January 13, 1879; died near Sligo, Montgomery County, Md., July 7, 1879; interment in the Danforth family lot adjacent to West Lawn Cemetery, Williamstown, Berkshire County, Mass.

**OLIN, Gideon** (father of Abram Baldwin Olin and uncle of Henry Olin), a Representative from Vermont; born in East Greenwich, Kent County, R.I., November 2, 1743; received a limited schooling; engaged in agricultural pursuits; moved to Vermont and settled in Shaftsbury in 1776; delegate to the Windsor convention of July 2-8, 1777 that re-declared Vermont an independent republic, and adopted a constitution; member of the Vermont house of representatives in 1778, 1780-1793, and in 1799, serving as speaker from 1788 to 1793; during the Revolutionary War served as a major in the Second Regiment; assistant judge of Bennington County Court, 1781-1798, and chief judge, 1807-1811; delegate to the State constitutional convention in 1791; member of the Governor's council, 1793-1798; elected as a Republican to the Eighth and Ninth Congresses (March 4, 1803-March 3, 1807); resumed agricultural pursuits; died in Shaftsbury, Bennington County, Vt., January 21, 1823; interment in Shaftsbury Center.

**OLIN, Henry** (nephew of Gideon Olin), a Representative from Vermont; born in Shaftsbury, Bennington County, Vt., May 7, 1768; attended the common schools; studied law; was admitted to the bar and practiced; moved to Leicester, Vt., in 1788; member of the Vermont State house of representatives, 1799-1804, 1806-1815, 1817-1819, and 1822-1824; delegate to the State constitutional conventions in 1814, 1822, and 1828; associate judge and afterwards chief judge of the Addison County Court, 1801-1824; member of the executive council in 1820 and 1821; elected to the Eighteenth Congress to fill the vacancy caused by the death of Charles Rich, and served from December 13, 1824 to March 3, 1825; Lieutenant Governor of Vermont, 1827-1830; died in Salisbury, Addison County, Vt., August 16, 1837; interment in Brookside Cemetery, Leicester, Vt.

**OLIN, James R.,** a Representative from Virginia; born in Chicago, Ill., February 28, 1920; attended Deep Springs (Calif.) College, 1938-1941; B.E.E., Cornell University, Ithaca, N.Y., 1943; served in the United States Army Signal Corps as an enlisted man and officer, 1943-1946; elected supervisor, Town of Rotterdam, N.Y., and county board of supervisors, Schenectady County, N.Y., 1953; employed by General Electric Co. until his retirement in January 1982 after serving as corporate vice president and general manager, industrial electronics division; elected as a Democrat to the Ninety-eighth and to the four succeeeding Congresses (January 3, 1983-January 3, 1993); was not a candidate for reelection in 1992 to the One Hundred Third Congress; is a resident of Roanoke, Va.

**OLIVER, Andrew,** a Representative from New York; born in Springfield, N.Y., January 16, 1815; was graduated from Union College, Schenectady, N.Y., in 1835; studied law; was admitted to the bar and commenced practice in Penn Yan, Yates County, N.Y., in 1838; judge of the court of common pleas 1843-1847; judge of the surrogate and county courts in 1846; elected as a Democrat to the Thirty-third and Thirty-fourth Congresses (March 4, 1853-March 3, 1857); chairman, Committee on Invalid Pensions (Thirty-fourth Congress); unsuccessful candidate on the American Party ticket for reelection in 1856 to the Thirty-fifth Congress; engaged in agricultural pursuits and also in the practice of law; again served as county judge and surrogate 1872-1877; died in Penn Yan, N.Y., March 6, 1889; interment in Lake View Cemetery.

**OLIVER, Daniel Charles,** a Representative from New York; born in New York City October 6, 1865; attended the public schools and graduated from the College of the City of New York; served twenty years as a member of the school board; importer of dry goods; member of the Commercial Travelers' Association; member of the State assembly in 1914 and 1915; elected as a Democrat to the Sixty-fifth Congress (March 4, 1917-March 3, 1919); did not seek renomination in 1918 to the Sixty-sixth Congress; resumed his former business pursuits in New York City, where he died March 26, 1924; interment in Calvary Cemetery, Long Island City, N.Y.

**OLIVER, Frank,** a Representative from New York; born in New York City October 2, 1883; attended the public schools and the Morris High School, Borough of the Bronx; was graduated from Fordham University at New York City in 1905; studied law at the New York Law School; was admitted to the bar in 1908 and commenced practice in New York City; appointed on December 1, 1908, chief of the bureau of licenses for New York City and served until April 16, 1911, when he resigned to become secretary to United States Senator James A. O'Gorman, of New York, in which capacity he served until his resignation on January 3, 1916; was appointed chief clerk to the magistrates' courts of New York City and served from January 3, 1916, until December 31, 1919; appointed assistant district attorney for Bronx County on January 1, 1920, and served until February 28, 1923, when he resigned, having been elected to Congress; elected as a Democrat to the Sixty-eighth and to the five succeeding Congresses and served from March 4, 1923, until his resignation on June 18, 1934; appointed on June 19, 1934, justice of the court of special sessions, in which capacity he served until his retirement April 6, 1952; died in the Bronx, N.Y., January 1, 1968; interment in Calvary Cemetery, New York City.

**OLIVER, George Tener,** a Senator from Pennsylvania; born January 26, 1848, in County Tyrone, Ireland, during a visit abroad of his parents, who at that time were residents of Pittsburgh, Pa.; attended the common schools and Pleasant Hill Academy, West Middletown, Pa.; graduated from Bethany (W.Va.) College 1868; taught school; studied law; was admitted to the bar of Allegheny County, Pa., in 1871 and practiced in Pittsburgh, Pa.; retired from his profession in 1881 and engaged in steel and wire manufacturing until 1901, when he disposed of his interests; president of the Pittsburgh Central Board of Education 1881-1884; presidential elector on the Republican ticket in 1884; engaged in the newspaper business in 1900 and became publisher of the Pittsburgh Gazette-Times and Pittsburgh Chronicle-Telegraph; declined the appointment as United States Senator in 1904 to fill the vacancy caused by the death of Matthew S. Quay; elected as a Republican to the United States Senate in 1909 to fill the vacancy caused by the resignation of Philander C. Knox; reelected in 1911 and served from March 17, 1909, to March 3, 1917; chairman, Committee on Transportation Routes to the Seaboard (Sixty-first Congress), Committee on Canadian Relations (Sixty-second Congress), Committee on Manufactures (Sixty-second Congress), Committee on Forest Reservations and Game Protection (Sixty-fourth Congress); declined to be a candidate for reelection; retired from public life and resided in Pittsburgh, Pa., until his death there January 22, 1919; interment in Allegheny Cemetery.

**Bibliography:** *DAB.*

**OLIVER, James Churchill,** a Representative from Maine; born in South Portland, Cumberland County, Maine, August 6, 1895; attended the public schools; Bowdoin College, Brunswick, Maine, A.B., 1917; during the First World War enlisted on June 4, 1917, attended the Plattsburg Barracks Training Camp, and was commissioned a captain on November 27, 1917; was promoted to major of Infantry on October 9, 1918, and transferred to the Inspector General's Department until honorably discharged on July 22, 1919; engaged in the general insurance business in Portland, Maine, 1930-1937; member of the board of aldermen of South Portland, Maine, in 1932 and 1933; elected as a Republican to the Seventy-fifth, Seventy-sixth, and Seventy-seventh Congresses (January 3, 1937-January 3, 1943); unsuccessful candidate for renomination in 1942; served as lieutenant commander in the United States Coast Guard from January 26, 1943, to April 23, 1946; in 1946 engaged in the real estate and insurance business in Maine and California; unsuccessful Democratic candidate for Governor in 1952; unsuccessful Democratic candidate for Congress in 1954 and 1956; unsuccessfully contested the election of Robert Hale to the Eighty-fifth Congress in 1956; elected as a Democrat to the Eighty-sixth Congress (January 3, 1959-January 3, 1961); unsuccessful candidate for reelection in 1960 to the Eighty-seventh Congress; delegate to Democratic National Convention, 1960; real estate developer in Cape Elizabeth, Maine; moved to Orlando, Fla., where he died December 25, 1986.

**OLIVER, Mordecai,** a Representative from Missouri; born in Anderson County, Ky., October 22, 1819; attended the common schools; studied law; was admitted to the bar in 1842 and commenced practice in Richmond, Mo.; prosecuting attorney for the fifth judicial circuit in 1848; elected as a Whig to the Thirty-third and Thirty-fourth Congresses (March 4, 1853-March 3, 1857); elected as a Unionist secretary of state of Missouri in 1861; resumed the practice of law in St. Louis, Mo.; judge of the criminal court 1889-1893; moved to Springfield, Greene County, Mo., where he died April 25, 1898; interment in Hazelwood Cemetery.

**OLIVER, Samuel Addison,** a Representative from Iowa; born near Washington, Washington County, Pa., on July 21, 1833; attended the common schools and West Alexandria Academy; was graduated from Washington (Pa.) College in 1851; moved to Arkansas, where he taught school; returned to Pennsylvania and engaged in agricultural pursuits; studied law; was admitted to the bar in 1857 and commenced practice in Onawa, Monona County, Iowa, in 1858; county supervisor in 1861; served as provost marshal during the Civil War; member of the State house of representatives in 1863 and 1864; delegate to the Republican National Convention in 1864; served in the State senate 1865-1867; judge of the fourth judicial circuit 1868-1875; elected as a Republican to the Forty-fourth and Forty-fifth Congresses (March 4, 1875-March 3, 1879); declined to be a candidate for renomination in 1878; mayor of

Onawa several times; again engaged in agricultural pursuits; died in Onawa, Monona County, Iowa, July 7, 1912; interment in Onawa Cemetery.

**OLIVER, William Bacon** (cousin of Sydney Parham Epes), a Representative from Alabama; born in Eutaw, Greene County, Ala., May 23, 1867; attended the common schools of his native city; was graduated from the Verner College Preparatory School at Tuscaloosa in 1883, the academic department of the University of Alabama at Tuscaloosa in 1887, and from its law department in 1889; took a special course at the law school of the University of Virginia at Charlottesville in 1889; was admitted to the bar in 1889 and commenced practice in Tuscaloosa, Ala.; appointed solicitor for the sixth judicial circuit of Alabama in 1898 and served until his resignation in 1909; dean of the law school of the University of Alabama from 1909 until 1913, when he resigned; chairman of the Democratic central committee of Tuscaloosa County for a number of years; delegate to the Democratic National Convention of 1924; elected as a Democrat to the Sixty-fourth and to the ten succeeding Congresses (March 4, 1915-January 3, 1937); was not a candidate for renomination in 1936 to the Seventy-fifth Congress; served as special assistant to the Attorney General at Washington, D.C., from July 22, 1939, to May 1, 1944, when he retired; died while on a visit in New Orleans, La., May 27, 1948; interment in Eutaw Cemetery, Eutaw, Ala.

**OLIVER, William Morrison,** a Representative from New York; born in Londonderry, N.H., October 15, 1792; received a limited schooling; moved to Cherry Valley, Otsego County, and thence to Penn Yan, Yates County, N.Y.; studied law; was admitted to the bar about 1812 and commenced practice in Penn Yan; first judge of the court of common pleas for Yates County 1823-1828; member of the State senate 1827-1830; Lieutenant Governor in 1830; again judge of the court of common pleas 1838-1845; elected as a Democrat to the Twenty-seventh Congress (March 4, 1841-March 3, 1843); clerk of the supreme court of New York about 1844; president of the Yates County Bank from the issuance of its charter until 1857; died in Penn Yan, N.Y., July 21, 1863; interment in Lake View Cemetery.

**OLMSTED, Marlin Edgar,** a Representative from Pennsylvania; born near Ulysses, Ulysses Township, Potter County, Pa., May 21, 1847; attended the common schools and Coudersport (Pa.) Academy; assistant corporation clerk and promoted to corporation clerk in charge of collection of corporate taxes under Pennsylvania's revenue system; studied law; was admitted to the bar November 25, 1878, and commenced practice in Harrisburg; elected to represent Dauphin County in the proposed constitutional convention in 1891; elected as a Republican to the Fifty-fifth and to the seven succeeding Congresses (March 4, 1897-March 3, 1913); chairman, Committee on Elections No. 2 (Fifty-seventh through Sixtieth Congresses), Committee on Insular Affairs (Sixty-first Congress); one of the managers appointed by the House of Representatives in 1905 to conduct the impeachment proceedings against Charles Swayne, judge of the United States District Court for the Northern District of Florida; was not a candidate for renomination in 1912 to the Sixty-third Congress; resumed the practice of his profession in Harrisburg, Pa.; died in New York City on July 19, 1913; interment in the Harrisburg Cemetery.

**Bibliography:** *DAB*.

**OLNEY, Richard,** a Representative from Massachusetts; born in Milton, Stafford County, N.H., January 5, 1871; attended the public schools and Leicester Academy; graduated from Brown University, Providence, R.I., in 1892; wool merchant; member of the Pennsylvania house of representatives in 1902; chairman of selectmen of Leicester in 1902 and 1903; unsuccessful candidate for Lieutenant Governor in 1903; member of the Massachusetts Minimum Wage Commission in 1911; delegate to the Democratic National Convention at Baltimore in 1912; elected as a Democrat to

the Sixty-fourth, Sixty-fifth, and Sixty-sixth Congresses (March 4, 1915-March 3, 1921); unsuccessful candidate for reelection in 1920 to the Sixty-seventh Congress; appointed a member of the World War Foreign Debt Commission in February 1923 and reappointed by President Coolidge in 1925; chairman of the Pennsylvania parole board 1932-1937; chairman of the Pennsylvania Commission of the Necessaries of Life from 1938 until his death at Boston, Mass., on January 15, 1939; interment in Cherry Valley Cemetery, Leicester, Mass.

**Bibliography:** Eggert, Gerald G. "Richard Olney and the Income Tax Cases." *Mississippi Valley Historical Review* 48 (June 1961): 24-41; James, Henry. *Richard Olney and his Public Service.* Boston: Houghton Mifflin, 1923.

**O'LOUGHLIN, Kathryn Ellen** (after election was married to Daniel M. McCarthy and thereupon served under the name of Kathryn O'Loughlin McCarthy), a Representative from Kansas; born near Hays, Ellis County, Kans., April 24, 1894; attended the rural schools; was graduated from the Hays (Kans.) High School in 1913, from the State Teachers College, Hays, Kans., in 1917, and from the law school of the University of Chicago, Chicago, Ill., in 1920; was admitted to the bar in 1921 and commenced practice in Chicago, Ill.; returned to Kansas in 1928 and continued the practice of law in Hays; delegate to the State Democratic conventions in 1930, 1931, 1932, 1934, and 1936, and to the Democratic National Conventions in 1940 and 1944; member of the State house of representatives in 1931 and 1932; elected as a Democrat to the Seventy-third Congress (March 4, 1933-January 3, 1935); was an unsuccessful candidate for reelection in 1934 to the Seventy-fourth Congress; resumed the practice of law; also owned and operated a large ranch and was part owner of an automobile agency at Hays and Ellis, Kans.; died in Hays, Kans., January 16, 1952; interment in St. Joseph's Cemetery.

**OLPP, Archibald Ernest,** a Representative from New Jersey; born in South Bethlehem, Northampton County, Pa., May 12, 1882; attended the public schools; was graduated from the Moravian School, Bethlehem, Pa., in 1899, Lehigh University, Bethlehem, Pa., in 1903, and from the medical department of the University of Pennsylvania at Philadelphia in 1908; instructor in chemistry at Lehigh University in 1903 and 1904; instructor in biological chemistry at the College of Physicians and Surgeons (Columbia University), New York City, in 1908 and 1909; began the practice of medicine in West Hoboken, N.J., in 1909; served as town physician 1912-1914; police surgeon and physician to public schools, Secaucus, N.J., 1916-1924; served as first lieutenant in the United States Medical Corps during the First World War; elected as a Republican to the Sixty-seventh Congress (March 4, 1921-March 3, 1923); was an unsuccessful candidate for reelection in 1922 to the Sixty-eighth Congress; resumed his medical profession; died in Cliffside Park, N.J., July 26, 1949; interment in Brookside Cemetery, Englewood, N.J.

**OLSEN, Arnold,** a Representative from Montana; born in Butte, Silver Bow County, Mont., December 17, 1916; attended Butte public schools, the Montana School of Mines, 1934-1936, and graduated from the Montana State University Law School in Missoula, Mont., in 1940; commenced the private practice of law in Butte in 1940; overseas duty in the United States Navy, 1942-1946; attorney general of Montana, 1948-1956; private law office in Helena, Mont., in 1956; elected as a Democrat to the Eighty-seventh and to the four succeeding Congresses (January 3, 1961-January 3, 1971); unsuccessful candidate for reelection in 1970 to the Ninety-second Congress; resumed the practice of his profession; unsuccessful candidate for election in 1972 to the Ninety-third Congress; unsuccessful candidate for nomination in 1974 to the Ninety-fourth Congress; appointed judge of the second judicial district by the Governor, February 2, 1975; was a resident of Butte, Mont.; died October 9, 1990.

**OLSON, Alec Gehard,** a Representative from Minnesota; born in Mamre Township, Kandiyohi County, Minn., September 11, 1930; attended the public schools and graduated from Willmar High School in 1948; engaged in farming, 1948-1955; employed as an insurance representative, 1955-1962; active in the Democrat-Farmer-Labor Party, 1952-1962, serving as district chairman for four years; delegate to the Democratic National Conventions of 1960, 1964, and 1968; elected as a Democrat-Farmer-Labor to the Eighty-eighth and Eighty-ninth Congresses (January 3, 1963-January 3, 1967); unsuccessful candidate for reelection in 1966 to the Ninetieth Congress; assistant in charge of defense mobilization planning to Secretary of Agriculture Orville L. Freeman, 1967; account executive with Kelley and Morey investment company; member, Minnesota State senate, 1969-1976; named Lieutenant Governor in 1976, and served from December 29, 1976 to January 3, 1979; is a resident of Spicer, Minn.

**OLVER, John Walter,** a Representative from Massachusetts; born in Honesdale, Wayne County, Pa., September 3, 1936; B.S., Rensselaer Polytechnic Institute, 1955; M.S., Tufts University, 1956; Ph.D., Massachusetts Institute of Technology, 1961; member, Massachusetts house of representatives, 1969-1973; member, Massachusetts senate, 1973-1991; elected as a Democrat to the One Hundred Second Congress, June 4, 1991, by special election to fill the vacancy caused by the death of Silvio O. Conte; reelected to the two succeeding Congresses, and served from June 4, 1991 to January 3, 1997; is a resident of Amherst, Mass.

**O'MAHONEY, Joseph Christopher,** a Senator from Wyoming; born in Chelsea, Suffolk County, Mass., November 5, 1884; attended the parochial and public schools and Columbia University, New York City; moved to Boulder, Colo., in 1908 and engaged as a reporter on the Boulder Herald; moved to Cheyenne, Wyo., in 1916 and served as city editor of the Cheyenne State Leader; executive secretary to Senator John B. Kendrick, 1917-1920; graduated from the Georgetown University Law School, Washington, D.C., in 1920; was admitted to the bar in 1920 and commenced practice in Cheyenne, Wyo., and Washington, D.C.; member of conference on uniform State laws, 1925-1926; city attorney of Cheyenne, Wyo., 1929-1931; Democratic national committeeman, 1929-1934; appointed First Assistant Postmaster General in 1933, and served until December 31, 1933, when he resigned to become a Senator; appointed as a Democrat to the United States Senate to fill the vacancy caused by the death of John B. Kendrick, and on November 6, 1934, was elected to fill this vacancy and also for the term commencing January 3, 1935; reelected in 1940 and again in 1946, and served from January 1, 1934 to January 3, 1953; chairman, Committee on Indian Affairs (Seventy-eighth and Seventy-ninth Congresses), Committee on Interior and Insular Affairs (Eighty-first and Eighty-second Congresses), co-chairman, Joint Committee on the Economic Report (Eighty-first and Eighty-second Congresses); unsuccessful candidate for reelection in 1952; elected on November 2, 1954, to fill the vacancy caused by the death of Lester C. Hunt, and also elected for the full term commencing January 3, 1955, and served from November 29, 1954 to January 3, 1961; was not a candidate for renomination in 1960; resumed the practice of law in Washington, D.C., and Cheyenne, Wyo.; died in Bethesda, Md., December 1, 1962; interment in Mount Olivet Cemetery, Cheyenne, Wyo.

**Bibliography:** Coombs, Frank Alan. "Joseph Christopher O'Mahoney: The New Deal Years." Ph.D. dissertation, University of Illinois, Urbana-Champaign, 1968; Ninneman, Thomas Richard. "Wyoming's Senator Joseph C. O'Mahoney." *Annals of Wyoming* 49 (Fall 1977): 193-222.

**O'MALLEY, Matthew Vincent,** a Representative from New York; born in Brooklyn, N.Y., June 26, 1878; attended the Parochial School of the Assumption and the grade and high schools of Brooklyn; secretary to the health officer of Brooklyn from 1894 to 1898; engaged in the real estate, insurance, and bonding business in 1899 and continued therein throughout the remainder of his life; secretary of the Citizens Publishing Co., of Brooklyn 1925-1931; elected as a Democrat to the Seventy-second Congress to fill the vacancy caused by the death of John F. Quayle and served from March 4, 1931, until his death, before the convening of Congress, in Brooklyn, N.Y., May 26, 1931; interment in Holy Cross Cemetery.

**O'MALLEY, Thomas David Patrick,** a Representative from Wisconsin; born in Milwaukee, Wis., March 24, 1903; attended the parochial schools; was graduated from Loyola Academy in 1920, after which he attended Loyola College, and the Y.M.C.A. College of Liberal Arts, Chicago, Ill.; engaged as a salesman, advertising writer, and as an author; delegate to the Democratic National Convention in 1932; unsuccessful candidate for election in 1928 to the Seventy-first Congress and in 1930 to the Seventy-second Congress; elected as a Democrat to the Seventy-third, Seventy-fourth, and Seventy-fifth Congresses (March 4, 1933-January 3, 1939); unsuccessful candidate for reelection in 1938 to the Seventy-sixth Congress; member of the Democratic national congressional committee 1933-1939; resumed advertising and public relations work; regional director of Wage and Hour and Public Contracts Division, United States Department of Labor, Chicago, Ill., 1939-1956; engaged in public relations and management counseling; was a resident of Chicago, Ill., until his death there on December 19, 1979; interment in Neenah, Wis.

**O'NEAL, Emmet,** a Representative from Kentucky; born in Louisville, Ky., on April 14, 1887; attended the public schools; was graduated from Centre College, Danville, Ky., in 1907, from Yale University in 1908, and from the law department of the University of Louisville, Ky., in 1910; was admitted to the bar in 1910 and commenced practice in Louisville; during the First World War served overseas in the United States Army as an enlisted man in the Fifth Field Artillery in the First Division, and as an officer in the One Hundred and Third Field Artillery in the Twenty-sixth Division, 1917-1919; resumed the practice of law in Louisville; also engaged in banking; elected as a Democrat to the Seventy-fourth and to the five succeeding Congresses (January 3, 1935-January 3, 1947); unsuccessful candidate for reelection in 1946 to the Eightieth Congress; appointed Ambassador to the Philippines on June 10, 1947 and served until April 1948; resumed the practice of law in Washington, D.C.; member and later chairman of the Corregidor-Bataan Memorial Commission; died in Washington, D.C., July 18, 1967; interment in Cave Hill Cemetery, Louisville, Ky.

**O'NEAL, Maston Emmett, Jr.,** a Representative from Georgia; born in Bainbridge, Decatur County, Ga., July 19, 1907; attended the public schools and Marion Military Institute; A.B., Davidson (N.C.) College, 1927; attended Lamar School of Law, Emory University; principal, Shellman High School, 1927-1928; admitted to practice law in Albany circuit, January 16, 1930; solicitor general, Albany Judicial Circuit, January 1, 1941, to May 1, 1964 (reelected five times to four-year terms without opposition, including one term *in absentia* while in naval service); served as lieutenant, United States Naval Reserve (Amphibs), Pacific Theater, 1944-1946; first president, Solicitors General Association of Georgia; former director, National Association of County and Prosecuting Attorney; elected as a Democrat to the Eighty-ninth and to the two succeeding Congresses (January 3, 1965-January 3, 1971); was not a candidate for reelection in 1970 to the Ninety-second Congress; was a resident of Bainbridge, Ga.; died January 9, 1990.

**O'NEALL, John Henry,** a Representative from Indiana; born in Newberry, Newberry County, S.C., October 30, 1838; was left an orphan when eight years of age and was reared by his grandfather, who resided in Daviess County, Ind.; attended country schools and was graduated from Indiana University at Bloomington in 1862; was graduated from the law department of the University of Michigan at Ann Arbor in 1864; was admitted to the bar the same year and practiced in Terre Haute and later in Washington, Ind.; served in the State legislature in 1866; appointed prosecuting attorney for the eleventh judicial circuit in 1873; elected to the office in 1874, but resigned before his term was completed; elected as a Democrat to the Fiftieth and Fifty-first Congresses (March 4, 1887-March 3, 1891); was not a candidate for renomination in 1890; resumed the practice of law in Washington, Ind.; school trustee of Washington for fifteen years; delegate to the Democratic National Convention in 1896; city attorney of Washington 1899-1907; organized the Federal Trust Co. in 1899 and was its president until 1902, when it was made a national bank; died in Washington, Daviess County, Ind., July 15, 1907; interment in St. John's Cemetery.

**O'NEIL, Joseph Henry,** a Representative from Massachusetts; born in Fall River, Bristol County, Mass., March 23, 1853; moved with his parents to Boston in 1854; attended the common schools; graduated from Quincy Grammar School, Boston; ten years at the carpenter's trade; member of the Boston school committee, 1874-1877; member of the Massachusetts house of representatives, 1878-1882 and in 1884; member of the board of directors for public institutions from 1880 to 1886, and was chairman of the board the last eighteen months; city clerk of Boston, 1887-1888; elected as a Democrat to the Fifty-first and to the two succeeding Congresses (March 4, 1889-March 3, 1895); unsuccessful candidate for renomination in 1894 to the Fifty-fourth Congress; assistant treasurer of the United States at Boston by appointment of President Grover Cleveland, 1895-1899; organized the Federal Trust Company of Boston in 1899 and served as its president until 1922, when it merged into the Federal National Bank, and then served as chairman of the board of directors until his death; member of the board of sinking fund commissioners, 1899-1909; delegate to the Democratic National Convention of 1916; died in Boston, Mass., February 19, 1935; interment in Holyhood Cemetery, Brookline, Mass.

**O'NEILL, Charles,** a Representative from Pennsylvania; born in Philadelphia, Pa., March 21, 1821; graduated from Dickinson College, Carlisle, Pa., in 1840; studied law; admitted to the bar in 1843 and commenced practice in Philadelphia; member of the Pennsylvania house of representatives 1850-1852 and in 1860; served in the Pennsylvania senate in 1853; elected as a Republican to the Thirty-eighth and to the three succeeding Congresses (March 4, 1863-March 3, 1871); unsuccessful candidate for reelection in 1870 to the Forty-second Congress; elected to the Forty-third and to the ten succeeding Congresses and served from March 4, 1873, until his death in Philadelphia, Pa., on November 25, 1893; interment in West Laurel Hill Cemetery, Montgomery County, Pa.

**O'NEILL, Edward Leo,** a Representative from New Jersey; born in Newark, N.J., July 10, 1903; attended the parochial schools; served in the United States Navy 1919-1923; became engaged in the real estate business in Newark, N.J.; unsuccessful candidate for election in 1934 to the Seventy-fourth Congress; elected as a Democrat to the Seventy-fifth Congress (January 3, 1937-January 3, 1939); unsuccessful candidate for reelection in 1938 to the Seventy-sixth Congress; lieutenant in the United States Naval Reserve in 1939 and 1940; served as a captain in the Quartermaster Corps, United States Army, in 1942 and 1943; commissioner of the Essex County Board of Taxation 1940-1945; realtor and mortgage broker in Newark, N.J., until his death December 12, 1948; interment in Holy Sepulchre Cemetery, East Orange, N.J.

**O'NEILL, Harry Patrick,** a Representative from Pennsylvania; born in Dunmore, Lackawanna County, Pa., February 10, 1889; left school at the age of ten and went to work as a slate picker in the O.S. Johnson Colliery, Dunmore, Pa.; worked evenings as an apprentice barber until the age of sixteen and at the age of eighteen purchased his employer's business; also engaged as an insurance broker; served in the Pennsylvania house of representatives 1929-1948; elected as a Democrat to the Eighty-first and Eighty-second Congresses (January 3, 1949-January 3, 1953); unsuccessful candidate for reelection in 1952 to the Eighty-third Congress; died in Scranton, Pa., June 24, 1953; interment in Cathedral Cemetery.

**O'NEILL, John,** a Representative from Ohio; born in Philadelphia, Pa., December 17, 1822; attended the common schools at Frederick, Md., and Georgetown College, Washington, D.C.; was graduated from Mount St. Mary's College, Emmitsburg, Md., and from the law department of Georgetown College, Washington, D.C., in 1841; was admitted to the bar in 1842; moved to Zanesville, Muskingum County, Ohio, in 1844 and commenced the practice of law; prosecuting attorney of Muskingum County in 1845; held various county offices; elected as a Democrat to the Thirty-eighth Congress (March 4, 1863-March 3, 1865); resumed the practice of his profession; member of the State senate 1883-1885; practiced law until his death in Zanesville, Ohio, May 25, 1905; interment in St. Thomas' Cemetery.

**O'NEILL, John Joseph,** a Representative from Missouri; born in St. Louis, Mo., June 25, 1846; attended the common schools; studied law; was admitted to the bar in 1870 and commenced practice in St. Louis; engaged in the manufacture of gold pens; member of the State house of representatives 1872-1878; member of the municipal assembly 1879-1881; elected as a Democrat to the Forty-eighth, Forty-ninth, and Fiftieth Congresses (March 4, 1883-March 3, 1889); chairman, Committee on Expenditures on Public Buildings (Forty-ninth Congress), Committee on Labor (Forty-ninth and Fiftieth Congresses); unsuccessful candidate for reelection in 1888 to the Fifty-first Congress; elected to the Fifty-second Congress (March 4, 1891-March 3, 1893); successfully contested the election of Charles F. Joy to the Fifty-third Congress and served from April 3, 1894, to March 3, 1895; was not a candidate for renomination in 1894; resumed the practice of law; died in St. Louis, Mo., February 19, 1898; interment in Calvary Cemetery.

**O'NEILL, Thomas Phillip, Jr. (Tip),** a Representative from Massachusetts; born in Cambridge, Mass., December 9, 1912; attended the parochial schools; graduated from St. John's High School in 1931; A.B., Boston College, 1936; engaged in the insurance and real estate business in Cambridge, Mass.; member of the Massachusetts house of representatives from 1936 until 1952, serving as minority leader in 1947 and 1948 and as speaker, 1949-1952; member of Massachusetts Democratic committee, 1942-1952; member of Cambridge School Committee in 1946 and 1947; elected as a Democrat to the Eighty-third and to the sixteen succeeding Congresses (January 3, 1953-January 3, 1987); chairman, Select Committee on Campaign Expenditures (Eighty-ninth through Ninety-second Congresses); majority whip (Ninety-second Congress), majority leader (Ninety-third and Ninety-fourth Congresses), Speaker of the House of Representatives (Ninety-fifth through Ninety-ninth Congresses); was not a candidate for reelection in 1986 to the One Hundredth Congress; was a resident of Washington, D.C., and Harwich Port, Mass., until his death in Boston, Mass., on January 5, 1994; interment in Mount Pleasant Cemetery, Harwich Port, Mass.

**Bibliography:** Clancy, Paul, and Shirley Elder. *Tip: A Biography of Thomas P. O'Neill, Speaker of the House.* New York: Macmillan, 1980; O'Neill, Thomas P., Jr., with William Novak. *Man* *of the House: The Life and Political Memoirs of Speaker Tip O'Neill.* New York: Random House, 1987.

**O'REILLY, Daniel,** a Representative from New York; born in Limerick, Ireland, June 3, 1838; pursued an academic course; immigrated to the United States in July 1856 with his parents, who settled in Brooklyn, N.Y.; member of the Brooklyn Board of Aldermen 1873-1875, 1878, and 1879; president pro tempore of the board of aldermen and acting mayor of the city; elected as an Independent Democrat to the Forty-sixth Congress (March 4, 1879-March 3, 1881); unsuccessful candidate for reelection in 1880 to the Forty-seventh Congress; studied law; was admitted to the bar in 1888 and commenced practice in Brooklyn, N.Y.; in charge of the transfer tax department of Kings County from 1898 until his death; died in Bayville, Long Island, N.Y., September 23, 1911; interment in Holy Cross Cemetery, Flatbush, Brooklyn, N.Y.

**ORMSBY, Stephen,** a Representative from Kentucky; born in County Sligo, Ireland, in 1759; immigrated to the United States when a boy and settled in Philadelphia, Pa.; pursued classical studies; studied law; was admitted to the bar in 1786 and commenced the practice of his profession in Danville, Ky.; deputy attorney general of Jefferson County in 1787; served in the early Indian wars, and as a brigadier general under General Josiah Harmar in the campaign of 1790; judge of the district court of Jefferson County in 1791; presidential elector in 1796; judge of the circuit court from 1802 until 1810; elected as a Republican to the Twelfth Congress (March 4, 1811-March 3, 1813); unsuccessful candidate for reelection in 1812 to the Thirteenth Congress; elected to the Thirteenth Congress to fill the vacancy caused by the death of Representative-elect John Simpson; reelected to the Fourteenth Congress and served from April 20, 1813, to March 3, 1817; unsuccessful candidate for reelection in 1816 to the Fifteenth Congress; appointed first president of the branch of the Bank of the United States of Louisville, Ky., in 1817; died near Louisville, Ky., in 1844; interment in the Ormsby Burial Ground (later the property of the Kentucky Military Institute) at Lyndon, near Louisville, Ky.

**ORR, Alexander Dalrymple** (nephew of William Grayson), a Representative from Kentucky; born in Alexandria, Loudoun County, Va., November 6, 1761; attended the local schools; about 1782 moved to Bourbon County, Ky. (then a part of Virginia), thence to a plantation on the Ohio River below Maysville, Mason County, Ky., and engaged in agricultural pursuits; member of the Virginia house of delegates in 1790; elected to the senate in 1792 and served until his election to Congress; upon the admission of Kentucky into the Union was elected to the Second Congress; reelected to the Third Congress and reelected as a Republican to the Fourth Congress and served from November 8, 1792, to March 3, 1797; resumed agricultural pursuits in Mason County near Maysville; died in Paris, Bourbon County, Ky., June 21, 1835; interment in Paris Cemetery.

**ORR, Benjamin,** a Representative from Massachusetts; born in Bedford, N.H., December 1, 1772; self-educated; apprenticed as a carpenter; attended Fryeburg (N.H.) Academy; taught school at Concord and New Milford, N.H.; graduated from Dartmouth College, Hanover, N.H., in 1798; studied law; was admitted to the bar in 1801 and commenced the practice of law in Brunswick, Maine (then a part of Massachusetts); moved to Topsham, Maine, the same year and continued the practice of law; overseer of Bowdoin College, Brunswick, Maine, and served as trustee from 1814 to 1828 and as treasurer in 1815 and 1816; elected as a Federalist to the Fifteenth Congress (March 4, 1817-March 3, 1819); was not a candidate for renomination in 1818; resumed the practice of law in Topsham, Maine; returned to Brunswick, Maine, in 1822 and continued the practice of law; died in Brunswick, Maine, on September 3, 1828; interment in Pine Grove Cemetery.

**ORR, Jackson,** a Representative from Iowa; born at Washington Court House, Fayette County, Ohio, September 21, 1832; moved with his parents to Benton, Elkhart County, Ind., in 1836; attended the common schools and Indiana University at Bloomington; moved to Jefferson, Greene County, Iowa, in 1856; served in the Union Army as captain of Company H, Tenth Regiment, Iowa Volunteer Infantry, 1861-1863; engaged in mercantile pursuits in Boone, Iowa; member of the State house of representatives in 1868; elected as a Republican to the Forty-second and Forty-third Congresses (March 4, 1871-March 3, 1875); chairman, Committee on Expenditures in the Department of the Interior (Forty-third Congress); was not a candidate for renomination in 1874; moved to Silverton, San Juan County, Colo., in 1875; elected county judge and served for three years; moved to Denver, Colo., and engaged in the practice of his profession and also in the real estate business; president of the Denver Fire and Police Board in 1893 and 1894; died in Denver, Colo., March 15, 1926; interment in Fairmount Cemetery.

**ORR, James Lawrence,** a Representative from South Carolina; born in Craytonville, Anderson County, S.C., May 12, 1822; attended the public schools; graduated from the University of Virginia at Charlottesville in 1842; studied law; admitted to the bar and commenced practice in Anderson, S.C., in 1843; engaged in newspaper work; member of the South Carolina State house of representatives, 1844-1847; elected as a Democrat to the Thirty-first and to the four succeeding Congresses (March 4, 1849-March 3, 1859); chairman, Committee on Indian Affairs (Thirty-third Congress); Speaker of the House of Representatives (Thirty-fifth Congress); was not a candidate for renomination in 1858 to the Thirty-sixth Congress; resumed the practice of law at Craytonville; member of the southern rights convention held in Charleston, S.C., in 1851; delegate to the Democratic National Convention at Charleston in 1860; member of the South Carolina secession convention in 1860; one of three commissioners sent to Washington, D.C., to treat with the Federal Government for the surrender of the forts in Charleston Harbor; member of the Confederate Senate in 1861; served in the Confederate Army during the Civil War; special commissioner sent to President Andrew Johnson to negotiate the establishment of a provisional government for the State of South Carolina in 1865; member of the State constitutional convention in 1865; elected Governor of South Carolina in 1865, and served until deposed in 1868 by an act of Congress; president of the State convention at Columbia in July 1866; delegate to the Union National Convention at Philadelphia in August 1866; judge of the eighth judicial circuit, 1868-1870; member of the Republican State convention in August 1872; delegate to the Republican National Convention of 1872; appointed by President Ulysses S. Grant as Minister to Russia on December 12, 1872; died in St. Petersburg, Russia, May 5, 1873; interment in the Presbyterian Cemetery, Anderson, S.C.

**Bibliography:** *DAB*; Foran, William A. "Attempted Conversion of James L. Orr." *Journal of Negro History* 39 (April 1954): 137-39; Leemhuis, Roger P. *James L. Orr and the Sectional Conflict.* Washington, D.C.: University Press of America, 1979.

**ORR, Robert, Jr.,** a Representative from Pennsylvania; born near Hannastown, Westmoreland County, Pa., March 5, 1786; attended the public schools; at an early age moved with his parents to Armstrong County; later moved to Kittanning; deputy sheriff of Armstrong County in 1805; studied surveying and was appointed deputy district surveyor; served in the War of 1812 and promoted to the rank of colonel; member of the Pennsylvania house of representatives 1817-1820; served in the Pennsylvania senate 1821-1826; elected to the Nineteenth Congress to fill the vacancy caused by the resignation of James Allison, Jr.; reelected to the Twentieth Congress and served from October 11, 1825, to March 3, 1829; retained his interest in military affairs, acquiring the rank and title of general; resided in Orrsville a short time in 1845, and later in Allegheny City 1848-1852; returned to Kittanning, Armstrong County, Pa., and died there May 22, 1876; interment in Kittanning Cemetery.

**ORTH, Godlove Stein,** a Representative from Indiana; born in Lebanon, Pa., April 22, 1817; attended Gettysburg (Pa.) College; studied law; was admitted to the bar in 1839 and commenced practice in Lafayette, Ind.; member of the Indiana State senate, 1843-1848, and served one year as president; presidential elector on the Whig ticket in 1848; delegate to the peace convention held in Washington, D.C., in 1861 in an effort to devise means to prevent the impending war; served as captain of a company of Volunteers during the Civil War; elected as a Republican to the Thirty-eighth and to the three succeeding Congresses (March 4, 1863-March 3, 1871); chairman, Committee on Private Land Claims (Fortieth and Forty-first Congresses), Committee on Foreign Affairs (Forty-third Congress); was not a candidate for reelection in 1870 to the Forty-second Congress; elected to the Forty-third Congress (March 4, 1873-March 3, 1875); was not a candidate for renomination in 1874 to the Forty-fourth Congress; appointed Envoy Extraordinary and Minister Plenipotentiary to Austria-Hungary on March 9, 1875, and served until March 1876; elected as a Republican to the Forty-sixth and Forty-seventh Congresses, and served from March 4, 1879 until his death in Lafayette, Tippecanoe County, Ind., December 16, 1882; interment in Springvale Cemetery.

Bibliography: *DAB*; Schauinger, J. Herman, ed. "The Letters of Godlove S. Orth, Hoosier American." *Indiana Magazine of History* 40 (March 1944): 51-66.

**ORTIZ, Solomon Porfirio,** a Representative from Texas; born in Robstown, Nueces County, Tex., June 3, 1937; attended the public schools of Robstown; attended Del Mar College, Corpus Christi, Tex., 1966-1968; officer's certificate, Institute of Applied Science, Chicago, Ill., 1962; officer's certificate, National Sheriffs Training Institute, 1977; served in the United States Army, specialist, fourth class, 1960-1962; insurance agent; Nueces County constable, 1965-1968; elected Nueces County Commissioner, 1969-1976; Nueces County Sheriff, 1976-1982; elected as a Democrat to the Ninety-eighth and to the six succeeding Congresses (January 3, 1983-January 3, 1997); is a resident of Corpus Christi, Tex.

**ORTON, William,** a Representative from Utah; born in North Ogden, Weber County, Utah, September 22, 1948; B.S., Brigham Young University, 1973; J.D., Brigham Young University School of Law, 1979; admitted to Utah bar, 1979; practicing attorney; elected as a Democrat to the One Hundred Second and to the two succeeding Congresses (January 3, 1991-January 3, 1997); is a resident of Sundance, Utah.

**OSBORN, Thomas Ward,** a Senator from Florida; born in Scotch Plains, Union County, N.J., March 9, 1836; moved to New York in 1842 with his parents, who settled in North Wilna; attended the common schools and graduated from Madison (now Colgate) University, Hamilton, N.Y., in 1860; studied law and was admitted to the bar in 1861; during the Civil War entered the Union Army in 1861 as lieutenant and became captain, major, and colonel of Battery D, First Regiment, New York Light Artillery; appointed assistant commissioner of the Bureau of Refugees and Freedmen for Florida 1865-1866; settled in Tallahassee, Fla., and commenced the practice of law; appointed register in bankruptcy in 1867; member of the State constitutional convention in 1868; moved to Pensacola, Fla.; member, State senate; upon the readmission of Florida to representation was elected as a Republican to the United States Senate and served from June 25, 1868, to March 3, 1873; was not a candidate for reelection; served as United States commissioner at the Centennial Exposition in Philadelphia, Pa., in 1876; moved to New York City and resumed the practice of law; also engaged in

literary pursuits; died in New York City, December 18, 1898; interment in Hillside Cemetery, North Adams, Berkshire County, Mass.

**OSBORNE, Edwin Sylvanus,** a Representative from Pennsylvania; born in Bethany, Wayne County, Pa., August 7, 1839; attended the public schools and the University of Northern Pennsylvania at Bethany; was graduated from the New York State and National Law School at Albany, N.Y., in 1860; was admitted to the bar and practiced law in Wilkes-Barre, Pa.; entered the Union Army on August 30, 1862, as captain of Company F, One Hundred and Forty-ninth Regiment, Pennsylvania Volunteer Infantry; was promoted to major of that regiment on February 25, 1865, and served until honorably discharged on July 25, 1865; appointed by Governor John W. Geary as major general of the National Guard, Third Division, of Pennsylvania in 1870; served as commander of the Department of Pennsylvania, Grand Army of the Republic, in 1883; elected as a Republican to the Forty-ninth and to the two succeeding Congresses (March 4, 1885-March 3, 1891); was not a candidate for renomination in 1890 to the Fifty-second Congress; delegate to the Republican National Convention of 1888; resumed the practice of law in Wilkes-Barre, Pa.; moved to Washington, D.C., in 1898 and lived in retirement until his death on January 1, 1900; interment in Arlington National Cemetery, Va.

**OSBORNE, Henry,** a Delegate from Georgia; born August 21, 1751, in Newton County, Lemardy, Ireland; emigrated to Pennsylvania in 1779 and admitted to the Philadelphia bar; judge advocate of the Pennsylvania militia, October 1780; state notary public, July 1781; removed from all state offices in June 1783 following supreme executive council's determination that he was a bigamist; settled near St. Mary's, Camden County, Ga., in December 1784; held various state offices; member of the Georgia Assembly, 1786-1788; elected as a Delegate to the Continental Congress in 1786 but did not attend; chief justice of Georgia March 1787-January 1789; judge of the superior court in the western district 1789-1791; was removed from office and convicted by the Georgia senate in December 1791 of election fraud in the election of Anthony Wayne to the United States House of Representatives; his citizenship was restored under the Georgia constitution of 1798; died on St. Simons Island, Ga., November 9, 1800.

**OSBORNE, Henry Zenas,** a Representative from California; born in New Lebanon, Columbia County, N.Y., October 4, 1848; attended the public schools; during the Civil War served in the One Hundred and Ninety-second Regiment, New York Volunteer Infantry; engaged in newspaper work as printer, reporter, editor, and publisher, with residences in New York City, Cincinnati, Memphis, New Orleans, Austin, Bodie, and Los Angeles; receiver of public moneys at Bodie, Calif., 1878-1884; collector of customs in Los Angeles 1890-1894; United States marshal, southern district of California, 1898-1906; delegate to the Republican National Convention in 1888; commissioner of the board of public works, Los Angeles, in 1914 and 1915; elected as a Republican to the Sixty-fifth, Sixty-sixth, and Sixty-seventh Congresses and served from March 4, 1917, until his death; had been reelected to the Sixty-eighth Congress; died in Los Angeles, Calif., February 8, 1923; interment in Rosedale Cemetery.

**OSBORNE, John Eugene,** a Representative from Wyoming; born in Westport, Essex County, N.Y., June 19, 1858; attended the common schools and was graduated from the high school at Westport; studied medicine and was graduated from the University of Vermont at Burlington in 1880; moved to Rawlins, Wyo., and engaged in the practice of medicine; later engaged in raising livestock on the open range; member of the Wyoming Territorial legislature, 1883-1885; served as chairman of the Territorial penitentiary building commission in 1888, and as mayor of the city of Rawlins the same year; elected Governor of Wyoming in 1892, by special election to fill the second half of the term left vacant by the resignation of Francis E. Warren; served as Governor from January 2, 1893 to January 7, 1895; was renominated in 1894 but declined; chairman of the Wyoming delegation to the Democratic National Convention of 1896; elected as a Democrat to the Fifty-fifth Congress (March 4, 1897-March 3, 1899); declined to be a candidate for renomination in 1898 to the Fifty-sixth Congress; member of the Democratic National Committee, 1900-1920; served as First Assistant Secretary of State from April 21, 1913 to December 1916; engaged in banking and stock raising; died in Rawlins, Wyo., April 24, 1943; interment in Cedar Hill Cemetery, Princeton, Ky.

**OSBORNE, Thomas Burr,** a Representative from Connecticut; born in Weston (now Easton), Conn., July 8, 1798; was graduated from Yale College in 1817; studied law; was admitted to the bar in 1820 and commenced practice in Fairfield, Conn.; clerk of the county and superior courts 1826-1839; member of the State house of representatives in 1836; elected as a Whig to the Twenty-sixth and Twenty-seventh Congresses (March 4, 1839-March 3, 1843); chairman, Committee on Patents (Twenty-seventh Congress); served in the State senate in 1844, and the same year was appointed judge of the Fairfield County Court, which office he held for several years; again a member of the State house of representatives in 1850; judge of probate for Fairfield district in 1851; moved to New Haven in 1854; professor in Yale Law School from 1855 until 1865, when he resigned; died in New Haven, Conn., on September 2, 1869; interment in Evergreen Cemetery.

**OSGOOD, Gayton Pickman,** a Representative from Massachusetts; born in Salem, Mass., July 4, 1797; was graduated from Harvard University in 1815; studied law; was admitted to the bar and commenced practice in Salem; moved to North Andover in 1819; member of the Massachusetts house of representatives, 1829-1831; elected as a Jacksonian to the Twenty-third Congress (March 4, 1833-March 3, 1835); unsuccessful candidate for renomination in 1834 to the Twenty-fourth Congress; retired from public life and engaged in agricultural pursuits; died in Andover, Essex County, Mass., June 26, 1861; interment in the Old North Parish Burying Ground, North Andover, Mass.

**OSGOOD, Samuel,** a Delegate from Massachusetts; born in Andover, Essex County, Mass., February 3, 1748; graduated from Harvard College in 1770; studied theology; engaged in mercantile pursuits; delegate to the Essex County convention in 1774; member of the Provincial Congress; entered the Revolutionary Army as captain and left the service as colonel and assistant quartermaster; Member of the Continental Congress 1781-1784; member of the Massachusetts senate in 1780; member of the Massachusetts house of representatives in 1784; first commissioner of the United States Treasury 1785-1789; appointed Postmaster General in the Cabinet of President George Washington on September 26, 1789, and served until his resignation on August 12, 1791; moved to New York City; member of the New York State assembly, 1800-1803; supervisor of New York State in 1801; appointed naval officer at the port of New York on May 10, 1803, and served until his death on August 12, 1813; interment in the Brick Presbyterian Church, Nassau and Beekman Streets (now Fifth Avenue and Thirty-seventh Street), New York City.

**Bibliography:** *DAB.*

**O'SHAUNESSY, George Francis,** a Representative from Rhode Island; born in Galway, Ireland, May 1, 1868; immigrated to the United States in 1872 with his parents, who settled in New York; attended St. Theresa's School, De La Salle Institute, and Columbia College Law School, New York City; was admitted to the bar in 1889 and practiced in New York City until 1907; deputy attorney general of New York in 1904 and 1905; assistant corporation counsel of New York City in 1906; resigned and moved to Providence, R.I., in 1907; was admitted to the Rhode Island bar the same year and practiced

in Providence; member of the State house of representatives in 1910; elected as a Democrat to the Sixty-second and to the three succeeding Congresses (March 4, 1911-March 3, 1919); did not seek renomination in 1918, but was an unsuccessful candidate for election to the United States Senate; appointed collector of internal revenue for Rhode Island October 1, 1919, and served until July 31, 1921; resumed the practice of law; died in Providence, R.I., November 28, 1934; interment in St. Francis Cemetery, Pawtucket, R.I.

**OSIAS, Camilo,** a Resident Commissioner from the Philippine Islands; born in Balaoan, La Union, Philippine Islands, March 23, 1889; attended school in Balaoan, Vigan, San Fernando, and was appointed government student to the United States in 1905; was graduated from the Western Illinois State Teachers College at Macomb in 1908; attended the University of Chicago, 1906-1907; was graduated from Columbia University in New York City, and from the Teachers College of New York City in 1910; returned to the Philippine Islands and taught school; first Filipino superintendent of schools, 1915-1916; assistant director of education, 1917-1921; member of the first Philippine mission to the United States, 1919-1920; lecturer at the University of the Philippines, 1919-1921; president of the National University, 1921-1936; elected a member of the Philippine Senate in 1925; elected as a Nationalist a Resident Commissioner to the United States in 1928; reelected in 1931, and served from March 4, 1929 until January 3, 1935, when his term expired in accordance with the new Philippine Commonwealth Government; unsuccessful candidate for election to the Philippine Senate in 1934; member of the Constitutional Convention in 1934; member of the first National Assembly in 1935; member of the Economic Mission to the United States in 1939; chairman of Educational Mission, 1938-1941; chairman of National Council of Education in 1941; director of publicity and propaganda until January 1942; chairman of the National Cooperative Administration in 1941; subsequently assistant commissioner of the Department of Education, Health, and Public Welfare, then Minister of Education of the Republic of the Philippines until 1945; chancellor of Osias Colleges; elected to the Philippine Senate in 1947 for the term expiring in 1953; served as minority and majority floor leader, and was then elected president of the Philippine Senate; Philippine representative to the Interparliamentary Union in Rome and to the International Trade Conference in Genoa in 1948; unsuccessful candidate for the Nationalist Party nomination for President of the Philippines in 1953; elected as a Liberal Party member to the Philippine Senate, 1961-1967, and served as president pro tempore; was a resident of Mandaluyong, Rizal, Philippines, until his death in Manila on May 20, 1976.

**Bibliography:** Bananal, Eduardo. *Camilo Osias: Educator and Statesman.* Quezon City: Manlapaz Publishing Co., 1974; Osias, Camilo. *The Story of a Long Career of Varied Tasks.* Quezon City: Manlapaz Publishing Co., 1971.

**OSMER, James H.,** a Representative from Pennsylvania; born in Tenterden (near London), England, January 23, 1832; when an infant his parents immigrated to the United States and settled near Bellefonte, Centre County, Pa.; attended private schools, Bellefonte Academy, Centre County, Pa., Mount Pleasant College, Westmoreland County, Pa., and Pennsylvania and Dickinson Seminary, Williamsport, Pa.; studied law at Elmira, N.Y.; admitted to the bar of the supreme court of New York at Cortland in 1858 and practiced at Horseheads, near Elmira, until 1865, when he moved to Franklin, Pa., where he was admitted to the bar and practiced; delegate to the Republican National Convention in 1876; delegate to several Pennsylvania conventions; elected as a Republican to the Forty-sixth Congress (March 4, 1879-March 3, 1881); was not a candidate for renomination in 1880; continued the practice of his profession in Franklin, Venango County, Pa., until his death, October 3, 1912; interment in Franklin Cemetery.

**OSMERS, Frank Charles, Jr.,** a Representative from New Jersey; born in Leonia, Bergen County, N.J., December 30, 1907; attended the public schools and Williams College, Williamstown, Mass.; engaged in the jewelry business; member of the Haworth, N.J., Borough Council 1930-1934; mayor of Haworth, N.J., in 1935 and 1936; member of the State house of assembly 1935-1937; elected as a Republican to the Seventy-sixth and to the Seventy-seventh Congress (January 3, 1939-January 3, 1943); while a member of the Seventy-seventh Congress enlisted as a private and was graduated from the Infantry School at Fort Benning, Ga., as a second lieutenant; placed on inactive list by Presidential directive and finished his term in Congress; was not a candidate for reelection in 1942 to the Seventy-eighth Congress; went on active duty as a second lieutenant in the Seventy-seventh Infantry Division on January 4, 1943, transferred to the Twenty-fourth Corps and served in the Pacific, and was discharged on February 22, 1946; major in Officers' Reserve Corps; resumed his former business pursuits; also interested in real estate, insurance, and publishing businesses; elected as a Republican to the Eighty-second Congress, by special election, November 6, 1951, to fill the vacancy caused by the resignation of Harry L. Towe; reelected to the six succeeding Congresses and served from November 6, 1951, to January 3, 1965; unsuccessful candidate for reelection in 1964 to the Eighty-ninth Congress; unsuccessful candidate for election in 1966 to the Ninetieth Congress; executive administrator, Bergen County, N.J., 1968-1970; engaged in real estate business in Englewood, N.J.; resided in Tenafly, N.J., where he died May 21, 1977; interment in Brookside Cemetery, Englewood, N.J.

**OSTERTAG, Harold Charles,** a Representative from New York; born in Attica, Wyoming County, N.Y., June 22, 1896; attended the public schools; was graduated from Chamberlain Military Institute at Perry, N.Y., in 1915; during the First World War enlisted in the Seventy-fourth Infantry, Twenty-seventh Division, and served in France with the Fifty-fifth Pioneer Infantry; employed with the New York Central Railroad 1917-1950, advancing to assistant to the vice president, traffic department; member of the State assembly 1932-1950; member of board of managers of the Council of State Governments 1935-1950; delegate to the Republican state conventions 1930-1958; delegate to the Republican National Conventions in 1952, 1956, and 1960; elected as a Republican to the Eighty-second and to the six succeeding Congresses (January 3, 1951-January 3, 1965); was not a candidate for renomination to the Eighty-ninth Congress; was a resident of Perry, N.Y., until his death on May 2, 1985, in Pompano Beach, Fla.

**O'SULLIVAN, Eugene Daniel,** a Representative from Nebraska; born on a cattle ranch near Kent, Reno County, Kans., May 31, 1883; attended the public schools of Kent, Kans.; was graduated from Christian Brothers College, St. Joseph, Mo., in 1903; attended St. Benedict's College, Atchison, Kans., in 1904 and 1905; graduated from Creighton University Law School, Omaha, Nebr., in 1910; was admitted to the bar in 1910 and commenced the practice of law in Omaha, Nebr.; unsuccessful Democratic candidate for the gubernatorial nomination in 1934; was unsuccessful as a write-in candidate for election to the United States Senate in 1934; delegate to the Democratic National Conventions in 1924, 1928, 1932, 1940, and 1944; elected as a Democrat to the Eighty-first Congress (January 3, 1949-January 3, 1951); unsuccessful candidate for reelection in 1950 to the Eighty-second Congress; resumed the practice of law; died in Omaha, Nebr., February 7, 1968; interment in Calvary Cemetery.

**O'SULLIVAN, Patrick Brett,** a Representative from Connecticut; born in Derby, New Haven County, Conn., August 11, 1887; attended the public schools; was graduated from Yale University in 1908, from Georgetown University, Washington, D.C., in 1909, and from Yale Law School in 1913; was admitted to the bar in 1913 and commenced practice in Derby; corporation counsel of Derby

1914-1917; delegate to the Democratic National Convention in 1916; member of the State senate and its minority leader in 1917; in 1918, during the First World War, resigned from the State senate to enlist in the United States Navy; elected as a Democrat to the Sixty-eighth Congress (March 4, 1923-March 3, 1925); unsuccessful candidate for reelection in 1924 to the Sixty-ninth Congress; resumed the practice of law; associate professor of law at the Yale Law School; judge of the Connecticut Superior Court 1931-1950, associate justice of Connecticut Supreme Court 1950-1957, and chief justice in 1957, serving until August 11 of that year when he reached the mandatory retirement age; continued serving as a State trial referee in New Haven; co-chairman, Constitutional Convention, 1965; resided in Orange, Conn., where he died November 10, 1978; interment in St. Lawrence Cemetery, West Haven, Conn.

**OTERO, Mariano Sabino** (nephew of Miguel Antonio Otero), a Delegate from the Territory of New Mexico; born in Peralta, Valencia County, N.Mex., August 29, 1844; attended private and parochial schools and St. Louis University, Missouri; engaged in commercial pursuits and stock raising, and subsequently became a banker; probate judge of Bernalillo County, 1871-1879; nominated by the Democratic State convention as a candidate for Delegate to the Forty-fourth Congress, but declined; elected as a Republican to the Forty-sixth Congress (March 4, 1879-March 3, 1881); declined to be a candidate for renomination in 1880 to the Forty-seventh Congress; engaged in his former business pursuits; commissioner of Bernalillo County, 1884-1886; unsuccessful candidate for election in 1888 to the Fifty-first Congress, and in 1890 to the Fifty-second Congress; moved to Albuquerque, N.Mex., in 1889; interested in the manufacture of sulphur and engaged in banking; died in Albuquerque, Bernalillo County, N.Mex., February 1, 1904; interment in Santa Barbara Cemetery.

**OTERO, Miguel Antonio** (uncle of Mariano Sabino Otero), a Delegate from the Territory of New Mexico; born in Valencia, N.Mex., June 21, 1829; attended private and parochial schools and St. Louis University, Missouri; was graduated from Pingree's College, Fishkill, N.Y., and later became a member of the faculty; returned to St. Louis, Mo.; studied law; was admitted to the bar in 1851 and commenced practice in Albuquerque, N.Mex., in 1852; member of the Territorial house of representatives, 1852-1854; attorney general for the Territory of New Mexico in 1854; successfully contested as a Democrat the election of José M. Gallegos to the Thirty-fourth Congress and served from July 23, 1856, to March 3, 1857; reelected to the Thirty-fifth and Thirty-sixth Congresses (March 4, 1857-March 3, 1861); was not a candidate for renomination in 1860 to the Thirty-seventh Congress; delegate to the Democratic National Convention at Charleston, S.C., in 1860; appointed by President Abraham Lincoln as secretary of the Territory of New Mexico and Acting Governor in 1861, and served for one year; engaged in mercantile pursuits at Westport Landing (now Kansas City), Mo., 1861-1864, and at several other places in the West until 1877; interested in the construction of railroads and engaged in banking; unsuccessful candidate for election in 1880 to the Forty-seventh Congress; died in Las Vegas, N.Mex., May 30, 1882; interment in Riverside Cemetery, Denver, Colo.

**OTEY, Peter Johnston,** a Representative from Virginia; was born in Lynchburg, Campbell County, Va., December 22, 1840; attended private schools in Lynchburg; was graduated from the Virginia Military Institute at Lexington in 1859; engaged in civil engineering; joined the Confederate Army in 1861 and served throughout the Civil War; organized and built the Lynchburg & Durham Railroad and became president of the company; engaged in banking and was general manager of the Rivermont Land Co.; elected as a Democrat to the Fifty-fourth and to the three succeeding Congresses and served from March 4, 1895, until his death; delegate to the Democratic National Convention in 1896; died in Lynchburg, Va., May 4, 1902; interment in the Presbyterian Cemetery.

**OTIS, Harrison Gray** (son of Samuel Allyne Otis), a Representative and a Senator from Massachusetts; born in Boston, Mass., on October 8, 1765; graduated from Harvard University in 1783; studied law; was admitted to the bar in 1786 and commenced practice in Boston; elected to the Massachusetts general court in 1794 and 1795; appointed by President George Washington as district attorney for the district of Massachusetts in 1796; elected as a Federalist to the Fifth and Sixth Congresses (March 4, 1797-March 3, 1801); was not a candidate for renomination in 1800 to the Seventh Congress; appointed United States district attorney for Massachusetts by President John Adams, 1801-1802; member and speaker of the Massachusetts house of representatives, 1802-1805; member, Massachusetts senate, 1805-1813, 1814-1817, and was its president, 1805-1806, 1808-1811; overseer of Harvard University, 1810-1823; delegate to the Hartford convention in 1814; judge of the court of common pleas, 1814-1818; elected as a Federalist to the United States Senate, and served from March 4, 1817 to May 30, 1822, when he resigned; unsuccessful candidate for mayor of Boston in 1822, and for governor of Massachusetts in 1823; fellow of Harvard University, 1823-1825; mayor of Boston, 1829-1832; retired from public life; died in Boston, Mass., October 28, 1848; interment in Mount Auburn Cemetery, Cambridge, Mass.

**Bibliography:** *DAB*; Morrison, Samuel Eliot. *Harrison Gray Otis, 1765-1848: The Urbane Federalist*. 1913. Reprint. Boston: Houghton Mifflin Co., 1969.

**OTIS, John,** a Representative from Maine; born in Leeds, Maine, August 3, 1801; attended the common schools, and was graduated from Bowdoin College, Brunswick, Maine, in 1823; studied law; was admitted to the bar and commenced practice in Hallowell, Maine, in 1826; member of the State house of representatives in 1841; appointed a member of the Northeastern Boundary Commission in 1842; served in the State senate in 1842; again a member of the State house of representatives in 1846 and 1847; elected as a Whig to the Thirty-first Congress (March 4, 1849-March 3, 1851); died in Hallowell, Kennebec County, Maine, October 17, 1856; interment in Hallowell Cemetery.

**OTIS, John Grant,** a Representative from Kansas; born near Danby, Rutland County, Vt., February 10, 1838; pursued an academic course at Burr Seminary, Manchester, Vt.; attended Williams College, Williamstown, Mass., and the law department of Harvard University; was admitted to the bar of Rutland County, Vt., in 1859; moved to Topeka, Kans., in May 1859 and commenced the practice of law; assisted in recruiting the first black regiment of Kansas in 1862; paymaster general of the Governor's military staff from February 1863 to 1865, with rank of colonel; engaged in agricultural pursuits and in the dairy business near Topeka; was State agent of the Grange 1873-1875; State lecturer for the Grange 1889-1891; elected as a Populist to the Fifty-second Congress (March 4, 1891-March 3, 1893); unsuccessful candidate for renomination in 1892; engaged in his former business pursuits until his death in Topeka, Kans., February 22, 1916; interment in Topeka Cemetery.

**OTIS, Norton Prentiss,** a Representative from New York; born in Halifax, Windham County, Vt., March 18, 1840; attended public schools of Halifax, Vt., and Albany, Hudson, and Yonkers, N.Y.; in early youth entered in business with his father and engaged in the manufacture of elevators for nearly fifty years; mayor of Yonkers, N.Y., 1880-1882; member of the State assembly in 1884; president of the New York State Commission to the World's Exposition at Paris, in 1900; president of St. John's Riverside Hospital of Yonkers; unsuccessful candidate for election in 1900 to the Fifty-seventh Congress; elected as a Republican to the Fifty-eighth Congress and served from March 4, 1903, until his death at Hudson Terrace,

Westchester County, N.Y., February 20, 1905; interment in Oakland Cemetery.

**OTIS, Samuel Allyne** (father of Harrison Gray Otis), a Delegate from Massachusetts; born in Barnstable, Barnstable County, Mass., November 24, 1740; graduated from Harvard College in 1759; engaged in mercantile pursuits in Boston; member of the Massachusetts house of representatives in 1776; member of the Board of War in 1776; collector of clothing for the Continental Army in 1777; member of the Massachusetts constitutional convention; again a member of the Massachusetts house of representatives 1784-1787 and elected speaker of the house in 1784; member of the Continental Congress in 1787 and 1788; elected Secretary of the United States Senate on April 8, 1789, and served until his death in Washington, D.C., April 22, 1814; interment in Congressional Cemetery.

**OTJEN, Theobald,** a Representative from Wisconsin; born in West China, St. Clair County, Mich., on October 27, 1851; attended the Marine City (Mich.) Academy and a private school in Detroit; employed as foreman in the rolling mill of the Milwaukee Iron Co. in Milwaukee 1870-1872; was graduated from the law department of the University of Michigan at Ann Arbor March 25, 1875; admitted to the bar at Ann Arbor in 1875 and commenced practice in Detroit, Mich.; moved to Milwaukee, Wis., in 1883; member of the common council of Milwaukee 1887-1894; trustee of the Milwaukee Public Library 1887-1891; trustee of the public museum 1891-1894; unsuccessful candidate for comptroller of the city in April 1892; unsuccessful candidate for election in 1892 to the Fifty-third Congress and in 1893 to the same Congress to fill the vacancy caused by the resignation of John L. Mitchell; elected as a Republican to the Fifty-fourth and to the five succeeding Congresses (March 4, 1895-March 3, 1907); unsuccessful candidate for renomination in 1906; resumed the practice of law in Milwaukee, Wis.; died in Milwaukee, Wis., April 11, 1924; interment in Forest Home Cemetery.

**O'TOOLE, Donald Lawrence,** a Representative from New York; born in Brooklyn, N.Y., August 1, 1902; attended the public and parochial schools; was graduated from St. James Academy, Brooklyn, N.Y., in 1916 and from the law department of Fordham University, New York City, in 1925; postgraduate student at Columbia University and New York University, New York City; was admitted to the bar in 1927 and commenced practice in New York City; member of the board of aldermen 1934-1936; elected as a Democrat to the Seventy-fifth and to the seven succeeding Congresses (January 3, 1937-January 3, 1953); unsuccessful candidate for reelection in 1952 to the Eighty-third Congress and for election in 1954 to the Eighty-fourth Congress; resumed the practice of law; executive director of New York State Department of Commerce and Industry 1955-1957, and commissioner of the department from August 1, 1958, to April 29, 1959; was a resident of Brooklyn, N.Y.; died in Ocala, Fla., September 12, 1964; interment in Holy Cross Cemetery, Brooklyn, N.Y.

**OTTINGER, Richard Lawrence,** a Representative from New York; born in New York City, January 27, 1929; attended the public schools of Scarsdale and the Loomis School, Windsor, Conn.; B.A., Cornell University, Ithaca, N.Y., 1950; LL.B., Harvard University Law School, 1953; took postgraduate study in international law, Georgetown University, 1960-1961; served in the United States Air Force, 1953-1955, and was discharged as a captain; was admitted to the New York bar in 1955; practiced international and corporate law, 1955-1960; member of the board of directors of the World Policy Institute, Overseas Development Council, The Democracy Project, The League of Conservation Voters and Peace PAC; contract manager for International Cooperation Administration in 1960 and 1961; a founder and second staff member of the Peace Corps, serving as director of programs for the West Coast of South America, 1961-1964; elected as a Democrat to the Eighty-ninth and to the two succeeding Congresses (January 3, 1965-January 3, 1971); was not a candidate in 1970 for reelection to the House of Representatives, but was an unsuccessful candidate for election to the United States Senate; organizer of Grassroots Action, Inc., in Washington, D.C., 1971-1972; unsuccessful candidate for election in 1972 to the Ninety-third Congress; represented New York interest groups in opposition to governmental regulation of communication, 1972-1974; elected as a Democrat to the Ninety-fourth and to the four succeeding Congresses (January 3, 1975-January 3, 1985); was not a candidate for reelection in 1984 to the Ninety-ninth Congress; dean and professor, Pace University Law School; is a resident of Mamaroneck, N.Y.

**OURY, Granville Henderson,** a Delegate from the Territory of Arizona; born in Abingdon, Washington County, Va., March 12, 1825; moved with his parents to Bowling Green, Mo., in 1836; pursued academic studies; studied law; was admitted to the bar in 1848 at Bowling Green, Mo.; moved to San Antonio, Tex., the same year, and in 1849 moved to Marysville, Calif., and engaged in mining; went to Tucson, Ariz., in 1856 and began the practice of law; presided as judge of the district court for Arizona and New Mexico at Mesilla, N.Mex.; elected delegate from Arizona to the Confederate Congress and took his seat on January 21, 1862; resigned in 1862 to serve as captain, Herbert's Battalion, Arizona Cavalry, Confederate Army; colonel on the staff of General Henry H. Sibley in Texas and Louisiana, 1862-1864; took the oath of allegiance at Fort Mason, Ariz., October 8, 1865, and then resumed the practice of law at Tucson; elected to the Territorial house of representatives in 1866; appointed Territorial attorney general in 1869; moved to Phoenix in 1871; appointed district attorney of Maricopa County and served from 1871 to 1873; again elected to the Territorial house of representatives in 1873 and 1875, serving as speaker in 1866 and 1873; unsuccessful candidate for election in 1878 to the Forty-sixth Congress; appointed district attorney of Pinal County in 1879; elected as a Democrat to the Forty-seventh and Forty-eighth Congresses (March 4, 1881-March 3, 1885); was not a candidate for renomination in 1884 to the Forty-ninth Congress; delegate to the Democratic National Convention of 1884; returned to Florence, Ariz., in 1885 and resumed the practice of law; district attorney for Pinal County, 1889-1890; died in Tucson, Ariz., January 11, 1891; interment in the Masonic Cemetery, Florence, Ariz.

**OUTHWAITE, Joseph Hodson,** a Representative from Ohio; born in Cleveland, Ohio, December 5, 1841; attended the public schools of Zanesville, Ohio; taught in the high school of Zanesville, 1862-1864; principal of a grammar school in Columbus, Ohio, 1864-1867; studied law while teaching; was admitted to the bar in 1866 and practiced from 1867 to 1871 at Osceola, Mo.; prosecuting attorney of Franklin County, Ohio, 1874-1878; trustee of the county children's home, 1879-1883; trustee of the sinking fund of the city of Columbus (instituted to pay off the principal of the city's debt) in 1883; reappointed in 1884 for a term of five years; elected as a Democrat to the Forty-ninth and to the four succeeding Congresses (March 4, 1885-March 3, 1895); chairman, Committee on Pacific Railroads (Fiftieth Congress), Committee on Military Affairs (Fifty-second and Fifty-third Congresses); appointed a member of the commission to codify the laws of the United States; civilian member of the Board of Ordnance and Fortification, 1895-1899; member of the board of trustees of Ohio State University at Columbus from December 1896 to January 1898; dean of the law school of Ohio State University from 1904 until his death in Columbus, Ohio, December 9, 1907; interment in Greenlawn Cemetery.

**OUTLAND, George Elmer,** a Representative from California; born in Santa Paula, Ventura County, Calif., October 8, 1906; attended the public schools; A.B., Whittier (Calif.) College, 1928; M.A., Harvard University, 1929; Ph.D., education, Yale University,

1937; also attended the University of Southern California at Los Angeles; served as assistant director of boy's work, Hale House, Boston, Mass., 1928-1930; director of boy's work, Denison House, Boston, Mass., 1929-1933, and of Neighborhood House, Los Angeles, Calif., in 1933 and 1934; supervisor of boys' welfare for Federal Transient Service of Southern California in 1934 and 1935; director of New Haven (Conn.) Community College in 1935 and 1936; instructor at Yale University 1935-1937; served on the faculty of Santa Barbara (Calif.) State College 1937-1942; delegate, California State Democratic Conventions, 1942-1950; elected as a Democrat to the Seventy-eighth and Seventy-ninth Congresses (January 3, 1943-January 3, 1947); unsuccessful candidate for reelection in 1946 to the Eightieth Congress; delegate to the Democratic National Conventions of 1944 and 1948; chairman, Democratic State policy committee, 1948-1950; lecturer, University of California at Berkeley, 1950; resided in Anacortes, Wash., where he died March 2, 1981; cremated; ashes interred at Santa Paula Cemetery, Santa Paula, Calif.

**OUTLAW, David** (cousin of George Outlaw), a Representative from North Carolina; born near Windsor, Bertie County, N.C., September 14, 1806; attended the private schools and academies of Bertie County; was graduated from the University of North Carolina at Chapel Hill in 1824; studied law; was admitted to the bar in 1825 and commenced practice in Windsor, N.C.; member of the State house of representatives 1831-1834, 1854, and 1858; delegate to the State constitutional convention at Raleigh in 1835; solicitor of the first judicial district 1836-1844; delegate to the Whig National Convention in 1844; colonel of the Bertie County Regiment of State militia; elected as a Whig to the Thirtieth, Thirty-first, and Thirty-second Congresses (March 4, 1847-March 3, 1853); unsuccessful candidate for reelection in 1852 to the Thirty-third Congress; resumed the practice of law in Windsor, Bertie County, N.C.; served in the State senate in 1860 and 1866; died in Windsor, N.C., October 22, 1868; interment in the Episcopal Cemetery.

**OUTLAW, George** (cousin of David Outlaw), a Representative from North Carolina; born near Windsor, Bertie County, N.C.; educated by private teachers and in the common schools; engaged in agricultural and mercantile pursuits; member of the State house of commons 1796-1797; served in the State senate in 1802, 1806-1808, 1810-1814, 1817, 1821, and 1822, and served as speaker in 1812, 1813, and 1814; elected to the Eighteenth Congress to fill the vacancy caused by the resignation of Hutchins G. Burton and served from January 19, 1825, to March 3, 1825; was not a candidate for reelection to the Nineteenth Congress; resumed agricultural and mercantile pursuits; died in Windsor, Bertie County, N.C., August 15, 1825; interment in the family cemetery.

**OVERMAN, Lee Slater,** a Senator from North Carolina; born in Salisbury, Rowan County, N.C., January 3, 1854; attended private schools and graduated from Trinity College (now Duke University), Durham, N.C., in 1874; taught school two years; private secretary to Governor Zebulon B. Vance, 1877-1879; studied law; was admitted to the bar in 1878 and began practice in Salisbury, N.C., in 1880; member of the North Carolina State house of representatives in 1883, 1885, 1887, 1893, 1899, and served as speaker in 1893; president of the North Carolina Railroad Co. in 1894; unsuccessful Democratic candidate for United States Senator in 1895; president of the Salisbury Savings Bank; member of the board of trustees of the University of North Carolina and Duke University; presidential elector on the Democratic ticket in 1900; elected as a Democrat to the United States Senate in 1903; reelected in 1909, 1914, 1920, and again in 1926, and served from March 4, 1903, until his death in Washington, D.C., December 12, 1930; chairman, Committee on Revolutionary Claims (Sixty-first Congress), Committee on Woman Suffrage (Sixty-second Congress), Committee on Rules (Sixty-third through Sixty-fifth Congresses), Committee on Engrossed Bills

(Sixty-sixth Congress); funeral services were held in the Chamber of the United States Senate; interment in Chestnut Hill Cemetery, Salisbury, N.C.

**Bibliography:** *DAB.*

**OVERMYER, Arthur Warren,** a Representative from Ohio; born near Lindsey, Sandusky County, Ohio, on May 31, 1879; attended the public schools and also Lima Lutheran College; taught school; was graduated from the Ohio Northern University Law School at Ada in 1902; was admitted to the bar in 1902 and commenced practice in Fremont, Ohio; clerk of the Fremont Board of Health, 1907-1910; city solicitor, 1910-1914; elected as a Democrat to the Sixty-fourth and Sixty-fifth Congresses (March 4, 1915-March 3, 1919); unsuccessful candidate for reelection in 1918 to the Sixty-sixth Congress; appointed judge of the court of common pleas by Governor Alvin Victor Donahey on April 10, 1926, and elected to that position in November of the same year; reelected in 1930 and served until his resignation on December 1, 1934, having been appointed by Governor George White to a vacancy in the Ohio Sixth District Court of Appeals; elected in 1936 for a six-year term; in 1942 was chosen as chief justice of the nine courts of appeals of Ohio; retired from the courts on February 8, 1943; resumed the private practice of law in Fremont, Ohio, until his retirement in 1951; died in North Royalton, Ohio, March 8, 1952; interment in Four-Mile House Cemetery, near Fremont, Ohio.

**OVERSTREET, James,** a Representative from South Carolina; born near Barnwell Court House, Barnwell District, S.C., February 11, 1773; attended the common schools; studied law; was admitted to the bar in 1798 and commenced practice in Barnwell District; member, State house of representatives, 1808-1813; elected to the Sixteenth and Seventeenth Congresses and served from March 4, 1819, until his death May 24, 1822, at China Grove, Rowan County, N.C., while en route to his home from Washington, D.C.; interment in Savitz Cemetery at Mount Zion Reformed Church, China Grove, N.C.

**OVERSTREET, James Whetstone,** a Representative from Georgia; born on a farm near Sylvania, Screven County, Ga., August 28, 1866; attended the rural schools and Sylvania High School; was graduated from Mercer (Ga.) University in 1888; studied law in Augusta; was admitted to the bar in 1892 and commenced practice in Sylvania, Ga.; member of the State house of representatives in 1898 and 1899; member of the Democratic executive committee in 1905 and 1906; appointed judge of the city court of Sylvania in December 1902 and served until October 1, 1906, when he resigned; elected as a Democrat to the Fifty-ninth Congress to fill the vacancy caused by the death of Rufus E. Lester and served from October 3, 1906, to March 4, 1907; resumed the practice of law in Sylvania; delegate to the Democratic National Convention in 1912; elected to the Sixty-fifth, Sixty-sixth, and Sixty-seventh Congresses (March 4, 1917-March 3, 1923); unsuccessful candidate for renomination in 1922; resumed the practice of law in Sylvania, Ga., where he died December 4, 1938; interment in Sylvania Cemetery.

**OVERSTREET, Jesse,** a Representative from Indiana; born in Franklin, Johnson County, Ind., December 14, 1859; attended the schools of his native city; was graduated from the Franklin High School in 1877 and from Franklin College in 1882; studied law; was admitted to the bar in 1886 and commenced practice in Franklin; member of the Republican State central committee of Indiana in 1892; elected as a Republican to the Fifty-fourth and to the six succeeding Congresses (March 4, 1895-March 3, 1909); chairman, Committee on Expenditures in the Department of Justice (Fifty-sixth and Fifty-seventh Congresses), Committee on the Post Office and Post Roads (Fifty-eighth through Sixtieth Congresses); unsuccessful candidate for reelection in 1908 to the Sixty-first Congress;

resumed the practice of his profession; died in Indianapolis, Ind., May 27, 1910; interment in the Columbus City Cemetery, Columbus, Ind.

**OVERTON, Edward, Jr.,** a Representative from Pennsylvania; born in Towanda, Bradford County, Pa., February 4, 1836; attended Susquehanna Collegiate Institute, Towanda, Pa., and was graduated from Princeton College in 1856; studied law; was admitted to the bar in 1858 and commenced practice in Towanda, Pa.; solicitor of Bradford County in 1861; during the Civil War entered the Union Army in September 1861 as a major in the Fiftieth Regiment, Pennsylvania Volunteer Infantry; promoted to lieutenant colonel in 1863 and from that time commanded the regiment until mustered out in October 1864; served as register in bankruptcy 1867-1876; elected as a Republican to the Forty-fifth and Forty-sixth Congresses (March 4, 1877-March 3, 1881); unsuccessful candidate for renomination in 1880; resumed the practice of law; president of the Citizens' National Bank of Towanda from 1897 until his death in Towanda, Pa., September 18, 1903; interment in Oak Hill Cemetery.

**OVERTON, John Holmes** (uncle of Overton Brooks), a Representative and a Senator from Louisiana; born in Marksville, Avoyelles Parish, La., September 17, 1875; attended the public schools; graduated from the Louisiana State University at Baton Rouge in 1895 and from the law department of Tulane University, New Orleans, La., in 1897; was admitted to the bar in 1898 and commenced practice in Alexandria, La.; member of the board of supervisors of Louisiana State University; elected as a Democrat to the Seventy-second Congress to fill the vacancy caused by the death of James B. Aswell and served from May 12, 1931, to March 3, 1933; did not seek renomination in 1932, having become a candidate for Senator; elected to the United States Senate in 1932; reelected in 1938, and again in 1944, and served from March 4, 1933, until his death in the naval hospital at Bethesda, Md., on May 14, 1948; chairman, Committee on Manufactures (Seventy-sixth through Seventy-ninth Congresses), Committee on Commerce (Seventy-ninth Congress), Committee on Irrigation and Reclamation (Seventy-ninth Congress); interment in Mount Olivet Cemetery, Pineville, La.

**Bibliography:** Hammond, Hilda. *Let Freedom Ring.* New York: Farrar and Rinehard, Inc., 1936.

**OVERTON, Walter Hampden,** a Representative from Louisiana; born near Louisa Court House, Va., in 1788; moved in infancy with his father to North Carolina, and thence to Tennessee in 1801; attended the common schools; entered the Army in 1808, and promoted through the ranks to major in the Third Rifles on February 21, 1814; transferred to the Artillery Corps on May 17, 1815; brevetted lieutenant colonel on December 23, 1814, for actions at the Battle of New Orleans, January 8, 1815; resigned October 31, 1815; commissioned major general of militia by the Louisiana Legislature; settled near Alexandria, Rapides Parish, La.; member of the courthouse building commission in 1820 and 1821; member of the commission on the navigation of Bayou Rapides in 1824; engaged in planting; elected as a Jacksonian to the Twenty-first Congress (March 4, 1829-March 3, 1831); was not a candidate for renomination in 1830 to the Twenty-second Congress; returned to his plantation near Alexandria, Rapides Parish, La.; died near Alexandria, December 24, 1845; interment in McNutt Hill Cemetery.

**OWEN, Allen Ferdinand,** a Representative from Georgia; born on a plantation near the Yadkin River, Wilkes County, N.C., October 9, 1816; moved to Talbotton, Talbot County, Ga.; studied under private teachers; was graduated from Franklin College, Athens, Ga., from Yale College in 1837, and from the Dane Law School of Harvard University in 1839; was admitted to the bar at Boston in 1839 and commenced practice in Talbotton, Ga., in 1840; member of the State house of representatives 1843-1847; clerk of the State house of representatives in 1848; delegate to the Whig National

Convention in 1848; elected as a Whig to the Thirty-first Congress (March 4, 1849-March 3, 1851); later became affiliated with the Democratic Party; consul at Havana, Cuba, from May to December 1851; resumed the practice of law in Talbotton, Ga.; died in Upatoi, Muscogee County, Ga., April 7, 1865, while on a visit with relatives; interment in Oak Hill Cemetery, Talbotton, Ga.

**OWEN, Emmett Marshall,** a Representative from Georgia; born on a farm near Hollonville, Pike County, Ga., October 19, 1877; attended the Hollonville grammar school; was graduated from Gordon Institute, Barnesville, Ga., in 1898 and from the law department of the University of Georgia at Athens in 1900; taught school in Butts County, Ga., in 1901 and 1902; was admitted to the bar in 1902 and commenced practice in Zebulon, Ga.; also operated a large peach farm; member of the State house of representatives 1902-1906; mayor of Zebulon 1905-1907; served as solicitor of the Pike County Court 1906-1909, as solicitor of the city court of Zebulon, Ga., 1909-1912, as solicitor general for the Flint judicial circuit 1913-1923, and as solicitor general for the Griffin judicial circuit 1923-1933; elected as a Democrat to the Seventy-third and to the three succeeding Congresses and served from March 4, 1933, until his death in Washington, D.C., on June 21, 1939; interment in East View Cemetery, Zebulon, Ga.

**OWEN, George Washington,** a Representative from Alabama; born in Brunswick County, Va., on October 20, 1796; moved with his parents to Tennessee; attended the common schools and was graduated from the University of Nashville Tennessee; studied law; was admitted to the bar in 1816 and commenced practice in Claiborne, Ala.; unsuccessful candidate for election in 1821 to the Seventeenth Congress; member of the State house of representatives 1819-1821 and served as speaker in 1821; elected to the Eighteenth, Nineteenth, and Twentieth Congresses (March 4, 1823-March 3, 1829); appointed collector of the port of Mobile by President Andrew Jackson and served from April 20, 1828, to July 20, 1836; elected mayor of Mobile in 1836 and held the position until his death, which occurred on his plantation near Mobile, Ala., August 18, 1837; interment in the Old Church Street Cemetery, Mobile, Ala.

**OWEN, James,** a Representative from North Carolina; born near Wilmington, Bladen County, N.C., on December 7, 1784; educated at Bingham's Academy, Pittsboro, N.C.; engaged in agricultural pursuits; member of the State house of commons 1808-1811; served as president of the Wilmington & Raleigh Railroad Co.; elected as a Republican to the Fifteenth Congress (March 4, 1817-March 3, 1819); died in Wilmington, N.C., September 4, 1865; interment in Oakdale Cemetery.

**OWEN, Robert Dale,** a Representative from Indiana; born in Glasgow, Scotland, November 7, 1801; studied under private teachers and attended the Emanuel von Fellenberg School at Hofwyl, near Berne, Switzerland, 1820-1823; immigrated to the United States in 1825 with his parents, who settled in Posey County, Ind.; aided his father in the establishment of the social community of New Harmony, Ind., and on the failure of that project he returned to Europe for further study; returned to the United States in 1827 and became a citizen; was the founder and editor of the Free Enquirer, published in New York, 1828-1832; returned to New Harmony in 1832; member of the Indiana State house of representatives, 1835-1838; unsuccessful candidate for election in 1838 to the Twenty-sixth Congress, and in 1840 to the Twenty-seventh Congress; elected as a Democrat to the Twenty-eighth and Twenty-ninth Congresses (March 4, 1843-March 3, 1847); chairman, Committee on Roads and Canals (Twenty-eighth Congress); unsuccessful candidate for reelection in 1846 to the Thirtieth Congress; member of the State constitutional convention in 1850; member of the State house of representatives in 1851; appointed by President Franklin Pierce as Chargé d'Affaires to the Two Sicilies on May 24,

1853, and as Minister Resident on June 29, 1854, serving until September 1858; was nominated on February 25, 1856 to be Envoy Extraordinary and Minister Plenipotentiary, but the nomination was withdrawn before the Senate acted on it; devoted the remainder of his life to writing on social problems; died at his summer home "Cosy Cove," at Crosbyside, on Lake George, N.Y., June 24, 1877; interment in the Village Cemetery at Lake George, Warren County, N.Y.

**Bibliography:** *DAB*; Leopold, Richard William. *Robert Dale Owen: A Biography*. Cambridge, Mass.: Harvard University Press, 1940; Pancoast, Elinor, and Anne E. Lincoln. *The Incorrigible Idealist: Robert Dale Owen in America*. Bloomington, Ind.: Principia Press, 1940.

**OWEN, Robert Latham,** a Senator from Oklahoma; born in Lynchburg, Campbell County, Va., February 2, 1856; attended private schools in Lynchburg, Va., and Baltimore, Md.; graduated from Washington and Lee University, Lexington, Va., in 1877; moved to Salina, Indian Territory, and taught school among the Cherokee Indians; studied law; was admitted to the bar in 1880 and commenced practice; federal Indian agent for the Five Civilized Tribes 1885-1889; member of the Democratic National Committee 1892-1896; organized the First National Bank of Muskogee in 1890 and was its president for ten years; upon the admission of Oklahoma as a State into the Union in 1907 was elected as a Democrat to the United States Senate for the term ending March 3, 1913; reelected in 1912, and again in 1918, and served from December 11, 1907, to March 3, 1925; declined to be a candidate for renomination in 1924; chairman, Committee on Indian Depredations (Sixty-second Congress), Committee on the Mississippi River and Its Tributaries (Sixty-second Congress), Committee on Pacific Railroads (Sixty-second Congress), Committee on Banking and Currency (Sixty-third through Sixty-fifth Congresses), Committee on the Five Civilized Tribes (Sixty-sixth Congress); resumed the practice of law in Washington, D.C.; organized and served as chairman of the National Popular Government League from 1913 until his death in Washington, D.C., July 19, 1947; interment in Spring Hill Cemetery, Lynchburg, Va.

**Bibliography:** *DAB*; Brown, Kenny. "A Progressive From Oklahoma: Senator Robert Latham Owen, Jr." *Chronicles of Oklahoma* 62 (Fall 1984): 232-65; Keso, Edward. *The Senatorial Career of Robert Latham Owen*. Gardenvale, Canada: Garden City Press, 1938.

**OWEN, Ruth Bryan** (later Mrs. Borge Rohde; daughter of William Jennings Bryan), a Representative from Florida; born in Jacksonville, Morgan County, Ill., October 2, 1885; moved to Lincoln, Nebr., with her parents in 1887; educated in the public schools; attended Monticello Seminary, Godfrey, Ill., and the University of Nebraska at Lincoln; spent three years in Jamaica, West Indies, 1910-1912, and three years in London, England, 1912-1915; member of the executive committee of the American Women's War Relief Fund in London; served as a war nurse in the Voluntary Aid Detachment in the Egypt-Palestine campaign, 1915-1918; returned to the United States in 1919 and settled in Miami, Fla.; Lyceum and Chautauqua lecturer from 1918 until 1928; vice president of the board of regents of the University of Miami, 1925-1928, and member of the faculty, 1926-1928; elected as a Democrat to the Seventy-first and Seventy-second Congresses (March 4, 1929-March 3, 1933); unsuccessful candidate for renomination in 1932 to the Seventy-third Congress; delegate to the Interparliamentary Union at London in 1930; appointed Minister to Denmark by President Franklin D. Roosevelt on April 13, 1933, and served until her resignation on August 30, 1936; special assistant in the Division of Public Liaison of the Department of State at the founding conference of the United Nations at San Francisco in 1945; member of the Advisory Board of the Federal Reformatory for Women, 1938-1954; member of the board of trustees of the Starr

Commonwealth for Boys, 1941-1954; engaged in literary work and lecturing and resided in Ossining, N.Y.; died while on a visit in Copenhagen, Denmark, July 26, 1954; remains were cremated and the ashes buried in Ordrup Cemetery, near Copenhagen, Denmark.

**Bibliography:** Vickers, Sarah Pauline. "The Life of Ruth Bryan Owen: Florida's First Congresswoman and America's First Woman Diplomat." Ph.D. dissertation, Florida State University, 1994.

**OWEN, William Dale,** a Representative from Indiana; born in Bloomington, Ind., on September 6, 1846; attended Indiana University at Bloomington in 1865 and entered upon the study of law; relinquished law for the ministry; pastor of the Logansport (Ind.) Christian Church until 1878; elected as a Republican to the Forty-ninth, Fiftieth, and Fifty-first Congresses (March 4, 1885-March 3, 1891); unsuccessful candidate for reelection in 1890 to the Fifty-second Congress; elected secretary of state of Indiana and served from January 16, 1895, to January 15, 1899; engaged in real estate speculation and interested in rubber plantations in Mexico; in 1906 went to Europe, where he died.

**OWENS, Douglas Wayne,** a Representative from Utah; born in Panguitch, Garfield County, Utah, May 2, 1937; educated in the public schools; graduated from Panguitch High School, 1955; attended the University of Utah, Salt Lake City, 1955-1957, 1960-1961; J.D., University of Utah Law School, 1964; missionary to France, Church of Jesus Christ of Latter-Day Saints, 1957-1960; admitted to the Utah bar in 1965 and commenced practice in Salt Lake City; western states coordinator for the presidential campaigns of Robert F. Kennedy in 1968 and Edward M. Kennedy in 1980; administrative assistant to Senator Edward M. Kennedy, majority whip's office, 1969-1971; administrative assistant to Senator Frank E. Moss of Utah, 1971-1972; delegate, Utah State Democratic conventions, 1964-1968; delegate to the Democratic National Conventions of 1968 and 1980; elected as a Democrat to the Ninety-third Congress (January 3, 1973-January 3, 1975); was not a candidate in 1974 for renomination to the House of Representatives, but was an unsuccessful candidate for election to the United States Senate; president of the Montreal, Canada Mission for the Church of Jesus Christ of Latter-Day Saints, 1975-1978; returned to the practice of law in Salt Lake City and Washington; elected as a Democrat to the One Hundredth and the two succeeding Congresses (January 3, 1987-January 3, 1993); was not a candidate for renomination in 1992 to the House of Representatives, but was an unsuccessful candidate for election to the United States Senate; president, Center for Middle East Peace and Economic Cooperation, Washington, D.C.; is a resident of Salt Lake City, Utah.

**OWENS, George Welshman,** a Representative from Georgia; born in Savannah, Ga., August 29, 1786; attended school in Harrow, England, and was graduated from Cambridge University; studied law in the office of Mr. Chitty in London; returned to Savannah, Ga.; was admitted to the bar and practiced; elected as a Jacksonian to the Twenty-fourth Congress and reelected as a Democrat to the Twenty-fifth Congress (March 4, 1835-March 3, 1839); resumed the practice of law; died in Savannah, Ga., March 2, 1856; interment in Laurel Grove Cemetery.

**OWENS, James W.,** a Representative from Ohio; born in Springfield Township, Franklin County, Ind., October 24, 1837; pursued academic studies; was graduated from Miami University, Oxford, Ohio, in 1862; during the Civil War enlisted in the Union Army as a private in the Twentieth Regiment, Ohio Volunteer Infantry, for three months' service; reenlisted and was made first lieutenant of Company A, Eighty-sixth Regiment, Ohio Volunteer Infantry, and on the reorganization of that regiment was made captain of Company K; attended the law department of the University of Michigan at Ann Arbor in 1864 and 1865; was admitted to the bar in 1865 and commenced practice in Newark,

Licking County, Ohio; elected prosecuting attorney of Licking County in 1867 and reelected in 1869; elected to the State senate in 1875; reelected in 1877, and served as president of that body; member of the board of trustees of Miami University 1878-1896; elected as a Democrat to the Fifty-first and Fifty-second Congresses (March 4, 1889-March 3, 1893); chairman, Committee on Expenditures in the Department of the Interior (Fifty-second Congress); was not a candidate for renomination in 1892; resumed the practice of his profession; died in Newark, Licking County, Ohio, on March 30, 1900; interment in Cedar Hill Cemetery.

**OWENS, Major Robert Odell,** a Representative from New York; born in Memphis, Tenn., June 28, 1936; attended Hamilton High School, Memphis, Tenn.; B.A., Morehouse College, 1956; M.S., Atlanta University, 1957; Columbia University (New York); chairman, Brooklyn Congress of Racial Equality; vice president, Metropolitan Council of Housing, 1964; community coordinator, Brooklyn Public Library, 1964-1966; executive director, Brownsville Community Council, 1966-1968; commissioner, New York City Community Development Agency, 1968-1973; director of the community media library program at Columbia University, 1973-1975; member, New York State senate, 1974-1982; served on the International Commission on Ways of Implementing Social Policy to Ensure Maximum Public Participation and Social Justice for Minorities at The Hague, Netherlands, 1972; elected as a Democrat to the Ninety-eighth and to the six succeeding Congresses (January 3, 1983-January 3, 1997); is a resident of Brooklyn, N.Y.

**OWENS, Thomas Leonard,** a Representative from Illinois; born in Chicago, Ill., December 21, 1897; attended the parochial schools, Northwestern University, and De Paul University, Chicago, Ill.; was graduated from Loyola University Law School, Chicago, Ill., in 1926; was admitted to the bar in 1927 and commenced practice in Chicago, Ill.; during the First World War served in the Students' Army Training Corps at Loyola University in 1918; elected as a Republican to the Eightieth Congress and served from January 3, 1947, until his death in Bethesda, Md., June 7, 1948; interment in All Saints' Cemetery, Chicago, Ill.

**OWENS, William Claiborne,** a Representative from Kentucky; born near Georgetown, Scott County, Ky., October 17, 1849; attended the common schools, also Kentucky Wesleyan College, Millersburg Ky., Transylvania University, Lexington, Ky., and graduated from Columbia Law College, New York City, in 1872; admitted to the bar in the same year and commenced practice in Georgetown, Ky.; prosecuting attorney for Scott County from 1874 to 1877, when he resigned; member of the Kentucky house of representatives 1877-1887 and served as speaker in 1882 and 1883; delegate to the Democratic National Convention in 1892; elected as a Democrat to the Fifty-fourth Congress (March 4, 1895-March 3, 1897); was not a candidate for renomination in 1896; became affiliated with the Republican Party in 1896; major in the Second Regiment, Kentucky Volunteers, during the Spanish-American War in 1898; moved to Louisville, Ky., in 1900 and resumed the practice of law; died in Louisville, Ky., November 18, 1925; interment in Georgetown Cemetery, Georgetown, Ky.

**OWSLEY, Bryan Young,** a Representative from Kentucky; born near Crab Orchard, Lincoln County, Ky., August 19, 1798; attended the common schools of Lincoln County; studied law and was admitted to the bar; moved to Jamestown, Ky.; clerk of the circuit court in 1827; elected as a Whig to the Twenty-seventh Congress (March 4, 1841-March 3, 1843); unsuccessful candidate for reelection in 1842 to the Twenty-eighth Congress; register of the United States land office, with residence in Frankfort, 1845-1849; died in Frankfort, Franklin County, Ky., on October 27, 1849.

**OXLEY, Michael Garver,** a Representative from Ohio; born in Findlay, Hancock County, Ohio, February 11, 1944; attended the city schools of Findlay; graduated, Findlay Senior High School, 1982; B.A., Miami University, Oxford, Ohio, 1966; J.D., Ohio State University College of Law, Columbus, 1969; Special Agent of the Federal Bureau of Investigation in Washington, D.C., Boston, and New York City, 1969-1972; admitted to the Ohio bar in 1969 and commenced practice in Findlay; member, Ohio State house of representatives, 1972-1981; delegate to Ohio State Republican conventions, 1972-1980; delegate to the Republican National Conventions of 1976 and 1984; elected as a Republican to the Ninety-seventh Congress, June 25, 1981, by special election to fill the vacancy caused by the death of Tennyson Guyer; reelected to the seven succeeding Congresses and served from June 25, 1981, to January 3, 1997; is a resident of Findlay, Ohio.

# P

**PACA, William,** a Delegate from Maryland; born at "Wye Hall," near Abingdon, Queen Anne (now Harford) County, Md., October 31, 1740; was graduated from Philadelphia College in 1759; studied law in Annapolis, Md., and in the Middle Temple, London, England; admitted to the bar in 1764; returned home and commenced the practice of his profession at Annapolis in 1764; member of the provincial assembly, 1771-1774; Member of the Continental Congress, 1774-1779; a signer of the Declaration of Independence; served in the Maryland State senate, 1777-1779; chief judge of the superior court of Maryland, 1778-1780; chief justice of the court of appeals in prize and admiralty cases, 1780-1782; Governor of Maryland from November 1782 to November 1785; was influential in establishing Washington College in Chestertown, Md., in 1786; delegate to the State convention in 1788 which ratified the Federal Constitution; appointed by President George Washington as judge of the United States Court for Maryland, and served from 1789 until his death at "Wye Hall," Queen Anne County, Md., October 23, 1799; interment in the family burial ground, Queen Anne County, Md.

**Bibliography:** *DAB*; Stiverson, Gregory A., and Phebe R. Jacobsen. *William Paca: A Biography*. Baltimore: Maryland Historical Society, 1976.

**PACE, Stephen,** a Representative from Georgia; born in Terrell County, Ga., near Dawson, March 9, 1891; attended the public schools and Georgia School of Technology at Atlanta; was graduated from the law department of the University of Georgia at Athens in 1914; was admitted to the bar the same year and commenced practice in Americus, Ga.; also engaged in agricultural pursuits; served in the State house of representatives 1917-1920; was a member of the State senate in 1923 and 1924; elected as a Democrat to the Seventy-fifth and to the six succeeding Congresses (January 3, 1937-January 3, 1951); did not seek renomination in 1950; resumed the practice of law in Americus, Ga., and practiced until his death there April 5, 1970; interment in Sunset Memorial Gardens.

**PACHECO, Romualdo,** a Representative from California; born in Santa Barbara, Calif., October 31, 1831; was instructed by private tutors; engaged in nautical pursuits and subsequently in agriculture; member of the California State senate in 1851 and again in 1861; member of the State assembly, 1853-1855, and 1868-1870; county judge, 1855-1859; State treasurer, 1863-1866; Lieutenant Governor, 1871-1875; became Governor of California when Governor Newton Booth was elected to the United States Senate, and served from February 27 to December 9, 1875; presented credentials as a Republican Member-elect to the Forty-fifth Congress, and served from March 4, 1877 to February 7, 1878, when he was succeeded by Peter D. Wigginton, who contested his election; elected as a Republican to the Forty-sixth and Forty-seventh Congresses (March 4, 1879-March 3, 1883); chairman, Committee on Private Land Claims (Forty-seventh Congress); appointed Envoy Extraordinary and Minister Plenipotentiary to the Central American States (resident at Guatemala) on December 11, 1890, serving to Costa Rica and Nicaragua until October 1891, to El Salvador until November 1891, and to Guatemala and Honduras until June 1893; died in Oakland, Calif., January 23, 1899; interment in Mountain View Cemetery.

**Bibliography:** *DAB*; Conmy, Peter Thomas. *Romualdo Pacheco: Distinguished Californian of the Mexican and American Periods*. San Francisco: Grand Parlor, Native Sons of the Golden West, 1957; Genini, Ronald, and Richard Hitchman. *Romualdo Pacheco: A Californian in Two Eras*. San Francisco: Book Club of California, 1985; Nicholson, Loren. *Romualdo Pacheco's California: The Mexican-American Who Won*. San Luis Obispo: California Heritage Publishing Associates, 1990.

**PACKARD, Jasper,** a Representative from Indiana; born in Austintown, Mahoning County, Ohio, February 1, 1832; moved with his parents to Indiana in 1835; attended the public schools and was graduated from the University of Michigan at Ann Arbor in 1855; taught school; settled in La Porte, Ind.; studied law and was admitted to the bar in 1861; during the Civil War enlisted in the Union Army as a private in the Forty-eighth Regiment, Indiana Volunteer Infantry, October 24, 1861; promoted to first lieutenant on January 1, 1862, and to captain on September 12, 1862; was wounded during the assault on Vicksburg, Miss., May 1863; commissioned lieutenant colonel of the One Hundred and Twenty-eighth Regiment, Indiana Volunteer Infantry, on March 17, 1864; appointed colonel on June 26, 1865; brevetted brigadier general, March 13, 1865, "for meritorious services"; mustered out on April 10, 1866; auditor of La Porte County from November 15, 1866 to March 1, 1869, when he resigned; elected as a Republican to the Forty-first and to the two succeeding Congresses (March 4, 1869-March 3, 1875); chairman, Committee on Expenditures in the Department of State (Forty-third Congress), Committee on Private Land Claims (Forty-third Congress); was not a candidate for renomination in 1874 to the Forty-fourth Congress; engaged in newspaper pursuits; appointed commandant of the State soldiers' home at Lafayette, Ind., on July 1, 1899, and died there on December 13, 1899; interment in the Soldiers' Home Cemetery.

**PACKARD, Ronald C.,** a Representative from California; born in Meridian, Ada County, Idaho, January 19, 1931; attended Meridian Elementary School, and graduated from Meridian High School, 1948; attended Brigham Young University, Provo, Utah, 1948-1950, Portland State University (Oreg.), 1952-1953; D.M.D., University of Oregon Dental School, Portland, 1953-1957; dentist; served as a lieutenant in the United States Navy Dental Corps, 1957-1959; chair, Carlsbad, Calif. School District Board, 1960-1972; member, Carlsbad, Calif. city council, 1976-1978; mayor of Carlsbad, 1978-1982; director, North County Transit District, 1978-1982; won as a write-in candidate in 1982 election to the United States House of Representatives; elected as a Republican to the Ninety-eighth and to the six succeeding Congresses (January 3, 1983-January 3, 1997); is a resident of Oceanside, Calif.

**PACKER, Asa,** a Representative from Pennsylvania; born in Mystic, New London County, Conn., December 29, 1805; attended the district schools; moved to Springfield, Pa., in 1820; learned the trade of carpenter; moved to Mauch Chunk, Pa., in 1833; engaged in mercantile pursuits, and established a boat yard for the construction of canal boats; became interested in the production of coal and also in railroads; member of the Pennsylvania house of representatives in 1842 and 1843; associate judge of Carbon County in 1843 and 1844; built the Lehigh Valley Railroad in 1852 and was president of the company at the time of his death; elected as a Democrat to the Thirty-third and Thirty-fourth Congresses (March 4, 1853-March 3, 1857); declined to be a candidate for renomination in 1856; resumed his former business interests; founded Lehigh University, Bethlehem, Pa.; unsuccessful candidate for Governor of Pennsylvania in

1869; died in Philadelphia, Pa., on May 17, 1879; interment in the Mauch Chunk Cemetery, Mauch Creek, Pa.

Bibliography: *DAB*.

**PACKER, Horace Billings**, a Representative from Pennsylvania; born in Wellsboro, Tioga County, Pa., on October 11, 1851; attended the common schools, the Wellsboro Academy, and Alfred (N.Y.) University; studied law; admitted to the bar of Tioga County in 1873 and commenced practice in Wellsboro; also engaged in the real estate business; district attorney of Tioga County 1875-1879; elected to the Pennsylvania house of representatives in 1884 and reelected in 1886; member of the Pennsylvania senate 1888-1892; served many years as a member of the borough council; presided over the Pennsylvania Republican conventions of 1893 and 1894; elected as a Republican to the Fifty-fifth and Fifty-sixth Congresses (March 4, 1897-March 3, 1901); was not a candidate for renomination in 1900; resumed the practice of law in Wellsboro, Pa.; also engaged in the real estate, banking, and lumber businesses; delegate to the Republican National Convention in 1924; died in Wellsboro, Pa., April 13, 1940; interment in Wellsboro Cemetery.

**PACKER, John Black**, a Representative from Pennsylvania; born in Sunbury, Northumberland County, Pa., March 21, 1824; received private instructions and later attended Sunbury (Pa.) Academy; member of the corps of engineers employed by Pennsylvania in the survey and construction of public improvements 1839-1842; studied law; admitted to the bar on August 6, 1844, and commenced the practice of his profession in Sunbury; also engaged in banking; deputy attorney general 1845-1847; served in the Pennsylvania house of representatives in 1850 and 1851; one of the organizers of the Susquehanna Railroad Co., in 1851; elected as a Republican to the Forty-first and to the three succeeding Congresses (March 4, 1869-March 3, 1877); chairman, Committee on Railways and Canals (Forty-second Congress), Committee on Post Office and Post Roads (Forty-third Congress); declined to be a candidate for renomination in 1876; resumed the practice of law in Sunbury, Pa.; also resumed his banking activities; died in Sunbury, Pa., July 7, 1891; interment in Pomfret Manor Cemetery.

**PACKWOOD, Robert William**, a Senator from Oregon; born in Portland, Multnomah County, Oreg., September 11, 1932; B.A., Willamette University, Salem, Oreg., 1954; LL.B., New York University School of Law, New York City, 1957; admitted to the bar in 1957 and commenced practice in Portland, Oreg.; member of the Oregon State house of representatives, 1963-1968; elected as a Republican to the United States Senate in 1968; reelected in 1974, 1980, 1986, and again in 1992, and served from January 3, 1969 until his resignation on October 1, 1995; chairman, Republican Senatorial Campaign Committee (Ninety-fifth and Ninety-seventh Congresses), Republican Conference (Ninety-sixth Congress), Committee on Commerce, Science and Transportation (Ninety-seventh and Ninety-eighth Congresses), Committee on Finance (Ninety-ninth and One Hundred Fourth Congresses); established a government consulting firm in Washington, D.C.; is a resident of Portland, Oreg.

**PADDOCK, Algernon Sidney**, a Senator from Nebraska; born at Glens Falls, Warren County, N.Y., November 9, 1830; attended the public schools, Glens Falls Academy, and Union College, Schenectady, N.Y.; taught school and studied law; moved to Omaha, Nebr., in 1857; was admitted to the bar in 1857 and commenced practice in Omaha; unsuccessful candidate for the Territorial house of representatives in 1858; delegate to the first Territorial convention in 1859; engaged in editorial work on the Nebraska Republican, 1858-1859; secretary of the Territory of Nebraska, 1861-1867, performing the duties of Acting Governor part of this time; unsuccessful candidate for election in 1866 to the Fortieth Congress; unsuccessful Republican candidate for United States Senator in 1867; declined to accept the position of Governor of the

Territory of Wyoming in 1868; moved to Beatrice, Gage County, Nebr., in 1872 and engaged in manufacturing and agricultural pursuits; elected as a Republican to the United States Senate, and served from March 4, 1875 to March 3, 1881; unsuccessful candidate for reelection; chairman, Committee on Agriculture (Forty-fifth Congress); member of the Federal commission having jurisdiction over elections in the Territory of Utah, 1882-1886; again elected as a Republican to the United States Senate, and served from March 4, 1887 to March 3, 1893; chairman, Committee on the Improvement of the Mississippi River and Its Tributaries (Fiftieth Congress), Committee on Agriculture and Forestry (Fifty-first and Fifty-second Congresses); engaged in the brokerage business; died in Beatrice, Nebr., on October 17, 1897; interment in Prospect Hill Cemetery, Omaha, Nebr.

Bibliography: *DAB*; Shepherd, Allen L. "Gentile in Zion: Algernon Sidney Paddock and the Utah Commission, 1882-1886." *Nebraska History* 57 (Fall 1976): 359-377.

**PADDOCK, George Arthur**, a Representative from Illinois; born in Winnetka, Cook County, Ill., March 24, 1885; attended the public schools; was graduated from Chicago (Ill.) Manual Training School in 1902 and from the University of Virginia at Charlottesville in 1906; studied law at the University of Virginia; was admitted to the bar in 1907 and commenced practice in Chicago, Ill.; during the First World War served as a captain and later as a major of the Three Hundred and Forty-second Infantry, Eighty-sixth Division, 1917-1919; resumed the practice of law at Chicago, Ill.; engaged as an investment banker in 1921; served as alderman of Evanston, Ill., 1931-1937 and as park commissioner 1929-1931, 1937, and 1938; delegate to the Republican State convention in 1936; member of the Soldiers' and Sailors' Service Commission of Illinois; member and treasurer of Cook County Republican Central Committee, 1938-1942; elected as a Republican to the Seventy-seventh Congress (January 3, 1941-January 3, 1943); unsuccessful candidate for renomination in 1942; resumed investment banking; was a resident of Evanston, Ill., until his death December 29, 1964; interment in Rosehill Cemetery, Chicago, Ill.

**PADGETT, Lemuel Phillips**, a Representative from Tennessee; born in Columbia, Maury County, Tenn., November 28, 1855; attended private schools in the county, and was graduated from Erskine College, Due West, S.C., in 1876; began the study of law in September 1876; was admitted to the bar in March 1877 and commenced practice in Columbia, Tenn., in January 1879; member of the State senate, 1899-1901; elected as a Democrat to the Fifty-seventh and to the ten succeeding Congresses and served from March 4, 1901, until his death in Washington, D.C., August 2, 1922; chairman, Committee on Naval Affairs (Sixty-second through Sixty-fifth Congresses); interment in Rose Hill Cemetery, Columbia, Tenn.

**PAGÁN, Bolívar**, a Resident Commissioner from Puerto Rico; born in Guayanilla, P.R., May 16, 1897; attended the public schools of Adjuntas, P.R., and Ponce (P.R.) High School; was graduated from the law department of the University of Puerto Rico at Río Piedras in 1921; was admitted to the bar the same year and commenced practice in San Juan, P.R.; judge of Fajardo, P.R., in 1922; member of the insular board of elections, 1923-1951; unsuccessful candidate for election to the Puerto Rican house of representatives in 1924; city treasurer of San Juan, P.R., 1925-1929; unsuccessful candidate for election to the Puerto Rican Senate in 1928; associate commissioner of the Public Service Commission of Puerto Rico, 1930-1933; member of the Puerto Rican senate, 1933-1939, and served as president pro tempore and majority floor leader; city manager of San Juan, P.R., in 1936 and 1937; member of the American Group of the Interparliamentary Union; also engaged as writer and editor; appointed by Governor William D. Leahy as a Coalitionist a Resident Commissioner to the United States on December 26, 1939, to fill the vacancy caused by the death of Santiago Iglesias for the term ending January 3, 1941; elected in 1940 for the term ending January 3, 1945; was not a candidate for renomination in 1944; again elected a member of the senate of Puerto Rico, and served from 1945 to 1953; practiced law in San Juan, P.R., until his death there February 9, 1961; interment in Puerto Rico Memorial Cemetery, Carolina, P.R.

PAGE, Carroll Smalley, a Senator from Vermont; born in Westfield, Orleans County, Vt., January 10, 1843; attended the common schools, People's Academy, Morrisville, Vt., and Lamoille Central Academy, Hyde Park, Lamoille County, Vt.; dealer in raw calfskins at Hyde Park, Vt.; president and director of several banks and corporations; member, Vermont State house of representatives, 1869-1872; member, State senate, 1874-1876; register of probate court, 1880-1891; savings bank examiner, 1884-1888; elected Governor of Vermont in 1890, and served from October 2, 1890 to October 6, 1892; elected as a Republican to the United States Senate in 1908 to fill the vacancy caused by the death of Redfield Proctor; reelected in 1910 and 1916, and served from October 21, 1908 to March 3, 1923; was not a candidate for reelection in 1922; chairman, Committee on Standards, Weights and Measures (Sixty-first Congress), Committee on Cuban Relations (Sixty-second Congress), Committee on the Disposition of Useless Executive Papers (Sixty-third Congress), Committee on Transportation and Sale of Meat Products (Sixty-fourth and Sixty-fifth Congresses), Committee on Naval Affairs (Sixty-sixth and Sixty-seventh Congresses); resided in Hyde Park, Vt., until his death on December 3, 1925; interment in Hyde Park Cemetery.

Bibliography: Barlow, Melvin L. *The Unconquerable Senator Page: The Struggle to Establish Legislation for Vocational Education.* Washington, D.C.: American Vocational Association, 1976.

PAGE, Charles Harrison, a Representative from Rhode Island; born in Gloucester, Providence County, R.I., July 19, 1843; attended the public schools; during the Civil War enlisted in the Union Army as a private at the age of nineteen in Company A, Twelfth Regiment, Rhode Island Volunteer Infantry, and was mustered out July 29, 1863; resumed studies in the Illinois State Normal School at Bloomington and at Southern Illinois College at Carbondale; returned to Rhode Island in 1869 and taught school in Scituate until the spring of 1870, when he entered the law department of the University of Albany, New York; was graduated in 1871; was admitted to the bar the same year and commenced practice in Scituate, and in Providence, R.I., in 1872; member of the State house of representatives in 1872 and 1873; served in the State senate in 1874, 1875, 1884, 1885, and 1890; unsuccessful candidate for election in 1876 to the Forty-fifth Congress; candidate for attorney general in 1879; delegate to the Democratic National Conventions in 1880, 1884, and 1888; contested as a Democrat the election of William A. Pirce to the Forty-ninth Congress, but the seat was declared vacant; subsequently elected at a special election to fill the vacancy thus caused and served from February 21 to March 3, 1887; elected to the Fifty-second Congress (March 4, 1891-March 3, 1893); reelected to the Fifty-third Congress at a special election (no candidate receiving a majority at the regular election), and served from April 5, 1893, to March 3, 1895; chairman, Committee on Manufactures (Fifty-second and Fifty-third Congresses); was not a candidate for renomination in 1894; resumed the practice of law until his death in Providence, R.I., July 21, 1912; interment in Swan Point Cemetery.

PAGE, Henry, a Representative from Maryland; born in Princess Anne, Somerset County, Md., June 28, 1841; received preparatory instruction at the school of Anthony Bolivar, West Chester, Pa.; attended the University of Virginia at Charlottesville; studied law; was admitted to the bar in 1864 and commenced practice in Princess Anne, Somerset County, Md.; member of the constitutional convention in 1867; State's attorney for Somerset County 1870-1884; elected as a Democrat to the Fifty-second Congress and served from March 4, 1891, until September 3, 1892, when he resigned to become a judge of the Maryland Court of Appeals; appointed chief judge of the first judicial district of Maryland in August 1892; elected to the position in November 1893 for a term of fifteen years; died in Princess Anne, Md., January 7, 1913; interment in Manokin Presbyterian Church Cemetery.

PAGE, Horace Francis, a Representative from California; born near Medina, Orleans County, N.Y., October 20, 1833; attended the public schools and Millville Academy; taught school in La Porte County, Ind., until 1854, when he moved to California and engaged in the sawmill business near Colfax; moved to Placerville and engaged in the livery-stable business; became engaged in mining and as a mail contractor and stage proprietor; studied law; was admitted to the bar and commenced practice in California; unsuccessful Republican candidate for the State senate in 1869; major in the California Militia; elected as a Republican to the Forty-third and to the four succeeding Congresses (March 4, 1873-March 3, 1883); chairman, Committee on Commerce (Forty-seventh Congress); unsuccessful candidate for reelection in 1882 to the Forty-eighth Congress; delegate to the Republican National Convention in 1884; resumed the practice of law in Washington, D.C.; died in San Francisco, Calif., August 23, 1890; interment in Mountain View Cemetery, Oakland, Calif.

PAGE, John, a Senator from New Hampshire; born in Haverhill, Grafton County, N.H., May 21, 1787; attended the public schools; engaged in agricultural pursuits; served as lieutenant in the War of 1812; assistant United States tax assessor in 1813, and assessor in 1815; member, New Hampshire State house of representatives, 1818-1820, and in 1835; register of deeds for Grafton County in 1827, and from 1829 until 1835; selectman of Haverhill for fourteen terms; served as town clerk; member of Governor's council 1836, 1838; elected as a Whig to the United States Senate to fill the vacancy caused by the resignation of Isaac Hill, and served from June 8, 1836 to March 3, 1837; unsuccessful candidate for reelection; chairman, Committee on Agriculture (Twenty-fourth Congress); resumed agricultural pursuits; elected Governor of New Hampshire in 1839, reelected in 1840 and 1841, and served from June 5, 1839 to June 2, 1842; died in Haverhill, N.H., September 8, 1865; interment in Ladd Street Cemetery.

PAGE, John (brother of Mann Page), a Representative from Virginia; born at "Rosewell," Gloucester County, Va., April 17, 1743; graduated from the College of William and Mary, Williamsburg, Va., in 1763; served under George Washington in an expedition against the French and Indians; delegate to the Virginia constitutional convention in 1776; Lieutenant Governor of Virginia, 1776-1779; raised a regiment of militia from Gloucester County; colonel in the Revolutionary Army; member of the Virginia house of delegates, 1781-1783, and 1785-1788; elected to the First Congress; reelected to the Second and Third Congresses, and as a Republican to the Fourth Congress (March 4, 1789-March 3, 1797); again a member of the Virginia house of delegates in 1797, 1798, 1800; and 1801; elected Governor of Virginia by the General Assembly, and served from December 1, 1802 to December 1, 1805; appointed United States commissioner of loans for Virginia, and held this office until his death in Richmond, Va., October 11, 1808; interment in St. John's Churchyard.

Bibliography: *DAB*; McCord, T.B., Jr. "John Page of Rosewell: Reason, Religion, and Republican Government from the Perspective of a Virginia Planter, 1743-1808." Ph.D. dissertation, American University, 1991.

PAGE, Mann (brother of John Page, of Virginia), a Delegate from Virginia; born at "Rosewell," Gloucester County, Va., in 1749; studied under a private teacher and graduated from the College of

William and Mary, Williamsburg, Va.; studied law; admitted to the bar and practiced; member of the Virginia house of burgesses; moved to Spotsylvania County; member of the Continental Congress in 1777; died on his estate, "Mansfield," near Fredericksburg, Spotsylvania County, Va., in 1781; interment near Fredericksburg.

**PAGE, Robert,** a Representative from Virginia; born at "North End," Gloucester (now Mathews) County, Va., February 4, 1765; received a liberal education from tutors at home; attended the College of William and Mary, Williamsburg, Va., which he left to join the Revolutionary Army, serving as a captain; studied law; was admitted to the bar and practiced in Frederick (now Clarke) and adjacent counties; planter; member of the council of state; member of the Virginia house of delegates in 1795; elected as a Federalist to the Sixth Congress (March 4, 1799-March 3, 1801); resumed former activities; died at "Janeville," Clarke County, Va., December 8, 1840; interment in Old Chapel Cemetery near Millwood, Clarke (then Frederick) County, Va.

**PAGE, Robert Newton,** a Representative from North Carolina; born in Cary, Wake County, N.C., October 26, 1859; attended the Cary High School and Bingham Military School, Mebane, N.C.; moved to Aberdeen, Moore County, N.C., in 1880 and engaged in the lumber business near Aberdeen until 1900; mayor of Aberdeen from 1890 until 1898; treasurer of the Aberdeen & Asheboro Railroad Co., 1894-1902; moved to Biscoe, Montgomery County, N.C., in 1897; member of the North Carolina State house of representatives in 1901 and 1902; elected as a Democrat to the Fifty-eighth and to the six succeeding Congresses (March 4, 1903-March 3, 1917); was not a candidate for renomination in 1916 to the Sixty-fifth Congress; returned to Aberdeen in 1920; unsuccessful candidate in 1920 for nomination for Governor of North Carolina; engaged in banking, and was president of the Page Trust Co.; died in Aberdeen, N.C., on October 3, 1933; interment in Old Bethesda Cemetery.

**Bibliography:** Abrams, Douglas Carl. "A Progressive-Conservative Duel: The 1920 Democratic Gubernatorial Primaries in North Carolina." *North Carolina Historical Review* 55 (Autumn 1978): 421-43.

**PAGE, Sherman,** a Representative from New York; born in Cheshire, Conn., May 9, 1779; attended the common schools; taught school in Coventry, N.Y., in 1799; studied law; was admitted to the bar in 1805 and commenced practice in Unadilla, Otsego County, N.Y.; member of the State assembly in 1827; judge of the court of common pleas in Otsego County; elected as a Jacksonian to the Twenty-third and Twenty-fourth Congresses (March 4, 1833-March 3, 1837); chairman, Committee on Public Expenditures (Twenty-fourth Congress); died in Unadilla, N.Y., September 27, 1853; interment in St. Matthew's Cemetery.

**PAIGE, Calvin DeWitt,** a Representative from Massachusetts; born in Southbridge, Worcester County, Mass., May 20, 1848; attended the public schools and graduated from the high school; president of the Central Cotton Mills Co., the Southbridge Savings Bank, and the Edwards Co.; served as selectman of Southbridge; member of the Massachusetts house of representatives in 1878 and 1879; delegate to the Republican National Convention in 1884; member of the Governor's council in 1906 and 1907; elected as a Republican to the Sixty-third Congress to fill the vacancy caused by the death of William H. Wilder; reelected to the Sixty-fourth and to the four succeeding Congresses and served from November 26, 1913, to March 3, 1925; voluntarily withdrew from public life, and engaged in banking in Southbridge, Mass., until his death there on April 24, 1930; interment in Oak Ridge Cemetery.

**PAIGE, David Raymond,** a Representative from Ohio; born in Madison, Lake County, Ohio, April 8, 1844; attended the public schools and Western Reserve Academy, Hudson, Ohio; was graduated from Union College, Schenectady, N.Y., in 1865; engaged in the hardware business in Akron, Ohio; treasurer of Summit County 1875-1879; elected as a Democrat to the Forty-eighth Congress (March 4, 1883-March 3, 1885); engaged in the contracting business; died in New York City June 30, 1901; interment in Evergreen Cemetery, Painesville, Lake County, Ohio.

**PAINE, Elijah,** a Senator from Vermont; born in Brooklyn, Conn., January 21, 1757; attended the public schools; served in the Revolutionary War; graduated from Harvard University in 1781; studied law; was admitted to the bar and commenced practice in Windsor, Vt.; practiced law and cultivated a farm; began a settlement at Williamstown; established a cloth factory and a saw and grist mill; secretary of the State constitutional convention 1786; member, State house of representatives 1787-1790; judge of the State supreme court 1791-1795; elected to the United States Senate in 1794; reelected as a Federalist in 1800 and served from March 4, 1795, to September 1, 1801, when he resigned; United States judge of the district of Vermont from 1801 until his death in Williamstown, Orange County, Vt., April 28, 1842; interment in Old Williamstown Cemetery.

**Bibliography:** *DAB.*

**PAINE, Ephraim,** a delegate from New York; was born in Canterbury, Conn., August 19, 1730; moved with his parents to Nine Partners, N.Y.; pursued preparatory studies; studied medicine and practiced in Amenia, Dutchess County, N.Y.; delegate to the Provincial Congress in 1775; county judge 1778-1781; member of the council of appointment in 1780; supervisor of Amenia in 1782 and 1783; served in the State senate 1780-1784; Member of the Continental Congress in 1784; died in Amenia, N.Y., August 10, 1785; interment in Red Meeting House Cemetery, near Amenia.

**PAINE, Halbert Eleazer,** a Representative from Wisconsin; born in Chardon, Geauga County, Ohio, February 4, 1826; attended the common schools; was graduated from the Western Reserve College, Hudson, Ohio, in 1845; taught school for a season in Mississippi; studied law; was admitted to the bar in 1848 and commenced practice in Cleveland, Ohio; moved to Milwaukee, Wis., in 1857 and continued the practice of law; entered the Union Army in May 1861 as colonel of the Fourth Regiment, Wisconsin Volunteers; promoted to the rank of brigadier general on March 13, 1863, and in the following June lost a leg at the siege of Port Hudson, La.; brevetted major general on March 13, 1865, and resigned on May 15, 1865; elected as a Republican to the Thirty-ninth and to the two succeeding Congresses (March 4, 1865-March 3, 1871); chairman, Committee on Militia (Fortieth Congress), Committee on Elections (Forty-first Congress); was not a candidate for renomination in 1870 to the Forty-second Congress; continued the practice of law in Washington, D.C.; through his efforts the taking of meteorological observations in the interior was inaugurated; appointed Commissioner of Patents by President Ulysses S. Grant and served from November 1, 1878, to May 7, 1880; died in Washington, D.C., April 14, 1905; interment in Arlington National Cemetery, Va.

**Bibliography:** *DAB.*

**PAINE, Robert Treat,** a Delegate from Massachusetts; born in Boston, Mass., March 11, 1731; attended the Boston Latin School and was graduated from Harvard College in 1749; studied theology; was chaplain of troops on the northern frontier in 1755; studied law; admitted to the bar in 1757 and commenced practice in Boston; moved to Taunton in 1761; delegate to the Massachusetts convention at Boston in 1768; member of the colonial house of representatives in 1773; delegate to the Provincial Congress in 1774 and 1775; member of the Continental Congress, 1774-1776; a signer of the Declaration of Independence; member of the Massachusetts house of representatives in 1777; attorney general of Massachusetts, 1777-1790; member of the Governor's council in 1779 and 1780;

delegate to the constitutional convention in 1779; moved to Boston in 1781; judge of the Massachusetts supreme court, 1790-1804; died in Boston, Mass., May 11, 1814.

**Bibliography:** *DAB*; Paine, Robert Treat. *The Papers of Robert Treat Paine*. 2 vols. to date. Edited by Stephen T. Riley and Edward W. Hanson. Boston: Massachusetts Historical Society, 1992-.

**PAINE, Robert Treat,** a Representative from North Carolina; born in Edenton, Chowan County, N.C., February 18, 1812; attended private schools and was graduated from Washington (now Trinity) College, Hartford, Conn.; studied law; was admitted to the bar and practiced; held several local offices; owned and operated shipyards and engaged in the shipping business; member of the North Carolina State house of commons in 1838, 1840, 1844, 1846 and 1848; served as colonel of a North Carolina regiment during the Mexican War, and as War Governor of Monterrey, Mexico, in 1846; member of the Mexican Claims Commission after the war; elected as a candidate of the American Party to the Thirty-fourth Congress (March 4, 1855-March 3, 1857); moved to Austin County, Tex., in 1860 and engaged in agricultural pursuits; died in Galveston, Tex., February 8, 1872; interment in Brenham Cemetery, Brenham, Tex.

**PAINE, William Wiseham,** a Representative from Georgia; born in Richmond, Va., on October 10, 1817; moved with his parents to Milledgeville, Baldwin County, Ga., in 1827; attended school in Mount Zion, Ga.; served in the Seminole Indian War in 1836; studied law in Washington, Wilkes County, Ga., and was admitted to the bar in 1838; moved to Telfair, Ga., in 1840 and commenced the practice of law; member of the Georgia State constitutional convention in 1850; served as private secretary to Governor Howell Cobb in 1851 and 1852; served in the Georgia State senate, 1857-1860; entered the Confederate Army and served as captain in the First Georgia Regiment throughout the Civil War; moved to Savannah, Ga., at the close of the Civil War and continued the practice of law; elected as a Democrat to the Forty-first Congress to fill the vacancy caused by the House declaring Joseph W. Clift not entitled to the seat, and served from December 22, 1870, to March 3, 1871; member of the Georgia State house of representatives, 1877-1879; curator of the Georgia Historical Society; died in Savannah, Ga., August 5, 1882; interment in Bonaventure Cemetery.

**PALEN, Rufus,** a Representative from New York; born in Palenville, Greene County, N.Y., February 25, 1807; moved with his parents to Fallsburg, where he received a limited schooling; engaged in the manufacture of leather; held several local offices; elected as a Whig to the Twenty-sixth Congress (March 4, 1839-March 3, 1841); died in New York City April 26, 1844; interment in the Old Cemetery, Palenville, N.Y.

**PALFREY, John Gorham,** a Representative from Massachusetts; born in Boston, Mass., May 2, 1796; completed preparatory studies in Phillips Exeter Academy, Exeter, N.H.; graduated from Harvard University in 1815; studied theology and was ordained minister of Brattle Square Unitarian Church, Boston, June 17, 1818; editor of the North American Review 1835-1843; member of the Massachusetts house of representatives in 1842 and 1843; secretary of state of Massachusetts 1844-1848; elected as a Whig to the Thirtieth Congress (March 4, 1847-March 3, 1849); unsuccessful candidate on the Free-Soil ticket for reelection in 1848 to the Thirty-first Congress; postmaster of Boston 1861-1867; devoted himself to literary pursuits; died in Cambridge, Mass., April 26, 1881; interment in Mount Auburn Cemetery.

**Bibliography:** *DAB*; Gattell, Frank Otto. *John Gorham Palfrey and the New England Conscience*. Cambridge, Mass.: Harvard University Press, 1963; Gattell, Frank Otto. "Palfrey's Vote, the Conscience Whigs, and the Election of Speaker Winthrop." *New England Quarterly* 31 (June 1958): 218-31.

**PALLONE, Frank, Jr.,** a Representative from New Jersey; born in Long Branch, Monmouth County, N.J., October 30, 1951; attended Long Branch schools; B.A., Middlebury College, 1973; M.A., Fletcher School of Law and Diplomacy, Tufts University, 1974; J.D., Rutgers University School of Law, 1978; admitted to Florida, New Jersey, New York and Pennsylvania bars; attorney, Marine Advisory Service; assistant professor, Cook College, Rutgers University Sea Grant Extension Program; counsel, Monmouth County, N.J. Protective Services for the Elderly; instructor, Monmouth County Community College; member, Long Branch City Council, 1982-1988; member, New Jersey State senate, 1984-1988; elected as a Democrat to the One Hundredth Congress, November 8, 1988, by special election to fill the vacancy caused by the death of James J. Howard, but was not sworn in because Congress had adjourned; elected at the same time to the One Hundred First Congress; reelected to the three succeeding Congresses, and served from November 8, 1988 to January 3, 1997; is a resident of Long Branch, N.J.

**PALMER, Alexander Mitchell,** a Representative from Pennsylvania; born near White Haven, Luzerne County, Pa., May 4, 1872; attended the public schools and prepared for college at the Moravian Parochial School, Bethlehem, Pa.; graduated from Swarthmore (Pa.) College in 1891; appointed offical stenographer of the forty-third judicial district of Pennsylvania in 1892; studied law; admitted to the bar in 1893 and practiced in Stroudsburg, Pa.; director of various banks and public service corporations; member of the Pennsylvania Democratic executive committee; elected as a Democrat to the Sixty-first and to the two succeeding Congresses (March 4, 1909-March 3, 1915); was not a candidate in 1914 for renomination to the House of Representatives, but was an unsuccessful candidate for the United States Senate; delegate to the Democratic National Conventions of 1912 and 1916; member of the Democratic National Committee, 1912-1920; appointed Alien Property Custodian on October 22, 1917, by President Woodrow Wilson, and served until March 4, 1919, when he resigned to become Attorney General of the United States, in which capacity he served from March 5, 1919 until March 4, 1921; engaged in the practice of law in Washington, D.C., and Stroudsburg, Pa.; died in Washington, D.C., May 11, 1936; interment in Laurelwood Cemetery, Stroudsburg, Pa.

**Bibliography:** *DAB*; Coben, Stanley. *A. Mitchell Palmer: Politician*. 1963. Reprint. New York: Da Capo Press, 1972; Johnson, Donald. "The Political Career of A. Mitchell Palmer." *Pennsylvania History* 25 (October 1958): 345-370.

**PALMER, Beriah,** a Representative from New York; born in Bristol County, Mass., in 1740; attended the common schools; moved to Cornwall, Orange County, N.Y., in 1769; studied law; was admitted to the bar and practiced in New York; engaged in surveying and farming near Burnt Hills; moved to Ballston Spa, Saratoga County, N.Y., in 1774; served in the Twelfth Regiment of the New York Militia during the Revolutionary War; served as assessor in 1779; commissioner of roads, district of Ballston, in 1780, 1783, and 1784; served as postmaster in 1784; member of the committee of safety of Albany County; supervisor of Saratoga County in 1790, 1791, and 1799; moderator of the first board of supervisors of Saratoga County in 1791; appointed judge of the court of common pleas in 1791; member of the State assembly in 1792-1795; delegate to the State constitutional convention in 1801; elected as a Republican to the Eighth Congress (March 4, 1803-March 3, 1805); surrogate of Saratoga County 1808-1812; died in Ballston Spa, N.Y., May 20, 1812; interment in the Village Cemetery.

**PALMER, Cyrus Maffet,** a Representative from Pennsylvania; born in Pottsville, Schuylkill County, Pa., February 12, 1887; educated in the public schools of Pottsville and attended the University of Pennsylvania at Philadelphia, Pa., in 1907; studied law; was admitted to the bar in 1911 and commenced practice in Pottsville, Pa.; served in the Pennsylvania house of representatives 1916-1920; district attorney of Schuylkill County, Pa., 1920-1927; elected as a Republican to the Seventieth Congress (March 4, 1927-March 3, 1929); unsuccessful candidate for renomination in 1928; resumed the practice of law; alternate delegate to the Republican National Convention at Philadelphia in 1940; elected judge of the common pleas court of Schuylkill County, twenty-first judicial district of Pennsylvania, in 1931; reelected in 1941 and again in 1951; became president judge of the court January 1, 1940, and served until his death in Pottsville, Pa., August 16, 1959; interment in Charles Baber Cemetery.

**PALMER, Francis Wayland,** a Representative from Iowa; born in Manchester, Dearborn County, Ind., October 11, 1827; moved with his parents to Jamestown, N.Y., in boyhood; learned the printing trade on the Jamestown Journal in 1841; owner of the Jamestown Journal 1848-1858; member of the State assembly in 1853 and again in 1854; moved to Dubuque, Iowa, in 1858, and became editor and one of the proprietors of the Dubuque Times; State printer of Iowa 1861-1869; settled in Des Moines in 1861 and was publisher and owner of the Iowa State Register; elected as a Republican to the Forty-first and Forty-second Congresses (March 4, 1869-March 3, 1873); was not a candidate for renomination in 1872; moved to Chicago, Ill., in 1873, purchased an interest in the Inter-Ocean and became its editor in chief; delegate to the Republican National Convention in 1876; postmaster of Chicago by appointment of President Rutherford B. Hayes from February 26, 1877, to May 5, 1885; Public Printer of the United States from May 7, 1889, to May 2, 1894, and again from March 31, 1897, until September 8, 1905, when he was removed; died in Chicago, Ill., December 3, 1907; interment in Graceland Cemetery.

**PALMER, George William** (nephew of John Palmer and cousin of William Elisha Haynes), a Representative from New York; born in Hoosick, Rensselaer County, N.Y., January 13, 1818; attended the common schools, the Schodack Academy, Schodack, N.Y., and Yale College; studied law; was admitted to the bar about 1840 and commenced practice in Plattsburgh, N.Y., surrogate of Clinton County, N.Y.; elected as a Republican to the Thirty-fifth and Thirty-sixth Congresses (March 4, 1857-March 3, 1861); chairman, Committee on Expenditures in the Post Office Department (Thirty-sixth Congress); was not a candidate for renomination in 1860; delegate to the Republican National Convention at Baltimore in 1864; appointed United States consul to Crete by President Abraham Lincoln; United States judge on the International Court for Suppression of Slave Trade on the West Coast of Africa from 1866 to 1870, when he resigned; member of the State assembly in 1884 and 1885; engaged in iron manufacturing at Clinton, N.Y.; died in Plattsburgh, N.Y.; March 2, 1916; interment in Riverside Cemetery.

**PALMER, Henry Wilber,** a Representative from Pennsylvania; born in Clifford, Susquehanna County, Pa., July 10, 1839; attended Wyoming Seminary, Kingston, Pa., and Fort Edward Institute, Fort Edward, N.Y.; graduated from the National Law School, Poughkeepsie, N.Y., in 1860; admitted to the bar in Peekskill, N.Y., the same year and in Wilkes-Barre, Pa., in 1861; prothonotary's clerk in 1861; served in the pay department of the Union Army at New Orleans in 1862 and 1863; member of the constitutional convention of Pennsylvania in 1872 and 1873; attorney general of Pennsylvania 1879-1883; elected as a Republican to the Fifty-seventh, Fifty-eighth, and Fifty-ninth Congresses (March 4, 1901-March 3, 1907); one of the managers appointed by the House of Representatives in 1905 to conduct the impeachment proceedings against Charles Swayne, judge of the United States Court for the Northern District of Florida; elected to the Sixty-first Congress (March 4, 1909-March 3, 1911); practiced law until his death in Wilkes-Barre, Pa., February 15, 1913; interment in Hollenback Cemetery.

**Bibliography:** *DAB.*

**PALMER, John** (uncle of George William Palmer), a Representative from New York; born in Hoosick, Rensselaer County, N.Y., January 29, 1785; completed preparatory studies; graduated from Williams College, Williamstown, Mass.; studied law; was admitted to the bar and commenced practice in Plattsburgh, N.Y., in 1810; served as paymaster in the Eighth Regiment, New York Militia, in 1812; elected as a Republican to the Fifteenth Congress (March 4, 1817-March 3, 1819); district attorney 1818-1832; member of the State assembly in 1832; judge of Clinton County from 1832 until 1837, when he resigned; elected as a Democrat to the Twenty-fifth Congress (March 4, 1837-March 3, 1839); was not a candidate for renomination; died in St. Bartholomew, French West Indies, December 8, 1840; interment in St. Bartholomew Cemetery.

**PALMER, John McAuley,** a Senator from Illinois; born at Eagle Creek, Scott County, Ky., September 13, 1817; moved with his family to Madison County, Ill., in 1831; attended the common schools of Kentucky and Illinois; in 1834 entered Alton (later Shurtleff) College, where he remained two years; taught school, peddled clocks, and studied law, 1835-1838; was admitted to the bar in 1839 and practiced in Carlinville, Ill., 1839-1861; probate judge of Macoupin County in 1843 and 1847; member of the Illinois State constitutional convention in 1847; county judge, 1849-1852; member, Illinois State senate, 1852-1854, and in 1856; unsuccessful Republican candidate for election in 1859 to the Thirty-sixth Congress; presidential elector on the Republican ticket in 1860; member of the peace convention of 1861 held in Washington, D.C., in an effort to devise means to prevent the impending war; during the Civil War was appointed colonel of the Fourteenth Regiment, Illinois Volunteer Infantry in 1861, and was mustered out as a major general in 1866; settled in Springfield, Ill., in 1867; elected as a Republican Governor of Illinois in 1868, and served from January 11, 1869 to January 13, 1873; unsuccessful Democratic candidate for Governor in 1888; elected as a Democrat to the United States Senate, and served from March 4, 1891 to March 3, 1897; chairman, Committee on Pensions (Fifty-third Congress); was not a candidate for reelection in 1896; resumed the practice of law; unsuccessful candidate for president of the United States in 1896 on the National Democratic Party (Gold Democrat) ticket; died in Springfield, Ill., September 25, 1900; interment in Carlinville City Cemetery, Carlinville, Ill.

**Bibliography:** *DAB*; Palmer, George T. *A Conscientious Turncoat: The Story of John M. Palmer 1817-1900.* New Haven: Yale University Press, 1941; Palmer, John M. *Personal Recollections of John M. Palmer: The Story of an Earnest Life.* Cincinnati: R. Clarke Co., 1901.

**PALMER, John William,** a Representative from Missouri; born on a farm near Macks Creek, Camden County, Mo., August 20, 1866; attended the local schools; taught school in Hickory County, Mo.; engaged in the drug business at Cross Timbers, Hickory County, Mo., in 1888 and in the general merchandise business at Climax Springs, Camden County, Mo., 1891-1909; attended the University Medical College at Kansas City, Mo., in 1894 and 1895; practiced medicine in Climax Springs 1895-1908; attended the law school of Lincoln-Jefferson University, Hammond, Ind., in 1896; was admitted to the bar in 1897 and commenced the practice of law in Climax Springs, Mo.; served as representative in the Fortieth and Forty-first General Assemblies of Missouri 1898-1902; moved to Linn Creek, Mo., in 1909; prosecuting attorney of Camden County 1909-1915; moved to Sedalia, Mo., in 1915 and continued the practice of law; unsuccessful candidate for State senator in 1904; elected as a Republican to the Seventy-first Congress (March 4, 1929-March 3, 1931); unsuccessful candidate for reelection in 1930 to the Seventy-second Congress, for election in 1931 to fill a vacancy in the Seventy-second Congress, and for election in 1932 to the

Seventy-third Congress; resumed the practice of law; died in Sedalia, Mo., November 3, 1958; interment in Crown Hill Cemetery.

**PALMER, Thomas Witherell,** a Senator from Michigan; born in Detroit, Mich., January 25, 1830; attended the public schools, Thompson's Academy in Palmer (now St. Clair), Mich., and the University of Michigan at Ann Arbor; traveled to Spain and South America; engaged in lumbering and agricultural pursuits; served on the Board of Estimates of Detroit in 1873; member, Michigan State senate, 1879-1880; elected as a Republican to the United States Senate, and served from March 4, 1883 to March 3, 1889; was not a candidate for reelection; chairman, Committee on Fisheries (Forty-ninth Congress), Committee on Agriculture and Forestry (Fiftieth Congress); appointed Minister to Spain on March 12, 1889 by President Benjamin Harrison, and served until April 1890; president of the National Commission of the World's Columbian Exposition at Chicago, 1890-1893; retired to his Wayne County farm near Detroit, Mich.; one of the founders of the Detroit Museum of Art; died in Detroit, Mich., June 1, 1913; interment in Elmwood Cemetery.

**Bibliography:** *DAB*; Burton, M. Agnes. "Thomas W. Palmer." *Michigan Pioneer and Historical Society Collections* 39 (1915): 208-217; Ziewacz, Lawrence E. "Thomas W. Palmer: A Political Biography." Ph.D. dissertation, Michigan State University, 1971.

**PALMER, William Adams,** a Senator from Vermont; born in Hebron, Conn., September 12, 1781; completed preparatory studies; moved to Chelsea, Vt., in 1802; studied law in Hebron and Chelsea; was admitted to the bar and commenced practice in various towns in Vermont; elected probate judge for Caledonia County, 1807-1808, 1811-1817; also served as clerk of the court from 1807 to 1815; member, Vermont State house of representatives, 1811-1812, 1818; judge of the State supreme court, 1816-1818; elected in 1818 as a Republican to the United States Senate to fill the vacancy caused by the resignation of James Fisk, as well as for the full term commencing in 1819; served from October 20, 1818 to March 3, 1825; was not a candidate for renomination in 1824; engaged in agricultural pursuits; member, State house of representatives, 1825-1826, 1829; delegate to the State constitutional conventions in 1828, 1836, and 1850; unsuccessful Anti-Mason candidate for election for Governor in 1830; elected as an Anti-Mason Governor of Vermont in 1831 by the Legislature, since no candidate had received a majority of the popular vote; reelected in 1832, 1833, 1834 and 1835, and served from October 18, 1831 to November 2, 1835; member, State senate, 1836-1837; died in Danville, Caledonia County, Vt., December 3, 1860; interment in Green Cemetery.

**Bibliography:** *DAB*.

**PALMISANO, Vincent Luke,** a Representative from Maryland; born in Termini Imerse, Italy, August 5, 1882; immigrated to the United States with his parents, who settled in Baltimore, Md., in 1887; attended parochial schools and studied law at the University of Maryland at Baltimore; was admitted to the bar in 1909 and commenced practice in Baltimore, Md.; member of the State house of delegates in 1914 and 1915; member of the city council 1915-1923; member of the Democratic State central committee of Baltimore 1923-1927; police examiner of Baltimore, Md., 1925-1927; elected as a Democrat to the Seventieth and to the five succeeding Congresses (March 4, 1927-January 3, 1939); chairman, Committee on Education (Seventy-fourth and Seventy-fifth Congresses), Committee on District of Columbia (Seventy-fifth Congress); unsuccessful for renomination in 1938; resumed the practice of law; served on the Baltimore Zoning Board until his resignation in 1952; disappeared from his home on January 12, 1953, and his body was recovered from the Baltimore Harbor on March 5, 1953; interment in New Cathedral Cemetery, Baltimore, Md.

**PANETTA, Leon Edward,** a Representative from California; born in Monterey, Monterey County, Calif., June 28, 1938; educated in the public schools of Monterey; graduated from Monterey Union High School, 1956; B.A., University of Santa Clara (Calif.), 1960; LL.B., Santa Clara Law School, 1963; admitted to the California bar in 1965 and commenced practice in Monterey; served in United States Army, 1963-1965; served as legislative assistant to Senator Thomas H. Kuchel of California, 1966-1969; director, Office of Civil Rights, United States Department of Health, Education, and Welfare, 1969-1970; executive assistant to Mayor John V. Lindsay of New York City, 1970-1971; engaged in private practice of law, 1971-1976; elected as a Democrat to the Ninety-fifth and to the eight succeeding Congresses, and served from January 3, 1977 until his resignation on January 22, 1993 to become director, Office of Management and Budget; appointed Chief of Staff, The White House, June 27, 1994; chairman, Committee on the Budget (One Hundred First and One Hundred Second Congresses); is a resident of Carmel Valley, Calif.

**PANTIN, Santiago Iglesias,** a Resident Commissioner from Puerto Rico. (*See* Iglesias, Santiago.)

**PAREDES, Quintin,** a Resident Commissioner from the Commonwealth of the Philippines; born in Bangued, Abra Province, Philippine Islands, September 9, 1884; attended the primary and seminary schools; was graduated from the law school of Manila in 1907; was admitted to the bar the same year and commenced practice in Manila; appointed fourth prosecuting attorney on July 9, 1908, first prosecuting attorney on November 1, 1913, and served until March 1, 1917; served on the faculty and became dean of the law school (Escuela de Derecho) of Manila 1913-1917; served as solicitor general in 1917 and 1918, as attorney general 1918-1920, and as secretary of justice in 1920 and 1921; member of the first parliamentary mission to the United States in 1919; resumed the practice of law at Manila, Philippine Islands, in 1921; elected a member of the Philippine House of Representatives in 1925, 1928, 1931, and 1934, serving as speaker 1929-1931 and again in 1934; member of the Philippine Assembly in 1935; appointed as a Nationalist on December 21, 1935, the first Resident Commissioner under the Tydings-McDuffie law creating the Philippine Commonwealth Government, and served from February 14, 1936, until his resignation on September 29, 1938; resumed the practice of law; again elected a member of the Philippine Assembly in 1938; member of the Philippine Senate 1941-1945; served as a member of the Philippine House of Representatives 1946-1949; member of the Philippine Senate in 1950; reelected in 1955 for the term ending in November 1961; resumed the practice of law; president, General Bank and Trust Co., 1963-1969; was a resident of Bangued, Abra Province, Philippines, until his death in Manila on January 30, 1973.

**Bibliography:** San Diego, Lourdes Paredes. *Don Quintin of Abra.* Quezon City: n.p., 1985.

**PARK, Frank,** a Representative from Georgia; born in Tuskegee, Macon County, Ala., March 3, 1864; attended the common schools and the University of Georgia at Athens; engaged in teaching from 1882 until 1885; railway civil engineer, 1885-1889; was graduated from the Atlanta Medical College in 1891; studied law; was admitted to the bar in 1891 and commenced practice in Atlanta, Ga.; chairman of the Democratic executive committee of Worth County, Ga., 1891-1902; judge of the county court, 1898-1903; chairman of the Democratic congressional committee for the second district of Georgia, 1902-1904; judge of the city court of Sylvester, Ga., 1903-1908; judge of the Albany judicial circuit, 1908-1913; chairman of the board of trustees of the State Agricultural and Mechanical School, Tifton, Ga., 1911-1915; elected as a Democrat to the Sixty-third Congress to fill the vacancy caused by the death of Seaborn A. Roddenbery; reelected to the Sixty-fourth and to the four succeeding Congresses and served from November 5, 1913, to March 3, 1925; chairman, Committee on Accounts (Sixty-fifth Congress); unsuccessful candidate for renomination in 1924 to the Sixty-ninth Congress; resumed the practice of law; died at Fort Lauderdale, Fla., November 20, 1925; interment in White Springs Cemetery, White Springs, Fla.

**PARKE, Benjamin,** a Delegate from the Territory of Indiana; born in New Jersey on September 22, 1777; received a limited schooling; moved to Lexington, Ky., in 1797; studied law and was admitted to the bar; moved to Vincennes, Territory of Indiana, in 1799 and practiced; attorney general of Indiana Territory, 1804-1808; member of the Territorial house of representatives in 1805; when the Territory was formed, was elected the first Delegate to the Ninth and Tenth Congresses and served from December 12, 1805, until March 1, 1808, when he resigned; served on the staff of Governor William Henry Harrison; Territorial judge, 1808-1817; judge of the United States District Court for Indiana, 1817-1835; was the first president of the Indiana Historical Society; died in Salem, Washington County, Ind., July 12, 1835; interment in Crown Hill Cemetery.

Bibliography: *DAB*.

**PARKER, Abraham X.,** a Representative from New York; born in Granville, Addison County, Vt., November 14, 1831; attended the St. Lawrence Academy and the Albany (N.Y.) Law School; was admitted to the bar in Albany, N.Y., in 1854 and in 1856 commenced practice in Potsdam, N.Y.; member of the New York State assembly in 1863 and 1864; postmaster of Potsdam in 1865 and 1866; president of the village of Potsdam; served in the New York State senate, 1868-1871; secretary of the State normal school at Potsdam; elected as a Republican to the Forty-seventh and to the three succeeding Congresses (March 4, 1881-March 3, 1889); was not a candidate for renomination in 1888 to the Fifty-first Congress; appointed by President Grover Cleveland a member of the first labor investigation commission; delegate to the Republican National Convention of 1892; First Assistant Attorney General from September 8, 1890, to March 4, 1893; returned to Potsdam, N.Y., and resumed the practice of law; president of the Thomas S. Clarkson Memorial School of Technology; died in Potsdam, St. Lawrence County, N.Y., on August 9, 1909; interment in Bayside Cemetery.

**PARKER, Amasa Junius,** a Representative from New York; born in Sharon, Litchfield County, Conn., June 2, 1807; moved with his parents to Hudson, N.Y., in 1816; taught by private tutors and graduated from Union College, Schenectady, N.Y., in 1825; principal of Hudson (N.Y.) Academy 1823-1827; studied law; was admitted to the bar in 1828 and commenced practice in Delhi, N.Y.; member of the State assembly in 1833 and 1834; regent of the State university 1835-1844; elected as a Democrat to the Twenty-fifth Congress (March 4, 1837-March 3, 1839); declined to be a candidate for renomination in 1838; resumed the practice of law; vice chancellor and circuit judge 1844-1847; moved to Albany, N.Y., in 1844; judge of the supreme court for the third district 1847-1855; unsuccessful candidate for reelection; unsuccessful candidate for Governor of New York in 1856 and 1858; one of the founders of the Albany (N.Y.) Law School in 1851; delegate to the State constitutional convention of 1867 and 1868; died in Albany, N.Y., May 13, 1890; interment in the Albany Rural Cemetery.

Bibliography: *DAB*.

**PARKER, Andrew,** a Representative from Pennsylvania; born in Cumberland County, Pa., May 21, 1805; attended the common schools; was graduated from Dickinson College, Carlisle, Pa., in 1824; studied law in Carlisle; was admitted to the bar in 1826 and commenced practice in Lewistown, Pa.; appointed deputy attorney general of Mifflin County; moved to Mifflintown in 1831, where he

practiced law; elected as a Democrat to the Thirty-second Congress (March 4, 1851-March 3, 1853); continued the practice of law in Mifflintown, Juniata County, Pa., until his death there on January 15, 1864; interment in the Presbyterian Cemetery.

**PARKER, Homer Cling,** a Representative from Georgia; born in Baxley, Appling County, Ga., September 25, 1885; attended the public schools; was graduated from Statesboro (Ga.) High School in 1904 and from the law department of Mercer University, Macon, Ga., in 1908; was admitted to the bar the same year and commenced practice in Statesboro, Ga.; served as solicitor of the city court from 1914 until 1917; served in the United States Army during the First World War as a cadet, First Officers' Training Camp, May 15 to August 15, 1917; captain of Infantry, August 15, 1917, to May 20, 1919; major and judge advocate, May 20, 1919, to September 16, 1920; captain, Judge Advocate General's Department, 1920 to 1922; resumed the practice of law in Statesboro in 1923; served as mayor from 1924 until 1927; appointed adjutant general of Georgia on June 28, 1927, and served until June 27, 1931; member of the Georgia National Guard and served as brigadier general, Adjutant General's Department, from July 12, 1927, to May 31, 1931; elected as a Democrat to the Seventy-second Congress to fill the vacancy caused by the death of Charles G. Edwards; reelected to the Seventy-third Congress and served from September 10, 1931, to January 3, 1935; chairman, Committee on Elections No. 1 (Seventy-third Congress); unsuccessful candidate for renomination in 1934 to the Seventy-fourth Congress; resumed the practice of law in Statesboro, Ga.; was appointed comptroller general of Georgia on June 16, 1936, and served until January 13, 1937; elected comptroller general of Georgia in 1940, in which capacity he served until his death in Atlanta, Ga., on June 22, 1946; interment in East Side Cemetery, Statesboro, Ga.

**PARKER, Hosea Washington,** a Representative from New Hampshire; born in Lempster, Sullivan County, N.H., May 30, 1833; pursued classical studies; attended Tufts College, Medford, Mass., and was graduated from the Green Mountain Liberal Institute, South Woodstock, Vt.; studied law; was admitted to the bar in 1859 and commenced practice in Lempster, N.H.; member of the State house of representatives in 1859 and 1860; moved to Claremont, N.H., in 1860; delegate to the Democratic National Convention in 1868, 1880, 1884, and 1888; elected as a Democrat to the Forty-second and Forty-third Congresses (March 4, 1871-March 3, 1875); unsuccessful candidate for reelection in 1874 to the Forty-fourth Congress; resumed the practice of his profession; member of the State constitutional convention in 1918; died in Claremont, Sullivan County, N.H., August 21, 1922; interment in Mountain View Cemetery.

**PARKER, Isaac,** a Representative from Massachusetts; born in Boston, Mass., June 17, 1768; attended the common schools and was graduated from Harvard University in 1786; studied law; was admitted to the bar and commenced practice in Castine, Maine (until 1820 a part of Massachusetts); held several local offices; moved to Portland, Maine, and continued the practice of law; elected as a Federalist to the Fifth Congress (March 4, 1797-March 3, 1799); appointed United States marshal for Maine district on March 5, 1799, and served until December 21, 1803; moved to Boston, Mass., having been appointed by Governor Caleb Strong an associate justice of the supreme court of Massachusetts on January 28, 1806, and presided as chief justice from August 24, 1814, until his death; professor of law at Harvard University, 1815-1827; served as president of the Massachusetts constitutional convention in 1820; served as a trustee of Bowdoin College for eleven years, and as an overseer of Harvard University for twenty years; died in Boston, Mass., July 25, 1830; interment in Copps Hill Cemetery.

Bibliography: *DAB*.

**PARKER, Isaac Charles,** a Representative from Missouri; born near Barnesville, Belmont County, Ohio, October 15, 1838; completed preparatory studies; attended Barnesville Academy; studied law and was admitted to the bar in 1859; moved to Missouri in 1859 and began practice in St. Joseph; during the Civil War was a corporal in Company A, Sixty-first Missouri Emergency Regiment; city attorney for St. Joseph, Mo., 1862-1864; elected circuit attorney in 1864 and resigned in 1867; elected circuit judge in 1868, but resigned in 1870 to become a candidate for Congress; elected as a Republican to the Forty-second and Forty-third Congresses (March 4, 1871-March 3, 1875); was the caucus nominee of his party for United States Senator in 1874; appointed judge of the United States District Court for Western Arkansas on March 19, 1875, and served until his death in Fort Smith, Sebastian County, Ark., November 17, 1896; interment in the National Cemetery, Fort Smith, Ark.

Bibliography: *DAB*; Croy, Homer. *He Hanged them High; An Authentic Account of the Fanatic Judge Who Hanged Eighty-eight Men.* New York: Duell, Sloan and Pearce, 1952; Harrington, Fred Harvey. *Hanging Judge.* Caldwell, Idaho: Caxton Printers, 1951; Stolberg, Mary M. "Politician, Populist, Reformer: A Reexamination of 'Hanging Judge' Isaac C. Parker." *Arkansas Historical Quarterly* 47 (Spring 1988): 3-28.

**PARKER, James,** a Representative from Massachusetts; born in Boston, Mass., in 1768; completed preparatory studies; studied medicine and began practice in Gardiner, Maine (then a part of Massachusetts); member of the Massachusetts senate in 1811 and 1812; elected as a Republican to the Thirteenth Congress (March 4, 1813-March 3, 1815); elected to the Sixteenth Congress (March 4, 1819-March 3, 1821); resumed the practice of medicine; died in Gardiner, Kennebee County, Maine, November 9, 1837; interment in Oak Grove Cemetery.

**PARKER, James** (grandfather of Richard Wayne Parker), a Representative from New Jersey; born in Bethlehem, N.J., March 3, 1776; moved to Perth Amboy, N.J., after the Revolution; was graduated from Columbia College, New York City, in 1793; engaged in the management and settlement of large landed properties left by his father, also as a land surveyor and as a lawyer, although never admitted to the bar; member of the State general assembly 1806-1810, 1812, 1813, 1815, 1816, 1818, and 1827; mayor of Perth Amboy in 1815 and again in 1850; collector of customs at Perth Amboy, N.J., 1829-1833; elected as a Jacksonian to the Twenty-third and Twenty-fourth Congresses (March 4, 1833-March 3, 1837); resumed his former activities; registrar of the board of proprietors of East Jersey; member of the different boundary commissions to obtain a settlement of the boundary question between the States of New York and New Jersey; delegate to the State constitutional convention in 1844; died in Perth Amboy, N.J., April 1, 1868; interment in St. Peter's Churchyard.

Bibliography: *DAB*.

**PARKER, James Southworth,** a Representative from New York; born in Great Barrington, Berkshire County, Mass., on June 3, 1867; attended the public schools and was graduated from Cornell University, Ithaca, N.Y., in 1887; taught at St. Paul's School, Concord, N.H., in 1887; moved to Salem, Washington County, N.Y., in 1888 and taught at St. Paul's School at Salem; engaged in agricultural pursuits in 1888; also interested in breeding harness racing horses; member of the State assembly in 1904, 1905, and 1908-1912; elected as a Republican to the Sixty-third and to the ten succeeding Congresses and served from March 4, 1913, until his death in Washington, D.C., December 19, 1933; chairman, Committee on Interstate and Foreign Commerce (Sixty-ninth through Seventy-first Congresses); interment in Evergreen Cemetery, Salem, N.Y.

**PARKER, John,** a Delegate from South Carolina; born in Charleston, S.C., June 24, 1759; attended school in Charleston, S.C., and later in Great Britain; was graduated from the Middle Temple, London; returned to South Carolina; was admitted to the bar in 1785 and commenced practice in Charleston, S.C.; also engaged in the cultivation of rice on his plantation near there; Member of the Continental Congress 1786-1788; resided at Charleston and also on his estates, "Hayes" and "Cedar Grove," and engaged in their cultivation; died near Charleston, S.C., April 20, 1832; interment in the family burying ground on the "Hayes" estate in St. James' Parish, Goose Creek, near Charleston, S.C.

**PARKER, John Mason,** a Representative from New York; born in Granville, N.Y., June 14, 1805; attended Granville Academy and was graduated from Middlebury College, Vermont, in 1828; studied law; was admitted to the bar and commenced practice in Owego, N.Y., in 1833; elected as a Whig to the Thirty-fourth and reelected as a Republican to the Thirty-fifth Congress (March 4, 1855-March 3, 1859); was not a candidate for renomination in 1858; justice of the supreme court of New York 1859-1873, and sat as a justice of the general term of the third department 1867-1873; member of the court of appeals; died in Owego, N.Y., December 16, 1873; interment in Evergreen Cemetery.

**PARKER, Josiah,** a Representative from Virginia; born in "Macclesfield," Isle of Wight County, Va., May 11, 1751; pursued preparatory studies; member of the committee of safety in 1775 and of the Virginia convention that held sessions in March, July, and December of that year; enlisted in the Revolutionary War and was commissioned major in the Fifth Virginia Regiment on February 13, 1776, lieutenant colonel on July 28, 1777, and colonel on April 1, 1778; served under General Charles Lee in Virginia until the fall of 1776, when he was transferred to General George Washington's army; resigned from the Army on July 12, 1778; member of the Virginia House of Delegates, 1778, 1779, 1782 and 1783; naval officer at Portsmouth, Va., in 1786; unsuccessful candidate for delegate to the Virginia convention in 1788; elected to the First and to the two succeeding Congresses, and reelected as a Federalist to the Fourth and to the two succeeding Congresses (March 4, 1789-March 3, 1801); engaged in agricultural pursuits; died in Macclesfield, Va., March 11, 1810; interment in the private burial ground on his estate, "Macclesfield," in Isle of Wight County, Va.

Bibliography: *DAB*.

**PARKER, Nahum,** a Senator from New Hampshire; born in Shrewsbury, Mass., March 4, 1760; during the Revolutionary War served in the Continental Army at the Battles of Saratoga, N.Y., September 17 and October 7, 1777; settled in Fitzwilliam, Cheshire County, N.H., in 1786; member of the board of selectmen, 1790-1794; clerk and town treasurer, 1792-1815; member, New Hampshire State house of representatives, 1794-1804, and 1806-1807; member of the Governor's council in 1804 and 1805; elected as Republican to the United States Senate and served from March 4, 1807, to June 1, 1810, when he resigned; justice of the court of common pleas for Cheshire and Sullivan Counties, 1807-1813; associate justice of the western circuit, 1813-1816; judge of the court of sessions, Cheshire County, in 1821 and of the court of common pleas, Hillsborough County, in 1822; member of the New Hampshire State senate and its president in 1828; died in Fitzwilliam, N.H., November 12, 1839; interment in the Town Cemetery.

**PARKER, Paul Michael (Mike),** a Representative from Mississippi; born in Laurel, Jones County, Miss., October 31, 1949; graduated, Franklin High School, Meadville, Miss., 1967; B.A., William Carey College, Hattiesburg, Miss., 1970; businessman; owner of two funeral homes and a livestock farm; elected as a Democrat to the One Hundred First and to the three succeeding Congresses (January 3, 1989-January 3, 1997); announced his affiliation with the Republican Party on November 10, 1995, and continued in office during the One Hundred Fourth Congress as a Republican; is a resident of Brookhaven, Miss.

**PARKER, Richard,** a Representative from Virginia; born in Richmond, Va., on December 22, 1810; completed preparatory studies; studied law; was admitted to the bar and commenced practice in Berryville, Clarke County, Va.; held several local offices; elected as a Democrat to the Thirty-first Congress (March 4, 1849-March 3, 1851); elected judge of the thirteenth judicial circuit of Virginia on January 15, 1851, and served until 1869; on November 2, 1859 he pronounced the sentence of death on John Brown, who was captured at Harpers Ferry, Jefferson County, Va. (now West Virginia) in October 1859 after his unsuccessful attempt to raise an insurrection there; resumed the practice of his profession in Winchester, Frederick County, Va., and died there on November 10, 1893; interment in Mount Hebron Cemetery.

**PARKER, Richard Elliott,** a Senator from Virginia; born at "Rock Spring," Westmoreland County, Va., December 27, 1783; attended the public schools and graduated from Washington College (now Washington and Lee University), Lexington, Va., in 1803; studied law; admitted to the bar in 1804 and practiced in Westmoreland County; member, Virginia house of delegates 1807-1809; served as a lieutenant-colonel with the 111th Regiment during the War of 1812; returned to practice in Westmoreland County; judge of the general court of Virginia 1817-1836; judge of the Virginia court of law and chancery 1831-1836; elected as a Jacksonian to the United States Senate to fill the vacancy caused by the resignation of Benjamin W. Leigh and served from December 12, 1836, to March 13, 1837, when he resigned; judge of the Virginia supreme court of appeals 1837-1840; died on his estate, "Soldier's Retreat," near Snickersville (now Bluemont, Loudoun County), Va., September 10, 1840; interment in the family cemetery near Warsaw, Richmond County, Va.

Bibliography: *DAB*.

**PARKER, Richard Wayne** (grandson of James Parker), a Representative from New Jersey; born in Morristown, Morris County, N.J., August 6, 1848; was graduated from Princeton College in 1867 and from the law school of Columbia College in 1869; was admitted to the bar of New Jersey in 1870 and commenced practice in Newark; member of the State house of assembly in 1885 and 1886; unsuccessful Republican candidate for election to the Fifty-third Congress; elected as a Republican to the Fifty-fourth and to the seven succeeding Congresses (March 4, 1895-March 3, 1911); chairman, Committee on the Judiciary (Sixty-first Congress); unsuccessful candidate for reelection in 1910 to the Sixty-second Congress; resumed the practice of law in Newark, N.J.; elected to the Sixty-third Congress to fill the vacancy caused by the resignation of Walter I. McCoy; reelected to the Sixty-fourth and Sixty-fifth Congresses and served from December 1, 1914, to March 3, 1919; unsuccessful candidate for reelection in 1918 to the Sixty-sixth Congress; delegate to the Republican National Convention in 1916; elected to the Sixty-seventh Congress (March 4, 1921-March 3, 1923); unsuccessful candidate for reelection in 1922 to the Sixty-eighth Congress; died in Paris, France, on November 28, 1923; interment in St. Peter's Churchyard, Perth Amboy, N.J.

**PARKER, Samuel Wilson,** a Representative from Indiana; born near Watertown, Jefferson County, N.Y., September 9, 1805; pursued academic studies; was graduated from Miami University, Oxford, Ohio, in 1828; studied law; was admitted to the bar in 1831 and commenced practice in Connersville, Fayette County, Ind.; served as prosecuting attorney of Fayette County from December 10, 1836, to December 10, 1838; member of the State house of representatives in 1839 and 1843; served in the State senate 1841-1843; unsuccessful candidate for election in 1849 to the Thirty-first Congress; elected as a Whig to the Thirty-second and Thirty-third Congresses (March 4, 1851-March 3, 1855); did not seek

renomination in 1855; died near Sackets Harbor, N.Y., February 1, 1859; interment in the private cemetery on the Old Elm farm, near Sackets Harbor.

**PARKER, Severn Eyre,** a Representative from Virginia; born near Eastville, Northampton County, Va., July 19, 1787; attended the common schools; studied law; admitted to the bar and practiced; member of the Virginia house of delegates 1809-1821; appointed deputy clerk of Northampton County March 8, 1813; captain of a rifle company in 1814; served in the Virginia senate 1817-1820; elected to the Sixteenth Congress (March 4, 1819-March 3, 1821); again a member of the Virginia house of delegates in 1828, 1829, and 1834-1836; died in Northampton County, Va., October 21, 1836; interment in the private cemetery on Kendall Grove farm, near Eastville, Va.

**PARKER, William Henry,** a Representative from South Dakota; born in Keene, Cheshire County, N.H., May 5, 1847; served in the Union Army from June 24, 1861, to October 16, 1866; was graduated from the law department of Columbian College (now George Washington University), Washington, D.C., in 1868 and was admitted to the bar of the supreme court of the District of Columbia the same year; appointed collector of internal revenue of Colorado Territory by President Ulysses S. Grant June 24, 1874; resigned in July 1876; appointed United States attorney of Colorado; moved to Deadwood, Territory of Dakota (now South Dakota), in July 1877 and practiced law; member of the constitutional convention of the proposed State of South Dakota June 30, 1885; elected a member of the State house of representatives in 1889; prosecuting attorney of Lawrence County 1903-1907; elected to the Sixtieth Congress and served from March 4, 1907, until his death in Deadwood, Lawrence County, S.Dak., on June 26, 1908; interment in Arlington National Cemetery, Va.

**PARKS, Gorham,** a Representative from Maine; born in Westfield, Mass., May 27, 1794; attended the common schools and was graduated from Harvard University in 1813; studied law; was admitted to the bar in 1819 and practiced; moved to Bangor, Maine, in 1823 and continued the practice of law; elected as a Jacksonian to the Twenty-third and Twenty-fourth Congresses (March 4, 1833-March 3, 1837); United States marshal for the district of Maine 1838-1841; United States attorney for the district of Maine 1843-1845; United States consul at Rio de Janeiro, Brazil, from 1845-1849; died in Bay Ridge, Kings County, N.Y., November 23, 1877; interment in Greenwood Cemetery, Brooklyn, N.Y.

**PARKS, Tilman Bacon,** a Representative from Arkansas; born near Lewisville, Lafayette County, Ark., May 14, 1872; attended the common schools, the University of Texas at Austin, and the University of Virginia at Charlottesville; studied law; was admitted to the bar in 1900 and commenced practice in Lewisville, Ark.; member of the State house of representatives in 1901, 1903, and 1909; temporary chairman of the Democratic State convention in 1910; prosecuting attorney of the eighth judicial circuit of Arkansas 1914-1918; in 1915 moved to Hope, Hempstead County, Ark., where he engaged in the practice of law; elected as a Democrat to the Sixty-seventh and to the seven succeeding Congresses (March 4, 1921-January 3, 1937); was not a candidate for renomination in 1936; continued the practice of law until his retirement; died in Washington, D.C., February 12, 1950; interment in the Congressional Cemetery.

**PARMENTER, William,** a Representative from Massachusetts; born in Boston, Mass., March 30, 1789; attended the public schools and the Boston Latin School; member of the Massachusetts house of representatives in 1829; served in the Massachusetts senate in 1836; selectman of Cambridge in 1836; manager and agent of the New England Crown Glass Co., 1824-1836; president of the Middlesex Bank; elected as a Democrat to the Twenty-fifth and to the three succeeding Congresses (March 4, 1837-March 3, 1845); chairman, Committee on Naval Affairs (Twenty-eighth Congress); naval officer at the port of Boston 1845-1849; died in East Cambridge, Mass., February 25, 1866; interment in Cambridge Cemetery.

**PARRAN, Thomas,** a Representative from Maryland; born near St. Leonard, Calvert County, Md., February 12, 1860; attended the public schools and Charlotte Hall (Md.) Academy; member of the State house of delegates 1884-1888; served as chief deputy collector for the Bureau of Internal Revenue, Baltimore district, 1889-1893; engaged in farming at St. Leonard, Md., in 1890; served in the State senate 1892-1894; assistant enrolling clerk 1895-1897; index clerk of the House of Representatives 1897-1901; clerk of the court of appeals of Maryland 1901-1907; delegate to the Republican National Conventions in 1888, 1904, and 1908; elected as a Republican to the Sixty-second Congress (March 4, 1911-March 3, 1913); unsuccessful candidate for reelection in 1912 to the Sixty-third Congress; member of the Maryland Road Commission 1913-1916; Immigration Commissioner in 1917 and 1918; resumed farming interests; member of the board of directors of the County Trust Co., in Prince Frederick, Md.; died in St. Leonard, Md., March 29, 1955; interment in Christ Church Cemetery, Port Republic, Md.

**PARRETT, William Fletcher,** a Representative from Indiana; born near Blairsville, Posey County, Ind., August 10, 1825; attended the public schools and the Indiana Asbury (now De Pauw) University at Greencastle; studied law; was admitted to the bar and practiced in Evansville, Ind., until 1852; moved to Oregon, where he practiced law for two and a half years; returned to Evansville in 1854, and moved to Boonville, Warrick County, Ind., in 1855; member of the State house of representatives in 1858 and served during the general and special sessions; appointed and subsequently elected judge of the fifteenth circuit and served from 1859 to 1865; returned to Evansville; reelected circuit judge and served from 1865 to 1871; appointed judge of the first circuit and elected in 1873, 1879, and 1884; resigned in December 1888; elected as a Democrat to the Fifty-first and Fifty-second Congresses (March 4, 1889-March 3, 1893); was not a candidate for renomination in 1892; resumed the practice of law until his death in Evansville, Ind., June 30, 1895; interment in Oak Hill Cemetery.

**PARRIS, Albion Keith** (cousin of Virgil Delphini Parris), a Representative from Massachusetts and a Senator from Maine; born in Hebron, Maine (at that time a part of Massachusetts), January 19, 1788; graduated from Dartmouth College, Hanover, N.H., in 1806; studied law; was admitted to the bar and commenced practice in Paris, Maine, in 1809; prosecuting attorney of Oxford County in 1811; member, Massachusetts house of representatives, 1813-1814; member, Massachusetts senate, 1814-1815; elected as a Republican from Massachusetts to the Fourteenth and Fifteenth Congresses and served from March 4, 1815, to February 3, 1818, when he resigned; judge of the District Court of the United States for the District of Maine, 1818-1820; delegate to the Maine constitutional convention in 1819; judge of probate for Cumberland County, Maine, 1820-1821; Governor of Maine from 1822 until 1827; elected to the United States Senate from Maine and served from March 4, 1827, to August 26, 1828, when he resigned; judge of the supreme court of Maine, 1828-1836; Second Comptroller of the United States Treasury from 1836 until 1850; mayor of Portland, Maine in 1852; was not a candidate for reelection; unsuccessful Democratic candidate for Governor in 1854; died in Portland, Maine, February 11, 1857; interment in Western Cemetery.

Bibliography: *DAB.*

**PARRIS, Stanford E.,** a Representative from Virginia; born in Champaign, Ill., September 9, 1929; attended the public schools of Illinois; B.S., University of Illinois, Champaign, 1950; J.D., George Washington University, Washington, D.C., 1958; served in the United States Air Force during the Korean conflict, 1950-1954; awarded Distinguished Flying Cross with cluster, Air Medal with clusters, Purple Heart, and United States and Korean Presidential Citations; admitted to the Virginia bar in 1958 and commenced practice in Alexandria; president, Woodbridge Chrysler-Plymouth Corp., 1965, and Flying Circus Aerodrome, 1971; commercial pilot; member of the Fairfax County Board of Supervisors, 1964-1967; member, Virginia house of delegates, 1969-1972; chairman, Joint Senate-House Republican caucus; elected as a Republican to the Ninety-third Congress (January 3, 1973-January 3, 1975); unsuccessful candidate for reelection in 1974 to the Ninety-fourth Congress; member, District of Columbia Law Revision Commission, 1975-1977; elected as a Republican to the Ninety-seventh and to the four succeeding Congresses (January 3, 1981-January 3, 1991); unsuccessful candidate for reelection in 1990 to the One Hundred Second Congress; unsuccessful candidate in 1995 for election to the Virginia senate; is a resident of Alexandria, Va.

**PARRIS, Virgil Delphini** (cousin of Albion Keith Parris), a Representative from Maine; born in Buckfield, Maine, February 18, 1807; attended the common schools, Hebron Academy, Hebron, Maine, and Colby College, Waterville, Maine; was graduated from Union College, Schenectady, N.Y., in 1827; studied law; was admitted to the bar in 1830 and commenced practice in Buckfield, Maine; assistant secretary of the Maine State senate in 1831; member of the Maine State house of representatives, 1832-1837; elected as a State Rights Democrat to the Twenty-fifth Congress to fill the vacancy caused by the death of Timothy J. Carter; reelected to the Twenty-sixth Congress and served from May 29, 1838, to March 3, 1841; unsuccessful candidate for renomination in 1840 to the Twenty-seventh Congress; member of the Maine State senate in 1842 and 1843, part of the time serving as president pro tempore and as Acting Governor of the State; United States marshal for the district of Maine from 1844 until 1848; special mail agent for New England in 1853; appointed naval storekeeper at Kittery Navy Yard in 1856; delegate to the Democratic National Conventions of 1852 and 1872; died in Paris, Oxford County, Maine, June 13, 1874; interment in the Rawson family knoll in the Old Cemetery.

**PARRISH, Isaac,** a Representative from Ohio; born near St. Clairsville, Belmont County, Ohio, in March 1804; resided in Cambridge, Guernsey County; studied law; was admitted to the bar and practiced; prosecuting attorney of Guernsey County in 1833; member of the State house of representatives in 1837; elected as a Democrat to the Twenty-sixth Congress (March 4, 1839-March 3, 1841); unsuccessful candidate for reelection in 1840 to the Twenty-seventh Congress; elected to the Twenty-ninth Congress (March 4, 1845-March 3, 1847); was not a candidate for renomination in 1846; resumed the practice of law and his former business pursuits in Sharon; also interested in the real estate business and engaged in freighting by steamboat on the Mississippi River; established the Harrison County Flag, published at Calhoun; died in Parrish City, Iowa, August 9, 1860; interment in Calhoun Cemetery, Calhoun, Harrison County, Iowa.

**PARRISH, Lucian Walton,** a Representative from Texas; born in Sister Grove, near Van Alstyne, Grayson County, Tex., January 10, 1878; moved with his parents to Clay County in 1887 and settled near Joy, Tex.; attended the public schools of Joy and Bowie, Tex., and the North Texas State Normal College at Denton, Tex.; taught school for two years; was graduated from the law department of the University of Texas at Austin in 1909; was admitted to the bar the same year and commenced practice in Henrietta, Tex.; elected as a Democrat to the Sixty-sixth and Sixty-seventh Congresses and served from March 4, 1919, until his death in Wichita Falls, Wichita County, Tex., March 27, 1922; interment in Hope Cemetery, Henrietta, Tex.

**PARROTT, John Fabyan,** a Representative and a Senator from New Hampshire; born in Portsmouth, N.H., August 8, 1767; attended the common schools; member, State house of representatives 1809-1814; held various local offices; unsuccessful candidate for election in 1812 to the Thirteenth Congress; elected to the Fifteenth Congress (March 4, 1817-March 3, 1819); elected to the United States Senate and served from March 4, 1819, to March 3, 1825; postmaster of Portsmouth, N.H., 1826; member, State senate 1830-1831; died in Greenland, Rockingham County, N.H., July 9, 1836; interment in the family burying ground on the Parrott estate.

**PARROTT, Marcus Junius,** a Delegate from Kansas; born in Hamburg, Aiken County, S.C., October 27, 1828; attended the common schools, and was graduated from Dickinson College, Carlisle, Pa., in 1849; studied law at Cambridge University; was admitted to the bar and commenced practice in Dayton, Ohio; member of the State house of representatives in 1853 and 1854; moved to Leavenworth, Kans., in 1855; court reporter of the first session of the Territorial supreme court in 1855; elected as a Republican to the Thirty-fifth and Thirty-sixth Congresses and served from March 4, 1857, to January 29, 1861, when the Territory of Kansas was admitted as a State into the Union; unsuccessful candidate for election on the Independent ticket to the Thirty-eighth Congress and on the Democratic ticket to the Forty-third Congress; engaged in agricultural pursuits near Leavenworth, Kans.; died in Dayton, Ohio, October 4, 1879; interment in Woodland Cemetery.

**PARSONS, Claude VanCleve,** a Representative from Illinois; born on a farm near McCormick, Pope County, Ill., October 7, 1895; attended the public schools; taught in the rural schools of Pope County, Ill., 1914-1922; was graduated from Southern Illinois State Normal School at Carbondale in 1923; moved to Golconda, Pope County, Ill., in 1922 to become county superintendent of schools, in which capacity he served until 1930; was also engaged as an editor and newspaper publisher from 1924 to 1930; elected on November 4, 1930, as a Democrat to the Seventy-first Congress to fill the vacancy caused by the resignation of Thomas S. Williams and on the same day was elected to the Seventy-second Congress; reelected to the Seventy-third and to the three succeeding Congresses and served from November 4, 1930, to January 3, 1941; unsuccessful candidate for reelection in 1940 to the Seventy-seventh Congress; appointed first assistant administrator of the United States Housing Authority February 14, 1941, and served until his death in Washington, D.C., May 23, 1941; interment in Zion Church Cemetery, near Ozark, Ill.

**PARSONS, Edward Young,** a Representative from Kentucky; born in Middletown, Jefferson County, Ky., December 12, 1842; attended the public schools at Louisville until twelve years of age; studied one year in the St. Louis High School; returned to Louisville and was graduated from the municipal university in 1861, where he taught school for three years; was graduated from the Louisville Law School in 1865 and practiced law in Louisville, Ky; elected as a Democrat to the Forty-fourth Congress and served from March 4, 1875, until his death in Washington, D.C., July 8, 1876; interment in Cave Hill Cemetery, Louisville, Ky.

**PARSONS, Herbert,** a Representative from New York; born in New York City, October 28, 1869; attended private schools in New York City, St. Paul's School, Concord, N.H., Yale University, the University of Berlin, Harvard Law School, and was graduated from Yale University in 1890; was admitted to the bar in 1894 and commenced practice in New York City; member of the board of aldermen of New York City 1900-1904; elected as a Republican to the Fifty-ninth, Sixtieth, and Sixty-first Congresses (March 4, 1905-March 3, 1911); unsuccessful candidate for reelection in 1910 to the Sixty-second Congress; resumed the practice of law in New York City; delegate to all Republican New York State conventions 1904-1920; delegate to the Republican National Conventions in 1908, 1912, 1916, and 1920; served on the general staff of the American Expeditionary Forces during the First World War; died in Pittsfield, Mass., September 16, 1925; interment in Lenox Cemetery, Lenox, Mass.

**PARSONS, Richard Chappel,** a Representative from Ohio; born in New London, Conn., October 10, 1826; pursued classical studies; moved to Norwalk, Ohio, in 1845; studied law; was admitted to the bar in 1851 and commenced practice at Cleveland; member of the city council in 1852 and 1853 and served as president in 1853; member of the State house of representatives 1858-1861 and served one term as speaker; appointed consul to Rio de Janeiro, Brazil, on March 27, 1862, but resigned, effective October 1, 1862; collector of internal revenue at Cleveland 1862-1866; marshal of the Supreme Court of the United States 1867-1872; elected as a Republican to the Forty-third Congress (March 4, 1873-March 3, 1875); unsuccessful Republican candidate for reelection to the Forty-fourth Congress; resumed the practice of law in Cleveland, Ohio; editor and part owner of the Cleveland Daily Herald in 1877; died in Cleveland, Ohio, January 9, 1899; interment in Lake View Cemetery.

**PARTRIDGE, Donald Barrows,** a Representative from Maine; born in Norway, Oxford County, Maine, June 7, 1891; attended the common and high schools and was graduated from Bates College, Lewiston, Maine, in 1914; principal of the high school, at Canton, Maine, 1914-1917; was elected clerk of the supreme judicial court for Oxford County in 1918 and served from 1919 to 1931; studied law; was admitted to the bar in 1924 and commenced practice in Norway, Maine, the same year; served as town clerk 1924-1931; member of the board of education of Norway 1926-1931; served as chairman of the Oxford County Republican committee for six years; elected as a Republican to the Seventy-second Congress (March 4, 1931-March 3, 1933); was not a candidate for renomination in 1932; resumed the practice of law in Norway, Maine; member of the Maine Industrial Accident Commission; died in Portland, Maine, June 5, 1946, while on a business trip; interment in Norway Pine Grove Cemetery, South Paris, Maine.

**PARTRIDGE, Frank Charles,** a Senator from Vermont; born in East Middlebury, Vt., May 7, 1861; attended the public schools and graduated from Amherst (Mass.) College in 1882 and from the Columbia University Law School at New York City in 1884; was admitted to the bar in 1885 and commenced practice in Rutland, Vt.; moved to Proctor, Vt., in 1886 and engaged in the marble industry; also served as president of other business corporations; town clerk, 1887-1889; member of the school committee, 1888-1889; private secretary to Secretary of War Redfield Proctor, 1889-1890; solicitor of the Department of State, 1890-1893; appointed United States Minister to Venezuela on January 25, 1893 and served until January 1894; consul general at Tangier, Morocco, 1897-1898; member, Vermont State senate, 1898-1900; member of the executive council of the American Society of International Law, 1906-1923; chairman of the commission to propose amendments to the Vermont constitution, 1909; member of the Vermont committee of public safety, 1917-1919; delegate of the United States to the Fifth Pan-American Conference at Santiago, Chile, 1923; member of the New England Council, 1925-1927; president of the Vermont Flood Credit Corporation; appointed as a Republican to the United States Senate to fill the vacancy caused by the death of Frank L. Greene and served from December 23, 1930, to March 31, 1931, when a successor was elected; unsuccessful candidate for the nomination to fill this vacancy; chairman, Committee on Enrolled Bills (Seventy-first Congress); resumed his former activities in the marble industry; died in Proctor, Vt., March 2, 1943; interment in Proctor Cemetery.

**PARTRIDGE, George,** a Delegate and a Representative from Massachusetts; born in Duxbury, Mass., February 8, 1740; graduated from Harvard College in 1762; taught school in Kingston, Mass.; studied theology; delegate to the Provincial Congress in 1774 and 1775; member of the Massachusetts house of representatives 1775-1779; sheriff of Plymouth County 1777-1812; member of the Continental Congress 1779-1785; member of the Massachusetts house of representatives in 1788; elected to the First Congress and served from March 4, 1789, to August 14, 1790, when he resigned; endowed Partridge Seminary in Duxbury; died in Duxbury, Plymouth County, Mass., on July 7, 1828; interment in Mayflower Cemetery.

**PARTRIDGE, Samuel,** a Representative from New York; born in Norwich, Windsor County, Vt., November 29, 1790; received a limited schooling; during the War of 1812 enlisted as a private in the Vermont Militia; later appointed a captain of Engineers in the Regular Army; served two terms as high sheriff of Windsor County; moved to New York and engaged in mercantile pursuits at Cold Spring in 1820; moved to Chemung County, N.Y., in 1830 and to Elmira in 1837 and again engaged in mercantile pursuits; elected as a Democrat to the Twenty-seventh Congress (March 4, 1841-March 3, 1843); engaged in agricultural pursuits and the real estate business; died in Elmira, Chemung County, N.Y., March 30, 1883; interment in Second Street Cemetery.

**PASCHAL, Thomas Moore,** a Representative from Texas; born in Alexandria, Rapides Parish, La., December 15, 1845; moved with his parents to San Antonio, Tex., in 1846; educated in private schools; attended St. Mary's College, San Antonio, Tex.; was graduated from Centre College, Danville, Ky., in 1866; studied law; was admitted to the bar in 1867 and commenced practice in San Antonio; city attorney in 1867; United States commissioner for the western district of Texas, 1867-1869; judge of the district criminal court for San Antonio in 1870 and 1871; moved to Castroville, Tex., in 1870; district attorney of the twenty-fourth district, 1871-1875; moved to Brackett, King County, in 1873; elected judge of the thirty-eighth judicial district in 1876; reelected in 1880 and 1884, and served until 1892; appointed by Governor Richard Coke as extradition agent between the United States and Mexico in 1876, and reappointed by Governor Oran M. Roberts in 1880; returned to Castroville in 1885; elected as a Democrat to the Fifty-third Congress (March 4, 1893-March 3, 1895); unsuccessful candidate for renomination in 1894 to the Fifty-fourth Congress; resumed the practice of law in San Antonio, Tex.; delegate to the Democratic National Convention of 1896; died in New York City, January 28, 1919; interment in Mission Burial Park, San Antonio, Tex.

**PASCO, Samuel,** a Senator from Florida; born in London, England, June 28, 1834; immigrated to the United States with his family and settled in Charlestown, Mass., in 1846; attended the public schools and graduated from Harvard University in 1858; moved to Florida in 1859 and was principal of Waukeenah Academy, near Monticello, 1860-1861; during the Civil War entered the Confederate Army as a private in the Third Florida Volunteers; wounded and captured at Mississippi Ridge, and remained in prison until March 1865, when he was paroled with the rank of sergeant; returned to Florida in 1865 and was again principal of Waukeenah Academy 1865-1866; clerk of the circuit court of Jefferson County 1866-1868; studied law; was admitted to the bar in 1868 and commenced practice in Monticello, Fla.; presidential elector on the Democratic ticket in 1880; president of the Florida State constitutional convention in 1885; member, Florida State house of representatives 1886-1887, and served as speaker in the latter year; elected as a Democrat to the United States Senate to fill the vacancy in the term beginning March 4, 1887; was appointed in 1893 and subsequently elected; again appointed in 1899 and served from May 19, 1887, to April 18, 1899, when a successor was elected; unsuccessful candidate for reelection in 1899; chairman, Committee on Claims (Fifty-third Congress); member of the Isthmian Canal Commission 1899-1905; retired and resided in Monticello; died in

Tampa, Fla., March 13, 1917; interment in Roseland Cemetery, Monticello, Fla.

**Bibliography:** *DAB*; Pasco, Samuel. "Jefferson County, Florida." *Florida Historical Society Quarterly* 7 (October 1928): 139-54, 7 (January 1929): 234-57; Pasco, Samuel, Jr. "Samuel Pasco." *Florida Historical Society Quarterly* 7 (October 1928): 135-38.

**PASHAYAN, Charles, Jr.,** a Representative from California; born in Fresno, Fresno County, Calif., March 27, 1941; graduated from Bullard High School, 1959; B.A., Pomona College, Claremont, Calif., 1963; J.D., University of California, San Francisco, 1968; captain, United States Army, Strategic Intelligence, The Pentagon, 1968-1970; admitted to the California bar in 1969, to the District of Columbia bar in 1972, and to the United States Supreme Court bar in 1977; special assistant to the general counsel of the United States Department of Health, Education, and Welfare, 1973-1975; M.Litt., Oxford University, England, 1977; elected as a Republican to the Ninety-sixth and to the five succeeding Congresses (January 3, 1979-January 3, 1991); unsuccessful candidate for reelection in 1990 to the One Hundred Second Congress; is a resident of Fresno, Calif.

**PASSMAN, Otto Ernest,** a Representative from Louisiana; born on a farm near Franklinton, Washington Parish, La., June 27, 1900; was graduated from Baton Rouge (La.) High School, and from Soule Business College at Bogalousa, La.; in 1929 engaged in the manufacture of commercial refrigerators, and as a distributor of hotel and restaurant supplies and electrical appliances at Monroe, La.; owner, Passman Investment Company; during the Second World War was commissioned a lieutenant in the United States Navy, and served from October 11, 1942 until his discharge as a lieutenant commander on September 5, 1944; resumed the mercantile business; delegate to the Democratic National Conventions of 1948, 1952 and 1956; elected as a Democrat to the Eightieth and to the fourteen succeeding Congresses (January 3, 1947-January 3, 1977); unsuccessful candidate for renomination in 1976 to the Ninety-fifth Congress; was a resident of Monroe, La., until his death there on August 13, 1988.

**Bibliography:** Jones, Randolph. "Otto Passman and Foreign Aid: The Early Years." *Louisiana History* 26 (Winter 1985): 53-62.

**PASTOR, Edward Lopez,** a Representative from Arizona; born in Claypool, Gila County, Ariz., June 28, 1943; attended public schools in Miami, Ariz.; B.A., Arizona State University, 1966; J.D., Arizona State College of Law, 1974; member, staff of Governor Raul Castro of Arizona; chemistry teacher; deputy director, Guadalupe Organization, Inc.; member, Maricopa County (Ariz.) board of supervisors, 1977-1991; elected as a Democrat to the One Hundred Second Congress, September 24, 1991, by special election to fill the vacancy caused by the resignation of Morris K. Udall; reelected to the two succeeding Congresses, and served from September 24, 1991 to January 3, 1997; is a resident of Phoenix, Ariz.

**PASTORE, John Orlando,** a Senator from Rhode Island; born in Providence, R.I., March 17, 1907; attended the public schools; LL.B., Northeastern University, Boston, Mass., 1931; was admitted to the bar in 1932 and commenced the practice of law at Providence, R.I.; member, Rhode Island house of representatives, 1935-1937; assistant attorney general of Rhode Island, 1937-1938; member of the Providence Charter Revision Commission, 1939-1940; again assistant attorney general, 1940-1944; elected Lieutenant Governor in 1944, and assumed the office of Governor of Rhode Island on October 6, 1945, filling the vacancy caused by the resignation of J. Howard McGrath for the term ending January 7, 1947; elected Governor in 1946, reelected in 1948, but resigned on December 18, 1950, having been elected as a Democrat to the United States Senate, November 7, 1950, to fill the vacancy caused by the resignation of J. Howard McGrath for the term ending January 3, 1953; reelected in 1952, 1958, 1964, and again in 1970, and served from December 19, 1950 until his resignation on December 28, 1976; delivered keynote address at the Democratic National Convention of 1964; was not a candidate for reelection in 1976; co-chairman, Joint Committee on Atomic Energy (Eighty-eighth, Ninetieth, Ninety-second, and Ninety-fourth Congresses); is a resident of Providence R. I.

Bibliography: Morgenthau, Ruth S. *Pride Without Prejudice: The Life of John O. Pastore.* With a foreword by Edward D. DiPrete. Providence: Rhode Island Historical Society, 1989.

PATERSON, John, a Representative from New York; born in New Britain, Hartford County, Conn., in 1744; attended the common schools; completed preparatory studies and was graduated from Yale College in 1762; studied law; was admitted to the bar and practiced in New Britain and Lenox, Mass.; member of the Berkshire convention of 1774 and of the general court that became the first Provincial Congress in 1774; raised a regiment and participated in the Revolutionary War; colonel of the regiment from April to December 1775; colonel of the Fifteenth Continental Infantry January 1, 1776; brigadier general February 21, 1777, and served until the close of the war; brevetted major general September 30, 1783; after the war returned to Lenox, Mass., and was commander of the Massachusetts troops in putting down Shays' Rebellion; moved to Lisle, Broome County, N.Y., in 1790; member of the State assembly in 1792 and 1793; county judge of Broome County in 1798 and 1806; member of the committee to revise the constitution of the State of New York in 1801; elected as a Republican to the Eighth Congress (March 4, 1803-March 3, 1805); from 1805 until his death he devoted himself to farming; died in Lisle, N.Y. (now Whitneys Point), July 19, 1808; interment in Lenox Cemetery.

Bibliography: *DAB*.

PATERSON, William, a Delegate and a Senator from New Jersey; born in County Antrim, Ireland, December 24, 1745; immigrated to the United States in 1747 with his parents, who settled in New Castle, Pa.; moved about through the colonies before settling in Princeton, N.J., in 1750; attended private schools; graduated from the College of New Jersey (later Princeton University) in 1763; studied law; was admitted to the bar in 1768 and commenced practice in New Bromley, N.J., in 1769; delegate and secretary to the Provincial Congress, 1775-1776; member, New Jersey State legislative council, 1776-1777; delegate to the New Jersey constitutional convention in 1776; attorney general of New Jersey from 1776 until 1783, when he resigned; moved to Raritan, N.J., in 1779; elected as a Delegate to the Continental Congress in 1780, but declined, owing to his duties as attorney general; moved to New Brunswick, N.J., in 1783; delegate to the Federal Constitutional Convention in Philadelphia in 1787 and one of the signers of the Constitution; again elected as a Delegate to the Continental Congress in 1787, but declined; elected to the United States Senate and served from March 4, 1789 to November 13, 1790, when he resigned, having been elected Governor of New Jersey by the Legislature; reelected Governor and served from October 30, 1790 until March 4, 1793, when he resigned to take a seat on the United States Supreme Court; nominated on March 4, 1793 by President George Washington as an Associate Justice of the United States Supreme Court; was confirmed by the Senate the same day and served until his death in Albany, N.Y., September 9, 1806; interment in the Van Rensselaer Manor House vault, near Albany, N.Y.; manor house was destroyed around 1900; reinterred in the Van Rensselaer lot, Albany Rural Cemetery, Albany, N.Y.

Bibliography: *DAB*; Haskett, Richard. "William Paterson, Counsellor at Law." Ph.D. dissertation, Princeton University, 1952; O'Connor, John E. *William Paterson: Lawyer and Statesman, 1745-1806.* New Brunswick, N.J.: Rutgers University Press, 1979.

PATMAN, John William Wright (father of William Neff Patman), a Representative from Texas; born at Patman's Switch near Hughes Springs, Cass County, Tex., August 6, 1893; attended the public schools; was graduated from Hughes Springs (Tex.) High School in 1912, and from the law department of Cumberland University, Lebanon, Tenn., in 1916; engaged in agricultural pursuits in Texas in 1913 and 1914; was admitted to the bar in 1916 and commenced practice in Hughes Springs, Tex.; assistant county attorney of Cass County, Tex., 1916-1917; during the First World War served as a private and later as a machine gun officer in the United States Army, 1917-1919; member, Texas State house of representatives, 1921-1924; district attorney of the fifth judicial district of Texas, 1924-1929; elected as a Democrat to the Seventy-first Congress; reelected to the twenty-three succeeding Congresses, and served from March 4, 1929 until his death in Bethesda, Md., March 7, 1976; chairman, Select Committee on Small Business (Eighty-first, Eighty-second, and Eighty-fourth through Eighty-seventh Congresses), Joint Economic Committee (Eighty-fifth, Eighty-seventh, Eighty-ninth, Ninety-first and Ninety-third Congresses), Joint Committee on Defense Production (Eighty-eighth, Ninetieth, Ninety-second, and Ninety-fourth Congresses), Committee on Banking and Currency (Eighty-eighth through Ninety-third Congresses); interment in Hillcrest Cemetery, Texarkana, Tex.

Bibliography: *DAB*; Schmelzer, Janet Louise. "The Early Life and Early Congressional Career of Wright Patman, 1894-1941." Ph.D. dissertation, Texas Christian University, 1978; Young, Nancy Beck. "Wright Patman: Congressman to the Nation, 1893-1953." Ph.D. dissertation, University of Texas, 1995.

PATMAN, William Neff (son of John William Wright Patman), a Representative from Texas; born in Texarkana, Bowie County, Tex., March 26, 1927; attended the public schools of Texarkana and Washington, D.C.; graduated from Kemper Military School, Boonville, Mo., 1944; B.B.A., University of Texas, Austin, 1953, and LL.B., 1953; served in the United States Marine Corps, private first class, 1945-1946, and in the United States Air Force Reserve, captain, 1953-1966; diplomatic courier, United States Foreign Service, 1949-1950; admitted to the Texas bar in 1953 and was legal examiner, Texas Railroad Commission, 1953-1955; commenced the private practice of law in 1955; city attorney of Ganado, Tex., from 1955 until 1960; served in the Texas State senate, 1961-1980; delegate, Texas State Democratic conventions, 1960-1978; elected as a Democrat to the Ninety-seventh and Ninety-eighth Congresses (January 3, 1981-January 3, 1985); unsuccessful candidate for reelection in 1984 to the Ninety-ninth Congress; is a resident of Ganado, Tex.

PATRICK, Luther, a Representative from Alabama; born near Decatur, Morgan County, Ala., January 23, 1894; attended the public schools, Louisiana State University at Baton Rouge, and Purdue University, Lafayette, Ind.; in 1918 was graduated from the law department of the University of Alabama at Tuscaloosa; during the First World War served as a private, assigned to the Army training detachment and to the Central Officers' Training School, from June 14, 1918, to December 4, 1918; was admitted to the bar in 1919 and commenced practice in Fairfield, Ala.; city attorney of Fairfield 1920-1922; author of many poems and books; began career of radio commentator in 1925; assistant attorney general of Alabama 1927-1929; assistant United States district attorney of the northern Alabama district in 1933 and 1934; elected as a Democrat to the Seventy-fifth, Seventy-sixth, and Seventy-seventh Congresses (January 3, 1937-January 3, 1943); unsuccessful candidate for renomination in 1942; served as a consultant to the War Production Board in 1943 and 1944; elected to the Seventy-ninth Congress (January 3, 1945-January 3, 1947); unsuccessful candidate for renomination in 1946; resumed law practice in Birmingham, Ala.;

delegate to the Democratic National Convention in 1956; died in Birmingham, Ala., May 26, 1957; interment in Elmwood Cemetery.

**PATTEN, Edward James,** a Representative from New Jersey; born in Perth Amboy, Middlesex County, N.J., August 22, 1905; attended the public schools of Perth Amboy; graduated from the Newark Normal School in 1927; LL.B., Newark State College (now Rutgers University) Law School, Newark, N.J., 1926, B.S., 1928; was admitted to the bar in 1927 and began the practice of law in Perth Amboy; teacher in the public schools of Elizabeth, N.J., 1927-1934; mayor of Perth Amboy, 1934-1940; county clerk, Middlesex County, 1940-1954; secretary of state, State of New Jersey, 1954-1962; director and counsel of the Woodbridge National Bank, 1935-1962; elected as a Democrat to the Eighty-eighth and to the eight succeeding Congresses (January 3, 1963-January 3, 1981); was not a candidate for reelection in 1980 to the Ninety-seventh Congress; was a resident of Perth Amboy, N.J.; died September 17, 1994.

**PATTEN, Harold Ambrose,** a Representative from Arizona; born in Husted, El Paso County, Colo., October 6, 1907; moved to Tucson, Pima County, Ariz., in 1916; graduated from the University of Arizona in 1930; coach and teacher of physical education in Tucson High School in 1931 and 1932; director of recreation for city of Tucson and city schools 1933-1939; State director of recreation in 1939 and 1940; entered military service with the Seventh Cavalry Regiment as a first lieutenant in August 1940; transferred to the Air Corps in 1941 and spent thirty-one months on foreign service in Africa and Italy; discharged as a major on November 21, 1945; retired July 1, 1960, as lieutenant colonel, Air Force Reserve; life insurance agent in Phoenix, 1946-1948; elected as a Democrat to the Eighty-first and to the two succeeding Congresses (January 3, 1949-January 3, 1955); was not a candidate for renomination in 1954 to the Eighty-fourth Congress; unsuccessful candidate for nomination in 1961 to fill a vacancy in the Eighty-seventh Congress; resumed his career in the insurance field; in 1965, appointed to head a Federal Job Corps Center in Oregon; organized and directed a Center at Malheur Wildlife Refuge and was director of Center offices in Portland, Oreg.; died in Tucson, Ariz., September 6, 1969; willed his body to the University of Arizona College of Medicine for research purposes.

**PATTEN, John,** a Delegate and a Representative from Delaware; born in Kent County, Del., April 26, 1746; attended the common schools; engaged in agricultural pursuits; entered the Revolutionary Army as a lieutenant; was promoted to the rank of major; Member of the Continental Congress in 1786; presented credentials as a Member-elect to the Third Congress and served from March 4, 1793, to February 14, 1794, when he was succeeded by Henry Latimer, who contested his election; elected as a Republican to the Fourth Congress (March 4, 1795-March 3, 1797); was not a candidate for renomination; engaged in farming until his death at "Tynhead Court," near Dover, Del., December 26, 1800; interment in the Presbyterian Churchyard.

**PATTEN, Thomas Gedney,** a Representative from New York; born in New York City September 12, 1861; attended Mount Pleasant Academy, Ossining, N.Y., Columbia College, New York City, 1877-1879, and Columbia Law School 1880-1882; engaged in the shipping business and subsequently operated a fleet of tugboats in New York Harbor; served as president of the New York & Long Branch Steamboat Co.; elected as a Democrat to the Sixty-second, Sixty-third, and Sixty-fourth Congresses (March 4, 1911-March 3, 1917); unsuccessful candidate for reelection in 1916 to the Sixty-fifth Congress; postmaster of New York City, 1917-1921; moved to Hollywood, Calif., in 1922 and served on the staff of the Motion Picture Producers and Distributors of America, Inc., until 1924, when he retired; died in Hollywood, Calif., February 23, 1939; interment in Forest Lawn Memorial Park, Los Angeles, Calif.

**PATTERSON, David Trotter,** a Senator from Tennessee; born at Cedar Creek, near Greeneville, Greene County, Tenn., February 28, 1818; attended the common schools and Greeneville College for two years; studied law; was admitted to the bar in 1841 and commenced practice in Greeneville, Tenn.; engaged in manufacturing; judge of the first circuit court of Tennessee 1854-1863; upon the readmission of the State of Tennessee to representation was elected as a Democrat to the United States Senate and served from May 4, 1865, to March 3, 1869; was not a candidate for reelection; engaged in the management of his extensive agricultural interests; died in Afton, near Greeneville, Tenn., November 3, 1891; interment in the Andrew Johnson National Cemetery, Greeneville, Tenn.

**PATTERSON, Edward White,** a Representative from Kansas; born in Pittsburg, Crawford County, Kans., October 4, 1895; attended the public schools; during the First World War served as a sergeant in the Thirty-fifth Division, American Expeditionary Forces, from May 1917 to March 1919; after the war attended the University of Chicago at Chicago, Ill.; was graduated from the law department of the University of Kansas at Lawrence in 1922; was admitted to the bar the same year and commenced practice in Pittsburg, Kans.; prosecuting attorney of Crawford County, Kans., 1926-1928; elected as a Democrat to the Seventy-fourth and Seventy-fifth Congresses (January 3, 1935-January 3, 1939); unsuccessful candidate for reelection in 1938 to the Seventy-sixth Congress; resumed the practice of law in Pittsburg, Kans., until his death in Weir, Kans., March 6, 1940; interment in Highland Park Cemetery, Pittsburg, Kans.

**PATTERSON, Elizabeth J.** (daughter of Olin D. Johnston), a Representative from South Carolina; born in Columbia, S.C., November 18, 1939; attended public schools in Kensington, Md., and Spartanburg, S.C.; B.A., Columbia (S.C.) College, 1961; graduate study, University of South Carolina, 1961-1962; recruiting officer for the Peace Corps, 1962-1964; recruiting officer for Volunteers In Service To America, 1965-1967; director of a Head Start program, 1967-1968; staff assistant for Representative James R. Mann of South Carolina, 1969-1970; served on the Spartanburg County Council, 1975-1976; South Carolina State senator, 1979-1986; elected as a Democrat to the One Hundredth and to the two succeeding Congresses (January 3, 1987-January 3, 1993); unsuccessful candidate for reelection in 1992 to the One Hundred Third Congress; is a resident of Spartanburg, S.C.

**PATTERSON, Ellis Ellwood,** a Representative from California; born in Yuba City, Sutter County, Calif., November 28, 1897; attended the public schools; was graduated from the University of California at Berkeley in 1921; during the First World War served as a seaman in the United States Navy in 1917 and 1918; taught school in Colusa County, Calif., 1922-1924; district superintendent of schools of South Monterey County, Calif., 1923-1932; studied law at Stanford University and at the University of California, 1931-1936; was admitted to the bar in 1937 and commenced practice in Sacramento and Los Angeles, Calif.; member of the California State assembly, 1932-1938; Lieutenant Governor, 1939-1943; elected as a Democrat to the Seventy-ninth Congress (January 3, 1945-January 3, 1947); did not seek renomination in 1946 to the House of Representatives, but was an unsuccessful candidate for nomination to the United States Senate; unsuccessful candidate for election in 1948 to the Eighty-first Congress; resumed the practice of law; was a resident of Los Angeles, Calif., until his death there on August 25, 1985.

**PATTERSON, Francis Ford, Jr.,** a Representative from New Jersey; born in Newark, N.J., July 30, 1867; moved with his parents to Woodbury, N.J., in 1874; attended the public schools; employed in a newspaper office at the age of thirteen; moved to Camden, N.J., in 1882; connected with the Camden Courier 1883-1890; New Jersey editor of the Philadelphia Record 1890-1894; owner and publisher of the Camden Post-Telegram 1894-1923; president of the West Jersey Trust Co. 1916-1925; director of the West Jersey Title Co. 1920-1925; member of the State house of assembly in 1900; county clerk of Camden County 1900-1920; delegate to the Republican National Convention in 1920; elected as a Republican to the Sixty-sixth Congress to fill the vacancy caused by the death of William J. Browning; reelected to the Sixty-seventh, Sixty-eighth, and Sixty-ninth Congresses and served from November 2, 1920, to March 3, 1927; unsuccessful candidate for renomination in 1926; engaged in banking, serving as president of the West Jersey Parkside Trust Co., of Camden, N.J., until his death in Merchantville, N.J., on November 30, 1935; interment in Colestown Cemetery, located between Merchantville and Moorestown, N.J.

**PATTERSON, George Robert,** a Representative from Pennsylvania; born in Lewistown, Mifflin County, Pa., November 9, 1863; attended the public schools and Lewistown (Pa.) Academy; engaged in mercantile pursuits in 1880; moved to Ashland, Schuylkill County, in 1886 and engaged in the wholesale grain and feed business; delegate to the Republican National Convention in 1900 and 1904; elected as a Republican to the Fifty-seventh, Fifty-eighth, and Fifty-ninth Congresses and served from March 4, 1901, until his death in Washington, D.C., March 21, 1906; interment in Citizens' Cemetery, Ashland, Pa.

**PATTERSON, George Washington** (brother of William Patterson and uncle of Augustus Frank), a Representative from New York; born in Londonderry, Rockingham County, N.H., November 11, 1799; completed preparatory studies, and was graduated from Pinkerton Academy; moved to New York and settled in Genesee County in 1818; engaged in the manufacture of fanning mills; settled in Leicester, N.Y., in 1825 and engaged in agricultural pursuits and the manufacture of farming implements; commissioner of highways of Leicester; justice of the peace; member of the State assembly 1832, 1833, and 1835-1840, and served as speaker in 1839 and 1840; basin commissioner at Albany in 1839 and 1840; moved to Westfield, N.Y., in 1841 to take charge of the Chautauqua land office; delegate to the State constitutional convention in 1846; elected Lieutenant Governor of New York in 1848; chairman of the harbor commission at New York 1855-1857; quarantine commissioner of the port of New York in 1859; supervisor and president of the board of education for many years; delegate to the Republican National Convention in 1856 and 1860; elected as a Republican to the Forty-fifth Congress (March 4, 1877-March 3, 1879); was not a candidate for renomination in 1878; died in Westfield, Chautauqua County, N.Y., October 15, 1879; interment in Westfield Cemetery.

**PATTERSON, Gilbert Brown,** a Representative from North Carolina; born near Maxton, Robeson County, N.C., May 29, 1863; attended Shoe Heel Academy, Shoe Heel (now Maxton), N.C., and the Lurinburg (N.C.) High School; was graduated from the University of North Carolina at Chapel Hill in 1886; studied law; was admitted to the bar in 1890 and commenced practice in Maxton, N.C.; member of the State house of representatives 1899-1901; elected as a Democrat to the Fifty-eighth and Fifty-ninth Congresses (March 4, 1903-March 3, 1907); resumed the practice of law; died in Maxton, N.C., January 26, 1922; interment in Maxton Cemetery.

**PATTERSON, James O'Hanlon,** a Representative from South Carolina; born in Barnwell, Barnwell County, S.C., June 25, 1857; attended private schools in Barnwell, S.C., and Augusta, Ga.; studied law; was admitted to the bar in 1886 and commenced practice in Barnwell, S.C.; probate judge of Barnwell County 1888-1892; member of the State house of representatives 1899-1904; elected as a Democrat to the Fifty-ninth, Sixtieth, and Sixty-first Congresses (March 4, 1905-March 3, 1911); resumed the practice of his profession in Barnwell, S.C., where he died on October 25, 1911; interment in the Episcopal Cemetery.

**PATTERSON, James Thomas,** a Representative from Connecticut; born in Naugatuck, New Haven County, Conn., on October 20, 1908; attended the public schools; was graduated from Peekskill (N.Y.) Military Academy in 1929 and from Georgetown University, Washington, D.C., in 1933; B.A., University of Miami (Fla.), 1934; LL.B., National University Law School (now George Washington University), Washington, D.C., 1939; while attending school worked for the Connecticut highway department from 1924 to 1933, for the United States Rubber Company in 1934, for the United States Department of Labor, 1934-1937, for the Social Security Board in 1937 and 1938, and for the United States Treasury, 1938-1940; served with the United States Marine Corps and the Office of Strategic Services from September 1941 until discharged as a major in July 1946, with overseas service in the African and European Theaters and in India, Burma, and China; elected as a Republican to the Eightieth and to the five succeeding Congresses (January 3, 1947-January 3, 1959); unsuccessful candidate for reelection in 1958 to the Eighty-sixth Congress; unsuccessful candidate for election in 1960 to the Eighty-seventh Congress, and for election in 1970 to the Ninety-second Congress; was a resident of Bethlehem, Conn.; died February 7, 1989.

**PATTERSON, James Willis,** a Representative and a Senator from New Hampshire; born in Henniker, N.H., July 2, 1823; pursued classical studies; graduated from Dartmouth College, Hanover, N.H., in 1848; principal of the Woodstock Academy, Conn., for two years; attended the Theological Seminary at New Haven, Conn.; studied law; professor of mathematics, astronomy, and meteorology at Dartmouth College, 1854-1865; member of the New Hampshire State house of representatives in 1862; elected as a Republican to the Thirty-eighth and Thirty-ninth Congresses (March 4, 1863-March 3, 1867); elected to the United States Senate, and served from March 4, 1867 to March 3, 1873; chairman, Committee on Enrolled Bills (Forty-first Congress), Committee on the District of Columbia (Forty-first and Forty-second Congresses); regent of the Smithsonian Institution; member, New Hampshire State house of representatives, 1877-1878; State superintendent of public instruction, 1881-1893; president of American Institute of Instruction; died in Hanover, N.H., May 4, 1893; interment in Dartmouth Cemetery.

**Bibliography:** *DAB.*

**PATTERSON, Jerry Mumford,** a Representative from California; born in El Paso, Tex., October 25, 1934; attended public schools in Tucson, Ariz.; B.A., California State University, Long Beach, 1960; J.D., University of California at Los Angeles Law School, 1966; engaged in graduate work, University of Southern California, Los Angeles, 1960-1963; admitted to the California bar in 1967 and commenced practice in Santa Ana; served in the United States Coast Guard, 1953-1957; city attorney, Placentia, Calif., 1973-1975; city councilman for Santa Ana, 1969-1973; mayor, Santa Ana, 1973-1975; delegate to the Democratic National Conventions of 1976, 1980, and 1984; elected as a Democrat to the Ninety-fourth and to the four succeeding Congresses (January 3, 1975-January 3, 1985); unsuccessful candidate for reelection in 1984 to the Ninety-ninth Congress; chairman, Select Committee on Committees (Ninety-sixth Congress); visiting professor, graduate center for public policy and administration, California State University, Long Beach, 1986 to present; resumed the practice of law in Costa Mesa, Calif., in 1986; city attorney, Cypress, Calif., 1987-1993; city attorney, Dana Point, Calif., 1989 to present; city attorney, Lake Forest, Calif., 1992 to present; is a resident of Fountain Valley, Calif.

**PATTERSON, John** (half brother of Thomas Patterson), a Representative from Ohio; born in Little Britain Township, Lancaster County, Pa., February 10, 1771; moved with his parents to Pattersons Mills, Cross Creek Township, Washington County, Pa., in 1778; attended the common schools; moved to St. Clairsville, Belmont County, Ohio; engaged in mercantile pursuits; first mayor of St. Clairsville in 1807 and 1808; member of the State house of representatives in 1807 and 1808; served in the State senate 1815-1818; associate judge of the court of common pleas of Belmont County from February 1810 to February 1815; elected to the Eighteenth Congress (March 4, 1823-March 3, 1825); engaged in the hardware business and in agricultural pursuits; died in St. Clairsville, Ohio, February 7, 1848; interment in Union Cemetery.

**PATTERSON, John James,** a Senator from South Carolina; born in Waterloo, Juniata County, Pa., August 8, 1830; attended the common schools and graduated from Jefferson College, Canonsburg, Pa., in 1848; engaged in newspaper work; publisher of the Juniata Sentinel in 1852 and became editor and part owner of the Harrisburg Telegraph in 1853; engaged in banking; member, State house of representatives 1854-1856; during the Civil War served in the Union Army as a captain in the Fifteenth United States Volunteer Infantry; unsuccessful candidate for election in 1862 to the Thirty-eighth Congress; engaged in banking 1863-1869; moved to Columbia, S.C., in 1869 and engaged in railroad construction; elected as a Republican to the United States Senate from South Carolina and served from March 4, 1873, to March 3, 1879; was not a candidate for reelection to the Senate; chairman, Committee on Education and Labor (Forty-fourth Congress), Committee on Territories (Forty-fifth Congress); resided in Washington, D.C., and engaged in various financial enterprises; moved to Mifflintown, Juniata County, Pa., in 1886; engaged in the construction of electric railways and electric lighting plants; died in Mifflintown, Pa., September 28, 1912; interment in Westminster Presbyterian Cemetery.

**PATTERSON, Josiah** (father of Malcolm Rice Patterson), a Representative from Tennessee; born in Morgan County, Ala., April 14, 1837; attended the common schools and Somerville (Ala.) Academy; studied law; was admitted to the bar and commenced the practice of law in Morgan County in 1859; entered the Confederate Army in September 1861; commissioned a first lieutenant in the First Regiment of Alabama Cavalry in 1862; promoted to the rank of captain, then to colonel, and subsequently assigned to the command of the Fifth Regiment of Alabama Cavalry; resumed the practice of law; settled in Florence, Ala., in January 1867; moved to Memphis, Tenn., in March 1872 and continued the practice of his profession; member of the State house of representatives, 1883-1885; elected as a Democrat to the Fifty-second, Fifty-third, and Fifty-fourth Congresses (March 4, 1891-March 3, 1897); unsuccessful candidate for reelection in 1896 to the Fifty-fifth Congress as a Gold Democrat; again resumed the practice of his profession; died in Memphis, Shelby County, Tenn., February 10, 1904; interment in Forest Hill Cemetery.

**Bibliography:** Faries, Clyde J. "Carmack Versus Patterson: The Genesis of a Political Feud." *Tennessee Historical Quarterly* 38 (Fall 1979): 332-47.

**PATTERSON, LaFayette Lee,** a Representative from Alabama; born near Delta, Clay County, Ala., August 23, 1888; attended the rural schools; engaged in agricultural pursuits and taught in the rural schools; was graduated from Jacksonville (Ala.) State Teachers' College in 1922, from Birmingham-Southern College, Birmingham, Ala., in 1924, and from Stanford University in 1927; superintendent of education of Tallapoosa County, Ala., 1924-1926; elected as a Democrat to the Seventieth Congress to fill the vacancy caused by the resignation of William B. Bowling; reelected to the two succeeding Congresses, and served from November 6, 1928 to March 3, 1933; unsuccessful candidate for renomination in 1932 to the Seventy-third Congress; moved to Gadsden, Etowah County, Ala., in 1931; field representative for the Agricultural Adjustment Administration, 1933-1943; special assistant to the War Food Administration, 1943-1945; special adviser to the Secretary of Agriculture 1945-1947; liaison officer for the Democratic National Committee in

1948; assistant professor of history at Jacksonville (Ala.) State College, 1948-1951; delegate at large to the Democratic National Convention of 1952; moved to Raleigh, N.C., in 1952 and engaged in the travel business; moved to Alabama and resumed his profession as a teacher in 1965; was a resident of Montgomery, Ala., until his death in Birmingham, Ala., on March 3, 1987; interment in Bethlehem Cemetery, New Site, Ala.

**PATTERSON, Malcolm Rice** (son of Josiah Patterson), a Representative from Tennessee; born in Somerville, Morgan County, Ala., June 7, 1861; attended the common schools; moved to Memphis, Tenn., with his parents in 1872; was graduated from the Christian Brothers' College, Memphis, Tenn., and subsequently took courses at Vanderbilt University, Nashville, Tenn.; studied law; was admitted to the bar in 1883 and commenced practice in Memphis, Tenn.; elected district attorney of Shelby County in 1894 for a term of eight years, but resigned on September 10, 1900, having been nominated as a candidate for Congress; elected as a Democrat to the Fifty-seventh and to the two succeeding Congresses, and served from March 4, 1901 to November 5, 1906, when he resigned, having been elected Governor of Tennessee; reelected Governor in 1908, and served from January 17, 1907 to January 26, 1911; resumed the practice of his profession in Memphis, Tenn.; unsuccessful candidate for election to the United States Senate in 1915; appointed in 1923 and subsequently elected judge of the first circuit court of Shelby County, Tenn., serving until his retirement September 1, 1934; unsuccessful candidate for nomination for Governor in 1932; died while on a visit to Sarasota, Fla., March 8, 1935; interment in Forest Hill Cemetery, Memphis, Tenn.

**PATTERSON, Roscoe Conkling,** a Representative and a Senator from Missouri; born in Springfield, Greene County, Mo., September 15, 1876; attended public and private schools, Drury College, Springfield, Mo., and the University of Missouri at Columbia; graduated from the law department of Washington University, St. Louis, Mo., in 1897; was admitted to the bar the same year and commenced practice in Springfield, Mo.; prosecuting attorney of Greene County, Mo., 1903-1907; elected as a Republican to the Sixty-seventh Congress (March 4, 1921-March 3, 1923); unsuccessful candidate for reelection in 1922 to the Sixty-eighth Congress; resumed the practice of law in Springfield, Mo.; presidential elector on the Republican ticket in 1924; moved to Kansas City, Mo., in 1925; United States district attorney for the western district of Missouri 1925-1929, when he resigned; elected as a Republican to the United States Senate and served from March 4, 1929, to January 3, 1935; unsuccessful candidate for reelection in 1934; chairman, Committee on Mines and Mining (Seventy-second Congress); resumed the practice of law in Springfield, Mo.; member of the Missouri Appellate Judicial Commission; died in Springfield, Mo., October 22, 1954; interment in Maple Park Cemetery, southeast of the city.

**PATTERSON, Thomas** (half brother of John Patterson), a Representative from Pennsylvania; born in Little Britain Township, Lancaster County, Pa., October 1, 1764; moved with his parents to Pattersons Mills, Cross Creek Township, Washington County, Pa., in 1778; completed preparatory studies; engaged in agricultural pursuits and operated a flour mill; served as a major general of militia in the War of 1812; elected as a Republican to the Fifteenth Congress and reelected to the three succeeding Congresses (March 4, 1817-March 3, 1825); did not seek renomination in 1824; resumed former business pursuits; died in Cross Creek Township, near Pattersons Mills, Washington County, Pa., on November 16, 1841; interment in West Middletown Cemetery, West Middletown, Pa.

**PATTERSON, Thomas J.,** a Representative from New York; born in that State about 1808; attended the public schools; elected as a Whig to the Twenty-eighth Congress (March 4, 1843-March 3, 1845); engaged as a land agent in Rochester, Monroe County, N.Y.

**PATTERSON, Thomas MacDonald,** a Delegate, a Representative, and a Senator from Colorado; born in County Carlow, Ireland, November 4, 1839; immigrated to the United States with his parents, who settled in New York City in 1849; attended the public schools; moved with his parents to Crawfordsville, Ind., in 1853; worked in a printing office for three years, and as a watchmaker and jeweler for five years; during the Civil War enlisted in the Eleventh Regiment, Indiana Volunteer Infantry, in 1861; attended the Indiana Asbury (now De Pauw) University, Greencastle, Ind., in 1862 and Wabash College, Crawfordsville, Ind., in 1863; studied law; was admitted to the bar in 1867 and commenced practice in Crawfordsville, Ind.; moved to Denver, Colo., in 1872 and continued the practice of law; city attorney of Denver, 1873-1874; elected as a Democrat to be a Delegate to the Forty-fourth Congress, and served from March 4, 1875 to August 1, 1876, when the Territory became a State; successfully contested the election of James B. Belford to the Forty-fifth Congress, and served from December 13, 1877 to March 3, 1879; was not a candidate for renomination in 1878 to the Forty-sixth Congress; resumed the practice of law in Denver; member of the Democratic National Committee, 1874-1880; purchased the Rocky Mountain News in 1890 and later the Denver Times; elected as a Democrat to the United States Senate, and served from March 4, 1901 to March 3, 1907; was not a candidate for reelection; unsuccessful Democratic candidate for Governor in 1888 and 1914; resumed his newspaper activities in Denver, Colo., and died there on July 23, 1916; interment in Fairmount Cemetery.

Bibliography: *DAB*; Downing, Sybil, and Robert E. Smith. *Tom Patterson: Crusader for Change, 1872-1916.* Niwot: University of Colorado Press, 1995.

**PATTERSON, Walter,** a Representative from New York; born in Columbia County, N.Y.; completed preparatory studies; member of the State assembly in 1818; served as supervisor of the town of Ancram 1821-1823; elected to the Seventeenth Congress (March 4, 1821-March 3, 1823); moved to Livingston, Columbia County, N.Y.; supervisor for the town of Livingston 1826-1828; associate justice of the Columbia County Court and served from 1828 to 1830.

**PATTERSON, William** (brother of George Washington Patterson and uncle of Augustus Frank), a Representative from New York; born in Londonderry, Rockingham County, N.H., June 4, 1789; attended the common schools; moved to Rensselaerville, Albany County, N.Y., in 1815, and in the following year to Lyons, Wayne County; engaged in the manufacture and sale of fanning mills; moved to a farm near Warsaw, N.Y., in 1822 and engaged in agricultural pursuits; settled in Warsaw, N.Y., in 1837; held several local offices; elected as a Whig to the Twenty-fifth Congress and served from March 4, 1837, until his death in Warsaw, Wyoming County, N.Y., August 14, 1838; interment in Warsaw Town Cemetery.

**PATTERSON, William,** a Representative from Ohio; born in Maryland in 1790; moved to Mansfield, Ohio; completed preparatory studies; studied law; was admitted to the bar and practiced; held several local offices; associate judge of the court of common pleas in 1820 and 1827; elected as a Jacksonian to the Twenty-third and Twenty-fourth Congresses (March 4, 1833-March 3, 1837); died in Van Wert, Van Wert County, Ohio, on August 17, 1868; interment in Mansfield Cemetery, Mansfield, Ohio.

**PATTISON, Edward Worthington,** a Representative from New York; born in Troy, Rensselaer County, N.Y., April 29, 1932; graduated from Albany (N.Y.) Academy, 1949; A.B., Cornell University, Ithaca, N.Y., 1953; LL.B., Cornell University School of Law, 1957; admitted to the New York bar in 1957 and commenced practice in Troy; served in the United States Army, 1954-1956; served as Rensselaer County (N.Y.) treasurer, 1970-1975; unsuccessful candidate for election in 1970 to the Ninety-second Congress; unsuccessful candidate for Rensselaer County Executive, 1973;

elected as a Democrat to the Ninety-fourth and Ninety-fifth Congresses (January 3, 1975-January 3, 1979); unsuccessful candidate for reelection in 1978 to the Ninety-sixth Congress; was a resident of West Sand Lake, N.Y.; died August 22, 1990.

**PATTISON, John M.,** a Representative from Ohio; born near Owensville, Clermont County, Ohio, June 13, 1847; during the Civil War entered the Union Army in 1864; was graduated from the Ohio Wesleyan University, Delaware, Ohio, in 1869; studied law; was admitted to the bar in 1872 and commenced practice in Cincinnati, Ohio; member of the State house of representatives in 1873; attorney for the committee of safety of Cincinnati 1874-1876; vice president and manager of the Union Central Life Insurance Co. of Cincinnati in 1881 and became president in 1891; member of the State senate in 1890; elected as a Democrat to the Fifty-second Congress (March 4, 1891-March 3, 1893); unsuccessful candidate for reelection; elected Governor of Ohio and served from January 8, 1906, until his death in Milford, Clermont County, Ohio, June 18, 1906; interment in Greenlawn Cemetery.

Bibliography: *DAB*.

**PATTON, Charles Emory** (son of John Patton and brother of John Patton, Jr.), a Representative from Pennsylvania; born in Curwensville, Clearfield County, Pa., July 5, 1859; attended the common schools and was graduated from Dickinson Seminary, Williamsport, Pa., in 1878; engaged in the lumber business; owned and operated the Curwensville Electric Co., and then engaged in the construction contracting business; director of the Curwensville National Bank; member of the school board, serving as president; member of the city council, and served as burgess; elected to the Sixty-second and Sixty-third Congresses (March 4, 1911-March 3, 1915); was not a candidate for renomination in 1914 to the Sixty-fourth Congress; appointed secretary of agriculture for the Commonwealth of Pennsylvania on October 15, 1915, and served in this capacity until January 22, 1920; retired to a farm near West Grove, Chester County, Pa., and resumed his interest in agricultural pursuits; died on his estate December 15, 1937; interment in Oak Hill Cemetery, Curwensville, Pa.

**PATTON, David Henry,** a Representative from Indiana; born in Flemingsburg, Fleming County, Ky., November 26, 1837; attended the Collegiate Institute, Waveland, Ind.; enlisted in the Thirty-eighth Indiana Regiment in 1861 and was mustered out in July 1865, after having attained the rank of colonel; was graduated from the Chicago Medical College in 1867 and practiced medicine in Remington, Jasper County, Ind.; pension examiner at Remington 1886-1890; delegate to the Democratic National Convention in 1892 and 1900; elected as a Democrat to the Fifty-second Congress (March 4, 1891-March 3, 1893); was not a candidate for renomination in 1892; moved to Woodward, Woodward County, Indian Territory (now Oklahoma), in 1893; appointed receiver of public lands for Oklahoma in 1893, and later resumed the practice of medicine; member of the district board of health of Woodward, Okla.; appointed pension examiner at Woodward; died in Otterbein, Benton County, Ind., on January 17, 1914; interment in Remington Cemetery, Remington, Ind.

**PATTON, John** (father of Charles Emory Patton and John Patton Jr., and uncle of William Irvin Swoope), a Representative from Pennsylvania; born in Covington, Tioga County, Pa., January 6, 1823; moved to Curwensville, Clearfield County, Pa., in 1828; attended the public schools; engaged in mercantile pursuits and in lumbering 1844-1860; organized the First National Bank of Curwensville in 1864 and was elected its president; organized the Curwensville Bank, and was elected its president; delegate to the Whig National Convention in 1852 and to the Republican National Convention in 1860; elected as a Republican to the Thirty-seventh Congress (March 4, 1861-March 3, 1863); declined to be a candidate for renomination in 1862; elected to the Fiftieth Congress (March 4,

1887-March 3, 1889); was not a candidate for renomination in 1888; resumed banking; died in Philadelphia, Pa., where he had gone for medical treatment, on December 23, 1897; interment in Oak Hill Cemetery, Curwensville, Pa.

**PATTON, John, Jr.** (son of John Patton and brother of Charles Emory Patton), a Senator from Michigan; born in Curwensville, Clearfield County, Pa., October 30, 1850; prepared for college at Phillips Academy, Andover, Mass.; graduated from Yale College in 1875 and from the law department of Columbia College, New York City, in 1877; moved to Grand Rapids, Mich., in 1878; was admitted to the bar the same year and commenced the practice of law; appointed as a Republican to the United States Senate to fill the vacancy caused by the death of Francis B. Stockbridge and served from May 5, 1894, to January 14, 1895, when a successor was elected and qualified; unsuccessful candidate for election in 1895 to fill the vacancy; banker; member and later president of the Board of Library Commissioners of Grand Rapids; died in Grand Rapids, Mich., on May 24, 1907; interment in Oak Hill Cemetery.

**PATTON, John Denniston,** a Representative from Pennsylvania; born in Indiana, Indiana County, Pa., November 28, 1829; attended the public schools; worked in a tannery for several years; engaged in mercantile pursuits in Indiana, Pa.; elected as a Democrat to the Forty-eighth Congress (March 4, 1883-March 3, 1885); declined to be a candidate for renomination in 1884; retired from public life; died in Indiana, Pa., February 22, 1904; interment in Oakland Cemetery.

**PATTON, John Mercer,** a Representative from Virginia; born in Fredericksburg, Va., August 10, 1797; attended Princeton College, and was graduated from the medical department of the University of Pennsylvania at Philadelphia in 1818, but never practiced; studied law; was admitted to the bar and commenced practice in Fredericksburg, Va.; elected as a Jacksonian to the Twenty-first Congress to fill the vacancy caused by the resignation of Philip P. Barbour; reelected to the Twenty-second through Twenty-fourth Congresses, and as a Democrat to the Twenty-fifth Congress, and served from November 25, 1830 to April 7, 1838, when he resigned; chairman, Committee on Territories (Twenty-fourth and Twenty-fifth Congresses); the senior member of the Virginia Council of State, he became Acting Governor of Virginia on March 18, 1841, following the resignation of Governor Thomas W. Gilmer; served as Governor until March 31, 1841; moved to Richmond, Va., and resumed the practice of law; died in Richmond, Va., October 29, 1858; interment in Shockee Cemetery.

Bibliography: *DAB.*

**PATTON, Nat,** a Representative from Texas; born on a farm near Tadmor, Houston County, Tex., February 26, 1884; attended the rural schools and Sam Houston Normal School, Huntsville, Tex.; taught in the rural and high schools from 1899 until 1918; also engaged in agricultural pursuits at Belott, Houston County, Tex., in 1915 and 1916; member of the Texas State house of representatives in 1912 and 1913; attended the law department of the University of Texas at Austin; was admitted to the bar in 1918 and commenced practice in Crockett, Houston County, Tex.; served as county judge of Houston County, Tex., 1918-1922; member of the Texas State senate from 1929 to 1934; delegate to the Democratic State conventions in 1924 and 1935; during the First World War enlisted in the United States Army on November 1, 1918, but was never sworn in due to the armistice being signed; elected as a Democrat to the Seventy-fourth and to the four succeeding Congresses (January 3, 1935-January 3, 1945); unsuccessful candidate for renomination in 1944 to the Seventy-ninth Congress; resumed the practice of law; died in Crockett, Tex., July 27, 1957; interment in Evergreen Memorial Park.

**PAUL, John** (father of John Paul [1883-1964]), a Representative from Virginia; born in Rockingham County, Va., June 30, 1839; attended the common schools, and taught school in Rockingham County, 1859-1860; attended Roanoke College, Salem, Va., from September 1860 until June 1861; during the Civil War entered the Confederate Army and became a captain in the First Virginia Cavalry; LL.B., University of Virginia School of Law, Charlottesville, 1867; was admitted to the bar in 1867 and commenced practice in Harrisonburg, Va.; Commonwealth attorney of Rockingham County, 1870-1877; served in the Virginia senate, 1877-1880; unsuccessful candidate for election in 1878 to the Forty-sixth Congress; elected as a Readjuster Democrat to the Forty-seventh Congress (March 4, 1881-March 3, 1883); presented credentials as a Member-elect to the Forty-eighth Congress, and served from March 4, 1883 until September 5, 1883, when he resigned, having been appointed to a judicial position; the election subsequently was successfully contested by Charles T. O'Farrall; appointed judge of the United States District Court for the Western District of Virginia by President Chester A. Arthur, and served from September 5, 1883 until his death in Harrisonburg, Va., November 1, 1901; interment in Woodbine Cemetery.

**PAUL, John** (son of John Paul [1839-1901]), a Representative from Virginia; born in Harrisonburg, Rockingham County, Va., December 9, 1883; attended private and public schools; B.A., Virginia Military Institute, Lexington, 1903, and was an instructor in that institution in 1903 and 1904; LL.B., University of Virginia School of Law, Charlottesville, 1906; was admitted to the bar and commenced practice in Harrisonburg, Va., in 1907; member of the Virginia senate, 1911-1915; unsuccessful candidate for election in 1916 to the Sixty-fifth Congress, and for election in 1918 to the Sixty-sixth Congress; entered the United States Army in May 1917 and served throughout the First World War with the Three Hundred and Thirteenth Field Artillery of the One Hundred and Fifty-fifth Field Artillery Brigade, being in the American Expeditionary Forces from May 1918 to May 1919; again served in the Virginia senate, 1919-1922; city attorney of Harrisonburg, 1919-1923; successfully contested as a Republican the election of Thomas W. Harrison to the Sixty-seventh Congress, and served from December 15, 1922 to March 3, 1923; unsuccessful candidate for reelection in 1922 to the Sixty-eighth Congress; special assistant to the Attorney General of the United States in 1923 and 1924; delegate to the Republican National Conventions of 1912, 1916, 1920, and 1924; resumed the private practice of law in 1924; United States district attorney for the western district of Virginia, 1929-1932; appointed United States district judge for the western district of Virginia in 1932, and served until his retirement in 1959; continued in service as a judge on an assigned basis, as well as operating his farm in Rockingham County, Va.; died at Ottobine, Rockingham County, Va., February 13, 1964; interment in Woodbine Cemetery, Harrisonburg, Va.

**PAUL, Ronald Ernest,** a Representative from Texas; born in Pittsburgh, Allegheny County, Pa., August 20, 1935; graduated from Dormont (Pa.) High School in 1953; B.A., Gettysburg (Pa.) College, 1957; M.D., Duke University Medical Center, Durham, N.C., 1961; internship and residency training, Henry Ford Hospital, Detroit, Mich., 1961 and 1962; specialty training in obstetrics and gynecology, University of Pittsburgh, 1965-1968; flight surgeon, United States Air Force, 1963-1965, and with United States Air National Guard, 1965-1968; delegate, Texas State Republican convention, 1974; unsuccessful candidate for election in 1974 to the Ninety-fourth Congress; elected as a Republican to the Ninety-fourth Congress, April 3, 1976, by special election to fill the vacancy caused by the resignation of Robert R. Casey and served from April 3, 1976, to January 3, 1977; unsuccessful candidate for reelection in 1976 to the Ninety-fifth Congress; resumed the practice of medicine; elected to the Ninety-sixth and to the two succeeding Congresses (January 3, 1979-January 3, 1985); was not a candidate in 1984 for reelection to the House of Representatives, but was an unsuccessful candidate for nomination to the United States Senate; returned to the practice of medicine; publisher of investment letter and political report; nominated by the Libertarian Party on September 5, 1987, for the presidency of the United States; candidate for election in 1996 to the One Hundred Fifth Congress; is a resident of Lake Jackson, Tex.

**PAULDING, William, Jr.,** a Representative from New York; born in Philipsburgh (now Tarrytown), N.Y., March 7, 1770; completed preparatory studies; studied law; was admitted to the bar and commenced practice in New York City; elected as a Republican to the Twelfth Congress (March 4, 1811-March 3, 1813); brigadier general of militia; served in the War of 1812; delegate to the State constitutional convention in 1821; adjutant general of the State of New York; mayor of New York City 1824-1826; died in Tarrytown, Westchester County, N.Y., February 11, 1854; interment in Old Dutch Burying Ground at Sleepy Hollow, Tarrytown.

**PAWLING, Levi,** a Representative from Pennsylvania; born in Fatland, near Norristown, Pa., July 25, 1773; attended the common schools and was graduated from the University of Pennsylvania at Philadelphia; moved to Norristown, Montgomery County, Pa., in November 1795; studied law; was admitted to the bar in 1795 and practiced in Norristown and Philadelphia; trustee of lands belonging to the University of Pennsylvania; appointed chairman of the commission to raise funds relative to lock navigation on the Schuylkill River in 1816; elected as a Federalist to the Fifteenth Congress (March 4, 1817-March 3, 1819); elected burgess of Norristown in 1818; president of the board of directors of the Bank of Montgomery County; died in Norristown, Pa., September 7, 1845; interment in St. John's Protestant Episcopal Cemetery.

**PAXON, Leon William (Bill)** (husband of Susan Molinari and son-in-law of Guy Victor Molinari), a Representative from New York; born in Buffalo, Erie County, N.Y., April 29, 1954; graduated, St. Joseph's Collegiate Institute, Buffalo, 1968; attended Fordham University; B.A., Canisius College, 1977; member, Erie County legislature, 1978-1982; member, New York State assembly, 1983-1988; elected as a Republican to the One Hundred First and to the three succeeding Congresses (January 3, 1989-January 3, 1997); is a resident of Williamsville, N.Y.

**PAYNE, Donald Milford,** a Representative from New Jersey; born in Newark, Essex County, N.J., July 16, 1934; graduated, Barringer High School, Newark, 1952; B.A., Seton Hall University, South Orange, N.J., 1957; business executive; president, Young Men's Christian Associations of the U.S.A., 1970-1973; chair, World Young Men's Christian Association Refugee and Rehabilitation Committee of Geneva, Switzerland, 1973-1981; member, Essex County Board of Chosen Freeholders, 1972-1978, director, 1977-1978; unsuccessful candidate for nomination in 1980 to the Ninety-seventh Congress; member, Newark Municipal Council, 1982-1988; unsuccessful candidate for nomination in 1986 to the One Hundredth Congress; elected as a Democrat to the One Hundred First and to the three succeeding Congresses (January 3, 1989-January 3, 1997); is a resident of Newark, N.J.

**PAYNE, Frederick George,** a Senator from Maine; born in Lewiston, Androscoggin County, Maine, July 24, 1904; attended the public schools of Lewiston, Maine, and the Bentley School of Accounting and Finance, Boston, Mass.; during his early school days worked as a newsboy, usher and doorman in a theater, and as a reporter for a weekly newspaper; engaged in automobile and farm machinery sales, and in theater auditing and managing, 1925-1935; industrial consultant, 1936-1940; mayor of Augusta, Maine, 1935-1941; unsuccessful Republican candidate for nomination for governor of Maine in 1940; Maine commissioner of finance and director of the budget, 1940-1942; during the Second World War entered the United States Air Force in 1942 as a captain, and served until inactivated to the Reserves in 1945 as a lieutenant colonel; business manager, Waldoboro Garage Co., 1945-1949; elected Governor of Maine in 1948, reelected in 1950, and served from January 5, 1949 until his resignation on December 25, 1952, having been elected Senator; elected as a Republican to the United States Senate in 1952, and served from January 3, 1953 to January 3, 1959; unsuccessful candidate for reelection in 1958; trustee of the Bentley School of Accounting and Finance; industrial consultant and district manager of Walsh Engineers, Inc.; resided in Waldoboro, Maine, where he died on June 15, 1978; interment in German Lutheran Cemetery.

**PAYNE, Henry B.** (grandfather of Frances P. Bolton and great-grandfather of Oliver Payne Bolton), a Representative and a Senator from Ohio; born in Hamilton, Madison County, N.Y., November 30, 1810; graduated from Hamilton College, Clinton, N.Y., in 1832; studied law; was admitted to the bar and practiced in Cleveland, Ohio, 1834-1846; city clerk 1836; founder of the Cleveland and Columbus Railroad; presidential elector on the Democratic ticket in 1848; member, State senate 1849-1851; unsuccessful Democratic candidate for election to the United States Senate in 1851 and for governor of Ohio in 1857; elected as a Democrat to the Forty-fourth Congress (March 4, 1875-March 3, 1877); unsuccessful candidate for reelection in 1876 to the Forty-fifth Congress; appointed a member of the Electoral Commission to decide the contests in various States in the presidential election of 1876; unsuccessful candidate for the Democratic presidential nomination in 1880 and again in 1884; elected as a Democrat to the United States Senate and served from March 4, 1885, to March 3, 1891; died in Cleveland, Cuyahoga County, Ohio, September 9, 1896; interment in Lake View Cemetery.

**Bibliography:** *DAB.*

**PAYNE, Lewis Franklin, Jr.,** a Representative from Virginia; born in Amherst, Amherst County, Va., on July 9, 1945; attended the public schools; graduated, Amherst High School, 1963; B.S., Virginia Military Institute, 1967; M.B.A., University of Virginia, 1973; served in the United States Army, 1969-1970, and in the United States Army Reserve, 1971-1973; staff engineering associate, Chesapeake and Potomac Telephone Co. of Virginia, 1970-1971; planning and development manager of Wintergreen, Wintergreen, Va., 1973-1975; chairman of the board, Wintergreen Development, Inc., 1985 to 1988; elected as a Democrat to the One Hundredth Congress, June 14, 1988, by special election to fill the vacancy caused by the death of Wilbur Clarence (Dan) Daniel; reelected to the four succeeding Congresses, and served from June 14, 1988 to January 3, 1997; was not a candidate for reelection in 1996 to the One Hundred Fifth Congress; announced September 16, 1996 that he was a candidate for Lieutenant Governor of Virginia; is a resident of Nellysford, Va.

**PAYNE, Sereno Elisha,** a Representative from New York; born in Hamilton, Madison County, N.Y., June 26, 1843; attended the Auburn (N.Y.) Academy and was graduated from the University of Rochester, N.Y., in 1864; studied law; was admitted to the bar in 1866 and practiced in Auburn, N.Y.; city clerk of Auburn in 1867 and 1868; supervisor in 1871 and 1872; district attorney of Cayuga County 1873-1879; president of the board of education of Auburn 1879-1882; appointed a member of the American-British Joint High Commission in January 1899; elected as a Republican to the Forty-eighth and Forty-ninth Congresses (March 4, 1883-March 3, 1887); elected to the Fifty-first Congress to fill the vacancy caused by the death of Newton W. Nutting; reelected to the Fifty-second and to the eleven succeeding Congresses and served from March 4, 1889, until his death in Washington, D.C., December 10, 1914; had been reelected to the Sixty-fourth Congress; chairman, Committee on Merchant Marine and Fisheries (Fifty-fourth and Fifty-fifth Congresses), Committee on Ways and Means (Fifty-fifth through

Sixty-first Congresses); majority leader (Fifty-seventh through Sixty-first Congresses); interment in Fort Hill Cemetery, Auburn, N.Y.

**Bibliography:** *DAB.*

**PAYNE, William Winter,** a Representative from Alabama; born at "Granville," near Warrenton, Fauquier County, Va., January 2, 1807; completed preparatory studies; studied law but never practiced; moved to Franklin County, Ala., in 1825 and engaged in planting; member of the State house of representatives in 1831; moved to Sumter County, Ala.; again a member of the State house of representatives 1834-1838 and in 1840; unsuccessful candidate for the State senate in 1839; elected as a Democrat to the Twenty-seventh, Twenty-eighth, and Twenty-ninth Congresses (March 4, 1841-March 3, 1847); chairman, Committee on Elections (Twenty-eighth Congress); unsuccessful candidate for reelection in 1846 to the Thirtieth Congress; returned to Virginia in 1847 and engaged in planting near Warrenton; chairman of the Democratic State convention in 1859; died in Warrenton, Va., September 2, 1874; interment in the City Cemetery.

**PAYNTER, Lemuel,** a Representative from Pennsylvania; born in Lewes, Sussex County, Del., in 1788; attended the common schools; moved to Philadelphia, Pa.; served in the War of 1812 and became major and lieutenant colonel of the Ninety-third Regiment, Pennsylvania Militia; member of the board of commissioners of the Southwark district for many years and also served as president of the board; member of the guardians of the poor and also school director; elected a member of the Pennsylvania senate in 1833; elected as a Democrat to the Twenty-fifth and Twenty-sixth Congresses (March 4, 1837-March 3, 1841); was not a candidate for renomination in 1840; again served as a member of the board of commissioners of the Southwark district; died in Philadelphia, Pa., August 1, 1863; interment in Union Sixth Street Cemetery.

**PAYNTER, Thomas Hanson,** a Representative and a Senator from Kentucky; born on a farm near Vanceburg, Lewis County, Ky., December 9, 1851; attended the common schools, Rand's Academy in Lewis County, Ky., and Centre College, Danville, Ky.; studied law; was admitted to the bar in 1872 and commenced practice in Greenup, Ky.; prosecuting attorney of Greenup County 1876-1882; resumed the practice of law in Greenup; elected as a Democrat to the Fifty-first, Fifty-second, and Fifty-third Congresses and served from March 4, 1889, until his resignation, effective January 5, 1895, having been elected to the judiciary; chairman, Committee on Expenditures in the Post Office Department (Fifty-third Congress); judge of the court of appeals of Kentucky from 1895-1906, when he resigned, having been elected Senator; elected as a Democrat to the United States Senate and served from March 4, 1907, to March 3, 1913; was not a candidate for reelection in 1912; chairman, Committee to Examine Branches of the Civil Service (Sixty-second Congress); moved to Frankfort, Ky., in 1913 and continued the practice of law; also interested in agricultural pursuits; died in Frankfort, Ky., March 8, 1921; interment in the State Cemetery.

**PAYSON, Lewis Edwin,** a Representative from Illinois; born in Providence, R.I., September 17, 1840; moved with his parents to Illinois in 1852; attended the common schools and Lombard University, Galesburg, Ill.; studied law; was admitted to the bar and commenced practice in Ottawa, Ill., in 1862; moved to Pontiac, Livingston County, Ill., in January 1865 and continued the practice of law; judge of the county court 1869-1873; elected as a Republican to the Forty-seventh and to the four succeeding Congresses (March 4, 1881-March 3, 1891); chairman, Committee on Public Lands (Fifty-first Congress); resumed the practice of law; died in Washington, D.C., October 4, 1909; interment in Rock Creek Cemetery.

**PEABODY, Nathaniel,** a Delegate from New Hampshire; born in Topsfield, Essex County, Mass., March 1, 1741; tutored by his father; studied medicine; commenced practice in Plaistow, N.H., in 1761; moved to Atkinson, N.H., in 1770; resigned a royal commission to enter the Revolutionary Army; elected a member of the committee of safety January 10, 1776, and was its chairman; member of the State house of representatives 1776-1779, 1781-1785, 1787-1790, and 1793-1796, serving as speaker in 1793; adjutant general of the New Hampshire Militia July 19, 1777, and commanded a brigade in Rhode Island in 1779; Member of the Continental Congress in 1779 and 1780; delegate to the State constitutional conventions of 1782 and 1783; again elected a Member of the Continental Congress in 1785 but did not take his seat; member of the State senate in 1785, 1786, and 1790-1793; chosen from the house in 1784 and from the senate in 1785 to serve as councilor; major general of militia 1793-1798; because of pecuniary embarrassment was confined within the limits of a debtor's prison for about twenty years; died in Exeter, Rockingham County, N.H., on June 27, 1823; interment probably in the Old Cemetery.

**Bibliography:** *DAB.*

**PEACE, Roger Craft,** a Senator from South Carolina; born in Greenville, Greenville County, S.C., May 19, 1899; attended the public schools and graduated from Furman University, Greenville, S.C., in 1919; newspaper reporter, sports editor, editor, business manager, and publisher in Greenville, S.C.; during the First World War served as an instructor in the United States Army at Camp Perry in 1918; colonel on the Governor's staff 1930-1934; trustee of Furman University 1938-1948; appointed as a Democrat to the United States Senate to fill the vacancy caused by the death of Alva M. Lumpkin, who had been appointed to fill the vacancy caused by the resignation of James F. Byrnes, and served from August 5, 1941, until November 4, 1941; was not a candidate for election to the vacancy; resumed his career of writing, publishing, and civic activities; at the time of his death was chairman of Multimedia, Inc.; died in Greenville, S.C., August 20, 1968; interment in Springwood Cemetery.

**PEARCE, Charles Edward,** a Representative from Missouri; born in Whitesboro, Oneida County, N.Y., May 29, 1842; attended Fairfield Seminary and was graduated from Union College, Schenectady, N.Y., in 1863; enlisted in the Union Army and was commissioned captain of Battery D, Sixteenth Regiment, New York Heavy Artillery, in 1863; promoted to the rank of major in June 1864; on the occupation of Wilmington was detailed as provost marshal general of the eastern district of North Carolina; resigned from the Army in the fall of 1865; settled in St. Louis, Mo., in 1866; studied law; was admitted to the bar in 1867 and commenced practice in St. Louis, Mo.; also interested in the manufacture of bagging, rope, and twine; organized and commanded the First Regiment of the Missouri National Guard in 1877; delegate to the Republican National Convention in 1888; appointed chairman of the commission to treat with the Sioux Indians of the Northwest in 1891; elected as a Republican to the Fifty-fifth and Fifty-sixth Congresses (March 4, 1897-March 3, 1901); declined to be a candidate for renomination in 1900; died in St. Louis, Mo., on January 30, 1902; interment in Fort Hill Cemetery, Auburn, N.Y.

**PEARCE, Dutee Jerauld,** a Representative from Rhode Island; born on the island of Prudence, R.I., April 3, 1789; was graduated from Brown University, Providence, R.I., in 1808; studied law; was admitted to the bar and commenced practice in Newport, R.I.; held various local offices; attorney general of Rhode Island 1819-1825; United States district attorney in 1824 and 1825; member of the State house of representatives; elected to the Nineteenth Congress; reelected to the Twentieth through Twenty-second Congresses and reelected as an Anti-Masonic candidate to the Twenty-third and

Twenty-fourth Congresses (March 4, 1825-March 3, 1837); chairman, Committee on Revisal and Unfinished Business (Twentieth and Twenty-first Congresses); unsuccessful candidate for reelection in 1836 to the Twenty-fifth Congress; died in Newport, R.I., May 9, 1849; interment in the Common Burial Ground.

**PEARCE, James Alfred,** a Representative and a Senator from Maryland; born in Alexandria, Va., December 14, 1805; attended a private academy in Alexandria; graduated from the College of New Jersey (now Princeton University) in 1822; studied law; was admitted to the bar and commenced practice in Cambridge, Dorchester County, Md., in 1824; moved to Louisiana in 1825 and engaged in sugar planting; returned to Maryland and settled in Kent County in 1828; resumed the practice of law in Chestertown; member, State house of delegates 1831-1835; elected as a Whig to the Twenty-fourth and Twenty-fifth Congresses (March 4, 1835-March 3, 1839); unsuccessful candidate for reelection in 1838 to the Twenty-sixth Congress; elected to the Twenty-seventh Congress (March 4, 1841-March 3, 1843); elected as a Whig to the United States Senate in 1843; reelected in 1849, 1855, and 1861, the last time as a Democrat, and served from March 4, 1843, until his death in Chestertown, Md., on December 20, 1862; chairman, Committee on the Library (Twenty-ninth through Thirty-seventh Congresses); interment in New Chester Cemetery.

**Bibliography:** *DAB*; Steiner, Bernard. "James Alfred Pearce." *Maryland Historical Magazine* 16 (December 1921): 319-39, 17 (March 1922): 33-47, 17 (June 1922): 177-90, 17 (September 1922): 269-83, 17 (December 1922): 348-63, 18 (March 1923): 38-52, 18 (June 1923): 134-50, 18 (September 1923): 257-73, 18 (December 1923): 341-57, 19 (March 1924): 13-29, 19 (June 1924): 162-78.

**PEARCE, John Jamison,** a Representative from Pennsylvania; born in Wilkes-Barre, Pa., February 28, 1826; completed preparatory studies; was ordained a minister in the Methodist Episcopal Church when eighteen years of age; joined the Baltimore Conference and served as pastor at Warriors Mark, Jersey Shore, and Lock Haven, Pa.; elected as a Republican to the Thirty-fourth Congress (March 4, 1855-March 3, 1857); declined to be a candidate for reelection in 1856 to the Thirty-fifth Congress; served as a pastor in various localities until he retired to Lock Haven in 1888; moved to Conneaut, Ashtabula County, Ohio, where he died May 26, 1912; interment in Highland Cemetery, Lock Haven, Pa.

**PEARRE, George Alexander,** a Representative from Maryland; born in Cumberland, Md., July 16, 1860; attended private schools; Allegany County Academy at Cumberland, St. James College near Hagerstown, Md., and Princeton College; was graduated from the West Virginia University at Morgantown in 1880 and from the law department of Maryland University at Baltimore in 1882; was admitted to the bar in 1882 and commenced practice in Cumberland, Md., in 1887; member of the Maryland National Guard and served as adjutant and lieutenant colonel 1887-1892; member of the State senate 1890-1892; prosecuting attorney of Allegany County 1895-1899; elected as a Republican to the Fifty-sixth and to the five succeeding Congresses (March 4, 1899-March 3, 1911); declined to be a candidate for reelection in 1910 to the Sixty-second Congress; engaged in the practice of his profession until his death in Cumberland, Md., on September 19, 1923; interment in Rose Hill Cemetery.

**PEARSON, Albert Jackson,** a Representative from Ohio; born in Centerville, Belmont County, Ohio, May 20, 1846; at an early age moved with his parents to Beallsville, Monroe County, Ohio; attended the common schools and the normal school at Lebanon, Ohio; served as a private in Company I, One Hundred and Eighty-sixth Regiment, Ohio Volunteer Infantry, during the Civil War; studied law; was admitted to the bar in 1868 and commenced practice in Woodsfield, Ohio; prosecuting attorney of Monroe County 1871-1877; member of the State senate in 1881 and 1882; probate judge of Monroe County 1884-1890; elected as a Democrat to the Fifty-second and Fifty-third Congresses (March 4, 1891-March 3, 1895); was not a candidate for reelection in 1894 to the Fifty-fourth Congress; resumed the practice of his profession; died in Woodsfield, Monroe County, Ohio, on May 15, 1905; interment in Woodsfield Cemetery.

**PEARSON, Herron Carney,** a Representative from Tennessee; born in Taylor, Williamson County, Tex., July 31, 1890; moved to Jackson, Tenn., in 1891; attended the public and high schools; was graduated from Union University, Jackson, Tenn., in 1910 and from the law department of Cumberland University, Lebanon, Tenn., in 1912; was admitted to the bar the same year and commenced practice in Jackson, Tenn.; served as municipal judge of the city of Jackson, Tenn., in 1915; city attorney of Jackson, Tenn., 1920-1923; elected as a Democrat to the Seventy-fourth and to the three succeeding Congresses (January 3, 1935-January 3, 1943); was not a candidate for renomination in 1942; resumed the practice of law; died in Jackson, Tenn., April 24, 1953; interment in Hollywood Cemetery.

**PEARSON, James Blackwood,** a Senator from Kansas; born in Nashville, Davidson County, Tenn., May 7, 1920; with his parents moved to Virginia in 1934 and attended the public schools; attended Duke University, Durham, N.C., 1940-1942; during the Second World War interrupted schooling to serve as a pilot in the Naval Air Transport of the United States Navy, 1943-1946, and was discharged as a lieutenant; LL.B., University of Virginia School of Law, Charlottesville, 1950; was admitted to the bar and commenced the practice of law in Mission, Kans., in 1950; assistant county attorney of Johnson County, Kans., 1952-1954; county probate judge, 1954-1956; member, Kansas State senate, 1956-1960; did not seek reelection, but returned to the practice of law; appointed January 31, 1962, as a Republican to the United States Senate to fill the vacancy caused by the death of Andrew F. Schoeppel; elected in November 1962 for the term ending January 3, 1967; reelected in 1966, and again in 1972, and served from January 31, 1962, until his resignation on December 23, 1978; was not a candidate for reelection in 1978; is a resident of Washington, D.C.

**Bibliography:** Pearson, James B. "Oversight: A Vital Yet Neglected Congressional Function." *Kansas Law Review* 23 (Winter 1975): 277-88.

**PEARSON, John James,** a Representative from Pennsylvania; born near Darby, Delaware County, Pa., October 25, 1800; moved with his parents to Mercer, Pa., in 1805; attended private schools and a grammar boarding school; studied law; was admitted to the bar in August 1822 and commenced practice in Mercer County; elected as a Whig to the Twenty-fourth Congress to fill the vacancy caused by the resignation of John Banks and served from December 5, 1836, to March 3, 1837; was not a candidate for renomination in 1836; resumed the practice of law; member of State senate 1838-1842; appointed president judge of Dauphin and Lebanon Counties, Pa., April 7, 1849, and served until January 1, 1882; died in Harrisburg, Pa., May 30, 1888; interment in Mount Kalmia Cemetery.

**PEARSON, Joseph,** a Representative from North Carolina; born in Rowan County, N.C., in 1776; completed preparatory studies; studied law; was admitted to the bar and commenced practice in Salisbury, N.C.; member of the North Carolina State house of commons; elected as a Federalist to the Eleventh and to the two succeeding Congresses (March 4, 1809-March 3, 1815); while in Congress fought a duel with John George Jackson, of Virginia, and on the second fire wounded his opponent in the hip; died in Salisbury, N.C., October 27, 1834.

**Bibliography:** Brown, Stephen W. "Satisfaction at Bladensburg: The Pearson-Jackson Duel of 1809." *North Carolina Historical Review* 58 (Winter 1981): 23-43.

**PEARSON, Richmond,** a Representative from North Carolina; born at "Richmond Hill," Yadkin County, N.C., January 26, 1852, attended Horner's School, Oxford, N.C., and was graduated from Princeton College in 1872; studied law; was admitted to the bar in 1874; in the same year was appointed United States consul to Verviers and Liege, Belgium; resigned in 1877; member of the North Carolina State house of representatives, 1884-1886; elected as a Republican to the Fifty-fourth and Fifty-fifth Congresses (March 4, 1895-March 3, 1899); successfully contested the election of William T. Crawford to the Fifty-sixth Congress, and served from May 10, 1900 to March 3, 1901; appointed by President Theodore Roosevelt as United States consul to Genoa, Italy, December 11, 1901; appointed Envoy Extraordinary and Minister Plenipotentiary to Persia on December 17, 1902, and served until November 1907; appointed Minister to Greece and Montenegro on July 11, 1907 and served until June 1909; resigned from the diplomatic service in 1909; died at "Richmond Hill," Asheville, N.C., September 12, 1923; interment in Riverside Cemetery.

Bibliography: Steelman, Joseph F. "Richmond Pearson, Roosevelt Republicans, and the Campaign of 1912 in North Carolina." *North Carolina Historical Review* 43 (Spring 1966): 122-39.

**PEASE, Donald James,** a Representative from Ohio; born in Toledo, Lucas County, Ohio, September 26, 1931; attended the public schools of Toledo; B.S., Ohio University, Athens, 1953, and M.A., 1955; Fulbright scholar, Kings College, University of Durham, England, 1954-1955; newspaperman; served in the United States Army, 1955-1957; coeditor and publisher, 1957-1968, editor, 1969-1976; member, Oberlin City Council, 1962-1965; served in the Ohio State senate, 1965-1967, 1975-1977; member of the Ohio State house of representatives, 1969-1975; elected as a Democrat to the Ninety-fifth and to the seven succeeding Congresses (January 3, 1977-January 3, 1993); was not a candidate for reelection in 1992 to the One Hundred Third Congress; is a resident of Oberlin, Ohio.

**PEASE, Henry Roberts,** a Senator from Mississippi; born in Winsted, Litchfield County, Conn., February 19, 1835; received a normal-school training; engaged in teaching 1848-1859; studied law; was admitted to the bar in 1859 and commenced practice in Washington, D.C.; during the Civil War entered the Union Army as a private in 1862 and attained the rank of captain; superintendent of education of Louisiana while that State was under military rule; appointed superintendent of education of freedmen in Mississippi in 1867; elected State superintendent of education of Mississippi in 1869; elected as a Republican to the United States Senate to fill the vacancy caused by the resignation of Adelbert Ames and served from February 3, 1874, to March 3, 1875; was not a candidate for reelection; postmaster of Vicksburg, Miss., 1875; established and edited the Mississippi Educational Journal; moved to Dakota in 1881 and settled in Watertown; receiver of the United States land office at Watertown 1881-1885; member, State senate 1904; died in Watertown, S.Dak., January 2, 1907; interment in Mount Hope Cemetery.

**PEASLEE, Charles Hazen,** a Representative from New Hampshire; born in Gilmanton, N.H., on February 6, 1804; attended Gilmanton Academy, and was graduated from Dartmouth College, Hanover, N.H., in 1824; studied law; was admitted to the bar in 1828 and commenced practice in Concord, N.H.; member of the State house of representatives 1833-1837; adjutant general of the State militia 1839-1847; elected as a Democrat to the Thirtieth, Thirty-first, and Thirty-second Congresses (March 4, 1847-March 3, 1853); chairman, Committee on Militia (Thirty-first and Thirty-second Congresses); was not a candidate for renomination in 1852; collector of the port of Boston by appointment of President Franklin Pierce 1853-1857; moved to Portsmouth, N.H., in 1860; died while

on a visit to St. Paul, Minn., on September 18, 1866; interment in Harmony Grove Cemetery, Portsmouth, N.H.

**PEAVEY, Hubert Haskell,** a Representative from Wisconsin; born in Adams, Mower County, Minn., on January 12, 1881; moved with his parents to Redwood Falls, Minn., in 1886; attended the public schools, the high school at Redwood Falls, and Pillsbury Academy, Owatonna, Minn.; pursued various activities in Nebraska, Kansas, and Oklahoma from 1900 until 1904, when he moved to South Dakota and engaged in the real estate business; moved to Washburn, Bayfield County, Wis., in 1909 and continued the real estate business; served as alderman in 1911 and as mayor of Washburn in 1912 and 1920-1922; member of the State assembly 1913-1915; became editor and publisher of the Washburn News in 1915; during the First World War recruited Company D, Sixth Infantry, Wisconsin National Guard, and served as captain; resumed his former newspaper activities in Washburn, Wis.; unsuccessful candidate for the Republican nomination in 1920 to the Sixty-seventh Congress; elected as a Republican to the Sixty-eighth and to the five succeeding Congresses (March 4, 1923-January 3, 1935); unsuccessful candidate for reelection in 1934 to the Seventy-fourth Congress; again engaged in the real estate business and also operated a fur ranch; died in Washburn, Wis., November 21, 1937; interment in Woodland Cemetery.

**PECK, Erasmus Darwin,** a Representative from Ohio; born in Stafford, Conn., September 16, 1808; attended the common schools of Munson, Mass., and was graduated from the medical department of Yale College in 1829; moved to Portage County, Ohio, in 1830 and practiced medicine; moved to Perrysburg, Wood County, Ohio, in 1834 and continued the practice of his profession; member of the State house of representatives 1856-1859; elected as a Republican to the Forty-first Congress to fill the vacancy caused by the death of Truman H. Hoag; reelected to the Forty-second Congress and served from April 23, 1870, to March 3, 1873; did not seek renomination in 1872; practiced medicine in Perrysburg, Ohio, until his death there December 25, 1876; interment in Fort Meigs Cemetery.

**PECK, George Washington,** a Representative from Michigan; born in New York City June 4, 1818; pursued classical studies; attended Yale College; studied law in New York City; moved to Michigan in 1839 and settled in Brighton, Livingston County; was admitted to the bar in 1842 and commenced practice in Brighton the same year; member of the State house of representatives in 1846 and 1847 and served as speaker the last term; moved to Lansing, Mich., when the State capital was located there in 1847; was the first postmaster of Lansing; secretary of state of Michigan in 1848 and 1849; editor and proprietor of the Lansing Journal; State printer 1852-1855; elected as a Democrat to the Thirty-fourth Congress (March 4, 1855-March 3, 1857); unsuccessful for reelection in 1856 to the Thirty-fifth Congress; mayor of Lansing in 1864; moved to East Saginaw, Mich., and engaged in the practice of law 1864-1873; moved to St. Louis, Mo., in 1873, to Hot Springs, Ark., in 1880, and to Bismarck, Mo., in 1882; died in Saginaw, Mich., June 30, 1905; interment in Brady Hill Cemetery.

Bibliography: *DAB*.

**PECK, Jared Valentine,** a Representative from New York; born in Port Chester, Westchester County, N.Y., September 21, 1816; attended the common schools; engaged in the lumber, brick, hardware, and building-material business; auditor for the town of Rye in 1844 and 1845; member of the New York State assembly in 1848; elected as a Democrat to the Thirty-third Congress (March 4, 1853-March 3, 1855); was not a candidate for renomination in 1854 to the Thirty-fourth Congress; resumed his former business pursuits; appointed warden of the port of New York by Governor Edwin D. Morgan in 1859, with residence in New York City, and served until 1865; one of the founders of the Union League Club; returned to Westchester County and settled in Rye; member of the town board of auditors; died in Rye, Westchester County, N.Y., December 25, 1891; interment in Greenwood Union Cemetery.

**PECK, Lucius Benedict,** a Representative from Vermont; born in Waterbury, Vt., November 17, 1802; pursued classical studies and attended the United States Military Academy, West Point, N.Y., for one year; studied law; was admitted to the bar and commenced practice in Barre, Washington County, Vt., in 1825; member of the State house of representatives in 1831; moved to Montpelier, Vt., in 1832, where he practiced his profession; elected as a Democrat to the Thirtieth and Thirty-first Congresses (March 4, 1847-March 3, 1851); chairman, Committee on Manufactures (Thirty-first Congress); did not seek renomination in 1850, having become a gubernatorial candidate; unsuccessful candidate for Governor of Vermont in 1850; resumed the practice of law; United States district attorney for Vermont by appointment of President Franklin Pierce 1853-1857; president of the Vermont & Canada Railroad from 1859 until his death in Lowell, Mass., December 28, 1866; interment in Green Mount Cemetery, Montpelier, Vt.

**PECK, Luther Christopher,** a Representative from New York; born in Connecticut in January 1800; completed preparatory studies; studied law; was admitted to the bar and practiced; moved to Allegheny County, Pa., and later to Pike, Wyoming County, N.Y., and continued the practice of law; held various local offices; elected as a Whig to the Twenty-fifth and Twenty-sixth Congresses (March 4, 1837-March 3, 1841); chairman, Committee on Revisal and Unfinished Business (Twenty-sixth Congress); affiliated with the Republican Party after it was formed; resumed the practice of his profession at Pike, N.Y.; moved to Nunda, N.Y., and continued the practice of law; died in Nunda, Livingston County, N.Y., February 5, 1876; interment in Oakwood Cemetery.

**PECKHAM, Rufus Wheeler,** a Representative from New York; was born in Rensselaerville, Albany County, N.Y., on December 20, 1809; completed preparatory studies; was graduated from Union College at Schenectady, N.Y., in 1827; studied law; was admitted to the bar in 1830 and commenced practice in Albany, N.Y.; district attorney of Albany County 1838-1841; elected as a Democrat to the Thirty-third Congress (March 4, 1853-March 3, 1855); chairman, Committee on Revolutionary Claims (Thirty-third Congress); resumed the practice of law; justice of the supreme court for the third judicial district and served from 1861 to 1869; associate judge of the court of appeals from May 17, 1870, until his death; lost at sea November 22, 1873, in a collision between two steamers in mid-ocean.

**PEDDIE, Thomas Baldwin,** a Representative from New Jersey; born in Edinburgh, Scotland, February 11, 1808; attended elementary schools; immigrated to the United States in 1833 and settled in Newark, N.J.; engaged in the manufacture of traveling bags and trunks; member of the State house of assembly in 1864 and 1865; mayor of Newark 1866-1869; served as president of the Newark Board of Trade in 1873; elected as a Republican to the Forty-fifth Congress (March 4, 1877-March 3, 1879); declined to be a candidate in 1878 for renomination; resumed his former manufacturing pursuits; vice president of the Essex County National Bank and president of the Security Savings Bank of Newark; died in Newark, N.J., February 16, 1889; interment in Mount Pleasant Cemetery.

**PEDEN, Preston Elmer,** a Representative from Oklahoma; born in Duke, Jackson County, Okla., June 28, 1914; moved to Altus, Okla., in 1920; attended the public schools; University of Oklahoma at Norman, A.B., 1936, and from the law school of the same university, LL.B., 1939; was admitted to the bar in 1939 and commenced practice in Altus, Okla.; attorney for the State insurance fund of the State of Oklahoma 1939-1942; enlisted in June 1942 as a private in the United States Army; promoted through the ranks to captain, being discharged May 5, 1946; awarded Bronze Star; while serving overseas sent a notification and declaration for the office of Congressman to the election board and subsequently received the nomination; elected as a Democrat to the Eightieth Congress (January 3, 1947-January 3, 1949); was an unsuccessful candidate for renomination in 1948; staff member of the Public Lands Committee of the United States House of Representatives in May 1949; appointed Alaskan regional counsel, Bureau of Land Management, Department of the Interior, in 1950; counsel to House Committee on Interior and Insular Affairs 1950-1952; director of governmental affairs of the Chicago Association of Commerce and Industry, 1954-1980; was a resident of La Grange, Ill.; moved to Walnut Creek, Calif., and lived there until his death on June 27, 1985.

**PEEK, Harmanus,** a Representative from New York; born in Albany, N.Y., June 24, 1782; completed preparatory studies; was graduated from Union College, Schenectady, N.Y., in 1804; studied law; was admitted to the bar and commenced practice in Schenectady; member of the State assembly in 1816 and 1817; elected to the Sixteenth Congress (March 4, 1819-March 3, 1821); chairman, Committee on Expenditures in the Department of State (Sixteenth Congress); was not a candidate for reelection; died in Schenectady, N.Y., September 27, 1838; interment in Dutch Church Cemetery; reinterred in Vale Cemetery.

**PEEL, Samuel West,** a Representative from Arkansas; born near Batesville, Independence County, Ark., September 13, 1831; attended the common schools; clerk of the circuit court of Carroll County, Ark., 1858-1860; entered the Confederate service in 1861 as a private; elected major of the Third Regiment, Arkansas Infantry, and later colonel of the Fourth Regiment, Arkansas Infantry; studied law; was admitted to the bar and commenced the practice of his profession in Carrollton, Ark., in 1865; moved to Bentonville, Benton County, in 1867 and continued the practice of law; prosecuting attorney of the fourth judicial circuit of Arkansas 1873-1876; elected as a Democrat to the Forty-eighth and to the four succeeding Congresses (March 4, 1883-March 3, 1893); chairman, Committee on Indian Affairs (Fiftieth and Fifty-second Congresses); unsuccessful candidate for renomination in 1892; resumed the practice of law in Bentonville, Ark., and before the Court of Claims at Washington, D.C., until 1915; died in Bentonville, Ark., December 18, 1924; interment in Bentonville Cemetery.

**PEELLE, Stanton Judkins,** a Representative from Indiana; born near Richmond, Wayne County, Ind., February 11, 1843; attended the common schools and Winchester Seminary; enlisted in Company G, Eighth Regiment, Indiana Volunteers, August 5, 1861 and served until near the close of the war; studied law; was admitted to the bar in 1866 and commenced practice in Winchester, Ind.; moved to Indianapolis in 1869; deputy district attorney of Marion County in 1872 and 1873; member of the State house of representatives 1877-1879; elected as a Republican to the Forty-seventh Congress (March 4, 1881-March 3, 1883); presented credentials as a Member-elect to the Forty-eighth Congress and served from March 4, 1883, to May 22, 1884, when he was succeeded by William E. English, who contested his election; delegate to the Republican National Convention in 1892; appointed judge of the United States Court of Claims in 1892 and served until January 1, 1906, when he was advanced to chief justice and served until February 11, 1913, when he resigned; professor of law at George Washington University (D.C.) 1901-1911; member of the board of trustees of Howard University, Washington, D.C., 1906-1925; president of the board of the Washington College of Law 1910-1925; resided in Washington, D.C., until his death there September 4, 1928; interment in Rock Creek Cemetery.

**PEERY, George Campbell,** a Representative from Virginia; born in Cedar Bluff, Tazewell County, Va., October 28, 1873; attended the common schools, and was graduated from Emory and Henry College, Emory, Va., in 1894; principal of Tazewell High School, 1894-1896; was graduated from the law department of Washington and Lee University, Lexington, Va., in 1897; was admitted to the bar the same year and commenced practice in Tazewell, Va.; delegate to the Democratic National Conventions of 1920 and 1924; local food administrator for Tazewell County during the First World War; elected as a Democrat to the Sixty-eighth and to the two succeeding Congresses (March 4, 1923-March 3, 1929); was not a candidate for renomination in 1928 to the Seventy-first Congress; resumed the practice of law and also engaged in the raising of livestock; temporary chairman of the Democratic State convention in 1928; member of the Virginia Corporation Commission, 1929-1933; elected Governor of Virginia in 1933, and served from January 17, 1934 to January 19, 1938; member of the board of trustees of Washington and Lee University and of Hollins College; died in Richlands, Va., October 14, 1952; interment in Maplewood Cemetery, Tazewell, Va.

Bibliography: Fry, Joseph A., and Brent Tarter. "The Redemption of the Ninth: The 1922 Congressional Election in the Ninth District of Virginia and the Origins of the Byrd Organization." *South Atlantic Quarterly* 77 (Summer 1978): 352-70.

**PEERY, William,** a Delegate from Delaware; settled with his father's family near Lewes, Del.; engaged in agricultural pursuits; during the Revolutionary War he raised and equipped an independent company at his own expense, and was commissioned its captain on April 13, 1777; member of the Delaware State house of representatives in 1782, 1784, 1787, 1793, and 1794; studied law; was admitted to the bar in 1785 and commenced practice in Sussex County; Member of the Continental Congress in 1786; treasurer of Sussex County from 1785 until 1796; died at Cool Spring, Sussex County, Del., December 17, 1800; interment in the churchyard of the Cool Spring Presbyterian Church.

**PEFFER, William Alfred,** a Senator from Kansas; born in Cumberland County, Pa., September 10, 1831; attended the public schools and commenced teaching at the age of fifteen; followed the gold rush to San Francisco, Calif., in 1850; moved to Indiana in 1853, Missouri in 1859, and Illinois in 1862; during the Civil War enlisted in the Union Army as a private, was promoted to second lieutenant, and served as regimental quartermaster and adjutant, post adjutant, judge advocate of the military commission, and department quartermaster in the engineering department at Nashville; mustered out of the service 1865; studied law while in the Army; was admitted to the bar in 1865 and commenced practice in Clarksville, Tenn.; moved to Fredonia, Kans., in 1870 and continued the practice of law; purchased and edited the Fredonia Journal; member, State senate 1874-1876; moved to Coffeyville, Kans. and edited the Coffeyville Journal in 1875 and also practiced law; presidential elector on the Republican ticket in 1880; editor of the Kansas Farmer at Topeka in 1881; elected as a Populist to the United States Senate and served from March 4, 1891, to March 3, 1897; unsuccessful candidate for reelection in 1896; chairman, Committee to Examine Branches of the Civil Service (Fifty-third and Fifty-fourth Congresses); unsuccessful candidate for Governor of Kansas in 1898; engaged in literary pursuits; died in Grenola, Kans., October 6, 1912; interment in Topeka Cemetery, Topeka, Kans.

Bibliography: *DAB*; Argersinger, Peter H. *Populism and Politics: William A. Peffer and the People's Party.* Lexington: University of Kentucky Press, 1974; Peffer, William A. "The United States Senate: Its Origin, Personnel and Organization." *North American Review* 167 (July 1898): 48-63.

**PEGRAM, John,** a Representative from Virginia; born at "Bonneville," in Dinwiddie County, Va., November 16, 1773; attended the common schools; held various local offices; member of the Virginia house of delegates 1797-1801; served in the Virginia senate, 1804-1808; major general of the Virginia militia in the War of 1812; again a member of the Virginia house of delegates, 1813-1815; elected as a Republican to the Fifteenth Congress to fill the vacancy caused by the death of Peterson Goodwyn and served from April 21, 1818, to March 3, 1819; appointed United States marshal for the eastern district of Virginia on April 23, 1821; lost his life during the burning of a boat on the Ohio River April 8, 1831, his body never being recovered.

**PEIRCE, Joseph,** a Representative from New Hampshire; born in Portsmouth, N.H., on June 25, 1748; attended school in Portsmouth; served during the Revolutionary War in Colonel Pierce Long's regiment in 1775 and 1776; was a member of the New Hampshire State house of representatives in 1788, 1789, 1792-1795, 1800, and 1801; town clerk from 1789 until 1794; elected as a Federalist to the Seventh Congress and served from March 4, 1801, until his resignation in 1802; engaged in agricultural pursuits; died in Alton, N.H., September 12, 1812.

**PEIRCE, Robert Bruce Fraser,** a Representative from Indiana; born in Laurel, Franklin County, Ind., February 17, 1843; attended the public schools and also educated by private tutors; served in the Civil War as second lieutenant of Company H, One Hundred and Thirty-fifth Regiment, Indiana Volunteers; was graduated from Wabash College, Crawfordsville, Ind., in 1866; studied law at Shelbyville, Ind.; was admitted to the bar in 1866 and commenced practice in Crawfordsville in 1867; elected prosecuting attorney of Montgomery County in 1868 and reelected in 1870 and 1872; elected as a Republican to the Forty-seventh Congress (March 4, 1881-March 3, 1883); unsuccessful candidate for reelection in 1882 to the Forty-eighth Congress; resumed the practice of law; appointed receiver for the Toledo, St. Louis & Western Railway; died in Indianapolis, Ind., December 5, 1898; interment in Oak Hill Cemetery, Crawfordsville, Ind.

**PELHAM, Charles,** a Representative from Alabama; born in Person County, N.C., March 12, 1835; moved with his parents to Alabama in 1838; attended the common schools; studied law; was admitted to the bar and commenced practice in Talladega, Ala., in 1858; entered the Confederate Army in 1862 and served as first lieutenant of Company C, Fifty-first Regiment, Alabama Infantry; judge of the tenth judicial circuit of Alabama 1868-1873; elected as a Republican to the Forty-third Congress (March 4, 1873-March 3, 1875); was not a candidate for renomination in 1874; resumed the practice of law in Washington, D.C.; late in life was appointed a clerk in the Treasury Department; moved to Poulan, Worth County, Ga., in 1907; died in Poulan, Ga., January 18, 1908; interment in the Presbyterian Cemetery.

**PELL, Claiborne de Borda** (son of Herbert Claiborne Pell, Jr., great-great-grandson of John Francis Hamtramck Claiborne, great-great-grandnephew of George Mifflin Dallas, great-great-great-grandnephew of William Charles Cole Claiborne and Nathaniel Herbert Claiborne), a Senator from Rhode Island; born in New York City, November 22, 1918; graduated, St. George's School, Middletown, RI, 1936; A.B., Princeton University, 1940; A.M., Columbia University, 1946; served in the United States Coast Guard, 1941-1945, and in the United States Coast Guard Reserve from 1945 until 1978; State Department and foreign service officer in Czechoslovakia, Italy, and Washington, D.C., 1945-1952; special assistant at the founding conference of the United Nations held at San Francisco, April-June 1945; businessman; served on a wide variety of government commissions and committees; consultant, Democratic National Committee, 1953-1960; elected as a Democrat to the United States Senate in 1960; reelected in 1966, 1972, 1978,

1984, and again in 1990, and served from January 3, 1961 to January 3, 1997; was not a candidate for reelection in 1996; chairman, Committee on Foreign Relations (One Hundredth through One Hundred Third Congresses); is a resident of Newport, R.I.

**PELL, Herbert Claiborne, Jr.** (great-grandson of John Francis Hamtramck Claiborne, great-great-grandnephew of William Charles Cole Claiborne and Nathaniel Herbert Claiborne, and father of Claiborne de Borda Pell), a Representative from New York; born in New York City, February 16, 1884; attended Pomfret (Conn.) School, Harvard University, and Columbia University, New York City; member of the Progressive committee of Orange County, N.Y., 1912-1914; elected as a Democrat to the Sixty-sixth Congress (March 4, 1919-March 3, 1921); unsuccessful candidate for reelection in 1920 to the Sixty-seventh Congress; chairman of the Democratic State committee, 1921-1926; delegate to the Democratic National Convention of 1924; occasional lecturer at Columbia University, Harvard University, and other institutions of learning; vice chairman of the Democratic National Campaign Committee in 1936; appointed Minister to Portugal on May 27, 1937 and served until February 1941; appointed Minister to Hungary on February 11, 1941, and served until January 1942, following the Hungarian declaration of war; United States representative on the United Nations War Crimes Commission from August 1943 to January 1945; died in Munich, Germany, July 17, 1961; remains cremated and the ashes committed off Beavertail, Jamestown, R.I.

**Bibliography:** Baker, Leonard. *Brahmin in Revolt; A Biography of Herbert C. Pell*. Garden City, N.Y.: Doubleday, 1972; Blayney, Michael Steward. *Democracy's Aristocrat: The Life of Herbert C. Pell*. Lanham, Md.: University Press of America, 1986.

**PELL, Philip,** a Delegate from New York; born in Pelham Manor, N.Y., July 7, 1753; was graduated from King's College (now Columbia University), New York City, in 1770; studied law; was admitted to the bar and practiced in New York City and Westchester County; lieutenant, New York Volunteers, in 1776; deputy judge advocate, Continental Army, in 1777; member of the State assembly 1779-1781; Judge Advocate General, United States Army, 1781-1783; member of General George Washington's staff at the evacuation of the city of New York in 1783; again a member of the State assembly 1784-1786; regent of the University of the State of New York 1784-1787; surrogate of Westchester County from March 13, 1787, to October 31, 1800; Member of the Continental Congress, 1789; died in Pelham Manor, N.Y., May 1, 1811; interment in St. Paul's Churchyard, Eastchester (now in the Bronx), N.Y.

**PELLY, Thomas Minor,** a Representative from Washington; born in Seattle, King County, Wash., August 22, 1902; attended the public schools, the University School, Victoria, B.C., and the Hoosac School, Hoosick, N.Y.; employed in real estate and the banking business, 1921-1930; officer of a printing and stationery company, 1930-1955; elected as a Republican to the Eighty-third and to the nine succeeding Congresses (January 3, 1953-January 3, 1973); was not a candidate for reelection in 1972 to the Ninety-third Congress; retired and resided in Seattle, Wash.; died in Ojai, Calif., November 21, 1973; interment in Evergreen Washelli Cemetery, Seattle, Wash.

**PELOSI, Nancy** (daughter of Thomas D'Alesandro, Jr.), a Representative from California; born in Baltimore, Md., March 26, 1940; attended the Institute of Notre Dame Grammar School, Baltimore, 1954, and graduated from the Institute of Notre Dame High School in 1958; A.B., Trinity College, Washington, D.C., 1962; public relations consultant; northern chair, California State Democratic Party, 1977-1981; chair, California State Democratic Party, 1981-1983; finance chairman, Democratic Senatorial Campaign Committee, 1985-1986; elected as a Democrat to the One Hundredth Congress, June 2, 1987, by special election to fill the vacancy caused by the death of Sala Burton; reelected to the four succeeding Congresses and served from June 2, 1987, to January 3, 1997; is a resident of San Francisco, Calif.

**PELTON, Guy Ray,** a Representative from New York; born near Great Barrington, Berkshire County, Mass., August 3, 1824; attended the common schools and the Connecticut Literary Institute, Suffield, Conn.; taught school; studied law; was admitted to the bar and commenced practice in New York City in 1851; held various local offices; elected as a Whig to the Thirty-fourth Congress (March 4, 1855-March 3, 1857); unsuccessful candidate for reelection in 1856 to the Thirty-fifth Congress; resumed the practice of law in Great Barrington; died while on a tour in an attempt to climb Mary's Mountain in the Yellowstone National Park, Wyo., July 24, 1890; interment in Mahaiwe Cemetery, Great Barrington, Mass.

**PENCE, Lafayette,** a Representative from Colorado; born in Columbus, Bartholomew County, Ind., December 23, 1857; attended the common schools; was graduated from Hanover (Ind.) College in 1877; studied law; was admitted to the bar in 1878 and practiced in Columbus, Ind., until September 1879, when he moved to Winfield, Kans.; moved to Rico, Dolores County, Colo., in 1881 and continued the practice of law until 1884; member of the State house of representatives in 1885; settled in Denver in 1885 and continued the practice of law; prosecuting attorney for Arapahoe County in 1887 and 1888; elected as a Populist to the Fifty-third Congress (March 4, 1893-March 3, 1895); unsuccessful candidate for reelection in 1894 to the Fifty-fourth Congress; moved to New York City and engaged in railroad work; returned to Denver and from there moved to San Francisco, Calif., and subsequently to Washington, D.C., and continued the practice of law; also engaged in hydraulic mining in Breckenridge, Colo., and Portland, Oreg.; died in Washington, D.C., October 22, 1923; interment in Garland Brook Cemetery, Columbus, Ind.

**PENDLETON, Edmund** (uncle of Nathaniel Pendleton and John Penn), a Delegate from Virginia; born in Caroline County, Va., September 9, 1721; completed preparatory studies; clerk, Caroline County Court, in 1740; studied law; was admitted to the bar in 1741 and practiced; justice of the peace in 1751; member of the Virginia House of Burgesses 1752-1774; member of the committee of correspondence in 1773 and of the provincial convention in 1774; Member of the Continental Congress in 1774 and 1775; president of the committee of safety in 1775; president of the Virginia conventions in 1775 and 1776; member of the Virginia house of delegates in 1776 and 1777; judge of the general court and the court of chancery in 1777; presiding judge of the court of appeals in 1779; member and president of the Virginia ratification convention in 1788; died in Richmond, Va., October 23, 1803; interment at Edmundsbury, eight miles southeast of Bowling Green, Va.; in 1907 was reinterred in Bruton Parish Church Cemetery, Williamsburg, Va.

**Bibliography:** *DAB*; Mays, David J. *Edmund Pendleton, 1721-1803: A Biography*. Cambridge: Harvard University Press, 1952; Pendleton, Edmund. *The Letters and Papers of Edmund Pendleton, 1734-1803*. 2 vols. Edited by David J. Mays. Charlottesville, Va.: University Press of Virginia, 1967.

**PENDLETON, Edmund Henry,** a Representative from New York; born in Savannah, Ga., in 1788; received a liberal schooling; studied law; was admitted to the bar and practiced for several years in Hyde Park, Dutchess County, N.Y.; county judge of Dutchess County 1830-1840; was elected as an Anti-Jacksonian to the Twenty-second Congress (March 4, 1831-March 3, 1833); died in New York City February 25, 1862; interment in St. James' Churchyard, Hyde Park, N.Y.

**PENDLETON, George Cassety,** a Representative from Texas; born near Viola, Warren County, Tenn., April 23, 1845; attended the country schools and the Hannah High School; moved with his parents to Ellis County, Tex., in 1857; settled in Belton, Tex., and engaged in mercantile and agricultural pursuits; during the Civil War entered the Confederate service as a private in Captain Forrest's Company, Watson's Regiment, Parson's Brigade, Texas Cavalry; at the close of the war attended Waxahachie Academy in Ellis County, Tex.; employed as a commercial traveler for twelve years; engaged in mercantile and agricultural pursuits; delegate to every Democratic State convention from 1876 to 1910; member of the State house of representatives 1882-1888 and served as speaker in 1886; Lieutenant Governor of Texas 1890-1892; delegate to the Democratic National Convention in 1896; elected as a Democrat to the Fifty-third and Fifty-fourth Congresses (March 4, 1893-March 3, 1897); declined to be a candidate for renomination in 1896; engaged in banking in Temple, Bell County, Tex.; studied law; was admitted to the bar in 1900 and practiced in Temple until his death there on January 19, 1913; interment in City Cemetery.

**PENDLETON, George Hunt** (son of Nathanael Greene Pendleton), a Representative and a Senator from Ohio; born in Cincinnati, Ohio, July 19, 1825; attended the local schools and Cincinnati College; attended Heidelberg University, Germany; studied law; was admitted to the bar in 1847 and commenced practice in Cincinnati; member, Ohio State senate, 1854-1856; unsuccessful candidate for election in 1854 to the Thirty-fourth Congress; elected as a Democrat to the Thirty-fifth and to the three succeeding Congresses (March 4, 1857-March 3, 1865); unsuccessful candidate for reelection in 1864 to the Thirty-ninth Congress; one of the managers appointed by the House of Representatives in 1862 to conduct the impeachment proceedings against West H. Humphreys, United States judge for the several districts of Tennessee; unsuccessful candidate for Vice President of the United States in 1864 on the Democratic ticket headed by George B. McClellan; unsuccessful candidate for election in 1866 to the Fortieth Congress; unsuccessful Democratic candidate for Governor of Ohio in 1869; president of the Kentucky Central Railroad, 1869-1879; elected as a Democrat to the United States Senate, and served from March 4, 1879 to March 3, 1885; unsuccessful candidate for renomination; sponsor of the Pendleton (Civil Service) Act of 1883, instituting merit-based examinations for the selection of some Federal workers, and establishing an independent civil service commission to regulate standards for Federal employment; appointed Envoy Extraordinary and Minister Plenipotentiary to Germany on March 23, 1885, and served until April 1889; died in Brussels, Belgium, November 24, 1889; interment in Spring Grove Cemetery, Cincinnati, Ohio.

Bibliography: *DAB*; Bloss, George. *Life and Speeches of George H. Pendleton.* Cincinnati: Miami Printing and Publishing Co., 1868.

**PENDLETON, James Monroe,** a Representative from Rhode Island; born in North Stonington, New London County, Conn., January 10, 1822; attended school in North Stonington and Suffield, Conn.; moved to Westerly, R.I., and engaged in mercantile pursuits and later in the insurance business and banking; served in the State senate 1862-1865; delegate to the Republican National Convention in 1868; elected as a Republican to the Forty-second and Forty-third Congresses (March 4, 1871-March 3, 1875); unsuccessful for reelection in 1874 to the Forty-fourth Congress; member of the State house of representatives 1879-1884; chairman of the State board of charities and corrections 1884-1889; died in Westerly, R.I., February 16, 1889; interment in River Bend Cemetery.

**PENDLETON, John Overton,** a Representative from West Virginia; born in Wellsburg, Brooke County, Va. (now West Virginia), July 4, 1851; moved with his parents to Wheeling, Va. (now West Virginia), in 1851; attended Aspen Hill Academy, Louisa County, Va.,

1865-1869, and Bethany College, West Virginia, 1869-1871; studied law; was admitted to the bar and commenced practice in Wheeling, W.Va., in 1874; unsuccessful Democratic candidate for State senator in 1886; presented credentials as a Democratic Member-elect to the Fifty-first Congress and served from March 4, 1889, to February 26, 1890, when he was succeeded by George W. Atkinson, who contested the election; elected as a Democrat to the Fifty-second and Fifty-third Congresses (March 4, 1891-March 3, 1895); chairman, Committee on Private Land Claims (Fifty-third Congress); unsuccessful candidate for renomination in 1894; resumed the practice of law in Wheeling, W.Va., and died there December 24, 1916; interment in Greenwood Cemetery.

**PENDLETON, John Strother,** a Representative from Virginia; born near Culpeper, Culpeper County, Va., March 1, 1802; pursued preparatory studies; studied law; was admitted to the bar in 1824 and practiced in Culpeper County; member of the Virginia house of delegates, 1830-1833, and 1836-1839; appointed Chargé d'Affaires to Chile on August 16, 1841 and served until June 1844; elected as a Whig to the Twenty-ninth and Thirtieth Congresses (March 4, 1845-March 3, 1849); appointed Chargé d'Affaires to the Argentine Confederation on February 27, 1851 and served until March 1854; empowered jointly with Robert C. Schenck, American Minister to Brazil, April 27, 1852, to negotiate a treaty of commerce with Paraguay and Uruguay; engaged in farming; died near Culpeper, Va., November 19, 1868; interment in the family burying ground, "Redwood," Culpeper, Va.

Bibliography: *DAB*.

**PENDLETON, Nathanael Greene** (father of George Hunt Pendleton), a Representative from Ohio; born in Savannah, Ga., August 25, 1793, moved to New York City with his parents; was graduated from Columbia College at New York City in 1813; studied law; was admitted to the bar; served in the War of 1812; moved to Cincinnati, Ohio, in 1818 and practiced law; member of the State senate 1825-1829; elected as a Whig to the Twenty-seventh Congress (March 4, 1841-March 3, 1843); did not seek renomination in 1842; died in Cincinnati, Ohio, June 16, 1861; interment in Spring Grove Cemetery.

**PENDLETON, Nathaniel** (nephew of Edmund Pendleton and cousin of John Penn), a Delegate from Georgia; born in New Kent County, Va., in 1756; entered the Revolutionary Army at the age of nineteen years; aide-de-camp to General Nathanael Greene in the campaigns in the Southern States; at the close of the war settled in Georgia and studied law, ultimately becoming a district judge; elected a delegate to the Federal Convention of 1787 but did not attend; appointed to a Federal judgeship in Georgia in 1789 and served until 1796 when he resigned; elected to the Continental Congress in 1789 but did not attend; moved to New York City in 1796 and practiced law; served as a second to Alexander Hamilton in Hamilton's duel with Aaron Burr fought at Weehawken, N.J. on July 11, 1804; died in Hyde Park, N.Y., October 20, 1821; interment in St. James' Churchyard.

**PENINGTON, John Brown,** a Representative from Delaware; born near New Castle, Del., December 20, 1825; pursued an academic course in New Castle and Newark, Del., and was graduated from Jefferson College, Canonsburg, Pa.; engaged in teaching in Indiana for several years; returned to Delaware; studied law; was admitted to the bar in 1857 and commenced practice in Dover, Del.; member of the Delaware State house of representatives, 1857; clerk of the Delaware State house of representatives in 1859, 1863, and 1871; delegate to the Democratic National Conventions at Charleston and Baltimore in 1860; appointed United States attorney for the district of Delaware in 1868 by President Andrew Johnson, and served until 1872; appointed attorney general of the State by Governor James Ponder in 1874, and served until 1878; elected as a Democrat to the Fiftieth and Fifty-first Congresses

(March 4, 1887-March 3, 1891); was not a candidate for renomination in 1890 to the Fifty-second Congress; resumed the practice of law at Dover, Del., where he died June 1, 1902; interment in the Presbyterian Cemetery.

**PENN, Alexander Gordon,** a Representative from Louisiana; born near Stella, Patrick County, Va., May 10, 1799; moved with his parents to Lexington, Ky.; completed preparatory studies and attended Emory and Henry College, Marion, Va.; moved to the parish of St. Tammany, La., in 1821 and engaged in planting near Covington; served in the State house of representatives; postmaster of New Orleans from December 19, 1843, to April 18, 1849; delegate to the Democratic National Conventions in 1844, 1852, 1856, and 1860; elected as a Democrat to the Thirty-first Congress to fill the vacancy caused by the death of John H. Harmanson; reelected to the Thirty-second Congress and served from December 30, 1850, to March 3, 1853; chairman, Committee on Expenditures in the Post Office Department (Thirty-second Congress); returned to St. Tammany Parish and engaged in planting and the operation of a lumber mill near Covington; at the conclusion of the Civil War returned to Washington, D.C., where he died May 7, 1866; interment in Glenwood Cemetery.

**PENN, John** (nephew of Edmund Pendleton and cousin of Nathaniel Pendleton), a Delegate from North Carolina; born near Port Royal, Caroline County, Va., May 17, 1741; was educated under private tutors; studied law; was admitted to the bar in 1762 and commenced practice in Bowling Green, Caroline County, Va.; moved to Granville County, N.C., in 1774; elected to the Provincial Congress which met in Hillsboro, N.C., in August 1775; Member of the Continental Congress, 1775-1780; a signer of the Declaration of Independence; one of the three representatives from North Carolina to ratify the Articles of Confederation on behalf of the State; member of board of war in North Carolina in 1780; receiver of taxes for North Carolina in 1784; resumed the practice of law; died near Williamsboro, Granville County, N.C., September 14, 1788; interment on his estate in Granville County, N.C.; reinterment at Guilford Battle Grounds, near Greensboro, N.C., in 1894.

**Bibliography:** *DAB.*

**PENNIMAN, Ebenezer Jenckes,** a Representative from Michigan; born in Lansingburgh, Rensselaer County, N.Y., January 11, 1804; attended the common schools; apprenticed as a printer; moved to New York City in 1822 and to Orwell, Addison County, Vt., where he engaged in business as a dry-goods merchant; moved to Plymouth, Mich., in 1840 and again engaged as a dry-goods merchant; supervisor of Plymouth Township, Wayne County; elected as a Whig to the Thirty-second Congress (March 4, 1851-March 3, 1853); was not a candidate for renomination in 1852 to the Thirty-third Congress; resumed mercantile pursuits until 1871, when he engaged in banking and served as president of the First National Bank of Plymouth; member of the convention that met under the oaks at Jackson, Mich., July 6, 1854, at the organization of the Republican Party in Michigan; died in Plymouth, Mich., April 12, 1890; interment in Riverside Cemetery.

**PENNINGTON, Alexander Cumming McWhorter** (cousin of William Pennington), a Representative from New Jersey; born in Newark, N.J., July 2, 1810; completed preparatory studies; attended the United States Military Academy, West Point, N.Y., 1826-1828; studied law; was admitted to the bar in 1833 and commenced practice in Newark; member of the New Jersey State general assembly in 1837 and 1838; alderman of Newark, 1837-1840; elected as a Whig to the Thirty-third and Thirty-fourth Congresses (March 4, 1853-March 3, 1857); chairman, Committee on Foreign Affairs (Thirty-fourth Congress); moved to New York City, where he died on January 25, 1867; interment in Mount Pleasant Cemetery, Newark, N.J.

**PENNINGTON, William** (cousin of Alexander Cumming McWhorter Pennington), a Representative from New Jersey; born in Newark, N.J., May 4, 1796; completed preparatory studies; was graduated from Princeton College in 1813; clerk of the United States district court from 1815 until 1826; studied law; was admitted to the bar and commenced practice in Newark in 1820; member of the New Jersey State general assembly in 1828; served as sergeant at law in 1834; elected Governor of New Jersey by the Legislature, and served from October 27, 1837 to October 27, 1843; appointed Governor of Minnesota Territory by President Millard Fillmore, but declined to accept; elected as a Republican to the Thirty-sixth Congress (March 4, 1859-March 3, 1861); Speaker of the House of Representatives (Thirty-sixth Congress); unsuccessful candidate for reelection in 1860 to the Thirty-seventh Congress; died in Newark, N.J., February 16, 1862; interment in Mount Pleasant Cemetery.

**Bibliography:** *DAB.*

**PENNY, Timothy Joseph,** a Representative from Minnesota; born in Albert Lea, Freeborn County, Minn., November 19, 1951; graduated from Kiester High School, 1969; B.A., Winona (Minn.) State University, 1974; graduate studies, University of Minnesota, Minneapolis, 1975; elected to the Minnesota State senate, 1976-1982; elected on the Democratic-Farmer-Labor ticket to the Ninety-eighth and to the five succeeding Congresses (January 3, 1983-January 3, 1995); was not a candidate for reelection in 1994 to the One Hundred Fourth Congress; is a resident of New Richland, Minn.

**Bibliography:** Penny, Timothy J., and Major Garrett. *Common Cents: A Retiring Six-Term Congressman Reveals How Congress Really Works—and What We Must Do to Fix It.* Boston: Little, Brown and Co., 1995.

**PENNYBACKER, Isaac Samuels** (cousin of Green Berry Samuels), a Representative and a Senator from Virginia; born at Pine Forge, near Newmarket, Shenandoah County, Va., September 3, 1805; attended an "old field" school and the Winchester Law School; was admitted to the bar and commenced practice in Harrisonburg, Rockingham County, Va.; elected as a Democrat to the Twenty-fifth Congress (March 4, 1837-March 3, 1839); judge of the United States District Court for the Western District of Virginia 1839-1845; declined the office of United States Attorney General offered him by President Martin Van Buren and that of justice of the supreme court of Virginia; elected as a Democrat to the United States Senate to fill the vacancy in the term beginning March 4, 1845, caused by the failure of the legislature to elect and served from December 3, 1845, until his death; chairman, Committee on Claims (Twenty-ninth Congress); regent of the Smithsonian Institution; died in Washington, D.C., January 12, 1847; interment in Woodbine Cemetery, Harrisonburg, Va.

**PENROSE, Boies,** a Senator from Pennsylvania; born in Philadelphia, Pa., November 1, 1860; attended the public schools and was prepared for college by private tutors; graduated from Harvard University in 1881; studied law; admitted to the bar in 1883 and commenced practice in Philadelphia; member, Pennsylvania house of representatives, 1884-1886; member of the Pennsylvania senate from 1886 until 1897, when he resigned, having been elected United States Senator; president pro tempore of the Pennsylvania senate, 1889-1891; unsuccessful candidate in 1895 for mayor of Philadelphia; elected as a member of the Republican National Committee in 1904, and reelected in 1908; elected as a Republican to the United States Senate in 1897; reelected in 1903, 1909, 1914, and 1920, and served from March 4, 1897, until his death in Washington, D.C., December 31, 1921; chairman, Committee on Immigration (Fifty-sixth and Fifty-seventh Congresses), Committee on Post Office and Post Roads (Fifty-eighth through Sixty-first Congresses), Committee on Education and Labor (Fifty-ninth Congress), Committee on Finance (Sixty-second, Sixty-sixth and Sixty-seventh Congresses), Committee on Additional Accommodations for the Library (Sixty-third through Sixty-fifth Congresses); interment in Laurel Hill Cemetery, Philadelphia, Pa.

**Bibliography:** *DAB*; Bowden, Robert D. *Boise Penrose: Symbol of an Era.* 1937. Reprint. Freeport, N.Y.: Books for Libraries, 1971; Davenport, Walter. *Power and Glory: Boise Penrose.* 1931. Reprint. New York: AMS Press, 1969.

**PEPPER, Claude Denson,** a Senator and a Representative from Florida; born on a farm near Dudleyville, Chambers County, Ala., September 8, 1900; attended the public schools of Camp Hill, Ala.; taught school in Dothan, Ala., and worked in a steel mill in Ensley, Ala., before attending college; served in the Students Army Training Corps, University of Alabama, in 1918; A.B., University of Alabama, Tuscaloosa, 1921; LL.B., Harvard University School of Law, 1924; taught law at the University of Arkansas, 1924-1925; was admitted to the bar in 1925 and commenced practice in Perry, Fla., 1925-1936; member of the Florida State house of representatives, 1929-1930; moved to Tallahassee, Fla., in 1930 and continued the practice of law; served on the Florida State board of public welfare, 1931-1932; member of the Florida State board of law examiners in 1933; elected as a Democrat to the United States Senate to fill the vacancy caused by the death of Duncan U. Fletcher; reelected in 1938 and again in 1944, and served from November 4, 1936, to January 3, 1951; chairman, Committee on Patents (Seventy-eighth and Seventy-ninth Congresses); unsuccessful candidate for renomination in 1950, and for nomination in 1958; engaged in the practice of law at Miami Beach, Coral Gables, and Tallahassee, Fla., and in Washington, D.C.; elected as a Democrat to the Eighty-eighth and to the thirteen succeeding Congresses and served from January 3, 1963, until his death in Washington, D.C., on May 30, 1989; chairman, Select Committee on Crime (Ninety-first through Ninety-sixth Congresses), Select Committee on Aging (Ninety-fifth through Ninety-seventh Congress), Committee on Rules (Ninety-eighth through One Hundred First Congresses); lay in state in the rotunda of the United States Capitol.

**Bibliography:** Kabat, Ric A. "From New Deal to Red Scare: The Political Odyssey of Senator Claude D. Pepper." Ph.D. dissertation, Florida State University, 1995; Pepper, Claude Denson, with Hays Gorey. *Pepper: Eyewitness to a Century.* New York: Harcourt Brace Jovanovich, 1987; Stoesen, Alexander Rudolph. "The Senatorial Career of Claude D. Pepper." Ph.D. dissertation, University of North Carolina at Chapel Hill, 1965.

**PEPPER, George Wharton,** a Senator from Pennsylvania; born in Philadelphia, Pa., March 16, 1867; prepared privately for college; graduated from the University of Pennsylvania at Philadelphia in 1887, and from that university's law department in 1889; admitted to the bar in 1889 and commenced practice in Philadelphia, Pa.; professor of law at the University of Pennsylvania, 1894-1910, and trustee of the university from 1911 until 1961; chairman of the Pennsylvania Council of National Defense during the First World War; lecturer at Yale University in 1915; member of the commission on constitutional revision in Pennsylvania, 1920-1921; appointed as a Republican and subsequently elected to the United States Senate to fill the vacancy caused by the death of Boies Penrose and served from January 9, 1922, to March 3, 1927; unsuccessful candidate for renomination in 1926; chairman, Committee on the Library (Sixty-eighth Congress), Committee on Printing (Sixty-ninth Congress); member, Republican National Committee, 1922-1928; resumed the practice of law in Philadelphia, Pa.; died in Devon, Pa., May 24, 1961; interment in Old St. David's Churchyard Cemetery, Wayne, Pa.

**Bibliography:** *DAB*; Pepper, George Wharton. *In the Senate.* Philadelphia: University of Pennsylvania Press, 1930; Zieger, Robert. "Senator George Wharton Pepper and Labor Issues in the 1920s." *Labor History* 9 (Spring 1968): 163-83.

**PEPPER, Irvin St. Clair,** a Representative from Iowa; born in Davis County, Iowa, June 10, 1876; attended the public schools; was graduated from Southern Iowa Normal School at Bloomfield in 1897; principal of the Atalissa High School and of the Washington School at Muscatine; secretary for Representative Martin J. Wade of Iowa, 1903-1905; graduated from the law department of George Washington University, Washington, D.C., in 1905; was admitted to the bar the same year and commenced practice in Muscatine, Iowa; served as prosecuting attorney of Muscatine County, 1906-1910; elected as a Democrat to the Sixty-second and Sixty-third Congresses and served from March 4, 1911, until his death in Clinton County, Iowa, December 22, 1913; chairman, Committee on Expenditures in the Post Office Department (Sixty-third Congress); interment in Shaul Cemetery, near Ottumwa, Wapello County, Iowa.

**PERCE, Legrand Winfield,** a Representative from Mississippi; born in Buffalo, N.Y., June 19, 1836; completed preparatory studies; attended Wesleyan College, Lima, N.Y., and was graduated from the Albany (N.Y.) Law School in 1857; was admitted to the bar the same year and commenced practice in Buffalo, N.Y.; enlisted in the Union Army in April 1861, at the outbreak of the Civil War; was commissioned a second lieutenant in the Sixth Regiment, Michigan Volunteer Infantry, in August 1861; promoted to the rank of captain in June 1862; appointed captain in the United States Volunteers in August 1863 and was brevetted lieutenant colonel and colonel in 1865; settled in Natchez, Miss.; appointed register in bankruptcy in June 1867; upon readmission of the State of Mississippi to representation was elected as a Republican to the Forty-first Congress; reelected to the Forty-second Congress and served from February 23, 1870, to March 3, 1873; chairman, Committee on Education and Labor (Forty-second Congress); was not a candidate for reelection in 1872; engaged in the practice of law and also in the real estate business at Chicago, Ill., where he died March 16, 1911; interment in Rose Hill Cemetery.

**PERCY, Charles Harting** (father-in-law of John D. Rockefeller IV), a Senator from Illinois; born in Pensacola, Escambia County, Fla., September 27, 1919; attended public schools in Chicago and Winnetka, Ill.; B.A., University of Chicago, 1941; joined the firm of Bell & Howell; during the Second World War enlisted in the United States Navy in 1943 as an apprentice seaman; became officer in charge of the Advance Base Aviation Training Units, received an admiral's commendation, and was honorably discharged in 1945 with the rank of lieutenant; after the war, rejoined the firm of Bell & Howell, eventually becoming president, chief executive officer, and chairman of the board; appointed as President Dwight D. Eisenhower's personal representative to presidential inaugurations in Peru and Bolivia with rank of special ambassador, 1956; unsuccessful candidate for Governor of Illinois in 1964; elected as a Republican to the United States Senate in 1966; reelected in 1972 and again in 1978, and served from January 3, 1967 to January 3, 1985; unsuccessful candidate for reelection in 1984; chairman, Committee on Foreign Relations (Ninety-seventh and Ninety-eighth Congresses); chairman and chief executive officer of the Hariri Foundation, USA, and chairman of Charles Percy and Associates, Inc.; serves on the boards of several foundations and committees; is a resident of Washington, D.C.

**Bibliography:** Hartley, Robert. *Charles H. Percy: A Political Perspective.* Chicago: Rand-McNally, 1975; Murray, David. *Charles Percy of Illinois.* New York: Harper and Row, 1968.

**PERCY, Le Roy,** a Senator from Mississippi; born near Greenville, Washington County, Miss., on November 9, 1860; attended the public schools; graduated from the University of the South, Sewanee, Tenn., in 1879 and from the law department of the University of Virginia at Charlottesville in 1881; was admitted to the bar in 1881 and commenced practice in Greenville, Miss.; also interested in agricultural pursuits; elected as a Democrat to the

United States Senate to fill the vacancy caused by the death of Anselm J. McLaurin and served from February 23, 1910, to March 3, 1913; unsuccessful candidate for renomination in 1912; member of the United States Joint Immigration Commission 1910; resumed the practice of law in Greenville, Miss.; also supervised his extensive land acreage holdings; director of the Federal Reserve Board branch at St. Louis, Mo., from 1914 until his death on December 24, 1929, in Memphis, Tenn., while en route to his home in Mississippi; interment in Greenville Cemetery, Greenville, Miss.

**Bibliography:** Baker, Lewis. *The Percys of Mississippi: Politics and Literature in the New South*. Baton Rouge: Louisiana State University Press, 1983.

**PEREA, Francisco** (cousin of Pedro Perea), a Delegate from the Territory of New Mexico; born in Los Padillas, N.Mex. (then in the Republic of Mexico), January 9, 1830; attended select schools in Bernalillo County and at Santa Fe 1836-1839; enrolled at the Jesuit College, St. Louis, Mo., 1843-1845 and received collegiate training at the Bank Street Academy in New York City 1847-1849; from 1850 to 1864 was engaged in stock raising and commercial pursuits and in carrying merchandise by mule train from St. Louis and Independence, Mo., to Mexico; member of the Territorial council in 1858, 1866, and 1884; during the Civil War served as lieutenant colonel of Perea's Battalion in 1861 and 1862; delegate to the Republican National Convention in 1864; elected as a Republican to the Thirty-eighth Congress (March 4, 1863-March 3, 1865); unsuccessful candidate for renomination in 1864; moved from Bernalillo County to Jemez Springs, Sandoval County, N.Mex., in 1881; proprietor of the springs and a hotel; postmaster of Jemez Springs 1894-1905; moved to Albuquerque, N.Mex., in 1906 and died there May 21, 1913; interment in Fairview Cemetery.

**PEREA, Pedro** (cousin of Francisco Perea), a Delegate from the Territory of New Mexico; born in Bernalillo, Sandoval County, N.Mex., April 22, 1852; attended St. Michael's College, Santa Fe, N.Mex., Georgetown University, Washington, D.C., and was graduated from the St. Louis University, St. Louis, Mo., in 1871; principally engaged in agricultural pursuits and sheep raising; president of the First National Bank of Santa Fe 1890-1894; member of the council of the New Mexico Legislature in 1889, 1891, and 1895; delegate to the Republican National Convention in 1896; elected as a Republican to the Fifty-sixth Congress (March 4, 1899-March 3, 1901); was not a candidate for renomination in 1900 to the Fifty-seventh Congress; engaged in banking and also interested in stock raising; appointed Territorial insurance commissioner in 1906 and served until his death in Bernalillo, N.Mex., January 11, 1906; interment in Bernalillo Cemetery.

**PERHAM, Sidney,** a Representative from Maine; born in Woodstock, Maine, on March 27, 1819; attended the common schools; engaged in agricultural pursuits; member of the Maine State house of representatives in 1854, and served as speaker; clerk of the courts of Oxford County, Maine, 1859-1863; elected as a Republican to the Thirty-eighth and to the two succeeding Congresses (March 4, 1863-March 3, 1869); chairman, Committee on Invalid Pensions (Thirty-ninth and Fortieth Congresses); was not a candidate for renomination in 1868 to the Forty-first Congress; elected Governor of Maine in 1870, reelected in 1871 and 1872, and served from January 4, 1871 to January 7, 1874; president of the board of trustees of Westbrook Seminary, Deering, Maine, 1865-1880, and of the Maine Industrial School at Hallowell, 1873-1898; served as secretary of state of Maine in 1875 to fill a vacancy; served as appraiser in the custom house at Portland, Maine, 1877-1885; member of the board of trustees of the Universalist General Convention for twenty-seven years and served as president of the board; died in Washington, D.C., April 10, 1907; interment in Lakeside Cemetery, Bryant Pond, Oxford County, Maine.

**PERKINS, Bishop,** a Representative from New York; born in Becket, Berkshire County, Mass., September 5, 1787; attended private school at East Granville, Mass., and was graduated from Williams College, Williamstown, Mass., in 1807; studied law; was admitted to the bar in 1812 and commenced practice in Lisbon, N.Y.; subsequently moved to Ogdensburg, St. Lawrence County, N.Y., and continued the practice of law; clerk of the board of supervisors of St. Lawrence County 1820-1852; appointed district attorney of St. Lawrence County February 24, 1821, and served until May 21, 1840; member of the State constitutional convention in 1846; member of the State assembly in 1846, 1847, and again in 1849; elected as a Democrat to the Thirty-third Congress (March 4, 1853-March 3, 1855); was not a candidate for renomination in 1854; returned to Ogdensburg, N.Y., and continued the practice of his profession until his death there November 20, 1866; interment in Ogdensburg Cemetery.

**PERKINS, Bishop Walden,** a Representative and a Senator from Kansas; born in Rochester, Lorain County, Ohio, October 18, 1841; attended the common schools and Knox College, Galesburg, Ill.; prospected for gold through California and New Mexico 1860-1862; served four years in the Union Army during the Civil War as sergeant, adjutant, and captain; studied law in Ottawa, Ill.; was admitted to the bar in 1867, and commenced the practice of law in Princeton, Ind.; moved to Oswego, Labette County, Kans., and continued practice; local county attorney for the Missouri, Kansas & Texas Railroad for two years; prosecuting attorney of Labette County 1869; judge of the probate court of Labette County 1870-1882; became editor of the Oswego Register in 1873; elected as a Republican to the Forty-eighth and to the three succeeding Congresses (March 4, 1883-March 3, 1891); unsuccessful candidate for reelection in 1890 to the Fifty-second Congress; appointed to the United States Senate as a Republican to fill the vacancy caused by the death of Preston B. Plumb and served from January 1, 1892, to March 3, 1893, when a successor was elected and qualified; resumed the practice of his profession in Washington, D.C., and died there June 20, 1894; interment in Rock Creek Cemetery.

**PERKINS, Carl Christopher** (son of Carl Dewey Perkins), a Representative from Kentucky; born in Washington, D.C., August 6, 1954; attended public schools in Fairfax County (Va.); B.A., Davidson College, (N.C.), 1976; J.D., University of Louisville (Ky.), 1978; practiced law in Kentucky, 1978-1984; member, Kentucky house of representatives, 1981-1984; elected as a Democrat to the Ninety-eighth Congress by special election November 6, 1984, to fill the vacancy caused by the death of his father, United States Representative Carl Dewey Perkins, and at the same time elected to the Ninety-ninth Congress; reelected to the three succeeding Congresses, and served from November 6, 1984 to January 3, 1993; was not a candidate for reelection in 1992 to the One Hundred Third Congress; is a resident of Leburn, Ky.

**PERKINS, Carl Dewey** (father of Carl Christopher Perkins), a Representative from Kentucky; born in Hindman, Knott County, Ky., October 15, 1912; attended the Knott County grade schools, Hindman High School, Caney Junior College (now Alice Lloyd College), Lees Junior College, and was graduated from Jefferson School of Law (now the University of Louisville Law School), Louisville, Ky., in 1935; was admitted to the bar in 1935 and commenced the practice of law in Hindman, Ky.; in 1939 served an unexpired term as commonwealth attorney from the thirty-first judicial district; member of Kentucky General Assembly from the ninety-ninth district in 1940; elected Knott County attorney in 1941, reelected in 1945, and resigned on January 1, 1948 to become counsel for the Department of Highways, Frankfort, Ky.; during the Second World War enlisted in the United States Army and saw service in the European Theater; elected as a Democrat to the Eighty-first and to the seventeen succeeding Congresses, and served from January 3, 1949 until his death in Lexington, Ky., August 3, 1984; chairman, Committee on Education and Labor (Ninetieth through Ninety-eighth Congresses); interment in Perkins Cemetery, Leburn, Ky.

**Bibliography:** Damron, Donald Reid. "The Contributions of Carl D. Perkins on Higher Education Legislation, 1948-1984." D.A. dissertation, Middle Tennesssee State University, 1990.

**PERKINS, Elias,** a Representative from Connecticut; born in Newent Society (now Lisbon), Conn., April 5, 1767; was graduated from Yale College in 1786; studied law; was admitted to the bar and commenced practice in New London, New London County, Conn.; member of the State house of representatives 1795-1800, 1814, and 1815 and served as speaker in 1798 and 1815; was assistant judge of the New London County Court in 1799 and chief justice of the same court 1807-1825; elected as a Federalist to the Seventh Congress (March 4, 1801-March 3, 1803); resumed the practice of law; member of the State senate 1817-1822; mayor of New London 1829-1832; died in New London, Conn., September 27, 1845; interment in Cedar Grove Cemetery.

**PERKINS, George Clement,** a Senator from California; born in Kennebunkport, York County, Maine, August 23, 1839; had limited educational advantages; at the age of twelve went to sea as a cabin boy; followed the sea for several years; subsequently engaged in banking, milling, mining, farming, ranching, whaling, and in operating steamships on the coasts of California, Oregon, Washington, British Columbia, Alaska, and Mexico; member, California State senate, 1869-1876; elected Governor of California in 1879, and served from January 8, 1880 to January 10, 1883; unsuccessful Republican candidate for the United States Senate in 1886; appointed in 1893 and subsequently elected as a Republican to the United States Senate to fill the vacancy caused by the death of Leland Stanford; reelected in 1897, 1903, and 1909 and served from July 26, 1893, to March 3, 1915; on account of ill health was not a candidate for reelection; chairman, Committee on Fisheries (Fifty-fourth through Fifty-sixth Congresses), Committee on Civil Service and Retrenchment (Fifty-seventh through Sixtieth Congresses), Committee on Naval Affairs (Sixty-first and Sixty-second Congresses), Committee on Railroads (Sixty-third Congress); returned to his home in Oakland, Calif., and lived in retirement until his death there on February 26, 1923; interment in Mountain View Cemetery.

**Bibliography:** *DAB.*

**PERKINS, George Douglas,** a Representative from Iowa; born in Holly, Orleans County, N.Y., February 29, 1840; attended the common schools; moved to Wisconsin and learned the printer's trade in Baraboo, Sauk County; moved to Iowa, established the Gazette in Cedar Falls in 1860, and continued that publication until 1866; enlisted as a private in Company B, Thirty-first Regiment, Iowa Volunteer Infantry, August 12, 1862, and served until January 12, 1863; went to Chicago, Ill., and was engaged as agent of the Northwestern Associated Press until 1869; moved to Sioux City, Iowa, in 1869 and became editor of the Journal; member of the Iowa State senate, 1874-1876; State commissioner of immigration, 1880-1882; appointed United States marshal for the northern district of Iowa by President Chester A. Arthur on January 29, 1883, and was removed by President Grover Cleveland in 1885; elected as a Republican to the Fifty-second and to the three succeeding Congresses (March 4, 1891-March 3, 1899); unsuccessful candidate for renomination in 1898 to the Fifty-sixth Congress; resumed his journalistic activities at Sioux City, Iowa; delegate to the Republican National Conventions of 1876, 1880, 1888, 1908, and 1912; editor and publisher of the Sioux City Journal; died in Sioux City, Woodbury County, Iowa, February 3, 1914; interment in Floyd Cemetery.

**Bibliography:** *DAB*; Wright, Luella M. "Henry A. and George D.

Perkins in the Campaign of 1860." *Iowa Journal of History and Politics* 42 (April 1944): 162-191.

**PERKINS, James Breck,** a Representative from New York; born at St. Croix Falls, Polk County, Wis., November 4, 1847; moved with his parents to Rochester, N.Y., in 1856; attended the public schools; was graduated from the University of Rochester (New York) in 1867; studied law; was admitted to the bar in 1868 and commenced practice in Rochester; city attorney 1874-1880; lived in Paris, France, from 1890 to 1895, and engaged in the study of European literature and in historical research; author of several historical works; returned to Rochester in 1895; served in the State assembly 1898-1900; elected as a Republican to the Fifty-seventh and to the four succeeding Congresses and served from March 4, 1901, until his death; chairman, Committee on Foreign Affairs (Sixty-first Congress); one of the managers appointed by the House of Representatives in 1905 to conduct the impeachment proceedings against Charles Swayne, judge of the United States District Court for the Northern District of Florida; died in Washington, D.C., March 11, 1910; interment in Mount Hope Cemetery, Rochester, N.Y.

**Bibliography:** *DAB.*

**PERKINS, Jared,** a Representative from New Hampshire; born in Unity, Sullivan County, N.H., January 5, 1793; attended the common schools of Unity and Claremont; studied theology; was ordained as a minister in 1824 and served for thirty years; State councilor 1846-1848; served in the State house of representatives in 1850; elected as a Whig to the Thirty-second Congress (March 4, 1851-March 3, 1853); unsuccessful candidate for reelection in 1852 to the Thirty-third Congress; nominated for Governor of New Hampshire in 1854 but died before the election; appointed justice of the peace in 1854 and served until his death in Nashua, N.H., October 15, 1854; interment in West Unity Cemetery, Unity, N.H.

**PERKINS, John, Jr.,** a Representative from Louisiana; born in Natchez, Miss., July 1, 1819; received his early education from private tutors; was graduated from Yale College in 1840 and from the law department of Harvard University in 1842; was admitted to the bar in 1843 and commenced practice in New Orleans, La.; engaged in cotton planting; appointed judge of the circuit court for the district comprising Tensas and Madison Parishes in 1851; elected as a Democrat to the Thirty-third Congress (March 4, 1853-March 3, 1855); was not a candidate for renomination in 1854; chairman of the State secession convention in 1861; served in the Confederate Senate 1862-1865; traveled extensively in Mexico and Europe; returned to the United States in 1878 and spent the remaining years of his life in Louisiana and Canada; died in Baltimore, Md., November 28, 1885; interment in Natchez Cemetery, Natchez, Miss.

**PERKINS, Randolph,** a Representative from New Jersey; born in Dunellen, Middlesex County, N.J., November 30, 1871; moved to Jersey City, N.J., with his parents in 1879; attended the grade and high schools, and Cooper Union School, New York City; studied law; was admitted to the bar in 1893 and commenced practice in Jersey City, N.J.; moved to Westfield, N.J., in 1902, to Woodcliff Lake, N.J., in 1909, and continued the practice of law; mayor of Westfield, 1903-1905; member of the State assembly from 1905 to 1911, serving as speaker in 1907; chairman of the Bergen County Republican committee 1911-1916; elected as a Republican to the Sixty-seventh and to the seven succeeding Congresses and served from March 4, 1921, until his death; chairman, Committee on Coinage, Weights, and Measures (Sixty-ninth through Seventy-first Congresses); was renominated for election to the Seventy-fifth Congress at the time of his death; one of the managers appointed by the House of Representatives in 1933 to conduct the impeachment proceedings against Harold Louderback, judge of the United States District Court for the Northern District of California, and again in 1936 to conduct the impeachment proceedings against Halsted L.

Ritter, judge of the United States District Court for the Southern District of Florida; died in Washington, D.C., May 25, 1936; interment in Fairview Cemetery, West New Brighton, Staten Island, N.Y.

**PERKY, Kirtland Irving,** a Senator from Idaho; born in Smithville, Wayne County, Ohio, February 8, 1867; attended the public schools and graduated from Ohio Northern University at Ada in 1888; studied law at the University of Iowa, Iowa City; was admitted to the bar in 1890 and commenced practice in Wahoo, Saunders County, Nebr.; moved to Albion, Idaho, in 1894; district judge of the fourth judicial district of the State of Idaho in 1901; moved to Boise, Idaho, and continued the practice of law; appointed as a Democrat to the United States Senate to fill the vacancy caused by the death of Weldon B. Heyburn and served from November 18, 1912, to February 5, 1913, when a successor was elected and qualified; resumed the practice of law in Boise; moved to Los Angeles, Calif., in 1923 and continued the practice of law until his death there on January 9, 1939; interment in Forest Lawn Cemetery, Glendale, Calif.

**PERLMAN, Nathan David,** a Representative from New York; born in Poland August 2, 1887; immigrated to the United States in 1891 with his mother, who settled in New York City; attended the public schools and the College of the City of New York; was graduated from New York University Law School in 1907; was admitted to the bar in 1909 and commenced practice in New York City; special deputy attorney general of the State of New York 1912-1914; member of the State assembly 1915-1917; elected as a Republican to the Sixty-sixth Congress to fill the vacancy caused by the resignation of Fiorello H. LaGuardia; reelected to the Sixty-seventh, Sixty-eighth, and Sixty-ninth Congresses and served from November 2, 1920, to March 3, 1927; unsuccessful candidate for reelection in 1926 to the Seventieth Congress; resumed the practice of law; delegate to the New York State Convention to repeal prohibition; magistrate of the city of New York May 1, 1935, to September 1, 1936; appointed justice of the court of special sessions of the city of New York November 26, 1936; reappointed July 1, 1945, and served until his death in New York City, June 29, 1952; interment in Mount Hebron Cemetery, Queens County, N.Y.

**PERRILL, Augustus Leonard,** a Representative from Ohio; born near Moorefield, Hardy County, Va. (now West Virginia), January 20, 1807; in 1816 moved to Ohio with his parents, who settled in Madison Township near Lithopolis, Pickaway County; attended the local schools; taught school near Circleville, Ohio, and then engaged in agricultural pursuits; appointed deputy sheriff in January 1833; elected sheriff in 1834 and served until 1837; member of the State house of representatives 1839-1841; elected as a Democrat to the Twenty-ninth Congress (March 4, 1845-March 3, 1847); unsuccessful candidate for reelection in 1846 to the Thirtieth Congress; resumed agricultural pursuits near Circleville, Ohio; member of the State senate 1858-1863; again served in the State house of representatives 1865-1867; died on his farm near Circleville, Pickaway County, Ohio, June 2, 1882; interment in Forest Cemetery, Circleville, Ohio.

**PERRY, Aaron Fyfe,** a Representative from Ohio; born in Leicester, Vt., January 1, 1815; attended the public schools and Yale Law School; was admitted to the bar of Connecticut in 1838; moved to Columbus, Ohio, where he was admitted to the bar in 1840 and commenced practice; member of the State house of representatives in 1847 and 1848; moved to Cincinnati, Ohio, in 1854 and continued the practice of law; declined appointment as Associate Justice of the United States Supreme Court in 1861 tendered by President Abraham Lincoln; delegate to the Republican National Convention in 1864; elected as a Republican to the Forty-second Congress and served from March 4, 1871, until his resignation in 1872; resumed the practice of his profession and also engaged in literary pursuits;

appointed chief counsel for the Government in the Crédit Mobilier case in 1873; appointed a member of the board of sinking-fund trustees of Cincinnati in 1877 and was president of the board from 1884 to 1892, when he resigned; died in Cincinnati, Ohio, March 11, 1893; interment in Spring Grove Cemetery.

**PERRY, Eli,** a Representative from New York; born in Cambridge, Washington County, N.Y., December 25, 1799; attended the common schools; engaged in business in Albany, N.Y., in 1827 and continued until 1852; member of the Board of Aldermen of Albany for two years; served in the State assembly in 1851; mayor of Albany 1851-1853, 1856-1860, 1862-1866; elected as a Democrat to the Forty-second and Forty-third Congresses (March 4, 1871-March 3, 1875); unsuccessful candidate for reelection in 1874 to the Forty-fourth Congress; died in Albany, Albany County, N.Y., May 17, 1881; interment in Albany Rural Cemetery.

**PERRY, John Jasiel,** a Representative from Maine; born in Portsmouth, N.H., August 2, 1811; moved with his parents to Hebron (now Oxford), Maine, in 1812; attended the common schools and Maine Wesleyan Seminary; deputy sheriff of Oxford County; member of the State house of representatives in 1840, 1842, 1843, and 1872; studied law; was admitted to the bar in 1844 and commenced practice in Oxford; member of the State senate in 1846 and 1847; clerk of the State house of representatives in 1854; elected as a Republican to the Thirty-fourth Congress (March 4, 1855-March 3, 1857); was not a candidate for renomination in 1856; elected to the Thirty-sixth Congress (March 4, 1859-March 3, 1861); was not a candidate for renomination in 1860; member of the peace convention in 1861 held in Washington, D.C., in an effort to devise means to prevent the impending war; editor of the Oxford Democrat from 1860 to 1875 and extensively connected with newspapers, both in and out of the State, as correspondent; member of the State executive council in 1866 and 1867; moved to Portland, Cumberland County, Maine, in 1875 and engaged in the practice of his profession until his death in that city on May 2, 1897; interment in Evergreen Cemetery.

**PERRY, Nehemiah,** a Representative from New Jersey; born in Ridgefield, Fairfield County, Conn., March 30, 1816; educated at the Wesleyan Seminary of Ridgefield; clerked in a store in Norwalk, Conn., and New York City; moved to Newark, N.J., in 1836; engaged in the manufacture of cloth and in the clothing business; member of the State house of assembly in 1850 and 1856 and served as speaker in the latter year; member of the common council in 1852; elected as a Democrat to the Thirty-seventh and Thirty-eighth Congresses (March 4, 1861-March 3, 1865); was not a candidate for renomination in 1864; resumed his former manufacturing pursuits; mayor of Newark in 1873; died in Newark, N.J., November 1, 1881; interment in Mount Pleasant Cemetery.

**PERRY, Thomas Johns,** a Representative from Maryland; born in Cumberland, Md., February 17, 1807; completed preparatory studies; studied law; was admitted to the bar in 1828 and commenced practice in Cumberland, Md.; member of the State house of delegates 1834-1836; elected as a Democrat to the Twenty-ninth Congress (March 4, 1845-March 3, 1847); was not a candidate for renomination in 1846; associate judge of the sixth judicial district of Maryland 1851-1861 and 1864-1871; delegate to the State constitutional convention in 1867; died in Cumberland, Allegany County, Md., June 27, 1871; interment in Rose Hill Cemetery.

**PERRY, William Hayne,** a Representative from South Carolina; born in Greenville, Greenville County, S.C., June 9, 1839; attended Greenville Academy, and was graduated from Furman University at Greenville in 1857; attended South Carolina College (now the University of South Carolina) at Columbia, and was graduated from Harvard University in 1859; studied law in

Greenville; was admitted to the bar in 1861 and commenced practice in Greenville; served as a private and subsequently as lieutenant in the Confederate Cavalry during the Civil War; resumed the practice of law in Greenville in 1865; member of the State constitutional convention in 1865; member of the State house of representatives in 1865 and 1866; solicitor of the eighth judicial circuit of South Carolina 1868-1872; served in the State senate 1880-1884; elected as a Democrat to the Forty-ninth, Fiftieth, and Fifty-first Congresses (March 4, 1885-March 3, 1891); declined to be a candidate for renomination in 1890; resumed the practice of law; died at his home, "San Souci," near Greenville, S.C., July 7, 1902; interment in Christ Church Cemetery, Greenville, S.C.

**PERSON, Seymour Howe,** a Representative from Michigan; born on a farm near Howell, Livingston County, Mich., February 2, 1879; attended the district schools and the Howell public schools; was graduated from the law department of the University of Michigan at Ann Arbor in 1901; was admitted to the bar the same year and commenced practice in Lansing, Mich.; member of the State house of representatives 1915-1921; served in the State senate 1927-1931; delegate to all State conventions for thirty years; elected as a Republican to the Seventy-second Congress (March 4, 1931-March 3, 1933); unsuccessful candidate for reelection in 1932 to the Seventy-third Congress; resumed the practice of his profession; died in Lansing, Mich., on April 7, 1957; interment in Deepdale Cemetery.

**PERSONS, Henry,** a Representative from Georgia; born near Smarrs, Monroe County, Ga., January 30, 1834; moved to Talbot County, Ga., in 1836; attended the Talbotton schools; was graduated from the University of Georgia at Athens in 1855; served as captain of Cavalry in the Third Georgia regiment of the Confederate Army during the Civil War; engaged in agricultural pursuits in Talbot County, Ga.; elected as an Independent Democrat to the Forty-sixth Congress (March 4, 1879-March 3, 1881); unsuccessful candidate for renomination in 1880; returned to Geneva, Ga.; studied law; was admitted to the bar in 1885 and commenced practice in Talbotton, Ga.; ordinary of Talbot County 1898-1910; trustee of the University of Georgia 1894-1910; died in Talbotton, Ga., June 17, 1910; interment in Rose Hill Cemetery.

**PESQUERA, José Lorenzo,** a Resident Commissioner from Puerto Rico; born in Bayamon, P.R., August 10, 1882; was graduated from Provincial Institute of Puerto Rico in 1897; attended the Keystone State Normal School, Kutztown, Pa., in 1901 and 1902; was graduated from the law department of West Virginia University at Morgantown in 1904; was admitted to the bar the same year and commenced practice in Puerto Rico; also engaged in agricultural pursuits and dairying; member of the Puerto Rico House of Representatives 1917-1920; director and president of the Agricultural Association of Puerto Rico; appointed as a Nonpartisan a Resident Commissioner to the United States to fill the vacancy caused by the resignation of Felix Cordova Davila and served from April 15, 1932, until March 3, 1933; was not a candidate for election in 1932; returned to his law practice and agricultural interests; died in Bayamon, P.R., July 25, 1950; interment in Municipal Cemetery.

**PETER, George,** a Representative from Maryland; born in Georgetown, Md. (now the District of Columbia), September 28, 1779; pursued classical studies and was graduated from Georgetown College; at the age of fifteen joined the Maryland troops in the campaign against the Whiskey Rebellion in 1794, but at the request of his parents, was sent home; entered the Army as second lieutenant in the Ninth Infantry in July 1799; transferred to the Artillery, and in May 1808 organized and commanded the first light battery of artillery in the United States; resigned on June 11, 1809; engaged in agricultural pursuits; served as a major of Volunteers in the War of 1812; elected as a Federalist to the Fourteenth Congress to fill the vacancy caused by the resignation of Alexander C. Hanson;

reelected to the Fifteenth Congress, and served from October 7, 1816 to March 3, 1819; served in the Maryland State house of delegates, 1819-1823; elected to the Nineteenth Congress (March 4, 1825-March 3, 1827); unsuccessful candidate for reelection in 1826 to the Twentieth Congress; resumed agricultural activities; commissioner of public works of Maryland in 1855; retired to his plantation; died near Darnestown, Montgomery County, Md., June 22, 1861; interment in Oak Hill Cemetery, Georgetown, D.C.

**PETERS, Andrew James,** a Representative from Massachusetts; born in West Roxbury, Mass., April 3, 1872; attended Hopkinson's and St. Paul's Schools; graduated from Harvard University in 1895 and from the Harvard Law School in 1898; admitted to the bar in 1897 and commenced practice in Boston, Mass.; member of the Massachusetts house of representatives in 1902; served in the Massachusetts senate in 1904 and 1905; served five years in the Massachusetts Militia; elected as a Democrat to the Sixtieth and to the three succeeding Congresses and served from March 4, 1907, until his resignation, effective August 15, 1914; appointed Assistant Secretary of the Treasury and served from August 17, 1914, to March 15, 1917; mayor of Boston 1918-1922; resumed the practice of law; president of the Boston Chamber of Commerce 1926-1928; died in Jamaica Plain, Mass., June 26, 1938; interment in Forest Hills Cemetery.

**PETERS, John Andrew** (uncle of John Andrew Peters [1864-1953]), a Representative from Maine; born in Ellsworth, Hancock County, Maine, October 9, 1822; attended Gorham Academy, and was graduated from Yale College in 1842; studied law; was admitted to the bar in 1844 and commenced practice in Bangor, Maine, in 1844; member of the State senate in 1862 and 1863; served in the State house of representatives in 1864; attorney general of the State 1864-1866; elected as a Republican to the Fortieth, Forty-first, and Forty-second Congresses (March 4, 1867-March 3, 1873); declined to be a candidate for renomination in 1872; judge of the supreme judicial court of Maine 1873-1883 and served as chief justice from 1883 until January 1, 1900, when he resigned; died in Bangor, Penobscot County, Maine, April 2, 1904; interment in Mount Hope Cemetery.

**Bibliography:** *DAB.*

**PETERS, John Andrew** (nephew of John Andrew Peters [1822-1904]), a Representative from Maine; born in Ellsworth, Hancock County, Maine, August 13, 1864; attended the common schools; was graduated from Bowdoin College, Brunswick, Maine, in 1885; studied law; was admitted to the bar and commenced practice in Ellsworth in 1887; judge of the municipal court of Ellsworth 1896-1908; member of the State house of representatives in 1909, 1911, and 1913, serving as speaker in 1913; elected as a Republican to the Sixty-third Congress to fill the vacancy caused by the death of Forrest Goodwin; reelected to the Sixty-fourth and to the three succeeding Congresses and served from September 8, 1913, until his resignation January 2, 1922, to become judge of the United States District Court for Maine, in which capacity he served until his resignation in 1947; delegate at large to the Republican National Convention in 1916; vice president of the board of trustees of Bowdoin College; died in Ellsworth, Maine, August 22, 1953; interment in Woodbine Cemetery.

**PETERS, Mason Summers,** a Representative from Kansas; born near Kearney, Clay County, Mo., September 3, 1844; attended the William Jewell College, Liberty, Mo.; taught in the grammar schools of Clay County, Mo., 1867-1870; clerk of the court of Clinton County, Mo., 1870-1874; studied law; was admitted to the bar in 1875 and commenced practice in Plattsburg, Mo.; moved to Wyandotte County, Kans., in 1886; organized the Union Live Stock Commission Co. in 1895; elected as a Populist to the Fifty-fifth Congress (March 4, 1897-March 3, 1899); was unsuccessful for reelection in 1898 to the Fifty-sixth Congress; resumed his business and professional pursuits in Kansas City, Kans.; died in Kansas City, Mo., February 14, 1914; interment in Forest Hill Cemetery.

**PETERS, Richard, Jr.,** a Delegate from Pennsylvania; born near Philadelphia, Pa., June 22, 1744; graduated from the University of Pennsylvania at Philadelphia in 1761; studied law; admitted to the bar and commenced practice in Philadelphia; register of the admiralty from 1771 until the Revolution; entered the Revolutionary Army and served as captain in 1771; served as secretary of the Continental Board of War from June 13, 1776, to June 8, 1781; member of the Continental Congress in 1782 and 1783; member of the Pennsylvania assembly 1787-1790 and served as speaker; served in the Pennsylvania senate in 1791 and was speaker; judge of the district court of Pennsylvania 1792-1828; died in Philadelphia, Pa., August 22, 1828; interment in St. Peter's Churchyard.

**Bibliography:** *DAB.*

**PETERS, Samuel Ritter,** a Representative from Kansas; born in Walnut Township, near Circleville, Pickaway County, Ohio, August 16, 1842; attended the common schools and the Ohio Wesleyan University at Delaware; enlisted in the Union Army as a private in Company E, Seventy-third Regiment, Ohio Volunteer Infantry, in October 1861 and was mustered out in June 1865, having held successively the ranks of sergeant, second lieutenant, first lieutenant, and captain; was graduated in law from the University of Michigan at Ann Arbor in 1867; was admitted to the bar the same year and commenced practice in Memphis, Mo.; editor of the Memphis Reveille 1868-1873; delegate to the Republican National Convention in 1872; mayor of Memphis in 1873; moved to Marion, Kans., in 1873 and resumed the practice of law; elected a member of the State senate in 1874 and served until his resignation in March 1875; appointed and subsequently elected judge of the ninth judicial district and served from 1875 until 1883, when he resigned; moved to Newton, Harvey County, Kans., in 1876; elected as a Republican to the Forty-eighth and to the three succeeding Congresses (March 4, 1883-March 3, 1891); was not a candidate for renomination in 1890; resumed the practice of law in Newton; member of the board of managers of the State reformatory 1895-1899; postmaster of Newton 1898-1910; editor of the Newton Daily Kansas-Republican in 1899; died in Newton, Kans., April 21, 1910; interment in Greenwood Cemetery.

**PETERSEN, Andrew Nicholas,** a Representative from New York; born near Thisted, Denmark, March 10, 1870; immigrated to the United States in 1873 with his parents, who settled in Boston, Mass.; moved to New York City in 1879; attended the public schools; learned the patternmaker's trade; president of the Brooklyn Foundry Co. 1900-1952; elected as a Republican to the Sixty-seventh Congress (March 4, 1921-March 3, 1923); unsuccessful candidate for reelection in 1922 to the Sixty-eighth Congress; resumed manufacturing pursuits in Brooklyn, N.Y.; died in East Rockaway, N.Y., September 28, 1952; interment in Cypress Hills Abbey, Brooklyn, N.Y.

**PETERSON, Collin Clark,** a Representative from Minnesota; born in Fargo, Cass County, N.D., June 29, 1944; graduated from Glyndon (Minn.) High School, 1962; B.A., Moorhead State University, 1966; entered active duty, United States Army in 1963; released as staff sergeant/specialist 6 in 1969 after service with One Hundred Sixty-eighth Army Band; certified public accountant; member, Minnesota State senate, 1977-1986; unsuccessful candidate for nomination in 1984 to the Ninety-ninth Congress, and in 1986 to the One Hundredth Congress; elected as a Democrat to the One Hundred Second and to the two succeeding Congresses (January 3, 1991-January 3, 1997); is a resident of Detroit Lakes, Minn.

**PETERSON, Douglas Brian (Pete),** a Representative from Florida; born in Omaha, Douglas County, Nebr., June 26, 1935; B.A., University of Tampa, 1976; University of Central Michigan, 1977; entered active duty, United States Air Force in 1954; released as colonel in 1980 after service as an F-4 fighter pilot during the Cuban Missile Crisis and Vietnam; shot down over An Doai, Vietnam, September 10, 1966, and held for six and one half years as a prisoner of war; businessman, CRT Computers, 1984-1990; administrator, specialized treatment program, Dozier School for Boys, 1985-1990; elected as a Democrat to the One Hundred Second and to the two succeeding Congresses (January 3, 1991-January 3, 1997); was not a candidate for reelection in 1996 to the One Hundred Fifth Congress; nominated by President William J. Clinton to be Ambassador to Vietnam, May 23, 1996; is a resident of Marianna, Fla.

**PETERSON, Hugh,** a Representative from Georgia; born on a farm near Ailey, Montgomery County, Ga., August 21, 1898; attended the public schools, Brewton Parker Institute, Mount Vernon-Ailey, Ga., and the University of Georgia at Athens; studied law; was admitted to the bar in 1921 and commenced practice in Mount Vernon, Ga.; also engaged in agricultural pursuits and editorial work; served as mayor of Ailey, Ga., in 1922; member of the State house of representatives 1923-1931; served in the State senate in 1931 and 1932; elected as a Democrat to the Seventh-fourth and to the five succeeding Congresses (January 3, 1935-January 3, 1947); chairman, Committee on Elections No. 3 (Seventy-seventh and Seventy-eighth Congresses), Committee on Territories (Seventy-ninth Congress); unsuccessful for renomination in 1946; practiced law in Ailey, Ga.; died in Sylva, N.C., October 3, 1961; interment in the Peterson family cemetery, Ailey, Ga.

**PETERSON, James Hardin,** a Representative from Florida; born in Batesburg, Lexington County, S.C., February 11, 1894; moved to Lakeland, Fla., in 1903; attended the public schools; was graduated from the law department of the University of Florida at Gainesville in 1914; admitted to the Florida bar in 1914 and commenced practice in Lakeland in 1915; law clerk in United States General Land Office in 1914; city attorney of Lakeland, Fla., in 1916, 1917, and 1919-1932, of Frostproof, Fla., 1918-1929, of Lake Wales, Fla., 1920-1930, and of Eagle Lake, Fla., 1923-1933; during the First World War served as a chief yeoman in the United States Navy, 1917-1919; prosecuting attorney and county solicitor of Polk County, Fla., 1921-1932; special counsel for the Florida State department of agriculture, 1930-1932; elected as a Democrat to the Seventy-third and to the eight succeeding Congresses (March 4, 1933-January 3, 1951); chairman, Committee on Public Lands (Seventy-eighth, Seventy-ninth, and Eighty-first Congresses); was not a candidate for renomination in 1950 to the Eighty-second Congress; resumed the practice of law in Lakeland, Fla.; special counsel for the Territorial Government of Guam; chairman of Commission on Federal Application of Laws to Guam; served as chairman and vice chairman of the board of directors, First State Bank of Lakeland; resided in Lakeland, Fla., where he died on March 28, 1978; interment in Roselawn Cemetery.

**PETERSON, John Barney** (cousin of Horatio Clifford Claypool and Harold Kile Claypool), a Representative from Indiana; born near Lowell, Lake County, Ind., July 4, 1850; attended the public schools; studied law; was admitted to the bar in 1870 and commenced practice in Crown Point, Lake County, Ind.; prosecuting attorney of the thirty-first judicial circuit 1880-1884; elected as a Democrat to the Sixty-third Congress (March 4, 1913-March 3, 1915); unsuccessful candidate for reelection in 1914 to the Sixty-fourth Congress; resumed the practice of law in Crown Point, Ind.; also engaged in banking and served as president of the Commercial Bank, Crown Point, Ind., and of the First Calumet Trust & Savings Bank of East Chicago, Ind., until 1939, when he retired; died in Crown Point, Ind., July 16, 1944; interment in Maplewood Cemetery.

**PETERSON, Morris Blaine,** a Representative from Utah; born in Ogden, Weber County, Utah, March 26, 1906; attended the public schools and Weber College; graduated from the University of Utah in 1931 and from Georgetown Law School in 1938; law clerk to Justice Eugene E. Pratt of the Utah State Supreme Court; engaged in the private practice of law in 1941; served in the State legislature 1955-1957; Weber County attorney; elected as a Democrat to the Eighty-seventh Congress (January 3, 1961-January 3, 1963); unsuccessful candidate for reelection in 1962 to the Eighty-eighth Congress; member, Great Salt Lake Authority, Utah, 1968-1969; chairman, Weber County, Utah, Taxpayers Association; special consultant to director of Food for Peace Program, 1963; was a resident of Ogden, Utah until his death there July 15, 1985; interment in Ogden City Cemetery, Utah.

**PETRI, Thomas Evert,** a Representative from Wisconsin; born in Marinette, Wis., May 28, 1940; attended the public schools of Fond du Lac, Wis.; graduated from Lowell P. Goodrich High School, 1958; B.A., Harvard University, 1962; J.D., Harvard University Law School, 1965; law clerk to United States Judge James E. Doyle, 1965; Peace Corps volunteer in Somalia, 1966-1967; director, crime studies, National Advisory Council on Executive Organization, 1969; admitted to the Wisconsin bar in 1965 and commenced practice in Fond du Lac in 1970; member, Wisconsin State senate, 1972-1979; delegate to the Republican State conventions, 1973 to present; unsuccessful candidate in 1974 for election to the United States Senate; elected as a Republican to the Ninety-sixth Congress, April 3, 1979, by special election to fill the vacancy caused by the death of William A. Steiger; reelected to the eight succeeding Congresses and served from April 3, 1979, to January 3, 1997; is a resident of Fond du Lac, Wis.

**PETRIE, George,** a Representative from New York; born at Little Falls, Herkimer County, N.Y., September 8, 1793; attended the common schools; elected as an Independent Democrat to the Thirtieth Congress (March 4, 1847-March 3, 1849); employed in the Post Office Department, Washington, D.C., from January 1, 1869, until August 31, 1875, when he resigned; died at Little Falls, N.Y., May 8, 1879; interment in Church Street Cemetery.

**PETRIKIN, David,** a Representative from Pennsylvania; born in Bellefonte, Centre County, Pa., December 1, 1788; completed preparatory studies; studied medicine and was admitted to practice; moved to Danville (then in Columbia County), Pa., and engaged in the practice of medicine; during the War of 1812 served as a surgeon with the Second Regiment of the Pennsylvania Riflemen; after the war returned to Danville, Pa., and continued the practice of medicine; also erected and operated a woolen mill; elected prothonotary of Columbia County March 15, 1821; member of the Pennsylvania house of representatives; served as postmaster of Danville from February 1, 1834, to March 21, 1837; elected as a Democrat to the Twenty-fifth and Twenty-sixth Congresses (March 4, 1837-March 3, 1841); chairman, Committee on Public Buildings and Grounds (Twenty-sixth Congress); died in Catawissa, Columbia County, Pa., March 1, 1847; interment in Petrikin Cemetery, Danville, Pa., which was later converted into a memorial park.

**PETTENGILL, Samuel Barrett,** (nephew of William Horace Clagett), a Representative from Indiana; born in Portland, Oreg., January 19, 1886; in 1892 moved to Vermont with his father, who settled on a farm in Grafton, Windham County; attended the common schools; was graduated from Vermont Academy at Saxtons River in 1904, from Middlebury College, Middlebury, Vt., in 1908, and from the law department of Yale University in 1911; was admitted to the bar in 1912 and commenced practice in South Bend, Ind.; member of the board of education of South Bend, 1926-1928;

elected as a Democrat to the Seventy-second and to the three succeeding Congresses (March 4, 1931-January 3, 1939); was not a candidate for renomination in 1938 to the Seventy-sixth Congress; resumed the practice of law; newspaper columnist 1939-1948; vice president and general counsel of the Transportation Association of America, 1943-1945; national radio commentator, 1946-1948; attorney for the Pure Oil Co., Chicago, Ill., 1949-1956; consultant, the Coe Foundation, 1956-1965; resided at his boyhood farm near Grafton, Vt.; died in Springfield, Vt., March 20, 1974; interment in Grafton Village Cemetery, Grafton, Vt.

**Bibliography:** Pettengill, Samuel Barrett. *My Story.* Edited by Helen M. Pettengill. Grafton, Vt.: H.M. Pettengill, 1979.

**PETTIBONE, Augustus Herman,** a Representative from Tennessee; born in Bedford, Cuyahoga County, Ohio, January 21, 1835; was graduated from Hiram College, Ohio, and from the University of Michigan at Ann Arbor in 1859; studied law; was admitted to the bar in 1860 and commenced practice in La Crosse, Wis.; enlisted in the Union Army as a private in 1861; promoted to second lieutenant, captain, and major in the Twentieth Regiment, Wisconsin Volunteer Infantry; continued the practice of law in Greeneville in 1865; alderman of Greeneville 1866-1868; attorney general for the first judicial circuit of Tennessee in 1869 and 1870; appointed assistant United States district attorney for the eastern district of Tennessee December 27, 1871, and served until 1880; unsuccessful candidate for election in 1878 to the Forty-sixth Congress; delegate to the Republican National Convention in 1880; elected as a Republican to the Forty-seventh, Forty-eighth, and Forty-ninth Congresses (March 4, 1881-March 3, 1887); was not a candidate for renomination in 1886; resumed the practice of law; member of the State house of representatives 1897-1899; appointed special agent of the General Land Office and served from July 17, 1899, to January 31, 1905, when he resigned; died in Nashville, Tenn., November 26, 1918; interment in Nashville National Cemetery, Madison, Davidson County, Tenn.

**PETTIGREW, Ebenezer,** a Representative from North Carolina; born near Plymouth, Tyrrell County, N.C., March 10, 1783; studied under tutors at home and later attended the University of North Carolina at Chapel Hill; engaged in planting; member of the North Carolina State senate in 1809 and 1810; elected as a Whig to the Twenty-fourth Congress (March 4, 1835-March 3, 1837); resumed agricultural pursuits; died at Magnolia plantation on Lake Scuppernong, Tyrrell County, N.C., July 8, 1848; interment in the family cemetery.

**Bibliography:** Wall, Bennett H. "Ebenezer Pettigrew's Efforts to Control the Marketing of his Crops." *Agricultural History* 27 (October 1953): 123-132.

**PETTIGREW, Richard Franklin,** a Delegate from the Territory of Dakota and a Senator from South Dakota; born in Ludlow, Windsor County, Vt., July 23, 1848; moved with his parents to Wisconsin in 1854; attended the public schools and the Evansville (Wis.) Academy; entered Beloit (Wis.) College in 1864; spent one year teaching school and studying law in Iowa; entered the law department of the University of Wisconsin at Madison in 1867; went to Dakota Territory in 1869 in the employ of a United States deputy surveyor; settled in Sioux Falls; was admitted to the bar about 1871; practiced law, engaged in surveying and the real estate business; member of the Territorial house of representatives in 1872; served in the Territorial council in 1877 and 1879; elected as a Republican a Delegate to the Forty-seventh Congress (March 4, 1881-March 3, 1883); unsuccessful candidate for reelection in 1882 to the Forty-eighth Congress; member of the Territorial council in 1885; upon the admission of South Dakota as a State into the Union was elected as a Republican to the United States Senate in 1889; reelected in 1895, and served from November 2, 1889 to March 3, 1901; unsuccessful candidate for reelection in 1900; chairman,

Committee on Indian Affairs (Fifty-fourth and Fifty-fifth Congresses); engaged in the practice of law in New York City; returned to Sioux Falls and was active in politics and business until his death there on October 5, 1926; interment in Woodlawn Cemetery.

**Bibliography:** *DAB*; Hendrickson, Kenneth E., Jr. "The Public Career of Richard F. Pettigrew of South Dakota, 1848-1926." Ph.D. dissertation, University of Oklahoma, 1962; Olson, Gary D. "Dakota Resources: The Richard F. Pettigrew Papers." *South Dakota History* 12 (Summer/Fall 1982): 182-187; Pettigrew, Richard F. *Imperial Washington: The Story of American Public Life from 1870 to 1920.* 1922. Reprint. New York: Arno Press, 1970.

**PETTIS, Jerry Lyle** (husband of Shirley Neil Pettis), a Representative from California; born in Phoenix, Maricopa County, Ariz., July 18, 1916; received an elementary and secondary education in Arizona and California; graduated from Pacific Union College, Angwin, Calif., in 1938; engaged in graduate work at the University of Southern California and the University of Denver, 1939-1941; founder of Magnetic Tape Duplicators of Los Angeles; founder of Audio-Digest Foundation, a subsidiary of California Medical Association; founder of a consultant firm for radio, television, and the motion picture industry; flight instructor, search and rescue pilot, Colorado Wing Civil Air Patrol; pilot with Air Transport Command, Pacific Theater, 1941-1946; professor of economics; vice president for development and chairman of the Board of Councilors, Loma Linda University, Loma Linda, Calif., 1948-1961; special assistant to the president of United Air Lines, Chicago, Ill.; ranch owner in Pauma Valley, Calif.; elected as a Republican to the Ninetieth Congress; reelected to the four succeeding Congresses, and served from January 3, 1967 until his death in a private aircraft crash in Banning, Calif., February 14, 1975; interment in Montecito Memorial Park, San Bernardino, Calif.

**Bibliography:** Wood, Miriam. *Congressman Jerry L. Pettis: His Story.* Mountain View, Calif.: Pacific Press Publishing Association, 1977.

**PETTIS, Shirley Neil** (wife of Jerry Lyle Pettis, now Shirley Pettis-Roberson), a Representative from California; born in Mountain View, Santa Clara County, Calif., July 12, 1924; attended the elementary schools, Berkeley, Calif., 1931-1932, and Berrien Springs, Mich., 1933-1937; graduated from Andrews University Academy, 1942; attended Andrews University, Berrien Springs, Mich., 1942-1943, and the University of California, Berkeley, 1944-1945; secretary-treasurer, Pettis, Inc., co-founder of Audio-Digest and Magnetic Duplicators, 1953-1967; Washington, D.C. correspondent and columnist for the San Bernardino (Calif.) Sun-Telegram, 1967-1970; elected as a Republican to the Ninety-fourth Congress, April 29, 1975, by special election to fill the vacancy caused by the death of her husband, Jerry L. Pettis; reelected to the Ninety-fifth Congress, and served from April 29, 1975 to January 3, 1979; was not a candidate for reelection in 1978 to the Ninety-sixth Congress; vice president, Women's Research and Education Institute, Washington, D.C., 1980-1981; member of the Arms Control and Disarmament Commission, 1981-1983, and the Commission on Presidential Scholars, 1990-1992; member, board of directors, Kemper National Insurance Companies, 1979 to present; is a resident of Rancho Mirage, Calif.

**PETTIS, Solomon Newton,** a Representative from Pennsylvania; born in Lenox, Ashtabula County, Ohio, October 10, 1827; completed preparatory studies; studied law; was admitted to the bar in 1848 and commenced practice in Meadville, Crawford County, Pa.; associate justice of the Territory of Colorado in 1861 and 1862; returned to Meadville, Pa., and continued the practice of his profession; elected as a Republican to the Fortieth Congress to fill the vacancy caused by the death of Darwin A. Finney, and served from December 7, 1868 to March 3, 1869; unsuccessful candidate for reelection in 1868 to the Forty-first Congress; resumed the practice of law in Meadville; appointed Minister to Bolivia on September 4, 1878, and served until November 1, 1879; again engaged in the practice of law until his death in Meadville, Pa., September 18, 1900; interment in Greendale Cemetery.

**PETTIS, Spencer Darwin,** a Representative from Missouri; born in Culpeper County, Va., in 1802; completed preparatory studies; studied law; was admitted to the bar about 1824 and commenced practice in Fayette, Howard County, Mo.; held various local offices; appointed secretary of state on July 22, 1826, and served until December 31, 1828, when he resigned; elected as a Jacksonian to the Twenty-first and Twenty-second Congresses, and served from March 4, 1829 until his death; during the campaign of 1830 his feeling regarding the United States bank issue precipitated a quarrel and subsequently a duel with Major Thomas Biddle, in which both fell mortally wounded; Pettis died the next day, August 28, 1831, in St. Louis; interment in the Old City Cemetery, St. Louis, Mo.

**PETTIT, Charles,** a Delegate from Pennsylvania; born near Amwell, Hunterdon County, N.J., in 1736; received an English training; studied law; was admitted to the bar in 1770 but did not commence practice until 1773; deputy secretary of the Province of New Jersey, 1769-1778; clerk of the council; clerk of the supreme court and of the pleas court; surrogate and keeper and register of the records of the Province of New Jersey; appointed aide-de-camp to Governor William Franklin, March 8, 1771; secretary of state of New Jersey and aide to Governor William Livingston, October 8, 1776; assistant adjutant general on the staff of General Nathanael Greene in the Revolutionary Army from 1778 until his resignation in 1781; became an importing merchant in Philadelphia; member of the Pennsylvania house of representatives in 1783 and 1784; Member of the Continental Congress from 1785 to 1787; died in Philadelphia, Pa., September 3, 1806.

**Bibliography:** *DAB.*

**PETTIT, John,** a Representative and a Senator from Indiana; born in Sackets Harbor, N.Y., June 24, 1807; completed preparatory studies; studied law and was admitted to the bar in 1831; moved to LaFayette, Tippecanoe County, Ind., where he commenced practice in 1838; member, Indiana State house of representatives, 1838-1839; United States district attorney, 1839-1843; elected as a Democrat to the Twenty-eighth and to the two succeeding Congresses (March 4, 1843-March 3, 1849); unsuccessful candidate for renomination in 1848 to the Thirty-first Congress; delegate to the State constitutional convention in 1850; presidential elector on the Democratic ticket in 1852; elected as a Democrat to the United States Senate to fill the vacancy caused by the death of James Whitcomb, and served from January 11, 1853 to March 3, 1855; unsuccessful candidate for reelection in 1854; chairman, Committee on Private Land Claims (Thirty-third Congress); chief justice of the United States courts in the Territory of Kansas, 1859-1861; judge of the supreme court of Indiana, 1870-1877; died in LaFayette, Ind., January 17, 1877; interment in Greenbush Cemetery.

**PETTIT, John Upfold,** a Representative from Indiana; born in Fabius, Onondaga County, N.Y., September 11, 1820; received an academic education; attended Hamilton College, Clinton, N.Y., and was graduated from Union College, Schenectady, N.Y., in 1839; studied law; was admitted to the bar in 1841 and commenced practice in Wabash, Wabash County, Ind.; American consul to Maranham, Brazil, 1850-1853; elected as a Republican to the Thirty-fourth, Thirty-fifth, and Thirty-sixth Congresses (March 4, 1855-March 3, 1861); chairman, Committee on Expenditures in the Post Office Department (Thirty-fourth Congress); member of the State house of representatives in 1865 and served as speaker; judge of the twenty-seventh judicial district of Indiana 1872-1880; died in Wabash, Ind., March 21, 1881; interment in Falls Cemetery.

**PETTUS, Edmund Winston,** a Senator from Alabama; born in Limestone County, Ala., July 6, 1821; attended the common schools of Alabama and Clinton College in Smith County, Tenn.; studied law; was admitted to the bar in 1842 and commenced practice in Gainesville, Ala.; elected solicitor for the seventh circuit in 1844; served as a lieutenant in the Mexican War; again solicitor 1853-1855; elected judge of the seventh circuit in 1855 but resigned in 1858 and moved to Dallas County; resumed the practice of law; served as envoy from Alabama to Mississippi during the formation of the Southern Confederacy; entered the Confederate Army as major in 1861; was made a brigadier general of Infantry in 1863 and served until the close of the Civil War; returned to Selma, Ala., and practiced law; elected as a Democrat to the United States Senate in 1897; reelected in 1903 and served from March 4, 1897, until his death at Hot Springs, Madison County, N.C., July 27, 1907; interment in Live Oak Cemetery, Selma, Ala.

**Bibliography:** *DAB.*

**PEYSER, Peter A.,** a Representative from New York; born in Cedarhurst, Long Island, N.Y., September 7, 1921; attended the Cedarhurst and New York City public schools; graduated from Dwight Preparatory School, 1939; B.A., Colgate University, Hamilton, N.Y., 1943; enlisted in the United States Army as a private in 1943 and served in the European Theater; nine months of combat with the Ninety-ninth Infantry Division in the Battles of the Bulge, December 1944, and Remagen, March 1945; occupation duty in Germany with First Infantry Division; discharged in 1946, accepted commission as second lieutenant with the Seventh Regiment, New York National Guard, and later with rank of captain; manager of an insurance agency in White Plains, N.Y., and New York City, 1956-1970; mayor of the Village of Irvington (N.Y.), 1963-1970; elected as a Republican to the Ninety-second and to the two succeeding Congresses (January 3, 1971-January 3, 1977); was not a candidate in 1976 for reelection to the House of Representatives, but was an unsuccessful candidate for nomination to United States Senate; announced his affiliation with the Democratic Party in April 1977; self-employed as a pension consultant; elected as a Democrat to the Ninety-sixth and Ninety-seventh Congresses (January 3, 1979-January 3, 1983); unsuccessful candidate for reelection in 1982 to the Ninety-eighth Congress; national director, Gabelli Asset Management Company; is a resident of Irvington, N.Y.

**PEYSER, Theodore Albert,** a Representative from New York; born in Charleston, W.Va., February 18, 1873; attended the public schools; engaged in various occupations until 1893, when he moved to Cincinnati, Ohio, and became employed as a traveling salesman, in which capacity he served until 1900; moved to New York City in 1900 and engaged in the life insurance business; elected as a Democrat to the Seventy-third and to the two succeeding Congresses, and served from March 4, 1933 until his death in New York City, August 8, 1937; interment in United Cemetery, Cincinnati, Ohio.

**PEYTON, Balie** (brother of Joseph Hopkins Peyton), a Representative from Tennessee; born near Gallatin, Tenn., November 26, 1803; completed preparatory studies; studied law; was admitted to the bar and commenced practice in Gallatin in 1824; elected as a Jacksonian to the Twenty-third Congress and reelected as a Hugh L. White supporter to the Twenty-fourth Congress (March 4, 1833-March 3, 1837); resumed the practice of law; moved to New Orleans in 1841, having been appointed United States attorney for the eastern district of Louisiana, which position he held for four years; served as aide-de-camp on the staff of General William J. Worth during the Mexican War; appointed as Minister to Chile by President Zachary Taylor and served from August 9, 1849, to September 14, 1853, when he resigned; moved to San Francisco, Calif., in 1853 and continued the practice of law; prosecuting attorney of San Francisco from 1853 until 1859; returned to Gallatin, Tenn., in 1859 and resumed the practice of law; presidential elector on the Constitutional Union ticket of John Bell and Edward Everett in 1860; unsuccessful candidate for election in 1866 to the Fortieth Congress; member of the Tennessee State senate, 1869-1871; resumed the practice of law; died on his farm near Gallatin, Sumner County, Tenn., August 18, 1878; interment in the family burying ground on his estate.

**PEYTON, Joseph Hopkins** (brother of Balie Peyton), a Representative from Tennessee; born near Gallatin, Sumner County, Tenn., May 20, 1808; completed preparatory studies and was graduated from college in 1837; studied medicine and practiced; held various local offices; member of the State senate of Tennessee in 1840; elected as a Whig to the Twenty-eighth and Twenty-ninth Congresses and served from March 4, 1843, until his death near Gallatin, Tenn., November 11, 1845; interment in the family burying ground near Gallatin, Sumner County, Tenn.

**PEYTON, Samuel Oldham,** a Representative from Kentucky; born in Bullitt County, Ky., January 8, 1804; completed preparatory studies; graduated from the medical department of Transylvania University, Lexington, Ky., in 1827 and began practice in Hartford, Ohio County, Ky.; member of the Kentucky house of representatives in 1835; elected as a Democrat to the Thirtieth Congress (March 4, 1847-March 3, 1849); unsuccessful candidate for reelection in 1848 to the Thirty-first Congress; elected to the Thirty-fifth and Thirty-sixth Congresses (March 4, 1857-March 3, 1861); unsuccessful candidate for renomination in 1860; resumed the practice of medicine; died in Hartford, Ky., January 4, 1870; interment in Oakwood Cemetery.

**PFEIFER, Joseph Lawrence,** a Representative from New York; born in Brooklyn, Kings County, N.Y., February 6, 1892; attended St. Nicholas Parochial School, St. Leonard's Academy, and St. Francis College, Brooklyn, N.Y.; was graduated from Long Island (N.Y.) Medical College in 1914; was licensed to practice the same year; lecturer and author on surgical topics; during the First World War served on the medical advisory board, instructing medical officers going overseas; elected as a Democrat to the Seventy-fourth and to the seven succeeding Congresses (January 3, 1935-January 3, 1951); unsuccessful candidate for renomination in 1950 to the Eighty-second Congress; resumed the practice of medicine; retired; resided in Brooklyn, N.Y., where he died April 19, 1974; interment in St. John's Cemetery, Middle Village, N.Y.

**PFEIFFER, William Louis,** a Representative from New York; born in Buffalo, Erie County, N.Y., May 29, 1907; attended the public schools and graduated from Tech High School; timekeeper, American Radiator Co.; studied accounting; chief aide to New York State Republican Congressional Committee in 1938; member of New York State journal clerk's staff in 1939 and 1940; secretary of Erie County New York Republican committee in 1941 and 1942; county personnel officer of Erie County Board of Supervisors in 1942 and 1943; executive assistant to New York State comptroller 1943-1946; deputy comptroller of New York State 1946-1948; elected as a Republican to the Eighty-first Congress (January 3, 1949-January 3, 1951); was not a candidate for renomination in 1950; chairman of New York State Republican committee 1949-1953; director and chairman of the executive committee, Bank of North America, New York City, 1952-1966; Albany Savings Bank, trustee, 1955-1982, president, 1967-1971, chairman and chief executive officer, 1971-1975; manager of the gubernatorial campaigns of Nelson Rockefeller, 1962 and 1966; was a resident of Kattskill Bay, N.Y., until his death in Glens Falls, N.Y., on July 22, 1985; interment in Pineview Cemetery, Glens Falls, N.Y.

**PFOST, Gracie Bowers,** a Representative from Idaho; born in Harrison, Boone County, Ark., March 12, 1906; moved with her parents to a farm in the Boise Valley, Idaho, in 1911; attended the public schools and graduated from Link's Business University, Boise, Idaho, in 1929; chemist for milk products company for two years; deputy county clerk, auditor, and recorder of Canyon County, Idaho, 1929-1939; treasurer of Canyon County 1941-1951; engaged in the real estate business in Nampa, Idaho, in 1951 and 1952; delegate to the Democratic National Conventions in 1944, 1948, 1952, 1956, and 1960; unsuccessful Democratic candidate for Congress in 1950; elected as a Democrat to the Eighty-third and to the four succeeding Congresses (January 3, 1953-January 3, 1963); was not a candidate for renomination in 1962 to the Eighty-eighth Congress, but was an unsuccessful candidate for the United States Senate; Special Assistant for Elderly Housing, Federal Housing Administration, Washington, D.C., from June 1963 until her death in Johns Hopkins Hospital, Baltimore, Md., August 11, 1965; interment in Meridian Cemetery, Meridian, Idaho.

**PHEIFFER, William Townsend,** a Representative from New York; born in Purcell, Indian Territory (now Oklahoma), July 15, 1898; attended the public schools of Purcell, Ardmore, and Oklahoma City, Okla., and the University of Southern California at Los Angeles; during the First World War served as a private in the Cavalry, United States Army, in 1918; LL.B., University of Oklahoma School of Law, Norman, 1919; was admitted to the bar the same year and practiced law in Sayre, Okla., 1923-1926; moved to Amarillo, Tex., in 1926 and continued the practice of law until 1939, when he moved to New York City; delegate to the Republican National Convention of 1932, and to the Republican State conventions in 1936 and 1942; elected as a Republican to the Seventy-seventh Congress (January 3, 1941-January 3, 1943); unsuccessful candidate for reelection in 1942 to the Seventy-eighth Congress; entered the United States Army as a captain of Cavalry and served from March 12, 1943, to April 22, 1944; appointed counsel for the Petroleum Administration for War, Washington, D.C., on August 1, 1944, and served until February 8, 1945, when he resumed the private practice of law; executive assistant to the chairman of the Republican National Committee, 1945-1948; appointed by President Dwight D. Eisenhower as Ambassador to the Dominican Republic on May 28, 1953, and served until June 1957; was a resident of New York City until his death there on August 16, 1986.

**PHELAN, James,** a Representative from Tennessee; born in Aberdeen, Monroe County, Miss., December 7, 1856; moved with his father to Memphis, Tenn., in 1867; attended private schools and the Kentucky Military Institute near Frankfort in 1871; entered the University of Leipzig, Saxony, in 1874 and was graduated in February 1878; returned to Memphis; studied law; was admitted to the bar and commenced practice in 1881; elected as a Democrat to the Fiftieth and Fifty-first Congresses and served from March 4, 1887, until his death in Nassau, Bahama Islands, on January 30, 1891; interment in Elmwood Cemetery, Memphis, Tenn.

**Bibliography:** *DAB.*

**PHELAN, James Duval,** a Senator from California; born in San Francisco, Calif., April 20, 1861; graduated from St. Ignatius University, San Francisco, in 1881; studied law at the University of California at Berkeley; engaged in banking; mayor of San Francisco from 1897 to 1902; president of Relief and Red Cross Funds after the San Francisco earthquake disaster of April 1906; elected as a Democrat to the United States Senate in 1914, and served from March 4, 1915 to March 3, 1921; unsuccessful candidate for reelection in 1920; chairman, Committee on Railroads (Sixty-fourth Congress), Committee on Irrigation and Reclamation of Arid Lands (Sixty-fifth Congress); traveled extensively in 1921 and 1922; chairman of the board of directors of the United Bank and Trust Company of San Francisco; art collector; died at his country estate "Villa Montalvo," Saratoga, Santa Clara County, Calif., August 7, 1930; interment in the family mausoleum in Holy Cross Cemetery, San Mateo County, near San Francisco, Calif.

**Bibliography:** *DAB*; Hennings, Robert E. *James D. Phelan and the Wilson Progressives of California.* New York: Garland Publishing Co., 1985; Walsh, James P. "James Phelan's Montalvo: Many Accepted, One Declined." *Southern California Quarterly* 58 (Spring 1976): 95-112.

**PHELAN, Michael Francis,** a Representative from Massachusetts; born in Lynn, Essex County, Mass., October 22, 1875; attended the public schools; graduated from Lynn Classical High School, from the academic department of Harvard University in 1897, and from the law department of the same university in 1900; was admitted to the bar in 1900 and commenced practice in Lynn; member of the Massachusetts house of representatives in 1905 and 1906; elected as a Democrat to the Sixty-third and to the three succeeding Congresses (March 4, 1913-March 3, 1921); chairman, Committee on Banking and Currency (Sixty-fifth Congress); unsuccessful candidate for reelection in 1920 to the Sixty-seventh Congress; practiced law in Lynn and Boston, Mass., and Washington, D.C.; member of the Merrimac Valley Sewage Commission in 1937; appointed a member of the Massachusetts Labor Relations Board in 1937 and served until his death in Boston, Mass., October 12, 1941; interment in St. Mary's Cemetery, Lynn, Mass.

**PHELPS, Charles Edward,** a Representative from Maryland; born in Guilford, Windham County, Vt., May 1, 1833; moved with his parents to New Jersey in 1837 and to Maryland in 1841; pursued classical studies in St. Timothy's Hall, near Catonsville, Md., and was graduated from Princeton College in 1852; attended the law department of Harvard University; was admitted to the bar and commenced practice in Baltimore, Md., in 1855; elected a member of the city council in 1860; entered the Union Army on August 20, 1862, as lieutenant colonel of the Seventh Regiment, Maryland Volunteers; was promoted to colonel, April 13, 1864; awarded the Congressional Medal of Honor on March 30, 1898, for action during the Spotsylvania (Va.) campaign, May 8, 1864; elected as an Unconditional Unionist to the Thirty-ninth Congress and as a Conservative to the Fortieth Congress (March 4, 1865-March 3, 1869); resumed the practice of law in Baltimore, Md.; served as commissioner of public schools; judge on the supreme bench of the city of Baltimore from 1882 until 1908; member of the law faculty of the University of Maryland, 1884-1907; died in Walbrook, Baltimore, Md., December 27, 1908; interment in Woodlawn Cemetery, Baltimore, Md.

**Bibliography:** *DAB.*

**PHELPS, Darwin,** a Representative from Pennsylvania; born in East Granby, Conn., April 17, 1807; was left an orphan at an early age and went to live with his grandparents in Portage, Ohio, where he completed preparatory studies; attended Western University, Pittsburgh, Pa.; studied law in Pittsburgh, Pa.; admitted to the bar and commenced practice in Kittanning, Pa., in 1835; member of the board of trustees of Kittanning Academy; member of the town council in 1841 and 1848; burgess in 1844, 1845, 1849, 1852, 1855, 1858, 1859, and 1861; unsuccessful Republican candidate for auditor general in 1856; delegate to the Republican National Convention in 1860; major of the Twenty-second Regiment, Pennsylvania Volunteer Militia, in 1862; member of the Pennsylvania house of representatives in 1865; elected as a Republican to the Forty-first Congress (March 4, 1869-March 3, 1871); was not a candidate for renomination in 1870; died in Kittanning, Pa., on December 14, 1879; interment in Kittanning Cemetery.

**PHELPS, Elisha** (father of John Smith Phelps), a Representative from Connecticut; born in Simsbury, Hartford County, Conn., November 16, 1779; was graduated from Yale College in 1800 and from Litchfield (Conn.) Law School; was admitted to the bar in 1803 and began practice in Simsbury; member of the State house of representatives in 1807, 1812, and 1814-1818; elected to the Sixteenth Congress (March 4, 1819-March 3, 1821); again a member of the State house of representatives in 1821 and served as speaker; served in the State senate 1822-1824; elected to the Nineteenth and Twentieth Congresses (March 4, 1825-March 3, 1829); declined to be a candidate for renomination in 1828; State comptroller 1831-1837; again a member of the State house of representatives in 1829 and 1835 and served as speaker in 1829; appointed a commissioner to revise and codify the State laws in 1835; died in Simsbury, Conn., April 6, 1847; interment in Hop Meadow Cemetery.

**PHELPS, James** (son of Lancelot Phelps), a Representative from Connecticut; born in Colebrook, Litchfield County, Conn., January 12, 1822; attended the public schools, the Episcopal Academy, Cheshire, Conn., Trinity College, Hartford, Conn., and the law department of Yale College; was admitted to the bar in 1845 and commenced practice in Essex, Conn.; member of the State house of representatives in 1853, 1854, and 1856; served in the State senate in 1858 and 1859; judge of the superior court of Connecticut 1863-1873; judge of the supreme court of errors of the State from 1873 until his resignation in 1875; elected as a Democrat to the Forty-fourth and to the three succeeding Congresses (March 4, 1875-March 3, 1883); declined to be a candidate for renomination in 1882; resumed the practice of law; again judge of the superior court 1885-1892; resumed the practice of his profession and also engaged in banking; delegate to several State conventions; died in Essex, Middlesex County, Conn., January 15, 1900; interment in River View Cemetery.

**PHELPS, John Smith** (son of Elisha Phelps), a Representative from Missouri; born in Simsbury, Hartford County, Conn., December 22, 1814; attended the common schools and was graduated from Trinity College, Hartford, Conn., in 1832; studied law; was admitted to the bar in 1835 and commenced practice in Simsbury; moved to Springfield, Greene County, Mo., in 1837; member of the Missouri State house of representatives in 1840; elected as a Democrat to the Twenty-ninth and to the eight succeeding Congresses (March 4, 1845-March 3, 1863); chairman, Committee on Ways and Means (Thirty-fifth Congress); was not a candidate for renomination in 1862 to the Thirty-eighth Congress; during the Civil War enlisted as a private in Captain Coleman's Company of Missouri Infantry; promoted to lieutenant colonel on October 2, 1861, and to colonel, December 19, 1861; mustered out on May 13, 1862; appointed by President Abraham Lincoln in July 1862 as Military Governor of Arkansas; resumed the practice of his profession in Springfield; unsuccessful Democratic candidate in 1868 for Governor of Missouri; elected Governor of Missouri in 1876, and served from January 8, 1877 to January 10, 1881; resumed the practice of his profession; died in St. Louis, Mo., November 20, 1886; interment in Hazelwood Cemetery, Springfield, Mo.

**Bibliography:** *DAB.*

**PHELPS, Lancelot** (father of James Phelps), a Representative from Connecticut; born in Windsor, Conn., November 9, 1784; moved with his father to Colebrook, Conn., in 1794; attended the common schools; studied medicine and commenced practice in Colebrook, Litchfield County, Conn.; also engaged in agricultural and mercantile pursuits in Hitchcockville (now Riverton), Conn.; returned to Colebrook; held various local offices; member of the State house of representatives in 1817, 1819-1821, 1824, 1827, 1828, and 1830; elected as a Jacksonian to the Twenty-fourth Congress and reelected as a Democrat to the Twenty-fifth Congress (March 4, 1835-March 3,

1839); died in Colebrook, Conn., September 1, 1866; interment in Center Cemetery, Winsted, Conn.

**PHELPS, Oliver,** a Representative from New York; born in Poquonock, Hartford County, Conn., October 21, 1749; completed preparatory studies; engaged in mercantile pursuits in Granville, Mass., in 1770; during the Revolution was deputy commissary in the Continental Army and served until the end of the war; settled in Suffield, Mass.; member of the State house of representatives 1778-1780; member of the constitutional convention in 1779 and 1780; served in the State senate in 1785; member of the Governor's council in 1786; assisted in the organization of the Phelps & Gorham syndicate in 1788 and acted as the representative of that company in the exploration of the Genesee country in western New York; first judge of Ontario County, N.Y., 1789-1793; moved to Canandaigua, N.Y., in 1802; elected as a Republican to the Eighth Congress (March 4, 1803-March 3, 1805); died in Canandaigua, N.Y., February 21, 1809; interment in West Avenue Cemetery.

**Bibliography:** *DAB.*

**PHELPS, Samuel Shethar,** a Senator from Vermont; born in Litchfield, Conn., May 13, 1793; graduated from Yale College in 1811; studied law; was admitted to the bar and commenced practice in Middlebury, Addison County, Vt., in 1812; served in the War of 1812 as paymaster; member, Vermont house of representatives 1821-1832; judge of the supreme court of Vermont 1832-1838; member, Vermont State senate 1838-1839; elected as a Whig to the United States Senate in 1839; reelected in 1845 and served from March 4, 1839, to March 3, 1851; chairman, Committee on the Militia (Twenty-seventh Congress), Committee on Revolutionary Claims (Twenty-seventh Congress), Committee on Pensions (Twenty-seventy Congress), Committee on Patents and the Patent Office (Twenty-eighth Congress), Committee on Territories (Twenty-eighth Congress); was appointed to the United States Senate to fill the vacancy caused by the death of William Upham and served from January 17, 1853, until March 16, 1854, when the Senate declared that he was not entitled to the seat; died in Middlebury, Addison County, Vt., on March 25, 1855; interment in West Cemetery.

**PHELPS, Timothy Guy,** a Representative from California; born in Oxford, Chenango County, N.Y., December 20, 1824; completed preparatory studies; moved to New York City and engaged in mercantile pursuits; returned to Chenango County and began the study of law but discontinued it; moved to San Francisco, Calif., in December 1849; engaged in mining in Tuolumne County; returned to San Francisco and resumed mercantile pursuits; engaged in the real estate business in 1853; unsuccessful candidate for the State assembly in 1854; member of the State assembly from 1855 to 1857; served in the State senate 1858-1861; unsuccessful candidate for Governor in 1861; elected as a Republican to the Thirty-seventh Congress (March 4, 1861-March 3, 1863); was not a candidate for renomination in 1862; resumed the real estate business until 1870; collector of customs at the port of San Francisco 1870-1872 and 1890-1893; engaged in agricultural pursuits; unsuccessful Republican candidate for Governor in 1875; moved to San Mateo County; regent of the University of California at Berkeley from December 6, 1880, until his death; chairman of the board of regents of Lick Observatory for nineteen years; died near San Carlos, San Mateo County, Calif., June 11, 1899, following an accident in which he was struck by two boys on a tandem bicycle; interment in Cypress Lawn Memorial Park Cemetery, Lawndale, San Mateo County, Calif.

**PHELPS, William Wallace,** a Representative from Minnesota; born in Oakland County, Mich., June 1, 1826; attended the country schools; was graduated from the University of Michigan at Ann Arbor in 1846; studied law; was admitted to the bar in 1848 and commenced practice; register of the United States land office at Red Wing, Goodhue County, Minn.; upon the admission of Minnesota as a State into the Union was elected as a Democrat to the Thirty-fifth

Congress and served from May 11, 1858, to March 3, 1859; resumed the practice of his profession in Red Wing, Minn.; died in Spring Lake, Ottawa County, Mich., August 3, 1873; interment in Oakwood Cemetery, Red Wing, Minn.

**PHELPS, William Walter,** a Representative from New Jersey; born in New York City, August 24, 1839; attended private schools near Bridgeport, Conn., and Mount Washington Institute, New York; was graduated from Yale College in 1860 and from the law department of Columbia College, New York City, in 1863; was admitted to the bar and commenced practice in New York City; retired from the practice of law in 1868; engaged in banking in New York City, with residence in Englewood, N.J.; also served as a director of numerous railroads; elected to the Forty-third Congress (March 4, 1873-March 3, 1875); unsuccessful candidate for reelection in 1874 to the Forty-fourth Congress; delegate to the Republican National Conventions of 1880 and 1884; appointed Envoy Extraordinary and Minister Plenipotentiary to Austria on May 5, 1881 and served until June 1882; elected as a Republican to the Forty-eighth and to the two succeeding Congresses (March 4, 1883-March 3, 1889); declined to be a candidate for renomination in 1888 to the Fifty-first Congress; appointed by President Benjamin Harrison one of the commissioners to represent the United States at the International Congress on the Samoan Question, which met in Berlin in 1889; appointed Envoy Extraordinary and Minister Plenipotentiary to Germany on June 20, 1889 and served until June 1893; appointed a special judge of the court of errors and appeals of the State of New Jersey in 1893; died in Englewood, Bergen County, N.J., June 17, 1894; interment in the City Cemetery, Simsbury, Conn.

**Bibliography:** *DAB.*

**PHILBIN, Philip Joseph,** a Representative from Massachusetts; born in Clinton, Worcester County, Mass., May 29, 1898; attended the public and high schools; during the First World War served as a seaman in the United States Navy 1917-1919; was graduated from Harvard University in 1920 and from Columbia University Law School, New York City, in 1924; was admitted to the bar the same year and commenced practice in Boston, Mass., and later in Clinton, Mass.; also engaged in the realty and fuel businesses and in agricultural pursuits; secretary, campaign manager, and personal representative at intervals for Senator David I. Walsh 1921-1940; special counsel for the United States Senate Committee on Education and Labor 1934-1936; referee in the United States Department of Labor in 1936 and 1937; member of the advisory board of the Massachusetts Unemployment Compensation Commission 1937-1940; in 1935 became chairman of the town of Clinton Finance Committee; elected as a Democrat to the Seventy-eighth and to the thirteen succeeding Congresses (January 3, 1943-January 3, 1971); chairman, Committee on Armed Services (Ninety-first Congress); unsuccessful candidate for renomination in 1970 to the Ninety-second Congress; died at his home, Philcrest Farms, Bolton, Mass., June 14, 1972; interment in St. John's Cemetery, Lancaster, Mass.

**PHILIPS, John Finis,** a Representative from Missouri; born in Thralls Prairie, Boone County, Mo., December 31, 1834; attended the common schools, the University of Missouri at Columbia, and was graduated from Centre College, Danville, Ky., in 1855; studied law; was admitted to the bar in 1857 and commenced practice in Georgetown, Pettis County, Mo.; member of the State constitutional convention in 1861; during the Civil War was commissioned colonel in 1862 and commanded the Seventh Regiment, Missouri Volunteer Cavalry; resumed the practice of his profession at Sedalia, Mo.; served as mayor; delegate to the Democratic National Convention in 1868; unsuccessful candidate for election in 1868 to the Forty-first Congress; elected as a Democrat to the Forty-fourth Congress (March 4, 1875-March 3, 1877); elected to the Forty-sixth Congress

to fill the vacancy caused by the death of Alfred M. Lay and served from January 10, 1880, to March 3, 1881; unsuccessful candidate for reelection in 1880 to the Forty-seventh Congress; moved to Kansas City, Mo., in 1881 and resumed the practice of law; commissioner of the Missouri Supreme Court 1883-1885; judge of the Kansas City Court of Appeals 1885-1888; appointed United States judge of the western district of Missouri by President Grover Cleveland in 1888 and served until 1910, when he retired from public life; died at Hot Springs, Ark., March 13, 1919; interment in Mount Washington Cemetery, Kansas City, Mo.

**Bibliography:** *DAB.*

**PHILLIPS, Alfred Noroton,** a Representative from Connecticut; born in Darien, Fairfield County, Conn., April 23, 1894; attended the public schools, Betts Academy, Stamford, Conn., and Hotchkiss School, Lakeville, Conn.; was graduated from Yale University in 1917; during the First World War served as a first lieutenant in the Field Artillery, United States Army, in 1917 and 1918, with overseas service; moved to Stamford, Conn., in 1918; served as major in the Connecticut National Guard Reserve 1928-1933; employed with the Charles H. Phillips Chemical Co. from early youth until 1923, and as publisher of a newspaper in Darien, Conn., after 1922; mayor of Stamford in 1923 and 1924, in 1927 and 1928, and 1935 and 1936; commander of the American Legion of Connecticut in 1919; member of the Democratic State Central committee; elected as a Democrat to the Seventy-fifth Congress (January 3, 1937-January 3, 1939); unsuccessful candidate for reelection in 1938 to the Seventy-sixth Congress; resumed his publishing business in Darien, Conn., and the management of his dairy farm in Cecilton, Md.; was commissioned as a captain, Military Police, United States Army, and served from July 17, 1942, to August 16, 1944, with service in North Africa; died in Stamford, Conn., January 18, 1970; interment in St. Stephen's Cemetery, Cecilton, Md.

**PHILLIPS, Dayton Edward,** a Representative from Tennessee; born in Shell Creek, Carter County, Tenn., March 29, 1910; raised on a farm; attended the country school and Cloudland High School, Roan Mountain, Tenn., Milligan (Tenn.) College 1929-1931, and the University of Tennessee at Knoxville, LL.B., 1934; taught school in Carter County, Tenn., in 1931 and 1932; was graduated from the National University Law School, Washington, D.C., J.D., 1936; was admitted to the bar in 1935 and commenced practice in Elizabethton, Tenn.; attorney for Carter County 1938-1942; district attorney general, first judicial circuit of Tennessee, 1942-1947; during the Second World War served as an enlisted man in the United States Army, with overseas service in the European Theater of Operations, 1943-1945; elected as a Republican to the Eightieth and Eighty-first Congresses (January 3, 1947-January 3, 1951); unsuccessful candidate for renomination in 1950; resumed the practice of law; chancellor of the First Chancery Court of Tennessee from 1952 until his death in Kingsport, Tenn., October 23, 1980; resided in Elizabethton, Tenn.; interment in Happy Valley Memorial Park.

**PHILLIPS, Fremont Orestes,** a Representative from Ohio; born in Lafayette, Medina County, Ohio, March 16, 1856; attended the public schools; moved to Medina, Ohio, in 1873; attended Medina High School, Medina Normal School, and Kenyon College, Gambier, Ohio; studied law; was admitted to the bar in 1880 and commenced practice in Medina, Ohio; justice of the peace; mayor of Medina 1886-1890; served as probate judge of Medina County 1892-1897; elected as a Republican to the Fifty-sixth Congress (March 4, 1899-March 3, 1901); unsuccessful candidate for renomination in 1900; resumed the practice of law in Medina, Ohio; chairman of the Medina County Republican Central committee 1916-1934; again elected probate judge of Medina County in 1924;

reelected in 1928 and served until 1932; died in Medina, Ohio, February 21, 1936; interment in Spring Grove Cemetery.

**PHILLIPS, Henry Myer,** a Representative from Pennsylvania; born in Philadelphia, Pa., June 30, 1811; attended the Philadelphia schools and Franklin Institute; studied law; was admitted to the bar in 1832 and commenced practice in Philadelphia; clerk of the court of common pleas of Philadelphia; elected as a Democrat to the Thirty-fifth Congress (March 4, 1857-March 3, 1859); unsuccessful candidate for reelection in 1858 to the Thirty-sixth Congress; resumed the practice of law in Philadelphia; trustee of Jefferson Medical College in 1862; appointed a member of the Board of Fairmount Park Commissioners in 1867 and elected its president in 1881; member of the Board of City Trusts in 1869, vice president of the board 1870-1878, and president 1878-1882; director of the Academy of Music in 1870 and its president in 1872, resigning in 1884; member of the commission to supervise the erection of the municipal buildings in Philadelphia in 1870, resigning in 1871; director of the Pennsylvania Railroad Co. in 1874; died in Philadelphia, August 28, 1884; interment in Mount Sinai Cemetery, Frankford (Philadelphia), Pa.

**PHILLIPS, John,** a Representative from California; born in Wilkes-Barre, Luzerne County, Pa., September 11, 1887; moved to St. David, Pa., in 1891; attended the public schools; was graduated from Haverford (Pa.) College in 1910; during the First World War served in the Adjutant General's Office and in Ordnance, 1917-1919; moved to California in 1924; business analyst and rancher; member of the city council of Banning, Calif., 1930-1932; served in the California State assembly, 1932-1936; member of the California State senate, 1936-1942; member of the United States delegation to the Eleventh World's Dairy Congress in Berlin in 1937; elected as a Republican to the Seventy-eighth and to the six succeeding Congresses (January 3, 1943-January 3, 1957); was not a candidate for renomination in 1956 to the Eighty-fifth Congress; delegate to the Republican National Conventions of 1944, 1948, 1952, 1956 and 1960; member of the American Battle Monuments Commission, 1952-1961; engaged as a public relations counselor; was a resident of Hemet, Calif., until his death in Palm Springs, Calif., December 18, 1983; interment in Desert Memorial Park, Cathedral City, Calif.

**PHILLIPS, John,** a Representative from Pennsylvania; was born in Chester County, Pa.; received a limited schooling; elected as a Federalist to the Seventeenth Congress (March 4, 1821-March 3, 1823).

**PHILLIPS, Philip,** a Representative from Alabama; born in Charleston, S.C., December 13, 1807; pursued classical studies; studied law; was admitted to the bar and commenced practice in Charleston, S.C., December 14, 1828; member of the State constitutional convention in 1832; member of the State house of representatives in 1833 and 1834; moved to Mobile, Ala., and continued the practice of law; member of the State house of representatives in 1844 and 1851; delegate to the Democratic National Convention in 1852; elected as a Democrat to the Thirty-third Congress (March 4, 1853-March 3, 1855); declined to be a candidate for renomination in 1854 to the Thirty-fourth Congress; resumed the practice of law in Washington, D.C., and died there on January 14, 1884; interment in Laurel Hill Cemetery, Savannah, Ga.

**Bibliography:** Morgan, David T. "Philip Phillips and Internal Improvements in Mid-Nineteenth-Century Alabama." *Alabama Review* 34 (April 1981): 83-93.

**PHILLIPS, Stephen Clarendon,** a Representative from Massachusetts; born in Salem, Mass., November 4, 1801; graduated from Harvard University in 1819; engaged in mercantile pursuits in Salem; member of the Massachusetts house of representatives 1824-1829; served in the Massachusetts senate in 1830; elected to

the Twenty-third Congress to fill the vacancy caused by the resignation of Rufus Choate; elected as a Whig to the Twenty-fourth and Twenty-fifth Congresses and served from December 1, 1834, to September 28, 1838, when he resigned; mayor of Salem 1838-1842; defeated as the Free-Soil candidate for Governor in 1848 and 1849; engaged in the lumber business in Canada; perished in the burning of the steamer *Montreal* on the St. Lawrence River June 26, 1857, and the remains were never recovered.

**PHILLIPS, Thomas Wharton** (father of Thomas Wharton Phillips, Jr.), a Representative from Pennsylvania; born near Mount Jackson in that section of Beaver County now included in Lawrence County, Pa., February 23, 1835; attended the common schools and was also privately instructed; engaged in the production of oil; president of the Producers' Protective Association 1887-1890; president of the Citizens' National Bank of New Castle; member of the board of trustees of Bethany College, West Virginia, and of Hiram College, Ohio; elected as a Republican to the Fifty-third and Fifty-fourth Congresses (March 4, 1893-March 3, 1897); chairman, Committee on Labor (Fifty-fourth Congress); did not seek renomination in 1896; resumed his former pursuits; appointed a member of the United States Industrial Commission by President William McKinley and served until its dissolution; delegate to the Republican National Convention in 1908; died in New Castle, Pa., July 21, 1912; interment in Oak Park Cemetery, New Castle, Pa.

**PHILLIPS, Thomas Wharton, Jr.** (son of Thomas Wharton Phillips), a Representative from Pennsylvania; born in New Castle, Lawrence County, Pa., November 21, 1874; attended the common schools; was graduated from Phillips Academy, Andover, Mass., in 1894 and from the Sheffield Scientific School, Yale University, in 1897; engaged in the petroleum, natural-gas, and coal businesses; delegate to the Republican National Convention in 1916; elected as a Republican to the Sixty-eighth and Sixty-ninth Congresses (March 4, 1923-March 3, 1927); did not seek renomination for Congress in 1926; was an unsuccessful candidate for the Republican nomination for Governor in 1926, 1930, and 1934; resumed his former occupation and was president of the Phillips Gas and Oil Co.; also a director of the Butler Consolidated Coal Co., and the Pennsylvania Investment and Real Estate Corp., of Butler; died at Phillips Hall, Penn Township, Butler County, Pa., January 2, 1956; interment in North Cemetery, Butler, Pa.

**PHILLIPS, William Addison,** a Representative from Kansas; born in Paisley, Scotland, January 14, 1824; attended the common schools of Paisley; immigrated to the United States in 1838 with his parents, who settled in Randolph County, Ill.; engaged in agricultural pursuits; employed as a newspaper correspondent 1845-1862; studied law; was admitted to the bar in 1855 and commenced practice in Lawrence, Kans.; first justice of the supreme court under the Leavenworth constitution; founded the city of Salina, Kans., in 1858; during the Civil War raised some of the first troops in Kansas in 1861; was afterward commissioned colonel and served as commander of the Cherokee Indian Regiment; prosecuting attorney of Cherokee County in 1865; served in the State house of representatives in 1865; attorney for the Cherokee Indians at Washington, D.C.; elected as a Republican to the Forty-third, Forty-fourth, and Forty-fifth Congresses (March 4, 1873-March 3, 1879); unsuccessful candidate for renomination in 1878; unsuccessful candidate for election in 1890 to the Fifty-second Congress; died at Fort Gibson, Muskogee County, Indian Territory (now Oklahoma), November 30, 1893; interment in Gypsum Hill Cemetery, Salina, Kans.

**Bibliography:** *DAB*.

**PHILSON, Robert,** a Representative from Pennsylvania; born in County Tyrone, Ireland, in 1759; immigrated to the United States and settled in Berlin, Pa., in 1785; received a limited schooling; engaged in agricultural pursuits; held various town and county offices; served as associate judge of Somerset County for twenty years; commissioned brigadier general of the Second Brigade, Tenth Division, Pennsylvania Militia, May 9, 1800; during the War of 1812 served as brigadier general of the Second Brigade, Twelfth Division, Pennsylvania Volunteers; elected to the Sixteenth Congress (March 4, 1819-March 3, 1821); retired from public life and active pursuits; died in Berlin, Pa., July 25, 1831; interment in Reformed Church Cemetery.

**PHIPPS, Lawrence Cowle,** a Senator from Colorado; born in Amityville, Pa., August 30, 1862; moved with his parents to Pittsburgh, Pa., in 1867; attended the common schools; entered the employ of the Carnegie Steel Co., advancing from clerk to first vice president; retired from active participation in the steel business in 1901; moved to Denver, Colo., and engaged in the investment business; donor of the Agnes Memorial Sanatorium in Denver; president of the Colorado Taxpayers' Protective League in 1913; chairman of the mountain division in the Red Cross campaign in 1917; member of the Colorado council of defense in 1917; elected as a Republican to the United States Senate in 1918; reelected in 1924, and served from March 4, 1919, to March 3, 1931; was not a candidate for reelection in 1930; chairman, Committee on Expenditures in the Department of State (Sixty-sixth Congress), Committee on Education and Labor (Sixty-eighth and Sixty-ninth Congresses), Committee on Irrigation and Reclamation (Sixty-ninth and Seventieth Congresses), Committee on the Post Office and Post Roads (Seventy-first Congress); engaged in railroad and electric power investments; died in Santa Monica, Calif., March 1, 1958; interment in Fairmount Mausoleum, Denver, Colo.

**PHISTER, Elijah Conner,** a Representative from Kentucky; born in Maysville, Mason County, Ky., October 8, 1822; attended the Seminary of Rand and Richardson, Maysville, Ky.; graduated from Augusta College, Kentucky, in August 1840; studied law; was admitted to the bar and commenced practice in 1844; mayor of Maysville in 1848; circuit judge 1856-1862; member of the Kentucky house of representatives 1867-1871; appointed one of the commissioners to revise the Kentucky statutes in 1872 but declined; elected as a Democrat to the Forty-sixth and Forty-seventh Congresses (March 4, 1879-March 3, 1883); resumed the practice of law; died in Maysville, Ky., May 16, 1887; interment in the City Cemetery.

**PHOENIX, Jonas Phillips,** a Representative from New York; born in Morristown, Morris County, N.J., January 14, 1788; received a limited schooling; became a merchant in New York City; alderman of the first ward in 1840, 1842, and 1847; appointed a commissioner of the Croton Aqueduct Works in 1842; elected as a Whig to the Twenty-eighth Congress (March 4, 1843-March 3, 1845); declined to be a candidate for renomination in 1844; unsuccessful candidate for election in 1846 to the Thirtieth Congress; chairman of the Whig General Committee in 1846 and 1847; member of the State assembly in 1848; elected to the Thirty-first Congress (March 4, 1849-March 3, 1851); renominated in 1850 but declined to be a candidate; died in New York City May 4, 1859; interment in the Presbyterian Cemetery, Morristown, N.J.

**PICKENS, Andrew** (grandfather of Francis Wilkinson Pickens), a Representative from South Carolina; born in Paxton, Bucks County, Pa., September 13, 1739; attended the common schools; moved with his parents to the Waxhaw settlement in South Carolina in 1752; served in the provincial militia in the campaign against the Cherokee Indians in 1760; entered the Revolutionary Army as captain of militia and attained the rank of brigadier general; commanded an expedition against the Cherokee Indians in 1782; member of the State house of representatives 1781-1794; one of the commissioners named to settle the boundary line between South Carolina and Georgia in 1787; member of the State constitutional convention in 1790; elected to the Third Congress (March 4, 1793-March 3, 1795); appointed major general of militia in 1795;

unsuccessful candidate for election to the United States Senate in 1797; member of the State house of representatives 1800-1812; declined the nomination for Governor in 1812; died in Tomassee, Pendleton District, S.C., August 11, 1817; interment in Old Stone Churchyard, near Pendleton, S.C.

**Bibliography:** *DAB*; Waring, Alice Noble. *The Fighting Elder: Andrew Pickens, 1739-1817.* Columbia: University of South Carolina Press, 1962.

**PICKENS, Francis Wilkinson** (grandson of Andrew Pickens), a Representative from South Carolina; born on a plantation on the Toogoodoo River, St. Paul's Parish, Colleton District, S.C., April 7, 1805; completed preparatory studies; attended Franklin College, Athens, Ga., and was graduated from South Carolina College (now the University of South Carolina) at Columbia; studied law; was admitted to the bar and commenced practice in Edgefield District in 1829; engaged in planting; member of the South Carolina State house of representatives, 1832-1833; elected as a Nullifier to the Twenty-third Congress to fill the vacancy caused by the resignation of George McDuffie; reelected to the Twenty-fourth and Twenty-fifth Congresses, and as a Democrat to the Twenty-sixth and Twenty-seventh Congresses, and served from December 8, 1834 to March 3, 1843; chairman, Committee on Foreign Affairs (Twenty-sixth Congress); member of the South Carolina State senate, 1844-1846; member of the Nashville southern convention in 1850; delegate to the Democratic National Convention of 1856; unsuccessful candidate for the United States Senate in 1857 to fill the vacancy caused by the death of Andrew P. Butler; appointed Minister to Russia on January 11, 1858 and served until September 1860; Governor of South Carolina from December 1860 to December 1862; died in Edgefield, S.C., January 25, 1869; interment in Edgefield Cemetery.

**Bibliography:** *DAB*; Edmunds, John B., Jr. *Francis W. Pickens and the Politics of Destruction.* Chapel Hill: University of North Carolina Press, 1986.

**PICKENS, Israel,** a Representative from North Carolina and a Senator from Alabama; born near Concord, Mecklenburg (now Cabarrus) County, N.C., January 30, 1780; moved to Burke County, N.C.; received instruction from private teachers and graduated from Jefferson College, Canonsburg, Pa., in 1802; studied law; was admitted to the bar and practiced; member, North Carolina State senate, 1808-1809; elected as a Republican from North Carolina to the Twelfth and to the two succeeding Congresses (March 4, 1811-March 3, 1817); register of the land office of Mississippi Territory (which included the present State of Alabama), 1817-1821; Governor of Alabama from November 9, 1821 to November 25, 1825; appointed to the United States Senate from Alabama to fill the vacancy caused by the death of Henry Chambers, and served from February 17, 1826 to November 27, 1826, when a successor was elected; was not a candidate for election to the vacancy; declined an appointment as judge of the United States Court for the District of Alabama in 1826; died near Matanzas, Cuba, on April 24, 1827; interment in the family cemetery near Greensboro, Hale County, Ala.

**Bibliography:** *DAB*; Bailey, Hugh C. "Israel Pickens, People's Politician." *Alabama Review* 27 (1964): 83-101.

**PICKERING, Timothy,** a Senator and a Representative from Massachusetts; born in Salem, Mass., July 17, 1745; attended the grammar school and graduated from Harvard College in 1763; clerk in the office of register of deeds in Salem; studied law; was admitted to the bar in 1768 and commenced practice in Salem; selectman and assessor from 1772 until 1777; member of Committee on State of Rights of Colonists in 1773; member of Committee of Correspondence and Safety, 1774-1775; held various local offices; elected to the Massachusetts legislature in 1776; entered the Revolutionary Army as colonel; appointed adjutant general and elected as a member of Board of War in 1777; became Quartermaster General of the Army in 1780; moved to Philadelphia in 1785 and to Wyoming County, Pa., in 1787; member of the Pennsylvania constitutional convention, 1789-1790; special government agent on missions to the Indians; Postmaster General in the Cabinet of President George Washington, August 12, 1791 to February 24, 1795; appointed Secretary of War and served from January 2 until December 10, 1795; appointed Secretary of State on December 10, 1795 and served until May 12, 1800; returned to Massachusetts in 1802; unsuccessful candidate for election in 1802 to the Eighth Congress; appointed chief justice of court of common pleas and general sessions of the peace in 1802; elected to the United States Senate as a Federalist in 1803 to fill the vacancy caused by the resignation of Dwight Foster; reelected and served from March 4, 1803, to March 3, 1811; unsuccessful candidate for reelection in 1811; censured by the Senate in 1811 for breach of confidence; member of the executive council of Massachusetts, 1812-1813; elected as a Federalist to the Thirteenth and Fourteenth Congresses (March 4, 1813-March 3, 1817); declined to be a candidate for renomination in 1816 to the Fifteenth Congress; returned to his farm near Wenham, Mass.; returned to Salem in 1820; unsuccessful candidate for election in 1820 to the Seventeenth Congress; died in Salem, Essex County, Mass., January 29, 1829; interment in Broad Street Cemetery.

Bibliography: *DAB*; Clarfield, Gerald. *Timothy Pickering and the American Republic*. Pittsburgh: University of Pittsburgh Press, 1980; Prentiss, Hervey. *Timothy Pickering as the Leader of New England Federalism, 1800-1815*. 1934. Reprint. New York: Da Capo Press, 1972.

**PICKETT, Charles Edgar,** a Representative from Iowa; born near Bonaparte, Van Buren County, Iowa, January 14, 1866; attended the common schools; was graduated from Iowa State University at Iowa City in 1888 and from its law department in 1890; was admitted to the bar in 1890 and commenced practice in Waterloo, Iowa; vice president of the Pioneer National Bank; regent of the State University of Iowa 1896-1909; elected as a Republican to the Sixty-first and Sixty-second Congresses (March 4, 1909-March 3, 1913); unsuccessful candidate for reelection in 1912 to the Sixty-third Congress; resumed the practice of law in Waterloo, Iowa; chairman of the Republican State conventions in 1899 and 1916; delegate at large to the Republican National Convention in 1920; unsuccessful candidate for the Republican nomination for United States Senator in 1926; died in Waterloo, Iowa, July 20, 1930; interment in Elmwood Cemetery.

**PICKETT, Owen Bradford,** a Representative from Virginia; born in Richmond, Va., August 31, 1930; attended the public schools and graduated from Henry Clay High School, Ashland, Va., 1947; B.S., Virginia Polytechnic Institute, Blacksburg, 1952; LL.B., University of Richmond Law School, 1955; admitted to the Virginia bar in 1955 and commenced practice in Richmond; certified public accountant; member of the Virginia Democratic central committee, 1980-1982; chairman, Second Congressional District Democratic committee, 1978-1982; member, Virginia house of delegates, 1972-1986; elected as a Democrat to the One Hundredth and to the four succeeding Congresses (January 3, 1987-January 3, 1997); is a resident of Virginia Beach, Va.

**PICKETT, Thomas Augustus,** a Representative from Texas; born in Travis, Falls County, Tex., August 14, 1906; attended the public schools of Palestine, Tex., and the University of Texas at Austin; studied law; was admitted to the bar in 1929 and commenced practice in Palestine, Tex.; county attorney of Anderson County 1931-1935; district attorney of the third judicial district of Texas 1935-1945; elected as a Democrat to the Seventy-ninth Congress; reelected to the three succeeding Congresses and served from January 3, 1945, until his resignation June 30, 1952; vice president of the National Coal Association from July 1, 1952, to March 31, 1961; vice president of the Association of American Railroads, April 1, 1961, to November 30, 1967; resided in Leesburg, Fla., until his death there June 7, 1980; cremated; ashes interred at St. James Episcopal Church.

**PICKLE, James Jarrell (Jake),** a Representative from Texas; born in Roscoe, Nolan County, Tex., October 11, 1913; educated in the public schools of Big Spring, Tex.; B.A., University of Texas, Austin, 1938; area director, National Youth Administration, 1938-1941; served three and a half years with the Navy in the Pacific during the Second World War; in 1946 entered the radio business in Austin, Tex.; engaged in public relations and advertising business, 1948-1956; director of the Texas State Democratic Executive committee, 1957-1960; appointed a member of the Texas Employment Commission in 1961, resigning September 27, 1963, to be a candidate for Congress; elected as a Democrat to the Eighty-eighth Congress, December 21, 1963, by special election to fill the vacancy caused by the resignation of Homer Thornberry; reelected to the fifteen succeeding Congresses, and served from December 21, 1963 to January 3, 1995; was not a candidate for reelection in 1994 to the One Hundred Fourth Congress; maintains an office in the law firm of Brown, McCarroll, Oaks and Hartline; is a resident of Austin, Tex.

**PICKLER, John Alfred,** a Representative from South Dakota; born near Salem, Washington County, Ind., January 24, 1844; moved with his father to Davis County, Iowa; attended the district school; during the Civil War entered the Union Army and served in the Third Regiment, Iowa Volunteer Cavalry and as major in the One Hundred and Thirty-eighth Regiment, Iowa Volunteer Cavalry; was graduated from the University of Iowa at Iowa City in 1870; attended the Chicago University Law School in 1871 and was graduated from the Ann Arbor (Mich.) Law School in 1872; was admitted to the bar and commenced practice in Kirksville, Mo.; elected district attorney of Adair County, Mo., in 1872; moved to Muscatine, Iowa, in 1874; member of the State legislature 1881-1883; moved to the Territory of Dakota in 1883; elected to the Dakota Legislature in 1884; upon the admission of South Dakota as a State into the Union was elected as a Republican to the Fifty-first and to the three succeeding Congresses and served from November 2, 1889, to March 3, 1897; chairman, Committee on Invalid Pensions (Fifty-fourth Congress); was not a candidate for renomination in 1896; resumed the practice of his profession; also engaged in the real estate business; died in Faulkton, Faulk County, S.Dak., on June 13, 1910; interment in Faulkton Cemetery.

**PICKMAN, Benjamin, Jr.,** a Representative from Massachusetts; born in Salem, Mass., September 30, 1763; graduated from Harvard University in 1784; studied law in Newburyport, Mass., and was admitted to the bar, but soon relinquished the practice of law and engaged in commercial pursuits; member of the Massachusetts house of representatives 1797-1802, 1812, and 1813; served in the Massachusetts senate in 1803; member of the executive council of the Commonwealth in 1805, 1808, 1813, 1814, and 1819-1821; elected as a Federalist to the Eleventh Congress (March 4, 1809-March 3, 1811); was not a candidate for renomination in 1810; member of the convention to revise the constitution of the Commonwealth of Massachusetts in 1820; overseer of Harvard University 1810-1818; president of the board of directors of the Theological School at Cambridge; died in Salem, Essex County, Mass., August 16, 1843; interment in Broad Street Cemetery.

**PIDCOCK, James Nelson** (cousin of Alvah Augustus Clark), a Representative from New Jersey; born in Whitehouse, Hunterdon County, N.J., February 8, 1836; attended the district schools and Lebanon Grammar School, Lebanon, N.J.; engaged in civil engineering 1850-1857; engaged in agricultural pursuits and was also a dealer in livestock after 1857; member of the State senate from Hunterdon County, N.J., 1877-1880; delegate to the Democratic National Conventions in 1884 and 1888; elected as a Democrat to the Forty-ninth and Fiftieth Congresses (March 4, 1885-March 3,

1889); was not a candidate for renomination in 1888; again resumed his agricultrual pursuits; built the Georgia Northern Railroad in southern Georgia, where he owned large timber tracts; served as president of the board of managers of the New Jersey State Hospital for the Insane 1891-1896; was an orchardist in New Jersey; died at Whitehouse Station, N.J., on December 17, 1899; interment in Elmwood Cemetery, Lebanon, Hunterdon County, N.J.

**PIERCE, Charles Wilson,** a Representative from Alabama; born in Benton, Yates County, N.Y., October 7, 1823; completed preparatory studies; moved with his father to Sandusky, Ohio, in 1829, and from there to Huntsville, Ohio, in 1847; moved to Havana, Ill., in 1855; during the Civil War enlisted in Company B, Eighty-fifth Regiment, Illinois Volunteer Infantry, and was elected first lieutenant; appointed quartermaster June 14, 1864; commissioned major in 1865; settled in Demopolis, Ala.; held various public offices; upon the readmission of Alabama to representation was elected as a Republican to the Fortieth Congress and served from July 21, 1868, to March 3, 1869; declined to be a candidate for renomination; moved to Nebraska in 1872; member of the Nebraska State constitutional convention in 1875; elected to the State senate in 1877 and reelected in 1880; resigned in 1881 to become register of the United States land office, which position he held until May 1886; returned to his farm; died in Hastings, Fla., February 18, 1907; interment in the family plot on the home farm near Waverly, Lancaster County, Nebr.

**PIERCE, Franklin,** a Representative and a Senator from New Hampshire and 14th President of the United States; born in Hillsborough, N.H., November 23, 1804; attended the academies of Hancock and Francestown, N.H.; prepared for college at Exeter and graduated from Bowdoin College, Brunswick, Maine, in 1824; studied law; was admitted to the bar and commenced practice in Hillsborough in 1827; member, New Hampshire State general court, 1829-1833, and served as speaker in 1832 and 1833; elected as a Democrat to the Twenty-third and Twenty-fourth Congresses (March 4, 1833-March 3, 1837); elected as a Democrat to the United States Senate, and served from March 4, 1837 to February 28, 1842, when he resigned; chairman, Committee on Pensions (Twenty-sixth Congress); resumed the practice of law in Concord, N.H.; district attorney for New Hampshire; declined the appointment as Attorney General of the United States tendered by President James K. Polk; served in the Mexican War as a colonel and brigadier general; member of the New Hampshire State constitutional convention in 1850 and served as its president; elected President of the United States on the Democratic ticket in 1852, and served from March 4, 1853 to March 3, 1857; resumed the practice of law; died in Concord, N.H., October 8, 1869; interment in Minat Inclosure, Old North Cemetery.

Bibliography: *DAB*; Hawthorne, Nathaniel. *The Life of Franklin Pierce.* 1852. Reprint. New York: Garrett Press, 1970; Nichols, Roy. *Franklin Pierce: Young Hickory of the Granite Hills.* 1931. Reprint. Philadelphia: University of Pennsylvania Press, 1958.

**PIERCE, Gilbert Ashville,** a Senator from North Dakota; born in East Otto, Cattaraugus County, N.Y., January 11, 1839; attended the public schools; moved to Indiana in 1854 and settled near Valparaiso; attended the University of Chicago Law School for two years; during the Civil War enlisted as a second lieutenant, rose to lieutenant colonel and chief quartermaster; was admitted to the bar and commenced practice in Valparaiso in 1865; member, Indiana State house of representatives, 1869; assistant financial clerk of the United States Senate, 1869-1871; resigned to accept an editorial position on the Chicago Inter-Ocean, serving as associate editor and managing editor for twelve years; became associated with the Chicago News in 1883; author of several books and plays; appointed Governor of Dakota Territory by President Chester A. Arthur on July 2, 1884, and served until November 15, 1886, when he resigned; upon the admission of North Dakota as a State into the Union was elected as a Republican to the United States Senate, and served from November 21, 1889 to March 3, 1891; unsuccessful candidate for reelection; moved to Minneapolis, Minn.; purchased the Minneapolis Tribune and became its editor in chief in 1891; moved to Florida, then Colorado; appointed Minister to Portugal by President Benjamin Harrison on January 6, 1893, but resigned on April 26, 1893, owing to poor health; died in Chicago, Ill., February 15, 1901; interment in Adams Cemetery, near Valparaiso, Ind.

Bibliography: *DAB.*

**PIERCE, Henry Lillie,** a Representative from Massachusetts; born in Stoughton, Norfolk County, Mass., August 23, 1825; pursued classical studies; attended the Massachusetts normal school at Bridgewater, Mass.; engaged in manufacturing; member of the Massachusetts house of representatives 1860-1862 and in 1866; member of the Boston Board of Aldermen in 1870 and 1871; mayor of Boston in 1873; elected as a Republican to the Forty-third Congress to fill the vacancy caused by the death of William Whiting; reelected to the Forty-fourth Congress and served from December 1, 1873, to March 3, 1877; declined to be a candidate for renomination; again mayor of Boston in 1878; died in Boston, Mass., December 17, 1896; interment in Dorchester Burying Ground, Dorchester, Mass.

Bibliography: *DAB.*

**PIERCE, Ray Vaughn,** a Representative from New York; born in Stark, Herkimer County, N.Y., August 6, 1840; attended public and private schools; was graduated from the Eclectic Medical College, Cincinnati, Ohio, in 1862; practiced medicine in Titusville, Pa., 1862-1866; moved to Buffalo, N.Y., in 1867; engaged in the manufacture and sale of proprietary medicines and established the Invalids' Hotel and Surgical Institute; member of the State senate 1877-1879; elected as a Republican to the Forty-sixth Congress and served from March 4, 1879, to September 18, 1880, when he resigned; was publisher of the Medical Adviser and also a manufacturer; died on St. Vincents Island, Fla., February 4, 1914; interment in Forest Lawn Cemetery, Buffalo, N.Y.

**PIERCE, Rice Alexander,** a Representative from Tennessee; born in Dresden, Weakley County, Tenn., July 3, 1848; attended the common schools in Tennessee; during the Civil War served in the Confederate States Army with the Eighth Tennessee Cavalry; after the war attended school in London, Canada; studied law in Halifax, N.C.; was admitted to the bar of the supreme court in Raleigh, N.C., in 1868 and commenced practice in Union City, Obion County, Tenn., in 1869; served as mayor in 1872; elected district attorney general of the twelfth judicial circuit in 1874; reelected in 1878 and served until 1883; elected as a Democrat to the Forty-eighth Congress (March 4, 1883-March 3, 1885); unsuccessful candidate for renomination in 1884; elected to the Fifty-first and Fifty-second Congresses (March 4, 1889-March 3, 1893); unsuccessful candidate for reelection in 1892 to the Fifty-third Congress; elected to the Fifty-fifth and to the three succeeding Congresses (March 4, 1897-March 3, 1905); unsuccessful candidate for reelection in 1904 to the Fifty-ninth Congress; resumed the practice of law in Union City, Tenn.; chairman of the Democratic State campaign committee in 1929; died in Union City, Tenn., July 12, 1936; interment in the City Cemetery.

**PIERCE, Wallace Edgar,** a Representative from New York; born in the town of Black Brook, Clinton County, N.Y., December 9, 1881; attended the rural schools; was graduated from Plattsburg (N.Y.) State Normal School in 1903; taught school in Clinton County and in Ogdensburg; served as secretary to Congressman George R. Malby 1909-1912 and to Congressman Edwin A. Merritt 1912-1914; studied law; was admitted to the bar in 1913 and commenced practice in Plattsburg, N.Y., in 1914; member of the State assembly 1916-1920; served as president of the board of visitors of the Plattsburg State Normal School 1926-1940; chairman of the Clinton

County Republican committee 1926-1940; member of the New York State Republican executive committee 1934-1940; elected as a Republican to the Seventy-sixth Congress and served from January 3, 1939, until his death in Washington, D.C., January 3, 1940; interment in Riverside Cemetery, Plattsburg, N.Y.

**PIERCE, Walter Marcus,** a Representative from Oregon; born on a farm near Morris, Grundy County, Ill., May 30, 1861; attended the common schools, Morris (Ill.) Academy, and the University of Michigan at Ann Arbor; taught school in Grundy County, Ill., 1877-1880, and in Franklin County, Kans., in 1881; moved to Oregon and taught school in Milton and Weston, Umatilla County, 1883-1890; superintendent of schools of Umatilla County, Oreg., 1886-1890; Umatilla County clerk, 1890-1894; was graduated from the law department of Northwestern University, Evanston, Ill., in 1896; was admitted to the bar and practiced in Pendleton, Oreg., 1895-1907; engaged in banking and in the power and light business, 1898-1907; operated stock and wheat farms, 1907-1937; served in the Oregon State senate, 1903-1907, and 1917-1921; unsuccessful candidate in 1918 for election for Governor; elected Governor of Oregon in 1922, and served from January 8, 1923 to January 10, 1927; unsuccessful candidate for reelection in 1926; member of the board of regents of Oregon State College, 1905-1927; delegate to all Democratic State conventions from 1890 to 1908; delegate to the Democratic National Conventions of 1920, 1932, and 1936; Democratic National committeeman from Oregon, 1932-1936; elected as a Democrat to the Seventy-third and to the four succeeding Congresses (March 4, 1933-January 3, 1943); unsuccessful candidate for reelection in 1942 to the Seventy-eighth Congress; died at his home in Eola Hills, west of Salem, Oreg., March 27, 1954; remains were cremated and the ashes deposited in Mount Crest Abbey Mausoleum, Salem, Oreg.

**Bibliography:** Pierce, Walter M. *Oregon Cattleman-Governor-Congressman: Memoirs and Times of Walter M. Pierce.* Edited by Arthur H. Bone. Portland: Oregon Historical Society, 1981; Schwartz, Gerald. "Walter M. Pierce and the Tradition of Progressive Reform: A Study of Eastern Oregon's Great Democrat." Ph.D. dissertation, Washington State University, 1969.

**PIERCE, William,** a Delegate from Georgia; born in that State in 1740; completed preparatory studies; served in the Continental Army during the Revolutionary War as aide-de-camp to General Nathanael Greene; engaged in mercantile pursuits in Savannah, Ga.; member of the State house of representatives in 1786; member of the Continental Congress in 1787; delegate from Georgia to the Federal Convention at Philadelphia in 1787; was an original member and vice president of the Society of the Cincinnati; trustee of Chatham County Academy at the time of his death; died in Savannah, Ga., December 10, 1789.

**PIERSON, Isaac,** a Representative from New Jersey; born in Orange, Essex County, N.J., August 15, 1770; attended private schools; was graduated from Princeton College in 1789; studied medicine; was graduated from the College of Physicians and Surgeons, New York City, and commenced practice in Orange, N.J.; elected assessor of Orange April 13, 1807, and served one year; sheriff of Essex County 1807-1809; president of the Medical Society of New Jersey in 1827; elected to the Twentieth and Twenty-first Congresses (March 4, 1827-March 3, 1831); unsuccessful candidate for reelection in 1830 to the Twenty-second Congress; died in Orange, N.J., September 22, 1833; interment in Old Burying Ground; reinterment in Rosedale Cemetery in 1840.

**PIERSON, Jeremiah Halsey,** a Representative from New York; born in Newark, N.J., September 13, 1766; moved with his parents to Richmond, Mass., in 1772; attended the public schools of Richmond and Stockbridge, Mass., and completed preparatory studies; studied law; was admitted to the bar and practiced in Massachusetts; moved to New York in 1795 and settled in Ramapo;

practiced law and engaged in mercantile pursuits and manufacturing; justice of the peace 1800-1811; associate justice of the court of common pleas in 1808; largely instrumental in securing the construction of the Erie Railroad; elected to the Seventeenth Congress (March 4, 1821-March 3, 1823); was not a candidate for renomination in 1822; resumed his former business pursuits; delegate to the National-Republican Convention at Baltimore in 1831; died in Ramapo, Rockland County, N.Y., December 12, 1855; interment in Ramapo Cemetery.

**PIERSON, Job,** a Representative from New York; born in East Hampton, Suffolk County, N.Y., September 23, 1791; attended the common schools; was graduated from Williams College in 1811; studied law in Salem and Schaghticoke; was admitted to the bar in 1815 and commenced practice in Rensselaer County; district attorney 1824-1833; elected as a Jacksonian to the Twenty-second and Twenty-third Congresses (March 4, 1831-March 3, 1835); unsuccessful candidate for reelection in 1834 to the Twenty-fourth Congress; resumed the practice of law; surrogate of Rensselaer County 1835-1840; delegate to the Democratic National Conventions in 1848, 1852, and 1856; died in Troy, N.Y., April 9, 1860; interment in Oakwood Cemetery.

**PIGOTT, James Protus,** a Representative from Connecticut; born in New Haven, Conn., September 11, 1852; attended the common schools and was graduated from Yale College in 1878 and from the law school of the same institution in 1880; was admitted to the bar in 1880 and commenced practice in New Haven, Conn.; served as city clerk of New Haven 1881-1884; member of the State house of representatives in 1885 and 1886; delegate to the Democratic National Conventions in 1888 and 1900; elected as a Democrat to the Fifty-third Congress (March 4, 1893-March 3, 1895); unsuccessful candidate for reelection to the Fifty-fourth Congress; resumed the practice of law; died in New Haven, Conn., July 1, 1919; interment in St. Lawrence Cemetery.

**PIKE, Austin Franklin,** a Representative and a Senator from New Hampshire; born in Hebron, N.H., October 16, 1819; pursued an academic course; studied law; was admitted to the bar of Merrimack County in 1845; member, State house of representatives 1850-1852, 1865-1866, and served as speaker during the last two years; member, State senate 1857-1858, serving as president the last year; elected as a Republican to the Forty-third Congress (March 4, 1873-March 3, 1875); unsuccessful candidate for reelection in 1874 to the Forty-fourth Congress; elected as a Republican to the United States Senate and served from March 4, 1883, until his death in Franklin, Merrimack County, N.H., October 8, 1886; chairman, Committee on Claims (Forty-eighth and Forty-ninth Congresses); interment in Franklin Cemetery.

**PIKE, Frederick Augustus,** a Representative from Maine; born in Calais, Maine, December 9, 1816; attended the common schools and the Washington Academy, East Machias, Maine; was graduated from Bowdoin College, Brunswick, Maine, in 1837; studied law; was admitted to the bar and commenced practice in Calais, Washington County, in 1840; mayor of Calais in 1852 and 1853; member of the State house of representatives 1858-1860 and served as speaker in 1860; elected as a Republican to the Thirty-seventh and to the three succeeding Congresses (March 4, 1861-March 3, 1869); chairman, Committee on Expenditures in the Department of State (Thirty-eighth and Thirty-ninth Congresses), Committee on Naval Affairs (Fortieth Congress); unsuccessful candidate for renomination in 1868; resumed the practice of law; again a member of the State house of representatives in 1870 and 1871; unsuccessful candidate for election in 1872 to the Forty-third Congress; died in Calais, Maine, December 2, 1886; interment in Calais Cemetery.

**PIKE, James,** a Representative from New Hampshire; born in Salisbury, Essex County, Mass., November 10, 1818; pursued classical studies; studied theology at the Wesleyan University, Connecticut, 1837-1839; served as a minister from 1841 to 1854; moved to Pembroke, N.H., in 1854; elected as the candidate of the American Party to the Thirty-fourth Congress and reelected as a Republican to the Thirty-fifth Congress (March 4, 1855-March 3, 1859); was not a candidate for renomination in 1858; during the Civil War served as colonel of the Sixteenth Regiment, New Hampshire Volunteer Infantry, from November 1, 1862, to August 20, 1863; unsuccessful candidate for Governor of New Hampshire in 1871; resumed preaching and became presiding elder of the Dover district; discontinued active duties in 1886 and lived in retirement until his death in Newfields, Rockingham County, N.H., July 26, 1895; interment in Locust Cemetery.

**PIKE, Otis Grey,** a Representative from New York; born in Riverhead, Suffolk County, N.Y., August 31, 1921; attended the public schools; A.B., Princeton University, 1946; J.D., Columbia University Law School, 1948; served as a Marine Corps pilot in the Pacific Theater, 1942-1946; awarded five air medals; justice of the peace of the town of Riverhead, 1954-1960; member of the Riverhead Town Board, 1954-1960; engaged in the practice of law in Riverhead, N.Y., 1949-1960; elected as a Democrat to the Eighty-seventh and to the eight succeeding Congresses (January 3, 1961-January 3, 1979); was not a candidate for reelection in 1978 to the Ninety-sixth Congress; chairman, Select Committee on Intelligence (Ninety-fourth Congress); president, South Oaks Hospital, Amityville, N.Y., 1982 to present; syndicated columnist, Newhouse newspapers, 1982 to present; is a resident of Vero Beach, Fla.

**PILCHER, John Leonard,** a Representative from Georgia; born on a farm near Meigs, Thomas County, Ga., August 27, 1898; attended the public schools; engaged in agricultural pursuits for thirty-five years; also operated general mercantile business, cotton gin, warehouses, fertilizer manufacturing plant, and syrup canning plant; mayor and councilman of Meigs, Ga.; member of the board of education and a county commissioner; member of the State house of representatives; member of the State senate 1940-1944; State purchasing agent in 1948 and 1949; delegate, each State and National Democratic Convention for thirty years; elected as a Democrat to the Eighty-third Congress to fill the vacancy caused by the death of E.E. Cox; reelected to the Eighty-fourth and the four succeeding Congresses and served from February 4, 1953, to January 3, 1965; was not a candidate for renomination in 1964 to the Eighty-ninth Congress; resided in Meigs, Ga., where he died August 20, 1981; interment in Meigs Sunset Cemetery.

**PILE, William Anderson,** a Representative from Missouri; born near Indianapolis, Ind., February 11, 1829; completed preparatory studies; studied theology and became a minister in the Methodist Episcopal Church and a member of the Missouri conference; during the Civil War entered the Union Army; commissioned chaplain of the First Regiment, Missouri Light Artillery, June 12, 1861; appointed lieutenant colonel of the Thirty-third Regiment, Missouri Infantry, on September 5, 1862, and colonel on December 23, 1862; commissioned brigadier general of Volunteers, December 26, 1863; commanded a division of United States Colored Troops in West Florida from February to April 1865; brevetted major general on April 9, 1865 for services rendered at Fort Blakely, Ala.; elected as a Republican to the Fortieth Congress (March 4, 1867-March 3, 1869); chairman, Committee on Expenditures in the Post Office Department (Fortieth Congress); unsuccessful candidate for reelection in 1868 to the Forty-first Congress; appointed Governor of New Mexico Territory by President Ulysses S. Grant, and served from August 16, 1869 until June 21, 1871, when he left the Territory to take a diplomatic post; appointed Minister Resident to Venezuela on May 23, 1871 and served until January

1874; died in Monrovia, Calif., July 7, 1889; interment in Live Oak Cemetery.

**PILES, Samuel Henry,** a Senator from Washington; born near Smithland, Livingston County, Ky., December 28, 1858; attended private schools in Smithland, Ky.; studied law; was admitted to the bar and commenced practice in Snohomish, Territory of Washington, in 1883; moved to Spokane, Wash., in 1886 and later in the same year to Seattle, where he engaged in the practice of law; assistant prosecuting attorney for the third judicial district of the Territory of Washington, 1887-1889; city attorney of Seattle, 1888-1889; general counsel of the Pacific Coast Co., 1895-1905; elected as a Republican to the United States Senate, and served from March 4, 1905 to March 3, 1911; was not a candidate for renomination in 1910; chairman, Committee on Coast and Insular Survey (Fifty-ninth through Sixty-first Congresses); resumed the practice of law in Seattle, Wash.; appointed by President Warren G. Harding as Envoy Extraordinary and Minister Plenipotentiary to Colombia on March 22, 1922, and served until September 1928; retired from active pursuits and moved to Los Angeles, Calif., where he died on March 11, 1940; interment in Lakeview Cemetery, Seattle, Wash.

**PILLION, John Raymond,** a Representative from New York; born in Conneaut, Ashtabula County, Ohio, August 10, 1904; moved to Lackawanna, N.Y., in 1907; attended the public schools of Lackawanna, South Park High School at Buffalo, and Cornell School of Engineering; LL.B., Cornell University, 1927; was admitted to the bar in 1928 and commenced the practice of law in Lackawanna, N.Y., in 1929; served as city court judge, 1932-1936; corporation counsel and tax attorney, city of Lackawanna, 1936-1941; president and treasurer of Bison Storage & Warehouse Corp., Buffalo, N.Y., 1945-1953; operator of a fruit and vegetable farm in Niagara County, beginning in 1935; member of the New York State assembly, 1941-1950; elected as a Republican to the Eighty-third and to the five succeeding Congresses (January 3, 1953-January 3, 1965); unsuccessful candidate for reelection in 1964 to the Eighty-ninth Congress; resumed the practice of law and practiced until 1968; unsuccessful candidate for election in 1968 to the Ninety-first Congress; resided in Hamburg, N.Y., until his death in Eden, N.Y., December 31, 1978; interment in Lakeside Memorial Park, Hamburg, N.Y.

**PILSBURY, Timothy,** a Representative from Texas; born in Newburyport, Mass., April 12, 1789; attended the common schools; employed in a store for about two years; became a sailor and during the War of 1812 commanded the privateer *Yankee;* engaged in shipping; settled in Eastport, Maine; member of the Maine house of representatives in 1825 and 1826; member of the executive council 1827-1836; unsuccessful candidate for election in 1836 to the Twenty-fifth Congress; moved to Ohio, thence to New Orleans, La., and later to Brazoria, Tex.; member of the house of representatives of the Republic of Texas in 1840 and 1841 and served in the senate of that Republic in 1842; chief justice of the county court; judge of probate for Brazoria County; again a member of the Texas senate in 1845; upon the admission of Texas as a State into the Union was elected as a Democrat to the Twenty-ninth and Thirtieth Congresses and served from March 30, 1846, to March 3, 1849; unsuccessful candidate for reelection in 1848 to the Thirty-first Congress; died in Henderson, Rusk County, Tex., November 23, 1858; interment in the City Cemetery.

**PINCKNEY, Charles** (father of Henry Laurens Pinckney), a Delegate, a Senator, and a Representative from South Carolina; born in Charles Town (now Charleston), S.C., October 26, 1757; pursued classical studies; was admitted to the bar and commenced practice in 1779; member of the South Carolina State house of representatives, 1779-1780, 1786-1789, 1792-1796, 1805, 1806, 1810-1814; fought in the Revolutionary War and was taken prisoner by the British in 1780; Member of the Continental Congress,

1785-1787; member of the Constitutional Convention in 1787; member of the State constitutional conventions in 1788 and 1790 and served as president; Governor of South Carolina, 1789-1792, and 1796-1798; was elected in 1798 as a Republican to the United States Senate to fill the vacancy caused by the resignation of John Hunter and also for the full term expiring March 3, 1805, and served from December 6, 1798, until his resignation in 1801; appointed Minister to Spain on June 6, 1801 and served until October 1804; again served in the State general assembly, and as Governor of South Carolina, 1806-1808; elected to the Sixteenth Congress (March 4, 1819-March 3, 1821); resumed the practice of law and also engaged in agricultural pursuits; died in Charleston, S.C., October 29, 1824; interment in St. Philip's Churchyard.

**Bibliography:** *DAB*; Bethea, Andrew. *The Contribution of Charles Pinckney to the Formation of the American Union.* Richmond: Garrett and Massis, Inc., 1937; Nott, Charles. *The Mystery of the Pinckney Draught.* New York: The Century Company, 1908.

**PINCKNEY, Henry Laurens** (son of Charles Pinckney), a Representative from South Carolina; born in Charleston, S.C., September 24, 1794; attended private schools; was graduated from South Carolina College (now the University of South Carolina) at Columbia in 1812; studied law; was admitted to the bar and commenced practice in Charleston; member of the South Carolina State house of representatives, 1816-1832; founded the Charleston Mercury in 1819 and was its sole editor for fifteen years; intendant (administrative official) of Charleston, 1830-1832; elected as a Nullifier to the Twenty-third and Twenty-fourth Congresses (March 4, 1833-March 3, 1837); unsuccessful candidate for renomination in 1836 to the Twenty-fifth Congress; mayor of Charleston, 1837-1840; collector of the port of Charleston in 1841 and 1842; tax collector of St. Philip's and St. Michael's parishes from 1845 to 1863; died in Charleston, S.C., February 3, 1863; interment in the Circular Congregational Church Burying Ground.

**Bibliography:** *DAB.*

**PINCKNEY, John McPherson,** a Representative from Texas; born in Grimes County, Tex., near the town of Hempstead, Waller County, May 4, 1845; attended the public schools and was privately instructed; enlisted as a private in the Confederate Army and served in Company D, Fourth Texas Brigade, until the close of the Civil War, attaining the rank of first lieutenant; studied law; was admitted to the bar in 1875 and commenced practice in Hempstead, Tex.; district attorney for the twenty-third judicial district of Texas 1890-1900; county judge of Waller County 1900-1903; elected as a Democrat to the Fifty-eighth Congress to fill the vacancy caused by the resignation of Thomas H. Ball; reelected to the Fifty-ninth Congress and served from November 17, 1903, until April 24, 1905, when he was assaulted and killed at Hempstead, Tex.; interment in the City Cemetery at Hempstead.

**PINCKNEY, Thomas,** a Representative from South Carolina; born in Charleston, S.C., October 23, 1750; attended Westminster School, Oxford, England, and was graduated from Oxford University, England; also attended the French Military College, Caen, France, for one year; studied law at the Inner Temple, London; was admitted to the bar in 1774 and commenced practice in Charleston, S.C.; captain of Engineers, First Regiment, Continental Army, in 1775; major in the Florida campaign in 1778; served under General Benjamin Lincoln in 1778 and 1779 and with Count d'Estaing in 1779; served in the defense of Charleston; Governor of South Carolina, 1787-1789; presided over the State ratification convention in 1788; member of the South Carolina State house of representatives in 1791; appointed the first United States Minister to Great Britain on January 12, 1792, and served until July 1796; appointed Envoy Extraordinary to Spain on November 24, 1794 and served until November 1795; negotiated the treaty settling the boundary

between the United States and East and West Florida, and between the United States and Louisiana; elected as a Federalist to the Fifth Congress to fill the vacancy caused by the resignation of William L. Smith; reelected to the Sixth Congress, and served from November 23, 1797 to March 3, 1801; one of the managers appointed by the House of Representatives in 1798 to conduct the impeachment proceedings against William Blount, a Senator from Tennessee; resumed the practice of law and also engaged in agricultural pursuits; appointed major general in the War of 1812 and served throughout the war; president general of the Society of the Cincinnati, 1825-1828; died in Charleston, S.C., November 2, 1828; interment in St. Philip's Churchyard.

**Bibliography:** *DAB.*

**PINDALL, James,** a Representative from Virginia; born in Monongalia County, Va. (now West Virginia), about 1783; attended the common schools; studied law; was admitted to the bar in 1803 and practiced in Morgantown; moved to Clarksburg (now West Virginia) and continued the practice of his profession; held various local offices; served in the Virginia senate 1808-1812; was colonel of militia; elected as a Federalist to the Fifteenth and Sixteenth Congresses and served from March 4, 1817, until his resignation on July 26, 1820; died in Clarksburg, Harrison County, Va. (now West Virginia), November 22, 1825; interment in what was known as the Daniel Davisson burial ground in Clarksburg, W.Va.

**PINDAR, John Sigsbee,** a Representative from New York; born in Sharon, Schoharie County, N.Y., November 18, 1835; attended the common schools and Richmondville Seminary; studied law; was admitted to the bar in 1865; president of the village of Cobleskill 1882-1884; chairman of the Democratic county committee for ten years; elected as a Democrat to the Forty-ninth Congress (March 4, 1885-March 3, 1887); delegate to the Democratic National Convention in 1888; resumed the practice of law in Cobleskill, N.Y.; unsuccessful candidate in 1888 for election to the Fifty-first Congress; subsequently elected to the Fifty-first Congress to fill the vacancy caused by the death of David Wilber and served from November 4, 1890, to March 3, 1891; resumed the practice of law; died in Cobleskill, Schoharie County, N.Y., June 30, 1907; interment in Cobleskill Cemetery.

**PINE, William Bliss,** a Senator from Oklahoma; born in Bluffs, Scott County, Ill., December 30, 1877; attended the public schools; taught school three years; employed as a salesman of harvesters; moved to Chanute, Kans., and was employed in the oil producing business, moved to Oklahoma in 1904 and continued in the oil industry; in 1909 located in Okmulgee, Okla., where he eventually became extensively engaged in the production of oil; elected as a Republican to the United States Senate, and served from March 4, 1925 to March 3, 1931; unsuccessful candidate for reelection in 1930; resumed his former business pursuits; unsuccessful candidate in 1934 for election for Governor of Oklahoma; died in Okmulgee, Okla., August 25, 1942; was the Republican nominee for the United States Senate at the time of his death; interment in Okmulgee Cemetery.

**Bibliography:** Hanson, Maynard J. "Senator William B. Pine and His Times." Ph.D. dissertation, Oklahoma State University, 1983; Jones, Stephen. *Once Before: The Political and Senatorial Careers of Oklahoma's First Two Republican United States Senators: John W. Harreld and W.B. Pine.* Enid, Okla.: Dougherty Press, 1986.

**PINERO, Jesús T.,** a Resident Commissioner from Puerto Rico; born in Carolina, P.R., April 16, 1897; attended the grade schools, Colegio Janer (a private school), Baltimore, Md., and the School of Engineering at the University of Pennsylvania at Philadelphia; was graduated from the College of Liberal Arts, University of Puerto Rico at Rio Piedras, in 1914; engaged in agricultural pursuits and in the sugarcane and dairy industries, 1920-1944; member and president of the municipal assembly at Carolina, P.R., 1928-1932; member of the Puerto Rico House of Representatives, 1940-1944; delegate to the Popular Democratic Convention at San Juan, P.R., in 1940; elected as a Popular Democrat a Resident Commissioner to the United States and served from January 3, 1945, until his resignation on September 2, 1946, having been appointed Governor of Puerto Rico, serving until December 1948; died in Loiza, P.R., November 19, 1952; interment in Carolina Cemetery, Carolina, P.R.

**PINKNEY, William,** a Representative and a Senator from Maryland; born in Annapolis, Md., March 17, 1764; pursued classical studies; studied medicine but did not practice; studied law; was admitted to the bar in 1786 and commenced practice in Harford County, Md.; member of the Maryland constitutional ratification convention in 1788; member, Maryland State house of delegates, 1789-1792; elected to the Second Congress and served from March 4, 1791, to November of that year, when he resigned due to questions of ineligibility; member, executive council of Maryland, 1792-1795; member, Maryland State house of delegates, 1795; appointed by President George Washington as one of the commissioners to London under the Jay Treaty, 1796-1804; attorney general of Maryland in 1805; appointed jointly with James Monroe as Commissioner Plenipotentiary and Extraordinary to Great Britain, 1806-1808; appointed Minister Plenipotentiary to Great Britain on February 26, 1808, and served until May 1811; returned to Baltimore, Md.; appointed Attorney General in the Cabinet of President James Madison, and served from December 11, 1811 until February 10, 1814; served as a major in the Maryland militia during the War of 1812 and was wounded at the Battle of Bladensburg, Md., in August 1814; elected to the Fourteenth Congress and served from March 4, 1815, to April 18, 1816, when he resigned to accept a diplomatic position; appointed Minister Plenipotentiary to Russia on March 7, 1816, and served until February 1818; elected as a Republican to the United States Senate to fill the vacancy caused by the death of Alexander Contee Hanson, and served from December 21, 1819 until his death in Washington, D.C., February 25, 1822; interment in Congressional Cemetery.

Bibliography: *DAB*; Ireland, Robert. *The Legal Career of William Pinkney, 1764-1822.* New York: Garland, 1986; Pinkney, William. *Life of William Pinkney.* 1853. Reprint. New York: Da Capo Press, 1969.

**PIPER, William,** a Representative from Pennsylvania; born at Bloody Run (now Everett), Bedford County, Pa., January 1, 1774; commanded a regiment during the War of 1812; adjutant general of Pennsylvania after the war; elected as a Republican to the Twelfth, Thirteenth, and Fourteenth Congresses (March 4, 1811-March 3, 1817); died in Hopewell Township, near Everett, Pa., in 1852; interment in the Piper Cemetery on his farm in Hopewell Township.

**PIPER, William Adam,** a Representative from California; born in Franklin County, Pa., May 21, 1826; attended the common schools; moved to St. Louis, Mo.; during the Mexican War served in Company A, Eighth Missouri Light Artillery, from June 8, 1846, to June 24, 1847; moved to California in 1848, and in 1849 settled in San Francisco, where he engaged in mercantile pursuits; elected as a Democrat to the Forty-fourth Congress (March 4, 1875-March 3, 1877); unsuccessful candidate for reelection in 1876 to the Forty-fifth Congress; continued business activities; died in San Francisco, Calif., August 5, 1899; interment in Odd Fellows Cemetery.

**PIRCE, William Almy,** a Representative from Rhode Island; born in Hope, Providence County, R.I., February 29, 1824; attended the common schools and Smithville Seminary (now Lapham Institute); taught school; manager of the store and countingroom of his father's cotton mill in Simmons Upper Village, R.I., for ten years; engaged in the manufacture of cotton goods 1854-1863; served in the State senate in 1855; member of the State house of representatives

in 1858 and 1862; assessor of internal revenue for the second district of Rhode Island 1862-1873; appointed paymaster with rank of major in the State militia in 1863; again a member of the State house of representatives 1879-1881; again served in the State senate in 1882; delegate to the Republican National Convention in 1880; member of the Republican National Committee in 1880 and 1884; presented credentials as a Republican Member-elect to the Forty-ninth Congress and served from March 4, 1885, to January 25, 1887, when the seat was declared vacant on account of irregularities in the election; justice of the peace and assessor of taxes in Johnston, R.I.; died in Johnston, R.I., March 5, 1891; interment in Swan Point Cemetery, R.I.

**PIRNIE, Alexander,** a Representative from New York; born in Pulaski, Oswego County, N.Y., April 16, 1903; graduated from Pulaski Academy in 1920, Cornell University in 1924, and from Cornell Law School in 1926; was admitted to the bar in 1926 and commenced the practice of law in Utica, N.Y.; in 1924 was commissioned a second lieutenant, Infantry, Officers Reserve Corps; during the Second World War, served in Europe and retired as a colonel; awarded Bronze Star and Legion of Merit; elected as a Republican to the Eighty-sixth and to the six succeeding Congresses (January 3, 1959-January 3, 1973); was not a candidate for reelection in 1972 to the Ninety-third Congress; member, Interparliamentary Union, 1965-1982; resumed the practice of law; presiding officer of a clothing firm, Mohawk, N.Y., 1977-1980; resided in Utica, N.Y. until his death in Canastota, N.Y. on June 12, 1982; interment in Pulaski Cemetery, Pulaski, N.Y.

**PITCHER, Nathaniel,** a Representative from New York; born in Litchfield, Conn., in 1777; received a limited schooling; moved to Sandy Hill, N.Y.; supervisor, 1804-1810; member of the New York State assembly in 1806 and 1815-1817; assessor of Kingsbury in 1812; surrogate of Washington County in 1812 and 1813; town clerk of Kingsbury in 1813 and 1814, and justice of the peace; studied law; was admitted to the bar and practiced; delegate to the State constitutional convention in 1821; Lieutenant Governor in 1826; became Governor of New York upon the death of Governor De Witt Clinton on February 11, 1828, and served until January 1, 1829; elected to the Sixteenth and Seventeenth Congresses (March 4, 1819-March 3, 1823); elected as a Jacksonian to the Twenty-second Congress (March 4, 1831-March 3, 1833); died in Sandy Hill (now Hudson Falls), Washington County, N.Y., May 25, 1836; interment in Wright Cemetery.

**PITKIN, Timothy,** a Representative from Connecticut; born in Farmington, Conn., on January 21, 1766; received private instruction and was graduated from Yale College in 1785; taught in the academy at Plainfield, Conn., for one year; studied law; was admitted to the bar in 1788 and commenced practice in Farmington; member of the State house of representatives in 1790, 1792, and 1794-1805, serving as clerk of the house 1800-1802 and as speaker 1803-1805; elected as a Federalist to the Ninth Congress to fill in part the vacancies caused by the resignations of Calvin Goddard and Roger Griswold; reelected to the Tenth and to the five succeeding Congresses and served from September 16, 1805, to March 3, 1819; was not a candidate for renomination in 1818; delegate to the convention which framed the new State constitution in 1818; resumed the practice of law and engaged in literary work; again a member of the State house of representatives 1819-1830; died in New Haven, Conn., December 18, 1847; interment in Grove Street Cemetery.

Bibliography: *DAB.*

**PITMAN, Charles Wesley,** a Representative from Pennsylvania; born in New Jersey; attended the common schools; was graduated from Dickinson College, Carlisle, Pa., in 1838; moved to Pottsville, Pa., the same year and conducted a school for boys, known as the Pottsville Academy; elected as a Whig to the

Thirty-first Congress (March 4, 1849-March 3, 1851); later became affiliated with the Republican Party; engaged extensively in the lumber business; elected sheriff of Schuylkill County in 1870 and served from January 1871 until his death in Pottsville, Schuylkill County, Pa., June 8, 1871; interment in Presbyterian Cemetery.

**PITNEY, Mahlon,** a Representative from New Jersey; born in Morristown, Morris County, N.J., February 5, 1858; attended the public schools; A.B., Princeton College, 1879, and A.M., 1882; studied law; was admitted to the bar in June 1882 and practiced in Dover and Morristown, N.J., 1882-1889; elected as a Republican to the Fifty-fourth and Fifty-fifth Congresses and served from March 4, 1895, to January 10, 1899, when he resigned; member of the New Jersey State senate, 1899-1901, and its president in 1901; associate justice of the supreme court of New Jersey 1901-1908; chancellor of New Jersey from 1908 to 1912, when he resigned; nominated on February 19, 1912 by President William Howard Taft as an Associate Justice of the United States Supreme Court; was confirmed by the Senate on March 13, 1912, and served from March 18, 1912, until December 31, 1922, when he resigned; died in Washington, D.C., December 9, 1924; interment in Evergreen Cemetery, Morristown, N.J.

**Bibliography:** *DAB.*

**PITTENGER, William Alvin,** a Representative from Minnesota; born on a farm near Crawfordsville, Montgomery County, Ind., December 29, 1885; attended rural schools; was graduated from Wabash College, Crawfordsville, Ind., in 1909, and from Harvard Law School in 1912; was admitted to the bar in 1912 and commenced practice in Duluth, Minn.; member of the State house of representatives 1917-1920; elected as a Republican to the Seventy-first and Seventy-second Congresses (March 4, 1929-March 3, 1933); unsuccessful candidate for reelection in 1932 to the Seventy-third Congress; resumed the practice of law in Duluth, Minn.; elected to the Seventy-fourth Congress (January 3, 1935-January 3, 1937); unsuccessful candidate for reelection in 1936 to the Seventy-fifth Congress; elected to the Seventy-sixth and to the three succeeding Congresses (January 3, 1939-January 3, 1947); unsuccessful candidate for reelection in 1946 to the Eightieth Congress; resumed the practice of law; died in Duluth, Minn., November 26, 1951; interment in Forest Hill Cemetery.

**PITTMAN, Key,** a Senator from Nevada; born near Vicksburg, Warren County, Miss., September 12, 1872; educated by private tutors; attended Southwestern Presbyterian University, Clarksville, Tenn., 1887-1890; moved to Seattle, Wash., in October 1890; studied law in the office of August Moore in Seattle and in Mt. Vernon, Wash., 1890-1893; joined in the gold rush to the fields of the Klondike, Alaska, in 1897 and worked as a miner in Dawson until 1899; elected city attorney of Nome, Alaska, September 13, 1899; moved to the silver boom-town of Tonopah, Nev., in January 1902 and continued the practice of law; invested in real estate and mining enterprises; appointed to represent the State of Nevada at the St. Louis Exposition, the Lewis and Clark Exposition, and the irrigation congress; chaired the committee on platform and resolutions at the Democratic National Convention of 1928; unsuccessful Democratic candidate for election to the United States Senate in 1910; elected as a Democrat to the United States Senate in 1913 to fill the vacancy caused by the death of George S. Nixon; reelected in 1916, 1922, 1928, and 1934, and served from January 29, 1913 until his death in Reno, Nev., November 10, 1940; had been reelected November 5, 1940 for the term beginning January 3, 1941; served as President pro tempore of the United States Senate during the Seventy-third through Seventy-sixth Congresses; chairman, Committee on Territories (Sixty-third through Sixty-fifth Congresses), Committee on Industrial Expositions (Sixty-sixth Congress), Committee on Foreign Relations (Seventy-third through Seventy-sixth Congresses); interment in Mountain View Cemetery, Reno, Nev.

**Bibliography:** *DAB*; Glad, Betty. *Key Pittman: The Tragedy of a Senate Insider.* New York: Columbia University Press, 1986; Israel, Fred. *Nevada's Key Pittman.* Lincoln: University of Nebraska Press, 1963.

**PLAISTED, Harris Merrill,** a Representative from Maine; born in Jefferson, Coos County, N.H., November 2, 1828; attended the common schools; was graduated from Waterville (Maine) College in 1853 and from the Albany (N.Y.) Law School in 1856; was admitted to the bar and commenced practice in Bangor, Maine, in 1856; during the Civil War served in the Union Army and was commissioned lieutenant colonel of the Eleventh Regiment, Maine Infantry, October 30, 1861, and colonel on May 12, 1862; brevetted brigadier general of Volunteers, February 21, 1865, and major general on March 13, 1865; member of the Maine State house of representatives in 1867 and 1868; delegate to the Republican National Convention of 1868; attorney general of Maine, 1873-1875; elected as a Republican to the Forty-fourth Congress to fill the vacancy caused by the death of Samuel F. Hersey, and served from September 13, 1875 to March 3, 1877; was not a candidate for renomination in 1876 to the Forty-fifth Congress; author of "Digest of Maine Reports from 1820 to 1880"; elected Governor of Maine in 1880, and served from January 13, 1881 to January 3, 1883; unsuccessful candidate for reelection in 1882; editor and publisher of the New Age, Augusta, from 1883 until his death in Bangor, Maine, January 31, 1898; interment in Mount Hope Cemetery.

**Bibliography:** *DAB.*

**PLANT, David,** a Representative from Connecticut; born in Stratford, Conn., March 29, 1783; attended the Episcopal Academy, Cheshire, Conn.; was graduated from Yale College in 1804; studied law in the Litchfield (Conn.) Law School; was admitted to the bar in 1804 and commenced practice in Stratford; judge of the probate court of Fairfield County; member of the Connecticut State house of representatives, 1817-1820, and served as speaker; served in the State senate, 1821-1822; Lieutenant Governor of Connecticut, 1823-1827; elected to the Twentieth Congress (March 4, 1827-March 3, 1829); was not a candidate for renomination in 1828 to the Twenty-first Congress; resumed the practice of law; died in Stratford, Conn., October 18, 1851; interment in the Congregational Burying Ground.

**PLANTS, Tobias Avery,** a Representative from Ohio; born at Sewickley, Beaver County, Pa., March 17, 1811; apprenticed to a saddler at the age of twelve; received a limited common school education; attended Beaver College, Meadville, Pa.; taught school, and while teaching studied law with Edwin M. Stanton in the office of Judge David Powell at Steubenville, Ohio; was admitted to the bar and commenced practice in Athens, Ohio, in 1846, but soon moved to Pomeroy; member of the State house of representatives 1858-1861; owner and publisher of the Pomeroy Weekly Telegraph about 1860; elected as a Republican to the Thirty-ninth and Fortieth Congresses (March 4, 1865-March 3, 1869); was not a candidate for renomination in 1868; judge of the court of common pleas in Meigs County from 1873 to 1875, when he resigned to resume the practice of law; president of the First City Bank of Pomeroy from 1878 until his death in Pomeroy, Meigs County, Ohio, June 19, 1887; interment in Beech Grove Cemetery.

**PLATER, George** (father of Thomas Plater), a Delegate from Maryland; born in Sotterly, near Leonardtown, St. Marys County, Md., November 8, 1735; was graduated from the College of William and Mary, Williamsburg, Va., in 1753; studied law; was admitted to the bar and commenced practice in Annapolis, Md.; member of the Maryland Assembly in 1758; naval officer at Patuxent, 1767-1771; judge of the provincial court, 1771-1773; member of the council in 1773 and 1774; represented St. Marys County in the Annapolis conventions of 1776; Member of the Continental Congress, 1778-1780; president of the State ratification convention in 1788; elected

Governor of Maryland by the General Assembly, and served from November 14, 1791 until his death in Annapolis, Md., February 10, 1792; interment in the garden of "Sotterly," his home, near Leonardtown, Md.

**Bibliography:** *DAB*.

**PLATER, Thomas** (son of George Plater), a Representative from Maryland; born in Annapolis, Md., May 9, 1769; attended the College of William and Mary, Williamsburg, Va.; studied law; was admitted to the bar and practiced; served as lieutenant colonel in the Maryland State militia in 1794 for duty during the Whiskey Rebellion; held several local offices; elected as a Federalist to the Seventh and Eighth Congresses (March 4, 1801-March 3, 1805); resumed the practice of law and resided at his estate overlooking Georgetown, Md. (now part of the District of Columbia); moved to Poolesville, Md., where he died on May 1, 1830.

**PLATT, Edmund,** a Representative from New York; born in Poughkeepsie, N.Y., February 2, 1865; attended a private school and Riverview Academy; was graduated from Eastman Business College, Poughkeepsie, N.Y.; learned the printer's trade; was graduated from Harvard University in 1888; taught school and studied law; moved to Wisconsin and edited the Superior (Wis.) Evening Telegram in 1890 and 1891; returned to Poughkeepsie in 1891 and engaged in editing and publishing the Poughkeepsie Eagle; member of the board of water commissioners of Poughkeepsie, N.Y.; elected as a Republican to the Sixty-third and to the three succeeding Congresses and served from March 4, 1913, to June 7, 1920, when he resigned to accept appointment by President Woodrow Wilson to the Federal Reserve Board; chairman, Committee on Banking and Currency (Sixty-sixth Congress); became vice governor of the board in August 1920 and served until 1930 when he resigned; returned to Poughkeepsie, N.Y., and engaged in an extensive banking business; died in Chazy, Clinton County, N.Y., while on a visit, August 7, 1939; interment in the Poughkeepsie Rural Cemetery, Poughkeepsie, N.Y.

**PLATT, James Henry, Jr.,** a Representative from Virginia; born in St. John's, Canada, July 13, 1837; moved to Burlington, Vt.; attended the common schools; completed preparatory studies and graduated from the medical department of the University of Vermont at Burlington in 1859; during the Civil War entered the Union Army as first sergeant of the Third Regiment, Vermont Volunteer Infantry; served as captain and lieutenant colonel; declined assignment to duty as chief quartermaster of the Sixth Corps; settled in Petersburg, Va., April 6, 1865; member of the Virginia constitutional convention in 1867; member of the city council in 1867 and 1868; moved to Norfolk, Va.; upon the readmission of Virginia to representation was elected as a Republican to the Forty-first, Forty-second, and Forty-third Congresses and served from January 26, 1870, to March 3, 1875; chairman, Committee on Public Buildings and Grounds (Forty-third Congress); unsuccessful candidate for reelection in 1874 to the Forty-fourth Congress; moved to New York in 1876 and engaged in the manufacture of oil products; moved to Colorado in 1887 and settled in Denver; engaged in the insurance business, paper manufacturing, and in mining; was drowned in Green Lake, near Georgetown, Colo., August 13, 1894; interment in Fairmont Cemetery, Denver, Colo.

**PLATT, Jonas** (son of Zephaniah Platt), a Representative from New York; born in Poughkeepsie, N.Y., June 30, 1769; attended a French academy at Montreal, Canada; studied law; was admitted to the bar in 1790 and practiced in Poughkeepsie; county clerk of Herkimer County 1791-1798 and of Oneida County 1798-1802; member of the State assembly in 1796; elected as a Federalist to the Sixth Congress (March 4, 1799-March 3, 1801); chairman, Committee on Revisal and Unfinished Business (Sixth Congress); resumed the practice of law; general of Cavalry in the State militia; was an unsuccessful candidate for Governor in 1810; member of the State senate 1810-1813; member of the council of appointment in 1813; served as associate justice of the supreme court of New York 1814-1821; delegate to the New York Constitutional Convention in 1821; resumed the practice of law; died in Peru, Clinton County, N.Y., February 22, 1834; interment in Riverside Cemetery, Plattsburg, N.Y.

**PLATT, Orville Hitchcock,** a Senator from Connecticut; born in Washington, Litchfield County, Conn., July 19, 1827; attended the common schools and graduated from the Gunnery Academy, Washington, Conn.; studied law in Litchfield, Conn.; was admitted to the bar in 1850 and commenced practice in Towanda, Pa.; moved to Meriden, Conn., in 1850 and continued the practice of his profession; clerk of the State senate 1855-1856; secretary of State of Connecticut 1857; member, State senate 1861-1862; member, State house of representatives in 1864, 1869, and served as speaker in the latter year; State's attorney for New Haven County 1877-1879; elected as a Republican to the United States Senate in 1879; reelected in 1885, 1891, 1897, and 1903 and served from March 4, 1879, until his death in Meriden, Conn., April 21, 1905; Republican caucus chairman 1902-1903; chairman, Committee on Patents (Forty-seventh through Forty-ninth and Fifty-fourth and Fifty-fifth Congresses), Committee on Pensions (Forty-seventh Congress), Committee on Territories (Fiftieth through Fifty-second Congresses), Committee on Cuban Relations (Fifty-sixth through Fifty-eighth Congresses), Republican Conference (Fifty-seventh Congress), Committee on the Judiciary (Fifty-eighth and Fifty-ninth Congresses); interment in Washington (Conn.) Cemetery on the Green.

**Bibliography:** *DAB*; Coolidge, Louis. *An Old Fashioned Senator: Orville H. Platt.* 1910. Reprint. Port Washington, N.Y.: Kennikat, 1971; Smith, Edwina C. "Conservatism in the Gilded Age: The Senatorial Career of Orville H. Platt." Ph.D. dissertation, University of North Carolina, 1976.

**PLATT, Thomas Collier,** a Representative and a Senator from New York; born in Owego, Tioga County, N.Y., July 15, 1833; was prepared for college in the Owego Academy and attended Yale College in 1849 and 1850; in 1852 engaged in business as a druggist and continued for twenty years; president of the Tioga National Bank; interested in the lumbering business in Michigan; clerk of Tioga County 1859-1861; elected as a Republican to the Forty-third and Forty-fourth Congresses (March 4, 1873-March 3, 1877); elected as a Republican to the United States Senate in 1881, and served from March 4, 1881, to May 16, 1881, when he resigned because of a disagreement with President James A. Garfield over federal appointments in New York; unsuccessful candidate for election to the United States Senate to succeed himself; chairman, Committee on Enrolled Bills (Forty-seventh Congress); secretary and director of the United States Express Co. in 1879 and elected president of the company in 1880; member and president of the Board of Quarantine Commissioners of New York 1880-1888; member of the Republican National Committee; elected to the United States Senate in 1896; reelected in 1903 and served from March 4, 1897, to March 3, 1909; chairman, Committee on Transportation Routes to the Seaboard (Fifty-fifth Congress), Committee on Printing (Fifty-sixth through Sixtieth Congresses), Committee on Cuban Relations (Fifty-ninth Congress), Committee on Interoceanic Canals (Fifty-ninth Congress); died in New York City, March 6, 1910; interment in Owego Cemetery, Owego, N.Y.

**Bibliography:** *DAB*; Gosnell, Harold. *Boss Platt and His New York Machine: A Study of the Political Leadership of Thomas C. Platt, Theodore Roosevelt, and Others.* 1924. Reprint. New York: AMS Press, 1969; Platt, Thomas Collier. *The Autobiography of Thomas Collier Platt.* 1910. Reprint. New York: Arno Press, 1974.

**PLATT, Zephaniah** (father of Jonas Platt), a Delegate from New York; born in Huntington, Long Island, Suffolk County, N.Y., May 27, 1735; received an English education; studied law; was admitted to the bar and commenced practice in Poughkeepsie, N.Y.; Member of the Provincial Congress 1775-1777; member of the council of safety in 1777; served in the State senate 1777-1783; Member of the Continental Congress in 1785 and 1786; member of the council of appointment in 1778 and 1781; county judge of Dutchess County 1781-1795; founded the town of Plattsburg in 1784; delegate to the State constitutional convention in 1788; moved to Plattsburg, N.Y., in 1798 and continued the practice of law; regent of the State university from 1791 until his death; one of the projectors of the Erie Canal; died in Plattsburg, N.Y., September 12, 1807; interment in Riverside Cemetery.

**PLAUCHÉ, Vance Gabriel,** a Representative from Louisiana; born in Plaucheville, Avoyelles Parish, La., August 25, 1897; attended private and public schools; B.S., College of St. Francis Xavier, 1914; LL.B., Loyola University, New Orleans, La., 1918; during the First World War served overseas as a private, first class; was admitted to the bar in 1918 and commenced practice in Lake Charles, La.; city attorney of Lake Charles, La., 1928-1932; district counsel for the Home Owners' Loan Corporation 1933-1935; served as secretary of the State Civil Service commission in 1940; delegate to the Democratic State convention at Baton Rouge, La., in 1940; elected as a Democrat to the Seventy-seventh Congress (January 3, 1941-January 3, 1943); was not a candidate for reelection in 1942 to the Seventy-eighth Congress; resumed the practice of law; died in Lake Charles, La., April 2, 1976; interment in Consolata Cemetery.

**PLEASANTS, James,** a Representative and a Senator from Virginia; born at "Cold Comfort," in Powhatan County, Va., October 24, 1769; pursued classical studies and graduated from the College of William and Mary, Williamsburg, Va.; studied law; admitted to the bar and commenced practice in Amelia County in 1791; member, Virginia house of delegates, 1797-1802; clerk of the Virginia house of delegates, 1803-1811; elected as a Republican to the Twelfth and to the four succeeding Congresses, and served from March 4, 1811 to December 14, 1819, when he resigned, having been elected a United States Senator on December 10, 1819; chairman, Committee on Public Expenditures (Thirteenth Congress), Committee on Expenditures in the Department of the Navy (Fifteenth Congress); elected as a Republican to the United States Senate to fill the vacancy caused by the resignation of John W. Eppes, and served from December 14, 1819 to December 15, 1822, when he resigned; chairman, Committee on Naval Affairs (Sixteenth and Seventeenth Congresses); elected Governor of Virginia by the General Assembly, and served from December 1, 1822 to December 1825; delegate to the Virginia constitutional conventions in 1829 and 1830; retired and lived on his estate, "Contention," near Goochland, Va., where he died on November 9, 1836; interment on his estate.

Bibliography: *DAB.*

**PLOESER, Walter Christian,** a Representative from Missouri; born in St. Louis, Mo., January 7, 1907; attended the public schools of St. Louis, Mo., Casper and Lusk, Wyo., and the City College of Law and Finance, St. Louis, Mo.; engaged in the insurance business in St. Louis, Mo., in 1922 and founded his own company in 1933; organizer and chairman of the board of Marine Underwriters Corp., 1935; served in the Missouri State house of representatives in 1931 and 1932; elected as a Republican to the Seventy-seventh and to the three succeeding Congresses (January 3, 1941-January 3, 1949); chairman, Select Committee on Small Business (Eightieth Congress); unsuccessful candidate for reelection in 1948 to the Eighty-first Congress; delegate to the Republican National Conventions of 1964 and 1968; resumed the insurance business; director of Webster Groves Trust Company; appointed Ambassador to Paraguay on August 5, 1957, and served until September 1959; chairman of board, Salvation Army, 1967-1969; appointed Ambassador to Costa Rica on April 8, 1970, and served until April 1972; is a resident of St. Louis, Mo.

**PLOWMAN, Thomas Scales,** a Representative from Alabama; born in Talladega, Talladega County, Ala., June 8, 1843; attended the common schools; joined the Confederate Army in May 1862 as a member of Company F, Fifty-first Alabama Cavalry; engaged in agricultural and mercantile pursuits in Talladega, Ala.; elected mayor in 1872 and served three terms; delegate to the Democratic National Convention in 1888; for a number of years president of the First National Bank of Talladega; presented credentials as a Democratic Member-elect to the Fifty-fifth Congress and served from March 4, 1897, to February 9, 1898, when he was succeeded by William F. Aldrich, who contested his election; member and chairman of the Talladega County Jury Commission in 1910 and 1911; member of the State senate in 1912; first president of the Bankhead Highway; died in Talladega, Ala., July 26, 1919; interment in Oak Hill Cemetery.

**PLUMB, Preston B.,** a Senator from Kansas; born in Delaware County, Ohio, October 12, 1837; attended a preparatory school; learned the trade of printing and afterward purchased and edited the Xenia News; moved to Lawrence, Kans., in 1856, to support the "Free-State" movement; was one of the founders of Emporia, Kans., where he established the Kansas News in 1857; secretary of the Free-State convention in 1857; member of the Leavenworth constitutional convention in 1859; studied law; as admitted to the bar in 1861; elected to the State house of representatives in 1862; reporter for the State supreme court; during the Civil War entered the Union Army in 1862 as second lieutenant, and served successively as captain, major, and lieutenant colonel; member, of the State house of representatives 1867-1868, and served as speaker in the latter year; prosecuting attorney of Lyon County; president of the Emporia National Bank in 1873; elected as a Republican to the United States Senate in 1877; reelected in 1883 and 1888 and served from March 4, 1877, until his death in Washington, D.C., December 20, 1891; chairman, Committee on Public Lands (Forty-seventh through Fifty-second Congresses); interment in Maplewood Cemetery, Emporia, Lyon County, Kans.

Bibliography: *DAB*; Connelley, William E. *The Life of Preston B. Plumb*. Chicago: Browne and Howell Company, 1913.

**PLUMB, Ralph,** a Representative from Illinois; born in Busti, Chautauqua County, N.Y., March 29, 1816; attended the common schools; engaged in mercantile pursuits; moved to Ohio; member of the State house of representatives in 1855; studied law; was admitted to the bar in 1857 and commenced practice in Oberlin, Lorain County, Ohio; during the Civil War served in the Union Army as captain and quartermaster of Volunteers 1861-1865; was brevetted lieutenant colonel; moved to Illinois in 1866 and settled in Streator; engaged in the mining of coal and the building of railroads; mayor of Streator, Ill., 1882-1885; elected as a Republican to the Forty-ninth and Fiftieth Congresses (March 4, 1885-March 3, 1889); engaged in banking until his death in Streator, Ill., April 8, 1903; interment in Riverview Cemetery.

**PLUMER, Arnold,** a Representative from Pennsylvania; born near Cooperstown, Venango County, Pa., June 6, 1801; was privately tutored at home; completed preparatory studies; sheriff of Venango County in 1823; prothonotary of the county in 1829, and clerk of the courts and recorder from 1830 until 1836; elected as a Democrat to the Twenty-fifth Congress (March 4, 1837-March 3, 1839); appointed marshal of the western district of Pennsylvania by President Martin Van Buren on May 20, 1839, and served until May 6, 1841; elected to the Twenty-seventh Congress (March 4, 1841-March 3, 1843); again appointed United States marshal for the western district of Pennsylvania on December 14, 1847, and served until April 3, 1848; when he resigned; treasurer of Pennsylvania in 1848; engaged in mining and banking enterprises; died in Franklin, Venango County, Pa., on April 28, 1869; interment in Franklin Cemetery.

**PLUMER, George,** a Representative from Pennsylvania; born near Pittsburgh, Pa., December 5, 1762; received a limited schooling; member of the Pennsylvania house of representatives 1812-1815 and again in 1817; elected to the Seventeenth, Eighteenth, and Nineteenth Congresses (March 4, 1821-March 3, 1827); declined to be a candidate for renomination; engaged in agricultural pursuits; died near West Newton, Westmoreland County, Pa., June 8, 1843; interment in Old Sewickley Presbyterian Church Cemetery.

**PLUMER, William** (father of William Plumer, Jr.), a Senator from New Hampshire; born in Newburyport, Mass., June 25, 1759; moved with his parents to Epping, N.H., in 1768; completed preparatory studies; Baptist exhorter; studied law; was admitted to the bar in 1787 and commenced practice in Epping, N.H.; held various local offices; member, New Hampshire State house of representatives, 1785-1786, 1788, 1790-1791, 1797-1800, and served as speaker in 1791 and 1797; member of the State constitutional conventions in 1791 and 1792; elected as a Federalist to the United States Senate to fill the vacancy caused by the resignation of James Sheafe, and served from June 17, 1802 to March 3, 1807; was not a candidate for reelection; member, State senate, 1810-1811, and chosen president of that body in both years; elected Governor of New Hampshire in 1812, and served from June 5, 1812 to June 3, 1813; unsuccessful candidate for reelection in 1813, and for election in 1814; again elected Governor in 1816, reelected in 1817 and 1818, and served from June 6, 1816 to June 3, 1819; presidential elector on the Democratic ticket in 1820; retired from public life and engaged in literary pursuits; one of the founders and the first president of the New Hampshire Historical Society; died in Epping, Rockingham County, N.H., December 22, 1850; interment in the family burial ground on his estate near Epping, N.H.

**Bibliography:** *DAB*; Plumer, William. *William Plumer's Memorandum of Proceedings in the United States Senate, 1803-1807.* Edited by Everett Brown. 1923. Reprint. New York: Da Capo Press, 1969; Turner, Lynn. *William Plummer of New Hampshire, 1759-1850.* Chapel Hill: University of North Carolina Press, 1962.

**PLUMER, William, Jr.** (son of William Plumer), a Representative from New Hampshire; born in Epping, Rockingham County, N.H., February 9, 1789; attended Phillips Exeter Academy, Exeter, N.H., and was graduated from Harvard University in 1809; studied law; was admitted to the bar in 1812 and commenced practice in Epping, N.H.; United States commissioner of loans in 1816 and 1817; member of the State house of representatives in 1818; elected to the Sixteenth, Seventeenth, and Eighteenth Congresses (March 4, 1819-March 3, 1825); member of the State senate in 1827 and 1828; engaged in literary pursuits; member of the State constitutional convention in 1850; died in Epping, N.H., September 18, 1854; interment in the family burial ground on his father's estate near Epping, N.H.

**Bibliography:** Plumer, William, Jr. *The Missouri Compromises and Presidential Politics, 1820-1825, from the Letters of William Plumer, Jr.* Edited by Evert Somerville Brown. St. Louis: Missouri Historical Society, 1926.

**PLUMLEY, Charles Albert** (son of Frank Plumley), a Representative from Vermont; born in Northfield, Washington County, Vt., April 14, 1875; attended the public schools; was graduated from Norwich University, Northfield, Vt., in 1896; assistant secretary of the State senate in 1894; principal and superintendent of the Northfield graded and high schools 1896-1900; assistant clerk and clerk of the State house of representatives 1900-1910; captain in the Vermont National Guard in 1901; colonel in the Officers' Reserve Corps; studied law; was admitted to the bar in 1903 and commenced practice in Northfield, Vt.; secretary of the French-Venezuela Mixed Commission in 1906; member of the State house of representatives 1912-1915, serving as speaker; commissioner of taxes for the State of Vermont 1912-1919; general counsel and tax attorney for a rubber company in Akron, Ohio, in 1919 and 1920; president of Norwich University 1920-1934; reading clerk of the Republican National Conventions of 1936 and 1940; also engaged in banking; elected as a Republican to the Seventy-third Congress to fill the vacancy caused by the resignation of Ernest W. Gibson; reelected to the Seventy-fourth and to the seven succeeding Congresses and served from January 16, 1934, to January 3, 1951; was not a candidate for renomination in 1950; resumed the practice of law in Northfield, Vt.; died in Barre, Vt., October 31, 1964; interment in Mount Hope Cemetery, Northfield, Vt.

**PLUMLEY, Frank** (father of Charles Albert Plumley), a Representative from Vermont; born in Eden, Lamoille County, Vt., December 17, 1844; attended the public schools and People's Academy; taught school near Morrisville, Vt.; studied law in Morrisville and in the University of Michigan at Ann Arbor; was admitted to the bar in Lamoille County, Vt., in May 1869 and commenced practice in Northfield; State's attorney of Washington County 1876-1880; elected to the State house of representatives in 1882; chairman of the Republican State convention in 1886; delegate to the Republican National Convention in 1888; United States district attorney for the district of Vermont 1889-1894; served in the State senate in 1894; member of the Vermont Court of Claims 1902-1904 and chief justice 1904-1908; appointed by President Theodore Roosevelt in 1903 as umpire of the mixed commissions of Great Britain and Venezuela, and the Netherlands and Venezuela, sitting in Caracas, Venezuela; was later selected by France and by Venezuela as umpire in the French-Venezuela mixed commission, which sat in Northfield, Vt., in 1905; trustee of Norwich University, Northfield, Vt.; elected as a Republican to the Sixty-first, Sixty-second, and Sixty-third Congresses (March 4, 1909-March 3, 1915); declined to be a candidate for renomination in 1914; resumed the practice of law in Northfield, Washington County, Vt.; was one of the four delegates from the Congress of the United States to the Interparliamentary Union of the World at Geneva, Switzerland, in 1912; died in Northfield, Vt., April 30, 1924; interment in Mount Hope Cemetery.

**Bibliography:** *DAB*.

**PLUMMER, Franklin E.,** a Representative from Mississippi; born in Massachusetts; completed preparatory studies; moved to Mississippi and taught school in Copiah County, Miss.; studied law; was admitted to the bar and commenced practice in Westville, Miss.; held various local offices; member of the State house of representatives; founded the town of Pittsburg (now part of Grenada); elected as a Jacksonian to the Twenty-second and Twenty-third Congresses (March 4, 1831-March 3, 1835); unsuccessful candidate for the United States Senate; died in Jackson, Miss., September 24, 1847.

**Bibliography:** Miles, Edwin A. "Franklin E. Plummer: Piney Woods Spokesman of the Jackson Era." *Journal of Mississippi History* 14 (January 1952): 2-34.

**POAGE, William Robert,** a Representative from Texas; born in Waco, McLennan County, Tex., December 28, 1899; in 1901 moved to Throckmorton County, Tex., with his parents, who settled near Woodson; attended the rural schools of Throckmorton County, Tex.; during the First World War served as an apprentice seaman in the United States Navy; attended the University of Texas in Austin and the University of Colorado at Boulder; A.B., Baylor University, Waco, Tex., 1921; engaged in agricultural pursuits, 1920-1922; instructor in geology at Baylor University, 1922-1924; LL.B., Baylor University law department, 1924; was admitted to the bar the same year and commenced practice in Waco, Tex.; instructor in law at Baylor University, 1924-1928; member of the Texas State house of representatives, 1925-1929; served in the State senate, 1931-1937; delegate, Texas State Democratic convention, 1922; delegate to the Democratic National Conventions of 1956, 1960, and 1964; elected as a Democrat to the Seventy-fifth and to the twenty succeeding Congresses, and served from January 3, 1937 until his resignation on December 31, 1978; chairman, Committee on Agriculture (Ninetieth through Ninety-third Congresses); was not a candidate for reelection in 1978 to the Ninety-sixth Congress; was a resident of Waco, Tex., until his death in Temple, Tex., January 3, 1987; interment in Oakwood Cemetery, Waco, Tex.

Bibliography: Poage, W.R. *My First 85 Years*. Waco, Tex.: Baylor University, 1985.

PODELL, Bertram L., a Representative from New York; born in Brooklyn, N.Y., December 27, 1925; attended Yeshiva of Flatbush and Abraham Lincoln High School; A.B., St. John's University, 1944; LL.B., Brooklyn Law School, 1950; admitted to the bar in 1950 and commenced practice in New York City; served in the United States Navy, 1944-1946; member of the New York State assembly, 1954-1968; elected as a Democrat to the Ninetieth Congress, February 20, 1968, by special election to fill the vacancy caused by the resignation of Abraham J. Multer; reelected to the three succeeding Congresses, and served from February 20, 1968 until January 3, 1975; unsuccessful candidate for renomination in 1974 to the Ninety-fourth Congress; resumed the practice of law in New York City where he is a resident.

POEHLER, Henry, a Representative from Minnesota; born in Hiddeson, Lippe-Detmold, Germany, August 22, 1833; attended his father's academy; immigrated to the United States in April 1848 and settled in Burlington, Iowa, where he attended the public schools; moved to St. Paul, Minn., in 1853 and to Henderson, Sibley County, Minn., in 1854; engaged in general merchandising and as a grain merchant; appointed postmaster at Henderson, Minn., February 25, 1856, and served until April 12, 1861; served in the State house of representatives in 1857, 1858, and 1865; county commissioner of Sibley County and chairman of the board from January 1865 to January 1868; member of the State senate in 1872 and 1873 and again in 1876 and 1877; elected as a Democrat to the Forty-sixth Congress (March 4, 1879-March 3, 1881); unsuccessful candidate for reelection in 1880 to the Forty-seventh Congress; unsuccessful candidate for treasurer of Minnesota; served as mayor of Henderson for several terms; moved to Minneapolis in 1889 and engaged in the general merchandise and grain business; moved to Los Angeles, Calif., in 1895; died in Henderson, Minn., while on a visit, on July 18, 1912; interment in Maj. James R. Browne's Cemetery.

POFF, Richard Harding, a Representative from Virginia; born in Radford, Montgomery County, Va., October 19, 1923; attended the Christiansburg, Va., public schools; engaged in undergraduate work at Roanoke College, Salem, Va.; during the Second World War, served as a bomber pilot with the Eighth Air Force in Great Britain; flew thirty-five successful missions over Europe; awarded the Distinguished Flying Cross; was inactivated from the service as a first lieutenant, serving from February 1943 to August 1945; LL.B., University of Virginia School of Law, Charlottesville, 1948; was admitted to the bar in June 1947, and commenced practice in Radford, Va., in 1948; delegate to the Republican National Convention of 1968; elected as a Republican to the Eighty-third and to the nine succeeding Congresses, and served from January 3, 1953 until his resignation on August 29, 1972; appointed a justice of the Supreme Court of Virginia by the General Assembly, and served from August 31, 1972 until his retirement on January 1, 1989; appointed Senior Justice of the Supreme Court of Virginia on January 1, 1989; is a resident of Midlothian, Va.

POINDEXTER, George, a Delegate, a Representative, and a Senator from Mississippi; born in Louisa County, Va., in 1779; had a sporadic education; studied law; was admitted to the bar in 1800 and commenced practice in Milton, Va.; moved to the Territory of Mississippi in 1802 and practiced law in Natchez; attorney general of the Territory; member, Territorial general assembly 1805; elected as a Delegate from Mississippi Territory to the Tenth and to the two succeeding Congresses (March 4, 1807-March 3, 1813); United States district judge for the Territory, 1813-1817; served in the War of 1812; upon the admission of Mississippi as a State into the Union was elected to the Fifteenth Congress, and served from December 10, 1817 to March 3, 1819; chairman, Committee on Public Lands (Fifteenth Congress); elected Governor of Mississippi in 1819, and served from January 5, 1820 to January 7, 1822; unsuccessful candidate for election in 1820 to the Seventeenth Congress, and in 1822 to the Eighteenth Congress; appointed in 1830 to the United States Senate to fill the vacancy caused by the death of Robert H. Adams; subsequently elected, and served from October 15, 1830 to March 3, 1835; unsuccessful candidate for reelection; served as President pro tempore of the Senate during the Twenty-third Congress; chairman, Committee on Private Land Claims (Twenty-second Congress), Committee on Public Lands (Twenty-third Congress); moved to Kentucky and resumed the practice of his profession in Lexington; returned to Jackson, Miss., and continued the practice of law until his death on September 5, 1853; interment in Jackson Cemetery.

Bibliography: *DAB*; Smith, Suanna. "George Poindexter: A Political Biography." Ph.D. dissertation, University of Southern Mississippi, 1980; Swearingen, Mack. *The Early Life of George Poindexter*. New Orleans: Tulane University Press, 1934.

POINDEXTER, Miles, a Representative and a Senator from Washington; born in Memphis, Tenn., April 22, 1868; attended the Fancy Hill Academy, Rockbridge County, Va., and Washington and Lee University, Lexington, Va., graduating in law from that university in 1891; settled in Walla Walla, Wash., in 1891; was admitted to the bar and began the practice of law; prosecuting attorney of Walla Walla County in 1892; moved to Spokane, Wash., in 1897 and continued the practice of law; assistant prosecuting attorney for Spokane County, 1898-1904; judge of the superior court, 1904-1908; elected as a Republican to the Sixty-first Congress (March 4, 1909-March 3, 1911); elected to the United States Senate in 1910; reelected in 1916, and served from March 4, 1911 to March 3, 1923; unsuccessful candidate for reelection in 1922; chairman, Committee on Expenditures in the Interior Department (Sixty-second Congress), Committee on Mines and Mining (Sixty-second, Sixty-sixth and Sixty-seventh Congresses), Committee on Pacific Islands and Puerto Rico (Sixty-second Congress), Committee on Expenditures in the War Department (Sixty-third and Sixty-fourth Congresses), Committee on Indian Depredations (Sixty-fifth Congress); appointed by President Warren G. Harding as Ambassador to Peru on February 19, 1923, and served until March 1928; unsuccessful candidate in 1928 for nomination to the United States Senate; returned to his home, "Elk Cliff," Greenlee, Rockbridge County, Va., where he died on September 21, 1946; interment in the Presbyterian Cemetery, Lexington, Va.

Bibliography: *DAB*; Allen, Howard. *Poindexter of Washington: A Study in Progressive Politics*. Carbondale: Southern Illinois University Press, 1981.

POINSETT, Joel Roberts, a Representative from South Carolina; born in Charleston, S.C., March 2, 1779; spent his early childhood in England; returned to America in 1788; attended private school at Greenfield Hill, Conn., and later in Wandsworth, near London, England; studied medicine at the University of Edinburgh, Scotland, and attended the military school in Woolwich, England; returned to Charleston, S.C., in 1800; studied law for a few months; traveled extensively in Europe from 1801 to 1809, returning to the United States for short intervals; sent to South America by President James Madison in 1809 to investigate the prospects of the revolutionists there in their struggle for independence from Spain;

returned to Charleston, S.C., in 1816; member of the South Carolina State house of representatives, 1816-1819, and 1830-1831; served as president of the board of public works; declined the offer of commissioner to South America by President James Monroe; elected to the Seventeenth and to the two succeeding Congresses, and served from March 4, 1821 to March 7, 1825, when he resigned to enter the diplomatic service; appointed Minister to Mexico on March 8, 1825, and served until he left his post on January 3, 1830, his recall having been requested by the Mexican government; Secretary of War in the Cabinet of President Martin Van Buren from March 7, 1837 until March 5, 1841; was instrumental in the development in the United States of the Poinsettia plant (*Euphorbia pulcherrima*) from plants found in Mexico; one of the founders in 1840 of the National Institute for the Promotion of Science and the Useful Arts; died near what is now Statesburg, Sumter County, S.C., December 12, 1851; interment in the Church of the Holy Cross (Episcopal) Cemetery.

**Bibliography:** *DAB*; Hruneni, George A., Jr. "Palmetto Yankee. The Public Life and Times of Joel Roberts Poinsett: 1824-1851." Ph.D. dissertation, University of California, Santa Barbara, 1972; Rippy, James Fred. *Joel R. Poinsett, Versatile American.* Durham, N.C.: Duke University Press, 1935.

**POLANCO-ABREU, Santiago,** a Resident Commissioner from Puerto Rico; born in Bayamón, P.R., October 30, 1920; attended elementary and high schools in Isabela, P.R.; B.A., University of Puerto Rico, 1941; LL.B., University of Puerto Rico School of Law, 1943; was admitted to the bar in 1943 and practiced law in Isabela and San Juan; legal adviser to the Tax Court of Puerto Rico, 1943-1944; member of the American Bar and Puerto Rico Bar Associations; one of the founders of the Institute for Democratic Studies in San José, Costa Rica; served in the House of Representatives, Commonwealth of Puerto Rico, 1949-1964; member of the Constitutional Convention of Puerto Rico in 1951-1952; appointed speaker of the house, 1963-1964; elected as a Popular Democrat to the United States House of Representatives, November 3, 1964, for a four-year term ending January 3, 1969; unsuccessful candidate for reelection in 1968; resumed the practice of law; was a resident of San Juan, P.R., until his death there on January 18, 1988; interment in Municipal Cemetery, Isabela, P.R.

**POLAND, Luke Potter,** a Senator and a Representative from Vermont; born in Westford, Vt., November 1, 1815; attended the common schools and Jericho Academy; taught school; studied law; was admitted to the bar in December 1836 and practiced in Morrisville, Vt.; register of probate 1839-1840; member of the State constitutional convention in 1843; prosecuting attorney of Lamoille County 1844-1845; judge of the supreme court of Vermont 1848-1860, chief justice 1860-1865; when he resigned; appointed and subsequently elected as a Republican to the United States Senate to fill the vacancy caused by the death of Jacob Collamer and served from November 21, 1865, to March 3, 1867; elected to the Fortieth and to the three succeeding Congresses (March 4, 1867-March 3, 1875); unsuccessful candidate for reelection to the Forty-fourth Congress; chairman, Committee on Revisal and Unfinished Business (Fortieth Congress), Committee on Revision of the Laws (Fortieth, Forty-first and Forty-third Congresses); member, of the Vermont house of representatives 1878; trustee of the University of Vermont at Burlington and of the State Agricultural College; president of the First National Bank of St. Johnsbury for twenty years; elected as a Republican to the Forty-eighth Congress (March 4, 1883-March 3, 1885); was not a candidate for renomination; died at his country home near Waterville, Lamoille County, Vt., July 2, 1887; interment in Mount Pleasant Cemetery, St. Johnsbury, Vt.

**Bibliography:** *DAB*.

**POLK, Albert Fawcett,** a Representative from Delaware; born in Frederica, Kent County, Del., October 11, 1869; attended public and private schools; was graduated from Delaware College (now the University of Delaware), Newark, Del., in 1889; studied law; was admitted to the bar in 1892 and began practice in Georgetown, Del.; attorney for the Delaware State senate in 1899; chairman of the Democratic county committee of Sussex County 1902-1908, 1915, and 1916; also a member of the Democratic State committee during the same periods; member of the Georgetown Board of Education 1905-1912; member and secretary of the Board of Law Examiners of Sussex County 1914-1921; elected as a Democrat to the Sixty-fifth Congress (March 4, 1917-March 3, 1919); was an unsuccessful candidate for reelection in 1918 to the Sixty-sixth Congress; resumed the practice of law; moved to Wilmington, Del., in 1921 and continued the practice of his profession; appointed United States Commissioner for the district of Delaware in 1929 and served until his retirement in 1951; died in Wilmington, Del., on February 14, 1955; interment in Union Cemetery, Georgetown, Del.

**POLK, James Gould,** a Representative from Ohio; born on a farm in Penn Township, Highland County, Ohio, October 6, 1896; attended elementary school in Highland, Ohio; graduated from New Vienna (Ohio) High School in 1915; during the First World War, while attending the Agricultural College of Ohio State University was inducted into the military service on September 5, 1918, and sent to Camp Sherman, Ohio; was discharged on September 19, 1918, due to a physical disability; graduated from Ohio State University in 1919; principal of New Vienna (Ohio) High School 1919-1920; superintendent of schools, New Vienna, 1920-1922; engaged in farming; graduated from Wittenberg College, Springfield, Ohio, in 1923; principal of Hillsboro (Ohio) High School 1923-1928; elected as a Democrat to the Seventy-second and to the four succeeding Congresses (March 4, 1931-January 3, 1941); was not a candidate for renomination in 1940; special assistant in the Department of Agriculture, Washington, D.C., from October 1942 to May 1946; elected as a Democrat to the Eighty-first and to the five succeeding Congresses and served from January 3, 1949, until his death in Washington, D.C., April 28, 1959; interment in Highland Cemetery, Highland, Ohio.

**POLK, James Knox** (brother of William Hawkins Polk), a Representative from Tennessee and 11th President of the United States; born near Little Sugar Creek, Mecklenburg County, N.C., November 2, 1795; moved to Tennessee in 1806 with his parents, who settled in what later became Maury County; attended the common schools and was tutored privately; was graduated from the University of North Carolina at Chapel Hill in 1818; studied law; was admitted to the bar in 1820 and commenced practice in Columbia, Tenn.; chief clerk of the Tennessee State senate, 1821-1823; member of the State house of representatives, 1823-1825; elected to the Nineteenth Congress; reelected as a Jacksonian to the Twentieth through Twenty-fourth Congresses, and as a Democrat to the Twenty-fifth Congress (March 4, 1825-March 3, 1839); chairman, Committee on Ways and Means (Twenty-third Congress); Speaker of the House of Representatives (Twenty-fourth and Twenty-fifth Congresses); was not a candidate for renomination in 1838 to the Twenty-sixth Congress, having become a candidate for Governor; elected Governor of Tennessee in 1839, and served from October 14, 1839 to October 15, 1841; unsuccessful candidate for reelection in 1841, and for election in 1843; elected President of the United States on the Democratic ticket in 1844; was inaugurated on March 4, 1845, and served until March 3, 1849; declined to be a candidate for renomination in 1848; died in Nashville, Tenn., June 15, 1849; interment within the grounds of the State capitol.

**Bibliography:** *DAB*; Polk, James Knox. *Correspondence of James K. Polk.* 6 vols. Edited by Herbert Weaver, Paul H. Bergeron, and Wayne Cutler. Nashville: Vanderbilt University Press, 1969; Sellers, Charles G., Jr. *James K. Polk.* 2 vols. Princeton: Princeton University Press, 1957-1966.

**POLK, Rufus King,** a Representative from Pennsylvania; born in Columbia, Maury County, Tenn., August 23, 1866; attended Webb's Academy, Culleoka, Tenn.; was graduated from Lehigh University, South Bethlehem, Pa., in 1887 and took a post-graduate course in mining engineering; settled in Danville, Montour County, Pa., and was employed as a chemist; held supervisory positions with several steel companies and ultimately became engaged in the manufacture of structural iron; served as first lieutenant of Company F, Twelfth Regiment, Pennsylvania Volunteer Infantry, in the Spanish-American War; delegate to the Democratic National Convention in 1900; elected as a Democrat to the Fifty-sixth and Fifty-seventh Congresses and served from March 4, 1899, until his death in Philadelphia, Pa., March 5, 1902; interment in Fairview Cemetery, Danville, Pa.

**POLK, Trusten,** a Senator from Missouri; born near Bridgeville, Sussex County, Del., May 29, 1811; attended the common schools and a private academy; graduated from Yale College in 1831; studied law; was admitted to the bar in 1835 and commenced practice in St. Louis, Mo.; served as city counselor of St. Louis in 1843; delegate to the Missouri State constitutional convention in 1845; presidential elector on the Democratic ticket in 1848; elected Governor of Missouri in 1856, and served from January 5, 1857 until his resignation on February 27, 1857, having been elected to the United States Senate; served from March 4, 1857 to January 10, 1862, when he was expelled for disloyalty to the Union; during the Civil War served as colonel in the Confederate Army; judge in the military courts of the department of Mississippi in 1864 and 1865, until taken prisoner; resumed the practice of law in St. Louis, Mo., and died there on April 16, 1876; interment in Bellefontaine Cemetery.

Bibliography: *DAB.*

**POLK, William Hawkins** (brother of James Knox Polk), a Representative from Tennessee; born in Maury County, Tenn., May 24, 1815; attended the city schools, Columbia, Tenn., and the University of North Carolina at Chapel Hill in 1832 and 1833; was graduated from the University of Tennessee at Knoxville; studied law; was admitted to the bar in 1839 and commenced practice in Columbia, Tenn.; member of the Tennessee State house of representatives, 1842-1845; appointed Minister to the Two Sicilies on March 13, 1845, and served until May 1847; served as major of the Third Dragoons in the Mexican War in 1847 and 1848; elected as an Independent Democrat to the Thirty-second Congress (March 4, 1851-March 3, 1853); resumed the practice of law; died in Nashville, Tenn., December 16, 1862; interment in Greenwood Cemetery, Columbia, Tenn.

Bibliography: Bergeron, Paul H., ed. "My Brother's Keeper: William H. Polk Goes to School." *North Carolina Historical Review* 44 (Spring 1967): 188-204.

**POLLARD, Ernest Mark,** a Representative from Nebraska; born in Nehawka, Cass County, Nebr., April 15, 1869; attended the district school in Nehawka and was graduated from Nebraska State University at Lincoln in 1893; engaged in agricultural pursuits near Nehawka, Nebr.; member of the Nebraska State house of representatives, 1896-1899; president of the Nebraska Republican League in 1900; elected as a Republican to the Fifty-ninth Congress to fill the vacancy caused by the resignation of Elmer J. Burkett; reelected to the Sixtieth Congress and served from July 18, 1905, to March 3, 1909; unsuccessful candidate for reelection in 1908 to the Sixty-first Congress; delegate to the Republican National Convention of 1912; member of the Nebraska State constitutional convention in 1920 and 1921; resumed agricultural pursuits; moved to Lincoln, Nebr., in 1929; appointed secretary of the Nebraska State department of welfare and labor by Governor Arthur J. Weaver in January 1929 and served until January 1931; died in Lincoln, Nebr., on September 24, 1939; interment in Mount Pleasant Cemetery, Nehawka, Nebr.

**POLLARD, Henry Moses,** a Representative from Missouri; born in Plymouth, Windsor County, Vt., June 14, 1836; attended the common schools; was graduated from Dartmouth College, Hanover, N.H., in 1857; moved to Milwaukee, Wis., where he studied law; was admitted to the bar in 1861; returned to Vermont and served during the Civil War in the Union Army as major in the Eighth Regiment, Vermont Volunteers; moved to Chillicothe, Mo., in 1865 and commenced the practice of law; mayor in 1874; county attorney in 1876; elected as a Republican to the Forty-fifth Congress (March 4, 1877-March 3, 1879); unsuccessful candidate for reelection to the Forty-sixth Congress; moved to St. Louis, Mo., in 1879 and continued the practice of law in that city until his death on February 24, 1904; interment in Edgewood Cemetery, Chillicothe, Mo.

**POLLOCK, Howard Wallace,** a Representative from Alaska; born in Chicago, Ill., April 11, 1920; attended Perkinston High School, Perkinston, Miss., 1935-1939; Junior College, Perkinston, Miss., 1939-1941; University of Santa Clara (Calif.) School of Law, 1952-1953; University of Houston (Tex.) School of Law, J.D., 1953-1955; postgraduate advanced studies, Massachusetts Institute of Technology, Cambridge, Mass., M.S., in industrial management; practicing attorney; enlisted as a seaman in the United States Navy in 1941, retired with rank of lieutenant commander in 1946; president, Alaska Gold and Other Products, Inc.; president, Falcon Alaska Oil Co.; chairman of the board, Alaskan Seafoods, Inc.; Territorial representative, Alaska Territorial Legislature, 1953-1955; Alaska State senator, 1961-1963, and 1965-1966, serving as minority whip, 1965-1966; member, Alaska Republican State Central committee, 1960-1966; committeeman, Republican South-central District, 1962-1966; elected as a Republican to the Ninetieth and Ninety-first Congresses (January 3, 1967-January 3, 1971); was not a candidate for reelection in 1970 to the Ninety-second Congress, but was an unsuccessful candidate for nomination for Governor of Alaska; deputy administrator, National Oceanic and Atmospheric Administration; delegate, United Nations Law of the Sea Conference; served as president, National Rifle Association; is a resident of Arlington, Va.

**POLLOCK, James,** a Representative from Pennsylvania; born in Milton, Pa., September 11, 1810; attended the Kirkpatrick Private School at Milton; was graduated from Princeton College in 1831; studied law; was admitted to the bar in Northumberland County, Pa., in 1833 and practiced in Milton, Pa.; appointed deputy attorney general for Northumberland County in 1836; judge of the court of common pleas; elected as a Whig to the Twenty-eighth Congress to fill the vacancy caused by the death of Henry Frick; reelected to the two succeeding Congresses, and served from April 5, 1844 to March 4, 1849; was not a candidate for renomination in 1848 to the Thirty-first Congress; appointed president judge of the eighth judicial district on January 15, 1851, and served until the judgeship became an elective office; elected Governor of Pennsylvania in 1854, and served from January 16, 1855 to January 19, 1858; declined to be a candidate for renomination in 1857; member of the peace convention of 1861 held in Washington, D.C., in an effort to devise means to prevent the impending war; Director of the Mint in Philadelphia, 1861-1866, and 1869-1873; was the originator of the motto "In God we trust" for all coins of the United States large enough to contain the same; naval officer at Philadelphia in 1879; appointed chief supervisor of election in 1886; died in Lock Haven, Clinton County, Pa., April 19, 1890; interment in Milton Cemetery; Milton, Pa.

Bibliography: *DAB.*

**POLLOCK, William Pegues,** a Senator from South Carolina; born near Cheraw, Chesterfield County, S.C., December 9, 1870; attended private and public schools, and the University of South Carolina at Columbia; graduated from the law department of that university in 1891; served as clerk of the Committee on the District of Columbia in the House of Representatives, 1891-1893; was admitted to the bar in 1893 and commenced practice in Cheraw, S.C.; also engaged in agricultural pursuits; member, South Carolina State house of representatives, 1894-1898; presidential elector on the Democratic ticket in 1900; elected to the State house of representatives in 1902, 1904, and 1906; unsuccessful candidate for election in 1910 to the Sixty-second Congress; elected as a Democrat to the United States Senate to fill the vacancy caused by the death of Benjamin R. Tillman, and served from November 6, 1918 to March 3, 1919; chairman, Committee on National Banks (Sixty-fifth Congress); resumed the practice of law in Cheraw, S.C., and died there on June 2, 1922; interment in St. David's Cemetery.

**POLSLEY, Daniel Haymond,** a Representative from West Virginia; born at Palatine, near Fairmont, Va. (now West Virginia), November 28, 1803; attended the country schools; completed preparatory studies; studied law; was admitted to the bar in 1827 and commenced practice in Wellsburg, Brooke County, Va. (now West Virginia); edited the Western Transcript 1833-1845; moved to Mason County in 1845 and engaged in agricultural pursuits and practiced law; member of the Wheeling loyal conventions of May 13 and June 11, 1861; chosen Lieutenant Governor of the "restored government" of the Commonwealth of Virginia in 1861; judge of the seventh judicial district of West Virginia 1863-1866; elected as a Republican to the Fortieth Congress (March 4, 1867-March 3, 1869); was not a candidate for renomination in 1868; resumed the practice of his profession; died in Point Pleasant, Mason County, W.Va., October 14, 1877; interment in Lone Oak Cemetery.

**POMBO, Richard William,** a Representative from California; born in Tracy, San Joaquin County, Calif., January 8, 1961; attended California State Polytechnic University at Pomona; partner, family beef cattle, trucking and ranching operations; member, San Joaquin County Citizens Land Alliance, vice president; member, San Joaquin County Republican central committee; member of the Tracy city council in 1990, and mayor pro tem of Tracy, 1991-1992; elected as a Republican to the One Hundred Third and One Hundred Fourth Congresses (January 3, 1993-January 3, 1997); is a resident of Tracy, Calif.

**POMERENE, Atlee,** a Senator from Ohio; born in Berlin, Holmes County, Ohio, December 6, 1863; attended the common schools and Vermillion Institute, Hayesville, Ohio; graduated from Princeton College in 1884 and from the Cincinnati Law School in 1886; was admitted to the bar in 1886 and commenced practice in Canton, Ohio; city solicitor, 1887-1891; prosecuting attorney of Stark County, 1897-1900; Ohio tax commissioner, 1906-1908; unsuccessful candidate for the Democratic nomination for Governor in 1908; elected Lieutenant Governor of Ohio in 1910 and served from January until April 1911, when he resigned to assume the duties of United States Senator; elected as a Democrat to the United States Senate in 1911; reelected in 1916, and served from March 4, 1911 to March 3, 1923; unsuccessful candidate for reelection in 1922, and for election in 1926; chairman, Committee on Civil Service and Retrenchment (Sixty-third and Sixty-fourth Congresses), Committee on Privileges and Elections (Sixty-fifth Congress), Committee on Corporations Organized in the District of Columbia (Sixty-sixth Congress); moved to Cleveland, Ohio, in 1923 and resumed the practice of law; delegate representing the United States at the Fifth Pan American Congress in Chile in 1923; appointed by President Calvin Coolidge in 1924 as special counsel for the United States to prosecute the Teapot Dome oil fraud cases; unsuccessful candidate for the Democratic nomination for President of the United States in 1928; appointed chairman of the Reconstruction Finance Corporation by President Herbert Hoover, 1932-1933; resumed the practice of law in Cleveland, Ohio, where he died on November 12, 1937; interment in West Lawn Cemetery, Canton, Ohio.

**Bibliography:** *DAB*; Shriver, Philip. "The Making of a Moderate Progressive: Atlee Pomerene." Ph.D. dissertation, Columbia University, 1954; Smith, Thomas. "The Senatorial Career of Atlee Pomerene of Ohio." Ph.D. dissertation, Kent State University, 1966.

**POMEROY, Charles,** a Representative from Iowa; born in Meriden, New Haven County, Conn., September 3, 1825; received an academic education; studied law and practiced; moved to Iowa in 1855 and engaged in agricultural pursuits; served as receiver of the United States land office at Fort Dodge, Iowa, from September 11, 1861, until March 3, 1869, when he resigned; elected as a Republican to the Forty-first Congress (March 4, 1869-March 3, 1871); unsuccessful candidate for renomination in 1870; was a claim agent until his death in Washington, D.C., February 11, 1891; interment in Oak Hill Cemetery.

**POMEROY, Earl Ralph,** a Representative from North Dakota; born in Valley City, Barnes County, N.Dak., September 2, 1952; B.A., University of North Dakota, 1974; University of Durham, England, graduate research in legal history, 1975-1976; J.D., University of North Dakota, 1979; attorney, 1979-1984; member, North Dakota State house of representatives, 1980-1984; North Dakota State insurance commissioner, 1985-1993; elected as a Democrat to the One Hundred Third and One Hundred Fourth Congresses (January 3, 1993-January 3, 1997); is a resident of Bismarck, N.Dak.

**POMEROY, Samuel Clarke,** a Senator from Kansas; born in Southampton, Mass., January 3, 1816; attended Amherst College, Massachusetts, 1836-1838; moved to New York State in 1838 and taught school; returned to Southampton, Mass., in 1842; held various local offices; member, Massachusetts house of representatives, 1852-1853; organizer and financial agent of the New England Emigrant Aid Co., which encouraged free-soilers to move to Kansas; traveled to Kansas in 1854 and settled in Lawrence; moved to Atchison, Kans.; mayor of Atchison, 1858-1859; member of the free State convention held at Lawrence in 1859; president of the relief committee during the famine in Kansas, 1860-1861; chaired a committee in the early months of 1864 to promote the presidential candidacy of Secretary of the Treasury Salmon P. Chase; upon the admission of Kansas as a State into the Union was elected as a Republican to the United States Senate; reelected in 1867, and served from April 4, 1861 to March 3, 1873; unsuccessful candidate for reelection in 1872; chairman, Committee on Public Lands (Thirty-ninth through Forty-second Congresses); resided in Washington, D.C., for several years; died in Whitinsville, Worcester County, Mass., August 27, 1891; interment in Forest Hills Cemetery, Boston, Mass.

**Bibliography:** *DAB*; Gambone, Joseph. "Samuel C. Pomeroy and the Senatorial Election of 1861, Reconsidered." *Kansas Historical Quarterly* 37 (Spring 1971): 15-32; Kitzhaber, Albert. "Gotterdammerung in Topeka: The Downfall of Senator Pomeroy." *Kansas Historical Quarterly* 18 (August 1950): 243-78.

**POMEROY, Theodore Medad,** a Representative from New York; born in Cayuga, N.Y., December 31, 1824; attended the common schools and Munro Collegiate Institute, Elbridge, N.Y.; was graduated from Hamilton College, Clinton, N.Y., in 1842; studied law; was admitted to the bar in 1846 and commenced practice in Auburn, N.Y.; district attorney of Cayuga County, 1850-1856; member of the New York State assembly in 1857; delegate to the Republican National Conventions of 1860 and 1876, and served as temporary chairman of the latter convention; elected as a Republican to the Thirty-seventh and to the three succeeding Congresses (March 4, 1861-March 3, 1869); chairman, Committee on Expenditures in the Post Office Department (Thirty-eighth Congress), Committee on Banking and Currency (Thirty-ninth and Fortieth Congresses); during the Fortieth Congress was elected Speaker of the House of Representatives on the last day of the session, March 3, 1869, serving one day only; declined to be a candidate for renomination in 1868 to the Forty-first Congress; first vice president and general counsel of the American Express Company in 1868; engaged in banking in Auburn, N.Y., after 1870; mayor of Auburn, 1875-1876; member of the State senate, 1878-1879; died in Auburn, N.Y., March 23, 1905; interment in Fort Hill Cemetery.

**POND, Benjamin,** a Representative from New York; born in Stockbridge, Mass., in 1768; attended the common schools; moved to Poultney, Vt., and thence to that part of the town of Crown Point (later Schroon) now comprised in the town of North Hudson, N.Y., in 1800; engaged in agricultural pursuits; justice of the peace and supervisor in 1804; judge of the court of common pleas of Essex County in 1808, with residence in Schroon; member of the New York State assembly, 1808-1810; elected as a Republican to the Twelfth Congress (March 4, 1811-March 3, 1813); served in the War of 1812 and participated in the siege and Battle of Plattsburgh in September 1814 as a volunteer in Captain Russell Walker's company of the Thirty-seventh Regiment, New York Militia; elected to the Fourteenth Congress but died of disease, incurred through exposure at the siege of Plattsburgh, in Schroon, N.Y., October 6, 1814, before the beginning of the congressional term; interment in Pine Ridge Cemetery, North Hudson, Essex County, N.Y.; reinterment in Riverside Cemetery, Elizabethtown, Essex County, N.Y., September 3, 1923.

**POOL, Joe Richard,** a Representative from Texas; born in Fort Worth, Tarrant County, Tex., February 18, 1911; attended the Dallas public schools and the University of Texas, 1929-1933; graduated from Southern Methodist University School of Law, Dallas, Tex., in 1937; was admitted to the Texas bar the same year and commenced the practice of law in Dallas, Tex.; served with the United States Army as a special investigator, Air Corps Intelligence, 1943-1945; member of State house of representatives, 1953-1958; unsuccessful candidate for the Eighty-sixth Congress in 1958 and the Eighty-seventh Congress in 1960; elected as a Democrat to the Eighty-eighth, Eighty-ninth, and Ninetieth Congresses, and served from January 3, 1963, until his death in Houston, Tex., July 14, 1968; interment in Laurel Land Memorial Park, Dallas, Tex.

**POOL, John** (uncle of Walter Freshwater Pool), a Senator from North Carolina; born near Elizabeth City, Pasquotank County, N.C., June 16, 1826; was tutored at home and graduated from the University of North Carolina at Chapel Hill in 1847; studied law; was admitted to the bar in 1847 and practiced in Elizabeth City, N.C., 1847-1856; also engaged in agricultural pursuits; member, State senate 1856, 1858, 1864-1865; unsuccessful Whig candidate for governor in 1860; delegate to the State constitutional convention in 1865; presented credentials dated December 29, 1865, as a Republican Senator-elect to the United States Senate on February 8, 1866, but was not permitted to take his seat because the State had not been readmitted to representation; upon the readmission of North Carolina was again elected to the United States Senate and served from July 4, 1868, to March 3, 1873; was not a candidate for reelection; chairman, Committee on Revolutionary Claims (Forty-second Congress); resumed the practice of law in Washington, D.C., where he died August 16, 1884; interment in Oak Hill Cemetery.

Bibliography: *DAB.*

**POOL, Walter Freshwater** (nephew of John Pool), a Representative from North Carolina; born at "Elm Grove," near Elizabeth City, Pasquotank County, N.C., October 10, 1850; attended the public school conducted by his family and the University of North Carolina at Chapel Hill; moved with his parents to Elizabeth City, N.C., in 1870; studied law; was admitted to the bar in 1873 and commenced practice in Elizabeth City; elected as a Republican to the Forty-eighth Congress and served from March 4, 1883, until his death in Elizabeth City, N.C., on August 25, 1883, before the

assembling of Congress; interment in the Pool Cemetery, near Elizabeth City, N.C.

**POOLE, Theodore Lewis,** a Representative from New York; born in Jordan, Onondaga County, N.Y., April 10, 1840; moved with his parents to Syracuse, N.Y., in 1842; attended the common schools; during the Civil War enlisted as quartermaster sergeant in the One Hundred and Twenty-second Regiment, New York Volunteers, in July 1862; discharged as captain and brevet major July 3, 1865; county clerk of Onondaga County 1868-1870; United States pension agent for the western district of New York 1879-1888; commander of the Department of New York, Grand Army of the Republic, in 1892; connected with various manufacturing industries and corporations; director of the Bank of Syracuse; elected as a Republican to the Fifty-fourth Congress (March 4, 1895-March 3, 1897); unsuccessful candidate for reelection in 1896 to the Fifty-fifth Congress; appointed United States marshal of New York in 1899 and served until his death in Syracuse, N.Y., December 23, 1900; interment in Oakwood Cemetery.

**POPE, James Pinckney,** a Senator from Idaho; born on a farm near Jonesboro, Jackson Parish, La., March 31, 1884; attended the common schools; graduated from Louisiana Polytechnic Institute, Ruston, La., in 1906 and from the law department of the University of Chicago, Chicago, Ill., in 1909; was admitted to the bar in 1909 and commenced practice in Boise, Idaho; deputy collector of internal revenue 1916; city attorney of Boise 1916-1917; assistant attorney general of Idaho 1918-1919; member of the board of education of Boise 1924-1929; mayor of Boise 1929-1933, when he resigned, having been elected to Congress; elected as a Democrat to the United States Senate and served from March 4, 1933, to January 3, 1939; unsuccessful candidate for renomination in 1938; appointed a director of the Tennessee Valley Authority by President Franklin D. Roosevelt 1939-1951; associated with law firm in Knoxville, Tenn.; member of board of directors, Federal Savings & Loan Association, Knoxville, Tenn.; moved to Alexandria, Va., in 1963, where he resided until his death there on January 23, 1966; interment in Lynnhurst Cemetery, Knoxville, Tenn.

Bibliography: Sims, Robert C. "James P. Pope, Senator from Idaho." *Idaho Yesterdays* 15 (Fall 1971): 9-15.

**POPE, John,** a Senator and a Representative from Kentucky; born in Prince William County, Va., in 1770; completed preparatory studies; studied law; moved to Springfield, Ky.; admitted to the bar and practiced in Washington, Shelby, and Fayette Counties; member, Kentucky house of representatives 1802, 1806-1807; elected as a Republican to the United States Senate and served from March 4, 1807, to March 3, 1813; served as President pro tempore of the Senate during the Eleventh Congress; member, Kentucky senate 1825-1829; Territorial Governor of Arkansas 1829-1835; resumed the practice of law in Springfield, Ky.; elected as a Whig to the Twenty-fifth, Twenty-sixth, and Twenty-seventh Congresses (March 4, 1837-March 3, 1843); unsuccessful candidate for reelection in 1842 to the Twenty-eighth Congress; died in Springfield, Washington County, Ky., on July 12, 1845; interment in the cemetery at Springfield, Ky.

Bibliography: Baylor, Orval. *John Pope: Kentuckian, His Life and Times 1770-1845.* Cynthiana, Ky.: The Hobson Press, 1943; Blakey, George T. "Rendezvous with Republicanism: John T. Pope vs. Henry Clay in 1816." *Indiana Magazine of History* 62 (September 1966): 233-50.

**POPE, Nathaniel,** a Delegate from Illinois Territory; born in Louisville, Ky., January 5, 1784; attended Transylvania University, Lexington, Ky.; studied law; was admitted to the bar; settled in Ste. Genevieve, Mo., in 1804, where he commenced the practice of his profession; moved to Springfield, Ill.; appointed secretary of Illinois Territory by President James Madison in 1809; reappointed in 1813, and served from March 7, 1809 until his resignation in 1816 to become Delegate; elected a Delegate to Congress on September 5, 1816 for a term of two years (Fourteenth and Fifteenth Congresses); appointed register of the land office at Edwardsville, Ill., on November 30, 1818 and served until March 3, 1819; appointed United States judge for the district of Illinois on March 3, 1819, and served in that capacity until his death in St. Louis, Mo., January 22, 1850; unsuccessful candidate for election to the United States Senate in 1824; interment in the Colonel O'Fallon Burying Ground, on the Bellefontaine Road.

**Bibliography:** *DAB*; Edstrom, James A. "With . . . candour and good faith: Nathaniel Pope and the Admission Enabling Act of 1818." *Illinois Historical Journal* 88 (Winter 1995): 241-262.

**POPE, Patrick Hamilton,** a Representative from Kentucky; born in Louisville, Ky., March 17, 1806; attended the common schools and was graduated from St. Joseph College, Bardstown, Ky.; studied law; was admitted to the bar in 1827 and commenced practice in Louisville; declined the position of secretary of state tendered by Governor John Breathitt in 1832; elected as a Jacksonian to the Twenty-third Congress (March 4, 1833-March 3, 1835); unsuccessful candidate for reelection in 1834 to the Twenty-fourth Congress; elected a member of the Kentucky house of representatives in 1836; resumed the practice of law; died in Louisville, Ky., May 4, 1841; interment in Cave Hill Cemetery.

**POPPLETON, Earley Franklin,** a Representative from Ohio; born in Belleville, Richland County, Ohio, September 29, 1834; pursued classical studies; educated at the Ohio Wesleyan University at Delaware; studied law; was admitted to the bar and commenced law practice in Elyria, Ohio; moved to Delaware, Ohio, in 1861 and continued the practice of his profession; member of the State senate in 1870; elected as a Democrat to the Forty-fourth Congress (March 4, 1875-March 3, 1877); unsuccessful candidate for reelection; resumed the practice of law; died in Delaware, Ohio, May 6, 1899; interment in Oak Grove Cemetery.

**PORTER, Albert Gallatin,** a Representative from Indiana; born in Lawrenceburg, Dearborn County, Ind., April 20, 1824; attended the public schools and the preparatory department of Hanover (Ind.) College, and was graduated from Indiana Asbury University (now De Pauw University), Greencastle, Ind., in 1843; studied law; was admitted to the bar in 1845 and commenced practice in Indianapolis; city attorney, 1851-1853; reporter of the Indiana Supreme Court, 1853-1857; member of the city council, 1857-1859; elected as a Republican to the Thirty-sixth and Thirty-seventh Congresses (March 4, 1859-March 3, 1863); declined to be a candidate for renomination in 1862 to the Thirty-eighth Congress; resumed the practice of law; appointed First Comptroller of the Treasury on March 5, 1878, and served until 1880; elected Governor of Indiana in 1880, and served from January 10, 1881 to January 1885; delegate to the Republican National Convention of 1888; appointed Minister to Italy on March 13, 1889 and served until July 1892; died in Indianapolis, Ind., May 3, 1897; interment in Crown Hill Cemetery.

**Bibliography:** *DAB*.

**PORTER, Alexander,** a Senator from Louisiana; born in County Donegal, Ireland, June 24, 1785; immigrated to the United States in 1801 with an uncle, who settled in Nashville, Tenn.; received a limited schooling; studied law; was admitted to the bar in 1807 and commenced practice in the Attakapas region of the Territory of Orleans; delegate to the convention which framed the first State constitution in 1812; member, lower branch of the Lousiana State legislature 1816-1818; judge of the State supreme court 1821-1833; elected as a Whig to the United States Senate to fill the vacancy caused by the death of Josiah S. Johnson and served from December 19, 1833, until January 5, 1837, when he resigned due to ill health; continued the practice of law in Attakapas; planter; again elected to the United States Senate for the term beginning March 4, 1843, but did not take his seat due to ill health; died in Attakapas, La., January 13, 1844; interment on Oakland plantation in Franklin, La.

**Bibliography:** *DAB*; Stephenson, Wendell. *Alexander Porter, Whig Planter of Old Louisiana.* 1934. Reprint. New York: Da Capo Press, 1969.

**PORTER, Augustus Seymour** (nephew of Peter Buell Porter), a Senator from Michigan; born in Canandaigua, N.Y., January 18, 1798; attended Canandaigua Academy, Canandaigua, N.Y.; graduated from Union College, Schenectady, N.Y., in 1818; studied law; was admitted to the bar and commenced practice in Detroit, Mich.; recorder of Detroit 1830; mayor of Detroit 1838; elected as a Whig to the United States Senate on January 20, 1840, for the term beginning March 4, 1839, and served until March 3, 1845; was not a candidate for renomination; chairman, Committee on Roads and Canals (Twenty-seventh and Twenty-eighth Congresses), Committee on Enrolled Bills (Twenty-seventh Congress); moved to his father's residence in Niagara Falls, N.Y., in 1848; died at Niagara Falls, N.Y., September 18, 1872; interment in Oakwood Cemetery.

**PORTER, Charles Howell,** a Representative from Virginia; born in Cairo, Greene County, N.Y., June 21, 1833; completed preparatory studies; was graduated from the law university at Albany, N.Y., in 1853; was admitted to the bar in 1854 and commenced practice in Ashland, Greene County, N.Y.; entered the Union Army in 1861 as a member of the First Regiment, New York Mounted Rifles; settled in Norfolk, Va.; served as city attorney for one year; Commonwealth attorney 1863-1867; moved to Richmond, Va., in 1867; member of the constitutional convention of Virginia in 1867 and 1868; upon the readmission of Virginia to representation was elected as a Republican to the Forty-first and Forty-second Congresses and served from January 26, 1870, to March 3, 1873; declined to be a candidate for renomination in 1872; engaged in the practice of law in New York City and Beacon, N.Y.; died in Cairo, N.Y., July 9, 1897; interment in Cairo Cemetery.

**PORTER, Charles Orlando,** a Representative from Oregon; born in Klamath Falls, Klamath County, Oreg., April 4, 1919; moved to Eugene, Lane County, Oreg., in 1923 and attended the public schools; B.A., Harvard University, 1941; LL.B., Harvard University Law School, 1947; served with the United States Air Force from private to first lieutenant,1941-1945, with overseas service in Europe; major in the Air Force Reserve (retired); law clerk, United States Court of Appeals, San Francisco, 1947-1948; was admitted to the bar in 1948; assistant to the director, American Bar Association Survey of the Legal Profession, Boston, Mass., 1948-1951; practiced law in Eugene, Oreg., 1951-1956; delegate at large to the Democratic National Conventions of 1960, 1964, 1968, and 1972; elected as a Democrat to the Eighty-fifth and Eighty-sixth Congresses (January 3, 1957-January 3, 1961); unsuccessful candidate for reelection in 1960 to the Eighty-seventh Congress; resumed the practice of law; consultant, Food for Peace, The White House, 1961; unsuccessful candidate for nomination in 1964 to the Eighty-ninth Congress, and for election in 1966 to the Ninetieth Congress; unsuccessful candidate for election in 1972 to the Ninety-third Congress, and for nomination in 1976 to the Ninety-fifth Congress; unsuccessful candidate for nomination in 1980 to the United States Senate; is a resident of Eugene, Oreg.

**PORTER, Gilchrist,** a Representative from Missouri; born in Windsor, near Fredericksburg, Va., November 1, 1817; received a limited schooling; studied law; was admitted to the bar and commenced practice in Bowling Green, Mo.; elected as a Whig to the Thirty-second Congress (March 4, 1851-March 3, 1853); unsuccessful candidate for reelection in 1852 to the Thirty-third Congress; elected to the Thirty-fourth Congress (March 4, 1855-March 3,

1857); chairman, Committee on Private Land Claims (Thirty-fourth Congress); circuit judge 1866-1880; resumed the practice of law; died in Hannibal, Marion County, Mo., November 1, 1894; interment in Riverside Cemetery.

**PORTER, Henry Kirke,** a Representative from Pennsylvania; born in Concord, N.H., November 24, 1840; attended public and private schools and was prepared for college at the New London Academy, New London, N.H.; was graduated from Brown University, Providence, R.I., in 1860; one of the founders of the Young Men's Christian Association in 1860; pursued professional studies in Newton Theological Seminary, Newton Center, Mass., and in Rochester Theological Seminary, Rochester, N.Y., 1861-1866; during the Civil War enlisted in the Forty-fifth Regiment, Massachusetts Volunteer Militia, in 1862 and was mustered out of service in July 1863; served on the United States Christian Commission in 1863; engaged with his father in the manufacture of light locomotives at Pittsburgh, Pa., in May 1866 and became president of the company; president of the Pittsburgh Y.M.C.A. 1868-1887; vice president of the Pittsburgh Chamber of Commerce 1892-1906; elected as an Independent Republican to the Fifty-eighth Congress (March 4, 1903-March 3, 1905); unsuccessful candidate for reelection to the Fifty-ninth Congress in 1904; member of the board of trustees and president of the board of directors of the Western Pennsylvania Institute for the Blind in 1904; resumed the manufacture of locomotives; member of the International Committee of the Y.M.C.A. 1875-1921; trustee of the Carnegie Institute 1890-1921; trustee of the Crozier Theological Seminary 1871-1921; member of the Board of Fellows of Brown University from 1899 until his death in Washington, D.C., April 10, 1921; interment in Allegheny Cemetery, Pittsburgh, Pa.

**PORTER, James,** a Representative from New York; born in Williamstown, Mass., April 18, 1787; was graduated from Williams College, Williamstown, Mass., in 1810; studied law; was admitted to the bar and commenced practice in Skaneateles, N.Y.; member of the State assembly in 1814 and 1815; elected as a Republican to the Fifteenth Congress (March 4, 1817-March 3, 1819); was not a candidate for renomination; resumed the practice of law; surrogate of Onondaga County 1822-1824; moved to Albany, N.Y., and served as register of the court of chancery until his death there February 7, 1839; interment in Greenwood Cemetery, Brooklyn, N.Y.

**PORTER, John,** a Representative from Pennsylvania; born in Pennsylvania; received a limited schooling; elected as a Republican to the Ninth Congress to fill the vacancy caused by the resignation of Michael Leib; reelected to the Tenth and Eleventh Congresses and served from December 8, 1806, to March 4, 1811.

**PORTER, John Edward,** a Representative from Illinois; born in Evanston, Cook County, Ill., June 1, 1935; attended the public schools and graduated from Evanston Township High School, 1953; attended the Massachusetts Institute of Technology, Cambridge, Mass., 1953-1954; B.S.B.A., Northwestern University, Evanston, Ill., 1957; J.D., University of Michigan Law School, Ann Arbor, Mich., 1961; served in United States Army Reserve, 1958-1964; admitted to the Illinois bar in 1961; attorney, United States Department of Justice, Washington, D.C., 1961-1963; private practice, Evanston, Ill., 1963-1979; member, Illinois State general assembly, 1973-1979; unsuccessful candidate for election in 1978 to the Ninety-sixth Congress; elected as a Republican to the Ninety-sixth Congress, January 22, 1980, by special election to fill the vacancy caused by the resignation of Abner J. Mikva; reelected to the eight succeeding Congresses and served from January 22, 1980, to January 3, 1997; is a resident of Wilmette, Ill.

**PORTER, Peter Augustus** (grandson of Peter Buell Porter), a Representative from New York; born at Niagara Falls, N.Y., October 10, 1853; taught by private teachers; attended St. Paul's Schools, Concord, N.H., 1865-1871 and was graduated from Yale College in 1874; engaged in banking and was an extensive landowner; president of the village of Niagara Falls, N.Y., in 1878; member of the State assembly in 1886 and 1887; elected as an Independent Republican to the Sixtieth Congress (March 4, 1907-March 3, 1909); declined to be a candidate for renomination; engaged in the study and writing of history of the Niagara frontier; died in Buffalo, N.Y., December 15, 1925; interment in Oakwood Cemetery, Niagara Falls, N.Y.

**PORTER, Peter Buell** (grandfather of Peter Augustus Porter and uncle of Augustus Seymour Porter), a Representative from New York; born in Salisbury, Conn., August 14, 1773; was graduated from Yale College in 1791; studied law in Litchfield, Conn.; was admitted to the bar and commenced practice in Canandaigua, N.Y., in 1793; clerk of Ontario County, 1797-1804; member of the New York State assembly in 1802, and again in 1828; moved to Buffalo, N.Y., in the fall of 1809; elected as a Republican to the Eleventh and Twelfth Congresses (March 4, 1809-March 3, 1813); declined to be a candidate for renomination in 1812 to the Thirteenth Congress; appointed a canal commissioner in 1811; served in the War of 1812; major general of New York Volunteers, 1812-1815; presented a gold medal under a joint resolution of Congress dated November 3, 1814, "for gallantry and good conduct in the several conflicts of Chippewa, Niagara, and Erie"; elected to the Fourteenth Congress and served from March 4, 1815, to January 23, 1816, when he resigned; secretary of state of New York in 1815 and 1816; unsuccessful candidate for Governor of New York in 1817; regent of the University of the State of New York, 1824-1830; appointed Secretary of War in the Cabinet of President John Quincy Adams, and served from June 21, 1828 to March 9, 1829; moved to Niagara Falls, N.Y. in 1836; presidential elector on the Whig ticket in 1840; died at Niagara Falls, Niagara County, N.Y., March 20, 1844; interment in Oakwood Cemetery.

**Bibliography:** *DAB*; Grande, Joseph A. "The Political Career of Peter Buell Porter, 1797-1829." Ph.D. dissertation, University of Notre Dame, 1971; Roland, Daniel Dean. "Peter Buell Porter and Self-Interest in American Politics." Ph.D. dissertation, Claremont Graduate School, 1990.

**PORTER, Stephen Geyer,** a Representative from Pennsylvania; born near Salem, Columbiana County, Ohio, May 18, 1869; moved to Pennsylvania with his parents, who settled in Allegheny (now Pittsburgh), Pa., in 1877; attended the common schools and Allegheny High School; studied medicine for two years, after which he studied law; admitted to the bar in December 1893 and commenced practice in Pittsburgh; city solicitor of Allegheny 1903-1906; chairman of the Pennsylvania Republican convention in 1912; elected as a Republican to the Sixty-second and to the nine succeeding Congresses and served from March 4, 1911, until his death; chairman, Committee on Foreign Affairs (Sixty-sixth through Seventy-first Congresses); unsuccessful candidate for mayor of Pittsburgh in 1913; appointed in 1921 to represent the House of Representatives on the advisory committee to the Washington conference on armament limitations; represented the United States at the centennial of Brazil's independence, in 1922; member and chairman of the American delegation to the Second International Conference on Opium, at Geneva in 1923 and 1924; chairman of the Foreign Service Buildings Commission 1926-1930; died in Pittsburgh, Pa., on June 27, 1930; interment in Highwood Cemetery.

**Bibliography:** *DAB*.

**PORTER, Timothy H.,** a Representative from New York; born in New Haven, Conn.; completed preparatory studies; moved to New York and settled in Cattaraugus County; member of the State assembly in 1816 and 1817; county judge of Cattaraugus County 1817-1820; studied law; was admitted to the bar of Tioga and Cattaraugus Counties in 1819 and commenced practice in Olean, N.Y.; first judge of the court of common pleas in 1819; district attorney for Cattaraugus County in 1819, 1820, and 1824; served in the State senate in 1823; elected to the Nineteenth Congress (March 4, 1825-March 3, 1827); resumed the practice of law in Olean, N.Y.; again a member of the State senate 1828-1831 and of the State assembly in 1838 and 1840; died in Olean Township, near the city of Olean, N.Y., about 1840; interment in Mount View Cemetery, Olean, N.Y.

**PORTMAN, Robert Jones,** a Representative from Ohio; born in Cincinnati, Ohio, December 19, 1955; graduated, Cincinnati Country Day School; B.A., Dartmouth College, 1979; J.D., University of Michigan School of Law, 1984; attorney, Washington, D.C., 1984-1986; practicing attorney, Cincinnati, 1987-1989 and 1992-1993; associate counsel, deputy assistant to the President then director, Office of Legislative Affairs, The White House, 1989-1991; elected as a Republican to the One Hundred Third Congress, May 4, 1993, by special election to fill the vacancy caused by the resignation of Willis D. Gradison, Jr.; reelected to the One Hundred Fourth Congress, and served from May 5, 1993 to January 3, 1997; is a resident of Hyde Park, Ohio.

**POSEY, Francis Blackburn,** a Representative from Indiana; born in Petersburg, Pike County, Ind., April 28, 1848; attended the public schools, Blythewood Academy, and Indiana Asbury (now De Pauw) University, Greencastle, Ind.; was graduated from the law department of the Indiana University at Bloomington in 1869; was admitted to the bar the same year and commenced practice in Petersburg, Ind.; delegate to the Republican National Convention of 1884; unsuccessful Republican candidate for election in 1888 to the Fifty-first Congress; was subsequently elected to the Fiftieth Congress to fill the vacancy caused by the resignation of Alvin P. Hovey and served from January 29, 1889, to March 3, 1889; resumed the practice of law in Evansville, Ind.; surveyor of the port of Evansville, 1903-1913; died in Rockport, Spencer County, Ind., on October 31, 1915; interment in Walnut Hills Cemetery, Petersburg, Ind.

**POSEY, Thomas,** a Senator from Louisiana; born in Fairfax County, Va., July 9, 1750; received a limited schooling; moved to the western frontier of Virginia in 1769; served in the Virginia militia in the French and Indian wars; member of the Virginia committee of correspondence; at the outbreak of the Revolutionary War was appointed captain in a Virginia regiment; promoted to the rank of major in 1778 and the following year was made colonel; was at the surrender of Yorktown, Va., by the British on October 19, 1781; held various county and militia offices; appointed brigadier general in 1793 and participated in campaigns against the Indians; moved to Kentucky in 1794; served in the Kentucky senate and was its presiding officer in 1805 and 1806; lieutenant governor of Kentucky for four years; major general of Kentucky levies after 1809; moved to the Attakapas region of Louisiana; appointed to the United States Senate from Louisiana to fill the vacancy caused by the resignation of John N. Destréhan and served from October 8, 1812, to February 4, 1813; unsuccessful candidate for election to fill the vacancy; appointed Governor of Indiana Territory by President James Madison on March 3, 1813, and served until 1816; upon the admission of Indiana as a State into the Union was an unsuccessful candidate for governor; appointed Indian agent in 1816 and held the position until his death in Shawneetown, Ill., on March 19, 1818; interment in Westwood Cemetery.

**Bibliography:** *DAB.*

**POSHARD, Glendal William (Glenn),** a Representative from Illinois; born in Herald, White County, Ill., October 30, 1945; graduated, Carmi Township (Ill.) High School, 1962; B.S., Southern Illinois University, Carbondale, 1970, M.S., 1974, and Ph.D., 1984; entered active duty, United States Army in 1962; released in 1965; farmer, teacher, and school administrator; member, Illinois State senate, 1984-1988; elected as a Democrat to the One Hundred First and to the three succeeding Congresses (January 3, 1989-January 3, 1997); is a resident of Carterville, Ill.

**POST, George Adams,** a Representative from Pennsylvania; born in Cuba, Allegany County, N.Y., September 1, 1854; pursued an academic course at Oswego Academy; moved to Susquehanna Depot, Pa.; secretary of the motive power department of the Erie Railway; elected burgess in February 1877 and served one year; studied law; admitted to the bar in 1881 and commenced practice in Montrose, Pa.; one of the owners and editors of the Montrose Democrat 1883-1889; elected as a Democrat to the Forty-eighth Congress (March 4, 1883-March 3, 1885); delegate to the Democratic National Convention in 1884; chairman of the Pennsylvania Democratic convention in 1885; moved to New York City in 1889; engaged as a writer for the New York World; engaged in the manufacture of railway equipment in 1892 and served as vice president and later president of the Standard Coupler Co.; founder and president of the Railway Business Association; chairman of the railroad committee of the United States Chamber of Commerce; died in Somerville, Somerset County, N.J., on October 31, 1925; interment in Evergreen Cemetery, Oswego, N.Y.

**Bibliography:** *DAB.*

**POST, James Douglass,** a Representative from Ohio; born near Milledgeville, Fayette County, Ohio, November 25, 1863; attended the common schools and was graduated from the National Normal University, Lebanon, Ohio, in 1882; engaged in teaching for five years; studied law; was admitted to the bar in 1887 and commenced practice at Washington Court House, Fayette County, Ohio; elected as a Democrat to the Sixty-second and Sixty-third Congresses (March 4, 1911-March 3, 1915); chairman, Committee on Elections No. 1 (Sixty-third Congress); was not a candidate for renomination in 1914; resumed the practice of law at Washington Court House, Ohio, and died there April 1, 1921; interment in Washington Cemetery.

**POST, Jotham, Jr.,** a Representative from New York; born near Westbury, Nassau County, N.Y., April 4, 1771; was graduated from Columbia College, New York City, in 1792; studied medicine but did not practice; engaged in the drug-importing business in New York City; member of the board of aldermen; served in the State assembly 1795 and 1805-1808; director of the New York Hospital 1798-1802; elected as a Federalist to the Thirteenth Congress (March 4, 1813-March 3, 1815); died in New York City, May 15, 1817.

**POST, Morton Everel,** a Delegate from the Territory of Wyoming; born in West Henrietta (near Rochester), Monroe County, N.Y., December 25, 1840; pursued an academic course in the Albion and Medina Academies, New York; moved to Denver, Colo., in 1860 and engaged in the freighting business between the Missouri River and Denver; engaged in mining in Alder Gulch, Mont., in 1864; delegate to the Democratic National Convention in 1864; moved in 1867 to that portion of Dakota which is now Wyoming; county commissioner of Laramie County 1870-1876; member of the Territorial legislative council 1878-1880; engaged in banking and stock raising near Cheyenne, Wyo.; elected as a Democrat to the Forty-seventh and Forty-eighth Congresses (March 4, 1881-March 3, 1885); declined to be a candidate for renomination in 1884; resumed banking and stock raising; moved to California in 1895 and engaged in farming and fruit growing near Cucamonga and Alhambra; retired in 1916 and resided in Los Angeles, Calif., until 1928 when he moved to Alhambra, Calif.; died in Alhambra, Calif., March 19, 1933; interment in Inglewood Park Cemetery, Inglewood, Calif.

**POST, Philip Sidney,** a Representative from Illinois; born in Florida, Orange County, N.Y., March 19, 1833; pursued classical studies and graduated from Union College, Schenectady, N.Y., in 1855; entered the Poughkeepsie Law School; admitted to the bar in Illinois in 1856; during the Civil War entered the Union Army and served with the Fifty-ninth Regiment, Illinois Infantry; promoted through the ranks to colonel; brevetted brigadier general of Volunteers on December 16, 1864; awarded a Congressional Medal of Honor, March 18, 1893, for action at the Battle of Nashville, Tenn., December 15-16, 1864; appointed consul to Vienna in 1866; promoted to consul general to Austria-Hungary in 1874; resigned in 1879; commander of the department of Illinois, Grand Army of the Republic, in 1886; elected as a Republican to the Fiftieth and to the four succeeding Congresses and served from March 4, 1887, until his death, before the close of the Fifty-third Congress, in Washington, D.C., on January 6, 1895; interment in Hope Cemetery, Galesburg, Ill.

**POSTON, Charles Debrille,** a Delegate from the Territory of Arizona; born near Elizabethtown, Hardin County, Ky., April 20, 1825; attended the public schools; clerk in the county clerk's office; clerk of the supreme court at Nashville, Tenn.; moved to California in 1850 and settled in San Francisco; clerk in the customhouse at San Francisco, 1850-1853; moved to Arizona in 1854 and became interested in silver mining; appointed by President Abraham Lincoln superintendent of Indian affairs in 1863 and was civilian aide to General Samuel P. Heintzelman the same year; when Arizona Territory was formed was elected as a Republican to the Thirty-eighth Congress and served from December 5, 1864, to March 3, 1865; unsuccessful candidate for reelection in 1864 to the Thirty-ninth Congress; studied law; was admitted to the bar in 1867 and commenced the practice of his profession in Washington, D.C.; appointed by President Rutherford B. Hayes as register of the United States land office at Florence, Ariz., in 1878; consular agent at El Paso, Tex., in 1890; died in Phoenix, Ariz., June 24, 1902; interment in Arizona Cemetery; reinterment under a rock cairn erected by the State of Arizona at the summit of Poston Butte, overlooking the town of Florence, Ariz., April 26, 1925.

Bibliography: *DAB*; Gressinger, A.W. *Charles D. Poston, Sunland Seer.* Globe, Ariz.: D.S. King, 1961; Poston, Lawrence, ed. "Poston vs. Goodwin: A Document on the Congressional Election of 1865." *Arizona and the West* 3 (Winter 1961): 351-54.

**POTTER, Allen,** a Representative from Michigan; born in Galloway, Saratoga County, N.Y., October 2, 1818; attended the common schools; moved to Adrian, Mich., in 1830 and to Jonesville, Mich., in 1838; learned the trade of tinsmith; moved to Kalamazoo, Mich., in 1845 and engaged in the retail hardware business until 1858, when he engaged in banking and in the manufacture of gas; member of the State house of representatives in 1857; president of the village council in 1859, 1863, 1870, and again in 1872; elected a member of the board of education in 1867, 1869, and 1871, serving as president in 1869; member of the board of water commissioners in 1872; unsuccessful Liberal candidate for election in 1872 to the Forty-third Congress; elected as a Democrat to the Forty-fourth Congress (March 4, 1875-March 3, 1877); was not a candidate for reelection in 1876; resumed banking activities; also financially interested in railroads and Colorado mining enterprises; member of the sewer commission 1880-1883; elected as the first mayor of Kalamazoo, in 1884; treasurer of the State asylum for the insane; died in Kalamazoo, Mich., May 8, 1885; interment in the City Cemetery.

**POTTER, Charles Edward,** a Representative and a Senator from Michigan; born in Lapeer, Mich., October 30, 1916; attended the public schools; graduated from Eastern Michigan University, Ypsilanti, Mich., in 1938; administrator of Bureau of Social Aid, Cheboygan County, Mich., 1938-1942; in 1942 enlisted as a private in the United States Army with combat service in the European Theater of Operations; seriously wounded in France in 1945, resulting in the loss of both legs; discharged from the service as a major in 1946; engaged as vocational rehabilitation representative for the Retraining and Reemployment Administration with the United States Labor Department until his resignation in 1947; elected as a Republican to the Eightieth Congress, August 26, 1947, by special election to fill the vacancy caused by the death of Frederick V. Bradley; reelected to the two succeeding Congresses and served from August 26, 1947, until his resignation November 4, 1952; elected to the United States Senate in 1952 to fill the vacancy caused by the death of Arthur H. Vandenberg and served from November 5, 1952, to January 3, 1953; also elected in 1952 for the term commencing January 3, 1953, and served until January 3, 1959; unsuccessful candidate for reelection in 1958; engaged as an industrial consultant and international securities executive; member of the American Battle Monuments Commission; resided in Queenstown, Md., until his death in Washington, D.C., November 23, 1979; interment in Arlington National Cemetery, Va.

Bibliography: *DAB*; Potter, Charles E. *Days of Shame*. New York: Coward-McCann, 1965.

**POTTER, Clarkson Nott,** a Representative from New York; born in Schenectady, N.Y., April 25, 1825; completed preparatory studies and was graduated from Union College, Schenectady, N.Y., in 1842 and from Rensselaer Polytechnic Institute as a civil engineer in 1843; served as a surveyor in Wisconsin in 1843; studied law; was admitted to the bar in 1846 and commenced practice in New York City in 1847; elected as a Democrat to the Forty-first, Forty-second, and Forty-third Congresses (March 4, 1869-March 3, 1875); declined to be a candidate for renomination in 1874; elected to the Forty-fifth Congress (March 4, 1877-March 3, 1879); chairman, Committee on Pacific Railroads (Forty-fifth Congress); declined to be a candidate for renomination in 1878; president of the Democratic State conventions in 1875 and 1877; delegate to the Democratic National Conventions in 1872 and 1876; unsuccessful candidate for Lieutenant Governor in 1879; trustee of Union College 1863-1882; president of the American Bar Association in 1881 and 1882; died in New York City on January 23, 1882; interment probably in the Vale Cemetery, Schenectady, N.Y.

Bibliography: *DAB*; Vazzano, Frank P. "The Louisiana Question Resurrected: The Potter Commission and the Election of 1876." *Louisiana History* 16 (Winter 1975): 39-57.

**POTTER, Elisha Reynolds** (father of Elisha Reynolds Potter [1811-1882]), a Representative from Rhode Island; born in Little Rest (now Kingston), R.I., November 5, 1764; learned the blacksmith's trade and also engaged in agricultural pursuits; served as a private in the Revolutionary War; attended Plainfield Academy; studied law; was admitted to the bar about 1789 and commenced practice in South Kingstown Township, R.I.; member of the Rhode Island house of representatives, 1793-1796, and served as speaker in 1795 and 1796; elected as a Federalist to the Fourth and Fifth Congresses to fill the vacancies caused by the resignation of Benjamin Bourn and served from November 15, 1796, until his resignation in 1797; again a member of the Rhode Island house of representatives, 1798-1808, and speaker in 1802 and 1806-1808; elected to the Eleventh and to the two succeeding Congresses (March 4, 1809-March 3, 1815); from 1816 to 1835 was a member of the Rhode Island house of representatives, except in the year 1818, when he was an unsuccessful candidate for Governor of Rhode Island; died in South Kingston, R.I., September 26, 1835; interment in the family burial ground at Kingston, R.I.

**POTTER, Elisha Reynolds** (son of Elisha Reynolds Potter [1764-1835]), a Representative from Rhode Island; born in Little Rest (now Kingston), R.I., June 20, 1811; attended the Kingston Academy and was graduated from Harvard University in 1830;

studied law; was admitted to the bar in 1832 and practiced in South Kingstown Township, R.I.; adjutant general of the State 1835-1836; member of the State house of representatives 1838-1840; elected as a Law and Order Party candidate to the Twenty-eighth Congress (March 4, 1843-March 3, 1845); chairman, Committee on Revisal and Unfinished Business (Twenty-eighth Congress); unsuccessful candidate for reelection in 1844 to the Twenty-ninth Congress; served in the State senate 1847-1852 and 1861-1863; State commissioner of public schools from 1849 to 1854, when he resigned; associate justice of the Rhode Island Supreme Court from March 16, 1868, until his death in Kingston, Washington County, R.I., April 10, 1882; interment in the family burial ground.

**Bibliography:** *DAB.*

**POTTER, Emery Davis,** a Representative from Ohio; born in Providence, R.I., October 7, 1804; attended the district school and the academy in Herkimer County, N.Y.; studied law in Cooperstown, N.Y.; was admitted to the New York State bar at Utica in 1833 and commenced practice in Cooperstown, N.Y.; moved to Toledo, Ohio, in 1834 and continued the practice of law; judge of the circuit court for the northern counties of Ohio; president judge of the court of common pleas from 1834 to 1843, when he resigned; elected as a Democrat to the Twenty-eighth Congress (March 4, 1843-March 3, 1845); was not a candidate for renomination; mayor of Toledo 1846-1848; member of the State house of representatives 1848-1850; elected to the Thirty-first Congress (March 4, 1849-March 3, 1851); chairman, Committee on Post Office and Post Roads (Thirty-first Congress); was not a candidate for renomination; resumed the practice of law in Toledo; declined the appointment of judge of the Territory of Utah in 1858; city solicitor of Toledo in 1861 and 1862; member of the board of education in 1864 and 1865; member of the State senate 1874-1876 and served as president; retired from active practice in 1880; died in Toledo, Ohio, February 12, 1896; interment in Forest Cemetery.

**POTTER, John Fox,** a Representative from Wisconsin; born in Augusta, Maine, May 11, 1817; attended the common schools and Phillips Exeter Academy, Exeter, N.H.; studied law; was admitted to the bar in 1837 and commenced practice in East Troy, Wis.; judge of Walworth County, 1842-1846; member of the Wisconsin State assembly in 1856; delegate to the Whig National Conventions of 1852 and 1856, and to the Republican National Conventions of 1860 and 1864; elected as a Republican to the Thirty-fifth and to the two succeeding Congresses (March 4, 1857-March 3, 1863); chairman, Committee on Revolutionary Pensions (Thirty-sixth Congress), Committee on Public Lands (Thirty-seventh Congress); unsuccessful candidate for reelection in 1862 to the Thirty-eighth Congress; consul general of the United States to the British Provinces in North America from 1863 to 1866, residing in Montreal, Canada; practiced law in East Troy, Wis., and died there on May 18, 1899; interment in Oak Ridge Cemetery.

**Bibliography:** Riley, Ben A. "The Pryor-Potter Affair: Nineteenth Century Civilian Conflict as Precursor to Civil War." *Journal of the West Virginia Historical Association* 8 (Spring 1984): 29-40.

**POTTER, Orlando Brunson,** a Representative from New York; born in Charlemont, Franklin County, Mass., March 10, 1823; attended the district school, Williams College, Williamstown, Mass., and the Dane Law School, Cambridge, Mass.; studied law; was admitted to the bar in 1848 and commenced practice in Boston, Mass.; engaged in manufacturing; moved to New York in 1853 and engaged in agricultural pursuits; unsuccessful for election in 1878 to the Forty-sixth Congress; elected as a Democrat to the Forty-eighth Congress (March 4, 1883-March 3, 1885); declined to be a candidate for renomination in 1884; member of the Rapid Transit Commission of New York City 1890-1894; died in New York City, January 2, 1894; interment in Greenwood Cemetery.

**POTTER, Robert,** a Representative from North Carolina; born in Granville County, near Williamsboro, N.C., about 1800; attended the common schools; midshipman in the United States Navy, 1815-1821; studied law; was admitted to the bar and practiced in Halifax, Halifax County, N.C.; member of the North Carolina State house of commons in 1826 and 1828; moved to Oxford, Granville County, N.C., in 1827 and continued the practice of law; elected as a Jacksonian to the Twenty-first and Twenty-second Congresses and served from March 4, 1829, until his resignation in November 1831; again a member of the State house of commons from 1834 until his expulsion in January 1835; moved to Harrison County, Tex., in 1835 and settled on a farm overlooking Lake Soda, near Marshall; member of the convention that declared the independence of Texas on March 2, 1836; during the Texas Revolution was secretary of the navy in the cabinet of the Provincial President, David G. Burnett; represented the Red River District in the Texas Congress, 1837-1841; participated in the Regulator-Moderator War in east Texas as a leader of the Harrison County Moderators; his home being surrounded by the Regulators on March 2, 1842, he ran to the edge of Lake Soda and dived in, his body sinking to the bottom riddled with bullets; interred at "Potter's Point," a bluff near his home; reinterred in the Texas State Cemetery, at Austin, in 1931.

**Bibliography:** *DAB*; Fisher, Ernest G. *Robert Potter: Founder of the Texas Navy.* Gretna, La.: Pelican, 1976; Shearer, Ernest Charles. *Robert Potter, Remarkable North Carolinian and Texan.* Houston: University of Houston Press, 1951.

**POTTER, Samuel John,** a Senator from Rhode Island; born in South Kingston Township, R.I., June 29, 1753; completed preparatory studies; studied law; was admitted to the bar and practiced; deputy governor of Rhode Island, 1790-1803; presidential elector in 1792 and 1796; elected as a Republican to the United States Senate and served from March 4, 1803, until his death in Washington, D.C., October 14, 1804; interment in the family burial ground, Kingston (formerly Little Rest), Washington County, R.I.

**POTTER, William Wilson,** a Representative from Pennsylvania; born at Potters Mills, Pa., December 18, 1792; completed preparatory studies in Bellefonte, Centre County, Pa., and was graduated from Dickinson College, Carlisle, Pa.; studied law; was admitted to the bar in 1814 and practiced his profession; elected as a Democrat to the Twenty-fifth and Twenty-sixth Congresses and served from March 4, 1837, until his death, before the assembling of the Twenty-sixth Congress, in Bellefonte, Pa., on October 28, 1839; interment in Union Cemetery, Bellefonte, Pa.

**POTTLE, Emory Bemsley,** a Representative from New York; born in Naples, Ontario County, N.Y., July 4, 1815; pursued classical studies at Penn Yan (N.Y.) Academy; studied law; was admitted to the bar at New York City in 1838 and commenced practice in Springfield, Clark County, Ohio; returned to Naples, N.Y., and continued the practice of law; member of the State assembly in 1847; elected as a Republican to the Thirty-fifth and Thirty-sixth Congresses (March 4, 1857-March 3, 1861); again resumed the practice of his profession; appointed by President Abraham Lincoln as a member of the commission which prepared a bill providing for a tariff on wool; died in Naples, N.Y., April 18, 1891; interment in Rose Ridge Cemetery.

**POTTS, David, Jr.,** a Representative from Pennsylvania; born at Warwick Furnace, about eight miles from Pottstown, Chester County, Pa., November 27, 1794; completed preparatory studies in Pottstown; became an ironmaster; owner and manager of Warwick Furnace; member of the Pennsylvania house of representatives 1824-1826; elected as an Anti-Masonic candidate to the Twenty-second and to the three succeeding Congresses (March 4, 1831-March 3, 1839); was not a candidate for renomination in 1838; resumed his former business pursuits; died at Warwick Furnace (now Warwick), Chester County, Pa., June 1, 1863; interment in Coventry Cemetery, near Warwick.

**POTTS, David Matthew,** a Representative from New York; born in New York City, March 12, 1906; attended the public schools and the College of the City of New York, 1927-1929; was graduated from Brooklyn Law School of St. Lawrence University in 1932; was admitted to the New York bar in 1933 and commenced practice in New York City; counsel to the New York Senate Committee on Affairs of the City of New York during the 1945 session; elected as a Republican to the Eightieth Congress (January 3, 1947-January 3, 1949); unsuccessful candidate for reelection in 1948 to the Eighty-first Congress; resumed the practice of law; appointed surrogate of Bronx County by Governor Thomas E. Dewey and served from November 1951 to January 1953; special referee, Appellate Division, First Department, Supreme Court of State of New York, June 1953 term; resumed the practice of law, and was a senior partner, Kadel, Wilson & Potts, until his death in Bronxville, N.Y., September 11, 1976; interment in Ferncliff Mausoleum, Hartsdale, N.Y.

**POTTS, Richard,** a Delegate and a Senator from Maryland; born in Upper Marlboro, Md., July 19, 1753; moved with his family to the Barbados Islands in 1757; returned to Maryland and settled in Annapolis in 1761; studied law; commenced practice in Frederick County, Md., in 1775; member of the committee of observation for Frederick County in 1776; clerk of the county court, 1777-1778; military aide to the Governor of Maryland in 1777; member, Maryland State house of delegates, 1779-1780; Member of the Continental Congress in 1781; prosecuting attorney for Frederick, Montgomery, and Washington Counties in 1784; member, State house of delegates, 1787-1788; declined the nomination for State senator in 1787; member of the Maryland convention which ratified the Constitution of the United States in 1788; appointed by President George Washington as United States attorney for Maryland, and served from 1789 to 1791; chief judge of the fifth judicial circuit of the State, 1791-1793; presidential elector in 1792; elected to the United States Senate to fill the vacancy caused by the resignation of Charles Carroll of Carrollton, and served from January 10, 1793 to October 24, 1796, when he resigned; again appointed chief judge of the fifth judicial circuit, 1796-1801; associate justice of the Maryland Court of Appeals, 1801-1804; resumed the practice of his profession; died in Frederick, Md., November 26, 1808; interment in All Saints' Parish Cemetery; reinterment in Mount Olivet Cemetery, Baltimore.

Bibliography: *DAB*; Steiner, Lewis H. "A Memoir of Hon. Richard Potts." *Maryland Historical Magazine* 5 (March 1910): 63-8.

**POU, Edward William** (cousin of James Paul Buchanan), a Representative from North Carolina; born in Tuskegee, Macon County, Ala., September 9, 1863; moved to North Carolina with his parents, who settled in Smithfield in 1867; received private instructions and attended the common schools and the University of North Carolina at Chapel Hill; studied law; was admitted to the bar in 1885 and practiced in Smithfield, Johnston County, N.C.; chairman of the Democratic executive committee of Johnston County in 1886; solicitor of the fourth judicial district of North Carolina 1890-1901; unsuccessful candidate for election in 1896 to the Fifty-fifth Congress; elected as a Democrat to the Fifty-seventh and to the sixteen succeeding Congresses and served from March 4, 1901, until his death; chairman, Committee on Claims (Sixty-second, Sixty-third, and Sixty-fourth Congresses), Committee on Rules (Sixty-fifth, Seventy-second, and Seventy-third Congresses); delegate to the Democratic National Convention in 1916; died in Washington, D.C., April 1, 1934; funeral services were held in the Chamber of the United States House of Representatives; interment in Riverside Cemetery, Smithfield, N.C.

Bibliography: *DAB*.

**POULSON, C. Norris,** a Representative from California; born and reared on a ranch near Haines, Baker County, Oreg., July 23, 1895; attended the public schools, Oregon State College at Corvallis, and Southwestern University, Los Angeles, Calif., 1923-1925; moved to Los Angeles, Calif., in 1923; became a certified public accountant in 1933; member of the California assembly 1938-1942; delegate to California State Republican conventions on seven occasions; delegate to Republican National Convention, 1956; elected as a Republican to the Seventy-eighth Congress (January 3, 1943-January 3, 1945); unsuccessful candidate for reelection in 1944 to the Seventy-ninth Congress; elected in 1946 to the Eightieth and to the three succeeding Congresses and served from January 3, 1947, until his resignation on June 11, 1953; elected mayor of Los Angeles, Calif., in 1953 and again in 1957 and served from June 1953 to June 1961; unsuccessful for reelection as mayor in 1961; California State Water Commissioner, June 1963 to April 1969; resided in Tustin, Calif., until his death in Orange, Calif., on September 25, 1982; cremated; ashes buried at Mount Hope Cemetery in Baker, Oreg.

**POUND, Thaddeus Coleman,** a Representative from Wisconsin; born in Elk, Warren County, Pa., December 6, 1833; moved with his parents to Monroe County, N.Y., in 1838; later moved to Rochester, N.Y.; attended the common schools, Milton (Wis.) Academy, and Rushford Academy, Allegany County, N.Y.; moved to Rock County, Wis., in May 1856; engaged in the manufacture of lumber; president of the Union Lumbering Co. and of the Chippewa Falls & Western Railway Co.; member of the State assembly in 1864, 1866, 1867, and 1869, and served the last year as speaker pro tempore; Lieutenant Governor of Wisconsin in 1870 and 1871; delegate to the Republican National Convention in 1872; elected as a Republican to the Forty-fifth, Forty-sixth, and Forty-seventh Congresses (March 4, 1877-March 3, 1883); chairman, Committee on Public Lands (Forty-seventh Congress); was not a candidate for renomination in 1882 to the Forty-eighth Congress; president of the Chippewa Spring Water Co.; died in a hospital in Chicago, Ill., on November 21, 1914; interment in Forest Hill Cemetery, Chippewa Falls, Wis.

**POWELL, Adam Clayton, Jr.,** a Representative from New York; born in New Haven, Conn., November 29, 1908; attended the public schools of New York City and graduated from Townsend Harris High School; attended the City College of New York; was graduated from Colgate University, Hamilton, N.Y., in 1930; M.A., Columbia University Teachers College, New York City, 1932; graduated from the theological department of Shaw University, Raleigh, N.C., in 1934; studied four months in Europe, North Africa, and Asia Minor; was ordained to the ministry and officiated in the Abyssinian Baptist Church, New York City, beginning in 1931; became senior minister in November 1937; member of the New York City Council in 1941; publisher and editor of The People's Voice, a newspaper in New York City, February 1942 to December 1946; instructor at Columbia University Extension School, Department of Religious Education, 1932-1940; active in campaigns against discrimination in employment in New York City; co-chair, Greater New York Coordinating Committee for Employment, 1938-1941; co-founder of the National Negro Congress; member of the Consumer Division, State of New York, Office of Price Administration, 1942-1944; member of the Manhattan Civilian Defense, 1942-1945; elected as a Democrat to the Seventy-ninth Congress; reelected to the eleven succeeding Congresses, and served from January 3, 1945 to February 28, 1967, at which time he was excluded from membership in the Ninetieth Congress pursuant to H. Res. 278; chairman, Committee on Education and Labor (Eighty-seventh through Eighty-ninth Congresses); elected as a Democrat to the Ninetieth Congress in a special election held on April 11, 1967 to fill the vacancy caused by his exclusion, but did not appear to be sworn in; reelected to the Ninety-first Congress on November 5, 1968, and served from January 3, 1969 to January 3,

1971; unsuccessful candidate for renomination in 1970 to the Ninety-second Congress; died in Miami, Fla., April 4, 1972; cremated; ashes scattered over South Bimini in the Bahamas.

**Bibliography:** Hamilton, Charles V. *Adam Clayton Powell, Jr.: The Political Biography of An American Dilemma.* New York: Atheneum, 1991; Haygood, Wil. *King of the Cats: The Life and Times of Adam Clayton Powell, Jr.* Boston: Houghton Mifflin, 1993; Powell, Adam Clayton. *Adam by Adam.* New York: The Dial Press, 1971.

**POWELL, Alfred H.,** a Representative from Virginia; born in Loudoun County, Va., March 6, 1781; graduated from Princeton College; studied law; admitted to the bar and commenced the practice of his profession in Winchester, Va., in 1800; member of the Virginia senate 1812-1819; elected to the Nineteenth Congress (March 4, 1825-March 3, 1827); delegate to the Virginia constitutional convention in 1830; died in Loudoun County, Va., in 1831.

**POWELL, Cuthbert** (son of Levin Powell), a Representative from Virginia; born in Alexandria, Va., March 4, 1775; completed preparatory studies; studied law; admitted to the bar and practiced in Alexandria; mayor of Alexandria; moved to Loudoun County; engaged in agricultural pursuits; held various local offices; served in the Virginia senate 1815-1819; member of the Virginia house of delegates in 1828 and 1829; elected as a Whig to the Twenty-seventh Congress (March 4, 1841-March 3, 1843); died in "Llangollen," Loudoun County, Va., May 8, 1849; interment in the private cemetery on his estate, "Llangollen," in Loudoun County, Va.

**POWELL, Joseph,** a Representative from Pennsylvania; born in Towanda, Bradford County, Pa., June 23, 1828; completed preparatory studies; engaged in mercantile pursuits; president of the First National Bank of Towanda 1870-1889; elected as a Democrat to the Forty-fourth Congress (March 4, 1875-March 3, 1877); unsuccessful candidate for reelection in 1876 to the Forty-fifth Congress; appointed special deputy collector of the port of Philadelphia in 1885 and served four years; sheriff of Bradford County 1889-1893; died in Towanda, Pa., April 24, 1904; interment in Oak Hill Cemetery.

**POWELL, Lazarus Whitehead,** a Senator from Kentucky; born near Henderson, Ky., October 6, 1812; attended the common schools; graduated from St. Joseph College, Bardstown, Ky., in 1833; studied law; was admitted to the bar and commenced practice at Henderson in 1835; member of the Kentucky house of representatives in 1836; presidential elector on the Democratic ticket in 1844; unsuccessful Democratic candidate for Governor in 1848; elected Governor of Kentucky in 1851, and served from September 1851 to September 2, 1855; elected as a Democrat to the United States Senate, and served from March 4, 1859 to March 3, 1865; resumed the practice of his profession; unsuccessful candidate for the United States Senate in 1867; died near Henderson, Ky., July 3, 1867; interment in Fernwood Cemetery.

**Bibliography:** *DAB*; Kentucky. General Assembly. *Biographical Sketch of Honorable Lazarus W. Powell.* Frankfort: Kentucky Yeoman Office, 1868; Morton, Jennie C. "Gov. Lazarus W. Powell." *Register of the Kentucky State Historical Society* 4 (January 1906): 11-14.

**POWELL, Leven** (father of Cuthbert Powell), a Representative from Virginia; born near Manassas, Prince William County, Va., in 1737; studied in private schools; deputy sheriff of Prince William County; moved to Loudoun County in 1763; engaged in mercantile pursuits; served as major in the Revolutionary Army in 1775; appointed lieutenant colonel of the Sixteenth Regiment of the Continental Line in 1777; resigned on account of ill health in 1778; member of the Virginia house of delegates in 1779; was delegate to the Virginia ratification convention in 1788; again a member of the Virginia house of delegates in 1787, 1788, 1791, and 1792; elected as a Federalist to the Sixth Congress (March 4, 1799-March 3, 1801);

helped to build a turnpike from Alexandria, Va., to the upper country; died in Bedford, Pa., on August 23, 1810; interment in Old Presbyterian Graveyard.

**Bibliography:** "Correspondence of Col. Leven Powell, M.C., Relating to the Election of 1800." *John P. Branch Historical Papers of Randolph-Macon College* 1 (1901): 54-63; Powell, Robert C., ed. *A Biographical Sketch of Col. Leven Powell.* Alexandria, Va.: G.H. Ramey and Son, 1877.

**POWELL, Paulus,** a Representative from Virginia; born in Amherst County, Va., in 1809; attended private schools and Amherst College, Amherst, Va.; held various local offices; member of the Virginia house of delegates 1843-1849, 1863, and 1864; elected as a Democrat to the Thirty-first and to the four succeeding Congresses (March 4, 1849-March 3, 1859); unsuccessful candidate for reelection in 1858 to the Thirty-sixth Congress; died in Amherst, Amherst County, Va., June 10, 1874; interment in the private burying ground of his brother-in-law on the estate, "Kenmore," near Amherst, Va.

**POWELL, Samuel,** a Representative from Tennessee; born in Norristown, Montgomery County, Pa., July 10, 1776; attended the common schools and Philadelphia (Pa.) College; studied law; was admitted to the bar in Norristown, Pa., prior to 1800; moved to Blountville, Sullivan County, Tenn., in 1800; established the first law school in Tennessee at his home; moved to Rogersville, Hawkins County, Tenn., in 1805 and practiced law; member of the superior court of law and equity 1807-1809; judge of the first circuit court of Tennessee in 1812 and 1813; elected as a Republican to the Fourteenth Congress (March 4, 1815-March 3, 1817); was not a candidate for renomination in 1816; resumed the practice of law; again judge of the first circuit court 1819-1841; died in Rogersville, Tenn., August 2, 1841; interment in the Old Presbyterian Cemetery.

**POWELL, Walter Eugene,** a Representative from Ohio; born in Hamilton, Butler County, Ohio, April 25, 1931; attended Hamilton public schools; A.B., Heidelberg College, Tiffin, Ohio, 1953; M.Ed., Miami (Ohio) University, 1961; educator in Butler County, Ohio, for twenty-four years; clerk, city of Fairfield, Ohio, 1956-1957; member, Fairfield City Council, 1958; member, Ohio State house of representatives, 1961-1967; Ohio State senator, 1967-1971; elected as a Republican to the Ninety-second and Ninety-third Congresses (January 3, 1971-January 3, 1975); was not a candidate for reelection in 1974 to the Ninety-fourth Congress; is a resident of Middletown, Ohio.

**POWER, Thomas Charles,** a Senator from Montana; born near Dubuque, Dubuque County, Iowa, May 22, 1839; attended the common schools and studied civil engineering at Sinsiniwa College, Wisconsin; practiced engineering and taught school three years; employed as a surveyor in Dakota in 1860; engaged in trade on the Missouri River, 1861-1867; president of a line of steamers; moved to Fort Benton, Mont.; settled in Helena in 1876; engaged in mercantile pursuits and in banking; member of the first constitutional convention of Montana in 1883; unsuccessful candidate for governor of Montana in 1889; upon the admission of Montana as a State into the Union was elected as a Republican to the United States Senate, and served from January 2, 1890 to March 3, 1895; was not a candidate for renomination; chairman, Committee to Examine Branches of the Civil Service (Fifty-second Congress); engaged in banking, stock raising, and mercantile pursuits; died in Helena, Mont., February 16, 1923; interment in Resurrection Cemetery.

**POWERS, Caleb,** a Representative from Kentucky; born near Williamsburg, Whitley County, Ky., February 1, 1869; attended the public schools, Union College, Barbourville, Ky., the University of Kentucky at Lexington, and Centre College, Danville, Ky.; was graduated from Valparaiso (Ind.) University; attended West Point Military Academy in 1890 and 1891; studied law; was admitted to the bar in 1894 and commenced practice at Barbourville, Ky.; superintendent of public schools for Knox County, 1894-1899; elected secretary of state of Kentucky in 1899, but was unseated after a contest; convicted of complicity in the assassination of Governor William Goebel in 1900 and sentenced to prison; was pardoned in 1908; elected as a Republican to the Sixty-second and to the three succeeding Congresses (March 4, 1911-March 3, 1919); was not a candidate for renomination in 1918 to the Sixty-sixth Congress; delegate to the Republican National Convention of 1912; moved to Washington, D.C., and served as assistant counsel for the United States Shipping Board from 1921 until his death in Baltimore, Md., July 25, 1932; interment in City Cemetery, Barbourville, Ky.

**POWERS, David Lane,** a Representative from New Jersey; born in Philadelphia, Pa., July 29, 1896; attended the public schools, and was graduated from Pennsylvania Military College at Chester in 1915; during the First World War was commissioned a second lieutenant on August 15, 1917; promoted to first lieutenant and served as battalion adjutant in the Eight Hundred and Seventh Pioneer Infantry; moved to Trenton, N.J., in 1919 and engaged in the building business; member of the State house of assembly 1928-1930; elected as a Republican to the Seventy-third and to the six succeeding Congresses and served from March 4, 1933, until his resignation on August 30, 1945, to become a member of the Public Utilities Commission of New Jersey, a post he held until retirement in 1967; died in Feasterville, Pa., March 28, 1968; interment in Riverview Cemetery, Trenton, N.J.

**POWERS, Gershom,** a Representative from New York; born in Croydon, Sullivan County, N.H., July 11, 1789; attended the common schools and was largely self-taught; taught school in the town of Sempronius, Cayuga County, N.Y., while attending the local law school, from which he graduated in 1810; was admitted to the bar the same year and commenced practice in Auburn, Cayuga County, N.Y.; appointed superintendent of Auburn prison in 1820; first judge of the court of common pleas of Cayuga County 1823-1828; elected as a Jacksonian to the Twenty-first Congress (March 4, 1829-March 3, 1831); chairman, Committee on District of Columbia (Twenty-first Congress); declined to be a candidate for renomination in 1830; appointed inspector of Auburn prison on April 2, 1830, and served until his death; died in Auburn, N.Y., June 25, 1831; interment in North Street Cemetery.

**POWERS, Horace Henry,** a Representative from Vermont; born in Morristown, Lamoille County, Vt., May 29, 1835; attended Peoples Academy; was graduated from the University of Vermont at Burlington in 1855; studied law; was admitted to the bar in 1858 and practiced in Hyde Park, Vt., 1859-1862; member of the State house of representatives in 1858; prosecuting attorney of Lamoille County in 1861 and 1862; member of the council of censors in 1869; member of the State constitutional convention in 1870; served in the State senate in 1872 and 1873; again a member of the State house of representatives in 1874 and served as speaker; judge of the supreme court of Vermont from December 1874 to December 1890; trustee of the University of Vermont from 1883 until his death; delegate to the Republican National Convention in 1892; elected as a Republican to the Fifty-second and to the four succeeding Congresses (March 4, 1891-March 3, 1901); chairman, Committee on Pacific Railroads (Fifty-fourth through Fifty-sixth Congresses); unsuccessful candidate for renomination in 1900; resumed the practice of law in Morrisville, Vt.; died in Morrisville, Vt., December 8, 1913; interment in Pleasant View Cemetery.

**POWERS, Llewellyn,** a Representative from Maine; born in Pittsfield, Somerset County, Maine, October 14, 1836; attended the common schools of Pittsfield and St. Albans Academy; was graduated from the Colburn Classical Institute; attended Colby College, Waterville, Maine, and was graduated from the law department of Union University, Albany, N.Y., in 1860; was admitted to the bar in Albany, N.Y., and Somerset, Maine, in 1860 and commenced practice in Houlton, Maine, in January 1861; prosecuting attorney for Aroostook County, 1864-1871; collector of customs for the district of Aroostook, 1868-1872; member of the Maine State house of representatives, 1873-1876, 1883, 1892, and 1895, and served as speaker during the last term; elected as a Republican to the Forty-fifth Congress (March 4, 1877-March 3, 1879); unsuccessful candidate for reelection in 1878 to the Forty-sixth Congress; elected Governor of Maine in 1896, reelected in 1898, and served from January 6, 1897 to January 2, 1901; elected as a Republican to the Fifty-seventh Congress to fill the vacancy caused by the resignation of Charles A. Boutelle; reelected to the Fifty-eighth to the two succeeding Congresses, and served from April 8, 1901 until his death in Houlton, Maine, July 28, 1908; interment in West Pittsfield Cemetery, near Pittsfield, Maine.

**POWERS, Samuel Leland,** a Representative from Massachusetts; born in Cornish, N.H., October 26, 1848; prepared for college at Kimball Union Academy, Meriden, N.H.; graduated from Dartmouth College, Hanover, N.H., in 1874; studied law in the law school of the University of the City of New York, and also in Worcester, Mass.; admitted to the bar in 1875 and commenced practice in Boston, Mass., in 1876; moved to Newton, Mass., in 1882; member of the Newton City Council 1883-1887, serving as president in 1885 and 1886; elected as a Republican to the Fifty-seventh and Fifty-eighth Congresses (March 4, 1901-March 3, 1905); declined to be a candidate for renomination in 1904; one of the managers appointed by the House of Representatives in 1905 to conduct the impeachment proceedings against Charles Swayne, judge of the United States District Court for the Northern District of Florida; resumed the practice of law in Boston and resided in Newton, Mass.; trustee of Dartmouth College 1905-1915; member of the Massachusetts Board of Education in 1915-1919; member of the Massachusetts constitutional convention in 1918 and 1919; served in the Massachusetts militia for ten years; trustee of the board of public control for the operation of the Boston Elevated Railway 1918-1928, serving as chairman 1923-1928; died in Newton, Mass., on November 30, 1929; interment in Newton Cemetery, Newton Center, Mass.

**POYDRAS, Julien de Lallande,** a Delegate from the Territory of Orleans; born in Nantes, France, April 3, 1740; completed preparatory studies; served in the French Navy in his youth; was captured by the British in 1760 and taken to England; escaped on board a West Indian merchantman to San Domingo, whence he immigrated to New Orleans, La., in 1768; wrote the first poetical work printed in Louisiana in 1779; president of the first legislative council of the Territory of Orleans; founded the Female Orphan Asylum in New Orleans; elected to the Eleventh Congress (March 4, 1809-March 3, 1811); president of the first State constitutional convention; presidential elector for James Madison in 1812; founded and endowed the Poydras Asylum; died in Pointe Coupee, La., June 14, 1824; interment in Old St. Francis Cemetery; reinterment in the grounds of the Poydras High School, New Roads, La.

**Bibliography:** *DAB*.

**PRACHT, Charles Frederick,** a Representative from Pennsylvania; born in Pitman, Schuylkill County, Pa., October 20, 1880; attended the public schools; associated in the toy novelty and notions business from 1897 until 1914; children's agent and investigator in the county commissioner's office from 1915 to 1929; served in the department of accounts under the clerk of quarter sessions in 1930 and 1931; personal property assessor in the board of revision department, 1932-1942; member of the Republican executive ward committee, beginning in 1904, and serving as chairman for twenty-five consecutive years; elected as a Republican to the Seventy-eighth Congress (January 3, 1943-January 3, 1945);

unsuccessful candidate for reelection in 1944 to the Seventy-ninth Congress; died in Philadelphia, Pa., December 22, 1950; interment in Lawnview Cemetery (Rockledge), Philadelphia, Pa.

**PRALL, Anning Smith,** a Representative from New York; born in Port Richmond, Staten Island, N.Y., September 17, 1870; attended the public schools and New York University; employed as a clerk in a New York City newspaper office; was in charge of a real estate department of a bank 1908-1918; served as clerk of the first district municipal court; appointed a member of the New York City Board of Education January 1, 1918, and served until December 31, 1921, and three times elected its president; commissioner of taxes and assessment in 1922 and 1923; delegate to the Democratic National Convention in 1924; elected as a Democrat to the Sixty-eighth Congress to fill the vacancy caused by the death of Daniel J. Riordan; reelected to the Sixty-ninth and to the four succeeding Congresses and served from November 6, 1923, to January 3, 1935; was not a candidate for renomination in 1934; served as a member and chairman of the Federal Communications Commission from January 15, 1935, until his death at his summer home in Boothbay Harbor, Maine, July 23, 1937; interment in Moravian Cemetery, New Dorp, Staten Island, N.Y.

**PRATT, Charles Clarence,** a Representative from Pennsylvania; born in New Milford, Susquehanna County, Pa., April 23, 1854; attended the rural schools in his community, Sedgwick Institute, Great Barrington, Mass.; graduated from the Pennsylvania normal school at Bloomsburg, Pa.; became engaged in the lumber and oil businesses at New Milford in 1879; served as assessor, school director, and justice of the peace; colonel on the respective staffs of Governors William A. Stone, Samuel W. Pennypacker, and John K. Tener, 1899-1907; elected as a Republican to the Sixty-first Congress (March 4, 1909-March 3, 1911); unsuccessful candidate for reelection in 1910 to the Sixty-second Congress; resumed his former business pursuits, residing in Binghamton, N.Y., during the winters and in New Milford, Pa., during the summers; died in Binghamton, N.Y., January 27, 1916; interment in New Milford Cemetery, New Milford, Pa.

**PRATT, Daniel Darwin,** a Senator from Indiana; born in Palermo, Maine, October 26, 1813; moved to New York with his parents, who settled in Fenner, Madison County; attended the public schools and Cazenovia Seminary; graduated from Hamilton College, Clinton, N.Y., in 1831; moved to Indiana in 1832 and taught school; settled in Indianapolis in 1834 and was employed in the office of the secretary of State; studied law; was admitted to the bar and commenced practice in Logansport, Ind., in 1836; member, State house of representatives in 1851, 1853; elected in 1868 as a Republican to the Forty-first Congress but resigned January 27, 1869, before the beginning of the congressional term, having been elected to the United States Senate; served as a Republican in the Senate from March 4, 1869, to March 3, 1875; chairman, Committee on Pensions (Forty-second and Forty-third Congresses); appointed by President Ulysses S. Grant as Commissioner of Internal Revenue 1875-1876; died in Logansport, Cass County, Ind., June 17, 1877; interment in Mount Hope Cemetery.

**Bibliography:** Holliday, Joseph E. "Daniel D. Pratt: Lawyer and Legislator." *Indiana Magazine of History* 57 (June 1961): 99-126.

**PRATT, Eliza Jane,** a Representative from North Carolina; born in Morven, Anson County, N.C., March 5, 1902; attended the public schools of Morven and Raeford, N.C., and Queens College at Charlotte, N.C.; newspaper editor at Troy, N.C., in 1923 and 1924; served as secretary to Members of Congress from the Eighth Congressional District of North Carolina 1924-1946; elected as a Democrat to the Seventy-ninth Congress to fill the vacancy caused by the death of William O. Burgin and served from May 25, 1946, to January 3, 1947; was not a candidate for renomination in 1946; employed with the Office of Alien Property, Washington, D.C., from

1947 to 1951; with Department of Agriculture from 1951 to 1954; with Library of Congress from 1954 to 1956; secretary to Representative Kitchin of North Carolina from 1957 to 1962; served as public relations head for North Carolina Telephone Company; resided in Wadesboro, N.C.; died in Charlotte, N.C. May 13, 1981; interment in Raeford City Cemetery, Raeford, N.C.

**PRATT, Harcourt Joseph,** a Representative from New York; born in Highland, Ulster County, N.Y., October 23, 1866; attended the public schools and Claverack Academy at Claverack, N.Y.; engaged in the lumber and coal business; also interested in banking; member of the Board of Supervisors of Ulster County, 1895-1897; member of the New York State assembly in 1897; director of the First National Bank of Highland, beginning in 1900, and of the Kingston Trust Co., beginning in 1921; was president of the Board of Education of Highland, N.Y., 1908-1926; elected as a Republican to the Sixty-ninth and to the three succeeding Congresses (March 4, 1925-March 3, 1933); was not a candidate for renomination in 1932 to the Seventy-third Congress; resumed his former business interests; died from injuries received in an automobile accident near Highland, N.Y., May 21, 1934; interment in Highland Cemetery.

**PRATT, Harry Hayt,** a Representative from New York; born in Corning, Steuben County, N.Y., November 11, 1864; attended Corning Union School and was graduated from Corning Free Academy in 1882; associate editor of the Corning Weekly Journal 1882-1891 and of the Corning Daily Journal 1891-1906; editor of the same and manager of the Corning Journal Publishing Co. 1906-1919; supervisor of Corning in 1898 and 1899; delegate to the Republican State conventions in 1908 and 1910; postmaster of Corning from September 8, 1905, to January 27, 1914; elected as a Republican to the Sixty-fourth and Sixty-fifth Congresses (March 4, 1915-March 3, 1919); unsuccessful candidate for renomination in 1918; engaged in publicity work for the United States Department of Labor and the War Risk Insurance Bureau 1919-1921; public relations counselor for the Erie Railroad Co. 1923-1928, and managing editor of the Erie Railroad Magazine; director of the Corning Free Library and the Chamber of Commerce; died in Corning, N.Y., November 13, 1932; interment in Hope Cemetery.

**PRATT, Henry Otis,** a Representative from Iowa; born in Foxcroft, Piscataquis County, Maine, February 11, 1838; attended the common schools and Foxcroft Academy; was graduated from the law department of Harvard University; moved to Charles City, Iowa, in 1862 and taught school; was admitted to the bar in Mason City, Iowa, in 1862; during the Civil War enlisted in the Union Army in August 1862 and served in Company B, Thirty-second Regiment, Iowa Volunteer Infantry, until March 1863, when he was discharged at Fort Pillow, Tenn.; commenced the practice of law in Charles City, Iowa, in 1864; Floyd County superintendent of public schools, 1868-1869; member of the Iowa State house of representatives, 1870-1872; elected as a Republican to the Forty-third and Forty-fourth Congresses (March 4, 1873-March 3, 1877); was not a candidate for renomination in 1876 to the Forty-fifth Congress; president of the Republican State convention at Des Moines, Iowa, in 1877; studied for the ministry; was ordained and entered the ministry of the Methodist Episcopal Church in October 1877, and continued his ministerial duties until he retired on account of age in October 1918; died in Cedar Rapids, Iowa, May 22, 1931; interment in Oak Hill Cemetery.

**PRATT, James Timothy,** a Representative from Connecticut; born in Cromwell, Conn., December 14, 1802; attended the common schools; engaged in mercantile and agricultural pursuits in Hartford, Conn.; enlisted in the "Horse Guard" in 1820; mayor 1826-1829; elected major of the First Regiment of Cavalry in 1834; colonel in 1836; brigadier general 1837-1839; major general 1839-1846; adjutant general in 1846; retired from mercantile pursuits and settled in Rocky Hill, Conn.; member of the State house of representatives in 1847, 1848, and 1850; served in the State senate in 1852; again a member of the State house of representatives in 1857 and 1862; elected as a Democrat to the Thirty-third Congress (March 4, 1853-March 3, 1855); unsuccessful candidate for reelection in 1854 to the Thirty-fourth Congress; unsuccessful candidate for election as Governor in 1858 and 1859; member of the peace convention of 1861 held in Washington, D.C., in an effort to devise means to prevent the impending war; again a member of the State house of representatives in 1870 and 1871; engaged in agricultural pursuits; died in Wethersfield, Hartford County, Conn., April 11, 1887; interment in Indian Hill Cemetery, Middletown, Conn.

**PRATT, Joseph Marmaduke,** a Representative from Pennsylvania; born in Paterson, Passaic County, N.J., September 4, 1891; moved with his parents to Philadelphia, Pa. in 1892; attended the public schools and business colleges; was graduated from Temple University, Philadelphia, Pa., in 1919; engaged in the manufacture of industrial and marine products; member of the Republican city committee of Philadelphia 1937-1946; elected as a Republican to the Seventy-eighth Congress to fill the vacancy caused by the resignation of James P. McGranery and served from January 18, 1944, to January 3, 1945; unsuccessful candidate for reelection in 1944 to the Seventy-ninth Congress; resumed his former business pursuits in Philadelphia, Pa.; received the Republican nomination for senator of the Commonwealth in the second senatorial district of Pennsylvania in 1946; died in Washington, D.C., on July 19, 1946, while on a business trip; interment in Arlington Cemetery, Upper Darby, Pa.

**PRATT, Le Gage,** a Representative from New Jersey; born in Sterling, Worcester County, Mass., December 14, 1852; educated in the common schools; in 1869 entered upon a commercial career in Boston; subsequently moved with his parents to Chicago, Ill.; engaged in newspaper work in Chicago 1884-1886; was employed for several years in the life-insurance business in Texas; was subsequently transferred to Illinois and Minnesota and continued in this business; in 1897 tendered his resignation and moved to East Orange, N.J., and in 1903 accepted a position with an insurance company at Newark, N.J., being elected vice president, which office he held until elected to Congress; elected as a Democrat to the Sixtieth Congress (March 4, 1907-March 3, 1909); unsuccessful candidate for reelection in 1908 to the Sixty-first Congress; resumed the insurance business and became connected with the Puritan Life Insurance Co., of Providence, R.I.; died in Newark, N.J., March 9, 1911; interment in Fairmount Cemetery.

**PRATT, Ruth Sears Baker,** a Representative from New York; born in Ware, Mass., August 24, 1877; attended private schools and Wellesley (Mass.) College; moved to Greenwich, Conn., in 1894 and to New York City in 1904; during the First World War chaired the Second Federal Reserve District's Woman's Liberty Loan Committee; elected Associate Leader of the Fifteenth Assembly District in January 1924; member of the board of aldermen of New York City in 1925, being the first woman to serve; reelected in 1927 and served until March 1, 1929; member of the Republican National Committee from 1929 to 1943; delegate to the Republican National Conventions of 1924, 1932, 1936, and 1940; delegate to the Republican State conventions in 1922, 1924, 1926, 1928, 1930, 1936, and 1938; served as president of the Woman's National Republican Club, 1943-1946; elected as a Republican to the Seventy-first and Seventy-second Congresses (March 4, 1929-March 3, 1933); unsuccessful candidate for reelection in 1932 to the Seventy-third Congress; was a resident of New York City; died at her home, "The Manor House," Glen Cove, N.Y., August 23, 1965; interment in the Pratt Mausoleum.

**PRATT, Thomas George,** a Senator from Maryland; born in Georgetown, Md. (now a part of Washington, D.C.), February 18, 1804; completed preparatory studies and attended Georgetown

University, Washington, D.C., and the College of New Jersey (now Princeton University); studied law; was admitted to the bar and commenced practice in Upper Marlboro, Md., in 1823; member, Maryland State house of delegates, 1832-1835; Whig presidential elector in 1836; appointed president of the executive council in 1836; member, State senate, 1838-1843; elected Governor of Maryland in 1844, and served from January 6, 1845 to January 3, 1848; moved to Annapolis, Md., in 1848 and resumed the practice of law; elected as a Whig to the United States Senate in 1849 to fill the vacancy caused by the resignation of Reverdy Johnson; reelected in 1851, and served from January 12, 1850 to March 3, 1857; moved to Baltimore, Md., in 1864 and again resumed the practice of his profession; unsuccessful candidate for election to the United States Senate in 1867; died in Baltimore, Md., November 9, 1869; interment in St. Anne's Cemetery, Annapolis, Md.

**Bibliography:** *DAB.*

**PRATT, Zadock,** a Representative from New York; born in Stephentown, N.Y., October 30, 1790; moved with his parents to Windham (later Jewett), Greene County, in 1802; received a limited schooling; engaged in tanning leather in Greene County, where he established a town called Prattsville; member of the State militia 1819-1823; justice of the peace in 1824; supervisor of the town of Windham in 1827; member of the State senate in 1830; elected as a Democrat to the Twenty-fifth Congress (March 4, 1837-March 3, 1839); elected to the Twenty-eighth Congress (March 4, 1843-March 3, 1845); chairman, Committee on Public Buildings and Grounds (Twenty-eighth Congress); resumed his former business activities; also engaged in banking and agricultural pursuits near Prattsville, Greene County, N.Y.; delegate to the Democratic National Convention in 1852; retired from active business pursuits in 1860; died in Bergen, N.J., on April 6, 1871; interment in the City Cemetery, Prattsville, N.Y.

**Bibliography:** *DAB.*

**PRAY, Charles Nelson,** a Representative from Montana; born in Potsdam, St. Lawrence County, N.Y., April 6, 1868; attended the public schools in Salisbury and Middlebury, Vt.; graduate of the Middlebury High School; attended Middlebury (Vt.) College 1886-1888 and was graduated from the Chicago College of Law; was admitted to the bar in 1892 and commenced practice at Fort Benton, Mont., in 1896; served as assistant prosecuting attorney of Chouteau County in 1897 and 1898; elected prosecuting attorney in 1898 and reelected in 1900, 1902, and 1904; elected as a Republican to the Sixtieth, Sixty-first, and Sixty-second Congresses (March 4, 1907-March 3, 1913); unsuccessful candidate for reelection in 1912 to the Sixty-third Congress; resumed the practice of law in Great Falls, Cascade County, Mont., January 1, 1914; unsuccessful candidate for election to the United States Senate in 1916; appointed judge of the United States District Court of Montana on January 21, 1924, in which capacity he served until his retirement in 1957; died in Great Falls, Mont., September 12, 1963; interment in Hillcrest Lawn Memorial Cemetery.

**PRENTISS, John Holmes** (brother of Samuel Prentiss), a Representative from New York; born in Worcester, Mass., April 17, 1784; attended local and private schools; foreman of the New York Evening Post in 1808; moved to Cooperstown, Otsego County, N.Y., in October 1808; established the Freeman's Journal in the same year and served as editor; appointed colonel of militia by Governor Clinton and served as division inspector on the staff of the commander in chief; postmaster of Cooperstown from April 24, 1833, to February 17, 1837; vice president of the Democratic State convention at Albany; elected as a Democrat to the Twenty-fifth and Twenty-sixth Congresses (March 4, 1837-March 3, 1841); was not a candidate for renomination in 1840 to the Twenty-seventh Congress; resumed his former newspaper pursuits; also served as president of the Bank of Cooperstown; resided in Cooperstown, N.Y., until his death in that city on June 26, 1861; interment in Lakewood Cemetery.

**PRENTISS, Samuel** (brother of John Holmes Prentiss), a Senator from Vermont; born in Stonington, Conn., March 31, 1782; moved to Northfield, Mass., in 1786; completed preparatory studies and was instructed in the classics by a private tutor; studied law in Northfield and in Brattleboro, Vt.; was admitted to the bar in 1802 and practiced in Montpelier, Vt. 1803-1822; member, State house of representatives 1824-1825; associate justice of the supreme court of Vermont; elected chief justice of the State supreme court in 1829; elected in 1831 as a Whig to the United States Senate; reelected in 1837 and served from March 4, 1831, to April 11, 1842, when he resigned to accept a judicial assignment; chairman, Committee on Patents and the Patent Office (Twenty-seventh Congress); originator and successful advocate of the law to suppress dueling in the District of Columbia; judge of the United States District Court of Vermont from 1842 until his death in Montpelier, Vt., January 15, 1857; interment in Green Mount Cemetery.

Bibliography: *DAB*; Binney, Charles. *Memoirs of Judge Samuel Prentiss of Montpelier, Vermont, and His Wife*. Boston: n.p., 1883.

**PRENTISS, Seargent Smith,** a Representative from Mississippi; born in Portland, Cumberland County, Maine, September 30, 1808; attended Gorham (Maine) Academy and was graduated from Bowdoin College, Brunswick, Maine, in 1826; studied law in Gorham, Maine, and in Cincinnati, Ohio; moved to Natchez, Adams County, Miss.; was admitted to the bar in 1829 and commenced practice in Vicksburg, Miss.; member of the State house of representatives 1836-1837; contested the election of John F.H. Claiborne to the Twenty-fifth Congress and the election was set aside by the House; subsequently elected to fill the vacancy caused by this action and served from May 30, 1838, to March 3, 1839; was not a candidate for renomination in 1838; unsuccessful candidate for the United States Senate in 1839-1840; resumed the practice of law at Vicksburg; moved to New Orleans, La, in 1845 and resumed the practice of law; died at "Longwood," near Natchez, Miss., July 1, 1850; interment in the private burying ground at "Longwood."

Bibliography: *DAB*; Dickey, Dallas C. *Seargent S. Prentiss, Whig Orator of the Old South*. Baton Rouge: Louisiana State University Press, 1945; Prentiss, George Lewis. *A Memoir of S.S. Prentiss*. 2 vols. New York: C. Scribner's Sons, 1886.

**PRESCOTT, Cyrus Dan,** a Representative from New York; born in New Hartford, Oneida County, N.Y., August 15, 1836; pursued an academic course and was graduated from Utica Free Academy; studied law in Utica and in Rome, N.Y.; was admitted to the bar in 1859 and commenced practice in Rome in 1860; moved to New York City in 1867 and was employed as a financial clerk in a wholesale house; returned to Rome, N.Y., in 1868 and continued the practice of law; member of the Board of Aldermen of Rome 1874-1876; served in the State assembly in 1878; elected as a Republican to the Forty-sixth and Forty-seventh Congresses (March 4, 1879-March 3, 1883); was not a candidate for renomination in 1882; resumed the practice of law in Rome, N.Y.; attorney for the New York Central Railroad Co. for over thirty years; died in Rome, Oneida County, N.Y., October 23, 1902; interment in Sauquoit Valley Cemetery, near Clayville, Oneida County, N.Y.

**PRESSLER, Larry Lee,** a Representative and a Senator from South Dakota; born in Humboldt, Minnehaha County, S.Dak., March 29, 1942; B.A., University of South Dakota, Vermillion, 1964; attended Oxford University, England, 1966, as a Rhodes scholar; M.A., John F. Kennedy School of Government, Harvard University, 1971; J.D., Harvard University Law School, 1971; admitted to District of Columbia bar in 1972 and commenced practice; lieutenant, United States Army, 1966-1968, with service in Vietnam; served in the Office of Legal Adviser to the Secretary of State,

1971-1974; elected as a Republican to the Ninety-fourth and Ninety-fifth Congresses (January 3, 1975-January 3, 1979); was not a candidate for reelection to the House of Representatives in 1978, but was elected to the United States Senate for the term commencing January 3, 1979; reelected in 1984, and again in 1990 for the term ending January 3, 1997; chairman, Committee on Commerce, Science, and Transportation (One Hundred Fourth Congress); is a resident of Humboldt, S.D.

**PRESTON, Francis** (father of William Campbell Preston and uncle of William Ballard Preston and William Preston), a Representative from Virginia; born in Greenfield, Botetourt County, Va., August 2, 1765; graduated from the College of William and Mary, Williamsburg, Va., in 1783; studied law; admitted to the bar and practiced in Montgomery and Washington Counties; member of the Virginia house of delegates in 1788 and 1789; elected to the Third Congress and reelected as a Republican to the Fourth Congress (March 4, 1793-March 3, 1797); declined to be a candidate for renomination; settled in Abingdon, Va., and resumed the practice of law; again a member of the Virginia house of delegates 1812-1814; colonel of Volunteers in the War of 1812; served in the Virginia senate 1816-1820; died at the home of his brother, William C. Preston, in Columbia, S.C., May 26, 1836; interment in Aspinvale Cemetery, near Seven Mile Ford, Va.

**PRESTON, Jacob Alexander,** a Representative from Maryland; born in Bel Air, Harford County, Md., March 12, 1796; attended the common schools; was graduated from the medical department of the University of Maryland at Baltimore in 1816; practiced his profession in Harford, Baltimore, and Cecil Counties; also engaged in agricultural pursuits; served with a Maryland regiment as lieutenant in the War of 1812; elected as a Whig to the Twenty-eighth Congress (March 4, 1843-March 3, 1845); was not a candidate for renomination in 1844; resumed the practice of medicine and also engaged in agricultural pursuits; died in Perryman, Harford County, Md., on August 2, 1868; interment in St. George's Churchyard, Spesutia Island, Md.

**PRESTON, Prince Hulon, Jr.,** a Representative from Georgia, born in Monroe, Walton County, Ga., July 5, 1908; attended the public schools of Statesboro, Ga.; was graduated from the law department of the University of Georgia at Athens in 1930; was admitted to the bar the same year and commenced practice in Statesboro, Ga.; member of the State house of representatives 1935-1938; during the Second World War enlisted in September 1942 as a private in the United States Army; was promoted through the ranks to captain, being discharged October 13, 1945; elected judge of the city court of Statesboro in 1946 but did not serve, having been elected to Congress; elected as a Democrat to the Eightieth and to the six succeeding Congresses (January 3, 1947-January 3, 1961); unsuccessful candidate for renomination in 1960; died in Savannah, Ga., February 8, 1961; interment in Eastside Cemetery, Statesboro, Ga.

**PRESTON, William** (nephew of Francis Preston), a Representative from Kentucky; born near Louisville, Ky., October 16, 1816; pursued preparatory studies and was graduated from St. Joseph's College, Kentucky; attended Yale College in 1835; was graduated from the law department of Harvard University in 1838; was admitted to the bar and commenced practice in Louisville, Ky., in 1839; served as lieutenant colonel of the Fourth Kentucky Volunteers in the war with Mexico, 1846-1848; delegate to the Kentucky constitutional convention in 1849; member of the Kentucky house of representatives in 1850; served in the Kentucky senate, 1851-1853; elected as a Whig to the Thirty-second Congress to fill the vacancy caused by the resignation of Humphrey Marshall; reelected to the Thirty-third Congress, and served from December 6, 1852 to March 3, 1855; unsuccessful candidate for reelection in 1854 to the Thirty-fourth Congress; appointed Envoy Extraordinary and

Minister Plenipotentiary to Spain on December 15, 1858, and served until May 1861; during the Civil War served in the Confederate Army and attained the rank of brigadier general on April 14, 1862; appointed Envoy Extraordinary and Minister Plenipotentiary from the Confederacy to Maximilian, Emperor of Mexico, on January 7, 1864; following the close of the Civil War he traveled in Mexico, the West Indies, Great Britain and Canada before returning to the United States in 1866; again a member of the Kentucky house of representatives in 1868 and 1869; died in Louisville, Ky., September 21, 1887; interment in Cave Hill Cemetery.

Bibliography: *DAB.*

**PRESTON, William Ballard** (nephew of Francis Preston), a Representative from Virginia; born in Smithfield, Va., November 25, 1805; graduated from the College of William and Mary, Williamsburg, Va., in 1823; studied law; graduated from the University of Virginia at Charlottesville; admitted to the bar and commenced practice in 1826; member of the Virginia house of delegates, 1830-1832; served in the Virginia senate, 1840-1844; again a member of the Virginia house of delegates in 1844 and 1845; elected as a Whig to the Thirtieth Congress (March 4, 1847-March 3, 1849); appointed Secretary of the Navy in the Cabinet of President Zachary Taylor, and served from March 8, 1849 to July 22, 1850; delegate to the Virginia constitutional convention in 1861; served in the Confederate States Congress; died in Smithfield, Va., on November 16, 1862; interment in Preston Cemetery on the former Smithfield Plantation, Blacksburg, Va.

Bibliography: *DAB.*

**PRESTON, William Campbell** (son of Francis Preston), a Senator from South Carolina; born in Philadelphia, Pa., on December 27, 1794; studied under private tutors; attended Washington College (later Washington and Lee University), Lexington, Va., and graduated from South Carolina College (later the University of South Carolina) at Columbia in 1812; traveled and studied in Europe for several years; studied law at the University of Edinburgh, Scotland; returned to the United States in 1819; was admitted to the bar in Virginia in 1820 and practiced; moved to Columbia, S.C., in 1822; unsuccessful candidate for election in 1828 to the Twenty-second Congress; member, State house of representatives 1828-1834; elected in 1833 as a Nullifier to the United States Senate to fill the vacancy caused by the resignation of Stephen D. Miller; reelected as a Whig in 1837 and served from November 26, 1833, until his resignation on November 29, 1842; chairman, Committee on the Library (Twenty-seventh Congress), Committee on Military Affairs (Twenty-seventh Congress); resumed the practice of law in Columbia, S.C.; president of South Carolina College 1845-1851, when he resigned due to ill health; died in Columbia, S.C., on May 22, 1860; interment in the Trinity Episcopal Churchyard, Columbia, S.C.

Bibliography: *DAB*; Green, Edwin. *William Campbell Preston.* Columbia: n.p., 1946; Preston, William. *Reminiscences of William C. Preston.* Edited by Minnie Yarborough. Chapel Hill: University of North Carolina Press, 1933.

**PREYER, Lunsford Richardson,** a Representative from North Carolina; born in Greensboro, Guilford County, N.C., January 11, 1919; attended Greensboro High School, and graduated from Woodberry Forest School, Woodberry Forest, Va.; A.B., Princeton University, 1941; LL.B., Harvard University Law School, 1949; during the Second World War served in United States Navy in the Pacific; awarded Bronze Star; city judge, 1953-1954; North Carolina State superior court judge, 1956-1961; United States judge for the middle district of North Carolina, 1961-1963; unsuccessful candidate in 1964 for nomination for governor of North Carolina; senior vice president, trust officer, city executive of North Carolina National Bank, Greensboro, N.C., 1964-1966; elected as a Democrat to the Ninety-first and to the five succeeding Congresses (January 3,

1969-January 3, 1981); chairman, Select Committee on Ethics (Ninety-fifth Congress); unsuccessful candidate for reelection in 1980 to the Ninety-seventh Congress; is a resident of Greensboro, N.C.

**PRICE, Andrew** (son-in-law of Edward James Gay), a Representative from Louisiana; born on Chatsworth plantation, near Franklin, St. Mary Parish, La., April 2, 1854; attended various private schools; was graduated from the law department of Cumberland University, Lebanon, Tenn., in 1875 and from the law department of Washington University, St. Louis, Mo., in 1877; was admitted to the bar and practiced in St. Louis until 1880, when he returned to Louisiana and engaged in sugar planting; delegate to the Democratic National Convention of 1888; elected as a Democrat to the Fifty-first Congress to fill the vacancy caused by the death of his father-in-law, Edward James Gay; reelected to the three succeeding Congresses, and served from December 2, 1889 to March 3, 1897; died at Acadia plantation, Lafourche Parish, La., on February 5, 1909; interment in Mount Olivet Cemetery, Nashville, Tenn.

**PRICE, Charles Melvin,** a Representative from Illinois; born in East St. Louis, St. Clair County, Ill., January 1, 1905; attended the parochial schools, St. Louis (Mo.) University High School, and St. Louis (Mo.) University; sports editor for the East St. Louis News-Review, 1925-1927; newspaper correspondent, East St. Louis Journal, 1927-1933; member of the St. Clair County Board of Supervisors, 1929-1931; secretary to Representative Edwin M. Schaefer, 1933-1943; enlisted in the United States Army in October 1943 and served in the Quartermaster Corps at Camp Lee, Va., until elected to Congress in 1944; director, Edgemont Bank and Trust, East St. Louis, Ill.; elected as a Democrat to the Seventy-ninth and to the twenty-one succeeding Congresses, and served from January 3, 1945 until his death in Camp Springs, Md., on April 22, 1988; chairman, Committee on Standards of Official Conduct (Ninetieth through Ninety-fourth Congresses), Joint Committee on Atomic Energy (Ninety-third Congress), Committee on Armed Services (Ninety-fourth through Ninety-eighth Congresses); interment in Mount Carmel Cemetery, Belleville, Ill.

**PRICE, David Eugene,** a Representative from North Carolina; born in Johnson City, Tenn., August 17, 1940; attended public schools; attended Mars Hill College, N.C., 1957-1959; B.A., University of North Carolina, Chapel Hill, 1961; B.D., Yale University, 1964; Ph.D., political science, Yale University, 1969; legislative aide to Senator Edward L. (Bob) Bartlett of Alaska, 1963-1967; professor, Duke University, Durham, N.C., 1973-1986; staff director, Commission on Presidential Nomination, Democratic National Committee, 1981-1982; member, Democratic National Committee, 1983-1984; chairman, North Carolina Democratic Party, 1983-1984; elected as a Democrat to the One Hundredth and to the three succeeding Congresses (January 3, 1987-January 3, 1995); unsuccessful candidate for reelection in 1994 to the One Hundred Fourth Congress; professor of political science and public policy, Duke University; candidate for election in 1996 to the One Hundred Fifth Congress; is a resident of Chapel Hill, N.C.

Bibliography: Price, David E. *The Congressional Experience: A View From the Hill.* Boulder, Colo.: Westview Press, 1992.

**PRICE, Emory Hilliard,** a Representative from Florida; born in Bostwick, Putnam County, Fla., December 3, 1899; attended the public schools of Duval County, Fla.; was graduated from Jacksonville (Fla.) Law College in 1936; was admitted to the bar the same year and commenced practice in Jacksonville, Fla.; member of the city council of Jacksonville, Fla., 1929-1932; supervisor of registration of Duval County, Fla., 1932-1942; elected as a Democrat to the Seventy-eighth and to the two succeeding Congresses (January 3, 1943-January 3, 1949); unsuccessful candidate for renomination in 1948 to the Eighty-first Congress; resumed the practice of law and real estate pursuits; died in Jacksonville, Fla., February 11, 1976; interment in Greenlawn Cemetery.

**PRICE, Hiram,** a Representative from Iowa; born in Washington County, Pa., January 10, 1814; attended the common schools; was engaged in agricultural pursuits on his father's farm for several years; employed as a bookkeeper for a large commission house near Pittsburgh, Pa., and equipped himself for mercantile life; moved to Davenport, Iowa, in 1844 and engaged in the mercantile business; served as collector, treasurer, and recorder of Scott County, Iowa; was president of the State Bank of Iowa from 1859 until 1866, and became president of the First National Bank of Davenport in 1873; during the early days of the Civil War was appointed by Governor Samuel J. Kirkwood as paymaster general of the Iowa troops, to whom he advanced large sums of money; elected as a Republican to the Thirty-eighth and to the two succeeding Congresses (March 4, 1863-March 3, 1869); chairman, Committee on Revolutionary Claims (Thirty-eighth Congress), Committee on Pacific Railroads (Thirty-ninth and Fortieth Congresses); declined to be a candidate for renomination in 1868 to the Forty-first Congress; president of the Davenport & St. Paul Railroad Co.; elected to the Forty-fifth and Forty-sixth Congresses (March 4, 1877-March 3, 1881); declined to be a candidate for renomination in 1880 to the Forty-seventh Congress; appointed chief clerk for the Indian Office on April 13, 1881; appointed United States Commissioner of Indian Affairs during the administration of President James A. Garfield and served from May 6, 1881, to March 27, 1885; lived in Washington, D.C., until his death in that city on May 30, 1901; interment in Oakdale Cemetery, Davenport, Iowa.

**Bibliography:** *DAB.*

**PRICE, Hugh Hiram** (son of William Thompson Price), a Representative from Wisconsin; born at Black River Falls, Jackson County, Wis., December 2, 1859; attended the grade and high schools, and the University of Wisconsin at Madison; engaged in milling and in the lumber business; member of the city council in 1885 and 1886, and of the Jackson County Board of Wisconsin in 1885 and 1886; secretary of the Jackson County Agricultural Society in 1885; elected as a Republican to the Forty-ninth Congress to fill the vacancy caused by the death of his father, William T. Price, and served from January 18 to March 3, 1887; resumed his former business pursuits; member of the Wisconsin State senate in 1889; moved to Silver City, N.Mex., in 1894 and engaged in silver mining; moved to Phoenix, Ariz., and served as surveyor general of Arizona Territory for two years; moved to Denver, Colo., and lived in retirement until his death on December 25, 1904; interment in Fairmont Cemetery.

**PRICE, Jesse Dashiell,** a Representative from Maryland; born in Whitehaven, Somerset (later Wicomico) County, Md., August 15, 1863; attended the public schools; engaged in mercantile and manufacturing enterprises and in banking; member of the city council of Salisbury in 1903; treasurer of Wicomico County, 1903-1907; member of the Maryland State senate, 1908-1916 and served as president of the senate and ex officio Lieutenant Governor from 1912 until 1916, when he resigned to enter Congress; elected as a Democrat to the Sixty-third Congress to fill the vacancy caused by the resignation of J. Harry Covington; reelected to the two succeeding Congresses, and served from November 3, 1914 to March 3, 1919; unsuccessful candidate for reelection in 1918 to the Sixty-sixth Congress; resumed his former business pursuits; member of the Maryland State tax commission, 1923-1935; died at Ocean City, Md., May 14, 1939; interment in Parsons Cemetery, Salisbury, Md.

**PRICE, Robert Dale,** a Representative from Texas; born in Reading, Lyon County, Kans., September 7, 1927; educated in the public schools of Reading, Kans.; B.S., Oklahoma State University, 1951; served four years active duty in the United States Air Force,

1951-1955; flew twenty-seven combat missions during the Korean conflict; awarded Air Medal; returned to Texas after his honorable discharge in 1955; owned and operated a ranch in Texas; delegate, Texas State Republican conventions, 1964, 1966, and 1968; delegate to the Republican National Convention of 1968; elected as a Republican to the Ninetieth and to the three succeeding Congresses (January 3, 1967-January 3, 1975); unsuccessful candidate for reelection in 1974 to the Ninety-fourth Congress, and for election in 1976 to the Ninety-fifth Congress; member, Texas State senate, 1978-1980; unsuccessful candidate for nomination in 1988 to the One Hundred First Congress; rancher; is a resident of Pampa, Tex.

**PRICE, Rodman McCamley,** a Representative from New Jersey; born in Newton, Sussex County, N.J., May 5, 1816; attended the public schools of New York City and the Lawrenceville (N.J.) Academy; pursued classical studies in Princeton College, but did not graduate; studied law; was admitted to the bar; appointed purser in the Navy in 1840 and was stationed in San Francisco; during the Mexican War served as an officer of the Navy; prefect and alcalde of Monterey in 1846, and the first American to exercise judicial functions in California; naval agent, 1848-1850; delegate to the first constitutional convention of California; returned to New Jersey; elected as a Democrat to the Thirty-second Congress (March 4, 1851-March 3, 1853); unsuccessful candidate for reelection in 1852 to the Thirty-third Congress; elected Governor of New Jersey in 1853, and served from January 17, 1854 to January 20, 1857; father of the public school system of New Jersey; established a ferry from Weehawken to New York; engaged in the quarrying business and in the reclamation of lands along the Hackensack River; delegate to the peace convention held at Washington, D.C., in 1861 in an effort to devise means to prevent the impending war; died in Oakland, Bergen County, N.J., June 7, 1894; interment in Reformed Cemetery, Mahwah, N.J.

**Bibliography:** *DAB.*

**PRICE, Samuel,** a Senator from West Virginia; born in Fauquier County, Va., July 28, 1805; moved with his parents to Preston County in 1815; received a preparatory training; studied law; admitted to the bar in 1832 and commenced the practice of his profession in Nicholas and Braxton Counties; served as county clerk of Nicholas County in 1830, and as prosecuting attorney in 1833; member, Virginia house of delegates, 1834-1836; moved to Wheeling, Va. (now West Virginia), in 1836 and to Lewisburg, Greenbrier County, in 1838; prosecuting attorney for Braxton County, 1836-1850; member, Virginia house of delegates, 1847-1850, 1852; delegate to the constitutional conventions in 1850, 1851, and 1861; elected lieutenant governor of Virginia in 1863 and served until the close of the Civil War; delegate to the constitutional convention of West Virginia in 1872 and was its president; appointed as a Democrat to the United States Senate to fill the vacancy caused by the death of Allen T. Caperton, and served from August 26, 1876 to January 26, 1877, when a successor was elected; unsuccessful candidate in 1876 for election to fill the vacancy; died in Lewisburg, Greenbrier County, W.Va., on February 25, 1884; interment in the Stuart Burying Ground at Stuart Manor, near Lewisburg, W.Va.

**PRICE, Sterling,** a Representative from Missouri; was born near Farmville, Prince Edward County, Va., on September 20, 1809; completed preparatory studies and attended Hampden-Sidney College, Virginia; studied law; was admitted to the bar and practiced; moved to Fayette and later to Keytesville, Mo.; member of the Missouri State house of representatives, 1840-1844, and served as speaker; elected as a Democrat to the Twenty-ninth Congress, and served from March 4, 1845 to August 12, 1846, when he resigned to participate in the Mexican War; appointed colonel of the Second Regiment, Missouri Infantry, August 12, 1846; promoted to brigadier general of Volunteers, July 20, 1847, and was honorably discharged on November 25, 1848; returned to Missouri and engaged in agricultural pursuits on the Bowling Green prairie; elected Governor of Missouri in 1852, and served from January 3, 1853 to January 5, 1857; State bank commissioner, 1857-1861; elected presiding officer, Missouri State convention, February 28, 1861; allied with the Confederacy and commanded the Missouri State Guard; appointed a major general in the Confederate Army on March 6, 1862; led cavalry into Missouri during "Price's Raid," September-October 1864; after the war went to Mexico but later returned to Missouri; died in St. Louis, Mo., September 29, 1867; interment in Bellefontaine Cemetery.

**Bibliography:** *DAB*; Castel, Albert. *General Sterling Price and the Civil War in the West*. Baton Rouge: Louisiana State University Press, 1968; Shalhope, Robert E. *Sterling Price, Portrait of a Southerner*. Columbia: University of Missouri Press, 1971.

**PRICE, Thomas Lawson,** a Representative from Missouri; born near Danville, Va., on January 19, 1809; attended the country schools; moved to Missouri in 1831 and settled in Jefferson City; conducted stage lines and engaged in manufacturing and mercantile pursuits; first mayor of Jefferson City, 1839-1842; unsuccessful candidate for the Missouri State senate in 1845; commissioned brevet major general of the Sixth Division of Missouri Militia in 1847; elected Lieutenant Governor in 1849; member of the State house of representatives, 1860-1862; was one of the incorporators of the Capital City Bank and president of the Jefferson Land Co.; actively engaged in the promotion of various railway lines; brigadier general of Volunteers in 1861 and 1862; elected as a Democrat to the Thirty-seventh Congress to fill the vacancy caused by the expulsion of John W. Reid, and served from January 21, 1862 to March 3, 1863; unsuccessful candidate for reelection in 1862 to the Thirty-eighth Congress; delegate to the Democratic National Conventions of 1864 and 1868; died in Jefferson City, Mo., July 15, 1870; interment in a private cemetery; reinterment in Riverview Cemetery, Jefferson City, Mo., in 1912.

**Bibliography:** *DAB*.

**PRICE, William Pierce,** a Representative from Georgia; born in Dahlonega, Lumpkin County, Ga., January 29, 1835; attended the common schools; was apprenticed to the printer's trade; moved to Greenville, S.C., in 1851; attended Furman University, Greenville, S.C., but left before graduating to take charge of the editorial department of the Southern Enterprise, a Greenville newspaper; studied law; was admitted to the bar in 1856 and commenced practice in Greenville, S.C.; during the Civil War served in the Confederate Army as orderly sergeant in Kershaw's Second South Carolina Regiment; member of the South Carolina house of representatives, 1864-1866; moved to Dahlonega, Ga., in 1866; member, Georgia State house of representatives, 1868-1870; elected as a Democrat to the Forty-first Congress to fill the vacancy caused by failure to elect; reelected to the Forty-second Congress, and served from December 22, 1870 to March 3, 1873; was not a candidate for renomination in 1872 to the Forty-third Congress; again a member of the State house of representatives, 1877-1879, of the State senate in 1880 and 1881, and of the State house of representatives in 1894 and 1895; delegate to the Democratic National Convention of 1880; resumed the practice of law; president of the board of trustees of North Georgia Agricultural College, 1870-1908; died in Dahlonega, Ga., November 4, 1908; interment in Hill Crest Cemetery.

**PRICE, William Thompson** (father of Hugh Hiram Price), a Representative from Wisconsin; born in Huntingdon County, Pa., June 17, 1824; attended the common schools; was a clerk in a store in Hollidaysburg, Pa., and also studied law; moved to Mount Pleasant, Iowa, in 1845, and in the following autumn moved to Black River Falls, Wis.; engaged in lumbering and agricultrual pursuits; deputy sheriff of Crawford County in 1849; member of the Wisconsin State assembly in 1851 and again in 1882; was admitted

to the bar in 1852 and engaged in the practice of law; in 1854 moved to La Crosse, Wis., and operated a stage line between La Crosse and Black River Falls; moved to Black River Falls and continued the practice of law until 1857; judge of Jackson County in 1854 and 1859; under sheriff of Crawford County in 1855; county treasurer in 1856 and 1857; served in the Wisconsin State senate in 1857, 1870, and 1878-1881, and was president of the Senate in 1879; collector of internal revenue, 1863-1865; elected as a Republican to the Forty-eighth and Forty-ninth Congresses, and served from March 4, 1883 until his death at Black River Falls, Jackson County, Wis., December 6, 1886; interment in Riverside Cemetery.

**PRIDEMORE, Auburn Lorenzo,** a Representative from Virginia; born in Scott County, Va., June 27, 1837; received a limited education; completed preparatory studies; during the Civil War raised a company of volunteer infantry for the Confederate Army and served as its captain until June 1862; promoted to major, lieutenant colonel of Infantry, and to colonel of Cavalry; commanded the Sixty-fourth Virginia Cavalry until the close of the war; was elected a member of the Virginia house of delegates in 1865 but the war prevented him from taking his seat; studied law; admitted to the bar in 1867 and commenced practice in Jonesville; member of the Virginia senate 1871-1875; elected as a Democrat to the Forty-fifth Congress (March 4, 1877-March 3, 1879); continued the practice of law in Jonesville, Lee County, Va., until his death there on May 17, 1900; interment in Hill Cemetery.

**PRIEST, James Percy,** a Representative from Tennessee; born in Carter's Creek, Maury County, Tenn., April 1, 1900; attended the public schools of Maury County, Tenn., Central High School, Columbia, Tenn., State Teachers' College, Murfreesboro, Tenn., George Peabody College for Teachers, Nashville, Tenn., and the University of Tennessee at Knoxville; teacher and athletic coach at the high school in Culleoka, Tenn., 1920-1926; member of the editorial staff of the Nashville Tennessean from May 1926 until September 1940; elected as an Independent Democrat to the Seventy-seventh Congress, and reelected as a Democrat to the seven succeeding Congresses, and served from January 3, 1941 until his death in Nashville, Tenn., October 12, 1956; had been renominated to the Eighty-fifth Congress in the August 2, 1956 primary election; majority whip (Eighty-first and Eighty-second Congresses); chairman, Committee on Interstate and Foreign Commerce (Eighty-fourth Congress); interment in Woodlawn Memorial Park.

**PRINCE, Charles Henry,** a Representative from Georgia; born in Buckfield, Oxford County, Maine, May 9, 1837; attended local schools; engaged in mercantile pursuits; appointed postmaster in 1861; during the Civil War was captain of Company C, Twenty-third Regiment, Maine Volunteer Infantry, from September 10, 1862, to July 15, 1863; settled in Augusta, Ga., in 1866 and was cashier of a bank; State superintendent of education; delegate to the State constitutional convention; upon the readmission of Georgia to representation was elected as a Republican to the Fortieth Congress and served from July 25, 1868, to March 3, 1869; presented credentials as a Member-elect to the Forty-first Congress but was not permitted to qualify; postmaster of Augusta 1870-1882; delegate to the Republican National Conventions in 1872, 1876, and 1880; returned to Buckfield, Oxford County, Maine, in 1882 and engaged in mercantile pursuits; also engaged in the insurance business and in the manufacture of brushes; member of the Maine State senate in 1901; died in Buckfield, Maine, April 3, 1912; interment in Buckfield Village Cemetery.

**PRINCE, George Washington,** a Representative from Illinois; born in Tazewell County, Ill., March 4, 1854; attended the public schools; was graduated from Knox College, Galesburg, Ill., in 1878; studied law; was admitted to the bar in 1880 and commenced practice in Galesburg, Knox County, Ill.; city attorney of Galesburg 1881-1883; chairman of the Republican county central committee of

Knox County in 1884; member of the State house of representatives in 1888; reelected in 1890; unsuccessful candidate for attorney general of Illinois on the Republican ticket in 1892; elected as a Republican to the Fifty-fourth Congress to fill the vacancy caused by the death of Philip Sidney Post; reelected to the Fifty-fifth and to the seven succeeding Congresses and served from December 2, 1895, to March 3, 1913; chairman, Committee on Ventilation and Acoustics (Fifty-sixth Congress), Committee on Levees and Improvements of the Mississippi River (Fifty-ninth and Sixtieth Congresses), Committee on Claims (Sixty-first Congress); unsuccessful candidate for reelection in 1912 to the Sixty-third Congress; moved to Los Angeles, Calif., in 1913 and continued the practice of law; retired from active business pursuits in 1917 and resided in Los Angeles, Calif., until his death in that city on September 26, 1939; interment in Inglewood Park Cemetery, Inglewood, Calif.

**PRINCE, Oliver Hillhouse,** a Senator from Georgia; born in Montville, Conn., in 1787; completed preparatory studies; moved to Georgia in 1796 with his parents, who settled in Washington, Wilkes County; engaged in newspaper work; studied law; was admitted to the bar in 1806 and commenced practice in Macon, Ga.; one of the five commissioners who laid out the town of Macon in 1824; member of the Georgia State senate in 1824; elected to the United States Senate to fill the vacancy caused by the resignation of Thomas W. Cobb, and served from November 7, 1828 to March 3, 1829; author and editor; presided over the first railroad convention in Georgia and was one of the first stockholders and directors of the Georgia Railroad Company; abandoned the practice of law to become editor of the Georgia Journal in 1830; retired to Athens, Ga., in 1835; perished in the wreck of the packet ship *Home* near Ocracoke Inlet, N.C., October 9, 1837, and the remains were never recovered.

**Bibliography:** Nirenstein, Virginia King. *With Kindly Voices: A Nineteenth Century Georgia Family*. Macon, Ga.: Tullous Books, 1984.

**PRINCE, William,** a Representative from Indiana; born in Ireland in 1772; immigrated to the United States and settled in Indiana; studied law; served in the Indiana State senate in 1816; delegate to the Indiana constitutional convention in 1816; served as captain in the Battle of Tippecanoe, November 7, 1811; member of the Indiana State house of representatives in 1821 and 1822; was elected to the Eighteenth Congress and served from March 4, 1823, until his death near Princeton, Gibson County, Ind., September 8, 1824; interment in the Old Cemetery, near Princeton, Ind.

**PRINDLE, Elizur H.,** a Representative from New York; born in Newtown, Conn., May 6, 1829; completed preparatory studies; attended the local academy at Homer, N.Y.; studied law; was admitted to the bar in 1854 and practiced; moved to New York and practiced law in Norwich, Chenango County; was district attorney of Chenango County, N.Y., 1859-1863; member of the State assembly in 1863; member of the State constitutional convention in 1867 and 1868; elected as a Republican to the Forty-second Congress (March 4, 1871-March 3, 1873); resumed the practice of law; died in Norwich, N.Y., October 7, 1890; interment in Mount Hope Cemetery.

**PRINGEY, Joseph Colburn,** a Representative from Oklahoma; born in Somerset, Somerset County, Pa., May 22, 1858; attended the common schools; moved to Missouri in 1870; attended a business college in Sedalia, Mo.; moved to Chandler, Lincoln County, Okla., in 1891; engaged in agricultural pursuits and in the loan and insurance business; member of the Territorial senate in 1893; member of the board of regents of the University of Oklahoma at Norman in 1893 and 1894; delegate to the Republican National Convention in 1900; county clerk of Lincoln County, Okla., 1912-1920; elected as a Republican to the Sixty-seventh Congress (March 4, 1921-March 3, 1923); unsuccessful candidate for reelection in 1922 to the Sixty-eighth Congress; acting postmaster of Chandler, Okla., in 1923 and 1924; resumed agricultural pursuits; died in Chandler, Okla., on February 11, 1935; interment in Oak Park Cemetery.

**PRINGLE, Benjamin,** a Representative from New York; born in Richfield Springs, Otsego County, N.Y., November 9, 1807; completed preparatory studies; studied law; was admitted to the bar in 1830 and practiced for a number of years; president of a bank in Batavia, Genesee County, N.Y.; judge of the Genesee County Court, 1841-1846; elected as a Whig to the Thirty-third and Thirty-fourth Congresses (March 4, 1853-March 3, 1857); chairman, Committee on Indian Affairs (Thirty-fourth Congress); unsuccessful candidate for reelection in 1856 to the Thirty-fifth Congress; member of the New York State assembly in 1863; appointed by President Abraham Lincoln in 1863 judge of the court of arbitration in Cape Town, Africa, under the treaty with Great Britain of April 7, 1862, for the suppression of the African slave trade; appointed a member of the board of trustees of the State Institution for the Blind in 1873; died in Hastings, Dakota County, Minn., June 7, 1887; interment in the Old Cemetery, Batavia, N.Y.

**PRITCHARD, George Moore** (son of Jeter Connelly Pritchard), a Representative from North Carolina; born near Mars Hill in Madison County, N.C., January 4, 1886; attended the public schools of Marshall, N.C., and Washington, D.C., Emerson Institute, Washington, D.C., the University of North Carolina at Chapel Hill, and the law department of the University of South Carolina at Columbia; was admitted to the bar in 1908 and commenced practice in Greenville, S.C.; moved to Marshall, N.C., in 1910 and continued the practice of law; member of the North Carolina State house of representatives in 1916 and 1917; elected trustee of the University of North Carolina in 1917; solicitor of the nineteenth judicial district 1919-1922; moved to Asheville, N.C., in 1919 and continued the practice of law; chairman of the Buncombe County Republican committee in 1928; elected as a Republican to the Seventy-first Congress (March 4, 1929-March 3, 1931); was not a candidate for renomination to the Seventy-second Congress, but was an unsuccessful candidate for election to the United States Senate in 1930; resumed the practice of law in Asheville and Marshall, N.C.; delegate to the Republican National Convention in 1932; was an unsuccessful candidate for Governor of North Carolina in 1948; died in Asheville, N.C., April 24, 1955; interment in Pritchard Cemetery, Marshall, N.C.

**PRITCHARD, Jeter Connelly** (father of George Moore Pritchard), a Senator from North Carolina; born in Jonesboro, Washington County, Tenn., July 12, 1857; apprenticed to the printer's trade; moved to Bakersville, Mitchell County, N.C., in 1873; became joint editor and owner of the Roan Mountain Republican; attended the Martins Creek Academy in Tennessee; presidential elector on the Republican ticket in 1880; elected to the State house of representatives in 1884, 1886, and 1890; studied law; was admitted to the bar in 1889 and commenced practice in Marshall, N.C.; unsuccessful candidate for lieutenant governor in 1888; unsuccessful Republican candidate for United States Senator in 1891; president of the North Carolina Protective Tariff League in 1891; unsuccessful candidate for election in 1892 to the Fifty-third Congress; elected as a Republican to the United States Senate in 1894 to fill the vacancy caused by the death of Zebulon B. Vance; reelected in 1897 and served from January 23, 1895, to March 3, 1903; chairman, Committee on Civil Service and Retrenchment (Fifty-fourth and Fifty-fifth Congresses), Committee on Patents (Fifty-sixth and Fifty-seventh Congresses); justice of the supreme court of the District of Columbia 1903-1904; judge of the United States Circuit Court of Appeals, Fourth Judicial Circuit from 1904 until his death in Asheville, N.C., on April 10, 1921; interment in Riverside Cemetery.

**Bibliography:** *DAB*.

**PRITCHARD, Joel McFee,** a Representative from Washington; born in Seattle, King County, Wash., May 5, 1925; attended the public schools; attended Marietta (Ohio) College, 1946-1947; served in the United States Army, 1944-1946, with rank of sergeant; employed, Griffin Envelope Co., Seattle, Wash., president, 1948-1971; member, Washington State house of representatives, 1953-1966; Washington State senator, 1966-1970; delegate to the Republican National Convention of 1956; elected as a Republican to the Ninety-third and to the five succeeding Congresses (January 3, 1973-January 3, 1985); was not a candidate for reelection in 1984 to the Ninety-ninth Congress; elected Lieutenant Governor of Washington in 1988, reelected in 1992, and served from January 11, 1989 to present; is a resident of Seattle, Wash.

**PROCTOR, Redfield,** a Senator from Vermont; born in Proctorsville, Windsor County, Vt., June 1, 1831; graduated from Dartmouth College, Hanover, N.H., in 1851 and from the Albany Law School in 1859; was admitted to the bar and practiced in Boston, Mass., in 1860 and 1861; during the Civil War enlisted in the Union Army as a major, promoted to colonel, and was mustered out in 1863; returned to Vermont, engaged in the practice of law, and became interested in the development of the marble industry; member, Vermont State house of representatives, 1867-1868; member of the State senate and president pro tempore, 1874-1875; Lieutenant Governor of Vermont, 1876-1878; elected Governor of Vermont in 1878, and served from October 3, 1878 to October 7, 1880; member of the State house of representatives in 1888; appointed Secretary of War in the Cabinet of President Benjamin Harrison, and served from March 5, 1889 until his resignation on November 5, 1891 to become Senator; appointed in 1891 and subsequently elected as a Republican to the United States Senate to fill the vacancy caused by the resignation of George F. Edmunds; reelected in 1892, 1898, and 1904, and served from November 2, 1891 until his death in Washington, D.C., March 4, 1908; chairman, Committee on Agriculture and Forestry (Fifty-fourth through Sixtieth Congresses), Committee on Military Affairs (Fifty-ninth Congress); interment in the City Cemetery, Proctor, Rutland County, Vt.

Bibliography: *DAB*; Bowie, Chester W. "Redfield Proctor: A Biography." Ph.D. dissertation, University of Wisconsin, 1980; Partridge, Frank. "Redfield Proctor." *Vermont Historical Society Proceedings* (1915): 59-123.

**PROFFIT, George H.,** a Representative from Indiana; born in New Orleans, La., September 4, 1807; completed preparatory studies; moved to Petersburg, Pike County, Ind., in 1828; engaged in mercantile pursuits in Petersburg and Portersville, Ind.; studied law; was admitted to the bar and commenced practice in Petersburg, Ind.; member of the Indiana State house of representatives in 1831, 1832, and 1836-1838; elected as a Whig to the Twenty-sixth and Twenty-seventh Congresses (March 4, 1839-March 3, 1843); was not a candidate for renomination in 1842 to the Twenty-eighth Congress; appointed by President John Tyler as Envoy Extraordinary and Minister Plenipotentiary to Brazil, and served from June 7, 1843 until August 1844, when he returned home, the Senate having refused to confirm his appointment; died in Louisville, Ky., September 7, 1847; interment in Walnut Hills Cemetery, Petersburg, Ind.

**PROKOP, Stanley A.,** a Representative from Pennsylvania; born in Throop, Lackawanna County, Pa., July 29, 1909; attended the public schools of Dickson City and Throop; graduated from Villanova (Pa.) University with B.A. and B.S. degrees; entered the Second World War as a private in the Thirtieth Infantry Division and was discharged as a captain; served as supervisor of Lackawanna, Pa.; member, North Pocono Joint School Board for ten years; commissioned an officer at the Adjutant General's Officer Candidate School, Fort Washington, Md.; elected as a Democrat to

the Eighty-sixth Congress (January 3, 1959-January 3, 1961); unsuccessful candidate for reelection in 1960 to the Eighty-seventh Congress; served as a member of Board of Assessment Appeals, Lackawanna County, Pa.; director of veterans' affairs for fourteen years, Lackawanna County; resided in Lake Ariel, Pa., where he died November 11, 1977; interment in St. Catherine's Cemetery, Moscow, Pa.

**PROSSER, William Farrand,** a Representative from Tennessee; born in Williamsport, Lycoming County, Pa., on March 16, 1834; received a limited schooling; taught school; studied law but never practiced; moved to California in 1854; engaged in mining; returned to Pennsylvania in 1861; entered the Union Army November 30, 1861, promoted through the ranks to colonel, and served throughout the Civil War; after the war settled on a farm near Nashville, Tenn.; elected to the State house of representatives, 1867-1869; elected as a Republican to the Forty-first Congress (March 4, 1869-March 3, 1871); unsuccessful candidate for reelection in 1870 to the Forty-second Congress; postmaster of Nashville 1872-1875; a director of the Tennessee, Edgefield & Kentucky Railroad; appointed in 1872 as one of the State commissioners to the Centennial Exposition at Philadelphia in 1876 and sent on a special mission in 1873 to assist in arranging participation of European countries in the exposition; published the Nashville Republican for several years; appointed by President Rutherford B. Hayes in 1879 as special agent of the Interior Department for Oregon, Washington, and Idaho and moved to Washington in the same year; delegate to the first State constitutional convention of Washington; chairman of the State harbor line commission; mayor of North Yakima; city treasurer of Seattle 1908-1910; died in Seattle, Wash., September 23, 1911; interment in Lakeview Cemetery.

**PROUTY, Solomon Francis,** a Representative from Iowa; born in Delaware, Ohio, January 17, 1854; moved with his father to Marion County, Iowa, in 1855; attended the public schools, Central University, Pella, Iowa, 1870-1873, Simpson College, Indianola, Iowa, 1873-1875, and was graduated from Central University in 1877; professor at Central University from 1878 until 1882; member of the Iowa State house of representatives in 1880 and 1881; studied law; was admitted to the bar in 1882 and commenced practice in Pella, Marion County, Iowa; moved to Des Moines, Iowa, in 1891 and engaged in the practice of law; judge of the district court in 1899; elected as a Republican to the Sixty-second and Sixty-third Congresses (March 4, 1911-March 3, 1915); was not a candidate for renomination in 1914 to the Sixty-fourth Congress; resumed the practice of his profession; trustee of the Central University of Iowa; died in Des Moines, Polk County, Iowa, July 16, 1927; interment in Glendale Cemetery.

**PROUTY, Winston Lewis,** a Representative and a Senator from Vermont; born in Newport, Orleans County, Vt., September 1, 1906; attended public schools, Bordentown (N.J.) Military Institute, and Lafayette College, Easton, Pa.; mayor of Newport from 1938 until 1941; member of the Vermont State house of representatives in 1941, 1945, 1947, serving as speaker in 1947; chairman of Vermont State Water Conservation Board, 1948-1950; officer and director of family-owned lumber and building material enterprises; elected as a Republican to the Eighty-second Congress; reelected to the three succeeding Congresses (January 3, 1951-January 3, 1959); was not a candidate in 1958 for renomination to the House of Representatives, but was elected to the United States Senate; reelected in 1964 and 1970, and served from January 3, 1959, until his death in Boston, Mass., September 10, 1971; interment in Pine Grove Cemetery, Newport, Vt.

**PROXMIRE, William,** a Senator from Wisconsin; born in Lake Forest, Lake County, Ill., November 11, 1915; attended the public schools of Lake Forest and the Hill School, Pottstown, Pa.; B.A., Yale University, 1938; M.B.A., Harvard University Business School,

1940; M.P.A., Harvard University Graduate School of Arts and Sciences, 1948; during the Second World War served in the Military Intelligence Service, 1941-1946; member, Wisconsin State assembly, 1951-1952; businessman; unsuccessful candidate in 1952, 1954 and 1956 for election for Governor of Wisconsin; elected as a Democrat to the United States Senate, August 27, 1957, by special election to fill the vacancy caused by the death of Joseph R. McCarthy; reelected in 1958, 1964, 1970, 1976, and again in 1982, and served from August 29, 1957 until January 3, 1989; chairman, Committee on Banking, Housing, and Urban Affairs (Ninety-fourth, Ninety-fifth, Ninety-sixth, and One Hundredth Congresses); was not a candidate for reelection in 1988; is a resident of Washington, D.C.

**Bibliography:** Sykes, Jay G. *Proxmire.* Washington: Robert B. Luce, 1972.

**PRUYN, John Van Schaick Lansing,** a Representative from New York; born in Albany, N.Y., June 22, 1811; pursued classical studies and was graduated from the Albany Academy in 1826; studied law; was admitted to the bar and commenced practice in Albany in 1832; held several local offices; appointed a regent of the University of the State of New York in 1844; unsuccessful candidate for election to the Thirty-fourth Congress in 1854; member of the State senate in 1861; elected as a Democrat to the Thirty-eighth Congress to fill the vacancy caused by the resignation of Erastus Corning and served from December 7, 1863, to March 3, 1865; elected to the Fortieth Congress (March 4, 1867-March 3, 1869); was not a candidate for renomination in 1864 and 1868; resumed the practice of law at Albany, N.Y.; chancellor of the University of the State of New York from 1868 until his death in Clifton Springs, Ontario County, N.Y., November 21, 1877; interment in Albany Rural Cemetery, Albany, N.Y.

**Bibliography:** *DAB.*

**PRYCE, Deborah D.,** a Representative from Ohio; born in Warren, Trumbull County, Ohio, July 29, 1951; B.A., Ohio State University, 1973; J.D., Capital University Law School, Columbus, 1976; admitted to Ohio bar; administrative law judge, Ohio Department of Insurance, 1976-1978; first assistant city prosecutor, senior assistant city attorney then assistant city attorney, Columbus, Ohio, 1978-1985; administrative and presiding judge, 1989, 1990 and 1992, Franklin County Municipal Court; elected as a Republican to the One Hundred Third and One Hundred Fourth Congresses (January 3, 1993-January 3, 1997); is a resident of Dublin, Ohio.

**PRYOR, David Hampton,** a Representative and a Senator from Arkansas; born in Camden, Ouachita County, Ark., August 29, 1934; attended the public schools of Camden; graduated, Camden High School, 1952; attended Henderson State Teachers College (now Henderson State University), Arkadelphia, Ark., 1953; B.A., University of Arkansas, 1957; LL.B., University of Arkansas Law School, 1964; admitted to the bar in 1964 and commenced practice in Camden; founder and publisher, Ouachita Citizen 1957-1960; member, Arkansas State house of representatives, 1961-1966; elected as a Democrat to the Eighty-ninth Congress, November 8, 1966, by special election, to fill the vacancy caused by the resignation of Oren Harris and at the same time elected to the Ninetieth Congress; reelected to the two succeeding Congresses and served from November 8, 1966, to January 3, 1973; was not a candidate for reelection in 1972 to the House of Representatives, but was an unsuccessful candidate for nomination for the United States Senate; elected Governor of Arkansas in 1974, reelected in 1976, and served from January 14, 1975 until his resignation January 3, 1979; elected as a Democrat to the United States Senate in 1978; reelected in 1984 and 1990, and served from January 3, 1979 to January 3, 1997; was not a candidate for reelection in 1996; chairman, Special Committee on Aging (One Hundred First through One Hundred Third Congresses); is a resident of Little Rock, Ark.

**PRYOR, Luke,** a Senator and a Representative from Alabama; born in Huntsville, Madison County, Ala., July 5, 1820; moved with his parents to Limestone County in 1824; pursued academic studies; studied law; was admitted to the bar in 1841 and commenced practice in Athens, Ala.; also engaged in agricultural pursuits; member, State house of representatives 1855-1856; appointed to the United States Senate to fill the vacancy caused by the death of George S. Houston and served from January 7 to November 23, 1880, when a successor was elected; elected as a Democrat to the Forty-eighth Congress (March 4, 1883-March 3, 1885); declined to be a candidate for reelection in 1884; chairman, Committee on Territories (Forty-eighth Congress); retired to his farm near Athens, Ala., where he died August 5, 1900; interment in the City Cemetery.

**PRYOR, Roger Atkinson,** a Representative from Virginia; born near Petersburg, Dinwiddie County, Va., July 19, 1828; was graduated from Hampden-Sidney College, Virginia, in 1845, and from the University of Virginia at Charlottesville in 1848; studied law; was admitted to the bar in 1849 and practiced a short time in Petersburg, but abandoned law on account of ill health; engaged on the editorial staff of the Washington Union in 1852, and the Richmond Enquirer in 1854; appointed special United States Minister to Greece in 1854; returned and established The South in 1857; associated himself with the staff of the Washington States; elected as a Democrat to the Thirty-sixth Congress to fill the vacancy caused by the death of William O. Goode, and served from December 7, 1859 to March 3, 1861; during the Civil War served in the Confederate Army as a colonel in 1861; commissioned brigadier general on April 16, 1862; resigned his commission on August 18, 1863 and reenlisted as a private soldier; member of the Virginia Confederate House of Representatives; captured by the Union troops near Petersburg, Va. on November 27, 1864 and confined in Fort Lafayette, but soon afterward was released; moved to New York City in September 1865 and practiced law from 1866 to 1890; delegate to the Democratic National Convention of 1876; judge of the court of common pleas of New York, 1890-1894; justice of the New York Supreme Court, 1894-1899; retired upon reaching the age limit; appointed official referee by the appellate division of the supreme court on April 10, 1912, and served until his death in New York City, March 14, 1919; interment in Princeton Cemetery, Princeton, N.J.

**Bibliography:** *DAB*; Holzman, Robert S. *Adapt or Perish; The Life of General Roger A. Pryor, C.S.A.* Hamden, Conn.: Archon Books, 1976; Riley, Ben A. "The Pryor-Potter Affair: Nineteenth Century Civilian Conflict as Precursor to Civil War." *Journal of the West Virginia Historical Association* 8 (Spring 1984): 29-40.

**PUCINSKI, Roman Conrad,** a Representative from Illinois; born in Buffalo, Erie County, N.Y., May 13, 1919; attended the public schools in Chicago, Ill., Northwestern University, 1938-1941, and John Marshall Law School, 1945-1949; staff reporter and writer for the Chicago Sun-Times, 1939-1959; enlisted as a private in the One Hundred and Sixth Cavalry on November 1, 1940; served with the Twentieth Global (Superfort) Air Force; led his bomber group on the first B-29 bombing raid over Tokyo in 1944; awarded the Distinguished Flying Cross and Air Medal with clusters; served as chief investigator in 1952 for a select committee of Congress investigating the 1940 massacre of Polish officers in the Katyn Forest near Smolensk in the western part of the former Soviet Union; elected as a Democrat to the Eighty-sixth and to the six succeeding Congresses (January 3, 1959-January 3, 1973); was not a candidate in 1972 for reelection to the House of Representatives, but was an unsuccessful candidate for election to the United States Senate; appointed to the National Advisory Council on Vocational Education in October 1974, and served until his reappointment, August 1979, for a three year term; Alderman, Chicago, Ill., 1973 to present; is a resident of Chicago, Ill.

**PUGH, George Ellis,** a Senator from Ohio; born in Cincinnati, Ohio, November 28, 1822; attended private schools; graduated from Miami University at Oxford, Ohio, in 1840; studied law; was admitted to the bar in 1843 and commenced practice the same year in Cincinnati, Ohio; served in the Mexican War as captain of the Fourth Regiment, Ohio Volunteer Infantry; returned to Cincinnati and resumed the practice of law; member, State house of representatives 1848-1850; city solicitor 1850; State attorney general 1852-1854; elected as a Democrat to the United States Senate and served from March 4, 1855, to March 3, 1861; unsuccessful candidate for reelection; resumed the practice of law in Cincinnati; unsuccessful Democratic candidate for election in 1863 as lieutenant governor and for election in 1864 to the Thirty-ninth Congress; delegate to the State constitutional convention in 1873 but withdrew from its deliberations; retired from public life; died in Cincinnati, Ohio, July 19, 1876; interment in Spring Grove Cemetery.

Bibliography: *DAB.*

**PUGH, James Lawrence,** a Representative and a Senator from Alabama; born in Burke County, Ga., December 12, 1820; moved with his parents to Alabama in 1824; pursued an academic course in Alabama and Georgia; studied law; was admitted to the bar in 1841 and commenced practice in Eufaula, Ala.; also engaged in agricultural pursuits; Democratic presidential elector in 1848, 1856, and 1876; elected to the Thirty-sixth Congress and served from March 4, 1859, to January 21, 1861, when he withdrew; during the Civil War joined the Eufaula Rifles, First Alabama Regiment, as a private; elected to the Confederate Congress in 1861 and reelected in 1863; after the war resumed the practice of law; member of the convention that framed the State constitution in 1875; presidential elector on the Democratic ticket in 1876; elected as a Democrat to the United States Senate to fill the vacancy caused by the death of George S. Houston; twice reelected, and served from November 24, 1880, to March 3, 1897; was not a candidate for reelection; chairman, Committee on the Judiciary (Fifty-third Congress), Committee on Revolutionary Claims (Fifty-fourth Congress); retired from active business and resided in Washington, D.C., until his death there on March 9, 1907; interment in the Fairview Cemetery, Eufaula, Barbour County, Ala.

**PUGH, John,** a Representative from Pennsylvania; born in Hilltown Township, Bucks County, Pa., June 2, 1761; attended the common schools; served in the Revolutionary Army as a private, ensign, and captain; engaged in agricultural and mercantile pursuits; justice of the peace; member of the Pennsylvania house of representatives 1800-1804; elected as a Republican to the Ninth and Tenth Congresses (March 4, 1805-March 3, 1809); unsuccessful candidate for reelection in 1808 to the Eleventh Congress; register of wills and recorder of deeds of Bucks County 1810-1821; died in Doylestown, Bucks County, Pa., on July 13, 1842; interment in the Presbyterian Churchyard.

**PUGH, John Howard,** a Representative from New Jersey; born in Unionville, Chester County, Pa., June 23, 1827; attended the common schools and the Friends' School, Westtown, Pa.; taught school in Marietta, Pa., in 1847; was graduated from the medical department of the University of Pennsylvania at Philadelphia in 1852; began the practice of his profession in Bristol, Pa., in 1852; moved to Burlington, Burlington County, N.J., in 1854 and continued the practice of medicine; during the Civil War served as a physician without compensation at the United States general hospital in Beverly, N.J.; president of the Mechanics' National Bank of Burlington for thirty-six years; elected as a Republican to the Forty-fifth Congress (March 4, 1877-March 3, 1879); unsuccessful candidate for reelection in 1878 to the Forty-sixth Congress; resumed the practice of medicine; member of the State board of

education; died in Burlington, N.J., April 30, 1905; interment in St. Mary's Churchyard.

**PUGH, Samuel Johnson,** a Representative from Kentucky; born in Greenup County, Ky., January 28, 1850; moved with his parents to Lewis County in 1852; attended Chandler's Select School, Rand's Academy, and Centre College, Danville, Ky.; studied law; was admitted to the bar and commenced practice in Vanceburg, Lewis County, Ky.; city attorney in 1872 and 1873; master commissioner of the circuit court 1874-1880; county attorney 1878-1886; county judge 1886-1890; delegate to the Kentucky constitutional convention in 1890 and 1891; member of the Kentucky senate in 1893 and 1894; elected as a Republican to the Fifty-fourth, Fifty-fifth, and Fifty-sixth Congresses (March 4, 1895-March 3, 1901); resumed the practice of law in Vanceburg, Ky., and died there April 17, 1922; interment in Greenlawn Cemetery.

**PUGSLEY, Cornelius Amory,** a Representative from New York; born in Peekskill, Westchester County, N.Y., July 17, 1850; attended the public schools and was instructed in higher education by a private tutor; clerk and assistant postmaster 1867-1870; engaged in the banking business in 1870; president of the board of trustees of the Peekskill Military Academy; elected as a Democrat to the Fifty-seventh Congress (March 4, 1901-March 3, 1903); unsuccessful candidate for reelection in 1902 to the Fifty-eighth Congress; resumed banking in Peekskill; president general of the Sons of the American Revolution in 1906 and 1907; delegate to the National Democratic Convention in 1908; president of the New York State Bankers' Association in 1913; president of the Westchester County National Bank, Peekskill, N.Y.; member of the Westchester County Park Commission; died in Peekskill, N.Y., on September 10, 1936; interment in Raymond Hill Cemetery, Carmel, N.Y.

**PUGSLEY, Jacob Joseph,** a Representative from Ohio; born in Dutchess County, N.Y., January 25, 1838; moved to Ohio with his parents in 1839; was graduated from Miami University, Oxford, Ohio; studied law; was admitted to the bar and commenced practice in Dayton, Ohio; moved to Hillsboro and continued the practice of law; member of the State house of representatives 1880-1883; served in the State senate in 1886 and 1887; elected as a Republican to the Fiftieth and Fifty-first Congresses (March 4, 1887-March 3, 1891); was not a candidate for renomination in 1890; resided in Hillsboro, Highland County, Ohio, where he died February 5, 1920; interment in Hillsboro Cemetery.

**PUJO, Arsène Paulin,** a Representative from Louisiana; born near Lake Charles, Calcasieu Parish, La., December 16, 1861; attended public and private schools; studied law; was admitted to the bar in 1886 and commenced practice in Lake Charles, La.; delegate to the State constitutional convention in 1898; elected as a Democrat to the Fifty-eighth and to the four succeeding Congresses (March 4, 1903-March 3, 1913); chairman, Committee on Banking and Currency (Sixty-second Congress); was not a candidate for renomination in 1912; resumed the practice of law in Lake Charles, La.; died in New Orleans, La., December 31, 1939, while on a visit for medical treatment; interment in Orange Grove Cemetery, Lake Charles, La.

**PULITZER, Joseph,** a Representative from New York; born in Makdo, near Budapest, Hungary, April 10, 1847; received his early training from a private tutor; immigrated to the United States in 1864; enlisted as a private in the Union Army at the age of seventeen in the First Regiment, New York (Lincoln) Cavalry, in Kingston, N.Y., September 30, 1864; mustered out in Alexandria, Va., June 5, 1865; resumed civil life in St. Louis, Mo.; studied law and was admitted to practice by the supreme court of Missouri; entered journalism in 1867 as a reporter on the St. Louis Westliche Post and became managing editor and part proprietor; elected to the Missouri legislature in 1869; delegate to the Reform Republican

Convention at Cincinnati in 1872; member of the State constitutional convention in 1874; founded the St. Louis Post-Dispatch December 10, 1878, and continued to own and publish it until his death; delegate to the Democratic National Convention in 1880; moved to New York City in the spring of 1883 and bought the New York World; elected as a Democrat to the Forty-ninth Congress and served from March 4, 1885, until April 10, 1886, when he resigned; died aboard his yacht in the harbor of Charleston, S.C., October 29, 1911; interment in Woodlawn Cemetery, New York City.

**Bibliography:** *DAB*; Juergens, George. *Joseph Pulitzer and the New York World*. Princeton: Princeton University Press, 1966; Swanberg, W.A. *Pulitzer*. New York: Charles Scribner's Sons, 1967.

**PURCELL, Graham Boynton, Jr.,** a Representative from Texas; born in Archer City, Tex., May 5, 1919; attended the public schools; B.S., Texas A&M College, 1946; LL.B., Baylor University Law School, Waco, Tex., 1949; entered the United States Army in 1941, serving as an Infantry officer in the Tunisian and Italian campaigns, and was discharged as a major in 1946; remained in active reserves; was admitted to the bar and commenced the practice of law in Big Spring, Tex., in 1949; judge of the Wichita County juvenile court, 1955-1962; judge of the Eighty-ninth Judicial District Court of Texas, 1955-1962; delegate to the Democratic National Conventions of 1960 and 1964; elected as a Democrat to the Eighty-seventh Congress, January 27, 1962, by special election to fill the vacancy caused by the resignation of Frank Ikard; reelected to the five succeeding Congresses, and served from January 27, 1962 to January 3, 1973; unsuccessful candidate for reelection in 1972 to the Ninety-third Congress; resumed the practice of law; is a resident of Wichita Falls, Tex.

**PURCELL, William Edward,** a Senator from North Dakota; born in Flemington, Hunterdon County, N.J., August 3, 1856; attended the common schools; studied law; was admitted to the bar of New Jersey in 1880 and commenced practice in Flemington, N.J.; moved to Wahpeton, Territory of Dakota, in 1881 and continued the practice of law; was appointed by President Grover Cleveland as United States attorney for the Territory of Dakota in 1888; resigned in 1889, having been elected a member of the constitutional convention for the new State of North Dakota; district attorney of Richland County, N.Dak., 1889-1891; member, North Dakota State senate, 1907-1909; appointed as a Democrat to the United States Senate to fill the vacancy caused by the death of Martin N. Johnson and the resignation of Fountain L. Thompson, and served from February 1, 1910 to February 1, 1911, when a successor was elected and qualified; unsuccessful candidate for election; continued the practice of law until his death; appointed chairman of the Food Conservation Commission in 1917; died in Wahpeton, Richland County, N.Dak., November 23, 1928; interment in Calvary Cemetery.

**PURDY, Smith Meade,** a Representative from New York; born in North Norwich, Chenango County, N.Y., July 31, 1796; attended the common schools; studied law; was admitted to the bar and commenced practice at Sherburne, N.Y., in 1819; moved to Norwich, N.Y., in 1827 and continued the practice of law; appointed judge of the court of common pleas and surrogate of Chenango County in 1833 and served until his resignation in 1837; elected as a Democrat to the Twenty-eighth Congress (March 4, 1843-March 3, 1845); was not a candidate for renomination in 1844; resumed the practice of law; elected judge and surrogate of Chenango County in 1847 and served until 1851; declined a renomination owing to poor health and retired from active pursuits; died in Norwich, N.Y., March 30, 1870; interment in Mount Hope Cemetery.

**PURMAN, William James,** a Representative from Florida; born in Millheim, Centre County, Pa., April 11, 1840; attended the common schools and completed his studies at Aaronsburg Academy, Centre County, Pa.; taught school; studied law at Lock Haven, Pa.;

during the Civil War entered the Union Army as a private and served on special duty at the War Department until transferred to Florida in 1865; was admitted to the bar in 1868 and commenced practice in Tallahassee, Fla.; member of the Florida State constitutional convention in 1868; served in the State senate, 1869-1872; appointed by Governor Harrison Reed and confirmed by the State senate as secretary of state in 1869, but declined; chairman of the Florida Commission in 1869 for entering into negotiations for transfer of West Florida to the State of Alabama, which transfer was not ratified by Alabama; assessor of United States internal revenue for the district of Florida, 1870-1872; chairman of the Republican State committee, 1870-1872; member of the Republican National Committee, 1876-1880; elected as a Republican to the Forty-third Congress, and served from March 4, 1873 to January 25, 1875, when he resigned; member of the State house of representatives for one session and resigned when elected to Congress; elected to the Forty-fourth Congress (March 4, 1875-March 3, 1877); unsuccessful candidate for reelection in 1876 to the Forty-fifth Congress; returned in 1878 to Millheim, Pa., and engaged in agricultural pursuits; moved to Boston, Mass., in 1883; moved to Washington, D.C., where he lived in retirement until his death on August 14, 1928; the remains were cremated and the ashes deposited in a vault at Glenwood Cemetery.

**PURNELL, Fred Sampson,** a Representative from Indiana; born on a farm near Veedersburg, Fountain County, Ind., October 25, 1882; attended the common schools and the high school at Veedersburg; was graduated from the law department of Indiana University at Bloomington in 1904; was admitted to the bar the same year and commenced practice in Attica, Fountain County, Ind.; city attorney of Attica 1910-1914; resumed the practice of his profession; unsuccessful candidate for election in 1914 to the Sixty-fourth Congress; elected as a Republican to the Sixty-fifth and to the seven succeeding Congresses (March 4, 1917-March 3, 1933); unsuccessful candidate for reelection in 1932 to the Seventy-third Congress and for election in 1934 to the Seventy-fourth Congress; resumed the practice of law in Attica, Ind.; moved to Washington, D.C., in April 1939 and served as an attorney in the General Accounting Office until his resignation on October 1, 1939; died in Washington, D.C., October 21, 1939; interment in Rockfield Cemetery, near Veedersburg, Ind.

**PURSELL, Carl Duane,** a Representative from Michigan; born in Imlay City, Lapeer County, Mich., December 19, 1932; educated in the public schools of Plymouth, Mich.; graduated from Plymouth High School in 1951; served in the United States Army, 1957-1959; teacher; businessman; member, Wayne County (Mich.) Board of Commissioners, 1969-1970; member, Michigan State senate, 1971-1977; elected as a Republican to the Ninety-fifth and to the seven succeeding Congresses (January 3, 1977-January 3, 1993); was not a candidate for reelection in 1992 to the One Hundred Third Congress; is a resident of Plymouth, Mich.

**PURTELL, William Arthur,** a Senator from Connecticut; born in Hartford, Conn., May 6, 1897; attended the public and parochial schools; during the First World War enlisted in the United States Army in 1918 and was discharged as a corporal in 1919; engaged as a salesman from 1919 until 1929; organizer, president, treasurer, and general manager of the Holo-Krome Screw Corp.; also was director and officer of many other business enterprises; unsuccessful candidate for the Republican nomination for governor in 1950; appointed as a Republican to the United States Senate on August 29, 1952, to fill the vacancy caused by the death of Brien McMahon, and served from August 29, 1952 to November 4, 1952, when a successor was duly elected; was not a candidate for election to the vacancy; elected to the United State Senate on November 4, 1952 for a full six-year term, and served from January 3, 1953 to January 3, 1959; unsuccessful candidate for reelection in 1958; resumed manufacturing interests; resided in West Hartford, Conn., where he died on May 31, 1978; interment in Fairview Cemetery.

**PURVIANCE, Samuel Anderson,** a Representative from Pennsylvania; born in Butler, Pa., January 10, 1809; after receiving a preliminary education, entered college and pursued a partial course and then studied law; admitted to the bar in 1827 and commenced practice in Butler, Pa.; moved to Warren County and was prosecuting attorney for two years; returned to Butler, where he continued the practice of law; delegate to the Pennsylvania constitutional convention of 1837 and 1838; member of the Pennsylvania house of representatives in 1838 and 1839; delegate to the Whig National Convention in 1844 and to the Republican National Convention in 1856, 1860, 1864, and 1868; elected as a Whig to the Thirty-fourth Congress and reelected as a Republican to the Thirty-fifth Congress (March 4, 1855-March 3, 1859); unsuccessful candidate for renomination in 1858; moved to Pittsburgh in 1859 and continued the practice of law; served as attorney general of Pennsylvania in 1861; resumed the practice of his profession in Pittsburgh until 1876, when he retired; member of the National Executive Committee of the Republican Party 1864-1868; member of the Pennsylvania constitutional convention of 1872; unsuccessful candidate for election in 1874 to the Forty-fourth Congress; died in Allegheny (now a part of Pittsburgh), Pa., February 14, 1882; interment in Highwood (formerly Bellevue) Cemetery.

**PURVIANCE, Samuel Dinsmore,** a Representative from North Carolina; born on Masonboro Sound at Castle Fin House, near Wilmington, New Hanover County, N.C., January 7, 1774; attended a private school; studied law; was admitted to the bar and practiced at Fayetteville, N.C.; also owned and operated a large plantation; member of the State house of commons in 1798 and 1799; member of the State senate from Cumberland County in 1801; trustee of Fayetteville Academy in 1803; elected as a Federalist to the Eighth Congress (March 4, 1803-March 3, 1805); continued the practice of law in Fayetteville; died on the Red River about 1806, while on an exploring expedition into the West.

**PURYEAR, Richard Clauselle,** a Representative from North Carolina; born in Mecklenburg County, Va., February 9, 1801; moved with his parents to Surry County, N.C.; pursued classical studies; engaged in planting near Huntsville, N.C.; colonel of militia; magistrate of Surry County; served in the State house of commons in 1838, 1844, 1846, and in 1852; member of the State senate; elected as a Whig to the Thirty-third Congress and reelected as an American Party candidate to the Thirty-fourth Congress (March 4, 1853-March 3, 1857); unsuccessful candidate for reelection in 1856 to the Thirty-fifth Congress; was a delegate to the Confederate Provisional Congress which assembled at Richmond in 1861; delegate to the peace congress held in Philadelphia after the Civil War; resumed agricultural pursuits; died on his plantation, "Shallow Ford," in Yadkin County, N.C., July 30, 1867; interment in the family burial ground.

**PUSEY, William Henry Mills,** a Representative from Iowa; born in Washington County, Pa., on July 29, 1826; attended the Washington and Jefferson College, Pennsylvania, and was graduated in 1847; studied law and was admitted to the bar but did not engage in extensive practice; moved to Iowa and engaged in banking; member of the State senate 1858-1862; elected as a Democrat to the Forty-eighth Congress (March 4, 1883-March 3, 1885); unsuccessful candidate for reelection in 1884 to the Forty-ninth Congress; resumed banking activities; died in Council Bluffs, Pottawattamie County, Iowa, November 15, 1900; interment in Walnut Hill Cemetery.

**PUTNAM, Harvey,** a Representative from New York; born in Brattleboro, Vt., January 5, 1793; attended the common schools; studied law; was admitted to the bar in 1816 and commenced practice in Attica, N.Y., in 1817; held several local offices; elected as a Whig to the Twenty-fifth Congress to fill the vacancy caused by the death of William Patterson and served from November 7, 1838, to March 3, 1839; appointed surrogate of Genessee County in 1840, which office he held until the division of the county, when he was appointed surrogate of Wyoming County, serving until 1842; member of the State senate 1843-1846; elected as a Whig to the Thirtieth and Thirty-first Congresses (March 4, 1847-March 3, 1851); was not a candidate for renomination in 1850; resumed the practice of law; died in Attica, Wyoming County, N.Y., September 20, 1855; interment in Forest Hill Cemetery.

**PYLE, Gladys,** a Senator from South Dakota; born in Huron, Beadle County, S.Dak., October 4, 1890; attended the public schools; graduated from Huron (S.Dak.) College in 1911; taught in the public high schools at Miller, Wessington, and Huron, S.Dak., 1912-1918; first woman member of the South Dakota State house of representatives, 1923-1927; served as secretary of State of South Dakota 1927-1931; unsuccessful candidate in 1930 for the Republican nomination for Governor; member of the South Dakota State securities commission, 1931-1933; engaged in the life insurance business; elected as a Republican to the United States Senate to fill the vacancy caused by the death of Peter Norbeck, and served from November 9, 1938, to January 3, 1939; was not a candidate for election in 1938 to the full term; resumed the life insurance business and also engaged in farm management; member of the South Dakota Board of Charities and Corrections, 1943-1957; agent for Northwestern Mutual Life Insurance Co.; was a resident of Huron, S.Dak.; died March 14, 1989.

# Q

**QUACKENBUSH, John Adam,** a Representative from New York; born in Schaghticoke, Rensselaer County, N.Y., October 15, 1828; attended the district schools and the local academy in Stillwater, N.Y.; engaged in agricultural pursuits and was also interested in the lumber business; supervisor of Schaghticoke, 1860-1862; chairman of the Board of Supervisors of Rensselaer County in 1862; member of the New York State assembly in 1862; sheriff of Rensselaer County, 1873-1876; elected as a Republican to the Fifty-first and Fifty-second Congresses (March 4, 1889-March 4, 1893); was an unsuccessful candidate for reelection in 1892 to the Fifty-third Congress; resumed agricultural pursuits; died in Schaghticoke, N.Y., May 11, 1908; interment in the City Cemetery.

**QUARLES, James Minor,** a Representative from Tennessee; born near Louisa Court House, Louisa County, Va., February 8, 1823; attended the common schools; in 1833 moved to Kentucky with his father who settled in Christian County; completed preparatory studies; studied law; was admitted to the bar in 1845 and commenced practice in Clarksville, Tenn.; elected attorney general for the tenth judicial circuit in 1853 and served until 1859, when he resigned, having been elected to Congress; elected as an Opposition Party candidate to the Thirty-sixth Congress (March 4, 1859-March 4, 1861); resumed the practice of law; during the Civil War served in the Confederate Army in the brigade of his brother, Brigadier General William A. Quarles, until the close of the war; moved to Nashville, Tenn., in 1872 and continued the practice of law; elected judge of the criminal court in 1878 and served until 1882, when he resigned; resumed the practice of law; died in Nashville, Tenn., March 3, 1901; interment in Mount Olivet Cemetery.

**QUARLES, Joseph Very,** a Senator from Wisconsin; born in Southport (now Kenosha), Kenosha County, Wis., December 16, 1843; attended the common schools and the University of Michigan at Ann Arbor; during the Civil War served in the Union Army in the Thirty-ninth Regiment, Wisconsin Volunteers, and was mustered out as first lieutenant; graduated from the University of Michigan in 1866 and from its law department in 1867; was admitted to the bar in 1868 and commenced practice in Kenosha; district attorney for Kenosha County, 1870-1876; served as mayor of Kenosha in 1876; member, Wisconsin State assembly, 1879; Wisconsin State senator, 1880-1882; moved to Racine, Wis., and six years later made Milwaukee his home; elected as a Republican to the United States Senate and served from March 4, 1899, to March 3, 1905; was not a candidate for reelection in 1905; chairman, Committee on Transportation Routes to the Seaboard (Fifty-sixth Congress), Committee on the Census (Fifty-seventh and Fifty-eighth Congresses); appointed United States District Judge for the eastern district of Wisconsin by President Theodore Roosevelt in 1905, and served until his death in Milwaukee, Wis., October 7, 1911; interment in the City Cemetery, Kenosha, Wis.

**QUARLES, Julian Minor,** a Representative from Virginia; born near Ruther Glen, Caroline County, Va., September 25, 1848; attended the primary schools in Caroline and Augusta Counties and Pine Hill and Aspen School Academies, Louisa County, Va.; taught school for three years, and then attended the University of Virginia at Charlottesville; studied law; was admitted to the bar and commenced practice in Staunton, Augusta County, Va., in September 1874; judge of the county court of Augusta County, Va., from January 1880 to June 1883, when he resigned; moved to Minneapolis, Minn., and practiced his profession for two years; returned to Staunton, Va., and continued the practice of law; elected as a Democrat to the Fifty-sixth Congress (March 4, 1899-March 4, 1901); was not a candidate for renomination in 1900 to the Fifty-seventh Congress; member of the Virginia constitutional convention in 1901; resumed the practice of law in Staunton, Va., until 1924; died in Staunton, Va., November 18, 1929; interment in Thornrose Cemetery.

**QUARLES, Tunstall,** a Representative from Kentucky; born in King William County, Va., about 1770; attended the local schools; moved with his parents to Woodford County, Ky., about 1790; studied law; was admitted to the bar and practiced; member of the Kentucky house of representatives in 1796; moved to Somerset, Pulaski County, Ky.; member of the Kentucky house of representatives in 1811 and 1812; during the War of 1812, at his own expense, armed and equipped a company of the Second Regiment, Kentucky Militia, which he commanded; appointed circuit judge by the Governor; elected as a Republican to the Fifteenth and Sixteenth Congresses and served from March 4, 1817, until his resignation effective June 15, 1820; appointed receiver of public moneys for the Cape Girardeau land district, with offices at Jackson, Mo., and served from May 1821 to July 1824; returned to Somerset, Ky., and engaged in agricultural pursuits and the practice of law; member and speaker of the Kentucky house of representatives in 1840; served in the Kentucky senate in 1840; died in Somerset, Ky., January 7, 1855; interment in the old Baptist Cemetery.

**QUAY, Matthew Stanley,** a Senator from Pennsylvania; born in Dillsburg, York County, Pa., September 30, 1833; attended Beaver and Indiana academies and graduated from Jefferson College, Canonsburg, Pa., in 1850; taught school; studied law; admitted to the bar in 1854 and commenced practice in Beaver, Pa.; prothonotary of Beaver County, 1856-1860; during the Civil War, served as a colonel of the One Hundred and Thirty-fourth Regiment, Pennsylvania Volunteers, lieutenant colonel, assistant commissary general, military state agent in Washington, private secretary to Governor Andrew G. Curtin, and major and chief of transportation and telegraphs; awarded the Congressional Medal of Honor; member, Pennsylvania house of representatives, 1865-1867; owned and edited the Beaver Radical, 1867-1872; secretary of the Common-

wealth of Pennsylvania 1872-1878, 1879-1882; recorder of the City of Philadelphia; Pennsylvania treasurer, 1885-1887; elected in 1887 as a Republican to the United States Senate; reelected in 1893 and served from March 4, 1887, to March 3, 1899; unsuccessful candidate for reelection in 1899; appointed to the United States Senate to fill the vacancy in the term commencing March 4, 1899, caused by the failure of the legislature to elect, but by resolution of the Senate on April 24, 1900, was declared not entitled to the seat; elected on January 15, 1901, to fill the existing vacancy, and served from January 16, 1901 until his death in Beaver, Pa., May 28, 1904; chairman, Committee to Examine Branches of the Civil Service (Fiftieth Congress), Committee on Transportation Routes to the Seaboard (Fifty-first and Fifty-second Congresses), Committee on the Library (Fifty-second Congress), Committee on Public Buildings and Grounds (Fifty-fourth and Fifty-fifth Congresses), Committee on the Organization, Conduct, and Expenditures of the Executive Departments (Fifty-seventh and Fifty-eighth Congresses); interment in Beaver Cemetery.

**Bibliography:** *DAB*; Kehl, James A. *Boss Rule in the Gilded Age: Matt Quay of Pennsylvania.* Pittsburgh: University of Pittsburgh Press, 1981; Oliver, John W. "Matthew Stanley Quay" *Western Pennsylvania Historical Magazine* 17 (March 1934): 1-12.

**QUAYLE, James Danforth (Dan),** a Representative and a Senator from Indiana and a Vice President of the United States; born in Indianapolis, Marion County, Ind., February 4, 1947; attended the public schools of Huntington, Ind.; B.A., DePauw University, Greencastle, Ind., 1969; J.D., Indiana University School of Law, Indianapolis, 1974; admitted to the Indiana bar in 1974 and commenced practice in Huntington; served in the Indiana National Guard, 1969-1975; associate publisher of the Huntington Herald Press, 1974-1976; elected as a Republican to the Ninety-fifth and Ninety-sixth Congresses (January 3, 1977-January 3, 1981); was not a candidate in 1980 for reelection to the House of Representatives, but was elected to the United States Senate; reelected to the Senate in 1986; chairman, Select Committee to Study the Committee System (Ninety-eighth Congress); served as a Senator from January 3, 1981, until his resignation on January 3, 1989, having been elected Vice President of the United States on the Republican ticket headed by George Bush in 1988; was inaugurated on January 20, 1989, and served until January 20, 1993; unsuccessful candidate for reelection in 1992 for Vice President; is a resident of Carmel, Ind.

**Bibliography:** Fenno, Richard F., Jr. *The Making of a Senator: Dan Quayle.* Washington: Congressional Quarterly Press, 1989; Quayle, Dan. *Standing Firm: A Vice-Presidential Memoir.* New York: HarperCollins Publishers, 1994.

**QUAYLE, John Francis,** a Representative from New York; born in Brooklyn, N.Y., on December 1, 1868; attended the public schools, St. James Academy, and St. Francis College, in Brooklyn; engaged in the retail butcher business; also became engaged in building construction in 1902; served as deputy collector of internal revenue for the first district of New York from November 12, 1914, until February 19, 1919, when he resigned to enter upon his duties as deputy city clerk of Brooklyn Borough, in which capacity he served from March 1919 to February 1923, when he resigned; elected as a Democrat to the Sixty-eighth and to the three succeeding Congresses and served from March 4, 1923, until his death in Brooklyn, N.Y., November 27, 1930; had been reelected to the Seventy-second Congress; interment in St. John's Cemetery.

**QUEZON, Manuel Luis,** a Resident Commissioner from the Philippine Islands; born in Baler, Province of Tayabas, Philippine Islands, August 19, 1878; attended the public schools and the College of San Juan de Letran, Manila; studied law at the University of Santo Thomas; was admitted to the bar in April 1903; major in the Philippine Army and detailed to General Emilio Aguinaldo's staff; under the American Government held the office of prosecuting attorney for the Province of Mindoro and was subsequently transferred to the Province of Tayabas; elected Provisional Governor of Tayabas and served from 1906 to 1907, when he resigned; delegate to the first Philippine Asssembly, and was the floor leader of his party in 1907 and 1908; elected by the Nationalist Party a Resident Commissioner to the United States in 1909; reelected in 1912 and served from November 23, 1909, to October 15, 1916, when he resigned, member and president of the Philippine Senate, 1916-1935; elected President of the Philippine Islands on September 17, 1935, and served from the inauguration of the Commonwealth of the Philippines on November 15, 1935, until his death; escaped from Luzon in the Philippine Islands on February 20, 1942, in a United States submarine after the Philippines had fallen to the Japanese; died in Saranac Lake, N.Y., on August 1, 1944; remains interred temporarily in a mausoleum at Arlington National Cemetery; subsequently reinterred in Cemeterio del Norte, Manila, Philippines.

Bibliography: *DAB*; Quezon, Manuel. *The Good Fight*. Introduction by Douglas MacArthur. 1946. Reprint. New York: AMS Press, 1974; Quirino, Carlos. *Quezon: Paladin of Philippine Freedom*. With an introduction by Alejandro R. Roces. Manila: Community Publishers, 1971.

QUIE, Albert Harold, a Representative from Minnesota; born on a farm in Wheeling Township, Rice County, near Dennison, Minn., September 18, 1923; attended the grade schools in Nerstrand and high school in Northfield; graduated from St. Olaf College, Northfield, Minn., in 1950; served as a pilot in the United States Navy, 1943-1945; owner and operator of a dairy farm; clerk of the District 43 School Board, 1949-1952; supervisor of the Rice County Soil Conservation District, 1950-1954; served in the Minnesota State senate, 1955-1958; elected as a Republican to the Eighty-fifth Congress, February 18, 1958, by special election to fill the vacancy caused by the death of August H. Andresen; reelected to the ten succeeding Congresses and served from February 18, 1958, to January 3, 1979; was not a candidate for reelection in 1978 to the Ninety-sixth Congress, but was elected Governor of Minnesota and served from January 1, 1979 to January 3, 1983; declined to be a candidate for reelection in 1982; appointed to the President's Commission on Excellence in Education, 1982; lecturer and teacher, 1983-1986; area director, Prison Fellowship, Minnesota and North Dakota, 1986-1987; executive vice president, Prison Fellowship USA, 1987; president, Prison Fellowship Ministries, Reston, Va., 1988-1989; chairman, U.S. History Standards Review Panel, 1995; chairman of the Tentmakers Youth Ministry, and of the Greater Twin Cities Billy Graham Crusade, 1996; is a resident of Minnetonka, Minn.

QUIGG, Lemuel Ely, a Representative from New York; born near Chestertown, Kent County, Md., on February 12, 1863; attended the public schools of Wilmington, Del.; moved to New York City in 1880 and engaged in journalism; editor of the Flushing (N.Y.) Times in 1883 and 1884; member of the editorial staff of the New York Tribune, 1884-1894; editor in chief of the New York Press in 1895; elected as a Republican to the Fifty-third Congress to fill the vacancy caused by the resignation of John R. Fellows; reelected to the Fifty-fourth and Fifty-fifth Congresses and served from January 30, 1894, to March 3, 1899; chairman, Committee on Expenditures in the Department of State (Fifty-fourth and Fifty-fifth Congresses); unsuccessful candidate for reelection in 1898 to the Fifty-sixth Congress; chairman of the Republican State conventions in 1896 and 1902; delegate to the Republican National Conventions of 1896, 1900 and 1904; president of the Republican county committee, 1896-1900; studied law; was admitted to the bar in 1903; delegate to the New York State constitutional convention in 1915; engaged in the practice of law in New York City until his death there, July 1, 1919; interment in Queens Cemetery, Flushing, Queens County, N.Y.

Bibliography: *DAB*.

QUIGLEY, James Michael, a Representative from Pennsylvania; born in Mount Carmel, Northumberland County, Pa., March 30, 1918; attended the parochial schools of Mount Carmel; graduated from Villanova College in 1939 and from Dickinson School of Law, Carlisle, Pa., in 1942; admitted to the bar in 1942 and commenced the practice of law in Harrisburg, Pa.; served in the United States Navy 1943-1946, engaged in the Philippine and Okinawa campaigns, and after V-J day served with the occupation forces in Korea and China; resumed law practice in Harrisburg, Pa.; unsuccessful candidate for election in 1950 to the Eighty-second Congress; elected as a Democrat to the Eighty-fourth Congress (January 3, 1955-January 3, 1957); unsuccessful candidate for reelection in 1956 to the Eighty-fifth Congress; in 1957 became administrative assistant to Senator Joseph S. Clark; assistant Commonwealth attorney general, Pennsylvania, 1958; elected to the Eighty-sixth Congress (January 3, 1959-January 3, 1961); unsuccessful candidate for reelection in 1960 to the Eighty-seventh Congress; appointed assistant Secretary of Health, Education, and Welfare for Federal and State Matters on February 24, 1961, serving until January 1966; appointed Commissioner, Federal Water Pollution Control Administration, January 1966-January 1968; vice president, United States Plywood-Champion Papers, Inc., 1968-1986; is a resident of Bethesda, Md.

QUILLEN, James Henry, a Representative from Tennessee; born near Gate City, Scott County, Va., January 11, 1916; moved to Kingsport, Tenn. in 1927; graduated from Dobyns-Bennett High School, Kingsport, in 1934; newspaper publisher in Kingsport and Johnson City, Tenn., 1934-1944; served in the United States Navy 1942-1946; real estate, mortgage loan and insurance corporation executive in Kingsport and Johnson City; director of the Kingsport National Bank, 1961-1982; member of the Tennessee Legislative Council, 1954-1961; member, Tennessee house of representatives, 1954-1962; delegate to the Republican National Conventions of 1956, 1964, 1968, 1972 and 1976; parliamentarian of the Republican National Conventions of 1980, 1984 and 1988; elected as a Republican to the Eighty-eighth and to the sixteen succeeding Congresses (January 3, 1963-January 3, 1997); was not a candidate for reelection in 1996 to the One Hundred Fourth Congress; is a resident of Kingsport, Tenn.

QUIN, Percy Edwards, a Representative from Mississippi; born near Liberty, Amite County, Miss., October 30, 1872; attended the public schools; was graduated from Gillsburg Collegiate Institute, Amite County, Miss., in 1890 and from Mississippi College, Clinton, Miss., in 1893; taught school in McComb City, Pike County, Miss., in 1893 and 1894; studied law; was admitted to the bar in 1894 and commenced practice in McComb City; city attorney in 1895; delegate to the Democratic State conventions in 1899 and 1912; member of the Mississippi State house of representatives, 1900-1902; unsuccessful candidate for nomination in 1910 to the Sixty-second Congress; elected as a Democrat to the Sixty-third and to the nine succeeding Congresses and served from March 4, 1913, until his death in Washington, D.C., February 4, 1932; chairman, Committee on Military Affairs (Seventy-second Congress); interment in the City Cemetery of Natchez, Miss.

QUINCY, Josiah, a Representative from Massachusetts; born in Boston, Mass., February 4, 1772; attended Phillips Academy, Andover, Mass., and was graduated from Harvard University in 1790; studied law; was admitted to the bar in 1793 and commenced the practice of his profession in Boston; unsuccessful candidate for election in 1800 to the Seventh Congress, and for election in 1802 to the Eighth Congress; served in the Massachusetts senate in 1804 and 1805; elected as a Federalist to the Ninth and to the three succeeding Congresses (March 4, 1805-March 3, 1813); was not a candidate for renomination in 1812 to the Thirteenth Congress;

again served in the Massachusetts senate, 1813-1820; member of the Massachusetts house of representatives in 1821 and 1822, serving the last year as speaker; delegate to the Massachusetts constitutional convention in 1820; judge of the Boston municipal court in 1822; served as mayor of Boston from 1823 to 1829; president of Harvard University from 1829 to 1845; died in Quincy, Norfolk County, Mass., on July 1, 1864; interment in Mount Auburn Cemetery, Cambridge, Middlesex County, Mass.

**Bibliography:** *DAB*; McCaughey, Robert A. *Josiah Quincy, 1772-1864, the Last Federalist.* Cambridge, Mass.: Harvard University Press, 1974; Quincy, Josiah. *Memoir of the Life of Josiah Quincy.* 1825. Reprint. New York: DaCapo Press, 1971.

**QUINN, James Leland,** a Representative from Pennsylvania; born in Emlenton, Venango County, Pa., September 8, 1875; moved to Braddock, Allegheny County, Pa., with his parents in 1880 and attended St. Thomas School; employed as a newspaper reporter, 1891-1896; became owner and publisher of the Braddock (Pa.) Journal in 1896; member of the Pennsylvania house of representatives, 1933-1935; elected as a Democrat to the Seventy-fourth and Seventy-fifth Congresses (January 3, 1935-January 3, 1939); unsuccessful candidate for reelection in 1938 to the Seventy-sixth Congress; resumed the newspaper publishing business; died in Braddock, Pa., November 12, 1960; interment in Braddock Catholic Cemetery.

**QUINN, John,** a Representative from New York; born in County Tipperary, Ireland, August 9, 1839; attended Clonmel College, Tipperary; immigrated to the United States in 1866 and settled in New York City; engaged in the real estate and building business; president of the West Side Electric Light and Power Company, and was one of the founders and a director of the Homestead Bank of New York; served as a member of the New York State assembly in 1882; member of the board of aldermen, 1885-1887; delegate to the Democratic National Conventions of 1884 and 1888; elected as a Democrat to the Fifty-first Congress (March 4, 1889-March 4, 1891); died in New York City on February 23, 1903; interment in Calvary Cemetery, Long Island City, N.Y.

**QUINN, John Francis (Jack),** a Representative from New York; born in Buffalo, N.Y., April 13, 1951; B.A., Siena College, Loudonville, N.Y., 1972; M.Ed., State University of New York at Buffalo, 1983; English teacher, football, basketball and track coach, Orchard Park Schools, N.Y.; Town of Hamburg (N.Y.) Council, 1982-1984; Hamburg town supervisor, 1985-1993; elected as a Republican to the One Hundred Third and One Hundred Fourth Congresses (January 3, 1993-January 3, 1997); is a resident of Hamburg, N.Y.

**QUINN, Peter Anthony,** a Representative from New York; born in New York City, May 10, 1904; attended the St. Brigid's and St. Raymond's School; was graduated from Manhattan Preparatory School in 1922, Manhattan College, New York City, in 1926, and from the law department of Fordham University, New York City, in 1929; was admitted to the bar in 1931 and commenced practice in New York City; member of the New York State assembly, 1936-1944; elected as a Democrat to the Seventy-ninth Congress January 3, 1945-January 3, 1947; unsuccessful candidate for reelection in 1946 to the Eightieth Congress; resumed the practice of law until January 1, 1949, when he became a justice of the Municipal Court of New York City; in 1955 was elected a justice, and in 1957 a chief justice of the City Court of New York City, serving until 1960; elected justice of the Supreme Court of the State of New York for a fourteen-year term; died in Bronx, N.Y., December 23, 1974; interment in St. Joseph's Cemetery, Hackensack, N.J.

**QUINN, Terence John,** a Representative from New York; born in Albany, N.Y., October 16, 1836; educated at a private school and the Boys' Academy in his native city; early in life entered the brewery business with his father and subsequently became senior member of the firm; at the outbreak of the Civil War was second lieutenant in Company B, Twenty-fifth Regiment, New York State Militia Volunteers, which was ordered to the defense of Washington, D.C., in April 1861 and assigned to duty at Arlington Heights; member of the common council of Albany, 1869-1872; elected a member of the New York State assembly in 1873; elected as a Democrat to the Forty-fifth Congress and served from March 4, 1877, until his death in Albany, N.Y., June 18, 1878; interment in St. Agnes' Cemetery.

**QUINN, Thomas Vincent,** a Representative from New York; born in Long Island City, Queens County, N.Y., March 16, 1903; attended the grade and high schools of Queens County, N.Y.; graduated from Fordham University Law School in 1924; was admitted to the bar in 1924 and commenced the practice of law in New York City in June 1925; assistant district attorney of Queens County from September 1931 to August 1934; assistant United States attorney, eastern district of New York, 1934-1947; Assistant Attorney General of the United States from July 21, 1947, until his resignation August 10, 1948; elected as a Democrat to the Eighty-first and Eighty-second Congresses and served from January 3, 1949, until his resignation December 30, 1951, to become district attorney of Queens County, N.Y., and served until December 31, 1955; unsuccessful candidate for the Democratic nomination for district attorney of Queens County in 1955; appointed a city magistrate, April 30, 1957, and served until that office merged with the criminal court of New York City in 1962; subsequently served as a judge of the criminal court until his retirement on September 15, 1972; was a resident of Venice, Fla., until his death there on March 1, 1982.

**QUITMAN, John Anthony,** a Representative from Mississippi; born in Rhinebeck, Dutchess County, N.Y., September 1, 1799; pursued classical studies and was graduated from Hartwick Seminary in 1816; instructor in Mount Airy College, Pennsylvania, in 1818; studied law; was admitted to the bar; moved to Chillicothe, Ohio, in 1820, and thence to Natchez, Miss., in 1821, where he practiced law; member of the Mississippi State house of representatives in 1826 and 1827; chancellor of the State from 1828 until 1835, when he resigned; member of the State constitutional convention in 1832; served in the Mississippi State senate in 1835 and 1836 and was made its president; as president of the State senate, he became Governor of Mississippi on December 3, 1835, filling the vacancy caused by the resignation of Governor Hiram G. Runnels, and served until January 7, 1836; judge of the high court of errors and appeals in 1838; during the Mexican War was appointed a brigadier general of Volunteers on July 1, 1846; commissioned a major general in the Regular Army on April 14, 1847, and honorably discharged July 20, 1848; elected Governor of Mississippi in 1849 and served from January 10, 1850, until his resignation February 3, 1851; elected as a Democrat to the Thirty-fourth and Thirty-fifth Congresses and served from March 4, 1855, until his death on his plantation, "Monmouth," near Natchez, Miss., July 17, 1858, presumably from the effects of National Hotel disease contracted in Washington, D.C., during the inauguration of President James Buchanan; chairman, Committee on Military Affairs (Thirty-fourth and Thirty-fifth Congresses); interment in the Natchez City Cemetery.

**Bibliography:** *DAB*; Claiborne, John Francis Hamtramck. *Life and Correspondence of John A. Quitman.* 2 vols. New York: Harper and Bros., 1860; Gonzales, John Edmond. "John Anthony Quitman in the United States House of Representatives." *Southern Quarterly* 4 (April 1966): 276-288; May, Robert E. *John A. Quitman: Old South Crusader.* Baton Rouge: Louisiana State University Press, 1985.

# R

**RABAUT, Louis Charles,** a Representative from Michigan; born in Detroit, Mich., December 5, 1886; attended parochial schools; was graduated from Detroit (Mich.) College in 1909, and from the Detroit College of Law in 1912; was admitted to the bar in 1912 and commenced practice in Detroit; also engaged in the building business; delegate to the Democratic National Conventions in 1936 and 1940; delegate to the Interparliamentary Union at Oslo, Norway, in 1939; elected as a Democrat to the Seventy-fourth and to the five succeeding Congresses (January 3, 1935-January 3, 1947); unsuccessful for reelection in 1946 to the Eightieth Congress; elected to the Eighty-first and to the six succeeding Congresses and served from January 3, 1949, until his death in Hamtramck, Mich., on November 12, 1961; interment in Mount Olivet Cemetery, Detroit, Mich.

**RABIN, Benjamin J.,** a Representative from New York; born in Rochester, Monroe County, N.Y., June 3, 1896; attended the public schools of his native city, and New York University until May 30, 1917, when he enlisted in the United States Navy as a seaman; was subsequently commissioned as an ensign and served until January 1919; discharged as an ensign from the Naval Reserve in May 1921; reentered New York University and was graduated from the law department in 1919; was admitted to the bar the same year and commenced practice in New York City; counsel to the New York State joint legislative committee investigating guaranteed mortgages in 1934 and 1935; counsel to the Mortgage Commission of the State of New York 1935-1937 and served as chairman 1937-1939; elected as a Democrat to the Seventy-ninth and Eightieth Congresses and served from January 3, 1945, until his resignation effective midnight December 31, 1947, having been elected a justice of the New York State Supreme Court and took the oath of office on January 5, 1948; designated by the Governor as associate justice of appellate division in January 1955 for the term ending December 31, 1961; reelected for a fourteen-year term; died in Palm Beach, Fla., February 22, 1969; interment in Riverside Cemetery, Rochelle Park, N.J.

**RACE, John Abner,** a Representative from Wisconsin; born in Fond du Lac, Wis., May 12, 1914; attended the public schools of Fond du Lac and the University of Wisconsin; employed in the machine-tool industry as a specialist, 1942-1965; member of the State Coordinating Committee for Higher Education, 1963-1964; member of the Wisconsin State Board of Vocational and Adult Education, 1960-1965; elected Fond du Lac County supervisor in 1958 and reelected in 1960 and 1962; chairman of Fond du Lac County Democratic Party, 1959-1965; vice chairman of the Sixth District Democratic Party, 1961-1964; elected as a Democrat to the Eighty-ninth Congress (January 3, 1965-January 3, 1967); unsuccessful candidate for reelection in 1966 to the Ninetieth Congress; unsuccessful candidate for Wisconsin State assembly in 1970; salesman, Central Electric Supply Co.; was a resident of Fond du Lac, Wis. until his death there November 9, 1983; interment in Estabrooks Cemetery, Fond du Lac, Wis.

**RADANOVICH, George Purdy,** a Representative from California; born in Mariposa, Calif., June 20, 1955; graduated, Mariposa County High School; B.S., California State Polytechnic University, San Luis Obispo, 1978; substitute teacher for elementary and secondary schools; carpenter, 1979-1980; assistant bank manager, 1980-1983; member, Mariposa County Planning Commission, 1982-1986, chair, 1985-1986; opened the first winery in Mariposa County in 1986; member, Mariposa County Board of Supervisors, 1988-1992, chair, 1991; unsuccessful candidate in 1992 for nomination to the One Hundred Third Congress; elected as a Republican to the One Hundred Fourth Congress (January 3, 1995-January 3, 1997); is a resident of Mariposa, Calif.

**RADCLIFFE, Amos Henry,** a Representative from New Jersey; born in Paterson, N.J., January 16, 1870; attended the public schools of Paterson; was graduated from the New York Trade School; blacksmith and ornamental and structural iron worker; sergeant in the National Guard of New Jersey, 1888-1893; in 1896 became associated with his father's firm and in 1907 was made secretary of James Radcliffe and Sons Co., a structural iron manufacturing company; member of the New Jersey State house of assembly, 1907-1912; delegate to the Republican State conventions in 1910, 1911, and 1912; sheriff of Passaic County, 1912-1915; fish and game commissioner, 1914-1919; mayor of Paterson, 1916-1919; elected as a Republican to the Sixty-sixth and Sixty-seventh Congresses (March 4, 1919-March 3, 1923); was an unsuccessful candidate for reelection in 1922 to the Sixty-eighth Congress; resumed active interests in Radcliffe and Sons Company, and was treasurer at the time of his death; founder and a former president of the Franklin Trust Company, of Paterson, and served as chairman of the board; in 1925 became a member of the Board of Standards and Appeals, Paterson, N.J.; died in Baleville, N.J., on December 29, 1950; interment in Cedar Lawn Cemetery, Paterson, N.J.

**RADCLIFFE, George Lovic Pierce,** a Senator from Maryland; born on a farm at Lloyds, near Cambridge, Dorchester County, Md., August 22, 1877; attended both public and private schools; graduated from Cambridge (Md.) Seminary in 1893, from Johns Hopkins University, Baltimore, Md., in 1897, from the graduate school of Johns Hopkins in 1900, and from the law department of the University of Maryland in Baltimore in 1903; principal of the Cambridge (Md.) Seminary, 1900-1901; teacher in the Baltimore City College, 1901-1902; was admitted to the bar in 1903 and commenced practice in Baltimore; also interested in banking and farming; member of the Liquor License Commission, Baltimore, 1916-1919; member of the Maryland State Council of Defense during the First World War; secretary of state of Maryland, 1919-1920; regional adviser of the Public Works Administration for Maryland, Delaware, Virginia, West Virginia, North Carolina, Tennessee, Kentucky, and the District of Columbia, 1933-1934; elected as a Democrat to the United States Senate in 1934; reelected in 1940, and served from January 3, 1935 to January 3, 1947; unsuccessful candidate for renomination in 1946; resumed banking and farming interests; actively involved in civic life; resided in Baltimore, Md., where he died on July 29, 1974; interment in Cambridge Cemetery, Cambridge, Md.

**RADFORD, William,** a Representative from New York; born in Poughkeepsie, Dutchess County, N.Y., June 24, 1814; received a limited schooling; moved to New York City in 1829 and engaged in mercantile pursuits; elected as a Democrat to the Thirty-eighth and Thirty-ninth Congresses (March 4, 1863-March 3, 1867); unsuccessful candidate for reelection in 1866 to the Fortieth Congress; resumed his former business pursuits; died in Yonkers, Westchester County, N.Y., January 18, 1870; interment in the Old Presbyterian Cemetery, Westfield, Union County, N.J.

**RADWAN, Edmund Patrick,** a Representative from New York; born in Buffalo, Erie County, N.Y., September 22, 1911; attended the public schools; graduated from the University of Buffalo Law School in 1934; athletic coach of East High School, Buffalo, N.Y., 1929-1934; was admitted to the bar in 1935 and commenced the practice of law in Buffalo, N.Y.; village attorney of Sloan, N.Y., 1938-1940; served as a corporal in the United States Army 1943-1945; member of the State senate from 1945 to December 31, 1950; elected as a Republican to the Eighty-second and to the three succeeding Congresses (January 3, 1951-January 3, 1959); was not a candidate for renomination in 1958; died in Buffalo, N.Y., September 7, 1959; interment in St. Stanislaus Cemetery.

**RAGON, Heartsill,** a Representative from Arkansas; born in Dublin, Logan County, Ark., March 20, 1885; attended the common schools, the Clarksville High School, the College of the Ozarks, Clarksville, Ark., and the University of Arkansas at Fayetteville; was graduated from the law department of Washington and Lee University, Lexington, Va.; was admitted to the bar in 1908 and commenced practice in Clarksville, Ark.; member of the State house of representatives 1911-1913; district attorney 1916-1920; secretary of the Democratic State convention in 1918; chairman of the Democratic State convention in 1920; delegate to the Democratic National Convention in 1920; elected as a Democrat to the Sixty-eighth and to the five succeeding Congresses and served from March 4, 1923, until his resignation effective June 16, 1933, having been appointed judge of the United States District Court for the Western District of Arkansas on May 12, 1933, in which capacity he served until his death in Fort Smith, Ark., September 15, 1940; interment in Forest Park Cemetery.

**RAGSDALE, James Willard,** a Representative from South Carolina; born in Timmonsville, Florence County, S.C., December 14, 1872; attended the public schools; employed in a railroad office at Wilmington, N.C., for several years; attended the University of South Carolina at Columbia; studied law; was admitted to the bar in 1898 and commenced practice in Florence, Florence County, S.C.; engaged in agricultural pursuits and banking; trustee of the South Carolina Industrial School; member of the State house of representatives 1899-1900; member of the State senate 1902-1904; unsuccessful candidate for attorney general of South Carolina and for election in 1910 to the Sixty-second Congress; elected as a Democrat to the Sixty-third and to the three succeeding Congresses and served from March 4, 1913, until his death in Washington, D.C., July 23, 1919; interment in Mount Hope Cemetery, Florence, S.C.

**RAHALL, Nick Joe, II,** a Representative from West Virginia; born in Beckley, Raleigh County, W.Va., May 20, 1949; attended the public schools of Beckley; graduated, Woodrow Wilson High School, 1967; A.B., Duke University, Durham, N.C., 1971; graduate studies, George Washington University, Washington, D.C., 1973; United States Air Force Civil Air Patrol service; served in the Office of the Majority Whip, United States Senate, 1971-1974; sales manager for a radio station in Beckley, 1974; member, Board of Directors, Rahall Communications Corp., of Beckley, 1974; president of a travel agency, 1975; delegate to the Democratic National Convention of 1972, and to the Democratic Mid-Term Convention of 1974; elected as a Democrat to the Ninety-fifth and to the nine succeeding Congresses (January 3, 1977-January 3, 1997); is a resident of Beckley, W.Va.

**RAILSBACK, Thomas Fisher,** a Representative from Illinois; born in Moline, Rock Island County, Ill., January 22, 1932; attended the public schools of Moline, Ill.; B.A., Grinnell (Iowa) College, 1954; J.D., Northwestern University School of Law, Chicago, Ill., 1957; served in the United States Army, 1957-1959; admitted to the bar in 1957 and commenced practice; member of the Illinois State house of representatives, 1962-1966; elected as a Republican to the Ninetieth and to the seven succeeding Congresses (January 3, 1967-January 3, 1983); was an unsuccessful candidate for renomination in 1982 to the Ninety-eighth Congress; practices law in Washington, D.C.; is a resident of Washington, D.C.

Bibliography: Nollen, Sheila H. "Thomas F. Railsback and His Congressional Papers." *Western Illinois Regional Studies* 9 (1986): 59-74.

**RAINES, John,** a Representative from New York; born in Canandaigua, Ontario County, N.Y., May 6, 1840; attended the public schools; taught school; studied law and was graduated from the Albany (N.Y.) Law School in 1861; was admitted to the bar the same year and commenced practice in Geneva, N.Y.; during the Civil War organized and was captain of Company G, Eighty-fifth Regiment, New York Volunteer Infantry, in 1861 and served in the Armies of the Potomac and North Carolina until July 1863; member of the State assembly 1881-1883 and in 1885; member of the State senate 1886-1889; president of the board of education of Canandaigua 1887-1909; delegate to the Republican National Convention in 1888; elected as a Republican to the Fifty-first and Fifty-second Congresses (March 4, 1889-March 3, 1893); was not a candidate for renomination in 1892; elected to the State senate in 1894 to fill an unexpired term; reelected and served continuously until his death; was president of the State senate after 1904; died in Canandaigua, N.Y., December 16, 1909; interment in Woodlawn Cemetery.

Bibliography: *DAB*.

**RAINEY, Henry Thomas,** a Representative from Illinois; born in Carrollton, Greene County, Ill., on August 20, 1860; attended the public schools and Knox Academy and Knox College, Galesburg, Ill.; was graduated from Amherst (Mass.) College in 1883 and from the Union College of Law, Chicago, Ill., in 1885; was admitted to the bar in 1885 and commenced practice in Carrollton, Ill.; master in chancery for Greene County, Ill., from 1887 to 1895, when he resigned; elected as a Democrat to the Fifty-eighth and to the eight succeeding Congresses (March 4, 1903-March 3, 1921); unsuccessfully contested the election of Guy L. Shaw to the Sixty-seventh Congress; engaged in agricultural pursuits; elected to the Sixty-eighth and to the five succeeding Congresses and served from March 4, 1923, until his death; majority leader (Seventy-second Congress), Speaker of the House of Representatives (Seventy-third Congress); died in St. Louis, Mo., on August 19, 1934; interment in the Carrollton Cemetery, Carrollton, Ill.

Bibliography: *DAB*; Block, Marvin W. "Henry T. Rainey of Illinois." *Journal of the Illinois State Historical Society* 65 (Summer 1972): 142-57; Waller, Robert A. *Rainey of Illinois: A Political Biography, 1903-34.* Urbana: University of Illinois Press, 1977.

**RAINEY, John William,** a Representative from Illinois; born in Chicago, Ill., December 21, 1880; attended the public schools of his native city, De La Salle Institute, and the Kent College of Law; was admitted to the bar in 1910 and commenced the practice of law in Chicago; assistant judge of the probate court of Cook County 1910-1912; clerk of the circuit court 1912-1916; elected as a Democrat to the Sixty-fifth Congress to fill the vacancy caused by the death of Charles Martin; reelected to the Sixty-sixth, Sixty-seventh, and Sixty-eighth Congresses and served from April 2, 1918, until his death in Chicago, Ill., on May 4, 1923; interment in Calvary Cemetery.

**RAINEY, Joseph Hayne,** a Representative from South Carolina; born in Georgetown, Georgetown County, S.C., June 21, 1832; received a limited schooling; followed the trade of barber until 1862, when upon being forced to work on the Confederate fortifications in Charleston, S.C., he escaped to the West Indies and remained there until the close of the war; delegate to the State constitutional convention in 1868; member of the State senate in 1870 but resigned; elected as a Republican to the Forty-first Congress to fill the vacancy caused by the action of the House of Representatives in declaring the seat of B. Franklin Whittemore vacant and was the first black to be elected to the House of Representatives; reelected to the Forty-second and to the three succeeding Congresses and served from December 12, 1870, to March 3, 1879; appointed internal-revenue agent of South Carolina on May 22, 1879, and served until July 15, 1881, when he resigned; engaged in banking and the brokerage business in Washington, D.C.; retired from all business activities in 1886, returned to Georgetown, S.C., and died there August 2, 1887; interment in the Baptist Cemetery.

Bibliography: *DAB*.

**RAINEY, Lilius Bratton,** a Representative from Alabama; born in Dadeville, Tallapoosa County, Ala., July 27, 1876; attended the common schools; moved to Fort Payne, De Kalb County, Ala.; was graduated from the Alabama Polytechnic Institute, Auburn, Ala., in 1899 and from the law department of the University of Alabama at Tuscaloosa in 1902; was admitted to the bar in the latter year and commenced practice in Gadsden, Ala.; elected a captain in the Alabama National Guard in 1903; reelected and commissioned in 1906, but resigned the command in 1907; city solicitor of Gadsden 1911-1917; elected as a Democrat to the Sixty-sixth Congress to fill the vacancy caused by the death of John L. Burnett; reelected to the Sixty-seventh Congress and served from September 30, 1919, to March 3, 1923; declined to be a candidate for renomination in 1922; trustee of the State department of archives and history, Montgomery, Ala.; resumed the practice of law in Gadsden, Ala., until his death there September 27, 1959; interment in Glenwood Cemetery, Fort Payne, Ala.

**RAINS, Albert M.,** a Representative from Alabama; born in Grove Oak, De Kalb County, Ala., March 11, 1902; attended the public schools, Snead Seminary, Boaz, Ala., State Teachers College, Jacksonville, Ala., and the University of Alabama at Tuscaloosa; studied law; was admitted to the bar in 1928 and commenced practice in Gadsden, Ala., in 1929; deputy solicitor for Etowah County, Ala., 1930-1935; city attorney for the city of Gadsden, Ala., 1935-1944; served as a member of the Alabama State house of representatives, 1941-1944; elected as a Democrat to the Seventy-ninth and to the nine succeeding Congresses (January 3, 1945-January 3, 1965); was not a candidate for renomination in 1964 to the Eighty-ninth Congress; chairman of board, First City National Bank (later First Alabama Bank of Gadsden) until becoming chairman emeritus in 1979; was a resident of Gadsden, Ala.; died March 22, 1991.

**RAKER, John Edward,** a Representative from California; born near Knoxville, Knox County, Ill., February 22, 1863; moved with his parents to Lassen County, Calif., in 1873; attended the public schools and the State normal school at San Jose 1882-1884; studied law; was admitted to the bar in 1885 and commenced practice in Susanville; moved to Alturas December 6, 1886; district attorney of Modoc County 1895-1899; judge of the superior court of Modoc County from January 5, 1903, to December 19, 1910, when he resigned; chairman of the Democratic State central committee 1908-1910; delegate to the Democratic National Convention at Denver in 1908; elected as a Democrat to the Sixty-second and to the seven succeeding Congresses and served from March 4, 1911, until his death in Washington, D.C., January 22, 1926; chairman, Committee on Expenditures in the Department of Justice (Sixty-fifth Congress), Committee on Woman Suffrage (Sixty-fifth Congress); interment in Susanville Cemetery, Susanville, Calif.

**RALSTON, Samuel Moffett,** a Senator from Indiana; born near New Cumberland, Tuscarawas County, Ohio, on December 1, 1857; attended the public schools; moved with his parents to Owen County, Ind., in 1865; taught school for several years; was graduated from the Central Normal College, Danville, Ind., in 1884; studied law; was admitted to the bar in 1886 and began practice in Lebanon, Ind.; presidential elector on the Democratic ticket in 1888 and in 1892; president of the Lebanon School Board, 1908-1911; elected Governor of Indiana in 1912, and served from January 13, 1913 to January 8, 1917; resumed the practice of law in Indianapolis; elected as a Democrat to the United States Senate and served from March 4, 1923, until his death near Indianapolis, Ind., October 14, 1925; interment in Oak Hill Cemetery, Lebanon, Ind.

**Bibliography:** *DAB.*

**RAMEY, Frank Marion,** a Representative from Illinois; born in Hillsboro, Montgomery County, Ill., September 23, 1881; attended the public schools and was graduated from Hillsboro High School in 1900; also attended Eastern Illinois Normal School at Charleston, Ill.; taught school in Hillsboro, Ill., 1902-1905; studied law; was admitted to the bar of Illinois in December 1907 and commenced practice in Hillsboro; served as city attorney of Hillsboro 1907-1911; State's attorney of Montgomery County, Ill., 1920-1928; elected as a Republican to the Seventy-first Congress (March 4, 1929-March 3, 1931); was not a candidate for renomination in 1930; served as assistant district attorney 1931-1934; unsuccessful candidate for election in 1934 to the Seventy-fourth Congress, in 1936 to the Seventy-fifth Congress, and in 1938 to the Seventy-sixth Congress; resumed the practice of law; was appointed an examiner for the Illinois Commerce Commission in 1942 and served until his death; died in Hillsboro, Ill., March 27, 1942; interment in Oak Grove Cemetery.

**RAMEY, Homer Alonzo,** a Representative from Ohio; born on a farm near Sparta, South Bloomfield Township, Morrow County, Ohio, March 2, 1891; attended the grade and high schools; was graduated from Park College, Parkville, Mo., in 1913 and from the law school of Ohio Northern University at Ada in 1916; was admitted to the bar in 1917 and commenced practice in Put-in-Bay, Ohio; member of the State house of representatives 1920-1924; served in the State senate in 1925 and 1926; judge of the municipal court of Toledo, Ohio, 1926-1943; unsuccessful candidate for election in 1938 to the Seventy-sixth Congress; elected as a Republican to the Seventy-eighth, Seventy-ninth, and Eightieth Congresses (January 3, 1943-January 3, 1949); unsuccessful candidate for reelection in 1948 to the Eighty-first Congress and for election in 1950 to the Eighty-second Congress; appointed in 1949 and subsequently elected judge of the municipal court of Toledo and served in that capacity until his death in Toledo, Ohio, April 13, 1960; interment in Ottawa Hills Memorial Park.

**RAMSAY, David** (brother of Nathaniel Ramsey), a Delegate from South Carolina; born in Dunmore, Lancaster County, Pa., April 2, 1749; attended the common schools, and was graduated from the College of New Jersey (now Princeton University) in 1765; was graduated from the medical department of the University of Pennsylvania at Philadelphia in 1773 and began practice in Cecil County, Md.; settled in Charleston, S.C., in 1773; member of the State house of representatives 1776-1783; served in the Revolutionary Army as surgeon of the Charleston Battalion of Artillery, State militia; captured at the fall of Charleston in May 1780 and imprisoned at St. Augustine, Fla., for eleven months; Member of the Continental Congress 1782-1783 and 1785-1786 and served as President pro tempore during the last term; unsuccessfully contested the election of William L. Smith to the First Congress (the first contested-election case); State historian and author of several historical works; member of the State senate of South Carolina and served as president of that body for seven years; shot by a maniac on May 6, 1815, in Charleston, S.C., and died in that city May 8, 1815.

**Bibliography:** *DAB*; Shaffer, Arthur H. *To Be an American: David Ramsay and the Making of the American Consciousness.* Columbia: University of South Carolina Press, 1991.

**RAMSAY, Robert Lincoln,** a Representative from West Virginia; born in Durham, England, March 24, 1877; immigrated to the United States in 1881 with his parents, who settled in New Cumberland, Hancock County, W.Va.; attended the public schools and was graduated from the law department of the West Virginia University at Morgantown in 1901; was admitted to the bar in 1901 and commenced practice in New Cumberland; moved to Wellsburg, Brooke County, W.Va., in 1905 and continued the practice of law; city attorney of Follansbee, Brooke County, from 1905 until 1930; prosecuting attorney of Brooke County, 1908-1912, and 1916-1920; member of the board of governors for West Virginia University, 1927-1930; elected as a Democrat to the Seventy-third and to the two succeeding Congresses (March 4, 1933-January 3, 1939);

unsuccessful candidate for reelection in 1938 to the Seventy-sixth Congress; resumed the practice of law in Wellsburg, W.Va.; elected to the Seventy-seventh Congress (January 3, 1941-January 3, 1943); unsuccessful candidate for reelection in 1942 to the Seventy-eighth Congress; special assistant to the United States Attorney General, 1943-1945; assistant attorney general of West Virginia, 1945-1948; elected to the Eighty-first and Eighty-second Congresses (January 3, 1949-January 3, 1953); unsuccessful candidate for renomination in 1952 to the Eighty-third Congress; resumed the practice of law and was assistant prosecuting attorney, 1952-1956; died in Wheeling, W.Va., November 14, 1956; interment in Oak Grove Cemetery, Follansbee, W.Va.

**RAMSEY, Alexander,** a Representative from Pennsylvania and a Senator from Minnesota; born near Harrisburg, Pa., September 8, 1815; attended the common schools and Lafayette College, Easton, Pa.; studied law; was admitted to the bar in 1839 and commenced practice in Harrisburg; secretary to the electoral college of Pennsylvania in 1840; clerk of the Pennsylvania house of representatives in 1841; elected from Pennsylvania as a Whig to the Twenty-eighth and Twenty-ninth Congresses (March 4, 1843-March 3, 1847); declined to be a candidate for renomination in 1846 to the Thirtieth Congress; Governor of Minnesota Territory, 1849-1853; mayor of St. Paul, Minn., in 1855; unsuccessful candidate for election as governor of Minnesota in 1857; elected Governor of Minnesota in 1859, reelected in 1861, and served from January 2, 1860 until his resignation on July 10, 1863; elected in 1863 as a Republican to the United States Senate; reelected in 1869, and served from March 4, 1863 to March 3, 1875; chairman, Committee on Post Office and Post Roads (Thirty-ninth through Forty-third Congresses), Committee on Revolutionary Claims (Thirty-ninth Congress); appointed Secretary of War in the Cabinet of President Rutherford B. Hayes and served from December 10, 1879 to March 5, 1881; chairman of the Edmunds Commission, dealing with the question of Mormonism and polygamy in Utah, from 1882 until 1886, when he resigned; president of the Minnesota Historical Society, 1849-1863, 1891-1903; delegate to the centennial celebration of the adoption of the Federal Constitution in 1887; died in St. Paul, Ramsey County, Minn., April 22, 1903; interment in Oakland Cemetery.

**Bibliography:** Hayland, John C. "Alexander Ramsey and the Republican Party, 1855-1875." Ph.D. dissertation, University of Nebraska, 1976; Ryland, William Jesse. *Alexander Ramsey: A Study of a Frontier Politician and the Transition of Minnesota From Territory to State.* Philadelphia: Harris and Partridge Co., 1941.

**RAMSEY, John Rathbone,** a Representative from New Jersey; born in Wyckoff, Bergen County, N.J., April 25, 1862; attended the public schools and a private school in Parkersburg, W.Va., where he lived from 1872 to 1879; studied law in Hackensack, N.J.; was admitted to the bar in 1883 and commenced practice in Hackensack, N.J.; Bergen County clerk, 1895-1910; delegate to the Republican National Convention in 1908; president of the Hackensack Brick Company, 1909-1933; director of several banks; elected as a Republican to the Sixty-fifth and Sixty-sixth Congresses (March 4, 1917-March 3, 1921); was an unsuccessful candidate for renomination in 1920 to the Sixty-seventh Congress; resumed the manufacture of brick; died in Hackensack, N.J., April 10, 1933; interment in Hackensack Cemetery.

**RAMSEY, Nathaniel** (brother of David Ramsay), a Delegate from Maryland; born in Lancaster County, Pa., May 1, 1741; was graduated from the College of New Jersey (now Princeton University) in 1767; a signer of the declaration of freemen of Maryland; delegate to the Maryland convention of 1775; appointed captain in Smallwood's Maryland Regiment January 14, 1776; joined the Continental Army in July 1776 and was promoted to lieutenant colonel of the Third Regiment, Maryland Line, December 10, 1776; retired from the Army January 1, 1781; practiced law in Cecil County, Md., 1781-1783 and in Baltimore 1783-1790; Member of the Continental Congress in 1786 and 1787; appointed United States marshal for Maryland by President George Washington and served from 1790 to 1798; naval officer of the port of Baltimore 1794-1817; died in Baltimore, Md., October 23, 1817; interment in the burial ground of the First Presbyterian Church.

**Bibliography:** *DAB.*

**RAMSEY, Robert,** a Representative from Pennsylvania; born in Warminster Township, Bucks County, Pa., February 15, 1780; attended the public schools of Hartsville; member of the Pennsylvania house of representatives 1825-1831; elected as a Jacksonian to the Twenty-third Congress (March 4, 1833-March 3, 1835); was not a candidate for reelection in 1834 to the Twenty-fourth Congress; elected as a Whig to the Twenty-seventh Congress (March 4, 1841-March 3, 1843); was not a candidate for reelection; engaged in agricultural pursuits; died in Warwick, Bucks County, Pa., December 12, 1849; interment in Neshaminy Cemetery.

**RAMSEY, William,** a Representative from Pennsylvania; born at Sterretts Gap, Cumberland County, Pa., September 7, 1779; attended the public schools; appointed surveyor for Cumberland County in 1803; clerk of the orphans' court of Cumberland County; studied law; was admitted to the bar and commenced practice in Carlisle, Pa.; elected to the Twentieth Congress; reelected as a Jacksonian to the Twenty-first and Twenty-second Congresses and served from March 4, 1827, until his death in Carlisle, Pa., September 29, 1831; interment in Ashland Cemetery.

**RAMSEY, William Sterrett,** a Representative from Pennsylvania; born in Carlisle, Cumberland County, Pa., June 12, 1810; pursued classical studies in the United States and Europe; attaché of the American Legation in London; elected as a Democrat to the Twenty-sixth Congress and served from March 4, 1839, until his death before the commencement of the Twenty-seventh Congress, to which he had been reelected; died in Baltimore, Md., October 17, 1840; interment in Ashland Cemetery, Carlisle, Pa.

**RAMSEYER, Christian William,** a Representative from Iowa; born near Collinsville, Butler County, Ohio, March 13, 1875; moved to Davis County, Iowa, in 1887 and settled near Pulaski; attended the public schools; was graduated from the Southern Iowa Normal School in 1897 and from Iowa State Teachers College, Cedar Falls, Iowa, in 1902; taught school for nine years; was principal and later superintendent of the Bloomfield High School; was graduated from the law department of the University of Iowa at Iowa City in 1906; was admitted to the bar the same year and commenced the practice of law in Bloomfield, Iowa; prosecuting attorney of Davis County 1911-1915; elected as a Republican to the Sixty-fourth and to the eight succeeding Congresses (March 4, 1915-March 3, 1933); unsuccessful candidate for renomination in 1932 to the Seventy-third Congress; served as commissioner for the United States Court of Claims, Washington, D.C., from 1933 until his death in Washington, D.C., on November 1, 1943; interment in Odd Fellows Cemetery, Bloomfield, Iowa.

**RAMSPECK, Robert C. Word,** a Representative from Georgia; born in Decatur, De Kalb County, Ga., September 5, 1890; attended the public schools and the Donald Fraser School at Decatur, Ga.; deputy clerk of the superior court of Georgia 1907-1911; chief clerk of the post office in the United States House of Representatives in 1911; secretary to Congressman William Schley Howard in 1912; deputy United States marshal for the northern district of Georgia 1914-1916; chief deputy United States marshal 1917-1919; engaged in the insurance and real estate business 1919-1921; was graduated from the Atlanta (Ga.) Law School in 1920; was admitted to the bar in 1920; engaged in the newspaper business in 1922; solicitor for the city court of Decatur, Ga., 1923-1927; city attorney of Decatur

1927-1929; member of the State house of representatives in 1929; elected as a Democrat to the Seventy-first Congress, by special election, October 2, 1929, to fill the vacancy caused by the death of Leslie J. Steele; reelected to the eight succeeding Congresses and served from October 2, 1929, until his resignation on December 31, 1945, to become executive vice president of the Air Transport Association; chairman, Committee on Civil Service (Seventy-fourth through Seventy-ninth Congresses); majority whip (Seventy-seventh through Seventy-ninth Congresses); chairman of the United States Civil Service Commission from March 7, 1951, until his resignation on December 31, 1952; vice president of Eastern Air Lines, Washington, D.C., January 1, 1953, to December 31, 1961; remained a consultant for Eastern Air Lines until his retirement in 1966; died while on a visit to Castor, La., September 10, 1972; interment in Decatur City Cemetery, Decatur, Ga.

**RAMSTAD, James,** a Representative from Minnesota; born in Jamestown, Stutsman County, N.Dak., May 6, 1946; B.A., University of Minnesota, 1968; J.D., George Washington University, 1973; entered active duty, United States Army in 1968; released in 1969; administrative assistant to L.L. Duxbury, Speaker of the Minnesota State house of representatives, 1969-1970; legislative assistant to Representative Thomas S. Kleppe of North Dakota, 1970; adjunct professor of government, American University, 1974-1978; assistant campaign manager to Representative William E. Frenzel of Minnesota, 1978; member, Minnesota State senate, 1981-1990; elected as a Republican to the One Hundred Second and to the two succeeding Congresses (January 3, 1991-January 3, 1997); is a resident of Minnetonka, Minn.

**RANDALL, Alexander,** a Representative from Maryland; born in Annapolis, Md., on January 3, 1803; educated under private tutors; was graduated from St. John's College, Annapolis, in 1822; studied law; was admitted to the bar and commenced practice in Annapolis, Md., in 1824; elected as a Whig to the Twenty-seventh Congress (March 4, 1841-March 3, 1843); declined to be a candidate for renomination in 1842; resumed the practice of law and also engaged in banking at Annapolis; auditor of the high court of chancery of Maryland 1844-1848; delegate to the State constitutional convention in 1850; attorney general of Maryland from 1864 to 1868; died in Annapolis, Anne Arundel County, Md., November 21, 1881; interment in St. Anne's Cemetery.

**RANDALL, Benjamin,** a Representative from Maine; born in Topsham, Maine (then a district of Massachusetts), November 14, 1789; pursued an academic course; was graduated from Bowdoin College, Brunswick, Maine, in 1809; studied law; was admitted to the bar in 1812 and commenced practice in Bath, Maine; served in the State militia in Colonel Reed's regiment stationed at Coxes Head in September 1814; member of the Maine senate in 1833, 1835, and 1838; elected as a Whig to the Twenty-sixth and Twenty-seventh Congresses (March 4, 1839-March 3, 1843); resumed the practice of law; appointed collector of customs for the port of Bath in 1849 and served until his death in Bath, Maine, October 11, 1859; interment in Maple Grove Cemetery.

**RANDALL, Charles Hiram,** a Representative from California; born in Auburn, Nemaha County, Nebr., July 23, 1865; attended the public schools; published newspapers at Kimball and Harrisburg, Nebr., 1885-1892; railway mail clerk 1892-1904; moved to Los Angeles, Calif., in 1904; engaged in newspaper work as editor and publisher; member of the Municipal Park Commission of Los Angeles in 1909 and 1910; member of the State assembly in 1911 and 1912; elected as a Prohibitionist to the Sixty-fourth, Sixty-fifth, and Sixty-sixth Congresses and served from March 4, 1915, to March 3, 1921; unsuccessful candidate for reelection in 1920 to the Sixty-seventh Congress; resumed work for the advancement of the prohibition movement; member of the city council of Los Angeles, Calif., from July 1, 1925, to July 1, 1933; unsuccessful candidate for

election in 1934 to the Seventy-fourth Congress; died in Los Angeles, Calif., February 18, 1951; interment in Forest Lawn Memorial Park, Glendale, Calif.

**RANDALL, Charles Sturtevant,** a Representative from Massachusetts; born in New Bedford, Bristol County, Mass., February 20, 1824; attended a private school, the Friends Academy, New Bedford, and also studied in France; joined the gold rush to California in 1849 but returned two years later to engage in the commission and shipping business, from which he retired in 1872; served in the Massachusetts senate in 1883 and 1884; elected as a Republican to the Fifty-first, Fifty-second, and Fifty-third Congresses (March 4, 1889-March 3, 1895); unsuccessful candidate for renomination in 1894; retired from his former business pursuits; died in New Bedford, Mass., August 17, 1904; interment in the Rural Cemetery.

**RANDALL, Clifford Ellsworth,** a Representative from Wisconsin; born in Troy Center, Walworth County, Wis., December 25, 1876; attended the public schools; was graduated from the public high school of East Troy, Wis., in 1894 and from the Whitewater Normal School in 1901; taught school at Lake Beulah, Troy Center, and Rochester, Wis.; was graduated from the law department of the University of Wisconsin at Madison in 1906; was admitted to the bar the same year and commenced the practice of law in Kenosha, Wis., judge of the municipal court 1909-1917; elected as a Republican to the Sixty-sixth Congress (March 4, 1919-March 3, 1921); unsuccessful candidate for renomination in 1920; resumed the practice of law in Kenosha, Wis.; elected city attorney in 1921 and served until 1930, continued the practice of law in Kenosha, Wis., until his death there on October 16, 1934; interment in Green Ridge Cemetery.

**RANDALL, Samuel Jackson,** a Representative from Pennsylvania; born in Philadelphia, Pa., October 10, 1828; attended the common schools and the University Academy in Philadelphia; engaged in mercantile pursuits; member of the common council of Philadelphia 1852-1855; member of the Pennsylvania senate in 1858 and 1859; served as a member of the First Troop of Philadelphia in 1861 and was in the Union Army three months of that year and again as captain in 1863; was promoted to provost marshal at Gettysburg; elected as a Democrat to the Thirty-eighth and to the thirteen succeeding Congresses and served from March 4, 1863, until his death; chairman, Committee on Appropriations (Forty-fourth, Forty-eighth, Forty-ninth, and Fiftieth Congresses), Committee on Public Expenditures (Forty-seventh Congress); Speaker of the House of Representatives (Forty-fourth through Forty-sixth Congresses); died in Washington, D.C., April 13, 1890; interment in Laurel Hill Cemetery, Philadelphia, Pa.

**Bibliography:** *DAB*; House, Albert V., Jr. "Contributions of Samuel J. Randall to the Rules of the National House of Representatives." *American Political Science Review* 29 (October 1935): 837-41; House, Albert V. "The Political Career of Samuel Jackson Randall." Ph.D. dissertation, University of Wisconsin, 1935.

**RANDALL, William Harrison,** a Representative from Kentucky; born near Richmond, Madison County, Ky., July 15, 1812; completed preparatory studies; studied law; was admitted to the bar and commenced practice in London, Laurel County, Ky., in 1835; clerk of the circuit court and county court of Laurel County 1836-1844; elected as an Unconditional Unionist to the Thirty-eighth and Thirty-ninth Congresses (March 4, 1863-March 3, 1867); district judge of the fifteenth Kentucky district 1870-1880; died in London, Ky., August 1, 1881; interment in the family cemetery at London, Ky.

**Bibliography:** Hood, James Larry. "For the Union: Kentucky's Unconditional Unionist Congressmen and the Development of the Republican Party in Kentucky, 1863-1865." *Register of the Kentucky Historical Society* 76 (July 1978): 197-215.

**RANDALL, William Joseph,** a Representative from Missouri; born in Independence, Jackson County, Mo., July 16, 1909; graduated from William Chrisman High School in 1927, Junior College of Kansas City, Mo., in 1929, University of Missouri in 1931, and Kansas City School of Law in 1936; was admitted to the bar in 1936 and commenced the practice of law in Independence, Mo.; served from March 1943 in the United States Army as a sergeant in the Southwest Pacific and the Philippines until discharged in December 1945; elected as judge of the Jackson County Court in 1946, reelected to six additional terms, and served until March 1959; elected as a Democrat to the Eighty-sixth Congress, by special election, March 3, 1959, to fill the vacancy caused by the death of George H. Christopher; reelected to the eight succeeding Congresses and served from March 3, 1959, to January 3, 1977; chairman, Select Committee on Aging (Ninety-fourth Congress); was not a candidate for reelection in 1976 to the Ninety-fifth Congress; resumed the practice of law; is a resident of Independence, Mo.

**RANDELL, Choice Boswell** (nephew of Lucius Jeremiah Gartrell), a Representative from Texas; born near Spring Place, Murray County, Ga., January 1, 1857; attended public and private schools and the North Georgia Agricultural College at Dahlonega; studied law; was admitted to the bar in 1878 and commenced practice in Denison, Grayson County, Tex., in January 1879; moved to Sherman, Tex., in 1882 and continued the practice of law; elected as a Democrat to the Fifty-seventh and to the five succeeding Congresses (March 4, 1901-March 3, 1913); unsuccessful candidate for nomination to the United States Senate in 1912; resumed the practice of law; died in Sherman, Tex., October 19, 1945; interment in West Hill Cemetery.

**RANDOLPH, Edmund Jenings** (nephew of Peyton Randolph), a Delegate from Virginia; born in Williamsburg, Va., August 10, 1753; graduated from the College of William and Mary, Williamsburg, Va.; studied law; was admitted to the bar and commenced practice in Williamsburg; served in the Revolutionary Army and was aide-de-camp to General George Washington; attorney general of Virginia in 1776; member of the Continental Congress in 1779, 1781, and 1782; elected Governor of Virginia in 1786, but resigned in 1788 to serve in the Virginia house of delegates in order that he might participate in the codification of the laws of Virginia in 1788 and 1789; delegate to the Federal Convention in Philadelphia in 1787; was appointed the first Attorney General of the United States, in the Cabinet of President George Washington, on September 26, 1789; transferred to the State Department as Secretary of State on January 2, 1794, and served until August 19, 1795, when he was requested to resign following charges (subsequently found to be false) preferred by Minister Joseph Fauchet of France; was the principal counsel for former Vice President Aaron Burr when the latter was tried for treason in 1807; died in Clarke County, Va., September 12, 1813; interment in the Old Chapel Cemetery, Millwood, Va.

Bibliography: *DAB*; Reardon, John J. *Edmund Randolph.* New York: Macmillan, 1975.

**RANDOLPH, James Fitz** (father of Theodore Fitz Randolph), a Representative from New Jersey; born in Middlesex County, N.J., June 26, 1791; received a limited schooling; learned the printing trade; edited the New Brunswick Fredonian 1812-1842; United States collector of internal revenue 1815-1846; clerk of the court of common pleas; member of the State house of assembly in 1823 and 1824; elected to the Twentieth Congress to fill the vacancy caused by the death of George Holcombe; reelected to the Twenty-first and Twenty-second Congresses and served from December 1, 1827, to March 3, 1833; president of a bank in New Brunswick, N.J.; died in Easton, Pa., January 25, 1872; interment in Easton Cemetery.

**RANDOLPH, James Henry,** a Representative from Tennessee; born near Dandridge, Jefferson County, Tenn., October 18, 1825; attended New Market Academy and was graduated from Holston College, New Market, Tenn.; studied law; was admitted to the bar in 1850 and commenced practice in Dandridge, Tenn.; member of the State house of representatives in 1857, 1858, 1860, and 1861; served in the State senate in 1865; elected judge of the second judicial circuit of Tennessee in 1869; reelected after the constitutional convention in 1870; elected as a Republican to the Forty-fifth Congress (March 4, 1877-March 3, 1879); engaged in agricultural pursuits and milling; died in Newport, Cocke County, Tenn., August 22, 1900; interment in Union Cemetery.

**RANDOLPH, Jennings,** a Representative and a Senator from West Virginia; born in Salem, Harrison County, W.Va., March 8, 1902; attended the public schools; graduated from the Salem (W.Va.) Academy in 1920; A.B., Salem (W.Va.) College, 1924; engaged in newspaper work in Clarksburg, W.Va., in 1924; associate editor of West Virginia Review at Charleston in 1925; head of the department of public speaking and journalism at Davis and Elkins College at Elkins, W.Va., 1926-1932; trustee of Salem College and Davis and Elkins College; unsuccessful candidate for election in 1930 to the Seventy-second Congress; elected as a Democrat to the Seventy-third and to the six succeeding Congresses (March 4, 1933-January 3, 1947); unsuccessful candidate for reelection in 1946 to the Eightieth Congress; chairman, Committee on the District of Columbia (Seventy-sixth through Seventy-ninth Congresses), Committee on Civil Service (Seventy-ninth Congress); professor of public speaking at Southeastern University, Washington, D.C., 1935-1953, and dean of School of Business Administration, 1952-1958; assistant to president and director of public relations, Capital Airlines, Washington, D.C., February 1947-April 1958; elected in 1958 as a Democrat to the United States Senate to fill the vacancy caused by the death of Matthew M. Neely; reelected in 1960, 1966, 1972, and again in 1978, and served from November 5, 1958 to January 3, 1985; was not a candidate for reelection in 1984; chairman, Committee on Public Works (Eighty-ninth through Ninety-fifth Congresses), Committee on Environment and Public Works (Ninety-fifth and Ninety-sixth Congresses); is a resident of Washington, D.C., and Elkins, W.Va.

**RANDOLPH, John,** a Representative and a Senator from Virginia; born in Cawsons, Prince George County, Va., June 2, 1773; known as "John Randolph of Roanoke" to distinguish him from kinsmen; studied under private tutors, at private schools, the College of New Jersey (now Princeton University), and Columbia College, New York City; studied law in Philadelphia, Pa., but never practiced; engaged in several duels; elected to the Sixth and to the six succeeding Congresses (March 4, 1799-March 3, 1813); one of the managers appointed by the House of Representatives in January 1804 to conduct the impeachment proceedings against John Pickering, judge of the United States District Court for New Hampshire, and in December of the same year against Samuel Chase, Associate Justice of the Supreme Court of the United States; unsuccessful candidate for election in 1812 to the Thirteenth Congress; chairman, Committee on Ways and Means (Seventh through Ninth Congresses); elected to the Fourteenth Congress (March 4, 1815-March 3, 1817); not a candidate for reelection in 1816 to the Fifteenth Congress; elected to the Sixteenth and to the three succeeding Congresses, and served from March 4, 1819, until his resignation, effective December 26, 1825; appointed to the United States Senate on December 8, 1825, to fill the vacancy in the term beginning March 4, 1821 caused by the resignation of James Barbour, and served from December 26, 1825 to March 3, 1827; unsuccessful candidate for reelection in 1827; elected to the Twentieth Congress (March 4, 1827-March 3, 1829); was not a candidate for reelection in 1828 to the Twenty-first Congress; chairman, Committee on Ways and Means (Twentieth Congress);

member of the Virginia constitutional convention at Richmond in 1829; appointed Minister to Russia by President Andrew Jackson on May 26, 1830, and served until September 1830, when he resigned; elected to the Twenty-third Congress, and served from March 4, 1833 until his death in Philadelphia, Pa., May 24, 1833; interment at his residence, "Roanoke," in Charlotte County, Va.; reinterment at "Hollywood," Richmond, Va.

**Bibliography:** *DAB*; Adams, Henry. *John Randolph and the History of the United States.* 1882. Reprint, with primary documents and introduction by Robert McColley. Armonk, N.Y.: M.E. Sharpe, 1996; Bruce, William Cabell. *John Randolph of Roanoke, 1773-1833.* 1922. Reprint. 2 vols. New York: Octagon Books, 1970.

**RANDOLPH, Joseph Fitz,** a Representative from New Jersey; born in New York City, March 14, 1803; in early childhood moved with his parents to Piscataway, Middlesex County, N.J.; educated by private tutors and in private schools; prepared for the class of 1825 in Rutgers College, New Brunswick, N.J., but did not enter; studied law; was admitted to the bar in 1825 and commenced practice in Freehold, N.J.; prosecuting attorney for Monmouth County about 1836; elected as a Whig to the Twenty-fifth and to the two succeeding Congresses (March 4, 1837-March 3, 1843); chairman, Committee on Revolutionary Claims (Twenty-sixth Congress); was not a candidate for renomination in 1842 to the Twenty-eighth Congress; moved to New Brunswick in 1843 and resumed the practice of law; delegate to the State constitutional convention in 1844; member of the committee appointed by Governor Daniel Haines in 1844 to revise the statutes of New Jersey; moved to Trenton in 1845; associate justice of the State supreme court, 1845-1852; member of the peace convention held in Washington, D.C., in 1861 in an effort to prevent the impending war; moved to Jersey City in 1864; died in Jersey City, N.J., on March 20, 1873; interment in Easton Cemetery, Easton, Pa.

**RANDOLPH, Peyton** (uncle of Edmund Jenings Randolph), a Delegate from Virginia; born at Tazewell Hall, Williamsburg, Va., in September 1721; received his early education under private tutors; was graduated from the College of William and Mary, Williamsburg, Va.; studied law at the Inner Temple, London, England, and was appointed King's attorney for Virginia in 1748; member of the Virginia House of Burgesses 1764-1774 and served as speaker in 1766; chairman of the committee of correspondence in 1773; president of the Virginia conventions of 1774 and 1775; Member of the Continental Congress in Philadelphia, Pa., September 5, 1774, and elected its President but resigned October 22, 1774, to attend the Virginia House of Burgesses; reelected to the Continental Congress, which met in Philadelphia in May 1775 and again served as President; died in Philadelphia, Pa., October 22, 1775; interment beneath the chapel of the College of William and Mary, Williamsburg, Va.

**Bibliography:** *DAB*.

**RANDOLPH, Theodore Fitz** (son of James Fitz Randolph), a Senator from New Jersey; born in Mansfield, Tioga County, Pa., June 24, 1826; attended the common schools of New Brunswick, N.J., engaged in the coal and iron business; moved to Vicksburg, Miss., and engaged in business in 1840; returned to New Jersey and settled in Jersey City in 1852; became interested in mining and the transportation of ores, and was president of the Morris and Essex Railroad; member of the New Jersey State house of assembly in 1859; member, State senate, 1862-1863; elected Governor of New Jersey in 1868, and served from January 19, 1869 to January 16, 1872; elected as a Democrat to the United States Senate, and served from March 4, 1875 to March 3, 1881; chairman, Committee on Military Affairs (Forty-sixth Congress); died in Morristown, Morris County, N.J., November 7, 1883; interment in Woodlawn Cemetery.

**Bibliography:** *DAB*.

**RANDOLPH, Thomas Mann** (son-in-law of Thomas Jefferson), a Representative from Virginia; born at "Tuckahoe," in Goochland County, Va., October 1, 1768; received his early education from private teachers; attended the College of William and Mary, Williamsburg, Va., and the University of Edinburgh, Scotland, 1785-1788; served in the Virginia senate in 1793 and 1794; elected as a Republican to the Eighth and Ninth Congresses (March 4, 1803-March 3, 1807); colonel of the Twentieth Infantry during the War of 1812; member of the Virginia house of delegates in 1819, 1820, and 1823-1825; elected Governor of Virginia by the General Assembly, and served from December 1, 1819 to December 1, 1822; died at "Monticello," the home of Thomas Jefferson on June 20, 1828; interment in the family burial ground.

**Bibliography:** *DAB*; Gaines, William Harris. *Thomas Mann Randolph: Jefferson's Son-in-Law.* Baton Rouge: Louisiana State University Press, 1966.

**RANEY, John Henry,** a Representative from Missouri; born in Gravelton, Wayne County, Mo., September 28, 1849; attended Union School, Des Arc, Mo., and Woods School, Virginia Settlement, Mo.; judge of the county court of Wayne County 1880-1882; studied law; was admitted to the bar in 1881 and commenced practice at Greenville, Mo.; also engaged in agricultural pursuits and as a stock raiser; prosecuting attorney of Wayne County 1882-1888; unsuccessful candidate for election in 1888 to the State house of representatives; delegate to all Republican State conventions 1884-1927; delegate to the Republican National Convention in 1892; one of the board of regents of the State normal school, Cape Girardeau, Mo., 1893-1895; elected as a Republican to the Fifty-fourth Congress (March 4, 1895-March 3, 1897); unsuccessful candidate for reelection in 1896 to the Fifty-fifth Congress; resumed the practice of law in Piedmont, Mo.; unsuccessful candidate for circuit judge of the twenty-first judicial district in 1898; again prosecuting attorney of Wayne County in 1921 and 1922; died near Patterson, Wayne County, Mo., January 23, 1928; interment in the Masonic Cemetery, Piedmont, Mo.

**RANGEL, Charles Bernard,** a Representative from New York; born in New York City June 11, 1930; attended the public schools of Harlem and DeWitt Clinton High School; B.S., New York University School of Commerce, Washington Square, N.Y., 1957; LL.B., St. John's Law School, Brooklyn, N.Y., 1960; entered United States Army in 1948 and was discharged as a staff sergeant in 1952; admitted to the New York bar in 1960 and commenced practice in New York City; assistant United States Attorney for the Southern District of New York, 1961-1962; counsel to speaker of the New York State assembly, 1965; counsel to the President's Commission to Revise the Draft Laws, 1966; secretary, New York State Penal Law and Code Revision Commission; counsel, New York City Housing and Redevelopment Board, Neighborhood Conservation Bureau; member, New York State assembly, 1966-1970; elected as a Democrat to the Ninety-second and to the twelve succeeding Congresses (January 3, 1971-January 3, 1997); chairman, Select Committee on Narcotics Abuse and Control (Ninety-eighth through One Hundred Third Congresses); is a resident of New York City.

**RANKIN, Christopher,** a Representative from Mississippi; born in Washington County, Pa., in 1788; completed preparatory studies at Canonsburg, Pa., moved to Georgia; taught a village school and studied law at the same time; was admitted to the bar in 1809 and commenced practice in Liberty, Amite County, Miss.; member of the Territorial legislature in 1813; moved to Natchez, Miss., in 1816 and practiced law; member of the State constitutional convention in 1817; unsuccessful candidate for United States Senator in 1817; held several local offices; elected to the Sixteenth and to the three succeeding Congresses and served from March 4, 1819, until his death in Washington, D.C., March 14, 1826;

chairman, Committee on Public Lands (Seventeenth through Nineteenth Congresses); interment in the Congressional Cemetery.

**RANKIN, Jeannette,** a Representative from Montana; born near Missoula, Missoula County, Mont., June 11, 1880; attended the public schools, and was graduated from the University of Montana at Missoula in 1902; student at the School of Philanthropy, New York City in 1908 and 1909; social worker in Seattle, Wash., in 1909; engaged in promoting the cause of woman suffrage in the State of Washington in 1910, in California in 1911, and in Montana 1912-1914; visited New Zealand in 1915 and worked as a seamstress in order to gain personal knowledge of social conditions; elected as a Republican to the Sixty-fifth Congress (March 4, 1917-March 3, 1919); was the first woman to be elected to the United States House of Representatives; did not seek renomination in 1918, but was an unsuccessful candidate for the Republican nomination for Senator; was also an unsuccessful candidate on an independent ticket for election to the United States Senate; engaged in social work; elected to the Seventy-seventh Congress (January 3, 1941-January 3, 1943); was not a candidate for renomination in 1942 to the Seventy-eighth Congress; resumed lecturing and ranching; member, National Consumers League; field worker, Women's International League for Peace and Freedom; member, National Council for Prevention of War; remained leader and lobbyist for peace and women's rights until her death in Carmel, Calif., May 18, 1973; cremated; ashes scattered on ocean, Carmel-by-the-Sea, Calif.

**Bibliography:** *DAB*; Josephson, Hannah. *Jeannette Rankin, First Lady in Congress; A Biography.* Indianapolis: Bobbs-Merrill, 1974; Schaffer, Ronald. "Jeannette Rankin, Progressive-Isolationist." Ph.D. dissertation, Princeton University, 1959.

**RANKIN, John Elliott,** a Representative from Mississippi; born near Bolanda, Itawamba County, Miss., March 29, 1882; attended the common and high schools; was graduated from the law department of the University of Mississippi at Oxford in 1910; was admitted to the bar the same year and commenced practice in West Point, Clay County, Miss.; moved to Tupelo, Miss., the following November and continued the practice of law; prosecuting attorney of Lee County 1911-1915; also engaged as a lecturer and newspaper writer; served in the United States Army during the First World War; delegate to the Democratic National Conventions in 1932, 1936, and 1940; elected as a Democrat to the Sixty-seventh and to the fifteen succeeding Congresses (March 4, 1921-January 3, 1953); chairman, Committee on World War Veterans' Legislation (Seventy-second through Seventy-ninth Congresses), Committee on Veterans' Affairs (Eighty-first and Eighty-second Congresses); co-author of bill to create the Tennessee Valley Authority; unsuccessful candidate for renomination in 1952; was an unsuccessful candidate for the Democratic nomination for United States Senator in 1947; resumed the practice of law; also interested in farming and real estate; died in Tupelo, Miss., November 26, 1960; interment in Greenwood Cemetery, West Point, Miss.

**Bibliography:** *DAB*.

**RANKIN, Joseph,** a Representative from Wisconsin; born in Passaic, N.J., September 25, 1833; pursued an academic course; moved to Mishicott, Manitowoc County, Wis., in 1854 and engaged in mercantile pursuits; member of the county board in 1859; member of the State assembly in 1860; during the Civil War enlisted in the Union Army in 1862 and was chosen captain of Company D, Twenty-sixth Regiment, Wisconsin Volunteer Infantry; after the war settled in Manitowoc, Wis.; city clerk of Manitowoc 1866-1871; again a member of the State assembly 1871-1874; served in the State senate 1877-1882; elected as a Democrat to the Forty-eighth and Forty-ninth Congresses and served from March 4, 1883, until his death in Washington, D.C., January 24, 1886; interment in Evergreen Cemetery, Manitowoc, Wis.

**RANNEY, Ambrose Arnold,** a Representative from Massachusetts; born in Townshend, Windham County, Vt., April 17, 1821; graduated from Dartmouth College, Hanover, N.H., in 1844; studied law in Woodstock, Vt.; admitted to the bar in 1848 and commenced practice in Boston, Mass.; corporation counsel for the city 1855-1857; member of the Massachusetts house of representatives in 1857, 1863, and 1864; elected as a Republican to the Forty-seventh, Forty-eighth, and Forty-ninth Congresses (March 4, 1881-March 3, 1887); unsuccessful candidate for reelection in 1886 to the Fiftieth Congress; resumed the practice of law; died in Boston, Mass., March 5, 1899; interment in Forest Hill Cemetery.

**RANSDELL, Joseph Eugene,** a Representative and a Senator from Louisiana; born in Alexandria, Rapides Parish, La., October 7, 1858; attended the public schools and graduated from Union College, Schenectady, N.Y., in 1882; studied law; was admitted to the bar in 1883 and practiced at Lake Providence, La., 1883-1889; district attorney for the eighth judicial district of Louisiana, 1884-1896; interested in cotton planting and pecan groves; member of the levee board, fifth levee district, 1896-1899; member of the State constitutional convention in 1898; elected as a Democrat to the Fifty-sixth Congress to fill the vacancy caused by the death of Samuel T. Baird; reelected to the Fifty-seventh and to the five succeeding Congresses, and served from August 29, 1899 to March 3, 1913; was not a candidate in 1912 for renomination to the House of Representatives, having become a candidate for the United States Senate; elected as a Democrat to the United States Senate in 1912, reelected in 1918 and 1924, and served from March 4, 1913 to March 3, 1931; unsuccessful candidate for renomination in 1930; chairman, Committee on Public Health and National Quarantine (Sixty-third through Sixty-fifth Congresses), Committee on Mississippi River and Its Tributaries (Sixty-sixth Congress); in 1920 founded a printing firm in Washington, D.C., and served as a director until 1931 when he returned to Lake Providence, La.; engaged in the real estate business, cotton planting, and pecan growing; member of the board of supervisors, Louisiana State University and Agricultural College at Baton Rouge, 1940-1944; died in Lake Providence, La., July 27, 1954; interment in Lake Providence Cemetery.

**Bibliography:** Flynn, George Q. "A Louisiana Senator and the Underwood Tariff." *Louisiana History* 10 (Winter 1969): 5-34; LaBorde, Andras P. *A National Southerner: Ransdell of Louisiana.* New York: Benziger, 1951; Marsala, Vincent J. "U.S. Senator Joseph E. Ransdell, Catholic Statesman: A Reappraisal." *Louisiana History* 35 (Winter 1994): 35-49.

**RANSIER, Alonzo Jacob,** a Representative from South Carolina; born in Charleston, S.C., January 3, 1834; received a limited schooling; employed as shipping clerk in 1850; following the close of the Civil War was appointed Registrar of Elections by General Daniel Sickles, military governor of the Carolinas; member of a convention of the Friends of Equal Rights at Charleston in 1868, and was deputed to present the memorial there framed to Congress; member, South Carolina State house of representatives, 1868-1869; member of the State constitutional convention in 1868 and 1869; presidential elector on the Republican ticket in 1868; Lieutenant Governor of South Carolina in 1870; president of the Southern States Convention at Columbia in 1871; delegate to the Republican National Convention of 1872; elected as a Republican to the Forty-third Congress (March 4, 1873-March 3, 1875); unsuccessful candidate for renomination in 1874 to the Forty-fourth Congress; United States internal revenue collector for the second district of South Carolina in 1875 and 1876; later employed as a night watchman at the Custom House, and as a municipal street sweeper; died in Charleston, S.C., on August 17, 1882; interment in Unity Friendship Cemetery.

**RANSLEY, Harry Clay,** a Representative from Pennsylvania; born in Philadelphia, Pa., February 5, 1863; attended the public and private schools; engaged in mercantile pursuits; served in the Pennsylvania house of representatives 1891-1894; member of the Select Council of Philadelphia for sixteen years and president for eight years; delegate to the Republican National Convention in 1912; sheriff of Philadelphia County 1916-1920; chairman of the Republican city committee 1916-1919; elected as a Republican to the Sixty-sixth Congress to fill the vacancy caused by the resignation of J. Hampton Moore; reelected to the Sixty-seventh and to the seven succeeding Congresses and served from November 2, 1920, to January 3, 1937; unsuccessful candidate for reelection in 1936 to the Seventy-fifth Congress; resumed his interest in mercantile pursuits until his death in Philadelphia, Pa., November 7, 1941; interment in West Laurel Hill Cemetery.

**RANSOM, Matt Whitaker** (cousin of Wharton Jackson Green), a Senator from North Carolina; born in Warren County, N.C., October 8, 1826; attended a private academy; graduated from the University of North Carolina at Chapel Hill in 1847; studied law; was admitted to the bar and commenced practice in Warrenton, N.C.; presidential elector on the Whig ticket in 1852; attorney general of North Carolina from 1852 until 1855, when he resigned; member, North Carolina State house of commons, 1858-1861; peace commissioner to the Provisional Congress at Montgomery, Ala., in 1861; entered the Confederate Army and served throughout the Civil War, attaining the rank of brigadier general on June 13, 1863; moved to Weldon, N.C., in 1866; planter and lawyer; elected as a Democrat to the United States Senate in 1872 to fill the vacancy in the term commencing March 4, 1871; reelected in 1876, 1883, and 1889, and served from January 30, 1872 to March 3, 1895; unsuccessful candidate for reelection; served as President pro tempore of the Senate during the Fifty-third Congress; chairman, Committee on Commerce (Forty-sixth and Fifty-third Congresses), Committee on Railroads (Forty-sixth Congress), Committee on Private Land Claims (Forty-ninth through Fifty-second Congresses); appointed Minister to Mexico on December 5, 1895 and served until February 1897; engaged in agricultural pursuits; died near Garysburg, Northampton County, N.C., on October 8, 1904; interment in the private burying ground on his estate, "Verona," near Weldon, Halifax County, N.C.

Bibliography: *DAB*.

**RANTOUL, Robert, Jr.,** a Senator and a Representative from Massachusetts; born in Beverly, Mass., August 13, 1805; attended the common schools and Phillips Andover Academy, Andover, Mass.; graduated from Harvard University in 1826; studied law; admitted to the bar in 1829 and commenced practice in Salem; moved to South Reading in 1830, to Gloucester in 1832, and to Boston in 1838, and practiced law; member, Massachusetts house of representatives 1835-1839; member of the commission to revise the laws of Massachusetts; member of the Massachusetts board of education 1837-1842; United States district attorney for Massachusetts 1846-1849; elected as a Democrat to the United States Senate to fill the vacancy caused by the resignation of Daniel Webster and served from February 1 to March 3, 1851; elected as a Democrat to the Thirty-second Congress and served from March 4, 1851, until his death in Washington, D.C., on August 7, 1852; interment in Central Cemetery, Beverly, Mass.

Bibliography: *DAB*; Bulkley, Robert D., Jr. "Robert Rantoul, Jr., 1805-1852: Politics and Reform in Antebellum Massachusetts." Ph.D. dissertation, Princeton University, 1971; Rantoul, Robert, Jr. *Memoirs, Speeches and Writings of Robert Rantoul, Jr.* Edited by Luther Hamilton. Boston: J.P. Jewett and Co., 1854.

**RAPIER, James Thomas,** a Representative from Alabama; born a free black in Florence, Lauderdale County, Ala., November 13, 1837; educated in Nashville, Tenn., and worked as a skilled laborer on the Mississippi River; settled in Buxton, Ontario, Canada, in 1856; attended a normal institute in Toronto, and received a teaching certificate in 1863; returned to Nashville in 1864 and traveled as a correspondent for a northern newspaper; became a cotton planter in Maury County, Tenn. in 1865; delegate to the Tennessee Negro Suffrage Convention in Nashville, 1865; moved to Alabama and resumed cotton planting; appointed a notary public by Governor Robert M. Patton of Alabama in 1866; member of the first Republican state convention held in Alabama, and was one of the committee that framed the platform; member of the State constitutional convention at Montgomery in 1867; attended the founding convention of the National Negro Labor Union in Washington, D.C., 1869, and was instrumental in organizing the Alabama Negro Labor Union; unsuccessful candidate for Alabama secretary of state in 1870; appointed assessor of internal revenue in 1871; appointed State commissioner to the Fifth International Exposition in Vienna by Governor David P. Lewis of Alabama in 1873; commissioner on the part of the United States to the World's Fair in Paris; elected as a Republican to the Forty-third Congress (March 4, 1873-March 3, 1875); unsuccessful candidate for reelection in 1874 to the Forty-fourth Congress, and for election in 1876 to the Forty-fifth Congress; appointed Collector of Internal Revenue for the Second District of Alabama on August 8, 1878, and served until his resignation in 1883 due to ill health; attended the Southern States Negro Convention in May 1879; appointed disbursing officer for a government building in Montgomery, Ala., where he died on May 31, 1883; interment in Calvary Cemetery, St. Louis, Mo.

Bibliography: Feldman, Eugene. *Black Power in Old Alabama: The Life and Stirring Times of James Rapier, Afro-American Congressman from Alabama, 1839-1883*. Chicago: Museum of African-American History, 1968; Schweninger, Loren. *James T. Rapier and Reconstruction*. Chicago: University of Chicago Press, 1978.

**RARICK, John Richard,** a Representative from Louisiana; born in Waterford, Elkhart County, Ind., January 29, 1924; attended Goshen (Ind.) High School; attended Ball State Teacher's College, Muncie, Ind., 1942 and 1944-1945, and Louisiana State University, 1943-1944; served in the United States Army for three years in the Second World War, during which time he participated in campaigns in the Rhineland and the Ardennes, for which he received two Battle Stars; was captured and later escaped from a German prison camp; awarded the Bronze Star and the Purple Heart; J.D., Tulane University School of Law, 1949; admitted to practice law in Louisiana in 1949; elected district judge of the Twentieth Judicial District, June 28, 1961; resigned from his judgeship on May 15, 1966, to declare his candidacy for Congress; elected as a Democrat to the Ninetieth and to the three succeeding Congresses (January 3, 1967-January 3, 1975); unsuccessful candidate for renomination in 1974 to the Ninety-fourth Congress; resumed the practice of law; unsuccessful candidate for the American Independent Party presidential nomination in 1976; unsuccessful Independent candidate for election in 1976 to the Ninety-fifth Congress; American Independent Party candidate for President of the United States in 1980; is a resident of St. Francisville, La.

**RARIDEN, James,** a Representative from Indiana; born near Cynthiana, Harrison County, Ky., February 14, 1795; received a limited schooling; moved to Brookville, Ind., and thence to Salisbury; deputy clerk of court; studied law; was admitted to the bar in 1818 and began practice in Centerville, Ind., in 1820; prosecuting attorney 1822-1825; served in the State senate in 1823; member of the State house of representatives in 1829, 1830, 1832, and 1833; elected as a Whig to the Twenty-fifth and Twenty-sixth Congresses (March 4, 1837-March 3, 1841); moved to Cambridge City, Ind., in 1846; delegate to the State constitutional convention in 1850; died in Cambridge City, Wayne County, Ind., October 20, 1856; interment in Riverside Cemetery.

**RATCHFORD, William Richard,** a Representative from Connecticut; born in Danbury, Fairfield County, Conn., May 24, 1934; attended the public schools of Danbury; B.A., University of Connecticut, Storrs, 1956; J.D., Georgetown University Law School, Washington, D.C., 1959; served in the Connecticut National Guard, 1959-1965; admitted to the Connecticut bar in 1959 and commenced practice in Danbury in 1960; served in the Connecticut State house of representatives, 1962-1974, and was speaker, 1969-1973; unsuccessful candidate for election in 1974 to the Ninety-fourth Congress; chairman, Governor's Blue Ribbon Committee on Nursing Homes, 1975-1976; commissioner on aging, 1977-1978; delegate, Connecticut State Democratic conventions, 1960-1974; delegate to the Democratic National Conventions of 1972 and 1984; elected as a Democrat to the Ninety-sixth and to the two succeeding Congresses (January 3, 1979-January 3, 1985); unsuccessful candidate for reelection in 1984 to the Ninety-ninth Congress; is a resident of Danbury, Conn.

**RATHBONE, Henry Riggs** (grandson of Ira Harris), a Representative from Illinois; born in Washington, D.C., February 12, 1870; was graduated from Phillips Academy, Andover, Mass., in 1887, from Yale University in 1892, and from the law department of the University of Wisconsin, Madison, in 1894; was admitted to the bar in 1895 and commenced practice in Chicago, Ill.; delegate to the Republican National Convention of 1916; elected as a Republican to the Sixty-eighth and to the two succeeding Congresses, and served from March 4, 1923 until his death in Chicago, Ill., on July 15, 1928; had been nominated for reelection in the April 1928 primary; chairman, Committee on Expenditures in the Department of Commerce (Sixty-ninth Congress); interment in Rosehill Cemetery.

**RATHBUN, George Oscar,** a Representative from New York; born in Scipioville, near Auburn, N.Y., in 1803; attended the Auburn schools and was graduated from Hamilton College; studied law; was admitted to the bar and commenced practice in Auburn; member of the State assembly; elected as a Democrat to the Twenty-eighth and Twenty-ninth Congresses (March 4, 1843-March 3, 1847); chairman, Committee on Revolutionary Pensions (Twenty-eighth Congress), Committee on the Judiciary (Twenty-ninth Congress); resumed the practice of his profession; died in Auburn, Cayuga County, N.Y., January 5, 1870; interment in Fort Hill Cemetery.

**RAUCH, George Washington,** a Representative from Indiana; born on a farm near Warren in Salamonie Township, Huntington County, Ind., February 22, 1876; attended the common schools and Valparaiso (Ind.) Normal School (now Valparaiso University); was graduated from the Northern Indiana Law School at Valparaiso in 1902; was admitted to the bar the same year and commenced the practice of law in Marion, Grant County, Ind.; elected as a Democrat to the Sixtieth and to the four succeeding Congresses (March 4, 1907-March 3, 1917); unsuccessful candidate for reelection in 1916 to the Sixty-fifth Congress; resumed the practice of his profession in Marion, Ind., served on the board of directors of the Motor Securities Corporation and as president and treasurer of the Davis Records Co.; appointed a Federal bank receiver for banks in Swayzee, Sheridan, and Marion, Ind., serving from 1930 to 1939; member of the city school board 1927-1933; died in Marion, Ind., November 4, 1940; interment in Masonic Cemetery, Warren, Ind.

**RAUM, Green Berry,** a Representative from Illinois; born in Golconda, Pope County, Ill., December 3, 1829; attended the common schools; studied law; was admitted to the bar in 1853 and practiced in Golconda 1853-1856; moved to Kansas in 1856 and practiced his profession for two years; returned to Illinois and settled in Harrisburg; during the Civil War served in the Union Army as major in the Fifty-sixth Regiment, Illinois Volunteer Infantry, and attained the rank of brigadier general; resigned his commission on May 6, 1865; engaged in railroad building; elected as a Republican to the Fortieth Congress (March 4, 1867-March 3,

1869); unsuccessful candidate for reelection in 1868 to the Forty-first Congress; United States Commissioner of Internal Revenue, 1876-1883; United States Commissioner of Pensions, 1889-1893; engaged in the practice of law in Chicago, Ill., until his death there on December 18, 1909; interment in Arlington National Cemetery, Va.

**Bibliography:** *DAB*; Barlow, William. "U.S. Commissioner of Pensions Green B. Raum of Illinois." *Journal of the Illinois State Historical Society* 60 (Autumn 1967): 297-312.

**RAVENEL, Arthur, Jr.,** a Representative from South Carolina; born in Charleston, S.C., March 29, 1927; graduated from St. Andrews High School, Charleston, in 1944; B.S., College of Charleston, 1950; served in the United States Marine Corps, 1945-1946; realtor and general contractor; member, South Carolina State house of representatives, 1953-1958; South Carolina State senator, 1980-1986; elected as a Republican to the One Hundredth and to the three succeeding Congresses (January 3, 1987-January 3, 1995); was not a candidate in 1994 for renomination to the One Hundred Fourth Congress, but was an unsuccessful candidate for nomination for Governor of South Carolina; chair, Charleston Naval Shipyard Redevelopment Authority; is a resident of Mount Pleasant, S.C.

**RAWLINS, Joseph Lafayette,** a Delegate from the Territory of Utah and a Senator from Utah; born at Mill Creek, Salt Lake County, Utah, March 28, 1850; attended the common schools and the University of Utah, Salt Lake City; pursued a classical course at Indiana University, Bloomington, Ind.; professor at the University of Deseret, Salt Lake City, Utah, 1873-1875; studied law; was admitted to the bar in 1875 and commenced practice in Salt Lake City, Utah; elected as a Democrat to the Fifty-third Congress (March 4, 1893-March 3, 1895); unsuccessful candidate for reelection in 1894 to the Fifty-fourth Congress; elected as a Democrat to the United States Senate and served from March 4, 1897, to March 3, 1903; unsuccessful candidate for renomination; continued the practice of law; withdrew from public life and active business in 1921; died in Salt Lake City, Utah, May 24, 1926; interment in Salt Lake City Cemetery.

**Bibliography:** Harrow, Joan. "Joseph L. Rawlins, Father of Utah Statehood." *Utah Historical Quarterly* 44 (Winter 1976): 59-75; Rawlins, Joseph L. *The Unfavored Son: The Autobiography of Joseph L. Rawlins.* n.p. 1956.

**RAWLS, Morgan,** a Representative from Georgia; born near Statesboro, Bulloch County, Ga., June 29, 1829; attended the common schools and pursued an academic course; engaged in agricultural pursuits; moved to Guyton, Ga., in 1856; unsuccessful Union candidate for delegate to the convention of 1860, which passed the ordinance of secession; enlisted in the Confederate Army as a captain of Infantry; elected colonel of the Fifty-fourth Regiment, Georgia Infantry, in 1863; member of the State house of representatives 1863-1865, 1868-1872, 1886-1889, and 1896-1904; member of the State reconstruction convention in 1865; presented credentials as a Democratic Member-elect to the Forty-third Congress and served from March 4, 1873, to March 24, 1874, when he was succeeded by Andrew Sloan, who contested his election; served in the office of the Clerk of the House of Representatives 1874-1882 and 1891-1895; engaged in agricultural pursuits; died in Guyton, Effingham County, Ga., October 18, 1906; interment in Guyton Cemetery.

**RAWSON, Charles Augustus,** a Senator from Iowa; born in Des Moines, Iowa, May 29, 1867; attended the public schools and Grinnell (Iowa) College; engaged in banking and the insurance business and also in the manufacture of clay products; member of the board of trustees of Grinnell College; State chairman of the war work council of the Young Men's Christian Association and served overseas with that organization during the First World War; appointed as a Republican to the United States Senate to fill the vacancy caused by the resignation of William S. Kenyon and served from February 24 to December 1, 1922, when a successor was elected and qualified; was not a candidate for election to fill this vacancy; member of the Republican National Committee 1924-1932; resumed the manufacture of clay products; also interested in banking; died in Des Moines, Iowa, September 2, 1936; interment in Woodland Cemetery.

**RAY, George Washington,** a Representative from New York; born in Otselic, Chenango County, N.Y., February 3, 1844; attended the common schools and Norwich Academy; private in Company B, Ninetieth New York Volunteers, and brigade clerk, First Brigade, First Division, Nineteenth Army Corps, during the Civil War; discharged at the close of the war; studied law and was admitted to the bar in November 1867; chairman of the Republican county committee of Chenango County; member of the Republican State committee in 1880; elected as a Republican to the Forty-eighth Congress (March 4, 1883-March 3, 1885); member of the board of education of Norwich Academy and Union Free School; elected to the Fifty-second and to the five succeeding Congresses and served from March 4, 1891, to September 11, 1902; chairman, Committee on Levees and Improvements of the Mississippi River (Fifty-fourth Congress), Committee on Invalid Pensions (Fifty-fifth Congress), Committee on the Judiciary (Fifty-sixth and Fifty-seventh Congresses); resigned from Congress to accept the United States judgeship for the northern district of New York, in which capacity he served until his death in Norwich, Chenango County, N.Y., January 10, 1925; interment in Mount Hope Cemetery.

**RAY, John Henry,** a Representative from New York; born in Mankato, Blue Earth County, Minn., September 27, 1886; attended the public schools; was graduated from the University of Minnesota in 1908, and from Harvard Law School in 1911; was admitted to the Minnesota bar in 1912 and commenced practice in Minneapolis, Minn.; assistant trust officer, Wells Dickey Trust Co., 1918-1919; served as a first lieutenant in the Judge Advocate General's Department, 1918-1919; assistant to special representative of Secretary of War Newton D. Baker in 1919, concerned with the adjustment of United States war claims against the governments of the Allies; member and vice president of the State Teachers College Board, 1921-1923; moved to Dongan Hills, N.Y., in 1924 and served as general attorney for the American Telephone & Telegraph Co.; vice president and general counsel, Western Electric Co., 1930-1936; vice president and general counsel, American Telephone & Telegraph Co., 1942-1951; resumed the practice of law in New York City; elected as a Republican to the Eighty-third and to the four succeeding Congresses (January 3, 1953-January 3, 1963); was not a candidate for reelection in 1962 to the Eighty-eighth Congress; resumed the practice of law; resided in Staten Island, N.Y., where he died on May 21, 1975; remains were cremated and ashes placed in his home.

**RAY, Joseph Warren,** a Representative from Pennsylvania; born near Nineveh, Morris Township, Greene County, Pa., May 25, 1849; attended the common schools and was graduated from Waynesburg (Pa.) College in 1874; studied law; was admitted to the bar in 1876 and commenced practice in Waynesburg, Greene County, Pa.; elected as a Republican to the Fifty-first Congress (March 4, 1889-March 3, 1891); unsuccessful candidate for renomination in 1890 to the Fifty-second Congress; resumed the practice of law in Waynesburg, Pa.; trustee of Waynesburg College from 1902 until his death; elected president judge of the thirteenth judicial district of Pennsylvania in 1915 and served until 1926; declined to be a candidate for reelection; again resumed the practice of law in Waynesburg, Pa., where he died on September 15, 1928; interment in Greenmont Cemetery.

**RAY, Ossian,** a Representative from New Hampshire; born in Hinesburg, Chittenden County, Vt., December 13, 1835; moved to Irasburg, Vt., in early childhood; attended the common schools and an academy in Derby, Vt.; studied law in Irasburg and in Lancaster, N.H., to which latter place he moved in 1854; was admitted to the bar in 1857, and practiced in Essex and Coos Counties; solicitor for Coos County, 1862-1872; member, New Hampshire State house of representatives, 1868-1869; delegate to the Republican National Convention of 1872; United States attorney for the district of New Hampshire from February 22, 1879 until December 23, 1880, when he resigned; elected as a Republican to the Forty-sixth Congress to fill the vacancy caused by the death of Evarts W. Farr; reelected to the Forty-seventh and Forty-eighth Congresses, and served from January 8, 1881 to March 3, 1885; was not a candidate for renomination in 1884 to the Forty-ninth Congress; died in Lancaster, N.H., January 28, 1892; interment in the Summer Street Cemetery.

**RAY, Richard Belmont,** a Representative from Georgia; born in Fort Valley, Crawford County, Ga., February 2, 1927; attended the public schools of Crawford County; graduated from Crawford County High School, Roberta, Ga., 1944; served in the United States Navy, 1944-1946; farmer, 1946-1950; owner and operator of a service firm, 1950-1962; southeast division manager, Getz, Inc., 1962-1972; member of the Perry, Ga., city council, 1962-1964; mayor of Perry, Ga., 1964-1970; president, Georgia Municipal Association, 1969-1970; administrative assistant to Senator Sam Nunn of Georgia, 1972-1982; elected as a Democrat to the Ninety-eighth and to the four succeeding Congresses (January 3, 1983-January 3, 1993); unsuccessful candidate for reelection in 1992 to the One Hundred Third Congress; is a resident of Perry, Ga.

**RAY, William Henry,** a Representative from Illinois; born in Amenia, Dutchess County, N.Y., December 14, 1812; moved to Oneida County, N.Y., in 1813 with his parents who settled in Utica; attended the common schools; moved to Rushville, Ill., in 1834; engaged in mercantile pursuits; also interested in banking; member of the first State board of equalization 1867-1869; elected as a Republican to the Forty-third Congress (March 4, 1873-March 3, 1875); resumed his former business pursuits in Rushville, Schuyler County, Ill., and died there January 25, 1881; interment in Rushville Cemetery.

**RAYBURN, Samuel Taliaferro,** a Representative from Texas; born near Kingston, Roane County, Tenn., January 6, 1882; moved to Fannin County, Tex., in 1887 with his parents, who settled near Windom; attended the rural schools and was graduated from the East Texas Normal College, Commerce, Tex., in 1903; studied law at the University of Texas at Austin; was admitted to the bar in 1908 and commenced practice in Bonham, Fannin County, Tex.; member of the Texas State house of representatives, 1907-1913, and served as speaker during the last two years; elected as a Democrat to the Sixty-third and to the twenty-four succeeding Congresses, and served from March 4, 1913 until his death in Bonham, Tex., November 16, 1961; chairman, Committee on Interstate and Foreign Commerce (Seventy-second, Seventy-third, and Seventy-fourth Congresses); majority leader (Seventy-fifth and Seventy-sixth Congresses), minority leader (Eightieth and Eighty-third Congresses); elected Speaker of the House of Representatives on September 16, 1940 to fill the vacancy caused by the death of Speaker William B. Bankhead; reelected Speaker in the Seventy-seventh, Seventy-eighth, Seventy-ninth, Eighty-first, Eighty-second, Eighty-fourth, Eighty-fifth, Eighty-sixth, and Eighty-seventh Congresses; interment in Willow Wild Cemetery, Bonham, Tex.

**Bibliography:** *DAB*; Champagne, Anthony. *Congressman Sam Rayburn.* New Brunswick, N.J.: Rutgers University Press, 1984; Hardeman, D.B., and Donald C. Bacon. *Rayburn: A Biography.* Austin: Texas Monthly Press, 1987.

**RAYFIEL, Leo Frederick,** a Representative from New York; born in New York City, March 22, 1888; attended the grade and high schools; was graduated from the New York University Law School in 1908; was admitted to the bar in 1918 and commenced practice in Brooklyn, N.Y.; member of the New York State assembly 1939-1944; elected as a Democrat to the Seventy-ninth Congress; reelected to the Eightieth Congress and served from January 3, 1945, until his resignation on September 13, 1947, having been appointed a judge of the United States District Court for the Eastern District of New York, in which capacity he served until his death; died in Wayne, N.J., November 18, 1978; interment in Wellward Cemetery, Farmingdale, N.Y.

**RAYMOND, Henry Jarvis,** a Representative from New York; born in Lima, Livingston County, N.Y., January 24, 1820; attended the common schools; was graduated from the University of Vermont at Burlington in 1840; moved to New York City and studied law; engaged in journalism; was connected with the New York Tribune, 1841-1848, with the Courier and Enquirer, 1848-1850, and with Harper's Magazine in 1850; member of the New York State assembly in 1850 and 1851, and served as speaker in the latter year; established the New-York Daily Times (now New York Times), which published its first issue on September 18, 1851; delegate to the Whig National Convention in 1852; Lieutenant Governor of New York in 1854; declined a renomination; delegate to the Republican National Convention of 1860; again a member of the State assembly in 1862, and served as speaker; elected as a Republican to the Thirty-ninth Congress (March 4, 1865-March 3, 1867); unsuccessful candidate for renomination in 1866 to the Fortieth Congress; resumed his newspaper activities with the New York Times; died in New York City, June 18, 1869; interment in Greenwood Cemetery, Brooklyn, N.Y.

**Bibliography:** *DAB*; Brown, Ernest Francis. *Raymond of the Times.* 1951. Reprint. Westport, Conn.: Greenwood Press, 1970; Dodd, Dorothy. *Henry J. Raymond and the New York Times During Reconstruction.* Chicago: University of Chicago Libraries, 1936; Maverick, Augustus. *Henry J. Raymond and the New York Press.* 1870. Reprint. New York: Arno Press, 1970.

**RAYMOND, John Baldwin,** a Delegate from the Territory of Dakota; born in Lockport, Niagara County, N.Y., December 5, 1844; moved with his parents to Tazewell County, Ill., in 1853; attended the public schools and the Poughkeepsie (N.Y.) Business College in 1865 and 1866; enlisted as a private in the Thirty-first Regiment, Illinois Infantry, in 1861; promoted to captain of Company E of that regiment after the siege of Vicksburg in 1863; served throughout the war and settled in Mississippi; published the Mississippi Pilot at Jackson, Miss., during the reconstruction of that State and until 1877; assistant State treasurer 1873-1875 appointed United States marshal of Dakota Territory in 1877, with headquarters at Yankton, later at Fargo, and served until 1882; declined a reappointment; elected as a Republican to the Forty-eighth Congress (March 4, 1883-March 3, 1885); unsuccessful candidate for renomination in 1884; engaged in wheat raising; died in Fargo, Dak. (now North Dakota), January 3, 1886; interment in the public vault in Rock Creek Cemetery, Washington, D.C.

**RAYNER, Isidor,** a Representative and a Senator from Maryland; born in Baltimore, Md., April 11, 1850; attended private schools, the University of Maryland at Baltimore, and the University of Virginia at Charlottesville; studied law; admitted to the Maryland bar in 1871; member, Maryland State house of delegates, 1878-1884; member, State senate, 1885-1886; elected as a Democrat to the Fiftieth Congress (March 4, 1887-March 3, 1889); unsuccessful candidate for reelection in 1888 to the Fifty-first Congress; elected to the Fifty-second and Fifty-third Congresses (March 4, 1891-March 3, 1895); declined to be a candidate for renomination in 1894 to the Fifty-fourth Congress; attorney general

of Maryland, 1899-1903; elected as a Democrat to the United States Senate in 1905; reelected in 1911, and served from March 4, 1905 until his death in Washington, D.C., November 25, 1912; chairman, Committee on Indian Depredations (Sixty-second Congress); interment in Rock Creek Cemetery.

**Bibliography:** *DAB*; Rayner, Isidor. *Essays of Isidor Rayner.* Compiled and edited by Jesse Frederick Essary and William B. Rayner. Baltimore: John Murphy Co., 1914.

**RAYNER, Kenneth,** a Representative from North Carolina; born in Bertie County, N.C., June 20, 1808; attended Tarborough Academy; studied law; was admitted to the bar in 1829; moved to Hertford County and practiced; member of the North Carolina State constitutional convention in 1835; member of the State house of commons in 1835, 1836, 1846, 1848, and 1850; elected as a Whig to the Twenty-sixth and to the two succeeding Congresses (March 4, 1839-March 3, 1845); was not a candidate for renomination in 1844 to the Twenty-ninth Congress; member of the State senate in 1854; appointed by President Ulysses S. Grant as commissioner of the court to settle the *Alabama* claims at its organization, and served until its dissolution; Solicitor of the United States Treasury from 1877 to 1884; died in Washington, D.C., March 4, 1884; interment in the Old City Cemetery, Raleigh, N.C.

**Bibliography:** *DAB*; Cantrell, Gregg. *Kenneth and John B. Rayner and the Limits of Southern Dissent.* Urbana: University of Illinois Press, 1993.

**REA, David,** a Representative from Missouri; born near New Marion, Ripley County, Ind., January 19, 1831; attended the common schools; moved to Missouri with his parents, who settled in Andrew County in 1842; engaged in agricultural pursuits near Rosendale; taught school in the country 1849-1854; studied law; was admitted to the bar in 1862 and commenced practice in Savannah, Mo., in 1863; during the Civil War enlisted in the Union Army and served successively as first lieutenant, captain, quartermaster, and lieutenant colonel; resumed the practice of his profession in Savannah; member of the board of education; elected as a Democrat to the Forty-fourth and Forty-fifth Congresses (March 4, 1875-March 3, 1879); was an unsuccessful candidate for reelection in 1878 to the Forty-sixth Congress; engaged in the practice of law in Savannah, Mo., until his death in that city on June 13, 1901; interment in the City Cemetery.

**REA, John,** a Representative from Pennsylvania; born at "Rea's Mansion," near Chambersburg, Pa., January 27, 1755; completed preparatory studies; served as lieutenant and captain with the Cumberland County (Pa.) Militia during the Revolutionary War; commissioned the first coroner of Franklin County, Pa., on October 20, 1784; member of the Pennsylvania house of representatives in 1785, 1786, 1789, 1790, 1792, 1793, 1801, and 1802; county auditor in 1793 and 1794; elected as a Republican to the Eighth and to the three succeeding Congresses (March 4, 1803-March 3, 1811); was an unsuccessful candidate for reelection in 1810 to the Twelfth Congress; served in the War of 1812 as major general of the Eleventh Division of Militia; elected to the Thirteenth Congress to fill the vacancy caused by the death of Robert Whitehill and served from May 11, 1813, to March 3, 1815; member of the Pennsylvania senate in 1823 and 1824, when he resigned; died in Chambersburg, Franklin County, Pa., February 26, 1829; interment in Rocky Spring Churchyard, near Chambersburg, Pa.

**READ, Almon Heath,** a Representative from Pennsylvania; born in Shelburne, Chittenden County, Vt., June 12, 1790; graduated from Williams College, Williamstown, Mass., in 1811; county clerk 1815-1820; studied law; admitted to the bar in 1816 and commenced practice in Montrose, Susquehanna County, Pa.; member of the Pennsylvania house of representatives 1827-1832; served in the Pennsylvania senate 1833-1837; Pennsylvania treasurer in 1840; elected as a Democrat to the Twenty-seventh Congress to fill the vacancy caused by the death of Davis Dimock, Jr.; reelected to the Twenty-eighth Congress and served from March 18, 1842, until his death in Montrose, Pa., June 3, 1844; interment in Montrose Cemetery.

**READ, George,** a Delegate and a Senator from Delaware; born near North East, Cecil County, Md., September 18, 1733; completed preparatory studies; studied law; was admitted to the bar and began practice in New Castle, Del., in 1752; attorney general for lower Delaware 1763-1774; member, provincial assembly 1765-1777; Member of the Continental Congress 1774-1777; a signer of the Declaration of Independence; president of the State constitutional convention in 1776; vice president of the State under this constitution; member, State house of representatives 1779-1780; judge of the United States Court of Appeals in admiralty cases 1782; representative at the Annapolis convention 1786; delegate from Delaware to the Federal Constitutional Convention; elected to the United States Senate in 1789, reelected in 1790, and served from March 4, 1789, to September 18, 1793, when he resigned, having been appointed chief justice of Delaware; served until his death in New Castle, Del., September 21, 1798; interment in Immanuel Churchyard.

**Bibliography:** *DAB*; Boughner, D. Terry, Jr. "George Read and the Founding of Delaware State, 1781-1798." Ph.D. dissertation, Catholic University, 1970; Read, William T. *Life and Correspondence of George Read*. Philadelphia: J.B. Lippincott and Co., 1870.

**READ, Jacob,** a Delegate and a Senator from South Carolina; born at "Hobcaw" plantation in Christ Church Parish, near Charleston, S.C., in 1752; completed preparatory studies; studied law and was admitted to the bar; studied in Great Britain 1773-1776; joined other Americans in London in 1774 in a petition against the Boston port bill; returned to the United States and served South Carolina in various military and civil capacities during the Revolutionary War; sent with other Americans as a prisoner of the British to St. Augustine 1780-1781; member, State assembly 1782, and of the privy council 1783; Member of the Continental Congress 1783-1785; member, South Carolina house of representatives and served as speaker; elected as a Federalist to the United States Senate and served from March 4, 1795, to March 3, 1801; unsuccessful candidate for reelection; served as President pro tempore of the Senate during the Fifth Congress; died in Charleston, S.C., July 17, 1816; interment in the family cemetery at "Hobcaw," in Christ Church Parish, near Charleston, S.C.

**Bibliography:** *DAB*.

**READ, Nathan,** a Representative from Massachusetts; born in Warren, Mass., July 2, 1759; attended the common schools and was graduated from Harvard University in 1781; taught school in Beverly and Salem and was elected a tutor in Harvard University, where he continued until 1787; opened an apothecary store in Salem; interested in an iron factory at Danvers, Mass.; elected as a Federalist to the Sixth Congress to fill the vacancy caused by the resignation of Samuel Sewall; reelected to the Seventh Congress and served from November 25, 1800, to March 3, 1803; was not a candidate for renomination in 1802; judge of the court of common pleas of Essex County in 1803; moved to Belfast, Maine, in 1807; judge of the county court of Hancock County in 1807; instrumental in establishing Belfast Academy and served as trustee for forty years; died near Belfast, Waldo County, Maine, January 20, 1849; interment in Grove Cemetery, Belfast, Maine.

**Bibliography:** *DAB*.

**READ, William Brown,** a Representative from Kentucky; born in Hardin County, near Hodgenville, Ky., December 14, 1817; completed preparatory studies; studied law; admitted to the bar and commenced practice in Hodgenville, Ky., in 1849; member of the

Kentucky senate 1857-1865; unsuccessful candidate for election as Lieutenant Governor of Kentucky in 1863; delegate to the Democratic National Conventions at Charleston and Baltimore in 1860 and at Chicago in 1864; member of the Kentucky house of representatives 1867-1869; elected as a Democrat to the Forty-second and Forty-third Congresses (March 4, 1871-March 3, 1875); unsuccessful candidate for renomination in 1874; resumed the practice of his profession; died in Hodgenville, Ky., August 5, 1880; interment in Red Hill Cemetery.

**READE, Edwin Godwin,** a Representative from North Carolina; born on a farm in Person County, N.C., November 13, 1812; completed preparatory studies; engaged in agricultural pursuits; studied law; was admitted to the bar in 1835 and commenced practice in Roxboro, Person County, N.C.; elected as the candidate of the American Party to the Thirty-fourth Congress (March 4, 1855-March 3, 1857); declined to be a candidate for renomination in 1856; served in the Confederate Senate in 1863 by appointment of Governor Vance; president of the reconstruction convention which met in Raleigh in 1865; associate justice of the supreme court of North Carolina 1868-1879; engaged in banking in Raleigh, N.C., and died there October 18, 1894; interment in Oakwood Cemetery.

**Bibliography:** *DAB*.

**READING, John Roberts,** a Representative from Pennsylvania; born in Somerton, Philadelphia County, Pa., November 1, 1826; completed preparatory studies; was graduated from the Jefferson Medical College, Philadelphia, Pa., in 1847 and began practice in Somerton, Pa.; later graduated from Hahnemann College, Philadelphia, Pa., and practiced homeopathy; presented credentials as a Democratic Member-elect to the Forty-first Congress and served from March 4, 1869, to April 13, 1870, when he was succeeded by Caleb N. Taylor, who contested his election; unsuccessful Democratic candidate for election in 1870 to the Forty-second Congress; died in Philadelphia, Pa., February 14, 1886; interment in the William Penn Cemetery, Somerton, Pa.

**READY, Charles** (uncle of William T. Haskell), a Representative from Tennessee; born in Readyville, Rutherford (now Cannon) County, Tenn., December 22, 1802; attended the common schools and was graduated from Greeneville (Tenn.) College; studied law; was admitted to the bar in 1825 and commenced practice in Murfreesboro, Tenn.; member of the Tennessee State house of representatives in 1835; elected as a Whig to the Thirty-third Congress, and reelected as a candidate of the American Party to the Thirty-fourth and Thirty-fifth Congresses (March 4, 1853-March 3, 1859); unsuccessful candidate for reelection in 1858 to the Thirty-sixth Congress; resumed the practice of law; died in Murfreesboro, Rutherford County, Tenn., June 4, 1878; interment in Evergreen Cemetery.

**REAGAN, John Henninger,** a Representative and a Senator from Texas; born in Sevierville, Sevier County, Tenn., October 8, 1818; attended the common schools and private academies; moved to Texas in 1839, joined the republic's army, and participated in campaigns against the Cherokee Indians; deputy State surveyor of the public lands 1839-1843; studied law; was admitted to the bar in 1848 and practiced in Buffalo and Palestine, Tex.; member, State house of representatives 1847-1849; judge of the district court 1852-1857, when he resigned; elected as a Democrat to the Thirty-fifth and Thirty-sixth Congresses (March 4, 1857-March 3, 1861); elected to the secession convention of Texas in 1861; deputy to the Provisional Congress of the Confederacy; postmaster general of the Confederacy from 1861 until the close of the war; also appointed Acting Secretary of the Treasury of the Confederacy for a short time preceding the close of the war; imprisoned at Fort Warren for several months after the war; member of the State constitutional convention in 1875; elected as a Democrat to the Forty-fourth and to the five succeeding Congresses (March 4, 1875-March 3, 1887); had been reelected to the Fiftieth Congress but resigned March 4, 1887, to become Senator; chairman, Committee on Commerce (Forty-fifth, Forty-sixth, Forty-eighth, and Forty-ninth Congresses); elected as a Democrat to the United States Senate and served from March 4, 1887, until June 10, 1891, when he resigned; returned to Texas and was appointed a member of the railroad commission of the State and served as chairman 1897-1903; died in Palestine, Anderson County, Tex., March 6, 1905; interment in East Hill Cemetery.

**Bibliography:** *DAB*; Proctor, Ben. *Not Without Honor: The Life of John H. Reagan*. Austin: University of Texas Press, 1962; Reagan, John H. *Memoirs with Special Reference to Secession and the Civil War*. Edited by Walter Flavius. 1906. Reprint. New York: AMS Press, 1973.

**REAMES, Alfred Evan,** a Senator from Oregon; born in Jacksonville, Jackson County, Oreg., February 5, 1870; attended the public schools, the University of the Pacific, San Jose, Calif., and the University of Oregon at Eugene; graduated from the law department of Washington and Lee University, Lexington, Va., in 1893; was admitted to the bar the same year and commenced practice in Eugene, Oreg., and in various places in the State; served as district attorney of Jackson, Josephine, Klamath, and Lake Counties, Oreg., 1900-1908; returned to Medford, Oreg., in 1908 and continued the practice of law; also engaged in mining; appointed as a Democrat to the United States Senate to fill the vacancy caused by the resignation of Frederick Steiwer and served from February 1, to November 8, 1938, when a successor was elected; was not a candidate for election in 1938 to fill the vacancy; resumed the practice of law; died in Medford, Oreg., on March 4, 1943; interment in Siskiyou Memorial Park.

**REAMS, Henry Frazier,** a Representative from Ohio; born in Franklin, Williamson County, Tenn., January 15, 1897; attended the public schools of Tennessee; during First World War enlisted as a private in 1918 and served with the Fifty-eighth Field Artillery, United States Army, until discharged as a lieutenant in 1919; graduated from the University of Tennessee at Knoxville in 1919 and from Vanderbilt University Law School, Nashville, Tenn., in 1922; was admitted to the Tennessee bar in 1920 and commenced the practice of law in Nashville; moved to Toledo, Ohio, in 1922, admitted to the Ohio bar in 1923, and continued the practice of law; delegate to Democratic National Conventions of 1928, 1932, 1936, 1940, 1944, 1948, and 1956; prosecuting attorney of Lucas County, Ohio, 1933-1937; member of Toledo Port Commission, 1939-1945; collector of internal revenue at Toledo, Ohio, 1942-1944; Ohio State director of public welfare, 1945-1946; president and treasurer of Community Broadcasting Co. 1937-1960; also interested in the banking business; trustee of Bowling Green State University, 1948-1957; delegate to the Council of Europe at Strasbourg in 1951, and to the Interparliamentary Union Conferences in Washington, D.C., in 1953, and in Vienna, Austria, in 1954; elected as an Independent to the Eighty-second and to the Eighty-third Congresses (January 3, 1951-January 3, 1955); unsuccessful candidate for reelection in 1954 to the Eighty-fourth Congress; resumed the practice of law; chairman of board, Reams Broadcasting Corp., beginning in 1965; died in Oakland, Calif., September 15, 1971; interment in Woodlawn Cemetery, Toledo, Ohio.

**REAVIS, Charles Frank,** a Representative from Nebraska; born in Falls City, Richardson County, Nebr., September 5, 1870; attended the public schools and Northwestern University, Evanston, Ill.; studied law; was admitted to the bar in 1892 and commenced practice in Falls City; prosecuting attorney of Richardson County, 1894-1896; elected as a Republican to the Sixty-fourth and to the three succeeding Congresses, and served from March 4, 1915 to June 3, 1922, when he resigned; appointed in June 1922 as special assistant to the Attorney General in the prosecution of so-called war fraud cases, and served until June 1, 1924; moved to Lincoln, Nebr.,

in 1924 and continued the practice of law; died in Lincoln, Nebr., May 26, 1932; interment in Steele Cemetery, Falls City, Nebr.

**REBER, John,** a Representative from Pennsylvania; born in South Manheim Township, Schuylkill County, Pa., February 1, 1858; attended the public schools, and was graduated from the Eastman Business College, Poughkeepsie, N.Y., in 1875; taught school for several years and was later employed as a bookkeeper; deputy county treasurer of Schuylkill County 1882-1884; engaged in the manufacture of hosiery in Pottsville 1885-1917 and also interested in banking; elected as a Republican to the Sixty-sixth and Sixty-seventh Congresses (March 4, 1919-March 3, 1923); chairman, Committee on Mileage (Sixty-seventh Congress); was not a candidate for renomination in 1922; resumed banking activities in Pottsville, Pa., and served as president of the Reber Investment Co.; died in Pottsville, Pa., on September 26, 1931; interment in the Charles Baber Cemetery.

**REDDEN, Monroe Minor,** a Representative from North Carolina; born in Hendersonville, Henderson County, N.C., September 24, 1901; attended the public schools; was graduated from the law school of Wake Forest College, Wake Forest, N.C., in 1923; was admitted to the bar the same year and commenced practice in Hendersonville, N.C.; chairman of the Henderson County Democratic committee, 1930-1946; chairman of the State Democratic executive committee from 1942 to 1944; elected as a Democrat to the Eightieth and to the two succeeding Congresses (January 3, 1947-January 3, 1953); was not a candidate for renomination in 1952 to the Eighty-third Congress; resumed the practice of law; president of the Southern Heritage Life Insurance Co., 1956-1959; chairman, board of directors of Home Bank and Trust Company; was a resident of Hendersonville, N.C.; died December 16, 1987.

**REDFIELD, William Cox,** a Representative from New York; born in Albany, N.Y., June 18, 1858; moved with his parents to Pittsfield, Mass., in 1867; attended the public schools and received home instruction; employed in the Pittsfield post office and later as a traveling salesman for a paper company; went to New York City at the age of nineteen and was employed in the stationery and printing business; leaving this in 1883, he became connected with the manufacture of steel and iron forgings in Brooklyn, N.Y.; interested in many other manufacturing concerns and banking and life insurance companies; delegate to the Gold Democrats National Convention at Indianapolis in 1896; unsuccessful candidate as a Gold Democrat for election in 1896 to the Fifty-fifth Congress; commissioner of public works for Brooklyn Borough in 1902 and 1903; elected as a Democrat to the Sixty-second Congress (March 4, 1911-March 3, 1913); unsuccessful candidate for nomination for Vice President of the United States in 1912, and therefore declined to be a candidate for renomination to the Sixty-third Congress; appointed Secretary of Commerce in the Cabinet of President Woodrow Wilson, and served from March 4, 1913 to November 1, 1919, when he resigned; engaged in banking and the investment and insurance business in New York City and Brooklyn, N.Y.; died in New York City, June 13, 1932; interment in the Albany Rural Cemetery, Albany, N.Y.

**Bibliography:** *DAB*.

**REDING, John Randall,** a Representative from New Hampshire; born in Portsmouth, N.H., October 18, 1805; attended the common schools; was apprenticed to the printer's trade and subsequently became an editor; elected as a Democrat to the Twenty-seventh and Twenty-eighth Congresses (March 4, 1841-March 3, 1845); naval storekeeper at Portsmouth 1853-1858; mayor of Portsmouth in 1860; member of the State house of representatives 1867-1870; died in Portsmouth, N.H., October 8, 1892; interment in Haverhill Cemetery, Haverhill, N.H.

**REDLIN, Rolland W.,** a Representative from North Dakota; born in Lambert, Richland County, Mont., February 29, 1920; educated in grade school in Lambert, Mont., high school in Minneapolis, Minn., the University of Washington, Seattle, Wash., and took extension courses at Minot (N.Dak.) State University; owns and operates a farm near Crosby, Divide County, N.Dak.; was a candidate for the North Dakota State house of representatives in 1952; North Dakota State senator, 1959-1963; elected as a Democrat to the Eighty-ninth Congress (January 3, 1965-January 3, 1967); unsuccessful candidate for reelection in 1966 to the Ninetieth Congress; war on hunger consultant, Agency for International Development, 1967; vice president and agricultural representative for Minot First Western Bank; North Dakota State senator, District 38, 1973 to present; is a resident of Minot, N.Dak.

**REECE, Brazilla Carroll** (husband of Louise G. Reece), a Representative from Tennessee; born on a farm near Butler, Johnson County, Tenn., December 22, 1889; attended the public schools, Watauga Academy, Carson-Newman College, New York University, and the University of London; assistant secretary and instructor in the New York University in 1916 and 1917; during the First World War enlisted in May 1917 and served with the American Expeditionary Forces from October 1917 to July 1919; was decorated with the Distinguished Service Cross, Distinguished Service Medal, Purple Heart, and the French Croix de Guerre with Palm; director of the School of Business Administration of New York University in 1919 and 1920; elected as a Republican to the Sixty-seventh and to the four succeeding Congresses (March 4, 1921-March 3, 1931); unsuccessful candidate for reelection in 1930 to the Seventy-second Congress; elected to the Seventy-third and to the six succeeding Congresses (March 4, 1933-January 3, 1947); was not a candidate for renomination in 1946; delegate to the Republican National Conventions in 1928, 1932, 1936, 1940, 1944, and 1948; lawyer, banker, and publisher; member of the Board of Regents of the Smithsonian Institution in 1945 and 1946; chairman of the Republican National Committee 1946-1948; unsuccessful candidate for election to the United States Senate in 1948; elected to the Eighty-second and to the five succeeding Congresses and served from January 3, 1951, until his death in Bethesda, Md., March 19, 1961; chairman, Special Committee on Tax Exempt Foundations (Eighty-third Congress); interment in Monte Vista Burial Park, Johnson City, Tenn.

Bibliography: *DAB*.

**REECE, Louise Goff** (wife of Brazilla Carroll Reece, daughter of Guy D. Goff, and granddaughter of Nathan Goff), a Representative from Tennessee; born in Milwaukee, Wis., November 6, 1898; educated at Miss Treat's School, Milwaukee Downer Seminary, and Miss Spence's School, New York City; member of the board of the First Peoples Bank, Johnson City, Tenn.; chairman of the board of Carter County Bank, Elizabethton, Tenn.; proprietor and manager of Goff Properties, Clarksburg, W.Va.; elected as a Republican to the Eighty-seventh Congress May 16, 1961, to fill the vacancy caused by the death of her husband, Brazilla Carroll Reece, and served until January 3, 1963; was not a candidate for renomination in 1962 to the Eighty-eighth Congress; remained active in State and national politics; businesswoman with wide interests in Tennessee and West Virginia; died in Johnson City, Tenn., May 14, 1970; interment in Monte Vista Burial Park.

**REED, Charles Manning,** a Representative from Pennsylvania; born in Erie, Pa., April 3, 1803; attended the public schools and was graduated from Washington College, Washington, Pa.; studied law; was admitted to the bar in Philadelphia in 1824 but did not practice; engaged in business in Erie with his father, an owner of vessels on the Great Lakes; appointed colonel of militia in 1831 and brigadier general at the expiration of his commission; member of the Pennsylvania house of representatives in 1837 and 1838; elected as a Whig to the Twenty-eighth Congress (March 4, 1843-March 3, 1845); unsuccessful candidate for reelection in 1844 to the Twenty-ninth Congress; resumed shipping on the Great Lakes; also engaged in banking, mercantile pursuits, and in the railroad business, 1846-1849; died in Erie, Pa., December 16, 1871; interment in Erie Cemetery.

**REED, Chauncey William,** a Representative from Illinois; born in West Chicago, Du Page County, Ill., June 2, 1890; attended the public schools and Northwestern University, Evanston, Ill.; city treasurer of West Chicago, Ill., in 1913 and 1914; was graduated from the Webster College of Law, Chicago, Ill., in 1915; was admitted to the bar the same year and commenced practice in Naperville, Ill.; during the First World War served as a sergeant of Infantry, Eighty-sixth Division; resumed practice of law at Naperville, Ill.; served as State's attorney of Du Page County from 1920 until 1935; chairman of the Du Page County Republican central committee, 1926-1934; elected as a Republican to the Seventy-fourth and to the ten succeeding Congresses, and served from January 3, 1935, until his death in Bethesda, Md., February 9, 1956; chairman, Committee on the Judiciary (Eighty-third Congress); interment in Glen Oak Cemetery, West Chicago, Ill.

**REED, Clyde Martin,** a Senator from Kansas; born near Champaign, Champaign County, Ill., October 19, 1871; moved with his family to Labette County, Kans., in 1875; attended the public schools; taught school one year; served in the railway mail service from 1889 until 1910, rising through all grades to field superintendent of divisions at Cleveland and Cincinnati, Ohio, New Orleans, La., Omaha, Nebr., and St. Paul, Minn., and superintendent, Railway Adjustment Division, Post Office Department; resigned in 1917 to manage and publish a newspaper at Parsons, Kans.; secretary to Governor Henry J. Allen of Kansas in 1919; member of the Kansas Industrial Court in 1920; chairman of the Kansas Public Utilities Commission, 1921-1924; elected Governor of Kansas in 1928, and served from January 14, 1929 to January 12, 1931; unsuccessful candidate for renomination in 1930; practiced extensively before the Interstate Commerce Commission; unsuccessful candidate for the gubernatorial nomination in 1942; elected as a Republican in 1938 to the United States Senate, reelected in 1944, and served from January 3, 1939, until his death in Parsons, Kans., on November 8, 1949; interment in Oakwood Cemetery.

Bibliography:

**REED, Daniel Alden,** a Representative from New York; born in Sheridan, Chautauqua County, N.Y., September 15, 1875; attended the public schools in Sheridan and in Silver Creek, N.Y.; was graduated from Cornell University, Ithaca, N.Y., in 1898; studied law; was admitted to the bar in 1900 and practiced in Silver Creek and later in Dunkirk, N.Y.; attorney for the excise department of the State of New York, 1903-1909; sent by the Government of the United States on a special mission to France in 1917 and 1918; director of the Dunkirk Trust Co.; lecturer on commercial and civic subjects; elected as a Republican to the Sixty-sixth and to the twenty succeeding Congresses and served from March 4, 1919, until his death in Washington, D.C., February 19, 1959; chairman, Committee on Industrial Arts and Expositions (Sixty-eighth Congress), Committee on Education (Sixty-ninth through Seventy-first Congresses), Committee on Ways and Means (Eighty-third Congress), Joint Committee on Internal Revenue Taxation (Eighty-third Congress); delegate to the Interparliamentary Union meeting in Rome, Italy, in 1948, and represented the United States at subsequent meetings in Sweden, Switzerland, and France; interment in Sheridan Cemetery, Sheridan, N.Y.

Bibliography: *DAB*; Bulkley, Peter B. "Daniel A. Reed: A Study in Conservatism." Ph.D. dissertation, Clark University, 1972.

**REED, David Aiken,** a Senator from Pennsylvania; born in Pittsburgh, Pa., December 21, 1880; attended private schools; graduated from Shadyside Academy, Pittsburgh, Pa., in 1896, from Princeton University, Princeton, N.J., in 1900, and from the University of Pittsburgh Law School in 1903; was admitted to the bar in 1903 and practiced in Pittsburgh, Pa., from 1903 until 1917; chairman of the Pennsylvania Industrial Accidents Commission, 1912-1915; during the First World War served as major in the field artillery, 1917-1919; resumed the practice of law in Pittsburgh in 1919; appointed as a Republican on August 8, 1922, and elected on November 7, 1922, to the United States Senate to fill the vacancy in the term ending March 3, 1923, caused by the death of William E. Crow, and on the same day was elected for the term commencing March 4, 1923; reelected in 1928, and served from August 8, 1922, to January 3, 1935; unsuccessful candidate for reelection in 1934; chairman, Committee on Expenditures in Executive Departments (Sixty-ninth Congress), Committee on Military Affairs (Seventieth through Seventy-second Congresses); resumed the practice of law in Pittsburgh, Pa.; died in Sarasota, Fla., February 10, 1953; interment in Arlington National Cemetery, Va.

**Bibliography:** *DAB.*

**REED, Edward Cambridge,** a Representative from New York; born in Fitzwilliam, N.H., March 8, 1793; attended the common schools; was graduated from Dartmouth College, Hanover, N.H., in 1812; served in the War of 1812 under Governor William L. Marcy; studied law in Troy, N.Y.; was admitted to the bar in 1816 and commenced practice in Homer, N.Y.; secretary of the board of trustees of Cortland Academy, Homer, N.Y., from 1822 until 1870; district attorney of Cortland County, 1827-1836; was admitted to the court of chancery in 1830; elected as a Jacksonian to the Twenty-second Congress (March 4, 1831-March 3, 1833); resumed the practice of law; associate judge of the court of common pleas of Cortland County, 1836-1840; again district attorney in 1856; moved to Ithaca, Tompkins County, N.Y., in 1875 and resumed the practice of his profession; died in Ithaca, N.Y., on May 1, 1883; interment in Glenwood Cemetery, Homer, Cortland County, N.Y.

**REED, Eugene Elliott,** a Representative from New Hampshire; born in Manchester, N.H., April 23, 1866; attended the public schools and received instruction from private tutors; studied law; director and officer of numerous New England and New York corporations and engaged in construction contracting business; alderman of Manchester, 1899-1903; mayor of Manchester, 1903-1911; Democratic National and State committeeman for twelve years; delegate to the Democratic National Conventions of 1908, 1912, 1916, and 1924; unsuccessful candidate for election in 1910 to the Sixty-second Congress; elected as a Democrat to the Sixty-third Congress (March 4, 1913-March 3, 1915); unsuccessful candidate for reelection in 1914 to the Sixty-fourth Congress; appointed by President Woodrow Wilson to the Philippine Commission, and served as secretary of commerce and police in 1916; negotiated the purchase and was first president under the Philippine ownership of Manila railroads; returned to the United States in 1918; unsuccessful candidate for United States Senator in 1918; engaged in the general export business in New York, 1919-1922; vice president of United Life & Accident Insurance Co., Concord, N.H., 1922-1931; National Recovery Administration director for New Hampshire in 1933 and 1934; State director, National Emergency Council and Federal Housing Agency, 1934-1939; member of the New Hampshire Emergency Flood Relief and Rehabilitation Committee in 1936; member of the New Hampshire Disaster Relief Committee in 1938; regional director for New England, Office of Government Reports, in 1939 and 1940; died at Manchester, N.H., December 15, 1940; interment in Pine Grove Cemetery.

**REED, Isaac,** a Representative from Maine; born in Waldoboro, Maine, August 22, 1809; prepared for college at Bloomfield Academy, but by preference became a merchant-ship builder; also engaged in banking; town clerk of Waldoboro, 1836-1838; served in the Maine State senate in 1839, 1840, 1850, and 1863; member of the State house of representatives in 1842, 1843, and 1846; president of the town board from 1843 until 1868; selectman, 1849-1853, 1855, and 1856; member of the State board of agriculture and a trustee of the Maine Insane Hospital; unsuccessful candidate for election in 1850 to the Thirty-second Congress; subsequently elected as a Whig to the Thirty-second Congress to fill the vacancy caused by the death of Charles Andrews and served from June 25, 1852, to March 3, 1853; unsuccessful candidate for Governor of Maine in 1854 and 1855; resumed shipbuilding; State treasurer in 1856; upon the dissolution of the Whig Party became a Democrat; again a member of the State house of representatives in 1870 and 1871; died in Waldoboro, Lincoln County, Maine, September 19, 1887; interment in Central Cemetery.

**REED, James Alexander,** a Senator from Missouri; born on a farm near Mansfield, Richland County, Ohio, November 9, 1861; moved with his parents to Cedar Rapids, Linn County, Iowa, in 1864; attended the public schools and Coe College, Cedar Rapids, Iowa; studied law; was admitted to the bar in 1885 and commenced practice in Cedar Rapids, Iowa; moved to Kansas City, Mo., in 1887 and continued the practice of law; counselor of Kansas City, 1897-1898; prosecuting attorney of Jackson County from 1898 until 1900, when he resigned; mayor of Kansas City, 1900-1904; elected as a Democrat to the United States Senate in 1910; reelected in 1916 and again in 1922 and served from March 4, 1911, to March 3, 1929; was not a candidate for renomination in 1928; chairman, Committee on Manufactures (Sixty-third through Sixty-fifth Congresses), Committee on Public Buildings and Grounds (Sixty-fifth Congress), Committee on Standards, Weights and Measures (Sixty-sixth Congress); resumed the practice of his profession in Kansas City, Mo.; died at his summer home near Fairview, Oscoda County, Mich., September 8, 1944; interment in Mount Washington Cemetery, near Kansas City, Mo.

**Bibliography:** *DAB*; Meriwether, Lee. *Jim Read, Senatorial Immortal.* Webster Groves, Mo.: International Mark Twain Society, 1948; Mitchell, Franklin D. "The Re-Election of Irreconcilable James A. Reed." *Missouri Historical Review* 60 (July 1966): 416-35.

**REED, James Byron,** a Representative from Arkansas; born near Lonoke, Lonoke County, Ark., January 2, 1881; attended the rural schools of his county and Hendrix College and was graduated from the law department of the University of Arkansas at Fayetteville in 1906; was admitted to the bar in 1906 and commenced the practice of law in Lonoke, Ark.; member of the Arkansas State house of representatives in 1907; prosecuting attorney of the seventeenth judicial district of Arkansas from 1912 until 1916; elected as a Democrat to the Sixty-eighth Congress to fill the vacancy caused by the death of Lewis E. Sawyer; reelected to the two succeeding Congresses, and served from October 20, 1923 to March 3, 1929; unsuccessful candidate for renomination in 1928 to the Seventy-first Congress; resumed the practice of law in Lonoke, Ark.; moved to Little Rock, Ark., in 1931 and continued the practice of law until his death there on April 27, 1935; interment in Lonoke Cemetery, Lonoke, Ark.

**REED, John** (father of John Reed [1781-1860]), a Representative from Massachusetts; born in Framingham, Mass., November 11, 1751; moved with his parents to Titicut Parish, in the northwestern part of Middleboro, Mass., in 1756; was graduated from Yale College in 1772; studied theology; was ordained as a Congregational minister in 1780; served as chaplain in the United States Navy for two years; moved to West Bridgewater, Mass., in 1780, where he became pastor of the First Congregational Society, which position he retained until his death; elected as a Federalist to the Fourth and to the two succeeding Congresses (March 4, 1795-March 3, 1801); was not a candidate for renomination in 1800 to the Seventh Congress; again resumed his ministerial duties; died in West Bridgewater, Plymouth County, Mass., on February 17, 1831; interment in the Old Graveyard.

REED, John (son of John Reed [1751-1831]), a Representative from Massachusetts; born in West Bridgewater, Mass., September 2, 1781; was graduated from Brown University, Providence, R.I., in 1803; tutor of languages in that institution for two years and principal of the Bridgewater (Mass.) Academy in 1806 and 1807; studied law; was admitted to the bar and commenced practice in Yarmouth, Mass.; elected as a Federalist to the Thirteenth and Fourteenth Congresses (March 4, 1813-March 3, 1817); elected to the Seventeenth through Twenty-third Congresses, elected as an Anti-Masonic candidate to the Twenty-fourth Congress, and elected as a Whig to the Twenty-fifth and Twenty-sixth Congresses (March 4, 1821-March 3, 1841); chairman, Committee on Revisal and Unfinished Business (Twenty-second Congress); declined to be candidate for reelection in 1840 to the Twenty-seventh Congress; Lieutenant Governor of Massachusetts, 1845-1851; died in West Bridgewater, Plymouth County, Mass., November 25, 1860.

REED, John Francis, a Representative from Rhode Island; born in Cranston, Providence County, R.I., November 12, 1949; graduated, La Salle Academy, Providence, R.I., 1967; B.S., United States Military Academy, 1971; M.P.P., John F. Kennedy School of Government, Harvard University, 1973; J.D., Harvard University Law School, 1982; admitted to Rhode Island bar, 1982; entered active duty, United States Army in 1967; released in 1979 as captain after service with Eighty-second Airborne Division; faculty at United States Military Academy, West Point, N.Y., department of social science, 1971-1979; United States Army Reserve, captain; practicing attorney, Washington, D.C., 1982-1983, and Providence, R.I., 1983-1990; member, Rhode Island State senate, 1985-1990; elected as a Democrat to the One Hundred Second and to the two succeeding Congresses (January 3, 1991-January 3, 1997); was not a candidate for reelection in 1996 to the House of Representatives, but was a candidate for election to the United States Senate; is a resident of Cranston, R.I.

REED, Joseph, a Delegate from Pennsylvania; was born in Trenton, N.J., August 27, 1741; attended Philadelphia Academy; graduated from the College of New Jersey (now Princeton University) in 1757; studied law; admitted to the bar in 1762; was a law student in the Temple in London; returned in 1767 and commenced practice in Trenton, N.J.; moved to Philadelphia, Pa., in October 1770; member of the committee of correspondence in 1774; president of the Pennsylvania convention in January 1775; accompanied General George Washington to Cambridge as his aide-de-camp and military secretary in July 1775; served during the campaign of 1776 as adjutant general of the Army from June 5, 1776, to January 22, 1777; Member of the Continental Congress in 1778; president of the supreme executive council of Pennsylvania, 1778-1781; trustee of the University of Pennsylvania, 1782-1785; died in Philadelphia, Pa., March 5, 1785; interment in the Arch Street Presbyterian Church Cemetery.

Bibliography: *DAB.*

REED, Joseph Rea, a Representative from Iowa; born in Ashland County, Ohio, March 12, 1835; attended the common schools and Vermillion Institution, Hayesville, Ohio, 1854-1857; moved to Adel, Dallas County, Iowa, in 1857; studied law; was admitted to the bar in 1859 and engaged in the practice of law at Adel until 1861; enlisted as first lieutenant in the Second Battery, Iowa Light Artillery, in July 1861, promoted to captain in October 1864, and served until June 10, 1865; resumed the practice of law in Adel; member of the Iowa State senate in 1866 and 1868; moved to

Council Bluffs, Iowa, in 1869; judge of the district court from 1872 until 1884; judge of the Iowa State supreme court, 1884-1889; elected as a Republican to the Fifty-first Congress (March 4, 1889-March 3, 1891); unsuccessful candidate for reelection in 1890 to the Fifty-second Congress; chief justice of the court of private land claims from 1891 to 1904; resumed the practice of law in Council Bluffs, Pottawattamie County, Iowa, where he died on April 2, 1925; interment in Walnut Hill Cemetery.

REED, Philip, a Senator and a Representative from Maryland; born near Chestertown, Kent County, Md., in 1760; completed preparatory studies; served in the Revolutionary Army, attaining the rank of captain of infantry; member of the Maryland State house of delegates in 1787; sheriff of Kent County, 1791-1794; member of the executive council, 1805-1806; elected as a Republican to the United States Senate in 1806 to fill the vacancy caused by the resignation of Robert Wright; reelected the same year, and served from November 25, 1806, to March 3, 1813; lieutenant colonel of the Twenty-first Regiment, Maryland Militia, in the War of 1812 and lieutenant colonel commandant of the First Regiment, Maryland Militia, in 1814; elected to the Fifteenth Congress (March 4, 1817-March 3, 1819); unsuccessful candidate for reelection in 1818 to the Sixteenth Congress; successfully contested the election of Jeremiah Cosden to the Seventeenth Congress, and served from March 19, 1822, to March 3, 1823; died in Huntingtown, Kent County, Md., November 2, 1829; interment in the cemetery of Christ Church, near Chestertown, Md.

REED, Robert Rentoul, a Representative from Pennsylvania; born in Washington, Pa., March 12, 1807; completed preparatory studies; was graduated from Washington and Jefferson College, Washington, Pa., in 1824, and from the medical department of the University of Pennsylvania in 1829; began the practice of medicine in Washington, Pa.; elected as a Whig to the Thirty-first Congress (March 4, 1849-March 3, 1851); member of the Pennsylvania house of representatives in 1863 and 1864; died near Washington, Washington County, Pa., on December 14, 1864; interment in Washington Cemetery.

REED, Stuart Felix, a Representative from West Virginia; born near Philippi, Barbour County, W.Va., January 8, 1866; attended the common schools; taught in country schools; was graduated from the Fairmont State Normal School in 1885, and from the law department of the University of West Virginia at Morgantown in 1889; founded and edited the Athenaeum (college journal) in 1889; editor of the Telegram in Clarksburg from 1890 until 1898; member of the West Virginia State senate, 1895-1899; postmaster of Clarksburg, 1897-1901; president of the board of trustees of Broaddus College, 1901-1908; member of the International Tax Conference at Louisville, Ky., in 1909; secretary of State of West Virginia from 1909 to 1917; president of the Association of American Secretaries of State in 1915; elected as a Republican to the Sixty-fifth and to the three succeeding Congresses (March 4, 1917-March 3, 1925); chairman, Committee on Expenditures in the Department of Justice (Sixty-seventh Congress), Committee on District of Columbia (Sixty-eighth Congress); declined to be a candidate for renomination in 1924 to the Sixty-ninth Congress; engaged in literary pursuits; resided in Washington, D.C., until his death there on July 4, 1935; interment in Elkview Masonic Cemetery, Clarksburg, W.Va.

REED, Thomas Brackett, a Representative from Maine; born in Portland, Cumberland County, Maine, October 18, 1839; attended the public schools; was graduated from Bowdoin College, Brunswick, Maine, in 1860; studied law; acting assistant paymaster, United States Navy, from April 19, 1864, to November 4, 1865; was admitted to the bar in 1865 and commenced practice in Portland, Maine; member of the Maine State house of representatives in 1868 and 1869; served in the State senate in 1870; attorney general of

Maine, 1870-1872; city solicitor of Portland, 1874-1877; elected as a Republican to the Forty-fifth and to the eleven succeeding Congresses and served from March 4, 1877, to September 4, 1899, when he resigned; chairman, Committee on the Judiciary (Forty-seventh Congress), Committee on Rules (Fifty-first, Fifty-fourth, and Fifty-fifth Congresses); Speaker of the House of Representatives (Fifty-first, Fifty-fourth, and Fifty-fifth Congresses); moved to New York City and engaged in the practice of his profession; died in Washington, D.C., on December 7, 1902; interment in Evergreen Cemetery, Portland, Maine.

**Bibliography:** *DAB*; Offenberg, Richard Stanley. "The Political Career of Thomas Brackett Reed." Ph.D. dissertation, New York University, 1963; Reed, Thomas Brackett. *Reed's Rules: A Manual of General Parliamentary Law*. Chicago: Rand McNally and Co., 1894; Robinson, William A. *Thomas B. Reed: Parliamentarian*. New York: Dodd, Mead, 1930.

**REED, Thomas Buck,** a Senator from Mississippi; born near Lexington, Ky., May 7, 1787; attended the public schools and the College of New Jersey (now Princeton University); studied law; was admitted to the bar and commenced practice in Lexington in 1808; moved to Natchez, Miss., in 1809; served as city clerk of Natchez in 1811; unsuccessful candidate for Delegate to Congress from Mississippi Territory in 1813; attorney general of Mississippi from 1821 until 1826; elected to the Mississippi State house of representatives in 1825, but declined to take his seat; elected to the United States Senate to fill the vacancy caused by the resignation of David Holmes, and served from January 28, 1826, to March 3, 1827; unsuccessful candidate for reelection in 1827; again elected to the United States Senate in 1828 and served from March 4, 1829, until his death in Lexington, Ky., November 26, 1829; interment in the Old Baptist Cemetery.

**REED, William,** a Representative from Massachusetts; born in Marblehead, Mass., June 6, 1776; received a limited education; engaged in mercantile pursuits; elected as a Federalist to the Twelfth and Thirteenth Congresses (March 4, 1811-March 3, 1815); member of the board of the Andover Theological Seminary; trustee of Dartmouth College, Hanover, N.H.; resumed mercantile pursuits; died in Marblehead, Essex County, Mass., February 18, 1837; interment in a private burying ground on Harris Street.

**REEDER, William Augustus,** a Representative from Kansas; born near Shippensburg, Cumberland County, Pa., August 28, 1849; moved with his parents to Ipava, Fulton County, Ill., in 1853; attended the public schools; taught school in Illinois 1863-1871; moved to Beloit, Mitchell County, Kans., in 1871; principal of the Beloit public schools 1871-1879; moved to Logan, Phillips County, Kans., in 1880 and engaged in banking; also interested in irrigation farming 1891-1901; elected as a Republican to the Fifty-sixth and to the five succeeding Congresses (March 4, 1899-March 3, 1911); chairman, Committee on Mileage (Fifty-seventh, Fifty-eighth, and Fifty-ninth Congresses), Committee on the Irrigation of Arid Lands (Sixtieth and Sixty-first Congresses); was an unsuccessful candidate for renomination in 1910; moved to Los Angeles, Calif., in 1911 and to Beverly Hills, Calif., in 1913, where he engaged in banking and in the real estate business until 1926; died in Beverly Hills, Calif., on November 7, 1929; interment in Hollywood Cemetery, Hollywood, Calif.

**REES, Edward Herbert,** a Representative from Kansas; born on a farm near Emporia, Lyon County, Kans., June 3, 1886; attended the public schools and the Kansas State Teachers' College at Emporia; taught school in Lyon County, Kans., 1909-1911; clerk of the court of Lyon County, Kans., 1912-1918; studied law; was admitted to the bar in 1915 and commenced practice in Emporia, Kans.; also engaged in agricultural pursuits; member of the Kansas State house of representatives, 1927-1933; served in the State senate, 1933-1935; member of the Kansas Judicial Council,

1933-1937; elected as a Republican to the Seventy-fifth and to the eleven succeeding Congresses (January 3, 1937-January 3, 1961); chairman, Committee on the Post Office and Civil Service (Eightieth and Eighty-third Congresses); was not a candidate for renomination in 1960 to the Eighty-seventh Congress; resumed the practice of law in Emporia, where he died on October 25, 1969; interment in Maplewood Cemetery.

**REES, Rollin Raymond,** a Representative from Kansas; born in Camden, Preble County, Ohio, January 10, 1865; moved with his parents to Ottawa County, Kans., in 1867; attended the public schools; was graduated from the agricultural college at Manhattan, Kans., in 1885; studied law; was admitted to the bar in 1887 and commenced practice in Minneapolis, Kans.; prosecuting attorney of Ottawa County, 1895-1899; member of the Kansas State house of representatives, 1899-1903; judge of the thirtieth judicial district, 1903-1910; resigned to become a candidate for Congress; elected as a Republican to the Sixty-second Congress (March 4, 1911-March 3, 1913); unsuccessful candidate for reelection in 1912 to the Sixty-third Congress; resumed the practice of law in Minneapolis, Ottawa County, Kans.; moved to California and engaged in banking and ranching; died in Anaheim, Calif., on May 30, 1935; interment in Fairhaven Cemetery, Orange, Calif.

**REES, Thomas Mankell,** a Representative from California; born in Los Angeles, Calif., on March 26, 1925; educated in local public schools; B.A., Occidental College, Los Angeles, 1950; attended University of California Law School, 1951; admitted to the California bar in 1973; served as a combat infantryman with General George S. Patton's Third Army during the Second World War; president of Compania del Pacifico, a Latin American export firm; member, California State assembly, 1954-1962; California State senator, 1962-1965; delegate to the Democratic National Conventions of 1956, 1960, 1964, and 1968; elected as a Democrat to the Eighty-ninth Congress, December 15, 1965, by special election to fill the vacancy caused by the resignation of James Roosevelt; reelected to the five succeeding Congresses, and served from December 15, 1965 to January 3, 1977; was not a candidate for reelection in 1976 to the Ninety-fifth Congress; commenced the practice of law in Washington, D.C., and San Jose, Calif.; president, Community Development and Management, San Jose, and proprietor, Vista Del Mare Vineyard, Santa Cruz; is a resident of Santa Cruz, Calif.

**REESE, David Addison,** a Representative from Georgia; born in Charlotte, N.C., March 3, 1794; attended the public schools and was instructed in the classics by a private tutor; studied medicine; was graduated from the Jefferson Medical College, Philadelphia, Pa., and commenced practice in Elberton, Ga.; moved to Monticello, Ga., and continued the practice of medicine; member of the State senate in 1829, 1830, 1834, 1835, and 1836; member of the board of trustees of the University of Georgia at Athens for twenty-five years; elected as a Whig to the Thirty-third Congress (March 4, 1853-March 3, 1855); moved to Auburn, Ala., and resumed the practice of medicine; died in Auburn December 16, 1871; interment in Hopewell Cemetery, West Point, Troup County, Ga.

**REESE, Seaborn,** a Representative from Georgia; born in Madison, Morgan County, Ga., November 28, 1846; attended a private school for boys in Hancock County and the University of Georgia at Athens, which institution he left in his senior year, 1868; studied law; was admitted to the bar in 1871 and commenced practice in Madison, Ga.; moved to Augusta and then to Sparta; member of the General Assembly of Georgia 1872-1874; solicitor general of the northern judicial circuit 1877-1880; elected as a Democrat to the Forty-seventh Congress to fill the vacancy caused by the resignation of Alexander H. Stephens; reelected to the Forty-eighth and Forty-ninth Congresses and served from December 4, 1882, to March 3, 1887; chairman, Committee on Expenditures in the Post Office Department (Forty-ninth Congress); judge of the northern judicial circuit 1893-1900; died in Sparta, Hancock County, Ga., March 1, 1907; interment in the Methodist Church Cemetery.

**REEVES, Albert Lee, Jr.,** a Representative from Missouri; born in Steelville, Crawford County, Mo., on May 31, 1906; attended the public schools of Kansas City, Mo.; was graduated from William Jewell College, Liberty, Mo., in 1927; taught at Baylor University in Waco, Tex., in 1927 and 1928; student at Harvard University in 1928 and 1929; was graduated from the University of Missouri Law School at Columbia in 1931; was admitted to the bar the same year and commenced practice in Kansas City, Mo.; entered on active duty in July 1942 as captain, Corps of Engineers, Missouri River Division, subsequently serving in India, Burma, and China; promoted through the ranks to lieutenant colonel and relieved from active duty April 23, 1946; resumed the practice of law; elected as a Republican to the Eightieth Congress (January 3, 1947-January 3, 1949); unsuccessful candidate for reelection in 1948 to the Eighty-first Congress; practiced law in Kansas City, Mo., and Washington, D.C.; senior vice president, Utah Construction & Mining Co., San Francisco, Calif.; director and secretary of Marcona Corporation and Affiliates; was a resident of Pauma Valley, Calif., until his death in La Jolla, Calif., on April 15, 1987; cremated; ashes buried at St. Francis Church, Pauma Valley.

**REEVES, Henry Augustus,** a Representative from New York; born in Sag Harbor, N.Y., December 7, 1832; attended private schools in Sag Harbor, the Southampton Academy, the University of Michigan at Ann Arbor for three years, and was graduated from Union College, Schenectady, N.Y., in 1852; studied law; was admitted to the bar; edited the Republican Watchman in Greenport from 1858 until his death; elected as a Democrat to the Forty-first Congress (March 4, 1869-March 3, 1871); resumed newspaper interests; supervisor of Southold Town 1872-1894; member of the State assembly in 1887; member of the State commission in lunacy 1889-1897; died in Greenport, Suffolk County, N.Y., March 4, 1916; interment in Southampton Cemetery, Southampton, N.Y.

Bibliography: Bethauser, Margaret O'Connor. "Henry A. Reeves: The Career of a Conservative Democratic Editor, 1858-1916." *Journal of Long Island History* 9 (Spring 1973): 34-43.

**REEVES, Walter,** a Representative from Illinois; born near Brownsville, Fayette County, Pa., September 25, 1848; moved with his parents to Illinois in 1856, where they settled upon a farm in La Salle County; attended the public schools; taught school; studied law; was admitted to the bar in Mount Vernon, Ill., in 1875, and commenced practice in Streator, Ill.; elected as a Republican to the Fifty-fourth and to the three succeeding Congresses (March 4, 1895-March 3, 1903); chairman, Committee on Patents (Fifty-seventh Congress); was not a candidate for renomination in 1902; unsuccessful candidate for the Republican nomination for Governor in 1900; resumed the practice of law; died in Streator, La Salle County, Ill., April 9, 1909; interment in Riverview Cemetery.

**REGAN, Kenneth Mills,** a Representative from Texas; born in Mount Morris, Ogle County, Ill., March 6, 1893; attended the public schools and Vincennes (Ind.) University; during the First World War served as a flyer in the United States Army Signal Corps; in 1920 engaged in the real estate business and as an oil operator in Pecos, Tex.; alderman of the city of Pecos; mayor of Pecos 1929-1932; member of the State senate 1933-1937; during the Second World War served as an intelligence officer in the Air Corps and was discharged with the rank of captain; moved to Midland, Tex., and continued oil operations; elected as a Democrat to the Eightieth Congress to fill the vacancy caused by the resignation of Robert Ewing Thomason; reelected to the Eighty-first, Eighty-second, and Eighty-third Congresses, and served from August 23, 1947, to January 3, 1955; unsuccessful candidate for renomination in 1954 to the Eighty-fourth Congress; representative of Texas railroads in

Washington, D.C.; died in Santa Fe, N.Mex., on August 15, 1959; interment in Resthaven Memorial Park, Midland, Tex.

**REGULA, Ralph Straus,** a Representative from Ohio; born in Beach City, Stark County, Ohio, December 3, 1924; attended the public schools; B.A., Mount Union College, Alliance, Ohio, 1948; LL.B., William McKinley School of Law, Canton, Ohio, 1952; served in the United States Navy, 1944-1946; school administrator, Stark County Board of Education, 1948-1955; admitted to the Ohio bar in 1952 and commenced practice in Navarre; member, Ohio State board of education, 1960-1964; member, Ohio State house of representatives, 1965-1966; member, Ohio State senate, 1967-1972; delegate to the Republican National Convention of 1972; elected as a Republican to the Ninety-third and to the eleven succeeding Congresses (January 3, 1973-January 3, 1997); is a resident of Navarre, Ohio.

**REID, Charles Chester,** a Representative from Arkansas; born in Clarksville, Johnson County, Ark., June 15, 1868; attended the public schools and the University of Arkansas at Fayetteville 1883-1885; was graduated from the law department of Vanderbilt University, Nashville, Tenn., in 1887; was admitted to the bar the same year and commenced practice in Morrillton, Ark.; prosecuting attorney of Conway County 1894-1898; voluntarily retired from office in 1898 and resumed the practice of law; elected as a Democrat to the Fifty-seventh and to the four succeeding Congresses (March 4, 1901-March 3, 1911); was not a candidate for renomination in 1910 to the Sixty-second Congress; again engaged in the practice of his profession in Little Rock, Ark., where he died on May 20, 1922; interment in Oakland Cemetery.

**REID, Charlotte Thompson,** a Representative from Illinois; born September 27, 1913, in Kankakee, Ill.; moved to Aurora, Ill.; attended the public schools of Aurora and Illinois College at Jacksonville, Ill.; professional singing career with the National Broadcasting Company under the name of Annette King; active in civic, community, and political affairs; elected as a Republican to the Eighty-eighth and to the four succeeding Congresses, and served from January 3, 1963 until her resignation on October 7, 1971, to become a member of the Federal Communications Commission, and served in that capacity until July 1976; member, President's Task Force on International Private Enterprise, 1983-1985; member, board of overseers, Hoover Institution, 1984 to 1988; is a resident of Frankfort, Mich.

**REID, David Settle** (nephew of Thomas Settle), a Representative and a Senator from North Carolina; born near Reidsville, Rockingham County, N.C., on April 19, 1813; attended the common schools and an academy; studied law; was admitted to the bar in 1833 and commenced practice in Wentworth, N.C., the following year; member, North Carolina State senate, 1835-1842; elected as a Democrat to the Twenty-eighth and Twenty-ninth Congresses (March 4, 1843-March 3, 1847); was not a candidate for renomination in 1846 to the Thirtieth Congress; unsuccessful candidate for Governor in 1848; elected Governor of North Carolina in 1850, reelected in 1852, and served from January 1, 1851 until his resignation on December 6, 1854, having been elected Senator; elected as a Democrat to the United States Senate to fill a vacancy in the term commencing March 4, 1853, caused by the failure of the legislature to elect, and served from December 6, 1854 until March 3, 1859; unsuccessful candidate for reelection; chairman, Committee on Patents and the Patent Office (Thirty-fifth Congress); delegate to the peace convention held at Washington, D.C., in 1861 in an effort to devise means to prevent the impending war; member of the State constitutional convention in 1875; practiced law at Reidsville, N.C., and died there on June 19, 1891; interment in Greenview Cemetery.

Bibliography: *DAB*; Reid, David Settle. *The Papers of David Settle Reid. 1829-1852*. Edited by Lindley S. Butler, Patricia R.

Johnson, E.T. Malone, Jr., and Ann Ward Little. Raleigh: Department of Cultural Resources, Division of Archives and History, 1993.

**REID, Frank R.,** a Representative from Illinois; born in Aurora, Kane County, Ill., April 18, 1879; attended the public schools, the University of Chicago, and the Chicago College of Law; was admitted to the bar in 1901 and commenced practice in Aurora, Ill.; prosecuting attorney of Kane County 1904-1908; State's attorney 1904-1908; assistant United States attorney at Chicago 1908-1910; member of the State house of representatives in 1911 and 1912; chairman of the Kane County Republican central committee 1914-1916; secretary of the League of Illinois Municipalities in 1916 and 1917; elected as a Republican to the Sixty-eighth and to the five succeeding Congresses (March 4, 1923-January 3, 1935); chairman, Committee on Flood Conrol (Sixty-ninth through Seventy-first Congresses); was not a candidate for renomination in 1934; engaged in the general practice of law at Chicago and Aurora, Ill.; died in Aurora, Ill., on January 25, 1945; interment in Spring Lake Cemetery.

**REID, Harry,** a Representative and a Senator from Nevada; born in Searchlight, Clark County, Nev., December 2, 1939; graduated, Basic High School, Henderson, Nev., 1957; A.A., Southern Utah State College, Cedar City, 1959; B.S., Utah State University, Logan, 1961; J.D., George Washington School of Law, Washington, D.C., 1964; United States Capitol police officer, 1961-1964; admitted to the Nevada bar in 1963 and practiced; city attorney, Henderson, Nev., 1964-1966; member of the Nevada State assembly, 1969-1970; lieutenant governor of Nevada, 1970-1974; unsuccessful candidate in 1974 for election to the United States Senate; chairman, Nevada Gaming Commission, 1977-1981; elected as a Democrat to the Ninety-eighth and Ninety-ninth Congresses (January 3, 1983-January 3, 1987); was not a candidate for reelection in 1986 to the House of Representatives, but was elected to the United States Senate for the term commencing January 2, 1987; reelected in 1992 for the term ending January 3, 1999; is a resident of Searchlight, Nev.

**REID, James Randolph,** a Delegate from Pennsylvania; born in Hamiltonban Township, York (now Adams) County, Pa., August 11, 1750; graduated from Princeton University with a bachelor of arts degree; served in the Revolutionary Army as a lieutenant and later was promoted to major in "Congress' Own" Regiment; received a land grant for services during the Revolution; Member of the Continental Congress 1787-1789; died in Middlesex, Cumberland County, Pa., January 25, 1789.

**REID, James Wesley,** a Representative from North Carolina; born in Wentworth, Rockingham County, N.C., June 11, 1849; pursued an academic course; was graduated from Emory and Henry College, Emory, Va., in 1869 and subsequently taught in the same college; studied law; was admitted to the bar in 1873 and commenced practice in Wentworth, N.C.; treasurer of Rockingham County 1874-1884; elected as a Democrat to the Forty-eighth Congress to fill the vacancy caused by the resignation of Alfred M. Scales; reelected to the Forty-ninth Congress and served from January 28, 1885, to December 31, 1886, when he resigned; moved to Lewiston, Idaho, in 1887 and engaged in the practice of law; member of the State constitutional convention in 1889 and vice president of that body; president of the board of trustees of the Lewiston State Normal College from 1893 until his death; delegate to the Democratic National Convention in 1896 and 1900; died in Lewiston, Nez Perce County, Idaho, January 1, 1902; interment in the Masonic Cemetery.

**REID, John William,** a Representative from Missouri; born near Lynchburg, Bedford County, Va., June 14, 1821; attended the common schools; moved to Missouri in 1840; taught school; studied law; was admitted to the bar and commenced practice in Jefferson City, Mo., in 1844; served as captain in the Mexican War; member, Missouri State house of representatives, 1854-1856; elected as a Democrat to the Thirty-seventh Congress, and served from March 4, 1861 to December 2, 1861; withdrew from the House of Representatives on August 3, 1861, and was expelled by the Thirty-seventh Congress on December 2, 1861, for having taken up arms against the Union; during the Civil War served in the Confederate Army as volunteer aide to General Sterling Price; appointed a commissioner to adjust claims against the Confederate Government; settled in Kansas City, Mo.; resumed the practice of his profession and engaged in banking; died at Lees Summit, Jackson County, Mo., November 22, 1881; interment in Elmwood Cemetery, Kansas City, Mo.

**REID, Ogden Rogers,** a Representative from New York; born in New York City, June 24, 1925; student, Deerfield Academy, 1940-1943; A.B., Yale University, 1949; fellow of Brandeis University and Bar-Ilan University, Israel; associated with the New York Herald-Tribune as president of Societe Anonyme and president, editor and director, 1953-1959; enlisted as a private in the United States Army in 1943 and discharged as a first lieutenant in 1946; captain, United States Army Reserve, inactive; appointed United States Ambassador to Israel on June 5, 1959, and served until January 1961; chairman, New York State Commission for Human Rights, 1961-1962; trustee, Hampton Institute; member of advisory council, School of International Affairs, Columbia University; vice president of National Institute of Social Sciences; director of Atlantic Council of the United States; elected as a Republican to the Eighty-eighth and to the four succeeding Congresses (January 3, 1963-January 3, 1973); announced his affiliation with the Democratic Party on March 22, 1972, and continued in office during the Ninety-second Congress as a Democrat; reelected as a Democrat to the Ninety-third Congress (January 3, 1973-January 3, 1975); was not a candidate for reelection in 1974 to the Ninety-fourth Congress, but was a candidate for nomination for Governor of New York until he withdrew from the race; commissioner of Environmental Conservation for the State of New York from January 1975 to May 1976; is a resident of Purchase, N.Y.

**REID, Robert Raymond,** a Representative from Georgia; born in Prince William Parish, Beaufort District, S.C., September 8, 1789; attended South Carolina College at Columbia; moved to Augusta, Ga.; studied law; was admitted to the bar and began practice in 1810; elected judge of the superior court of Georgia in 1816, and served until he was elected to Congress; elected as a Republican to the Fifteenth Congress to fill the vacancy caused by the resignation of John Forsyth; reelected to the Sixteenth and Seventeenth Congresses and served from February 18, 1819, to March 3, 1823; was not a candidate for renomination in 1822 to the Eighteenth Congress; judge of the middle circuit court of Georgia, 1823-1825; judge of the city court of Augusta, 1827-1832; United States judge for the district of east Florida, 1832-1839; appointed Governor of the Territory of Florida by President Martin Van Buren on December 2, 1839, and served until March 1841; president of the convention which framed a constitution for the State of Florida; died in Blackwood, near Tallahassee, Leon County, Fla., July 1, 1841.

**REIFEL, Benjamin,** a Representative from South Dakota; born on the Rosebud Indian Reservation near Parmelee, Todd County, S.Dak., September 19, 1906; attended Todd County rural schools; B.S., South Dakota State College, 1932; M.A., Harvard University, 1949, Ph.D., economics, 1952; served in the United States Army as a lieutenant colonel from 1942 to 1945, with service in Europe; employed by the Department of the Interior from 1933 until his resignation as Aberdeen area administrator in the Bureau of Indian Affairs in March 1960; elected as a Republican to the Eighty-seventh and to the four succeeding Congresses (January 3, 1961-January 3, 1971); was not a candidate for reelection in 1970 to the Ninety-second Congress; was a resident of Aberdeen, S.Dak.; died January 2, 1990.

**REILLY, James Bernard,** a Representative from Pennsylvania; born in Pinedale, West Brunswick Township, Schuylkill County, Pa., August 12, 1845; attended the public schools and was graduated from the Bunker Hill School, Pottsville, Pa., in 1862; studied law; was admitted to the bar in 1869 and commenced practice in Pottsville; district attorney of Schuylkill County 1871-1875; elected as a Democrat to the Forty-fourth and Forty-fifth Congresses (March 4, 1875-March 3, 1879); resumed the practice of law in Pottsville, Pa.; delegate to the Democratic National Convention in 1880; unsuccessful candidate for law judge of Schuylkill County in 1881 and again in 1882; unsuccessful Democratic candidate for election in 1884 to the Forty-ninth Congress; elected to the Fifty-first, Fifty-second, and Fifty-third Congresses (March 4, 1889-March 3, 1895); chairman, Committee on Pacific Railroads (Fifty-second and Fifty-third Congresses); unsuccessful candidate for reelection in 1894 to the Fifty-fourth Congress; United States marshal for the eastern district of Pennsylvania 1896-1900; again resumed the practice of law in Pottsville, Pa.; unsuccessful candidate for justice of the superior court in 1913; died in Pottsville, Schuylkill County, Pa., May 14, 1924; interment in St. Patrick's No. 3 Cemetery.

**REILLY, John,** a Representative from Pennsylvania; born in Abnerville, Indiana County, Pa., February 22, 1836; received home instruction and attended the public schools; entered the service of the Pennsylvania Railroad Co. April 10, 1854; appointed superintendent of transportation April 1, 1865; served until his resignation in 1875, having been elected to Congress; president of the Bells Gap Railroad Co. 1871-1873; president of the board of city commissioners of Altoona in 1872 and 1873; elected as a Democrat to the Forty-fourth Congress (March 4, 1875-March 3, 1877); unsuccessful candidate for reelection in 1876 to the Forty-fifth Congress; again superintendent of transportation of the Pennsylvania Railroad Co. and served from 1877 until his resignation in 1885; moved to Philadelphia, Pa., in 1881; interested in various business enterprises; died in Philadelphia, Pa., April 19, 1904; interment in West Laurel Hill Cemetery.

**REILLY, Michael Kieran,** a Representative from Wisconsin; born in Empire, Fond du Lac County, Wis., July 15, 1869; attended the public schools; was graduated from Oshkosh Normal School in 1889, from the University of Wisconsin at Madison in 1894, and from the law department of the latter university in 1895; was admitted to the bar the same year and commenced practice in Fond du Lac, Wis.; district attorney of Fond du Lac County in 1899 and 1900; city attorney 1905-1910; delegate to the Democratic National Conventions in 1908 and 1924; elected as a Democrat to the Sixty-third and Sixty-fourth Congresses (March 4, 1913-March 3, 1917); unsuccessful candidate for reelection in 1916 to the Sixty-fifth Congress; resumed the practice of law; again elected to the Seventy-first Congress to fill the vacancy caused by the death of Florian Lampert; reelected to the Seventy-second and to the three succeeding Congresses and served from November 4, 1930, to January 3, 1939; unsuccessful candidate for reelection in 1938 to the Seventy-sixth Congress; resumed the practice of his chosen profession; died in a hospital in Neptune, N.J., October 14, 1944; interment in Woodlawn Cemetery, Woodlawn, N.Y.

**REILLY, Thomas Lawrence,** a Representative from Connecticut; was born in New Britain, Hartford County, Conn., September 20, 1858; attended the common schools and was graduated from the Connecticut State Normal School in 1876; assistant town clerk of New Britain in 1876; moved with his parents to Meriden, Conn., in 1877; studied law for a year; employed as a bookkeeper for several years; engaged as a newspaper correspondent until 1886; one of the founders of the Meriden Journal in 1886 and became the city editor;

member of the Meriden Board of Education 1896-1903; chairman of the town committee in 1900; mayor of Meriden 1906-1912; elected as a Democrat to the Sixty-second and Sixty-third Congresses (March 4, 1911-March 3, 1915); unsuccessful candidate for reelection in 1914 to the Sixty-fourth Congress; employed in the Internal Revenue Service in 1916 and 1917; elected sheriff of New Haven County in 1918; reelected and served until his death in New Haven, Conn., July 6, 1924; interment in Sacred Heart Cemetery, Meriden, Conn.

**REILLY, Wilson,** a Representative from Pennsylvania; was born in Waynesboro, Franklin County, Pa., August 8, 1811; attended the common schools; engaged as a hatter in Waynesboro and Chambersburg, Pa.; studied law; was admitted to the bar in 1837 and commenced practice in Chambersburg, Pa.; prosecuting attorney of Franklin County 1842-1845; unsuccessful Democratic candidate for election in 1854 to the Thirty-fourth Congress; elected to the Thirty-fifth Congress (March 4, 1857-March 3, 1859); chairman, Committee on Expenditures in the Department of War (Thirty-fifth Congress); unsuccessful candidate for reelection in 1858 to the Thirty-sixth Congress; became captain of the McClure Rifles, which joined the Pennsylvania Reserve Corps at Camp Curtin, Harrisburg, Pa.; resumed the practice of law; died in Chambersburg, Franklin County, Pa., August 26, 1885; interment in Falling Spring Cemetery.

**REILY, Luther,** a Representative from Pennsylvania; born in Myerstown, Pa., October 17, 1794; completed preparatory studies; studied medicine and began practice in Harrisburg; held various local offices; in the War of 1812 served as a private in Capt. R.M. Crane's company of Pennsylvania Volunteers from August 3 to September 7, 1814, and as surgeon's mate in Major General R. Watson's company from September 7 to December 5, 1814; resumed the practice of medicine; elected as a Democrat to the Twenty-fifth Congress (March 4, 1837-March 3, 1839); again resumed the practice of his profession; died in Harrisburg, Pa., on February 20, 1854; interment in Harrisburg Cemetery.

**REINECKE, Edwin,** a Representative from California; born in Medford, Jackson County, Oreg., January 7, 1924; attended the public schools of Beverly Hills, Calif.; B.S., California Institute of Technology, Pasadena, 1950; enlisted in the United States Navy in November 1942 and was discharged as a radio technician second class in February 1946; was in officers' training (V-12) at time of discharge; professional mechanical engineer in California since 1952; president of Febco, Inc., manufacturers of lawn irrigation equipment, 1964; elected as a Republican to the Eighty-ninth and to the two succeeding Congresses, and served from January 3, 1965, until his resignation, January 21, 1969; appointed Lieutenant Governor of California on January 8, 1969, and served until October 2, 1974; unsuccessful candidate in 1974 for nomination for Governor of California; vice-chairman, California Republican party, 1981-1983, chairman, 1983-1985; is a resident of Lake Tahoe, Calif.

**RELFE, James Hugh,** a Representative from Missouri; born in Virginia October 17, 1791; moved to Washington County, Mo., about 1816 with his father, who settled in Caledonia; received a limited schooling; studied medicine and practiced in Caledonia, Mo.; appointed a member of the commission to adjust Spanish land claims to fill the vacancy occasioned by the resignation of Dr. Lewis F. Linn; member of the State house of representatives 1835-1844; served in the Black Hawk War; appointed United States marshal for the district of Missouri February 17, 1841; elected as a Democrat to the Twenty-eighth and Twenty-ninth Congresses (March 4, 1843-March 3, 1847); continued the practice of medicine in Caledonia, Washington County, Mo., until his death there September 14, 1863; interment in the Methodist Cemetery.

**REMANN, Frederick,** a Representative from Illinois; born in Vandalia, Fayette County, Ill., May 10, 1847; attended the common schools of Vandalia and the Mifflin (Pa.) Academy; was graduated from the Iron City Business College, Pittsburgh, Pa., in April 1865; during the Civil War served as corporal in Company E, One Hundred and Forty-third Regiment, Illinois Volunteer Infantry; again attended Mifflin Academy in 1866 and 1867 and was graduated from Illinois College at Jacksonville in 1868; returned to Vandalia and engaged in mercantile pursuits; served as county supervisor of Fayette County and as alderman of Vandalia; delegate to numerous Republican State conventions; member of the State house of representatives in 1877 and 1878; elected as a Republican to the Fifty-fourth Congress and served from March 4, 1895, until his death in Vandalia, Ill., July 14, 1895, before the convening of Congress; interment in South Hill Cemetery.

**RENCHER, Abraham,** a Representative from North Carolina; born near Raleigh, Wake County, N.C., August 12, 1798; tutored at home and attended the common schools and Pittsboro (N.C.) Academy; was graduated from the University of North Carolina at Chapel Hill in 1822; studied law; was admitted to the bar in 1825 and commenced practice in Pittsboro, Chatham County, N.C.; elected as a Jacksonian to the Twenty-first and Twenty-second Congresses, as an Anti-Jacksonian to the Twenty-third and Twenty-fourth Congresses, and as a Whig to the Twenty-fifth Congress (March 4, 1829-March 3, 1839); declined to be a candidate for renomination in 1838 to the Twenty-sixth Congress; elected to the Twenty-seventh Congress (March 4, 1841-March 3, 1843); declined to be candidate for renomination in 1842 to the Twenty-eighth Congress on account of ill health; appointed Minister to Portugal on September 22, 1843 and served until November 1847; appointed Governor of New Mexico Territory by President James Buchanan, and served from 1857 to 1861; retired to his home in Pittsboro, N.C.; died in Chapel Hill, N.C., July 6, 1883; interment in St. Bartholomew's Protestant Episcopal Churchyard, Pittsboro, N.C.

**RESA, Alexander John,** a Representative from Illinois; born in Chicago, Ill., August 4, 1887; attended the public schools of Chicago, Ill., and St. Joseph's College, Kirkwood, Mo.; was graduated from the John Marshall Law School, Chicago, Ill., in 1911; was admitted to the bar the same year and commenced practice in Chicago, Ill., assistant corporation counsel of the city of Chicago, serving as head of the appeals division and public improvement division 1937-1944; member of the faculty of the John Marshall Law School 1918-1942; elected as a Democrat to the Seventy-ninth Congress (January 3, 1945-January 3, 1947); unsuccessful candidate for reelection in 1946 to the Eightieth Congress; returned to practice of law and retired December 31, 1959; died in Evanston, Ill., July 4, 1964; interment in Calvary Cemetery.

**RESNICK, Joseph Yale,** a Representative from New York; born in Ellenville, Ulster County, N.Y., July 13, 1924; educated in electronics; during the Second World War served as a radio officer in the United States Merchant Marine; founder and chairman of the board of Channel Master Corp.; engaged in electronics and plastic research and development; member of Ellenville School Board; elected as a Democrat to the Eighty-ninth and Ninetieth Congresses (January 3, 1965-January 3, 1969); was not a candidate for reelection to the House of Representatives in 1968 but was an unsuccessful candidate for nomination to the United States Senate; returned to business interests; died in Las Vegas, Nev., while enroute to California on a business trip, October 6, 1969; interment in Hebrew Aid Society Cemetery, Wawarsing, N.Y.

**REUSS, Henry Schoellkopf,** a Representative from Wisconsin; born in Milwaukee, Wis., February 22, 1912; attended Milwaukee schools; A.B., Cornell University, Ithaca, N.Y., 1933; LL.B., Harvard University Law School, 1936; was admitted to the bar in 1936 and commenced the practice of law in Milwaukee, Wis.; assistant

corporation counsel for Milwaukee County, 1939-1940; assistant general counsel for the Office of Price Administration, Washington, D.C., 1941-1942; entered the United States Army as a private in January 1943; commissioned a second lieutenant in November 1943, and served with the Sixty-third and Seventy-fifth Infantry Divisions until 1945; chief of price control, Office of Military Government for Germany, in 1945; awarded the Bronze Star Medal; engaged in private law practice from 1936 until 1955; deputy general counsel for the European Recovery Program (Marshall Plan) in Paris, 1949; special prosecutor, Milwaukee County Grand Jury, 1950; lecturer at Wisconsin State College, 1950-1951; member of the Milwaukee School Board, 1953-1954; personal counsel to the secretary of state for reapportionment and redistricting case in 1953; president of White Elm Nursery Co., Hartland, Wis., 1949-1953; director of Marshall & Ilsley Bank, Milwaukee, Wis., 1946-1948, and Niagara Share Corp., Buffalo, N.Y., 1947-1949; member of legal advisory committee, National Resources Board, Washington, D.C., 1948-1952; unsuccessful candidate for mayor of Milwaukee in 1960; elected as a Democrat to the Eighty-fourth and to the thirteen succeeding Congresses (January 3, 1955-January 3, 1983); was not a candidate for reelection in 1982 to the Ninety-eighth Congress; chairman, Committee on Banking, Currency, and Housing (Ninety-fourth Congress), Committee on Banking, Finance, and Urban Affairs (Ninety-fifth and Ninety-sixth Congresses); Joint Economic Committee (Ninety-seventh Congress); is a resident of Belvedere, Calif.

**Bibliography:** Reuss, Henry S. "Reflections of a Wisconsin Congressman of German Descent." *Yearbook of German-American Studies* 19 (1984): 17-22.

**REVELS, Hiram Rhodes,** a Senator from Mississippi; born of free parents in Fayetteville, Cumberland County, N.C., September 27, 1827; attended various schools and seminaries and Knox College, Galesburg, Ill.; barber; ordained a minister in the African Methodist Episcopal Church at Baltimore, Md., in 1845; carried on religious work in Indiana, Illinois, Kansas, Kentucky, Tennessee, and Missouri; accepted a pastorate in Baltimore, Md., in 1860; at the outbreak of the Civil War assisted in recruiting two regiments of African-Americans in Maryland; served in Vicksburg, Miss., as chaplain of an African-American regiment, and organized African-American churches in that State; established a school for freedmen in St. Louis, Mo., in 1863; settled in Natchez, Miss., in 1866; elected alderman in 1868; member of the Mississippi State senate in 1870; upon the readmission of Mississippi to representation was elected as a Republican to the United States Senate, and served from February 23, 1870 to March 3, 1871; first African-American Senator; secretary of State ad interim of Mississippi in 1873; president of the Alcorn Agricultural College (now Alcorn State University), Rodney, Miss., the first land-grant college in the United States for African-American students, from 1876 until his retirement in 1882; moved to Holly Springs, Marshall County, Miss.; continued his religious work as a district superintendent of the African Methodist Episcopal Church, and as a teacher of theology at Shaw (later Rust) College in Holly Springs; died in Aberdeen, Miss., January 16, 1901; interment in Hill Crest Cemetery, Holly Springs, Miss.

**Bibliography:** *DAB*; Gibbs, Warmoth. "Hiram R. Revels and His Times." *Quarterly Review of Higher Education Among Negroes* 8 (January 1940): 25-37, 8 (April 1940): 64-91; Thompson, Julius. *Hiram R. Revels, 1827-1901: A Biography.* New York: Arno Press, 1982.

**REVERCOMB, William Chapman,** a Senator from West Virginia; born in Covington, Alleghany County, Va., July 20, 1895; attended the public schools at Covington, Va.; attended Washington and Lee University, Lexington, Va., 1914-1916; graduated from law department of the University of Virginia at Charlottesville in 1919; was admitted to the bar the same year and practiced in Covington, Va.; during the First World War enlisted in the United States Army and served as a corporal 1917-1919; moved to Charleston, W.Va., in 1922 and continued the practice of law; chairman of the State judicial convention of 1936; elected as a Republican to the United States Senate in 1942 and served from January 3, 1943, to January 3, 1949; unsuccessful candidate for reelection in 1948 and for election in 1952; chairman, Committee on Public Works (Eightieth Congress), Special Committee on the Roof and Sky Lights (Eightieth Congress); elected to the United States Senate in 1956 to fill the vacancy caused by the death of Harley M. Kilgore and served from November 7, 1956, to January 3, 1959; unsuccessful candidate for reelection in 1958 and for the gubernatorial nomination in 1960; resumed the practice of law; resided in Charleston, W.Va., where he died October 6, 1979; interment in Sunset Memorial Park, South Charleston, W.Va.

**REYBURN, John Edgar** (father of William Stuart Reyburn), a Representative from Pennsylvania; born in New Carlisle, Clark County, Ohio, February 7, 1845; was instructed by a private tutor and attended Saunders Institute, West Philadelphia, Pa.; studied law; admitted to the bar in 1870 and commenced practice in Philadelphia; member of the Pennsylvania house of representatives in 1871 and 1874-1876; member of the Pennsylvania senate 1876-1892 and served as president pro tempore during the session of 1883; elected as a Republican to the Fifty-first Congress to fill the vacancy caused by the death of William D. Kelley; reelected to the Fifty-second, Fifty-third, and Fifty-fourth Congresses and served from February 18, 1890, to March 3, 1897; unsuccessful candidate for renomination in 1896; elected to the Fifty-ninth Congress to fill the vacancy caused by the death of Robert Adams; reelected to the Sixtieth Congress and served from November 6, 1906, to March 31, 1907, when he resigned, having been elected mayor of Philadelphia, Pa.; served as mayor from April 1, 1907, to December 4, 1911; engaged in manufacturing in Philadelphia, but retained a residence in Washington, D.C., where he died on January 4, 1914; interment in Laurel Hill Cemetery, Philadelphia, Pa.

**REYBURN, William Stuart** (son of John Edgar Reyburn), a Representative from Pennsylvania; born in Philadelphia, Pa., December 17, 1882; attended the Hill School, Pottstown, Pa.; graduated from Yale University in 1904 and from the law department of Georgetown University, Washington, D.C.; admitted to the bar in 1908 and commenced practice in Washington, D.C.; member of Secretary of War William Howard Taft's party which visited the Philippines, Japan, and China in 1905; served in the Pennsylvania house of representatives from 1909 until May 25, 1911, when he resigned; elected as a Republican to the Sixty-second Congress to fill the vacancy caused by the death of Joel Cook, and served from May 23, 1911, to March 3, 1913; declined to be a candidate for renomination in 1912 to the Sixty-third Congress; resumed the practice of his profession in Washington, D.C., and subsequently retired from active business pursuits; resided in Aiken, S.C., and later moved to his estate "Black Hill," Old Lyme, Conn.; died in New Haven, Conn., on July 25, 1946; interment in Laurel Hill Cemetery, Philadelphia, Pa.

**REYNOLDS, Edwin Ruthvin,** a Representative from New York; born at Fort Ann, N.Y., February 16, 1816; pursued classical studies; was principal of Albion Academy, Orleans County, N.Y., for six years; was county superintendent 1843-1845; studied law; was admitted to the bar in 1843 and commenced practice in Albion, N.Y., in 1846; elected as a Republican to the Thirty-sixth Congress to fill the vacancy caused by the death of Silas M. Burroughs and served from December 5, 1860, to March 3, 1861; judge and surrogate of Orleans County 1864-1868; resumed the practice of law; died in Albion, N.Y., July 4, 1908; interment in Mount Albion Cemetery.

**REYNOLDS, Gideon,** a Representative from New York; born in Petersburg, N.Y., August 9, 1813; educated in private schools; moved with his father to Hoosick in 1836 and engaged in agricultural pursuits; member of the State assembly in 1839; sheriff of Rensselaer County, N.Y., 1843-1846; elected as a Whig to the Thirtieth and Thirty-first Congresses (March 4, 1847-March 3, 1851); was not a candidate for renomination in 1850; resumed agricultural pursuits in Rensselaer County; delegate to the Republican National Conventions in 1856 and 1860; member of the Republican State central committee; was appointed internal revenue collector for the fifteenth district of New York on September 9, 1862, and served until March 31, 1865, when he resigned; member of the board of supervisors of Hoosick in 1875; died in Hoosick, Rensselaer County, N.Y., July 13, 1896; interment in the Hoosick Rural Cemetery.

**REYNOLDS, James B.,** a Representative from Tennessee; born in County Antrim, Ireland, in 1779; attended the common schools; immigrated to the United States and settled in Clarksville, Tenn.; studied law; was admitted to the bar in 1804 and practiced; elected as a Republican to the Fourteenth Congress (March 4, 1815-March 3, 1817); elected to the Eighteenth Congress (March 4, 1823-March 3, 1825); resumed the practice of law; died in Clarksville, Tenn., June 10, 1851; interment in the City Cemetery.

**REYNOLDS, John,** a Representative from Illinois; born in Montgomery County, near Philadelphia, Pa., February 26, 1788; moved to Illinois in 1800 with his parents, who settled in the vicinity of Kaskaskia; pursued classical studies; studied law; was admitted to the bar and commenced practice in Cahokia, Ill., in 1812; elected a justice of the Illinois Supreme Court in 1818; unsuccessful candidate for election to the United States Senate in 1823; member of the Illinois State house of representatives, 1827-1829; elected Governor of Illinois in 1830, and served from December 6, 1830 to November 17, 1834, when he resigned, having been elected to Congress; in 1832 took the field as commander of the State militia in the Black Hawk War; elected as a Jacksonian to the Twenty-third Congress to fill the vacancy caused by the death of Charles Slade; reelected to the Twenty-fourth Congress, and served from December 1, 1834 to March 3, 1837; unsuccessful candidate for reelection in 1836 to the Twenty-fifth Congress; elected as a Democrat to the Twenty-sixth and Twenty-seventh Congresses (March 4, 1839-March 3, 1843); again a member of the State house of representatives in 1846 and 1852, and served during the latter term as speaker; unsuccessful candidate for election to the State senate in 1848; unsuccessful candidate for State superintendent of schools in 1858; engaged in newspaper work; died in Belleville, St. Clair County, Ill., May 8, 1865; interment in Walnut Hill Cemetery.

**Bibliography:** *DAB*; Harper, Josephine L. "John Reynolds, The 'Old Ranger' of Illinois, 1788-1865." Ph.D. dissertation, University of Illinois Urbana-Champaign, 1949.

**REYNOLDS, John Hazard,** a Representative from New York; born in Moriah, N.Y., June 21, 1819; attended the public schools in Sandy Hill (now Hudson Falls), N.Y., and Bennington, Vt.; engaged in civil engineering; was graduated from Kinderhook Academy in 1840; studied law; was admitted to the bar and began practice in Kinderhook in 1843; moved to Albany in 1851 and continued the practice of law; elected as an Anti-Lecompton Democrat to the Thirty-sixth Congress (March 4, 1859-March 3, 1861); was not a candidate for renomination in 1860; resumed the practice of his profession; appointed a judge of the commission of appeals of the State in 1873, which position he held until the expiration of the court by limitation July 1, 1875; died in Kinderhook, Columbia County, N.Y., September 24, 1875; interment in Kinderhook Cemetery.

**REYNOLDS, John Merriman,** a Representative from Pennsylvania; born near Quarryville, Lancaster County, Pa., March 5, 1848; attended the public schools; graduated from the first Pennsylvania normal school in 1867 and from Columbian (now George Washington) University, Washington, D.C., in 1895; principal of public schools of Bedford, Pa., 1867-1869; studied law; admitted to the bar on February 15, 1870, and commenced practice in Bedford, Pa.; publisher of the Bedford Gazette, 1872-1880; member of the Pennsylvania house of representatives in 1873 and 1874; prosecuting attorney of Bedford County, 1875-1879; president of the board of education of Bedford, 1884-1900; delegate to the Democratic National Conventions of 1888 and 1892; engaged in the banking business in 1893; Assistant Secretary of the Interior from April 15, 1893 to June 1, 1897; elected as a Republican to the Fifty-ninth and to the two succeeding Congresses, and served from March 4, 1905 to January 17, 1911, when he resigned to accept the office of Lieutenant Governor of Pennsylvania, which office he held from 1911 to 1915; resumed the practice of law and again engaged in banking in Bedford, Pa.; member of the commission to revise the banking laws of the Commonwealth of Pennsylvania, 1917-1925; died in Bedford, Pa., September 14, 1933; interment in Bedford Cemetery.

**REYNOLDS, Joseph,** a Representative from New York; born in Easton, Washington County, N.Y., September 14, 1785; completed academic studies; moved to Virgil, N.Y., in 1809; engaged in agricultural pursuits; organized a company of riflemen for service in the War of 1812; was major, colonel, and brigadier general in the State troops; justice of the peace 1815-1837; member of the State assembly in 1818; judge of Cortland County 1821-1839; supervisor of the town of Cortlandville 1825-1835; elected as a Jacksonian to the Twenty-fourth Congress (March 4, 1835-March 3, 1837); first president of the village of Cortland in 1864; died in Cortland, Cortland County, N.Y., September 24, 1864; interment in the Cortland Rural Cemetery.

**REYNOLDS, Melvin Jay,** a Representative from Illinois; born in Mound Bayou, Bolivar County, Miss., January 8, 1952; A.A., Chicago City College, 1972; B.A., University of Illinois, 1974; LL.B., Oxford University, 1979, and M.A., 1981; M.P.A., John F. Kennedy School of Government, Harvard University; assistant professor, Roosevelt University, Chicago; executive director, Community Economic Development and Education Foundation; radio talk show host; member, executive committee, Chicago chapter of the National Association for the Advancement of Colored People; special assistant to the vice president, academic affairs, University of Illinois; founder and former president, American Scholars Against World Hunger; unsuccessful candidate for nomination in 1988 to the One Hundred First Congress and in 1990 to the One Hundred Second Congress; elected as a Democrat to the One Hundred Third and One Hundred Fourth Congresses, and served from January 3, 1993 until his resignation on October 1, 1995; is a resident of Chicago, Ill.

**REYNOLDS, Robert Rice,** a Senator from North Carolina; born in Asheville, Buncombe County, N.C., June 18, 1884; attended the public schools, Weaverville (N.C.) College, and the University of North Carolina at Chapel Hill; studied law; was admitted to the bar in 1907 and commenced practice in Asheville, N.C.; served as prosecuting attorney of the fifteenth judicial district of North Carolina 1910-1914; unsuccessful candidate for nomination for lieutenant governor in 1924 and for United States Senator in 1926; presidential elector in 1928 on the Democratic ticket; elected as a Democrat on November 8, 1932, to the United States Senate to fill the vacancy caused by the death of Lee S. Overman for the term ending March 3, 1933, and on the same day was elected for the term beginning March 4, 1933; reelected in 1938 and served from December 5, 1932, to January 3, 1945; was not a candidate for renomination in 1944; chairman, Committee on the District of Columbia (Seventy-seventh Congress), Committee on Military Affairs (Seventy-seventh and Seventy-eighth Congresses); unsuccessful candidate for the United States Senate in 1950; practiced law in Washington, D.C., and operated a large estate near Asheville,

N.C.; died in Asheville, N.C., February 13, 1963; interment in Riverside Cemetery.

**Bibliography:** *DAB*; Pleasants, Julian. "The Senatorial Career of Robert Rice Reynolds." Ph.D. dissertation, University of North Carolina, 1971.

**REYNOLDS, Samuel Williams,** a Senator from Nebraska; born in Omaha, Douglas County, Nebr., August 11, 1890; attended the public schools; engaged in the wholesale coal business in Omaha, Nebr., in 1908; served in the Air Service during the First World War 1917-1918; during the Second World War served as a colonel in the Army Specialist Corps as director of corps activities in Omaha 1942-1943; appointed as a Republican to the United States Senate to fill the vacancy caused by the death of Hugh Butler and served from July 3, 1954, to November 7, 1954; was not a candidate for election to fill the vacancy; resumed wholesale coal business; member, Omaha City Council, 1957-1958; a resident of Omaha, Nebr., until his death there on March 20, 1988; interment in Forest Lawn Memorial Park.

**RHEA, John,** a Representative from Tennessee; born in the parish of Langhorn, County Londonderry, Ireland, in 1753; immigrated to the United States in 1769 with his parents, who settled in Philadelphia, Pa.; moved to Piney Creek, Md., in 1771 and to eastern Tennessee in 1778; completed preparatory studies and was graduated from Princeton College in 1780; member of the Patriot force in the Battle of King's Mountain, S.C., October 7, 1780; clerk of the Sullivan County Court in the proposed State of Franklin and subsequently in North Carolina, 1785-1790; member of the house of commons of North Carolina; was a delegate to the North Carolina State convention that ratified the Federal Constitution in 1789; studied law; was admitted to the bar in 1789; delegate to the constitutional convention of Tennessee in 1796; attorney general of Greene County, Tenn., in 1796; member of the Tennessee State house of representatives in 1796 and 1797; elected as a Republican to the Eighth and to the five succeeding Congresses (March 4, 1803-March 3, 1815); chairman, Committee on the Post Office and Post Roads (Tenth through Thirteenth Congresses), Committee on Pensions and Revolutionary Claims (Fifteenth through Seventeenth Congresses); appointed United States commissioner to treat with the Choctaw Nation in 1816; elected to the Fifteenth and to the two succeeding Congresses (March 4, 1817-March 3, 1823); actively connected with higher education in Tennessee; retired from active pursuits and resided on the Rhea plantation near Blountville, Sullivan County, Tenn., where he died May 27, 1832; interment in the Blountville Cemetery.

**Bibliography:** *DAB*; Hamer, Marguerite B. "John Rhea of Tennessee." *East Tennessee Historical Society's Publications* 4 (January 1932): 35-44.

**RHEA, John Stockdale,** a Representative from Kentucky; born in Russellville, Logan County, Ky., March 9, 1855; pursued preparatory studies; attended Bethel College, Russellville, Ky., and Washington and Lee University, Lexington, Va.; studied law; was admitted to the bar and commenced practice in 1873; prosecuting attorney for Logan County in 1878 and 1882; presidential elector on the Democratic ticket in 1884 and 1888; delegate to the Democratic National Conventions in 1892 and 1896; elected as a Democrat to the Fifty-fifth and Fifty-sixth Congresses (March 4, 1897-March 3, 1901); presented credentials as a Member-elect to the Fifty-seventh Congress and served from March 4, 1901, to March 25, 1902, when he was succeeded by J. McKenzie Moss, who contested his election; elected to the Fifty-eighth Congress (March 4, 1903-March 3, 1905); was not a candidate for renomination in 1904; resumed the practice of his profession in Russellville; appointed circuit court judge in 1913 and subsequently elected in 1915 and served until January 1, 1922; died in Russellville, Ky., on July 29, 1924; interment in Maple Grove Cemetery.

**RHEA, William Francis,** a Representative from Virginia; born on a farm near Bristol, Washington County, Va., April 20, 1858; attended rural and private schools; graduated from King College, Bristol, Tenn., in 1878; studied law; was admitted to the bar in 1879 and commenced practice in Bristol, Va.; judge of the Washington County Court 1880-1885; member of the Virginia senate 1885-1888; judge of the city court of Bristol; resigned in 1895 and resumed the practice of law; elected as a Democrat to the Fifty-sixth and Fifty-seventh Congresses (March 4, 1899-March 3, 1903); unsuccessful candidate for reelection in 1902 to the Fifty-eighth Congress; resumed the practice of law in Bristol, Va.; moved to Richmond, Va., when appointed a member of the Virginia corporation commission in 1908 and served until 1925; died in Richmond, Va., March 23, 1931; interment in Hollywood Cemetery.

**RHETT, Robert Barnwell** a Representative and a Senator from South Carolina; born Robert Barnwell Smith in Beaufort, S.C., December 21, 1800; completed preparatory studies; studied law; was admitted to the bar and commenced practice in Beaufort in 1824; elected to the State house of representatives for St. Bartholomew's Parish in 1826, 1828, 1830, and 1832; elected attorney general of South Carolina in 1832; elected as a Democrat to the Twenty-fifth and to the five succeeding Congresses (March 4, 1837-March 3, 1849); changed his name to Robert Barnwell Rhett in 1838; member of the Nashville convention in 1850; elected as a Democrat to the United States Senate to fill the vacancy caused by the death of John C. Calhoun and served from December 18, 1850, until his resignation effective May 7, 1852; delegate to the South Carolina secession convention in 1860; delegate to the Confederate Provisional Congress in 1861; chairman of the committee which reported the constitution of the Confederate States; moved to St. James Parish, La., in 1867; died in St. James Parish, La., on September 14, 1876; interment in Magnolia Cemetery, Charleston, S.C.

Bibliography: *DAB*; Barnwell, John. "Hamlet to Hotspur: Letters of Robert Woodward Barnwell to Robert Barnwell Rhett." *South Carolina Historical Magazine* 77 (October 1976): 236-56; White, Laura. *Robert Barnwell Rhett, Father of Secession.* 1931. Reprint. Gloucester, Mass.: P. Smith, 1965.

**RHINOCK, Joseph Lafayette,** a Representative from Kentucky; born in Owenton, Owen County, Ky., January 4, 1863; moved to Covington, Ky.; attended the Covington public schools; engaged in the oil-refining business; president of the Covington Public Library Board two terms; member of the city council of Covington; mayor 1893-1900; elected as a Democrat to the Fifty-ninth, Sixtieth, and Sixty-first Congresses (March 4, 1905-March 3, 1911); was not a candidate for renomination in 1910; for twenty-two years was connected with theatrical enterprises in New York City and Cincinnati, Ohio, serving as vice president, secretary, and treasurer of the Shubert theatrical companies; vice president of the Loew theatrical enterprises; became actively interested in horse racing and racetrack corporations; died at his home, "Bonnie Crest," New Rochelle, Westchester County, N.Y., on September 20, 1926; interment in Highland Cemetery, Covington, Ky.

**RHOADS, Samuel,** a Delegate from Pennsylvania; born in Philadelphia, Pa., in 1711; received a limited schooling and became a carpenter and builder; member of the city council in 1741; member of the provincial assembly 1761-1764 and 1771-1774; commissioner to a conference of western Indians and the Six Nations at Lancaster, Pa., in 1761; Member of the Continental Congress in 1774; mayor of Philadelphia in 1774; founder and member of board of managers of the Pennsylvania Hospital 1751-1781; director of the Philadelphia Library; died in Philadelphia, Pa., April 7, 1784.

**RHODES, George Milton,** a Representative from Pennsylvania; born in Reading, Berks County, Pa., February 24, 1898; attended Reading public schools; during the First World War served in the United States Army; printer, Reading Eagle Co., 1913-1927;

business manager, Reading Labor Advocate, 1927-1942; A.F. of L. labor representative; editor and manager of The New Era, 1942-1949; president of the Federated Trades Council, American Federation of Labor Central Labor Union, 1928-1951; member of the Reading Housing Authority, 1938-1948; delegate to Socialist National Conventions in 1928 and 1932; delegate to the Democratic National Conventions of 1952 and 1956; elected as a Democrat to the Eighty-first and to the nine succeeding Congresses (January 3, 1949-January 3, 1969); was not a candidate for reelection in 1968 to the Ninety-first Congress; resided in Reading, Pa., where he died on October 23, 1978; interment in Forest Hills Memorial Park, Reiffton, Pa.

**RHODES, John Jacob** (father of John Jacob Rhodes III), a Representative from Arizona; born in Council Grove, Morris County, Kans., September 18, 1916; attended the public schools; B.S., Kansas State University, Manhattan, 1938; LL.B., Harvard University Law School, 1941; was admitted to the Kansas bar in 1942, and to the Arizona bar in 1945; commenced the practice of law in Mesa, Ariz., in 1946; served in the United States Army Air Corps, September 5, 1941, to June 28, 1946; on the staff of the judge advocate, Arizona National Guard, 1947-1952; vice chairman, Arizona Board of Public Welfare, 1951-1952; delegate to the Republican National Conventions of 1952, 1964, and 1968; elected as a Republican to the Eighty-third and to the fourteen succeeding Congresses (January 3, 1953-January 3, 1983); was not a candidate for reelection in 1982 to the Ninety-eighth Congress; minority leader (Ninety-third through Ninety-sixth Congresses); returned to the practice of law; is a resident of Mesa, Ariz.

Bibliography: Rhodes, John, with Dean Smith. *John Rhodes: I Was There.* Foreword by Barry Goldwater. Salt Lake City: Northwest Publishing, 1995.

**RHODES, John Jacob, III** (son of John Jacob Rhodes), a Representative from Arizona; born in Mesa, Ariz., September 8, 1943; graduated from Landon School, Bethesda, Md., 1961; B.A., Yale University, 1965; J.D., University of Arizona College of Law, Tucson, 1968; admitted to the Arizona State bar in 1968 and commenced practice in Mesa; admitted to the District of Columbia bar in August 1995; captain, United States Army, 1968-1970, with service in Vietnam; member, Mesa Board of Education, 1973-1976; served with the Central Arizona Water Conservation District, 1983-1986; elected as a Republican to the One Hundredth and to the two succeeding Congresses (January 3, 1987-January 3, 1993); unsuccessful candidate for reelection in 1992 to the One Hundred Third Congress; resumed the practice of law as special counsel to Hunton & Williams, Washington, D.C.; is a resident of Washington, D.C.

**RHODES, Marion Edwards,** a Representative from Missouri; born on a farm near Glen Allen, Bollinger County, Mo., January 4, 1868; attended the public schools and Will Mayfield College; was graduated from the State normal school at Cape Girardeau, Mo., in 1891 and from Stansbury College in 1893; taught school; studied law; was admitted to the bar in 1896 and commenced practice in Potosi, Washington County, Mo., in 1898; delegate to all Republican State conventions from 1896 to 1920; prosecuting attorney of Washington County, 1900-1904; elected as a Republican to the Fifty-ninth Congress (March 4, 1905-March 3, 1907); was an unsuccessful candidate for reelection in 1906 to the Sixtieth Congress; mayor of Potosi in 1908 and 1909; member, Missouri State house of representatives, 1908-1910; delegate to the Republican National Convention of 1908; member of the Missouri State Board of Law Examiners, 1912-1914; elected to the Sixty-sixth and Sixty-seventh Congresses (March 4, 1919-March 3, 1923); chairman, Committee on Mines and Mining (Sixty-seventh Congress); unsuccessful candidate for reelection in 1922 to the Sixty-eighth Congress; appointed assistant to the United States Comptroller of the

Currency in Washington, D.C., and served from April 1, 1923 until his death in that city, December 25, 1928; interment in the Masonic Cemetery, Potosi, Mo.

**RIBICOFF, Abraham Alexander,** a Representative and a Senator from Connecticut; born in New Britain, Hartford County, Conn., April 9, 1910; attended the public schools and New York University; LL.B., University of Chicago Law School, 1933; admitted to the bar in 1933; member, Connecticut State legislature, 1938-1942; judge of the Hartford Police Court, 1941-1943, and 1945-1947; chairman, assembly of municipal court judges for the State of Connecticut in 1941 and 1942; member of the Charter Revision Commission of the city of Hartford in 1945 and 1946; hearing examiner, Connecticut Fair Employment Practices Act, 1937-1939; elected as a Democrat to the Eighty-first and Eighty-second Congresses (January 3, 1949-January 3, 1953); was not a candidate for renomination in 1952 to the House of Representatives, and was unsuccessful for election to fill a vacancy in the United States Senate; elected Governor of Connecticut in 1954, reelected in 1958, and served from January 5, 1955 until his resignation on January 21, 1961, to accept a Cabinet portfolio; appointed Secretary of Health, Education, and Welfare in the Cabinet of President John F. Kennedy, and served from January 21, 1961 until July 30, 1962; elected to the United States Senate in 1962; reelected in 1968 and again in 1974, and served from January 3, 1963, to January 3, 1981; was not a candidate for reelection in 1980; chairman, Committee on Government Operations (Ninety-fourth and Ninety-fifth Congresses), Committee on Governmental Affairs (Ninety-fifth and Ninety-sixth Congresses); practices law in New York City; is a resident of Cornwall Bridge, Conn.

Bibliography: Ribicoff, Abraham. *America Can Make It!* New York: Atheneum, 1972; Ribicoff, Abraham. *Politics: The American Way.* Boston: Allyn and Bacon, 1973.

**RICAUD, James Barroll,** a Representative from Maryland; born in Baltimore, Md., February 11, 1808; attended the common schools and was graduated from Washington College, Chestertown, Kent County, Md., in 1828; studied law; was admitted to the bar in 1829 and commenced practice in Chestertown; member of the Maryland State house of delegates in 1834; served in the Maryland State senate, 1836-1844; presidential elector on the Whig tickets in 1840 and 1844; elected as the candidate of the American Party to the Thirty-fourth and Thirty-fifth Congresses (March 4, 1855-March 3, 1859); resumed the practice of his profession; appointed associate judge of the second Maryland judicial district in 1864 by Governor Augustus W. Bradford and served during the May term; died in Chestertown, Md., on January 24, 1866; interment in St. Paul's Church Cemetery.

**RICE, Alexander Hamilton,** a Representative from Massachusetts; born in Newton Lower Falls, Mass., August 30, 1818; was graduated from Union College in 1844; engaged in the manufacture of paper at Boston; mayor of Boston in 1856 and 1857; elected as a Republican to the Thirty-sixth and to the three succeeding Congresses (March 4, 1859-March 3, 1867); chairman, Committee on Naval Affairs (Thirty-eighth and Thirty-ninth Congresses); was not a candidate for renomination in 1866 to the Fortieth Congress; resumed his former business pursuits in Boston; delegate to the Philadelphia Loyalist Convention in 1866; delegate to the Republican National Convention of 1868; elected Governor of Massachusetts in 1875, reelected in 1876 and 1877, and served from January 6, 1876 to January 2, 1879; died in Boston, Mass., July 22, 1895; interment in Newton Cemetery, Newton, Mass.

Bibliography: *DAB.*

**RICE, Americus Vespucius,** a Representative from Ohio; born in Perryville, Ashland County, Ohio, on November 18, 1835; pursued classical studies; attended Antioch College and was graduated from

Union College, Schenectady, N.Y., in 1860; studied law; commissioned as captain in the Twenty-first Ohio Infantry on April 27, 1861, and promoted through the ranks to lieutenant colonel on February 8, 1862; commissioned colonel May 24, 1863, during the siege of Vicksburg, Miss.; lost a leg at the Battle of Kennesaw Mountain, Ga., June 27, 1864; appointed brigadier general on May 31, 1865; manager of a private banking house in Ottawa, Ohio; delegate to the Democratic National Convention of 1872; elected as a Democrat to the Forty-fourth and Forty-fifth Congresses (March 4, 1875-March 3, 1879); chairman, Committee on Invalid Pensions (Forty-fifth Congress); was not a candidate for renomination in 1878 to the Forty-sixth Congress; president of A.V. Rice and Co., a banking concern of Ottawa; director in various business enterprises; appointed pension agent for Ohio in 1893, and served from May 1, 1894 until the fall of 1898; moved to Washington, D.C., in 1899 and engaged in banking and various other enterprises; appointed purchasing agent of the United States Census Bureau, which position he held at the time of his death in Washington, D.C., on April 4, 1904; interment in Arlington National Cemetery, Va.

**RICE, Benjamin Franklin,** a Senator from Arkansas; born in East Otto, Cattaraugus County, N.Y., on May 26, 1828; attended private schools; studied law; was admitted to the bar and practiced in Irvine, Estill County, Ky.; member, State house of representatives 1855-1856; presidential elector on the Republican ticket in 1856; moved to Minnesota in 1860; during the Civil War served in the Union Army as a captain and was promoted to judge advocate in the Minnesota Volunteers; settled in Little Rock, Ark., in 1864 and resumed the practice of law; active in organizing the Republican Party in Arkansas; appointed chairman of the committee to prepare a code of practice for the State in 1868; upon the readmission of the State of Arkansas to representation was elected as a Republican to the United States Senate and served from June 23, 1868, to March 3, 1873; chairman, Committee on Mines and Mining (Forty-second Congress); resumed the practice of law in Arkansas; because of ill health moved to Colorado in 1875; moved to Washington, D.C., in 1882, where he continued the practice of law until his death; died in Tulsa, Okla., January 19, 1905; interment in Oak Hill Cemetery, Washington, D.C.

**RICE, Edmund** (brother of Henry Mower Rice), a Representative from Minnesota; born in Waitsfield, Vt., February 14, 1819; attended the common schools; moved to Kalamazoo, Mich., in November 1838; studied law; was admitted to the bar in 1842 and commenced practice in Kalamazoo; register of the court of chancery in 1841; master in chancery in 1845; enlisted to serve in the Mexican War in 1847; commissioned first lieutenant of Company A, First Regiment, Michigan Volunteers; moved to St. Paul, Minn., in July 1849; clerk of the State supreme court, third circuit, in 1849; member of the Territorial house of representatives in 1851; practiced law until 1856; elected commissioner of Ramsey County in 1856; president of the Minnesota & Pacific Railroad Co. 1857-1863 and of the St. Paul & Pacific Railroad 1863-1872 and trustee of the latter in 1879; president of the St. Paul & Chicago Railroad 1863-1877; served in the State senate 1864-1866 and 1874-1876; member of the State house of representatives in 1867, 1872, 1877, and 1878; elected mayor of St. Paul and served from 1881 to 1883; again elected mayor in 1885 and served until February 1887, when he resigned; elected as a Democrat to the Fiftieth Congress (March 4, 1887-March 3, 1889); was an unsuccessful candidate for reelection in 1888 to the Fifty-first Congress; retired from public and political activities; died at White Bear Lake, Ramsey County, Minn., on July 11, 1889; interment in Oakland Cemetery, St. Paul, Minn.

Bibliography: *DAB.*

**RICE, Edward Young,** a Representative from Illinois; born near Russellville, Logan County, Ky., February 8, 1820; pursued classical studies; studied law; was admitted to the bar in 1844;

moved to Montgomery County, Ill., and commenced practice in Hillsboro, Montgomery County, Ill.; elected county recorder in 1847; member of the State house of representatives in 1849 and 1850; judge of the Montgomery County Court in 1851 and 1852; master in chancery 1853-1857; elected judge of the eighteenth circuit of Illinois in 1857 and reelected in 1861 and 1867; member of the State constitutional convention in 1869 and 1870; elected as a Democrat to the Forty-second Congress (March 4, 1871-March 3, 1873); unsuccessful candidate for renomination in 1872; resumed the practice of law in Hillsboro and Springfield, Ill.; died in Hillsboro, Ill., April 16, 1883; interment in Oak Grove Cemetery.

**RICE, Henry Mower** (brother of Edmund Rice), a Delegate and a Senator from Minnesota; born in Waitsfield, Vt., November 29, 1816; attended common schools and academies in Detroit and Kalamazoo, Mich.; resided in the Territories of Iowa and Wisconsin; moved to the Territory of Minnesota in 1839; post sutler for the United States Army at Fort Atkinson, Iowa; engaged in the fur business; negotiated a treaty with the Winnebago and Chippewa Indians in 1847; settled in St. Paul in 1848; through his personal influence secured the consent of the objecting Sioux Indians to confirmation of the treaty of 1851, whereby all of Minnesota west of the Mississippi River and south of Ojibway County was opened to white settlers; elected as a Democrat a Delegate to the Thirty-third and Thirty-fourth Congresses (March 4, 1853-March 3, 1857); was not a candidate for renomination in 1856 to the Thirty-fifth Congress; upon the admission of Minnesota as a State into the Union was elected as a Democrat to the United States Senate, and served from May 11, 1858 to March 3, 1863; was not a candidate for reelection in 1862; member of the board of regents of the University of Minnesota, 1851-1859; unsuccessful candidate in 1865 for election for Governor of Minnesota; president of the State historical society; president of the board of public works; treasurer of Ramsey County, 1878-1884; United States commissioner in making several Indian treaties, 1887-1888; died in San Antonio, Tex., while on a visit, January 15, 1894; interment in Oakland Cemetery, St. Paul, Minn.

**Bibliography:** *DAB*; Marshall, William. "Henry Mower Rice." *Minnesota Historical Society Collections* 9 (1901): 654-58.

**RICE, John Birchard,** a Representative from Ohio; born in Fremont, Sandusky County, Ohio, June 23, 1832; attended the common schools of Lower Sandusky (now Fremont) and Oberlin College, Ohio; was graduated from the medical department of the University of Michigan at Ann Arbor in 1857; took a post-graduate course at Jefferson Medical College, Philadelphia, Pa., and at Bellevue Hospital, New York City, in 1859; lecturer on military surgery and obstetrics in the Charity Hospital Medical College and the medical department of the University of Wooster in Cleveland, Ohio; served on the medical staff during the Civil War as assistant surgeon of the Tenth and surgeon of the Seventy-second Regiment, Ohio Volunteer Infantry; also surgeon in chief of a division in the Fifteenth Army Corps and of the district of Memphis; appointed a trustee of the State hospital, Toledo, Ohio; member of the Board of Health of Fremont, Ohio; elected as a Republican to the Forty-seventh Congress (March 4, 1881-March 3, 1883); was not a candidate for renomination in 1882; engaged in the practice of medicine in Fremont, Ohio; died in Fremont, Ohio, January 14, 1893; interment in Oakwood Cemetery.

**RICE, John Blake,** a Representative from Illinois; born in Easton, Talbot County, Md., May 28, 1809; received a limited schooling; went on the stage in New York in 1839; moved to Chicago, Ill., in 1847 and was manager of a theater; also managed theaters in Bangor, Maine, Buffalo, N.Y., and Milwaukee, Wis.; retired from the stage in 1857 and from theatrical management in 1861; mayor of Chicago 1865-1869; elected as a Republican to the Forty-third Congress and served from March 4, 1873, until his death in Norfolk, Va., December 17, 1874; interment in Rosehill Cemetery, Chicago, Ill.

**RICE, John Hovey,** a Representative from Maine; born in Mount Vernon, Maine, February 5, 1816; attended the common schools; clerk in the office of the register of deeds, Augusta, Maine, 1831-1841; engaged in the mercantile business; deputy sheriff; aide-de-camp to General Bachelor in the "Aroostook War," the northeastern boundary dispute with Great Britain, in 1838; moved to Piscataquis County, Maine, in 1843; studied law; was admitted to the bar and commenced practice in Piscataquis County in 1848; prosecuting attorney for Piscataquis County 1852-1860; delegate to the Republican National Convention in 1856; elected as a Republican to the Thirty-seventh, Thirty-eighth, and Thirty-ninth Congresses (March 4, 1861-March 3, 1867); chairman, Committee on Public Buildings and Grounds (Thirty-eighth and Thirty-ninth Congresses); declined to be a candidate for renomination; United States collector of customs at the port of Bangor, Maine, 1861-1871; moved to Washington, D.C., where he practiced law for twelve years; thence to New York City in 1884 and practiced until 1899; moved to Chicago, Ill., in May 1899 and remained there until his death on March 14, 1911; interment in Oakwood Cemetery.

**RICE, John McConnell,** a Representative from Kentucky; born in Prestonsburg, Floyd County, Ky., February 19, 1831; received a limited schooling; graduated from a Louisville law school in 1852; admitted to the bar in 1853 and commenced practice in Pikeville, Ky.; superintendent of schools of Pike County in 1854; elected prosecuting attorney of Pike County in 1856; member of the Kentucky house of representatives in 1858; moved to Louisa, Lawrence County, Ky., in 1860; again a member of the Kentucky house of representatives in 1861; elected as a Democrat to the Forty-first and Forty-second Congresses (March 4, 1869-March 3, 1873); was not a candidate for renomination in 1872; resumed the practice of law in Louisa, Ky.; appointed judge of the Lawrence County criminal court in 1883; was elected to the same office in 1884; reelected in 1890 and served until his death in Louisa, Ky., September 18, 1895; interment in Pine Hill Cemetery.

**RICE, Theron Moses,** a Representative from Missouri; born in Mecca, Trumbull County, Ohio, on September 21, 1829; attended the academy in Chester, Ohio; taught in the district school during the winter months; studied law; was admitted to the bar in June 1854 and practiced for about three years in Mahoning County, Ohio; moved in the spring of 1858 to California, Moniteau County, Mo.; served during the Civil War, 1861-1865, in the United States Infantry Volunteer Service from Missouri; received gradual promotions from first lieutenant to colonel; returned to Missouri in the spring of 1866 and resumed the practice of his profession in Tipton, Moniteau County, Mo.; was circuit judge 1868-1874; elected as a Greenbacker to the Forty-seventh Congress (March 4, 1881-March 3, 1883); was not a candidate for renomination in 1882; resumed the practice of law in Boonville, Mo., until his death in that city November 7, 1895; interment in Tipton Cemetery, Tipton, Mo.

**RICE, Thomas,** a Representative from Massachusetts; born in Pownalborough (now Wiscasset), Maine (then a part of Massachusetts), March 30, 1768; graduated from Harvard University in 1791; studied law; admitted to the bar in Suffolk County, Mass., in 1794 and commenced practice in Winslow, Maine, the following year; appointed in 1807 by the supreme judicial court of Maine one of the examiners of counselors and attorneys for Kennebec County; member of the Massachusetts house of representatives in 1814; elected as a Federalist to the Fourteenth and Fifteenth Congresses (March 4, 1815-March 3, 1819); unsuccessful candidate for reelection in 1818 to the Sixteenth Congress; resumed the practice of law; died in Winslow, Kennebec County, Maine, August 25, 1854; interment in Pine Grove Cemetery, Waterville, Maine.

**RICE, William Whitney,** a Representative from Massachusetts; born in Deerfield, Franklin County, Mass., on March 7, 1826; attended Gorham Academy, Maine, and graduated from Bowdoin College, Brunswick, Maine, in 1846; preceptor in Leicester Academy, Massachusetts, 1847-1851; studied law in Worcester; admitted to the bar in 1854 and commenced practice in that city; appointed judge of insolvency for Worcester County in 1858; mayor of the city of Worcester in 1860; district attorney for the middle district of Massachusetts 1869-1874; member of the Massachusetts house of representatives in 1875; elected as a Republican to the Forty-fifth and to the four succeeding Congresses (March 4, 1877-March 3, 1887); unsuccessful candidate for reelection in 1886 to the Fiftieth Congress; resumed the practice of law in Worcester, Mass., and died there March 1, 1896; interment in the Rural Cemetery.

**RICH, Carl West,** a Representative from Ohio; born in Cincinnati, Hamilton County, Ohio, September 12, 1898; attended Walnut Hills High School; University of Cincinnati College of Liberal Arts, A.B., 1922, and from the college of law of the same university, LL.B., 1924; was admitted to the bar in 1924 and commenced the practice of law in Cincinnati; instructor on the faculty of the University of Cincinnati; assistant city solicitor and assistant prosecutor of Cincinnati, 1925-1929; served three terms as prosecuting attorney of Hamilton County, 1938-1947; served nine years in the city council of Cincinnati, serving as mayor for three terms, 1947-1956; judge of the Common Pleas Court of Hamilton County; president and chairman of the board of the Cincinnati Royals Professional Basketball Team; elected as a Republican to the Eighty-eighth Congress (January 3, 1963-January 3, 1965); unsuccessful candidate for reelection in 1964 to the Eighty-ninth Congress; resumed the practice of law; died in Cincinnati, Ohio, June 26, 1972; interment in Spring Grove Cemetery.

**RICH, Charles,** a Representative from Vermont; born in Warwick, Hampshire County, Mass., on September 13, 1771; received a limited schooling; moved to Shoreham, Addison County, Vt., in 1787; member of the State house of representatives 1800-1811; was county judge for six years; elected as a Republican to the Thirteenth Congress (March 4, 1813-March 3, 1815); elected to the Fifteenth and to the three succeeding Congresses and served from March 4, 1817, until his death in Shoreham, Vt., on October 15, 1824; interment in the family vault on his farm near Shoreham, Vt.

**RICH, John Tyler,** a Representative from Michigan; born in Conneautville, Crawford County, Pa., April 23, 1841; moved with his parents to Addison County, Vt., in 1846 and to Elba, Lapeer County, Mich., in 1848; attended the public schools; engaged in agricultural pursuits; member and chairman of the board of supervisors of Lapeer County, 1869-1872; member of the Michigan State house of representatives, 1873-1881, and served as speaker during the last two terms; delegate to the Republican State conventions in 1873, 1875, and 1878; served in the State senate from January 1 until March 21, 1881, when he resigned, having been elected to Congress; elected as a Republican to the Forty-seventh Congress to fill the vacancy caused by the resignation of Omar D. Conger, and served from April 5, 1881 to March 3, 1883; unsuccessful candidate for reelection in 1882 to the Forty-eighth Congress; State railroad commissioner, 1887-1891; delegate to the Republican National Conventions of 1884 and 1892; elected Governor of Michigan in 1892, reelected in 1894, and served from January 1, 1893 to January 1, 1897; United States collector of customs at Detroit from February 16, 1898 to January 30, 1906; was elected State treasurer of Michigan to fill a vacancy, and served from January 23, 1908 to January 1, 1909; collector of customs at Port Huron, Mich., from December 11, 1908 to May 30, 1913; died in St. Petersburg, Fla., March 28, 1926; interment in Mount Hope Cemetery, Lapeer, Mich.

**RICH, Robert Fleming,** a Representative from Pennsylvania; born in Woolrich, Clinton County, Pa., June 23, 1883; attended the public schools, Dickinson Seminary, Williamsport, Pa., and Williamsport (Pa.) Commercial College; was graduated from Mercersburg (Pa.) Academy in 1902, and attended Dickinson College, Carlisle, Pa., from 1903 until 1906; engaged in the woolen-mills business in 1906; also engaged in banking and became financially interested in various business and manufacturing enterprises; delegate to the Republican National Conventions of 1924, 1952, and 1956; member of the board of trustees of Dickinson College, 1912-1958, of Lock Haven (Pa.) Teachers College, 1918-1928, of Lock Haven (Pa.) Hospital, 1920-1951, and of Lycoming College, 1931-1963; elected as a Republican to the Seventy-first Congress to fill the vacancy caused by the death of Edgar R. Kiess; reelected to the Seventy-second and to the five succeeding Congresses and served from November 4, 1930, to January 3, 1943; was not a candidate for renomination in 1942 to the Seventy-eighth Congress; elected to the Seventy-ninth and to the two succeeding Congresses (January 3, 1945-January 3, 1951); was not a candidate for renomination in 1950 to the Eighty-second Congress; general manager of Woolrich Woolen Mills, 1930-1959, president, 1959-1964, and chairman of the board from 1964 until 1966, when he became honorary chairman; died at Jersey Shore, Pa., April 28, 1968; interment in Woolrich Cemetery, Woolrich, Pa.

**RICHARD, Gabriel,** a Delegate from Michigan Territory; born in La Ville de Saintes, France, October 15, 1767; pursued classical studies; studied theology in the seminary of Augers, France, and in Paris, and was ordained as a priest on October 15, 1790; immigrated to the United States in 1792 and settled in Baltimore, Md.; professor of mathematics in St. Mary's College, Maryland; sent by Bishop Carroll as a missionary to the Indians in the Northwest Territory and was stationed in what is now Kaskaskia, Ill., and later as a missionary in Detroit, Mich.; published a periodical in the French language entitled "Essais du Michigan"; was elected to the Eighteenth Congress (March 4, 1823-March 3, 1825); unsuccessful candidate for reelection in 1824 to the Nineteenth Congress; returned to Detroit and officiated as grand vicar; died in Detroit, Mich., September 13, 1832; interment in the cemetery of the Roman Catholic Church of St. Anne.

Bibliography: *DAB*; Pargellis, Stanley McCrory. *Father Gabriel Richard.* (Cass Lectureship Series, 1948). Detroit: Wayne University Press, 1950.

**RICHARDS, Charles Lenmore,** a Representative from Nevada; born in Austin, Lander County, Nev., October 3, 1877; attended the public schools in Nevada and Pennsylvania and was graduated from the law department of Stanford University, California, in 1901; studied law; was admitted to the bar and commenced practice in Tonopah, Nev., in 1901; served as district attorney of Nye County in 1903 and 1904; member of the State house of representatives in 1919; moved to Reno, Nev., in 1919; chairman of the Democratic State committee in 1922; councilor from Nevada to the United States Chamber of Commerce from March 29, 1923, to May 20, 1924; elected as a Democrat to the Sixty-eighth Congress (March 4, 1923-March 3, 1925); unsuccessful candidate for reelection in 1924 to the Sixty-ninth Congress; practiced law in Reno, Nev., until his death there on December 22, 1953; interment in Mountain View Cemetery.

**RICHARDS, Jacob,** a Representative from Pennsylvania; born near Chester, Delaware County, Pa., in 1773; was graduated from the University of Pennsylvania at Philadelphia in 1794; studied law; was admitted to the bar in 1795 and commenced practice in Philadelphia; elected as a Republican to the Eighth, Ninth, and Tenth Congresses (March 4, 1803-March 3, 1809); was commissioned as colonel of militia in Delaware County, Pa.; engaged in the practice of law until his death near Chester, Pa., July 20, 1816.

**RICHARDS, James Alexander Dudley,** a Representative from Ohio; born in Boston, Mass., March 22, 1845; spent his early life in Boston and New York City, where he received a common-school education; moved to New Philadelphia, Tuscarawas County, Ohio, in 1861; studied law; was admitted to the bar in 1867 and commenced practice in New Philadelphia; elected as a Democrat to the Fifty-third Congress (March 4, 1893-March 3, 1895); chairman, Committee on Expenditures in the Post Office Department (Fifty-third Congress); unsuccessful candidate for reelection in 1894 to the Fifty-fourth Congress; resumed the practice of law in Washington, D.C., and subsequently returned to New Philadelphia, Ohio, and continued the practice of his profession; died in New Philadelphia, on December 4, 1911; interment in the East Fair Street Cemetery.

**RICHARDS, James Prioleau,** a Representative from South Carolina; born in Liberty Hill, Kershaw County, S.C., August 31, 1894; attended the county schools and Clemson College, Clemson, S.C.; during the First World War served overseas as a private, corporal, sergeant, and second lieutenant in the Trench Mortar Battery, Headquarters Company, One Hundred and Eighteenth Regiment, Thirtieth Division, 1917-1919; was graduated from the law department of the University of South Carolina at Columbia in 1921; was admitted to the bar the same year and commenced practice in Lancaster, S.C.; judge of the probate court of Lancaster County, S.C., 1923-1933; elected as a Democrat to the Seventy-third and to the eleven succeeding Congresses (March 4, 1933-January 3, 1957); chairman, Committee on Foreign Affairs (Eighty-second and Eighty-fourth Congresses); was not a candidate for reelection in 1956 to the Eighty-fifth Congress; delegate to the Japanese Peace Conference of September 1951, and United States delegate to the United Nations in 1953; special assistant to President Dwight D. Eisenhower for the Middle East, January 1957-January 1958, with the rank of ambassador; resumed the practice of law; resided in Lancaster, S.C., where he died on February 21, 1979; interment in Liberty Hill Presbyterian Church Cemetery, Liberty Hill, S.C.

Bibliography: Lee, Joseph Edward. "'America Comes First with Me': The Political Career of Congressman James P. Richards, 1932-1957." Ph.D. dissertation, University of South Carolina, 1987.

**RICHARDS, John,** a Representative from New York; born in Wales April 13, 1765; immigrated to the United States and settled in Johnsburg, Warren County, N.Y.; received a limited schooling; member of the State assembly from January 29, 1811, to April 8, 1811; State surveyor 1810-1812; delegate to the State constitutional convention in 1821; elected to the Eighteenth Congress (March 4, 1823-March 3, 1825); died at Lake George, Warren County, N.Y., April 18, 1850.

**RICHARDS, John** (brother of Matthias Richards), a Representative from Pennsylvania; born in New Hanover, Philadelphia County, Pa., April 18, 1753; educated under private tutors; served as magistrate during the Revolutionary War; appointed justice of the peace for Philadelphia County June 6, 1777, and served until his death; judge of the court of common pleas for Montgomery County in 1784; delegate to the Federal Constitutional Convention in 1787; elected as a Republican to the Fourth Congress (March 4, 1795-March 3, 1797); was not a candidate for renomination in 1796; was an ironmaster and also engaged in mercantile and agricultural pursuits; member of the Pennsylvania senate 1801-1807; died in New Hanover, Pa., November 13, 1822; interment in Faulkner Swamp (Lutheran) Church Cemetery.

**RICHARDS, Mark,** a Representative from Vermont; born in Waterbury, Conn., July 15, 1760; received a limited schooling; enlisted during the Revolutionary War in 1776; settled in Boston after the Revolution and engaged in mercantile and mechanical pursuits; moved to Westminster, Vt., in 1796; member of the State house of representatives 1801-1805; sheriff of Windham County 1806-1810; member of the Governor's council in 1816; elected as a Republican to the Fifteenth and Sixteenth Congresses (March 4, 1817-March 3, 1821); again a member of the State house of representatives 1824-1826, 1828, and 1832-1834; Lieutenant Governor of Vermont in 1830 and 1831; died in Westminster, Vt., August 10, 1844; interment in the Bradley tomb, Old Cemetery.

**RICHARDS, Matthias** (brother of John Richards), a Representative from Pennsylvania; born near Pottstown, New Hanover Township, Montgomery County, Pa., on February 26, 1758; completed preparatory studies under private tutoring; served during the Revolutionary War as a private in Colonel Daniel Udree's second battalion, Berks County (Pa.) Militia, from August 5, 1777, until January 5, 1778; major of the Fourth Battalion, Philadelphia County Militia, in 1780; appointed justice of the peace in 1788 and held this office for forty years; judge of the Berks County (Pa.) Courts, 1791-1797; inspector of customs in 1801 and 1802; elected as a Republican to the Tenth and Eleventh Congresses (March 4, 1807-March 3, 1811); was not a candidate for renomination in 1810 to the Twelfth Congress; appointed collector of revenue for the ninth district of Pennsylvania in 1813; clerk of the orphans' court for Berks County in 1823; was appointed associate judge of Berks County Courts by Governor John A. Shulze; engaged in mercantile pursuits in Reading, Pa., until his death in that city on August 4, 1830; interment in the Charles Evans Cemetery.

**RICHARDSON, David Plunket,** a Representative from New York; born in Macedon, Wayne County, N.Y., May 28, 1833; attended the common school and the local academy at Macedon; was graduated from Yale College in 1856; studied law in Rochester, N.Y.; was admitted to the bar in 1859, and practiced; entered the Union Army in 1861, and served over three years; moved to Angelica, N.Y., in 1866; elected as a Republican to the Forty-sixth and Forty-seventh Congresses (March 4, 1879-March 3, 1883); was not a candidate for reelection in 1882; resumed the practice of law in Angelica, N.Y., where he died on June 21, 1904; interment in Angelica Cemetery.

**RICHARDSON, George Frederick,** a Representative from Michigan; born in Jamestown, Ottawa County, Mich., July 1, 1850; attended the common schools; engaged in agricultural and mercantile pursuits; elected township clerk eight years in succession; member of the State house of representatives 1885-1887, 1891, and 1892, and served as speaker in the two last-named years; moved to Grand Rapids, Mich., in 1893; elected as a Democrat to the Fifty-third Congress (March 4, 1893-March 3, 1895); declined to be a candidate for renomination in 1894; operated a dairy farm in Grand Rapids; moved to Kennewick, Wash., in 1904 and engaged in agricultural pursuits and in the transfer, livery, and fuel business; was twice elected mayor of Kennewick and also served as chairman of the school board; moved to Ellensburg, Wash., and in 1916 engaged in agricultural pursuits; retired to private life in 1919 and made his home in Bellevue, Wash., where he died on March 1, 1923; interment in the Odd Fellows Cemetery, Ellensburg, Wash.

**RICHARDSON, Harry Alden,** a Senator from Delaware; born in Camden, Kent County, Del., January 1, 1853; moved with his parents to Dover, Kent County, in 1856; attended the common schools and the academy in East Greenwich, R.I.; worked in his father's canning and packing establishment at Dover, Del., became a partner, and assumed entire control in 1894; elected Delaware State senator in 1888; president of the First National Bank of Dover; also interested in public service corporations; unsuccessful Republican candidate for Governor of Delaware in 1890; elected as a Republican to the United States Senate in 1907, and served from March 4, 1907 to March 3, 1913; was not a candidate for reelection; chairman, Committee to Examine Branches of the Civil Service (Sixty-first Congress), Committee on Pacific Islands and Puerto Rico (Sixty-second Congress), Committee on Printing (Sixty-second Congress);

again engaged in the manufacture of canned food products; died in Dover, Del., June 16, 1928; interment in Lakeside Cemetery.

**RICHARDSON, James Daniel,** a Representative from Tennessee; born in Rutherford County, Tenn., March 10, 1843; attended the country schools and Franklin College, near Nashville; during the Civil War entered the Confederate Army before graduating from college and served nearly four years, the first year as a private and the remaining three years as adjutant of the Forty-fifth Regiment, Tennessee Infantry; studied law; was admitted to the bar and commenced practice on January 1, 1867, in Murfreesboro, Tenn.; member of the Tennessee State house of representatives, 1871-1873; served in the State senate, 1873-1875; delegate to the Democratic National Conventions of 1876, 1896 and 1900; presided as permanent chairman at the last-named convention; chairman of the Democratic congressional committee in 1900; editor and compiler of the Government publication entitled "Messages and Papers of the Presidents"; elected as a Democrat to the Forty-ninth and to the nine succeeding Congresses (March 4, 1885-March 3, 1905); minority leader (Fifty-seventh Congress); died in Murfreesboro, Tenn., July 24, 1914; interment in Evergreen Cemetery.

**Bibliography:** *DAB*.

**RICHARDSON, James Montgomery,** a Representative from Kentucky; born in Mobile, Ala., July 1, 1858; moved to Glasgow, Ky., in early youth and resided with his uncle; attended the common schools; became editor of the Glasgow (Ky.) Times in 1878; delegate to the Democratic National Convention in 1896; member of the Kentucky house of representatives in 1896; served as prison commissioner from 1900 to 1905, when he resigned, having been elected to Congress; elected as a Democrat to the Fifty-ninth Congress (March 4, 1905-March 3, 1907); unsuccessful candidate for reelection; resumed newspaper activities; postmaster at Glasgow from May 22, 1913, to May 9, 1922; died in Glasgow, Ky., February 9, 1925; interment in Glasgow Cemetery.

**RICHARDSON, John Peter,** a Representative from South Carolina; born at Hickory Hill, S.C., April 14, 1801; was graduated from South Carolina College at Columbia in 1819; studied law; was admitted to the bar and commenced practice in Fulton, S.C.; member of the South Carolina State house of representatives, 1825-1833; judge of the circuit court; elected as a Jacksonian to the Twenty-fourth Congress to fill the vacancy caused by the death of Richard I. Manning; reelected as a Democrat to the Twenty-fifth Congress, and served from December 19, 1836 to March 3, 1839; elected Governor of South Carolina by the Legislature, and served from December 10, 1840 to December 1842; died in Fulton (later Pinewood), Sumter County, S.C., January 24, 1864.

**RICHARDSON, John Smythe,** a Representative from South Carolina; born on the Bloomhill plantation, near Sumter, Sumter County, S.C., February 29, 1828; pursued an academic course in Cokesbury, S.C., and was graduated from South Carolina College (now the University of South Carolina) at Columbia in 1850; studied law; was admitted to the bar in 1852 and began practice in Sumter, S.C.; during the Civil War entered the Confederate Army as a captain of Infantry; later promoted to adjutant of the Twenty-third Regiment, South Carolina Infantry, and served until the close of the war in 1865; member of the State house of representatives 1865-1867; appointed agent of the State of South Carolina in 1866 to apply for and receive the land script donated to South Carolina by Congress; delegate to the Democratic National Convention in 1876; elected as a Democrat to the Forty-sixth and Forty-seventh Congresses (March 4, 1879-March 3, 1883); master in equity for Sumter County 1884-1893; died at his country home, "Shadyside," near Sumter, S.C., February 24, 1894; interment in Sumter Cemetery.

**RICHARDSON, Joseph,** a Representative from Massachusetts; born in Billerica, Mass., February 1, 1778; attended public and private schools; graduated from Dartmouth College, Hanover, N.H., in 1802; teacher in Charlestown 1804-1806; studied theology; was ordained a minister and assigned to the first parish of the Unitarian Church in Hingham July 2, 1806; delegate to the Massachusetts constitutional convention in 1820; member of the Massachusetts house of representatives in 1821 and 1822; served in the Massachusetts senate in 1823, 1824, and 1826; elected to the Twentieth and Twenty-first Congresses (March 4, 1827-March 3, 1831); declined to be a candidate for renomination in 1830 to the Twenty-second Congress; resumed his ministerial duties; died in Hingham, Plymouth County, Mass., on September 25, 1871; interment in Old Ship Cemetery.

**RICHARDSON, William,** a Representative from Alabama; born in Athens, Limestone County, Ala., May 8, 1839; attended the public schools; during the Civil War served in the Confederate Army; paroled in April 1865 in Marietta, Ga.; member of the Alabama house of representatives 1865-1867; studied law; was admitted to the bar in 1867 and commenced practice in Huntsville, Ala.; judge of the probate and county courts of Madison County, Ala., 1875-1886; delegate to the Democratic National Convention in 1904; elected as a Democrat to the Fifty-sixth Congress to fill the vacancy caused by the resignation of Joseph Wheeler; reelected to the Fifty-seventh and to the six succeeding Congresses and served from August 6, 1900, until his death in Atlantic City, N.J., where he had gone for the benefit of his health, on March 31, 1914; chairman, Committee on Pensions (Sixty-second and Sixty-third Congresses); interment in Maple Hill Cemetery, Huntsville, Ala.

**RICHARDSON, William Alexander,** a Representative and a Senator from Illinois; born near Lexington, Fayette County, Ky., January 16, 1811; attended an academy at Walnut Hill, Ky., Centre College at Danville, Ky., and Transylvania University at Lexington, Ky.; taught school; studied law; was admitted to the bar in 1831 and commenced practice in Shelbyville, Ill.; State's attorney 1834-1835; member, State house of representatives 1836-1838, 1844-1846, and served as speaker in 1844; member, State senate 1838-1842; presidential elector on the Democratic ticket in 1844; during the Mexican War enlisted as a captain and was promoted to the rank of major; moved to Quincy, Ill., in 1849; elected as a Democrat to the Thirtieth Congress to fill the vacancy caused by the resignation of Stephen A. Douglas; reelected to the Thirty-first and to the three succeeding Congresses and served from December 6, 1847, to August 25, 1856, when he resigned; chairman, Committee on Territories (Thirty-second and Thirty-third Congresses); elected to the Thirty-seventh Congress and served from March 4, 1861, until his resignation on January 29, 1863, having previously been elected Senator; elected as a Democrat to the United States Senate in 1863 to fill the vacancy caused by the death of Stephen A. Douglas and served from January 30, 1863, to March 3, 1865; was not a candidate for renomination in 1864; engaged in newspaper work; died in Quincy, Adams County, Ill., December 27, 1875; interment in Woodland Cemetery.

**Bibliography:** Thavenet, Dennis. "William Alexander Richardson, 1811-1875." Ph.D. dissertation, University of Nebraska, 1967.

**RICHARDSON, William Blaine,** a Representative from New Mexico; born in Pasadena, Los Angeles County, Calif., November 15, 1947; attended the schools of Mexico City, Mexico; graduated from Middlesex School, Concord, Mass., 1966; B.A., Tufts University, Medford, Mass., 1970; M.A., Fletcher School of Law and Diplomacy, Tufts University, 1971; served on the staff of the House of Representatives 1971-1972, served in the congressional relations office of the Department of State 1973-1975; staff of the Senate Foreign Relations Committee 1975-1978; executive director, New Mexico State Democratic Party and Bernalillo County, N.Mex.,

Democratic Party, 1978; international business consultant, 1978-1982; unsuccessful candidate for election in 1980 to the Ninety-seventh Congress; elected as a Democrat to the Ninety-eighth and to the six succeeding Congresses (January 3, 1983-January 3, 1997); is a resident of Santa Fe, N.Mex.

**RICHARDSON, William Emanuel,** a Representative from Pennsylvania; born on a farm (the old Daniel Boone homestead) near Stonersville, in Exeter Township, Berks County, Pa., on September 3, 1886; moved to Bernville, Berks County, Pa., with his parents at an early age, where he attended the public schools; was graduated from Princeton University in 1910, and from the law department of Columbia University, New York City, in 1913; was admitted to the bar the same year and commenced practice in Reading, Pa., in 1914; served with Ambulance Americaine, in Belgium and France in 1915, and with Squadron A, New York Cavalry, on the Mexican border in 1916; during the First World War was commissioned a second lieutenant on August 15, 1917, and served with the Eightieth Cavalry Division, United States Army, and later with the Seventh Machine Gun Battalion, Third Division, and was discharged a first lieutenant on September 15, 1919; after the war resumed the practice of law in Reading, Pa.; elected as a Democrat to the Seventy-third and Seventy-fourth Congresses (March 4, 1933-January 3, 1937); unsuccessful candidate for renomination in 1936; attended the Interparliamentary Union Conference in Budapest, Hungary, in 1936; again practiced law in Reading, Pa.; died in Wyomissing, Pa., November 3, 1948; interment in Schwartzwald Cemetery, Jacksonwald, Pa.

**RICHARDSON, William Merchant,** a Representative from Massachusetts; born in Pelham, Hillsborough County, N.H., January 4, 1774; was graduated from Harvard University in 1797; studied law; was admitted to the bar and commenced practice in Groton, Mass., in 1804; elected as a Republican to the Twelfth Congress to fill the vacancy caused by the resignation of Joseph B. Varnum; reelected to the Thirteenth Congress and served from November 4, 1811, to April 18, 1814, when he resigned; moved to Portsmouth, Rockingham County, N.H., in 1814; United States attorney in 1814; appointed chief justice of New Hampshire in 1816 and served until his death; died in Chester, Rockingham County, N.H., March 15, 1838; interment in the Old Cemetery.

**Bibliography:** *DAB.*

**RICHMOND, Frederick William,** a Representative from New York; born in Mattapan, Mass., November 15, 1923; attended Mattapan (Mass.) Elementary School; graduated from Roxbury (Mass.) Memorial High School, 1940; attended Harvard University, 1942-1943; B.A., Boston University, 1945; served in the United States Navy in the Pacific Theater, Radioman Third Class, 1943-1945; pursued a career in business; chairman, National Urban League Equal Opportunity Conference, 1955-1956; served as deputy finance chairman, Democratic National Committee, 1958-1960; president, Greater New York Urban League, 1959-1964; chairman of the board, Walco National Corp., 1960-1978, Carnegie Hall Corporation, 1960-1978, and Frederick W. Richmond Foundation, 1960 to present; budget director, New York State Council on the Arts, 1965-1975; New York City human rights commissioner, 1964-1970; New York City taxi and limousine commissioner, 1970-1972; member, New York City council, 1973-1974; delegate to the Democratic National Convention of 1964; elected as a Democrat to the Ninety-fourth and to the three succeeding Congresses, and served from January 3, 1975 until his resignation on August 25, 1982; president, US Systems; is a resident of North Egremont, Mass.

**RICHMOND, Hiram Lawton,** a Representative from Pennsylvania; born in Chautauqua, Chautauqua County, N.Y., May 17, 1810; received his early education from a private instructor and in the common schools; studied medicine for two years with his father; attended Allegheny College, Meadville, Pa., in 1834 and 1835 but did not graduate; studied law; was admitted to the bar in 1838 and commenced the practice of law in Meadville, Crawford County, Pa.; in early manhood was a staunch Whig, but united with the Republican Party upon its organization; elected as a Republican to the Forty-third Congress (March 4, 1873-March 3, 1875); was not a candidate for renomination in 1874 to the Forty-fourth Congress; member of the board of trustees of Allegheny College for many years; resumed the practice of law; died in Meadville, Pa., February 19, 1885; interment in Greendale Cemetery.

**RICHMOND, James Buchanan,** a Representative from Virginia; born in Turkey Cove, Lee County, Va., February 27, 1842; attended Emory and Henry College, Emory, Va.; studied law; admitted to the bar and practiced in the circuit and county courts of Lee, Scott, and Wise Counties, Va., and in the court of appeals at Wytheville, Va.; served as orderly sergeant and promoted to captain of Company A, Fiftieth Regiment, Virginia Infantry; afterward major in the Sixty-fourth Virginia Regiment for a time, and was subsequently promoted to the rank of lieutenant colonel of the same regiment; member of the Virginia house of delegates in 1874 and 1875; was elected as a Democrat to the Forty-sixth Congress (March 4, 1879-March 3, 1881); county judge of Scott County, 1886-1892; delegate to the Virginia constitutional convention at Richmond in 1901 and 1902; chief counsel of the South Atlantic & Ohio Railroad for a number of years; also engaged in banking; died in Baltimore, Md., April 30, 1910; interment in Estil Cemetery, Gate City, Va.

**RICHMOND, Jonathan,** a Representative from New York; born in Dartmouth, Mass., July 31, 1774; completed preparatory studies; moved to western New York in 1813 and settled in Aurora, Cayuga County; sheriff of Cayuga County, N.Y., from 1808 to 1812; United States internal revenue collector; elected to the Sixteenth Congress (March 4, 1819-March 3, 1821); died in Aurora, Cayuga County, N.Y., July 28, 1853; interment in Aurora Cemetery.

**RICKETTS, Edwin Darlington,** a Representative from Ohio; born near Maxville, Perry County, Ohio, August 3, 1867; attended the public schools; for twelve years was a teacher and superintendent of schools; studied law; was admitted to the bar in 1899 and commenced practice in Logan, Hocking County, Ohio; elected as a Republican to the Sixty-fourth Congress (March 4, 1915-March 3, 1917); was an unsuccessful candidate for reelection in 1916 to the Sixty-fifth Congress; elected to the Sixty-sixth and Sixty-seventh Congresses (March 4, 1919-March 3, 1923); was an unsuccessful candidate for reelection in 1922 to the Sixty-eighth Congress; resumed the practice of law; delegate to the Republican National Convention in 1928; died in Logan, Ohio, on July 3, 1937; interment in Oak Grove Cemetery.

**RIDDICK, Carl Wood,** a Representative from Montana; born in Wells, Faribault County, Minn., February 25, 1872; attended the common schools; was graduated from Menominee (Mich.) High School in 1890; attended Albion (Mich.) College and Lawrence University, Appleton, Wis.; editor and publisher of the Winamac (Ind.) Republican, 1899-1910; secretary of the Indiana Republican State central committee, 1906-1908; moved to Montana and settled on a homestead in Fergus County in 1910; engaged in wheat and cattle raising from 1910 until 1918; assessor of Fergus County, Mont., 1915-1918; elected as a Republican to the Sixty-sixth and Sixty-seventh Congresses (March 4, 1919-March 3, 1923); was not a candidate in 1922 for renomination to the House of Representatives, but was an unsuccessful candidate for election to the United States Senate; former president of the National Republic, a magazine published in Washington, D.C.; owned and operated a home development at Sylvan Shores on the South River, Riva, Md.; moved to Florida; died in Fort Lauderdale, Fla., July 9, 1960; interment in Hillcrest Memorial Cemetery, Annapolis, Md.

**RIDDLE, Albert Gallatin,** a Representative from Ohio; was born in Monson, Mass., May 28, 1816; moved with his parents to Newbury, in the Western Reserve of Ohio, in 1817; completed preparatory studies; studied law; was admitted to the bar in 1840 and began practice in Geauga County; prosecuting attorney of that county 1840-1846; member of the State house of representatives 1848-1850; moved to Cleveland, Ohio, in 1856; elected as a Republican to the Thirty-seventh Congress (March 4, 1861-March 3, 1863); was not a candidate for renomination in 1862; consul at Matanzas, Cuba, in 1863 and 1864; returned to Washington, D.C., and again engaged in the practice of law; was retained by the State Department to aid in the prosecution of John H. Surratt as one of the accomplices in the murder of President Abraham Lincoln; law officer of the District of Columbia 1877-1889; died in Washington, D.C., May 16, 1902; interment in Rock Creek Cemetery.

**Bibliography:** *DAB*; Riddle, Albert G. *Recollections of War Times: Reminiscences of Men and Events in Washington, 1860-1865.* G.P. Putnam's Sons, 1895.

**RIDDLE, George Read,** a Representative and a Senator from Delaware; born in New Castle, Del., in 1817; pursued classical studies and attended Delaware College; studied civil engineering and engaged in the construction of railroads and canals; studied law; was admitted to the bar in 1848 and commenced practice in Wilmington, Del., the same year; commissioner to retrace the Mason and Dixon line in 1849; deputy attorney general 1849-1850; elected as a Democrat to the Thirty-second and Thirty-third Congresses (March 4, 1851-March 3, 1855); unsuccessful candidate for reelection in 1854 to the Thirty-fourth Congress; chairman, Committee on Engraving (Thirty-third Congress); elected to the United States Senate to fill the vacancy caused by the resignation of James A. Bayard and served from February 2, 1864, until his death in Washington, D.C., on March 29, 1867; interment in the Wilmington and Brandywine Cemetery, Wilmington, Del.

**RIDDLE, Haywood Yancey,** a Representative from Tennessee; born in Van Buren, Hardeman County, Tenn., June 20, 1834; completed preparatory studies and was graduated from Union University, Murfreesboro, Tenn., in 1854; adjunct professor of mathematics and languages at that institution; was graduated from the law department of Cumberland University, Lebanon, Tenn., in 1857 and was admitted to the bar in Ripley, Miss., the same year; moved to Smith County, Tenn., in 1858 and engaged in agricultural pursuits; enlisted in the Confederate Army as a private in 1861 and served throughout the war, the last year on the staffs of Brigadier Generals Wright and William W. Mackall; moved to Lebanon, Wilson County, Tenn., in 1865 to practice law, but was employed as a deputy clerk in the chancery clerk's office for five years; appointed clerk for a term of six years in 1870, and served until December 31, 1875; elected as a Democrat to the Forty-fourth Congress to fill the vacancy caused by the death of Samuel M. Fite; reelected to the Forty-fifth Congress, and served from December 14, 1875 to March 3, 1879; died in Lebanon, Tenn., March 28, 1879; interment in Cedar Grove Cemetery.

**RIDDLEBERGER, Harrison Holt,** a Senator from Virginia; born in Edinburg; Shenandoah County, Va., October 4, 1844; attended the common schools; served three years during the Civil War in the Confederate Army as second and first lieutenant of Infantry and as captain of Cavalry; returned to Edinburg and became editor of the Tenth Legion Banner; studied law; admitted to the bar and commenced practice in Woodstock, Va.; member, Virginia house of delegates 1871-1875; Commonwealth attorney of Shenandoah County 1876-1880; member, Virginia senate 1879-1882; editor of the Shenandoah Democrat and later of the Virginian at Woodstock; presidential elector on the Democratic ticket in 1876 and on the Readjuster ticket in 1880; elected as a Readjuster to the United States Senate in 1881 and served from March 4, 1883, to March 3, 1889; chairman, Committee on Manufactures (Forty-eighth through Fiftieth Congresses); died in Woodstock, Va., January 24, 1890; interment in Cedarwood Cemetery, Edinburg, Shenandoah County, Va.

**RIDER, Ira Edgar,** a Representative from New York; born in Jersey City, N.J., November 17, 1868; attended the public schools and the College of the City of New York; was graduated from the St. Lawrence University, Canton, N.Y.; studied law; was admitted to the bar and commenced practice in New York City; secretary to the president of Manhattan Borough 1898-1902; elected as a Democrat to the Fifty-eighth Congress (March 4, 1903-March 3, 1905); owing to ill health was not a candidate for renomination in 1904; resumed the practice of law; died in New York City, May 29, 1906; interment in Calvary Cemetery.

**RIDGE, Thomas Joseph,** a Representative from Pennsylvania; born in Munhall, Allegheny County, Pa., August 26, 1945; attended St. Andrew's School, Erie, Pa.; graduated from Cathedral Prep School, Erie, 1963; B.A., Harvard University, 1967; J.D., Dickinson School of Law, Carlisle, Pa., 1972; served in the United States Army as a staff sergeant, 1968-1970; admitted to the Pennsylvania bar in 1972 and commenced practice in Erie; assistant district attorney, Erie County, 1972-1982; delegate, Pennsylvania Republican convention, 1983; delegate to the Republican National Convention of 1984; elected as a Republican to the Ninety-eighth and to the five succeeding Congresses (January 3, 1983-January 3, 1995); was not a candidate in 1994 for renomination to the One Hundred Fourth Congress, but was elected Governor of Pennsylvania for a four-year term beginning January 17, 1995; is a resident of Erie, Pa.

**RIDGELY, Edwin Reed,** a Representative from Kansas; born near Lancaster, Wabash County, Ill., May 9, 1844; attended district school in the winter months; during the Civil War enlisted as a private in Company C, One Hundred and Fifteenth Regiment, Illinois Volunteer Infantry, in 1862; promoted to sergeant and served until the end of the war; moved to Girard, Kans., in 1869 and engaged in general merchandising and in agricultural pursuits; left the Republican Party in 1876 because of its financial policy; lived in Ogden, Utah, from 1889 to 1893 and then returned to Kansas; elected as a Populist to the Fifty-fifth and Fifty-sixth Congresses (March 4, 1897-March 3, 1901); was not a candidate for renomination in 1900; resumed agricultural pursuits in Mulberry, Crawford County, Kans.; died in Girard, Kans., April 23, 1927; interment in Girard Cemetery.

**RIDGELY, Henry Moore,** a Representative and a Senator from Delaware; born in Dover, Del., August 6, 1779; completed preparatory studies; studied law; was admitted to the bar in 1802 and began practice in Dover; secretary of State of Delaware 1817-1827; elected as a Federalist to the Twelfth and Thirteenth Congresses (March 4, 1811-March 3, 1815); was not a candidate for renomination in 1814; returned to Dover, Del., and resumed the practice of law; elected to the United States Senate to fill the vacancy caused by the death of Nicholas Van Dyke and served from January 12, 1827, to March 3, 1829; was not a candidate for reelection; continued the practice of law; died in Dover, Del., August 6, 1847; interment in the Episcopal Cemetery.

**RIDGELY, Richard,** a Delegate from Maryland; born in Queen Caroline Parish, Anne Arundel County, Md., August 3, 1755; attended St. John's College, Annapolis, Md.; assistant clerk of the council of safety in 1776, and later clerk; studied law; was admitted to the bar in 1780 and commenced practice in Baltimore; advocate in the Maryland Court of Chancery; elected a Member of the Continental Congress in 1784 and 1785, but did not attend; served in the State senate 1786-1791; resumed the practice of law in Baltimore; appointed judge of the county court July 30, 1811, which position he held until his death in Howard County, Md., February

25, 1824; interment on the "Dorsey Hall" estate, near Columbia, Howard County, Md.

**RIDGWAY, Joseph,** a Representative from Ohio; born on Staten Island, N.Y., May 6, 1783; attended the public schools; learned the trade of carpenter; moved to Cayuga County, N.Y., in 1811 and engaged in the manufacture of plows; settled in Columbus, Franklin County, Ohio, in 1822 and established an iron foundry; member of the State house of representatives 1828-1832; elected as a Whig to the Twenty-fifth, Twenty-sixth, and Twenty-seventh Congresses (March 4, 1837-March 3, 1843); unsuccessful candidate for reelection in 1842 to the Twenty-eighth Congress; member of the State board of equalization; director of the Clinton Bank for twenty years; member of the city council; died in Columbus, Ohio, February 1, 1861; interment in Greenlawn Cemetery.

**RIDGWAY, Robert,** a Representative from Virginia; born in Lynchburg, Amherst County, Va., April 21, 1823; attended Emory and Henry College, Emory, Va.; was graduated from the University of Virginia at Charlottesville; studied law; was admitted to the bar and commenced practice in Liberty (now Bedford), Va.; edited the Bedford Sentinel; moved to Richmond, Va., in 1853; edited the Richmond Whig until the outbreak of the Civil War, when he retired to Amherst; elected as a Whig to the Fortieth Congress, but as reconstruction measures were not completed was not permitted to qualify; elected as a Conservative to the Forty-first Congress in July 1869; took his seat January 27, 1870, and served until his death at Cool Well, Amherst County, Va., October 16, 1870; interment in the family cemetery at Amherst, Va.

**RIEGLE, Donald Wayne, Jr.,** a Representative and a Senator from Michigan; born in Flint, Genesee County, Mich., February 4, 1938; attended the public schools of Flint, Mich., Flint Junior College and Western University; B.A., University of Michigan, 1960; M.B.A., Michigan State University, 1961; pursued doctoral studies at Harvard Business School, 1964-1966; financial analyst, IBM Corp., 1961-1964; faculty member, Michigan State University, Boston University, and Harvard University; elected as a Republican to the Ninetieth and to the three succeeding Congresses (January 3, 1967-January 3, 1975); announced his affiliation with the Democratic Party on February 27, 1973, and continued in office during the Ninety-third Congress as a Democrat; reelected as a Democrat to the Ninety-fourth Congress, and served from January 3, 1975 until his resignation December 30, 1976; was not a candidate in 1976 for reelection to the House of Representatives, but was elected to the United States Senate for the term commencing January 3, 1977; subsequently appointed by the Governor, December 30, 1976, to fill the vacancy caused by the death of Philip A. Hart for the term ending January 3, 1977; reelected in 1982 and in 1988, and served from December 30, 1976 to January 3, 1995; was not a candidate for reelection in 1994; chairman, Committee on Banking, Housing and Urban Affairs (One Hundred First through One Hundred Third Congresses); chairman, Shandwick Public Affairs, Washington, D.C.; is a resident of Traverse City, Mich.

**RIEHLMAN, Roy Walter,** a Representative from New York; born in Otisco, Onondaga County, N.Y., August 26, 1899; attended the public schools of Tully, N.Y.; was graduated from the Manlius Military Academy, Manlius, N.Y., in 1919 and the Central City Business School, Syracuse, N.Y., in 1921; operated a general store and served as postmaster of Nedrow, N.Y., 1921-1923; in 1923 became owner and operator of a bakery at Tully, N.Y.; member of Tully Board of Education 1933-1938; member of the board of supervisors of Onondaga County 1938-1943; county clerk of Onondaga County 1943-1946; member of the advisory board of the Marine Midland Trust Co., Tully, N.Y.; area board of directors, Lynchburg College, Va.; elected as a Republican to the Eightieth and to the eight succeeding Congresses (January 3, 1947-January 3, 1965); unsuccessful candidate for reelection in 1964 to the

Eighty-ninth Congress; vice president, Lu-Mar Enterprises, Inc.; resided in Ormond Beach, Fla., until his death there July 16, 1978; interment in Tully Cemetery, Tully, N.Y.

**RIFE, John Winebrenner,** a Representative from Pennsylvania; born in Middletown, Dauphin County, Pa., August 14, 1846; attended the common schools; learned the trade of tanner; enlisted July 15, 1864, as a private in Company D, One Hundred and Ninety-fourth Regiment, Pennsylvania Volunteer Infantry, and served until honorably discharged on November 6, 1864; member of the city council in 1871; burgess of Middletown, Pa., in 1877 and 1878; member of the Pennsylvania house of representatives in 1885 and 1886; president of the Middletown & Hummelstown Railroad Co.; elected as a Republican to the Fifty-first and Fifty-second Congresses (March 4, 1889-March 3, 1893); was not a candidate for renomination; died in Middletown, Pa., April 17, 1908; interment in Middletown Cemetery.

**RIGGS, Frank Duncan,** a Representative from California; born in Louisville, Ky., September 5, 1950; graduated, San Rafael (Calif.) High School; B.A. Golden Gate University, 1980; United States Army service; real estate developer; police officer and deputy sheriff; coordinator, campaigns of Ronald Reagan for President in 1984, and George Deukmejian for Governor, 1982, 1986; member, Windsor Union School District, board president; elected as a Republican to the One Hundred Second Congress (January 3, 1991-January 3, 1993); unsuccessful candidate for reelection in 1992 to the One Hundred Third Congress; elected to the One Hundred Fourth Congress (January 3, 1995-January 3, 1997); is a resident of Windsor, Calif.

**RIGGS, James Milton,** a Representative from Illinois; born on a farm near Winchester, Scott County, Ill., April 17, 1839; attended the common schools and Eureka (Ill.) College in 1862 and 1863; engaged in agricultural pursuits and taught school; sheriff of Scott County from December 1, 1864, to December 1, 1866; studied law; was admitted to the bar December 28, 1867, and commenced practice in Winchester, Scott County, Ill.; secretary of the Winchester School Board 1868-1884 and served as president 1889-1892; member of the State house of representatives in 1871 and 1872; State's attorney for Scott County 1872-1876; mayor of Winchester in 1876 and 1877; was elected as a Democrat to the Forty-eighth and Forty-ninth Congresses (March 4, 1883-March 3, 1887); was not a candidate for renomination in 1886; resumed the practice of law in Winchester, Ill.; president of the State bar association in 1891; delegate to several State conventions; was elected judge of Scott County in 1922; reelected in 1926 and served until 1930 when he retired from active pursuits; died in Winchester, Ill., November 18, 1933; interment in Winchester Cemetery.

**RIGGS, Jetur Rose,** a Representative from New Jersey; born near Drakesville (now Ledgewood), Morris County, N.J., June 20, 1809; received an academic education; was graduated from the New York College of Physicians and Surgeons in 1837 and commenced practice in Newfoundland, N.J.; member of the New Jersey State general assembly in 1836; one of the founders of the District Medical Society of Passaic County, N.J., in 1844 and served as president, 1846-1848; moved to California in 1849 and was in charge of the hospital at Sutters Fort; returned to New Jersey and settled in Paterson in 1852; member of the State senate, 1855-1858; elected as an Anti-Lecompton Democrat to the Thirty-sixth Congress (March 4, 1859-March 3, 1861); was not a candidate for renomination in 1860 to the Thirty-seventh Congress; resumed the practice of medicine in Paterson, Passaic County, N.J., later moved to Drakesville (now Ledgewood), N.J., and died there on November 5, 1869; interment in the Presbyterian Cemetery, Succasunna, Morris County, N.J.

**RIGGS, Lewis,** a Representative from New York; born in Norfolk, Conn., January 16, 1789; attended the common schools and schools of Latin and Greek; was apprenticed to the carpenter's trade; studied medicine in the village of Torringford, Litchfield County, Conn., and received his diploma in May 1812; also attended medical lectures given by Dr. Benjamin Rush at the University of Pennsylvania, Philadelphia, Pa., in 1812; practiced in East Winsted, Conn.; moved to Vernon, Oneida County, N.Y., in 1813 and later to Homer, N.Y., continuously practicing his profession; also engaged in business as a retail druggist and in 1828 in the sale of dry goods; served as secretary of the Cortland County Medical Society 1820-1823 and as president in 1825 and 1826; appointed postmaster of Homer by President Andrew Jackson on April 25, 1829, and served until August 7, 1839; was elected as a Democrat to the Twenty-seventh Congress (March 4, 1841-March 3, 1843); resumed the practice of medicine; also operated a flour mill; died in Homer, Cortland County, N.Y., November 6, 1870; interment in Glenwood Cemetery.

**RIGNEY, Hugh McPheeters,** a Representative from Illinois; born in Arthur, Moultrie County, Ill., July 31, 1873; attended the local schools and was graduated from the high school of his native city; apprenticed to the printer's trade and worked as a journeyman; editor and owner of the Arthur (Ill.) Graphic-Clarion 1900-1925; served as city treasurer 1910-1911; member of the school board 1910-1916; chairman of Moultrie County Democratic central committee 1930-1934 and reelected chairman in 1942; member of the State house of representatives 1935-1937; elected as a Democrat to the Seventy-fifth Congress (January 3, 1937-January 3, 1939); unsuccessful candidate for reelection in 1938 to the Seventy-sixth Congress; engaged in the real estate brokerage business 1939-1943; appointed to a position in the office of the secretary of state on September 15, 1943, and served until his death in Springfield, Ill., October 12, 1950; interment in Arthur Cemetery, Arthur, Ill.

**RIKER, Samuel,** a Representative from New York; born in Newtown, Long Island, N.Y., April 8, 1743; attended the common schools; member of the Newtown committee of correspondence in 1774; was supervisor of Suffolk County in 1783; lieutenant of Light Horse in the Revolution; member of the State assembly in 1784; elected as a Republican to the Eighth Congress to fill the vacancy caused by the resignation of John Smith and served from November 5, 1804, to March 3, 1805; elected to the Tenth Congress (March 4, 1807-March 3, 1809); died in Newtown, Long Island, N.Y., May 19, 1823; interment in the Dutch Reformed Cemetery.

**RILEY, Corinne Boyd** (wife of John Jacob Riley), a Representative from South Carolina; born in Piedmont, Greenville County, S.C., July 4, 1893; attended the public schools and graduated from Converse College, Spartanburg, S.C., in 1915; taught in the secondary schools of South Carolina for thirteen years, 1915-1937; field representative, South Carolina State Text Book Commission, 1938-1942; associated with Civilian Personnel Office, Shaw Air Force Base, Sumter, S.C., 1942-1944; elected as a Democrat to the Eighty-seventh Congress, by special election, April 10, 1962, to fill the vacancy caused by the death of her husband, John J. Riley, and served from April 10, 1962, to January 3, 1963; was not a candidate for reelection in 1962 to the Eighty-eighth Congress; resided in Sumter, S.C., where she died on April 12, 1979; cremated; ashes interred in Sumter Cemetery.

**RILEY, John Jacob,** (husband of Corinne Boyd Riley) a Representative from South Carolina; born on a farm near Orangeburg, S.C., February 1, 1895; attended the public schools in Orangeburg County; was graduated from Wofford College, Spartanburg, S.C., in 1915; taught in the Orangeburg city schools 1915-1917, and at Clemson (S.C.) Agricultural and Mechanical College in 1917 and 1918; during the First World War served in the United States Navy as a seaman, second class, and as a yeoman,

third class, in 1918 and 1919; engaged in the real estate and insurance business in Sumter, S.C., 1919-1945; secretary of a building and loan association 1923-1945; delegate to Democratic State conventions 1928-1944; elected as a Democrat to the Seventy-ninth and Eightieth Congresses (January 3, 1945-January 3, 1949); unsuccessful candidate for renomination in 1948; elected to the Eighty-second and to the five succeeding Congresses and served from January 3, 1951, until his death at Surfside, near Myrtle Beach, S.C., January 1, 1962; interment in Sumter Cemetery, Sumter, S.C.

**RINAKER, John Irving,** a Representative from Illinois; born in Baltimore, Md., November 1, 1830; moved with his parents to Springfield, Ill., in December 1836; attended the Illinois College for one term and was graduated from McKendree College, Lebanon, Ill., in 1851; studied law; was admitted to the bar in 1854 and commenced practice in Carlinville, Ill.; raised and organized the One Hundred and Twenty-second Regiment, Illinois Volunteer Infantry, in 1862; commissioned colonel September 4, 1862; commanded a brigade in the Sixteenth Corps of the Army of the Tennessee, and was brevetted brigadier general February 13, 1865; delegate to the Republican National Conventions in 1876 and 1884; chairman of the Board of Railroad and Warehouse Commissioners of Illinois 1885-1889; successfully contested as a Republican the election of Finis E. Downing to the Fifty-fourth Congress and served from June 5, 1896, to March 3, 1897; unsuccessful candidate for reelection in 1896 to the Fifty-fifth Congress; returned to Carlinville, Ill., and resumed the practice of law; died in Eustis, Lake County, Fla., January 15, 1915; interment in the City Cemetery, Carlinville, Ill.

**RINALDO, Matthew John,** a Representative from New Jersey; born in Elizabeth, Union County, N.J., September 1, 1931; B.S., Rutgers University, New Brunswick, N.J., 1953; M.B.A., Seton Hall University Graduate School of Business Administration, South Orange, N.J., 1959; D.P.A., New York University, School of Public Administration, 1979; member of the Union Township Zoning Board of Adjustment, 1962-1963, and of the Union County Board of Freeholders, 1963-1964; New Jersey State senator, 1967-1972; elected as a Republican to the Ninety-third and to the nine succeeding Congresses (January 3, 1973-January 3, 1993); was not a candidate for reelection in 1992 to the One Hundred Third Congress; is a resident of Union, N.J.

**RINGGOLD, Samuel,** a Representative from Maryland; born in Chestertown, Md., January 15, 1770; received a limited schooling; moved to Washington County, Md., and settled at Fountain Rock, near Hagerstown; engaged in agricultural pursuits; member of the State house of delegates in 1795; served in the State senate 1801-1806; judge of the levy court of Washington County 1806-1810 and 1822-1826; appointed a brigadier general in the Maryland Militia on July 7, 1810; elected as a Republican to the Eleventh Congress to fill the vacancy caused by the resignation of Roger Nelson; reelected to the Twelfth and Thirteenth Congresses and served from October 15, 1810, to March 3, 1815; served in the War of 1812; elected to the Fifteenth and Sixteenth Congresses (March 4, 1817-March 3, 1821); resumed agricultural pursuits; died in Frederick, Frederick County, Md., October 18, 1829; interment in Fountain Rock Cemetery, near Hagerstown, Washington County, Md.

**RIORDAN, Daniel Joseph,** a Representative from New York; born in New York City July 7, 1870; attended the public schools until 1886, when he entered Manhattan College, from which he graduated in 1890; engaged in the real-estate business; elected as a Democrat to the Fifty-sixth Congress (March 4, 1899-March 3, 1901); elected a member of the State senate in 1902 and again in 1904; elected to the Fifty-ninth Congress to fill the vacancy caused by the resignation of Timothy D. Sullivan and on the same day was elected to the Sixtieth Congress; reelected to the Sixty-first and to the seven succeeding Congresses and served from November 6, 1906, until his death in Washington, D.C., April 28, 1923; interment in Calvary Cemetery, Long Island City, N.Y.

**RIPLEY, Eleazar Wheelock** (brother of James Wheelock Ripley), a Representative from Louisiana; born in Hanover, N.H., April 15, 1782; was graduated from Dartmouth College, Hanover, N.H., in 1800; studied law; was admitted to the bar and commenced practice in Waterville, Maine (a district of Massachusetts until 1820); was a member of the Massachusetts house of representatives in 1807 and 1811 and served as speaker the last term; moved to Portland, Maine, in 1812; member of the Massachusetts senate; served in the War of 1812, being commissioned lieutenant colonel of the Twenty-first Infantry March 12, 1812; colonel March 12, 1813; brigadier general April 15, 1814; brevetted major general on July 25, 1814; by a resolution of Congress dated November 3, 1814, was presented a gold medal in honor of his military service; resigned from the Army February 1, 1820, and settled in Jackson, La., where he resumed the private practice of law; member of the State senate; elected as a Jacksonian to the Twenty-fourth Congress; reelected as a Democrat to the Twenty-fifth Congress and served from March 4, 1835, until his death in West Feliciana Parish, La., on March 2, 1839; interment in a private cemetery at St. Francisville, La.

Bibliography: *DAB*.

**RIPLEY, James Wheelock** (brother of Eleazar Wheelock Ripley), a Representative from Maine; born in Hanover, N.H., March 12, 1786; attended the common schools and Fryeburg (Maine) Academy; studied law; was admitted to the bar and commenced practice in Fryeburg, Maine (until 1820 a part of Massachusetts); served in the War of 1812; member of the Massachusetts house of representatives 1814-1819; elected from Maine to the Nineteenth Congress to fill the vacancy caused by the resignation of Enoch Lincoln and on the same day was elected to the Twentieth Congress; reelected as a Jacksonian to the Twenty-first Congress and served from September 11, 1826, to March 12, 1830, when he resigned; resumed the practice of law; collector of customs for the district of Passamaquoddy, Maine, from December 16, 1830, until his death in Fryeburg, Oxford County, Maine, June 17, 1835; interment in the Village Cemetery.

**RIPLEY, Thomas C.,** a Representative from New York; born in Schaghticoke, N.Y.; received a limited schooling; studied law; was admitted to the bar and practiced in Harts Falls, N.Y.; elected as a Whig to the Twenty-ninth Congress to fill the vacancy caused by the death of Richard P. Herrick and served from December 7, 1846, to March 3, 1847; was not a candidate for renomination in 1846.

**RISENHOOVER, Theodore Marshall,** a Representative from Oklahoma; born in East Liberty near Stigler, Haskell County, Okla., November 3, 1934; attended public schools in Yuma, Ariz., and Stigler; attended the University of Alabama, 1960-1961; B.A., Northeastern State University, Tahlequah, Okla., 1965; served in the United States Air Force, 1955-1963; pursued career as a newspaper publisher; in 1965 became part owner and president of printing businesses in Tahlequah, Okla.; served as Oklahoma crime commissioner, second district, 1970-1974; delegate to the Democratic National Mid-term Convention of 1974; elected as a Democrat to the Ninety-fourth and Ninety-fifth Congresses (January 3, 1975-January 3, 1979); unsuccessful candidate for renomination in 1978 to the Ninety-sixth Congress; agent with Funeral Directors Life Insurance Company, Abilene, Tex.; is a resident of Tulsa, Okla.

**RISK, Charles Francis,** a Representative from Rhode Island; born in Central Falls, Providence County, R.I., August 19, 1897; attended the public and high schools; worked in textile plants; during the First World War served in the United States Army as a private at Camp Meigs in 1918; was employed in the Treasury Department, Washington, D.C., 1919-1922; was graduated from the law department of Georgetown University, Washington, D.C., in 1922; was admitted to the bar in 1923 and commenced practice in Central Falls, R.I., the same year; served as probate judge of Central Falls 1929-1931, as coroner of Lincoln, R.I., in 1931 and 1932, and as judge of the eleventh district court of Rhode Island 1932-1935; delegate to the Republican State conventions in 1936, 1940, and 1942; elected as a Republican to the Seventy-fourth Congress to fill the vacancy caused by the resignation of Francis B. Condon and served from August 6, 1935, to January 3, 1937; unsuccessful candidate for reelection in 1936 to the Seventy-fifth Congress; elected to the Seventy-sixth Congress (January 3, 1939-January 3, 1941); unsuccessful candidate for reelection in 1940 to the Seventy-seventh Congress; resumed the practice of law in Pawtucket, R.I.; died in Saylesville, in the township of Lincoln, R.I., December 26, 1943; interment in St. Francis Cemetery, Pawtucket, R.I.

**RISLEY, Elijah,** a Representative from New York; born in Connecticut on May 7, 1787; completed preparatory studies; moved to Fredonia, Chautauqua County, N.Y., in 1807; engaged in mercantile pursuits; sheriff of Chautauqua County 1825-1828; supervisor of town of Pomfret in 1835; engaged in the culture of garden seeds 1833-1853; elected as a Whig to the Thirty-first Congress (March 4, 1849-March 3, 1851); was not a candidate for renomination in 1850; major general in the State militia; died in Fredonia, Chautauqua County, N.Y., January 9, 1870; interment in the East Main Street Cemetery.

**RITCHEY, Thomas,** a Representative from Ohio; born in Bedford County, Pa., January 19, 1801; moved to Somerset, Ohio; attended the common schools; engaged in agricultural pursuits; treasurer of Perry County in 1835, 1837, and 1839; elected as a Democrat to the Thirtieth Congress (March 4, 1847-March 3, 1849); elected to the Thirty-third Congress (March 4, 1853-March 3, 1855); engaged in agricultural pursuits near Somerset, Perry County, Ohio, until his death on March 9, 1863; interment in the Zion Methodist Episcopal Cemetery, Madison Township, Perry County, Ohio.

**RITCHIE, Byron Foster** (son of James Monroe Ritchie), a Representative from Ohio; born in Grafton, Lorain County, Ohio, January 29, 1853; moved with his parents to Toledo, Ohio, in 1860; was graduated from the Toledo High School in 1870; studied law; was admitted to the bar in 1874 and commenced practice in Toledo; elected as a Democrat to the Fifty-third Congress (March 4, 1893-March 3, 1895); unsuccessful candidate for reelection in 1894 to the Fifty-fourth Congress; resumed the practice of law in Toledo, Ohio; elected judge of the court of common pleas of Lucas County, Ohio, in 1914; reelected in 1916 and again in 1922, and served until his death in Toledo, Ohio, August 22, 1928; interment in Woodlawn Cemetery.

**RITCHIE, David,** a Representative from Pennsylvania; born in Canonsburg, Washington County, Pa., August 19, 1812; was graduated from Jefferson College, Canonsburg, Pa., in 1829, and subsequently at Heidelberg, Germany; studied law; was admitted to the bar in 1835 and commenced practice in Pittsburgh, Pa.; elected as a Whig to the Thirty-third and Thirty-fourth Congresses and elected as a Republican to the Thirty-fifth Congress (March 4, 1853-March 3, 1859); chairman, Committee on Revolutionary Claims (Thirty-fourth Congress); was appointed associate judge of the court of common pleas of Allegheny County in 1862 and served nine months; resumed the practice of his profession; died in Pittsburgh, Pa., January 24, 1867.

**RITCHIE, James Monroe** (father of Byron Foster Ritchie), a Representative from Ohio; born in Dunfermline, Scotland, July 28, 1829; immigrated to the United States in 1832 with his parents, who settled in St. Lawrence County, N.Y.; his early schooling was limited and he received instruction at home from his father and mother;

studied law; was admitted to the bar in 1858 and commenced practice in Toledo, Ohio; delegate to the Republican National Convention in 1880; elected as a Republican to the Forty-seventh Congress (March 4, 1881-March 3, 1883); was not a candidate for renomination in 1882; again resumed the practice of his profession in Toledo, Ohio, and died there August 17, 1918; interment in Grafton Cemetery, Grafton, Lorain County, Ohio.

**RITCHIE, John,** a Representative from Maryland; born in Frederick, Frederick County, Md., August 12, 1831; completed preparatory studies at the Frederick Academy; commenced the study of medicine but abandoned it for law; attended the law department of Harvard University; was admitted to the bar and began practice in Frederick in 1854; captain of the Junior Defenders (militia) and was ordered by President James Buchanan to the scene of John Brown's raid at Harpers Ferry in October 1859; served as State's attorney for Frederick County, 1867-1871; elected as a Democrat to the Forty-second Congress (March 4, 1871-March 3, 1873); unsuccessful candidate for reelection in 1872 to the Forty-third Congress; resumed the practice of law in Frederick; appointed by Governor William T. Hamilton on March 16, 1881, chief judge of the sixth judicial circuit and associate justice of the court of appeals to fill the unexpired term of Judge Richard Bowie; elected in November 1881 to this office for a term of fifteen years, and served until his death in Frederick, Md., October 27, 1887; interment in Mount Olivet Cemetery.

**RITTER, Burwell Clark** (uncle of Walter Evans), a Representative from Kentucky; born near Russellville, Barren County, Ky., January 6, 1810; received a limited schooling; member of the Kentucky house of representatives in 1842 and 1850; elected as a Democrat to the Thirty-ninth Congress (March 4, 1865-March 3, 1867); was not a candidate for renomination in 1866 to the Fortieth Congress; engaged in agricultural pursuits; died in Hopkinsville, Christian County, Ky., October 1, 1880; interment in Hopewell (later known as Riverside) Cemetery.

**RITTER, Donald Lawrence,** a Representative from Pennsylvania; born in New York City, October 21, 1940; attended the Bronx High School of Science, N.Y.; B.S., Lehigh University, Bethlehem, Pa., 1961; M.S., Massachusetts Institute of Technology, Cambridge, 1963, and Sc.D., 1966; research assistant, Massachusetts Institute of Technology, 1961-1966; scientific exchange fellow, United States National Academy of Sciences-Soviet Academy of Sciences, Baikov Institute, Moscow, U.S.S.R., 1967-1968; assistant professor, California State Polytechnic University, San Luis Obispo, and contract consultant, private industry, 1968-1969; metallurgy professor and assistant to the vice president for research, Lehigh University, 1969-1976; manager of research program development, Lehigh University, 1976-1978; engineering consultant to industry; elected as a Republican to the Ninety-sixth and to the six succeeding Congresses (January 3, 1979-January 3, 1993); unsuccessful candidate for reelection in 1992 to the One Hundred Third Congress; chairman, National Environmental Policy Institute; is a resident of Coopersburg, Pa., and Washington, D.C.

**RITTER, John,** a Representative from Pennsylvania; born in Exeter, Pa., February 6, 1779; received a limited schooling; apprenticed as a printer; member of the Pennsylvania constitutional convention in 1836; elected as a Democrat to the Twenty-eighth and Twenty-ninth Congresses (March 4, 1843-March 3, 1847); was not a candidate for renomination in 1846 to the Thirtieth Congress; editor and publisher of the Adler, a German newspaper, at Reading; died in Reading, Berks County, Pa., November 24, 1851; interment in the Charles Evans Cemetery.

**RIVERA, Luis Muñoz,** a Resident Commissioner from Puerto Rico; born in Barranquitas, P.R., July 17, 1859; attended the common schools; engaged in commerce and general business; founded La Democracia, a daily newspaper, in Ponce, P.R., in 1889; was sent to Madrid in 1896 as a special representative to confer with the Liberal Party of Spain on establishing home rule in Puerto Rico; one of the founders of the Liberal Party in Puerto Rico in 1897; appointed secretary of state under the home-rule government and president of the cabinet in 1897; created and organized the insular police; resigned in 1898, when American sovereignty was declared, but his resignation not being accepted, he continued to serve until 1899; representative of his party to Washington, D.C., regarding the establishment of free-trade relations between the United States and Puerto Rico; organized the Federal Party in 1900, and on its dissolution in 1902 organized the Unionist Party; founded the Porto Rico Journal in 1900; published the Porto Rico Herald in New York City in 1901; served in the Puerto Rico House of Delegates, 1906-1910; presided over a special commission of the house of delegates which was sent to Washington, D.C., in 1909; elected as a Unionist a Resident Commissioner to the United States in 1910; reelected in 1912 and 1914 and served from March 4, 1911, until his death in San Juan, P.R., November 15, 1916; interment in San Antonio de Padua's Cemetery, Barranquitas, P.R.

**RIVERS, Lucius Mendel,** a Representative from South Carolina; born in Gumville, Berkeley County, S.C., September 28, 1905; attended the public schools, the College of Charleston, Charleston, S.C., and the University of South Carolina at Columbia; studied law; was admitted to the bar in 1932 and commenced practice in Charleston, S.C.; member, South Carolina State house of representatives, 1933-1936; delegate to the Democratic National Convention of 1936; elected as a Democrat to the Seventy-seventh and to the fifteen succeeding Congresses, and served from January 3, 1941 until his death in Birmingham, Ala., December 28, 1970; chairman, Committee on Armed Services (Eighty-ninth through Ninety-first Congresses); interment in St. Stephen Episcopal Church Cemetery, St. Stephen, S.C.

**Bibliography:** Huntley, Will F. "Mighty Rivers of Charleston." Ph.D. dissertation, University of South Carolina, 1993; Ravenel, Marion Rivers. *Rivers Delivers.* Charleston, S.C.: Wyrick and Co., 1995.

**RIVERS, Lynn Nancy,** a Representative from Michigan; born in Au Gres, Arenac County, Mich., December 19, 1956; attended the public schools and graduated, Au Gres-Sims High School, 1975; B.A., University of Michigan, 1987; J.D., Wayne State University, 1992; Ann Arbor board of education; member, Michigan State house of representatives, 1993-1994; elected as a Democrat to the One Hundred Fourth Congress (January 3, 1995-January 3, 1997); is a resident of Ann Arbor, Mich.

**RIVERS, Ralph Julian,** a Representative from Alaska; born in Seattle, King County, Wash., May 23, 1903; attended grammar school in Flat, Alaska, and Franklin High School, Seattle, Wash.; gold miner, Flat, Alaska, 1921-1923; graduated from the University of Washington at Seattle, LL.B., 1929; was admitted to Washington State bar in 1930; practiced law in Seattle, Wash., in 1930 and 1931; was admitted to the Alaska bar in 1931 and practiced law in Fairbanks, Alaska, 1931-1933; United States district attorney, fourth judicial division, district of Alaska, from 1933 until his resignation in 1944; elected attorney general of Alaska in 1945 and served until 1949; chairman of Employment Security Commission of Alaska 1950-1952; mayor of Fairbanks 1952-1954; president, League of Alaskan Cities, in 1954; member of Alaska Territorial senate in 1955; second vice president of Alaska Constitutional Convention at College, Alaska, in 1955 and 1956; delegate, Democratic National Conventions in 1960, 1964, and 1968; United

States Representative-elect under Alaska-Tennessee Plan, Washington, D.C., provisional basis, pending statehood, in 1957 and 1958; upon the admission of Alaska as a State into the Union was elected as a Democrat to the Eighty-sixth and to the three succeeding Congresses (January 3, 1959-January 3, 1967); unsuccessful candidate for reelection in 1966 to the Ninetieth Congress; resumed law practice at Fairbanks, 1967-1969; died in Chehalis, Wash., August 14, 1976; cremated; ashes interred at Sunset Memorial Gardens.

**RIVERS, Thomas,** a Representative from Tennessee; born in Franklin County, Tenn., September 18, 1819; received an academic education and attended La Grange College, Alabama; studied law; was admitted to the bar in 1839 and commenced practice in Somerville, Tenn.; served for many years in the State militia ranking as brigadier general; elected as the candidate of the American Party to the Thirty-fourth Congress (March 4, 1855-March 3, 1857); was not a candidate for renomination in 1856; continued the practice of law until his death on his plantation near Somerville, Tenn., March 18, 1863; interment in the Somerville Cemetery.

**RIVES, Francis Everod,** a Representative from Virginia; born in Prince George County, near Petersburg, Dinwiddie County, Va., January 14, 1792; completed preparatory studies; engaged in planting and in the building and management of railways in Virginia and North Carolina; member of the Virginia house of delegates 1821-1831; served in the Virginia senate 1831-1836, 1848-1851; elected as a Democrat to the Twenty-fifth and Twenty-sixth Congresses (March 4, 1837-March 3, 1841); chairman, Committee on Elections (Twenty-sixth Congress); declined to be a candidate for renomination; mayor of Petersburg, Va., from May 6, 1847, to May 5, 1848; died in Petersburg, Va., December 26, 1861; interment in Blandford Cemetery.

**RIVES, William Cabell,** a Representative and a Senator from Virginia; born at "Union Hill," Amherst County, Va., May 4, 1793; attended Hampden-Sidney College in Virginia and graduated from the College of William and Mary, Williamsburg, Va., in 1809; studied law; was admitted to the bar about 1814 and commenced practice in Charlottesville, Albemarle County; delegate to the Virginia constitutional convention in 1816; member, Virginia house of delegates, 1817-1820, 1822-1823; moved to "Castle Hill," Albemarle County, in 1821; elected to the Eighteenth and to the three succeeding Congresses, and served from March 4, 1823 until his resignation in 1829 to accept a diplomatic post; appointed Minister to France on April 18, 1829 and served until September 1832; elected as a Jacksonian to the United States Senate to fill the vacancy caused by the resignation of Littleton W. Tazewell, and served from December 10, 1832 to February 22, 1834, when he resigned; again elected to the United States Senate to fill the vacancy caused by the resignation of John Tyler, and served from March 4, 1836 to March 3, 1839; chairman, Committee on Naval Affairs (Twenty-fourth and Twenty-fifth Congresses); subsequently reelected as a Whig on January 18, 1841, for the term beginning March 4, 1839, and served until March 3, 1845; chairman, Committee on Foreign Relations (Twenty-seventh Congress); appointed Minister to France on July 20, 1849 and served until May 1853; member of the peace convention of 1861 held in Washington, D.C., in an effort to devise means to prevent the impending war; delegate from Virginia to the Confederate Provisional Congress in Montgomery, Ala., and Richmond, Va., in 1861; member of the house of representatives from Virginia in the Second Confederate Congress; died on his plantation, "Castle Hill," near Charlottesville, Va., April 25, 1868; interment in the private burial ground on the family estate.

**Bibliography:** DAB; Dingledine, Raymond C. "The Political Career of William Cabell Rives." Ph.D. dissertation, University of Virginia, 1947; Wingfield, Russell S. "William Cabell Rives."

*Richmond College Historical Papers* 1 (June 1915): 57-72.

**RIVES, Zeno John,** a Representative from Illinois; born near Greenfield, Hancock County, Ind., February 22, 1874; moved with his parents to Litchfield, Montgomery County, Ill., in 1880; attended the public schools; studied law; was admitted to the bar in 1901 and commenced practice in Litchfield, Ill.; appointed city clerk in June 1903; elected as a Republican to the Fifty-ninth Congress (March 4, 1905-March 3, 1907); unsuccessful candidate for reelection in 1906 to the Sixtieth Congress; resumed the practice of law in Litchfield, Ill.; was postmaster of Litchfield 1912-1916; moved to Decatur, Macon County, Ill., in 1919, and engaged in the practice of law and also the real estate business; died in Decatur, Ill., September 2, 1939; interment in Graceland Cemetery.

**RIXEY, John Franklin,** a Representative from Virginia; born in Culpeper County, Va., August 1, 1854; attended the common schools, Bethel Academy, and the University of Virginia at Charlottesville; studied law; was admitted to the bar in 1876 and commenced practice in Culpeper, Va.; Commonwealth attorney for Culpeper County, Va., 1879-1891; elected as a Democrat to the Fifty-fifth and to the four succeeding Congresses and served from March 4, 1897, until his death in Washington, D.C., February 8, 1907, before the close of the Fifty-ninth Congress; had been reelected to the Sixtieth Congress; interment in Fairview Cemetery, Culpeper, Va.

**RIZLEY, Ross,** a Representative from Oklahoma; born on a farm near Beaver, Okla., July 5, 1892; attended the public schools; taught in the rural schools of Beaver County, Okla., in 1909 and 1910; served as a deputy register of deeds of Beaver County, Okla., in 1911 and 1912; was graduated from the law department of the University of Kansas City, Kansas City, Mo., in 1915; was admitted to the bar the same year and commenced practice in Beaver, Okla.; elected county attorney of Beaver County in 1918 and served until 1920, when he resigned and moved to Guymon, Texas County, Okla., and resumed the practice of law; member of the Guymon Board of Education 1924-1932; city attorney of Guymon 1928-1938; member of the State senate 1931-1934; unsuccessful candidate for election as Governor of Oklahoma in 1938; elected as a Republican to the Seventy-seventh and to the three succeeding Congresses (January 3, 1941-January 3, 1949); chairman, Special Committee on Campaign Expenditures (Eightieth Congress); delegate to the Republican National Conventions in 1932, 1936, and 1948; was not a candidate for renomination in 1948 but was unsuccessful for election to the United States Senate; solicitor for the Post Office Department, Washington, D.C., from March to December 1953; Assistant Secretary of Agriculture from December 1953 until his resignation December 16, 1954; member of the Civil Aeronautics Board from February 25, 1955, until April 15, 1956, when he resigned; judge of the United States District Court for the western district of Oklahoma from 1956 until his death in Oklahoma City, Okla., March 4, 1969; interment in Elmhurst Cemetery, Guymon, Okla.

**ROACH, Sidney Crain,** a Representative from Missouri; born at Linn Creek, Camden County, Mo., on July 25, 1876; attended the public schools and the St. Louis Law School (now Washington University) in St. Louis; was admitted to the bar in 1897 and commenced practice at Linn Creek, Mo.; prosecuting attorney for Camden County, 1898-1909; member of the board of directors of the National Bank of Linn Creek, 1900-1924; member of the Missouri State house of representatives, 1909-1913; delegate to the Republican National Convention of 1912; elected as a Republican to the Sixty-seventh and Sixty-eighth Congresses (March 4, 1921-March 3, 1925); chairman, Committee on Expenditures in the Department of Justice (Sixty-eighth Congress); unsuccessful candidate for reelection in 1924 to the Sixty-ninth Congress; moved to St. Louis, Mo., December 27, 1924, and resumed the practice of law; died at Kansas City, Mo., June 29, 1934; interment in Roach Cemetery near Roach, Mo.

**ROACH, William Nathaniel,** a Senator from North Dakota; born in Washington, D.C., September 25, 1840; attended the public schools and Georgetown University, Washington, D.C.; clerk in the quartermaster's department during the Civil War; moved to Dakota Territory in 1879 and settled in Larimore; interested in mail contracts for several years; member of the Territorial house of representatives in 1885; unsuccessful Democratic candidate for Governor at the first State election in 1889, and again in 1891; elected as a Democrat to the United States Senate, and served from March 4, 1893 to March 3, 1899; unsuccessful candidate for reelection; discontinued active business pursuits and lived in retirement in Washington, D.C.; died in New York City on September 7, 1902; interment in the Congressional Cemetery, Washington, D.C.

**Bibliography:** Schlup, Leonard. "William N. Roach: North Dakota Isolationist and Gilded Age Senator." *North Dakota History* 57 (Fall 1990): 2-11.

**ROANE, John** (father of John Jones Roane), a Representative from Virginia; born at "Uppowac," King William County, Va., February 9, 1766; completed preparatory studies; member of the Virginia house of delegates 1788-1790 and in 1792; delegate to the Virginia constitutional convention in 1788; elected as a Republican to the Eleventh, Twelfth, and Thirteenth Congresses (March 4, 1809-March 3, 1815); engaged in agricultural pursuits; elected to the Twentieth Congress and reelected as a Jacksonian to the Twenty-first Congress (March 4, 1827-March 3, 1831); elected to the Twenty-fourth Congress (March 4, 1835-March 3, 1837); died at his residence, "Uppowac," King William County, Va., November 15, 1838; interment in the family burying ground, Rumford, Va.

**ROANE, John Jones** (son of John Roane), a Representative from Virginia; born in Essex County, Va., October 31, 1794; completed preparatory studies; attended Rumford Academy in King William County, Va., and Princeton College, New Jersey, but did not graduate; engaged in agricultural pursuits; served in the War of 1812 as a private in the Fourth Regiment, Virginia Militia; member of the Virginia house of delegates 1820-1823; elected as a Jacksonian to the Twenty-second Congress (March 4, 1831-March 3, 1833); clerk in the United States Patent Office 1836-1851; special agent in the Treasury Department 1855-1867; died in Washington, D.C., December 18, 1869; interment in Glenwood Cemetery.

**ROANE, William Henry** (grandson of Patrick Henry), a Representative and a Senator from Virginia; born in Virginia, September 17, 1787; completed preparatory studies; member, Virginia house of delegates 1812-1815; elected as a Republican to the Fourteenth Congress (March 4, 1815-March 3, 1817); was not a candidate for renomination; member of the executive council of Virginia; elected as a Democrat to the United States Senate to fill the vacancy caused by the resignation of Richard E. Parker and served from March 14, 1837, to March 3, 1841; chairman, Committee on the District of Columbia (Twenty-fifth Congress); unsuccessful candidate for reelection in 1841; engaged in agricultural pursuits; died in Tree Hill, near Richmond, Va., May 11, 1845; interment in the private cemetery of the Lyons family in Hanover County, Va.

**ROARK, Charles Wickliffe,** a Representative from Kentucky; born in Greenville, Muhlenberg County, Ky., January 22, 1887; attended the public schools and the Greenville Seminary; founder and president of the Greenville Milling Co.; served as president of the Kentucky Retail Lumbermen in 1908 and of the Tri-State Lumber Dealers' Association in 1909; elected mayor of Greenville and served from 1918 to 1922; elected as a Republican to the Seventy-first Congress and served from March 4, 1929, until his death, before the convening of Congress; died in Louisville, Ky., April 5, 1929; interment in the family lot in Evergreen Cemetery, Greenville, Ky.

**ROBB, Charles Spittal** (son-in-law of Lyndon Baines Johnson), a Senator from Virginia; born in Phoenix, Ariz., June 26, 1939; graduated from Mount Vernon High School, Fairfax, Va., 1957; attended Cornell University, Ithaca, N.Y., 1957-1958; B.B.A., University of Wisconsin, 1961; J.D., University of Virginia Law School, 1973; entered active duty, United States Marine Corps in 1961, released in 1970; admitted to the Virginia bar in 1973; law clerk, United States Court of Appeals, 1973-1974; practicing attorney, 1974-1977; Lieutenant Governor of Virginia, 1978-1982; elected Governor of Virginia in 1981, and served from January 16, 1982 to January 18, 1986; practicing attorney, 1986-1988; chair, Democratic Leadership Council, 1986-1988; elected as a Democrat to the United States Senate in 1988 for the term beginning January 3, 1989; reelected in 1994 for the term ending January 3, 2001; chairman, Democratic Senatorial Campaign Committee (One Hundred Second Congress); is a resident of McLean, Va.

**ROBB, Edward,** a Representative from Missouri; born in Brazeau, Perry County, Mo., March 19, 1857; attended the common schools, Brazeau (Mo.) Academy, Fruitland (Mo.) Normal Institute, and the University of Missouri at Columbia; was graduated from the law department of the University of Missouri in March 1879; was admitted to the bar in 1879 and commenced practice in Perryville; elected prosecuting attorney of Perry County in 1880 and reelected in 1882; member, Missouri State house of representatives, 1884-1886; assistant attorney general of Missouri, 1889-1893; elected as a Democrat to the Fifty-fifth and to the three succeeding Congresses (March 4, 1897-March 3, 1905); unsuccessful candidate for reelection in 1904 to the Fifty-ninth Congress; delegate to the Democratic National Convention of 1908; resumed the practice of law until his death in Perryville, Mo., March 13, 1934; interment in Home Cemetery.

**ROBBINS, Asher,** a Senator from Rhode Island; born in Wethersfield, Conn., October 26, 1757; graduated from Yale College in 1782; tutor in Rhode Island College (now Brown University) 1782-1790; studied law; was admitted to the bar in 1792 and began practice in Providence, R.I.; moved to Newport in 1795; appointed United States district attorney in 1812; member, State assembly 1818-1825; elected as a Whig to the United States Senate in 1825 to fill the vacancy caused by the resignation of James De Wolf; reelected in 1827 and 1833 and served from October 31, 1825, to March 3, 1839; chairman, Committee on Engrossed Bills (Twenty-second Congress); member, State assembly 1840-1841; postmaster of Newport, Newport County, R.I., from 1841 until his death in that city February 25, 1845; interment in Burial Ground Common.

**ROBBINS, Edward Everett,** a Representative from Pennsylvania; born at Robbins Station, Westmoreland County, Pa., September 27, 1860; attended the public schools, Indiana (Pa.) Normal School, and Eldersridge (Pa.) Academy; graduated from Washington and Jefferson College, Washington, Pa., in 1881 and from the law department of Columbia College, New York City, in 1884; admitted to the bar in 1884 and commenced practice in Greensburg, Pa.; also engaged in banking and coal-mining enterprises; member of the Pennsylvania senate 1888-1892; chairman of the Republican county committee in 1885; member of the Pennsylvania National Guard; served as major of Volunteers in the Spanish-American War in 1898; elected as a Republican to the Fifty-fifth Congress (March 4, 1897-March 3, 1899); was not a candidate for renomination in 1898; resumed the practice of his profession in Greensburg, Pa.; elected to the Sixty-fifth Congress and served from March 4, 1917, until his death; had been reelected to the Sixty-sixth Congress; died in Somerset, Somerset County, Pa., January 25, 1919; interment in St. Clair Cemetery, Greensburg, Pa.

**ROBBINS, Gaston Ahi,** a Representative from Alabama; born in Goldsboro, Wayne County, N.C., September 26, 1858; moved to Randolph County, N.C.; attended Trinity College at Durham and was graduated from the University of North Carolina at Chapel Hill in 1879; studied law; was admitted to the bar in 1880 and commenced practice in Selma, Ala.; elected as a Democrat to the Fifty-third Congress (March 4, 1893-March 3, 1895); presented credentials as a Member-elect to the Fifty-fourth Congress and served from March 4, 1895, to March 13, 1896, when he was succeeded by William F. Aldrich, who contested his election; presented credentials to the Fifty-sixth Congress and served from March 4, 1899, to March 8, 1900, when he was again succeeded by William F. Aldrich, who contested his election; resumed the practice of law in New York City, where he died on February 22, 1902; interment in Oakwood Cemetery, Statesville, N.C.

**ROBBINS, George Robbins,** a Representative from New Jersey; born near Allentown, Monmouth County, N.J., September 24, 1808; received a good literary education; was graduated from the Jefferson Medical College at Philadelphia in 1837 and commenced the practice of medicine in Falsington, Bucks County, Pa.; moved to Hamilton Square, N.J., the same year and continued the practice of medicine; elected as a Whig to the Thirty-fourth Congress and reelected as a Republican to the Thirty-fifth Congress (March 4, 1855-March 3, 1859); was not a candidate for renomination; resumed the practice of his profession; died in Hamilton Square, N.J., February 22, 1875; interment in the Presbyterian Church Cemetery.

**ROBBINS, John,** a Representative from Pennsylvania; born in Bustleton (now a part of Philadelphia), near Lower Dublin, Pa., in 1808; attended the public schools; student at the Gunmere Academy in Burlington, N.J.; moved to Philadelphia in 1836 and engaged in the manufacture of steel; member of the board of commissioners of the district of Kensington and served as president several years; elected as a Democrat to the Thirty-first, Thirty-second, and Thirty-third Congresses (March 4, 1849-March 3, 1855); declined to be a candidate for renomination in 1854; unsuccessful candidate for office of mayor of Philadelphia in 1862; resumed the steel manufacturing business and held several municipal offices; elected to the Forty-fourth Congress (March 4, 1875-March 3, 1877); declined to be a candidate for renomination in 1876; member of the board of education and served as president for many years; president and director of the Kensington National Bank; died in Philadelphia, Pa., April 27, 1880; interment in Laurel Hill Cemetery.

**ROBBINS, William McKendree,** a Representative from North Carolina; born in the old homestead near Trinity, Randolph County, N.C., October 26, 1828; pursued classical studies; attended Old Trinity College and was graduated from Randolph-Macon College, Virginia, about 1850; studied law; was admitted to the bar in 1854 and commenced practice the same year in Eufaula, Ala.; served four years as major in the Fourth Alabama Regiment of the Confederate Army during the Civil War; member of the Alabama State senate in 1868 and 1872; elected as a Democrat to the Forty-third and to the two succeeding Congresses (March 4, 1873-March 3, 1879); chairman, Committee on Expenditures in the Department of War (Forty-fourth Congress); appointed by President Grover Cleveland as the southern commissioner on the Gettysburg Battle Field Commission in 1894, which position he held until his death in Salisbury, Rowan County, N.C., on May 5, 1905; interment in Oakwood Cemetery, Statesville, N.C.

**ROBERDEAU, Daniel,** a Delegate from Pennsylvania; born on the island of St. Christopher, West Indies, in 1727; immigrated to the United States and settled in Philadelphia, Pa., in boyhood; completed preparatory studies; engaged in the lumber business; member of the Pennsylvania assembly 1756-1760; manager of the Pennsylvania Hospital 1756-1758 and 1766-1776; member of the council of safety; first brigadier general of Pennsylvania troops in 1776; Member of the Continental Congress from 1777 to 1779; moved to Alexandria, Va., in 1785; died in Winchester, Frederick County, Va., on January 5, 1795; interment in Mount Hebron Cemetery.

**Bibliography:** *DAB.*

**ROBERTS, Anthony Ellmaker** (grandfather of Robert Grey Bushong), a Representative from Pennsylvania; born near Barneston Station, Chester County, Pa., on October 29, 1803; received a limited schooling; engaged in mercantile pursuits in New Holland, Lancaster County, Pa., 1816-1839; moved to Lancaster, Pa., in 1839; sheriff of Lancaster County 1839-1842; unsuccessful candidate for election in 1842 to the Twenty-eighth Congress; was appointed United States marshall for the eastern district of Pennsylvania on May 16, 1850, and served until March 29, 1853; elected as an Independent Whig to the Thirty-fourth Congress and reelected as a Republican to the Thirty-fifth Congress (March 4, 1855-March 3, 1859); was not a candidate for renomination in 1858; was active in organization of the Republican Party in Pennsylvania; engaged in operating his real estate holdings in Lancaster and was executor for various estates; died in Lancaster, Pa., on January 23, 1885; interment in the Lancaster Cemetery.

**ROBERTS, Brigham Henry,** a Representative from Utah; born in Warrington, Lancashire, England, March 13, 1857; immigrated to the United States in 1866 with his parents, who settled in Bountiful, Davis County, Utah; attended the district schools; was graduated from Deseret University, Salt Lake City, in 1878; taught school for several years and later worked as associate and editor in chief of the Salt Lake Herald; member of the State constitutional convention which framed the organic law of Utah in 1894; unsuccessful Democratic candidate for election in 1895 to the Fifty-fifth Congress; presented credentials as a Democratic Member-elect to the Fifty-sixth Congress, and served from March 4, 1899 to January 25, 1900, when the seat was declared vacant because he was a polygamist; author of numerous historical, biographical, and doctrinal works; served on the State board of equalization tax department in 1916 and subsequently ordained as a minister of the gospel; during the First World War served as chaplain of the One Hundred and Forty-fifth Regiment, Field Artillery; served as president of the Eastern States Mission of the Church of Jesus Christ of Latter-Day Saints in Brooklyn, N.Y.; died in Salt Lake City, Utah, September 27, 1933; interment in Centerville Ward Cemetery, Centerville, Davis County, Utah.

**Bibliography:** *DAB*; White, William Griffin, Jr. "The Feminist Campaign for the Exclusion of Brigham Henry Roberts from the Fifty-sixth Congress." *Journal of the West* 17 (January 1978): 45-52.

**ROBERTS, Charles Boyle,** a Representative from Maryland; born in Uniontown, Carroll County, Md., on April 19, 1842; was graduated from Calvert College, New Windsor, Md., in 1861; studied law; was admitted to the bar in 1864 and commenced practice in Westminster, Carroll County, Md.; elected as a Democrat to the Forty-fourth and Forty-fifth Congresses (March 4, 1875-March 3, 1879); chairman, Committee on Accounts (Forty-fourth and Forty-fifth Congresses); elected attorney general of Maryland in 1883, serving one term; elected associate judge of the fifth judicial district in 1891; appointed chief judge of the district to fill the vacancy caused by the death of Judge Miller and in 1893 was elected for the full term of fifteen years; died in Westminster, Md., September 10, 1899; interment in the Catholic Cemetery.

**ROBERTS, Charles Patrick (Pat),** a Representative from Kansas; born in Topeka, Shawnee County, Kans., April 20, 1936; attended the public schools; graduated from Holton High School, 1954; B.A., Kansas State University, Manhattan, 1958; teaching certificate, Arizona State University, 1962-1964; entered the United States Marine Corps in 1958, released as a captain, 1962; newspaper publisher, Avondale, Ariz., 1962-1967; administrative assistant to Senator Frank Carlson of Kansas, 1967-1968; administrative assistant to Representative Keith G. Sebelius of Kansas, 1968-1980; elected as a Republican to the Ninety-seventh and to the seven succeeding Congresses (January 3, 1981-January 3, 1997); chairman, Committee on Agriculture (One Hundred Fourth Congress); was not a candidate in 1996 for reelection to the House of Representatives, but was a candidate for election to the United States Senate; is a resident of Dodge City, Kans.

**ROBERTS, Clint Ronald,** a Representative from South Dakota; born in Presho, Lyman County, S.Dak., January 30, 1935; attended the public schools; graduated from Presho High School, 1952; attended Black Hills State College, Spearfish, S.Dak., 1952-1953; farmer and rancher; owner of a clothing store; served in the South Dakota State senate, 1972-1978; unsuccessful candidate in 1978 for election for Governor of South Dakota; South Dakota secretary of agriculture, 1979-1980; elected as a Republican to the Ninety-seventh Congress (January 3, 1981-January 3, 1983); unsuccessful candidate for reelection in 1982 to the Ninety-eighth Congress; commissioner, South Dakota Office of Energy Policy, 1987-1989; executive administrator of the Conservation Reserve Enhancement Program of South Dakota, 1989 to present; is a resident of Presho, S.Dak.

**ROBERTS, Edwin Ewing,** a Representative from Nevada; born in Pleasant Grove, Sutter County, Calif., December 12, 1870; attended the public schools and was graduated from the State normal school at San Jose, Calif., in 1891; taught school at Hollister, Calif., 1891-1897, and at Empire, Nev., 1897-1899; studied law; was admitted to the bar in 1899 and commenced practice in Carson City, Nev.; also engaged in the newspaper publishing business; district attorney of Ormsby County 1900-1910; elected as a Republican to the Sixty-second and to the three succeeding Congresses (March 4, 1911-March 3, 1919); did not seek renomination in 1918, but was an unsuccessful candidate for the United States Senate; delegate to the Republican National Convention in 1912 and 1924; resumed the practice of law in Reno, Nev., in 1920; elected mayor of Reno in 1923; reelected in 1927 and again in 1931 and served until his death; unsuccessful candidate for nomination as United States Senator in 1926 and for Governor in 1930; died in Reno, Nev., December 11, 1933; interment in the Odd Fellows Cemetery.

**ROBERTS, Ellis Henry,** a Representative from New York; born in Utica, Oneida County, N.Y., September 30, 1827; attended the common schools and the Whitestown (N.Y.) Seminary; was graduated from Yale College in 1850; principal of Utica Free Academy in 1850 and 1851; editor and proprietor of the Utica Morning Herald 1851-1889; delegate to the Republican National Conventions in 1864, 1868, and 1876; member of the State assembly in 1866; elected as a Republican to the Forty-second and Forty-third Congresses (March 4, 1871-March 3, 1875); unsuccessful candidate for reelection in 1874 to the Forty-fourth Congress; resumed his former newspaper activities in Utica, N.Y.; Assistant Treasurer of the United States 1889-1893; president of the Franklin National Bank of New York City 1893-1897; appointed Treasurer of the United States on July 1, 1897, and served until June 30, 1905, when he resigned; again engaged in banking; died in Utica, N.Y., January 8, 1918; interment in Forest Hill Cemetery.

**Bibliography:** *DAB.*

**ROBERTS, Ernest William,** a Representative from Massachusetts; born in East Madison, Maine, November 22, 1858; attended the public schools in Chelsea, Mass.; graduated from Highland Military Academy, Worcester, Mass., in 1877, and from the law school of Boston University; admitted to the bar in 1881 and commenced practice in Boston; member of the city council of Chelsea in 1887 and 1888; member of the Massachusetts house of representatives in 1894 and 1896; served in the Massachusetts senate in 1897 and 1898; elected as a Republican to the Fifty-sixth

and to the eight succeeding Congresses (March 4, 1899-March 3, 1917); chairman, Committee on Private Land Claims (Sixty-first Congress); unsuccessful candidate for renomination in 1916; after retiring from public life practiced law in Washington, D.C., until his death on February 27, 1924; interment in Woodlawn Cemetery, Everett, Middlesex County, Mass.

**ROBERTS, Herbert Ray,** a Representative from Texas; born near McKinney, Collin County, Tex., March 28, 1913; graduated from McKinney High School; attended Texas A.&M. University, 1930-1931, North Texas State University, 1931-1932, and the University of Texas, 1933-1935; served on the staff of Speaker Sam Rayburn of the House of Representatives, Washington, D.C., 1941-1942; served in the United States Navy as a lieutenant commander from 1942 to 1945 in the Pacific and European theaters; recalled to active duty in the Korean conflict; captain, United States Naval Reserve; businessman with diversified interests, including farming; served in the Texas State senate, 1955-1962, and was president pro tempore, 1961; elected as a Democrat to the Eighty-seventh Congress, January 30, 1962, by special election to fill the vacancy caused by the death of Sam Rayburn; reelected to the nine succeeding Congresses and served from January 30, 1962, to January 3, 1981; chairman, Committee on Veterans' Affairs (Ninety-fourth through Ninety-sixth Congresses); was not a candidate for reelection in 1980 to the Ninety-seventh Congress; was a resident of Denton, Tex.; died April 13, 1992.

**ROBERTS, Jonathan,** a Representative and a Senator from Pennsylvania; born near Norristown, Pa., August 16, 1771; privately tutored; apprenticed as a wheelwright; member, Pennsylvania house of representatives, 1799-1800; member, Pennsylvania senate, 1807-1811; elected as a Republican to the Twelfth and Thirteenth Congresses, and served from March 4, 1811 to February 24, 1814, when he resigned, having been elected Senator; elected as a Republican to the United States Senate to fill the vacancy caused by the resignation of Michael Leib; reelected in 1815, and served from February 24, 1814 to March 3, 1821; chairman, Committee on Claims (Fourteenth through Sixteenth Congresses), Committee to Audit and Control the Contingent Expense (Sixteenth Congress), Committee on Public Buildings (Sixteenth Congress); again a member of the Pennsylvania house of representatives, 1823-1826; collector of customs at the port of Philadelphia, 1841-1842; died on his farm, "Robertsville," King of Prussia, Montgomery County, Pa., July 24, 1854; interment in the Roberts family cemetery near Norristown, Pa.

**Bibliography:** *DAB*; Roberts, Jonathan. "Memoirs of a Senator from Pennsylvania: Jonathan Roberts, 1771-1854." Edited by Robert Klein. *The Pennsylvania Magazine of History and Biography* 61 (October 1937): 446-74, 62 (January 1938): 64-97, 62 (July 1938): 213-48, 62 (July 1938): 361-409, 62 (October 1938): 502-51.

**ROBERTS, Kenneth Allison,** a Representative from Alabama; born in Piedmont, Calhoun County, Ala., November 1, 1912; attended the public schools and Samford College, Birmingham, Ala.; was graduated from the University of Alabama Law School in 1935; was admitted to the bar in 1936 and commenced the practice of law in Anniston, Ala.; practiced law in Talladega, Ala., 1937-1942; elected to the Alabama State senate in 1942, but resigned the same year to enter the United States Navy, and served until discharged as a lieutenant in 1945 with service in both Atlantic and Pacific Theaters; president, Piedmont Development Co., 1945-1950; member of the Alabama State Board of Veterans Affairs, and city attorney of Piedmont, Ala., 1948-1950; elected as a Democrat to the Eighty-second and to the six succeeding Congresses (January 3, 1951-January 3, 1965); wounded March 1, 1954 when three Puerto Rican Nationalists fired about thirty shots into a crowd of representatives on the floor of the House; unsuccessful candidate for reelection in 1964 to the Eighty-ninth Congress; resumed the practice of law until his retirement in 1979; counsel, Vehicle Equipment Safety Commission, 1965-1971; member, National Highway Safety Advisory Committee, 1966-1969; was a resident of Anniston, Ala.; died May 9, 1989.

**ROBERTS, Robert Whyte,** a Representative from Mississippi; born in Kent County, Del., November 28, 1784; received a liberal education; studied law; was admitted to the bar; shortly after reaching his majority moved to Tennessee, where he was elected a circuit judge; moved to Limestone County, Ala. in 1822, and to Scott County, Miss., in 1826, and settled near Hillsboro; engaged in agricultural pursuits; commenced the practice of law in Hillsboro; circuit judge of Scott County 1830-1838; member of the State house of representatives 1838-1844 and served as speaker in 1842 and 1843; elected as a Democrat to the Twenty-eighth and Twenty-ninth Congresses (March 4, 1843-March 3, 1847); resumed the practice of law; also engaged in planting; died on his plantation, "Long Avenue," near Hillsboro, Miss., January 4, 1865; interment in a private cemetery on the Roberts plantation.

**ROBERTS, William Randall,** a Representative from New York; born in County Cork, Ireland, February 6, 1830; immigrated to the United States in July 1849; received a limited schooling; merchant in New York City until 1869, when he retired; president of the Fenian Brotherhood in 1865, and aided in the foray into Canada the following year, for which he was arrested by the Government; elected as a Democrat to the Forty-second and Forty-third Congresses (March 4, 1871-March 3, 1875); member of the board of aldermen of New York City in 1877; unsuccessful candidate for sheriff in 1879; appointed as Envoy Extraordinary and Minister Plenipotentiary to Chile by President Grover Cleveland on April 2, 1885, and served until August 1889; died in New York City on August 9, 1897; interment in Calvary Cemetery, Long Island City, N.Y.

**Bibliography:** *DAB.*

**ROBERTSON, Absalom Willis,** a Representative and a Senator from Virginia; born in Martinsburg, Berkeley County, W.Va., May 27, 1887; moved to Lynchburg, Va., with his parents in 1891; attended the public schools of Lynchburg and Rocky Mount, Va.; graduated from the University of Richmond, Richmond, Va., in 1907, and from its law department in 1908; was admitted to the bar in 1908 and commenced practice in Buena Vista, Rockbridge County, Va.; moved to Lexington, Rockbridge County, Va., in 1919 and continued the practice of law; member, Virginia senate, 1916-1922; during the First World War served in the United States Army as assistant camp adjutant at Camp Lee, Va., and in the Adjutant General's Office, Washington, D.C., with the rank of major, 1917-1919; served as Commonwealth's attorney for Rockbridge County from 1922 until 1928; chairman of the Virginia commission of game and inland fisheries, 1926-1932; elected as a Democrat to the Seventy-third Congress; reelected to the six succeeding Congresses and served from March 4, 1933, until November 5, 1946, when he resigned; was nominated to the Eightieth Congress in 1946 but withdrew, having received the nomination for United States Senator; elected in 1946 as a Democrat to the United States Senate to fill the vacancy in the term ending January 3, 1949, caused by the death of Carter Glass; reelected in 1948, 1954, and 1960, and served from November 6, 1946, until his resignation December 30, 1966; unsuccessful candidate for renomination in 1966; co-chairman, Joint Committee on Defense Production (Eighty-fifth, Eighty-seventh, and Eighty-ninth Congresses), chairman, Committee on Banking and Currency (Eighty-sixth through Eighty-ninth Congresses); served as consultant to the International Bank for Reconstruction and Development, 1966-1968; retired and resided in Lexington, Va., until his death there on November 1, 1971; interment in Stonewall Jackson Memorial Cemetery.

**ROBERTSON, Alice Mary,** a Representative from Oklahoma; born at Tullahassee Mission, Creek Nation, Indian Territory (now Tullahassee, Okla.), January 2, 1854; self-taught in early life under the supervision of missionary parents; attended Elmira College, Elmira, N.Y.; clerk in the Office of Indian Affairs, Washington, D.C., 1873-1879; returned to Indian Territory and taught in the school at Tullahassee and later in the Carlisle Indian School, Carlisle, Pa., 1880-1882; again returned to Indian Territory and established Nuyaka Mission; engaged in teaching at Okmulgee, Okla., and had charge of a boarding school for Indian girls, which developed into Henry Kendall College (now the University of Tulsa); government supervisor of Creek Indian schools 1900-1905; postmaster of Muskogee, Okla., 1905-1913; operated a dairy farm and cafeteria in Muskogee; elected as a Republican to the Sixty-seventh Congress (March 4, 1921-March 3, 1923); became the first woman to preside over a session of the House of Representatives, June 20, 1921; was an unsuccessful candidate for reelection in 1922 to the Sixty-eighth Congress; appointed by President Warren G. Harding a welfare worker at Veterans' Hospital No. 90 at Muskogee in May 1923; died in Muskogee, Okla., on July 1, 1931; interment in Greenhill Cemetery.

**Bibliography:** *DAB*; James, Louise B. "Alice Mary Robertson-Anti-Feminist Congresswoman." *Chronicles of Oklahoma* 55 (Winter 1977-1978): 454-62; Stanley, Ruth M. "Alice M. Robertson, Oklahoma's First Congresswoman." *Chronicles of Oklahoma* 45 (Autumn 1967): 259-89.

**ROBERTSON, Charles Raymond,** a Representative from North Dakota; born on a farm near Madison, Wis., on September 5, 1889; assisted his father on a grain and stock farm in Columbia County, Wis., while attending public schools at Arlington and Poynette, Wis.; was graduated from Parker College, Winnebago, Minn.; held executive positions in wholesale and retail department stores throughout Minnesota and the Dakotas; delegate to the Republican National Convention of 1940; member of the Republican State executive committee; elected as a Republican to the Seventy-seventh Congress (January 3, 1941-January 3, 1943); unsuccessful candidate for renomination in 1942 to the Seventy-eighth Congress; engaged in the retail business in Bismarck, N.Dak.; elected to the Seventy-ninth and Eightieth Congresses (January 3, 1945-January 3, 1949); unsuccessful candidate for renomination in 1948 to the Eighty-first Congress; resumed the merchandising business in Bismarck, N.Dak., and paint manufacturing in Washington, D.C.; advisory member, Commission on Organization of the Executive Branch of the Government (Hoover Commission); died in Bismarck, N.Dak., February 18, 1951; interment in Lakewood Cemetery, Minneapolis, Minn.

**ROBERTSON, Edward Vivian,** a Senator from Wyoming; born in Cardiff, Wales, May 27, 1881; attended schools in Wales; served in the Third Battalion of the Welsh Regiment during the Boer War 1899-1902; engaged in mechanical and electric power engineering 1902-1912; immigrated to the United States in 1912 and settled in Park County, Wyo.; engaged in the raising of livestock and the mercantile business at Cody, Wyo., 1912-1942; elected as a Republican to the United States Senate in 1942, and served from January 3, 1943, to January 3, 1949; unsuccessful candidate for reelection in 1948; retired from political and public life; was a resident of Cody, Wyo., until 1958 when he moved to Pendleton, Oreg., where he died April 15, 1963; interment in Mount Hope Cemetery, Baker, Oreg.

**ROBERTSON, Edward White** (father of Samuel Matthews Robertson), a Representative from Louisiana; born near Nashville, Davidson County, Tenn., on June 13, 1823; moved with his parents to Iberville Parish, La., in 1825; attended the country schools and the preparatory department of Centenary College, Jackson, La.; attended Augusta College, Kentucky, in 1842; entered Nashville

(Tenn.) University and commenced the study of law in 1845; served in the War with Mexico in 1846 as orderly sergeant in the Second Regiment, Louisiana Volunteers; member of the State house of representatives 1847-1849; was graduated from the law department of the University of Louisiana in 1850; was admitted to the bar the same year and practiced in Iberville and East Baton Rouge Parishes; again elected to the State house of representatives in 1853; State auditor of public accounts 1857-1862; entered the Confederate service in March 1862 as captain of a company which he had raised for the Twenty-seventh Regiment, Louisiana Infantry; resumed the practice of law in Baton Rouge; elected as a Democrat to the Forty-fifth, Forty-sixth, and Forty-seventh Congresses (March 4, 1877-March 3, 1883); chairman, Committee on the Mississippi Levees (Forty-fifth Congress), Committee on Levees and Improvements of the Mississippi River (Forty-sixth Congress); unsuccessful candidate for renomination in 1882 to the Forty-eighth Congress; elected to the Fiftieth Congress and served from March 4, 1887, until his death in Baton Rouge, La., on August 2, 1887, before the Congress assembled; interment in Magnolia Cemetery.

**ROBERTSON, George,** a Representative from Kentucky; born near Harrodsburg, Mercer County, Ky., November 18, 1790; pursued preparatory studies and attended Transylvania University, Lexington, Ky., until 1806; studied law; was admitted to the bar in 1809 and commenced practice in Lancaster, Ky.; elected as a Republican to the Fifteenth and to the two succeeding Congresses, and served from March 4, 1817 until his resignation in 1821, before the convening of the Seventeenth Congress; chairman, Committee on Private Land Claims (Fifteenth Congress); member of the Kentucky house of representatives, 1822-1827, serving four years as speaker; declined the appointment as Governor of Arkansas Territory tendered by President James Monroe, and the diplomatic posts of United States Minister to Colombia in 1824 and to Peru in 1828; secretary of state of Kentucky in 1828; appointed associate justice of the court of appeals of Kentucky in 1829, and served as chief justice from 1829 to 1834, when he resigned; resumed the practice of law in Lexington, Ky.; professor of law in Transylvania University, 1834-1857; elected as a Whig a member of the Kentucky house of representatives in 1848, 1851, and 1852, and served as speaker in the two last-named years; justice of the court of appeals for the second district of Kentucky, 1864-1871, and acting chief justice part of the time; died in Lexington, Ky., May 16, 1874; interment in Lexington Cemetery.

Bibliography: *DAB.*

**ROBERTSON, John** (brother of Thomas Bolling Robertson), a Representative from Virginia; born at "Bellefield," near Petersburg, Dinwiddie County, Va., April 13, 1787; completed preparatory studies and graduated from the College of William and Mary, Williamsburg, Va.; studied law; admitted to the bar and practiced in Richmond, Va.; attorney general of Virginia; elected to the Twenty-third Congress to fill the vacancy caused by the resignation of Andrew Stevenson; reelected as a Whig to the Twenty-fourth and Twenty-fifth Congresses and served from December 8, 1834, to March 3, 1839; judge of the circuit court of chancery for Henrico County, Va., for several years; delegate to the peace convention held at Washington, D.C., in 1861 in an effort to devise means to prevent the impending war; member of the Virginia senate, 1861-1863; died at "Mount Athos," near Lynchburg, Va., July 5, 1873; interment in a private cemetery at "Mount Athos."

Bibliography: *DAB.*

**ROBERTSON, Samuel Matthews** (son of Edward White Robertson), a Representative from Louisiana; born in Plaquemine, Iberville Parish, La., January 1, 1852; attended Magruder's Collegiate Institute, Baton Rouge, La., and was graduated from the Louisiana State University in 1874; studied law; was admitted to the bar in 1874 and commenced practice in Baton Rouge, La.;

elected a member of the State house of representatives in 1879; member of the faculty of the Louisiana State University and Agriculture and Mechanical College in 1880; elected as a Democrat to the Fiftieth Congress to fill the vacancy caused by the death of his father, Edward White Robertson; reelected to the Fifty-first and to the eight succeeding Congresses and served from December 5, 1887, to March 3, 1907; chairman, Committee on Levees and Improvements of the Mississippi River (Fifty-second Congress); unsuccessful candidate for renomination in 1906; resumed the practice of law in Baton Rouge; superintendent of the Louisiana School for the Deaf and Dumb 1908-1911; died in Baton Rouge, La., December 24, 1911; interment in Magnolia Cemetery.

**ROBERTSON, Thomas Austin,** a Representative from Kentucky; born in Hodgenville, Larue County, Ky., September 9, 1848; pursued preparatory studies; graduated from Cecilian College and afterwards from the law department of the University of Louisville; admitted to the bar in 1871 and commenced practice at Hodgenville, Ky.; county attorney of Larue County 1874-1877; member of the Kentucky house of representatives in 1877 and 1878; Commonwealth attorney of the eighteenth judicial district 1878-1883; elected as a Democrat to the Forty-eighth and Forty-ninth Congresses (March 4, 1883-March 3, 1887); chairman, Committee on Expenditures in the Department of War (Forty-ninth Congress); unsuccessful candidate for renomination in 1886; resumed the practice of law at Elizabethtown, Hardin County, Ky., and died there July 18, 1892; interment in Red Hill Cemetery, Hodgenville, Ky.

**ROBERTSON, Thomas Bolling** (brother of John Robertson), a Representative from Louisiana; born at "Bellefield," near Petersburg, Dinwiddie County, Va., February 27, 1779; was graduated from the College of William and Mary, Williamsburg, Va.; studied law; was admitted to the bar in 1806 and commenced practice in Petersburg, Va.; moved to the Territory of Orleans in 1807; appointed by President Thomas Jefferson as secretary of the Territory of Louisiana, and served from 1807 to 1811; upon the admission of the Territory into the Union as a State was elected as a Republican to the Twelfth and to the three succeeding Congresses, and served from April 30, 1812 until April 20, 1818, when he resigned; chairman, Committee on Public Lands (Fourteenth and Fifteenth Congresses); elected Governor of Louisiana in 1820, and served from December 18, 1820 until his resignation on November 15, 1824; attorney general of Louisiana in 1822; judge of the United States Court for the District of Louisiana, 1825-1827; returned to Petersburg, Va.; died at White Sulphur Springs, Va. (now West Virginia), October 5, 1828; interment in Copeland Hill Cemetery.

Bibliography: *DAB.*

**ROBERTSON, Thomas James,** a Senator from South Carolina; born near Winnsboro, Fairfield County, S.C., August 3, 1823; completed preparatory studies and graduated from South Carolina College (now the University of South Carolina) at Columbia in 1843; engaged in planting; member of the State constitutional convention in 1865; upon the readmission of the State of South Carolina to representation in 1868 was elected as a Republican to the United States Senate; reelected in 1871 and served from July 15, 1868, to March 3, 1877; was not a candidate for reelection; chairman, Committee on Manufactures (Forty-second through Forty-fourth Congresses); retired from public life and active business due to ill health; died in Columbia, S.C., October 13, 1897; interment in Elmwood Cemetery.

**ROBERTSON, William Henry,** a Representative from New York; born in Bedford, N.Y., October 10, 1823; attended the common schools and Bedford Union Academy, at Bedford; studied law; was admitted to the bar in 1847 and commenced practice at White Plains, N.Y.; member of the State assembly in 1849 and 1850; served in the State senate in 1854 and 1855; judge of Westchester County, N.Y., 1855-1867; inspector of the Seventh Brigade New York State

Militia 1860-1866; elected as a Republican to the Fortieth Congress (March 4, 1867-March 3, 1869); was not a candidate for renomination; unsuccessful candidate for the gubernatorial nomination in 1872 and 1879; again a member of the State senate 1872-1881 and president pro tempore 1874-1881; collector of the port of New York 1881-1885; again a member of the State senate in 1888 and 1889; died in Katonah, N.Y., December 6, 1898; interment in Union Cemetery, Bedford, N.Y.

**Bibliography:** *DAB.*

**ROBESON, Edward John, Jr.,** a Representative from Virginia; born in Waynesville, Haywood County, N.C., August 9, 1890; moved from Wythe County, Va., with his parents to Cartersville, Ga., in 1891; attended the public schools in Quitman, Marietta, and Sparta, Ga.; graduated from the University of Georgia at Athens in 1910; civil engineer in Bay Minette, Ala., and Ironwood, Mich., 1910-1915; employed with the Newport News (Va.) Shipbuilding & Dry Dock Co. from 1915 until his retirement April 30, 1950, as vice president and personnel manager; elected as a Democrat to the Eighty-first Congress to fill the vacancy caused by the death of Schuyler Otis Bland; reelected to the Eighty-second and to the three succeeding Congresses and served from May 2, 1950, to January 3, 1959; unsuccessful candidate for renomination in 1958; was a resident of Newport News, Va., until 1964, at which time he returned to Waynesville, N.C.; died in Pascagoula, Miss., on March 10, 1966; interment in Green Hill Cemetery, Waynesville, N.C.

**ROBESON, George Maxwell** (nephew of George Clifford Maxwell), a Representative from New Jersey; born at Oxford Furnace, near Belvidere, Warren County, N.J., March 16, 1829; pursued an academic course and was graduated from Princeton College in 1847; studied law; was admitted to the bar in 1850 and practiced in Newark and subsequently in Camden; appointed prosecuting attorney for Camden County in 1858; was active in organizing the New Jersey State troops for service in the Civil War and was commissioned brigadier general by Governor Joel Parker; elected attorney general of New Jersey in 1867 and served until his resignation June 22, 1869; appointed Secretary of the Navy in the Cabinet of President Ulysses S. Grant, and served from June 26, 1869 to March 12, 1877; resumed the practice of law in Camden, N.J.; elected as a Republican to the Forty-sixth and Forty-seventh Congresses (March 4, 1879-March 3, 1883); chairman, Committee on Expenditures in the Department of the Navy (Forty-seventh Congress); unsuccessful candidate for reelection in 1882 to the Forty-eighth Congress; resumed the practice of law in Trenton, N.J., where he died on September 27, 1897; interment in Belvidere Cemetery, Belvidere, N.J.

**Bibliography:** *DAB.*

**ROBIE, Reuben,** a Representative from New York; born in Corinth, Orange County, Vt., July 15, 1799; attended the common schools; at the age of twenty moved to Bath, Steuben County, N.Y.; engaged in mercantile pursuits in 1822; town clerk 1825-1830; supervisor in 1831 and 1832; appointed postmaster in 1837, holding the office for four years; treasurer of Steuben County 1844-1847; elected as a Democrat to the Thirty-second Congress (March 4, 1851-March 3, 1853); was not a candidate for renomination in 1852; resumed mercantile pursuits in Bath, Steuben County, N.Y., where he died January 21, 1872; interment in Grove Cemetery.

**ROBINSON, Arthur Raymond,** a Senator from Indiana, born in Pickerington, Fairfield County, Ohio, on March 12, 1881; attended the common schools; graduated from the Ohio Northern University at Ada in 1901, the Indiana Law School at Indianapolis in 1910, and the University of Chicago, Chicago, Ill., in 1913; was admitted to the bar in 1910 and commenced practice in Indianapolis, Ind.; member, State senate 1914-1918, and was the Republican floor leader during the entire period; during the First World War served in the army as a first lieutenant, captain, and major; served in France in the Army of Occupation; resumed the practice of law; judge of Marion County Superior Court 1921-1922; resumed the practice of law in Indianapolis, Ind., in 1922; appointed as a Republican to the United States Senate and subsequently elected on November 2, 1926, to fill the vacancy caused by the death of Samuel M. Ralston; reelected in 1928, and served from October 20, 1925, to January 3, 1935; was an unsuccessful candidate for reelection in 1934; chairman, Committee on Pensions (Seventieth through Seventy-second Congresses); practiced law in Indianapolis, Ind., until his death there on March 17, 1961; interment in Washington Park Cemetery East.

**ROBINSON, Christopher,** a Representative from Rhode Island; born in Providence, R.I., on May 15, 1806; was graduated from Brown University, Providence, R.I., in 1825; studied law; was admitted to the bar in 1833 and commenced practice in Woonsocket, R.I.; attorney general of Rhode Island in 1854; elected as a Republican to the Thirty-sixth Congress (March 4, 1859-March 3, 1861); unsuccessful candidate for reelection in 1860 to the Thirty-seventh Congress; appointed Minister to Peru on June 8, 1861 and served until December 1865; delegate from Rhode Island to the Loyalist Convention held in Philadelphia in 1866; died in Woonsocket, R.I., October 3, 1889; interment in Oak Hill Cemetery.

**Bibliography:** *DAB.*

**ROBINSON, Edward,** a Representative from Maine; born in Cushing, Maine, November 25, 1796; self-educated while engaged in seafaring; engaged in mercantile pursuits at Thomaston, Maine, in 1837; member of the State senate in 1836 and 1837; elected as a Whig to the Twenty-fifth Congress to fill the vacancy caused by the death of Jonathan Cilley and served from April 28, 1838, to March 3, 1839; engaged in mercantile pursuits, banking, and shipbuilding until his death in Thomaston, Knox County, Maine, February 19, 1857; interment in Thomaston Cemetery.

**ROBINSON, George Dexter,** a Representative from Massachusetts; born in Lexington, Mass., January 20, 1834; attended Lexington Academy and Hopkins Classical School, Cambridge, Mass., and was graduated from Harvard University in 1856; principal teacher at the Chicopee High School from 1856 until 1865; studied law; was admitted to the bar in Cambridge, Mass., in 1866 and commenced practice in Chicopee, Hampden County, Mass.; member of the Massachusetts house of representatives in 1874; served in the Massachusetts senate in 1876; elected as a Republican to the Forty-fifth and to the three succeeding Congresses, and served from March 4, 1877 to January 7, 1884, when he resigned, having been elected Governor; elected Governor of Massachusetts in 1883, reelected in 1884 and 1885, and served from January 3, 1884 to January 6, 1887; resumed the practice of his profession in Springfield, Mass.; died in Chicopee, Mass., February 22, 1896; interment in Fairview Cemetery.

**ROBINSON, James Carroll,** a Representative from Illinois; born near Paris, Edgar County, Ill., August 19, 1823; moved to Clark County, Ill., with his parents in 1825; received a limited schooling; engaged in agricultural pursuits; served as a corporal during the Mexican War; studied law; was admitted to the bar in 1850 and commenced practice in Marshall, Clark County, Ill.; elected as a Democrat to the Thirty-sixth and to the two succeeding Congresses (March 4, 1859-March 3, 1865); was not a candidate for renomination in 1864 to the Thirty-ninth Congress, but was an unsuccessful candidate for Governor of Illinois; resumed the practice of law in Marshall; moved to Sangamon County, Ill., in 1869 and continued the practice of law in Springfield; elected to the Forty-second and Forty-third Congresses (March 4, 1871-March 3, 1875); chairman, Committee on Mileage (Thirty-seventh and Thirty-eighth Congresses); declined to be a candidate for renomination in 1874 to the Forty-fourth Congress; resumed the practice of law; appointed a member of the Illinois Board of Livestock Commissioners in 1886;

died in Springfield, Ill., November 3, 1886; interment in Oak Ridge Cemetery.

**ROBINSON, James Kenneth,** a Representative from Virginia; born in Winchester, Frederick County, Va., May 14, 1916; attended the public schools of Winchester, Va.; B.S., Virginia Polytechnic Institute, Blacksburg, 1937; served as an infantryman in the United States Army, 1941-1945; discharged with the rank of major; elected to the Virginia senate in 1965; reelected to a four-year term in 1967; chairman of the Republican delegation to the 1968 and 1969 Virginia general assembly; orchardist and fruit packer with real estate and other business interests in the Winchester area; elected as a Republican to the Ninety-second and to the six succeeding Congresses (January 3, 1971-January 3, 1985); was not a candidate for reelection in 1984 to the Ninety-ninth Congress; was a resident of Winchester, Va.; died April 8, 1990.

**ROBINSON, James McClellan,** a Representative from Indiana; born on a farm near Fort Wayne, Allen County, Ind., May 31, 1861; attended the public schools; studied law; was admitted to the bar in 1882 and commenced practice in Fort Wayne, Ind.; prosecuting attorney for the thirty-eighth judicial circuit of Indiana 1886-1890; resumed the practice of law; elected as a Democrat to the Fifty-fifth and to the three succeeding Congresses (March 4, 1897-March 3, 1905); unsuccessful candidate for reelection in 1904 to the Fifty-ninth Congress; continued the practice of law in Fort Wayne, Ind., until 1908; moved to Los Angeles, Calif., in 1911; died in Los Angeles, January 16, 1942; interment in Lindenwood Cemetery, Fort Wayne, Ind.

**ROBINSON, James Sidney,** a Representative from Ohio; born near Mansfield, Richland County, Ohio, October 14, 1827; attended the common schools; acquired the art of printing; moved to Kenton, Ohio, December 31, 1845; edited and published the Kenton Republican; chief clerk of the Ohio house of representatives in 1856; enlisted in Company G, Fourth Regiment, Ohio Volunteer Infantry, April 17, 1861, and rose through the ranks to colonel; chairman of the Republican State executive committee of Ohio 1877-1879; appointed commissioner of railroads and telegraphs in Ohio in January 1880; elected as a Republican to the Forty-seventh and Forty-eighth Congresses and served from March 4, 1881, to January 12, 1885, when he resigned; secretary of state of Ohio 1885-1889; died in Kenton, Ohio, January 14, 1892; interment in Grove Cemetery.

**ROBINSON, James Wallace,** a Representative from Ohio; born in the township of Carby, near Unionville Center, Union County, Ohio, on November 26, 1826; attended the common schools and Marysville Academy; was graduated from Jefferson College, Canonsburg, Pa., in 1848 and from the Cincinnati Law School in 1851; was admitted to the bar in the latter year and commenced practice in London, Ohio; prosecuting attorney of Union County for two terms; moved to Marysville, Ohio, in 1855; member of the State house of representatives 1860-1862, and in 1864 was elected to fill an unexpired term; elected as a Republican to the Forty-third Congress (March 4, 1873-March 3, 1875); unsuccessful candidate for reelection in 1874 to the Forty-fourth Congress; resumed the practice of his profession; died in Marysville, Union County, Ohio, June 28, 1898; interment in Oakdale Cemetery.

**ROBINSON, James William,** a Representative from Utah; born in Coalville, Summit County, Utah, January 19, 1878; attended public schools; graduated from Brigham Young University, Provo, Utah, and from the law school of the University of Chicago in 1912; principal of Uinta Academy, Vernal, Utah, and of the Wasatch High School, Heber, Utah; admitted as member of the bar of the State of Utah in 1912; engaged in practice of law in Provo, Utah County, Utah, 1912-1933; county attorney of Utah County 1918-1921; Democratic candidate for attorney general of Utah in 1924; member of the board of regents of the University of Utah 1925-1935; elected as a Democrat to the Seventy-third and to the six succeeding Congresses (March 4, 1933-January 3, 1947); chairman, Committee on Public Lands (Seventy-sixth and Seventy-seventh Congresses), Committee on Roads (Seventy-eighth and Seventy-ninth Congresses); unsuccessful candidate for reelection in 1946 to the Eightieth Congress; served as director of grazing in the Office of Land Management, Interior Department, Washington, D.C., from January 3, 1947, to January 31, 1949; returned to Salt Lake City, Utah; died in Escondido, Calif., December 2, 1964; interment in Provo City Cemetery, Provo, Utah.

**ROBINSON, John Buchanan,** a Representative from Pennsylvania; born in Allegheny City, Pa., May 23, 1846; studied with a private tutor at the University of Pittsburgh, and Amherst (Mass.) College; enlisted in the Union Army in 1864, but resigned to accept an appointment to the United States Naval Academy at Annapolis, Md., from which he was graduated in 1868, and served in the Navy until he resigned in 1875; studied law; was admitted to the bar in 1876 and commenced practice in Philadelphia, Pa.; moved to Media, Pa., in 1878 and continued the practice of law; editor of the Delaware County Gazette, 1881-1882; newspaper correspondent; owner of the Media Ledger; member of the Pennsylvania house of representatives, 1885-1887; served in the Pennsylvania senate in 1889; elected as a Republican to the Fifty-second and to the two succeeding Congresses (March 4, 1891-March 3, 1897); unsuccessful candidate for reelection in 1896 to the Fifty-fifth Congress; president of the League of Republican Clubs of Pennsylvania, 1891-1897; member of the Board of Visitors to the United States Naval Academy in 1893; delegate to the Republican National Conventions of 1892, 1896, and 1908; United States marshal for the eastern district of Pennsylvania, 1900-1914; resided in Philadelphia, Pa., where he died on January 28, 1933; interment in Allegheny Cemetery, Pittsburgh, Pa.

**ROBINSON, John Larne,** a Representative from Indiana; born near Maysville, Mason County, Ky., May 3, 1813; attended the public schools; moved to Rush County, Ind.; engaged in the mercantile business in Milroy, Ind.; county clerk of Rush County, Ind., 1841-1845; elected as a Democrat to the Thirtieth, Thirty-first, and Thirty-second Congresses (March 4, 1847-March 3, 1853); chairman, Committee on Roads and Canals (Thirty-first and Thirty-second Congresses); appointed by President Franklin Pierce as United States marshal for the southern district of Indiana in 1853; reappointed by President James Buchanan in 1858 and served until his death; appointed brigade inspector of the fourth military district of Indiana in 1854; trustee of Indiana University at Bloomington 1856-1859; died at Rushville, Ind., March 21, 1860; interment in East Hill Cemetery.

**ROBINSON, John McCracken,** a Senator from Illinois; born near Georgetown, Scott County, Ky., April 10, 1794; attended the common schools and graduated from Transylvania University at Lexington, Ky.; studied law; was admitted to the bar and began practice in Carmi, Ill., in 1818; judge of the State supreme court; served as general in the State militia; elected in 1830 as a Jacksonian to the United States Senate to fill the vacancy caused by the death of John McLean; reelected in 1835 and served from December 11, 1830, to March 3, 1841; was not a candidate for reelection; chairman, Committee on Engrossed Bills (Twenty-second Congress), Committee on Militia (Twenty-second through Twenty-fourth Congresses), Committee on Post Office and Post Roads (Twenty-fourth through Twenty-sixth Congresses); elected an associate justice of the State supreme court in 1843 and served until his death two months later in Ottawa, Ill., April 25, 1843; interment in the Old Graveyard, Carmi, Ill.

**ROBINSON, John Seaton,** a Representative from Nebraska; born in Wheeling, W.Va., May 4, 1856; attended the public schools; studied law; was admitted to the bar by the supreme court of West Virginia in 1880; moved to Madison, Nebr., in 1884; prosecuting attorney of Madison County 1886-1888 and 1890-1892; judge of the ninth judicial district 1893-1895; elected as a Democrat to the Fifty-sixth and Fifty-seventh Congresses (March 4, 1899-March 3, 1903); was an unsuccessful candidate for reelection in 1902; died in Madison, Nebr., on May 25, 1903; interment in Crownhill Cemetery.

**ROBINSON, Jonathan** (brother of Moses Robinson), a Senator from Vermont; born in Hardwick, Mass., August 11, 1756; received a limited schooling; moved to Bennington, Vt., in 1761; studied law; was admitted to the bar in 1796 and commenced practice in Bennington, Vt.; town clerk 1795-1801; member, State house of representatives 1789-1802; judge of the Vermont probate court 1795-1798; chief justice of the supreme court of Vermont 1801-1807; elected in 1807 as a Republican to the United States Senate to fill the vacancy caused by the resignation of Israel Smith; reelected in 1809 and served from October 10, 1807, to March 3, 1815; was not a candidate for reelection in 1814; again judge of the probate court 1815-1819; member, State house of representatives in 1818; died in Bennington, Vt., on November 3, 1819; interment in the Old Cemetery, Old Bennington, Vt.

**ROBINSON, Joseph Taylor,** a Representative and a Senator from Arkansas; born on a farm near Lonoke, Lonoke County, Ark., August 26, 1872; attended the common schools, the University of Arkansas at Fayetteville, and the law department of the University of Virginia at Charlottesville; was admitted to the bar in 1895 and commenced practice in Lonoke, Ark.; member of the Arkansas State general assembly in 1895; presidential elector on the Democratic ticket in 1900; elected as a Democrat to the Fifty-eighth and to the four succeeding Congresses, and served from March 4, 1903 to January 14, 1913, when he resigned, having been elected Governor; chairman, Committee on Public Lands (Sixty-second Congress); elected Governor of Arkansas in 1912, and served from January 15 to March 10, 1913, when he resigned, having been elected Senator; elected to the United States Senate in 1913 to fill the vacancy caused by the death of Jeff Davis; reelected in 1918, 1924, 1930, and 1936, and served from March 4, 1913 until his death in Washington, D.C., July 14, 1937; minority leader (Sixty-eighth through Seventy-second Congresses); majority leader (Seventy-third, Seventy-fourth, and Seventy-fifth Congresses); chairman, Committee on Expenditures in the Treasury Department (Sixty-third and Sixty-fourth Congresses), Committee on Claims (Sixty-fifth Congress); unsuccessful candidate for Vice President of the United States in 1928 on the Democratic ticket headed by Alfred E. Smith; funeral services were held in the Chamber of the United States Senate; interment in Roselawn Memorial Park in Little Rock, Ark.

**Bibliography:** *DAB*; Bacon, Donald C. "Joseph Taylor Robinson: The Good Soldier." In *First Among Equals: Outstanding Senate Leaders of the Twentieth Century*, edited by Richard A. Baker and Roger H. Davidson, pp. 63-97. Washington: Congressional Quarterly, Inc., 1991; Weller, Cecil Edward, Jr. "Always A Loyal Democrat: The Life of Senate Majority Leader Joseph Taylor Robinson." Ph.D. dissertation, Texas Christian University, 1993.

**ROBINSON, Leonidas Dunlap,** a Representative from North Carolina; born in Gulledge Township, Anson County, N.C., April 22, 1867; attended the common schools; moved to Wadesboro in 1888; studied law; was admitted to the bar in 1889 and practiced in Wadesboro; delegate to every Democratic State convention 1888-1941; mayor of Wadesboro 1890-1893; member of the State house of representatives in 1894 and 1900; appointed solicitor of the thirteenth judicial district in 1901; elected to the same office in 1902 and served in that capacity until 1910, when he resigned; became president of the Bank of Wadesboro in 1910; delegate to the

Democratic National Conventions in 1912, 1920, and 1924; elected as a Democrat to the Sixty-fifth and Sixty-sixth Congresses (March 4, 1917-March 3, 1921); declined to be a candidate for renomination; resumed banking and also engaged in agricultural pursuits; died in Wadesboro, N.C., November 7, 1941; interment in Eastview Cemetery.

**ROBINSON, Milton Stapp,** a Representative from Indiana; born in Versailles, Ripley County, Ind., April 20, 1832; received a limited schooling; studied law; was admitted to the bar in 1851 and began practice in Anderson, Ind.; presidential elector on the Republican ticket in 1856; appointed a director of the Indiana State Penitentiary at Michigan City in 1861, but resigned after a few months; entered the Union Army in September 1861 as lieutenant colonel of the Forty-seventh Regiment, Indiana Volunteer Infantry and served until March 29, 1864; brevetted brigadier general on March 13, 1865; served in the Indiana State senate, 1866-1870; delegate to the Republican National Convention of 1872; elected as a Republican to the Forty-fourth and Forty-fifth Congresses (March 4, 1875-March 3, 1879); was not a candidate for renomination in 1878 to the Forty-sixth Congress; resumed the practice of law; appointed associate justice of the appellate court of Indiana in March 1891; subsequently appointed chief justice and served until his death in Anderson, Ind., July 28, 1892; interment in Maplewood Cemetery.

**ROBINSON, Moses** (brother of Jonathan Robinson), a Senator from Vermont; born in Hardwick, Mass., on March 22, 1741; pursued classical studies; moved to Bennington, Vt., in 1761; town clerk of Bennington from 1762 until 1781; studied law and practiced; member of the Vermont council of safety; colonel of militia during the Revolutionary War; served on the Governor's council, 1778-1785; chief justice of Vermont, 1778-1789, save one year; sent to the Continental Congress as State agent to adjust the controversy with New York in 1782; Governor of Vermont, 1789-1790; upon the admission of Vermont as a State into the Union was elected to the United States Senate, and served from October 17, 1791 until his resignation on October 15, 1796; member of the Vermont State house of representatives in 1802; resumed the practice of his profession at Bennington, Vt., where he died on May 26, 1813; interment in the Old Bennington Cemetery.

**Bibliography:** *DAB*.

**ROBINSON, Orville,** a Representative from New York; born in Richfield, Oswego County, N.Y., October 28, 1801; completed preparatory studies; studied law; was admitted to the bar in 1827 and commenced practice in Mexico, N.Y.; justice of the peace of Mexico, N.Y., in 1828; town clerk in 1829; surrogate of Oswego County 1830-1838; member of the State assembly in 1834, 1836, and 1837; district attorney of Oswego County 1841-1843; supervisor of the town of Mexico in 1843; elected as a Democrat to the Twenty-eighth Congress (March 4, 1843-March 3, 1845); moved to Oswego, N.Y., in 1847; recorder of Oswego in 1853; again a member of the State assembly in 1856 and served as speaker; collector of customs for the district of Oswego 1858-1860; died in Oswego, N.Y., December 1, 1882; interment in Riverside Cemetery.

**ROBINSON, Thomas, Jr.,** a Representative from Delaware; born in Georgetown, Sussex County, Del., in 1800; attended the common schools and was graduated from Princeton College; studied law; was admitted to the bar in 1823 and commenced practice in Georgetown, Del.; treasurer of Sussex County in 1825; levy court commissioner in 1831 and 1832; elected as a Democrat to the Twenty-sixth Congress (March 4, 1839-March 3, 1841); died in Georgetown, Del., October 28, 1843; interment in the Old Cemetery of St. George's Chapel.

**ROBINSON, Thomas John Bright,** a Representative from Iowa; born in New Diggings, Lafayette County, Wis., August 12, 1868; moved with his parents to Hampton, Iowa, in 1870; attended the public schools and the Hampton High School; engaged in agricultural pursuits; president of the Citizens National Bank of Hampton 1907-1923; member of the Hampton Board of Education and board of trustees of Cornell College, Mount Vernon, Iowa; member of the State senate 1912-1916; delegate to many Republican State conventions; elected as a Republican to the Sixty-eighth and to the four succeeding Congresses (March 4, 1923-March 3, 1933); unsuccessful candidate for reelection in 1932 to the Seventy-third Congress; engaged in the real estate and investment business; died in Hampton, Iowa, January 27, 1958; interment in Hampton Cemetery.

**ROBINSON, Tommy Franklin,** a Representative from Arkansas; born in Little Rock, Ark., March 7, 1942; attended North Little Rock public schools and the Arkansas State Police Training Academy; B.A., University of Little Rock, 1976; served in the United States Navy, 1959-1963; served with the North Little Rock Police Department and the Arkansas State Police, 1963-1971; United States Marshal Service, 1971-1974; director of public safety, University of Arkansas Medical Sciences, 1974-1975; police chief, city of Jacksonville, Ark., 1975-1979; director of public safety, State of Arkansas, 1979-1980; sheriff of Pulaski County, Ark., 1980-1984; elected as a Democrat to the Ninety-ninth and to the two succeeding Congresses (January 3, 1985-January 3, 1991); announced his affiliation with the Republican Party on July 28, 1989, and continued in office during the One Hundred First Congress as a Republican; was not a candidate for reelection in 1990 to the One Hundred Second Congress, but was an unsuccessful candidate for nomination for Governor of Arkansas; is a resident of Jacksonville, Ark.

**ROBINSON, William Erigena,** a Representative from New York; born in Unagh, near Cookstown, County Tyrone, Ireland, May 6, 1814; attended the classical school in Cookstown and Belfast College in 1834; immigrated to the United States and settled in New York City in November 1836; was graduated from Yale College in 1841; connected for two years with the Yale Law School; engaged in lecturing before literary associations; assistant editor of the New York Tribune in 1843 and its only Washington correspondent, writing under the name of "Richelieu"; also wrote Washington correspondence for other papers; was admitted to the New York bar in 1854 and practiced law in New York City; appointed by President Abraham Lincoln assessor of internal revenue for the third district of New York in 1862; elected as a Democrat to the Fortieth Congress (March 4, 1867-March 3, 1869); resumed the practice of law; elected to the Forty-seventh and Forty-eighth Congresses (March 4, 1881-March 3, 1885); died in Brooklyn, N.Y., on January 23, 1892; interment in Greenwood Cemetery.

**ROBISON, David Fullerton** (nephew of David Fullerton), a Representative from Pennsylvania; born in Antrim Township, near Greencastle, Franklin County, Pa., May 28, 1816; attended the public schools; taught school; studied law; was admitted to the Franklin County bar in 1843 and commenced practice in Chambersburg, Pa., elected as a Whig to the Thirty-fourth Congress (March 4, 1855-March 3, 1857); was not a candidate for renomination; continued the practice of law in Chambersburg, Pa., until his death there June 24, 1859, presumably from the effects of poison secretly placed in food served at a banquet in Washington, D.C., during the inauguration of President James Buchanan; interment in Cedar Hill Cemetery, Greencastle, Franklin County, Pa.

**ROBISON, Howard Winfield,** a Representative from New York; born in Owego, Tioga County, N.Y., October 30, 1915; attended the public schools of Owego, N.Y.; graduated from Cornell University in 1937 and from the law school of the same university in 1939; was admitted to the bar in 1939 and commenced the practice of law in Owego, N.Y.; served in the United States Army Counter Intelligence Corps 1942-1946; county attorney of Tioga County from 1946 until elected to Congress; elected as a Republican to the Eighty-fifth Congress, by special election, January 14, 1958, to fill the vacancy caused by the resignation of W. Sterling Cole; reelected to the eight succeeding Congresses and served from January 14, 1958, to January 3, 1975; was not a candidate for reelection in 1974 to the Ninety-fourth Congress; vice president for congressional relations, American Railroad Association, 1975-1987; was a resident of Rehoboth Beach, Del., until his death there on September 26, 1987; interment in Evergreen Cemetery, Owego, N.Y.

**ROBSION, John Marshall** (father of John Marshall Robsion, Jr.), a Representative and a Senator from Kentucky; born near Berlin, Bracken County, Ky., January 2, 1873; attended the common schools, the National Northern University, Ada, Ohio, and Holbrook College, Knoxville, Tenn.; graduated from the National Normal University, Lebanon, Ohio, and from the law department of Centre College, Danville, Ky., in 1900; taught in the public schools of Kentucky for several years and in Union College, Barbourville, Ky.; was admitted to the bar in 1898 and commenced practice at Barbourville, Ky., president of the First National Bank of Barbourville, Ky.; elected as a Republican to the Sixty-sixth and to the five succeeding Congresses and served from March 4, 1919, until January 10, 1930, when he resigned to serve as United States Senator; chairman, Committee on Mines and Mining (Sixty-eighth through Seventy-first Congresses); appointed as a Republican to the Senate to fill the vacancy caused by the resignation of Frederick M. Sackett and served from January 11 to November 30, 1930; unsuccessful candidate for election to the vacancy and also for the full term in 1930; resumed the practice of law; elected to the Seventy-fourth and to the six succeeding Congresses and served from January 3, 1935, until his death in Barbourville, Ky., February 17, 1948; interment in Barbourville Cemetery.

**ROBSION, John Marshall, Jr.** (son of John Marshall Robsion), a Representative from Kentucky; born in Barbourville, Knox County, Ky., August 28, 1904; graduated from Union College Academy, Barbourville, in 1919; J.D., George Washington University, Washington, D.C., 1926; attended Georgetown University, Washington, D.C., and the National War College; congressional secretary from 1919 until 1928; was admitted to the bar in 1926; settled in Louisville, Ky., in 1928; chief of law division, United States Bureau of Pensions, 1929-1935; returned to Louisville and engaged in the practice of law; served in the United States Army, 1942-1946, with overseas service in Africa, Italy, and Austria; served as a special circuit judge in Kentucky by appointment of both political parties, 1946-1952; general counsel of Kentucky Republicans, 1938-1942; delegate to the Republican National Conventions of 1952, 1956 and 1960; elected as a Republican to the Eighty-third and to the two succeeding Congresses (January 3, 1953-January 3, 1959); unsuccessful candidate for reelection in 1958 to the Eighty-sixth Congress; unsuccessful candidate in 1959 for election for Governor of Kentucky; trustee for the Kentucky Jockey Club, and engaged in the practice of law; was a resident of Louisville, Ky.; died February 14, 1990.

**ROCHESTER, William Beatty,** a Representative from New York; born in Hagerstown, Md., January 29, 1789; attended the public schools and was graduated from Charlotte Hall, St. Marys County, Md.; was aide-de-camp to General McClure in the War of 1812; studied law; was admitted to the bar and began practice in Bath, N.Y.; moved to Angelica, N.Y.; member of the New York State assembly in 1816-1818; elected to the Seventeenth and Eighteenth Congresses, and served from March 4, 1821 until his resignation in 1823; State circuit judge for the eighth circuit from April 21, 1823, until 1826, when he resigned; unsuccessful Van Buren Republican candidate in 1826 for election for Governor of New York; secretary to special Envoy Extraordinary and Minister Plenipotentiary, Colombia, in 1826; appointed Chargé d'Affaires to the Republic of Central America on March 3, 1827, but returned to the United States without having presented his credentials; settled in Buffalo, N.Y., in 1828; president of the branch bank of the United States at Buffalo, N.Y.; president of the Bank of Pensacola, Fla.; director of the Alabama & Florida Railroad Co. in 1837 and 1838; was lost in the wreck of the steamer *Pulaski* off the coast of North Carolina on June 14, 1838.

**ROCKEFELLER, John Davison (Jay)** (nephew of Nelson Aldrich Rockefeller, great-grandson of Nelson Wilmarth Aldrich, and son-in-law of Charles Harting Percy), a Senator from West Virginia; born in New York City, June 18, 1937; graduated, Phillips Exeter Academy, Exeter, N.H., 1954; attended International Christian University, Tokyo, Japan, 1957-1960; A.B., Harvard University, 1961; Yale University Institute of Far Eastern Languages; operations officer for the United States Peace Corps in the Philippines, 1962-1963; Indonesian operations officer, United States Department of State, 1963-1964; served with Volunteers In Service To America, Action for Appalachia Youth Program, Emmons, W.Va., 1964-1966; member, West Virginia State house of delegates, 1966-1968; secretary of state of West Virginia, 1968-1972; unsuccessful candidate in 1972 for election for Governor of West Virginia; president, West Virginia Wesleyan College, Buckhannon, 1973-1976; elected Governor of West Virginia in 1976, reelected in 1980, and served from January 17, 1977 to January 14, 1985; elected as a Democrat to the United States Senate in 1984 for the term commencing January 3, 1985, but, preferring to continue as Governor, did not assume his senatorial duties until January 15, 1985; reelected in 1990 for the term ending January 3, 1997; is a resident of Charleston, W.Va.

**ROCKEFELLER, Lewis Kirby,** a Representative from New York; born in Schenectady, N.Y., November 25, 1875; attended the public schools; was graduated from New York State College, Albany, N.Y., in 1898; principal of grammar school at North Germantown, N.Y.; employed in finance bureau of New York State Department of Public Instruction from 1898 until 1904; chief accountant, municipal accounts bureau, in the State comptroller's office, 1905-1915; deputy State tax commissioner 1915-1921; deputy State commissioner of taxation and finance, 1921-1933; engaged in the accounting and auditing business in 1933; delegate to the Republican National Convention of 1936; elected as a Republican to the Seventy-fifth Congress to fill the vacancy caused by the death of Philip A. Goodwin; reelected to the Seventy-sixth and Seventy-seventh Congresses and served from November 2, 1937, to January 3, 1943; was not a candidate for renomination in 1942 to the Seventy-ninth Congress; resumed activities as an accountant and tax consultant in Chatham, N.Y.; died in Canaan, N.Y., on September 18, 1948; interment in Kinderhook Cemetery, Kinderhook, N.Y.

**ROCKEFELLER, Nelson Aldrich** (grandson of Nelson Wilmarth Aldrich and uncle of John Davison Rockefeller), a Vice President of the United States; born in Bar Harbor, Hancock County, Maine, July 8, 1908; attended Lincoln School of Teachers' College at Columbia University, New York, N.Y., 1926; graduated, Dartmouth College, 1930; engaged in the oil, real estate, and banking businesses, and in family philanthropic activities; served variously as trustee, treasurer, president, and chairman of the board of the Museum of Modern Art in New York City, 1932-1975; director, Office of Inter-American Affairs, 1940-1944; Assistant Secretary of State for Latin American Affairs, 1944-1945; returned to family philanthropic activities and helped establish the American International Association; member and chairman of President's Advisory Committee on Government Organization, 1953-1958; Under Secretary of the United States Department of Health, Education, and

Welfare, 1953-1954; Special Assistant to the President for Foreign Affairs, 1954-1955; elected Governor of New York in 1958; reelected in 1962, 1966, and again in 1970, and served from January 1, 1959 until his resignation on December 18, 1973; unsuccessful candidate for the Republican presidential nomination in 1964 and 1968; nominated by President Gerald R. Ford on August 20, 1974, under the provisions of the twenty-fifth amendment to the Constitution, to be the Forty-first Vice President of the United States; confirmed by the Congress and took the oath of office on December 19, 1974, and served until January 20, 1977, when the term ended; returned to family philanthropic activities and worked extensively on his art collection in New York City, where he died on January 26, 1979; cremated; ashes interred at the family estate, Pocantico Hills, N.Y.

**Bibliography:** *DAB*; Kramer, Michael, and Sam Roberts. *"I Never Wanted to be Vice President of Anything:" An Investigative Biography of Nelson Rockefeller.* New York: Basic Books, 1976; Persico, Joseph. *The Imperial Rockefeller.* New York: Simon and Schuster, 1982.

**ROCKHILL, William,** a Representative from Indiana; born in Burlington, N.J., February 10, 1793; attended the public schools; moved to Fort Wayne, Ind., in 1822; engaged in agricultural pursuits; commissioner of Allen County, Ind., in 1825 justice of the peace; member of the first city council of Fort Wayne and also city assessor; member of the State house of representatives 1834-1837; served in the State senate 1844-1847; elected as a Democrat to the Thirtieth Congress (March 4, 1847-March 3, 1849); resumed agricultural pursuits; died at Fort Wayne, Allen County, Ind., January 15, 1865; interment in Lindenwood Cemetery.

**ROCKWELL, Francis Williams** (son of Julius Rockwell), a Representative from Massachusetts; born in Pittsfield, Berkshire County, Mass., on May 26, 1844; attended the public schools and Edwards Place School, Stockbridge, Mass.; graduated from Amherst (Mass.) College in 1868 and from the law department of Harvard University in 1871; commenced the practice of law in Pittsfield in 1871; appointed one of the special justices of the district court of central Berkshire in 1873, resigning in 1875; served in the Massachusetts house of representatives in 1879; served in the Massachusetts senate in 1881 and 1882; elected as a Republican to the Forty-eighth Congress to fill the vacancy caused by the resignation of George D. Robinson; reelected to the Forty-ninth, Fiftieth, and Fifty-first Congresses and served from January 17, 1884, to March 3, 1891; unsuccessful candidate for reelection in 1890 to the Fifty-second Congress; resumed the practice of law in Pittsfield, Mass., until 1916 when he retired; president of the City Savings Bank 1893-1916; delegate to the Republican National Convention in 1900; member of the Greylock Reservation Commission 1898-1926; died in Pittsfield, Mass., June 26, 1929; interment in Pittsfield Cemetery.

**ROCKWELL, Hosea Hunt,** a Representative from New York; born in Lawrenceville, Tioga County, Pa., on May 31, 1840; attended the common schools; served as a private in the Twenty-third Regiment, New York Volunteers, in 1861 and 1862; studied law; was admitted to the bar in 1869 and commenced practice in Elmira, N.Y.; member of the State assembly in 1877; city attorney of Elmira; elected as a Democrat to the Fifty-second Congress (March 4, 1891-March 3, 1893); was not a candidate for renomination in 1892; delegate to the Democratic National Convention in 1896; chairman of the Democratic State convention in 1896; resumed the practice of law in Elmira, N.Y.; died in Elmira, Chemung County, N.Y., December 18, 1918; interment in Woodlawn Cemetery.

**ROCKWELL, John Arnold,** a Representative from Connecticut; born in Norwich, Conn., August 27, 1803; attended the common schools; was graduated from Yale College in 1822; studied law; was admitted to the bar and practiced in Norwich; member of the State senate in 1839; judge of the county court; elected as a Whig to the

Twenty-ninth and Thirtieth Congresses (March 4, 1845-March 3, 1849); chairman, Committee on Claims (Thirtieth Congress); unsuccessful candidate for reelection in 1848 to the Thirty-first Congress; engaged in the practice of law before the court of claims of the United States at Washington, D.C., until his death in that city on February 10, 1861; interment in Yantic Cemetery, Norwich, Conn.

**ROCKWELL, Julius** (father of Francis Williams Rockwell), a Representative and a Senator from Massachusetts; born in Colebrook, Conn., April 26, 1805; attended private schools; graduated from Yale College in 1826; studied law; admitted to the bar and commenced practice in Pittsfield, Mass., in 1830; member, Massachusetts house of representatives 1834-1838, and served three years as speaker; Massachusetts bank commissioner 1838-1840; elected as a Whig to the Twenty-eighth and to the three succeeding Congresses (March 4, 1843-March 3, 1851); was not a candidate for renomination in 1850; delegate to the Massachusetts constitutional convention in 1853; appointed to the United States Senate to fill the vacancy caused by the resignation of Edward Everett and served from June 3, 1854, to January 31, 1855, when a successor was elected; presidential elector on the Republican ticket in 1856; member, Massachusetts house of representatives 1858, and served as speaker; appointed a judge of the superior court of Massachusetts in 1859 and resigned in 1886; died in Lenox, Berkshire County, Mass., May 19, 1888; interment in Lenox Cemetery.

**ROCKWELL, Robert Fay,** a Representative from Colorado; born in Cortland, N.Y., February 11, 1886; attended the public schools of New York State, the Hill School, Pottstown, Pa., and Princeton University; moved to Paonia, Colo., in 1907 and engaged in cattle raising and fruit growing; member of the Colorado State house of representatives, 1916-1920; served in the State senate, 1920-1924, and 1938-1941; Lieutenant Governor, 1922-1924; unsuccessful candidate for Governor in 1930; member of the State board of agriculture, 1932-1946; elected as a Republican to the Seventy-seventh Congress to fill the vacancy caused by the death of Edward T. Taylor; reelected to the Seventy-eighth and to the two succeeding Congresses, and served from December 9, 1941 to January 3, 1949; unsuccessful candidate for reelection in 1948 to the Eighty-first Congress; resumed cattle ranching in Colorado; chairman of the board of directors of Tuttle and Rockwell Co., Hornell, N.Y., and Rockwell Co., Corning, N.Y.; died in Maher, Colo., September 29, 1950; interment in Hornell Cemetery, Hornell, N.Y.

**RODDENBERY, Seaborn Anderson,** a Representative from Georgia; born near Bainbridge, Decatur County, Ga., January 12, 1870; moved to Thomas County in early childhood; attended the common schools and Mercer University, Macon, Ga., for three years; taught at South Georgia College one year; member of the State house of representatives in 1892 and 1893 and declined to be a candidate for reelection; studied law; was admitted to the bar in 1894 and commenced practice in Thomasville, Thomas County, Ga.; president of the board of education of Thomas County 1895-1898; appointed judge of the county court of Thomas County in 1897 and served four years; declined reappointment; mayor of Thomasville in 1903 and 1904; elected as a Democrat to the Sixty-first Congress to fill the vacancy caused by the death of James M. Griggs; reelected to the Sixty-second and Sixty-third Congresses and served from February 16, 1910, until his death in Thomasville, Ga., September 25, 1913; interment in Laurel Hill Cemetery.

**RODENBERG, William August,** a Representative from Illinois; born near Chester, Randolph County, Ill., October 30, 1865; attended the public schools; was graduated from Central Wesleyan College, Warrenton, Mo., in 1884; taught for seven years; attended the St. Louis Law School; was admitted to the bar in 1893 and commenced practice in East St. Louis, St. Clair County, Ill.; delegate to the Republican National Conventions in 1896, 1908, 1916, and

1920; elected as a Republican to the Fifty-sixth Congress (March 4, 1899-March 3, 1901); unsuccessful candidate for reelection in 1900 to the Fifty-seventh Congress; appointed a member of the United States Civil Service Commission by President William McKinley March 25, 1901, and served until April 1, 1902, when he resigned; resumed the practice of law in East St. Louis, also financially interested in various business enterprises; elected to the Fifty-eighth and to the four succeeding Congresses (March 4, 1903-March 3, 1913); chairman, Committee on Industrial Arts and Expositions (Sixty-first Congress); unsuccessful candidate for reelection in 1912 to the Sixty-third Congress; elected to the Sixty-fourth and to the three succeeding Congresses (March 4, 1915-March 3, 1923); chairman, Committee on Flood Control (Sixty-sixth and Sixty-seventh Congresses); engaged in the practice of law in Washington, D.C.; died in Alpena, Mich., while on a visit, September 10, 1937; interment in Rock Creek Cemetery, Washington, D.C.

**RODEY, Bernard Shandon,** a Delegate from the Territory of New Mexico; born in County Mayo, Ireland, March 1, 1856; immigrated with his parents to Canada in 1862; attended the public schools at Sherbrooke, Province of Quebec, Canada; studied law in Boston, Mass.; moved to Albuquerque, N.Mex., in 1881; was private secretary to the general manager of the A.&P. Railroad; court stenographer of the second district of New Mexico in 1882; was admitted to the bar in 1883 and commenced practice in Albuquerque; city attorney of Albuquerque in 1887 and 1888; member of the Territorial senate in 1889; member of the constitutional convention of New Mexico in 1890; elected as a Republican to the Fifty-seventh and Fifty-eighth Congresses (March 4, 1901-March 3, 1905); unsuccessful candidate for reelection in 1904 to the Fifty-ninth Congress; delegate to the Republican National Convention of 1908; judge of the Federal Court of Puerto Rico, 1906-1910; United States attorney for the second division of Alaska, 1910-1913; appointed on March 6, 1912, as special assistant United States attorney, western district of Washington, to assist in the prosecution of coal frauds in Alaska, and served until December 16, 1913; resumed the practice of law; died in Albuquerque, Bernalillo County, N.Mex., March 10, 1927; interment in Fairview Cemetery.

**RODGERS, Robert Lewis,** a Representative from Pennsylvania; born in El Dorado, Butler County, Kans., June 2, 1875; raised on a farm near Jamestown, Mercer County, Pa.; attended district school and Fredonia (Pa.) Institute; during the War with Spain enlisted in Company K, Fifteenth Regiment, Pennsylvania Volunteer Infantry; taught in the district schools; engaged in agricultural pursuits; moved to Erie, Erie County, Pa., in 1914 and engaged in the insurance, real estate, and mortgage business; elected as a Republican to the Seventy-sixth and to the three succeeding Congresses (January 3, 1939-January 3, 1947); unsuccessful candidate for renomination in 1946 to the Eightieth Congress; resided in Erie, Pa., until his death there May 9, 1960; interment in Rocky Glen Cemetery, Adamsville, Pa.

**RODINO, Peter Wallace, Jr.,** a Representative from New Jersey; born in Newark, Essex County, N.J., June 7, 1909; attended the McKinley Grammar School and Barringer High School; graduated from the University of Newark and from the New Jersey Law School in 1937; was admitted to the bar in 1938 and commenced the practice of law in Newark; teacher, public speaking and citizenship classes, Young Men's Christian Association and Federation of Clubs, Newark, N.J., 1930-1932; managing editor of the Jersey Review in 1934 and 1935; enlisted in the United States Army on March 10, 1941, and served with the First Armored Division in North Africa and Italy, and on military missions with the Italian Army; discharged as a captain in April 1946; awarded Bronze Star for military operations, War Cross, and Knight of Order of Crown from Italy; unsuccessful candidate for election in 1946 to the Eightieth Congress; elected as a Democrat to the Eighty-first and to the nineteen succeeding Congresses (January 3, 1949-January 3, 1989); chairman, Committee on the Judiciary (Ninety-third through One Hundredth Congresses); was not a candidate for reelection in 1988 to the One Hundred First Congress; is a resident of Newark, N.J.

**RODMAN, William,** a Representative from Pennsylvania; born in Bensalem Township, near Bristol, Bucks County, Pa., October 7, 1757; completed preparatory studies; served in the Revolutionary War as a private and subsequently as brigade quartermaster; commanded a company during the Whisky Rebellion in 1794; justice of the peace 1791-1800; member of the Pennsylvania senate 1804-1808; elected as a Republican to the Twelfth Congress (March 4, 1811-March 3, 1813); died at "Flushing" near Bristol, Bucks County, Pa., July 27, 1824; interment in the Episcopal Cemetery (later known as the St. James Burying Ground).

**RODNEY, Caesar** (brother of Thomas Rodney, uncle of Caesar Augustus Rodney, and cousin of George Brydges Rodney), a Delegate from Delaware; born in Dover, Del., October 7, 1728; completed preparatory studies; engaged in agricultural pursuits; high sheriff of Kent County, 1755-1758; justice of the peace; judge of all lower courts; captain in the Kent County Militia in 1756; superintendent of the printing of Delaware currency in 1759; member of the Delaware assembly, 1762-1769; superintendent of the loan office in 1769; associate justice of the Delaware Supreme Court, 1769-1777; Member of the Continental Congress, 1774-1776; on July 1, 1776, he rode horseback from his farm near Dover to Philadelphia, arriving in time to vote for the Declaration of Independence and break a tie between Delaware's delegates to the Continental Congress; a signer of the Declaration of Independence; served in the Revolutionary Army as a brigadier general; elected President of Delaware and served from 1778 to 1782; elected to the Continental Congress in 1782 and 1783, but did not serve; died in Dover, Del., June 26, 1784; interment on his farm, "Byfield," near Dover; reinterment in Christ Churchyard, Dover, Del.

**Bibliography:** *DAB*; Frank, William, and Hancock, Harold. "Caesar Rodney's Two Hundred and Fiftieth Anniversary: An Evaluation." *Delaware History* 18 (Fall-Winter 1976): 63-76; Rodney, Caesar. *Letters To and From Caesar Rodney, 1756-1784*. Edited by George Ryden. 1933. Reprint. New York: Da Capo Press, 1970.

**RODNEY, Caesar Augustus** (son of Thomas Rodney, cousin of George Brydges Rodney, and nephew of Caesar Rodney), a Representative and a Senator from Delaware; born in Dover, Del., January 4, 1772; completed preparatory studies and graduated from the University of Pennsylvania at Philadelphia in 1789; studied law; was admitted to the bar and began practice in Wilmington, Del., in 1793; member, Delaware State house of representatives, 1796-1802; elected as a Republican to the Eighth Congress (March 4, 1803-March 3, 1805); was not a candidate for renomination in 1804 to the Ninth Congress; one of the managers appointed by the House of Representatives in January 1804 to conduct the impeachment proceedings against John Pickering, judge of the United States District Court for New Hampshire, and in December of the same year against Samuel Chase, Associate Justice of the Supreme Court of the United States; Attorney General in the Cabinets of Presidents Thomas Jefferson and James Madison from January 20, 1807 until December 5, 1811, when he resigned; served in the War of 1812; member of the Delaware Committee of Safety in 1813; member, Delaware State senate, 1815-1816; was sent to South America by President James Monroe as one of the commissioners to investigate and report on the propriety of recognizing the independence of the South American Republics; elected to the Seventeenth Congress, and served from March 4, 1821 to January 24, 1822, when he resigned; elected to the United States Senate, and served from January 24, 1822 to January 29, 1823, when he resigned; appointed Minister Plenipotentiary to Argentina on January 27, 1823, and

served until his death in Buenos Aires, June 10, 1824; interment in British Cemetery, Victoria district; reinterred, 1923, in British Cemetery, Charcarita district, Buenos Aires, Argentina.

**Bibliography:** *DAB*.

**RODNEY, Daniel,** a Representative and a Senator from Delaware; born in Lewes, Sussex County, Del., September 10, 1764; received a limited schooling; engaged in mercantile pursuits; associate judge of the court of common pleas from 1793 until 1806; presidential elector on the Federalist ticket in 1808; unsuccessful Federalist candidate for Governor in 1810; elected Governor of Delaware in 1813, and served from January 1814 to January 1817; elected to the Seventeenth Congress to fill the vacancy caused by the resignation of Caesar A. Rodney, and served from October 1, 1822 to March 3, 1823; appointed to the United States Senate to fill the vacancy caused by the death of Nicholas Van Dyke, and served from November 8, 1826 to January 12, 1827, when a successor was elected; died in Lewes, Del., on September 2, 1846; interment in St. Peter's Churchyard.

**Bibliography:** Turner, D.H.B., ed. *Rodney's Diary and Other Delaware Records*. Philadelphia: Allen, Lane and Scott, 1911.

**RODNEY, George Brydges** (cousin of Caesar Rodney, Caesar Augustus Rodney, and Thomas Rodney), a Representative from Delaware; born in Lewes, Del., April 2, 1803; received a liberal education and was graduated from Princeton College in 1820; register in chancery and clerk of the orphans' court of Sussex County, 1826-1830; studied law; was admitted to the bar in 1828 and engaged in practice in New Castle; elected as a Whig to the Twenty-seventh and Twenty-eighth Congresses (March 4, 1841-March 3, 1845); resumed the practice of law; delegate to the peace convention held in Washington, D.C., in 1861 in an effort to prevent the impending war; died in New Castle, New Castle County, Del., June 18, 1883; interment in the Immanuel Churchyard.

**RODNEY, Thomas** (father of Caesar Augustus Rodney, brother of Caesar Rodney, and cousin of George Brydges Rodney), a Delegate from Delaware; born near Dover, Kent County, Del., June 4, 1744; justice of the peace in 1770 and 1784; member of the assembly to elect delegates in 1774; member of the council of safety in 1775; colonel of Delaware Militia during the Revolutionary War; chief justice of Kent County Court in 1778; register of wills in 1779; Member of the Continental Congress 1781-1782 and 1786; member of the State assembly in 1787 and served as speaker; superintendent of Kent County Almshouse in 1802; appointed an associate justice of the supreme court of Delaware on December 17, 1802, and served until August 1803, when he resigned, having been appointed United States judge for Mississippi Territory; died in Natchez, Miss., January 2, 1811.

**Bibliography:** *DAB*; Rodney, Thomas. *Anglo-American Law on the Frontier: Thomas Rodney and His Territorial Cases*. Edited by William Baskerville Hamilton. Durham, N.C.: Duke University Press, 1953.

**ROE, Dudley George,** a Representative from Maryland; born in Sudlersville, Queen Annes County, Md., March 23, 1881; attended the public schools; was graduated from Washington College, Chestertown, Md., in 1903, and from the law department of the University of Maryland at Baltimore in 1905; was admitted to the bar in 1905 and commenced practice in Baltimore, Md.; served in the Maryland State house of delegates, 1907-1909; member of the State senate, 1923-1935, and 1939-1943, serving as Democratic floor leader from 1939 until 1943; delegate to the Democratic National Convention of 1928; elected as a Democrat to the Seventy-ninth Congress (January 3, 1945-January 3, 1947); unsuccessful candidate for reelection in 1946 to the Eightieth Congress; farmer, banker, and grain dealer in Sudlersville, Md.; director and later president of the Sudlersville Bank of Maryland; resigned in 1967, but continued as chairman of the board of directors until his death in Chestertown, Md., January 4, 1970; interment in Sudlersville Cemetery, Sudlersville, Md.

**ROE, James A.,** a Representative from New York; born in Flushing, Queens County, N.Y., July 9, 1896; attended the public and parochial schools; studied law, engineering, and accounting; was graduated from the United States School of Military Aeronautics, Cornell University, Ithaca, N.Y., in August 1917; during the First World War enlisted on September 17, 1917, as a private in the United States Army Air Corps, was promoted to lieutenant and instructor of advanced flying, and was discharged on January 4, 1919; real estate and insurance broker; also interested in the contracting and engineering business; director of Flushing National Bank; chairman of the Democratic County Committee of Queens County, 1939-1952; delegate to the Democratic National Conventions of 1940, 1948, and 1960; entered the United States Army in July 1943 with rank of major, and was assigned to duty with the Corps of Engineers, and served until January 1945, when he was honorably discharged with the rank of lieutenant colonel to enter Congress; elected as a Democrat to the Seventy-ninth Congress (January 3, 1945-January 3, 1947); was not a candidate for renomination in 1946 to the Eightieth Congress; resumed his former business pursuits; died in Hollywood, Fla., April 22, 1967; interment in Mount St. Mary's Cemetery, Flushing, N.Y.

**ROE, Robert A.,** a Representative from New Jersey; born in Wayne, Passaic County, N.J., February 28, 1924; attended local schools and Oregon State and Washington State Universities; during the Second World War served with Army Infantry communications and reconnaissance forces in the European Theater; chairman, board of directors, Morris Canal & Banking Co.; committeeman, Wayne Township, 1955-1956; mayor, Wayne Township, 1956-1961; Passaic County Freeholder, 1959-1963; director, board of Chosen Freeholders, 1962-1963; member of Governor Richard J. Hughes' cabinet as New Jersey Commissioner of Conservation and Economic Development, 1963-1969; elected as a Democrat to the Ninety-first Congress, by special election, November 4, 1969, to fill the vacancy caused by the resignation of Charles S. Joelson; reelected to the eleven succeeding Congresses and served from November 4, 1969, to January 3, 1993; chairman, Committee on Science, Space, and Technology (One Hundredth and One Hundred First Congresses), Committee on Public Works and Transportation (One Hundred Second Congress); unsuccessful candidate in 1977 for nomination for governor of New Jersey; was not a candidate for renomination in 1992 to the One Hundred Third Congress; is a resident of Wayne, N.J.

**ROEMER, Charles Elson, III (Buddy),** a Representative from Louisiana; born in Shreveport, Caddo Parish, La., October 4, 1943; attended the public schools; graduated from Bossier High School, 1960; B.S., Harvard University, 1964, and M.A., 1967; businessman, farmer, banker; elected delegate, Louisiana Constitutional convention, 1972; delegate, Louisiana State Democratic convention, 1979; delegate to the Democratic National Convention of 1972; elected as a Democrat to the Ninety-seventh and to the three succeeding Congresses, and served from January 3, 1981 until his resignation on March 14, 1988, having been elected Governor; elected Governor of Louisiana in 1987, and served from March 14, 1988 to January 13, 1992; while serving as Governor announced his affiliation with the Republican Party on March 11, 1991; unsuccessful candidate for renomination in 1991; unsuccessful candidate in 1995 for election for Governor; is a resident of Bossier City, La.

**ROEMER, Timothy John** (son-in-law of John Bennett Johnston, Jr.), a Representative from Indiana; born in South Bend, St. Joseph County, Ind., October 30, 1956; graduated, Penn High School, Mishawaka, Ind., 1975; B.A., University of California, San Diego, 1979; M.A., University of Notre Dame, 1982, Ph.D., 1985;

legislative assistant to Senator Dennis DeConcini of Arizona, 1987-1989; instructor, American University, Washington, D.C.; elected as a Democrat to the One Hundred Second and to the two succeeding Congresses (January 3, 1991-January 3, 1997); is a resident of South Bend, Ind.

**ROGERS, Andrew Jackson,** a Representative from New Jersey; born in Hamburg, Sussex County, N.J., July 1, 1828; attended the common schools; employed as clerk in a hotel and in a country store; engaged in teaching for two years; studied law; was admitted to the bar in 1852 and commenced practice in La Fayette, Sussex County, N.J.; moved to Newton, N.J., in 1857 and continued the practice of law; elected as a Democrat to the Thirty-eighth and Thirty-ninth Congresses (March 4, 1863-March 3, 1867); unsuccessful candidate for reelection in 1866 to the Fortieth Congress; moved to New York City in 1867 and became counsel for the city in important litigation; moved to Denver, Colo., in 1892; served as police commissioner of the city of Denver; returned to New York City in 1896 and died there on May 22, 1900; interment in Woodlawn Cemetery.

**ROGERS, Anthony Astley Cooper,** a Representative from Arkansas; born in Clarksville, Sumner County, Tenn., February 14, 1821; received a limited schooling; engaged in mercantile pursuits; moved to Arkansas in 1854; candidate of the Union supporters for delegate to the State convention in 1861; opposed secession; arrested for his loyalty, was imprisoned, and forced to give bond to answer the charge of "treason against the Confederate Government"; elected to the Thirty-eighth Congress but was not allowed to take his seat, his State not having been readmitted; moved to Chicago, Ill., in 1864 and engaged in the real estate business; returned to Arkansas in 1868; elected as a Democrat to the Forty-first Congress (March 4, 1869-March 3, 1871); unsuccessful candidate for reelection in 1870 to the Forty-second Congress; postmaster at Pine Bluff, Ark., from January 7, 1881, to July 24, 1885; again engaged in mercantile pursuits; moved to Los Angeles, Calif., in 1888 and died there July 27, 1899; interment in Rosedale Cemetery.

**ROGERS, Byron Giles,** a Representative from Colorado; born in Greenville, Hunt County, Tex., August 1, 1900; moved with his parents to Oklahoma in April 1902; attended the public schools of Checotah, Okla.; during the First World War served as a private in the Infantry, United States Army; attended the University of Arkansas in 1918, the University of Oklahoma 1919-1922, and the University of Colorado 1923 and 1924; was graduated from the law school of the University of Denver, LL.B., 1925, and commenced the practice of law in Las Animas, Colo.; city attorney of Las Animas 1929-1933; member of the State house of representatives 1932-1935, serving as speaker in 1933; county attorney of Bent County, Colo., in 1933; on legal staff of Agricultural Adjustment Administration and National Recovery Administration, Washington, D.C., in 1933 and 1934; assistant United States attorney of Colorado 1934-1936, and attorney general 1936-1941; public member War Labor Board 1942-1945; elected as a Democrat to the Eighty-second and to the ten succeeding Congresses (January 3, 1951-January 3, 1971); unsuccessful candidate for renomination in 1970 to the Ninety-second Congress; was a resident of Denver, Colo. until his death there December 31, 1983; interment in Mount Lindo Cemetery near Tiny Town, Colo.

**ROGERS, Charles,** a Representative from New York; born in Northumberland, Saratoga County, N.Y., April 30, 1800; attended Granville Academy and was graduated from Union College, Schenectady, N.Y., in 1818; studied law; was admitted to the bar but did not engage in extensive practice; served in the State assembly in 1833 and 1837; unsuccessful candidate for election to the State senate; elected as a Whig to the Twenty-eighth Congress (March 4, 1843-March 3, 1845); chairman, Committee on Expenditures in the Department of State (Twenty-eighth Congress); was not a candidate for renomination in 1844; retired from public life; affiliated with the Republican Party; died in Sandy Hill (now Hudson Falls), Washington County, N.Y., January 13, 1874; interment in Union Cemetery, near Sandy Hill.

**ROGERS, Dwight Laing** (father of Paul Grant Rogers), a Representative from Florida; born near Reidsville, Tattnall County, Ga., August 17, 1886; attended the public schools and Locust Grove Institute at Locust Grove, Ga.; was graduated from the University of Georgia at Athens in 1909 and from the law department of Mercer University, Macon, Ga., in 1910; was admitted to the bar in 1910 and commenced practice in Ocilla, Ga.; moved to Fort Lauderdale, Fla., in 1925 and continued the practice of law; member of the State house of representatives 1930-1938, serving as speaker pro tempore in 1933; elected as a Democrat to the Seventy-ninth and to the four succeeding Congresses and served from January 3, 1945, until his death; had been reelected to the Eighty-fourth Congress; died in Fort Lauderdale, Fla., December 1, 1954; interment in Lauderdale Memorial Park.

**ROGERS, Edith Nourse** (wife of John Jacob Rogers), a Representative from Massachusetts; born in Saco, York County, Maine, March 19, 1881; attended the common schools; moved with her family in 1895 to Lowell, Mass.; was graduated from the Rogers Hall School, Lowell, and from Madame Julien's School, Paris, France; inspected field hospitals with the Women's Overseas Service and served with the American Red Cross in the care of disabled soldiers of the First World War, 1917-1922; appointed a personal representative of President Warren G. Harding in the care of disabled veterans in 1922, and was reappointed by President Calvin Coolidge in 1923; president, board of trustees, Rogers Hall School, Lowell, Mass.; elected as a Republican to the Sixty-ninth Congress to fill the vacancy caused by the death of her husband, John Jacob Rogers; reelected to the Seventieth and to the sixteen succeeding Congresses and served from June 30, 1925, until her death in Boston, Mass., September 10, 1960; chairman, Committee on Veterans' Affairs (Eightieth and Eighty-third Congresses); interment in Lowell Cemetery, Lowell, Mass.

Bibliography: *DAB*.

**ROGERS, Edward,** a Representative from New York; born in Cornwall, Conn., on May 30, 1787; completed preparatory studies and was graduated from Williams College, Williamstown, Mass., in 1809; moved to New York State about the close of the War of 1812; was graduated from Yale College; studied law; was admitted to the bar and commenced practice in Madison, N.Y.; delegate to the State convention to revise the constitution in 1822; judge of the court of common pleas for Madison County; elected as a Democrat to the Twenty-sixth Congress (March 4, 1839-March 3, 1841); resumed the practice of law; also engaged in literary pursuits; died in Galway, Saratoga County, N.Y., May 29, 1857; interment in Madison Cemetery, Madison, N.Y.

**ROGERS, George Frederick,** a Representative from New York; born in Harwood, Ontario, Canada, March 19, 1887; attended the public schools in Canada and Rochester, N.Y.; immigrated to the United States in 1899 and settled in Rochester, N.Y.; food merchant in Rochester, N.Y., 1911-1943; supervisor of Monroe County, N.Y., in 1934 and 1935; served in the State senate in 1937 and 1938; member of the Genesee State Park Commission 1942-1948; elected as a Democrat to the Seventy-ninth Congress (January 3, 1945-January 3, 1947); unsuccessful candidate for reelection in 1946 to the Eightieth Congress and for election in 1948 to the Eighty-first Congress; retired and resided in Rochester, N.Y.; died in Coburg, Ontario, Canada, November 20, 1948; interment in Riverside Cemetery, Rochester, N.Y.

**ROGERS, Harold Dallas,** a Representative from Kentucky; born in Barrier, Wayne County, Ky., December 31, 1937; attended the public schools; graduated from Wayne County High School, 1955; attended Western Kentucky University, Bowling Green, 1956-1957; A.B., University of Kentucky, Lexington, 1962; LL.B., University of Kentucky Law School, 1964; served in the Kentucky and North Carolina Army National Guard, 1956-1964; admitted to the Kentucky bar in 1964 and commenced practice in Somerset; commonwealth attorney, Pulaski and Rockcastle Counties, 1969-1980; delegate to the Republican National Conventions of 1972, 1976, 1980 and 1984; elected as a Republican to the Ninety-seventh and to the seven succeeding Congresses (January 3, 1981-January 3, 1997); is a resident of Somerset, Ky.

**ROGERS, James,** a Representative from South Carolina; born in what is now Goshen Hill Township, Union County, S.C., October 24, 1795; completed preparatory studies and was graduated from South Carolina College (now the University of South Carolina) at Columbia in 1813; studied law; was admitted to the bar and began practice in Yorkville (now York), S.C.; held various local offices; elected as a Jacksonian to the Twenty-fourth Congress (March 4, 1835-March 3, 1837); unsuccessful candidate for reelection in 1836 to the Twenty-fifth Congress; elected as a Democrat to the Twenty-sixth and Twenty-seventh Congresses (March 4, 1839-March 3, 1843); died in South Carolina on December 21, 1873; interment in what was formerly called the Irish Graveyard at Kings Creek A.R.P. Church near Newberry, S.C.

**ROGERS, John,** a Delegate from Maryland; born in Annapolis, Anne Arundel County, Md., in 1723; received a liberal schooling; studied law; was admitted to the bar and commenced practice; member of the committee of safety in 1774 and 1775; member of the Maryland provincial conventions in 1774, 1775, and 1776; one of the trustees of the Lower Marlboro Academy in 1775; second major of battalion, Prince Georges County; Member of the Continental Congress in 1775 and 1776; judge of the court of admiralty in 1776; member of the executive council on the organization of the State government in February 1777; chancellor of Maryland from March 10, 1778, until his death in Upper Marlboro, Prince Georges County, Md., September 23, 1789.

**ROGERS, John,** a Representative from New York; born in Caldwell, N.Y., May 9, 1813; completed preparatory studies; moved to Black Brook, Clinton County, in 1832 and engaged in the manufacture of iron; supervisor of the town of Black Brook for ten years and held other local offices; elected as a Democrat to the Forty-second Congress (March 4, 1871-March 3, 1873); resumed manufacturing activities; died at the "Rogers Place," near Fort Edward, Washington County, N.Y., May 11, 1879; interment in the family burial ground on his estate at Moreau, near Fort Henry, N.Y.

**ROGERS, John Henry,** a Representative from Arkansas; born near Roxobel, Bertie County, N.C., October 9, 1845; moved to Mississippi in 1852 with his parents, who settled near Madison Station; attended the common schools; joined the Ninth Mississippi Volunteer Regiment, Confederate service, as a private in March 1862; promoted to first lieutenant in the same regiment and served throughout the war; attended Centre College, Danville, Ky., and was graduated from the law department of the University of Mississippi at Oxford in 1868; was admitted to the bar in 1868 and commenced practice in Canton, Miss.; moved to Fort Smith, Ark., in 1869 and practiced law; elected circuit judge in 1877; reelected in 1878 and resigned in May 1882; elected as a Democrat to the Forty-eighth and to the three succeeding Congresses (March 4, 1883-March 3, 1891); chairman, Committee on Mileage (Fiftieth Congress); declined to be a candidate for renomination; resumed the practice of law in Fort Smith, Ark.; member of the Democratic State convention in 1892; delegate to the Democratic National Convention in 1892; appointed United States district judge for the western district of Arkansas by

President Grover Cleveland on November 27, 1896, and served until his death in Little Rock, Ark., on April 16, 1911; interment in Oak Cemetery, Fort Smith, Sebastian County, Ark.

**ROGERS, John Jacob** (husband of Edith Nourse Rogers), a Representative from Massachusetts; born in Lowell, Middlesex County, Mass., August 18, 1881; attended the public schools, and was graduated from Harvard University in 1904 and from the law department of that university in 1907; was admitted to the bar the same year and commenced practice in Lowell in 1908; member of the Lowell city government in 1911; school commissioner in 1912; elected as a Republican to the Sixty-third and to the six succeeding Congresses and served from March 4, 1913, until his death; during the First World War enlisted on September 12, 1918, as a private with the Twenty-ninth Training Battery, Tenth Training Battalion, Field Artillery, Fourth Central Officers' Training School, and served until honorably discharged on November 29, 1918; died in Washington, D.C., March 28, 1925; interment in Lowell Cemetery, Lowell, Mass.

**ROGERS, Paul Grant,** (son of Dwight Laing Rogers), a Representative from Florida; born in Ocilla, Irwin County, Ga., June 4, 1921; at the age of four years moved with his parents to Fort Lauderdale, Fla.; attended the public schools; B.A., University of Florida, Gainesville, 1942; during the Second World War served in the Field Artillery, United States Army, with service in the European Theater; studied law at George Washington University, Washington, D.C., in 1946; LL.B., University of Florida, 1948; was admitted to the bar in 1948 and commenced the practice of law in West Palm Beach, Fla.; elected as a Democrat to the Eighty-fourth Congress, January 11, 1955, by special election to fill the vacancy caused by the death of his father, Dwight L. Rogers; reelected to the eleven succeeding Congresses, and served from January 11, 1955 to January 3, 1979; was not a candidate for reelection in 1978 to the Ninety-sixth Congress; resumed the practice of law with the firm of Hogan and Hartson; chairman of the board of trustees, Scripps Research Institute; is a resident of Washington, D.C.

**ROGERS, Sion Hart,** a Representative from North Carolina; born near Raleigh, Wake County, N.C., September 30, 1825; attended the common schools, and was graduated from the University of North Carolina at Chapel Hill in 1846; studied law; was admitted to the bar in 1848 and commenced practice in Raleigh; elected as a Whig to the Thirty-third Congress (March 4, 1853-March 3, 1855); declined to be a candidate for renomination in 1854; solicitor of the Raleigh district of the superior court; served in the Confederate Army as a lieutenant in the Fourteenth Regiment of North Carolina State Troops in 1861; was commissioned colonel of the Forty-seventh North Carolina Infantry April 8, 1862; resigned January 5, 1863, upon being elected attorney general of the State of North Carolina; served in that capacity until 1866; unsuccessful candidate for election in 1868 to the Forty-first Congress; elected as a Democrat to the Forty-second Congress (March 4, 1871-March 3, 1873); unsuccessful candidate for reelection in 1872 to the Forty-third Congress; died in Raleigh, Wake County, N.C., on August 14, 1874; interment in the City Cemetery.

**ROGERS, Thomas Jones** (father of William Findlay Rogers), a Representative from Pennsylvania; born in Waterford, Ireland, in 1781; immigrated to the United States in 1784 with his parents, who settled in Easton, Pa.; learned the printing trade; editor and owner of the Northampton Farmer, 1805-1814; elected as a Republican to the Fifteenth Congress to fill the vacancy caused by the resignation of John Ross; reelected to the Sixteenth, Seventeenth, and Eighteenth Congresses and served from March 3, 1818, to April 20, 1824, when he resigned; trustee of Lafayette College, 1826-1832; register and recorder of deeds for Northampton County, Pa., from 1828 to 1830; served as brigadier general in the Pennsylvania militia; United States naval officer at the port of Philadelphia; died

in New York City December 7, 1832; interment in the graveyard of the New Market Street Baptist Church, Philadelphia, Pa., reinterment in Glenwood Cemetery in 1851.

**ROGERS, Walter Edward,** a Representative from Texas; born in Texarkana, Miller County, Ark., July 19, 1908; attended the public schools in McKinney, Tex.; attended Austin College, Sherman, Tex., in 1926, and the law school of the University of Texas at Austin until 1935; was admitted to the bar in 1935 and commenced the practice of law in 1936 in Pampa, Tex.; city attorney of Pampa, 1938-1940; district attorney of the thirty-first judicial district of Texas, 1943-1947; delegate to Texas State Democratic conventions, 1950-1956, and 1960; delegate to National Democratic Conventions from 1952 to 1964; elected as a Democrat to the Eighty-second and to the seven succeeding Congresses (January 3, 1951-January 3, 1967); was not a candidate for reelection in 1966 to the Ninetieth Congress; resumed the practice of law; president, Independent Natural Gas Association of America; is a resident of Chevy Chase, Md.

**ROGERS, Will,** a Representative from Oklahoma; born on a farm near Bessie, Washita County, Oklahoma Territory (now Oklahoma), December 12, 1898; attended the public schools, and Southwestern Teachers College, Weatherford, Okla.; B.S., Central Teachers College, Edmond, Okla., 1926, and A.B., 1929; M.S., University of Oklahoma at Norman, 1930; teacher in the public schools of Bessie, Okla., 1917-1919; principal of the public schools at Bartlesville, Okla., 1919-1923; superintendent of schools in several Oklahoma school districts, 1923-1932; elected as a Democrat to the Seventy-third and to the four succeeding Congresses (March 4, 1933-January 3, 1943); chairman, Committee on Indian Affairs (Seventy-fourth through Seventy-seventh Congresses); while serving as a Representative at large was an unsuccessful candidate for nomination in 1941 to fill the vacancy caused by the death of Sam C. Massingale in the Seventh District for the Seventy-seventh Congress; was not a candidate for renomination in 1942 to the Seventy-eighth Congress; admitted to the Oklahoma bar in 1942; unsuccessful candidate for the Democratic nomination for secretary of state of Oklahoma in 1943; employed by the Department of the Interior, 1943-1945; assistant to the Secretary of Agriculture, Washington, D.C., in 1946 and 1947; hearing examiner in the Department of Agriculture from May 1947 until his retirement in 1968; engaged in building and real estate management; was a resident of McLean, Va. until his death in Falls Church, Va., on August 3, 1983; cremated, ashes interred at National Memorial Park, Falls Church, Va.

**ROGERS, William Findlay** (son of Thomas Jones Rogers), a Representative from New York; born in Forks Township, near the borough of Easton, Pa., March 1, 1820; moved with his parents to Philadelphia, where he attended the common schools; returned to Easton, Pa., and entered a printing office in 1832; returned to Philadelphia in 1834 and continued working at his trade; established a paper at Honesdale, Pa., in 1840; moved to Buffalo, N.Y., in 1846; was foreman in the office of the Buffalo Daily Courier; established and managed the Buffalo Republic in 1850; member of Company D, Buffalo City Guard, in 1846; served in the Civil War as colonel of the Twenty-first Regiment, New York Volunteers; mustered out in 1863; comptroller of the city of Buffalo in 1867 and mayor in 1869; secretary and treasurer of the park commissioners in 1871; nominated for the State senate in 1878, but declined; elected as a Democrat to the Forty-eighth Congress (March 4, 1883-March 3, 1885); was not a candidate for renomination in 1884; superintendent of the Soldiers' and Sailors' Home at Bath, N.Y., from 1887 to 1897; died in Buffalo, N.Y., on December 16, 1899; interment in Forest Lawn Cemetery.

**ROGERS, William Nathaniel,** a Representative from New Hampshire; born in Sanbornville, Carroll County, N.H., January 10, 1892; attended the public schools, Brewster Free Academy, Wolfeboro, N.H., and Dartmouth College, Hanover, N.H.; was graduated from the law department of the University of Maine at Orono in 1916; was admitted to the bar the same year and practiced in Sanbornville and Rochester, N.H.; member of the State house of representatives in 1917, 1919, and 1921; elected as a Democrat to the Sixty-eighth Congress (March 4, 1923-March 3, 1925); unsuccessful candidate for reelection in 1924 to the Sixty-ninth Congress; resumed the practice of his profession in Concord, N.H.; moderator of the town of Wakefield, N.H., 1928-1945; elected January 5, 1932, to fill the vacancy in the Seventy-second Congress caused by the death of Fletcher Hale; reelected to the Seventy-third and Seventy-fourth Congresses and served from January 5, 1932, to January 3, 1937; was not a candidate for renomination, but was an unsuccessful candidate for election to the United States Senate in 1936; resumed the practice of law in Concord, N.H., until 1943, when he moved to Sanbornville, N.H., and continued practice until his death in Wolfeboro, N.H., September 25, 1945; interment in Lovell Lake Cemetery, Sanbornville, N.H.

**ROGERS, William Vann, Jr.,** a Representative from California; born in New York City October 20, 1911; attended the grade and high schools at Beverly Hills, Calif.; B.A., Stanford University, Palo Alto, Calif., 1935; owner and publisher, Beverly Hills Citizen, 1935-1953; second lieutenant in the Field Artillery, Reserve Officers Training Corps 1935-1940; enlisted as a private in the United States Army in June 1942; commissioned a second lieutenant of Field Artillery in July 1942; assigned to the Eight Hundred and Ninety-ninth Tank Destroyer Battalion and served until December 1942; elected as a Democrat to the Seventy-eighth Congress and served from January 3, 1943, until his resignation May 23, 1944, to return to the United States Army, serving as a lieutenant in the Eight Hundred and Fourteenth Tank Destroyer Battalion until March 1, 1946; unsuccessful candidate in 1946 for election to the United States Senate; delegate to the Democratic National Conventions of 1948, 1952 and 1956; writer, active in radio and television programs; member, California State Park Commission 1958-1960, chairman, 1960-1962; appointed Special Assistant to the Commissioner of Indian Affairs, 1967-1969; was a resident of Beverly Hills, Calif.; died July 9, 1993.

**ROHRABACHER, Dana Tyrone,** a Representative from California; born in Coronado, San Diego County, Calif., June 21, 1947; graduated, Palos Verdes (Calif.) High School, 1965; attended Los Angeles Harbor College, 1965-1967; B.A., California State University at Long Beach, 1969; M.A., University of Southern California, 1975; Los Angeles County high school chair, Youth for Reagan gubernatorial campaign, 1966; assistant to press secretary, President Ronald Reagan's presidential campaigns, 1976 and 1980; editorial writer, Orange County Register; staff, KFWB Radio and Radio New West-City News Service, Los Angeles; speechwriter, The White House, 1981-1987; special assistant to President Ronald Reagan and speechwriter, 1987-1988; elected as a Republican to the One Hundred First and to the three succeeding Congresses (January 3, 1989-January 3, 1997); is a resident of Huntington Beach, Calif.

**ROHRBOUGH, Edward Gay,** a Representative from West Virginia; born in 1874, near Buckhannon, Upshur County, W.Va.; attended the public schools and West Virginia Wesleyan College at Buckhannon; graduated from Allegheny College, Meadville, Pa., in 1900 and from Harvard University in 1906; later studied at the University of Chicago; instructor at West Virginia Wesleyan College and at West Virginia University at Morgantown; taught school in Brookville, Pa., in 1900 and 1901, and at Glenville, W.Va. State Normal School, 1901-1907; vice president of Fairmont, W.Va. State Teachers College, 1907-1908; president of Glenville, W.Va. State Teachers College from 1908 until 1942; also engaged in banking; elected as a Republican to the Seventy-eighth Congress (January 3, 1943-January 3, 1945); was an unsuccessful candidate for reelection in 1944 to the Seventy-ninth Congress; elected in 1946 to the Eightieth Congress (January 3, 1947-January 3, 1949); unsuccessful candidate for reelection in 1948 to the Eighty-first Congress; died in Washington, D.C., December 12, 1956; interment in Stalnaker Cemetery, Glenville, W.Va.

**ROLLINS, Edward Henry,** a Representative and a Senator from New Hampshire; born in Somersworth (Rollinsford), Strafford County, N.H., October 3, 1824; attended the common schools and academies in Dover, N.H., and South Berwick, Maine; engaged in mercantile pursuits at Concord, N.H.; member, New Hampshire State house of representatives, 1855-1857, and served as speaker; elected as a Republican to the Thirty-seventh and to the two succeeding Congresses (March 4, 1861-March 3, 1867); was not a candidate for renomination in 1866 to the Fortieth Congress; chairman, Committee on Accounts (Thirty-eighth and Thirty-ninth Congresses); secretary and treasurer of the Union Pacific Railroad Company; elected in 1876 as a Republican to the United States Senate, and served from March 4, 1877 to March 3, 1883; unsuccessful candidate for reelection; chairman, Committee on Manufactures (Forty-fifth Congress), Committee on Enrolled Bills (Forty-seventh Congress), Committee on Public Buildings and Grounds (Forty-seventh Congress); president of the Boston, Concord and Montreal Railroad Company, 1886-1889; founder of the First National Bank of Concord, N.H., and of the banking house of E.H. Rollins and Sons, of Boston, Mass.; died on the Isle of Shoals, N.H., July 31, 1889; interment in Blossom Hill Cemetery, Concord, N.H.

**Bibliography:** *DAB*; Lyford, James. *Life of Edward H. Rollins.* Boston: D. Estes and Company, 1906.

**ROLLINS, James Sidney,** a Representative from Missouri; born in Richmond, Madison County, Ky., April 19, 1812; completed preparatory studies; attended Centre College, Danville, Ky., and was graduated from the University of Indiana at Bloomington in 1830; studied law; was admitted to the bar in 1834 and commenced practice in Columbia, Mo.; served as major in the Black Hawk War; member of the State house of representatives 1838-1840, 1854, and 1867; delegate to the Whig National Convention in 1844; served in the State senate 1846-1848; unsuccessful candidate for Governor in 1848 and 1857; elected as a Constitutional Unionist to the Thirty-seventh Congress and reelected as a Unionist to the Thirty-eighth Congress (March 4, 1861-March 3, 1865); resumed the practice of his profession; delegate to the Philadelphia Union Convention in 1866; president of the board of curators of the University of Missouri from 1869 to 1886, when he resigned; died in Columbia, Boone County, Mo., January 9, 1888; interment in Columbia Cemetery.

**Bibliography:** *DAB*; Wood, James M., Jr. "James Sidney Rollins of Missouri: A Political Biography." Ph.D. dissertation, Stanford University, 1952.

**ROLPH, Thomas,** a Representative from California; born in San Francisco, Calif., January 17, 1885; attended the public schools; graduated from Humboldt Evening High School; in 1912 founded a building materials sales agency, which he headed until his death; elected as a Republican to the Seventy-seventh and Seventy-eighth Congresses (January 3, 1941-January 3, 1945); unsuccessful candidate for reelection in 1944 to the Seventy-ninth Congress; returned to his building material sales agency; died in San Francisco, Calif., May 10, 1956; interment in Cypress Lawn Memorial Park, Colma, San Mateo County, Calif.

**ROMAN, James Dixon,** a Representative from Maryland; born in Chester County, Pa., August 11, 1809; attended the common schools and a private school at West Nottingham (now Nottingham); moved to Cecil County, Md.; studied law in Frederick, Md.; was admitted to the bar in 1834 and commenced practice in Hagerstown, Md.; member of the State senate in 1847; elected as a Whig to the Thirtieth Congress (March 4, 1847-March 3, 1849); presidential elector on the Whig ticket in 1848 and on the Democratic ticket in 1856; again resumed the practice of law in Hagerstown; president of the Old Hagerstown Bank from 1851 until his death; member of the peace convention held in Washington, D.C., in 1861 in an effort to devise means to prevent the impending war; died near Hagerstown, Washington County, Md., January 19, 1867; interment in Rose Hill Cemetery.

**ROMEIS, Jacob,** a Representative from Ohio; born in Weisenbach, Bavaria, Germany, December 1, 1835; attended the village schools; immigrated in 1847 to the United States with his parents, who settled in Erie County, N.Y., and attended the public and select schools of Buffalo, N.Y.; engaged in the shipping business and railroading; moved to Toledo, Ohio, in 1856; elected to the board of aldermen of the city of Toledo in 1874; reelected in 1876 and served as president of the board in 1877; mayor of Toledo 1879-1885; elected as a Republican to the Forty-ninth and Fiftieth Congresses (March 4, 1885-March 3, 1889); unsuccessful candidate for reelection in 1888 to the Fifty-first Congress; engaged in fruit growing near Toledo; died in Toledo, Lucas County, Ohio, March 8, 1904; interment in Woodlawn Cemetery.

**ROMERO, Trinidad,** a Delegate from the Territory of New Mexico; born in Santa Fe, Santa Fe County (then a part of the Republic of Mexico), N.Mex., June 15, 1835; educated by private tutors; engaged in merchandising, freighting with ox teams from Kansas City to Santa Fe, and later in stock raising; member of the New Mexico Territorial house of representatives in 1863; probate judge of San Miguel County, N.Mex., in 1869 and 1870; elected as a Republican to the Forty-fifth Congress (March 4, 1877-March 3, 1879); was not a candidate for renomination in 1878 to the Forty-sixth Congress; appointed United States marshal by President Benjamin Harrison and served from November 13, 1889, to May 30, 1893; engaged in mercantile pursuits and stock raising on his ranch near Wagon Mound, N.Mex.; died in Las Vegas, San Miguel County, N.Mex., August 28, 1918; interment in Calvary Cemetery.

**ROMERO-BARCELÓ, Carlos Antonio,** a Resident Commissioner from Puerto Rico; born in San Juan, P.R., September 4, 1932; B.A., Yale University, 1953; LL.B., University of Puerto Rico School of Law, 1956; practicing attorney, San Juan; mayor of San Juan, 1969-1976; Governor of Puerto Rico, 1977-1984; elected as a Democrat to the United States House of Representatives November 3, 1992, for a four-year term commencing January 3, 1993; is a resident of San Juan, P.R.

**ROMJUE, Milton Andrew,** a Representative from Missouri; born in Love Lake, Macon County, Mo., December 5, 1874; attended the public schools and the Kirksville State Normal School; was graduated from the law department of the University of Missouri at Columbia in 1904; was admitted to the bar the same year and commenced practice in Macon, Macon County, Mo.; city attorney of Higbee, Randolph County, Mo., in 1904 and 1905; judge of the Macon County probate court, 1907-1915; delegate to Democratic State conventions from 1920 to 1940; delegate to the Democratic National Convention in 1928; elected as a Democrat to the Sixty-fifth and Sixty-sixth Congresses (March 4, 1917-March 3, 1921); unsuccessful candidate for reelection in 1920 to the Sixty-seventh Congress; elected to the Sixty-eighth and to the nine succeeding Congresses (March 4, 1923-January 3, 1943); chairman, Committee on the Post Office and Post Roads (Seventy-sixth and

Seventy-seventh Congresses); unsuccessful candidate for reelection in 1942 to the Seventy-eighth Congress; resumed the practice of law and also engaged in farming and stock raising; died in Macon, Mo., January 23, 1968; interment in Oakwood Cemetery.

**ROMULO, Carlos Peña,** a Resident Commissioner from the Commonwealth of the Philippines; born in Camiling, Tarlac, Philippine Islands, January 14, 1899; was graduated from the University of the Philippines at Manila in 1918, from Columbia University at New York City in 1921, and from Notre Dame (Ind.) University in 1935; member of the faculty of the University of the Philippines, 1923-1928; author, editor, and publisher at Manila, Philippine Islands, 1922-1941; also interested in a broadcasting corporation; secretary to Manuel L. Quezon, president of the Philippine Senate, in 1922; member of the independence missions to the United States in 1921, 1924, 1928, 1929, 1933, and 1937; member of the Board of Regents of the University of the Philippines, 1929-1941; secretary of Information and Public Relations and member of the President's war cabinet in 1943 and 1944; member of the Filipino Rehabilitation Commission, 1944-1946; secretary of public instruction from October 1944 to February 1945; aide-de-camp to General Douglas MacArthur at Bataan, Corregidor, and Australia; promoted to brigadier general in the Philippine Army in September 1944; appointed Resident Commissioner to the United States on August 10, 1944, to fill the vacancy caused by the resignation of Joaquin M. Elizalde, and served until July 4, 1946, when the office of Resident Commissioner was terminated; appointed by President Manuel Roxas on July 9, 1946, as permanent delegate of the Republic of the Philippines to the United Nations; Ambassador to the United States, 1952-1953, and 1955-1962; secretary of foreign affairs, 1949-1951; president of the United Nations General Assembly in 1949 and 1950, and of United Nations Security Council in 1957; president, University of Philippines and concurrently secretary of education, 1962-1968; president, Philippine Academy of Arts and Science, 1962; secretary of foreign affairs, 1969-1984; was a resident of Manila, Philippines, until his death there on December 15, 1985; interment in Heroes' Cemetery.

**Bibliography:** Romulo, Carlos Peña. *I Walked With Heroes.* New York: Holt, Rinehart and Winston, 1961.

**RONAN, Daniel John,** a Representative from Illinois; born in Chicago, Ill., July 13, 1914; attended parochial schools; graduated from St. Ignatius High School in 1933, from Loyola University, Chicago, Ill., in 1938, and was engaged in postgraduate work at Loyola University, 1939-1941, and 1947-1948; served in United States Army Air Corps communications in the China-Burma-India Theater, 1942-1945; member of the Illinois State house of representatives, 1948-1952; alderman from 1951 until 1964; was appointed acting ward committeeman in 1959, elected in 1960, and reelected in 1964; member of the Chicago Planning Commission, 1959-1964; elected as a Democrat to the Eighty-ninth and to the two succeeding Congresses, and served from January 3, 1965 until his death in Chicago, Ill., August 13, 1969; interment in Queen of Heaven Mausoleum, Hillside, Ill.

**RONCALIO, Teno,** a Representative from Wyoming; born in Rock Springs, Sweetwater County, Wyo., March 23, 1916; attended the public schools; employee of the United States Senate Library under the patronage of Senator Joseph C. O'Mahoney, 1940-1941; enlisted in the United States Army (Infantry), and served overseas in North Africa, Sicily, and Europe in the First Division from December 1941 until March 1946; LL.B., University of Wyoming, Laramie, 1947; admitted to the Wyoming bar in 1947 and commenced the practice of law in Cheyenne, Wyo.; deputy prosecuting attorney of Laramie County, 1950-1956; chairman of the Wyoming Democratic Central committee, 1957-1961; delegate to the Democratic National Conventions of 1956, 1960, 1964, and 1968; member, Democratic National Committee, 1969-1970; engaged in banking; member of the International Joint Commission, United States and Canada, 1961-1964; elected as a Democrat to the Eighty-ninth Congress (January 3, 1965-January 3, 1967); was not a candidate in 1966 for renomination to the House of Representatives, but was an unsuccessful candidate for election to the United States Senate; elected to the Ninety-second and to the three succeeding Congresses, and served from January 3, 1971 until his resignation December 30, 1978; was not a candidate for reelection in 1978 to the Ninety-sixth Congress; resumed the practice of law; served as Special Master in Wyoming's Big Horn adjudication of Indian Water Rights, 1979-1982; is a resident of Cheyenne, Wyo.

**RONCALLO, Angelo Dominick,** a Representative from New York; born in Port Chester, Westchester County, N.Y., May 28, 1927; attended the public schools, and Peekskill (N.Y.) Military Academy, 1943; B.A., Manhattan College, 1950; J.D., Georgetown University School of Law, Washington, D.C., 1953; served in the United States Army, 1944-1945; admitted to the New York bar in 1955 and commenced practice in Massapequa; councilman, town of Oyster Bay, 1965-1967; comptroller, Nassau County, 1968-1972; delegate, New York State Republican convention, 1968; delegate to the Republican National Convention of 1972; elected as a Republican to the Ninety-third Congress (January 3, 1973-January 3, 1975); unsuccessful candidate for reelection in 1974 to the Ninety-fourth Congress; justice, New York State supreme court, Tenth Judicial District, since his election in November 1977; is a resident of Massapequa, N.Y.

**ROONEY, Frederick Bernard,** a Representative from Pennsylvania; born in Bethlehem, Northampton County, Pa., November 6, 1925; attended the public schools; graduated from the Bethlehem High School in 1944; served in the United States Army from February 1944 to April 1946, with service in Europe as a paratrooper; B.A., University of Georgia at Athens, 1950; engaged in the real estate and insurance business in 1950; elected to two terms in the Pennsylvania senate and served from November 5, 1958, until his resignation August 6, 1963; elected as a Democrat, by special election, July 30, 1963, to the Eighty-eighth Congress to fill the vacancy caused by the death of Francis E. Walter; reelected to the seven succeeding Congresses, and served from July 30, 1963, to January 3, 1979; unsuccessful candidate for reelection in 1978 to the Ninety-sixth Congress; established a consulting business; is a resident of Washington, D.C.

**ROONEY, John James,** a Representative from New York; born in Brooklyn, N.Y., November 29, 1903; attended the parochial schools and St. Francis Preparatory School and College; the law department of Fordham University, New York, N.Y., LL.B., 1925; was admitted to the bar in 1926 and commenced practice in Brooklyn, N.Y.; served as assistant district attorney in Brooklyn 1940-1944; elected as a Democrat to the Seventy-eighth Congress, by special election June 6, 1944, to fill the vacancy caused by the death of Thomas H. Cullen; reelected to the fifteen succeeding Congresses and served from June 6, 1944, until his resignation on December 31, 1974; was not a candidate for reelection in 1974 to the Ninety-fourth Congress; resided in Washington, D.C., until his death there on October 26, 1975; interment in Holy Cross Cemetery, Brooklyn, N.Y.

**ROOSEVELT, Franklin Delano, Jr.** (son of President Franklin Delano Roosevelt and brother of James Roosevelt), a Representative from New York; born in Campobello, New Brunswick, Canada, August 17, 1914; graduated from Groton School, Harvard University in 1937, and the University of Virginia Law School at Charlottesville in 1940; was admitted to the bar in 1942; was called from the Naval Reserve on March 13, 1941, to active duty as an ensign in the United States Navy and served in North Africa, Europe, and the Pacific; discharged from active duty in January 1946; awarded the Purple Heart Medal and the Silver Star; member of a law firm in New York City, beginning in 1946; vice president of President Harry S Truman's Committee on Civil Rights in 1947 and 1948; chairman of Mayor William O'Dwyer's committee on unity in New York City in 1948 and 1949; delegate to the Democratic National Conventions of 1952 and 1956; elected as a Liberal Party candidate to the Eighty-first Congress to fill the vacancy caused by the death of Sol Bloom; reelected as a Democrat to the Eighty-second and Eighty-third Congresses, and served from May 17, 1949 to January 3, 1955; was not a candidate for reelection in 1954 to the Eighty-fourth Congress, but was an unsuccessful candidate for nomination for Governor of New York; unsuccessful candidate for election for attorney general of New York in 1954; resumed the practice of law in New York City; engaged in the automobile import business; appointed by President John F. Kennedy as chairman of Appalachian Regional Commission, 1963; appointed by President Kennedy as Undersecretary of Commerce, 1963; appointed by President Lyndon B. Johnson as first Chairman of the Equal Employment Opportunity Commission, 1965; unsuccessful Liberal Party candidate for Governor of New York in 1966; businessman and farmer; was a resident of Millbrook, N.Y.; died August 17, 1988.

**ROOSEVELT, James** (son of President Franklin Delano Roosevelt and brother of Franklin Delano Roosevelt, Jr.), a Representative from California; born in New York City, December 23, 1907; attended schools in New York and St. Albans School of Washington, D.C.; was graduated from Groton School in 1926 and from Harvard University in 1930; in 1930 became an insurance broker in Boston, Mass.; organized Roosevelt & Sargent, Inc., and served as president until January 1937; secretary to his father, President Franklin D. Roosevelt, in 1937 and 1938; vice president, United Artists motion picture studios, 1939; went on active duty as a captain in the United States Marine Corps in November 1940; promoted to colonel April 13, 1944, and served in the Pacific Theater; released from active duty in August 1945; brigadier general, United States Marine Corps Reserve, retired; rejoined Roosevelt & Sargent, Inc., as executive vice president and established an office in Los Angeles, Calif., in June 1946; served as chairman of the board, Roosevelt & Haines, Inc.; unsuccessful candidate in 1950 for election for Governor of California; delegate to the Democratic National Conventions of 1948, 1952, 1956 and 1960; elected as a Democrat to the Eighty-fourth and to the five succeeding Congresses and served from January 3, 1955, to September 30, 1965; unsuccessful candidate for Democratic nomination for mayor of Los Angeles, Calif., in April 1965; resigned from Congress effective September 30, 1965, to become United States representative to United Nations Economic and Social Council, resigning in December 1966; public relations consultant; was a resident of Newport Beach, Calif.; died August 13, 1991.

**ROOSEVELT, James I.** (uncle of Robert Barnwell Roosevelt), a Representative from New York; born in New York City December 14, 1795; was graduated from Columbia College, New York City, in 1815; studied law; was admitted to the bar in 1818 and commenced practice in New York City; councilman; member of the New York State assembly in 1835 and 1840; elected as a Democrat to the Twenty-seventh Congress (March 4, 1841-March 3, 1843); declined to be a candidate for renomination in 1842 to the Twenty-eighth Congress; studied foreign law in the courts of Great Britain, the Netherlands, and France; justice of the supreme court of the State of New York from 1851 until 1859; served one term as ex officio judge of the State court of appeals in 1859; appointed United States district attorney for southern New York by President James Buchanan and served in 1860 and 1861; engaged in agricultural pursuits; died in New York City on April 5, 1875; interment in Greenwood Cemetery, Brooklyn, N.Y.

**ROOSEVELT, Robert Barnwell** (nephew of James I. Roosevelt and uncle of Theodore Roosevelt), a Representative from New York; born in New York City, August 7, 1829; completed preparatory studies; studied law; was admitted to the bar in 1850 and commenced practice in New York City; served as fish commissioner of the State of New York from 1868 until 1888; for several years edited the New York Citizen; elected as a Democrat to the Forty-second Congress (March 4, 1871-March 3, 1873); appointed by President Grover Cleveland as Minister to The Netherlands on May 16, 1888 and served until May 1889; treasurer of the Democratic National Committee in 1892; member of the Board of Aldermen of New York City; served as trustee representing the city of New York for the New York and Brooklyn Bridge from 1879 to 1882; died in Sayville, N.Y., on June 14, 1906; interment in Greenwood Cemetery, Brooklyn, N.Y.

**Bibliography:** *DAB*.

**ROOSEVELT, Theodore, Jr.** (great-great-grandson of Archibald Bulloch, father-in-law of Nicholas Longworth, and nephew of Robert Barnwell Roosevelt), a Vice President and 26th President of the United States; born in New York City, October 27, 1858; privately tutored; graduated from Harvard University in 1880; studied law; traveled abroad; member of the New York State assembly from 1882 to 1884; moved to North Dakota and lived on his ranch; returned to New York City in 1886; appointed by President Benjamin Harrison a member of the United States Civil Service Commission in 1889 and served until his resignation in 1895 to become president of the New York Board of Police Commissioners; resigned this position upon his appointment by President William McKinley as Assistant Secretary of the Navy in 1897, and served until 1898, when he resigned to enter the war with Spain; organized the First Regiment, United States Volunteer Cavalry, popularly known as Roosevelt's Rough Riders; elected Governor of New York in 1898, and served from January 1, 1899 to January 1, 1901; elected Vice President of the United States on the Republican ticket headed by William McKinley in 1900, and was inaugurated March 4, 1901; upon the death of President McKinley on September 14, 1901, became President of the United States; elected President of the United States in 1904, was inaugurated March 4, 1905, and served until March 3, 1909; awarded the Nobel Peace Prize in 1906 for his mediation of the Russian-Japanese conflict; unsuccessful candidate of the Progressive Party for President of the United States in 1912; engaged in literary pursuits; died at Oyster Bay, N.Y., January 6, 1919; interment in Young's Memorial Cemetery.

**Bibliography:** *DAB*; Blum, John Morton. *The Republican Roosevelt.* Cambridge, Mass.: Harvard University Press, 1977; Morris, Edmund. *The Rise of Theodore Roosevelt.* New York: Coward, McCann and Geoghegan, 1979.

**ROOT, Elihu,** a Senator from New York; born in Clinton, Oneida County, N.Y., February 15, 1845; attended the common schools; graduated from Hamilton College, Clinton, N.Y., in 1864; taught in the Rome (N.Y.) Academy in 1865; was graduated from the law school of the University of the City of New York in 1867; was admitted to the bar in the same year and commenced practice in New York City; United States attorney for the southern district of New York, 1883-1885; delegate to the New York State constitutional convention in 1894; appointed Secretary of War by President William McKinley, and served from August 1, 1899 to January 31, 1904; appointed Secretary of State by President Theodore Roosevelt on July 7, 1905, and served until January 27, 1909; elected as a Republican to the United States Senate and served from March 4, 1909 to March 3, 1915; declined to be a candidate for reelection; chairman, Committee on Expenditures in the Department of State (Sixty-first Congress), Committee on Industrial Expositions (Sixty-second Congress); resumed the practice of law in New York City; author; awarded the Nobel Peace Prize in 1912 for his work with the Carnegie Endowment for International Peace, of which organization

he served as president from 1910 until 1925; president of The Hague Tribunal of Arbitration between Great Britain, France, Spain, and Portugal, concerning church property, in 1913; president of the New York State constitutional convention in 1915; appointed by President Woodrow Wilson to be Ambassador Extraordinary at the head of a special diplomatic mission from the United States to Russia in 1917; Commissioner Plenipotentiary to the Conference on Limitation of Armament at Washington, D.C., 1921-1922; member of the Committee of International Jurists, which, on invitation of the Council of the League of Nations, reported the plan for a new Permanent Court of International Justice in 1921; died in New York City, February 7, 1937; interment in Hamilton College Cemetery, Clinton, N.Y.

**Bibliography:** *DAB*; Jessup, Philip. *Elihu Root.* 1938. Reprint. 2 vols. Hamden, Conn.: Archon Books, 1964; Leopold, Richard. *Elihu Root and the Conservative Tradition.* Boston: Little, Brown and Company, 1954.

**ROOT, Erastus,** a Representative from New York; born in Hebron, Conn., March 16, 1773; was graduated from Dartmouth College, Hanover, N.H., in 1793; taught school for several years; studied law; was admitted to the bar in 1796 and commenced practice in Delhi, N.Y.; member of the State assembly 1798-1802; elected as a Republican to the Eighth Congress (March 4, 1803-March 3, 1805); resumed the practice of law; elected to the Eleventh Congress (March 4, 1809-March 3, 1811); chairman, Committee on Claims (Eleventh Congress); appointed in 1811 a member of the commission to revise and codify the laws of New York State; served in the State senate 1812-1815; successfully contested the election of John Adams to the Fourteenth Congress and served from December 26, 1815, to March 3, 1817; chairman, Committee on Expenditures in the Department of War (Fourteenth Congress); again a member of the State assembly 1818-1822; member of the State constitutional convention of 1821; Lieutenant Governor of New York State 1822-1824; unsuccessful candidate for reelection in 1824; again became a member of the State assembly 1826-1828, and in 1830, and served as speaker during the terms in 1827 and 1828; elected as a Jacksonian to the Twenty-second Congress (March 4, 1831-March 3, 1833); chairman, Committee on Agriculture (Twenty-second Congress); unsuccessful Whig candidate for election in 1838 to the Twenty-sixth Congress; again served in the State senate 1840-1844; died in New York City December 24, 1846; interment in the Old (High Street) Cemetery, Delhi, N.Y.

**Bibliography:** *DAB*.

**ROOT, Jesse,** a Delegate from Connecticut; born in Coventry, Tolland County, Conn., December 28, 1736; was graduated from Princeton College in 1756; studied theology in Andover; was ordained as a minister and preached from 1758 to 1763; studied law; was admitted to the bar in 1763 and commenced practice in Hartford, Conn.; captain, lieutenant colonel, and adjutant general in the Revolutionary Army; Member of the Continental Congress, 1778-1782; State's attorney, 1785-1789; appointed a judge of the superior court in 1789, and served as chief justice from 1796 to 1807, when he resigned; member of the State house of representatives, 1807-1809; delegate to the State constitutional convention in 1818; died in Coventry, Conn., March 29, 1822; interment in Nathan Hale Cemetery, South Coventry, Tolland County, Conn.

**Bibliography:** *DAB*.

**ROOT, Joseph Mosley,** a Representative from Ohio; born in Brutus, Cayuga County, N.Y., October 7, 1807; pursued classical studies; studied law in Auburn, N.Y.; moved to Ohio in 1829; was admitted to the bar in 1830 and commenced practice in Norwalk, Huron County, Ohio; elected prosecuting attorney of Huron County in 1837; member of the State senate in 1840 and 1841; elected as a Whig to the Twenty-ninth Congress; reelected to the Thirtieth Congress and reelected as a Free-Soil candidate to the Thirty-first

Congress (March 4, 1845-March 3, 1851); chairman, Committee on Expenditures in the Department of the Treasury (Thirtieth Congress); presidential elector on the Republican ticket in 1860; appointed United States attorney for the northern district of Ohio in 1861; again a member of the State senate in 1869; Democratic delegate to the State constitutional convention in 1873; unsuccessful Democratic candidate for probate judge of Erie County in 1875; died in Sandusky, Erie County, Ohio, April 7, 1879; interment in Oakland Cemetery.

**ROOTS, Logan Holt,** a Representative from Arkansas; born near Tamaroa, Perry County, Ill., March 26, 1841; completed preparatory studies and was graduated from the Illinois State Normal University in 1862; assisted in recruiting the Eighty-first Illinois Volunteers and served in the Army until the close of the Civil War; settled in Arkansas and engaged in planting and trading; upon the readmission of Arkansas to representation was elected as a Republican to the Fortieth Congress; reelected to the Forty-first Congress and served from June 22, 1868, to March 3, 1871; unsuccessful candidate for reelection in 1870 to the Forty-second Congress; served as president of the First National Bank of Little Rock, Ark., until his death in that city May 30, 1893; interment in Oakland Cemetery.

**ROS-LEHTINEN, Ileana C.,** a Representative from Florida; born in Havana, Cuba, July 15, 1952; A.A., Miami-Dade Community College, 1972; B.A., Florida International University, 1975, and M.S., 1986; University of Miami, currently doctoral candidate in educational administration; teacher; founder and former owner, Eastern Academy; member, Florida State house of representatives, 1982-1986; member, Florida State senate, 1986-1989; elected as a Republican to the One Hundred First Congress, August 29, 1989, by special election to fill the vacancy caused by the death of Claude D. Pepper; reelected to the three succeeding Congresses, and served from August 29, 1989 to January 3, 1997; is a resident of Miami, Fla.

**ROSE, Charles Grandison, III** (son-in-law of Willie Gathrel (Bill) Hefner), a Representative from North Carolina; born in Fayetteville, Cumberland County, N.C., August 10, 1939; attended the public schools; graduated, Fayetteville Senior High School, 1957; A.B., Davidson (N.C.) College, 1961; LL.B., University of North Carolina Law School, Chapel Hill, 1964; admitted to the North Carolina bar in 1964 and commenced practice in Raleigh; chief district court prosecutor for the Twelfth Judicial District, 1967-1970; elected as a Democrat to the Ninety-third and to the eleven succeeding Congresses (January 3, 1973-January 3, 1997); chairman, Joint Committee on Printing (One Hundred Second Congress), Committee on House Administration (One Hundred Second and One Hundred Third Congresses); was not a candidate for reelection in 1996 to the One Hundred Fifth Congress; is a resident of Fayetteville, N.C.

**ROSE, John Marshall,** a Representative from Pennsylvania; born in Johnstown, Cambria County, Pa., May 18, 1856; attended the public schools; was graduated from Washington and Jefferson College, Washington, Pa., in 1880; taught school; studied law; was admitted to the bar in 1884 and commenced practice in Johnstown; member of the Pennsylvania house of representatives in 1889; declined to be a candidate for reelection; elected as a Republican to the Sixty-fifth and to the two succeeding Congresses (March 4, 1917-March 3, 1923); declined to be a candidate for renomination in 1922 to the Sixty-eighth Congress; died in Washington, D.C., April 22, 1923; interment in Grandview Cemetery, Johnstown, Pa.

**ROSE, Robert Lawson** (son of Robert Selden Rose and son-in-law of Nathaniel Allen), a Representative from New York; born in Geneva, N.Y., October 12, 1804; received a limited schooling; moved to Allens Hill, N.Y., and engaged in agricultural pursuits; held several local offices; elected as a Whig to the Thirtieth and

Thirty-first Congresses (March 4, 1847-March 3, 1851); resumed agricultural pursuits; returned to Geneva, Ontario County, N.Y.; subsequently moved to Pleasant Grove, near Funkstown, Washington County, Md., in 1868 and engaged in the manufacture of paper until his death there on March 14, 1877; interment in Rose Hill Cemetery, Hagerstown, Washington County, Md.

**ROSE, Robert Selden** (father of Robert Lawson Rose), a Representative from New York; born in Amherst County, Va., February 24, 1774; attended the common schools; moved to Seneca County, N.Y., in 1803 and settled at Fayette, near Geneva, N.Y.; engaged in agricultural pursuits; member of the New York State assembly in 1811, 1820, and 1821; member of the State constitutional convention in 1821 at Albany; elected to the Eighteenth and Nineteenth Congresses (March 4, 1823-March 3, 1827); elected as an Anti-Masonic candidate to the Twenty-first Congress (March 4, 1829-March 3, 1831); later affiliated with the Whig Party; again resumed agricultural pursuits; died in Waterloo, Seneca County, N.Y., while attending a session of the circuit court, on November 24, 1835; interment in the Old Pulteney Street Cemetery; reinterment in Glenwood Cemetery, Geneva, Ontario County, N.Y.

**ROSECRANS, William Starke,** a Representative from California; born in Kingston, Ross County, Ohio, September 6, 1819; completed preparatory studies; was appointed to the United States Military Academy at West Point in 1838 and graduated in 1842; brevetted second lieutenant, United States Corps of Engineers, July 1, 1842; second lieutenant on April 3, 1843; assistant professor of engineering at the United States Military Academy, 1843-1847; in charge of various Government surveys and improvements, 1843-1853; resigned from the Army on April 1, 1854; engaged as an architect and civil engineer, with residence in Cincinnati; president of the Coal River Navigation Co., Kanawha County, Va. (now West Virginia), in 1856; organized the Preston Coal Oil Co. in 1857 and engaged in the manufacture of kerosene; during the Civil War reentered the service on June 7, 1861, as colonel of the Twenty-third Regiment, Ohio Volunteer Infantry; commissioned brigadier general, United States Army, May 16, 1861; major general, United States Volunteers, March 21, 1862; commanded the Army of the Cumberland during the Tullahoma campaign, and at the battles of Stone's River and Chickamauga; resigned from the United States Army on March 28, 1867; moved to California and settled in Los Angeles; appointed Minister to Mexico on July 27, 1868 and served until June 1869; again engaged in civil engineering; president of the Safety Powder Co., Los Angeles, Calif., in 1875; elected as a Democrat to the Forty-seventh and Forty-eighth Congresses (March 4, 1881-March 3, 1885); chairman, Committee on Military Affairs (Forty-eighth Congress); was not a candidate for renomination in 1884 to the Forty-ninth Congress; regent of the State university, 1884-1885; Register of the Treasury, 1885-1893; reappointed brigadier general on the retired list, United States Army (act of Congress, February 27, 1889), and retired March 1, 1889; died near Redondo, Los Angeles County, Calif., March 11, 1898; interment in Rosedale Cemetery; reinterment in the Arlington National Cemetery on May 17, 1902.

**Bibliography:** *DAB*; Lamers, William M. *The Edge of Glory: A Biography of General William S. Rosecrans.* New York: Harcourt, Brace, 1961.

**ROSENBLOOM, Benjamin Louis,** a Representative from West Virginia; born in Braddock, Allegheny County, Pa., June 3, 1880; attended the public schools; was graduated from the North Braddock High School; attended the University of West Virginia at Morgantown; studied law; was admitted to the bar in 1904 and commenced practice in Wheeling, Ohio County, W.Va., in 1905; member of the State senate 1914-1918; elected as a Republican to the Sixty-seventh and Sixty-eighth Congresses (March 4, 1921-March 3, 1925); was not a candidate for renomination in 1924, having become a candidate for the United States Senate; unsuccessful candidate for the Republican nomination for United States Senator in 1924; resumed the practice of his profession in Wheeling; weekly newspaper publisher 1933-1935; councilman and vice mayor of Wheeling, W.Va., 1935-1939; retired from law practice in 1951; died in Cleveland, Ohio, March 22, 1965.

**ROSENTHAL, Benjamin Stanley,** a Representative from New York; born in New York City June 8, 1923; attended public schools, Long Island University, and City College; served in the United States Army, 1943-1946; LL.B., Brooklyn Law School, 1949; LL.M., New York University, 1952; admitted to the New York bar in 1949 and commenced practice in New York City; admitted to the Supreme Court bar in 1954; elected as a Democrat to the Eighty-seventh Congress, by special election, on February 20, 1962, to fill the vacancy caused by the resignation of Lester Holtzman; reelected to the eleven succeeding Congresses, and served from January 20, 1962 until his death on January 4, 1983 in Washington, D.C.; interment at Beth-David Cemetery, Elmont, N.Y.

**ROSIER, Joseph,** a Senator from West Virginia; born in Wilsonburg, Harrison County, W.Va., January 24, 1870; attended the public schools; graduated from Salem (W.Va.) College in 1895; teacher of the village school at Bristol, W.Va., 1890; principal of the public schools of Salem, W.Va., 1891-1892; superintendent of schools of Harrison County, W.Va., 1893-1894; member of the faculty of Salem (W.Va.) College 1894-1896; teacher in the State normal school at Glenville, W.Va., 1896-1897; member of the faculty of the State Teachers' College, Fairmont, W.Va., 1897-1900; superintendent of schools of Fairmont, W.Va., 1900-1915; president of Fairmont State College, Fairmont, W.Va., 1915-1945, and then president emeritus; during the First World War served as county food administrator 1917-1918; consultant on education for the Works Progress Administration 1933-1937; appointed as a Democrat to the United States Senate to fill the vacancy caused by the resignation of Matthew M. Neely and served from January 13, 1941, to November 17, 1942, when a duly elected successor qualified; unsuccessful candidate for election to the unexpired term; resumed his former pursuits; elected to the State house of delegates in 1946; died in Fairmont, W.Va., October 7, 1951; interment in I.O.O.F. Cemetery, Salem, W.Va.

**Bibliography:** Maddox, Robert F. "The Martin-Rosier Affair," *Capitol Studies* 5 (Spring 1977): 57-69.

**ROSS, David,** a Delegate from Maryland; born in Prince Georges County, Md., February 12, 1755; appointed major of Grayson's additional Continental regiment by General George Washington January 1, 1777, and served until December 20, 1777, when he resigned; upon the death of his father devoted his time to the management of the family estate; studied law; was admitted to the bar in 1783 and commenced the practice of his profession in Frederick County, Md.; Member of the Continental Congress 1787-1789; died in Frederick County, Md., in 1800.

**ROSS, Edmund Gibson,** a Senator from Kansas; born in Ashland, Ohio, December 7, 1826; apprenticed as a printer in Sandusky, Ohio; moved to Milwaukee, Wis., in 1849 and was connected with the Milwaukee Sentinel; moved to Topeka, Kans., in 1856, to lead the "free state" movement; published the Topeka Tribune, 1856-1858, and established the Kansas State Record, 1859; member of the Kansas constitutional convention, 1859-1861; promoter and director of the Atchison, Topeka & Santa Fe Railway; during the Civil War entered the Union Army as a private in 1862 and was mustered out as a major in 1865; editor of the Kansas Tribune, 1865-1866; appointed and subsequently elected as a Republican to the United States Senate to fill the vacancy caused by the death of James H. Lane and served from July 19, 1866, to March 3, 1871; unsuccessful candidate for reelection; chairman, Committee on Enrolled Bills (Fortieth Congress), Committee on Engrossed Bills

(Forty-first Congress); his vote against the impeachment of President Andrew Johnson on May 16 and May 26, 1868 was considered the one vote essential for the President's acquittal, and Ross was vilified by Republicans for his stand; affiliated with the Democratic party after 1872; publisher of several newspapers, 1871-1893; unsuccessful Democratic candidate for Governor in 1880; moved to Albuquerque, N.Mex., in 1882; appointed Governor of the Territory of New Mexico by President Grover Cleveland in May 1885, and served until his removal by President Benjamin Harrison in April 1889; died in Albuquerque, Bernalillo County, N.Mex., May 8, 1907; interment in Fairview Cemetery.

**Bibliography:** *DAB*; Kubicek, Earl C. "Pioneer, Soldier and Statesman: The Story of Edmund Gibson Ross." *Lincoln Herald* 84 (Fall 1982: 147-154; Robbins, Richard W. "The Life of Senator Edmund G. Ross of Kansas." *Kansas Historical Quarterly* 33 (Spring 1967): 90-116; Ross, Edmund G. *History of the Impeachment Trial of Andrew Johnson.* 1896. Reprint. New York: Burt Franklin, 1965.

**ROSS, George,** a Delegate from Pennsylvania; born in New Castle, Del., May 10, 1730; completed preparatory studies; studied law; admitted to the bar in 1750 and commenced practice in Lancaster, Pa.; member of the colonial assembly 1768-1776; delegate to the Pennsylvania convention in 1774; Member of the Continental Congress 1774-1777; a signer of the Declaration of Independence; appointed judge of the court of admiralty for Pennsylvania in April 1779 and served in that capacity until his death near Philadelphia, Pa., July 14, 1779; interment in Christ Church Burying Ground, Philadelphia, Pa.

**Bibliography:** *DAB*.

**ROSS, Henry Howard,** a Representative from New York; born in Essex, N.Y., May 9, 1790; instructed by private tutors; was graduated from Columbia College, New York City, in 1808; studied law; was admitted to the bar and commenced practice in Essex, N.Y.; during the War of 1812 served as second lieutenant and adjutant in the Thirty-seventh Infantry Regiment, New York State Militia, at the Battle of Boquet River, Willsboro, N.Y., and at the Battle of Plattsburgh, N.Y., September 1814; subsequently rose to the rank of major general; elected to the Nineteenth Congress (March 4, 1825-March 3, 1827); resumed the practice of law in Essex, N.Y.; county judge of Essex County in 1847 and 1848; presidential elector on the Whig ticket in 1848; resumed the practice of his profession; died in Essex, N.Y., September 14, 1862; interment in a vault on his family place, "Hickory Hill," Essex, N.Y.

**ROSS, James,** a Senator from Pennsylvania; born near Delta, Peachbottom Township, York County, Pa., July 12, 1762; attended a classical school near Delta and later became an instructor of Latin in what is now Washington and Jefferson College, Washington, Pa.; studied law; admitted to the bar in 1784 and commenced practice in Washington, Washington County, Pa.; delegate to the Pennsylvania constitutional convention in 1789 and 1790; elected as a Federalist to the United States Senate in 1794 to fill the vacancy caused by the Senate declaring the election of Albert Gallatin void; reelected and served from April 24, 1794, to March 3, 1803; served as President pro tempore of the Senate during the Fifth Congress; moved to Pittsburgh in 1795; unsuccessful candidate for governor of Pennsylvania in 1799, 1802, and 1808; resumed the practice of law; died in Pittsburgh, Pa., November 27, 1847; interment in Allegheny Cemetery.

**Bibliography:** *DAB*; Brownson, James I. *The Life and Times of Senator James Ross.* Washington, Pa.: Historical Society of Washington, 1910.

**ROSS, John** (father of Thomas Ross), a Representative from Pennsylvania; born in Solebury, Bucks County, Pa., February 24, 1770; studied law in West Chester, Pa.; admitted to the bar in 1792 and engaged in practice in Easton, Pa.; member of the Pennsylvania house of representatives in 1800; clerk of the orphans' court and recorder 1800-1803; county register 1800-1809; burgess of Easton in 1804; elected as a Republican to the Eleventh Congress (March 4, 1809-March 3, 1811); elected to the Fourteenth and Fifteenth Congresses and served from March 4, 1815, to February 24, 1818, when he resigned to become president judge of the seventh judicial district of Pennsylvania; was transferred to the Pennsylvania supreme bench in 1830 and served until his death in Easton, Northampton County, Pa., January 31, 1834; interment in a private cemetery on the family estate, "Ross Common," Ross Township, Pa.

ROSS, Jonathan, a Senator from Vermont; born in Waterford, Caledonia County, Vt., April 30, 1826; attended the public schools and St. Johnsbury (Vt.) Academy; graduated from Dartmouth College, Hanover, N.H., in 1851; principal of the Chelsea and Craftsbury Academies 1851-1856; studied law; was admitted to the bar in 1856 and practiced in St. Johnsbury until 1870; State's attorney for Caledonia County 1862-1863; appointed a member of the State board of education 1866-1870; member, State house of representatives 1865-1867; member, State senate 1870; judge of the supreme court of Vermont 1870-1890; chief justice of the State of Vermont 1890-1899; appointed as a Republican to the United States Senate to fill the vacancy caused by the death of Justin S. Morrill and served from January 11, 1899, to October 18, 1900, when a successor was elected; was not an active candidate for reelection in 1900; chairman, Committee to Examine Branches of the Civil Service (Fifty-sixth Congress); chairman of the board of State railroad commissioners 1900-1902; died in St. Johnsbury, Vt., February 23, 1905; interment in Mount Pleasant Cemetery.

ROSS, Lewis Winans, a Representative from Illinois; born near Seneca Falls, Seneca County, N.Y., December 8, 1812; moved to Illinois and settled in Lewistown; completed preparatory studies and attended Illinois College at Jacksonville in 1837; studied law; was admitted to the bar in 1839 and commenced practice in Lewistown, Ill.; member of the State house of representatives in 1840, 1841, 1844, and 1845; member of the State constitutional conventions in 1861 and 1870; elected as a Democrat to the Thirty-eighth, Thirty-ninth, and Fortieth Congresses (March 4, 1863-March 3, 1869); was not a candidate for renomination in 1868; resumed the practice of law; died in Lewistown, Ill., October 20, 1895; interment in Oak Hill Cemetery.

ROSS, Miles, a Representative from New Jersey; born in Raritan Township, Middlesex County, N.J., April 30, 1827; received a practical English training; engaged with his father in the transportation of freight by water and in the coal business; one of the chosen freeholders of New Brunswick, N.J., 1859-1864; member of the State house of assembly in 1863 and 1864; director of several banks; member of the board of street commissioners in 1865 and 1866; mayor of New Brunswick 1867-1869; elected as a Democrat to the Forty-fourth and to the three succeeding Congresses (March 4, 1875-March 3, 1883); chairman, Committee on Militia (Forty-fifth and Forty-sixth Congresses); unsuccessful candidate for reelection in 1882 to the Forty-eighth Congress; delegate at large to the Democratic National Conventions in 1884, 1888, and 1892; engaged in the wholesale and retail coal business; died in New Brunswick, Middlesex County, N.J., on February 22, 1903; interment in Elmwood Cemetery.

ROSS, Robert Tripp, a Representative from New York; born in Washington, Beaufort County, N.C., June 4, 1903; attended the public schools; moved to New York City in 1929 and engaged as a druggist; for seventeen years associated with a large drug firm in managerial and executive positions; elected as a Republican to the Eightieth Congress (January 3, 1947-January 3, 1949); unsuccessful candidate for reelection in 1948 to the Eighty-first Congress; engaged in the manufacture of clothing and athletic equipment; unsuccessful candidate for election in 1950 to the Eighty-second

Congress; subsequently elected to the Eighty-second Congress in a special election to fill the vacancy caused by the resignation of T. Vincent Quinn and served from February 19, 1952, to January 3, 1953; unsuccessful candidate for reelection in 1952 to the Eighty-third Congress; Deputy Assistant Secretary of Defense for Legislative Affairs from March 1954 to March 1956; Assistant Secretary of Defense for Legislative and Public Affairs from March 1956 to March 1957; assistant borough works commissioner, Queens, N.Y., from March 1957 to January 1958; vice president, Merchandising Apparel Company, 1959-1968; resided in Jackson Heights, N.Y., until his death there on October 1, 1981; interment at Oakdale Cemetery, Washington, N.C.

ROSS, Sobieski, a Representative from Pennsylvania; born in Coudersport, Potter County, Pa., May 16, 1828; attended the common schools and Coudersport Academy; engaged in civil engineering and the real estate business; also interested in agricultural pursuits; appointed associate judge in 1852; elected as a Republican to the Forty-third and Forty-fourth Congresses (March 4, 1873-March 3, 1877); declined to be a candidate for renomination in 1876; resumed the real estate business; died in Coudersport, Pa., October 24, 1877; interment in Eulalia Cemetery.

ROSS, Thomas (son of John Ross), a Representative from Pennsylvania; born in Easton, Northampton County, Pa., December 1, 1806; attended the Doylestown, Pa., schools; graduated from Princeton College in 1823; studied law; admitted to the bar in 1829 and commenced practice in Doylestown, Pa.; appointed deputy attorney general of the Pennsylvania for Bucks County in 1829; frequently a candidate of the Democratic Party and also affiliated with the Anti-Masonic Party; elected as a Democrat to the Thirty-first and Thirty-second Congresses (March 4, 1849-March 3, 1853); resumed the practice of law in Doylestown, Bucks County, Pa.; died July 7, 1865; interment in Doylestown Cemetery.

ROSS, Thomas Randolph, a Representative from Ohio; born in New Garden Township, Chester County, Pa., October 26, 1788; completed preparatory studies; studied law; was admitted to the bar and began practice in Lebanon, Warren County, Ohio, in 1810; elected to the Sixteenth, Seventeenth, and Eighteenth Congresses (March 4, 1819-March 3, 1825); chairman, Committee on Revisal and Unfinished Business (Seventeenth and Eighteenth Congresses); unsuccessful candidate for reelection in 1824 to the Nineteenth Congress; resumed the practice of law in Lebanon; lost his eyesight in 1866; died on his farm near Lebanon, Ohio, June 28, 1869; interment in Lebanon Cemetery.

ROSSDALE, Albert Berger, a Representative from New York; born in New York City October 23, 1878; attended the public schools; clerk in the New York post office 1900-1910; president of the New York Federation of Post Office Clerks in 1906 and 1907 and vice president of the national organization in 1908 and 1909; engaged in the wholesale jewelry business in 1910; elected as a Republican to the Sixty-seventh Congress (March 4, 1921-March 3, 1923); unsuccessful candidate for reelection in 1922 to the Sixty-eighth Congress and for election in 1924 to the Sixty-ninth Congress; delegate to the Republican State conventions in 1922 and 1924; delegate to the Republican National Convention in 1924; again engaged in the wholesale jewelry business; moved to Sandy Hook, Conn., in 1939 and to Bronxville, N.Y., in 1946; died in Eastchester, Westchester County, N.Y., April 17, 1968; interment in Maimonides Cemetery, Elmont, N.Y.

ROSTENKOWSKI, Daniel David, a Representative from Illinois; born in Chicago, Ill., January 2, 1928; graduated from St. John's Military Academy in 1946 and attended Loyola University; served in Korea with the United States Infantry, 1946-1948; served in the Illinois State house of representatives in the sixty-eighth general assembly in 1952; delegate to the Illinois State Democratic convention every four years since 1952; delegate to every Democratic National Convention from 1960 to 1992; member of the Illinois State senate, 1954-1956; elected as a Democrat to the Eighty-sixth and to the seventeen succeeding Congresses (January 3, 1959-January 3, 1995); chairman, Committee on Ways and Means (Ninety-seventh through One Hundred Third Congresses), Joint Committee on Taxation (Ninety-seventh through One Hundred First Congresses); unsuccessful candidate for reelection in 1994 to the One Hundred Fourth Congress; is a resident of Chicago, Ill.

**ROTH, Tobias Anton (Toby),** a Representative from Wisconsin; born in Strasburg, Emmons County, N.Dak., October 10, 1938; graduated from St. Mary's High School, Menasha, Wis., 1957; B.A., Marquette University, Milwaukee, 1961; served in the United States Army Reserve, 1962-1969, with the rank of first lieutenant; realtor; member, Wisconsin State assembly, 1972-1978; elected as a Republican to the Ninety-sixth and to the eight succeeding Congresses (January 3, 1979-January 3, 1997); was not a candidate for reelection in 1996 to the One Hundred Fifth Congress; is a resident of Appleton, Wis.

**ROTH, William Victor, Jr.,** a Representative and a Senator from Delaware; born in Great Falls, Cascade County, Mont., July 22, 1921; attended the public schools of Helena, Mont.; B.A., University of Oregon, Eugene, 1944; M.B.A., Harvard University Business School, 1947; LL.B., Harvard University Law School, 1949; admitted to the California bar in 1950 and to the Delaware bar in 1958; entered the United States Army as a private, 1943, released as a captain, 1946, following service in the Pacific Theater during the Second World War; chairman, Delaware Republican Committee 1961-1964; member, Republican National Committee 1961-1964; elected as a Republican to the Ninetieth and Ninety-first Congresses and served from January 3, 1967, until his resignation December 31, 1970; was not a candidate for reelection to the House of Representatives, but was elected in 1970 to the United States Senate for the term commencing January 3, 1971; subsequently appointed January 1, 1971, to fill the vacancy caused by the resignation of John J. Williams for the term ending January 3, 1971; reelected in 1976, 1982, 1988, and in 1994 for the term ending January 3, 2001; chairman, Committee on Governmental Affairs (Ninety-seventh through Ninety-ninth Congresses, One Hundred Fourth Congress), Committee on Finance (One Hundred Fourth Congress); Joint Committee on Taxation (One Hundred Fourth Congress); is a resident of Wilmington, Del.

**ROTHERMEL, John Hoover,** a Representative from Pennsylvania; born in Richmond Township, Berks County, Pa., March 7, 1856; attended the common schools and pursued an academic course at Brunner's Business College, Reading, Pa.; taught school in Blandon Township 1876-1881; served as a member of the faculty at Brunner's Scientific Academy; studied law; was admitted to the bar in 1881 and commenced practice in Reading, Pa.; assistant district attorney of Reading, Pa., 1886-1889; county solicitor of Berks County 1895-1898; unsuccessful candidate for judge of the court of common pleas in 1899; elected as a Democrat to the Sixtieth and to the three succeeding Congresses (March 4, 1907-March 3, 1915); chairman, Committee on Expenditures in the Department of Commerce and Labor (Sixty-second Congress), Committee on Expenditures in the Department of Commerce (Sixty-third Congress); unsuccessful candidate for reelection in 1914; resumed the practice of law; died in Reading, Pa., in August 1922; interment in the Charles Evans Cemetery.

**ROTHWELL, Gideon Frank,** a Representative from Missouri; born near Fulton, Callaway County, Mo., on April 24, 1836; was graduated from the University of Missouri at Columbia; studied law; was admitted to the bar in 1864 and commenced practice in Huntsville, Randolph County, Mo.; elected as a Democrat to the Forty-sixth Congress (March 4, 1879-March 3, 1881); unsuccessful

candidate for renomination in 1880; resumed the practice of law in Moberly, Mo.; appointed in 1889 a member of the board of curators of the University of Missouri, and served as its president 1890-1894; died in Moberly, Mo., on January 18, 1894; interment in Oakland Cemetery.

**ROUDEBUSH, Richard Lowell,** a Representative from Indiana; born on a farm in Hamilton County, near Noblesville, Ind., January 18, 1918; attended Hamilton County schools; B.S., Butler University, Indianapolis, Ind., 1941; served in the United States Army from November 18, 1941, to August 12, 1944, as a demolition specialist for the Ordnance Department in Middle Eastern, North African, and Italian Campaigns; farmer; partner in livestock commission company; National Commander of Veterans of Foreign Wars in 1957-1958; chairman of Indiana Veterans Commission, 1954-1960; elected as a Republican to the Eighty-seventh and to the four succeeding Congresses (January 3, 1961-January 3, 1971); was not a candidate in 1970 for reelection to the House of Representatives, but was an unsuccessful candidate for election to the United States Senate; administrator of Veterans Affairs, Veterans Administration, 1974-1977; was a resident of Noblesville, Ind.; died January 28, 1995.

**ROUKEMA, Margaret Scafati,** a Representative from New Jersey; born in Newark, Essex County, N.J., September 19, 1929; attended the public schools; graduated from West Orange High School, 1947; B.A., Montclair State College, Montclair, N.J., 1951; engaged in graduate work, Montclair State College, 1951-1953, and attended Rutgers University, New Brunswick, N.J., 1975; teacher, 1951-1955; vice president, Ridgewood, N.J., Board of Education, 1970-1973; president, Ridgewood Republican Club, 1977-1978; elected as a Republican to the Ninety-seventh and to the seven succeeding Congresses (January 3, 1981-January 3, 1997); is a resident of Ridgewood, N.J.

**ROUSE, Arthur Blythe,** a Representative from Kentucky; born in Burlington, Boone County, Ky., June 20, 1874; attended the public schools; graduated from Hanover College, Indiana, in 1896 and from the Louisville Law School in 1900; admitted to the bar in 1900 and commenced practice in Burlington; in 1907 became the first secretary of the Kentucky Racing Commission and served four years; served as Kentucky revenue commissioner under Governor Ruby Laffoon; secretary to Representatives Daniel L. Gooch and Joseph L. Rhinoch of Kentucky; member of the Kentucky Democratic executive committee from 1903 to 1910; elected as a Democrat to the Sixty-second and to the seven succeeding Congresses (March 4, 1911-March 3, 1927); was not a candidate for renomination in 1926 to the Seventieth Congress; chairman of the Democratic National Congressional Committee from 1921 until he resigned in December 1924; resumed the practice of law in Erlanger, Ky.; operated several bus companies; appointed clerk of the United States District Court for the Eastern District of Kentucky on October 8, 1935, and served until his resignation due to ill health in January 1953; died in Lexington, Ky., January 25, 1956; interment in Lexington Cemetery.

**ROUSH, John Edward,** a Representative from Indiana; born in Barnsdall, Osage County, Okla., September 12, 1920; moved with parents to Huntington, Ind., in 1924; attended the public schools in Huntington; A.B., Huntington College, 1942; served as an Infantry officer with the United States Army, 1942-1946; J.D., Indiana University School of Law, 1949; was admitted to the bar in 1949 and commenced the practice of law in Huntington, Ind.; served one term in the Indiana State house of representatives in 1949; in 1950 was recalled to active duty in the United States Army, and served as a Counterintelligence Corps agent until separated from the service in June 1952; prosecuting attorney of Huntington County, 1955-1958; vice president of the board of trustees of Huntington College, 1958-1960; elected as a Democrat to the Eighty-sixth and to the four succeeding Congresses (January 3, 1959-January 3, 1969); unsuccessful candidate for reelection in 1968 to the Ninety-first Congress; resumed the practice of law; elected to the Ninety-second and to the two succeeding Congresses (January 3, 1971-January 3, 1977); unsuccessful candidate for reelection in 1976 to the Ninety-fifth Congress; Director, regional and intergovernmental operations for the Environmental Protection Agency, 1977-1979; resumed the practice of law in 1979; chairman of the board of Huntington College, 1981-1987; is a resident of Huntington, Ind.

**ROUSSEAU, Lovell Harrison,** a Representative from Kentucky; born near Stanford, Lincoln County, Ky., August 4, 1818; attended the common schools; studied law; was admitted to the bar in 1841 and began practice in Bloomfield, Ind.; member of the Indiana State house of representatives, 1844-1845; captain in the Mexican War; served in the Indiana State senate, 1847-1849; returned to Kentucky in 1849 and resumed the practice of law in Louisville; member of the Kentucky senate, 1860-1861; served as a colonel, brigadier general, and major general in the Union Army during the Civil War and resigned November 17, 1865; elected as an Unconditional Unionist to the Thirty-ninth Congress, and served from March 4, 1865 to July 21, 1866, when he resigned, after having made an assault upon Representative Josiah B. Grinnell of Iowa in the portico on the East Front of the Capitol Building; censured by the House of Representatives on July 17, 1866, for his assault on Grinnell, and on July 21 was compelled to stand at the bar of the House and submit to a public reprimand by the Speaker; was subsequently reelected to fill the vacancy caused by his own resignation, took his seat December 3, 1866, and served until March 3, 1867; appointed a brigadier general in the Regular Army with the brevet rank of major general on March 27, 1867, and assigned to duty in Alaska; on July 28, 1868, was placed in command of the Department of Louisiana and served in that capacity until his death in New Orleans, La., January 7, 1869; interment in Arlington National Cemetery, Va.

Bibliography: *DAB*; Dawson, Joseph G. "General Lovell H. Rousseau and Louisiana Reconstruction." *Louisiana History* 20 (Fall 1979): 373-91.

**ROUSSELOT, John Harbin,** a Representative from California; born in Los Angeles, Calif., November 1, 1927; attended the public schools of San Marino and South Pasadena, Calif.; A.B., Principia College, Elsah, Ill., 1949; life insurance underwriter, 1949-1952; assistant to public relations director, Pacific Finance Corp., Los Angeles, Calif., 1954-1955; operated a public relations consultant firm in Los Angeles, Calif., 1954-1958; Director of public information, Federal Housing Administration, Washington, D.C., 1958-1960; deputy to chairman of Board of Equalization, State of California, 1956; delegate to the Republican National Convention of 1956; member of executive committee, Republican State central committee, 1956-1957; vice chairman, Los Angeles County Republican Central committee, 1956-1958; elected as a Republican to the Eighty-seventh Congress (January 3, 1961-January 3, 1963); unsuccessful candidate for reelection in 1962 to the Eighty-eighth Congress; management consultant in the fields of marketing, management systems, and government relations, 1967-1970; elected to the Ninety-first Congress, by special election, June 30, 1970, to fill the vacancy caused by the death of Glenard P. Lipscomb; reelected to the six succeeding Congresses and served from January 3, 1971, to January 3, 1983; was an unsuccessful candidate for reelection in 1982 to the Ninety-eighth Congress; special assistant to President Ronald Reagan, 1983; president, National Council of Savings Institutions, 1985 to 1989; appointed by Governor Pete Wilson as a Commissioner, Board of Prison Terms, for the year 1993; management consultant in the field of marketing and government relations, 1994 to present; is a resident of Pasadena, Calif.

**ROUTZOHN, Harry Nelson,** a Representative from Ohio; born in Dayton, Ohio, November 4, 1881; attended the public grade schools; served one year at the blacksmith trade; became court page in common pleas court of Montgomery County, Ohio; studied law; was admitted to the bar in 1904 and commenced practice in Dayton, Ohio; assistant county prosecutor of Montgomery County, Ohio, 1906-1909; taught law at the University of Dayton, Dayton, Ohio, 1923-1930; probate judge, 1917-1929; assistant United States district attorney, 1930-1932; delegate to the Republican National Conventions of 1928 and 1932; captain in the Officers' Reserve Corps, 1925-1935; elected as a Republican to the Seventy-sixth Congress (January 3, 1939-January 3, 1941); was an unsuccessful candidate for reelection in 1940 to the Seventy-seventh Congress; resumed the practice of law in Dayton, Ohio; appointed Solicitor for the Department of Labor, Washington, D.C., and served from March 6, 1953 until his death in Washington, D.C., April 14, 1953; interment in Memorial Park Cemetery, Dayton, Ohio.

**ROWAN, John** (uncle of Robert Todd Lytle), a Representative and a Senator from Kentucky; born near York, Pa., July 12, 1773; moved to Kentucky around 1783; received a classical training; studied law in Lexington; admitted to the bar in 1795 and commenced practice in Louisville; member of the second Kentucky constitutional convention held at Frankfort in 1799; secretary of State of Kentucky, 1804-1806; elected as a Republican to the Tenth Congress (March 4, 1807-March 3, 1809); member, Kentucky house of representatives, 1813-1817, 1822, 1824; judge of the court of appeals, 1819-1821; elected to the United States Senate, and served from March 4, 1825 to March 3, 1831; chairman, Committee on the Judiciary (Twenty-first Congress); appointed commissioner for carrying out the treaty of 1839 with the Republic of Mexico; president of the Kentucky Historical Society from 1838 until his death in Louisville, Ky., July 13, 1843; interment in the family burial ground at Federal Hill, near Bardstown, Nelson County, Ky.

Bibliography: *DAB*; Fackler, Stephen. "John Rowan and the Demise of Jeffersonian Republicanism in Kentucky, 1819-1831." *Register of the Kentucky Historical Society* 78 (Winter 1980): 1-26.

**ROWAN, Joseph,** a Representative from New York; born in New York City September 8, 1870; attended the public schools; was graduated from Columbia College Law School in 1891; was admitted to the bar in 1892 and commenced the practice of law in New York City; elected as a Democrat to the Sixty-sixth Congress (March 4, 1919-March 3, 1921); was not a candidate for renomination in 1920; continued the practice of his profession in New York City until his death there on August 3, 1930; interment in Woodlawn Cemetery.

**ROWAN, William A.,** a Representative from Illinois; born in Chicago, Cook County, Ill., November 24, 1882; was graduated from St. Patrick Grade School and St. Patrick High School and attended the University of Chicago; employed in a steel plant after graduation; associated with a daily community newspaper in Chicago, becoming city editor and editor, 1907-1927; served as alderman of the tenth ward of Chicago 1927-1942; elected as a Democrat to the Seventy-eighth and Seventy-ninth Congresses (January 3, 1943-January 3, 1947); unsuccessful candidate for reelection in 1946 to the Eightieth Congress; appointed United States Comptroller of Customs at Chicago, Ill., on January 21, 1947, in which capacity he served until 1953; died in Chicago, Ill., May 31, 1961; interment in Holy Sepulchre Cemetery, Worth, Ill.

**ROWBOTTOM, Harry Emerson,** a Representative from Indiana; born in Aurora, Dearborn County, Ind., November 3, 1884; moved with his parents to Ludlow, Ky., in 1885; attended the common schools; was graduated from Ludlow High School in 1901; attended Kentucky State College at Lexington 1902-1904; salesman of lubricating oils 1904-1907; attended the Cincinnati Business College and was graduated in accountancy in 1907; engaged as an auditor in Cincinnati 1907-1910 and in Chicago 1910-1912; moved to Evansville, Ind., in 1913 and was employed as chief clerk for the Indiana Refining Co. 1913-1918; member of the Indiana State house of representatives 1919-1923; elected as a Republican to the Sixty-ninth, Seventieth, and Seventy-first Congresses (March 4, 1925-March 3, 1931); unsuccessful for reelection in 1930 to the Seventy-second Congress; engaged as commercial agent for a truck line; died in Evansville, Ind., March 22, 1934; interment in Locust Hill Cemetery.

**ROWE, Edmund,** a Representative from Ohio; born in Sherrodsville, Carroll County, Ohio, December 21, 1892; attended the public schools; worked in the coal mines 1905-1909, in the rubber industry 1909-1913, and at the machinist trade 1913-1916; during the First World War served in the United States Navy, 1917-1919; owner of a bowling academy 1919-1929; engaged in the real estate business in 1920 and the insurance business in 1928; organizer of the Rowe Oil & Chemical Co. in 1936; member of the city council of Akron, Ohio, 1928-1942, serving one term as president; elected as a Republican to the Seventy-eighth Congress (January 3, 1943-January 3, 1945); was an unsuccessful candidate for reelection in 1944 to the Seventy-ninth Congress and for election in 1948 to the Eighty-first Congress; member of the Ohio General Assembly 1955-1959; unsuccessful candidate for mayor of Akron in 1957; real estate broker; resided in Akron, Ohio, where he died October 4, 1972; interment in Glendale Cemetery.

**ROWE, Frederick William,** a Representative from New York; born at Wappingers Falls, Dutchess County, N.Y., March 19, 1863; attended the common schools; was graduated from De Garmo Institute in 1882 and from Colgate University, Hamilton, N.Y., in 1887; studied law; was admitted to the bar in New York City in 1889 and practiced in Brooklyn and New York City until 1904, when he became interested in the development of real estate in Brooklyn; president of several companies, including a street railway company; director of the Dime Savings Bank of Brooklyn; elected as a Republican to the Sixty-fourth, Sixty-fifth, and Sixty-sixth Congresses (March 4, 1915-March 3, 1921); was not a candidate for renomination in 1920; resumed his former business activities in New York City; died in Rockville Centre, Nassau County, N.Y., June 20, 1946; interment in Greenwood Cemetery, Brooklyn, N.Y.

**ROWE, Peter,** a Representative from New York; born in Crescent, Saratoga County, N.Y., March 10, 1807; completed preparatory studies and was graduated from Schenectady (N.Y.) Academy; engaged in mercantile pursuits; chief auditor of the New York Central Railroad; mayor of Schenectady 1846-1850; elected as a Democrat to the Thirty-third Congress (March 4, 1853-March 3, 1855); died in Schenectady, N.Y., April 17, 1876; interment in Vale Cemetery.

**ROWELL, Jonathan Harvey,** a Representative from Illinois; born in Haverhill, Grafton County, N.H., February 10, 1833; attended Rock Creek School; was graduated from Eureka College, Illinois; during the Civil War served as a company officer in the Seventeenth Regiment, Illinois Volunteer Infantry; studied law; was admitted to the bar in 1866 and commenced practice in Bloomington, Ill.; State's attorney of the eighth judicial circuit of Illinois 1868-1872; elected as a Republican to the Forty-eighth and to the three succeeding Congresses (March 4, 1883-March 3, 1891); chairman, Committee on Elections (Fifty-first Congress); unsuccessful candidate for reelection in 1890 to the Fifty-second Congress; resumed the practice of law; died in Bloomington, McLean County, Ill., May 15, 1908; interment in Evergreen Cemetery.

**ROWLAND, Alfred,** a Representative from North Carolina; born in Lumberton, Robeson County, N.C., February 9, 1844; attended the common schools; entered the Confederate Army in May 1861 and served as a lieutenant in Company D, Eighteenth Regiment of North Carolina State Troops, until May 12, 1864; imprisoned at Fort Delaware until June 1865; studied law; was admitted to the bar in 1867 and commenced practice in Lumberton; register of deeds for Robeson County in 1867; member of the State house of representatives in 1876, 1877, 1880, and 1881; elected as a Democrat to the Fiftieth and Fifty-first Congresses (March 4, 1887-March 3, 1891); was not a candidate for renomination in 1890; resumed the practice of law; died in Lumberton, N.C., August 2, 1898; interment in Meadow Brook Cemetery.

**ROWLAND, Charles Hedding,** a Representative from Pennsylvania; born in Hancock, Washington County, Md., December 20, 1860; moved to Huntingdon County, Pa., in 1866 and to Houtzdale, Pa., in 1874; attended the public schools; president of the Moshannon Coal Mining Co. and of the Pittsburgh & Susquehanna Railroad Co.; elected as a Republican to the Sixty-fourth and Sixty-fifth Congresses (March 4, 1915-March 3, 1919); declined to be a candidate for renomination in 1918; died in Philipsburg, Centre County, Pa., on November 24, 1921; interment in the Philipsburg Cemetery.

**ROWLAND, James Roy, Jr.,** a Representative from Georgia; born in Wrightsville, Johnson County, Ga., February 3, 1926; attended Wrightsville Primary School; graduated from Wrightsville High School, 1943; attended Emory at Oxford, Oxford, Ga., 1943; South Georgia College, Douglas, 1946; University of Georgia, Athens, 1946-1948; M.D., Medical College of Georgia, Augusta, 1952; served in the United States Army, sergeant, 1944-1946; physician; elected to the Georgia State house of representatives, 1976-1982; elected as a Democrat to the Ninety-eighth and to the five succeeding Congresses (January 3, 1983-January 3, 1995); was not a candidate for reelection in 1994 to the One Hundred Fourth Congress; is a resident of Dublin, Ga.

**ROWLAND, John Grosvenor,** a Representative from Connecticut; born in Waterbury, Conn., May 24, 1957; graduated from Holy Cross High School, Waterbury, 1975; B.S., Villanova University (Pa.), 1979; insurance agent; member, Connecticut general assembly, 1981-1984; elected as a Republican to the Ninety-ninth and to the two succeeding Congresses (January 3, 1985-January 3, 1991); was not a candidate for reelection in 1990 to the One Hundred Second Congress, but was an unsuccessful candidate for election for Governor of Connecticut; elected Governor of Connecticut in 1994 for a four-year term beginning January 4, 1995; is a resident of Waterbury, Conn.

**ROY, Alphonse,** a Representative from New Hampshire; born in St. Simon, Province of Quebec, Canada, October 26, 1897; moved to Manchester, N.H., in 1901; attended the parochial schools; engaged in the real estate business; served as alderman 1925-1931; member of the State house of representatives 1925-1931; served as executive councilor of New Hampshire 1933-1937; successfully contested as a Democrat the election of Arthur B. Jenks to the Seventy-fifth Congress and served from June 9, 1938, to January 3, 1939; unsuccessful candidate for reelection in 1938 to the Seventy-sixth Congress and for election in 1940 to the Seventy-seventh Congress; appointed sealer of weights and measures of Manchester, N.H., in 1943 and served until his resignation in 1945; United States marshal for the district of New Hampshire 1945-1953; unsuccessful candidate for election in 1958 to the Eighty-sixth Congress; unsuccessful candidate for nomination for the United States Senate in 1960; engaged in the real estate business until his death in Manchester, N.H., October 5, 1967; interment in Mount Calvary Cemetery.

**ROY, William Robert,** a Representative from Kansas; born in Bloomington, McLean County, Ill., February 23, 1926; attended the Lexington, Ill., public schools; B.S., Illinois Wesleyan University, Bloomington, 1945; B.M., Northwestern University Medical School, Chicago, 1948, and M.D., 1949; J.D., Washburn University Law

School, Topeka, Kans., 1970; served in the United States Air Force, 1953-1955; discharged with rank of captain; practiced medicine in Topeka, Kans., 1955-1970; elected as a Democrat to the Ninety-second and to the Ninety-third Congresses (January 3, 1971-January 3, 1975); was not a candidate in 1974 for reelection to the House of Representatives, but was an unsuccessful candidate for election to the United States Senate; unsuccessful candidate for election to the United States Senate in 1978; resumed the practice of medicine in Topeka; nominated for election to the United States Senate in the August 7, 1990 primary despite his earlier withdrawal from the race, but he declined the nomination nine days later; is a resident of Topeka, Kans.

**ROYBAL, Edward Ross** (father of Lucille Roybal-Allard), a Representative from California; born in Albuquerque, Bernalillo County, N.Mex., February 10, 1916; moved to Los Angeles, Calif., in 1922; attended the public schools; graduated from Roosevelt High School in 1934; joined the Civilian Conservation Corps until April 1, 1935; trained in business administration at the University of California in Los Angeles and at Southwestern University in Los Angeles; public health educator with the California Tuberculosis Association, 1942-1944; served in the United States Army from April 1944 to December 1945; director of health education for the Los Angeles County Tuberculosis and Health Association, 1945-1949; member of the city council of Los Angeles, 1949-1962, and served as president pro tempore from July 1961; president of Eastland Savings & Loan Association, 1958-1968; elected as a Democrat to the Eighty-eighth and to the fourteen succeeding Congresses (January 3, 1963-January 3, 1993); chairman, Select Committee on Aging (Ninety-eighth through One Hundred Second Congresses); was not a candidate for reelection in 1992 to the One Hundred Third Congress; is a resident of Pasadena, Calif.

**ROYBAL-ALLARD, Lucille** (daughter of Edward Ross Roybal), a Representative from California; born in Boyle Heights, Los Angeles County, Calif., June 12, 1941; B.A., California State University, Los Angeles, 1965; member, California State assembly, 1987-1993; elected as a Democrat to the One Hundred Third and One Hundred Fourth Congresses (January 3, 1993-January 3, 1997); is a resident of Bell Gardens, Calif.

**ROYCE, Edward Randall,** a Representative from California; born in Los Angeles, Calif., October 12, 1951; B.A., California State University, Fullerton, 1977; member, California State senate, 1983-1993; elected as a Republican to the One Hundred Third and One Hundred Fourth Congresses (January 3, 1993-January 3, 1997); is a resident of Fullerton, Calif.

**ROYCE, Homer Elihu,** a Representative from Vermont; born in East Berkshire, Franklin County, Vt., June 14, 1819; attended the local academies of St. Albans and Enosburg, Vt.; studied law; was admitted to the bar and commenced practice in East Berkshire, Vt., in 1844; member of the Vermont State house of representatives, 1846-1847; State prosecuting attorney in 1848; served in the State senate, 1849-1851, 1861, and 1868; elected as a Republican to the Thirty-fifth and Thirty-sixth Congresses (March 4, 1857-March 3, 1861); was not a candidate for renomination in 1860 to the Thirty-seventh Congress; again a member of the State senate in 1861 and 1868; elected associate justice of the supreme court of Vermont in 1870; was appointed chief justice of that court in 1882, and served until 1890, when he resigned; died in St. Albans, Vt., April 24, 1891; interment in Calvary Cemetery, East Berkshire, Vt.

**ROYER, William Howard,** a Representative from California; born in Jerome, Idaho, April 11, 1920; attended the public schools; graduated from Sequoia High School, Redwood City, Calif., 1938; B.S., Santa Clara (Calif.) University, 1941; pursued graduate studies at Oklahoma A.&M. College (now Oklahoma State University), Stillwater, Okla., 1943; served in the United States Army Air Corps, 1943-1945; realtor; city councilman, Redwood City, Calif., 1950-1966; mayor, Redwood City, Calif., 1956-1960; member, San Mateo County, Calif., board of supervisors, 1972-1979; elected as a Republican to the Ninety-sixth Congress, April 3, 1979, by special election to fill the vacancy caused by the death of Leo J. Ryan, and served from April 3, 1979 to January 3, 1981; unsuccessful candidate for reelection in 1980 to the Ninety-seventh Congress; regional representative, United States Department of Transportation, 1981-1982; is a resident of Redwood City, Calif.

**ROYSE, Lemuel Willard,** a Representative from Indiana; born near Pierceton, Kosciusko County, Ind., January 19, 1847; attended the common schools; studied law; was admitted to the bar in 1874 and commenced practice in Warsaw, Kosciusko County, Ind.; prosecuting attorney for the thirty-third judicial circuit of Indiana in 1876; mayor of Warsaw 1885-1891; member of the Republican State central committee from 1886 to 1890; delegate to the Republican National Convention in 1892; elected as a Republican to the Fifty-fourth and Fifty-fifth Congresses (March 4, 1895-March 3, 1899); chairman, Committee on Elections No. 2 (Fifty-fifth Congress); unsuccessful candidate for renomination in 1898; resumed the practice of law in Warsaw, Ind.; judge of the Kosciusko County Circuit Court 1904-1908; resumed the practice of his profession; reelected circuit judge and served from 1920 to 1932; again resumed the practice of law until his retirement in 1940; died in Warsaw, Ind., December 18, 1946; interment in Oakwood Cemetery.

**RUBEY, Thomas Lewis,** a Representative from Missouri; born in Lebanon, Laclede County, Mo., September 27, 1862; attended the common schools; was graduated from the University of Missouri at Columbia in 1885; superintendent of schools of Lebanon, Mo., 1886-1891; teacher in the Missouri School of Mines, 1891-1898; member of the Missouri State house of representatives in 1891 and 1892; moved to La Plata, Macon County, Mo., in 1898 and organized a bank; served in the Missouri State senate, 1901-1903; elected president of the State senate in 1903, and upon the resignation of Lieutenant Governor John A. Lee in that year became Lieutenant Governor, serving in that capacity until 1905; returned to Lebanon in 1905 and engaged in banking; president of the State Bank, Lebanon, Mo., from 1914 until his death; elected as a Democrat to the Sixty-second and to the four succeeding Congresses (March 4, 1911-March 3, 1921); unsuccessful candidate for reelection in 1920 to the Sixty-seventh Congress; elected to the Sixty-eighth and to the two succeeding Congresses and served from March 4, 1923, until his death in Lebanon, Mo., on November 2, 1928; interment in Lebanon Cemetery.

**RUCKER, Atterson Walden,** a Representative from Colorado; born in Harrodsburg, Mercer County, Ky., April 3, 1847; moved in early youth with his parents to Missouri; attended the common schools; served four years in the Confederate Army during the Civil War; studied law; was admitted to the bar in 1868 and commenced practice in Lexington, Mo., the following year; moved to Baxter Springs, Kans., in 1873 and resumed the practice of law; moved to Leadville, Colo., in 1879 and continued the practice of his profession; was also interested in mining; judge of the court of records of Lake County in 1881 and 1882; moved to Aspen, Pitkin County, Colo., in 1885 and became largely interested in the development of mining projects; elected as a Democrat to the Sixty-first and Sixty-second Congresses (March 4, 1909-March 3, 1913); unsuccessful candidate for renomination in 1912; returned to Colorado and settled in Denver; resumed the practice of his profession; died near Mount Morrison, Jefferson County, Colo., on July 19, 1924; interment in the Littleton Cemetery, Littleton, Arapahoe County, Colo.

**RUCKER, Tinsley White,** a Representative from Georgia; born near Farm Hill, Elbert County, Ga., March 24, 1848; attended the public schools, Princeton College, and the Georgia Military Academy at Marietta; served in the Confederate Army from March 24, 1864, until the close of the Civil War; returned to Athens; was graduated from the law department of the University of Georgia at Athens in 1868; was admitted to the bar in 1871 and commenced practice in Athens, Clarke County, Ga.; was appointed by President Grover Cleveland as assistant United States district attorney for the northern district of Georgia in 1893 and resided in Atlanta; returned to Athens in 1912 and continued the practice of law; elected as a Democrat to the Sixty-fourth Congress to fill the vacancy caused by the death of Samuel J. Tribble and served from January 11 to March 3, 1917; was not a candidate for renomination in 1916; engaged in the practice of law until his death in Athens, Ga., November 18, 1926; interment in Oconee Cemetery.

**RUCKER, William Waller,** a Representative from Missouri; born near Covington, Alleghany County, Va., February 1, 1855; moved with his parents to western Virginia in 1861; attended the common schools; moved to Chariton County, Mo., in 1873; engaged in teaching in the district schools; studied law; was admitted to the bar in 1876 and commenced practice in Keytesville, Chariton County, Mo.; prosecuting attorney of Chariton County 1886-1892; judge of the twelfth circuit 1892-1899; elected as a Democrat to the Fifty-sixth and to the eleven succeeding Congresses (March 4, 1899-March 3, 1923); chairman, Committee on Election of President, Vice President, and Representatives (Sixty-second through Sixty-fifth Congresses); unsuccessful candidate for reelection in 1922 to the Sixty-eighth Congress; resumed the practice of law in Keytesville, Mo.; also engaged in agricultural pursuits; died in Keytesville, Mo., May 30, 1936; interment in the City Cemetery.

**RUDD, Eldon Dean,** a Representative from Arizona; born in Camp Verde, Yavapai County, Ariz., July 15, 1920; attended the public schools of Arizona; graduated from Clarkdale (Ariz.) High School, 1939; B.A., Arizona State University, Tempe, 1947; J.D., University of Arizona, Tucson, 1949; admitted to the Arizona bar in 1949 and commenced practice in Tucson; served in the United States Marine Corps as a carrier-based fighter pilot, 1942-1946; special agent, Federal Bureau of Investigation, 1950-1970; member, Maricopa County, Ariz., Board of Supervisors, 1972-1976; delegate, Arizona State Republican conventions, 1973-1976; elected as a Republican to the Ninety-fifth and to the four succeeding Congresses (January 3, 1977-January 3, 1987); was not a candidate for reelection in 1986 to the One Hundredth Congress; resumed the practice of law in Phoenix, Ariz., 1987-1994; director of the Southern Pacific Transportation Company, and of the Salt River Project; president, Eldon Rudd Consultancy, Inc.; is a resident of Scottsdale, Ariz.

**RUDD, Stephen Andrew,** a Representative from New York; born in Brooklyn, N.Y., December 11, 1874; attended the public schools and the New York Preparatory School; studied law at the Brooklyn Law School of St. Lawrence University, Brooklyn, N.Y.; was admitted to the bar in 1914 and commenced practice in Brooklyn; member of the New York City Board of Aldermen, 1922-1930; elected as a Democrat to the Seventy-second Congress to fill the vacancy caused by the death of David J. O'Connell; reelected to the Seventy-third and Seventy-fourth Congresses and served from March 4, 1931 until his death in Brooklyn, N.Y., March 31, 1936; interment in Evergreen Cemetery.

**RUDMAN, Warren Bruce,** a Senator from New Hampshire; born in Boston, Suffolk County, Mass., May 18, 1930; attended the public schools of Nashua, N.H.; graduated, Valley Forge Military School, Wayne, Pa., 1948; B.S., Syracuse (N.Y.) University, 1952; LL.B., Boston (Mass.) College Law School, 1960; served in the United States Army Infantry, 1952-1954; admitted to the New Hampshire bar in 1960 and commenced practiced in Nashua; served as legal counsel to Governor Walter Peterson of New Hampshire in 1970; attorney general of New Hampshire, 1970-1976; practiced law in Manchester, N.H., 1976-1980; elected as a Republican to the

United States Senate, November 4, 1980, for the six-year term commencing January 3, 1981; subsequently appointed by the Governor, December 29, 1980, to fill the vacancy caused by the resignation of John A. Durkin for the term ending January 3, 1981; reelected in 1986 and served from December 29, 1980 to January 3, 1993; was not a candidate for reelection in 1992; chairman, Select Committee on Ethics (Ninety-ninth Congress); is a resident of Nashua, N.H.

**Bibliography:** Rudman, Warren B. *Combat: Twelve Years in the U.S. Senate.* New York: Random House, 1996.

**RUFFIN, James Edward,** a Representative from Missouri; born on a farm near Covington, Tipton County, Tenn., July 24, 1893; in 1905 moved to Missouri with his parents, who settled in Aurora, Lawrence County; attended the grade schools; was graduated from the Aurora High School in 1912 and from Drury College, Springfield, Mo., in 1916; taught school at Nickerson (Kans.) College in 1917; during the First World War was commissioned a first lieutenant on November 27, 1917; served in the Fifty-third Regiment, Pioneer Infantry, overseas with the First and Thirty-fifth Divisions, and was discharged on June 3, 1919; was graduated from the law department of Cumberland University, Lebanon, Tenn., in 1920; was admitted to the bar the same year and commenced practice in Springfield, Mo.; served as assistant city attorney 1926-1928; elected as a Democrat to the Seventy-third Congress (March 4, 1933-January 3, 1935); unsuccessful candidate for renomination in 1934 to the Seventy-fourth Congress; appointed special assistant to the Attorney General of the United States on May 9, 1935, assigned to the criminal division of the Department of Justice, and served until August 1953; resumed the practice of law in Springfield, Mo., where he died April 9, 1977; interment in East Lawn Cemetery.

**RUFFIN, Thomas,** a Representative from North Carolina; born in Louisburg, Franklin County (formerly a part of Edgecombe County), N.C., September 9, 1820; attended the common schools; was graduated from the law department of the University of North Carolina at Chapel Hill in 1841; was admitted to the bar the same year and commenced practice in Goldsboro, N.C.; circuit attorney of the seventh judicial district of the State of Missouri 1844-1848; returned to Goldsboro, N.C., in 1850; elected as a Democrat to the Thirty-third and to the three succeeding Congresses (March 4, 1853-March 3, 1861); delegate to the Confederate Provisional Congress at Richmond in July 1861; during the Civil War served in the Confederate Army as colonel of the First North Carolina Cavalry; mortally wounded in action at Bristoe Station, near Alexandria, Va., and died while a prisoner of war at Alexandria on October 13, 1863; interment in the private cemetery on the Ruffin homestead, near Louisburg, N.C.

**RUGGLES, Benjamin,** a Senator from Ohio; born in Abington, Windham County, Conn., February 21, 1783; completed preparatory studies; studied law; was admitted to the bar and began practice in Marietta, Ohio, in 1807; moved to St. Clairsville, Ohio; presiding judge of the court of common pleas for the third judicial circuit, 1810-1815; elected as a Republican to the United States Senate in 1815; reelected in 1821 and again in 1827, and served from March 4, 1815 to March 3, 1833; was not a candidate for renomination in 1832; chairman, Committee on the Militia (Fifteenth Congress), Committee on Claims (Seventeenth, Eighteenth, and Twentieth through Twenty-second Congresses); presidential elector on the Whig ticket in 1836; resumed the practice of law and was also interested in agricultural pursuits; died in St. Clairsville, Belmont County, Ohio, September 2, 1857; interment in Union Cemetery.

**RUGGLES, Charles Herman,** a Representative from New York; born in New Milford, Conn., February 10, 1789; completed preparatory studies; studied law; was admitted to the bar and began practice in Kingston, N.Y.; member of the State assembly in 1820; elected to the Seventeenth Congress (March 4, 1821-March 3, 1823);

circuit judge and vice chancellor of the second judicial district of New York 1833-1846; moved to Poughkeepsie, Dutchess County, N.Y.; member of the State constitutional convention in 1846; judge of the Dutchess County court; again elected a member of the State assembly; judge of the court of appeals 1847-1855; died in Poughkeepsie, N.Y., June 16, 1865.

**RUGGLES, John,** a Senator from Maine; born in Westboro, Mass., October 8, 1789; attended the common schools; graduated from Brown University, Providence, R.I., in 1813; studied law; was admitted to the bar and commenced practice in Skowhegan, Maine, in 1815; moved to Thomaston, Maine, in 1817; member, State house of representatives 1823-1831, and served as speaker 1825-1829, 1831; justice of the supreme judicial court of Maine 1831-1834; elected as a Jacksonian to the United States Senate to fill the vacancy caused by the resignation of Peleg Sprague, and at the same time was elected for the full term beginning March 4, 1835, and served from January 20, 1835, to March 3, 1841; was an unsuccessful candidate for reelection in 1840; chairman, Committee on Patents and Patent Office (Twenty-fifth Congress); framer of the bill for the reorganization of the United States Patent Office in 1836; resumed the practice of law in Thomaston, Knox County, Maine; also engaged as an inventor, orator, and writer; died in Thomaston, Maine, on June 20, 1874; interment in Elm Grove Cemetery.

**RUGGLES, Nathaniel,** a Representative from Massachusetts; born in Roxbury, Mass., November 11, 1761; pursued preparatory studies; was graduated from Harvard University in 1781; studied law; was admitted to the bar and practiced law in Roxbury, Mass.; appointed judge of the general sessions in 1807; chief justice of Massachusetts in 1808; was elected as a Federalist to the Thirteenth, Fourteenth, and Fifteenth Congresses (March 4, 1813-March 3, 1819); died in Roxbury, Mass., December 19, 1819.

**RUMPLE, John Nicholas William,** a Representative from Iowa; born near Fostoria, Seneca County, Ohio, March 4, 1841; attended the public schools, Western College, Iowa, and the Iowa State University; enlisted in Company H, Second Iowa Cavalry, in August 1861 and remained in the Army until October 1865, when mustered out as captain; studied law; was admitted to the bar in 1867 and commenced practice in Marengo, Iowa County, Iowa; member of the State senate 1873-1878; member of the board of regents of the State University of Iowa 1880-1886; curator of the State Historical Society of Iowa 1881-1885; member of the city council; mayor of Marengo, Iowa, in 1885 and 1886; attorney for the city council of Marengo 1896-1900; member of the school board; elected as a Republican to the Fifty-seventh Congress and served from March 4, 1901, until his death in Chicago, Ill., January 31, 1903; interment in the Odd Fellows Cemetery, Marengo, Iowa.

**RUMSEY, Benjamin,** a Delegate from Maryland; born in Bohemia Manor, Cecil County, Md., October 6, 1734; attended Princeton College; member of the Maryland convention of December 29, 1775; was appointed by the provincial convention colonel of the Lower Battalion of Harford County in 1776; member of the council of safety in 1776; Member of the Continental Congress 1776-1777; chief justice of the Maryland Court of Appeals from 1778 to 1805, when he resigned; died in Joppa, Harford County, Md., March 7, 1808; interment in the Old St. John's Cemetery.

**RUMSEY, David,** a Representative from New York; born in Salem, Washington County, N.Y., December 25, 1810; attended school at Auburn, N.Y., and Hobart College at Geneva, N.Y.; studied law; was admitted to the bar in 1831 and commenced practice in Bath, N.Y.; surrogate of Steuben County 1840-1844; held many local offices; elected as a Whig to the Thirtieth and Thirty-first Congresses (March 4, 1847-March 3, 1851); delegate to the State constitutional convention in 1867; member of the commission to propose amendments to the State constitution in 1872; appointed in

1873 as an associate justice of the State supreme court to fill a vacancy; elected to the same office in the fall of that year; died in Bath, Steuben County, N.Y., March 12, 1883; interment in private cemetery on the Rumsey place.

**RUMSEY, Edward,** a Representative from Kentucky; born in Botetourt County, Va., November 5, 1796; moved when a child with his parents to Christian County, Ky.; completed preparatory studies in Hopkinsville; moved to Greenville, Ky.; studied law; admitted to the bar and commenced practice in Greenville; held several local offices; member of the Kentucky house of representatives in 1822; elected as a Whig to the Twenty-fifth Congress (March 4, 1837-March 3, 1839); again resumed the practice of his profession; died in Greenville, Muhlenberg County, Ky., on April 6, 1868; interment in the Old Caney Station Cemetery, near Greenville, Ky.

**RUMSFELD, Donald Henry,** a Representative from Illinois; born in Chicago, Ill., July 9, 1932; A.B., Princeton University, 1954; received a commission in the United States Navy and served as a naval aviator and flight instructor, 1954-1957; administrative assistant to Representative David S. Dennison of Ohio in 1958, and on the staff of Representative Robert P. Griffin of Michigan in 1959; investment broker in Chicago, Ill., 1960-1962; elected as a Republican to the Eighty-eighth and to the three succeeding Congresses and served from January 3, 1963, until his resignation May 25, 1969, to join the Cabinet of President Richard M. Nixon as an Assistant to the President, member of the Cabinet, and Director of the Office of Economic Opportunity, and served until 1970; Counsellor to President Nixon, 1970-1973; appointed Director of the Cost of Living Council in October 1971; United States Permanent Representative on the council of the North Atlantic Treaty Organization, with the rank of Ambassador, 1973-1974; White House chief of staff, 1974-1975; appointed Secretary of Defense in the Cabinet of President Gerald R. Ford, and served from November 20, 1975 to January 20, 1977; chief executive officer, G.D. Searle and Co., Skokie, Ill., 1977-1985; senior adviser, William Blair and Co., Chicago, 1985 to 1990; chairman and chief executive officer, General Instrument Corp., 1990-1993; chairman of the board of trustees of the RAND Corp., 1995 to present; member, President's General Advisory Committee on Arms Control, and advisor to the government on national security affairs, 1983-1984; Special Presidential Ambassador to the Middle East, 1983-1984; is a resident of Chicago, Ill.

**RUNK, John,** a Representative from New Jersey; born in Milltown (now Idell), Hunterdon County, N.J., July 3, 1791; attended the district schools; took charge of the mills and general store on his father's property in Milltown, N.J.; member of the board of chosen freeholders from Kingwood 1825-1833; unsuccessful candidate for sheriff in 1830; high sheriff of Hunterdon County 1836-1838; elected as a Whig to the Twenty-ninth Congress (March 4, 1845-March 3, 1847); unsuccessful candidate for reelection in 1846 to the Thirtieth Congress; unsuccessful candidate for Governor of New Jersey in 1850; moved to Lambertville, Hunterdon County, N.J., in 1854; and engaged in the milling business and mercantile pursuits; died in Lambertville, September 22, 1872; interment in Rosemont Cemetery, Rosemont, Hunterdon County, N.J.

**RUNNELS, Harold Lowell (Mud),** a Representative from New Mexico; born in Dallas, Tex., March 17, 1924; attended the Dallas public schools, and Cameron State Agricultural College, Lawton, Okla.; enlisted in the United States Army Air Force Reserve as a private, December 1942-July 1943; employed by the Federal Bureau of Investigation, Washington, D.C., in 1942; manager, Magnolia Amusement Company, Magnolia, Ark., 1945-1951; moved to Lovington, N.Mex., in 1951 and became a partner in the Southland Supply Company in 1952; formed the Runnels Mud Company in 1953, and RunCo Acidizing and Fracturing Company in 1964; a founder of the Permian Basin Petroleum Association, 1960; member, New Mexico

State senate, 1960-1970; delegate to New Mexico State Democratic conventions, 1960-1979; elected as a Democrat to the Ninety-second and to the four succeeding Congresses, and served from January 3, 1971 until his death in New York City on August 5, 1980; interment in Rest Haven Memorial Gardens, Lovington, N.Mex.

**RUPLEY, Arthur Ringwalt,** a Representative from Pennsylvania; born in West Fairview, Cumberland County, Pa., November 13, 1868; attended the Harrisburg Academy and the Cumberland Valley State Normal School, Shippensburg, Pa.; graduated from the Dickinson School of Law, Carlisle, Pa., in 1890; admitted to the bar in 1891 and practiced; chairman of the Republican county committee 1895-1898; district attorney of Cumberland County 1895-1899; county and city solicitor 1900-1906; delegate to the Pennsylvania Republican convention in 1910 and to the Republican National Convention in 1912; elected as a Republican to the Sixty-third Congress (March 4, 1913-March 3, 1915); resumed the practice of law and specialized in public-service work; died in Carlisle, Pa., on November 11, 1920; interment in Ashland Cemetery.

**RUPPE, Philip Edward,** a Representative from Michigan; born in Laurium, Houghton County, Mich., September 29, 1926; graduated from high school in 1944; Navy V-12 program, Central Michigan University and University of Michigan, 1944-1946; B.A., Yale University, 1948; served in the United States Navy during the Korean conflict as lieutenant (junior grade); president, Bosch Brewing Co., 1955-1965; director, Houghton National Bank, Commercial National Bank of L'Anse, and R.L. Polk and Co.; elected as a Republican to the Ninetieth and to the five succeeding Congresses (January 3, 1967-January 3, 1979); was not a candidate for reelection in 1978 to the Ninety-sixth Congress; unsuccessful candidate for the United States Senate in 1982; president of Woodlak Company until 1986; is a resident of Bethesda, Md.

**RUPPERT, Jacob, Jr.,** a Representative from New York; born in New York City, August 5, 1867; attended the Columbia Grammar School; engaged in the brewing business with his father in 1887; served as a private in the Seventh Regiment, National Guard of New York, 1886-1889; appointed a colonel on the staff of Governor David B. Hill, serving as aide-de-camp; subsequently served as senior aide on the staff of Governor Roswell P. Flower from 1892 until 1895; elected as a Democrat to the Fifty-sixth and to the three succeeding Congresses (March 4, 1899-March 3, 1907); was not a candidate for renomination in 1906 to the Sixtieth Congress; resumed his activities in the brewing business and became president of his father's company in 1915; served as president of the United States Brewers Association from 1911 until 1914; financially interested in various business and real estate holdings; served as president of the Astoria Silk Works; purchased and became president of the New York Yankees professional baseball team on December 31, 1914, and served in that capacity until his death in New York City, January 13, 1939; interment in Kensico Cemetery, Valhalla, Westchester County, N.Y.

**RUSH, Benjamin,** a Delegate from Pennsylvania; born in Byberry Township, near Philadelphia, Pa., January 4, 1746; educated under private tutors and at a private school in Nottingham, Md.; was graduated from Princeton College in 1760; studied medicine in Philadelphia, Edinburgh, London, and Paris, and commenced practice in Philadelphia in August 1769; held several professorships in the Philadelphia Medical College; Member of the Continental Congress in 1776 and 1777; a signer of the Declaration of Independence; entered the Revolutionary Army as surgeon general of the Middle Department in April 1777; made physician general in July 1777; resigned in February 1778; resumed the practice of medicine; delegate to the Pennsylvania ratification convention, 1787; founder of the Pennsylvania Hospital in Philadelphia; president of the Philadelphia Medical Society; vice president and one of the founders of the Philadelphia Bible Society; one of the founders of Dickinson College at Carlisle, Pa.; assisted in the establishment of the Philadelphia dispensary in 1786; treasurer of the United States Mint at Philadelphia from 1799 until his death in that city April 19, 1813; interment in Christ Church Burying Ground.

**Bibliography:** *DAB*; Goodman, Nathan G. *Benjamin Rush, Physician and Citizen, 1746-1813.* Philadelphia: University of Pennsylvania Press, 1934; Hawke, David F. *Benjamin Rush, Revolutionary Gadfly.* Indianapolis: Bobbs-Merrill, 1971.

**RUSH, Bobby Lee,** a Representative from Illinois; born in Albany, Dougherty County, Ga., November 23, 1946; B.A., Roosevelt University, 1974; University of Illinois, completed core courses and thesis for M.A. in political science; entered active duty, United States Army in 1963; released in 1968; Democratic Ward Committee, Second Ward, 1984 and 1988; Illinois Democratic Central Committee, First Congressional District, 1990; deputy chair, Illinois Democratic Party, 1990; Chicago city council, 1983-1993; elected as a Democrat to the One Hundred Third and One Hundred Fourth Congresses (January 3, 1993-January 3, 1997); is a resident of Chicago, Ill.

**RUSK, Harry Welles,** a Representative from Maryland; born in Baltimore, Md., October 17, 1852; attended private schools; was graduated from the Baltimore City College in 1866 and from the Maryland University Law School at Baltimore in 1882; was admitted to the bar in 1873 and commenced practice in Baltimore; member of the State house of delegates in 1876, 1878, and 1880; served in the State senate 1882-1884; delegate to the Democratic National Convention in 1884; elected as a Democrat to the Forty-ninth Congress to fill the vacancy caused by the death of William H. Cole; reelected to the Fiftieth and to the four succeeding Congresses and served from November 2, 1886, to March 3, 1897; chairman, Committee on Accounts (Fifty-second and Fifty-third Congresses); declined to be a candidate for renomination in 1896; chairman of the Democratic State central committee for Baltimore from 1898 to 1908, when he resigned; resumed the practice of law in Baltimore, Md., where he died on January 28, 1926; interment in Greenmount Cemetery.

**RUSK, Jeremiah McLain,** a Representative from Wisconsin; born in Malta, Morgan County, Ohio, June 17, 1830; received a limited schooling; moved to Vernon County, Wis., in 1853 and engaged in agricultural pursuits; sheriff of Viroqua, Wis., 1855-1857; coroner in 1857; member of the Wisconsin State assembly in 1862; became major in the Twenty-fifth Regiment, Wisconsin Volunteer Infantry, August 14, 1862; lieutenant colonel September 16, 1863; mustered out June 7, 1865; bank comptroller of Wisconsin, 1866-1869; elected as a Republican to the Forty-second and to the two succeeding Congresses (March 4, 1871-March 3, 1877); chairman, Committee on Invalid Pensions (Forty-third Congress); was not a candidate for renomination in 1876 to the Forty-fifth Congress; elected Governor of Wisconsin in 1881, reelected in 1884 and 1886, and served from January 2, 1882 to January 7, 1889; appointed Secretary of Agriculture in the Cabinet of President Benjamin Harrison, and served from March 5, 1889 to March 5, 1893; died in Viroqua, Vernon County, Wis., on November 21, 1893; interment in Viroqua Cemetery.

**Bibliography:** *DAB*.

**RUSK, Thomas Jefferson,** a Senator from Texas; born in Pendleton District, S.C., December 5, 1803; self-taught; studied law; was admitted to the bar and commenced practice in Georgia; moved to Nacogdoches, Tex., in 1835; delegate to the convention which declared for the independence of Texas in 1836; first Secretary of War of the new Republic; at the Battle of San Jacinto, April 21, 1836, took command of the forces and retained command until October

1836, when he resumed his duties as Secretary of War; member of the Second Congress of the Republic of Texas; chief justice of the supreme court of Texas, 1838-1842; appointed major general of militia of the Republic of Texas in 1843; president of the convention that confirmed the annexation of Texas to the United States in 1845; upon the admission of Texas as a State into the Union was elected as a Democrat to the United States Senate; reelected in 1851 and 1857 and served from February 21, 1846, until his death; served as President pro tempore of the Senate during the Thirty-fifth Congress; chairman, Committee on Enrolled Bills (Thirtieth and Thirty-first Congresses), Committee on the Militia (Thirtieth Congress), Committee on Engrossed Bills (Thirtieth Congress), Committee on Post Office and Post Roads (Thirty-first through Thirty-fourth Congresses); committed suicide in Nacogdoches, Tex., July 29, 1857; interment in Oak Grove Cemetery.

**Bibliography:** *DAB*; Clarke, Mary. *Thomas J. Rusk: Soldier, Statesman, Jurist*. Austin: Jenkins Publishing Company, 1971; Huston, Cleburne. *Towering Texan: A Biography of Thomas J. Rusk*. Waco: Texian Press, 1971.

**RUSS, John,** a Representative from Connecticut; was born in Ipswich, Mass., on October 29, 1767; completed preparatory studies; moved to Hartford, Conn.; engaged in mercantile pursuits; elected to the Sixteenth and Seventeenth Congresses (March 4, 1819-March 3, 1823); was not a candidate for reelection in 1823; unsuccessful candidate for election in 1823 to the State house of representatives; elected to the State house of representatives in 1824; elected judge of the Hartford Probate Court in 1824 and served until 1830; resumed his former business pursuits; died in Hartford, Conn., June 22, 1833; interment in the Old North Cemetery.

**RUSSELL, Benjamin Edward** (cousin of Rienzi Melville Johnston), a Representative from Georgia; born in Monticello, Jefferson County, Fla., on October 5, 1845; moved with his parents to Decatur County, Ga., in 1854; attended the common schools; entered the Confederate Army as a drummer boy in the First Georgia Regiment; upon the disbanding of this regiment he immediately enlisted in the Eighth Florida Regiment and continued with it during the last three years of the war, with the rank of first lieutenant; entered the printing business; editor of the Bainbridge (Ga.) Democrat; delegate to the State constitutional convention in 1877; delegate to the Democratic National Convention in 1880; mayor of Bainbridge in 1881 and 1882; member of the State house of representatives in 1882 and 1883; postmaster of Bainbridge 1885-1890; elected as a Democrat to the Fifty-third and Fifty-fourth Congresses (March 4, 1893-March 3, 1897); was not a candidate for renomination in 1896; resumed the publication of the Bainbridge Democrat; died in Bainbridge, Decatur County, Ga., December 4, 1909; interment in Oak City Cemetery.

**RUSSELL, Charles Addison,** a Representative from Connecticut; born in Worcester, Mass., March 2, 1852; attended the public schools; was graduated from Yale College in 1873; city editor of the Worcester Press from 1873 until 1879, and associate editor of the Worcester Spy in 1879 and 1880; moved to Killingly, Conn., in 1879 and engaged in the manufacture of woolen products; aide-de-camp on the staff of Governor Hobart B. Bigelow in 1881; member of the Connecticut State house of representatives in 1883; secretary of state of Connecticut in 1885 and 1886; was elected as a Republican to the Fiftieth and to the seven succeeding Congresses and served from March 4, 1887, until his death in Killingly, Conn., October 23, 1902; chairman, Committee on Expenditures in the Department of War (Fifty-seventh Congress); had been renominated to the Fifty-eighth Congress at the time of his death; interment in the High Street Cemetery, Dayville, Killingly, Conn.

**RUSSELL, Charles Hinton,** a Representative from Nevada; born in Lovelock, Pershing County, Nev., December 27, 1903; attended the public schools; was graduated from Elko County High School in 1922 and the University of Nevada at Reno in 1926; taught school in Ruby Valley, Nev. in 1926 and 1927; employed in a mine office in Ruth, Nev., in 1928 and 1929; publisher of the Ely (Nev.) Record in 1929; served in the Nevada State assembly, 1935-1940; member of the Nevada State senate, 1941-1946, resigning in 1946 to become a candidate for Congress; served as president pro tempore of the State senate in 1943; elected as a Republican to the Eightieth Congress (January 3, 1947-January 3, 1949); unsuccessful candidate for reelection in 1948 to the Eighty-first Congress; member of the staff of the Joint Congressional Committee on Foreign Economic Cooperation in Washington, D.C., in 1949 and 1950; elected Governor of Nevada in 1950, reelected in 1954, and served from January 1, 1951, to January 5, 1959; unsuccessful candidate for reelection in 1958; director of an International Cooperation Administration mission to Paraguay, serving from December 15, 1959 until July 1, 1963; assistant to the president of University of Nevada, August 1963 to January 1, 1968; was a resident of Carson City, Nev., until his death there on September 13, 1989; interment in Dayton Cemetery, Dayton, Nev.

**RUSSELL, Daniel Lindsay,** a Representative from North Carolina; born on Winnabow plantation, Brunswick County, near Wilmington, N.C., on August 7, 1845; received his early education from private teachers and attended the Bingham School in Orange County, N.C.; entered the University of North Carolina at Chapel Hill, but left upon the outbreak of the Civil War; served as a captain in the Confederate Army; member of the North Carolina State house of commons, 1864-1866; studied law, was admitted to the bar in 1866 and commenced practice in Wilmington, N.C.; judge of the superior courts for the fourth judicial circuit, 1868-1874; elected as a delegate to the State constitutional convention in 1871; member of the State house of representatives in 1876; delegate to the Republican National Convention of 1876; elected as a Greenbacker to the Forty-sixth Congress (March 4, 1879-March 3, 1881); was not a candidate for renomination in 1880 to the Forty-seventh Congress; elected as a Republican Governor of North Carolina in 1896, and served from January 12, 1897 to January 15, 1901; resumed the practice of law and also engaged in agricultural pursuits; died on Belville plantation, near Wilmington, N.C., May 14, 1908; interment in the family burying ground, Hickory Hill, Onslow County, N.C.

**Bibliography:** Crow, Jeffrey J., and Robert F. Durden. *Maverick Republican in the Old North State: A Political Biography of Daniel L. Russell*. Baton Rouge: Louisiana State University Press, 1977.

**RUSSELL, David Abel,** a Representative from New York; born in Petersburg, N.Y., in 1780; completed preparatory studies; studied law; was admitted to the bar and commenced practice in Salem, N.Y.; appointed justice of the peace in 1807; admitted to practice as counselor in 1809; district attorney for the northern judicial district of New York in 1813; member of the State assembly in 1816, 1830, and 1833; elected as a Whig to the Twenty-fourth, Twenty-fifth, and Twenty-sixth Congresses (March 4, 1835-March 3, 1841); chairman, Committee on Claims (Twenty-sixth Congress); died in Salem, Washington County, N.Y., November 24, 1861; interment in Evergreen Cemetery.

**RUSSELL, Donald Stuart,** a Senator from South Carolina; born in Lafayette Springs, Lafayette County, Miss., February 22, 1906; moved with his family to Chester, S.C., in 1914; attended the public schools; A.B., University of South Carolina, Columbia, 1925; LL.B., University of South Carolina School Law, 1928; was admitted to the bar and commenced the practice of law in Union, S.C., in 1928; engaged in graduate work in law at the University of Michigan in 1929; moved to Spartanburg, S.C., in 1930 and continued law practice until 1942; went to Washington, D.C., and worked in the War Department, and as assistant to Director of Economic Stabilization James F. Byrnes, 1942-1943; entered upon active duty in the United States Army, and was released as a major in 1944 after assignment with Supreme Headquarters, Allied Expeditionary Force; Deputy Director, Office of War Mobilization and Reconversion, 1945; Assistant Secretary of State for Administration, 1945-1947; resumed law practice in Spartanburg, S.C.; president of the University of South Carolina, 1952-1957; elected Governor of South Carolina in 1962, and served from January 15, 1963 until his resignation on April 22, 1965; appointed as a Democrat to the United States Senate to fill the vacancy caused by the death of Olin D. Johnston, and served from April 22, 1965 until November 8, 1966; unsuccessful candidate for nomination in 1966 to complete the term; judge of the United States District Court for the District of South Carolina, 1966-1971; judge of the United States Court of Appeals for the Fourth Circuit, 1971 to present; is a resident of Spartanburg, S.C.

**RUSSELL, Gordon James,** a Representative from Texas; born in Huntsville, Madison County, Ala., December 22, 1859; attended the common schools, the Sam Bailey Institute, Griffin, Ga., and Crawford High School, Dalton, Ga.; was graduated from the University of Georgia at Athens in 1877; taught school in Dalton, Ga.; studied law; was admitted to the bar in 1878 and commenced practice in Dalton; moved to Texas in 1879 and later, in 1884, settled in Van Zandt County; elected county judge in 1890 and at the end of one term relinquished the office to resume the practice of law in Willsport, Tex.; district attorney of the seventh judicial district 1892-1896; judge of the seventh judicial district 1896-1904; elected as a Democrat to the Fifty-seventh Congress to fill the vacancy caused by the death of Reese C. de Graffenreid; reelected to the Fifty-eighth and to the three succeeding Congresses and served from November 4, 1902, to June 14, 1910, when he resigned to become United States district judge of the eastern district of Texas, which office he held until his death in Kerrville, Kerr County, Tex., September 14, 1919; interment in Oakwood Cemetery, Tyler, Smith County, Tex.

**RUSSELL, James McPherson** (father of Samuel Lyon Russell), a Representative from Pennsylvania; born in York, Pa., November 10, 1786; moved with his parents to a farm near Gettysburg, Adams County, Pa.; attended the classical academy of James Ross in Chambersburg; studied law; admitted to the bar of Franklin County in 1807; admitted to the Bedford County bar in 1808 and commenced practice in Bedford, Pa.; first burgess of Bedford Borough in 1818 and 1819; member of the Pennsylvania constitutional convention in 1837; elected as a Whig to the Twenty-seventh Congress to fill the vacancy caused by the death of Henry Black and served from December 21, 1841, to March 3, 1843; was not a candidate for renomination in 1842; resumed the practice of law; trustee of the Bedford Academy and secretary of the Chambersburg & Bedford Turnpike Co.; died in Bedford, Pa., November 14, 1870; interment in Bedford Cemetery.

**RUSSELL, Jeremiah,** a Representative from New York; born in Saugerties, N.Y., January 26, 1786; received a limited schooling; engaged in mercantile pursuits, the real estate business, and banking; served several times as supervisor; member of the State assembly in 1842; elected as a Democrat to the Twenty-eighth Congress (March 4, 1843-March 3, 1845); unsuccessful candidate for reelection in 1844 to the Twenty-ninth Congress; resumed banking; died in Saugerties, Ulster County, N.Y., September 30, 1867; interment in Mountain View Cemetery.

**RUSSELL, John,** a Representative from New York; born in Branford, Conn., September 7, 1772; attended the public school; moved to New York State; studied medicine and practiced a short time in Cooperstown, N.Y.; county clerk of Otsego County 1801-1804; elected as a Republican to the Ninth and Tenth Congresses (March 4, 1805-March 3, 1809); presidential elector on the Clinton ticket in 1812; engaged in mercantile pursuits; died in Cooperstown, Otsego County, N.Y., August 2, 1842; interment in Christ Churchyard.

**RUSSELL, John Edwards,** a Representative from Massachusetts; born in Greenfield, Franklin County, Mass., January 20, 1834; was instructed by private tutors; returned to Massachusetts and became interested in mail transportation west of the Mississippi River and in steamship lines on the Pacific coast; engaged in agricultural pursuits; elected secretary of the Massachusetts Board of Agriculture in 1880; reelected five times; elected as a Democrat to the Fiftieth Congress (March 4, 1887-March 3, 1889); delegate to the Democratic National Convention in 1892; unsuccessful candidate for Governor of Massachusetts in 1893 and 1894; member of the Deep Waterways Commission; died in Leicester, Worcester County, Mass., October 28, 1903; interment in Pine Grove Cemetery.

**RUSSELL, Jonathan,** a Representative from Massachusetts; born in Providence, R.I., February 27, 1771; was graduated from Brown University (then Rhode Island College), Providence, R.I., in 1791; studied law; was admitted to the bar, but did not practice; engaged in mercantile pursuits; appointed by President James Madison to be Chargé d'Affaires to France, and served from September 1810 until November 1811; appointed Chargé d'Affaires to Great Britain in July 1811, and served until July 29, 1812, when he suspended his official functions after having received notice of the declaration of war against Great Britain; Minister to Norway and Sweden from January 18, 1814, to October 16, 1818; one of the five commissioners that negotiated the Treaty of Ghent with Great Britain in 1814; returned to the United States in 1818 and settled in Mendon, Mass.; writer and orator; member of the Massachusetts house of representatives in 1820; elected to the Seventeenth Congress (March 4, 1821-March 3, 1823); chairman, Committee on Foreign Affairs (Seventeenth Congress); died in Milton, Norfolk County, Mass., February 17, 1832; interment in the family plot on his estate in Milton.

**Bibliography:** *DAB.*

**RUSSELL, Joseph,** a Representative from New York; born in that State and resided in Warrensburg, N.Y.; received a limited schooling; sheriff of Warren County from November 1834 to November 1837; member of the State assembly in 1840; elected as a Democrat to the Twenty-ninth Congress (March 4, 1845-March 3, 1847); again elected to the Thirty-second Congress (March 4, 1851-March 3, 1853).

**RUSSELL, Joseph James,** a Representative from Missouri; born near Charleston, Mississippi County, Mo., August 23, 1854; attended the public schools and Charleston Academy; was admitted to the bar in 1876 and commenced practice in Charleston, Mo.; graduated from the law department of the University of Missouri at Columbia in 1880; school commissioner for Mississippi County in 1878 and 1879; prosecuting attorney 1880-1884; delegate to the Democratic National Convention in 1884; member of the State house of representatives 1886-1890 and served as speaker pro tempore of the house in 1886 and as speaker in 1888; elected as a Democrat to the Sixtieth Congress (March 4, 1907-March 3, 1909); unsuccessful candidate for reelection in 1908 to the Sixty-first Congress; elected to the Sixty-second and to the three succeeding Congresses (March 4, 1911-March 3, 1919); was not a candidate for renomination; died in Charleston, Mo., October 22, 1922; interment in the Odd Fellows Cemetery.

**RUSSELL, Joshua Edward,** a Representative from Ohio; born near Sidney, Shelby County, Ohio, on August 9, 1867; attended the common schools and Sidney High School; studied law; was admitted to the bar in 1893 and commenced practice in Sidney; member of the city board of education in 1894 and 1895; city solicitor 1895-1899; member of the State senate 1905-1908; elected as a Republican to the Sixty-fourth Congress (March 4, 1915-March 3, 1917); was an unsuccessful candidate for reelection in 1916 to the Sixty-fifth Congress; resumed the practice of law; died in Sidney, Ohio, June 21, 1953; interment in Graceland Cemetery.

RUSSELL, Leslie W., a Representative from New York; born in Canton, St. Lawrence County, N.Y., April 15, 1840; attended the common schools; studied law; was admitted to the bar in 1861 and commenced practice in Canton; delegate to the State constitutional convention of 1867; district attorney of St. Lawrence County in 1869; member of the board of regents of the University of the State of New York 1878-1891; county judge of St. Lawrence County 1877-1881; attorney general of New York 1881-1883; practiced law in New York City 1883-1891; elected to the Fifty-second Congress and served from March 4, 1891, to September 11, 1891, when he resigned, having been elected justice of the supreme court of the State of New York; resigned as justice on October 1, 1902; died in New York City on February 3, 1903; interment in Evergreen Cemetery, Canton, N.Y.

RUSSELL, Richard Brevard, Jr., a Senator from Georgia; born in Winder, Barrow County, Ga., November 2, 1897; attended the public schools; graduated from the Seventh District Agricultural and Mechanical School, Powder Springs, Ga., in 1914; B.A., Gordon Institute, Barnesville, Ga., 1915; LL.B., University of Georgia School of Law, Athens, 1918; was admitted to the bar and commenced practice at Winder, Ga., in 1919; served with the United States Naval Reserve in 1918; member, Georgia State house of representatives, 1921-1931, serving as speaker from 1927 to 1931; elected Governor of Georgia in 1930, and served from June 27, 1931 until his resignation on January 10, 1933; elected as a Democrat to the United States Senate on January 12, 1933, to fill the vacancy caused by the death of William J. Harris; reelected in 1936, 1942, 1948, 1954, 1960, and 1966 and served from January 12, 1933, until his death in Washington, D.C., on January 21, 1971; served as President pro tempore of the Senate during the Ninety-first and Ninety-second Congresses; chairman, Committee on Immigration (Seventy-fifth through Seventy-ninth Congresses), Committee on Manufactures (Seventy-ninth Congress), Committee on Armed Services (Eighty-second and Eighty-fourth through Ninetieth Congresses), Committee on Appropriations (Ninety-first Congress); interment in Russell Memorial Park, Winder, Ga.

Bibliography: Fite, Gilbert C. *Richard B. Russell, Jr.: Senator from Georgia.* Chapel Hill: University of North Carolina Press, 1991; Kelly, Karen. "Richard B. Russell: Democrat From Georgia." Ph.D. dissertation, University of North Carolina, 1979; Potenziani, David D. "Look to the Past: Richard B. Russell and the Defense of Southern White Supremacy." Ph.D. dissertation, University of Georgia, 1981.

RUSSELL, Richard Manning, a Representative from Massachusetts; born in Cambridge, Mass., March 3, 1891; attended the Middlesex School, Concord, Mass.; graduated from Harvard University in 1914, and from Harvard Law School in 1917; during the First World War served from August 15, 1917, as a second lieutenant in the Three Hundred and Third Field Artillery and as a first lieutenant and communications officer of the One Hundred and Fifty-first Field Artillery Brigade, with service in France, and was discharged on February 20, 1919; was admitted to the bar in 1919 and commenced practice in Boston, Mass.; member of the Cambridge City Council in 1926 and 1927; mayor of Cambridge, 1930-1935; elected as a Democrat to the Seventy-fourth Congress (January 3, 1935-January 3, 1937); unsuccessful candidate for reelection in 1936 to the Seventy-fifth Congress, for election in 1950 to fill a vacancy in the Eighty-first Congress, and for election in 1950 to the Eighty-second Congress; resumed the practice of law in Boston, Mass.; resided in Essex, Mass., where he died on February 27, 1977; interment in Pine Hill Cemetery, Tewksbury, Mass.

RUSSELL, Sam Morris, a Representative from Texas; born on a farm near Stephenville, Erath County, Tex., August 9, 1889; attended the rural schools and the John Tarleton College, Stephenville, Tex.; taught school in Erath County, Tex., 1913-1918; also engaged in agricultural pursuits; during the First World War served as a private in the Forty-sixth Machine Gun Company, United States Army, in 1918 and 1919; studied law; was admitted to the bar in 1919 and commenced practice in Stephenville, Tex.; served as county attorney of Erath County, Tex., 1919-1924; district attorney of the twenty-ninth judicial district 1924-1928; served as judge of the twenty-ninth judicial district 1928-1940; elected as a Democrat and to the Seventy-seventh and to the two succeeding Congresses (January 3, 1941-January 3, 1947); was not a candidate for renomination in 1946 to the Eightieth Congress; resumed the practice of law, Democratic county chairman, 1953-1955; resided in Stephenville, Tex., until his death there October 19, 1971; interment in East Memorial Cemetery.

RUSSELL, Samuel Lyon (son of James McPherson Russell), a Representative from Pennsylvania; born in Bedford, Pa., July 30, 1816; attended the common schools and Bedford Academy; graduated from Washington College, Pennsylvania, in 1834; studied law; admitted to the bar in 1837 and commenced practice in Bedford; prosecuting attorney of Bedford County during the 1840s; elected as a Whig to the Thirty-third Congress (March 4, 1853-March 3, 1855); was not a candidate for renomination; resumed the practice of law in Bedford, Bedford County, Pa.; became a Republican upon the organization of that party in 1856; member of the Pennsylvania constitutional convention in 1873; member of the town council and the school board; died in Bedford, Pa., September 27, 1891; interment in Bedford Cemetery.

RUSSELL, William, a Representative from Ohio; born in Ireland in 1782; immigrated to the United States and settled in West Union, Ohio; received a limited schooling; held several local offices; member of the State house of representatives in 1809, 1810, and 1811-1813; served in the State senate 1819-1821; elected as a Jacksonian to the Twentieth, Twenty-first, and Twenty-second Congresses (March 4, 1827-March 3, 1833); unsuccessful candidate for reelection in 1832 to the Twenty-third Congress; moved to Portsmouth, Scioto County, Ohio; was elected as a Whig to the Twenty-seventh Congress (March 4, 1841-March 3, 1843); was not a candidate for renomination in 1842; retired to his farm on Scioto Brush Creek, where he died September 28, 1845; interment in the old section of Rushtown Cemetery, Rushtown, Scioto County, Ohio.

RUSSELL, William Augustus, a Representative from Massachusetts; born at Wells River, Orange County, Vt., April 22, 1831; pursued an academic course in Franklin, N.H.; engaged in the manufacture of paper in Exeter, N.H., in 1852; moved to Lawrence, Mass., in 1852, where he continued in that business; member of the Massachusetts house of representatives in 1869; delegate to the Republican National Conventions in 1868 and 1876; elected as a Republican to the Forty-sixth, Forty-seventh, and Forty-eighth Congresses (March 4, 1879-March 3, 1885); after leaving Congress devoted his time to the manufacture of paper; died in Boston, Mass., January 10, 1899; interment in Bellevue Cemetery, Lawrence, Essex County, Mass.

RUSSELL, William Fiero, a Representative from New York; born in Saugerties, Ulster County, N.Y., January 14, 1812; completed preparatory studies; engaged in mercantile pursuits and banking; founder and president of the Saugerties Bank; served as postmaster of Saugerties from October 19, 1836, to January 25, 1841; member of the State assembly in 1851; elected as a Democrat to the Thirty-fifth Congress (March 4, 1857-March 3, 1859); appointed as naval agent for the port of New York City in 1859; resumed the banking business; died in Saugerties, N.Y., April 29, 1896; interment in Mountain View Cemetery.

**RUSSO, Martin Anthony,** a Representative from Illinois; born in Chicago, Ill., January 23, 1944; graduated from St. Ignatius, Chicago, 1961; B.A., DePaul University, Chicago, 1965; J.D., DePaul University School of Law, 1967; admitted to the Illinois bar in 1967 and commenced practice in Chicago; served as assistant State's attorney, Cook County, Ill., 1971-1973; elected as a Democrat to the Ninety-fourth and to the eight succeeding Congresses (January 3, 1975-January 3, 1993); unsuccessful candidate for renomination in 1992 to the One Hundred Third Congress; is a resident of South Holland, Ill.

**RUST, Albert,** a Representative from Arkansas; was born in Virginia; completed preparatory studies; studied law; was admitted to the bar and commenced practice in El Dorado, Union County, Ark.; member of the State house of representatives 1842-1848 and 1852-1854; elected as a Democrat to the Thirty-fourth Congress (March 4, 1855-March 3, 1857); unsuccessful candidate for reelection in 1856 to the Thirty-fifth Congress; elected to the Thirty-sixth Congress (March 4, 1859-March 3, 1861); brigadier general in the Confederate Army during the Civil War; resumed the practice of his profession; died in El Dorado, Ark., April 3, 1870; interment in the Old Methodist Cemetery.

**RUTH, Earl Baker,** a Representative from North Carolina; born in Spencer, Rowan County, N.C., February 7, 1916; graduated from Central High School, Charlotte, N.C., 1934; A.B., University of North Carolina, 1938, M.A., 1942, Ph.D., education, 1955; teacher and coach, Chapel Hill, N.C., and Charlotte, N.C., 1938-1940; entered the United States Navy as an ensign, resigned as lieutenant; served three terms on the City Council of Salisbury, N.C., 1963-1968; served as mayor pro tempore, June 1967 to November 1968; elected as a Republican to the Ninety-first and to the two succeeding Congresses (January 3, 1969-January 3, 1975); unsuccessful candidate for reelection in 1974 to the Ninety-fourth Congress; appointed Governor of American Samoa by Secretary of the Interior, Rogers C.B. Morton, and served from February 1975 to September 1976; was a resident of Salisbury, N.C.; died August 15, 1989.

**RUTHERFORD, Albert Greig,** a Representative from Pennsylvania; born in Watford, Ontario Province, Canada, January 3, 1879; immigrated to the United States in 1883 with his parents, who settled in Carbondale, Pa.; attended the public schools, Blair Academy, Blairstown, N.J., and Scranton-Lackawanna Business College; was graduated from the law department of the University of Pennsylvania at Philadelphia in 1904; was admitted to the bar October 10, 1904, and commenced practice in Scranton, Pa.; affiliated with the Democratic Party; served as deputy prothonotary of Lackawanna County, Pa., 1907-1914; moved to Honesdale, Wayne County, Pa., in 1918 and continued the practice of law; enlisted in the Pennsylvania National Guard in 1904; served as a lieutenant colonel of the Second Pennsylvania Reserve Militia in 1918; elected as a Republican to the Seventy-fifth, Seventy-sixth, and Seventy-seventh Congresses and served from January 3, 1937, until his death in Washington, D.C., on August 10, 1941; interment in Glen Dyberry Cemetery, Honesdale, Pa.

**RUTHERFORD, J.T.,** a Representative from Texas; born in Hot Springs, Ark., May 30, 1921; moved to Odessa, Tex., in 1934 and attended the public schools; served as an enlisted man in the United States Marine Corps, 1942-1946, with twenty-eight months overseas; awarded the Purple Heart Medal; retired as a major in the United States Marine Corps Reserve; student at San Angelo (Tex.) College, 1946-1947, and Sul Ross State College, Alpine, Tex., 1947-1948; attended Baylor University Law School, Waco, Tex., 1948-1950; partner in an industrial electrical construction firm and owner of an advertising company; served in the Texas State house of representatives, 1948-1952; member of the State senate, 1952-1954; elected as a Democrat to the Eighty-fourth and to the three succeeding Congresses (January 3, 1955-January 3, 1963); unsuccessful candidate for reelection in 1962 to the Eighty-eighth Congress; consultant; is a resident of Odessa, Tex., and Arlington, Va.

**RUTHERFORD, Robert,** a Representative from Virginia; born in Scotland, October 20, 1728; completed preparatory studies and was educated at the Royal College of Edinburgh; immigrated to the United States and settled in Berks County, Tenn., and subsequently moved to Virginia; delegate to the conventions in Richmond and Williamsburg, July and December 1775 and May 1776; served in the Virginia senate 1776-1790; elected to the Third Congress and reelected as a Republican to the Fourth Congresses (March 4, 1793-March 3, 1797); unsuccessful candidate for reelection in 1796 to the Fifth Congress; settled on his estate "Flowing Spring" near Charles Town, Va. (now West Virginia) and resided there until his death in October 1803; interment on "Flowing Spring" estate near Charles Town.

**RUTHERFORD, Samuel,** a Representative from Georgia; born near Culloden, Crawford County, Ga., March 15, 1870; attended the public schools at Culloden and Washington and Lee University, Lexington, Va.; was graduated from the law department of the University of Georgia at Athens in 1894; was admitted to the bar the same year and commenced practice in Forsyth, Monroe County, Ga.; mayor of Forsyth for three consecutive years; member of the State house of representatives in 1896 and 1897; solicitor of the city court of Forsyth 1898-1900; interested in banking 1901-1916; served in the State senate in 1909 and 1910; resumed the practice of law and also engaged in agricultural pursuits; again a member of the State house of representatives 1921-1924; elected as a Democrat to the Sixty-ninth and to the three succeeding Congresses and served from March 4, 1925, until his death in Washington, D.C., on February 4, 1932; chairman, Committee on Election of President, Vice President, and Representatives (Seventy-second Congress); interment in Oakland Cemetery, Forsyth, Ga.

**RUTHERFURD, John,** a Senator from New Jersey; born in New York City on September 20, 1760; graduated from the College of New Jersey (now Princeton University) in 1779; studied law; was admitted to the bar and commenced practice in New York City in 1784; moved to a farm near Allamuchy, Warren County, N.J., in 1787; presidential elector in 1788; member, State general assembly 1788-1789; elected in 1790 to the United States Senate; reelected in 1796 and served from March 4, 1791, to December 5, 1798, when he resigned; president of the Board of Proprietors of East Jersey 1804-1840; appointed by the New York legislature as commissioner to lay out the city of New York north of Fourteenth Street 1807-1811; moved to a large farm on the banks of the Passaic River in 1808, which he called "Edgerston"; appointed by the New Jersey legislature as commissioner to determine the route and cost of a canal to connect the Delaware and Raritan Rivers in 1816; served as a commissioner to determine the boundary lines between the States of New Jersey and New York and New Jersey and Pennsylvania 1826-1833; died at his home, "Edgerston," New Jersey, February 23, 1840; interment in the family vault in the burying ground of Christ Church, Belleville, Essex County, N.J.

**RUTLEDGE, Edward** (brother of John Rutledge and uncle of John Rutledge, Jr.), a Delegate from South Carolina; born in Christ Church Parish, S.C., November 23, 1749; completed preparatory studies; studied law at the Middle Temple in London; returned to South Carolina; was admitted to the bar and commenced practice in 1773; Member of the Continental Congress, 1774-1776; a signer of the Declaration of Independence; was a delegate to the first provincial congress in 1775, and to the second provincial congress, 1775-1776; appointed a member of the first board of war in June 1776; member of the general assembly in 1778; elected a Member of the Continental Congress in 1779 but did not take his seat; captain in the Charleston Battalion of Artillery in the Militia of South

Carolina in the Revolution; taken prisoner when the British captured Charleston May 12, 1780, imprisoned at St. Augustine until July 1781, when he was exchanged; member of the State house of representatives in 1782, 1786, 1788, and 1792; member of the State constitutional convention in 1790 and was author of the act abolishing the law of primogeniture in 1791; was tendered the appointment of Associate Justice of the United States Supreme Court in 1794 by President George Washington, but did not accept; elected Governor of South Carolina by the Legislature, and served from December 6, 1798 until his death in Charleston, S.C., January 23, 1800; interment in St. Philip's Churchyard.

Bibliography: *DAB*.

RUTLEDGE, John (brother of Edward Rutledge and father of John Rutledge, Jr.), a Delegate from South Carolina; born in Christ Church Parish, S.C., in 1739; pursued classical studies; studied law in Charleston and later at the Middle Temple in London; returned to Charleston, S.C., and commenced practice in 1761; elected to the provincial assembly in 1762; attorney general pro tempore in 1764 and 1765; delegate to the Stamp Act Congress at New York City in 1765; continued the practice of law; Member of the Continental Congress, 1774-1775; served as President and commander in chief of South Carolina, 1776-1778, and as Governor, 1779-1782; again a Member of the Continental Congress in 1782 and 1783; elected one of the State chancellors in 1784; delegate to the Constitutional Convention in 1787; member of the South Carolina ratification convention in 1788; received the electoral vote of South Carolina for Vice President in 1789; nominated on September 24, 1789 by President George Washington to be an Associate Justice of the United States Supreme Court, confirmed by the Senate on September 26, 1789, and served until his resignation in February 1791; elected chief justice of South Carolina in 1790 and served until 1795, when he resigned; nominated on July 1, 1795 by President Washington to be Chief Justice of the United States and presided at the August term, but the Senate, on December 15, 1795, refused to confirm him; died in Charleston, S.C., June 21, 1800; interment in St. Michael's Churchyard.

Bibliography: *DAB*; Barry, Richard H. *Mr. Rutledge of South Carolina*. 1942. Reprint. Freeport, N.Y.: Books for Libraries Press, 1971.

RUTLEDGE, John, Jr. (son of John Rutledge and nephew of Edward Rutledge), a Representative from South Carolina; born in Charleston, S.C., in 1766; received private instruction and also attended school in Charleston and Philadelphia; studied law with his father; was admitted to the bar about 1787 and practiced in Charleston, S.C.; also engaged as a planter; member of the State house of representatives 1788-1794 and in 1811; unsuccessful candidate for election in 1794 to the Fourth Congress; elected as a Federalist to the Fifth, Sixth, and Seventh Congresses (March 4, 1797-March 3, 1803); unsuccessful candidate for election to the Thirteenth Congress; commanded a company of the Twenty-eighth Regiment, South Carolina Militia, in 1799; promoted to major and in 1804 succeeded to the command of the regiment and served as its commander in the War of 1812; commanded the Seventh Brigade from 1816 until his death; died in Philadelphia, Pa., September 1, 1819.

Bibliography: Furlong, Patrick J. "John Rutledge, Jr., and the Election of a Speaker of the House in 1799." *William and Mary Quarterly* 3rd ser., 24 (July 1967): 432-36; Ratzlaff, Robert K. "John Rutledge, Jr., South Carolina Federalist, 1766-1819." Ph.D. dissertation, University of Kansas, 1975.

RYALL, Daniel Bailey, a Representative from New Jersey; born in Trenton, N.J., January 30, 1798; completed preparatory studies at Trenton, N.J.; attended Trenton Academy; studied law; was admitted to the bar in 1820 and commenced practice in Freehold, N.J.; member of the State general assembly 1831 and 1833-1835 and

served as speaker 1833-1835; elected as a Democrat to the Twenty-sixth Congress (March 4, 1839-March 3, 1841); resumed the practice of law; died in Freehold, Monmouth County, N.J., December 17, 1864; interment in Maplewood Cemetery.

RYAN, Elmer James, a Representative from Minnesota; born in Rosemount, Dakota County, Minn., May 26, 1907; attended the public schools; was graduated from the law department of the University of Minnesota at Minneapolis in 1929; was admitted to the bar the same year and commenced practice in South St. Paul, Minn.; city attorney of South St. Paul 1933-1934; delegate to the Democratic National Conventions in 1936 and 1940; elected as a Democrat to the Seventy-fourth, Seventy-fifth, and Seventy-sixth Congresses (January 3, 1935-January 3, 1941); unsuccessful candidate for reelection in 1940 to the Seventy-seventh Congress; resumed the practice of law; entered active duty in the United States Army on June 23, 1942, as a lieutenant in the Selective Service; was promoted to captain and transferred to the Judge Advocate General's department, later promoted to major and was discharged on October 1, 1945; again resumed the practice of law in South St. Paul, Minn.; died in an automobile accident on Highway 35, five miles north of Somerset, Wis., February 1, 1958; interment in Rosemount Cemetery, Rosemount, Minn.

RYAN, Harold Martin, a Representative from Michigan; born in Detroit, Wayne County, Mich., February 6, 1911; graduated from St. Joseph's High School in 1929; attended Ferris Institute from 1929 to 1930, and Michigan State College from 1930 to 1932; J.D., University of Detroit Law School, 1935; admitted to the bar in 1935 and commenced the practice of law in Detroit; assistant prosecuting attorney of Wayne County in 1944 and 1945; served in the Michigan State senate, 1948-1962, and was minority leader from 1956 to 1962; delegate to State conventions every two years, 1940-1970; delegate to the Democratic National Conventions of 1952, 1956, 1960 and 1964; elected as a Democrat to the Eighty-seventh Congress, February 13, 1962, by special election to fill the vacancy caused by the death of Louis C. Rabaut; reelected to the Eighty-eighth Congress, and served from February 13, 1962 until January 3, 1965; was an unsuccessful candidate for renomination in 1964 to the Eighty-ninth Congress; resumed the practice of law; circuit court judge, Wayne County, Mich., 1976-1985; visiting judge, circuit court of Michigan, 1985 to present; is a resident of St. Clair Shores, Mich.

RYAN, James Wilfrid, a Representative from Pennsylvania; born in Norwegian Township, Schuylkill County, Pa., October 16, 1858; moved to Mahanoy City with his parents, where he attended the public schools; was graduated from the high school of Frackville, Pa.; engaged in teaching in the public schools; studied law; was admitted to the bar in 1884 and commenced practice in Pottsville, Pa.; elected district attorney in 1892 and served until January 1896; elected as a Democrat to the Fifty-sixth Congress (March 4, 1899-March 3, 1901); resumed the practice of law; died in Mahanoy City, Pa., on February 26, 1907; interment in the Holy Rosary Cemetery, Frackville, Pa.

RYAN, Leo Joseph, a Representative from California; born in Lincoln, Lancaster County, Nebr., May 5, 1925; attended schools in Illinois, New York, Florida, Massachusetts, and Wisconsin; A.B., Creighton University, Omaha, Nebr., 1949; M.S., same university, 1951; served in the United States Navy in ComSubPac, Pacific Theater, 1943-1946; teacher and school administrator; city councilman, 1956-1962; served as mayor, South San Francisco, Calif., 1962; member, California State assembly, 1962-1972; delegate to California State Democratic conventions, 1956-1972; delegate to Democratic National Conventions, 1964-1968; elected as a Democrat to the Ninety-third and to the three succeeding Congresses and served from January 3, 1973, until his death November 18, 1978, in an ambush at the airstrip of Port Kaituma, Guyana; interment in Golden Gate National Cemetery, San Bruno, Calif.

**RYAN, Thomas,** a Representative from Kansas; born in Oxford, Chenango County, N.Y., November 25, 1837; moved with his parents to Bradford County, Pa.; attended Dickson Seminary in Williamsport, Pa.; studied law; was admitted to the bar in 1861; during the Civil War served in the Union Army, 1862-1864; moved to Topeka, Kans., in 1865; prosecuting attorney of Shawnee County, 1865-1873; assistant United States attorney for Kansas, 1873-1877; elected as a Republican to the Forty-fifth and to the six succeeding Congresses, and served from March 4, 1877 to April 4, 1889, when he resigned to accept a diplomatic post; appointed Minister to Mexico on March 30, 1889 and served until May 1893; appointed First Assistant Secretary of the Interior by President William McKinley in 1897, reappointed by President Theodore Roosevelt, and served in that capacity until 1907, when he was sent to Muskogee, Okla., as the personal resident representative of the Secretary of the Interior; died in Muskogee, Okla., April 5, 1914; interment in Topeka Cemetery, Topeka, Kans.

**RYAN, Thomas Jefferson,** a Representative from New York; born in New York City June 17, 1890; attended the public schools and the College of the City of New York; was graduated from the scientific school of Fordham University, New York City, in 1908 and from the law department of that institution in 1911; was admitted to the bar in 1912 and commenced practice in New York City; was wounded while serving as an aviator in France during the First World War; elected as a Republican to the Sixty-seventh Congress (March 4, 1921-March 3, 1923); unsuccessful candidate for reelection in 1922 to the Sixty-eighth Congress; delegate to the State convention in 1922; resumed the practice of law; delegate to the Republican National Convention in 1924; special deputy attorney general of New York in 1925; served as counsel to the Alien Property Custodian 1925-1930; affiliated with the Democratic Party in 1926; resumed the practice of law and was a special deputy attorney of New York; retired in 1950 to Coral Gables, Fla.; died in Miami, Fla., November 10, 1968; interment in Calvary Cemetery, Long Island City, N.Y.

**RYAN, William,** a Representative from New York; born in Tipperary, Ireland, March 8, 1840; immigrated to the United States with his parents, who settled in Stanwich, Conn., in 1844; attended the district schools; in the spring of 1859 went to the Rocky Mountains and engaged in prospecting, mining, and also in campaigns against the Indians until 1861, when he returned East and settled in Port Chester, Westchester County, N.Y.; engaged in agricultural pursuits and teaching and later in mercantile pursuits; supervisor of the town of Rye 1883-1885; member of the State assembly in 1891 and 1892; elected as a Democrat to the Fifty-third Congress (March 4, 1893-March 3, 1895); unsuccessful candidate for reelection in 1894 to the Fifty-fourth Congress; resumed business as a merchant in Port Chester, N.Y.; president of the Port Chester Savings Bank and president of the village of Port Chester in 1912; died in Crescent City, Fla., February 18, 1925; interment in St. Mary's Cemetery, Greenwich, Conn.

**RYAN, William Fitts,** a Representative from New York; born in Albion, Orleans County, N.Y., June 28, 1922; attended the Albion schools; graduated from Princeton University in 1947 and from Columbia Law School in 1949; was admitted to the bar and commenced the practice of law in New York City in 1949; assistant district attorney, New York County, 1950-1957 and 1957-1961; served in the United States Army in the Thirty-second Infantry Division as an artillery officer with the rank of first lieutenant from 1943 to 1946, in the South Pacific; delegate, Democratic National Convention, 1968; elected as a Democrat to the Eighty-seventh Congress; reelected to the five succeeding Congresses and served from January 3, 1961, until his death in New York City, September 17, 1972; interment in St. Thomas Church Cemetery, Croom, Md.

**RYAN, William Henry,** a Representative from New York; born in Hopkinton, Middlesex County, Mass., May 10, 1860; moved to Buffalo, N.Y., with his parents in 1866; attended the grade and high schools; engaged in the retail shoe business and later in the general insurance and bonding business; elected to the board of supervisors of Erie County in 1894; reelected in 1897, and served as chairman in 1898; elected as a Democrat to the Fifty-sixth and to the four succeeding Congresses (March 4, 1899-March 3, 1909); unsuccessful candidate for renomination in 1908; delegate to the Democratic National Conventions in 1904 and 1924; resumed the insurance and bonding business in Buffalo, N.Y., and also engaged in banking; member of the grade crossing and terminal commission 1919-1939; member of the Allegany State Park Commission 1930-1939; died in Buffalo, N.Y., November 18, 1939; interment in Mount Calvary Cemetery, at Pine Hill, near Buffalo, N.Y.

**RYON, John Walker,** a Representative from Pennsylvania; born in Elkland, Tioga County, Pa., March 4, 1825; attended the common schools, Millville Academy, Orleans County, N.Y., and Wellsboro Academy, Wellsboro, Pa.; studied law; was admitted to the bar in 1847 and commenced practice in Lawrenceville, Pa.; district attorney of Tioga County, 1850-1856; during the Civil War assisted in the organization of Company A of the famous Bucktail Regiment; appointed by Governor Andrew G. Curtin as paymaster with the rank of major in the reserve corps; moved to Pottsville, Pa., and resumed the practice of law; elected as a Democrat to the Forty-sixth Congress (March 4, 1879-March 3, 1881); president of the Pennsylvania National Bank for several years; also interested in various other business enterprises; died in Pottsville, Schuylkill County, Pa., March 12, 1901; interment in St. Patrick's (No. 3) Cemetery.

**RYTER, Joseph Francis,** a Representative from Connecticut; born in Hartford, Conn., February 4, 1914; attended the parochial schools and St. Thomas Seminary, Bloomfield, Conn.; was graduated from Trinity College, Hartford, Conn., in 1935 and from Hartford (Conn.) College of Law in 1938; was admitted to the bar in 1938 and commenced practice in Hartford, Conn.; assistant clerk of Hartford Police Court 1939-1941, and of Hartford City Court 1941-1943; delegate to the Democratic National Convention in 1940; president of Pulaski Federation of Democratic Clubs of Connecticut 1939-1942; elected as a Democrat to the Seventy-ninth Congress (January 3, 1945-January 3, 1947); was an unsuccessful candidate for reelection in 1946 to the Eightieth Congress; resumed the practice of his profession; resided in West Hartford, Conn., where he died February 5, 1978; interment in Mount Saint Benedict Cemetery, Bloomfield, Conn.

# S

**SABATH, Adolph Joachim,** a Representative from Illinois; born in Zabori, Czechoslovakia, April 4, 1866; attended the schools of his native town; immigrated to the United States in 1881 and settled in Chicago, Ill.; was graduated from the Chicago College of Law in 1891; was admitted to the bar in 1892 and commenced practice in Chicago, Ill.; ward committeeman and district leader in Chicago from 1892 until 1944; appointed justice of the peace for the city of Chicago in 1895; police magistrate, 1897-1906; member of the central and executive committees of the Democratic Party from 1909 to 1920; delegate to all the Democratic State conventions, 1890-1952; delegate to all Democratic National Conventions, 1896-1944; elected as a Democrat to the Sixtieth and to the twenty-three succeeding Congresses, but died before the convening of the Eighty-third Congress; served from March 4, 1907 until his death in Bethesda, Md., November 6, 1952; chairman, Committee on Alcohol Liquor Traffic (Sixty-third through Sixty-fifth Congresses), Committee on Rules (Seventy-sixth through Seventy-ninth and Eighty-first and Eighty-second Congresses); interment in Forest Home Cemetery, Forest Park, Ill.

**Bibliography:** *DAB*; Boxerman, Burton A. "Adolph Joachim Sabath in Congress: The Early Years, 1907-1932." *Journal of the Illinois State Historical Society* 66 (Autumn 1973): 327-40; Boxerman, Burton A. "Adolph Joachim Sabath in Congress: The Roosevelt and Truman Years." *Journal of the Illinois State Historical Society* 66 (Winter 1973): 428-43.

**SABIN, Alvah,** a Representative from Vermont; born in Georgia, Franklin County, Vt., October 23, 1793; attended the common schools and Burlington College; member of the Vermont State militia and served during the War of 1812; studied theology in Philadelphia; was graduated from Columbian College (now George Washington University), Washington, D.C., in 1821; was ordained a minister and preached at Cambridge, Westfield, and Underhill until 1825, when he returned to Georgia, Vt.; was pastor of the Georgia Baptist Church over forty years; member of the Vermont State house of representatives, 1826-1835, 1838-1840, 1847-1849, 1851, 1861, and 1862; served in the Vermont State senate in 1841, 1843, and 1845; secretary of state of Vermont in 1841; elected as a Whig to the Thirty-third and Thirty-fourth Congresses (March 4, 1853-March 3, 1857); chairman, Committee on Revisal and Unfinished Business (Thirty-fourth Congress); was not a candidate for renomination in 1856 to the Thirty-fifth Congress; delegate to the first Anti-Slavery National Convention; county commissioner of Franklin County in 1861 and 1862; moved to Sycamore, De Kalb County, Ill., in 1867 and continued his ministerial duties; died in Sycamore, Ill., January 22, 1885; interment in Georgia Plain Cemetery, Georgia Plain, Vt.

**SABIN, Dwight May,** a Senator from Minnesota; born near Marseilles, La Salle County, Ill., April 25, 1843; moved to Connecticut with his parents in 1857; attended the country schools and Phillips Academy, Andover, Mass.; served in the Union Army during the Civil War; employed as a clerk in Washington, D.C.; returned to Connecticut in 1864 and engaged in agricultural pursuits and also the lumber business; moved to Stillwater, Minn., in 1868; engaged in lumbering and the general manufacture of railroad cars and agricultural machinery; member, Minnesota State senate 1872-1875; served in the State house of representatives in 1878 and 1881; chairman of the Republican National Committee 1883-1884; elected as a Republican to the United States Senate and served from March 4, 1883, to March 3, 1889; unsuccessful candidate for renomination in 1886; chairman, Committee to Examine Branches of the Civil Service (Forty-ninth Congress), Committee on Railroads (Fiftieth Congress); engaged in the coal, lumber, and manufacturing business; died in Chicago, Ill., on December 22, 1902; interment in Fairview Cemetery, Stillwater, Washington County, Minn.

**SABINE, Lorenzo,** a Representative from Massachusetts; born in New Concord (now Lisbon), N.H., February 28, 1803; moved to Boston, Mass., with his parents in 1811 and to Hampden, Maine, in 1814; completed preparatory studies; at the age of eighteen moved to Eastport, Maine, and became employed as a clerk and afterward engaged in mercantile pursuits; editor of the Eastport Sentinel; founder of the Eastport Lyceum; incorporator of Eastport Academy and Eastport Athenaeum; member of the Maine State house of representatives in 1833 and 1834; deputy collector of customs at Eastport, 1841-1843; moved to Framingham, Mass., in 1848, having been appointed trial justice; elected as a Whig to the Thirty-second Congress to fill the vacancy caused by the death of Benjamin Thompson and served from December 13, 1852, to March 3, 1853; was not a candidate for renomination in 1852 to the Thirty-third Congress; moved to Roxbury, Mass., having been appointed secretary of the Boston Board of Trade; also served as special agent of the United States Treasury Department; died in Roxbury, Mass., April 14, 1877; interment in Hillside Cemetery, Eastport, Washington County, Maine.

**Bibliography:** *DAB*.

**SABO, Martin Olav,** a Representative from Minnesota; born in Crosby, Divide County, N.Dak., February 28, 1938; attended the Alkabo, N.Dak. public schools and graduated from Alkabo High School in 1955; B.A., Augsburg College, Minneapolis, Minn., 1959; graduate studies, University of Minnesota, Minneapolis, 1960; served in the Minnesota State house of representatives, 1960-1978; served as house minority leader, 1969-1972; speaker of the house, 1973-1978; Presidential appointee on the National Advisory Commission on Intergovernmental Relations; president, National Conference of State Legislatures; president, National Legislative Conference; elected as a Democrat to the Ninety-sixth and to the eight succeeding Congresses (January 3, 1979-January 3, 1997); chairman, Committee on the Budget (One Hundred Third Congress); is a resident of Minneapolis, Minn.

**SACKETT, Frederic Mosley,** a Senator from Kentucky; born in Providence, R.I., December 17, 1868; attended the public schools; graduated from Brown University at Providence, R.I. in 1890 and from the law department of Harvard University in 1893; admitted to the bar in 1893 and commenced practice in Columbus, Ohio, the same year; moved to Cincinnati, Ohio, in 1897, to Louisville, Ky., in 1898, and continued the practice of his profession until 1907; was also interested in the mining of coal and the manufacture of cement; president of the Louisville Gas Co. and of the Louisville Lighting Co. 1907-1912; member of the Board of Trade of Louisville, serving as president in 1917, 1922, and 1923; director of the Louisville Branch of the Federal Reserve Bank 1917-1924; during the First World War served from 1917 to 1919 as federal food administrator for Kentucky; member of the Kentucky Board of Charities and Corrections 1919-1924; elected as a Republican to the United States Senate in 1924, and served from March 4, 1925 until his resignation on January 9, 1930 to accept a diplomatic position; appointed Ambassador to Germany by President Herbert Hoover, and served from January 1930 to March 1933, when he resigned; chairman, Committee on Expenditures in Executive Departments (Seventieth and Seventy-first Congresses); resumed his former business activities; died in Baltimore, Md., on May 18, 1941; interment in Cave Hill Cemetery, Louisville, Ky.

**Bibliography:** Burke, Bernard. "Senator and Diplomat: The Public Career of Frederic M. Sackett." *Filson Club History Quarterly* 61 (April 1987): 185-216.

**SACKETT, William Augustus,** a Representative from New York; born in Aurelius, near Auburn, N.Y., November 18, 1811; attended private schools and Aurora Academy; moved to Seneca Falls, Seneca County, N.Y., in 1831; studied law; was admitted to the bar in 1834 and commenced practice at Seneca Falls; elected as a Whig to the Thirty-first and Thirty-second Congresses (March 4, 1849-March 3, 1853); resumed the practice of law at Seneca Falls, N.Y.; moved to Saratoga Springs in 1857; register in bankruptcy during the term of the 1867 bankruptcy law; died at Saratoga Springs, N.Y., September 6, 1895; interment in Greenridge Cemetery.

**SACKS, Leon,** a Representative from Pennsylvania; born in Philadelphia, Pa., October 7, 1902; attended the public schools; graduated from the Wharton School of the University of Pennsylvania at Philadelphia in 1923, and from the law department of the University of Pennsylvania in 1926; admitted to the bar in 1926 and commenced the practice of law in Philadelphia, Pa.; appointed deputy attorney general of Pennsylvania in February 1935 and served until January 1937; elected as a member of the Pennsylvania Democratic committee in 1936 and served until 1942; elected as a Democrat to the Seventy-fifth and to the two succeeding Congresses (January 3, 1937-January 3, 1943); was an unsuccessful candidate for reelection in 1942 to the Seventy-eighth Congress; served at Army Air Forces Eastern Flying Training Command, with the rank of lieutenant colonel, from January 4, 1943, to January 10, 1946; resumed the practice of his profession; member of Pennsylvania Veterans Commission 1951-1969; chairman, registration commission of Philadelphia 1952-1965; member of Military Reservations Commission 1957-1967; died in Philadelphia, Pa., March 11, 1972; interment in Shalom Memorial Park.

**SADLAK, Antoni Nicholas,** a Representative from Connecticut; born in Rockville, Tolland County, Conn., June 13, 1908; attended the parochial school; was graduated from George Sykes Manual Training and High School in 1926, and from the Georgetown University School of Law, Washington, D.C., in 1931; special inspector for the Department of Justice from July 1941 to December 1942; assistant secretary-treasurer of the Farmers' Production Credit Association, Hartford, Conn., 1944-1946; secretary to Representative Boleslaus J. Monkiewicz of Connecticut in 1939, 1940, 1943, and 1944; served in the United States Naval Reserve in New Guinea, the Philippines, and China from March 1944 to April 1946; educational supervisor in the Connecticut Department of Education from July 1, 1946, to September 15, 1946; elected as a Republican to the Eightieth and to the five succeeding Congresses (January 3, 1947-January 3, 1959); unsuccessful candidate for reelection in 1958 to the Eighty-sixth Congress; regional assistant manager, Veterans' Administration, Hartford, Conn., from March 30, 1959, to May 2, 1960; engaged in lecturing and legislative consultation; elected judge of probate for the Ellington-Vernon District in 1966 and served until his death in Rockville, Conn., October 18, 1969; interment in St. Bernard's Cemetery.

**SADLER, Thomas William,** a Representative from Alabama; born near Russellville, Franklin County, Ala., April 17, 1831; moved with his parents to Jefferson County, Ala., in 1833; pursued an academic course; moved to Autauga County, Ala., in 1855 and engaged in mercantile pursuits; during the Civil War volunteered and served in the division of the Confederate Army commanded by General Joseph Wheeler; engaged in agricultural pursuits; studied law; was admitted to the bar in 1867 and commenced practice in Prattville, Ala.; served as Autauga County superintendent of education from 1875 until 1884; elected as a Democrat to the Forty-ninth Congress (March 4, 1885-March 3, 1887); unsuccessful candidate for renomination in 1886 to the Fiftieth Congress; resumed the practice of law; died in Prattville, Autauga County, Ala., October 29, 1896; interment in Oak Hill Cemetery.

**SADOWSKI, George Gregory,** a Representative from Michigan; born in Detroit, Mich., March 12, 1903; attended the Ferry School, Detroit, Mich., and high school in Foley, Ala.; was graduated from Northeastern High School, Detroit, Mich., in 1920 and from the law department of the University of Detroit in 1924; was admitted to the bar in 1926 and commenced practice in Detroit; also interested in the real estate and building businesses; member of the Michigan State senate in 1931 and 1932; member of the State Democratic central committee, 1930-1936; delegate to the Democratic National Conventions of 1932, 1936, 1940, 1944, and 1948; elected as a Democrat to the Seventy-third and to the two succeeding Congresses (March 4, 1933-January 3, 1939); unsuccessful candidate for renomination in 1938 to the Seventy-sixth Congress; elected to the Seventy-eighth and to the three succeeding Congresses (January 3, 1943-January 3, 1951); unsuccessful candidate for renomination in 1950 to the Eighty-second Congress; owner of two golf clubs in Michigan; died in Utica, Mich., on October 9, 1961; interment in Mount Olivet Cemetery, Detroit, Mich.

**SAGE, Ebenezer,** a Representative from New York; born in Chatham (now Portland), Conn., August 16, 1755; received his early education from a private tutor and was graduated from Yale College in 1778; studied medicine; commenced practice in Easthampton, Suffolk County, N.Y., in 1784; moved to Sag Harbor, N.Y., about 1801; elected as a Republican to the Eleventh, Twelfth, and Thirteenth Congresses (March 4, 1809-March 3, 1815); was not a candidate for reelection; credentials of his election to the Sixteenth Congress were presented but he did not qualify, and on January 14, 1820, James Guyon, Jr., successfully contested his election; resumed the practice of medicine at Sag Harbor, N.Y.; delegate to the State constitutional convention of 1821; died at Sag Harbor, Suffolk County, N.Y., January 20, 1834; interment in the Old Burying Ground; reinterment in Oakland Cemetery.

**Bibliography:** Harmond, Richard. "Ebenezer Sage of Sag Harbor: An Old Republican in Young America, 1812-1834." *New-York Historical Society Quarterly* 57 (October 1973): 309-25; Harmond, Richard J. "A Reluctant War Hawk: Ebenezer Sage of Sag Harbor, Long Island, and the Coming of the War of 1812." *Journal of Long Island History* 14 (Fall 1977): 48-53.

**SAGE, Russell,** a Representative from New York; born in Shenandoah, Oneida County, N.Y., August 4, 1816; moved with his parents to Durhamville in 1818; attended the public schools; engaged in mercantile pursuits in Troy, N.Y.; treasurer of Rensselaer County 1844-1851; alderman of Troy 1845-1848; delegate to the Whig National Convention in 1848; elected as a Whig to the Thirty-third and Thirty-fourth Congresses (March 4, 1853-March 3, 1857); was not a candidate for renomination in 1856; moved to New York City in 1863; became president and director of several railroad companies and financial institutions; died in Lawrence, Long Island, N.Y., July 22, 1906; interment in Oakwood Cemetery, Troy, N.Y.

**Bibliography:** *DAB*; Sarnoff, Paul. *Russell Sage: The Money King*. New York: Ivan Obolensky, Inc., 1965.

**SAIKI, Patricia Fukuda,** a Representative from Hawaii; born in Hilo, Hawaii, May 28, 1930; attended public schools; B.S., University of Hawaii, 1952; teacher; member, Hawaii State house of representatives, 1968-1974; member, Hawaii State senate, 1974-1982; elected as a Republican to the One Hundredth and One Hundred First Congresses (January 3, 1987-January 3, 1991); was not a candidate for renomination in 1990 to the House of Representatives, but was an unsuccessful candidate for election to the United States Senate; is a resident of Honolulu, Hawaii.

**SAILLY, Peter,** a Representative from New York; born in Lorraine, France, April 20, 1754; immigrated to the United States in 1783 and settled in Plattsburgh, N.Y.; engaged in mercantile pursuits and as a fur trader; also engaged in the manufacture of potash and in the shipping of lumber; associate justice of the court of common pleas, 1788-1796; commissioner of highways and school commissioner in 1797 and 1798; supervisor of schools in 1799 and 1800; member of the New York State assembly in 1803; judge of Clinton County, 1804-1806; elected as a Republican to the Ninth Congress (March 4, 1805-March 3, 1807); declined to be a candidate for renomination in 1806 to the Tenth Congress; collector of customs at Plattsburgh from 1807 until his death there on March 16, 1826; interment in Riverside Cemetery.

**SALINGER, Pierre Emil George,** a Senator from California; born in San Francisco, Calif., June 14, 1925; attended San Francisco State College during 1942 and 1943; graduated from the University of San Francisco in 1947; employed on the editorial staff of the San Francisco Chronicle, 1942-1943; resigned to enlist in the United States Navy; commanded a subchaser in the Pacific Theater of Operations during the Second World War and was honorably discharged with the rank of lieutenant (junior grade) in 1946; returned to the editorial staff of the San Francisco Chronicle, 1946-1955; lecturer in journalism at Mills College, Oakland, Calif., 1951-1955; west coast editor and contributing editor of Collier's Magazine, 1955-1956; investigator, Senate Select Committee To Investigate Improper Activities in Labor-Management Relations, 1957-1959; joined the staff of Senator John F. Kennedy in 1959 and served as his press officer in the 1960 presidential campaign;

appointed press secretary to President John F. Kennedy on January 20, 1961, and continued in this capacity for President Lyndon B. Johnson until his resignation March 19, 1964, to run for the United States Senate; appointed as a Democrat to the United States Senate to fill the vacancy caused by the death of Clair Engle and served from August 4, 1964, until his resignation December 31, 1964; was an unsuccessful candidate in 1964 for election to the full term; corporate executive; a correspondent for the French news magazine, L'Express; chief foreign correspondent and senior editor, ABC News, Paris, France; vice chairman, Burson Marsteller, Washington, D.C.

**Bibliography:** Salinger, Pierre. *P.S.: A Memoir.* New York: St. Martin's Press, 1995.

**SALMON, Joshua S.,** a Representative from New Jersey; born at Mount Olive, Morris County, N.J., February 2, 1846; at an early age moved with his parents to the village of Bartley; attended the district school; taught school for two years; completed an academic course at the Charlotteville (N.Y.) Seminary and at Schooley's Mountain Seminary, New Jersey, where he afterward became an instructor; was graduated from the Albany (N.Y.) Law School in 1873; was admitted to the New York bar in 1873, to the New Jersey bar in 1875, and commenced practice in Jersey City, N.J.; moved to Boonton, Morris County, and practiced there and in Morristown; held several county offices; member of the State house of assembly in 1877 and 1878; prosecuting attorney of Morris County 1893-1898; delegate to the Democratic National Convention in 1900; elected as a Democrat to the Fifty-sixth and Fifty-seventh Congresses and served from March 4, 1899, until his death in Boonton, N.J., May 6, 1902; interment in Greenwood Cemetery.

**SALMON, Matthew James,** a Representative from Arizona; born in Salt Lake City, Utah, January 21, 1958; graduated from Mesa (Ariz.) High School, 1976; B.A., Arizona State University, Tempe, 1981; M.P.A., Brigham Young University, 1986; risk management office then business and community affairs manager, US West Communications; member, Arizona State senate, 1991-1994; elected as a Republican to the One Hundred Fourth Congress (January 3, 1995-January 3, 1997); is a resident of Mesa, Ariz.

**SALMON, William Charles,** a Representative from Tennessee; born near Paris, Henry County, Tenn., on April 3, 1868; attended the public schools, Edgewood Normal School, Dickson College, and Valparaiso University at Valparaiso, Ind.; was graduated in law from Cumberland University, Lebanon, Tenn., in 1897; was admitted to the bar the same year and commenced practice in Columbia, Maury County, Tenn.; taught in public and private schools for six years and also engaged in agricultural pursuits; served as special circuit judge of the eleventh judicial circuit of Tennessee in 1908; president of the Columbia Board of Education 1912-1922; commanded an Artillery battery during the First World War; elected as a Democrat to the Sixty-eighth Congress (March 4, 1923-March 3, 1925); died in Washington, D.C., on May 13, 1925; interment in Rose Hill Cemetery, Columbia, Tenn.

**SALTONSTALL, Leverett** (great-grandfather of Leverett Saltonstall [1892-1979]); a Representative from Massachusetts; born in Haverhill, Mass., June 13, 1783; pursued classical studies; attended Phillips Exeter Academy, Exeter, N.H., and was graduated from Harvard University in 1802; studied law; was admitted to the bar and commenced practice in Salem in 1805; unsuccessful candidate for election in 1820 to the Seventeenth Congress; delegate to the Massachusetts constitutional convention in 1820; member of the Massachusetts house of representatives in 1813, 1814, 1816, 1822, 1829, and 1834; served in the Massachusetts senate, 1817-1819, 1831, and 1832, and was its president in 1831 and 1832; first mayor of Salem, Mass., 1836-1838; elected as a Whig to the Twenty-fifth Congress to fill the vacancy caused by the resignation of Stephen C. Phillips; reelected to the two succeeding Congresses, and served from December 5, 1838 to March 3, 1843; chairman, Committee on Expenditures in the Department of the Navy (Twenty-sixth Congress), Committee on Manufactures (Twenty-seventh Congress); unsuccessful candidate for reelection in 1842 to the Twenty-eighth Congress; again a member of the Massachusetts house of representatives in 1844; overseer of Harvard University from 1835 until 1845; died in Salem, Essex County, Mass., May 8, 1845; interment in Harmony Grove Cemetery.

**Bibliography:** Saltonstall, Leverett. *The Papers of Leverett Saltonstall.* Boston: Massachusetts Historical Society, 1978.

**SALTONSTALL, Leverett** (great-grandson of Leverett Saltonstall [1783-1845]), a Senator from Massachusetts; born in Chestnut Hill, Middlesex County, Mass., September 1, 1892; attended the public schools and Noble and Greenough School, Dedham, Mass.; graduated from Harvard University in 1914 and from its law school in 1917; during the First World War served in the United States Army as a first lieutenant, 1917-1919; was admitted to the bar in 1919, and commenced practice in Boston, Mass.; member of the board of aldermen of Newton, Mass., 1920-1922; assistant district attorney of Middlesex County, Mass., 1921-1922; member, Massachusetts house of representatives, 1923-1936, serving as speaker from 1929 until 1936; unsuccessful candidate for lieutenant governor of Massachusetts in 1936; elected Governor of Massachusetts in 1938, reelected in 1940 and 1942, and served from January 5, 1939 to January 3, 1945; chairman of the National Governors' Conference in 1944; elected as a Republican to the United States Senate, November 7, 1944, to fill the vacancy caused by the resignation of Henry Cabot Lodge, Jr. in the term ending January 3, 1949, but did not assume office until January 4, 1945, after completion of his term as Governor; reelected in 1948, 1954, and again in 1960, and served from January 4, 1945 to January 3, 1967; was not a candidate for reelection in 1966; Republican whip (Eighty-first through Eighty-fourth Congresses); chairman, Committee on Armed Services (Eighty-third Congress), Republican Conference (Eighty-fifth through Eighty-ninth Congresses); trustee and director of several mutual investment funds and charities; resided in Dover, Mass., where he died on June 17, 1979; interment in Harmony Grove Cemetery, Salem, Mass.

**Bibliography:** *DAB*; Saltonstall, Leverett. *Salty: Recollections of a Yankee in Politics.* Boston: The Boston Globe, 1976.

**SAMFORD, William James,** a Representative from Alabama; born in Greenville, Meriwether County, Ga., September 16, 1844; moved in early childhood with his parents to Chambers County, Ala.; attended a private school in Auburn, Ala., and the University of Georgia at Athens in 1860; enlisted in the Confederate Army in 1862 as a private in the Forty-sixth Alabama Regiment; promoted to first lieutenant and was in command of a company at the close of the war; studied law; was admitted to the bar in 1867 and commenced practice in Opelika, Lee County, Ala., in 1867; delegate to the Alabama State constitutional convention in 1875; elected as a Democrat to the Forty-sixth Congress (March 4, 1879-March 3, 1881); was not a candidate for renomination in 1880 to the Forty-seventh Congress; again resumed the practice of his profession; member of the Alabama State house of representatives in 1882; served in the Alabama State senate, 1884-1886, and in 1892, and was its president in 1886; president of the board of trustees of the University of Alabama; elected Governor of Alabama in 1900, and served from December 26, 1900 until his death in Tuscaloosa, Ala., June 11, 1901; interment in Rosemere Cemetery, Opelika, Ala.

**SAMMONS, Thomas** (grandfather of John Henry Starin), a Representative from New York; born in Shamenkop, Ulster County, N.Y., October 1, 1762; attended the rural schools; served as an officer in the Revolutionary War; engaged in agricultural pursuits; delegate to the State constitutional convention in 1801; member of the council of appointment; served as lieutenant, captain, and major in the State militia; elected as a Republican to the Eighth and Ninth

Congresses (March 4, 1803-March 3, 1807); unsuccessful Democratic candidate for reelection; elected to the Eleventh and Twelfth Congresses (March 4, 1809-March 3, 1813); resumed agricultural pursuits; died on the Sammons homestead, in Montgomery County, near Johnstown, N.Y., November 20, 1838; interment on the homestead in the Simeon Sammons Cemetery.

**SAMPLE, Samuel Caldwell,** a Representative from Indiana; born in Elkton, Cecil County, Md., on August 15, 1796; attended the rural school; learned the trade of carpenter and assisted his father, who was a contractor; moved with his father's family to Connersville, Ind., about 1823; studied law; was admitted to the bar in 1833 and commenced practice in South Bend, St. Joseph County, Ind.; elected prosecuting attorney in 1834; elected judge of the ninth judicial circuit in 1836 and served until 1843, when he resigned; was the first president of the First National Bank of South Bend; elected as a Whig to the Twenty-eighth Congress (March 4, 1843-March 3, 1845); unsuccessful candidate for reelection in 1844 to the Twenty-ninth Congress; resumed the practice of his profession in South Bend, Ind., and died there December 2, 1855; interment in the City Cemetery.

**SAMPSON, Ezekiel Silas,** a Representative from Iowa; born in Huron County, Ohio, December 6, 1831; moved to Keokuk County, Iowa, in 1843; attended the public schools, Howe's Academy in Mount Pleasant, Iowa, and Knox College, Illinois; studied law; was admitted to the bar in 1856 and commenced practice in Sigourney, Keokuk County, Iowa; prosecuting attorney 1856-1858; enlisted in the Union Army as captain in the Fifth Regiment, Iowa Volunteer Infantry, in 1861 and was lieutenant colonel of the same regiment when mustered out in 1864; returned to the practice of law in Sigourney, Iowa; member of the State senate in 1866; judge of the sixth district of Iowa from January 1867 to January 1875; elected as a Republican to the Forty-fourth and Forty-fifth Congresses (March 4, 1875-March 3, 1879); unsuccessful candidate for reelection in 1878 to the Forty-sixth Congress; resumed the practice of his profession; died in Sigourney, Keokuk County, Iowa, October 7, 1892; interment in West Cemetery.

**SAMPSON, Zabdiel,** a Representative from Massachusetts; born in Plympton, Mass., August 22, 1781; pursued classical studies and was graduated from Brown University, Providence, R.I., in 1803; studied law; was admitted to the bar in 1806 and commenced practice in Plymouth; elected as a Republican to the Fifteenth and Sixteenth Congresses and served from March 4, 1817, to July 26, 1820, when he resigned; appointed collector of customs at Plymouth, Mass., July 26, 1820, and served until his death there July 19, 1828; interment in Burial Hill Cemetery.

**SAMUEL, Edmund William,** a Representative from Pennsylvania; born in Blaenavon, Wales, on November 27, 1857; immigrated to the United States with his parents, who settled in Ashland, Schuylkill County, Pa., in 1859; attended the public schools; engaged in coal mining; learned the drug business and began the study of medicine; was graduated from the Jefferson Medical College at Philadelphia March 13, 1880, and commenced practice in Mount Carmel, Pa.; school director of Mount Carmel 1890-1894; elected as a Republican to the Fifty-ninth Congress (March 4, 1905-March 3, 1907); unsuccessful candidate for reelection in 1906 to the Sixtieth Congress and for election in 1908 to the Sixty-first Congress; resumed the practice of medicine in Mount Carmel, Pa.; president and general manager of the Shamokin-Mount Carmel Transit Co. 1908-1924; retired in 1925 and moved to Brooklyn, N.Y.; died in Mount Carmel, Pa., on March 7, 1930; interment in Mount Carmel Cemetery.

**SAMUELS, Green Berry** (cousin of Isaac Samuels Pennybacker), a Representative from Virginia; born near Red Banks, Shenandoah County, Va., February 1, 1806; pursued classical studies; studied law; admitted to the Pennsylvania bar in 1827 and commenced the practice of law; resided at Woodstock, Va.; elected as a Democrat to the Twenty-sixth Congress (March 4, 1839-March 3, 1841); resumed the practice of law; member of the Virginia constitutional convention in 1850 and 1851; elected judge of the circuit court in 1850 and of the court of appeals in 1852; died in Richmond, Va., on January 5, 1859; interment in the Old Lutheran Graveyard, Woodstock, Shenandoah County, Va.

**SANBORN, John Carfield,** a Representative from Idaho; born in Chenoa, McLean County, Ill., September 28, 1885; attended the public schools; was graduated from Oberlin (Ohio) College in 1908, and from Columbia University Law School, New York City, in 1912; engaged in agricultural pursuits; trustee of the Hagerman Independent School District, 1921-1924; served in the Idaho State house of representatives from 1921 until 1929; member of the Idaho State senate, 1939-1941; elected as a Republican to the Eightieth and Eighty-first Congresses (January 3, 1947-January 3, 1951); was not a candidate for renomination in 1950 to the House of Representatives, but was an unsuccessful candidate for nomination to the United States Senate; unsuccessful candidate in 1956 for nomination to the United States Senate; resumed agricultural pursuits; president of Hagerman Farms, Inc.; member of board of directors of Idaho Farm Bureau Federation; legislative representative before the 1959 and 1961 sessions of Idaho legislature; died in Boise, Idaho, May 16, 1968; interment in Hagerman Cemetery, Hagerman, Idaho.

**SANDAGER, Harry,** a Representative from Rhode Island; born in Providence, R.I., April 12, 1887; attended the public schools at Cranston, R.I., and Georgetown University, Washington, D.C.; graduated from George Washington University, Washington, D.C., in 1922; newspaper reporter 1905-1918; secretary to Representative Walter R. Stiness 1918-1922; returned to Providence, R.I., and served as an office executive 1922-1931; member of the State house of representatives 1928-1936; moved to Cranston, R.I., in 1931 and engaged in business as an automobile dealer; elected as a Republican to the Seventy-sixth Congress (January 3, 1939-January 3, 1941); unsuccessful candidate for reelection in 1940 to the Seventy-seventh Congress and for election in 1942 to the Seventy-eighth Congress; resumed the automobile business until his death; member of the Republican National Committee 1941-1944; died in Cranston, R.I., December 24, 1955; interment in St. Francis Cemetery, Pawtucket, R.I.

**SANDERS, Archie Dovell,** a Representative from New York; born in Stafford, Genesee County, N.Y., June 17, 1857; attended the common schools, Le Roy Academy and Buffalo Central High School; in 1873 became a partner with his father in the produce business at Stafford, N.Y.; elected highway commissioner of Stafford in 1894 and supervisor in 1895; member of the New York State assembly in 1895 and 1896; delegate to many State conventions; delegate to the Republican National Conventions of 1896 and 1924; appointed by President William McKinley as collector of internal revenue for the twenty-eighth district of New York in 1898 and served until 1913; Republican State committeeman for the Thirtieth Congressional District in 1900 and 1901; member of the New York State senate in 1914 and 1915; elected as a Republican to the Sixty-fifth and to the seven succeeding Congresses (March 4, 1917-March 3, 1933); chairman, Committee on the Post Office and Post Roads (Seventy-first Congress); was not a candidate for renomination in 1932 to the Seventy-third Congress; returned to Stafford, N.Y.; was serving as chairman of the Genesee County Republican Committee at the time of his death in Rochester, N.Y., on July 15, 1941; interment in Stafford Rural Cemetery, Stafford, N.Y.

**SANDERS, Bernard,** a Representative from Vermont; born in Brooklyn, N.Y., September 8, 1941; graduated from Madison High School, Brooklyn, N.Y.; B.A., University of Chicago, 1964; freelance writer, youth counselor, and carpenter; director, American People's History Society, 1975-1981; director, Vermont League of Cities and Towns, 1981-1989; independent candidate for election in 1972 and 1974 to the United States Senate; independent candidate for election for Governor of Vermont in 1972, 1976 and 1986; mayor of Burlington, Vt., 1981-1989; visiting lecturer, John F. Kennedy School of Government, Institute of Politics, Harvard University, 1989; visiting professor of sociology, Hamilton College, N.Y., 1989; unsuccessful independent candidate in 1988 to the One Hundred First Congress; elected as an independent to the One Hundred Second and to the two succeeding Congresses (January 3, 1991-January 3, 1997); is a resident of Burlington, Vt.

**SANDERS, Everett,** a Representative from Indiana; born near Coalmont, Clay County, Ind., March 8, 1882; attended the public schools and the Indiana State Normal School at Terre Haute; was graduated from the law department of Indiana University at Bloomington in 1907; was admitted to the bar the same year and practiced his profession in Terre Haute, Ind.; elected as a Republican to the Sixty-fifth and to the three succeeding Congresses (March 4, 1917-March 3, 1925); declined to be a candidate for renomination in 1924 to the Sixty-ninth Congress; was director of the speakers' bureau of the Republican National Committee in 1924; appointed secretary to President Calvin Coolidge on March 4, 1925, and served until March 4, 1929; served as Republican National Chairman from 1932 to 1934; resumed the practice of law in Washington, D.C., where he died on May 12, 1950; interment in Highland Lawn Cemetery, Terre Haute, Ind.

**SANDERS, Jared Young** (father of Jared Young Sanders, Jr.), a Representative from Louisiana; born near Morgan City, St. Mary Parish, La., January 29, 1869; attended the public schools; was graduated from the law department of Tulane University, New Orleans, La., in 1893; was admitted to the bar the same year and commenced practice in New Orleans; elected as an anti-lottery member of the Louisiana State house of representatives in 1892 and served until 1904, being elected speaker in 1900; member of the Louisiana State constitutional convention in 1898; Lieutenant Governor, 1904-1908; elected Governor of Louisiana in 1908 and served from May 12, 1908 to May 14, 1912; elected to the United States Senate on July 6, 1910, to fill the vacancy caused by the death of Samuel D. McEnery, but did not qualify, preferring to finish his term as Governor; elected as a Democrat to the Sixty-fifth and Sixty-sixth Congresses (March 4, 1917-March 3, 1921); was not a candidate for renomination in 1920 to the Sixty-seventh Congress; member of the Louisiana State constitutional convention in 1921; resumed the practice of law; unsuccessful candidate for the Democratic nomination for United States Senator in 1920 and 1926; died in Baton Rouge, La., March 23, 1944; interment in Franklin Cemetery, Franklin, La.

**SANDERS, Jared Young, Jr.** (son of Jared Young Sanders), a Representative from Louisiana; born in Franklin, St. Mary Parish, La., April 20, 1892; attended the public schools, Dixon Academy, Covington, La., and Washington and Lee University, Lexington, Va.; was graduated from the Louisiana State University at Baton Rouge in 1912, and from the law department of Tulane University, New Orleans, La., in 1914; was admitted to the bar in 1914 and commenced practice in Baton Rouge, La.; during the First World War served in the United States Army from May 1917 to April 1919 as captain of the Three Hundred and Forty-sixth Infantry, Eighty-seventh Division; member of the Louisiana State house of representatives, 1928-1932; elected to the Louisiana State senate in 1932, and served until elected to Congress; elected as a Democrat to the Seventy-third Congress to fill the vacancy caused by the death of

Bolivar E. Kemp; reelected to the Seventy-fourth Congress and served from May 1, 1934, to January 3, 1937; unsuccessful candidate for renomination in 1936 to the Seventy-fifth Congress; resumed the practice of law; delegate to the Democratic National Conventions of 1940 and 1944; elected to the Seventy-seventh Congress (January 3, 1941-January 3, 1943); was an unsuccessful candidate for renomination in 1942 to the Seventy-eighth Congress; resumed the practice of law; also interested in banking; died in Baton Rouge, La., November 29, 1960; interment in Roselawn Memorial Park.

**SANDERS, Morgan Gurley,** a Representative from Texas; born near Ben Wheeler, Van Zandt County, Tex., on July 14, 1878; attended the public schools; graduated from the Alamo Institute and taught school for three years; owned and published a weekly newspaper; studied law at the University of Texas at Austin; was admitted to the bar in 1901 and commenced practice in Canton, Tex.; member of the Texas State house of representatives, 1902-1906; prosecuting attorney of Van Zandt County, 1910-1914; district attorney of the seventh judicial district of Texas in 1915 and 1916; voluntarily retired and resumed the practice of law in Canton, Van Zandt County, Tex.; delegate to many Democratic State conventions; elected as a Democrat to the Sixty-seventh and to the eight succeeding Congresses (March 4, 1921-January 3, 1939); unsuccessful candidate for renomination in 1938 to the Seventy-sixth Congress; resumed the practice of law in Canton, Tex., until his death in Corsicana, Tex., January 7, 1956; interment in Hillcrest Cemetery, Canton, Tex.

**SANDERS, Newell,** a Senator from Tennessee; born on a farm near Bloomington, Owen County, Ind., July 12, 1850; attended the rural schools; graduated from Indiana University at Bloomington in 1873; owned and operated a book store in Bloomington, Ind., 1873-1877; moved to Chattanooga, Tenn., in 1877 and became a manufacturer of agricultural implements; member of the school board 1881-1882; alderman 1882-1886; president of the Chattanooga Plow Co. 1882-1901; member of the board of directors of the Nashville, Chattanooga & St. Louis Railway; appointed as a Republican to the United States Senate to fill the vacancy caused by the death of Robert L. Taylor and served from April 11, 1912, to January 24, 1913, when a successor was elected; was not a candidate for election; chairman, Committee on National Banks (Sixty-second Congress); continued his former manufacturing pursuits in Chattanooga until 1927, when he retired from active pursuits; died at his home on Lookout Mountain, Tenn., January 26, 1939; interment in Forest Hills Cemetery, Chattanooga, Tenn.

**Bibliography:** Terral, Rufus. *Newell Sanders: A Biography.* Kingsport, Tenn.: Kingsport Press, 1935.

**SANDERS, Wilbur Fiske,** a Senator from Montana; born in Leon, Cattaraugus County, N.Y., May 2, 1834; attended the common schools; taught school in New York; moved to Ohio in 1854, where he continued teaching; studied law in Akron, Ohio, and was admitted to the bar in 1856; during the Civil War recruited a company of infantry and a battery of artillery in the summer of 1861 and was commissioned a first lieutenant in the Sixty-fourth Regiment, Ohio Infantry, of which regiment he was made adjutant; assisted in 1862 in the construction of defenses along the railroads south of Nashville; settled in that part of Idaho which later became Montana; engaged in the practice of law and also became interested in mining and stock raising; unsuccessful Republican candidate for election in 1864, 1867, 1880, and 1886 as a Delegate to Congress; member, Territorial house of representatives of Montana 1873-1879; upon the admission of Montana as a State into the Union was elected as a Republican to the United States Senate and served from January 1, 1890, to March 3, 1893; unsuccessful candidate for reelection; chairman, Committee on Enrolled Bills (Fifty-second Congress);

died in Helena, Mont., July 7, 1905; interment in Forestvale Cemetery.

Bibliography: *DAB*.

SANDFORD, James T., a Representative from Tennessee; born in Virginia; attended the common schools; moved to Columbia, Tenn.; engaged in agricultural pursuits; elected to the Eighteenth Congress (March 4, 1823-March 3, 1825); unsuccessful candidate for reelection in 1825 to the Nineteenth Congress; contributed a part of his wealth to the establishment of Jackson College at Columbia, Tenn.

SANDFORD, Thomas, a Representative from Kentucky; born in Westmoreland County, Va., in 1762; pursued classical studies; served in the Revolutionary War; settled on the highlands back of Covington, Ky., in 1792 and engaged in agricultural pursuits; delegate to the Kentucky constitutional convention in 1799; member of the Kentucky senate 1800-1802; served in the Kentucky house of representatives in 1802; elected as a Republican to the Eighth and Ninth Congresses (March 4, 1803-March 3, 1807); drowned in the Ohio River near Covington, Ky., on December 10, 1808; interment in Highland Cemetery, Fort Mitchell, near Covington, Kenton County, Ky.

SANDIDGE, John Milton, a Representative from Louisiana; born near Carnesville, Franklin County, Ga., January 7, 1817; moved to Louisiana and became a planter; served as colonel in the Mexican War; member of the Louisiana State house of representatives, 1846-1855, and served two years as speaker; delegate to the Louisiana constitutional convention in 1852; elected as a Democrat to the Thirty-fourth and Thirty-fifth Congresses (March 4, 1855-March 3, 1859); chairman, Committee on Private Land Claims (Thirty-fifth Congress); served throughout the Civil War as colonel of Bossier Cavalry; surrendered the archives of the State to the Federal authorities in the absence of Governor Henry W. Allen; died in Bastrop, Morehouse Parish, La., on March 30, 1890; interment in Christ Church Cemetery.

SANDLIN, John Nicholas, a Representative from Louisiana; born near Minden, Webster Parish, La., February 24, 1872; attended the public schools; studied law, was admitted to the bar in 1896 and commenced practice in Minden, La.; prosecuting attorney for the second district of Louisiana, 1904-1910; judge of the second judicial district of Louisiana from 1910 until 1920; delegate to the Democratic National Convention of 1916; elected as a Democrat to the Sixty-seventh and to the seven succeeding Congresses (March 4, 1921-January 3, 1937); was not a candidate in 1936 for renomination to the House of Representatives, but was an unsuccessful candidate for nomination to the United States Senate; engaged in the practice of law; died in Minden, La., December 25, 1957; interment in Minden Cemetery.

SANDMAN, Charles William, Jr., a Representative from New Jersey; born in Philadelphia, Pa., October 23, 1921; graduated from Cape May (N.J.) High School; graduated, Temple University, Philadelphia, Pa., and Rutgers University Law School, Newark, N.J.; admitted to New Jersey bar in 1949; served as solicitor for Cape May City, N.J.; served as a navigator in the Army Air Corps, European Theater, during the Second World War; elected to the New Jersey State senate in November 1955, reelected in 1959 and 1963; delegate to the Republican National Conventions of 1956, 1960, 1964, and 1968; majority leader of the New Jersey State senate in 1964 and 1965; chairman of the New Jersey State Narcotics Investigating Committee, 1962-1967; delegate to the New Jersey Constitutional convention, March-April 1966; elected as a Republican to the Ninetieth and to the three succeeding Congresses (January 3, 1967-January 3, 1975); unsuccessful candidate for Governor of New Jersey in 1973; unsuccessful candidate for reelection in 1974 to the Ninety-fourth Congress; was a resident of Cape May Court House, N.J., until his death there on August 26, 1985; interment in Cold Spring Presbyterian Cemetery.

SANDS, Joshua, a Representative from New York; born in Cow Neck (now Sands Point), Queens County, Long Island, N.Y., October 12, 1757; received a limited schooling; served as captain in the American Army during the Revolutionary War; engaged in mercantile pursuits; member of the State senate 1792-1799; collector of customs at the port of New York in 1797; elected as a Federalist to the Eighth Congress (March 4, 1803-March 3, 1805); was not a candidate for renomination; president of the board of trustees of the village of Brooklyn in 1824; elected to the Nineteenth Congress (March 4, 1825-March 3, 1827); died in Brooklyn, N.Y., September 13, 1835; interment in St. Paul's Church Cemetery, Eastchester, N.Y.; reinterment in Greenwood Cemetery, Brooklyn, N.Y., in 1852.

SANFORD, John (father of Stephen Sanford and grandfather of John Sanford [1851-1939]), a Representative from New York; born in Roxbury, Conn., June 3, 1803; received a good education; moved to Amsterdam, N.Y., in 1821; taught school in Amsterdam and afterward in Mayfield, where he also engaged in mercantile pursuits; returned to Amsterdam and continued in commercial pursuits until 1840; elected as a Democrat to the Twenty-seventh Congress (March 4, 1841-March 3, 1843); founder of a carpet manufacturing firm in New York, but the factory was destroyed by fire in 1849, whereupon he retired from active business; died in Amsterdam, Montgomery County, N.Y., on October 4, 1857; interment in Green Hill Cemetery.

SANFORD, John (son of Stephen Sanford and grandson of John Sanford [1803-1857]), a Representative from New York; born in Amsterdam, Montgomery County, N.Y., January 18, 1851; attended the common schools, Amsterdam Academy, and Poughkeepsie Military Institute; was graduated from Yale College in 1872; engaged with his father in the carpet manufacturing industry in Amsterdam, N.Y.; elected as a Republican to the Fifty-first and Fifty-second Congresses (March 4, 1889-March 3, 1893); was not a candidate for renomination in 1892; resumed former business pursuits; delegate to the Republican National Convention in 1892; interested in the breeding of race horses and owner of the Sanford Racing Stable; member of the New York Racing Commission; died in Saratoga, N.Y., September 26, 1939; interment in Green Hill Cemetery, Amsterdam, N.Y.

SANFORD, John W.A., a Representative from Georgia; born near Milledgeville, Baldwin County, Ga., August 28, 1798; attended the Baldwin County schools, and Yale University; engaged in agricultural pursuits; elected as a Union Democrat to the Twenty-fourth Congress and served from March 4, 1835, to July 25, 1835, when he resigned, before the convening of Congress, to assist in the removal of the Cherokee Indians; served in the Cherokee War in 1836 with the rank of major general; elected to the State senate in 1837, but resigned before taking his seat; served as secretary of state of Georgia 1841-1843; member of the State convention of 1850; died in Milledgeville, Ga., September 12, 1870; interment in Milledgeville Cemetery.

SANFORD, Jonah (great-grandfather of Rollin Brewster Sanford), a Representative from New York; born in Cornwall, Vt., November 30, 1790; attended the district schools; moved to Hopkinton, N.Y., in 1811; enlisted as a volunteer and participated in the battle at Plattsburgh, September 11, 1814; appointed justice of the peace in 1818 and served for twenty-two years; studied law; was admitted to the bar and practiced in Franklin County; supervisor of Hopkinton 1823-1826; commissioned a captain of Volunteer Cavalry in 1827; promoted to lieutenant colonel in 1828, colonel in 1831, and brigadier general of State militia in 1832 and 1833; member of the State assembly in 1829 and 1830; elected as a Jacksonian to the Twenty-first Congress to fill the vacancy caused by the resignation of Silas Wright, Jr., and served from November 3, 1830, to March 3, 1831; judge of the court of common pleas 1831-1837; delegate to the convention to revise the State constitution in 1846; became a Republican upon the formation of that party in 1856; raised a regiment during the Civil War and was elected its colonel; died in Hopkinton, St. Lawrence County, N.Y., on December 25, 1867; interment in Hopkinton Cemetery.

**SANFORD, Marshall Clement, Jr. (Mark),** a Representative from South Carolina; born in Fort Lauderdale, Broward County, Fla., May 28, 1960; attended high school in Beaufort, S.C.; B.A., Furman University, Greenville, S.C., 1983; M.B.A., Colgate W. Darden School of Business, University of Virginia, 1988; owner of a real estate investment firm; farmer; elected as a Republican to the One Hundred Fourth Congress (January 3, 1995-January 3, 1997); is a resident of Charleston, S.C.

**SANFORD, Nathan,** a Senator from New York; born in Bridgehampton, Long Island, N.Y., November 5, 1777; completed preparatory studies; studied law; was admitted to the bar in 1799 and commenced practice in New York City; United States commissioner in bankruptcy in 1802; United States attorney for the district of New York 1803-1816; member, State assembly 1808-1809, 1811, and served as speaker in the latter year; member, State senate 1812-1815; elected as a Democrat to the United States Senate and served from March 4, 1815, to March 3, 1821; chairman, Committee on Commerce and Manufactures (Fifteenth and Sixteenth Congresses), Committee on Naval Affairs (Fifteenth Congress), Committee on Finance (Sixteenth Congress); delegate to the State constitutional convention in 1821; chancellor of New York 1823-1826, when he resigned, having been elected Senator; elected to the United States Senate to fill the vacancy in the term commencing March 4, 1825, and served from January 14, 1826, to March 3, 1831; was not a candidate for reelection; chairman, Committee on Foreign Relations (Nineteenth Congress); resumed the practice of law in Flushing, Queens County, N.Y., and died there October 17, 1838.

**Bibliography:** *DAB*.

**SANFORD, Rollin Brewster** (great-grandson of Jonah Sanford), a Representative from New York; born in Nicholville, St. Lawrence County, N.Y., May 18, 1874; attended the public schools; was graduated from the Albany (N.Y.) High School in 1893, from Tufts College, Medford, Mass., in 1897, and from the Albany Law School in 1899; was admitted to the bar in 1899 and commenced practice in Albany, N.Y.; member of the New York National Guard 1901-1906; prosecuting attorney of Albany County 1908-1914; elected as a Republican to the Sixty-fourth, Sixty-fifth, and Sixty-sixth Congresses (March 4, 1915-March 3, 1921); declined to be a candidate for reelection in 1920; resumed the practice of law; member of the New York State Board of Law Examiners 1921-1940; died in Loudonville (town of Colonie), Albany, N.Y., May 16, 1957; interment in Albany Rural Cemetery, Cemetery Avenue, Menands, Albany, N.Y.

**SANFORD, Stephen** (son of John Sanford [1803-1857] and father of John Sanford [1851-1939]), a Representative from New York; born in Mayfield, Fulton County, N.Y., May 26, 1826; attended the common schools and local academy at Amsterdam, N.Y., Georgetown College, Washington, D.C., for two years, and the United States Military Academy at West Point, N.Y.; engaged in the carpet manufacturing business from 1844 until his death; elected as Republican to the Forty-first Congress (March 4, 1869-March 3, 1871); declined to be a candidate for renomination; delegate to the Republican National Convention in 1876; died in Amsterdam, N.Y., February 13, 1913; interment in Green Hill Cemetery.

**SANFORD, Terry,** a Senator from North Carolina; born in Laurinburg, Scotland County, N.C., August 20, 1917; attended Presbyterian Junior College; A.B., University of North Carolina, Chapel Hill, 1939; J.D., University of North Carolina School of Law, 1946; special agent, Federal Bureau of Investigation, 1941-1942; served in the Five Hundred Seventeenth Infantry Parachute Combat Team, United States Army, from 1942 until 1945, and was discharged as a first lieutenant after service in the European Theater; served in the North Carolina National Guard, 1948-1960; assistant director, Institute of Government, University of North Carolina, 1946-1948; lawyer in private practice, 1948-1960, 1965-1969 and 1985-1986; North Carolina State senator, 1953-1955; elected Governor of North Carolina in 1960 and served from January 5, 1961 to January 8, 1965; president of Duke University, Durham, N.C., from 1969 until 1985; unsuccessful candidate for the Democratic presidential nomination in 1972 and 1976; elected as a Democrat to the United States Senate, November 4, 1986, for the vacancy in the term ending January 3, 1987, caused by the death of John P. East, and for the term ending January 3, 1993; unsuccessful candidate for reelection in 1992; chairman, Select Committee on Ethics (One Hundred Second Congress); is a resident of Durham, N.C.

**Bibliography:** Sanford, Terry. *A Danger of Democracy: The Presidential Nominating Process.* Boulder, Colo.: Westview Press, 1981; Sanford, Terry. *Storm Over the States.* New York: McGraw-Hill, 1967.

**SANGMEISTER, George Edward,** a Representative from Illinois; born in Joliet, Will County, Ill., February 16, 1931; graduated, Joliet Township (Ill.) High School, 1949; student, Joliet Junior College, 1949-1951; B.A., Elmhurst (Ill.) College, 1957; LL.B., John Marshall Law School, Chicago, 1960, and J.D., 1970; United States Army service, 1951-1953; admitted to Illinois bar, 1960; attorney; Justice of the Peace, Will County, 1961-1963; Magistrate of Circuit Court, 1963-1964; Illinois State's attorney, 1964-1968; member, board of trustees, School District 210, 1970-1973; member, Illinois state house of representatives, 1973-1976; member, Illinois state senate, 1977-1987; elected as a Democrat to the One Hundred First and to the two succeeding Congresses (January 3, 1989-January 3, 1995); was not a candidate for reelection in 1994 to the One Hundred Fourth Congress; is a resident of Mokena, Ill.

**SANTANGELO, Alfred Edward,** a Representative from New York; born in New York City June 4, 1912; attended public schools; A.B., City College of New York, 1935; LL.B, Columbia University School of Law, 1938; admitted to the New York bar in 1939 and commenced practice in New York City; assistant district attorney, 1945; New York State senator, 1947-1950 and 1953-1956; elected as a Democrat to the Eighty-fifth and to the two succeeding Congresses (January 3, 1957-January 3, 1963); unsuccessful candidate for reelection in 1962 to the Eighty-eighth Congress; resumed the practice of law; delegate to New York State Constitutional convention, 1967; resided in Bronx, N.Y.; died in Orlando, Fla., March 30, 1978; interment in Calvary Cemetery, Woodside, N.Y.

**SANTINI, James David,** a Representative from Nevada; born in Reno, Washoe County, Nev., August 13, 1937; graduated from Manogue High School, Reno, 1955; B.S., University of Nevada, Reno, 1959; J.D., Hastings College of Law, San Francisco, Calif., 1962; admitted to the Nevada bar in 1962 and commenced practice in Las Vegas; admitted to the California bar in 1963, and to the Arizona bar in 1965; served in the United States Army, 1963-1966; Clark County, Nev., deputy district attorney, 1966-1968; Clark County public defender, 1968-1970; served as Las Vegas, Nev., justice of the peace, 1970-1972; district court judge of Clark County, 1972-1974; owner and teacher, Nevada Bar Review, 1969-1974; elected as a Democrat to the Ninety-fourth and to the three succeeding Congresses (January 3, 1975-January 3, 1983); was not a candidate in 1982 for reelection to the House of Representatives, but was an unsuccessful candidate for the Democratic nomination to the United States Senate; unsuccessful Republican candidate for election to the United States Senate in 1986; resumed the practice of law in Washington, D.C.; is a resident of Potomac, Md.

**SANTORUM, Richard John,** a Representative and a Senator from Pennsylvania; born in Winchester, Va., May 10, 1958; graduated Carmel High School, 1976; B.A., Pennsylvania State University, 1980; M.B.A., University of Pittsburgh, 1981; J.D., Dickinson School of Law, Carlisle, Pa., 1986; practicing attorney; administrative assistant to Pennsylvania senator J. Doyle Corman, 1981-1986; director, Pennsylvania senate local government committee, 1981-1984; director, Pennsylvania senate transportation committee, 1984-1986; practicing attorney in Pittsburgh, Pa., 1986-1989; elected as a Republican to the One Hundred Second and One Hundred Third Congresses (January 3, 1991-January 3, 1995); was not a candidate in 1994 for renomination to the House of Representatives, but was elected to the United States Senate for the term ending January 3, 2001; is a resident of Mt. Lebanon, Pa.

**SAPP, William Fletcher** (nephew of William R. Sapp), a Representative from Iowa; born in Danville, Knox County, Ohio, November 20, 1824; attended the public schools and Martinsburg Academy; studied law; was admitted to the bar in 1850 and commenced practice in Mount Vernon, Ohio; unsuccessful candidate for prosecuting attorney of Knox County in 1850; elected prosecuting attorney of Knox County in 1854 and 1856; moved to Omaha, Nebr., in 1860; appointed adjutant general of Nebraska Territory in 1861; member of the Territorial legislative council; entered the Union Army in 1862 as lieutenant colonel of the Second Nebraska Cavalry and served until mustered out; moved to Council Bluffs, Iowa, and resumed the practice of law; member of the State house of representatives in 1865; United States district attorney for Iowa 1869-1873; elected as a Republican to the Forty-fifth and Forty-sixth Congresses (March 4, 1877-March 3, 1881); was not a candidate for renomination in 1880; resumed the practice of law; died in Council Bluffs, Iowa, November 22, 1890; interment in Mound View Cemetery, Mount Vernon, Ohio.

**SAPP, William Robinson** (uncle of William F. Sapp), a Representative from Ohio; born at Cadiz, Ohio, March 4, 1804; moved to Knox County, where he attended the public schools; engaged in the mercantile business in Danville; studied law; was admitted to the bar in 1833 and commenced practice at Millersburg, Holmes County, Ohio; prosecuting attorney of Holmes County; moved to Mount Vernon, Knox County, in 1846; elected as a Whig to the Thirty-third Congress and reelected as a Republican to the Thirty-fourth Congress (March 4, 1853-March 3, 1857); unsuccessful candidate for reelection; assessor of internal revenue for the thirteenth district 1869-1872; collector of internal revenue from 1872 until his death in Mount Vernon, Knox County, Ohio, January 3, 1875; interment in Mound View Cemetery.

**SARASIN, Ronald Arthur,** a Representative from Connecticut; born in Fall River, Bristol County, Mass., December 31, 1934; attended the public schools of Connecticut; B.S., University of Connecticut, Storrs, 1960; J.D., University of Connecticut Law School, 1963; served in the United States Navy during the Korean conflict, 1952-1956; attained rank of petty officer, second class; admitted to the Connecticut bar in 1963 and commenced practice in New Haven; served as town counsel for Beacon Falls, 1963-1972; assistant professor of law at New Haven College, 1963-1966; member, Connecticut State house of representatives, 1968-1972; assistant minority leader, 1970-1972; delegate, Connecticut State Republican conventions, 1968, 1970, 1972, and 1974, serving as convention chairman in 1974; delegate to the Republican National Convention of 1976; elected as a Republican to the Ninety-third and

to the two succeeding Congresses (January 3, 1973-January 3, 1979); was not a candidate for reelection in 1978 to the Ninety-sixth Congress, but was an unsuccessful candidate for election for Governor of Connecticut; president, National Beer Wholesalers Association; is a resident of Vienna, Va.

**SARBACHER, George William, Jr.,** a Representative from Pennsylvania; born in Philadelphia, Pa., September 30, 1919; attended the public schools; was graduated from Olney High School in 1938 and from Temple University, Philadelphia, Pa., in 1942; enlisted in the United States Marine Corps in 1941, and served with the Second Marine Division from January 1942 to January 1947; was commissioned a lieutenant and later a captain and served overseas in the Southwest Pacific for two and a half years; while serving on active duty was elected to Congress; elected as a Republican to the Eightieth Congress (January 3, 1947-January 3, 1949); unsuccessful candidate for reelection in 1948 to the Eighty-first Congress, and for election in 1950 to the Eighty-second Congress; director of highway safety for Pennsylvania; president and chairman of board of directors of the National Scientific Laboratories, Inc., Washington, D.C., and NSL Electronics, Ltd., Hamilton, Ontario, Canada; served as an industry consultant; served as chairman of the Postal Service management advisory team from 1970 until his death in Bethesda, Md., on March 4, 1973.

**SARBANES, Paul Spyros,** a Representative and a Senator from Maryland; born in Salisbury, Wicomico County, Md., February 3, 1933; attended the public schools of Salisbury; graduated Wicomico Senior High School, 1950; B.A., Princeton University, 1954; attended Balliol College, Oxford, England, as a Rhodes scholar, 1954-1957; LL.B., Harvard University Law School, 1960; admitted to the Maryland bar in 1960 and commenced practice in Baltimore; law clerk, United States Court of Appeals, Fourth Judicial Circuit, 1960-1961; legislative draftsman, Maryland Department of Legislative Reference, Maryland General Assembly, 1961; administrative assistant to Walter W. Heller, chairman of the President's Council of Economic Advisers, 1962-1963; executive director, Charter Revision Commission of Baltimore City, 1963-1964; member, Maryland State house of delegates, 1967-1971; elected as a Democrat to the Ninety-second and to the two succeeding Congresses (January 3, 1971-January 3, 1977); was not a candidate in 1976 for reelection to the House of Representatives, but was elected to the United States Senate for the term commencing January 3, 1977; reelected in 1982, 1988, and again in 1994 for the term ending January 3, 2001; chairman, Joint Economic Committee (One Hundredth through One Hundred Second Congress); is a resident of Baltimore, Md.

**SARGENT, Aaron Augustus,** a Representative and a Senator from California; born in Newburyport, Essex County, Mass., September 28, 1827; attended the common schools; apprenticed to a cabinetmaker; worked as a printer in Philadelphia, Pa.; moved to Washington, D.C., in 1847 and became secretary to a Member of Congress; moved to California in 1849 and settled in Nevada City in 1850; employed on the staff of the Nevada Daily Journal and later became owner of the paper; studied law; was admitted to the bar in 1854 and commenced practice in Nevada City, Calif.; district attorney for Nevada County, 1855-1856; member, California State senate, 1856; elected as a Republican to the Thirty-seventh Congress (March 4, 1861-March 3, 1863); declined to be a candidate for renomination in 1862 to the Thirty-eighth Congress; elected as a Republican to the Forty-first and Forty-second Congresses (March 4, 1869-March 3, 1873); was not a candidate in 1872 for renomination to the House of Representatives, having become a candidate for United States Senator; elected as a Republican to the United States Senate and served from March 4, 1873, to March 3, 1879; was not a candidate for reelection; chairman, Committee on Mines and Mining (Forty-fourth Congress), Committee on Naval Affairs (Forty-fifth

Congress); engaged in the practice of law in San Francisco, 1879-1882; appointed Envoy Extraordinary and Minister Plenipotentiary to Germany on March 2, 1882, and served until June 1884; declined to accept the appointment of Minister to Russia; returned to California in 1884 and resumed the practice of law; unsuccessful candidate for the Republican nomination for Senator in 1885; died in San Francisco, Calif., August 14, 1887; interment in Laurel Hill Cemetery.

Bibliography: *DAB.*

**SARPALIUS, William,** a Representative from Texas; born in Los Angeles, January 10, 1948; grew up on Cal Farley's Boys Ranch near Amarillo, Tex.; A.S., Clarendon (Tex.) Junior College, 1970; B.A., Texas Tech University, 1972; M.A., West Texas State University, 1978; agricultural consultant; vocational agriculture teacher, Cal Farley's Boys Ranch, 1972-1977; district office manager to Texas State Representative, 1977-1979; director of business development, Cepex, Inc., 1979-1988; member, Texas State senate, 1981-1988; elected as a Democrat to the One Hundred First and to the two succeeding Congresses (January 3, 1989-January 3, 1995); unsuccessful candidate for reelection in 1994 to the One Hundred Fourth Congress; president, CCCI; is a resident of Stevensville, Md.

**SASSCER, Lansdale Ghiselin,** a Representative from Maryland; born in Upper Marlboro, Prince Georges County, Md., September 30, 1893; attended the public schools, Central High School, Washington, D.C., and Tome School, Port Deposit, Md.; was graduated from Dickinson Law School, Carlisle, Pa., in 1914; was admitted to the bar the same year and commenced practice in Upper Marlboro, Md.; served during the First World War, 1917-1919, being overseas for thirteen months as a first lieutenant in the Fifty-ninth Artillery; resumed the practice of law; member of the Maryland State senate from 1922 until 1938, serving as president in 1935 and 1937; delegate to the Democratic National Conventions of 1924 and 1936; vice chairman of the committee on reorganization of the State government in 1939; elected as a Democrat to the Seventy-sixth Congress to fill the vacancy caused by the death of Stephen W. Gambrill; reelected to the Seventy-seventh and to the five succeeding Congresses and served from February 3, 1939, to January 3, 1953; was not a candidate in 1952 for renomination to the House of Representatives, but was an unsuccessful candidate for nomination to the United States Senate; resumed the practice of law; was a resident of Upper Marlboro, Md., until his death there on November 5, 1964; interment in Trinity Cemetery.

**SASSER, James Ralph,** a Senator from Tennessee; born in Memphis, Shelby County, Tenn., September 30, 1936; attended the public schools of Nashville, and the University of Tennessee, 1954-1955; B.A., Vanderbilt University, Nashville, 1958; J.D., Vanderbilt University Law School, 1961; admitted to the Tennessee bar in 1961 and commenced practice in Nashville; served in the United States Marine Corps Reserve from 1957 to 1963; chairman, Tennessee Democratic Party, 1973-1976; elected as a Democrat to the United States Senate in 1976; reelected in 1982 and 1988, and served from January 3, 1977 to January 3, 1995; unsuccessful candidate for reelection in 1994; chairman, Committee on the Budget (One Hundred First and One Hundred Second Congresses); nominated by President William J. Clinton as Ambassador to China, September 25, 1995, confirmed by the Senate December 14, 1995, and took the oath of office on January 10, 1996; is a resident of Nashville, Tenn.

**SATTERFIELD, David Edward, Jr**. (father of David E. Satterfield III), a Representative from Virginia; born in Richmond, Va., September 11, 1894; attended the public schools; was graduated from the law department of the University of Richmond, in 1916; was admitted to the bar the same year and commenced practice in Richmond, Va.; during the First World War enlisted in the United States Navy in 1917; was transferred to the Naval Flying Corps and commissioned as a first lieutenant; lieutenant commander, United States Naval Reserve Force, 1917-1919; Commonwealth's attorney for Richmond, Va., 1922-1933; resigned to return to the private practice of law; elected as a Democrat to the Seventy-fifth Congress to fill the vacancy caused by the death of Andrew J. Montague; reelected to the Seventy-sixth and to the three succeeding Congresses and served from November 2, 1937, until his resignation on February 15, 1945, to become general counsel and executive director of the Life Insurance Association of America, New York City; died in Richmond, Va., December 27, 1946; interment in Hollywood Cemetery.

**SATTERFIELD, David Edward, III** (son of David Edward Satterfield, Jr.), a Representative from Virginia; born in Richmond, Va., December 2, 1920; educated in the public schools, St. Christopher's Preparatory School, the University of Richmond, and the University of Virginia; served in the United States Navy from January 1942 to December 1945; member of the Naval Air Reserve; LL.B., University of Virginia School of Law, 1948; was admitted to the bar in 1948 and commenced the practice of law in Richmond, Va.; assistant United States attorney for the eastern district of Virginia, 1950-1953; councilman, city of Richmond, 1954-1956; served in the Virginia house of delegates, 1960-1964; elected as a Democrat to the Eighty-ninth and to the seven succeeding Congresses (January 3, 1965-January 3, 1981); was not a candidate for reelection in 1980 to the Ninety-seventh Congress; resumed the practice of law in Washington, D.C.; was a resident of Richmond, Va.; died September 30, 1988.

**SAUERHERING, Edward,** a Representative from Wisconsin; born in Mayville, Dodge County, Wis., June 24, 1864; attended the public schools; was graduated from the Chicago College of Pharmacy in 1885; engaged in the drug business in Chicago, Ill., for three years; returned to Mayville, Wis., and continued in the same business; elected as a Republican to the Fifty-fourth and Fifty-fifth Congresses (March 4, 1895-March 3, 1899); was not a candidate for renomination in 1898 to the Fifty-sixth Congress; superintendent of the commission of public works of Mayville 1909-1918; engaged in the construction of waterworks; justice of the peace 1912-1920; died in Mayville, Wis., on March 1, 1924; interment in Graceland Cemetery.

**SAULSBURY, Eli** (brother of Willard Saulsbury, uncle of Willard Saulsbury, Jr.), a Senator from Delaware; born in Mispillion Hundred, Kent County, Del., December 29, 1817; attended the common schools and Dickinson College, Carlisle, Pa.; member, State house of representatives 1853-1854; moved to Dover, Del., in 1856; studied law; was admitted to the bar in 1857 and practiced in Dover; elected as a Democrat to the United States Senate in 1870; reelected in 1876 and again in 1883 and served from March 4, 1871, to March 3, 1889; unsuccessful candidate for reelection; chairman, Committee on Privileges and Elections (Forty-sixth Congress), Committee on Engrossed Bills (Forty-seventh through Fiftieth Congresses); resumed the practice of his profession; died in Dover, Kent County, Del., March 22, 1893; interment in Silver Lake Cemetery.

Bibliography: *DAB.*

**SAULSBURY, Willard, Jr.** (son of Willard Saulsbury, Sr., nephew of Eli Saulsbury), a Senator from Delaware; born in Georgetown, Sussex County, Del., April 17, 1861; attended private schools and the University of Virginia at Charlottesville; studied law; was admitted to the bar in 1882 and commenced practice in Wilmington, Del.; president of the New Castle Bar Association and chairman of the board of censors; interested in banking and sundry business organizations; member of the Democratic National Committee 1908-1920; unsuccessful Democratic candidate for United States Senator in 1899, 1901, 1903, 1905, 1907, and 1911; elected as a Democrat to the United States Senate in 1913 and served from March 4, 1913, to March 3, 1919; unsuccessful candidate for reelection in 1918; served as President pro tempore of the Senate during the Sixty-fourth and Sixty-fifth Congresses; chairman, Committee on Coast and Insular Survey (Sixty-third through Sixty-fifth Congresses), Committee on Pacific Inlands and Puerto Rico (Sixty-fifth Congress); member of the advisory committee of the Conference on Limitation of Armaments in Washington, D.C., 1921-1922; member of the Pan American Conference in Santiago, Chile, in 1923; engaged in the practice of law in Wilmington, Del., and Washington, D.C., until his death in Wilmington, Del., February 20, 1927; interment in Christ Episcopal Churchyard, Dover, Del.

**Bibliography:** *DAB*

**SAULSBURY, Willard, Sr.** (brother of Eli Saulsbury, father of Willard Saulsbury, Jr.), a Senator from Delaware; born in Mispillion Hundred, Kent County, Del., June 2, 1820; attended the common schools, Dickinson College, Carlisle, Pa., and Delaware College (now the University of Delaware), Newark, Del.; studied law; was admitted to the bar and commenced practice in Georgetown, Del.; attorney general of Delaware 1850-1855; elected as a Democrat to the United States Senate in 1858; reelected in 1864 and served from March 4, 1859, to March 3, 1871; unsuccessful candidate for reelection; resumed the practice of law; chancellor of the State from 1874 until his death in Dover, Del., April 6, 1892; interment in Christ Episcopal Churchyard.

**Bibliography:** *DAB*.

**SAUND, Dalip Singh,** a Representative from California; born in Amritsar, India, September 20, 1899; educated in boarding schools; A.B., University of Punjab, 1919; came to the United States in 1920 to attend the University of California at Berkeley, and received an M.A. degree in 1922; Ph.D., mathematics, University of California, Berkeley, 1924; lettuce farmer in the Imperial Valley of California, 1930-1953; also distributor of chemical fertilizer in Westmoreland, Calif.; became a citizen of the United States in 1949 and less than a year later was elected judge of the Justice Court, Westmoreland Judicial District, Imperial County, but was denied his seat, not having been a citizen one year when elected; elected judge of the same court in 1952 and served until his resignation January 1, 1957; delegate to the Democratic National Conventions of 1952, 1956 and 1960; elected as a Democrat to the Eighty-fifth and to the two succeeding Congresses (January 3, 1957-January 3, 1963); unsuccessful candidate for reelection in 1962 to the Eighty-eighth Congress; died in Hollywood, Calif., April 22, 1973; interment in Forest Lawn Cemetery, Glendale, Calif.

**Bibliography:** Saund, Dalip Singh. *Congressman From India.* New York: Dutton, 1960.

**SAUNDERS, Alvin** (grandfather of William Henry Harrison), a Senator from Nebraska; born in Fleming County, Ky., July 12, 1817; attended the common schools and pursued an academic course; moved with his father to Illinois in 1829 and to Mount Pleasant, Iowa (then a part of Wisconsin Territory), in 1836; postmaster of Mount Pleasant for seven years; studied law but never entered upon its practice; engaged in mercantile pursuits and banking; delegate to the Iowa constitutional convention in 1846; member, Iowa State senate, 1854-1856, 1858-1860; one of the commissioners appointed by Congress to organize the Pacific Railroad Co.; appointed Governor of the Territory of Nebraska by President Abraham Lincoln on March 26, 1861 and served until March 27, 1867; elected as a Republican to the United States Senate and served from March 5, 1877, to March 3, 1883; chairman, Committee on Territories (Forty-seventh Congress); died in Omaha, Nebr., November 1, 1899; interment in Forest Lawn Cemetery.

**Bibliography:** *DAB*.

**SAUNDERS, Edward Watts,** a Representative from Virginia; born near Rockymount, Franklin County, Va., October 20, 1860; received his early education under private teachers; attended Bellevue High School, Bedford County, Va., and was graduated from the University of Virginia at Charlottesville in 1882; studied law; was admitted to the bar and commenced practice in Rockymount, Va., in 1883; member of the Virginia house of delegates from 1887 until 1901, and served as speaker in 1899; elected judge of the Fourth Circuit Court of Virginia in 1901 and judge of the seventh circuit in 1904; elected as a Democrat to the Fifty-ninth Congress to fill the vacancy caused by the resignation of Claude A. Swanson; reelected to the Sixtieth and to the six succeeding Congresses, and served from November 6, 1906 to February 29, 1920, when he resigned, having been elected judge of the Virginia supreme court of appeals, which position he held until his death in Rockymount, Va., on December 16, 1921; interment in High Street Cemetery.

**SAUNDERS, Romulus Mitchell,** a Representative from North Carolina; born near Milton, Caswell (then Orange) County, N.C., March 3, 1791; attended the common schools and the University of North Carolina at Chapel Hill, 1809-1811; studied law; was admitted to the bar in Nashville, Tenn., in 1812 and commenced practice in Milton, N.C.; member of the North Carolina State house of commons in 1815, 1817, and 1819, and served two years as speaker; trustee of the University of North Carolina from 1819 until 1864; moved to Raleigh, N.C., in 1823; elected as a Republican to the Seventeenth and to the two succeeding Congresses (March 4, 1821-March 3, 1827); declined to be a candidate for reelection in 1826 to the Twentieth Congress; attorney general of North Carolina, 1828-1831; judge of the superior court, 1835-1840; unsuccessful candidate in 1840 for Governor of North Carolina; elected as a Democrat to the Twenty-seventh and Twenty-eighth Congresses (March 4, 1841-March 3, 1845); chairman, Committee on the Judiciary (Twenty-eighth Congress); unsuccessful candidate for reelection in 1844 to the Twenty-ninth Congress; unsuccessful candidate for the United States Senate in 1842 and 1852; appointed Minister to Spain on February 25, 1846 and served until September 1849; again a member of the State house of commons, 1850-1852; judge of the superior court of North Carolina, 1852-1856; member of the board of commissioners to revise the laws of North Carolina; died in Raleigh, N.C., April 21, 1867; interment in Old City Cemetery.

**Bibliography:** *DAB*.

**SAUTHOFF, Harry,** a Representative from Wisconsin; born in Madison, Dane County, Wis., June 3, 1879; attended the public schools; was graduated from the University of Wisconsin at Madison in 1902; taught school at Lake Geneva (Wis.) High School from 1902 until 1905, and at Northern Illinois State Normal School at De Kalb in 1905 and 1906; was graduated from the law department of the University of Wisconsin in 1909; was admitted to the bar the same year and commenced practice in Madison, Wis.; district attorney of Dane County, Wis., 1915-1919; secretary to Governor John J. Blaine in 1921; delegate to the International Conference on the St. Lawrence Deep Waterway between the United States and Canada, in 1921, and to the Mississippi Valley Conference on Mississippi River Improvement, in 1921; served in the Wisconsin State senate, 1925-1929; elected as a Progressive to the Seventy-fourth and Seventy-fifth Congresses (January 3, 1935-January 3, 1939); unsuccessful candidate for reelection in 1938 to the Seventy-sixth Congress; elected to the Seventy-seventh and Seventy-eighth Congresses (January 3, 1941-January 3, 1945); was not a candidate for renomination in 1944 to the House of Representatives, but was an unsuccessful candidate for election to the United States Senate on the Progressive ticket; resumed the practice of law until his retirement in 1955; died in Madison, Wis., June 16, 1966; interment in Forest Hill Cemetery.

**SAVAGE, Charles Raymon,** a Representative from Washington; born on a farm at La Farge, Vernon County, Wis., April 12, 1906; attended the public schools; took special courses in mechanics, building construction, business law, and salesmanship; moved to Washington State and engaged in the building construction and logging businesses; member of the Washington State house of representatives, 1939-1945, 1951-1959, 1963-1967, and 1969-1976; delegate to State Democratic conventions twelve times from 1938 to 1970; delegate to the Democratic National Convention of 1944; elected as a Democrat to the Seventy-ninth Congress (January 3, 1945-January 3, 1947); unsuccessful candidate for reelection in 1946 to the Eightieth Congress, and also unsuccessful in a special election in June 1947 to the Eightieth Congress; unsuccessful candidate for election in 1948 to the Eighty-first Congress; unsuccessful candidate for nomination in 1958 to the Eighty-sixth Congress; continued his logging pursuits; district manager of an insurance society; engaged in real estate business; resided in Shelton, Wash., where he died on January 14, 1976; interment in Shelton Memorial Park.

**SAVAGE, Gus,** a Representative from Illinois; born in Detroit, Mich., October 30, 1925; attended the public schools of Chicago; graduated from Wendell Phillips High School, Chicago, Ill., 1943; B.A., Roosevelt College, Chicago, 1951; served in the United States Army, 1943-1946; engaged in graduate work at Roosevelt College, 1952; attended Chicago-Kent College of Law, Chicago, 1952-1953; worked as a journalist, 1954-1979, and was editor and publisher, Citizen Community Newspapers, 1965-1979; a founder and chief strategist of black political independent movement in Midwest; campaign manager, Midwest League of Negro Voters, 1960; chairman, Protest at the Polls, 1963; chairman, Southend Voters Conference, Chicago, 1960; chairman, Committee for a Black Mayor, Chicago, 1976; unsuccessful candidate for election in 1970 to the Ninety-first Congress; elected as a Democrat to the Ninety-seventh and to the five succeeding Congresses (January 3, 1981-January 3, 1993); chairman, Minority Business Braintrust, Congressional Black Caucus, 1987-1992; unsuccessful candidate for renomination in 1992 to the One Hundred Third Congress; is a resident of Chicago, Ill.

**SAVAGE, John,** a Representative from New York; born in Salem, Washington County, N.Y., February 22, 1779; attended the common schools; was graduated from Union College, Schenectady, N.Y., in 1799; studied law; was admitted to the bar in 1800 and commenced practice in Salem, N.Y.; district attorney for the fourth New York district from 1806 until 1811, and in 1812 and 1813; member of the New York State assembly in 1814; elected as a Republican to the Fourteenth and Fifteenth Congresses (March 4, 1815-March 3, 1819); chairman, Committee on Revisal and Unfinished Business (Fifteenth Congress); district attorney of Washington County, 1818-1820; State comptroller, 1821-1823; chief justice of the State supreme court, 1823-1836; appointed Treasurer of the United States in 1828, but did not accept; presidential elector on the Democratic ticket in 1844; died in Utica, N.Y., October 19, 1863; interment in Forest Hill Cemetery.

**SAVAGE, John Houston,** a Representative from Tennessee; born in McMinnville, Tenn., on October 9, 1815; attended the common schools; served as a private in the Seminole War; studied law; was admitted to the bar and commenced practice in Smithville, Tenn.; colonel of State militia; attorney general of the fourth Tennessee district from 1841 until 1847; major of the Fourteenth United States Infantry during the Mexican War, and subsequently promoted to lieutenant colonel; elected as a Democrat to the Thirty-first and Thirty-second Congresses (March 4, 1849-March 3, 1853); declined to be a candidate for reelection in 1852 to the Thirty-third Congress; elected to the Thirty-fourth and Thirty-fifth Congresses (March 4, 1855-March 3, 1859); colonel of the Sixteenth Regiment Tennessee Infantry, in the Confederate Army during the Civil War; member of the Tennessee State house of representatives, 1877-1879, and 1887-1891; Tennessee State senator, 1879-1881; died in McMinnville, Tenn., on April 5, 1904; interment in Riverside Cemetery.

**SAVAGE, John Simpson,** a Representative from Ohio; born in Clermont County, Ohio, October 30, 1841; attended the public schools; taught school; studied law; was admitted to the bar in 1865 and commenced practice in Wilmington, Clinton County, Ohio, the same year; elected as a Democrat to the Forty-fourth Congress (March 4, 1875-March 3, 1877); unsuccessful candidate for reelection in 1876 to the Forty-fifth Congress; resumed the practice of law; died in Wilmington, Ohio, November 24, 1884; interment in Sugar Grove Cemetery.

**SAWTELLE, Cullen,** a Representative from Maine; born in Norridgewock, Maine, September 25, 1805; received his early education under private tutors and was graduated from Bowdoin College, Brunswick, Maine, in 1825; studied law; was admitted to the bar in 1828 and practiced in Norridgewock until 1841; register of probate 1830-1838; member of the State senate 1842-1844; elected as a Democrat to the Twenty-ninth Congress (March 4, 1845-March 3, 1847); chairman, Committee on Revisal and Unfinished Business (Twenty-ninth Congress); elected to the Thirty-first Congress (March 4, 1849-March 3, 1851); chairman, Committee on Revolutionary Claims (Thirty-first Congress); attorney and credit manager for several mercantile firms in New York City 1852-1882; died in Englewood, Bergen County, N.J., November 10, 1887; interment in Brookside Cemetery.

**SAWYER, Frederick Adolphus,** a Senator from South Carolina; born in Bolton, Worcester County, Mass., December 12, 1822; attended the public schools; graduated from Harvard University in 1844; taught school in New England from 1844 until 1859; took charge of the State normal school at Charleston, S.C., in 1859; returned to the North during the Civil War; returned to Charleston in February 1865 and was active in advancing reconstruction measures; appointed collector of internal revenue in the second South Carolina district in 1865; upon the readmission of the State of South Carolina to representation was elected as a Republican to the United States Senate, and served from July 16, 1868 to March 3, 1873; chairman, Committee on Education (Forty-first Congress), Committee on Education and Labor (Forty-second Congress); Assistant Secretary of the Treasury, 1873-1874; employed in the United States Coast Survey, 1874-1880; special agent of the War Department, 1880-1887; conducted a preparatory school in Ithaca, N.Y., and gave private instruction to students at Cornell University; moved to Tennessee and became president of a company at Cumberland Gap to promote the sale of agricultural lands in that vicinity; died suddenly at Shawnee, Tenn., July 31, 1891; interment in "Sawyer Heights," on the property of his land company, near East Cumberland Gap, Tenn.

**SAWYER, Harold Samuel,** a Representative from Michigan; born in San Francisco, Calif., March 21, 1920; attended the public schools of the San Francisco Bay area; graduated from Marin Junior College (now College of Marin), Kentfield, Calif., in 1940; B.A., University of California, Berkeley, 1940; J.D., Hastings College of Law, University of California, San Francisco, 1943; admitted to the California bar in 1943, the Michigan bar in 1946, and commenced practice in Grand Rapids, Mich.; served in the United States Navy, 1941-1945; practiced law in Grand Rapids from 1945 until 1975; member, Michigan Law Revision Commission, 1968-1976; Kent County (Mich.) prosecuting attorney, 1975-1976; elected as a Republican to the Ninety-fifth and to the three succeeding Congresses (January 3, 1977-January 3, 1985); was not a candidate for reelection in 1984 to the Ninety-ninth Congress; resumed the practice of law in Grand Rapids; is a resident of Rockford, Mich.

**SAWYER, John Gilbert,** a Representative from New York; born in Brandon, Rutland County, Vt., June 5, 1825; attended the common schools and Millville (N.Y.) Academy; moved to Albion, N.Y., in 1845; superintendent of schools for Orleans County, N.Y., 1848-1851; studied law; was admitted to the bar in 1850 and commenced practice in Albion, N.Y.; justice of the peace of Barre, Orleans County, N.Y., 1851-1862; prosecuting attorney of Orleans County 1862-1865; judge and surrogate of Orleans County 1867-1883; delegate to several Republican State conventions; elected as a Republican to the Forty-ninth, Fiftieth, and Fifty-first Congresses (March 4, 1885-March 3, 1891); chairman, Committee on Expenditures in the Department of the Navy (Fifty-first Congress); was not a candidate for renomination in 1890; resumed the practice of his profession in Albion, N.Y., and died there September 5, 1898; interment in Mount Albion Cemetery.

**SAWYER, Lemuel,** a Representative from North Carolina; born in Camden County, near Elizabeth City, N.C., in 1777; attended Flatbush Academy, Long Island, N.Y., and was graduated from the University of North Carolina at Chapel Hill in 1799; attended the University of Pennsylvania at Philadelphia for a time; studied law; was admitted to the bar in 1804 and commenced practice in Elizabeth City, N.C.; member of the State house of commons in 1800 and 1801; elected as a Republican to the Tenth, Eleventh, and Twelfth Congresses (March 4, 1807-March 3, 1813); elected to the Fifteenth, Sixteenth, and Seventeenth Congresses (March 4, 1817-March 3, 1823); unsuccessful candidate for reelection in 1822 to the Eighteenth Congress; elected to the Nineteenth and Twentieth Congresses (March 4, 1825-March 3, 1829); unsuccessful candidate for reelection in 1828 to the Twenty-first Congress; department clerk in Washington, D.C., until his death in that city on January 9, 1852; interment in the family burying ground at Lambs Ferry, Camden County, about four miles from Elizabeth City, Pasquotank County, N.C.

**Bibliography:** *DAB.*

**SAWYER, Lewis Ernest,** a Representative from Arkansas; born in Shelby County, Ala., June 24, 1867; moved with his parents to Lee County, Miss.; attended the public schools and was graduated from the University of Mississippi at Oxford; studied law; was admitted to the bar and commenced practice at Friars Point, Miss., in 1895; mayor of Friars Point from 1896 until he enlisted in the Spanish-American War in June 1898; served in the Philippine Islands during the war; resumed the practice of law in Iuka, Miss., in 1900; moved to Hot Springs, Ark., in 1908 and continued the practice of his profession; member of the State house of representatives in 1913 and 1915 and was its speaker in the latter year; elected as a Democrat to the Sixty-eighth Congress and served from March 4, 1923, until his death at Hot Springs, Ark., May 5, 1923; interment in Hollywood Cemetery.

**SAWYER, Philetus,** a Representative and a Senator from Wisconsin; born in Whiting, Rutland County, Vt., September 22, 1816; moved with his parents to Crown Point, N.Y., in 1817; attended the common schools; moved to Fond du Lac County, Wis., in 1847 and engaged in the lumber business; member, Wisconsin assembly 1857, 1861; mayor of Oshkosh 1863-1864; elected as a Republican to the Thirty-ninth and to the four succeeding Congresses (March 4, 1865-March 3, 1875); declined to be a candidate for renomination in 1874; chairman, Committee on Public Expenditures (Forty-second Congress), Committee on Pacific Railroads (Forty-third Congress); elected as a Republican to the United States Senate in 1881; reelected in 1887 and served from March 4, 1881, to March 3, 1893; was not a candidate for reelection; chairman, Committee on Railroads (Forty-eighth and Forty-ninth Congresses), Committee on Post Office and Post Roads (Fiftieth through Fifty-second Congresses); resumed his former business pursuits; died in Oshkosh, Winnebago County, Wis., March 29, 1900; interment in the family vault at Riverside, Oshkosh.

**Bibliography:** *DAB*; Current, Richard N. *Pine Logs and Politics: A Life of Philetus Sawyer, 1816-1900.* Madison: State Historical Society of Wisconsin, 1950.

**SAWYER, Samuel Locke,** a Representative from Missouri; born in Mount Vernon, N.H., November 27, 1813; was graduated from Dartmouth College, Hanover, N.H., in 1833; studied law; was admitted to the bar in Amherst, N.H., in 1836; moved to Lexington, Mo., in 1838 and practiced law; elected circuit attorney of the sixth judicial circuit of Missouri in 1848, and reelected in 1852; delegate to the Missouri constitutional convention in 1861; delegate to the Democratic National Convention of 1868; elected judge of the twenty-fourth judicial circuit, and served from 1871 until February 15, 1876, when he resigned; elected as an Independent Democrat to the Forty-sixth Congress (March 4, 1879-March 3, 1881); was not a candidate for renomination in 1880 to the Forty-seventh Congress; practiced law and engaged in banking; died in Independence, Mo., March 29, 1890; interment in Woodlawn Cemetery.

**SAWYER, Samuel Tredwell,** a Representative from North Carolina; born in Edenton, Chowan County, N.C., in 1800; attended Edenton Academy and the University of North Carolina at Chapel Hill; studied law; was admitted to the bar and commenced practice in Edenton; member of the State house of representatives 1829-1832; served in the State senate in 1834; elected as a Whig to the Twenty-fifth Congress (March 4, 1837-March 3, 1839); chairman, Committee on Expenditures on Public Buildings (Twenty-fifth Congress); unsuccessful candidate for reelection to the Twenty-sixth Congress; moved to Norfolk, Va., and resumed the practice of law; editor of the Norfolk Argus for several years; appointed collector of customs at Norfolk on May 16, 1853, and served until April 6, 1858; moved to Washington, D.C.; during the Civil War was appointed, September 17, 1861, commissary with the rank of major in the Confederate service and served until August 2, 1862; died in Bloomfield, Essex County, N.J., November 29, 1865.

**SAWYER, Thomas Charles,** a Representative from Ohio; born in Akron, Summit County, Ohio, August 15, 1945; attended public schools; graduated, Buchtel High School, Akron, 1963; B.A., University of Akron, 1968, M.A., 1970; public school teacher and administrator; legislative agent, Public Utilities Commission; member, Ohio State house of representatives, 1977-1983; mayor of Akron, 1984-1986; elected as a Democrat to the One Hundredth and to the four succeeding Congresses (January 3, 1987-January 3, 1997); is a resident of Akron, Ohio.

**SAWYER, William,** a Representative from Ohio; born in Montgomery County, Ohio, August 5, 1803; apprenticed to a blacksmith in 1818 and worked in Dayton, Ohio, and near Grand Rapids, Mich.; moved to Miamisburg, Ohio, in 1829; member of the Ohio State house of representatives, 1832-1835, and served as speaker in 1835; unsuccessful candidate for election to the Twenty-sixth and Twenty-seventh Congresses; moved to St. Marys, Ohio, in 1843; elected as a Democrat to the Twenty-ninth and Thirtieth Congresses (March 4, 1845-March 3, 1849); was not a candidate for renomination in 1848 to the Thirty-first Congress; delegate to the State constitutional convention, 1850-1851; again a member of the State house of representatives in 1856; receiver of the land office of the Otter Trail district in Minnesota, 1855-1861; trustee of Ohio Agricultural and Mechanical College (later Ohio State University), 1870-1874; mayor and justice of the peace of St. Marys, 1870-1877; died at St. Marys, Auglaize County, Ohio, September 18, 1877; interment in Elm Grove Cemetery.

**SAXBE, William Bart,** a Senator from Ohio; born in Mechanicsburg, Champaign County, Ohio, June 24, 1916; attended the public schools in Mechanicsburg; enlisted in Ohio National Guard in 1937; active military duty, Second World War, 1941-1945, and the Korean conflict, 1951-1952; A.B., Ohio State University, 1940; LL.B., Ohio State University School of Law, 1948; was admitted to the bar in 1948 and commenced practice in Columbus, Ohio; member, Ohio State house of representatives, 1947-1954; Ohio attorney general, 1957-1958, 1963-1968; chairman, Ohio Crime Commission, 1967-1968; elected as a Republican to the United States Senate in 1968, and served from January 3, 1969 until his resignation on January 3, 1974 to accept a Cabinet portfolio; Attorney General in the Cabinets of Presidents Richard M. Nixon and Gerald R. Ford from January 4, 1974 to February 2, 1975; appointed Ambassador to India by President Gerald R. Ford on February 3, 1975, and served until November 1976; resumed the practice of law; is a resident of Mechanicsburg, Ohio.

**SAXTON, Hugh James,** a Representative from New Jersey; born in Nicholson, Wyoming County, Pa., January 22, 1943; attended public schools; graduated Lackawanna Trail High School, Factoryville, Pa., 1961; B.A., East Stroudsburg (Pa.) State College, 1965; engaged in graduate work, Temple University, Philadelphia, Pa., 1967-1968; public school teacher, 1965-1968; entered the real estate business in 1965 and owned a realty company in New Jersey; member, New Jersey State assembly, 1976-1981; member, New Jersey State senate, 1982-1984; elected as a Republican to the Ninety-eighth Congress, November 6, 1984, by special election to fill the vacancy caused by the death of Edwin B. Forsythe, and at the same time elected to the Ninety-ninth Congress; reelected to the five succeeding Congresses and served from November 6, 1984, to January 3, 1997; is a resident of Mount Holly, N.J.

**SAY, Benjamin,** a Representative from Pennsylvania; born in Philadelphia, Pa., August 28, 1755; attended the Friends schools; was graduated from the medical department of the University of Pennsylvania at Philadelphia in 1780 and practiced in that city; was also an apothecary; served in the Revolutionary War; was a fellow of the College of Physicians of Philadelphia, of which he was one of the founders in 1787, and was treasurer from 1791 to 1809; member of the Pennsylvania Prison Society and president of the Pennsylvania Humane Society; elected as a Republican to the Tenth Congress to fill the vacancy caused by the resignation of Joseph Clay; reelected to the Eleventh Congress and served from November 16, 1808, until his resignation in June 1809; died in Philadelphia, Pa., April 23, 1813.

**Bibliography:** *DAB.*

**SAYERS, Joseph Draper,** a Representative from Texas; born in Grenada, Grenada County, Miss., September 23, 1841; moved with his father to Bastrop, Tex., in 1851; attended Bastrop Military Institute; entered the Confederate Army in 1861 and served throughout the Civil War, attaining the rank of major; taught school; studied law; was admitted to the bar in 1866 and commenced practice in Bastrop, Tex.; member of the Texas State senate, 1873-1879; chairman of the Democratic State executive committee, 1875-1878; Lieutenant Governor of Texas in 1879 and 1880; elected as a Democrat to the Forty-ninth and to the six succeeding Congresses, and served from March 4, 1885 until his resignation on January 16, 1899; chairman, Committee on Appropriations (Fifty-third Congress); elected Governor of Texas in 1898, reelected in 1900, and served from January 17, 1899 to January 20, 1903; resumed the practice of his profession in Austin, Travis County, Tex.; member of the State board of regents of the University of Texas at Austin in 1913; chairman of the State industrial accident board, 1914-1915; member of the State board of legal examiners, 1923-1925; appointed a member of the State pardon board in 1927

and served until his death in Austin, Tex., on May 15, 1929; interment in Fairview Cemetery, Bastrop, Tex.

**SAYLER, Henry Benton** (cousin of Milton Sayler), a Representative from Indiana; born in Montgomery County, Ohio, March 31, 1836; moved to Clinton County, Ind.; attended the common schools of the county; studied law; was admitted to the bar in 1856 and commenced practice in Eaton, Preble County, Ohio; during the Civil War served in the Union Army as lieutenant, captain, and major; elected as a Republican to the Forty-third Congress (March 4, 1873-March 3, 1875); was not a candidate for renomiantion in 1874; judge of the Twenty-eighth judicial circuit court of Indiana 1875-1900; died in Huntington, Huntington County, Ind., June 18, 1900; interment in Mount Hope Cemetery.

**SAYLER, Milton** (cousin of Henry Benton Sayler), a Representative from Ohio; born in Lewisburg, Preble County, Ohio, November 4, 1831; attended the public schools; pursued classical studies and was graduated from Miami University, Oxford, Ohio, in 1852; studied law at the Cincinnati Law School; was admitted to the bar and commenced practice in Cincinnati, Ohio; member of the State house of representatives in 1862 and 1863; member of the city council of Cincinnati in 1864 and 1865; elected as a Democrat to the Forty-third, Forty-fourth, and Forty-fifth Congresses (March 4, 1873-March 3, 1879); chairman, Committee on Public Lands (Forty-fourth Congress); unsuccessful candidate for reelection in 1878 to the Forty-sixth Congress; moved to New York City and resumed the practice of his profession; died in that city November 17, 1892; interment in Spring Grove Cemetery, Cincinnati, Ohio.

**SAYLOR, John Phillips,** a Representative from Pennsylvania; born in Conemaugh Township, Somerset County, Pa., July 23, 1908; attended the public schools in Johnstown, Pa.; was graduated from Mercersburg Academy in 1925, Franklin and Marshall College, Lancaster, Pa., in 1929, and Dickinson College Law School, Carlisle, Pa., in 1933; was admitted to the bar in 1934 and commenced the practice of law in Johnstown, Pa.; elected city solicitor of Johnstown, Pa., in 1938 and served until 1940; enlisted in the United States Navy on August 6, 1943, commissioned a lieutenant (junior grade) in 1943, and was discharged in January 1946; elected as a Republican to the Eighty-first Congress, September 13, 1949, by special election to fill the vacancy caused by the death of Robert L. Coffey; reelected to the twelve succeeding Congresses, and served from September 13, 1949 until his death in Houston, Tex., on October 28, 1973; interment in Grandview Cemetery, Johnstown, Pa.

**SCALES, Alfred Moore,** a Representative from North Carolina; born in Reidsville, Rockingham County, N.C., November 26, 1827; pursued classical studies; attended the Caldwell Institute, Greensboro, N.C., and the University of North Carolina at Chapel Hill in 1845 and 1846; studied law; was admitted to the bar in 1851 and practiced in Madison, N.C.; solicitor of Rockingham County in 1853; member of the North Carolina State house of commons in 1852, 1853, 1856, and 1857; elected as a Democrat to the Thirty-fifth Congress (March 4, 1857-March 3, 1859); presidential elector on the Southern Democratic ticket of John C. Breckinridge and Joseph Lane in 1860; volunteered as a private in the Confederate Army and served throughout the Civil War, attaining the rank of brigadier general on June 13, 1863; resumed the practice of law in Greensboro, N.C.; member of the State house of representatives, 1866-1869; elected as a Democrat to the Forty-fourth and to the four succeeding Congresses, and served from March 4, 1875 to December 30, 1884, when he resigned, having been elected Governor; chairman, Committee on Indian Affairs (Forty-fourth through Forty-sixth Congresses); elected Governor of North Carolina in 1884, and served from January 21, 1885 to January 17, 1889; engaged in banking in Greensboro, N.C., and died there on February 9, 1892; interment in Green Hill Cemetery.

**SCAMMAN, John Fairfield,** a Representative from Maine; born in Wells, Maine (then a district of Massachusetts), October 24, 1786; attended the common schools; engaged in mercantile pursuits; member of the Massachusetts house of representatives in 1817; member of the Maine house of representatives in 1820 and 1821; collector of customs in Saco, Maine, 1829-1841; elected as a Democrat to the Twenty-ninth Congress (March 4, 1845-March 3, 1847); chairman, Committee on Expenditures in the Department of the Treasury (Twenty-ninth Congress); served in the State senate in 1855; died in Saco, York County, Maine, May 22, 1858; interment in Laurel Hill Cemetery.

**SCANLON, Thomas Edward,** a Representative from Pennsylvania; born in Pittsburgh, Pa., September 18, 1896; attended the public schools, Forbes School, and Duquesne University, Pittsburgh, Pa.; learned the pressman's trade and was employed on Pittsburgh newspapers 1914-1936; during the First World War served as a private, first class, in the United States Army from September 6, 1918, to May 14, 1919; delegate to the Pittsburgh Central Labor Union 1920-1940; member of the Allegheny County Board for the Assessment and Revision of Taxes 1936-1941; elected as a Democrat to the Seventy-seventh and Seventy-eighth Congresses (January 3, 1941-January 3, 1945); unsuccessful candidate for reelection in 1944 to the Seventy-ninth Congress; member of the Boards of Viewers of Allegheny County, Pa.; died in Pittsburgh, Pa., August 9, 1955; interment in North Side Catholic Cemetery.

**SCARBOROUGH, Charles Joseph,** a Representative from Florida; born in Atlanta, Ga., April 9, 1963; graduated, Catholic High School, Pensacola, Fla., 1981; B.A., University of Alabama, 1985; J.D., University of Florida School of Law, 1990; attorney; businessman; elected as a Republican to the One Hundred Fourth Congress (January 3, 1995-January 3, 1997); is a resident of Pensacola, Fla.

**SCARBOROUGH, Robert Bethea,** a Representative from South Carolina; born in Chesterfield, Chesterfield County, S.C., October 29, 1861; attended the common schools and Mullins (S.C.) Academy; taught school; studied law; was admitted to the bar in 1884 and commenced practice in Conway, S.C.; county attorney of Horry County, 1885-1893; served as clerk of the county board from 1885 until 1890; member of the South Carolina State senate in 1897 and 1898 and was elected president pro tempore in 1898; Lieutenant Governor of South Carolina in 1899; elected as a Democrat to the Fifty-seventh and Fifty-eighth Congresses (March 4, 1901-March 3, 1905); declined to be a candidate for renomination in 1904 to the Fifty-ninth Congress; resumed the practice of law in Conway, S.C., and was also interested in banking; served as chairman of the board of regents of the South Carolina State Hospital; died in Conway, Horry County, S.C., on November 23, 1927; interment in Lake Side Cemetery.

**SCHADEBERG, Henry Carl,** a Representative from Wisconsin; born in Manitowoc, Manitowoc County, Wis., October 12, 1913; graduated from Manitowoc public schools; B.A., Carroll College, Waukesha, Wis., 1938; B.D., Garrett Biblical Institute, Evanston, Ill., 1941; clergyman in the Congregational Church; served in the United States Navy as a chaplain from 1943 to 1946, and in the Korean conflict from 1952 to 1953; captain in the United States Naval Reserve until his retirement in 1969; elected as a Republican to the Eighty-seventh and Eighty-eighth Congresses (January 3, 1961-January 3, 1965); unsuccessful candidate for reelection in 1964 to the Eighty-ninth Congress; delegate to Republican State conventions, beginning in 1960; delegate to the Republican National Convention of 1964; elected to the Ninetieth and Ninety-first Congresses (January 3, 1967-January 3, 1971); unsuccessful candidate for reelection in 1970 to the Ninety-second Congress; was a resident of Rockbridge Baths, Va., until his death there on December 11, 1985; ashes buried at Hill-Valley Ranch.

**SCHAEFER, Daniel,** a Representative from Colorado; born in Guttenberg, Clayton County, Iowa, January 25, 1936; attended public schools; B.A., Niagara University, Niagara Falls, N.Y., 1961; attended Potsdam State (N.Y.) University, 1961-1964; served in the United States Marine Corps, sergeant, 1955-1957; public relations consultant, 1967-1983; member, Colorado State general assembly, 1977-1978; member, Colorado State senate, 1979-1983; delegate, Colorado State Republican conventions, 1972-1982; secretary, Jefferson County Republican Party, 1975-1976; elected as a Republican to the Ninety-eighth Congress, March 29, 1983, by special election to fill the vacancy caused by the death of Representative-elect John L. Swigert; reelected to the Ninety-ninth and to the five succeeding Congresses and served from March 29, 1983, to January 3, 1997; is a resident of Lakewood, Colo.

**SCHAEFER, Edwin Martin,** a Representative from Illinois; born in Belleville, St. Clair County, Ill., May 14, 1887; attended the public schools, Western Military Academy, Alton, Ill., and the University of Illinois at Urbana; was graduated from Washington University, St. Louis, Mo., in 1910; chemical engineer with Morris & Co., packers, East St. Louis, Ill., 1913-1916, assistant general superintendent 1916-1918, and general superintendent 1919-1928; assistant recorder of deeds of St. Clair County, Ill., 1928-1930; county treasurer of St. Clair County, Ill., 1930-1932; delegate to the Democratic State conventions in 1928, 1932, and 1936; elected as a Democrat to the Seventy-third and to the four succeeding Congresses (March 4, 1933-January 3, 1943); was not a candidate for renomination in 1942; member of the board of directors of Griesediech-Western Brewery Co., Belleville, Ill., at the time of his death; died in St. Louis, Mo., November 8, 1950; interment in Walnut Hill Cemetery, Belleville, Ill.

**SCHAFER, John Charles,** a Representative from Wisconsin; born in Milwaukee, Wis., May 7, 1893; attended the public schools of Wauwatosa and West Allis High School; employed in the office of the Allis-Chalmers Co.; during the First World War enlisted in the Thirteenth Engineers on May 24, 1917, and served twenty-two months in France; engaged as a locomotive engineer on the Chicago & North Western Railroad; member of Wauwatosa School Board, district No. 11; member of the Wisconsin State assembly in 1921; elected as a Republican to the Sixty-eighth and to the four succeeding Congresses (March 4, 1923-March 3, 1933); unsuccessful candidate for reelection in 1932 to the Seventy-third Congress; unsuccessful candidate for election in 1934 to the Seventy-fourth Congress, and in 1936 to the Seventy-fifth Congress; elected to the Seventy-sixth Congress (January 3, 1939-January 3, 1941); unsuccessful candidate for reelection in 1940 to the Seventy-seventh Congress, and for election in 1942 to the Seventy-eighth Congress; unsuccessfully contested the election of Thaddeus F.B. Wasielewski in the Seventy-eighth Congress; unsuccessful candidate for election in 1952 to the Eighty-third Congress, in 1954 to the Eighty-fourth Congress, and in 1957 for nomination to the United States Senate to fill the vacancy caused by the death of Joseph R. McCarthy; engaged in the sale of automotive electrical equipment and in the insurance business in Oak Park, Ill.; died in Pewaukee, Wis., June 9, 1962; interment in Arlington Park, Milwaukee, Wis.

**SCHALL, Thomas David,** a Representative and a Senator from Minnesota; born in Reed City, Osceola County, Mich., June 4, 1878; moved with his mother to Campbell, Minn., in 1884; attended the common schools, but ran away to join the circus; attended Hamline University, St. Paul, Minn., 1898-1899; graduated from the University of Minnesota at Minneapolis in 1902 and from St. Paul College of Law in 1904; was admitted to the bar in 1904 and commenced practice at Minneapolis; in 1907 lost his sight as the result of an electric shock but continued the practice of his profession; unsuccessful candidate for election in 1912 to the Sixty-third Congress; elected as a Republican to the Sixty-fourth and to the four succeeding Congresses (March 4, 1915-March 3, 1925); was not a candidate in 1924 for renomination to the House of Representatives, having become a candidate for the United States Senate; chairman, Committee on Alcohol Liquor Traffic (Sixty-seventh Congress), Committee on Flood Control (Sixty-eighth Congress); elected in 1924 as a Republican to the United States Senate; reelected in 1930, and served from March 4, 1925 until his death in Washington, D.C., December 22, 1935, as the result of being struck by an automobile in Cottage City, Md., near his home in Berwyn Heights, Md.; chairman, Committee on Interoceanic Canals (Seventy-first and Seventy-second Congresses); interment in Lakewood Cemetery, Minneapolis, Minn.

**Bibliography:** *DAB.*

**SCHELL, Richard,** a Representative from New York; born in Rhinebeck, Rhinebeck County, N.Y., May 15, 1810; completed preparatory studies; engaged in mercantile pursuits; moved to New York City in 1830 and became a wholesale dry-goods merchant; member of the State senate in 1857; elected as a Democrat to the Forty-third Congress to fill the vacancy caused by the death of David B. Mellish and served from December 7, 1874, to March 3, 1875; resumed mercantile pursuits; died in New York City, November 10, 1879; interment in the Old Dutch Cemetery, Rhinebeck, N.Y.

**SCHENCK, Abraham Henry** (uncle of Isaac Teller), a Representative from New York; born in Matteawan, Dutchess County, N.Y., January 22, 1775; received a thorough English education; became engaged in the manufacture of machinery; member of the State assembly 1804-1806; elected as a Republican to the Fourteenth Congress (March 4, 1815-March 3, 1817); engaged in the manufacture of cotton goods; died in Fishkill, Dutchess County, N.Y., June 1, 1831; interment in the Dutch Reform Churchyard, Beacon (formerly Fishkill Landing), N.Y.

**SCHENCK, Ferdinand Schureman,** a Representative from New Jersey; born in Millstone, Somerset County, N.J., February 11, 1790; completed preparatory studies; studied medicine at the College of Physicians and Surgeons of New York, graduating in 1814; commenced practice at Six-Mile Run (now Franklin Park), N.J.; member of the State general assembly 1829-1831; elected as a Jacksonian to the Twenty-third and Twenty-fourth Congresses (March 4, 1833-March 3, 1837); was not a candidate for renomination; trustee of Rutgers College, New Brunswick, N.J., 1841-1861; member of the State constitutional convention in 1844; judge of the State court of errors and appeals 1845-1857; unsuccessful Republican candidate for the State senate in 1856; continued the practice of medicine; died in Camden, N.J., May 16, 1860; interment in a private cemetery at Pleasant Plains (near Franklin Park), N.J.

**SCHENCK, Paul Fornshell,** a Representative from Ohio; born in Miamisburg, Montgomery County, Ohio, April 19, 1899; moved to Dayton, Ohio, in 1908 and graduated from Steele High School in 1917; two years of college training; teacher in Steele High School 1917-1919; automotive service business from 1919 to 1923; automotive training teacher and faculty manager of athletics at Roosevelt High School, 1923 to 1929; director of recreation, city of Dayton, 1929-1935; established own real estate, mortgage loan, and insurance business in September 1935; member of the board of education 1941-1950, serving as president for seven years; vice chairman of the Dayton Safety Council in 1946 and 1947; president Dayton Real Estate Board 1947-1949; elected as a Republican to the Eighty-second Congress to fill the vacancy caused by the resignation of Edward F. Breen; reelected to the Eighty-third and to the five succeeding Congresses (November 6, 1951-January 3, 1965); unsuccessful candidate in 1964 for reelection to the Eighty-ninth Congress; died in Dayton, Ohio, November 30, 1968; interment in Woodland Cemetery.

**SCHENCK, Robert Cumming,** a Representative from Ohio; born in Franklin, Ohio, October 4, 1809; attended the rural schools and was graduated from Miami University, Oxford, Ohio, in 1827; was a professor in that university from 1827 until 1829; studied law; was admitted to the bar in 1833 and commenced practice in Dayton, Ohio; member of the Ohio State house of representatives, 1839-1843; elected as a Whig to the Twenty-eighth and to the three succeeding Congresses (March 4, 1843-March 3, 1851); chairman, Committee on Roads and Canals (Thirtieth Congress); was not a candidate for renomination; appointed Minister to Brazil on March 12, 1851; served until October 1853, and was also accredited to Uruguay, the Argentine Confederation, and Paraguay; entered the Union Army on May 17, 1861, and served as brigadier general of Volunteers; promoted to major general September 18, 1862, to date from August 30, 1862; resigned his commission in the Army on December 3, 1863, to take his seat in Congress; elected as a Republican to the Thirty-eighth and to the three succeeding Congresses and served from March 4, 1863, to January 5, 1871, when he resigned to accept a position in the diplomatic service; chairman, Committee on Military Affairs (Thirty-eighth and Thirty-ninth Congresses), Committee on Ways and Means (Fortieth and Forty-first Congresses); unsuccessful candidate for reelection in 1870 to the Forty-second Congress; appointed Minister to Great Britain on December 22, 1870 and served until March 1876, when he resigned; delegate to the Philadelphia Loyalist Convention in 1866; member of the *Alabama* Claims Commission in 1871; resumed the practice of law in Washington, D.C., where he died on March 23, 1890; interment in Woodland Cemetery, Dayton, Ohio.

**Bibliography:** *DAB*; Joyner, Fred B. "Robert Cumming Schenck, First Citizen and Statesman of the Miami Valley." *Ohio State Archaeological and Historical Quarterly* 58 (July 1949): 286-97.

**SCHENK, Lynn,** a Representative from California; born in the Bronx, New York City, October 15, 1945; graduated from Hamilton High School, Los Angeles, Calif., 1962; B.A., University of California, Los Angeles, 1967; J.D., University of San Diego, 1970; London School of Economics, post-graduate studies in international law; deputy attorney general, California; attorney, San Diego Gas and Electric Co., 1972-1978; White House Fellow and special assistant to Vice Presidents Nelson A. Rockefeller and Walter F. Mondale, 1976-1977; deputy secretary then secretary of California State Business, Transportation and Housing, 1980-1983; attorney in private practice, 1983-1993; commissioner and vice chair of board, San Diego Unified Port District, 1990-1993; elected as a Democrat to the One Hundred Third Congress (January 3, 1993-January 3, 1995); unsuccessful candidate for reelection in 1994 to the One Hundred Fourth Congress; is a resident of San Diego, Calif.

**SCHERER, Gordon Harry,** a Representative from Ohio; born in Cincinnati, Hamilton County, Ohio, December 26, 1906; Salmon P. Chase College of Law, LL.B., in 1929 and attended the University of Cincinnati; was admitted to the Ohio bar in 1929 and commenced the practice of law in Cincinnati; assistant prosecuting attorney of Hamilton County 1933-1941; director of safety in Cincinnati in 1943 and 1944; member of the city planning commission in 1945 and 1946; member of the city council 1945-1949; elected as a Republican to the Eighty-third and to the four succeeding Congresses (January 3, 1953-January 3, 1963); was not a candidate for renomination in 1962 to the Eighty-eighth Congress; resumed the practice of law; delegate to the Republican National Conventions of 1964 and 1968; chairman, Hamilton County, Ohio, Republican Party, 1962-1968; member, U.S. National Commission for the United Nations Educational, Scientific and Cultural Organization, 1970-1973, and served on the executive board, 1974-1975; United States representative to the United Nations, 1972-1973; was a resident of Cincinnati, Ohio, until his death there on August 13, 1988.

**SCHERLE, William Joseph,** a Representative from Iowa; born in Little Falls, Herkimer County, N.Y., March 14, 1923; graduated from St. Mary's Academy in New York; attended Southern Methodist University of Dallas, Tex., 1945-1947; served in the Second World War, 1942-1946, and in the United States Naval Reserve, 1947-1954; assistant division manager with George D. Barnard Co., Dallas, Tex., 1947; became a grain and livestock farmer in 1948; chairman, Mills County (Iowa) Republican Central committee, 1956-1964; member, Iowa State house of representatives, 1960-1966; elected as a Republican to the Ninetieth and the three succeeding Congresses (January 3, 1967-January 3, 1975); unsuccessful candidate for reelection in 1974 to the Ninety-fourth Congress; deputy admnistrator, United States Department of Agriculture, 1975-1977; president of a consulting firm in Washington, D.C., 1977-1987; is a resident of Henderson, Iowa.

**SCHERMERHORN, Abraham Maus,** a Representative from New York; born in Schenectady, N.Y., December 11, 1791; completed preparatory studies and was graduated from Union College, Schenectady, in 1810; studied law; was admitted to the bar in 1812; moved to Rochester, N.Y., in 1813; engaged in banking; supervisor of Rochester in 1834; mayor in 1837; member of State assembly in 1848; elected as a Whig to the Thirty-first and Thirty-second Congresses (March 4, 1849-March 3, 1853); died at Savin Rock, near New Haven, Conn., August 22, 1855; interment in Mount Hope Cemetery, Rochester, N.Y.

**SCHERMERHORN, Simon Jacob,** a Representative from New York; born in Rotterdam, Schenectady County, N.Y., September 25, 1827; attended the common schools; engaged in agricultural pursuits; supervisor of the town of Rotterdam in 1856; served two terms as school commissioner; member of the State assembly in 1862 and 1865; a director and trustee in local banks; elected as a Democrat to the Fifty-third Congress (March 4, 1893-March 3, 1895); was not a candidate for renomination in 1894; retired to his farm in Rotterdam, N.Y., and died there July 21, 1901; interment in Viewland Cemetery.

**SCHEUER, James Haas,** a Representative from New York; born in New York City February 6, 1920; attended the New York Fieldston and Ethical Culture schools; A.B., Swarthmore (Pa.) College, 1946; LL.B., Columbia University Law School, New York City, 1948; graduated, Harvard University School of Business Administration, 1943; was admitted to the bar in 1948 and began the practice of law in 1949; served as a flight instructor in the United States Army, 1943-1945; economist for the Foreign Economic Administration in 1945 and 1946; member of the legal staff for the Office of Price Stabilization, 1951-1957; writer and lecturer; unsuccessful candidate for the Democratic nomination to the Eighty-eighth Congress in 1962; elected as a Democrat-Liberal to the Eighty-ninth and to the three succeeding Congresses (January 3, 1965-January 3, 1973); unsuccessful candidate for renomination in 1972 to the Ninety-third Congress; served as president, National Alliance for Safer Cities, 1972-1973; president, National Housing Conference, 1972-1974; elected as a Democrat-Liberal to the Ninety-fourth and to the eight succeeding Congresses (January 3, 1975-January 3, 1993); was not a candidate for renomination in 1992 to the One Hundred Third Congress; chairman, Select Committee on Population (Ninety-fifth Congress); is a resident of Douglaston, N.Y.

**SCHIFF, Steven Harvey,** a Representative from New Mexico; born in Chicago, Ill., March 18, 1947; B.A., University of Illinois, Chicago, 1968; J.D., University of New Mexico Law School, 1972; New Mexico Air National Guard service as lieutenant colonel; admitted to New Mexico bar, 1972; attorney, private practice, 1977-1979; assistant district attorney of Bernalillo County, N.Mex., 1972-1974; trial attorney, 1977-1979; assistant city attorney and counsel for Albuquerque police department, 1979-1981; district attorney of Bernalillo County, 1980-1988; elected as a Republican to the One Hundred First and to the three succeeding Congresses (January 3, 1989-January 3, 1997); is a resident of Albuquerque, N.Mex.

**SCHIFFLER, Andrew Charles,** a Representative from West Virginia; born in Wheeling, W.Va., August 10, 1889; attended the public schools; studied law in law offices in Wheeling, W.Va.; was admitted to the bar and commenced practice in Wheeling in 1913; referee in bankruptcy, northern district of West Virginia, 1918-1922; prosecuting attorney of Ohio County, W.Va., 1925-1932; chairman of the Ohio County Republican committee 1936-1938; elected as a Republican to the Seventy-sixth Congress (January 3, 1939-January 3, 1941); unsuccessful candidate for reelection in 1940 to the Seventy-seventh Congress; elected to the Seventy-eighth Congress (January 3, 1943-January 3, 1945); unsuccessful candidate for reelection in 1944 to the Seventy-ninth Congress; resumed the practice of law in Wheeling, W.Va., and remained active in his profession until his death there March 27, 1970; interment in Mount Calvary Cemetery.

**SCHIRM, Charles Reginald,** a Representative from Maryland; born in Baltimore, Md., August 12, 1864; attended the public schools; commenced, but did not complete, an apprenticeship at iron molding; attended Washington and Jefferson College, Washington, Pa.; taught school in Pennsylvania and Maryland; studied law; was admitted to the Baltimore County bar in 1896 and practiced; member of the State house of delegates 1898-1900; counsel to the board of police commissioners of the city of Baltimore in 1899 and 1900; elected as a Republican to the Fifty-seventh Congress (March 4, 1901-March 3, 1903); unsuccessful candidate for reelection in 1902 to the Fifty-eighth Congress; delegate to the Bull Moose National Convention in 1912; continued the practice of law in Baltimore, Md., until his death there on November 2, 1918; interment in Loudon Park Cemetery.

**SCHISLER, Darwin Gale,** a Representative from Illinois; born on a farm in Indian Point Township, Knox County, Ill., March 2, 1933; attended Indian Point public schools; graduated from Abingdon High School in 1951; served in the United States Air Force, 1952-1955, serving ten months overseas in France; B.S., Western Illinois University, Macomb, 1959; began teaching and coaching at London Mills (Ill.) Junior High School in 1959, and then was employed as principal from 1960 until 1964; M.A., Northeast Missouri State Teachers College, Kirksville, 1962; elected as a Democrat to the Eighty-ninth Congress (January 3, 1965-January 3, 1967); unsuccessful candidate for reelection in 1966 to the Ninetieth Congress; appointed by Governor Otto Kerner to head the Illinois Office of Intergovernmental Cooperation, 1967-1969; member, Illinois State general assembly, 1969-1981; partner, Gray-Schisler Real Estate Agency, 1979-1982; administrative assistant, State's Attorney Appellate Prosecutor, and consultant, Shea, Rogal and Associates, Ltd., 1981-1986; retired; is a resident of London Mills, Ill.

**SCHLEICHER, Gustave,** a Representative from Texas; was born in Darmstadt, Germany, on November 19, 1823; attended the University of Giessen; became a civil engineer and was employed in the construction of several European railroads; immigrated to the United States in 1847 and settled in San Antonio, Tex., in 1850; member of the State house of representatives in 1853 and 1854; served in the State senate 1859-1861; elected as a Democrat to the Forty-fourth and Forty-fifth Congresses and served from March 4, 1875, until his death; chairman, Committee on Railways and Canals (Forty-fifth Congress); had been reelected in 1878 to the Forty-sixth Congress; died in Washington, D.C., January 10, 1879; interment in the United States National Cemetery, San Antonio, Tex.

**SCHLEY, William,** a Representative from Georgia; born in Frederick, Frederick County, Md., December 15, 1786; in childhood moved with his parents to Georgia; completed preparatory studies; attended the local academies in Louisville and Augusta, Ga.; studied law; was admitted to the bar and commenced practice in Augusta, Ga., in 1812; served as judge of the superior court, 1825-1828; member of the Georgia State house of representatives in 1830; elected as a Jacksonian to the Twenty-third and Twenty-fourth Congresses, and served from March 4, 1833 to July 1, 1835, when he resigned, having been nominated for Governor; elected Governor of Georgia in 1835, and served from November 4, 1835 to November 8, 1837; unsuccessful candidate for reelection in 1837; president of the Georgia Medical College at Augusta; died near Augusta, Ga., on November 20, 1858; interment in the family burying ground at Richmond Hill, near Augusta, Ga.

**SCHMIDHAUSER, John Richard,** a Representative from Iowa; born in the Bronx, New York City, January 3, 1922; attended public schools in New York and Maryland; moved to Salisbury, Md., with parents in 1934; served in the United States Navy from August 1941 to December 1945; B.A., University of Delaware, Newark, 1949; M.A., University of Virginia, Charlottesville, 1952, and Ph.D., political science, 1954; professor of constitutional law at the State University of Iowa from 1954 until 1964; precinct committeeman and Democratic county chairman of Johnson County, Iowa; elected as a Democrat to the Eighty-ninth Congress (January 3, 1965-January 3, 1967); unsuccessful candidate for reelection in 1966 to the Ninetieth Congress, and for election in 1968 to the Ninety-first Congress; unsuccessful candidate for nomination in 1972 to the Ninety-third Congress; Democratic central committee member, Santa Barbara County, Calif., 1986 to present; taught constitutional law at the University of Iowa, 1967-1973; professor of political science, University of Southern California, 1973-1992, and professor emeritus of political science, 1992 to present; is a resident of Carpinteria, Calif.

**SCHMITT, Harrison Hagan,** a Senator from New Mexico; born in Santa Rita, Grant County, N.Mex., July 3, 1935; attended the public schools; B.S., California Institute of Technology, Pasadena, 1957; Fulbright fellowship student at the University of Oslo (Norway), 1957-1958; Ph.D., geology, Harvard University, 1964; geologist, United States Geological Survey, Department of the Interior, 1964-1965; astronaut, National Aeronautics and Space Administration, 1965-1975; elected as a Republican to the United States Senate in 1976, and served from January 3, 1977 to January 3, 1983; unsuccessful candidate for reelection in 1982; consultant and writer in science, technology and public policy, 1983 to present; adjunct professor of engineering, University of Wisconsin, Madison; acting president and chief executive officer, The Lovelace Institutes; chair and president, The Annapolis Center; is a resident of Albuquerque, N.Mex.

**SCHMITZ, John George,** a Representative from California; born in Milwaukee, Wis., August 12, 1930; graduated from Marquette University High School, 1948; B.S., Marquette University, 1952; M.A., California State College, Long Beach, 1960; served as a Marine Corps jet fighter and helicopter pilot, 1952-1960; lieutenant colonel, United States Marine Corps Reserve, 1960-1983; instructor in philosophy and political science, Santa Ana (now Rancho Santiago) College, 1960-1990; California State senator, 1964-1970; elected as a Republican to the Ninety-first Congress, June 30, 1970, by special election to fill the vacancy caused by the death of James B. Utt; reelected to the Ninety-second Congress, and served from June 30, 1970 to January 3, 1973; unsuccessful candidate for renomination in 1972 to the Ninety-third Congress; American Party candidate for election for President of the United States in 1972; unsuccessful candidate for nomination in 1976 to the Ninety-fifth Congress; California State senator, 1978-1982; presi-dent, Chapelle Charlemagne Vineyards, 1995 to present; is a resident of Washington, Va.

**Bibliography:** Schmitz, John G. *Stranger in the Arena.* Santa Ana, Calif.: Rayline Printing Co., 1974.

**SCHNEEBELI, Gustav Adolphus,** a Representative from Pennsylvania; born in Neusalz, Germany, May 23, 1853; immigrated to the United States with his parents, who settled in Bethlehem, Pa.; attended the Moravian Parochial School; later moved to Nazareth, Pa., and entered upon a mercantile career; founded the knit-goods industry of the Nazareth Waist Co.; in 1888 he established a lace manufacturing company, of which he became sole owner; elected as a Republican to the Fifty-ninth Congress (March 4, 1905-March 3, 1907); unsuccessful candidate for reelection in 1906 to the Sixtieth Congress; continued in the lace manufacturing business until his death in Nazareth, Northampton County, Pa., February 6, 1923; interment in Moravian Cemetery.

**SCHNEEBELI, Herman Theodore,** a Representative from Pennsylvania; born in Lancaster, Lancaster County, Pa., July 7, 1907; attended the public schools; graduated from Mercersburg Academy in 1926, Dartmouth College in 1930, and Amos Tuck School in 1931; commission distributor, Gulf Oil Corporation and automobile dealer in Williamsport, Pa.; served as a captain, Ordnance Department, 1942-1946; elected as a Republican to the Eighty-sixth Congress, by special election, April 26, 1960, to fill the vacancy caused by the death of United States Representative Alvin R. Bush; reelected to the eight succeeding Congresses and served from April 26, 1960, to January 3, 1977; was not a candidate for reelection in 1976 to the Ninety-fifth Congress; resided in Willliamsport, Pa., until his death in Philadelphia, Pa., on May 6, 1982; interment in Wildwood Cemetery, Williamsport, Pa.

**SCHNEIDER, Claudine,** a Representative from Rhode Island; born in Clairton, Allegheny County, Pa., March 25, 1947; attended parochial schools; studied at the University of Barcelona, Spain, and Rosemont College (Pa.); B.A., Windham College (Vt.), 1969; attended the University of Rhode Island School of Community Planning; founder, Rhode Island Committee on Energy, 1973; executive director, Conservation Law Foundation, 1974; federal coordinator, Rhode Island Coastal Zone Management Program, 1978; producer and host of public affairs television program, Providence, R.I., 1978-1979; elected as a Republican to the Ninety-seventh and to the four succeeding Congresses (January 3, 1981-January 3, 1991); was not a candidate for reelection in 1990 to the One Hundred Second Congress, but was an unsuccessful candidate for election to the United States Senate; is a resident of Narragansett, R.I.

**SCHNEIDER, George John,** a Representative from Wisconsin; born in the town of Grand Chute, Outagamie County; Wis., October 30, 1877; moved to Appleton with his parents, attended the public schools of Appleton, Wis.; learned the trade of paper making; vice president of the International Brotherhood of Paper Makers from 1909 until 1927; member of the executive board of the Wisconsin State Federation of Labor, 1921-1928; elected as a Republican to the Sixty-eighth and to the four succeeding Congresses (March 4, 1923-March 3, 1933); unsuccessful candidate for reelection in 1932 to the Seventy-third Congress; elected as a Progressive to the Seventy-fourth and Seventy-fifth Congresses (January 3, 1935-January 3, 1939); unsuccessful candidate for reelection in 1938 to the Seventy-sixth Congress; resumed labor activities, and died in Toledo, Ohio, March 12, 1939, while attending a labor meeting; interment in Riverside Cemetery, Appleton, Wis.

**SCHOEPPEL, Andrew Frank,** a Senator from Kansas; born on a farm in Barton County, near Chaflin, Kans., November 23, 1894; attended the district schools in Ness County; attended the University of Kansas from 1916 until 1918; left school during the First World War and enlisted in the Naval Air Service; following the armistice entered the University of Nebraska Law School and graduated in 1922; was admitted to the Kansas bar in 1923 and commenced practice in Ness City, Kans.; county attorney of Ness County; mayor of Ness City; chairman of the Corporation Commission of the State of Kansas, 1939-1942; elected Governor of Kansas in 1942, reelected in 1944 and served from January 11, 1943 to January 13, 1947; practiced law in Wichita, Kans.; elected as a Republican to the United States Senate in 1948; reelected in 1954, and again in 1960 and served from January 3, 1949, until his death in the naval hospital at Bethesda, Md., on January 21, 1962; interment in Old Mission Cemetery, Wichita, Kans.

**Bibliography:** *DAB*; Koppes, Clayton R. "Oscar L. Chapman and McCarthyism." *Colorado Magazine* 56 (Winter-Spring 1979): 35-44.

**SCHOOLCRAFT, John Lawrence,** a Representative from New York; born in Albany, N.Y., in 1804; received a limited schooling; engaged in mercantile pursuits; elected as a Whig to the Thirty-first and Thirty-second Congresses (March 4, 1849-March 3, 1853); was not a candidate for renomination in 1852; chosen president of the Commercial Bank at Albany, N.Y., and served from 1854 until his death; delegate to the Republican National Convention in 1860; died while returning to his home from the convention at Chicago, in St. Catherines, Ontario, Canada, July 7, 1860; interment in the Rural Cemetery, Albany, N.Y.

**SCHOONMAKER, Cornelius Corneliusen** (grandfather of Marius Schoonmaker), a Representative from New York; born in Shawangunk (now Wallkill), Ulster County, N.Y., in June 1745; received a limited schooling; became a surveyor and engaged in agricultural pursuits; member of the committees of vigilance and safety during the Revolutionary War; served in the State assembly 1777-1790; member of the State ratification convention in 1788; elected to the Second Congress (March 4, 1791-March 3, 1793); again a member of the State assembly in 1795; died in Shawangunk, N.Y., in the spring of 1796; interment in Old Shawangunk Churchyard at Bruynswick, in Shawangunk (now Wallkill), Ulster County, N.Y.

**SCHOONMAKER, Marius** (grandson of Cornelius Corneliusen Schoonmaker), a Representative from New York; born in Kingston, Ulster County, N.Y., April 24, 1811; attended the common schools, Kingston Academy, and was graduated from Yale College in 1830; was admitted to the bar in 1833 and commenced practice in Kingston, N.Y.; member of the State senate in 1850 and 1851; elected as a Whig to the Thirty-second Congress (March 4, 1851-March 3, 1853); declined to be a candidate for renomination in 1852; resumed the practice of law in Kingston, N.Y.; auditor of the canal department of New York State in 1854 and 1855; superintendent of the banking department 1854-1856; president of the Kingston Board of Education for nine years; president of the village of Kingston in 1866, 1869, and 1870; delegate to the State constitutional convention in 1867; president of the board of directors of Kingston; died in Kingston, N.Y., January 5, 1894; interment in Wiltwyck Rural Cemetery.

**SCHROEDER, Patricia Scott,** a Representative from Colorado; born in Portland, Multnomah County, Oreg., July 30, 1940; attended the public schools of Texas, Ohio, and Iowa; B.A., University of Minnesota, Minneapolis, 1961; J.D., Harvard University Law School, 1964; admitted to the Colorado bar in 1964 and commenced practice in Denver; lecturer and law instructor, 1969-1972; counsel, Colorado Planned Parenthood, 1970-1972; hearing officer, Colorato State personnel department, 1971-1972; elected as a Democrat to the Ninety-third and to the eleven succeeding Congresses (January 3, 1973-January 3, 1997); was not a candidate for reelection in 1996 to the One Hundred Fifth Congress; chairman, Select Committee on Children, Youth and Families (One

Hundred Second and One Hundred Third Congresses); is a resident of Denver, Colo.

**SCHUETTE, Bill,** a Representative from Michigan; born in Midland, Mich., October 13, 1953; attended public schools; B.S.F.S., Georgetown University, Washington, D.C., 1976; attended the University of Aberdeen, Scotland, 1974-1975; J.D., University of San Francisco School of Law, 1979; admitted to the Michigan bar and commenced practice in Midland in 1979; delegate to Michigan State Republican conventions, 1972, 1974, and 1982; elected as a Republican to the Ninety-ninth and to the two succeeding Congresses (January 3, 1985-January 3, 1991); was not a candidate in 1990 for reelection to the House of Representatives, but was an unsuccessful candidate for election to the United States Senate; director, Michigan Department of Agriculture, 1991-1994; elected to the Michigan State senate, District 35, in November 1994 for a four-year term beginning in January 1995; is a resident of Midland, Mich.

**SCHUETZ, Leonard William,** a Representative from Illinois; born in Posen, Germany (later Poland), November 16, 1887; in 1888 immigrated to the United States with his father, who settled in Chicago, Ill.; attended the public schools, Lane Technical High School, and Bryant and Stratton Business College, Chicago, Ill.; engaged as a stenographer and secretary until 1906, when he became associated with Swift & Co. in an executive capacity; organized the Schuetz Construction Co. in 1923 and served as its president and treasurer; elected as a Democrat to the Seventy-second and to the six succeeding Congresses and served from March 4, 1931, until his death in Washington, D.C., on February 13, 1944; interment in St. Adabert's Cemetery, Chicago, Ill.

**SCHULTE, William Theodore,** a Representative from Indiana; born in St. Bernard, Platte County, Nebr., August 19, 1890; attended the public schools of St. Bernard, Nebr.; moved with his parents to Hammond, Ind., where he attended high school and received a business training; engaged in the theatrical business until 1918; also interested in agricultural pursuits; member of the city council of Hammond, Ind., 1918-1922; resumed the theatrical business until 1932; elected as a Democrat to the Seventy-third and to the four succeeding Congresses (March 4, 1933-January 3, 1943); unsuccessful candidate for renomination in 1942 to the Seventy-eighth Congress, coordinator of field operations in the labor division of the War Production Board, Washington, D.C., 1942-1944; returned to Lake County, Ind., and engaged in agricultural pursuits, engaged in the automobile business at Michigan City, Ind., from October 1947 to March 1949; sales representative of a construction machinery firm; died in Hammond, Ind., on December 7, 1966; interment in St. Andrew's Cemetery.

**SCHULZE, Richard Taylor,** a Representative from Pennsylvania; born in Philadelphia, Pa., August 7, 1929; graduated from Haverford High School, February 1948; attended University of Houston, 1948-1949; extension student, Villanova (Pa.) University, Temple University, Philadelphia, Pa., 1968; entered the appliance business in Paoli, Pa., in 1950; served in the United States Army, 1951-1953; served as register of wills and clerk of orphans court in Chester County, Pa., 1967-1969; member, Pennsylvania house of representatives, 1969-1974; elected as a Republican to the Ninety-fourth and to the eight succeeding Congresses (January 3, 1975-January 3, 1993); was not a candidate for renomination in 1992 to the One Hundred Third Congress; senior legislative adviser, Valis Associates, Washington, D.C.; is a resident of Arlington, Va.

**SCHUMAKER, John Godfrey,** a Representative from New York; born in Claverack, Columbia County, N.Y., June 27, 1826; completed preparatory studies in the Lenox (Mass.) Academy; studied law; was admitted to the bar and commenced practice in 1847; moved to Brooklyn, N.Y., in 1853 and continued the practice of law; district attorney for Kings County 1856-1859; corporation counsel for the city of Brooklyn 1862-1864; member of the State constitutional conventions in 1862, 1867, and 1894; delegate to the Democratic National Convention in 1864; elected as a Democrat to the Forty-first Congress (March 4, 1869-March 3, 1871); was not a candidate for renomination in 1870; elected to the Forty-third and Forty-fourth Congresses (March 4, 1873-March 3, 1877); was not a candidate for renomination in 1876 to the Forty-fifth Congress; resumed the practice of law; died in Brooklyn, N.Y., on November 23, 1905; interment in Greenwood Cemetery.

**SCHUMER, Charles Ellis,** a Representative from New York; born in Brooklyn, N.Y., November 23, 1950; attended the public schools; graduated from Madison High School, Brooklyn, 1967; B.A., Harvard University, 1971; J.D., Harvard University Law School, 1974; admitted to the New York bar in 1975; staff aide to Senator Claiborne Pell of Rhode Island, 1973; member, New York State assembly, 1975-1980; elected as a Democrat to the Ninety-seventh and to the seven succeeding Congresses (January 3, 1981-January 3, 1997); is a resident of Brooklyn, N.Y.

**SCHUNEMAN, Martin Gerretsen,** a Representative from New York; born in Catskill, Albany (now Greene) County, N.Y., February 10, 1764; educated by his father; justice of the peace of Albany County in 1792; engaged in mercantile pursuits and owned an inn at Madison; supervisor for Catskill in Albany and Greene Counties in 1797, 1799, and 1802; member of the State assembly from Ulster County 1798-1800 and from Greene County in 1803; delegate from Greene County to the State constitutional convention in 1801; elected as a Republican to the Ninth Congress (March 4, 1805-March 3, 1807); resumed his former business pursuits; died in Catskill, N.Y., February 21, 1827; interment in the Old Cemetery, Madison (now Leeds), N.Y.

**SCHUREMAN, James,** a Delegate, a Representative, and a Senator from New Jersey; born in New Brunswick, N.J., February 12, 1756; attended the common schools, and graduated from Rutgers College, New Brunswick, N.J., in 1775; engaged in mercantile pursuits; served in the Revolutionary Army; member, State general assembly 1783-1785, 1788; delegate to the Provincial Congress of New Jersey in 1786; Member of the Continental Congress in 1786 and 1787; elected to the First Congress (March 4, 1789-March 3, 1791); president of New Brunswick in 1792; elected to the Fifth Congress (March 4, 1797-March 3, 1799); elected to the United States Senate as a Federalist on February 14, 1799, to fill the vacancy caused by the resignation of John Rutherfurd, but did not qualify until later, preferring to serve out his term in the House; served as Senator from March 4, 1799, to February 16, 1801, when he resigned; mayor of New Brunswick 1801-1813; member of the State council 1808-1810; elected to the Thirteenth Congress (March 4, 1813-March 3, 1815); was not a candidate for renomination in 1814; again elected mayor and served from 1821 until his death; died in New Brunswick, January 22, 1824; interment in First Reformed Church Cemetery.

**SCHURZ, Carl,** a Senator from Missouri; born in Liblar, near Cologne, Germany, March 2, 1829; was educated at the gymnasium of Cologne and the University of Bonn; having taken part in the German revolutionary movement of 1848, he was compelled to flee from Germany to Switzerland; was a newspaper correspondent in Paris and later taught school in London; immigrated to the United States in 1852 and settled in Philadelphia, Pa.; moved to Watertown, Wis., in 1855; studied law; was admitted to the bar and practiced in Milwaukee, Wis.; unsuccessful candidate for lieutenant governor and governor of Wisconsin; appointed Minister to Spain on March 28, 1861 but resigned in December 1861; during the Civil War was appointed brigadier general of volunteers in the Union Army on April 15, 1862; served as chief of staff to General Henry W. Slocum, resigning on May 6, 1865; engaged in newspaper work after

the war in St. Louis, Mo.; elected as a Republican to the United States Senate, and served from March 4, 1869 to March 3, 1875; was not a candidate for reelection in 1874; served in the Cabinet of President Rutherford B. Hayes as Secretary of the Interior, March 12, 1877 to March 4, 1881; editor of the New York Evening Post, 1881-1884; contributor to Harper's Weekly, 1892-1898; president of the National Civil Service Reform League, 1892-1901; engaged in literary pursuits; died in New York City, May 14, 1906; interment in Sleepy Hollow Cemetery, Tarrytown, N.Y.

**Bibliography:** *DAB*; Schurz, Carl. *Reminiscences.* 3 vols. New York: The McClure Company, 1907-1908; Trefousse, Hans L. *Carl Schurz: A Biography.* Knoxville: University of Tennessee Press, 1982.

**SCHUYLER, Karl Cortlandt,** a Senator from Colorado; born in Colorado Springs, Colo., April 3, 1877; attended the Colorado Springs public schools; worked on the Colorado Midland Railroad; graduated from the law school of the University of Denver in 1898; was admitted to the bar the same year and commenced practice in Colorado Springs; in 1905 moved to Denver, Colo., where he continued the practice of law; trustee of the University of Denver and of Colorado Woman's College at Denver, Colo.; unsuccessful candidate for the Republican nomination for United States Senator in 1920; elected on November 8, 1932, as a Republican to the United States Senate to fill the vacancy caused by the death of Charles W. Waterman and served from December 7, 1932, to March 3, 1933; at the same election was an unsuccessful candidate for the full term beginning March 4, 1933; resumed the practice of law in Denver; was struck by an automobile and killed in New York City, July 31, 1933; interment in Fairmount Cemetery, Denver, Colo.

**SCHUYLER, Philip Jeremiah** (son of Philip John Schuyler), a Representative from New York; born in Albany, N.Y., January 21, 1768; received a limited schooling under private tutors; engaged in agriculture in Dutchess County; member of the State assembly in 1798; elected as a Federalist to the Fifteenth Congress (March 4, 1817-March 3, 1819); was not a candidate for reelection in 1818; resumed agricultural pursuits; died in New York City February 21, 1835; interment on the Schuyler estate near Rhinebeck, Dutchess County, N.Y.; reinterment in Poughkeepsie Rural Cemetery, Poughkeepsie.

**SCHUYLER, Philip John** (father of Philip Jeremiah Schuyler), a Delegate and a Senator from New York; born in Albany, N.Y., November 20, 1733; attended the common schools of Albany and studied under a private tutor in New Rochelle, N.Y.; served in the British Army and was commissioned captain in 1755; appointed chief commissary in 1756; resigned from the British Army in 1757; rejoined in 1758 as a major; sent to England to settle colonial claims in 1758; returned in 1763 and engaged in the lumber business in Saratoga, N.Y.; built the first flax mill in America; member, New York assembly 1768; Member of the Continental Congress 1775, 1777, and 1779-1780; appointed one of the four major generals in the Continental Army in 1775 and resigned in 1779; member, New York State senate 1780-1784, 1786-1790; elected to the United States Senate and served from March 4, 1789, to March 3, 1791; unsuccessful candidate for reelection; member, State senate 1792-1797; elected to the United States Senate and served from March 4, 1797, to January 3, 1798, when he resigned because of ill health; died in Albany, N.Y., November 18, 1804; interment in Albany Rural Cemetery.

**Bibliography:** *DAB*; Bush, Martin. *Revolutionary Enigma: A Re-Appraisal of General Philip Schuyler.* Port Washington, N.Y.: I.J. Friedman, 1969; Loosing, Benson. *The Life and Times of Philip Schuyler.* 1893. Reprint. New York: Da Capo Press, 1973.

**SCHWABE, George Blaine** (brother of Max Schwabe), a Representative from Oklahoma; born in Arthur, Vernon County, Mo., July 26, 1886; attended the country and town schools of Pettis County, Mo., and Sedalia (Mo.) High School; in 1910 was graduated from the law department of the University of Missouri at Columbia; was admitted to the bar the same year and commenced practice in Columbia, Mo.; moved to Nowata, Okla., in 1911 and continued the practice of law; mayor of Nowata, Okla., in 1913 and 1914; member of the Nowata Board of Education 1918-1922; member of the State house of representatives from Nowata County 1918-1922, serving as speaker in 1921 and 1922; moved to Tulsa, Okla., in 1922 and continued the practice of law; chairman of the Republican county committee of Tulsa County, Okla., 1928-1936; delegate to all Republican State conventions after 1912 and to the Republican National Convention in 1936; elected as a Republican to the Seventy-ninth and Eightieth Congresses (January 3, 1945-January 3, 1949); unsuccessful candidate for reelection in 1948 to the Eighty-first Congress; elected to the Eighty-second Congress and served from January 3, 1951, until his death in Alexandria, Va., April 2, 1952; interment in Memorial Park Cemetery, Tulsa, Okla.

**SCHWABE, Max** (brother of George Blaine Schwabe), a Representative from Missouri; born on a farm near Columbia, Boone County, Mo., December 6, 1905; attended the public schools and the University of Missouri at Columbia; engaged in the life insurance business in Columbia, Mo. from 1926 until 1942; elected as a Republican to the Seventy-eighth and to the two succeeding Congresses (January 3, 1943-January 3, 1949); unsuccessful candidate for reelection in 1948 to the Eighty-first Congress; Missouri State director, Farmers Home Administration, United States Department of Agriculture, 1953-1961; operated a livestock farm in Columbia; was a resident of Columbia, Mo.; died July 31, 1983.

**SCHWARTZ, Henry Herman (Harry),** a Senator from Wyoming; born on a farm near Fort Recovery, Mercer County, Ohio, May 18, 1869; educated in the public schools of Mercer County and Cincinnati, Ohio; engaged in the newspaper business at Fort Recovery, Ohio, 1892-1894, and at Sioux Falls, S.Dak., 1894-1896; studied law; was admitted to the bar in 1895 and commenced practice in Sioux Falls; member, South Dakota State house of representatives, 1896-1897; chief of the field division of the United States General Land Office, at Spokane, Wash., and Helena, Mont., 1897-1907; special assistant to the Attorney General in 1907; chief of the field service, General Land Office, Washington, D.C., 1907-1910; moved to Casper, Wyo., in 1915; president of the Casper Board of Education and the Natrona County High School Board from 1928 until 1934; member, Wyoming State senate, 1933-1935; unsuccessful candidate for election to the United States Senate in 1930; elected as a Democrat to the United States Senate in 1936 and served from January 3, 1937, to January 3, 1943; unsuccessful candidate for reelection in 1942; chairman, Committee on Pensions (Seventy-seventh Congress); appointed by President Franklin D. Roosevelt to the National Mediation Board in 1943, and served until 1947; resumed the practice of law in Casper, Wyo., until his death there on April 24, 1955; interment in Highland Cemetery.

**SCHWARTZ, John,** a Representative from Pennsylvania; born in Sunbury, Northumberland County, Pa., October 27, 1793; received a limited schooling; at the age of ten years was apprenticed to a merchant in Reading, Pa., and became a partner at the expiration of his apprenticeship; served in the War of 1812 as a major; engaged in the manufacture of iron products; elected as an Anti-Lecompton Democrat to the Thirty-sixth Congress and served from March 4, 1859, until his death in Washington, D.C., June 20, 1860; interment in Charles Evans Cemetery, Reading, Berks County, Pa.

**SCHWEIKER, Richard Schultz,** a Representative and a Senator from Pennsylvania; born in Norristown, Montgomery County, Pa., June 1, 1926; B.A., Pennsylvania State University, 1950; during the Second World War, enlisted in the United States Navy and served aboard an aircraft carrier, 1944-1946; ten years of business experience as manufacturing and sales executive; elected as a Republican to the Eighty-seventh and to the three succeeding Congresses (January 3, 1961-January 3, 1969); was not a candidate in 1968 for reelection to the House of Representatives, but was elected to the United States Senate; reelected in 1974, and served from January 3, 1969 to January 3, 1981; was former Governor Ronald Reagan's designated choice for Vice President of the United States, July 26, 1976; was not a candidate for reelection in 1980; Secretary of Health and Human Services in the Cabinet of President Ronald Reagan, January 21, 1981 to January 13, 1983; president, American Council of Life Insurance, 1983 to 1994; is a resident of McLean, Va.

**Bibliography:** Landes, Burton R. *The Making of a Senator, 1974: A Biography of Richard S. Schweiker.* Trappes, Pa.: Landes, 1976.

**SCHWELLENBACH, Lewis Baxter,** a Senator from Washington; born in Superior, Douglas County, Wis., September 20, 1894; moved to Spokane, Wash., with his parents in 1902; attended the grade and high schools in Spokane and graduated from the law department of the University of Washington at Seattle in 1917; assistant instructor at the University of Washington, 1916-1917; during the First World War served from 1918, as a private in the Twelfth Regiment, United States Infantry, until discharged as a corporal in 1919; was admitted to the bar in 1919 and commenced practice in Seattle, Wash.; unsuccessful candidate for nomination for governor in 1932; delegate to the Interparliamentary Union at The Hague in 1938; elected as a Democrat to the United States Senate, and served from January 3, 1935 to December 16, 1940, when he resigned; was not a candidate for renomination in 1940, having been appointed United States district judge for the eastern district of Washington, in which capacity he served until his resignation to accept a Cabinet portfolio; appointed Secretary of Labor by President Harry S Truman, and served from July 1, 1945 until his death in Washington, D.C., June 10, 1948; interment in Washelli Cemetery, Seattle, Wash.

**Bibliography:** *DAB*; Libby, Justin H. "Anti-Japanese Sentiment in the Pacific Northwest: Senator Schwellenbach and Congressman Coffee Attempt to Embargo Japan, 1937-1941." *Mid-America* 58 (October 1976): 167-174.

**SCHWENGEL, Frederic Delbert,** a Representative from Iowa; born on a farm near Sheffield, Franklin County, Iowa, May 28, 1906; attended the rural schools in West Fork Township, and high schools in Chapin and Sheffield, Iowa; B.S., Northeast Missouri Teachers College, Kirksville, 1930; attended Iowa University graduate school, 1933-1935; athletic coach and instructor of history and political science in the public schools of Shelbina and Kirksville, Mo., 1930-1937; engaged in the insurance business in Davenport, Iowa, from 1937 to 1954; served in the Missouri National Guard, 1929-1936; member of the Iowa State house of representatives, 1945-1955; member, Iowa Development Commission, 1949-1955; elected as a Republican to the Eighty-fourth and to the four succeeding Congresses (January 3, 1955-January 3, 1965); unsuccessful candidate for reelection in 1964 to the Eighty-ninth Congress; elected as a Republican to the Ninetieth and to the two succeeding Congresses (January 3, 1967-January 3, 1973); unsuccessful candidate for reelection in 1972 to the Ninety-third Congress; founder and president, Republican Heritage Foundation; founder and president of the United States Capitol Historical Society from 1962 until 1992, and served as chairman of the board until his death in Arlington, Va., on April 1, 1993.

**Bibliography:** Schwengel, Fred. *The Republican Party: Its Heritage and History.* Foreword by Gerald R. Ford. Washington: Acropolis Books Ltd., 1987.

**SCHWERT, Pius Louis,** a Representative from New York; born in Angola, Erie County, N.Y., November 22, 1892; attended the public schools in Angola and Lafayette High School, Buffalo, N.Y.; was graduated from Wharton School of Commerce, University of Pennsylvania, Philadelphia, Pa., in 1914; played professional baseball with the New York American League Ball Club 1914-1917; during the First World War served in the United States Navy as a yeoman, first class, and later was commissioned as an ensign; engaged in mercantile and banking pursuits in Angola; president of the Bank of Angola, N.Y., 1921-1931; member of the first salary survey committee of Erie County in 1932; moved to Buffalo, N.Y., and served as county clerk 1933-1938; elected as a Democrat to the Seventy-sixth and Seventy-seventh Congresses and served from January 3, 1939, until his death in Washington, D.C., March 11, 1941; interment in Forest Avenue Cemetery, Angola, N.Y.

**SCOBLICK, James Paul,** a Representative from Pennsylvania; born in Archbald, Lackawanna County, Pa., May 10, 1909; attended the public school and St. Thomas High School, Scranton, Pa.; B.S., Fordham University, New York City, 1930; engaged in postgraduate work at Columbia University, New York City; member of the Lackawanna County (Pa.) Department of Public Assistance Board; elected as a Republican to the Seventy-ninth Congress to fill the vacancy caused by the resignation of John W. Murphy; elected at the same time to the Eightieth Congress, and served from November 5, 1946 to January 3, 1949; unsuccessful candidate for renomination in 1948 to the Eighty-first Congress; resumed his former business pursuits; engaged as consultant to the food industry; was a resident of Archbald, Pa., until his death there on December 4, 1981; interment in Mother of Sorrows Cemetery, Finch Hill, Pa.

**SCOFIELD, Glenni William,** a Representative from Pennsylvania; born in Dewittville, Chautauqua County, N.Y., on March 11, 1817; attended the common schools; learned the printing trade; returned to classical study and was graduated from Hamilton College, Clinton, N.Y., in 1840; engaged in teaching; studied law; was admitted to the bar in 1842 and commenced practice in Warren, Pa.; district attorney, 1846-1848; member of the Pennsylvania house of representatives, 1849-1851; affiliated with the Republican Party in 1856; served in the Pennsylvania senate, 1857-1859; appointed president judge of the eighteenth judicial district of Pennsylvania in 1861; elected as a Republican to the Thirty-eighth and to the five succeeding Congresses (March 4, 1863-March 3, 1875); chairman, Committee on Revisal and Unfinished Business (Thirty-ninth Congress), Committee on Naval Affairs (Forty-first, Forty-second, and Forty-third Congresses); was not a candidate for renomination in 1874 to the Forty-fourth Congress; resumed the practice of law in Warren; appointed Register of the Treasury by President Rutherford B. Hayes and served from 1878 to 1881; associate justice of the United States Court of Claims, 1881-1891; died in Warren, Warren County, Pa., August 30, 1891; interment in Oakland Cemetery.

**SCOTT, Byron Nicholson,** a Representative from California; born in Council Grove, Morris County, Kans., March 21, 1903; attended the public schools; was graduated from the University of Kansas at Lawrence in 1924, from the University of Southern California at Los Angeles in 1930, and from the National University School of Law in 1949; taught school at Tucson, Ariz., 1924-1926; moved to Long Beach, Los Angeles County, Calif., in 1926 and taught school until 1934; delegate to the California Democratic State Conventions 1934-1940; delegate to the Democratic National Convention of 1936; elected as a Democrat to the Seventy-fourth and Seventy-fifth Congresses (January 3, 1935-January 3, 1939); unsuccessful candidate for reelection in 1938 to the Seventy-sixth Congress, and for election in 1940 to the Seventy-seventh Congress; secretary of the California State Highway Commission, 1939-1940; engaged in the construction business in 1941 and 1942; served with the War Production Board in Washington, D.C., 1942-1945; admitted to the District of Columbia bar in 1949 and practiced law in Washington, D.C., until his retirement in 1979; is a resident of Sun City, Calif.

**SCOTT, Charles Frederick,** a Representative from Kansas; born near Iola, Allen County, Kans., on September 7, 1860; attended the common schools; was graduated from the University of Kansas at Lawrence in 1881; went to Colorado, New Mexico, and Arizona, and was engaged chiefly in clerical work; returned to Iola, Kans., in 1882 and edited the Iola Register; appointed regent of the University in 1891-1900; member of the State senate 1892-1896; elected as a Republican to the Fifty-seventh and to the four succeeding Congresses (March 4, 1901-March 3, 1911); chairman, Committee on Agriculture (Sixtieth and Sixty-first Congresses); unsuccessful candidate for reelection in 1910 to the Sixty-second Congress; appointed one of five delegates to the International Institute of Agriculture at Rome in 1911; lectured on Chautauqua platform in 1913, 1915, and 1916; delegate to the Republican National Conventions in 1916 and 1932; unsuccessful candidate for nomination to the United States Senate in 1918 and again in 1928; resumed newspaper work until his death in Iola, Kans., on September 18, 1938; interment in Iola Cemetery.

**SCOTT, Charles Lewis,** a Representative from California; born in Richmond, Henrico County, Va., January 23, 1827; attended the public schools and Richmond Academy and was graduated from the College of William and Mary, Williamsburg, Va., in 1846; studied law; was admitted to the bar in 1847 and commenced practice in Richmond, Va.; moved to California in 1849 and engaged in gold mining; resumed the practice of his profession in Sonora, Calif., in 1851; member of the California State assembly, 1854-1856; elected as a Democrat to the Thirty-fifth and Thirty-sixth Congresses (March 4, 1857-March 3, 1861); was not a candidate for reelection in 1860 to the Thirty-seventh Congress; during the Civil War served as a major in the Fourth Regiment, Alabama Volunteer Infantry, of the Confederate Army; after the war engaged in agricultural pursuits in Wilcox County, Ala., and from 1869 to 1879 was engaged in journalism; was a delegate to every Democratic National Convention from the end of the Civil War to 1896; appointed by President Grover Cleveland on August 10, 1885, Minister Resident to Venezuela and consul general at Caracas and served until his resignation, effective March 8, 1889; returned to the United States and engaged in agricultural pursuits until his death near Mount Pleasant, Monroe County, Ala., April 30, 1899; interment in the private cemetery of Mrs. Robert G. Scott at Cedar Hill, Ala.

**SCOTT, David,** a Representative from Pennsylvania; elected in 1816 to the Fifteenth Congress, but resigned in 1817, before the Congress assembled, having been appointed president and judge of the court of common pleas.

**SCOTT, Frank Douglas,** a Representative from Michigan; born in Alpena, Alpena County, Mich., on August 25, 1878; attended the public schools; was graduated from the law department of the University of Michigan at Ann Arbor in 1901; was admitted to the bar the same year and commenced practice in Alpena; city attorney of Alpena in 1903 and 1904; city prosecutor 1906-1910; member of the State senate 1911-1914 and served as president pro tempore in 1913 and 1914; elected as a Republican to the Sixty-fourth and to the five succeeding Congresses (March 4, 1915-March 3, 1927); chairman, Committee on Merchant Marine and Fisheries (Sixty-ninth Congress); unsuccessful candidate for renomination in 1926; resumed the practice of his profession in Washington, D.C.; died in Palm Beach, Fla., February 12, 1951; interment in Evergreen Cemetery, Alpena, Mich.

SCOTT, George Cromwell, a Representative from Iowa; born near East Kendall (now Morton), Monroe County, N.Y., August 8, 1864; moved to Iowa in 1880; attended the country schools and the high school at Dallas Center, Iowa; studied law; was admitted to the bar in 1887 and commenced practice in Le Mars, Iowa, in 1888; moved to Sioux City in 1901 and continued the practice of law; elected as a Republican to the Sixty-second Congress to fill the vacancy caused by the death of Elbert H. Hubbard; reelected to the Sixty-third Congress and served from November 5, 1912, to March 3, 1915; unsuccessful candidate for reelection in 1914 to the Sixty-fourth Congress; elected to the Sixty-fifth Congress (March 4, 1917-March 3, 1919); was not a candidate for renomination in 1918 to the Sixty-sixth Congress; resumed the practice of law in Sioux City; appointed by President Warren G. Harding judge of the United States District Court for the Northern District of Iowa and served from March 4, 1922, until his retirement on November 1, 1943; died in Sioux City, Iowa, October 6, 1948; interment in Graceland Park Cemetery.

SCOTT, Gustavus (grandfather of William Lawrence Scott), a Delegate from Maryland; born at "Westwood," Prince William County, Va., in 1753; went with his brother to Scotland in 1765 and studied at King's College, Aberdeen, Scotland; entered the Middle Temple, London, England, in 1767, and completed his law studies in 1771; returned to Maryland in the latter year and settled in Somerset County, Md., where he practiced law; delegate to the Annapolis convention in 1774 and 1775; member of the Association of the Freemen of Maryland; member of the first State constitutional convention in 1776; moved to Dorchester County; member of the house of delegates in 1780; elected to the Continental Congress in 1784, but did not attend; resumed the practice of law; moved to Montgomery County in 1794; one of the commissioners to superintend the erection of the public buildings in Washington, D.C., 1794-1800; died in Washington, D.C., December 25, 1800; interment on his farm in Virginia.

Bibliography: *DAB.*

SCOTT, Hardie (son of John Roger Kirkpatrick Scott), a Representative from Pennsylvania; born in Cynwyd, Montgomery County, Pa., June 7, 1907; was graduated from Taft School, Watertown, Conn., in 1926, from Yale University in 1930, and from the University of Pennsylvania Law School at Philadelphia in 1934; was admitted to the bar in 1935 and commenced practice in Philadelphia, Pa.; elected as a Republican to the Eightieth and to the two succeeding Congresses (January 3, 1947-January 3, 1953); was not a candidate for renomination in 1952 to the Eighty-third Congress; resumed the practice of law; is a resident of Edgemont, Pa.

SCOTT, Harvey David, a Representative from Indiana; born near Ashtabula, Union County, Ohio, October 18, 1818; attended the public schools and the Asbury (now De Pauw) University at Greencastle, Ind.; studied law; was admitted to the bar and commenced practice in Terre Haute, Ind.; held several local offices; elected as a Republican to the Thirty-fourth Congress (March 4, 1855-March 3, 1857); resumed the practice of law; judge of the circuit court of Vigo County 1881-1884; moved to California in 1887; died in Pasadena, Calif., July 11, 1891; interment in Mountain View Cemetery.

SCOTT, Hugh Doggett, Jr., a Representative and a Senator from Pennsylvania; born in Fredericksburg, Spotsylvania County, Va., on November 11, 1900; attended public and private schools; A.B., Randolph-Macon College, Ashland, Va., 1919; LL.B., University of Virginia School of Law, Charlottesville, 1922; was admitted to the bar in 1922 and commenced practice in Philadelphia, Pa.; during the First World War enrolled in the Student Reserve Officers' Training Corps and the Students' Army Training Corps; assistant district attorney of Philadelphia, Pa., 1926-1941; member of the

Governor's Commission on Reform of the Magistrates System, 1938-1940; during the Second World War was on active duty for two years with the United States Navy with the final rank of commander; author; vice president of the United States Delegation to the Interparliamentary Union; elected as a Republican to the Seventy-seventh Congress; reelected to the Seventy-eighth Congress (January 3, 1941-January 3, 1945); unsuccessful candidate for reelection in 1944 to the Seventy-ninth Congress; resumed the practice of law; chairman of the Republican National Committee, 1948-1949; elected to the Eightieth and to the five succeeding Congresses (January 3, 1947-January 3, 1959); was not a candidate for reelection in 1958 to the House of Representatives, but was elected to the United States Senate; reelected in 1964 and again in 1970, and served from January 3, 1959 to January 3, 1977; was not a candidate for reelection in 1976; Republican whip (Ninety-first Congress); minority leader (Ninety-first through Ninety-fifth Congresses); chairman, Select Committee on Secret and Confidential Documents (Ninety-second Congress); practiced law in Washington, D.C. until his retirement in 1987; died in Falls Church, Va. on July 21, 1994; interment in Arlington National Cemetery, Va.

Bibliography: Scott, Hugh D., Jr. *Come to the Party.* Englewood Cliffs, N.J.: Prentice-Hall, 1968; Scott, Hugh D., Jr. *How to Run for Public Office and Win!* Washington, D.C.: National Press, 1968.

SCOTT, John, a Delegate and a Representative from Missouri; born in Hanover County, Va., May 18, 1785; moved with his parents to Indiana Territory in 1802; was graduated from Princeton College in 1805; studied law; was admitted to the bar and commenced practice in Ste. Genevieve, Mo., in 1806; presented credentials as a Delegate-elect to the Fourteenth Congress from the Territory of Missouri, and served from August 6, 1816 to January 13, 1817, when the election was declared illegal and the seat vacant; elected as a Delegate to the Fifteenth and Sixteenth Congresses, and served from August 4, 1817 to March 3, 1821; upon the admission of Missouri as a State into the Union was elected to the Seventeenth and to the two succeeding Congresses, and served from August 10, 1821 to March 3, 1827; chairman, Committee on Public Lands (Nineteenth Congress); unsuccessful candidate for reelection in 1826 to the Twentieth Congress; resumed the practice of law; died in Ste. Genevieve, Mo., on October 1, 1861.

Bibliography: Weiner, Alan S. "John Scott, Thomas Hart Benton, David Barton and the Presidential Election of 1824: A Case Study in Pressure Politics." *Missouri Historical Review* 60 (July 1966): 460-494.

SCOTT, John (father of John Scott [1824-1896]), a Representative from Pennsylvania; born at Marsh Creek, near Gettysburg, Pa., December 25, 1784; moved to Alexandria, Pa., in 1806; engaged as tanner and shoemaker; served as major in the War of 1812; member of the Pennsylvania house of representatives in 1819 and 1820; elected as a Jacksonian to the Twenty-first Congress (March 4, 1829-March 3, 1831); unsuccessful candidate for reelection to the Twenty-second Congress; resumed his former business pursuits; retired from business in 1842; died in Alexandria, Huntingdon County, Pa., on September 22, 1850; interment in Alexandria Cemetery.

SCOTT, John (son of John Scott [1784-1850]), a Senator from Pennsylvania; born in Alexandria, Huntingdon County, Pa., July 24, 1824; attended the common schools and Marshall College, Chambersburg, Pa.; studied law; was admitted to the bar in 1846 and practiced in Huntingdon, Pa., 1846-1869; prosecuting attorney 1846-1849; member of the revenue commission in 1851; member, State house of representatives 1862; elected as a Republican to the United States Senate and served from March 4, 1869, to March 3, 1875; was not a candidate for reelection in 1875; chairman, Committee on Claims (Forty-third Congress); moved to Pittsburgh, Pa., in 1875; general counsel of the Pennsylvania Railroad

1875-1877 and general solicitor 1877-1895; died in Philadelphia, Pa., November 29, 1896; interment in Woodlands Cemetery.

**SCOTT, John Guier,** a Representative from Missouri; born in Philadelphia, Pa., December 26, 1819; completed preparatory studies; was graduated from Bethlehem Academy, Pennsylvania, in civil engineering; moved to Missouri in 1842; general manager of the Iron Mountain Co. at Iron Mountain; established the Irondale Iron Co. at Irondale in 1858; unsuccessful Democratic candidate for election in 1862 to the Thirty-eighth Congress; subsequently elected as a Democrat to the Thirty-eighth Congress to fill the vacancy caused by the death of John W. Noell and served from December 7, 1863, to March 3, 1865; engaged in the drug business in St. Louis; resumed mining, and built furnaces, at Scotia, Crawford County, Mo., in 1868 and at Nova Scotia a year later; returned in 1870 to St. Louis; moved to east Tennessee about 1880; died at Oliver Springs, Roane County, Tenn., May 16, 1892; interment in Bellefontaine Cemetery, St. Louis, Mo.

**SCOTT, John Morin,** a Delegate from New York; born in New York City in 1730; attended the common schools; was graduated from Yale College in 1746; studied law; was admitted to the bar in 1752 and commenced practice in New York City; one of the founders of the Sons of Liberty; alderman 1756-1761; member of the New York General Committee in 1775; member of the Provincial Congress 1775-1777; brigadier general in the Revolutionary War; member of the committee to draw up a constitution for the State of New York in 1776; elected associate justice of the supreme court of New York in 1777, but declined to accept the position; member of the State senate 1777-1782; secretary of state of New York 1778-1784; Member of the Continental Congress 1780 and 1782; died in New York City September 14, 1784; interment at the north entrance of Trinity Church.

Bibliography: *DAB.*

**SCOTT, John Roger Kirkpatrick** (father of Hardie Scott), a Representative from Pennsylvania; born in Bloomsburg, Columbia County, Pa., July 6, 1873; moved with his parents to Wilkes-Barre, Pa., and later to Philadelphia; attended the public schools; was graduated from the Central High School of Philadelphia in 1893; attended the law school of the University of Pennsylvania at Philadelphia; was admitted to the bar in December 1895 and commenced the practice of law in Philadelphia; member of the State house of representatives in 1899 and again in 1909, 1911, and 1913; elected as a Republican to the Sixty-fourth and Sixty-fifth Congresses and served from March 4, 1915, until his resignation, effective January 5, 1919; resumed the practice of his profession; died in Philadelphia, Pa., December 9, 1945; interment in West Laurel Hills Cemetery.

**SCOTT, Lon Allen,** a Representative from Tennessee; born on a farm near Cypress Inn, Wayne County, Tenn., September 25, 1888; moved with his parents to Savannah, Hardin County, Tenn.; attended the public schools and Savannah (Tenn.) Institute; was graduated from the law department of Cumberland University, Lebanon, Tenn., in 1915; engaged in mercantile pursuits and the real estate and lumber business; member of the State house of representatives 1913-1917 and served as minority floor leader in 1915 and 1917; represented Tennessee in the prosecution of Attorney General Estes in an impeachment proceeding before the State senate; resigned as a State representative and enlisted as a private in the United States Marine Corps during the First World War; was promoted to a lieutenancy; elected as a Republican to the Sixty-seventh Congress (March 4, 1921-March 3, 1923); unsuccessful candidate for reelection in 1922 to the Sixty-eighth Congress; resumed his former business pursuits and resided in Savannah, Tenn., until his death there on February 11, 1931; interment in Savannah Cemetery.

**SCOTT, Nathan Bay,** a Senator from West Virginia; born near Quaker City, Guernsey County, Ohio, December 18, 1842; attended the common schools; engaged in mining near Colorado Springs, Colo., 1859-1862; during the Civil War entered the Union Army in 1863 as a corporal; appointed sergeant in 1864, promoted to regimental commissary sergeant in 1865, and mustered out in 1865; engaged in the manufacture of glass in Wheeling, W.Va.; also engaged in banking; member of the city council 1881-1883 and served as president 1881-1883; member, State senate 1883-1890; member of the Republican National Committee in 1888; appointed Commissioner of Internal Revenue by President William McKinley in 1898, and served until February 1899, when he resigned to become Senator; elected as a Republican to the United States Senate in 1899; reelected in 1905 and served from March 4, 1899, to March 3, 1911; unsuccessful candidate for renomination; chairman, Committee on Mines and Mining (Fifty-seventh through Fifty-ninth Congresses), Committee on Public Buildings and Grounds (Fifty-ninth through Sixty-first Congresses); appointed a member of the Lincoln Memorial Commission in 1911; engaged in banking in Washington, D.C., until his death on January 2, 1924; remains were cremated and the ashes deposited in a mausoleum in Rock Creek Cemetery.

**SCOTT, Owen,** a Representative from Illinois; born on a farm in Jackson Township, Effingham County, Ill., July 6, 1848; attended the common schools, a private school in Kinmundy, and the State normal school in Normal, Ill.; taught school; superintendent of schools for Effingham County, Ill., 1873-1881; studied law; was admitted to the bar in 1873 and commenced practice in Effingham, Ill.; engaged in newspaper work; published the Effingham Democrat; mayor of Effingham in 1882; city attorney in 1883 and 1884; moved to Bloomington, Ill., in 1884 and became proprietor and manager of the Bloomington Daily and Weekly Bulletins; deputy collector of internal revenue by appointment of President Grover Cleveland, 1885-1889; chairman of the Illinois Democratic convention at Springfield, Ill., in 1888; elected as a Democrat to the Fifty-second Congress (March 4, 1891-March 3, 1893); unsuccessful candidate for reelection in 1892 to the Fifty-third Congress; moved to Decatur, Ill., in 1899 and managed the Decatur Herald until 1904, when he engaged in the insurance business; retired from the insurance business in 1921 to become secretary of the Masonic Grand Lodge of Illinois, which position he held until his death in Decatur, Ill., December 21, 1928; interment in Oak Ridge Cemetery, Effingham, Ill.

**SCOTT, Ralph James,** a Representative from North Carolina; born in Surry County, near Pinnacle, N.C., October 15, 1905; educated in the public schools; Wake Forest College, LL.B., 1930; was admitted to the bar in 1930 and commenced the practice of law in Danbury, N.C.; member of the State house of representatives, 1936-1937; delegate to State Democratic conventions, 1936-1968; chairman, Democratic Executive Committee of Stokes County, 1936-1970; solicitor of the twenty-first judicial district of North Carolina 1938-1956; elected as a Democrat to the Eighty-fifth and to the four succeeding Congresses (January 3, 1957-January 3, 1967); was not a candidate for reelection in 1966 to the Ninetieth Congress; resumed the practice of law; was a resident of Danbury, N.C., until his death there August 5, 1983; interment in Pannacle Baptist Church cemetery.

**SCOTT, Robert Cortez,** a Representative from Virginia; born in Washington, D.C., April 30, 1947; graduated from Groton High School; B.A., Harvard University, 1969; J.D., Boston College School of Law, 1973; served in the Massachusetts National Guard; attorney in Newport News, Va., since 1973; member, Virginia House of Delegates, 1978-1982; member, Virginia Senate, 1982-1993; unsuccessful candidate for election in 1986 to the One Hundredth Congress; elected as a Democrat to the One Hundred Third and One

Hundred Fourth Congresses (January 3, 1993-January 3, 1997); is a resident of Newport News, Va.

**SCOTT, Thomas,** a Representative from Pennsylvania; born in Chester County, Pa., in 1739; as a child moved with his parents to Lancaster County; attended the rural schools; studied law; admitted to the bar and practiced; moved to Westmoreland County in 1770 and settled on Dunlaps Creek, near the Monongahela River; justice of the peace in 1773; member of the first Pennsylvania Assembly in 1776; member of the supreme council in 1777; upon the formation of Washington County in 1781 was appointed prothonotary and served until March 28, 1789, when he resigned, having been elected to Congress; commissioned a justice of Washington County on November 21, 1786; member of the Pennsylvania ratification convention in 1787; elected to the First Congress (March 4, 1789-March 3, 1791); declined to be a candidate for reelection in 1790; again a member of the Pennsylvania assembly in 1791; elected to the Third Congress (March 4, 1793-March 3, 1795); died in Washington, Pa., March 2, 1796; interment in the old graveyard on First Walnut Street; reinterment in Washington Cemetery.

**SCOTT, William Kerr,** a Senator from North Carolina; born in Haw River, Alamance County, N.C., April 17, 1896; attended the public schools of Hawfields, N.C.; graduated from North Carolina State College at Raleigh in 1917; during the First World War served as a private in the Field Artillery, United States Army, in 1918; farmer and dairyman; Alamance County farm agent 1920-1930; master, North Carolina State Grange, 1930-1933; regional director, Farm Debt Adjustment Program of Resettlement Administration, 1934-1936; North Carolina State Commissioner of Agriculture, 1937-1948; elected Governor of North Carolina in 1948, and served from January 6, 1949 to January 8, 1953; elected as a Democrat to the United States Senate November 2, 1954, to fill the vacancy caused by the death of Willis Smith, and at the same time was elected to a full term beginning January 3, 1955; served from November 29, 1954, until his death in Burlington, N.C., April 16, 1958; interment in Hawfields Presbyterian Church Cemetery, near Mebane, N.C.

**Bibliography:** *DAB.*

**SCOTT, William Lawrence** (grandson of Gustavus Scott), a Representative from Pennsylvania; born in Washington, D.C., July 2, 1828; attended the common schools and Hampden-Sidney Academy in Virginia; page in the House of Representatives from 1840 until 1846; moved to Erie, Pa., in 1846 and was employed as a shipping clerk until 1850; was subsequently engaged in shipping, coal mining, iron manufacturing, banking, and railroad construction; had extensive land holdings and was interested in the raising of cattle; mayor of Erie in 1866 and again in 1871; unsuccessful candidate for election in 1866 to the Fortieth Congress, and in 1876 to the Forty-fifth Congress; elected a member of the Democratic National Committee in 1876, 1880, and 1884; delegate to the Democratic National Conventions of 1876, 1880, and 1888; elected as a Democrat to the Forty-ninth and Fiftieth Congresses (March 4, 1885-March 3, 1889); chairman, Committee on Expenditures in the Department of the Navy (Fiftieth Congress); was nominated in 1888 to the Fifty-first Congress, and in 1890 to the Fifty-second Congress, but each time declined to be a candidate because of the condition of his health; director in a number of railroad companies and president of the Erie & Pittsburgh Railroad; died in Newport, R.I., September 19, 1891; interment in Erie Cemetery, Erie, Pa.

**Bibliography:** *DAB.*

**SCOTT, William Lloyd,** a Representative and a Senator from Virginia; born in Williamsburg, Va., July 1, 1915; J.D., George Washington University, 1938; employed by the federal government from 1934 until 1961, principally as a trial attorney with the Department of Justice; engaged in the private practice of law,

Fairfax, Va., 1961-1966; elected as a Republican to the Ninetieth and to the two succeeding Congresses (January 3, 1967-January 3, 1973); was not a candidate in 1972 for reelection to the House of Representatives, but was elected to the United States Senate; served from January 3, 1973 until his resignation on January 1, 1979; was not a candidate for reelection in 1978; is a resident of Fairfax Station, Va.

**SCOVILLE, Jonathan,** a Representative from New York; born in Salisbury, Litchfield County, Conn., July 14, 1830; attended various educational institutions in Massachusetts, including the scientific department of Harvard University; engaged in business in Canaan, Conn., in 1854 as an iron manufacturer and mine owner; moved to Buffalo, N.Y., in 1860 and established a car-wheel foundry, and the next year established another in Toronto, Canada; elected as a Democrat to the Forty-sixth Congress to fill the vacancy caused by the resignation of Ray V. Pierce; reelected to the Forty-seventh Congress and served from November 12, 1880, to March 3, 1883; was not a candidate for renomination in 1882; mayor of Buffalo in 1884 and 1885; died in New York City, March 4, 1891; interment in Salisbury Cemetery, Salisbury, Conn.

**SCRANTON, George Whitfield** (second cousin of Joseph Augustine Scranton), a Representative from Pennsylvania; born in Madison, New Haven County, Conn., May 11, 1811; attended the common schools and Lee's Academy; moved to Belvidere, N.J., in 1828 and became a teamster; subsequently engaged in mercantile pursuits; from 1835 to 1839 was interested in agricultural pursuits and in the latter year engaged in the manufacture of iron, and began experimenting with the practicability of smelting ore by means of anthracite coal in Slocum (now Scranton), Pa.; founder of the Lackawanna Iron & Coal Co. and the city of Scranton, Pa.; projected and constructed the Northumberland division of the Lackawanna Railroad; president of two railroad companies; elected as a Republican to the Thirty-sixth and Thirty-seventh Congresses and served from March 4, 1859, until his death in Scranton, Pa., March 24, 1861; interment in Dunmore Cemetery.

**Bibliography:** *DAB.*

**SCRANTON, Joseph Augustine** (second cousin of George Whitfield Scranton), a Representative from Pennsylvania; born in Madison, New Haven County, Conn., July 26, 1838; moved with his parents to Pennsylvania in 1847; attended Phillips Academy, Andover, Mass.; attended Yale College, 1857-1861; collector of internal revenue from 1862 until 1866; founded the Scranton Daily Republican in 1867; delegate to the Republican National Convention of 1872; postmaster of Scranton from March 19, 1874, to May 5, 1881; elected as a Republican to the Forty-seventh Congress (March 4, 1881-March 3, 1883); unsuccessful candidate for reelection in 1882 to the Forty-eighth Congress; elected to the Forty-ninth Congress (March 4, 1885-March 3, 1887); unsuccessful candidate for reelection in 1886 to the Fiftieth Congress; elected to the Fifty-first Congress (March 4, 1889-March 3, 1891); chairman, Committee on Expenditures in the Department of State (Fifty-first Congress); unsuccessful candidate for reelection in 1890 to the Fifty-second Congress; resumed the newspaper business in Scranton; elected to the Fifty-third and Fifty-fourth Congresses (March 4, 1893-March 3, 1897); chairman, Committee on Territories (Fifty-fourth Congress); was not a candidate for renomination in 1896 to the Fifty-fifth Congress; resumed the publication and editorship of the Scranton Republican; treasurer of Lackawanna County, 1901-1903; died in Scranton, Lackawanna County, Pa., October 12, 1908; interment in Forest Hill Cemetery.

**SCRANTON, William Warren,** a Representative from Pennsylvania; born in Madison, New Haven County, Conn., July 19, 1917; attended the Hotchkiss school; B.A., Yale University, 1939; LL.B., Yale University Law School, 1946; served as a pilot (captain) in the United States Army Air Corps, with overseas service in Africa, the

Middle East, and South America, 1941-1945, retired as lieutenant colonel; associated with the International Textbook Co., and Haddon Craftsman, Inc., 1947-1952, rising to position of vice president; president of the Scranton-Lackawanna Trust Co., 1954-1956; chairman of the board of Northeastern Pennsylvania Broadcasting, Inc., 1953-1959; special assistant to Secretary of State Christian A. Herter, 1959 and 1960; elected as a Republican to the Eighty-seventh Congress (January 3, 1961-January 3, 1963); was not a candidate for renomination in 1962 to the Eighty-eighth Congress, but was elected Governor of Pennsylvania and served from January 15, 1963, to January 17, 1967; candidate for Republican presidential nomination in 1964; delegate and chairman of Judiciary Committee, Pennsylvania Constitutional Convention, 1967-1968; vice chairman, President's Commission on Insurance for Riot-torn Areas, 1967; United States Ambassador, 1969; member, President's Advisory Committee on Arms Limitation and Disarmament; Representative of the United States to the United Nations, March 15, 1976, to January 19, 1977; is a resident of Dalton, Pa.

**Bibliography:** Wolf, George D. *William Warren Scranton: Pennsylvania Statesman.* University Park: Pennsylvania State University Press, 1981.

**SCRIVNER, Errett Power,** a Representative from Kansas; born in Newton, Harvey County, Kans., March 20, 1898; attended the grade schools and was graduated from Manual Training High School, Kansas City, Mo.; during the First World War enlisted in Battery B, One Hundred and Twenty-ninth Field Artillery, in July 1917; served overseas in 1918 and 1919; awarded the Silver Star and Purple Heart Medals; was graduated from the law department of the University of Kansas at Lawrence in 1925; was admitted to the bar the same year and commenced practice in Kansas City, Kans.; elected as a Republican to the Seventy-eight Congress, by special election, September 14, 1943, to fill the vacancy caused by the death of Ulysses S. Guyer; reelected to the seven succeeding Congresses and served from September 14, 1943 to January 3, 1959; unsuccessful candidate for reelection in 1958 to the Eighty-sixth Congress; special assistant to the comptroller, Department of Defense, Washington, D.C., from January 1959 to March 1960; Deputy Assistant Secretary of Defense, Public Affairs, from March 7, 1960 to January 20, 1961; city commissioner, Cocoa Beach, Fla., 1970; resided in Cocoa Beach, Fla., until his death there on May 5, 1978; cremated; entombment in a crypt at Florida Memorial Gardens, Rockledge, Fla.

**SCROGGY, Thomas Edmund,** a Representative from Ohio; born in Harveysburg, Warren County, Ohio, March 18, 1843; attended the public schools; engaged in manufacturing; enlisted in July 1861 as a private in Company H, Thirty-ninth Regiment, Ohio Volunteer Infantry, and served in that capacity and as corporal; honorably discharged and mustered out at Camp Dennison in March 1865; in June 1865 engaged in the retail business in Xenia, Ohio; was elected justice of the peace in 1869 and served one term; studied law; was admitted to the bar September 8, 1871, and commenced practice in Xenia, Ohio; served three terms as clerk and three terms as solicitor of the city of Xenia; common pleas judge in 1898, and again elected for a term of five years beginning February 1904 from which he resigned upon his election to Congress; elected as a Republican to the Fifty-ninth Congress (March 4, 1905-March 3, 1907); was not a candidate for renomination in 1906; resumed the practice of his profession; moved to Tulsa, Okla., in 1912, where he died March 6, 1915; interment in Woodlawn Cemetery, Xenia, Ohio.

**SCRUGHAM, James Graves,** a Representative and a Senator from Nevada; born in Lexington, Fayette County, Ky., January 19, 1880; attended the public schools and graduated from the engineering department of the University of Kentucky at Lexington in 1906; served in an engineering capacity successively in Cincinnati, Ohio, Chicago, Ill., and San Francisco, Calif.; professor of mechanical engineering, Engineering College, University of Nevada, Reno, from 1903 until 1914, and dean from 1914 to 1917; commissioned as a major in the United States Army in 1917 and was promoted to the rank of lieutenant colonel in 1918; State engineer of Nevada, 1917-1923; Nevada State public service commissioner, 1919-1923; elected Governor of Nevada in 1922, and served from January 1, 1923 to January 3, 1927; unsuccessful candidate for reelection in 1926; editor and publisher of the Nevada State Journal, 1927-1932; special adviser to Secretary of the Interior Hubert Work on Colorado River development projects in 1927; elected as a Democrat to the Seventy-third and to the four succeeding Congresses, and served from March 4, 1933 to December 7, 1942, when he resigned to become a Senator; elected as a Democrat to the United States Senate on November 3, 1942, to fill the vacancy caused by the death of Key Pittman for the term ending January 3, 1947, and served from December 7, 1942 until his death at the United States Naval Hospital in San Diego, Calif., on June 23, 1945; interment in Mountain View Cemetery, Reno, Nev.

**Bibliography:** Cox, Thomas R. "Before the Casino: James G. Scrugham, State Parks, and Nevada's Quest for Tourism." *Western Historical Quarterly* 24 (August 1993): 333-350.

**SCUDDER, Henry Joel** (uncle of Townsend Scudder), a Representative from New York; born in Northport, Suffolk County, N.Y., on September 18, 1825; attended the district school and Huntington Academy; was graduated from Trinity College, Hartford, Conn., in 1846; studied law; was admitted to the bar in 1848 and practiced in New York City; commissioned captain in the Thirty-seventh Regiment, New York National Guard, in 1862 and served throughout the Civil War; elected as a Republican to the Forty-third Congress (March 4, 1873-March 3, 1875); declined to be a candidate for renomination in 1874; trustee of Trinity College for over twenty years; resumed the practice of law in New York City, where he died February 10, 1886; interment in the family cemetery at Northport, Suffolk County, N.Y.

**SCUDDER, Hubert Baxter,** a Representative from California; born in Sebastopol, Sonoma County, Calif., November 5, 1888; graduated from the public schools; supplemented school training with correspondence courses, night schools, and reading of law; superintendent of utilities for the city of Sebastopol from July 1, 1912, to November 4, 1920; served in the United States Coast Artillery from May to December 1918; engaged in the insurance and real estate business in November 1920; elected city councilman of Sebastopol in April 1924 and mayor in 1926; member of the California State assembly from January 1925 to January 1940; appointed real estate commissioner of the State of California in January 1943 and resigned March 1, 1948; president of the National Association of License Law Officials from November 1947 to September 1948; elected as a Republican to the Eighty-first and to the four succeeding Congresses (January 3, 1949-January 3, 1959); was not a candidate for renomination in 1958; engaged in the real estate and insurance business; died in Sebastopol, Calif., July 4, 1968; interment in Sebastopol Cemetery.

**SCUDDER, Isaac Williamson,** a Representative from New Jersey; born in Elizabethtown (now Elizabeth), N.J., in 1816; completed preparatory studies; studied law; was admitted to the bar in 1838 and commenced practice in Elizabeth, N.J.; moved to Jersey City; prosecutor of the pleas of Hudson County 1845-1855; appointed as a member of the first police commission of Jersey City, in 1866; elected director and counsel of the New Jersey Railroad & Transportation Co. May 14, 1866, and director of the United New Jersey Railroad & Canal Co. May 21, 1872; elected as a Republican to the Forty-third Congress (March 4, 1873-March 3, 1875); was not a candidate for reelection in 1874; appointed solicitor of the Pennsylvania Railroad Co. for Hudson County, N.J., June 23, 1875;

died in Jersey City September 10, 1881; interment in St. John's Churchyard, Elizabeth, Union County, N.J.

**SCUDDER, John Anderson,** a Representative from New Jersey; born in Freehold, Monmouth County, N.J., March 22, 1759; completed preparatory studies, and was graduated from Princeton College in 1775; studied medicine and commenced practice in Monmouth County, N.J.; during the Revolutionary War served as surgeon's mate in the First Regiment of Monmouth County, in 1777; secretary of the New Jersey Medical Society in 1788 and 1789; member of the State general assembly 1801-1807; elected as a Republican to the Eleventh Congress to fill the vacancy caused by the death of James Cox and served from October 31, 1810, to March 3, 1811; was not a candidate for renomination to the Twelfth Congress; resumed the practice of medicine; moved to Kentucky after 1810 and to Daviess County, Ind., in 1819; died in Washington, Daviess County, Ind., November 6, 1836; interment in the Old City Cemetery.

**SCUDDER, Nathaniel,** a Delegate from New Jersey; born at Monmouth Court House, Monmouth County, N.J., May 10, 1733; was graduated from Princeton College in 1751; studied medicine and commenced practice in Monmouth County, N.J.; member of the committee of safety; delegate to the Provincial Congress of New Jersey in 1774; member of the New Jersey State general assembly, serving as speaker in 1776; lieutenant colonel of the New Jersey Militia in 1776, and colonel in 1781; Member of the Continental Congress, 1778-1779; trustee of Princeton College, 1778-1781; was killed at Blacks Point, near Shrewsbury, Monmouth County, N.J., October 17, 1781, while resisting an invading party of the British Army; interment in Tennent Church Graveyard, Tennent, N.J.

Bibliography: *DAB.*

**SCUDDER, Townsend** (nephew of Henry Joel Scudder), a Representative from New York; born in Northport, Suffolk County, N.Y., July 26, 1865; attended preparatory schools in Europe; was graduated from Columbia Law School, New York City, in 1888; was admitted to the bar in 1889 and commenced practice in New York City; corporation counsel for Queens County, N.Y., 1893-1899; elected as a Democrat to the Fifty-sixth Congress (March 4, 1899-March 3, 1901); declined to be a candidate for renomination in 1900 to the Fifty-seventh Congress, and resumed the practice of law; elected to the Fifty-eighth Congress (March 4, 1903-March 3, 1905); was not a candidate for renomination in 1904 to the Fifty-ninth Congress; justice of the New York State supreme court for the second judicial district, 1907-1920; again resumed the practice of his profession in New York City; New York State park commissioner and vice president of the Long Island State Park Commission, 1924-1927; appointed to the New York State supreme court by Governor Alfred E. Smith in February 1927; subsequently nominated by the two major political parties to succeed himself for the full term of fourteen years; elected on November 8, 1927, and served until January 1, 1936, when he retired; died in Greenwich, Conn., February 22, 1960; interment in Putnam Cemetery.

**SCUDDER, Tredwell,** a Representative from New York; born in Islip, Suffolk County, N.Y., January 1, 1778; attended the public schools; engaged in agricultural pursuits; town supervisor of Islip in 1795, 1796, and 1804-1815; member of the State assembly in 1802, 1810, 1811, 1814, and 1815; elected as a Republican to the Fifteenth Congress (March 4, 1817-March 3, 1819); was not a candidate for renomination in 1818; resumed agricultural pursuits; again served in the State assembly in 1822 and 1828; again town supervisor of Islip 1824-1833; died in Islip, N.Y., October 31, 1834; interment in that village.

**SCUDDER, Zeno,** a Representative from Massachusetts; born in Osterville, Barnstable County, Mass., August 18, 1807; completed preparatory studies; studied law; admitted to the bar in 1836 and commenced practice in Falmouth, Mass.; member of the Massachusetts senate 1846-1848, serving as president; elected as a Whig to the Thirty-second and Thirty-third Congresses and served from March 4, 1851, until his resignation on March 4, 1854, because of an accident, from the effects of which he never recovered; died in Barnstable, Mass., June 26, 1857; interment in Hillside Cemetery, Osterville, Mass.

**SCULL, Edward,** a Representative from Pennsylvania; born in Pittsburgh, Pa., February 5, 1818; attended the common schools and pursued an academic course; studied law; admitted to the bar in 1844; moved to Somerset, Pa., in 1846 and practiced until 1857, prothonotary and clerk of the court for three years; appointed collector of internal revenue by President Abraham Lincoln in 1863; removed by President Andrew Johnson in September 1866; delegate to the Republican National Conventions of 1864, 1876 and 1884; appointed assessor of internal revenue by President Ulysses S. Grant in April 1869; again appointed collector, on March 22, 1873, and served until August 1883, when the district was consolidated with another; published and edited the Somerset Herald from 1852 until 1887; elected as a Republican to the Fiftieth and to the two succeeding Congresses (March 4, 1887-March 3, 1893); died in Somerset, Somerset County, Pa., July 10, 1900; interment in Union Cemetery.

**SCULLY, Thomas Joseph,** a Representative from New Jersey; born in South Amboy, Middlesex County, N.J., September 19, 1868; attended the public schools, and Seton Hall College, South Orange, N.J.; engaged in the towing and transportation business; member of the board of education 1893-1895; mayor of South Amboy, N.J., in 1909 and 1910; elected as a Democrat to the Sixty-second and to the four succeeding Congresses (March 4, 1911-March 3, 1921); delegate to the Democratic National Convention in 1912; again mayor of South Amboy, from 1921 until his death in that city December 14, 1921; interment in St. Mary's Cemetery.

**SCURRY, Richardson,** a Representative from Texas; born in Gallatin, Sumner County, Tenn., November 11, 1811; educated by private tutors; studied law; was admitted to the bar about 1830 and commenced practice in Covington, Tipton County, Tenn.; moved to Texas and settled in Clarksville, where he continued the practice of law; delegate to the State convention at Washington, Tex., which issued the Texas declaration of independence; a pioneer in the formation of State government; took an active part in the Texan War; elected as a Democrat to the Thirty-second Congress (March 4, 1851-March 3, 1853); resumed the practice of law; died in Hempstead, Waller (formerly Austin) County, Tex., April 9, 1862; interment in Hempstead Cemetery.

**SEAMAN, Henry John,** a Representative from New York; born in Marshland (now Greenridge), Staten Island, N.Y., April 16, 1805; engaged in agricultural pursuits; promoter of Richmond village in 1836; elected as the candidate of the American Party to the Twenty-ninth Congress (March 4, 1845-March 3, 1847); director of the Staten Island Railroad in 1851; secretary of the Plank Road Co. in 1856; constructed the bridge over Fresh Kills; died on Staten Island, N.Y., May 3, 1861; interment in Woodlawn Cemetery, New York City.

**SEARING, John Alexander,** a Representative from New York; born in North Hempstead, N.Y., May 14, 1805; completed preparatory studies; sheriff of Queens County, N.Y., 1843-1846; member of the State assembly in 1854; elected as a Democrat to the Thirty-fifth Congress (March 4, 1857-March 3, 1859); chairman, Committee on Accounts (Thirty-fifth Congress); declined to be a candidate for renomination in 1858; died in Mineola, Nassau

County, N.Y., May 6, 1876; interment in Greenfield Cemetery, Hempstead, N.Y.

**SEARLE, James,** a Delegate from Pennsylvania; born in New York City in 1730; completed preparatory studies; engaged in business at Madeira in 1757; moved to Philadelphia, Pa., in 1762; one of the managers of the United States lottery 1776-1778; member of the Navy board in 1778; Member of the Continental Congress 1778-1780; trustee of the University of Pennsylvania at Philadelphia 1779-1781; was commissioner to France and the Netherlands to negotiate a loan for the Commonwealth of Pennsylvania 1780-1782, but was unsuccessful; located in New York City in 1784 as agent for an importing house; returned to Pennsylvania in 1785; died in Philadelphia, Pa., on August 7, 1797; interment in St. Peter's Churchyard.

**Bibliography:** *DAB.*

**SEARS, William Joseph,** a Representative from Florida; born in Smithville, Lee County, Ga., December 4, 1874; moved with his parents to Ellaville, Ga., and thence to Kissimmee, Osceola County, Fla., in January 1881; attended the public schools; was graduated from Florida State College at Lake City in 1895 and from Mercer University, Macon, Ga., in 1896; studied law; was admitted to the bar in 1905 and commenced practice in Kissimmee, Fla.; mayor of Kissimmee 1907-1911; superintendent of public instruction of Osceola County 1905-1915; elected as a Democrat to the Sixty-fourth and to the six succeeding Congresses (March 4, 1915-March 3, 1929); chairman, Committee on Education (Sixty-fifth Congress); unsuccessful candidate for renomination in 1928; resumed the practice of his legal profession at Kissimmee, Fla.; moved to Jacksonville, Fla., and continued the practice of law; elected to the Seventy-third and Seventy-fourth Congresses (March 4, 1933-January 3, 1937); was an unsuccessful candidate for renomination in 1936; associate member of the Board of Veterans' Appeals of the Veterans' Administration in Washington, D.C., from 1937 until his retirement in October 1942; died in Kissimmee, Fla., March 30, 1944; interment in Rose Hill Cemetery.

**SEARS, Willis Gratz,** a Representative from Nebraska; born in Willoughby, Lake County, Ohio, August 16, 1860; attended the common schools; moved to Nebraska in 1879 and studied law at the University of Kansas at Lawrence; was admitted to the bar in 1884 and commenced the practice of his profession in Tekamah, Burt County, Nebr.; prosecuting attorney for Burt County 1895-1901; member of the State house of representatives 1901-1904, serving as speaker in 1901; elected as judge of the fourth judicial district of Nebraska, November 6, 1903, and served until March 10, 1923, when he resigned, having been elected to Congress; elected as a Republican to the Sixty-eighth and to the three succeeding Congresses (March 4, 1923-March 3, 1931); chairman, Committee on Expenditures in the Department of Justice (Sixty-ninth Congress), Committee on Elections No. 3 (Seventy-first Congress); was an unsuccessful candidate for renomination in 1930 to the Seventy-second Congress; resumed the practice of law; again elected judge of the fourth judicial district of Nebraska and served from 1932 to 1948; died in Omaha, Nebr., on June 1, 1949; interment in Tekamah Cemetery, Tekamah, Nebr.

**SEASTRAND, Andrea H.,** a Representative from California; born in Chicago, Ill., August 5, 1941; B.A., De Paul University, 1963; teacher; California Federation of Republican Women, president; member, California State assembly, 1991-1994; elected as a Republican to the One Hundred Fourth Congress (January 3, 1995-January 3, 1997); is a resident of Shell Beach, Calif.

**SEATON, Frederick Andrew,** a Senator from Nebraska; born in Washington, D.C., December 11, 1909; attended the public schools in Manhattan, Kans., and Kansas State College at Manhattan; president of Seaton Publishing Co., Hastings, Nebr., and publisher of Hastings Daily Tribune; also interested in several daily and weekly newspapers and operating radio and television stations; member, Nebraska State senate, 1945-1949; chairman of the legislative council, 1947-1949; secretary to Republican presidential candidate Alfred M. Landon in 1936; trustee of Hastings College and University of Nebraska Foundation; appointed as a Republican to the United States Senate, December 10, 1951, to fill the vacancy caused by the death of Kenneth S. Wherry, and served from December 10, 1951 to November 4, 1952; was not a candidate for election to the vacancy; Assistant Secretary of Defense, 1953-1955; administrative assistant to President Dwight D. Eisenhower from February to June 1955, then made deputy assistant, in which capacity he served until May 1956; appointed Secretary of the Interior in the Cabinet of President Eisenhower, and served from June 8, 1956 until January 20, 1961; resumed the publishing business; died in Minneapolis, Minn., January 16, 1974; interment in Parkview Cemetery, Hastings, Nebr.

**SEAVER, Ebenezer,** a Representative from Massachusetts; born in Roxbury, Mass., July 5, 1763; graduated from Harvard University in 1784; engaged in agricultural pursuits; member of the Massachusetts house of representatives 1794-1802; elected as a Republican to the Eighth and to the four succeeding Congresses (March 4, 1803-March 3, 1813); unsuccessful candidate for reelection in 1812 to the Thirteenth Congress; member of the Massachusetts constitutional convention in 1820; again a member of the Massachusetts house of representatives in 1822, 1823, and 1826; died in Roxbury, Mass., March 1, 1844.

**SEBASTIAN, William King,** a Senator from Arkansas; born in Centerville, Hickman County, Tenn., in 1812; graduated from Columbia College, Tennessee, about 1834; studied law; was admitted to the bar and commenced practice in Helena, Ark., in 1835; later became a cotton planter; prosecuting attorney 1835-1837; circuit judge, 1840-1843; associate justice of the Arkansas State supreme court, 1843-1845; member and president of the Arkansas State senate, 1846-1847; presidential elector on the Democratic ticket in 1846; appointed in 1848 and subsequently elected as a Democrat to the United States Senate to fill the vacancy caused by the death of Chester Ashley; reelected in 1853 and 1859, and served from May 12, 1848 to July 11, 1861, when he was expelled for support of the Confederacy; chairman, Committee on Manufactures (Thirty-first and Thirty-second Congresses), Committee on Indian Affairs (Thirty-third through Thirty-sixth Congresses); returned to Helena, Ark., where he resided during the Civil War and practiced law; after federal troops occupied Helena, Ark., moved to Memphis, Tenn., in 1864 and resumed the practice of law; died in Memphis, Tenn., May 20, 1865; interment near Helena, Ark., in the Dunn Family burying ground; in 1877 the Senate revoked the resolution of expulsion and paid the full amount of compensation to Sebastian's children.

**SEBELIUS, Keith George,** a Representative from Kansas; born in Almena, Norton County, Kans., September 10, 1916; attended Almena grade and high schools; A.B., Fort Hays Kansas State College, 1941; J.D., George Washington University Law School, 1939; admitted to practice in Kansas and District of Columbia; served in the Armed Forces of the United States as private to master sergeant, lieutenant to major (AUS), Second World War and Korean conflict, USAR (retired); city councilman, mayor, city attorney; State senator, 1962-1968; legislative counsel, 1964-1968; elected as a Republican to the Ninety-first and to the five succeeding Congresses (January 3, 1969-January 3, 1981); was not a candidate for reelection in 1980 to the Ninety-seventh Congress; resided in Norton, Kans. until his death there on August 5, 1982; interment at Norton Cemetery.

**SECCOMBE, James,** a Representative from Ohio; born in Mineral City, Tuscarawas County, Ohio, February 12, 1893; moved with his parents to Canton, Ohio, in 1906; attended the public schools in Mineral City and Canton, Ohio; during the First World War served in the United States Army from July 17, 1917, with service overseas, until discharged April 10, 1919; worked in various factories as machinist and foreman from 1913 to 1932; attended the Y.M.C.A. night school of automobile engineering in 1930 and 1931; member of the Canton City Council 1928-1933, serving as vice president, president, and mayor; delegate to the Republican State conventions at Canton, Ohio, in 1932, 1934, and 1936; elected mayor of Canton in 1935 and served until his resignation in December 1938; elected as a Republican to the Seventy-sixth Congress (January 3, 1939-January 3, 1941); was an unsuccessful candidate for reelection in 1940 to the Seventy-seventh Congress; served as State tax examiner, Canton, Ohio, in 1941 and 1942; director of Stark County Board of Elections, 1942-1970; president of the Ohio Association of Election Officials in 1959; died in Canton, Ohio, August 23, 1970; interment in North Lawn Cemetery.

**SECREST, Robert Thompson,** a Representative from Ohio; born on a farm near Senecaville, Noble County, Ohio, January 22, 1904; attended the public schools; A.B., Muskingum College, New Concord, Ohio, 1926; LL.B., Washington, D.C., College of Law, 1938; completed work for an M.A. degree, Columbia University, 1943; pursued studies at the British School of Civil Affairs, Wimbledon, England, 1943; principal of Senecaville (Ohio) High School 1926-1930; superintendent of schools of Murray City, Ohio, in 1931 and 1932; member of the Ohio State house of representatives in 1931 and 1932; elected as a Democrat to the Seventy-third and to the four succeeding Congresses and served from March 4, 1933, until his resignation on August 3, 1942; lieutenant commander in the United States Navy, later promoted to commander, and served until February 28, 1946, in Great Britain, Africa, Italy, and the Pacific as a military government officer; unsuccessful candidate for election in 1946 to the Eightieth Congress; engaged as a legal supervisor at the Library of Congress from December 15, 1946, until his resignation in June 1947; elected to the Eighty-first and to the two succeeding Congresses and served from January 3, 1949, until his resignation September 26, 1954; had been renominated in the primary election May 4, 1954, to the Eighty-fourth Congress; member of Federal Trade Commission 1954-1961; director of commerce, State of Ohio, January 15, 1962, to August 31, 1962; elected to the Eighty-eighth and Eighty-ninth Congresses (January 3, 1963-January 3, 1967); unsuccessful candidate for reelection in 1966 to the Ninetieth Congress; elected in 1969 to the Ohio State senate for the term ending in January 1973; member, national council, American Legion, 1978-1987; was a resident of Cambridge, Ohio; died May 15, 1994.

**SEDDON, James Alexander,** a Representative from Virginia; born in Falmouth, Va., July 13, 1815; studied under private tutors and was graduated from the law department of the University of Virginia at Charlottesville in 1835; was admitted to the bar about 1838 and commenced practice in Richmond, Va.; elected as a Democrat to the Twenty-ninth Congress (March 4, 1845-March 3, 1847); declined to be a candidate for renomination in 1846 to the Thirtieth Congress; elected to the Thirty-first Congress (March 4, 1849-March 3, 1851); declined to be a candidate for renomination in 1850 to the Thirty-second Congress; member of the peace convention held in Washington, D.C., in 1861 in an effort to devise means to prevent the impending war; delegate from Virginia to the Provisional Confederate Congress at Richmond, Va., in July 1861; appointed Secretary of War in the Cabinet of the Confederate States on November 20, 1862; retired in January 1865; died at "Sabot Hill," Goochland County, Va., August 19, 1880; interment in Hollywood Cemetery, Richmond, Va.

**Bibliography:** *DAB*; Curry, Roy W. "James A. Seddon, A Southern Prototype." *Virginia Magazine of History and Biography* 63 (April 1955): 123-50; O'Brien, Gerald F.J. "James A. Seddon, Statesman of the Old South." Ph.D. dissertation, University of Maryland, 1963.

**SEDGWICK, Charles Baldwin,** a Representative from New York; born in Pompey, Onondaga County, N.Y., March 15, 1815; attended Pompey Hill Academy, and Hamilton College, Clinton, N.Y.; studied law; was admitted to the bar in 1848 and commenced practice in Syracuse, N.Y.; elected as a Republican to the Thirty-sixth and Thirty-seventh Congresses (March 4, 1859-March 3, 1863); chairman, Committee on Naval Affairs (Thirty-seventh Congress); unsuccessful candidate for renomination in 1862; engaged for the next two years in codifying naval laws for the Navy Department at Washington, D.C.; resumed the practice of law in Syracuse, N.Y., where he died February 3, 1883; interment in Oakwood Cemetery.

**Bibliography:** Field, Earle. "Charles B. Sedgwick's Letters From Washington, 1859-1861." *Mid-America* 49 (April 1967): 129-39.

**SEDGWICK, Theodore,** a Delegate, a Representative, and a Senator from Massachusetts; born in West Hartford, Conn., May 9, 1746; attended Yale College; studied theology and law; admitted to the bar in 1766 and commenced practice in Great Barrington, Mass.; moved to Sheffield, Mass.; during the Revolutionary War served in the expedition against Canada in 1776; member, Massachusetts house of representatives, 1780, 1782-1783; member, Massachusetts senate, 1784-1785; Member of the Continental Congress in 1785, 1786, and 1788; member, Massachusetts house of representatives, 1787-1788, and served as speaker; delegate to the Massachusetts convention that adopted the Federal Constitution in 1788; elected to the First and to the three succeeding Congresses, and served from March 4, 1789 until his resignation in June 1796; elected as a Federalist to the United States Senate to fill the vacancy caused by the resignation of Caleb Strong, and served from June 11, 1796 to March 3, 1799; served as President pro tempore of the Senate during the Fifth Congress; elected to the Sixth Congress (March 4, 1799-March 3, 1801); Speaker of the House of Representatives (Sixth Congress); judge of the supreme court of Massachusetts, 1802-1813; died in Boston, Mass., January 24, 1813; interment in the family cemetery, Stockbridge, Mass.

**Bibliography:** *DAB*; Welch, Richard. *Theodore Sedgwick, Federalist: A Political Portrait*. Middletown, Conn.: Wesleyan University Press, 1965.

**SEELEY, John Edward,** a Representative from New York; born in Ovid, Seneca County, N.Y., August 1, 1810; attended Ovid Academy and was graduated from Yale College in 1835; studied law; was admitted to the bar and commenced practice in Monroe, Mich.; returned to Ovid, N.Y., in 1839; supervisor of Ovid in 1842; county judge and surrogate of Seneca County, N.Y., 1851-1855; delegate to the Republican National Convention in 1856; elected as a Republican to the Forty-second Congress (March 4, 1871-March 3, 1873); resumed the practice of his profession in Ovid, N.Y., and died there March 30, 1875; interment on his farm near Ovid.

**SEELY-BROWN, Horace, Jr.,** a Representative from Connecticut; born in Kensington, Montgomery County, Md., May 12, 1908; attended the public schools of Hoosick, N.Y.; was graduated from Hamilton College, Clinton, N.Y., in 1929; student at Yale University in 1929 and 1930; taught school in Hoosick, N.Y., 1930-1932 and in New Lebanon, N.Y., 1932-1934; moved to Pomfret, Conn., in 1934 and taught school until 1942; delegate to the Republican State conventions in 1938, 1940, and 1942; served as Air Operations Officer, Carrier Aircraft Service Unit No. 2, from February 1943 to January 1946; engaged in agricultural pursuits in 1946; elected as a Republican to the Eightieth Congress (January 3, 1947-January 3,

1949); unsuccessful candidate for reelection in 1948 to the Eighty-first Congress; elected to the Eighty-second and to the three succeeding Congresses (January 3, 1951-January 3, 1959); unsuccessful candidate for reelection in 1958 to the Eighty-sixth Congress; elected in 1960 to the Eighty-seventh Congress (January 3, 1961-January 3, 1963); was not a candidate in 1962 for renomination to the House of Representatives, but was an unsuccessful candidate for election to the United States Senate; resumed agricultural pursuits; resided in Pomfret Center, Conn., until his death in Boca Raton, Fla., April 9, 1982; interment in Christ Episcopal Church Cemetery, Pomfret Center, Conn.

**SEELYE, Julius Hawley,** a Representative from Massachusetts; born in Bethel, Fairfield County, Conn., September 14, 1824; was graduated from Amherst (Mass.) College in 1849; studied theology, and was graduated from Auburn Theological Seminary in 1852; ordained as a minister in 1853 and became pastor of the First Reformed Protestant Dutch Church, Schenectady, N.Y., 1853-1858; professor of mental and moral philosophy in Amherst College 1858-1876; accepted an invitation to deliver a course of lectures in India in 1872; elected as an Independent to the Forty-fourth Congress (March 4, 1875-March 3, 1877); declined to be a candidate for reelection; member of the commission to revise the tax laws of Massachusetts; president of Amherst College 1876-1890; died in Amherst, Mass., May 12, 1895; interment in Wildwood Cemetery.

**Bibliography:** *DAB.*

**SEERLEY, John Joseph,** a Representative from Iowa; born on a farm near Toulon, Stark County, Ill., March 13, 1852; in 1854 moved to Iowa with his parents, who settled on a farm in Keokuk County; attended the common schools; was graduated from the University of Iowa at Iowa City in 1875; principal of the Iowa City High School in 1876; was graduated from the law department of the University of Iowa in 1877; was admitted to the bar in 1877 and commenced practice in Burlington, Des Moines County, Iowa; city solicitor of Burlington 1885-1890 and 1893-1895; unsuccessful Democratic candidate for election in 1888 to the Fifty-first Congress; elected as a Democrat to the Fifty-second Congress (March 4, 1891-March 3, 1893); unsuccessful candidate for reelection in 1892 to the Fifty-third Congress; resumed the practice of law in Burlington, Iowa; also interested in banking and agricultural pursuits; delegate to the Democratic National Convention in 1920; died in Burlington, Iowa, on February 23, 1931; interment in Aspin Grove Cemetery.

**SEGAR, Joseph Eggleston,** a Representative from Virginia; born in King William County, Va., June 1, 1804; attended the common schools; studied law; admitted to the bar and practiced; held several local offices; member of the Virginia house of delegates 1836-1838, 1848-1852, and 1855-1861; presented credentials as a Unionist Member-elect to the Thirty-seventh Congress from an election held on October 24, 1861, but the House on February 11, 1862, decided he was not entitled to the seat; subsequently elected to the same Congress and served from March 15, 1862, to March 3, 1863; presented credentials as a Member-elect to the Thirty-eighth Congress, but was declared not entitled to the seat by resolution of May 17, 1864, presented credentials on February 17, 1865, as a United States Senator-elect to fill the vacancy in the term commencing March 4, 1863, caused by the death of Lemuel J. Bowden, but was not permitted to take his seat; presented credentials as a Member-elect to the Forty-first Congress, but was not permitted to qualify; unsuccessful Republican candidate for election in 1876 to the Forty-fifth Congress; member of Spanish Claims Commission, 1877-1880; died on a steamer while en route from Norfolk, Va., to Washington, D.C., April 30, 1880; interment in St. John's Cemetery, Hampton, Va.

**SEGER, George Nicholas,** a Representative from New Jersey; born in New York City January 4, 1866; attended the public schools; settled in Passaic, N.J., in 1899 and engaged in the building business; member of the board of education of Passaic 1906-1911; mayor of Passaic 1911-1919; delegate to the Republican National Convention in 1916; president of the New Jersey League of Municipalities in 1917 and 1918; city director of finance 1919-1923; member of the Council of National Defense during the First World War; elected as a Republican to the Sixty-eighth and to the eight succeeding Congresses and served from March 4, 1923, until his death in Washington, D.C., on August 26, 1940; interment in Greenwood Cemetery, Brooklyn, N.Y.

**SEIBERLING, Francis** (cousin of John Frederick Seiberling), a Representative from Ohio; born in Des Moines, Iowa, September 20, 1870; moved with his parents to Wadsworth, Summit County, Ohio, in 1873; attended the public schools and Wittenberg College, Springfield, Ohio, and was graduated from the College of Wooster (Ohio) in 1892; studied law; was admitted to the bar in 1894 and commenced practice in Akron, Ohio; also interested in the manufacture of rubber and tires and served as a director in various manufacturing companies; served as a trustee of Wittenberg College; elected as a Republican to the Seventy-first and Seventy-second Congresses (March 4, 1929-March 3, 1933); unsuccessful candidate for reelection in 1932 to the Seventy-third Congress; resumed the practice of law; died in Akron, Ohio, February 1, 1945; interment in Rose Hill Cemetery.

**SEIBERLING, John Frederick** (cousin of Francis Seiberling), a Representative from Ohio; born in Akron, Summit County, Ohio, September 8, 1918; attended the public schools of Akron, and Staunton Military Academy, Virginia; A.B., Harvard University, 1941; LL.B., Columbia Law School, New York City, 1949; enlisted as a private in the United States Army and served from March 1942 to March 1946, rising to rank of major; admitted to the New York bar in 1950 and commenced practice in New York; associate with New York firm, 1949-1954; volunteer service with New York Legal Aid Society, 1950; corporate attorney, private industry, 1954-1970; member, Tri-County Regional Planning Commission, Akron, Ohio, 1964-1970; elected as a Democrat to the Ninety-second and to the seven succeeding Congresses (January 3, 1971-January 3, 1987); was not a candidate for reelection in 1986 to the One Hundredth Congress; resumed the practice of law; professor, University of Akron School of Law, 1987 and 1990; director of peace studies, University of Akron, 1991-1996; is a resident of Akron, Ohio.

**SELBY, Thomas Jefferson,** a Representative from Illinois; born in Delaware County, Ohio, December 4, 1840; attended the common schools; studied law; was admitted to the bar in 1869 and commenced the practice of his profession in 1875; sheriff of Jersey County, Ill., 1864-1866; published the Jersey County Democrat 1866-1870; county clerk 1869-1877; mayor of Jerseyville, Ill., two terms; State attorney for Calhoun County 1888-1900; elected as a Democrat to the Fifty-seventh Congress (March 4, 1901-March 3, 1903); resumed the practice of law; State's attorney; died in Hardin, Calhoun County, Ill., March 10, 1917; interment in Hardin Cemetery.

**SELDEN, Armistead Inge, Jr.,** a Representative from Alabama; born in Greensboro, Hale County, Ala., February 20, 1921; attended the public schools; graduated from Greensboro High School in 1938 and from the University of the South, Sewanee, Tenn., in 1942; served in the United States Navy from August 1942 until March 1946, with thirty-one months aboard ship, primarily in the North Atlantic, and was discharged as a lieutenant; lieutenant commander in the United States Naval Reserve; entered the University of Alabama School of Law and graduated in 1948; was admitted to the bar in 1948 and commenced practice in Greensboro, Ala.; member of the Alabama State house of representatives,

1951-1952; elected as a Democrat to the Eighty-third and to the seven succeeding Congresses (January 3, 1953-January 3, 1969); was not a candidate in 1968 for reelection to the House of Representatives, but was an unsuccessful candidate for nomination to the United States Senate; resumed the practice of law until October 1970; Principal Deputy Assistant Secretary of Defense (International Security Affairs), October 1970-February 1973; appointed Ambassador to New Zealand, Fiji, The Kingdom of Tonga, and Western Samoa on March 1, 1974, and served until April 1979; unsuccessful Republican candidate in 1980 for nomination to the United States Senate; president, American League for Exports and Security Assistance, 1980-1985; was a resident of Greensboro, Ala., and Falls Church, Va., until his death in Birmingham, Ala., November 14, 1985; interment in Greensboro City Cemetery, Greensboro, Ala.

**SELDEN, Dudley,** a Representative from New York; was graduated from Union College, Schenectady, N.Y., in 1819; studied law; was admitted to the bar and commenced the practice of his profession in New York City in 1831; member of the State assembly in 1831; elected as a Jacksonian to the Twenty-third Congress and served from March 4, 1833, to July 1, 1834, when he resigned; died in Paris, France, November 7, 1855; interment in Greenwood Cemetery, Brooklyn, N.Y.

**SELDOMRIDGE, Harry Hunter,** a Representative from Colorado; born in Philadelphia, Pa., October 1, 1864; attended the public schools of Philadelphia; moved to Colorado Springs, Colo., in February 1878; was graduated from Colorado College at Colorado Springs in 1885; city editor of the Colorado Springs Gazette, 1886-1888; engaged in the grain and hay business in 1888; delegate to the Democratic National Convention of 1896; member of the Colorado State senate, 1896-1904; member and president of the State charter convention at Colorado Springs in 1909; elected as a Democrat to the Sixty-third Congress (March 4, 1913-March 3, 1915); unsuccessful candidate for reelection in 1914 to the Sixty-fourth Congress; resumed his former business pursuits; receiver of the Mercantile National Bank of Pueblo, 1915-1923; appointed public trustee of El Paso County, Colo., by Governor William E. Sweet; died at Colorado Springs, El Paso County, Colo., November 2, 1927; interment in Evergreen Cemetery.

**SELLS, Sam Riley,** a Representative from Tennessee; born in Bristol, Sullivan County, Tenn., August 2, 1871; attended the rural schools and King College in Bristol, Tenn., 1885-1890; studied law; was admitted to the bar and commenced practice in Blountville, Tenn.; served as a private in Company F, Third Regiment, Tennessee Volunteer Infantry, during the Spanish-American War; moved to Johnson City, Tenn., and engaged in the lumber business; member of the State senate 1909-1911; elected as a Republican to the Sixty-second and to the four succeeding Congresses (March 4, 1911-March 3, 1921); chairman, Committee on Pensions (Sixty-sixth Congress); unsuccessful candidate for renomination in 1920; delegate to the Republican National Conventions in 1912 and 1916; resumed the lumber business in Johnson City, Tenn.; also engaged in the manufacture of shale brick and in numerous other business enterprises; died in Johnson City, Tenn., November 2, 1935; interment in Oak Hill Cemetery.

**SELVIG, Conrad George,** a Representative from Minnesota; born in Rushford, Fillmore County, Minn., October 11, 1877; attended the public schools and was graduated from Rushford High School in 1895; in the war with Spain served as a private with the Twelfth Minnesota Volunteer Infantry; taught in rural and village schools; was graduated from the University of Minnesota at Minneapolis in 1907; superintendent of schools at Harmony and Glencoe, Minn., 1901-1910; delegate to the Republican State convention in 1908; was appointed director of the University of Minnesota Northwest School of Agriculture and Experiment Station, Crookston, Minn., in 1910; president of various Red River Valley farm and community development organizations; elected as a Republican to the Seventieth and to the two succeeding Congresses (March 4, 1927-March 3, 1933); unsuccessful candidate for reelection in 1932 to the Seventy-third Congress; moved to Santa Monica, Calif., in 1935; vice president of the National Hearing Society and was the society's legislative chairman; died in Santa Monica, Calif., August 2, 1953; interment in Oakdale Cemetery, Crookston, Minn.

**Bibliography:** Selvig, Conrad George. *Tale of Two Valleys: An Autobiography*. Los Angeles: C. Jones Press, 1951.

**SELYE, Lewis,** a Representative from New York; born in Chittenango, Madison County, N.Y., July 11, 1803; attended the common schools; learned the blacksmith trade; moved to Rochester, N.Y., in 1824 and engaged in the manufacture of iron; member of the Board of Supervisors of Monroe County several terms; elected alderman in 1841; member of the common council in 1843, 1856, and 1871; treasurer of Monroe County, 1848-1851, and in 1854; elected as an Independent Republican to the Fortieth Congress (March 4, 1867-March 3, 1869); in 1868 established the Rochester Daily Chronicle, which was merged with the Rochester Democrat and Chronicle in 1870; trustee of the Monroe County Savings Bank; died in Rochester, N.Y., January 27, 1883; interment in Mount Hope Cemetery.

**SEMMES, Benedict Joseph,** a Representative from Maryland; born in Charles County, Md., November 1, 1789; attended the rural schools and a medical college in Philadelphia; was graduated from Baltimore Medical School in 1811; commenced practice in Piscataway, Prince Georges County, Md., and later engaged in farming; member of the State house of delegates 1825-1828 and served as speaker; served in the State senate; elected to the Twenty-first and Twenty-second Congresses (March 4, 1829-March 3, 1833); again a member of the State house of delegates in 1842 and 1843; lived in retirement until his death at Oak Lawn, Prince Georges County, Md., February 10, 1863.

**SEMPLE, James,** a Senator from Illinois; born in Green County, Ky., January 5, 1798; moved with his parents to Clinton County; received private instruction and attended the common schools; enlisted in the Army in 1814; ensign in the Kentucky Militia in 1816; moved to Edwardsville, Ill., in 1818 and to Chariton, Mo., in 1819, where he engaged in business; elected as a commissioner of the loan office; studied law in Louisville, Ky.; was admitted to the bar and commenced practice in Clinton County, Ky.; returned to Edwardsville, Ill., in 1827 and continued the practice of law; member, Illinois State house of representatives 1828-1833, serving as speaker four years; served as a private, adjutant, and judge advocate during the Black Hawk War; attorney general of Illinois in 1833; unsuccessful candidate for election in 1836 to the United States Senate; moved to Alton, Ill., in 1837; Chargé d'Affaires to Colombia 1837-1842; judge of the State supreme court 1842-1843; appointed and subsequently elected as a Democrat to the United States Senate to fill the vacancy caused by the death of Samuel McRoberts and served from December 4, 1843, to March 3, 1847; was not a candidate for renomination in 1846; chairman, Committee on Revolutionary Claims (Twenty-ninth Congress); returned to Alton and engaged in the real estate business; moved to Jersey County, Ill., in 1853 and founded the town of Elsah; continued in the real estate business; also engaged in literary pursuits; died in Elsah, Ill., December 20, 1866; interment in Bellefontaine Cemetery, St. Louis, Mo.

**SENER, James Beverley,** a Representative from Virginia; born in Fredericksburg, Spotsylvania County, Va., May 18, 1837; attended private schools and in 1859 was graduated from the University of Virginia at Charlottesville; was graduated in law from Washington College (now Washington and Lee University) at Lexington in 1860; was admitted to the bar the same year and commenced practice in Fredericksburg, Va.; sheriff of Fredericksburg in 1860; sergeant of the city of Fredericksburg, 1863-1865; army correspondent of the Southern Associated Press with the army of General Robert E. Lee; became editor of the Fredericksburg (Va.) Ledger in 1865; delegate to the Republican National Convention of 1872; elected as a Republican to the Forty-third Congress (March 4, 1873-March 3, 1875); chairman, Committee on Expenditures in the Department of Justice (Forty-third Congress); unsuccessful candidate for reelection in 1874 to the Forty-fourth Congress; resumed the practice of his profession; served as chief justice of Wyoming Territory from 1878 until 1882; died in Washington, D.C., November 18, 1903; interment in Citizens Cemetery, Fredericksburg, Va.

**SENEY, George Ebbert,** a Representative from Ohio; born in Uniontown, Fayette County, Pa., May 29, 1832; moved with his parents to Tiffin, Seneca County, Ohio, in November 1832; attended Norwalk (Ohio) Seminary; studied law; was admitted to the bar in 1853 and practiced in Tiffin; judge of the court of common pleas in 1857; in July 1862, enlisted in the One Hundred and First Regiment, Ohio Volunteer Infantry; was subsequently commissioned first lieutenant and acted as quartermaster of the regiment until near the close of the Civil War; delegate to the Democratic National Convention in 1876; elected as a Democrat to the Forty-eighth and to the three succeeding Congresses (March 4, 1883-March 3, 1891); was not a candidate for renomination in 1890; resumed the practice of his profession in Tiffin, Seneca County, Ohio, where he died June 11, 1905; interment in Greenlawn Cemetery.

**SENEY, Joshua,** a Delegate and a Representative from Maryland; born near Church Hill, Queen Annes County, Md., March 4, 1756; attended the common schools, and was graduated from the University of Pennsylvania at Philadelphia in 1773; studied law; was admitted to the bar and practiced; high sheriff of Queen Annes County in 1779; member of the State house of delegates 1785-1787; Member of the Continental Congress in 1788; engaged in agricultural pursuits; elected to the First and Second Congresses and served from March 4, 1789, until his resignation May 1, 1792, to accept a judicial appointment; chief justice of the third judicial district of Maryland, 1792-1796; died near Church Hill, Queen Annes County, Md., October 20, 1798; interment in a private cemetery on the Everett farm, between Church Hill and Sudlersville, Md.

**SENNER, George Frederick, Jr.,** a Representative from Arizona; born in Miami, Gila County, Ariz., November 24, 1921; graduated from Miami High School in 1940; studied at Arizona State University in Tempe and graduated from the University of Arizona Law School in Tucson in 1952; enlisted in the United States Marine Corps in May 1942, served twenty-seven months in the South Pacific, and was discharged in October 1945 with the rank of sergeant; was admitted to the bar in October 1952 and engaged in the practice of law in Miami, Ariz.; assistant attorney, city of Miami, 1952-1954; county attorney, Gila County, 1954-1957; member of Arizona Corporation Commission from August 1957 to January 1963, serving as chairman, 1958-1961; elected as a Democrat to the Eighty-eighth and Eighty-ninth Congresses (January 3, 1963-January 3, 1967); unsuccessful candidate for reelection in 1966 to the Ninetieth Congress; resumed the practice of law; is a resident of Lukeville, Ariz.

**SENSENBRENNER, Frank James, Jr.,** a Representative from Wisconsin; born in Chicago, Ill., June 14, 1943; graduated from Milwaukee Country Day School (high school), 1961; A.B., Stanford University, California, 1965; J.D., University of Wisconsin Law School, Madison, 1968; staff member to Representative J. Arthur Younger, California, 1965; admitted to the Wisconsin bar in 1968 and commenced practice in Cedarburg; private practice of law, 1970-1975; member, Wisconsin State assembly, 1969-1975; member, Wisconsin State senate, 1975-1979 and was assistant minority leader, 1977-1979; delegate, Wisconsin State Republican conventions, 1965-1988; Waukesha County Republican Party; elected as a Republican to the Ninety-sixth and to the eight succeeding Congresses (January 3, 1979-January 3, 1997); is a resident of Menomonee Falls, Wis.

**SENTER, William Tandy,** a Representative from Tennessee; born at Bean Station, Grainger County, Tenn., May 12, 1801; attended the common schools; held several local offices; engaged in agricultural pursuits; minister in the Methodist Episcopal Church South, Holston Conference; member of the State constitutional convention which met at Nashville from May 19 to August 30, 1834; elected as a Whig to the Twenty-eighth Congress (March 4, 1843-March 3, 1845); resumed agricultural pursuits and ministerial work; died at Panther Springs, Hamblen County, Tenn., August 28, 1848; interment in Senter Memorial Church Cemetery.

**SERGEANT, John** (son of Jonathan Dickinson Sergeant, grandfather of John Sergeant Wise and Richard Alsop Wise, and great-grandfather of John Crain Kunkel), a Representative from Pennsylvania; born in Philadelphia, Pa., December 5, 1779; attended the common schools and the University of Pennsylvania at Philadelphia; graduated from Princeton College in 1795; studied law; admitted to the bar in 1799 and practiced in Philadelphia for fifty years; deputy attorney general for Philadelphia in 1800; commissioner of bankruptcy for Pennsylvania in 1801; member of the Pennsylvania house of representatives, 1808-1810; elected as a Federalist to the Fourteenth Congress to fill the vacancy caused by the death of Jonathan Williams; reelected to the three succeeding Congresses, and served from October 10, 1815 to March 3, 1823; chairman, Committee on the Judiciary (Sixteenth and Seventeenth Congresses); was not a candidate for reelection in 1822 to the Eighteenth Congress; president of the Pennsylvania Board of Canal Commissioners in 1825; envoy to the Panama Congress in 1826; elected to the Twentieth Congress (March 4, 1827-March 3, 1829); unsuccessful candidate for reelection in 1828 to the Twenty-first Congress; unsuccessful candidate in 1832 for election as Vice President of the United States on the National Republican ticket headed by Henry Clay; president of the Pennsylvania constitutional convention in 1838; elected as a Whig to the Twenty-fifth and to the two succeeding Congresses, and served from March 4, 1837 until his resignation on September 15, 1841; chairman, Committee on the Judiciary (Twenty-sixth Congress); died in Philadelphia, Pa., November 23, 1852; interment in Laurel Hill Cemetery.

**Bibliography:** *DAB.*

**SERGEANT, Jonathan Dickinson** (father of John Sergeant), a Delegate from New Jersey; born in Newark, N.J., in 1746; moved with his parents to Princeton, N.J., in 1758; completed preparatory studies; was graduated from Princeton College in 1762 and from the University of Pennsylvania at Philadelphia in 1763; studied law; was admitted to the bar in 1767 and commenced practice in Princeton, N.J.; surrogate of Somerset County, N.J., in 1769; secretary of the State provincial convention in 1774; member of the New Jersey Provincial Congress, 1775 and 1776; secretary from May 24 to May 30, 1775, treasurer from August 17 to October 3, 1775, and member of the committee of safety from August 17 to October 3, 1775; appointed as a member of the committee that drafted the first constitution of New Jersey in 1776; Member of the Continental Congress from February 14 to June 22, 1776, when he resigned; again elected a Member of the Continental Congress on November 30, 1776, and served until his resignation on September 6, 1777, to accept the office of attorney general of Pennsylvania; moved to Philadelphia, Pa., in 1777; member of the council of safety of Pennsylvania in 1777; attorney general of Pennsylvania 1777-1780; counsel for the State in the Wyoming land controversy with Connecticut in 1782; died in Philadelphia, Pa., October 8, 1793;

interment in the Presbyterian Churchyard, then located at Fourth and Pine Streets; reinterment in Laurel Hill Cemetery in 1878.

**Bibliography:** *DAB.*

**SERRANO, José Enrique,** a Representative from New York; born in Mayaguez, Puerto Rico, October 24, 1943; attended Dodge Vocational High School, Bronx, N.Y., and Lehman College, City University of New York; entered active duty, United States Army in 1964; released in 1966 after service with the Medical Corps; Manufacturers Hanover Bank, New York City, 1961-1969; administrative positions with Community School District 7, 1969-1974; member, New York State assembly, 1975-1990; elected as a Democrat to the One Hundred First Congress, March 20, 1990, by special election to fill the vacancy caused by the resignation of Robert Garcia; reelected to the three succeeding Congresses, and served from March 20, 1990 to January 3, 1997; is a resident of the Bronx, N.Y.

**SESSINGHAUS, Gustavus,** a Representative from Missouri; born in Koela, Prussia, November 8, 1838; pursued preparatory studies; immigrated to the United States and settled in St. Louis, Mo.; during the Civil War served as a private in Company A, Fifth Regiment, United States Reserve Corps, Missouri Volunteer Infantry; member of the school board 1878-1880; successfully contested as a Republican the election of Richard G. Frost to the Forty-seventh Congress and served two days only, March 2 and 3, 1883; unsuccessful candidate for reelection in 1882 to the Forty-eighth Congress; engaged in the milling business; died in St. Louis, Mo., November 16, 1887; interment in Bellefontaine Cemetery.

**SESSIONS, Walter Loomis,** a Representative from New York; born in Brandon, Rutland County, Vt., October 4, 1820; as a child was brought to Chautauqua County, N.Y.; attended the common schools of the county and Westfield (N.Y.) Academy; studied law; was admitted to the bar in 1849 and commenced the practice of his profession in Panama, Chautauqua County, N.Y.; engaged in teaching; commissioner of schools for several years; member of the State assembly in 1853 and 1854; served in the State senate in 1860, 1861, 1866, and 1867; supervisor of the town of Harmony, Chautauqua County, N.Y., 1870-1872; elected as a Republican to the Forty-second and Forty-third Congresses (March 4, 1871-March 3, 1875); unsuccessful candidate for reelection in 1874 to the Forty-fourth Congress; resumed the practice of law; elected to the Forty-ninth Congress (March 4, 1885-March 3, 1887); unsuccessful candidate for renomination in 1886 and for the nomination in 1890; engaged in the practice of his profession in Jamestown and Panama, N.Y.; appointed commissioner of the State of New York to the World's Columbian Exposition at Chicago, Ill., in 1893; died in Panama, N.Y., on May 27, 1896; interment in Forest Hill Cemetery.

**SETTLE, Evan Evans,** a Representative from Kentucky; born in Frankfort, Ky., December 1, 1848; attended the public schools; was graduated from Louisville High School in June 1864; studied law; admitted to the bar in 1870 and commenced practice in Owenton, Owenton County, Ky.; elected prosecuting attorney of Owenton County in 1878, 1882, and 1886; resigned in 1887; member of the Kentucky house of representatives 1887-1890; delegate to the Democratic National Convention in 1888; elected as a Democrat to the Fifty-fifth and Fifty-sixth Congresses and served from March 3, 1897, until his death in Owenton, Ky., November 16, 1899; interment in Odd Fellows Cemetery.

**SETTLE, Thomas,** (grandfather of Thomas Settle [1865-1919] and uncle of David Settle Reid), a Representative from North Carolina; born near Reidsville, Rockingham County, N.C., March 9, 1789; educated by private tutors; studied law; was admitted to the bar in 1812 and commenced practice in Wentworth, N.C.; member of the State house of commons in 1816; elected as a Republican to the Fifteenth and Sixteenth Congresses (March 4, 1817-March 3, 1821); declined to be a candidate for reelection; resumed the practice of law; again a member of the State house of commons, in 1826 and 1827, and served as speaker in the last session; judge of the superior courts of North Carolina in 1832; died in Rockingham County, N.C., August 5, 1857; interment in the Settle family graveyard, near Reidsville, N.C.

**SETTLE, Thomas** (grandson of Thomas Settle [1789-1857]), a Representative from North Carolina; born near Wentworth, Rockingham County, N.C., March 10, 1865; attended the public schools and Georgetown College, District of Columbia; studied law in Greensboro, N.C.; was admitted to the bar in 1885 and commenced practice at Wentworth, N.C.; solicitor of the ninth judicial district 1886-1894; elected as a Republican to the Fifty-third and Fifty-fourth Congresses (March 4, 1893-March 3, 1897); chairman, Committee on Expenditures on Public Buildings (Fifty-fourth Congress); unsuccessful candidate for reelection in 1896 to the Fifty-fifth Congress; resumed the practice of his profession in Asheville, N.C.; appointed by the Department of Justice as special attorney to the United States Court of Customs in New York City in 1909, and served in that capacity until 1910; unsuccessful candidate for Governor of North Carolina in 1912; died in Asheville, N.C., January 20, 1919; interment in Oakdale Cemetery, Wilmington, N.C.

**SEVERANCE, Luther,** a Representative from Maine; born in Montague, Mass., October 26, 1797; moved with his parents to Cazenovia, N.Y., in 1799; attended the common schools; learned the printer's trade in Peterboro, N.Y.; established the Kennebec Journal in Augusta, Maine, in 1825; member of the State house of representatives in 1829, 1839, 1840, 1842, and 1848; served in the State senate in 1835 and 1836; elected as a Whig to the Twenty-eighth and Twenty-ninth Congresses (March 4, 1843-March 3, 1847); vice president of the Whig National Convention in 1848; United States commissioner to the Sandwich Islands 1850-1854; died in Augusta, Maine, January 25, 1855; interment in Forest Grove Cemetery.

**SEVIER, Ambrose Hundley** (cousin of Henry Wharton Conway), a Delegate and a Senator from Arkansas; born in Greene County, Tenn., November 4, 1801; completed preparatory studies; moved to Missouri in 1820 and to Little Rock, Ark., in 1821; clerk of the Territorial house of representatives; studied law; was admitted to the bar in 1823 and practiced; member, Territorial house of representatives, 1823-1827, serving as speaker in 1827; elected as a Delegate to the Twentieth Congress to fill the vacancy caused by the death of Henry W. Conway; reelected to the Twenty-first and to the three succeeding Congresses, and served from February 13, 1828 to June 15, 1836, when the Territory was admitted as a State into the Union; elected as a Democrat to the United States Senate in 1836; reelected in 1837 and 1843, and served from September 18, 1836 until his resignation on March 15, 1848; served as President pro tempore of the Senate during the Twenty-ninth Congress; chairman, Committee on Indian Affairs (Twenty-sixth and Twenty-ninth Congresses), Committee on Foreign Relations (Twenty-ninth and Thirtieth Congresses); appointed Minister to Mexico to negotiate the Treaty of Guadalupe Hidalgo in 1848, which ended hostilities between Mexico and the United States; died on his plantation near Little Rock, Pulaski County, Ark., December 31, 1848; interment in Mount Holly Cemetery, where the State erected a monument to his memory.

**Bibliography:** *DAB*; Walton, Brian. "Ambrose Hundley Sevier in the United States Senate, 1836-1848." *Arkansas Historical Quarterly* 32 (Spring 1973): 25-60.

**SEVIER, John,** a Representative from North Carolina and from Tennessee; born near Harrisonburg, Rockingham County, Va., September 23, 1745; attended the common schools and the academy at Fredericksburg, Va.; moved with his brothers to Watauga County, N.C., in 1773 and settled on the Holston River, N.C. (now Tennessee); county clerk and district judge, 1777-1780; elected Governor of the "State of Franklin" in March 1785 and served for three years; elected from North Carolina to the First Congress, and served from June 16, 1790 until March 3, 1791; appointed in 1791 as brigadier general of militia for the Washington district of the territory south of the Ohio; upon the admission of Tennessee as a State into the Union in 1796 was elected Governor; reelected in 1797 and 1799, and served from March 30, 1796 to September 23, 1801; again elected Governor of Tennessee in 1803, reelected in 1805 and 1807, and served from September 23, 1803 to September 20, 1809; appointed in 1798 as brigadier general of the Provisional Army; served one term in the Tennessee State senate, 1810-1811; appointed in 1815 as one of the commissioners to determine the boundary between Georgia and the Creek territory in Alabama; elected as a Republican from Tennessee to the Twelfth and to the two succeeding Congresses, and served from March 4, 1811 until his death near Fort Decatur, Ala., September 24, 1815; interment at Fort Decatur, Ala.; reinterred in Knoxville, Tenn., in 1889.

**Bibliography:** *DAB*; Driver, Carl S. "John Sevier, A Pioneer of the Old Southwest." Ph.D. dissertation, Vanderbilt University, 1929.

**SEWALL, Charles S.,** a Representative from Maryland; born in Queen Annes County, Md., in 1779; attended the common schools; served in the Forty-second Regiment, Maryland Militia, in the War of 1812; served in the State house of delegates; was member of the State senate; elected as a Jacksonian to the Twenty-second Congress to fill the vacancy caused by the death of George E. Mitchell and served from October 1, 1832, to March 3, 1833; elected as a Democrat to the Twenty-seventh Congress to fill the vacancy which was caused by the death of James W. Williams and served from January 2 to March 3, 1843; moved to Harford County, Md.; died at Rose Hill, Harford County, Md., on November 3, 1848.

**SEWALL, Samuel,** a Representative from Massachusetts; born in Boston, Mass., December 11, 1757; attended the common schools and graduated from Harvard College in 1776; studied law; admitted to the bar and commenced practice in Marblehead, Mass.; member of the Massachusetts house of representatives 1784 and 1788-1796; elected as a Federalist to the Fourth Congress to fill the vacancy caused by the resignation of Benjamin Goodhue; reelected to the Fifth and Sixth Congresses and served from December 7, 1796, until his resignation on January 10, 1800; one of the managers appointed by the House of Representatives in 1798 to conduct the impeachment proceedings against William Blount, a Senator from Tennessee; associate judge of the supreme court of Massachusetts 1801-1813 and served as chief justice in 1813 and 1814; died in Wiscasset, Maine, June 8, 1814; interment in Ancient Cemetery; reinterment in the family tomb at Marblehead, Mass.

**SEWARD, James Lindsay,** a Representative from Georgia; born in Dublin, Laurens County, Ga., on October 30, 1813; attended the common schools; moved with his parents to Thomas County in 1826; studied law; was admitted to the bar in 1835 and commenced practice in Thomasville, Thomas County, Ga.; member of the State house of representatives 1835-1839, 1847, 1848, 1851, and 1852; elected as a Democrat to the Thirty-third, Thirty-fourth, and Thirty-fifth Congresses (March 4, 1853-March 3, 1859); was not a candidate for renomination in 1858; resumed the practice of law and also engaged as a planter; delegate to the Democratic State conventions in 1858, 1859, and 1860; served in the State senate 1859-1865; delegate to the Democratic National Conventions at Charleston and Baltimore in 1860; member of the board of trustees of Young's Female College 1860-1886 and of the University of Georgia at Athens 1865-1886; delegate to the reconstruction constitutional convention in 1865; delegate to the Democratic

Conservative Convention in 1870; delegate to the State constitutional convention in 1877; died in Thomasville, Ga., on November 21, 1886; interment in Laurel Hill Cemetery.

**SEWARD, William Henry,** a Senator from New York; born in Florida, Orange County, N.Y., on May 16, 1801; after preparatory studies, graduated from Union College in 1820; studied law; was admitted to the bar and commenced practice in Auburn, N.Y., in 1823; member, New York State senate, 1830-1834; unsuccessful Whig candidate for election for governor in 1834; elected Governor of New York in 1838, reelected in 1840, and served from January 1, 1839 to January 1, 1843; elected as a Whig to the United States Senate in 1849; reelected as a Republican in 1855 and served from March 4, 1849, to March 3, 1861; unsuccessful candidate for the Republican nomination for president in 1860; Secretary of State in the Cabinets of Presidents Abraham Lincoln and Andrew Johnson, March 5, 1861 to March 4, 1869; concluded the convention with Great Britain for the settlement of claims for damages caused by the *Alabama* during the Civil War while that ship was in the service of the Confederacy; concluded on March 30, 1867 the treaty with Russia for the purchase of Alaska; died in Auburn, Cayuga County, N.Y., October 10, 1872; interment in Fort Hill Cemetery.

**Bibliography:** *DAB*; Seward, William Henry. *William Henry Seward*. Edited by Frederick Seward. 3 vols. New York: Derby and Miller, 1891; Van Deusen, Glyndon. *William Henry Seward*. New York: Oxford University Press, 1967.

**SEWELL, William Joyce,** a Senator from New Jersey; born in Castlebar, Ireland, December 6, 1835; immigrated to the United States in 1851; engaged in mercantile pursuits in Chicago, Ill.; moved to Camden, N.J., in 1860; during the Civil War, served with the New Jersey Volunteers, beginning as a captain on August 28, 1861; brevetted brigadier general and major general in 1865; awarded the Congressional Medal of Honor on March 25, 1896, "for having assumed command of a brigade at Chancellorsville, Va., May 3, 1863"; after the war became connected with railroads in New Jersey; member, New Jersey State senate, 1872-1881, serving as president in 1876 and 1879-1880; elected as a Republican to the United States Senate, and served from March 4, 1881 to March 3, 1887; unsuccessful candidate for reelection in 1887, and for election to the United States Senate in 1889 and 1893; chairman, Committee on Enrolled Bills (Forty-seventh and Forty-eighth Congresses), Committee on Military Affairs (Forty-ninth Congress), Committee on the Library (Forty-ninth Congress); one of the national commissioners for New Jersey to the World's Columbian Exposition in Chicago in 1893; was in command of the Second Brigade of the National Guard of New Jersey; appointed a member of the Board of Managers of the National Home for Disabled Volunteer Soldiers; again elected to the United States Senate in 1895; reelected in 1901, and served from March 4, 1895 until his death in Camden, N.J., December 27, 1901; chairman, Committee on Enrolled Bills (Fifty-fourth through Fifty-seventh Congresses); interment in Harleigh Cemetery.

**Bibliography:** *DAB*.

**SEXTON, Leonidas,** a Representative from Indiana; born in Rushville, Rush County, Ind., May 19, 1827; attended the public schools of his native county and was graduated from Jefferson College, Canonsburg, Pa., in 1847; studied law in Rushville and in 1848 and 1849 attended the Cincinnati Law School; was admitted to the Indiana bar in 1850 and commenced the practice of his profession in Rushville, Ind.; member of the State house of representatives in 1856; elected Lieutenant Governor of Indiana and served from January 1873 to January 1877; elected as a Republican to the Forty-fifth Congress (March 4, 1877-March 3, 1879); unsuccessful candidate for reelection in 1878 to the Forty-sixth Congress; died in Parsons, Labette County, Kans., July 4, 1880; interment in East Hill Cemetery, Rushville, Ind.

**SEYBERT, Adam,** a Representative from Pennsylvania; born in Philadelphia, Pa., May 16, 1773; attended the common schools; completed the medical course at the University of Pennsylvania at Philadelphia in 1793 and continued studies in Europe, where he attended schools in Edinburgh, Gottingen, and Paris; returned to Philadelphia and devoted himself to chemistry and mineralogy; elected as a member of the American Philosophical Society in 1797; elected as a Republican to the Eleventh Congress to fill the vacancy caused by the resignation of Benjamin Say; reelected to the Twelfth and Thirteenth Congresses and served from October 10, 1809, to March 3, 1815; chairman, Committee on Revisal and Unfinished Business (Twelfth Congress); elected to the Fifteenth Congress (March 4, 1817-March 3, 1819); visited Europe 1819-1821 and again in 1824 and settled in Paris, France, where he died May 2, 1825.

**Bibliography:** *DAB.*

**SEYMOUR, David Lowrey,** a Representative from New York; born in Wethersfield, Conn., December 2, 1803; pursued preparatory studies; was graduated from Yale College in 1826; tutor at Yale College 1828-1830; studied law; was admitted to the bar in 1829 and commenced the practice of his profession in Troy, N.Y.; member of the State assembly in 1836; district attorney of Rensselaer County from October 14, 1839, to October 14, 1842; master in chancery in 1839; elected as a Democrat to the Twenty-eighth Congress (March 4, 1843-March 3, 1845); chairman, Committee on Revolutionary Pensions (Twenty-eighth Congress); unsuccessful candidate for reelection in 1844 to the Twenty-ninth Congress; elected to the Thirty-second Congress (March 4, 1851-March 3, 1853); chairman, Committee on Commerce (Thirty-second Congress); unsuccessful candidate for reelection in 1852 to the Thirty-third Congress; resumed the practice of his profession; unsuccessful candidate in 1858 to the Thirty-sixth Congress; member of the constitutional convention of New York in 1867; died in Lanesboro, Berkshire County, Mass., on October 11, 1867; interment in Mount Ida Cemetery, Troy, N.Y.

**SEYMOUR, Edward Woodruff** (son of Origen Storrs Seymour), a Representative from Connecticut; born in Litchfield, Conn., August 30, 1832; attended the public schools and was graduated from Yale College in 1853; studied law; was admitted to the bar in 1856 and practiced in Litchfield and Bridgeport, Conn.; member of the State house of representatives in 1859, 1860, 1870, and 1871; served in the State senate in 1876; elected as a Democrat to the Forty-eighth and Forty-ninth Congresses (March 4, 1883-March 3, 1887); resumed the practice of his profession; appointed as a judge of the Connecticut Supreme Court in 1889; died in Litchfield, Conn., on October 16, 1892; interment in East Cemetery.

**SEYMOUR, Henry William,** a Representative from Michigan; born in Brockport, Monroe County, N.Y., July 21, 1834; attended the public schools, Brockport Collegiate Institute, and Canandaigua Academy and was graduated from Williams College, Williamstown, Mass., in 1855; studied law in Albany, N.Y., taking lectures at Albany Law School; was admitted to the bar in May 1856, but never practiced; engaged in mercantile pursuits in Brockport; moved to Michigan in 1872 and settled in Sault Ste. Marie, where he engaged in the manufacture of reapers and subsequently in the manufacture of lumber and in agricultural pursuits; member of the State house of representatives 1880-1882; member of the State senate 1882-1884 and 1886-1888; elected as a Republican to the Fiftieth Congress to fill the vacancy caused by the death of Seth C. Moffatt and served from February 14, 1888, to March 3, 1889; unsuccessful candidate for renomination in 1888; died, while on a visit, in Washington, D.C., April 7, 1906; interment in Lakeview Cemetery, Brockport, N.Y.

**SEYMOUR, Horatio** (uncle of Origen Storrs Seymour), a Senator from Vermont; born in Litchfield, Conn., May 31, 1778; attended the common schools and graduated from Yale College in 1797; taught school in Cheshire, Conn.; pursued legal studies in Litchfield Law School; was admitted to the bar in 1800 and commenced the practice of law in Middlebury, Vt.; postmaster of Middlebury 1800-1809; member, State executive council 1809-1814; State's attorney for Addison County 1810-1813, 1815-1819; elected to the United States Senate in 1821; reelected in 1827 and served from March 4, 1821, to March 3, 1833; was not a candidate for reelection; chairman, Committee to Audit and Control the Contingent Expense (Eighteenth and Nineteenth Congresses), Committee on Agriculture (Twenty-second Congress); unsuccessful Whig candidate for Governor of Vermont in 1836; judge of the probate court 1847-1856; died in Middlebury, Addison County, Vt., November 21, 1857; interment in West Cemetery.

**SEYMOUR, John,** a Senator from California; born in Chicago, Ill., December 3, 1937; graduated Mt. Lebanon (Pa.) High School, 1955; B.S., University of California, Los Angeles, 1962; United States Marine Corps service, sergeant; realtor, Seymour Realty, 1962-1981; Anaheim (Calif.) city council, 1974-1978; mayor of Anaheim, 1978-1982; member, California State senate, District 35, from April 1982 until appointed to the United States Senate; Republican caucus chairman, 1983-1987; State chair of Senator Pete Wilson's reelection campaign in 1988; unsuccessful candidate in 1990 for nomination for Lieutenant Governor; appointed as a Republican to the United States Senate, January 2, 1991, to fill the vacancy caused by the resignation of Peter B. (Pete) Wilson, and served from January 10, 1991 until his resignation on November 10, 1992; unsuccessful candidate in 1992 for election to the remainder of the term ending January 3, 1995; is a resident of Anaheim, Calif.

**SEYMOUR, Origen Storrs** (father of Edward Woodruff Seymour and nephew of Horatio Seymour), a Representative from Connecticut; born in Litchfield, Conn., February 9, 1804; attended the public schools and was graduated from Yale College in 1824; studied law; was admitted to the bar in 1826 and commenced practice in Litchfield, Conn.; served as county clerk 1836-1844; member of the State house of representatives in 1842, 1849, and 1850, and served as speaker in 1850; elected as a Democrat to the Thirty-second and Thirty-third Congresses (March 4, 1851-March 3, 1855); judge of the superior court of Connecticut 1855-1863; unsuccessful Democratic candidate for Governor in 1864 and 1865; judge of the State supreme court in 1870, chief justice in 1873, and served until retired by age limitation in 1874; chairman of the commission to settle the boundary dispute between Connecticut and New York in 1876; again a member of the State house of representatives in 1880; died in Litchfield, Conn., August 12, 1881; interment in East Cemetery.

**SEYMOUR, Thomas Hart,** a Representative from Connecticut; born in Hartford, Conn., September 29, 1807; attended the public schools, and was graduated from Middletown (Conn.) Military Academy in 1829; studied law; was admitted to the bar in 1833 and commenced practice in Hartford, Conn.; editor of the Jeffersonian in 1837 and 1838; judge of probate, 1836-1838; elected as a Democrat to the Twenty-eighth Congress (March 4, 1843-March 3, 1845); declined to be a candidate for renomination in 1844 to the Twenty-ninth Congress; served in the Mexican War; commissioned major in the Connecticut Infantry on March 16, 1846, and in the Ninth United States Infantry on April 9, 1847; commissioned lieutenant colonel of the Twelfth Infantry on August 12, 1847; unsuccessful candidate for election for Governor of Connecticut in 1849; elected Governor of Connecticut in 1850, reelected in 1851, 1852 and 1853, and served from May 4, 1850 until his resignation on October 13, 1853, to accept a diplomatic post; appointed Minister to Russia on May 24, 1853 and served until July 1858; again an unsuccessful candidate for election for Governor in 1863; died in Hartford, Conn., September 3, 1868; interment in Cedar Hill Cemetery.

**Bibliography:** *DAB.*

**SEYMOUR, William,** a Representative from New York; born in Connecticut about 1780; moved to Windsor, Broome County, N.Y., about 1793; attended the public schools; studied law; was admitted to the bar in 1806 and commenced practice in Binghamton, N.Y.; returned to Windsor in 1807; justice of the peace 1812-1828; in 1833, upon his appointment as first judge of the court of common pleas of Broome County, returned to Binghamton; elected as one of the first trustees of the village in 1834; elected as a Jacksonian to the Twenty-fourth Congress (March 4, 1835-March 3, 1837); again served as first judge of the court of common pleas in Broome County until 1847; resumed the practice of his profession in Binghamton, where he died December 28, 1848; interment in Binghamton Cemetery.

**SHACKELFORD, John Williams,** a Representative from North Carolina; born in Richlands, Onslow County, N.C., November 16, 1844; attended the common schools and Richlands (N.C.) Academy; during the Civil War entered the Confederate Army at the age of seventeen and served throughout the war, attaining the rank of lieutenant; member of the State house of representatives 1872-1878; served in the State senate 1878-1880; was elected to preside over the convention that nominated him for Congress in 1880; elected as a Democrat to the Forty-seventh Congress, and served from March 4, 1881, until his death in Washington, D.C., January 18, 1883; interment in the Wallace Graveyard, Richlands, N.C.

**SHACKLEFORD, Dorsey William,** a Representative from Missouri; born near Sweet Springs, Saline County, Mo., August 27, 1853; attended the public schools and William Jewell College, Liberty, Mo.; taught school 1877-1879; studied law; was admitted to the bar in 1878 and commenced practice in Boonville, Mo.; prosecuting attorney of Cooper County, Mo., 1882-1886 and 1890-1892; judge of the fourteenth judicial circuit of Missouri from June 1, 1892, until his resignation on September 9, 1899, having been elected to Congress; elected as a Democrat to the Fifty-sixth Congress to fill the vacancy caused by the death of Richard P. Bland; reelected to the Fifty-seventh and to the eight succeeding Congresses, and served from August 29, 1899, to March 3, 1919; chairman, Committee on Roads (Sixty-third through Sixty-fifth Congresses); was an unsuccessful candidate for renomination in 1918 to the Sixty-sixth Congress; moved to Jefferson City, Mo., in 1919 and continued the practice of law; died in Jefferson City, Mo., on July 15, 1936; interment in Walnut Grove Cemetery, Boonville, Mo.

**SHADEGG, John B.,** a Representative from Arizona; born in Phoenix, Ariz., October 22, 1949; graduated from Camelback High School; B.A., University of Arizona, 1972; J.D., University of Arizona School of Law, 1975; served in the Arizona Air National Guard; special assistant attorney general, 1983-1990; special counsel to the Republican caucus, Arizona State house of representatives, 1991-1992; Arizona Republican Caucus, chair, 1985-1987; elected as a Republican to the One Hundred Fourth Congress (January 3, 1995-January 3, 1997); is a resident of Phoenix, Ariz.

**SHAFER, Jacob K.,** a Delegate from the Territory of Idaho; born near Broadway, Rockingham County, Va., December 26, 1823; was graduated from Washington College, Lexington, Va., in 1843; and from the law school of L.P. Thompson in Staunton, Va., in 1846; moved to Stockton, Calif., in 1849; was admitted to the bar and practiced; district attorney of the fifth judicial district of California in 1850; served as mayor of Stockton in 1852; judge of the San Joaquin County Court, 1853-1862; moved in 1862 to what later became Idaho Territory; elected as a Democrat to the Forty-first Congress (March 4, 1869-March 3, 1871); unsuccessful candidate for renomination in 1870 to the Forty-second Congress; resumed the practice of law; moved to Eureka, Nev., where he died November 22, 1876; interment in the Masonic Cemetery.

**SHAFER, Paul Werntz,** a Representative from Michigan; born in Elkhart, Ind., April 27, 1893; moved with his parents to Three Rivers, Mich., and attended the public schools; student at Ferris Institute, Big Rapids, Mich., and studied law by correspondence with the Blackstone Institute of Chicago, Ill.; reporter, editor, and publisher of newspapers in Elkhart, Ind., Battle Creek, Mich., and Bronson, Mich.; member of Indiana State Militia in 1916 and 1917; municipal judge in Battle Creek, Mich., 1929-1936; elected as a Republican to the Seventy-fifth and to the eight succeeding Congresses, and served from January 3, 1937 until his death in Washington, D.C, August 17, 1954; had been renominated to the Eighty-fourth Congress in the Republican primary election of August 3, 1954; interment in Memorial Park Cemetery, Battle Creek, Mich.

**SHAFFER, Joseph Crockett,** a Representative from Virginia; born near Wytheville, Wythe County, Va., January 19, 1880; attended the Wytheville public schools; was graduated from Plummer College, Wytheville, Va., in 1902 and from the law department of the University of Virginia at Charlottesville in 1904; was admitted to the bar in 1904 and commenced practice in Wytheville, Va.; served as Commonwealth attorney of Wythe County 1908-1912; assistant United States district attorney 1920-1924 and served as United States district attorney for the western district of Virginia 1924-1929; elected as a Republican to the Seventy-first Congress (March 4, 1929-March 3, 1931); unsuccessful candidate for reelection in 1930 to the Seventy-second Congress; United States district attorney for the western district of Virginia from 1931 until his resignation in 1932; resumed the practice of law; stockholder and officer in Wythe County National Bank; delegate to the Republican National Convention in 1940; died in Abingdon, Va., October 19 1958; interment in St. John's Church Cemetery, Wytheville, Va.

**SHAFROTH, John Franklin,** a Representative and a Senator from Colorado; born in Fayette, Mo., June 9, 1854; attended the common schools and graduated from the University of Michigan at Ann Arbor in 1875; studied law; was admitted to the bar in 1876 and commenced practice in Fayette, Mo.; moved to Denver, Colo., in 1879 and continued law practice; city attorney, 1887-1891; elected as a Republican to the Fifty-fourth Congress; reelected as a Silver Republican to the Fifty-fifth and to the two succeeding Congresses; presented credentials as a Democratic Member-elect to the Fifty-eighth Congress, and served from March 4, 1895 until his resignation on February 15, 1904, when he declared his conviction that his opponent, Robert W. Bonynge, had been duly elected; elected Governor of Colorado in 1908, reelected in 1910, and served from January 12, 1909 to January 14, 1913; elected as a Democrat to the United States Senate in 1912, and served from March 4, 1913 to March 3, 1919; unsuccessful candidate for reelection in 1918; chairman, Committee on Pacific Islands and Puerto Rico (Sixty-third through Sixty-fifth Congresses); Committee on the Philippines (Sixty-fifth Congress); chairman of the War Minerals Relief Commission from 1919 to 1921; died in Denver, Colo., February 20, 1922; interment in Fairmount Cemetery.

**Bibliography:** *DAB.*

**SHALLENBERGER, Ashton Cokayne,** a Representative from Nebraska; born in Toulon, Stark County, Ill., December 23, 1862; attended the common schools and the University of Illinois at Urbana; moved to Stromsburg, Polk County, Nebr., in 1881, to Osceola, Polk County, Nebr., in 1883, and to Alma, Harlan County, Nebr., in 1887; engaged in banking and also in stock raising; temporary chairman of the Democratic State conventions in 1897 and 1919; elected as a Democrat to the Fifty-seventh Congress (March 4, 1901-March 3, 1903); unsuccessful candidate for reelection in 1902 to the Fifty-eighth Congress; unsuccessful candidate in 1906 for Governor; elected Governor of Nebraska in 1908, and served from January 7, 1909 to January 5, 1911; unsuccessful Democratic candidate for election in 1912 to the United States Senate; elected to the Sixty-fourth and Sixty-fifth Congresses (March 4, 1915-March 3, 1919); unsuccessful candidate for reelection in 1918 to the Sixty-sixth Congress; delegate to the Democratic National Convention of 1920; elected to the Sixty-eighth and to the two succeeding Congresses (March 4, 1923-March 3, 1929); unsuccessful candidate for reelection in 1928 to the Seventy-first Congress; elected to the Seventy-second and Seventy-third Congresses (March 4, 1931-January 3, 1935); unsuccessful candidate for renomination in 1934 to the Seventy-fourth Congress; resumed banking and also engaged in agricultural pursuits and the breeding of shorthorn cattle; died in Franklin, Nebr., while on a visit, February 22, 1938; interment in Alma Cemetery, Alma, Nebr.

**SHALLENBERGER, William Shadrack,** a Representative from Pennsylvania; born in Mount Pleasant, Westmoreland County, Pa., November 24, 1839; attended the public schools and Mount Pleasant Academy; was graduated from Lewisburg University (now Bucknell University), Lewisburg, Pa., in 1862; engaged in mercantile pursuits; during the Civil War enlisted in the Union Army in 1862 in the One Hundred and Fortieth Regiment, Pennsylvania Volunteer Infantry, and soon afterward was appointed adjutant of the regiment; mustered out of the service in October 1864 and again engaged in mercantile pursuits in Rochester, Pa.; chairman of the Beaver County Republican committee in 1872 and 1874; elected as a Republican to the Forty-fifth and to the two succeeding Congresses (March 4, 1877-March 3, 1883); chairman, Committee on Public Buildings and Grounds (Forty-seventh Congress); appointed by President William McKinley as Second Assistant Postmaster General and served from 1897 to 1907; died in Washington, D.C., April 15, 1914; interment in Arlington National Cemetery, Va.

**SHAMANSKY, Robert Norton,** a Representative from Ohio; born in Columbus, Franklin County, Ohio, April 18, 1927; attended the public schools; B.A., Ohio State University, Columbus, 1947; LL.B., Harvard University School of Law, 1950; served in the United States Army Counter-Intelligence Corps, special agent, 1950-1952; admitted to Ohio bar in 1950 and commenced practice in Columbus; unsuccessful candidate for election in 1966 to the Ninetieth Congress; elected as a Democrat to the Ninety-seventh Congress (January 3, 1981-January 3, 1983); unsuccessful candidate for reelection in 1982 to the Ninety-eighth Congress; resumed the practice of law; is a resident of Columbus, Ohio.

**SHANKLIN, George Sea,** a Representative from Kentucky; born in Jessamine County, Ky., December 23, 1807; attended a private school at Nicholasville, Ky.; studied law; admitted to the bar and commenced practice in Nicholasville; member of the Kentucky house of representatives in 1838 and 1844; appointed Commonwealth attorney in 1854; again a member of the Kentucky house of representatives, and served from 1861 to 1865; elected as a Democrat to the Thirty-ninth Congress (March 4, 1865-March 3, 1867); retired to his farm in Jessamine County, where he died April 1, 1883; interment in Lexington Cemetery, Lexington, Ky.

**SHANKS, John Peter Cleaver,** a Representative from Indiana; born in Martinsburg, Va. (now West Virginia), June 17, 1826; pursued an academic course; studied law; was admitted to the bar in 1848 and commenced practice in Portland, Ind., in 1849; prosecuting attorney of Jay County in 1850 and 1851; member of the State house of representatives in 1855; during the Civil War served in the Union Army as a colonel and aide-de-camp; elected as a Republican to the Thirty-seventh Congress (March 4, 1861-March 3, 1863); unsuccessful candidate for reelection in 1862 to the Thirty-eighth Congress; elected to the Fortieth and to the three succeeding Congresses (March 4, 1867-March 3, 1875); chairman, Committee on Militia (Forty-first Congress); Committee on Indian Affairs (Forty-second Congress); unsuccessful candidate for renomination in 1874;

resumed the practice of his profession; was again a member of the State house of representatives in 1879; died in Portland, Jay County, Ind., January 23, 1901; interment in Green Park Cemetery.

**SHANLEY, James Andrew,** a Representative from Connecticut; born in New Haven, Conn., April 1, 1896; attended the public schools; graduate of Battery Commander School at Fort Sill, Ark., in 1917; during the First World War served as a lieutenant in the Forty-fifth Field Artillery, United States Army, in 1917 and 1918; was graduated from Yale University in 1920; taught mathematics at Carlton Academy, Summit, N.J., in 1920 and 1921 and in New Haven, Conn., 1921-1934; educational and athletic adviser of the New Haven Boys Club, 1926-1928; graduated from the law department of Yale University in 1928; was admitted to the bar in 1928 and commenced practice in New Haven; captain in the Artillery Reserves, 1923-1935; adjutant in the Connecticut National Guard, 1929-1935; major on the staff of Governor Wilbur L. Cross, 1931-1935; lecturer at the Catholic University of America in Washington, D.C., 1941-1945; elected as a Democrat to the Seventy-fourth and to the three succeeding Congresses (January 3, 1935-January 3, 1943); unsuccessful candidate for reelection in 1942 to the Seventy-eighth Congress; receiver for the Hartford Empire Co. from 1942 to 1946; resumed the practice of law; elected November 5, 1949, as judge of probate for the towns of New Haven, East Haven, North Haven, Orange, and Woodbridge, Conn., and served until his death in New Haven, Conn., April 4, 1965; interment in St. Lawrence Cemetery, West Haven, Conn.

**SHANNON, James Michael,** a Representative from Massachusetts; born in Methuen, Essex County, Mass., April 4, 1952; attended parochial school in Lawrence, Mass.; graduated from Phillips Academy, Andover, 1969; B.A., Johns Hopkins University, Baltimore, Md., 1973; J.D., George Washington University, Washington, D.C., 1975; admitted to the Massachusetts bar in 1975, and to the Washington, D.C., bar in 1976; commenced practice in Lawrence, Mass., in 1976; aide to Representative Michael Harrington and intern to Representative F. Bradford Morse; elected as a Democrat to the Ninety-sixth and to the two succeeding Congresses (January 3, 1979-January 3, 1985); was not a candidate for reelection in 1984 to the House of Representatives, but was an unsuccessful candidate for nomination to the United States Senate; resumed the practice of law; attorney general of Massachusetts, 1987-1991; is a resident of Lawrence, Mass.

**SHANNON, Joseph Bernard,** a Representative from Missouri; born in St. Louis, Mo., March 17, 1867; attended the public schools of St. Louis and Spalding Business College, Kansas City, Mo.; moved with his parents to Girard, Kans., in early youth; upon the death of his father moved to Kansas City, Mo., in 1879; became constable in the justice court in 1890; was city market-master in 1892 and served two years; studied law; was admitted to the bar in 1905 and commenced practice in Kansas City, Mo.; chairman of the Democratic State committee in 1910; delegate to the Democratic National Conventions of 1908, 1912, 1920, 1924, 1928, 1932, and 1940; member of the Missouri constitutional conventions in 1922 and 1923; elected as a Democrat to the Seventy-second and the five succeeding Congresses (March 4, 1931-January 3, 1943); was not a candidate for renomination in 1942 to the Seventy-eighth Congress; died in Kansas City, Mo., March 28, 1943; interment in Calvary Cemetery.

**Bibliography:** Blackmore, Charles P. "Joseph B. Shannon, Political Boss and Twentieth-Century 'Jeffersonian'." Ph.D. dissertation, Columbia University, 1953.

**SHANNON, Richard Cutts,** a Representative from New York; born in New London, Conn., February 12, 1839; was graduated from the grammar and high schools at Biddeford, Maine, and from Waterville College (now Colby College), Waterville, Maine; during the Civil War enlisted in Company H, Fifth Regiment, Maine

Volunteer Infantry, June 24, 1861; appointed first lieutenant on October 10, 1861; aide-de-camp to General Henry W. Slocum on March 15, 1862; captain and assistant adjutant general of Volunteers on October 2, 1862; honorably discharged on February 10, 1866; appointed secretary of the United States legation at Rio de Janeiro, Brazil, in 1871, and served until March 1875, when he resigned; took charge of the Botanical Garden Railroad Co. in 1876, an American enterprise in Brazil, of which he subsequently became the vice president, general manager, and president; returned to the United States in 1883 and was graduated from the law department of Columbia College, New York City, in 1885; was admitted to the New York bar in 1886 and commenced practice in New York City; appointed Envoy Extraordinary and Minister Plenipotentiary to Nicaragua, El Salvador, and Costa Rica on August 8, 1891, and served until April 1893; elected as a Republican to the Fifty-fourth and Fifty-fifth Congresses (March 4, 1895-March 3, 1899); declined to be a candidate for renomination in 1898 to the Fifty-sixth Congress; resumed the practice of his profession in New York City; retired in 1903 and moved to Brockport, Monroe County, N.Y., where he died on October 5, 1920; interment in Lake View Cemetery.

**SHANNON, Thomas** (brother of Wilson Shannon), a Representative from Ohio; born in Washington County, Pa., November 15, 1786; attended the public schools; moved to Ohio with his parents, who settled in Belmont County in 1800; engaged in agricultural pursuits; moved to Barnesville, Belmont County, Ohio, in 1812 and engaged in mercantile pursuits; during the War of 1812 served as captain of Belmont County Company in Colonel Delong's regiment; member of the Ohio house of representatives 1819-1822, 1824, and 1825; elected to the Nineteenth Congress to fill the vacancy caused by the resignation of David Jennings and served from December 4, 1826, to March 3, 1827; was not a candidate for renomination in 1827; returned to Barnesville, Ohio, and became a leaf-tobacco merchant; served in the State senate 1829 and 1837-1841; died in Barnesville, Belmont County, Ohio, March 16, 1843; interment in Green Mount Cemetery.

**SHANNON, Thomas Bowles,** a Representative from California; born in Westmoreland County, Pa., September 21, 1827; attended the public schools; moved to Illinois in 1844 and to California in 1849; engaged in mercantile pursuits; member of the California State assembly in 1859, 1860, and 1862; elected as a Republican to the Thirty-eighth Congress (March 4, 1863-March 3, 1865); chairman, Committee on Expenditures in the Department of the Interior (Thirty-eighth Congress); was not a candidate for renomination in 1864 to the Thirty-ninth Congress; appointed surveyor at the port of San Francisco on August 11, 1865, and served four years; again a member of the State assembly in 1871 and 1872, and served as speaker the first year; appointed by President Ulysses S. Grant as collector of customs at San Francisco, Calif., and served from July 1, 1872, to August 10, 1880; resumed mercantile pursuits; died in San Francisco, Calif., February 21, 1897; interment in the Masonic Cemetery.

**SHANNON, Wilson** (brother of Thomas Shannon), a Representative from Ohio; born at Mount Olivet, Belmont County, Ohio, February 24, 1802; attended Ohio University, Athens, Ohio, 1820-1822 and Transylvania College, Lexington, Ky., in 1823; studied law; was admitted to the bar in 1830 and began practice in St. Clairsville, Ohio; unsuccessful candidate for election in 1832 to the Twenty-third Congress; prosecuting attorney for Belmont County, 1833-1835; State prosecuting attorney in 1835; elected Governor of Ohio in 1838 and served from December 13, 1838 to December 16, 1840; unsuccessful candidate for reelection in 1840; elected Governor of Ohio in 1842 and served from December 14, 1842 until his resignation on April 15, 1844 to accept a diplomatic position; unsuccessful candidate for the United States Senate in 1842; appointed United States Minister to Mexico on April 9, 1844

and served until he left his post on May 14, 1845, Mexico having severed diplomatic relations with the United States; elected as a Democrat to the Thirty-third Congress (March 4, 1853-March 3, 1855); was not a candidate for renomination in 1854 to the Thirty-fourth Congress; appointed Governor of Kansas Territory by President Franklin Pierce on August 10, 1855, and served until his resignation August 18, 1856; engaged in the practice of law in Lawrence, Kans., where he died on August 30, 1877; interment in Oak Hill Cemetery.

    **Bibliography:** *DAB*; Day, Donald Eugene. "A Life of Wilson Shannon, Governor of Ohio, Diplomat, Territorial Governor of Kansas." Ph.D. dissertation, Ohio State University, 1978.

**SHARON, William,** a Senator from Nevada; born in Smithfield, Jefferson County, Ohio, January 9, 1821; attended Athens College; moved to St. Louis, Mo.; studied law; was admitted to the bar and practiced; engaged in mercantile pursuits in Carrollton, Greene County, Ill.; moved to California in 1849 and engaged in business in Sacramento; moved to San Francisco in 1850 and was a dealer in real estate; moved to Virginia City, Storey County, Nev., in 1864 as manager of the branch of the Bank of California and became interested in silver mining; elected as a Republican to the United States Senate and served from March 4, 1875, to March 3, 1881; chairman, Committee on Mines and Mining (Forty-fifth Congress); resided in San Francisco, Calif., until his death on November 13, 1885; interment in Laurel Hill Cemetery.

    **Bibliography:** Kroninger, Robert. *Sarah and the Senator.* Berkeley, Calif.: Howell-North, 1964.

**SHARP, Edgar Allan,** a Representative from New York; born in Patchogue, Suffolk County, N.Y., June 3, 1876; attended the public and high schools; engaged as a clerk in the post office at Patchogue, N.Y., 1898-1906 and served as assistant postmaster 1906-1918; in charge of construction work for the Knights of Columbus in France and England from April 1918 to January 1920; engaged in the real estate and insurance business in Patchogue, N.Y., and as real estate appraiser for Suffolk County 1920-1944; auctioneer 1929-1944; also interested in banking; member of the zoning and planning board of Brookhaven, N.Y., 1930-1933; supervisor of Brookhaven, N.Y., 1935-1943; elected as a Republican to the Seventy-ninth Congress (January 3, 1945-January 3, 1947); was not a candidate for renomination in 1946; resumed his former business pursuits; died in Patchogue, N.Y., November 27, 1948; interment in Holy Sepulchre Cemetery, Coram, N.Y.

**SHARP, Philip Riley,** a Representative from Indiana; born in Baltimore, Md., July 15, 1942; attended Washington Elementary School, Elwood, Ind.; graduated from Wendell Willkie High School, Elwood, 1960; attended DePauw University, Greencastle, Ind., 1961; B.S., Georgetown University School of Foreign Service, Washington, D.C., 1964; engaged in graduate work, Exeter College, Oxford University, 1966; Ph.D., Georgetown University, 1974; aide to Senator Vance Hartke of Indiana, 1964-1969; assistant and later associate professor, Ball State University, Muncie, Ind., 1969-1974; elected as a Democrat to the Ninety-fourth and to the nine succeeding Congresses (January 3, 1975-January 3, 1995); was not a candidate for reelection in 1994 to the One Hundred Fourth Congress; director, Institute of Politics, John F. Kennedy School of Government, Harvard University; chair, energy board, Keystone Center; is a resident of Muncie, Ind.

**SHARP, Solomon P.,** a Representative from Kentucky; born in Abingdon, Washington County, Va., in 1780; moved with his parents to Kentucky; pursued preparatory studies; engaged in agricultural pursuits; studied law; was admitted to the bar in 1809 and began practice in Russellville, Ky.; member of the Kentucky house of representatives, 1809-1811, 1817, and 1818; entered the War of 1812 as captain of a company which he organized and later was made a colonel of militia; elected as a Republican to the Thirteenth and Fourteenth Congresses (March 4, 1813-March 3, 1817); chairman, Committee on Private Land Claims (Fourteenth Congress); again a member of the Kentucky house of representatives in 1817 and 1818; resumed the practice of law; moved to Frankfort, Ky., in 1820; attorney general of Kentucky, 1820-1824; again served in the Kentucky house of representatives in 1825; assassinated in Frankfort, Ky., November 7, 1825; interment in the State Cemetery.

**SHARP, William Graves,** a Representative from Ohio; born in Mount Gilead, Morrow County, Ohio, March 14, 1859; moved with his parents to Elyria, Ohio; was graduated from the public schools and from the law department of the University of Michigan at Ann Arbor in 1881; was admitted to the bar the same year and commenced practice in Elyria, Ohio; served as prosecuting attorney of Lorain County, Ohio, 1885-1888; also interested in the manufacture of charcoal, pig iron, and chemicals; unsuccessful Democratic candidate for election in 1900 to the Fifty-seventh Congress; delegate to the Democratic National Convention of 1904; elected as a Democrat to the Sixty-first and to the two succeeding Congresses, and served from March 4, 1909 to July 23, 1914, when he resigned to become Ambassador to France, in which capacity he served until April 14, 1919; returned to Elyria, Lorain County, Ohio, and engaged in literary pursuits; died in Elyria, Ohio, November 17, 1922; interment in Ridgelawn Cemetery.

**Bibliography:** *DAB.*

**SHARPE, Peter,** a Representative from New York; born in that State; completed preparatory studies; member of the Columbia County Medical Society in 1807; represented New York County as a member of the State assembly 1814-1821, and served as speaker in 1820 and 1821; delegate to the State constitutional convention in 1821; credentials of his election to the Seventeenth Congress were presented, but he did not qualify, and on December 12, 1821, Cadwallader D. Colden successfully contested his election; elected to the Eighteenth Congress (March 4, 1823-March 3, 1825); unsuccessful candidate for reelection in 1824 to the Nineteenth Congress.

**SHARPE, William,** a Delegate from North Carolina; born near Rock Church, Cecil County, Md., December 13, 1742; pursued classical studies; studied law; was admitted to the bar and commenced practice in Mecklenburg County, N.C. in 1763; also engaged in surveying; moved to Rowan (now Iredell) County; member of the Provincial Congress in 1775; aide to General Rutherford in the Indian campaign in 1776 and was one of four commissioners appointed by Governor Richard Caswell to form a treaty with the Indians in 1777; delegate to the convention in Halifax in 1776 and helped to frame the first constitution of the State; Member of the Continental Congress, 1779-1781; member of the North Carolina State house of representatives in 1781 and 1782; died near Statesville, Iredell County, N.C., on July 1, 1818; interment in Snow Creek Graveyard.

**SHARTEL, Cassius McLean,** a Representative from Missouri; born in Crawford County, Pa., April 27, 1860; moved with his parents to Knox County, Mo., and resided there until 1873; moved with his parents to Chautauqua County, Kans.; attended the common schools and Kansas State Agricultural College at Manhattan; taught school; studied law; was admitted to the bar in 1881 and commenced practice in Sedan, Kans.; moved to Nevada, Mo., in 1887 and then to Neosho, Newton County, Mo., the same year and continued the practice of law; delegate to the Republican National Conventions in 1900 and 1936; elected as a Republican to the Fifty-ninth Congress (March 4, 1905-March 3, 1907); was not a candidate for renomination in 1906; interested in farm loans; president of the Missouri constitutional convention in 1922 and 1923; died in Neosho, Mo., September 27, 1943; interment in Odd Fellows Cemetery.

**SHATTUC, William Bunn,** a Representative from Ohio; born in North Hector, Schuyler County, N.Y., June 11, 1841; moved to Ohio in 1852 with his parents, who settled near Sandusky; attended the public schools; enlisted in Company I, Second Regiment, Ohio Volunteer Cavalry, August 13, 1861, as second lieutenant; mustered out February 21, 1863, as first lieutenant; assistant and afterward general passenger agent of the Ohio & Mississippi Railway Co. 1865-1894; member of the State senate in 1895; elected as a Republican to the Fifty-fifth, Fifty-sixth and Fifty-seventh Congresses (March 4, 1897-March 3, 1903); chairman, Committee on Immigration and Naturalization (Fifty-sixth and Fifty-seventh Congresses); was not a candidate for renomination in 1902; died in Madisonville, near Cincinnati, Ohio, July 13, 1911; interment in Spring Grove Cemetery, Cincinnati, Ohio.

**SHAW, Aaron,** a Representative from Illinois; born near Goshen, Orange County, N.Y., December 19, 1811; attended Montgomery Academy, New York; studied law in Goshen, N.Y.; was admitted to the bar in 1833 and commenced practice in Lawrenceville, Ill.; delegate to the first Internal Improvement Convention of Illinois; elected State's attorney by the Legislature of Illinois in 1842; member of the State house of representatives in 1850; elected as a Democrat to the Thirty-fifth Congress (March 4, 1857-March 3, 1859); was not a candidate for renomination in 1858; again a member of the State house of representatives in 1860; circuit judge of the fourth judicial district of Illinois 1863-1869; elected to the Forty-eighth Congress (March 4, 1883-March 3, 1885); was not a candidate for renomination in 1884; resumed the practice of law; died in Olney, Richland County, Ill., January 7, 1887; interment in Haven Hill Cemetery.

**SHAW, Albert Duane,** a Representative from New York; born in Lyme, Jefferson County, N.Y., December 21, 1841; attended Belleville and Union Academies and St. Lawrence University, Canton, N.Y.; enlisted as a private in Company A, Thirty-fifth Regiment, New York Volunteers, in June 1861 and served out the term of enlistment; appointed a special agent of the War Department in 1863, stationed at provost marshal's headquarters in Watertown, N.Y., and served until the close of the war; member of the State assembly in 1866; appointed colonel of the Thirty-sixth Regiment, New York National Guard, in 1867, and resigned to accept the position of United States consul at Toronto, Canada, in 1868; promoted to United States consul at Manchester, England, in 1878; elected department commander of the Grand Army of the Republic of New York in 1896; unanimously elected commander in chief at the national encampment in 1899; elected as a Republican to the Fifty-sixth Congress to fill the vacancy caused by the death of Charles A. Chickering; reelected to the Fifty-seventh Congress and served from November 6, 1900, until his death in Washington, D.C., on February 10, 1901, before the close of the Fifty-sixth Congress; interment in Brookside Cemetery, Watertown, Jefferson County, N.Y.

**SHAW, Eugene Clay, Jr.,** a Representative from Florida; born in Miami, Dade County, Fla., April 19, 1939; attended the public schools; graduated from Miami Edison Senior High School, 1957; B.A., Stetson University, Deland, Fla., 1961; M.B.A., University of Alabama, Tuscaloosa, 1963; J.D., Stetson University College of Law, 1966; admitted to the Florida bar in 1966 and commenced practice in Fort Lauderdale; assistant city attorney, Fort Lauderdale, 1968; chief city prosecutor, 1968-1969; associate municipal judge, 1969-1971; city commissioner, 1971-1973; vice mayor, 1973-1975; mayor, 1975-1980; member, Republican National Committee, executive committee; elected as a Republican to the Ninety-seventh and to the seven succeeding Congresses (January 3, 1981-January 3, 1997); is a resident of Fort Lauderdale, Fla.

**SHAW, Frank Thomas,** a Representative from Maryland; born in Woodsboro, Frederick County, Md., October 7, 1841; attended the common schools and was graduated from the medical department of the University of Maryland at Baltimore in 1864; engaged in the practice of medicine in Uniontown, Carroll County, Md., until November 1873; elected clerk of the circuit court for Carroll County in 1873; reelected in 1879 and served until 1885, when he resigned; elected as a Democrat to the Forty-ninth and Fiftieth Congresses (March 4, 1885-March 3, 1889); chairman, Committee on Accounts (Fiftieth Congress); unsuccessful candidate for renomination in 1888 to the Fifty-first Congress; member of the Maryland State house of delegates in 1890; State tax commissioner, 1890-1894; appointed by President Grover Cleveland as collector of customs for the port of Baltimore, and served from May 5, 1894 to May 24, 1898; adviser to the clerk of the circuit court, 1915-1921; resided in Westminster, Carroll County, Md., until his death on February 24, 1923; interment in Westminster Cemetery.

**SHAW, George Bullen,** a Representative from Wisconsin; born in Alma, Allegany County, N.Y., on March 12, 1854; moved to Eau Claire, Wis., in 1856 with his father; attended the public schools and was graduated from the International Business College, Chicago, Ill., in 1871; engaged in the lumber manufacturing business; member of the Common Council of Eau Claire 1876-1887; mayor of Eau Claire in 1888 and 1889; delegate to the Republican National Convention in 1884; supreme chancellor of the Knights of Pythias of the World from July 1890 to August 1892; elected as a Republican to the Fifty-third Congress and served from March 4, 1893, until his death in Eau Claire, Wis., August 27, 1894; interment in Lake View Cemetery.

**SHAW, Guy Loren,** a Representative from Illinois; born on a farm near Summer Hill, Pike County, Ill., May 16, 1881; attended the public schools and the College of Agriculture of the University of Illinois at Urbana; engaged in agricultural pursuits and the development of overflow lands along the Illinois River; delegate to the State constitutional convention in 1920; elected as a Republican to the Sixty-seventh Congress (March 4, 1921-March 3, 1923); unsuccessful candidate for reelection in 1922 to the Sixty-eighth Congress; engaged in the real estate business in Beardstown, Cass County, Ill., and Urbana, Champaign County, Ill.; moved to Normal, McLean County, Ill., and continued agricultural pursuits, farm management, and the real estate business; died in Normal, Ill., May 19, 1950; interment in Bloomington Cemetery, Bloomington, Ill.

**SHAW, Henry** (son of Samuel Shaw), a Representative from Massachusetts; born near Putney, Windham County, Vt., in 1788; completed preparatory studies; studied law; admitted to the bar and commenced practice in Albany, N.Y., in 1810; moved to Lanesboro, Mass., in 1813; elected as a Republican to the Fifteenth and Sixteenth Congresses (March 4, 1817-March 3, 1821); unsuccessful candidate for renomination in 1820; member of the Massachusetts house of representatives 1824-1830 and 1833; served in the Massachusetts senate in 1835; unsuccessful candidate for Governor of Massachusetts in 1845; moved to New York City in 1848; member of the Board of Education of New York City in 1849; member of the New York City Common Council 1850-1851; member of the New York State Assembly in 1853; moved to Newburgh, N.Y., in 1854; died in Peekskill, Westchester County, N.Y., October 17, 1857; interment in the Lower Cemetery, Lanesboro, Mass.

**SHAW, Henry Marchmore,** a Representative from North Carolina; born in Newport, R.I., November 20, 1819; completed preparatory studies; was graduated from the medical department of the University of Pennsylvania at Philadelphia in 1838 and began practice in Indiantown, Camden County, N.C.; elected as a Democrat to the Thirty-third Congress (March 4, 1853-March 3, 1855); unsuccessful candidate for reelection in 1854 to the Thirty-fourth Congress; elected to the Thirty-fifth Congress (March 4, 1857-March 3, 1859); unsuccessful candidate for reelection in 1858 to the Thirty-sixth Congress; served as a colonel in the Confederate Army during the Civil War and was killed near New Bern, N.C., November 1, 1864; interment in the cemetery at Shawboro, Currituck County, N.C.

**SHAW, John Gilbert,** a Representative from North Carolina; born near Fayetteville, Cumberland County, N.C., January 16, 1859; attended the common schools; engaged in the naval-stores business; studied law; was admitted to the bar in 1888 and commenced practice in Fayetteville; member of the State house of representatives in 1888; prosecuting attorney for Cumberland County 1890-1894; elected as a Democrat to the Fifty-fourth Congress (March 4, 1895-March 3, 1897); unsuccessful candidate for reelection in 1896 to the Fifty-fifth Congress; resumed the practice of law in Fayetteville, N.C., until his death in that city on July 21, 1932; interment in Cross Creek Cemetery.

**SHAW, Samuel** (father of Henry Shaw), a Representative from Vermont; born in Dighton, Mass., in December 1768; received a limited schooling; moved to Putney, Vt.; studied medicine and commenced practice in Castleton, Vt., in 1789; member of the State house of representatives 1800-1807; elected as a Republican to the Tenth Congress to fill the vacancy caused by the resignation of James Witherell; reelected to the Eleventh and Twelfth Congresses and served from September 6, 1808, to March 3, 1813; served in the United States Army as hospital surgeon from April 6, 1813, to June 15, 1815, when he was honorably discharged; reinstated on September 13, 1815; appointed post surgeon April 18, 1818, and resigned on December 31, 1818; died in Clarendon Springs, Rutland County, Vt., October 23, 1827; interment in Castleton Cemetery, Castleton, Vt.

**SHAW, Tristram,** a Representative from New Hampshire; born in Hampton, Rockingham County, N.H., May 23, 1786; completed preparatory studies; held several local offices in Exeter, N.H.; elected as a Democrat to the Twenty-sixth and Twenty-seventh Congresses (March 4, 1839-March 3, 1843); died in Exeter, Rockingham County, N.H., March 14, 1843; interment in Bride Hill Cemetery, Hampton, N.H.

**SHAYS, Christopher H.,** a Representative from Connecticut; born in Stamford, Fairfield County, Conn., October 18, 1945; attended public schools in Darien, Conn.; graduated Darien High School, 1964; B.A., Principia College, Elsah, Ill., 1968; M.B.A., New York University, 1974; M.P.A., New York University, 1978; served in the Peace Corps as a teacher in the Fiji Islands, 1968-1970; executive aide to Trumbull (Conn.) first selectman Larry Heimann, 1971-1972; member, Connecticut State house of representatives, 1975-1987; elected as a Republican to the One Hundredth Congress, August 18, 1987, by special election to fill the vacancy caused by the death of Stewart B. McKinney; reelected to the One Hundred First and to the three succeeding Congresses, and served from August 18, 1987 to January 3, 1997; is a resident of Stamford, Conn.

**SHEAFE, James,** a Representative and a Senator from New Hampshire; born in Portsmouth, N.H., November 16, 1755; completed preparatory studies and graduated from Harvard College in 1774; engaged in mercantile pursuits; member, State house of representatives 1788-1790; member, State senate 1791, 1793, 1799; member, State executive council 1799; elected as a Federalist to the Sixth Congress (March 4, 1799-March 3, 1801); elected to the United States Senate and served from March 4, 1801, until his resignation on June 14, 1802; unsuccessful candidate for governor of New Hampshire in 1816; died in Portsmouth, Rockingham County, N.H., December 5, 1829; interment in St. John's Church Cemetery.

**SHEAKLEY, James,** a Representative from Pennsylvania; born in Sheakleyville, Mercer County, Pa., April 24, 1829; attended the common schools and Meadville (Pa.) Academy; learned the trade of cabinetmaker; moved to California in 1851 and engaged in the mining of gold; returned to Pennsylvania and settled in Greenville in 1855; engaged in mercantile pursuits and in 1864 in the production and shipment of petroleum; school director of Greenville, Pa., 1864-1868; elected as a Democrat to the Forty-fourth Congress (March 4, 1875-March 3, 1877); unsuccessful candidate for reelection in 1876 to the Forty-fifth Congress; appointed United States commissioner of schools of Alaska by President Grover Cleveland in July 1887 and served five years; studied law and was admitted to the bar in the United States District Court of Alaska in 1888; delegate to the Democratic National Convention of 1892; Governor of Alaska Territory, 1893-1897; again returned to Greenville, Pa., in 1898; mayor of Greenville, 1909-1913; elected justice of the peace in 1914 and served until his death in Greenville, Pa., on December 10, 1917; interment in Shenango Valley Cemetery.

**SHEATS, Charles Christopher,** a Representative from Alabama; born in Walker County, Ala., April 10, 1839; attended the common schools; elected a member of the secession convention in 1860, but refused to sign the ordinance of secession; member of the Alabama State house of representatives in 1861, and was expelled in 1862 for his adherence to the Union; was imprisoned on a charge of treason by the Confederate authorities, but could not obtain a trial, and was not released until after the close of the Civil War; unsuccessful candidate for election in 1864 to the Thirty-ninth Congress; member of the constitutional convention in 1865; studied law; was admitted to the bar in 1867 and commenced practice in Decatur; appointed by President Ulysses S. Grant as consul at Elsinore, Denmark, on May 31, 1869, and served until elected to Congress; elected as a Republican to the Forty-third Congress (March 4, 1873-March 3, 1875); unsuccessful candidate for reelection in 1874 to the Forty-fourth Congress; died in Decatur, Morgan County, Ala., May 27, 1904; interment in McKendree Cemetery, near Decatur.

**SHEEHAN, Timothy Patrick,** a Representative from Illinois; born in Chicago, Ill., February 21, 1909; attended St. Pius Grammar School and Joseph Medill High School; B.S.C., Northwestern University, 1931; began work with food importers and wholesalers in 1932; elected as a Republican to the Eighty-second and to the three succeeding Congresses (January 3, 1951-January 3, 1959); unsuccessful candidate for reelection in 1958 to the Eighty-sixth Congress; unsuccessful Republican candidate for election for mayor of Chicago in 1959; unsuccessful candidate for election in 1960 to the Eighty-seventh Congress; resumed his importing and wholesale business; delegate to Republican National Conventions, 1964-1984; chairman, Cook County Republican Party, 1964-1968; president, 1971-1983, and chairman of the board, 1984 to present, Peerless Federal Savings and Loan Assoc.; is a resident of Chicago, Ill.

**SHEFFER, Daniel,** a Representative from Pennsylvania; born in York, Pa., May 24, 1783; attended the common schools and Harvard University; studied medicine in Philadelphia and commenced practice at York Springs, Adams County, Pa.; associate judge of Adams County, Pa., 1813-1837; elected as a Democrat to the Twenty-fifth Congress (March 4, 1837-March 3, 1839); unsuccessful candidate for reelection in 1838 to the Twenty-sixth Congress; resumed the practice of his profession; was a delegate to the Democratic National Convention in 1848; died at York Springs, Pa., February 16, 1880; interment in the Old Lutheran Cemetery.

**SHEFFEY, Daniel,** a Representative from Virginia; born in Frederick, Frederick County, Md., in 1770; pursued classical studies; apprenticed as a shoemaker in his father's shop; moved to Wytheville, Va., in 1791; worked at his trade and at the same time studied law; admitted to the bar July 1, 1802, and commenced the practice of his profession in Wytheville; moved to Abbeville and later to Staunton, where he continued the practice of law; member of the Virginia house of delegates 1800-1804; served in the Virginia senate 1804-1808; elected as a Federalist to the Eleventh and to the three succeeding Congresses (March 4, 1809-March 3, 1817); again a member of the Virginia house of delegates in 1822 and 1823; died in Staunton, Augusta County, Va., December 3, 1830.

**SHEFFIELD, William Paine** (father of William Paine Sheffield [1857-1919]), a Representative and a Senator from Rhode Island; born in New Shoreham, Block Island, Newport County, R.I., August 30, 1820; completed preparatory studies; attended Kingston Academy, Rhode Island, and graduated from the law department of Harvard University in 1843; was admitted to the bar in 1844 and commenced practice in Newport, R.I.; delegate to the State constitutional conventions in 1841 and 1842; member, State house of representatives 1842-1845, 1849-1853, 1857-1861; moved to Tiverton, R.I.; returned to Newport, R.I.; elected as a Republican to the Thirty-seventh Congress (March 4, 1861-March 3, 1863); resumed the practice of law; appointed in 1871 one of the commissioners to revise the State laws; member, State house of representatives 1875-1884; appointed as a Republican to the United States Senate to fill the vacancy caused by the death of Henry B. Anthony and served from November 19, 1884, to January 20, 1885; resumed the practice of his profession; died in Newport, R.I., June 2, 1907; interment in the Island Cemetery.

**SHEFFIELD, William Paine** (son of William Paine Sheffield [1820-1907]), a Representative from Rhode Island; born in Newport, R.I., June 1, 1857; attended Phillips Academy, Andover, Mass., from 1869 until 1873, and was graduated from Brown University, Providence, R.I., in 1877; studied law at the University of Paris and the law department of Harvard University; was admitted to the bar in 1880 and commenced practice in Newport, R.I.; commissioner to extend citizenship to the Narragansett Tribe of Indians in 1880; appointed colonel on the staff of Governor George Peabody Wetmore; member of the Rhode Island State house of representatives, 1885-1887, 1889, 1890, 1894-1896, and 1899-1901; member of the commission to revise the Rhode Island constitution in 1897; elected as a Republican to the Sixty-first Congress (March 4, 1909-March 3, 1911); unsuccessful candidate for reelection in 1910 to the Sixty-second Congress, and for election in 1912 to the Sixty-third Congress; member of the Republican National Committee in 1913; member of the committee to revise the Rhode Island constitution in 1918; died in Exeter, Washington County, R.I., October 19, 1919; interment in the Island Cemetery, Newport, R.I.

**SHELBY, Richard C.,** a Representative and a Senator from Alabama; born in Birmingham, Ala., May 6, 1934; attended the public schools; A.B., University of Alabama, 1957; LL.B., University of Alabama School of Law, 1963; admitted to the Alabama bar in 1961 and commenced practice in Tuscaloosa; city prosecutor of Tuscaloosa, 1963-1971; United States Commissioner, Northern District of Alabama, 1966-1970; member of the Alabama State senate 1970-1978; elected as a Democrat to the Ninety-sixth and to the three succeeding Congresses (January 3, 1979-January 3, 1987); was not a candidate in 1986 for reelection to the House of Representatives, but was elected to the United States Senate for the term commencing January 2, 1987; reelected in 1992 for the term ending January 3, 1999; announced his affiliation with the Republican Party on November 9, 1994; is a resident of Tuscaloosa, Ala.

**SHELDEN, Carlos Douglas,** a Representative from Michigan; born in Walworth, Walworth County, Wis., June 10, 1840; moved with his parents to Houghton County, Mich., in 1847; attended the Union School, Ypsilanti, Mich., and returned to his home in the fall of 1861; served throughout the Civil War as captain in the Twenty-third Regiment, Michigan Volunteer Infantry; at the end of his service returned to Houghton and engaged in mining and the real estate business; member of the State house of representatives in 1892; served in the State senate in 1894; elected as a Republican to the Fifty-fifth, Fifty-sixth, and Fifty-seventh Congresses (March 4, 1897-March 3, 1903); unsuccessful candidate for renomination in 1902; died in Houghton, Mich., June 24, 1904; interment in Forest Hill Cemetery.

**SHELDON, Lionel Allen,** a Representative from Louisiana; born in Worcester, Otsego County, N.Y., August 30, 1828; moved with his parents to Lagrange, Ohio; attended the district school and Oberlin College, Ohio, 1848-1850 and was graduated from the Fowler Law School, Poughkeepsie, N.Y., in 1853; was admitted to the bar the same year and commenced practice in Elyria, Lorain County, Ohio; probate judge of Lorain County, Ohio, in 1856 and 1857; delegate to the Republican National Conventions of 1856, 1880 and 1896; commissioned brigadier general of the militia by Governor Salmon P. Chase; served in the Union Army during the Civil War; appointed lieutenant colonel of the Forty-second Regiment, Ohio Volunteer Infantry, November 27, 1861, and promoted to the rank of colonel on March 14, 1862; settled in New Orleans, La., and practiced law, 1864-1879; elected as a Republican to the Forty-first and to the two succeeding Congresses (March 4, 1869-March 3, 1875); chairman, Committee on Militia (Forty-second Congress); unsuccessful candidate for reelection in 1874 to the Forty-fourth Congress; returned to Ohio in 1879; Governor of the Territory of New Mexico, 1881-1885; one of the receivers of the Texas and Pacific Railway, 1885-1887; moved to Los Angeles, Calif., in 1888 and engaged in the practice of law; moved to Pasadena, Calif., and died in that city January 17, 1917; remains were cremated.

**SHELDON, Porter,** a Representative from New York; born in Victor, Ontario County, N.Y., on September 29, 1831; completed preparatory studies; studied law; was admitted to the bar in 1854 at Batavia, N.Y., and commenced practice in Randolph, Cattaraugus County, N.Y.; moved to Rockford, Ill., in 1857 and continued the practice of law; member of the Illinois constitutional convention in 1861; returned to Jamestown, N.Y., in 1865 and continued the practice of law; elected as a Republican to the Forty-first Congress (March 4, 1869-March 3, 1871); unsuccessful candidate for renomination in 1870; resumed the practice of his profession; died in Jamestown, Chautauqua County, N.Y., on August 15, 1908; interment in Lakeview Cemetery.

**SHELL, George Washington,** a Representative from South Carolina; born near Laurens, Laurens County, S.C., November 13, 1831; attended the common schools and Laurens Academy; engaged in agricultural pursuits; entered the Confederate Army as a private in April 1861 and served throughout the Civil War, attaining the rank of captain; resumed agricultural pursuits; member of the State Democratic executive committee in 1886 and 1887; chosen president of the State Farmers' Association in 1888; clerk of court of Laurens County 1888-1896; elected as a Democrat to the Fifty-second and Fifty-third Congresses (March 4, 1891-March 3, 1895); chairman, Committee on Ventilation and Acoustics (Fifty-third Congress); was not a candidate for renomination in 1894; retired to his plantation near Laurens, Laurens County, S.C., and died there December 15, 1899; interment in Chestnut Ridge Cemetery.

**SHELLABARGER, Samuel,** a Representative from Ohio; born near Enon, Clark County, Ohio, on December 10, 1817; attended the county schools and was graduated from Miami University, Oxford, Ohio, in 1841; studied law; was admitted to the bar and commenced practice in Springfield, Ohio, in 1846; member of the Ohio State house of representatives in 1852 and 1853; elected as a Republican to the Thirty-seventh Congress (March 4, 1861-March 3, 1863); unsuccessful candidate for reelection in 1862 to the Thirty-eighth Congress; elected to the Thirty-ninth and Fortieth Congresses (March 4, 1865-March 3, 1869); declined to be a candidate for

renomination in 1868 to the Forty-first Congress; served as Minister to Portugal from April 21 to December 31, 1869; elected to the Forty-second Congress (March 4, 1871-March 3, 1873); chairman, Committee on Commerce (Forty-second Congress); was not a candidate for renomination in 1872 to the Forty-third Congress; member of the United States Civil Service Commission in 1874 and 1875; continued the practice of law until his death in Washington, D.C., August 7, 1896; interment in Ferncliff Cemetery, Springfield, Ohio.

**SHELLEY, Charles Miller,** a Representative from Alabama; born in Sullivan County, Tenn., December 28, 1833; moved with his father to Selma, Ala., in 1836; received a limited schooling; became an architect and builder; entered the Confederate Army in February 1861 as a lieutenant, and was stationed first at Fort Morgan and afterward attached to the Fifth Alabama Regiment; was commissioned brigadier general; elected as a Democrat to the Forty-fifth and Forty-sixth Congresses (March 4, 1877-March 3, 1881); presented credentials as a Member-elect to the Forty-seventh Congress, but the election was contested by James Q. Smith, and the seat was declared vacant on July 20, 1882; subsequently elected to fill the vacancy thus caused and served from November 7, 1882 to March 3, 1883; presented credentials as a Member-elect to the Forty-eighth Congress, and served from March 4, 1883 to January 9, 1885, when he was succeeded by George H. Craig, who contested the election; returned to Birmingham, Jefferson County, Ala., and engaged in promoting the industrial interests of that region until his death in that city on January 20, 1907; interment in Oak Hill Cemetery, Talladega, Ala.

**SHELLEY, John Francis,** a Representative from California; born in San Francisco, Calif., September 3, 1905; attended the parochial and public schools; graduated from the law school of the University of San Francisco in 1932; was admitted to the bar and commenced the practice of law in California; elected to the California State senate in 1938, and reelected in 1942, serving as Democratic floor leader from 1938 to 1946; unsuccessful Democratic candidate for Lieutenant Governor in 1946; president of the San Francisco Labor Council from January 1937 to May 1949, and then became secretary; elected president of the California American Federation of Labor in 1947, reelected in 1948 and 1949; delegate to the Democratic National Conventions of 1940, 1944, 1948, 1952, 1956, and 1960; served in temporary service, United States Coast Guard, during the Second World War on detached duty; elected as a Democrat to the Eighty-first Congress, November 8, 1949, by special election to fill the vacancy caused by the death of Richard J. Welch; reelected to the seven succeeding Congresses, and served from November 8, 1949 until his resignation on January 7, 1964, having been elected mayor of San Francisco, taking office January 8, 1964, and serving until January 8, 1968; legislative advocate for San Francisco at the State legislature from February 1969 until his death in San Francisco, Calif., on September 1, 1974; interment in Holy Cross Cemetery, Colma, Calif.

**SHELTON, Samuel Azariah,** a Representative from Missouri; born near Waterloo, Lauderdale County, Ala., September 3, 1858; moved with his widowed mother to Webster County, Mo., in 1869; attended the common schools, Mountain Dale Academy, and the Seymour and Marshfield High Schools; taught school; engaged in agricultural pursuits 1881-1930; clerk of the circuit court of Webster County 1895-1899; studied law; was admitted to the bar in 1901 and commenced practice in Marshfield, Webster County, Mo.; postmaster of Marshfield 1906-1910; prosecuting attorney of Webster County 1914-1916; chairman of the Republican county committee for four terms; elected as a Republican to the Sixty-seventh Congress (March 4, 1921-March 3, 1923); declined to be a candidate for reelection; resumed the practice of law in Marshfield, Mo., where he died September 13, 1948; interment in Marshfield Cemetery.

**SHEPARD, Charles Biddle,** a Representative from North Carolina; born in New Bern, Craven County, N.C., December 5, 1808; attended private schools of his native city and was graduated from the University of North Carolina at Chapel Hill in 1827; studied law; was admitted to the bar in 1828 and commenced practice in New Bern, N.C.; elected to the State house of representatives to fill out the unexpired term of Charles Spaight and served in 1831 and 1832; elected as a Whig to the Twenty-fifth Congress and reelected as a Democrat to the Twenty-sixth Congress (March 4, 1837-March 3, 1841); resumed the practice of his profession; died in New Bern, N.C., October 25, 1843; interment in Cedar Grove Cemetery.

**SHEPARD, William,** a Representative from Massachusetts; born in Westfield, Mass., December 1, 1737; attended the common schools; engaged in agricultural pursuits; served in the French and Indian wars for six years; member of the committee of correspondence for Westfield in 1774; lieutenant colonel of Minutemen in April 1775; entered the Continental Army in May 1775 as lieutenant colonel; commissioned colonel of the Fourth Massachusetts Regiment October 6, 1776, and served throughout the Revolutionary War; member of the Massachusetts house of representatives in 1785 and 1786; selectman for Westfield, Mass., 1784-1787; chosen major general of the Fourth Division, Massachusetts Militia, in 1786 and defended Springfield Arsenal during Shays' Rebellion; member of the Governor's council of Massachusetts 1792-1796; appointed in 1796 to treat with the Penobscot Indians and in 1797 with the Six Nations; elected as a Federalist to the Fifth, Sixth, and Seventh Congresses (March 4, 1797-March 3, 1803); resumed his agricultural pursuits; died in Westfield, Mass., November 16, 1817; interment in the Mechanic Street Cemetery.

Bibliography: *DAB*.

**SHEPARD, William Biddle,** a Representative from North Carolina; born in New Bern, N.C., May 14, 1799; completed preparatory studies; attended the University of North Carolina at Chapel Hill in 1813; was graduated from the University of Pennsylvania at Philadelphia; studied law; was admitted to the bar and commenced practice in Camden County, later removing to Elizabeth City, Pasquotank County, N.C.; also engaged in banking; elected to the Twenty-first through Twenty-third Congresses and elected as a Whig to the Twenty-fourth Congress (March 4, 1829-March 3, 1837); chairman, Committee on District of Columbia (Twenty-fourth Congress); was not a candidate for renomination in 1836; member of the State senate 1838-1840 and 1848-1850; member of the board of trustees of the University of North Carolina 1838-1852; died in Elizabeth City, N.C., June 20, 1852; interment in St. Paul's Churchyard, Edenton, N.C.

**SHEPHERD, Karen,** a Representative from Utah; born in Silver City, Grant County, N.Mex., July 5, 1940; graduated, Provo (Utah) High School; M.A., Brigham Young University, 1963; high school and college English teacher in Utah, Washington, Egypt and Brigham Young University; Utah County coordinator for Wayne Owens for Senate; assistant director, Salt Lake County social services, 1975-1976 then director, 1976-1978; director of continuing education, Westminster College; stockholder in *network* magazine, 1978-1984, editor ten years; helped found Webster Publishing Co.; director of development and community relations, David Eccles School of Business, University of Utah, 1988; member, Utah State senate, 1990-1993; elected as a Democrat to the One Hundred Third Congress (January 3, 1993-January 3, 1995); unsuccessful candidate for reelection in 1994 to the One Hundred Fourth Congress; fellow at the Institute of Politics, John F. Kennedy School of Government, Harvard University; is a resident of Salt Lake City, Utah.

**SHEPLER, Matthias,** a Representative from Ohio; born in Westmoreland County, Pa., November 11, 1790; received a limited schooling; served in the War of 1812; moved to Ohio in April 1818 and settled in Bethlehem Township, Stark County; engaged in agricultural pursuits; justice of the peace for thirty years; county commissioner for two terms; member of the State house of representatives in 1829; served in the State senate in 1832; elected as a Democrat to the Twenty-fifth Congress (March 4, 1837-March 3, 1839); chairman, Committee on Revisal and Unfinished Business (Twenty-fifth Congress); declined to be a candidate for renomination in 1838; moved to Navarre, Stark County, Ohio, in 1860, where he died April 7, 1863; interment in Shepler Church Cemetery, near Navarre, Ohio.

**SHEPLEY, Ether,** a Senator from Maine; born in Groton, Mass., November 2, 1789; attended Groton Academy and graduated from Dartmouth College, Hanover, N.H., in 1811; studied law; was admitted to the bar in 1814 and began practice in Saco, Maine (until 1820 a district of Massachusetts); member, Massachusetts general court 1819; delegate to the Maine constitutional convention in 1820; United States attorney for the district of Maine 1821-1833; moved to Portland, Maine; elected as a Jacksonian to the United States Senate and served from March 4, 1833, to March 3, 1836, when he resigned; chairman, Committee on Engrossed Bills (Twenty-third and Twenty-fourth Congresses); justice of the supreme court of Maine 1836-1848, chief justice 1848-1855; was not a candidate for renomination in 1854; appointed sole commissioner to revise the public laws of Maine in 1856; resumed the practice of his profession; died in Portland, Cumberland County, Maine, January 15, 1877; interment in Evergreen Cemetery.

Bibliography: *DAB*.

**SHEPPARD, Harry Richard,** a Representative from California; born in Mobile, Ala., January 10, 1885; attended the public schools; studied law; employed in transportation department of the Santa Fe Railroad; active committee member of the Brotherhood of Railroad Trainmen; engaged in the copper business in Alaska; president and general manager of King's Beverage and King's Laboratories Corps. of California until 1934; elected as a Democrat to the Seventy-fifth and to the thirteen succeeding Congresses (January 3, 1937-January 3, 1965); was not a candidate for renomination in 1964 to the Eighty-ninth Congress; died in Washington, D.C., April 28, 1969; interment in National Memorial Park, Falls Church, Va.

**SHEPPARD, John Levi** (father of Morris Sheppard and great-grandfather of Connie Mack, III), a Representative from Texas; born in Bluffton, Chambers County, Ala., April 13, 1852; moved with his mother to Morris County, Tex.; attended the common schools; studied law; was admitted to the bar and commenced practice in Daingerfield, Morris County, Tex., in 1879; district attorney of the fifth judicial district of Texas 1882-1888; district judge of the same district 1888-1896; temporary chairman of the Democratic State convention in 1892; appointed delegate to the Bimetallic Convention in Chicago in 1893; delegate to the Democratic National Convention in 1896; elected as a Democrat to the Fifty-sixth and Fifty-seventh Congresses and served from March 4, 1899, until his death in Texarkana, Bowie County, Tex., October 11, 1902; interment in Rose Hill Cemetery.

**SHEPPARD, Morris** (son of John Levi Sheppard), a Representative and a Senator from Texas; born in Wheatville, Morris County, Tex., May 28, 1875; attended the common schools of various Texas towns; graduated from the University of Texas at Austin in 1895, from the law department of the same university in 1897, and from the law department of Yale University in 1898; was admitted to the bar and commenced practice in Pittsburg, Camp County, Tex., in 1898; moved to Texarkana in 1899 and continued the practice of his profession; elected as a Democrat to the Fifty-seventh Congress to fill the vacancy caused by the death of his father, John L. Sheppard; reelected to the Fifty-eighth and to the four succeeding Congresses and served from November 15, 1902, to February 3, 1913, when he resigned; chairman, Committee on Public Buildings and Grounds (Sixty-second Congress); elected as a Democrat to the United States Senate on January 29, 1913, to fill the vacancy in the term ending March 3, 1913, caused by the resignation of Joseph W. Bailey, and on the same day was also elected for the term commencing March 4, 1913; reelected in 1918, 1924, 1930, and again in 1936, and served from February 3, 1913, until his death in Washington, D.C., April 9, 1941; Democratic whip 1929-1933; chairman, Committee on Expenditures in the Department of Agriculture (Sixty-third and Sixty-fourth Congresses), Committee on the Census (Sixty-fourth and Sixty-fifth Congresses), Committee on Revolutionary Claims (Sixty-sixth Congress), Committee on Military Affairs (Seventy-third through Seventy-seventh Congresses); co-sponsor of the Sheppard-Towner Act of 1921, designating funding to enable states to improve their maternal and child care services; interment in Hillcrest Cemetery, Texarkana, Tex.

**Bibliography:** Bailey, Richard. "Morris Sheppard of Texas: Southern Progressive and Prohibitionist." Ph.D. dissertation, Texas Christian University, 1980; Dude, Escal F. "Political Career of Morris Sheppard, 1875-1941." Ph.D. dissertation, University of Texas, 1958.

**SHEPPERD, Augustine Henry,** a Representative from North Carolina; born in Rockford, Surry County, N.C., February 24, 1792; completed preparatory studies; studied law; was admitted to the bar and commenced practice in Surry County, N.C.; member of the State house of representatives 1822-1826; elected to the Twentieth through Twenty-third Congresses and elected as a Whig to the Twenty-fourth and Twenty-fifth Congresses (March 4, 1827-March 3, 1839); chairman, Committee on Expenditures in the Department of the Navy (Twenty-first Congress), Committee on Expenditures in the Department of War (Twenty-second Congress), Committee on Expenditures in the Department of State (Twenty-third and Twenty-fourth Congresses); unsuccessful candidate for reelection in 1838 to the Twenty-sixth Congress; elected as a Whig to the Twenty-seventh Congress (March 4, 1841-March 3, 1843); chairman, Committee on Public Expenditures (Twenty-seventh Congress); elected as a Whig to the Thirtieth and Thirty-first Congresses (March 4, 1847-March 3, 1851); declined to be a candidate for reelection in 1850; resumed the practice of his profession; died at "Good Spring," Salem (now Winston-Salem), Forsyth County, N.C., July 11, 1864; interment in Salem Cemetery.

**SHERBURNE, John Samuel,** a Representative from New Hampshire; born in Portsmouth, N.H., in 1757; was graduated from Dartmouth College, Hanover, N.H., in 1776 and from the law department of Harvard University; was admitted to the bar and commenced practice in Portsmouth, N.H., in 1776; served in the Revolutionary Army and attained the rank of brigade major of staff; elected to the Third Congress and reelected as a Republican to the Fourth Congress (March 4, 1793-March 3, 1797); United States district attorney for New Hampshire 1801-1804; appointed judge of the United States District Court for the District of New Hampshire and served from May 1804 until his death in Portsmouth, N.H., August 2, 1830.

**SHEREDINE, Upton,** a Representative from Maryland; born near Baltimore, Baltimore County, Md., in 1740; moved to a farm near Liberty, Frederick County, Md., in 1754; pursued academic studies; delegate to the State constitutional convention in 1776; member of the State house of delegates in 1777; served in the State senate 1776-1781; judge of the county court of appeals in 1777; member of the special court which tried, convicted, and sentenced Tories July 25, 1781; judge of the orphans court of Frederick County in 1777 and served many years; associate judge of the fifth judicial district in 1791; elected to the Second Congress (March 4, 1791-March 3, 1793); appointed in 1798 commissioner of the fourth division of Maryland for the valuation of land and houses and the enumeration of slaves; died on his estate, "Midhill," near Liberty, Frederick County, Md., January 14, 1800; interment in a private cemetery on his estate.

**SHERIDAN, George Augustus,** a Representative from Louisiana; born in Millbury, Mass., February 22, 1840; moved with his parents to Chicago, Ill., in 1858; completed preparatory studies; engaged in the publishing business; during the Civil War enlisted in the Union Army and served as captain of Company D, Eighty-eighth Regiment, Illinois Volunteer Infantry, until October 28, 1864, when he resigned; moved to New Orleans, La., in 1866; served as brigadier general of militia on Governor Warmouth's staff; sheriff of Carroll Parish, La., in 1867; elected as a Liberal Republican to the Forty-third Congress (March 4, 1873-March 3, 1875); appointed recorder of deeds for the District of Columbia May 17, 1878; and served until May 17, 1881, when he resigned; died in the National Soldiers' Home, Virginia, October 7, 1896; interment in the Arlington National Cemetery.

**SHERIDAN, John Edward,** a Representative from Pennsylvania; born in Waterbury, New Haven County, Conn., September 15, 1902; attended the public schools; was graduated from the University of Pennsylvania at Philadelphia in 1925 and from the law department of Temple University, Philadelphia, Pa., in 1931; was admitted to the bar in 1931 and commenced practice in Philadelphia, Pa.; served as deputy attorney general of Pennsylvania 1934-1937; member of the Board of Revision of Taxes of Philadelphia County in 1937; Pennsylvania counsel for Delaware River Bridge Commission in 1938 and 1939; delegate to the Democratic National Conventions in 1932, 1936, 1940, and 1944; elected as a Democrat to the Seventy-sixth Congress to fill the vacancy caused by the death of J. Burrwood Daly; reelected to the Seventy-seventh, Seventy-eighth, and Seventy-ninth Congresses and served from November 7, 1939, to January 3, 1947; was not a candidate for reelection in 1946 to the Eightieth Congress; resumed the practice of law; colonel, United States Air Force (retired), 1954-1962; member of County Board of Law Examiners 1954-1965; consul general, Principality de Monaco (Philadelphia); was a resident of Philadelphia, Pa., until his death there on November 12, 1987; interment in Arlington National Cemetery, Va.

**SHERLEY, Joseph Swagar,** a Representative from Kentucky; born in Louisville, Jefferson County, Ky., November 28, 1871; attended the public schools; was graduated from the Louisville High School in 1889 and from the law department of the University of Virginia at Charlottesville in 1891; was admitted to the bar the same year and commenced practice in Louisville, Ky.; elected as a Democrat to the Fifty-eighth and to the seven succeeding Congresses (March 4, 1903-March 3, 1919); chairman, Committee on Appropriations (Sixty-fifth Congress); unsuccessful candidate for reelection in 1918 to the Sixty-sixth Congress; director of the division of finance of the United States Railroad Administration from April 1919 to September 1920, when he resigned; resumed the practice of law in Washington, D.C.; died while on a visit in Louisville, Ky., February 13, 1941; interment in Cave Hill Cemetery.

**SHERMAN, James Schoolcraft,** a Representative from New York and a Vice President of the United States; born in Utica, N.Y., October 24, 1855; attended the public schools; pursued academic and collegiate courses and graduated from Hamilton College, Clinton, N.Y., in 1878; studied law; was admitted to the bar in 1880 and commenced practice in Utica, N.Y.; president of the Utica Trust and Deposit Company and of the New Hartford Canning Company; elected mayor of Utica in 1884 and served until 1886; chairman of the State Republican convention in 1895, 1900 and 1908; elected as a Republican to the Fiftieth and Fifty-first Congresses (March 4, 1887-March 3, 1891); unsuccessful candidate for reelection in 1890 to the Fifty-second Congress; elected to the Fifty-third and to the seven succeeding Congresses (March 4, 1893-March 3, 1909); was not a candidate for reelection in 1908 to the Sixty-first Congress, having been nominated as the Republican candidate for Vice President on the ticket with William Howard Taft; elected Vice President of the United States, November 3, 1908, and served from March 4, 1909 until his death; had been renominated for Vice President in June 1912; died in Utica, Oneida County, N.Y., October 30, 1912; interment in Forest Hill Cemetery.

**Bibliography:** *DAB.*

**SHERMAN, John,** a Representative and a Senator from Ohio; born in Lancaster, Fairfield County, Ohio, on May 10, 1823; attended the common schools and an academy in Ohio; left school to work as an engineer on canal projects; studied law; was admitted to the bar in 1844 and began practice in Mansfield, Ohio; moved to Cleveland, Ohio, in 1853; elected as a Republican to the Thirty-fourth and to the three succeeding Congresses and served from March 4, 1855, to March 21, 1861, when he resigned; chairman, Committee on Ways and Means (Thirty-sixth Congress); elected in 1861 as a Republican to the United States Senate to fill the vacancy caused by the resignation of Salmon P. Chase; reelected in 1866 and 1872 and served from March 21, 1861, until his resignation on March 8, 1877; chairman, Committee on Agriculture (Thirty-eighth and Thirty-ninth Congresses), Committee on Finance (Thirty-eighth and Fortieth through Forty-fourth Congresses); appointed Secretary of the Treasury in the Cabinet of President Rutherford B. Hayes in March 1877, and served until March 1881; elected as a Republican to the United States Senate in 1881 in the place of James A. Garfield, who had been elected President of the United States; reelected in 1886 and 1892 and served from March 4, 1881, until his resignation on March 4, 1897; Republican caucus chairman, 1893-1897; served as President pro tempore during the Forty-ninth Congress; chairman, Committee on the Library (Forty-seventh through Forty-ninth Congresses), Committee on Foreign Relations (Forty-ninth through Fifty-second and Fifty-fourth Congresses); sponsor of the Sherman Anti-Trust Act of 1890, which declared that trusts restraining trade or commerce between States or with foreign countries were illegal; appointed Secretary of State in the Cabinet of President William McKinley, and served from March 5, 1897 until his resignation on April 27, 1898; retired to private life; died in Washington, D.C., October 22, 1900; interment in Mansfield Cemetery, Mansfield, Richland County, Ohio.

**Bibliography:** *DAB*; Burton, Theodore. *John Sherman.* 1906. Reprint. New York: AMS Press, 1972; Sherman, John. *Recollections of Forty Years in the House, Senate, and Cabinet.* 1895. Reprint. 2 vols. New York: Greenwood Press, 1968.

**SHERMAN, Judson W.,** a Representative from New York; born in that State in 1808; completed preparatory studies; held several local offices in Angelica, N.Y., where he resided; clerk of Allegany County, N.Y., 1831-1837; deputy treasurer of the State of New York about 1850; elected as a Republican to the Thirty-fifth Congress (March 4, 1857-March 3, 1859); appointed captain and commissary of subsistence of Volunteers on September 7, 1861, was assigned to duty with Brigadier General Wood's brigade, and resigned his commission November 9, 1861; died at Angelica, Allegany County, N.Y., on November 12, 1881; interment in Until the Day Dawn Cemetery.

**SHERMAN, Lawrence Yates,** a Senator from Illinois; born near Piqua, Miami County, Ohio, November 8, 1858; moved with his parents to Illinois in 1859; attended the common schools, Lee's Academy in Coles County, and McKendree College, Lebanon, Ill.; studied law; was admitted to the bar in 1882 and commenced practice in Macomb, Ill.; city attorney 1885-1887; judge in McDonough County 1886-1890; member, State house of representatives 1897-1905, and served as speaker 1899-1903; lieutenant governor and ex officio president of the State senate 1905-1909; president of the State board of administration of public charities 1909-1913; continued the practice of law in Springfield, Ill.; elected in 1913 as a Republican to the United States Senate to fill the vacancy caused by the unseating of William Lorimer; reelected in 1914 and served from March 26, 1913, to March 3, 1921; chairman, Committee on the District of Columbia (Sixty-sixth Congress); resumed the practice of law in Springfield, Ill.; moved to Daytona Beach, Fla., in 1924 and continued the practice of law; also engaged in the investment business; retired from active business pursuits in 1933; died in Daytona Beach, Fla., September 15, 1939; interment in Montrose Cemetery, Effingham County, Ill.

**SHERMAN, Roger** (grandfather of William Evarts), a Delegate, a Representative, and a Senator from Connecticut; born in Newton, Mass., April 19, 1721; moved with his parents to Stoughton (now Canton), Mass., in 1723; attended the public schools; learned the shoemaker's trade; moved to New Milford, Conn., in 1743; surveyor of New Haven County in 1745; studied law; was admitted to the bar in 1754 and practiced; member, Connecticut assembly, 1755-1756, 1758-1761, 1764-1766; justice of the peace for Litchfield County, 1755-1761, and of the quorum, 1759-1761; moved to New Haven, Conn. in June 1761; justice of the peace and member of the court, 1765-1766; member, Connecticut senate, 1766-1785; judge of the superior court, 1766-1767, and 1773-1788; member of the council of safety, 1777-1779; Member of the Continental Congress, 1774-1781, and 1784; a signer of the Declaration of Independence and a member of the committee which drafted it; member of the committee to prepare the Articles of Confederation; the only Member of the Continental Congress who signed the Declaration of 1774, the Declaration of Independence, the Articles of Confederation, and the Federal Constitution; mayor of New Haven from 1784 until his death; delegate to the Federal Constitutional Convention at Philadelphia in 1787; elected to the First Congress (March 4, 1789-March 3, 1791); elected to the United States Senate to fill the vacancy caused by the resignation of William S. Johnson, and served from June 13, 1791 until his death in New Haven, Conn., July 23, 1793; interment in the New Haven City Burying Ground.

**Bibliography:** *DAB*; Boardman, Roger S. *Roger Sherman, Signer and Statesman.* 1938. Reprint. New York: Da Capo Press, 1971; Collier, Christopher. *Roger Sherman's Connecticut: Yankee Politics and the American Revolution.* Middletown, Conn.: Wesleyan University Press, 1971; Rommel, John G. *Connecticut's Yankee Patriot: Roger Sherman.* Hartford: American Revolution Bicentennial Commission of Connecticut, 1980.

**SHERMAN, Socrates Norton,** a Representative from New York; born in Barre, Washington County, Vt., July 22, 1801; attended the grade schools and high school; studied medicine and was graduated from Mount Castleton Medical College in 1824; moved to Ogdensburg, St. Lawrence County, N.Y., in 1825 and engaged in the practice of medicine; elected as a Republican to the Thirty-seventh Congress (March 4, 1861-March 3, 1863); declined to be a candidate for renomination in 1862; during the Civil War was mustered into the service as major and surgeon of the Thirty-fourth Regiment, New York Volunteer Infantry, and was mustered out October 7, 1865, as brevet lieutenant colonel, United States Volunteers; resumed the practice of medicine at Ogdensburg, N.Y., where he died February 1, 1873; interment in Ogdensburg Cemetery.

**SHERRILL, Eliakim,** a Representative from New York; born in Greenville, Ulster County, N.Y., February 16, 1813; attended the public schools; tanner and farmer; held several local offices; major in the State militia; elected as a Whig to the Thirtieth Congress (March 4, 1847-March 3, 1849); member of the State senate in 1854; during the Civil War organized the One Hundred and Twenty-sixth New York Volunteer Regiment and became its colonel; commanded the Third Brigade, Third Division, Second Army Corps, after Colonel Willard's death on July 2, 1863, at the Battle of Gettysburg, until he was mortally wounded on July 3, 1863, and died the next day; interment in the Washington Street Cemetery, Geneva, Ontario County, N.Y.

**SHERROD, William Crawford,** a Representative from Alabama; born in Courtland, Lawrence County, Ala., August 17, 1835; attended the common schools, a preparatory school at Edgefield, N.C., and the University of North Carolina at Chapel Hill in 1851 and 1852; returned to Courtland and engaged in planting; member of the Alabama State house of representatives in 1859 and 1860; delegate to the Democratic National Convention at Charleston, S.C., in 1860; during the Civil War served as a colonel under General Nathan Bedford Forrest in the Confederate Army; elected as a Democrat to the Forty-first Congress (March 4, 1869-March 3, 1871); was not a candidate for renomination in 1870 to the Forty-second Congress; again engaged in planting; member of the Alabama State senate in 1875; moved to Wichita Falls, Wichita County, Tex., in 1893, engaged in farming and ranching, and died there on March 24, 1919; interment in Riverside Cemetery.

**SHERWIN, John Crocker,** a Representative from Illinois; born in Gouverneur, St. Lawrence County, N.Y., February 8, 1838; was educated in the common schools, Gouverneur Wesleyan Seminary in New York, and Lombard College, Galesburg, Ill.; studied law; was admitted to the bar and practiced; county clerk of Kane County, Ill.; served as city attorney of Aurora, Ill.; enlisted in the Union Army during the Civil War in the Eighty-ninth Regiment, Illinois Volunteer Infantry, and served until the close of the war; elected as a Republican to the Forty-sixth and Forty-seventh Congresses (March 4, 1879-March 3, 1883); was not a candidate for renomination in 1882; resumed the practice of law; died at Benton Harbor, Mich., January 1, 1904; interment in Spring Lake Cemetery, Aurora, Ill.

**SHERWOOD, Henry,** a Representative from Pennsylvania; born in Bridgeport, Conn., October 9, 1813; moved with his parents to Catharine, Chemung County, N.Y., in 1817; attended the common schools; during the Texas war for independence served in the Texas Army under Sam Houston in 1836 and 1837; moved to Tioga County and settled in Wellsboro, Pa., in 1840; studied law; was admitted to the bar in 1847 and practiced his profession in Wellsboro; elected burgess of Wellsboro; elected as a Democrat to the Forty-second Congress (March 4, 1871-March 3, 1873); unsuccessful candidate for reelection in 1872 to the Forty-third Congress; president of the Wellsboro & Lawrenceville Railroad and of the Pennsylvania division of the Pine Creek road; died in Wellsboro, Tioga County, Pa., on November 10, 1896; interment in the Wellsboro Cemetery.

**SHERWOOD, Isaac R.,** a Representative from Ohio; born in Stanford, Dutchess County, N.Y., August 13, 1835; attended the common schools, the Hudson River Institute, Claverack, N.Y., Antioch College, Yellow Springs, Ohio, and the Ohio Law College, Poland, Ohio; editor of the Williams County Gazette, Bryan, Ohio, in 1857; elected probate judge of Williams County in October 1860; resigned at the beginning of the Civil War and enlisted April 22, 1861, as a private in the Fourteenth Regiment, Ohio Volunteer Infantry, and promoted through the ranks to lieutenant colonel; honorably mustered out June 27, 1865; settled in Toledo, Ohio, and was editor of the Toledo Daily Commercial; political editorial writer on the Cleveland Leader; secretary of state of Ohio in 1868 and 1870; organized and established the Bureau of Statistics of the State of Ohio in 1869; elected as a Republican to the Forty-third Congress (March 4, 1873-March 3, 1875); was not a candidate for renomination in 1874; proprietor and editor of the Toledo Journal 1875-1884; elected probate judge of Lucas County in 1878 and 1881; editor of the Canton News-Democrat 1885-1895; elected as a Democrat to the Sixtieth and to the six succeeding Congresses (March 4, 1907-March 3, 1921); chairman, Committee on Invalid Pensions (Sixty-second

through Sixty-fifth Congresses); unsuccessful candidate for reelection in 1920 to the Sixty-seventh Congress; again elected to the Sixty-eighth Congress (March 4, 1923-March 3, 1925); unsuccessful candidate for reelection in 1924 to the Sixty-ninth Congress; retired from public life and returned to Toledo, Ohio, where he died October 15, 1925; interment in Woodlawn Cemetery.

**Bibliography:** *DAB.*

**SHERWOOD, Samuel,** a Representative from New York; born in Kingsbury, Washington County, N.Y., April 24, 1779; completed preparatory studies; began the study of law at the age of fifteen in Kingston, Ulster County, and in 1798 moved to Delhi, Delaware County, N.Y., where he continued his legal studies; was admitted to the bar in 1800 and practiced in Delhi, N.Y.; elected as a Federalist to the Thirteenth Congress (March 4, 1813-March 3, 1815); was not a candidate for renomination to the Fourteenth Congress; resumed the practice of his profession in Delhi and in New York City, where he moved in 1830; retired from active practice in 1858; died in New York City on October 31, 1862; interment in Woodlawn Cemetery, Delhi, N.Y.

**SHERWOOD, Samuel Burr,** a Representative from Connecticut; born in Northfield Society (later Weston), Conn., November 26, 1767; graduated from Yale College in 1786; studied law; was admitted to the bar and began practice in that part of Fairfield which is now Westport, Conn.; member of the State house of representatives 1809-1815; served in the State senate in 1816; elected as a Federalist to the Fifteenth Congress (March 4, 1817-March 3, 1819); resumed the practice of his profession until 1831, when he retired from professional life; died in Westport, Fairfield County, Conn., on April 27, 1833; interment in Evergreen Cemetery.

**SHIEL, George Knox,** a Representative from Oregon; born in Ireland in 1825; immigrated to the United States and settled in New Orleans, La.; moved to Ohio; studied law; was admitted to the bar and practiced; moved to Oregon in 1854 and practiced law in Salem; successfully contested as a Democrat the election of Andrew J. Thayer to the Thirty-seventh Congress and served from July 30, 1861, to March 3, 1863; was not a candidate for renomination in 1862 to the Thirty-eighth Congress; was barred from practicing law, as he would not take the oath of allegiance, and lived in retirement until he was accidentally killed in Salem, Marion County, Oreg., December 12, 1893; interment in the Odd Fellows Cemetery.

**SHIELDS, Benjamin Glover,** a Representative from Alabama; born in Abbeville, S.C., in 1808; moved with his father to Clarke County, Ala.; resided in Demopolis, Marengo County, Ala.; completed preparatory studies; member of the Alabama State house of representatives in 1834; elected as a Democrat to the Twenty-seventh Congress (March 4, 1841-March 3, 1843); appointed on March 14, 1845 by President James K. Polk as United States Chargé d'Affaires to Venezuela, where he remained until January 7, 1850; moved to Texas and engaged in planting until his death.

**SHIELDS, Ebenezer J.,** a Representative from Tennessee; born in Georgia, December 22, 1778; moved to Tennessee in 1809 and settled on Robertson Fork Creek near Lynnville, Giles County; completed preparatory studies; was graduated from the University of Nashville, Tennessee, in 1827; studied law; was admitted to the bar and commenced practice in Pulaski, Tenn.; member of the Tennessee State house of representatives, 1833-1835; elected as a Hugh L. White supporter to the Twenty-fourth Congress and reelected as a Whig to the Twenty-fifth Congress (March 4, 1835-March 3, 1839); unsuccessful candidate for reelection in 1838 to the Twenty-sixth Congress; resumed the practice of law in Pulaski, Tenn.; moved to Memphis, Tenn., in 1844 and continued the practice of his profession; died near La Grange, Fayette County, Tex., April 21, 1846.

**SHIELDS, James** (nephew of James Shields [1762-1831]), a Senator from Illinois, Minnesota, and Missouri; born in Altmore, County Tyrone, Ireland, in either 1806 or 1810; attended a hedge school, private schools, and pursued classical studies; immigrated to the United States about 1826; studied law; was admitted to the bar in 1832 and commenced practice in Kaskaskia, Randolph County, Ill.; member, Illinois State house of representatives, 1836; Illinois State auditor in 1839; judge of the supreme court of Illinois, 1843; Commissioner of the General Land Office, 1845-1847; during the Mexican War was commissioned brigadier general of Volunteers in 1846, brevetted major general in 1847, and honorably discharged in 1848; appointed Governor of Oregon Territory by President James K. Polk in 1848 and resigned in 1849; elected as a Democrat to the United States Senate from Illinois for the term commencing March 4, 1849; upon his appearance to take his seat on March 5, 1849, a resolution was presented raising the question of his eligibility; took his seat on March 6, 1849, but on March 15, 1849, the Senate declared his election void on the ground that he had not been a citizen of the United States the number of years required by the Constitution; immediately elected for the same term and served from October 27, 1849, to March 3, 1855; unsuccessful candidate for reelection; chairman, Committee on the District of Columbia (Thirty-second and Thirty-third Congresses), Committee on Military Affairs (Thirty-second and Thirty-third Congresses); moved to Minnesota in 1855; upon the admission of Minnesota as a State into the Union was elected as a Democrat to the United States Senate and served from May 11, 1858, to March 3, 1859; unsuccessful candidate for reelection; chairman, Committee on Revolutionary Claims (Thirty-fifth Congress); moved to California; during the Civil War served in the Union Army as brigadier general of volunteers from 1861 to 1863, when he resigned and returned to California; moved to Carrollton, Mo., and resumed the practice of law; member, Missouri State house of representatives, 1874, 1879; adjutant general of Missouri in 1877; served as railroad commissioner; elected as a Democrat to the United States Senate from Missouri on January 22, 1879, to fill the vacancy caused by the death of Lewis V. Bogy and served from January 27, 1879, to March 3, 1879; declined to be a candidate for renomination; died in Ottumwa, Wapello County, Iowa, June 1, 1879; interment in St. Mary's Cemetery, Carrollton, Carroll County, Mo.

Bibliography: *DAB*; Condon, William, *Life of Major General James Shields*. Chicago: Press of Blakely Printing Co., 1900; Curran, Judith. "The Career of James Shields, an Immigrant Irishman in Nineteenth Century America." Ph.D. dissertation, Columbia University Teachers College, 1980.

**SHIELDS, James** (uncle of James Shields [1810-1879]), a Representative from Ohio; born in Banbridge, County Down, Ireland, April 13, 1762; received a common school education; entered the University of Glasgow, Scotland, in 1782 and was graduated in 1786; attended medical college for two years; immigrated to the United States in July 1791 and settled in Frederick County, Va., where he taught school; moved to Butler County, Ohio, in 1801; returned to Virginia and became a citizen of the United States in 1804; returned to Ohio in 1807; member of the Ohio State house of representatives, 1806-1827; elected as a Jacksonian to the Twenty-first Congress (March 4, 1829-March 3, 1831); was killed near Venice, Butler County, Ohio, on August 13, 1831, when the stagecoach in which he was riding accidentally overturned; interment in Venice Cemetery, Venice, Ohio.

**SHIELDS, John Knight,** a Senator from Tennessee; born at "Clinchdale," near Bean's Station, Grainger County, Tenn., August 15, 1858; was educated by private tutors; studied law; was admitted to the bar in 1879 and practiced in Grainger and adjoining counties until 1893; chancellor of the twelfth chancery division 1893-1894; resumed the practice of law in Morristown, Hamblen County, Tenn.; associate justice of the supreme court of Tennessee 1902-1910, chief justice 1910-1913, when he resigned, having been nominated as a candidate for Senator; elected as a Democrat to the United States Senate in 1913; reelected in 1918 and served from March 4, 1913, to March 3, 1925; unsuccessful candidate for renomination in 1924; chairman, Committee on Canadian Relations (Sixty-third and Sixty-fourth Congresses), Committee on Interoceanic Canals (Sixty-fifth Congress), Committee on Transportation and Sale of Meat Products (Sixty-sixth Congress); resumed the practice of law in Knoxville, Tenn.; died at his country estate, "Clinchdale," near Knoxville, September 30, 1934; interment in Memorial Cemetery, Knoxville, Tenn.

Bibliography: *DAB*.

**SHINN, William Norton,** a Representative from New Jersey; born in Burlington County, N.J., October 24, 1782; attended the public schools; engaged in agricultural pursuits; sheriff of Burlington County 1825-1828; member of the State general assembly in 1828; served in the State council 1829-1831; chairman of the Democratic State central committee in 1832; elected as a Jacksonian to the Twenty-third and Twenty-fourth Congresses (March 4, 1833-March 3, 1837); resumed agricultural pursuits; president of the Burlington Agricultural Association in 1853 and 1854; elected a director of the Camden & Amboy Railroad Co.; died in Mount Holly, Burlington County, N.J., on August 18, 1871; interment in Mount Holly Cemetery.

**SHIPHERD, Zebulon Rudd,** a Representative from New York; born in Granville, Washington County, N.Y., November 15, 1768; completed preparatory studies; studied law; was admitted to the bar and commenced practice in Granville, N.Y.; was elected as a Federalist to the Thirteenth Congress (March 4, 1813-March 3, 1815); resumed the practice of his profession in Granville; trustee of Middlebury College, Middlebury, Vt., 1819-1841; moved to Moriah, Essex County, about 1830, where he died November 1, 1841; interment in the Moriah Corners Cemetery.

**SHIPLEY, George Edward,** a Representative from Illinois; born in Richland County, near Olney, Ill., April 21, 1927; attended the East Richland High School, Olney, Ill., and graduated from Olney (Ill.) High School in 1950; served as a private in the United States Marine Corps from December 1944 until discharged in May 1947, with service in the South Pacific; chief deputy sheriff of Richland County, Ill., 1950-1954, and sheriff, 1954-1958; owner of a restaurant in Olney, Ill.; elected as a Democrat to the Eighty-sixth and to the nine succeeding Congresses (January 3, 1959-January 3, 1979); was not a candidate for reelection in 1978 to the Ninety-sixth Congress; is a resident of Olney, Ill.

**SHIPPEN, William,** a Delegate from Pennsylvania; born in Philadelphia, Pa., October 1, 1712; pursued preparatory studies; studied medicine and practiced his profession in Philadelphia; was one of the founders of the Public Academy and a trustee in 1749; was one of the twenty-four founders of the College of Philadelphia, which afterward became the University of Pennsylvania, and a trustee 1749-1779; one of the founders of the College of New Jersey (now Princeton University) and a trustee from 1765 to 1796; was a member of the American Philosophical Society, of which he was vice president in 1768 and for many years thereafter; Member of the Continental Congress 1779-1780; resumed the practice of medicine in Philadelphia; died in Germantown, Pa., November 4, 1801; interment in the First Presbyterian Church Cemetery, Philadelphia, Pa.

**SHIPSTEAD, Henrik,** a Senator from Minnesota; born in Burbank, Kandiyohi County, Minn., January 8, 1881; attended the public schools at New London, Minn., and the State normal school at St. Cloud, Minn.; graduated from the dental department of Northwestern University, Chicago, Ill., in 1903 and practiced dentistry in Glenwood, Minn., 1904-1920; mayor of Glenwood

1911-1913; member, State house of representatives 1917; moved to Minneapolis in 1920 and resumed the practice of dentistry; unsuccessful candidate for the United States Congress in 1918 and for governor in 1920; elected on the Farmer-Labor ticket in 1922 to the United States Senate; reelected in 1928, 1934, and as a Republican in 1940 and served from March 4, 1923, to January 3, 1947; unsuccessful candidate for renomination in 1946; chairman, Committee on Printing (Seventieth through Seventy-second Congresses); died in Alexandria, Minn., June 26, 1960; interment in Kinkead Cemetery.

Bibliography: *DAB*; Lorentz, Sister Mary Rene. "Henrik Shipstead: Minnesota Independent, 1923-1946." Ph.D. dissertation, Catholic University, 1963; Ross, Martin. *Shipstead of Minnesota.* Chicago: Packard and Company, 1940.

SHIRAS, George, III, a Representative from Pennsylvania; born in Allegheny, Pa., January 1, 1859; attended the public schools and Phillips Academy, Andover, Mass.; graduated from Cornell University, Ithaca, N.Y., in 1881 and from the law department of Yale College in 1883; admitted to the Connecticut and Pennsylvania bars in 1883 and commenced the practice of his profession in Pittsburgh, Pa.; member of the Pennsylvania house of representatives in 1889 and 1890; unsuccessful candidate for the Republican nomination for Congress in 1890; elected as an Independent Republican to the Fifty-eighth Congress (March 4, 1903-March 3, 1905); did not seek renomination in 1904 to the Fifty-ninth Congress; engaged in biological research and wildlife photography; died in Marquette, Mich., March 24, 1942; interment in Park Cemetery.

SHIVELY, Benjamin Franklin, a Representative and a Senator from Indiana; born near Osceola, St. Joseph County, Ind., March 20, 1857; attended the common schools and the Northern Indiana Normal School at Valparaiso, Ind.; taught school 1874-1880; engaged in journalism 1880-1884; secretary of the National Anti-Monopoly Association in 1883; president of the board of Indiana University in 1884; elected as a National Anti-Monopolist to the Forty-eighth Congress to fill the vacancy caused by the resignation of William H. Calkins and served from December 1, 1884, to March 3, 1885; graduated from the law department of the University of Michigan at Ann Arbor in 1886; was admitted to the bar and commenced practice in South Bend, Ind.; elected as a Democrat to the Fiftieth, Fifty-first, and Fifty-second Congresses (March 4, 1887-March 3, 1893); was not a candidate for renomination in 1892; resumed the practice of law in South Bend, Ind.; unsuccessful Democratic candidate for governor of Indiana in 1896; unsuccessful candidate for election in 1906 to the Sixtieth Congress; elected as a Democrat to the United States Senate in 1909; reelected in 1914 and served from March 4, 1909, until his death in Washington, D.C., March 14, 1916; chairman, Committee on Pacific Railroads (Sixty-second Congress), Committee on Pensions (Sixty-third and Sixty-fourth Congresses); interment in the Brookville Cemetery, Brookville, Pa.

SHOBER, Francis Edwin (father of Francis Emanuel Shober), a Representative from North Carolina; born in Salem (now Winston-Salem), N.C., March 12, 1831; attended the common schools and the Moravian School, Bethlehem, Pa.; was graduated from the University of North Carolina at Chapel Hill in 1851; studied law; was admitted to the bar in 1853 and commenced practice in Salisbury, N.C., in 1854; member of the State house of commons in 1862 and 1864; served in the State senate in 1865; elected as a Democrat to the Forty-first and Forty-second Congresses (March 4, 1869-March 3, 1873); was not a candidate for renomination in 1872; delegate to the State constitutional convention in 1875; county judge of Rowan County in 1877 and 1878; appointed Chief Clerk of the United States Senate in the Forty-fifth Congress; upon the death of Secretary John C. Burch in the

Forty-seventh Congress was appointed Acting Secretary of the Senate and served from October 24, 1881, to March 3, 1883; delegate to the Democratic National Conventions in 1880 and 1884; again a member of the State senate in 1887; resumed the practice of his profession; died in Salisbury, Rowan County, N.C., May 29, 1896; interment in Oakdale Cemetery.

SHOBER, Francis Emanuel (son of Francis Edwin Shober), a Representative from New York; born in Salisbury, N.C., October 24, 1860; studied under private tutors; was graduated from St. Stephen's College, Annandale, N.Y., in 1880; engaged in ministerial and educational work in Dutchess County, N.Y.; reporter on the News-Press of Poughkeepsie; pastor of St. John's Episcopal Church at Barrytown, N.Y., 1880-1891; editor of the Rockaway Journal at Far Rockaway, N.Y.; member of the editorial staff of the New York World; elected as a Democrat to the Fifty-eighth Congress (March 4, 1903-March 3, 1905); unsuccessful candidate for renomination in 1904; deputy tax appraiser of the State of New York in 1907 and 1908; resumed newspaper work; editor of the New York American until his death in New York City October 7, 1919; interment in Worcester Cemetery, Danbury, Fairfield County, Conn.

SHOEMAKER, Francis Henry, a Representative from Minnesota; born on a farm in Flora Township, Renville County, Minn., April 25, 1889; self-educated with mother's assistance; engaged in agricultural pursuits and worked for many farm and labor organizations; charter member and organizer of the Minnesota Farmer-Labor Party; assisted in organizing the Federated Farmer-Labor Party at Chicago in 1924; was nominated for Vice President of the United States in 1924, but declined; editor and publisher of the People's Voice, Green Bay, Wis., 1921-1927, and of the Organized Farmer, Red Wing, Minn., in 1928; elected as a Farmer-Laborite to the Seventy-third Congress (March 4, 1933-January 3, 1935); was not a candidate in 1934 for renomination to the House of Representatives, but was an unsuccessful candidate for nomination to the United States Senate; then became an unsuccessful Independent candidate for reelection to the Seventy-fourth Congress; unsuccessful candidate for election in 1942 to the Seventy-eighth Congress; resumed agricultural pursuits near North Redwood, Minn.; died in Minneapolis, Minn., July 24, 1958; interment in Zion Cemetery, Flora Township, Renville County, Minn.

Bibliography: Johnson, Frederick L. "From Leavenworth to Congress: The Improbable Journey of Francis H. Shoemaker." *Minnesota History* 51 (Spring 1989): 166-185.

SHOEMAKER, Lazarus Denison, a Representative from Pennsylvania; born in Kingston, Luzerne County, Pa., November 5, 1819; attended Nazareth Hall, Nazareth, Pa., and Kenyon College, Gambier, Ohio; graduated from Yale College in 1840; studied law; admitted to the bar in 1842 and commenced practice in Wilkes-Barre, Pa.; member of the Pennsylvania senate 1866-1870; elected as a Republican to the Forty-second and Forty-third Congresses (March 4, 1871-March 3, 1875); chairman, Committee on Revolutionary Pensions (Forty-third Congress); was not a candidate for renomination in 1874; resumed the practice of his profession; also engaged in banking; died in Wilkes-Barre, Pa., September 9, 1893; interment in Forty Fort Cemetery, Forty Fort, Luzerne County, Pa.

SHONK, George Washington, a Representative from Pennsylvania; born in Plymouth, Luzerne County, Pa., April 26, 1850; attended the public schools and Wyoming Seminary, Kingston, Pa.; was graduated from Wesleyan University, Middletown, Conn., in 1873; studied law; was admitted to the bar of Luzerne County, Pa., on September 29, 1876, and commenced the practice of law in Wilkes-Barre; elected as a Republican to the Fifty-second Congress (March 4, 1891-March 3, 1893); declined to be a candidate for renomination in 1892 to the Fifty-third Congress; again resumed the practice of his profession in Wilkes-Barre; was also interested in coal mining in Pennsylvania; died in Washington, D.C., while on a business trip, August 14, 1900; interment in Shawnee Cemetery, Plymouth, Pa.

**SHORT, Dewey Jackson,** a Representative from Missouri; born in Galena, Stone County, Mo., April 7, 1898; attended the public school, Galena High School, and Marionville (Mo.) College; during the First World War served in the Infantry; was graduated from Baker University, Baldwin City, Kans., in 1919, and from Boston (Mass.) University in 1922; attended Harvard University, Heidelberg University, the University of Berlin, Germany, and Oxford University, Oxford, England; professor of ethics, psychology, and political philosophy at Southwestern College, Winfield, Kans., in 1923, 1924, and 1926-1928; pastor of the Grace Methodist Episcopal Church, Springfield, Mo., in 1927; elected as a Republican to the Seventy-first Congress (March 4, 1929-March 3, 1931); unsuccessful candidate for reelection in 1930 to the Seventy-second Congress; resumed his former professional pursuits; delegate to the Republican National Convention of 1932; unsuccessful candidate in 1932 for nomination to the United States Senate; elected to the Seventy-fourth and to the ten succeeding Congresses (January 3, 1935-January 3, 1957); chairman, Committee on Armed Services (Eighty-third Congress); unsuccessful candidate for reelection in 1956 to the Eighty-fifth Congress; congressional delegate to inspect concentration camps in Germany in 1945; Assistant Secretary of the Army from March 15, 1957 to January 20, 1961; was president emeritus, National Rivers and Harbors Congress, and a lecturer; resided in Washington, D.C., where he died on November 19, 1979; interment in Galena Cemetery, Galena, Mo.

**Bibliography:** Wiley, Robert S. *Dewey Short: Orator of the Ozarks*. Crane, Mo.: R.S. Wiley, 1985.

**SHORT, Don Levingston,** a Representative from North Dakota; born in Le Mars, Plymouth County, Iowa, June 22, 1903; moved with his parents to a ranch in Billings County, near Medora, N.Dak., in February 1904; attended Medora public schools and St. James School, Faribault, Minn.; studied an agricultural short course at Montana State College at Bozeman in 1918 and 1919; graduated from Pillsbury Military Academy, Owatonna, Minn., in 1921; student at the University of Minnesota, 1922-1926; farmer and rancher; county supervisor, Farm Security Administration, 1937-1938; member of the North Dakota State assembly in 1957; elected as a Republican to the Eighty-sixth and to the two succeeding Congresses (January 3, 1959-January 3, 1965); unsuccessful candidate for reelection in 1964 to the Eighty-ninth Congress; resumed cattle ranching until retirement; was a resident of Beach, N.Dak., until his death in Dickinson, N.Dak., on May 10, 1982; interment in Medora Cemetery, Medora, N.Dak.

**SHORTER, Eli Sims,** a Representative from Alabama; born in Monticello, Jasper County, Ga., March 15, 1823; attended the common schools and was graduated in law from Yale College in 1844; was admitted to the bar and commenced practice in Eufaula, Ala., in 1844; also engaged in agricultural pursuits; elected as a Democrat to the Thirty-fourth and Thirty-fifth Congresses (March 4, 1855-March 3, 1859); resumed the practice of law in Eufaula, Ala.; during the Civil War served in the Confederate Army as colonel of the Eighteenth Regiment, Alabama Volunteer Infantry; died in Eufaula, Ala., April 29, 1879; interment in Fairview Cemetery.

**SHORTRIDGE, Samuel Morgan,** a Senator from California; born in Mount Pleasant, Henry County, Iowa, August 3, 1861; moved to California with his parents, who settled in San Jose in 1875; attended the public schools and the Hastings College of Law at San Francisco, Calif.; was admitted to the bar in 1884 and commenced the practice of law in San Francisco, Calif.; presidential elector on the Republican ticket in 1888, 1900, and again in 1908; elected as a Republican to the United States Senate in 1920; reelected in 1926 and served from March 4, 1921, to March 3, 1933; unsuccessful candidate for renomination in 1932; chairman,

Committee on Privileges and Elections (Seventieth through Seventy-second Congresses), Committee on Naval Affairs (Seventy-second Congress); resumed the practice of law; special attorney with the United States Department of Justice, Washington, D.C., from 1939 until 1943; died in Atherton, Calif., January 15, 1952; interment in Oak Hill Cemetery, San Jose, Calif.

**SHOTT, Hugh Ike,** a Representative and a Senator from West Virginia; born in Staunton, Augusta County, Va., September 3, 1866; attended the Staunton public schools; apprenticed as a printer; later became a reporter and editorial writer; moved to Bluefield, W.Va., in 1893; served as a clerk in the railway mail service in 1895; became publisher and editor of the Bluefield Daily Telegraph in 1896; postmaster of Bluefield 1903-1912; member of the West Virginia Semicentennial Commission in 1912 and 1913; elected as a Republican to the Seventy-first and Seventy-second Congresses (March 4, 1929-March 3, 1933); was an unsuccessful candidate for reelection in 1932 and for election to the United States Senate in 1936; elected as a Republican to the United States Senate to fill the vacancy caused by the resignation of Matthew M. Neely and served from November 18, 1942, to January 3, 1943; was not a candidate for the full term; continued as editor and publisher of the Bluefield Daily Telegraph until his death in Bluefield, W.Va., October 12, 1953; interment in Monte Vista Cemetery.

**SHOUP, George Laird,** a Senator from Idaho (great-grandfather of Richard Gardner Shoup); born in Kittanning, Armstrong County, Pa., June 15, 1836; attended the public schools of Freeport and Slate Lick; moved to Illinois in 1852; engaged in agricultural pursuits and stock raising near Galesburg, Ill., until 1858; moved to Colorado in 1859; engaged in mining and mercantile pursuits until 1861; during the Civil War enlisted in an independent company of scouts and soon thereafter was commissioned a second lieutenant; scouted throughout New Mexico and Colorado and on the Canadian, Pecos, Arkansas and Red Rivers; promoted to first lieutenant; given leave of absence to attend the convention to prepare a constitution for the proposed State of Colorado in 1864; returned to active duty, commissioned colonel, and mustered out in Denver in 1864; engaged in mercantile pursuits in Virginia City, Mont., in 1866 and later in Salmon City, Idaho; Lemhi county treasurer and superintendent of schools; member, Territorial house of representatives, 1874; member, Territorial council, 1878; member of the Republican National Committee, 1880-1884, 1888-1892; United States commissioner for Idaho at the World's Cotton Centennial Exposition in New Orleans, La., in 1884 and 1885; appointed Governor of Idaho Territory by President Benjamin Harrison on April 1, 1889, and served until July 3, 1890, when Idaho was admitted as a State into the Union; elected the first Governor of Idaho, October 1, 1890, but resigned in December of that year, having been elected Senator; elected as a Republican to the United States Senate in 1890; reelected in 1895 and served from December 18, 1890, to March 3, 1901; unsuccessful candidate for reelection in 1900; chairman, Committee on Education and Labor (Fifty-fourth Congress), Committee on Territories (Fifty-fifth and Fifty-sixth Congresses); died in Boise, Idaho, December 21, 1904; interment in the Masonic Cemetery.

**Bibliography:** *DAB*; Crowder, David L. "George Laird Shoup." *Idaho Yesterdays* 33 (Winter 1990): 18-23; Mathews, W.B. *Sketch of the Life and Services of the Hon. George L. Shoup*. Washington, D.C.: B.S. Adams, 1900.

**SHOUP, Richard Gardner** (great-grandson of George Laird Shoup), a Representative from Montana; born in Salmon, Lemhi County, Idaho, November 29, 1923; attended the public schools of Salmon and Idaho State University; B.S., University of Montana, Missoula, 1950; served in the United States Army, European Theater, Field Artillery, 1943-1946; served in the Korean conflict, 1951-1952; employed in agriculture service department, Montana

Flour Mills, 1953-1954; moved to Missoula, Mont. in 1955; secretary and manager of Moose Lodge, 1957-1960; part owner-operator, laundry and dry cleaning business, 1960-1967; elected to the Missoula City Council, representing the Fourth Ward, in 1963, and also served as Council president from 1965 to 1967; elected mayor of Missoula in 1966 and served from May 1967 until his resignation in June 1970, having been nominated for Congress; member of the Governor's (Montana) Crime Commission, 1969-1970, and of the Montana League of Cities and Towns, 1967-1970; elected as a Republican to the Ninety-second and Ninety-third Congresses (January 3, 1971-January 3, 1975); unsuccessful candidate for reelection in 1974 to the Ninety-fourth Congress; director, Union Pacific Railroad, Washington, D.C., from 1975 until his resignation in 1984; returned to Missoula, Mont., and resided there until his death on November 25, 1995.

**SHOUSE, Jouett,** a Representative from Kansas; born in Midway, Woodford County, Ky., December 10, 1879; moved with his parents to Mexico, Mo., in 1892; attended the public schools and the University of Missouri at Columbia; moved to Lexington, Ky., in 1898 and engaged in newspaper work until 1911; moved to Kinsley, Kans., in 1911 and engaged in agricultural pursuits and livestock raising; vice president and treasurer of the Mexican lines of the Kansas, Mexico & Orient Railroad; director of the Kinsley Bank; member of the State senate 1913-1915; elected as a Democrat to the Sixty-fourth and Sixty-fifth Congresses (March 4, 1915-March 3, 1919); unsuccessful candidate for reelection; Assistant Secretary of the Treasury from March 5, 1919, to November 15, 1920; delegate to the Democratic National Conventions in 1920, 1924, and 1932; chairman, Democratic National Executive Committee, 1929-1932; engaged in the practice of law in Kansas City, Mo., and Washington, D.C.; in 1953 became chairman of the board of Anton Smit and Co., Inc., of New York; retired in 1965; died in Washington, D.C., June 2, 1968; cremated and interred in Lexington Cemetery, Lexington, Ky.

**SHOWALTER, Joseph Baltzell,** a Representative from Pennsylvania; born near Smithfield, Fayette County, Pa., February 11, 1851; attended the public schools and Georges Creek Academy at Smithfield; taught school in West Virginia, Indiana, and Illinois 1867-1873; moved to Chicora, Pa., in 1873 and engaged in the production of petroleum and natural gas; studied medicine at Long Island College Hospital, Brooklyn, N.Y., in 1883; graduated from the College of Physicians and Surgeons, Baltimore, Md., in 1884; practiced medicine in Chicora, Pa., from 1884 to 1890, when he again engaged in the production of petroleum and natural gas; member of the Pennsylvania house of representatives in 1887 and 1888; served in the Pennsylvania senate 1889-1892; elected as a Republican to the Fifty-fifth Congress to fill the vacancy caused by the death of James J. Davidson; reelected to the Fifty-sixth and Fifty-seventh Congresses and served from April 20, 1897, to March 3, 1903; was not a candidate for reelection; resumed his former business pursuits and resided in Butler, Pa.; moved to Pittsburgh, Pa., and then to Washington, D.C.; also engaged in the development of land in southern Florida; died in Washington, D.C., December 3, 1932; interment in North Cemetery, Butler, Pa.

**SHOWER, Jacob,** a Representative from Maryland; born in Manchester, Baltimore County, Md., February 22, 1803; was a drummer boy in the War of 1812; attended private schools at Emmitsburg, Md., and was graduated from the medical department of the University of Maryland at Baltimore in 1825; commenced the practice of his profession in Carroll County, Md.; charter member of the first Andrew Jackson Club in the State in 1824; Democratic member of the State house of delegates 1834-1840; clerk of the circuit court of Carroll County 1842-1850; delegate to the State constitutional convention in 1851; elected as a Democrat to the Thirty-third Congress (March 4, 1853-March 3, 1855); resumed medical practice; died in Manchester, Md., May 25, 1879.

**SHREVE, Milton William,** a Representative from Pennsylvania; born in Chapmanville, Venango County, Pa., May 3, 1858; attended the Edinboro State Normal School and Allegheny College, Meadville, Pa.; graduated from Bucknell University, Lewisburg, Pa., in 1884; studied law; admitted to the bar in Erie County and commenced practice in Erie, Pa.; district attorney of Erie County 1899-1902; member of the Pennsylvania house of representatives 1907-1912 and in the session of 1911 succeeded to the speakership; elected as a Republican to the Sixty-third Congress (March 4, 1913-March 3, 1915); unsuccessful candidate for reelection in 1914 to the Sixty-fourth Congress; resumed the practice of law in Erie; also engaged in banking and interested in several manufacturing plants; elected as a Republican to the Sixty-sixth Congress; reelected as an Independent Republican to the Sixty-seventh Congress and as a Republican to the Sixty-eighth through Seventy-second Congresses (March 4, 1919-March 3, 1933); unsuccessful candidate for reelection in 1932 to the Seventy-third Congress; resumed the practice of law in Erie, Pa., until his death there on December 23, 1939; interment in Erie Cemetery.

**SHRIVER, Garner E.,** a Representative from Kansas; born in Towanda, Butler County, Kans., July 6, 1912; attended the public schools of Towanda and Wichita; moved to Wichita, Kans., in 1925; B.A., University of Wichita, 1934 (postgraduate study at University of Southern California in 1936); LL.B., Washburn Law School, 1940 and J.D., 1970; worked for a drug company in Wichita, 1934-1936; teacher at South Haven High School in 1936 and 1937; was admitted to the bar in Wichita in February 1940; served for three years in the United States Navy as an enlisted man and officer, 1943-1946; member, Kansas State house of representatives, 1947-1951; Kansas State senator, 1953-1960; elected as a Republican to the Eighty-seventh and to the seven succeeding Congresses (January 3, 1961-January 3, 1977); unsuccessful candidate for reelection in 1976 to the Ninety-fifth Congress; minority staff director and legal counsel for the Senate Veterans' Affairs Committee, Washington, D.C., 1977-1980, and general counsel, 1981-1982; resumed the practice of law; is a resident of Wichita, Kans.

**SHUFORD, Alonzo Craig,** a Representative from North Carolina; born on a farm near Newton, Catawba County, N.C., March 1, 1858; attended the common schools and Newton College; engaged in agricultural pursuits; joined the Farmers Alliance in 1889 and was a county and district lecturer; delegate to the labor conference at St. Louis, Mo., in February 1892; also a delegate to the Populist convention at Omaha, Nebr., in July 1892; elected vice president of the State Alliance in 1894; elected as a Populist to the Fifty-fourth and Fifty-fifth Congresses (March 4, 1895-March 3, 1899); unsuccessful candidate for renomination in 1898; resumed agricultural pursuits near Newton, N.C.; presidential elector on the Progressive ticket in 1924; retired from active business pursuits in 1928 and moved to Chapel Hill, N.C., where he died on February 8, 1933; interment in Chapel Hill Cemetery.

**SHUFORD, George Adams,** a Representative from North Carolina; born in Asheville, Buncombe County, N.C., September 5, 1895; attended the public schools and the University of North Carolina 1913-1915; graduated from the University of Georgia at Athens in 1917; was admitted to the Georgia bar in 1917; during the First World War entered the first officers' training camp at Fort McPherson, Ga., in May 1917; was commissioned a second lieutenant in August 1917 and assigned to the One Hundred and Nineteenth Infantry Regiment of the Thirtieth Combat Division; commissioned a first lieutenant in January 1918 and served in the United States and France; was discharged at Camp Jackson, S.C., April 28, 1919; was admitted to the North Carolina bar in August 1920 and commenced practice in Asheville, N.C.; chairman of Buncombe County board of elections 1940-1942; served in the North

Carolina State house of representatives 1945-1947; State superior court judge 1947-1949; elected as a Democrat to the Eighty-third and to the two succeeding Congresses (January 3, 1953-January 3, 1959); had been renominated for the Eighty-sixth Congress in the May 1958 primary election, but withdrew on July 27, 1958 because of ill health; resumed the practice of law; resided in Asheville, N.C., until his death there on December 8, 1962; interment in Riverside Cemetery.

**SHULL, Joseph Horace,** a Representative from Pennsylvania; born at Martins Creek, Northampton County, Pa., August 17, 1848; attended the public schools and Blair Hall, Blairstown, N.J.; took a special course at Lafayette College, Easton, Pa.; graduated from the University of New York and in 1873 from the Bellevue Hospital Medical College, both in New York City; taught in the public schools of Pennsylvania for four years; studied law; admitted to the bar in 1879 and commenced practice in Stroudsburg, Monroe County, Pa.; editor of the Monroe Democrat 1881-1886; member of the Pennsylvania senate 1886-1891; elected as a Democrat to the Fifty-eighth Congress (March 4, 1903-March 3, 1905); unsuccessful candidate for renomination in 1904; resumed the practice of law and medicine; was a contract surgeon during the First World War; died in Stroudsburg, Pa., August 9, 1944; interment in Stroudsburg Cemetery.

**SHULTZ, Emanuel,** a Representative from Ohio; born in Stouchsburg, Berks County, Pa., July 25, 1819; attended the public schools; apprenticed to the trade of shoemaker; moved to Miamisburg, Montgomery County, Ohio, in 1838; engaged in mercantile pursuits, banking, and the manufacture of paper; member of the State constitutional convention in 1873; member of the State house of representatives 1875-1877; elected as a Republican to the Forty-seventh Congress (March 4, 1881-March 3, 1883); unsuccessful candidate for renomination in 1882; again engaged in paper making; appointed postmaster of Miamisburg and served from August 2, 1889, to January 17, 1894; died in Miamisburg, Ohio, November 5, 1912; interment in Hill Grove Cemetery.

**SHUMWAY, Norman David,** a Representative from California; born in Phoenix, Maricopa County, Ariz., July 28, 1934; educated in the Stockton public schools; graduated from Stockton High School, 1952; A.A., Stockton (Calif.) College, 1954; B.S., University of Utah, Salt Lake City, 1960; J.D., Hastings College of Law, University of California, San Francisco, 1963; admitted to the California bar in 1964 and commenced practice in Downey, Calif.; appointed to the San Joaquin County Board of Supervisors by Governor Ronald Reagan in 1974; elected in 1974, and reelected in 1976; elected as a Republican to the Ninety-sixth and to the five succeeding Congresses (January 3, 1979-January 3, 1991); was not a candidate for renomination in 1990 to the One Hundred Second Congress; appointed by Governor Pete Wilson to the California Public Utilities Commission in 1991; is a resident of Stockton, Calif.

**SHUSTER, E.G. (Bud),** a Representative from Pennsylvania; born in Glassport, Allegheny County, Pa., January 23, 1932; attended the public schools of Glassport; B.S., University of Pittsburgh, 1954; M.B.A., Duquesne University, Pittsburgh, 1960; Ph.D., economics and management, American University, Washington, D.C., 1967; served in the Infantry, United States Army, 1954-1956; vice president, computer division, RCA Corporation; founder and chair of a computer software company; delegate to the Republican National Conventions of 1976, 1980, 1984 and 1988; elected as a Republican to the Ninety-third and to the eleven succeeding Congresses (January 3, 1973-January 3, 1997); chairman, Committee on Transportation and Infrastructure (One Hundred Fourth Congress); is a resident of Everett, Pa.

**SIBAL, Abner Woodruff,** a Representative from Connecticut; born in Ridgewood, Queens County, N.Y., April 11, 1921; graduated from Norwalk High School in 1938; A.B., Wesleyan University, 1943; LL.B., St. John's Law School, 1949; enlisted in the United States Army in March 1943, served in the European and Pacific Theaters, and was discharged as a first lieutenant in September 1946; was admitted to the Connecticut bar in 1949 and to the Federal bar in 1965; prosecuting attorney in Norwalk City Court, 1951-1955; corporation counsel, city of Norwalk, 1959-1960; member of the Connecticut State senate, 1956-1960, serving as minority leader the last two years; chairman of the Connecticut Commission on Corporation Law in 1959; delegate to each Connecticut Republican State Convention from 1952 to 1968; delegate to the Republican National Convention of 1964; elected as a Republican to the Eighty-seventh and Eighty-eighth Congresses (January 3, 1961-January 3, 1965); was an unsuccessful candidate for reelection in 1964 to the Eighty-ninth Congress; general counsel, United States Equal Employment Opportunity Commission, 1975-1978; resumed the practice of law in Connecticut, and in Washington, D.C.; is a resident of Avon, Conn.

**SIBLEY, Henry Hastings** (son of Solomon Sibley), a Delegate from the Territories of Wisconsin and Minnesota; born in Detroit, Mich., February 20, 1811; attended the Detroit Academy and also studied under private tutors; studied law; moved to Sault Ste. Marie in 1828 and engaged in mercantile pursuits until 1829, when he moved to Mackinac and entered the service of the American Fur Co.; justice of the peace in 1831; moved to the mouth of the Minnesota River in 1834 and engaged in fur trading; elected as a Delegate from the Territory of Wisconsin to the Thirtieth Congress to fill the vacancy caused by the disqualification of John H. Tweedy and served from October 30, 1848, to March 3, 1849; upon the formation of the Territory of Minnesota was elected as a Delegate to the Thirty-first and Thirty-second Congresses and served from July 7, 1849, to March 3, 1853; declined to be a candidate for renomination in 1852 to the Thirty-third Congress; member of the Territorial Legislature of Minnesota in 1855; member of the constitutional convention of Minnesota in 1857, and served as president; elected the first Governor of the State of Minnesota in 1857 and served from May 24, 1858 to January 2, 1860; regent of the State university, 1860-1869, and president of the board of regents, 1876-1891; served in the Union Army as brigadier general of Volunteers from 1862 until he was honorably mustered out April 30, 1866; moved to St. Paul, Minn.; interested in banking, railroads, and other public corporations; president of the St. Paul Gas Co. in 1866; president of the Minnesota Historical Society, 1879-1891; unsuccessful candidate for election in 1880 to the Forty-seventh Congress; appointed by President Chester A. Arthur in 1883 as president of the commission to settle damage claims of the Ojibway Indians resulting from the construction of national reservoirs; died in St. Paul, Minn., February 18, 1891; interment in Oakland Cemetery.

Bibliography: *DAB*; Jorstad, Erling T. "The Life of Henry Hastings Sibley." Ph.D. dissertation, University of Wisconsin, 1957.

**SIBLEY, Jonas,** a Representative from Massachusetts; born in Sutton, Mass., on March 7, 1762; completed preparatory studies; served as selectman during 1801-1803, and again in 1819; town moderator from 1802 to 1827; town treasurer, 1806-1816; member of the Massachusetts house of representatives, 1806-1822, and 1827-1829; member of the Massachusetts senate in 1826; delegate to the Massachusetts constitutional convention in 1820; elected to the Eighteenth Congress (March 4, 1823-March 3, 1825); unsuccessful candidate for reelection in 1824 to the Nineteenth Congress; engaged in agricultural pursuits; died in Sutton, Worcester County, Mass., February 5, 1834; interment in Center Cemetery.

**SIBLEY, Joseph Crocker,** (granduncle of Edwin Arthur Hall), a Representative from Pennsylvania; born in Friendship, Allegany County, N.Y., February 18, 1850; in 1859 moved with his parents to Boston, N.Y.; attended the county schools and the local academies at Springville and Friendship; taught school and studied medicine; engaged in the oil refining business in Franklin, Pa., and also in manufacturing and agricultural pursuits; mayor of Franklin, Pa., in 1879; elected as a Democrat to the Fifty-third Congress (March 4, 1893-March 3, 1895); unsuccessful candidate of the Democratic and Populist Parties for reelection in 1894 to the Fifty-fourth Congress, and for election in 1896 to the Fifty-fifth Congress; elected as a Democrat to the Fifty-sixth Congress (March 4, 1899-March 3, 1901); elected as a Republican to the Fifty-seventh and to the two succeeding Congresses (March 4, 1901-March 3, 1907); chairman, Committee on Manufactures (Fifty-eighth and Fifty-ninth Congresses); declined to be a candidate for renomination in 1906 to the Sixtieth Congress; was nominated to the Sixty-second Congress in 1910, but declined to conduct the campaign because of ill health; chairman of the Republican State convention in 1902; resumed his former manufacturing and agricultural pursuits; died at his home, "River Ridge Farm," near Franklin, Pa., on May 19, 1926; interment in Franklin Cemetery.

Bibliography: *DAB.*

**SIBLEY, Mark Hopkins,** a Representative from New York; born in Great Barrington, Mass., in 1796; completed preparatory studies; studied law; was admitted to the bar and commenced practice in Canandaigua, N.Y., in 1814; member of the State assembly in 1834 and 1835; elected as a Whig to the Twenty-fifth Congress (March 4, 1837-March 3, 1839); member of the State senate in 1841; judge of Ontario County 1847-1851; resumed the practice of his profession; died in Canandaigua, Ontario County, N.Y., September 8, 1852; interment in West Avenue Cemetery.

**SIBLEY, Solomon** (father of Henry Hastings Sibley), a Delegate from the Territory of Michigan; born in Sutton, Mass., October 7, 1769; completed preparatory studies, and in 1794 was graduated from the College of Rhode Island at Providence; studied law; was admitted to the bar in 1795 and commenced practice in Marietta, Ohio; moved to Detroit, Mich., in 1797 and continued the practice of law; was a member of the Territorial legislature of Northwest Territory in 1799; mayor of Detroit, Mich., in 1806; president of the board of trustees of Detroit in 1815; auditor of Michigan Territory, 1814-1817; United States attorney, Michigan Territory, by appointment of President James Madison, 1815-1823; elected to the Sixteenth Congress to fill the vacancy caused by the resignation of William W. Woodbridge; reelected to the Seventeenth Congress and served from November 20, 1820, to March 3, 1823; was not a candidate for reelection in 1822 to the Eighteenth Congress; judge of the supreme court of Michigan Territory, 1824-1837; resumed the practice of law; died in Detroit, Mich., April 4, 1846; interment in Elmwood Cemetery.

**SICKLES, Carlton Ralph,** a Representative from Maryland; born in Hamden, New Haven County, Conn., June 15, 1921; graduated from Roosevelt High School, Washington, D.C., in 1939; B.S.S., Georgetown University, 1943; J.D., Georgetown University School of Law, 1948; served with the Chinese Combat Command, United States Army, 1943-1946, with service in India and China; served as a captain in 1951 and 1952, during the Korean conflict, with the United States Air Force in the Office of Special Investigations; admitted to the bar in 1949 and began the practice of law in Washington, D.C., and Maryland; taught at Georgetown University Law School, 1960-1966; served in the Maryland State house of delegates, 1955-1962; member, joint commission to establish regional transit compact, Washington Metropolitan Transit Authority, 1955-1966, chairman, 1960-1966; delegate to the Democratic National Conventions of 1964, 1968, and 1972; elected

as a Democrat to the Eighty-eighth and Eighty-ninth Congresses (January 3, 1963-January 3, 1967); was not a candidate for reelection in 1966 to the Ninetieth Congress, but was an unsuccessful candidate for nomination for Governor of Maryland; resumed the practice of law; delegate, Maryland Constitutional Convention, 1967-1968; president, Carday Associates, Inc.; member, Maryland State Planning Commission; member, Washington Metropolitan Area Transit Authority, 1967-1973, 1975-1978, and 1981 to present; was an unsuccessful candidate in 1986 for nomination to the One Hundredth Congress; pension consultant and administrator; is a resident of Rockville, Md.

**SICKLES, Daniel Edgar,** a Representative from New York; born in New York City, October 20, 1819; attended New York University; apprenticed as a printer; studied law; was admitted to the bar in 1846 and commenced practice in New York City; member of the New York State assembly in 1847; corporation attorney in 1853; secretary of the legation at London by appointment of President Franklin Pierce, 1853-1855; member of the New York State senate in 1856 and 1857; elected as a Democrat to the Thirty-fifth and Thirty-sixth Congresses (March 4, 1857-March 3, 1861); was not a candidate for renomination in 1860 to the Thirty-seventh Congress; served in the Civil War as colonel of the Seventeenth Regiment, New York Volunteer Infantry, and brigadier general and major general of Volunteers; retired with rank of major general on April 14, 1869; awarded the Congressional Medal of Honor on October 30, 1897, for action at the Battle of Gettysburg, July 2, 1863; intrusted with a special mission to the South American Republics in 1865; named Minister Resident to the Netherlands on May 13, 1866, but declined the appointment; appointed Envoy Extraordinary and Minister Plenipotentiary to Spain on May 15, 1869, and served until January 1874; chairman of the New York State Civil Service Commission in 1888 and 1889; sheriff of New York City in 1890; elected as a Democrat to the Fifty-third Congress (March 4, 1893-March 3, 1895); unsuccessful candidate for reelection in 1894 to the Fifty-fourth Congress; resided in New York City until his death there on May 3, 1914; interment in Arlington National Cemetery, Va.

Bibliography: *DAB*; Swanberg, W.A. *Sickles the Incredible.* New York: Scribner, 1956.

**SICKLES, Nicholas,** a Representative from New York; born in Kinderhook, Ulster County, N.Y., September 11, 1801; attended private schools and Kinderhook Academy; studied law; was admitted to the bar in 1823 and commenced practice in Kingston, N.Y.; elected as a Jacksonian to the Twenty-fourth Congress (December 7, 1835-March 3, 1837); prosecuting attorney of Ulster County, N.Y., in 1836 and 1837; served as surrogate of Ulster County from January 1, 1844, until his death in Kingston, Ulster County, N.Y., May 13, 1845; interment in Houghtaling Burying Ground.

**SIEGEL, Isaac,** a Representative from New York; born in New York City April 12, 1880; attended the public schools and pursued a supplementary course of study in New York City; was graduated from New York University Law School in 1901; was admitted to the bar May 26, 1902, and commenced practice in New York City; was appointed special deputy attorney general for the prosecution of election frauds in 1909 and 1910; elected as a Republican to the Sixty-fourth and to the three succeeding Congresses (March 4, 1915-March 3, 1923); chairman, Committee on the Census (Sixty-sixth and Sixty-seventh Congresses); was not a candidate for renomination in 1922 to the Sixty-eighth Congress; during the First World War was a member of the overseas commission which visited France and Italy during July and August 1918; delegate to the Republican National Conventions in 1916, 1920, 1924, and 1936; resumed the practice of law; appointed as a magistrate of New York City on July 4, 1939, and served until September 14, 1940, when he was appointed to the bench; justice of the domestic relations court of New York City until his death in that city on June 29, 1947; interment in Field Cemetery, Brooklyn, N.Y.

**SIEMINSKI, Alfred Dennis,** a Representative from New Jersey; born in Jersey City, Hudson County, N.J., August 23, 1911; attended the public schools, New York Military Academy, Cornwall-on-the-Hudson, N.Y. and Hun School, Princeton, N.J.; was graduated from Princeton University in 1934; student, Harvard Law School in 1935 and 1936; comptroller and vice president of Brunswick Laundry, Jersey City, N.J., beginning in 1937; entered the United States Army as a private in 1942; served in Italian campaign with the Ninety-second Buffalo Division in 1944 and 1945; captain, Military Government Division in Austria, in 1945 and 1946; served with the Tenth Corps in Korea in 1950, and was elected to Congress while on active duty; discharged to the Infantry Reserve as a major in 1950, and promoted to lieutenant colonel in 1956; elected as a Democrat to the Eighty-second and to the three succeeding Congresses (January 3, 1951-January 3, 1959); unsuccessful candidate for renomination in 1958 to the Eighty-sixth Congress; administrative vice president of the Hun School; engaged in administrative education and project development; worked at the Medical and General Reference Library, Veterans Administration, Washington, D.C., 1962-1973; was a resident of Vienna, Va.; died December 13, 1990.

**SIKES, Robert Lee Fulton,** a Representative from Florida; born in Isabella, near Sylvester, Worth County, Ga., June 3, 1906; attended the public schools; B.S., University of Georgia, Athens, 1927; M.S., University of Florida, Gainesville, 1929; published the Okaloosa (Fla.) News-Journal, Crestview, Fla., 1933-1946; president of the Florida Press Association in 1937; served in the Florida State house of representatives, 1936-1940; elected as a Democrat to the Seventy-seventh and Seventy-eighth Congresses, and served from January 3, 1941 until his resignation on October 19, 1944, to enter the United States Army during the Second World War; delegate to the Interparliamentary Conference in Warsaw, 1959; elected to the Seventy-ninth and to the sixteen succeeding Congresses (January 3, 1945-January 3, 1979); was not a candidate for reelection in 1978 to the Ninety-sixth Congress; was a resident of Crestview, Fla., until his death there on September 28, 1994.
**Bibliography:** Sikes, Bob. *He-Coon: The Bob Sikes Story.* Pensacola, Fla.: Perdido Bay Press, 1984.

**SIKORSKI, Gerald Edward,** a Representative from Minnesota; born in Breckenridge, Wilkin County, Minn., April 26, 1948; graduated from Breckenridge High School, 1966; B.A., University of Minnesota, Minneapolis, 1970; J.D., University of Minnesota Law School, Minneapolis, 1973; admitted to the Minnesota bar, 1973 and commenced practice in Stillwater, 1974; Minnesota State senator, 1976-1982; elected as a Democratic-Farmer-Labor candidate to the Ninety-eighth and to the four succeeding Congresses (January 3, 1983-January 3, 1993); unsuccessful candidate for reelection in 1992 to the One Hundred Third Congress; is a resident of Stillwater, Minn.

**SILER, Eugene,** a Representative from Kentucky; born in Williamsburg, Whitley County, Ky., June 26, 1900; attended the public schools; graduated from Cumberland College, Williamsburg, Ky., in 1920 and from the University of Kentucky at Lexington in 1922; law student at Columbia University in 1922 and University of Kentucky until 1924; was admitted to the bar in 1923 and commenced the practice of law in Williamsburg, Ky.; during the First World War served as an enlisted man in the United States Navy, and in the Second World War served as a captain in the United States Army 1942-1945; elected judge of the Court of Appeals of Kentucky in 1945 and served until January 1, 1949; unsuccessful Republican candidate for Governor of Kentucky in 1951; trustee of Cumberland College; director of the Bank of Williamsburg and

Kingsport Grocery Co.; elected as a Republican to the Eighty-fourth and to the four succeeding Congresses (January 3, 1955-January 3, 1965); was not a candidate in 1964 for renomination to the Eighty-ninth Congress; was a resident of Williamsburg, Ky., until his death in Louisville, Ky., on December 5, 1987; interment in Highland Cemetery, Williamsburg.

**SILJANDER, Mark Deli,** a Representative from Michigan; born in Chicago, Cook County, Ill., June 11, 1951; attended the public schools; graduated from Oak Park-River Forest High School, 1969; B.S., Western Michigan University, Kalamazoo, 1972, and M.A., 1973; trustee, Fabius Township Board, St. Joseph County, 1972-1976; real estate broker; served in the Michigan State house of representatives, 1977-1981; delegate to the Republican National Convention of 1980; elected as Republican to the Ninety-seventh Congress, April 21, 1981, by special election to fill the vacancy caused by the resignation of David A. Stockman; reelected to the two succeeding Congresses, and served from April 21, 1981 to January 3, 1987; unsuccessful candidate for renomination in 1986 to the One Hundredth Congress; delegate to the United Nations General Assembly, September 1987-September 1988; president of a consulting firm in Washington, D.C., and operates an import-export firm; radio commentator; is a resident of Reston, Va.

**SILL, Thomas Hale,** a Representative from Pennsylvania; born in Windsor, Conn., October 11, 1783; completed preparatory studies; graduated, Brown University, Providence, R.I., in 1804; studied law; admitted to the bar in 1809 and commenced practice in Lebanon, Ohio; moved to Erie, Pa., in 1813 and resumed the practice of law; member of the staff of General Wallace and also a member of the Minutemen of the Pennsylvania militia; deputy United States marshal 1816-1818; deputy attorney general in 1819; member of the Pennsylvania house of representatives in 1823; elected to the Nineteenth Congress to fill the vacancy caused by the death of Patrick Farrelly and served from March 14, 1826, to March 3, 1827; elected to the Twenty-first Congress (March 4, 1829-March 3, 1831); declined to be a candidate for renomination in 1830; president of the United States branch bank at Erie, Pa., in 1837; member of the Pennsylvania constitutional convention in 1837 and 1838; presidential elector on the Whig ticket in 1848; postmaster of Erie, Pa., 1847-1853; served as a director of the Erie Academy for more than thirty years; engaged in the practice of his profession until his death in Erie, Pa., on February 7, 1856; interment in Erie Cemetery.

**SILSBEE, Nathaniel,** a Representative and a Senator from Massachusetts; born in Salem, Mass., on January 14, 1773; attended private schools; went to sea and became a sea captain, ship owner and merchant; held several local offices in Salem and Boston; elected to the Fifteenth and Sixteenth Congresses (March 4, 1817-March 3, 1821); was not a candidate for renomination; elected to the Massachusetts house of representatives in 1821; member, Massachusetts senate 1823-1825, serving as president; presidential elector in 1824; elected to the United States Senate in 1826 to fill the vacancy caused by the resignation of James Lloyd; reelected in 1829 and served from May 31, 1826, to March 3, 1835; declined to be a candidate for reelection; chairman, Committee on Commerce (Twenty-third Congress); Whig presidential elector in 1836; resumed mercantile pursuits in Salem, Mass., where he died on July 14, 1850; interment in Harmony Grove Cemetery.
**Bibliography:** *DAB.*

**SILVESTER, Peter** (grandfather of Peter Henry Silvester), a Representative from New York; born at Shelter Island, Long Island, N.Y., in 1734; completed preparatory studies; studied law; was admitted to the bar in 1763 and practiced in Albany, N.Y.; member of the Albany Common Council in 1772; member of the committee of safety in 1774; served in the First and Second Provincial Congresses in 1775 and 1776; moved to Kinderhook, N.Y., and practiced law; appointed judge of the court of common pleas of Columbia County in

1786; regent of the University of the State of New York 1787-1808; elected to the First and Second Congresses (March 4, 1789-March 3, 1793); served in the State assembly in 1788; member of the State senate 1796-1800; again served in the State assembly 1803-1806; retired from public life; died in Kinderhook, Columbia County, N.Y., October 15, 1808; interment in Old Van Schaack Cemetery, over which the Reformed Dutch Church was built in 1814.

**SILVESTER, Peter Henry** (grandson of Peter Silvester), a Representative from New York; born in Kinderhook, Columbia County, N.Y., February 17, 1807; attended Kinderhook Academy, and was graduated from Union College, Schenectady, N.Y., in 1827; studied law; was admitted to the bar in 1830 and practiced his profession in Coxsackie, N.Y.; elected as a Whig to the Thirtieth and Thirty-first Congresses (March 4, 1847-March 3, 1851); retired and lived on one of his farms in Coxsackie, Greene County, N.Y., until his death on November 29, 1882; interment in Kinderhook Cemetery, Kinderhook, Columbia County, N.Y.

**SIMKINS, Eldred,** a Representative from South Carolina; born in Edgefield, S.C., August 30, 1779; attended a private academy at Willington, Abbeville District, S.C., and was graduated from South Carolina College (now the University of South Carolina) at Columbia; attended Litchfield (Conn.) Law School for three years; was admitted to the bar in 1805 and commenced practice in Edgefield, S.C., in 1806; member of the State house of representatives; served in the State senate 1810-1812; Lieutenant Governor of the State 1812-1814; elected as a Republican to the Fifteenth Congress to fill the vacancy caused by the resignation of John C. Calhoun; reelected to the Sixteenth Congress and served from January 24, 1818, to March 3, 1821; chairman, Committee on Public Expenditures (Sixteenth Congress); declined to be a candidate for renomination; again a member of the State house of representatives, 1828-1829; resumed the practice of his profession and also engaged in planting; died in Edgefield, Edgefield County, S.C., November 17, 1831; interment in Cedar Fields, the family burial ground, near Edgefield, S.C.

**SIMMONS, Furnifold McLendel,** a Representative and a Senator from North Carolina; born on his father's plantation near Polloksville, Jones County, N.C., January 20, 1854; attended a private school and Wake Forest (N.C.) College; graduated from Trinity College (now Duke University), Durham, N.C., in 1873; studied law; was admitted to the bar in 1875; moved to New Bern, Craven County, N.C., in 1876 and commenced the practice of law; elected as a Democrat to the Fiftieth Congress (March 4, 1887-March 3, 1889); unsuccessful candidate for reelection in 1888 to the Fifty-first Congress, and for election in 1890 to the Fifty-second Congress; resumed the practice of his profession in New Bern; appointed by President Grover Cleveland as collector of internal revenue for the fourth district of North Carolina, 1893-1897; elected as a Democrat to the United States Senate in 1900; reelected in 1906, 1912, 1918, and again in 1924, and served from March 4, 1901 to March 3, 1931; unsuccessful candidate for renomination in 1930; chairman, Committee on Disposition of Useless Executive Papers (Sixty-first Congress), Committee on Engrossed Bills (Sixty-first and Sixty-second Congresses), Committee on Finance (Sixty-third through Sixty-fifth Congresses), Committee on Additional Accommodations for the Library of Congress (Sixty-sixth Congress); resided in New Bern, N.C., until his death there on April 30, 1940; interment in Cedar Grove Cemetery.

Bibliography: *DAB*; Rippy, J. Fred, ed. *F.M. Simmons: Statesman of the New South.* Durham: Duke University Press, 1936; Watson, Richard L., Jr. "Furnifold M. Simmons and the Politics of White Supremacy." Chap. 5 in *Race, Class, and Politics in Southern History.* Edited by Jeffrey J. Crow, Paul D. Escott, and Charles L. Flynn, Jr. Baton Rouge: Louisiana State University Press, 1989.

**SIMMONS, George Abel,** a Representative from New York; born in Lyme, N.H., September 8, 1791; attended the district school; was graduated from Dartmouth College, Hanover, N.H., in 1816; moved to Lansingburg, Rensselaer County, N.Y., and was principal of the local academy; studied law; was admitted to the bar in 1825 and commenced practice in Keeseville, Essex County, N.Y.; member of the State assembly 1840-1842; member of the State constitutional convention in 1846; elected as a Whig to the Thirty-third and Thirty-fourth Congresses (March 4, 1853-March 3, 1857); chairman, Committee on the Judiciary (Thirty-fourth Congress); was not a candidate for reelection in 1856; resumed the practice of his profession in Keeseville, N.Y., where he died October 27, 1857; interment in Evergreen Cemetery.

**SIMMONS, James Fowler,** a Senator from Rhode Island; born on a farm near Little Compton, Newport County, R.I., September 10, 1795; attended a private school in Newport, R.I.; moved to Providence, R.I., in 1812; employed in various manufacturing concerns in Rhode Island and Massachusetts; engaged in the manufacture of yarn at Simmonsville, N.H., in 1822; moved to Johnston, R.I., in 1827 and resumed the manufacture of yarns and engaged in agricultural pursuits; member, State house of representatives 1828-1841; elected as a Whig to the United States Senate and served from March 4, 1841, to March 3, 1847; unsuccessful candidate for reelection in 1846 and for election in 1850 to the United States Senate; chairman, Committee on Manufactures (Twenty-seventh and Twenty-eighth Congresses), Committee on Printing (Twenty-seventh and Twenty-eighth Congresses); returned to Johnston, R.I., and resumed his former pursuits; again elected to the United States Senate as a Republican and served from March 4, 1857, to August 15, 1862, when he resigned; chairman, Committee on Patents and the Patent Office (Thirty-seventh Congress); resumed his former manufacturing pursuits; died in Johnston, R.I., July 10, 1864; interment in North End Cemetery, Providence, R.I.

**SIMMONS, James Samuel** (nephew of Milton George Urner), a Representative from New York; born near Liberty, Frederick County, Md., November 25, 1861; attended the public schools and the local academy at Liberty; was graduated from Frederick College; moved to Roanoke, Va., in 1880 and engaged in the real estate business; moved to Niagara Falls, N.Y., in 1894 and continued in the real estate business; chairman of the Republican city committee in 1907 and 1908; elected as a Republican to the Sixty-first and Sixty-second Congresses (March 4, 1909-March 3, 1913); unsuccessful candidate for reelection in 1912 to the Sixty-third Congress; delegate to the Republican National Convention in 1912; resumed the real estate business in Niagara Falls, N.Y., and also, in 1927, in St. Petersburg, Fla., where he died November 28, 1935; interment in Riverdale Cemetery, Lewiston, N.Y.

**SIMMONS, Robert Glenmore,** a Representative from Nebraska; born in Scotts Bluff County, near Scottsbluff, Nebr., December 25, 1891; attended the public schools and Hastings (Nebr.) College, 1909-1911; was graduated from the law college of the University of Nebraska at Lincoln in 1915; was admitted to the bar the same year and commenced practice in Gering, Nebr.; elected prosecuting attorney of Scotts Bluff County in 1916; during the First World War enlisted in the Army on October 15, 1917, and was commissioned as a second lieutenant in the Air Service, March 12, 1918, being discharged on January 14, 1919; elected as a Republican to the Sixty-eighth and to the four succeeding Congresses (March 4, 1923-March 3, 1933); unsuccessful candidate for reelection in 1932 to the Seventy-third Congress; unsuccessful candidate for election to the United States Senate in 1934 and again in 1936; resumed the practice of law in Lincoln, Nebr.; elected chief justice of Nebraska in 1938, and served until his retirement in January 1963; deputy judge, administrative tribunal of the International Labor Organization, Geneva, Switzerland, in 1955; returned to private law practice in Lincoln, Nebr., where he died on December 27, 1969; interment in Fairview Cemetery, Scottsbluff, Nebr.

**SIMMS, Albert Gallatin** (husband of Ruth Hanna McCormick), a Representative from New Mexico; born in Washington, Hempstead County, Ark., October 8, 1882; attended private schools and the University of Arkansas at Fayetteville; moved to Monterrey, Mexico, in 1906 and was employed as an accountant; moved to Silver City, N.Mex., in 1912; studied law; was admitted to the bar in 1915 and practiced law at Albuquerque, N.Mex., until 1919; member of the city council 1920-1922; member and chairman of the board of county commissioners of Bernalillo County, 1920-1922; engaged in banking, serving as president of a national bank in Albuquerque, 1920-1924, and as president of a mortgage company in 1924; member of the New Mexico house of representatives 1925-1927; elected as a Republican to the Seventy-first Congress (March 4, 1929-March 3, 1931); unsuccessful candidate for reelection in 1930 to the Seventy-second Congress; member of the Republican National Committee 1932-1934; banker, farmer, and rancher; was a resident of Albuquerque, N.Mex., where he died December 29, 1964; interment in Fairview Park Cemetery.

**SIMMS, William Emmett,** a Representative from Kentucky; born near Cynthiana, Harrison County, Ky., January 2, 1822; attended the public schools, and was graduated from the law department of Transylvania University, Lexington, Ky., in 1846; was admitted to the bar in 1846 and commenced practice in Paris, Bourbon County, Ky.; served as captain throughout the Mexican War; member of the Kentucky house of representatives, 1849-1851; was elected as a Democrat to the Thirty-sixth Congress (March 4, 1859-March 3, 1861); unsuccessful candidate for reelection in 1860 to the Thirty-seventh Congress; on October 21, 1861, was appointed to the temporary rank of colonel in the Confederate Army; appointed lieutenant colonel in the Provisional Army of the Confederate States, December 24, 1861, and was assigned to the First Battalion, Kentucky Cavalry; resigned February 17, 1862, having been chosen Senator from Kentucky to the Confederate States Congress; member of the Senate of the First and Second Confederate Congresses; engaged in agricultural pursuits; died on his estate, "Mount Airy," near Paris, Bourbon County, Ky., June 25, 1898; interment in Paris Cemetery.

**SIMON, Joseph,** a Senator from Oregon; born in Bechtheim, Germany, February 7, 1851; immigrated to the United States with his parents, who settled in Portland, Oreg., in 1857; attended the public schools; studied law; was admitted to the bar in 1872 and commenced practice in Portland, Oreg.; member of the city council 1877-1880; member, State senate 1880-1898, frequently serving as president; member of the National Republican Committee 1892-1896; elected as a Republican to the United States Senate October 8, 1898, to fill the vacancy in the term commencing March 4, 1897, and served until March 3, 1903; was not a candidate for reelection; chairman, Committee on Irrigation and Reclamation of Arid Lands (Fifty-sixth and Fifty-seventh Congresses); mayor of Portland 1909-1911; resumed the practice of law; died in Portland, February 14, 1935; interment in Beth Israel Cemetery.

**SIMON, Paul Martin,** a Representative and a Senator from Illinois; born in Eugene, Lane County, Oreg., November 29, 1928; attended the public schools of Eugene and Concordia Academy High School, Portland, Oreg.; attended the University of Oregon, Eugene, 1945-1946 and Dana College, Blair, Nebr., 1946-1948; pursued a career as a newspaper editor and publisher in Troy, Ill., eventually building a chain of fourteen weeklies; served in the United States Army from 1951 until 1953; teacher at Sangamon State University, Springfield, Ill., 1972-1973, and John F. Kennedy School of Government, Harvard University, in 1973; member, Illinois State house of representatives, 1955-1963; member, Illinois State senate, 1963-1968; Lieutenant Governor of Illinois, 1969-1973; author;

elected as a Democrat to the Ninety-fourth and to the four succeeding Congresses (January 3, 1975-January 3, 1985); was not a candidate for reelection in 1984 to the House of Representatives, but was elected to the United States Senate; reelected in 1990, and served from January 3, 1985 to January 3, 1997; was not a candidate for reelection in 1996; unsuccessful candidate for the Democratic presidential nomination in 1988; is a resident of Makanda, Ill.

**SIMONDS, William Edgar,** a Representative from Connecticut; born in Collinsville, town of Canton, Hartford County, Conn., November 24, 1842; attended the public school and Collinsville High School, and was graduated from Connecticut State Normal School at New Britain in 1860; taught school; enlisted as a private in Company A, Twenty-fifth Regiment, Connecticut Volunteer Infantry, August 18, 1862; promoted to sergeant major before being mustered into the United States service; promoted to second lieutenant of Company I of his regiment April 24, 1863; awarded the Congressional Medal of Honor February 25, 1899 for action April 14, 1863; was graduated from Yale Law School in 1865; was admitted to the bar and commenced practice in Hartford, Conn.; member of the Connecticut State house of representatives in 1883 and 1885, and served as speaker in the latter year; elected as a Republican to the Fifty-first Congress (March 4, 1889-March 3, 1891); unsuccessful candidate for reelection in 1890 to the Fifty-second Congress; United States Commissioner of Patents, 1891-1893; resumed the practice of his profession; died in Hartford, Conn., March 14, 1903; interment in Canton Center Cemetery, Canton, Conn.

**SIMONS, Samuel,** a Representative from Connecticut; born in Bridgeport, Conn., in 1792; pursued an academic course; held several local offices; taught school; studied medicine and commenced practice in Bridgeport, Fairfield County, Conn.; member of the State house of representatives in 1830; director of the Housatonic Railroad; trustee of the Bridgeport Savings Bank; elected as a Democrat to the Twenty-eighth Congress (March 4, 1843-March 3, 1845); chairman, Committee on Engraving (Twenty-eighth Congress); resumed the practice of medicine in Bridgeport, Conn., where he died January 13, 1847; interment in Mountain Grove Cemetery.

**SIMONTON, Charles Bryson,** a Representative from Tennessee; born in Tipton County, Tenn., September 8, 1838; was graduated from Erskine College, Due West, S.C., in August 1859; enlisted as a private in Company C, Ninth Tennessee Infantry, Confederate Army, in 1861; subsequently became second lieutenant and then captain; was severely wounded in the Battle of Perryville, Ky., October 8, 1862, and disabled from any further active duty during the war; elected clerk of the circuit court of Tipton County in March 1870; studied law; was admitted to the bar in 1873 and commenced practice in Covington, Tenn.; member of the Tennessee State house of representatives in 1877-1879; editor of the Tipton Record in Covington, Tipton County, Tenn.; elected as a Democrat to the Forty-sixth and Forty-seventh Congresses (March 4, 1879-March 3, 1883); chairman of the Democratic State convention in 1886; president of the Covington city school board, 1892-1903; United States district attorney for the district of Tennessee, 1895-1898; died in Covington, Tenn., June 10, 1911; interment in Munford Cemetery.

**SIMONTON, William,** a Representative from Pennsylvania; born in West Hanover Township, near Harrisburg, Pa., February 12, 1788; received his early education from his mother and later attended a private school; was graduated from the medical department of the University of Pennsylvania at Philadelphia in 1810 and practiced his profession while residing on his farm near Hummelstown, Dauphin County, Pa.; elected auditor of Dauphin County in 1823 and served three years; one of the original supporters of the free-school system established by the act of 1834; elected as a Whig to the Twenty-sixth and Twenty-seventh

Congresses (March 4, 1839-March 3, 1843); died in South Hanover, Pa., May 17, 1846; interment in the Old Hanover Cemetery, north of Shellsville, Pa.

**SIMPKINS, John,** a Representative from Massachusetts; born in New Bedford, Bristol County, Mass., June 27, 1862; attended the public schools of Yarmouth and St. Mark's School, Southboro, Mass.; graduated from Harvard University in 1885; served in the Massachusetts senate in 1890 and 1891; president of the Republican Club of Massachusetts in 1892 and 1893; member of the Massachusetts Republican committee 1892-1894; elected as a Republican to the Fifty-fourth and Fifty-fifth Congresses and served from March 4, 1895, until his death in Washington, D.C., on March 27, 1898; interment in Woodside Cemetery, Yarmouth, Barnstable County, Mass.

**SIMPSON, Alan Kooi** (son of Milward Lee Simpson), a Senator from Wyoming; born in Denver, Colo., September 2, 1931; attended the public schools of Cody, Wyo.; graduated, Cody High School, 1949; B.S., University of Wyoming, Laramie, 1954; LL.B., University of Wyoming Law School, 1958; admitted to the Wyoming bar in 1958 and commenced practice in Cody; served in the United States Army, Infantry, 1954-1956; assistant attorney general of Wyoming, 1958-1959; city attorney, Cody, Wyo., and United States Commissioner, 1959-1969; member, Wyoming State house of representatives, 1964-1977; majority whip, 1973-1975, majority leader, 1975-1977, speaker pro tempore, 1977; elected as a Republican to the United States Senate, November 7, 1978, for the six-year term commencing January 3, 1979; subsequently appointed by the Governor, January 1, 1979, to fill the vacancy caused by the resignation of Clifford P. Hansen for the term ending January 3, 1979; reelected in 1984 and again in 1990, and served from January 1, 1979 to January 3, 1997; was not a candidate for reelection in 1996; Republican whip (Ninety-ninth through One Hundred Third Congresses); chairman, Committee on Veterans' Affairs (One Hundred Fourth Congress); is a resident of Cody, Wyo.

**SIMPSON, Edna Oakes** (wife of Sidney E. Simpson), a Representative from Illinois; born in Carrollton, Greene County, Ill., October 26, 1891; elected as a Republican to the Eighty-sixth Congress (January 3, 1959-January 3, 1961); did not seek renomination in 1960; was a resident of Carrollton, Ill., until her death in Alton, Ill., on May 15, 1984.

**SIMPSON, James, Jr.,** a Representative from Illinois; born in Chicago, Ill., January 7, 1905; attended St. Paul's School in Concord, N.H., 1919-1922, Westminster School, Salisbury, Conn., 1922-1925, and later a student at Harvard University; director of Marshall Field & Co., 1931-1960; elected as a Republican to the Seventy-third Congress (March 4, 1933-January 3, 1935); unsuccessful candidate for renomination in 1934; was admitted to the Illinois bar in 1939; owner and operator of farms near Wadsworth, Lake County, Ill., and Rapidan, Culpeper County, Va.; entered the United States Marine Corps in 1943 and served thirty-six months, with twenty-four months in the Pacific area, and was discharged as a captain; civilian aide to Secretary of the Army Robert Stevens in 1953 and 1954; died at his farm near Wadsworth, Ill., February 29, 1960; interment in Graceland Cemetery, Chicago, Ill.

**SIMPSON, Jeremiah,** a Representative from Kansas; born on Prince Edward Island, Canada, March 31, 1842; moved with his parents to Oneida County, N.Y., in 1848; attended the public schools; at the age of fourteen became a sailor and followed nautical pursuits from 1856 to 1879; served in the Civil War in Company A, Twelfth Regiment, Illinois Volunteer Infantry; moved to Barber County, Kans., in 1878 and settled near Medicine Lodge; engaged in farming and stock raising; on two occasions was an unsuccessful candidate for election on the Independent ticket to the Kansas house of representatives from Barber County; elected as a Populist to the

Fifty-second and Fifty-third Congresses (March 4, 1891-March 3, 1895); unsuccessful candidate for reelection in 1894 to the Fifty-fourth Congress; elected to the Fifty-fifth Congress (March 4, 1897-March 3, 1899); unsuccessful candidate for reelection in 1898 to the Fifty-sixth Congress; resumed his former pursuits; died in Wichita, Kans., October 23, 1905; interment in Maple Grove Cemetery.

**Bibliography:** *DAB*; Bicha, Karel Denis. "Jerry Simpson: Populist Without Principle." *Journal of American History* 54 (September 1967): 291-306.

**SIMPSON, Kenneth Farrand,** a Representative from New York; born in New York City May 4, 1895; attended private schools in New York City and Hill School, Pottstown, Pa.; was graduated from Yale University, in 1917 and from the law department of Harvard University in 1922; during the First World War served as captain, Three Hundred and Second Field Artillery, with one year of overseas service; commandant, American School Detachment University of Aix-Marseilles, in 1919; was admitted to the bar in 1922 and commenced practice in New York City; assistant United States attorney, southern district of New York, 1925-1927; chairman of Republican county committee 1935-1940; member of Republican National Conventions in 1936 and 1940; elected as a Republican to the Seventy-seventh Congress and served from January 3, 1941, until his death in New York City, January 25, 1941; interment in Hudson City Cemetery, Hudson, N.Y.

**SIMPSON, Milward Lee** (father of Alan Kooi Simpson), a Senator from Wyoming; born in Jackson, Teton County, Wyo., November 12, 1897; attended the public schools of Wood River, Meeteetse, and Cody; B.S., University of Wyoming, Laramie, 1921; attended Harvard University Law School, 1921-1925; during the First World War served as a second lieutenant in the Infantry, United States Army; admitted to the bar in 1926 and practiced law in Cody, Wyo., until 1955; member, Wyoming State house of representatives, 1926-1927; unsuccessful candidate in 1940 for election to the United States Senate; elected Governor of Wyoming in 1954 and served from January 3, 1955 to January 5, 1959; unsuccessful candidate for reelection in 1958; resumed law practice in 1959; appointed member of the board of trustees of University of Wyoming in 1939, and served as president, 1943-1954; member of the National Association of Governing Boards of State Universities and Allied Institutions in 1950, and served as president in 1952 and 1953; elected as a Republican to the United States Senate, November 6, 1962, to fill the vacancy caused by the death of Senator-elect Keith Thomson in the term ending January 3, 1967; was not a candidate for reelection in 1966; retired; was a resident of Cody, Wyo.; died June 10, 1993.

**SIMPSON, Richard Franklin,** a Representative from South Carolina; born in Laurens, S.C., March 24, 1798; was graduated from South Carolina College (now the University of South Carolina) at Columbia in 1816; studied law; was admitted to the bar in 1819 and began practice in Pendleton, S.C.; held several local offices; served as major during the Seminole War in 1835; member of the State senate 1835-1841; elected as a Democrat to the Twenty-eighth, Twenty-ninth, and Thirtieth Congresses (March 4, 1843-March 3, 1849); declined to be a candidate for renomination in 1848; engaged in agricultural pursuits; member of the secession convention in 1860 and signed the ordinance of secession; died in Pendleton, Anderson County, S.C., October 28, 1882; interment in the family cemetery near that city.

**SIMPSON, Richard Murray,** a Representative from Pennsylvania; born in Huntingdon, Pa., August 30, 1900; attended the public schools; graduated from the University of Pittsburgh, Pittsburgh, Pa., in 1923 and from Georgetown Law School, Washington, D.C., in 1942; during the First World War served as a private in the Three Hundred and First Company, Tank Corps;

engaged in the insurance business 1923-1937; served in the Pennsylvania house of representatives 1935-1937; elected as a Republican to the Seventy-fifth Congress to fill the vacancy caused by the death of Benjamin K. Focht; reelected to the Seventy-sixth and to the ten succeeding Congresses and served from May 11, 1937, until his death in Bethesda, Md., January 7, 1960; interment in Riverview Cemetery, Huntingdon, Pa.

**SIMPSON, Sidney Elmer** (husband of Edna Oakes Simpson), a Representative from Illinois; born in Carrollton, Greene County, Ill., September 20, 1894; attended the public schools and was graduated from Carrollton High School; during the First World War served in the United States Army, with overseas service; owner of Simpson Motor Co. and Simpson Bus Co.; served as chairman of the Greene County Republican Committee; member of the executive committee of the County Chairman's Association of Illinois; city treasurer of Carrollton, Ill., for one term; member of Carrollton Board of Education; elected as a Republican to the Seventy-eighth and to the seven succeeding Congresses and served from January 3, 1943, until his death; chairman, Committee on District of Columbia (Eighty-third Congress); had been renominated to the Eighty-sixth Congress; died in Pittsfield, Ill., October 26, 1958; interment in Carrollton City Cemetery, Carrollton, Ill.

**SIMS, Alexander Dromgoole** (nephew of George Coke Dromgoole), a Representative from South Carolina; born near Randals Ordinary, Brunswick County, Va., June 12, 1803; attended the rural schools of his native county and at the age of sixteen entered the University of North Carolina at Chapel Hill; was graduated from Union College, Schenectady, N.Y., in 1823; read law with General Dromgoole in Brunswick County, Va., and later was admitted to practice; moved to South Carolina in 1826 and settled in Darlington; assumed charge of Darlington (S.C.) Academy in 1827; was admitted to the bar of South Carolina in 1829 and practiced in Darlington; also engaged in literary pursuits; member, South Carolina State house of representatives, 1840-1843; elected as a Democrat to the Twenty-ninth and Thirtieth Congresses, and served from March 4, 1845 until his death in Kingstree, Williamsburg County, S.C., November 22, 1848; had been reelected to the Thirty-first Congress; interment in First Baptist Cemetery, Darlington, S.C.

**SIMS, Hugo Sheridan, Jr.,** a Representative from South Carolina; born in Orangeburg, S.C., October 14, 1921; attended the public schools; graduated from Wofford College, Spartanburg, S.C., in 1941; editor of the Times and Democrat, daily newspaper, Orangeburg, S.C., in 1941 and 1942; enlisted in the United States Army as a private in April 1942; commissioned a captain in November 1944 and commanded Company A, Five Hundred and First Parachute Infantry, One Hundred and First Airborne Division; discharged in October 1945 after serving overseas from January 1944 to September 1945; awarded the Distinguished Service Cross and Silver Star; graduated from the law school of the University of South Carolina at Columbia in 1947; was admitted to the bar August 28, 1947, and commenced the practice of law in Orangeburg, S.C.; member of the South Carolina State house of representatives in 1947 and 1948; elected as a Democrat to the Eighty-first Congress (January 3, 1949-January 3, 1951); unsuccessful candidate for renomination in 1950 to the Eighty-second Congress; reentered the Army on January 3, 1951, as a captain and served until December 1951; resumed the practice of law from 1951 until 1965; president of Management and Investment Corporation, 1965-1983; chairman and chief executive officer, Orangeburg National Bank, and Community Bankshares, Inc.; is a resident of Orangeburg, S.C.

**SIMS, Leonard Henly,** a Representative from Missouri; born in Burke County, N.C., February 6, 1807; received a limited schooling; moved to Rutherford County, Tenn., in 1830 and engaged in agricultural pursuits; member of the Tennessee State house of representatives for two terms; settled near Springfield, Green

County, Mo., in 1839 and continued agricultural pursuits; member, Missouri State house of representatives, 1842-1846; elected as a Democrat to the Twenty-ninth Congress (March 4, 1845-March 3, 1847); returned to Rutherford County, Tenn., in 1847 and continued farming; moved to Independence County, Ark., in 1859, settled on a farm near Batesville, and engaged in cotton raising and farming; served in the Arkansas State senate, 1866-1870, and 1874-1878; died on his plantation near Batesville, Independence County, Ark., February 28, 1886; interment in the family plot on his farm.

**SIMS, Thetus Willrette,** a Representative from Tennessee; born near Waynesboro, Wayne County, Tenn., April 25, 1852; attended a private school at Martins Mills; moved with his parents to Savannah, Hardin County, Tenn., in 1862; attended Savannah (Tenn.) College and was graduated from the law department of Cumberland University, Lebanon, Tenn., in June 1876; was admitted to the bar the same year and commenced practice in Linden, Perry County, Tenn.; superintendent of public instruction for Perry County, Tenn., 1882-1884; elected as a Democrat to the Fifty-fifth and to the eleven succeeding Congresses (March 4, 1897-March 3, 1921); chairman, Committee on War Claims (Sixty-second Congress), Committee on Interstate and Foreign Commerce (Sixty-fifth Congress); unsuccessful candidate for renomination in 1920 to the Sixty-seventh Congress; resumed the practice of law in Lexington, Henderson County, Tenn.; retired from active business pursuits in 1930 and moved to Washington, D.C., where he died on December 17, 1939; interment in Rock Creek Cemetery.

**SINCLAIR, James Herbert,** a Representative from North Dakota; born near St. Marys, Ontario, Canada, October 9, 1871; moved with his parents to Cooperstown, Griggs County, N.Dak., in 1883; attended the public schools and was graduated from Mayville (N.Dak.) State Normal School; superintendent of schools of Cooperstown, N.Dak., 1896-1898; register of deeds of Griggs County 1899-1905; organized the First National Bank of Binford and served as cashier 1905-1908; moved to Kenmare, Ward County, in March 1908; engaged in agricultural pursuits and in the real estate business; member of the State house of representatives 1915-1919; elected as a Republican to the Sixty-sixth and to the seven succeeding Congresses (March 4, 1919-January 3, 1935); unsuccessful candidate for renomination in 1934; Republican member of the Special Mexican Claims Commission 1936-1939; died in Miami, Fla., September 5, 1943; the remains were cremated and the ashes deposited under a red flowering hibiscus on the grounds of his home.

**SINGISER, Theodore Frelinghuysen,** a Delegate from the Territory of Idaho; born in Churchtown, Cumberland County, Pa., March 15, 1845; attended the common schools; learned the art of printing; enlisted in the Union Army as a private in Company E, Sixth Regiment, Pennsylvania Reserves, June 6, 1861; assistant assessor of internal revenue in 1866 and 1867; engaged in mercantile and editorial pursuits; studied law; was admitted to the bar in Washington, D.C., in 1878; employed in the United States Treasury from June 1, 1875, to May 31, 1879; appointed receiver of public moneys at Oxford, Idaho, in February 1879; engaged in mining in Idaho and Utah; secretary of the Territory of Idaho in 1880; Acting Governor of Idaho during the winter of 1881-1882; elected as a Republican to the Forty-eighth Congress (March 4, 1883-March 3, 1885); unsuccessful candidate for reelection in 1884 to the Forty-ninth Congress; receiver of public moneys at Mitchell, Dak. (now South Dakota), 1885-1889; again engaged in mining, and resided at Salt Lake City, Utah, until his death in Chicago, Ill., on January 23, 1907; interment in Chestnut Hill Cemetery, Mechanicsburg, Cumberland County, Pa.

**SINGLETON, James Washington,** a Representative from Illinois; born in Paxton, Frederick County, Va., November 23, 1811; attended Winchester (Va.) Academy; moved to Mount Sterling,

Brown County, Ill., in 1834; studied medicine and practiced; studied law; was admitted to the bar in 1838 and commenced practice in Mount Sterling; engaged in agricultural pursuits; elected brigadier general of the Illinois Militia in 1844, and took a conspicuous part in the so-called "Mormon War"; delegate to the Illinois State constitutional conventions in 1847 and 1861; member of the Illinois State house of representatives, 1850-1854; moved to Quincy, Adams County, Ill., in 1854; was again a member of the State house of representatives in 1861; was appointed in 1862 by Governor Richard Yates as a member of the commission to confer with the British and Canadian authorities on the establishment of continuous water communication between the United States and Canada; unsuccessful candidate for election in 1868 to the Forty-first Congress; constructed the Quincy & Toledo and the Quincy, Alton & St. Louis Railroads and served as president of both companies; elected as a Democrat to the Forty-sixth and Forty-seventh Congresses (March 4, 1879-March 3, 1883); returned to his farm near Quincy, Ill., and engaged in farming; moved to Baltimore, Md., about 1891, and died there on April 4, 1892; interment in Mount Hebron Cemetery, Winchester, Frederick County, Va.

Bibliography: *DAB*.

**SINGLETON, Otho Robards,** a Representative from Mississippi; born near Nicholasville, Jessamine County, Ky., October 14, 1814; attended the common schools; was graduated from St. Joseph's College, Bardstown, Ky., and from the law department of the University of Lexington; was admitted to the bar in 1838 and commenced practice in Canton, Madison County, Miss.; member of the State house of representatives in 1846 and 1847; served in the State senate 1848-1854; elected as a Democrat to the Thirty-third Congress (March 4, 1853-March 3, 1855); unsuccessful candidate for reelection; elected to the Thirty-fifth and Thirty-sixth Congresses and served from March 4, 1857, until January 12, 1861, when he withdrew; Representative from Mississippi in the Confederate Congress 1861-1865; elected as a Democrat to the Forty-fourth and to the five succeeding Congresses (March 4, 1875-March 3, 1887); was not a candidate for renomination in 1886; died in Washington, D.C., January 11, 1889; interment in Canton Cemetery, Canton, Madison County, Miss.

**SINGLETON, Thomas Day,** a Representative from South Carolina; born near Kingstree, S.C.; attended the common schools; member, State house of representatives, 1826-1833; elected as a Nullifier to the Twenty-third Congress and served without having qualified, from March 3, 1833, until his death in Raleigh, N.C., November 25, 1833, while en route to Washington, D.C.; interment in Congressional Cemetery, Washington, D.C.

**SINNICKSON, Clement Hall** (grandnephew of Thomas Sinnickson [1744-1817]), a Representative from New Jersey; born in Salem, Salem County, N.J., September 16, 1834; attended private schools, and the Polytechnic Institute at Troy, N.Y.; was graduated from Union College, New York, in 1855; studied law; was admitted to the bar in 1858 and commenced the practice of law in Salem, N.J.; during the Civil War served as captain in the Union Army; elected as a Republican to the Forty-fourth and Forty-fifth Congresses (March 4, 1875-March 3, 1879); resumed the practice of law in Salem; delegate to the Republican National Convention in 1880; appointed judge of the court of common pleas in 1896 and reappointed in 1901 and 1906; died in Salem, N.J., on July 24, 1919; interment in St. John's Episcopal Cemetery.

**SINNICKSON, Thomas** (granduncle of Clement Hall Sinnickson and uncle of Thomas Sinnickson [1786-1873]), a Representative from New Jersey; born near Salem, Salem County, N.J., December 21, 1744; completed preparatory studies; engaged in mercantile pursuits; served as captain in the Revolutionary Army; held several local offices; member of the State general assembly in 1777, 1782, 1784, 1785, 1787, and 1788; elected to the First Congress (March 4,

1789-March 3, 1791); elected as a Federalist to the Fifth Congress (March 4, 1797-March 3, 1799); died in Salem, N.J., May 15, 1817; interment in St. John's Episcopal Cemetery.

**SINNICKSON, Thomas** (nephew of Thomas Sinnickson [1744-1817]), a Representative from New Jersey; born in Salem, Salem County, N.J., December 13, 1786; completed preparatory studies; engaged in mercantile pursuits; judge of the court of errors and appeals of New Jersey; member of the State general assembly; judge of the court of common pleas for twenty years; elected to the Twentieth Congress to fill the vacancy caused by the death of Hedge Thompson and served from December 1, 1828, to March 3, 1829; died in Salem, Salem County, N.J., February 17, 1873; interment in St. John's Episcopal Cemetery.

**SINNOTT, Nicholas John,** a Representative from Oregon; born in The Dalles, Wasco County, Oreg., December 6, 1870; attended the public schools and Wasco Independent Academy at The Dalles; was graduated from the University of Notre Dame, Indiana, in 1892; studied law; was admitted to the bar in 1895 and commenced practice at The Dalles, Oreg.; elected to the State senate in 1909 and 1911; elected as a Republican to the Sixty-third and to the seven succeeding Congresses and served from March 4, 1913, until his resignation effective May 31, 1928; chairman, Committee on Public Lands (Sixty-sixth through Seventieth Congresses), Committee on Patents (Seventieth Congress); appointed by President Calvin Coolidge on April 18, 1928, as a judge of the United States Court of Claims, at Washington, D.C., in which capacity he served until his death in Washington, D.C., July 20, 1929; interment in St. Peters Cemetery, The Dalles, Oreg.

**SIPE, William Allen,** a Representative from Pennsylvania; born near Harrisonville, Fulton County, Pa., July 1, 1844; attended the public schools, and Cassville Academy, Cassville, Huntingdon County, Pa.; enlisted in the Union Army in 1862 and served in Company K, One Hundred and Forty-ninth Regiment, Pennsylvania Volunteer Infantry; was discharged for disability the same year; studied law; was admitted to the bar in August 1865 and practiced in Huntingdon, Pa.; moved to Indianapolis, Ind., in January 1867, to Pittsburgh, Pa., in December 1868, and continued the practice of law; elected as a Democrat to the Fifty-second Congress to fill the vacancy caused by the death of Alexander K. Craig; reelected to the Fifty-third Congress and served from December 5, 1892, to March 3, 1895; unsuccessful candidate for reelection in 1894 to the Fifty-fourth Congress; resumed the practice of law in Pittsburgh, Pa., until he retired in 1921; moved to San Diego, Calif., where he died on September 10, 1935; interment in Highwood Cemetery, Pittsburgh, Pa.

**SIROVICH, William Irving,** a Representative from New York; born in York, York County, Pa., March 18, 1882; moved to New York City with his parents in 1888; attended the public schools; was graduated from the College of the City of New York in 1902 and from the College of Physicians and Surgeons of Columbia University, New York City, in 1906; commenced the practice of medicine in New York City in 1906; also engaged as a lecturer, editor, and playwright, several of his plays being produced on Broadway; member of the fifth district school board 1906-1926; appointed as a member of the commission to inquire into the subject of widows' pensions and of the State pension commission in 1913; appointed a member of the State charities convention in 1914; served as superintendent of Peoples Hospital, New York City, 1910-1927; appointed commissioner of child welfare in 1919 and served until 1931; unsuccessful candidate for election in 1924 to the Sixty-ninth Congress; elected as a Democrat to the Seventieth and to the six succeeding Congresses and served from March 4, 1927, until his death; chairman, Committee on Patents (Seventy-second through Seventy-sixth Congresses); president of the Industrial National Bank, New York City, 1929-1932; delegate to the Interparliamentary Union Congress held at Bucharest, Rumania, in 1931; died in New York City December 17, 1939; interment in Mount Hebron Cemetery, Flushing, Long Island, N.Y.

**SISISKY, Norman,** a Representative from Virginia; born in Baltimore, Md., June 9, 1927; attended Belview Elementary School, Richmond, Va.; graduated from John Marshall High School, Richmond, 1944; B.S., Virginia Commonwealth University, Richmond, 1949; served in the United States Navy, 1945-1946; executive, soft drink bottling industry, 1949-1982; elected to the Virginia house of delegates, 1974-1982; elected as a Democrat to the Ninety-eighth and to the six succeeding Congresses (January 3, 1983-January 3, 1997); is a resident of Petersburg, Va.

**SISK, Bernice Frederic,** a Representative from California; born in Montague, Tex., December 14, 1910; at the age of six years moved with his parents to Donley County, Tex.; attended the Whitefish School and high school at Abernathy and Meadow, Tex.; attended Abilene (Tex.) Christian College, 1929-1931; assisted his father in the operation of a cotton farm; moved to the San Joaquin Valley of California in 1937 and was employed in a food processing plant until 1941; served as a civilian flight dispatcher at the Sequoia Air Force training field, Visalia, Calif., from 1941 to 1945; employed with LeMoss-Smith Tire Co. in Fresno, Calif., 1945-1954; elected as a Democrat to the Eighty-fourth and to the eleven succeeding Congresses (January 3, 1955-January 3, 1979); was not a candidate for reelection in 1978 to the Ninety-sixth Congress; was a resident of Fresno, Calif., until his death there on October 25, 1995.

**Bibliography:** Sisk, B.F. *A Congressional Record: The Memoir of Bernie Sisk*. Fresno, Calif.: Panorama West, 1980.

**SISSON, Frederick James,** a Representative from New York; born in Wells Bridge, Otsego County, N.Y., March 31, 1879; attended the public schools at Unadilla, N.Y.; was graduated from Hamilton College, Clinton, N.Y., in 1904; principal of Vernon (N.Y.) High School 1904-1910; studied law; was admitted to the bar in 1911 and commenced practice in Utica, N.Y.; sheriff's attorney in 1913 and corporation counsel for the city of Utica in 1914; unsuccessful candidate for election in 1922 to the Sixty-eighth Congress and in 1928 to the Seventy-first Congress; member of the Whitesboro (N.Y.) Board of Education 1925-1933, serving as president 1926-1930; elected as a Democrat to the Seventy-third and Seventy-fourth Congresses (March 4, 1933-January 3, 1937); unsuccessful candidate for reelection in 1936 to the Seventy-fifth Congress; continued the practice of law in Utica, N.Y., and Washington, D.C., until his retirement in 1945; died in Washington, D.C., October 20, 1949; interment in Mount Olivet Cemetery, Whitesboro, N.Y.

**SISSON, Thomas Upton,** a Representative from Mississippi; born near McCool, Attala County, Miss., September 22, 1869; moved with his father to Choctaw County, Miss.; attended the common schools and the French Camp Academy, Mississippi; was graduated from Southwestern Presbyterian University, Clarkesville, Tenn., in 1889; principal of Carthage High School in 1889 and 1890 and of the graded schools of Kosciusko, Attala County, Miss., 1890-1892; studied law at the University of Mississippi at Oxford and was graduated from the law department of Cumberland University, Lebanon, Tenn.; was admitted to the bar at Memphis, Tenn., in 1894 and commenced practice in Winona, Montgomery County, Miss.; member of the State senate in 1898; district attorney of the fifth judicial district 1903-1907; elected as a Democrat to the Sixty-first and to the six succeeding Congresses (March 4, 1909-March 3, 1923); unsuccessful candidate for reelection in 1922 to the Sixty-eighth Congress; died in Washington, D.C., September 26, 1923; interment in Oak Hill Cemetery, Winona, Miss.

**SITES, Frank Crawford,** a Representative from Pennsylvania; born in Shippensburg, Cumberland County, Pa., December 24, 1864; moved with his parents to Harrisburg, Pa., in 1875; attended the public schools; learned the trade of watchmaker and jeweler; and afterward engaged in that business at Harrisburg; director on the Harrisburg school board 1903-1912; appointed postmaster of Harrisburg June 3, 1913, and served until his successor was appointed June 20, 1922; elected as a Democrat to the Sixty-eighth Congress (March 4, 1923-March 3, 1925); unsuccessful candidate for reelection in 1924 to the Sixty-ninth Congress; returned to Harrisburg and engaged in the bond business; died in Harrisburg, Pa., May 23, 1935; interment in East Harrisburg Cemetery.

**SITGREAVES, Charles,** a Representative from New Jersey; born in Easton, Pa., April 22, 1803; moved with his parents to New Jersey in 1806; pursued classical studies; studied law; was admitted to the bar in Easton in 1824 and commenced practice in Phillipsburg, Warren County, N.J.; member of the State general assembly 1831-1833; major commandant in the State militia 1828-1838; member of the town council in 1834 and 1835; served in the State senate 1851-1854; president of the Belvidere & Delaware Railroad Co.; mayor of Phillipsburg, N.J., in 1861 and 1862; president of the National Bank of Phillipsburg 1856-1878; elected as a Democrat to the Thirty-ninth and Fortieth Congresses (March 4, 1865-March 3, 1869); was not a candidate for renomination in 1868; engaged in banking and railroading; died in Phillipsburg, N.J., March 17, 1878; interment in Seventh Street Cemetery, Easton, Pa.

**SITGREAVES, John,** a Delegate from North Carolina; born in England in 1757; attended Eton College; immigrated to the United States and settled in New Bern, N.C.; studied law; was admitted to the bar and commenced practice in New Bern, N.C.; during the Revolutionary War attained the rank of lieutenant, later serving as military aide to General Caswell; commissioner in charge of confiscated property; assistant clerk, first State senate of North Carolina in 1777; clerk of the State senate in 1778 and 1779; Member of the Continental Congress in 1785; member of the State house of commons in 1784, 1786, 1787, and 1788, serving as speaker in 1787 and 1788; United States district judge for North Carolina from December 20, 1790, until his death in Halifax, N.C., March 4, 1802; interment in the Colonial Cemetery.

**SITGREAVES, Samuel,** a Representative from Pennsylvania; born in Philadelphia, Pa., March 16, 1764; pursued classical studies; studied law; admitted to the bar in Philadelphia, Pa., September 3, 1783, and began practice in Easton, Pa., in 1786; delegate to the Pennsylvania constitutional convention in 1790; elected as a Federalist to the Fourth and Fifth Congresses, and served from March 4, 1795 until his resignation in 1798; one of the managers appointed by the House of Representatives in 1798 to conduct the impeachment proceedings against Senator William Blount; appointed United States commissioner to Great Britain under the Jay Treaty, regarding British claims, August 11, 1798; burgess of Easton, 1804-1807; treasurer of Northampton County, 1816-1819; resumed the practice of law; president of the Easton Bank, 1815-1827; died in Easton, Pa., April 4, 1827; interment in Easton Cemetery.

**SITTLER, Edward Lewis, Jr.,** a Representative from Pennsylvania; born in Greensburg, Westmoreland County, Pa., April 21, 1908; moved with his parents to Uniontown, Fayette County, Pa., in August 1908; attended the public schools; A.B., Brown University, Providence, R.I., in 1930; salesman for an ice cream company 1931-1937; elected to the Uniontown School Board in 1934 and served as president of the board in 1936 and 1937; became field underwriter for Mutual Life Insurance Co. of New York in 1937; enlisted as a private in the United States Army in February 1943 and served in the Ordnance Department in the European Theater until released to the Inactive Reserve as a captain in August 1946;

mayor of Uniontown 1948-1951; elected as a Republican to the Eighty-second Congress (January 3, 1951-January 3, 1953); unsuccessful candidate for reelection in 1952 to the Eighty-third Congress; resumed insurance business; served as Pennsylvania Republican committeeman for Fayette County, 1960-1972; minority Fayette County Commissioner, 1968-1971; resided in Uniontown, Pa., until his death in Pittsburgh, Pa., December 26, 1978; interment in Sylvan Heights Cemetery, Uniontown, Pa.

**SKAGGS, David Evans,** a Representative from Colorado; born in Cincinnati, Ohio, February 22, 1943; B.A., Wesleyan University, Middletown, Conn., 1964; attended University of Virginia Law School, Charlottesville; LL.B., Yale University Law School, 1967; served in the United States Marine Corps, 1968-1971; major, United States Marine Corps Reserve, 1971-1977; admitted to the New York State bar in 1968, and to the Colorado State bar in 1971; practiced law in Boulder, Colo.; aide to Representative Timothy E. Wirth, 1975-1977; member, Colorado State house of representatives, 1980-1986, Democratic leader, 1982-1985; elected as a Democrat to the One Hundredth and to the four succeeding Congresses (January 3, 1987-January 3, 1997); is a resident of Boulder, Colo.

**SKEEN, Joseph Richard,** a Representative from New Mexico; born in Roswell, Chaves County, N.Mex., June 30, 1927; attended public and parochial schools; graduated from O'Dea High School, Seattle, Wash., 1944; B.S., Texas A&M University, College Station, 1950; served in the United States Navy, 1945-1946, and in the United States Air Force Reserve, 1949-1952; engineer, 1951; businessman, 1952-1960; member, New Mexico State senate, 1960-1970, minority leader six years; chairman, New Mexico Republican Party, 1962-1965; delegate, New Mexico State Republican conventions, 1960-1970; delegate to the Republican National Convention of 1964; unsuccessful candidate in 1970 for Lieutenant Governor and in 1974 and 1978 for Governor of New Mexico; won as a write-in candidate in 1980 election to the United States House of Representatives after the courts denied him a position on the ballot; elected as a Republican to the Ninety-seventh and to the seven succeeding Congresses (January 3, 1981-January 3, 1997); is a resident of Picacho, N.Mex.

**SKELTON, Charles,** a Representative from New Jersey; born in Buckingham Township, Bucks County, Pa., April 19, 1806; moved to Trenton, N.J., about 1829; attended the country schools and Trenton Academy; engaged in mercantile pursuits; moved to Philadelphia, Pa., in 1835; was graduated from Jefferson Medical College at Philadelphia in 1838 and commenced the practice of his profession in that city; returned to Trenton, N.J., in 1841; superintendent of the public schools of Trenton in 1848; elected as a Democrat to the Thirty-second and Thirty-third Congresses (March 4, 1851-March 3, 1855); member of the common council 1873-1875; died in Trenton, N.J., May 20, 1879; interment in City Cemetery, Hamilton Square, Mercer County, N.J.

**SKELTON, Isaac Newton, IV,** a Representative from Missouri; born in Lexington, Lafayette County, Mo., December 20, 1931; attended the public schools of Lexington and the Wentworth Military Academy, Lexington; graduated from Lexington High School, 1949; A.B., University of Missouri, Columbia, 1953, LL.B., 1956; attended the University of Edinburgh, Scotland, 1953; admitted to the Missouri bar in 1957 and commenced practice in Lexington; served as Lafayette County prosecuting attorney, 1957-1960; special assistant State attorney general, 1961-1963; served in the Missouri State senate, 1971-1977; elected as a Democrat to the Ninety-fifth and to the nine succeeding Congresses (January 3, 1977-January 3, 1997); is a resident of Lexington, Mo.

**SKILES, William Woodburn,** a Representative from Ohio; born in Stoughstown, Cumberland County, Pa., December 11, 1849, moved with his parents to Richland County, Ohio, in 1854; attended the district schools; taught school for several years; was graduated from Baldwin University, Berea, Ohio, in 1876; studied law; was admitted to the bar July 24, 1878, and commenced the practice of his profession in Shelby, Ohio; interested as a stockholder and director in various manufacturing enterprises; president of the Citizens Bank from 1893 until his death; president and member of the city school board 1885-1904; member of the Republican State central committee 1900-1904; elected as a Republican to the Fifty-seventh and Fifty-eighth Congresses and served from March 4, 1901, until his death in Shelby, Richland County, Ohio, January 9, 1904; chairman, Committee on Patents (Fifty-eighth Congress); interment in Oakland Cemetery.

**SKINNER, Charles Rufus,** a Representative from New York; born in Union Square, Oswego County, N.Y., August 4, 1844; attended the common schools and Clinton Liberal Institute; was graduated from Mexico Academy, N.Y., in 1866; taught in the common schools; editor of the Watertown Daily Times 1870-1874; member of the board of education of Watertown, N.Y., 1875-1884; member of the State assembly 1877-1881; elected as a Republican to the Forty-seventh Congress to fill the vacancy caused by the resignation of Warner Miller; reelected to the Forty-eighth Congress and served from November 8, 1881, to March 3, 1885; was not a candidate for renomination in 1884; member of the Board of Visitors to the United States Military Academy at West Point in 1884; editor of the Watertown Daily Republican 1885-1886; city editor of the Watertown Daily Times 1886; deputy State superintendent of public instruction 1886-1892; supervisor of teachers' training classes and teachers' institutes in the State department of public instruction 1892-1895; State superintendent of public instruction 1895-1904; elected president of the National Education Association in 1897; assistant appraiser of merchandise for the port of New York 1906-1911; librarian of the State assembly in 1913 and 1914 and served as legislative librarian 1915-1925; died in Pelham Manor, N.Y., June 30, 1928; remains were cremated and the ashes interred in Brookside Cemetery, Watertown, N.Y.

**Bibliography:** *DAB*; Skinner, Charles R. "How Congress Acted Forty Years Ago: Reminiscences of a Member from New York State." *State Service* 8 (December 1924): 104-110.

**SKINNER, Harry** (brother of Thomas Gregory Skinner), a Representative from North Carolina; born near Hertford, Perquimans County, N.C., May 25, 1855; attended Hertford Academy and was graduated from the law department of the University of Kentucky at Lexington; was admitted to the bar in 1876 and commenced practice in Greenville, Pitt County, N.C.; member of the town council in 1878; member of Governor Jarvis' staff and served as aide-de-camp 1879-1886; chairman of the Democratic executive committee of the First Congressional District 1880-1890; chairman of the Democratic executive committee of Pitt County 1880-1892; member of the State house of representatives in 1891 and 1892; chairman of the Populist executive committee of Pitt County 1892-1896; member of the State central committee 1892-1896; trustee of the University of North Carolina at Chapel Hill 1890-1896; elected as a Populist to the Fifty-fourth and Fifty-fifth Congresses (March 4, 1895-March 3, 1899); unsuccessful candidate for reelection in 1898 to the Fifty-sixth Congress; United States district attorney for the eastern district of North Carolina 1902-1910; resumed the practice of his profession in Greenville, N.C.; died in Greenville, N.C., May 19, 1929; interment in Cherry Hill Cemetery.

**Bibliography:** *DAB*.

**SKINNER, Richard,** a Representative from Vermont; born in Litchfield, Conn., May 30, 1778; completed preparatory studies and was graduated from Litchfield Law School; was admitted to the bar in 1800 and commenced practice in Manchester, Vt.; State's attorney for Bennington County, 1801-1813, and 1819; judge of probate for the Manchester district, 1806-1813; elected as a Republican to the Thirteenth Congress (March 4, 1813-March 3, 1815); unsuccessful candidate for reelection in 1814 to the Fourteenth Congress; resumed the practice of law; assistant judge of the Vermont State supreme court in 1815 and 1816; declined the office of chief justice in 1817; member of the State house of representatives in 1815 and 1818, serving as speaker in the latter year; elected Governor of Vermont in 1820, reelected in 1821 and 1822, and served from October 13, 1820 to October 10, 1823; chief justice of the supreme court of Vermont from 1823 until 1828, when he retired; interested in public education and served as president of the northeastern branch of the American Educational Society; trustee of Middlebury College; died in Manchester, Bennington County, Vt., May 23, 1833; interment in Dellwood Cemetery.

**SKINNER, Thomas Gregory** (brother of Harry Skinner), a Representative from North Carolina; born near Hertford, Perquimans County, N.C., January 22, 1842; attended private schools, Friends Academy, Belvidere, N.C., Horners Military School, Oxford, N.C., and the University of North Carolina at Chapel Hill; entered the Confederate Army in May 1861 and served with the First Regiment, North Carolina Volunteers, until the close of the Civil War, attaining the rank of lieutenant; studied law; was admitted to the bar in 1868 and commenced practice in Hertford, N.C.; elected as a Democrat to the Forty-eighth Congress on November 20, 1883, to fill the vacancy caused by the death of Walter F. Pool; reelected to the Forty-ninth Congress and served from November 20, 1883, to March 3, 1887; again elected to the Fifty-first Congress (March 4, 1889-March 3, 1891); declined to be a candidate for renomination in 1890 to the Fifty-second Congress; resumed the practice of his profession in Hertford, N.C.; delegate to the Democratic National Convention in 1892 and 1904; member of the State senate in 1899 and 1900; died in Baltimore, Md., on December 22, 1907; interment in Holy Trinity Churchyard, Hertford, N.C.

**SKINNER, Thomson Joseph,** a Representative from Massachusetts; born in Colchester, Conn., May 24, 1752; completed preparatory studies; moved to Massachusetts; member of the Massachusetts house of representatives in 1781, 1785, 1789, 1800, and 1801; served in the Massachusetts senate 1786-1788, 1790-1797, 1802, and 1803; delegate to the Massachusetts ratification convention in 1788; judge of the court of common pleas 1788-1807; Massachusetts treasurer in 1806 and 1807; elected as a Republican to the Fourth Congress to fill the vacancy caused by the resignation of Theodore Sedgwick; reelected to the Fifth Congress and served from January 27, 1797, to March 3, 1799; elected to the Eighth Congress and served from March 4, 1803, to August 10, 1804, when he resigned; died in Boston, Mass., on January 20, 1809.

**SKUBITZ, Joe,** a Representative from Kansas; born in Frontenac, Crawford County, Kans., May 6, 1906; attended grade school in Ringo, Kans., and high schools in Girard and Frontenac, Kans.; B.S., Kansas State College, Pittsburg, 1929, and M.S., 1934; attended law school at Washburn University, Topeka, Kans., in 1938; LL.B., George Washington University, Washington, D.C., 1944; was admitted to the bar in 1944 and commenced practice in Kansas and the District of Columbia; administrative assistant to Senator Clyde M. Reed, 1939-1949, and Senator Andrew F. Schoeppel, 1949-1962; delegate to the Republican National Convention of 1960; elected as a Republican to the Eighty-eighth and to the seven succeeding Congresses, and served from January 3, 1963 until his resignation on December 31, 1978; was not a candidate for reelection in 1978 to the Ninety-sixth Congress; is a resident of Wichita, Kans.

**SLACK, John Mark, Jr.,** a Representative from West Virginia; born in Charleston, Kanawha County, W.Va., March 18, 1915; attended the public schools in Charleston, W.Va., and Virginia Military Institute at Lexington; member of Kanawha County Court 1948-1952; Kanawha County assessor 1952-1958; elected as a Democrat to the Eighty-sixth and to the ten succeeding Congresses and served from January 3, 1959, until his death March 17, 1980, in Alexandria, Va.; interment in Cunningham Memorial Park, St. Albans, W.Va.

**SLADE, Charles,** a Representative from Illinois; born in England; immigrated to the United States with his parents, who settled in Alexandria, Va.; attended the public schools; moved to Carlyle, St. Clair County, Ill.; engaged in mercantile pursuits; held several local offices; member of the State house of representatives in 1820 and 1826; elected as a Jacksonian to the Twenty-third Congress and served from March 4, 1833, until his death near Vincennes, Ind., July 26, 1834.

**SLADE, William,** a Representative from Vermont; born in Cornwall, Vt., May 9, 1786; attended the public schools, and was graduated from Middlebury (Vt.) College in 1807; studied law; was admitted to the bar in 1810 and commenced practice in Middlebury; engaged in editorial work; established and was the editor of the Columbian Patriot, 1814-1816; secretary of state of Vermont, 1815-1822; judge of the Addison County Court; clerk in the Department of State, Washington, D.C., 1823-1829; elected as an Anti-Masonic candidate to the Twenty-second Congress to fill the vacancy caused by the death of Rollin C. Mallary; reelected as an Anti-Masonic candidate to the Twenty-third and Twenty-fourth Congresses, and as a Whig to the Twenty-fifth through Twenty-seventh Congresses, and served from November 1, 1831 to March 3, 1843; reporter of decisions of the Vermont State supreme court, 1843-1844; elected Governor of Vermont in 1844, reelected in 1845, and served from October 11, 1844 to October 9, 1846; corresponding secretary of the Board of National Popular Education, 1846-1859; died in Middlebury, Addison County, Vt., on January 18, 1859; interment in West Cemetery.

**Bibliography:** *DAB.*

**SLATER, James Harvey,** a Representative and a Senator from Oregon; born near Springfield, Sangamon County, Ill., December 28, 1826; attended the common schools; moved to California in 1849; settled in Corvallis, Oreg., in 1850; studied law; was admitted to the bar in 1854; clerk of the district court of the Territory of Oregon for Benton County 1853-1856; member, Territorial assembly 1857-1858; member, State house of representatives 1859; published the Oregon Weekly Union at Corvallis 1859-1861; district attorney for the fifth judicial district of Oregon in 1868; presidential elector on the Democratic ticket in 1868; elected as a Democrat to the Forty-second Congress (March 4, 1871-March 3, 1873); elected as a Democrat to the United States Senate and served from March 4, 1879, to March 3, 1885; resumed the practice of law in La Grande, Oreg.; member of the State railroad commission 1889-1891; died in La Grande, Oreg., January 28, 1899; interment in Masonic Cemetery.

**SLATTERY, James Charles,** a Representative from Kansas; born in Good Intent, Atchison County, Kans., August 4, 1948; attended public schools in Atchison, Kans., and graduated from Maur Hill High School in 1966; attended the Netherlands School of International Business and Economics, 1969; B.S., Washburn University, Topeka, Kans., 1970; J.D., Washburn University Law School, 1974; realtor; admitted to the Kansas bar in 1975 and commenced practice in Topeka; elected to the Kansas State house of representatives, 1972-1978; elected as a Democrat to the Ninety-eighth and to the five succeeding Congresses (January 3, 1983-January 3, 1995); was not a candidate in 1994 for renomination to the One Hundred Fourth Congress, but was an unsuccessful candidate for election for Governor of Kansas; is a resident of Topeka, Kans.

**SLATTERY, James Michael,** a Senator from Illinois; born in Chicago, Ill., July 29, 1878; attended the parochial schools and St. Ignatius College, Chicago, Ill.; employed as a secretary with the building departments of the city of Chicago in 1905; graduated from Illinois College of Law at Chicago in 1908; was admitted to the bar the same year and commenced practice in Chicago, Ill.; member of the faculty, Illinois College of Law, 1909-1912; superintendent of public service, Cook County, Ill., 1910-1912; secretary of Webster College of Law, Chicago, Ill., 1912-1914; counsel for the Lincoln Park Commission, 1933-1934, and for the Chicago Park District, 1934-1936; chairman, Illinois Commerce Commission, 1936-1939; appointed as a Democrat to the United States Senate to fill the vacancy caused by the death of James Hamilton Lewis and served from April 14, 1939, to November 21, 1940, when a duly elected successor qualified; was an unsuccessful candidate for election to fill the vacancy; resumed the practice of law in Chicago, Ill.; died at his summer home at Lake Geneva, Wis., August 28, 1948; interment in Calvary Cemetery, Evanston, Ill.

**SLAUGHTER, D. French, Jr.,** a Representative from Virginia; born in Culpeper, Va., May 20, 1925; attended public schools in Culpeper County; attended the Virginia Military Institute, Lexington, 1941-1943; B.A., University of Virginia, 1949; LL.B., University of Virginia School of Law, 1953; served in the United States Army in the European Theater of Operations, 1943-1947; awarded the Purple Heart; was admitted to the bar and practiced law in Culpeper; member, Virginia house of delegates, 1958-1978; member, board of visitors, University of Virginia, 1978-1982, and served as rector, 1980-1982; aide to Secretary of the Army John O. Marsh, Jr., 1981-1984; elected as a Republican to the Ninety-ninth and to the three succeeding Congresses, and served from January 3, 1985 until his resignation on November 5, 1991; is a resident of Culpeper, Va.

**SLAUGHTER, Louise M.,** a Representative from New York; born Louise McIntosh in Lynch, Harlan County, Ky., August 14, 1929; B.S., University of Kentucky, 1951, M.S., 1953; member, New York State Democratic Committee, 1971-1982; served in the Monroe County (N.Y.) legislature, 1976-1979; regional coordinator for the New York Department of State, 1976-1979; cordinator, regional office of New York lieutenant governor, 1979-1982; member, New York State assembly, 1982-1986; elected as a Democrat to the One Hundredth and to the four succeeding Congresses (January 3, 1987-January 3, 1997); is a resident of Fairport, N.Y.

**SLAUGHTER, Roger Caldwell,** a Representative from Missouri; born near Odessa, Lafayette County, Mo., July 17, 1905; attended the public schools at Independence, Mo.; A.B., Princeton University, 1928; read law in the office of Hon. Henry L. Jost, Kansas City, Mo., and attended the Kansas City School of Law; was admitted to the bar in 1932 and commenced practice in Kansas City; served as assistant prosecutor of Jackson County, Mo., 1932-1936; member of the board of directors of the school district of Kansas City, Mo., 1940-1942; elected as a Democrat to the Seventy-eighth and to the Seventy-ninth Congresses (January 3, 1943-January 3, 1947); unsuccessful candidate for renomination in 1946 to the Eightieth Congress; member, State Democratic Committee, 1960-1962; resumed the practice of law in Kansas City, Mo.; appointed magistrate judge of Lafayette County in 1972; died on his farm near Odessa, Mo., June 2, 1974; interment in Greenton Cemetery, Odessa, Mo.

**SLAYDEN, James Luther** (uncle of Maury Maverick), a Representative from Texas; born in Mayfield, Graves County, Ky., June 1, 1853; upon the death of his father in 1869 moved with his mother to New Orleans, La.; attended the common schools and Washington and Lee University, Lexington, Va.; moved to San Antonio, Tex., in 1876; became a cotton merchant and ranchman; member of the State house of representatives in 1892; declined to be a candidate for renomination; engaged in agricultural pursuits and mining; appointed by Andrew Carnegie as one of the original trustees of the Carnegie Endowment for International Peace in October 1910; president of the American Peace Society for several years; elected as a Democrat to the Fifty-fifth and to the ten succeeding Congresses (March 4, 1897-March 3, 1919); was not a candidate for renomination in 1918 to the Sixty-sixth Congress; managed an orchard in Virginia, a ranch in Texas, and mines in Mexico; died in San Antonio, Tex., February 24, 1924; interment in Mission Park Cemetery.

**Bibliography:** Pohl, James W. "Slayden's Defeat: A Texas Congressman Loses Bid as Wilson's Secretary of War." *Military History of Texas and the Southwest* 10 (1972): 43-56.

**SLAYMAKER, Amos,** a Representative from Pennsylvania; born in London Lands, Lancaster County, Pa., on March 11, 1755; received a limited schooling; engaged in agricultural pursuits; built and operated a hotel on the Lancaster and Philadelphia pike; during the Revolutionary War served as an ensign in the company of Capt. John Slaymaker; member of an association formed for the suppression of Tory activities in Lancaster County; justice of the peace of Salisbury Township; county commissioner 1806-1810; served in the Pennsylvania senate in 1810 and 1811; elected as a Federalist to the Thirteenth Congress to fill the vacancy caused by the resignation of James Whitehill and served from October 11, 1814, to March 3, 1815; died in Salisbury, Lancaster County, Pa., June 12, 1837.

**SLEMONS, William Ferguson,** a Representative from Arkansas; born near Dresden, Weakley County, Tenn., March 15, 1830; attended Bethel College; moved to Arkansas in 1852; studied law; was admitted to the bar in 1855 and practiced in Monticello, Drew County; member of the Arkansas State convention in 1861; entered the Confederate Army in July 1861 and served as colonel in General Sterling Price's Cavalry throughout the Civil War; resumed the practice of law; district attorney 1866-1868; elected as a Democrat to the Forty-fourth, Forty-fifth, and Forty-sixth Congresses (March 4, 1875-March 3, 1881); was not a candidate for renomination in 1880; resumed the practice of his profession in Monticello, Ark.; county and probate judge of Drew County 1903-1907; justice of the peace 1908-1918; died in Monticello, Ark., December 10, 1918; interment in Union Ridge Cemetery, near Monticello, Ark.

**SLEMP, Campbell** (father of Campbell Bascom Slemp), a Representative from Virginia; born near Turkey Cove, Lee County, Va., December 2, 1839; attended a private school and Emory and Henry College, Emory, Va.; interested in agricultural pursuits and also engaged in the real estate business; during the Civil War served in the Confederate Army as captain and lieutenant colonel of the Twenty-first Virginia Battalion and colonel of the Sixty-fourth Regiment, composed of Infantry and Cavalry; member of the Virginia house of delegates 1879-1882; unsuccessful Republican candidate for Lieutenant Governor in 1889; elected as a Republican to the Fifty-eighth, Fifty-ninth, and Sixtieth Congresses and served from March 4, 1903, until his death in Big Stone Gap, Wise County, Va., October 13, 1907; interment in the family cemetery in Lee County, Va.

**SLEMP, Campbell Bascom** (son of Campbell Slemp), a Representative from Virginia; born at Turkey Cove, Lee County, Va., September 4, 1870; attended the public schools; was graduated from Virginia Military Institute at Lexington in 1891; studied law in the University of Virginia at Charlottesville; admitted to the bar in 1901 and commenced practice at Big Stone Gap, Wise County, Va.; commandant of cadets at Marion Military Institute for one year; professor of mathematics at Virginia Military Institute for several years, resigning in 1901 to enter professional and business life at Big Stone Gap, Va.; was chairman of the Virginia Republican committee from 1905 to 1918, when he was elected a member of the Republican National Committee; was elected as a Republican to the Sixtieth Congress to fill the vacancy caused by the death of his father, Campbell Slemp; was reelected to the Sixty-first and to the six succeeding Congresses and served from December 17, 1907, to March 3, 1923; declined to be a candidate for reelection in 1922; was appointed secretary to President Calvin Coolidge on September 4, 1923, and served until March 4, 1925, when he resigned; continued the practice of his profession in Big Stone Gap, Va., and in Washington, D.C., until 1932, when he retired and resided at Big Stone Gap, Va.; died August 7, 1943, in Knoxville, Tenn.; interment in the family cemetery at Turkey Cove, Va.

**Bibliography:** *DAB*; Hathorn, Guy B. "The Political Career of C. Bascom Slemp." Ph.D. dissertation, Duke University, 1950.

**SLIDELL, John,** a Representative and a Senator from Louisiana; born in New York City in 1793; graduated from Columbia College (later Columbia University), New York City, in 1810; studied law; was admitted to the bar in New York City; practiced law and engaged in business; moved to New Orleans around 1819 and engaged in law and business; unsuccessful candidate for election in 1828 to the Twenty-first Congress; United States district attorney, 1829-1833; unsuccessful candidate for the United States Senate in 1834, 1836, and 1848; elected as a Democrat to the Twenty-eighth and Twenty-ninth Congresses, and served from March 4, 1843 until his resignation on November 10, 1845; chairman, Committee on Private Land Claims (Twenty-eighth Congress); appointed Minister to Mexico on November 10, 1845, but that government refused to accept him, and he left his post in March 1846; appointed Minister to Central America on March 29, 1853, but declined the appointment; elected as a Democrat to the United States Senate in 1853 to fill the vacancy caused by the resignation of Pierre Soule; was reelected, and served from December 5, 1853 until his resignation on February 4, 1861; chairman, Committee on Roads and Canals (Thirty-fourth Congress); on November 8, 1861, while on a diplomatic mission from the Confederate States to England and France, was taken from the British mail steamer *Trent*, sailing from Havana to England, and placed under arrest by Captain Charles Wilkes of the U.S.S. *San Jacinto*; confined in Fort Warren, Boston Harbor; was later released and sailed for Paris; died in Cowes, Isle of Wight, England, July 9, 1871; interment in the private cemetery of the Saint-Roman family at Villejuif, near Paris, France, in the Département de la Seine.

**Bibliography:** *DAB*; Diket, Albert L. *Senator John Slidell and the Community He Represented in Washington, 1853-1861.* Washington, D.C.: University Press of America, 1982; Sears, Louis. *John Slidell.* Durham: Duke University Press, 1925.

**SLINGERLAND, John I.,** a Representative from New York; born in Jerusalem, Albany County, N.Y., March 1, 1804; attended the public schools; engaged in agricultural pursuits; member of the State assembly in 1843 and 1844; elected as a Whig to the Thirtieth Congress (March 4, 1847-March 3, 1849); was not a candidate for renomination in 1848; resumed agricultural pursuits; again a member of the State assembly, in 1860 and 1861; died in Slingerland, N.Y., October 26, 1861; interment in the Slingerland family mausoleum.

**SLOAN, Andrew,** a Representative from Georgia; born in McDonough, Henry County, Ga., June 10, 1845; attended the common schools, Marshall College, Griffin, Ga., and Bethany (W.Va.) College; studied law; was admitted to the bar in 1866 and practiced; solicitor of Henry County in 1866; moved to Savannah, Ga.; deputy collector of customs in 1867; resigned, and resumed the practice of law; assistant United States district attorney in 1869; later appointed district attorney and served until 1872, when he resigned, acting at the same time as local counsel for the United States in regard to the cotton claims and also with the mixed commission on British and American claims; successfully contested as a Republican the election of Morgan Rawls to the Forty-third Congress and served from March 24, 1874, to March 3, 1875; moved to New Mexico in 1881 and settled in Silver City, where he died September 22, 1883; interment in the City Cemetery.

**SLOAN, Andrew Scott** (brother of Ithamar Conkey Sloan), a Representative from Wisconsin; born in Morrisville, Madison County, N.Y., June 12, 1820; attended the public schools and Morrisville Academy; studied law; was admitted to the bar in 1842 and commenced practice in Morrisville, N.Y.; clerk of the Madison County Court 1847-1849; moved to Wisconsin in 1854 and settled at Beaver Dam, Dodge County, where he continued the practice of law; member of the State assembly in 1857; mayor of Beaver Dam in 1857, 1858, and again in 1879; appointed in 1858 as judge of the circuit court for the third district; elected as a Republican to the Thirty-seventh Congress (March 4, 1861-March 3, 1863); was not a candidate for renomination in 1862; resumed the practice of law; unsuccessful candidate of the Union Party for election in 1864 to the Thirty-ninth Congress; clerk of the United States District Court for Wisconsin 1864-1866; judge of the Dodge County Court 1868-1874; attorney general of Wisconsin 1874-1878; judge of the circuit court for the thirteenth judicial district from January 1882 until his death; died at Beaver Dam, Wis., on April 8, 1895; interment in Oakwood Cemetery.

**SLOAN, Charles Henry,** a Representative from Nebraska; born in Monticello, Jones County, Iowa, May 2, 1863; attended the public schools and was graduated from the Iowa State Agricultural College at Ames in 1884; moved to Fairmont, Nebr., the same year; superintendent of the city schools 1884-1887; studied law; was admitted to the bar in 1887 and commenced practice in Fairmont; moved to Geneva, Fillmore County, in 1891 and continued the practice of law; director of the Geneva State Bank; prosecuting attorney of Fillmore County 1890-1894; member of the State senate 1894-1896; chairman of the Republican State convention in 1903; elected as a Republican to the Sixty-second and to the three succeeding Congresses (March 4, 1911-March 3, 1919); did not seek renomination in 1918; elected to the Seventy-first Congress (March 4, 1929-March 3, 1931); unsuccessful for reelection in 1930 to the Seventy-second Congress; resumed the practice of law in Geneva, Nebr., and also engaged in banking; died in Geneva, Nebr., on June 2, 1946; interment in Geneva Cemetery.

**SLOAN, Ithamar Conkey** (brother of Andrew Scott Sloan), a Representative from Wisconsin; born in Morrisville, Madison County, N.Y., May 9, 1822; attended the common schools; studied law; was admitted to the bar in Oneida County, N.Y. in 1848 and commenced practice; moved to Janesville, Wis., in 1854 and resumed the practice of his profession; district attorney of Rock County, Wis., 1858-1862; elected as a Republican to the Thirty-eighth and Thirty-ninth Congresses (March 4, 1863-March 3, 1867); moved to Madison, Wis., in 1875; dean of the law department of the University of Wisconsin; special counsel for the State of Wisconsin 1874-1879 in the Granger law cases; died in Janesville, Rock County, Wis., December 24, 1898; interment in Oak Hill Cemetery.

**SLOAN, James,** a Representative from New Jersey; born in that State; engaged in agricultural pursuits; assessor of Newton township for several years; held several other local offices; elected as a Republican to the Eighth and to the two succeeding Congresses (March 4, 1803-March 3, 1809); was not a candidate for renomination in 1808 to the Eleventh Congress; died in Elmira, N.Y., on September 7, 1811.

**SLOANE, John,** a Representative from Ohio; born in York, Pa., in 1779; moved to Ohio in early youth; completed preparatory studies; member of the State house of representatives 1803-1805 and in 1807; colonel of militia in the War of 1812; United States receiver of public moneys at Canton, Ohio, 1808-1816 and at Wooster 1816-1819; elected to the Sixteenth and to the four succeeding Congresses (March 4, 1819-March 3, 1829); chairman, Committee on Elections (Seventeenth through Twentieth Congresses); appointed clerk of the court of common pleas of Wayne County in 1831 and served several years; secretary of state of Ohio 1841-1844; Treasurer of the United States from November 27, 1850, to April 6, 1853; died in Wooster, Ohio, May 15, 1856; interment in Oak Hill Cemetery.

**SLOANE, Jonathan,** a Representative from Ohio; born in Pelham, Mass., in November 1785; completed preparatory studies and was graduated from Williams College, Williamstown, Mass., in 1812; studied law; was admitted to the bar in 1816 and commenced practice in Ravenna, Ohio; was also general agent of the Tappan family for the sale of lands; prosecuting attorney of Portage County in 1819; member of the State house of representatives 1820-1822; served in the State senate in 1826 and 1827; elected as an Anti-Masonic candidate to the Twenty-third Congress and reelected as a Whig to the Twenty-fourth Congress (March 4, 1833-March 3, 1837); declined to be a candidate for renomination in 1836; retired from business activities on account of ill health; died in Ravenna, Portage County, Ohio, April 25, 1854; interment in Evergreen Cemetery.

**SLOCUM, Henry Warner,** a Representative from New York; born in Delphi, Onondaga County, N.Y., September 24, 1827; was graduated from the United States Military Academy at West Point and commissioned as a second lieutenant, First Artillery, July 1, 1852; served in the Seminole War and was promoted to first lieutenant March 3, 1855; resigned his commission October 31, 1856; settled in Syracuse, N.Y.; studied law while in the Army; was admitted to the bar in 1858 and practiced in Syracuse, N.Y.; member of the State assembly in 1859; entered the Union Army as colonel of the Twenty-eighth New York Volunteers in May 1861; promoted to major general and resigned his commission September 28, 1865, and settled in Brooklyn, N.Y., where he continued the practice of law; unsuccessful Democratic candidate for secretary of state of New York; elected as a Democrat to the Forty-first and Forty-second Congresses (March 4, 1869-March 3, 1873); was not a candidate for renomination in 1872; resumed the practice of law; was appointed president of the department of city works in 1876; elected as a Representative at Large from New York to the Forty-eighth Congress (March 4, 1883-March 3, 1885); died in Brooklyn, N.Y., April 14, 1894; interment in Greenwood Cemetery.

Bibliography: *DAB.*

**SLOCUMB, Jesse,** a Representative from North Carolina; born in Spring Bank, Dobbs (later Wayne) County, N.C., in 1780; completed preparatory studies; engaged in agricultural pursuits; held several local offices; member of the court of pleas and quarter sessions of the county; register of deeds 1802-1808; elected as a Federalist to the Fifteenth and Sixteenth Congresses and served from March 4, 1817, until his death in Washington, D.C., December 20, 1820; interment in Congressional Cemetery.

**SLOSS, Joseph Humphrey,** a Representative from Alabama; born in Somerville, Ala., October 12, 1826; completed preparatory studies; studied law; was admitted to the bar and commenced practice in St. Louis, Mo.; moved to Edwardsville, Ill., in 1849; member of the Illinois State house of representatives in 1858 and 1859; returned to Alabama; during the Civil War served in the Confederate Army; mayor of Tuscumbia, Ala.; elected as a Democrat to the Forty-second and Forty-third Congresses (March 4, 1871-March 3, 1875); unsuccessful candidate for reelection in 1874 to the Forty-fourth Congress; appointed United States marshal for the northern district of Alabama February 10, 1877, and served until September 6, 1882; clerk of the Federal court at Huntsville, Ala.; engaged in agricultural pursuits near Huntsville; moved to Memphis, Tenn., where he died January 27, 1911; interment in Maple Hill Cemetery, Huntsville, Ala.

**SMALL, Frank, Jr.,** a Representative from Maryland; born on a farm in Temple Hills, Prince Georges County, Md., July 15, 1896; attended the public schools and received technical education at the National Automobile College in 1914 and 1915; operated several farms; engaged in banking and the automobile business 1923-1957; served in the State house of delegates in 1927 and 1928; member of the board of county commissioners 1930-1934; member of the Republican State Central committee 1934-1942, serving as chairman for four years; member of the Maryland Racing Commission 1937-1952, serving as chairman in 1951 and 1952; president of Clinton Bank, Clinton, Md., 1928-1972; delegate, Republican Conventions, 1940, 1944, and 1956; elected as a Republican to the Eighty-third Congress (January 3, 1953-January 3, 1955); was unsuccessful for reelection in 1954 to the Eighty-fourth Congress; engaged in real estate, 1954-1973; Maryland Commissioner of Motor Vehicles from April 29, 1955, to April 15, 1957; vice president of the Equitable Trust Co. of Baltimore; died in Washington, D.C., October 24, 1973; interment in Resurrection Cemetery, Clinton, Md.

**SMALL, John Humphrey,** a Representative from North Carolina; born in Washington, Beaufort County, N.C., August 29, 1858; attended private schools and Trinity College (later Duke University), Durham, N.C.; taught school 1876-1880; studied law; was admitted to the bar in 1881 and commenced practice in Washington, N.C.; elected reading clerk of the State senate in 1881; superintendent of public instruction of Beaufort County, N.C., in 1881; solicitor of the inferior court of Beaufort County 1882-1885; editor of the Washington Gazette 1883-1886; attorney of the Board of Commissioners of Beaufort County 1888-1896; member of the city council 1887-1890; mayor of Washington, N.C., in 1889 and 1890; delegate to all Democratic State conventions from 1889 to 1920; elected as a Democrat to the Fifty-sixth and to the ten succeeding Congresses (March 4, 1899-March 3, 1921); chairman, Committee on Rivers and Harbors (Sixty-fifth Congress); declined to be a candidate for renomination in 1920; resumed the practice of his profession in Washington, D.C., until 1931; returned to Washington, N.C., where he died on July 13, 1946; interment in Oakdale Cemetery.

**SMALL, William Bradbury,** a Representative from New Hampshire; born in Limington, Maine, May 17, 1817; moved with his parents to Ossipee, N.H.; attended the public schools and Phillips Exeter Academy, Exeter, N.H.; studied law; was admitted to the bar in 1846 and commenced practice in Newmarket, N.H.; solicitor of Rockingham County, N.H.; member of the State house of representatives in 1865; served in the State senate in 1870; elected as a Republican to the Forty-third Congress (March 4, 1873-March 3, 1875); was not a candidate for renomination in 1874; resumed the practice of law and also engaged in banking; died in Newmarket, N.H., April 7, 1878; interment in Riverside Cemetery.

**SMALLS, Robert,** a Representative from South Carolina; born in Beaufort, S.C., April 5, 1839; moved to Charleston, S.C. in 1851, and worked on the waterfront as a stevedore, foreman, sailmaker, rigger and sailor; pilot of boats along the coasts of South Carolina and Georgia; piloted the cotton steamer *Planter* past Confederate coastal defenses and into possession of the Union fleet, May 13, 1862; appointed pilot in the United States Navy and served throughout the Civil War; member of the State constitutional convention in 1868; served in the South Carolina State house of representatives, 1868-1870; member of the State senate, 1870-1874; delegate to the Republican National Conventions of 1864, 1872 and

1876; elected as a Republican to the Forty-fourth and Forty-fifth Congresses (March 4, 1875-March 3, 1879); unsuccessful candidate for reelection in 1878 to the Forty-sixth Congress; successfully contested the election of George D. Tillman to the Forty-seventh Congress, and served from July 19, 1882 to March 3, 1883; unsuccessful candidate for reelection in 1882; elected to the Forty-eighth Congress to fill the vacancy caused by the death of Edmund W.M. Mackey; reelected to the Forty-ninth Congress, and served from March 18, 1884 to March 3, 1887; unsuccessful candidate for reelection in 1886 to the Fiftieth Congress; collector of the port of Beaufort, S.C., from 1889 until June 1913; died in Beaufort, S.C., February 22, 1915; interment in the Tabernacle Baptist Church Cemetery.

**Bibliography:** *DAB*; Miller, Edward A. *Gullah Statesman: Robert Smalls from Slavery to Congress, 1839-1915*. Columbia: University of South Carolina Press, 1995; Uya, Okun Edet. *From Slavery to Political Service: Robert Smalls, 1839-1915*. New York: Oxford University Press, 1971.

**SMART, Ephraim Knight,** a Representative from Maine; born in Prospect (now Searsport), Maine, September 3, 1813; attended the common schools; completed preparatory studies under private tutors and attended Maine Wesleyan Seminary at Readfield; studied law; was admitted to the bar in 1838 and commenced practice in Camden, Knox County, Maine; appointed postmaster of Camden in 1838; member of the Maine State senate in 1841 and 1842; appointed aide-de-camp with the rank of lieutenant colonel on the staff of Governor John Fairfield in 1842; moved to Missouri in 1843 and continued the practice of his profession; returned to Camden, Maine, the following year and resumed the practice of law; again appointed postmaster of Camden in 1845; elected as a Democrat to the Thirtieth Congress (March 4, 1847-March 3, 1849); elected to the Thirty-second Congress (March 4, 1851-March 3, 1853); collector of customs at Belfast, 1853-1858; established the Maine Free Press in 1854, and served as editor for three years; member of the Maine State house of representatives in 1858; unsuccessful candidate in 1860 for election for Governor of Maine; again served in the Maine State senate in 1862; moved to Biddeford, York County, Maine, in 1869 and established the Maine Democrat; died in Camden, Maine, September 29, 1872; interment in the Mountain Street Cemetery.

**SMART, James Stevenson,** a Representative from New York; born in Baltimore, Md., June 14, 1842; moved with his parents to Coila, Washington County, N.Y., in 1849; attended Cambridge (N.Y.) Academy and Union College, Schenectady, N.Y., and was graduated from Jefferson College, Canonsburg, Pa., in 1863; entered the Union Army in January 1864 as first lieutenant in the Sixteenth Regiment of New York Heavy Artillery; promoted to a captaincy, and was honorably discharged in August 1865; engaged in newspaper work at Cambridge, N.Y., in 1865 and published the Washington County Post; elected as a Republican to the Forty-third Congress (March 4, 1873-March 3, 1875); was not a candidate for renomination in 1874; appointed collector of internal revenue for the northern district of New York and served from March 31, 1883, until November 9, 1885; member of the Republican State central committee for many years; died in Cambridge, Washington County, N.Y., September 17, 1903; interment in Woodland Cemetery.

**SMATHERS, George Armistead** (nephew of William Howell Smathers), a Representative and a Senator from Florida; born in Atlantic City, N.J., November 14, 1913; moved to Miami, Fla., in 1919; attended the public schools of Dade County, Fla.; attended the University of Louisville; B.A., University of Florida, 1936, and LL.B., 1938; was admitted to the bar in 1938 and commenced practice in Miami, Fla.; assistant United States district attorney, 1940-1942; during the Second World War served in the United States Marine Corps from May 1942 until discharged as a major in October 1945; special assistant to United States attorney general

Tom C. Clark from October 1945 until his resignation in January 1946 to begin his campaign for the United States House of Representatives; elected as a Democrat to the Eightieth and Eighty-first Congresses (January 3, 1947-January 3, 1951); was not a candidate in 1950 for renomination to the House of Representatives, but was elected to the United States Senate; reelected in 1956 and again in 1962, and served from January 3, 1951, until January 3, 1969; was not a candidate for reelection in 1968; chairman, Special Committee on Aging (Eighty-eighth and Eighty-ninth Congresses), Select Committee on Small Business (Ninetieth Congress); resumed the practice of law in Washington, D.C., and Miami, Fla.; is a resident of Washington, D.C., and Miami, Fla.

**SMATHERS, William Howell** (uncle of George Armistead Smathers), a Senator from New Jersey; born on a plantation near Waynesville, Haywood County, N.C., January 7, 1891; attended the public schools and Washington and Lee University, Lexington, Va.; graduated from the law department of the University of North Carolina at Chapel Hill in 1911; was admitted to the bar in 1912 and commenced practice in Atlantic City, N.J.; judge of the common pleas court of Atlantic City, N.J., 1922-1932; member of the State supreme court commission, beginning in 1923; special master in chancery in 1924; first assistant attorney general of New Jersey, 1934-1936; elected to the State senate in 1935; elected as a Democrat to the United States Senate for the term beginning January 3, 1937, but was not sworn in until April 15, 1937, being a member of the State senate until that time, and served until January 3, 1943; unsuccessful candidate for reelection in 1942; engaged in the practice of law in Atlantic City, N.J., until his retirement; returned to Waynesville, N.C., where he resided until his death in Asheville, N.C., September 24, 1955; interment in Green Hill Cemetery, Waynesville, N.C.

**SMELT, Dennis,** a Representative from Georgia; born near Savannah, Ga., about 1750; received a limited schooling; participated in the Revolutionary War; elected as a Republican to the Ninth Congress to fill the vacancy caused by the resignation of Joseph Bryan; reelected to the Tenth and Eleventh Congresses and served from September 1, 1806, to March 3, 1811; was not a candidate for reelection to the Twelfth Congress.

**SMILIE, John,** a Representative from Pennsylvania; born in Ireland in 1741; immigrated to the United States and settled in Pennsylvania in 1760; attended the public schools; served in the Revolutionary War; moved to Fayette, Pa., in 1780; was a member of the Pennsylvania house of representatives 1784-1786; member of the Pennsylvania constitutional convention in 1790; served in the Pennsylvania senate from 1790 to 1793, when he resigned; elected to the Third Congress (March 4, 1793-March 3, 1795); elected as a Republican to the Sixth and to the six succeeding Congresses and served from March 4, 1799, until his death; had been reelected to the Thirteenth Congress, but died in Washington, D.C., December 30, 1812, before the close of the Twelfth Congress; interment in the Congressional Cemetery.

**SMITH, Abraham Herr,** a Representative from Pennsylvania; born near Millersville, Manor Township, in Lancaster County, Pa., March 7, 1815; attended Professor Beck's Academy at Lititz, Lancaster County, Pa.; graduated from Dickinson College, Carlisle, Pa., in 1840; studied law; admitted to the bar in 1842 and commenced practice in Lancaster, Lancaster County, Pa.; member of the Pennsylvania house of representatives in 1843 and 1844; served in the Pennsylvania senate in 1845; elected as a Republican to the Forty-third and to the five succeeding Congresses (March 4, 1873-March 3, 1885); chairman, Committee on Mileage (Forty-seventh Congress); unsuccessful for renomination in 1884; resumed the practice of law; died in Lancaster, Pa., February 16, 1894; interment in Woodward Hill Cemetery.

**SMITH, Addison Taylor,** a Representative from Idaho; born near Cambridge, Guernsey County, Ohio, September 5, 1862; attended the public schools of Cambridge, Ohio; was graduated from the Cambridge High School in 1882, from the Iron City Commercial College, Pittsburgh, Pa., in 1883, from the law department of George Washington University, Washington, D.C., in 1895, and from the National Law School, Washington, D.C., in 1896; was admitted to the District of Columbia bar in 1899 and to the Idaho bar in 1905; secretary to Senator George Laird Shoup 1891-1901 and to Senator Weldon B. Heyburn 1903-1912; secretary to the Republican State central committee of Idaho 1904-1911; register of the United States land office at Boise, Idaho, in 1907 and 1908; member of the Republican National congressional committee 1917-1927; elected as a Republican to the Sixty-third and to the nine succeeding Congresses (March 4, 1913-March 3, 1933); chairman, Committee on Alcohol Liquor Traffic (Sixty-sixth and Sixty-seventh Congresses), Committee on Irrigation of Arid Lands (Sixty-seventh and Sixty-eighth Congresses), Committee on Irrigation and Reclamation (Sixty-ninth through Seventy-first Congresses); unsuccessful candidate for reelection in 1932 to the Seventy-third Congress; associate member of the Board of Veterans' Appeals of the Veterans' Administration from 1934 until his retirement in 1942; director of the Columbia Institution for the Deaf (now Gallaudet College), Washington, D.C., from 1937 until his death; died in Washington, D.C., July 5, 1956; interment in Rock Creek Cemetery.

**SMITH, Albert,** a Representative from Maine; born in Hanover, Mass., January 3, 1793; attended the common schools and was graduated from Brown University, Providence, R.I., in 1813; studied law; was admitted to the bar and commenced practice in Portland, Maine, in 1817; member of the State house of representatives in 1820; was United States marshal for the district of Maine 1830-1838; elected as a Democrat to the Twenty-sixth Congress (March 4, 1839-March 3, 1841); unsuccessful candidate for reelection in 1840 to the Twenty-seventh Congress; died in Boston, Mass., on May 29, 1867; interment in Mount Auburn Cemetery, Cambridge, Mass.

**SMITH, Albert,** a Representative from New York, born in Cooperstown, Otsego County, N.Y., June 22, 1805; completed preparatory studies; moved to Batavia, Genesee County, N.Y.; studied law; was admitted to the bar and practiced; held several local offices; member of the State assembly in 1840; elected as a Whig to the Twenty-eighth and Twenty-ninth Congresses (March 4, 1843-March 3, 1847); moved to Milwaukee, Wis., in 1849 and resumed the practice of law; justice of the peace 1851-1859; judge of the Milwaukee County Court 1859-1870; died in Milwaukee, Wis., August 27, 1870; interment in Forest Home Cemetery.

**SMITH, Albert Lee, Jr.,** a Representative from Alabama; born in Birmingham, Jefferson County, Ala., August 31, 1931; attended the public schools; B.S., Auburn (Ala.) University, 1954; served in the United States Navy, as a lieutenant (junior grade), 1954-1956; life insurance underwriter; delegate, Alabama State Republican convention, 1968; delegate to the Republican National Conventions of 1968, 1972, 1976 and 1984; unsuccessful candidate for election in 1978 to the Ninety-sixth Congress; elected as a Republican to the Ninety-seventh Congress (January 3, 1981-January 3, 1983); unsuccessful candidate for reelection in 1982 to the Ninety-eighth Congress; unsuccessful candidate in 1984 for election to the United States Senate; appointed by President Ronald Reagan to the Federal Council on the Aging in 1985; is a resident of Birmingham, Ala.

**SMITH, Arthur,** a Representative from Virginia; born at "Windsor Castle," near Smithfield, Isle of Wight County, Va., November 15, 1785; attended an academy at Smithfield, Va., and graduated from the College of William and Mary, Williamsburg, Va.; studied law; admitted to the bar in 1808 and commenced practice in Smithfield, Va.; also engaged in agricultural pursuits; served as colonel in the War of 1812; member of the Virginia house of delegates 1818-1820; elected to the Seventeenth and Eighteenth Congresses (March 4, 1821-March 3, 1825); was not a candidate for renomination in 1824; resumed the practice of law; member of the house of delegates 1836-1841; died in Smithfield, Va., March 30, 1853; interment in the family burying ground on "Windsor Castle" estate, near Smithfield, Va.

**SMITH, Ballard,** a Representative from Virginia; born in Hanover County, Va.; served as lieutenant in the Army during the Revolutionary War; member of the Virginia house of delegates 1810-1813; elected as a Republican to the Fourteenth, Fifteenth, and Sixteenth Congresses (March 4, 1815-March 3, 1821); again a member of the Virginia house of delegates 1824-1826, 1836, and 1837.

**SMITH, Benjamin A., II,** a Senator from Massachusetts; born in Gloucester, Essex County, Mass., March 26, 1916; attended Gloucester public schools and graduated from Governor Dummer Academy; B.S., Harvard University, 1939; during the Second World War served as a lieutenant in the United States Navy with service in the Pacific Theater, 1941-1945; president of Merchants Box Factory, Cape Ann Fisheries, Inc., United Fisheries Co., Gloucester By-Products, Inc., and Gloucester Community Pier Association, Inc.; mayor of Gloucester, Mass., 1954-1955; appointed as a Democrat to the United States Senate on December 27, 1960, to fill the vacancy caused by the resignation of John F. Kennedy and served until November 6, 1962; was not a candidate for election to fill the vacancy in 1962; was a resident of Gloucester, Mass; died September 26, 1991.

**SMITH, Bernard,** a Representative from New Jersey; born in Morristown, N.J., July 5, 1776; completed preparatory studies; collector of customs in 1809 and 1810; postmaster of New Brunswick, N.J., 1810-1819; elected to the Sixteenth Congress (March 4, 1819-March 3, 1821); was not a candidate for renomination in 1820 to the Seventeenth Congress; appointed register of the land office at Little Rock, Arkansas Territory, in 1821, and settled in that Territory; secretary to Governor George Izard of Arkansas Territory, 1825-1828; appointed by Governor Izard as sub-agent of the Quapaw Indians in 1825, and served until his death in Little Rock, Ark., July 16, 1835; interment in Mount Holly Cemetery.

**SMITH, Caleb Blood,** a Representative from Indiana; born in Boston, Mass., April 16, 1808; moved with his parents to Ohio in 1814; attended Miami University, Oxford, Ohio, 1825-1826; studied law; was admitted to the bar in 1828 and commenced practice in Connersville, Fayette County, Ind.; founded and edited the Indiana Sentinel in 1832; member of the Indiana State house of representatives, 1833-1837, 1840, and 1841, and served as speaker in 1836; unsuccessful candidate for the Twenty-seventh Congress in 1841; elected as a Whig to the Twenty-eighth and to the two succeeding Congresses (March 4, 1843-March 3, 1849); chairman, Committee on Territories (Thirtieth Congress); appointed by President Zachary Taylor a member of the board to investigate claims of American citizens against Mexico; moved to Cincinnati, Ohio, and practiced his profession; member of the peace convention of 1861 held in Washington, D.C., in an effort to devise means to prevent the impending war; appointed Secretary of the Interior in the Cabinet of President Abraham Lincoln, and served from March 5, 1861 to January 1, 1863, when he resigned to become judge of the United States District Court for the District of Indiana, in which capacity he served until his death in Indianapolis, Marion County, Ind., January 7, 1864; interment in the City Cemetery, Connersville, Ind.

**Bibliography:** *DAB*; Bochin, Hal W. "Caleb B. Smith's Opposition to the Mexican War." *Indiana Magazine of History* 69 (June 1973): 95-114; Thomas, Richard J. "Caleb Blood Smith: Whig Orator and Politician-Lincoln's Secretary of Interior." Ph.D. dissertation, Indiana University, 1969.

**SMITH, Charles Bennett,** a Representative from New York; born in Sardinia, Erie County, N.Y., September 14, 1870; attended the district schools, and was graduated from Arcade Academy in 1886; engaged in agricultural pursuits, subsequently became a railroad telegraph operator, and later pursued newspaper work in Buffalo; reporter on the Buffalo Courier 1890-1893; became managing editor of the Buffalo Times in 1894; editor of the Buffalo Evening Enquirer and the Buffalo Morning Courier; appointed a member of the Buffalo Board of School Examiners and served two years as its chairman; elected as a Democrat to the Sixty-second and to the three succeeding Congresses (March 4, 1911-March 3, 1919); chairman, Committee on Foreign Affairs (Sixty-second Congress), Committee on Expenditures in the Department of Commerce (Sixty-fourth Congress), Committee on Patents (Sixty-fifth Congress); unsuccessful candidate for reelection in 1918 to the Sixty-sixth Congress; engaged in commercial and industrial pursuits in Buffalo, N.Y.; superintendent of Standards and Purchases, Albany, N.Y., from 1935 until his death in Wilmington Notch, Essex County, N.Y., May 21, 1939; interment in Mount Olivet Cemetery, Tonawanda, Erie County, N.Y.

**SMITH, Charles Brooks,** a Representative from West Virginia; born in Elizabeth, Wirt County, Va. (now West Virginia), February 24, 1844; attended a private school at Parkersburg; enlisted on March 1, 1864, in Company I of the First West Virginia Cavalry of the Union Army; promoted to second lieutenant of the company March 5, 1864, and was honorably discharged on July 8, 1865; engaged in the mercantile business; recorder of Wood County in 1875; member of the city council of Parkersburg, W.Va., in 1876; mayor of Parkersburg 1878-1880; sheriff and treasurer of Wood County 1880-1884; delegate at large to the Republican National Convention in 1888; successfully contested as a Republican the election of James Monroe Jackson to the Fifty-first Congress and served from February 3, 1890, to March 3, 1891; unsuccessful candidate for reelection to the Fifty-second Congress in 1890; became engaged in the fire insurance business; died in Parkersburg, Wood County, W.Va., December 7, 1899; interment in Mount Olivet Cemetery.

**SMITH, Christopher Henry,** a Representative from New Jersey; born in Rahway, Union County, N.J., March 4, 1953; graduated from St. Mary's High School, Perth Amboy, 1971; B.A., Trenton (N.J.) State College, 1975; attended Worcester College, England, 1974; businessman; executive director, New Jersey Right-to-Life Committee, Inc., 1976-1978; legislative agent, New Jersey State legislature, 1979; unsuccessful candidate for election in 1978 to the Ninety-sixth Congress; elected as a Republican to the Ninety-seventh and to the seven succeeding Congresses (January 3, 1981-January 3, 1997); is a resident of Robbinsville, N.J.

**SMITH, Clyde Harold** (husband of Margaret Chase Smith), a Representative from Maine; born on a farm near Harmony, Somerset County, Maine, June 9, 1876; moved with his parents to Hartland, Maine, in 1891; attended the rural schools and Hartland (Maine) Academy; taught school; served in the State house of representatives 1899-1903 and 1919-1923; engaged in the retail clothing and hardware business in 1901; superintendent of schools of Hartland 1903-1906; member of the board of selectmen of Hartland 1904-1907; moved to Skowhegan, Maine, having been elected sheriff of Somerset County and served from 1905 to 1909; engaged in the retail sales of automobiles, the hardware and plumbing business, and the newspaper publishing business in Skowhegan; later engaged in banking and the real estate business; member of the board of selectmen of Skowhegan 1914-1932; served in the State senate 1923-1929; chairman of the State highway commission 1928-1932; member of the Governor's council 1933-1937; elected as a Republican to the Seventy-fifth and Seventy-sixth Congresses and served from January 3, 1937, until his death in Washington, D.C., April 8, 1940; interment in Pine Grove Cemetery, Hartland, Maine.

**SMITH, Daniel,** a Senator from Tennessee; born in Stafford County, Va., October 29, 1748; attended the College of William and Mary, Williamsburg, Va.; became a surveyor; moved to Augusta County, Va.; deputy surveyor of Augusta County in 1773; fought in the Indian wars 1774; major of the Washington County militia; high sheriff of Augusta County in 1780; commissioned colonel in the Second Battalion and fought in several battles of the Revolution; moved to Sumner County, Tenn., at the close of the war; laid out the town of Nashville; member of the North Carolina convention which ratified the United States Constitution 1789; appointed by President George Washington secretary of the territory south of the Ohio River in 1790; member of the constitutional convention of 1796 to draw up a constitution for the new State of Tennessee; made the first map of Tennessee; general of State militia; appointed as a Republican to the United States Senate to fill the vacancy caused by the resignation of Andrew Jackson and served from October 6, 1798, to March 3, 1799; elected as a Republican to the United States Senate and served from March 4, 1805, to March 31, 1809, when he resigned; engaged in agricultural pursuits; died at his home, "Rock Castle," near Hendersonville, Sumner County, Tenn., June 16, 1818; interment in the family burial ground near his home.

**Bibliography:** Durham, Walter. *Daniel Smith: Frontier Statesman.* Gallatin, Tenn.: Sumner County Library Board, 1976; Sioussat, St. George, ed. "The Journal of Daniel Smith." *Tennessee Historical Magazine* (March 1915): 40-65.

**SMITH, David Highbaugh,** a Representative from Kentucky; born near Hammonville, Hart County, Ky., December 19, 1854; attended the public schools and the colleges at Horse Cave, Leitchfield, and Hartford, Ky.; studied law; admitted to the bar in 1876 and commenced practice in Hodgenville, Larue County, Ky.; superintendent of common schools for Larue County in 1878; county attorney for Larue County 1878-1881; member of the Kentucky house of representatives 1881-1883; served in the Kentucky senate 1885-1893, and as president pro tempore 1891-1893; elected as a Democrat to the Fifty-fifth and to the four succeeding Congresses (March 4, 1897-March 3, 1907); was not a candidate for renomination in 1906; one of the managers appointed by the House of Representatives in 1905 to conduct the impeachment proceedings against Charles Swayne, judge of the United States District Court for the Northern District of Florida; resumed the practice of law; president of the Farmers' National Bank of Hodgenville, Ky.; died in Hodgenville, Ky., December 17, 1928; interment in Red Hill Cemetery.

**SMITH, Delazon,** a Senator from Oregon; born in New Berlin, Chenango County, N.Y., October 5, 1816; graduated from Oberlin College, Ohio, in 1837; studied law and was admitted to the bar; in 1838 established the New York Watchman in Rochester, N.Y., of which he was editor for two years; published and edited the True Jeffersonian and the Western Herald in Rochester in 1840, and in 1841 founded the Western Empire in Dayton, Ohio; special United States commissioner to Quito, Ecuador, 1842-1845; moved to the Territory of Iowa in 1846 and entered the ministry; moved to the Territory of Oregon in 1852; edited the Oregon Democrat; member, Territorial house of representatives 1854-1856; delegate to the State constitutional convention in 1857; upon the admission of Oregon as a State into the Union was elected as a Democrat to the United States Senate and served from February 14 to March 3, 1859; unsuccessful candidate for reelection; died in Portland, Oreg., on November 19, 1860; interment in the City Cemetery, Albany, Linn County, Oreg.

**SMITH, Dennis Alan (Denny)** (cousin of Steven Douglas Symms), a Representative from Oregon; born in Ontario, Malheur County, Oreg., January 19, 1938; attended the public schools;

graduated from Grant Union High School, 1956; B.A., Willamette University, Salem, Oreg., 1961; served in the United States Air Force, 1958-1960 and 1962-1967, with service in Vietnam; pilot, Oregon Air National Guard, 1960-1962; co-pilot and flight engineer for Pan American Airways, 1967-1976; elected as a Republican to the Ninety-seventh and to the four succeeding Congresses (January 3, 1981-January 3, 1991); unsuccessful candidate for reelection in 1990 to the One Hundred Second Congress; is a resident of Salem, Oreg.

**SMITH, Dietrich Conrad,** a Representative from Illinois; born in Ost Friesland, Hanover, Germany, April 4, 1840; immigrated to the United States with his parents, who settled in Pekin, Tazewell County, Ill., about 1850; attended the public schools of Pekin, Ill., and Quincy College, Quincy, Ill.; during the Civil War served in the Union Army as lieutenant in Company I, Eighth Regiment, Illinois Volunteer Infantry; left the service as captain of Company C, One Hundred and Thirty-ninth Regiment, Illinois Volunteer Infantry; organizer of the German College at Mount Pleasant in 1874; member of board of trustees of that institution for many years; member of the State house of representatives 1876-1878; engaged in banking and manufacturing and also in the construction and management of railroads in Illinois; elected as a Republican to the Forty-seventh Congress (March 4, 1881-March 3, 1883); unsuccessful candidate for reelection in 1882 to the Forty-eighth Congress; again engaged in banking; died in Pekin, Ill., April 18, 1914; interment in Lakeside Cemetery.

**SMITH, Edward Henry,** a Representative from New York; born in Smithtown, Long Island, Suffolk County, N.Y., May 5, 1809; attended private schools; engaged in agricultural pursuits; served as justice of the peace in the township of Smithtown 1833-1843, assessor 1840-1843, and supervisor 1856-1860; elected as a Democrat to the Thirty-seventh Congress (March 4, 1861-March 3, 1863); was not a candidate for renomination in 1862; resumed farming in Suffolk County, N.Y.; died in Smithtown, N.Y., August 7, 1885; interment in St. James' Protestant Episcopal Cemetery, St. James, Long Island, N.Y.

**SMITH, Ellison DuRant,** a Senator from South Carolina; born in Lynchburg, Sumter (now Lee) County, S.C., August 1, 1864; attended the private and public schools of Lynchburg, Stewart's School at Charleston, S.C., and the University of South Carolina at Columbia; graduated from Wofford College at Spartanburg, S.C., in 1889; member, State house of representatives 1896-1900; unsuccessful candidate for the United States Congress 1901; engaged in mercantile and agricultural pursuits; one of the principal figures in the organization of the Southern Cotton Association in 1905; field agent and general organizer in the cotton protective movement 1905-1908 and became known as "Cotton Ed"; elected as a Democrat to the United States Senate in 1908; reelected in 1914, 1920, 1926, 1932, and again in 1938, and served from March 4, 1909, until his death; unsuccessful candidate for renomination in 1944; chairman, Committee on Transportation Routes to the Seaboard (Sixty-second Congress), Committee on Immigration (Sixty-third through Sixty-fifth Congresses), Committee on Interstate Commerce (Sixty-fifth and Sixty-eighth Congresses), Committee on Conservation of Natural Resources (Sixty-sixth Congress), Committee on Agriculture and Forestry (Seventy-third through Seventy-eighth Congresses); died in Lynchburg, S.C., on November 17, 1944; interment in St. Lukes Cemetery.

**Bibliography:** Smith, Selden K. "Ellison DuRant Smith: A Southern Progressive 1909-1929." Ph.D. dissertation, University of South Carolina, 1970.

**SMITH, Francis Ormand Jonathan,** a Representative from Maine; born in Brentwood, N.H., November 23, 1806; attended Phillips Exeter Academy, Exeter, N.H.; studied law; was admitted to the bar and commenced practice in Portland, Maine, in 1826;

division advocate of the fifth division of the circuit court-martial in Maine 1829-1834; served in the State house of representatives in 1831; member of the State senate in 1833 and served as its president; elected as a Jacksonian to the Twenty-third and Twenty-fourth Congresses and as a Democrat to the Twenty-fifth Congress (March 4, 1833-March 3, 1839); chairman, Committee on Commerce (Twenty-fifth Congress); unsuccessful candidate for reelection in 1838 to the Twenty-sixth Congress; assisted Professor Samuel F.B. Morse in perfecting and introducing the electric telegraph; again a member of the State house of representatives in 1863 and 1864; died in Deering (later Woodfords), Maine, October 14, 1876; interment on his estate, "Forest Home"; reinterment in Evergreen Cemetery, Portland, Maine.

**Bibliography:** Gaffney, Thomas L. "Maine's Mr. Smith: A Study of the Career of Francis O. J. Smith, Politician and Entrepreneur." Ph.D. dissertation, University of Maine, 1979.

**SMITH, Francis Raphael,** a Representative from Pennsylvania; born in Philadelphia, Pa., September 25, 1911; attended the parochial school and graduated from Roman Catholic High School, Philadelphia, Pa., in 1929, from St. Joseph's College, Philadelphia, Pa., in 1933, and from the law department of Temple University, Philadelphia, Pa., in 1938; bank examiner with Pennsylvania Banking Department in 1938 and 1939; unsuccessful candidate for election in 1938 to the Pennsylvania house of representatives; elected as a Democrat to the Seventy-seventh Congress (January 3, 1941-January 3, 1943); unsuccessful candidate for reelection in 1942 to the Seventy-eighth Congress; United States marshal for the eastern district of Pennsylvania from January 29, 1943, until his resignation on April 30, 1945; was appointed collector of internal revenue at Philadelphia on May 1, 1945, and served in that capacity until 1952; insurance commissioner, Commonwealth of Pennsylvania, 1955-1963; chairman of Democratic City Committee of Philadelphia 1965 to 1968; elected member of Board of Revision of Taxes of Philadelphia and member of Board of View of Philadelphia; was a resident of Philadelphia, Pa., until his death there on December 9, 1982; interment in Holy Sepulchre Cemetery.

**SMITH, Frank Ellis,** a Representative from Mississippi; born in Sidon, Leflore County, Miss., February 21, 1918; attended the public schools of Sidon and Greenwood, Miss.; was graduated from Sunflower Junior College, Moorhead, Miss., in 1936, and from the University of Mississippi in 1941; entered the United States Army as a private on February 9, 1942; graduate of Field Artillery officers candidate school; served in Europe as a captain with the Two Hundred and Forty-third Field Artillery Battalion, Third Army; awarded Bronze Star; was discharged to Reserves as a major of Field Artillery on February 13, 1946; managing editor of the Greenwood Morning Star in 1946 and 1947; student at American University, Washington, D.C., in 1946; legislative assistant to Senator John C. Stennis of Mississippi, 1947-1949; Mississippi State senator, 1948-1950; elected as a Democrat to the Eighty-second and to the five succeeding Congresses, and served from January 3, 1951, until his resignation November 14, 1962; unsuccessful candidate for renomination in 1962 to the Eighty-eighth Congress; member, Board of Directors, Tennessee Valley Authority, November 14, 1962, to May 18, 1972; associate director, Illinois State Board of Higher Education, 1973-1974; visiting professor, Virginia Polytechnic Institute, 1977-1979; special assistant to Governor William Winter of Mississippi, 1980-1983; elected life fellow, Southern Regional Council, 1984; is a resident of Jackson, Miss.

**Bibliography:** Mitchell, Dennis J. "Frank E. Smith: Mississippi Liberal." *Journal of Mississippi History* 48 (May 1986): 85-104; Smith, Frank E. *Congressman from Mississippi.* New York: Pantheon Books, 1964; Smith, Frank E. *The Politics of Conservation.* New York: Pantheon Books, 1966.

**SMITH, Frank Leslie,** a Representative and a Senator-elect from Illinois; born in Dwight, Livingston County, Ill., November 24, 1867; attended the public schools of Dwight; taught school for several years; engaged in banking, real estate, insurance, and agricultural pursuits; served as Dwight village clerk in 1894; unsuccessful candidate for lieutenant governor in 1904; internal revenue collector, 1905-1909; elected as a Republican to the Sixty-sixth Congress (March 4, 1919-March 3, 1921); was not a candidate in 1920 for renomination to the House of Representatives, but was an unsuccessful candidate for nomination to the United States Senate; resumed his former business pursuits; chairman of the Illinois Commerce Commission, 1921-1926; appointed as a Republican to the United States Senate in 1926 to fill the vacancy caused by the death of William B. McKinley in the term ending March 3, 1927; presented credentials as a Senator-designate but was not permitted to qualify, due to charges of "fraud and corruption" in his campaign; presented credentials as a Senator-elect to the United States Senate for the term beginning March 4, 1927, but again was not permitted to qualify, and subsequently tendered his resignation on February 9, 1928; unsuccessful candidate for election in 1930 to the Seventy-second Congress; member of the Republican National Committee in 1932; continued in the real estate and insurance business, and with agricultural pursuits; chairman of the board of directors of the First National Bank of Dwight, Ill., until his death there on August 30, 1950; interment in Oak Lawn Cemetery.

Bibliography: *DAB*; Wooddy, Carroll H. *The Case of Frank L. Smith: A Study in Representative Government.* 1931. Reprint. New York: Arno Press, 1974.

**SMITH, Frank Owens,** a Representative from Maryland; born in Smithville, Calvert County, Md., August 27, 1859; attended the private and public schools of the county, North Mount Institute, West Virginia, and Bethel Military Academy, Virginia; served in the United States Revenue Service at Baltimore, Md., during the first administration of President Grover Cleveland, 1885-1889; organized the Calumet Canning Co. in 1889 and engaged in a general merchandise business in 1890; engaged in manufacturing flour and feed, 1898-1910; appointed Maryland State tobacco inspector by Governor Edwin Warfield in 1904 and reappointed in 1906; unsuccessful candidate for election to the Maryland State senate in 1911; chief engrossing clerk of the State senate in 1911; elected as a Democrat to the Sixty-third Congress (March 4, 1913-March 3, 1915); unsuccessful candidate for renomination in 1914 to the Sixty-fourth Congress; engaged in fruit growing in Dunkirk, Calvert County, Md., until his death on January 29, 1924; interment in Mount Zion Cemetery, Lothian, Anne Arundel County, Md.

**SMITH, Frederick Cleveland,** a Representative from Ohio; born in Shanesville, Tuscarawas County, Ohio, July 29, 1884; attended the public schools; graduated in osteopathy at Kirksville, Ohio, and practiced there for several years; went abroad and continued his study of medicine in Frankfurt, Germany, and in Vienna, Austria; in 1917 was licensed to practice medicine and surgery in the State of Ohio and commenced practice at Marion, Ohio; mayor of Marion, Ohio, from January 1936 until January 1, 1939, when he resigned; elected as a Republican to the Seventy-sixth and to the five succeeding Congresses (January 3, 1939-January 3, 1951); was not a candidate for renomination in 1950; resumed his medical profession; died in Marion, Ohio, July 16, 1956; interment in Marion Cemetery.

**SMITH, George,** a Representative from Pennsylvania; elected as a Republican to the Eleventh and Twelfth Congresses (March 4, 1809-March 3, 1813).

**SMITH, George Joseph,** a Representative from New York; born in Kingston, Ulster County, N.Y., November 7, 1859; attended the public schools; engaged in banking and the manufacturing business in New York City and Kingston; chairman of the Republican county committee in 1898; treasurer of the Republican State committee in 1899; delegate to the Republican National Convention in 1909; elected as a Republican to the Fifty-eighth Congress (March 4, 1903-March 3, 1905); declined to be a candidate for reelection; engaged in the real estate and wholesale grocery business in New York City; died in Atlantic City, N.J., December 24, 1913; interment in Wiltwyck Cemetery, Kingston, N.Y.

**SMITH, George Luke,** a Representative from Louisiana; born in New Boston, Hillsboro County, N.H., December 11, 1837; completed preparatory studies and attended Union College, Schenectady, N.Y.; during the Civil War served in the Union Army; at the close of the war moved to Shreveport, La., and engaged in mercantile pursuits; held several local offices; member of the State house of representatives 1870-1872; proprietor of the Shreveport Southwestern Telegram; president of the Shreveport Savings Bank & Trust Co.; elected as a Republican to the Forty-third Congress to fill the vacancy caused by the death of Representative-elect Samuel Peters and served from November 24, 1873, to March 3, 1875; unsuccessful candidate for reelection in 1874 to the Forty-fourth Congress; appointed collector of customs at the port of New Orleans by President Rutherford B. Hayes and served from May 4, 1878, to February 20, 1879; moved to Hot Springs, Ark., and engaged in the real estate business until his death in that city on July 9, 1884; interment in the West Street Cemetery, Milford, N.H.

**SMITH, George Ross,** a Representative from Minnesota; born in St. Cloud, Stearns County, Minn., May 28, 1864; attended the public schools and Sauk Centre (Minn.) Academy; was graduated from the law school of the University of Minnesota at Minneapolis in 1893; was admitted to the bar in 1893 and commenced practice in Minneapolis; member of the State house of representatives in 1903; judge of the probate court of Hennepin County, Minn., 1907-1913; elected as a Republican to the Sixty-third and Sixty-fourth Congresses (March 4, 1913-March 3, 1917); unsuccessful candidate for reelection in 1916 to the Sixty-fifth Congress; resumed the practice of law and taught law classes at Minneapolis-Minnesota Law School; died in Minneapolis, Minn., November 7, 1952; interment in St. Mary's Cemetery.

**SMITH, George Washington,** a Representative from Illinois; born in Putnam County, Ohio, August 18, 1846; moved with his father to Wayne County, Ill., in 1850; learned the blacksmith trade; attended the common schools and was graduated from the literary department of McKendree College, Lebanon, Ill., in 1868; studied law in Fairfield, Ill.; was graduated from the law department of the Indiana University at Bloomington in 1870; was admitted to the bar the same year and commenced practice in Murphysboro, Jackson County, Ill.; master in chancery from 1880 until 1888; elected as a Republican to the Fifty-first and to the nine succeeding Congresses, and served from March 4, 1889 until his death in Murphysboro, Ill., November 30, 1907, before the convening of the Sixtieth Congress; chairman, Committee on Private Land Claims (Fifty-fourth through Fifty-ninth Congresses); interment in the City Cemetery.

**SMITH, Gerrit,** a Representative from New York; born in Utica, N.Y., March 6, 1797; moved to Peterboro in 1806; attended an academy in Clinton, N.Y.; graduated from Hamilton College, Clinton, N.Y., in 1818; studied law; engaged in the management of a large estate which he inherited; delegate to the State conventions in 1824 and 1828; unsuccessful Liberty Party candidate for governor in 1840; unsuccessful presidential candidate in 1848; was admitted to the bar in 1853 and commenced practice in Peterboro, N.Y.; elected as a Free-Soil candidate to the Thirty-third Congress and served from March 4, 1853, until August 7, 1854, when he resigned; resumed the practice of his profession, and was a publicist and philanthropist; he revived the Anti-Dramshop Party, but was a delegate to the Republican National Convention in 1872 and supported Ulysses S. Grant; died in New York City December 28, 1874; interment in Peterboro Cemetery, Peterboro, Madison County, N.Y.

**Bibliography:** *DAB*; Harlow, Ralph V. *Gerrit Smith, Philanthropist and Reformer.* New York: H. Holt and Co., 1939.

**SMITH, Gomer Griffith,** a Representative from Oklahoma, born on a farm near Kansas City, Jackson County, Mo., July 11, 1896; attended the common and high schools of Missouri; was graduated from Rockingham Academy, Kansas City, Mo., in 1915; taught in a country school near Excelsior Springs, Clay County, Mo., 1916-1918; studied law; was admitted to the Missouri bar in 1920, to the Oklahoma bar in 1922, and commenced practice in Oklahoma City, Okla.; elected as a Democrat to the Seventy-fifth Congress to fill the vacancy caused by the death of Robert P. Hill and served from December 10, 1937, to January 3, 1939; was not a candidate for renomination in 1938, but was an unsuccessful candidate for the Democratic nomination for United States Senator; resumed the practice of law in Oklahoma City, where he died May 26, 1953; interment in Rose Hill Mausoleum.

**SMITH, Green Clay** (son of John Speed Smith), a Representative from Kentucky; born in Richmond, Madison County, Ky., July 4, 1826; pursued academic studies; served in the Mexican War; commissioned second lieutenant in the First Regiment, Kentucky Volunteer Infantry, June 9, 1846; graduated from Transylvania University, Lexington, Ky., in 1849; studied law; admitted to the bar in 1852 and commenced practice in Covington, Ky.; was school commissioner, 1853-1857; member of the Kentucky house of representatives, 1861-1863; commissioned colonel of the Fourth Regiment, Kentucky Volunteer Cavalry, April 4, 1862; brigadier general of Volunteers July 2, 1862; resigned on December 1, 1863; brevetted major general of Volunteers on March 13, 1865; elected as an Unconditional Unionist to the Thirty-eighth and Thirty-ninth Congresses and served from March 4, 1863, until his resignation in 1866; chairman, Committee on Militia (Thirty-ninth Congress); appointed by President Andrew Johnson as Governor of Montana Territory and served from July 13, 1866, until April 9, 1869, when he resigned; moved to Washington, D.C., where he was ordained to the Baptist ministry; was the candidate of the National Prohibition Party in 1876 for President of the United States; pastor of the Metropolitan Baptist Church in Washington, D.C., from 1890 until his death on June 29, 1895; interment in Arlington National Cemetery, Va.

**Bibliography:** Hood, James Larry. "For the Union: Kentucky's Unconditional Unionist Congressmen and the Development of the Republican Party in Kentucky, 1863-1865." *Register of the Kentucky Historical Society* 76 (July 1978): 197-215.

**SMITH, H. Allen,** a Representative from California; born in Dixon, Lee County, Ill., October 8, 1909; attended the public schools; moved to Los Angeles, Calif., in 1924 and attended Hollywood High School and the University of California at Los Angeles; A.B., University of Southern California, 1930; LL.B., University of Southern California School of Law, 1933; was admitted to the bar in 1934 and practiced law in Los Angeles, Calif., until December 1935; special agent for the Federal Bureau of Investigation from December 1935 until August 1942; manager of plant protection, Lockheed Aircraft Corp., from August 1942 to August 1944; resumed the practice of law in Los Angeles, Calif., in 1944; member of the California State assembly, 1948-1956; delegate to every State Republican convention, beginning in 1948; delegate to the Republican National Conventions of 1960, 1964, and 1968, and served as parliamentarian at the 1968 convention; elected as a Republican to the Eighty-fifth and to the seven succeeding Congresses (January 3, 1957-January 3, 1973); was not a candidate for reelection in 1972 to the Ninety-third Congress; is a resident of Glendale, Calif.

**SMITH, Henry,** a Representative from Wisconsin; born in Baltimore, Md., July 22, 1838; moved with his parents to Massillon, Stark County, Ohio, and later, in 1844, to Milwaukee, Wis.; attended the public schools; became a millwright; member of the common council of Milwaukee 1868-1872; served in the State assembly in 1878; again a member of the common council 1880-1882 and 1884-1887; city comptroller 1882-1884; elected as a Labor Party candidate to the Fiftieth Congress (March 4, 1887-March 3, 1889); unsuccessful candidate for reelection in 1888 to the Fifty-first Congress; was an architect and builder; elected a member of the board of aldermen of Milwaukee, Wis., in 1898 and served until his death in Milwaukee, Wis., September 16, 1916; remains were cremated and the ashes interred in Union Cemetery.

**SMITH, Henry Cassorte,** a Representative from Michigan; born in Canandaigua, Ontario County, N.Y., June 2, 1856; moved with his father to a farm near Palmyra, Lenawee County, Mich., in 1857; attended the common schools; graduated from Adrian (Mich.) College in 1878; taught school; studied law; was admitted to the bar on September 25, 1880, and commenced practice in Adrian, Mich.; city attorney of Adrian; delegate to the Republican National Convention of 1896; elected as a Republican to the Fifty-sixth and Fifty-seventh Congresses (March 4, 1899-March 3, 1903); unsuccessful candidate for renomination in 1902 to the Fifty-eighth Congress; resumed the practice of law in Adrian, Mich., and died there on December 7, 1911; interment in Oakwood Cemetery.

**SMITH, Henry P., III,** a Representative from New York; born in North Tonawanda, Niagara County, N.Y., September 29, 1911; attended the public schools and the Nichols School of Buffalo; A.B., Dartmouth College, Hanover, N.H., 1933; LL.B., Cornell University Law School, Ithaca, N.Y., 1936; was admitted to the bar in 1936 and practiced law in Ithaca until 1941, and then in North Tonawanda; elected mayor of North Tonawanda in November 1961 and served until his resignation in January 1963 to accept appointment as Niagara County judge, surrogate and family court judge for one year; elected as a Republican to the Eighty-ninth and to the four succeeding Congresses (January 3, 1965-January 3, 1975); was not a candidate for reelection in 1974 to the Ninety-fourth Congress; chairman, United States section, International Joint Commission, United States and Canada, 1975-1978; executive director and chairman, Association to Unite the Democracies; was a resident of Washington, D.C., until his death there on October 1, 1995.

**SMITH, Hezekiah Bradley,** a Representative from New Jersey; born in Bridgewater, Windsor County, Vt., July 24, 1816; attended the common schools; learned the trade of cabinetmaker; settled in Lowell, Mass., about 1840 and engaged in the manufacture of woodworking machinery; took out more than forty patents for original inventions; moved to Smithville, Burlington County, N.J., in 1865 and continued the manufacture of wood-working machinery; also manufactured the Star bicycle; made the first steam-driven vehicle operated in New Jersey; elected as a Democrat to the Forty-sixth Congress (March 4, 1879-March 3, 1881); unsuccessful candidate for reelection in 1880 to the Forty-seventh Congress; resumed his former business activities; member of the New Jersey State senate, 1883-1885; died in Smithville, N.J., November 3, 1887; interment in the Pine Street Cemetery, Mount Holly, N.J.

**SMITH, Hiram Ypsilanti,** a Representative from Iowa; born in Piqua, Miami County, Ohio, March 22, 1843; moved with his parents to Rock Island, Ill., in 1850, and to Des Moines, Iowa, in 1854; attended the public schools; in 1861 enlisted in the State militia for service against the Indians; appointed a clerk in the Post Office Department, Washington, D.C., and served from January 1862 to February 1864; transferred to the Treasury Department, from which he resigned in August 1865; was graduated from the Albany (N.Y.) Law School in 1866; was admitted to the bar the same year and commenced practice in Des Moines, Iowa; district attorney of the fifth judicial district of Iowa, 1875-1879; member of the Iowa State senate, 1882-1884; elected as a Republican to the Forty-eighth Congress to fill the vacancy caused by the resignation of John A. Kasson, and served from December 2, 1884 to March 3, 1885; was not a candidate for reelection in 1884 to the Forty-ninth Congress; resumed the practice of law; died in Des Moines, Iowa, November 4, 1894; interment in Woodland Cemetery.

**SMITH, Hoke,** a Senator from Georgia; born in Newton, Catawba County, N.C., September 2, 1855; educated principally by his father, a professor at the University of North Carolina at Chapel Hill; studied law in Atlanta, Ga.; was admitted to the bar in 1873 and commenced practice in Atlanta, Ga.; became owner of the Atlanta Evening Journal in 1887 and served as editor and president until 1900; appointed Secretary of the Interior in the Cabinet of President Grover Cleveland, and served from March 6, 1893 to September 1, 1896; resumed the practice of law in Atlanta, Ga.; president of the Atlanta Board of Education, 1896-1907; elected Governor of Georgia in 1906, and served from June 29, 1907 to June 26, 1909; unsuccessful candidate for renomination in 1908; again elected Governor in 1910, and served from July 1, 1911 until his resignation on November 16, 1911, having previously been elected Senator; elected as a Democrat to the United States Senate on July 12, 1911, to fill the vacancy caused by the death of Alexander S. Clay, but did not assume these duties until later, preferring to continue as Governor; reelected to the Senate in 1914, and served from November 16, 1911 to March 3, 1921; unsuccessful candidate for renomination in 1920; chairman, Committee on Education and Labor (Sixty-third through Sixty-fifth Congresses), Committee on Expenditures in the Treasury Department (Sixth-sixth Congress); resumed the practice of his profession in Washington, D.C., and Atlanta, Ga.; died in Atlanta, Ga., November 27, 1931; interment in Oakland Cemetery.

Bibliography: *DAB*; Carageorge, Ted. "An Evaluation of Hoke Smith and Thomas E. Watson as Georgia Reformers." Ph.D. dissertation, University of Georgia, 1963; Grantham, Dewey. *Hoke Smith and the Politics of the New South.* Baton Rouge: Louisiana State University Press, 1958.

**SMITH, Horace Boardman,** a Representative from New York; born in Whitingham, Windham County, Vt., August 18, 1826; pursued classical studies and was graduated from Williams College, Williamstown, Mass., in 1847; studied law; was admitted to the bar in 1850 and began practice in Elmira, N.Y.; held several local offices; judge of Chemung County in 1859 and 1860; elected as a Republican to the Forty-second and Forty-third Congresses (March 4, 1871-March 3, 1875); chairman, Committee on Elections (Forty-third Congress); was not a candidate for renomination in 1874; resumed the practice of law in Elmira, Chemung County, N.Y., until 1883; justice of the supreme court of New York State 1883-1888; retired to his home at Elmira, where he died on December 26, 1888; interment in Woodlawn Cemetery.

**SMITH, Howard Alexander** (uncle of Peter Hoyt Dominick), a Senator from New Jersey; born in New York City, January 30, 1880; attended the Cutler School in New York City; graduated from Princeton University in 1901 and from the law department of Columbia University in 1904; was admitted to the bar the same year and commenced practice in New York City; moved to Colorado Springs, Colo., in 1905 and continued the practice of law until 1917; during the First World War served in the United States Food Administration in Colorado and Washington, D.C.; member of postwar relief organizations in 1918; moved to Princeton, N.J., in 1919 and served as executive secretary of Princeton University until 1927; lecturer in the department of politics at Princeton University, 1927-1930; resumed the practice of law in New York City from 1932 to 1941; member of the Republican National Committee, 1942-1943; elected in 1944 as a Republican to the United States Senate to fill the vacancy in the term ending January 3, 1947, caused by the death of W. Warren Barbour; reelected in 1946 and again in 1952, and served from December 7, 1944 to January 3, 1959; was not a candidate for renomination in 1958; chairman, Committee on Labor and Public Welfare (Eighty-third Congress); special consultant on foreign affairs to the Secretary of State, 1959-1960; died in Princeton, N.J., October 27, 1966; interment in Princeton Cemetery.

Bibliography: Leary, William, Jr. "Smith of New Jersey: A Biography of H. Alexander Smith, United States Senator From New Jersey, 1944-1959." Ph.D. dissertation, Princeton University, 1966.

**SMITH, Howard Worth,** a Representative from Virginia; born in Broad Run, Fauquier County Va., February 2, 1883; attended the public schools; was graduated from Bethel Military Academy, near Warrenton, Va., in 1901, and from the law department of the University of Virginia at Charlottesville in 1903; moved to Alexandria, Va., in May 1904 and commenced the practice of law; served on the Alexandria City council (second ward), 1908-1918, and was its president, 1912-1918; part owner of the Alexandria Gazette, 1911-1921; assistant general counsel, Alien Property Custodian, 1917 and 1918; served as Commonwealth attorney of Alexandria, Va., 1918-1922; judge of the corporation court of Alexandria, 1922-1928; judge of the sixteenth judicial circuit of Virginia, 1928-1930; president of the Alexandria National Bank, 1928-1958; also engaged in farming and dairying; elected as a Democrat to the Seventy-second and to the seventeen succeeding Congresses (March 4, 1931-January 3, 1967); chairman, Committee on Rules (Eighty-fourth through Eighty-ninth Congresses); sponsor of the Smith Act of 1940, requiring aliens to be registered and outlawing promotion of the overthrow of the United States government and the advocacy of subversive acts; unsuccessful candidate for renomination in 1966 to the Ninetieth Congress; resumed the practice of law in Alexandria, Va., where he died on October 3, 1976; interment in Georgetown Cemetery, Broad Run, Va.

Bibliography: *DAB*; Dierenfield, Bruce J. *Keeper of the Rules; Congressman Howard W. Smith of Virginia.* Charlottesville: The University Press of Virginia, 1987.

**SMITH, Isaac,** a Representative from New Jersey; born in Trenton, N.J., in 1740; was graduated from Princeton College in 1755; teacher in that institution 1755-1758; studied medicine and commenced practice in Trenton, N.J.; colonel in the Hunterdon County Militia in 1776 and 1777; elected as a Federalist to the Fourth Congress (March 4, 1795-March 3, 1797); appointed by President George Washington a commissioner to treat with the Seneca Indians in 1797; associate justice of the supreme court of New Jersey 1777-1804; first president of the Trenton Banking Co. 1805-1807; died in Trenton, Mercer County, N.J., on August 29, 1807; interment in the First Presbyterian Churchyard.

**SMITH, Isaac,** a Representative from Pennsylvania; born in Chester County, Pa., January 4, 1761; attended the common schools; engaged in agricultural pursuits near Level Corners, Lycoming County, Pa.; member of the Pennsylvania house of representatives 1806-1808; elected as a Republican to the Thirteenth Congress (March 4, 1813-March 3, 1815); resumed agricultural pursuits and also engaged in the occupation of millwright; died on his farm at Level Corners, near Jersey Shore, Lycoming County, Pa., April 4, 1834; interment in the Pine Creek Presbyterian Churchyard; reinterment in Jersey Shore Cemetery, Jersey Shore, Lycoming County, Pa.

**SMITH, Israel,** a Representative and a Senator from Vermont; born in Suffield, Conn., April 4, 1759; graduated from Yale College in 1781; studied law; was admitted to the bar and commenced practice in Rupert, Vt.; member, Vermont State house of representatives, 1785, 1788-1791; moved to Rutland, Vt.; delegate to the State constitutional convention in 1791; upon the admission of Vermont as a State into the Union was elected to the Second Congress; reelected to the Third and Fourth Congresses, and served from October 17, 1791 to March 3, 1797; unsuccessful candidate for reelection in 1796 to the Fifth Congress; member of the State house of representatives in 1797; chief justice of the State supreme court, 1797-1798; unsuccessful candidate in 1806 for election for Governor; elected to the Seventh Congress (March 4, 1801-March 3, 1803); did not seek renomination in 1802 to the House of Representatives, having become a candidate for Senator; elected as a Republican to the United States Senate, and served from March 4, 1803 until his resignation on October 1, 1807, having been elected Governor; elected Governor of Vermont in 1807, and served from October 9, 1807 to October 14, 1808; unsuccessful candidate for reelection in 1808; died in Rutland, Vt., December 2, 1810; interment in the West Street Cemetery.

**Bibliography:** *DAB.*

**SMITH, James,** a Delegate from Pennsylvania; born in Ireland in 1713; immigrated to the United States with his father in 1727 and settled in Pennsylvania; pursued classical studies; attended the Philadelphia Academy (now the University of Pennsylvania); worked as a surveyor in Cumberland County; studied law; admitted to the bar in 1745 and began practice in Shippensburg, Pa.; moved to York, Pa., and engaged in the manufacture of iron; delegate to the provisional conference in Philadelphia; delegate to the Pennsylvania convention in January 1775; organized the Pennsylvania Militia and the two regiments of the Flying Camp in Perth Amboy, N.J., in 1776; Member of the Continental Congress 1776-1778; a signer of the Declaration of Independence; member of the Pennsylvania house of representatives in 1780; brigadier general of Pennsylvania militia; Pennsylvania councilor; resumed the practice of his profession in York, Pa., and died there on July 11, 1806; interment in the First Presbyterian Churchyard.

**Bibliography:** *DAB.*

**SMITH, James, Jr.,** a Senator from New Jersey; born in Newark, N.J., June 12, 1851; attended private schools and St. Mary's College, Wilmington, Del.; engaged in the dry-goods and importing business, later becoming a manufacturer of leather in Newark, N.J.; member of the board of aldermen of Newark 1883-1887; declined the nomination for mayor of Newark in 1884; president of the first board of works of Newark; elected as a Democrat to the United States Senate and served from March 4, 1893, to March 3, 1899; chairman, Committee on the Organization, Conduct and Expenditures of Executive Departments (Fifty-third Congress); resumed the manufacture of leather, and also engaged in banking and newspaper publishing; unsuccessful candidate for election to the United States Senate in 1911; died in Newark, N.J., April 1, 1927; interment in Holy Sepulcher Cemetery.

**Bibliography:** *DAB.*

**SMITH, James Strudwick,** a Representative from North Carolina; born near Hillsboro, Orange County, N.C., October 15, 1790; attended a private school near Hillsboro and Hillsboro Academy; was graduated from Jefferson Medical College, Philadelphia, Pa., in 1818, and practiced medicine near Hillsboro and later near Chapel Hill, Orange County; elected as a Republican to the Fifteenth and Sixteenth Congresses (March 4, 1817-March 3, 1821); chairman, Committee on Accounts (Sixteenth Congress); unsuccessful candidate for renomination; resumed the practice of medicine; member of the State house of commons in 1821 and 1822; delegate to the State constitutional convention in 1835; died near Chapel Hill, N.C., in August 1859; interment in a private cemetery on his farm.

**SMITH, James Vernon,** a Representative from Oklahoma; born in Oklahoma City, Okla., July 23, 1926; educated in Tuttle public schools and attended Oklahoma College of Liberal Arts at Chickasha, Okla.; engaged in farming and cattle raising; served as member, board of regents, Oklahoma Four-Year Colleges; elected as a Republican to the Ninetieth Congress (January 3, 1967-January 3, 1969); unsuccessful candidate for reelection in 1968 to the Ninety-first Congress; nominated by President Richard M. Nixon to be Administrator of Farmers Home Administration, confirmed by the Senate on March 16, 1969, and served until his resignation in 1973; died in a wheat field fire at his farm northwest of Chickasha, June 23, 1973; interment in Fairlawn Cemetery, Chickasha, Okla.

**SMITH, Jedediah Kilburn,** a Representative from New Hampshire; born in Amherst, N.H., November 7, 1770; completed preparatory studies; studied law; was admitted to the bar and commenced practice at Amherst in 1800; member of the State house of representatives in 1803; member of the State senate 1804-1806 and 1809; elected as a Republican to the Tenth Congress (March 4, 1807-March 3, 1809); unsuccessful candidate for the United States Senate in 1810; councilor 1810-1815; postmaster at Amherst from May 19, 1819, until his successor was appointed on March 15, 1826; associate justice of the court of common pleas 1816-1821, and of the court of sessions 1821-1823; chief justice of the court of sessions 1823-1825; died in Amherst, Hillsborough County, N.H., December 17, 1828.

**SMITH, Jeremiah** (brother of Samuel Smith, of New Hampshire, and uncle of Robert Smith), a Representative from New Hampshire; born in Peterboro, N.H., November 29, 1759; received instruction from a private tutor; attended Harvard College in 1777; during the Revolutionary War served under General John Stark in the Battle of Bennington, N.Y., August 16, 1777; entered Queen's (now Rutgers) College, New Jersey, from which he was graduated in 1780; studied law; was admitted to the bar in 1786 and commenced practice in Peterboro, N.H.; member of the New Hampshire State house of representatives, 1788-1791; member of the constitutional convention in 1791 and 1792; elected to the Second and Third Congresses and elected as a Federalist to the Fourth and Fifth Congresses and served from March 4, 1791, until his resignation on July 26, 1797; chairman, Committee on Revisal and Unfinished Business (Fifth Congress); moved to Exeter, N.H.; United States district attorney for New Hampshire from 1797 to 1800; judge of probate of Rockingham County, 1800-1802; appointed, under authority of the act of February 13, 1801, by President John Adams as judge of the United States circuit court February 20, 1801, and served until March 8, 1802, when the court was abolished by the act of that date; chief justice of the Superior Court of Judicature of New Hampshire, 1802-1809; elected Governor of New Hampshire in 1809, and served from June 8, 1809 to June 7, 1810; unsuccessful candidate for reelection in 1810, and for election as Governor in 1811; Chief Justice of the Supreme Judicial Court of New Hampshire, 1813-1816; resumed the practice of law, from which he retired in 1820; president of a bank and treasurer of Phillips Exeter Academy; moved to Dover, N.H. and died there September 21, 1842; interment in Winter Street (also called Old) Cemetery, Exeter, N.H.

**Bibliography:** *DAB.*

**SMITH, John,** a Representative and a Senator from New York; born in Mastic, Long Island, N.Y., February 12, 1752; completed preparatory studies; member, State assembly 1784-1799; delegate to the State convention which adopted the Federal Constitution in 1788; elected to the Sixth Congress to fill the vacancy caused by the death of Jonathan N. Havens; reelected to the Seventh and Eighth Congresses and served from February 6, 1800, until his resignation, effective February 23, 1804; elected as a Republican on February 4, 1804, to the United States Senate to fill the vacancy caused by the resignation of De Witt Clinton; reelected, and served from February 23, 1804, to March 3, 1813; United States marshal for the district of New York 1813-1815; major general of the New York Militia at the time of his death in Mastic, Long Island, N.Y., August 12, 1816; interment in the family cemetery on Smiths Point, N.Y.

**SMITH, John,** a Senator from Ohio; born in either Virginia or Ohio around 1735; prepared for the ministry, and was pastor in various Baptist congregations in Virginia and Ohio by 1790; member of the Northwest Territorial legislature 1799-1803; upon the admission of Ohio as a State into the Union was elected as a Republican to the United States Senate and served from April 1, 1803, to April 25, 1808, when he resigned; died in St. Francisville, Louisiana, July 30, 1824.

Bibliography: *DAB*; Wilhelmy, Robert W. "Senator John Smith and the Aaron Burr Conspiracy." *Cincinnati Historical Society Bulletin* 28 (Spring 1970): 39-60.

**SMITH, John** (father of Worthington Curtis Smith), a Representative from Vermont; born in Barre, Mass., August 12, 1789; attended the common schools; moved to St. Albans, Vt.; studied law; was admitted to the bar in 1810 and commenced practice in St. Albans, Vt.; State's attorney for Franklin County 1826-1832; member of the State house of representatives 1827-1837, and served as speaker from 1831 to 1833; elected as a Democrat to the Twenty-sixth Congress (March 4, 1839-March 3, 1841); unsuccessful candidate for reelection in 1840 to the Twenty-seventh Congress; engaged in the construction of railroads; died in St. Albans, Vt., November 26, 1858; interment in Greenwood Cemetery.

**SMITH, John,** a Representative from Virginia; born at "Shooter's Hill," near Locust Hill, Middlesex County, Va., May 7, 1750; moved to Frederick County, Va., in 1773 and engaged in planting at "Hackwood," near Winchester; commissioned a justice of the peace in 1773; served in Lord Dunmore's War with the Indians in 1774, the Revolutionary War, and the War of 1812; member of the Virginia house of delegates 1779-1783; served in the Virginia senate 1791-1794; elected as a Republican to the Seventh and to the six succeeding Congresses (March 4, 1801-March 3, 1815); resumed agricultural pursuits; died at "Rockville," near Middletown, Frederick County, Va., on March 5, 1836; interment in the family burying ground at "Hackwood," near Winchester, Va.; reinterred in Mount Hebron Cemetery, Winchester, Va., in 1890.

**SMITH, John Ambler,** a Representative from Virginia; born at Village View, near Dinwiddie Court House, Dinwiddie County, Va., September 23, 1847; attended the rural school and was educated at David Turner's high school at Richmond; graduated from the law department of the Richmond (Va.) College; admitted to the bar in 1867 and commenced the practice of law in Richmond, Va.; appointed commissioner in chancery of the courts of Richmond in 1868; served as Commonwealth attorney of Charles City and New Kent Counties; member of the Virginia senate in 1869; elected as a Republican to the Forty-third Congress (March 4, 1873-March 3, 1875); unsuccessful candidate for renomination in 1874; resumed the practice of law in Washington, D.C.; member of the immigration commission to London; died in Washington, D.C., on January 6, 1892; interment in Glenwood Cemetery.

**SMITH, John Armstrong,** a Representative from Ohio; born in Hillsboro, Ohio, September 23, 1814; pursued classical studies and was graduated from Miami University, Oxford, Ohio, in 1834; studied law; was admitted to the bar in 1835 and commenced practice in Hillsboro, Ohio; served in the State house of representatives in 1841; member of the State constitutional convention of Ohio in 1850; elected as a Republican to the Forty-first and Forty-second Congresses (March 4, 1869-March 3, 1873); resumed the practice of law; member of the State constitutional convention of 1873; died in Hillsboro, Ohio, March 7, 1892; interment in Hillsboro Cemetery.

**SMITH, John Cotton,** a Representative from Connecticut; born in Sharon, Conn., on February 12, 1765; completed preparatory studies; was graduated from Yale College in 1783; studied law; was admitted to the bar and began practice in Sharon, Conn., in 1787; member of the Connecticut State house of representatives in 1793, 1796, and 1800, and served as speaker in 1800; elected as a Federalist to the Sixth Congress to fill the vacancy caused by the resignation of Jonathan Brace; reelected to the Seventh and to the two succeeding Congresses, and served from November 17, 1800 until his resignation in August 1806; chairman, Committee on Claims (Seventh through Ninth Congresses); judge of the supreme court of Connecticut in 1809; Lieutenant Governor in 1810; elected Governor of Connecticut on the Federalist ticket in 1813, reelected in 1814, 1815 and 1816, and served from October 25, 1812 to May 8, 1817; unsuccessful candidate for reelection in 1817; president of the American Board of Commissioners for Foreign Missions; president of the Connecticut Bible Society; retired to his estate near Sharon, Litchfield County, Conn., where he died on December 7, 1845; interment in Hillside Cemetery.

Bibliography: *DAB*.

**SMITH, John Hyatt,** a Representative from New York; born in Saratoga, N.Y., April 10, 1824; taught by his father; employed for a time as a clerk in Detroit, Mich., and later as a bank clerk in Albany, N.Y., and while in the latter position studied theology; after ordination his first pastorate was in Poughkeepsie, N.Y., in 1848; officiated in Cleveland, Ohio, for three years, in Buffalo, N.Y., from 1855 until 1860, and in Philadelphia, Pa., from 1860 until 1866; during the Civil War served in Virginia with the United States Christian Commission in 1862; chaplain of the Forty-seventh Regiment, National Guard of New York, in 1869; continued his ministerial duties in Brooklyn, N.Y., from 1866 until 1880; elected as an Independent candidate to the Forty-seventh Congress (March 4, 1881-March 3, 1883); appointed by President Chester A. Arthur as a commissioner to inspect the Pacific Railroad, after which he resumed a pastorate in Brooklyn, N.Y., where he died on December 7, 1886; interment in Greenwood Cemetery.

**SMITH, John Joseph,** a Representative from Connecticut; born in Waterbury, New Haven County, Conn., January 25, 1904; attended the public schools; B.A., Yale University, 1925; law department of the same university, LL.B., 1927; research fellow, Yale Law School, 1927-1928; was admitted to the bar in 1927 and commenced practice in Waterbury, Conn.; served in the Field Artillery Reserves 1925-1935; elected as a Democrat to the Seventy-fourth Congress; reelected to the three succeeding Congresses and served from January 3, 1935, until his resignation on November 4, 1941, having been appointed a United States district judge for the district of Connecticut; appointed judge for the Second Circuit Court of the United States on September 2, 1960, and served until November 6, 1971, when he retired to become a senior judge; resided in West Hartford, Conn., until his death in Waterbury, Conn., February 16, 1980; interment in Calvary Cemetery, Waterbury.

**SMITH, John M.C.,** a Representative from Michigan; born in Belfast, Ireland, February 6, 1853; immigrated to the United States in 1855 with his parents, who settled near Plymouth, Ohio; attended the public schools; moved to Charlotte, Mich., in 1867; engaged in agricultural pursuits and also worked as a mason; was graduated from the academic department of the University of Michigan at Ann Arbor in 1879 and from the law department in 1880; was admitted to the bar in 1882 and commenced practice in Detroit; prosecuting attorney of Eaton County, 1885-1888; president of the First National Bank of Charlotte in 1898; also engaged in manufacturing and agricultural pursuits; member of the board of aldermen in 1903; member of the State constitutional convention in 1908; elected as a Republican to the Sixty-second and to the four succeeding

Congresses (March 4, 1911-March 3, 1921); chairman, Committee on Labor (Sixty-sixth Congress); was not a candidate for renomination in 1920 to the Sixty-seventh Congress, but was later elected to that Congress to fill the vacancy caused by the death of William H. Frankhouser; reelected to the Sixty-eighth Congress, and served from June 28, 1921 until his death in Charlotte, Mich., March 30, 1923; interment in Maple Hill Cemetery.

**SMITH, John Quincy,** a Representative from Ohio; born near Waynesville, Warren County, Ohio, November 5, 1824; attended the common schools and Miami University, Oxford, Ohio; engaged in agricultural pursuits; member of the State senate in 1860 and 1861; served in the State house of representatives in 1862 and 1863; again a member of the State house of representatives in 1872 and 1873; elected as a Republican to the Forty-third Congress (March 4, 1873-March 3, 1875); unsuccessful candidate for reelection in 1874 to the Forty-fourth Congress; United States Commissioner of Indian Affairs 1875-1877; appointed United States consul general to Montreal, Canada, and served from 1878 until he resigned in 1882; died in Oakland, Clinton County, Ohio, December 30, 1901; interment in Miami Cemetery, Waynesville, Ohio.

**SMITH, John Speed** (father of Green Clay Smith), a Representative from Kentucky; born near Nicholasville, Jessamine County, Ky., July 1, 1792; attended a private school in Mercer County; studied law; admitted to the bar in 1812 and commenced practice in Richmond, Ky.; during the War of 1812 enlisted as a private, and subsequently promoted to major; aide-de-camp to General William Henry Harrison with the rank of colonel; member of the State house of representatives in 1819; elected to the Seventeenth Congress to fill the vacancy caused by the resignation of George Robertson and served from August 6, 1821, to March 3, 1823; was not a candidate for renomination in 1822; again a member of the Kentucky house of representatives in 1827, 1830, 1839, 1841, and 1845, and served as speaker in 1827; United States district attorney for Kentucky 1828-1832; member of the Kentucky senate 1846-1850; died in Richmond, Ky., June 6, 1854; interment in Richmond Cemetery.

**SMITH, John T.,** a Representative from Pennsylvania; born in Philadelphia, Pa.; attended the common schools of his native city; elected as a Democrat to the Twenty-eighth Congress (March 4, 1843-March 3, 1845).

**SMITH, John Walter,** a Representative and a Senator from Maryland; born at Snow Hill, Md., February 5, 1845; attended private schools and Union Academy; engaged in the lumber business in Maryland, Virginia, and North Carolina; president of the First National Bank of Snow Hill and director in many business and financial institutions; elected to the Maryland State senate in 1889, 1893, and 1897, and served as president in 1894; elected as a Democrat to the Fifty-sixth Congress, and served from March 4, 1899 until his resignation on January 12, 1900; elected Governor of Maryland in 1899, and served from January 10, 1900 to January 13, 1904; elected as a Democrat to the United States Senate to fill the vacancy caused by the death of William Pinkney Whyte; reelected in 1909 and 1914, and served from March 25, 1908 to March 3, 1921; unsuccessful for reelection in 1920; chairman, Committee to Investigate Trespassers Upon Land (Sixty-second Congress), Committee on the District of Columbia (Sixty-third through Sixty-fifth Congresses), Committee to Examine Branches of the Civil Service (Sixty-sixth Congress); retired to private life and died in Baltimore, Md., on April 19, 1925; interment in the Presbyterian Cemetery, Snow Hill, Md.

**SMITH, Jonathan Bayard,** a Delegate from Pennsylvania; born in Philadelphia, Pa., February 21, 1742; received an English education, and was graduated from Princeton College in 1760; secretary of the Philadelphia Committee of Safety 1775-1777;

Member of the Continental Congress in 1777 and 1778; prothonotary of the court of common pleas in 1777 and 1778; appointed justice of the court of common pleas in 1778; one of the founders in 1779 of the University of the State of Pennsylvania and a member of its board of trustees until its consolidation in 1791 with the College of Philadelphia into the University of Pennsylvania, serving as a trustee of the latter institution until his death; also a trustee of Princeton College from 1779 until 1808; served on the board of aldermen of Philadelphia 1792-1794; auditor general of Pennsylvania in 1794; died in Philadelphia, Pa., June 16, 1812; interment in the graveyard of the Second Presbyterian Church.

**Bibliography:** *DAB.*

**SMITH, Joseph Francis,** a Representative from Pennsylvania; born in Philadelphia, Philadelphia County, Pa., January 24, 1920; attended St. Anne's Parochial School, Philadelphia; graduated from Northeast Catholic High School, Philadelphia, 1939; attended St. Joseph's College, Philadelphia, 1940-1942; served in the United States Army, sergeant, 1942-1945; accountant; administrative assistant to Representative James A. Byrne of Pennsylvania, 1965-1970; served in the Pennsylvania legislature, 1970-1981; elected as a Republican and Independent to the Ninety-seventh Congress, July 21, 1981, by special election to fill the vacancy caused by the resignation of Raymond F. Lederer, and served from July 21, 1981, to January 3, 1983; unsuccessful candidate for renomination as a Democrat in 1982 to the Ninety-eighth Congress; Democratic City chairman, Philadelphia, 1983-1986; is a resident of Philadelphia, Pa.

**SMITH, Joseph Luther,** a Representative from West Virginia; born in Marshes (now Glen Daniel), Raleigh County, W.Va., May 22, 1880; attended public and private schools; editor and owner of the Raleigh Register, Beckley, W.Va., until 1911; also engaged in the real estate and banking business; mayor of Beckley 1904-1929; member of the State senate 1909-1913; elected as a Democrat to the Seventy-first and to the seven succeeding Congresses (March 4, 1929-January 3, 1945); chairman, Committee on Mines and Mining (Seventy-second through Seventy-eighth Congresses); was not a candidate for renomination in 1944; engaged in banking administrative business, and was a resident of Beckley, W.Va., until his death on August 23, 1962; interment in Sunset Memorial Park.

**SMITH, Joseph Showalter,** a Representative from Oregon; born in Connellsville, Fayette County, Pa., June 20, 1824; attended the common schools; moved to Oregon City in the spring of 1844; moved to Salem, Oreg., and taught school; studied law and was admitted to the bar; moved to Olympia, Wash., in 1853; was elected to the Territorial house of representatives in 1856, and served as speaker; was appointed United States attorney for Washington Territory by President James Buchanan on March 12, 1857; returned to Salem, Oreg., in 1858 and practiced law for twelve years; elected as a Democrat to the Forty-first Congress (March 4, 1869-March 3, 1871); moved to Portland, Oreg., in 1870 and resumed the practice of his profession; unsuccessful Democratic candidate for Governor of Oregon in 1882; died in Portland, Oreg., July 13, 1884; interment in Riverview Cemetery.

**SMITH, Josiah,** a Representative from Massachusetts; born in Pembroke, Mass., February 26, 1738; graduated from Harvard College in 1774; studied law; admitted to the bar and practiced; member of the Massachusetts house of representatives in 1789 and 1790; served in the Massachusetts senate 1792-1794 and in 1797; Massachusetts treasurer in 1797; elected as a Republican to the Seventh Congress (March 4, 1801-March 3, 1803); was not a candidate for renomination in 1802; died in Pembroke, Plymouth County, Mass., April 4, 1803; interment in Pembroke Cemetery.

**SMITH, Lamar Seeligson,** a Representative from Texas; born in San Antonio, Tex., November 19, 1947; graduated from the Texas Military Institute, San Antonio, 1965; B.A., Yale University, 1969; J.D., Southern Methodist University School of Law, Dallas, Tex., 1975; intern, Small Business Administration, Washington, D.C., 1969-1970; business and financial writer, The Christian Science Monitor, 1970-1972; admitted to the Texas State bar in 1975 and commenced practice in San Antonio; chair, Bexar County Republican Party, 1978-1982; member, Texas State house of representatives, 1981-1982; Bexar County (Tex.) commissioner, 1982-1985; elected as a Republican to the One Hundredth and to the four succeeding Congresses (January 3, 1987-January 3, 1997); is a resident of San Antonio, Tex.

**SMITH, Larkin I.,** a Representative from Mississippi; born in Poplarville, Pearl River County, Miss., June 26, 1944; graduated from Poplarville High School in 1962; A.A., Pearl River Junior College, 1964; B.A., William Carey College, Hattiesburg, Miss., 1979; joined sheriff's department of Pearl River County in 1966; chief investigator, Harrison County (Miss.) sheriff's department, 1972-1977; Harrison County sheriff, 1984-1988; elected as a Republican to the One Hundred First Congress, and served from January 3, 1989 until his death in an airplane crash in the DeSoto National Forest near Janice, Miss., August 13, 1989; interment in Floral Hills Memorial Gardens, Gulfport, Miss.

**SMITH, Lawrence Henry,** a Representative from Wisconsin; born in Racine, Boone County, Wis., September 15, 1892; attended the public schools and the State Teachers College, Milwaukee, Wis.; graduated from the Marquette University Law School, Milwaukee, Wis., in 1923; was admitted to the bar the same year and commenced the practice of law in Racine, Wis.; during the First World War served as a first lieutenant of Infantry, Thirty-second Division, 1917-1919; elected as a Republican to the Seventy-seventh Congress to fill the vacancy caused by the death of Stephen Bolles; reelected to the Seventy-eighth and to the seven succeeding Congresses and served from August 29, 1941, until his death in the United States Capitol, Washington, D.C., January 22, 1958; interment in West Lawn Memorial Park, Racine, Wis.

**SMITH, Lawrence Jack,** a Representative from Florida; born in Brooklyn, Kings County, N.Y., April 25, 1941; attended public schools in East Meadow, N.Y.; attended New York University, New York City, 1958-1961; LL.B. and J.D., Brooklyn (N.Y.) Law School, 1964; admitted to the bar in 1964 and commenced practice in New York City; admitted to the Florida bar, 1972; served in the Florida State house of representatives, 1978-1982; elected as a Democrat to the Ninety-eighth and to the four succeeding Congresses (January 3, 1983-January 3, 1993); was not a candidate for renomination in 1992 to the One Hundred Third Congress; resumed a governmental relations practice; is a resident of Hollywood, Fla.

**SMITH, Linda A.,** a Representative from Washington; born in La Junta, Otero County, Colo., July 16, 1950; graduated, Fort Vancouver High School, Vancouver, Wash., 1968; manager of tax consulting and tax preparation businesses in Vancouver; member, Washington State house of representatives, 1983-1987; member, Washington State senate, 1987-1995; elected as a Republican to the One Hundred Fourth Congress (January 3, 1995-January 3, 1997); is a resident of Hazel Dell, Wash.

**SMITH, Madison Roswell,** a Representative from Missouri; born on a farm near Glenallen, Bollinger County, Mo., July 9, 1850; attended the public schools and Central College in Fayette, Mo.; studied law and was admitted to the bar in 1874; taught school; began the practice of law at Marble Hill, Bollinger County, Mo., in 1877; prosecuting attorney of Bollinger County, 1878-1882; served in the Missouri State senate, 1884-1888; declined to be a candidate for reelection; served as editor of reports for the St. Louis court of appeals for four years and resigned; delegate to the Democratic National Conventions of 1896 and 1912; elected as a Democrat to the Sixtieth Congress (March 4, 1907-March 3, 1909); unsuccessful candidate for reelection in 1908 to the Sixty-first Congress; organizer and secretary of the Federal Trust Co., of St. Louis, 1909-1912; appointed Minister to Haiti on August 15, 1913 and served until July 1914; continued the practice of his profession in Farmington, Mo., where he died on June 18, 1919; interment in the Masonic Cemetery.

**SMITH, Marcus Aurelius,** a Delegate and a Senator from Arizona; born near Cynthiana, Harrison County, Ky., January 24, 1851; attended the common schools; taught school in Bourbon County, Ky.; graduated from Transylvania University, Lexington, Ky., in 1872 and from the law department of the University of Kentucky at Lexington; was admitted to the bar and practiced; prosecuting attorney for the city of Lexington; moved to San Francisco and practiced law 1879-1881; moved to Tombstone, Ariz., in 1881 and continued the practice of law; prosecuting attorney for the Tombstone district 1882; elected as a Democrat a Delegate to the Fiftieth and to the three succeeding Congresses (March 4, 1887-March 3, 1895); elected to the Fifty-fifth Congress (March 4, 1897-March 3, 1899); elected to the Fifty-seventh Congress (March 4, 1901-March 3, 1903); elected to the Fifty-ninth and Sixtieth Congresses (March 4, 1905-March 3, 1909); was not a candidate for election to the Fifty-fourth, Fifty-sixth, and Fifty-eighth Congresses; upon the admission of Arizona as a State into the Union was elected as a Democrat in 1912 to the United States Senate for the term ending March 3, 1915; reelected in 1914 and served from March 27, 1912 to March 3, 1921; unsuccessful candidate for reelection in 1920; chairman, Committee on Conservation of Natural Resources (Sixty-third Congress), Committee on Irrigation and Reclamation of Arid Lands (Sixty-third and Sixty-fourth Congresses), Committee on Printing (Sixty-fifth Congress), Committee on the Geological Survey (Sixty-sixth Congress); appointed in 1921 by President Woodrow Wilson as a member of the International Joint Commission created to prevent disputes regarding the use of the boundary waters between the United States and Canada, and served until his death in Washington, D.C., April 7, 1924; interment in Battle Grove Cemetery, Cynthiana, Ky.

**Bibliography:** Fazio, Steven A. "Marcus Aurelius Smith: Arizona Delegate and Senator." *Arizona and the West* 12 (Spring 1970): 23-62.

**SMITH, Margaret Chase** (wife of Clyde Harold Smith), a Representative and a Senator from Maine; born December 14, 1897, in Skowhegan, Somerset County, Maine; attended the public schools and graduated from Skowhegan High School in 1916; taught primary school in Skowhegan in 1916 and 1917; telephone operator and commercial manager of a telephone company, circulation manager for a country weekly newspaper, office manager for a woolen company, and treasurer of a waste process company, 1919-1930; secretary to her husband while he was a member of the House of Representatives, 1937-1940; lieutenant colonel, Air Force Reserve, 1950-1958; elected as a Republican to the Seventy-sixth Congress, June 3, 1940, by special election to fill the vacancy caused by the death of her husband, Clyde H. Smith; reelected to the four succeeding Congresses, and served from June 3, 1940 to January 3, 1949; was not a candidate in 1948 for reelection to the House of Representatives, but was elected to the United Sates Senate; reelected in 1954, 1960, and again in 1966, and served from January 3, 1949, until January 3, 1973; unsuccessful candidate for reelection in 1972; chairwoman, Special Committee on Rates of Compensation (Eighty-third Congress), Senate Republican Conference (Ninetieth through Ninety-second Congresses); visiting professor for the Woodrow Wilson National Fellowship Foundation, 1973-1976; active in the affairs of the Margaret Chase Smith Library Center,

Northwood Institute, Skowhegan; was a resident of Skowhegan, Maine, until her death there on May 29, 1995.

**Bibliography:** Sherman, Janann Margaret. "Margaret Chase Smith: The Making of a Senator." Ph.D. dissertation, Rutgers University, 1993; Smith, Margaret Chase. *Declaration of Conscience.* Edited by William C. Lewis, Jr. New York: Doubleday, 1972; Wallace, Patricia Ward. *The Politics of Conscience: A Biography of Margaret Chase Smith.* Westport, Conn.: Praeger, 1995.

**SMITH, Martin Fernard,** a Representative from Washington; born in Chicago, Ill., May 28, 1891; attended the public schools, Lewis Institute, Chicago, Ill., and Northwestern University, Evanston, Ill.; moved to Hoquiam, Wash., in 1911 and completed law studies commenced in Chicago; was admitted to the bar in 1912 and commenced practice in Hoquiam, Wash.; served as municipal judge of Hoquiam 1914-1917; during the First World War served as a private in the Coast Artillery Corps from October 9, 1918, to December 15, 1918; member of the city council 1926-1928; mayor of Hoquiam 1928-1930; elected as a Democrat to the Seventy-third and to the four succeeding Congresses (March 4, 1933-January 3, 1943); chairman, Committee on Pensions (Seventy-sixth and Seventy-seventh Congresses); unsuccessful candidate for reelection in 1942 to the Seventy-eighth Congress; delegate to the Democratic National Convention in 1936; appointed a member of the Board of Immigration Appeals, Justice Department, on April 1, 1943, and served until his resignation on April 29, 1944; unsuccessful candidate in 1944 for the Democratic nomination for United States Senator; appointed special assistant to the Attorney General of the United States on September 26, 1944, and served until his death in Bethesda, Md., October 25, 1954; interment in Arlington National Cemetery, Va.

**SMITH, Melancton,** a Delegate from New York; born in Jamaica, Long Island, N.Y., May 7, 1744; was educated by his parents; engaged in business in Poughkeepsie, N.Y.; delegate to the First Provincial Congress in New York, May 22, 1775; served in the Continental Line Regiment which was organized June 30, 1775; organized and became captain of the Dutchess County Minutemen; secret service commissioner and sheriff of Dutchess County, N.Y., in 1777 and 1778; moved to New York City in 1785 and engaged in mercantile pursuits; Member of the Continental Congress 1785-1787; member of the State ratification convention at Poughkeepsie in 1788; served in the State assembly in 1791; died in New York City July 29, 1798; interment in Jamaica Cemetery, Jamaica, Queens County, N.Y.

**SMITH, Meriwether,** a Delegate from Virginia; born at "Bathurst," near Dunnsville, Essex County, Va., in 1730; completed preparatory studies; was a signer of the Westmoreland Association in 1766; member of Essex Committee on Safety in 1774; member of the Virginia house of burgesses in 1774 and 1775; delegate to the Revolutionary conventions of 1775 and 1776; member of the Virginia house of delegates 1776-1778; member of the Continental Congress 1778-1779 and 1781; again a member of the Virginia house of delegates in 1781, 1782, 1785, and 1788; delegate to the Virginia ratification convention in 1788; died at "Marigold," near Ozeana, Essex County, Va., January 25, 1790; interment on his estate at "Bathurst," near Dunnsville, Essex County, Va.

**SMITH, Nathan** (brother of Nathaniel Smith and uncle of Truman Smith), a Senator from Connecticut; born in Woodbury, Conn., January 8, 1770; received a modest education; read law; was admitted to the bar in 1792 and commenced the practice of his profession in New Haven, Conn.; prosecuting attorney for New Haven County, 1817-1835; delegate to the State constitutional convention in 1818; unsuccessful candidate for governor of Connecticut in 1825; appointed United States attorney for the district of Connecticut, 1828-1829; elected as a Whig to the United States Senate, and served from March 4, 1833 until his death in

Washington, D.C., December 6, 1835; interment in the Grove Street Cemetery, New Haven, Conn.

**Bibliography:** *DAB*; Smith, Emily, ed. *Life and Letters of Nathan Smith.* New Haven: Yale University Press, 1914.

**SMITH, Nathaniel** (brother of Nathan Smith and uncle of Truman Smith), a Representative from Connecticut; born in Woodbury, Conn., January 6, 1762; attended the common schools; engaged in agricultural pursuits and was also a cattle dealer; studied law; was admitted to the bar in 1787 and commenced the practice of his profession in Woodbury, Conn.; member of the State house of representatives 1789-1795; elected as a Federalist to the Fourth and Fifth Congresses (March 4, 1795-March 3, 1799); declined to be a candidate for renomination in 1798; served in the State senate 1800-1805; judge of the supreme court of Connecticut 1806-1819; delegate to the Hartford Convention of 1814; died in Woodbury, Litchfield County, Conn., March 9, 1822; interment in the Episcopal Church Cemetery.

**Bibliography:** *DAB*.

**SMITH, Neal Edward,** a Representative from Iowa; born in Hedrick, Keokuk County, Iowa, March 23, 1920; attended the public schools of Packwood, Iowa, the Missouri University College of Liberal Arts in 1945 and 1946, and the Syracuse University Schools of Public and Business Administration from 1946 until 1948; LL.B., Drake University Law School, Des Moines, Iowa, 1950; was admitted to the bar in 1950 and commenced the practice of law in Des Moines; also lives on and operates a farm in Polk County; served in the Army Air Force from 1942 to 1945; awarded nine battle stars, Air Medal, four oak leaf clusters, and Order of the Purple Heart; assistant county attorney for Polk County, Iowa, in 1951 and 1952; national president, Young Democratic Clubs of America, 1953-1955; chairman, Polk County Welfare Board, 1953-1954; elected as a Democrat to the Eighty-sixth and to the seventeen succeeding Congresses (January 3, 1959-January 3, 1995); chairman, Special Committee on Campaign Expenditures (Ninety-third Congress), Committee on Small Business (Ninety-fifth and Ninety-sixth Congresses); unsuccessful candidate for reelection in 1994 to the One Hundred Fourth Congress; resumed the practice of law in Des Moines; is a resident of Altoona, Iowa.

**Bibliography:** Smith, Neal. *Mr. Smith Went to Washington: From Eisenhower to Clinton.* Ames: Iowa State University Press, 1996.

**SMITH, Nicholas Hart (Nick),** a Representative from Michigan; born in Addison, Hillsdale County, Mich., November 5, 1934; attended Addison community schools; B.A., Michigan State University, 1957; M.S., University of Delaware, 1959; entered active duty, United States Air Force in 1959; released in 1961; served Addison Township as trustee, supervisor and County board member; State chairman, Agriculture Stabilization and Conservation Service; director, Michigan Farm Bureau; National Director of Energy for the United States Department of Agriculture; member, Michigan State house of representatives, 1978-1982; member, Michigan State senate, 1983-1993; elected as a Republican to the One Hundred Third and One Hundred Fourth Congresses (January 3, 1993-January 3, 1997); is a resident of Addison, Mich.

**SMITH, O'Brien,** a Representative from South Carolina; born in Ireland about 1756; came to South Carolina following the Revolutionary War, taking the oath of allegiance to the Government of the United States July 31, 1784; member of the State assembly, 1791-1799; served in the State senate in 1803; elected as a Republican to the Ninth Congress (March 4, 1805-March 3, 1807); died April 27, 1811; interment in the burial ground of the colonial Chapel of Ease of St. Bartholomew's Parish, Colleton County, near Jacksonboro, S.C.

**SMITH, Oliver Hampton,** a Representative and a Senator from Indiana; born on Smith's Island, near Trenton, N.J., October 23, 1794; attended the common schools; moved west, eventually settling in Lawrenceburg, Ind., in 1818; studied law; was admitted to the bar in 1820 and commenced practice in Connersville, Ind.; member, State house of representatives 1822-1824; prosecuting attorney for the third judicial district 1824-1825; elected to the Twentieth Congress (March 4, 1827-March 3, 1829); unsuccessful candidate for reelection in 1828; elected as a Whig to the United States Senate and served from March 4, 1837, to March 3, 1843; chairman, Committee on Engrossed Bills (Twenty-sixth Congress), Committee on Public Lands (Twenty-seventh Congress); unsuccessful candidate for reelection; moved to Indianapolis, Ind., and resumed the practice of law; declined to be a candidate for governor of Indiana in 1845; engaged in the railroad business in Indianapolis; died in Indianapolis, Ind., March 19, 1859; interment in Crown Hill Cemetery.

**Bibliography:** *DAB.*

**SMITH, Perry,** a Senator from Connecticut; born in Woodbury, Conn., May 12, 1783; completed preparatory studies; studied law at the Litchfield Law School; was admitted to the bar and commenced the practice of law in New Milford, Conn., in 1807; member of the State house of representatives in 1822-1823, 1835-1836; judge of probate court 1833-1835; postmaster of New Milford 1829-1837; elected as a Democrat to the United States Senate and served from March 4, 1837, to March 3, 1843; chairman, Committee on Agriculture (Twenty-fifth Congress), Committee on Revolutionary Claims (Twenty-sixth Congress); died in New Milford, Litchfield County, Conn., on June 8, 1852; interment in Center Cemetery.

**SMITH, Peter P.,** a Representative from Vermont; born in Boston, Mass., October 31, 1943; B.A., Princeton University, 1968; M.A., Harvard Graduate School of Education, 1970, and Ph.D., 1984; educator; assisted in founding the Community College of Vermont; member, Vermont State senate, 1981-1982; Lieutenant Governor of Vermont, 1983-1986; unsuccessful Republican candidate in 1986 for election for Governor of Vermont; elected as a Republican to the One Hundred First Congress (January 3, 1989-January 3, 1991); unsuccessful candidate for reelection in 1990 to the One Hundred Second Congress; president, California State University at Monterey Bay, January 1995 to present; is a resident of Seaside, Calif.

**SMITH, Ralph Tyler,** a Senator from Illinois; born in Granite City, Madison County, Ill., October 6, 1915; attended public schools in Granite City; A.B., Illinois College, Jacksonville, 1937; J.D., Washington University Law School, St. Louis, 1940; was admitted to the bar in 1940 and commenced practice in Granite City; enlisted in the United States Naval Reserve immediately after Pearl Harbor, ordered to active duty in July 1942, commissioned an ensign in October 1942 and served until January 1946; resumed the practice of law in Alton, Ill., in 1946; elected to the Illinois State general assembly in 1954, and was reelected for seven succeeding terms; majority whip in 1963; elected speaker in 1967 and reelected in 1969; appointed as a Republican September 17, 1969, to fill the vacancy in the United States Senate created by the death of Everett McKinley Dirksen, and served until November 3, 1970; unsuccessful candidate in 1970 for election to fill the unexpired term; resumed the practice of law; died in Alton, Ill., August 13, 1972; interment in Sunset Hill Cemetery Mausoleum, Edwardsville, Ill.

**SMITH, Richard,** a Delegate from New Jersey; born in Burlington, N.J., March 22, 1735; educated under private teachers and in Friends' schools; studied law; was admitted to the bar in 1762 and practiced in Philadelphia, Pa., and later in Burlington, N.J.; commissioned county clerk of Burlington on December 7, 1762; Member of the Continental Congress from July 23, 1774, to June 12, 1776, when he resigned; member of the State council in 1776; elected treasurer of New Jersey and served from 1776 to February 15, 1777, when he resigned; moved to Laurens, N.Y., in 1790 and thence to Philadelphia in 1799; died near Natchez, Miss., September 17, 1803; interment in Natchez Cemetery.

**Bibliography:** *DAB.*

**SMITH, Robert** (nephew of Jeremiah Smith and Samuel Smith of New Hampshire), a Representative from Illinois; born in Peterborough, Hillsboro County, N.H., June 12, 1802; attended the public schools and New Ipswich Academy; taught school; engaged in mercantile pursuits in 1822 and in the manufacturing of textile goods in Northfield, N.H., in 1823; studied law; was admitted to the bar and practiced; moved to Illinois and settled in Alton in 1832 and again engaged in mercantile pursuits; elected captain in the State militia in 1832; extensive land owner and engaged in the real estate business; member of the State house of representatives 1836-1840; elected enrolling and engrossing clerk of the State house of representatives in 1840 and 1842; elected as a Democrat to the Twenty-eighth and Twenty-ninth Congresses and as an Independent Democrat to the Thirtieth Congress (March 4, 1843-March 3, 1849); chairman, Committee on Roads and Canals (Twenty-ninth Congress); elected as a Democrat to the Thirty-fifth Congress (March 4, 1857-March 3, 1859); chairman, Committee on Mileage (Thirty-fifth Congress); served as paymaster during the Civil War; died in Alton, Ill., December 21, 1867; interment in Alton City Cemetery.

**SMITH, Robert Barnwell,** a Representative and a Senator from South Carolina. (*See* RHETT, Robert Barnwell.)

**SMITH, Robert C.,** a Representative and a Senator from New Hampshire; born in Trenton, N.J., March 30, 1941; attended the public schools of Allentown, N.J.; graduated Hamilton High East High School, Trenton, N.J., 1959; B.S., Lafayette College, Easton, Pa., 1965; attended Long Beach State College, Long Beach, Calif., 1967-1969; served two years active duty in the United States Navy from 1965 to 1967, with one year of duty in Vietnam, and also served five years in the Naval Reserve from 1962-1965 and 1967-1969; taught history, civics and English, 1968-1974; owned and managed a real estate business; unsuccessful candidate in 1982 for election to the Ninety-eighth Congress; elected as a Republican to the Ninety-ninth and to the two succeeding Congresses; served from January 3, 1985, until his resignation on December 7, 1990; appointed to the United States Senate, December 7, 1990, to fill vacancy caused by the resignation of Gordon J. Humphrey, and served for the remainder of the term ending January 3, 1991; elected to the United States Senate in 1990 for the term beginning January 3, 1991 and ending January 3, 1997; is a resident of Tuftonboro, N.H.

**SMITH, Robert Freeman,** a Representative from Oregon; born in Portland, Multnomah County, Oreg., June 16, 1931; attended public schools in Burns, Oreg.; B.A., Willamette University, Salem, Oreg., 1953; rancher; businessman; member, Oregon State house of representatives, 1960-1972; Oregon State senator, 1972-1982; Oregon's representative on the President's Public Land Review Commission, 1965-1969; delegate to the Republican National Convention of 1980; elected as a Republican to the Ninety-eighth and the five succeeding Congresses (January 3, 1983-January 3, 1995); was not a candidate for reelection in 1994 to the One Hundred Fourth Congress; founder of a political and public affairs consulting firm; candidate for election in 1996 to the One Hundred Fifth Congress; is a resident of Medford, Oreg.

**SMITH, Samuel,** a Representative and a Senator from Maryland; born in Carlisle, Pa., July 27, 1752; moved with his family to Baltimore, Md., in 1759; attended a private academy; engaged in mercantile pursuits; served in the Revolutionary War as captain, major, and lieutenant colonel; engaged in the shipping business; member, State house of delegates 1790-1792; at the time of the threatened war with France in 1794 was appointed brigadier general of militia and commanded Maryland's quota during the Whisky Rebellion; during the War of 1812 served as major general of militia in the defense of Baltimore; elected to the Third and to the four succeeding Congresses (March 4, 1793-March 3, 1803); did not seek renomination in 1802, having become a candidate for Senator; chairman, Committee on Commerce and Manufactures (Fifth through Seventh Congresses); elected to the United States Senate as a Republican in 1802, reelected in 1808, and served from March 4, 1803, to March 3, 1815; served as President pro tempore of the Senate during the Ninth and Tenth Congresses; elected to the Fourteenth Congress to fill the vacancy caused by the resignation of Nicholas R. Moore; reelected to the Fifteenth, Sixteenth, and Seventeenth Congresses and served from January 31, 1816, to December 17, 1822, when he resigned, having been elected Senator; chairman, Committee on Expenditures in the Department of the Treasury (Fourteenth Congress), Committee on Ways and Means (Fifteenth through Seventeenth Congresses); elected to the United States Senate to fill the vacancy caused by the death of William Pinkney; reelected in 1826 and served from December 17, 1822, to March 3, 1833; served as President pro tempore of the Senate during the Twentieth and Twenty-first Congresses); chairman, Committee on Finance (Eighteenth and Twentieth through Twenty-second Congresses); mayor of Baltimore, Md., 1835-1838; retired from public life; died in Baltimore, April 22, 1839; interment in the Old Westminster Burying Ground.

**Bibliography:** Cassell, Frank A. *Merchant Congressman in the Young Republic.* Madison: University of Wisconsin Press, 1971; Pancake, John. *Samuel Smith and the Politics of Business, 1782-1839.* University, Ala.: University of Alabama Press, 1972.

**SMITH, Samuel** (brother of Jeremiah Smith and uncle of Robert Smith), a Representative from New Hampshire; born in Peterboro, N.H., November 11, 1765; attended Phillips Exeter Academy, Exeter, N.H., and Phillips Academy, Andover, Mass.; engaged in mercantile pursuits; served as moderator in town meetings 1794-1811; elected as a Federalist to the Thirteenth Congress (March 4, 1813-March 3, 1815); was not a candidate for renomination in 1814; resumed his former business pursuits, and in 1828 engaged in the manufacture of paper and cotton goods; died in Peterboro, N.H., April 25, 1842; interment in the Village Cemetery.

**SMITH, Samuel,** a Representative from Pennsylvania; associate judge of Erie County, Pa., from 1803 to 1805, when he resigned; elected as a Republican to the Ninth Congress to fill the vacancy caused by the resignation of John B. C. Lucas; reelected to the Tenth and Eleventh Congresses and served from November 7, 1805, to March 3, 1811; unsuccessful candidate for reelection in 1810 to the Twelfth Congress.

**SMITH, Samuel A.,** a Representative from Pennsylvania; born in Harrow, Nockamixon Township, Bucks County, Pa., in 1795; attended the common schools; commissioned justice of the peace for the Rockhill-Milford district before he was twenty-one years of age; register of wills for Bucks County, 1824-1829; was brigade inspector of militia for the Bucks and Montgomery County district; resigned in 1832; elected as a Jacksonian to the Twenty-first Congress to fill in part the vacancies caused by the resignations of George Wolf and Samuel D. Ingham; reelected to the Twenty-second Congress and served from October 13, 1829, to March 3, 1833; member of the Pennsylvania senate, 1841-1843; was appointed associate judge of the courts of Bucks County by Governor David R. Porter in 1844 and served until 1849; engaged in mercantile pursuits in Doylestown, Pa., and later in Point Pleasant, Pa.; died in Point Pleasant, Bucks County, Pa., May 15, 1861; interment in the Presbyterian Churchyard, Doylestown, Pa.

**SMITH, Samuel Axley,** a Representative from Tennessee; born in Monroe County, Tenn., June 26, 1822; received a limited education; taught school; studied law; was admitted to the bar in 1845 and commenced practice in Cleveland, Tenn.; district attorney general, 1845-1850; delegate to the Democratic National Convention of 1848; elected as a Democrat to the Thirty-third and to the two succeeding Congresses (March 4, 1853-March 3, 1859); unsuccessful candidate for reelection in 1858 to the Thirty-sixth Congress; appointed by President James Buchanan to be Commissioner of the General Land Office, and served from January 18 to February 12, 1860, when he resigned; appointed by Governor Isham G. Harris of Tennessee on November 16, 1861, as an agent to collect arms for the Confederate Army; died at Ladd Springs, Polk County, Tenn., November 25, 1863; interment in Amos Ladd's Burial Ground.

**SMITH, Samuel William,** a Representative from Michigan; born in Independence Township, Oakland County, Mich., August 23, 1852; attended the common schools in Clarkston and Detroit; began teaching school in 1869; served as superintendent of schools in Waterford Township, Mich., in 1875 and at the same time served as principal of the school at Waterford, Mich.; studied law; was admitted to the bar in 1877 and was graduated from the law department of the University of Michigan at Ann Arbor in 1878; commenced the practice of law in Pontiac, Mich.; prosecuting attorney of Oakland County, 1880-1884; served in the Michigan State senate, 1885-1887; elected as a Republican to the Fifty-fifth and to the eight succeeding Congresses (March 4, 1897-March 3, 1915); chairman, Committee on District of Columbia (Sixtieth and Sixty-first Congresses); was not a candidate for reelection in 1914 to the Sixty-fourth Congress; moved to Detroit in 1913 and continued the practice of law; died in Detroit, Mich., June 19, 1931; interment in Oak Hill Cemetery, Adrian, Mich.

**SMITH, Sylvester Clark,** a Representative from California; born near Mount Pleasant, Henry County, Iowa, August 26, 1858; attended the district schools and Howe's Academy at Mount Pleasant; taught school in Winfield, Iowa; moved to California in 1879 and engaged in agricultural pursuits; taught school in Colusa and Kern Counties in 1883; studied law; was admitted to the bar in 1885 and commenced practice in Bakersfield, Calif.; edited the Kern County Echo; resumed the practice of law; member of the State senate 1894-1902; unsuccessful candidate for election in 1902 to the Fifty-eighth Congress; elected as a Republican to the Fifty-ninth and to the three succeeding Congresses and served from March 4, 1905, until his death in Los Angeles, Calif., January 26, 1913; interment in Union Cemetery.

**SMITH, Thomas,** a Representative from Indiana; born in Fayette County, Pa., May 1, 1799; moved to Rising Sun, Ind., in 1818; learned the trade of tanner; moved to Versailles, Ind., in 1821 and established a tanyard; became a colonel in the militia; member of the State house of representatives in 1829, 1830, and 1833-1836; served in the State senate 1836-1839; elected as a Democrat to the Twenty-sixth Congress (March 4, 1839-March 3, 1841); unsuccessful candidate for election in 1840 to the Twenty-seventh Congress; elected to the Twenty-eighth and Twenty-ninth Congresses (March 4, 1843-March 3, 1847); was not a candidate for renomination in 1846; delegate to the State constitutional convention in 1850; died in Versailles, Ripley County, Ind., April 12, 1876; interment in Cliff Hill Cemetery.

**SMITH, Thomas,** a Delegate from Pennsylvania; born near Cruden, Aberdeenshire, Scotland, in 1745; pursued preparatory studies; attended the University of Edinburgh, Scotland; immigrated to the United States and settled in Bedford, Pa., February 9, 1769; deputy surveyor in 1769; studied law; admitted to the bar and commenced the practice of his profession in 1772; deputy register of wills and prothonotary in 1773; justice of the peace in 1774; member of the committee of correspondence in 1775; served in the Revolutionary Army as a deputy colonel of militia; delegate to the Pennsylvania constitutional convention in 1776; member of the Pennsylvania house of representatives 1776-1780; Member of the

Continental Congress 1781-1782; judge of the court of common pleas in 1791; judge of the Pennsylvania Supreme Court 1794-1809; died in Philadelphia, Pa., on March 31, 1809; interment in Christ Churchyard.

**SMITH, Thomas,** a Representative from Pennsylvania; born in Pennsylvania; resided in Tinicum Township, Delaware County, Pa.; member of the State house of representatives in 1806 and 1807; elected as a Federalist to the Fourteenth Congress (March 4, 1815-March 3, 1817); moved to Darby Township (later Darby Borough) in 1815; justice of the peace at the time of his death in Darby, Delaware County, Pa., on January 29, 1846; interment in St. James's (Old Swedes) Cemetery, Paschall (now a part of Philadelphia), Pa.

**SMITH, Thomas Alexander,** a Representative from Maryland; born near Greenwood, Sussex County, Del., September 3, 1850; moved with his parents to Ridgely, Md., in 1856; attended the public schools and Denton (Md.) Academy; taught school in Delaware, Maryland, and Michigan; returned to Ridgely, Md., where he was postmaster from August 4, 1885, to November 25, 1889; engaged in the mercantile business; member of the board of school commissioners for Caroline County 1889-1893; member of the State senate in 1894 and 1896; was chief of the Maryland Bureau of Statistics and Information 1900-1904; first vice president of the National Association of Labor Statisticians in 1903 and 1904; member of the board of State aid and charities in 1904 and 1905; one of the founders of the Bank of Ridgely and served as its first president; elected as a Democrat to the Fifty-ninth Congress (March 4, 1905-March 3, 1907); unsuccessful candidate for reelection in 1906 to the Sixtieth Congress; was a delegate to the Farmers' National Congress of the United States held at Madison, Wis., in 1908 and at Lincoln, Nebr., in 1910; land commissioner of Maryland 1908-1912; appointed internal revenue agent for the district of Maryland in 1915 and served until January 1, 1920; retired in 1922, and resided in Ridgely, Caroline County, Md.; died in Newark, Del., May 1, 1932; interment in Denton Cemetery, Ridgely, Md.

**SMITH, Thomas Francis,** a Representative from New York; born in New York City, July 24, 1865; attended the common schools, St. Francis Xavier College, Manhattan College, and the New York Law School from 1899 to 1901; reporter on the New York World and the New York Tribune; clerk of the city court 1898-1917; was admitted to the bar in 1911 and commenced practice in New York City; delegate to the State constitutional convention in 1915 and to the Democratic National Convention in 1916; elected as a Democrat to the Sixty-fifth Congress to fill the vacancy caused by the death of Michael F. Conry; reelected to the Sixty-sixth Congress and served from April 12, 1917, to March 3, 1921; was not a candidate for renomination in 1920; public administrator of New York from April 1, 1921, until his death in a taxicab accident in New York City April 11, 1923; interment in Calvary Cemetery, Long Island City, N.Y.

**SMITH, Thomas Vernor,** a Representative from Illinois; born in Blanket, Brown County, Tex., April 26, 1890; attended the public schools; was graduated from the University of Texas at Austin in 1915 and from the University of Chicago, Chicago, Ill., in 1922; during the First World War entered the military service September 3, 1918, and served as a private in the United States Army until discharged on January 28, 1919; member of the faculty of Texas Christian University, 1916-1918, the University of Texas, 1919-1921, and the University of Chicago, 1923-1948; author of numerous books; editor of the International Journal of Ethics, 1931-1948; member of the Illinois State senate, 1935-1938; chairman of the Illinois Legislative Council in 1937 and 1938; elected as a Democrat to the Seventy-sixth Congress (January 3, 1939-January 3, 1941); unsuccessful candidate for reelection in 1940 to the Seventy-seventh Congress; served in the United States Army as a lieutenant colonel and later as a colonel, from 1943 to 1946; served as director of

education of the Allied Control Commission in Italy from November 24, 1943, to November 11, 1944; in 1948 resumed his profession as a writer and teacher at the University of Syracuse, Syracuse, N.Y., until his retirement in 1959; resided in Hyattsville, Md., until his death there on May 24, 1964; interment in Arlington National Cemetery, Va.

**Bibliography:** *DAB.*

**SMITH, Truman** (nephew of Nathan Smith and Nathaniel Smith), a Representative and a Senator from Connecticut; born in Roxbury, Conn., November 27, 1791; completed preparatory studies; graduated from Yale College in 1815; studied law; was admitted to the bar in 1818 and commenced practice in Litchfield, Conn.; member, Connecticut State house of representatives, 1831-1832, 1834; elected as a Whig to the Twenty-sixth and Twenty-seventh Congresses (March 4, 1839-March 3, 1843); declined to be a candidate for renomination in 1842 to the Twenty-eighth Congress; presidential elector on the Whig ticket in 1844; elected to the Twenty-ninth and Thirtieth Congresses (March 4, 1845-March 3, 1849); declined the appointment of Secretary of the Interior in the Cabinet of President Zachary Taylor; elected to the United States Senate as a Whig and served from March 4, 1849, until his resignation May 24, 1854; resumed the practice of his profession in New York City in 1854, with residence in Stamford, Conn.; appointed by President Abraham Lincoln as judge of the court of arbitration, under the treaty of 1862 with Great Britain for the suppression of the slave trade, 1862-1870; retired from active business life in 1872; died in Stamford, Fairfield County, Conn., May 3, 1884; interment in Woodland Cemetery.

**Bibliography:** *DAB.*

**SMITH, Virginia Dodd,** a Representative from Nebraska; born in Randolph, Fremont County, Iowa, June 30, 1911; attended Manti Rural School (elementary) in Fremont County, Iowa; graduated from Shenandoah (Iowa) High School; B.A., University of Nebraska, Lincoln, 1936; lecturer before agricultural and civic groups; member, United States Department of Agriculture's Home Economics Research Advisory Committee, 1950-1960; delegate to White House Conference on Children and Youth, 1960; chairwoman, Presidential Task Force on Rural Development, 1971-1972; served on Advisory Board, Educational Resources Information Center, Clearinghouse on Rural Education and Small Schools, United States Department of Health, Education, and Welfare, 1972-1974; served on Census Advisory Committee on Agricultural Statistics, United States Department of Commerce, 1973; delegate to Republican National Conventions, 1956-1972; elected as a Republican to the Ninety-fourth and to the seven succeeding Congresses (January 3, 1975-January 3, 1991); was not a candidate for renomination in 1990 to the One Hundred Second Congress; is a resident of Chappell, Nebr.

**SMITH, Walter Inglewood,** a Representative from Iowa; born in Council Bluffs, Pottawattamie County, Iowa, July 10, 1862; attended the common schools; studied law; was admitted to the bar in 1882 and commenced practice in Council Bluffs, Iowa; judge of the fifteenth judicial district of Iowa, 1890-1900; elected as a Republican to the Fifty-sixth Congress to fill the vacancy caused by the resignation of Smith McPherson, and on the same day was elected to the Fifty-seventh Congress; reelected to the Fifty-eighth and to the four succeeding Congresses and served from December 3, 1900, to March 15, 1911, when he resigned to accept an appointment on the bench; appointed by President William Howard Taft to be United States circuit judge for the eighth judicial circuit and served from March 16, 1911, until his death in Council Bluffs, Iowa, on January 27, 1922; interment in Fairview Cemetery.

**Bibliography:** *DAB.*

**SMITH, William,** a Delegate and a Representative from Maryland; born in Donegal Township, Lancaster County, Pa., April 12, 1728; moved to Baltimore, Md., May 1, 1761; appointed a member of the committee of correspondence in 1774; member of the committee of observation in 1775; one of a committee appointed by Congress to constitute a naval board in 1777; Member of the Continental Congress in 1777; engaged in mercantile pursuits; elected to the First Congress (March 4, 1789-March 3, 1791); First Auditor of the United States Treasury July 16 to November 27, 1791; member of the State senate in 1801; died in Baltimore, Md., on March 27, 1814; interment in the Old Westminster Graveyard.

**SMITH, William,** a Representative from South Carolina; born in Bucks County, Pa., September 20, 1751; removed to South Carolina with his father in 1765; planter, of Spartan District; fought in the Revolutionary War; county court judge, 1785-1797; South Carolina senate from Spartan District 1790-1796; elected as a Republican to Fifth Congress (March 4, 1797-March 3, 1799); again a member of the South Carolina senate from Spartan District 1810-1818; died in Spartan District June 22, 1837; probably buried in Glenn Springs section of Spartanburg.

**SMITH, William,** a Senator from South Carolina; born around 1762, probably in North Carolina; attended several private academies; studied law and was admitted to the bar in 1784; settled in Pinckneyville, S.C., and later in Yorkville (now York), S.C., and practiced law; also was engaged as a planter; member, South Carolina State senate, 1802-1808, and served as president of that body, 1806-1808; judge of the South Carolina Circuit Court, 1808-1816; elected as a Republican to the United States Senate, December 4, 1816, to fill the vacancy caused by the resignation of John Taylor; on the same day was elected for the term commencing March 4, 1817, and served from December 4, 1816 to March 3, 1823; unsuccessful candidate for reelection; chairman, Committee on the Judiciary (Sixteenth and Seventeenth Congresses); member, State house of representatives, 1824-1825; again elected to the United States Senate to fill the vacancy caused by the death of John Gaillard, and served from November 29, 1826 to March 3, 1831; unsuccessful candidate for reelection in 1830; chairman, Committee on Private Land Claims (Twentieth Congress); again a member of the State senate, 1831-1832; moved to Louisiana in 1832, and to a farm near Huntsville, Madison County, Ala., in 1833; member, Alabama State house of representatives, 1836-1840; declined the appointment of Associate Justice of the Supreme Court of the United States tendered by President Andrew Jackson in 1829 and 1836; presidential elector on the Democratic ticket in 1836; died at his estate "Calhoun Place," on the Maysville Pike, near Huntsville, Ala., June 26, 1840; interment in the family burial ground on the estate; reinterment in Maple Hill Cemetery, Huntsville, Ala.

Bibliography: *DAB*; Davis, Richard W. "William Smith: A Study in the Politics of Dissent." Ph.D. dissertation, Columbia University, 1964; Smith, Caroline. "Jacksonian Conservative: The Later Years of William Smith, 1826-1840." Ph.D. dissertation, Auburn University, 1977.

**SMITH, William,** a Representative from Virginia; born in Marengo, King George County, Va., September 6, 1797; attended private schools in Virginia and Plainfield Academy in Connecticut; studied law; was admitted to the bar and commenced practice in Culpeper, Culpeper County, Va., in 1818; established a line of United States mail and passenger post coaches through Virginia, the Carolinas, and Georgia in 1831; known as "Extra Billy" because of the large number of extra payments granted to his post coach line by the Federal government; member of the Virginia senate from 1836 to 1841, when he resigned; successfully contested as a Democrat the election of Linn Banks to the Twenty-seventh Congress, and served from March 4, 1841 to March 3, 1843; unsuccessful candidate for reelection in 1842 to the Twenty-eighth Congress; moved to

Fauquier County; elected Governor of Virginia by the General Assembly, and served from January 1, 1846 to January 1, 1849, and was an unsuccessful candidate for election to the United States Senate during that period; moved to California in April 1849; president of the first Virginia Democratic convention in 1850; returned to Virginia in December 1852; elected to the Thirty-third and to the three succeeding Congresses (March 4, 1853-March 3, 1861); during the Civil War served in the Confederate Army as colonel of the Forty-ninth Regiment of Virginia Infantry; commissioned brigadier general on April 23, 1863, and major general on August 12, 1863; served in the Confederate Congress in 1862; elected Governor of Virginia in 1863, and served from January 1, 1864 until the close of the war in Virginia in April 1865; returned to his estate, "Monterosa," near Warrenton, Va., in June 1865; engaged in agricultural pursuits; member of the Virginia house of delegates, 1877-1879; died in Warrenton, Va., May 18, 1887; interment in Hollywood Cemetery, Richmond, Va.

Bibliography: *DAB*; Fahrner, Alvin A. "The Public Career of William 'Extra Billy' Smith." Ph.D. dissertation, University of North Carolina, 1953.

**SMITH, William,** a Representative from Virginia; born in Chesterfield, Va.; completed preparatory studies; member of the Virginia house of delegates in 1782; elected to the Seventeenth, Eighteenth, and Nineteenth Congresses (March 4, 1821-March 3, 1827).

**SMITH, William Alden,** a Representative and a Senator from Michigan; born in Dowagiac, Cass County, Mich., May 12, 1859; attended the common schools; moved with his parents to Grand Rapids in 1872; appointed a page in the Michigan State house of representatives in 1875; studied law; was admitted to the bar and commenced practice in Grand Rapids in 1883; general counsel of the Chicago and West Michigan Railway, and the Detroit Lansing and Northern Railroad; assistant secretary of the Michigan State senate in 1883; State game warden, 1887-1891; constructed a railroad in Michigan in 1898 and became owner of the Lowell and Hastings Railroad in 1900; owner and publisher of the Grand Rapids Herald in 1906; chairman of the board of directors of a transit company operating a line of steamboats from Chicago to various Lake Michigan ports; elected as a Republican to the Fifty-fourth and to the six succeeding Congresses, and served from March 4, 1895 until his resignation, effective February 9, 1907, having been elected Senator; chairman, Committee on Expenditures in the Department of State (Fifty-sixth Congress), Committee on Pacific Railroads (Fifty-seventh and Fifty-eighth Congresses); elected as a Republican to the United States Senate, January 15, 1907, for the term beginning March 4, 1907; subsequently elected on February 6, 1907 to fill the vacancy in the term ending March 3, 1907, caused by the death of Russell A. Alger; reelected in 1913, and served from February 9, 1907 to March 3, 1919; was not a candidate for renomination in 1918; chairman, Committee on Canadian Relations (Sixty-first Congress), Committee on Territories (Sixty-second Congress), Committee to Examine Branches of the Civil Service (Sixty-third through Sixty-fifth Congresses); died in Grand Rapids, Mich., on October 11, 1932; interment in Woodlawn Cemetery.

Bibliography: Wade, Wyn Craig. "The Senator and the Shipwreck." *Michigan History* 63 (November/December 1979): 10-19.

**SMITH, William Alexander,** a Representative from North Carolina; born in Warren County, N.C., January 9, 1828; attended the common schools; engaged in agricultural pursuits; member of the State constitutional convention in 1865; member of the State senate in 1870; president of the North Carolina Railroad in 1868 and of the Yadkin River Railroad; elected as a Republican to the Forty-third Congress (March 4, 1873-March 3, 1875); died in Richmond, Va., May 16, 1888; interment in Hollywood Cemetery.

**SMITH, William Ephraim,** a Representative from Georgia; born in Augusta, Richmond County, Ga., March 14, 1829; pursued an academic course; studied law; was admitted to the bar in 1846, under a special act of the legislature, and practiced in Albany, Ga.; also a planter; ordinary of Dougherty County, Ga., in 1853; solicitor general of the southwest circuit 1858-1860; during the Civil War enlisted in the Confederate Army as a first lieutenant in the Fourth Georgia Volunteer Infantry; elected captain in April 1862; elected to the house of representatives of the Second Confederate Congress in 1863; declined the office of circuit judge of Georgia in 1874; elected as a Democrat to the Forty-fourth, Forty-fifth, and Forty-sixth Congresses (March 4, 1875-March 3, 1881); was not a candidate for renomination in 1880; resumed the practice of law; president of the Democratic State convention in 1886; served in the State senate 1886-1888; died in Albany, Dougherty County, Ga., March 11, 1890; interment in Oakview Cemetery.

**SMITH, William Jay,** a Representative from Tennessee; born in Birmingham, England, September 24, 1823; immigrated to the United States and settled in Orange County, N.Y.; attended the common schools; learned the printing trade; moved to Tennessee in 1846; during the Mexican War, in 1847, served in a regiment from that State; moved to Hardeman County, Tenn., and engaged in horticulture; during the Civil War served in the Union Army 1861-1865; delegate to the State constitutional convention in 1865; member of the State house of representatives, 1865-1867; served in the State senate, 1867-1869 and 1885-1887; surveyor of the port of Memphis, Tenn., 1871-1883; elected as a Republican to the Forty-first Congress (March 4, 1869-March 3, 1871); unsuccessful candidate for reelection; engaged in the real estate business and in banking; delegate to the Republican National Convention in 1876; died in Memphis, Tenn., November 29, 1913; interment in Elmwood Cemetery.

**SMITH, William Loughton,** a Representative from South Carolina; born in Charleston, S.C., in 1758; attended preparatory schools in England from 1770 until 1774; studied law in the Middle Temple at London, England, in 1774; pursued higher studies in Geneva, Switzerland, 1774-1778; returned to Charleston, S.C., in 1783; was admitted to the bar in 1784 and commenced practice in Charleston; engaged in agricultural pursuits on his estate near Charleston; member of the privy council in 1784; member of the South Carolina State house of representatives, 1787-1788; warden of the city of Charleston in 1786; elected to the First, Second and Third Congresses, and elected as a Federalist to the Fourth and Fifth Congresses, and served from March 4, 1789 until July 10, 1797, when he resigned; chairman, Committee on Elections (Third Congress), Committee on Ways and Means (Fourth and Fifth Congresses); appointed United States Minister to Portugal and Spain on July 10, 1797, and served until September 9, 1801, when he took leave of absence; commissioned Minister to the Ottoman Porte on February 11, 1799, but did not reach that court; returned to Charleston; unsuccessful Federalist candidate for election in 1804 to the Ninth Congress, in 1806 to the Tenth Congress, and in 1808 to the Eleventh Congress; lieutenant in the State militia in 1808; again a member of the State house of representatives in 1808; president of the Santee Canal Co.; vice president of the Charleston Library Society and of the St. Cecilia Society; died in Charleston, S.C., December 19, 1812; interment in St. Philip's Churchyard.

**Bibliography:** *DAB*; Rogers, George C. *Evolution of a Federalist: William Loughton Smith of Charleston 1758-1812.* Columbia: University of South Carolina Press, 1962.

**SMITH, William Nathan Harrell,** a Representative from North Carolina; born in Murfreesboro, N.C., September 24, 1812; attended the common schools in Murfreesboro, N.C., Kingston, R.I., and Colchester and East Lyme, Conn.; was graduated from Yale College in 1834 and from Yale Law School in 1836; was admitted to the bar and commenced practice in Murfreesboro, N.C., in 1839; held several local offices; was a member of the North Carolina State house of commons in 1840, 1858, 1865, and 1866; served in the State senate in 1848; solicitor of the first judicial district of North Carolina for eight years; elected as an Opposition Party candidate to the Thirty-sixth Congress (March 4, 1859-March 3, 1861); served in the Confederate Congress, 1862-1865; delegate to the Democratic National Convention of 1868; chief justice of the North Carolina Supreme Court, 1878-1889; died in Raleigh, N.C., November 14, 1889; interment in Oakwood Cemetery.

**Bibliography:** *DAB*.

**SMITH, William Orlando,** a Representative from Pennsylvania; born in Reynoldsville, Jefferson County, Pa., June 13, 1859; attended the public schools; learned the printing trade; publisher of the Reynoldsville Herald 1876-1879; worked in the Government Printing Office, Washington, D.C., 1879-1884; returned to Punxsutawney, Pa., in 1884 and successively edited the Punxsutawney Tribune and the Punxsutawney Spirit; member of the Pennsylvania house of representatives 1889-1898; editor of the Bradford (Pa.) Daily Era in 1891; purchased a half interest in the Punxsutawney Spirit in January 1892; elected as a Republican to the Fifty-eighth and Fifty-ninth Congresses (March 4, 1903-March 3, 1907); was not a candidate for renomination in 1906; resumed newspaper interests in Punxsutawney, Jefferson County, Pa.; died in Cleveland, Ohio, May 12, 1932; interment in Circle Hill Cemetery, Punxsutawney, Pa.

**SMITH, William Robert,** a Representative from Texas; born near Tyler, Smith County, Tex., August 18, 1863; attended the country schools, and was graduated from Sam Houston Normal Institute, Huntsville, Tex., in 1883; studied law; was admitted to the bar in 1885 and practiced in Tyler until February 1888; moved to Colorado, Mitchell County, Tex., and continued the practice of law; judge of the thirty-second judicial district of Texas 1897-1903; was elected as a Democrat to the Fifty-eighth and to the six succeeding Congresses (March 4, 1903-March 3, 1917); chairman, Committee on Irrigation of Arid Lands (Sixty-second through Sixty-fourth Congresses); unsuccessful candidate for renomination in 1916; moved to El Paso, Tex., in October 1916 and practiced his profession; appointed United States district judge for the western district of Texas and served from April 12, 1917, until his death in El Paso, Tex., August 16, 1924; interment in Evergreen Cemetery.

**SMITH, William Russell,** a Representative from Alabama; born in Russellville, Ky., March 27, 1815; moved at an early age to Huntsville, Ala.; pursued classical studies and attended the University of Alabama at Tuscaloosa; studied law; was admitted to the bar and commenced practice in Greensboro, Ala., in 1835; served as captain of Alabama State troops in the campaign against the Creek Indians in 1836; moved to Tuscaloosa, Ala., where he continued the practice of law and also engaged in newspaper work; founded and edited the Mirror; mayor of Tuscaloosa in 1839; author of several books and plays; member, Alabama State house of representatives, 1841-1843; elected brigadier general of the militia in 1845; judge of the seventh judicial circuit, 1850-1851; elected as a Unionist to the Thirty-second Congress, as a Democrat to the Thirty-third Congress, and as an American Party candidate to the Thirty-fourth Congress (March 4, 1851-March 3, 1857); unsuccessful candidate for reelection in 1856 to the Thirty-fifth Congress; member of the State constitutional convention in 1861 and voted against secession; during the Civil War served in the Confederate Army as colonel of the Twenty-sixth Alabama Regiment; Representative in the First and Second Confederate Congresses; president of the University of Alabama, 1869-1871; resumed the practice of his profession and engaged in historical and literary pursuits; died in Washington, D.C., on February 26, 1896; interment in Tuscaloosa, Ala.; reinterment in Mount Olivet Cemetery, Washington, D.C.

**Bibliography:** *DAB; Easby-Smith, Anne. William Russell Smith* *of Alabama: His Life and Works*. Foreword by George H. Denny. Philadelphia: The Dolphin Press, 1931; Smith, William R., Sr. *Reminiscences of A Long Life; Historical, Political, Personal and Literary*. Washington: Published by William R. Smith, Sr., 1889.

**SMITH, William Stephens,** a Representative from New York; born on Long Island, N.Y., November 8, 1755; graduated from the College of New Jersey (now Princeton University) in 1774; studied law for a short time; served in the Revolutionary Army as aide-de-camp to General Sullivan in 1776; was on the staff of General Lafayette in 1780 and 1781, and then transferred to the staff of General George Washington; secretary of the Legation at London in 1784; returned to America in 1788; appointed by President George Washington to be United States marshal for the district of New York in 1789, and later supervisor of revenue; one of the originators of the Society of the Cincinnati, and served as its president 1795-1797; appointed by President John Adams surveyor of the port of New York in 1800; moved to Lebanon, N.Y., in 1807; elected as a Federalist to the Thirteenth Congress (March 4, 1813-March 3, 1815); presented credentials of his election to the Fourteenth Congress, but he did not qualify, and on December 13, 1815, Westel Willoughby, Jr., successfully contested his election; died in Smith Valley, town of Lebanon, Madison County, N.Y., on June 10, 1816; interment in the Lines Hill Cemetery, between Smyrna and Sherburne, N.Y.

    **Bibliography:** *DAB*.

**SMITH, Willis,** a Senator from North Carolina; born in Norfolk, Va., December 19, 1887; at the death of his father, moved with his mother to North Carolina in 1889 and attended the public schools in Elizabeth City; graduated from Atlantic Collegiate Institute, Elizabeth City, N.C., in 1905, Trinity College (now Duke University), Durham, N.C., in 1910, and from the law school of Duke University in 1912; was admitted to the bar in 1912 and commenced the practice of law in Raleigh, N.C.; during the First World War served in the United States Army at Fort Monroe, Va.; inheritance tax attorney of North Carolina, 1915-1920; member, North Carolina State house of representatives, 1928-1932, serving as speaker in 1931; member of commission preparing rules for federal courts in North Carolina in 1933; observer at the trial of major war criminals at Nuremberg, Germany, in 1946; United States delegate to the Interparliamentary Union in Istanbul, Turkey, in 1951, and served as chairman of the American delegation to the Interparliamentary Union in Bern, Switzerland, in 1952; elected as a Democrat to the United States Senate on November 7, 1950, to fill the vacancy caused by the death of J. Melville Broughton, and served from November 27, 1950 until his death in the naval hospital at Bethesda, Md., June 26, 1953; interment in Oakwood Cemetery, Raleigh, N.C.

**SMITH, Wint,** a Representative from Kansas; born in Mankato, Jewell County, Kans., October 7, 1892; attended the public schools and was graduated from the Mankato High School; during the First World War served in the United States Army as a combat Infantry officer from May 11, 1917, to September 4, 1919, with twenty-four months' service overseas; A.B., University of Kansas, Lawrence, 1920; LL.B., Yale University Law School, 1922; was admitted to the bar in 1923 and commenced practice in Kansas City, Kans.; was admitted to practice in all Federal courts, including the United States Supreme Court in 1934; assistant attorney general, 1931-1940; attorney for the Kansas Highway Commission, 1932-1940; during the Second World War served as lieutenant colonel and commanding officer of the Six Hundred and Thirty-fifth Tank Destroyer Battalion from May 1941 to December 1945, with twenty-two months' service overseas; retired as brigadier general; resumed the practice of law; elected as a Republican to the Eightieth and to the six succeeding Congresses (January 3, 1947-January 3, 1961); was not a candidate for renomination in 1960 to the

Eighty-seventh Congress; returned to his home in Mankato and engaged in farming and ranching; died in Wichita, Kans., April 27, 1976; interment in Mount Hope Cemetery, Mankato, Kans.

**SMITH, Worthington Curtis** (son of John Smith, of Vermont), a Representative from Vermont; born in St. Albans, Franklin County, Vt., April 23, 1823; pursued classical studies, and was graduated from the University of Vermont at Burlington in 1843; studied law, but did not practice; engaged in the iron trade; during the Civil War assisted in raising the First Regiment, Vermont Volunteer Infantry; member of the State house of representatives in 1863; served in the State senate in 1864 and 1865, and was elected president pro tempore of that body in 1865; elected as a Republican to the Fortieth, Forty-first, and Forty-second Congresses (March 4, 1867-March 3, 1873); president of St. Albans Foundry Co.; died in St. Albans, Vt., January 2, 1894; interment in Greenwood Cemetery.

**SMITHERS, Nathaniel Barratt,** a Representative from Delaware; born in Dover, Del., October 8, 1818; was graduated from Lafayette College, Pennsylvania, in 1836; studied law; was admitted to the bar and commenced practice in Dover, Del., in 1840; secretary of State of Delaware January 20 to November 23, 1863; elected as an Unconditional Unionist to the Thirty-eighth Congress to fill the vacancy caused by the death of William Temple and served from December 7, 1863, to March 3, 1865; unsuccessful candidate for reelection in 1864 to the Thirty-ninth Congress; resumed the practice of law in Dover; delegate to the Republican National Convention in 1864; died in Dover, Kent County, Del., January 16, 1896; interment in the Old Methodist Cemetery.

**SMITHWICK, John Harris,** a Representative from Florida; born near Orange, Cherokee County, Ga., July 17, 1872; attended the public schools; was graduated from Reinhardt Normal College, Waleska, Ga., in 1895 and from the law department of Cumberland University, Lebanon, Tenn., in 1897; was admitted to the bar in 1898 and commenced the practice of his profession in Moultrie, Ga.; moved to Pensacola, Fla., in 1906 and continued the practice of his profession; elected as a Democrat to the Sixty-sixth and to the three succeeding Congresses (March 4, 1919-March 3, 1927); unsuccessful candidate for renomination in 1926 to the Seventieth Congress; engaged in the real estate business in Fort Myers, Lee County, Fla., and in Washington, D.C.; retired in 1932 and resided in Moultrie, Ga., until his death on December 2, 1948; interment in Westview Cemetery.

**SMOOT, Reed,** a Senator from Utah; born in Salt Lake City, Utah, January 10, 1862; moved with his parents to Provo, Utah County, Utah, in 1874; attended Mormon church schools and academies and graduated from the Brigham Young Academy (now Brigham Young University) at Provo in 1879; engaged in banking, mining, livestock raising, and in the manufacture of woolen goods; elected as a Republican to the United States Senate in 1902; reelected in 1908, 1914, 1920, and again in 1926, and served from March 4, 1903 to March 3, 1933; unsuccessful candidate for reelection in 1932; chairman, Committee on Patents (Sixtieth Congress), Committee on Printing (Sixty-first and Sixty-second Congresses), Committee on Public Lands (Sixty-second and Sixty-sixth Congresses), Committee on Expenditures in the Interior Department (Sixty-third through Sixty-fifth Congresses), Committee on Public Lands and Surveys (Sixty-seventh Congress), Committee on Finance (Sixty-eighth through Seventy-second Congresses); co-sponsor of the Smoot-Hawley Tariff Act of 1930; moved to Salt Lake City, Utah, in 1933 and retired from active business pursuits; served as one of the twelve apostles of the Church of Jesus Christ of Latter-Day Saints (Mormon Church) and at the time of his death was next in line to succeed the president of the quorum and third to succeed the president; died in St. Petersburg, Fla., February 9, 1941; interment in Provo Burial Park, Provo, Utah.

    **Bibliography:** Allen, James B. "The Great Protectionist,

Senator Reed Smoot of Utah." *Utah Historical Quarterly* 45 (Fall 1977): 325-45; Morrill, Milton R. *Reed Smoot: Apostle in Politics.* Foreword by M. Judd Harmon and an introduction by F. Ross Peterson. Logan: Utah State University Press, 1990.

**SMYSER, Martin Luther,** a Representative from Ohio; born on a farm in Plaine Township, Wayne County, Ohio, April 3, 1851; attended the common schools and was graduated from Wittenberg College, Springfield, Ohio, in 1870; studied law; was admitted to the bar in 1872 and practiced in Wooster; elected prosecuting attorney of Wayne County in 1872 and served one term; delegate to the Republican National Conventions in 1884 and 1888; elected to the Fifty-first Congress (March 4, 1889-March 3, 1891); unsuccessful candidate for reelection in 1890 to the Fifty-second Congress; resumed the practice of law in Wooster; elected to the Fifty-ninth Congress (March 4, 1905-March 3, 1907); unsuccessful candidate for reelection in 1906 to the Sixtieth Congress; continued the practice of law in Wooster, Ohio, until his death in that city May 6, 1908; interment in Wooster Cemetery.

**SMYTH, Alexander,** a Representative from Virginia; born on the Island of Rathlin, Ireland, in 1765; immigrated to the United States and settled in Botetourt County, Va., in 1775; completed preparatory studies; studied law; admitted to the bar and commenced practice in Abingdon, Va.; moved to Wythe County, Va.; member of the Virginia house of delegates in 1792, 1796, 1801, 1802, and 1804-1808; served in the Virginia senate in 1808 and 1809; served in the United States Army from 1808 to 1813; resumed the practice of his profession; again a member of the Virginia house of delegates in 1816, 1817, 1826, and 1827; elected as a Republican to the Fifteenth Congress and reelected to the three succeeding Congresses (March 4, 1817-March 3, 1825); elected to the Twentieth and Twenty-first Congresses and served from March 4, 1827, until his death in Washington, D.C., April 17, 1830; interment in the Congressional Cemetery.

Bibliography: *DAB.*

**SMYTH, George Washington,** a Representative from Texas; born in North Carolina, May 16, 1803; moved with his parents to Alabama, and later to Murfreesboro, Tenn.; attended the common schools and the college at Murfreesboro; moved to Texas, then a part of the Republic of Mexico, in 1828, and settled in the municipality of Bevell, Zavalas Colony (now Jasper County); appointed by the Mexican Government as surveyor, and later made commissioner of titles; delegate to the General Consultation of Texas at San Felipe de Austin in 1835; member of the Texas State convention and a signer of the declaration of independence of Texas in 1836; also a signer of the constitution of the Republic of Texas; appointed by President Mirabeau B. Lamar, of Texas, as commissioner in charge of the boundary line between the Republic of Texas and the United States; engaged in agricultural pursuits; deputy in the Congress of the Republic of Texas in 1845, and assisted in framing the constitution of the State of Texas; elected commissioner of the general land office of the State in 1848; elected as a Democrat to the Thirty-third Congress (March 4, 1853-March 3, 1855); declined to be a candidate for renomination in 1854 to the Thirty-fourth Congress; served in the Confederate Army during the Civil War; member of the Texas State constitutional convention in 1866; died in Austin, Tex., February 21, 1866, while attending a session of the convention; interment in the State Cemetery.

**SMYTH, William,** a Representative from Iowa; born in Eden, County Tyrone, Ireland, January 3, 1824; attended the rural schools; completed preparatory studies; immigrated to the United States in 1838 with his parents, who settled in Pennsylvania; moved to Iowa in 1844; attended the University of Iowa at Iowa City; studied law; was admitted to the bar in 1847 and commenced practice in Marion, Iowa; prosecuting attorney of Linn County 1848-1853; was appointed judge of the district court for the fourth judicial district of Iowa in 1853 and served until his resignation in 1857; resumed the practice of law; in 1858 served as chairman of the commission to codify and revise the State laws; during the Civil War served in the Union Army for two years as colonel of the Thirty-first Regiment, Iowa Volunteer Infantry; elected as a Republican to the Forty-first Congress and served from March 4, 1869, until his death; renominated in 1870 and was a candidate for reelection at the time of his death; died in Marion, Iowa, September 30, 1870; interment in Oak Shade Cemetery.

**SNAPP, Henry** (father of Howard Malcolm Snapp), a Representative from Illinois; born in Livonia, Livingston County, N.Y., June 30, 1822; moved with his parents to Rochester, N.Y., in 1825; attended the common schools of that city; moved to Homer, Will County, Ill., in 1833, where he completed his common-school education; studied law; was admitted to the bar in 1843 and commenced practice in Joliet, Will County, Ill.; member of the State senate from 1869 to 1871; elected as a Republican to the Forty-second Congress to fill the vacancy caused by the resignation of Burton C. Cook and served from December 4, 1871, to March 3, 1873; declined to be a candidate for renomination in 1872; resumed the practice of his profession in Joliet, Ill., where he died on November 26, 1895; interment in Oakwood Cemetery.

**SNAPP, Howard Malcolm** (son of Henry Snapp), a Representative from Illinois; born in Joliet, Will County, Ill., September 27, 1855; attended the Eastern Avenue school and Forest University in Chicago, Ill., 1872-1875; studied law; was admitted to the bar in 1878 and commenced practice in Globe, Ariz.; returned to Joliet, Ill., and continued the practice of law; master in chancery for Will County, Ill., from 1884 to 1903; elected chairman of the Will County Republican central committee in 1893; delegate to the Republican National Conventions in 1896 and 1908; was elected as a Republican to the Fifty-eighth and to the three succeeding Congresses (March 4, 1903-March 3, 1911); was not a candidate for renomination in 1910; resumed the practice of law in Joliet, Ill.; died in Joliet, Ill., August 14, 1938; interment in Elmhurst Cemetery.

**SNEED, William Henry,** a Representative from Tennessee; born in Davidson County, Tenn., August 27, 1812; completed preparatory studies; moved with his father's family to Rutherford County, Tenn.; studied law; was admitted to the bar in 1834 and commenced practice in Murfreesboro, Tenn.; member of the Tennessee State senate, 1843-1845; moved to Knoxville, Tenn., in 1845 and resumed the practice of law; elected as the candidate of the American Party to the Thirty-fourth Congress (March 4, 1855-March 3, 1857); chairman, Committee on Mileage (Thirty-fourth Congress); declined to be a candidate for renomination in 1856 to the Thirty-fifth Congress, and also declined to be a candidate for nomination as circuit judge; resumed the practice of law; died in Knoxville, Tenn., September 18, 1869; interment in the Old Gray Cemetery.

**SNELL, Bertrand Hollis,** a Representative from New York; born in Colton, St. Lawrence County, N.Y., December 9, 1870; attended the public schools; was graduated from the State normal school at Potsdam, N.Y., in 1889 and from Amherst (Mass.) College in 1894; began work as a bookkeeper and afterward became secretary and manager of a paper company in Potsdam; in 1904 organized the Canton Lumber Co. in Potsdam; president and manager of cheese manufacturing company of New York City; owner of a power plant in Higley Falls, N.Y.; director of the Northern New York Trust Co., the Agricultural Insurance Co. of Watertown, N.Y., and Gould Pumps, Inc., Seneca Falls, N.Y.; vice president of the Northern New York Development League 1908-1910; member of the Republican State committee 1914-1944; delegate to all Republican National Conventions 1916-1940, serving as chairman in 1932 and 1936; president, board of trustees of Clarkson College, Potsdam, N.Y., 1920-1945; elected as a Republican to the Sixty-fourth

Congress to fill the vacancy caused by the death of Edwin A. Merritt, Jr.; reelected to the Sixty-fifth and to the ten succeeding Congresses and served from November 2, 1915, to January 3, 1939; chairman, Committee on War Claims (Sixty-seventh Congress), Committee on Rules (Sixty-eighth through Seventy-first Congresses); minority leader (Seventy-second through Seventy-fifth Congresses); was not a candidate for renomination in 1938; publisher of the Potsdam Courier-Freeman newspaper 1934-1949; in 1941 became owner and manager of New York State Oil Co., of Kansas; died in Potsdam, N.Y., February 2, 1958; interment in Bayside Cemetery.

**Bibliography:** *DAB*; Barone, Louis A. "Republican House Minority Leader Bertrand H. Snell and the Coming of the New Deal, 1931-1939." Ph.D. dissertation, State University of New York at Buffalo, 1969.

**SNIDER, Samuel Prather,** a Representative from Minnesota; born in Mount Gilead, Morrow County, Ohio, October 9, 1845; attended the public schools, the local high school at Mount Gilead, Ohio, and Oberlin College, Ohio; during the Civil War enlisted as a private soldier in the Sixty-fifth Regiment, Ohio Volunteer Infantry; after the war engaged in commercial pursuits in New York; moved to Minnesota in 1876 and settled in Minneapolis; organized and built the Midland Railway in southern Minnesota; engaged in agricultural pursuits and the mining of iron ore; member of the State house of representatives 1884-1888; elected as a Republican to the Fifty-first Congress (March 4, 1889-March 3, 1891); unsuccessful candidate for reelection in 1890 to the Fifty-second Congress; delegate to the Republican National Convention in 1892; retired and resided in Minneapolis, Minn., until his death September 24, 1928; interment in Lakewood Cemetery.

**SNODGRASS, Charles Edward** (nephew of Henry Clay Snodgrass), a Representative from Tennessee; born near Sparta, White County, Tenn., December 28, 1866; attended the common schools; studied law; was admitted to the bar and commenced practice in Crossville, Tenn., in 1888; elected as a Democrat to the Fifty-sixth and Fifty-seventh Congresses (March 4, 1899-March 3, 1903); unsuccessful candidate for renomination in 1902; judge of the fifth judicial circuit of Tennessee; appointed and subsequently elected judge of the court of appeals upon the reorganization of that court and served from 1925 to 1934; retired to private life in Crossville, Tenn., where he died August 3, 1936; interment in the Crossville City Cemetery.

**SNODGRASS, Henry Clay** (uncle of Charles Edward Snodgrass), a Representative from Tennessee; born near Sparta, White County, Tenn., March 29, 1848; attended Sparta Academy; studied law at Cumberland University, Lebanon, Tenn.; was admitted to the bar in 1870 and commenced practice in Sparta, Tenn.; also engaged in agricultural pursuits; during the Civil War served as a private in the Confederate Army; attorney general of the fifth judicial circuit 1878-1884; elected as a Democrat to the Fifty-second and Fifty-third Congresses (March 4, 1891-March 3, 1895); unsuccessful candidate for reelection in 1894 to the Fifty-fourth Congress; delegate to the Democratic National Convention in 1896; resumed the practice of his profession in Sparta, White County, Tenn.; moved to Gould, Okla., and engaged in agricultural pursuits; died in Altus, Okla., April 22, 1931; interment in Altus Cemetery.

**SNODGRASS, John Fryall,** a Representative from Virginia; born in Berkeley County, Va. (now West Virginia), March 2, 1804; completed preparatory studies; studied law; admitted to the bar in 1843 and commenced practice in Parkersburg, Va.; delegate to the Virginia constitutional convention in 1850 and 1851; elected as a Democrat to the Thirty-third Congress and served from March 4, 1853, until his death in Parkersburg, Va. (now West Virginia), June 5, 1854.

**SNOOK, John Stout,** a Representative from Ohio; born near Antwerp, Paulding County, Ohio, on December 18, 1862; was graduated from the Antwerp grade schools in 1881; attended the Ohio Wesleyan University, Delaware, Ohio; was graduated from the law school of Cincinnati College in May 1887; was admitted to the bar the same year and began practice in Antwerp, Ohio; moved to Paulding, Ohio, in 1890 and continued the practice of his profession; elected as a Democrat to the Fifty-seventh and Fifty-eighth Congresses (March 4, 1901-March 3, 1905); was not a candidate for renomination in 1904; resumed the practice of law in Paulding; delegate to the Democratic National Conventions in 1912 and 1932; judge of the court of common pleas 1913-1915; elected to the Sixty-fifth Congress (March 4, 1917-March 3, 1919); was an unsuccessful candidate for reelection in 1918 to the Sixty-sixth Congress; again engaged in the practice of his profession; judge of the court of common pleas from 1930 to 1938, when he retired; died in Paulding, Ohio, September 19, 1952; interment in Live Oak Cemetery.

**SNOVER, Horace Greeley,** a Representative from Michigan; born in Romeo, Macomb County, Mich., September 21, 1847; attended the public schools and Dickenson Institute at Romeo; was graduated from the academic department of the University of Michigan at Ann Arbor in 1869 and from the law department in 1871; was admitted to the bar and practiced in Wichita, Kans., in 1871 and 1872; moved to Romeo, Mich., in 1873 and to Port Austin, Huron County, Mich., in 1874 and continued the practice of law; also engaged in banking; principal of the public schools of Port Austin for two years; probate judge of Huron County from January 1, 1881, to January 1, 1885; elected as a Republican to the Fifty-fourth and Fifty-fifth Congresses (March 4, 1895-March 3, 1899); was not a candidate for renomination in 1898; moved to Port Huron, Mich., where he died July 21, 1924; interment in Lakeside Cemetery.

**SNOW, Donald Francis,** a Representative from Maine; born in Bangor, Penobscot County, Maine, September 6, 1877; attended the public schools of his native city; was graduated from Bowdoin College, Brunswick, Maine, in 1901 and from the law school of the University of Maine at Orono in 1904; was admitted to the bar in 1904 and commenced practice in Bangor, Maine; city solicitor of Bangor 1906-1910 and prosecuting attorney of Penobscot County 1911-1913; elected as a Republican to the Seventy-first and Seventy-second Congresses (March 4, 1929-March 3, 1933); unsuccessful candidate for renomination in 1932; engaged in literary work in Washington, D.C., 1933-1935; moved to Gorham, Cumberland County, Maine, in 1936 and engaged in poultry farming until 1945; secretary for the E.C. Jones Insurance Corp., Portland, Maine, and later had his own insurance business; died in Gorham, Maine, February 12, 1958; interment in Evergreen Cemetery, Portland, Maine.

**SNOW, Herman Wilber,** a Representative from Illinois; born in Michigan City, La Porte County, Ind., July 3, 1836; moved with his parents to Madisonville, Ky.; attended the public schools; moved to Sheldon, Iroquois County, Ill.; taught school several years; studied law; was admitted to the bar and practiced; during the Civil War enlisted as a private in the One Hundred and Thirty-ninth Regiment, Illinois Volunteer Infantry; rose to the rank of captain; reenlisted in the One Hundred and Fifty-first Regiment, Illinois Volunteer Infantry, and was promoted to the rank of lieutenant colonel; provost marshal general of Georgia on Major General Steedman's staff; at the expiration of his service taught in the Chicago High School for three years; returned to Sheldon and engaged in banking; member of the State house of representatives 1872-1874; elected as a Democrat to the Fifty-second Congress (March 4, 1891-March 3, 1893); unsuccessful candidate for reelection in 1892 to the Fifty-third Congress; Sergeant at Arms of the House of Representatives during the Fifty-third Congress; moved to

Kankakee, Kankakee County, Ill., and resumed banking; died in Kankakee, Ill., August 25, 1914; interment in Mound Grove Cemetery.

**SNOW, William W.,** a Representative from New York; born in Heath, Franklin County, Mass., April 27, 1812; attended the public schools; learned the trade of wool-carder and cloth dresser; moved to Oneonta, Otsego County, N.Y., in 1831; engaged in the wool-carding business in 1841 and the following year entered the tin and hardware business; also engaged in agricultural pursuits; member of the State assembly in 1844; elected as a Democrat to the Thirty-second Congress (March 4, 1851-March 3, 1853); again a member of the State assembly in 1870; served as supervisor of the town of Oneonta in 1873 and 1874; served as State excise commissioner in 1877; member of the village board of trustees; engaged in banking; died in Oneonta, N.Y., September 3, 1886; interment in Riverside Cemetery.

**SNOWE, Olympia Jean** (wife of John Rettie McKernan, Jr.), a Representative and a Senator from Maine; born in Augusta, Kennebec County, Maine, February 21, 1947; attended St. Basil's Academy, Garrison, N.Y., 1962; graduated from Edward Little High School, Auburn, Maine, 1965; B.A., University of Maine, Orono, 1969; businesswoman; district office manager for Representative William S. Cohen, 1973; member, Auburn Board of Voter Registration, 1971-1973; member, Maine State house of representatives, 1973-1976; member, Maine State senate, 1976-1978; delegate, Maine State Republican convention, 1976; delegate to the Republican National Convention of 1976; Auburn Republican Committee, chair; Governor's Commission on Alcoholism, Drug Abuse and Treatment; elected as a Republican to the Ninety-sixth and to the seven succeeding Congresses (January 3, 1979-January 3, 1995); was not a candidate in 1994 for renomination to the House of Representatives, but was elected to the United States Senate for the term ending January 3, 2001; is a resident of Auburn, Maine.

**SNYDER, Adam Wilson,** a Representative from Illinois; born in Connellsville, Fayette County, Pa., October 6, 1799; attended the common schools; moved to Cahokia, Ill., in 1817; studied law; was admitted to the bar in 1820 and commenced practice in Cahokia; appointed prosecuting attorney for the first judicial district in 1822 and served until his resignation in 1823; engaged in agricultural pursuits from 1824 to 1832; member of the Illinois State senate in 1830; reelected in 1832; served as a captain throughout the Black Hawk War; moved to Belleville, Ill., in 1833; unsuccessful candidate for election in 1834 to the Twenty-fourth Congress; elected as a Democrat to the Twenty-fifth Congress (March 4, 1837-March 3, 1839); was not a candidate for renomination in 1838 to the Twenty-sixth Congress; elected to the State senate in 1840, and resigned in 1841; nominated as a candidate for Governor of Illinois, but died in Belleville, St. Clair County, Ill., May 14, 1842, before the election; interment in Green Mount Cemetery, near Belleville, Ill.

**SNYDER, Charles Philip,** a Representative from West Virginia; born in Charleston, Kanawha County, Va. (now West Virginia), June 9, 1847; pursued an academic course; studied law; was admitted to the bar and practiced; prosecuting attorney of Kanawha County, W.Va., 1876-1884; elected as a Democrat to the Forty-eighth Congress to fill the vacancy caused by the resignation of John E. Kenna; reelected to the Forty-ninth and Fiftieth Congresses and served from May 15, 1883, to March 3, 1889; judge of the criminal court of Kanawha County 1890-1896; United States consul to Ciudad Porfirio Diaz, Mexico, 1897-1901; died in Vineland, Cumberland County, N.J., August 21, 1915; interment in Spring Hill Cemetery, Charleston, W.Va.

**SNYDER, Homer Peter,** a Representative from New York; born in Amsterdam, Amsterdam County, N.Y., December 6, 1863; attended the common schools; was employed in various capacities in knitting mills until 1887; moved to Little Falls, N.Y., in 1887 and continued employment in knitting mills; engaged in the manufacture of knitting machinery in 1890 and, later, of bicycles and other wheeled vehicles; director and vice president of the Little Falls National Bank; served one term as school commissioner in 1895 and two terms as fire and police commissioner of Little Falls in 1910 and 1911; unsuccessful candidate for election in 1912 to the Sixty-third Congress; elected as a Republican to the Sixty-fourth and to the four succeeding Congresses (March 4, 1915-March 3, 1925); chairman, Committee on Indian Affairs (Sixty-sixth through Sixty-eighth Congresses), Committee on World War Veterans' Legislation (Sixty-eighth Congress); was not a candidate for reelection in 1924; delegate to the Republican National Conventions in 1916 and 1920; resumed his former manufacturing pursuits; died in Little Falls, N.Y., December 30, 1937; interment in the Church Street Cemetery.

**SNYDER, John,** a Representative from Pennsylvania; born in Selinsgrove, Snyder County, Pa., January 29, 1793; attended the rural schools; served in the War of 1812 as captain of Selinsgrove Rifle Volunteers, Pennsylvania Militia; connected with the Snyder Spring Oil Co. and paper mills; elected to the Twenty-seventh Congress (March 4, 1841-March 3, 1843); unsuccessful candidate for reelection to the Twenty-eighth Congress; resumed former business pursuits; died in Selinsgrove, Snyder County, Pa. August 15, 1850; interment in the New Lutheran Cemetery.

**SNYDER, John Buell,** a Representative from Pennsylvania; born on a farm in Upper Turkeyfoot Township, Somerset County, Pa., July 30, 1877; attended the public schools, and the summer sessions of Harvard University, and Columbia University, New York City; graduated from Lock Haven (Pa.) Teachers College; principal of schools at Stoyestown, Rockwood, and Berlin, Somerset County, 1901-1906, and of Perry Township Union High School 1906-1912; western Pennsylvania manager for an educational publisher, 1912-1932; member of the board of education of Perry Township, Pa., 1922-1932; legislative representative for Pennsylvania school directors during sessions of the Pennsylvania legislature 1921-1923; member of the National Commission of One Hundred for Study and Survey of Rural Schools in the United States 1922-1924; elected as a Democrat to the Seventy-third and to the six succeeding Congresses and served from March 4, 1933, until his death in Pittsburgh, Pa., on February 24, 1946; interment in Mount Washington Cemetery, Perryopolis, Pa.

**SNYDER, Marion Gene,** a Representative from Kentucky; born in Louisville, Jefferson County, Ky., January 26, 1928; attended the public schools; graduated from duPont Manual High School; studied at the University of Louisville; LL.B. and J.D., Jefferson School of Law (now part of the University of Louisville School of Law), 1950; was admitted to the bar and commenced the practice of law in Louisville, Ky., in 1950; city attorney of Jeffersontown, Ky., 1954-1958; elected magistrate of the first district of Jefferson County for two terms, January 1958 to January 1962; engaged in farming, real estate, insurance, and also in the residential construction business; delegate to the Republican National Conventions of 1968, 1976, 1980, and 1984; elected as a Republican to the Eighty-eighth Congress (January 3, 1963-January 3, 1965); unsuccessful candidate for reelection in 1964 to the Eighty-ninth Congress; elected to the Ninetieth and to the nine succeeding Congresses (January 3, 1967-January 3, 1987); was not a candidate for reelection in 1986 to the One Hundredth Congress; is a resident of Pewee Valley, Ky., and Naples, Fla.

**SNYDER, Melvin Claude,** a Representative from West Virginia; born in Albright, Preston County, W.Va., October 29, 1898; attended the public schools; during the First World War enlisted in the United States Army and served as a private in 1918; was graduated in 1923 from the West Virginia University Law School at Morgantown; was admitted to the bar the same year and commenced practice in Kingwood, W.Va.; mayor of Kingwood in 1926; prosecuting attorney for Preston County, W.Va., 1929-1944; served in the United States Army from January 6, 1941, until his discharge as a colonel on January 30, 1946; director of Surplus Property for Division of Territories and Island Possessions, Department of Interior, in 1946; was elected as a Republican to the Eightieth Congress (January 3, 1947-January 3, 1949); unsuccessful candidate for reelection in 1948 to the Eighty-first Congress and for election in 1950 to the Eighty-second Congress; circuit court judge, eighteenth judicial circuit, West Virginia, January 1, 1953-October 1, 1971; served as a member of the West Virginia Judicial Council and had served as president of the West Virginia Judicial Association; resided in Kingwood, W.Va., where he died on August 5, 1972; interment in Maplewood Cemetery.

**SNYDER, Oliver P.,** a Representative from Arkansas; born in Missouri November 13, 1833; completed preparatory studies; moved to Arkansas in 1853; engaged in scientific and literary pursuits and at the same time studied law; was admitted to the bar and practiced in Pine Bluff; member of the State house of representatives in 1864 and 1865; delegate to the State constitutional convention in 1867; served in the State senate 1868-1871; member of the committee to revise and rearrange the statutes of Arkansas in 1868; elected as a Republican to the Forty-second and Forty-third Congresses (March 4, 1871-March 3, 1875); unsuccessful candidate for renomination in 1874; resumed the practice of his profession; elected treasurer of Jefferson County in 1882 and served until his death in Pine Bluff, Jefferson County, Ark., November 22, 1882; interment in Bellewood Cemetery.

**SOLARZ, Stephen Joshua,** a Representative from New York; born in New York City, September 12, 1940; attended public schools in New York City; B.A., Brandeis University, Waltham, Mass., 1962; M.A., public law and government, Columbia University, New York, 1967; taught political science at Brooklyn (N.Y.) College, 1967-1968; served in the New York State assembly, 1969-1974; delegate, Democratic National Mid-term Convention, 1974; elected as a Democrat to the Ninety-fourth and to the eight succeeding Congresses (January 3, 1975-January 3, 1993); unsuccessful candidate for renomination in 1992 to the One Hundred Third Congress; nominated as Ambassador to India, but the nomination was withdrawn on March 17, 1994; President's Special Representative on Sudan; is a resident of Brooklyn, N.Y.

**SOLLERS, Augustus Rhodes,** a Representative from Maryland; born near Prince Frederick, Calvert County, Md., May 1, 1814; studied law; was admitted to the bar in 1836 and commenced practice in Prince Frederick; elected as a Whig to the Twenty-seventh Congress (March 4, 1841-March 3, 1843); resumed the practice of law; delegate to the State constitutional convention in 1851; elected to the Thirty-third Congress (March 4, 1853-March 3, 1855); resumed the practice of law at Prince Frederick, and died near there November 26, 1862; interment in St. Paul's Churchyard, near Prince Frederick, Md.

**SOLOMON, Gerald Brooks Hunt,** a Representative from New York; born in Okeechobee, Fla., August 14, 1930; attended the public schools of Delmar, N.Y., and graduated from Bethlehem Central High School; attended Siena College, Albany, N.Y., 1949-1950; attended St. Lawrence University, Canton, N.Y., 1953-1954; served in United States Marine Corps, 1951-1952; founding partner of insurance and investment firm, 1963; Queensbury town supervisor and Warren County legislator, 1968-1972; member, New York State assembly, 1973-1978; delegate, New York State Republican convention, 1974; delegate, Republican National Convention, 1976; elected as a Republican to the Ninety-sixth and to the eight succeeding

Congresses (January 3, 1979-January 3, 1997); chairman, Committee on Rules (One Hundred Fourth Congress); is a resident of Queensbury, N.Y.

**SOMERS, Andrew Lawrence,** a Representative from New York; born in Brooklyn, N.Y., March 21, 1895; attended St. Teresa's Academy in Brooklyn, Brooklyn College Preparatory School, Manhattan College, and New York University in New York City; engaged in dry color and chemical business; during the First World War enlisted on July 18, 1917, as a hospital apprentice, second class, United States Naval Reserve Force; subsequently served as ensign in the Naval Reserve Flying Corps and was then appointed a naval aviator on September 17, 1918; proceeded to foreign service on September 30, 1918, and served until honorably discharged March 4, 1919; delegate to the Democratic National Convention in 1928; elected as a Democrat to the Sixty-ninth and to the twelve succeeding Congresses and served from March 4, 1925, until his death in St. Albans, Long Island, N.Y., April 6, 1949; chairman, Committee on Coinage, Weights, and Measures (Seventy-second through Seventy-eighth Congresses), Committee on Mines and Mining (Seventy-ninth Congress), Committee on Public Lands (Eighty-first Congress); interment in Holy Cross Cemetery, Brooklyn, N.Y.

**SOMERS, Peter J.,** a Representative from Wisconsin; born at Menominee Falls, Waukesha County, Wis., April 12, 1850; attended the common schools, the Whitewater Normal School, and the Waukesha Academy; studied law; was admitted to the bar in 1874 and commenced practice in Milwaukee, Wis.; Milwaukee city attorney, 1882-1884; elected to the Milwaukee common council in 1890, and upon its organization became its president; mayor of Milwaukee, 1890-1893; elected as a Democrat to the Fifty-third Congress to fill the vacancy caused by the resignation of John L. Mitchell, and served from August 27, 1893 to March 3, 1895; was not a candidate for renomination in 1894 to the Fifty-fourth Congress; resumed the practice of law in Milwaukee; moved to Reno, Nev., in 1905 and continued the practice of law; chairman of the State Democratic central committee, 1907-1909; appointed district judge of Esmeralda County in 1908, and elected in 1910 for the term ending January 1, 1914; again engaged in the practice of law; died in Los Angeles, Calif., February 15, 1924; interment in Calvary Cemetery.

**SOMES, Daniel Eton,** a Representative from Maine; born in Meredith (now Laconia), N.H., May 20, 1815; received an academic education; moved to Biddeford, Maine, in 1846; established the Eastern Journal, later known as the Union and Journal; engaged in the manufacture of loom harnesses, reed twine, and varnishes; mayor of Biddeford 1855-1857; president of the City Bank of Biddeford 1856-1858; elected as a Republican to the Thirty-sixth Congress (March 4, 1859-March 3, 1861); member of the peace convention of 1861 held in Washington, D.C., in an effort to devise means to prevent the impending war; engaged in the practice of patent law in Washington, D.C., until his death in that city on February 13, 1888; interment in Rock Creek Cemetery.

**SORG, Paul John,** a Representative from Ohio; born in Wheeling, Va. (now West Virginia), September 23, 1840; attended the common schools; moved with his parents to Cincinnati, Ohio, in 1852; apprenticed to the molder's trade; attended night school in Cincinnati; engaged in the tobacco manufacturing industry in 1864; served in the Union Army during the Civil War; elected as a Democrat to the Fifty-third Congress to fill the vacancy caused by the death of George W. Houk; reelected to the Fifty-fourth Congress and served from May 21, 1894, to March 3, 1897; was not a candidate for renomination in 1896; settled in Middletown, Ohio, and resumed his former business activities; died in Middletown, Ohio, on May 28, 1902; interment in Woodside Cemetery.

**SOSNOWSKI, John Bartholomew,** a Representative from Michigan; born in Detroit, Mich., December 8, 1883; attended the parochial and Army schools; during the Spanish-American War enlisted as a private in the Seventh Regiment, United States Cavalry, and served in Cuba and the Philippine Islands; after the close of the war continued in the service and was on detached duty at the United States Military Academy, West Point, N.Y.; was honorably discharged on December 26, 1906; returned to Detroit, Mich., and engaged in the real estate and brokerage business; captain and adjutant in the Thirty-first Regiment, Infantry, National Guard of Michigan, from 1909 to 1916, with service on the Mexican border in 1916; member and chairman of the board of water commissioners of the city of Detroit 1918-1924; elected as a Republican to the Sixty-ninth Congress (March 4, 1925-March 3, 1927); unsuccessful candidate for renomination in 1926; resumed the real estate and brokerage business in Detroit, Mich.; delegate to the Republican National Conventions in 1932, 1936, 1940, and 1944; unsuccessful candidate for election in 1942 to the Seventy-eighth Congress, in 1944 to the Seventy-ninth Congress, and in 1946 to the Eightieth Congress; hearing examiner, Michigan Liquor Control Commission, 1947-1951; died in Detroit, Mich., July 16, 1968; interment in Sweetest Heart of Mary Cemetery.

**SOUDER, Mark Edward,** a Representative from Indiana; born in Fort Wayne, Allen County, Ind., July 18, 1950; graduated from Leo High School, 1968; B.S., Indiana University, 1972; M.B.A., University of Notre Dame, 1974; executive for a furniture manufacturing company; worked in Souder's General Store; economic liaison to Representative Dan Coats; staff director, House Select Committee on Children, Youth and Families; legislative director, 1989-1990, and deputy chief of staff, to Senator Dan Coats; elected as a Republican to the One Hundred Fourth Congress (January 3, 1995-January 3, 1997); is a resident of Fort Wayne, Ind.

**SOULE, Nathan,** a Representative from New York; born in that State; resided at Fort Plain; completed preparatory studies; elected as a Jacksonian to the Twenty-second Congress (March 4, 1831-March 3, 1833); member of the State assembly in 1837.

**SOULÉ, Pierre,** a Senator from Louisiana; born in Castillon-en-Couserans, near Bordeaux, France, August 31, 1801; attended the Jesuit College at Toulouse and later an academy in Bordeaux; exiled to Navarre at the age of fifteen for anti-Bourbon activity, and worked as a shepherd boy in the Pyrennes for a year; pardoned in 1818 and returned to school in Bordeaux; studied law in Paris and practiced; engaged in journalism; imprisoned for publishing revolutionary articles in 1825, but escaped to England; went to Haiti in 1825, and then to the United States; after travelling around the nation, commenced the practice of law in New Orleans, La.; member of the Louisiana State senate in 1846; elected as a Democrat in 1846 to the United States Senate to fill the vacancy caused by the death of Alexander Barrow, and served from January 21 to March 3, 1847; again elected to the United States Senate, and served from March 3, 1849 to April 11, 1853, when he resigned to accept a diplomatic post; chairman, Committee on Agriculture (Thirty-second Congress); appointed Minister to Spain on April 7, 1853 and served until February 1855; author of the "Ostend Manifesto" of October 1854, a memorandum outlining the attitude the United States should take in regard to Cuba; resumed the practice of law in New Orleans, La.; was opposed to secession, but abided by the action of his State; when New Orleans was captured in April 1862 he was arrested and imprisoned in Fort Lafayette, N.Y., for several months; paroled to Boston and fled to the Bahamas; travelled to Richmond, Va., to aid the Confederacy; moved to Havana, Cuba, but subsequently returned to New Orleans, La., and died there on March 26, 1870; interment in St. Louis Cemetery No. 2.

Bibliography: Freeman, Arthur. "The Early Career of Pierre Soulé." *Louisiana Historical Quarterly* 25 (October 1942): 970-1127;

Moore, J. Preston. "Pierre Soulé: Southern Expansionist and Promoter." *Journal of Southern History* 21 (May 1955): 203-223; Moore, J. Preston, ed. "Correspondence of Pierre Soulé: The Louisiana Tehuantepec Company." *Hispanic American Historical Review* 32 (February 1952): 59-72.

**SOUTH, Charles Lacy,** a Representative from Texas; born on a farm near Damascus, Washington County, Va., July 22, 1892; moved with his parents to Callahan County, Tex., in 1898 and to Coleman County, Tex., in 1914; attended the public schools and Simmons University at Abilene, Tex., in 1915 and 1916; taught in the Coleman County, Tex., public schools 1914-1920; served as superintendent of schools of Coleman County 1921-1925; studied law and was admitted to the bar in 1925; served as county judge 1925-1931 and as district attorney for the thirty-fifth judicial district 1930-1934; elected as a Democrat to the Seventy-fourth and to the three succeeding Congresses (January 3, 1935-January 3, 1943); unsuccessful candidate for renomination in the first primary in 1942 and later withdrew; engaged in the practice of law in Coleman, Tex.; member of the State house of representatives in 1947 and 1948; was a resident of Austin, Tex., from 1948 until his death there on December 20, 1965; interment in Coleman Cemetery, Coleman, Tex.

**SOUTHALL, Robert Goode,** a Representative from Virginia; born at Amelia Court House, Amelia County, Va., December 26, 1852; attended the Washington Academy and High School of Amelia County; deputy clerk of Nottaway County in 1873 and 1874; graduated from the law department of the University of Virginia at Charlottesville in 1876; admitted to the bar in 1877 and commenced practice at Amelia Court House; prosecuting attorney for Amelia County, Va., 1884-1902; delegate to the Democratic National Conventions in 1888 and 1896; member of the Virginia house of delegates 1899-1904; elected as a Democrat to the Fifty-eighth and Fifty-ninth Congresses (March 4, 1903-March 3, 1907); resumed the practice of his profession in Amelia County, Va.; served as a judge of the fourth judicial circuit court of Virginia from January 1912, until his death in Baltimore, Md., May 25, 1924; interment in Amelia Cemetery, Amelia Court House, Va.

**SOUTHARD, Henry** (father of Isaac Southard and Samuel Lewis Southard), a Representative from New Jersey; born in Hempstead, Long Island, N.Y., October 7, 1747; moved with his parents to Basking Ridge, N.J., in 1755; attended the common schools and worked on a farm; served as a private and later as wagon master during the Revolutionary War; engaged in agricultural pursuits; justice of the peace from 1787 until 1792; member of the New Jersey State general assembly, 1797-1799, and in 1811; elected as a Republican to the Seventh and to the four succeeding Congresses (March 4, 1801-March 3, 1811); chairman, Committee on Revisal and Unfinished Business (Eleventh Congress); elected to the Fourteenth and to the two succeeding Congresses (March 4, 1815-March 3, 1821); resumed farming; died in Basking Ridge, Somerset County, N.J., May 22, 1842; interment in Basking Ridge Cemetery.

**SOUTHARD, Isaac** (son of Henry Southard and brother of Samuel Lewis Southard), a Representative from New Jersey; born in Basking Ridge, Somerset County, N.J., August 30, 1783; educated at the classical school of his native city; engaged in the general merchandise business until 1814; appointed deputy collector of internal revenue for Somerset County; appointed a major of the Second Battalion, Second Regiment, Somerset Brigade, on February 17, 1815; was a director in the State bank at Morristown, N.J.; appointed one of the lay judges of the court of common pleas of Somerset on November 13, 1820; commissioned a justice of the peace on November 16, 1820; moved to Somerville, N.J.; county clerk of Somerset County from 1820 until 1830; elected as an Anti-Jacksonian to the Twenty-second Congress (March 4, 1831-March 3, 1833); unsuccessful candidate for reelection in 1832 to the

Twenty-third Congress; appointed a master and examiner in chancery by Governor Elias P. Seeley in 1833; colonel in the New Jersey State Militia; State treasurer of New Jersey, 1837-1843; resided in Trenton, N.J., for several years; lived in retirement until his death in Somerville, N.J., September 18, 1850; interment in the Old Cemetery.

**SOUTHARD, James Harding,** a Representative from Ohio; born near Toledo, Washington Township, Lucas County, Ohio, January 20, 1851; attended the public schools and was graduated from Cornell University, Ithaca, N.Y., in 1874; studied law; was admitted to the bar in 1877 and commenced practice in Toledo, Ohio; appointed assistant prosecuting attorney of Lucas County in 1882; twice elected prosecuting attorney of the county, and served in that office six years; elected as a Republican to the Fifty-fourth and to the five succeeding Congresses (March 4, 1895-March 3, 1907); chairman, Committee on Coinage, Weights, and Measures (Fifty-sixth through Fifty-ninth Congresses); unsuccessful candidate for reelection in 1906 to the Sixtieth Congress; resumed the practice of law in Toledo, Ohio, until his death there on February 20, 1919; interment in Woodlawn Cemetery.

**SOUTHARD, Milton Isaiah,** a Representative from Ohio; born in Hanover, Licking County, Ohio, October 20, 1836; completed preparatory studies; was graduated from the Denison University, Granville, Ohio; studied law; was admitted to the bar in 1863 and commenced practice in Toledo, Ohio; prosecuting attorney for Muskingum County, Ohio, from 1867 until 1871; elected as a Democrat to the Forty-third and to the two succeeding Congresses (March 4, 1873-March 3, 1879); chairman, Committee on Territories (Forty-fourth Congress); moved to New York City and resumed the practice of law; died in Zanesville, Muskingum County, Ohio, May 4, 1905; interment in Woodlawn Cemetery.

**SOUTHARD, Samuel Lewis** (son of Henry Southard and brother of Isaac Southard), a Senator from New Jersey; born in Basking Ridge, Somerset County, N.J., June 9, 1787; attended the village school; graduated from the College of New Jersey (now Princeton College) in 1804; engaged as tutor by a family near Fredericksburg, Va., in 1805; studied law and was admitted to the bar in Virginia in 1809; returned to New Jersey and commenced practice in Flemington in 1811; member, New Jersey State general assembly, 1815; associate justice of the New Jersey Supreme Court, 1815-1820; moved to Trenton, N.J.; appointed and subsequently elected as a Republican to the United States Senate to fill the vacancy caused by the resignation of James J. Wilson and served from January 26, 1821, to March 3, 1823, when he resigned, having been tendered a Cabinet portfolio; appointed Secretary of the Navy in the Cabinet of President James Monroe, and served from September 16, 1823 to March 3, 1829; Secretary of the Treasury ad interim in 1825; attorney general of New Jersey, 1829-1833; elected Governor of New Jersey by the Legislature and served from October 26, 1832 until February 1833, when he resigned to become Senator; elected as a Whig to the United States Senate in 1833; reelected in 1838, and served from March 4, 1833, until his death; served as President pro tempore of the Senate during the Twenty-seventh Congress; chairman, Committee on Naval Affairs (Twenty-third and Twenty-fourth Congresses); died in Fredericksburg, Va., June 26, 1842; interment in the Congressional Cemetery, Washington, D.C.

Bibliography: *DAB*; Birkner, Michael. *Samuel L. Southard: Jeffersonian Whig.* Rutherfurd, N.J.: Farleigh Dickinson University Press, 1984; Ershkowitz, Herbert. "Samuel L. Southard: A Case Study of Whig Leadership in the Age of Jackson." *New Jersey History* 88 (Spring 1970): 5-24.

**SOUTHGATE, William Wright,** a Representative from Kentucky; born in Newport, Campbell County, Ky., November 27, 1800; educated in private schools and by private tutors; graduated from Transylvania College, Lexington, Ky.; moved to Covington, Kenton County, Ky.; studied law; admitted to the bar in 1821 and commenced practice in Lexington, Ky.; prosecuting attorney 1825-1827; member of the Kentucky house of representatives in 1827, 1832, and 1836; elected as a Whig to the Twenty-fifth Congress (March 4, 1837-March 3, 1839); resumed the practice of law; died in Covington, Ky., December 26, 1849; interment in Linden Grove Cemetery.

**SOUTHWICK, George Newell,** a Representative from New York; born in Albany, N.Y., March 7, 1863; attended private and public schools; was graduated from the Albany High School in 1879 and from Williams College, Williamstown, Mass., in 1884; attended the Albany Law School; began work for the Albany Morning Express in 1885; official reporter of the legislature for the Associated Press 1886-1888; in 1888 became managing editor of the Morning Express and in 1889 of the Albany Evening Journal; chairman of the Republican State convention in 1896; elected as a Republican to the Fifty-fourth and Fifty-fifth Congresses (March 4, 1895-March 3, 1899); unsuccessful candidate for reelection in 1898 to the Fifty-sixth Congress; elected to the Fifty-seventh and to the four succeeding Congresses (March 4, 1901-March 3, 1911); chairman, Committee on Education (Fifty-eighth through Sixtieth Congresses); was not a candidate for renomination in 1910; died in Albany, N.Y., October 17, 1912; interment in Albany Rural Cemetery.

**SOWDEN, William Henry,** a Representative from Pennsylvania; born in Liskeard, England, June 6, 1840; immigrated to the United States in 1846 with his father, who settled in Philadelphia; later went to live with friends in Allentown, Pa.; attended the public schools and Allentown Academy; served in the Civil War as a corporal in Company D, One Hundred and Twenty-eighth Pennsylvania Volunteer Infantry, and served from August 13, 1862, to May 19, 1863; studied law; was admitted to the bar in 1864, and after graduation from Harvard Law School in 1865 commenced practice in Allentown, Pa.; served as solicitor of Lehigh County in 1868; district attorney in 1872-1874; unsuccessful candidate for Lieutenant Governor in 1874; unsuccessful candidate for election in 1876 to the Forty-fifth Congress; delegate to the Democratic National Convention in 1884; city solicitor of Allentown in 1886; elected as a Democrat to the Forty-ninth and Fiftieth Congresses (March 4, 1885-March 3, 1889); was not a candidate for reelection in 1888; resumed the practice of law; city solicitor of Allentown 1900-1902; delegate to the Democratic National Convention in 1900; unsuccessful Republican candidate to the Fifty-ninth Congress in 1904; elected solicitor of Lehigh County in 1906; died in Allentown, Pa., March 3, 1907; interment in Union Cemetery.

**SPAIGHT, Richard Dobbs** (father of Richard Dobbs Spaight, Jr., and grandfather of Richard Spaight Donnell), a Delegate and a Representative from North Carolina; born in New Bern, N.C., March 25, 1758; received his early schooling in Ireland and attended the University of Glasgow in Scotland; returned home in 1778 and joined the Continental Army as aide-de-camp to General Richard Caswell; member of the North Carolina House of Commons, 1779-1783; Member of the Continental Congress, 1783-1785; delegate to the Constitutional Convention at Philadelphia in 1787 and to the State ratification convention in 1788; elected Governor of North Carolina by the General Assembly, and served from December 14, 1792 to November 19, 1795; elected as a Republican to the Fifth Congress to fill the vacancy caused by the death of Nathan Bryan; reelected to the Sixth Congress, and served from December 10, 1798 to March 3, 1801; member of the State senate in 1801 and 1802; was wounded in a duel with John Stanly, his successor in Congress, from the effects of which he died in New Bern, N.C., September 6, 1802; interment in the family sepulchre at "Clermont," near New Bern, N.C.

Bibliography: *DAB*; Wheeler, John Hill. *Sketch of the Life of Richard Dobbs Spaight of North Carolina.* Baltimore: W.K. Boyle, 1880.

**SPAIGHT, Richard Dobbs, Jr**. (son of Richard Dobbs Spaight), a Representative from North Carolina; born in New Bern, N.C., in 1796; attended the New Bern Academy, and was graduated from the University of North Carolina at Chapel Hill in 1815; studied law; was admitted to the bar in 1818 and commenced practice in New Bern; member of the North Carolina State house of commons from November 15 until December 25, 1819; elected to the Eighteenth Congress (March 4, 1823-March 3, 1825); unsuccessful candidate for reelection in 1824 to the Nineteenth Congress; member of the State senate, 1820-1822, and 1825-1835; elected Governor of North Carolina by the General Assembly, and served from December 10, 1835 to December 31, 1836; unsuccessful candidate for reelection in 1836; delegate to the Democratic State convention in 1835; engaged in agricultural pursuits; died in New Bern, N.C., November 17, 1850; interment in the family sepulchre at "Clermont," near New Bern, N.C.

**SPALDING, Burleigh Folsom,** a Representative from North Dakota; born on a farm near Craftsbury, Orleans County, Vt., December 3, 1853; attended the Lyndon Literary Institute, Lyndon, Vt., and was graduated from Norwich University, Northfield, Vt., in 1877; studied law in Montpelier, Vt.; was admitted to the bar in 1880 and commenced practice in Fargo, Dak. (now North Dakota); superintendent of public instruction of Cass County, Dak., 1882-1884; member of the commission to relocate the capital of the Territory of Dakota and build the capitol in 1883; member of the North Dakota constitutional convention in 1889; chairman of the Republican State central committee of North Dakota 1892-1894 and of the Cass County Republican committee 1896-1898; elected as a Republican to the Fifty-sixth Congress (March 4, 1899-March 3, 1901); did not seek renomination in 1900; elected to the Fifty-eighth Congress (March 4, 1903-March 3, 1905); unsuccessful candidate for renomination in 1904; appointed in 1907 and elected in 1908 an associate justice of the North Dakota Supreme Court; became chief justice in 1911 and served until 1915; resumed the practice of law in Fargo, N.Dak., in 1915; delegate to most Republican Territorial and State conventions 1888-1933; delegate to the Republican National Convention in 1924; died in Fargo, N.Dak., March 17, 1934; interment in Riverside Cemetery.

**SPALDING, George,** a Representative from Michigan; born in Blairgowrie, Perthshire, Scotland, on November 12, 1836; immigrated to the United States in 1843 with his parents, who settled in Buffalo, N.Y.; attended the public schools; moved to Monroe, Mich.; taught school in 1860 and 1861; entered the United States Army June 20, 1861, as a private in Company A, Fourth Regiment, Michigan Volunteer Infantry, and was promoted through the ranks to colonel, Twelfth Tennessee Cavalry; appointed postmaster of Monroe, Mich., July 27, 1866, and served until December 15, 1870; special agent of the Treasury Department 1871-1875; mayor of Monroe in 1876; president of the board of education; studied law, and was admitted to the bar in 1878; member of the board of control of the State Industrial Home for Girls 1885-1897; was elected as a Republican to the Fifty-fourth and Fifty-fifth Congresses (March 4, 1895-March 3, 1899); unsuccessful candidate for renomination in 1898; again appointed postmaster of Monroe, Mich., on February 20, 1899, and served until February 13, 1907; resumed the practice of law and also engaged in agricultural pursuits; president of the First National Bank of Monroe, Mich., until his death there September 13, 1915; interment in Woodlawn Cemetery.

**SPALDING, Rufus Paine,** a Representative from Ohio; born in West Tisbury, Mass., May 3, 1798; was graduated from Yale College in 1817; studied law and was admitted to the bar; moved to Little Rock, Ark., in 1820 and commenced practice; moved to Warren, Ohio, in 1821 and practiced his profession until 1835, when he moved to Ravenna, Ohio, and continued the practice of law; member, Ohio State house of representatives, 1839-1842, and served one

term as speaker; associate judge of the Ohio Supreme Court, 1849-1852; resumed the practice of law in Cleveland, Ohio; elected as a Republican to the Thirty-eighth and to the two succeeding Congresses (March 4, 1863-March 3, 1869); was not a candidate for renomination in 1868 to the Forty-first Congress; resumed the practice of law; died in Cleveland, Ohio, August 29, 1886; interment in Lake View Cemetery.

**SPALDING, Thomas,** a Representative from Georgia; born in Frederica, St. Simons Island, Glynn County, Ga., March 26, 1774; attended the common schools of Georgia and Florida and a private school in Massachusetts; studied law; was admitted to the bar about 1790, but did not practice; engaged extensively in agricultural pursuits; member of the State house of representatives in 1794; member of the State constitutional convention in 1798; moved to McIntosh County, Ga., in 1803; served in the State senate; successfully contested as a Republican the election of Cowles Mead to the Ninth Congress and served from December 24, 1805, until his resignation in 1806; trustee of the McIntosh County Academy in 1807; one of the founders of the Bank of Darien and of the branch in Milledgeville, Ga., and president for many years; engaged in the planting of sea-island cotton, residing on Sapelo Island, Ga.; commissioner on the part of the State of Georgia to determine the boundary line between Georgia and the Territory of Florida in 1826; commissioner from the Federal Government to Bermuda to negotiate relative to property taken or destroyed in the South by the British in the War of 1812; president of the convention at Milledgeville, Ga., in 1850 which resolved that the State of Georgia would resist any act of Congress abolishing slavery and died, while en route home, at the residence of his son, near Darien, Ga., January 5, 1851; interment in St. Andrew's Cemetery.

Bibliography: *DAB*; Coulter, E. Merton. *Thomas Spalding of Sapelo.* University, La.: Louisiana State University Press, 1940.

**SPANGLER, David,** a Representative from Ohio; born in Sharpsburg, Washington County, Md., on December 2, 1796; moved with his parents to Zanesville, Ohio, in 1802; attended the public schools; worked at the blacksmith's trade; engaged in mercantile pursuits; studied law; was admitted to the bar in 1824 and commenced practice in Zanesville; unsuccessful candidate for election to the Ohio State house of representatives in 1830; moved to Coshocton, Ohio, in 1832 and continued the practice of law; elected as an Anti-Jacksonian to the Twenty-third Congress and reelected as a Whig to the Twenty-fourth Congress (March 4, 1833-March 3, 1837); declined to be a candidate for renomination in 1836 to the Twenty-fifth Congress; declined to be a candidate for the nomination for Governor of Ohio in 1844; died in Coshocton, Ohio, October 18, 1856; interment in South Lawn Cemetery.

**SPANGLER, Jacob,** a Representative from Pennsylvania; born in York, Pa., November 28, 1767; attended the York County Academy; engaged in surveying; served as a trumpeter in Captain McClellan's light horse company of York in 1799; county commissioner in 1800; postmaster of York 1795-1812; deputy surveyor of York County 1796-1815; again county commissioner in 1814; elected as a Republican to the Fifteenth Congress and served from March 4, 1817, until his resignation on April 20, 1818; surveyor general of Pennsylvania 1818-1821; commander, Pennsylvania militia, with title of general; chief escort of General Lafayette from York to Harrisburg on his visit to the United States in 1825; clerk of York County Court until 1830; again surveyor general of Pennsylvania from 1830 to 1836; died in York, Pa., June 17, 1843; interment in Prospect Hill Cemetery.

**SPARKMAN, John Jackson,** a Representative and a Senator from Alabama; born on a farm near Hartselle, Morgan County, Ala., December 20, 1899; attended the rural schools and helped on the family farm; during the First World War was a member of the Students Army Training Corps; A.B., University of Alabama, Tuscaloosa, 1921; LL.B., University of Alabama School of Law, 1923, A.M., 1924; was admitted to the bar in 1925 and commenced practice in Huntsville, Madison County, Ala.; instructor at Huntsville (Ala.) College, 1925-1928; elected as a Democrat to the Seventy-fifth and to the five succeeding Congresses and served from January 3, 1937, to November 5, 1946, when he resigned; majority whip in 1946; was reelected to the Eightieth Congress on November 5, 1946, and at the same time was elected to the United States Senate to fill the vacancy caused by the death of John H. Bankhead II for the term ending January 3, 1949; following the election resigned from the House of Representatives and began duties in the Senate on November 6, 1946; reelected in 1948, 1954, 1960, 1966, and again in 1972, and served from November 6, 1946, to January 3, 1979; was not a candidate for reelection in 1978; chairman, Select Committee on Small Business (Eighty-first, Eighty-second, and Eighty-fourth through Ninetieth Congresses), co-chairman, Joint Committee on Inaugural Arrangements (Eighty-sixth Congress), chairman, Committee on Banking and Currency (Ninetieth and Ninety-first Congresses), co-chairman, Joint Committee on Defense Production (Ninety-first and Ninety-third Congresses), Committee on Banking, Housing, and Urban Affairs (Ninety-second and Ninety-third Congresses), Committee on Foreign Relations (Ninety-fourth and Ninety-fifth Congresses); representative of the United States to the Fifth General Assembly of the United Nations in 1950; unsuccessful candidate in 1952 for Vice President of the United States on the Democratic ticket headed by Adlai E. Stevenson; died in Huntsville, Ala., November 16, 1985; interment in Maple Hill Cemetery, Huntsville, Ala.

**Bibliography:** Sparkman, John. "The Role of the Senate in Determining Foreign Policy." In *The Senate Institution.* Edited by Nathaniel Preston. pp. 31-39. New York: Van Nostrant Reinhold, 1969. Sparkman, Mrs. Ivo Hall. *Journeys With the Senator.* Huntsville, Ala.: Strode Publishers, 1977.

**SPARKMAN, Stephen Milancthon,** a Representative from Florida; born on a farm in Hernando County, Fla., July 29, 1849; attended the common schools; taught school from 1867 until 1870; studied law; was admitted to the bar in 1872 and commenced practice in Tampa, Fla.; State's attorney for the sixth judicial circuit, 1878-1887; declined the position of circuit judge for the sixth judicial circuit in 1888, and also the appointment of associate justice of the Florida State supreme court in 1891; member of the county Democratic executive committee, 1890-1894, and served as chairman in 1890 and 1891; member of the Florida State Democratic executive committee, 1892-1896, serving as chairman; delegate to the Democratic National Convention of 1892; elected as a Democrat to the Fifty-fourth and to the ten succeeding Congresses (March 4, 1895-March 3, 1917); chairman, Committee on Rivers and Harbors (Sixty-second through Sixty-fourth Congresses); was not a candidate for renomination in 1916 to the Sixty-fifth Congress; resumed the practice of law in Tampa, Fla.; president of the board of port commissioners until 1920; died in Washington, D.C., September 26, 1929; interment in Woodlawn Cemetery, Tampa, Fla.

**SPARKS, Charles Isaac,** a Representative from Kansas; born on a farm near Ontario, in Jackson Township, Boone County, Iowa, December 20, 1872; educated in the rural schools and Simpson College, Indianola, Iowa; was graduated from the law department of the State University of Iowa at Iowa City in 1896; was admitted to the bar the same year and commenced practice in Boone, Iowa; served as prosecuting attorney of Boone County 1899-1902; chairman of the Republican county committee in 1898; moved to Goodland, Sherman County, Kans., in 1907 and continued the practice of law; served as city attorney and was a member of the Goodland School Board; judge of the thirty-fourth judicial district of Kansas 1915-1929; elected as a Republican to the Seventy-first and

Seventy-second Congresses (March 4, 1929-March 3, 1933); unsuccessful candidate for reelection in 1932 to the Seventy-third Congress; resumed the practice of law in Goodland, Kans., until his death there on April 30, 1937; interment in the Goodland Cemetery.

**SPARKS, William Andrew Jackson,** a Representative from Illinois; born near New Albany, Ind., November 19, 1828; moved with his parents to Illinois in 1836; attended the public schools; taught school and was graduated from McKendree College, Lebanon, Ill., in 1850; studied law; was admitted to the bar in 1851 and commenced practice in Carlyle, Ill.; United States land receiver for the Edwardsville (Ill.) land office, 1853-1856; member of the Illinois State house of representatives, 1856-1857; served in the State senate, 1863-1864; delegate to the Democratic National Convention of 1868; elected as a Democrat to the Forty-fourth and to the three succeeding Congresses (March 4, 1875-March 3, 1883); chairman, Committee on Expenditures in the Department of the Interior (Forty-fifth Congress), Committee on Military Affairs (Forty-sixth Congress); was not a candidate for renomination in 1882 to the Forty-eighth Congress; resumed the practice of law; appointed by President Grover Cleveland as Commissioner of the United States General Land Office, and served from March 26, 1885 to March 26, 1888; resumed the practice of law at Carlyle and Springfield, Ill.; died in St. Louis, Mo., May 7, 1904; interment in St. Mary's Catholic Cemetery, Carlyle, Ill.

**Bibliography:** *DAB;* Schlup, Leonard. "Prairie Politician: William Andrew Jackson Sparks and the Politics of Honor during the Gilded Age." *Illinois Historical Journal* 88 (Summer 1995): 117-134.

**SPAULDING, Elbridge Gerry,** a Representative from New York; born in Summer Hill, Cayuga County, N.Y., on February 24, 1809; completed preparatory studies; studied law; was admitted to the bar in 1836 and commenced practice in Batavia, Genesee County, N.Y.; moved to Buffalo, N.Y., in 1834; mayor of Buffalo in 1847; member of the State assembly in 1848; elected as a Whig to the Thirty-first Congress (March 4, 1849-March 3, 1851); was not a candidate for renomination in 1850; treasurer of the State of New York in 1854 and 1855; elected as a Republican to the Thirty-sixth and Thirty-seventh Congresses (March 4, 1859-March 3, 1863); was not a candidate for renomination in 1862 to the Thirty-eighth Congress; organized the Farmers & Mechanics' National Bank in Buffalo in 1864; died in Buffalo, N.Y., May 5, 1897; interment in Forest Lawn Cemetery.

**Bibliography:** *DAB.*

**SPAULDING, Oliver Lyman,** a Representative from Michigan; born in Jaffrey, Cheshire County, N.H., August 2, 1833; completed preparatory studies, and was graduated from Oberlin (Ohio) College in 1855; moved to Michigan and taught school; studied law; was admitted to the bar in 1858 and commenced practice in St. Johns, Mich.; regent of the University of Michigan at Ann Arbor, 1858-1864; during the Civil War served in the Union Army as a captain in the Twenty-third Regiment, Michigan Volunteers and promoted to colonel; resumed the practice of law in St. Johns, Mich.; secretary of state of Michigan, 1866-1870; member of the Republican State committee, 1871-1878; declined the position of United States district judge of the Territory of Utah in 1871; special agent of the United States Treasury Department, 1875-1881; elected as a Republican to the Forty-seventh Congress (March 4, 1881-March 3, 1883); unsuccessful candidate for reelection in 1882 to the Forty-eighth Congress; chairman of the commission sent to the Sandwich Islands to investigate alleged violations of the Hawaiian reciprocity treaty in 1883; again a special agent of the United States Treasury in 1885, 1889, and 1890; Assistant Secretary of the Treasury, 1890-1893, and 1897-1903; president of the first International American Customs Congress, held in New York City in January 1903; again a special agent of the United States Treasury, 1903-1909; customs agent,

1909-1916; died in Washington, D.C., July 30, 1922; interment in Arlington National Cemetery, Va.

**Bibliography:** *DAB.*

**SPEAKS, John Charles,** a Representative from Ohio; born in Canal Winchester, Franklin County, Ohio, February 11, 1859; attended the public schools; engaged in milling and the lumber business; fish, game, and conservation officer of Ohio 1907-1918; member of the Ohio National Guard for more than forty years, advancing from private to brigadier general; during the Spanish-American War served as major of the Fourth Regiment, Ohio Volunteer Infantry, participating in the Puerto Rican campaign; commanded the Second Brigade of the Ohio National Guard on the Mexican Border in 1916; during the First World War commanded the Seventy-third Brigade, Thirty-seventh Division; unsuccessful candidate for election in 1918 to the Sixty-sixth Congress; elected as a Republican to the Sixty-seventh and to the four succeeding Congresses (March 4, 1921-March 3, 1931); unsuccessful candidate for reelection in 1930 to the Seventy-second Congress, and for election in 1932 to the Seventy-third Congress, and in 1934 to the Seventy-fourth Congress; died in Columbus, Ohio, November 6, 1945; interment in Union Grove Cemetery, Canal Winchester, Ohio.

**SPEARING, James Zacharie,** a Representative from Louisiana; born in Alto, Cherokee County, Tex., April 23, 1864; moved with his parents to New Orleans, La., in 1866; attended the public schools; left school and went to work in 1877; was graduated from the law department of Tulane University, New Orleans, La., in 1886; was admitted to the bar in 1886 and commenced practice in New Orleans; member of the Orleans Parish school board 1908-1912; member of the State board of education 1912-1916; again a member of the Orleans Parish school board 1916-1920, serving as president in 1919 and 1920; alternate delegate to the Democratic National Convention in 1912; elected as a Democrat to the Sixty-eighth Congress to fill the vacancy caused by the death of H. Garland Dupré; reelected to the Sixty-ninth, Seventieth, and Seventy-first Congresses and served from April 22, 1924, to March 3, 1931; unsuccessful candidate for renomination in 1930; resumed the practice of law in New Orleans, La., where he died November 2, 1942; interment in Metairie Cemetery.

**SPECTER, Arlen,** a Senator from Pennsylvania; born in Wichita, Sedgwick County, Kans., February 12, 1930; attended the public schools; graduated, Russell (Kans.) High School, 1947; University of Oklahoma, 1947-1948; B.A., University of Pennsylvania, 1951; LL.B., Yale University Law School, 1956; served in the United States Air Force from 1951 until 1953; admitted to the Pennsylvania bar in 1956 and commenced practice in Philadelphia; assistant district attorney of Philadelphia, 1959-1964; assistant counsel, Warren Commission, Washington, D.C., 1964; unsuccessful candidate in 1967 for election as mayor of Philadelphia; district attorney of Philadelphia, 1966-1974; unsuccessful candidate in 1976 for nomination to the United States Senate, and in 1978 for nomination for Governor of Pennsylvania; resumed the practice of law from 1974 to 1980; admitted to the New Jersey bar in 1979 and to the District of Columbia bar in 1983; elected as a Republican to the United States Senate in 1980 for the term commencing January 3, 1981; reelected in 1986 and again in 1992 for the term ending January 3, 1999; chairman, Select Committee on Intelligence (One Hundred Fourth Congress); unsuccessful candidate for the Republican presidential nomination in 1996; is a resident of Philadelphia, Pa.

**SPEED, Thomas,** a Representative from Kentucky; born in Charlotte County, Va., October 25, 1768; taught by his father; moved with his parents to Kentucky in 1782; employed in the office of the clerk of the general court; engaged in mercantile pursuits at Danville and Bardstown in 1790; also engaged in agricultural pursuits; clerk of the Bullitt and Nelson circuit courts; served as

major of Volunteers in the War of 1812; elected as a Republican to the Fifteenth Congress (March 4, 1817-March 3, 1819); unsuccessful candidate for reelection in 1818 to the Sixteenth Congress; resumed agricultural pursuits; contributed articles to the National Intelligencer, Washington, D.C.; member of the Kentucky house of representatives in 1821, 1822, and again in 1840; was a member of the Whig Party when it was organized; died on his farm, near Bardstown, Nelson County, Ky., February 20, 1842; interment on his farm, "Cottage Grove," near Bardstown, Ky.

**SPEER, Emory,** a Representative from Georgia; born in Culloden, Monroe County, Ga., September 3, 1848; pursued classical studies and was graduated from the University of Georgia at Athens in 1869; entered the Confederate Army at the age of sixteen as a volunteer in the Fifth Kentucky Regiment, Lewis brigade, and remained with that command throughout the Civil War; studied law; was admitted to the bar in 1869 and commenced practice in Athens, Ga.; solicitor general of Georgia, 1873-1876; unsuccessful candidate for election in 1877 to the Forty-fifth Congress to fill the unexpired term of Benjamin H. Hill; elected as an Independent Democrat to the Forty-sixth and Forty-seventh Congresses (March 4, 1879-March 3, 1883); unsuccessful candidate for reelection in 1882 to the Forty-eighth Congress; United States attorney for the northern district of Georgia, 1883-1885; United States judge for the southern district of Georgia, 1885-1918; dean of Mercer University Law School, Macon, Ga., 1893-1918; died in Macon, Ga., December 13, 1918; interment in Riverside Cemetery.

**Bibliography:** *DAB.*

**SPEER, Peter Moore,** a Representative from Pennsylvania; born near Oil City, Venango County, Pa., December 29, 1862; attended the country schools, Allegheny College, Meadville, Pa., and the Westminster College, New Wilmington, Pa.; graduated from Washington and Jefferson College, Washington, Pa., in 1887; studied law; admitted to the bar in 1889 and commenced practice in Oil City, Venango County, Pa.; district attorney of Venango County 1891-1893; city solicitor of Oil City 1895-1906; member of the Pennsylvania house of representatives in 1897 and 1898; elected as a Republican to the Sixty-second Congress (March 4, 1911-March 3, 1913); unsuccessful candidate for reelection in 1910 to the Sixty-third Congress; resumed the practice of law in Oil City, Pa.; moved to New York City in 1918 and continued the practice of law; assistant general counsel for the Standard Oil Co. 1918-1922, general counsel and member of the board of directors 1922-1928, and vice president 1928-1932; retired from active business pursuits in 1932; died in New York City, August 3, 1933; interment in Kensico Cemetery, near White Plains, N.Y.

**SPEER, Robert Milton,** a Representative from Pennsylvania; born in Cassville, Huntingdon County, Pa., September 8, 1838; attended Cassville Academy; taught school; studied law; admitted to the bar in 1859 and commenced practice in Huntingdon, Pa.; elected assistant clerk of the Pennsylvania house of representatives in 1863; elected as a Democrat to the Forty-second and Forty-third Congresses (March 4, 1871-March 3, 1875); was not a candidate for renomination in 1874; delegate to the Democratic National Conventions in 1872 and 1880; resumed the practice of law and in 1876 became one of the proprietors of the Huntingdon Monitor; unsuccessful candidate for election in 1880 to the Forty-seventh Congress; died in New York City January 17, 1890; interment in Riverview Cemetery, Huntingdon, Pa.

**SPEER, Thomas Jefferson,** a Representative from Georgia; born in Monroe County, Ga., August 31, 1837; attended the common schools; engaged in mercantile pursuits and as a planter; elected justice of the peace in 1861 and reelected in 1865; appointed collector of Confederate taxes for Pike County in June 1863, serving until the cessation of hostilities; elected justice of the inferior court for Pike County in 1865, serving until July 1868; delegate to the

State constitutional convention 1867-1868; member of the State senate 1868-1870; elected as a Republican to the Forty-second Congress and served from March 4, 1871, until his death in Barnesville, Lamar County, Ga., August 18, 1872; interment in Zebulon Street Cemetery.

**SPEIGHT, Jesse,** a Representative from North Carolina and a Senator from Mississippi; born in Greene County, N.C., September 22, 1795; attended the country schools; member of the North Carolina State house of commons in 1820, and served as speaker; member, State senate, 1823-1827; elected from North Carolina to the Twenty-first and to the three succeeding Congresses (March 4, 1829-March 3, 1837); was not a candidate for renomination in 1836 to the Twenty-fifth Congress; moved to Plymouth, Miss.; member, Mississippi State senate, 1841-1844, and served as president; elected as a Democrat to the United States Senate from Mississippi, and served from March 4, 1845 until his death in Columbus, Miss., May 1, 1847; chairman, Committee on Engrossed Bills (Twenty-ninth Congress), Committee to Audit and Control the Contingent Expense (Twenty-ninth Congress); interment in Friendship Cemetery.

**SPELLMAN, Gladys Noon,** a Representative from Maryland; born in New York City, March 1, 1918; attended public schools in New York City and Washington, D.C.; attended George Washington University, Washington, D.C.; graduate school, United States Department of Agriculture; taught in Prince Georges (Md.) County schools; member, Prince Georges County Board of Commissioners, 1962-1970; councilwoman at large, 1971-1974; appointed by President Lyndon B. Johnson to Advisory Commission on Intergovernmental Relations, 1967; president, National Association of Counties, 1972; elected as a Democrat to the Ninety-fourth Congress; reelected to the three succeeding Congresses and served from January 3, 1975, until removed from Congress by H. Res. 80, February 24, 1981, due to an incapacitating illness; was a resident of Laurel, Md., until her death in Rockville, Md., on June 19, 1988; interment in Arlington National Cemetery, Va.

**SPENCE, Brent,** a Representative from Kentucky; born in Newport, Campbell County, Ky., December 24, 1874; attended public and private schools; was graduated from the law department of the University of Cincinnati, Cincinnati, Ohio, in 1895; was admitted to the bar the same year and commenced practice in Newport, Ky.; member of the Kentucky senate, 1904-1908; city solicitor of Newport, Ky., 1916-1924; elected as a Democrat to the Seventy-second and to the fifteen succeeding Congresses (March 4, 1931-January 3, 1963); chairman, Committee on Banking and Currency (Seventy-eighth, Seventy-ninth, Eighty-first, Eighty-second, and Eighty-fourth through Eighty-seventh Congresses); was not a candidate for renomination in 1962 to the Eighty-eighth Congress; resided in Fort Thomas, Ky., until his death there on September 18, 1967; interment in Evergreen Cemetery, Southgate, Ky.

**Bibliography:** Hedlund, Richard. "Brent Spence and the Bretton Woods Legislation." *Register of the Kentucky Historical Society* 79 (Winter 1981): 40-56.

**SPENCE, Floyd Davidson,** a Representative from South Carolina; born in Columbia, Richland County, S.C., April 9, 1928; attended the public schools of Lexington, S.C. and graduated, Lexington High School; A.B., University of South Carolina, Columbia, 1952, LL.B., 1956; editor, South Carolina Law Quarterly; enlisted in the United States Naval Reserve, and commissioned upon graduation from college, attained rank of captain, United States Naval Reserve, former group commander, Naval Reserve units, Columbia, S.C., 1953-1985; admitted to the South Carolina bar in 1956 and commenced practice in West Columbia; member, South Carolina State house of representatives, 1956-1962; member, South Carolina State senate, 1966-1970, and served as minority leader; delegate, South Carolina State Republican conventions, 1964 to present; delegate to the Republican National Conventions of 1964, 1968, 1972, 1976, 1980 and 1984; elected as a Republican to the Ninety-second and to the twelve succeeding Congresses (January 3, 1971-January 3, 1997); chairman, Committee on National Security (One Hundred Fourth Congress); is a resident of Lexington, S.C.

**SPENCE, John Selby** (uncle of Thomas Ara Spence), a Representative and a Senator from Maryland; born near Snow Hill, Worcester County, Md., February 29, 1788; attended the common schools; graduated from the medical department of the University of Pennsylvania at Philadelphia in 1809 and practiced in Worcester County, Md.; member, State house of delegates; member, State senate; elected to the Eighteenth Congress (March 4, 1823-March 3, 1825); elected as a Whig in 1836 to the Twenty-second Congress (March 4, 1831-March 3, 1833); elected as a Whig to the United States Senate to fill the vacancy caused by the death of Robert H. Goldsborough; reelected in 1837, and served from December 31, 1836, until his death near Berlin, Worcester County, Md., October 24, 1840; interment in the Episcopal Churchyard.

**SPENCE, Thomas Ara** (nephew of John Selby Spence), a Representative from Maryland; born near Accomac Court House, Accomac County, Va., February 20, 1810; pursued academic studies and attended a local academy; was graduated from Yale College in 1829; studied law; was admitted to the bar and commenced practice at Snow Hill, Md.; elected as a Whig to the Twenty-eighth Congress (March 4, 1843-March 3, 1845); was not a candidate for renomination; later affiliated with the Republican Party; owned large iron-ore properties in Worcester County; judge for Worcester County and the twelfth judicial circuit 1857-1867; practiced law in Salisbury, Wicomico County, Md.; assistant attorney general for the Post Office Department 1872-1877; died in Washington, D.C., on November 10, 1877; interment in Makamie Memorial Church Cemetery, Snow Hill, Worcester County, Md.

**SPENCER, Ambrose** (father of John Canfield Spencer), a Representative from New York; born in Salisbury, Litchfield County, Conn., December 13, 1765; attended Yale College, and was graduated from Harvard University in 1783; studied law; was admitted to the bar and commenced practice in Hudson, Columbia County, N.Y.; city clerk 1786-1793; member of the State assembly 1793-1795; served in the State senate 1795-1804; assistant attorney general in 1796; attorney general of New York 1802-1804; justice of the State supreme court 1804-1819 and chief justice 1819-1823; resumed the practice of law in Albany, N.Y.; elected to the Twenty-first Congress (March 4, 1829-March 3, 1831); chairman, Committee on Agriculture (Twenty-first Congress); unsuccessful candidate for reelection; one of the managers appointed by the House of Representatives in 1830 to conduct the impeachment proceedings against James H. Peck, United States judge for the district of Missouri; mayor of Albany 1824-1826; moved to Lyons, N.Y., in 1839 and engaged in agricultural pursuits; president of the Whig National Convention at Baltimore in 1844; died in Lyons, N.Y., March 13, 1848; interment in Lyons Rural Cemetery.

**Bibliography:** *DAB.*

**SPENCER, Elijah,** a Representative from New York; born in Columbia County, N.Y., in 1775; received a limited education; moved to Jerusalem (later Benton), N.Y., in 1791 and engaged in agricultural pursuits; supervisor of the town of Benton 1810-1819; member of the State assembly in 1819; elected to the Seventeenth Congress (March 4, 1821-March 3, 1823); again supervisor of Benton 1826-1828; member of the State constitutional convention in 1846; resumed agricultural pursuits; died in Benton, N.Y., December 15, 1852; interment in Lake View Cemetery, Penn Yan, N.Y.

**SPENCER, George Eliphaz,** a Senator from Alabama; born in Champion, Jefferson County, N.Y., November 1, 1836; pursued classical studies; attended Montreal College, Canada; moved to Iowa; secretary of the State senate in 1856; studied law; was admitted to the bar in 1857 and practiced; during the Civil War entered the Union Army as a captain, and when he resigned in 1865 was brevetted brigadier general for gallantry on the field; resumed the practice of law in Decatur, Ala.; appointed register in bankruptcy for the fourth district of Alabama 1867; upon the readmission of Alabama to representation in 1868 was elected as a Republican to the United States Senate; reelected in 1872, and served from July 13, 1868, to March 3, 1879; chairman, Committee on the District of Columbia (Forty-fourth Congress), Committee on Military Affairs (Forty-fifth Congress); retired to his ranch in Nevada; died in Washington, D.C., February 19, 1893; interment in Arlington National Cemetery, Va.

**Bibliography:** Woolfolk, Sarah Van V. "George E. Spencer: A Carpetbagger in Alabama." *Alabama Review* 19 (January 1966): 41-52.

**SPENCER, George Lloyd,** a Senator from Arkansas; born in Sarcoxie, Jasper County, Mo., March 27, 1893; moved to Okolona, Ark., in 1902; attended the public schools, Peddie School at Hightstown, N.J., and Henderson College at Arkadelphia, Ark.; during the First World War served in the United States Navy as a seaman, second class, in 1918; lieutenant commander in the United States Naval Reserve 1931-1943; moved to Hope, Ark., in 1921 and engaged in banking and farming; appointed as a Democrat to the United States Senate to fill the vacancy caused by the resignation of John E. Miller and served from April 1, 1941, to January 3, 1943; was not a candidate for nomination to the full term; during the Second World War served in the United States Navy in 1943; director, Arkansas-Louisiana Gas Co., Shreveport, La.; commissioner, Southwest Arkansas Water District; Arkansas executive vice president of Red River Valley Association; chairman of board and former president of First National Bank of Hope, Ark.; died in Hope, Ark., January 14, 1981; interment in Rosehill Gardens.

**SPENCER, James Bradley,** a Representative from New York; born in Salisbury, Conn., April 26, 1781; received a limited education; moved to Franklin County, N.Y., and settled in Fort Covington; raised a company for the War of 1812, and served as Captain in the Twenty-ninth United States Infantry; appointed a local magistrate in 1814; surrogate of Franklin County 1828-1837; appointed loan commissioner in 1829; member of the State assembly in 1831 and 1832; elected as a Democrat to the Twenty-fifth Congress (March 4, 1837-March 3, 1839); died in Fort Covington, N.Y., March 26, 1848; interment probably in the Old Cemetery near Fort Covington.

**SPENCER, James Grafton,** a Representative from Mississippi; born near Port Gibson, Claiborne County, Miss., September 13, 1844; attended private schools and Oakland College in 1861; during the Civil War enlisted in the Confederate Army as a private in Cowan's battery of Light Artillery; served until the close of the Civil War in the Army of Mississippi and Tennessee; returned to his home and engaged in agricultural pursuits; member of the State house of representatives 1892-1894; elected as a Democrat to the Fifty-fourth Congress (March 4, 1895-March 3, 1897); engaged in the real estate and insurance business; died in Port Gibson, Miss., February 22, 1926; interment in Wintergreen Cemetery.

**SPENCER, John Canfield** (son of Ambrose Spencer), a Representative from New York; born in Hudson, N.Y., January 8, 1788; was graduated from Union College, Schenectady, N.Y., in 1806; studied law; was admitted to the bar in 1809 and commenced practice in Canandaigua, N.Y.; served in the War of 1812; Judge Advocate General in 1813; postmaster of Canandaigua, N.Y.; assistant attorney general for western New York in 1815; elected as

a Republican to the Fifteenth Congress (March 4, 1817-March 3, 1819); was not a candidate for renomination in 1818 to the Sixteenth Congress; member of the New York State assembly, 1820-1821, and served one year as speaker; served in the State senate, 1824-1828; special attorney general to prosecute the abductors of William Morgan of Batavia, N.Y.; again a member of the State assembly, 1831-1832; secretary of state of New York in 1839; appointed Secretary of War by President John Tyler on October 12, 1841, and served until March 3, 1843; Secretary of the Treasury from March 3, 1843 to May 2, 1844, when he resigned; nominated by President Tyler as an Associate Justice of the United States Supreme Court on January 9, 1844, but the Senate, on January 31, 1844, refused to confirm the nomination; died in Albany, N.Y., May 17, 1855; interment in Albany Rural Cemetery.

**Bibliography:** *DAB.*

**SPENCER, Joseph,** a Delegate from Connecticut; born in East Haddam, Conn., October 3, 1714; completed preparatory studies; studied law; admitted to the bar and practiced; held several local offices; judge of probate in 1753; served in the French and Indian war in 1758; member of the Connecticut Council in 1776; brigadier general in the Continental Army; commissioned major general August 9, 1776, and resigned June 14, 1778, because Congress had ordered an investigation of his military conduct in 1777; Member of the Continental Congress in 1779; again a member of the Connecticut Council in 1780 and was annually reelected until his death in East Haddam, Conn., on January 13, 1789; interment in Millington Green Cemetery; reinterment in Nathan Hale Park in 1904.

**Bibliography:** *DAB.*

**SPENCER, Richard,** a Representative from Maryland; born at "Spencer Hall," Talbot County, Md., October 29, 1796; attended the common schools; studied law in Baltimore and was admitted to the Talbot County bar in 1819; moved to his farm, "Solitude," near St. Michaels, Md., in 1822 and engaged in agricultural pursuits; member of the State house of delegates 1823-1825; engaged in literary pursuits and in 1828 he contributed to the establishment of the Eastern Shore Whig and controlled that paper until 1834; elected as a Jacksonian to the Twenty-first Congress (March 4, 1829-March 3, 1831); unsuccessful candidate for reelection in 1830 to the Twenty-second Congress; again a member of the State house of delegates in 1833 and 1834; was an unsuccessful candidate for reelection in 1835; moved to Georgia in 1837 and engaged in cotton planting; moved to Alabama in 1852 and settled at "Cottage Hill," near Mobile, where he died September 3, 1868; interment probably on his estate, "Cottage Hill."

**SPENCER, Selden Palmer,** a Senator from Missouri; born in Erie, Pa., September 16, 1862; attended the public schools of Erie; graduated from Yale College in 1884 and from the Washington University Law School, St. Louis, Mo., in 1886; was admitted to the bar in 1886 and commenced practice in St. Louis; professor of medical jurisprudence in the Missouri Medical College at St. Louis in 1886; member, Missouri State house of representatives, 1895-1896; judge of the circuit court of St. Louis, 1897-1903; captain in the Missouri Home Guard and chairman of the draft board, 1917-1918; elected as a Republican to the United States Senate to fill the vacancy caused by the death of William J. Stone; reelected in 1920, and served from November 6, 1918 until his death at Walter Reed Hospital, Washington, D.C., on May 16, 1925; chairman, Committee on Claims (Sixty-sixth and Sixty-seventh Congresses), Committee on Indian Affairs (Sixty-seventh Congress), Committee on Privileges and Elections (Sixty-seventh through Sixty-ninth Congresses); interment in Bellefontaine Cemetery, St. Louis, Mo.

**Bibliography:** Margulies, Herbert F. "Selden P. Spencer, Senate Moderates and the League of Nations." *Missouri Historical Review* 83 (July 1989): 373-394; Schlup, Leonard. "The Unknown Senator:

Selden Palmer Spencer of Missouri and the League of Nations." *Research Journal of Philosophy and Social Sciences* (1991): 15-23.

**SPENCER, William Brainerd,** a Representative from Louisiana; born on "Home Plantation," in Catahoula Parish, La., February 5, 1835; received his early schooling under private tutors; was graduated from Centenary College, Jackson, La., in 1855 and from the law department of the University of Louisiana at New Orleans in 1857; was admitted to the bar in 1857 and commenced practice in Harrisonburg, La.; served in the Confederate Army, with the rank of captain, until 1863, when he was captured; remained a prisoner of war at Johnsons Island, Ohio, until the close of the Civil War; resumed the practice of law in Vidalia, La., in 1866; successfully contested as a Democrat the election of Frank Morey to the Forty-fourth Congress and served from June 8, 1876, to January 8, 1877, when he resigned to accept a judicial appointment; appointed associate justice of the Louisiana Supreme Court January 9, 1877, which position he held until his resignation April 3, 1880; again resumed the practice of law in New Orleans, La.; died in Jalapa, Mexico, February 12, 1882; interment in Magnolia Cemetery, Baton Rouge, La.

**SPERRY, Lewis,** a Representative from Connecticut; born at East Windsor Hill, town of South Windsor, Conn., January 23, 1848; attended the district school and Monson Academy, Monson, Mass.; was graduated from Amherst College, Amherst, Mass., in 1873; studied law; was admitted to the bar in March 1875 and commenced practice in Hartford, Conn.; member of the State house of representatives in 1876; elected as a Democrat to the Fifty-second and Fifty-third Congresses (March 4, 1891-March 3, 1895); unsuccessful candidate for reelection in 1894 to the Fifty-fourth Congress; again resumed the practice of his profession in Hartford, Conn.; died at East Windsor Hill, town of South Windsor, Hartford County, Conn., June 22, 1922; interment in South Windsor Cemetery.

**SPERRY, Nehemiah Day,** a Representative from Connecticut; born in Woodbridge, New Haven County, Conn., July 10, 1827; attended the common schools and a private school in New Haven; engaged in agricultural pursuits and worked in a mill; taught school for several years; became a member of a building and contracting firm; member of the common council in 1853; alderman of the city in 1854; secretary of state of Connecticut in 1855 and 1856; delegate to the Republican National Conventions of 1856, 1864, and 1888; member and secretary of the national and executive committees; chairman of the Republican State committee for a number of years; chairman of the recruiting committee of New Haven during the Civil War; appointed July 16, 1861, by President Abraham Lincoln as postmaster of New Haven; reappointed and served until removed by President Grover Cleveland on January 20, 1886; again postmaster at New Haven, and served from January 9, 1890 until March 15, 1894; elected as a Republican to the Fifty-fourth and to the seven succeeding Congresses (March 4, 1895-March 3, 1911); chairman, Committee on Alcohol Liquor Traffic (Fifty-sixth through Sixty-first Congresses); was not a candidate for renomination in 1910 to the Sixty-second Congress; died in New Haven, Conn., on November 13, 1911; interment in Evergreen Cemetery.

Bibliography: *DAB.*

**SPIGHT, Thomas,** a Representative from Mississippi; born near Ripley, Tippah County, Miss., October 25, 1841; attended the common schools, Ripley Academy, Purdy (Tenn.) College, and the La Grange (Tenn.) Synodical College; enlisted in the Confederate Army as a private in 1861; promoted to the rank of lieutenant the same year; in 1862 became captain of Company B, Thirty-fourth Regiment, Mississippi Volunteer Infantry, and served until the close of the war; taught school and also engaged in agricultural pursuits; studied law; was admitted to the bar in 1875 and commenced practice in Ripley, Miss.; member of the State house of representatives 1874-1880; established the Southern Sentinel in 1879, retiring from the newspaper business five years later; prosecuting attorney of the third judicial district 1884-1892; elected as a Democrat to the Fifty-fifth Congress to fill the vacancy caused by the resignation of William V. Sullivan; reelected to the Fifty-sixth and to the five succeeding Congresses and served from July 5, 1898, to March 3, 1911; unsuccessful candidate for renomination in 1910; again resumed the practice of his profession and also engaged in religious work until his death in Ripley, Miss., January 5, 1924; interment in Ripley Cemetery.

**SPINK, Cyrus,** a Representative from Ohio; born in Berkshire County, Mass., March 24, 1793; moved to Stark County, Ohio, in 1815; taught school for several years in Kendall, Stark County, Ohio; appointed deputy surveyor of Wayne County in October 1815 and served until December 1816; county surveyor from 1816 to 1821, serving also for a time as district surveyor; county auditor in 1820 and 1821; member of the Ohio State house of representatives in 1821 and 1822; employed in the register's office at Wooster, 1822-1824; appointed register by President James Monroe in 1824; reappointed by President John Quincy Adams in 1828 and served until 1832; engaged in mercantile pursuits in Wooster; member of the Ohio State board of equalization in 1846; delegate to the Whig National Convention of 1852; appointed by Governor Salmon P. Chase as one of the directors of the Ohio Penitentiary in 1856; elected as a Republican to the Thirty-sixth Congress and served from March 4, 1859, until his death in Wooster, Wayne County, Ohio, on May 31, 1859; interment in Wooster Cemetery.

**SPINK, Solomon Lewis,** a Delegate from the Territory of Dakota; born in Whitehall, Washington County, N.Y., March 20, 1831; completed preparatory studies and graduated from Castleton (Vt.) Seminary; taught school several years; studied law; admitted to the bar in 1856 and commenced practice in Burlington, Iowa; moved to Paris, Ill., in 1860 and became the editor and publisher of the Prairie Beacon; member of the State house of representatives in 1864; moved to Yankton, Dak., in 1865, having been appointed by President Abraham Lincoln, as secretary of the Territory of North Dakota, in which position he served until 1869; was elected as a Republican to the Forty-first Congress (March 4, 1869-March 3, 1871); unsuccessful candidate for reelection in 1870 to the Forty-second Congress; resumed the practice of his profession in Yankton, S.Dak.; unsuccessful candidate for election in 1876 to the Forty-fifth Congress; died in Yankton, S.Dak., September 22, 1881; interment in the City Cemetery.

**SPINNER, Francis Elias,** a Representative from New York; born in Mohawk, German Flats, Herkimer County, N.Y., January 21, 1802; educated by his father; served an apprenticeship at both harness making and candy making; engaged in mercantile pursuits in 1824; entered the State militia and was subsequently promoted to the rank of major general; appointed deputy sheriff in 1829; sheriff of Herkimer County 1834-1837; appointed one of the commissioners for the construction of the State lunatic asylum at Utica in 1838; engaged in banking as cashier and later president of the Mohawk Bank; State inspector of turnpikes; commissioner and supervisor of schools; appointed auditor and deputy naval officer in charge of the port of New York in 1845 and served four years; elected as a Democrat to the Thirty-fourth Congress and as a Republican to the Thirty-fifth and Thirty-sixth Congresses (March 4, 1855-March 3, 1861); chairman, Committee on Accounts (Thirty-sixth Congress); was not a candidate for renomination in 1860 to the Thirty-seventh Congress; appointed by President Abraham Lincoln as Treasurer of the United States and served from March 16, 1861, until his resignation on July 1, 1875; successfully urged the employment of women in the Treasury Department; died in Jacksonville, Fla., December 31, 1890; interment in Mohawk Cemetery, Mohawk, N.Y.

Bibliography: *DAB.*

**SPINOLA, Francis Barretto,** a Representative from New York; born at Stony Brook, Long Island, N.Y., March 19, 1821; attended Quaker Hill Academy in Dutchess County; studied law; was admitted to the bar in 1844 and commenced practice in Brooklyn, N.Y.; elected alderman of the second ward in Brooklyn in 1846 and 1847; reelected in 1849 and served for four years; member of the State assembly in 1855; served in the State senate 1858-1861; delegate to the Democratic National Convention at Charleston in 1860; harbor commissioner; during the Civil War was appointed brigadier general of Volunteers October 2, 1862; honorably discharged from the service in August 1865; engaged in the insurance business and banking; elected as a Democrat to the Fiftieth, Fifty-first, and Fifty-second Congresses and served from March 4, 1887, until his death in Washington, D.C., April 14, 1891; interment in Greenwood Cemetery, Brooklyn, N.Y.

**SPONG, William Belser, Jr.,** a Senator from Virginia; born in Portsmouth, Va., September 29, 1920; attended the public schools of Portsmouth; attended Hampden-Sydney College, the University of Virginia, and the University of Edinburgh, Scotland; studied law; served in the Army Air Corps, Eighth Air Force, 1942-1945; admitted to the bar in 1947 and commenced the practice of law in Portsmouth, Va.; lecturer in law and government, College of William and Mary, 1948-1949; member, Virginia house of delegates, 1954-1955; member, Virginia senate, 1956-1966; chairman of the Virginia Commission on Public Education, 1958-1962; elected as a Democrat to the United States Senate in 1966 for the six-year term commencing January 3, 1967; subsequently appointed by the Governor, December 31, 1966, to fill the vacancy caused by the resignation of A. Willis Robertson for the term ending January 3, 1967; served from December 31, 1966, to January 3, 1973; unsuccessful candidate for reelection in 1972; law professor and dean, Marshall-Wythe School of Law, College of William and Mary, 1976-1985; president, Old Dominion University, Norfolk, Va., 1988-1990; lawyer, Cooper, Spong and Davis, 1990 to present; is a resident of Portsmouth, Va.

**SPOONER, Henry Joshua,** a Representative from Rhode Island; born in Providence, R.I., August 6, 1839; attended the common schools and was graduated from Brown University, Providence, R.I., in 1860; studied law; entered the Union Army in 1862 as second lieutenant in the Fourth Regiment, Rhode Island Volunteer Infantry; served in the Armies of the Potomac and the James, mostly in the Ninth Army Corps; was admitted to the bar in 1865 and commenced practice in Providence, R.I.; commander of the department of Rhode Island, Grand Army of the Republic, in 1877; member of the State house of representatives 1875-1881, serving as speaker 1879-1881; elected as a Republican to the Forty-seventh Congress to fill the vacancy caused by the resignation of Nelson W. Aldrich; reelected to the Forty-eighth and to the three succeeding Congresses and served from December 5, 1881, to March 3, 1891; chairman, Committee on Accounts (Fifty-first Congress); unsuccessful candidate for reelection in 1890 to the Fifty-second Congress; again a member of the State house of representatives in 1902; resumed the practice of law in Providence, R.I., and died in that city February 9, 1918; interment in Swan Point Cemetery.

**SPOONER, John Coit,** a Senator from Wisconsin; born in Lawrenceburg, Dearborn County, Ind., January 6, 1843; moved to Wisconsin with his parents, who settled in Madison in 1859; attended the common schools and graduated from the University of Wisconsin at Madison, in 1864; during the Civil War enlisted as a private and was brevetted major at the close of the war; private and military secretary to the Governor of Wisconsin; studied law; was admitted to the bar in 1867 and served as assistant attorney general of Wisconsin until 1870; moved to Hudson, Wis., and practiced law from 1870 until 1884; member, Wisconsin State assembly, 1872; member of the board of regents of Wisconsin University; elected as a Republican to the United States Senate and served from March 4, 1885, to March 3, 1891; unsuccessful candidate for reelection; chairman, Committee on Claims (Forty-ninth through Fifty-first Congresses); unsuccessful Republican candidate for governor of Wisconsin in 1892; moved to Madison in 1893; again elected to the United States Senate in 1897; reelected in 1903 and served from March 4, 1897, until his resignation, effective April 30, 1907; chairman, Committee on Relations with Canada (Fifty-fifth Congress), Committee on Rules (Fifty-fifth through Fifty-ninth Congresses); engaged in the practice of law in New York City; declined the positions of Secretary of the Interior and Attorney General in the Cabinet of President William McKinley in 1898 and 1901; declined the position of Secretary of State in the Cabinet of President William Howard Taft; practiced law in New York City; died in New York City, June 11, 1919; interment in Forest Hill Cemetery, Madison, Wis.

**Bibliography:** *DAB*; Fowler, Dorothy. *John Coit Spooner: Defender of Presidents.* New York: University Publishers, 1961; Parker, James. "Senator John C. Spooner, 1887-1907." Ph.D. dissertation, University of Maryland, 1972.

**SPRAGUE, Charles Franklin** (grandson of Peleg Sprague [1793-1880]), a Representative from Massachusetts; born in Boston, Mass., June 10, 1857; attended the public schools; graduated from Harvard University in 1879; studied law at the Harvard Law School and the Boston University and was admitted to the bar in Boston; member of the Boston Common Council in 1889 and 1890; member of the Massachusetts house of representatives in 1891 and 1892; served as chairman of the board of park commissioners of the city of Boston in 1893 and 1894; served in the Massachusetts senate in 1895 and 1896; elected as a Republican to the Fifty-fifth and Fifty-sixth Congresses (March 4, 1897-March 3, 1901); declined to be a candidate for renomination in 1900 to the Fifty-seventh Congress; died in Providence, R.I., on January 30, 1902; interment in Mount Auburn Cemetery, Watertown, Mass.

**SPRAGUE, Peleg** (grandfather of Charles Franklin Sprague), a Representative and a Senator from Maine; born in Duxbury, Mass., April 27, 1793; graduated from Harvard University in 1812; studied law at Litchfield, Conn.; was admitted to the bar in 1815 and commenced practice in Augusta, Maine; moved to Hallowell, Kennebec County, Maine, in 1817 and continued the practice of law; member, Maine house of representatives 1821-1822; corporate member of the Maine Historical Society; elected to the Nineteenth, Twentieth, and Twenty-first Congresses and served from March 4, 1825, until his resignation, effective March 3, 1829, having been elected Senator; elected to the United States Senate and served from March 4, 1829, to January 1, 1835, when he resigned; again resumed the practice of law in Boston, Mass., in 1840; presidential elector on the Whig ticket in 1840; United States district judge of Massachusetts 1841-1865; died in Boston, Mass., October 13, 1880; interment in Mount Auburn Cemetery, Cambridge, Mass.

**Bibliography:** *DAB*; Sprague, Peleg. *Speeches and Addresses.* Boston: Sampson and Co., 1858.

**SPRAGUE, Peleg,** a Representative from New Hampshire; born in Rochester, Mass., December 10, 1756; clerked in a store in Littleton, Mass.; attended Harvard College, and was graduated from Dartmouth College, Hanover, N.H., in 1783; studied law; was admitted to the bar in 1785 and commenced practice in Winchendon, Mass.; moved to Keene, N.H., in 1787; selectman 1789-1791; county solicitor for Cheshire County in 1794; member of the State house of representatives in 1797; elected as a Federalist to the Fifth Congress to fill the vacancy caused by the resignation of Jeremiah Smith and served from December 15, 1797, to March 3, 1799; declined to be a candidate for renomination in 1798; died in Keene, N.H., April 20, 1800; interment in the Washington Street Cemetery.

**SPRAGUE, William,** a Representative from Michigan; born in Providence, R.I., February 23, 1809; attended the public schools; moved to Michigan and settled in Kalamazoo; studied theology and was ordained as a minister; presiding elder of the Methodist Episcopal Church, Kalamazoo district, 1844-1848; elected as a Whig to the Thirty-first Congress (March 4, 1849-March 3, 1851); retired to his farm near Oshtemo, Kalamazoo County, Mich.; died in Kalamazoo, Mich., September 19, 1868; interment in Mountain Home Cemetery.

**SPRAGUE, William** (uncle of William Sprague [1830-1915]), a Representative and a Senator from Rhode Island; born in Cranston, R.I., November 3, 1799; pursued classical studies; engaged in mercantile pursuits; member, Rhode Island house of representatives, serving as speaker, 1832-1835; elected as a Whig to the Twenty-fourth Congress (March 4, 1835-March 3, 1837); declined to be a candidate for renomination in 1836 to the Twenty-fifth Congress; elected Governor of Rhode Island in 1838, reelected in 1839 and served from May 2, 1838 to May 1, 1839; elected as a Whig to the United States Senate to fill the vacancy caused by the death of Nathan F. Dixon and served from February 18, 1842, to January 17, 1844, when he resigned; chairman, Committee on Enrolled Bills (Twenty-seventh Congress); presidential elector on the Whig ticket in 1848; engaged in the manufacture of cotton and paint; died in Providence, R.I., on October 19, 1856; interment in Swan Point Cemetery.

**SPRAGUE, William** (nephew of William Sprague [1799-1856]), a Senator from Rhode Island; born in Cranston, R.I., September 12, 1830; attended the common schools and Irving Institute, Tarrytown, N.Y.; engaged in the calico-printing business and the manufacture of locomotives; elected Governor of Rhode Island in 1860, reelected in 1861 and 1862 and served from May 29, 1860, until his resignation March 3, 1863, having been elected United States Senator; head of a Rhode Island regiment that was one of the first to answer the call for troops in 1861; tendered a commission as brigadier general in 1861, but declined; elected as a Republican to the United States Senate in 1862; reelected in 1868 and served from March 4, 1863, to March 3, 1875; was not a candidate for renomination; chairman, Committee on Manufactures (Thirty-eighth through Fortieth Congresses), Committee on Public Lands (Forty-third Congress); unsuccessful candidate in 1883 for election for Governor of Rhode Island; engaged in agricultural pursuits near Narragansett Pier, R.I.; died in Paris, France, September 11, 1915; interment in Swan Point Cemetery, Providence, R.I.

Bibliography: *DAB*; Belden, Thomas. *So Fell the Angels*. Boston: Little Brown, 1956.

**SPRAGUE, William Peter,** a Representative from Ohio; born near Malta, Morgan County, Ohio, May 21, 1827; attended the country schools; engaged in mercantile pursuits when quite young and continued in active business until 1864; member of the State senate 1860-1863; moved to McConnelsville, Ohio, in 1866, and engaged in banking; elected as a Republican to the Forty-second and Forty-third Congresses (March 4, 1871-March 3, 1875); was not a candidate for renomination in 1874; resumed the banking business at Malta, Ohio; died in McConnelsville, Morgan County, Ohio, March 3, 1899; interment in Riverview Cemetery.

**SPRATT, John McKee, Jr.,** a Representative from South Carolina; born in Charlotte, Mecklenburg County, N.C., November 1, 1942; attended York (S.C.) Elementary School; graduated from York High School, 1960; A.B., Davidson (N.C.) College, 1964; attended Corpus Christi College; M.A., Oxford University, Oxford, England, 1966; LL.B., Yale University Law School, 1969; served in the United States Army, 1969-1971; admitted to the South Carolina bar in 1969 and commenced practice in 1971 in York; banker; delegate, South Carolina State Democratic convention, 1972-1980; delegate to the Democratic National Convention of 1964; elected as a

Democrat to the Ninety-eighth and to the six succeeding Congresses (January 3, 1983-January 3, 1997); is a resident of York, S.C.

**SPRIGG, James Cresap** (brother of Michael Cresap Sprigg), a Representative from Kentucky; born in Frostburg, Md., in 1802; completed preparatory studies; moved to Shelbyville, Shelby County, Ky.; studied law; admitted to the bar and practiced; held several local offices; member of the Kentucky house of representatives 1830-1834 and 1837-1840; elected as a Whig to the Twenty-seventh Congress (March 4, 1841-March 3, 1843); unsuccessful candidate as an Independent for reelection in 1842 to the Twenty-eighth Congress; resumed the practice of law; again a member of the Kentucky house of representatives in 1852, and served until his death in Shelbyville, Ky., October 3, 1852; interment in Grove Hill Cemetery.

**SPRIGG, Michael Cresap** (brother of James Cresap Sprigg), a Representative from Maryland; born in Frostburg, Md., July 1, 1791; completed preparatory studies; held a number of local offices; member of the State house of delegates in 1821, 1823, 1837, 1840, and 1844; president of the Chesapeake & Ohio Canal Co. in 1841 and 1842; elected as a Jacksonian to the Twentieth and Twenty-first Congresses (March 4, 1827-March 3, 1831); chairman, Committee on Expenditures on Public Buildings (Twentieth and Twenty-first Congresses); died in Cumberland, Allegany County, Md., December 18, 1845; interment in Rose Hill Cemetery.

**SPRIGG, Richard, Jr.** (nephew of Thomas Sprigg), a Representative from Maryland; born in Prince Georges County, Md.; member of the State house of delegates in 1792 and 1793; elected as a Republican to the Fourth Congress to fill the vacancy caused by the resignation of Gabriel Duval; reelected to the Fifth Congress and served from May 5, 1796, to March 3, 1799; elected to the Seventh Congress and served from March 4, 1801, until his resignation February 11, 1802; appointed associate judge of the Maryland Court of Appeals on January 27, 1806.

**SPRIGG, Thomas** (uncle of Richard Sprigg, Jr.), a Representative from Maryland; born in Prince Georges County, Md., in 1747; served during the Revolutionary War as ensign in the Maryland Battalion of the Flying Camp from September to December 1776; appointed the first register of wills of Washington County, Md., in 1777, and served until September 29, 1780, when he resigned; appointed lieutenant of Washington County by the Governor and Council of Maryland December 21, 1779; elected to the Third Congress and reelected as a Republican to the Fourth Congress (March 4, 1793-March 3, 1797); died in Washington County, Md., December 13, 1809.

**SPRIGGS, John Thomas,** a Representative from New York; born in Peterborough, Northamptonshire, England, April 5, 1825; immigrated to the United States with his parents, who settled in Whitesboro, Oneida County, N.Y., in 1836; attended Hamilton College, Clinton, N.Y., and was graduated from Union College, Schenectady, N.Y., in 1848; studied law; was admitted to the bar in 1848 and commenced practice in Whitesboro, N.Y.; prosecuting attorney of Oneida County in 1853; county treasurer in 1854; delegate to the Democratic National Convention at Baltimore in 1860; mayor of Utica 1868-1880; delegate to the Democratic National Convention in 1872 and 1880; elected as a Democrat to the Forty-eighth and Forty-ninth Congresses (March 4, 1883-March 3, 1887); chairman, Committee on Accounts (Forty-ninth Congress); unsuccessful candidate for reelection in 1886 to the Fiftieth Congress; resumed the practice of law; died in Utica, N.Y., December 23, 1888; interment in Whitesboro Cemetery, Whitesboro, N.Y.

**SPRINGER, Raymond Smiley,** a Representative from Indiana; born on a farm in Rush County, near Dunreith, Ind., April 26, 1882; attended the public schools, Earlham College, Richmond, Ind., and Butler University, Indianapolis, Ind.; was graduated from the Indiana Law School at Indianapolis in 1904; was admitted to the bar in 1904 and commenced practice in Connersville, Fayette County, Ind.; county attorney of Fayette County, Ind., 1908-1914; judge of the thirty-seventh judicial circuit of Indiana 1916-1922; during the First World War served as a captain of Infantry, Eighty-fourth Division, in 1918; lieutenant colonel of the Officers' Reserve Corps 1918-1946; unsuccessful candidate for Governor of Indiana in 1932 and 1936; elected as a Republican to the Seventy-sixth and to the four succeeding Congresses and served from January 3, 1939, until his death in Connersville, Ind., August 28, 1947; interment in Dale Cemetery.

**SPRINGER, William Lee,** a Representative from Illinois; born in Sullivan, Ind., April 12, 1909; attended the public schools of Sullivan and Culver Military Academy at Culver, Ind.; B.A., DePauw University, Greencastle, Ind., 1931; LL.B., University of Illinois School of Law, 1935; was admitted to the bar in 1935 and commenced the practice of law in 1936 in Champaign, Ill.; State's attorney of Champaign County, Ill., 1940-1942; served in the United States Navy from March 1942 as an officer, with nineteen months' foreign duty, until discharged as a lieutenant in the Naval Reserve on September 22, 1945; county judge of Champaign County 1946-1950; elected as a Republican to the Eighty-second and to the ten succeeding Congresses (January 3, 1951-January 3, 1973); was not a candidate for reelection in 1972 to the Ninety-third Congress; member of the Federal Power Commission, May 1973-December 1975; member of the Federal Election Commission from May 1976 to March 1979; was a resident of Champaign, Ill.; died September 20, 1992.

**SPRINGER, William McKendree,** a Representative from Illinois; born near New Lebanon, Sullivan County, Ind., May 30, 1836; moved to Jacksonville, Ill., with his parents in 1848; attended the public schools in New Lebanon and Jacksonville and the Illinois College at Jacksonville; was graduated from the University of Indiana at Bloomington in 1858; studied law; was admitted to the bar in 1859 and practiced in Lincoln and Springfield, Ill.; secretary of the Illinois State constitutional convention in 1862; traveled in Europe, 1868-1871; member of the State house of representatives, 1871-1872; elected as a Democrat to the Forty-fourth and to the nine succeeding Congresses (March 4, 1875-March 3, 1895); chairman, Committee on Expenditures in the Department of State (Forty-fourth and Forty-fifth Congresses), Committee on Elections (Forty-sixth Congress), Committee on Expenditures in the Department of Justice (Forty-eighth Congress), Committee on Claims (Forty-ninth Congress), Committee on Territories (Fiftieth Congress), Committee on Ways and Means (Fifty-second Congress), Committee on Banking and Currency (Fifty-third Congress); was an unsuccessful candidate for reelection in 1894 to the Fifty-fourth Congress; again resumed the practice of law in Washington, D.C., in 1895; United States judge for the northern district of Indian Territory, and chief justice of the United States Court of Appeals of Indian Territory, by appointment of President Grover Cleveland, 1895-1900; again engaged in the practice of his profession in Washington, D.C., where he died on December 4, 1903; interment in Oak Ridge Cemetery, Springfield, Ill.

Bibliography: *DAB.*

**SPROUL, Elliott Wilford,** a Representative from Illinois; born in Apohaqui, Kings County, New Brunswick, Canada, December 28, 1856; attended the public schools; moved to Boston, Mass., in 1879 and to Chicago, Ill., in 1880, and engaged in the building and contracting business; was naturalized in 1886; member of the Chicago City Council 1896-1899; delegate to the Republican National Convention in 1920; member of the board of directors of the Chicago Public Library 1919-1921; elected as a Republican to the Sixty-seventh and to the four succeeding Congresses (March 4, 1921-March 3, 1931); unsuccessful candidate for reelection in 1930 to the Seventy-second Congress; resided in Chicago, Ill., until his death there on June 22, 1935; interment in Mount Hope Cemetery.

**SPROUL, William Henry,** a Representative from Kansas; born on a farm near Livingston, Overton County, Tenn., October 14, 1867; attended the public schools and Alpine Academy in Overton County, Tenn.; in 1883 moved to Kansas with his parents, who settled in Cherokee County; worked on a farm and in the mines; attended high school at Columbus, Kans., and the Kansas Normal College at Fort Scott; taught school at Columbus 1888-1892; was graduated from the Kansas State University Law School in 1894; was admitted to the bar in 1894 and commenced practice in Sedan, Kans.; prosecuting attorney of Chautauqua County 1897-1901; mayor of Sedan 1921-1923; engaged in agricultural pursuits and stock raising; was also interested in the oil and gas business; elected as a Republican to the Sixty-eighth and to the three succeeding Congresses (March 4, 1923-March 3, 1931); chairman, Committee on Mines and Mining (Seventy-first Congress); was not a candidate for renomination, but was an unsuccessful candidate for nomination for United States Senator in 1930; resumed his former business pursuits; died in a hospital in Kansas City, Mo., December 27, 1932; interment in Greenwood Cemetery, Sedan, Kans.

**SPRUANCE, Presley,** a Senator from Delaware; born in Kent County, Del., September 11, 1785; pursued preparatory studies; engaged in manufacturing and mercantile pursuits in Smyrna, Del.; delegate to the State constitutional convention in 1831; member, State senate 1828, 1840, 1846, and served as its president; elected as a Whig to the United States Senate and served from March 4, 1847, to March 3, 1853; was not a candidate for renomination in 1852; resumed his business pursuits; died in Smyrna, Del., February 13, 1863; interment in the Presbyterian Cemetery.

**SQUIRE, Watson Carvosso,** a Senator from Washington; born in Cape Vincent, Jefferson County, N.Y., May 18, 1838; attended the public schools, Falley Seminary, Fulton, N.Y., and Fairfield Seminary, Herkimer County, N.Y.; graduated from Wesleyan University, Middletown, Conn., in 1859; principal of the Moravia (N.Y.) Institute; during the Civil War enlisted in Company F, Nineteenth Regiment, New York Volunteer Infantry, in 1861; promoted to the rank of first lieutenant, and was mustered out the same year; graduated from the Cleveland (Ohio) Law School in 1862; was admitted to the bar the same year and commenced practice in Cleveland, Ohio; raised a company of sharpshooters, of which he was commissioned captain; made judge advocate of the district of Tennessee, with headquarters in Nashville; discharged with the rank of captain in 1865 and subsequently brevetted major, lieutenant colonel, and colonel; subsequently employed with the Remington Arms Co.; purchased large holdings in the Territory of Washington in 1876 and moved to Seattle in 1879; appointed Governor of the Territory of Washington by President Chester A. Arthur on July 2, 1884 and served until April 1887; upon the admission of Washington as a State into the Union in 1889 was elected as a Republican to the United States Senate; reelected in 1891, and served from November 20, 1889, to March 3, 1897; unsuccessful candidate for reelection in 1897; chairman, Committee on Coast Defenses (Fifty-second and Fifty-fourth Congresses), Committee on Transportation Routes to the Seaboard (Fifty-second Congress); retired from the practice of law and devoted his time to management of his properties in Seattle; organizer and president of the Union Trust Co. and the Squire Investment Co.; died in Seattle, Wash., June 7, 1926; interment in Washelli Cemetery.

Bibliography: *DAB.*

**STACK, Edmund John,** a Representative from Illinois; born in Chicago, Ill., January 31, 1874; attended the grammar and high schools of Chicago; was graduated from the law department of Lake Forest (Ill.) University in 1895; was admitted to the bar the same year and commenced the practice of his profession in Chicago, Ill.; appointed assistant corporation counsel of Chicago and, later, chief trial attorney; unsuccessful candidate for election in 1906 to the Sixtieth Congress; elected as a Democrat to the Sixty-second Congress (March 4, 1911-March 3, 1913); unsuccessful candidate for renomination in 1912; resumed the practice of law; died in Chicago, Ill., April 12, 1957; interment in Calvary Cemetery, Evanston, Ill.

**STACK, Edward John,** a Representative from Florida; born in Bayonne, Hudson County, N.J., April 29, 1910; attended James Madison High School, Brooklyn, N.Y.; B.A., Lehigh University, Bethlehem, Pa., 1931; J.D., University of Pennsylvania Law School, Philadelphia, 1934; M.A., Columbia University, New York City, 1938; instructor in law, Hunter College of the University of the City of New York; builder, real estate investor, banker, and restaurateur; admitted to the New York bar in 1934 and commenced practice in New York City; served in the United States Coast Guard, 1942-1946; city commissioner and mayor, Pompano Beach, Fla., 1965-1969; sheriff of Broward County, Fla., 1968-1978; affiliated with the Democratic Party in 1975; delegate, Florida State Democratic conventions, 1977-1978; member, Democratic National Finance Council, 1976-1978; elected as a Democrat to the Ninety-sixth Congress (January 3, 1979-January 3, 1981); unsuccessful candidate for renomination in 1980 to the Ninety-seventh Congress; resumed the practice of law; unsuccessful candidate for election in 1982 to the Ninety-eighth Congress; administrator, Broward County Court alcohol rehabilitation program; was a resident of Pompano Beach, Fla., until his death in Fort Lauderdale, Fla., November 3, 1989; interment in Queen of Heaven Cemetery, North Lauderdale, Fla.

**STACK, Michael Joseph,** a Representative from Pennsylvania; born in Listowel, County Kerry, Ireland, September 29, 1888; attended the national school of his native city; immigrated to the United States in 1903 and settled in Philadelphia, Pa.; attended St. Joseph's College, Philadelphia, Pa., and was graduated from St. Mary's University, Baltimore, Md., in 1910; employed by a railroad company at Detroit, Mich., 1910-1917; during the First World War enlisted on July 17, 1917, as a private in the Medical Detachment, Three Hundred and Sixtieth Infantry; after the war became engaged in the real estate business in Philadelphia, Pa.; elected as a Democrat to the Seventy-fourth and Seventy-fifth Congresses (January 3, 1935-January 3, 1939); unsuccessful Democratic candidate for renomination in 1938 and was an unsuccessful Royal Oak candidate for reelection in 1938 to the Seventy-sixth Congress; resumed the real estate business; died in Philadelphia, Pa., December 14, 1960; interment in St. Denis Cemetery, Havertown, Pa.

**STACKHOUSE, Eli Thomas,** a Representative from South Carolina; born in Little Rock, Marion County, S.C., March 27, 1824; attended the common schools; worked on his father's farm; taught school for several years; later engaged in agricultural pursuits; enlisted in the Confederate Army January 9, 1861, and served throughout the Civil War, attaining the rank of colonel of the Eighth Regiment, South Carolina Volunteers; member of the State house of representatives 1863, 1865-1866; member of the first board of trustees of Clemson Agricultural and Mechanical College of South Carolina in 1887; first president of the South Carolina State Farmers' Alliance in 1888; elected as a Democrat to the Fifty-second Congress and served from March 4, 1891, until his death in Washington, D.C., June 14, 1892; interment in Little Rock Cemetery, Little Rock, S.C.

**STAEBLER, Neil Oliver,** a Representative from Michigan; born in Ann Arbor, Washtenaw County, Mich., July 11, 1905; attended the public schools; graduated from Ann Arbor High School in 1922; A.B., University of Michigan, 1926; treasurer, Staebler-Kempf Oil Co., 1926-1951; engaged in real estate and land development, beginning in 1946; chief of the building materials branch, Office of Price Administration, 1942-1943; served as a lieutenant in the United States Navy, 1943-1945; consultant to Federal Housing Expediter in 1946; chairman of Democratic State Central committee of Michigan, 1950-1961; member of Democratic National Committee, 1961-1964, and 1965-1968; visiting professor, University of Massachusetts, 1962; elected as a Democrat to the Eighty-eighth Congress (January 3, 1963-January 3, 1965); was not a candidate in 1964 for reelection to the Eighty-ninth Congress, but was an unsuccessful candidate for election for Governor of Michigan; member of the Federal Election Commission from April 1975 to October 1978; is a resident of Ann Arbor, Mich.

**Bibliography:** Staebler, Neil. *Out of the Smoke-Filled Room: A Story of Michigan Politics.* Ann Arbor, Mich.: Wahr Publishing Co., 1991; Weideman, Christine. *Neil Staebler: His Career and Legacy.* Ann Arbor, Mich.: Michigan Historical Collections, 1987.

**STAFFORD, Robert Theodore,** a Representative and a Senator from Vermont; born in Rutland, Vt., August 8, 1913; educated in the public schools of Rutland; B.S., Middlebury (Vt.) College, 1935; attended the University of Michigan Law School; LL.B., Boston University Law School, 1938; Rutland County prosecuting attorney, 1938-1942; during the Second World War served on active duty in the United States Navy as a lieutenant commander, 1942-1946, and during the Korean conflict, 1951-1953; captain in the United States Navy Reserve; Rutland County State's attorney, 1947-1951; deputy State attorney general, 1953-1955; State attorney general, 1955-1957; Lieutenant Governor, 1957-1959; elected Governor of Vermont in 1958 and served from January 8, 1959 to January 5, 1961; elected as a Republican to the Eighty-seventh and to the five succeeding Congresses and served from January 3, 1961, until his resignation on September 16, 1971, to accept appointment the same day to the United States Senate to fill the vacancy caused by the death of Winston L. Prouty; elected by special election, January 7, 1972, to complete the unexpired term ending January 3, 1977; reelected in 1976 and again in 1982, and served from September 16, 1971 to January 3, 1989; was not a candidate for reelection in 1988; chairman, Committee on Environment and Public Works (Ninety-seventh through Ninety-ninth Congresses); is a resident of Rutland, Vt.

**STAFFORD, William Henry,** a Representative from Wisconsin; born in Milwaukee, Wis., October 12, 1869; attended the public schools, and was graduated from Harvard University Law School in 1893; was admitted to the bar in 1894 and commenced practice in Milwaukee, Wis.; elected as a Republican to the Fifty-eighth and to the three succeeding Congresses (March 4, 1903-March 3, 1911); unsuccessful candidate for renomination in 1910 to the Sixty-second Congress; resumed the practice of his profession in Milwaukee, Wis.; elected to the Sixty-third and to the two succeeding Congresses (March 4, 1913-March 3, 1919); unsuccessful candidate for reelection in 1918 to the Sixty-sixth Congress; elected to the Sixty-seventh Congress (March 4, 1921-March 3, 1923); unsuccessful candidate for reelection in 1922 to the Sixty-eighth Congress, and for election in 1926 to the Seventieth Congress; elected to the Seventy-first and Seventy-second Congresses (March 4, 1929-March 3, 1933); unsuccessful candidate for renomination in 1932 to the Seventy-third Congress, and for the Republican nomination for United States Senator in 1938; resumed the practice of law; died in Milwaukee, Wis., April 22, 1957; interment in Forest Home Cemetery.

**STAGGERS, Harley Orrin** (father of Harley Orrin Staggers, Jr.), a Representative from West Virginia; born in Keyser, Mineral County, W.Va., August 3, 1907; attended the public schools of Mineral County, W.Va.; was graduated from Emory and Henry College, Emory, Va., in 1931; engaged in graduate work at Duke University in 1935; coach and teacher of science at Norton (Va.) High School 1931-1933; head coach of Potomac State College, Keyser, W.Va., 1933-1935; sheriff of Mineral County, W.Va., 1937-1941; right-of-way agent, State Road Commission of West Virginia, in 1941 and 1942; West Virginia State Director, Office of Government Reports (later Office of War Information) in 1942; lieutenant commander in the United States Naval Air Corps with service as a navigator in the Atlantic and Pacific Theaters of War 1942-1946; elected as a Democrat to the Eighty-first and to the fifteen succeeding Congresses (January 3, 1949-January 3, 1981); chairman, Committee on Interstate and Foreign Commerce (Eighty-ninth through Ninety-sixth Congresses); was not a candidate for reelection in 1980 to the Ninety-seventh Congress; was a resident of Keyser, W.Va.; died August 20, 1991.

**STAGGERS, Harley Orrin, Jr.** (son of Harley Orrin Staggers), a Representative from West Virginia; born in Washington, D.C., on February 22, 1951; graduated from Keyser High School, 1969; B.A., Harvard University, 1974; J.D., West Virginia University School of Law, Morgantown, 1977; admitted to West Virginia bar in 1977 and commenced practice as an assistant attorney general in Charleston; administrative assistant, Democratic National Convention, 1976; West Virginia State senator, 1980-1982; elected as a Democrat to the Ninety-eighth and to the four succeeding Congresses (January 3, 1983-January 3, 1993); unsuccessful candidate for renomination in 1992 to the One Hundred Third Congress; is a resident of Keyser, W.Va.

**STAHLE, James Alonzo,** a Representative from Pennsylvania; born in West Manchester Township, York County, Pa., January 11, 1829; attended the common schools and York Academy; learned the printing trade; later became a merchant tailor; organized the Ellsworth Zouaves in 1861 and in August of that year, together with his company of forty recruits, enlisted as Company A in the Eighty-seventh Regiment, Pennsylvania Volunteers, and served until his discharge October 13, 1864; deputy collector of internal revenue at York, Pa., from May 3, 1869, to July 3, 1885; engaged in agricultural pursuits; elected as a Republican to the Fifty-fourth Congress (March 4, 1895-March 3, 1897); was not a candidate for renomination in 1896; resumed agricultural pursuits; died on his estate near York, Pa., December 21, 1912; interment in Prospect Hill Cemetery, York, Pa.

**STAHLNECKER, William Griggs,** a Representative from New York; born in Auburn, Cayuga County, N.Y., June 20, 1849; moved with his parents to Brooklyn and later to New York City; pursued an academic course and attended the University of New York in New York City; studied law; was admitted to practice; engaged in mercantile pursuits; member of the New York Produce Exchange; moved to Yonkers in 1880; mayor of Yonkers, N.Y., 1884-1886; delegate to the Democratic State convention at Saratoga in June 1884; delegate to the Democratic National Convention in 1884; elected as a Democrat to the Forty-ninth and to the three succeeding Congresses (March 4, 1885-March 3, 1893); engaged in the practice of law; died in Yonkers, N.Y., March 26, 1902; interment in Sleepy Hollow Cemetery, Tarrytown, N.Y.

**STALBAUM, Lynn Ellsworth,** a Representative from Wisconsin; born on a farm near Waterford, Racine County, Wis., May 15, 1920; attended the public schools; graduated from the Racine County Agricultural School in 1936; employed with the United States Department of Agriculture in Racine County from 1936 until 1944, serving as administrative officer from 1937; served in the United States Navy, 1944-1946; feed salesman, 1946-1951; secretary-treasurer of the Racine Milk Producers Cooperative Association and manager of the Harmony Dairy Co., 1951-1964; elected to the Wisconsin State senate in 1954 and reelected in 1958 and 1962; served as caucus chairman in 1957, 1959, and 1961, and as assistant minority leader in 1963; elected as a Democrat to the Eighty-ninth Congress (January 3, 1965-January 3, 1967); unsuccessful candidate for reelection in 1966 to the Ninetieth Congress, and for election in 1968 to the Ninety-first Congress; legislative consultant to rural electric and dairy cooperatives, 1968; owner of income tax preparation business; is a resident of Bethesda, Md.

**STALKER, Gale Hamilton,** a Representative from New York; born in Long Eddy, Sullivan County, N.Y., November 7, 1889; attended the grade and high schools, Scranton (Pa.) Business College, and the night schools of New York City; moved to Elmira, Chemung County, N.Y., and engaged in the lumber business and also in banking; elected as a Republican to the Sixty-eighth and to the five succeeding Congresses (March 4, 1923-January 3, 1935); was not a candidate for renomination in 1934; was a resident of Palm Bay, Fla., until his death November 4, 1985; interment in Hillside Cemetery, Ormond Beach, Fla.

**STALLINGS, Jesse Francis,** a Representative from Alabama; born near Manningham, Butler County, Ala., April 4, 1856; completed preparatory studies and was graduated from the University of Alabama at Tuscaloosa in 1877; studied law at that university; was admitted to the bar in April 1880 and commenced practice in Greenville, Ala.; elected by the legislature of Alabama as solicitor for the second judicial circuit in November 1886 and served until his resignation in September 1892; delegate to the Democratic National Convention in 1888; elected as a Democrat to the Fifty-third and to the three succeeding Congresses (March 4, 1893-March 3, 1901); was not a candidate for renomination in 1900; resumed the practice of his profession in Birmingham, Ala.; president of the Lincoln Reserve Life Insurance Co. 1912-1928: died in Birmingham, Ala., on March 18, 1928; interment in Elmwood Cemetery.

**STALLINGS, Richard Howard,** a Representative from Idaho; born in Ogden, Weber County, Utah, October 7, 1940; attended public schools in Ogden; was on a mission for the Church of Jesus Christ of Latter-Day Saints to New Zealand, 1960-1962; B.S., Weber State College, Ogden, 1965; M.S., Utah State University, Logan, 1968; pursued graduate studies at Colorado College, Colorado Springs, Colo., 1968; professor of history at Ricks College, Rexburg, Idaho, 1969-1984; elected as a Democrat to the Ninety-ninth and to the three succeeding Congresses (January 3, 1985-January 3, 1993); was not a candidate in 1992 for renomination to the House of Representatives, but was an unsuccessful candidate for election to the United States Senate; is a resident of Rexburg, Idaho.

**STALLWORTH, James Adams,** a Representative from Alabama; born in Evergreen, Conecuh County, Ala., April 7, 1822; attended Old Field Piney Woods Schools; engaged as a planter; studied law; was admitted to the bar in 1848 and commenced practice in Evergreen, Ala.; member of the State house of representatives 1845-1848; solicitor for the second judicial circuit of Alabama in 1850 and 1855; unsuccessful candidate for election in 1854 to the Thirty-fourth Congress; elected as a Democrat to the Thirty-fifth and Thirty-sixth Congresses and served from March 4, 1857, to January 21, 1861, when he withdrew; died near Evergreen, Conecuh County, Ala., August 31, 1861; interment in Evergreen Cemetery.

**STANARD, Edwin Obed,** a Representative from Missouri; born in Newport, Sullivan County, N.H., January 5, 1832; moved with his parents to the Territory of Iowa in 1836; completed preparatory studies; moved to St. Louis, Mo., in 1853; taught school in Illinois in 1854 and 1855; was graduated from St. Louis (Mo.) Commercial

College in 1855; engaged in the commission business in 1856 and later in the milling business at St. Louis; Lieutenant Governor of Missouri 1869-1871; elected as a Republican to the Forty-third Congress (March 4, 1873-March 3, 1875); unsuccessful candidate for reelection in 1874 to the Forty-fourth Congress; engaged in the manufacture of flour; died in St. Louis, Mo., March 12, 1914; interment in Bellefontaine Cemetery.

**STANBERY, William,** a Representative from Ohio; born in Essex County, N.J., August 10, 1788; received an academic education; studied law in New York City and was admitted to the bar; moved to Ohio in 1809; settled in Newark, Licking County, and practiced law; member of the Ohio State senate, 1824-1825; elected to the Twentieth Congress to fill the vacancy caused by the death of William Wilson; reelected as a Jacksonian to the Twenty-first Congress and as an Anti-Jacksonian to the Twenty-second Congress, and served from October 9, 1827 to March 3, 1833; censured by the Twenty-second Congress on July 11, 1832, for use of unparliamentary language; unsuccessful candidate for renomination in 1832 to the Twenty-third Congress; resumed the practice of law; died in Newark, Ohio, January 23, 1873; interment in Cedar Hill Cemetery.

**STANDIFER, James,** a Representative from Tennessee; born in the Sequatchie Valley, near Dunlap, Tenn.; attended the common schools and was graduated from the University of Tennessee at Knoxville; elected to the Eighteenth Congress (March 4, 1823-March 3, 1825); elected as a Jacksonian to the Twenty-first through Twenty-third Congresses, as a Hugh L. White supporter to the Twenty-fourth Congress, and as a Whig to the Twenty-fifth Congress, and served from March 4, 1829 until his death near Kingston, Tenn., August 20, 1837, while on his way to Washington, D.C.; interment in the Baptist Cemetery, Kingston, Tenn.

**Bibliography:** Byas, Stephen D. "James Standifer, Sequatchie Valley Congressman." *Tennessee Historical Quarterly* 50 (Summer 1991): 90-97.

**STANDIFORD, Elisha David,** a Representative from Kentucky; born near Louisville, Jefferson County, Ky., December 28, 1831; attended the common schools and St. Mary's College, near Lebanon, Ky.; graduated from the Kentucky School of Medicine and commenced practice in Louisville; abandoned the practice of medicine and engaged in agricultural pursuits and other enterprises; member of the Kentucky senate in 1868 and 1871; elected as a Democrat to the Forty-third Congress (March 4, 1873-March 3, 1875); declined a renomination in 1874 to the Forty-fourth Congress; president of the Louisville & Nashville Railroad Co. 1875-1879; engaged in banking and agricultural pursuits; died in Louisville, Ky., July 26, 1887; interment in Cave Hill Cemetery.

**STANFIELD, Robert Nelson,** a Senator from Oregon; born in Umatilla, Umatilla County, Oreg., July 9, 1877; attended the public schools and the State normal school at Weston, Oreg.; engaged in the livestock industry and also interested in banking in Echo and Baker, Oreg.; member, State house of representatives 1913-1917, serving as speaker in 1917; elected as a Republican to the United States Senate in 1920 and served from March 4, 1921, to March 3, 1927; unsuccessful candidate for reelection on the Independent ticket in 1926; chairman, Committee to Examine Branches of the Civil Service (Sixty-eighth Congress), Committee on Public Lands and Surveys (Sixty-ninth Congress); resumed his former business pursuits; died in Weiser, Idaho, April 13, 1945: interment in Hillcrest Cemetery.

**STANFILL, William Abner,** a Senator from Kentucky; born in Barbourville, Knox County, Ky., January 16, 1892; attended the public schools and Union College; graduated from the law department of the University of Kentucky at Lexington in 1912; was admitted to the bar the same year and commenced practice in Barbourville, Ky.; moved to Hazard, Ky., in 1916 and continued the practice of law; member of the board of regents of Morehead State Teachers College 1927-1931; member of the board of governors of the Kentucky Children's Home at Lyndon, Ky., 1933-1936; appointed as a Republican to the United States Senate, November 19, 1945, to fill the vacancy caused by the resignation of Albert B. Chandler and served from November 19, 1945, to November 5, 1946, when a successor was elected; was not a candidate for nomination to the vacancy in 1946; resumed the practice of law; retired; resided in Lexington, Ky., where he died June 12, 1971; interment in Hillcrest Memorial Park.

**STANFORD, Leland,** a Senator from California; born in Watervliet, N.Y., March 9, 1824; pursued an academic course; studied law; was admitted to practice in 1848; moved to Port Washington, Wis., the same year and engaged in the practice of law; moved to California in 1852 and opened a general store for miners first in Cold Springs, and then in 1855 moved to Sacramento and engaged in mercantile pursuits on a large scale; one of the "big four" who built the Central Pacific Railroad, serving as its president in 1863; involved in several railroads in the West; founder of Leland Stanford Junior University; unsuccessful candidate in 1859 for election for Governor; elected Governor of California in 1861, and served from January 10, 1862 to December 10, 1863; returned to private business; elected as a Republican to the United States Senate in 1885; reelected in 1891 and served from March 4, 1885, until his death in Palo Alto, Calif., June 21, 1893; chairman, Committee on Public Buildings and Grounds (Fiftieth through Fifty-second Congresses); interment in a masoleum on the grounds of Stanford University.

**Bibliography:** *DAB*; Clark, George. *Leland Stanford, War Governor of California and Founder of Stanford University.* Stanford: Stanford University Press, 1931; Lewis, Oscar. *The Big Four: The Story of Huntington, Stanford, Hopkins, and Crocker, and of the Building of the Central Pacific.* 1938. Reprint. New York: Arno Press, 1981; Tutorow, Norman. *Leland Stanford: Man of Many Careers.* Menlo Park, Calif.: Pacific Coast Publishers, 1971.

**STANFORD, Richard** (grandfather of William Robert Webb), a Representative from North Carolina; born near Vienna, Md., March 2, 1767; completed preparatory studies; moved to Hawfields, N.C., about 1793 and established an academy; elected as a Republican to the Fifth and to the nine succeeding Congresses and served from March 4, 1797, until his death in Georgetown, D.C., April 9, 1816; chairman, Committee on Revisal and Unfinished Business (Thirteenth Congress); interment in Congressional Cemetery, Washington, D.C.

**STANGELAND, Arlan Ingehart,** a Representative from Minnesota; born in Fargo, Cass County, N.Dak., February 8, 1930; moved to Minnesota in 1936; educated in the public schools of Moorhead, Minn.; graduated from Moorhead High School, 1948; farmer, Wilkin County, Minn.; member, Barnesville (Minn.) School Board, 1976-1977; served in the Minnesota State house of representatives from 1966 until 1975; delegate, Minnesota State Republican conventions, 1964-1968; elected as a Republican to the Ninety-fifth Congress, February 22, 1977, by special election to fill the vacancy caused by the resignation of Robert S. Bergland; reelected to the six succeeding Congresses, and served from February 22, 1977 to January 3, 1991; unsuccessful candidate for reelection in 1990 to the One Hundred Second Congress; is a resident of Barnesville, Minn.

**STANLEY, Augustus Owsley,** a Representative and a Senator from Kentucky; born in Shelbyville, Ky., May 21, 1867; attended the State college at Lexington, Ky., and graduated from Centre College, Danville, Ky., in 1889; professor of belles-lettres at Christian College and principal of the Mackville Academy, 1891-1893; studied law; was admitted to the bar in 1894 and commenced practice in Flemingsburg, Ky.; presidential elector on the Democratic ticket in

1900; elected as a Democrat to the Fifty-eighth and to the five succeeding Congresses (March 4, 1903-March 3, 1915); unsuccessful candidate for reelection to the Sixty-fourth Congress; elected Governor of Kentucky in 1915, and served from December 7, 1915 until May 19, 1919, when he resigned, having been elected Senator; elected as a Democrat to the United States Senate in 1918 to fill the vacancy caused by the death of Ollie James for the term commencing March 4, 1919, but, preferring to continue as Governor, did not qualify until May 19, 1919, and served until March 3, 1925; unsuccessful candidate for reelection in 1924; resumed the practice of law in Washington, D.C.; member of the International Joint Commission created to regulate the use of the boundary waters between the United States and Canada, 1930-1933, and served as chairman from 1933 to 1954; died in Washington, D.C., August 12, 1958; interment in Frankfort Cemetery, Frankfort, Ky.

**Bibliography:** *DAB*; Ramage, Thomas. "Augustus Owsley Stanley: Early Twentieth-Century Kentucky Democrat." Ph.D. dissertation, University of Kentucky, 1968.

**STANLEY, Thomas Bahnson,** a Representative from Virginia; born on a farm near Spencer, Henry County, Va., July 16, 1890; attended the local public schools and Eastman Business College, Poughkeepsie, N.Y.; engaged in furniture manufacturing, beginning in 1924; dairy farmer and livestock breeder; member of the Virginia house of delegates, 1930-1946, serving as speaker 1942-1946; elected as a Democrat to the Seventy-ninth Congress to fill the vacancy caused by the resignation of Thomas G. Burch, and at the same time was elected to the Eightieth Congress; reelected to the three succeeding Congresses, and served from November 5, 1946 until his resignation on February 3, 1953, having entered the campaign for Governor; chairman, Committee on House Administration (Eighty-second Congress); elected Governor of Virginia in 1953, and served from January 20, 1954 to January 11, 1958; trustee of Randolph-Macon College; vice president and director of First National Bank, Bassett, Va.; chairman, Commission on State and Local Revenues and Expenditures (a tax study commission); resumed his business of furniture manufacturing; died in Martinsville, Va., July 10, 1970; interment in Roselawn Burial Park.

**STANLEY, Winifred Claire,** a Representative from New York; born in New York City, August 14, 1909; attended the public schools in New York City and Buffalo, N.Y., and graduated from Lafayette High School, Buffalo; B.A., University of Buffalo, 1930; LL.B., J.D., University of Buffalo School of Law, 1933; was admitted to the bar in 1934 and commenced practice in the law office of Elmer E. Finck, Buffalo, N.Y.; appointed an assistant district attorney of Erie County, N.Y., and served from 1938 until 1942; elected as a Republican to the Seventy-eighth Congress (January 3, 1943-January 3, 1945); was not a candidate for renomination in 1944 to the Seventy-ninth Congress; appointed counsel to the New York State Employees' Retirement System on January 1, 1945 and served until April 1, 1955; assistant attorney general, Appeals and Opinions Bureau, New York State Law Department, Albany, N.Y., 1955-1979; engaged in the practice of law in Albany, N.Y., 1980-1981, and in Kenmore, N.Y., 1981-1986; was a resident of Kenmore, N.Y., until her death on February 29, 1996; interment in Mount Olivet Cemetery, Tonawanda, N.Y.

**STANLY, Edward** (son of John Stanly), a Representative from North Carolina; born in New Bern, N.C., January 10, 1810; attended New Bern Academy and was graduated from the American Literary, Scientific, and Military Academy, Norwich University, in 1829; studied law; was admitted to the bar in 1832 and commenced practice in Washington, Beaufort County, N.C.; elected as a Whig to the Twenty-fifth and to the two succeeding Congresses (March 4, 1837-March 3, 1843); chairman, Committee on Expenditures on Public Buildings (Twenty-sixth Congress), Committee on Military Affairs (Twenty-seventh Congress); unsuccessful candidate for

reelection in 1842 to the Twenty-eighth Congress; member of the North Carolina State house of representatives, 1844-1846, 1848, and 1849, serving as speaker in 1844-1846; attorney general of North Carolina in 1847; elected to the Thirty-first and Thirty-second Congresses (March 4, 1849-March 3, 1853); unsuccessful candidate for reelection in 1852 to the Thirty-third Congress; moved to California in 1853 and practiced law in San Francisco; unsuccessful Republican candidate for Governor of California in 1857; during the Civil War was appointed Military Governor of eastern North Carolina on May 26, 1862, with rank of brigadier general, and served until March 2, 1863, when he resigned; returned to California and resumed the practice of law; died in San Francisco, Calif., July 12, 1872; interment in Mountain View Cemetery, Oakland, Calif.

**Bibliography:** *DAB*; Brown, Norman D. *Edward Stanly: Whiggery's Tarheel "Conqueror."* University, Ala.: University of Alabama Press, 1974.

**STANLY, John** (father of Edward Stanly), a Representative from North Carolina; born in New Bern, N.C., April 9, 1774; received his early education from private tutors; attended Princeton University; studied law; was admitted to the bar in 1799 and practiced; clerk and master in equity; member of the State house of commons in 1798 and 1799; elected as a Federalist to the Seventh Congress (March 4, 1801-March 3, 1803); elected to the Eleventh Congress (March 4, 1809-March 3, 1811); resumed the practice of his profession; again a member of the State house of commons 1812-1815, 1818, 1819, 1823-1825, and 1826; died in New Bern, N.C., August 2, 1834; interment in Episcopal Cemetery.

**STANTON, Benjamin,** a Representative from Ohio; born in Mount Pleasant, Jefferson County, Ohio, June 4, 1809; pursued academic studies; learned the tailor's trade; studied law; was admitted to the bar in 1834 and commenced practice in Bellefontaine, Ohio; member of the State senate in 1841 and 1843; delegate to the State constitutional convention in 1850; elected as a Whig to the Thirty-second Congress (March 4, 1851-March 3, 1853); elected as a Republican to the Thirty-fourth, Thirty-fifth, and Thirty-sixth Congresses (March 4, 1855-March 3, 1861); chairman, Committee on Military Affairs (Thirty-sixth Congress); Lieutenant Governor of Ohio in 1862; moved to Martinsburg, W.Va., in 1865, and practiced law; moved to Wheeling, W.Va., in 1867 and continued the practice of law; died in Wheeling, W.Va., June 2, 1872; interment in Greenwood Cemetery.

**STANTON, Frederick Perry,** a Representative from Tennessee; born in Alexandria, Va., December 22, 1814; pursued classical studies, and was graduated from Columbian College (now George Washington University), Washington, D.C., in 1833; taught school; studied law; was admitted to the bar and commenced practice in Memphis, Tenn.; elected as a Democrat to the Twenty-ninth and to the four succeeding Congresses (March 4, 1845-March 3, 1855); chairman, Committee on Naval Affairs (Thirty-first and Thirty-second Congresses), Committee on the Judiciary (Thirty-third Congress); Acting Governor of Kansas Territory from November 1857 until December 19, 1857, when he was removed from office by order of President James Buchanan; moved to Virginia and subsequently settled in Florida; died in Stanton, Fla., June 4, 1894; interment in South Lake Weir Cemetery, South Lake Weir, Fla.

**Bibliography:** *DAB*.

**STANTON, James Vincent,** a Representative from Ohio; born in Cleveland, Cuyahoga County, Ohio, February 27, 1932; attended Ohio parochial schools; served in the United States Air Force, 1950-1954; A.B., University of Dayton (Ohio), 1958; J.D., Cleveland-Marshall College of Law, 1961; admitted to the Ohio bar in 1961 and commenced practice in Cleveland; member, Cleveland City Council, 1959-1970, serving as president from 1964 to 1970; elected as a

Democrat to the Ninety-second and to the two succeeding Congresses (January 3, 1971-January 3, 1977); was not a candidate in 1976 for reelection to the House of Representatives, but was an unsuccessful candidate for nomination to the United States Senate; resumed the practice of law in Washington, D.C., 1977-1981; executive vice president of Delaware North Companies in Buffalo, N.Y., 1981-1988; resumed the practice of law in Washington, D.C., in 1988; is a resident of Potomac, Md.

STANTON, John William, a Representative from Ohio; born in Painesville, Lake County, Ohio, February 20, 1924; attended St. Mary's grade school; graduated from Culver (Ind.) Military Academy in 1942; entered the School of Foreign Service at Georgetown University, Washington, D.C., in July 1942; left his studies and entered the United States Army in December 1942; served in the Pacific Theater; discharged January 1, 1946, with the rank of captain; B.S., Georgetown University, 1949; engaged in the retail automobile business; president, J.W. Stanton, Inc., 1949-1963; Lake County Commissioner, 1956-1964; elected as a Republican to the Eighty-ninth and to the eight succeeding Congresses (January 3, 1965-January 3, 1983); was not a candidate for reelection in 1982 to the Ninety-eighth Congress; counselor to the president of the International Bank for Reconstruction and Development (World Bank); is a resident of Washington, D.C.

STANTON, Joseph, Jr., a Senator and a Representative from Rhode Island; born in Charlestown, R.I., July 19, 1739; served in the expedition against Canada in 1759; member, State house of representatives 1768-1774; served as colonel in the Revolutionary Army; delegate to the State constitutional convention in 1790; elected to the United States Senate and served from June 7, 1790, to March 3, 1793; member, State house of representatives 1794-1800; elected as a Republican to the Seventh, Eighth, and Ninth Congresses (March 4, 1801-March 3, 1807); died in Charlestown, R.I., in 1807; interment in the family cemetery.

STANTON, Richard Henry, a Representative from Kentucky; born in Alexandria, Va., September 9, 1812; completed preparatory studies; attended Alexandria Academy; studied law; was admitted to the bar and began practice in Maysville, Ky., in 1835; editor of the Maysville Monitor 1835-1842; postmaster of Maysville; elected as a Democrat to the Thirty-first, Thirty-second, and Thirty-third Congresses (March 4, 1849-March 3, 1855); chairman, Committee on Public Buildings and Grounds (Thirty-first and Thirty-second Congresses), Committee on Elections (Thirty-third Congress); unsuccessful candidate for reelection in 1854 to the Thirty-fourth Congress; State's attorney 1858-1861; delegate to the Democratic National Convention in 1868; district judge 1868-1874; resumed the practice of law until his retirement in 1885; died in Maysville, Ky., March 20, 1891; interment in Maysville Cemetery.

**Bibliography:** *DAB*.

STANTON, William Henry, a Representative from Pennsylvania; born in New York City July 28, 1843; moved with his parents to Carbondale, Pa., and subsequently to Archbald, Pa.; attended the public schools in Archbald and St. John's College, near Montrose, Pa.; studied law; admitted to the bar in Scranton, Pa., in 1868 and commenced practice in that city; prosecuting attorney of the mayor's court of Scranton 1872-1874; served in the Pennsylvania senate in 1875 and 1876; elected as a Democrat to the Forty-fourth Congress to fill the vacancy caused by the resignation of Winthrop W. Ketchum and served from November 7, 1876, to March 3, 1877; was not a candidate for election to the Forty-fifth Congress; elected judge of the Luzerne County Court of Common Pleas in 1877; served with Judges Harding and Handley at the organization of the courts of the newly created county of Lackawanna October 24, 1878; resigned in 1879; resumed the practice of law in Scranton, Pa., and died there March 28, 1900; interment in West Side Catholic Cemetery.

STARIN, John Henry (grandson of Thomas Sammons), a Representative from New York; born in Sammonsville, Fulton County (then a part of Montgomery County), N.Y., August 27, 1825; pursued an academic course in Esperance, N.Y.; began the study of medicine in 1842; established and conducted a drug and medicine business in Fultonville 1845-1858; postmaster of Fultonville, N.Y., 1848-1852; founder and president of the Starin City River & Harbor Transportation Co.; director of the North River Bank, New York City, and the Mohawk River National Bank; also interested in agriculture and stock raising; elected as a Republican to the Forty-fifth and Forty-sixth Congresses (March 4, 1877-March 3, 1881); president of Fultonville National Bank 1883-1909; engaged in railroading; member of the New York City Rapid Transit Commission; died in New York City March 21, 1909; interment in Starin mausoleum, Fultonville Cemetery, Fultonville, N.Y.

**Bibliography:** *DAB*.

STARK, Benjamin, a Senator from Oregon; born in New Orleans, La., June 26, 1820; pursued classical studies and graduated from Union School, New London, Conn., and Hebron Academy; engaged in mercantile pursuits in New York City 1835-1848, and also studied law; moved to San Francisco, Calif., and engaged in mercantile pursuits in 1849 and 1850, moving to Portland, Oreg., the latter year; was admitted to the bar in 1850 and commenced practice in Portland, Oreg.; member, Territorial house of representatives 1852; served in the Oregon Indian hostilities in 1853 with the rank of colonel; member, State house of representatives 1860; appointed as a Democrat to the United States Senate to fill the vacancy caused by the death of Edward D. Baker and served from October 29, 1861, to September 12, 1862, when a successor was elected; was not a candidate for election; resumed the practice of law; moved to New London, Conn.; member of the board of aldermen of New London, Conn., 1873-1874; member, State house of representatives 1874; member of the Connecticut State Prison Commission; died in New London, Conn., October 10, 1898; interment in Cedar Grove Cemetery.

STARK, Fortney Hillman, Jr. (Pete), a Representative from California; born in Milwaukee, Wis., November 11, 1931; attended the public schools of Wisconsin and graduated from Wauwatosa (Wis.) High School in 1949; B.S., Massachusetts Institute of Technology, Cambridge, 1953; M.B.A., University of California, Berkeley, 1960; served in the United States Air Force, 1955-1957, with the rank of captain; banker; founder, Beacon Savings and Loan Association, Antioch, Calif., 1961; founder and president, Security National Bank, Walnut Creek, Calif., 1963-1972; chairman of the board, Security Capital Corp., 1963-1972; delegate, California State Democratic convention, 1972; alternate delegate to the Democratic National Convention of 1972; elected as a Democrat to the Ninety-third and to the eleven succeeding Congresses (January 3, 1973-January 3, 1997); chairman, Committee on the District of Columbia (One Hundred Third Congress); is a resident of Hayward, Calif.

STARK, William Ledyard, a Representative from Nebraska; born in Mystic, New London County, Conn., July 29, 1853; was graduated from Mystic Valley Institute, Mystic, Conn., in 1872; moved to Wyoming, Stark County, Ill.; taught school and clerked in a store; attended the Union College of Law, Chicago, Ill.; was admitted to the bar by the supreme court of Illinois in January 1878; moved to Aurora, Nebr., in February 1878; served as superintendent of city schools; deputy district attorney; judge of the Hamilton County Court; served as a major and judge advocate general of the Nebraska National Guard; unsuccessful Populist candidate for election in 1895 to the Fifty-fourth Congress; elected as a Populist to the Fifty-fifth, Fifty-sixth, and Fifty-seventh Congresses (March 4, 1897-March 3, 1903); unsuccessful Fusionist candidate for reelection in 1902 to the Fifty-eighth Congress; retired and resided in Aurora,

Nebr.; died at Tarpon Springs, Fla., November 11, 1922; interment in the City Cemetery, Aurora, Nebr.

**STARKEY, Frank Thomas,** a Representative from Minnesota; born in St. Paul, Ramsey County, Minn., February 18, 1892; attended the public schools; business representative of the Milk Drivers Union 1917-1933 and 1942-1944; member of the State house of representatives 1923-1933, serving as chief clerk in 1933; member of the State Industrial Commission 1933-1939; vice president of the Minnesota State Federation of Labor for twelve years, serving as director of its research division 1939-1942; member of the Ramsey County Civil Service Commission 1942-1944; elected as a Democrat to the Seventy-ninth Congress (January 3, 1945-January 3, 1947); unsuccessful for reelection in 1946 to the Eightieth Congress; writer for trade magazines; commissioner, Department of Employment Security, St. Paul, Minn., 1955-1965; died in St. Paul, Minn., May 14, 1968; cremated; ashes interred in Calvary Cemetery.

**STARKWEATHER, David Austin,** a Representative from Ohio; born in Preston, Conn., January 21, 1802; received an academic education; studied law; was admitted to the bar in 1825 and commenced practice in Mansfield, Ohio; moved to Canton, Ohio, in 1827 and continued the practice of law; judge of one of the higher courts in Stark County, Ohio; member of the Ohio State house of representatives, 1833-1835; served in the State senate, 1836-1838; elected as a Democrat to the Twenty-sixth Congress (March 4, 1839-March 3, 1841); resumed the practice of law in Cleveland, Ohio; elected to the Twenty-ninth Congress (March 4, 1845-March 3, 1847); unsuccessful candidate for reelection in 1846 to the Thirtieth Congress; chairman of the Democratic National Convention of 1852; appointed Minister to Chile on June 29, 1854 and served until August 1857; lived in retirement until his death in Cleveland, Ohio, on July 12, 1876; interment in Lake View Cemetery.

**STARKWEATHER, George Anson,** a Representative from New York; born in Preston, Conn., May 19, 1794; attended the common schools and was graduated from Union College, Schenectady, N.Y., in 1819; studied law; was admitted to the bar and practiced in Cooperstown, N.Y.; elected as a Democrat to the Thirtieth Congress (March 4, 1847-March 3, 1849); again resumed the practice of his profession in Milwaukee, Wis., 1853-1868; died in Cooperstown, N.Y., October 15, 1879; interment in Lakewood Cemetery.

**STARKWEATHER, Henry Howard,** a Representative from Connecticut; born in Preston, Conn., April 29, 1826; attended the common schools; studied law; was admitted to the bar and commenced practice in Norwich, Conn.; member of the State house of representatives in 1856; delegate to the Republican National Conventions in 1860 and 1868; postmaster of Norwich, Conn., 1861-1865; elected as a Republican to the Fortieth and to the four succeeding Congresses and served from March 4, 1867, until his death in Washington, D.C., on January 28, 1876; chairman, Committee on District of Columbia (Forty-second Congress); interment in Yantic Cemetery, Norwich, Conn.

**STARNES, Joe,** a Representative from Alabama; born in Guntersville, Marshall County, Ala., March 31, 1895; attended the public schools; taught school in Marshall County, Ala., 1912-1917; during the First World War served overseas as a second lieutenant in the Fifty-third Infantry, Sixth Division, in 1918 and 1919; was graduated from the law department of the University of Alabama at Tuscaloosa in 1921; was admitted to the bar the same year and commenced practice at Guntersville, Ala.; member of the One Hundred and Sixty-Seventh Infantry, Alabama National Guard, beginning in 1923, advancing through the ranks to colonel; member of the Alabama State board of education, 1933-1949, and became vice chairman in January 1948; elected as a Democrat to the Seventy-fourth and to the four succeeding Congresses (January 3,

1935-January 3, 1945); unsuccessful candidate for renomination in 1944 to the Seventy-ninth Congress; served as a colonel of Infantry in the European Theater of Operations, and in the Army of Occupation from January 4, 1945, until discharged on February 22, 1946; resumed the practice of law in Guntersville, Ala.; died in Washington, D.C., January 9, 1962; interment in City Cemetery, Guntersville, Ala.

**STARR, John Farson,** a Representative from New Jersey; born in Philadelphia, Pa., March 25, 1818; completed preparatory studies; moved to Camden, N.J., in 1844; one of the founders of the Camden Iron Works; engaged in mercantile pursuits; president of the First National Bank of Camden for over thirty years, up to the time of his death; elected as a Republican to the Thirty-eighth and Thirty-ninth Congresses (March 4, 1863-March 3, 1867); was not a candidate for renomination in 1866; died in Atlantic City, N.J., August 9, 1904; interment in Harleigh Cemetery, Camden, N.J.

**STATON, David Michael (Mick),** a Representative from West Virginia; born in Parkersburg, Wood County, W.Va., February 11, 1940; attended the public schools; graduated from Parkersburg High School, 1958; attended Concord College, Athens, W.Va., 1961-1963; served in the United States Army National Guard, 1957-1965; data processing manager; vice president, Kanawha Valley Bank, Charleston, W.Va., 1972-1980; delegate, West Virginia State Republican conventions, 1976-1980; delegate to the Republican National Convention of 1980; unsuccessful candidate for election in 1978 to the Ninety-sixth Congress; elected as a Republican to the Ninety-seventh Congress (January 3, 1981-January 3, 1983); unsuccessful candidate for reelection in 1982 to the Ninety-eighth Congress; president, Mick Staton Associates, Washington, D.C., 1982-1984; chief political adviser, United States Chamber of Commerce, 1984-1990; executive vice president, Delchamps Associates, Washington, D.C., 1990-1992; president, Capitol Link, Reston, Va., 1992 to present; is a resident of Inwood, W.Va.

**STAUFFER, Simon Walter,** a Representative from Pennsylvania; born in Walkersville, Frederick County, Md., August 13, 1888; attended the public schools; attended Conway Hall, Carlisle, Pa., in 1906 and 1907; graduated from Dickinson College, Carlisle, Pa., in 1912; moved to York, Pa., in 1915; engaged in the manufacture of lime, crushed stone, and refractory dolomite 1916-1936; trustee of Dickinson College from 1930 until his death; president of National Lime Association, Washington, D.C., 1936-1946; chairman of York City Housing Authority 1949-1952; vice president and chairman of executive committee, York County Gas Co., 1950-1960; owner of a large tract of woodland and engaged in timbering operations 1947-1960; elected as a Republican to the Eighty-third Congress (January 3, 1953-January 3, 1955); was an unsuccessful candidate for reelection in 1954 to the Eighty-fourth Congress; elected to the Eighty-fifth Congress (January 3, 1957-January 3, 1959); unsuccessful candidate for reelection in 1958 to the Eighty-sixth Congress; resided in York, Pa., where he died September 26, 1975; interment in Prospect Hill Cemetery.

**STEAGALL, Henry Bascom,** a Representative from Alabama; born in Clopton, Dale County, Ala., May 19, 1873; attended the common schools and the Southeast Alabama Agricultural School at Abbeville; was graduated from the law department of the University of Alabama at Tuscaloosa in 1893; was admitted to the bar the same year and commenced practice in Ozark, Ala.; county solicitor of Dale County, 1902-1908; member of the Alabama State house of representatives in 1906 and 1907; member of the State Democratic executive committee, 1906-1910; prosecuting attorney of the third judicial circuit, 1907-1914; delegate to the Democratic National Convention of 1912; elected as a Democrat to the Sixty-fourth and to the fourteen succeeding Congresses, and served from March 4, 1915 until his death in Washington, D.C., November 22, 1943; chairman, Committee on Banking and Currency (Seventy-second through

Seventy-eighth Congresses); co-sponsor of the Glass-Steagall Act of 1933, which established the Federal Deposit Insurance Corporation to safeguard deposits and revive public confidence in the banking system; interment in the City Cemetery, Ozark, Ala.

Bibliography: *DAB*; Key, Jack Brien. "Henry B. Steagall: The Conservative as a Reformer." *Alabama Review* 17 (July 1964): 198-209.

STEARNS, Asahel, a Representative from Massachusetts; born in Lunenburg, Mass., June 17, 1774; was graduated from Harvard University in 1797; studied law; was admitted to the bar and commenced the practice of law in Chelmsford, Mass.; member of the Massachusetts senate in 1813; moved to Charlestown, Mass., in 1815; elected as a Federalist to the Fourteenth Congress (March 4, 1815-March 3, 1817); served in the Massachusetts house of representatives in 1817; professor of law at Harvard University from 1817 to 1829; again served as a member of the Massachusetts senate in 1830 and 1831; died in Cambridge, Mass., February 5, 1839; interment in Mount Auburn Cemetery.

Bibliography: *DAB*.

STEARNS, Clifford Bundy, a Representative from Florida; born in Washington, D.C., April 16, 1941; graduated, Woodrow Wilson High School, Washington, D.C., 1959; B.S., George Washington University, 1963; University of California at Los Angeles, graduate work, 1965; entered active duty, United States Air Force in 1963; released as captain in 1967; motel company executive; elected as a Republican to the One Hundred First and to the three succeeding Congresses (January 3, 1989-January 3, 1997); is a resident of Ocala, Fla.

STEARNS, Foster Waterman, a Representative from New Hampshire; born in Hull, Plymouth County, Mass., July 29, 1881; attended the public schools; was graduated from Amherst (Mass.) College in 1903, Harvard University in 1906, and Boston College in 1915; librarian of the Museum of Fine Arts, Boston, Mass., 1913-1917; State librarian of Massachusetts in 1917; during the First World War served as a first lieutenant with the Sixteenth Infantry, First Division, and at the General Headquarters of the American Expeditionary Forces in France from November 27, 1917, until discharged August 5, 1919; assistant military attaché to Belgium in 1919; served in the Department of State, Washington, D.C., 1920-1921; third secretary of the American Embassy, attached to the United States High Commission in Constantinople (now Istanbul), 1921-1923; second secretary of the United States Embassy at Paris, 1923-1924; librarian of Holy Cross College, Worcester, Mass., 1925-1930; moved to Hancock, N.H., in 1927; member, New Hampshire State house of representatives, 1937-1938; delegate to the Republican National Conventions of 1940 and 1948; Regent of the Smithsonian Institution, 1941-1945; elected as a Republican to the Seventy-sixth and to the two succeeding Congresses (January 3, 1939-January 3, 1945); was not a candidate in 1944 for renomination to the House of Representatives, but was an unsuccessful candidate for nomination to the United States Senate; engaged in foreign educational work; in 1942 became a director of the Rumford Printing Co. of Concord, N.H.; moved to Exeter, N.H., in 1948, where he died on June 4, 1956; interment in Exeter Cemetery.

STEARNS, Ozora Pierson, a Senator from Minnesota; born in De Kalb, St. Lawrence County, N.Y., January 15, 1831; moved to Ohio in 1833 with his parents, who settled in Lake County; attended Oberlin (Ohio) College, and graduated from the University of Michigan in 1858 and from the law department of that university in 1860; was admitted to the bar in 1860 and commenced practice in Rochester, Minn.; elected prosecuting attorney of Olmstead County in 1861; mayor of Rochester, 1866-1868; served in the Union Army during the Civil War as a lieutenant, and then colonel; elected as a

Republican to the United States Senate on January 18, 1871, to fill the vacancy caused by the death of Daniel S. Norton, and served from January 23 to March 3, 1871; was not a candidate for reelection; moved to Duluth, Minn., in 1872 and practiced law; judge of the eleventh judicial district of Minnesota, 1874-1895; regent of the University of Minnesota at Minneapolis, 1890-1895; died in Pacific Beach, Calif., June 2, 1896; remains were cremated in Los Angeles and the ashes interred in Forest Hill Cemetery, Duluth, St. Louis County, Minn.

STEBBINS, Henry George, a Representative from New York; born in Ridgefield, Conn., September 15, 1811; attended private schools; moved to New York; engaged in banking; colonel of the Twelfth Regiment; president of the Dramatic Fund Association; president of the Academy of Music; elected as a Democrat to the Thirty-eighth Congress and served from March 4, 1863, until his resignation on October 24, 1864; engaged as a stock broker; president of the New York Stock Exchange; appointed president of the Central Park Commission; died in New York City December 9, 1881; interment in Greenwood Cemetery, Brooklyn, N.Y.

STECK, Daniel Frederic, a Senator from Iowa; born in Ottumwa, Wapello County, Iowa, December 16, 1881; attended the common schools; graduated from the law department of the University of Iowa at Iowa City in 1906; was admitted to the bar the same year and commenced practice in Ottumwa; during the First World War, served in France as a captain; resumed the practice of law in Ottumwa; successfully contested as a Democrat the election of Smith W. Brookhart to the United States Senate and served from April 12, 1926, to March 3, 1931; was an unsuccessful candidate for reelection in 1930; resumed the practice of his profession; special assistant to the United States Attorney General 1933-1947; retired; died in Ottumwa, Iowa, December 31, 1950; interment in Ottumwa Cemetery.

STEDMAN, Charles Manly, a Representative from North Carolina; born in Pittsboro, Chatham County, N.C., January 29, 1841; moved with his parents to Fayetteville, N.C., in 1853; attended Pittsboro Academy and Donaldson Academy at Fayetteville; was graduated from the University of North Carolina at Chapel Hill in 1861; during the Civil War served as a private in the Fayetteville Independent Light Infantry Company, First North Carolina Regiment, and later as major in the Forty-fourth North Carolina Regiment; returned to Chatham County and taught school at Pittsboro one year; studied law; was admitted to the bar in 1865 and commenced practice in Wilmington, N.C., in 1867; delegate to the Democratic National Convention in 1880; Lieutenant Governor of North Carolina 1884-1888; unsuccessful candidate for nomination as Governor in 1888 and again in 1903; moved to Asheville, N.C., in 1891, to Greensboro, N.C., in 1898, and continued the practice of law; president of the North Carolina Bar Association in 1900 and 1901; director of the North Carolina Railroad in 1909 and 1910, during which time he served as president; trustee of the University of North Carolina 1899-1915; elected as a Democrat to the Sixty-second and to the nine succeeding Congresses and served from March 4, 1911, until his death in Washington, D.C., September 23, 1930; interment in Cross Creek Cemetery, Fayetteville, N.C.

STEDMAN, William, a Representative from Massachusetts; born in Cambridge, Mass., January 21, 1765; graduated from Harvard University in 1784; studied law; admitted to the bar in 1787 and practiced in Lancaster, Charlestown, and Worcester; appointed justice of the peace in 1790; town clerk of Lancaster 1795-1800; member of the Massachusetts house of representatives in 1802; executive chancellor of Lancaster, 1803-1807; elected as a Federalist to the Eighth and to the three succeeding Congresses and served from March 4, 1803, until his resignation July 16, 1810; clerk of Worcester County Courts 1810-1816; late in life moved to

Newburyport, Essex County, Mass., where he died August 31, 1831; interment in Old Hill Burying Ground.

**STEED, Thomas Jefferson (Tom),** a Representative from Oklahoma; born on a farm near Rising Star, Eastland County, Tex., March 2, 1904; attended the public schools of Konawa, Okla.; connected with Oklahoma daily newspapers for twenty years, including four years as managing editor of Shawnee News and Star; enlisted on October 29, 1942, as a private in Antiaircraft Artillery and released from active duty in May 1944 with rank of second lieutenant; joined Office of War Information July 1, 1944, and served with information division in the India-Burma Theater until December 1945; elected as a Democrat to the Eighty-first and to the fifteen succeeding Congresses (January 3, 1949-January 3, 1981); chairman, Committee on Small Business (Ninety-fourth Congress); was not a candidate for reelection in 1980 to the Ninety-seventh Congress; was a resident of Shawnee, Okla., until his death on June 8, 1983; interment at Resthaven Cemetery, Shawnee, Okla.

**STEELE, George Washington,** a Representative from Indiana; born near Connersville, Fayette County, Ind., December 13, 1839; attended the common schools and Ohio Wesleyan University at Delaware; studied law; was admitted to the bar and commenced practice in Hartford City, Ind.; during the Civil War served with the Twelfth Indiana Regiment and the One Hundred and First Indiana Regiment from May 1861, until the close of the war; commissioned and served in the Fourteenth Regiment, United States Infantry, from February 23, 1866, to February 1, 1876; resigned and engaged in agricultural pursuits and pork packing until 1882; appointed Governor of Oklahoma Territory by President Benjamin Harrison in 1890; resigned on October 3, 1891, but continued to serve until November 8, 1891; elected as a Republican to the Forty-seventh and to the three succeeding Congresses (March 4, 1881-March 3, 1889); member of the Board of Managers of the National Military Home from April 21, 1890, to December 10, 1904; elected to the Fifty-fourth and to the three succeeding Congresses (March 4, 1895-March 3, 1903); chairman, Committee on Manufactures (Fifty-seventh Congress); governor of the National Military Home in Marion, Ind., from December 11, 1904, to May 31, 1915, when he resigned; died in Marion, Grant County, Ind., July 12, 1922; interment in Odd Fellows Cemetery.

**STEELE, Henry Joseph,** a Representative from Pennsylvania; born in Easton, Northampton County, Pa., May 10, 1860; attended the public schools, graduated from Stevens College of Business in 1875; studied law; admitted to the bar on May 16, 1881, and commenced practice in Easton, Pa.; member of the board of education 1889-1893; city solicitor 1889-1895; delegate to the Pennsylvania constitutional convention in 1891; president of the Pennsylvania Bar Association in 1914; elected as a Democrat to the Sixty-fourth, Sixty-fifth, and Sixty-sixth Congresses (March 4, 1915-March 3, 1921); declined to be a candidate for renomination in 1920; resumed the practice of law in Easton, Pa.; served as a director of the Lehigh Valley Transit Co. and of the Pennsylvania Motor Co.; died in Easton, Pa., March 19, 1933; interment in Easton Cemetery.

**STEELE, John,** a Representative from North Carolina; born in Salisbury, N.C., November 16, 1764; attended Clio's Nursery, near Statesville, N.C., and the English School, Salisbury, N.C.; farmer; assessor in 1784; town commissioner in 1787; member of the State house of commons in 1787, 1788, 1794, 1795, 1806, and 1811-1813; delegate to the Hillsborough convention in 1788; special commissioner from North Carolina to treat with the Cherokee and Chickasaw Indians from 1788 to 1790; delegate to ratification convention in Fayetteville, 1789; elected to the First and Second Congresses and served from April 19, 1790, until March 3, 1793; appointed Comptroller of the Treasury July 1, 1796; reappointed by both President John Adams and President Thomas Jefferson and served until December 15, 1802, when he resigned; member of the board of commissioners to determine the boundary line between North Carolina and Georgia 1805-1814; died August 14, 1815, in Salisbury, N.C., having been on the same day again elected to the State house of commons; interment in Chestnut Hill Cemetery.

**Bibliography:** *DAB*; West, William Shepherd. "John Steele: Portrait of a Moderate Southern Federalist." Ph.D. dissertation, University of North Carolina at Chapel Hill, 1972.

**STEELE, John Benedict,** a Representative from New York; born in Delhi, N.Y., March 28, 1814; attended Delaware Academy at Delhi and was graduated in law from Williams College, Williamstown, Mass.; was admitted to the bar of Otsego County in 1839 and commenced practice in Cooperstown, N.Y.; district attorney of Otsego County, 1841-1847; moved to Kingston in 1847; elected special judge of Ulster County in 1850; elected as a Democrat to the Thirty-seventh and Thirty-eighth Congresses (March 4, 1861-March 3, 1865); was an unsuccessful candidate for renomination in 1864 to the Thirty-ninth Congress; was a candidate for nomination in 1866 to the Fortieth Congress, but died on the eve of the primary; was accidentally killed in Rondout, near Kingston, N.Y., September 24, 1866; interment in Wiltwyck Cemetery, Kingston, N.Y.

**STEELE, John Nevett,** a Representative from Maryland; born in Weston, Dorchester County, Md., February 22, 1796; resided on an estate called "Indian Town," near Vienna, Md.; completed preparatory studies; studied law; was admitted to the bar in 1819 and commenced practice in Dorchester County, Md.; member of the State house of delegates 1822-1824, 1829, and 1830; elected as an Anti-Jacksonian to the Twenty-third Congress to fill the vacancy caused by the death of Littleton P. Dennis; reelected to the Twenty-fourth Congress and served from May 29, 1834, to March 3, 1837; unsuccessful Whig candidate for Governor of Maryland in 1838; engaged in agricultural pursuits; died in Cambridge, Md., August 13, 1853; interment in Christ Protestant Episcopal Church Cemetery.

**STEELE, Leslie Jasper,** a Representative from Georgia; born near Decatur, De Kalb County, Ga., November 21, 1868; attended the public and private schools of Decatur and was graduated from Emory College, Oxford, Ga., in 1893; taught school 1893-1898; was graduated from the law department of Georgia University, Athens, Ga., in 1899; was admitted to the bar the same year and commenced practice in Decatur, Ga.; member of the De Kalb County Board of Education 1902-1921; mayor of Decatur 1915-1920; served in the State house of representatives 1915-1919; city and county attorney 1921-1925; elected as a Democrat to the Seventieth and Seventy-first Congresses and served from March 4, 1927, until his death in Washington, D.C., on July 24, 1929; interment in Decatur Cemetery, Decatur, Ga.

**STEELE, Robert Hampton,** a Representative from Connecticut; born in Hartford, Conn., November 3, 1938; attended the Wethersfield, Conn., public schools; B.A., Amherst (Mass.) College, 1960; M.A., Columbia University, 1963; securities analyst, The Travelers Insurance Company, 1968-1970; elected as a Republican to the Ninety-first Congress, November 3, 1970, by special election to fill the vacancy caused by the death of William L. St. Onge, and at the same time elected to the Ninety-second Congress; reelected to the Ninety-third Congress, and served from November 3, 1970 to January 3, 1975; was not a candidate in 1974 for reelection to the Ninety-fourth Congress, but was an unsuccessful candidate for election for Governor of Connecticut; is a resident of Ledyard, Conn.

**STEELE, Thomas Jefferson,** a Representative from Iowa; born near Rushville, Rush County, Ind., March 19, 1853; attended the public schools and Axline Seminary, Fairfax, Iowa; taught school in central and western Iowa; studied law at Sheldon, Iowa; engaged in the hardware business and in banking at Wayne, Nebr.; county clerk of Wayne County, Nebr., 1884-1886; moved to Sioux City, Iowa, in 1897 and became a livestock commission merchant; elected as a Democrat to the Sixty-fourth Congress (March 4, 1915-March 3, 1917); unsuccessfully contested the election of George C. Scott to the Sixty-fifth Congress; resumed business as commission merchant; unsuccessful candidate for election in 1918 to the Sixty-sixth Congress; died in Sioux City, Iowa, March 20, 1920; interment in Graceland Park Cemetery.

**STEELE, Walter Leak,** a Representative from North Carolina; born at Steeles Mills (later Littles Mills), near Rockingham, Richmond County, N.C., April 18, 1823; attended the common schools, Randolph-Macon College, Lynchburg, Va., and Wake Forest (N.C.) College; was graduated from the University of North Carolina at Chapel Hill in 1844; member of the State house of commons in 1846, 1848, 1850, and 1854; trustee of the University of North Carolina from 1852 until his death; served in the State senate in 1852 and 1858; delegate to the Democratic National Conventions at Charleston and Baltimore in 1860; secretary of the State convention in 1861 which passed the ordinance of secession; studied law; was admitted to the bar in 1865 and commenced practice in Rockingham, N.C.; elected as a Democrat to the Forty-fifth and Forty-sixth Congresses (March 4, 1877-March 3, 1881); declined to be a candidate for renomination in 1880 to the Forty-seventh Congress; engaged in cotton manufacturing and banking; died in Baltimore, Md., on October 16, 1891; interment in Leak Cemetery, near Rockingham, Richmond County, N.C.

**STEELE, William Gaston,** a Representative from New Jersey; born in Somerville, Somerset County, N.J., December 17, 1820; attended the public schools and Somerville Academy; engaged in banking; elected as a Democrat to the Thirty-seventh and Thirty-eighth Congresses (March 4, 1861-March 3, 1865); engaged in the brokerage business; died in Somerville, Somerset County, N.J., April 22, 1892; interment in Somerville City Cemetery.

**STEELE, William Randolph,** a Delegate from the Territory of Wyoming; born in New York City, July 24, 1842; received an academic education; studied law; was admitted to the bar and practiced; during the Civil War served in the Second Army Corps from 1861 to 1865; discharged with the rank of captain and brevet lieutenant colonel; moved to the Territory of Wyoming in 1869 and engaged in the practice of law in Cheyenne; elected as a member of the Territorial legislative council in 1871 and served until March 4, 1873, when he resigned, having been elected to Congress; elected as a Democrat to the Forty-third and Forty-fourth Congresses (March 4, 1873-March 3, 1877); unsuccessful candidate for reelection in 1876 to the Forty-fifth Congress; moved to Deadwood, S.Dak., and resumed the practice of law; mayor of Deadwood 1894-1896; died in Deadwood November 30, 1901; interment in Mount Moriah Cemetery.

**STEELMAN, Alan Watson,** a Representative from Texas; born in Little Rock, Pulaski County, Ark., March 15, 1942; attended the public schools of Arkansas; B.A., Baylor University, Waco, Tex., 1964; M.L.A., Southern Methodist University, Dallas, Tex., 1971; Visiting Fellow, John F. Kennedy Institute of Politics, Harvard University, November 1972; group president, Asia-Pacific, Alexander Proudfoot PLC, 1977 to present; executive director, President's Advisory Council on Minority Business Enterprise, 1969-1972; delegate to Texas State Republican conventions, 1968, 1972; elected as a Republican to the Ninety-third and Ninety-fourth Congresses (January 3, 1973-January 3, 1977); was not a candidate in 1976 for reelection to the House of Representatives, but was an unsuccessful candidate for election to the United States Senate; is a resident of Dallas, Tex., and the Republic of Singapore.

**STEENERSON, Halvor,** a Representative from Minnesota; born at Pleasant Springs, near Madison, Dane County, Wis., June 30, 1852; moved with his parents to Sheldon, Houston County, Minn., in 1853; attended the county schools and the high school in Rushford, Minn.; studied law at the Union College of Law in Chicago; was admitted to the bar in 1878 and commenced practice in Lanesboro, Minn.; moved to Crookston, Polk County, Minn., in 1880; prosecuting attorney of Polk County, 1881-1883; city attorney of Crookston; member of the Minnesota State senate, 1883-1887; delegate to the Republican National Conventions of 1884 and 1888; elected as a Republican to the Fifty-eighth and to the nine succeeding Congresses (March 4, 1903-March 3, 1923); chairman, Committee on Militia (Sixtieth and Sixty-first Congresses), Committee on Post Office and Post Roads (Sixty-sixth and Sixty-seventh Congresses); unsuccessful candidate for reelection in 1922 to the Sixty-eighth Congress; vice president of the American group of the Interparliamentary Union; resumed the practice of law in Crookston, Minn., and died there on November 22, 1926; interment in Oakdale Cemetery.

**STEENROD, Lewis,** a Representative from Virginia; born near Wheeling, Ohio County, Va. (now West Virginia), May 27, 1810; attended the common schools; studied law; admitted to the bar in 1835 and commenced practice in Wheeling; elected as a Democrat to the Twenty-sixth, Twenty-seventh, and Twenty-eighth Congresses (March 4, 1839-March 3, 1845); served in the Virginia senate from 1853 to 1856; resumed the practice of his profession; died near Wheeling, Ohio County, Va. (now West Virginia), October 3, 1862; interment in Stone Church Cemetery, Elm Grove, Va.

**STEERS, Newton Ivan, Jr.,** a Representative from Maryland; born in Glen Ridge, Essex County, N.J., January 13, 1917; attended the public schools of White Plains, N.Y.; graduated from the Hotchkiss School, Lakeville, Conn., 1935; B.A., Yale University, 1939; Certificate of Advanced Meteorology, Massachusetts Institute of Technology, 1943; J.D., Yale University School of Law, 1948; admitted to the New York bar in 1958 and the District of Columbia bar in 1967; served in United States Army Air Corps, 1941-1946; employed by E.I. du Pont, 1939-1941, GAF Corp., 1948-1951, and the United States Atomic Energy Commission, 1951-1953; president of several investment companies in New York, 1953-1965; Maryland State insurance commissioner, 1967-1970; in 1970, became Maryland Assistant Secretary, Licensing and Regulation; member, Maryland State senate, 1971-1977; delegate to the Republican National Conventions of 1964 and 1984; elected as a Republican to the Ninety-fifth Congress (January 3, 1977-January 3, 1979); unsuccessful candidate for reelection in 1978 to the Ninety-sixth Congress; was a resident of Bethesda, Md.; died February 11, 1993.

**STEFAN, Karl,** a Representative from Nebraska; born on a farm near Zebrakov, Bohemia, March 1, 1884; immigrated to the United States in 1885 with his parents, who settled in Omaha, Douglas County, Nebr.; attended the public schools in Omaha, Nebr., and later the Y.M.C.A. night school; private in the Illinois National Guard; lieutenant in the Nebraska National Guard; served as inspector of telegraph in Philippine Constabulary 1904-1906; moved to Norfolk, Nebr., in 1909; served as telegrapher and later as city editor of the Norfolk Daily News until 1924; radio commentator and contributor to newspapers and magazines until 1934; president of the Stefan Co., publishers' agent for magazines and newspapers; member of congressional committee aiding inauguration of Philippine Commonwealth Government, Manila, P. I., 1935; delegate to the Interparliamentary Union, Oslo, Norway, in 1939; official adviser, United Nations Conference, San Francisco, Calif., in 1945; elected as a Republican to the Seventy-fourth and to the eight succeeding Congresses and served from January 3, 1935, until his death in Washington, D.C., October 2, 1951; interment in Prospect Hill Cemetery, Norfolk, Nebr.

**STEIGER, Sam,** a Representative from Arizona; born in New York City, March 10, 1929; attended grade and high schools in New York City; attended Cornell University, Ithaca, N.Y., 1946-1948; B.S., Colorado A.&M., Fort Collins, 1950; was a commissioned officer in the United States Army serving as a tank platoon leader in Korea; was awarded the Silver Star and the Purple Heart; engaged in ranching and horse breeding in Prescott, Ariz.; Arizona State senator, 1960-1964; was Vietnam war correspondent for two local newspapers in 1965; elected as a Republican to the Ninetieth and to the four succeeding Congresses (January 3, 1967-January 3, 1977); was not a candidate in 1976 for reelection to the House of Representatives, but was an unsuccessful candidate for election to the United States Senate; special assistant to Governor Evan Mecham, 1987-1988; is a resident of Prescott, Ariz.

**STEIGER, William Albert,** a Representative from Wisconsin; born in Oshkosh, Winnebago County, Wis., May 15, 1938; attended Rose C. Swart Campus School and Oshkosh High School; B.S., University of Wisconsin, 1960; chairman College Service Committee, Young Republican National Federation, 1959-1961; member of the Wisconsin State assembly from the first district of Winnebago County, 1960-1966; president, Steiger-Rathke Development Co.; member, board of directors, Oshkosh Motor Lodge, Inc.; assistant chief page at the Republican National Convention of 1960; delegate to the Republican National Convention of 1968; elected as a Republican to the Ninetieth and to the six succeeding Congresses, and served from January 3, 1967 until his death in Washington, D.C., on December 4, 1978; interment in Lake View Memorial Park, Oshkosh, Wis.

**STEIWER, Frederick,** a Senator from Oregon; born on a farm near Jefferson, Marion County, Oreg., October 13, 1883; attended the public schools; graduated from Oregon State Agricultural College at Corvallis in 1902 and from the University of Oregon at Eugene in 1906; studied law; was admitted to the bar in 1908 and commenced practice in Pendleton, Umatilla County, in 1909; also interested in agricultural pursuits; deputy district attorney, 1909-1910, district attorney, 1912-1916; member, Oregon State senate, 1916-1917; enlisted in the United States Army during the First World War and served from 1917 to 1919 in the Sixty-fifth Field Artillery, with rank of first lieutenant; elected as a Republican to the United States Senate in 1926; reelected in 1932, and served from March 4, 1927 until January 31, 1938, when he resigned; chairman, Committee on Expenditures in Executive Departments (Seventy-second Congress); continued the practice of law in Washington, D.C., until his death there on February 3, 1939; interment in Arlington National Cemetery, Va.

**STENGER, William Shearer,** a Representative from Pennsylvania; born in Fort London, Franklin County, Pa., February 13, 1840; attended the public schools; was graduated from Franklin and Marshall College, Lancaster, Pa., in 1858; studied law; was admitted to the bar in 1860 and commenced practice in Chambersburg, Pa.; executive director of the Philadelphia Record; district attorney of Franklin County 1862-1871; elected as a Democrat to the Forty-fourth and Forty-fifth Congresses (March 4, 1875-March 3, 1879); unsuccessful candidate for reelection in 1878 to the Forty-sixth Congress; resumed the practice of his profession; secretary of the Commonwealth of Pennsylvania 1883-1887; died in Philadelphia, Pa., March 29, 1918; interment in Falling Spring Presbyterian Church Cemetery.

**STENGLE, Charles Irwin,** a Representative from New York; born in Savageville, Accomack County, Va., December 5, 1869; attended the public schools; graduated from Goldey College, Wilmington, Del., in 1890; chaplain of the Delaware house of representatives in 1898; engaged in newspaper work in Norfolk and Fredericksburg, Va., and in New York City 1910-1917; secretary of the municipal civil service commission of New York City from

January 1, 1918, to January 1, 1923, when he resigned; elected as a Democrat to the Sixty-eighth Congress (March 4, 1923-March 3, 1925); was not a candidate for renomination in 1924 to the Sixty-ninth Congress; appointed by President Calvin Coolidge in 1925 as a lieutenant colonel, Specialist Reserves, attached to The Adjutant General's Office; editor of the National Farm News; legislative representative of the American Federation of Government Employees from 1934 until his retirement in August 1953; died at Shaftos Corner, New Shrewsbury, N.J., November 23, 1953; interment in Monmouth Memorial Park.

**STENHOLM, Charles Walter,** a Representative from Texas; born in Stamford, Jones County, Tex., October 26, 1938; attended the public schools of Stamford and graduated from Stamford High School in 1957; A.S., Tarleton State Junior College, Stephenville, 1959; B.S., Texas Tech University, Lubbock, 1961, M.S., 1962; farmer; teacher, vocational agriculture, Avoca, Tex., 1962-1965; executive vice president of an agriculture commodity promotion group, 1966-1968; general manager of a rural electric cooperative, 1968-1977; Texas State Democratic executive committeeman, Thirtieth senatorial district, 1974-1977; delegate to the Democratic National Convention of 1972; elected as a Democrat to the Ninety-sixth and to the eight succeeding Congresses (January 3, 1979-January 3, 1997); is a resident of Avoca, Tex.

**STENNIS, John Cornelius,** a Senator from Mississippi; born near De Kalb, Kemper County, Miss., August 3, 1901; attended the county schools; B.S., Mississippi State College, 1923; LL.B., University of Virginia Law School, 1928; admitted to the bar in 1928 and commenced practice in De Kalb, Miss.; member, Mississippi State house of representatives, 1928-1932; prosecuting attorney for the sixteenth judicial district of Mississippi, 1932-1937; circuit judge, 1937-1947; elected as a Democrat to the United States Senate on November 4, 1947, to fill the vacancy caused by the death of Theodore G. Bilbo; reelected in 1952, 1958, 1964, 1970, 1976, and again in 1982, and served from November 5, 1947 to January 3, 1989; declined to be a candidate for reelection in 1988; President pro tempore of the Senate during the One Hundreth Congress; chairman, Select Committee on Standards and Conduct (Eighty-ninth through Ninety-third Congresses), Committee on Armed Services (Ninety-first through Ninety-sixth Congresses), Committee on Appropriations (One Hundredth Congress); executive in residence, Mississippi State University, Starkville; was a resident of Madison, Miss., until his death in Jackson, Miss., on April 23, 1995; interment in De Kalb Cemetery.

**Bibliography:** Dazey, Mary Ann Tharp. "A Stylistic Study of the Public Addresses of Senator John Stennis of Mississippi." Ph.D. dissertation, University of Southern Mississippi, 1981; Downs, Michael Scott. "Advise and Consent: John Stennis and the Vietnam War, 1954-1973." *Journal of Mississippi History* 55 (May 1993): 87-114.

**STEPHENS, Abraham P.,** a Representative from New York; born near New City, Rockland County, N.Y., February 18, 1796; justice of the peace; elected as a Democrat to the Thirty-second Congress (March 4, 1851-March 3, 1853); died in Nyack, Rockland County, N.Y., November 25, 1859; interment in Oak Hill Cemetery.

**STEPHENS, Alexander Hamilton** (great-great-uncle of Robert Grier Stephens, Jr.), a Representative from Georgia; born near Crawfordville, Taliaferro County, Ga., on February 11, 1812; attended private and public schools; was graduated from the University of Georgia at Athens in 1832; taught school eighteen months; studied law; was admitted to the bar in Crawfordville in 1834; member of the Georgia State house of representatives, 1836-1841; served in the State senate in 1842; elected as a Whig to the Twenty-eighth Congress to fill the vacancy caused by the resignation of Mark A. Cooper; reelected as a Whig to the Twenty-ninth through Thirty-first Congresses, as a Unionist to the

Thirty-second Congress, as a Whig to the Thirty-third Congress, and as a Democrat to the Thirty-fourth and Thirty-fifth Congresses, and served from October 2, 1843 to March 3, 1859; chairman, Committee on Territories (Thirty-fifth Congress); was not a candidate for renomination in 1858 to the Thirty-sixth Congress; member of the secession convention of Georgia in 1861, which elected him to the Confederate Congress, and was chosen by that Congress as Vice President of the provisional government; elected Vice President of the Confederacy; one of the commissioners representing the Confederacy at the Hampton Roads conference in February 1865; after the Civil War was imprisoned in Fort Warren, Boston Harbor, for five months, until October 1865; elected to the United States Senate in 1866 by the first legislature convened under the new State constitution, but did not present his credentials, as the State had not been readmitted to representation; elected as a Democrat to the Forty-third Congress to fill the vacancy caused by the death of Ambrose R. Wright; reelected to the Forty-fourth and to the three succeeding Congresses, and served from December 1, 1873 until his resignation on November 4, 1882; chairman, Committee on Coinage, Weights, and Measures (Forty-fourth through Forty-sixth Congresses); elected Governor of Georgia in 1882, and served from November 4, 1882 until his death in Atlanta, Ga., March 4, 1883; interment in a vault in Oakland Cemetery; reinterment on his estate, "Liberty Hall," near Crawfordville, Ga.

Bibliography: *DAB*; Schott, Thomas E. *Alexander H. Stephens of Georgia: A Biography*. Baton Rouge: Louisiana State University Press, 1988; Von Abele, Rudolph R. *Alexander H. Stephens, A Biography*. New York: Knopf, 1946.

**STEPHENS, Ambrose Everett Burnside,** a Representative from Ohio; born in Crosby Township, Hamilton County, Ohio, June 3, 1862; attended the public schools and Chickering's Institute of Cincinnati; studied law; was admitted to the bar in 1902 and commenced practice in Cincinnati; captain in the Ohio National Guard 1901-1903 and colonel in 1910 and 1911; clerk of the Hamilton County Courts 1911-1917; elected as a Republican to the Sixty-sixth and to the three succeeding Congresses and served from March 4, 1919, until his death; had been reelected to the Seventieth Congress; died in North Bend, Ohio, February 12, 1927; interment in Maple Grove Cemetery, Cleves, Hamilton County, Ohio.

**STEPHENS, Dan Voorhees,** a Representative from Nebraska; born in Bloomington, Monroe County, Ind., on November 4, 1868; attended the common schools and Valparaiso College, Indiana; settled in Fremont, Dodge County, Nebr., in 1887; studied law; taught school; county superintendent of schools in Dodge County 1890-1894; author of books on education; engaged in agricultural pursuits, manufacturing, publishing, and banking; delegate to the Democratic National Conventions in 1904, 1908, 1920, 1924, and 1932; elected as a Democrat to the Sixty-second Congress to fill the vacancy caused by the death of James P. Latta; elected to the Sixty-third, Sixty-fourth, and Sixty-fifth Congresses and served from November 7, 1911, to March 3, 1919; unsuccessful candidate for reelection in 1918 to the Sixty-sixth Congress; resumed his former business pursuits; member of the State board of education of Nebraska 1923-1926; died in Fremont, Nebr., January 13, 1939, and the remains were cremated.

**STEPHENS, Hubert Durrett,** a Representative and a Senator from Mississippi; born in New Albany, Union County, Miss., July 2, 1875; attended the public schools and graduated from the law department of the University of Mississippi at Oxford in 1896; was admitted to the bar the same year and commenced practice in New Albany; district attorney for the second district of Mississippi 1907-1910; elected as a Democrat to the Sixty-second and to the four succeeding Congresses (March 4, 1911-March 3, 1921); was not a candidate for reelection in 1920 to the Sixty-seventh Congress;

chairman, Committee on Elections (Sixty-fourth Congress), Committee on Claims (Sixty-fifth Congress); resumed the practice of law in New Albany; elected as a Democrat to the United States Senate in 1922; reelected in 1928 and served from March 4, 1923, to January 3, 1935; unsuccessful candidate for renomination in 1934; chairman, Committee on Commerce (Seventy-third Congress); director of the Reconstruction Finance Corporation 1935-1936; continued the practice of law in Washington, D.C., until 1941, when he retired to his farm in Union County, Miss., and engaged in agricultural pursuits; died March 14, 1946, at his country home near New Albany, Miss.; interment in Pythian Cemetery.

**STEPHENS, John Hall,** a Representative from Texas; was born in Shelby County, Tex., on November 22, 1847; attended the common schools in Mansfield, Tarrant County, Tex.; was graduated from Mansfield College, and from the law department of Cumberland University, Lebanon, Tenn., in 1872; was admitted to the bar in 1873 and practiced in Montague, Montague County, and Vernon, Wilbarger County, Tex.; member of the State senate 1886-1888; resumed the practice of law in Vernon, Tex.; elected as a Democrat to the Fifty-fifth and to the nine succeeding Congresses (March 4, 1897-March 3, 1917); chairman, Committee on Indian Affairs (Sixty-second through Sixty-fourth Congresses); unsuccessful candidate for renomination in 1916; moved to Monrovia, Los Angeles County, Calif., in 1917, and died there November 18, 1924; interment in East View Cemetery, Vernon, Tex.

**STEPHENS, Philander,** a Representative from Pennsylvania; born near Montrose, Susquehanna County, Pa., in 1788; received a limited education; engaged in agricultural and mercantile pursuits; coroner in 1815; county commissioner in 1818; sheriff in 1821; member of the Pennsylvania house of representatives in 1824 and 1825; elected as a Jacksonian to the Twenty-first and Twenty-second Congresses (March 4, 1829-March 3, 1833); chairman, Committee on Expenditures in the Department of the Treasury (Twenty-second Congress); was not a candidate for renomination in 1832; resumed agricultural and mercantile pursuits; died probably in Springville, Susquehanna County, Pa., July 8, 1842; interment in Stephens Burying Ground, Dimock Township, Susquehanna County, Pa.

**STEPHENS, Robert Grier, Jr.** (great-great-nephew of Alexander Hamilton Stephens), a Representative from Georgia; born in Atlanta, Fulton County, Ga., August 14, 1913; attended the public schools; graduated from Boys High School in 1931; A.B., University of Georgia, 1935, and M.A., 1937; LL.B., University of Georgia Law School, 1941; attended the University of Hamburg, Germany, on an exchange student scholarship during 1935-1936; taught history at the University of Georgia, 1936-1940; served in the United States Army, with overseas duty, September 1941 to March 1946; released from active duty with rank of lieutenant colonel, the last assignment being on the legal staff of Justice Robert H. Jackson at the Nuremberg trials of major Nazi war criminals, 1945-1946; resumed teaching career, 1946-1947, at University of Georgia and University of Georgia Law School; engaged in the practice of law in Athens, Ga., 1946-1961; city attorney of Athens, 1947-1950; member of the Georgia State senate, 1951-1953; member of the State house of representatives, 1953-1959; delegate to the Democratic National Convention of 1964; elected as a Democrat to the Eighty-seventh and to the seven succeeding Congresses (January 3, 1961-January 3, 1977); was not a candidate for reelection in 1976 to the Ninety-fifth Congress; is a resident of Athens, Ga.

**STEPHENS, William Dennison,** a Representative from California; born in Eaton, Preble County, Ohio, December 26, 1859; attended the public schools and was graduated from Eaton High School; taught country school; studied law; engaged in the construction and operation of railroads in Ohio, Indiana, Iowa, and Louisiana from 1880 to 1887; moved to Los Angeles, Calif., in 1887; engaged in the wholesale and retail grocery business from 1888 until 1909; was a member of the board of education in 1906; major and commissary of the First Brigade, California National Guard, 1904-1914; president of the Los Angeles Chamber of Commerce in 1907; mayor of Los Angeles in 1909; elected as a Republican to the Sixty-second Congress; reelected to the Sixty-third Congress and reelected as a Progressive to the Sixty-fourth Congress and served from March 4, 1911, to July 22, 1916, when he resigned; appointed Lieutenant Governor of California and served from January 2 to March 15, 1917, when he became Governor upon the resignation of Governor Hiram W. Johnson; elected Governor of California in 1918, and served from March 15, 1917 until January 9, 1923; was admitted to the bar in 1920; resided in Los Angeles, Calif., until his death on April 25, 1944; interment in Rosedale Cemetery.

**STEPHENSON, Benjamin,** a Delegate from Illinois Territory; born in Kentucky; moved to Illinois Territory in 1809 and settled in Randolph County; appointed as the first sheriff of Randolph County by Governor Ninian Edwards on June 28, 1809; moved to Edwardsville, Madison County, and engaged in the general mercantile business; appointed adjutant general of the Territory in 1813; served as a colonel in two campaigns during the War of 1812; elected on September 3, 1814, to Congress for a term of two years (Thirteenth and Fourteenth Congresses); was not a candidate for renomination in 1816 to the Fifteenth Congress; served as receiver of public moneys in the land office at Edwardsville from April 29, 1816, until his death; delegate to the convention at Kaskaskia in 1818 which framed the first State constitution of Illinois; president of the Bank of Edwardsville in 1819; died in Edwardsville, Ill., October 10, 1822.

**STEPHENSON, Isaac** (brother of Samuel Merritt Stephenson), a Representative and a Senator from Wisconsin; born in Yorkton near Fredericton, in York County, New Brunswick, Canada, June 18, 1829; attended the common schools; settled in Marinette, Wis., in 1858 and engaged in the lumber business; held various local offices; member, Wisconsin State assembly 1866, 1868; founder and president of the Stephenson Banking Co. in 1873; elected as a Republican to the Forty-eighth, Forty-ninth, and Fiftieth Congresses (March 4, 1883-March 3, 1889); was not a candidate for renomination in 1888; resumed the lumber business in Marinette, Wis.; elected in 1907 as a Republican to the United States Senate to fill the vacancy caused by the resignation of John C. Spooner; reelected in 1909 and served from May 17, 1907, to March 3, 1915; chairman, Committee on Expenditures in the Department of Agriculture (Sixty-first Congress), Committee on Enrolled Bills (Sixty-second Congress), Committee to Investigate Trespassers Upon Indian Lands (Sixty-third Congress); died in Marinette, Wis., on March 15, 1918; interment in Forest Home Cemetery.

**Bibliography:** *DAB*; Stephenson, Isaac. *Recollections of a Long Life, 1829-1915*. Chicago: Donnelley Company, 1915.

**STEPHENSON, James,** a Representative from Virginia; born in Gettysburg, Pa., March 20, 1764; moved to Martinsburg, Va. (now West Virginia); volunteer rifleman under General Arthur St. Clair in his Indian expedition in 1791; brigade inspector; member of the Virginia house of delegates 1800-1803; elected as a Federalist to the Eighth Congress (March 4, 1803-March 3, 1805); again a member of the Virginia house of delegates in 1806 and 1807; elected to the Eleventh Congress (March 4, 1809-March 3, 1811); elected to the Seventeenth Congress to fill the vacancy caused by the death of Thomas Van Swearingen; reelected to the Eighteenth Congress and served from October 28, 1822, to March 3, 1825; died in Martinsburg, Va. (now West Virginia), August 7, 1833.

**STEPHENSON, Samuel Merritt** (brother of Isaac Stephenson), a Representative from Michigan; born in Hartland, in Carleton County, New Brunswick, Canada, December 23, 1831; moved with his parents to Maine, and in 1846 to Delta County, Mich., and engaged in lumbering; moved to Menominee, Mich., in 1858;

interested in real estate, lumbering, general merchandising, and agricultural pursuits; was chairman of the board of supervisors of Menominee County for several years; member, Michigan State house of representatives, 1877-1878; served in the State senate in 1879, 1880, 1885, and 1886; delegate to the Republican National Conventions of 1884 and 1888; elected as a Republican to the Fifty-first and to the three succeeding Congresses (March 4, 1889-March 3, 1897); resumed the lumber business; died in Menominee, Mich., on July 31, 1907; interment in Riverside Cemetery.

**STERETT, Samuel,** a Representative from Maryland; born in Carlisle, Pa., in 1758; moved with his parents to Baltimore, Md., in 1761; completed preparatory studies; was graduated from the University of Pennsylvania at Philadelphia; held several local offices; member of the independent company (military) of Baltimore merchants in 1777; appointed private secretary to the President of Congress in November 1782; member of the Maryland State senate in 1789; elected to the Second Congress (March 4, 1791-March 3, 1793); secretary of the Maryland Society for Promoting the Abolition of Slavery in 1791; member of the Baltimore committee of safety in 1812; served as captain of an independent company at the Battle of North Point, September 12, 1814; grand marshal at Baltimore at the laying of the foundation stone of the Baltimore & Ohio Railroad, July 4, 1828; died in Baltimore, Md., July 12, 1833; interment in the burying ground of Westminster Church.

**STERIGERE, John Benton,** a Representative from Pennsylvania; born in Upper Dublin Township, near Ambler, Montgomery County, Pa., July 31, 1793; worked on a farm and attended school; taught at Puffs Church School; appointed justice of the peace in 1818; member of the Pennsylvania house of representatives 1821-1824; studied law; was admitted to the bar November 17, 1829, and commenced practice in Norristown, Pa.; elected to the Twentieth Congress and reelected as a Jacksonian to the Twenty-first Congress (March 4, 1827-March 3, 1831); chairman, Committee on Private Land Claims (Twenty-first Congress); delegate to the Pennsylvania convention to revise the constitution in 1838; member of the Pennsylvania senate 1839 and 1843-1846; delegate to the Democratic National Convention in 1852; edited the Register; appointed by the Pennsylvania assembly as chairman of a commission to improve the town of Norristown; died in Norristown, Montgomery County, Pa., October 13, 1852; interment in Upper Dublin Lutheran Church Cemetery, Ambler, Pa.

**STERLING, Ansel** (brother of Micah Sterling), a Representative from Connecticut; born in Lyme, New London County, Conn., February 3, 1782; attended the common schools; studied law; was admitted to the bar in 1805 and commenced practice in Salisbury, Conn.; moved to Sharon, Litchfield County, in 1808 and continued the practice of his profession; member of the State house of representatives in 1815, 1818-1821, 1825, 1826, 1829, and 1835-1837, and served as clerk of the house in the sessions of 1815 and 1818-1820; elected to the Seventeenth and Eighteenth Congresses (March 4, 1821-March 3, 1825); resumed legal practice; chief justice of the court of common pleas of Litchfield County 1838-1840; died in Sharon, Conn., November 6, 1853; interment in Sharon Burying Ground.

**STERLING, Bruce Foster,** a Representative from Pennsylvania; born in Masontown, Fayette County, Pa., September 28, 1870; attended the public schools of Masontown and the California State Normal School, California, Pa.; graduated from the University of West Virginia at Morgantown in 1895; studied law; admitted to the bar in 1896 and commenced practice in Uniontown, Pa.; member of the Pennsylvania house of representatives in 1906; delegate to the Democratic National Conventions in 1912, 1920, and 1924; elected as a Democrat to the Sixty-fifth Congress (March 4, 1917-March 3, 1919); unsuccessful candidate for reelection in 1918 to the

Sixty-sixth Congress; resumed the practice of law; elected register of wills and clerk of the orphans court of Fayette County, Pa., in 1935, 1939, and 1943; died at Uniontown, Pa., on April 26, 1945; interment in Oak Grove Cemetery.

**STERLING, John Allen** (brother of Thomas Sterling), a Representative from Illinois; born near Le Roy, McLean County, Ill., February 1, 1857; attended the public schools, and was graduated from the Illinois Wesleyan University at Bloomington in 1881; superintendent of the public schools of Lexington, Ill., 1881-1883; studied law; was admitted to the bar in December 1884 and commenced practice in Bloomington, Ill.; State's attorney of McLean County 1892-1896; member of the Republican State central committee 1896-1898; elected as a Republican to the Fifty-eighth and to the four succeeding Congresses (March 4, 1903-March 3, 1913); one of the managers appointed by the House of Representatives in 1912 to conduct the impeachment proceedings against Robert W. Archbald, judge of the United States Commerce Court; unsuccessful candidate for reelection to the Sixty-third Congress; elected to the Sixty-fourth and Sixty-fifth Congresses and served from March 4, 1915, until his death near Pontiac, Ill., as the result of an automobile accident, October 17, 1918; interment in Park Hill Cemetery, Bloomington, Ill.

**STERLING, Micah** (brother of Ansel Sterling), a Representative from New York; born in Lyme, Conn., November 5, 1784; was graduated from Yale College in 1804; studied law at the Litchfield (Conn.) Law School; was admitted to the bar in 1809 and commenced the practice of law in Adams, Jefferson County, N.Y.; moved to Watertown, N.Y., in 1809 and continued the practice of his profession; held several local offices; treasurer of the village of Watertown in 1816; served as a director of the Jefferson County Bank; elected to the Seventeenth Congress (March 4, 1821-March 3, 1823); resumed the practice of law; member of the State senate 1836-1839; died in Watertown, N.Y., April 11, 1844; interment in Brookside Cemetery.

**STERLING, Thomas** (brother of John Allen Sterling), a Senator from South Dakota; born near Amanda, Fairfield County, Ohio, February 21, 1851; moved with his parents to McLean County, Ill., in 1854; attended the public schools and graduated from Illinois Wesleyan University at Bloomington in 1875; superintendent of schools of Bement, Ill., 1875-1877; studied law; was admitted to the bar in 1878 and commenced practice in Springfield, Ill.; city prosecuting attorney 1880-1881; moved to the Territory of Dakota and located in Northville, Spink County, in 1882; moved to Redfield in 1886 and continued the practice of law; district attorney of Spink County, Dak., 1886-1888; member of the State constitutional convention in 1889; member, State senate 1890; dean of the college of law of the University of South Dakota at Vermillion 1901-1911; elected in 1913 as a Republican to the United States Senate; reelected in 1918, and served from March 4, 1913, to March 3, 1925; unsuccessful candidate for renomination in 1924; chairman, Committee on Civil Service and Retrenchment (Sixty-sixth Congress), Committee on Civil Service (Sixty-seventh Congress), Committee on Post Office and Post Roads (Sixty-eighth Congress); engaged in the practice of law in Washington, D.C., and also served on the faculty of National University Law School; appointed by President Calvin Coolidge in 1925 as field secretary of the Commission for the Celebration of the Two Hundredth Anniversary of the Birth of George Washington; died in Washington, D.C., August 26, 1930; interment in Cedar Hill Cemetery.

**STETSON, Charles,** a Representative from Maine; born in New Ipswich, Hillsborough County, N.H., November 2, 1801; moved with his parents to Hampden, Penobscot County, Maine, in 1802; attended Hampden Academy and was graduated from Yale College in 1823; studied law; was admitted to the bar and commenced practice in Hampden in 1826; admitted to the bar of the United States Supreme Court in 1828; held various local offices; moved to Bangor, Maine, in 1833; judge of the Bangor Municipal Court 1834-1839; member of the common council of Bangor in 1843 and 1844; member of the State executive council 1845-1848; elected as a Democrat to the Thirty-first Congress (March 4, 1849-March 3, 1851); unsuccessful candidate for renomination in 1850 to the Thirty-second Congress; resumed the practice of his profession; affiliated with the Republican Party in 1860; died in Bangor, Maine, March 27, 1863; interment in Mount Hope Cemetery.

**STETSON, Lemuel,** a Representative from New York; born in Champlain, Clinton County, N.Y., March 13, 1804; attended the public schools and Plattsburgh Academy; studied law; was admitted to the bar in 1824 and commenced practice in Keeseville, Essex County, N.Y.; member of the New York State assembly in 1835, 1836, and 1842; district attorney of Clinton County, 1838-1843; elected as a Democrat to the Twenty-eighth Congress (March 4, 1843-March 3, 1845); chairman, Committee on District of Columbia (Twenty-eighth Congress); member of the New York State constitutional convention in 1846; again a member of the State assembly in 1846; moved to Plattsburgh, N.Y., in 1847; judge of Clinton County, 1847-1851; delegate to the Democratic National Convention at Baltimore in 1860; resumed the practice of law; died in Plattsburgh, N.Y., May 17, 1868; interment in Riverside Cemetery.

**STEVENS, Aaron Fletcher,** a Representative from New Hampshire; born in Londonderry, Rockingham County, N.H., August 9, 1819; attended Pinkerton Academy, Derry, N.H., and Crosby's Nashua Literary Institute, Nashua, N.H.; at the age of sixteen was apprenticed to the trade of machinist and worked as a journeyman for several years; studied law; was admitted to the bar and commenced practice in Nashua, Hillsborough County, N.H.; member of the New Hampshire State house of representatives in 1845; held several local offices; during the Civil War served in the Union Army as major of the First Regiment, New Hampshire Volunteer Infantry, as colonel of the Thirteenth New Hampshire Volunteer Infantry, and was brevetted brigadier general; delegate to the Whig National Convention of 1852; president of the common council of Nashua in 1853 and 1854; solicitor of Hillsborough County from 1856 until 1861; city solicitor of Nashua in 1859, 1860, 1865, 1872, and 1875-1877; elected as a Republican to the Fortieth and Forty-first Congresses (March 4, 1867-March 3, 1871); unsuccessful candidate for reelection in 1870 to the Forty-second Congress; again a member of the State house of representatives, 1876-1884; resumed the practice of law; died in Nashua, N.H., May 10, 1887; interment in Nashua Cemetery.

**STEVENS, Bradford Newcomb,** a Representative from Illinois; born in Boscawen, Merrimack County, N.H., January 3, 1813; attended schools in New Hampshire and at Montreal, Canada, and was graduated from Dartmouth College, Hanover, N.H., in 1835; taught school six years in Hopkinsville, Ky., and New York City; moved to Bureau County, Ill., in 1846; engaged in mercantile and agricultural pursuits; county surveyor; mayor of Tiskilwa, Ill.; elected as a Democrat to the Forty-second Congress (March 4, 1871-March 3, 1873); resumed mercantile and agricultural pursuits; died in Tiskilwa, Bureau County, Ill., November 10, 1885; interment in Mount Bloom Cemetery.

**STEVENS, Charles Abbot** (brother of Moses Tyler Stevens and cousin of Isaac Ingalls Stevens), a Representative from Massachusetts; born in North Andover (then a part of Andover), Essex County, Mass., August 9, 1816; attended Franklin Academy at North Andover; manufacturer of flannels and broadcloths at Ware, Hampshire County, Mass., in 1841; member of the Massachusetts house of representatives in 1853; delegate to the Republican National Conventions of 1860 and 1868; served as a member of the Governor's council from 1867 until 1870; unsuccessful candidate for election in 1874 to the Forty-fourth Congress; was subsequently elected as a Republican to the Forty-third Congress to fill the vacancy caused by the death of Alvah Crocker and served from January 27 to March 3, 1875; resumed the manufacturing business; died in New York City, April 7, 1892; interment in Aspen Grove Cemetery, Ware, Mass.

**STEVENS, Frederick Clement,** a Representative from Minnesota; born in Boston, Mass., January 1, 1861; moved with his parents to Searsport, Maine; attended the common schools of Rockland; was graduated from Bowdoin College, Brunswick, Maine, in 1881, and from the law department of the University of Iowa at Iowa City in 1884; was admitted to the bar in 1884 and commenced practice in St. Paul, Minn.; member of the Minnesota State house of representatives, 1888-1891; elected as a Republican to the Fifty-fifth and to the eight succeeding Congresses (March 4, 1897-March 3, 1915); unsuccessful candidate for reelection in 1914 to the Sixty-fourth Congress; engaged in the practice of law until his death in St. Paul, Minn., July 1, 1923, interment in Oakland Cemetery.

**STEVENS, Hestor Lockhart,** a Representative from Michigan; born in Lima, Livingston County, N.Y., October 1, 1803; attended the common schools; studied law; was admitted to the bar and commenced practice in Rochester, N.Y.; major general of militia of western New York; moved to Pontiac, Mich.; elected as a Democrat to the Thirty-third Congress (March 4, 1853-March 3, 1855); resumed the practice of law in Washington, D.C.; died in Georgetown, D.C., May 7, 1864; interment in Oak Hill Cemetery.

**STEVENS, Hiram Sanford,** a Delegate from the Territory of Arizona; born in Weston, Windsor County, Vt., March 20, 1832; received a limited education; farmer; in 1851 enlisted in Company I, First United States Dragoons, for service in New Mexico; participated in engagements against the Apaches in 1852 and 1854; honorably discharged at Fort Thorn, N.Mex., in 1856, moving to Tucson, Ariz., where he engaged in general merchandising and the supplying of forage for the Army; elected to the Arizona Territorial house of representatives in 1868; served on the Territorial council from 1871 until 1873; assessor and supervisor of Pima County; served as treasurer of Tucson in 1871; elected as a Democrat to the Forty-fourth and Forty-fifth Congresses (March 4, 1875-March 3, 1879); unsuccessful candidate for renomination in 1878 to the Forty-sixth Congress; engaged in mercantile pursuits and cattle raising; died in Tucson, Ariz., March 22, 1893; interment in Old Tucson Cemetery; reinterment in Evergreen Cemetery.

**STEVENS, Isaac Ingalls** (cousin of Charles Abbot Stevens and Moses Tyler Stevens), a Delegate from the Territory of Washington; born in North Andover (then a part of Andover), Essex County, Mass., March 25, 1818; attended Phillips Academy, Andover, Mass., and was graduated from the United States Military Academy at West Point in 1839; entered the Corps of Engineers and served on the staff of General Winfield Scott in Mexico; assistant in charge of the Coast Survey Office in Washington, D.C.; engaged in engineering work along the coast of New England; organized and commanded the northern Pacific exploration party which explored and surveyed the route for a railway from St. Paul to Puget Sound in 1853; resigned his commission as major in the Corps of Engineers to become Governor; appointed Governor of the Territory of Washington by President Franklin Pierce on March 17, 1853 and served until 1857; was a candidate for the Democratic nomination to Congress in 1855, but withdrew; elected as a Democrat to the Thirty-fifth and Thirty-sixth Congresses (March 4, 1857-March 3, 1861); was not a candidate for renomination in 1860 to the Thirty-seventh Congress; delegate to the Democratic National Conventions at Charleston and Baltimore in 1860; during the Civil War entered the Union Army as a colonel of the Seventy-ninth New York Highlanders, July 30, 1861; appointed brigadier general, September 28, 1861, and major general, July 4, 1862, in command of a division; killed at the Battle of Chantilly, Virginia, September 1, 1862; interment in Island Cemetery, Newport, R.I.

**Bibliography:** *DAB*; Hazard, Joseph Taylor. *Companion of Adventure: A Biography of Isaac Ingalls Stevens, First Governor of Washington Territory.* Portland, Ore.: Binfords and Mort, 1952; Mills, Hazel E. "Governor Isaac I. Stevens and the Washington Territorial Library." *Pacific Northwest Quarterly* 53 (January 1962): 1-16; Richards, Kent D. *Isaac I. Stevens: Young Man in a Hurry.* Provo, Utah: Brigham Young University Press, 1979.

**STEVENS, James,** a Representative from Connecticut; born in that part of Stamford which is now the town of New Canaan, Fairfield County, Conn., July 4, 1768; studied law; was admitted to the bar and commenced practice in Stamford, Conn.; member of the Connecticut State house of representatives, 1804, 1805, 1808-1810, 1814, 1815, 1817, and 1818; judge of probate, Stamford district, in 1819; elected to the Sixteenth Congress (March 4, 1819-March 3, 1821); justice of the peace at Stamford from 1819 until 1826; postmaster of Stamford, Conn., from May 17, 1822 to October 5, 1829; judge of the Fairfield County Court in 1823; resumed the practice of law in Stamford, Conn., and died there on April 4, 1835; interment in St. John's and St. Andrew's Episcopal Cemetery.

**STEVENS, John,** a Delegate from New Jersey; born in Perth Amboy, N.J., in 1715; merchant and shipowner; engaged in trading with the West Indies and Madeira; large landowner and mine owner in Hunterdon, Union, and Somerset Counties; member of the general colonial assembly in 1751; was a member of the defense committee to protect New York and New Jersey against Indian depredations; commissioner to the Indians in 1758; paymaster of Colonel Schuyler's regiment, the "Old Blues," 1756-1760; as a resident of New York City in 1765 was one of the committee of four who prevented the issue of stamps; in 1774 was appointed a commissioner to define the boundary line between New York and New Jersey; vice president of the council of New Jersey from 1770 until 1782; served as president of the council of East Jersey proprietors in 1783; Member of the Continental Congress in 1784; presided over the State ratification convention, December 18, 1787; died in Hoboken, Hudson County, N.J., May 10, 1792; interment in the Frame Meeting House Cemetery, Hunterdon County, N.J.

**STEVENS, Moses Tyler** (brother of Charles Abbot Stevens and cousin of Isaac Ingalls Stevens), a Representative from Massachusetts; born in North Andover (then a part of Andover), Essex County, Mass., October 10, 1825; attended Franklin Academy at North Andover; was graduated from Phillips Academy, Andover, in 1842; attended Dartmouth College, Hanover, N.H., in 1842 and 1843; engaged in the manufacture of woolen goods in North Andover; served as president of the Andover National Bank; member of the Massachusetts house of representatives in 1861; served in the Massachusetts senate in 1868; elected as a Democrat to the Fifty-second and Fifty-third Congresses (March 4, 1891-March 3, 1895); was not a candidate for renomination in 1894 to the Fifty-fourth Congress; resumed his interests in the manufacturing business; died in North Andover, Mass., March 25, 1907; interment in Ridgewood Cemetery.

**STEVENS, Raymond Bartlett,** a Representative from New Hampshire; born in Binghamton, Broome County, N.Y., June 18, 1874; moved with his parents to Lisbon, Grafton County, N.H., in 1876; attended the public schools, Boston Latin School, Harvard University, and Harvard Law School; was admitted to the bar in 1899 and commenced practice in Lisbon, N.H.; member of the New Hampshire State house of representatives in 1909, 1911, 1913, and 1923; member of the State constitutional convention in 1912; elected as a Democrat to the Sixty-third Congress (March 4, 1913-March 3, 1915); was not a candidate in 1914 for renomination to the House of Representatives, but was an unsuccessful candidate for election to the United States Senate; special counsel of the Federal Trade

Commission, 1915-1917; United States representative to the Allied Maritime Transport Council in 1917 and 1918; vice chairman of the United States Shipping Board, 1917-1920; delegate to the Democratic National Conventions of 1920 and 1924; appointed adviser in foreign affairs to King Prajadhipok of Siam (Thailand) in January 1926, in which capacity he served until 1935, except for a six-month period during 1933 when he was a member of the Federal Trade Commission; member of the Federal Tariff Commission from 1935 until 1942, serving as chairman, 1937-1942; died at Indianapolis, Ind., May 18, 1942; interment on the grounds of the family residence at Landaff, N.H.

**STEVENS, Robert Smith,** a Representative from New York; born in Attica, Wyoming County, N.Y., March 27, 1824; prepared for college under a tutor; pursued an academic course; studied law; was admitted to the bar in 1846; moved to Kansas, and engaged in the practice of law; subsequently became extensively interested in real estate, in the development of coal lands, and in the management and building of railroads; member of the Kansas State house of representatives; retired from active business pursuits in 1880 and returned to New York; engaged in agricultural pursuits; elected as a Democrat to the Forty-eighth Congress (March 4, 1883-March 3, 1885); unsuccessful candidate for reelection in 1884 to the Forty-ninth Congress; resumed agricultural pursuits; died in Attica, Wyoming County, N.Y., on February 23, 1893; interment in Forest Hill Cemetery.

**STEVENS, Thaddeus,** a Representative from Pennsylvania; born in Danville, Caledonia County, Vt. April 4, 1792; attended Peacham Academy and the University of Vermont at Burlington; graduated from Dartmouth College, Hanover, N.H., in 1814; moved to Pennsylvania in 1814; studied law; admitted to the bar in 1816 and commenced practice in Gettysburg; member of the Pennsylvania house of representatives, 1833-1835, 1837, and 1841; delegate to the Pennsylvania constitutional convention in 1838; appointed as a canal commissioner in 1838; moved to Lancaster, Pa., in 1842; elected as a Whig to the Thirty-first and Thirty-second Congresses (March 4, 1849-March 3, 1853); elected as a Republican to the Thirty-sixth and to the four succeeding Congresses and served from March 4, 1859, until his death in Washington, D.C., August 11, 1868; chairman, Committee on Ways and Means (Thirty-seventh and Thirty-eighth Congresses), Committee on Appropriations (Thirty-ninth and Fortieth Congresses); chairman of the managers appointed by the House of Representatives in 1868 to conduct the impeachment proceedings against President Andrew Johnson; interment in Shreiner's Cemetery, Lancaster, Pa.

**Bibliography:** *DAB*; Brodie, Fawn. *Thaddeus Stevens, Scourge of the South.* New York: Norton, 1959; Current, Richard N. *Old Thad Stevens, A Story of Ambition.* 1942. Reprint. Westport, Conn.: Greenwood Press, 1980.

**STEVENS, Theodore Fulton (Ted),** a Senator from Alaska; born in Indianapolis, Marion County, Ind., November 18, 1923; attended Oregon State College and Montana State College; B.A., University of California, Los Angeles, 1947; LL.B., Harvard University Law School, 1950; served in the United States Air Force in the Second World War in China, 1943-1946; admitted to the California bar in 1950, to the District of Columbia bar in 1951, and to the Alaska bar in 1957; practiced law in Fairbanks, Alaska, 1953; legislative counsel, Department of Interior, Washington, D.C., 1956-1957; assistant to Secretary of the Interior Frederick A. Seaton, 1958-1959; chief counsel, Department of the Interior, 1960; returned to Anchorage, Alaska, in 1961 and practiced law; elected to the Alaska State house of representatives in 1964, reelected in 1966, serving as speaker pro tempore and majority leader; appointed as a Republican to the United States Senate, December 24, 1968, to fill the vacancy caused by the death of E.L. Bartlett, and was subsequently elected on November 3, 1970, to complete the unexpired term ending January 3, 1973; reelected in 1972, 1978, 1984, and again in 1990 for the term ending January 3, 1997; Republican whip (Ninety-fifth through Ninety-eighth Congresses); chairman, Republican Senatorial Campaign Committee (Ninety-fourth Congress), Select Committee on Ethics (Ninety-eighth and Ninety-ninth Congresses), Committee on Rules and Administration (One Hundred Fourth Congress), Committee on Governmental Affairs (One Hundred Fourth Congress); is a resident of Girdwood, Alaska.

**STEVENSON, Adlai Ewing** (great-grandfather of Adlai Ewing Stevenson III), a Representative from Illinois and a Vice President of the United States; born in Christian County, Ky., October 23, 1835; moved with his parents to Bloomington, Ill., in 1852; attended Illinois Wesleyan University at Bloomington and Centre College, Danville, Ky., studied law; was admitted to the bar in 1858 and commenced practice in Metamora, Woodford County, Ill.; master in chancery, 1860-1864; presidential elector on the Democratic ticket in 1864; district attorney from 1865 until 1868; elected as a Democrat to the Forty-fourth Congress (March 4, 1875-March 3, 1877); unsuccessful candidate for reelection in 1876 to the Forty-fifth Congress; elected to the Forty-sixth Congress (March 4, 1879-March 3, 1881); unsuccessful candidate for reelection in 1880 to the Forty-seventh Congress; First Assistant Postmaster General, 1885-1889; elected Vice President of the United States, November 8, 1892, on the Democratic ticket headed by Grover Cleveland; was inaugurated March 4, 1893, and served until March 3, 1897; was an unsuccessful Democratic candidate for Vice President of the United States in 1900 on the ticket headed by William Jennings Bryan; unsuccessful candidate for election for Governor of Illinois in 1908; retired from public and political activities and resided in Bloomington, Ill.; died in Chicago, Ill., June 14, 1914; interment in Bloomington Cemetery, Bloomington, Ill.

**Bibliography:** *DAB*; Schlup, Leonard C. "The Political Career of the First Adlai E. Stevenson." Ph.D. dissertation, University of Illinois at Urbana-Champaign, 1973; Stevenson, Adlai. *Something of Men I Have Known With Some Papers of a General Nature, Political, Historical and Retrospective.* Chicago; A.C. McClurg and Co., 1909.

**STEVENSON, Adlai Ewing, III** (great-grandson of Adlai Ewing Stevenson), a Senator from Illinois; born in Chicago, Cook County, Ill., October 10, 1930; attended grammar schools in Illinois, and Milton Academy, Massachusetts; A.B., Harvard University, 1952; LL.B., Harvard University School of Law, 1957; entered the United States Marine Corps as a private in 1952 and served as a tank platoon commander in Korea; discharged as a first lieutenant in 1954, and from the Reserves in 1961 with the rank of captain; law clerk to justice of Illinois Supreme Court, 1957-1958; was admitted to the bar in 1957 and commenced practice in Chicago, Ill.; member, Illinois State house of representatives, 1965-1967; treasurer, State of Illinois, 1967-1970; elected as a Democrat to the United States Senate on November 3, 1970, to fill the vacancy caused by the death of Everett McKinley Dirksen; reelected in 1976, and served from November 17, 1970, to January 3, 1981; was not a candidate for reelection in 1980; chairman, Select Committee on the Senate Committee System (Ninety-fourth Congress), Select Committee on Ethics (Ninety-fifth and Ninety-sixth Congresses); resumed the practice of law; unsuccessful Democratic candidate for Governor of Illinois in 1982 and 1986; president, SCM International Ltd., Chicago, Ill., 1991 to present; is a resident of Hanover, Ill.

**STEVENSON, Andrew** (father of John White Stevenson), a Representative from Virginia; born in Culpeper County, Va., January 21, 1784; pursued classical studies; attended the College of William and Mary, Williamsburg, Va.; studied law; was admitted to the bar and commenced practice in Richmond, Va.; member of the Virginia house of delegates, 1809-1816, and 1818-1821, and served as speaker from 1812 to 1815; unsuccessful candidate for election in

1814 to the Fourteenth Congress, and for election in 1816 to the Fifteenth Congress; elected to the Seventeenth Congress; reelected to the Eighteenth through Twentieth Congresses, and reelected as a Jacksonian to the Twenty-first through Twenty-third Congresses, and served from March 4, 1821 until his resignation on June 2, 1834; Speaker of the House of Representatives (Twentieth through Twenty-third Congresses); nominated by President Andrew Jackson as Minister to Great Britain on May 20, 1834, but the Senate refused to confirm him; again nominated Minister to Great Britain on February 1, 1836, confirmed by the Senate, and served until October 1841; engaged in agricultural pursuits at "Blenheim," Albemarle County, Va.; in 1845 was elected a member of the board of visitors of the University of Virginia at Charlottesville, and in 1856 was elected rector; died at his home, "Blenheim," January 25, 1857; interment in Enniscothy Cemetery, Albemarle County, Va.

**Bibliography:** *DAB*; Wayland, Francis Fry. *Andrew Stevenson, Democrat and Diplomat, 1785-1857.* Philadelphia: University of Pennsylvania Press, 1949.

**STEVENSON, James S.,** a Representative from Pennsylvania; born in York County, Pa., in 1780; completed preparatory studies; studied law; admitted to the bar and practiced; member of the Pennsylvania house of representatives in 1822 and 1823; president of the board of canal commissioners of the Commonwealth, which position he held until the time of his death; elected to the Nineteenth and Twentieth Congresses (March 4, 1825-March 3, 1829); unsuccessful candidate for reelection in 1828 to the Twenty-first Congress; engaged in manufacturing in Pittsburgh, Pa., until his death in that city October 16, 1831; interment in First Presbyterian Cemetery.

**STEVENSON, Job Evans,** a Representative from Ohio; born in Yellow Bud, Ross County, Ohio, February 10, 1832; completed preparatory studies; studied law; was admitted to the bar and commenced the practice of his profession in Chillicothe, Ohio; also engaged in agricultural pursuits; member of the State senate 1863-1865; solicitor of Chillicothe 1859-1862; unsuccessful candidate for election in 1864 to the Thirty-ninth Congress; moved to Cincinnati, Ohio, in 1865; was elected as a Republican to the Forty-first and Forty-second Congresses (March 4, 1869-March 3, 1873); resumed the practice of law in Cincinnati, Ohio; resided in Lexington and Corinth, Ky.; died in Corinth, Ky., July 24, 1922; interment in Yellowbud Cemetery, Yellowbud, Ohio.

**STEVENSON, John White** (son of Andrew Stevenson), a Representative and a Senator from Kentucky; born in Richmond, Va., May 4, 1812; attended Hampden-Sidney Academy, Virginia, and graduated from the University of Virginia at Charlottesville in 1832; studied law; admitted to the bar and commenced practice in Vicksburg, Miss; moved to Covington, Kenton County, Ky., in 1841; county attorney; member, Kentucky house of representatives, 1845-1849; delegate to the Kentucky constitutional convention in 1849; one of three commissioners appointed to revise the civic and criminal code of Kentucky, 1850-1851; presidential elector on the Democratic ticket in 1852 and 1856; elected as a Democrat to the Thirty-fifth and Thirty-sixth Congresses (March 4, 1857-March 3, 1861); unsuccessful candidate for reelection in 1860 to the Thirty-seventh Congress; Lieutenant Governor of Kentucky in 1867; became Governor on September 13, 1867, upon the death of Governor John L. Helm; was subsequently elected Governor in 1868 and served until his resignation on March 4, 1871, having been elected a Senator; elected as a Democrat to the United States Senate, and served from March 4, 1871 to March 3, 1877; was not a candidate for reelection; chairman, Committee on Revolutionary Claims (Forty-fourth Congress); professor in the Cincinnati Law School; president of the American Bar Association, 1884-1885; died in Covington, Ky., August 10, 1886; interment in Spring Grove Cemetery, Cincinnati, Ohio.

**Bibliography:** *DAB*.

**STEVENSON, William Francis,** a Representative from South Carolina; born in what is now Loray, near Statesville, Iredell County, N.C., November 23, 1861; attended the public schools and was tutored by his father; teacher in the public schools in 1879 and 1880; was graduated from Davidson College, Davidson, N.C., in 1885; again engaged in teaching in Cheraw, S.C., 1885-1887, studying law at the same time; was admitted to the bar in 1887 and commenced practice in Chesterfield, S.C., the same year; moved to Cheraw in 1892 and continued the practice of law; member of the Democratic executive committee of Chesterfield County 1888-1914, serving as chairman 1896-1902; mayor of Cheraw in 1895 and 1896; member of the State house of representatives 1897-1902, serving as speaker 1900-1902; declined to be a candidate for reelection; interested in various business enterprises in Chesterfield County; district counsel for the Seaboard Air Line Railway 1900-1917; member of the Democratic State executive committee 1901-1942; general counsel for the State dispensary commission 1907-1911; again a member of the State house of representatives 1911-1914; elected as a Democrat to the Sixty-fifth Congress to fill the vacancy caused by the death of Representative-elect David E. Finley; reelected to the Sixty-sixth and to the six succeeding Congresses and served from March 4, 1917, to March 3, 1933; was an unsuccessful candidate for renomination in 1932 to the Seventy-third Congress; member of the Federal Home Loan Bank Board, Washington, D.C., 1933-1939, serving as chairman in 1933; died in Washington, D.C., on February 12, 1942; interment in St. David's Episcopal Church Cemetery, Cheraw, S.C.

**STEVENSON, William Henry,** a Representative from Wisconsin; born in Kenosha, Wis., September 23, 1891; moved to La Crosse, Wis., with his parents in 1894; attended the grade and high schools; was graduated from Teachers College, La Crosse, Wis., in 1912; taught in the high schools of Holmen, Neillsville, and Madison, Wis., 1912-1916; was graduated from the University of Wisconsin at Madison in 1919 and from its law department in 1920; was admitted to the bar in 1920 and commenced practice in Richland Center, Wis.; appointed circuit court commissioner and divorce counsel of Richland County in 1922 and served until 1924; district attorney of Richland County 1924-1926; moved to La Crosse, Wis., in 1930 and continued the practice of his profession; served as district attorney of La Crosse County, Wis., 1935-1941; elected as a Republican to the Seventy-seventh and to the three succeeding Congresses (January 3, 1941-January 3, 1949); was an unsuccessful candidate for renomination in 1948 to the Eighty-first Congress; admitted to practice before United States Supreme Court in 1946; resumed the practice of law; resided in Onalaska, Wis., until his death in La Crosse, Wis., March 19, 1978; cremated; ashes interred in Onalaska Cemetery.

**STEWARD, Lewis,** a Representative from Illinois; born near Hollisterville, Wayne County, Pa., November 21, 1824; attended the common schools; in 1838 moved with his parents to Kendall County, Ill.; studied law; was admitted to the bar about 1860 but never practiced; engaged in agricultural pursuits and became an extensive landowner; also engaged in the manufacture of harvesters, mowers, and binders at Plano and later at West Pullman; unsuccessful Democratic candidate for Governor of Illinois in 1876; elected as a Democrat to the Fifty-second Congress (March 4, 1891-March 3, 1893); unsuccessful candidate for reelection in 1892 to the Fifty-third Congress and for election in 1894 to the Fifty-fourth Congress; resumed his former manufacturing activities; also interested in agricultural pursuits; died in Plano, Kendall County, Ill., August 27, 1896; interment in Plano Cemetery.

**STEWART, Alexander,** a Representative from Wisconsin; born in Fredericton, York County, New Brunswick, Canada, September 12, 1829; attended the common schools of his native city; moved to Marathon County, Wis., in 1849, and settled where the city of

Wausau is now located; engaged in the lumber business; delegate to the Republican National Convention in 1884; elected as a Republican to the Fifty-fourth, Fifty-fifth, and Fifty-sixth Congresses (March 4, 1895-March 3, 1901); was not a candidate for renomination in 1900 to the Fifty-seventh Congress; resided in Washington, D.C., until his death on May 24, 1912; interment in Pine Grove Cemetery, Wausau, Wis.

**STEWART, Andrew** (father of Andrew Stewart [1836-1903]), a Representative from Pennsylvania; born near Uniontown, Fayette County, Pa., on June 11, 1791; received a good education; taught school; graduated from Washington College (now Washington and Jefferson College), Washington, Pa.; studied law; admitted to the bar in 1815 and commenced practice in Uniontown; member of the Pennsylvania house of representatives 1815-1818; was appointed by President James Monroe as United States attorney for the western district of Pennsylvania and served from 1818 to 1820, when he resigned; elected to the Seventeenth and to the three succeeding Congresses (March 4, 1821-March 3, 1829); elected as an Anti-Masonic candidate to the Twenty-second and Twenty-third Congresses (March 4, 1831-March 3, 1835); unsuccessful candidate for reelection in 1834 to the Twenty-fourth Congress; was elected as a Whig to the Twenty-eighth, Twenty-ninth, and Thirtieth Congresses (March 4, 1843-March 3, 1849); chairman, Committee on Manufactures (Thirtieth Congress); declined to be a candidate for renomination; affiliated with the Republican Party; unsuccessful candidate for election in 1870 to the Forty-second Congress; largely interested in building and real estate until his death in Uniontown, Fayette County, Pa., July 16, 1872; interment in Union Cemetery.

Bibliography: *DAB*.

**STEWART, Andrew** (son of Andrew Stewart [1791-1872]), a Representative from Pennsylvania; born in Uniontown, Fayette County, Pa., April 6, 1836; attended Sewickley Academy, Sewickley, Pa., and Madison College, Uniontown, Pa.; studied medicine and attended Jefferson Medical College, Philadelphia, Pa.; during the Civil War enlisted as a private in the Eighty-fifth Regiment, Pennsylvania Volunteer Infantry, and served throughout the war; unsuccessful candidate for election in 1874 to the Forty-fourth Congress; presented credentials as a Republican Member-elect to the Fifty-second Congress and served from March 4, 1891, to February 26, 1892, when he was succeeded by Alexander K. Craig, who contested his election; unsuccessful candidate for election to the Fifty-second Congress to fill the vacancy caused by the death of Alexander K. Craig; engaged in the manufacture of paper pulp and lumber; died in Stewarton, Fayette County, Pa., November 9, 1903; interment in Union Cemetery, Uniontown, Pa.

**STEWART, Arthur Thomas (Tom)**, a Senator from Tennessee; born in Dunlap, Sequatchie County, Tenn., January 11, 1892; attended the public schools, Pryor Institute, Jasper, Tenn., and Emory (Ga.) College; graduated from the law department of Cumberland University, Lebanon, Tenn.; was admitted to the bar in 1913 and commenced practice in Birmingham, Ala.; returned to Jasper, Tenn., in 1915; moved to Winchester, Tenn., in 1919 and continued the practice of law; attorney general of the Tennessee Eighteenth Judicial District (Winchester) from 1923 until 1939, when he resigned, having previously been elected Senator; one of the attorneys representing the State of Tennessee during the trial of John T. Scopes for violation of the statute prohibiting the teaching of the theory of evolution, Dayton, Tenn., July 1925; elected as a Democrat to the United States Senate on November 8, 1938, for the term ending January 3, 1943, to fill the vacancy caused by the death of Nathan L. Bachman, but, preferring to continue as district attorney general, did not assume his senatorial duties until January 16, 1939; reelected in 1942, and served from January 16, 1939 to January 3, 1949; unsuccessful candidate for renomination in 1948;

chairman, Committee on Interoceanic Canals (Seventy-ninth Congress); moved to Nashville, Tenn. in 1948 and resumed the practice of law; died in Nashville, Tenn., October 10, 1972; interment in Memorial Park Cemetery, Winchester, Tenn.

**STEWART, Bennett McVey**, a Representative from Illinois; born in Huntsville, Madison County, Ala., August 6, 1912; attended the public schools in Huntsville and Birmingham; B.A., Miles College, Birmingham, 1936; assistant principal, Irondale High School, Birmingham, 1936-1938; associate professor of sociology, Miles College, 1938-1940; insurance executive beginning in 1940; Illinois state director, insurance company, 1950-1968; inspector, Chicago Building Department, 1968; rehabilitation specialist, Chicago Department of Urban Renewal, 1968; alderman, Chicago City Council, Twenty-first ward, 1971-1978; Democratic ward committeeman, Twenty-first ward, 1972-1978; delegate, Illinois State Democratic conventions, 1971-1978; delegate to the Democratic National Conventions of 1972 and 1976; elected as a Democrat to the Ninety-sixth Congress (January 3, 1979-January 3, 1981); unsuccessful candidate for renomination in 1980 to the Ninety-seventh Congress; interim director, Chicago Department of Inter-Governmental Affairs, 1981-1983; was a resident of Chicago, Ill., until his death there on April 26, 1988.

**STEWART, Charles**, a Delegate from New Jersey; born in Gortlea, County Donegal, Ireland, in 1729; immigrated to the United States in 1750; engaged in agricultural pursuits; was commissioned lieutenant colonel of militia in Hunterdon County, N.J., April 10, 1771; commissioned colonel of a battalion of Minutemen on February 15, 1776; appointed commissary general of issues by the Continental Congress on June 18, 1777; Member of the Continental Congress in 1784 and 1785; died in Flemington, N.J., on June 24, 1800; interment in Old Stone Church, Bethlehem Township, Hunterdon County, N.J.

**STEWART, Charles**, a Representative from Texas; born in Memphis, Tenn., May 30, 1836; moved to Texas in 1845 with his parents, who settled in Galveston; attended the common schools; studied law; was admitted to the bar in 1854 and commenced the practice of law in Marlin, Falls County, Tex.; prosecuting attorney for the thirteenth judicial district from 1856 to 1860; delegate to the secession convention in 1861; enlisted in the Confederate Army and served throughout the Civil War, first in the Tenth Regiment of Texas Infantry and later in Baylor's Cavalry; moved to Houston in 1866 and resumed the practice of law; was city attorney of Houston 1874-1876; member of the State senate 1878-1882; elected as a Democrat to the Forty-eighth and to the four succeeding Congresses (March 4, 1883-March 3, 1893); was not a candidate for renomination in 1892; resumed the practice of his profession in Houston, Tex.; died in San Antonio, Tex., September 21, 1895; interment in Glenwood Cemetery, Houston, Tex.

**STEWART, David**, a Senator from Maryland; born in Baltimore, Md., September 13, 1800; completed preparatory studies; attended the College of New Jersey (now Princeton University), and graduated from Union College, Schenectady, N.Y., in 1819; studied law; was admitted to the bar about 1821 and commenced practice in Baltimore, Md.; appointed as a Whig to the United States Senate to fill the vacancy caused by the resignation of Reverdy Johnson and served from December 6, 1849, to January 12, 1850, when a successor was elected; was not a candidate for election to fill the vacancy; resumed the practice of his profession in Baltimore, Md., where he died January 5, 1858; interment in the Stewart vault in "Old Westminster" Burying Ground.

**STEWART, David Wallace**, a Senator from Iowa; born in New Concord, Muskingum County, Ohio, January 22, 1887; attended the common schools; graduated from Geneva College, Beaver Falls, Pa., in 1911; high school teacher and athletic coach 1911-1914;

graduated from the law department of the University of Chicago in 1917; was admitted to the bar the same year and commenced practice in Sioux City, Iowa; during the First World War served overseas as a first sergeant 1918-1919; discharged; resumed the practice of law in Sioux City, Iowa; president of the Sioux City Chamber of Commerce in 1925; appointed August 7, 1926, as a Republican to the United States Senate to fill the vacancy caused by the death of Albert B. Cummins, and was subsequently elected November 2, 1926, to complete the unexpired term ending March 3, 1927, and served from August 7, 1926, until March 3, 1927; was not a candidate for renomination in 1926; resumed the practice of his profession; president of the board of trustees of Morningside College 1938-1962; died in Sioux City, Iowa, February 10, 1974; interment in Logan Park Cemetery.

**STEWART, Donald Wilbur,** a Senator from Alabama; born in Munford, Talladega County, Ala., February 8, 1940; attended the Munford and Anniston public schools; B.S., University of Alabama, Tuscaloosa, 1962; J.D., University of Alabama School of Law, 1965; admitted to the Alabama bar in 1965 and commenced practice in Anniston; served in the United States Army, first lieutenant, 1965; United States magistrate from 1967 until 1970; member, Alabama State house of representatives, 1970-1974; member, State senate, 1974-1978; elected as a Democrat to the United States Senate, November 7, 1978, to complete the unexpired term of James B. Allen ending January 3, 1981; served from November 8, 1978 until his resignation on January 2, 1981; unsuccessful candidate for reelection in 1980; currently president of the law firm of Stewart, Cody and Smith, with offices in Anniston, Birmingham and Tuscaloosa, Ala.; is a resident of Anniston, Ala.

**STEWART, Jacob Henry,** a Representative from Minnesota; born in Clermont, Columbia County, N.Y., January 15, 1829; moved with his parents to Peekskill, N.Y.; attended the common schools and was graduated from Phillips Academy, Peekskill; attended Yale College; studied medicine and was graduated from the University Medical College of New York City in 1851; commenced the practice of medicine in Peekskill, N.Y.; moved to St. Paul, Minn., in 1855; medical officer of Ramsey County in 1856; member of the State senate in 1858 and 1859; during the Civil War served as a surgeon in the Union Army in 1861; surgeon general of the State of Minnesota 1857-1863; mayor of St. Paul in 1864, 1868, and 1872-1874; postmaster of St. Paul 1865-1870; elected as a Republican to the Forty-fifth Congress (March 4, 1877-March 3, 1879); was not a candidate for renomination in 1878; surveyor general of Minnesota 1879-1882; resumed the practice of medicine in St. Paul, Minn., and died there August 25, 1884; interment in Oakland Cemetery.

**STEWART, James,** a Representative from North Carolina; born in Scotland November 11, 1775; received a liberal education; immigrated to the United States and settled near Stewartsville, Richmond County, N.C.; engaged in mercantile and agricultural pursuits; member of the State house of commons in 1798 and 1799; served in the State senate 1802-1804 and 1813-1815; elected as a Federalist to the Fifteenth Congress to fill the vacancy caused by the death of Alexander McMillan and served from January 5, 1818, to March 3, 1819; resumed mercantile and agricultural pursuits; died near Laurinburg, Richmond County, N.C., on December 29, 1821; interment in the Old Stewartsville Cemetery, near Laurinburg.

**STEWART, James Augustus,** a Representative from Maryland; born at "Tobacco Stick" (now Madison), Dorchester County, Md., November 24, 1808; attended the local schools; studied law in Baltimore, Md.; was admitted to the bar in 1829 and commenced practice in Cambridge, Dorchester County, Md.; also engaged in the building of ships and houses; unsuccessful candidate for election in 1838 to the Twenty-sixth Congress; member of the State house of delegates 1843-1845; elected as a Democrat to the Thirty-fourth,

Thirty-fifth, and Thirty-sixth Congresses (March 4, 1855-March 3, 1861); chairman, Committee on Patents (Thirty-fifth Congress); was not a candidate for renomination in 1860; resumed the practice of his profession in Cambridge; member of the Court of Appeals of Maryland and chief justice of the circuit court from 1867 until his death in Cambridge, Md., April 3, 1879; interment in Christ Protestant Episcopal Church Cemetery.

**STEWART, James Fleming,** a Representative from New Jersey; born in Paterson, N.J., June 15, 1851; attended the public and private schools of Paterson; was graduated from the law department of the University of New York at New York City in 1870; was admitted to the bar the same year and commenced the practice of law in New York City; returned to Paterson, N.J., and continued the practice of law in 1875; recorder (criminal magistrate) of the city of Paterson 1890-1895; elected as a Republican to the Fifty-fourth and to the three succeeding Congresses (March 4, 1895-March 3, 1903); chairman, Committee on Expenditures in the Department of the Navy (Fifty-fifth through Fifty-seventh Congresses); was an unsuccessful candidate for reelection in 1902 to the Fifty-eighth Congress; resumed the practice of law in Paterson, N.J., where he died on January 21, 1904; interment in Cedar Lawn Cemetery.

**STEWART, John,** a Representative from Connecticut; born in Chatham, Conn., February 10, 1795; completed preparatory studies; became engaged in shipbuilding and in the mercantile business in Middle Haddam; member of the State house of representatives in 1830; served in the State senate 1832-1837; judge of the county court of Middletown; elected as a Democrat to the Twenty-eighth Congress (March 4, 1843-March 3, 1845); unsuccessful candidate for reelection in 1844 to the Twenty-ninth Congress; resumed shipbuilding pursuits; again a member of the State senate in 1846; again served in the house of representatives in 1854; died in Chatham, Middlesex County, Conn., September 16, 1860; interment in Union Hill Cemetery at Middle Haddam, Chatham, Conn.

**STEWART, John,** a Representative from Pennsylvania; completed preparatory studies; member of the Pennsylvania house of representatives 1789-1796; elected as a Republican to the Sixth Congress to fill the vacancy caused by the death of Thomas Hartley; reelected to the Seventh and Eighth Congresses and served from January 15, 1801, to March 3, 1805; died in Elmwood, near York, Spring Garden Township, Pa., in 1820; interment on his estate near Elmwood.

**STEWART, John David,** a Representative from Georgia; born near Fayetteville, Fayette County, Ga., August 2, 1833; attended the common schools and Marshall College, Griffin, Ga.; taught school two years in Griffin, Spalding County, Ga.; studied law; was admitted to the bar in 1856 and commenced practice in Griffin, Ga.; probate judge of Spalding County 1858-1860; lieutenant and captain in the Thirteenth Georgia Regiment during the Civil War; member of the State house of representatives 1865-1867; studied theology; was ordained as a minister of the Baptist Church in 1871; mayor of Griffin in 1875 and 1876; judge of the superior court from November 7, 1879, to January 1, 1886, when he resigned to become a candidate for Congress; elected as a Democrat to the Fiftieth and Fifty-first Congresses (March 4, 1887-March 3, 1891); unsuccessful candidate for renomination in 1890; engaged in the practice of his profession until his death in Griffin, Ga., January 28, 1894; interment in Oak Hill Cemetery.

**STEWART, John George,** a Representative from Delaware; born in Wilmington, New Castle County, Del., June 2, 1890; attended the public schools of Wilmington and the University of Delaware at Newark; engaged in the landscape construction business 1919-1942; member of the Delaware Athletic Commission 1931-1934; commissioner on the Delaware Emergency Relief Commission in 1934; elected as a Republican to the Seventy-fourth

Congress (January 3, 1935-January 3, 1937); unsuccessful candidate for reelection in 1936 to the Seventy-fifth Congress; member of the staff of the United States Senate Committee on the District of Columbia 1947-1951; special engineer to the lands division of the Department of Justice and Corps of Engineers in 1952 and 1953; civil engineer in Hollywood, Fla., in 1954; appointed Architect of the Capitol August 16, 1954; assumed duties October 1, 1954, and served until his death in Washington, D.C., May 24, 1970; interment in Lower Brandywine Cemetery, Centerville, New Castle County, Del.

**STEWART, John Knox,** a Representative from New York; born in Perth, Fulton County, N.Y., October 20, 1853; moved with his parents to Amsterdam in 1860; attended the public schools and Amsterdam Academy; engaged in the manufacture of paper until 1885, when he engaged in the manufacture of textiles; sewer commissioner of the city 1885-1890; a director of the Farmers' National Bank of Amsterdam and of the Chuctanunda Gas Light Co.; vice president of the Amsterdam Board of Trade; member of the State assembly in 1889; elected as a Republican to the Fifty-sixth and Fifty-seventh Congresses (March 4, 1899-March 3, 1903); unsuccessful candidate for renomination in 1902; resumed the manufacture of textiles and continued in that business until his death in Amsterdam, N.Y., June 27, 1919; interment in Greenhill Cemetery.

**STEWART, John Wolcott,** a Representative and a Senator from Vermont; born in Middlebury, Addison County, Vt., November 24, 1825; graduated from the Middlebury Academy in 1846; studied law; was admitted to the bar in 1850 and commenced practice in Middlebury, Vt.; prosecuting attorney of Addison County, 1852-1854; member, Vermont State house of representatives, 1856, 1865-1867, and 1876, serving as speaker, 1865-1867 and in 1876; member, State senate, 1861-1862; elected Governor of Vermont in 1870, and served from October 6, 1870 to October 3, 1872; elected as a Republican to the Forty-eighth and to the three succeeding Congresses (March 4, 1883-March 3, 1891); declined to be a candidate for renomination in 1890 to the Fifty-second Congress; engaged in the banking business at Middlebury; appointed as a Republican to the United States Senate, March 24, 1908, to fill the vacancy caused by the death of Redfield Proctor, and served from March 24 to October 21, 1908, when a successor was elected; retired from political life and active business pursuits and resided in Middlebury, Vt., until his death on October 29, 1915; interment in West Cemetery.

**STEWART, Paul,** a Representative from Oklahoma; born in Clarksville, Johnson County, Ark., February 27, 1892; moved with his parents to Poteau, Indian Territory, in 1894 and to Red River County, Choctaw Nation, Indian Territory (now a part of McCurtain County, Okla.) in 1897; self-educated; entered the mercantile business at the age of thirteen at Spencerville, Indian Territory; in 1910 moved his mercantile business to Haworth, Okla., where he continued its operation until 1919; was admitted to the bar in 1915 and commenced the practice of law; postmaster at Haworth 1914-1922; served in the Oklahoma State house of representatives 1922-1926; moved to Antlers Okla., in 1929; editor, owner, and publisher of the Antlers (Okla.) American, a weekly newspaper, 1929-1950; member of the State senate 1926-1942, serving as Democratic floor leader in 1929 and 1930 and as president pro tempore in 1933 and 1934; Acting Governor in 1933; engaged in cattle raising, farming, and hotel business; elected as a Democrat to the Seventy-eighth and Seventy-ninth Congresses (January 3, 1943-January 3, 1947); was not a candidate for renomination in 1946 to the Eightieth Congress; resumed newspaper publishing business until his death in Antlers, Okla., on November 13, 1950; interment in City Cemetery.

**STEWART, Percy Hamilton,** a Representative from New Jersey; born in Newark, Essex County, N.J., January 10, 1867; attended the public schools; was graduated from Yale College in 1890 and from Columbia Law School, New York City in 1893; was admitted to the bar the same year and commenced practice in New York City; mayor of Plainfield, N.J., in 1912 and 1913; chairman of the Union County Democratic committee in 1914 and of the Washington Rock Park Commission of New Jersey 1915-1921; member of the New Jersey State Board of Education 1919-1921 and of the New Jersey State Highway Commission 1923-1929; delegate to the Democratic National Conventions in 1920 and 1928; elected as a Democrat to the Seventy-second Congress to fill the vacancy caused by the death of Ernest R. Ackerman and served from December 1, 1931, to March 3, 1933; was not a candidate for renomination in 1932, but was an unsuccessful candidate for election to the United States Senate; resumed the practice of law until his retirement in 1941; died in Plainfield, N.J., June 30, 1951; interment in Hillside Cemetery.

**STEWART, Thomas Elliott,** a Representative from New York; born in New York City September 22, 1824; completed preparatory studies; studied law; was admitted to the bar in 1847 and commenced practice in New York City; member of the board of education in 1854; served in the State assembly in 1865 and 1866; member of the Republican State committee 1866-1868; elected as a Conservative Republican to the Fortieth Congress (March 4, 1867-March 3, 1869); was not a candidate for renomination in 1868 to the Forty-first Congress; resumed the practice of his profession in New York City; chairman of the Liberal Republican general committee of New York City in 1872; park commissioner of New York City 1874-1876; died in New York City on January 9, 1904; interment in Center Cemetery, New Milford, Litchfield County, Conn.

**STEWART, William,** a Representative from Pennsylvania; born in Mercer, Mercer County, Pa., September 10, 1810; attended the public schools; graduated from Jefferson College, Canonsburg, Pa.; studied law; admitted to the bar and commenced practice in Mercer, Pa.; member of the Pennsylvania senate; elected as a Republican to the Thirty-fifth and Thirty-sixth Congresses (March 4, 1857-March 3, 1861); chairman, Committee on Expenditures in the Department of War (Thirty-sixth Congress); resumed the practice of law; died in Mercer, Pa., on October 17, 1876; interment in Mercer Cemetery.

**STEWART, William Morris,** a Senator from Nevada; born in Galen, near Lyons, Wayne County, N.Y., August 9, 1827; moved with his parents to Mesopotamia Township, Trumbull County, Ohio; attended Lyons Union School and West Farmington Academy; teacher of mathematics at Lyons Union School; attended Yale College, 1849-1850; moved to San Francisco, Calif., in 1850 and engaged in gold mining in Nevada County; studied law; was admitted to the bar in 1852 and commenced practice in Nevada City, Calif.; served as district attorney in 1852; attorney general of California in 1854; moved to Virginia City, Nev., in 1860; involved in early mining litigation and in the development of the Comstock lode; member of the Territorial council in 1861; member of the State constitutional convention in 1863; upon the admission of Nevada as a State into the Union was elected as a Republican to the United States Senate in 1864; reelected in 1869, and served from December 15, 1864 to March 3, 1875; was not a candidate for reelection; chairman, Committee on Pacific Railroads (Forty-second Congress), Committee on Railroads (Forty-third Congress); resumed the practice of law in Nevada and California; again elected as a Republican to the United States Senate in 1887; reelected in 1893 and 1899, as a Silver Republican, and served from March 4, 1887 to March 3, 1905; chairman, Committee on Mines and Mining (Fiftieth through Fifty-sixth Congresses), Committee on Indian Affairs (Fifty-seventh and Fifty-eighth Congresses); declined to be a candidate for reelection in 1905; died in Washington, D.C., April 23, 1909; remains were cremated and the ashes deposited in Laurel Hill Cemetery, San Francisco, Calif.

**Bibliography:** *DAB*; Elliott, Russell R. *Servant of Power: A Political Biography of Senator William M. Stewart.* Reno: University of Nevada Press, 1983; Stewart, William M. *Reminiscences of Senator William M. Stewart of Nevada.* New York: Neale Publishing Co., 1908.

**ST. CLAIR, Arthur,** a Delegate from Pennsylvania; born in Thurso, Caithness, Scotland, March 23, 1734 (old style); attended the University of Edinburgh and studied medicine; purchased a commission as ensign in the Sixtieth Foot, May 13, 1757, and came to America; served under General Jeffrey Amherst at the capture of Louisbourg, Nova Scotia, July 26, 1758, and under General James Wolfe at Quebec in 1759; resigned April 16, 1762; settled in Ligonier Valley, Pa., in 1764, where he erected mills; surveyor of the district of Cumberland in 1770; justice of the court of quarter sessions and of common pleas; member of the proprietary council, justice, recorder, and clerk of the orphans' court; prothonotary of Bedford and Westmoreland Counties; served in the Pennsylvania Militia and Continental Army during the Revolutionary War; commissioned major general, February 19, 1777; retired from the Continental Army on November 3, 1783; was a member of the Pennsylvania council of censors in 1783; Member of the Continental Congress, 1786-1787, and its President in 1787; selected by Congress to be Governor of the Northwest Territory on October 5, 1787, and served until his removal from office on November 22, 1802; named commander of Federal Troops, March 4, 1791; returned to Ligonier Valley, Pa., and engaged in the iron business; died near his old home, "Hermitage," near Youngstown, Pa., August 31, 1818; interment in General Arthur St. Clair Cemetery, Greensburg, Pa.

**Bibliography:** *DAB*; Smith, William H. *The St. Clair Papers. The Life and Public Services of Arthur St. Clair, Soldier of the Revolutionary War; President of the Continental Congress; the Governor of the Northwestern Territory, with his correspondence and other papers.* 1882. Reprint. New York: Da Capo Press, 1971.

**ST. GEORGE, Katharine Price Collier,** a Representative from New York; born July 12, 1894, in Bridgnorth, England; at the age of two came to United States with her parents, who had been living abroad, and resided in Tuxedo, Orange County, N.Y.; attended private schools; at the age of eleven returned to Europe and was educated in England, France, and Germany; returned to Tuxedo, N.Y., in 1914; member of the town board of Tuxedo Park from 1926 until 1949; member, treasurer, vice chairman, and chairman of the Orange County Republican committee, 1942-1948; delegate to the Republican National Convention of 1944; member of the Tuxedo Park Board of Education from 1926 to 1946, serving as president, 1930-1946; elected as a Republican to the Eightieth and to the eight succeeding Congresses (January 3, 1947-January 3, 1965); was an unsuccessful candidate for reelection in 1964 to the Eighty-ninth Congress; chairman, Tuxedo town committee; was a resident of Tuxedo Park, N.Y., until her death there on May 2, 1983; interment in St. Mary's-in-Tuxedo Church Cemetery.

**ST GERMAIN, Fernand Joseph,** a Representative from Rhode Island; born in Blackstone, Worcester County, Mass., January 9, 1928; attended parochial schools in Woonsocket, R.I., and graduated from Our Lady of Providence Seminary High School in 1945; Ph.B., Providence (R.I.) College, 1948; LL.B., Boston University Law School, 1955; served in the United States Army, 1949-1952, with service in the Korean conflict; member, Rhode Island State house of representatives, 1952-1961; was admitted to the bar and commenced the practice of law in Rhode Island in 1956; elected as a Democrat to the Eighty-seventh and to the thirteen succeeding Congresses (January 3, 1961-January 3, 1989); chairman, Committee on Banking, Finance, and Urban Affairs (Ninety-seventh

through One Hundredth Congresses); unsuccessful candidate for reelection in 1988 to the One Hundred First Congress; is a resident of St. Petersburg, Fla., and Newport, R.I.

**STIGLER, William Grady,** a Representative from Oklahoma; born in Stigler, Haskell County, Indian Territory (now Oklahoma), July 7, 1891; attended the public schools; was graduated from Northeastern State College, Tahlequah, Okla., in 1912; attended the law school of the University of Oklahoma at Norman; during the First World War served as a second lieutenant in the Three Hundred and Fifty-seventh Infantry of the Ninetieth Division in 1918 and 1919, with overseas service; attended the University of Grenoble, France, in 1919; was admitted to the Oklahoma bar in 1920 and commenced practice in Stigler, Haskell County, Okla.; city attorney of Stigler, Okla., 1920-1924; served in the Oklahoma State senate, 1924-1932, serving as president pro tempore in 1931; lieutenant colonel in the Forty-fifth Division of the Oklahoma National Guard, 1925-1938; elected as a Democrat to the Seventy-eighth Congress to fill the vacancy caused by the resignation of Jack Nichols; reelected to the Seventy-ninth and to the three succeeding Congresses and served from March 28, 1944, until his death in Stigler, Okla., August 21, 1952; interment in Stigler Cemetery.

**Bibliography:** *DAB*.

**STILES, John Dodson,** a Representative from Pennsylvania; born in Town Hill, Luzerne County, Pa., January 15, 1822; completed preparatory studies; studied law; was admitted to the bar in 1844 and practiced in Allentown, Lehigh County; elected district attorney of Lehigh County in 1853 and served three years; delegate to the Democratic National Convention in 1856, 1864, and 1868; was also a delegate to the Union National Convention at Philadelphia in 1866; elected as a Democrat to the Thirty-seventh Congress to fill the vacancy caused by the death of Thomas B. Cooper; reelected to the Thirty-eighth Congress and served from June 3, 1862, to March 3, 1865; elected to the Forty-first Congress (March 4, 1869-March 3, 1871); was not a candidate for renomination in 1870; resumed the practice of law; died in Allentown, Pa., October 29, 1896; interment in Fairview Cemetery.

**STILES, William Henry** (grandson of Joseph Clay), a Representative from Georgia; born in Savannah, Ga., January 1, 1808; completed preparatory studies; studied law at Yale College; was admitted to the bar in 1831 and commenced practice in Savannah, Ga.; solicitor general for the eastern district of Georgia, 1833-1836; elected as a Democrat to the Twenty-eighth Congress (March 4, 1843-March 3, 1845); appointed on April 19, 1845, by President James K. Polk as Chargé d'Affaires to Austria and served until October 1849; resumed the practice of law in Savannah; member of the Georgia State house of representatives and served as speaker in 1858; delegate from the State at large to the commercial congress held at Montgomery, Ala., in 1858; delegate to the Democratic National Convention at Baltimore in 1860; served as colonel in the Confederate Army during the Civil War; engaged in literary pursuits; died in Savannah, Ga., December 20, 1865; interment in Laurel Grove Cemetery.

**Bibliography:** Harwell, Christopher L. "William Stiles: Georgia Gentleman-Politician." Ph.D. dissertation, Emory University, 1959.

**STILWELL, Thomas Neel,** a Representative from Indiana; born in Stilwell, Ohio, August 29, 1830; received a thorough English education; attended Oxford and College Hill Colleges; studied law; was admitted to the bar in 1852 and began practice in Anderson, Ind.; member of the Indiana State house of representatives in 1856; served in the Union Army during the Civil War; elected as a Republican to the Thirty-ninth Congress (March 4, 1865-March 3, 1867); was not a candidate for renomination in 1866 to the Fortieth Congress; appointed Minister Resident to Venezuela on August 30, 1867, and served until June 1868; served as president of the First

National Bank of Anderson until his death as the result of a gunshot wound in Anderson, Ind., January 14, 1874; interment in Maplewood Cemetery.

**STINESS, Walter Russell,** a Representative from Rhode Island; born in Smithfield, Providence County, R.I., March 13, 1854; attended the public schools and was a student at Brown University, Providence, R.I., in 1873 and 1874; served in the city council in 1875; was graduated from Boston University Law School in 1877; was admitted to the bar the same year and commenced practice in Providence, R.I.; member of the Rhode Island State house of representatives, 1878-1881; clerk of the justice court of Providence, 1879-1885; aide-de-camp on the staff of Governor Augustus O. Bourn, 1883-1885; Rhode Island State railroad commissioner, 1888-1891; assistant judge advocate general of Rhode Island, 1888-1898; judge advocate general, 1898-1913; member of the Rhode Island State senate, 1904-1909; chairman of the commission to revise the statutes of Rhode Island in 1909; United States attorney for the district of Rhode Island, 1911-1914; elected as a Republican to the Sixty-fourth and to the three succeeding Congresses (March 4, 1915-March 3, 1923); was not a candidate for renomination in 1922 to the Sixty-eighth Congress; lived in retirement in Warwick, R.I., until his death there March 17, 1924; interment in Swan Point Cemetery, Providence, R.I.

**STINSON, K. William,** a Representative from Washington; born in Grand Rapids, Kent County, Mich., April 20, 1930; attended the public schools and Grand Rapids Junior College for two years; graduated in 1952 from the University of Michigan at Ann Arbor; entered the executive training program of Westinghouse Electric Corp.; enlisted in the United States Navy in January 1953, attended Officers' Candidate School, and served until June 1956; employed with Westinghouse Electric Corp., Seattle, Wash., 1956-1959; manufacturer's representative to the marine and sporting goods business, 1959-1962; elected as a Republican to the Eighty-eighth Congress (January 3, 1963-January 3, 1965); unsuccessful candidate for reelection in 1964 to the Eighty-ninth Congress; is a resident of Battle Ground, Wash.

**STIRK, Samuel,** a Delegate from Georgia; born in Savannah, Ga.; clerk of executive council in 1777; lieutenant colonel in Georgia militia 1778-1779; elected as a Delegate to the Continental Congress on August 16, 1781, but did not attend; attorney general of Georgia in 1781 and reelected in 1783; justice of Chatham County 1786-1789.

**STIVERS, Moses Dunning,** a Representative from New York; born near Beemerville, Sussex County, N.J., December 30, 1828; attended common and private schools and Mount Retirement Seminary in Wantage, Sussex County, N.J.; moved with his father to Ridgebury, N.Y., in 1845 and completed his education; taught school; engaged in mercantile pursuits in Ridgebury and later in Middletown, N.Y., 1855-1864; clerk of Orange County 1864-1867 and resided in Goshen, N.Y.; returned to Middletown and became proprietor of the Orange County Press in 1868 and was also one of the proprietors and editors of the Middletown Daily Press; appointed by President Ulysses S. Grant as United States collector of internal revenue for the eleventh district of New York in 1869 and served until 1883; delegate to the Republican National Convention in 1880; engaged in banking; unsuccessful Republican candidate for election in 1884 to the Forty-ninth Congress to fill the vacancy caused by the death of Lewis Beach and for election in 1886 to the Fiftieth Congress; elected as a Republican to the Fifty-first Congress (March 4, 1889-March 3, 1891); was not a candidate for renomination in 1890; engaged in banking; died in Middletown, N.Y., February 2, 1895; interment in Hillside Cemetery.

**ST. JOHN, Charles,** a Representative from New York; born at Mount Hope, Orange County, N.Y., October 8, 1818; attended the common schools and Goshen and Newburgh (N.Y.) Academies; engaged in lumbering on the Delaware River and in mercantile pursuits and banking at Port Jervis, N.Y.; served as internal revenue collector and later as president of the Barrett Bridge Co.; elected as a Republican to the Forty-second and Forty-third Congresses (March 4, 1871-March 3, 1875); resumed his former business activities; died in Port Jervis, N.Y., July 6, 1891; interment in Laurel Grove Cemetery.

**ST. JOHN, Daniel Bennett,** a Representative from New York; born in Sharon, Conn., October 8, 1808; engaged in mercantile pursuits and the real estate business at Monticello, N.Y., in 1831; member of the State assembly in 1840; elected as a Whig to the Thirtieth Congress (March 4, 1847-March 3, 1849); moved to Newburgh, N.Y.; delegate to the Constitutional-Union National Convention in 1860; unsuccessful Democratic candidate for election to the Thirty-seventh Congress in 1860; member of the State senate in 1875; delegate to the Democratic National Convention in 1876; chief registrar in the banking department of New York State; died in New York City February 18, 1890; interment in Woodlawn Cemetery, Newburgh, Orange County, N.Y.

**ST. JOHN, Henry,** a Representative from Ohio; born in Washington County, Vt., July 16, 1783; received a limited schooling; served during the War of 1812; moved to Wooster, Ohio, in 1815, to Crawford County, Ohio, in 1828, and in 1837 to Seneca County, where he engaged in agricultural pursuits, milling, and storekeeping near Tiffin, Ohio; elected as a Democrat to the Twenty-eighth and Twenty-ninth Congresses (March 4, 1843-March 3, 1847); was not a candidate for renomination; resumed agricultural pursuits; resided in Tiffin, Ohio, where he died in May 1869.

**ST. MARTIN, Louis,** a Representative from Louisiana; born in St. Charles Parish, La., on May 17, 1820; attended St. Mary's College, Missouri, and Jefferson College, Louisiana; entered a notarial office and studied law until appointed a clerk in the post office at New Orleans; elected a member of the Louisiana State house of representatives in 1840; appointed by President James K. Polk as register of the United States land office for the southeastern district of Louisiana in 1846 and served until 1849; member of the Louisiana State house of representatives, 1846-1850; elected as a Democrat to the Thirty-second Congress (March 4, 1851-March 3, 1853); was not a candidate for reelection in 1852 to the Thirty-third Congress; engaged in mercantile pursuits; appointed register of voters for the city of New Orleans by Governor Robert C. Wickliffe and reappointed by Governor Thomas O. Moore; credentials of election to the Thirty-ninth Congress were presented, but as the State had not been readmitted to representation, did not qualify; presented credentials as a Member-elect to the Forty-first Congress, but the House decided that no valid election had been held; delegate to the Democratic National Conventions of 1852, 1868, 1876, and 1880; again engaged in mercantile pursuits; elected as a Democrat to the Forty-ninth Congress (March 4, 1885-March 3, 1887); was connected with the office of public accounts in the city hall at the time of his death; died in New Orleans, La., February 9, 1893; interment in St. Vincent de Paul Cemetery.

**STOBBS, George Russell,** a Representative from Massachusetts; born in Webster, Worcester County, Mass., February 7, 1877; attended the public schools of Webster, and Phillips Exeter Academy, Exeter, N.H.; graduated from Harvard University, in 1899 and from its law department in 1902; admitted to the bar in 1902 and commenced practice in Worcester, Mass.; special justice for the central district court of Worcester 1909-1916; captain in the State Guard of Massachusetts 1917-1920; assistant district attorney for the middle district of Massachusetts 1917-1921; elected as a Republican to the Sixty-ninth, Seventieth, and Seventy-first

Congresses (March 4, 1925-March 3, 1931); was not a candidate for renomination in 1930; one of the managers appointed by the House of Representatives in 1926 to conduct the impeachment proceedings against George W. English, judge of the United States District Court for the Eastern District of Illinois; major and subsequently lieutenant colonel in the Judge Advocate General's Department, Officers' Reserve Corps, 1927-1942; delegate to the Interparliamentary Congress, London, England, in 1930; delegate to the Republican National Convention in 1932, and to the Massachusetts Republican conventions in 1940 and 1942; resumed the practice of law in Worcester, Mass.; died in Worcester, Mass., December 23, 1966; interment in Rural Cemetery.

**STOCKBRIDGE, Francis Brown,** a Senator from Michigan; born in Bath, Maine, April 9, 1826; attended the common schools; clerk in a wholesale house in Boston 1843-1847; moved to Chicago, Ill., and opened a lumber yard; moved to Saugatuck, Allegan County, Mich., in 1851 and engaged in the operation of sawmills; also interested in mercantile pursuits; moved to Kalamazoo, Mich., in 1863 and engaged in the lumber business; member, State house of representatives 1869; member, State senate 1871; elected as a Republican to the United States Senate in 1887; reelected in 1893 and served from March 4, 1887, until his death in Chicago, Ill., on April 30, 1894; chairman, Committee on Fisheries (Fiftieth through Fifty-second Congresses); interment in Mountain Home Cemetery, Kalamazoo, Mich.

**STOCKBRIDGE, Henry, Jr.,** a Representative from Maryland; born in Baltimore, Md., September 18, 1856; attended public and private schools and Williston Academy, Easthampton, Mass.; was graduated from Amherst (Mass.) College in 1877 and from the law school of the University of Maryland at Baltimore in 1878; was admitted to the bar in the latter year and commenced practice in Baltimore; employed on the editorial staff of the Baltimore Herald and later with the Baltimore American; appointed as an examiner in equity by the supreme bench of Baltimore in December 1882; elected as a Republican to the Fifty-first Congress (March 4, 1889-March 3, 1891); declined to be a candidate for renomination in 1890; served as United States commissioner of immigration for the port of Baltimore 1891-1893; elected judge of the supreme bench of Baltimore in November 1896 and served until 1911; regent of the University of Maryland 1907-1920; appointed judge of the Maryland Court of Appeals on April 13, 1911, and was elected in November 1911 for a term of fifteen years; died in Baltimore, Md., March 22, 1924; interment in Loudon Park Cemetery.

**Bibliography:** *DAB.*

**STOCKDALE, Thomas Ringland,** a Representative from Mississippi; born near West Union Church, Greene County, Pa., March 28, 1828; was graduated from Jefferson College, Canonsburg, Pa., in 1856; moved to Pike County, Miss., in 1857 and taught school; was graduated from the University of Mississippi at Oxford in 1859; studied law; was admitted to the bar in 1859 and practiced in Woodville, Miss., 1859-1861; during the Civil War enlisted in the Confederate Army as a private in the Sixteenth Mississippi Infantry in 1861, being promoted successively to lieutenant, adjutant, and major of that regiment; at the close of the war resumed the practice of law in Summit, Miss.; delegate to the Democratic National Convention in 1868; elected as a Democrat to the Fiftieth and to the three succeeding Congresses (March 4, 1887-March 3, 1895); was an unsuccessful candidate for renomination; appointed judge of the State supreme court December 1, 1896; died in Summit, Pike County, Miss., January 8, 1899; interment in Woodlawn Cemetery.

**Bibliography:** *DAB.*

**STOCKMAN, David Alan,** a Representative from Michigan; born in Fort Hood, Bell County, Tex., November 10, 1946; educated in the public schools of St. Joseph, Mich., and graduated from

Lakeshore High School in 1964; B.A., Michigan State University, East Lansing, 1968; pursued graduate studies, Harvard University, 1968-1970, 1974-1975; served as special assistant to Representative John B. Anderson of Illinois, 1970-1972; executive director, United States House of Representatives Republican Conference, 1972-1975; elected as a Republican to the Ninety-fifth and to the two succeeding Congresses, and served from January 3, 1977 until his resignation on January 27, 1981; director of the Office of Management and Budget, 1981-1985; managing director, Salomon Brothers, Inc., New York City, 1985-1988; senior managing director, The Blackstone Group, New York City; is a resident of Greenwich, Conn.

**STOCKMAN, Lowell,** a Representative from Oregon; born on a farm near Helix, Umatilla County, Oreg., April 12, 1901; attended the public schools at Pendleton, Oreg.; was graduated from Oregon State University at Corvallis in 1922; engaged in agricultural pursuits in 1922; member of the Pendleton School Board and the Oregon Liquor Control Commission; elected as a Republican to the Seventy-eighth and to the four succeeding Congresses (January 3, 1943-January 3, 1953); was not a candidate for renomination in 1952 to the Eighty-third Congress; resumed farming until 1959; member of the Theodore Roosevelt Centennial Commission, 1956-1959; vice president of Oregon Fiber Products, Inc., and treasurer of Pilot Rock Lumber Co.; moved to Bellevue, Wash., in 1959 and operated a trailer court until his death on August 9, 1962; interment on University of Washington property near Pack Forest, Wash.

**STOCKMAN, Stephen E.,** a Representative from Texas; born in Bloomfield Hills, Oakland County, Mich., November 14, 1956; graduated, Dondero High School, Royal Oak, Mich., 1975; moved to Texas in 1979 and attended San Jacinto College, Pasadena, Tex., 1985-1986; B.S., University of Houston, Clear Lake, 1990; accountant, McKee Environmental Health; unsuccessful candidate in 1990 for nomination to the One Hundred Second Congress, and in 1992 for election to the One Hundred Third Congress; elected as a Republican to the One Hundred Fourth Congress (January 3, 1995-January 3, 1997); is a resident of Friendswood, Tex.

**STOCKSLAGER, Strother Madison,** a Representative from Indiana; born in Mauckport, Harrison County, Ind., May 7, 1842; attended the common schools, Corydon High School, and Indiana University at Bloomington; taught school; served in the Union Army during the Civil War as second lieutenant and captain in the Thirteenth Indiana Volunteer Cavalry, which he had assisted to organize; was mustered out as captain and returned to Mauckport; deputy county auditor of Harrison County, 1866-1868; deputy county clerk of Harrison County, 1868-1870; appointed by President Andrew Johnson as assessor of internal revenue in 1867, but was not confirmed by the United States Senate; studied law; was admitted to the bar in Corydon, Ind., in 1871 and practiced in Indiana and Kentucky; member of the Indiana State senate, 1874-1878; editor of the Corydon Democrat, 1879-1882; elected as a Democrat to the Forty-seventh and Forty-eighth Congresses (March 4, 1881-March 3, 1885); chairman, Committee on Public Buildings and Grounds (Forty-eighth Congress); was an unsuccessful candidate for renomination in 1884 to the Forty-ninth Congress; resumed the practice of law in Corydon; appointed assistant commissioner of the General Land Office on October 1, 1885, and commissioner on March 27, 1888; resigned March 4, 1889, but remained in charge until June 20, 1889; continued the practice of law in Washington, D.C.; unsuccessful candidate for election in 1894 to the Fifty-fourth Congress; delegate to the Democratic National Convention of 1896; served as legal expert in the Department of Labor in 1918; resumed the practice of law in Washington, D.C., until his death there on June 1, 1930; interment in Arlington National Cemetery, Va.

**STOCKTON, John Potter** (son of Robert Field Stockton, grandson of Richard Stockton [1764-1828], great-grandson of Richard Stockton [1730-1781]), a Senator from New Jersey; born in

Princeton, N.J., August 2, 1826; attended private schools and graduated from the College of New Jersey (now Princeton University) in 1843; studied law; was admitted to the bar in 1846 and practiced in Princeton and Trenton, N.J.; State reporter to the court of chancery, 1852-1858; appointed Minister Resident at Rome (Holy See) on June 15 1858, and served until May 1861; nominated to be Minister to Austria, but the nomination was rejected by the Senate; practiced law in Trenton, N.J.; presented credentials as a Democratic Senator-elect to the United States Senate, and served from March 15, 1865 to March 27, 1866, when, the election being in dispute, the Senate declared the seat vacant; again elected as a Democrat to the United States Senate, and served from March 4, 1869 to March 3, 1875; resumed the practice of his profession; attorney general of New Jersey, 1877-1897; died in New York City, January 22, 1900; interment in Princeton Cemetery, Princeton, N.J.

**Bibliography:** *DAB*; Stockton, Thomas Coates. *The Stockton Family of New Jersey*. Washington, D.C.: Carnahan Press, 1911.

**STOCKTON, Richard** (father of Richard Stockton [1764-1828], grandfather of Richard Stockton Field and Robert Field Stockton, and great-grandfather of John Potter Stockton), a Delegate from New Jersey; born at "Morven," near Princeton, Somerset County, N.J., October 1, 1730; attended Nottingham Academy in Cecil County, Md., and was graduated in the first class from Princeton College, in 1748; studied law; was admitted to the bar in 1754 and commenced practice in Princeton, N.J.; member of the executive council of New Jersey from November 2, 1768 to June 17, 1776; associate justice of the State supreme court from February 28, 1774 to June 17, 1776; Member of the Continental Congress in 1776; a signer of the Declaration of Independence; unsuccessful candidate for Governor of New Jersey on August 31, 1776; elected chief justice of the State supreme court on August 31, 1776, but declined the office; resumed the practice of law; died at "Morven," near Princeton, N.J., February 28, 1781; interment in Stoney Brook Meeting House Burial Ground near Princeton, N.J.

**Bibliography:** *DAB*.

**STOCKTON, Richard** (son of Richard Stockton [1730-1781], father of Robert Field Stockton, and grandfather of John Potter Stockton), a Senator and a Representative from New Jersey; born in Princeton, N.J., April 17, 1764; tutored privately; graduated from the College of New Jersey (now Princeton University) in 1779; studied law; was admitted to the bar in 1784 and commenced practice in Princeton, N.J.; elected as a Federalist to the United States Senate to fill the vacancy caused by the resignation of Frederick Frelinghuysen, and served from November 12, 1796 to March 3, 1799; declined to be a candidate for reelection; unsuccessful candidate for Governor of New Jersey in 1801, 1803, and 1804; elected as a Federalist to the Thirteenth Congress (March 4, 1813-March 3, 1815); declined to be a candidate for renomination in 1814 to the Fourteenth Congress; resumed the practice of his profession; died at "Morven," near Princeton, Mercer County, N.J., March 7, 1828; interment in Princeton Cemetery, Princeton, N.J.

**Bibliography:** *DAB*; Stockton, Thomas Coates. *The Stockton Family of New Jersey*. Washington, D.C.: Carnahan Press, 1911.

**STOCKTON, Robert Field** (son of Richard Stockton [1764-1828], father of John Potter Stockton, grandson of Richard Stockton [1730-1781]), a Senator from New Jersey; born in Princeton, N.J., August 20, 1795; was privately tutored; attended the College of New Jersey (now Princeton University); entered the United States Navy in 1811, served in the War of 1812, the war with Algiers, and the Mexican War; was sent to the Pacific coast in 1845 and, in cooperation with the land forces, captured the Mexican capital of California and organized a civil government; attained the rank of commodore; returned home and resigned his commission in 1850; elected as a Democrat to the United States Senate and served from March 4, 1851, until his resignation on January 10, 1853; president

of the Delaware & Raritan Canal 1853-1866; member of the peace convention of 1861 held in Washington, D.C., in an effort to devise means to prevent the impending war; retired from public life; died in Princeton, N.J., October 7, 1866; interment in Princeton Cemetery.

**Bibliography:** *DAB*; Bayard, Samuel. *A Sketch of the Life of Com. Robert F. Stockton*. New York: Derby and Jackson, 1856; Stockton, Thomas Coates. *The Stockton Family of New Jersey*. Washington, D.C.: Carnahan Press, 1911.

**STODDARD, Ebenezer,** a Representative from Connecticut; born in Union, Tolland County, Conn., May 6, 1785; attended Woodstock Academy in 1802 and in 1803, and was graduated from Brown University, Providence, R.I., in 1807; studied law; was admitted to the bar in 1810 and commenced practice in West Woodstock, Conn.; elected to the Seventeenth and Eighteenth Congresses (March 4, 1821-March 3, 1825); served in the Connecticut State senate, 1825-1827; Lieutenant Governor of Connecticut in 1833, and 1835-1837; practiced law; died in West Woodstock, Conn., on August 19, 1847; interment in Bungay Cemetery.

**STODDERT, John Truman,** a Representative from Maryland; born in Smith Point, Nanjemoy, Charles County, Md., October 1, 1790; studied under private teachers and was graduated from Princeton College in 1810; studied law; was admitted to the bar and practiced; served in the War of 1812; member of the State house of delegates in 1820; elected as a Jacksonian to the Twenty-third Congress (March 4, 1833-March 3, 1835); engaged in agricultural pursuits; died at the "Wicomico House," West Hatton estate, in Charles County, Md., July 19, 1870; interment in the family burying ground on his estate.

**STOKELY, Samuel,** a Representative from Ohio; born in Washington, Pa., January 25, 1796; attended private schools; was graduated from Washington College (now Washington and Jefferson College), Washington, Pa., in 1813; studied law; was admitted to the bar and commenced practice in Steubenville, Ohio, in 1817; United States land receiver in 1827 and 1828; member of the State senate in 1837 and 1838; elected as a Whig to the Twenty-seventh Congress (March 4, 1841-March 3, 1843); resumed the practice of law in Steubenville, Jefferson County, Ohio, where he died May 23, 1861; interment in Union Cemetery.

**STOKES, Edward Lowber,** a Representative from Pennsylvania; born in Philadelphia, Pa., September 29, 1880; attended the public schools, graduated from St. Paul's School, Concord, N.H.; employed as a clerk for a trust company and later engaged as an investment dealer; unsuccessful candidate for election to the Pennsylvania house of representatives in 1930; elected as a Republican to the Seventy-second Congress to fill the vacancy caused by the death of George S. Graham; reelected to the Seventy-third Congress and served from November 3, 1931, to January 3, 1935; was not a candidate for renomination but was a gubernatorial candidate in 1934, a candidate for Congress in 1950, and a candidate for mayor and councilman at large in 1952; engaged in investment banking until his retirement in 1955; resident of Newtown Square, Pa.; died November 8, 1964; interment in St. David's Church Burial Grounds, Radnor Township, Pa.

**STOKES, James William,** a Representative from South Carolina; born near Orangeburg, S.C., December 12, 1853; attended the common schools and was graduated from Washington and Lee University, Lexington, Va., in 1876; taught school for twelve years; was graduated in medicine from Vanderbilt University, Nashville, Tenn.; engaged in agricultural pursuits in 1889; president of the State Farmers' Alliance; member of the State senate in 1890; delegate to the Democratic National Convention in 1892; unsuccessful candidate for election in 1892 to the Fifty-third Congress; presented credentials as a Democratic Member-elect to the Fifty-fourth Congress and served from March 4, 1895, to June 1,

1896, when the seat was declared vacant; elected to fill the vacancy thus caused; reelected to the Fifty-fifth, Fifty-sixth, and Fifty-seventh Congresses and served from November 3, 1896, until his death in Orangeburg, Orangeburg County, S.C., July 6, 1901; interment in Sunnyside Cemetery.

**STOKES, Louis,** a Representative from Ohio; born in Cleveland, Cuyahoga County, Ohio, February 23, 1925; educated at Cleveland College of Case Western Reserve University, 1946-1948; J.D., Cleveland Marshall Law School, 1948-1953; served in the United States Army, 1943-1946; was admitted to the bar in 1953 and commenced practice in Cleveland, Ohio; lecturer and writer for universities and bar associations; elected as a Democrat to the Ninety-first and to the thirteen succeeding Congresses (January 3, 1969-January 3, 1997); chairman, Select Committee on Assassinations (Ninety-fifth Congress), Committee on Standards of Official Conduct (Ninety-seventh, Ninety-eighth and One Hundred Second Congresses), Permanent Select Committee on Intelligence (One Hundredth Congress); is a resident of Shaker Heights, Ohio.

**STOKES, Montfort,** a Senator from North Carolina; born in Lunenburg County, Va., March 12, 1762; served in the Revolutionary War in the Continental Navy; was captured by the British and confined for seven months on the British prison ship *Jersey* in New York Harbor; after the Revolutionary War settled in North Carolina and engaged in planting; clerk of the North Carolina State senate, 1786-1791; clerk of the superior court of Rowan County, N.C.; elected as United States Senator in 1804, but declined; trustee of the University of North Carolina at Chapel Hill, 1805-1838; about 1812 settled in Wilkesboro, N.C.; elected in 1816 to the United States Senate to fill the vacancy caused by the resignation of James Turner; elected at same time for the full term, and served from December 4, 1816 to March 3, 1823; chairman, Committee on Post Office and Post Roads (Fifteenth through Seventeenth Congresses); member of the State senate in 1826; member, State house of representatives, 1829-1830; elected Governor of North Carolina by the General Assembly, and served from December 18, 1830 to December 6, 1832; appointed by President Andrew Jackson in 1832 as a member of the Board of Indian Commissioners, and resided at Fort Gibson in what was then unorganized Indian Territory (now Oklahoma); was later appointed as a commissioner to negotiate treaties with various tribes of Indians in the West and Southwest; appointed agent for the Cherokee Indians and served from 1837 to 1842, when he was made sub-agent for the Senecas, Shawnees, and Quapaws; died at Fort Gibson, Indian Territory, on November 4, 1842; interment in Fort Gibson Cemetery.

**Bibliography:** *DAB*; Foster, William. "The Career of Montfort Stokes in North Carolina." *North Carolina Historical Review* 16 (1939): 237-72.

**STOKES, William Brickly,** a Representative from Tennessee; born in Chatham County, N.C., September 9, 1814; attended the common schools; moved to Tennessee; engaged in agricultural pursuits; member of the State house of representatives 1849-1852; served in the State senate in 1855 and 1856; elected as an Opposition Party candidate to the Thirty-sixth Congress (March 4, 1859-March 3, 1861); entered the Union Army May 15, 1862, as major of Tennessee Volunteers; promoted to colonel and subsequently brevetted major general; honorably discharged March 10, 1865; studied law; was admitted to the bar in 1867 and commenced practice in Alexandria, De Kalb County, Tenn.; upon the readmission of the State of Tennessee to representation was elected as an Unconditional Unionist to the Thirty-ninth Congress and reelected as a Republican to the Fortieth and Forty-first Congresses and served from July 24, 1866, to March 3, 1871; unsuccessful candidate for reelection in 1870 to the Forty-second Congress; supervisor of internal revenue for Tennessee; resumed the practice of law; died in

Alexandria, Tenn., March 14, 1897; interment in East View Cemetery.

**STOLL, Philip Henry,** a Representative from South Carolina; born in Little Rock, Marion (now Dillon) County, S.C., November 5, 1874; attended the public schools; was graduated from Wofford College, Spartanburg, S.C., in 1897; teacher in the public schools 1897-1901; studied law; was admitted to the bar in 1901 and commenced practice in Kingstree, Williamsburg County, S.C.; member of the State house of representatives 1905-1906; solicitor of the third judicial circuit from 1908 to 1917, when he resigned; chairman of the Democratic county committee and member of the Democratic State committee 1908-1918; commissioned as a major in the Judge Advocate General's Department of the United States Army in 1917; promoted to the rank of lieutenant colonel in 1918 and served throughout the First World War; elected as a Democrat to the Sixty-sixth Congress to fill the vacancy caused by the death of J. Willard Ragsdale; reelected to the Sixty-seventh Congress and served from October 7, 1919, to March 3, 1923; unsuccessful candidate for renomination in 1922; resumed the practice of law; again a member, State house of representatives, 1929-1931; elected as a judge of the third judicial circuit of South Carolina in 1931 and served until December 6, 1946, when he retired; died in Columbia, S.C., October 29, 1958; interment in Williamsburg Presbyterian Cemetery, Kingstree, S.C.

**STONE, Alfred Parish,** a Representative from Ohio; born in Worthington, Mass., June 28, 1813; attended the common schools; moved to Columbus, Ohio, in 1832 and engaged in mercantile pursuits; elected as a Democrat to the Twenty-eighth Congress to fill the vacancy caused by the death of Heman A. Moore and served from October 8, 1844, to March 3, 1845; was not a candidate for renomination in 1844 to the Twenty-ninth Congress; appointed Ohio State treasurer by Governor Salmon P. Chase in 1857 to fill the vacancy caused by the resignation of W.H. Gibson; was elected and reelected to the same office and served until 1862; appointed as collector of internal revenue for the Columbus district of Ohio in 1862 and served until his death in Columbus, Ohio, August 2, 1865; interment in Greenlawn Cemetery.

**STONE, Charles Warren,** a Representative from Pennsylvania; born in Groton, Middlesex County, Mass., June 29, 1843; attended Lawrence Academy at Groton; graduated from Williams College, Williamstown, Mass., in 1863; moved to Pennsylvania in 1863 and settled in Warren; superintendent of schools of Warren County in 1865; studied law; admitted to the bar in 1867 and commenced practice in Warren; trustee of Pennsylvania State College; member of the Pennsylvania house of representatives in 1870 and 1871; served in the Pennsylvania senate in 1877 and 1878; Lieutenant Governor of Pennsylvania 1879-1883; appointed secretary of the Commonwealth on January 18, 1887, and served until his resignation to accept nomination for Congress; elected as a Republican to the Fifty-first Congress to fill the vacancy caused by the death of Lewis F. Watson; reelected to the Fifty-second and to the three succeeding Congresses and served from November 4, 1890, to March 3, 1899; chairman, Committee on Coinage, Weights, and Measures (Fifty-fourth and Fifty-fifth Congresses); unsuccessful candidate for reelection in 1898 to the Fifty-sixth Congress; unsuccessful candidate for Governor of Pennsylvania in 1898; resumed the practice of law; died at his home near Warren, Pa., August 15, 1912; interment in Oakland Cemetery, Pleasant Township, Warren County, Pa.

**STONE, Claudius Ulysses,** a Representative from Illinois; born on a farm in Menard County, near Greenview, Ill., May 11, 1879; attended the rural school and Western Normal College, Bushnell, Ill.; at the age of seventeen taught in the Bee Grove rural school in Menard County for one year; principal of Brimfield (Ill.) Public Schools for two years; during the Spanish-American War served as a corporal in Company K, Fourth Illinois Volunteer Infantry, from May 1898 to May 1899 with service in Cuba; studied law at the University of Michigan at Ann Arbor and at George Washington University, Washington, D.C.; elected superintendent of schools for Peoria County, Ill., in 1902, reelected in 1906 and served until 1910; president of the Association of County Superintendents of Schools of Illinois in 1909; was admitted to the bar in 1909 and commenced practice in Peoria, Ill.; elected as a Democrat to the Sixty-second, Sixty-third, and Sixty-fourth Congresses (March 4, 1911-March 3, 1917); unsuccessful candidate for reelection in 1916 to the Sixty-fifth Congress; postmaster of Peoria from 1917 until he resigned in October 1920 to practice law; master in chancery of the circuit court of Peoria County from June 5, 1928, to January 20, 1945; editor and publisher of the Peoria Star from 1938 until 1949; died in Peoria, Ill., November 13, 1957; interment in Parkview Memorial Cemetery.

**STONE, David,** a Representative and a Senator from North Carolina; born at "Hope," near Windsor, Bertie County, N.C., February 17, 1770; attended Windsor Academy and graduated from the College of New Jersey (now Princeton University) in 1788; studied law; was admitted to the bar in 1790 and commenced practice in Halifax, N.C.; member, North Carolina State house of commons, 1791-1794; judge of the supreme court of North Carolina, 1794-1798; elected to the Sixth Congress (March 4, 1799-March 3, 1801); elected as a Republican to the United States Senate, and served from March 4, 1801 until his resignation about February 17, 1807; once again a judge; elected Governor of North Carolina by the General Assembly, and served from December 12, 1808 to December 5, 1810; member, State house of commons, 1811-1812; again elected to the United States Senate, and served from March 4, 1813 until his resignation on December 24, 1814; resumed the practice of law; died on his plantation near Raleigh, Wake County, N.C., October 7, 1818; interment in the family burial ground on the banks of the Neuse River, near Raleigh, N.C.

Bibliography: *DAB.*

**STONE, Eben Francis,** a Representative from Massachusetts; born in Newburyport, Essex County, Mass., August 3, 1822; attended North Andover Academy; graduated from Harvard University in 1843 and from Harvard Law School in 1846; admitted to the bar in 1847 and commenced practice in Newburyport, Mass.; president of the common council in 1851; served in the Massachusetts senate in 1857, 1858, and 1861; enlisted in the Union Army during the Civil War and commanded the Forty-eighth Regiment, Massachusetts Volunteer Militia; mayor of Newburyport in 1867; member of the Massachusetts house of representatives in 1867, 1877, 1878, and 1880; elected as a Republican to the Forty-seventh, Forty-eighth, and Forty-ninth Congresses (March 4, 1881-March 3, 1887); was not a candidate for renomination in 1886; resumed the practice of law in Newburyport, Mass., where he died January 22, 1895; interment in Oakhill Cemetery.

**STONE, Frederick** (grandson of Michael Jenifer Stone), a Representative from Maryland; born in Charles County, Md., February 7, 1820; was graduated from St. John's College, Annapolis, Md., in 1839; studied law; was admitted to the bar in 1841 and began practice in Port Tobacco, Md.; appointed by the legislature in 1852 as one of the commissioners to revise the rules of pleading and practice in the State courts; member of the State house of delegates in 1864 and 1865; elected as a Democrat to the Fortieth and Forty-first Congresses (March 4, 1867-March 3, 1871); unsuccessful candidate for reelection in 1870 to the Forty-second Congress; associate judge of the court of appeals 1881-1890; died near La Plata, Md., October 17, 1899; interment in Mount Rest Cemetery, La Plata, Md.

**STONE, James W.,** a Representative from Kentucky; born in Taylorsville, Spencer County, Ky., in 1813; attended the common schools; studied law; admitted to the bar and practiced; held several local offices; member of the Kentucky house of representatives in 1837 and 1839; elected as a Democrat to the Twenty-eighth Congress (March 4, 1843-March 3, 1845); unsuccessful candidate for reelection in 1844 to the Twenty-ninth Congress; elected to the Thirty-second Congress (March 4, 1851-March 3, 1853); unsuccessful candidate for reelection in 1852 to the Thirty-third Congress; died in Taylorsville, Ky., October 13, 1854.

**STONE, John Wesley,** a Representative from Michigan; born in Wadsworth, Medina County, Ohio, July 18, 1838; attended the public schools and Spencer (Ohio) Academy; moved to Allegan County, Mich., in 1856; elected county clerk of Allegan County in 1860; studied law; was admitted to the bar in January 1862 and practiced; reelected county clerk in 1862; prosecuting attorney 1864-1870; president of Allegan Village in 1872; circuit judge of the twentieth judicial circuit of Michigan from April 1873 until his resignation on November 1, 1874; moved to Grand Rapids, Mich., and practiced law; elected as a Republican to the Forty-fifth and Forty-sixth Congresses (March 4, 1877-March 3, 1881); was not a candidate for renomination in 1880; appointed by President Chester A. Arthur as United States attorney for the western Michigan district in 1882; moved to Houghton, Mich., in 1887 and resumed the practice of law; elected circuit judge of the twenty-fifth Michigan circuit in April 1890 and served until December 31, 1909; elected justice of the State supreme court in April 1909 for the term ending December 31, 1917; reelected in 1916 and served until his death in Lansing, Mich., March 24, 1922; interment in Park Cemetery, Marquette, Mich.

Bibliography: *DAB.*

**STONE, Joseph Champlin,** a Representative from Iowa; born in Westport, Essex County, N.Y., July 30, 1829; moved to Iowa Territory in 1844; attended the public schools; was graduated from the medical department of St. Louis University, Missouri, in 1854 and practiced; during the Civil War enlisted as a private in the Union Army and was made adjutant of the First Iowa Cavalry; promoted to captain and assistant adjutant general of Volunteers in 1862 and served until the end of the war; resumed the practice of medicine in Burlington, Iowa; elected as a Republican to the Forty-fifth Congress (March 4, 1877-March 3, 1879); again engaged in the practice of his profession; died in Burlington, Iowa, December 3, 1902; interment in Aspen Grove Cemetery.

**STONE, Michael Jenifer** (brother of Thomas Stone and grandfather of Frederick Stone), a Representative from Maryland; born at "Equality," near Port Tobacco, Charles County, Md., in 1747; completed preparatory studies; member of the State house of delegates 1781-1783; member of the State ratification convention in 1788; elected to the First Congress (March 4, 1789-March 3, 1791); appointed judge of the first judicial district of Maryland in 1791; died in Charles County, Md., in 1812; interment on his estate, "Equality," near Port Tobacco, Charles County, Md.

**STONE, Richard Bernard,** a Senator from Florida; born in New York City, September 22, 1928; attended Dade County, Fla., public schools; B.A., Harvard University, 1949; LL.B., Columbia University Law School, 1954; admitted to the Florida bar in 1955 and commenced practice in Miami; city attorney of Miami, 1966-1967; member, Florida State senate, 1967-1970; Florida secretary of State, 1970-1974; elected as a Democrat to the United States Senate in 1974, for the six-year term commencing January 3, 1975; subsequently appointed by the Governor, January 1, 1975, to fill the vacancy caused by the resignation of Edward Gurney for the term ending January 3, 1975; served from January 1, 1975, until his resignation December 31, 1980; unsuccessful candidate for reelection in 1980; Ambassador at Large and Special Envoy to Central

America, 1983-1984; nominated as Ambassador to Denmark, November 12, 1991, confirmed by the Senate on November 20, 1991, and served until October 1993; attorney and banker; is a resident of Washington, D.C.

**STONE, Thomas** (brother of Michael Jenifer Stone), a Delegate from Maryland; born at Poynton Manor, Charles County, Md., in 1743; completed preparatory studies; studied law; was admitted to the bar in 1764 and commenced practice in Frederick, Md.; moved to Charles County, Md., in 1771; member of the State senate 1779-1783; Member of the Continental Congress in 1775, 1776, 1778, and 1784; a signer of the Declaration of Independence; died in Alexandria, Va., October 5, 1787; interment in the garden of his estate, Habre de Venture, Port Tobacco, Charles County, Md.

**Bibliography:** *DAB*.

**STONE, Ulysses Stevens,** a Representative from Oklahoma; born on a farm near Weldon, De Witt Township, De Witt County, Ill., December 17, 1878; moved with his parents to Jones, Okla., in 1894; attended the country schools and the University of Oklahoma at Norman; engaged in the banking business at Jones, Okla., 1894-1905 and as an oil operator at Norman and Oklahoma City in 1905; was an unsuccessful candidate for Governor of Oklahoma in 1918 and for election to the United States Senate in 1926; elected as a Republican to the Seventy-first Congress (March 4, 1929-March 3, 1931); was an unsuccessful candidate for reelection in 1930 to the Seventy-second Congress and for election in 1934 to the Seventy-fourth Congress; resumed activities as an oil operator and also interested in investments and real estate; died in Oklahoma City, Okla., December 8, 1962; remains were cremated; interment in Rose Hill Abbey.

**STONE, William,** a Representative from Tennessee; born in Sevier County, Tenn. (then North Carolina), January 26, 1791; completed preparatory studies; held several local offices; was a captain in the Creek War of 1813-1814, and served with General Andrew Jackson in the Battle of New Orleans, January 8, 1815; was presented a cane by Congress for bravery in the Battle of Tippecanoe, November 7, 1811; unsuccessful Whig candidate for election in 1836 to the Twenty-fifth Congress; subsequently elected to the Twenty-fifth Congress to fill the vacancy caused by the death of James Standifer and served from September 14, 1837, to March 3, 1839; unsuccessful candidate for reelection to the Twenty-sixth Congress; died in Delphi (later Davis), Sequatchie County, Tenn., February 18, 1853; interment in the family burying ground at Delphi.

**STONE, William Alexis,** a Representative from Pennsylvania; born near Wellsboro, Delmar Township, Tioga County, Pa., April 18, 1846; attended the public schools and the State normal school at Mansfield, Tioga County, Pa.; served in the Civil War as second lieutenant of Company A, One Hundred and Eighty-seventh Regiment, Pennsylvania Volunteer Infantry; after the war became a lieutenant colonel in the Pennsylvania National Guard; studied law in Wellsboro, Pa.; admitted to the bar in 1870 and practiced in Wellsboro and Pittsburgh, Pa.; district attorney of Tioga County from 1874 to 1876, when he resigned and moved to Pittsburgh, Pa.; served as United States attorney for the western district of Pennsylvania, 1880-1886; elected as a Republican to the Fifty-second and to the three succeeding Congresses, and served from March 4, 1891 until his resignation on November 9, 1898; elected Governor of Pennsylvania in 1898, and served from January 17, 1899 to January 20, 1903; resumed the practice of his profession in Pittsburgh, Pa.; prothonotary of the eastern district of Pennsylvania, and served from January 1, 1916 until his death in Philadelphia, Pa., on March 1, 1920; interment in Wellsboro Cemetery, Wellsboro, Pa.

**STONE, William Henry,** a Representative from Missouri; born in Shawangunk, N.Y., November 7, 1828; attended the common schools; moved to St. Louis, Mo., in 1848 and engaged in the manufacture of iron; became president of the St. Louis Hot Pressed Nut & Bolt Company upon its organization in 1867; served in the Missouri State house of representatives; member of the St. Louis Board of Water Commissioners from July 5, 1871, to November 15, 1873, when he resigned, having been elected to Congress; elected as a Democrat to the Forty-third and Forty-fourth Congresses (March 4, 1873-March 3, 1877); chairman, Committee on Expenditures in the Post Office Department (Forty-fourth Congress), Committee on Manufactures (Forty-fourth Congress); was not a candidate for renomination in 1876 to the Forty-fifth Congress; resumed business interests; died in Asbury Park, N.J., July 9, 1901; interment in Bellefontaine Cemetery, St. Louis, Mo.

**STONE, William Joel,** a Representative and a Senator from Missouri; born near Richmond, Madison County, Ky., May 7, 1848; attended the public schools of Richmond, Ky.; graduated from the University of Missouri at Columbia in 1867; studied law; was admitted to the bar in 1869 and commenced practice in Bedford, Ind.; moved to Columbia, Mo., where he was city attorney for a few months in 1870, and later in the same year moved to Nevada, Mo., and continued the practice of law; prosecuting attorney of Vernon County, Mo., 1873-1874; presidential elector on the Democratic ticket in 1876; elected as a Democrat to the Forty-ninth and to the two succeeding Congresses (March 4, 1885-March 3, 1891); was not a candidate for renomination in 1890 to the Fifty-second Congress; chairman, Committee on War Claims (Fiftieth Congress); elected Governor of Missouri in 1892, and served from January 9, 1893 to January 11, 1897; member of the Democratic National Committee, 1896-1904, serving as vice chairman, 1900-1904; moved to St. Louis in 1897 and continued the practice of law; returned to Jefferson City in 1903; elected as a Democrat to the United States Senate in 1902; reelected in 1908 and again in 1914, and served from March 4, 1903 until his death in Washington, D.C., April 14, 1918; chairman, Committee on Additional Accommodations for the Library (Sixty-second Congress), Committee on Revolutionary Claims (Sixty-second Congress), Committee on Corporations Organized in the District of Columbia (Sixty-second Congress), Committee on Foreign Relations (Sixty-third through Sixty-fifth Congresses), Committee on Indian Affairs (Sixty-third Congress); interment in Deepwood Cemetery, Nevada, Mo.

**Bibliography:** Towne, Ruth Warner. *Senator William J. Stone and the Politics of Compromise.* Port Washington, N.Y.: Kennikat Press, 1979.

**STONE, William Johnson,** a Representative from Kentucky; born in Kuttawa, Caldwell (now Lyon) County, Ky., June 26, 1841; attended the common schools and Q.M. Tyler's Collegiate Institute in Cadiz, Trigg County; studied law; during the Civil War served as captain in the Confederate Army; engaged in agricultural pursuits; member of the Kentucky house of representatives in 1867, 1875, and 1883, serving as speaker in 1875; elected as a Democrat to the Forty-ninth and to the four succeeding Congresses (March 4, 1885-March 3, 1895); chairman, Committee on War Claims (Fiftieth Congress); engaged in mercantile pursuits in Kuttawa, Lyon County; Confederate pension commissioner of Kentucky in 1912 and served until his death in Frankfort, Ky., March 12, 1923; interment in New Bethel Cemetery, Lyon County, Ky.

**ST. ONGE, William Leon,** a Representative from Connecticut; born in Putnam, Windham County, Conn., October 9, 1914; attended the secondary schools of Putnam; graduated from Tufts University, Medford, Mass., in 1941 and from the University of Connecticut School of Law at Hartford in 1948; enlisted in the United States Army in 1942, serving in the Army Air Corps in North Africa and Europe, and was discharged as a flight engineer in September 1945;

was admitted to the bar in 1948 and commenced the practice of law in Putnam in 1948; judge of probate court, 1948-1962; served in the State house of representatives, 1941-1942; mayor of the city of Putnam, 1961-1962; judge of city court of Putnam, 1955-1961; prosecutor of city court of Putnam, 1949-1951; member of board of education of Putnam, 1939-1941; chairman and executive director of redevelopment agency of city of Putnam, 1956-1958; corporation counsel of Putnam; elected as a Democrat to the Eighty-eighth and to the three succeeding Congresses, and served from January 3, 1963, until his death in Groton, Conn., May 1, 1970; interment in St. Mary's Cemetery, Putnam, Conn.

**STORER, Bellamy** (father of Bellamy Storer [1847-1922]), a Representative from Ohio; was born in Portland, Maine, March 26, 1796; attended private schools in his native city; entered Bowdoin College, Brunswick, Maine, in 1809; studied law in Boston; was admitted to the bar in Portland in 1817 and commenced practice in Cincinnati, Ohio, the same year; elected as a Whig to the Twenty-fourth Congress (March 4, 1835-March 3, 1837); declined to be a candidate for renomination in 1836 to the Twenty-fifth Congress; professor in Cincinnati Law School 1855-1874; judge of the superior court of Cincinnati from its organization in 1854 until 1872, when he resigned; resumed the practice of law, and died in Cincinnati, Ohio, on June 1, 1875; interment in Spring Grove Cemetery.

**STORER, Bellamy** (son of Bellamy Storer [1796-1875] and uncle of Nicholas Longworth), a Representative from Ohio; born in Cincinnati, Ohio, August 28, 1847; attended the common schools of that city and Dixwell's private Latin school, Boston, Mass.; was graduated from Harvard University in 1867, and from the law school of Cincinnati College in 1869; was admitted to the bar in 1869 and commenced practice in Cincinnati; assistant United States attorney for the southern district of Ohio, 1869-1870; elected as a Republican to the Fifty-second and Fifty-third Congresses (March 4, 1891-March 3, 1895); was not a candidate for renomination in 1894 to the Fifty-fourth Congress; resumed the practice of law; Assistant Secretary of State in 1897; appointed Minister to Belgium on May 4, 1897, and served until May 1899; Minister to Spain from April 12, 1899 to December 1902; Minister to Austria-Hungary from September 26, 1902 until February 1906; resumed the practice of law; died in Paris, France, November 12, 1922; interment in Le Cimetière Neuf, Marvejols, France.

**Bibliography:** *DAB*; Storer, Maria Longworth. *In Memoriam: Bellamy Storer*. Boston: The Merrymount Press, 1923.

**STORER, Clement,** a Representative and a Senator from New Hampshire; born in Kennebunk, Maine, September 20, 1760; completed preparatory studies; studied medicine in Portsmouth, N.H., and in Europe; engaged in the practice of medicine in Portsmouth; captain of militia and held successive ranks to that of major general; member, State house of representatives 1810-1812, serving one year as speaker; elected as a Republican to the Tenth Congress (March 4, 1807-March 3, 1809); elected as a Republican to the United States Senate to fill the vacancy caused by the resignation of Jeremiah Mason and served from June 27, 1817, to March 3, 1819; chairman, Committee on the Militia (Fifteenth Congress); high sheriff of Rockingham County 1818-1824; died in Portsmouth, N.H., November 21, 1830; interment in North Cemetery.

**STORKE, Thomas More,** a Senator from California; born in Santa Barbara, Calif., November 23, 1876; attended the public schools; graduated from Stanford University, Palo Alto, Calif., 1898; editor and publisher of Santa Barbara News-Press and its predecessors; rancher and citrus fruit grower; postmaster, Santa Barbara, Calif., 1914-1921; appointed as a Democrat to the United States Senate to fill the vacancy caused by the resignation of William Gibbs McAdoo and served from November 9, 1938, to January 3, 1939; was not a candidate for election for the full term; resumed newspaper business; member, California Crime Commission 1951-1952; member of the board of regents of University of California 1955-1960; died in Santa Barbara, Calif., October 12, 1971; interment in Santa Barbara Cemetery.

**Bibliography:** Storke, Thomas. *California Editor.* Los Angeles: Westernlore Press, 1958; Storke, Thomas. *I Write for Freedom.* Fresno: McNally and Loftin, 1963.

**STORM, Frederic,** a Representative from New York; born in Alsace, France, July 2, 1844; immigrated to the United States in 1846 with his parents, who settled in New York City; attended the public schools of New York City; engaged in the cigar manufacturing business; member of the State constitutional convention in 1894; elected to the State assembly in 1895; member of the Queens County Republican committee 1894-1900 and was three times its chairman; founder of Flushing Hospital; elected as a Republican to the Fifty-seventh Congress (March 4, 1901-March 3, 1903); unsuccessful candidate for reelection in 1902 to the Fifty-eighth Congress; after leaving Congress engaged in banking in Bayside; founded the Bayside National Bank in 1905 and was its president until his resignation in 1920; resided in Bayside, Flushing, N.Y., until his death in that city on June 9, 1935; interment in Flushing Cemetery, Flushing, N.Y.

**STORM, John Brutzman,** a Representative from Pennsylvania; born in Hamilton Township, Monroe County, Pa., September 19, 1838; attended the common schools, and was graduated from Dickinson College, Carlisle, Pa., in 1861; studied law; was admitted to the bar in 1863 and commenced practice in Stroudsburg, Monroe County; county superintendent of public schools for seven years; elected as a Democrat to the Forty-second and Forty-third Congresses (March 4, 1871-March 3, 1875); was not a candidate for renomination in 1874; elected to the Forty-eighth and Forty-ninth Congresses (March 4, 1883-March 3, 1887); was not a candidate for renomination in 1886; resumed the practice of law; president judge of the forty-third judicial district of Pennsylvania; died in Stroudsburg, Monroe County, Pa., on August 13, 1901; interment in Stroudsburg Cemetery.

**STORRS, Henry Randolph** (brother of William Lucius Storrs), a Representative from New York; born in Middletown, Conn., September 3, 1787; was graduated from Yale College in 1804; studied law; was admitted to the bar in 1807 and commenced practice in Champion, Jefferson County, N.Y.; later practiced in Whitesboro and Utica, N.Y.; elected as a Federalist to the Fifteenth and Sixteenth Congresses (March 4, 1817-March 3, 1821); unsuccessful candidate for renomination in 1820; elected to the Eighteenth and to the three succeeding Congresses (March 4, 1823-March 3, 1831); chairman, Committee on Naval Affairs (Nineteenth Congress); one of the managers appointed by the House of Representatives in 1830 to conduct the impeachment proceedings against James H. Peck, United States judge for the district of Missouri; presiding judge of the court of common pleas of Oneida County 1825-1829; moved to New York City and practiced law; died in New Haven, Conn., July 29, 1837; interment in Grove Street Cemetery.

**STORRS, William Lucius** (brother of Henry Randolph Storrs), a Representative from Connecticut; born in Middletown, Conn., March 25, 1795; was graduated from Yale College in 1814; studied law and was admitted to the bar in Whitestown, N.Y., in 1817; returned to Connecticut the same year and commenced practice in Middletown; member of the State house of representatives 1827-1829 and again in 1834; served as speaker in 1834; elected to the Twenty-first and Twenty-second Congresses (March 4, 1829-March 3, 1833); was not a candidate for renomination in 1832; elected as a Whig to the Twenty-sixth Congress and served from March 1839 until his resignation in June 1840; appointed associate judge of the

Connecticut Supreme Court in 1840 and promoted to chief justice in 1856, in which capacity he served until his death; professor of law in the Wesleyan University at Middletown 1841-1846; professor of law at Yale College in 1846 and 1847; died in Hartford, Conn., June 25, 1861; interment in Old North Cemetery.

**STORY, Joseph,** a Representative from Massachusetts; born in Marblehead, Mass., September 18, 1779; attended Marblehead Academy; was graduated from Harvard University in 1798; studied law; was admitted to the bar in 1801 and commenced practice in Salem; member of the Massachusetts house of representatives, 1805-1807; elected as a Republican to the Tenth Congress to fill the vacancy caused by the death of Jacob Crowninshield and served from May 23, 1808, to March 3, 1809; was not a candidate for renomination in 1808 to the Eleventh Congress; again a member of the Massachusetts house of representatives in 1811, and served as speaker; published commentaries on the Constitution, and also other works; elected as an overseer of Harvard University in 1818 and as professor of law in the same institution in 1829, a position which he held until his death; delegate to the Massachusetts constitutional convention in 1820; declined the position of chief justice of the Massachusetts Supreme Court in 1831; nominated on November 15, 1811 by President James Madison as an Associate Justice of the United States Supreme Court; was confirmed by the Senate on November 18, 1811, and served until his death in Cambridge, Mass., September 10, 1845; interment in Mount Auburn Cemetery.

Bibliography: *DAB*; Dunne, Gerald T. *Justice Joseph Story and the Rise of the Supreme Court.* New York: Simon and Schuster, 1970; Story, Joseph. *Joseph Story; A Collection of Writings By and About An Eminent American Jurist.* Edited by Mortimer D. Schwartz and John C. Hogan. New York: Oceana Publications, 1959.

**STOUGHTON, William Lewis,** a Representative from Michigan; born in Bangor, N.Y., March 20, 1827; attended Kirkland, Painesville, and Madison Academies in Ohio; studied law in Ohio, Indiana, and Michigan 1849-1851; was admitted to the bar and commenced practice in Sturgis, Mich., in 1851; prosecuting attorney 1855-1859; delegate to the Republican National Convention in 1860; appointed by President Abraham Lincoln as United States district attorney for the Michigan district in March 1861, but resigned a few months later to enter the Union Army; served as colonel and brigadier general and was promoted to the rank of major general by brevet; resigned in August 1864 because of ill health and resumed the practice of his profession in Sturgis, St. Joseph County, Mich., in 1865; member of the Michigan State Constitutional convention in 1867; attorney general of Michigan in 1867 and 1868; elected as a Republican to the Forty-first and Forty-second Congresses (March 4, 1869-March 3, 1873); again engaged in the practice of his profession in May 1874; died in Sturgis, Mich., on June 6, 1888; interment in Oak Lawn Cemetery.

**STOUT, Byron Gray,** a Representative from Michigan; born in Richmond, Ontario County, N.Y., January 12, 1829; moved with his parents to Michigan in 1831; attended the common schools; was graduated from the University of Michigan at Ann Arbor in 1851; studied law; superintendent and principal of Pontiac High School in 1853 and 1854; member of the State house of representatives in 1855 and 1857, serving as speaker in the latter year; member of the State senate in 1860 and served as president pro tempore; member of the Union Convention of Conservatives at Philadelphia in 1866; delegate to the Democratic National Conventions in 1868, 1880, and 1888; engaged in private banking prior to 1869; elected as a Democrat to the Fifty-second Congress (March 4, 1891-March 3, 1893); was not a candidate for reelection in 1892 to the Fifty-third Congress; president of the Oakland County Bank 1893-1896; died in Pontiac, Oakland County, Mich., June 19, 1896; interment in Oak Hill Cemetery.

**STOUT, Lansing,** a Representative from Oregon; born in Watertown, Jefferson County, N.Y., March 27, 1828; attended the public schools; studied law; was admitted to the bar; moved to Placer County, Calif., in 1852 and commenced the practice of law; member of the California assembly in 1855; moved to Portland, Oreg., in 1857 and continued the practice of his profession; judge of the Multnomah County Court in 1858; was elected as a Democrat to the Thirty-sixth Congress (March 4, 1859-March 3, 1861); was not a candidate for renomination in 1860; resumed the practice of his profession in Portland; elected to the Oregon senate in June 1868 and served until his death in Portland, Multnomah County, Oreg., March 4, 1871; interment in Riverview Cemetery.

**STOUT, Tom,** a Representative from Montana; born in New London, Ralls County, Mo., May 20, 1879; attended the common schools, Warrenburg (Mo.) State Normal School, and the University of Missouri at Columbia; taught school; studied law; was admitted to the Missouri bar in 1901 but did not practice; moved to Lewistown, Mont., in 1902; engaged in the newspaper business and was editor and publisher of the Fergus County Democrat 1902-1916 and the Lewistown Democrat News 1916-1946; delegate to the Democratic National Convention in 1908 and to all State conventions from 1904 to 1946; member of the State senate of Montana 1911-1913; elected as a Democrat to the Sixty-third and Sixty-fourth Congresses (March 4, 1913-March 3, 1917); chairman, Committee on Expenditures in the Department of the Interior (Sixty-fourth Congress); was not a candidate for renomination in 1916; member of the Montana Public Service commission 1930-1932; elected to the State house of representatives in 1942, 1944, and 1946; editoral writer for the Billings (Mont.) Gazette from 1947 to 1960; resided in Billings, Mont., until his death there on December 26, 1965; interment in Mountview Cemetery.

**STOVER, John Hubler,** a Representative from Missouri; born in Aaronsburg, Centre County, Pa., April 24, 1833; completed preparatory studies at Bellefonte Academy; studied law; was admitted to the bar in 1857 and commenced practice in Bellefonte, Pa.; held several local offices; district attorney of Center County 1860-1862; enlisted in the Union Army in 1861 as a private, and was successively a captain and a major; commissioned as a colonel of the One Hundred and Eighty-fourth Regiment, Pennsylvania Volunteer Infantry; after the war moved to Versailles, Morgan County, Mo., and resumed the practice of law; district attorney of Morgan County from 1866 to 1868; elected as a Republican to the Fortieth Congress to fill the vacancy caused by the resignation of Joseph W. McClurg and served from December 7, 1868, to March 3, 1869; was not a candidate for renomination in 1868 to the Forty-first Congress; resumed the practice of his profession; engaged in the real estate business and was also interested in mining pursuits at Versailles, Mo.; delegate to the Centennial Exposition at Philadelphia in 1876; unsuccessful candidate for election in 1876 to the Forty-fifth Congress; died at Aurora Springs, Mo., October 27, 1889; interment in the City Cemetery, Versailles, Morgan County, Mo.

**STOW, Silas,** a Representative from New York; born in Middlefield, Middlesex County, Conn., December 21, 1773; attended the common schools; studied law, but never practiced; moved to Lowville, Lewis County, N.Y., and engaged in agricultural pursuits; became land agent for Nicholas Low and moved to Oneida County in 1797; appointed judge of Oneida County, January 28, 1801; returned to Lewis County; elected as a Republican to the Twelfth Congress (March 4, 1811-March 3, 1813); sheriff of Lewis County in 1814 and 1815; judge of the same county 1815-1823; died in Lowville, N.Y., January 19, 1827; interment in East State Street Burying Ground.

**STOWELL, William Henry Harrison,** a Representative from Virginia; born in Windsor, Vt., July 26, 1840; attended the public schools in Boston, Mass., and was graduated from Boston Latin School in 1860; engaged in mercantile pursuits; moved to Virginia in

1865; collector of internal revenue for the fourth district in 1869; elected as a Republican to the Forty-second, Forty-third, and Forty-fourth Congresses (March 4, 1871-March 3, 1877); was not a candidate for renomination in 1876; delegate to the Republican National Convention in 1876; moved to Appleton, Wis., in 1880 and engaged in paper manufacturing; moved to Duluth, Minn., in 1886 and engaged in paper and steel manufacturing; president of the Manufacturers Bank of West Duluth 1889-1895; correspondent in Paris, France, for various newspapers; moved to Amherst, Mass., in 1914, where he died on April 27, 1922; interment in Woodlawn Cemetery, New York City.

**STOWER, John G.,** a Representative from New York; born in Madison, Madison County, N.Y.; completed preparatory studies; elected as a Jacksonian to the Twentieth Congress (March 4, 1827-March 3, 1829); member of the State senate in 1833 and 1834.

**STRADER, Peter Wilson,** a Representative from Ohio; born in Shawnee, Warren County, N.J., November 6, 1818; moved with his parents to Lebanon, Ohio, in 1819; attended the common schools; worked in a printing office for three years; moved to Cincinnati, Ohio, in 1835; connected with the steamboat interests on the Ohio and Mississippi Rivers as a clerk and an engineer 1835-1848; general ticket agent of the Little Miami Railroad 1848-1867; elected as a Democrat to the Forty-first Congress (March 4, 1869-March 3, 1871); was not a candidate for renomination in 1870; resumed his former business interests; moved to Ashtabula, Ohio, in 1876, where he died February 25, 1881; interment in Spring Grove Cemetery, Cincinnati, Ohio.

**STRAIT, Horace Burton,** a Representative from Minnesota; born in Potter County, Pa., January 26, 1835; attended the common schools; moved with his parents to Indiana in 1846; settled near Jordan, Minn., in 1855 and engaged in agricultural pursuits; moved to Shakopee, Minn., in 1860 and conducted a general store; entered the Union Army in 1862 as captain in the Ninth Regiment, Minnesota Volunteer Infantry, being promoted to major in 1864; served at the close of the war as inspector general on the staff of General McArthur; honorably discharged in 1865; trustee of the Minnesota Hospital for the Insane in 1866; mayor of Shakopee in 1870, 1871, and 1872; engaged in mercantile pursuits, manufacturing, and banking; elected as a Republican to the Forty-third and to the two succeeding Congresses (March 4, 1873-March 3, 1879); unsuccessful candidate for reelection in 1878 to the Forty-sixth Congress; elected to the Forty-seventh and to the two succeeding Congresses (March 4, 1881-March 3, 1887); chairman, Committee on Militia (Forty-seventh Congress); resumed banking at Shakopee and also engaged in agricultural pursuits; died February 25, 1894, on a train at Juarez, Mexico, en route to the United States; interment in Valley Cemetery, Shakopee, Minn.

**STRAIT, Thomas Jefferson,** a Representative from South Carolina; born in Chester District, S.C., December 25, 1846; attended the common schools of Mayesville, S.C., and Cooper Institute, Mississippi; during the Civil War entered the Confederate Army in 1862 and served throughout the war, first in Company A, Sixth Regiment of Infantry, and later as sergeant in Company H, Twenty-fourth Regiment, Gist's brigade; engaged in agricultural pursuits; taught school in Ebenezer, York County, S.C., in 1880; was graduated from South Carolina Medical College at Charleston in 1885 and practiced medicine; member of the State senate 1890-1893; elected as a Democrat to the Fifty-third, Fifty-fourth, and Fifty-fifth Congresses (March 4, 1893-March 3, 1899); unsuccessful candidate for renomination in 1898 to the Fifty-sixth Congress; resumed the practice of his profession in Lancaster, S.C., and died there on April 18, 1924; interment in Westside Cemetery.

**STRANAHAN, James Samuel Thomas,** a Representative from New York; born in Peterboro, Madison County, N.Y., April 25, 1808; attended the common schools and Cazenovia Seminary; founded the town of Florence, Oneida County, N.Y., in 1832; engaged in the lumber business; postmaster of Florence; member of the State assembly in 1838; moved to Newark, N.J., in 1840; engaged in building railroads; moved to Brooklyn, N.Y., in 1845; elected alderman of that city in 1848; elected as a Whig to the Thirty-fourth Congress (March 4, 1855-March 3, 1857); unsuccessful candidate for reelection in 1856 to the Thirty-fifth Congress; appointed as a member of the metropolitan police commission on January 1, 1857; presidential elector on the Republican tickets in 1860 and 1888; president of the board of trustees of Prospect Park, Brooklyn, N.Y.; director of the first Brooklyn Bridge and presided at its dedication May 28, 1884; died at his summer home at Saratoga Springs, N.Y., September 3, 1898; interment in Greenwood Cemetery, Brooklyn, N.Y.

Bibliography: *DAB.*

**STRANG, Michael Lathrop,** a Representative from Colorado; born in Bucks County, Pa., June 17, 1929; tutored at home; A.B., Princeton University, 1956; engaged in graduate work at the University of Geneva, Switzerland, 1956-1957; served as a second lieutenant, United States Army, 1950-1953; rancher; investment banker, 1957-1985; elected as a Republican to the Ninety-ninth Congress (January 3, 1985-January 3, 1987); was an unsuccessful candidate for reelection in 1986 to the One Hundredth Congress; resumed horse and cattle ranching; consultant on natural resources and taxes; is a resident of Carbondale, Colo.

**STRANGE, Robert,** a Senator from North Carolina; born in Manchester, Va., September 20, 1796; attended private schools in Virginia, New Oxford Academy, and Washington College (now Washington and Lee University), Lexington, Va.; graduated from Hampden-Sidney College, Virginia; moved to Fayetteville, N.C., in 1815; studied law; was admitted to the bar and practiced in Fayetteville; member, State house of commons 1821-1823, 1826; judge of the superior court of North Carolina 1827-1836; elected as a Democrat to the United States Senate to fill the vacancy caused by the resignation of Willie P. Mangum and served from December 5, 1836, to November 16, 1840, when he resigned; chairman, Committee on Patents and the Patent Office (Twenty-sixth Congress); resumed the practice of law in Fayetteville, Cumberland County, N.C.; solicitor for the fifth judicial district of North Carolina; engaged in literary pursuits; died in Fayetteville, N.C., February 19, 1854; interment in the family burial ground at "Myrtle Hill," near Fayetteville, N.C.

**STRATTON, Charles Creighton** (uncle of Benjamin Franklin Howey), a Representative from New Jersey; born in Swedesboro, Gloucester County, N.J., March 6, 1796; attended the common schools; was graduated from Rutgers College, New Brunswick, N.J., in 1814; engaged in agricultural pursuits; member of the New Jersey State general assembly in 1821, 1823, and again in 1829; elected as a Whig to the Twenty-fifth Congress (March 4, 1837-March 3, 1839); presented credentials as a Member-elect to the Twenty-sixth Congress, but the House declined to seat him; reelected to the Twenty-seventh Congress (March 4, 1841-March 3, 1843); was not a candidate for renomination in 1842 to the Twenty-eighth Congress; member of the State constitutional convention in 1844; elected Governor of New Jersey in 1844, and served from January 21, 1845 to January 18, 1848; resumed agricultural pursuits; resided in Europe in 1857 and 1858; died in Swedesboro, N.J., March 30, 1859; interment in the Episcopal Cemetery.

**STRATTON, John,** a Representative from Virginia; born at "Old Castle," near Eastville, Northampton County, Va., August 19, 1769; attended the common schools; studied law; admitted to the bar and practiced; member of the Virginia house of delegates 1789-1792; elected as a Federalist to the Seventh Congress (March 4, 1801-March 3, 1803); died in Norfolk, Va., May 10, 1804; interment in St. Paul's Church Cemetery.

**STRATTON, John Leake Newbold,** a Representative from New Jersey; born in Mount Holly, Burlington County, N.J., November 27, 1817; attended private schools at Mount Holly; prepared for college at Mendham; was graduated from Princeton College in 1836; studied law; was admitted to the bar in 1839 and commenced practice in Mount Holly; elected as a Republican to the Thirty-sixth and Thirty-seventh Congresses (March 4, 1859-March 3, 1863); was not a candidate for renomination in 1862; resumed the practice of law; delegate to the Union National Convention of Conservatives at Philadelphia in 1866; president of the Farmers' National Bank of Mount Holly in 1875; died in Mount Holly, N.J., on May 17, 1899; interment in St. Andrews Cemetery.

**STRATTON, Nathan Taylor,** a Representative from New Jersey; born in Pilesgrove Township, Salem County, N.J., near Swedesboro, March 17, 1813; attended the common schools; moved to Mullica Hill, N.J., in 1829 and clerked in a store, becoming a partner of his employer in 1835; conducted his own business 1840-1886; member of the State general assembly 1843-1844; justice of the peace 1844-1847; also engaged in the real estate business and in agricultural pursuits; held several local offices; elected as a Democrat to the Thirty-second and Thirty-third Congresses (March 4, 1851-March 3, 1855) was not a candidate for renomination in 1854; again engaged in mercantile pursuits; elected as a member of the Harrison Township committee in 1865; served as State tax commissioner; trustee of the State reform school for boys at Jamesburg, N.J., 1865-1887; delegate to the Union National Convention of Conservatives at Philadelphia in 1866; unsuccessful candidate for election in 1880 to the Forty-seventh Congress; died in Mullica Hill, N.J., March 9, 1887; interment in the Baptist Cemetery.

**STRATTON, Samuel Studdiford,** a Representative from New York; born in Yonkers, Westchester County, N.Y., September 27, 1916; at age of three months moved with parents to Schenectady, N.Y.; attended the public schools of Schenectady and Rochester, N.Y., and Blair Academy, Blairstown, N.J.; A.B., University of Rochester, 1937; M.A., Haverford (Pa.) College, 1938; M.A., Harvard University, 1940; executive secretary to Representative Thomas H. Eliot of Massachusetts, 1940-1942; commissioned an ensign in the United States Naval Reserve on June 26, 1942; served in the Southwest Pacific Theater as naval combat intelligence officer on the staff of General Douglas MacArthur; separated from the service as a lieutenant in 1946; twice awarded the Bronze Star Medal with combat V; at the close of the war interrogated Japanese supreme commander in the Philippines, General Tomoyuki Yamashita, who was later hanged as a war criminal; deputy secretary-general of the Far Eastern Commission, Washington, D.C., 1946-1948; elected city councilman of Schenectady, N.Y., in 1949, reelected in 1953 and served until 1956; recalled to active naval duty as a lieutenant commander and served as an instructor at the Naval Intelligence School, Washington, D.C., 1951-1953; captain, United States Naval Reserve; member of the Schenectady Municipal Housing Authority, 1950-1955, serving as chairman in 1951; mayor of Schenectady, 1956-1959; registered representative with the First Albany Corporation, 1957-1958; elected as a Democrat to the Eighty-sixth and to the fourteen succeeding Congresses (January 3, 1959-January 3, 1989); unsuccessful candidate in 1962 for nomination for Governor of New York; unsuccessful candidate in 1964 for nomination to the United States Senate; was not a candidate for reelection in 1988 to the One Hundred First Congress; was a resident of Schenectady, N.Y.; died September 13, 1990.

**Bibliography:** Cross, Wilber. *Samuel S. Stratton: A Story of Political Gumption.* New York: James H. Heineman, 1964.

**STRATTON, William Grant,** a Representative from Illinois; born in Ingleside, Lake County, Ill., February 26, 1914; attended the public schools and was graduated from the University of Arizona at Tucson in 1934; elected as a Republican to the Seventy-seventh Congress (January 3, 1941-January 3, 1943); was not a candidate for renomination in 1942 to the Seventy-eighth Congress; State treasurer of Illinois in 1943 and 1944, and 1950-1952; served as a lieutenant in the United States Navy in 1945 and 1946; elected in 1946 to the Eightieth Congress (January 3, 1947-January 3, 1949); was not a candidate for renomination in 1948 to the Eighty-first Congress; delegate to the Republican National Conventions of 1952, 1956, 1960, and 1976; elected governor of Illinois in 1952; reelected in 1956, and served from January 12, 1953 to January 9, 1961; was an unsuccessful candidate for reelection in 1960, and for nomination for Governor in 1968; engaged in livestock farming at Cantrall, Ill.; vice president, Canteen Corporation; vice president, Associated Bank Chicago; is a resident of Chicago, Ill.

**Bibliography:** Kenney, David. *A Political Passage: The Career of Stratton of Illinois.* Carbondale: Southern Illinois University Press, 1990.

**STRAUB, Christian Markle,** a Representative from Pennsylvania; born in Milton, Pa., in 1804; studied law; admitted to the bar; prothonotary of Schuylkill County in 1845; sheriff of Schuylkill County in 1849; elected as a Democrat to the Thirty-third Congress (March 4, 1853-March 3, 1855); member of the Pennsylvania senate 1856-1858; died in Washington, D.C.; interment in Pottsville, Pa.

**STRAUS, Isidor,** a Representative from New York; born in Otterberg, Rhenish Bavaria, Germany, February 6, 1845; immigrated to the United States in 1854 and settled in Talbotton, Ga.; attended Collinsworth Institute; moved to New York City in 1865 and engaged in mercantile pursuits and later became owner of R.H. Macy and Company; elected as a Democrat to the Fifty-third Congress to fill the vacancy caused by the resignation of Ashbel P. Fitch and served from January 30, 1894, to March 3, 1895; was not a candidate for reelection in 1894 to the Fifty-fourth Congress; resumed the mercantile business in New York City; member of the New York and New Jersey Bridge Commission; perished with about 1,500 other passengers in the wreck of the Royal Mail Steamer *Titanic* on April 15, 1912; the body was subsequently recovered and interred in the family vault in Beth-El Cemetery, Fresh Pond Road, Brooklyn, N.Y.

**Bibliography:** *DAB.*

**STRAWBRIDGE, James Dale,** a Representative from Pennsylvania; born in Liberty Township, Montour County, Pa., April 7, 1824; attended the common schools; was graduated from Princeton College in 1844 and from the medical department of the University of Pennsylvania at Philadelphia in 1847; engaged in the practice of medicine at Danville, Pa.; during the Civil War entered the Army as a brigade surgeon of Volunteers and served throughout the war; resumed the practice of medicine at Danville; elected as a Republican to the Forty-third Congress (March 4, 1873-March 3, 1875); again engaged in the practice of his profession; died in Danville, Pa., July 19, 1890; interment in Fairview Cemetery.

**STREET, Randall S.,** a Representative from New York; born in Catskill, N.Y., in 1780; pursued classical studies; studied law; was admitted to the bar and began practice in Poughkeepsie; district attorney for the second judicial district from February 1810 to February 1811 and from March 1813 to February 1815; lieutenant colonel of militia in the War of 1812; elected to the Sixteenth Congress (March 4, 1819-March 3, 1821); moved to Monticello, N.Y., about 1825; continued the practice of law until his death in Monticello, N.Y., November 21, 1841; interment in Poughkeepsie, N.Y.

**STRICKLAND, Randolph,** a Representative from Michigan; born in Dansville, N.Y., February 4, 1823; attended the common schools; moved to Michigan in 1844 and taught school in Ingham County; studied law; was admitted to the bar in 1849 and commenced practice in De Witt, Clinton County, Mich.; moved to St. Johns, Clinton County, and continued the practice of law; elected prosecuting attorney for Clinton County in 1852, 1854, 1856, 1858, and 1862; member of the Michigan State senate in 1861 and 1862; provost marshal of the Sixth Congressional District, 1863-1865; delegate to the Republican National Conventions of 1856 and 1868; elected as a Republican to the Forty-first Congress (March 4, 1869-March 3, 1871); was an unsuccessful candidate for renomination in 1870 to the Forty-second Congress; resumed the practice of law; died in Battle Creek, Mich., May 5, 1880; interment in De Witt Cemetery, De Witt, Mich.

**STRICKLAND, Ted,** a Representative from Ohio; born in Portsmouth, Scioto County, Ohio, August 4, 1941; graduated from Northwest High School, Lucasville, Ohio, 1959; B.A., Asbury College, 1963; M.Div., Asbury Theological Seminary, 1967; Ph.D., University of Kentucky, 1980; church worker; campus director, Methodist Children's Home; unsuccessful candidate for election in 1976 to the Ninety-fourth Congress, in 1978 to the Ninety-fifth Congress, and in 1980 to the Ninety-sixth Congress; professor of psychology, Shawnee State University, Portsmouth, Ohio, and consulting psychologist at a maximum security prison; Democratic district committeeman, 1988-1992; elected as a Democrat to the One Hundred Third Congress (January 3, 1993-January 3, 1995); unsuccessful candidate for reelection in 1994 to the One Hundred Fourth Congress; resumed teaching at Shawnee State University; is a resident of Lucasville, Ohio.

**STRINGER, Lawrence Beaumont,** a Representative from Illinois; born near Atlantic City, N.J., February 24, 1866; moved with his parents to Lincoln, Ill., in 1876; attended the public schools; was graduated from Lincoln University (later Lincoln College) in 1887; reporter on a local paper; member of the State house of representatives 1890-1892; entered the Chicago College of Law (law department of Lake Forest University), and was graduated in 1896; returned to Lincoln, Ill., in 1898 and commenced practice; delegate to the Democratic State convention in 1900 and served as chairman; member of the State senate 1900-1904; unsuccessful Democratic candidate for Governor of Illinois in 1904; appointed chief justice of the Illinois State Court of Claims in 1905 and served until 1913; unsuccessful candidate for the Democratic nomination for United States Senator in 1908; elected as a Democrat to the Sixty-third Congress (March 4, 1913-March 3, 1915); did not seek renomination in 1914, but was an unsuccessful candidate for United States Senator; resumed the practice of law; unsuccessful candidate for justice of the supreme court of Illinois in 1924; elected judge of Logan County in 1918 and served until his death in Lincoln, Ill., December 5, 1942; interment in Union Cemetery.

**Bibliography:** Lindstrom, Andrew F. "Lawrence Stringer: A Wilson Democrat." *Journal of the Illinois State Historical Society* 66 (Spring 1973): 20-40.

**STRINGFELLOW, Douglas R.,** a Representative from Utah; born in Draper, Utah, September 24, 1922; attended the public schools; moved to Odgen, Utah, in 1935 and graduated from high school in 1941; attended Weber College in 1941 and 1942, Ohio State University in 1943, and the University of Cincinnati in 1943 and 1944; entered the military service on November 4, 1942; separated as a private first class, on November 8, 1945; awarded the Purple Heart Medal; Utah State chairman of the Young Republican League in 1946; served a Latter-Day Saint's Mission in Northern California in 1947 and 1948; announcer and executive for a radio station from 1949 until 1952; elected as a Republican to the Eighty-third Congress (January 3, 1953-January 3, 1955); renominated to the Eighty-fourth Congress but withdrew on October 18, 1954, two days after acknowledging that his account of heroic exploits during his service in the Second World War had been a fabrication; engaged as a newscaster, Mutual Broadcasting System, Intermountain Network; was a resident of San Clemente, Calif., until his death in Long Beach, Calif., October 19, 1966; interment in Memorial Gardens of the Wasatch, Ogden, Utah.

**Bibliography:** Jonas, Frank H. *The Story of a Political Hoax.* Institute of Government. University of Utah. Research Monographs. Salt Lake City: University of Utah, 1966.

**STRODE, Jesse Burr,** a Representative from Nebraska; born in Farmers Township, Fulton County, Ill., February 18, 1845; attended the public and high schools and was graduated from Abingdon (Ill.) College; during the Civil War enlisted in Company G, Fiftieth Regiment, Illinois Volunteer Infantry, September 10, 1861, and served throughout the war; principal of the graded schools of Abingdon 1865-1873; was twice elected mayor and six times councilman of Abingdon; studied law; moved to Plattsmouth, Nebr., May 1, 1879; was admitted to the bar in November 1879 and commenced practice in Plattsmouth; district attorney 1882-1888; moved to Lincoln in 1887 and practiced law; judge of the district court in 1892; elected as a Republican to the Fifty-fourth and Fifty-fifth Congresses (March 4, 1895-March 3, 1899); was not a candidate for renomination in 1898; resumed the practice of law; prosecuting attorney for the third district of Nebraska; department commander of the Grand Army of the Republic in 1919 and 1920; died in Lincoln, Nebr., on November 10, 1924; interment in Wyuka Cemetery.

**STROHM, John,** a Representative from Pennsylvania; born in Little Britain (later Fulton) Township, near Centerville, Lancaster County, Pa., October 16, 1793; attended the public schools; taught school for several years; moved to Providence, Pa.; member of the Pennsylvania house of representatives 1831-1833; served in the Pennsylvania senate 1834-1842, being speaker in 1842; elected as a Whig to the Twenty-ninth and Thirtieth Congresses (March 4, 1845-March 3, 1849); surveyor and justice of the peace in Providence Township for several years; delegate to the Whig National Convention in 1852; delegate to the Pennsylvania convention in 1869; died in Lancaster, Pa., September 12, 1884; interment in the Mennonite Cemetery.

**STRONG, Caleb,** a Senator from Massachusetts; born in Northampton, Mass., January 9, 1745; studied under private tutors; graduated from Harvard College in 1764; studied law; was admitted to the bar and commenced practice in 1772; Northampton selectman; member of the committee of correspondence and safety throughout the Revolution; member, Massachusetts house of representatives, 1776-1778; member, Massachusetts senate, 1780-1788; county attorney, 1776-1800; elected to the Continental Congress in 1780, but did not attend; member of the convention in Philadelphia which framed the Constitution of the United States; member of the Massachusetts constitutional convention which ratified the Constitution of the United States; elected to the United States Senate in 1789; reelected in 1793, and served from March 4, 1789 to June 1, 1796, when he resigned; elected Governor of Massachusetts on the Federalist ticket in 1800, reelected every year until 1807, and served from May 30, 1800 to May 29, 1807; unsuccessful candidate for reelection in 1807; again elected Governor in 1812, reelected in 1813, 1814 and 1815, and served from June 1812 to May 30, 1816; died in Northampton, Mass., November 7, 1819; interment in Bridge Street Cemetery.

**Bibliography:** *DAB*; Bradford, Alden. *Biography of the Hon. Caleb Strong, Several Years Governor of the State of Massachusetts.* Boston: West, Richardson and Lord, 1820; Lodge, Henry Cabot. *A Memoir of Caleb Strong, United States Senator and Governor of Massachusetts.* Cambridge, Mass.: Press of J. Wilson and Son, 1879.

**STRONG, James,** a Representative from New York; born in Windham, Conn., in 1783; was graduated from the University of Vermont at Burlington in 1806; moved to Hudson, Columbia County, N.Y.; elected to the Sixteenth Congress (March 4, 1819-March 3, 1821); elected to the Eighteenth and to the three succeeding Congresses (March 4, 1823-March 3, 1831); chairman, Committee on Territories (Nineteenth and Twentieth Congresses); died in Chester, Morris County, N.J., on August 8, 1847.

**STRONG, James George,** a Representative from Kansas; born in Dwight, Livingston County, Ill., April 23, 1870; attended the public schools of Dwight, Ill., 1876-1879, the Episcopal Mission of Greenwood Agency, S.Dak., 1879-1880, the public school at St. Marys, Kans., 1882-1887, and Baker University, Baldwin, Kans., 1887-1889; moved to Blue Rapids, Kans., in 1891; engaged in the real estate, loan, and insurance businesses; also studied law; was admitted to the bar in 1895 and commenced practice in Blue Rapids; also interested in mercantile and agricultural pursuits; city attorney 1896-1911; organized the Blue Rapids Telephone Co. in 1905; assistant attorney general of Marshall County in 1911 and 1912; delegate to the Republican National Conventions in 1912 and 1928; organized and developed the Marshall County Power & Light Co. in 1912; member of the school board 1913-1916; prosecuting attorney of Marshall County in 1916 and 1917; elected as a Republican to the Sixty-sixth and to the six succeeding Congresses (March 4, 1919-March 3, 1933); chairman, Committee on War Claims (Sixty-eighth through Seventy-first Congresses); unsuccessful for renomination in 1932; appointed first assistant treasurer of the Home Owners' Loan Corporation in 1933 and served until his death in Washington, D.C., on January 11, 1938; interment in Fairmount Cemetery, Blue Rapids, Kans.

**STRONG, Jedediah,** a Delegate from Connecticut; born in Litchfield, Conn., November 7, 1738; was graduated from Yale College in 1761; studied law; was admitted to the bar in 1764 and commenced the practice of his profession in Litchfield; member of the State house of representatives 1771-1801; town clerk 1773-1789; member of the committee on inspection in 1774 and 1775, and was made commissary of supplies for the Army in 1775; clerk of the State house of representatives 1779-1788; associate judge of the Litchfield County Court 1780-1791; elected to the Continental Congress in 1782, 1783, and 1784, but did not attend; delegate to the Connecticut ratification convention in 1788; served as a member of the Governor's council, or upper house, in 1789 and 1790; died in Litchfield, Conn., August 21, 1802; interment in the West Burying Ground.

**STRONG, Julius Levi,** a Representative from Connecticut; born in Bolton, Tolland County, Conn., November 8, 1828; attended Wesleyan University, Middletown, Conn., and Union College, Schenectady, N.Y.; member of the State house of representatives in 1852; served in the State senate in 1853; studied law at National Law School, Balston Spa, N.Y.; was admitted to the bar in 1853 and commenced practice in Hartford, Conn.; again a member of the State house of representatives in 1855; prosecuting attorney in 1864 and 1865; president of the common council; elected as a Republican to the Forty-first and Forty-second Congresses and served from March 4, 1869, until his death in Hartford, Conn., September 7, 1872; interment in Cedar Hill Cemetery.

**STRONG, Luther Martin,** a Representative from Ohio; born near Tiffin, Seneca County, Ohio, June 23, 1838; attended the common schools and Aaron Schuyler's Academy, Republic, Ohio; taught school; enlisted in the Forty-ninth Regiment, Ohio Volunteer Infantry, in 1861 and served until March 13, 1865; studied law; was admitted to the bar by the supreme court of Ohio on January 30, 1867; moved to Kenton, Hardin County, Ohio and practiced his profession; member of the board of education; was elected to the Ohio State senate in 1879 and 1881; appointed judge of the court of common pleas by Governor Charles Foster in 1883 to fill an unexpired term; elected as a Republican to the Fifty-third and Fifty-fourth Congresses (March 4, 1893-March 3, 1897); unsuccessful candidate for renomination in 1896 to the Fifty-fifth Congress; engaged in agricultural pursuits; died in Kenton, Ohio, April 26, 1903; interment in Grove Cemetery.

**STRONG, Nathan Leroy,** a Representative from Pennsylvania; born in Troy (now Summerville), Jefferson County, Pa., November 12, 1859; attended the public schools; was a telegraph operator and railroad agent 1877-1894; studied law; was admitted to the bar in 1891 and commenced practice in Brookville, Jefferson County, Pa., in 1893; district attorney of Jefferson County 1895-1900; engaged in the development of mineral lands in Jefferson and Armstrong Counties 1901-1916; president of the Mohawk Mining Co.; engaged in banking; elected as a Republican to the Sixty-fifth and to the eight succeeding Congresses (March 4, 1917-January 3, 1935); unsuccessful candidate for reelection in 1934 to the Seventy-fourth Congress; resumed his former business activities; died in Brookville, Pa., December 14, 1939; interment in Brookville Cemetery.

**STRONG, Selah Brewster,** a Representative from New York; born in Brookhaven, Suffolk County, N.Y., May 1, 1792; received a preliminary education and was graduated from Yale College in 1811; studied law; was admitted to the bar in 1814 and began practice in New York City; during the War of 1812 was commissioned as an ensign and quartermaster in the Tenth Regiment, Third Brigade, New York City and County Troops, and in 1815 was promoted successively to lieutenant and captain; master in chancery in 1817; moved to Brookhaven in 1820; district attorney for Suffolk County from 1821 to 1847, except for nine months in 1830; appointed judge advocate of the First Division of the New York State Infantry in 1825; elected as a Democrat to the Twenty-eighth Congress (March 4, 1843-March 3, 1845); was not a candidate for renomination in 1844; resumed the practice of law; judge of the supreme court for the second judicial district from June 7, 1847, to January 1, 1860; member of the State constitutional convention in 1867; died in Setauket, Long Island, N.Y., November 29, 1872; interment on his estate.

**STRONG, Solomon,** a Representative from Massachusetts; born in Amherst, Mass., March 2, 1780; graduated from Williams College, Williamstown, Mass., in 1798; studied law; admitted to the bar in Northampton, Mass., in 1800 and commenced the practice of law; member of the Massachusetts senate in 1812 and 1813; judge of the circuit court of common pleas in 1818 and judge of the court of common pleas from 1821 until his resignation in 1842; elected as a Federalist to the Fourteenth and Fifteenth Congresses (March 4, 1815-March 3, 1819); was not a candidate for renomination in 1818; again a member of the Massachusetts senate in 1843 and 1844; died in Leominster, Mass., on September 16, 1850; interment in Evergreen Cemetery.

**STRONG, Stephen,** a Representative from New York; born in Lebanon, Conn., October 11, 1791; moved to New York; attended Hamilton College, Clinton, N.Y.; studied law; was admitted to the bar in 1822 and practiced; district attorney of Tioga County 1836-1838 and 1844-1847; judge of Tioga County 1838-1843; elected as a Democrat to the Twenty-ninth Congress (March 4, 1845-March 3, 1847); chairman, Committee on Expenditures in the Department of State (Twenty-ninth Congress); resumed the practice of law in Owego, N.Y.; again judge of Tioga County 1855-1859; moved to Watertown, Jefferson County, N.Y., in 1861 and practiced law; died in Watertown, N.Y., April 15, 1866.

**STRONG, Sterling Price,** a Representative from Texas; born on a farm near Jefferson City, Cole County, Mo., August 17, 1862; moved to Texas in 1871 with his parents, who settled in Montague County; attended the rural schools of Montague County, Tex., and was graduated from Eastman's National Business College, Poughkeepsie, N.Y., in 1884; county clerk of Montague County, 1884-1888, and 1898-1904; engrossing clerk of the Texas State senate in 1889; county and district clerk of Hale County, 1889-1892; engaged as a traveling salesman, 1892-1898, and from 1911 until 1932; cashier in the National Bank of Bowie, Tex., 1908-1911; member of Texas State Democratic executive committee, 1900-1902; unsuccessful candidate for Lieutenant Governor of Texas in 1930; elected as a Democrat to the Seventy-third Congress (March 4, 1933-January 3, 1935); unsuccessful candidate for renomination in 1934 to the Seventy-fourth Congress; died in Dallas, Tex., March 28, 1936; interment in Old Oak Cliff Cemetery.

**STRONG, Theron Rudd** (cousin of William Strong of Pennsylvania), a Representative from New York; born in Salisbury, Conn., November 7, 1802; attended the common schools; studied law at Litchfield Law School; was admitted to the bar in 1821 and commenced practice in Palmyra, Wayne County, N.Y.; master and examiner in chancery for several years; held several local offices; district attorney of Wayne County from 1835 to 1839; elected as a Democrat to the Twenty-sixth Congress (March 4, 1839-March 3, 1841); member of the State assembly in 1842; associate justice of the supreme court of New York 1851-1859 and judge of the court of appeals in 1859; moved to Rochester, N.Y., in 1860 and resumed the practice of his profession; returned to New York City in 1867 and continued the practice of law until his death May 14, 1873; interment in Mount Hope Cemetery, Rochester, N.Y.

**STRONG, William** (cousin of Theron Rudd Strong), a Representative from Pennsylvania; born in Somers, Conn., May 6, 1808; attended Munson Academy, Mass.; B.A., Yale College, 1828, M.A., 1831; taught school in New Haven, Conn.; studied law; was admitted to the bar in 1832 and commenced practice in Reading, Pa.; elected as a Democrat to the Thirtieth and Thirty-first Congresses (March 4, 1847-March 3, 1851); chairman, Committee on Elections (Thirty-first Congress); was not a candidate for renomination in 1850 to the Thirty-second Congress; associate justice of the supreme court of Pennsylvania, 1857-1868; practiced law in Philadelphia, Pa.; vice president, American Bible Society, 1871-1895; president, American Tract Society, 1873-1895; nominated on February 7, 1870 by President Ulysses S. Grant as an Associate Justice of the United States Supreme Court; was confirmed by the Senate on February 18, 1870, and served until December 1880, when he retired; resumed the practice of law; president, American Sunday School Union, 1883-1895; died at Lake Minnewassa, N.Y., August 19, 1895; interment in Charles Evans Cemetery, Reading, Pa.

Bibliography: *DAB.*

**STRONG, William,** a Representative from Vermont; born in Lebanon, Conn., in 1763; moved with his parents to Hartford, Vt.; in 1764; self-educated; engaged extensively in land surveying; member of the State house of representatives in 1798, 1799, 1801, and 1802; sheriff of Windsor County from 1802 to 1810; elected as a Republican to the Twelfth and Thirteenth Congresses (March 4, 1811-March 3, 1815); again a member of the State house of representatives 1815-1818; judge of the supreme court of Windsor County 1819-1821; elected to the Sixteenth Congress (March 4, 1819-March 3, 1821); member of the council of censors in 1834; died in Hartford, Windsor County, Vt., January 28, 1840; interment in Quechee Cemetery.

**STROTHER, George French** (father of James French Strother [1811-1860] and great-grandfather of James French Strother [1868-1930]), a Representative from Virginia; born in Stevensburg, Culpeper County, Va., in 1783; attended the College of William and Mary, Williamsburg, Va.; studied law; admitted to the bar and commenced practice in Culpeper; member of the Virginia house of delegates 1806-1809; elected as a Republican to the Fifteenth and Sixteenth Congresses and served from March 4, 1817, until his resignation February 10, 1820; receiver of public moneys at St. Louis, Mo.; died in St. Louis November 28, 1840; interment in Christ Church Cemetery; reinterment in Bellefontaine Cemetery in 1860.

**STROTHER, James French** (son of George French Strother and grandfather of James French Strother [1868-1930]), a Representative from Virginia; born in Culpeper, Va., September 4, 1811; completed preparatory studies and attended St. Louis University, Missouri; studied law; admitted to the bar and commenced practice in Washington, Rappahannock County, Va.; member of the Virginia house of delegates 1840-1851, serving as speaker in 1851; delegate to the Virginia constitutional convention in 1850; elected as a Whig to the Thirty-second Congress (March 4, 1851-March 3, 1853); resumed the practice of law in Culpeper, Va.; died near Culpeper, Va., September 20, 1860; interment in the Masonic Cemetery.

**STROTHER, James French** (grandson of James French Strother [1811-1860] and great-grandson of George French Strother), a Representative from West Virginia; born near Pearisburg, Giles County, Va., June 29, 1868; attended the public schools, Pearisburg Academy, and Virginia Agricultural and Mechanical College at Blacksburg; deputy collector of internal revenue at Lynchburg, Va., 1890-1893; studied law at the University of Virginia at Charlottesville; was admitted to the bar in 1894 and commenced practice in Pearisburg; settled in Welch, McDowell County, W.Va., in 1895 and continued the practice of law; United States commissioner, 1897-1901; appointed judge of the criminal court of McDowell County by Governor Albert B. White on January 1, 1905; was thrice elected and served until September 30, 1924, when he resigned, having been nominated for Congress; elected as a Republican to the Sixty-ninth and Seventieth Congresses (March 4, 1925-March 3, 1929); was not a candidate for renomination in 1928 to the Seventy-first Congress; died in Welch, W.Va., April 10, 1930; interment in Monte Vista Cemetery, Bluefield, W.Va.

**STROUSE, Myer,** a Representative from Pennsylvania; born in Oberstrau, Bavaria, Germany, December 16, 1825; immigrated to the United States in 1832 with his father, who settled in Pottsville, Schuylkill County, Pa.; attended private schools; edited the North American Farmer in Philadelphia 1848-1852; studied law; was admitted to the bar in 1855 and commenced practice in Pottsville; elected as a Democrat to the Thirty-eighth and Thirty-ninth Congresses (March 4, 1863-March 3, 1867); was not a candidate for renomination in 1866; resumed the practice of law; was attorney and solicitor for the "Molly Maguires," a secret organization in the mining regions of Pennsylvania, in 1876 and 1877; died in Pottsville, Pa., February 11, 1878; interment in Odd Fellows Cemetery.

**STROWD, William Franklin,** a Representative from North Carolina; born near Chapel Hill, Orange County, N.C., December 7, 1832; attended the country schools, Bingham private school at Melvane, the local academy at High Hill, and Graham Institute; moved to Chatham County in 1861 and engaged in agricultural pursuits; during the Civil War served as a private in the Confederate Army; member of the State constitutional convention in 1875; unsuccessful Populist candidate for election in 1892 to the Fifty-third Congress; elected as a Populist to the Fifty-fourth and Fifty-fifth Congresses (March 4, 1895-March 3, 1899); was not a candidate for renomination in 1898; resumed agricultural pursuits in Chatham County; discontinued activities in 1908 and lived in retirement until his death December 12, 1911, in Chapel Hill, N.C.; interment in Chapel Hill Cemetery.

**STRUBLE, Isaac S.,** a Representative from Iowa; born near Fredericksburg, Va., November 3, 1843; moved to Iowa with his parents, who settled in Johnson County; attended the common schools; during the Civil War enlisted at the age of seventeen and served three years as a private in Company F, Twenty-second Iowa Regiment, Volunteer Infantry; attended the University of Iowa in Iowa City; studied law; was admitted to the bar in 1870 and commenced practice in Ogle County, Ill.; settled in Le Mars, Plymouth County, Iowa, in 1872; elected as a Republican to the Forty-eighth and to the three succeeding Congresses (March 4, 1883-March 3, 1891); chairman, Committee on Territories (Fifty-first Congress); unsuccessful candidate for renomination in 1890; resumed the practice of law; died in Le Mars, Iowa, on February 17, 1913; interment in Le Mars Cemetery.

**STRUDWICK, William Francis,** a Representative from North Carolina; born at "Stag Park," near Wilmington, New Hanover County, N.C.; received a limited education; engaged in agricultural pursuits; delegate to the State convention in 1789; served in the State senate 1792-1797; held several local offices; elected as a Federalist to the Fourth Congress to fill the vacancy caused by the resignation of Absalom Tatom and served from November 28, 1796, to March 3, 1797; member of the State house of representatives 1801-1803; resumed agricultural interests; died in North Carolina in 1812; interment in a private cemetery on his estate at "Hawfields," Orange County, N.C.

**STUART, Alexander Hugh Holmes** (cousin of Archibald Stuart), a Representative from Virginia; born in Staunton, Va., April 2, 1807; attended Staunton Academy and the College of William and Mary, Williamsburg, Va.; was graduated from the University of Virginia at Charlottesville in 1828; studied law; was admitted to the bar in 1828 and commenced practice in Staunton; member of the Virginia house of delegates, 1836-1839; elected as a Whig to the Twenty-seventh Congress (March 4, 1841-March 3, 1843); unsuccessful candidate for reelection in 1842 to the Twenty-eighth Congress; served as Secretary of the Interior in the Cabinet of President Millard Fillmore from September 16, 1850 to March 6, 1853; member of the Virginia senate, 1857-1861; member of the Virginia secession convention in 1861; delegate to the National Convention of Conservatives at Philadelphia in 1866; presented credentials as a Member-elect to the Thirty-ninth Congress in 1865 but was not admitted; chairman of the committee of nine, which was instrumental in restoring Virginia to the Union in 1870; member of the Virginia house of delegates from 1874 to 1877; rector of the University of Virginia from 1874 to 1882; president of the Virginia Historical Society; resumed the practice of law; died in Staunton, Va., February 13, 1891; interment in Thornrose Cemetery.

**Bibliography:** *DAB*; Robertson, Alexander F. *Alexander Hugh Holmes Stuart, 1807-1891: A Biography.* Richmond: The William Byrd Press, 1925.

**STUART, Andrew,** a Representative from Ohio; born near Pittsburgh, Pa., August 3, 1823; moved to Pittsburgh with his mother in 1834; received limited schooling; worked in a newspaper office; moved to Steubenville, Ohio, in 1850; was editor of the American Union 1850-1857; elected as a Democrat to the Thirty-third Congress (March 4, 1853-March 3, 1855); unsuccessful candidate for reelection; engaged in the shipping business on the Gulf of Mexico and in the transportation of mails and supplies from Leavenworth, Kans., to Santa Fe, N.Mex.; resided in Washington, D.C., from 1869 until his death, April 30, 1872; interment in Union Cemetery, Steubenville, Ohio.

**STUART, Archibald** (cousin of Alexander Hugh Holmes Stuart), a Representative from Virginia; born in Lynchburg, Va., December 2, 1795; attended private schools and completed preparatory studies; served as an officer in the War of 1812; studied law; admitted to the bar and practiced in Lynchburg, Campbell County,

Va.; member of the Virginia house of delegates in 1830 and 1831; delegate to the Virginia conventions of 1829, 1830, 1850, and 1851; elected as a Democrat to the Twenty-fifth Congress (March 4, 1837-March 3, 1839); unsuccessful candidate for reelection in 1838 to the Twenty-sixth Congress; resumed the practice of law; served in the Virginia senate 1852-1854; died at his home, "Laurel Hill," Patrick County, Va., September 20, 1855; interment in the Stuart family cemetery at Laurel Hill, Patrick County, Va.

**STUART, Charles Edward,** a Representative and a Senator from Michigan; born near Waterloo, Columbia County, N.Y., November 25, 1810; studied law; was admitted to the bar in 1832 and commenced practice in Waterloo; moved to Michigan in 1835 and settled in Kalamazoo; member, State house of representatives 1842; elected as a Democrat to the Thirtieth Congress to fill the vacancy caused by the death of Edward Bradley, who never qualified, and served from December 6, 1847, to March 3, 1849; unsuccessful candidate for reelection in 1848; elected to the Thirty-second Congress (March 4, 1851-March 3, 1853); chairman, Committee on Expenditures in the Department of State (Thirty-second Congress); elected as a Democrat to the United States Senate and served from March 4, 1853, to March 3, 1859; was not a candidate for renomination; served as President pro tempore of the Senate during the Thirty-fourth Congress; chairman, Committee on Public Lands (Thirty-fourth and Thirty-fifth Congresses); resumed the practice of law; during the Civil War raised and equipped the Thirteenth Regiment, Michigan Volunteer Infantry, of which he was commissioned colonel, but resigned because of ill health; died in Kalamazoo, Mich., May 19, 1887; interment in Mountain Home Cemetery.

**STUART, David,** a Representative from Michigan; born in Brooklyn, N.Y., March 12, 1816; studied law; was admitted to the bar and commenced practice in Detroit, Mich.; elected as a Democrat to the Thirty-third Congress (March 4, 1853-March 3, 1855); chairman, Committee on Expenditures in the Department of the Treasury (Thirty-third Congress); unsuccessful candidate for reelection in 1854 to the Thirty-fourth Congress; moved to Chicago, Ill.; enlisted in the Union Army and was commissioned lieutenant colonel of the Forty-second Regiment, Illinois Volunteer Infantry, July 22, 1861; colonel of the Fifty-fifth Regiment, Illinois Volunteer Infantry, October 31, 1861; appointed brigadier general of Volunteers November 29, 1862, but the Senate declined to confirm the nomination March 11, 1863; resigned April 3, 1863; resumed the practice of law in Detroit, Mich., and died there September 12, 1868; interment in Elmwood Cemetery.

**STUART, John Todd,** a Representative from Illinois; born near Lexington, Ky., November 10, 1807; was graduated from Centre College, Danville, Ky., in 1826; studied law; was admitted to the bar in 1828 and commenced practice in Springfield, Sangamon County, Ill.; subsequently became a law partner of Abraham Lincoln; major in the Black Hawk War in 1832; member of the Illinois State house of representatives, 1832-1836; unsuccessful candidate for election in 1836 to the Twenty-fifth Congress; elected as a Whig to the Twenty-sixth and Twenty-seventh Congresses (March 4, 1839-March 3, 1843); was not a candidate for renomination in 1842 to the Twenty-eighth Congress; member of the State senate, 1848-1852; was the unsuccessful Constitutional Union candidate for Governor of Illinois in 1860; elected as a Democrat to the Thirty-eighth Congress (March 4, 1863-March 3, 1865); resumed the practice of law; died in Springfield, Sangamon County, Ill., November 23, 1885; interment in Oak Ridge Cemetery.

**Bibliography:** *DAB.*

**STUART, Philip,** a Representative from Maryland; born near Fredericksburg, Va., in 1760; completed his preparatory education; moved to Maryland; served in the Revolutionary Army as a lieutenant in the Third Continental Dragoons; wounded at Eutaw

Springs September 8, 1781; transferred to Baylor's dragoons November 9, 1782; lieutenant, Second Artillerists and Engineers, June 5, 1798; resigned November 15, 1800; served in the War of 1812; elected as a Federalist to the Twelfth and to the three succeeding Congresses (March 4, 1811-March 3, 1819); died in Washington, D.C., August 14, 1830; interment in the Congressional Cemetery.

**STUBBLEFIELD, Frank Albert,** a Representative from Kentucky; born in Murray, Calloway County, Ky., April 5, 1907; attended the public schools; student at University of Arizona in 1927; B.S., University of Kentucky College of Commerce, 1932; engaged in the retail drug business in Murray, Ky., in 1933; member of city council, Murray, Ky., 1939-1942; served as a lieutenant in the United States Navy from 1944 until September 1945; member of the Kentucky Railroad Commission, 1951-1955; reelected to four-year term in 1955, but resigned December 31, 1958, to run for Congress; elected as a Democrat to the Eighty-sixth and to the seven succeeding Congresses and served from January 3, 1959, until his resignation December 31, 1974; unsuccessful candidate for renomination in 1974 to the Ninety-fourth Congress; resided in Murray, Ky., where he died October 14, 1977; interment in Murray City Cemetery.

**STUBBS, Henry Elbert,** a Representative from California; born in Nampa, Coleman County, Tex., March 4, 1881; attended the public schools in Groesbeck, Tex., and Phillips University, Enid, Okla.; was ordained a minister of the Christian Church in 1911 and served as pastor of the Christian Church in Frederick, Okla., 1911-1914, and 1918-1921, and in Kingfisher, Okla., 1914-1917; moved to California in 1921 and served as pastor of the Christian Church in Tulare, 1921-1923, and of the Santa Maria Christian Church from 1923 until elected to Congress; elected as a Democrat to the Seventy-third and to the two succeeding Congresses, and served from March 4, 1933 until his death in Washington, D.C., February 28, 1937; interment in Santa Maria Cemetery, Santa Maria, Calif.

**STUCKEY, Williamson Sylvester, Jr.,** a Representative from Georgia; born in Eastman, Dodge County, Ga., May 25, 1935; attended Woodward Academy; B.B.A., University of Georgia, 1956; LL.B., University of Georgia School of Law, 1959; president, Stuckey's Stores, Inc., 1958-1966, Stuckey Pecan Co., 1958-1966, Stuckey Investments, Inc., 1958-1966; Stuckey Timberlands, Inc., 1958-1966; elected as a Democrat to the Ninetieth and to the four succeeding Congresses (January 3, 1967-January 3, 1977); was not a candidate for reelection in 1976 to the Ninety-fifth Congress; chairman of the board, Stuckey's Inc., 1985 to present; is a resident of Eastman, Ga., and Washington, D.C.

**STUDDS, Gerry Eastman,** a Representative from Massachusetts; born in Mineola, Nassau County, N.Y., May 12, 1937; attended the public schools in Cohasset, and the Derby Academy in Hingham, Mass.; B.A., Yale University, 1959, M.A.T., history, 1961; Foreign Service Officer, United States Department of State, 1961-1962; member, President John F. Kennedy's White House staff, 1962-1963; legislative assistant to Senator Harrison A. Williams, Jr., 1964; teacher at St. Paul's School, Concord, N.H., 1965-1969; Massachusetts Coordinator of Senator Eugene McCarthy's presidential primary campaign, 1968; delegate to the Democratic National Convention of 1968; office of the President, University of Massachusetts, 1971; elected as a Democrat to the Ninety-third and to the eleven succeeding Congresses (January 3, 1973-January 3, 1997); was not a candidate for reelection in 1996 to the One Hundred Fifth Congress; censured by the Ninety-eighth Congress pursuant to H.Res. 265, passed July 20, 1983; chairman, Committee on Merchant Marine and Fisheries (One Hundred Third Congress); is a resident of Cohasset, Mass.

**STUDLEY, Elmer Ebenezer,** a Representative from New York; born on a farm near East Ashford, Cattaraugus County, N.Y., September 24, 1869; attended the district schools; was graduated from Cornell University, Ithaca, N.Y., in 1894; reporter on Buffalo newspapers in 1894 and 1895; commissioned as a first lieutenant in the Two Hundred and Second Regiment, New York Volunteer Infantry, serving in Cuba in 1898 and 1899; studied law; was admitted to the bar in 1895 and practiced in Buffalo, N.Y., 1895-1898; moved to Raton, Colfax County, N.Mex., in 1899 and practiced law until 1917; served as a Republican in the Territorial house of representatives in 1907; member of the New Mexico Statutory Revision Commission in 1907; district attorney of Colfax and Union Counties, N.Mex., in 1909 and 1910; delegate to the Progressive National Convention at Chicago in 1916; moved to New York City in 1917 and continued the practice of law; deputy attorney general of New York in 1924; United States commissioner for the eastern district of New York in 1925 and 1926; elected as a Democrat to the Seventy-third Congress (March 4, 1933-January 3, 1935); was not a candidate for renomination in 1934; resumed the practice of law; appointed by President Franklin D. Roosevelt in February 1935 as a member of the Board of Veterans' Appeals and served until his death in Flushing, Long Island, N.Y., on September 6, 1942; interment in Flushing Cemetery.

**STULL, Howard William,** a Representative from Pennsylvania; born on a farm near Johnstown, Cambria County, Pa., April 11, 1876; attended the public schools, Johnstown High School, and State Normal School (later State Teachers' College), Indiana, Pa.; employed as a store clerk 1887-1894 and as a railroad clerk in 1894 and 1895; taught school at Ferndale and Dale, Pa., 1895-1897; served as post office clerk at Johnstown in 1897 and 1898 and as assistant postmaster 1899-1904; moved to Washington, D.C., in 1905 and served as an assistant division chief in the United States Treasury Department 1905-1908; graduated from the law department of George Washington University, Washington, D.C., in 1908; admitted to the bar the same year and commenced practice in Colville, Stevens County, Wash., in 1909; prosecuting attorney of Stevens County, Wash., in 1911, 1912, 1915, and 1916; delegate to the Pennsylvania Republican convention in 1916; returned to Johnstown, Pa., in 1917 and continued the practice of law; elected as a Republican to the Seventy-second Congress to fill the vacancy caused by the resignation of J. Russell Leech and served from April 26, 1932, to March 3, 1933; was not a candidate for renomination in 1932; resumed the practice of law; died in Johnstown, Pa., April 22, 1949; interment in Grandview Cemetery.

**STUMP, Herman,** a Representative from Maryland; born on Oakington farm, Harford County, Md., August 8, 1837; pursued classical studies; studied law; was admitted to the bar in 1856 and commenced practice in Bel Air, Md.; also interested in agricultural pursuits; elected to the Maryland State senate in 1878, serving as president in 1880; chairman of the Democratic State convention in 1879; elected as a Democrat to the Fifty-first and Fifty-second Congresses (March 4, 1889-March 3, 1893); was not a candidate for renomination in 1892 to the Fifty-third Congress; appointed Superintendent of Immigration by President Grover Cleveland on April 8, 1893, and served until July 16, 1897; resumed the practice of law in Bel Air, Md.; died at his home near Bel Air, Md., January 9, 1917; interment in St. Mary's Cemetery, Emmorton, Md.

**STUMP, Robert Lee (Bob),** a Representative from Arizona; born in Phoenix, Maricopa County, Ariz., April 4, 1927; attended the public schools in Phoenix, and graduated from Tolleson (Ariz.) High School in 1947; B.S., Arizona State University, Tempe, 1951; cotton farmer; served in the United States Navy, 1943-1946; member, Arizona State house of representatives, 1959-1967; member, Arizona State senate, 1967-1976, serving as president, 1975-1976; elected as a Democrat to the Ninety-fifth and to the two succeeding Congresses

(January 3, 1977-January 3, 1981); announced his affiliation with the Republican Party, September 24, 1981, and continued in office during the Ninety-seventh Congress as a Republican; reelected as a Republican to the Ninety-eighth and to the six succeeding Congresses (January 3, 1983-January 3, 1997); chairman, Committee on Veterans' Affairs (One Hundred Fourth Congress); is a resident of Tolleson, Ariz.

**STUPAK, Bart T.,** a Representative from Michigan; born in Milwaukee, Wis., February 29, 1952; graduated, Gladstone (Mich.) High School, 1970; A.A., Northwestern Michigan Community College, 1972; B.S., Saginaw Valley State College, 1977; J.D., Thomas M. Cooley Law School, 1981; patrolman, Escanaba, Mich. city police department, 1972-1973; trooper, Michigan Department of State Police, 1973-1978; practicing attorney, 1981-1984, 1984-1988, and 1991 to present; member, Michigan State house of representatives, 1989-1990; elected as a Democrat to the One Hundred Third and One Hundred Fourth Congresses (January 3, 1993-January 3, 1997); is a resident of Menominee, Mich.

**STURGEON, Daniel,** a Senator from Pennsylvania; born in Mount Pleasant, York (later Adams) County, Pa., October 27, 1789; attended the common schools; moved to western Pennsylvania in 1804 with his parents, who settled near Pittsburgh; graduated from Jefferson College, Canonsburg, Pa. (later Washington and Jefferson College), and Jefferson Medical College, Philadelphia, Pa.; commenced the practice of medicine in Uniontown, Pa., in 1813; appointed county coroner; member, Pennsylvania house of representatives 1818-1824; member, Pennsylvania senate 1825-1830, serving as president 1828-1830; auditor general of Pennsylvania 1830-1836; Pennsylvania treasurer 1838-1839; elected as a Democrat to the United States Senate to fill the vacancy in the term commencing March 4, 1839, caused by the failure of the legislature to elect; reelected in 1844 and served from January 14, 1840, to March 3, 1851; was not a candidate for reelection; chairman, Committee on Patents and the Patent Office (Twenty-sixth Congress), Committee on Agriculture (Twenty-ninth through Thirty-first Congresses); appointed by President Franklin Pierce as treasurer of the United States Mint in Philadelphia, Pa., 1853-1858; engaged in banking; died in Uniontown, Fayette County, Pa., July 3, 1878; interment in Oak Grove Cemetery.

**STURGES, Jonathan** (father of Lewis Burr Sturges), a Delegate and a Representative from Connecticut; born in Fairfield, Conn., August 23, 1740; was graduated from Yale College in 1759; was admitted to the bar in May 1772 and commenced practice in Fairfield, Conn.; member of the State house of representatives in 1772 and 1773-1784; justice of the peace in 1773; Member of the Continental Congress in 1786; judge of the probate court for the district of Fairfield in 1775; again a member of the State house of representatives in 1786; elected to the First and Second Congresses (March 4, 1789-March 3, 1793); associate justice of the State supreme court 1793-1805; died in Fairfield, Fairfield County, Conn., October 4, 1819; interment in the Old Burying Ground.

**STURGES, Lewis Burr** (son of Jonathan Sturges), a Representative from Connecticut; born in Fairfield, Conn., March 15, 1763; was graduated from Yale College in 1782; engaged in mercantile pursuits in New Haven; returned to Fairfield, Conn., in 1786; clerk of the probate court for the district of Fairfield 1787-1791; member of the State house of representatives 1794-1803; elected as a Federalist to the Ninth Congress to fill in part the vacancies caused by the resignations of Calvin Goddard and Roger Griswold; reelected to the Tenth and to the four succeeding Congresses and served from September 16, 1805, to March 3, 1817; moved to Norwalk, Huron County, Ohio, where he died March 30, 1844; interment in St. Paul's Episcopal Churchyard.

**STURGISS, George Cookman,** a Representative from West Virginia; born in Poland, Mahoning County, Ohio, August 16, 1842; attended country schools; moved to Morgantown, Va. (now West Virginia), in 1859; attended Monongalia Academy, Morgantown, W.Va., and taught in that school for a short time; studied law; was admitted to the bar in 1863 and commenced practice at Morgantown; during the Civil War served as a clerk under Major James V. Boughner, paymaster of United States Volunteers; Monongalia County superintendent of free schools, 1865-1869; member of the West Virginia State house of delegates, 1870-1872; prosecuting attorney of Monongalia County, 1872-1880; unsuccessful candidate in 1880 for election for Governor of West Virginia; appointed by President Benjamin Harrison as United States attorney for the district of West Virginia in 1889 and served four years; first president of the West Virginia State board of trade, and of the West Virginia State association for the promotion of good roads; elected as a Republican to the Sixtieth and Sixty-first Congresses (March 4, 1907-March 3, 1911); unsuccessful candidate for reelection in 1910 to the Sixty-second Congress; trustee of American University, Washington, D.C.; was instrumental in the construction of the Morgantown and Kingwood Railroad; judge of the circuit court, 1912-1920; engaged in the practice of law at Morgantown, W.Va., until his death on February 26, 1925; interment in Oak Grove Cemetery.

**STURTEVANT, John Cirby,** a Representative from Pennsylvania; born in Spring Township, Crawford County, Pa., February 20, 1835; attended the common schools; engaged in teaching and farming; officer in the Pennsylvania house of representatives at Harrisburg in 1861, 1862, and 1864; delegate to seven Pennsylvania Republican conventions from 1865 to 1890; member of the Pennsylvania house of representatives in 1865 and in 1866; moved to Conneautville, Pa., in 1867; engaged in the hardware business until 1873, and in manufacturing and milling until 1888; also engaged in banking, serving as cashier and president of the First National Bank of Conneautville; elected as a Republican to the Fifty-fifth Congress (March 4, 1897-March 3, 1899); was not a candidate for renomination in 1898; resumed banking interests in Conneautville, Crawford County, Pa., and died there December 20, 1912; interment in Conneautville Cemetery.

**SULLIVAN, Christopher Daniel,** a Representative from New York; born in New York City, July 14, 1870; attended the public schools, St. James Parochial School, and St. Mary's Academy, in New York City; engaged in the real-estate business in 1904; elected as a member of the State senate in 1906; reelected in 1908, 1910, 1912, and 1914, and served until 1916, when he was elected to Congress; was elected as a Democrat to the Sixty-fifth and to the eleven succeeding Congresses (March 4, 1917-January 3, 1941); chairman, Committee on Expenditures in the Department of Labor (Sixty-fifth Congress); was not a candidate for renomination in 1940; resided in New York City, until his death there August 3, 1942; interment in Calvary Cemetery, Woodside, Long Island, N.Y.

**SULLIVAN, George** (son of John Sullivan and nephew of James Sullivan), a Representative from New Hampshire; born in Durham, N.H., August 29, 1771; was graduated from Harvard University in 1790; studied law; was admitted to the bar and commenced practice in Exeter, Rockingham County, N.H., in 1793; member of the State house of representatives in 1805; attorney general of New Hampshire in 1805 and 1806; elected as a Federalist to the Twelfth Congress (March 4, 1811-March 3, 1813); again a member of the State house of representatives in 1813; served in the State senate in 1814 and 1815; again attorney general of the State 1816-1835; died in Exeter, N.H., April 14, 1838; interment in the Old Cemetery (Winter Street).

**Bibliography:** *DAB.*

**SULLIVAN, James** (brother of John Sullivan and uncle of George Sullivan), a Delegate from Massachusetts; born in Berwick, Maine (then a part of Massachusetts), April 22, 1744; completed preparatory studies; studied law; was admitted to the bar about 1782 and commenced practice in Biddeford; King's attorney for York County; active in pre-Revolutionary movements; member of the Provincial Congress of Massachusetts in 1774 and 1775; member of the general court in 1775 and 1776; justice of the superior court, 1776-1782; elected to the Continental Congress in 1782 and 1783 but did not attend; member of the executive council in 1787; judge of probate for Suffolk County in 1788; Massachusetts attorney general, 1790-1807; unsuccessful candidate for Governor in 1797, 1798, 1804, and 1805; elected Governor of Massachusetts in 1807, and served from May 29, 1807 until his death in Boston, Mass., December 10, 1808; had been an unsuccessful candidate for reelection in 1808; interment in Central Boston Common Cemetery.

Bibliography: *DAB*.

**SULLIVAN, John** (brother of James Sullivan and father of George Sullivan), a Delegate from New Hampshire; born in Somersworth, N.H., February 17, 1740; received a limited education; studied law; was admitted to the bar and commenced practice in Durham in 1760; Member of the Continental Congress in 1774 and 1775; during the Revolution was appointed as a brigadier general; later promoted to major general, and from June 1775 until early in 1780; again a Member of the Continental Congress in 1780 and 1781; attorney general of New Hampshire 1782-1786; President of New Hampshire in 1786 and 1787; member of the state ratification convention in 1788; speaker of the State house of representatives; again chosen President of New Hampshire; appointed by President George Washington judge of the United States District Court of New Hampshire in September 1789 and held that office until his death in Durham, N.H., January 23, 1795; interment in the Sullivan family cemetery.

Bibliography: *DAB*; Sullivan, John. *Letters and Papers of Major General John Sullivan, Continental Army*. 3 vols. Edited by Otis G. Hammond. Concord, N.H.: New Hampshire Historical Society, 1930-39.

**SULLIVAN, John Andrew**, a Representative from Massachusetts; born in Boston, Mass., May 10, 1868; attended the common and high schools; graduated from the Boston University Law School in 1896; admitted to the bar the same year and commenced practice in Boston, Mass.; member of the Massachusetts senate 1900-1902; elected as a Democrat to the Fifty-eighth and Fifty-ninth Congresses (March 4, 1903-March 3, 1907); declined to be a candidate for renomination; resumed the practice of law in Boston, Mass.; appointed a member of the Boston Finance Commission in July 1907 and served until the commission expired; in June 1909 became chairman of the permanent finance commission; resigned in 1914 to become corporation counsel of Boston; lecturer on municipal government in Harvard University in 1912 and 1913; lecturer at Boston University Law School 1920-1925; resumed the practice of his profession in Boston; died in Scituate, Mass., May 31, 1927; interment in Holy Cross Cemetery, Malden, Mass.

**SULLIVAN, John Berchmans** (husband of Leonor Kretzer Sullivan), a Representative from Missouri; born in Sedalia, Pettis County, Mo., October 10, 1897; attended St. Patrick's parochial school in Sedalia, Mo.; moved to St. Louis, Mo., in 1910; was graduated from Gonzaga Hall (St. Louis University High School) in 1914 and from St. Louis University in 1918; during the First World War enlisted in the United States Army and served as a private in the Infantry; was graduated from the law department of the St. Louis University in 1922; was admitted to the bar in 1921 and commenced practice in St. Louis, Mo.; delegate to the Democratic State conventions in 1928, 1932, and 1940; associate city counselor of St. Louis 1936-1938; secretary to the mayor of St. Louis

1938-1940; elected as a Democrat to the Seventy-seventh Congress (January 3, 1941-January 3, 1943); unsuccessful candidate for reelection in 1942 to the Seventy-eighth Congress; elected to the Seventy-ninth Congress (January 3, 1945-January 3, 1947); unsuccessful candidate for reelection in 1946 to the Eightieth Congress; special assistant to the United States Attorney General in 1947 and 1948; elected to the Eighty-first and Eighty-second Congresses and served from January 3, 1949, until his death in Bethesda, Md., January 29, 1951; interment in Calvary Cemetery, St. Louis, Mo.

**SULLIVAN, Leonor Kretzer** (wife of John Berchmans Sullivan), a Representative from Missouri; born August 21, 1902, in St. Louis, Mo.; attended public and private schools; also attended Washington University, St. Louis, Mo., night classes for training in selected and special subjects; taught business arithmetic and accounting and also served as director of the St. Louis Comptometer School; served as administrative aide to her husband, John B. Sullivan, 1942-1951, and as secretary to Representative Theodore L. Irving of Missouri until May 1952, when she resigned to campaign for congressional nomination; elected as a Democrat to the Eighty-third and to the eleven succeeding Congresses (January 3, 1953-January 3, 1977); chairman, Committee on Merchant Marine and Fisheries (Ninety-third and Ninety-fourth Congresses); was not a candidate for reelection in 1976 to the Ninety-fifth Congress; was a resident of St. Louis, Mo.; died September 1, 1988.

**SULLIVAN, Maurice Joseph**, a Representative from Nevada; born in San Rafael, Marin County, Calif., December 7, 1884; attended the parochial school and Sacred Heart College, San Francisco, Calif.; Lieutenant Governor of Nevada, 1915-1926, and 1939-1942; during the First World War was adjutant general of Nevada, disbursing officer of the United States Government, and draft executive of Nevada; colonel in the United States Army from 1922 until 1932; was admitted to the bar in 1923 and commenced practice in Carson City, Nev.; also a mining operator; principal owner of the Wood-Sullivan Hardware Company; elected as a Democrat to the Seventy-eighth Congress (January 3, 1943-January 3, 1945); unsuccessful candidate for renomination in 1944 to the Seventy-ninth Congress; resumed the practice of law in Reno, Nev., until his death there on August 9, 1953; interment in Mater Dolorosa Cemetery.

**SULLIVAN, Patrick Joseph**, a Representative from Pennsylvania; born in Pittsburgh, Allegheny County, Pa., October 12, 1877; attended public and parochial schools; employed in the Homestead Axle Works, Homestead, Pa., 1890-1900, and in the steel mills at Pittsburgh, Pa., 1900-1909; member of the city council 1906-1909; served as alderman 1910-1929; police magistrate 1916-1923; member of the board of assessment and tax revision, Allegheny County, Pa., 1923-1929; elected as a Republican to the Seventy-first and Seventy-second Congresses (March 4, 1929-March 3, 1933); unsuccessful candidate for renomination in 1932; city police magistrate in Pittsburgh, Pa., from 1936 until his death there December 31, 1946; interment in Calvary Cemetery.

**SULLIVAN, Patrick Joseph**, a Senator from Wyoming; born on a farm west of Bantry, County Cork, Ireland, March 17, 1865; immigrated to America in 1888, landed in New York, and moved on to the Territory of Wyoming; engaged in sheep raising in Rawlins, Carbon County; moved to Casper, Natrona County, in 1892; interested in banking, the production of oil, and various other enterprises; member, State house of representatives 1894-1896, 1898-1900; mayor of Casper 1897-1898; appointed as a Republican to the United States Senate to fill the vacancy caused by the death of Francis E. Warren and served from December 5, 1929, to November 20, 1930, when a successor was elected and qualified; was not a candidate for election to fill the vacancy; continued his former business pursuits until his death in Santa Barbara, Calif., April 8, 1935; interment in Highland Cemetery, Casper, Wyo.

**SULLIVAN, Timothy Daniel,** a Representative from New York; born in New York City, July 23, 1863; attended the public schools; worked as a bundler of newspapers, bootblack, and as a wholesale news dealer; engaged in the vaudeville circuit theater business, and was also financially interested in amusement parks, athletic clubs, nickelodeons and racetracks; elected to the New York State assembly in 1886 and served until 1893; member of the New York State senate, 1893-1902; elected as a Democrat to the Fifty-eighth and Fifty-ninth Congresses, and served from March 4, 1903 to July 27, 1906, when he resigned; served in the New York State senate in 1908 and 1910; elected in 1912 to the Sixty-third Congress but never took his seat; committed on January 10, 1913, to a sanitarium in Yonkers, N.Y.; escaped from the care of three nurses at his brother's home in Eastchester, N.Y., and was struck and killed by a locomotive near Pelham Parkway, New York City, on August 31, 1913; interment in Calvary Cemetery, Long Island City, N.Y.

Bibliography: *DAB*; Czitrom, Daniel. "Underworlds and Underdogs: Big Tim Sullivan and Metropolitan Politics in New York, 1889-1917." *Journal of American History* 78 (September 1991): 536-558.

**SULLIVAN, William Van Amberg,** a Representative and a Senator from Mississippi; born near Winona, Montgomery County, Miss., December 18, 1857; attended the common schools in Panola County and the University of Mississippi at Oxford; graduated from Vanderbilt University, Nashville, Tenn., in 1875; was admitted to the bar in 1875 and commenced practice in Austin, Tunica County; moved to Oxford, Lafayette County, Miss., in 1877; member of the board of city aldermen; elected as a Democrat to the Fifty-fifth Congress and served from March 4, 1897, to May 31, 1898, when he resigned, having been appointed Senator; appointed and subsequently elected as a Democrat to the United States Senate to fill the vacancy caused by the death of Edward C. Walthall and served from May 31, 1898, to March 3, 1901; retired from active business and resided in Washington, D.C.; died in Oxford, Miss., March 21, 1918; interment in St. Peter's Cemetery.

**SULLOWAY, Cyrus Adams,** a Representative from New Hampshire; born in Grafton, Grafton County, N.H., June 8, 1839; attended the common schools, Colby Academy, and Kimball Academy; studied law in Franklin, N.H.; was admitted to the bar in 1863 and commenced practice in Manchester, N.H.; member of the State house of representatives in 1872, 1873, and 1887-1893; elected as a Republican to the Fifty-fourth and to the eight succeeding Congresses (March 4, 1895-March 3, 1913); chairman, Committee on Expenditures in the Department of Justice (Fifty-fifth Congress), Committee on Invalid Pensions (Fifty-sixth through Sixty-second Congresses); unsuccessful candidate for reelection in 1912 to the Sixty-third Congress; elected to the Sixty-fourth and Sixty-fifth Congresses and served from March 4, 1915, until his death in Washington, D.C., March 11, 1917; interment in the City Cemetery, Franklin, N.H.

**SULZER, Charles August** (brother of William Sulzer), a Delegate from the Territory of Alaska; born in Roselle, Union County, N.J., February 24, 1879; attended the public schools, Pingry School, Elizabeth, N.J., Berkeley Academy, New York City, and the United States Military Academy, West Point, N.Y.; during the Spanish-American War served with the Fourth Regiment, New Jersey Volunteer Infantry; moved to Alaska in 1902 and engaged in mining; member of the Alaska Territorial senate in 1914; presented credentials as a Democratic Delegate-elect to the Sixty-fifth Congress and served from March 4, 1917, to January 7, 1919, when he was succeeded by James Wickersham, who contested his election; presented credentials as a Delegate-elect to the Sixty-sixth Congress and served from March 4, 1919, until his death in Sulzer, Alaska, April 28, 1919, before the convening of Congress; interment in Evergreen Cemetery, Elizabeth, N.J.

**SULZER, William** (brother of Charles August Sulzer), a Representative from New York; born in Elizabeth, N.J., March 18, 1863; spent his early years on his father's farm near Elizabeth; ran away to sea in 1875 and served as a cabin boy for one year; attended the public schools and Columbia College, New York City; worked as a clerk at a wholesale grocery house while studying law; was admitted to the bar in 1884 and commenced practice in New York City; member of the New York State assembly, 1889-1894, serving as speaker in 1893; delegate to the Democratic National Conventions of 1892, 1896, 1900, 1904, 1908, and 1912; elected as a Democrat to the Fifty-fourth and to the eight succeeding Congresses, and served from March 4, 1895 until his resignation on December 31, 1912, having been elected Governor; chairman, Committee on Foreign Affairs (Sixty-second Congress); elected Governor of New York in 1912, and served from January 1, 1913 until October 18, 1913, when he was removed from office by the legislature; elected as an independent to the State assembly in November 1913; unsuccessful American Party and Prohibition Party candidate for election for Governor in 1914; declined the nomination for President in 1916 by the American Party; engaged in the practice of law in New York City until his death there on November 6, 1941; interment in Evergreen Cemetery, Hillside, N.J.

Bibliography: *DAB*; Wesser, Robert F. "Impeachment of a Governor: William Sulzer and the Politics of Excess." *New York History* 60 (October 1979): 407-38.

**SUMMERS, George William,** a Representative from Virginia; born near Alexandria, Va., March 4, 1804; attended school at Charleston, Va. (now West Virginia) and Washington College (now Washington and Lee University), Lexington, Va.; graduated from the Ohio University at Athens in 1826; studied law; admitted to the bar in 1827 and commenced practice in Charleston, Va.; member of the Virginia house of delegates 1830-1832 and 1834-1836; elected as a Whig to the Twenty-seventh and Twenty-eighth Congresses (March 4, 1841-March 3, 1845); unsuccessful candidate for reelection in 1844 to the Twenty-ninth Congress; elected as a delegate to the Virginia constitutional convention in 1850; unsuccessful Whig candidate for Governor in 1851; judge of the eighteenth judicial circuit of Virginia 1852-1858; member of the peace conference held at Washington, D.C., in 1861 in an effort to devise means to prevent the impending war; delegate to the secession convention in 1861 at Richmond, Va.; resumed the practice of his profession; died in Charleston, W.Va., September 19, 1868; interment in Walnut Grove Cemetery, Putnam County, W.Va.

Bibliography: *DAB*.

**SUMMERS, John William,** a Representative from Washington; born near Valeene, Orange County, Ind., April 29, 1870; attended the public schools; was graduated from the Southern Indiana Normal College at Mitchell, Ind., in 1889 and from the Kentucky School of Medicine at Louisville in 1892; pursued postgraduate studies in the Louisville Medical College and in New York, London, Berlin, and the University of Vienna, Austria; commenced the practice of medicine in Mattoon, Ill.; moved to Walla Walla, Wash., in 1908 and continued the practice of medicine; also engaged in agricultural pursuits and fruit raising; member of the State house of representatives in 1917; elected as a Republican to the Sixty-sixth and to the six succeeding Congresses (March 4, 1919-March 3, 1933); unsuccessful candidate for reelection in 1932 to the Seventy-third Congress, and for election in 1934 to the Seventy-fourth Congress and in 1936 to the Seventy-fifth Congress; resumed former pursuits; died in Walla Walla, Wash., on September 25, 1937; interment in Mountain View Cemetery.

**SUMNER, Charles,** a Senator from Massachusetts; born in Boston, Mass., January 6, 1811; attended the Boston Latin School; graduated from Harvard University in 1830 and from the Harvard Law School in 1833; was admitted to the bar the following year and commenced the practice of law in Boston, Mass.; lectured at the Harvard Law School 1836-1837; traveled extensively in Europe 1837-1840; declined the Whig nomination in 1846 for election to the Thirtieth Congress; one of the founders of the Free-Soil Party in 1848; unsuccessful candidate for election in 1848 on the Free-Soil ticket to the Thirty-first Congress; elected to the United States Senate in 1851 as a Free-Soiler; reelected as a Republican in 1857, 1863, and 1869 and served from April 24, 1851, until his death; as a result of his inflamatory "Crime Against Kansas" speech, was assaulted by Representative Preston Brooks of South Carolina, May 22, 1856, while in his seat in the Senate, and was absent on account of injuries received until December 1859; chairman, Committee on Foreign Relations (Thirty-seventh through Forty-first Congresses), Committee on Privileges and Elections (Forty-second Congress); removed as chairman of the Committee on Foreign Relations in 1871 as a result of differences with President Ulysses S. Grant over policy in Santo Domingo; died in Washington, D.C., March 11, 1874; interment in Mount Auburn Cemetery, Cambridge, Mass.

**Bibliography:** *DAB*; Donald, David Herbert. *Charles Sumner.* With a new introduction by the author. 1960, 1970. Reprint. New York: Da Capo Press, 1996.

**SUMNER, Charles Allen,** a Representative from California; born in Great Barrington, Mass., on August 2, 1835; attended Trinity College, Hartford, Conn.; studied law; was admitted to the bar and engaged in patent practice; moved to California in 1856 and settled in San Francisco; editor of the Herald and Mirror in 1861; during the Civil War was appointed November 26, 1862, to be captain and assistant quartermaster of United States Volunteers, and served until his resignation on March 30, 1864; moved to Virginia City, Nev.; member of the State senate 1865-1868 and served as president pro tempore for one session; returned to San Francisco in 1868 and became editor of the Herald; was elected as a Democrat to the Forty-eighth Congress (March 4, 1883-March 3, 1885); unsuccessful candidate for reelection in 1884 to the Forty-ninth Congress; resumed the practice of law; died in San Francisco, Calif., January 31, 1903; interment in the George H. Thomas Post plot at the Presidio.

**SUMNER, Daniel Hadley,** a Representative from Wisconsin; born in Malone, Franklin County, N.Y., September 15, 1837; moved to Michigan in 1843 with his parents, who settled in Richland; attended the common schools and Prairie Seminary, Richland, Mich.; studied law; was admitted to the bar in 1868 and commenced practice in Kalamazoo, Mich.; moved to Oconomowoc, Wis., in 1868 and practiced law; also published the La Belle Mirror; moved to Waukesha, Wis., in 1870 and continued the practice of his profession; town superintendent of schools; member of the county board of supervisors; district attorney of Waukesha County in 1876 and 1877; elected as a Democrat to the Forty-eighth Congress (March 4, 1883-March 3, 1885); was not a candidate for renomination in 1884; resumed the practice of law; died in Waukesha, Wis., May 29, 1903; interment in Prairie Home Cemetery.

**SUMNER, Jessie,** a Representative from Illinois; born in Milford, Iroquois County, Ill., July 17, 1898; attended the public schools; was graduated from Girton School, Winnetka, Ill., in 1916 and Smith College, Northampton, Mass., in 1920; studied law at the University of Chicago, Columbia University, New York City, and Oxford University, England; also studied briefly at the University of Wisconsin at Madison and New York University School of Commerce in New York City; was admitted to the bar in 1923 and practiced in Chicago, Ill.; employed at the Chase National Bank in New York City in 1928; returned to Milford, Ill., in 1932 and resumed the practice of law; served as county judge of Iroquois County, Ill., in 1937; director of Sumner National Bank, Sheldon, Ill.; elected as a Republican to the Seventy-sixth and to the three succeeding Congresses (January 3, 1939-January 3, 1947); was not a candidate

for renomination in 1946 to the Eightieth Congress; resumed position as vice president and later president of Sumner National Bank; was a resident of Milford, Ill.; died August 10, 1994.

**SUMNERS, Hatton William,** a Representative from Texas; born near Fayetteville, Lincoln County, Tenn., May 30, 1875; moved to Garland, Dallas County, Tex., in 1893; studied law; was admitted to the bar in 1897 and commenced practice in Dallas, Tex.; elected prosecuting attorney of Dallas County in 1900 and served two terms; president of the district and county attorney's association of Texas in 1906 and 1907; elected as a Democrat to the Sixty-third and to the sixteen succeeding Congresses (March 4, 1913-January 3, 1947); chairman, Committee on the Judiciary (Seventy-second through Seventy-ninth Congresses); was not a candidate for renomination in 1946 to the Eightieth Congress; retired from public activities; was a resident of Dallas, Tex., until his death there on April 19, 1962; interment in Knights of Pythias Cemetery, Garland, Tex.

**Bibliography:** *DAB*; Law, Ron C. "Congressman Hatton W. Sumners of Dallas, Texas: His Life and Congressional Career, 1875-1937." Ph.D. dissertation, Texas Christian University, 1990; Patenaude, Lionel V. "Garner, Sumners, and Connally: The Defeat of the Roosevelt Court Bill in 1937." *Southwestern Historical Quarterly* 74 (July 1970): 36-51; Porter, David. "The Battle of the Texas Giants: Hatton Sumners, Sam Rayburn, and the Logan-Walter Bill of 1939." *Texana* 12 (1973): 349-61.

**SUMTER, Thomas** (grandfather of Thomas De Lage Sumter), a Representative and a Senator from South Carolina; born near Charlottesville, Va., August 14, 1734; received a limited schooling; fought in skirmishes against the Indians; moved to South Carolina about 1760 and opened a crossroads store near Nelson's Ferry; justice of the peace; served with the South Carolina troops throughout the Revolution; elected to the privy council in 1782; elected a Delegate to the Continental Congress in 1783, but declined to accept; served several terms in the State house of representatives; delegate to the State convention which ratified the Constitution, which he opposed; planter; elected to the First and Second Congresses (March 4, 1789-March 3, 1793); defeated for reelection in 1792; elected as a Republican to the Fifth, Sixth, and Seventh Congresses and served from March 4, 1797, to December 15, 1801, when he resigned; elected as a Republican to the United States Senate in December 1801 to fill the vacancy caused by the resignation of Charles Pinckney; reelected in 1805 and served from December 15, 1801, until his resignation on December 16, 1810; retired from public life and lived on his plantation, "South Mount," near Stateburg, S.C.; died at "South Mount," June 1, 1832; interment in the private burial ground on the family estate.

**Bibliography:** *DAB*; Bass, Robert. *Gamecock: The Life and Campaigns of General Thomas Sumter.* New York: Holt, Rinehart and Winston, 1961; Gregorie, Anne. *Thomas Sumter.* Columbia, S.C.: The R.L. Bryon Co., 1931.

**SUMTER, Thomas De Lage** (grandson of Thomas Sumter), a Representative from South Carolina; born in Germantown, Pa., November 14, 1809; attended the common schools at Edgehill, near Stateburg, S.C.; was graduated from the United States Military Academy at West Point, N.Y., in 1835; entered the United States Army as first lieutenant the same year and served until 1841, attaining the rank of colonel; engaged in the war against the Seminole Indians; moved to Stateburg, S.C.; elected as a Democrat to the Twenty-sixth and Twenty-seventh Congresses (March 4, 1839-March 3, 1843); was not a candidate for renomination; engaged in teaching, surveying, and agricultural pursuits; connected as agent with the South Carolina Railroad Co.; died on his plantation, "South Mount," near Stateburg, S.C., July 2, 1874; interment in the private burial ground on his estate.

**SUNDQUIST, Donald Kenneth,** a Representative from Tennessee; born in Moline, Rock Island County, Ill., March 15, 1936; attended public schools and graduated from Moline High School in 1954; B.A., Augustana College, Rock Island, Ill., 1957; served in the United States Navy, 1957-1959, and in the United States Naval Reserve, 1959-1963; businessman; delegate to the Republican National Conventions of 1976 and 1980; elected as a Republican to the Ninety-eighth and to the five succeeding Congresses (January 3, 1983-January 3, 1995); was not a candidate in 1994 for reelection to the One Hundred Fourth Congress, but was elected Governor of Tennessee for a four-year term beginning January 21, 1995; is a resident of Memphis, Tenn.

**SUNDSTROM, Frank Leander,** a Representative from New Jersey; born in Massena, St. Lawrence County, N.Y., January 5, 1901; attended the public schools; newspaper reporter and editor 1918-1920; was graduated from Cornell University, Ithaca, N.Y., in 1924; football coach at Indiana University at Bloomington in 1924; engaged in the banking and brokerage business in New York City in 1925-1969; chairman of the East Orange (N.J.) Republican Committee 1940-1946; elected as a Republican to the Seventy-eighth, Seventy-ninth, and Eightieth Congresses (January 3, 1943-January 3, 1949); unsuccessful candidate for reelection in 1948 to the Eighty-first Congress; vice president and director, Schenley Distillers, 1954-1969; vice president and director of public relations, Schenley Industries, Inc., 1955-1969; vice president of the Tobacco Institute, 1969-1976; consultant for a group of United States distillers, 1976-1980; resided in Chatham, N.J., until his death in Summit, N.J., May 23, 1980; interment in Restland Memorial Park, East Hanover, N.J.

**SUNIA, Fofó Iosefa Fiti,** the first Delegate from American Samoa; born in Fagasá, Pago Pago, American Samoa, March 13, 1937; attended the public schools in Samoa; B.A., University of Hawaii, Honolulu, 1960; administrative officer, Samoan affairs-liaison functions for Governor, translator, interpreter, 1961-1966; election commissioner, American Samoa, 1962-1970; founder, Samoan News, 1964; director, tourism for Government of American Samoa, 1966-1972; senator, Legislature of American Samoa, 1970-1978; delegate at large to Washington, D.C., 1979-1980; president and chairman, American Samoan Development Corporation, 1965-1971; elected as a Democrat to the Ninety-seventh and to the three succeeding Congresses and served from January 3, 1981 until his resignation on September 6, 1988; is a resident of Pago Pago, American Samoa.

**SUTHERLAND, Daniel Alexander,** a Delegate from the Territory of Alaska; born in Pleasant Bay on Cape Breton Island, Canada, April 17, 1869; moved with his parents to Essex, Mass., in 1876; attended the public schools; was employed as a grocer's clerk, and subsequently engaged in the fish business; moved to Circle City, Alaska, in 1898, to Nome in 1900, and thence to Juneau in 1909; engaged in mining and fishing; member of the Territorial senate 1912-1920, serving as president in 1915; during the First World War enrolled in the United States Naval Reserve; elected as a Republican to the Sixty-seventh and to the four succeeding Congresses (March 4, 1921-March 3, 1931); was not a candidate for renomination in 1930; purchasing agent for the Ogontz (Pa.) School 1931-1950; died in Abington, Pa., March 24, 1955; remains were cremated and deposited in St. Paul's Church Cemetery, Elkins Park, Pa.

**SUTHERLAND, George,** a Representative and a Senator from Utah; born in Buckinghamshire, England, March 25, 1862; immigrated to the United States in 1863 with his parents, who were Mormon converts, and settled in Springville, Utah County, Utah; received a common-school education; miner; studied law at the University of Michigan at Ann Arbor; was admitted to the bar in 1883 and commenced practice in Provo, Utah; unsuccessful candidate for mayor of Provo, Utah, in 1890; unsuccessful candidate for Territorial representative in Congress in 1892; member, Utah State senate, 1897-1901; elected as a Republican to the Fifty-seventh Congress (March 4, 1901-March 3, 1903); declined to be a candidate for reelection in 1902 to the Fifty-eighth Congress; elected as a Republican to the United States Senate in 1904; reelected in 1910, and served from March 4, 1905, to March 3, 1917; unsuccessful candidate for reelection in 1916; chairman, Committee on Cuban Relations (Sixty-first Congress), Committee on Public Buildings and Grounds (Sixty-second Congress), Committee on Expenditures in the Department of Justice (Sixty-third and Sixty-fourth Congresses); president of the American Bar Association, 1916-1917; nominated on September 5, 1922 by President Warren G. Harding as an Associate Justice of the United States Supreme Court; was confirmed by the Senate the same day and served until his retirement on January 18, 1938; died in Stockbridge, Mass., July 18, 1942; interment in the Abbey Mausoleum, Arlington, Va.; remains subsequently moved to Cedar Hill Cemetery, Washington, D.C.

**Bibliography:** *DAB*; Paschal, Joel. *Mr. Justice Sutherland, A Man Against the State.* 1951. Reprint. New York: Greenwood Press, 1969; Sutherland, George. *Constitutional Power and World Affairs.* 1919. Reprint. New York: Johnson Reprint Corp., 1970.

**SUTHERLAND, Howard,** a Representative and a Senator from West Virginia; born near Kirkwood, St. Louis County, Mo., September 8, 1865; attended the public schools of the county and the city of St. Louis; graduated from Westminster College, Fulton, Mo., in 1889; edited a daily and weekly newspaper at Fulton; moved to Washington, D.C., in 1890; employed in the Census Office; studied law at Columbian (now George Washington) University, Washington, D.C.; moved to Elkins, Randolph County, W.Va., in 1893; engaged in the coal and railroad business and later in the coal and timberland business; member, State senate 1908-1912; elected as a Republican to the Sixty-third and Sixty-fourth Congresses (March 4, 1913-March 3, 1917); did not seek renomination in 1916, having become a candidate for Senator; elected as a Republican to the United States Senate in 1916 and served from March 4, 1917, to March 3, 1923; unsuccessful candidate for reelection in 1922; chairman, Committee on the Census (Sixty-sixth Congress), Committee on Enrolled Bills (Sixty-seventh Congress); resumed his former business activities in Elkins, W.Va.; vice president of the West Virginia Board of Trade; chairman of the West Virginia Good Roads Commission; member of the board of trustees of Davis and Elkins Presbyterian College; appointed Alien Property Custodian by President Calvin Coolidge 1925-1933, when he resigned and retired from public life; was a resident of Washington, D.C., until his death March 12, 1950; interment in Maplewood Cemetery, Elkins, W.Va.

**Bibliography:** Casdorph, Paul D. "Howard Sutherland's 1920 Bid for the Presidency." *West Virginia History* 35 (1973-1974): 1-25.

**SUTHERLAND, Jabez Gridley,** a Representative from Michigan; born in Van Buren, Onondaga County, N.Y., October 6, 1825; completed preparatory studies; studied law; was admitted to the bar in 1848 and commenced practice in Saginaw, Mich.; prosecuting attorney of Saginaw County, Mich., in 1848 and 1849; delegate to the State constitutional conventions in 1850 and 1867; member of the State house of representatives in 1853; judge of the tenth circuit court of Michigan from 1863 to 1871, when he resigned to enter Congress; elected as a Democrat to the Forty-second Congress (March 4, 1871-March 3, 1873); was not a candidate for renomination in 1872; moved to Salt Lake City in 1873; resumed the practice of law; a member of the faculty of what is now the University of Utah in 1889; president of the Territorial Bar Association in 1894 and 1895; moved to California in 1897; died in Berkeley, Calif., November 20, 1902; interment in Mount Olivet Cemetery, Salt Lake City, Utah.

**SUTHERLAND, Joel Barlow,** a Representative from Pennsylvania; born in Gloucester County, N.J., February 26, 1792; attended the common schools; graduated from the University of Pennsylvania at Philadelphia in 1812; served in the War of 1812 as assistant surgeon to the "Junior Artillerists of Philadelphia," transferred to the line, and was appointed in 1814 lieutenant colonel of rifles in the Pennsylvania militia; member of the Pennsylvania house of representatives 1813-1816; founder of Jefferson Medical College at Philadelphia; served in the Pennsylvania senate in 1816 and 1817; abandoned medicine for the practice of law; elected as a Jacksonian to the Twentieth and to the four succeeding Congresses (March 4, 1827-March 3, 1837); chairman, Committee on Commerce (Twenty-third and Twenty-fourth Congresses); unsuccessful Whig candidate for reelection in 1836 to the Twenty-fifth Congress and for election in 1838 to the Twenty-sixth Congress; associate judge of the court of common pleas of Philadelphia, Pa., in 1833 and 1834; died in Philadelphia, Pa., November 15, 1861; interment in the Old Pine Street Presbyterian Church Cemetery.

Bibliography: *DAB.*

**SUTHERLAND, Josiah,** a Representative from New York; born in the township of Stanford, near the village of Stissing, Dutchess County, N.Y., June 12, 1804; attended the district school, and was graduated from Union College, Schenectady, N.Y., in 1824; studied law in Waterford and Hudson; was admitted to the bar in 1828 and commenced practice in the village of Johnstown, Livingston Township, N.Y.; district attorney for Columbia County 1832-1843; moved to Hudson, N.Y., in 1838 and continued the practice of law; elected as a Democrat to the Thirty-second Congress (March 4, 1851-March 3, 1853); was not a candidate for renomination; moved to New York City in 1857 and continued the practice of law; associate justice of the supreme court of New York 1857-1871; member and presiding judge of the court of general sessions 1872-1878; resumed the practice of law in New York City and died there May 25, 1887; interment in Woodlawn Cemetery.

**SUTHERLAND, Roderick Dhu,** a Representative from Nebraska; born in Scotch Grove, Jones County, Iowa, April 27, 1862; attended the common schools and Amity College, College Springs, Iowa; taught school; studied law; was admitted to the bar in 1888 and commenced practice in Nelson, Nuckolls County, Nebr.; prosecuting attorney of Nuckolls County, 1890-1896; served as chairman of the Populist State convention in 1899; appointed by Governor William A. Poynter as a delegate to the trust conference held in Chicago in September 1899; elected as a Populist to the Fifty-fifth and Fifty-sixth Congresses (March 4, 1897-March 3, 1901); unsuccessful candidate for reelection in 1900 to the Fifty-seventh Congress; delegate to the Populist National Convention of 1900; delegate to the Democratic National Conventions of 1900 and 1908; resumed the practice of his profession in Nelson, Nebr.; died in Kansas City, Kans., October 18, 1915; interment in Evergreen Cemetery, Nelson, Nebr.

**SUTPHIN, William Halstead,** a Representative from New Jersey; born in Browntown, Middlesex County, N.J., August 30, 1887; attended the public schools of Matawan, N.J., and the Woods Business College, Brooklyn, N.Y.; attended the officers training camp at Plattsburgh, N.Y., in 1915; mayor of Matawan, Monmouth County, N.J., 1915-1916 and 1921-1926; served on the Mexican border in 1916 with B Troop, First Squadron, New Jersey Cavalry; during the First World War served in France from December 1917 to May 1919; discharged as captain in the Air Service; factory representative for asphalt roofing 1920-1931; elected as a Democrat to the Seventy-second and to the five succeeding Congresses (March 4, 1931-January 3, 1943); unsuccessful candidate for reelection in 1942 to the Seventy-eighth Congress; vice president of the M.J. Merkin Paint Co., in New York City; retired in 1951 and resided in Berlin, Md.; died in Salisbury, Md., October 14, 1972; interment in Arlington National Cemetery, Va.

**SUTTON, James Patrick,** a Representative from Tennessee; born on a farm near Wartrace, Bedford County, Tenn., October 31, 1915; attended the public schools of Wartrace, Tenn., and Cumberland University Law School, Lebanon, Tenn.; graduated from Middle Tennessee State College at Murfreesboro in 1939; served in the United States Navy, 1942-1946; awarded the Distinguished Service Cross, Silver Star, Purple Heart with oak leaf cluster; elected as a Democrat to the Eighty-first and to the two succeeding Congresses (January 3, 1949-January 3, 1955); was not a candidate in 1954 for reelection to the House of Representatives, but was an unsuccessful candidate for nomination to the United States Senate; investment securities broker.

**SWAN, Samuel,** a Representative from New Jersey; born near Scotch Plains, Somerset County, N.J., in 1771; studied medicine, and practiced in Boundbrook, N.J., 1800-1806 and in Somerville, N.J., 1806-1809; commissioned as sheriff of Somerset County October 13, 1804, for two years; county clerk 1809-1820; elected to the Seventeenth and to the four succeeding Congresses (March 4, 1821-March 3, 1831); did not seek renomination in 1830 to the Twenty-second Congress; affiliated with the Whig Party; resumed the practice of medicine; died at Boundbrook, N.J., August 24, 1844; interment in the De Groot vault in the Presbyterian Cemetery.

**SWANK, Fletcher B.,** a Representative from Oklahoma; born near Bloomfield, Davis County, Iowa, April 24, 1875; moved with his parents to Beef Creek, Indian Territory, in 1888; attended an academy in Noble, Okla., and University of Oklahoma at Norman; superintendent of schools of Cleveland County, Okla., 1903-1907; private secretary to Representative Scott Ferris of Oklahoma in 1907 and 1908; attended the law department of Georgetown University, Washington, D.C., in 1907 and 1908, and was graduated from Cumberland University, Lebanon, Tenn., in 1909; was admitted to the bar in 1909 and commenced practice in Norman, Cleveland County, Okla.; judge of the county court of Cleveland County, Okla., 1911-1915; judge of the fourteenth judicial district of Oklahoma from 1915 to September 1920, when he resigned; elected as a Democrat to the Sixty-seventh and to the three succeeding Congresses (March 4, 1921-March 3, 1929); unsuccessful candidate for reelection in 1928 to the Seventy-first Congress; elected to the Seventy-second and Seventy-third Congresses (March 4, 1931-January 3, 1935); unsuccessful candidate for renomination in 1934 to the Seventy-fourth Congress; died in Norman, Okla., March 16, 1950; interment in Odd Fellows Cemetery.

**SWANN, Edward,** a Representative from New York, born near Madison, Madison County, Fla., March 10, 1862; attended the common schools and was graduated from the law department of Columbia College (now University), New York City, in 1886; was admitted to the bar the same year and commenced practice in New York City; elected as a Democrat to the Fifty-seventh Congress to fill the vacancy caused by the death of Amos J. Cummings and served from November 4, 1902, to March 3, 1903; was not a candidate for renomination in 1902; resumed the practice of law in New York City; elected judge of the court of general sessions, New York City, and served from January 1, 1908, until his resignation in 1916; district attorney for New York County 1916-1922; retired from public and political activities; died in Sewalls Point, Jensen Beach, Fla., September 19, 1945; interment in St. Peters Episcopal Cemetery, Fernandina, Fla.

**SWANN, John,** a Delegate from North Carolina; born in Pasquotank County, N.C., in 1760; attended the College of William and Mary, Williamsburg, Va., about 1780; appointed a Delegate to the Continental Congress to fill the vacancy caused by the resignation of John Baptista Ashe and served from March 22 to

November 1, 1788; engaged in agricultural pursuits; urged the adoption by North Carolina of the proposed Constitution of the United States; died in 1793; interment on the grounds of his plantation, "The Elms," in Pasquotank County, N.C.

**SWANN, Thomas,** a Representative from Maryland; born in Alexandria, Va., February 3, 1809; attended Columbian College (now George Washington University), Washington, D.C., and the University of Virginia at Charlottesville; studied law; was appointed by President Andrew Jackson as secretary of the United States Neapolitan Commission; moved to Baltimore, Md., in 1834; director and president of the Baltimore and Ohio Railroad, 1847-1853; president of the Northwestern Virginia Railroad; mayor of Baltimore, 1856-1860; elected by the Union Republican Party as Governor of Maryland in 1864, and served from January 10, 1866 to January 13, 1869; elected as a Democrat to the United States Senate in 1866, but did not serve, preferring to continue as Governor; elected as a Democrat to the Forty-first and to the four succeeding Congresses (March 4, 1869-March 3, 1879); chairman, Committee on Foreign Affairs (Forty-fourth and Forty-fifth Congresses); died on his estate, "Morven Park," near Leesburg, Va., July 24, 1883; interment in Greenmount Cemetery, Baltimore, Md.

**Bibliography:** *DAB.*

**SWANSON, Charles Edward,** a Representative from Iowa; born on a farm near Galesburg, Knox County, Ill., January 3, 1879; in 1890 moved to Iowa with his parents, who settled on a farm in Ringgold County; attended the public schools of Galesburg, Ill., and Clearfield, Iowa; was graduated from Knox College, Galesburg, Ill., in 1902, and from the law department of Northwestern University, Evanston, Ill., in 1907; principal of schools, Altona, Ill., 1902-1904; was admitted to the bar in 1907 and commenced practice in Council Bluffs, Iowa; prosecuting attorney of Pottawattamie County, Iowa, 1915-1922; elected as a Republican to the Seventy-first and to the Seventy-second Congresses (March 4, 1929-March 3, 1933); unsuccessful candidate for reelection in 1932 to the Seventy-third Congress and for election in 1934 to the Seventy-fourth Congress; resumed the practice of law; chairman, City Board of Tax Review, 1949-1968; died in Council Bluffs, Iowa, August 22, 1970; interment in Walnut Hill Cemetery.

**SWANSON, Claude Augustus,** a Representative and a Senator from Virginia; born in Swansonville, Va., March 31, 1862; attended the public schools; taught school; attended the Virginia Agricultural and Mechanical College (now the Virginia Polytechnic Institute and State University) at Blacksburg; graduated from Randolph-Macon College, Ashland, Va., in 1885 and from the law department of the University of Virginia at Charlottesville in 1886; was admitted to the bar in 1886 and commenced practice in Chatham, Pittsylvania County, Va.; elected as a Democrat to the Fifty-third and to the six succeeding Congresses and served from March 4, 1893, until his resignation, effective January 30, 1906; unsuccessful candidate for nomination as governor in 1901; elected Governor of Virginia in 1905, and served from February 1, 1906 to February 1, 1910; appointed as a Democrat to the United States Senate in August 1910 to fill the vacancy in the term ending March 3, 1911, caused by the death of John W. Daniel; again appointed, on February 28, 1911, and subsequently elected to fill the vacancy caused by the death of John W. Daniel, who had been reelected for the term commencing March 4, 1911; reelected in 1916, 1922, and in 1928, and served from August 1, 1910 until March 3, 1933, when he resigned to accept a Cabinet portfolio; chairman, Committee on Public Buildings and Grounds (Sixty-third through Sixty-fifth Congresses), Committee on Naval Affairs (Sixty-fifth Congress), Committee on Expenditures in the Department of the Navy (Sixty-sixth Congress); Secretary of the Navy in the Cabinet of President Franklin D. Roosevelt from March 4, 1933 until his death at Rapidan Camp in the Blue Ridge Mountains, near Criglersville, Madison County, Va., July 7, 1939;

funeral services were held in the Chamber of the United States Senate; interment in Hollywood Cemetery, Richmond, Va.

**Bibliography:** *DAB*; Ferrell, Henry C. Jr. *Claude A. Swanson: A Political Biography.* Lexington: University Press of Kentucky, 1985.

**SWANWICK, John,** a Representative from Pennsylvania; born in 1740; engaged in mercantile pursuits in Philadelphia, Pa., and was also interested in literature, having published a volume of poetry; elected as a Republican to the Fourth and Fifth Congresses and served from March 4, 1795, until his death in Philadelphia, Pa., August 1, 1798; chairman, Committee on Commerce and Manufactures (Fourth Congress); interment in St. Peter's Churchyard.

**Bibliography:** Baumann, Ronald M. "John Swanwick: Spokesman for 'Merchant-Republicanism' in Philadelphia, 1790-1798." *Pennsylvania Magazine of History and Biography* 97 (April 1973): 131-82.

**SWART, Peter,** a Representative from New York; born in Schoharie, N.Y., July 5, 1752; attended the common schools; studied law; was admitted to the New York bar and commenced the practice of law in Schoharie; judge of the court of common pleas of Schoharie County in 1795; member of the New York State assembly in 1798 and 1799; elected as a Republican to the Tenth Congress (March 4, 1807-March 3, 1809); sheriff of Schoharie County in 1810 and 1813; served in the New York State senate 1817-1820; resumed the practice of his profession in Schoharie, N.Y., and died there on November 3, 1829; interment in the Old Stone Fort Cemetery.

**SWARTZ, Joshua William,** a Representative from Pennsylvania; born in Lower Swatara Township, Dauphin County, Pa., June 9, 1867; raised on his father's farm; attended the rural schools, Lebanon Valley College, and Williamsport Commercial School; graduated from the law department of Dickinson College, Carlisle, Pa., in 1892; admitted to the bar the same year and commenced practice in Harrisburg, Pa.; member of the Pennsylvania house of representatives 1915-1917; elected as a Republican to the Sixty-ninth Congress (March 4, 1925-March 3, 1927); declined to become a candidate for reelection in 1926; resumed the practice of law until his death in Harrisburg, Pa., May 27, 1959; interment in Paxtang Cemetery, Paxtang, Pa.

**SWASEY, John Philip,** a Representative from Maine; born in Canton, Oxford County, Maine, September 4, 1839; attended the Canton public schools, Dearborn Academy, Hebron Academy, Maine State Seminary, and Tufts College, Medford, Mass.; during the Civil War enlisted in the Union Army and was appointed first lieutenant of Company K, Seventeenth Regiment, Maine Volunteer Infantry; studied law; was admitted to the bar in 1863 and commenced practice in Canton; town clerk and treasurer of Canton in 1866 and 1867; county attorney of Oxford County, Maine, 1868-1870; assessor of internal revenue in 1869 and 1870; member of the State house of representatives in 1874; served in the State senate in 1875 and 1876; member of Governor Robie's council in 1883 and 1884; elected on November 3, 1908, as a Republican to the Sixtieth Congress to fill the vacancy caused by the resignation of Charles E. Littlefield and at the same time was elected to the Sixty-first Congress and served from November 3, 1908, to March 3, 1911; unsuccessful candidate for reelection in 1910 to the Sixty-second Congress; resumed the practice of his profession at Canton, Maine, where he died May 27, 1928; interment in Pine Grove Cemetery.

**SWEARINGEN, Henry,** a Representative from Ohio; born in the Panhandle of Virginia about 1792; moved to Ohio and settled near Steubenville; sheriff of Jefferson County, Ohio, 1824-1828 and 1830-1832; elected as a Democrat to the Twenty-fifth Congress to fill the vacancy caused by the resignation of Daniel Kilgore; reelected to the Twenty-sixth Congress and served from December 3, 1838, to March 3, 1841; died on board ship while en route to his home from the State of California and was buried at sea.

SWEAT, Lorenzo De Medici, a Representative from Maine; born in Parsonsfield, Maine, May 26, 1818; was graduated from Bowdoin College, Brunswick, Maine, in 1837 and from the law department of Harvard University in 1840; was admitted to the bar and commenced practice in New Orleans, La., in 1841; returned to Maine and settled in Portland; held several local offices, including city solicitor, 1856-1860; member of the State senate in 1862; elected as a Democrat to the Thirty-eighth Congress (March 4, 1863-March 3, 1865); unsuccessful candidate for reelection in 1864 to the Thirty-ninth Congress and for election in 1866 to the Fortieth Congress; delegate to the Union National Convention at Philadelphia in 1868; while attending the Democratic National Convention in 1872 was chosen a member of the National committee and served four years; honorary commissioner to the World's Expositions at Paris in 1867 and at Vienna in 1873; died in Portland, Maine, July 26, 1898; interment in Evergreen Cemetery.

SWEENEY, David McCann (Mac), a Representative from Texas; born in Wharton, Tex., September 15, 1955; attended public schools; B.A., University of Texas, 1978; attended University of Texas School of Law, 1979-1981; served on the staff of Senator John Tower, 1977-1978, and Governor John B. Connally, 1979-1980; director of administrative operations at the White House, 1981-1983; elected as a Republican to the Ninety-ninth and to the One Hundredth Congresses (January 3, 1985-January 3, 1989); unsuccessful candidate for reelection in 1988 to the One Hundred First Congress; is a resident of Wharton, Tex.

SWEENEY, Martin Leonard (father of Robert E. Sweeney), a Representative from Ohio; born in Cleveland, Cuyahoga County, Ohio, April 15, 1885; attended the parochial and public schools; was graduated from the Cleveland Law School of Baldwin-Wallace College, Cleveland, Ohio, in 1914; employed as a laborer, 1901-1903; as a hoisting engineer, 1904-1908, and as a salesman, 1910-1913; member of the Ohio State house of representatives in 1913 and 1914; was admitted to the bar in 1914 and commenced practice in Cleveland, Ohio; judge of the municipal court of Cleveland from 1924 until 1932; delegate to the Democratic National Convention of 1932; elected as a Democrat to the Seventy-second Congress to fill the vacancy caused by the death of Charles A. Mooney; reelected to the Seventy-third and to the four succeeding Congresses and served from November 3, 1931, to January 3, 1943; unsuccessful candidate for renomination in 1942 to the Seventy-eighth Congress; unsuccessful candidate for the Democratic nomination for mayor of Cleveland, Ohio, in 1933 and in 1941, and for the gubernatorial nomination in 1944; practiced law in Cleveland, Ohio, until his death there on May 1, 1960; interment in Calvary Cemetery.

Bibliography: *DAB.*

SWEENEY, Robert E. (son of Martin Leonard Sweeney), a Representative from Ohio; born in Cleveland, Cuyahoga County, Ohio, November 4, 1924; attended St. Ignatius High School in Cleveland; Georgetown University, Washington, D.C.; Baldwin-Wallace College, Berea, Ohio, and Cleveland-Marshall Law School, Cleveland, Ohio; studied law; served in the United States Army, 1943-1946; was admitted to the bar in 1951 and commenced the practice of law in Cleveland, Ohio; assistant director of law, city of Cleveland, 1951-1954; special counsel to the attorney general of Ohio, 1958-1962; Democratic candidate for election for attorney general of Ohio in 1962 and 1966; elected as a Democrat to the Eighty-ninth Congress (January 3, 1965-January 3, 1967); was not a candidate for reelection in 1966 to the Ninetieth Congress; resumed the practice of law; appointed in 1976 as Commissioner of Cuyahoga County for an unexpired term ending in 1977; elected to a full term beginning in 1977; unsuccessful candidate for reelection in 1980; is a resident of Bay Village, Ohio.

SWEENEY, William Northcut, a Representative from Kentucky; born in Liberty, Casey County, Ky., May 5, 1832; attended the common schools and Bethany (W.Va.) College; studied law; was admitted to the bar in 1853 and commenced practice in Liberty, Ky.; moved to Owensboro, Daviess County, in 1853; prosecuting attorney of Daviess County, 1854-1858; presidential elector on the Democratic ticket of Stephen A. Douglas and Herschel V. Johnson in 1860; elected as a Democrat to the Forty-first Congress (March 4, 1869-March 3, 1871); was renominated in 1870 to the Forty-second Congress, but declined to accept the nomination; resumed the practice of law in Owensboro, Ky., and died there on April 21, 1895; interment in Elmwood Cemetery.

SWEENY, George, a Representative from Ohio; born near Gettysburg, Pa., February 22, 1796; pursued academic studies and was graduated from Dickinson College, Carlisle, Pa.; studied law; was admitted to the bar and commenced practice in Gettysburg in 1820; moved to Bucyrus, Crawford County, Ohio, in 1830; prosecuting attorney of Crawford County in 1838; elected as a Democrat to the Twenty-sixth and Twenty-seventh Congresses (March 4, 1839-March 3, 1843); was not a candidate for renomination in 1842; resumed the practice of his profession; moved to Geneseo, Henry County, Ill., in 1853, and continued the practice of law; returned to Bucyrus, Ohio, in 1856; was again elected prosecuting attorney of Crawford County; retired from the practice of his profession and engaged in literary and scientific pursuits; died in Bucyrus, Ohio, October 10, 1877; interment in Oakwood Cemetery.

SWEET, Burton Erwin, a Representative from Iowa; born on a farm near Waverly, Bremer County, Iowa, December 10, 1867; attended the common schools and the Iowa State Normal School at Cedar Falls; was graduated from Cornell College, Mount Vernon, Iowa, in 1893 and from the law department of the University of Iowa at Iowa City in 1895; was admitted to the bar in 1895 and commenced practice in Waverly, Iowa; city solicitor of Waverly 1896-1899; member of the State house of representatives 1900-1904; delegate to the Republican National Convention in 1904; member of the Republican State central committee 1902-1906; elected as a Republican to the Sixty-fourth and to the three succeeding Congresses (March 4, 1915-March 3, 1923); did not seek renomination in 1922, having become a candidate for Senator; unsuccessful candidate for United States Senator in the Republican primary election of 1922 and again in 1924; resumed the practice of law; died in Waverly, Iowa, January 3, 1957; interment in Harlington Cemetery.

SWEET, Edwin Forrest, a Representative from Michigan; born in Dansville, Livingston County, N.Y., November 21, 1847; attended the common schools; was graduated from the literary department of Yale College in 1871, and from the law department of Michigan University at Ann Arbor in 1874; was admitted to the bar in 1874 and commenced practice in Grand Rapids, Mich., in 1876; member of the board of education from 1899 to 1906; mayor of Grand Rapids, 1904-1906; elected as a Democrat to the Sixty-second Congress (March 4, 1911-March 3, 1913); unsuccessful candidate for reelection in 1912 to the Sixty-third Congress; Assistant Secretary of Commerce, 1913-1921; unsuccessful candidate for Governor of Michigan in 1916; member of the board of education of Grand Rapids, 1923-1926; member of the Grand Rapids city commission, 1926-1928; operated a grain and stock ranch in North Dakota; resided in Grand Rapids, Mich., until 1928 when he retired and moved to Ojai, Calif., where he died on April 2, 1935; interment in Oakhill Cemetery, Grand Rapids, Mich.

SWEET, John Hyde, a Representative from Nebraska; born in Milford, Otsego County, N.Y., September 1, 1880; moved to Palmyra, Nebr., with his parents in 1885; attended the Palmyra grade and high schools, the University of Nebraska at Lincoln, and the Lincoln

(Nebr.) Business College; employed as a court reporter in western Nebraska in 1899 and 1900; wholesale grocer in Nebraska City 1902-1909; engaged in the newspaper publishing business at Nebraska City, Nebr., in 1909; delegate to the Progressive National Convention in 1912; elected as a Republican to the Seventy-sixth Congress to fill the vacancy caused by the death of George H. Heinke and served from April 9, 1940, to January 3, 1941; was not a candidate for renomination in 1940; resumed the newspaper publishing business in Nebraska City, Nebr., until his death in Community Hospital, Wickenburg, Ariz., April 4, 1964; interment in Wyuka Cemetery, Nebraska City, Nebr.

**SWEET, Thaddeus C.,** a Representative from New York; born in Phoenix, Oswego County, N.Y., November 16, 1872; attended the public schools; was graduated from Phoenix Academy and High School; entered business and for two years served as a traveling salesman; in 1895 began the manufacture of paper and was president of the Sweet Paper Manufacturing Co.; also engaged in banking; town clerk of Phoenix 1896-1899; member, New York State assembly, 1910-1920, serving as speaker 1914-1920; elected as a Republican to the Sixty-eighth Congress to fill the vacancy caused by the death of Luther W. Mott; reelected to the Sixty-ninth and Seventieth Congresses and served from November 6, 1923, until his death as the result of an airplane accident at Whitney Point, Broome County, N.Y., May 1, 1928; chairman, Committee on Expenditures in the Department of War (Sixty-ninth Congress); interment in the Rural Cemetery, Phoenix, N.Y.

**SWEET, Willis,** a Representative from Idaho; born at Alburg Springs, Vt., January 1, 1856; attended the common schools and the University of Nebraska at Lincoln; learned the printer's trade in Lincoln, Nebr.; moved to Moscow, Latah County, Idaho, in September 1881; studied law; was admitted to the bar in 1889 and commenced practice in Moscow; appointed United States attorney for Idaho in May 1888; judge of the first judicial district of Idaho from November 19, 1889, to January 1, 1890; appointed associate justice of Idaho Supreme Court November 25, 1889; first president of the board of regents of the University of Idaho 1889-1893; upon the admission of Idaho as a State into the Union was elected as a Republican to the Fifty-first Congress; reelected to the Fifty-second and Fifty-third Congresses and served from October 1, 1890, to March 3, 1895; was not a candidate for renomination in 1894; unsuccessful candidate for election to the United States Senate in 1896; resumed the practice of his profession in Coeur d'Alene, Kootenai County, Idaho; attorney general for Puerto Rico 1903-1905; editor of a newspaper in San Juan, P.R., from 1913 until his death there July 9, 1925; interment in Santurce Cemetery.

**SWEETSER, Charles,** a Representative from Ohio; born in Dummerston, Vt., January 22, 1808; moved with his parents to Delaware, Ohio, in 1817; attended the public schools; engaged in mercantile pursuits; studied law; was admitted to the bar in 1832 and commenced practice in Delaware, Delaware County, Ohio; elected as a Democrat to the Thirty-first and Thirty-second Congresses (March 4, 1849-March 3, 1853); chairman, Committee on Public Expenditures (Thirty-second Congress); resumed the practice of law; died in Delaware, Ohio, April 14, 1864; interment in Oak Grove Cemetery.

**SWENEY, Joseph Henry,** a Representative from Iowa; born in Warren County, Pa., October 2, 1845; attended the public schools of Pennsylvania and Iowa; was graduated from the law department of the University of Iowa at Iowa City in 1880; was admitted to the bar the same year and commenced practice in Osage, Mitchell County, Iowa; also engaged in banking and agricultural pursuits; during the Civil War enlisted in the Union Army and served as sergeant in Company K, Twenty-seventh Regiment, Iowa Volunteer Infantry; colonel of the Sixth Regiment National Guard of Iowa for four years and brigadier and inspector general of the State; member of the

State senate 1883-1891, serving as president pro tempore in 1886; elected as a Republican to the Fifty-first Congress (March 4, 1889-March 3, 1891); unsuccessful candidate for reelection in 1890 to the Fifty-second Congress; resumed the practice of law in Osage, Iowa; died while on a visit in Norfolk, Va., November 11, 1918; interment in Osage Cemetery, Osage, Iowa.

**SWETT, Richard** (son-in-law of Thomas Peter Lantos), a Representative from New Hampshire; born in Bryn Mawr, Montgomery County, Pa., May 1, 1957; graduated from Laconia (N.H.) High School, 1975; B.A., Yale University, 1979; architect; elected as a Democrat to the One Hundred Second and One Hundred Third Congresses (January 3, 1991-January 3, 1995); unsuccessful candidate for reelection in 1994 to the One Hundred Fourth Congress; resumed architectural and energy consulting practice; candidate in 1996 for election to the United States Senate; is a resident of Bow, N.H.

**SWICK, Jesse Howard,** a Representative from Pennsylvania; born near New Brighton, Beaver County, Pa., August 6, 1879; attended the public schools and Geneva College, Beaver Falls, Pa.; taught school in Beaver County, Pa., 1895-1900; graduated from Hahnemann Medical College of Philadelphia in 1906; moved to Beaver Falls, Pa., in 1906 and commenced the practice of medicine; president of the Beaver Falls Bureau of Health 1907-1914; during the First World War served as a first lieutenant and later as a captain in the Medical Corps of the United States Army, with overseas service, from August 31, 1917, to May 9, 1919; resumed the practice of medicine in Beaver Falls, Pa.; also interested in banking and the manufacturing of steel products; member of the Beaver Falls City Council 1925-1927; elected as a Republican to the Seventieth and to the three succeeding Congresses (March 4, 1927-January 3, 1935); was an unsuccessful candidate for reelection in 1934 to the Seventy-fourth Congress; resumed the practice of medicine until August 1945, when he retired; died in Beaver Falls, Pa., November 17, 1952; interment in Concord Cemetery, North Sewickley Township, Beaver County, Pa.

**SWIFT, Allan Byron,** a Representative from Washington; born in Tacoma, Pierce County, Wash., September 12, 1935; attended the Pierce County public schools; graduated from Lincoln High School, Tacoma, 1953; attended Whitman College, Walla Walla, 1953-1955; B.A., Central Washington University, Ellensburg, Wash., 1957; broadcaster; public affairs director, KVOS-TV; administrative assistant to Representative Lloyd Meeds of Washington, 1965-1969; member, Bellingham City Charter Revision; chairman and member, Bellingham Citizens' Advisory Committee on Schools; member, Bellingham Housing Authority; elected as a Democrat to the Ninety-sixth and to the seven succeeding Congresses (January 3, 1979-January 3, 1995); was not a candidate for reelection in 1994 to the One Hundred Fourth Congress; is a resident of Alexandria, Va.

**SWIFT, Benjamin,** a Representative and a Senator from Vermont; born in Amenia, N.Y., April 3, 1781; moved with his father to Bennington, Vt., in 1786; completed preparatory studies; studied law; was admitted to the bar in 1806 and commenced practice in Bennington; moved to Manchester and then to St. Albans in 1809; practiced law and also engaged in banking and agricultural pursuits; member of the Vermont house of representatives in 1813, 1825, 1826; elected to the Twentieth and Twenty-first Congresses (March 4, 1827-March 3, 1831); was not a candidate for renomination in 1830 to the Twenty-second Congress; elected as a Whig to the United States Senate, and served from March 4, 1833 to March 3, 1839; was not a candidate for renomination in 1839; resumed the practice of law and agricultural pursuits; died in St. Albans, Vt., November 11, 1847; interment in the Old Cemetery, South Main Street.

**SWIFT, George Robinson,** a Senator from Alabama; born at Swift Post Office, Baldwin County, Ala., December 19, 1887; attended the public schools of Baldwin County, Ala., the University Military School, Mobile, Ala., and the University of Alabama at Tuscaloosa; engaged in the lumber industry in Alabama; member, Alabama State house of representatives, 1931-1935; Alabama State senator, 1935-1939; State highway director, 1943-1946; appointed as a Democrat to the United States Senate to fill the vacancy caused by the death of John H. Bankhead II and served from June 15, 1946, to November 5, 1946, when a successor was elected; was not a candidate for election to the vacancy; again served as an Alabama State senator, 1947-1951; president of the Southern Pine Association, 1954-1955; president, Swift-Hunter Lumber Co., Atmore, Ala.; retired and resided in Atmore, Ala.; died in New Orleans, La., September 10, 1972; interment in Oak Hill Cemetery, Atmore, Ala.

**SWIFT, Oscar William,** a Representative from New York; born in Paines Hollow, Herkimer County, N.Y., April 11, 1869; moved to Michigan with his parents, who settled in Adrian in 1877; attended the public schools and the University of Michigan at Ann Arbor; was graduated from the New York Law School, New York City, in 1896; was admitted to the bar in 1897 and commenced practice in New York City; elected as a Republican to the Sixty-fourth and Sixty-fifth Congresses (March 4, 1915-March 3, 1919); unsuccessful candidate for reelection in 1918 to the Sixty-sixth Congress; resumed law practice in New York City; died in Brooklyn, N.Y., June 30, 1940; interment in Kensico Cemetery, Valhalla, N.Y.

**SWIFT, Zephaniah,** a Representative from Connecticut; born in Wareham, Plymouth County, Mass., February 27, 1759; moved with his parents to Lebanon, New London County, Conn.; completed preparatory studies; was graduated from Yale College in 1778; studied law; was admitted to the bar and commenced practice in Windham, Conn.; member of the Connecticut State house of representatives, 1787-1793, serving as speaker in 1792; clerk of the house for four sessions; elected to the Third Congress and reelected as a Federalist to the Fourth Congress (March 4, 1793-March 3, 1797); resumed the practice of law at Windham; also engaged in literary pursuits; secretary of the French mission in 1800; judge of the supreme court in 1801, and chief justice from 1806 until 1819; member of the Hartford Convention in 1814; again a member of the State house of representatives, 1820-1822; died in Warren, Trumbull County, Ohio, September 27, 1823; interment in Oakwood Cemetery.
Bibliography: *DAB*.

**SWINBURNE, John,** a Representative from New York; born at Deer River, Lewis County, N.Y., May 30, 1820; attended the public schools and academies in Denmark and Lowville, Lewis County, and in Fairfield, Herkimer County; was graduated from the Albany Medical College in 1847 and commenced practice as a physician and surgeon; during the Civil War was appointed a medical officer; appointed by Governor Horatio Seymour in 1864 as health officer of the port of New York, and reappointed by Governor Reuben E. Fenton in 1866, holding the position six years; in charge of the American Ambulance Corps during the siege of Paris by the Prussians in 1870 and 1871; elected mayor of Albany in 1882 and counted out, but after fourteen months' litigation was awarded the office by the courts; elected as a Republican to the Forty-ninth Congress (March 4, 1885-March 3, 1887); resumed the practice of his profession; died in Albany, N.Y., March 28, 1889; interment in Albany Rural Cemetery.

**SWINDALL, Charles,** a Representative from Oklahoma; born at College Mound, near Terrell, Kaufman County, Tex., February 13, 1876; attended the public schools and Vanderbilt University, Nashville, Tenn.; was graduated from the law department of Cumberland University, Lebanon, Tenn., in 1897; was admitted to the bar the same year and commenced practice in Woodward, Okla.; prosecuting attorney of Day (later Ellis) County 1898-1900; returned to Woodward in 1900 and continued the practice of law; delegate to the Republican National Convention in 1916; elected as a Republican to the Sixty-sixth Congress to fill the vacancy caused by the death of Dick T. Morgan, and served from November 2, 1920, to March 3, 1921; unsuccessful candidate for renomination in 1920 to the Sixty-seventh Congress; resumed the practice of law in Woodward, Okla.; appointed April 26, 1924, judge of the twentieth judicial district of Oklahoma, in which capacity he served until 1929; justice of the State supreme court 1929-1934; resumed the practice of law in Oklahoma City, Okla., until his death there June 19, 1939; interment in Memorial Park Cemetery.

**SWINDALL, Patrick Lynn,** a Representative from Georgia; born in Gadsden, Ala., October 18, 1950; attended public schools; B.A., University of Georgia, 1972; J.D., University of Georgia School of Law, 1975; practiced law in Atlanta, Ga., 1975-1984; elected as a Republican to the Ninety-ninth and One Hundredth Congresses (January 3, 1985-January 3, 1989); unsuccessful candidate for reelection in 1988 to the One Hundred First Congress; is a resident of Stone Mountain, Ga.

**SWING, Philip David,** a Representative from California; born in San Bernardino, Calif., November 30, 1884; attended the public schools and was graduated from Stanford University in 1905; first lieutenant in the California National Guard, 1906-1908; studied law; was admitted to the bar in 1907 and commenced practice in San Bernardino; city attorney of Brawley, Calif., in 1908 and 1909; deputy district attorney of Imperial County, 1908-1911, and district attorney, 1911-1915; chief counsel of the Imperial Irrigation District, 1916-1919; judge of the superior court of Imperial County, 1919-1921; delegate to the Republican State conventions at Sacramento, Calif., 1920-1932, serving as chairman in 1926; during the First World War served as a private in the Officers Training Camp at Camp Taylor, Ky., in 1918; elected as a Republican to the Sixty-seventh and to the five succeeding Congresses (March 4, 1921-March 3, 1933); chairman, Committee on Expenditures in the Post Office Department (Sixty-ninth Congress); was not a candidate for renomination in 1932 to the Seventy-third Congress; resumed law practice; appointed a member of the California State Water Resources Board (now California Water Commission) in 1945; reappointed in 1950 and served until 1958; died in San Diego, Calif., August 8, 1963; interment in Greenwood Memorial Park.
Bibliography: Moeller, Beverley B. *Phil Swing and Boulder Dam*. Berkeley: University of California Press, 1971.

**SWITZER, Robert Mauck,** a Representative from Ohio; born near Gallipolis, Gallia County, Ohio, March 6, 1863; attended the district schools, Gallia Academy, and Rio Grande College; taught school 1883-1887; deputy sheriff of Gallia County 1888-1892; attended the law departments of the University of Virginia at Charlottesville and the Ohio State University of Columbus; was admitted to the bar in 1892 and commenced practice in Gallipolis, Ohio; prosecuting attorney of Gallia County 1893-1900; delegate to the Republican National Conventions in 1900 and 1920; elected as a Republican to the Sixty-second and to the three succeeding Congresses (March 4, 1911-March 3, 1919); was an unsuccessful candidate for renomination in 1918 to the Sixty-sixth Congress; resumed the practice of law; city solicitor of Gallipolis, Ohio; died in Gallipolis, Ohio, on October 28, 1952; interment in Mound Hill Cemetery.

**SWOOPE, Jacob,** a Representative from Virginia; born in Philadelphia, Pa.; attended the common schools; moved to Staunton, Va., in 1789 and engaged in the mercantile business; held several local offices; elected the first mayor of Staunton under the new charter of 1801; reelected in 1804; elected as a Federalist to the Eleventh Congress (March 4, 1809-March 3, 1811); declined to be a candidate for renomination in 1810; died in Staunton, Va., in 1832; interment in Trinity Episcopal Churchyard.

**SWOOPE, William Irvin** (nephew of John Patton), a Representative from Pennsylvania; born in Clearfield, Clearfield County, Pa., October 3, 1862; attended the public schools, Hill School, Pottstown, Pa., and Phillips Academy, Andover, Mass.; was graduated from the law department of Harvard University in 1886; was admitted to the bar December 6, 1886, and practiced law in Minnesota, Nebraska, and also at Bellefonte, Pa. where he was elected burgess; returned to Clearfield, Pa., in 1892 and continued the practice of law; county chairman and district attorney for Clearfield County 1901-1907; delegate to the Republican National Convention in 1916; deputy attorney general for Pennsylvania 1919-1923; elected as a Republican to the Sixty-eighth and Sixty-ninth Congresses (March 4, 1923-March 3, 1927); chairman, Committee on Invalid Pensions (Sixty-ninth Congress); declined to be a candidate for renomination in 1926; resumed the practice of law in Clearfield, Pa., until his death there October 9, 1930; interment in Hillcrest Cemetery.

**SWOPE, Guy Jacob,** a Representative from Pennsylvania; born in Meckville, Berks County, Pa., December 26, 1892; attended the public schools, Keystone State Teachers College, Kutztown, Pa., and Columbia University School of International Affairs; taught school in Lebanon County, Pa., 1909-1913; served as a United States internal revenue agent, 1913-1918; engaged as a public accountant from 1919 until 1934; budget secretary of Pennsylvania, 1935-1937; elected as a Democrat to the Seventy-fifth Congress (January 3, 1937-January 3, 1939); unsuccessful candidate for reelection in 1938 to the Seventy-sixth Congress; engaged as an accountant in 1939; auditor of Puerto Rico from January 15, 1940, to February 2, 1941; Governor of Puerto Rico from February 3 until August 6, 1941; director of the Division of Territories and Island Possessions, Interior Department, from August 7, 1941, to October 15, 1942; district director, Office of Price Administration, Harrisburg, Pa., from October 16, 1942, to July 27, 1943; served as a lieutenant commander and later as a commander in the United States Naval Reserve, Military Government Branch, 1943 to 1946; engaged as a civilian chief, National Government Division, General Headquarters, Tokyo, Japan, from February 12, 1947, to March 9, 1948; special assistant to the Pennsylvania treasurer from August 1, 1948, to May 3, 1949; served as special assistant to the American High Commissioner in Germany from July 1949 to March 1954; was an unsuccessful candidate for election in 1956 to the Eighty-fifth Congress; certified public accountant; director and comptroller of Lake Asphalt & Petroleum Co. of Pennsylvania, 1956-1961; deputy treasurer, Commonwealth of Pennsylvania, from May 1, 1961 until May 3, 1965; died in New York City, July 25, 1969; interment in Old Klopp's Church Cemetery, Hamlin, Pa.

**SWOPE, John Augustus,** a Representative from Pennsylvania; born in Gettysburg, Adams County, Pa., December 25, 1827; attended the common schools at Gettysburg, Pa., and Mount St. Mary's Academy, Emmitsburg, Md.; graduated from Princeton College in 1847 and from the medical department of the University of Pennsylvania at Philadelphia, but discontinued the practice of medicine after a few years and engaged in mercantile pursuits in Baltimore; returned to Gettysburg and became president of the Gettysburg National Bank in 1879; also engaged in manufacturing and agricultural pursuits; elected in 1884 as a Democrat to the Forty-eighth Congress to fill the vacancy caused by the death of William A. Duncan and served from December 23, 1884, to March 3, 1885; subsequently elected in 1885 to the Forty-ninth Congress to fill the vacancy caused by the death of William A. Duncan, who had been reelected, and served from November 3, 1885, to March 3, 1887; was not a candidate for renomination in 1886; moved to Washington, D.C., and engaged in banking until his death there on December 6, 1910; interment in Evergreen Cemetery, Gettysburg, Pa.

**SWOPE, King,** a Representative from Kentucky; born in Danville, Boyle County, Ky., August 10, 1893; attended the common schools; graduated from Centre College, Danville, Ky., in 1914 and from the law department of the University of Kentucky at Lexington in 1916; admitted to the bar in 1915 and commenced practice in Lexington, Ky.; enlisted and served during the First World War as captain of Infantry; elected as a Republican to the Sixty-sixth Congress to fill the vacancy caused by the death of Harvey Helm and served from August 2, 1919, to March 3, 1921; unsuccessful candidate for reelection in 1920 to the Sixty-seventh Congress; appointed aide-de-camp with the rank of colonel on the staff of Governor Edwin P. Morrow in 1919; resumed the practice of law; chairman of the Republican executive committee of Fayette County, Ky., 1928-1931; appointed and subsequently elected a judge of the circuit court of the twenty-second judicial district of Kentucky and served from 1931 to 1940; unsuccessful Republican candidate for Governor in 1935 and 1939; delegate to the Republican National Conventions of 1936, 1940, and 1944; chairman of the Kentucky Republican convention in 1936; member of the judicial council of Kentucky, 1931-1940; died in Lexington, Ky., April 23, 1961; interment in Lexington Cemetery.

**SWOPE, Samuel Franklin,** a Representative from Kentucky; born in Bourbon County, Ky., March 1, 1809; attended the rural schools of Bourbon and Scott Counties and the Georgetown (Ky.) College; studied law; admitted to the bar March 1, 1830, and commenced practice in Georgetown, Ky.; moved to Falmouth, Pendleton County, Ky., in 1832 and continued the practice of law; member of the Kentucky house of representatives 1837-1839 and in 1841; served in the Kentucky senate 1844-1848; elected as a candidate of the American Party to the Thirty-fourth Congress (March 4, 1855-March 3, 1857); was not a candidate for renomination in 1856; affiliated with the Republican Party in 1856; engaged in the practice of law at Falmouth, Ky., until his death April 19, 1865; interment in Riverside Cemetery.

**SYKES, George,** a Representative from New Jersey; born near Sykesville, Burlington County, N.J., September 20, 1802; educated by private teachers; became a surveyor and conveyancer; elected as a Democrat to the Twenty-eighth Congress (March 4, 1843-March 3, 1845); elected to the Twenty-ninth Congress to fill the vacancy caused by the death of Samuel G. Wright, and served from November 4, 1845, to March 3, 1847; resumed his former pursuits; member of the council of properties of West Jersey; member of the State assembly 1877-1879; died near Columbia, Mansfield Township, Burlington County, N.J., February 25, 1880; interment in Upper Springfield Cemetery, near Wrightstown, N.J.

**Bibliography:** *DAB.*

**SYKES, James,** a Delegate from Delaware; born in 1725; studied law; was admitted to the bar and commenced practice; lieutenant in Capt. Caesar Rodney's company of Dover Militia in 1756; member of the council of safety in 1776; delegate to the State constitutional convention held at New Castle, Del., in 1776; member of the Continental Congress in 1777; clerk of the peace 1777-1792; prothonotary of Kent County 1777-1793; served in the State council in 1780; member of the State legislature which ratified the Federal Constitution on December 7, 1787; again a delegate to the State constitutional convention in 1790; judge of the High Court of Errors and Appeals of Delaware; died in Dover, Del., April 4, 1792; interment in the burial ground of Christ Church.

**SYMES, George Gifford,** a Representative from Colorado; born in Ashtabula County, Ohio, April 28, 1840; attended the common schools; studied law; was admitted to the bar and practiced; during the Civil War enlisted as a private in Company B, Second Regiment, Wisconsin Volunteers, April 12, 1861; adjutant of the Twenty-fifth Regiment, Wisconsin Infantry; commissioned colonel of the Forty-fourth Regiment, Wisconsin Volunteers, in August 1864; practiced law in Paducah, Ky.; associate justice of the supreme court of Montana Territory 1869-1871; resumed the practice of law in Helena, Mont.; moved to Denver, Colo., in 1874; elected as a Republican to the Forty-ninth and Fiftieth Congresses (March 4, 1885-March 3, 1889); engaged in the management of his estate and in the practice of law; died in Denver, Colo., November 3, 1893; interment in Fairmount Cemetery.

**SYMINGTON, James Wadsworth** (son of Stuart Symington), a Representative from Missouri; born in Rochester, Monroe County, New York, September 28, 1927; attended St. Bernard's School in New York City, St. Louis Country Day School and Deerfield Academy; B.A., Yale University, 1950; LL.B., Columbia University Law School, 1954; served in the United States Marine Corps, private first class, 1945-1946; assistant city counselor of St. Louis, Mo., 1954-1955; practiced law in St. Louis, Mo., 1955-1958; United States Foreign Service, London, England, 1958-1960; resumed the practice of law in Washington, D.C., 1960-1961; deputy director, Food for Peace, The White House, 1961-1962; administrative assistant to Attorney General Robert F. Kennedy, 1962-1963; director, President's Committee on Juvenile Delinquency, 1965-1966; consultant, President's Commission on Law Enforcement and Administration of Justice, 1965-1966; Chief of Protocol, Department of State with rank of Ambassador, March 22, 1966 to March 31, 1968; elected as a Democrat to the Ninety-first and to the three succeeding Congresses (January 3, 1969-January 3, 1977); was not a candidate in 1976 for reelection to the House of Representatives, but was an unsuccessful candidate for nomination to the United States Senate; resumed the practice of law; is a resident of Washington, D.C.

**SYMINGTON, Stuart,** (father of James Wadsworth Symington), a Senator from Missouri; born in Amherst, Hampshire County, Mass., June 26, 1901; soon after his birth the family moved to Baltimore, Md.; attended the public schools; enlisted as a private in the United States Army at seventeen years of age and was discharged as a second lieutenant; A.B., Yale University, 1923; worked summers as a reporter on a Baltimore newspaper; went to Rochester, N.Y., and worked as an iron moulder and lathe operator, 1923-1926, studying mechanical and electrical engineering at night and by correspondence; executive with several radio and steel companies, 1926-1937; moved to St. Louis, Mo., and became president of the Emerson Electric Manufacturing Company, 1938-1945; chairman of the Surplus Property Board, 1945; Surplus Property Administrator, 1945-1946; Assistant Secretary of War for Air, 1946-1947; served as first Secretary of the Air Force, September 18, 1947 to April 24, 1950; chairman of National Security Resources Board, 1950-1951; Reconstruction Finance Corporation Administrator, 1951-1952, from which office he resigned to run for nomination as United States Senator; elected as a Democrat to the United States Senate in 1952; reelected in 1958, 1964, and again in 1970, and served from January 3, 1953 until his resignation on December 27, 1976; was not a candidate for reelection in 1976; unsuccessful candidate for the Democratic presidential nomination in 1960; was a resident of New Canaan, Conn.; died December 14, 1988.

**Bibliography:** Green, Murray. "Stuart Symington and the B-36." Ph.D. dissertation, American University, 1960; Wellman, Paul Iselin. *Stuart Symington: Portrait of a Man with a Mission.* Garden City, N.Y.: Doubleday and Co., 1960.

**SYMMES, John Cleves,** a Delegate from New Jersey; born in Riverhead, Long Island, N.Y., July 21, 1742; completed preparatory studies; moved to New Jersey; chairman of the committee of safety of Sussex County in 1774; member of the State council in 1778; served in the Revolutionary Army; chief justice of the State supreme court 1777-1787; Member of the Continental Congress in 1785 and 1786; moved to the Northwest Territory and settled in North Bend, below Cincinnati; appointed one of the three judges of the Northwest

Territory in 1788 and held the position until Ohio was admitted into the Union; died in Cincinnati, Ohio, February 26, 1814; interment in Congress Green Cemetery, North Bend, Ohio.

**Bibliography:** *DAB.*

**SYMMS, Steven Douglas** (cousin of Dennis Alan Smith), a Representative and a Senator from Idaho; born in Nampa, Canyon County, Idaho, April 23, 1938; attended the public schools; B.S., University of Idaho, 1960; served in the United States Marine Corps, 1960-1963; private pilot; fruit rancher; co-editor of the Idaho Compass, 1969-1972; elected as a Republican to the Ninety-third and to the three succeeding Congresses (January 3, 1973-January 3, 1981); was not a candidate in 1980 for renomination to the House of Representatives, but was elected to the United States Senate; reelected in 1986, and served from January 3, 1981 to January 3, 1993; was not a candidate for reelection in 1992; is a resident of Caldwell, Idaho.

**SYNAR, Michael Lynn,** a Representative from Oklahoma; born in Vinita, Craig County, Okla., October 17, 1950; attended the public schools of Muskogee, Okla., and graduated from Muskogee High School in 1968; B.S., University of Oklahoma, Norman, 1972; LL.B., University of Oklahoma Law Center, 1977; Rotary International Scholar, Graduate School of Economics, University of Edinburgh, Scotland, 1973; M.A., Northwestern University, Evanston, Ill., 1974; rancher; real estate broker; admitted to the Oklahoma bar in 1976 and commenced practice in Muskogee; elected as a Democrat to the Ninety-sixth and to the seven succeeding Congresses (January 3, 1979-January 3, 1995); unsuccessful candidate for renomination in 1994 to the One Hundred Fourth Congress; chairman of the Campaign for America Project, and of the National Bankruptcy Review Commission; was a resident of Washington, D.C., until his death there on January 9, 1996; interment in Memorial Park Cemetery, Muskogee, Okla.

**SYPHER, Jacob Hale,** a Representative from Louisiana; born near Millerstown, Perry County, Pa., June 22, 1837; received a liberal education, and was graduated from Alfred (N.Y.) University in 1859; taught school in Cleveland, Ohio; entered the Union Army as a private in Company A, First Ohio Light Artillery, and later served as colonel of the Eleventh United States Colored Heavy Artillery; after the war bought a plantation in northern Louisiana, but about two years later commenced the study of law; was admitted to the bar and practiced in New Orleans, La.; delegate to the Republican National Convention of 1868; upon readmission of the State of Louisiana to representation was elected as a Republican to the Fortieth Congress, and served from July 18, 1868 to March 3, 1869; contested the election of Louis St. Martin to the Forty-first Congress, but the House decided that neither was entitled to the seat; subsequently elected to the Forty-first Congress to fill the vacancy thus created; reelected to the Forty-second Congress, and served from November 7, 1870 to March 3, 1873; presented credentials as a Member-elect to the Forty-third Congress, and served from March 4, 1873 to March 3, 1875, when he was succeeded by Effingham Lawrence, who contested the election; chairman, Committee on Expenditures in the Department of the Treasury (Forty-third Congress); unsuccessful candidate for election in 1874 to the Forty-fourth Congress; resumed the practice of law in Washington, D.C.; died in Baltimore, Md., May 9, 1905; interment in the Arlington National Cemetery.

# T

**TABER, John,** a Representative from New York; born in Auburn, Cayuga County, N.Y., May 5, 1880; attended the public schools; was graduated from Yale University in 1902 and from New York Law School in 1904; was admitted to the bar November 15, 1904, and commenced practice in Auburn, N.Y.; supervisor of Cayuga County in 1905 and 1906; special judge of the county court

1910-1918; delegate to the Republican National Conventions in 1920, 1924, and 1936; chairman of the Cayuga County Republican committee 1920-1925; president of the Auburn Chamber of Commerce in 1922; elected as a Republican to the Sixty-eighth and to the nineteen succeeding Congresses (March 4, 1923-January 3, 1963); chairman, Committee on Appropriations (Eightieth and Eighty-third Congresses); was not a candidate for renomination in 1962 to the Eighty-eighth Congress; practiced law in Auburn, N.Y., where he died November 22, 1965; interment in Fort Hill Cemetery.

**Bibliography:** *DAB*; Henderson, Cary S. "Congressman John Taber of Auburn: Politics and Federal Appropriations, 1923-1962." Ph.D. dissertation, Duke University, 1964.

**TABER, Stephen** (son of Thomas Taber II), a Representative from New York; born in Dover, Dutchess County, N.Y., March 7, 1821; completed preparatory studies; moved to Queens County and engaged in agricultural pursuits; member of the State assembly in 1860 and 1861; elected as a Democrat to the Thirty-ninth and Fortieth Congresses (March 4, 1865-March 3, 1869); assisted in organizing the Long Island North Shore Transportation Co. in 1861 and served as its president for several years; director of the Long Island Railroad Co.; became the first president of the Roslyn Savings Bank in 1876 and served in this capacity for a number of years; died in New York City April 23, 1886; interment in Roslyn Cemetery, Roslyn, Long Island, N.Y.

**TABER, Thomas, II** (father of Stephen Taber), a Representative from New York; born in Dover, Dutchess County, N.Y., May 19, 1785; attended the common schools; engaged in agricultural pursuits; member of the State assembly in 1826; elected as a Jacksonian to the Twentieth Congress to fill the vacancy caused by the resignation of Thomas J. Oakley and served from November 5, 1828, to March 3, 1829; died in Roslyn, Long Island, N.Y., March 21, 1862; interment in the Friends Cemetery, Westbury, Long Island, N.Y.

**TABOR, Horace Austin Warner,** a Senator from Colorado; born in Holland, Orleans County, Vt., November 26, 1830; attended the common schools; worked at the stonecutter's trade in Maine and Vermont; moved to Kansas in 1855 and settled in Riley County; engaged in agricultural pursuits; member of the Kansas legislature, 1856-1857; in 1859 joined the Pike's Peak gold rush and moved to Denver, Colo.; followed gold discoveries around the West; discovered silver instead and made several important strikes; settled in Leadville, Colo.; engaged in mining and mercantile pursuits; postmaster of Leadville in 1878; mayor of Leadville, 1878-1879; treasurer of Lake County; lieutenant governor of Colorado, 1879-1883; elected as a Republican to the United States Senate to fill the vacancy caused by the resignation of Henry M. Teller, and served from January 27 to March 3, 1883; was not a candidate for reelection; postmaster of Denver, Colo., from 1898 until his death on April 10, 1899; interment in Mount Calvary Cemetery.

**Bibliography:** *DAB*; Gandy, Lewis. *The Tabors: A Footnote of Western History.* New York: Press of the Pioneers, 1934; Smith, Duane. *Horace Tabor: His Life and Legend.* Boulder: Associated University Press, 1973.

**TACKETT, Boyd Anderson,** a Representative from Arkansas; born near Black Springs, Montgomery County, Ark., May 9, 1911; moved with his parents to Glenwood, Pike County, Ark., and attended the public schools; student at Arkansas Polytechnic College at Russellville, 1930-1932, Ouachita College, Arkandelphia, Ark., 1932-1933, and graduated from the University of Arkansas Law School at Fayetteville in 1935; was admitted to the bar in 1935 and practiced law in Glenwood, Murfreesboro, and Nashville, Ark.; member of the Arkansas State legislature, 1937-1941; elected prosecuting attorney of the ninth judicial circuit of Arkansas, and served from January 1, 1941 until enlistment in the Armed Services; served as a corporal in the United States Army Signal Corps from

October 4, 1943 until discharged on November 5, 1944; resumed law practice in Nashville, Ark.; State police commissioner, Little Rock, Ark., 1945-1948; elected as a Democrat to the Eighty-first and Eighty-second Congresses (January 3, 1949-January 3, 1953); was not a candidate for renomination in 1952 to the Eighty-third Congress, but was an unsuccessful candidate for nomination for Governor of Arkansas; resumed the practice of law in Texarkana, Ark., until his retirement in 1980; was a resident of Nashville, Ark., from 1983 until his death there on February 23, 1985; interment in Restland Memorial Park.

**TAFFE, John,** a Representative from Nebraska; born in Indianapolis, Ind., January 30, 1827; completed preparatory studies; studied law; was admitted to the bar in Indianapolis, Ind.; moved to Nebraska in 1856; member of the Territorial house of representatives in 1858 and 1859; member of the Territorial council in 1860 and 1861 and served as president; during the Civil War enlisted in the Union Army and served as major in the Second Regiment, Nebraska Volunteer Cavalry; returned to Omaha, Nebr.; elected as a Republican to the Fortieth, Forty-first, and Forty-second Congresses (March 4, 1867-March 3, 1873); chairman, Committee on Territories (Forty-second Congress); resumed the practice of law; receiver of the public land office in North Platte, Nebr., where he died March 14, 1884; interment in Prospect Hill Cemetery, Omaha, Nebr.

**TAFT, Charles Phelps** (brother of President William Howard Taft, uncle of Robert Alphonso Taft, and granduncle of Robert Taft, Jr.), a Representative from Ohio; born in Cincinnati, Ohio, December 21, 1843; attended the common schools and was graduated from Phillips Academy, Andover, Mass., in 1860, from Yale College in 1864, and from Columbia College Law School of New York in 1866; was admitted to the bar in 1866; went to Germany and was graduated from the University of Heidelberg in 1867; commenced the practice of law in Cincinnati, Ohio, in 1869; member of the Ohio State house of representatives, 1871-1873; became owner and editor of the Cincinnati Times-Star in 1879; member, board of trustees, city of Cincinnati sinking fund (instituted to pay off the principal of the city's debt) for sixteen years, and served as president, 1898-1908; elected as a Republican to the Fifty-fourth Congress (March 4, 1895-March 3, 1897); was not a candidate for renomination in 1896 to the Fifty-fifth Congress; resumed the newspaper business in Cincinnati; delegate to the Republican National Conventions of 1908 and 1912; died in Cincinnati, Ohio, December 31, 1929; interment in Spring Grove Cemetery.

**Bibliography:** *DAB*.

**TAFT, Kingley Arter,** a Senator from Ohio; born in Cleveland, Cuyahoga County, Ohio, July 19, 1903; attended the public schools of Cleveland; graduated from Amherst College, Amherst, Mass., in 1925 and from the law school of Harvard University in 1928; was admitted to the bar in 1928; practiced law in Cleveland, Ohio, through 1948; member, Ohio State house of representatives, 1933-1934; member, Shaker Heights board of education, 1940-1942, serving as president in 1942; during the Second World War was commissioned as a captain in the United States Army in 1942; promoted to major in 1945; separated from the service in 1946; trustee of Baldwin-Wallace College and the Welfare Federation of Cleveland; elected as a Republican to the United States Senate on November 5, 1946, to fill the vacancy in the term ending January 3, 1947, caused by the resignation of Harold H. Burton; served from November 6, 1946 until January 3, 1947; was not a candidate for election to the full term; justice of the Ohio State supreme court, 1948-1962, and chief justice from 1962 until his death in Columbus, Ohio, March 28, 1970; interment in Lakeview Cemetery, Cleveland, Ohio.

**TAFT, Robert, Jr.** (son of Robert Alphonso Taft, grandson of President William Howard Taft, and grandnephew of Charles Phelps Taft), a Representative and a Senator from Ohio; born in Cincinnati, Hamilton County, Ohio, February 26, 1917; attended Cincinnati public and private schools; B.A., Yale University, 1939; LL.B., Harvard University Law School, 1942; during the Second World War served as an officer in the United States Navy, 1942-1946; was admitted to the bar in 1946 and commenced the practice of law in Cincinnati, Ohio; elected to the Ohio State house of representatives in 1955, 1957, 1959 and 1961, and was majority floor leader 1961-1962; elected as a Republican to the Eighty-eighth Congress (January 3, 1963-January 3, 1965); was not a candidate for renomination in 1964 to the House of Representatives, but was an unsuccessful candidate for election to the United States Senate; elected to the Ninetieth and Ninety-first Congresses (January 3, 1967-January 3, 1971); was not a candidate in 1970 for reelection to the House of Representatives, but was elected to the United States Senate; served from January 3, 1971 until his resignation on December 28, 1976; unsuccessful candidate for reelection in 1976; practiced law in Cincinnati and Washington, D.C.; was a resident of Cincinnati; died December 7, 1993.

**TAFT, Robert Alphonso** (son of President William Howard Taft, nephew of Charles Phelps Taft, and father of Robert Taft, Jr.), a Senator from Ohio; born in Cincinnati, Ohio, September 8, 1889; attended the public schools of Cincinnati, Ohio, and of Manila, Philippine Islands, and Taft School, Watertown, Conn.; graduated from Yale University in 1910 and from Harvard University Law School in 1913; was admitted to the Ohio bar in 1913 and commenced practice in Cincinnati, Ohio; director in a number of business enterprises in Cincinnati; assistant counsel, United States Food Administration, 1917-1918; counsel, American Relief Administration, 1919; member, Ohio State house of representatives, 1921-1926, serving as speaker and majority leader in 1926; Ohio State Senator, 1931-1932; elected as a Republican to the United States Senate in 1938; reelected in 1944 and again in 1950, and served from January 3, 1939 until his death; majority leader (Eighty-third Congress); co-chairman, Joint Committee on the Economic Report (Eightieth Congress), chairman, Committee on Labor and Public Welfare (Eightieth Congress), Republican Policy Committee (Eightieth through Eighty-second Congresses); co-sponsor of the Taft-Hartley Act of 1947, imposing certain restrictions on the internal affairs and political activities of labor unions, and on their use of certan varieties of boycotts, strikes and other forms of economic pressure; unsuccessful candidate for the Republican presidential nomination in 1940, 1948 and 1952; died in New York City, July 31, 1953; memorial services were held in the rotunda of the Capitol; interment in Indian Hill Episcopal Church Cemetery, Cincinnati, Ohio.

Bibliography: *DAB*; Merry, Robert W. "Robert A. Taft: A Study in the Accumulation of Legislative Power." In *First Among Equals: Outstanding Senate Leaders of the Twentieth Century*, edited by Richard A. Baker and Roger H. Davidson, pp. 163-198. Washington: Congressional Quarterly, Inc., 1991; Patterson, James T. *Mr. Republican: A Biography of Robert A. Taft*. Boston: Houghton Mifflin, 1972.

**TAGGART, Joseph,** a Representative from Kansas; born near Waukon, Allamakee County, Iowa, June 15, 1867; attended the district school; moved to Salina, Kans., in 1885; was graduated from the Salina Normal University in 1890; taught school in Bavaria, Kans., in 1892 and 1893; studied law; was admitted to the bar in 1893 and commenced the practice of his profession in Salina, Kans., moving shortly thereafter to Kansas City, Kans.; prosecuting attorney of Wyandotte County 1907-1911; elected as a Democrat to the Sixty-second Congress to fill the vacancy caused by the death of Alexander C. Mitchell; reelected to the Sixty-third and Sixty-fourth Congresses and served from November 7, 1911, to March 3, 1917;

unsuccessful candidate for reelection in 1916 to the Sixty-fifth Congress; served as captain in the Quartermaster Corps of the United States Army during the First World War; resumed the practice of law in Kansas City, Kans.; appointed judge of the Kansas Court of Industrial Relations in 1924; died in Wadsworth, Kans., on December 3, 1938; interment in Mount Vernon Cemetery, Atchison, Kans.

**TAGGART, Samuel,** a Representative from Massachusetts; born in Londonderry, N.H., March 24, 1754; completed preparatory studies; was graduated from Dartmouth College, Hanover, N.H., in 1774; studied theology and was licensed to preach in 1776; was ordained to the Presbyterian ministry on February 19, 1777, and installed as pastor of a church in Colrain, Mass.; journeyed as a missionary through western New York; elected as a Federalist to the Eighth and to the six succeeding Congresses (March 4, 1803-March 3, 1817); was not a candidate for renomination in 1816; continued his service as pastor of the Colrain Presbyterian Church until October 28, 1818, when he resigned; died on his farm in Colrain, Franklin County, Mass., April 25, 1825; interment in Chandler Hill Cemetery.

Bibliography: Taggart, Samuel. "Letters of Samuel Taggart: Representative in Congress, 1803-1814." Edited by George H. Haynes. *Proceedings of the American Antiquarian Society* 33 (April 1923): 113-226.

**TAGGART, Thomas,** a Senator from Indiana; born in County Monaghan, Ireland, November 17, 1856; immigrated to the United States in 1861 with his parents, who settled in Xenia, Greene County, Ohio; attended the common schools while working on the railroad; moved to Garrett, Ind., in 1874 and to Indianapolis, Ind., in 1877 and was employed in a restaurant and later engaged in the restaurant and hotel business; auditor of Marion County 1886-1894; mayor of Indianapolis 1895-1901; member of the Democratic National Committee 1900-1916, and served as chairman 1900-1908; president of the French Lick Hotel Co.; appointed as a Democrat to the United States Senate to fill the vacancy caused by the death of Benjamin F. Shively and served from March 20 to November 7, 1916; unsuccessful candidate for election in 1916 to fill the vacancy; chairman, Committee on Forest Reservations and Game Protection (Sixty-fourth Congress); resumed his former business pursuits in Indianapolis and French Lick, Ind.; banker; died in Indianapolis, Ind., on March 6, 1929; interment in Crown Hill Cemetery.

Bibliography: *DAB*.

**TAGUE, Peter Francis,** a Representative from Massachusetts; born in Boston, Mass., June 4, 1871; attended the public schools; engaged in the blacksmith and contractor supply business and later in the manufacture of chemicals; member of the Boston Common Council, 1894-1896; member of the Massachusetts house of representatives, 1897-1898, and in 1913-1914; served in the Massachusetts senate, 1899-1900; elected as a Democrat to the Sixty-fourth and Sixty-fifth Congresses (March 4, 1915-March 3, 1919); successfully contested the election of John F. Fitzgerald to the Sixty-sixth Congress; unsuccessful candidate for mayor of Boston in 1917; elected to the Sixty-seventh and Sixty-eighth Congresses, and served from October 23, 1919 to March 3, 1925; was an unsuccessful candidate for reelection in 1924 to the Sixty-ninth Congress; resumed the manufacture of chemicals in Boston, Mass.; appointed assessor of Boston in 1930; chairman of the election commission of Boston in 1930; appointed postmaster in 1936 and served until his death in Boston, Mass., September 17, 1941; interment in Holy Cross Cemetery, Malden, Mass.

**TAIT, Charles,** a Senator from Georgia; born near the present town of Hanover, Hanover County, Va., February 1, 1768; moved to Georgia in 1783 with his parents, who settled near Petersburg; completed preparatory studies; attended Wilkes Academy, Washington, Ga., 1786-1787, and Cokesbury College, Abingdon, Md., 1788; professor of French in Cokesburg College 1789-1794; studied law while teaching and was admitted to the Georgia bar in 1795; rector and professor at Richmond Academy, Augusta, Ga., 1795-1798; commenced the practice of law in Elbert County in 1798; presiding judge of the western circuit court of Georgia 1803-1809; elected as a Republican to the United States Senate to fill the vacancy caused by the resignation of John Milledge; was reelected in 1813 and served from November 27, 1809, to March 3, 1819; chairman, Committee on Naval Affairs (Fourteenth and Fifteenth Congresses); moved to Wilcox County, Ala., in 1819; appointed by President James Monroe as United States district judge for Alabama 1820-1826, when he resigned; engaged as a planter near Claiborne, Ala.; declined a mission to Great Britain in 1828; died near Claiborne, Ala., October 7, 1835; interment in Dry Forks Cemetery on his country estate, Wilcox County, Ala.

Bibliography: *DAB*; Moffat, Charles. *Charles Tait: Planter, Politician, and Scientist of the Old South.* Nashville: n.p., 1948.

**TALBERT, William Jasper,** a Representative from South Carolina; born near Edgefield, S.C., October 6, 1846; attended the common schools in Greenwood and Due West Academy at Abbeville, and was graduated from Erskine College, Due West, S.C.; served in the Confederate Army as a private, Company F, Fifth South Carolina Reserves, as a substitute for his father B.M. Talbert, who was discharged on December 17, 1862; enlisted at Richmond, Va., September 15, 1864, as a private, Company B, Infantry Regiment, Hampton Legion, South Carolina; engaged in agricultural pursuits near Parksville, McCormick County, S.C.; member of the South Carolina State house of representatives, 1880-1883; served in the State senate, 1884-1888; superintendent of the State penitentiary, 1891-1893; delegate to the Democratic National Convention in 1892; mayor of Parksville, 1895-1900; president of the Democratic State convention in 1899; held various positions in the Farmers' Alliance; elected as a Democrat to the Fifty-third and to the four succeeding Congresses (March 4, 1893-March 3, 1903); was not a candidate in 1902 for renomination to the Fifty-eighth Congress, but was an unsuccessful candidate in the second primary for nomination for Governor of South Carolina; resumed agricultural pursuits near Parksville, McCormick County, S.C.; moved to McCormick, S.C., in 1927, and lived in retirement until his death in Greenwood, S.C., February 5, 1931; interment in Parksville Cemetery, Parksville, S.C.

**TALBOT, Isham,** a Senator from Kentucky; born near Talbot, Bedford County, Va., in 1773; moved with his father to Harrodsburg, Ky.; completed preparatory studies; studied law; admitted to the bar and commenced practice in Versailles, Ky.; moved to Frankfort, Ky., and continued the practice of law; member, Kentucky senate 1812-1815; elected as a Republican to the United States Senate to fill the vacancy caused by the resignation of Jesse Bledsoe and served from January 3, 1815, to March 3, 1819; again elected to the United States Senate to fill the vacancy caused by the resignation of William Logan and served from October 19, 1820, to March 3, 1825; resumed the practice of law; died near Frankfort, Ky., September 25, 1837; interment in the State Cemetery, Frankfort, Ky.

**TALBOT, Joseph Edward,** a Representative from Connecticut; born in Naugatuck, New Haven County, Conn., March 18, 1901; attended the public schools; was graduated from Dartmouth College, Hanover, N.H., in 1922 and from Yale Law School in 1925; was admitted to the bar in 1925 and commenced practice in Naugatuck and Waterbury, Conn.; prosecuting attorney, Naugatuck, Conn., 1928-1933 and judge 1935-1937; State treasurer 1939-1941; workmen's compensation commissioner for the fifth district of Connecticut in 1941 and 1942; elected as a Republican to the Seventy-seventh Congress in a special election to fill the vacancy caused by the resignation of J. Joseph Smith; reelected to the Seventy-eighth and Seventy-ninth Congresses and served from

January 20, 1942, to January 3, 1947; was not a candidate for renomination in 1946; unsuccessful candidate for the gubernatorial nomination in 1946; unsuccessful candidate for election to the United States Senate in 1950; appointed a member of the United States Tariff Commission in April 1953; reappointed in May 1959 and again on July 14, 1965, serving as vice chairman 1953-1959 and as chairman from 1959; chairman, Committee on Reciprocity Information, from 1959 until his death in Washington, D.C., April 30, 1966; interment in St. James Cemetery, Naugatuck, Conn.

**TALBOT, Silas,** a Representative from New York; born in Dighton, Bristol County, Mass., January 11, 1751; completed preparatory studies; went to sea on a coasting vessel; engaged in mercantile pursuits in Providence, R.I.; lieutenant and captain in the Revolutionary Army; promoted to the rank of major October 10, 1777, and to lieutenant colonel October 29, 1778; commissioned captain in the Continental Navy September 17, 1779; captured by the British in November 1780 and imprisoned in England until 1781, when he was exchanged and sent to Cherbourg, France; returned to America and resided in Philadelphia, Pa.; moved to Albany, N.Y., and engaged in agricultural pursuits; member of the State assembly in 1792 and 1793; elected to the Third Congress (March 4, 1793-March 3, 1795); again commissioned by President John Adams, May 11, 1798, a captain in the United States Navy; resigned September 21, 1801; died in New York City on June 30, 1813; interment in Trinity Churchyard.

Bibliography: *DAB*.

**TALBOTT, Albert Gallatin** (uncle of William Clayton Anderson), a Representative from Kentucky; born near Paris, Bourbon County, Ky., April 4, 1808; moved with his parents to Clark County in 1813 and to Jessamine County in 1818; attended Forrest Hill Academy, Jessamine County, Ky.; studied law, but did not practice; engaged in agricultural pursuits and general trading in 1831; moved to Mercer County in 1838 and engaged in the real estate business; moved to Danville, Boyle County, Ky., in 1846; delegate to the Kentucky constitutional convention in 1849; member of the Kentucky house of representatives in 1850; elected as a Democrat to the Thirty-fourth and Thirty-fifth Congresses (March 4, 1855-March 3, 1859); chairman, Committee on Expenditures in the Post Office Department (Thirty-fifth Congress); resumed real estate pursuits; served in the State senate 1869-1873; again a member of the Kentucky house of representatives in 1883; moved to Pennsylvania and settled near Chestnut Hill, and engaged in agricultural pursuits; died in Philadelphia on September 9, 1887; interment in Bellevue Cemetery, Danville, Ky.

**TALBOTT, Joshua Frederick Cockey,** a Representative from Maryland; born near Lutherville, Baltimore County, Md., July 29, 1843; attended the public schools; began the study of law in 1862; joined the Confederate Army in 1864 and served as a private in the Second Maryland Cavalry throughout the remainder of the Civil War; was admitted to the bar in 1866 and began the practice of law in Towson, Baltimore County, Md.; prosecuting attorney for Baltimore County 1871-1875; unsuccessful candidate for reelection; delegate to the Democratic National Convention in 1876, 1904, and 1908; elected as a Democrat to the Forty-sixth, Forty-seventh, and Forty-eighth Congresses (March 4, 1879-March 3, 1885); was not a candidate for reelection in 1884; appointed insurance commissioner of Maryland in October 1889 and resigned in January 1893, having been elected to Congress; elected to the Fifty-third Congress (March 4, 1893-March 3, 1895); unsuccessful candidate for reelection in 1894 to the Fifty-fourth Congress; resumed the practice of law in Towson; unsuccessful candidate for election in 1900 to the Fifty-seventh Congress; elected to the Fifty-eighth and to the seven succeeding Congresses and served from March 4, 1903, until his death in Lutherville, Md., on October 5, 1918; interment in Sherwood Cemetery, Cockeysville, Baltimore County, Md.

**TALCOTT, Burt Lacklen,** a Representative from California; born in Billings, Yellowstone County, Mont., February 22, 1920; attended the public schools and Great Falls High School; B.A., Stanford University, Palo Alto, Calif., 1942; LL.B., Stanford University Law School, 1948; worked as a journeyman carpenter while attending high school and college; enlisted in the Army Air Corps in 1942, became a bomber pilot and on a mission over Austria was shot down, wounded, and held for fourteen months in a German prison camp; was discharged in 1945 as a first lieutenant and awarded the Air Medal and Purple Heart with clusters; was admitted to the bar in 1948 and commenced the practice of law the same year in Salinas, Calif.; member of the County Board of Surpervisors from the Salinas-Alisal district, 1954-1962, serving as chairman of the board in 1962; elected as a Republican to the Eighty-eighth and to the six succeeding Congresses (January 3, 1963-January 3, 1977); unsuccessful candidate for reelection in 1976 to the Ninety-fifth Congress; associate, Louis C. Kramp and Associates, 1978-1981; president and consultant for legislative affairs, Talcott, McCabe and Associates, 1981-1986; associate deputy administrator for congressional affairs, Veterans Administration, 1986-1989; is a resident of Bethesda, Md., and Salinas, Calif.

**TALCOTT, Charles Andrew,** a Representative from New York; born in Oswego, Oswego County, N.Y., June 10, 1857; attended the public schools and Utica Free Academy; was graduated from Princeton University in 1879; studied law; was admitted to the bar in 1881 and commenced practice in Utica, N.Y.; clerk of the city court, 1881-1883; city counsel of Utica in 1886; member of the board of police and fire commissioners, 1888-1892; trustee of the Utica Public Library, 1893-1901; mayor of the city of Utica, 1902-1906; elected as a Democrat to the Sixty-second and Sixty-third Congresses (March 4, 1911-March 3, 1915); unsuccessful candidate for reelection in 1914 to the Sixty-fourth Congress; engaged in the practice of law until his death in Utica, N.Y., February 27, 1920; interment in Forest Hill Cemetery.

**TALENT, James Michael,** a Representative from Missouri; born in Des Peres, Mo., October 18, 1956; graduated, Kirkwood (Mo.) High School, 1973; B.A., Washington University, St. Louis, Mo., 1978; J.D., University of Chicago Law School, 1981; law clerk to Judge Richard A. Posner, United States Court of Appeals for the Seventh Circuit; adjunct professor of law, Washington University; attorney, St. Louis, Mo.; member, Missouri State house of representatives, 1985-1993, minority leader, 1989-1993; elected as a Republican to the One Hundred Third and One Hundred Fourth Congresses (January 3, 1993-January 3, 1997); is a resident of Chesterfield, Mo.

**TALIAFERRO, Benjamin,** a Representative from Georgia; born in Virginia in 1750; completed preparatory studies; served in the Revolutionary War as a lieutenant in the rifle corps commanded by General Daniel Morgan; was promoted to captain; captured by the British at Charleston in 1780; settled in Georgia in 1785; member of the Georgia State senate and its president; delegate to the State constitutional convention in 1798; elected as a Federalist to the Sixth Congress; reelected as a Republican to the Seventh Congress, and served from March 4, 1799 until his resignation in 1802; judge of the superior court; trustee of Georgia University; died in Wilkes County, Ga., September 3, 1821.

**TALIAFERRO, James Piper,** a Senator from Florida; born in Orange, Orange County, Va., September 30, 1847; attended the common schools and the William Dinwiddie School in Greenwood, Va.; during the Civil War enlisted in the Confederate Army in 1864 and served until the close of the war; resumed his studies in college; moved to Jacksonville, Fla., in 1866; engaged in the lumber business and other commercial enterprises; also engaged in the building of railroads; president of the First National Bank of Tampa; elected as a Democrat to the United States Senate to fill the vacancy in the term beginning March 4, 1899; appointed and subsequently reelected in 1905 and served from April 20, 1899, to March 3, 1911; was an unsuccessful candidate for reelection in 1910; chairman, Committee on Revolutionary Claims (Sixtieth Congress), Committee on Corporations Organized in the District of Columbia (Sixty-first Congress); again resumed his former business and commercial pursuits in Jacksonville, Duval County, Fla., until 1920 when he retired from active business pursuits; died in Jacksonville, Fla., October 6, 1934; interment in Evergreen Cemetery.

**TALIAFERRO, John,** a Representative from Virginia; born on the estate, "Hays," near Fredericksburg, King George County, Va., in 1768; attended the common schools; studied law; was admitted to the bar and commenced practice in Fredericksburg, Va.; elected as a Republican to the Seventh Congress (March 4, 1801-March 3, 1803); successfully contested the election of John P. Hungerford to the Twelfth Congress and served from November 29, 1811, to March 3, 1813; unsuccessfully contested the election of John P. Hungerford to the Thirteenth Congress; elected to the Eighteenth Congress to fill the vacancy caused by the death of William L. Ball; reelected to the Nineteenth, Twentieth, and Twenty-first Congresses and served from March 24, 1824, to March 3, 1831; elected as a Whig to the Twenty-fourth and to the three succeeding Congresses (March 4, 1835-March 3, 1843); chairman, Committee on Revolutionary Pensions (Twenty-sixth and Twenty-seventh Congresses); librarian of the United States Treasury Department from 1850 until his death at his residence, "Hagley," near Fredericksburg, King George County, Va., August 12, 1852; interment on his farm, "Hagley."

**TALLE, Henry Oscar,** a Representative from Iowa; born on a farm near Albert Lea, Freeborn County, Minn., January 12, 1892; educated in rural schools and Luther Academy, Albert Lea, Minn.; was graduated from Luther College, Decorah, Iowa, in 1917; engaged in graduate work at the University of Minnesota, Boston University, Emerson College (Boston), and the University of Chicago; during the First World War served in the United States Navy, 1917-1919; teacher and superintendent of schools, Rugby and Rolette, N.Dak., in 1919 and 1920; teacher in Luther Academy, Albert Lea, Minn., in 1920 and 1921; professor of economics, Luther College, Decorah, Iowa, 1921-1938; treasurer of Luther College, 1932-1938; elected as a Republican to the Seventy-sixth and to the nine succeeding Congresses (January 3, 1939-January 3, 1959); unsuccessful candidate for reelection in 1958 to the Eighty-sixth Congress; assistant administrator for program policy of the Housing and Home Finance Agency, Washington, D.C., from February 2, 1959 until February 19, 1961; resided in Chevy Chase, Md., until his death in Washington, D.C., March 14, 1969; interment in Arlington National Cemetery, Va.

**TALLMADGE, Benjamin** (father of Frederick Augustus Tallmadge), a Representative from Connecticut; born in Brookhaven, Long Island, N.Y., February 25, 1754; moved to Litchfield, Conn., in 1783; was graduated from Yale College in 1773; superintendent of Wethersfield High School 1773-1776; commissioned lieutenant in the Continental Line June 20, 1776; promoted to captain of dragoons December 15, 1776, major April 7, 1777, and colonel September 5, 1779; was appointed postmaster at Litchfield, Conn., in 1792; first president of the Phoenix Branch Bank; treasurer and later president of the Society of the Cincinnati; elected as a Federalist to the Seventh and to the seven succeeding Congresses (March 4, 1801-March 3, 1817); declined to be a candidate for renomination; engaged in mercantile pursuits and was an importer; also interested in banking; died in Litchfield, Conn., March 7, 1835; interment in the East Cemetery.

Bibliography: *DAB*; Tallmadge, Benjamin. *Memoir of Colonel Benjamin Tallmadge.* 1858. Reprint. New York: New York Times, 1968.

**TALLMADGE, Frederick Augustus** (son of Benjamin Tallmadge), a Representative from New York; born in Litchfield, Conn., August 29, 1792; completed preparatory studies and was graduated from Yale College in 1811; studied law in the Litchfield Law School; was admitted to the bar in 1811 and commenced practice in New York City in 1813; served as captain in the War of 1812; member of the board of aldermen of New York City in 1834; served as common councilman in 1836; member of the State senate 1837-1840, and during the last session served as president pro tempore; recorder of the city of New York 1841-1846; elected as a Whig to the Thirtieth Congress (March 4, 1847-March 3, 1849); was not a candidate for renomination in 1848; again recorder of the city of New York 1848-1851; superintendent of the Metropolitan police 1857-1862; clerk of the New York Court of Appeals 1862-1865; resumed the practice of law in New York City; returned to Litchfield, Conn., in 1869, and died there on September 17, 1869; interment in the East Cemetery.

**TALLMADGE, James, Jr.,** a Representative from New York; born in Stanfordville, Dutchess County, N.Y., January 28, 1778; was graduated from Brown University, Providence, R.I., in 1798; secretary to Governor George Clinton from 1798 until 1800; studied law; was admitted to the bar in 1802 and practiced in Poughkeepsie, N.Y., and in New York City; served in the War of 1812 and commanded a company of home guards in defense of New York; elected as a Republican to the Fifteenth Congress to fill the vacancy caused by the death of Henry B. Lee, and served from June 6, 1817 to March 3, 1819; author of the "Tallmadge Amendment," passed by the House on February 17, 1819, prohibiting further introduction of slaves into Missouri; declined to be a candidate for renomination in 1818 to the Sixteenth Congress; delegate to the State constitutional conventions of 1821 and 1846; member of the New York State assembly in 1824; Lieutenant Governor of New York, 1824-1826; president of New York University from 1830 until 1846; died in New York City, September 29, 1853; interment in Marble Cemetery.

Bibliography: *DAB*.

**TALLMADGE, Nathaniel Pitcher,** a Senator from New York; born in Chatham, Columbia County, N.Y., February 8, 1795; graduated from Union College, Schenectady, N.Y., in 1815; studied law; was admitted to the bar in 1818 and commenced practice in Poughkeepsie, N.Y.; member, New York State assembly, 1828; member, New York State senate, 1830-1833; elected as a Jacksonian to the United States Senate in 1833; reelected as a Democrat in 1839, and served from March 4, 1833, to June 17, 1844, when he resigned, having been appointed by President John Tyler to be Governor of Wisconsin Territory, with residence in Fond du Lac; served as Governor of Wisconsin Territory from June 21, 1844, until his removal from office on April 8, 1845; devoted himself to writing religious tracts; died in Battle Creek, Mich., November 2, 1864; interment in Rienzi Cemetery, Fond du Lac, Wis.

**TALLMAN, Peleg,** a Representative from Massachusetts; born in Tiverton, R.I., July 24, 1764; attended the public schools; served in the Revolutionary War on the privateer *Trumbull,* and lost an arm in an engagement in 1780; was captured and imprisoned in England and Ireland 1781-1783; engaged in mercantile pursuits in Bath, Maine (until 1820 a district of Massachusetts); elected as a Republican to the Twelfth Congress (March 4, 1811-March 3, 1813); declined to be a candidate for renomination; overseer of Bowdoin College, Brunswick, Maine, 1802-1840; member of the Maine senate in 1821 and 1822; died in Bath, Maine, March 12, 1840; interment in Maple Grove Cemetery; reinterment in Forest Hills Cemetery, Roxbury, Mass.

**TALLON, Robert Mooneyhan, Jr. (Robin),** a Representative from South Carolina; born in Hemingway, Williamsburg County, S.C., August 8, 1946; attended public schools; attended the University of South Carolina, Columbia, 1964-1968; clothing business owner and real estate broker; delegate, White House Conference on Small Business, 1979-1980; elected, South Carolina house of representatives, 1980-1982; elected as a Democrat to the Ninety-eighth and to the four succeeding Congresses (January 3, 1983-January 3, 1993); was not a candidate for renomination in 1992 to the One Hundred Third Congress; is a resident of Dillon, S.C.

**TALMADGE, Herman Eugene,** a Senator from Georgia; born on a farm near McRae, Telfair County, Ga., August 9, 1913; attended the public schools in McRae; LL.B., University of Georgia, Athens, 1936; was admitted to the bar in 1936 and commenced the practice of law in Atlanta, Ga.; volunteered for service in the United States Navy in 1941; saw extensive action in the Pacific theater, attained rank of lieutenant commander and was discharged in November 1945; upon the death of his father, Governor-elect Eugene Talmadge, was elected to the governorship by the Georgia State legislature on January 14, 1947; vacated the office on March 18, 1947 due to a decision of the State supreme court; elected on September 8, 1948 to fill the unexpired term; reelected in 1950, and served from November 17, 1948 until January 11, 1955; farmer; elected as a Democrat to the United States Senate in 1956; reelected in 1962, 1968, and again in 1974, and served from January 3, 1957 to January 3, 1981; unsuccessful candidate for reelection in 1980; denounced by the Senate on October 11, 1979 for financial misconduct; chairman, Committee on Agriculture and Forestry (Ninety-second through Ninety-fifth Congresses), Committee on Agriculture, Nutrition, and Forestry (Ninety-fifth and Ninety-sixth Congresses); resumed the practice of law; is a resident of Hampton, Ga.

Bibliography: Talmadge, Herman E., with Mark Royden Winchell. *Talmadge: A Political Legacy, A Politician's Life.* Atlanta: Peachtree Publishers, 1987; Talmadge, Herman E. *You and Segregation.* Birmingham: The Vulcan Press, 1955.

**TANNEHILL, Adamson,** a Representative from Pennsylvania; born in Frederick County, Md., May 23, 1750; attended the public schools; served in the Revolutionary War as captain of riflemen; moved to Pennsylvania and engaged in agricultural pursuits near Pittsburgh; held several local offices; brigadier general of Pennsylvania Volunteers in the United States service from September 25 to December 31, 1812; elected as a Republican to the Thirteenth Congress (March 4, 1813-March 3, 1815); unsuccessful candidate for reelection in 1814 to the Fourteenth Congress; resumed farming; died near Pittsburgh, Allegheny County, Pa., December 23, 1820; interment in the churchyard of the First Presbyterian Church; reinterment in Allegheny Cemetery, Pittsburgh, Pa., in 1849.

**TANNER, Adolphus Hitchcock,** a Representative from New York; born in Granville, Washington County, N.Y., May 23, 1833; completed preparatory studies; studied law; was admitted to the bar in 1854 and commenced practice in Whitehall, N.Y.; during the Civil War entered the Union Army in 1862 as a captain; was subsequently commissioned lieutenant colonel of the One Hundred and Twenty-third Regiment, New York Volunteer Infantry, and served until the close of the war; elected as a Republican to the Forty-first Congress (March 4, 1869-March 3, 1871); resumed the practice of law in Whitehall, Washington County, N.Y., and died there January 14, 1882; interment in Evergreen Cemetery, Salem, N.Y.

**TANNER, John S.,** a Representative from Tennessee; born at Dyersburg Army Air Base, Halls, Lauderdale County, Tenn., September 22, 1944; attended public schools of Union City, Tenn.; B.S., University of Tennessee, Knoxville, 1966, and J.D., 1968; entered active duty, United States Navy in 1968; released in 1972 after service in Judge Advocate General's Corps; Tennessee National Guard service as lieutenant colonel, 1974 to present; attorney, Union City, Tenn.; member, Tennessee State house of representatives, 1976-1988; elected as a Democrat to the One Hundred First and to the three succeeding Congresses (January 3, 1989-January 3, 1997); is a resident of Union City, Tenn.

**TAPPAN, Benjamin,** a Senator from Ohio; born in Northampton, Mass., May 25, 1773; attended the public schools; apprenticed as printer and engraver; traveled to the West Indies; studied painting with Gilbert Stuart; studied law; was admitted to the bar in Hartford, Conn., and commenced practice in Ravenna, Ohio, in 1799; member, Ohio State senate, 1803-1805; moved to Steubenville, Ohio, in 1809 and continued the practice of law; served in the War of 1812; held several local offices; county judge; judge of the fifth Ohio Circuit Court of Common Pleas, 1816-1823; presidential elector on the Democratic ticket in 1832; United States district judge of Ohio in 1833; elected as a Democrat to the United States Senate, and served from March 4, 1839 to March 3, 1845; chairman, Committee to Audit and Control the Contingent Expense (Twenty-seventh and Twenty-eighth Congresses), Committee on the Library (Twenty-seventh Congress); censured by the Senate on May 10, 1844 for breach of confidence for delivering President John Tyler's terms for an annexation treaty with Texas to editors of the New York Evening Post; died in Steubenville, Jefferson County, Ohio, April 20, 1857; interment in Union Cemetery.

Bibliography: *DAB*; Ratcliffe, Donald J., ed. "The Autobiography of Benjamin Tappan." *Ohio History* 85 (Spring 1976): 109-57.

**TAPPAN, Mason Weare,** a Representative from New Hampshire; born in Newport, Sullivan County, N.H., October 20, 1817; moved to Bradford, N.H., with his parents; attended private schools and the Hopkinton and Meriden Academies; studied law; was admitted to the bar in 1841 and commenced practice in Bradford, N.H.; served in the State house of representatives 1853-1855; elected as a candidate of the American Party to the Thirty-fourth Congress and reelected as a Republican to the Thirty-fifth and Thirty-sixth Congresses (March 4, 1855-March 3, 1861); chairman, Committee on Claims (Thirty-sixth Congress); was not a candidate for renomination in 1860; during the Civil War served in the Union Army as colonel of the First Regiment, New Hampshire Volunteer Infantry; again a member of the State house of representatives in 1860 and 1861; resumed the practice of law; appointed attorney general of the State in 1876, which position he held until his death in Bradford, Merrimack County, N.H., October 25, 1886; interment in Pleasant Hill Cemetery.

**TARBOX, John Kemble,** a Representative from Massachusetts; born in Methuen, near Lawrence, Mass., May 6, 1838; pursued classical studies; engaged in newspaper work; studied law; admitted to the bar in 1860 and practiced; during the Civil War served in the Union Army as first lieutenant in the Eighth Regiment, Massachusetts Volunteer Infantry; member of the Massachusetts house of representatives in 1868, 1870, and 1871; served in the Massachusetts senate in 1872; mayor of Lawrence in 1873 and 1874; elected as a Democrat to the Forty-fourth Congress (March 4, 1875-March 3, 1877); unsuccessful candidate for reelection in 1876 to the Forty-fifth Congress; city solicitor of Lawrence, Mass., in 1882 and 1883; Massachusetts insurance commissioner 1884-1887; died in Boston, Mass., May 28, 1887; interment in Bellevue Cemetery, Lawrence, Mass.

**TARR, Christian,** a Representative from Pennsylvania; born in Baltimore, Md., May 25, 1765; received a limited schooling; moved to Westmoreland County, Pa., in 1794 and engaged in agricultural pursuits; engaged in the manufacture of pottery in Fayette County, Pa.; elected as a Republican to the Fifteenth and Sixteenth Congresses (March 4, 1817-March 3, 1821); member of the Pennsylvania house of representatives in 1821 and 1822; appointed on October 31, 1827, superintendent of the road which had been built by the United States Government from Cumberland, Md., to Wheeling, Va. (now West Virginia), and served until March 20, 1829;

died in Washington Township, Fayette County, Pa., February 24, 1833; interment in the Methodist Graveyard, Brownsville, Pa.

**TARSNEY, John Charles,** a Representative from Missouri; born in Medina, Lenawee County, Mich., November 7, 1845; attended the common schools; during the Civil War enlisted in the Fourth Regiment, Michigan Volunteer Infantry, in August 1862; mustered out of the service in June 1865; attended high school in Hudson, Mich.; was graduated from the law department of the University of Michigan at Ann Arbor in 1869; was admitted to the bar the same year and commenced practice in Hudson, Mich.; moved to Kansas City, Mo., in 1872; city attorney of Kansas City in 1874 and 1875; elected as a Democrat to the Fifty-first and to the two succeeding Congresses (March 4, 1889-March 3, 1895); chairman, Committee on Labor (Fifty-second Congress); presented credentials as a Member-elect to the Fifty-fourth Congress, and served from March 4, 1895 to February 27, 1896, when he was succeeded by Robert T. Van Horn, who contested his election; appointed by President Grover Cleveland as an associate justice of the supreme court of Oklahoma Territory in 1896, and served until 1899; returned to Kansas City, Mo., in 1899 and resumed the practice of law; died in Kansas City, Mo., September 4, 1920; interment in Mount St. Mary's Cemetery.

**TARSNEY, Timothy Edward,** a Representative from Michigan; born in Ransom, Hillsdale County, Mich., February 4, 1849; attended the common and high schools; worked on the Government roads in Tennessee until the close of the Civil War, when he returned to Michigan and settled in Saginaw; was employed as an engineer in a sawmill; became a marine engineer in 1867; was graduated from the law department of the University of Michigan at Ann Arbor in 1872; was admitted to the bar the same year and commenced practice in East Saginaw, Mich.; elected justice of the peace in 1873; city attorney from 1875 to 1878, when he resigned; unsuccessful candidate for election in 1880 to the Forty-seventh Congress; delegate at large to the Democratic National Convention in 1884; elected as a Democrat to the Forty-ninth and Fiftieth Congresses (March 4, 1885-March 3, 1889); unsuccessful candidate for reelection in 1888 to the Fifty-first Congress; moved to Detroit, Mich., in 1893 and resumed the practice of law; corporation counsel of Detroit 1900-1908; died in Detroit, Mich., June 8, 1909; interment in Calvary Cemetery, Saginaw, Mich.

**TARVER, Malcolm Connor,** a Representative from Georgia; born in Rural Vale, Whitfield County, Ga., September 25, 1885; attended the public schools; was graduated from the law department of Mercer University, Macon, Ga., in 1904; was admitted to the bar the same year and commenced practice in Dalton, Ga.; member of the State house of representatives 1909-1912; served in the State senate in 1913 and 1914; judge of the superior courts, Cherokee Circuit, Ga., 1917-1927; elected as a Democrat to the Seventieth and to the nine succeeding Congresses (March 4, 1927-January 3, 1947); unsuccessful candidate for renomination in 1946; resumed the practice of law; died in Dalton, Ga., March 5, 1960; interment in West Hill Cemetery.

**TATE, Farish Carter,** a Representative from Georgia; born in Jasper, Pickens County, Ga., November 20, 1856; attended the common schools and North Georgia Agricultural College in Dahlonega, Ga.; studied law; was admitted to the bar in 1880 and commenced practice at Jasper, Ga.; member of the general assembly of Georgia, 1882-1887; member of the Democratic State executive committee, 1884-1887 and 1890-1892; delegate to the Democratic State convention in 1888; elected as a Democrat to the Fifty-third and to the five succeeding Congresses (March 4, 1893-March 3, 1905); unsuccessful candidate for renomination in 1904 to the Fifty-ninth Congress; appointed United States district attorney for the northern district of Georgia by President Theodore Roosevelt; reappointed by President William Howard Taft, and served from

1905 to 1913; resumed the practice of law in Jasper, Ga., and died there February 7, 1922; interment in the Tate family cemetery.

**TATE, Magnus,** a Representative from Virginia; born in Berkeley County, Va. (now West Virginia), in 1760; studied law; was admitted to the bar and practiced; engaged in agricultural pursuits; appointed justice of the Berkeley County Court May 19, 1798; sheriff of Berkeley County in 1819 and 1820; member of the house of delegates of Virginia in 1797, 1803, 1809, and 1810; elected as a Federalist to the Fourteenth Congress (March 4, 1815-March 3, 1817); died near Martinsburg, Va. (now West Virginia), March 30, 1823.

**TATE, Randy J.,** a Representative from Washington; born in Puyallup, Pierce County, Wash., November 23, 1965; A.A., Tacoma Community College, 1986; B.A., Western Washington University, Bellingham, 1988; member, Washington State house of representatives, 1989-1995; elected as a Republican to the One Hundred Fourth Congress (January 3, 1995-January 3, 1997); is a resident of Puyallup, Wash.

**TATGENHORST, Charles, Jr.,** a Representative from Ohio; born in Cincinnati, Hamilton County, Ohio, August 19, 1883; educated in the public schools of Cincinnati; was graduated from Cincinnati Law School in 1910; was admitted to the bar the same year and commenced practice in Cincinnati; assistant city solicitor for Cincinnati 1914-1919; moved to Cleves, Ohio, in 1919 and continued the practice of law; elected as a Republican to the Seventieth Congress to fill the vacancy caused by the death of Ambrose E.B. Stephens and served from November 8, 1927, to March 3, 1929; was not a candidate for renomination in 1928; again resumed the practice of his profession in Cincinnati, Ohio; elected judge of the court of appeals of the first appellate district of Ohio on November 3, 1936, and served until February 8, 1937; Ohio State bar examiner 1938-1942; in January 1941 became a member of the Ohio State Banking Board; director of Cincinnati Street Railway Co. and Sullivan Electric Co.; died in Cincinnati, Ohio, January 13, 1961; interment in Spring Grove Cemetery.

**TATOM, Absalom,** a Representative from North Carolina; born in that State in 1742; sergeant in the Greenville (N.C.) Militia in 1763; during the Revolutionary War was commissioned first lieutenant in the First North Carolina Continental Regiment on September 1, 1775; promoted to the rank of captain on June 29, 1776; resigned from the Continental Army on September 19, 1776; enlisted as assistant quartermaster and keeper of the arsenal in the State service at Hillsborough, N.C., August 15, 1778; was contractor for Hillsborough in 1778; major of detachment of the North Carolina Light Horse February 12, 1779; was clerk of Randolph County Court in 1779; elected to the North Carolina State house of commons, but was unseated because he already held the office of county clerk; was district auditor for Hillsborough in 1781; one of three commissioners appointed by Congress to survey lands granted to Continental soldiers in the western territory (later Tennessee) in 1782; private secretary to Governor Thomas Burke in 1782; State tobacco agent in 1782; elected surveyor of North Carolina by the Continental Congress in May 1785; commissioner to sign State paper money in December 1785; served as a delegate to the constitutional convention in 1788; elected as a Republican to the Fourth Congress and served from March 4, 1795, to June 1, 1796, when he resigned; again served in the North Carolina State house of commons, 1797-1802; died in Raleigh, N.C., on December 20, 1802; interment in the Old City Cemetery.

**TATTNALL, Edward Fenwick,** a Representative from Georgia; born in Savannah, Ga., in 1788; educated in England; held several local offices; solicitor general from November 1816 to September 1817, when he resigned; member of the State house of representatives in 1818 and 1819; elected to the Seventeenth and to the three succeeding Congresses and served from March 4, 1821, until his resignation in 1827 before the convening of the Twentieth Congress; first captain of the Savannah Volunteer Guards; died in Savannah, Chatham County, Ga., November 21, 1832; interment in Bonaventure Cemetery.

**TATTNALL, Josiah,** a Senator from Georgia; born at Bonaventure, near Savannah, Ga., in 1762; completed preparatory studies; went with his father to England at the outbreak of the Revolutionary War and attended Eaton College; ran away from England and enlisted in the Continental Army in 1782; colonel of a regiment of Georgia State troops in 1793 for protection against the Indians, and was promoted to brigadier general in 1801; member, Georgia State house of representatives, 1795-1796; elected as a Republican to the United States Senate to fill the vacancy caused by the resignation of James Jackson, and served from February 20, 1796 to March 3, 1799; elected Governor of Georgia by the Legislature, and served from November 7, 1801 to November 4, 1802; died in Nassau, New Providence, British West Indies, on June 6, 1803; interment in Bonaventure Cemetery, Savannah, Ga.

**TAUKE, Thomas Joseph,** a Representative from Iowa; born in Dubuque, Iowa, October 11, 1950; attended the Dubuque County private schools; graduated from Wahlert High School, 1968; B.A., Loras College, Dubuque, 1972; J.D., University of Iowa College of Law, Iowa City, 1974; admitted to the Iowa bar and commenced practice in Dubuque in 1974; served in the Iowa general assembly, 1975-1978; delegate, Iowa State Republican conventions, 1972-1978; delegate to the Republican National Convention of 1976; elected as a Republican to the Ninety-sixth and to the five succeeding Congresses (January 3, 1979-January 3, 1991); was not a candidate in 1990 for reelection to the House of Representatives, but was an unsuccessful candidate for election to the United States Senate; is a resident of Dubuque, Iowa.

**TAUL, Micah** (grandfather of Taul Bradford), a Representative from Kentucky; born in Bladensburg, Md., May 14, 1785; moved to Kentucky with his parents in 1787; attended private school; studied law; was admitted to the bar in 1801 and commenced practice in Monticello, Ky.; clerk of Wayne County Courts in 1801; served as a colonel of Wayne County Volunteers in the War of 1812; elected as a Republican to the Fourteenth Congress (March 4, 1815-March 3, 1817); declined to be a candidate for renomination in 1816; resumed the practice of law; moved to Winchester, Tenn., in 1826 and continued the practice of law; moved to Mardisville, Talladega County, Ala., in 1846 and engaged in agricultural pursuits until his death there on May 27, 1850; interment on his plantation at Mardisville.

**TAULBEE, William Preston,** a Representative from Kentucky; born near Mount Sterling, in Morgan County, Ky., October 22, 1851; attended the common schools and was tutored by his father; was ordained for the ministry and admitted to the Kentucky conference of the Methodist Episcopal Church South; elected clerk of the Magoffin County Court in 1878 and reelected in 1882; studied law and was admitted to the bar in 1881; elected as a Democrat to the Forty-ninth and Fiftieth Congresses (March 4, 1885-March 3, 1889); was not a candidate for renomination; was shot by Charles E. Kincaid, a reporter for the Louisville Times, in the Capitol Building, Washington, D.C., February 28, 1890, and died from the effects of the wounds at Providence Hospital, in that city, March 11, 1890; interment in the family burying ground near Mount Sterling, Ky.

**Bibliography:** Klotter, James C. "Sex, Scandal, and Suffrage in the Gilded Age." *Historian* 42 (February 1980): 225-243.

**TAURIELLO, Anthony Francis,** a Representative from New York; born in Buffalo, Erie County, N.Y., August 14, 1899; attended the public schools; was graduated from the law school of Cumberland University, Lebanon, Tenn., in 1929; was admitted to the Tennessee bar in 1929 and commenced the practice of law in Nashville, Tenn.; member of the Erie County (N.Y.) Board of Supervisors from October 1933 to December 1937, and Buffalo Common Council 1938-1941; deputy city treasurer 1942-1945; examiner for Reconstruction Finance Corporation, Buffalo, N.Y., from April 1946 to November 1946 and with War Assets Administration from November 1946 to May 1947; again a member of the Buffalo Common Council in 1948; delegate to the Democratic National Convention in 1936; elected as a Democrat to the Eighty-first Congress (January 3, 1949-January 3, 1951); was an unsuccessful candidate for reelection in 1950 to the Eighty-second Congress, and for election in 1952 to the Eighty-third Congress; retail liquor dealer; again elected a member of Buffalo Common Council and served from 1954 to 1957; appointed to Buffalo Municipal Housing Authority in November 1961 on which he served until 1973; was a resident of Buffalo, N.Y., until his death there December 21, 1983; interment in United German and French Cemetery, Buffalo, N.Y.

**TAUZIN, Wilbert Joseph (Billy),** a Representative from Louisiana; born in Chackbay, Lafourche Parish, La., June 14, 1943; attended the public schools and graduated from Thibodaux (La.) High School, 1961; B.A., Nicholls State University, Thibodaux, 1964; J.D., Louisiana State University, Baton Rouge, 1967; legislative aide, Louisiana State senate, 1963-1967; admitted to the Louisiana bar in 1968 and commenced practice in Houma; served in the Louisiana State house of representatives, 1972-1980; elected as a Democrat, May 17, 1980, by special election, to the Ninety-sixth Congress to fill the vacancy caused by the resignation of David C. Treen; reelected to the eight succeeding Congresses and served from May 17, 1980, to January 3, 1997; announced his affiliation with the Republican Party on August 6, 1995, and continued in office during the One Hundred Fourth Congress as a Republican; is a resident of Thibodaux, La.

**TAVENNER, Clyde Howard,** a Representative from Illinois; born in Cordova, Rock Island County, Ill., February 4, 1882; attended the common schools; learned the printer's trade; engaged as editorial writer; director of publicity for the Democratic National Congressional Committee in 1910 and 1912; elected as a Democrat to the Sixty-third and Sixty-fourth Congresses (March 4, 1913-March 3, 1917); chairman, Committee on Expenditures in the Post Office Department (Sixty-fourth Congress); unsuccessful candidate for reelection in 1916 to the Sixty-fifth Congress; founded a monthly magazine, the Philippine Republic, in Washington, D.C., in 1923, and also engaged in the publishing business; visited Europe, the Near East, and the Far East in 1931 and 1932 as a member of a mission from the Philippine Islands; legislative analyst to the House Committee on Rules in 1939; died in Washington, D.C., February 6, 1942; interment in the Congressional Cemetery.

**TAWNEY, James Albertus,** a Representative from Minnesota; born in Mount Pleasant Township, near Gettysburg, Adams County, Pa., January 3, 1855; apprenticed with his father as a blacksmith; subsequently learned the trade of machinist; moved to Winona, Minn., August 1, 1877, where he was employed as a blacksmith and machinist until January 1, 1881; attended the law department of the University of Wisconsin at Madison; was admitted to the bar in 1882 and commenced practice in Winona, Winona County, Minn.; member of the Minnesota State senate in 1890; elected as a Republican to the Fifty-third and to the eight succeeding Congresses (March 4, 1893-March 3, 1911); majority whip (Fifty-fifth through Fifty-eighth Congresses); chairman, Committee on Appropriations (Fifty-ninth through Sixty-first Congresses); unsuccessful candidate for renomination in 1910 to the Sixty-second Congress; member of the International Joint Commission, created to prevent disputes regarding the use of boundary waters between the United States and Canada, from March 11, 1911, until his death, serving as

chairman of the United States section from September 17, 1911 to December 1, 1914; died at Excelsior Springs, Clay County, Mo., June 12, 1919; interment in Woodlawn Cemetery, Winona, Minn.

**Bibliography:** *DAB*; Wyman, Roger E. "Insurgency in Minnesota: The Defeat of James A. Tawney in 1910." *Minnesota History* 40 (Fall 1967): 317-329.

**TAYLER, Robert Walker,** a Representative from Ohio; born in Youngstown, Mahoning County, Ohio, November 26, 1852; attended the public schools, and was graduated from Western Reserve College, Cleveland, Ohio, in 1872; taught in the high school in New Lisbon (now Lisbon), Ohio; superintendent of schools 1873-1875; editor of the Buckeye State, in New Lisbon, Ohio, 1875-1876; was admitted to the bar in April 1877 and commenced practice in East Liverpool, Columbiana County, Ohio; prosecuting attorney of Columbiana County 1880-1885; resumed the practice of law in Lisbon, Ohio; moved to New York in 1890; returned to Lisbon in 1892; elected as a Republican to the Fifty-fourth and to the three succeeding Congresses (March 4, 1895-March 3, 1903); chairman, Committee on Elections No. 1 (Fifty-fifth through Fifty-seventh Congresses); declined to be a candidate in 1902 for renomination; resumed the practice of law in Youngstown, Ohio; appointed by President Theodore Roosevelt to be United States district judge for the northern district of Ohio February 2, 1905; moved to Cleveland, Ohio, and died there November 25, 1910; interment in Lisbon Cemetery, Lisbon, Ohio.

**TAYLOR, Abner,** a Representative from Illinois; born in Bangor, Penobscot County, Maine, in 1829; moved with his parents to Champaign County, Ohio, in 1832, thence to Fort Dodge, Iowa, and subsequently to Chicago, Ill., in 1860; engaged in extensive contracting, building, and mercantile pursuits, and participated in the construction of the Texas State capitol; member of the Illinois house of representatives from 1884 to 1886; delegate to the Republican National Convention in 1884; elected as a Republican to the Fifty-first and Fifty-second Congresses (March 4, 1889-March 3, 1893); was not a candidate for renomination in 1892; resumed the building and contracting business; died in Washington, D.C., April 13, 1903; interment in Rock Creek Cemetery.

**TAYLOR, Alexander Wilson,** a Representative from Pennsylvania; born in Indiana, Indiana County, Pa., March 22, 1815; pursued classical studies; attended the Indiana Academy and Jefferson College, Canonsburg, Pa., graduated from the law school at Carlisle, Pa.; admitted to the bar in 1841 and commenced practice in Indiana, Pa.; clerk of the court of Indiana County 1845-1848; member of the Pennsylvania house of representatives in 1859 and 1860; elected as a Republican to the Forty-third Congress (March 4, 1873-March 3, 1875); again resumed the practice of law; died in Indiana, Pa., May 7, 1893; interment in Greenwood Cemetery.

**TAYLOR, Alfred Alexander** (son of Nathaniel Green Taylor and brother of Robert Love Taylor), a Representative from Tennessee; born in Happy Valley, Carter County, Tenn., August 6, 1848; attended Duffield Academy, Elizabethton, Tenn., Buffalo Institute (later Milligan College), Tennessee, and the schools of Edge Hill and Pennington Seminary, New Jersey; studied law; was admitted to the bar in 1874 and commenced practice in Jonesboro, Washington County, Tenn.; member of the Tennessee State house of representatives, 1875-1877; unsuccessful Republican candidate for Governor in 1886, being defeated by his brother Robert; delegate to the Republican National Convention of 1888; elected as a Republican to the Fifty-first and to the two succeeding Congresses (March 4, 1889-March 3, 1895); declined to be a candidate for renomination in 1894 to the Fifty-fourth Congress; engaged in the practice of law in Johnson City, Tenn.; engaged as a lecturer and also interested in agricultural pursuits; elected Governor of Tennessee in 1920, and served from January 15, 1921 to January 16, 1923; unsuccessful candidate for reelection in 1922; again engaged in lecturing and in agricultural pursuits; resided at Milligan College, Carter County, Tenn.; died while on a visit in Johnson City, Tenn., November 25, 1931; interment in Monta Vista Cemetery.

**Bibliography:** *DAB*; Taylor, Robert L., Jr. "Apprenticeship in the First District: Bob and Alf Taylor's Early Congressional Races." *Tennessee Historical Quarterly* 28 (Spring 1969): 24-41.

**TAYLOR, Arthur Herbert,** a Representative from Indiana; born at Caledonia Springs, Canada, February 29, 1852; moved with his parents to Yates County, N.Y., in 1856; attended the local school; taught school for several years; moved to Indianapolis, Ind., in 1869; studied law; was admitted to the bar in 1873 and commenced practice in Indianapolis, Ind.; moved to Petersburg, Ind., in 1874 and continued the practice of law; prosecuting attorney for the eleventh judicial circuit of Indiana 1880-1884; elected as a Democrat to the Fifty-third Congress (March 4, 1893-March 3, 1895); unsuccessful candidate for reelection in 1894 to the Fifty-fourth Congress; resumed the practice of law in Petersburg, Ind., until his death February 20, 1922; interment in Walnut Hills Cemetery.

**TAYLOR, Benjamin Irving,** a Representative from New York; born in New York City December 21, 1877; attended the public schools; was graduated from the high school in New Rochelle, N.Y., and from Columbia Law School in New York City in 1899; was admitted to the bar the same year and commenced practice in Port Chester, Westchester County, N.Y.; supervisor of Harrison, Westchester County, 1905-1913; elected as a Democrat to the Sixty-third Congress (March 4, 1913-March 3, 1915); unsuccessful candidate for reelection in 1914 to the Sixty-fourth Congress; resumed the practice of law in Port Chester, N.Y.; again elected supervisor of Harrison, N.Y., in 1921, and served in that capacity, with the exception of two years, until December 1945; died in Harrison, N.Y., September 5, 1946; interment in Kensico Cemetery, Valhalla, N.Y.

**TAYLOR, Caleb Newbold,** a Representative from Pennsylvania; born near Newportville, Bristol Township, Bucks County, Pa., July 27, 1813; completed preparatory studies; engaged in agricultural pursuits; delegate to the Pennsylvania Whig convention at Harrisburg in 1832; unsuccessful candidate for election to Congress in 1848, 1850, and again in 1852; delegate to the Republican National Convention in 1860; elected as a Republican to the Fortieth Congress (March 4, 1867-March 3, 1869); successfully contested the election of John R. Reading to the Forty-first Congress and served from April 13, 1870, to March 3, 1871; engaged in banking; president of the Farmers' National Bank of Bucks County, Bristol, Pa., from 1875 until his death at his home, "Sunbury Farm," near Newportville, Bristol Township, Pa., November 15, 1887; interment in the Friends Burying Ground, Bristol, Pa.

**TAYLOR, Charles Hart,** a Representative from North Carolina; born in Brevard, Transylvania County, N.C., January 23, 1941; graduated from Brevard High School; B.A., Wake Forest University, 1963; J.D., Wake Forest University School of Law, 1967; tree farmer; member, North Carolina State house of representatives, 1967-1971; member, North Carolina State senate, 1973-1975; unsuccessful candidate in 1988 for election to the One Hundred First Congress; elected as a Republican to the One Hundred Second and to the two succeeding Congresses (January 3, 1991-January 3, 1997); is a resident of Brevard, N.C.

**TAYLOR, Chester William** (son of Samuel Mitchell Taylor), a Representative from Arkansas; born in Verona, Lee County, Miss., July 16, 1883; moved to Pine Bluff, Ark., with his parents; attended the public schools in Pine Bluff, Ark.; studied law at Georgetown University Law School, Washington, D.C.; deputy State auditor 1908-1910; deputy secretary of state in 1911; deputy State treasurer in 1911 and 1912; secretary to his father 1913-1921; elected as a Democrat to the Sixty-seventh Congress to fill the vacancy caused by the death of his father, Samuel M. Taylor, and served from October 31, 1921, to March 3, 1923; was not a candidate for renomination in 1922; engaged in the general insurance business at Pine Bluff, Ark., and later as an official in the State department of conservation at Little Rock, until his death in Pine Bluff, Ark., July 17, 1931; interment in Bellewood Cemetery.

**TAYLOR, Dean Park,** a Representative from New York; born in Troy, Rensselaer County, N.Y., January 1, 1902; attended the public schools and Colgate University, Hamilton, N.Y.; was graduated from Union University Department of Law, Schenectady, N.Y., in 1926; was admitted to the bar the same year and commenced practice in Troy, N.Y.; served as assistant United States attorney, northern district of New York, 1927-1930; chairman of the Rensselaer County Republican Committee, 1938-1952; delegate to the Republican National Convention in 1940; chairman, New York State Republican Committee, 1953-1954; trustee of Russell Sage College; director of the Union National Bank and of the Niagara Mohawk Power Co.; elected as a Republican to the Seventy-eighth and to the eight succeeding Congresses (January 3, 1943-January 3, 1961); was not a candidate for renomination in 1960 to the Eighty-seventh Congress; resumed the practice of law; died in Albany, N.Y., October 16, 1977; interment in Oakwood Cemetery, Troy, N.Y.

**TAYLOR, Edward Livingston, Jr.,** a Representative from Ohio; born in Columbus, Ohio, August 10, 1869; attended the public schools and was graduated from the Columbus High School; studied law; was admitted to the bar in 1891 and commenced practice in Columbus; prosecuting attorney of Franklin County 1899-1904; elected as a Republican to the Fifty-ninth and to the three succeeding Congresses (March 4, 1905-March 3, 1913); unsuccessful candidate for reelection in 1912 to the Sixty-third Congress; continued the practice of law in Columbus, Ohio, until his death there March 10, 1938; interment in Greenlawn Cemetery.

**TAYLOR, Edward Thomas,** a Representative from Colorado; born on a farm near Metamora, Woodford County, Ill., June 19, 1858; attended the common schools of Illinois and Kansas, and was graduated from the high school at Leavenworth, Kans., in 1881; moved to Leadville, Lake County, Colo.; principal of Leadville High School in 1881 and 1882; was graduated from the law department of the University of Michigan at Ann Arbor in 1884; was admitted to the bar the same year and commenced the practice of law in Leadville, Colo.; superintendent of schools of Lake County in 1884; deputy district attorney in 1885; moved to Glenwood Springs, Colo., in 1887; resumed the practice of his profession; district attorney of the ninth judicial district 1887-1889; member of the State senate 1896-1908, and served as president pro tempore for one term; city attorney 1896-1900; county attorney in 1901 and 1902; elected as a Democrat to the Sixty-first and to the sixteen succeeding Congresses and served from March 4, 1909, until his death in Denver, Colo., September 3, 1941; chairman, Committee on Irrigation of Arid Lands (Sixty-fifth Congress), Committee on Appropriations (Seventy-fifth through Seventy-seventh Congresses); interment in a mausoleum in Rosebud Cemetery, Glenwood Springs, Colo.

**TAYLOR, Ezra Booth,** a Representative from Ohio; born in Nelson, Portage County, Ohio, July 9, 1823; attended the common and select schools and academies; studied law; was admitted to the bar and commenced practice in Portage County in 1845; elected prosecuting attorney in 1854; moved to Warren, Trumbull County, Ohio, in 1861; enrolled as a private in Company A, One Hundred and Seventy-first Ohio Infantry, on April 27, 1864; was mustered into service on May 5, 1864, and was honorably discharged on August 20, 1864; elected judge of the court of common pleas for the ninth judicial district of Ohio and served from March 1877 to September 1880, when he resigned; elected as a Republican to the Forty-sixth Congress to fill the vacancy caused by the resignation of James A. Garfield; reelected to the Forty-seventh and to the five succeeding Congresses and served from December 13, 1880, to March 3, 1893; chairman, Committee on the Judiciary (Fifty-first Congress); declined to be a candidate for renomination in 1892; resumed the practice of his profession; died in Warren, Trumbull County, Ohio, January 29, 1912; interment in the Warren mausoleum at Oakwood Cemetery.

**TAYLOR, Gary Eugene (Gene),** a Representative from Mississippi; born in New Orleans, La., September 17, 1953; graduated from De LaSalle High School, New Orleans, 1971; B.A., Tulane University, 1976; attended University of Mississippi, 1978-1980; United States Coast Guard Reserve service, 1971-1984; member, Bay St. Louis city council, 1981-1983; member, Mississippi State senate, 1984-1989; unsuccessful candidate for election in 1988 to the One Hundred First Congress; elected as a Democrat to the One Hundred First Congress, October 17, 1989, by special election to fill the vacancy caused by the death of Larkin I. Smith; reelected to the One Hundred Second and to the two succeeding Congresses, and served from October 18, 1989 to January 3, 1997; is a resident of Bay St. Louis, Miss.

**TAYLOR, Gene,** a Representative from Missouri; born near Sarcoxie, Jasper County, Mo., February 10, 1928; attended the public schools; attended Southwest Missouri State College, Springfield, 1945-1947; served in the One Hundred and Eighth Cavalry, Missouri National Guard, 1948-1949; teacher; automobile dealer, Gene Taylor Ford Sales, Inc., 1958-1973; mayor of Sarcoxie, Mo., 1954-1960; Republican National committeeman, 1966-1972; delegate, Missouri State Republican conventions, 1960, 1964, 1968, and 1972; delegate to the Republican National Conventions of 1960, 1964 and 1968; elected as a Republican to the Ninety-third and to the seven succeeding Congresses (January 3, 1973-January 3, 1989); was not a candidate for reelection in 1988 to the One Hundred First Congress; is a resident of Sarcoxie, Mo.

**TAYLOR, George,** a Representative from New York; born in Wheeling, Va. (now West Virginia), October 19, 1820; completed preparatory studies; studied medicine and law; was admitted to the bar and practiced in Indiana; moved to Alabama in 1844, and to Brooklyn, N.Y., in 1848, where he continued the practice of law; held several local offices; elected as a Democrat to the Thirty-fifth Congress (March 4, 1857-March 3, 1859); unsuccessful candidate for reelection in 1858 to the Thirty-sixth Congress; resumed the practice of law in Washington, D.C., until his death there January 18, 1894; interment in Rock Creek Cemetery.

**TAYLOR, George,** a Delegate from Pennsylvania; born in Ireland in 1716; pursued academic studies; immigrated to the United States in 1736 and settled at Warwick Furnace and later at Coventry Forge, Chester County, Pa.; engaged in the manufacture of iron; moved to Durham, Pa., in 1755; justice of the peace in 1757, 1761, and 1763; moved to Easton, Pa., in 1763; member of the provincial assembly 1764-1769; justice of the peace for Northampton County 1764-1772; appointed judge of the county court in 1770; again a member of the provincial assembly in 1775; colonel of Pennsylvania Militia in 1775; returned to Durham in 1775; Member of the Continental Congress in 1776; signer of the Declaration of Independence; member of the First Supreme Executive Council in 1777; returned to Easton, Pa., in 1780, where he died February 23, 1781; interment in St. John's Lutheran Church Cemetery; reinterment in the Easton Cemetery.

**Bibliography:** *DAB.*

**TAYLOR, George Washington,** a Representative from Alabama; born on "Roselawn" plantation near Montgomery, Montgomery County, Ala., January 16, 1849; attended private schools; while a schoolboy in Columbia, S.C., enlisted in the Confederate Army in November 1864, and served until the end of the war; was graduated from the University of South Carolina at Columbia in 1867; taught

school in Mobile, Ala., and studied law; was admitted to the bar in Mobile, Ala., in November 1871 and commenced practice in Butler, Choctaw County, Ala., in 1872; member of the State house of representatives in 1878 and 1879; State solicitor for the first judicial circuit of Alabama 1880-1892; declined a third term; moved to Demopolis, Marengo County, Ala., in 1883; elected as a Democrat to the Fifty-fifth and to the eight succeeding Congresses (March 4, 1897-March 3, 1915); was not a candidate for renomination in 1914; resumed the practice of law in Demopolis, Ala.; chairman of the State Democratic convention which called the constitutional convention in 1901; was a delegate to the Democratic National Convention in 1920; died in Rome, Ga., while on a visit in that city, on December 21, 1932; interment in Oakwood Cemetery, Montgomery, Ala.

**TAYLOR, Glen Hearst,** a Senator from Idaho; born in Portland, Oreg., April 12, 1904; moved to a homestead near Kooskia, Idaho, as a child; attended the public schools of Idaho; joined a dramatic stock company in 1919; owned and managed various entertainment enterprises from 1926 until 1944; country-western singer; unsuccessful Democratic candidate for election to the United States Senate in 1940 and 1942; elected as a Democrat to the United States Senate in 1944, and served from January 3, 1945 to January 3, 1951; unsuccessful candidate for renomination in 1950; unsuccessful candidate in 1948 for Vice President of the United States on the Progressive Party ticket headed by Henry A. Wallace; unsuccessful Democratic candidate for election to the United States Senate in 1954, and for nomination to the United States Senate in 1956; president of Coryell Construction Co., 1950-1952, and of Taylor Topper, Inc.; died in Millbrae, Calif., April 28, 1984; interment in Skylawn Cemetery, San Mateo, Calif.

**Bibliography:** Peterson, Frank Ross. *Prophet Without Honor: Glen Taylor and the Fight for American Liberalism.* Lexington: University Press of Kentucky, 1974; Taylor, Glen Hearst. *The Way It Was With Me.* Secaucus, N.J.: L. Stuart, 1979.

**TAYLOR, Herbert Worthington,** a Representative from New Jersey; born in Belleville, Essex County, N.J., February 19, 1869; attended the public schools, and was graduated from the law school of the University of New York, New York City, in 1891; was admitted to the New York bar the same year and to the New Jersey bar in 1897, and practiced in New York City and Newark, N.J.; member of the common council of Newark 1899-1903; member of the State assembly in 1904 and 1905; chairman of the Essex County Republican committee 1913-1917; delegate to the Republican National Convention in 1916; county counsel of Essex County 1916-1921; elected as a Republican to the Sixty-seventh Congress (March 4, 1921-March 3, 1923); unsuccessful candidate for renomination in 1922; resumed the practice of law in Newark, N.J.; elected to the Sixty-ninth Congress (March 4, 1925-March 3, 1927); unsuccessful candidate for reelection in 1926; resumed the practice of law in Newark, N.J., where he died on October 15, 1931; interment in East Ridgelawn Cemetery, Delawanna, N.J.

**TAYLOR, Isaac Hamilton,** a Representative from Ohio; born near New Harrisburg (later Hibbetts), Carroll County, Ohio, April 18, 1840; attended the common schools and completed an academic course; studied law; was admitted to the bar in 1867 and commenced practice in Carrollton, Ohio; clerk of court in Carroll County, Ohio, 1870-1877; elected as a Republican to the Forty-ninth Congress (March 4, 1885-March 3, 1887); was not a candidate for renomination in 1886; moved to Canton, Ohio, and resumed the practice of law; delegate to the Republican National Convention in 1892; judge of the court of common pleas from 1889 to 1901, when he resigned; engaged in the practice of his profession in Canton, Ohio, until 1922; died at Congress Lake, near Hartville, Stark County, Ohio, December 18, 1936; interment in Westlawn Cemetery, Canton, Ohio.

**TAYLOR, James Alfred,** a Representative from West Virginia; born near Ironton, Lawrence County, Ohio, September 25, 1878; attended the public schools; employed in a printing office in Ironton, Ohio; moved to Alderson, W.Va., and engaged in the newspaper business; moved from Greenbrier County to Fayette County in 1905; served as a noncommissioned officer in the West Virginia National Guard 1908-1911; member of the State house of representatives 1916-1918, 1920-1922, 1930-1932, and 1936-1938, serving as speaker 1930-1932; elected as a Democrat to the Sixty-eighth and Sixty-ninth Congresses (March 4, 1923-March 3, 1927); was an unsuccessful candidate for reelection in 1926 to the Seventieth Congress; resumed the newspaper publishing business; unsuccessful Democratic candidate for the gubernatorial nomination in 1928; served as secretary of the West Virginia Liquor Commission 1941-1945; elected a member of the Fayette County Board of Education in 1946 for a six-year term; died in Montgomery, W.Va., on June 9, 1956; interment in Huse Memorial Park, Fayetteville, W.Va.

**TAYLOR, James Willis,** a Representative from Tennessee; born near Lead Mine Bend, Union County, Tenn., August 28, 1880; attended the public schools, Holbrook Normal College, Fountain City, Tenn., and the American Temperance University, Harriman, Tenn.; taught school for several years; was graduated from the law department of Cumberland University, Lebanon, Tenn., in 1902; was admitted to the bar the same year; moved to La Follette, Campbell County, Tenn., and commenced practice; postmaster at La Follette 1904-1909; served as mayor 1910-1913 and in 1918 and 1919; insurance commissioner for the State of Tennessee in 1913 and 1914; chairman of the Republican State executive committee in 1917 and 1918; elected as a Republican to the Sixty-sixth and to the ten succeeding Congresses and served from March 4, 1919, until his death; chairman, Committee on Expenditures in the Department of State (Sixty-eighth and Sixty-ninth Congresses); member of the Republican National Executive Committee 1929-1939; died in La Follette, Tenn., November 14, 1939; interment in Woodlawn Cemetery.

**TAYLOR, John,** a Representative from South Carolina; member, South Carolina State house of representatives, 1802-1805; elected as a Republican to the Fourteenth Congress (March 4, 1815-March 3, 1817); unsuccessful candidate for reelection in 1816 to the Fifteenth Congress, and for election in 1820 to the Seventeenth Congress.

**TAYLOR, John,** a Representative and a Senator from South Carolina; born near Granby, S.C., May 4, 1770; attended Mount Zion Institute, Columbia, S.C., and was graduated from the College of New Jersey (now Princeton University) in 1790; studied law; was admitted to the bar in 1793 and commenced practice in Columbia, S.C.; also engaged in planting; member, South Carolina State house of representatives, 1796-1802, and 1804-1805; circuit court solicitor, 1805-1806; served as first intendant (administrative official) of Columbia, 1806-1807; elected as a Republican to the Tenth and Eleventh Congresses, and served from March 4, 1807 until his resignation on December 30, 1810; elected as a Republican to the United States Senate on December 19, 1810, to fill the vacancy caused by the resignation of Thomas Sumter; was also elected on December 20, 1810, for the full term beginning March 4, 1811, and served from December 31, 1810 until his resignation in November 1816; member, State senate, 1818-1826; elected Governor of South Carolina by the Legislature, and served from December 1826 to December 1828; trustee of South Carolina College (now the University of South Carolina) at Columbia and director of the Columbia Theological Seminary (Presbyterian); died at Camden, Kershaw County, S.C., on April 16, 1832; interment in the family burial ground at Columbia, S.C.

**TAYLOR, John,** a Senator from Virginia; known as "John Taylor of Caroline" to distinguish him from others of the same name; born in either Orange or Caroline County, Va., probably on December 19, 1753; educated by private tutors; studied at the College of William and Mary, Williamsburg, Va., 1770-1772; studied law; was admitted to the bar and commenced practice in Caroline County in 1774; served in the Revolutionary War as major and colonel; member, Virginia house of delegates, 1779-1785, with the exception of 1782, and 1796-1800; retired from the practice of law and engaged in agricultural pursuits; elected in 1792 to the United States Senate to fill the vacancy caused by the resignation of Richard Henry Lee; reelected in 1793, and served from October 18, 1792 until his resignation on May 11, 1794; presidential elector in 1797; appointed to the United States Senate as a Republican to fill the vacancy caused by the death of Stevens T. Mason, and served from June 4 to December 7, 1803, when a successor was elected; was not a candidate for election to fill the vacancy; elected in 1822 to the United States Senate to fill the vacancy caused by the resignation of James Pleasants; reelected in 1823, and served from December 18, 1822 until his death in Caroline County, Va., August 21, 1824; political theorist; interment on "Hazelwood" farm, near Port Royal, Caroline County, Va.

**Bibliography:** *DAB*; Hill, Charles William, Jr. *The Political Theory of John Taylor of Caroline.* Rutherfurd, N.J.: Fairleigh Dickinson University Press, 1976; Shalhope, Robert E. *John Taylor of Caroline.* Columbia, S.C.: University of South Carolina Press, 1980.

**TAYLOR, John Clarence,** a Representative from South Carolina; born in Honea Path, Anderson County, S.C., March 2, 1890; attended the public schools and Fruitland Institute, Hendersonville, N.C.; was graduated from the law department of the University of South Carolina at Columbia in 1919; during the First World War attended the Officers' Training School at Camp Johnston, Fla., in 1918 and was discharged into the Reserves at the end of the war; was admitted to the bar in 1919; engaged in agricultural pursuits; clerk of court and register of deeds for Anderson County, S.C., from 1920 until elected to Congress; elected as a Democrat to the Seventy-third, Seventy-fourth, and Seventy-fifth Congresses (March 4, 1933-January 3, 1939); was an unsuccessful candidate for renomination in 1938 to the Seventy-sixth Congress; resumed his former business pursuits; member, South Carolina State senate, 1951-1954 and 1959-1962; resident of Anderson, S.C., until his death there March 25, 1983; interment in Garden of Memories, Honea Path, S.C.

**TAYLOR, John James,** a Representative from New York; born in Leominster, Worcester County, Mass., April 27, 1808; attended the common schools, New Ipswich Academy, and Groton Academy; was graduated from Harvard University in 1829; engaged in teaching for a short time; moved to Troy, N.Y., in 1830; studied law; was admitted to the bar in 1834 and commenced practice in Greene, Chenango County, N.Y.; moved to Owego, N.Y., in 1834 and continued the practice of law; appointed district attorney of Tioga County in 1838, and served until 1843, when he resigned; member of the village board of trustees in 1839, 1843, and 1848; first chief engineer of the fire department in 1844; member of the State constitutional convention in 1846; unsuccessful candidate for election in 1850 to the Thirty-second Congress; elected as a Democrat to the Thirty-third Congress (March 4, 1853-March 3, 1855); resumed the practice of his profession; tendered the appointment of commissioner to settle the northwestern boundary of the United States by President Franklin Pierce, but declined the position; unsuccessful Democratic candidate for Lieutenant Governor of New York in 1858; president of the village of Owego in 1859; engaged in banking; elected vice president and later president of the Southern Central Railway Co., later the Auburn division of the

Lehigh Valley Railroad Co.; died in Owego, Tioga County, N.Y., July 1, 1892; interment in Evergreen Cemetery.

**TAYLOR, John Lampkin,** a Representative from Ohio; born in Stafford County, near Fredericksburg, Va., March 7, 1805; completed preparatory studies; studied law in Washington, D.C.; was admitted to the bar in 1828 and commenced practice in Chillicothe, Ross County, Ohio, in 1829; major general in the State militia for several years; elected as a Whig to the Thirtieth and to the three succeeding Congresses (March 4, 1847-March 3, 1855); served as a clerk in the Interior Department from May 1, 1870, until his sudden death at his desk in Washington, D.C., September 6, 1870; interment in the family burying ground on the Taylor ancestral estate, "Mansfield," near Louisa, Louisa County, Va.

**TAYLOR, John May,** a Representative from Tennessee; born in Lexington, Henderson County, Tenn., May 18, 1838; attended the Male Academy in Lexington and the Union University, Murfreesboro, Tenn.; was graduated from the law department of Cumberland University, Lebanon, Tenn., in 1861; was admitted to the bar the same year and commenced practice in Lexington; enlisted in the Confederate Army; was elected first lieutenant in June 1861 and promoted to captain; elected major in the Twenty-seventh Tennessee Regiment in 1862; mayor of Lexington in 1869 and 1870; delegate to the Tennessee State constitutional convention in 1870; attorney general of the eleventh judicial circuit of Tennessee, 1870-1878; delegate to the Democratic National Convention of 1880; member of the Tennessee State house of representatives, 1881-1882; elected as a Democrat to the Forty-eighth and Forty-ninth Congresses (March 4, 1883-March 3, 1887); chairman, Committee on Expenditures in the Department of the Navy (Forty-ninth Congress); member of the State senate in 1892; resumed the practice of law; was appointed judge of the criminal court for the eleventh judicial circuit in 1895 and subsequently elected for a six-year term, serving until the court was abolished; elected in August 1902 as a judge of the Court of Chancery Appeals (name changed to Court of Civil Appeals by the Legislature); reelected in 1910 for a period of eight years, and served until his death in Lexington, Tenn., February 17, 1911; interment in Lexington Cemetery.

**TAYLOR, John W.,** a Representative from New York; born in Charlton, N.Y., March 26, 1784; received his early education at home; was graduated from Union College, Schenectady, N.Y., in 1803; studied law; was admitted to the bar in 1807 and commenced practice in Ballston Spa, N.Y.; organized the Ballston Center Academy; justice of the peace in 1808; member of the New York State assembly in 1812 and 1813; elected as a Republican to the Thirteenth Congress, and reelected to the nine succeeding Congresses (March 4, 1813-March 3, 1833); chairman, Committee on Elections (Fourteenth and Fifteenth Congresses), Committee on Revisal and Unfinished Business (Fifteenth Congress), Committee on Elections (Sixteenth Congress); Speaker of the House of Representatives (Sixteenth and Nineteenth Congresses); unsuccessful candidate for reelection in 1832 to the Twenty-third Congress; resumed the practice of law in Ballston Spa, N.Y.; member of the State senate in 1840 and 1841, but resigned in consequence of a paralytic stroke; moved to Cleveland, Ohio, in 1843, and died there on September 18, 1854; interment in the City Cemetery, Ballston Spa, Saratoga County, N.Y.

Bibliography: *DAB*; Johnson, William R. "Prelude to the Missouri Compromise: A New York Congressman's Effort to Exclude Slavery from Arkansas Territory." *New-York Historical Society Quarterly* 48 (January 1964): 31-50; Spann, Edward K. "John W. Taylor, The Reluctant Partisan, 1784-1854." Ph.D. dissertation, New York University, 1957.

**TAYLOR, Jonathan,** a Representative from Ohio; born near Mansfield, Conn., in 1796; moved to Newark, Ohio; completed an academic course; studied law; was admitted to the bar and commenced practice in Newark; appointed by the Governor a commissioner to settle the boundary dispute between Ohio and Michigan; brigadier general in the State militia; member of the Ohio State house of representatives, 1831-1833; served in the State senate, 1833-1836; elected as a Democrat to the Twenty-sixth Congress (March 4, 1839-March 3, 1841); unsuccessful candidate for reelection in 1840 to the Twenty-seventh Congress; died in Newark, Licking County, Ohio, in April 1848; interment in the Old Cemetery; reinterment in Cedar Hill Cemetery.

**TAYLOR, Joseph Danner,** a Representative from Ohio; born in Goshen Township, Belmont County, Ohio, November 7, 1830; attended the common schools and Madison College at Antrim; taught school 1854-1856, and was principal of the Fairview High School in 1857; studied law in Cincinnati, Ohio, and was admitted to the bar in 1859; was graduated from the Cincinnati Law College in 1860 and commenced practice in Cambridge, Guernsey County, Ohio, the same year; owner of the Guernsey Times 1861-1871; during the Civil War entered the Union Army as a captain in the Eighty-eighth Regiment, Ohio Volunteer Infantry; was judge advocate of the Department of Indiana in 1863 and 1864; citizen judge advocate in Indianapolis, Ind., in 1865; prosecuting attorney of Guernsey County, Ohio, 1863-1866; delegate to the Philadelphia Loyalist Convention in 1866; member of the Cambridge School Board 1870-1877; delegate to the Republican National Conventions in 1876 and 1880; elected as a Republican to the Forty-seventh Congress to fill the vacancy caused by the death of Jonathan T. Updegraff; reelected to the Forty-eighth Congress and served from January 2, 1883, to March 3, 1885; unsuccessful candidate for reelection in 1884 to the Forty-ninth Congress; elected to the Fiftieth, Fifty-first, and Fifty-second Congresses (March 4, 1887-March 3, 1893); died in Cambridge, Ohio, September 19, 1899; interment in the South Cemetery.

**TAYLOR, Miles,** a Representative from Louisiana; born in Saratoga Springs, N.Y., July 16, 1805; received a liberal education; moved to Bayou Lafourche, La.; studied medicine, but never practiced; studied law; was admitted to the bar and commenced practice in Donaldsonville, Ascension Parish, La.; moved to New Orleans, La., about 1847; held several local offices; appointed by Governor Isaac Johnson in 1849 as a member of a committee to revise the Civil Code, the Code of Procedure, and the Statutes of Louisiana; elected as a Democrat to the Thirty-fourth and to the two succeeding Congresses, and served from March 4, 1855 to February 5, 1861, when he bade formal adieu and withdrew; chairman of the Douglas National Executive Committee in 1869; resumed the practice of law in New Orleans, La.; died in Saratoga Springs, N.Y., September 23, 1873; interment on the family plantation, "Front Scattery," near Belle Alliance, Assumption Parish, La.

**TAYLOR, Nathaniel Green** (father of Alfred Alexander Taylor and Robert Love Taylor), a Representative from Tennessee; born in Happy Valley, Carter County, Tenn., December 29, 1819; was educated in private schools and Washington College, near Jonesboro, Tenn.; was graduated from Princeton College in 1840; studied law; was admitted to the bar in 1841 and commenced practice in Elizabethton, Carter County, Tenn.; elected as a Whig to the Thirty-third Congress to fill the vacancy caused by the death of Brookins Campbell, who never qualified, and served from March 30, 1854, to March 3, 1855; unsuccessful candidate for reelection in 1854 to the Thirty-fourth Congress; presidential elector on the Constitutional Union ticket of Bell and Everett in 1860; member of the relief association formed for the aid of war sufferers in east Tennessee and lectured in their behalf throughout the East; upon the readmission of Tennessee to representation was elected as a Unionist to the Thirty-ninth Congress and served from July 24, 1866, to March 3, 1867; was not a candidate for renomination in 1866, Commissioner of Indian Affairs from March 26, 1867, to April

21, 1869, when he retired, and devoted himself to farming and preaching; died in Happy Valley, Carter County, Tenn., April 1, 1887; interment in the old Taylor private cemetery.

**TAYLOR, Nelson,** a Representative from New York; born in South Norwalk, Conn., June 8, 1821; attended the common schools; enlisted for the Mexican War as a captain in the First Regiment, New York Volunteer Infantry, August 1, 1846, and was sent to California in 1846 just before the outbreak of the war; was honorably mustered out September 18, 1848; remained in California and engaged in business at Stockton; member of the State senate 1850-1856; president of the board of trustees of the State insane asylum 1850-1856; elected sheriff of San Joaquin County in 1855; moved to New York City; was graduated from the law department of Harvard University in 1860; was admitted to the bar and practiced; unsuccessful Democratic candidate for election in 1860 to the Thirty-seventh Congress; was commissioned colonel of the Seventy-second Regiment, New York Volunteer Infantry, July 23, 1861; brigadier general of Volunteers September 7, 1862; resigned from the service January 19, 1863; resumed the practice of law in New York City; elected as a Democrat to the Thirty-ninth Congress (March 4, 1865-March 3, 1867); unsuccessful candidate for reelection in 1866 to the Fortieth Congress; moved to South Norwalk, Conn., in 1869 and continued the practice of law; served several times as city attorney; died in South Norwalk, Fairfield County, Conn., January 16, 1894; interment in Riverside Cemetery.

**TAYLOR, Robert,** a Representative from Virginia; born at Orange Court House, Va., April 29, 1763; completed preparatory studies; studied law; admitted to the bar in 1783 and commenced practice at Orange Court House, Va.; held several local offices; member of the Virginia senate 1804-1815, and served as president pro tempore; elected to the Nineteenth Congress (March 4, 1825-March 3, 1827); was not a candidate for renomination in 1826; devoted his attention to the management of his plantation; died on his estate, "Meadow Farm," in Orange County, Va., July 3, 1845; interment in the family burying ground at "Meadow Farm."

**TAYLOR, Robert Love** (son of Nathaniel Green Taylor and brother of Alfred Alexander Taylor), a Representative and a Senator from Tennessee; born in Happy Valley, Carter County, Tenn., July 31, 1850; attended Pennington Seminary in New Jersey, and Buffalo Institute, Milligan, Tenn.; studied law in Jonesboro, Tenn.; was admitted to the bar in 1878 and practiced in Elizabethton and Jonesboro; elected as a Democrat to the Forty-sixth Congress (March 4, 1879-March 3, 1881); unsuccessful candidate for reelection in 1880 to the Forty-seventh Congress, and for election in 1882 to the Forty-eighth Congress; practiced law and also engaged in the newspaper business in Johnson City, Tenn., in 1880; presidential elector on the Democratic ticket in 1884 and 1892; pension agent at Knoxville, Tenn., 1885-1887; elected Governor of Tennessee in 1886, reelected in 1888, and served from January 17, 1887 to January 19, 1891; resumed the practice of law in Chattanooga, Tenn.; lecturer; elected Governor of Tennessee in 1896, and served from January 21, 1897 to January 16, 1899; elected as a Democrat to the United States Senate in 1907, and served from March 4, 1907 until his death in Washington, D.C., March 31, 1912; chairman, Committee on the Geological Survey (Sixty-second Congress); interment in the Old Gray Cemetery, Knoxville, Tenn.; reinterred in Monta Vista Cemetery, Johnson City, Tenn., in 1938.

**Bibliography:** *DAB*; Robinson, Daniel. *Bob Taylor and the Agrarian Revolt in Tennessee.* Chapel Hill: University of North Carolina Press, 1935; Taylor, James. *The Life and Career of Senator Robert Love Taylor (Our Bob).* Nashville: The Bob Taylor Publishing Co., 1913.

**TAYLOR, Roy Arthur,** a Representative from North Carolina; born in Vader, Lewis County, Wash., January 31, 1910; moved to Candler, N.C., in 1910 and attended the public schools of Buncombe County, N.C.; graduated from Asheville-Biltmore College in 1929; A.B., Maryville (Tenn.) College, 1931; graduated from Asheville University Law School in 1936; was admitted to the bar in January 1936 and commenced the practice of law in Asheville, N.C.; during the Second World War served in the United States Navy from 1943 until discharged as a lieutenant in 1946, following service as a commanding officer of a tank landing ship; member, North Carolina State general assembly, 1947-1949, and 1951-1953; Buncombe County attorney, 1949-1960; member of the board of trustees, Asheville-Biltmore College, 1949-1960; elected as a Democrat to the Eighty-sixth Congress, June 25, 1960, by special election to fill the vacancy caused by the death of David M. Hall; reelected to the eight succeeding Congresses, and served from June 25, 1960 to January 3, 1977; was not a candidate for reelection in 1976 to the Ninety-fifth Congress; was a resident of Black Mountain, N.C., until his death on February 28, 1995.

**TAYLOR, Samuel Mitchell** (father of Chester William Taylor), a Representative from Arkansas; born near Fulton, Itawamba County, Miss., May 25, 1852; attended the public schools; studied law; was admitted to the bar in Tupelo, Miss., and commenced practice in 1876; member of the State house of representatives in 1879 and 1880; moved to Pine Bluff, Jefferson County, Ark., in 1887, where he continued the practice of law; prosecuting attorney of the eleventh judicial district of Arkansas 1888-1892; delegate to the Democratic National Convention in 1896; elected as a Democrat to the Sixty-third Congress; subsequently elected to the Sixty-second Congress to fill the vacancy caused by the resignation of Joseph T. Robinson; reelected to the Sixty-fourth and to the three succeeding Congresses and served from January 15, 1913, until his death in Washington, D.C., September 13, 1921; interment in Bellewood Cemetery, Pine Bluff, Ark.

**TAYLOR, Vincent Albert,** a Representative from Ohio; born in Bedford, Cuyahoga County, Ohio, December 6, 1845; attended the common schools; enlisted in Company H, One Hundred and Fiftieth Regiment, Ohio Volunteer Infantry, in May 1864 and in August of the same year in Company H, One Hundred and Seventy-seventh Regiment, Ohio Volunteer Infantry, and served until the close of the Civil War; engaged in manufacturing pursuits; member of the Ohio senate 1888-1890; elected as a Republican to the Fifty-second Congress (March 4, 1891-March 3, 1893); was not a candidate for renomination in 1892; president of the Taylor Chair Co., and a resident of Bedford, Ohio, until his death there December 2, 1922; interment in Bedford Cemetery.

**TAYLOR, Waller,** a Senator from Indiana; born in Lunenburg County, Va., before 1786; attended the common schools; studied law; was admitted to the bar and practiced in Virginia; member, Virginia house of delegates 1800-1802; moved to Vincennes, Ind., in 1804 and continued the practice of law; appointed chancellor of Indiana Territory in 1807; appointed major in the Territorial militia in 1807; served in the Army during the War of 1812 and was promoted to adjutant general in 1814; upon the admission of Indiana as a State into the Union in 1816 was elected as a Republican to the United States Senate; reelected, and served from December 11, 1816, to March 3, 1825; died in Lunenburg County, Va., August 26, 1826; interment in the family burial ground near Lunenburg, Va.

**TAYLOR, William,** a Representative from New York; born in Suffield, Hartford County, Conn., October 12, 1791; moved with his parents to Onondaga County, N.Y.; attended the public schools; studied medicine and was admitted to practice; elected as a Jacksonian to the Twenty-third Congress; reelected to the Twenty-fourth Congress and as a Democrat to the Twenty-fifth Congress (March 4, 1833-March 3, 1839); chairman, Committee on Invalid Pensions (Twenty-fifth Congress); resumed the practice of his chosen profession; member of the State assembly in 1841 and 1842; delegate to the State constitutional convention in 1846; died in

Manlius, N.Y., September 16, 1865; interment in Christ Church Cemetery.

**TAYLOR, William,** a Representative from Virginia; born in Alexandria, Va. (then included in the District of Columbia), April 5, 1788; completed preparatory studies; studied law; admitted to the bar and commenced practice in Staunton, Va.; moved to Lexington, Va., in 1813; became a member of the bar; Commonwealth attorney for the county court of Rockbridge 1817-1843; Commonwealth attorney for the circuit court of Pocahontas County 1817-1843; member of the Virginia house of delegates in 1821; elected as a Democrat to the Twenty-eighth and Twenty-ninth Congresses and served from March 4, 1843, until his death in Washington, D.C., January 17, 1846; chairman, Committee on Accounts (Twenty-eighth and Twenty-ninth Congresses); interment in the Congressional Cemetery.

**TAYLOR, William Penn,** a Representative from Virginia; born in Fredericksburg, Spotsylvania County, Va.; received a limited schooling; held several local offices; elected as an Anti-Jacksonian to the Twenty-third Congress (March 4, 1833-March 3, 1835); was an unsuccessful candidate for reelection in 1834 to the Twenty-fourth Congress; died at "Hayfield," Caroline County, Va., near Fredericksburg, Va.; interment in the family graveyard at "Hayfield."

**TAYLOR, Zachary,** a Representative from Tennessee; born near Brownsville, Haywood County, Tenn., May 9, 1849; attended J.I. Hall's School near Covington, Tenn., and was graduated from the Virginia Military Institute at Lexington as senior captain July 4, 1872, and from the law department of Cumberland University, Lebanon, Tenn., in January 1874; was admitted to the bar and commenced practice in Covington, Tenn., in 1878; served in the State senate, 1881-1883; postmaster of Covington, Tenn., from July 1, 1883, to January 1, 1885, when he resigned; elected as a Republican to the Forty-ninth Congress (March 4, 1885-March 3, 1887); unsuccessful candidate for reelection in 1886 to the Fiftieth Congress; moved to Memphis, Tenn., and engaged in the general life insurance business; delegate to the Republican National Convention in 1896; moved to San Antonio, Tex.; died in Ellendale, Shelby County, Tenn., February 19, 1921; interment in Zachary Taylor National Cemetery, Springfield, Ky.

**TAZEWELL, Henry** (father of Littleton Waller Tazewell), a Senator from Virginia; born in Brunswick County, Va., November 27, 1753; attended the rural schools; graduated from the College of William and Mary at Williamsburg in 1770; studied law; admitted to the bar and commenced practice in 1773; member, provincial house of burgesses 1775; raised and was commissioned captain of a troop of cavalry in the Revolutionary War; delegate to the Virginia constitutional convention of 1775 and 1776; member, General Assembly 1778-1785; judge of the Virginia supreme court 1785-1793, chief justice 1789-1793; judge of the high court of appeals 1793; elected in 1794 to the United States Senate to fill the vacancy caused by the resignation of John Taylor, reelected in 1798, and served from December 29, 1794, until his death; served as President pro tempore of the Senate during the Third and Fourth Congresses; died in Philadelphia, Pa., January 24, 1799; interment in Christ Church Cemetery.

**Bibliography:** *DAB.*

**TAZEWELL, Littleton Waller** (son of Henry Tazewell), a Representative and a Senator from Virginia; born in Williamsburg, Va., December 17, 1774; privately tutored; graduated from the College of William and Mary at Williamsburg in 1791; studied law; was admitted to the bar in 1796 and commenced practice in James City County; member, Virginia house of delegates, 1798-1800; elected to the Sixth Congress to fill the vacancy caused by the resignation of John Marshall, and served from November 26, 1800 to March 3, 1801; moved to Norfolk, Va., in 1802; member, Virginia

general assembly, 1804-1806; member, Virginia house of delegates, 1816-1817; one of the commissioners of claims by United States citizens against Spain, such claims being assumed by the United States under the Adams-Onís Treaty of 1819; elected in 1824 to the United States Senate to fill the vacancy caused by the death of John Taylor; reelected in 1829, and served from December 7, 1824 to July 16, 1832, when he resigned; served as President pro tempore of the Senate during the Twenty-second Congress; chairman, Committee on Foreign Relations (Twentieth through Twenty-second Congresses); delegate to the Virginia convention in 1829; Governor of Virginia from 1834 until his resignation in 1836; retired from public life; died in Norfolk, Va., May 6, 1860; interment on his estate on the Eastern Shore of Virginia; reinterment in 1866 in Elmwood Cemetery, Norfolk, Va.

**Bibliography:** *DAB*; Grigsby, Hugh. *Discourse on the Life and Character of Honorable Littleton Waller Tazewell.* Norfolk: J.D. Ghiselin, Jr., 1860; Peterson, Norma L. *Littleton Waller Tazewell.* Charlottesville: University of Virginia Press, 1983.

**TEAGUE, Charles McKevett,** a Representative from California; born in Santa Paula, Ventura County, Calif., September 18, 1909; attended the public schools; was graduated from Stanford University in 1931 and from Stanford Law School in 1934; was admitted to the bar in 1934 and commenced the practice of law in Los Angeles and Ventura, Calif.; served in the United States Air Force 1942-1946; awarded Air Force commendation ribbon; director of McKevett Corp. and Teague-McKevett Co.; elected as a Republican to the Eighty-fourth and to the nine succeeding Congresses, and served from January 3, 1955, until his death January 1, 1974, in Santa Paula, Calif.; cremated; ashes interred in family plot in Santa Paula Cemetery.

**TEAGUE, Olin Earl,** a Representative from Texas; born in Woodward, Woodward County, Okla., April 6, 1910; attended elementary and high school in Mena, Ark.; B.A., Texas Agricultural and Mechanical College at College Station, 1932; employed in the post office at College Station, Tex., 1932-1940; enlisted, on October 5, 1940, in the United States Army, being commissioned a first lieutenant; commanded the First Battalion, Three Hundred and Fourteenth Infantry, Seventy-ninth Division; awarded the Silver Star with two clusters, Bronze Star, and the Purple Heart with two clusters; was discharged as a colonel at Walter Reed General Hospital September 6, 1946; elected as a Democrat to the Seventy-ninth Congress, by special election, August 24, 1946, to fill the vacancy caused by the resignation of Luther A. Johnson; reelected to the sixteen succeeding Congresses and served from August 24, 1946, until his resignation December 31, 1978; chairman, Select Committee on Education, Training, and Loan Programs of World War II Veterans (Eighty-first and Eighty-second Congresses), Committee on Veterans' Affairs (Eighty-fourth through Ninety-second Congresses), Committee on Science and Astronautics (Ninety-third Congress), Committee on Science and Technology (Ninety-fourth and Ninety-fifth Congresses); was not a candidate for reelection in 1978 to the Ninety-sixth Congress; resided in Washington, D.C., until his death in Bethesda, Md., January 23, 1981; interment in Arlington National Cemetery, Va.

**TEESE, Frederick Halstead,** a Representative from New Jersey; born in Newark, N.J., October 21, 1823; was graduated from Princeton College in 1843; studied law; was admitted to the bar in 1846 and commenced practice in Newark, N.J.; member of the State house of assembly in 1860 and 1861, serving as speaker in 1861; presiding judge of the court of common pleas of Essex County from 1864 until his resignation in 1872; elected as a Democrat to the Forty-fourth Congress (March 4, 1875-March 3, 1877); declined the nomination for reelection in 1876 to the Forty-fifth Congress; resumed the practice of law; died in New York City January 7, 1894; interment in Mount Pleasant Cemetery, Newark, N.J.

**TEIGAN, Henry George,** a Representative from Minnesota; born in Forest City, Winnebago County, Iowa, August 7, 1881; attended the public schools, Luther Academy, Albert Lea, Minn., and Central College, Pella, Iowa; was graduated from Valparaiso (Ind.) University in 1908; taught in the Iowa rural schools 1900-1904, at Des Lacs, N.Dak., in 1909 and 1910, and at Logan, N.Dak., 1912-1913; secretary of North Dakota State Socialist Party 1913-1916; moved to Minneapolis, Minn., in 1917; secretary of National Nonpartisan League 1916-1923; secretary to Senator Magnus Johnson 1923-1925; editor and newspaper writer 1923-1933; served in the State senate 1933-1935; elected as a Farmer-Laborite to the Seventy-fifth Congress (January 3, 1937-January 3, 1939); unsuccessful candidate for reelection in 1938 to the Seventy-sixth Congress and in 1940 for election to the Seventy-seventh Congress; resumed newspaper and editorial work in Minneapolis, Minn., until his death on March 12, 1941; interment in Hillside Cemetery.

**TEJEDA, Frank Mariano,** a Representative from Texas; born in San Antonio, Tex., October 2, 1945; attended Harlandale High School; B.A., St. Mary's University, 1970; J.D., University of California at Berkeley, 1974; M.P.A., Harvard University, 1980; LL.D., Yale University, 1989; United States Marine Corps service, 1963-1967, during Vietnam conflict as sergeant; United States Marine Corps Reserve service as major; member, Texas State house of representatives, 1976-1986; member, Texas State senate, 1986-1993; elected as a Democrat to the One Hundred Third and One Hundred Fourth Congresses (January 3, 1993-January 3, 1997); is a resident of San Antonio, Tex.

**TELFAIR, Edward** (father of Thomas Telfair), a Delegate from Georgia; born in "Town Head," Scotland, in 1735; was graduated from the Kirkcudbright Grammar School and subsequently acquired a thorough commercial training; immigrated to the United States in 1758 as agent of a commercial house and settled in Virginia; moved to Halifax, N.C.; established a commission house in Savannah, Ga., in 1766; member of the council of safety in 1775 and 1776; delegate to the Provincial Congress at Savannah in 1776; member of the committee of intelligence and other important committees in 1776; Member of the Continental Congress, 1778, 1780, 1781, and 1782; one of the signers of the Articles of Confederation and a delegate to the State ratification convention; commissioner to treat with the Cherokee Indians in 1783; designated agent on the part of Georgia to settle the northern boundary of the Commonwealth in February 1783; Governor of Georgia in 1786; elected Governor of Georgia by the Legislature, and served from November 9, 1789 to November 7, 1793; died in Savannah, Ga., September 17, 1807; interment in Bonaventure Cemetery.

**Bibliography:** *DAB*; Coulter, E. Merton. "Edward Telfair." *Georgia Historical Quarterly* 20 (June 1936): 99-124.

**TELFAIR, Thomas** (son of Edward Telfair), a Representative from Georgia; born in Savannah, Ga., March 2, 1780; was graduated from Princeton College in 1805; studied law; was admitted to the bar and commenced practice in Savannah, Ga.; elected as a Republican to the Thirteenth and Fourteenth Congresses (March 4, 1813-March 3, 1817); died in Savannah, Ga., February 18, 1818; interment in Bonaventure Cemetery.

**TELLER, Henry Moore,** a Senator from Colorado; born in Granger, Allegany County, N.Y., May 23, 1830; attended Rushford and Alfred Academies in New York; taught school; studied law and was admitted to the bar in Binghamton, N.Y., in 1858; moved to Illinois in 1858 and to Colorado in 1861; major general of Colorado militia, 1862-1864; involved in railroad and real estate development; upon the admission of Colorado as a State into the Union in 1876 was elected as a Republican to the United States Senate; reelected, and served from November 15, 1876, until his resignation on April 17, 1882, to accept a Cabinet position; chairman, Committee on Civil Service and Retrenchment (Forty-fifth Congress), Committee on Pensions (Forty-seventh Congress); appointed Secretary of the Interior in the Cabinet of President Chester A. Arthur, and served from April 17, 1882 until March 4, 1885; elected as a Republican to the United States Senate in 1885 and 1891, as a Silver Republican in 1897, and as a Democrat in 1903, and served from March 4, 1885 to March 3, 1909; declined to be a candidate for renomination; chairman, Committee on Mines and Mining (Forty-ninth Congress), Committee on Patents (Fiftieth through Fifty-second Congresses), Committee on Privileges and Elections (Fifty-second Congress), Committee on Claims (Fifty-fourth and Fifty-fifth Congresses), Committee on Private Land Claims (Fifty-sixth through Sixtieth Congresses); member of the United States Monetary Commission, 1908-1912; engaged in the practice of law until his death in Denver, Colo., February 23, 1914; interment in Fairmount Cemetery.

**Bibliography:** *DAB*; Ellis, Elmer. *Henry Moore Teller: Defender of the West.* Caldwell, Idaho: Caxton Printers, 1941; Holsinger, M. Paul. "Henry M. Teller and the Edmunds-Tucker Act." *Colorado Magazine* 48 (Winter 1971): 1-14.

**TELLER, Isaac** (nephew of Abraham Henry Schenck), a Representative from New York; born in Matteawan, Dutchess County, N.Y., February 7, 1799; completed preparatory studies; held several local offices; elected as a Whig to the Thirty-third Congress to fill the vacancy caused by the resignation of Gilbert Dean and served from November 7, 1854, to March 3, 1855; engaged in agricultural pursuits; died in Matteawan (now Beacon), N.Y., April 30, 1868; interment in the Rural Cemetery, Fishkill, Dutchess County, N.Y.

**TELLER, Ludwig,** a Representative from New York; born in New York City (Borough of Manhattan), N.Y., June 22, 1911; educated in the public schools; graduated from New York University in 1936 and from the law school of the same university in 1935; was admitted to the bar in 1936 and commenced the practice of law in New York City; expert consultant to Labor Relations Board, War Department, in 1942; trial examiner, New York State Labor Relations Board, 1942-1946; served as a senior lieutenant in the United States Navy as communications officer in Atlantic convoy, and as labor relations officer, Ninth Naval District, Chicago, Ill., 1943-1945; lieutenant commander, United States Naval Reserve; served on the faculty of New York University Law School 1947-1950 and professor of law at New York Law School in 1950; member of the State assembly 1950-1956; elected as a Democrat to the Eighty-fifth and Eighty-sixth Congresses (January 3, 1957-January 3, 1961); was unsuccessful for the Democratic nomination in 1960 and also for election as a Liberal candidate to the Eighty-seventh Congress; resumed the practice of law in New York City until his death October 4, 1965; interment in Union Fields Cemetery, Jamaica, Queens County, N.Y.

**TEMPLE, Henry Wilson,** a Representative from Pennsylvania; born in Belle Center, Logan County, Ohio, March 31, 1864; attended the common schools; was graduated from Geneva College, Beaver Falls, Pa., in 1883, and from the Covenanter Theological Seminary, Allegheny, Pa., in 1887; pastor of churches at Baxter, Leechburg, and Washington, Pa.; professor of political science at Washington and Jefferson College, Washington, Pa., 1898-1913; elected as a Progressive to the Sixty-third Congress (March 4, 1913-March 3, 1915); unsuccessful candidate for reelection in 1914 to the Sixty-fourth Congress; elected as a Republican to the Sixty-fourth Congress to fill the vacancy caused by the death of William M. Brown; reelected to the Sixty-fifth and to the seven succeeding Congresses, and served from November 2, 1915 to March 3, 1933; unsuccessful candidate for reelection in 1932 to the Seventy-third Congress; professor of international relations in Washington and Jefferson College from 1933 until his retirement in 1947; died in

Washington, Pa., January 11, 1955; interment in Washington Cemetery.

**TEMPLE, William,** a Representative from Delaware; born in Queen Anne County, Md., February 28, 1814; completed preparatory studies; moved to Smyrna, Del., and engaged in mercantile pursuits; member of the Delaware State house of representatives in 1844, and served as speaker; served in the State senate, 1845-1854; became Acting Governor of Delaware following the death of Governor Joseph Maull, and served from May 1, 1846 to January 1847; elected as a Democrat to the Thirty-eighth Congress, and served from March 4, 1863 until his death in Smyrna, Del., May 28, 1863, before Congress had convened; interment in the Episcopal Cemetery.

**TEMPLETON, Thomas Weir,** a Representative from Pennsylvania; born in Plymouth, Luzerne County, Pa., November 8, 1867; attended the public schools and was graduated from Wyoming Seminary, Kingston, Pa.; studied law; was admitted to the bar in 1899 but did not practice; prothonotary of Luzerne County 1904-1907; engaged in business as a florist at Kingston; elected as a Republican to the Sixty-fifth Congress (March 4, 1917-March 3, 1919); was not a candidate for renomination in 1918; superintendent of grounds and buildings at the Pennsylvania capitol in 1920-1923; resumed the florist business in Kingston, Pa.; died in Plymouth, Pa., September 5, 1935; interment in Edgehill Cemetery, West Nanticoke, Pa.

**TENER, John Kinley,** a Representative from Pennsylvania; born in County Tyrone, Ireland, July 25, 1863; immigrated to the United States with his parents, who settled in Pittsburgh, Pa., in 1872; attended the public and high schools; was employed by manufacturing firms and corporations in and about Pittsburgh; engaged as a professional baseball player from 1885 until 1890; entered the banking business in Charleroi, Pa., in 1901, serving as cashier and later as president of the First National Bank; elected as a Republican to the Sixty-first Congress and served from March 4, 1909, to January 16, 1911, when he resigned, having been elected Governor; elected Governor of Pennsylvania in 1910 and served from January 17, 1911 to January 19, 1915; president of the National League of Professional Baseball Clubs, 1914-1918; elected as director of the Philadelphia National League Baseball Club in 1931; engaged in the insurance business until his death; died in Pittsburgh Pa., May 19, 1946; interment in Howewood Cemetery.

**TENEROWICZ, Rudolph Gabriel,** a Representative from Michigan; born in Budapest, June 14, 1890; immigrated to the United States in 1892 with his parents, who settled in Adrian, Pa.; attended the parochial schools in that city, St. Cyril and Methodius Seminary, Orchard Lake, Mich., St. Bonaventure's College, Allegany, N.Y., and St. Ignatius College, Chicago, Ill.; was graduated in medicine from Loyola University, Chicago, Ill., in 1912; practiced medicine in Chicago, Ill., 1912-1923; during the First World War served from September 10, 1917; as a first lieutenant in the Medical Corps of the United States Army until his discharge on December 26, 1918; captain in the Medical Reserve Corps 1919-1934; postgraduate course in surgery at Illinois Post Graduate School at Chicago, Ill., moved to Hamtramck, Wayne County, Mich., in 1923 and continued the practice of medicine; mayor of Hamtramck 1928-1932 and 1936-1938; member of the Wayne County Board of Supervisors for seven years; elected as a Democrat to the Seventy-sixth and Seventy-seventh Congresses (January 3, 1939-January 3, 1943); unsuccessful candidate for renomination in 1942 and for election as a Republican in 1948, 1950, 1952, and 1954; resumed practice in Hamtramck, Mich.; died in Hamtramck, Mich., August 31, 1963; interment in Arlington National Cemetery, Va.

**TEN EYCK, Egbert,** a Representative from New York; born in Schodack, Rensselaer County, N.Y., April 18, 1779; was graduated from Williams College, Williamstown, Mass., in 1799; studied law; was admitted to the bar in 1807 and commenced practice in Watertown, N.Y.; member of the State assembly in 1812 and 1813 and served as speaker; supervisor of Jefferson County in 1816; trustee of the village of Watertown in 1816; one of the incorporators of the Jefferson County National Bank; first secretary of the Jefferson County Agricultural Society in 1817; president of the village of Watertown in 1820; delegate to the State constitutional convention in 1822; elected to the Eighteenth Congress (March 4, 1823-March 3, 1825); presented credentials as a Member-elect to the Nineteenth Congress and served from March 4 to December 15, 1825, when he was succeeded by Daniel Hugunin, Jr., who contested his election; was judge of the Jefferson County courts for nine years; died in Watertown, Jefferson County, N.Y., April 11, 1844; interment in Brookside Cemetery.

**TEN EYCK, John Conover,** a Senator from New Jersey; born in Freehold, Monmouth County, N.J., March 12, 1814; completed preparatory studies under private tutors; studied law; was admitted to the bar in 1835 and commenced practice in Burlington, N.J.; prosecuting attorney for Burlington County 1839-1849; delegate to the State constitutional convention in 1844; elected as a Republican to the United States Senate and served from March 4, 1859, to March 3, 1865; unsuccessful candidate for reelection; appointed a member of a commission to revise the New Jersey constitution in 1875, and for a time was president of the commission; died in Mount Holly, N.J., August 24, 1879; interment in St. Andrew's Cemetery.

**TEN EYCK, Peter Gansevoort,** a Representative from New York; born in Bethlehem, Albany County, N.Y., November 7, 1873; was educated in the common schools in Normansville, the Albany Academy, and the Rensselaer Polytechnic Institute, Troy, N.Y.; engaged in civil and signal engineering for fifteen years; signal engineer of the New York Central Lines; chief engineer of the Federal Railway Signal Co. in 1903 and later its vice president and general manager; served seven years in the Third Signal Corps, Third Brigade, National Guard of New York; elected as a Democrat to the Sixty-third Congress (March 4, 1913-March 3, 1915); unsuccessful candidate for reelection in 1914 to the Sixty-fourth Congress; delegate to the Democratic National Convention in 1920; elected to the Sixty-seventh Congress (March 4, 1921-March 3, 1923); declined to be a candidate for renomination in 1922; engaged in agricultural pursuits near Albany, N.Y.; died at his summer residence at Altamont, N.Y., September 2, 1944; interment in the Rural Cemetery, Albany, N.Y.

**TENNEY, Samuel,** a Representative from New Hampshire; born in Byfield, Mass., November 27, 1748; attended Dummer Academy, Byfield, Mass.; was graduated from Harvard College in 1772; taught school in Andover, Mass.; studied medicine and began practice in Exeter, N.H.; surgeon in the Revolutionary War; returned to Exeter at the close of the war and continued the practice of his profession; delegate to the State constitutional convention in 1788; judge of probate for Rockingham County 1793-1800; elected as a Federalist to the Sixth Congress to fill the vacancy caused by the resignation of William Gordon; reelected to the Seventh, Eighth, and Ninth Congresses and served from December 8, 1800, to March 3, 1807; chairman, Committee on Revisal and Unfinished Business (Eighth and Ninth Congresses); pursued literary, historical, and scientific studies; died in Exeter, N.H., February 6, 1816; interment in the Old Cemetery.

**TENZER, Herbert,** a Representative from New York; born in New York City, November 1, 1905; attended public schools; graduated from New York University Law School in 1927; was admitted to the bar in 1929 and commenced the practice of law in the same year; January 1, 1937, organized and became senior partner in a law firm in New York City; elected as a Democrat to the Eighty-ninth and Ninetieth Congresses (January 3, 1965-January 3, 1969); was not a candidate for reelection in 1968 to the Ninety-first Congress; trustee of Yeshiva University; chairman, Nassau County board of ethics, 1969-1983; vice chairman, New York State special advisory committee on medical malpractice, 1975; chairman, New York State board of social welfare, 1977-1983; was a resident of Lawrence, Long Island, N.Y.; died March 24, 1993.

**TERRELL, George Butler,** a Representative from Texas; born in Alto, Cherokee County, Tex., December 5, 1862; attended the public schools, Sam Houston Teachers' College, Huntsville, Tex., and Baylor University, Waco, Tex.; taught school in Cherokee County, Tex., 1886-1903; member of the State teachers' examining board in 1897 and 1902, and of the State textbook commission in 1903; engaged in agricultural pursuits and in stock raising near Alto, Tex., in 1903; member of the State house of representatives 1898-1902, 1906-1912, 1916-1920, 1930-1932; elected commissioner of agriculture of Texas in 1920, serving by reelection until 1931; elected as a Democrat to the Seventy-third Congress (March 4, 1933-January 3, 1935); was not a candidate for renomination in 1934; resumed agricultural pursuits and resided at Alto, Tex., until his death there on April 18, 1947; interment in the Old Palestine Cemetery, near Alto, Tex.

**TERRELL, James C.,** a Representative from Georgia; born in Franklin County, Ga., November 7, 1806; studied law; was admitted to the bar by an act of the legislature and practiced in Carnesville, Ga.; member of the State house of representatives 1830-1834; elected on a Union ticket to the Twenty-fourth Congress and served from March 4 to July 8, 1835, when he resigned, before Congress convened, on account of ill health; died at Carnesville, Franklin County, Ga., December 1, 1835.

**TERRELL, Joseph Meriwether,** a Senator from Georgia; born in Greenville, Meriwether County, Ga., June 6, 1861; attended the common schools; studied law; was admitted to the bar in 1882 and commenced practice in Greenville, Ga.; member, Georgia State house of representatives, 1884-1887; member of the State senate in 1890; attorney general of Georgia from 1892 until 1902; elected Governor of Georgia in 1902, reelected in 1904, and served from October 25, 1902 to June 29, 1907; resumed the practice of law in Atlanta, Ga.; appointed as a Democrat to the United States Senate to fill the vacancy caused by the death of Alexander S. Clay, and served from November 17, 1910 to July 14, 1911, when he resigned; again resumed the practice of his profession in Atlanta, Ga., and died there on November 17, 1912; interment in the City Cemetery, Greenville, Ga.

**TERRELL, William,** a Representative from Georgia; born in Fairfax County, Va., in 1778; moved with his parents to Georgia; pursued classical studies; was graduated from the medical department of the University of Pennsylvania at Philadelphia and commenced practice in Sparta, Hancock County, Ga.; member of the State house of representatives 1810-1813; held various local offices; elected as a Republican to the Fifteenth and Sixteenth Congresses (March 4, 1817-March 3, 1821); declined to be a candidate for renomination in 1820; resumed the practice of medicine; died in Sparta, Ga., July 4, 1855; interment in Sparta Cemetery.

**TERRY, David Dickson** (son of William Leake Terry), a Representative from Arkansas; born in Little Rock, Pulaski County, Ark., January 31, 1881; attended the public schools, the Bethel Military Academy in Fauquier County, Va., and the University of Virginia at Charlottesville; was graduated from the law department of the University of Arkansas at Fayetteville in 1903; later attended the University of Chicago, Chicago, Ill.; was admitted to the bar in 1903 and commenced practice in Little Rock, Ark.; during the First World War enlisted on June 5, 1918, later commissioned a second

lieutenant of Infantry, and was discharged on December 20, 1918; member of the Little Rock School Board from 1929 to 1933; member of the Arkansas State house of representatives in 1933; elected as a Democrat to the Seventy-third Congress to fill the vacancy caused by the resignation of Heartsill Ragon; reelected to the Seventy-fourth and to the three succeeding Congresses, and served from December 19, 1933 to January 3, 1943; was not a candidate in 1942 for renomination to the House of Representatives, but was an unsuccessful candidate for nomination for United States Senator; engaged in the practice of law; director of the Division of Flood Control Water and Soil Conservation of the Arkansas Resources and Development Commission from 1945 until 1953; died in Little Rock, Ark., October 6, 1963; interment in Mount Holly Cemetery.

**TERRY, John Hart,** a Representative from New York; born in Syracuse, Onondaga County, N.Y., November 14, 1924; attended public and private schools in Syracuse; B.A., University of Notre Dame, 1945; LL.B. (J.D.), Syracuse University, 1948; entered the United States Army in September 1943 as a private and served in European Theater of Operations with rank of regimental sergeant major; received Bronze Star with clusters, and Purple Heart; discharged with rank of first lieutenant, 1946; admitted to the New York bar in 1950 and commenced practice in Syracuse; admitted to the bar of the United States Supreme Court and the District of Columbia; member, Onondaga County Board of Supervisors, 1948-1958; appointed assistant secretary to Governor Nelson A. Rockefeller of New York, 1959-1961; member, Inter-Group Relations Advisory Council of New York State Division of Housing and Community Renewal, 1961-1962; member, New York State assembly, 1963-1970; chairman, New York State United Services Organization, 1970; assistant secretary, New York State Republican convention, 1958, and delegate in 1962; elected as a Republican to the Ninety-second Congress (January 3, 1971-January 3, 1973); was not a candidate for reelection in 1972 to the Ninety-third Congress; senior vice president, general counsel and secretary, Niagara Mohawk Power Corp., 1973-1987; resumed the practice of law in Syracuse; is a resident of Syracuse and Vero Beach, Fla.

**TERRY, Nathaniel,** a Representative from Connecticut; born in Enfield, Conn., January 30, 1768; attended the common schools, Dartmouth College, and was graduated from Yale College in 1786; studied law; was admitted to the bar in 1790 and commenced practice in Enfield; moved to Hartford in 1796; commander of the Governor's Foot Guard of Hartford from 1802 until 1813; judge of the Hartford County Court from 1807 to 1809, when he resigned; member of the Connecticut State house of representatives, 1804-1815; elected as a Federalist to the Fifteenth Congress (March 4, 1817-March 3, 1819); member of the State constitutional convention in 1818; president of the Hartford Fire Insurance Co., 1810-1835; president of the Hartford Bank, 1819-1828; mayor of Hartford from 1824 until 1831; served as a general in the State militia; died in New Haven, Conn., June 14, 1844; interment in Old North (Spring Grove) Cemetery, Hartford, Conn.

**TERRY, William,** a Representative from Virginia; born in Amherst County, Va., August 14, 1824; attended an "old field school" in Amherst County; was graduated from the University of Virginia at Charlottesville in 1848; taught school; studied law; was admitted to the bar in 1851 and commenced practice in Wytheville, Va.; engaged in newspaper work; served in the Confederate Army as a lieutenant in the Fourth Regiment, Virginia Infantry; promoted to major in 1862, colonel in February 1864, and commissioned brigadier general on May 20, 1864; resumed the practice of law in Wytheville; elected as a Democrat to the Forty-second Congress (March 4, 1871-March 3, 1873); unsuccessful candidate for renomination in 1872 to the Forty-third Congress; elected to the Forty-fourth Congress (March 4, 1875-March 3, 1877); unsuccessful candidate for renomination in 1876 to the Forty-fifth Congress;

delegate to the Democratic National Convention of 1880; resumed the practice of law; drowned while trying to ford Reed Creek, near Wytheville, Va., September 5, 1888; interment in East End Cemetery, Wytheville, Va.

**TERRY, William Leake** (father of David Dickson Terry), a Representative from Arkansas; born near Wadesboro, Anson County, N.C., September 27, 1850; moved with his parents to Tippah County, Miss., in 1857 and to Pulaski County, Ark., in 1861; attended Bingham's Military Academy, North Carolina, and was graduated from Trinity College, North Carolina, in June 1872; studied law; was admitted to the bar in Novmeber 1873 and practiced; member of the city council, 1877-1879; member of the Arkansas State senate in 1878 and 1879, serving as president of the senate in the session of 1879; city attorney of Little Rock, Ark., 1879-1885; unsuccessful candidate for election in 1886 to the Fiftieth Congress; elected as a Democrat to the Fifty-second and to the four succeeding Congresses (March 4, 1891-March 3, 1901); unsuccessful candidate for renomination in 1900 to the Fifty-seventh Congress; resumed the practice of law in Little Rock, Ark., where he died on November 4, 1917; interment in Calvary Cemetery.

**TEST, John,** a Representative from Indiana; born in Salem, N.J., November 12, 1771; moved with his parents to Philadelphia, Pa., and attended the common schools; moved to Fayette County, Pa., and operated Fayette Chance Furnace for several years; moved to Cincinnati, Ohio, and then to Brookville, Franklin County, Ind., and operated a grist mill; studied law; was admitted to the bar and began practice in Brookville, Ind.; held several local offices; judge of the third district circuit 1816-1819; elected to the Eighteenth and Nineteenth Congresses (March 4, 1823-March 3, 1827); unsuccessful candidate for reelection in 1826 to the Twentieth Congress; elected to the Twenty-first Congress (March 4, 1829-March 3, 1831); presiding judge of the Indiana circuit court; moved to Mobile, Ala., and resumed the practice of law; died near Cambridge City, Wayne County, Ind., October 9, 1849; interment in Cambridge City, Ind.

**TEWES, Donald Edgar,** a Representative from Wisconsin; born in Merrill, Lincoln County, Wis., August 4, 1916; was graduated from Trinity Lutheran School, Merrill High School, Valparaiso (Ind.) University in 1938, and from University of Wisconsin Law School in 1940; was admitted to the bar and commenced the practice of law in Merrill, Wis.; entered the service as a private in 1942; became combat intelligence officer with the Fourteenth United States Air Force's Flying Tigers with twenty-five combat missions in the China-Burma-India Theater, and was discharged as a major in 1946; president of Tewes Plastics Corp., Waukesha, Wis., since 1947; elected as a Republican to the Eighty-fifth Congress (January 3, 1957-January 3, 1959); unsuccessful candidate for reelection in 1958 to the Eighty-sixth Congress; is a resident of Waukesha, Wis.

**THACHER, Thomas Chandler,** a Representative from Massachusetts; born in Yarmouth Port, Mass., July 20, 1858; attended the public schools; was graduated from Adams Academy, Quincy, Mass., in 1878 and from Harvard University in 1882; became engaged in the wool business at Boston in 1882; president of the Barnstable County Agricultural Society; president of the Cape Cod Pilgrim Memorial Association; chairman of the Yarmouth Port Planning Board; served as chairman of the Provincetown Tercentenary Commission in 1920; elected as a Democrat to the Sixty-third Congress (March 4, 1913-March 3, 1915); unsuccessful candidate for reelection in 1914; writer on business topics and also engaged in his former business pursuits; died in Boston, Mass., April 11, 1945; interment in Woodside Cemetery, Yarmouth Port, Mass.

**THATCHER, George,** a Delegate and a Representative from Massachusetts; born in Yarmouth, in the county of Barnstable, Mass., April 12, 1754; prepared for college by a private instructor; was graduated from Harvard College in 1776; studied law; was admitted to the bar in 1778 and commenced practice in York, Maine; moved to Biddeford, Maine, in 1782; Member of the Continental Congress 1787-1789; elected to the First Congress; reelected to the Second and Third Congresses and reelected as a Federalist to the Fourth through Sixth Congresses (March 4, 1789-March 3, 1801); chairman, Committee on Revisal and Unfinished Business (Fifth Congress); did not seek renomination in 1800, having accepted a judicial appointment; district judge in Maine 1792-1800; associate judge of the supreme court of Massachusetts 1800-1820; delegate in 1819 to the constitutional convention of Maine, which until 1820 was a district of Massachusetts; again a judge of the supreme court of Maine 1820-1824; died in Biddeford, Maine, April 6, 1824; interment in Woodlawn Cemetery.

**Bibliography:** *DAB.*

**THATCHER, Maurice Hudson,** a Representative from Kentucky; born in Chicago, Cook County, Ill., August 15, 1870; moved to Butler County, Ky., and settled near Morgantown in 1874; attended public and private schools; engaged in agricultural pursuits; was employed in a newspaper office and in various county offices; elected clerk of the circuit court of Butler County in 1892, and served from January 1, 1893 until his resignation in 1896; studied law in Frankfort, Ky.; was admitted to the bar in 1898 and commenced practice in Frankfort; assistant attorney general of Kentucky, 1898-1900; moved to Louisville, Ky., in 1900; assistant United States attorney for the western district of Kentucky, 1901-1906; inspector and examiner for Kentucky, 1908-1910; member of the Isthmian Canal Commission and civil governor of the Canal Zone, 1910-1913; resumed the practice of law in Louisville, Ky.; member of the board of public safety, 1917-1919, and department counsel, 1919-1923 for the city of Louisville; elected as a Republican to the Sixty-eighth and to the four succeeding Congresses (March 4, 1923-March 3, 1933); in 1932 was nominated for the House of Representatives, but subsequently relinquished that nomination to become his party's candidate for the United States Senate but was unsuccessful; resumed the practice of law in Washington, D.C.; vice president and general counsel of the Gorgas Memorial Institute of Tropical and Preventative Medicine, Inc., Washington, D.C., 1939-1969, honorary president and general counsel, 1969-1972; died in Washington, D.C., January 6, 1973; interment in Frankfort Cemetery, Frankfort, Ky.

**Bibliography:** DuVal, Miles P. "Maurice H. Thatcher: Benefactor of Kentucky and the Isthmus of Panama." *Filson Club History Quarterly* 30 (January 1956): 19-22; Thatcher, Maurice Hudson. *Autobiography in Poetry.* New York: R. Speller, 1974.

**THATCHER, Samuel,** a Representative from Massachusetts; born in Cambridge, Mass., July 1, 1776; was graduated from Harvard University in 1793; studied law; was admitted to the bar in 1797 and commenced practice in New Gloucester, Maine (then a district of Massachusetts); moved to Warren in 1800; member of the Massachusetts house of representatives 1801-1811; was elected as a Federalist to the Seventh Congress to fill the vacancy caused by the resignation of Silas Lee; reelected to the Eighth Congress and served from December 6, 1802, to March 3, 1805; was an unsuccessful candidate for reelection in 1804 to the Ninth Congress; sheriff of Lincoln County, Maine, 1814-1821; member of the Maine house of representatives in 1824; moved to Bangor, Maine, in 1860, and died there July 18, 1872; interment in Mount Hope Cemetery.

**THAYER, Andrew Jackson,** a Representative from Oregon; born in Lima, Livingston County, N.Y., November 27, 1818; attended the common schools; studied law; admitted to the bar in 1849 and commenced practice in Lima; crossed the continent in 1853 and settled on a farm near Corvallis, Benton County, Oreg.; resumed the practice of law and also engaged in agricultural pursuits; appointed by President James Buchanan United States attorney for the district of Oregon on March 2, 1859, and resigned after six months' service, having become a candidate for Congress; presented credentials as a Democratic Member-elect to the Thirty-seventh Congress and served from March 4 to July 30, 1861, when he was succeeded by George K. Shiel, who contested his election; district attorney for the second district of Oregon 1862-1864; served as circuit judge of the second judicial district of Oregon from 1870 until his death in Corvallis, Oreg., April 28, 1873; interment in Crystal Lake Cemetery.

**THAYER, Eli** (father of John Alden Thayer), a Representative from Massachusetts; born in Mendon, Worcester County, Mass., June 11, 1819; attended the common schools, the academies in Bellingham and Amherst, Mass., and the Worcester Manual Labor School; taught school in Douglas, Mass., in 1835 and 1836 and in Hopkington, R.I., in 1842; had charge of the boys' high school in Providence, R.I., in 1844; graduated from Brown University at Providence in 1845 and was an instructor in Worcester Academy 1845-1848; studied law and was admitted to the bar, but did not practice; founded the Oread Collegiate Institute, a school for young women, in 1848; member of the Worcester School Board in 1852; alderman of Worcester in 1852 and 1853; member of the Massachusetts house of representatives in 1853 and 1854; while in the legislature secured a charter, and originated and organized the New England Emigrant Aid Co., which had for its purpose the sending out of an advance colony of antislavery settlers to Kansas; elected as a Republican to the Thirty-fifth and Thirty-sixth Congresses (March 4, 1857-March 3, 1861); chairman, Committee on Public Lands (Thirty-sixth Congress); unsuccessful candidate for reelection in 1860 to the Thirty-seventh Congress; delegate accredited from Oregon to the Republican National Convention in 1860; engaged in railroad and other business pursuits; unsuccessful candidate for election in 1872 to the Forty-third Congress; died in Worcester, Mass., April 15, 1899; interment in Hope Cemetery.

**Bibliography:** *DAB*; Andrews, Horace. "Kansas Crusade: Eli Thayer and the New England Emigrant Aid Company." *New England Quarterly* 35 (December 1962): 497-514.

**THAYER, Harry Irving,** a Representative from Massachusetts; born in Pembroke, Plymouth County, Mass., September 10, 1869; attended the public schools of Hanover, Mass.; engaged in the leather business; organizer and president of the Thayer-Ross Co.; president of the New England Shoe and Leather Association 1916-1921; was president of the Tanners' Council of the United States in 1920 and 1921; was a delegate to the Republican National Convention in 1924; elected as a Republican to the Sixty-ninth Congress and served from March 4, 1925, until his death in Wakefield, Middlesex County, Mass., March 10, 1926; interment in Lakeside Cemetery.

**THAYER, John Alden** (son of Eli Thayer), a Representative from Massachusetts; born in Worcester, Mass., December 22, 1857; attended the grade and high schools of Worcester; was graduated from Harvard University in 1879; taught school; studied law at Columbia College of Law at New York City; was admitted to the bar in 1889 and commenced practice in Worcester; clerk of the central district court of Worcester 1892-1897; elected as a Democrat to the Sixty-second Congress (March 4, 1911-March 3, 1913); unsuccessful candidate for reelection in 1912 to the Sixty-third Congress; delegate to the Democratic National Convention in 1912; appointed postmaster of Worcester, Mass., in February 1915, and served until his death in Worcester, Mass., July 31, 1917; interment in Hope Cemetery.

**THAYER, John Milton** (uncle of Arthur Laban Bates), a Senator from Nebraska; born in Bellingham, Mass., January 24, 1820; graduated from Brown University, Providence, R.I., in 1841; studied law; was admitted to the bar and practiced; editor of a journal; moved to Nebraska in 1854, engaged in agricultural pursuits, and practiced law in Omaha; brigadier general and major

general of the Territorial forces operating against the Pawnee Indians, 1855-1861; member, Nebraska Territorial senate, 1860; delegate to the Nebraska constitutional convention in 1860; during the Civil War served in the Union Army as colonel and then brigadier general of the First Regiment, Nebraska Volunteer Infantry; brevetted major general of Volunteers in 1865; member of the Nebraska constitutional convention in 1866; upon the admission of Nebraska as a State into the Union was elected as a Republican to the United States Senate and served from March 1, 1867, to March 3, 1871; unsuccessful candidate for reelection in 1871; chairman, Committee on Enrolled Bills (Forty-first Congress); appointed by President Ulysses S. Grant as Governor of the Territory of Wyoming on February 10, 1875, and served until May 29, 1878; elected Governor of Nebraska in 1886, reelected in 1888 and served from January 15, 1887 to January 15, 1891; challenged the election of James E. Boyd as Governor on the grounds that Boyd had been born in Ireland and was not a citizen of the United States; following Boyd's removal by the Nebraska State supreme court on May 5, 1891, Thayer returned to office and served as Governor until February 8, 1892; resumed the practice of law in Lincoln, Nebr., and died there March 19, 1906; interment in Wyuka Cemetery.

**Bibliography:** *DAB*; Curtis, Earl G. "John Milton Thayer." *Nebraska History* 29 (March/June 1948): 134-50.

**THAYER, John Randolph,** a Representative from Massachusetts; born in Douglas, Worcester County, Mass., March 9, 1845; attended the common schools and Nichols Academy in Dudley, Worcester County; graduated from Yale College in 1869; studied law; admitted to the bar in 1871 and commenced practice in Worcester, Mass.; served in the city council 1874-1876 and as alderman 1878-1880; was one of the trustees of Nichols Academy for fifteen years; was an unsuccessful candidate for district attorney in 1876; member of the Massachusetts house of representatives in 1880 and 1881; unsuccessful candidate for mayor of Worcester in 1886; served in the Massachusetts senate in 1890 and 1891; unsuccessful candidate for election in 1892 to the Fifty-third Congress; elected as a Democrat to the Fifty-sixth, Fifty-seventh, and Fifty-eighth Congresses (March 4, 1899-March 3, 1905); was not a candidate for renomination in 1904; resumed the practice of law in Worcester, Mass., where he died December 19, 1916; interment in the Rural Cemetery.

**THAYER, Martin Russell,** a Representative from Pennsylvania; born in Dinwiddie County, near the city limits of Petersburg, Va., January 27, 1819; attended the Mount Pleasant Classical Institute in Amherst, Mass., and Amherst College; moved with his father to Philadelphia, Pa., in 1837; was graduated from the University of Pennsylvania at Philadelphia in 1840; studied law; was admitted to the bar in 1842 and commenced practice in Philadelphia; commissioner to revise the revenue laws of Pennsylvania in 1862; elected as a Republican to the Thirty-eighth and Thirty-ninth Congresses (March 4, 1863-March 3, 1867); chairman, Committee on Private Land Claims (Thirty-eighth and Thirty-ninth Congresses); declined to be a candidate for renomination in 1866; resumed the practice of law; judge of the district court of Philadelphia 1867-1874; president judge of the court of common pleas of Philadelphia from 1874 until his resignation in 1896; elected by the judges of the common pleas court prothonotary of Philadelphia in 1896; also engaged in literary pursuits; died in Philadelphia, Pa., October 14, 1906; interment in St. James the Less Church Cemetery.

**THEAKER, Thomas Clarke,** a Representative from Ohio; born in York County, Pa., February 1, 1812; attended the common schools; moved to Bridgeport, Belmont County, Ohio, in 1830; became a machinist and wheelwright; was elected as a Republican to the Thirty-sixth Congress (March 4, 1859-March 3, 1861); was an unsuccessful candidate for reelection in 1860 to the Thirty-seventh

Congress; member of the board of commissioners to investigate the Patent Office in 1864, and later was appointed a member of the board of examiners in chief; served as Commissioner of Patents from August 17, 1865, to January 20, 1868; engaged in the practice of patent law in Washington, D.C., until his death in Oakland, Md., July 16, 1883; interment in Weeks Cemetery, near Bridgeport, Ohio.

**THIBODEAUX, Bannon Goforth,** a Representative from Louisiana; born on St. Bridget plantation, near Thibodeaux, Terrebonne Parish, La., December 22, 1812; attended the country schools; studied law in Hagerstown, Md.; was admitted to the bar and commenced practice in Lafourche and Terrebonne Parishes, La.; member of the State constitutional conventions in 1845 and 1852; held several local offices; elected to the Twenty-ninth and Thirtieth Congresses (March 4, 1845-March 3, 1849); resumed the practice of law in Terrebonne and Lafourche Parishes, La.; sugar planter and manufacturer; died in Terrebonne Parish, La., March 5, 1866; interment in the Half-way Cemetery, near Houma, La.

**THILL, Lewis Dominic,** a Representative from Wisconsin; born in Milwaukee, Wis., October 18, 1903; attended the public and parochial schools and was graduated from Marquette University, Milwaukee, Wis., in 1926; attended Harvard Graduate School, and Northwestern University, Evanston, Ill.; was graduated from the law department of the University of Wisconsin at Madison in 1931; was admitted to the bar in 1932 and commenced practice in Milwaukee, Wis.; elected as a Republican to the Seventy-sixth and the Seventy-seventh Congresses (January 3, 1939-January 3, 1943); unsuccessful candidate for reelection in 1942 to the Seventy-eighth Congress and for election in 1944 to the Seventy-ninth Congress; engaged in real estate and investment business; resided in San Diego, Calif., where he died May 6, 1975; entombment in Holy Cross Mausoleum.

**THISTLEWOOD, Napoleon Bonaparte,** a Representative from Illinois; born near Harrington, Kent County, Del., March 30, 1837; attended the public schools; moved to Mason, Ill., in 1858 and engaged in mercantile pursuits; enlisted in the Union Army in 1862; captain of Company C, Ninety-eighth Regiment, Illinois Volunteer Infantry; served in the Army of the Cumberland, in Wilder's brigade, and with Wilson's Cavalry Corps; returned to Cairo, Ill., and engaged in business pursuits; moved to Cairo, Ill., and engaged in the commission business; mayor of Cairo, Ill., 1879-1883 and again 1897-1901; department commander of the Grand Army of the Republic for Illinois in 1901; elected as a Republican to the Sixtieth Congress to fill the vacancy caused by the death of George W. Smith; reelected to the Sixty-first and Sixty-second Congresses and served from February 15, 1908, to March 3, 1913; unsuccessful candidate for reelection in 1912 to the Sixty-third Congress; retired and was a resident of Cairo, Ill., until his death in that city September 15, 1915; interment in Beech Grove Cemetery, Mounds, Ill.

**THOM, William Richard,** a Representative from Ohio; born in Canton, Stark County, Ohio, July 7, 1885; attended the public schools; engaged as a newspaper reporter, 1905-1909; attended Western Reserve University, Cleveland, Ohio, 1909-1911; served as private secretary to Representative John J. Whitacre of Ohio, 1911-1913; member of the United States House of Representatives Press Galleries in 1915 and 1916; was graduated from the law department of Georgetown University, Washington, D.C., in 1916; was admitted to the bar in 1917 and commenced practice in Canton, Ohio; member of the park commission of Canton, 1920-1932; unsuccessful candidate for nomination in 1920 to the Sixty-seventh Congress; elected as a Democrat to the Seventy-third and to the two succeeding Congresses (March 4, 1933-January 3, 1939); unsuccessful candidate for reelection in 1938 to the Seventy-sixth Congress; resumed the practice of law; elected to the Seventy-seventh Congress (January 3, 1941-January 3, 1943); unsuccessful candidate for reelection in 1942 to the Seventy-eighth Congress; elected to the

Seventy-ninth Congress (January 3, 1945-January 3, 1947); unsuccessful candidate for reelection in 1946 to the Eightieth Congress; resumed the practice of law; delegate to the Democratic National Convention of 1956; died in Canton, Ohio, August 28, 1960; interment in West Lawn Cemetery.

**THOMAS, Albert** (husband of Lera Millard Thomas), a Representative from Texas; born in Nacogdoches, Tex., April 12, 1898; attended the public schools; during the First World War served as a second lieutenant in the United States Army; was graduated from Rice Institute, Houston, Tex., in 1920 and from the law department of the University of Texas at Austin in 1926; was admitted to the bar in 1927 and began practice in Nacogdoches, Tex.; county attorney of Nacogdoches County, Tex., 1927-1930; assistant United States district attorney for the southern district of Texas 1930-1936; elected as a Democrat to the Seventy-fifth and to the fourteen succeeding Congresses, serving from January 3, 1937, until his death in Washington, D.C., on February 15, 1966; chairman, Committee on Elections No. 3 (Seventy-sixth Congress); interment in Veterans' Administration Cemetery, Houston, Tex.

**THOMAS, Benjamin Franklin,** a Representative from Massachusetts; born in Boston, Mass., February 12, 1813; moved with his parents to Worcester in 1819; attended Lancaster Academy, and was graduated from Brown University, Providence, R.I., in 1830; studied law in Cambridge, Mass.; was admitted to the bar in 1833 and commenced practice in Worcester, Mass.; held several local offices; member of the Massachusetts house of representatives in 1842; commissioner of bankruptcy in 1842; judge of probate, 1844-1848; presidential elector on the Whig ticket in 1848; judge of the Massachusetts Supreme Court from 1853 to 1859, when he resigned; continued the practice of law in Boston, Mass.; elected as a Unionist to the Thirty-seventh Congress to fill the vacancy caused by the resignation of Charles Francis Adams and served from June 11, 1861, to March 3, 1863; declined to be a candidate for renomination in 1862 to the Thirty-eighth Congress; again engaged in the practice of law; nominated by Governor Alexander H. Bullock for chief justice of the supreme court of Massachusetts in 1868, but the nomination was not confirmed by the council; died at his home in Beverly Farms, Mass., September 27, 1878; interment in Forrest Hill Cemetery, Boston, Mass.

**THOMAS, Charles Randolph** (father of Charles Randolph Thomas [1861-1931]), a Representative from North Carolina; born in Beaufort, Carteret County, N.C., February 7, 1827; attended a private school in Hillsboro, N.C., and was graduated from the University of North Carolina at Chapel Hill in 1849; studied law; was admitted to the bar in 1850 and commenced practice in Beaufort, N.C.; moved to New Bern, N.C., and continued the practice of law; member of the State constitutional convention in 1861; secretary of state of North Carolina in 1864; appointed by Governor Jonathan Worth as president of the Atlantic & North Carolina Railroad in 1867; judge of the superior court, 1868-1870; elected as a Republican to the Forty-second and Forty-third Congresses (March 4, 1871-March 3, 1875); unsuccessful candidate for renomination in 1874 to the Forty-fourth Congress; resumed the practice of law in New Bern, N.C., and died there on February 18, 1891; interment in Cedar Grove Cemetery.

**THOMAS, Charles Randolph** (son of Charles Randolph Thomas [1827-1891]), a Representative from North Carolina; born in Beaufort, Carteret County, N.C., August 21, 1861; attended New Bern (N.C.) Academy and Emerson Institute, Washington, D.C.; was graduated from the University of North Carolina at Chapel Hill in 1881; studied law with his father and at the law school of Judges R.P. Dick and John H. Dillard at Greensboro, N.C.; was admitted to the bar in 1882 and commenced practice in New Bern, N.C.; member of the North Carolina State house of representatives in 1887; attorney for Craven County, 1890-1896; elected by the State legislature a trustee of the University of North Carolina in 1893; member of the Democratic State executive committee; elected as a Democrat to the Fifty-sixth and to the five succeeding Congresses (March 4, 1899-March 3, 1911); declined to be a candidate for renomination in 1910 to the Sixty-second Congress; resumed the practice of law in New Bern, N.C.; delegate to the Democratic National Convention of 1924; moved to Waynesville, Haywood County, N.C., in 1925 and practiced law; appointed in September 1926 as emergency judge of the superior court by Governor Angus W. McLean of North Carolina; resumed the practice of law in Waynesville, N.C.; died in Norfolk, Va., March 8, 1931; interment in Cedar Grove Cemetery, New Bern, N.C.

**THOMAS, Charles Spalding,** a Senator from Colorado; born in Darien, McIntosh County, Ga., December 6, 1849; attended private schools in Georgia and Connecticut; served briefly in the Confederate Army; graduated from the law department of the University of Michigan at Ann Arbor in 1871; was admitted to the bar in 1871; moved to Colorado and commenced practice in Denver, Colo.; Denver city attorney, 1875-1876; member of the Democratic National Committee from 1884 until 1896; unsuccessful candidate for election to the House of Representatives in 1884, to the Senate in 1888 and 1895, and for Governor in 1894; elected Governor of Colorado on the Fusion ticket in 1898, and served from January 10, 1899 to January 8, 1901; elected as a Democrat to the United States Senate in 1913 to fill the vacancy caused by the death of Charles J. Hughes, Jr.; reelected in 1914, and served from January 15, 1913 to March 3, 1921; unsuccessful candidate on the Nationalist ticket for reelection in 1920; chairman, Committee on Woman Suffrage (Sixty-third and Sixty-fourth Congresses), Committee on Coast Defenses (Sixty-fifth Congress), Committee on Pacific Railroads (Sixty-sixth Congress); resumed the practice of law; died in Denver, Colo., June 24, 1934; the remains were cremated and the ashes interred in Fairmount Cemetery.

**Bibliography:** *DAB*; Thomas, Sewell. *Silhouettes of Charles S. Thomas, Colorado Governor and U.S. Senator.* Caldwell, Idaho: Caxton Printers, 1959.

**THOMAS, Christopher Yancy,** a Representative from Virginia; born in Pittsylvania County, Va., March 24, 1818; attended the common schools; graduated from a private academy in 1838; studied law; admitted to the bar in 1844 and commenced practice in Martinsville, Henry County, Va.; served in the State senate 1860-1864; member of the commission to settle the boundary line between Virginia and North Carolina; treasurer of Henry County; prosecuting attorney for Henry County; member of the Virginia constitutional convention in 1868; elected to the Virginia house of delegates in 1869; successfully contested as a Republican the election of Alexander M. Davis to the Forty-third Congress and served from March 5, 1874, to March 3, 1875; unsuccessful candidate for reelection in 1874 to the Forty-fourth Congress; resumed the practice of law; died in Martinsville, Va., February 11, 1879; interment in the family cemetery at Leatherwood, Henry County, Va.

**THOMAS, Craig Lyle,** a Representative and a Senator from Wyoming; born in Cody, Park County, Wyo., February 17, 1933; graduated from Cody High School; B.A., University of Wyoming, 1955; entered active duty, United States Marine Corps in 1955, released as a captain in 1959; small businessman; exeutive vice president, Wyoming Farm Bureau, 1959-1966; general manager, American Farm Bureau, 1966-1975; general manager, Wyoming Rural Electric Association, 1975-1989; member, Wyoming State house of representatives, 1985-1988; elected as a Republican to the One Hundred First Congress, April 26, 1989, by special election to fill the vacancy caused by the resignation of Richard B. Cheney; reelected to the One Hundred Second and One Hundred Third Congresses, and served from April 26, 1989 to January 3, 1995; was not a candidate in 1994 for renomination to the House of Representatives, but was elected to the United States Senate for the term ending January 3, 2001; is a resident of Casper, Wyo.

**THOMAS, David,** a Representative from New York; born in Pelham, Mass., June 11, 1762; completed preparatory studies; served as a volunteer in 1777; joined the Fifth Massachusetts Regiment as a corporal in 1781, and later became sergeant in the Third Massachusetts Regiment; moved to Salem, Washington County, N.Y., in 1784, where he conducted a tavern for several years; commissioned captain in the State militia in 1786; rose to the rank of major general of the northern division of the Militia of New York in 1805; engaged in mercantile pursuits; member of the State assembly 1794 and 1798-1800; supervisor of the town of Salem 1797-1800; justice of the peace 1798-1801, 1804, and 1811; elected as a Republican to the Seventh and to the three succeeding Congresses and served from March 4, 1801, to May 1, 1808, when he resigned; served as treasurer of the State of New York from February 5, 1808, to February 8, 1810, and again from February 18, 1812, to February 10, 1813; moved to Providence, R.I., where he died November 27, 1831; interment in Evergreen Cemetery, Salem, N.Y.

**Bibliography:** *DAB*.

**THOMAS, Elbert Duncan,** a Senator from Utah; born in Salt Lake City, Utah, June 17, 1883; attended the public schools; graduated from the University of Utah at Salt Lake City in 1906 and from the graduate department of the University of California, Berkeley, 1924; served as a missionary of the Church of Latter-Day Saints in Japan 1907-1912; student traveler in Asia and Europe 1912-1913; instructor of Latin and Greek at the University of Utah 1914-1916 and secretary of board of regents 1917-1922; served as major, inspector general's department, Utah National Guard, and United States Reserves 1917-1926; professor of political science at the University of Utah 1924-1933; author; elected as a Democrat to the United States Senate in 1932; reelected in 1938 and again in 1944 and served from March 4, 1933, to January 3, 1951; unsuccessful candidate for reelection in 1950; chairman, Committee on Education and Labor (Seventy-fifth through Seventy-eighth Congresses), Committee on Military Affairs (Seventy-ninth Congress), Committee on Labor and Public Welfare (Eighty-first Congress); appointed high commissioner of United States trust territories of the Pacific and served from 1951, until his death in Honolulu, Hawaii, February 11, 1953; interment in City Cemetery, Salt Lake City, Utah.

**Bibliography:** *DAB*; Thomas, Elbert D. *The Four Fears.* Chicago: Ziff-Davis Company, 1944; Thomas, Elbert D. "The Senate During and Since the War." *Parliamentary Affairs* 3 (Winter 1949): 114-26.

**THOMAS, Elmer,** a Representative and a Senator from Oklahoma. (*See* THOMAS, John William Elmer.)

**THOMAS, Francis,** a Representative from Maryland; born in that part of Frederick County, Md., close to South Mountain, known as Merryland tract, February 3, 1799; attended St. John's College, Annapolis, Md.; studied law; was admitted to the bar in 1820 and commenced practice in Frankville, Md.; member of the Maryland State house of delegates in 1822, 1827, and 1829, and served the last year as speaker; elected as a Jacksonian to the Twenty-second through Twenty-fourth Congresses, and as a Democrat to the Twenty-fifth and Twenty-sixth Congresses (March 4, 1831-March 3, 1841); chairman, Committee on the Judiciary (Twenty-fourth and Twenty-fifth Congresses), Committee on Naval Affairs (Twenty-sixth Congress); president of the Chesapeake & Ohio Canal Co., 1839-1840; elected Governor of Maryland in 1841, and served from January 3, 1842 to January 6, 1845; unsuccessful candidate for reelection in 1844; member of the Maryland State Constitutional convention in 1850; elected as a Unionist to the Thirty-seventh

Congress, as an Unconditional Unionist to the Thirty-eighth and Thirty-ninth Congresses, and as a Republican to the Fortieth Congress (March 4, 1861-March 3, 1869); served as a delegate to the Loyalist Convention at Philadelphia in 1866; collector of internal revenue, 1870-1872; appointed Minister to Peru on May 25, 1872 and served until July 1875; retired from public and professional life and devoted his time to agricultural pursuits; was killed by a locomotive while walking on the railroad tracks near Frankville, Md., January 22, 1876; interment in a vault in Rose Hill Cemetery, Cumberland, Md.

**Bibliography:** *DAB.*

**THOMAS, George Morgan,** a Representative from Kentucky; born near Poplar Flat, Lewis County, Ky., November 23, 1828; educated in the common schools; taught school two years; was school commissioner from 1850 to 1859; studied law; was admitted to the bar in 1851 and practiced; elected prosecuting attorney of Lewis County in 1854 and served for four years; a member of the Kentucky house of representatives, 1859-1863; Commonwealth attorney for the tenth judicial district, 1862-1868; county judge in 1868; unsuccessful Republican candidate for Lieutenant Governor of Kentucky in 1871; again a member of the Kentucky house of representatives in 1872 and 1873; circuit judge of the fourteenth judicial district, 1874-1880; United States district attorney, 1881-1885; elected as a Republican to the Fiftieth Congress (March 4, 1887-March 3, 1889); appointed Solicitor of Internal Revenue by President William McKinley on May 20, 1897, and served until May 31, 1901; died in Vanceburg, Lewis County, Ky., January 7, 1914; interment in Greenlawn Cemetery.

**THOMAS, Henry Franklin,** a Representative from Michigan; born in Tompkins, Jackson County, Mich., December 17, 1843; attended the common schools and Albion (Mich.) College in 1859; enlisted in 1862 during the Civil War as a private in the Seventh Regiment, Michigan Volunteer Cavalry; was promoted to first sergeant of Company D, and in July 1864 to second lieutenant; renewed his studies in the Ypsilanti Normal School; was graduated from the medical department of Michigan University at Ann Arbor in 1868 and commenced practice in Constantine, St. Joseph County, Mich.; moved to Allegan, Mich., in 1870; member of the State house of representatives in 1873 and 1874; served in the State senate in 1875 and 1876; delegate to the Republican National Convention in 1884; elected as a Republican to the Fifty-third and Fifty-fourth Congresses (March 4, 1893-March 3, 1897); chairman, Committee on Expenditures in the Department of the Navy (Fifty-fourth Congress); was an unsuccessful candidate for renomination in 1896; surgeon in the Michigan Soldiers' Home in 1907 and 1908; member of the Michigan pardon board in 1909 and 1910; died in Allegan, Mich., April 16, 1912; interment in Oak Hill Cemetery, Ann Arbor, Mich.

**THOMAS, Isaac,** a Representative from Tennessee; born in Sevierville, Tenn., November 4, 1784; after the death of his parents he moved to Winchester, Tenn., in 1800; self-educated; studied law; was admitted to the bar in 1808 and practiced in Winchester; elected as a Republican to the Fourteenth Congress (March 4, 1815-March 3, 1817); moved to Alexandria, Rapides Parish, La., in 1819; resumed the practice of law; purchased vast tracts of land adjoining Alexandria and became one of the largest landowners and slaveholders in Louisiana; was the first man to introduce the cultivation of sugar cane in central Louisiana; also engaged in mercantile pursuits and in the operation of sawmills and steamboats; served as brigadier general of the Louisiana Militia; served in the State senate 1823-1827; moved to California in 1849; returned to Alexandria, La., where he died on February 2, 1859; interment in the Flint lot, in Rapides Cemetery, Pineville, La.

**THOMAS, James Houston,** a Representative from Tennessee; born in Iredell County, N.C., September 22, 1808; attended the rural schools; was graduated from Jackson College, Columbia Tenn., in 1830; studied law; was admitted to the bar in 1831 and commenced practice in Columbia, Tenn.; attorney general of Tennessee 1836-1842; elected as a Democrat to the Thirtieth and Thirty-first Congresses (March 4, 1847-March 3, 1851); unsuccessful candidate for reelection in 1850 to the Thirty-second Congress; elected to the Thirty-sixth Congress (March 4, 1859-March 3, 1861); resumed the practice of law in Columbia, Tenn.; died near Fayetteville, Lincoln County, Tenn., on August 4, 1876; interment in St. John's Cemetery, Ashwood, Maury County, Tenn.

**THOMAS, Jesse Burgess,** a Delegate from Indiana Territory and a Senator from Illinois; born in Shepherdstown, Va. (now West Virginia) in 1777; studied law in Mason County, Ky., where he also served as county clerk until 1803; moved to Lawrenceburg, Indiana Territory in 1803 and practiced law; appointed deputy attorney general of Indiana Territory in 1805; member, Territorial house of representatives 1805-1808, and served as speaker 1805-1808; elected as a Delegate from Indiana Territory to the Tenth Congress to fill the vacancy caused by the resignation of Benjamin Parke and served from October 22, 1808, to March 3, 1809; moved to Kaskaskia in 1809, then to Cahokia, and later to Edwardsville, Ill.; upon the organization of Illinois Territory was appointed judge of the United States court for the northwestern judicial district 1809-1818; delegate to the State constitutional convention in 1818 and served as president of that body; upon the admission of Illinois as a State into the Union in 1818 was elected as a Republican to the United States Senate; reelected in 1823, and served from December 3, 1818, to March 3, 1829; declined to be a candidate for reelection in 1829; chairman, Committee on Public Lands (Sixteenth and Seventeenth Congresses); moved to Mount Vernon, Ohio, in 1829; committed suicide in Mount Vernon, Ohio, May 3, 1853; interment in Mound View Cemetery.

**Bibliography:** *DAB*; Suppiger, Joseph E. "Jesse Burgess Thomas: Illinois' Pro-Slavery Advocate." Ph.D. dissertation, University of Tennessee, 1970.

**THOMAS, John,** a Senator from Idaho; born on a farm in Phillips County, Kans., January 4, 1874; attended the rural schools and the Central Normal College at Great Bend, Kans.; taught school, serving as superintendent of schools of Phillips County, Kans., 1898-1903; register of land office at Colby, Kans., 1906-1909; moved to Gooding, Idaho, in 1909; engaged in banking and livestock business; mayor of Gooding 1917-1919; member of the Republican National Committee 1925-1933; appointed and subsequently elected as a Republican to the United States Senate to fill the vacancy caused by the death of Frank R. Gooding and served from June 30, 1928, to March 3, 1933; unsuccessful candidate for reelection in 1932; chairman, Committee on Irrigation and Reclamation (Seventy-first and Seventy-second Congresses); resumed former business pursuits; again appointed and subsequently elected to the United States Senate to fill the vacancy caused by the death of William E. Borah; reelected in 1942, and served from January 27, 1940, until his death in Washington, D.C., November 10, 1945; interment in Elmwood Cemetery, Gooding, Idaho.

**THOMAS, John Chew,** a Representative from Maryland; born in Perryville, Cecil County, Md., October 15, 1764; attended private schools; was graduated from the University of Pennsylvania at Philadelphia in 1783; moved to "Fairland," in Anne Arundel County, Md., about 1789; studied law; admitted to the bar in Philadelphia, Pa., December 15, 1787, but did not engage in extensive practice; elected as a Federalist to the Sixth Congress (March 4, 1799-March 3, 1801); declined to be a candidate for reelection in 1800 to the

Seventh Congress; moved to Pennsylvania; died near Leiperville, Pa., May 10, 1836; interment in the Friends Cemetery, near Chester, Pa.

**THOMAS, John Lewis, Jr.,** a Representative from Maryland; born in Baltimore, Md., May 20, 1835; completed preparatory studies; studied law; was admitted to the bar in 1856 and commenced practice in Cumberland, Md.; city counselor of Cumberland in 1856 and 1857; moved to Baltimore, Md., in 1857 and continued the practice of law; city solicitor of Baltimore 1860-1862; delegate to the State constitutional convention in 1863; State's attorney 1863-1865; elected as an Unconditional Unionist to the Thirty-ninth Congress to fill the vacancy caused by the resignation of Edwin H. Webster and served from December 4, 1865, to March 3, 1867; was an unsuccessful Republican candidate for reelection in 1866 to the Fortieth Congress; collector of the port of Baltimore, Md., from 1869 to 1873, and from 1877 to 1882; died in Baltimore, Md., on October 15, 1893; interment in Greenmount Cemetery.

**THOMAS, John Parnell,** a Representative from New Jersey; born in Jersey City, Hudson County, N.J., January 16, 1895; attended the public schools of Allendale, N.J., the high school at Ridgewood, N.J., and the University of Pennsylvania at Philadelphia; during the First World War served overseas as a second lieutenant in Company B, Three Hundred and Sixth Infantry, and first lieutenant and captain in Headquarters, Regimental Staff of the Fiftieth Infantry, 1917-1919; engaged in investment securities pursuits from 1920 until 1938, and in the insurance business in New York City, beginning in 1938; member of the borough council of Allendale, N.J., in 1925; mayor of Allendale, 1926-1930; member of the New Jersey State house of assembly, 1935-1937; elected as a Republican to the Seventy-fifth and to the six succeeding Congresses; served from January 3, 1937 until his resignation on January 2, 1950, having pleaded no contest to charges of salary fraud, November 30, 1949, before the United States District Court for the District of Columbia; chairman, Committee on Un-American Activities (Eightieth Congress); editor and publisher of three weekly newspapers in Bergen County, N.J., 1951-1955; real estate solicitor in 1955 and 1956; unsuccessful candidate for nomination in 1954 to the Eighty-fourth Congress; engaged in investment securities; moved to St. Petersburg, Fla., where he died on November 19, 1970; cremated; ashes interred in Elmgrove Cemetery, Mystic, Conn.

**Bibliography:** Carlson, Lewis H. "J. Parnell Thomas and the House Committee on Un-American Activities, 1938-1948." Ph.D. dissertation, Michigan State University, 1967.

**THOMAS, John Robert,** a Representative from Illinois; born in Mount Vernon, Jefferson County, Ill., October 11, 1846; attended the common schools and Hunter Collegiate Institute, Princeton, Ind.; served in the Union Army during the Civil War, and rose from the rank of private to that of captain of Company D, One Hundred and Twentieth Regiment, Indiana Volunteer Infantry; studied law; was admitted to the bar in 1869 and practiced; city attorney of Metropolis, Ill., 1869 and 1870; served as State's attorney, 1871-1874; elected as a Republican to the Forty-sixth and to the four succeeding Congresses (March 4, 1879-March 3, 1889); chairman, Committee on Levees and Improvements of the Mississippi River (Forty-seventh Congress); was not a candidate for renomination in 1888 to the Fifty-first Congress; resumed the practice of law in Muskogee, Okla.; United States judge in the Indian Territory from June 30, 1897 to June 30, 1901; nominated for judge of the supreme court by the first Republican State convention of Oklahoma, but declined the nomination; member of the Oklahoma State Code Commission, 1908-1910; resumed the practice of law in Muskogee, Okla.; died in McAlester, Okla., January 19, 1914; interment in Green Hill Cemetery, Muskogee, Okla.; reinterment in Arlington National Cemetery, Va.

**Bibliography:** Clark, J. Stanley. "The Career of John R.

Thomas." *Chronicles of Oklahoma* 52 (Summer 1979): 152-179.

**THOMAS, John William Elmer,** a Representative and a Senator from Oklahoma; born on a farm near Greencastle, Putnam County, Ind., September 8, 1876; attended the common schools; graduated from the Central Normal College (now Canterbury), Danville, Ind., in 1897 and from the graduate department of DePauw University, Greencastle, Ind., in 1900; studied law; was admitted to the Indiana bar in 1897 and to the Oklahoma bar in 1900, and commenced practice in Oklahoma City, Okla.; moved to Lawton, Okla., in 1901 and continued the practice of law; member, Oklahoma State senate, 1907-1920, serving as president pro tempore, 1910-1913; unsuccessful candidate for election in 1920 to the Sixty-seventh Congress; elected as a Democrat to the Sixty-eighth and Sixty-ninth Congresses (March 4, 1923-March 3, 1927); was not a candidate in 1926 for renomination to the House of Representatives, but was elected to the United States Senate; reelected in 1932, 1938, and again in 1944, and served from March 4, 1927 to January 3, 1951; unsuccessful candidate for renomination in 1950; chairman, Committee on Indian Affairs (Seventy-fourth through Seventy-seventh Congresses), Committee on Agriculture and Forestry (Seventy-eighth, Seventy-ninth and Eighty-first Congresses), Committee on Indian Affairs (Seventy-eighth Congress); engaged in the practice of law in Washington, D.C., until August 1957; returned to Lawton, Okla., where he died on September 19, 1965; interment in Highland Cemetery.

**Bibliography:** *DAB*; Manheimer, Eric. "The Public Career of Elmer Thomas." Ph.D. dissertation, University of Oklahoma, 1953; Thomas, Elmer. *Autobiography of an Enigma*. New York: Pageant Press, 1965.

**THOMAS, Lera Millard** (wife of Albert Thomas), a Representative from Texas; born in Nacogdoches, Tex., August 3, 1900; attended Brenau College, Gainesville, Ga., and the University of Alabama; member of the Houston (Tex.) League of Women Voters; elected as a Democrat to the Eighty-ninth Congress, March 26, 1966, by special election to fill the vacancy caused by the death of her husband, Albert Thomas, and served from March 26, 1966 until January 3, 1967; was not a candidate for renomination in 1966 to the Ninetieth Congress; special liaison for the Houston Chronicle to members of the armed services in Vietnam, 1968; was a resident of Nacogdoches, Tex., until her death there on July 23, 1993; interment in Oak Grove Cemetery.

**THOMAS, Lot,** a Representative from Iowa; born near Markleysburg, Fayette County, Pa., October 17, 1843; attended the public schools and Vermillion Institute, Hayesville, Ohio; moved to Iowa in 1868; taught school in New Virginia, Warren County; attended the law department of the University of Iowa at Iowa City, and was admitted to the bar in 1870; moved to Buena Vista County and settled at Storm Lake in 1870; practiced law; judge of the fourteenth judicial district of Iowa from 1885 until his resignation on August 26, 1898, having become a candidate for Congress; elected as a Republican to the Fifty-sixth and to the two succeeding Congresses (March 4, 1899-March 3, 1905); unsuccessful candidate for renomination in 1904 to the Fifty-ninth Congress; died on a train near Yuma, Ariz., March 17, 1905, while en route to Los Angeles, Calif.; interment in Storm Lake Cemetery, Storm Lake, Iowa.

**THOMAS, Ormsby Brunson,** a Representative from Wisconsin; born in Sandgate, Bennington County, Vt., August 21, 1832; moved with his parents to Wisconsin in 1836; attended the common schools and Burr Seminary, Manchester, Vt.; was graduated from the National Law School, Poughkeepsie, N.Y., in 1856; was admitted to the bar in Albany, N.Y., in 1856 and commenced practice in Prairie du Chien, Wis.; district attorney of Crawford County, Wis.; served in the Union Army during the Civil War as captain of Company D, Thirty-first Regiment, Wisconsin Volunteer Infantry; member of the State assembly in 1862, 1865, and 1867; served in the

State senate in 1880 and 1881; elected as a Republican to the Forty-ninth, Fiftieth, and Fifty-first Congresses (March 4, 1885-March 3, 1891); chairman, Committee on War Claims (Fifty-first Congress); was an unsuccessful candidate for reelection in 1890 to the Fifty-second Congress; resumed the practice of law in Prairie du Chien, Wis., and died there October 24, 1904; interment in Evergreen Cemetery.

**THOMAS, Philemon,** a Representative from Louisiana; born in Orange County, Va., February 9, 1763; attended the common schools; served in the Revolutionary War; moved to Kentucky in 1783 and settled in Mason County; delegate to the convention which framed the constitution of the Commonwealth of Kentucky; member of the Kentucky house of representatives, 1796-1799; served in the Kentucky senate, 1800-1803; moved to Louisiana in 1806 and settled on the banks of the lower Mississippi River; member of the Louisiana house of representatives; leader of an uprising against the Spanish authorities, who exercised authority over what is now Mississippi and Louisiana, and commanded the forces which captured the Spanish fort at Baton Rouge in 1810; major general of Louisiana Militia in 1814 and 1815 and served in that capacity in the War of 1812; moved to Baton Rouge, La.; elected to the Twenty-second and Twenty-third Congresses (March 4, 1831-March 3, 1835); died in Baton Rouge, La., November 17, 1847; interment in the Old American Graveyard; reinterment in the National Cemetery at Baton Rouge, La.
**Bibliography:** Sterkx, Henry Eugene, and Brooks Thompson. "Philemon Thomas and the West Florida Revolution." *Florida Historical Quarterly* 39 (April 1961): 378-386.

**THOMAS, Phillip Francis,** a Representative from Maryland; born in Easton, Talbot County, Md., September 12, 1810; attended the academy in Easton, and was graduated from Dickinson College, Carlisle, Pa., in 1830; studied law; was admitted to the bar in 1831 and commenced practice in Easton, Md.; delegate to the Maryland State constitutional convention in 1836; member of the Maryland State house of delegates in 1838, 1843, and 1845; elected as a Democrat to the Twenty-sixth Congress (March 4, 1839-March 3, 1841); declined to be a candidate for renomination in 1840 to the Twenty-seventh Congress; resumed the practice of law; elected Governor of Maryland in 1847, and served from January 3, 1848 to January 6, 1851; judge of the land office court of eastern Maryland; Comptroller of the United States Treasury, 1851-1853; collector of the port of Baltimore, Md., 1853-1860; United States Commissioner of Patents from February 16 to December 10, 1860; appointed Secretary of the Treasury in the Cabinet of President James Buchanan, and served from December 10, 1860 until his resignation on January 11, 1861; again a member of the State house of delegates in 1863; presented credentials as a Senator-elect to the United States Senate for the term beginning March 4, 1867, but was not seated; elected as a Democrat to the Forty-fourth Congress (March 4, 1875-March 3, 1877); declined to be a candidate for renomination in 1876 to the Forty-fifth Congress; unsuccessful candidate for election to the United States Senate in 1878; again elected a member of the State house of delegates in 1878 and 1883; delegate to the Democratic State convention in 1883; resumed the practice of law in Easton, Md.; died in Baltimore, Md., October 2, 1890; interment in Spring Hill Cemetery, Easton, Md.
**Bibliography:** *DAB*.

**THOMAS, Richard,** a Representative from Pennsylvania; born in West Whiteland, Pa., December 30, 1744; educated at home by private teachers; served in the Revolutionary Army as colonel of the First Regiment, Chester County Volunteers; elected as a Federalist to the Fourth, Fifth, and Sixth Congresses (March 4, 1795-March 3, 1801); engaged in agricultural pursuits; died in Philadelphia, Pa., January 19, 1832; interment in the Friends Western Burial Ground.

**THOMAS, Robert Lindsay,** a Representative from Georgia; born in Patterson, Pierce County, Ga., November 20, 1943; attended public schools; B.A., University of Georgia, Athens, 1965; served in the Georgia National Guard, 1966-1972; investment banker; farmer; elected as a Democrat to the Ninety-eighth and to the four succeeding Congresses (January 3, 1983-January 3, 1993); was not a candidate for renomination in 1992 to the One Hundred Third Congress; director of state government relations, Atlanta Committee for the Olympic Games; is a resident of Screven, Ga.

**THOMAS, Robert Young, Jr.,** a Representative from Kentucky; born near Russellville, Logan County, Ky., July 13, 1855; attended the common schools; graduated from Bethel College, Russellville, Ky., in 1878; studied law; admitted to the bar in 1881 and commenced practice in Central City, Ky.; also engaged in journalism; member of the Kentucky house of representatives in 1886 and 1887; elected Commonwealth attorney for the seventh judicial district of Kentucky in 1903 for a term of six years; elected as a Democrat to the Sixty-first and to the eight succeeding Congresses and served from March 4, 1909, until his death at Red Boiling Springs, Macon County, Tenn., September 3, 1925; interment in Evergreen Cemetery, Greenville, Ky.

**THOMAS, William Aubrey,** a Representative from Ohio; born in Y Bynea, near Llanelly, Wales, June 7, 1866; immigrated to the United States in 1868 with his parents, who settled in Niles, Ohio; attended the public schools of Niles, Mount Union College, Alliance, Ohio, and Rensselaer Polytechnic Institute, Troy, N.Y.; analytical chemist at Niles 1886-1888; engaged in the iron and steel business; president of the Mahoning Steel Co.; secretary and director of the Niles Fire Brick Co.; elected as a Republican to the Fifty-eighth Congress to fill the vacancy caused by the resignation of Charles W.F. Dick; reelected to the Fifty-ninth, Sixtieth, and Sixty-first Congresses and served from November 8, 1904, to March 3, 1911; unsuccessful candidate for reelection in 1910 to the Sixty-second Congress; moved to Jenifer, Ala., in 1918, and continued his interest in the manufacture of iron, steel, and firebrick; president of the Jenifer Iron Co.; died in Talladega, Ala., September 8, 1951; interment in Oakhill Cemetery, Youngstown, Ohio.

**THOMAS, William David,** a Representative from New York; born in Middle Granville, Washington County, N.Y., March 22, 1880; attended the grade and high schools; was graduated from the Albany College of Pharmacy, Albany, N.Y., in 1904; moved to Hoosick Falls, Rensselaer County, N.Y., in 1905 and was employed as a pharmacist, later engaging in the retail drug business; also interested in banking; served as town clerk 1917-1925; member of the State assembly in 1925 and 1926; served as treasurer of Rensselaer County 1927-1933; chairman of the Republican county committee 1927-1934; elected as a Republican to the Seventy-third Congress to fill the vacancy caused by the death of James S. Parker; reelected to the Seventy-fourth Congress and served from January 30, 1934, until his death in Washington, D.C., May 17, 1936; interment in Maple Grove Cemetery, Hoosick Falls, N.Y.

**THOMAS, William Marshall,** a Representative from California; born in Wallace, Shoshone County, Idaho, December 6, 1941; attended the public schools of San Pedro and Garden Grove, Calif., and graduated from Garden Grove High School in 1959; A.A., Santa Ana Community College, 1961; B.A., San Francisco State University, 1963; M.A., San Francisco State University, 1965; professor, Bakersfield Community College, 1965-1974; member, California State assembly, 1974-1978; elected as a Republican to the Ninety-sixth and to the eight succeeding Congresses (January 3, 1979-January 3, 1997); chairman, Committee on House Oversight (One Hundred Fourth Congress), Joint Committee on Printing (One Hundred Fourth Congress); is a resident of Bakersfield, Calif.

**THOMASON, Robert Ewing,** a Representative from Texas; born in Shelbyville, Bedford County, Tenn., May 30, 1879; moved to Gainesville, Cooke County, Tex., with his parents in 1880; attended the public schools; was graduated from Southwestern University, Georgetown, Tex., in 1898 and from the law department of the University of Texas at Austin, LL.D., 1900; was admitted to the bar in 1901 and commenced practice in Gainesville, Tex.; prosecuting attorney of Cooke County, Tex., 1902-1906; moved to El Paso, Tex., in 1911 and continued the practice of law; member of the State house of representatives 1917-1921, and served as speaker in 1920 and 1921; mayor of El Paso 1927-1930; elected as a Democrat to the Seventy-second Congress; reelected to the eight succeeding Congresses and served from March 4, 1931, until his resignation on July 31, 1947, having been appointed United States district judge for the western district of Texas; retired as senior judge; resided in El Paso, Tex., until his death there November 8, 1973; interment in Restlawn Cemetery.

**THOMASSON, William Poindexter,** a Representative from Kentucky; born in New Castle, Henry County, Ky., October 8, 1797; completed preparatory studies; served in Captain Duncan's company in the War of 1812; studied law; admitted to the bar and commenced practice in Corydon, Ind., before he was twenty-one years of age; member of the Kentucky house of representatives 1818-1820; prosecuting attorney of Corydon in 1818; moved to Louisville, Ky., in 1841; elected as a Whig to the Twenty-eighth and Twenty-ninth Congresses (March 4, 1843-March 3, 1847); declined to be a candidate for renomination; moved to Chicago, Ill., and resumed the practice of law; during the Civil War served in the Union Army in the Seventy-first Regiment, New York Volunteer Infantry; died near La Grange, Oldham County, Ky., December 29, 1882; interment in Cave Hill Cemetery, Louisville, Ky.

**THOMPSON, Albert Clifton,** a Representative from Ohio; born in Brookville, Jefferson County, Pa., January 23, 1842; attended the common schools and Jefferson College, Canonsburg, Pa.; studied law; served in the Union Army during the Civil War as second lieutenant of Company B, One Hundred and Fifth Regiment, Pennsylvania Volunteer Infantry; promoted to captain of Company K in the same regiment, November 28, 1861, and served until March 23, 1863, when he was discharged on account of wounds received during the second Battle of Bull Run in August 1862; resumed the study of law; was admitted to the bar December 13, 1864, and commenced practice in Portsmouth, Ohio, in 1865; elected probate judge of Scioto County, Ohio, in October 1869; elected common pleas judge of the seventh judicial district of Ohio in October 1881; elected as a Republican to the Forty-ninth and to the two succeeding Congresses (March 4, 1885-March 3, 1891); unsuccessful candidate for renomination in 1890 to the Fifty-second Congress; resumed the practice of law; appointed by President William McKinley chairman of the commission to revise and codify the criminal and penal laws of the United States, June 21, 1897; appointed United States judge for the southern district of Ohio on September 13, 1898, and served until his death in Cincinnati, Ohio, on January 26, 1910; interment in Greenlawn Cemetery, Portsmouth, Ohio.

**THOMPSON, Benjamin,** a Representative from Massachusetts; born in Charlestown, Mass., August 5, 1798; attended the public schools; engaged in mercantile pursuits; member of the Massachusetts house of representatives 1830-1831 and 1833-1836; served in the Massachusetts senate in 1841; elected as a Whig to the Twenty-ninth Congress (March 4, 1845-March 3, 1847); declined to be a candidate for renomination in 1846; elected to the Thirty-second Congress and served from March 4, 1851, until his death in Charlestown, Mass., September 24, 1852; interment in the Congressional Cemetery, Washington, D.C.

**THOMPSON, Bennie G.,** a Representative from Mississippi; born in Bolton, Hinds County, Miss., January 28, 1948; B.A., Tougaloo College, 1968; M.S., Jackson State University, 1972; teacher; Bolton board of aldermen, 1969-1973; mayor of Bolton, 1973-1979; Hinds County supervisor, 1980-1993; elected as a Democrat to the One Hundred Third Congress, April 13, 1993, by special election to fill the vacancy caused by the resignation of A. Michael Espy; reelected to the One Hundred Fourth Congress, and served from April 13, 1993 to January 3, 1997; is a resident of Bolton, Miss.

**THOMPSON, Charles James,** a Representative from Ohio; born in Wapakoneta, Auglaize County, Ohio, January 24, 1862; attended the public schools and the Ohio Wesleyan University, Delaware, Ohio; learned the art of printing 1876-1879; worked as a journeyman printer in various cities in Ohio, Indiana, and Illinois 1879-1884; returned to Wapakoneta in 1885 and was employed as a bookkeeper until 1889; moved to Defiance, Ohio, in 1889 and was owner and publisher of the Defiance Express until 1902; member of the Republican State central committee in 1893 and 1894; postmaster of Defiance 1898-1915; unsuccessful candidate for mayor in 1915; elected as a Republican to the Sixty-sixth and to the five succeeding Congresses (March 4, 1919-March 3, 1931); unsuccessful candidate for reelection in 1930 to the Seventy-second Congress; retired from business pursuits; died in Albuquerque, N.Mex., while on a visit, March 27, 1932; interment in Riverside Cemetery, Defiance, Ohio.

**THOMPSON, Charles Perkins,** a Representative from Massachusetts; born in Braintree, Norfolk County, Mass., July 30, 1827; attended the public schools, the Hollis Institute of Braintree, and Amherst (Mass.) College; studied law; admitted to the bar in 1854 and commenced practice in Gloucester, Mass., in 1857; United States assistant district attorney from 1855 to 1857; member of the Massachusetts house of representatives in 1871 and 1872; delegate to the Democratic National Convention in 1872; elected as a Democrat to the Forty-fourth Congress (March 4, 1875-March 3, 1877); unsuccessful candidate for reelection in 1876 to the Forty-fifth Congress; resumed the practice of law; city solicitor of Gloucester, Mass., in 1874, 1875, 1877, and 1879; unsuccessful Democratic candidate for Governor of Massachusetts in 1880 and again in 1881; served as judge of the superior court of Massachusetts from 1885 until his death in Gloucester, Mass., January 19, 1894; interment in Oak Grove Cemetery.

**THOMPSON, Charles Winston,** a Representative from Alabama; born near Tuskegee, Macon County, Ala., December 30, 1860; attended the common schools and Park High School in Tuskegee, Ala.; was graduated from Bryant and Stratton's Business College, Louisville, Ky., in 1878; engaged in mercantile pursuits; president of the Bank of Tuskegee, Ala.; county superintendent of education for Macon County, 1886-1888; appointed in 1896 lieutenant colonel on the staff of Governor Joseph F. Johnston and served in that capacity until the end of the Governor's term in 1900; member of the Alabama State senate in 1898; elected as a Democrat to the Fifty-seventh and Fifty-eighth Congresses and served from March 4, 1901, until his death in Washington, D.C., March 20, 1904; interment in the City Cemetery, Tuskegee, Ala.

**THOMPSON, Chester Charles,** a Representative from Illinois; born in Rock Island, Ill., September 19, 1893; attended the grade and high schools; engaged in the plastering contracting business from 1910 until 1932; during the First World War served as a corporal in Headquarters Company of the Twenty-fifth Coast Artillery in 1918 and 1919; treasurer of Rock Island County, Ill., 1922-1926; mayor of Rock Island, 1927-1933; member of the Democratic State central committee, 1930-1932; elected as a Democrat to the Seventy-third and to the two succeeding Congresses (March 4, 1933-January 3, 1939); unsuccessful candidate for reelection in 1938 to the Seventy-sixth Congress; appointed on November 15, 1939, as president and chairman of the board of the Inland Waterways Corporation, and served until his resignation on August 15, 1944; president of the American Waterways Operators, Inc., from August 1944 until his retirement in 1957; member and chairman, Jury Commission of Rock Island County, beginning in 1961; member and committee chairman, Board of Supervisors, Rock Island County, from 1965 until his death in Rock Island, Ill., January 30, 1971; interment in Chippiannock Cemetery.

**THOMPSON, Clark Wallace,** a Representative from Texas; born in La Crosse, Wis., August 6, 1896; moved to Oregon in 1901 with his parents, who settled in Cascade Locks; attended the common schools and the University of Oregon at Eugene; during the First World War enlisted as a private on May 25, 1917, in the United States Marine Corps; promoted to corporal on December 20, 1917, and served until honorably discharged on December 15, 1918; commissioned a second lieutenant in the Marine Corps Reserve on December 16, 1918; moved to Galveston, Tex., in 1919; engaged in the insurance business until 1920 and the retail dry goods business 1920-1931, when he was engaged as a public relations counsel; elected as a Democrat to the Seventy-third Congress to fill the vacancy caused by the death of Clay Stone Briggs, serving from June 24, 1933, to January 3, 1935; was not a candidate for renomination in 1934; resumed activities as a public relations counsel; delegate to the Texas State Democratic convention in 1936; organized the Fifteenth Battalion, Marine Corps Reserve, in Galveston County, Tex., in 1936 and was called to active duty on November 1, 1940; served as a lieutenant colonel with the Second Marine Division in the Pacific and later returned to Marine Headquarters to head Division of Reserve; promoted to colonel on October 18, 1942, and placed on the retired list on June 1, 1946; resumed his activities as a public relations counsel; elected to the Eightieth Congress to fill the vacancy caused by the death of Joseph J. Mansfield; reelected to the Eighty-first and to the eight succeeding Congresses and served from August 23, 1947, to January 3, 1967; was not a candidate for reelection in 1966 to the Ninetieth Congress; director, Washington, D.C., office, Tenneco, Inc., 1968-1974; resided in Galveston, Tex., until his death there on December 16, 1981; interment in Galveston Memorial Park Cemetery.

**THOMPSON, Fountain Land,** a Senator from North Dakota; born near Scottsville, Macoupin County, Ill., November 18, 1854; moved to Girard, Ill., in 1865; attended the public schools in Girard; studied law and was admitted to the bar, but did not engage in extensive practice; member of the board of supervisors of Macoupin County; engaged in mercantile pursuits; moved to Dakota Territory and settled on a farm near Cando, Towner County, in 1888; judge of Towner County Court 1890-1894; engaged in the real estate business and banking in Cando and also in agricultural pursuits; school director; member of the Cando Board of Aldermen; mayor of Cando; appointed as a Democrat to the United States Senate to fill the vacancy caused by the death of Martin N. Johnson and served from November 10, 1909, to January 31, 1910, when he resigned; resumed his former business activities in Cando, until his retirement in 1921; moved to Los Angeles, Calif., where he resided until his death on February 4, 1942; interment in Hollywood Cemetery.

**THOMPSON, Frank, Jr.,** a Representative from New Jersey; born in Trenton, Mercer County, N.J., July 26, 1918; attended parochial and public schools and Wake Forest (N.C.) College, 1941 and the Wake Forest Law School; served in the United States Navy, 1941-1948; received three combat decorations for action at Iwo Jima and Okinawa; commanded the United States Naval Reserve Battallion 4-22 and completed a seventeen-month tour of active duty, from August 1950 to January 1952, on the staff of the commander, Eastern Sea Frontier, and released from active duty

January 1, 1952; was admitted to the bar in 1948 and commenced the practice of law in Trenton, N.J.; member of the New Jersey State house of assembly, 1950-1954, serving as assistant minority leader in 1950 and minority leader in 1954; elected as a Democrat to the Eighty-fourth Congress; reelected to the twelve succeeding Congresses and served from January 3, 1955, until his resignation December 29, 1980; chairman, Joint Committee on Printing (Ninety-fourth and Ninety-sixth Congresses), Committee on House Administration (Ninety-fourth, Ninety-fifth, and Ninety-sixth Congresses); unsuccessful candidate for reelection in 1980 to the Ninety-seventh Congress; was a resident of Alexandria, Va.; died July 22, 1989.

**Bibliography:** Wilson, Augusta E. *Liberal Leader in the House: Frank Thompson, Jr.* Washington: Acropolis Books, 1968.

**THOMPSON, Fred Dalton,** a Senator from Tennessee; born in Sheffield, Colbert County, Ala., August 19, 1942; graduated, Lawrence County High School, Lawrenceburg, Tenn., 1960; B.S., Memphis State University, 1964; J.D., Vanderbilt University School of Law, 1967; shoe salesman; truck driver; factory worker; practiced law in Lawrenceburg, Tenn., Nashville, Tenn., and Washington, D.C.; assistant United States Attorney for Middle Tennessee, 1969; Middle Tennessee Campaign manager for Senator Howard Baker; special counsel, Senate Intelligence and Foreign Relations Committees; minority counsel, Senate Select Committee on Presidential Campaign Activities; actor; elected as a Republican to the United States Senate, November 8, 1994, for the remainder of term ending January 3, 1997, and took his seat December 9, 1994 to fill the vacancy caused by the resignation of Harlan Mathews; is a resident of Nashville, Tenn.

**THOMPSON, George Western,** a Representative from Virginia; born in St. Clairsville, Ohio, May 14, 1806; was graduated from Jefferson (now Washington and Jefferson) College, Pa., in 1824; studied law in Richmond, Va.; was admitted to the bar in 1826 and commenced practice in St. Clairsville, Ohio, in 1828; moved to western Virginia in 1837; appointed deputy postmaster at Wheeling in 1838; appointed to a commission to settle jurisdiction of the Ohio River between Virginia and Ohio; United States attorney for the western district of Virginia by appointment of President James K. Polk, 1848-1850; elected as a Democrat to the Thirty-second Congress and served from March 4, 1851, until his resignation on July 30, 1852; was elected judge of the circuit court of Virginia in 1852 and reelected in 1860; was removed from office in 1861 on refusal to take the oath of office to support what he believed unconstitutional action to set up the present State of West Virginia; retired from the practice of his profession and resided on his estate near Wheeling, Ohio County, W.Va., until his death on February 24, 1888; interment in Elm Grove Cemetery, Wheeling, W.Va.

**THOMPSON, Hedge,** a Representative from New Jersey; born in Salem, N.J., January 28, 1780; pursued an academic course; was graduated from the medical department of the University of Pennsylvania at Philadelphia in 1802 and practiced his profession in Salem; member of the General Assembly of New Jersey in 1805; served in the State council in 1819; appointed associate judge of Salem County, N.J., in 1815 and again in 1824; served as collector for Salem County from 1826 to 1828; elected to the Twentieth Congress and served from March 4, 1827, until his death in Salem, N.J., on July 23, 1828; interment in St. John's Protestant Episcopal Churchyard.

**THOMPSON, Jacob,** a Representative from Mississippi; born in Leasburg, Caswell County, N.C., May 15, 1810; attended the public schools and Bingham Academy in Orange County; was graduated from the University of North Carolina at Chapel Hill in 1831; member of the faculty of the University of North Carolina in 1831 and 1832; studied law; was admitted to the bar in 1834 and commenced practice in Pontotoc, Miss., in 1835; elected as a

Democrat to the Twenty-sixth and to the five succeeding Congresses (March 4, 1839-March 3, 1851); chairman, Committee on Indian Affairs (Twenty-ninth Congress); unsuccessful candidate for reelection in 1850 to the Thirty-second Congress; appointed to the United States Senate in 1845, but never received the commission; appointed Secretary of the Interior in the Cabinet of President James Buchanan, and served from March 6, 1857 to January 8, 1861, when he resigned; served as inspector general in the Confederate Army during the Civil War; confidential agent of the Confederacy to Canada in 1864 and 1865; settled in Memphis, Tenn., in 1868 and managed the affairs of his extensive holdings; died in Memphis, Tenn., March 24, 1885; interment in Elmwood Cemetery.

**Bibliography:** *DAB.*

**THOMPSON, James,** a Representative from Pennsylvania; born in Middlesex, Butler County, Pa., October 1, 1806; completed preparatory studies; learned the printer's trade; studied law; admitted to the bar in 1829 and commenced practice in Erie, Pa.; member of the Pennsylvania house of representatives 1832-1834 and in 1855 and served as speaker in 1834; delegate to the Pennsylvania constitutional convention in 1838; presiding judge of sixth judicial district court 1838-1844; elected as a Democrat to the Twenty-ninth, Thirtieth, and Thirty-first Congresses (March 4, 1845-March 3, 1851); chairman, Committee on the Judiciary (Thirty-second Congress); was not a candidate for renomination in 1850; resumed the practice of his profession; associate justice of the supreme court of Pennsylvania from 1857 to 1866, and served as chief justice of that court from 1866 to 1872; again engaged in the practice of law; died in Philadelphia, Pa., January 28, 1874; interment in Woodlands Cemetery.

**THOMPSON, Joel,** a Representative from New York; born in Stanford, Dutchess County, N.Y., October 3, 1760; attended the common schools in Smyrna, N.Y.; studied law; was admitted to the bar and practiced in Duanesburg, and Sherburne, N.Y.; served in the Revolutionary Army in 1779 and 1780; member of the State assembly in 1798, 1803, and 1804, serving one term as member from Albany County and two terms as member from Chenango County; assistant justice of the court of common pleas of Chenango County from July 1799 to June 1807, when he became judge of Chenango County, serving until March 16, 1814; elected as a Federalist to the Thirteenth Congress (March 4, 1813-March 3, 1815); resumed the practice of law in Sherburne, N.Y.; died in Brooklyn, N.Y., February 8, 1843; interment in Greenwood Cemetery.

**THOMPSON, John,** a Representative from New York; born in Litchfield, Conn., March 20, 1749; attended the common schools; at the age of fourteen moved with his parents to Stillwater, N.Y.; appointed justice of Stillwater Township in 1788; member of the New York State assembly in 1788 and 1789; elected as a Republican to the Sixth Congress (March 4, 1799-March 3, 1801); delegate to the New York State Constitutional Convention in 1801; was appointed by Governor George Clinton in 1791 as first judge of Saratoga County, and held this office until 1809; elected to the Tenth and Eleventh Congresses (March 4, 1807-March 3, 1811); died in Stillwater, Saratoga County, N.Y., in 1823; interment in a cemetery at Stillwater, N.Y.

**Bibliography:** *DAB.*

**THOMPSON, John,** a Representative from New York; born in Rhinebeck, Dutchess County, N.Y., July 4, 1809; was graduated from Union College, Schenectady, N.Y., and later from Yale College; studied law; was admitted to the bar and commenced practice in Poughkeepsie, N.Y.; elected as a Republican to the Thirty-fifth Congress (March 4, 1857-March 3, 1859); resumed the practice of law; died in New Hamburg, Dutchess County, N.Y., June 1, 1890; interment in Poughkeepsie Rural Cemetery, Poughkeepsie, N.Y.

**THOMPSON, John Burton,** a Representative and a Senator from Kentucky; born near Harrodsburg, Ky., December 14, 1810; completed preparatory studies; studied law; admitted to the bar and practiced in Harrodsburg, Ky.; Commonwealth attorney; member, Kentucky senate 1829-1833; member, Kentucky house of representatives 1835, 1837; elected as a Whig to the Twenty-sixth Congress to fill the vacancy caused by the death of Simeon H. Anderson; reelected to the Twenty-seventh Congress and served from December 7, 1840, to March 3, 1843; elected to the Thirtieth and Thirty-first Congresses (March 4, 1847-March 3, 1851); chairman, Committee on the Militia (Thirtieth Congress); lieutenant governor of Kentucky 1852; elected by the American party to the United States Senate and served from March 4, 1853, to March 3, 1859; died in Harrodsburg, Mercer County, Ky., January 7, 1874; interment in Spring Hill Cemetery.

**THOMPSON, John McCandless** (brother of William George Thompson), a Representative from Pennsylvania; born near Butler, Butler County, Pa., January 4, 1829; attended the common schools and Witherspoon Institute; studied law; admitted to the bar in 1854 and began practice in Butler, Pa.; member of the Pennsylvania house of representatives in 1859 and 1860, and served one year as speaker; entered the Union Army during the Civil War and served as major and subsequently as lieutenant colonel of the One Hundred and Thirty-fourth Regiment, Pennsylvania Volunteer Infantry; delegate to the Republican National Convention in 1868; elected as a Republican to the Forty-third Congress to fill the vacancy caused by the resignation of Ebenezer McJunkin and served from December 22, 1874, to March 3, 1875; elected to the Forty-fifth Congress (March 4, 1877-March 3, 1879); was not a candidate for renomination in 1878; resumed the practice of his profession; died in Butler, Pa., September 3, 1903; interment in Butler Cemetery.

**THOMPSON, Joseph Bryan,** a Representative from Oklahoma; born near Sherman, Grayson County, Tex., April 29, 1871; attended the public schools, and was graduated from Savoy College in Fannin County, Tex., in 1890; studied law; was admitted to the bar in 1892 and commenced practice in Purcell, Indian Territory; moved to Ardmore, Indian Territory; appointed commissioner for the United States court in 1893 and returned to Purcell, Indian Territory; resigned in 1897; moved to Pauls Valley and resumed the practice of law; delegate to the Democratic National Conventions in 1900, 1904, and 1908; member of the Democratic Territorial committee 1896-1904; chairman of the Democratic State committee in 1906 and 1908; served in the State senate 1910-1914; elected as a Democrat to the Sixty-third and to the three succeeding Congresses and served from March 4, 1913, until his death on a train near Martinsburg, W.Va., while en route to his home at Pauls Valley, Okla., September 18, 1919; interment in Mount Olivet Cemetery, Pauls Valley, Okla.

**THOMPSON, Philip,** a Representative from Kentucky; born on Shawnee Run, near Harrodsburg, Mercer County, Ky., August 20, 1789; received a limited education; served as a lieutenant in the War of 1812; held several local offices; studied law; admitted to the bar and commenced practice in Hartford, Ohio County, Ky.; moved to Owensboro, Daviess County, Ky.; member of the Kentucky house of representatives; elected to the Eighteenth Congress (March 4, 1823-March 3, 1825); resumed the practice of law in Owensburg, Ky., where he died November 25, 1836; interment in the Moseley burying ground on Firth Street; reinterment in Rural Hill (later Elmwood) Cemetery in 1856.

**THOMPSON, Philip Burton, Jr.,** a Representative from Kentucky; born in Harrodsburg, Mercer County, Ky., October 15, 1845; attended the common schools and the University of Kentucky at Lexington; during the Civil War entered the Confederate Army at the age of sixteen and served throughout the war; studied law; was admitted to the bar in 1866 and commenced practice in Harrodsburg; was city attorney of Harrodsburg 1867-1869; was appointed in 1869 and subsequently elected Commonwealth attorney for the thirteenth judicial district of Kentucky, serving until 1874; reelected in 1874 and served until 1878, when he resigned, having been elected to Congress; elected as a Democrat to the Forty-sixth, Forty-seventh, and Forty-eighth Congresses (March 4, 1879-March 3, 1885); chairman, Committee on Expenditures in the Department of War (Forty-eighth Congress); delegate to the Democratic National Convention in 1884; moved to New York City and resumed the practice of law; died in Washington, D.C., December 15, 1909; interment in Spring Hill Cemetery, Harrodsburg, Ky.

**THOMPSON, Philip Rootes,** a Representative from Virginia; born near Fredericksburg, Va., March 26, 1766; educated by private tutors; graduated from the College of William and Mary, Williamsburg, Va.; studied law; admitted to the bar and commenced practice in Fairfax, Va.; member of the Virginia house of delegates 1793-1797; elected as a Republican to the Seventh, Eighth, and Ninth Congresses (March 4, 1801-March 3, 1807); resumed the practice of law; died in Kanawha County, Va. (now West Virginia), July 27, 1837; interment at Coals Mouth (now St. Albans), W.Va.

**THOMPSON, Richard Wigginton,** a Representative from Indiana; born near Culpeper Court House, Culpeper County, Va., June 9, 1809; pursued classical studies; moved to Louisville, Ky., in 1831; clerked in a store; moved to Lawrence County, Ind., in 1831; taught school; studied law; was admitted to the bar in 1834 and began practice in Bedford, Lawrence County, Ind.; member of the Indiana State house of representatives, 1834-1836; served in the Indiana State senate, 1836-1838, and for a short time as president pro tempore; elected as a Whig to the Twenty-seventh Congress (March 4, 1841-March 3, 1843); was not a candidate for renomination in 1842 to the Twenty-eighth Congress; moved to Terre Haute, Ind., in 1843; city attorney in 1846 and 1847; elected as a Whig to the Thirtieth Congress (March 4, 1847-March 3, 1849); chairman, Committee on Elections (Thirtieth Congress); declined to be a candidate for renomination in 1848 to the Thirty-first Congress; commander of Camp Thompson, Ind., and provost marshal, 1861-1865; appointed by President Abraham Lincoln collector of internal revenue for the seventh district of Indiana and served one term; delegate to the Republican National Conventions of 1868 and 1876; judge of the fifth Indiana circuit court, 1867-1869; appointed Secretary of the Navy in the Cabinet of President Rutherford B. Hayes, and served from March 13, 1877 until his resignation on December 20, 1880; chairman of the American Committee of the Panama Canal Co. in 1881; director of the Panama Railroad Co., 1881-1888; died in Terre Haute, Ind., February 9, 1900; interment in High Lawn Cemetery.

**Bibliography:** *DAB*; Neely, Mark E. "Richard W. Thompson: The Persistent Know Nothing." *Indiana Magazine of History* 72 (June 1976): 95-122; Roll, Charles. *Colonel Dick Thompson: The Persistent Whig*. Indianapolis: Indiana Historical Bureau, 1948.

**THOMPSON, Robert Augustine** (father of Thomas Larkin Thompson), a Representative from Virginia; born near Culpeper Court House, Culpeper County, Va., February 14, 1805; attended a private school at Gallipolis, Ohio, and the University of Virginia at Charlottesville, Va.; studied law; was admitted to the bar in 1826 and commenced practice in Charleston, Kanawha County, Va. (now West Virginia); member of the Virginia senate, 1839-1846; elected as a Democrat to the Thirtieth Congress (March 4, 1847-March 3, 1849); declined to be a candidate for reelection in 1848 to the Thirty-first Congress; delegate to the Democratic National Convention of 1852; member of the board of visitors to the University of Virginia in 1852; moved to San Francisco, Calif., in 1853; appointed in 1853 a member of a commission to settle private land claims in California; appointed by Governor Henry H. Haight as a reporter of

the California Supreme Court in 1870; member of the justices' court of San Francisco from 1870 until his death in San Francisco, Calif., on August 31, 1876; interment in Laurel Hill Cemetery.

**THOMPSON, Ruth,** a Representative from Michigan; born in Whitehall, Muskegon County, Mich., September 15, 1887; attended the public schools; graduated from Muskegon Business College in 1905; studied law while employed in a law office 1918-1924; was admitted to the bar; registrar of probate court of Muskegon County for eighteen years; judge of probate, Muskegon County, 1925-1937; member of the State house of representatives 1939-1941; with Social Security Board, Washington, D.C., in 1941 and 1942, Labor Department in 1942, Adjutant General's Office 1942-1945; Headquarters Command, Frankfurt, Germany, and Copenhagen, Denmark, in 1945 and 1946; member and chairman State Prison Commission for Women for four years; private practice of law in Michigan; elected as a Republican to the Eighty-second, Eighty-third, and Eighty-fourth Congresses (January 3, 1951-January 3, 1957); unsuccessful candidate for renomination in 1956 to the Eighty-fifth Congress; returned to Whitehall, Mich.; from 1965 to 1970, a patient at Plainwell Sanitorium, Allegan County, where she died April 5, 1970; interment in Oakhurst Cemetery, Whitehall, Mich.

**THOMPSON, Standish Fletcher,** a Representative from Georgia; born in College Park, Fulton County, Ga., February 5, 1925; attended the public schools and Russell High School in East Point, Ga., graduated from Emory University in 1949 and from Woodrow Wilson College of Law in 1957; was admitted to the bar in 1958 and commenced the practice of law in East Point, Ga.; president of an insurance firm; served in the United States Army Medical Corps in 1943; served as navigator with the Air Rescue Service in the United States Army Air Corps, 1944-1946; during the Korean conflict, 1950-1953, served as pilot with the United States Air Force; elected to the Georgia general assembly as State senator from the thirty-fourth senatorial district in 1964; elected as a Republican to the Ninetieth and to the two succeeding Congresses (January 3, 1967-January 3, 1973); was not a candidate in 1972 for reelection to the United States House of Representatives but was an unsuccessful candidate for election to the United States Senate; resumed the practice of law in Atlanta; owns and operates a trucking company; member, Atlanta Regional Commission, 1985; is a resident of Marietta, Ga.

**THOMPSON, Theo Ashton,** a Representative from Louisiana; born in Ville Platte, Evangeline Parish, La., March 31, 1916; attended the public schools and the Louisiana State University 1932-1934, completing course in higher accounting; traveling auditor for State highway commission 1934-1940; transferred to State reorganization plan; Louisiana representative at the national assembly of the States in the development of the civil defense program in Chicago, Ill., in 1942; served in the United States Army Air Force 1942-1946; served as State budget officer and financial adviser to the Louisiana Legislature, 1948-1952; chairman of the board of trustees of the State employees retirement system 1947-1953; represented the United States Department of State in Louisiana in training foreign representatives in principles of democracy in 1950 and 1951; elected as a Democrat to the Eighty-third and to the six succeeding Congresses and served from January 3, 1953, until his death July 1, 1965, in an automobile accident in Gastonia, N.C.; interment in Evangeline Memorial Park Cemetery, Ville Platte, La.

**THOMPSON, Thomas Larkin** (son of Robert Augustine Thompson), a Representative from California; born in Charleston, Va. (now West Virginia), May 31, 1838; attended the common schools and Buffalo Academy, Virginia (now West Virginia); moved to California in 1855 and settled in Sonoma County; established the Petaluma Journal the same year; purchased the Sonoma Democrat in 1860, and was the editor of that paper; delegate to the Democratic National Conventions of 1880 and 1892; secretary of state of California, 1882-1886; declined to be a candidate for renomination; elected as a Democrat to the Fiftieth Congress (March 4, 1887-March 3, 1889); unsuccessful candidate for reelection in 1888 to the Fifty-first Congress; appointed on April 4, 1891, commissioner from California to the World's Fair at Chicago; appointed Minister to Brazil on April 24, 1893 and served until July 1897; died in Santa Rosa, Sonoma County, Calif., February 1, 1898; interment in the Rural Cemetery.

**Bibliography:** *DAB.*

**THOMPSON, Thomas Weston,** a Representative and a Senator from New Hampshire; born in Boston, Mass., March 15, 1766; attended Dummer Academy, Byfield, Mass.; graduated from Harvard University in 1786; studied law; was admitted to the bar in 1791 and practiced in Salisbury, N.H., 1791-1810; postmaster of Salisbury, N.H., 1798-1803; trustee of Dartmouth College, Hanover, N.H., 1801-1821; moved to Concord, N.H., in 1810 and continued the practice of law; member, State house of representatives 1807-1808, 1813-1814, and served as speaker 1813-1814; elected as a Federalist to the Ninth Congress (March 4, 1805-March 3, 1807); State treasurer of New Hampshire 1809-1811; elected to the United States Senate to fill the vacancy caused by the death of Nicholas Gilman and served from June 24, 1814, to March 3, 1817; died in Concord, N.H., on October 1, 1821; interment in the Old North Cemetery.

**THOMPSON, Waddy, Jr.,** a Representative from South Carolina; born in Pickensville (now Pickens), Ninety-sixth District, S.C., January 8, 1798; moved to Greenville with his parents in his infancy; received his early education in neighboring schools, and was graduated from South Carolina College (now the University of South Carolina), at Columbia in 1814; studied law; was admitted to the bar in 1819 and began practice in Edgefield, S.C.; moved to Greenville, S.C., and continued the practice of law; member of the South Carolina State house of representatives, 1826-1829; elected solicitor of the western circuit in 1830; brigadier general of militia in 1832; elected as an Anti-Jacksonian to the Twenty-fourth Congress to fill the vacancy caused by the death of Warren R. Davis; reelected as a Whig to the Twenty-fifth and Twenty-sixth Congresses, and served from September 10, 1835 to March 3, 1841; chairman, Committee on Military Affairs (Twenty-sixth Congress); was not a candidate for renomination in 1840 to the Twenty-seventh Congress; appointed Envoy Extraordinary and Minister Plenipotentiary to Mexico on February 10, 1842, and served until March 1844; moved to Madison, Fla., and engaged in cotton planting; appointed solicitor general of a circuit in 1868; died while on a visit to Tallahassee, Fla., November 23, 1868; interment in the Episcopal Cemetery.

**Bibliography:** *DAB.*

**THOMPSON, Wiley,** a Representative from Georgia; born in Amelia County, Va., September 23, 1781; moved to Elberton, Elbert County, Ga.; served as a commissioner of the Elbert County Academy in 1808; served in the State senate 1817-1819; was appointed major general of the Fourth Division of the Georgia Militia in November 1817 and served until November 1824, when he resigned; elected to the Seventeenth through Nineteenth Congresses and elected as a Jacksonian to the Twentieth through Twenty-second Congresses (March 4, 1821-March 3, 1833); was a delegate to the State constitutional convention in 1833; agent to Seminole Indians; appointed in 1834 to superintend the removal of Seminoles from Florida; killed by a band of Seminoles led by Osceola at Fort King, Fla., on December 28, 1835; interment in the private burial ground on his estate at Elberton, Ga.

**Bibliography:** *DAB.*

**THOMPSON, William,** a Representative from Iowa; born in Fayette County, Pa., November 10, 1813; attended the common schools; moved to Iowa and settled in Mount Pleasant; member of the Territorial house of representatives in 1843; secretary of the State constitutional convention in 1846; elected as a Democrat to the Thirtieth Congress (March 4, 1847-March 3, 1849); presented credentials as a Member-elect to the Thirty-first Congress and served from March 4, 1849, to June 29, 1850, when the seat was declared vacant; chairman, Committee on Expenditures in the Post Office Department (Thirty-first Congress); served in the Union Army during the Civil War; commissioned captain in the First Iowa Volunteer Cavalry on July 31, 1861; promoted to major on May 18, 1863, and colonel on June 20, 1864; brevetted brigadier general of Volunteers on March 13, 1865, recommissioned captain in the Seventh Cavalry, Regular Army, on July 28, 1866, and retired from the Army on December 15, 1875; editor of the Iowa State Gazette; died in Tacoma, Pierce County, Wash., on October 6, 1897; interment in Tacoma Cemetery.

**Bibliography:** Schmidt, Louis B. "The Miller-Thompson Election Contest." *Iowa Journal of History* 12 (January 1914): 34-127.

**THOMPSON, William George** (brother of John McCandless Thompson), a Representative from Iowa; born near Butler, Butler County, Pa., January 17, 1830; attended the common schools and the Witherspoon Institute in Butler, Pa.; studied law and was admitted to the bar in 1853; moved to Iowa the same year and settled in Marion, Linn County, where he commenced the practice of law; prosecuting attorney of Linn County 1854-1856; member of the State senate 1856-1860; served during the Civil War as major of the Twentieth Regiment, Iowa Volunteer Infantry, in 1862; district attorney for the eighth judicial district for six years; appointed chief justice of the Territory of Idaho and served from January 13, 1879, until his resignation in April of that year; elected as a Republican to the Forty-sixth Congress to fill the vacancy caused by the death of Rush Clark; reelected to the Forty-seventh Congress and served from October 14, 1879, to March 3, 1883; declined to be a candidate for renomination in 1882; served on the city council of Marion; member of the State house of representatives 1885-1887; judge of the eighteenth judicial district of Iowa 1894-1906; moved to Kenwood Park, Linn County, Iowa, in 1896 and died there April 2, 1911; interment in Oak Shade Cemetery, Marion, Iowa.

**THOMPSON, William Henry,** a Senator from Nebraska; born in Perrysville, Ashland County, Ohio, December 14, 1853; attended the common schools and received private instruction; attended Upper Iowa University at Fayette, 1872-1875, and graduated from the law department of the State University of Iowa at Iowa City in 1877; was admitted to the bar the same year and commenced practice at Brush Creek (now Arlington), Iowa; moved to Grand Island, Hall County, Nebr., in 1881 and continued the practice of law; also interested in banking; city attorney of Grand Island, 1887-1888; unsuccessful candidate for election in 1890 to the Fifty-second Congress; member of the board of trustees of Grand Island College in 1893; mayor of Grand Island, 1895-1898; member of the Democratic National Committee, 1896-1900, and 1920-1924; unsuccessful candidate for governor of Nebraska in 1902; member of the State commission for construction of a new capitol; judge of the supreme court of Nebraska, 1924-1931; appointed as a Democrat to the United States Senate to fill the vacancy caused by the death of Robert B. Howell, and served from May 24, 1933 to November 6, 1934, when a successor was elected; was not a candidate for election to this vacancy; retired to private life; died in Grand Island, Nebr., June 6, 1937; interment in Grand Island Cemetery.

**THOMPSON, William Howard,** a Senator from Kansas; born in Crawfordsville, Montgomery County, Ind., October 14, 1871; moved with his parents to Nemaha County, Kans., in 1880; attended the public schools; graduated from the Seneca Normal School in

1886 and from the Lawrence Business College in 1891; official court reporter of the twenty-second judicial district of Kansas 1891-1894; studied law; was admitted to the bar in 1894 and commenced practice in Seneca; clerk of the Kansas Court of Appeals in Topeka and practiced law 1897-1901; moved to Iola, Kans., in 1901 and continued the practice of law; county attorney of Allen County; moved to Garden City in 1905; judge of the thirty-second judicial district of Kansas 1906-1913, when he resigned, having been elected Senator; elected as a Democrat to the United States Senate in 1912 and served from March 4, 1913, to March 3, 1919; unsuccessful candidate for reelection to the United States Senate in 1918; chairman, Committee on Expenditures in the Departments of Commerce and Labor (Sixty-third Congress), Committee on Expenditures in the Department of Commerce (Sixty-third and Sixty-fourth Congresses), Committee to Audit and Control the Contingent Expense (Sixty-fifth Congress); resumed the practice of law at Kansas City, Kans., in 1919; moved to Tulsa, Okla., in 1923 and practiced law in Kansas City and Tulsa; moved to Washington, D.C., in 1927, where he continued the practice of law, and died there on February 9, 1928; interment in Glenwood Cemetery.

**THOMSON, Alexander,** a Representative from Pennsylvania; born in Franklin County, Pa., January 12, 1788; apprenticed as a sickle maker; moved to Bedford, Pa.; received a limited schooling; studied law; admitted to the bar in 1816 and commenced practice in Chambersburg, Franklin County, Pa.; held several local offices; member of the Pennsylvania house of representatives; elected to the Eighteenth Congress to fill the vacancy caused by the resignation of John Tod; reelected to the Nineteenth Congress and served from December 6, 1824, to May 1, 1826, when he resigned; mayor of Lancaster, Pa.; president judge of the sixteenth judicial district of Pennsylvania 1827-1841; professor in the law school of Marshall College, Lancaster, Pa.; died in Chambersburg, Pa., August 2, 1848; interment in Falling Spring Presbyterian Cemetery.

**THOMSON, Charles Marsh,** a Representative from Illinois; born in Chicago, Ill., February 13, 1877; attended the public schools and the Chicago Manual Training School; was graduated from Washington and Jefferson College, Washington, Pa., in 1899 and from the Northwestern University Law School, Evanston, Ill., in 1902; was admitted to the bar in the latter year and commenced practice in Chicago, Ill.; elected a member of the city council in 1908, 1910, and again in 1912; elected as a Progressive to the Sixty-third Congress (March 4, 1913-March 3, 1915); unsuccessful candidate for reelection in 1914 to the Sixty-fourth Congress; elected judge of the circuit court of Cook County in 1915; reelected in 1921; appointed justice of the Appellate Court of Illinois in 1917; reappointed in 1921 and served until June 1927; resumed the practice of his profession in Chicago; trustee of the Chicago and Eastern Illinois Railroad Company from 1933 to 1939, when he was appointed trustee of the Chicago and North Western Railroad, in which capacity he served until his death in Chicago, Ill., December 30, 1943; interment in Rosehill Cemetery.

**THOMSON, Edwin Keith,** a Representative from Wyoming; born in New Castle, Weston County, Wyo., February 8, 1919; attended the public schools in Beulah, Wyo., and Spearfish, S.Dak.; was graduated from the University of Wyoming Law School in 1941; called to active duty on March 24, 1941; commanded Second Battalion, Three Hundred and Sixty-second Infantry Regiment, Ninety-first Division; released from active duty as a lieutenant colonel on January 24, 1946; was admitted to the bar in 1941 and commenced the practice of law in Cheyenne, Wyo., in February 1946; delegate to the Republican National Convention in 1952; member of the State house of representatives 1952-1954; elected as a Republican to the Eighty-fourth, Eighty-fifth, and Eighty-sixth Congresses and served from January 3, 1955, until his death; did not seek renomination to the Eighty-seventh Congress but was

elected to the United States Senate on November 8, 1960, for the term commencing January 3, 1961; died in Cody, Wyo., December 9, 1960; interment in Arlington National Cemetery, Va.

**THOMSON, John,** a Representative from Ohio; born in Ireland, November 20, 1780; immigrated with his parents to the United States in 1787; completed preparatory studies; studied medicine, and in 1806 moved to New Lisbon, Ohio, and practiced; served in the State senate in 1814, 1815, and 1817-1820; member of the State house of representatives in 1816; elected to the Nineteenth Congress (March 4, 1825-March 3, 1827); unsuccessful candidate for reelection in 1826 to the Twentieth Congress; elected as a Jacksonian to the Twenty-first and to the three succeeding Congresses (March 4, 1829-March 3, 1837); was not a candidate for renomination in 1836; resumed the practice of medicine; died in New Lisbon (now Lisbon), Columbiana County, Ohio, December 2, 1852; interment in New Lisbon Cemetery.

**THOMSON, John Renshaw,** a Senator from New Jersey; born in Philadelphia, Pa., September 25, 1800; attended the common schools in Princeton, N.J., and the College of New Jersey (now Princeton University); went to China in 1817 and became a merchant in Canton; United States consul at the port of Canton, 1823-1825; returned to the United States and settled in Princeton, N.J.; director and secretary of the Delaware and Raritan Canal Company; connected with the Philadelphia and Trenton Railroad Company as president and later as treasurer; member of the State constitutional convention in 1844; unsuccessful Democratic candidate for governor of New Jersey in 1844; elected as a Democrat to the United States Senate to fill the vacancy caused by the resignation of Robert F. Stockton; reelected in 1857, and served from March 4, 1853 until his death in Princeton, N.J., September 12, 1862; chairman, Committee on Patents and the Patent Office (Thirty-sixth Congress), Committee on Pensions (Thirty-sixth Congress); interment in the Princeton Cemetery.

**THOMSON, Mark,** a Representative from New Jersey; born in Norriton Township, near Norristown, Montgomery County, Pa., in 1739; engaged in milling; was justice of the peace of Sussex County in 1773; member of the provincial convention in 1774 and of the Provincial Congress in 1775; was commissioned lieutenant colonel of the First Regiment, Sussex County (N.J.) Militia, July 22, 1775; lieutenant colonel in Colonel Charles Stewart's Battalion of Minutemen, February 15, 1776; colonel of the First Regiment, Sussex County Militia, July 10, 1776; colonel of the Battalion of Detached New Jersey Militia, July 18, 1776; member of the New Jersey State general assembly in 1779; served in the State council, 1786-1788; appointed lieutenant colonel and aide-de-camp on the staff of Governor Richard Howell, of New Jersey, June 10, 1793; elected as a Federalist to the Fourth and Fifth Congresses (March 4, 1795-March 3, 1799); died in Marksboro, Sussex (later Warren) County, N.J., December 14, 1803; interment in the Presbyterian Church Cemetery.

**THOMSON, Vernon Wallace,** a Representative from Wisconsin; born in Richland Center, Richland County, Wis., November 5, 1905; graduated from Richland Center High School in 1923; attended Carroll College in Waukesha, Wis., 1923-1925; graduated from University of Wisconsin in 1927; taught at Viroqua High School, 1927-1929; graduated from the University of Wisconsin Law School in 1932; engaged in the private practice of law, Richland Center, Wis., 1932-1951; assistant district attorney of Richland County, 1933-1935, and city attorney, 1933-1937, and 1942-1944; mayor of Richland Center from April 1944 to February 1951; member of the Wisconsin State assembly, 1935-1951, serving as speaker, 1939-1945, and as Republican floor leader, 1945-1951; State attorney general, 1951-1957; elected Governor of Wisconsin in 1956, and served from January 7, 1957 to January 5, 1959; unsuccessful candidate for reelection in 1958; delegate to the

Republican National Conventions of 1936, 1940, 1952 and 1956; elected as a Republican to the Eighty-seventh and to the six succeeding Congresses, and served from January 3, 1961 until his resignation on December 31, 1974; unsuccessful candidate for reelection in 1974 to the Ninety-fourth Congress; member, Federal Election Commission, April 1975 to June 1979, and January to December 1981; was a resident of McLean, Va. until his death in Washington, D.C., on April 2, 1988; interment in Richland Center Cemetery, Richland Center, Wis.

**THONE, Charles,** a Representative from Nebraska; born in Hartington, Cedar County, Nebr., January 4, 1924; J.D., University of Nebraska Law School, Lincoln, 1950; admitted to the Nebraska bar in 1950 and commenced practice in Lincoln; president, Nebraska Junior Chamber of Commerce, 1952; Infantry noncommissioned officer and officer during the Second World War; administrative assistant to Senator Roman L. Hruska of Nebraska, 1954-1959; chairman, Lincoln Human Rights Commission, 1966-1969; chairman of the Nebraska Republican Party, 1959-1962; delegate at large to the Republican National Conventions of 1952, 1956, 1972, 1976, 1980, 1984, 1988, and 1992; elected as a Republican to the Ninety-second and to the three succeeding Congresses (January 3, 1971-January 3, 1979); was not a candidate for reelection in 1978 to the Ninety-sixth Congress, but was elected Governor of Nebraska, and served from January 4, 1979 to January 6, 1983; was an unsuccessful candidate for reelection in 1982; president-elect, Nebraska State Bar Foundation, and district governor of Rotary International; is a resident of Lincoln, Nebr.

**THORINGTON, James,** a Representative from Iowa; born in Wilmington, N.C., May 7, 1816; moved with his parents to Montgomery, Ala., in 1827; attended the common schools, the military school in Fayetteville, N.C., 1830-1832, and the University of Alabama at Tuscaloosa 1832-1835; studied law in Montgomery, Ala.; engaged in trading and trapping on the upper Missouri and Columbia Rivers 1837-1839; moved to Davenport, Iowa, in 1839; was admitted to the bar in 1844 and commenced practice in Davenport; mayor of Davenport 1843-1847; probate judge of Scott County 1843-1851; clerk of the district court of Scott County 1846-1854; elected as a Whig to the Thirty-fourth Congress (March 4, 1855-March 3, 1857); was not a candidate for renomination in 1856; affiliated with the Republican Party; sheriff of Scott County 1859-1863; recorder 1864-1868; was appointed consul at Aspinwall, Colombia, January 21, 1873; appointed commercial agent at the same city May 27, 1873, and served in both positions until October 21, 1882; died while on a visit to his daughter at Santa Fe, N.Mex., June 13, 1887; interment in Oakdale Cemetery, Davenport, Iowa.

**THORKELSON, Jacob,** a Representative from Montana; born in Egersund, Norway, September 24, 1876; attended elementary schools; immigrated to the United States in 1892 and studied navigation; engaged as a navigator in 1896 and served as master of ocean-going ships 1900-1907; served with the Virginia Naval Reserve 1897-1899; was graduated from the College of Physicians and Surgeons, University of Maryland, at Baltimore in 1911, and served as a member of the faculty 1911-1913; moved to Dillon, Beaverhead County, Mont., in 1913, to Warmsprings, Deer Lodge County, Mont., in 1915, and to Butte, Silver Bow County, Mont., in 1920, and practiced medicine and surgery; served in the United States Naval Reserve 1936-1939 with rank of lieutenant commander; elected as a Republican to the Seventy-sixth Congress (January 3, 1939-January 3, 1941); unsuccessful candidate for renomination in 1940; resumed the practice of medicine and surgery; unsuccessful candidate for the Republican nomination for United States Senator in 1942 and for Governor in 1944; died in Butte, Mont., November 20, 1945; interment in Holy Cross Cemetery.

**THORNBERRY, William Homer,** a Representative from Texas; born in Austin, Travis County, Tex., January 9, 1909; attended the public schools; served as a page in the Texas legislature, 1923; graduated from Austin High School in 1927; B.B.A., University of Texas, 1932; LL.B., University of Texas School of Law, 1936; was admitted to the bar in 1936 and commenced the practice of law in Austin, Tex. until 1941; member of the Texas State house of representatives, 1937-1941; district attorney of the fifty-third judicial district of Texas (Travis County) from 1941 until his resignation in 1942 to serve in the United States Navy; served in the United States Navy from July 1942 until discharged as a lieutenant commander in February 1946; member of the Austin City Council, 1946-1948, serving as mayor pro tempore in 1947 and 1948; delegate at large to the Democratic National Conventions of 1956 and 1960; elected as a Democrat to the Eighty-first and to the seven succeeding Congresses and served from January 3, 1949, until his resignation December 20, 1963; sworn in as United States district judge for the western district of Texas on December 21, 1963, serving until he was sworn in as United States circuit judge of the United States Court of Appeals of the Fifth Judicial Circuit on July 3, 1965; took senior status December 21, 1978; nominated to the United States Supreme Court on June 26, 1968, but the nomination was withdrawn at his request when a vacancy in the position to which he was nominated failed to occur; was a resident of Austin, Tex., until his death there on December 12, 1995; interment in Texas State Cemetery.

**THORNBERRY, William McClellan (Mac),** a Representative from Texas; born in Clarendon, Donley County, Tex., July 15, 1958; attended the public schools and graduated, Clarendon High School; B.A., Texas Tech University, Lubbock, 1980; J.D., University of Texas School of Law, 1983; legislative counsel to Representative Thomas G. Loeffler, 1983-1985; chief of staff to Representative Larry Combest, 1985-1988; Deputy Assistant Secretary of State for Legislative Affairs, Department of State, 1988-1989; entered the family ranching business in Donley County, 1989-present; commenced the practice of law in Amarillo; member, Texas State Republican Executive committee, 1990, 1993; elected as a Republican to the One Hundred Fourth Congress (January 3, 1995-January 3, 1997); is a resident of Amarillo, Tex.

**THORNBURGH, Jacob Montgomery,** a Representative from Tennessee; born in New Market, Jefferson County, Tenn., July 3, 1837; completed preparatory studies; studied law; was admitted to the bar in 1861 and commenced practice in Jefferson County; during the Civil War entered the Union Army as a private and was promoted to lieutenant colonel of the Fourth Regiment, Tennessee Volunteer Cavalry, July 11, 1863; returned to Jefferson County, Tenn., and practiced law; moved to Knoxville, Tenn., in 1867; appointed attorney general of the third judicial circuit of Tennessee in 1866, and elected in 1868 and 1870; United States commissioner at the International Exposition held at Vienna, Austria, in 1872; elected as a Republican to the Forty-third, Forty-fourth, and Forty-fifth Congresses (March 4, 1873-March 3, 1879); was not a candidate for renomination in 1878; delegate to the Republican National Conventions in 1872, 1876, and 1880; retired from public life and resumed the practice of law in Knoxville, Tenn., where he died September 19, 1890; interment in the Old Gray Cemetery.

**THORNTON, Anthony,** a Representative from Illinois; born near Paris, Bourbon County, Ky., November 9, 1814; attended the common schools and Centre College, Danville, Ky.; was graduated from Miami University, Ohio, in 1834; studied law; was admitted to the bar and commenced practice in Shelbyville, Ill., in 1836; major of militia during the war with Mexico; delegate to the State constitutional conventions in 1847 and 1862; member of the State house of representatives in 1850; elected as a Democrat to the Thirty-ninth Congress (March 4, 1865-March 3, 1867); was not a candidate for renomination in 1866; resumed the practice of law; justice of the supreme court of Illinois from 1870 to 1873, when he resigned; president of the State bar association for four terms; chairman of the State board of arbitration 1895-1897; died in Shelbyville, Shelby County, Ill., on September 10, 1904; interment in Glenwood Cemetery.

**THORNTON, John Randolph,** a Senator from Louisiana; born on Notoway plantation, near Bayou Goula, Iberville Parish, La., August 25, 1846; moved with his parents to Rapides Parish, La., in 1853; attended Parker Seminary, Pineville, La., the McGruder Institute, Baton Rouge, La., and the Louisiana Seminary (afterwards the State university) at Pineville until 1863; enlisted in the Confederate Army and served until the close of the Civil War in Company B, Second Louisiana Cavalry; engaged in agricultural pursuits until 1877; studied law; was admitted to the bar in 1877 and commenced practice in Rapides Parish; judge of Rapides Parish 1878-1880; delegate to the State constitutional convention in 1898; member of the board of supervisors of the State university 1904-1910; appointed as a Democrat to the United States Senate on August 27, 1910, and subsequently elected to fill the vacancy caused by the death of Samuel D. McEnery and served from December 7, 1910, to March 3, 1915; was not a candidate for reelection to the Senate; chairman, Committee on Fisheries (Sixty-third Congress); appointed by President Woodrow Wilson a member of the Board of Ordnance and Fortification and served from 1915 to 1917; resumed the practice of law in Alexandria, Rapides Parish, La., and died there December 28, 1917; interment in Rapides Cemetery, Pineville, La.

**THORNTON, Matthew,** a Delegate from New Hampshire; born in Ireland in 1714; immigrated to the United States in 1716 with his father, who settled in Wiscasset, Maine; moved to Worcester, Mass.; completed preparatory studies; studied medicine and commenced practice in Londonderry, N.H., in 1740; surgeon of New Hampshire troops in the expedition against Cape Breton; member of the New Hampshire Assembly when it was organized in 1758 and again in 1760 and 1761; justice of the peace; delegate to the first Provincial Congress in 1775 and served as its president; chairman of the committee of safety in 1775; speaker of the general assembly from January 5 to September 12, 1776; colonel of the State militia during the Revolutionary War; Member of the Continental Congress in 1776 and 1777; a signer of the Declaration of Independence; chief justice of the court of common pleas; judge of the superior court of New Hampshire 1776-1782; moved to Exeter, N.H., in 1779; member of the general assembly in 1783; served in the State senate in 1784; State councilor in 1785; moved to Merrimack, N.H., in 1789, where he purchased a farm and spent his remaining years in literary pursuits; died in Newburyport, Mass., June 24, 1803; interment in Thornton's Ferry Cemetery, Merrimack, N.H.

**Bibliography:** *DAB.*

**THORNTON, Raymond Hoyt, Jr. (Ray),** a Representative from Arkansas; born in Conway, Faulkner County, Ark., July 16, 1928; attended public schools at Leola and Sheridan, Grant County, Ark.; attended the University of Arkansas, 1945-1947; B.A., Yale University, 1950; attended law school at the University of Texas, 1950-1951; J.D., University of Arkansas, 1956; served in the United States Navy during the Korean conflict, 1951-1954, attained the rank of lieutenant; admitted to the Arkansas bar in 1956 and commenced practice in Sheridan and Little Rock; served as deputy prosecuting attorney, Pulaski and Perry Counties, 1956-1957; delegate from Grant and Jefferson Counties to the Seventh Constitutional Convention of Arkansas, 1969-1970; attorney general of Arkansas, 1971-1973; elected as a Democrat to the Ninety-third, Ninety-fourth and Ninety-fifth Congresses (January 3, 1973-January 3, 1979); was not a candidate in 1978 for reelection to the United States House of Representatives but was an unsuccessful

candidate for nomination to the United States Senate; director, Ouachita Baptist University-Henderson State University Joint Educational Consortium, 1979-1980; president, Arkansas State University, 1980-1984; president, University of Arkansas, 1984-1990; elected to the One Hundred Second and to the two succeeding Congresses (January 3, 1991-January 3, 1997); was not a candidate for reelection in 1996 to the One Hundred Fifth Congress; candidate in 1996 for election to the Arkansas State supreme court; is a resident of Little Rock, Ark.

**THORP, Robert Taylor,** a Representative from Virginia; born near Oxford, Granville County, N.C., March 12, 1850; attended Horner Academy, Oxford, N.C., and was graduated from the law department of the University of Virginia at Charlottesville in 1870; was admitted to the bar in 1870 and commenced practice in Boydton, Mecklenburg County, Va., in 1871; Commonwealth attorney for that county 1877-1895; successfully contested as a Republican the election of William R. McKenney to the Fifty-fourth Congress and served from May 2, 1896, to March 3, 1897; successfully contested the election of Sydney P. Epes to the Fifty-fifth Congress and served from March 23, 1898, to March 4, 1899; unsuccessful candidate for reelection in 1898 to the Fifty-sixth Congress; moved to Norfolk, Va., and continued the practice of law; moved to Virginia Beach, Va., in 1934 and died November 26, 1938; interment in Forest Lawn Cemetery, Norfolk, Va.

**THORPE, Roy Henry,** a Representative from Nebraska; born near Greensburg, Decatur County, Ind., December 13, 1874; attended the country schools and Greensburg (Ind.) High School; studied pharmacy, medicine, and law; engaged in evangelistic work and was known as "The boy tramp orator of 1896"; was employed as a salesman in Du Quoin, Ill., 1897-1904, and in Shenandoah, Iowa, 1905-1919; engaged in secret-service work in the State of Iowa in 1917 and 1918; moved to Nebraska in 1919 and settled in Lincoln, where he resumed the occupation of salesman; elected as a Republican to the Sixty-seventh Congress to fill the vacancy caused by the resignation of C. Frank Reavis and served from November 7, 1922, to March 3, 1923; was not a candidate for renomination to the Sixty-eighth Congress; unsuccessful candidate for election in 1924 to the Sixty-ninth Congress; traveled as a sales organizer and later engaged in the insurance business; died in Lincoln, Nebr., September 19, 1951; interment in Wyuka Cemetery.

**THROCKMORTON, James Webb,** a Representative from Texas; born in Sparta, White County, Tenn., on February 1, 1825; attended the common schools; moved with his father to Collin County, Tex., in 1841; studied medicine in Princeton, Ky., and practiced in Collin County; served as surgeon during the Mexican War; studied law; was admitted to the bar and commenced practice in McKinney, Collin County, Tex.; member of the Texas State house of representatives, 1851-1856; served in the Texas State senate, 1856-1861; member of the secession convention of Texas in 1861; during the Civil War served as captain and major in the Confederate Army from the spring of 1861 until November 1863; brigadier general of State troops in 1864 and commander on the northwest border of the State; again a member of the State senate in 1865; delegate to the reconstruction convention under President Andrew Johnson's proclamation, and chosen the presiding officer of that body in 1866; elected Governor of Texas and was inaugurated August 8, 1866; removed by order of General Philip H. Sheridan on August 9, 1867; resumed the practice of law in Collin County, Tex.; elected as a Democrat to the Forty-fourth and Forty-fifth Congresses (March 4, 1875-March 3, 1879); chairman, Committee on Pacific Railroads (Forty-fifth Congress); was not a candidate for renomination in 1878 to the Forty-sixth Congress; resumed the practice of his profession; elected to the Forty-eighth and Forty-ninth Congresses (March 4, 1883-March 3, 1887); chairman, Committee on Pacific Railroads (Forty-ninth Congress); declined to be a candidate for renomination in 1886 to the Fiftieth Congress; unsuccessful candidate in 1881 for election as United States Senator; resumed the practice of law; delegate to the Democratic National Convention of 1892; died in McKinney, Collin County, Tex., April 21, 1894; interment in Pecan Grove Cemetery.

**Bibliography:** Elliott, Claude. *Leathercoat: The Life History of a Texas Patriot.* San Antonio, Tex.: Standard Printing Co., 1938.

**THROOP, Enos Thompson,** a Representative from New York; born in Johnstown, Montgomery County, N.Y., August 21, 1784; attended the common schools; studied law; was admitted to the bar in 1806 and commenced practice in Auburn, N.Y.; clerk of Cayuga County, 1811-1815; elected as a Republican to the Fourteenth Congress and served from March 4, 1815, to June 4, 1816, when he resigned; unsuccessful candidate for reelection in 1816 to the Fifteenth Congress; circuit judge of New York 1823-1827; elected Lieutenant Governor of New York in 1828; became Governor on March 12, 1829, when Martin Van Buren was appointed Secretary of State of the United States; elected Governor of New York in 1830 and served from March 12, 1829 to January 1, 1833; naval officer of the port of New York 1833-1838; appointed Chargé d'Affaires to the Two Sicilies on February 6, 1838, and served until January 12, 1842; engaged in the management of his large estate and resided in Kalamazoo, Mich., from 1847 until 1867; returned to his estate "Willowbrook," near Auburn, Cayuga County, N.Y., and died there November 1, 1874; interment in St. Peter's Churchyard, Auburn, N.Y.

**Bibliography:** *DAB.*

**THROPP, Joseph Earlston,** a Representative from Pennsylvania; born in Valley Forge, Chester County, Pa., October 4, 1847; attended the public schools and Friends Central High School, Philadelphia, Pa., and was graduated as a civil engineer from the Polytechnic College of Pennsylvania in 1868; went to the Middle Northwest and engaged in his profession, constructing docks at Duluth and Fond du Lac, Wis., attaining the position of railroad division engineer; moved to Conshohocken, Pa., in 1870 and engaged in the manufacture of pig iron; subsequently became owner of the Earlston Furnaces, Everett, Pa., in 1888; elected as a Republican to the Fifty-sixth Congress (March 4, 1899-March 3, 1901); was an unsuccessful candidate for reelection in 1900 to the Fifty-seventh Congress; retired from active business pursuits and resided in Washington, D.C., and Miami, Fla.; died while on a visit in Quebec, Canada, July 27, 1927; interment in West Laurel Hill Cemetery, Philadelphia, Pa.

**THRUSTON, Buckner,** a Senator from Kentucky; born in Petsoe Parish, Gloucester County, Va., February 9, 1763; pursued preparatory studies; graduated from the College of William and Mary at Williamsburg, Va.; studied law; moved to Lexington, Fayette County, Va. (now Kentucky), in 1788; was admitted to the bar and began the practice of law; member, Virginia assembly 1789; after Kentucky was organized as a Commonwealth was elected clerk of the first Kentucky senate in 1792; appointed one of Kentucky's three commissioners to settle the boundary dispute between the Commonwealths of Kentucky and Virginia; district judge of Kentucky 1791; judge of the circuit court 1802-1803; appointed United States judge of the court of the Territory of Orleans in 1804, but declined; elected as a Republican to the United States Senate and served from March 4, 1805, to December 18, 1809, when he resigned, having been appointed to a judicial position; appointed judge of the United States Circuit Court for the District of Columbia and served from January 1810, until his death in Washington, D.C., on August 30, 1845; interment in the Congressional Cemetery.

**THURMAN, Allen Granberry,** a Representative and a Senator from Ohio; born in Lynchburg, Va., November 13, 1813; moved with his parents to Chillicothe, Ohio, in 1819; attended the Chillicothe

Academy; private secretary to Governor Robert Lucas in 1834; studied law; was admitted to the bar in 1835 and practiced in Ross County, Ohio; elected as a Democrat to the Twenty-ninth Congress (March 4, 1845-March 3, 1847); declined to be a candidate for renomination in 1846 to the Thirtieth Congress; resumed the practice of law; associate justice of the supreme court of Ohio, 1851-1854, chief justice, 1854-1856; unsuccessful candidate in 1867 for election for Governor of Ohio; elected as a Democrat to the United States Senate in 1868; reelected in 1874, and served from March 4, 1869, to March 3, 1881; served as President pro tempore of the Senate during the Forty-sixth Congress; chairman, Committee on Private Land Claims (Forty-second through Forty-fifth Congresses), Committee on the Judiciary (Forty-sixth Congress); appointed a member of the Electoral Commission to decide the contests in various States in the presidential election of 1876; unsuccessful candidate for reelection to the United States Senate in 1881; resumed the practice of law in Columbus, Ohio; appointed by President James A. Garfield a member of the international monetary conference in Paris in 1881; unsuccessful candidate for Vice President of the United States in 1888 on the Democratic ticket headed by President Grover Cleveland; died in Columbus, Franklin County, Ohio, December 12, 1895; interment in Greenlawn Cemetery.

**Bibliography:** *DAB*; Hare, John S. "Allen G. Thurman: A Political Study." Ph.D. dissertation, Ohio State University, 1933.

**THURMAN, John Richardson,** a Representative from New York; born in New York City October 6, 1814; was graduated from Columbia College in 1835; moved to Warren County, near Chestertown, N.Y., and engaged in agricultural pursuits; held several local offices; elected as a Whig to the Thirty-first Congress (March 4, 1849-March 3, 1851); declined to be a candidate for renomination in 1850; devoted his attention to the management of his estate; died at Friends Lake, Chester Township, Warren County, N.Y., July 24, 1854; interment in the family cemetery; reinterment in Oakwood Cemetery, Troy, Rensselaer County, N.Y.

**THURMAN, Karen L.,** a Representative from Florida; born in Rapid City, Pennington County, S.Dak., January 12, 1951; graduated, Satellite High School, Satellite Beach, Fla., 1969; A.A., Santa Fe Community College, 1970; B.A., University of Florida, 1973; teacher; Dunnellon, Fla., City Council, 1975-1983; mayor of Dunnellon, 1979-1981; member, Florida State senate, 1983-1993; elected as a Democrat to the One Hundred Third and One Hundred Fourth Congresses (January 3, 1993-January 3, 1997); is a resident of Dunnellon, Fla.

**THURMOND, James Strom,** a Senator from South Carolina; born in Edgefield, S.C., December 5, 1902; attended the public schools; B.S., Clemson College, 1923; taught in South Carolina high schools, 1923-1929; Edgefield County superintendent of education, 1929-1933; studied law and was admitted to the South Carolina bar in 1930; city and county attorney, 1930-1938; member, South Carolina State senate, 1933-1938; circuit judge, 1938-1946; served in the United States Army, 1942-1946, in Europe and in the Pacific; major general, United States Army Reserve; elected Governor of South Carolina in 1946 and served from January 21, 1947 to January 16, 1951; unsuccessful States' Rights candidate for President of the United States in 1948; unsuccessful candidate in 1950 for nomination to the United States Senate; practiced law in Aiken, S.C., 1951-1955; appointed as a Democrat to the United States Senate to complete the term of Charles E. Daniel, who resigned, and served from December 24, 1954, to January 3, 1955; had been previously elected as a write-in candidate in November 1954 for the term commencing January 3, 1955, and ending January 3, 1961, but due to a promise made to the voters in the 1954 election, he resigned as of April 4, 1956; again elected as a Democrat in November 1956 to fill the vacancy caused by his own resignation and served from November 7, 1956, to January 3, 1961; reelected in 1960; announced his affiliation with the Republican Party on September 16, 1964; reelected in 1966, 1972, 1978, 1984, and again in 1990 for the term ending January 3, 1997; President pro tempore of the Senate (Ninety-seventh through Ninety-ninth Congresses, One Hundred Fourth Congress); chairman, Committee on the Judiciary (Ninety-seventh through Ninety-ninth Congresses), Committee on Armed Services (One Hundred Fourth Congress); on March 8, 1996 he became, at ninety-three, the oldest person ever to serve in the Senate; is a resident of Aiken, S.C.

**Bibliography:** Cohodas, Nadine. *Strom Thurmond and the Politics of Southern Change*. New York: Simon and Schuster, 1993.

**THURSTON, Benjamin Babock,** a Representative from Rhode Island; born in Hopkinton, R.I., June 29, 1804; attended the common schools; engaged in mercantile pursuits; member of the Rhode Island house of representatives, 1831-1837; Lieutenant Governor of Rhode Island in 1838; elected as a Democrat to the Thirtieth Congress (March 4, 1847-March 3, 1849); unsuccessful candidate for reelection in 1848 to the Thirty-first Congress; elected as a Democrat to the Thirty-second and Thirty-third Congresses and as a candidate of the American Party to the Thirty-fourth Congress (March 4, 1851-March 3, 1857); chairman, Committee on Expenditures in the Department of the Treasury (Thirty-second Congress), Committee on Patents (Thirty-third Congress), Committee on Accounts (Thirty-fourth Congress); was not a candidate for renomination in 1856 to the Thirty-fifth Congress; after leaving Congress moved to New London, Conn.; member of the board of aldermen in 1862 and 1863; member of the Connecticut State house of representatives in 1869 and 1870; resumed mercantile pursuits; died in New London, Conn., May 17, 1886; interment in Cedar Grove Cemetery.

**THURSTON, John Mellen,** a Senator from Nebraska; born in Montpelier, Vt., August 21, 1847; moved with his parents to Madison, Wis., in 1854 and two years later to Beaver Dam, Wis.; attended the public schools and graduated from Wayland University, Beaver Dam, Wis.; studied law; was admitted to the bar in 1869 and commenced practice in Omaha, Nebr.; member, city council 1872-1874; city attorney of Omaha 1874-1877; member, State house of representatives 1875-1877; appointed assistant attorney of the Union Pacific Railroad in 1877 and general solicitor in 1888; presidential elector on the Republican ticket in 1880; unsuccessful Republican candidate for United States Senator in 1893; elected as a Republican to the United States Senate and served from March 4, 1895, to March 3, 1901; was not a candidate for reelection; chairman, Committee on Indian Affairs (Fifty-sixth Congress); appointed United States commissioner to the St. Louis Exposition in 1901; moved to Washington, D.C., and resumed the practice of law; returned to Omaha, Nebr., and practiced law until his death August 9, 1916; remains were cremated at Forest Lawn Cemetery, Omaha, Nebr., and the ashes interred in the Congressional Cemetery, Washington, D.C.

**THURSTON, Lloyd,** a Representative from Iowa; born in Osceola, Clarke County, Iowa, March 27, 1880; attended the public schools; during the Spanish-American War enlisted on June 13, 1898, as a private in Company I, Fifty-first Regiment, Iowa Volunteer Infantry; served with this company during the Philippine Insurrection, and was honorably discharged on November 2, 1899; was graduated from the law department of the University of Iowa at Iowa City in 1902; was admitted to the bar the same year and commenced practice in Osceola, Clarke County, Iowa; captain in the National Guard of Iowa, 1902-1906; prosecuting attorney of Clarke County, 1906-1910; during the First World War served with the rank of captain in Company C, Twenty-sixth Battalion, United States Guards, at Fort Crook, Nebr.; member of the Iowa State senate, 1920-1924; elected as a Republican to the Sixty-ninth and to the six

succeeding Congresses (March 4, 1925-January 3, 1939); was not a candidate in 1938 for renomination to the House of Representatives, but was an unsuccessful candidate for nomination to the United States Senate; resumed the practice of law in Osceola, Iowa; died in Des Moines, Iowa, on May 7, 1970; interment in Maple Hill Cemetery, Osceola, Iowa.

**THURSTON, Samuel Royal,** a Delegate from the Territory of Oregon; born in Monmouth, Kennebec County, Maine, April 15, 1816; attended Wesleyan Seminary, Readfield, Maine, and Dartmouth College, Hanover, N.H.; was graduated from Bowdoin College, Brunswick, Maine, in 1843; studied law; was admitted to the bar in 1844 and commenced practice in Brunswick, Cumberland County, Maine; moved to Burlington, Iowa, in 1845 and continued the practice of law; editor of the Iowa Gazette; moved to Oregon City, Oreg., in 1849 and engaged in the practice of his profession; when the Territory of Oregon was formed was elected as a Democrat to the Thirty-first Congress (March 4, 1849-March 3, 1851); died while at sea April 9, 1851, en route to his home from Washington, D.C., and was buried in Acapulco, Mexico; reinterment in the Odd Fellows Cemetery, Salem, Marion County, Oreg.

**THYE, Edward John,** a Senator from Minnesota; born on a farm near Frederick, Brown County, S.Dak., April 26, 1896; moved in early childhood to Minnesota with his parents, who settled on a farm near Northfield, Rice County; attended the public schools and business college; during the First World War enlisted as a private in the United States Army Air Corps in 1917 and promoted through the ranks to second lieutenant with overseas service; farmer and tractor expert, Minneapolis, Minn.; salesman, 1920-1922; appraiser for a Federal land bank, 1933-1934; deputy commissioner of agriculture for State of Minnesota, 1939-1942; elected Lieutenant Governor of Minnesota in 1942; became Governor on April 27, 1943, upon the resignation of Governor Harold E. Stassen; elected Governor in 1944 and served until January 8, 1947; elected as a Republican to the United States Senate in 1946, reelected in 1952, and served from January 3, 1947, to January 3, 1959; unsuccessful candidate for reelection in 1958; chairman, Select Committee on Small Business (Eighty-third Congress); resumed his agricultural interests and maintained an active interest in Republican politics and civic affairs; died in Northfield, Minn., August 28, 1969; interment in Oaklawn Cemetery.

**TIAHRT, Todd,** a Representative from Kansas; born in Vermillion, Clay County, S.Dak., June 15, 1951; attended the public schools and the South Dakota School of Mines and Technology, Rapid City; B.A., Evangel College, Springfield, Mo., 1975; M.B.A., Southwest Missouri State University, 1989; teacher, Kansas Newman College and Evangel College; proposal manager, Boeing Co.; unsuccessful candidate in 1990 for the Kansas State house of representatives; member, Kansas State senate; elected as a Republican to the One Hundred Fourth Congress (January 3, 1995-January 3, 1997); is a resident of Goddard, Kans.

**TIBBATTS, John Wooleston,** a Representative from Kentucky; born in Lexington, Ky., June 12, 1802; pursued classical studies; studied law; was admitted to the bar in 1826 and commenced practice in Newport, Campbell County, Ky.; held several local offices; elected as a Democrat to the Twenty-eighth and Twenty-ninth Congresses (March 4, 1843-March 3, 1847); served as colonel in the Mexican War; resumed the practice of law in Newport, Ky., and died there July 5, 1852; interment in Evergreen Cemetery.

**TIBBITS, George,** a Representative from New York; born in Warwick, R.I., January 14, 1763; pursued classical studies; engaged in business in Lansingburg, N.Y., in 1784; moved to Troy, N.Y., in 1797 and became engaged in extensive mercantile pursuits; member of the State assembly in 1800; elected as a Federalist to the Eighth Congress (March 4, 1803-March 3, 1805); was not a candidate for renomination in 1804; member of the State senate 1815-1818; unsuccessful Federalist candidate for Lieutenant Governor of New York in 1816; was a member of the commission on State prisons which rendered a favorable report on the Auburn Prison system in 1824; member of the commission which had charge of the construction of Sing Sing Prison; mayor of Troy, N.Y., from 1830 to 1836; died in Troy, Rensselaer County, N.Y., July 19, 1849; interment in Oakwood Cemetery.

**TIBBOTT, Harve,** a Representative from Pennsylvania; born near Ebensburg, Cambria County, Pa., May 27, 1885; attended the public schools; graduated from the school of pharmacy of the University of Pittsburgh in 1906; engaged in the retail drug business and as a pharmacist in Ebensburg, Pa., in 1906; treasurer of the William Penn Highway Association, 1913-1915; treasurer of Cambria County, Pa., 1932-1935; member of the Pennsylvania Republican committee in 1936 and 1937; president of the First National Bank of Ebensburg, beginning in 1938; elected as a Republican to the Seventy-sixth and to the four succeeding Congresses (January 3, 1939-January 3, 1949); unsuccessful candidate for reelection in 1948 to the Eighty-first Congress; returned to Ebensburg and resumed his banking career as president and chairman of the board of the First National Bank; died in Ebensburg, Pa., December 31, 1969; interment in Lloyd Cemetery.

**TICHENOR, Isaac,** a Senator from Vermont; born in Newark, N.J., February 8, 1754; completed preparatory studies; graduated from the College of New Jersey (now Princeton University) in 1775; studied law in Schenectady, N.Y.; appointed assistant commissary general in 1777 and was stationed in Bennington, Vt.; was admitted to the bar and commenced practice in Bennington, Vt., at the close of the Revolutionary War; member, Vermont State house of representatives, 1781-1785, serving as speaker, 1783-1784; agent from the State to the Continental Congress to present Vermont's claim for admission into the Union, 1782-1789; State councilor, 1786-1791; one of the commissioners to settle the boundary question with New York in 1790; unsuccessful candidate for Governor in 1793, 1794 and 1795; associate justice of the State supreme court, 1791-1796, and chief justice, 1794-1796; elected in 1796 as a Federalist to the United States Senate to fill the vacancy caused by the resignation of Moses Robinson; reelected for the term commencing March 4, 1797, and served from October 18, 1796 to October 17, 1797, when he resigned, having been elected Governor; elected Governor of Vermont in 1797, reelected every year from 1798 to 1806, and served from October 16, 1797 to October 9, 1807; unsuccessful candidate for reelection in 1807; again elected Governor in 1808, and served from October 14, 1808 to October 14, 1809; unsuccessful candidate for reelection in 1809, and for election in 1810; again elected as a Federalist to the United States Senate, and served from March 4, 1815 to March 3, 1821; resumed the practice of his profession; died in Bennington, Vt., December 11, 1838; interment in the Village Cemetery, Old Bennington, Vt.

**Bibliography:** *DAB.*

**TIERNAN, Robert Owens,** a Representative from Rhode Island; born in Providence, R.I., February 24, 1929; attended LaSalle Academy; A.B., Providence (R.I.) College, 1953; J.D., Catholic University School of Law, Washington, D.C., 1956; was admitted to the bar in 1956 and commenced practice in Providence, R.I.; elected to the Rhode Island general assembly, 1960, and reelected in 1962, 1964, and 1966; elected as a Democrat to the Ninetieth Congress, March 28, 1967, by special election to fill the vacancy caused by the death of John E. Fogarty; reelected to the three succeeding Congresses, and served from March 28, 1967 until January 3, 1975; unsuccessful candidate for renomination in 1974 to the Ninety-fourth Congress; member, Federal Election Commission, April 1975 to November 1981; practiced law in Washington, D.C.,

and Rhode Island, 1981-1986; resumed the practice of law in Providence, R.I., 1986 to present; is a resident of South Kingston, R.I.

**TIERNEY, William Laurence,** a Representative from Connecticut; born in Norwalk, Fairfield County, Conn., August 6, 1876; attended the public schools; was graduated from Fordham University, New York City, in 1898 and from New York Law School in 1900; was admitted to the bar in 1900 and commenced practice in New York City; moved to Denver, Colo., in 1905 and to Greenwich, Conn., in 1912, continuing the practice of law; judge of Greenwich court 1912-1914; elected as a Democrat to the Seventy-second Congress (March 4, 1931-March 3, 1933); unsuccessful candidate for reelection in 1932 to the Seventy-third Congress; resumed the practice of law in Greenwich, Conn., and New York City; State counsel for the Home Owners' Loan Corporation in 1934 and 1935; engaged in banking and the practice of law in Greenwich, Conn., until his death there April 13, 1958; interment in St. Mary's Cemetery.

**TIFFIN, Edward,** a Senator from Ohio; born in Carlisle, England, June 19, 1766; attended the common schools; studied medicine; immigrated to the United States in 1784 and settled in Charles Town, Va. (now West Virginia); attended lectures at the Jefferson Medical College in Philadelphia; practiced medicine in Charles Town; entered the ministry of the Methodist Episcopal Church in 1792; moved to Chillicothe, Ohio, in 1796 and engaged in preaching and the practice of medicine; member, Territorial house of representatives, 1799-1801, serving as speaker; president of the convention that formed the constitution of Ohio in 1802; elected the first Governor of the State of Ohio in 1803, reelected in 1805, and served from March 3, 1803 until his resignation on March 4, 1807, having been elected Senator; elected as a Republican to the United States Senate, and served from March 4, 1807 to March 3, 1809, when he resigned; member, Ohio State house of representatives, 1809-1810, 1810-1811, serving as speaker; resumed the practice of medicine in Chillicothe, Ohio; appointed by President James Madison as the first Commissioner of the General Land Office, and served from 1812 to 1814; with the consent of the President and the Senate he exchanged offices with Josiah Meigs and became surveyor general of the Northwest Territory, which position he held until removed by President Andrew Jackson in 1829; died in Chillicothe, Ross County, Ohio, on August 9, 1829; interment in Grandview Cemetery.

**Bibliography:** *DAB*; Comegys, Cornelius G. *Reminiscences of the Life and Public Services of Edward Tiffin, Ohio's First Governor.* Chillicothe: J.R.S. Bond and Son, 1869; Gilmore, William E. *Life of Edward Tiffin, First Governor of Ohio.* Chillicothe: Horney and Son, 1897.

**TIFT, Nelson,** a Representative from Georgia; born in Groton, Conn., July 23, 1810; attended the village school; moved to Key West, Fla., with his father in 1826, to Charleston, S.C., in 1830, and engaged in the mercantile business; moved to Georgia and engaged in mercantile pursuits at Augusta, Richmond County, in 1835, at Hawkinsville, Pulaski County, in March 1836, and at Albany, Baker (now Dougherty) County, in October 1836; founder of the Augusta (Ga.) Guards in 1835; founder of the city of Albany, Ga., in 1836; served as justice of the peace; delegate from Baker County to the convention held in Milledgeville, Ga., in 1839, to reduce the membership of the State legislature; elected to the Baker County Inferior Court on July 5, 1840; reelected in January 1841 and again in 1849; elected colonel of the Baker County (Ga.) Militia in 1840; member of the Georgia State house of representatives in 1841, 1847, and 1851-1852; founder in 1845 of the Albany Patriot, and served as editor and publisher until 1858; during the Civil War was connected with the Confederate States Navy Supply Department with the rank of captain; upon the readmission of Georgia to representation was elected as a Democrat to the Fortieth Congress, and served from

July 25, 1868 to March 3, 1869; presented credentials as a Member-elect to the Forty-first Congress, but was not permitted to qualify; contested the subsequent election of Richard H. Whiteley to the Forty-first Congress, but no action was taken thereon; operated an extensive plantation, as well as lumber, flour, and corn-meal mills; also instrumental in promoting the building of several railroads, serving as president; delegate to the State constitutional convention in 1877; died in Albany, Dougherty County, Ga., on November 21, 1891; interment in Oakview Cemetery.

**TILDEN, Daniel Rose,** a Representative from Ohio; born in Lebanon, Conn., November 5, 1804; attended the public schools; resided several years in Virginia and South Carolina; moved to Garrettsville, Ohio, about 1828, and thence to Warren, Ohio; studied law; was admitted to the bar in 1836 and commenced practice in Ravenna, Portage County, Ohio; prosecuting attorney of Portage County 1838-1841; elected as a Whig to the Twenty-eighth and Twenty-ninth Congresses (March 4, 1843-March 3, 1847); delegate to the Whig National Convention in 1848 and 1852; moved to Cleveland, Ohio, in 1852; elected probate judge of Cuyahoga County and served from 1855 to 1888; died in Cleveland, Ohio, March 4, 1890; remains were cremated at Buffalo, N.Y., and the ashes deposited in the Buffalo Crematory.

**TILGHMAN, Matthew,** a Delegate from Maryland; born at the "Hermitage," near Centerville, Queen Annes County, Md., February 17, 1718; was tutored privately; justice of the peace for Talbot County; member of the Maryland House of Delegates 1751-1777, serving as speaker 1773-1775; president of the Revolutionary convention that directed the affairs of the colony 1774-1777; member of the committee appointed to draw up the protest against the Stamp Act; chairman of the committee of correspondence in 1774; Member of the Continental Congress 1774-1776; was summoned from his seat in Congress to attend the convention at Annapolis, Md., convening June 21, 1776, and served as president of that body; chairman of the committee of safety in 1775; chairman of the committee which prepared the first declaration and charter of rights and plan of government (constitution) for the State of Maryland; elected as a member of the State senate in 1777; reelected, but resigned before the expiration of his term; was an extensive land owner and engaged in planting; died at his home "Rich Neck," near Claiborne, Talbot County, Md., May 4, 1790; interment in the family cemetery at "Rich Neck."

Bibliography: *DAB.*

**TILLINGHAST, Joseph Leonard** (cousin of Thomas Tillinghast), a Representative from Rhode Island; was born in Taunton, Mass., in 1791; moved to Rhode Island and pursued classical studies; published the Providence Gazette in 1809; studied law; was admitted to the bar in 1811 and began practice in Providence, R.I.; member of the State house of representatives 1826-1833, serving as speaker 1829-1832; elected as a Whig to the Twenty-fifth, Twenty-sixth, and Twenty-seventh Congresses (March 4, 1837-March 3, 1843); was not a candidate for renomination; trustee of Brown University at Providence 1833-1844; died in Providence, R.I., December 30, 1844; interment in North Burial Ground.

**TILLINGHAST, Thomas** (cousin of Joseph Leonard Tillinghast), a Representative from Rhode Island; born in East Greenwich, R.I., August 21, 1742; completed preparatory studies; member of the State house of representatives in 1772 and 1773; held several offices under Revolutionary authorities; again a member of the State house of representatives 1778-1780; judge of the court of common pleas in 1779; member of the council of war; associate justice of the State supreme court 1780-1797; elected as a Federalist to the Fifth Congress to fill the vacancy caused by the resignation of Elisha R. Potter and served from November 13, 1797, to March 3, 1799; elected as a Republican to the Seventh Congress (March 4,

1801-March 3, 1803); died in East Greenwich, R.I., August 26, 1821; interment in Tillinghast Cemetery.

**TILLMAN, Benjamin Ryan** (brother of George Dionysius Tillman), a Senator from South Carolina; born near Trenton, Edgefield County, S.C., August 11, 1847; pursued an academic course; left school in 1864 to join the Confederate Army, but was stricken with a severe illness; engaged in agricultural pursuits; elected Governor of South Carolina in 1890, reelected in 1892 and served from December 4, 1890 to December 1894; established Clemson College and Winthrop College while Governor; member of the South Carolina State constitutional convention in 1895; elected as a Democrat to the United States Senate in 1894; reelected in 1901, 1907, and 1913, and served from March 4, 1895 until his death in Washington, D.C., on July 3, 1918; censured by the Senate on February 28, 1902 after physically assaulting his colleague from South Carolina, John L. McLaurin, on the Senate floor; chairman, Committee on Revolutionary Claims (Fifty-seventh through Fifty-ninth Congresses), Committee on Five Civilized Tribes of Indians (Sixty-first and Sixty-second Congresses), Committee on Naval Affairs (Sixty-third through Sixty-fifth Congresses); interment in Ebenezer Cemetery, Trenton, S.C.

Bibliography: Neal, Diane. "Benjamin Ryan Tillman: The South Carolina Years, 1847-1894." Ph.D. dissertation, Kent State University, 1976; Simkins, Francis. *Pitchfork Ben Tillman: South Carolinian.* 1944. Reprint. Baton Rouge: Louisiana State University Press, 1967.

**TILLMAN, George Dionysius** (brother of Benjamin Ryan Tillman), a Representative from South Carolina; born near Curryton, Edgefield County, S.C., August 21, 1826; pursued an academic course in Penfield, Ga., and in Greenwood, S.C.; attended Harvard University, but did not graduate; studied law; was admitted to the bar in 1848 and commenced practice in Edgefield, S.C.; member of the South Carolina State house of representatives, 1854-1855 and 1864; enlisted during the Civil War and served in the Third Regiment of South Carolina State troops in 1862; shortly after its disbandment entered the Second Regiment of South Carolina Artillery, in which he served until the close of the war; again a member of the State house of representatives in 1864; member of the State constitutional convention in 1865, held under the reconstruction proclamation of President Andrew Johnson; served in the South Carolina State senate in 1865; unsuccessful candidate for election in 1876 to the Forty-fifth Congress; elected as a Democrat to the Forty-sixth Congress (March 4, 1879-March 3, 1881); presented credentials as a Member-elect to the Forty-seventh Congress and served from March 4, 1881, to June 19, 1882, when he was succeeded by Robert Smalls, who contested the election; elected to the Forty-eighth and to the four succeeding Congresses (March 4, 1883-March 3, 1893); chairman, Committee on Patents (Fifty-second Congress); unsuccessful candidate for renomination in 1892 to the Fifty-third Congress; engaged in agricultural pursuits and also as a publicist; member of the State constitutional convention in 1895; unsuccessful candidate in 1898 for election for Governor of South Carolina; died in Clarks Hill, McCormick County, S.C., February 2, 1902; interment in the Bethlehem Baptist Church Community Cemetery.

**TILLMAN, John Newton,** a Representative from Arkansas; born near Springfield, Greene County, Mo., December 13, 1859; attended the common schools; was graduated from the University of Arkansas at Fayetteville in 1880; taught school; studied law; was admitted to the bar in 1883 and commenced practice in Fayetteville, Washington County, Ark.; clerk of the circuit court of Washington County 1884-1889; served in the State senate 1888-1892; prosecuting attorney of the fourth judicial circuit 1892-1898; judge of the same circuit court 1900-1905; president of the University of Arkansas 1905-1912; elected as a Democrat to the Sixty-fourth and to the six succeeding Congresses (March 4, 1915-March 3, 1929); one of the managers appointed by the House of Representatives in 1926 to conduct the impeachment proceedings against George W. English, judge of the United States District Court for the Eastern District of Illinois; did not seek renomination in 1928; died in Fayetteville, Ark., March 9, 1929; interment in Evergreen Cemetery.

**TILLMAN, Lewis** (nephew of Barclay Martin), a Representative from Tennessee; born near Shelbyville, Bedford County, Tenn., August 18, 1816; attended the common schools and pursued an academic course; served in the Seminole War as a private; engaged in agricultural pursuits; clerk of the circuit court of Bedford County 1852-1860; colonel of State militia before the Civil War; editor of a newspaper in Shelbyville, Tenn.; clerk and master of the chancery court 1865-1869; elected as a Republican to the Forty-first Congress (March 4, 1869-March 3, 1871); was not a candidate for renomination in 1870; engaged in agricultural pursuits; died in Shelbyville, Bedford County, Tenn., May 3, 1886; interment in Willow Mount Cemetery.

**TILLOTSON, Thomas,** a Representative from New York; born in Maryland in 1750; received a thorough education; studied medicine and practiced; during the Revolutionary War was commissioned first lieutenant in the Maryland Militia in 1776; appointed by Congress as physician and surgeon general of the Northern Department of the Army in 1780 and served until the close of the war; settled in New York and engaged in the practice of medicine; member of the State assembly from Red Hook, Dutchess County, from 1788 to 1790; served in the State senate 1791-1799; member of the council of appointment in 1791; elected to the Seventh Congress, but did not qualify or take his seat and resigned August 10, 1801; secretary of state of New York from August 10, 1801, to March 15, 1806, and from February 16, 1807, to June 31, 1808; died in Rhinebeck, Dutchess County, N.Y., May 5, 1832; interment in the vault in the rear of Rhinebeck Reformed Dutch Church.

**TILSON, John Quillin,** a Representative from Connecticut; born in Clearbranch, Unicoi County, Tenn., April 5, 1866; attended public and private schools at Flag Pond, in his native county, and also at Mars Hill, Madison County, N.C.; was graduated from Carson-Newman College, Jefferson City, Tenn., in 1888, from Yale University, New Haven, Conn., in 1891, and from the law department of the same university in 1893; was admitted to the bar in 1897 and commenced practice in New Haven, Conn.; enlisted as a volunteer during the war with Spain and served as second lieutenant in the Sixth Regiment, United States Volunteer Infantry; member of the State house of representatives 1904-1908, serving as speaker the last two years; elected as a Republican to the Sixty-first and Sixty-second Congresses (March 4, 1909-March 3, 1913); unsuccessful candidate for reelection in 1912 to the Sixty-third Congress; served on the Mexican border as lieutenant colonel of the Second Infantry, Connecticut National Guard, in 1916; elected to the Sixty-fourth and to the eight succeeding Congresses and served from March 4, 1915, until his resignation on December 3, 1932; majority leader (Sixty-ninth, Seventieth, and Seventy-first Congresses); was not a candidate for renomination in 1932; delegate to the Republican National Convention in 1932; resumed practice of law in Washington, D.C., and New Haven, Conn.; special lecturer at Yale University on parliamentary law and procedure; died in New London, N.H., August 14, 1958; interment in private burial grounds on the family farm, Clearbranch, Tenn.

Bibliography: *DAB*; Sweeting, Orville J. "John Q. Tilson and the Re-Apportionment Act of 1929." *Western Political Quarterly* 9 (June 1956): 434-53.

**TILTON, James,** a Delegate from Delaware; born in Kent County, Del., June 1, 1745; attended Nottingham Academy, Maryland; was graduated from the medical department of the University of Pennsylvania in 1771 and commenced practice in Dover, Del.; entered the Revolutionary Army as surgeon, and in 1777 was in charge of the military hospital at Princeton, N.J.; after peace was declared resumed the practice of his profession in Dover, Del.; Member of the Continental Congress 1783-1784; moved to Wilmington, Del.; Government commissioner of loans 1785-1801; served several years as a member of the State house of representatives; Surgeon General of the United States Army 1813-1815; died near Wilmington, Del., May 14, 1822; interment in Wilmington and Brandywine Cemetery.

Bibliography: *DAB*.

**TIMBERLAKE, Charles Bateman,** a Representative from Colorado; born in Wilmington, Clinton County, Ohio, September 25, 1854; attended the common schools and Earlham College, Richmond, Ind., 1871-1874; taught school; moved to Colorado in 1885, and settled near Holyoke, Phillips County; engaged in agricultural pursuits and stock raising; member of the Republican State committee 1892-1910; superintendent of schools of Phillips County 1889-1895; county clerk 1895-1897; appointed receiver of the United States land office at Sterling, Colo., on July 1, 1897, and served until April 30, 1914; elected as a Republican to the Sixty-fourth and to the eight succeeding Congresses (March 4, 1915-March 3, 1933); unsuccessful candidate for renomination in 1932; engaged in banking in Sterling, Colo., until his death there on May 31, 1941; interment in Grand View Cemetery, Fort Collins, Colo.

**TINCHER, Jasper Napoleon,** a Representative from Kansas; born near Browning, Sullivan County, Mo., November 2, 1878; moved with his parents to Medicine Lodge, Barber County, Kans., in 1892; attended the common and high schools; taught school in Hardtner, Kans., from 1896 until February 1899; worked and studied in a law office and was admitted to the bar in May 1899; commenced the practice of law in Medicine Lodge, Kans.; also interested in farming and stock raising; elected as a Republican to the Sixty-sixth and to the three succeeding Congresses (March 4, 1919-March 3, 1927); was not a candidate for renomination in 1926; moved to Hutchinson, Kans., in 1926 and practiced law until his death there on November 6, 1951; interment in Memorial Park Cemetery.

**TINKHAM, George Holden,** a Representative from Massachusetts; born in Boston, Suffolk County, Mass., October 29, 1870; attended the public and private schools; graduated from Harvard University in 1894; member of the Boston Common Council in 1897 and 1898; studied law at Harvard Law School; admitted to the bar in 1899 and commenced practice in Boston; member of the board of aldermen 1900-1902; served in the Massachusetts senate 1910-1912; served overseas during the First World War; elected as a Republican to the Sixty-fourth and to the thirteen succeeding Congresses (March 4, 1915-January 3, 1943); was not a candidate for renomination in 1942; continued the practice of law in Boston, Mass., until his retirement; died in Cramerton, N.C., August 28, 1956; interment in Forest Hills Cemetery, Boston, Mass.

Bibliography: *DAB*.

**TIPTON, John,** a Senator from Indiana; born near Sevierville, Sevier County, Tenn., August 14, 1786; received a limited schooling; moved to Harrison County, Ind., in 1807 and engaged in agricultural pursuits; served with the "Yellow Jackets" in the Tippecanoe campaign and subsequently attained the rank of brigadier general of militia; sheriff of Harrison County, Ind., 1816-1819; member, State house of representatives 1819-1823; one of the commissioners to select a site for a new capital for Indiana in 1820; commissioner to determine the boundary line between Indiana and Illinois 1821; appointed United States Indian agent for the Pottawatamie and Miami tribes 1823; laid out the city of Logansport, Ind., in 1828; elected as a Democrat to the United States Senate on December 9,

1831, to fill the vacancy caused by the death of James Noble; reelected in 1832 and served from January 3, 1832, to March 3, 1839; due to poor health declined to be a candidate for reelection in 1838; chairman, Committee on Roads and Canals (Twenty-fifth Congress), Committee on Indian Affairs (Twenty-fifth Congress); died in Logansport, Cass County, Ind., on April 5, 1839; interment in Mount Hope Cemetery.

**Bibliography:** *DAB*; Blackburn, Glen A. "The Papers of John Tipton." Ph.D. dissertation, Indiana University, 1928; Robertson, Nellie and Dorothy Riker, eds. *The John Tipton Papers*. 3 vols. Indianapolis: The Indiana Historical Bureau, 1942.

**TIPTON, Thomas Foster,** a Representative from Illinois; born near Harrisburg, Franklin County, Ohio, August 29, 1833; attended the public schools; moved with his parents to McLean County, Ill., in 1843; studied law; was admitted to the bar in 1854 and commenced the practice of law; State attorney for the eighth judicial district of Illinois in 1867 and 1868; elected circuit judge of the eighth judicial circuit in 1870, and upon the reorganization of the circuit court under the new constitution was reelected circuit judge of the fourteenth judicial circuit; elected as a Republican to the Forty-fifth Congress (March 4, 1877-March 3, 1879); unsuccessful candidate for reelection in 1878 to the Forty-sixth Congress; again elected circuit judge and served from 1891 to 1897; resumed the practice of law; died in Bloomington, McLean County, Ill., February 7, 1904; interment in Evergreen Cemetery.

**TIPTON, Thomas Weston,** a Senator from Nebraska; born in Cadiz, Ohio, August 5, 1817; attended Allegheny College, Meadville, Pa.; pursued classical studies and graduated from Madison College, Pennsylvania, in 1840; studied law; was admitted to the bar in 1844 and commenced the practice of law; member, State house of representatives 1845; appointed to a position in the United States Land Office 1849-1852; resumed the practice of law in McConnelsville, Ohio, in 1853; was ordained a minister of the Methodist Episcopal Church in 1856; moved to Brownsville, Nebr., about 1859 and joined the Congregational Church; member of the Nebraska constitutional convention in 1859; member, Territorial council 1860; during the Civil War was appointed chaplain of the First Regiment, Nebraska Volunteer Infantry, 1861-1865; assessor of internal revenue for Nebraska in 1865; member of the State constitutional convention in 1867; upon the admission of Nebraska as a State into the Union was elected as a Republican to the United States Senate; reelected in 1869 and served from March 1, 1867, to March 3, 1875; resumed the practice of law; unsuccessful candidate for Governor of Nebraska in 1880; died in Washington, D.C., November 26, 1899; interment in Rock Creek Cemetery.

**Bibliography:** Tipton, Thomas. *Forty Years of Nebraska At Home and In Congress*. Lincoln: State Journal Co., 1902.

**TIRRELL, Charles Quincy,** a Representative from Massachusetts; born in Sharon, Norfolk County, Mass., December 10, 1844; attended the common schools; graduated from Dartmouth College, Hanover, N.H., in 1866; served as principal of Peacham (Vt.) Academy for one year and of the high school at St. Johnsbury, Vt., for two years; studied law; admitted to the bar in 1870 and commenced practice in Boston, Mass.; member of the Massachusetts house of representatives in 1872; moved to Natick, Mass., in 1873; served in the State senate in 1881 and 1882; elected as a Republican to the Fifty-seventh and to the four succeeding Congresses and served from March 4, 1901, until his death in Natick, Mass., July 31, 1910; interment in Dell Park Cemetery.

**TITUS, Obadiah,** a Representative from New York; born in what is now Millbrook, Dutchess County, N.Y., January 20, 1789; studied law; was admitted to the bar and commenced practice in the town of Washington, Dutchess County; served as captain of Infantry in the War of 1812; elected county judge; elected sheriff of Dutchess

County in 1828; elected as a Democrat to the Twenty-fifth Congress (March 4, 1837-March 3, 1839); unsuccessful candidate for reelection in 1838 to the Twenty-sixth Congress; resumed the practice of law; died in the town of Washington, Dutchess County, N.Y., September 2, 1854; interment in Nine Partners (Friends) Burial Ground at Millbrook, N.Y.

**TOBEY, Charles William,** a Representative and a Senator from New Hampshire; born in Roxbury, Mass., July 22, 1880; attended the public schools and Roxbury (Mass.) Latin School; moved to Temple, N.H., in 1903 and engaged in the raising of poultry; also engaged in insurance, agriculture, banking, and manufacturing; member, New Hampshire State house of representatives 1915-1916, 1919-1920, 1923-1924, serving as speaker 1919-1920; member, New Hampshire State senate, serving as president 1925-1926; elected Governor of New Hampshire in 1928 and served from January 3, 1929 to January 1, 1931; trustee of Colby Junior College, New London, N.H.; elected as a Republican to the Seventy-third and to the two succeeding Congresses (March 4, 1933-January 3, 1939); was not a candidate for renomination in 1938 to the House of Representatives, but was elected to the United States Senate; reelected in 1944 and again in 1950 and served from January 3, 1939, until his death in the naval hospital at Bethesda, Md., July 24, 1953; chairman, Committee on Banking and Currency (Eightieth Congress), Committee on Interstate and Foreign Commerce (Eighty-third Congress); United States adviser to the United Nations Educational, Scientific and Cultural Organization Conference in Paris, 1952; member of the United States delegation to the International Monetary Conference held in Bretton Woods, N.H., in 1944; interment in Miller Cemetery, Temple, N.H.

**Bibliography:** *DAB*.

**TOD, John,** a Representative from Pennsylvania; born in Hartford, Conn., in 1779; attended the common schools and Yale College; moved to Bedford, Pa., in 1800; taught school while studying law; admitted to the bar in 1803 and commenced practice in Bedford, Pa.; clerk to the county commissioners of Bedford County in 1806 and 1807; member of the Pennsylvania house of representatives 1810-1813, serving twice as speaker; served in the Pennsylvania senate and acted as president 1814-1816; elected to the Seventeenth and Eighteenth Congresses and served from March 4, 1821, until his resignation in 1824; chairman, Committee on Manufactures (Seventeenth and Eighteenth Congresses); presiding judge of the court of common pleas for the sixteenth judicial district 1824-1827; appointed associate judge of the Pennsylvania supreme court in 1827; died in Bedford, Bedford County, Pa., March 27, 1830; interment in Bedford Cemetery.

**Bibliography:** *DAB*.

**TODD, Albert May,** a Representative from Michigan; born near Nottawa, St. Joseph County, Mich., June 3, 1850; attended the district school and was graduated from Sturgis (Mich.) High School; studied at Northwestern University, Evanston, Ill.; moved to Kalamazoo, Mich.; engaged in business as a manufacturing chemist; unsuccessful Prohibition candidate for Governor in 1894; elected as a Democrat to the Fifty-fifth Congress (March 4, 1897-March 3, 1899); unsuccessful Democratic candidate for reelection in 1898 to the Fifty-sixth Congress; resumed his former manufacturing pursuits in Kalamazoo; founded a museum of art and a library of ten thousand rare books and illuminated manuscripts; died in Kalamazoo, Mich., October 6, 1931; interment in Mountain Home Cemetery.

**TODD, John Blair Smith,** a Delegate from the Territory of Dakota; born in Lexington, Ky., April 4, 1814; moved with his parents to Illinois in 1827; attended private schools; was graduated from the United States Military Academy, West Point, N.Y., in 1837; commissioned second lieutenant in the Sixth Infantry July 1, 1837, first lieutenant December 10, 1837, and captain November 8, 1843;

served in the Seminole War 1837-1842 and in the war with Mexico; resigned from the Army September 16, 1856; became an Indian trader and settled in Fort Randall, Dak.; studied law; was admitted to the bar in 1861 and commenced the practice of law in Yankton, Dak.; appointed brigadier general of Volunteers in the Union Army September 19, 1861, which appointment expired July 17, 1862; when the Territory of Dakota was formed was elected as a Democrat to the Thirty-seventh Congress and served from December 9, 1861, to March 3, 1863; successfully contested the election of William Jayne to the Thirty-eighth Congress and served from June 17, 1864, to March 3, 1865; unsuccessful candidate for reelection in 1864 to the Thirty-ninth Congress; engaged in mercantile pursuits and the practice of his profession; served as speaker of the Territorial house of representatives in 1866 and 1867; unsuccessful candidate for election in 1868 to the Forty-first Congress; died in Yankton County, Dak. (now South Dakota), January 5, 1872; interment in Yankton Cemetery.

**Bibliography:** Wilson, Wesley C. "General John B.S. Todd, First Delegate, Dakota Territory." *North Dakota History* 31 (July 1964): 189-194.

**TODD, Lemuel,** a Representative from Pennsylvania; born in Carlisle, Pa., July 29, 1817; pursued classical studies, and was graduated from Dickinson College, Carlisle, Pa., in 1839; studied law; was admitted to the bar in 1841 and commenced practice in Carlisle; elected as a Republican to the Thirty-fourth Congress (March 4, 1855-March 3, 1857); unsuccessful candidate for reelection in 1856 to the Thirty-fifth Congress; during the Civil War served in the Union Army as major of the First Regiment, Pennsylvania Volunteer Reserve Corps; inspector general of Pennsylvania on the Governor's staff; elected as a Republican to the Forty-third Congress (March 4, 1873-March 3, 1875); was not a candidate for renomination in 1874; resumed the practice of law; died in Carlisle, Cumberland County, Pa., May 12, 1891; interment in Ashland Cemetery.

**TODD, Paul Harold, Jr.,** a Representative from Michigan; born in Kalamazoo, Mich., September 22, 1921; attended Kalamazoo schools; graduated from Cornell University, Ithaca, N.Y., in 1943; founder of Kalamazoo Spice Extraction Co. in 1958; elected as a Democrat to the Eighty-ninth Congress (January 3, 1965-January 3, 1967); unsuccessful candidate for reelection in 1966 to the Ninetieth Congress; executive officer, Planned Parenthood Association, 1967-1970; president of a spice company since 1970; unsuccessful candidate for election in 1974 to the Ninety-fourth Congress; is a resident of Kalamazoo, Mich.

**TOLAN, John Harvey,** a Representative from California; born in St. Peter, Nicollet County, Minn., January 15, 1877; attended the public schools; moved to Anaconda, Mont., in 1897; was graduated from the law department of the University of Kansas at Lawrence in 1902; was admitted to the bar the same year and commenced the practice of law in Anaconda, Mont.; attorney of Deer Lodge County, Mont., 1904-1906; moved to Oakland, Calif., in 1914 and continued the practice of law; elected as a Democrat to the Seventy-fourth and to the five succeeding Congresses (January 3, 1935-January 3, 1947); was not a candidate for renomination in 1946 to the Eightieth Congress; died in Westwood, Calif., on June 30, 1947; interment in Holy Sepulchre Cemetery, Hayward, Calif.

**TOLAND, George Washington,** a Representative from Pennsylvania; born in Philadelphia, Pa., February 8, 1796; attended the common schools; was graduated from Princeton College in 1816; held several local offices; elected as a Whig to the Twenty-fifth, Twenty-sixth, and Twenty-seventh Congresses (March 4, 1837-March 3, 1843); died in Philadelphia, Pa., January 30, 1869; interment in Laurel Hill Cemetery.

**TOLL, Herman,** a Representative from Pennsylvania; born in Kiev, Russia, March 15, 1907; graduated from Temple University School of Law, Philadelphia, Pa.; admitted to the bar and commenced the practice of law in Philadelphia, Pa., in 1930; member of the Pennsylvania Prison Society, Philadelphia Housing Association, and the board of directors of the Crusader Savings & Loan Association; in 1950 was elected to the Pennsylvania legislature from the sixteenth legislative district in Philadelphia and reelected in 1952, 1954, and 1956; elected as a Democrat to the Eighty-sixth and to the three succeeding Congresses (January 3, 1959-January 3, 1967); was not a candidate for reelection in 1966 to the Ninetieth Congress; died in Philadelphia, Pa., July 26, 1967; interment in Roosevelt Memorial Park.

**TOLLEFSON, Thor Carl,** a Representative from Washington; born in Perley, Norman County, Minn., May 2, 1901; moved to Tacoma, Wash., in 1912; attended the public schools; was graduated from Lincoln High School in 1924 and from the University of Washington Law School at Seattle in 1930; was admitted to the bar in 1930 and commenced practice in Tacoma, Wash.; prosecutor of Pierce County from 1938 until 1946; delegate to the Republican State conventions in 1936, 1938, 1940, 1942, and 1944; elected as a Republican to the Eigthtieth and to the eight succeeding Congresses (January 3, 1947-January 3, 1965); unsuccessful candidate for reelection in 1964 to the Eighty-eighth Congress; appointed director of fisheries for the State of Washington; special assistant to the Governor in charge of international fisheries negotiations; was resident of Tacoma, Wash., until his death there on December 30, 1982; interment in Mountain View Memorial Park.

**TOLLEY, Harold Sumner,** a Representative from New York; born in Honesdale, Wayne County, Pa., January 16, 1894; moved with his parents to Binghamton, N.Y., in 1903; attended the public schools; was graduated from Syracuse University, New York, in 1916; studied for the ministry and took a postgraduate course at Drew Theological Seminary, Madison, N.J.; director of religious education at the Metropolitan (Methodist Episcopal) Temple, New York City, in 1916 and 1917; abandoned the ministry to enlist in the military forces of the United States during the First World War and served from May 13, 1917, to July 25, 1919, attaining the rank of captain of Infantry; was commissioned a captain in the United States Officers' Reserve Corps; engaged in the retail shoe business; elected as a Republican to the Sixty-ninth Congress (March 4, 1925-March 3, 1927); unsuccessful candidate for renomination in 1926; delegate to the Republican State convention in 1926; resumed his former business pursuits; commissioner of public welfare, city of Binghamton, from January 1932 to April 1937; in 1937 was appointed area director for New York State Department of Social Welfare, assigned to the western New York area, and served until his death; died in Kenmore, N.Y., May 20, 1956; interment in Forest Lawn Cemetery, Buffalo, N.Y.

**TOMLINSON, Gideon,** a Representative and a Senator from Connecticut; born in Stratford, Conn., December 31, 1780; completed preparatory studies and graduated from Yale College in 1802; studied law; was admitted to the bar and commenced practice in Fairfield, Conn., in 1807; clerk of the Connecticut State house of representatives in 1817; member of the State house of representatives in 1818, serving as speaker; elected to the Sixteenth and to the three succeeding Congresses (March 4, 1819-March 3, 1827); chairman, Committee on Commerce (Nineteenth Congress); elected Governor of Connecticut in 1827, reelected in 1828, 1829 and 1830, and served from May 2, 1827 until March 1831, when he resigned, having been elected Senator; elected to the United States Senate, and served from March 4, 1831 to March 3, 1837; chairman, Committee on Pensions (Twenty-third and Twenty-fourth Congresses); trustee of Trinity College, 1832-1836; retired to private life;

died in Fairfield, Conn., October 8, 1854; interment in the Old Congregational Cemetery, Stratford, Conn.

**TOMLINSON, Thomas Ash,** a Representative from New York; born in New York City in March 1802; attended the schools of Champlain and Plattsburgh, N.Y.; studied law; was admitted to the bar and commenced practice in Keeseville, N.Y., in 1823; mill owner and dealer in lands; served as colonel in the State militia; member of the New York State assembly in 1835 and 1836; elected as a Whig to the Twenty-seventh Congress (March 4, 1841-March 3, 1843); resumed the practice of law and also engaged in the real estate business; unsuccessful candidate for election to the United States Senate in 1859; died in Keeseville, N.Y., June 18, 1872; interment in Evergreen Cemetery.

**TOMPKINS, Arthur Sidney,** a Representative from New York; born in Middleburg, Schoharie County, N.Y., August 26, 1865; moved with his parents to West Nyack, N.Y., in 1866; attended the public schools of Clarkstown and Nyack until 1878; studied law; was admitted to the bar in 1886 and commenced practice in Nyack, Rockland County, N.Y.; police justice of Nyack, N.Y., 1887-1889; elected chairman of the Rockland County Republican committee in 1888; member of the State assembly in 1890; delegate to all Republican State conventions from 1888 to 1906; delegate or alternate to all Republican National Conventions from 1888 to 1900; county judge and surrogate of Rockland County 1893-1898; elected as a Republican to the Fifty-sixth and Fifty-seventh Congresses (March 4, 1899-March 3, 1903); was not a candidate for renomination in 1902; resumed the practice of law in Nyack, N.Y.; elected justice of the supreme court of New York in 1906; reelected in 1920 and 1934; raised to the appellate division of the supreme court of New York in January 1930 and served until his retirement in 1936; died in Nyack, N.Y., January 20, 1938; interment in Oak Hill Cemetery.

**TOMPKINS, Caleb** (brother of Daniel D. Tompkins), a Representative from New York; born near Scarsdale, Westchester County, N.Y., December 22, 1759; member of the State assembly 1804-1806; judge of the court of common pleas and county court of Westchester County 1807-1811 and 1820-1824; elected as a Republican to the Fifteenth and Sixteenth Congresses (March 4, 1817-March 3, 1821); died in Scarsdale, Westchester County, N.Y., January 1, 1846; interment in the First Presbyterian Church Cemetery, White Plains, N.Y.

**TOMPKINS, Christopher,** a Representative from Kentucky; born in Green County, Ky., March 24, 1780; completed preparatory studies; studied law; admitted to the bar and commenced practice in Glasgow; member of the Kentucky house of representatives in 1805; elected as an Anti-Jacksonian to the Twenty-second and Twenty-third Congresses (March 4, 1831-March 3, 1835); again a member of the Kentucky house of representatives in 1835 and 1836; presidential elector on the Whig ticket in 1837; resumed the practice of law; died in Glasgow, Barren County, Ky., August 9, 1858; interment in the family burying ground at Glasgow.

**Bibliography:** Doutrich, Paul E., III. "A Pivotal Decision: The 1824 Gubernatorial Election in Kentucky." *Filson Club Historical Quarterly* 56 (January 1982): 14-29.

**TOMPKINS, Cydnor Bailey** (father of Emmett Tompkins), a Representative from Ohio; born near St. Clairsville, Belmont County, Ohio, November 8, 1810; moved with his parents to Morgan County in 1831 and settled near McConnelsville; completed preparatory studies, and was graduated from the Ohio University at Athens in 1835; studied law; was admitted to the bar in 1837 and commenced practice in McConnelsville, Morgan County, Ohio; served as recorder of McConnelsville in 1840; prosecuting attorney of Morgan County 1848-1851; street commissioner of McConnelsville in 1850; member of the Republican State convention in 1855;

elected as a Republican to the Thirty-fifth and Thirty-sixth Congresses (March 4, 1857-March 3, 1861); chairman, Committee on Militia (Thirty-sixth Congress); unsuccessful candidate for renomination in 1860; resumed the practice of law; died in McConnelsville, Ohio, July 23, 1862; interment in McConnelsville Cemetery.

**TOMPKINS, Daniel D.** (brother of Caleb Tompkins), a Representative from New York and a Vice President of the United States; born in Fox Meadows (later Scarsdale), Westchester County, N.Y., June 21, 1774; completed preparatory studies; graduated from Columbia College, New York City, in 1795; studied law; was admitted to the bar in 1797 and began practice in New York City; delegate to the New York State constitutional convention in 1801; member, New York State assembly, 1803; elected to the Ninth Congress, but resigned before the beginning of the congressional term to accept an appointment as associate justice of the New York State supreme court, in which capacity he served from 1804 to 1807; elected Governor of New York in 1807, reelected in 1810, 1813 and 1816 and served from July 1, 1807 until his resignation on February 24, 1817, having previously been elected Vice President; declined an appointment as Secretary of State of the United States tendered by President James Madison; elected Vice President of the United States on the ticket with James Monroe in 1816; reelected in 1820, and served from March 4, 1817 to March 3, 1825; delegate to the New York State constitutional convention in 1821, serving as its president; died in Tompkinsville, Staten Island, N.Y., June 11, 1825; interment in the Minthorne vault in St. Mark's Churchyard, New York City.

**Bibliography:** *DAB*; Irwin, Ray W. *Daniel D. Tompkins: Governor of New York and Vice President of the United States.* New York: New-York Historical Society, 1968.

**TOMPKINS, Emmett** (son of Cydnor Bailey Tompkins), a Representative from Ohio; born in McConnelsville, Morgan County, Ohio, September 1, 1853; moved to Athens County, Ohio, in 1865; attended the public schools and Ohio University at Athens; studied law; was admitted to the bar in 1875 and commenced practice in Athens, Ohio; city solicitor in 1876 and 1877; mayor of Athens 1877-1879; prosecuting attorney of Athens County in 1879; delegate to the Republican State conventions in 1879, 1881, and 1883; member of the State house of representatives 1886-1890; moved to Columbus, Ohio, in 1889; member of the board of trustees of Ohio University; elected as a Republican to the Fifty-seventh Congress (March 4, 1901-March 3, 1903); resumed the practice of law in Columbus, Ohio; appointed trustee of Ohio University in 1908; died in Columbus, Ohio, December 18, 1917; remains were cremated in Cincinnati, Ohio, and the ashes returned to his home in Columbus, Ohio.

**TOMPKINS, Patrick Watson,** a Representative from Mississippi; born in Kentucky in 1804; received a limited education; studied law; was admitted to the bar and commenced practice in Vicksburg, Warren County, Miss.; judge of the circuit court; elected as a Whig to the Thirtieth Congress (March 4, 1847-March 3, 1849); chairman, Committee on Expenditures in the Department of the Navy (Thirtieth Congress); moved to California during the gold rush of 1849; died in San Francisco, Calif., May 8, 1853; interment in Yerba Buena Cemetery.

**TONGUE, Thomas H.,** a Representative from Oregon; born in Lincolnshire, England, June 23, 1844; attended the public schools in England; immigrated to the United States with his parents, who settled in Washington County, Oreg., November 23, 1859; attended Tualatin (Wash.) Academy, and was graduated from the Pacific University, Forest Grove, Washington County, Oreg., in 1868; moved to Hillsboro, Washington County, Oreg., in 1868; studied law; was admitted to the bar in 1870 and commenced practice in Hillsboro; chairman of the Republican State convention in 1890; served in the State senate 1888-1892; delegate to the Republican National

Convention in 1892; again chairman of the Republican State convention, in 1894; elected as a Republican to the Fifty-fifth, Fifty-sixth and Fifty-seventh Congresses and served from March 4, 1897, until his death; chairman, Committee on Irrigation of Arid Lands (Fifty-sixth and Fifty-seventh Congresses); had been reelected to the Fifty-eighth Congress; died in Washington, D.C., January 11, 1903; interment in the private family cemetery adjoining the Masonic Cemetery at Hillsboro, Oreg.

**TONRY, Richard Alvin,** a Representative from Louisiana; born in New Orleans, Orleans Parish, La., June 25, 1935; attended the Catholic schools of New Orleans, and graduated from Jesuit High School in 1953; A.B., Springfield College, Mobile, Ala., 1960, and M.A., 1962; pursued graduate studies at Georgetown University, Washington, D.C., 1962; J.D., Loyola University, New Orleans, 1967; admitted to the Louisiana bar in 1967 and commenced practice in Arabi; engaged in private practice of law in Arabi and Chalmette, La., 1967-1976; served in Louisiana State house of representatives in 1976; elected as a Democrat to the Ninety-fifth Congress and served from January 3, 1977, until he resigned on May 4, 1977, following allegations of receiving illegal campaign contributions; returned to Louisiana to campaign in the special election to fill his own seat, but was an unsuccessful candidate for renomination in the June 25, 1977 special primary; unsuccessful candidate for the Louisiana State house of representatives in 1983; resumed the practice of law; is a resident of Arabi, La.

**TONRY, Richard Joseph,** a Representative from New York; born in Brooklyn, N.Y., September 30, 1893; educated in the public schools, Randolph Military Academy, Montclair, N.J., and Pratt Institute, Brooklyn, N.Y.; during the First World War served as a sergeant in the United States Marine Corps, 1917-1921; engaged in the real estate and the insurance brokerage business in 1921; served in the New York State assembly, 1922-1929; member of the New York City Board of Aldermen, 1930-1934; elected as a Democrat to the Seventy-fourth Congress (January 3, 1935-January 3, 1937); unsuccessful candidate for renomination in 1936 to the Seventy-fifth Congress; delegate to the Democratic State conventions in 1938, 1940, 1942, and 1946; journal clerk of the House of Representatives, 1943-1946; in 1947 was appointed a commissioner of appraisal for the corporation counsel in the city of New York; real estate and insurance broker; died in Brooklyn, N.Y., January 17, 1971; interment in United States Military Cemetery, Long Island, N.Y.

**TOOLE, Joseph Kemp,** a Delegate from the Territory of Montana; born in Savannah, Andrew County, Mo., May 12, 1851; attended the public schools in St. Joseph, Mo., and the Western Military Academy, Newcastle, Ky.; moved to Helena, Mont., in 1870; studied law; was admitted to the bar in 1871 and commenced practice in Helena, Mont.; district attorney of the third judicial district of Montana, 1872-1876; member of the Territorial house of representatives, 1879-1881; member and president of the Territorial council, 1881-1883; delegate to the Montana constitutional conventions at Helena in 1884 and 1889; elected as a Democrat to the Forty-ninth and Fiftieth Congresses (March 4, 1885-March 3, 1889); did not seek renomination in 1888 to the Fifty-first Congress, having become a gubernatorial candidate; elected as the first Governor of the State of Montana in 1889, and served from November 8, 1889 until January 1, 1893; resumed the practice of law in Helena; delegate to the Democratic National Conventions of 1892 and 1904; again elected Governor in 1900; reelected in 1904, and served from January 7, 1901 until April 1, 1908, when he resigned on account of ill health; lived in retirement, dividing his time between his home in Helena, Mont., and San Francisco, Calif.; died in Helena, Mont., March 11, 1929; interment in Resurrection Cemetery.

**Bibliography:** *DAB.*

**TOOMBS, Robert Augustus,** a Representative and a Senator from Georgia; born in Wilkes County, Ga., July 2, 1810; attended the University of Georgia at Athens and graduated from Union College, Schenectady, N.Y., in 1828; studied law at the University of Virginia at Charlottesville; was admitted to the bar and commenced practice in Washington, Wilkes County, Ga., in 1830; commanded a company in the Creek War in 1836; member, Georgia State house of representatives, 1837-1840, 1841-1843; elected as a Whig to the Twenty-ninth and to the three succeeding Congresses (March 4, 1845-March 3, 1853); elected as a Democrat to the United States Senate in 1852; reelected in 1858, and served from March 4, 1853 to February 4, 1861, when he withdrew in support of the Confederacy; his seat was declared vacant and his name omitted from the roll by a resolution of March 14, 1861; member of the State sovereignty convention at Milledgeville, Ga., in 1861; during the Civil War served in the Confederate Provisional Congress; Secretary of State of the Confederate States; commissioned a brigadier general in the Confederate Army on July 19, 1861, resigning March 4, 1863; in order to avoid arrest at the end of the Civil War, fled to Havana and then to London; returned to his home in Washington, Ga., in 1867; delegate to the State constitutional convention in 1877; died in Washington, Ga., December 15, 1885; interment in Rest Haven Cemetery.

**Bibliography:** *DAB*; Phillips, Ulrich. *The Life of Robert Toombs.* 1913. Reprint. New York: Burt Franklin, 1968; Thompson, William Y. *Robert Toombs of Georgia.* Baton Rouge: Louisiana State University Press, 1966.

**TORKILDSEN, Peter Gerard,** a Representative from Massachusetts; born in Milwaukee, Wis., January 28, 1958; B.A., University of Massachusetts, 1980; M.P.A., John F. Kennedy School of Government, Harvard University, 1990; service coordinator, Visiting Nurse Association of Boston, 1982-1984; member, Massachusetts house of representatives, 1985-1990; commissioner, Massachusetts Department of Labor and Industries, 1991-1992; Massachusetts co-chair of the campaign of Governor William F. Weld and Lieutenant Governor Argeo P. Cellucci in 1990; elected as a Republican to the One Hundred Third and One Hundred Fourth Congresses (January 3, 1993-January 3, 1997); is a resident of Danvers, Mass.

**TORRENS, James H.,** a Representative from New York; born in New York City, September 12, 1874; elected as a Democrat to the Seventy-eighth Congress to fill the vacancy caused by the resignation of Joseph A. Gavagan; reelected to the Seventy-ninth Congress, and served from February 29, 1944 to January 3, 1947; was not a candidate for renomination in 1946 to the Eightieth Congress; died in New York City, April 5, 1952; interment in Gate of Heaven Cemetery, Mount Pleasant, N.Y.

**TORRES, Esteban Edward,** a Representative from California; born in Miami, Gila County, Ariz., January 27, 1930; attended the public schools of East Los Angeles, Calif., and graduated from James A. Garfield High School in 1949; attended Los Angeles Art Center, 1953; A.A. East Los Angeles College, 1959; B.A., California State University at Los Angeles, 1963; attended the University of Maryland, College Park, 1965, and American University, Washington, D.C., 1966; served in the United States Army, sergeant, first class, 1949-1953, with service during the Korean conflict; United Auto Workers representative and international labor consultant, 1954-1968; community affairs organizer, 1968-1974; United Auto Workers official, 1975-1976; consultant, Office of Technology Assessment, 1976-1977; United States Ambassador to the United Nations Educational, Scientific and Cultural Organization, Paris, 1977-1979; Special Assistant to the President, The White House, 1979-1981; delegate, California State Democratic conventions, 1968-1983; delegate to the Democratic National Conventions of 1984 and 1988; unsuccessful candidate for election in 1974 to the

Ninety-fourth Congress; elected as a Democrat to the Ninety-eighth and to the six succeeding Congresses (January 3, 1983-January 3, 1997); is a resident of West Covina, Calif.

**TORRICELLI, Robert Guy,** a Representative from New Jersey; born in Paterson, Passaic County, N.J., August 26, 1951; graduated from Storm King School, Cornwall on Hudson, N.Y., 1970; A.B., Rutgers University, New Brunswick, N.J., 1974; J.D., Rutgers University School of Law, 1977; M.P.A., Harvard University, 1980; admitted to the New Jersey bar in 1978; assistant to Governor Brendan T. Byrne of New Jersey, 1975-1977; counsel to Vice President Walter F. Mondale, 1978-1980; elected as a Democrat to the Ninety-eighth and to the six succeeding Congresses (January 3, 1983-January 3, 1997); was not a candidate in 1996 for reelection to the House of Representatives, but was a candidate for election to the United States Senate; is a resident of Englewood, N.J.

**TOUCEY, Isaac,** a Representative and a Senator from Connecticut; born in Newtown, Fairfield County, Conn., November 15, 1792; pursued classical studies; studied law; was admitted to the bar in 1818 and began practice in Hartford, Conn.; prosecuting attorney of Hartford County, 1822-1835; elected as a Democrat to the Twenty-fourth and Twenty-fifth Congresses (March 4, 1835-March 3, 1839); unsuccessful candidate for reelection in 1838 to the Twenty-sixth Congress; prosecuting attorney of Hartford County, 1842-1844; unsuccessful candidate for election for Governor of Connecticut in 1845, but was elected to that office by the Legislature in 1846, and served from May 6, 1846 to May 5, 1847; unsuccessful candidate for reelection in 1846; appointed Attorney General in the Cabinet of President James K. Polk, and served from June 29, 1848 until March 7, 1849; member of the Connecticut State senate in 1850; member of the State house of representatives in 1852; elected as a Democrat to the United States Senate for the term commencing March 4, 1851, and served from May 12, 1852 to March 3, 1857; declined to be a candidate for reelection; appointed Secretary of the Navy in the Cabinet of President James Buchanan, and served from March 7, 1857 to March 6, 1861; resumed the practice of his profession; died in Hartford, Conn., July 30, 1869; interment in Cedar Hill Cemetery.

Bibliography: *DAB.*

**TOU VELLE, William Ellsworth,** a Representative from Ohio; born in Celina, Mercer County, Ohio, November 23, 1862, attended the public schools and was graduated from Celina High School in 1879; appointed postmaster of Celina, Ohio, on May 27, 1885, and served until June 14, 1888, when a successor was appointed; was graduated from Cincinnati Law School in 1889; was admitted to the bar the same year and commenced practice in Celina; elected as a Democrat to the Sixtieth and Sixty-first Congresses (March 4, 1907-March 3, 1911); was not a candidate for renomination in 1910 to the Sixty-second Congress; resumed the practice of law; president of the First National Bank of Celina; died in Celina, Ohio, August 14, 1951; interment in North Grove Cemetery.

**TOWE, Harry Lancaster,** a Representative from New Jersey; born in Jersey City, N.J., November 3, 1898; attended the public schools of Passaic, N.J., and the United States Naval Academy, 1918-1920; was graduated from New Jersey Law School at Newark in 1925; was admitted to the bar the same year and commenced practice in Rutherford, N.J.; United States commissioner, 1929-1931; special assistant attorney general of New Jersey, 1931-1934; member of the New Jersey State house of assembly in 1941 and 1942; elected as a Republican to the Seventy-eighth and to the four succeeding Congresses and served from January 3, 1943, until his resignation September 7, 1951, to become an assistant attorney general of New Jersey, in which capacity he served until his resignation October 31, 1953; engaged in the practice of law in Hackensack, N.J.; secretary and general counsel of the publishing

firm of Medical Economics, Inc., Oradel, N.J., from 1960 to 1969; was a resident of Kinnelon, N.J.; died February 8, 1991.

**TOWELL, David Gilmer,** a Representative from Nevada; born in Bronxville, Westchester County, N.Y., June 9, 1937; attended Bronxville and New York City schools; B.A., University of Pacific, Stockton, Calif., 1960; served in the Nevada Air National Guard, 1960-1966; real estate broker and manager; elected chairman, Douglas County Republican Central Committee, 1970; delegate, Nevada State Republican conventions, 1968, 1970, and 1972; elected as a Republican to the Ninety-third Congress (January 3, 1973-January 3, 1975); unsuccessful candidate for reelection in 1974 to the Ninety-fourth Congress; unsuccessful candidate in 1976 for election to the United States Senate; resumed real estate business; is a resident of Gardnerville, Nev.

**TOWER, John Goodwin,** a Senator from Texas; born in Houston, Harris County, Tex., September 29, 1925; educated in the public schools of Houston and Beaumont, Tex.; enlisted in the Navy during the Second World War in 1943, saw action in the Pacific, and was discharged with the rank of seaman first class in 1946; B.A., Southwestern University, Georgetown, Tex., 1948; M.A., Southern Methodist University, Dallas, Tex., 1953; attended the London School of Economics and Political Science during 1952; assistant professor of political science, Midwestern University, Wichita Falls, Tex., 1951-1960; unsuccessful candidate in 1960 for election to the United States Senate; elected as a Republican to the United States Senate, May 27, 1961, to fill the vacancy caused by the resignation of Lyndon B. Johnson for the term ending January 3, 1967; reelected in 1966, 1972, and again in 1978, and served from June 15, 1961 to January 3, 1985; declined to be a candidate for reelection in 1984; chairman, Republican Policy Committee (Ninety-third through Ninety-eighth Congresses), Committee on Armed Services (Ninety-seventh and Ninety-eighth Congresses); appointed a member of the United States arms negotiation team in Geneva, Switzerland, by President Ronald Reagan in 1985; chairman, President's Special Review Board ("Tower Commission"), 1987; nominated by President-elect George Bush to be Secretary of Defense on December 16, 1988, but the Senate, on March 9, 1989, declined to confirm the appointment; was a resident of Washington, D.C.; died April 5, 1991.

Bibliography: Tower, John G. *Consequences: A Personal and Political Memoir.* Boston: Little, Brown, 1991; Tower, John G. *A Program for Conservatives.* New York: MacFadden-Bartell Corp., 1962.

**TOWEY, Frank William, Jr.,** a Representative from New Jersey; born in Jersey City, Hudson County, N.J., November 5, 1895; attended Manresa Hall Grammar School and St. Peters High School, Jersey City, N.J.; was graduated from Holy Cross College, Worcester, Mass., in 1916 and from the law department of Fordham University, New York City in 1919; commissioned as a second lieutenant of Infantry, United States Army, in September 1918, and served until honorably discharged in January 1919; was admitted to the bar in 1920 and commenced practice in Newark, N.J.; elected as a Democrat to the Seventy-fifth Congress (January 3, 1937-January 3, 1939); unsuccessful candidate for reelection in 1938 to the Seventy-sixth Congress; resumed the practice of law; member of State of New Jersey Selective Appeal Board from October 1940 to April 1947; assistant to the Attorney General of the United States, Department of Justice, at New York City, 1943-1955; resided in Caldwell, N.J.; died in Montclair N.J., September 4, 1979; interment in Acacia Memorial Park, Seattle, Wash.

**TOWNE, Charles Arnette,** a Representative and a Senator from Minnesota and a Representative from New York; born near Pontiac, Oakland County, Mich., on November 21, 1858; attended the common schools; graduated from the University of Michigan at Ann Arbor in 1881; studied law; was admitted to the bar in 1885 and commenced practice in Marquette, Mich.; moved to Duluth, Minn., in 1890 and continued the practice of law; judge advocate general of Minnesota, 1893-1895; elected as a Republican to the Fifty-fourth Congress (March 4, 1895-March 3, 1897); unsuccessful Independent candidate for reelection in 1896 to the Fifty-fifth Congress, and for election in 1898 to the Fifty-sixth Congress; declined the nomination for Vice President of the United States by the national conventions of the Populist and Silver Republican Parties in 1900; appointed as a Democrat to the United States Senate to fill the vacancy caused by the death of Cushman K. Davis, and served from December 5, 1900 to January 28, 1901, when a successor was elected and qualified; moved to New York City in 1901 and resumed the practice of law; elected as a Democrat from New York to the Fifty-ninth Congress (March 4, 1905-March 3, 1907); died in Tucson, Ariz., October 22, 1928; interment in Evergreen Cemetery, Tucson, Ariz.

**Bibliography:** *DAB*; Schlup, Leonard. "Charles A. Towne and the Vice-Presidential Question of 1900." *North Dakota History* 44 (Winter 1977): 14-20.

**TOWNER, Horace Mann,** a Representative from Iowa; born in Belvidere, Boone County, Ill., October 23, 1855; attended the public and high schools of Belvidere, the University of Chicago, and Union College of Law; was admitted to the bar in 1877 and commenced practice in Prescott, Adams County, Iowa; moved to Corning, Adams County, Iowa, in 1880, having been elected county superintendent of schools, in which capacity he served until 1884, when he resumed the practice of law; elected judge of the third judicial district of Iowa in 1890, and served until January 1, 1911; lectured on constitutional law in the University of Iowa, 1902-1911; elected as a Republican to the Sixty-second and to the six succeeding Congresses, and served from March 4, 1911 to April 1, 1923, when he resigned to become Governor of Puerto Rico, in which capacity he served until his resignation on September 29, 1929; chairman, Committee on Insular Affairs (Sixty-sixth and Sixty-seventh Congress); co-sponsor of the Sheppard-Towner Act of 1921, designating funding to enable States to improve their maternal and child care services; resumed the practice of law in Corning, Iowa, until his death on November 23, 1937; interment in Walnut Grove Cemetery.

**TOWNS, Edolphus,** a Representative from New York; born in Chadbourn, Columbus County, N.C. July 21, 1934; attended the public schools of Chadbourn, N.C., and graduated from West Side High School in 1961; B.S., North Carolina A&T, Greensboro, 1956; M.S.W., Adelphi University, Garden City, N.Y., 1973; served in the United States Army as a private, 1956-1958; teacher, public schools, New York, N.Y. and Medgar Evers College, Brooklyn, N.Y.; hospital administrator, 1965-1971; deputy president, Borough of Brooklyn, N.Y., 1976-1982; member, New York State Democratic Committee, 1972-present; elected as Democrat to the Ninety-eighth and to the six succeeding Congresses (January 3, 1983-January 3, 1997); is a resident of Brooklyn, N.Y.

**TOWNS, George Washington Bonaparte,** a Representative from Georgia; born in Wilkes County, Ga., May 4, 1801; received a limited education; studied law; was admitted to the bar in 1824 and began practice in Montgomery, Ala.; returned to Georgia in 1826 and continued the practice of law at Talbotton; member of the Georgia State house of representatives in 1829 and 1830; served in the State senate, 1832-1834; elected as a Jacksonian to the Twenty-fourth Congress, and served from March 4, 1835 to September 1, 1836, when he resigned; reelected as a Democrat to the Twenty-fifth Congress (March 4, 1837-March 3, 1839); chairman, Committee on Public Buildings and Grounds (Twenty-fifth Congress); was not a candidate for reelection in 1838 to the Twenty-sixth Congress; elected as a Democrat to the Twenty-ninth Congress to fill the vacancy caused by the resignation of Washington Poe, and served from January 5, 1846 to March 3, 1847; unsuccessful candidate for reelection in 1846 to the Thirtieth Congress; elected Governor of Georgia in 1847, reelected in 1849, and served from November 3,

1847 to November 5, 1851; resumed the practice of law; died in Macon, Ga., July 15, 1854; interment in Rose Hill Cemetery.

**Bibliography:** *DAB*.

**TOWNSEND, Amos,** a Representative from Ohio; born in Brownsville, Fayette County, Pa., in 1821; attended the common schools of Pittsburgh, Pa.; clerked in a store in Pittsburgh; moved to Mansfield, Ohio, in 1839 and engaged in mercantile pursuits; served as United States marshal during the Kansas troubles; moved to Cleveland, Ohio, in 1858 and engaged in the wholesale grocery business; member of the city council 1866-1876, serving as president for seven years; member of the State constitutional convention in 1873; elected as a Republican to the Forty-fifth, Forty-sixth, and Forty-seventh Congresses (March 4, 1877-March 3, 1883); chairman, Committee on Railways and Canals (Forty-seventh Congress); declined renomination; member of a wholesale foodpacking firm; died while on a visit to St. Augustine, Fla., March 17, 1895; interment in Lake View Cemetery, Cleveland, Ohio.

**TOWNSEND, Charles Champlain,** a Representative from Pennsylvania; born in Allegheny (now a part of Pittsburgh), Pa., November 24, 1841; attended the common schools and Western University, Pittsburgh, Pa.; manufacturer of wire rivets and nails; served two years in the Union Army during the Civil War as a private in Company A, Ninth Regiment, Pennsylvania Volunteer Reserve Corps, and later as adjutant of the First Pennsylvania Volunteer Cavalry; elected as a Republican to the Fifty-first Congress (March 4, 1889-March 3, 1891); was not a candidate for renomination in 1890 to the Fifty-second Congress; again engaged in manufacturing; died in New Brighton, Beaver County, Pa., on July 10, 1910; interment in Grove Cemetery.

**TOWNSEND, Charles Elroy,** a Representative and a Senator from Michigan; born near Concord, Jackson County, Mich., August 15, 1856; attended the common schools in Concord and Jackson, and the University of Michigan at Ann Arbor; taught school at Concord, 1881-1886; register of deeds from 1886 until 1897; studied law; was admitted to the bar in 1895 and commenced the practice of his profession in Jackson, Mich.; elected as a Republican to the Fifty-eighth and to the three succeeding Congresses (March 4, 1903-March 3, 1911); was not a candidate in 1910 for reelection to the House of Representatives, but was elected to the United States Senate; reelected in 1916, and served from March 4, 1911 to March 3, 1923; unsuccessful candidate for reelection in 1922; chairman, Committee on Coast and Insular Survey (Sixty-second Congress), Committee on Expenditures in the War Department (Sixty-fifth Congress), Committee on Post Office and Post Roads (Sixty-sixth and Sixty-seventh Congresses); appointed in 1923 as a member of the International Joint Commission created to regulate the use of the boundary waters between the United States and Canada, in which capacity he served until his death in Jackson, Mich., August 3, 1924; interment in Maple Grove Cemetery, Concord, Mich.

**TOWNSEND, Dwight,** a Representative from New York; born in New York City September 26, 1826; was educated at the grammar school of Columbia College, New York City; engaged in the sugar business in the early sixties; member of the original board of the Equitable Life Assurance Society from 1859 to 1865; elected as a Democrat to the Thirty-eighth Congress to fill the vacancy caused by the resignation of Henry G. Stebbins and served from December 5, 1864, to March 3, 1865; elected to the Forty-second Congress (March 4, 1871-March 3, 1873); resumed his former business pursuits in 1875; died in New York City October 29, 1899; interment in Greenwood Cemetery, Brooklyn, N.Y.

**TOWNSEND, Edward Waterman,** a Representative from New Jersey; born in Cleveland, Ohio, February 10, 1855; attended private and public schools in that city; went to San Francisco, Calif., in 1875 and engaged in newspaper and literary work; moved to New

York City in 1893 and continued his reportorial and literary pursuits; in 1900 became a resident of Montclair, Essex County, N.J.; author of novels, plays, short stories, as well as a textbook on the Constitution of the United States; elected as a Democrat to the Sixty-second and Sixty-third Congresses (March 4, 1911-March 3, 1915); unsuccessful candidate for reelection in 1914 to the Sixty-fourth Congress; served as postmaster of Montclair, N.J., 1915-1923; moved to New York City in 1924 and resumed newspaper and literary pursuits; member of the National Institute of Arts and Letters; died in New York City March 15, 1942; interment in Forest Hills Cemetery, Utica, N.Y.

**TOWNSEND, George,** a Representative from New York; born in Lattingtown, township of Oyster Bay, Queens County, N.Y., in 1769; engaged in agricultural pursuits; elected as a Republican to the Fourteenth and Fifteenth Congresses (March 4, 1815-March 3, 1819); died in Lattingtown, township of Oyster Bay, Queens County, N.Y., August 17, 1844.

**TOWNSEND, Hosea,** a Representative from Colorado; born in Greenwich, Huron County, Ohio, June 16, 1840; attended the common schools and Western Reserve College, Cleveland, Ohio, in 1860; enlisted in the Second Regiment, Ohio Volunteer Cavalry, in 1861; promoted to lieutenant, but resigned in 1863 on account of disability; studied law; was admitted to the bar in Cleveland, Ohio, in 1864 and commenced practice in Memphis, Tenn., in 1865; member of the State house of representatives in 1869; moved to Colorado in 1879 and settled in Silver Cliff in 1881; elected as a Republican to the Fifty-first and Fifty-second Congresses (March 4, 1889-March 3, 1893); unsuccessful for renomination in 1892; delegate to the Republican National Convention in 1892; United States judge for the southern district of the Indian Territory 1897-1907; died in Ardmore, Okla., March 4, 1909; interment in Woodlawn Cemetery, Norwalk, Huron County, Ohio.

**TOWNSEND, John Gillis, Jr.,** a Senator from Delaware; born on a farm in Worcester County, Md., near Selbyville, Del., May 31, 1871; attended the rural schools; moved to Selbyville, Sussex County, Del., in 1895 and engaged in banking; also interested in manufacturing and agricultural pursuits; member, Delaware State house of representatives, 1901-1903; elected Governor of Delaware in 1916, and served from January 17, 1917 to January 18, 1921; elected as a Republican to the United States Senate in 1928; reelected in 1934, and served from March 4, 1929 to January 3, 1941; unsuccessful candidate for reelection in 1940; chairman, Committee to Audit and Control the Contingent Expense (Seventy-second Congress); member of the Mount Rushmore National Memorial Commission, 1939-1940; trustee of several colleges and universities; resumed banking, agricultural pursuits, and the raising and processing of poultry and vegetables; was a resident of Selbyville, Del.; died in Philadelphia, Pa., on April 10, 1964; interment in Red Men's Cemetery, Selbyville, Del.

**TOWNSEND, Martin Ingham,** a Representative from New York; born in Hancock, Mass., February 6, 1810; moved with his parents to Williamstown, Mass, in 1816; attended the common schools, and was graduated from Williams College, Williamstown, Mass., in 1833; studied law; was admitted to the bar in 1836 and commenced practice in Troy, N.Y.; district attorney of Rensselaer County 1842-1845; delegate to the State constitutional convention in 1867 and 1868; regent of New York University 1873-1903; elected as a Republican to the Forty-fourth and Forty-fifth Congresses (March 4, 1875-March 3, 1879); declined to be a candidate for renomination in 1878; United States district attorney for the northern district of New York 1879-1887; member of the State constitutional convention in 1890; retired from legal practice in 1901; died in Troy, N.Y., March 8, 1903; interment in Oakwood Cemetery.

**TOWNSEND, Washington,** a Representative from Pennsylvania; born in West Chester, Chester County, Pa., January 20, 1813; attended a private school and West Chester Academy; engaged as a bank teller 1828-1844; studied law; was admitted to the bar in 1844 and commenced practice in West Chester, Pa.; prosecuting attorney of Chester County in 1848; deputy attorney under Attorneys General Darragh and Cooper; cashier of the Bank of Chester County 1849-1857; delegate to the Whig National Convention in 1852; delegate to the Republican National Convention in 1860; elected as a Republican to the Forty-first and to the three succeeding Congresses (March 4, 1869-March 3, 1877); chairman, Committee on Public Lands (Forty-third Congress); was not a candidate for renomination in 1876; again resumed the practice of his profession in West Chester, Chester County, Pa.; president of the Bank of Chester County 1879-1894; died in West Chester, Pa., March 18, 1894; interment in Oakland Cemetery, near West Chester.

**TOWNSHEND, Norton Strange,** a Representative from Ohio; born in Clay-Coaton, Northamptonshire, England, December 25, 1815; in 1830 immigrated to the United States with his parents, who settled in Avon, Ohio; educated himself by the use of his father's library; taught a district school for a short time; was graduated from the University of Physicians and Surgeons in New York in 1840; delegate to the World's Antislavery Convention in London, England, in 1840; studied medicine in the hospitals of London, Paris, Edinburgh, and Dublin; engaged in the practice of medicine in Avon, Ohio, in 1841; moved to Elyria, Ohio; member of the State house of representatives in 1848 and 1849; delegate to the State constitutional convention in 1850; elected as a Democrat to the Thirty-second Congress (March 4, 1851-March 3, 1853); member of the State senate in 1854 and 1855; medical inspector of the United States Army with the rank of lieutenant colonel 1863-1865; engaged in agricultural pursuits near Avon, Ohio; director of the State board of agriculture 1858-1869 and 1886-1889; professor of agriculture in Iowa Agricultural College in 1869; appointed in 1870 as one of the first trustees of Ohio Agricultural and Mechanical College; resigned in 1873 to become professor of agriculture in the new State college and served until his resignation in 1892, when he became professor emeritus; died in Columbus, Ohio, July 13, 1895; interment in Protestant Cemetery, Avon Center, Ohio.

**TOWNSHEND, Richard Wellington,** a Representative from Illinois; born near Upper Marlboro, Prince Georges County, Md., April 30, 1840; moved to Washington, D.C., in 1846; attended public and private schools; page in the House of Representatives; moved to Cairo, Alexander County, Ill., in 1858; taught school in Fayette County; studied law; was admitted to the bar in 1862 and commenced practice in McLeansboro, Ill.; clerk of the circuit court of Hamilton County 1863-1868; prosecuting attorney for the twelfth judicial circuit of Illinois 1868-1872; member of the Democratic State central committee in 1864, 1865, 1874, and 1875; delegate to the Democratic National Convention in 1872; moved to Shawneetown, Gallatin County, Ill., in 1873 and resumed the practice of law; elected as a Democrat to the Forty-fifth and to the six succeeding Congresses and served from March 4, 1877, until his death in Washington, D.C., March 9, 1889; chairman, Committee on Expenditures in the Department of the Navy (Forty-sixth Congress), Committee on Military Affairs (Fiftieth Congress); interment in Rock Creek Cemetery.

**TRACEWELL, Robert John,** a Representative from Indiana; born near Front Royal, Warren County, Va., May 7, 1852; moved with his parents to Corydon, Harrison County, Ind., in 1854; attended the public schools of Corydon and was graduated from Hanover (Ind.) College in 1874; studied law; was admitted to the bar in 1875 and commenced practice in Corydon, Ind.; elected as a Republican to the Fifty-fourth Congress (March 4, 1895-March 3, 1897); unsuccessful candidate for reelection in 1896 to the Fifty-fifth

Congress; appointed by President William McKinley as Comptroller of the Treasury and served from March 4, 1897, to June 15, 1914, when he resigned; moved to Evansville, Ind., in 1914 and resumed the practice of law; elected judge of the superior court of Vanderburg County, Ind., in 1918; renominated in 1922, but died in Evansville, Ind., on July 28, 1922, before the election; interment in Cedar Hill Cemetery, Corydon, Harrison County, Ind.

**TRACEY, Charles,** a Representative from New York; born in Albany, N.Y., May 27, 1847; was graduated from the Albany Academy in 1866; served in the Papal Zouaves at Rome, Italy, during portions of the years 1867 to 1870; appointed aide-de-camp to Governor Samuel J. Tilden, of New York, January 1, 1877; appointed manager of the House of Refuge in Hudson, N.Y., by Governor Grover Cleveland and reappointed by Governor David B. Hill in 1886; engaged in the distilling business; elected as a Democrat to the Fiftieth Congress to fill the vacancy caused by the death of Nicholas T. Kane; reelected to the Fifty-first and to the two succeeding Congresses and served from November 8, 1887, to March 3, 1895; was an unsuccessful candidate for reelection in 1894 to the Fifty-fourth Congress; resumed business activities in Albany and Rochester, N.Y.; died at Watkins Glen, Schuyler County, N.Y., on March 24, 1905; interment in St. Agnes Cemetery, Albany, N.Y.

**TRACEY, John Plank,** a Representative from Missouri; born in Wayne County, Ohio, September 18, 1836; attended the public schools of Ohio and Indiana; studied law; taught school; moved to Missouri in 1858; enlisted as a private in the Union Army March 1, 1862, and served until March 10, 1865, when he was mustered out with the rank of first lieutenant; commissioned lieutenant colonel of Missouri Enrolled Militia in April 1865; was admitted to the bar in May 1865 and commenced practice in Stockton, Cedar County, Mo.; moved to Springfield, Greene County, Mo., in 1874 and engaged in journalism; unsuccessful candidate for railroad commissioner in 1878; commissioned United States marshal for the western district of Missouri February 4, 1890, and served until March 4, 1894; elected as a Republican to the Fifty-fourth Congress (March 4, 1895-March 3, 1897); unsuccessful candidate for reelection in 1896 to the Fifty-fifth Congress; member of the State house of representatives in 1903 and 1904; superintendent of the Soldiers' Home at St. James, Mo., in 1909 and 1910; engaged in newspaper work in Springfield, Mo., where he died July 24, 1910; interment in Hazelwood Cemetery.

**TRACY, Albert Haller** (brother of Phineas Lyman Tracy), a Representative from New York; born in Norwich, Conn., June 17, 1793; pursued classical studies; studied medicine; moved to New York State in 1811; abandoned medicine and studied law; was admitted to the bar and commenced practice in Buffalo, N.Y., in 1815; elected to the Sixteenth, Seventeenth, and Eighteenth Congresses (March 4, 1819-March 3, 1825); chairman, Committee on Expenditures in the Department of the Treasury (Seventeenth Congress); member of the State senate 1830-1837; unsuccessful Whig candidate for election to the United States Senate in 1839; died in Buffalo, N.Y., September 19, 1859.

**TRACY, Andrew,** a Representative from Vermont; born in Hartford, Vt., December 15, 1797; attended Royalton and Randolph Academies, and also Dartmouth College, Hanover, N.H., for two years; taught school; studied law; was admitted to the bar in 1826 and commenced practice in Quechee, Windsor County, Vt.; moved to Woodstock, Vt., in 1838 and continued the practice of law; member of the State house of representatives 1833-1837; served in the State senate in 1839; was an unsuccessful candidate for election in 1840 to the Twenty-seventh Congress; again a member of the State house of representatives 1843-1845 and served as speaker; elected as a Whig to the Thirty-third Congress (March 4, 1853-March 3, 1855); declined to be a candidate for renomination in 1854 to the Thirty-fourth Congress; resumed the practice of his profession; died

in Woodstock, Vt., on October 28, 1868; interment in Old Cemetery on River Street.

**TRACY, Henry Wells,** a Representative from Pennsylvania; born in Ulster Township, Bradford County, Pa., September 24, 1807; completed preparatory studies; attended Angelica Seminary in Allegany County, N.Y.; studied law; engaged in mercantile pursuits and as a road contractor in Standing Stone, Pa., Havre de Grace, Md., and Towanda, Pa.; delegate to the Republican National Convention in 1860; member of the Pennsylvania house of representatives in 1861 and 1862; elected as an Independent Republican to the Thirty-eighth Congress (March 4, 1863-March 3, 1865); collector of the port of Philadelphia in 1866; resumed mercantile pursuits; died at Standing Stone, Bradford County, Pa., April 11, 1886; interment in the Brick Church Cemetery, Wysox, Pa.

**TRACY, Phineas Lyman** (brother of Albert Haller Tracy), a Representative from New York; born in Norwich, Conn., on December 25, 1786; was graduated from Yale College in 1806; engaged in teaching for two years; studied law; was admitted to the bar in 1811 and commenced practice in the village of Madison, Madison County, N.Y.; moved to Batavia, Genesee County, about 1815 and continued the practice of law; elected to the Twentieth Congress to fill the vacancy caused by the resignation of David E. Evans; reelected as an Anti-Masonic candidate to the Twenty-first and Twenty-second Congresses and served from November 5, 1827, to March 3, 1833; declined to be a candidate for renomination; appointed presiding judge of Genesee County Court in 1841, and continued in that office until 1846, when he retired from public life; died in Batavia, N.Y., December 22, 1876; interment in Batavia Cemetery.

**TRACY, Uri,** a Representative from New York; born in Norwich, West Farms (later Franklin), Conn., February 8, 1764; was graduated from Yale College in 1789; became a Presbyterian clergyman and missionary to the Indians; moved to Oxford, N.Y., in 1791; first principal of Oxford Academy in 1794; first sheriff of Chenango County and served from 1798 until his resignation in August 1801; elected county clerk and served from 1801 to 1815; member of the State assembly in 1803; first postmaster of Oxford 1802-1805; elected as a Republican to the Ninth Congress (March 4, 1805-March 3, 1807); elected to the Eleventh and Twelfth Congresses (March 4, 1809-March 3, 1813); appointed first judge of Chenango County July 8, 1819, and served until February 1823; died in Oxford, N.Y., July 21, 1838; interment in Riverview Cemetery.

**TRACY, Uriah,** a Representative and a Senator from Connecticut; born in Franklin, Conn., February 2, 1755; graduated from Yale College in 1778; studied law; was admitted to the bar in 1781 and commenced practice in Litchfield, Conn.; major general of militia; member, State general assembly 1788-1793, serving as speaker 1793; State's attorney for Litchfield County 1794-1799; elected to the Third and Fourth Congresses and served from March 4, 1793, until his resignation, effective October 13, 1796; elected as a Federalist to the United States Senate to fill the vacancy caused by the resignation of Jonathan Trumbull; reelected in 1801 and 1807, and served from October 13, 1796, until his death; served as President pro tempore of the Senate during the Sixth Congress; chairman, Committee on Claims (Third and Fourth Congresses); died in Washington, D.C., July 19, 1807; interment in Congressional Cemetery.

**Bibliography:** *DAB.*

**TRAEGER, William Isham,** a Representative from California; born in Porterville, Tulare County, Calif., February 26, 1880; attended the grammar and high schools of Porterville; during the Spanish-American War served as a private in Company E, First Battalion, California Infantry, later known as Sixth Regiment,

California Volunteer Infantry, and served from May 11 to December 15, 1898; was graduated from Stanford University in 1901; moved to Los Angeles in 1902 and engaged as athletic coach at Pomona College and later at the University of California; attended the law department of the University of Southern California at Los Angeles; deputy United States marshal 1903-1906; deputy sheriff of Los Angeles County 1907-1911; was admitted to the bar in 1909 and commenced the practice of law; deputy clerk of the California Supreme Court 1911-1921; sheriff of Los Angeles County 1921-1932; elected as a Republican to the Seventy-third Congress (March 4, 1933-January 3, 1935); unsuccessful candidate for reelection in 1934 to the Seventy-fourth Congress; died in Los Angeles, Calif., January 20, 1935; interment in Rosedale Cemetery.

**TRAFICANT, James A., Jr.,** a Representative from Ohio; born in Youngstown, Ohio, May 8, 1941; attended public and parochial schools in Youngstown and graduated from Cardinal Mooney High School in 1959; B.S., University of Pittsburgh, 1963; M.S., 1973, and M.S., Youngstown State University, 1976; executive director, Mahoning County Drug Program, Inc., 1971-1981; served as sheriff of Mahoning County from 1981 until 1985; elected as a Democrat to the Ninety-ninth and to the five succeeding Congresses (January 3, 1985-January 3, 1997); is a resident of Poland, Ohio.

**TRAFTON, Mark,** a Representative from Massachusetts; born in Bangor, Maine (then a district of Massachusetts), August 1, 1810; completed preparatory studies; studied theology and was ordained pastor of a church in Westfield, Mass.; elected as the candidate of the American Party to the Thirty-fourth Congress (March 4, 1855-March 3, 1857); unsuccessful candidate for reelection in 1856 to the Thirty-fifth Congress; resumed his ministerial duties and was pastor of a church in Mount Wollaston, Norfolk County, Mass.; died in West Somerville, Middlesex County, Mass., March 8, 1901; interment in Peabody Cemetery, Springfield, Mass.

**TRAIN, Charles Russell,** a Representative from Massachusetts; born in Framingham, Mass., October 18, 1817; attended the common schools, Framingham Academy, and was graduated from Brown University, Providence, R.I., in 1837; studied law at Harvard University; was admitted to the bar and commenced practice in Framingham, Mass., in 1841; member of the Massachusetts house of representatives, 1847-1848; district attorney, 1848-1854; declined the appointment of Associate Justice of the Supreme Court of the United States in 1852; delegate to the Massachusetts constitutional convention in 1853; delegate to the Republican National Conventions of 1856 and 1864; member of the Governor's council, 1857-1858; elected as Republican to the Thirty-sixth and Thirty-seventh Congresses (March 4, 1859-March 3, 1863); chairman, Committee on Public Buildings and Grounds (Thirty-sixth and Thirty-seventh Congresses); was not a candidate for renomination in 1862 to the Thirty-eighth Congress; one of the managers appointed by the House of Representatives in 1862 to conduct the impeachment proceedings against West H. Humphreys, United States judge for the several districts of Tennessee; during the Civil War served in the Union Army as a volunteer aide-de-camp to General George B. McClellan; moved to Boston, Mass.; again served in the Massachusetts house of representatives, 1868-1871; attorney general of Massachusetts, 1871-1878; resumed the practice of law; died while on a visit in Conway, Carroll County, N.H., July 28, 1885; interment in Edgell Grove Cemetery, Framingham, Mass.

**TRAMMELL, Park,** a Senator from Florida; born in Macon County, Ala., April 9, 1876; moved to Florida with his parents who settled on a farm near Lakeland, Polk County; attended the common schools in Florida; studied law at Vanderbilt University, Nashville, Tenn., and graduated from Cumberland University, Lebanon, Tenn., in 1899; was admitted to the bar in 1899 and commenced practice in Lakeland, Fla.; engaged as a fruit grower and owned and edited a newspaper; mayor of Lakeland, 1899-1903; member of the Florida

State house of representatives in 1902; member, Florida State senate, 1904-1908, serving as president in 1905; attorney general of Florida, 1909-1913; elected Governor of Florida in 1912 and served from January 7, 1913 to January 2, 1917; elected in 1916 as a Democrat to the United States Senate; reelected in 1922, 1928, and again in 1934, and served from March 4, 1917, until his death in Washington, D.C., May 8, 1936; chairman, Committee on Expenditures in the Treasury Department (Sixty-fifth Congress), Committee on Naval Affairs (Seventy-third and Seventy-fourth Congresses); interment in Roselawn Cemetery, Lakeland, Fla.

**Bibliography:** Kerber, Stephen. "Park Trammell of Florida: A Political Biography." Ph.D. dissertation, University of Florida, 1979.

**TRANSUE, Andrew Jackson,** a Representative from Michigan; born in Clarksville, Ionia County, Mich., January 12, 1903; graduated, Clarksville-Ionia County High School; J.D., Detroit (Mich.) College of Law, 1926; was admitted to the bar in 1926 and commenced the practice of law in Detroit, Mich., in 1926 and Flint, Mich., in 1927; prosecuting attorney of Genesee County, 1933-1937; elected as a Democrat to the Seventy-fifth Congress (January 3, 1937-January 3, 1939); unsuccessful candidate for reelection in 1938 to the Seventy-sixth Congress; Genesee County chairman for the presidential campaign of John F. Kennedy in 1960; resumed the practice of law; was a resident of Flint, Mich. until his death there on June 24, 1995; interment in Glenwood Cemetery.

**TRAPIER, Paul,** a Delegate from South Carolina; born in Prince George's Parish, Winyah, near Georgetown, S.C., in 1749; educated in England, where he attended Eton College 1763-1765; admitted pensioner, St. John's College, Cambridge, March 20, 1766; admitted to the Middle Temple, London, February 17, 1767; member of the Provincial Congress and the committee of safety for Georgetown, S.C.; member of the South Carolina general assembly in 1776; justice of the peace in 1776; served in the Revolutionary War as captain of the Georgetown Artillery; elected to the Continental Congress in 1777, but did not attend; died at his home near Georgetown, S.C., on July 8, 1778; interment in the churchyard of Prince George, Winyah, Georgetown, S.C.

**TRAXLER, Jerome Bob,** a Representative from Michigan; born in Kawkawlin, Bay County, Mich., July 21, 1931; attended the public schools in Bay City, Mich.; B.A., Michigan State University, East Lansing, 1953; LL.B., Detroit College of Law, 1959; admitted to the Michigan bar in 1960 and commenced practice in Bay City; served in the United States Army, 1953-1955; served as assistant Bay County prosecutor, 1960-1962; elected to the Michigan State house of representatives, 1962-1974; served as majority floor leader in the Michigan house, 1965-1966; elected as a Democrat to the Ninety-third Congress, April 16, 1974, by special election to fill the vacancy caused by the resignation of James Harvey; reelected to the nine succeeding Congresses, and served from April 16, 1974 to January 3, 1993; was not a candidate for reelection in 1992 to the One Hundred Third Congress; is a resident of Bay City, Mich.

**TRAYNOR, Philip Andrew,** a Representative from Delaware; born in Wilmington, New Castle County, Del., May 31, 1874; attended the public schools, Goldey Business College, Wilmington, Del., and the University of Delaware at Newark; was graduated in 1895 from the dental department of the University of Pennsylvania at Philadelphia, and commenced the practice of dentistry in Wilmington, Del.; member of the Delaware State board of dentistry from 1918 until 1943, serving as chairman of the board, beginning in 1922; delegate to the State Democratic convention in 1936; vice president and member of the board of trustees of Ferris Industrial School for Boys, 1938-1942; elected as a Democrat to the Seventy-seventh Congress (January 3, 1941-January 3, 1943); unsuccessful candidate for reelection in 1942 to the Seventy-eighth Congress; resumed the practice of his profession; elected as a Democrat to the Seventy-ninth Congress (January 3, 1945-January

3, 1947); unsuccessful candidate for reelection in 1946 to the Eightieth Congress; resumed the practice of dentistry at Wilmington, Del., where he died on December 5, 1962; interment in Cathedral Cemetery.

**TREADWAY, Allen Towner,** a Representative from Massachusetts; was born in Stockbridge, Berkshire County, Mass., on September 16, 1867; attended the public schools; graduated from Amherst (Mass.) College in 1886; engaged in the hotel business; member of the Massachusetts house of representatives in 1904; member of the Massachusetts senate 1908-1911, and served as president 1909-1911; elected as a Republican to the Sixty-third and to the fifteen succeeding Congresses (March 4, 1913-January 3, 1945); was not a candidate for renomination in 1944; resided in Stockbridge, Mass., and Washington, D.C.; died in Washington, D.C., February 16, 1947; interment in Stockbridge Cemetery, Stockbridge, Mass.

**TREADWELL, John,** a Delegate from Connecticut; born in Farmington, Hartford County, Conn., November 23, 1745; completed preparatory studies; was graduated from Yale College in 1767; studied law; was admitted to the bar and commenced practice in Farmington, Conn.; member of the Connecticut State house of representatives, 1776-1785; clerk of the court of probate, 1777-1784; member of the Governor's council in 1785; elected to the Continental Congress in 1784, 1785, and 1787, but did not attend; member of the State council, 1786-1797; judge of the court of common pleas; delegate to the State ratification convention in 1788; judge of probate and the supreme court of errors, 1789-1809; Lieutenant Governor of Connecticut from 1798 until 1809; became Governor of Connecticut on August 7, 1809, following the death of Governor Jonathan Trumbull; elected Governor by the Legislature in 1810, and served from August 7, 1809 to May 9, 1811; unsuccessful candidate for reelection in 1811; delegate to the State constitutional convention in 1818; died in Farmington, Conn., August 18, 1823; interment in the Old Cemetery.

**TREDWAY, William Marshall,** a Representative from Virginia; born near Farmville, Prince Edward County, Va., August 24, 1807; completed preparatory studies; graduated from Hampden-Sidney College, Prince Edward County, Va., in 1827; studied law; admitted to the bar in 1830 and commenced practice in Danville, Va.; elected as a Democrat to the Twenty-ninth Congress (March 4, 1845-March 3, 1847); unsuccessful candidate for reelection in 1846 to the Thirtieth Congress; delegate to the Virginia Democratic convention in 1850; member of the secession convention of Virginia in 1861; judge of the circuit court of Virginia 1870-1879; resumed the practice of law in Chatham, Va., and died there May 1, 1891; interment in Chatham Cemetery.

**TREDWELL, Thomas** (grandfather of Thomas Treadwell Davis), a Representative from New York; born in Smithtown, Long Island, N.Y., February 6, 1743; was graduated from Princeton College in 1764; studied law; was admitted to the bar and began practice in Plattsburgh, N.Y.; delegate to the Provincial Congress of New York in 1774 and 1775; delegate to the New York State constitutional convention in 1776 and 1777; member of the New York State assembly, 1777-1783; judge of the court of probate, 1778-1787; served in the New York State senate, 1786-1789; surrogate of Suffolk County, 1787-1791; delegate to the New York State ratification convention in 1788; elected to the Second Congress to fill the vacancy caused by the death of James Townsend; reelected to the Third Congress and served from May 1791 to March 3, 1795; delegate to the New York State constitutional convention in 1801; again a member of the State senate, 1803-1807; surrogate of Clinton County from 1807 until 1831; died in Plattsburgh, Clinton County, N.Y., December 30, 1831; interment in a private burial ground in Beekmantown, N.Y.

**TREEN, David Conner,** a Representative from Louisiana; born in Baton Rouge, La., July 16, 1928; attended public grammar schools in East Baton Rouge, Jefferson, and Orleans Parishes; graduated from Fortier High School, New Orleans, La., 1945; B.A., Tulane University, New Orleans, 1948; J.D., Tulane University Law School, 1950; served in the United States Air Force, 1951-1952; admitted to the Louisiana bar in 1950 and commenced practice in New Orleans; member, State Republican Central Committee, 1962-1973; unsuccessful Republican candidate for election in 1962 to the Eighty-eighth Congress, in 1964 to the Eighty-ninth Congress, and in 1968 to the Ninety-first Congress; unsuccessful candidate in 1972 for election for Governor of Louisiana; delegate to each Republican National Convention, 1964-1984; Republican National Committeeman for Louisiana, 1972-1974; elected as a Republican to the Ninety-third and to the three succeeding Congresses and served from January 3, 1973, until his resignation on March 10, 1980, having been elected Governor; elected Governor of Louisiana in 1979, and served from March 10, 1980 to March 12, 1984; unsuccessful candidate for reelection in 1983; chairman, Garrison Diversion Unit Commission, 1984; nominated to the United States Court of Appeals, Fifth Circuit, July 22, 1987; is a resident of Mandeville, La.

**TRELOAR, William Mitchellson,** a Representative from Missouri; born near Linden, Iowa County, Wis., September 21, 1850; attended the common schools; moved to Mount Pleasant, Iowa, in 1864 and attended the high school and the Iowa Wesleyan University at Mount Pleasant; moved to Missouri in 1872; taught at Mount Pleasant College, Huntsville, Mo., 1872-1875; moved to Mexico, Audrain County, Mo., in 1875 and taught in the Synodical Female College in Fulton, Hardin College in Mexico, Mo., and the public schools of Mexico, Mo.; delegate to the Republican State convention in 1894; elected as a Republican to the Fifty-fourth Congress (March 4, 1895-March 3, 1897); unsuccessful candidate for reelection in 1896 to the Fifty-fifth Congress; postmaster of Mexico, Mo., in 1898 and served until March 16, 1904; engaged in the music publishing business at Kansas City, Mo., in 1905; moved to St. Louis, Mo., in 1915 and continued the music publishing business; also engaged in teaching and composing music; served as election judge 1920-1924; died in St. Louis, Mo., July 3, 1935; interment in Bellefontaine Cemetery.

**TREMAIN, Lyman,** a Representative from New York; born in Durham, Greene County, N.Y., June 14, 1819; attended the common schools and Kinderhook Academy; studied law; was admitted to the bar in 1840 and commenced practice in Durham, N.Y.; elected supervisor of Durham in 1842; appointed district attorney in 1844; elected surrogate and county judge of Greene County in 1846; unsuccessful candidate for reelection in 1851; moved to Albany, N.Y., in 1853 and practiced law; elected, as a Democrat, attorney general of New York in 1858; unsuccessful candidate for reelection in 1860; unsuccessful Republican candidate for Lieutenant Governor of New York in 1862; member of the State assembly 1866-1868, serving as speaker in 1867; elected as a Republican to the Forty-third Congress (March 4, 1873-March 3, 1875); was not a candidate for renomination in 1874; resumed the practice of law in Albany; died in New York City, while on a visit, November 30, 1878; interment in the Rural Cemetery, Albany, N.Y.

**TREZVANT, James,** a Representative from Virginia; born in Sussex County, Va.; completed preparatory studies; studied law; admitted to the bar and commenced practice in Jerusalem, Va.; attorney general of Virginia; delegate to the Virginia constitutional convention in 1820; served in the Virginia house of delegates; elected to the Nineteenth and Twentieth Congresses and as a Jacksonian to the Twenty-first Congress (March 4, 1825-March 3, 1831); chairman, Committee on Military Pensions (Twenty-first Congress); died in Southampton County, Va., September 2, 1841.

**TRIBBLE, Samuel Joelah,** a Representative from Georgia; born on a farm near Carnesville, Franklin County, Ga., November 15, 1869; attended the common schools and the University of George at Athens; studied law; was admitted to the bar in 1891 and commenced practice in Athens, Ga.; solicitor of the city court 1899-1904; solicitor general of the western circuit of Georgia 1904-1908; continued the practice of law in Athens until elected to Congress; elected as a Democrat to the Sixty-second, Sixty-third, and Sixty-fourth Congresses and served from March 4, 1911, until his death; had been reelected in 1916 to the Sixty-fifth Congress; died in Washington, D.C., December 8, 1916; interment in Oconee Cemetery, Athens, Ga.

**TRIBLE, Paul Seward, Jr.,** a Representative and Senator from Virginia; born in Baltimore, Md., December 29, 1946; attended public and private schools in New Orleans, La., and Clark's Summit, Pa.; B.A., Hampden-Sydney (Va.) College, 1968; J.D., Washington and Lee Law School, Lexington, Va., 1971; admitted to the Virginia bar in 1971 and commenced practice in Alexandria; served as law clerk to Judge Albert V. Bryan, Jr., United States District Court for Eastern Virginia, 1971-1972; assistant United States attorney for the Eastern District of Virginia, 1972-1974; Commonwealth's attorney, Essex County, Va., 1974-1976; appointed to Virginia Law Enforcement Officers Training and Standards Commission in 1976; elected as a Republican to the Ninety-fifth and to the two succeeding Congresses (January 3, 1977-January 3, 1983); was not a candidate in 1982 for reelection to the House of Representatives, but was elected to the United States Senate for the term ending January 3, 1989; was not a candidate for reelection in 1988; is a resident of Tappahannock, Va.

**TRIGG, Abram** (brother of John Johns Trigg), a Representative from Virginia; born on his father's estate, near Old Liberty (now Bedford), Va., in 1750; completed academic studies; studied law; was admitted to the bar and commenced practice in Montgomery County, Va.; lived on his estate, "Buchanan's Bottom," on New River; held local offices, such as clerk and judge, and various other offices in Montgomery County; served in the Revolutionary War as lieutenant colonel of militia in 1782 and later as general of militia in Virginia; delegate to the Virginia ratification convention of 1788; elected as a Republican to the Fifth and to the five succeeding Congresses (March 4, 1797-March 3, 1809); died and was buried on the family estate.

**TRIGG, Connally Findlay,** a Representative from Virginia; born in Abingdon, Washington County, Va., September 18, 1847; attended the common schools; studied law; was admitted to the bar in 1870 and commenced practice in Abingdon, Va.; during the Civil War was a private in the First Virginia Cavalry and also served in the Confederate States Navy; elected Commonwealth attorney for Washington County in 1872, which position he held until he resigned in 1884 to become a candidate for Congress; elected as a Democrat to the Forty-ninth Congress (March 4, 1885-March 3, 1887); resumed the practice of law; died in Abingdon, Va., April 23, 1907; interment in Sinking Spring Cemetery.

**TRIGG, John Johns** (brother of Abram Trigg), a Representative from Virginia; born on his father's estate near Old Liberty (now Bedford), Va., in 1748; received a liberal schooling; engaged in agricultural pursuits; raised a company of militia in Bedford County, Va., in 1775; was commissioned captain on March 23, 1778; promoted to the rank of major in 1781, and served throughout the Revolution; served under Washington at the siege of Yorktown, Va.; member of the Virginia ratification convention in 1788; lieutenant colonel of militia in 1791; major of the Second Battalion, Tenth Regiment of Militia, in 1793; justice of the peace of Bedford County; served as a member of the Virginia house of delegates, 1784-1792; elected as a Republican to the Fifth and to the three succeeding Congresses and served from March 4, 1797, until his death on his estate, near Old Liberty, Bedford County, Va., on May 17, 1804; interment in burial grounds on his estate.

**TRIMBLE, Carey Allen,** a Representative from Ohio; born in Hillsboro, Highland County, Ohio, September 13, 1813; attended Pestalostian School in Philadelphia, Pa., and Stubb's Classical School in Newport, Ky.; was graduated from Ohio University at Athens in 1833 and from Cincinnati Medical College in 1836; taught for four years; practiced medicine in Chillicothe, Ohio; elected as a Republican to the Thirty-sixth and Thirty-seventh Congresses (March 4, 1859-March 3, 1863); unsuccessful candidate for reelection in 1862 to the Thirty-eighth Congress; resumed medical practice; moved to Columbus, Ohio, where he died on May 4, 1887; interment in Grandview Cemetery, Chillicothe, Ohio.

**TRIMBLE, David,** a Representative from Kentucky; born in Frederick County, Va., in June 1782; was graduated from the College of William and Mary, Williamsburg, Va., in 1799; studied law; was admitted to the bar and commenced legal practice in Mount Sterling, Ky.; served in the War of 1812 as brigade quartermaster of the First Brigade, Kentucky Mounted Militia, and later as a private in the Battalion of Kentucky Mounted Infantry Volunteers commanded by Major Dudley; elected as a Republican to the Fifteenth Congress and reelected to the four succeeding Congresses (March 4, 1817-March 3, 1827); chairman, Committee on Expenditures in the Department of the Treasury (Sixteenth Congress), Committee on Elections (Sixteenth Congress); was an unsuccessful candidate for reelection in 1826 to the Twentieth Congress; died at Trimble's Furnace, Greenup County, Ky., October 20, 1842.

**TRIMBLE, James William,** a Representative from Arkansas; born in Osage, Carroll County, Ark., February 3, 1894; attended the public schools; was graduated from the University of Arkansas at Fayetteville in 1917; was admitted to the bar in 1925 and commenced practice in Berryville, Carroll County, Ark.; during the First World War served in the United States Army as a private and was assigned to the Adjutant General's Office, Little Rock, Ark.; county official of Carroll County, Ark., 1920-1928; prosecuting attorney of the fourth judicial circuit of Arkansas, 1930-1938; judge of the fourth judicial circuit of Arkansas, 1938-1944; elected as a Democrat to the Seventy-ninth and to the ten succeeding Congresses (January 3, 1945-January 3, 1967); chairman, Special Committee on Chamber Improvements (Eighty-first and Eighty-second Congresses); unsuccessful candidate for reelection in 1966 to the Ninetieth Congress; resided in Berryville, Ark.; died in Eureka Springs, Ark., March 10, 1972; interment in Berryville Memorial Park, Berryville, Ark.

**Bibliography:** Rothrock, Thomas. "Congressman James Trimble." *Arkansas Historical Quarterly* 28 (Spring 1969): 76-85.

**TRIMBLE, John,** a Representative from Tennessee; born in Roane County, Tenn., February 7, 1812; pursued classical studies under a private tutor and at the University of Nashville; studied law; was admitted to the bar and commenced practice in Nashville, Tenn.; attorney general of Tennessee from 1836 until 1842; member of the Tennessee State house of representatives in 1843 and 1844; served in the State senate in 1845 and 1846, and in 1859 and 1861, when he resigned because of the secession of the State; United States attorney from April 1862 until August 1864, when he resigned; served in the State senate from 1865 to 1867; elected as a Republican to the Fortieth Congress (March 4, 1867-March 3, 1869); died in Nashville, Tenn., February 23, 1884.

**TRIMBLE, Lawrence Strother,** a Representative from Kentucky; born near Flemingsburg, Fleming County, Ky., August 26, 1825; completed preparatory studies; studied law; was admitted to the bar in 1847 and commenced practice in Paducah, Ky.; member of the Kentucky house of representatives in 1851 and 1852; judge of the equity and criminal court of the first judicial circuit of Kentucky, 1856-1860; president of the New Orleans and Ohio Railroad Company, 1860-1865; unsuccessful candidate for election in 1868 to the Thirty-eighth Congress; elected as a Democrat to the Thirty-ninth and to the two succeeding Congresses (March 4, 1865-March 3, 1871); unsuccessful candidate for renomination in 1870 to the Forty-second Congress; resumed the practice of law; moved to Albuquerque, N.Mex., in 1879 and continued the practice of law until 1889, when he retired; died in Albuquerque, N.Mex., August 9, 1904; interment in Fairview Cemetery.

**TRIMBLE, South,** a Representative from Kentucky; born near Hazel Green, Wolfe County, Ky., April 13, 1864; attended the public schools of Frankfort and Excelsior Institute; engaged in agricultural pursuits near Frankfort, Ky.; member of the Kentucky house of representatives, 1898-1900, serving as speaker in 1900; elected as a Democrat to the Fifty-seventh and to the two succeeding Congresses (March 4, 1901-March 3, 1907); was not a candidate for renomination in 1906 to the Sixtieth Congress, but was an unsuccessful Democratic candidate for Lieutenant Governor of Kentucky; Clerk of the House of Representatives from April 4, 1911 to May 18, 1919; retired from public life and operated a plantation near Selma, Ala.; served as Clerk of the House of Representatives from December 7, 1931 until his death in Washington, D.C., November 23, 1946; interment in Frankfort Cemetery, Frankfort, Ky.

**TRIMBLE, William Allen,** a Senator from Ohio; born in Woodford, Ky., April 4, 1786; graduated from Transylvania College, Lexington, Ky.; studied law; was admitted to the bar in 1811 and commenced practice in Highland County, Ohio; adjutant in the campaign against the Pottawatomie Indians in 1812; served as major of Ohio Volunteers in 1812, and as major of the Twenty-sixth United States Infantry in 1813; brevetted lieutenant colonel in 1814, and in the same year was commissioned lieutenant colonel of the First United States Infantry; transferred to the Eighth United States Infantry in 1815 and resigned in 1819; elected to the United States Senate, and served from March 4, 1819 until his death in Washington, D.C., December 13, 1821; interment in the Congressional Cemetery.

**TRIPLETT, Philip,** a Representative from Kentucky; born in Madison County, Ky., December 24, 1799; attended the common schools of central Kentucky near Franklin, and in Scott County; studied law in Owensboro, Daviess County, Ky.; was admitted to the bar and commenced practice in Owensboro in 1824; member of the Kentucky house of representatives in 1824; elected as a Whig to the Twenty-sixth and Twenty-seventh Congresses (March 3, 1839-March 3, 1843); was not a candidate for reelection in 1842; delegate to the State constitutional convention in 1849; died in Owensboro, Ky., March 30, 1852; interment in Elwood Cemetery.

**TRIPPE, Robert Pleasant,** a Representative from Georgia; born near Monticello, Jasper County, Ga., December 21, 1819; moved with his father to Monroe County and settled near Culloden; attended Randolph-Macon College, Ashland, Va., and was graduated from Franklin College (later the University of Georgia) at Athens in 1839; studied law; was admitted to the bar in 1840 and commenced practice in Forsyth, Ga.; member of the State house of representatives 1849-1852; unsuccessful candidate for election in 1852 to the Thirty-third Congress; elected as a candidate of the American Party to the Thirty-fourth and Thirty-fifth Congresses (March 4, 1855-March 3, 1859); was not a candidate for renomination in 1858 having become a candidate for State senator; served in the State senate in 1859 and 1860; Member of the First Confederate Congress; served in the Confederate Army 1862-1865; resumed the practice of law in Forsyth, Ga.; associate judge of the State supreme court from 1873 until 1875, when he resigned; again resumed the practice of law in Atlanta, Ga., and died there July 22, 1900; interment in Forsyth Cemetery, Forsyth, Ga.

**TROTTER, James Fisher,** a Senator from Mississippi; born in Brunswick County, Va., November 5, 1802; moved to eastern Tennessee; attended private schools; studied law; was admitted to the bar in 1820 and commenced practice in Hamilton, Monroe County, Miss., in 1823; member, State house of representatives 1827-1829; member, State senate 1829-1833; judge of the circuit court of Mississippi in 1833; appointed as a Democrat to the United States Senate to fill the vacancy caused by the resignation of John Black and served from January 22 to July 10, 1838, when he resigned; judge of the supreme court of Mississippi 1839-1842, when he resigned; moved to Holly Springs, Marshall County, Miss., and resumed the practice of law in 1840; vice chancellor of the northern district of Mississippi 1855-1857; professor of law at the University of Mississippi 1860-1862; appointed circuit judge in 1866 and served until his death in Holly Springs, Miss., March 9, 1866; interment in Hill Crest Cemetery.

**TROTTI, Samuel Wilds,** a Representative from South Carolina; born in Barnwell, S.C., July 18, 1810; attended the common schools; was graduated from South Carolina College (now University of South Carolina) at Columbia in 1832; studied law; was admitted to the bar and practiced; served in the Seminole War; member of the State house of representatives, 1840-1841, 1852-1855; elected as a Democrat to the Twenty-seventh Congress to fill the vacancy caused by the resignation of Sampson H. Butler and served from December 17, 1842, to March 3, 1843; resumed the practice of law; died in Buckhead, Fairfield District (now county), S.C., June 24, 1856.

**TROUP, George Michael,** a Representative and a Senator from Georgia; born at McIntosh Bluff, on the Tombigbee River, Ala. (then a part of Georgia), September 8, 1780; received preliminary education at home and in the schools of Savannah, Ga.; attended Erasmus Hall, Flatbush, N.Y., and graduated from the College of New Jersey (now Princeton University) in 1797; studied law; was admitted to the bar and commenced practice in Savannah, Ga., in 1799; member, Georgia State house of representatives, 1803-1805; elected as a Republican to the Tenth and to the three succeeding Congresses (March 4, 1807-March 3, 1815); was not a candidate for renomination in 1814 to the Fourteenth Congress; retired to his plantation in Laurens County; elected as a Republican to the United States Senate for the term beginning March 4, 1817; subsequently elected to fill the vacancy in the term ending March 3, 1817, caused by the resignation of William W. Bibb, and served from November 13, 1816 until September 23, 1818, when he resigned; chairman, Committee on Military Affairs (Fifteenth Congress); unsuccessful candidate for Governor in 1819 and 1821; elected Governor of Georgia, and served from November 7, 1823 to November 7, 1827; again elected to the United States Senate, and served from March 4, 1829 to November 8, 1833, when he resigned; chairman, Committee on Indian Affairs (Twenty-second Congress); died while on a visit to one of his plantations in Montgomery County, Ga., April 26, 1856; interment on the Rosemont plantation, Montgomery County, Ga.

**Bibliography:** *DAB*; Fortune, Porter L. "George M. Troup: Leading State Rights Advocate." Ph.D. dissertation, University of North Carolina, 1949; Harden, Edward. *Life of George Michael Troup.* Savanah: E.J. Purse, 1859.

**TROUT, Michael Carver,** a Representative from Pennsylvania; born in Hickory Township, Mercer County, Pa., September 30, 1810; received a very limited education; employed as a hatter for three years and then became a carpenter and contractor; served as president of the Hickory Township School Board for twenty years; elected burgess of Sharon in 1841; recorder of Mercer County, Pa., 1842-1845; prothonotary 1846-1851; elected as a Democrat to the Thirty-third Congress (March 4, 1853-March 3, 1855); unsuccessful candidate for reelection; engaged in iron manufacturing, banking, and coal mining; died in Hickory Township, Pa., June 25, 1873; interment in Morefield Cemetery, Hickory Township, near Sharon, Pa.

**TROUTMAN, William Irvin,** a Representative from Pennsylvania; born in Shamokin, Northumberland County, Pa., January 13, 1905; attended the public schools; graduated from Franklin and Marshall College, Lancaster, Pa., in 1927, and from the University of Pennsylvania Law School at Philadelphia in 1930; admitted to the bar in 1930 and commenced practice in Shamokin; special attorney for Pennsylvania 1939-1943; elected as a Republican to the Seventy-eighth Congress and served from January 3, 1943, until his resignation on January 2, 1945; did not seek renomination in 1944 to the Seventy-ninth Congress; member of the Pennsylvania senate in 1945; elected judge of the Court of Common Pleas of Northumberland County, Pa., for a ten-year term and assumed his duties on January 7, 1946; reelected in November 1955 for term ending January 1966; was not a candidate for reelection; became a senior judge, and served in the Court of Common Pleas, Philadelphia, Pa., died in Shamokin, Pa., January 27, 1971; interment in Odd Fellows Cemetery.

**TROWBRIDGE, Rowland Ebenezer,** a Representative from Michigan; born in Horseheads, Chemung County, N.Y., June 18, 1821; moved with his parents in 1821 to Oakland County, Mich.; was graduated from Kenyon College, Gambier, Ohio, in 1841; engaged in agricultural pursuits; member of the State senate 1856-1860; elected as a Republican to the Thirty-seventh Congress (March 4, 1861-March 3, 1863); unsuccessful candidate for reelection; elected to the Thirty-ninth and Fortieth Congresses (March 4, 1865-March 3, 1869); chairman, Committee on Agriculture (Fortieth Congress); unsuccessful candidate for renomination; resumed agricultural pursuits; Commissioner of Indian Affairs in 1880 and 1881; died in Birmingham, Mich., April 20, 1881; interment in Greenwood Cemetery.

**TRUAX, Charles Vilas,** a Representative from Ohio; born on a farm near Sycamore, Wyandot County, Ohio, February 1, 1887; attended the public schools and was graduated from Sycamore High School; engaged in the implement business and afterward in agricultural pursuits; editor of the Swine World from 1916 until 1921; appointed director of agriculture of Ohio by Governor Alvin Victor Donahey in 1913 and served until 1929; unsuccessful candidate for election to the United States Senate in 1928; engaged in the life insurance business in Columbus, Ohio, in 1928; was elected as a Democrat to the Seventy-third and Seventy-fourth Congresses and served from March 4, 1933, until his death in Washington, D.C., August 9, 1935; interment in Pleasant View Cemetery, Sycamore, Ohio.

**TRUMAN, Harry S,** a Senator from Missouri, a Vice President, and 33rd President of the United States; born in Lamar, Barton County, Mo., May 8, 1884; moved with his parents to Independence, Mo., in 1890; attended the public schools and graduated from Independence High School in 1901; attended Spalding's Commercial College in Kansas City, Mo. during 1901 and 1902; employed as a newspaper wrapper, timekeeper for a company engaged in railroad construction work, and as a clerk for banks in Kansas City; engaged in agricultural pursuits in Grandview, Mo., 1906-1917; during the First World War was commissioned a first lieutenant, later a captain, and served with Battery D, One Hundred and Twenty-ninth Field Artillery, United States Army, with service overseas; discharged as a major in 1919; colonel of Field Artillery, United States Army Reserve Corps, 1927-1945; engaged in the haberdashery business in Kansas City, 1919-1922; studied law at Kansas City (Mo.) Law School; eastern judge of the Jackson County Court, 1923-1925, and presiding judge, 1927-1934; elected as a Democrat to the United States Senate in 1934; reelected in 1940, and served from January 3, 1935 until his resignation on January 17, 1945, having

been elected Vice President; chairman of the Special Committee to Investigate the National Defense Program (Seventy-seventh and Seventy-eighth Congresses), formed at Truman's initiative and widely known as the "Truman Committee," which called nationwide attention to military contracting procedures; elected Vice President of the United States on the Democratic ticket headed by President Franklin D. Roosevelt in 1944; inaugurated on January 20, 1945, and upon the death of President Roosevelt, April 12, 1945, became President of the United States; elected in 1948 for the term ending January 20, 1953; returned to his home in Independence, Mo.; engaged in writing his memoirs and took an active interest in the creation of the Truman Library; died in Kansas City, Mo., December 26, 1972; interment in the Rose Garden at the Truman Library, Independence, Mo.

**Bibliography:** Miller, Richard L. *Truman: The Rise to Power.* New York: McGraw Hill, 1986; Truman, Harry S. *Memoirs: Year of Decisions.* Vol. I, Garden City, N.Y.: Doubleday, 1955.

**TRUMBO, Andrew Alkire,** a Representative from Kentucky; born in Montgomery (now Bath) County, Ky., September 15, 1797; attended the common schools; employed in the county clerk's office; studied law; was admitted to the bar and commenced practice in Owingsville, Ky., in 1824; served as clerk of Bath County in 1830; Commonwealth attorney for Bath County in 1830; elected as a Whig to the Twenty-ninth Congress (March 4, 1845-March 3, 1847); presidential elector on the Democratic ticket in 1848; resumed the practice of law; moved to Franklin County, Ky.; died in Frankfort, Ky., August 21, 1871; interment in the City Cemetery, Owingsville, Ky.

**Bibliography:** Trumbo, Andrew. *Andrew Trumbo Letters.* Compiled by Conrad W. Feltner. Middlesboro, Ky.: C.W. Feltner, 1981.

**TRUMBULL, Jonathan Jr.** (brother of Joseph Trumbull), a Representative and a Senator from Connecticut; born in Lebanon, Conn., March 26, 1740; graduated from Harvard College in 1759; member, State legislature 1774-1775, 1779-1780, 1788, and served as speaker of the house in 1788; served in the Continental Army as a paymaster; comptroller of the treasury 1778-1779; appointed secretary and aide-de-camp to General George Washington in 1781; elected to the First, Second, and Third Congresses (March 4, 1789-March 3, 1795); did not seek reelection, having become a candidate for Senator; Speaker of the House of Representatives, Second Congress; elected to the United States Senate and served from March 4, 1795, to June 10, 1796, when he resigned; lieutenant governor of Connecticut from 1796 until the death of the Governor in December 1797, when he became the Governor; was reelected for eleven consecutive terms, and served from 1797 until his death in Lebanon, Conn., August 7, 1809; interment in the East Cemetery.

**Bibliography:** *DAB;* Ifkovic, John. *Connecticut's Nationalist Revolutionary: Jonathan Trumbull, Jr.* Hartford: American Revolution Bicentennial Commission of Connecticut, 1977. Trumbull, Jonathan. *Jonathan Trumbull: Governor of Connecticut.* Boston: Little, Brown and Co., 1919.

**TRUMBULL, Joseph** (brother of Jonathan Trumbull, Jr.), a Delegate from Connecticut; born in Lebanon, Conn., March 11, 1737; was graduated from Harvard College in 1756; elected to the Continental Congress in 1774, but did not attend; served in the Continental Army as commissary general with the rank of colonel from July 19, 1775, to August 2, 1777; was commissioner of the board of war from 1777 until his resignation in April 1778 on account of ill health; died in Lebanon, Conn., July 23, 1778; interment in the East Cemetery.

**Bibliography:** *DAB.*

**TRUMBULL, Joseph,** a Representative from Connecticut; born in Lebanon, Conn., December 7, 1782; completed preparatory studies; was graduated from Yale College in 1801; studied law; was admitted to the bar in 1803 at Windham, Conn., and commenced practice in Hartford, Conn.; in 1828 became president of the Hartford Bank and later of the Providence, Hartford & Fishkill Railroad Co.; member of the Connecticut State house of representatives in 1832; elected to the Twenty-third Congress to fill the vacancy caused by the resignation of William W. Ellsworth, and served from December 1, 1834 to March 3, 1835; resigned the presidency of the bank in November 1839; elected as a Whig to the Twenty-sixth and Twenty-seventh Congresses (March 4, 1839-March 3, 1843); again a member of the State house of representatives in 1848; elected Governor of Connecticut in 1849, and served from May 2, 1849 to May 4, 1850; again elected to the State house of representatives in 1851; died in Hartford, Conn., August 4, 1861; interment in the East Cemetery, Lebanon, Conn.

**TRUMBULL, Lyman,** a Senator from Illinois; born in Colchester, Conn., October 12, 1813; attended Bacon Academy; taught school in Connecticut from 1829 to 1833; studied law; was admitted to the bar and commenced practice in Greenville, Ga.; moved to Belleville, Ill., 1837; member, Illinois State house of representatives, 1840-1841; secretary of State of Illinois in 1841 and 1843; justice of the supreme court of Illinois, 1848-1853; elected as a Republican in 1854 to the Thirty-fourth Congress, but before the beginning of the Congress was elected to the United States Senate; reelected in 1861 and again in 1867, and served from March 4, 1855 to March 3, 1873; was at various times a Democrat, then Republican, then Liberal Republican, then Democrat; chairman, Committee on the Judiciary (Thirty-seventh through Forty-second Congresses); resumed the practice of law in Chicago, Ill.; unsuccessful Democratic candidate for Governor of Illinois in 1880; died in Chicago, Ill., June 25, 1896; interment in Oakwoods Cemetery.

**Bibliography:** *DAB*; DiNunzio, Mario. "Lyman Trumbull, United States Senator." Ph.D. dissertation, Clark University, 1969; Krug, Mark M. *Lyman Trumbull, Conservative Radical.* New York: A.S. Barnes, 1965; Roske, Ralph J. *His Own Counsel: The Life and Times of Lyman Trumbull.* Reno: University of Nevada Press, 1979.

**TSONGAS, Paul Efthemios,** a Representative and a Senator from Massachusetts; born in Lowell, Middlesex County, Mass., February 14, 1941; attended the public schools of Lowell; B.A., Dartmouth College, Hanover, N.H., 1962; J.D., Yale University School of Law, 1967; attended the John F. Kennedy School of Government at Harvard University, 1973-1974; lawyer; admitted to the Massachusetts bar in 1968 and commenced practice in Lowell; served as Peace Corps Volunteer in Ethiopia, 1962-1964, and in the West Indies, 1967-1968; deputy assistant attorney general of Massachusetts, 1969-1971; served as Lowell city councillor, 1969-1972; Middlesex County (Mass.) commissioner, 1973-1974; elected as a Democrat to the Ninety-fourth and Ninety-fifth Congresses (January 3, 1975-January 3, 1979); was not a candidate in 1978 for reelection to the House of Representatives, but was elected to the United States Senate; served from January 3, 1979 to January 3, 1985; declined to be a candidate for reelection in 1984; unsuccessful candidate for the Democratic presidential nomination in 1992; is a resident of Lowell, Mass.

**Bibliography:** Tsongas, Paul. *Journey of Purpose: Reflections on the Presidency, Multiculturalism, and Third Parties.* New Haven: Yale University Press, 1995; Tsongas, Paul. *Heading Home.* New York: Knopf, 1984; Tsongas, Paul. *The Road From Here: Liberalism and Realities in the 1980s.* New York: Knopf, 1981.

**TUCK, Amos,** a Representative from New Hampshire; born in Parsonsfield, Maine, August 2, 1810; attended Effingham and Hampton Academies; was graduated from Dartmouth College, Hanover, N.H., in 1835; studied law; was admitted to the bar in 1838 and commenced practice in Exeter, N.H.; trustee of Dartmouth College; principal of the Hampton Academy, 1836-1838; member of the New Hampshire State house of representatives in 1842; elected

as an Independent to the Thirtieth Congress, as a Free-Soil candidate to the Thirty-first Congress, and as a Whig to the Thirty-second Congress (March 4, 1847-March 3, 1853); unsuccessful candidate for reelection in 1852 to the Thirty-third Congress; delegate to the Republican National Conventions of 1856 and 1860; delegate to the peace convention held in Washington, D.C., in 1861 in an effort to devise means to prevent the impending war; naval officer of the port of Boston, 1861-1865; resumed the practice of law and also engaged in railroad building; died in Exeter, N.H., December 11, 1879; interment in Exeter Cemetery.

**Bibliography:** *DAB*; Gregg, Hugh, and Georgi Hippauf, comps. *Birth of the Republican Party: A Summary of Historical Research on Amos Tuck and the Birthplace of the Republican Party at Exeter, New Hampshire.* Nashua, N.H.: Resources of New Hampshire, 1995.

**TUCK, William Munford,** a Representative from Virginia; born near High Hill, Halifax County, Va., September 28, 1896; attended the public schools; during the First World War served in the United States Marines from June 1918 to July 1919; attended the College of William and Mary; graduated from Washington and Lee University, Lexington, Va., in 1921; admitted to the bar the same year and commenced practice in South Boston, Va.; chairman of the Virginia Democratic Central Committee in 1952; delegate to the Democratic National Conventions of 1948 and 1952; member of the Virginia house of delegates, 1924-1932; served in the Virginia senate, 1932-1942; Lieutenant Governor of Virginia, 1942-1946; elected Governor of Virginia in 1945, and served from January 16, 1946 to January 18, 1950; resumed the practice of law; elected as a Democrat to the Eighty-third Congress to fill the vacancy caused by the resignation of Thomas B. Stanley; reelected to the seven succeeding Congresses, and served from April 14, 1953 until January 3, 1969; was not a candidate for reelection in 1968 to the Ninety-first Congress; was a resident of South Boston, Va., until his death on June 9, 1983; interment at Oak Ridge Cemetery, South Boston, Va.

**Bibliography:** Crawley, William B. *Bill Tuck: A Political Life in Harry Byrd's Virginia.* Charlottesville: University Press of Virginia, 1978.

**TUCKER, Ebenezer,** a Representative from New Jersey; born at Tuckers Beach, Burlington County, N.J., November 15, 1758; attended the common schools; served in the Revolution under General Washington at the Battle of Long Island, N.Y., August 27, 1776, and other engagements; judge of the court of common pleas, justice of the court of quarter sessions, and judge of the orphans' court of Burlington County from 1820 to 1825; moved to what is now Tuckerton, N.J., which was named after him, where he engaged in mercantile pursuits and shipbuilding; postmaster of Tuckerton from 1806 to 1825, when he resigned to take up his duties in Congress; elected to the Nineteenth and Twentieth Congresses (March 4, 1825-March 3, 1829); was not a candidate for renomination in 1828 to the Twenty-first Congress; first collector of revenue of the port of Tuckerton; again postmaster of Tuckerton, N.J. from 1831 until his death there on September 5, 1845; interment in the Old Methodist Cemetery.

**TUCKER, George** (cousin of Henry St. George Tucker), a Representative from Virginia; born in St. Georges, Bermuda, on August 20, 1775; immigrated to Virginia about 1790; was graduated from the College of William and Mary, Williamsburg, Va., in 1797; studied law with Judge St. George Tucker at the College of William and Mary; was admitted to the bar and commenced practice in Richmond, Va.; moved to Pittsylvania County, Va., and was elected Commonwealth attorney of the county; member of the Virginia house of delegates in 1815; moved to Lynchburg, Va., in 1818 and continued the practice of law; elected to the Sixteenth, Seventeenth, and Eighteenth Congresses (March 4, 1819-March 3, 1825); chairman, Committee on Expenditures in the Department of War

(Seventeenth and Eighteenth Congresses); was appointed by Thomas Jefferson as the first professor of moral philosophy at the University of Virginia; resigned as professor in 1845 and moved to Philadelphia; author on finance, economics, banking, and historical subjects; died in Sherwood, Albemarle County, Va., April 10, 1861; interment in the University of Virginia Cemetery, Albemarle County, Va.

**Bibliography:** *DAB*; McLean, Robert Colin. *George Tucker: Moral Philosopher and Man of Letters*. Chapel Hill: University of North Carolina Press, 1961; Snavely, Tipton Ray. *George Tucker as Political Economist*. Charlottesville: University Press of Virginia, 1964.

**TUCKER, Henry St. George** (father of John Randolph Tucker, grandfather of Henry St. George Tucker [1853-1932], cousin of George Tucker, and nephew of Thomas Tudor Tucker), a Representative from Virginia; born in Williamsburg, Va., December 29, 1780; pursued classical studies; was graduated from the College of William and Mary, Williamsburg, Va., in 1798; later studied law under his father, St. George Tucker, and was graduated in 1801; was admitted to the bar and commenced practice in Winchester, Va.; captain of Cavalry in the War of 1812; elected as a Republican to the Fourteenth and Fifteenth Congresses (March 4, 1815-March 3, 1819); chairman, Committee on District of Columbia (Fourteenth Congress), Committee on Expenditures on Public Buildings (Fifteenth Congress); was not a candidate for renomination in 1818; member, State senate, 1819-1823; chancellor of the fourth judicial district of Virginia 1824-1831; maintained a private law school; president of the court of appeals of Virginia 1831-1841; professor of law at the University of Virginia at Charlottesville from 1841 to 1845, when he resigned; was the author in 1842 of the honor system for students adopted at the university; author of Tucker's Commentaries and of a treatise on natural law and on the formation of the Constitution of the United States; died in Winchester, Va., August 28, 1848; interment in Mount Hebron Cemetery.

**Bibliography:** *DAB*.

**TUCKER, Henry St. George** (son of John Randolph Tucker and grandson of Henry St. George Tucker [1780-1848]), a Representative from Virginia; born in Winchester, Frederick County, Va., April 5, 1853; attended private schools in Richmond and Middleburg, Va.; was graduated from the law department of Washington and Lee University, Lexington, Va., in 1876; was admitted to the bar the same year and commenced practice in Staunton, Va.; elected as a Democrat to the Fifty-first and to the three succeeding Congresses (March 4, 1889-March 3, 1897); was not a candidate for renomination in 1896 to the Fifty-fifth Congress; elected professor of constitutional law and equity in Washington and Lee University in 1897; dean of the law school of the same university in 1900, and dean of the school of law and diplomacy in George Washington University, Washington, D.C., in 1905; president of the Jamestown Exposition Co., 1905-1907; president of the American Bar Association in 1905; unsuccessful Democratic candidate for the nomination for Governor in 1909, and again in 1921; elected as a Democrat to the Sixty-seventh Congress to fill the vacancy caused by the death of Henry D. Flood; reelected to the Sixty-eighth and to the four succeeding Congresses, and served from March 21, 1922 until his death in Lexington, Va., July 23, 1932; interment in the Presbyterian Cemetery.

**Bibliography:** *DAB*; Hohner, Robert A. "Prohibition and Virginia Politics: William Hodges Mann Versus Henry St. George Tucker, 1909." *Virginia Magazine of History and Biography* 74 (January 1966): 88-107.

**TUCKER, James Guy, Jr. (Jim),** a Representative from Arkansas; born in Oklahoma City, Okla., June 13, 1943; educated in the public schools of Little Rock, Ark.; B.A., Harvard University, 1964; J.D., University of Arkansas, Fayetteville, 1968; admitted to the Arkansas bar in 1968 and commenced practice in Little Rock; served in United States Marine Corps Reserve, 1964; served as free lance reporter in Vietnam, 1965, 1967; engaged in the private practice of law in Little Rock, 1968-1970; prosecuting attorney, Sixth Judicial District of Arkansas, 1971-1972; member, Arkansas Criminal Code Revision Commission, 1973-1975; served as Arkansas attorney general, 1973-1977; delegate to the Democratic National Convention of 1972; elected as a Democrat to the Ninety-fifth Congress (January 3, 1977-January 3, 1979); was not a candidate in 1978 for reelection to the House of Representatives, but was an unsuccessful candidate for nomination to the United States Senate; resumed the practice of law; unsuccessful candidate for nomination for Governor in 1982; elected Lieutenant Governor of Arkansas in 1990; upon the resignation of Governor William J. Clinton became Governor on December 12, 1992; elected to a full term as Governor in 1994, and served from January 10, 1995 until his resignation on July 15, 1996; is a resident of Little Rock, Ark.

**TUCKER, John Randolph** (son of Henry St. George Tucker [1780-1848] and father of Henry St. George Tucker [1853-1932]), a Representative from Virginia; born in Winchester, Frederick County, Va., on December 24, 1823; attended a private school and Richmond Academy, and was graduated from the University of Virginia at Charlottesville in 1844; was admitted to the bar in 1845 and commenced practice in Winchester, Va.; attorney general of Virginia 1857-1865; professor of equity and public law at Washington and Lee University, Lexington, Va., in 1870; elected as a Democrat to the Forty-fourth and to the five succeeding Congresses (March 4, 1875-March 3, 1887); chairman, Committee on Ways and Means (Forty-sixth Congress), Committee on the Judiciary (Forty-eighth and Forty-ninth Congresses); declined to be a candidate for renomination in 1886; elected professor of constitutional law at Washington and Lee University in 1888, and served until his death; president of the American Bar Association in 1894; died in Lexington, Va., February 13, 1897; interment in Mount Hebron Cemetery, Winchester, Va.

**Bibliography:** *DAB*; Davis, J.W. "John Randolph Tucker: The Man and His Work." In *John Randolph Tucker Lectures*. Lexington, Va.: Washington and Lee University, 1952, 11-36.

**TUCKER, Starling,** a Representative from South Carolina; born in Halifax County, N.C., in 1770; moved to Mountain Shoals (now Enoree), S.C.; received a limited education; held several local offices; member of the State house of representatives; elected as a Republican to the Fifteenth Congress; reelected to the Sixteenth through Nineteenth Congresses and reelected as a Jacksonian to the Twentieth and Twenty-first Congresses (March 4, 1817-March 3, 1831); died in Mountain Shoals (now Enoree), S.C., January 3, 1834; interment in the private burial ground on the family estate west of Enoree, S.C.

**TUCKER, Thomas Tudor** (uncle of Henry St. George Tucker [1780-1848]), a Delegate and a Representative from South Carolina; born in Port Royal, Bermuda, June 25, 1745; attended the common schools; studied medicine at the University of Edinburgh, Scotland; moved to South Carolina and practiced medicine; served as a surgeon in the Revolutionary War; member of the Virginia assembly, 1776, 1782-1783, 1785 and 1787-1788; Member of the Continental Congress in 1787 and 1788; elected to the First and Second Congresses (March 4, 1789-March 3, 1793); appointed United States Treasurer by President Thomas Jefferson, and served from December 1, 1801 until his death in Washington, D.C., May 2, 1828; interment in Congressional Cemetery.

**Bibliography:** Dowdy, Diana Dru. "'A School for Stoicism': Thomas Tudor Tucker and the Republican Age." *South Carolina Historical Magazine* 96 (April 1995): 102-118.

**TUCKER, Tilghman Mayfield,** a Representative from Mississippi; born near Lime Stone Springs, N.C., February 5, 1802; completed preparatory studies; engaged in agricultural pursuits; moved to Hamilton, Miss.; studied law; was admitted to the bar and commenced practice in Columbus, Miss.; member of the Mississippi State house of representatives, 1831-1835; served in the State senate, 1838-1841; elected Governor of Mississippi in 1841, and served from January 10, 1842 to January 10, 1844; elected as a Democrat to the Twenty-eighth Congress (March 4, 1843-March 3, 1845); retired to his plantation home, "Cottonwood," in Louisiana; died at the home of his father near Bexar, Marion County, Ala., April 3, 1859.

**TUCKER, Walter Rayford, III,** a Representative from California; born in Compton, Los Angeles County, Calif., May 28, 1957; graduated, Compton High School, 1974; attended Princeton University, 1974-1976; B.A., University of Southern California at Los Angeles, 1978; J.D., Georgetown University Law Center, Washington, D.C., 1981; admitted to California Bar in 1982; attorney, Washington, D.C., and Compton; deputy district attorney, County of Los Angeles, 1984-1986; mayor of Compton, 1991-1993; ordained minister; Democratic National Convention, credentials committee, 1992; elected as a Democrat to the One Hundred Third and One Hundred Fourth Congresses, and served from January 3, 1993 until his resignation on December 15, 1995; is a resident of Compton, Calif.

**TUFTS, John Quincy,** a Representative from Iowa; born near Aurora, Dearborn County, Ind., July 12, 1840; moved to Iowa in 1852 with his parents, who settled in Muscatine County; attended the common schools and Cornell College, Mount Vernon, Iowa; moved to Cedar County, Iowa, in 1858; engaged in agricultural pursuits; member of the State house of representatives in 1870, 1872, and 1874; elected as a Republican to the Forty-fourth Congress (March 4, 1875-March 3, 1877); United States Indian agent of Indian Territory 1879-1887; moved to Los Angeles, Calif.; engaged in the real estate business; president of the Los Angeles Board of Aldermen 1892-1896; died in Los Angeles, Calif., August 10, 1908; interment in Rosedale Cemetery.

**TULLY, Pleasant Britton,** a Representative from California; born in Henderson County, Tenn., on March 21, 1829; moved to Arkansas with his father, who settled in Phillips County in 1838; attended public and private schools; moved to California in 1853 and engaged in mining; resided in Gilroy, Calif., after 1857; studied law; was admitted to the bar and practiced; delegate at large to the State constitutional convention in 1879; elected as a Democrat to the Forty-eighth Congress (March 4, 1883-March 3, 1885); resumed the practice of law; died in Gilroy, Santa Clara County, Calif., March 24, 1897; interment in the Masonic Cemetery.

**TUMULTY, Thomas James,** a Representative from New Jersey; born in Jersey City, Hudson County, N.J., March 2, 1913; graduated from Xavier High School and attended Holy Cross University; graduated from Fordham University, New York City, in 1935, from Seton Hall, South Orange, N.J., in 1938 and from John Marshall Law School, Jersey City, N.J., in 1938; admitted to the bar in 1940 and commenced the practice of law in Jersey City, N.J.; professor at Seton Hall in 1940 and 1941; taught at St. Aloysius High School in Jersey City in 1949 and 1950; served in the United States Army as an enlisted man in 1943 and 1944; served in the State house of assembly 1944-1952, serving as minority leader in 1951; assistant corporation counsel for Jersey City 1943-1954; delegate to the Democratic National Convention in 1952; secretary to the mayor of Jersey City in 1952 and 1953; elected as a Democrat to the Eighty-fourth Congress (January 3, 1955-January 3, 1957); unsuccessful for reelection to the Eighty-fifth Congress; special counsel Urban Renewal for Jersey City in 1957; deputy mayor of Jersey City 1958-1960; resumed the practice of law; judge of the Superior Court of New Jersey, 1967-1972; was a resident of Jersey City, N.J., until his death there November 23, 1981; interment at Holy Name Cemetery.

**TUNNELL, James Miller,** a Senator from Delaware; born in Clarksville, Sussex County, Del., August 2, 1879; attended the public schools; graduated from Franklin College (now combined with Muskingum College at New Concord, Ohio) in 1900; taught in the public schools, advancing to principal of schools at Frankford, Selbyville, and Ocean View, Del., 1903-1907; studied law; was admitted to the bar in 1907 and commenced practice in Georgetown, Del.; president of the board of education of Georgetown, Del., 1919-1932; unsuccessful Democratic candidate for election to the United States Senate in 1924; elected as a Democrat to the United States Senate in 1940 and served from January 3, 1941, to January 3, 1947; unsuccessful candidate for reelection in 1946; chairman, Committee on Pensions (Seventy-eighth and Seventy-ninth Congresses); banker; owned and operated a number of farms in Sussex County, Del.; died in Philadelphia, Pa., November 14, 1957; interment in Blackwater Church Cemetery, near Clarksville, Del.

**TUNNEY, John Varick,** a Representative and a Senator from California; born in New York City, June 26, 1934; B.A., Yale University, 1956; attended the Academy of International Law at The Hague, Netherlands, in 1957; LL.B., University of Virginia School of Law, Charlottesville, 1959; was admitted to the Virginia and New York bars in 1959 and commenced practice in New York City; joined the United States Air Force as a judge advocate and served until discharged as a captain in April 1963; taught business law at the University of California at Riverside in 1961 and 1962; admitted to practice law in California in 1963; special adviser to the President's Committee on Juvenile Delinquency and Youth Crime, 1963-1968; elected as a Democrat to the Eighty-ninth and to the two succeeding Congresses and served from January 3, 1965, until his resignation January 2, 1971; was not a candidate in 1970 for reelection to the House of Representatives, but was elected to the United States Senate for the six-year term commencing January 3, 1971; subsequently appointed by the Governor, January 2, 1971, to fill the vacancy caused by the resignation of George Murphy for the term ending January 3, 1971; served from January 2, 1971, until his resignation on January 1, 1977; unsuccessful candidate for reelection in 1976; resumed the practice of law in Los Angeles; is a resident of Beverly Hills, Calif.

**Bibliography:** Tunney, John. *The Changing Dream.* Garden City, N.Y.: Doubleday, 1975.

**TUPPER, Stanley Roger,** a Representative from Maine; born in Boothbay Harbor, Lincoln County, Maine, January 25, 1921; educated in Boothbay Harbor public schools, the Hebron (Maine) Academy, Middlebury (Vt.) College, and LaSalle Extension University, Chicago, Ill.; served in the United States Navy from September 1944 until March 1946; member of board of selectmen of Boothbay Harbor in 1948, and served as chairman in 1949; was admitted to the bar and commenced the practice of law in Maine in 1949, in the Federal district court in 1950, and before the bar of the United States Supreme Court in 1952; member, Maine State legislature, 1953; assistant State attorney general, 1959-1960; State Commissioner of the Department of Sea and Shore Fisheries, 1953-1957; elected as a Republican to the Eighty-seventh and to the two succeeding Congresses (January 3, 1961-January 3, 1967); was not a candidate for reelection in 1966 to the Ninetieth Congress; appointed United States Commissioner General, with the rank of Ambassador, to the Canadian World Exhibition of 1967; resumed the practice of law in 1968; United State Commissioner, International Commission for Northeast Atlantic Fisheries, 1975-1976; is a resident of Boothbay Harbor, Maine.

**TURLEY, Thomas Battle,** a Senator from Tennessee; born in Memphis, Tenn., April 5, 1845; attended the public schools; served throughout the Civil War as a private in the Confederate Army; graduated from the law department of the University of Virginia at Charlottesville in 1867; was admitted to the bar in 1870 and commenced practice in Memphis, Tenn.; appointed as a Democrat and subsequently elected to the United States Senate to fill the vacancy caused by the death of Isham G. Harris and served from July 20, 1897, to March 3, 1901; declined to be a candidate for renomination and resumed the practice of law in Memphis, Tenn.; died in Memphis, Tenn., July 1, 1910; interment in Elmwood Cemetery.

**TURNBULL, Robert,** a Representative from Virginia; born in Lawrenceville, Brunswick County, Va., January 11, 1850; attended Rock Spring Academy; graduated from the law department of the University of Virginia at Charlottesville in 1871; admitted to the bar in 1871 and commenced practice in Lawrenceville, Va.; clerk of Brunswick County 1891-1910; member of the Virginia senate 1894-1898; delegate to the Virginia constitutional convention in 1901; delegate to the Democratic National Conventions in 1896 and 1904; elected as a Democrat to the Sixty-first Congress to fill the vacancy caused by the death of Francis R. Lassiter; reelected to the Sixty-second Congress and served from March 8, 1910, to March 3, 1913; unsuccessful candidate for renomination in 1912; resumed the practice of law in Lawrenceville; clerk of the circuit court of Brunswick County from 1916 until his death, January 22, 1920; interment in Lawrenceville Cemetery, Lawrenceville, Va.

**TURNER, Benjamin Sterling,** a Representative from Alabama; born near Weldon, Halifax County, N.C., March 17, 1825; raised as a slave; received no early education; moved to Alabama in 1830 and by clandestine study obtained a fair education; settled in Selma, Dallas County, Ala., where he owned a livery stable and engaged in mercantile pursuits; elected tax collector of Dallas County in 1867; councilman of the city of Selma in 1869; elected as a Republican to the Forty-second Congress (March 4, 1871-March 3, 1873); unsuccessful candidate for reelection in 1872 to the Forty-third Congress; delegate to the Republican National Convention of 1880; engaged in agricultural pursuits; died in Selma, Ala., March 21, 1894; interment in Live Oak Cemetery.

**TURNER, Charles, Jr.,** a Representative from Massachusetts; born in Duxbury, Mass., June 20, 1760; received a common-school education at Duxbury and Scituate, Mass.; was commissioned an adjutant in the Massachusetts Militia in 1787; promoted to major in 1790, and held the rank of lieutenant colonel commandant 1798-1812; appointed first postmaster of Scituate, Mass., in 1800; justice of the peace; member of the Massachusetts house of representatives in 1803 and 1805-1808; successfully contested as a Republican the election of William Baylies to the Eleventh Congress; reelected to the Twelfth Congress and served from June 28, 1809, to March 3, 1813; chairman, Committee on Accounts (Twelfth Congress); unsuccessful candidate for reelection to the Thirteenth Congress; served in the Massachusetts senate in 1816; again a member of the Massachusetts house of representatives in 1817, 1819, and 1823; appointed steward of the Marine Hospital at Chelsea, Mass.; delegate to the Massachusetts constitutional convention in 1820; engaged in agricultural pursuits; died in Scituate, Plymouth County, Mass., May 16, 1839; interment in the burial ground of the First Parish of Norwell (formerly Scituate).

**TURNER, Charles Henry,** a Representative from New York; born in Wentworth, Grafton County, N.H., May 26, 1861; attended the common schools; moved to New York City in November 1879; attended Columbia College, New York City, 1886-1888; engaged in the ice business; unsuccessful candidate for State senator in 1888; elected as a Democrat to the Fifty-first Congress to fill the vacancy caused by the resignation of Frank T. Fitzgerald and served from December 9, 1889, to March 3, 1891; was not a candidate for renomination in 1890; Doorkeeper in the House of Representatives 1891-1893; studied law; was admitted to the bar in 1897 and commenced practice in Washington, D.C.; appointed assistant district attorney for the District of Columbia July 16, 1903, and served until his resignation September 1, 1911; appointed special assistant to the United States attorney for the District of Columbia November 27, 1911, and served until his death in Wentworth, N.H., August 31, 1913; interment in Wentworth Cemetery.

**TURNER, Clarence Wyly,** a Representative from Tennessee; born on a farm near Clydeton, Humphreys County, Tenn., October 22, 1866; attended the public schools, a preparatory school in Edgewood, Dickson County, Tenn., and National Normal Institute, Lebanon, Ohio; was graduated from the law department of Northern Indiana Normal College at Valparaiso in 1904; was admitted to the bar the same year and commenced practice at Waverly, Humphreys County, Tenn.; editor of the Waverly Sentinel; chairman of the Democratic committee of Humphreys County for fifteen years; member of the State senate 1900, 1901, and 1909-1912; delegate to the Democratic National Convention in 1920; elected mayor of Waverly, Tenn., in 1920; city attorney; elected as a Democrat to the Sixty-seventh Congress to fill the vacancy caused by the death of Lemuel P. Padgett and served from November 7, 1922, to March 3, 1923; was not a candidate for reelection in 1922 to the Sixty-eighth Congress; returned to Waverly, Tenn., and engaged in banking and agricultural pursuits; served as county judge of Humphreys County 1924-1933; elected to the Seventy-third and to the three succeeding Congresses and served from March 4, 1933, until his death in Washington, D.C., March 23, 1939; interment in Marable Cemetery, Waverly, Tenn.

**TURNER, Daniel** (son of James Turner), a Representative from North Carolina; born near Warrenton, Warren County, N.C., September 21, 1796; completed preparatory studies; was graduated from the United States Military Academy at West Point in 1814, and commissioned second lieutenant of Artillery the same year; served in the War of 1812 as acting assistant engineer; resigned his commission May 17, 1815; student for two years at the College of William and Mary, Williamsburg, Va.; moved to North Carolina; member of the North Carolina house of commons 1819-1823; elected to the Twentieth Congress (March 4, 1827-March 3, 1829); was not a candidate for renomination; principal of the Warrenton (N.C.) Female Seminary; superintending engineer of the construction of public works at the Mare Island (Calif.) Navy Yard from September 16, 1854, until his death there July 21, 1860; interment in Mare Island Naval Cemetery.

**TURNER, Erastus Johnson,** a Representative from Kansas; born in Lockport, Erie County, Pa., December 26, 1846; attended college in Henry, Ill., in 1859 and 1860; moved to Bloomfield, Iowa, in 1860; enlisted in Company E, Thirteenth Regiment, Iowa Volunteer Infantry, in 1864 and served until the close of the Civil War; attended Adrian (Mich.) College 1866-1868; was admitted to the bar in 1871 and commenced practice at Bloomfield, Iowa; moved to Hoxie, Sheridan County, Kans., in 1879 and resumed the practice of law; member of the State house of representatives 1881-1885; secretary of the Kansas Board of Railroad Commissioners from April 1, 1883, to August 1, 1886; elected as a Republican to the Fiftieth and Fifty-first Congresses (March 4, 1887-March 3, 1891); was not a candidate for renomination in 1890; practiced law several years in Washington, D.C.; moved to Seattle, Wash., in 1905 and continued the practice of law; retired from active pursuits in 1916 and moved to Los Angeles, Calif., where he died February 10, 1933; interment in Forest Lawn Mausoleum, Glendale, Calif.

**TURNER, George,** a Senator from Washington; born in Edina, Knox County, Mo., February 25, 1850; attended the common schools; served as United States military telegraph operator with the Union forces during the Civil War 1861-1865; studied law; was admitted to the bar in 1869 and commenced practice in Mobile, Ala.; United States marshal for the southern and middle districts of Alabama, 1876-1880; associate justice of the supreme court for the Territory of Washington, 1885-1888; resumed the practice of law in Spokane, Wash., in 1888; also interested in mining; member of the Territorial convention in 1889 that framed the constitution of the new State of Washington; unsuccessful candidate for election as a Republican to the United States Senate in 1889 and 1893; elected on a fusionist ticket with Silver Republicans, Democrats, and Populists to the United States Senate and served from March 4, 1897, to March 3, 1903; was not a candidate for reelection; resumed the practice of law in Spokane, Wash.; member of the Alaska Boundary Tribunal in 1903; unsuccessful Democratic candidate for governor in 1904; counsel for the United States at The Hague in the northeastern fisheries arbitration with Great Britain in 1910; appointed by President William Howard Taft as a member of the International Joint Commission, created to prevent disputes regarding the use of boundary waters between the United States and Canada, 1911-1914; counsel for the United States before the International Joint Commission, 1918-1924; practiced law in Spokane, Wash.; died in Spokane, January 26, 1932; interment in Greenwood Cemetery.

**Bibliography:** *DAB*; Johnson, Claudius. *George Turner, Attorney-at-Law*. Pullman: State College of Washington, 1943.

**TURNER, Henry Gray,** a Representative from Georgia; born near Henderson, Franklin County, N.C., March 20, 1839; attended the common schools and the University of Virginia at Charlottesville in 1857; moved to Brooks County, Ga., in 1859 and taught school; enlisted in the Confederate Army as a private in 1861, and served throughout the Civil War, attaining the rank of captain; studied law; was admitted to the bar in 1865 and commenced practice in Quitman, Ga.; member of the State house of representatives 1874-1876; delegate to the Democratic National Convention in 1876; again served in the State house of representatives in 1878 and 1879; elected as a Democrat to the Forty-seventh and to the seven succeeding Congresses (March 4, 1881-March 3, 1897); chairman, Committee on Elections (Forty-eighth and Forty-ninth Congresses), Committee on Expenditures in the Department of the Interior (Fifty-third Congress); declined to be a candidate for renomination in 1896; resumed the practice of law in Quitman, Ga.; appointed associate justice of the supreme court of Georgia in 1903; died in Raleigh, N.C., June 9, 1904; interment in West End Cemetery, Quitman, Ga.

**TURNER, James,** a Representative from Maryland; born near Bel Air, Harford County, Md., November 7, 1783; completed preparatory studies at the Classic Academy of Madonna, Maryland; captain of militia in the War of 1812; moved to Parkton, Baltimore County, in 1811 and established a dairy farm; collector of State and county taxes in 1817; served as a justice of the peace in 1824; member of the State house of delegates 1824-1833; elected as a Jacksonian to the Twenty-third and Twenty-fourth Congresses (March 4, 1833-March 3, 1837); unsuccessful candidate for reelection; again served in the State house of delegates in 1837 and 1838; member of the State senate 1855-1859; engaged in farming at Parkton, Md., until his death March 28, 1861; interment in Bethel Cemetery, near Madonna, Harford County, Md.

**TURNER, James** (father of Daniel Turner), a Senator from North Carolina; born in Southampton County, Va., December 20, 1766; moved to Warren County, N.C., in 1770; attended the common schools; engaged in planting; served as a private in a company of North Carolina Volunteers during the Revolutionary War; member, North Carolina State house of commons, 1797-1800; member, State senate, 1801-1802; elected Governor of North Carolina by the General Assembly, and served from December 6, 1802 to December 10, 1805; elected as a Republican to the United States Senate in 1805; reelected in 1811, and served from March 4, 1805 to November 21, 1816, when he resigned due to ill health; died on his plantation, "Bloomsbury," near Warrenton, Warren County, N.C., January 15, 1824; interment in Bloomsbury Cemetery.

**TURNER, Oscar** (father of Oscar Turner [1867-1902]), a Representative from Kentucky; born in New Orleans, La., February 3, 1825; moved with his parents to Fayette County, Ky., in 1826; completed preparatory studies; moved to Ballard County, Ky., in 1843; graduated from the law department of Transylvania University, Lexington, Ky., in 1847; Commonwealth attorney 1851-1855; admitted to the bar and practiced until 1861; served in the Kentucky senate 1867-1871; elected as an Independent Democrat to the Forty-sixth Congress, as a Democrat to the Forty-seventh Congress, and as an Independent Democrat to the Forty-eighth Congress (March 4, 1879-March 3, 1885); resumed the practice of law; died in Louisville, Ky., on January 22, 1896; interment in Cave Hill Cemetery.

**TURNER, Oscar** (son of Oscar Turner [1825-1896]), a Representative from Kentucky; born in Woodlands, Ballard County, Ky., October 19, 1867; attended the public schools of Washington, D.C., and Louisville (Ky.) Rugby School; studied law at the University of Louisville, and graduated from the University of Virginia in 1886; was admitted to the bar and commenced practice in Louisville, Ky., in 1891; elected as a Democrat to the Fifty-sixth Congress (March 4, 1899-March 3, 1901); declined to be a candidate for renomination in 1900; resumed the practice of law; died in Louisville, Ky., July 17, 1902; interment in Cave Hill Cemetery.

**TURNER, Smith Spangler,** a Representative from Virginia; born in Warren County, Va., November 21, 1842; cadet at the Virginia Military Institute, Lexington, Va., when the Civil War commenced, and was subsequently given an honorary diploma; enlisted in the Confederate Army in 1861; served with General Thomas Jonathan "Stonewall" Jackson as drill officer; an officer of Major General George E. Pickett's division during the remainder of the war; taught mathematics in a female seminary in Winchester, Va., 1865-1867; studied law; was admitted to the bar in 1869 and commenced practice in Front Royal, Va.; member of the Virginia house of delegates, 1869-1872; prosecuting attorney for Warren County, Va., from 1874 until 1879; member of the board of visitors of the Virginia Military Institute for eight years; elected as a Democrat to the Fifty-third Congress to fill the vacancy caused by the resignation of Charles T. O'Ferrall; reelected to the Fifty-fourth Congress and served from January 30, 1894, to March 3, 1897; was not a candidate for renomination in 1896 to the Fifty-fifth Congress; died in Front Royal, Va., April 8, 1898; interment in Prospect Hill Cemetery.

**TURNER, Thomas,** a Representative from Kentucky; born in Richmond, Madison County, Ky., September 10, 1821; attended the Richmond Academy; graduated from Centre College, Danville, Ky., in September 1840; studied law at the Transylvania Law School, Lexington, Ky.; admitted to the bar in 1842 and commenced practice in Richmond, Ky.; Commonwealth attorney 1845-1846; served in the Mexican War as a private in Captain Stone's company of Col. Roger Hanson's regiment; moved to Mount Sterling, Montgomery County, Ky., in November 1854 and continued the practice of law; member of the Kentucky house of representatives 1861-1863; elected as a Democrat to the Forty-fifth and Forty-sixth Congresses (March 4, 1877-March 3, 1881); unsuccessful candidate for reelection in 1880 to the Forty-seventh Congress; resumed the practice of law; died in Mount Sterling, Ky., on September 11, 1900; interment in Macpelah Cemetery.

**TURNER, Thomas Johnston,** a Representative from Illinois; born in Trumbull County, Ohio, April 5, 1815; completed preparatory studies; moved with his parents to Butler County, Pa., in 1825; moved to Lake County, Ind., in 1837 and to Freeport, Ill., in 1838; studied law; was admitted to the bar in 1840 and commenced practice in Freeport; judge of the probate court of Stephenson County in 1842; postmaster of Freeport in 1844; State district attorney in 1845; established the first weekly newspaper (Prairie Democrat) in Stephenson County; elected as a Democrat to the Thirtieth Congress (March 4, 1847-March 3, 1849); member of the State house of representatives in 1854, serving as speaker; elected first mayor of Freeport, Ill., in 1855; delegate to the peace convention held in Washington, D.C., in 1861 in an effort to devise means to prevent the impending war; enlisted in the Union Army May 24, 1861, and served as colonel of the Fifteenth Regiment, Illinois Volunteer Infantry; resigned on account of ill health in 1862; member of the constitutional convention in 1863; unsuccessful Democratic candidate for United States Senator in 1871; moved to Chicago in 1871 and resumed the practice of law; died at Hot Springs, Ark., April 4, 1874; interment in the City Cemetery, Freeport, Ill.

**TURNEY, Hopkins Lacy,** a Representative and a Senator from Tennessee; born at Dixon Springs, Smith County, Tenn., October 3, 1797; apprenticed to the tailor's trade; served in the Seminole War in 1818; studied law; was admitted to the bar and commenced practice in Jasper, Tenn.; moved to Winchester, Tenn., and continued the practice of law; member, State house of representatives 1828-1838; elected as a Democrat to the Twenty-fifth, Twenty-sixth, and Twenty-seventh Congresses (March 4, 1837-March 3, 1843); elected to the United States Senate and served from March 4, 1845, to March 3, 1851; chairman, Committee on Retrenchment (Twenty-ninth and Thirtieth Congresses), Committee on Patents and the Patent Office (Thirty-first Congress); resumed the practice of law; died in Winchester, Tenn., August 1, 1857; interment in Winchester Cemetery.

**TURNEY, Jacob,** a Representative from Pennsylvania; born in Greensburg, Westmoreland County, Pa., February 18, 1825; completed preparatory studies and attended Greensburg Academy; apprenticed as a printer; studied law; admitted to the bar in 1849 and commenced practice in Greensburg, Pa.; district attorney for Westmoreland County 1850-1855; member of the Pennsylvania senate 1858-1860 and was elected president in 1859; unsuccessful candidate for Pennsylvania senator in 1871; elected as a Democrat to the Forty-fourth and Forty-fifth Congresses (March 4, 1875-March 3, 1879); again resumed the practice of law; died in Greensburg, Pa., on October 4, 1891; interment in St. Clair Cemetery.

**TURPIE, David,** a Senator from Indiana; born in Hamilton County, Ohio, July 8, 1828; graduated from Kenyon College, Gambier, Ohio, in 1848; studied law; was admitted to the bar in 1849 and commenced practice in Logansport, Cass County, Ind.; member, State house of representatives 1852, 1858; judge of the court of common pleas 1854-1856; judge of the circuit court 1856; elected as a Democrat to the United States Senate to fill the vacancy caused by the expulsion of Jesse D. Bright and served from January 14 to March 3, 1863; moved to Indianapolis, Ind., in 1872 and continued the practice of law; member, State house of representatives, serving as speaker 1874-1875; one of the three commissioners to revise the laws of Indiana in 1878 and 1881; United States district attorney for Indiana 1886-1887; again elected as a Democrat to the United States Senate in 1887; reelected in 1893 and served from March 4, 1887, to March 3, 1899; unsuccessful candidate for reelection; chairman, Committee on Census (Fifty-third Congress); retired from public life; died in Indianapolis, Ind., April 21, 1909; interment in Crown Hill Cemetery.

**Bibliography:** Turpie, David. *Sketches of My Own Time.* 1903. Reprint. New York: AMS Press, 1975.

**TURPIN, Charles Murray,** a Representative from Pennsylvania; born in Kingston, Luzerne County, Pa., March 4, 1878; attended the public and high schools and Wyoming Seminary, Kingston, Pa.; served as a corporal in the United States Army during the Spanish-American War in Company F, Ninth Pennsylvania Volunteer Infantry; member of the Pennsylvania National Guard 1896-1901, serving as second lieutenant, first lieutenant, and captain; employed as a carpenter, grocery clerk, and a steamboat captain before graduating from the dental department of the University of Pennsylvania at Philadelphia in 1904; commenced the practice of dentistry in Kingston, Pa., in 1905; member of the board of education 1916-1922; burgess of Kingston 1922-1926, and prothonotary of Luzerne County 1926-1929; elected as a Republican to the Seventy-first Congress to fill the vacancy caused by the death of John J. Casey; reelected to the Seventy-second, Seventy-third, and Seventy-fourth Congresses and served from June 4, 1929, to January 3, 1937; unsuccessful candidate for reelection in 1936 to the Seventy-fifth Congress; appointed assistant chief clerk, Luzerne County assessor's office, Wilkes-Barre, Pa.; died in Kingston, Pa., June 4, 1946; interment in Forty Fort Cemetery, Forty Fort, Pa.

**TURPIN, Louis Washington,** a Representative from Alabama; born in Charlottesville, Albemarle County, Va., February 22, 1849; his parents having died he moved to Alabama with his sister and settled in Perry County in 1858; self-educated; engaged in agricultural pursuits; tax assessor of Hale County 1873-1880; chairman of the Democratic committee of Hale County for six years; unsuccessful candidate for nomination to the Forty-eighth Congress; presented credentials as a Democratic Member-elect to the Fifty-first Congress and served from March 4, 1889, to June 4, 1890, when he was succeeded by John V. McDuffie, who contested his election; elected to the Fifty-second and Fifty-third Congresses (March 4, 1891-March 3, 1895); unsuccessful candidate for renomination; retired from politics and engaged in planting; died in Greensboro, Ala., February 3, 1903; interment in the City Cemetery.

**TURRILL, Joel,** a Representative from New York; born in Shoreham, Vt., February 22, 1794; attended the common school; was graduated from Middlebury College in 1816; studied law in Newburgh, N.Y.; moved to Oswego, Oswego County, N.Y.; was admitted to the bar in 1819 and commenced practice in Oswego; justice of the peace; county judge 1828-1833; member of the State assembly in 1831; elected as a Jacksonian to the Twenty-third and Twenty-fourth Congresses (March 4, 1833-March 3, 1837); was not a candidate for reelection in 1836; district attorney for Oswego County 1838-1840; surrogate of Oswego County in 1843; United States consul to the Sandwich Islands 1845-1850; died in Oswego, N.Y., December 28, 1859; interment in Riverside Cemetery.

**TUTEN, James Russell,** a Representative from Georgia; born on a farm in Appling County, Ga., July 23, 1911; educated in county public schools, South Georgia College at Douglas, and Georgia Southern College at Statesboro; engaged in farming, also as a teacher, bricklayer, businessman, and building contractor; city commissioner of Brunswick, Ga., from 1956 until 1962; mayor of Brunswick in 1958 and 1962; chairman, board of trustees, Brewton Parker College, Mount Vernon, Ga.; elected as a Democrat to the Eighty-eighth and Eighty-ninth Congresses (January 3, 1963-January 3, 1967); unsuccessful candidate for renomination in 1966 to the Ninetieth Congress; appointed as cochairman of the Coastal Plains Regional Commission in 1967; died in Falls Church, Va., August 16, 1968; interment in Palmetto Cemetery, Brunswick, Ga.

**TUTHILL, Joseph Hasbrouck** (nephew of Selah Tuthill), a Representative from New York; born in Blooming Grove, Orange County, N.Y., February 25, 1811; attended common and private schools; moved with his parents to Shawangunk, Ulster County, N.Y., in 1824; engaged in mercantile and agricultural pursuits; moved to New York City in 1828, and continued his mercantile pursuits; moved to Ulsterville, N.Y., in 1832, where he engaged in business; moved to Ellenville, N.Y., in 1834; member of the Ulster County Board of Supervisors in 1842, 1843, 1861, 1862, 1865-1870; clerk of Ulster County 1843-1847; served as president of the Ellenville Glass Works; unsuccessful candidate for election in 1866 to Congress; elected as a Democrat to the Forty-second Congress (March 4, 1871-March 3, 1873); died in Ellenville, N.Y., July 27, 1877; interment in Fantinekill Cemetery, near Ellenville, N.Y.

**TUTHILL, Selah** (uncle of Joseph Hasbrouck Tuthill), a Representative from New York; born in Blooming Grove, Orange County, N.Y., October 26, 1771; attended public and private schools; member of the State assembly from Ulster County in 1805 and from Orange County in 1820; elected to the Seventeenth Congress and served from March 4, 1821, until his death in Goshen, N.Y., September 7, 1821; interment in Riverside Cemetery, Marlboro, Ulster County, N.Y.

**TUTTLE, William Edgar, Jr.,** a Representative from New Jersey; born in Horseheads, Chemung County, N.Y., December 10, 1870; was graduated from Horseheads High School and Elmira Free Academy in 1887 and attended Cornell University, Ithaca, N.Y., for two years; was engaged in the lumber business in Westfield, N.J.; delegate to the Democratic National Convention in 1908 and 1916; elected as a Democrat to the Sixty-second and Sixty-third Congresses (March 4, 1911-March 3, 1915); unsuccessful candidate for reelection in 1914 to the Sixty-fourth Congress; resumed the lumber business; United States commissioner to the Panama Exposition in 1916; president of the State board of conservation and development in 1919; State commissioner of banking and insurance in 1921; died in Westfield, Union County, N.J., February 11, 1923; interment in Maple Grove Cemetery, Horseheads, N.Y.

**TWEED, William Magear,** a Representative from New York; born in New York City, April 3, 1823; completed preparatory studies; learned the trade of chair maker, and was later engaged as a saddler, bookkeeper, and clerk; one of the founders of Fire Company No. 6 (Americus Engine Company) in 1848; elected alderman of the Seventh Ward in New York City in 1851; elected as a Democrat to the Thirty-third Congress (March 4, 1853-March 3, 1855); unsuccessful candidate for reelection in 1854 to the Thirty-fourth Congress; member of the Board of Education in 1856 and 1857; member of the board of supervisors for New York County in 1856; unsuccessful candidate for sheriff in 1861; chairman of the Democratic general committee of New York County; deputy street commissioner, 1861-1870; elected to the New York State senate in 1867 and 1869, serving four years; again elected in 1871, but was not permitted to take his seat; commissioner of the department of public works in 1870; tried in 1873 on charges of official embezzlement, but the trial ended in a hung jury; tried a second time, found guilty, and sentenced to twelve years' imprisonment; escaped to New Jersey on December 4, 1875, while on a visit to his family; traveled to Florida and Cuba and was captured in Spain; brought back to the United States on a man-of-war; again confined in prison in New York City from November 23, 1876 until his death on April 12, 1878; interment in Greenwood Cemetery, Brooklyn, N.Y.

Bibliography: *DAB*; Hershkowitz, Leo. *Tweed's New York: Another Look.* Garden City, N.Y.: Anchor Press-Doubleday, 1977; Lynch, Denis Tilden. *"Boss" Tweed: The Story of a Grim Generation.* 1927. Reprint. New York: Arno Press, 1974.

**TWEEDY, John Hubbard,** a Delegate from the Territory of Wisconsin; born in Danbury, Fairfield County, Conn., November 9, 1814; was graduated from Yale College in 1834 and from the Yale Law School in 1836; was admitted to the bar in July 1836; moved to Milwaukee, Wis., in October 1836 and commenced practice; commissioner and receiver of canal lands 1839-1841; member of the Territorial council in 1842; delegate to the State constitutional convention in 1846; elected as a Whig to the Thirtieth Congress and served from March 4, 1847, until that portion of the Territory of Wisconsin in which he resided was admitted as a State into the Union on May 29, 1848; was not a candidate for renomination in 1848; unsuccessful Whig candidate for Governor in 1848; member of the State assembly in 1853; engaged in railroad development and served as director of the Milwaukee & Mississippi Railroad and the Milwaukee & Watertown Railroad; died in Milwaukee, Wis., November 12, 1891; interment in Wooster Cemetery, Danbury, Conn.

**TWEEDY, Samuel,** a Representative from Connecticut; born at Nine Partners, Dutchess County, N.Y., March 8, 1776; moved to Danbury, Fairfield County, Conn.; member of the State house of representatives in 1818, 1820, and 1824; served in the State senate 1826-1828; held many local offices; elected as an Anti-Jacksonian to the Twenty-third Congress (March 4, 1833-March 3, 1835); died in Danbury, Conn., on July 1, 1868; interment in Wooster Cemetery.

**TWICHELL, Ginery,** a Representative from Massachusetts; born in Athol, Mass., August 26, 1811; attended the common schools; proprietor of several stagecoach lines; in 1848 engaged in railroading; president of the Boston & Worcester Railway in 1857; delegate to the Republican National Convention in 1864; elected as a Republican to the Fortieth, Forty-first, and Forty-second Congresses (March 4, 1867-March 3, 1873); was not a candidate for renomination in 1872; president of the Atchison, Topeka & Santa Fe Railway Co. 1870-1874; president of the Boston, Barre & Gardner Railroad Co. 1873-1878; died in Brookline, Norfolk County, Mass., July 23, 1883; interment in the Rural Cemetery, Worcester, Mass.

**TWYMAN, Robert Joseph,** a Representative from Illinois; born in Indianapolis, Marion County, Ind., June 18, 1897; attended Georgetown University, Washington, D.C.; employed in foreign service by the Department of State; during the First World War served as an ensign in the United States Navy; employed by a public utility company in Guatemala, Central America, in 1919; accepted a commission in the United States Navy in February 1941 and served until September 1945; engaged in manufacturing and distributing construction machinery; elected as a Republican to the Eightieth Congress (January 3, 1947-January 3, 1949); unsuccessful candidate for reelection in 1948 to the Eighty-first Congress; resumed business interests until retirement; died in West Palm Beach, Fla., June 28, 1976; interment in Rosehill Cemetery, Chicago, Ill.

**TYDINGS, Joseph Davies** (adoptive son of Millard Evelyn Tydings), a Senator from Maryland; born in Asheville, Buncombe County, N.C., May 4, 1928; attended the public schools of Aberdeen, Md.; graduated from McDonogh School in 1946; B.A., University of Maryland, 1950; LL.B., University of Maryland School of Law, 1953; served in the Army of Occupation, European Theater of Operations, after the Second World War as a corporal, Sixth Constabulary Regiment; was admitted to the bar in 1952 and commenced the practice of law; member, Maryland State house of delegates, 1955-1961; United States attorney for Maryland, 1961-1963; United States representative at the Interpol Conference in Helsinki, Finland, and at the International Penal Conference in Bellagio, Italy, in 1963; elected as a Democrat to the United States Senate in 1964, and served from January 3, 1965 to January 3, 1971; unsuccessful candidate for reelection in 1970; chairman, Committee on the District of Columbia (Ninety-first Congress); unsuccessful candidate for nomination in 1976 to the United States Senate; resumed the practice of law; is a resident of Havre de Grace, Md.

**TYDINGS, Millard Evelyn** (father of Joseph Davies Tydings), a Representative and a Senator from Maryland; born in Havre de Grace, Harford County, Md., April 6, 1890; attended the public schools of Harford County; graduated from Maryland Agricultural College (now the University of Maryland) in 1910; engaged in civil engineering with the Baltimore & Ohio Railroad in West Virginia in 1911; studied law at the University of Maryland Law School, Baltimore, Md.; was admitted to the bar and commenced practice in Havre de Grace in 1913; member, Maryland State house of delegates, 1916-1921, serving as speaker of the house from 1920 to 1922; served as a private on the Mexican border at Eagle Pass, Tex., 1916; enlisted as a private in the First World War in 1917; promoted to lieutenant colonel and division machine-gun officer in 1918; served in Germany with the Army of Occupation; discharged from the service in 1919; author; member, State senate, 1922-1923; elected as a Democrat to the Sixty-eighth and Sixty-ninth Congresses (March 4, 1923-March 3, 1927); was not a candidate for renomination in 1926, having become a candidate for United States Senator; elected as a Democrat to the United States Senate in 1926, 1932, 1938, and again in 1944, and served from March 4, 1927 to January 3, 1951; was an unsuccessful candidate for reelection in 1950; chairman, Committee on Territories and Insular Possessions (Seventy-third through Seventy-ninth Congresses), Committee on Armed Services (Eighty-first Congress); nominated in 1956 as Democratic candidate for the United States Senate but withdrew before election due to ill health; engaged in the practice of law in Washington, D.C., and Baltimore, Md.; died at his farm, "Oakington," near Havre de Grace, Md., February 9, 1961; interment in Angel Hill Cemetery.

**Bibliography:** *DAB*; Alexander, Holmes. "Millard E. Tydings: The Man From Maryland." In *The American Politician*. Edited by John Salter. pp. 124-37. Chapel Hill: University of North Carolina Press, 1938; Keith, Caroline H. *For Hell and a Brown Mule: The Biography of Senator Millard E. Tydings*. Lanham, Md.: Madison Books, 1991.

**TYLER, Asher,** a Representative from New York; born in Bridgewater, Oneida County, N.Y., May 10, 1798; was graduated from Hamilton College, Clinton, N.Y., in 1817; studied law; was admitted to the bar and commenced practice in Ellicottville, Cattaraugus County, N.Y., in 1836; agent of the Devereaux Land Co., with headquarters at Ellicottville, and subsequently served in a like capacity for the Erie Co.; held several local offices; elected as a Whig to the Twenty-eighth Congress (March 4, 1843-March 3, 1845); moved to Elmira in 1846 and engaged in railroad operations; one of the incorporators of the Elmira Rolling Mill Co.; died in Elmira, N.Y., August 1, 1875; interment in Woodlawn Cemetery.

**TYLER, David Gardiner** (son of John Tyler), a Representative from Virginia; born in East Hampton, Long Island, N.Y., July 12, 1846; completed preparatory studies in a private school in Charles City County, Va., and entered Washington College (now Washington and Lee University), Lexington, Va., in 1862, leaving there in 1863 to join the Confederate Army; served as a private in the Rockbridge Artillery, First Virginia Battalion, Army of Northern Virginia, surrendering at Appomattox; went to Europe in October 1865 and for two years attended the Polytechnic School at Karlsruhe, Grand Duchy of Baden; graduated from the law department of Washington College in 1869; was admitted to the bar in 1870 and commenced practice in Richmond, Va.; director of the Virginia lunatic asylum in Williamsburg, Va., 1884-1887; served in the Virginia senate in 1891 and 1892; member of the board of visitors of the College of William and Mary; elected as a Democrat to the Fifty-third and Fifty-fourth Congresses (March 4, 1893-March 3, 1897); unsuccessful candidate for renomination in 1896; resumed the practice of his profession;

again served in the Virginia senate 1900-1904; elected judge of the fourteenth judicial circuit of Virginia in 1904; reelected in 1908 and 1912, and served until his death; died at "Sherwood Forest," Charles City County, Va., September 5, 1927; interment in Hollywood Cemetery, Richmond, Va.

**TYLER, James Manning,** a Representative from Vermont; born in Wilmington, Windham County, Vt., April 27, 1835; attended the Brattleboro Academy and was graduated from the Law University of Albany, N.Y.; was admitted to the bar in September 1860 and commenced practice in Wilmington, Vt.; member of the State house of representatives in 1863 and 1864; State's attorney in 1866 and 1867; trustee of the Vermont Asylum for the Insane 1875-1926; elected as a Republican to the Forty-sixth and Forty-seventh Congresses (March 4, 1879-March 3, 1883); declined to be a candidate for renomination in 1882; resumed the practice of his profession in Brattleboro, Vt.; appointed a judge of the supreme court of the State in September 1887 and served until his resignation December 1, 1908; president of the Vermont National Bank 1917-1923; president of the Vermont-Peoples' National Bank in 1923 and 1924; died in Brattleboro, Windham County, Vt., October 13, 1926; interment in Prospect Hill Cemetery.

**TYLER, John** (father of David Gardiner Tyler), a Representative and a Senator from Virginia, a Vice President and 10th President of the United States; born in Charles City County, Va., March 29, 1790; attended private schools; graduated from the College of William and Mary, Williamsburg, Va., in 1807; studied law; was admitted to the bar in 1809 and commenced practice in Charles City County; captain of a military company in 1813; member, Virginia house of delegates, 1811-1816; member of the council of Virginia in 1816; elected as a Republican to the Fourteenth Congress to fill the vacancy caused by the death of John Clopton; reelected to the two succeeding Congresses, and served from December 16, 1817 to March 3, 1821; declined to be a candidate for renomination in 1820 to the Seventeenth Congress because of impaired health; member, Virginia house of delegates, 1823-1825; elected Governor of Virginia by the General Assembly and served from December 10, 1825 to March 4, 1827; elected to the United States Senate in 1827; reelected in 1833, and served from March 4, 1827 to February 29, 1836, when he resigned; served as President pro tempore of the Senate during the Twenty-third Congress; chairman, Committee on the District of Columbia (Twenty-third and Twenty-fourth Congresses), Committee on Manufactures (Twenty-third Congress); member of the Virginia constitutional convention in 1829 and 1830; member, Virginia house of delegates, 1839; received forty-seven electoral votes as the Whig candidate for Vice President of the United States in 1836; elected Vice President in 1840 on the Whig ticket headed by William Henry Harrison; was inaugurated March 4, 1841, and served until the death of President Harrison on April 4, 1841; took the oath of office as President of the United States on April 6, 1841, and served until March 3, 1845; was not a candidate for election in 1844; delegate to and president of the peace convention held in Washington, D.C., in 1861 in an effort to devise means to prevent the impending war; delegate to the Confederate Provisional Congress in 1861; elected to the House of Representatives of the Confederate Congress, but died in Richmond, Va., January 18, 1862, before the assembling of the Congress; interment in Hollywood Cemetery.

**Bibliography:** *DAB*; Chitwood, Oliver. *John Tyler: Champion of the Old South*. 1939. Reprint. Newton, Conn.: American Political Biography Press, 1990; Peterson, Norma Lois. *The Presidencies of William Henry Harrison and John Tyler*. Lawrence: University Press of Kansas, 1989; Tyler, Lyon, ed. *The Letters and the Times of the Tylers*. 3 vols. 1884-1896. Reprint. New York: Da Capo Press, 1970.

**TYNDALL, William Thomas,** a Representative from Missouri; born in Sparta, Christian County, Mo., January 16, 1862; attended the public schools, Henderson Academy at Sparta, and Sparta Academy; engaged in teaching at Sparta, 1884-1895; studied law; was admitted to the bar in 1893 and commenced practice in Sparta; appointed postmaster of Sparta, Mo., by President Benjamin Harrison and served from March 23, 1891, to November 14, 1893; again appointed postmaster by President William McKinley, and served from December 8, 1897, to January 7, 1905; elected as a Republican to the Fifty-ninth Congress (March 4, 1905-March 3, 1907); unsuccessful candidate for reelection in 1906 to the Sixtieth Congress; resumed the practice of law in Sparta, Mo.; moved to Bartlesville, Okla., in 1912 and continued the practice of law until his death there on November 26, 1928; interment in a mausoleum in White Rose Cemetery.

**TYNER, James Noble,** a Representative from Indiana; born in Brookville, Franklin County, Ind., January 17, 1826; pursued an academic course, and was graduated from Brookville Academy in 1844; spent ten years in business; studied law; was admitted to the bar in 1857 and commenced practice in Peru, Ind.; secretary of the Indiana State senate, 1857-1861; special agent of the Post Office Department, 1861-1866; elected as a Republican to the Forty-first Congress to fill the vacancy caused by the resignation of Representative-elect Daniel D. Pratt; reelected to the Forty-second and Forty-third Congresses, and served from March 4, 1869 to March 3, 1875; appointed Second Assistant Postmaster General, serving from February 26, 1875 to July 11, 1876; Postmaster General in the Cabinet of President Ulysses S. Grant from July 12, 1876 to March 11, 1877; appointed First Assistant Postmaster General, and served from March 16, 1877 until his resignation on October 29, 1881; delegate to the International Postal Congress at Paris in 1878 and at Washington in 1897; Assistant Attorney General for the Post Office Department from March 21, 1889 to May 27, 1893, and again from May 6, 1897 to April 27, 1903; died in Washington, D.C., December 5, 1904; interment in Oak Hill Cemetery.

**TYSON, Jacob,** a Representative from New York; born in Staten Island, N.Y., October 8, 1773; attended the common schools; moved to Richmond, N.Y.; studied law; was admitted to the bar and practiced; supervisor of the town of Castletown, Richmond County, 1811-1821; served as judge of Richmond County 1822-1840; elected to the Eighteenth Congress (March 4, 1823-March 3, 1825); member of the State senate in 1828; died in Staten Island, N.Y., July 16, 1848; interment in the Reformed Protestant Dutch Church Cemetery, Port Richmond, Staten Island, N.Y.

**TYSON, Job Roberts,** a Representative from Pennsylvania; born in Philadelphia, Pa., February 8, 1803; completed preparatory studies; taught school in Hamburg, Pa.; studied law; admitted to the bar in 1827 and commenced practice in Philadelphia, Pa.; also engaged in literary pursuits; held several local offices; served in the Pennsylvania house of representatives; elected as a Whig to the Thirty-fourth Congress (March 4, 1855-March 3, 1857); died on his estate, "Woodlawn," Montgomery County, Pa., June 27, 1858; interment in South Laurel Hill Cemetery, Philadelphia, Pa.

**TYSON, John Russell,** a Representative from Alabama; born in Lowndes County, Ala., November 28, 1856; attended the public schools; was graduated from Howard College, Marion, Ala., in 1877 and from Washington and Lee University, Lexington, Va., in 1879; studied law; was admitted to the Alabama bar in 1879 and commenced the practice of law in Hayneville, Ala.; member of the Alabama State house of representatives in 1880; moved to Montgomery, Ala., in 1884 and resumed the practice of law; elected a member of the city council in May 1889 and its president in May 1891, resigning in October 1892, having been appointed to the circuit court; served as judge of the circuit court 1892-1898;

associate justice of the supreme court of Alabama 1898-1906, and served as chief justice from November 1906 to February 28, 1909, when he resigned; resumed the practice of law in Montgomery, Ala.; elected as a Democrat to the Sixty-seventh and Sixty-eighth Congresses, and served from March 4, 1921, until his death in Rochester, Minn., on March 27, 1923; interment in Oakwood Cemetery, Montgomery, Ala.

**TYSON, Lawrence Davis,** a Senator from Tennessee; born on a farm near Greenville, Pitt County, N.C., July 4, 1861; attended the county schools and Greenville Academy, and graduated from the United States Military Academy at West Point in 1883; took part in campaigns against the Apache Indians; professor of military science and tactics in the University of Tennessee at Knoxville 1891-1895, and graduated in law from that university in 1894; resigned his commission, was admitted to the bar in 1894 and commenced practice in Knoxville; volunteered in 1898 for service during the Spanish-American War, and was appointed colonel of the Sixth Regiment, United States Volunteer Infantry, which he recruited, trained, and took to Puerto Rico; was mustered out in 1899; engaged in the practice of law at Knoxville and later in manufacturing; brigadier general and inspector general of the National Guard of Tennessee 1902-1908; member, State house of representatives and served as speaker 1903-1905; was an unsuccessful candidate for election to the United States Senate in 1913; volunteered for service at the outbreak of the First World War and was commissioned brigadier general in command of all National Guard troops of Tennessee; later commissioned by President Woodrow Wilson as a brigadier general and assigned to the Fifty-ninth Brigade, Thirtieth Division; trained troops at Camp Sevier, Greenville, S.C.; fought in France and Belgium and was discharged in 1919; resumed newspaper pursuits; was an unsuccessful candidate for the Democratic nomination for Vice President in 1920; elected as a Democrat to the United States Senate and served from March 4, 1925, until his death in a sanitarium at Strafford, Pa., on August 24, 1929; interment in Old Gray Cemetery, Knoxville, Tenn.

**Bibliography:** *DAB*.

# U

**UDALL, Morris King** (brother of Stewart Lee Udall), a Representative from Arizona; born in St. Johns, Apache County, Ariz., June 15, 1922; attended the public schools; enlisted as a private in the United States Army in 1942, and was discharged as a captain in the United States Army Air Corps, with service in the Twentieth Air Force in the Pacific Theater in 1946; LL.B., University of Arizona School of Law, 1949; began practice in Tucson in 1949; county attorney for Pima County in 1953 and 1954; lecturer on labor law, University of Arizona College of Law, 1956-1957; co-founder of the Bank of Tucson and the Catalina Savings and Loan Association; elected as a Democrat to the Eighty-seventh Congress, May 2, 1961, by special election to fill the vacancy caused by the resignation of his brother, Stewart L. Udall; reelected to the fifteen succeeding Congresses, and served from May 2, 1961 until his resignation on May 4, 1991; chairman, Committee on Interior and Insular Affairs (Ninety-fifth through One Hundred Second Congresses); unsuccessful candidate for the Democratic presidential nomination in 1976; is a resident of Tucson, Ariz.

**Bibliography:** Udall, Morris K. *Education of a Congressman: The Newsletters of Morris K. Udall.* Edited by Robert L. Peabody with the assistance of Tim Wyngaard and Michael Alonge. Indianapolis: Bobbs-Merrill, 1972.

**UDALL, Stewart Lee** (brother of Morris King Udall), a Representative from Arizona; born in St. Johns, Apache County, Ariz., January 31, 1920; attended the public schools and the Eastern Arizona Junior College for one year; during the Second World War enlisted and engaged in combat operations over Europe as a gunner with the Fifteenth Air Force until 1944; graduated from the law school of the University of Arizona at Tucson in 1948; was admitted to the bar in 1948 and commenced the practice of law in Tucson, Ariz.; trustee of School District 16 in 1954; elected as a Democrat to the Eighty-fourth and to the three succeeding Congresses, and served from January 3, 1955 until his resignation January 18, 1961; appointed Secretary of the Interior by President John F. Kennedy, took the oath of office January 21, 1961, and served until January 23, 1969; consultant; author; resumed the practice of law; is a resident of Phoenix, Ariz.

**Bibliography:** Leunes, Barbara Laverne Blythe. "The Conservation Philosophy of Stewart L. Udall, 1961-1968." Ph.D. dissertation, Texas A&M University, 1977; Udall, Stewart L. *The Quiet Crisis*. New York: Holt, Rinehart and Winston, 1963.

**UDREE, Daniel,** a Representative from Pennsylvania; born in Philadelphia, Pa., August 5, 1751; attended the common schools; moved to Berks County and engaged in mercantile pursuits; member of the Pennsylvania house of representatives from 1799 until 1805; elected as a Republican to the Thirteenth Congress to fill the vacancy caused by the resignation of John M. Hyneman and served from October 12, 1813, to March 3, 1815; unsuccessful candidate for reelection in 1814 to the Fourteenth Congress; elected to the Sixteenth Congress to fill the vacancy caused by the resignation of Joseph Hiester and served from December 26, 1820, to March 3, 1821; elected to the Eighteenth Congress; subsequently elected to the Seventeenth Congress to fill the vacancy caused by the death of Ludwig Worman and served from December 10, 1822, to March 3, 1825; was not a candidate for renomination in 1824 to the Nineteenth Congress; resumed mercantile pursuits; died in Reading, Pa., July 15, 1828; interment in Oley Cemetery, Oley, Pa.

**ULLMAN, Albert Conrad,** a Representative from Oregon; born in Great Falls, Cascade County, Mont., March 9, 1914; attended the public schools in Snohomish, Wash; graduated from Whitman College, Walla Walla, Wash., in 1935; taught in Port Angeles (Wash.) High School, 1935-1937; M.A., Columbia University, 1939; commissioned an ensign in the United States Navy in 1942, and served as communications officer in the South and Southwest Pacific until December 1945; captain, United States Naval Reserve; engaged in business in Baker, Oreg., beginning in 1946; elected as a Democrat to the Eighty-fifth and to the eleven succeeding Congresses (January 3, 1957-January 3, 1981); chairman, Joint Committee on Budget Control (Ninety-second and Ninety-third Congresses), Committee on Budget (Ninety-third Congress), Committee on Ways and Means (Ninety-fourth through Ninety-sixth Congresses), Joint Committee on Internal Revenue Taxation (Ninety-fourth Congress), Joint Committee on Taxation (Ninety-fifth and Ninety-sixth Congresses); unsuccessful candidate for reelection in 1980 to the Ninety-seventh Congress; established a consulting firm in Washington, D.C.; was a resident of Falls Church, Va., until his death in Bethesda, Md., on October 11, 1986.

**UMSTEAD, William Bradley,** a Representative and a Senator from North Carolina; born on a farm in Mangum Township, Durham County, N.C., May 13, 1895; attended the county public schools and graduated from the University of North Carolina at Chapel Hill in 1916; taught school in Kinston, N.C., in 1916 and 1917; during the First World War served as a lieutenant in the United States Army from 1917 until 1919, with service overseas; studied law at Trinity College (now Duke University), 1919-1921; was admitted to the bar in 1920 and commenced practice in Durham, N.C., in 1921; prosecuting attorney of the Durham County Recorders Court, 1922-1926; solicitor of the tenth judicial district, 1927-1933; member of the board of trustees of the University of North Carolina; elected as a Democrat to the Seventy-third and to the two succeeding Congresses (March 4, 1933-January 3, 1939); was not a candidate for renomination in 1938 to the Seventy-sixth Congress; resumed the practice of law in Durham, N.C.; appointed to the United States

Senate to fill the vacancy caused by the death of Josiah W. Bailey and served from December 18, 1946, to December 30, 1948; was an unsuccessful candidate for the nomination to fill the vacancy and also for the full term; resumed the practice of law; elected Governor of North Carolina in 1952 and served from January 8, 1953 until his death in Durham, N.C., November 7, 1954; interment in Mount Tabor Church Cemetery in Mangum Township, Durham County, N.C.

**Bibliography:** Umstead, William. *Public Addresses, Letters and Papers of William Bradley Umstead.* Raleigh: Council of State, 1957.

**UNDERHILL, Charles Lee,** a Representative from Massachusetts; born in Richmond, Henrico County, Va., July 20, 1867; moved to Massachusetts in 1872 with his parents, who settled in Somerville; attended the common schools; was office boy, coal teamster, and blacksmith; subsequently engaged in the manufacture and sale of hardware in Somerville, Middlesex County, Mass.; served in the Massachusetts house of representatives in 1902, 1903, 1908-1913, 1917, and 1918; member of the Massachusetts constitutional convention in 1917 and 1918; elected as a Republican to the Sixty-seventh and to the five succeeding Congresses (March 4, 1921-March 3, 1933); chairman, Committee on Claims (Sixty-ninth and Seventieth Congresses), Committee on Accounts (Seventy-first Congress); was not a candidate for renomination in 1932 to the Seventy-third Congress; engaged in real estate development in Washington, D.C., from 1933 until he retired in 1941; died in New York City, January 28, 1946; interment in Mount Auburn Cemetery, Cambridge, Mass.

**UNDERHILL, Edwin Stewart,** a Representative from New York; born in Bath, Steuben County, N.Y., October 7, 1861; attended the common schools of his native city and Haverling High School at Bath; was graduated from Yale College in 1881; engaged in journalism and became editor of the Steuben Farmers' Advocate at Bath; presidential elector on the Democratic ticket in 1888; became editor and publisher of the Corning (N.Y.) Daily Democrat (later the Corning Evening Leader) in 1899; elected as a Democrat to the Sixty-second and Sixty-third Congresses (March 4, 1911-March 3, 1915); chairman, Committee on Industrial Arts and Expositions (Sixty-third Congress); was not a candidate for renomination in 1914 to the Sixty-fourth Congress; resumed the newspaper publishing business in Corning, N.Y.; engaged in banking, serving as vice president of the Farmers & Mechanics' Trust Co., Bath, N.Y.; delegate to the Democratic National Convention of 1928; died as the result of an automobile accident in Coopers, Steuben County, N.Y., February 7, 1929; interment in Grove Cemetery, Bath, N.Y.

**UNDERHILL, John Quincy,** a Representative from New York; born in New Rochelle, Westchester County, N.Y., February 19, 1848; attended private and public schools and the College of the City of New York; engaged in the insurance business; village trustee of New Rochelle in 1877; elected village president in 1878 and reelected in 1880; served as town auditor; member of the board of education for several years; connected with the Westchester Fire Insurance Co. for nineteen years, serving as president and treasurer; elected as a Democrat to the Fifty-sixth Congress (March 4, 1899-March 3, 1901); was not a candidate for renomination in 1900 to the Fifty-seventh Congress; discontinued active business pursuits and lived in retirement; died in New Rochelle, N.Y., May 21, 1907; interment in Beechwoods Cemetery.

**UNDERHILL, Walter,** a Representative from New York; born in New York City, September 12, 1795; completed preparatory studies; trustee of the house of refuge; treasurer of New York City for several years; served on the board of managers of the Society for the Reformation of Juvenile Delinquents in the city of New York from 1845 until 1866, serving as treasurer from 1858 to 1866; elected as a Whig to the Thirty-first Congress (March 4, 1849-March 3, 1851); was not a candidate for renomination in 1850 to the Thirty-second

Congress; president of the Mechanics & Traders' Insurance Co., New York City, from 1853 until his death in Whitestone, Long Island, N.Y., August 17, 1866; interment in Woodlawn Cemetery, New York City.

**UNDERWOOD, John William Henderson,** a Representative from Georgia; born in Ellenton, Ga., November 20, 1816; completed preparatory studies; studied law; was admitted to the bar in 1835 and commenced practice in Clarkesville, Ga.; solicitor general of the western judicial circuit of Georgia, 1843-1847; delegate to the State constitutional convention in 1850; delegate to the Democratic State convention in 1857; member of the Georgia State house of representatives, 1857-1859, and served as speaker; elected as a Democrat to the Thirty-sixth Congress and served from March 4, 1859, to January 23, 1861, when he withdrew and joined the Confederacy; served as brigade inspector during the Civil War; resumed the practice of law in Rome, Ga.; judge of the superior court of Georgia, 1867-1869, and 1873-1882; delegate to the Democratic National Convention of 1868; appointed by President Chester A. Arthur in 1884 a member of the first United States Tariff Commission; died in Rome, Floyd County, Ga., on July 18, 1888; interment in Myrtle Hill Cemetery.

**UNDERWOOD, Joseph Rogers** (brother of Warner Lewis Underwood and grandfather of Oscar Wilder Underwood), a Representative and a Senator from Kentucky; born in Goochland County, Va., October 24, 1791; moved to Barren County, Ky., in 1803 and lived with his uncle; attended the common schools and graduated from Transylvania College, Lexington, Ky., in 1811; studied law in Lexington; served in the War of 1812 as a lieutenant in the Thirteenth Regiment, Kentucky Infantry; was admitted to the bar in 1813 and commenced the practice of law in Glasgow, Ky.; served as town trustee and county auditor until 1823; member, Kentucky house of representatives, 1816-1819; moved to Bowling Green, Ky., in 1823; member, Kentucky house of representatives, 1825-1826; unsuccessful candidate for lieutenant governor of Kentucky in 1828; judge of the court of appeals from 1828 until 1835; elected as a Whig to the Twenty-fourth and to the three succeeding Congresses (March 4, 1835-March 3, 1843); declined to be a candidate for renomination in 1842 to the Twenty-eighth Congress; resumed the practice of law; presidential elector on the Whig ticket in 1844; member of the Kentucky house of representatives in 1846, and served as speaker; elected as a Whig to the United States Senate and served from March 4, 1847, to March 3, 1853; was not a candidate for reelection; member, Kentucky house of representatives, 1861-1863; resumed the practice of law and also engaged in agricultural pursuits; died near Bowling Green, Ky., August 23, 1876; interment in Fairview Cemetery, Bowling Green, Ky.

**Bibliography:** *DAB*; Priest, Nancy L. "Joseph Rogers Underwood: Nineteenth Century Kentucky Orator." *Register of the Kentucky Historical Society* 75 (October 1977): 386-403; Stickles, Arndt M., ed. "Joseph R. Underwood's Fragmentary Journal of the New and Old Court Contest in Kentucky." *Filson Club History Quarterly* 13 (October 1939): 202-10.

**UNDERWOOD, Mell Gilbert,** a Representative from Ohio; born at Rose Farm, Morgan County, Ohio, January 30, 1892; attended the public schools and was graduated from the New Lexington High School in 1911; taught in the public schools of New Lexington for several years; studied law at the Ohio State University at Columbus; was admitted to the bar in 1915 and commenced practice in New Lexington, Perry County, Ohio; prosecuting attorney of Perry County, 1917-1921; unsuccessful Democratic candidate for election in 1920 to the Sixty-seventh Congress; elected as a Democrat to the Sixty-eighth and to the six succeeding Congresses, and served from March 4, 1923 to April 10, 1936, when he resigned, having been appointed a judge of the

United States District Court for the Southern District of Ohio, and served until his retirement on June 30, 1967; chairman, Committee on Invalid Pensions (Seventy-second through Seventy-fourth Congresses); died on his farm near New Lexington, Ohio, March 8, 1972; interment in Maplewood Cemetery.

**UNDERWOOD, Oscar Wilder** (grandson of Joseph Rogers Underwood), a Representative and a Senator from Alabama; born in Louisville, Jefferson County, Ky., May 6, 1862; attended the common schools, the Rugby School, Louisville, Ky., and the University of Virginia at Charlottesville; studied law; was admitted to the bar in 1884 and commenced practice in Birmingham, Ala.; presented credentials as a Democratic Member-elect to the Fifty-fourth Congress, and served from March 4, 1895 to June 9, 1896, when he was succeeded by Truman H. Aldrich, who contested his election; elected as a Democrat to the Fifty-fifth and to the eight succeeding Congresses (March 4, 1897-March 3, 1915); majority leader 1911-1915; chairman, Committee on Ways and Means (Sixty-second and Sixty-third Congresses); unsuccessful candidate for the Democratic presidential nomination in 1912 and 1924; was not a candidate in 1914 for renomination to the House of Representatives, but was elected to the United States Senate; reelected in 1920, and served from March 4, 1915 to March 3, 1927; declined to be a candidate for reelection in 1926; minority leader (Sixty-sixth and Sixty-seventh Congresses); chairman, Committee on Cuban Relations (Sixty-fourth and Sixty-fifth Congresses); represented the United States as a member of the Conference on Limitation of Armaments in 1921 and 1922; represented the United States as a delegate to the Sixth International Conference of American States at Havana, Cuba, in 1928; retired to his estate, "Woodlawn Mansion," near Accotink, Fairfax County, Va., and engaged in literary pursuits until his death there on January 25, 1929; interment in Woodlawn Cemetery, Birmingham, Ala.

**Bibliography:** *DAB*; Johnson, Evans. *Oscar W. Underwood: A Political Biography*. Baton Rouge: Louisiana State University Press, 1980; Underwood, Oscar W. *Drifting Sands of Party Politics*. New York: The Century Co., 1928.

**UNDERWOOD, Robert Anacletus,** a Delegate from Guam; born in Tamuning, Guam, July 13, 1948; graduated from John F. Kennedy High School, 1965; B.A., California State University, Los Angeles, 1969, M.A., 1971, and Secondary Teaching Credential, 1972; University of Guam, certificate in education administration, 1976; D.Ed., University of Southern California, 1987; stockboy, Marianas Sales, Inc., 1963; library aide, Nieves Flores Library, 1964; loader and sorter, United Parcel Service, Los Angeles, Calif., 1966-1972; teacher, George Washington High School, 1972-1974; curriculum writer (part-time), Guam Bilingual Education Project, 1973-1976; assistant principal for business and student personnel, George Washington High School, 1974-1976; assistant and acting principal, Inarajan Junior High School, 1976; instructor and director of Bilingual Bicultural Training Program, 1976-1981, and assistant professor, 1981-1983, both at University of Guam; director of Project BEAM (Bilingual Education Assistance for Micronesia), 1983-1988; dean, College of Education, 1988-1990, academic vice president, University of Guam; elected as a Democrat a Delegate to the One Hundred Third and One Hundred Fourth Congresses (January 3, 1993-January 3, 1997); is a resident of Agana, Guam.

**UNDERWOOD, Thomas Rust,** a Representative and a Senator from Kentucky; born in Hopkinsville, Christian County, Ky., March 3, 1898; attended the public schools; graduated from the University of Kentucky at Lexington in 1917; started his newspaper career in 1917; during the First World War served in the Students Army Training Corps at the University of Kentucky in 1918; general manager of Lexington (Ky.) Herald, 1931-1935, and editor, 1935-1956; member of the Kentucky planning board, 1931-1935; secretary of the Kentucky racing commission, 1931-1943, 1947-1948; secretary of the National Association of State Racing Commissioners, 1934-1948; assistant to James F. Byrnes, Director and Chairman of the Economic Stabilization Board, 1943; elected as a Democrat to the Eighty-first and Eighty-second Congresses and served from January 3, 1949, until his resignation March 17, 1951; appointed to the United States Senate as a Democrat to fill the vacancy in the term ending January 3, 1955, caused by the death of Virgil M. Chapman, and served from March 19, 1951, to November 4, 1952; unsuccessful candidate for election in 1952 to fill the vacancy; resumed editorial duties with the Lexington Herald; died in Lexington, Ky., June 29, 1956; interment in Lexington Cemetery.

**UNDERWOOD, Warner Lewis** (brother of Joseph Rogers Underwood), a Representative from Kentucky; born in Goochland County, Va., on August 7, 1808; completed preparatory studies; moved to Kentucky in 1825; graduated from the University of Virginia at Charlottesville in 1829; studied law; admitted to the bar and commenced practice in Bowling Green; Ky., in 1830; moved to Texas in 1834; attorney general for the eastern district of Texas; returned to Bowling Green, Ky., in 1840; member of the Kentucky house of representatives in 1848; served in the Kentucky senate 1849-1853; elected as the candidate of the American Party to the Thirty-fourth and Thirty-fifth Congresses (March 4, 1855-March 3, 1859); was not a candidate for renomination; United States consul to Glasgow, Scotland, from July 17, 1862, until September 30, 1864; returned to the United States and practiced law in San Francisco, Calif.; returned to Kentucky in 1866 and resumed the practice of law; died near Bowling Green, Ky., March 12, 1872; interment in Fairview Cemetery, Bowling Green, Ky.

**UNSOELD, Jolene,** a Representative from Washington; born in Corvallis, Benton County, Oreg., December 3, 1931; graduated from Vancouver (Wash.) High School, 1949; student, Shanghai, China, 1938-1940; attended Oregon State University, 1949-1951; independent citizen lobbyist; director, English Language Institute, Kathmandu, Nepal, 1965-1967; member, Washington State house of representatives, 1984-1988; member, Democratic National Committee, 1980-1988; co-chair, Citizen's Toxic Cleanup Campaign (Initiative 97); elected as a Democrat to the One Hundred First and to the two succeeding Congresess (January 3, 1989-January 3, 1995); unsuccessful candidate for reelection in 1994 to the One Hundred Fourth Congress; is a resident of Olympia, Wash.

**UPDEGRAFF, Jonathan Taylor,** a Representative from Ohio; born near Mount Pleasant, Jefferson County, Ohio, May 13, 1822; attended private schools and Franklin College; studied medicine; was graduated from the University of Pennsylvania at Philadelphia in 1845 and later from medical schools in Edinburgh and Paris; practiced his profession, but devoted a large share of his time to agricultural pursuits; served as a surgeon in the Union Army during the Civil War; served in the State senate in 1872 and 1873; delegate to the Republican State convention in 1873 and to the Republican National Convention in 1876; elected as a Republican to the Forty-sixth and Forty-seventh Congresses and served from March 4, 1879, until his death in Mount Pleasant, Ohio, November 30, 1882; chairman, Committee on Education and Labor (Forty-seventh Congress); had been reelected to the Forty-eighth Congress; interment in Updegraff Cemetery, near Mount Pleasant, Ohio; reinterment in Short Creek Cemetery, west of Mount Pleasant, in 1926.

**UPDEGRAFF, Thomas,** a Representative from Iowa; born in Tioga County, Pa., April 3, 1834; attended private schools, the University of Notre Dame, South Bend, Ind., and an academy in Binghamton, N.Y.; clerk of the district court of Clayton County, Iowa, from 1856 until 1860; studied law; was admitted to the bar in 1860 and commenced practice in McGregor, Iowa; member of the Iowa State house of representatives in 1878; elected as a Republican to the Forty-sixth and Forty-seventh Congresses (March 4,

1879-March 3, 1883); unsuccessful candidate for reelection in 1882 to the Forty-eighth Congress; member of the board of education and city solicitor of McGregor, Iowa; delegate to the Republican National Convention of 1888; elected to the Fifty-third and to the two succeeding Congresses (March 4, 1893-March 3, 1899); unsuccessful candidate for renomination in 1898 to the Fifty-sixth Congress; engaged in the practice of his profession until his death in McGregor, Iowa, on October 4, 1910; interment in Pleasant Grove Cemetery.

**UPDIKE, Ralph Eugene,** a Representative from Indiana; born in Brookville, Franklin County, Ind., May 27, 1894; attended the public schools of Whitcomb and Brookville, Dodds Army and Navy Academy, Washington, D.C., Columbia University, New York City, and Purdue University, Lafayette, Ind.; during the First World War served overseas as a sergeant with the Seventy-fourth Company, Sixth Regiment, Second Division, United States Marines, 1916-1919; studied law; was admitted to the bar in 1920; was graduated from the law department of Indiana University in 1923 and commenced practice in Indianapolis, Ind.; member of the State house of representatives 1923-1925; special judge of the city of Indianapolis in 1923 and 1924; special judge of the superior court of Marion County in 1925 and 1926; elected as a Republican to the Sixty-ninth and Seventieth Congresses (March 4, 1925-March 3, 1929); unsuccessful candidate for reelection in 1928 to the Seventy-first Congress; special attorney in the Bureau of Internal Revenue 1929-1933; resumed the practice of law in Indianapolis, Ind., and Washington, D.C., until March 2, 1942, when he was commissioned a captain in the United States Marine Corps Reserve; served overseas in the South Pacific with the First Marine Division, Fleet Marine Force, and was inactivated June 15, 1945; resumed the practice of law in Indianapolis, Ind., and Washington, D.C., until his retirement; died in Arlington, Va., September 16, 1953; interment in Arlington National Cemetery.

**UPHAM, Charles Wentworth** (cousin of George Baxter Upham and Jabez Upham), a Representative from Massachusetts; born in St. John, New Brunswick, Canada, May 4, 1802; served as an apothecary's apprentice; worked on a farm in Nova Scotia, immigrated to the United States in 1816 and settled in Boston, Mass.; graduated from the theological department of Harvard University in 1821; ordained to the ministry and officiated in Salem, Mass., 1824-1844; member of the Massachusetts house of representatives 1840-1849; unsuccessful Whig candidate for election to the Thirty-second Congress; mayor of Salem, Mass., in 1852; delegate to the Massachusetts constitutional convention in 1853; elected as a Whig to the Thirty-third Congress (March 4, 1853-March 3, 1855); unsuccessful candidate for reelection in 1854 to the Thirty-fourth Congress; member of the Massachusetts senate in 1857 and 1858, serving as president; again a member of the Massachusetts house of representatives in 1859 and 1860; died in Salem, Mass., on June 15, 1875; interment in Harmony Grove Cemetery.

**Bibliography:** *DAB.*

**UPHAM, George Baxter** (brother of Jabez Upham and cousin of Charles Wentworth Upham), a Representative from New Hampshire; born in Brookfield, Mass., December 27, 1768; attended the common schools and Phillips Exeter Academy, Exeter, N.H.; was graduated from Harvard University in 1789; studied law; was admitted to the bar in 1792 and commenced practice in Claremont, N.H.; solicitor for Cheshire County from 1796 until 1804; elected as a Federalist to the Seventh Congress (March 4, 1801-March 3, 1803); declined to be a candidate for reelection in 1802 to the Eighth Congress; member of the New Hampshire State house of representatives, 1804-1813, and again in 1815, serving as speaker of the house in 1809 and 1815; served in the New Hampshire State senate in 1814; resumed the practice of law and was also interested in banking; died in Claremont, N.H., on February 10, 1848; interment in Pleasant Street Cemetery.

**UPHAM, Jabez** (brother of George Baxter Upham, and cousin of Charles Wentworth Upham), a Representative from Massachusetts; born in Brookfield, Mass., August 23, 1764; graduated from Harvard University in 1785; studied law; was admitted to the bar and commenced practice in Sturbridge, Mass.; moved to Claremont, N.H., and thence to Brookfield, Mass., where he continued the practice of law; member of the Massachusetts house of representatives 1804-1806 and in 1811; elected as a Federalist to the Tenth and Eleventh Congresses, and served from March 4, 1807, until his resignation in 1810; died in Brookfield, Mass., November 8, 1811; interment in New Cemetery, West Brookfield, Mass.

**UPHAM, Nathaniel,** a Representative from New Hampshire; born in Deerfield, N.H., June 9, 1774; pursued classical studies and attended the Phillips Exeter Academy, Exeter, N.H., in 1793; engaged in mercantile pursuits at Gilmanton in 1794, at Deerfield in 1796, at Portsmouth in 1801, and at Rochester in 1802 and afterward; member of the New Hampshire State house of representatives, 1807-1809; governor's counselor in 1811 and 1812; elected as a Republican to the Fifteenth Congress and reelected to the Sixteenth and Seventeenth Congresses (March 4, 1817-March 3, 1823); declined to be a candidate for renomination in 1822 to the Eighteenth Congress; returned to Rochester, N.H., and became interested in educational work; died in Rochester, N.H., July 10, 1829; interment in Old Rochester Cemetery.

**UPHAM, William,** a Senator from Vermont; born in Leicester, Mass., August 5, 1792; moved with his father to Montpelier, Vt., in 1802; attended the district schools, the Montpelier Academy, and was privately tutored; studied law; was admitted to the bar in 1811 and commenced practice in Montpelier, Vt., in 1812; member, State house of representatives 1827-1828; State's attorney for Washington County 1829; member, State house of representatives 1830; elected as a Whig to the United States Senate in 1843; reelected in 1849 and served from March 4, 1843, until his death in Washington, D.C., January 14, 1853; chairman, Committee on Agriculture (Twenty-eighth Congress), Committee on Pensions (Twenty-ninth Congress); interment in the Congressional Cemetery.

**UPSHAW, William David,** a Representative from Georgia; born near Newnan, Coweta County, Ga., October 15, 1866; attended the country schools, the public schools of Atlanta, Ga., and Mercer University, Macon, Ga.; engaged in agricultural and mercantile pursuits until physically incapacitated by an accident; founded The Golden Age magazine at Atlanta, Ga., February 22, 1906; elected as a Democrat to the Sixty-sixth and to the three succeeding Congresses (March 4, 1919-March 3, 1927); unsuccessful candidate for renomination in 1926; vice chairman of the Scandinavian Commercial Commission; nominated for President by the Prohibition Party in 1932; unsuccessful candidate for the Democratic nomination for United States Senator in 1942; resumed his former pursuits as a lecturer, evangelist, and writer; vice president of the Linda Vista Baptist Bible College and Seminary and member of the faculty, San Diego, Calif.; at the age of seventy-two was ordained a minister of the Baptist Church; died in Glendale, Calif., November 21, 1952; interment in Forest Lawn Cemetery.

Bibliography: *DAB.*

**UPSON, Charles,** a Representative from Michigan; born in Southington, Conn., March 19, 1821; attended the district and select schools of Southington; taught school in Farmington, Conn., from 1840 until 1842; studied law at the Yale Law School in 1844; removed to Constantine, St. Joseph County, Mich., in 1845; taught school in 1846 and 1847; deputy county clerk of St. Joseph County in 1847; admitted to the bar in 1847 and commenced practice in Kalamazoo, Mich.; county clerk in 1848 and 1849; prosecuting

attorney, 1852-1854; member of the Michigan State senate in 1855 and 1856; moved to Coldwater, Mich., in 1856 and continued the practice of law; member of the Michigan State board of railroad commissioners in 1857; attorney general of Michigan in 1861 and 1862; elected as a Republican to the Thirty-eighth and to the two succeeding Congresses (March 4, 1863-March 3, 1869); chairman, Committee on Expenditures in the Department of the Navy (Fortieth Congress); was not a candidate for renomination in 1868 to the Forty-first Congress; judge of the fifteenth circuit court from 1869 until his resignation on December 31, 1872; member of the commission to revise the State constitution in 1873; declined appointment as Commissioner of Indian Affairs in 1876; mayor of the city of Coldwater in 1877; again a member of the State senate in 1880; resumed the practice of his profession; died in Coldwater, Mich., September 5, 1885; interment in Oak Grove Cemetery.

**UPSON, Christopher Columbus,** a Representative from Texas; born near Syracuse, Onondaga County, N.Y., October 17, 1829; attended the common schools and Williams College, Williamstown, Mass.; studied law; was admitted to the bar in 1851 and commenced practice in Syracuse, N.Y., in 1851; moved to San Antonio, Tex., in 1854 and engaged in the practice of law; during the Civil War served in the Confederate Army as a volunteer aide, with the rank of colonel, on the staff of General William H.C. Whiting; appointed by the Confederacy as associate justice of Arizona in 1862; elected as a Democrat to the Forty-sixth Congress to fill the vacancy caused by the death of Gustave Schleicher; reelected to the Forty-seventh Congress and served from April 15, 1879, to March 3, 1883; unsuccessful candidate for renomination in 1882 to the Forty-eighth Congress; resumed the practice of law in San Antonio, Tex., and died there February 8, 1902; interment in Confederate Cemetery.

**UPSON, William Hanford,** a Representative from Ohio; born in Worthington, Franklin County, Ohio, on January 11, 1823; attended Tallmadge Academy, pursued classical studies, and was graduated from Western Reserve College, Hudson, Ohio, in 1842; studied law one year in the law department of Yale College and in Painesville, Ohio; was admitted to the bar in 1845 and commenced practice in Akron, Ohio, in 1846; prosecuting attorney of Summit County, 1848-1850; member of the Ohio State senate, 1853-1855; delegate to the Republican National Conventions of 1864 and 1876; elected as a Republican to the Forty-first and Forty-second Congresses (March 4, 1869-March 3, 1873); chairman, Committee on Private Land Claims (Forty-second Congress); was not a candidate for renomination in 1872 to the Forty-third Congress; appointed associate justice of the supreme court of Ohio in 1883; elected judge of the circuit court of Ohio in 1884 and served until 1894; resumed the practice of law; died in Akron, Ohio, April 13, 1910; interment in Glendale Cemetery.

**UPTON, Charles Horace,** a Representative from Virginia; born in Salem, Mass., August 23, 1812; attended the public schools; was graduated from Bowdoin College, Brunswick, Maine, in 1834; moved to Falls Church, Va., in 1836 and engaged in agricultural and literary pursuits; held several local offices; presented credentials as a Unionist Member-elect to the Thirty-seventh Congress under an election held on May 23, 1861, and served until February 27, 1862, when the House declared he was not entitled to the seat; appointed by President Abraham Lincoln in 1863 United States consul to Switzerland and served from July 9, 1863, until his death in Geneva, Switzerland, June 17, 1877; interment in the Congressional Cemetery, Washington, D.C.

**UPTON, Frederick Stephen,** a Representative from Michigan; born in St. Joseph, Mich., April 23, 1953; attended St. Joseph public schools and graduated from Shattuck School, Fairbault, Minn., in 1971; B.A., University of Michigan, Ann Arbor, 1975; aide to Representative David Stockman, 1976-1980; legislative assistant,

1981-1983, and director of legislative affairs, 1983-1985, Office of Management and Budget; elected as a Republican to the One Hundredth and to the four succeeding Congresses (January 3, 1987-January 3, 1997); is a resident of St. Joseph, Mich.

**UPTON, Robert William,** a Senator from New Hampshire; born in Boston, Mass., February 3, 1884; attended the public schools; graduated from Boston University Law School in 1907; admitted to the Massachusetts and New Hampshire bars in 1907 and commenced practice in Concord, N.H.; member of the New Hampshire State house of representatives in 1911; delegate to the New Hampshire State Constitutional Conventions in 1918, 1930, 1938, and 1948, serving as president in 1948; appointed as a Republican to the United States Senate to fill the vacancy caused by the death of Charles W. Tobey, and served from August 14, 1953 to November 7, 1954; unsuccessful candidate for nomination to fill the vacancy; resumed the practice of law; member, Mixed Board, Clemency and Parole, Bonn, Germany, 1956; special ambassador to Liberia in 1956; retired from his law practice in 1970; died in Concord, N.H., April 28, 1972; interment in Blossom Hill Cemetery.

**Bibliography:** Upton, William. "Robert W. Upton: A Recollection." *Historical New Hampshire* 27 (Summer 1972): 108-14.

**URNER, Milton George** (uncle of James Samuel Simmons), a Representative from Maryland; born in the Liberty district, Frederick County, Md., July 29, 1839; attended the common schools, Freeland Seminary, Montgomery County, Pa., and Dickinson Seminary, Williamsport, Pa.; engaged in teaching in his native county from 1859 until 1862; studied law; was admitted to the bar in 1863 and commenced practice in Frederick, Md.; State's attorney for Frederick County, 1871-1875; elected as a Republican to the Forty-sixth and Forty-seventh Congresses (March 4, 1879-March 3, 1883); chairman, Committee on Accounts (Forty-seventh Congress); was not a candidate for renomination in 1882 to the Forty-eighth Congress; resumed the practice of his profession in Frederick, Md.; became local attorney for the Pennsylvania Railroad Co. in 1887; member of the Maryland State senate, 1888-1890; appointed naval officer at the port of Baltimore by President Benjamin Harrison in 1890; engaged in banking and other business enterprises; trustee of several educational institutions; died in Frederick, Md., February 9, 1926; interment in Mount Olivet Cemetery.

**UTT, James Boyd,** a Representative from California; born in Tustin, Orange County, Calif., March 11, 1899; attended the public schools of Orange County, student at Santa Ana Junior College in 1942 and 1943; engaged in agricultural and citrus processing; member, California State assembly, 1932-1936; inheritance tax appraiser in the State controller's office from 1936 until 1952; graduated from the University of Southern California Law School in 1946; was admitted to the bar in 1947 and commenced the practice of law in Santa Ana, Calif.; elected as a Republican to the Eighty-third and to the eight succeeding Congresses, and served from January 3, 1953 until his death in Bethesda, Md., March 1, 1970; interment in Fairhaven Memorial Park, Santa Ana, Calif.

**UTTER, George Herbert,** a Representative from Rhode Island; born in Plainfield, Union County, N.J., July 24, 1854; moved with his parents to Westerly, R.I., in 1861; attended the public schools of Westerly and Alfred (N.Y.) Academy; was graduated from Amherst College, Massachusetts, in 1877; engaged as a printer and newspaper publisher in Westerly, R.I.; personal aide on the staff of Governor Augustus O. Bourn, 1883-1885; member of the Rhode Island house of representatives, 1885-1889, serving as speaker the last year; served in the Rhode Island senate, 1889-1891; secretary of state of Rhode Island 1891-1894; Lieutenant Governor in 1904; elected Governor of Rhode Island in 1904, reelected in 1905 and served from January 3, 1905 to January 1, 1907; unsuccessful candidate for reelection in 1906; elected as a Republican to the Sixty-second Congress and served from March 4, 1911, until his death in Westerly, R.I., November 3, 1912; interment in Riverbend Cemetery.

**UTTERBACK, Hubert** (cousin of John Gregg Utterback), a Representative from Iowa; born on a farm near Hayesville, Keokuk County, Iowa, June 28, 1880; attended the rural schools and Hedrick (Iowa) Normal and Commercial College; was graduated from Drake University, Des Moines, Iowa, in 1908; studied law; was admitted to the bar in 1906 and commenced practice in Des Moines, Iowa; instructor in the law department of Drake University 1908-1935; lecturer on law, Still College, Des Moines, Iowa, 1911-1933; judge of police court of Des Moines 1912-1914; judge of the ninth Iowa judicial district 1915-1927; member of the Iowa State Conference of Social Work and served as chairman of the legislative committee 1923-1925; served as an associate justice of the State supreme court from December 5, 1932, to April 16, 1933; elected as a Democrat to the Seventy-fourth Congress (January 3, 1935-January 3, 1937); was not a candidate for renomination but was an unsuccessful candidate for nomination as United States Senator in 1936; chairman of the State parole board 1937-1940; State Democratic National committeeman 1937-1940; died in Des Moines, Iowa, on May 12, 1942; interment in Glendale Cemetery.

**UTTERBACK, John Gregg** (cousin of Hubert Utterback), a Representative from Maine; born in Franklin, Johnson County, Ind., July 12, 1872; attended the public schools of his native city; employed in a carriage factory, 1889-1892; engaged as a traveling salesman from 1892 to 1905, during which time he resided in Jackson, Mich., Rochester, N.Y., and Winchester, Mass.; settled in Bangor, Maine, in 1905 and engaged in the retail sale of carriages and later in the retail sale of automobiles; served as councilman in 1912 and 1913, as alderman in 1913 and 1914, and as mayor of Bangor in 1914 and 1915; chairman of the Maine Motor Vehicle Conference Committee in 1930; delegate to the Democratic National Convention of 1932; elected as a Democrat to the Seventy-third Congress (March 4, 1933-January 3, 1935); unsuccessful candidate for reelection in 1934 to the Seventy-fourth Congress; appointed a United States marshal for the district of Maine in 1935 and served until his resignation in 1944; resumed the automobile business and was president of the Utterback Corp.; died in Bangor, Maine, July 11, 1955; interment in Mount Hope Cemetery.

# V

**VAIL, George,** a Representative from New Jersey; born in Morristown, Morris County, N.J., July 21, 1809; completed preparatory studies; attended Morris Academy at Morristown; engaged in the manufacture of telegraph instruments; member of the New Jersey State general assembly, 1843-1844; appointed by the Governor of New Jersey to represent the State at the World's Fair in London, England, in 1851; unsuccessful candidate for election in 1850 to the Thirty-second Congress; elected as a Democrat to the Thirty-third and Thirty-fourth Congresses (March 4, 1853-March 3, 1857); appointed by President James Buchanan as consul to Glasgow, Scotland, on February 3, 1858, and served until August 10, 1861; returned to the United States and settled in Morristown, N.J., where he engaged in literary pursuits; member of the court of pardons; judge of the New Jersey Court of Errors and Appeals, 1865-1871; died in Morristown, N.J., May 23, 1875; interment in First Presbyterian Church Cemetery.

**VAIL, Henry,** a Representative from New York; born near Milbrook, Dutchess County, N.Y., in 1782; received a limited schooling; engaged in the retail mercantile business 1806-1815 and in wholesale mercantile pursuits 1815-1832; elected as a Democrat to the Twenty-fifth Congress (March 4, 1837-March 3, 1839); unsuccessful candidate for reelection in 1838 to the Twenty-sixth Congress; resumed his former business pursuits in Troy, Rensselaer

County, N.Y., and died there June 25, 1853; interment in Oakwood Cemetery.

**VAIL, Richard Bernard,** a Representative from Illinois; born in Chicago, Cook County, Ill., August 31, 1895; attended the public schools, the School of Commerce, the Chicago Technical College, and the John Marshall Law School; during the First World War served in the United States Army as a lieutenant of Infantry; engaged in the manufacture of steel products; elected as a Republican to the Eightieth Congress (January 3, 1947-January 3, 1949); unsuccessful candidate for reelection in 1948 to the Eighty-first Congress; elected to the Eighty-second Congress (January 3, 1951-January 3, 1953); unsuccessful candidate for reelection in 1952 to the Eighty-third Congress and for election in 1954 to the Eighty-fourth Congress; chairman of the board of directors of the Vail Manufacturing Co., Chicago, Ill.; died in Chicago, Ill., July 29, 1955; interment in Holy Sepulchre Cemetery, Worth, Ill.

**VAILE, William Newell,** a Representative from Colorado; born in Kokomo, Howard County, Ind., June 22, 1876; moved with his parents to Denver, Colo., in 1881; attended the public schools and was graduated from Yale University in 1898; during the Spanish-American War served as a private in the First Regiment of the Connecticut Volunteer Field Artillery from May 19, 1898, to October 25, 1898; studied law at the University of Colorado and Harvard Law School; was admitted to the bar in 1901 and commenced the practice of law in Denver, Colo.; served on the Mexican border from June 28 to December 1, 1916, as a second lieutenant in the First Separate Battalion, National Guard of Colorado; elected as a Republican to the Sixty-sixth and to the four succeeding Congresses and served from March 4, 1919, until his death in Rocky Mountain National Park, Colo., on July 2, 1927; chairman, Committee on Expenditures in the Department of the Treasury (Sixty-eighth Congress); interment in Fairmount Cemetery, Denver, Colo.

**VALENTINE, Edward Kimble,** a Representative from Nebraska; born in Keosauqua, Van Buren County, Iowa, June 1, 1843; attended the common schools; learned the trade of a printer; during the Civil War enlisted in the Union Army and served in the Sixty-seventh Regiment, Illinois Volunteer Infantry; promoted to second lieutenant and honorably discharged; in the spring of 1863 reenlisted as a private in the Seventh Iowa Volunteer Cavalry; promoted to adjutant of the regiment and served until June 1866; settled in Omaha, Nebr., in 1866; appointed register of the United States land office at West Point, Nebr., and served from May 17, 1869, to September 30, 1871; studied law; was admitted to the bar in 1869 and commenced practice at West Point, Nebr.; elected judge of the sixth judicial district in 1875; elected as a Republican to the Forty-sixth and to the two succeeding Congresses (March 4, 1879-March 3, 1885); chairman, Committee on Agriculture (Forty-seventh Congress); declined to be a candidate for renomination in 1884 to the Forty-ninth Congress; Sergeant-at-Arms of the United States Senate from June 30, 1890, to August 6, 1893; resumed the practice of law in West Point, Nebr.; moved to Chicago, Ill., in 1908 and lived in retirement until his death on April 11, 1916; interment in Union Ridge Cemetery, Norwood Park, Ill.

**VALENTINE, Itimous Thaddeus, Jr. (Tim),** a Representative from North Carolina; born in Rocky Mount, Nash County, N.C., March 15, 1926; attended public schools in Nashville, N.C.; A.B., The Citadel, Charleston, S.C., 1948; LL.B., University of North Carolina, Chapel Hill, N.C., 1952; served in the United States Air Force, 1944-1946; admitted to the North Carolina bar, 1952 and commenced practice in Nashville; member of the North Carolina state house of representatives, 1955-1960; chairman, North Carolina Democratic executive committee, 1966-1968; delegate to the Democratic National Convention of 1968; elected as a Democrat to the Ninety-eighth and to the five succeeding Congresses (January 3,

1983-January 3, 1995); was not a candidate for reelection in 1994 to the One Hundred Fourth Congress; is a resident of Nashville, N.C.

**VALK, William Weightman,** a Representative from New York; born in Charleston, S.C., October 12, 1806; attended the local school and was graduated from the University of South Carolina at Columbia in 1830; studied medicine and commenced practice in Bridgeport, Conn.; served as assistant surgeon on the United States frigate *Constellation*; traveled to California about 1849 during the gold rush; finally settled in Flushing, Long Island, N.Y., and continued the practice of medicine until elected to Congress; elected as a candidate of the American Party to the Thirty-fourth Congress (March 4, 1855-March 3, 1857); unsuccessful candidate for reelection in 1856 to the Thirty-fifth Congress; during the Civil War was surgeon in the Second Regiment, Maryland Volunteer Infantry; appointed a clerk in the United States Pension Office at Washington, D.C., in 1867 and served until his death in that city on September 20, 1879; interment in Flushing Cemetery, Flushing, Queens County, N.Y.

**VALLANDIGHAM, Clement Laird** (uncle of John A. McMahon), a Representative from Ohio; born in New Lisbon, Columbiana County, Ohio, July 29, 1820; attended a classical school conducted by his father and Jefferson College, Canonsburg, Pa.; moved to Maryland and for two years was a preceptor in Union Academy at Snow Hill; moved to New Lisbon, Ohio, in 1840; studied law; was admitted to the bar in 1842 and commenced practice in Dayton, Ohio; member of the Ohio State house of representatives in 1845 and 1846; edited the Western Empire, 1847-1849; was an unsuccessful candidate for election in 1852 to the Thirty-third Congress and in 1854 to the Thirty-fourth Congress; delegate to the Democratic National Conventions of 1856, 1864, and 1868; successfully contested as a Democrat the election of Lewis D. Campbell to the Thirty-fifth Congress; reelected to the Thirty-sixth and Thirty-seventh Congresses and served from May 25, 1858, to March 3, 1863; unsuccessful candidate for reelection in 1862 to the Thirty-eighth Congress; arrested in Dayton by the Union military authorities on May 4, 1863 for treasonable utterance, and banished to the Confederate States; went from Wilmington, N.C., to Bermuda and thence to Canada, where he remained until June 1864; during his exile was an unsuccessful Democratic candidate for Governor of Ohio in 1863; unsuccessful candidate for election to the United States Senate in 1869; died in Lebanon, Ohio, June 17, 1871; interment in Woodland Cemetery, Dayton, Ohio.

**Bibliography:** *DAB*; Klement, Frank L. *The Limits of Dissent: Clement L. Vallandigham and the Civil War.* Lexington: University Press of Kentucky, 1970.

**VAN AERNAM, Henry,** a Representative from New York; born in Marcellus, Onondaga County, N.Y., March 11, 1819; pursued an academic course; studied medicine at the Geneva and Willoughby Medical Colleges and practiced his profession; member of the State assembly in 1858; served in the Union Army as a surgeon in the One Hundred and Fifty-fourth Regiment, New York Volunteer Infantry, from September 26, 1862, to November 5, 1864; elected as a Republican to the Thirty-ninth and Fortieth Congresses (March 4, 1865-March 3, 1869); appointed as Commissioner of Pensions May 1, 1869, and served until May 31, 1871, when he resigned; elected to the Forty-sixth and Forty-seventh Congresses (March 4, 1879-March 3, 1883); resumed the practice of medicine in Franklinville, Cattaraugus County, N.Y., and died there June 1, 1894; interment in Mount Prospect Cemetery.

**VAN ALEN, James Isaac** (half brother of Martin Van Buren), a Representative from New York; born in Kinderhook, Columbia County, N.Y., in 1776; attended the common schools; city clerk of Kinderhook 1797-1801; member of the State constitutional conventions in 1801 and 1803; justice of the peace 1801-1804; member of the State assembly in 1804; surrogate of Columbia County

1804-1808 and 1815-1822; elected as a Republican to the Tenth Congress (March 4, 1807-March 3, 1809); died in Newburgh, N.Y., on December 23, 1870; interment in Kinderhook Cemetery, Kinderhook, N.Y.

**VAN ALEN, John Evert,** a Representative from New York; born in Kinderhook, Columbia County, N.Y., in 1749; completed preparatory studies; moved to De Freestville in 1778 and engaged in extensive farming operations; surveyed the town of Greenbush in 1790 and conducted a general store there; engaged in civil engineering and surveying; assistant court justice in Rensselaer County in 1791; elected to the Third Congress and reelected as a Federalist to the Fourth and Fifth Congresses and served from March 4, 1793, to March 3, 1799; member of the State assembly in 1800 and 1801; died in March 1807.

**VAN ALSTYNE, Thomas Jefferson,** a Representative from New York; born in Richmondville, Schoharie County, N.Y., July 25, 1827; attended the common schools, Moravia (N.Y.) Academy, and Hartwick (N.Y.) Seminary, and was graduated from Hamilton College, Clinton, N.Y., in 1848; studied law in Albany, N.Y.; was admitted to the bar in 1849 and commenced practice in that city; served as judge advocate with the rank of major during the Civil War; judge of Albany County 1871-1882; elected as a Democrat to the Forty-eighth Congress (March 4, 1883-March 3, 1885); unsuccessful candidate for reelection in 1884 to the Forty-ninth Congress; resumed the practice of law; mayor of Albany, N.Y., 1898-1900; died in Albany, N.Y., October 26, 1903; interment in the Rural Cemetery.

**VAN AUKEN, Daniel Myers,** a Representative from Pennsylvania; born in Montague, Sussex County, N.J., January 15, 1826; attended the common schools and Deckertown Academy; was graduated from Union College, Schenectady, N.Y., in 1852; studied law; was admitted to the Pennsylvania bar in 1855 and commenced the practice of law in Milford, Pa.; served as prosecuting attorney of Pike County 1855-1859; elected as a Democrat to the Fortieth and Forty-first Congresses (March 4, 1867-March 3, 1871); was not a candidate for reelection in 1870 to the Forty-second Congress; resumed the practice of law in Milford, Pa.; served as district attorney of Pike County, Pa., 1893-1896 and 1899-1903; continued the practice of law until his death in Milford, Pa., on November 7, 1908; interment in Milford Cemetery.

**VAN BUREN, John,** a Representative from New York; born in Kingston, Ulster County, N.Y., May 13, 1799; was graduated from Union College, Schenectady, N.Y., in 1818; studied law; was admitted to the bar and commenced practice in Kingston, N.Y.; member of the State assembly in 1831; judge of Ulster County 1836-1841; elected as a Democrat to the Twenty-seventh Congress (March 4, 1841-March 3, 1843); chairman, Committee on Expenditures in the Department of State (Twenty-seventh Congress); resumed the practice of law; district attorney of Ulster County 1846-1850; died in Kingston, N.Y., January 16, 1855; interment in Old Houghtaling Cemetery.

**VAN BUREN, Martin** (half brother of James Isaac Van Alen), a Senator from New York and a Vice President and 8th President of the United States; born in Kinderhook, Columbia County, N.Y., December 5, 1782; attended the village schools; studied law; was admitted to the bar and commenced practice in Kinderhook, N.Y., in 1803; moved to Hudson, N.Y., in 1809; surrogate of Columbia County, 1808-1813; member, New York State senate 1813-1820; attorney general of New York, 1816-1819; delegate to the State constitutional convention in 1821; elected to the United States Senate; reelected in 1827, and served from March 4, 1821 until December 20, 1828, when he resigned, having been elected Governor; chairman, Committee on the Judiciary (Eighteenth through Twentieth Congresses); elected Governor of New York in 1828, and served from January 1 to March 12, 1829, when he

resigned to enter the Cabinet; appointed Secretary of State in the Cabinet of President Andrew Jackson on March 6, 1829, and served until his resignation in March 1831; appointed Minister to Great Britain on August 1, 1831; the Senate rejected his nomination in January 1832, and he returned to the United States; elected Vice President of the United States in 1832 on the Democratic ticket headed by Andrew Jackson, and served from March 4, 1833 to March 4, 1837; elected President of the United States in 1836, and served from March 4, 1837 to March 4, 1841; unsuccessful candidate for reelection as President on the Democratic ticket in 1840; unsuccessful candidate for election as President on the Free Soil ticket in 1848; withdrew from political life and retired to his country home, "Lindenwald," in Kinderhook, N.Y., where he died on July 24, 1862; interment in Kinderhook Cemetery.

**Bibliography:** *DAB*; Cole, Donald. *Martin Van Buren and the American Political System.* Princeton: Princeton University Press, 1984; Niven, John. *Martin Van Buren: The Romantic Age of American Politics.* New York: Oxford University Press, 1983; Wilson, Major L. *The Presidency of Martin Van Buren.* Lawrence: University Press of Kansas, 1984.

**VANCE, John Luther,** a Representative from Ohio; born in Gallipolis, Gallia County, Ohio, July 19, 1839; attended the public schools and Gallia Academy, Ohio; was graduated from the Cincinnati Law School in April 1861, and was admitted to the bar the same year; enlisted in April 1861 in the Union Army and served successively as captain, major, and lieutenant colonel in the Fourth Regiment, West Virginia Volunteer Infantry; mustered out in December 1864; established and published the Gallipolis Bulletin in 1867; commenced the practice of law in Gallipolis, Ohio, in 1870; delegate to the Democratic National Convention in 1872; elected as a Democrat to the Forty-fourth Congress (March 4, 1875-March 3, 1877); unsuccessful candidate for reelection in 1876 to the Forty-fifth Congress; resumed his former newspaper pursuits; president of the Ohio River Improvement Association from shortly after 1877 until his death; died in Gallipolis, Ohio, on June 10, 1921; interment in Pine Street Cemetery.

**VANCE, Joseph,** a Representative from Ohio; born in Catfish (now Washington), Washington County, Pa., March 21, 1786; moved with his father to Vanceburg, Ky., in 1788, and to Urbana, Ohio, in 1805; engaged in agricultural pursuits; captain of a rifle company in 1811 and 1812; during the War of 1812 served successively as major, colonel, brigadier general, and major general of the Ohio Militia; member of the Ohio State house of representatives, 1812-1813, 1815-1816, and 1818-1819; delegate to the State constitutional convention in 1820; engaged in mercantile pursuits at Urbana and Perrysburg, Ohio; laid out the city of Findlay in Hancock County; elected to the Seventeenth Congress; reelected to the Eighteenth through Twenty-second Congresses, and reelected as an Anti-Jacksonian to the Twenty-third Congress (March 4, 1821-March 3, 1835); chairman, Committee on Military Affairs (Nineteenth Congress); unsuccessful candidate for reelection in 1834 to the Twenty-fourth Congress; elected Governor of Ohio in 1836, and served from December 12, 1836 to December 13, 1838; unsuccessful candidate for reelection in 1838; member of the State senate, 1840-1841; elected as a Whig to the Twenty-eighth and Twenty-ninth Congresses (March 4, 1843-March 3, 1847); chairman, Committee on Claims (Twenty-eighth and Twenty-ninth Congresses), Committee on Manufactures (Twenty-ninth Congress); was not a candidate for renomination in 1846 to the Thirtieth Congress; delegate to the Whig National Convention in 1848; delegate to the State constitutional convention in 1851; died near Urbana, Champaign County, Ohio, August 24, 1852; interment in Oak Dale Cemetery.

**VANCE, Robert Brank** (uncle of Robert Brank Vance [1828-1899] and Zebulon Baird Vance), a Representative from North Carolina; born on Reems Creek, near Asheville, Buncombe County, N.C., in 1793; attended the common schools and Newton Academy, Asheville, N.C.; studied medicine at the medical school of Dr. Charles Harris in Cabarrus County, N.C.; commenced the practice of medicine in Asheville, N.C., in 1818; held several local offices; elected to the Eighteenth Congress (March 4, 1823-March 3, 1825); unsuccessful candidate for reelection in 1824 to the Nineteenth Congress and for election in 1826 to the Twentieth Congress; was mortally wounded by Samuel P. Carson, the successful candidate, who challenged him to a duel, fought at Saluda Gap, N.C., because of a derogatory remark made during the campaign of 1826, to the effect that the latter's father had turned Tory during the Revolutionary War; died the following day near Saluda Gap, N.C., 1827; interment in the family burial ground on Reems Creek, near Asheville, N.C.

**VANCE, Robert Brank** (nephew of Robert Brank Vance [1793-1827] and brother of Zebulon Baird Vance), a Representative from North Carolina; born on Reems Creek, near Asheville, Buncombe County, N.C., April 24, 1828; attended the common schools; engaged in mercantile and agricultural pursuits; clerk of the court of pleas and quarter sessions from 1848 until 1856; during the Civil War was elected captain of a company in the Confederate Army; twice elected colonel of the Twenty-ninth North Carolina Regiment; appointed brigadier general on April 23, 1863; taken prisoner on January 14, 1865 at Cosby Creek, Tenn., and paroled March 14, 1865; elected as a Democrat to the Forty-third and to the five succeeding Congresses (March 4, 1873-March 3, 1885); chairman, Committee on Patents (Forty-fourth through Forty-sixth and Forty-eighth Congresses); unsuccessful candidate for renomination in 1884 to the Forty-ninth Congress; United States Assistant Commissioner of Patents from April 11, 1885, to April 4, 1889, when he resigned; returned to North Carolina and settled in Alexander; member of the North Carolina State house of representatives, 1894-1896; died in Alexander, near Asheville, N.C., November 28, 1899; interment in Riverside Cemetery, Asheville, N.C.

**VANCE, Robert Johnstone,** a Representative from Connecticut; born in New York City, March 15, 1854; attended the common schools; moved to New Britain, Conn., in 1870; attended the high school; city clerk of New Britain from 1878 until his resignation in 1887, having been elected a Representative; became editor and publisher of the New Britain Herald in 1881; member of the State house of representatives in 1886; elected as a Democrat to the Fiftieth Congress (March 4, 1887-March 3, 1889); unsuccessful candidate for reelection in 1888 to the Fifty-first Congress; resumed his former business pursuits; labor commissioner of Connecticut 1893-1895; mayor of New Britain, Conn., in 1896 and 1897; delegate to the State constitutional convention in 1902; died in Montreat, N.C., June 15, 1902; interment in Fairview Cemetery, New Britain, Conn.

**VANCE, Zebulon Baird** (nephew of Robert Brank Vance [1793-1827] and brother of Robert Brank Vance [1828-1899]), a Representative and a Senator from North Carolina; born on Reems Creek, near Asheville, Buncombe County, N.C., May 13, 1830; attended the common schools of Buncombe County, and Washington (Tenn.) College; studied law at the University of North Carolina at Chapel Hill; was admitted to the bar in 1852 and commenced practice in Asheville, N.C.; elected prosecuting attorney of Buncombe County in 1852; member of the North Carolina State house of commons in 1854; elected as a Democrat to the Thirty-fifth Congress to fill the vacancy caused by the resignation of Thomas L. Clingman; reelected to the Thirty-sixth Congress, and served from December 7, 1858 to March 3, 1861; during the Civil War entered the Confederate Army as a captain, and was promoted to the rank of

colonel in August 1861; elected Governor of North Carolina in 1862, reelected in 1864, and served from September 8, 1862 until removed from office on May 29, 1865; arrested and imprisoned in Washington, D.C., in 1865 for Confederate activities; elected as a Democrat to the United States Senate in November 1870, but did not present his credentials; unsuccessful Democratic candidate for election to the United States Senate in 1872; elected Governor of North Carolina in 1876, and served from January 1, 1877 until his resignation on February 5, 1879; elected as a Democrat to the United States Senate in 1879; reelected in 1884 and 1890, and served from March 4, 1879 until his death in Washington, D.C., April 14, 1894; chairman, Committee on Enrolled Bills (Forty-sixth Congress), Committee on Privileges and Elections (Fifty-third Congress); funeral services were held in the Chamber of the United States Senate; interment in Riverside Cemetery, Asheville, N.C.

**Bibliography:** *DAB*; Shirley, Franklin. *Zebulon Vance, Tarheel Spokesman.* Charlotte, N.C.: McNally and Loftin, 1963; Tucker, Glenn. *Zeb Vance: Champion of Personal Freedom.* Indianapolis: Bobbs Merrill, 1966.

**VAN CORTLANDT, Philip** (brother of Pierre Van Cortlandt, Jr.), a Representative from New York; born in New York City, August 21, 1749; pursued classical studies; attended Coldenham Academy and was graduated from King's College (later Columbia University) in 1768; engaged as a civil engineer; member of the Provincial Congress in 1775; during the Revolutionary War served as lieutenant colonel and was mustered out of the service with the rank of brigadier general for gallant conduct at the siege of Yorktown, Va. under General Lafayette; delegate to the New York State ratification convention in 1788; served as supervisor of the town of Cortland, and as school commissioner and road master; member of the New York State assembly, 1788-1790; served in the New York State senate, 1791-1793; elected to the Third Congress and reelected as a Republican to the seven succeeding Congresses (March 4, 1793-March 3, 1809); engaged in agricultural pursuits; was a charter member of the Society of the Cincinnati; died at Van Cortlandt Manor, Croton-on-Hudson, Westchester County, N.Y., on November 21, 1831; interment in Hillside Cemetery, Peekskill, N.Y.

**VAN CORTLANDT, Pierre, Jr.** (brother of Philip Van Cortlandt), a Representative from New York; born at Van Cortlandt Manor, Croton, Westchester County, N.Y., August 29, 1762; pursued classical studies; was graduated from Queen's College (later Rutgers College), New Brunswick, N.J., in 1783; studied law in the office of Alexander Hamilton; was admitted to the bar and commenced practice; retired from his law practice and devoted his time managing his estate in Westchester County; member of the State assembly in 1811 and 1812; elected as a Republican to the Twelfth Congress (March 4, 1811-March 3, 1813); presidential elector on the Harrison ticket in 1840; founded and was president of the Westchester County Bank at Peekskill, N.Y., from 1833 until his death there July 13, 1848; interment in Hillside Cemetery.

**Bibliography:** *DAB.*

**VAN DEERLIN, Lionel,** a Representative from California; born in Los Angeles, Los Angeles County, Calif., July 25, 1914; attended the public schools of Oceanside, Calif.; B.A., University of Southern California, Los Angeles, 1937; studied journalism; served with the Field Artillery and Stars and Stripes newspaper, United States Army, as a staff sergeant from 1941 to 1945, with overseas service in the Mediterranean Theater; engaged in work as a newsman from 1937 until 1951; radio and television news editor and analyst, 1952-1961; delegate to the Democratic National Convention of 1964; elected as a Democrat to the Eighty-eighth and to the eight succeeding Congresses (January 3, 1963-January 3, 1981); unsuccessful candidate for reelection in 1980 to the Ninety-seventh Congress; professor emeritus, San Diego State University; columnist, San Diego Union-Tribune; is a resident of San Diego, Calif.

**VANDENBERG, Arthur Hendrick,** a Senator from Michigan; born in Grand Rapids, Mich., March 22, 1884; attended the public schools and studied law at the University of Michigan at Ann Arbor; editor and publisher of the Grand Rapids Herald from 1906 until 1928; author; appointed as a Republican to the United States Senate on March 31, 1928, to fill the vacancy caused by the death of Woodbridge N. Ferris, and on November 6, 1928 was elected to fill this vacancy, and also for the term ending January 3, 1935; reelected in 1934, 1940, and again in 1946, and served from March 31, 1928 until his death in Grand Rapids, Mich., April 18, 1951; unsuccessful candidate for the Republican presidential nomination in 1940; served as President pro tempore of the Senate during the Eightieth Congress; chairman, Committee on Enrolled Bills (Seventy-second Congress), Republican Conference (Seventy-ninth Congress), Committee on Foreign Relations (Eightieth Congress); delegate to the United Nations Conference at San Francisco in 1945; delegate to the United Nations General Assembly at London and New York in 1946; United States adviser to the Council of Foreign Ministers at London, Paris, and New York in 1946; delegate to Pan American Conference at Rio de Janeiro, Brazil, in 1947; interment in Oak Hill Cemetery, Grand Rapids, Mich.

**Bibliography:** *DAB*; Tompkins, C. David. *Senator Arthur H. Vandenberg: The Evolution of a Modern Republican, 1884-1945.* Lansing: Michigan State University Press, 1970; Vandenberg, Arthur H., Jr., and Morris, Joseph A., eds. *The Private Papers of Senator Vandenberg.* 1952. Reprint. Westport, Conn.: Greenwood Press, 1974.

**VANDERGRIFF, Tommy Joe (Tom),** a Representative from Texas; born in Carrollton, Dallas County, Tex., January 29, 1926; attended the public schools of Carrollton and Arlington, Tex., and graduated from Arlington High School in 1943; B.A., University of Southern California, Los Angeles, 1947; automobile dealer and owner-president of an insurance agency; mayor of Arlington, Tex., 1951-1977; member of the Presidential Commission on Urban Problems, 1967-1968; elected as a Democrat to the Ninety-eighth Congress (January 3, 1983-January 3, 1985); unsuccessful candidate for reelection in 1984 to the Ninety-ninth Congress; County Judge of Tarrant County, Tex., January 1, 1991 to present; is a resident of Arlington, Tex.

**VANDER JAGT, Guy Adrian,** a Representative from Michigan; born in Cadillac, Wexford County, Mich., August 26, 1931; attended Cadillac High School, 1945-1949; B.A., Hope College, Holland, Mich., 1953; B.D., Yale University, 1955; attended Bonn University on a Rotary Fellowship, 1956; LL.B., University of Michigan, 1960; practiced law in Grand Rapids, Mich., from 1960 until 1964; Michigan State senator, District 36, 1965-1966; elected as a Republican to the Eighty-ninth Congress, November 8, 1966, by special election to fill the vacancy caused by the resignation of Robert P. Griffin, and at the same time elected to the Ninetieth Congress; reelected to the twelve succeeding Congresses and served from November 8, 1966, to January 3, 1993; unsuccessful candidate for renomination in 1992 to the One Hundred Third Congress; is a resident of Luther, Mich.

**Bibliography:** Ried, Paul E. *The Orator: Guy Vander Jagt on the Hustings.* Ottawa, Ill.: Green Hill Publishers, 1984.

**VANDERPOEL, Aaron,** a Representative from New York; born in Kinderhook, Columbia County, N.Y., February 5, 1799; pursued classical studies; studied law; was admitted to the bar in 1820 and commenced practice in Kinderhook, N.Y.; member of the New York State assembly, 1826-1830; elected as a Jacksonian to the Twenty-third and Twenty-fourth Congresses (March 4, 1833-March 3, 1837); unsuccessful candidate for reelection in 1836 to the Twenty-fifth Congress; elected as a Democrat to the Twenty-sixth Congress (March 4, 1839-March 3, 1841); retired from Congress and settled in New York City; judge of the superior court from 1842 until

1850; died in New York City, July 18, 1870; interment in Woodlawn Cemetery.

**VANDER VEEN, Richard Franklin,** a Representative from Michigan; born in Grand Rapids, Kent County, Mich., November 26, 1922; attended the public schools and graduated from Muskegon (Mich.) High School in 1940; B.S., University of South Carolina, Columbia, 1946; LL.B., Harvard University Law School, 1949; enlisted in the United States Navy in January 1941 and served until 1946, with active duty in the South Pacific Theater; also served in the Korean Conflict, lieutenant (junior grade), 1950-1952; admitted to the Michigan bar in 1949 and commenced practice in Grand Rapids; chairman, Michigan Fifth District Democratic Party, 1959; delegate, Michigan State Democratic conventions, 1962, 1964; chairman, Michigan State Democratic convention, 1960; member of the East Grand Rapids Board of Education, 1969-1974; served on the Michigan State Mental Health Commission, 1958-1963, and the Michigan State Highway Commission, 1964-1969; elected as a Democrat to the Ninety-third Congress, February 18, 1974, by special election to fill the vacancy caused by the resignation of Gerald R. Ford; reelected to the Ninety-fourth Congress, and served from February 18, 1974 until January 3, 1977; unsuccessful candidate for reelection in 1976 to the Ninety-fifth Congress; unsuccessful candidate in 1978 for nomination to the United States Senate; member, Michigan State Waterways commission, 1984 to present; president, Resource Energy Company; is a resident of Grand Rapids, Mich.

**VANDERVEER, Abraham,** a Representative from New York; born in Kings County, N.Y., in 1781; attended the common schools; county clerk of Kings County, 1816-1821, and 1822-1837; upon its organization was elected treasurer of the Brooklyn Savings Bank; elected as a Democrat to the Twenty-fifth Congress (March 4, 1837-March 3, 1839); was not a candidate for renomination in 1838 to the Twenty-sixth Congress; died in Brooklyn, N.Y., July 21, 1839; interment in Reformed Dutch Cemetery.

**VANDEVER, William,** a Representative from Iowa and from California; born in Baltimore, Md., March 31, 1817; attended the common schools and pursued an academic course; moved to Illinois in 1839 and to Iowa in 1851; studied law; was admitted to the bar in 1852 and commenced practice in Dubuque, Iowa; elected as a Republican to the Thirty-sixth and Thirty-seventh Congresses, and served from March 4, 1859 until September 24, 1861, when he was mustered into the Union Army as colonel of the Ninth Regiment, Iowa Volunteer Infantry, never having resigned his seat in Congress; promoted to brigadier general of Volunteers in 1862 and brevetted a major general in 1865; member of the peace convention of 1861 held in Washington, D.C., in an effort to devise means to prevent the impending war; resumed the practice of law in Dubuque, Iowa; appointed United States Indian inspector by President Ulysses S. Grant in 1873, and served until 1877; moved to San Buenaventura, Calif., in 1884; elected as a Republican from California to the Fiftieth and Fifty-first Congresses (March 4, 1887-March 3, 1891); was not a candidate for renomination in 1890 to the Fifty-second Congress; died in Ventura, Calif., July 23, 1893; interment in Ventura Cemetery.

**VANDIVER, Willard Duncan,** a Representative from Missouri; born near Moorefield, Hardy County, Va. (now West Virginia), March 30, 1854; moved to Missouri with his parents, who settled on a farm in Boone County in 1857, and to Fayette in 1872; attended the common schools, and was graduated from Central College, Fayette, Mo., in 1877; studied law; professor of natural science in Bellevue Institute, Caledonia, Mo., 1877-1880, and served as its president 1880-1889; accepted the chair of science in the State normal school at Cape Girardeau, Mo., in 1889, and became its president in 1893 and served until 1897; delegate to the Democratic State conventions in 1896, 1898, 1918, and 1920 and served as chairman in 1918;

elected as a Democrat to the Fifty-fifth and to the three succeeding Congresses (March 4, 1897-March 3, 1905); was not a candidate for renomination in 1904; chairman of the State executive committee in 1904; State insurance commissioner of Missouri 1905-1909; vice president of the Central States Life Insurance Co. 1910-1912; Assistant Treasurer of the United States 1913-1921; settled on a farm near Columbia, Mo., and engaged in agricultural pursuits and lecturing; is credited with the authorship of the famous expression "I'm from Missouri, you've got to show me"; died in Columbia, Mo., May 30, 1932; interment in the Columbia Cemetery.

**VAN DUZER, Clarence Dunn,** a Representative from Nevada; born near Mountain City, Nev., May 4, 1866; attended public and private schools in Nevada and California, and the University of California at Berkeley; was graduated from the State University of Nevada at Reno in 1889, and from the law department of Georgetown University, Washington, D.C., in 1893; was admitted to practice before the supreme court of the District of Columbia in 1893; appointed by Governor R.K. Colcord of Nevada in 1892 as State land agent, with residence in Washington, D.C., and served until 1897; served as private secretary to Senator Francis G. Newlands of Nevada for five years; returned to Nevada and became interested in mining; elected district attorney of Humboldt County in 1898; member of the Nevada State house of representatives, 1900-1902, and served as speaker; elected as a Democrat to the Fifty-eighth and Fifty-ninth Congresses (March 4, 1903-March 3, 1907); was not a candidate for renomination in 1906 to the Sixtieth Congress; resumed his mining interests until 1922 when he moved to Passaic, N.J., and engaged in newspaper work; died in Passaic, N.J., September 28, 1947; remains were cremated and the ashes scattered on the Humboldt River near Winnemucca, Nev.

**VAN DYKE, Carl Chester,** a Representative from Minnesota; born in Alexandria, Douglas County, Minn., February 18, 1881; attended the common and high schools of Alexandria; taught school in Douglas County 1899-1901; during the Spanish-American War served as a private in Company B, Fifteenth Regiment, Minnesota Volunteer Infantry; was graduated from the St. Paul Law School; was admitted to the bar at St. Paul in 1916, but did not engage in extensive practice; elected commander in chief of the United Spanish War Veterans September 6, 1918; elected as a Democrat to the Sixty-fourth, Sixty-fifth, and Sixty-sixth Congresses and served from March 4, 1915, until his death in Washington, D.C., May 20, 1919; interment in a mausoleum in Forest Cemetery, St. Paul, Minn.

**VAN DYKE, John,** a Representative from New Jersey; born in Lamington, Somerset County, N.J., April 3, 1807; completed preparatory studies; studied law; was admitted to the bar in 1836 and commenced practice in New Brunswick, N.J.; prosecuting attorney of Middlesex County in 1841; mayor of New Brunswick in 1846 and 1847; president of the Bank of New Jersey at New Brunswick; elected as a Whig to the Thirtieth and Thirty-first Congresses (March 4, 1847-March 3, 1851); declined to be a candidate for renomination in 1850; resumed the practice of law; delegate to the Republican National Convention in 1856; judge of the New Jersey Supreme Court 1859-1866; moved to Minnesota in 1868 and settled in Wabasha, Wabasha County; member of the State senate in 1872 and 1873; judge of the third judicial district of Minnesota 1873-1878; died in Wabasha, Minn., December 24, 1878; interment in Riverview Cemetery.

**Bibliography:** *DAB.*

**VAN DYKE, Nicholas** (father of Nicholas Van Dyke), a Delegate from Delaware; born in New Castle County, Del., September 25, 1738; studied law in Philadelphia, Pa.; was admitted to the bar in 1765 and commenced practice in New Castle County; delegate to the State constitutional convention in July 1776; elected a member of the Council of Delaware in 1777, serving as speaker in 1779; appointed judge of admiralty February 21, 1777; Member of the Continental Congress 1777-1781; a signer of the Articles of Confederation; served as President of Delaware from February 1, 1783, to October 27, 1786; died in New Castle County, Del., February 19, 1789; interment in Immanuel Churchyard, New Castle, Del.

**Bibliography:** *DAB.*

**VAN DYKE, Nicholas** (son of Nicholas Van Dyke), a Representative and a Senator from Delaware; born in New Castle, Del., December 20, 1770; graduated from the College of New Jersey (now Princeton University) in 1788; studied law; was admitted to the bar in New Castle, Del., in 1792 and commenced the practice of law; member, State house of representatives 1799; elected as a Federalist to the Tenth Congress to fill the vacancy caused by the resignation of James M. Broom; reelected to the Eleventh Congress, and served from October 6, 1807, to March 3, 1811; member, State senate 1815-1816; elected as a Federalist to the United States Senate in 1817; reelected in 1823, and served from March 4, 1817, until his death in New Castle, Del., on May 21, 1826; chairman, Committee on Pensions (Sixteenth Congress); interment in Immanuel Churchyard.

**VAN EATON, Henry Smith,** a Representative from Mississippi; born in Anderson Township, Hamilton County, Ohio, September 14, 1826; was graduated from Illinois College, Jacksonville, Ill., in 1848; moved to Woodville, Miss., in 1848; taught school; studied law; was admitted to the bar in 1855 and commenced practice in Woodville, Wilkinson County; elected district attorney in 1857; member of the Mississippi State house of representatives in 1859; enlisted in the Confederate Army and served throughout the Civil War; resumed the practice of law in Woodville, Miss., in 1865; appointed chancellor of the tenth Mississippi district in 1880; elected as a Democrat to the Forty-eighth and Forty-ninth Congresses (March 4, 1883-March 3, 1887); appointed by President Grover Cleveland a member of the Board of Visitors to the United States Naval Academy at Annapolis in 1887; member of a commission to examine and report upon the last completed portion of the Northern Pacific Railroad in 1888; died in Woodville, Miss., May 30, 1898; interment in Evergreen Cemetery.

**VAN GAASBECK, Peter,** a Representative from New York; born in Ulster County, N.Y., September 27, 1754; attended the grammar schools and became a man of prominence in the county and State; engaged in mercantile pursuits in Kingston, N.Y.; was a captain and major in the Ulster County Militia during the Revolutionary War; elected to the Third Congress (March 4, 1793-March 3, 1795); died in Kingston, N.Y., in 1797; interment in First Reformed Dutch Churchyard.

**VAN HORN, Burt,** a Representative from New York; born in Newfane, Niagara County, N.Y., October 28, 1823; was raised on a farm; attended the common schools, Yates Academy in Orleans County, Hamilton College (now Colgate University), Hamilton, N.Y.; engaged in agricultural pursuits in Niagara County, and later in the manufacture of cloth; member of the State assembly 1858-1860; elected as a Republican to the Thirty-seventh Congress (March 4, 1861-March 3, 1863); elected to the Thirty-ninth and Fortieth Congresses (March 4, 1865-March 3, 1869); was not a candidate for renomination in 1868; moved to Lockport, N.Y., in 1867; resumed farming and also engaged in the loaning of money; collector of internal revenue at Rochester, N.Y., 1877-1882; died in Lockport, N.Y., April 1, 1896; interment in Glenwood Cemetery.

**VAN HORN, George,** a Representative from New York; born in Otsego, Otsego County, N.Y., February 5, 1850; attended the common schools, the Cooperstown Seminary, and the New Berlin Academy; studied law; was admitted to the bar in February 1871 and practiced in Cooperstown, N.Y.; elected clerk of Otsego County in 1881 and reelected in 1884; elected supervisor of Otsego, and twice reelected; member of the Democratic county committee; elected as a Democrat to the Fifty-second Congress (March 4, 1891-March 3, 1893); unsuccessful candidate for reelection in 1892 to the Fifty-third Congress; engaged in banking, and was vice president of the Second National Bank of Cooperstown, N.Y., until his death there on May 3, 1904; interment in Lakewood Cemetery.

**VAN HORN, Robert Thompson,** a Representative from Missouri; born in East Mahoning, Indiana County, Pa., May 19, 1824; attended the common schools; apprenticed to a printer; moved to Ohio in 1844 and settled in Pomeroy; studied law; was admitted to the bar about 1850 and commenced practice in Pomeroy, Ohio; moved to Kansas City, Mo., in 1855; member of the board of aldermen in 1857; postmaster of Kansas City 1857-1861; established and edited the Kansas City Journal; elected mayor of Kansas City in 1861 and again in 1864; enlisted in the Union Army during the Civil War and served as lieutenant colonel of the Twenty-fifth Regiment, Missouri Volunteer Infantry; member of the State senate 1862-1864; elected as a Republican to the Thirty-ninth, Fortieth, and Forty-first Congresses (March 4, 1865-March 3, 1871); was not a candidate for renomination in 1870; chairman of the Republican State central committee 1874-1876; collector of internal revenue for the sixth district of Missouri 1875-1881; delegate to the Republican National Conventions in 1864, 1868, 1872, 1876, 1880, and 1884; member of the Republican National Committee in 1872 and 1884; elected as a Republican to the Forty-seventh Congress (March 4, 1881-March 3, 1883); successfully contested the election of John C. Tarsney to the Fifty-fourth Congress and served from February 27, 1896, to March 3, 1897; unsuccessful candidate for renomination in 1896; retired from editorship of the Kansas City Journal in 1897; died on his estate, "Honeywood," at Evanston Station, near Kansas City, Mo., January 3, 1916; interment in Mount Washington Cemetery, Kansas City, Mo.

Bibliography: *DAB.*

**VAN HORNE, Archibald,** a Representative from Maryland; appointed adjutant of the Fourteenth Regiment of the Maryland Militia, April 18, 1798; commissioned captain May 26, 1802; member of the State house of delegates 1801-1803 and 1805, and served as speaker in the latter year; resigned November 11, 1805; elected as a Republican to the Tenth and Eleventh Congresses (March 4, 1807-March 3, 1811); chairman, Committee on District of Columbia (Eleventh Congress); again a member of the State house of delegates 1814-1816; elected to the State senate in 1816 and served until his death in Prince Georges County, Md., in 1817.

**VAN HORNE, Espy,** a Representative from Pennsylvania; born in Lycoming County, Pa., in 1795; elected to the Nineteenth and Twentieth Congresses (March 4, 1825-March 3, 1829); died in Williamsport, Pa., August 25, 1829.

**VAN HORNE, Isaac,** a Representative from Pennsylvania; born in Tollbury Township, Bucks County, Pa., January 13, 1754; apprenticed as a carpenter and cabinetmaker; elected ensign of a company of militia in 1775; appointed ensign in the Continental Army by the committee of safety and in January 1776 was assigned to Captain John Beatty's Company in Colonel Samuel McGaw's Regiment; held as a prisoner of war from November 1776 to May 1778 when he was exchanged; served as first lieutenant, captain lieutenant, and captain until the close of the Revolutionary War; justice of the peace for Tollbury Township for several years; coroner of Bucks County four years; member of the Pennsylvania house of representatives in 1796 and 1797; declined to be a candidate for reelection; elected as a Republican to the Seventh and Eighth Congresses (March 4, 1801-March 3, 1805); moved to Zanesville, Muskingum County, Ohio, in 1805; receiver of the land office at Zanesville from 1805 until December 1826, when he resigned; died in Zanesville, Ohio, February 2, 1834; interment in Woodlawn Cemetery.

**VAN HOUTEN, Isaac B.,** a Representative from New York; born in Clarkstown (now New City), Rockland County, N.Y., June 4, 1776; attended the common schools; engaged in milling and agricultural pursuits; member of the State assembly 1833-1835; elected as a Jacksonian to the Twenty-third Congress (March 4, 1833-March 3, 1835); resumed his former business pursuits; died in Clarkstown (now New City), N.Y., August 16, 1850; interment in the family burying ground on his estate near Clarkstown.

**VANIK, Charles Albert,** a Representative from Ohio; born in Cleveland, Cuyahoga County, Ohio, April 7, 1913; attended the public schools; A.B., Adelbert College of Western Reserve University, Cleveland, Ohio, 1933; LL.B., Western Reserve University Law School, 1936; was admitted to the bar in 1936 and commenced the practice of law in Cleveland, Ohio; member of Cleveland City Council in 1938 and 1939; served in the Ohio State senate, 1940-1941; member of the Cleveland Board of Education in 1941 and 1942; enlisted in the United States Naval Reserve as an ensign in 1942 and served with amphibious forces of the Atlantic and Pacific Fleets; released from active duty as a lieutenant in December 1945; appointed a member of the Cleveland Library Board in January 1946; elected judge of the Cleveland Municipal Court in 1947 and reelected in 1949 for a six-year term, but resigned in March 1954 to campaign for Congress; served as referee with the Ohio Industrial Commission; legal adviser to the Ohio highway director; elected as a Democrat to the Eighty-fourth and to the twelve succeeding Congresses (January 3, 1955-January 3, 1981); was not a candidate for reelection in 1980 to the Ninety-seventh Congress; resumed the practice of law in Washington, D.C.; is a resident of Arlington, Va.

**VANMETER, John Inskeep,** a Representative from Ohio; born near Moorefield, Hardy County, Va. (now West Virginia), in February 1798; attended the College of William and Mary, Williamsburg, Va., and was graduated from Princeton College in 1821; studied law at the school of Judge Gould in Litchfield, Conn.; was admitted to the bar of Virginia in 1822 and commenced practice in Moorefield, Va.; member of the Virginia house of delegates in 1824; retired from practice; moved to Pike County, Ohio, in 1826 and engaged in agricultural pursuits; member of the State house of representatives in 1836; served in the State senate in 1838; elected as a Whig to the Twenty-eighth Congress (March 4, 1843-March 3, 1845); unsuccessful candidate for reelection in 1844 to the Twenty-ninth Congress; affiliated with the Democratic Party in 1856; moved to Chillicothe, Ross County, Ohio, in 1855, where he resided until his death August 3, 1875; interment in Grandview Cemetery.

**VAN NESS, John Peter,** a Representative from New York; born in Ghent (formerly Claverly), Columbia County, N.Y., in 1770; completed preparatory studies and attended Columbia College in New York City; studied law and was admitted to the bar, but never practiced; elected as a Republican to the Seventh Congress to fill the vacancy caused by the resignation of John Bird and served from October 6, 1801, to January 17, 1803, when his seat was declared forfeited, as he had accepted and exercised the office of major of militia in the District of Columbia bestowed on him by President Thomas Jefferson; he then made Washington his home; president of the second council in 1803; promoted to the rank of lieutenant colonel commandant of the first legion of militia in 1805, brigadier general in 1811, and major general in 1813; alderman of the city of Washington in 1829; mayor 1830-1834; second vice president of the Washington National Monument Society in 1833; president of the commissioners of the Washington Canal in 1834; president of the branch bank of the United States at Washington, D.C.; first president of the National Metropolitan Bank from 1814 until his death in Washington, D.C., March 7, 1846; interment in a mausoleum at Oak Hill Cemetery.

**VAN NUYS, Frederick,** a Senator from Indiana; born in Falmouth, Rush County, Ind., April 16, 1874; attended the public schools; graduated from Earlham College, Richmond, Ind., in 1898 and from the Indiana Law School at Indianapolis, Ind., in 1900; was admitted to the bar in 1900 and commenced practice in Shelbyville, Ind., moving shortly afterward to Anderson, Ind.; prosecuting attorney of Madison County, Ind., 1906-1910; member, State senate 1913-1916, serving as president pro tempore in 1915; moved to Indianapolis, Ind., in 1916 and continued the practice of law; United States attorney, district of Indiana 1920-1922; elected as a Democrat to the United States Senate in 1932; reelected in 1938, and served from March 4, 1933, until his death on a farm near Vienna, Fairfax County, Va., on January 25, 1944; chairman, Committee on Expenditures in Executive Departments (Seventy-sixth Congress), Committee on the Judiciary (Seventy-seventh and Seventy-eighth Congresses); interment in East Maplewood Cemetery, Anderson, Ind.

**VAN PELT, William Kaiser,** a Representative from Wisconsin; born in Glenbeulah, Sheboygan County, Wis., March 10, 1905; moved with his parents to Fond du Lac, Wis., and attended the public schools, graduating from high school in 1924; owner and operator of City Fuel Co., Fond du Lac, Wis., from 1939 until 1952; chairman of the Fond du Lac County Republican Committee, 1944-1950; delegate to the Republican National Covention of 1944; elected as a Republican to the Eighty-second and to the six succeeding Congresses (January 3, 1951-January 3, 1965); was an unsuccessful candidate for reelection in 1964 to the Eighty-ninth Congress; is a resident of Fond du Lac, Wis.

**VAN RENSSELAER, Henry Bell** (son of Stephen Van Rensselaer), a Representative from New York; born at the Manor House in Albany, N.Y., May 14, 1810; was graduated from the United States Military Academy at West Point in 1831; commissioned brevet second lieutenant of the Fifth Regiment, United States Infantry, July 1, 1831, and resigned January 27, 1832; engaged in agricultural pursuits near Ogdensburg, N.Y.; elected as a Whig to the Twenty-seventh Congress (March 4, 1841-March 3, 1843); was associated with mining enterprises; upon the outbreak of the Civil War reentered the military service with the rank of brigadier general in the Union Army and was appointed chief of staff under General Winfield Scott; served as inspector general with the rank of colonel from 1862 until his death; died in Cincinnati, Ohio, March 23, 1864; interment in Grace Episcopal Churchyard, Jamaica, Long Island, N.Y.

**VAN RENSSELAER, Jeremiah** (father of Solomon Van Vechten Van Rensselaer and cousin of Killian Killian Van Rensselaer), a Representative from New York; born in that State August 27, 1738; completed preparatory studies at the manor house, "Rensselaerswyck," and in private schools in Albany; was graduated from Princeton College in 1758; took an active interest in the Revolutionary War and was a member of the Albany Committee of Safety; elected to the First Congress (March 4, 1789-March 3, 1791); unsuccessful candidate for reelection in 1790 to the Second Congress; member of the New York State assembly in 1789; member of the first board of directors of the Bank of Albany in 1792, and president of that bank, 1798-1806; Lieutenant Governor of New York, 1801-1804; curator of the Evangelical Lutheran Seminary at Albany in 1804; died in Albany, N.Y., February 19, 1810; interment in the Dutch Reformed Cemetery.

**VAN RENSSELAER, Killian Killian** (cousin of Jeremiah Van Rensselaer and uncle of Solomon Van Vechten Van Rensselaer), a Representative from New York; born in Greenbush, Rensselaer County, N.Y., June 9, 1763; completed preparatory studies and attended Yale College; studied law; was admitted to the bar in 1784 and commenced practice in Claverack, N.Y.; private secretary to General Philip Schuyler; elected as a Federalist to the Seventh and

to the four succeeding Congresses (March 4, 1801-March 3, 1811); resumed the practice of law; died in Albany, N.Y., on June 18, 1845; interment in a private cemetery at Greenbush, N.Y.

**VAN RENSSELAER, Solomon Van Vechten** (son of Jeremiah Van Rensselaer and nephew of Killian Killian Van Rensselaer), a Representative from New York; born in Greenbush, Rensselaer County, N.Y., August 6, 1774; completed preparatory studies; entered the United States Army; was promoted to captain of a volunteer company, and later, on January 8, 1799, to major; was mustered out in June 1800; adjutant general of State militia in 1801, 1810, and 1813; served in the War of 1812 as lieutenant colonel of New York Volunteers; elected as a Federalist to the Sixteenth and Seventeenth Congresses, and served from March 4, 1819 to January 14, 1822, when he resigned; postmaster of Albany, N.Y., 1822-1839 and 1841-1843; delegate from New York at the opening of the Erie Canal on November 4, 1825; died near Albany, N.Y., April 23, 1852; interment in North Dutch Church Cemetery, Albany, N.Y.; reinterment in Albany Rural Cemetery.

**Bibliography:** *DAB.*

**VAN RENSSELAER, Stephen** (father of Henry Bell Van Rensselaer), a Representative from New York; born in New York City November 1, 1764; completed preparatory studies and attended Princeton College; was graduated from Harvard University in 1782; major of militia in 1786, colonel in 1788, and major general in 1801; member of the State assembly 1789-1791, 1798, and 1818; served in the State senate 1791-1796; elected Lieutenant Governor of New York in 1795; served as major general of Volunteers in the War of 1812; member of the canal commission 1816-1839, and served fourteen years as its president; member of the State constitutional convention in 1821; founded the Rensselaer Polytechnic Institute at Troy in 1824; was a supporter of John Quincy Adams and was elected to the Seventeenth Congress to fill the vacancy caused by the resignation of Solomon Van Vechten Van Rensselaer; reelected to the Eighteenth, Nineteenth, and Twentieth Congresses and served from February 27, 1822, to March 3, 1829; chairman, Committee on Agriculture (Eighteenth through Twentieth Congresses); was not a candidate for reelection; devoted his time to landed interests and to educational and public welfare matters; regent of the University of New York 1819-1839; died in Albany, N.Y., January 26, 1839; interment in the family burying ground; reinterment in Albany Rural Cemetery.

**VAN SANT, Joshua,** a Representative from Maryland; born in Millington, Kent County, Md., December 31, 1803; moved with his parents to Wilmington, Del., in 1807 and to Philadelphia, Pa., in 1812; attended the common schools; moved to Baltimore, Md.; engaged in hat making in 1817, became journeyman, and continued at that trade until 1835; unsuccessful candidate as a Jackson Democrat to the State house of delegates in 1833 and 1834; delegate to the State constitutional convention in 1836; postmaster of Baltimore 1839-1841; member of the State house of delegates in 1845; commissioner of Baltimore finances March 1, 1846, to March 1, 1855; trustee of the city and county almshouse 1847-1853 and in 1861; commissioner of public schools 1852-1854, and served as president in 1854; elected as a Democrat to the Thirty-third Congress (March 4, 1853-March 3, 1855); unsuccessful candidate for reelection to the Thirty-fourth Congress in 1854; presidential elector on the Democratic ticket of Breckinridge and Lane in 1860; delegate to the State constitutional convention in 1867; director of the Maryland State Penitentiary 1867-1869, serving two years as president; member of the board of trustees of the McDonough Educational Fund and Institute 1867-1871, serving as president in 1871; member and president of the board for Bay View Asylum 1868-1870; mayor of Baltimore 1871-1875; declined to be a candidate for renomination; appointed city comptroller of Baltimore in July 1876 and served until January 1881; was afterward elected to that office and served until his death in Baltimore, Md., April 8, 1884; interment in Greenmount Cemetery.

**VAN SCHAICK, Isaac Whitbeck** (uncle of Aaron Van Schaick Cochrane), a Representative from Wisconsin; born in Coxsackie, Greene County, N.Y., December 7, 1817; attended the common schools; engaged extensively in the manufacture of glue; moved to Chicago in 1857, and to Wisconsin in 1861 and engaged in the flour-milling business in Milwaukee; elected to the Milwaukee Common Council in 1871; member of the State assembly 1873-1875; served in the State senate 1877-1882; elected as a Republican to the Forty-ninth Congress (March 4, 1885-March 3, 1887); declined to be a candidate for renomination in 1886; elected to the Fifty-first Congress (March 4, 1889-March 3, 1891); was not a candidate for renomination in 1890; unsuccessful candidate for State senator in 1890; moved to Catonsville, Baltimore County, Md., in 1894, where he lived in retirement until his death there August 22, 1901; interment in Athens Cemetery, Athens, N.Y.

**VAN SWEARINGEN, Thomas,** a Representative from Virginia; born near Shepherdstown, Jefferson County, Va. (now West Virginia), May 5, 1784; attended the common schools; member of the Virginia house of delegates 1814-1816; elected to the Sixteenth and Seventeenth Congresses and served from March 4, 1819, until his death in Shepherdstown, Va., August 19, 1822; interment in Elmwood Cemetery.

**VAN TRUMP, Philadelph,** a Representative from Ohio; born in Lancaster, Fairfield County, Ohio, November 15, 1810; attended the public schools; learned the art of printing and subsequently became editor of the Gazette and Enquirer at Lancaster; studied law; was admitted to the bar and commenced practice in Lancaster on May 14, 1838; delegate to the Whig National Convention in 1852; unsuccessful candidate of the American Party for Governor in 1856; delegate to the Bell and Everett State convention in 1860 and served as president; judge of the court of common pleas 1862-1867; unsuccessful candidate for supreme judge of Ohio in 1863, 1864, and 1865; elected as a Democrat to the Fortieth, Forty-first, and Forty-second Congresses (March 4, 1867-March 3, 1873); was not a candidate for renomination in 1872; served as president of the Democratic State convention in 1869; resumed the practice of law in Lancaster, Ohio, and died there on July 31, 1874; interment in Elmwood Cemetery.

**VAN VALKENBURGH, Robert Bruce,** a Representative from New York; born in Prattsburg, Steuben County, N.Y., September 4, 1821; attended Franklin Academy, Prattsburg, N.Y.; studied law; was admitted to the bar and commenced practice in Bath, N.Y.; member of the New York State assembly in 1852, and again in 1857 and 1858; was in command of the recruiting depot in Elmira, N.Y., and organized seventeen regiments for the Civil War; elected as a Republican to the Thirty-seventh and Thirty-eighth Congresses (March 4, 1861-March 3, 1865); chairman, Committee on Militia (Thirty-seventh and Thirty-eighth Congresses); served as colonel of the One Hundred and Seventh Regiment, New York Volunteer Infantry, and was its commander at the Battle of Antietam, Md., September 17, 1862; Acting Commissioner of Indian Affairs in 1865; appointed Minister Resident to Japan on January 18, 1866, and served until November 1869; settled in Florida; appointed associate justice of the Florida State supreme court on May 20, 1874, and served until his death in Suwanee Springs, near Live Oak, Suwanee County, Fla., August 1, 1888; interment in Old St. Nicholas Cemetery, on the south side of the St. Johns River, south of Jacksonville, Fla.

**VAN VOORHIS, Henry Clay,** a Representative from Ohio; born in Nashport, Muskingum County, Ohio, May 11, 1852; attended the public schools and Denison University, Granville, Ohio; studied law and was admitted to the bar in 1874; was graduated from the Cincinnati Law School in 1875 and commenced practice in Zanesville, Ohio, the same year; delegate to the Republican National Conventions in 1884 and 1916; president of the Citizens' National Bank of Zanesville 1885-1893; elected as a Republican to the Fifty-third and to the five succeeding Congresses (March 4, 1893-March 3, 1905); declined to be a candidate for renomination in 1904; again became president of the Citizens' National Bank of Zanesville, Ohio, in 1905; member of the board of trustees of Marietta (Ohio) College; died in Zanesville, Ohio, December 12, 1927; interment in Greenwood Cemetery.

**VAN VOORHIS, John,** a Representative from New York; born in Decatur, Otsego County, N.Y., on October 22, 1826; pursued an academic course; studied law; was admitted to the bar in 1851 and commenced practice in Elmira, Chemung County, N.Y.; member of the board of education in 1857; city attorney in 1859; appointed collector of internal revenue for the twenty-eighth district of New York and served from September 1, 1862, to March 31, 1863; delegate to the Republican National Convention in 1864; elected as a Republican to the Forty-sixth and Forty-seventh Congresses (March 4, 1879-March 3, 1883); chairman, Committee on Mines and Mining (Forty-seventh Congress); unsuccessful candidate for reelection in 1882 to the Forty-eighth Congress; resumed the practice of law in Rochester, N.Y.; elected to the Fifty-third Congress (March 4, 1893-March 3, 1895); unsuccessful candidate for renomination in 1894 to the Fifty-fourth Congress; resumed the practice of law in Rochester, N.Y., and died there on October 20, 1905; interment in Mount Hope Cemetery.

**VAN VORHES, Nelson Holmes,** a Representative from Ohio; born in Washington County, Pa., January 23, 1822; moved to Athens County, Ohio, in 1832 and engaged in agricultural pursuits; apprenticed to a printer for six years; editor and proprietor of the Athens Messenger 1844-1861; member of the State house of representatives 1850-1872 and served four years as speaker; elected probate judge in 1854, but resigned; unsuccessful candidate for election in 1858 to the Thirty-sixth Congress; delegate to the Republican National Convention in 1860; entered the Union Army as a private in 1861 and was mustered out as colonel; elected as a Republican to the Forty-fourth and Forty-fifth Congresses (March 4, 1875-March 3, 1879); unsuccessful candidate for reelection in 1878 to the Forty-sixth Congress; died in Athens, Athens County, Ohio, December 4, 1882; interment in West Union Street Cemetery.

**VAN WINKLE, Marshall** (grandnephew of Peter G. Van Winkle), a Representative from New Jersey; born in Jersey City, N.J., September 28, 1869; attended the public schools; studied law; was admitted to the bar in 1890 and commenced practice in Hoboken, N.J.; appointed counsel to the county tax board in 1895, holding this position until his resignation to accept an appointment as the assistant prosecutor of the pleas of Hudson County, N.J.; unsuccessful candidate for election in 1900 to the Fifty-seventh Congress; assistant prosecutor of pleas from 1902 to 1905, when he resigned to become a candidate for Congress; elected as a Republican to the Fifty-ninth Congress (March 4, 1905-March 3, 1907); was not a candidate for renomination in 1906; resumed the practice of law in Jersey City, N.J.; advisory master in chancery, matrimonial division, 1933-1939; wrote and published law reference books; died in Oceanport, N.J., May 10, 1957; interment in Fairview Mausoleum, Fairview, N.J.

**VAN WINKLE, Peter Godwin** (granduncle of Marshall Van Winkle), a Senator from West Virginia; born in New York City, September 7, 1808; completed preparatory studies; studied law; was admitted to the bar and commenced practice in Parkersburg, Va. (now West Virginia), in 1835; president of the town board of trustees 1844-1850; member of the Virginia constitutional convention in 1850; treasurer and later president of the Northwestern Virginia Railroad Co. in 1852; member of the Wheeling reorganization convention in 1861; delegate to the convention which framed the constitution of West Virginia; member, West Virginia house of delegates 1863; upon the admission of West Virginia as a State into the Union was elected as a Unionist to the United States Senate and served from August 4, 1863, to March 3, 1869; chairman, Committee on Pensions (Fortieth Congress); delegate to the Southern Loyalist Convention at Philadelphia, Pa., in 1866; resided in Parkersburg, W.Va., where he died April 15, 1872; interment in River View Cemetery.

**Bibliography:** *DAB*; Bayless, R.W. "Peter G. Van Winkle and Waitman Willey in the Impeachment Trial of Andrew Johnson." *West Virginia History* 13 (January 1952): 75-89; Howard, Thomas W. "Peter G. Van Winkle's Vote in the Impeachment of President Andrew Johnson: A West Virginian as a Profile in Courage." *West Virginia History* 35 (July 1974): 290-95.

**VAN WYCK, Charles Henry,** a Representative from New York and a Senator from Nebraska; born in Poughkeepsie, Dutchess County, N.Y., May 10, 1824; completed preparatory studies and graduated from Rutgers College, New Brunswick, N.J., in 1843; studied law; was admitted to the bar in 1847 and commenced the practice of law; moved to Bloomingburg, Sullivan County, N.Y.; district attorney 1850-1856; elected as a Republican from New York to the Thirty-sixth and Thirty-seventh Congresses (March 4, 1859-March 3, 1863); chairman, Committee on Mileage (Thirty-sixth Congress), Committee on Revolutionary Pensions (Thirty-seventh Congress); entered the Union Army as colonel of the Fifty-sixth Regiment, New York Volunteers, and commanded it during the Civil War; brevetted brigadier general for services during the war; elected to the Fortieth Congress (March 4, 1867-March 3, 1869); successfully contested the election of George W. Greene to the Forty-first Congress and served from February 17, 1870, to March 3, 1871; moved to Nebraska in 1874, settled on a farm in Otoe County, and engaged in agricultural pursuits; delegate to the State constitutional convention in 1875; elected to the State senate 1877, 1879, 1881; elected as a Republican to the United States Senate from Nebraska and served from March 4, 1881, to March 3, 1887; unsuccessful candidate for reelection; chairman, Committee on the Mississippi River and Its Tributaries (Forty-seventh Congress), Committee on the Improvement of the Mississippi River and Tributaries (Forty-eighth and Forty-ninth Congresses); unsuccessful Populist candidate for governor of Nebraska in 1892; retired from political life and active business pursuits; died in Washington, D.C., October 24, 1895; interment in Milford Cemetery, Milford, Pa.

**Bibliography:** *DAB*; Harmar, M.U. and J.L. Sellers. "Charles Henry Van Wyck." *Nebraska Historical Magazine* 12 (April-June 1929): 80-129, 12 (July-September 1929): 190-246, 12 (October-December 1929): 322-73.

**VAN WYCK, William William,** a Representative from New York; born near Fishkill, Dutchess County, N.Y., August 9, 1777; attended the public schools and Fishkill Academy; engaged in agricultural pursuits; elected to the Seventeenth and Eighteenth Congresses (March 4, 1821-March 3, 1825); chairman, Committee on Expenditures in the Post Office Department (Eighteenth Congress); moved to Sudley, Fairfax County, Va., and engaged in planting; returned to Dutchess County, N.Y., and died in Fishkill, N.Y., August 27, 1840; interment in the Dutch Reformed Churchyard.

**VAN ZANDT, James Edward,** a Representative from Pennsylvania; born in Altoona, Blair County, Pa., December 18, 1898; attended the public schools and the Pennsylvania Railroad Apprentice School, Altoona, Pa.; served in various departments until 1938, when he became district passenger agent; during the First World War enlisted as an apprentice seaman in the United States Navy on April 30, 1917, and served two years overseas; member of the United States Naval Reserve, 1919-1943, with rank of lieutenant; national commander of the Veterans of Foreign Wars,

1934-1936; elected as a Republican to the Seventy-sixth and to the two succeeding Congresses, and served from January 3, 1939 until his resignation September 24, 1943; while a Member of Congress was called to active duty in September 1941 and served until January 1942 with the Pacific Fleet and in escort convoy duty in the North Atlantic; reentered the service in September 1943 as a lieutenant commander and was assigned to the Pacific area until discharged as a captain, January 25, 1946, and retired as rear admiral, United States Naval Reserve, January 1, 1959; elected to the Eightieth and to the seven succeeding Congresses (January 3, 1947-January 3, 1963); was not a candidate in 1962 for renomination to the House of Representatives, but was an unsuccessful candidate for election to the United States Senate; special representative of the governor of Pennsylvania until 1971; resided in Arlington, Va., where he died on January 6, 1986; interment in Arlington National Cemetery.

**VARDAMAN, James Kimble,** a Senator from Mississippi; born near Edna, Jackson County, Tex., July 26, 1861; moved to Mississippi in 1868 with his parents, who settled in Yalobusha County; attended the public schools; studied law in Carrollton, Miss.; was admitted to the bar in 1881 and commenced practice in Winona, Miss.; became editor of the Winona Advance; moved to Greenwood, Miss., where he continued the practice of law and also engaged in the newspaper business; member, Mississippi State house of representatives, 1890-1896, and served as speaker in 1894; unsuccessful candidate for governor of Mississippi in 1895 and again in 1899; served in Cuba during the Spanish-American War; presidential elector on the Democratic ticket in 1892 and 1896; publisher of the Greenwood Commonwealth, 1896-1903, and the Issue, 1908-1912; elected Governor of Mississippi in 1903 and served from January 19, 1904 to January 21, 1908; unsuccessful candidate for election to the United States Senate in 1907 and 1910; elected as a Democrat to the United States Senate in 1912 and served from March 4, 1913, to March 3, 1919; unsuccessful candidate for renomination in 1918, and for nomination in 1922; chairman, Committee on the Conservation of Natural Resources (Sixty-third through Sixty-fifth Congresses), Committee on Expenditures in the Post Office Department (Sixty-third Congress), Committee on Manufacturers (Sixty-fifth Congress); retired from active business pursuits in 1922 and moved to Birmingham, Ala., where he died on June 25, 1930; interment in Lakewood Memorial Park, Jackson, Miss.

**Bibliography:** *DAB*; Fortenberry, Joseph E. "James Kimble Vardaman and American Foreign Policy, 1913-1919." *Journal of Mississippi History* 35 (May 1973): 127-40; Holmes, William. *The White Chief: James Kimble Vardaman.* Baton Rouge: Louisiana State University Press, 1970.

**VARE, William Scott,** a Representative and a Senator from Pennsylvania; born in Philadelphia, Pa., December 24, 1867; attended the public schools; at the age of fifteen years entered the mercantile business and became a general contractor in 1893; member of the select council of Philadelphia 1898-1901; recorder of deeds for Philadelphia 1902-1912; elected to the Pennsylvania senate in 1912, and at the same time was elected as a Republican to the Sixty-second Congress to fill the vacancy caused by the death of Henry H. Bingham; reelected to the Sixty-third and to the four succeeding Congresses and served from April 24, 1912, until January 2, 1923, when he resigned; member, Pennsylvania senate 1923; elected to the Sixty-eighth and Sixty-ninth Congresses (March 4, 1923-March 3, 1927); was not a candidate for reelection in 1926, having become a candidate for United States Senator; presented credentials as a Republican Senator-elect to the United States Senate for the term beginning March 4, 1927, but was not permitted to qualify, eventually being unseated on December 6, 1929, due to charges of corruption and fraud concerning his election; resumed his former business and political activities; died in Atlantic City, N.J.,

August 7, 1934; interment in West Laurel Hill Cemetery, Philadelphia, Pa.

**Bibliography:** *DAB*; Salter, John. *The People's Choice: Philadelphia's William S. Vare.* New York: Exposition Press, 1971; Vare, William. *My Forty Years in Politics.* Philadelphia: Roland Swain Co., 1933.

**VARNUM, James Mitchell** (brother of Joseph Bradley Varnum), a Delegate from Rhode Island; born in Dracut, Middlesex County, Mass., December 17, 1748; was graduated from the College of Rhode Island, Warren, R.I. (later Brown University, Providence, R.I.), in 1769; studied law; was admitted to the bar in 1771 and commenced practice in East Greenwich, R.I.; served in the Revolutionary Army, and was colonel of the "Kentish Guards" in 1774 and of Varnum's Rhode Island Regiment in 1775; commissioned colonel of the Ninth Continental Infantry in 1776; brigadier general of State troops December 12, 1776; brigadier general in the Continental Army February 21, 1777, and was honorably discharged March 5, 1779; appointed major general of State militia in May 1779; resumed the practice of law in East Greenwich, R.I.; Member of the Continental Congress 1780-1781, and 1787; appointed a judge of the United States Court in the Northwest Territory in 1787; moved to Marietta, Ohio, in 1788, and died there January 10, 1789; interment in Mound Cemetery.

**Bibliography:** *DAB*.

**VARNUM, John,** a Representative from Massachusetts; born in Dracut, Middlesex County, Mass., June 25, 1778; was graduated from Harvard University in 1798; studied law; was admitted to the bar and commenced practice in Haverhill, Mass., in 1802; was elected as a Federalist to the State senate in 1811; moved to Lowell, Mass.; elected to the Nineteenth, Twentieth, and Twenty-first Congresses (March 4, 1825-March 3, 1831); returned to Lowell, Mass., and later moved to Niles, Berrien County, Mich., where he died July 23, 1836; interment in Silverbrook Cemetery.

**VARNUM, Joseph Bradley** (brother of James Mitchell Varnum), a Representative and a Senator from Massachusetts; born in Dracut, Middlesex County, Mass., January 29, 1750 or 1751; largely self-taught; farmer; served in the Revolutionary Army; member, Massachusetts house of representatives 1780-1785; member, Massachusetts senate 1786-1795; delegate to the Massachusetts convention that ratified the Federal Constitution in 1788; justice of the court of common pleas; chief justice of the court of general sessions; elected to the Fourth and to the eight succeeding Congresses and served from March 4, 1795, to June 29, 1811, when he resigned, having been elected Senator; Speaker of the House during the Tenth and Eleventh Congresses; chairman, Committee on Elections (Fifth Congress); elected as a Republican to the United States Senate in 1811 to fill the vacancy in the term commencing March 4, 1811, and served from June 29, 1811, to March 3, 1817; served as President pro tempore of the Senate during the Thirteenth Congress; chairman, Committee on Militia (Fourteenth Congress); delegate to the Massachusetts constitutional convention in 1820; member, Massachusetts senate 1817-1821; died in Dracut, Mass., September 21, 1821; interment in Varnum Cemetery.

**Bibliography:** *DAB*; Varnum, Joseph. "Autobiography of General Joseph B. Varnum." *Magazine of American History* 20 (November 1888): 405-14.

**VAUGHAN, Horace Worth,** a Representative from Texas; born near Jefferson, Marion County, Tex., December 2, 1867; attended the common schools of Linden, Cass County, Tex.; studied law; was admitted to the bar in 1885 and commenced practice in Texarkana, Tex., in 1886; city attorney of Texarkana 1890-1898; prosecuting attorney of Bowie County 1898-1906; district attorney for the fifth judicial district of Texas 1906-1910; member of the State senate in 1910; elected as a Democrat to the Sixty-third Congress (March 4,

1913-March 3, 1915); unsuccessful candidate for reelection in 1914 to the Sixty-fourth Congress; appointed by President Woodrow Wilson as United States district attorney at Honolulu, Hawaii, and served from December 22, 1915, to March 22, 1916; United States district judge in Hawaii from May 15, 1916, to April 4, 1922; died in Honolulu, Hawaii, November 10, 1922; interment in Nuuanu Cemetery.

**VAUGHAN, William Wirt,** a Representative from Tennessee; born in LaGuardo (now Martha), Wilson County, Tenn., July 2, 1831; attended the common schools and was graduated from Cumberland University, Lebanon, Tenn.; studied law; was admitted to the bar in 1860 and commenced practice in Brownsville, Tenn.; elected as a Democrat to the Forty-second Congress (March 4, 1871-March 3, 1873); unsuccessful candidate for reelection in 1872 to the Forty-third Congress; resumed the practice of law in Brownsville; one of the prime movers in the building of the Chesapeake & Ohio Railroad branch from Brownsville to Newbern, and was president of the system at the time of his death; became a candidate for election in 1878 to the Forty-sixth Congress, but died in Crockett Mills, near Alamo, Crockett County, Tenn., August 19, 1878, while canvassing the district; interment in Oakwood Cemetery, Brownsville, Tenn.

**VAUGHN, Albert Clinton, Sr.,** a Representative from Pennsylvania; born in West Catasauqua, Lehigh County, Pa., October 9, 1894; attended the public schools in Whitehall Township; was graduated from Whitehall High School in 1910 and from Allentown (Pa.) Business College in 1911; also completed an extension course in business administration; during the First World War served as a yeoman in the United States Navy; for twenty-five years engaged in private industry, including engineering, administrative, and sales positions; elected a school director in Whitehall Township in 1929 for a six-year term; executive assistant to Representative Charles L. Gerlach of Pennsylvania in 1945, and to Representative Franklin H. Lichtenwalter of Pennsylvania in 1947, and served until taking his seat in Congress; elected as a Republican to the Eighty-second Congress and served from January 3, 1951, until his death in Fullerton, Lehigh County, Pa., September 1, 1951; interment in Fairview Cemetery, West Catasauqua, Pa.

**VAUX, Richard,** a Representative from Pennsylvania; born in Philadelphia, Pa., December 19, 1816; educated by private tutors at the Friends Select School in Philadelphia and Bolmar's French School, Westchester, Pa.; studied law and was admitted to the bar in Philadelphia in 1837; secretary of legation under Andrew Stevenson, United States Minister to Great Britain, for one year; returned to Philadelphia in 1839; member of the Pennsylvania house of representatives in 1839; delegate to the Pennsylvania Democratic convention in 1840; commenced the practice of law in Philadelphia in 1840; recorder of deeds of Philadelphia, 1842-1849; appointed by the Pennsylvania supreme court as inspector of the Pennsylvania penitentiary for the eastern district of Pennsylvania in 1842, and served as secretary and later as president of the board of inspectors until his death; unsuccessful candidate for mayor of Philadelphia in 1842, 1845, and 1854; elected mayor of Philadelphia in 1856; member of the board of city trusts, 1859-1866, serving as president from 1863 until 1865; elected as a Democrat to the Fifty-first Congress to fill the vacancy caused by the death of Samuel J. Randall, and served from May 20, 1890 to March 3, 1891; unsuccessful candidate for reelection in 1890 to the Fifty-second Congress; died in Philadelphia, Pa., March 22, 1895; interment in Laurel Hill Cemetery.

**Bibliography:** *DAB*.

**VEEDER, William Davis,** a Representative from New York; born in Guilderland, Albany County, N.Y., May 19, 1835; completed preparatory studies; studied law; was admitted to the bar and commenced the practice of law in Brooklyn, N.Y., in 1858; served in the State assembly in 1865 and 1866; delegate to the Democratic

State conventions in 1875 and 1877; member of the State constitutional convention in 1867 and 1868; surrogate of Kings County, N.Y., 1867-1877; elected as a Democrat to the Forty-fifth Congress (March 4, 1877-March 3, 1879); was not a candidate for renomination in 1878; resumed the practice of law in Brooklyn; member of the State constitutional convention in 1887 and 1888; died in Brooklyn, N.Y., December 2, 1910; interment in Voorheesville Cemetery, Voorheesville, N.Y.

**VEHSLAGE, John Herman George,** a Representative from New York; born in New York City December 20, 1842; attended the public schools; left school to become a clerk in the retail grocery business; engaged in the coal and wood business; joined the Third Cavalry, New York National Guard, in 1863 and was commissioned a captain by Governor Horatio Seymour on February 15, 1864; appointed inspector of rifle practice with the rank of captain and continued in service until 1880, when the regiment was mustered out by order of Governor Alonzo B. Cornell; remained as supernumerary until November 12, 1883, when he received an honorable discharge from Governor Grover Cleveland; member of the New York State assembly, 1894-1896; elected as a Democrat to the Fifty-fifth Congress (March 4, 1897-March 3, 1899); unsuccessful candidate for renomination in 1898 to the Fifty-sixth Congress; died in New York City on July 21, 1904; interment in the Lutheran Cemetery, Brooklyn, N.Y.

**VELÁZQUEZ, Nydia M.,** a Representative from New York; born in Yabucoa, Puerto Rico, March 28, 1953; B.A., University of Puerto Rico, 1974; M.A., New York University, 1976; faculty, University of Puerto Rico, 1976-1981; adjunct professor, Hunter College of City University of New York, 1981-1983; special assistant to Representative Edolphus Towns of New York, 1983; member, New York City council, 1984-1986; national director, Migration Division, Department of Labor and Human Resources of Puerto Rico, 1986-1989; elected as a Democrat to the One Hundred Third and One Hundred Fourth Congresses (January 3, 1993-January 3, 1997); is a resident of Brooklyn, N.Y.

**VELDE, Harold Himmel,** a Representative from Illinois; born on a farm near Parkland, Tazewell County, Ill., April 1, 1910; attended rural grade and high schools; student at Bradley University, Peoria, Ill., 1927-1929; was graduated from Northwestern University, Evanston, Ill., in 1931 and from the University of Illinois Law School at Champaign in 1937; athletic coach and teacher at Hillsdale (Ill.) Community High School, 1931-1935; was admitted to the bar in 1937 and commenced the practice of law in Pekin, Ill.; served as a private in the Signal Corps of the United States Army in 1942 and 1943; special agent of the Federal Bureau of Investigation in the sabotage and counter-espionage division, 1943-1946; elected county judge of Tazewell County in 1946 and served until 1949; elected as a Republican to the Eighty-first and to the three succeeding Congresses (January 3, 1949-January 3, 1957); chairman, Committee on Un-American Activities (Eighty-third Congress); was not a candidate for renomination in 1956 to the Eighty-fifth Congress; engaged in the practice of law in Urbana, Ill., and Washington, D.C., until May 5, 1969; became regional counsel, General Services Administration, Lansing, Ill., in 1969; was a resident of Sun City, Ariz., from 1974 until his death there on September 1, 1985; cremated; ashes interred in Pekin, Ill.

**VENABLE, Abraham Bedford** (uncle of Abraham Watkins Venable), a Representative and a Senator from Virginia; born on "State Hill" farm, near Prince Edward Court House (now Worsham), Prince Edward County, Va., November 20, 1758; attended Hampden-Sidney (Va.) College and graduated from the College of New Jersey (now Princeton University) in 1780; engaged as a planter in his native county; studied law; was admitted to the bar in 1784 and commenced practice at Prince Edward Court House; elected to the Second and to the three succeeding Congresses (March 4,

1791-March 3, 1799); was not a candidate for renomination in 1798 to the Sixth Congress; chairman, Committee on Elections (Fourth Congress); elected as a Republican to the United States Senate to fill the vacancy caused by the death of Stevens T. Mason, and served from December 7, 1803 to June 7, 1804, when he resigned to become president of the first national bank organized in Virginia; perished at the burning of a theater in Richmond, Va., December 26, 1811; interment of ashes, with those of other fire victims, under a stone in front of the altar in Monumental Church, Richmond, Va.

**VENABLE, Abraham Watkins** (nephew of Abraham Bedford Venable), a Representative from North Carolina; born in Springfield, Prince Edward County, Va., October 17, 1799; was graduated from Hampden-Sidney (Va.) College in 1816; studied medicine for two years; was graduated from Princeton College in 1819; studied law; was admitted to the bar in 1821 and commenced practice in Prince Edward and Mecklenburg Counties, Va.; moved to North Carolina in 1829; elected as a Democrat to the Thirtieth and to the two succeeding Congresses (March 4, 1847-March 3, 1853); unsuccessful candidate for renomination in 1852 to the Thirty-third Congress; presidential elector on the Southern Democratic ticket of Breckinridge and Lane in 1860; delegate from the State of North Carolina to the Provisional Confederate Congress in 1861; member of the house of representatives of the Confederate Congress, 1862-1864; died in Oxford, N.C., on February 24, 1876; interment in the Shiloh Presbyterian Churchyard, Granville County, N.C.

**VENABLE, Edward Carrington,** a Representative from Virginia; born near Farmville, Prince Edward County, Va., January 31, 1853; attended the local school, McCabe's University High School, Petersburg, Va., and the University of Virginia at Charlottesville; taught school for three years; moved to Petersburg, Va., in 1876 and engaged in mercantile pursuits; delegate to the Virginia Democratic convention in 1886; presented credentials as a Democratic Member-elect to the Fifty-first Congress and served from March 4, 1889, to September 23, 1890, when he was succeeded by John M. Langston, who successfully contested his election; resumed his former business pursuits; died in Baltimore, Md., December 8, 1908; interment in Blandford Cemetery, Petersburg, Va.

**VENABLE, William Webb,** a Representative from Mississippi; born in Clinton, Hinds County, Miss., September 25, 1880; moved with his parents to Memphis, Tenn., returned to Clinton, Miss., in 1891; attended public and private schools; was graduated from Mississippi College at Clinton in 1898, from the University of Mississippi at Oxford in 1899, and from the law department of Cumberland University, Lebanon, Tenn., in 1905; was admitted to the bar in 1905 and commenced practice in Meridian, Miss.; prosecuting attorney of Lauderdale County from April to October 1910, when he was appointed district attorney; served in the latter capacity until January 1, 1915, when he resigned; judge of the tenth judicial district of Mississippi from 1915 until his resignation in December 1916; elected as a Democrat to the Sixty-fourth Congress to fill the vacancy caused by the death of Samuel A. Witherspoon; reelected to the Sixty-fifth and Sixty-sixth Congresses and served from January 4, 1916, to March 3, 1921; unsuccessful for renomination; practiced law Clarksdale, Miss.; died in New Orleans, La., August 2, 1948; interment in Magnolia Cemetery, Meridian, Miss.

**VENTO, Bruce Frank,** a Representative from Minnesota; born in St. Paul, Ramsey County, Minn., October 7, 1940; attended the public schools of St. Paul and graduated from Johnson High School in 1958; attended St. Thomas College, St. Paul, 1958-1959; A.A., University of Minnesota, Minneapolis, 1961; B.S., Wisconsin State University, River Falls, 1965; graduate studies, University of Minnesota, 1966; taught in the public schools of Minneapolis, Minn., 1965-1976; member, Minnesota State house of representatives, 1971-1976; elected as a Democrat-Farmer-Labor candidate to the

Ninety-fifth and to the nine succeeding Congresses (January 3, 1977-January 3, 1997); is a resident of St. Paul, Minn.

**VERPLANCK, Daniel Crommelin** (father of Gulian Crommelin Verplanck), a Representative from New York; born in New York City March 19, 1762; was educated under private tutors; was graduated from Columbia College (now Columbia University), New York City, in 1788; studied law; was admitted to the bar and commenced practice in New York City in 1789; also engaged in banking; elected as a Republican to the Eighth Congress to fill the vacancy caused by the death of Isaac Bloom; reelected to the Ninth and Tenth Congresses and served from October 17, 1803, to March 3, 1809; was not a candidate for renomination in 1808; resumed the practice of law; judge of the court of common pleas of Dutchess County 1828-1830; died at his home, "Mount Gulian," near Fishkill, Dutchess County, N.Y., March 29, 1834; interment in Trinity Church Cemetery, Fishkill, N.Y.

**VERPLANCK, Gulian Crommelin** (son of Daniel Crommelin Verplanck), a Representative from New York; born in New York City, August 6, 1786; pursued classical studies, and was graduated from Columbia College (now Columbia University), New York City, in 1801; studied law and was admitted to the bar in 1807; member of the New York State assembly, 1820-1823; professor at General Theological Seminary, New York City, 1821-1824; elected to the Nineteenth and Twentieth Congresses, and elected as a Jacksonian to the Twenty-first and Twenty-second Congresses (March 4, 1825-March 3, 1833); chairman, Committee on Ways and Means (Twenty-second Congress); was not a candidate for renomination in 1832 to the Twenty-third Congress; unsuccessful Whig candidate for mayor of New York City in 1834; member of the State senate, 1838-1841; governor of the city hospital from 1823 until 1865; regent of the State university, 1826-1870, and vice chancellor, 1858-1870; president of the board of commissioners of immigration, 1846-1870; member of the State constitutional convention in 1867 and 1868; died in New York City on March 18, 1870; interment in Trinity Churchyard, Fishkill, Dutchess County, N.Y.

**Bibliography:** *DAB*; July, Robert William. *Essential New Yorker: Gulian Crommelin Verplanck.* Durham, N.C.: Duke University Press, 1951.

**VERREE, John Paul,** a Representative from Pennsylvania; born at "Verree Mills," on Pennypack Creek, near what is now Fox Chase Station, Philadelphia, Pa., March 9, 1817; completed preparatory studies; engaged in the manufacture of iron and subsequently was a dealer in edged tools and also in iron and steel; member of the select council of Philadelphia 1851-1857, serving as president 1853-1857; elected as a Republican to the Thirty-sixth and Thirty-seventh Congresses (March 4, 1859-March 3, 1863); declined to be a candidate for renomination in 1862; resumed his former manufacturing pursuits; also interested in life insurance and served as president of a company; president of the Philadelphia Union League in 1875 and 1876; retired from active business pursuits; died at "Verree Mills," Philadelphia, Pa., June 27, 1889; interment in Cedar Hill Cemetery, Frankford (now a part of Philadelphia), Pa.

**VEST, George Graham,** a Senator from Missouri; born in Frankfort, Franklin County, Ky., December 6, 1830; graduated from Centre College, Danville, Ky., in 1848 and from the law department of Transylvania University, Lexington, Ky., in 1853; was admitted to the bar in 1853 and commenced practice in Georgetown, Mo.; moved to Boonville, Mo., in 1856; Democratic presidential elector in 1860; member, State house of representatives 1860-1861; judge advocate with the Confederate forces in Missouri in 1862; served in the house of representatives of the Confederate Congress from February 1862 to January 1865, when he resigned, having been appointed to fill a vacancy in the Confederate Senate; resumed the practice of law in Sedalia, Mo., in 1865; moved to Kansas City in 1877; elected as a Democrat to the United States Senate; reelected in 1885, 1891, and

1897, and served from March 4, 1879, to March 3, 1903; chairman, Committee on Public Buildings and Grounds (Fifty-third Congress), Committee on Epidemic Diseases (Fifty-fourth Congress), Committee on Public Health and National Quarantine (Fifty-fourth through Fifty-seventh Congresses); due to ill health, retired from public life and resided at Sweet Springs, Saline County, Mo., until his death August 9, 1904; interment in Bellefontaine Cemetery, St. Louis, Mo.

**Bibliography:** *DAB*; Holsinger, M. Paul. "Senator George Graham Vest and the 'Menace' of Mormonism, 1882-1887." *Missouri Historical Review* 65 (October 1970): 23-36.

**VESTAL, Albert Henry,** a Representative from Indiana; born on a farm near Frankton, Madison County, Ind., January 18, 1875; attended the common schools; worked in steel mills and factories; attended the Indiana State Normal School at Terre Haute; taught school for several years; was graduated from the law department of the Valparaiso (Ind.) University in 1896; was admitted to the bar the same year and commenced practice in Anderson, Ind.; prosecuting attorney of the fiftieth judicial circuit 1900-1906; unsuccessful candidate for the Republican nomination for Congress in 1908; unsuccessful candidate for election in 1914 to the Sixty-fourth Congress; elected as a Republican to the Sixty-fifth and to the seven succeeding Congresses and served from March 4, 1917, until his death; chairman, Committee on Coinage, Weights, and Measures (Sixty-sixth through Sixty-eighth Congresses), Committee on Patents (Sixty-ninth through Seventy-first Congresses); majority whip (Sixty-eighth through Seventy-first Congresses); died in Washington, D.C., April 1, 1932; interment in East Maplewood Cemetery, Anderson, Ind.

**VEYSEY, Victor Vincent,** a Representative from California; born in Los Angeles, Calif., April 14, 1915; B.S., California Institute of Technology, Pasadena, 1936; M.B.A., Harvard University, 1938; engaged in graduate work at Stanford University, Palo Alto, Calif.; industrial relations and plant manager, Rocket Developmental Project, California Institute of Technology, and works manager in a private industry rocket plant during the Second World War; professor at the California Institute of Technology, 1938-1940, and 1941-1946; professor, Stanford University, 1940-1941; member, Brawley School District Board, 1955-1962; member, Imperial Valley College Board, 1960-1962; served on advisory commission, United States Department of Agriculture, 1959-1963; member, California State assembly, January 1963-January 1971; rancher; delegate, California State conventions, 1960-1970; delegate to the Republican National Convention of 1972; elected as a Republican to the Ninety-second and to the Ninety-third Congresses (January 3, 1971-January 3, 1975); unsuccessful candidate for reelection in 1974 to the Ninety-fourth Congress; Assistant Secretary for Civil Works, United States Army, 1975-1977; director, industrial relations center, California Institute of Technology, 1977-1983; secretary for industrial relations, State of California, 1983; is a resident of Pasadena, Calif.

**VIBBARD, Chauncey,** a Representative from New York; born in Galway, Saratoga County, N.Y., November 11, 1811; attended the common schools and was graduated from Mott's Academy for Boys, Albany, N.Y.; clerk in a wholesale grocery store in Albany, N.Y.; moved to New York City, and in 1834 went to Montgomery, Ala.; returned to New York and settled in Schenectady; was appointed chief clerk of the Utica & Schenectady Railroad Co. in 1836; became a railroad freight and ticket agent in 1848; consolidated the many little railroads of western New York into the New York Central Railroad Co., serving as its first general superintendent from 1853 until 1865; elected as a Democrat to the Thirty-seventh Congress (March 4, 1861-March 3, 1863); declined to be a candidate for renomination in 1862 to the Thirty-eighth Congress; during the Civil War served as director and superintendent of military railroads in 1862; first president of the Family Fund Insurance Co.,

1864-1867; moved to New York City in 1865 and became involved in the business of steamship lines and elevated railroads; interested in the development of southern railroads and South and Central American enterprises at the time of his retirement in 1889; died in Macon, Ga., June 5, 1891; interment in Riverside Cemetery.

**Bibliography:** *DAB.*

**VICKERS, George,** a Senator from Maryland; born in Chestertown, Kent County, Md., November 19, 1801; pursued an academic course; employed in the county clerk's office for several years; studied law; was admitted to the bar in 1832 and commenced practice in Chestertown, Md.; major general of the State militia in 1861; presidential elector on the Democratic ticket in 1864; vice president of the Union National Convention of Conservatives in Philadelphia in 1866; member, Maryland State senate, 1866-1867; elected as a Democrat to the United States Senate to fill the vacancy caused by the action of the Senate in declining to permit Philip F. Thomas to qualify, and served from March 7, 1868, to March 3, 1873; resumed the practice of law in Chestertown, Md., and died there on October 8, 1879; interment in Chester Cemetery.

**VIDAL, Michel,** a Representative from Louisiana; born in the city of Carcassonne, Languedoc, France, October 1, 1824; attended college; immigrated to the Republic of Texas; moved to Louisiana when Texas was annexed to the United States; engaged in literary and scientific pursuits; engaged as associate editor with several American and French papers of this country and Canada; moved to Opelousas, La., in 1867; founded and became editor of the St. Landry Progress; editor of the New York Courrier des États-Unis and the New Orleans Picayune; at the close of the Civil War was appointed by General Philip H. Sheridan a registrar for the city of New Orleans; delegate to the State constitutional convention in 1867 and 1868; upon the readmission of the State of Louisiana to representation was elected as a Republican to the Fortieth Congress and served from July 18, 1868, to March 3, 1869; appointed a United States commissioner under the convention concluded with Peru in 1868 for the adjustment of claims of citizens of either country; appointed by President Ulysses S. Grant as United States consul at Tripoli and served from April 5, 1870, to October 12, 1876.

**VIELE, Egbert Ludoricus,** a Representative from New York; born in Waterford, Saratoga County, N.Y., June 17, 1825; attended Albany (N.Y.) Academy; was graduated from the United States Military Academy, West Point, N.Y., July 1, 1847; commissioned a brevet second lieutenant in the Second United States Infantry; served in the Mexican War in 1847 and 1848; promoted to second lieutenant, First United States Infantry, on September 8, 1847; promoted to first lieutenant in 1850; resigned in 1853; became a civil and military engineer; appointed State engineer of New Jersey in 1855; appointed engineer in chief of Central Park, New York City, in 1856; appointed engineer of Prospect Park, Brooklyn, in 1860; appointed captain of the Engineer Corps of the Seventh New York Regiment in 1860; appointed brigadier general of United States Volunteers in August 1861; military governor of Norfolk, Va., from July 22, 1862 until August 1, 1863; supervised the drafting of men in northern Ohio into the Union forces until his resignation on October 20, 1863; engaged in civil engineering; appointed president of the department of public parks in New York City, 1883-1884; elected as a Democrat to the Forty-ninth Congress (March 4, 1885-March 3, 1887); unsuccessful candidate for reelection in 1886 to the Fiftieth Congress; resumed his former business pursuits and also engaged in literary work; died in New York City, April 22, 1902; interment in Post Cemetery, West Point, Orange County, N.Y.

**Bibliography:** *DAB.*

**VIGORITO, Joseph Phillip,** a Representative from Pennsylvania; born in Niles, Trumbull County, Ohio, November 10, 1918; moved with his parents to Erie, Pa., in 1931, attended the Erie

County schools, and graduated from the Strong Vincent High School in 1938; served in the United States Army from April 1942 to August 1945, first lieutenant, and was awarded the Purple Heart; B.S., Wharton School of Finance, University of Pennsylvania, 1947; M.B.A., University of Denver, 1949; engaged as a certified public accountant in 1954; assistant professor, Pennsylvania State University, 1949-1964; elected as a Democrat to the Eighty-ninth and to the five succeeding congresses (January 3, 1965-January 3, 1977); unsuccessful candidate for reelection in 1976 to the Ninety-fifth Congress; taught at Georgetown University, Washington, D.C., 1977-1978; unsuccessful candidate for election in 1978 to the Ninety-sixth Congress; is a resident of McLean, Va.

**VILAS, William Freeman,** a Senator from Wisconsin; born in Chelsea, Orange County, Vt., July 9, 1840; moved with his parents to Madison, Dane County, Wis., in 1851; attended the common schools; graduated from the University of Wisconsin at Madison in 1858 and from the law department of the University of Albany, New York, in 1860; was admitted to the bar and commenced practice in Madison, Wis., in 1860; enlisted in the Union Army during the Civil War; captain of Company A, Twenty-third Regiment, Wisconsin Volunteer Infantry, and afterward major and lieutenant colonel of the regiment; professor of law at the University of Wisconsin; regent of the university, 1880-1885; one of three revisers appointed by the Wisconsin Supreme Court in 1875 to prepare a revised body of the statute law; member, Wisconsin State assembly, 1885; Postmaster General in the Cabinet of President Grover Cleveland from March 7, 1885 until January 16, 1888, when he became Secretary of the Interior, and served until March 6, 1889; elected as a Democrat to the United States Senate in 1891, and served from March 4, 1891 to March 3, 1897; unsuccessful candidate for renomination in 1896; chairman, Committee on Post Office and Post Roads (Fifty-third Congress); regent of the University of Wisconsin, 1898-1905; resumed the practice of law; member of the commission to provide for the construction of the State capitol in 1907; died in Madison, Wis., August 27, 1908; interment in Forest Hill Cemetery.

**Bibliography:** *DAB*; Merrill, Horace Samuel. *William Freeman Vilas, Doctrinaire Democrat.* Madison: State Historical Society of Wisconsin, 1954.

**VINCENT, Beverly Mills,** a Representative from Kentucky; born in Brownsville, Edmonson County, Ky., March 28, 1890; attended the public schools, Western Kentucky State Teachers College at Bowling Green, and the law department of the University of Kentucky at Lexington; admitted to the bar in 1915 and commenced practice in Brownsville, Ky.; county judge of Edmonson County, Ky., 1916-1918; during the First World War served as a private in Battery A, Seventy-second Field Artillery, from August 27, 1918, to January 9, 1919; assistant attorney general of Kentucky in 1919 and 1920; member of the Kentucky senate 1929-1933; presidential elector on the Democratic ticket in 1932; attorney general of Kentucky from 1936 until his resignation in March 1937; elected as a Democrat to the Seventy-fifth Congress to fill the vacancy caused by the death of Glover H. Cary; reelected to the Seventy-sixth, Seventy-seventh, and Seventy-eighth Congresses and served from March 3, 1937, to January 3, 1945; was not a candidate for renomination in 1944; pursued agricultural interests, and resumed the practice of law; was a resident of Brownsville, Ky., until his death there on August 15, 1980.

**VINCENT, Bird J.,** a Representative from Michigan; born near Clarkston, Oakland County, Mich., March 6, 1880; attended the public schools of Oakland and Midland Counties and Ferris Institute; was graduated from the law department of the University of Michigan at Ann Arbor in 1905; was admitted to the bar the same year and commenced practice in Saginaw; assistant prosecuting attorney of Saginaw County 1909-1914 and prosecuting attorney from 1915 to 1917, when he resigned to enter the Army; during the

First World War served ten months in France as first lieutenant of the Sixth Train Headquarters and in the Three Hundred and Second Train Headquarters; city attorney of Saginaw 1919-1923; elected as a Republican to the Sixty-eighth and to the four succeeding Congresses and served from March 4, 1923, until his death July 18, 1931, on board the transport *Henderson,* while en route to the United States from Honolulu, Hawaii; chairman, Committee on Elections No. 2 (Sixty-ninth through Seventy-first Congresses); interment in Forest Lawn Cemetery, Saginaw, Mich.

**VINCENT, Earl W.,** a Representative from Iowa; born in Washington County, near Keota, Iowa, March 27, 1886; attended the rural schools; was graduated from Keota High School in 1904, from Monmouth (Ill.) College in 1909, and from the law department of the University of Iowa at Iowa City in 1912; was admitted to the bar in 1912 and commenced practice in Guthrie Center, Iowa; prosecuting attorney of Guthrie County 1919-1922; member of the Iowa house of representatives 1923-1927; elected as a Republican to the Seventieth Congress to fill the vacancy caused by the resignation of William R. Green and served from June 4, 1928, to March 3, 1929; unsuccessful candidate for renomination in 1928; resumed the practice of law in Guthrie Center, Iowa; delegate to the Republican State convention in 1930; appointed judge of the fifth judicial district of Iowa in February 1945, and served until his death in Guthrie Center, Iowa, May 22, 1953; interment in Union Cemetery.

**VINCENT, William Davis,** a Representative from Kansas; born near Dresden, Weakley County, Tenn., October 11, 1852; moved with his parents to Riley County, Kans., in 1858 and to Manhattan, Kans., in 1864; attended the public schools and the State agricultural college in Manhattan, Kans.; engaged in business in Manhattan 1872-1876; moved to Clay Center, Kans., in 1878 and engaged in mercantile pursuits; elected as a member of the city council in 1880; member of the State board of railroad commissioners in 1893 and 1894; elected as a Populist to the Fifty-fifth Congress (March 4, 1897-March 3, 1899); engaged in the hardware business in Clay Center, Clay County, Kans., until his death in St. Louis, Mo., February 28, 1922; interment in Greenwood Cemetery, Clay Center, Kans.

**VINING, John,** a Delegate, a Representative, and a Senator from Delaware; born in Dover, Kent County, Del., December 23, 1758; studied law; was admitted to the bar in 1782 and commenced practice in New Castle County; Member of the Continental Congress 1784-1785; member, State house of representatives 1787-1788; elected to the First and Second Congresses (March 4, 1789-March 3, 1793); was not a candidate for renomination in 1792; member, State senate 1793; elected to the United States Senate and served from March 4, 1793, to January 19, 1798, when he resigned; died in Dover, Del., in February 1802; interment in Episcopal Cemetery.

**VINSON, Carl** (grand-uncle of Samuel Augustus Nunn), a Representative from Georgia; born in Milledgeville, Baldwin County, Ga., November 18, 1883; attended the Georgia Military College at Milledgeville, and was graduated from Mercer University Law School, Macon, Ga., in 1902; was admitted to the bar in 1902 and commenced practice in Milledgeville; prosecuting attorney of Baldwin County, Ga., 1906-1909; member of the Georgia State house of representatives, 1909-1912, serving as speaker pro tempore in 1911 and 1912; appointed judge of the county court of Baldwin County, and served from October 3, 1912 to November 2, 1914, when he resigned, having been elected to Congress; elected as a Democrat to the Sixty-third Congress to fill the vacancy caused by the resignation of Thomas W. Hardwick; reelected to the Sixty-fourth and to the twenty-four succeeding Congresses, and served from November 3, 1914 to January 3, 1965; chairman, Committee on Naval Affairs (Seventy-second through Seventy-ninth Congresses), Committee on Armed Services (Eighty-first, Eighty-second and Eighty-fourth through Eighty-eighth Congresses); was not a

candidate for renomination in 1964 to the Eighty-ninth Congress; resided in Milledgeville, Ga., where he died on June 1, 1981; interment in Memory Hill Cemetery.

**Bibliography:** Enders, Calvin William. "The Vinson Navy." Ph.D. dissertation, Michigan State University, 1970; Walter, John C. "Congressman Carl Vinson and Franklin D. Roosevelt: Naval Preparedness and the Coming of World War II, 1932-40." *Georgia Historical Quarterly* 64 (Fall 1980): 294-305.

**VINSON, Frederick Moore,** a Representative from Kentucky; born in Louisa, Lawrence County, Ky., January 22, 1890; attended the public schools; A.B., Centre College, Danville, Ky., 1909, LL.B., 1911; was admitted to the bar the same year and commenced practice in Louisa; city attorney of Louisa in 1914 and 1915; served in the United States Army during the First World War; Commonwealth attorney for the thirty-second judicial district of Kentucky, 1921-1924; elected as a Democrat to the Sixty-eighth Congress to fill the vacancy caused by the resignation of William J. Fields; reelected to the Sixty-ninth and Seventieth Congresses, and served from January 12, 1924 to March 3, 1929; unsuccessful candidate for reelection in 1928 to the Seventy-first Congress; resumed the practice of law in Kentucky; elected to the Seventy-second and to the three succeeding Congresses, and served from March 4, 1931 to May 12, 1938, when he resigned, having been appointed by President Franklin D. Roosevelt an associate justice of the United States Court of Appeals for the District of Columbia, and subsequently designated by Chief Justice Harlan Fiske Stone on March 2, 1942, as chief judge of the United States Emergency Court of Appeals; served in each capacity until his resignation on May 27, 1943, to become Director of the Office of Economic Stabilization, in which capacity he served until March 5, 1945; Federal Loan Administrator from March 6 to April 3, 1945; director of War Mobilization and Reconversion from April 4 to July 22, 1945; appointed Secretary of the Treasury by President Harry S Truman, and served from July 23, 1945 to June 23, 1946; nominated on June 6, 1946 by President Truman as Chief Justice of the United States; was confirmed by the Senate on June 20, 1946, and served until his death in Washington, D.C., September 8, 1953; interment in Pinehill Cemetery, Louisa, Ky.

**Bibliography:** *DAB;* Bolner, James. "Fred M. Vinson: 1890-1938, The Years of Relative Obscurity." *Register of the Kentucky Historical Society* 63 (January 1965): 3-16; Hatcher, John H. "Fred Vinson: Congressman from Kentucky, A Political Biography: 1890-1938." Ph.D. dissertation, University of Cincinnati, 1967.

**VINTON, Samuel Finley,** a Representative from Ohio; born in South Hadley, Mass., September 25, 1792; was graduated from Williams College, Williamstown, Mass., in 1814; studied law; was admitted to the bar in 1816 and commenced practice in Gallipolis, Ohio; held several local offices; elected to the Eighteenth through Twenty-second Congresses, elected as an Anti-Jacksonian to the Twenty-third Congress, and elected as a Whig to the Twenty-fourth Congress (March 4, 1823-March 3, 1837); declined to be a candidate for renomination in 1836; elected as a Whig to the Twenty-eighth and to the three succeeding Congresses (March 4, 1843-March 3, 1851); chairman, Committee on Ways and Means (Thirtieth Congress); was not a candidate for renomination in 1850; unsuccessful candidate for election as Governor of Ohio in 1851; appointed by President Abraham Lincoln in 1862 to appraise the slaves emancipated in the District of Columbia; died in Washington, D.C., May 11, 1862; interment in Pine Street Cemetery, Gallipolis, Gallia County, Ohio.

**Bibliography:** *DAB.*

**VISCLOSKY, Peter J.,** a Representative from Indiana; born in Gary, Ind., August 13, 1949; graduated, Andrean High School, Merrillville, Ind., 1967; B.S., Indiana University, Gary, 1970; J.D., University of Notre Dame Law School, 1973; LL.M., Georgetown

University Law Center, Washington, D.C., 1982; admitted to the Indiana State bar in 1974 and practiced law 1974-1976; staff, United States House of Representatives, Committee on Appropriations, 1977-1980, and Committee on the Budget, 1980-1982; practiced law in Merrillville, Ind., 1983-1984; elected as a Democrat to the Ninety-ninth and to the five succeeding Congresses (January 3, 1985-January 3, 1997); is a resident of Merrillville, Ind.

**VIVIAN, Weston Edward,** a Representative from Michigan; born in Newfoundland, Canada, October 25, 1924; moved to the United States with his parents on September 5, 1929, and settled in Cranston, R.I.; attended the Cranston schools; served in the United States Navy as an enlisted man and officer, 1943-1946; graduated from Union College, Schenectady, N.Y., in 1945, and from the Massachusetts Institute of Technology, Cambridge, Mass., in 1949; Ph.D., engineering, University of Michigan, Ann Arbor, 1959; candidate for city council, Ann Arbor, Mich., 1958-1959; research engineer and lecturer at the University of Michigan from 1951 until 1959; chairman of Ann Arbor City Democratic Committee in 1959-1960; electronics engineer and consultant for various firms and institutions; elected as a Democrat to the Eighty-ninth Congress (January 3, 1965-January 3, 1967); unsuccessful candidate for reelection in 1966 to the Ninetieth Congress; vice president, Vicom Industries, Inc., Ann Arbor, Mich., November 1969 to present; lecturer, Institute of Public Policy Studies, University of Michigan; telecommunications consultant; is a resident of Ann Arbor, Mich.

**VOIGT, Edward,** a Representative from Wisconsin; born in Bremen, Germany, December 1, 1873; in 1883 immigrated to the United States with his parents, who settled in Milwaukee, Wis.; attended the public schools; employed in law and insurance office for several years; was graduated from law department of the University of Wisconsin at Madison in 1899; was admitted to the bar the same year and commenced practice in Sheboygan, Wis.; district attorney of Sheboygan County 1905-1911; city attorney for Sheboygan 1913-1917; elected as a Republican to the Sixty-fifth and to the four succeeding Congresses (March 4, 1917-March 3, 1927); was not a candidate for reelection in 1926 to the Seventieth Congress; delegate to the Republican National Convention in 1924; resumed the practice of law in Sheboygan, Wis.; elected in 1928 as a judge of the fourth judicial circuit of Wisconsin; reelected in 1934, and served from January 1929 until his death at his summer home at Crystal Lake, near Sheboygan, Wis., August 26, 1934; interment in Forest Home Cemetery, Milwaukee, Wis.

**VOLK, Lester David,** a Representative from New York; born in Brooklyn, N.Y., September 17, 1884; attended the public and high schools; was graduated from Long Island Medical School in 1906 and from St. Lawrence University Law School in 1911; in 1906 engaged in the practice of medicine; editor of the Medical Economist; was admitted to the bar in 1913 and engaged in the practice of law; elected as a Progressive to the New York Assembly in 1912; declined to be a candidate for renomination; coroner's physician in 1914; during the First World War served as first lieutenant in the Medical Corps with the American Expeditionary Forces in 1918 and 1919; was largely instrumental in securing the soldiers' bonus granted by the State of New York; judge advocate of the Veterans of Foreign Wars for the State of New York in 1922; delegate to the Republican State conventions in 1920, 1924, 1942, and 1946; elected as a Republican to the Sixty-sixth Congress to fill the vacancy caused by the resignation of Reuben L. Haskell; reelected to the Sixty-seventh Congress and served from November 2, 1920, to March 3, 1923; unsuccessful candidate for reelection in 1922 to the Sixty-eighth Congress; member from New York City on the American Waterways Commission in 1924; assistant attorney general of New York State from March 1, 1943, to January 15, 1958; died in Brooklyn, N.Y., April 30, 1962; interment in Bayside Cemetery, Ozone Park, N.Y.

**VOLKMER, Harold Lee,** a Representative from Missouri; born in Jefferson City, Cole County, Mo., April 4, 1931; graduated from St. Peter's High School, Jefferson City; attended Jefferson City Junior College and St. Louis (Mo.) University; LL.B., University of Missouri School of Law, Columbia, 1955; admitted to the Missouri bar in 1955; served in the United States Army, 1955-1957; served as assistant attorney general of Missouri, 1955; in 1958, commenced private practice of law in Hannibal, Mo.; prosecuting attorney, Marion County, Mo., 1960-1966; member, Missouri State house of representatives, 1967-1976; elected as a Democrat to the Ninety-fifth and to the nine succeeding Congresses (January 3, 1977-January 3, 1997); is a resident of Hannibal, Mo.

**VOLLMER, Henry,** a Representative from Iowa; born in Davenport, Iowa, July 28, 1867; attended the public and high schools of Davenport; distributing clerk of the Fiftieth Congress in 1887 and 1888; studied law at the University of Iowa at Iowa City and Georgetown University, Washington, D.C.; was admitted to the bar in 1889 and commenced practice in Davenport, Iowa; member of the board of aldermen of Davenport in 1889; served as mayor of Davenport from 1893 to 1897; member of the board of education 1898-1901; corporation counsel in 1913 and 1914; elected as a Democrat to the Sixty-third Congress to fill the vacancy caused by the death of Irvin S. Pepper and served from February 10, 1914, to March 3, 1915; unsuccessful candidate for reelection in 1914 to the Sixty-fourth Congress; resumed the practice of his profession; died in Piedmont, Calif., August 25, 1930; the remains were cremated and the ashes placed in a crypt in the California Crematorium.

**VOLSTEAD, Andrew John,** a Representative from Minnesota; born near Kenyon, Goodhue County, Minn., October 31, 1860; attended the public schools of the district and St. Olaf's College, Northfield, Minn.; was graduated from Decorah Institute, Decorah, Iowa, in 1881; studied law; was admitted to the bar in 1883 and commenced practice in Lac qui Parle County, Minn.; moved to Grantsburg, Wis., in 1885, and in the following year to Granite Falls, Yellow Medicine County, Minn.; member of the board of education and served as president; city attorney of Granite Falls; prosecuting attorney of Yellow Medicine County, 1886-1902; mayor of Granite Falls, 1900-1902; elected as a Republican to the Fifty-eighth and to the nine succeeding Congresses (March 4, 1903-March 3, 1923); chairman, Committee on the Judiciary (Sixty-sixth and Sixty-seventh Congresses); sponsor of the Volstead Act of 1919 providing for Federal enforcement of the Eighteenth Amendment to the Constitution; unsuccessful candidate for reelection in 1922 to the Sixty-eighth Congress; resumed the practice of law, and resided in Granite Falls, Minn., until his death there on January 20, 1947; interment in City Cemetery.

Bibliography: DAB.

**VOORHEES, Charles Stewart** (son of Daniel Wolsey Voorhees), a Delegate from the Territory of Washington; born in Covington, Fountain County, Ind., June 4, 1853; attended Wabash College, Crawfordsville, Ind., and was graduated from Georgetown College, Washington, D.C., June 26, 1873; studied law; was admitted to the bar in 1875 and commenced practice in Terre Haute, Ind.; moved to the Territory of Washington in 1882 and settled in Colfax; prosecuting attorney for Whitman County 1882-1885; elected as a Democrat to the Forty-ninth and Fiftieth Congresses (March 4, 1885-March 3, 1889); unsuccessful candidate for reelection in 1888; resumed the practice of law in Colfax, Wash.; moved to Spokane, Wash., and continued the practice of law until his death there December 26, 1909; interment in Greenwood Cemetery.

**VOORHEES, Daniel Wolsey** (father of Charles Stewart Voorhees), a Representative and a Senator from Indiana; born in Liberty Township, Butler County, Ohio, September 26, 1827; moved with his parents to Indiana in early childhood; attended the common schools of Veedersburg, Ind.; graduated from Indiana Asbury (now

De Pauw) University at Greencastle in 1849; studied law; was admitted to the bar in 1851 and commenced practice in Covington, Ind.; moved to Terre Haute and continued the practice of law; unsuccessful candidate for election in 1856 to the Thirty-fifth Congress; United States district attorney for Indiana 1858-1861; elected as a Democrat to the Thirty-seventh and Thirty-eighth Congresses (March 4, 1861-March 3, 1865); presented credentials as a Member-elect to the Thirty-ninth Congress and served from March 4, 1865, to February 23, 1866, when he was succeeded by Henry D. Washburn, who contested the election; elected to the Forty-first and Forty-second Congresses (March 4, 1869-March 3, 1873); unsuccessful candidate for reelection in 1872 to the Forty-third Congress; appointed and subsequently elected as a Democrat to the United States Senate to fill the vacancy caused by the death of Oliver H.P.T. Morton; reelected in 1885 and again in 1891, and served from November 6, 1877, to March 3, 1897; unsuccessful candidate for reelection; chairman, Committee on the Library (Forty-sixth Congress), Committee on Finance (Fifty-third Congress); died in Washington, D.C., April 10, 1897; interment in Highland Lawn Cemetery, Terre Haute, Ind.

**Bibliography:** *DAB*; Jordan, Henry D. "Daniel Wolsey Voorhees." *Mississippi Valley Historical Review* 6 (March 1920): 532-55; Kenworthy, Leonard S. *The Tall Sycamore of the Wabash, Daniel Voorhees*. Boston: B. Humphries, 1936.

**VOORHIS, Charles Henry,** a Representative from New Jersey; born in Spring Valley, Bergen County, N.J., March 13, 1833; attended the district schools; was graduated from Rutgers College, New Brunswick, N.J., in 1853; moved to Jersey City; studied law; was admitted to the bar in 1856 and commenced practice in Jersey City, N.J.; delegate to the Republican National Convention of 1864; presiding judge of Bergen County, N.J., in 1868 and 1869; one of the organizers of the Hackensack Improvement Commission in 1869 and also of the Hackensack Academy; organized and served as first president of the Hackensack Water Co. in 1873; became interested in banking; elected as a Republican to the Forty-sixth Congress (March 4, 1879-March 3, 1881); was not a candidate for reelection in 1880 to the Forty-seventh Congress; resumed his former business pursuits; died in Jersey City, N.J., April 15, 1896; interment in New York Cemetery, Hackensack, Bergen County, N.J.

**VOORHIS, Horace Jeremiah (Jerry),** a Representative from California; born in Ottawa, Franklin County, Kans., April 6, 1901; attended the public schools in Ottawa, Kans., Oklahoma City, Okla., Peoria, Ill., and Pontiac, Mich; was graduated from Yale University in 1923, and from Claremont (Calif.) College in 1928; worked in a factory, handled freight on the railroads, and worked as a cowboy in Wyoming; traveling representative for the Young Men's Christian Association in Germany in 1923 and 1924; worked in an automobile assembling plant in Charlotte, N.C., in 1924 and 1925; teacher in Allendale Farm School, Lake Villa, Ill., in 1925 and 1926, and at the Dray Cottage Home for Boys, Laramie, Wyo., in 1926 and 1927; headmaster and trustee of the Voorhis School for Boys, San Dimas, Calif., 1928-1938; lecturer at Pomona College, Claremont, Calif., 1930-1935; unsuccessful candidate for the California State assembly in 1934; elected as a Democrat to the Seventy-fifth and to the four succeeding Congresses (January 3, 1937-January 3, 1947); unsuccessful candidate for reelection in 1946 to the Eightieth Congress; author; executive director of the Cooperative League of the United States of America, 1947-1967; became secretary, Group Health Association of America, in 1947; resided in Claremont, Calif., until his death there on September 11, 1984; interment in Mountain View Cemetery, Pasadena, Calif.

**Bibliography:** Bullock, Paul. *Jerry Voorhis, The Idealist as Politician*. New York: Vantage, 1978; Voorhis, Jerry. *Confessions of a Congressman*. 1947. Reprint. Westport, Conn.: Greenwood Press, 1970.

**VORYS, John Martin,** a Representative from Ohio; born in Lancaster, Fairfield County, Ohio, June 16, 1896; attended the public schools in Lancaster and Columbus, Ohio; during the First World War served overseas as a pilot in the United States Naval Air Service, retiring to inactive service in 1919 with rank of lieutenant; was graduated from Yale University in 1919 and from Ohio State University Law School at Columbus in 1923; teacher in the College of Yale, Changsha, China, in 1919 and 1920; assistant secretary, American delegation, Conference on Limitation of Armament, Washington, D.C., in 1921 and 1922; was admitted to the bar in 1923 and commenced practice in Columbus, Ohio; member of the State house of representatives in 1923 and 1924; served in the State senate in 1925 and 1926; director of aeronautics of Ohio in 1929 and 1930; elected as a Republican to the Seventy-sixth and to the nine succeeding Congresses (January 3, 1939-January 3, 1959); did not seek renomination in 1958; delegate to the United Nations Assembly in 1951; regent of Smithsonian Institution 1949-1959; resumed the practice of law; died in Columbus, Ohio, August 25, 1968; interment in Greenlawn Cemetery.

**Bibliography:** Livingston, Jeffery C. "Ohio Congressman John M. Vorys: A Republican Conservative Nationalist and Twentieth Century American Foreign Policy." Ph.D. dissertation, University of Toledo, 1989.

**VOSE, Roger,** a Representative from New Hampshire; born in Milton, Norfolk County, Mass., February 24, 1763; moved to New Hampshire in 1766 with his parents, who settled near Walpole, Cheshire County; was graduated from Harvard University in 1790; studied law; was admitted to the bar in 1793 and commenced practice in Walpole, N.H.; member of the State senate in 1809, 1810, and 1812; elected as a Federalist to the Thirteenth and Fourteenth Congresses (March 4, 1813-March 3, 1817); member of the State house of representatives in 1818; chief justice of the court of common pleas 1818-1820; chief justice of the court of sessions 1820-1825; resumed the practice of law; died in Walpole, N.H., October 26, 1841; interment in the Village Cemetery.

**VREELAND, Albert Lincoln,** a Representative from New Jersey; born in East Orange, Essex County, N.J., July 2, 1901; attended the public schools; served as ambulance driver for the American Red Cross in 1918 and 1919; was graduated from the New York Electrical School in New York City in 1919, the Peddie School, Hightstown, N.J., in 1922, and the New Jersey Law School at Newark in 1925; was admitted to the bar in 1927 and commenced practice in East Orange, N.J.; assistant city counsel and city prosecutor of East Orange 1929-1934; judge of the recorder's court of East Orange 1934-1938; elected as a Republican to the Seventy-sixth and Seventy-seventh Congresses (January 3, 1939-January 3, 1943); was a captain in the United States Army Reserve and on December 9, 1941, was granted leave of absence from the House of Representatives to go on active duty and assigned to the Military Intelligence Section of the War Department; transferred to the Seventy-sixth Infantry Division in April 1942; commissioned a major in Infantry on July 17, 1942, and on July 18, 1942, by Presidential directive, was ordered back to the House of Representatives; was not a candidate for renomination in 1942 to the Seventy-eighth Congress; reentered the Army on January 4, 1943, and served two years in Australia and New Guinea; commissioned a lieutenant colonel on August 27, 1944, and ordered to inactive duty August 27, 1945; colonel, A.I., USAR (retired); police commissioner of East Orange, N.J., 1945-1951; public relations officer for the Celanese Corporation of America 1945-1946; resumed the practice of law; died in Orange, N.J., May 3, 1975; interment in Glendale Cemetery, Bloomfield, N.J.

**VREELAND, Edward Butterfield,** a Representative from New York; born in Cuba, Allegany County, N.Y., December 7, 1856; was graduated from Friendship Academy in 1877; moved to Salamanca,

Cattaraugus County, N.Y., in 1869; superintendent of the public schools at Salamanca, N.Y., 1877-1882; studied law; was admitted to the bar in 1881, but did not engage in active practice; engaged in banking and in the oil and insurance business; became president of the Salamanca Trust Co. in 1891, served as postmaster of Salamanca 1889-1893; was elected as a Republican to the Fifty-sixth Congress to fill the vacancy caused by the resignation of Warren B. Hooker; reelected to the Fifty-seventh and to the five succeeding Congresses and served from November 7, 1899, to March 3, 1913; chairman, Committee on Banking and Currency (Sixty-first Congress); declined to be a candidate for renomination in 1912; appointed a member of the National Monetary Commission, serving as vice chairman 1909-1912; resumed former business pursuits in Salamanca, N.Y., until January 1, 1936, when he retired from active business; died in Salamanca, N.Y., May 8, 1936; interment in Wildwood Cemetery.

**VROOM, Peter Dumont,** a Representative from New Jersey; born in Hillsboro, Somerset County, N.J., December 12, 1791; attended the common schools and the Somerville (N.J.) Academy; was graduated from Columbia College, New York City, in 1808; studied law; was admitted to the bar in 1813 and commenced practice in Hillsboro; moved to Somerville in 1821; member of the New Jersey State general assembly in 1826, 1827, and 1829; became a sergeant at law in 1828; elected Governor of New Jersey by the Legislature as a Jacksonian in 1829, reelected in 1830 and 1831, and served from November 6, 1829 to October 26, 1832; unsuccessful candidate for reelection in 1832; again elected Governor in 1833, reelected in 1834, 1835, and 1836, and served from October 25, 1833 to October 28, 1836; on account of ill health declined to become a candidate for renomination; was appointed a commissioner to adjust the claims of the Choctaw Indians in 1837; elected as a Democrat to the Twenty-sixth Congress (March 4, 1839-March 3, 1841); unsuccessful candidate for reelection in 1840 to the Twenty-seventh Congress; moved to Trenton, N.J., and resumed the practice of law; delegate to the State constitutional convention in 1844; appointed chief justice of the supreme court of New Jersey in 1853, but declined; appointed Minister to Prussia on May 24, 1853 and served until August 1857; again resumed the practice of law; delegate to the peace convention held in Washington, D.C., in 1861 in an effort to devise means to prevent the impending war; reporter of the supreme court of New Jersey, 1862-1872; commissioner of the sinking fund of New Jersey (instituted to pay off the principal of the State's debt) from 1864 until his death in Trenton, N.J., November 18, 1873; interment in the cemetery of the First Reformed Dutch Church, Somerville, N.J.

**Bibliography:** *DAB.*

**VUCANOVICH, Barbara Farrell,** a Representative from Nevada; born in Camp Dix, New Jersey, June 22, 1921; attended Miss Quinn's School, Albany, N.Y.; graduated from Albany Academy for Girls, Albany, 1938; attended, Manhattan College of Sacred Heart, New York City, 1938-1939; businesswoman; district staff assistant for Senator Paul Laxalt of Nevada, 1974-1982; delegate, Nevada State Republican conventions, 1952-1980; delegate to the Republican National Conventions of 1976 and 1980; elected as a Republican to the Ninety-eighth and to the six succeeding Congresses (January 3, 1983-January 3, 1997); was not a candidate for reelection in 1996 to the One Hundred Fifth Congress; is a resident of Reno, Nev.

**VURSELL, Charles Wesley** (cousin of Carl Bert Albert), a Representative from Illinois; born in Salem, Marion County, Ill., February 8, 1881; attended the public schools of Marion County, Ill.; hardware merchant in 1904; sheriff of Marion County 1910-1914; member of the State house of representatives 1914-1916; owner and publisher of the Salem Republican 1916-1948; elected as a Republican to the Seventy-eighth and to the seven succeeding

Congresses (January 3, 1943-January 3, 1959); unsuccessful candidate for reelection in 1958 to the Eighty-sixth Congress; retired and resided in Salem, Ill., where he died September 21, 1974; interment in East Lawn Cemetery.

# W

**WACHTER, Frank Charles,** a Representative from Maryland; born in Baltimore, Md., September 16, 1861; attended private schools and St. Paul's Evangelical School at Baltimore, Md.; learned the trade of clothing cutter and in 1892 engaged in the cloth-shrinking business; member of the jail board of Baltimore 1896-1898; unsuccessful candidate for police commissioner of Baltimore in 1898; elected as a Republican to the Fifty-sixth and to the three succeeding Congresses (March 4, 1899-March 3, 1907); was not a candidate for renomination in 1906; resumed his former business pursuits in Baltimore; member of the board of managers of Maryland Penitentiary from 1909 until his death in Baltimore, Md., on July 1, 1910; interment in Loudon Park Cemetery.

**WADDELL, Alfred Moore,** a Representative from North Carolina; born in Hillsboro, Orange County, N.C., September 16, 1834; attended Bingham's School and Caldwell Institute in Hillsboro; was graduated from the University of North Carolina at Chapel Hill in 1853; studied law; was admitted to the bar in 1855 and began practice in Wilmington, New Hanover County, N.C.; clerk of a court of equity 1858-1861; delegate to the Constitutional Union National Convention at Baltimore in 1860; engaged in newspaper work; edited the Wilmington Daily Herald in 1860 and 1861; served as lieutenant colonel of the Third Cavalry, Forty-first North Carolina Regiment, during the Civil War; elected as a Democrat to the Forty-second and to the three succeeding Congresses (March 4, 1871-March 3, 1879); chairman, Committee on Post Office and Post Roads (Forty-fifth Congress); unsuccessful candidate for reelection in 1878 to the Forty-sixth Congress; resumed the practice of law and also engaged in literary pursuits; editor of the Charlotte Journal-Observer in 1881 and 1882; delegate to the Democratic National Conventions in 1880 and 1896; mayor of Wilmington 1898-1904; died in Wilmington, N.C., March 17, 1912; interment in Oakdale Cemetery.

**Bibliography:** *DAB.*

**WADDILL, Edmund, Jr.,** a Representative from Virginia; born in Charles City County, Va., May 22, 1855; educated by private tutors and attended Norwood Academy; deputy clerk of the courts of Charles City, New Kent, Hanover, and Henrico Counties and of the circuit court of the city of Richmond; studied law privately and at the University of Virginia at Charlottesville; admitted to the bar in 1877 and commenced the practice of law in Richmond in 1878; judge of the Henrico County Court in 1880; resigned in 1883 to accept the position of United States attorney for the eastern district of Virginia, which he held until 1885; member of the Virginia house of delegates from 1886 to March 4, 1889, when he resigned; unsuccessful Republican candidate for election in 1886 to the Fiftieth Congress; successfully contested as a Republican the election of George D. Wise to the Fifty-first Congress and served from April 12, 1890, to March 3, 1891; was not a candidate for renomination in 1890; resumed the practice of law in Richmond, Va.; delegate to the Republican National Conventions in 1892 and 1896; appointed judge of the District Court of the United States for the Eastern District of Virginia, March 22, 1908, and served until June 2, 1921, when he was appointed as judge of the United States Circuit Court of Appeals for the fourth circuit and was presiding judge at the time of his death in Richmond, Va., April 9, 1931; interment in Hollywood Cemetery.

**WADDILL, James Richard,** a Representative from Missouri; born in Springfield, Greene County, Mo., November 22, 1842; attended private schools and Springfield College; during the Civil

War enlisted as a private in the Union Army and served from 1861 to 1863, when he resigned, having attained the rank of first lieutenant; studied law; was admitted to the bar in 1864 and commenced practice in Springfield, Mo.; prosecuting attorney of Greene County 1874-1876; elected as a Democrat to the Forty-sixth Congress (March 4, 1879-March 3, 1881); resumed the practice of law and also engaged in mining operations near Joplin, Mo.; died in Deming, Luna County, N.Mex., June 14, 1917; interment in Mountain View Cemetery.

**WADE, Benjamin Franklin** (brother of Edward Wade), a Senator from Ohio; born in Feeding Hills, near Springfield, Hampden County, Mass., October 27, 1800; received his early education from his mother; moved with his parents to Andover, Ohio, in 1821; taught school; studied medicine in Albany, N.Y., 1823-1825; returned to Ohio; studied law; was admitted to the bar in 1828 and commenced practice in Jefferson, Ashtabula County, Ohio; prosecuting attorney of Ashtabula County, 1835-1837; Ohio State senator, 1837-1838 and 1841-1842; judge of the third judicial court of Ohio, 1847-1851; elected as a Whig to the United States Senate to fill the vacancy in the term commencing March 4, 1851, caused by the failure of the legislature to elect; reelected as a Republican in 1856 and again in 1863, and served from March 15, 1851 to March 3, 1869; unsuccessful candidate for renomination in 1868; served as President pro tempore of the Senate during the Thirty-ninth and Fortieth Congresses; chairman, Committee on Territories (Thirty-seventh, Thirty-eighth, and Thirty-ninth Congresses); co-sponsor of the Wade-Davis Bill of 1864, establishing requirements (such as abolition of slavery and administration of loyalty oaths) for the readmission of former Confederate states into the Union; unsuccessful Republican candidate for the vice presidential nomination in 1868; resumed the practice of law in Jefferson, Ohio, in 1869; appointed a government director of the Union Pacific Railroad; member of the Santo Domingo Commission in 1871; died in Jefferson, Ashtabula County, Ohio, on March 2, 1878; interment in Oakdale Cemetery.

**Bibliography:** *DAB*; Shover, Kenneth. "The Life of Benjamin F. Wade." Ph.D. dissertation, University of California, Berkeley, 1962; Trefousse, Hans L. *Benjamin Franklin Wade: Radical Republican From Ohio.* New York: Twayne Publishers, 1963.

**WADE, Edward** (brother of Benjamin Franklin Wade), a Representative from Ohio; born in West Springfield, Hampden County, Mass., November 22, 1802; received a limited schooling; moved to Andover, Ashtabula County, Ohio, in 1821; studied law; was admitted to the bar in 1827 and commenced practice in Jefferson, Ashtabula County, Ohio; justice of the peace of Ashtabula County in 1831; moved to Unionville in 1832; prosecuting attorney of Ashtabula County in 1833; moved to Cleveland in 1837; elected as a Free-Soil candidate to the Thirty-third Congress, and reelected as a Republican to the three succeeding Congresses (March 4, 1853-March 3, 1861); was not a candidate for renomination in 1860 to the Thirty-seventh Congress; died in East Cleveland, Cuyahoga County, Ohio, August 13, 1866; interment in Woodland Cemetery, Cleveland, Ohio.

**WADE, Martin Joseph,** a Representative from Iowa; born in Burlington, Chittenden County, Vt., October 20, 1861; moved to Iowa with his parents at an early age; attended the common schools and St. Joseph's College (later Columbia University), Dubuque, Iowa; was graduated from the law department of the University of Iowa at Iowa City in 1886; was admitted to the bar the same year and practiced in Iowa City, Johnson County, Iowa, 1886-1893; judge of the eighth judicial district of Iowa, 1893-1903; lecturer in the law department of the University of Iowa, 1891-1903, and professor of medical jurisprudence, 1895-1905; president of the Iowa State Bar Association in 1897 and 1898; elected as a Democrat to the Fifty-eighth Congress (March 4, 1903-March 3, 1905); unsuccessful

candidate for reelection in 1904 to the Fifty-ninth Congress; resumed the practice of his profession in Iowa City, Iowa; delegate to the Democratic National Conventions of 1904 and 1912; appointed judge of the United States District Court for the Southern District of Iowa in 1915, and served until his death in Los Angeles, Calif., April 16, 1931, while on a visit; interment in St. Joseph's Cemetery, Iowa City, Iowa.

**Bibliography:** *DAB*.

**WADE, William Henry,** a Representative from Missouri; born near Springfield, Clark County, Ohio, November 3, 1835; attended the common schools, Grove Academy, and Antioch College, Yellow Springs, Ohio; engaged in agricultural pursuits; during the Civil War enlisted in the Union Army April 17, 1861, and was mustered out on April 26, 1866; moved to Missouri in May 1866 and resumed agricultural pursuits; member, Missouri State house of representatives, 1881-1884; elected as a Republican to the Forty-ninth and to the two succeeding Congresses (March 4, 1885-March 3, 1891); chairman, Committee on Labor (Fifty-first Congress); unsuccessful candidate for reelection in 1890 to the Fifty-second Congress; again engaged in agricultural pursuits; died in Springfield, Greene County, Mo., January 13, 1911; interment in Maple Park Cemetery.

**WADLEIGH, Bainbridge,** a Senator from New Hampshire; born in Bradford, Merrimack County, N.H., January 4, 1831; attended the common schools and Kimball Union Academy, Plainfield, N.H.; studied law; was admitted to the bar in 1850 and commenced practice in Milford, Hillsborough County, N.H.; served six terms as town moderator; member, State house of representatives 1855-1856, 1859-1860, 1869-1872; elected as a Republican to the United States Senate and served from March 4, 1873, to March 3, 1879; unsuccessful candidate for reelection in 1878; chairman, Committee on Patents (Forty-fourth and Forty-fifth Congresses), Committee on Privileges and Elections (Forty-fifth Congress); resumed the practice of law in Boston, Mass., where he died January 24, 1891; interment in West Street Cemetery, Milford, N.H.

**WADSWORTH, James,** a Delegate from Connecticut; born in Durham, Middlesex County, Conn., July 8, 1730; received a thorough English training and was graduated from Yale College in 1748; studied law and was admitted to the bar; town clerk 1756-1786; justice of the peace in 1762; appointed judge of the New Haven County Court in 1773 and promoted to presiding judge five years later; member of the committee of safety; served in the Revolutionary Army as a colonel and brigadier general of Connecticut Militia, and as a second major general 1777-1779; Member of the Continental Congress 1784; member of the State executive council 1785-1789; State comptroller in 1786 and 1787; member of the State ratification convention in 1788 and opposed adoption of the Constitution; died in Durham, Conn., September 22, 1817; interment in the Old Cemetery.

**WADSWORTH, James Wolcott** (father of James Wolcott Wadsworth, Jr.), a Representative from New York; born in Philadelphia, Pa., October 12, 1846; attended Hopkins Grammar School, New Haven, Conn.; served in the Civil War as captain on the staff of General Gouverneur K. Warren and was made brevet major; after the war settled in Geneseo, N.Y., and engaged in agricultural pursuits; supervisor of Geneseo from 1873 until 1876; member of the New York State assembly in 1878 and 1879; New York State comptroller in 1880 and 1881; elected as a Republican to the Forty-seventh Congress to fill the vacancy caused by the resignation of Eldridge G. Lapham; reelected to the Forty-eighth Congress and served from November 8, 1881, to March 3, 1885; elected to the Fifty-second and to the seven succeeding Congresses (March 4, 1891-March 3, 1907); chairman, Committee on Agriculture (Fifty-fourth through Fifty-ninth Congresses); unsuccessful candidate for reelection in 1906 to the Sixtieth Congress; elected president of the board of managers for the National Home for Disabled Volunteer

Soldiers; engaged in agricultural pursuits and interested in livestock; member of the New York State Constitutional Convention in 1914; president of the Genesee Valley National Bank; died in Washington, D.C., December 24, 1926; interment in the family plot in Temple Hill Cemetery, Geneseo, N.Y.

**WADSWORTH, James Wolcott, Jr.** (son of James Wadsworth), a Senator and a Representative from New York; born in Geneseo, N.Y., August 12, 1877; received preparatory education at St. Mark's School, Southboro, Mass.; graduated from Yale University in 1898; during the Spanish-American War served as a private in the Puerto Rican campaign in 1898; engaged in livestock and agricultural pursuits near Geneseo, N.Y., and as manager of a ranch in Texas from 1911 to 1915; member, New York State assembly, 1905-1910, serving as speaker, 1906-1910; elected as a Republican to the United States Senate in 1914; reelected in 1920, and served from March 4, 1915 to March 3, 1927; unsuccessful candidate for reelection in 1926; chairman, Committee on Military Affairs (Sixty-sixth through Sixty-ninth Congresses); Republican whip 1915; resumed agricultural pursuits; elected to the Seventy-third and to the eight succeeding Congresses (March 4, 1933-January 3, 1951); was not a candidate for renomination in 1950 to the Eighty-second Congress; appointed by President Harry S Truman as chairman of the National Security Training Commission in 1951, and served until his death in Washington, D.C., June 21, 1952; interment in Temple Hill Cemetery, Geneseo, N.Y.

Bibliography: *DAB*; Fausold, Martin. *James W. Wadsworth, Jr.: The Gentleman From New York*. Syracuse: Syracuse University Press, 1975; Holthusen, Henry. *James W. Wadsworth, Jr.: A Biographical Sketch*. New York: G.P. Putnam's Sons, 1926.

**WADSWORTH, Jeremiah,** a Delegate and a Representative from Connecticut; born in Hartford, Conn., July 12, 1743; attended the common schools; went to sea in 1761; became first mate of a vessel and subsequently master; served as deputy and commissary general 1775-1778 during the Revolution; Member of the Continental Congress in 1788; member of the Connecticut ratification convention in 1788; elected to the First, Second, and Third Congresses (March 4, 1789-March 3, 1795); was not a candidate for reelection; member of the State house of representatives in 1795 and of the State executive council 1795-1801; engaged in agricultural pursuits; died in Hartford, Conn., April 30, 1804; interment in Ancient Burying Ground.

Bibliography: *DAB*; Destler, Chester McArthur. "The Gentleman Farmer and the New Agriculture: Jeremiah Wadsworth." *Agricultural History* 46 (January 1972): 135-53; Platt, John D.R. "Jeremiah Wadsworth: Federalist Entrepreneur." Ph.D. dissertation, Columbia University, 1955.

**WADSWORTH, Peleg,** a Representative from Massachusetts; born in Duxbury, Mass., May 6, 1748; attended public and private schools, and was graduated from Harvard College in 1769; engaged in mercantile pursuits in Kingston, Mass.; served in the Revolutionary Army as an aide to General Artemas Ward in 1776; engineer under General Thomas in 1776 and 1777; brigadier general of militia in 1777; adjutant general of Massachusetts in 1778; moved to Portland, Maine (then a district of Massachusetts), in 1784 and became a land agent; served in the Massachusetts senate in 1792; elected to the Third Congress and reelected as a Federalist to the six succeeding Congresses (March 4, 1793-March 3, 1807); moved to Oxford County, Maine, in 1807 to survey and improve a large tract of land granted to him by the Government; died in Hiram, Oxford County, Maine, November 12, 1829; interment in the family cemetery at Wadsworth Hall.

Bibliography: *DAB*; Wadsworth, Peleg. *Letters of General Peleg Wadsworth to His Son John, Student at Harvard College, 1796-1798; Biographical Chapter and Notes by George and Margaret Rose*. Portland, Maine: Maine Historical Society, 1961.

**WADSWORTH, William Henry,** a Representative from Kentucky; born in Maysville, Mason County, Ky., July 4, 1821; attended town and county private schools; was graduated from Augusta College, Bracken County, Ky., in 1841; studied law; was admitted to the bar in 1844 and commenced practice in Maysville, Ky.; member of the Kentucky senate, 1853-1856; presidential elector on the Constitutional Union ticket in 1860; elected as a Unionist to the Thirty-seventh and Thirty-eighth Congresses (March 4, 1861-March 3, 1865); was not a candidate for renomination in 1864 to the Thirty-ninth Congress; during the Civil War served as aide to General Nelson, with the rank of colonel, at the Battle of Ivy Mountain; appointed United States commissioner to Mexico, under the treaty of Washington for the adjustment of claims, by President Ulysses S. Grant in 1869; elected as a Republican to the Forty-ninth Congress (March 4, 1885-March 3, 1887); was not a candidate for renomination in 1886 to the Fiftieth Congress; resumed the practice of law; died in Maysville, Mason County, Ky., April 2, 1893; interment in Maysville Cemetery.

**WAGENER, David Douglas,** a Representative from Pennsylvania; born in Easton, Pa., October 11, 1792; attended the common schools; captain of the Easton Union Guards 1816-1829; engaged in mercantile pursuits; elected as a Jacksonian to the Twenty-third and Twenty-fourth Congresses and elected as a Democrat to the Twenty-fifth and Twenty-sixth Congresses (March 4, 1833-March 3, 1841); chairman, Committee on Militia (Twenty-fifth Congress); established the Easton Bank in 1852 and was its president until his death in Easton, Northampton County, Pa., October 1, 1860; interment in Easton Cemetery.

**WAGGAMAN, George Augustus,** a Senator from Louisiana; born in Caroline County, Md., in 1782; completed preparatory studies under private tutors; studied law; was admitted to the bar in Caroline County, Md., in 1811; served in the War of 1812 under General Andrew Jackson at New Orleans; settled in Baton Rouge, La., and commenced the practice of law in 1813; attorney general of the third district of Louisiana in 1813; judge of the third judicial circuit court in 1818; assistant judge of the criminal court in New Orleans in 1819; interested in sugarcane growing; secretary of state of Louisiana 1830-1832; elected to the United States Senate to fill the vacancy caused by the resignation of Edward Livingston and served from November 15, 1831, to March 3, 1835; resumed the practice of law in New Orleans and also again engaged in sugarcane planting; participated as a principal in a duel and received injuries from which he died in New Orleans, La., March 31, 1843; interment in Girod Cemetery.

**WAGGONNER, Joseph David, Jr.,** a Representative from Louisiana; born near Plain Dealing, Bossier Parish, La., September 7, 1918; B.A., Louisiana Polytechnic Institute, Ruston, La., 1941; served as a lieutenant commander in the United States Navy, January 1942 to November 1945, and also in the Korean conflict, May 1951 to November 1952; member of the Bossier Parish School Board, 1954-1961, serving as president, 1956-1957; member, Louisiana State Board of Education (Third Public Service Commission District), 1960-1961; elected president of the United Schools Committee of Louisiana and president of Louisiana School Boards Association in 1961; operator of a wholesale petroleum products distribution agency for North Bossier Parish, 1952 to present; elected as a Democrat to the Eighty-seventh Congress, December 19, 1961, by special election to fill the vacancy caused by the death of Overton Brooks; reelected to the eight succeeding Congresses, and served from December 19, 1961 to January 3, 1979; was not a candidate for reelection in 1978 to the Ninety-sixth Congress; is a resident of Plain Dealing, La.

Bibliography: Childs, David W. "Congressman Joe D. Waggonner: A Study in Political Influence." *North Louisiana Historical Association Journal* 13 (Fall 1982): 118-130.

**WAGNER, Earl Thomas,** a Representative from Ohio; born in Cincinnati, Hamilton County, Ohio, April 27, 1908; attended parochial and public schools; was graduated from the Salmon P. Chase College of Law, Cincinnati, Ohio, in 1930; was admitted to the bar in September 1930 and commenced the practice of law in Cincinnati, Ohio; district counsel of Home Owners Loan Corporation, 1933-1934; special counsel to the attorney general of Ohio, 1937-1938; city solicitor of Sharonville, Ohio, 1938-1939; member of the board of education of the Cincinnati School district, 1944-1947; elected as a Democrat to the Eighty-first Congress (January 3, 1949-January 3, 1951); unsuccessful candidate for reelection in 1950 to the Eighty-second Congress; unsuccessful candidate for election in 1952 to the Eighty-third Congress, and for election in 1954 to the Eighty-fourth Congress; resumed the practice of law; city solicitor of Addyston, Ohio, in 1952 and 1953; general counsel for a savings and loan bank in Cincinnati; was a resident of Cincinnati until his death there on March 6, 1990; interment in St. Joseph New Cemetery, Delhi Township, Ohio.

**WAGNER, Peter Joseph,** a Representative from New York; born at Wagners Hollow in the town of Palatine, Montgomery County, N.Y., August 14, 1795; moved to Fort Plain, N.Y., with his parents in 1805; completed preparatory studies; attended Fairfield Academy in 1810 and 1811; was graduated from Union College, Schenectady, N.Y., in 1816; studied law; was admitted to the bar in September 1819 and commenced practice at Fort Plain, N.Y.; also engaged in agricultural pursuits and banking; unsuccessful candidate for election in 1834 to the Twenty-fourth Congress; elected as a Whig to the Twenty-sixth Congress (March 4, 1839-March 3, 1841); chairman, Committee on Expenditures in the Department of War (Twenty-sixth Congress); continued the practice of law at Fort Plain until May 1873, when he retired; died at Fort Plain, Montgomery County, N.Y., September 13, 1884; interment in Fort Plain Cemetery.

**WAGNER, Robert Ferdinand,** a Senator from New York; born in Nastatten, Province Hessen-Nassau, Germany, June 8, 1877; immigrated with his parents to the United States in 1885 and settled in New York City; attended the public schools; graduated from the College of the City of New York in 1898 and from New York Law School in 1900; was admitted to the bar in 1900 and commenced practice in New York City; member, State assembly 1905-1908; member, State senate 1909-1918, the last eight years as Democratic floor leader; chairman of the State Factory Investigating Committee 1911-1915; delegate to the New York constitutional conventions in 1915 and 1938; justice of the supreme court of New York 1919-1926; elected as a Democrat to the United States Senate in 1926; reelected in 1932, 1938, and again in 1944, and served from March 4, 1927, until his resignation on June 28, 1949, due to ill health; chairman, Committee on Patents (Seventy-third Congress), Committee on Public Lands and Surveys (Seventy-third and Seventy-fourth Congresses), Committee on Banking and Currency (Seventy-fifth through Seventy-ninth Congresses); sponsor of the Wagner (National Labor Relations) Act of 1935, affirming the right of workers to be represented by labor unions and to engage in collective bargaining with employers, and establishing the National Labor Relations Board; delegate to the United Nations Monetary and Financial Conference at Bretton Woods in 1944; died in New York City, May 4, 1953; interment in Calvary Cemetery, Queens, New York City.

Bibliography: *DAB*; Bryne, Thomas. "The Social Thought of Senator Robert F. Wagner." Ph.D. dissertation, Georgetown University, 1951; Huthmacher, J. Joseph. *Senator Robert F. Wagner and the Rise of Urban Liberalism*. New York: Atheneum, 1968.

**WAGONER, George Chester Robinson,** a Representative from Missouri; born in Cincinnati, Ohio, September 3, 1863; attended the public schools and Beaumont Hospital Medical College,

St. Louis, Mo.; president of the Wagoner Undertaking Co. and secretary and treasurer of the H.H. Wagoner Realty Co., St. Louis, Mo.; successfully contested as a Republican the election of James J. Butler to the Fifty-seventh Congress and served from February 26, 1901, to March 3, 1903; declined to be a candidate for renomination in 1904; resumed business activities; died in St. Louis, Mo., April 27, 1946; interment in Bellefontaine Cemetery.

**WAINWRIGHT, Jonathan Mayhew,** a Representative from New York; born in New York City December 10, 1864; was graduated from Columbia College and Columbia School of Political Science, New York City, in 1884, and from Columbia Law School in 1886; was admitted to the bar the same year and practiced in New York City and in Westchester County, N.Y.; served in the Twelfth Infantry of the New York National Guard from 1889 until 1903; also served in the war with Spain as captain of the Twelfth Regiment, New York Volunteers; member of the New York State assembly, 1902-1908; served in the New York State senate, 1909-1913; appointed as a member of the first New York State Workmen's Compensation Commission in 1914 and served until 1915; served as lieutenant colonel, inspector general's department, New York National Guard, on the Mexican border in 1916; during the First World War served as a lieutenant colonel in the Twenty-seventh Division, 1917-1919; Assistant Secretary of War from March 14, 1921, to March 4, 1923, when he resigned; elected as a Republican to the Sixty-eighth and to the three succeeding Congresses (March 4, 1923-March 3, 1931); was not a candidate for renomination in 1930 to the Seventy-second Congress; resumed the practice of law; member of the Westchester County Park Commission, 1930-1937; died in Rye, N.Y., June 3, 1945; interment in Greenwood Union Cemetery.

**WAINWRIGHT, Stuyvesant, II,** a Representative from New York; born in New York City, March 16, 1921; moved to East Hampton, N.Y., in 1927; graduated from Westminster School, Simsbury, Conn.; interrupted his legal studies at Yale University when twenty years of age to enlist as a private in the United States Army on January 30, 1942; attended officers candidate school; went overseas on December 30, 1943, rose through the ranks, and was commanding officer of the Office of Strategic Services units of the First Army; returned to the United States on June 10, 1945, and spent the last three months of his service as adviser on intelligence coordination in the War Department in Washington, D.C.; was discharged as a captain on December 13, 1945; lieutenant colonel in the Active Army Reserve; resumed legal studies and graduated from Yale University Law School in 1947; was admitted to the bar in 1948 and commenced practice in New York City; elected as a Republican to the Eighty-third and to the three succeeding Congresses (January 3, 1953-January 3, 1961); unsuccessful candidate for reelection in 1960 to the Eighty-seventh Congress; political science instuctor at Rutgers University, 1960-1961; resumed the practice of law; president, 1975-1979, and director, 1975-1985, Miltope Corp.; is a resident of Wainscott, N.Y.

**WAIT, John Turner,** a Representative from Connecticut; born in New London, Conn., August 27, 1811; moved with his mother to Norwich, Conn.; attended the common schools and Trinity College, Hartford, Conn., for two years; engaged in mercantile pursuits; studied law; was admitted to the bar in 1836 and began practice in Norwich; State's attorney for the county of New London 1842-1844 and 1846-1854; unsuccessful candidate for election as Lieutenant Governor in 1854, 1855, 1856, and 1857; served in the State senate in 1865 and 1866, the latter year as president pro tempore; member of the State house of representatives in 1867, 1871, and 1873, serving as speaker in 1867; elected as a Republican to the Forty-fourth Congress to fill the vacancy caused by the death of Henry H. Starkweather; reelected as a Republican to the Forty-fifth and to the four succeeding Congresses and served from April 12, 1876, to March 3, 1887; was not a candidate for renomination in

1886; resumed the practice of his profession; died in Norwich, Conn., April 21, 1899; interment in Yantic Cemetery.

**WAKEFIELD, James Beach,** a Representative from Minnesota; born in Winsted, Conn., March 21, 1825; attended the public schools at Westfield, Mass., and Jonesville, N.Y.; was graduated from Trinity College, Hartford, Conn., in 1846; studied law in Painesville, Lake County, Ohio; was admitted to the bar and commenced practice in Delphi, Ind., in 1852; moved to Shakopee, Minn., in 1854; first judge of the probate court of Faribault County, Minn.; elected as a member of the Minnesota State house of representatives in 1858, 1863, and 1866, serving as speaker in the session of 1866; member of the State senate, 1867-1869; appointed receiver of the United States Land Office at Winnebago City, Minn., on June 1, 1869, and served until January 15, 1875, when he resigned; Lieutenant Governor of Minnesota, 1875-1877; elected as a Republican to the Forty-eighth and Forty-ninth Congresses (March 4, 1883-March 3, 1887); retired from public life; died at Blue Earth, Faribault County, Minn., August 25, 1910; interment in Evergreen Cemetery, Painesville, Ohio.

**WAKEMAN, Abram,** a Representative from New York; born in Greenfield Hill, Fairfield County, Conn., May 31, 1824; completed preparatory studies and was graduated from Herkimer Academy, New York; studied law at Little Falls, N.Y.; was admitted to the bar and commenced practice in New York City in 1847; member of the State assembly in 1850 and 1851; elected as a Whig to the Thirty-fourth Congress (March 4, 1855-March 3, 1857); unsuccessful Republican candidate for reelection in 1856 to the Thirty-fifth Congress; delegate to the Republican National Convention in 1856; at the outbreak of the Civil War raised the Eighty-first Pennsylvania Volunteers; postmaster of New York City from March 21, 1862, to September 18, 1864; surveyor of the port of New York City; resumed the practice of law; died in New York City June 29, 1889; interment in Greenwood Cemetery, Brooklyn, N.Y.

**WAKEMAN, Seth,** a Representative from New York; born in Franklin, Vt., January 15, 1811; attended the common schools; moved to Batavia, N.Y., where he studied law; was admitted to the bar and commenced the practice of law; district attorney for Genesee County 1850-1856; member of the State assembly in 1856 and 1857; member of the State constitutional convention in 1867 and 1868; elected as a Republican to the Forty-second Congress (March 4, 1871-March 3, 1873); was not a candidate for renomination in 1872; resumed the practice of law; died in Batavia, Genesee County, N.Y., January 4, 1880; interment in Elmwood Cemetery.

**WALBRIDGE, David Safford,** a Representative from Michigan; born in Bennington, Vt., July 30, 1802; attended the common schools; moved to New York in 1820; engaged in mercantile and agricultural pursuits at Geneseo from 1820 to 1826, and at Jamestown from 1826 to 1842; moved to Kalamazoo, Mich., in 1842; again engaged in mercantile pursuits; became a large landowner and stock raiser; member of the Michigan State house of representatives in 1848; served two terms in the State senate; served as permanent chairman of the convention that met under the oaks at Jackson, Mich., July 6, 1854, at the organization of the Republican Party in Michigan; elected as a Republican to the Thirty-fourth and Thirty-fifth Congresses (March 4, 1855-March 3, 1859); resumed his former pursuits; appointed postmaster of Kalamazoo by President Andrew Johnson; died in Kalamazoo, Mich., June 15, 1868; interment in Mountain Home Cemetery.

**WALBRIDGE, Henry Sanford** (cousin of Hiram Walbridge), a Representative from New York; born in Norwich, Conn., April 8, 1801; attended school in Bennington, Vt.; moved to Ithaca, Tompkins County, N.Y., in 1820; studied law; was admitted to the bar and commenced practice in Ithaca; clerk of the board of supervisors of Tompkins County in 1824; member of the State assembly in 1829; president of the village council of Ithaca, Tompkins County, in 1829 and again in 1842; again a member of the State assembly in 1846; elected as a Whig to the Thirty-second Congress (March 4, 1851-March 3, 1853); declined to be a candidate for renomination in 1852; trustee of Ithaca Academy 1858-1868; judge and surrogate of Tompkins County 1859-1868; moved to Leonia, N.J., in 1868 and practiced law in New York City; killed in a railroad accident at Bergen Tunnel near Hoboken, N.J., January 27, 1869; interment in Ithaca City Cemetery, Ithaca, N.Y.

**WALBRIDGE, Hiram** (cousin of Henry Sanford Walbridge), a Representative from New York; born in Ithaca, Tompkins County, N.Y., February 2, 1821; moved to Ohio with his parents, who settled in Toledo in 1836; attended the public schools and the University of Ohio at Athens; studied law; was admitted to the bar in 1842 and commenced practice in Toledo; appointed brigadier general of militia in 1843; moved to New York and engaged in mercantile pursuits at Buffalo; member of the board of aldermen; moved to New York City in 1847 and continued mercantile pursuits; elected as a Democrat to the Thirty-third Congress (March 4, 1853-March 3, 1855); declined to be a candidate for renomination in 1854; resumed his former pursuits in New York City; unsuccessful Union candidate for election in 1862 to the Thirty-eighth Congress; president of the International Commercial Convention held in Detroit, Mich., July 11, 1865; elected as a delegate to the Southern Loyalist Convention at Philadelphia in 1866; died in New York City December 6, 1870; interment in Glenwood Cemetery, Washington, D.C.

**WALCOTT, Frederic Collin,** a Senator from Connecticut; born in New York Mills, Oneida County, N.Y., February 19, 1869; attended the public schools of Utica, N.Y.; graduated from Lawrenceville (N.J.) School in 1886, from Phillips Academy, Andover, Mass., in 1887, and from Yale University in 1891; moved to New York City in 1907 and engaged in the manufacture of cotton cloth and in banking; moved to Norfolk, Conn., in 1910, but continued his business connections in New York City; during the First World War served with the United States Food Administration; president of the Connecticut Board of Fisheries and Game 1923-1928; chairman of the Connecticut Water Commission 1925-1928; member, State senate 1925-1929, serving as president pro tempore 1927-1929; elected as a Republican to the United States Senate and served from March 4, 1929, to January 3, 1935; unsuccessful candidate for reelection in 1934; commissioner of welfare of Connecticut 1935-1939; member of the advisory committee of the Human Welfare Group of Yale University 1920-1948; regent of the Smithsonian Institution 1941-1948; died in Stamford, Conn., on April 27, 1949; interment in Center Cemetery, Norfolk, Conn.

**WALDEN, Hiram,** a Representative from New York; born in Pawlet, Vt., August 21, 1800; attended the district schools; moved to Berne, Albany County, N.Y., in 1818 and to Waldenville, Schoharie County, N.Y., in 1821; engaged in the manufacture of axes; major general of militia; member of the State assembly in 1836; was one of the supervisors of the town of Wright in 1842; elected as a Democrat to the Thirty-first Congress (March 4, 1849-March 3, 1851); chairman, Committee on Patents (Thirty-first Congress); was not a candidate for renomination in 1850 to the Thirty-second Congress; resumed his former manufacturing pursuits; was also employed in the customhouse in New York City; lived in retirement until his death in Waldenville, N.Y., July 21, 1880; interment in Pine Grove Cemetery, Berne, Albany County, N.Y.

**WALDEN, Madison Miner,** a Representative from Iowa; born near Scioto, Brush Creek, Adams County, Ohio, October 6, 1836; moved to Iowa in 1852; attended Denmark Academy, Lee County, Iowa, and Wesleyan College, Mount Pleasant, Iowa, and was graduated from Wesleyan University, Delaware, Ohio, in 1859; served in the Union Army as captain in the Sixth Regiment, Iowa

Volunteer Infantry, and the Eighth Regiment, Iowa Volunteer Cavalry, from May 1861 to May 1865; taught school; published the Centerville (Iowa) Citizen 1865-1874; member of the State house of representatives in 1866 and 1867; served in the State senate in 1868 and 1869; Lieutenant Governor of Iowa in 1870; elected as a Republican to the Forty-second Congress (March 4, 1871-March 3, 1873); unsuccessful candidate for renomination in 1872; engaged in agricultural pursuits and coal mining in Centerville, Appanoose County, Iowa; was appointed chief clerk in the office of the Solicitor of the Treasury in 1889 and served until his death in Washington, D.C., July 24, 1891; interment in Oakland Cemetery, Centerville, Iowa.

**WALDHOLTZ, Enid Greene,** a Representative from Utah; born in San Rafael, Marin County, Calif., October 5, 1958; graduated from East High School; B.S., University of Utah, 1980; J.D., Brigham Young University, 1983; admitted to the bar and commenced practice in Salt Lake City, Utah; deputy chief of staff to Governor Norman H. Bangerter; chair, Young Republican National Federation; unsuccessful candidate in 1992 for election to the One Hundred Third Congress; elected as a Republican to the One Hundred Fourth Congress (January 3, 1995-January 3, 1997); was not a candidate for reelection in 1996 to the One Hundred Fifth Congress; is a resident of Salt Lake City, Utah.

**WALDIE, Jerome Russell,** a Representative from California; born in Antioch, Calif., February 15, 1925; attended Antioch public schools; A.B., University of California, 1950; LL.B., University of California School of Law (Boalt), 1953; member of the California State assembly, 1959-1966; majority leader of the assembly, 1961-1966; elected as a Democrat to the Eighty-ninth Congress, June 7, 1966, by special election to fill the vacancy caused by the death of John F. Baldwin; reelected to the four succeeding Congresses and served from June 7, 1966, to January 3, 1975; was not a candidate for reelection in 1974 to the Ninety-fourth Congress, but was an unsuccessful candidate for the Democratic nomination for Governor of California; lobbyist for the National Association of Letter Carriers and the Recording Association of America, 1975-1978, and the Friends of the Earth, 1975-1978, both of Washington, D.C.; chairman, Federal Mine Safety and Health Review Commission, 1978-1979; executive director, White House Conference on Aging, 1980; member, California Agricultural Relations Board, 1981-1985; is a resident of Placerville, Calif.

**WALDO, George Ernest,** a Representative from New York; born in Brooklyn, N.Y., January 11, 1851; attended the public schools of Scotland, Conn., and Brooklyn, N.Y., Doctor Fitch's Academy, South Windham, Conn., Natchaug High School, Willimantic, Conn., and studied two years in Cornell University, Ithaca, N.Y., class of 1872; studied law in New York City; was admitted to the bar in Poughkeepsie, N.Y., in 1876 and practiced in New York City 1876-1883 and in Ulysses, Nebr., 1883-1889; village attorney of Ulysses, Nebr., for several years; for four years a member of the board of trustees and school director of Ulysses High School; returned to New York City in 1889; member of the New York assembly in 1896; commissioner of records of Kings County, N.Y., 1899-1904; delegate to the Republican National Convention in 1900; elected as a Republican to the Fifty-ninth and Sixtieth Congresses (March 4, 1905-March 3, 1909); was not a candidate for renomination in 1908; resumed the practice of law in New York City; moved to Los Angeles, Calif., in 1913, to Pasadena, Calif., in 1918, and continued the practice of his profession; died in Pasadena, Calif., June 16, 1942; remains were cremated and the ashes deposited in the New Cemetery, Scotland, Conn.

**WALDO, Loren Pinckney,** a Representative from Connecticut; born in Canterbury, Conn., February 2, 1802; attended the common schools; taught school; engaged in agricultural pursuits; moved to Tolland, Conn., in 1823; studied law; was admitted to the bar in

1825 and commenced practice in Somers; superintendent of schools; postmaster of Somers in 1829 and 1830; returned to Tolland in 1830; member of the Connecticut State house of representatives, 1832-1834, and in 1839; clerk of the Connecticut State house of representatives in 1833; State's attorney 1837-1849; judge of probate for Tolland district in 1842 and 1843; member in 1847 of the committee to revise the statutes; again a member of the State house of representatives in 1847 and 1848; elected as a Democrat to the Thirty-first Congress (March 4, 1849-March 3, 1851); chairman, Committee on Revolutionary Pensions (Thirty-first Congress); unsuccessful candidate for reelection in 1850 to the Thirty-second Congress; commissioner of the school fund of Connecticut; Commissioner of Pensions under President Franklin Pierce from March 17, 1853, until January 10, 1856, when he resigned to become a judge; judge of the superior court of Connecticut, 1856-1863; moved to Hartford, Conn., and resumed the practice of his profession; again a member of a committee to revise the statutes, in 1864; died in Hartford, Conn., September 8, 1881; interment in Cedar Hill Cemetery.

**WALDON, Alton Ronald, Jr.,** a Representative from New York; born in Lakeland, Fla., December 21, 1936; B.S., John Jay College, 1968; J.D., New York Law School, 1973; deputy commissioner, New York State division of human rights, 1975-1981; counsel, Office of Mental Retardation and Developmental Disabilities; member, New York State assembly, 1982-1986; elected as a Democrat to the Ninety-ninth Congress, June 10, 1986, by special election to fill the vacancy caused by the death of Joseph P. Addabbo, and served from June 10, 1986 to January 3, 1987; unsuccessful candidate for renomination in 1986 to the One Hundredth Congress; member of the New York State investigation commission, 1987-1990; New York State senator, District 10, 1991 to present; is a resident of Cambria Heights, N.Y.

**WALDOW, William Frederick,** a Representative from New York; born in Buffalo, N.Y., August 26, 1882; attended the common schools; apprenticed as a plumber and later engaged as a plumbing contractor; elected a member of the board of aldermen of Buffalo in 1912 and 1913; member of the New York Republican State committee in 1916; elected as a Republican to the Sixty-fifth Congress (March 4, 1917-March 3, 1919); unsuccessful for reelection in 1918 to the Sixty-sixth Congress; resumed former business pursuits; delegate to the Republican National Convention in 1920; sheriff of Erie County, N.Y., 1921-1923; died in Snyder (a suburb of Buffalo), N.Y., April 16, 1930; interment in Forest Lawn Cemetery.

**WALDRON, Alfred Marpole,** a Representative from Pennsylvania; born in Philadelphia, Pa., September 21, 1865; educated in the public schools of Philadelphia; engaged in the insurance business; member of the Philadelphia Select Council 1911-1924; member of the Republican city committee 1916-1936; delegate to the Republican National Conventions in 1924, 1928, and 1932; elected as a Republican to the Seventy-third Congress (March 4, 1933-January 3, 1935); did not seek renomination in 1934; resumed the insurance business; died in Philadelphia, Pa., June 28, 1952; interment in North Cedar Hill Cemetery.

**WALDRON, Henry,** a Representative from Michigan; born in Albany, N.Y., October 11, 1819; attended Albany Academy, and was graduated from Rutgers College, New Brunswick, N.J., in 1836; moved to Michigan in 1837 and was employed as a civil engineer in railroad work; settled in Hillsdale, Mich., in 1839; member of the State legislature in 1843; a director of the Michigan Southern Railroad 1846-1848; active in promoting the construction of the Detroit, Hillsdale & Southwestern Railroad and served as its first president; president of the Second National Bank of Hillsdale from the date of its organization until 1876; presidential elector on the Whig ticket in 1848; elected as a Republican to the Thirty-fourth, Thirty-fifth, and Thirty-sixth Congresses (March 4, 1855-March 3,

1861); chairman, Committee on Expenditures in the Department of the Treasury (Thirty-fourth Congress); was not a candidate for renomination in 1860; elected to the Forty-second, Forty-third, and Forty-fourth Congresses (March 4, 1871-March 3, 1877); chairman, Committee on Mines and Mining (Forty-second Congress); declined to be a candidate for renomination in 1876; elected president of the First National Bank of Hillsdale in 1876 and served until his death in Hillsdale, Hillsdale County, Mich., September 13, 1880; interment in Oak Grove Cemetery.

**WALES, George Edward,** a Representative from Vermont; born in Westminster, Windham County, Vt., May 13, 1792; attended the common schools; studied law in Westminster and Woodstock, Vt.; was admitted to the bar in 1812 and commenced practice at Hartford, Vt.; treasurer of the White River Bridge Co. in 1818; member of the State house of representatives 1822-1824 and served as speaker; elected to the Nineteenth and Twentieth Congresses (March 4, 1825-March 3, 1829); unsuccessful candidate for reelection in 1828 to the Twenty-first Congress; resumed the practice of his profession; town clerk of Hartford, Windsor County, Vt., 1840-1860; judge of probate for the Hartford district 1847-1850; died in Hartford, Vt., January 8, 1860; interment in Hartford Cemetery.

**WALES, John,** a Senator from Delaware; born in New Haven, Conn., July 31, 1783; pursued preparatory studies and was graduated from Yale College in 1801; studied law; was admitted to the bar in 1801 and commenced the practice of law at New Haven, Conn.; moved to Philadelphia, Pa., and continued his practice; moved to Baltimore, Md., in 1813, where he remained until 1815; moved to Wilmington, Del., in 1815 and was president of the National Bank of Wilmington and Brandywine; secretary of State of Delaware 1845-1849; elected as a Whig to the United States Senate to fill the vacancy caused by the resignation of John M. Clayton and served from February 3, 1849, to March 3, 1851; unsuccessful candidate for reelection in 1851; one of the founders of Delaware College, Newark, Del.; died in Wilmington, Del., on December 3, 1863; interment in Wilmington and Brandywine Cemetery.

**WALGREN, Douglas,** a Representative from Pennsylvania; born in Rochester, Monroe County, N.Y., December 28, 1940; attended the public schools of Mount Lebanon, Pa. and graduated from Mount Lebanon High School in 1958; B.A., Dartmouth College, Hanover, N.H., 1963; LL.B., Stanford (Calif.) University, 1966; admitted to the California bar in 1966 and commenced practice in Menlo Park; staff attorney, Neighborhood Legal Services, Pittsburgh, Pa., 1967-1968; engaged in private practice in Pittsburgh, 1969-1972; corporate counsel, Behavioral Research Laboratories, Inc., Palo Alto, Calif., 1973-1975; elected as a Democrat to the Ninety-fifth and to the six succeeding Congresses (January 3, 1977-January 3, 1991); unsuccessful candidate for reelection in 1990 to the One Hundred Second Congress; is a resident of Pittsburgh, Pa.

**WALKER, Amasa,** a Representative from Massachusetts; born in East Woodstock, Conn., May 4, 1799; moved with his parents to North Brookfield, Mass.; attended the district school; in 1814 entered commercial life in North Brookfield; in 1825 moved to Boston, where he engaged in mercantile pursuits until 1840; delegate to the Democratic National Convention in 1836; delegate to the first international peace conference at London in 1843 and at Paris in 1849; lecturer on political economy at Oberlin College, Ohio, 1842-1848; member of the Massachusetts house of representatives in 1849; served in the Massachusetts senate in 1850; secretary of state of Massachusetts in 1851 and 1852; member of the Massachusetts constitutional convention in 1853; lecturer on political economy at Harvard University 1853-1860; again a member of the Massachusetts house of representatives in 1860; elected as a Republican to the Thirty-seventh Congress to fill the vacancy caused by the death of Goldsmith F. Bailey and served from December 1,

1862, to March 3, 1863; was not a candidate for election to the Thirty-eighth Congress; lecturer on political economy at Amherst College, Amherst, Mass., 1859-1869; author of several books on political economy; died in North Brookfield, Mass., October 29, 1875; interment in Maple Street Cemetery.

**Bibliography:** *DAB*; Mick, Laura A. "The Life of Amasa Walker." Ph.D. dissertation, Ohio State University, 1940.

**WALKER, Benjamin,** a Representative from New York; born in London, England, in 1753; attended the Blue-Coat School; immigrated to the United States and settled in New York City; served in the Revolutionary War as aide-de-camp to General Freidrich von Steuben and subsequently as a member of the staff of General George Washington; naval officer of customs at the port of New York from March 21, 1791, to February 20, 1798; moved to Fort Schuyler (now Utica), N.Y., in 1797; agent of the great landed estate of the Earl of Bath; elected as a Federalist to the Seventh Congress (March 4, 1801-March 3, 1803); declined to be a candidate for renomination in 1802; died in Utica, N.Y., January 13, 1818; interment in the Old Village Burying Ground on Water Street; reinterment, June 17, 1875, in Forest Hill Cemetery.

**WALKER, Charles Christopher Brainerd,** a Representative from New York; was born in Drewsville, near Keene, N.H., June 27, 1824; completed preparatory studies; moved to Corning, Steuben County, N.Y., in 1848; postmaster of Corning 1856-1860; was a contractor and also engaged in the hardware and lumber business; during the Civil War served as brigade quartermaster with the rank of captain in the New York State Militia; delegate to the Democratic National Conventions at Charleston in 1860 and at Baltimore in 1872; elected as a Democrat to the Forty-fourth Congress (March 4, 1875-March 3, 1877); resumed former business activities; member of the board of control of the New York Agricultural Experiment Station from June 10, 1885, until his death in Corning, N.Y., January 26, 1888; interment in Palmyra Cemetery, Palmyra, Wayne County, N.Y.

**WALKER, David** (brother of George Walker and grandfather of James David Walker), a Representative from Kentucky; born in Brunswick County, Va.; attended public and private schools; served in the Revolutionary War as a private under General Lafayette; was at the surrender of General George Cornwallis at Yorktown, Va., October 19, 1781; moved to Logan County, Ky.; clerk of county and circuit courts; member of the Kentucky house of representatives, 1793-1796; served as major on the staff of Governor Isaac Shelby of Kentucky in the Battle of the Thames, Ontario, Canada, October 5, 1813; elected as a Republican to the Fifteenth Congress, reelected to the Sixteenth Congress and served from March 4, 1817, until his death in Washington, D.C., March 1, 1820; interment in the Congressional Cemetery.

**WALKER, E.S. Johnny,** a Representative from New Mexico; born in Fulton, Ky., June 18, 1911; attended the public schools; moved with his family to Albuquerque, N.Mex., in 1926; graduated from Albuquerque High School; attended the University of New Mexico in Albuquerque, and the National University (now George Washington University) in Washington, D.C.; served in the North African and European Theaters of Operation, 1942-1945; member of the New Mexico State house of representatives, 1949-1952 (majority whip); commissioner, State Land Office, 1953-1956, and 1961-1964; commissioner of the State Bureau of Revenue, 1960; organizer, director, and member of the State Oil and Gas Accounting Commission; elected as a Democrat to the Eighty-ninth and Ninetieth Congresses (January 3, 1965-January 3, 1969); unsuccessful candidate for reelection in 1968 to the Ninety-first Congress; president of a financial institution; is a resident of Albuquerque, N.Mex.

**WALKER, Felix,** a Representative from North Carolina; born on the south branch of the Potomac River, in Hampshire County, Va. (now West Virginia), July 19, 1753; attended country school on the Congaree River, near Columbia, S.C., and in Burke County, N.C.; moved with his father to what became Lincoln County, N.C., and in 1768, to what became Rutherford County, N.C.; was employed as a merchant's clerk at Charleston, S.C., in 1769; also engaged in agricultural pursuits; in company with Daniel Boone and others formed the settlement of Boonsboro, Ky., in 1775; clerk of the court of Washington district (most of which is now in Tennessee) in 1775 and 1776 and of the county court of Washington County (now chiefly in Tennessee) in 1777 and 1778; fought in the Revolutionary and Indian wars; clerk of court of Rutherford County, N.C., 1779-1787; member of the State house of commons in 1792, 1799-1802, and 1806; resumed agricultural pursuits and was also a trader and land speculator in Haywood County, N.C.; elected as a Republican to the Fifteenth Congress and reelected to the Sixteenth and Seventeenth Congresses (March 4, 1817-March 3, 1823); unsuccessful candidate for reelection in 1822 to the Eighteenth Congress; moved to Mississippi about 1824 and engaged in agricultural pursuits and trading; died in Clinton, Hinds County, Miss., in 1828; interment probably in a private cemetery.

**WALKER, Francis** (brother of John Walker), a Representative from Virginia; born at "Castle Hill," near Cobham, Albemarle County, Va., June 22, 1764; magistrate of Albemarle County; colonel of the Eighty-eighth Regiment, Virginia Militia; member of the Virginia house of delegates 1788-1791 and 1797-1801; elected to the Third Congress (March 4, 1793-March 3, 1795); died at "Castle Hill," near Cobham, Va., in March 1806; interment in the family cemetery at "Castle Hill."

**WALKER, Freeman,** a Senator from Georgia; born in Charles City, Va., October 25, 1780; attended the common schools; moved to Augusta, Ga., in 1797; studied law; was admitted to the bar in 1802 and commenced practice in Augusta; member, State house of representatives 1807-1811; mayor of Augusta 1818-1819; elected to the United States Senate to fill the vacancy caused by the resignation of John Forsyth and served from November 6, 1819, to August 6, 1821, when he resigned; mayor of Augusta 1823; died in Augusta, Richmond County, Ga., September 23, 1827; interment in Spring Hill Cemetery.

**WALKER, George** (brother of David Walker and great uncle of James David Walker), a Senator from Kentucky; born in Culpeper County, Va., in 1763; attended the common schools; served in the Revolutionary War; moved to Jessamine County, Ky., in 1794; studied law; was admitted to the bar and commenced practice in Nicholasville, Ky., in 1799; a commissioner of the Kentucky River Co. in 1801; member, Kentucky senate 1810-1814; appointed to the United States Senate to fill the vacancy caused by the resignation of George M. Bibb and served from August 30 to December 16, 1814, when a successor was elected; died in Nicholasville, Ky., in 1819; interment on his estate near Nicholasville.

**WALKER, Gilbert Carlton,** a Representative from Virginia; born in South Gibson, Susquehanna County, Pa., August 1, 1833; graduated from Hamilton College, Clinton, N.Y., in 1854; studied law; was admitted to the bar in 1855 and practiced in Owego, Broome County, N.Y., 1855-1859 and in Chicago, Ill., 1859-1864; moved to Norfolk, Va., in 1864 and continued the practice of law; also engaged in banking; elected Governor of Virginia in 1869, and served from September 21, 1869 to January 1, 1874; elected as a Democrat to the Forty-fourth and Forty-fifth Congresses (March 4, 1875-March 3, 1879); chairman, Committee on Education and Labor (Forty-fourth Congress); was not a candidate for renomination in 1878 to the Forty-sixth Congress; settled in Binghamton, N.Y., in 1879 and practiced law; moved to New York City in 1881 and continued the practice of law; served as president of the New York Underground Railroad Company; died in New York City, May 11, 1885; interment in Spring Forest Cemetery, Binghamton, N.Y.

**Bibliography:** *DAB.*

**WALKER, Isaac Pigeon,** a Senator from Wisconsin; born near Wheeling, Va. (now West Virginia), November 2, 1815; moved to Danville, Ill., in early youth; attended the common schools; was employed as a clerk in a store; studied law; was admitted to the bar in 1834 and commenced practice in Springfield; served one term in the State house of representatives; presidential elector on the Democratic ticket in 1840; moved to Wisconsin Territory in 1841, settled in Milwaukee, and continued the practice of law; member, Territorial legislature 1847-1848; upon the admission of Wisconsin as a State into the Union was elected as a Democrat to the United States Senate; reelected in 1849 and served from June 8, 1848, to March 3, 1855; chairman, Committee to Audit and Control the Contingent Expense (Thirtieth Congress), Committee on Revolutionary Claims (Thirty-first through Thirty-third Congresses), Committee on Agriculture (Thirty-second Congress), Committee on Indian Affairs (Thirty-second Congress); engaged in agricultural pursuits in Waukesha County; returned to Milwaukee and resumed the practice of law; died there March 29, 1872; interment in Forest Home Cemetery.

**WALKER, James Alexander,** a Representative from Virginia; born near Mount Meridian, Augusta County, Va., August 27, 1832; attended private schools, and was graduated from Virginia Military Institute, Lexington, Va., in 1852; studied law in the University of Virginia at Charlottesville in 1854 and 1855; was admitted to the bar in 1856 and commenced practice in Newbern, Pulaski County, Va., in 1856; attorney for the Commonwealth in 1860; entered the Confederate Army in April 1861 as captain of the Pulaski Guards, afterwards Company C, Fourth Virginia Infantry, Stonewall Brigade; promoted to lieutenant colonel and assigned to the Thirteenth Virginia Infantry in July 1861, becoming colonel in March 1862; was promoted to brigadier general and assigned as commander of the Stonewall Brigade in May 1863; member of the house of delegates of Virginia in 1871 and 1872; elected Lieutenant Governor of Virginia in 1877; until 1893 was a member of the Democratic Party; elected as a Republican to the Fifty-fourth and Fifty-fifth Congresses (March 4, 1895-March 3, 1899); chairman, Committee on Elections No. 3 (Fifty-fifth Congress); unsuccessful candidate for reelection in 1898 to the Fifty-sixth Congress; resumed the practice of his profession; died in Wytheville, Wythe County, Va., October 21, 1901; interment in East End Cemetery.

**Bibliography:** Caldwell, Willie Walker. *Stonewell Jim: A Biography of General James A. Walker, C.S.A.* Elliston, Va.: Northcross House, 1990.

**WALKER, James David** (grandson of David Walker, nephew of John McLean (1791-1830) and Finis Ewing McLean, cousin of Wilkinson Call, and great nephew of George Walker), a Senator from Arkansas; born near Russellville, Logan County, Ky., December 13, 1830; attended private schools in Kentucky and Ozark Institute and Arkansas College, Fayetteville, Ark.; moved to Arkansas in 1847; studied law; was admitted to the bar in 1850 and commenced practice in Fayetteville, Washington County, Ark.; judge of the circuit court, fourth judicial district; during the Civil War served as colonel of the First Regiment, Arkansas Infantry, Confederate Army; captured at Oak Hills, Mo., in 1861 and imprisoned for two years; resumed the practice of law in Fayetteville, Ark., in 1865; solicitor general of the State of Arkansas; presidential elector on the Democratic ticket in 1876; elected as a Democrat to the United States Senate and served from March 4, 1879, to March 3, 1885; declined to be a candidate for reelection in 1884; resumed the practice of law in Fayetteville, Ark., and died there on October 17, 1906; interment in the Walker family cemetery.

**WALKER, James Peter,** a Representative from Missouri; born near Memphis, Lauderdale County, Tenn., March 14, 1851; attended the public schools and the boys' college at Durhamville, Tenn.; employed in early youth as a clerk in a country store; moved to Missouri in 1867 and settled near Kennett, Dunkin County; engaged in agricultural pursuits; moved to Point Pleasant, New Madrid County, in 1871 and engaged in transportation on the Mississippi River; engaged in the dry-goods business at Dexter, Mo., in 1876, and later, in 1882, in the buying and selling of grain; delegate to the Democratic National Convention in 1880; unsuccessful candidate for the Democratic nomination for Congress in 1884; elected as a Democrat to the Fiftieth and Fifty-first Congresses and served from March 4, 1887, until his death; had been unanimously nominated as the Democratic candidate for reelection to the Fifty-second Congress on the day of his death; died July 19, 1890, in Dexter, Stoddard County, Mo.; interment in Dexter Cemetery.

**WALKER, John** (brother of Francis Walker), a Delegate and a Senator from Virginia; born at "Castle Hill," near Cobham, Albemarle County, Va., February 13, 1744; received private schooling and graduated from the College of William and Mary, Williamsburg, Va., in 1764; moved to "Belvoir," Albemarle County, and engaged in planting; commissioned with his father to make special terms with the Indians at Fort Pitt, Pa., so as to retain their friendship during the Revolutionary War; served as an aide to General George Washington in 1777 with the rank of colonel; Delegate to the Continental Congress 1780; studied law; was admitted to the bar and commenced the practice of law; appointed to the United States Senate to fill the vacancy caused by the death of William Grayson and served from March 31 to November 9, 1790, when a successor was elected; was not a candidate for reelection; resumed his agricultural pursuits; died near Madison Mills, Orange County, Va., December 2, 1809; interment in the family cemetery on the Belvoir estate near Cismont, Va.

**WALKER, John Randall,** a Representative from Georgia; born near Blackshear, Pierce County, Ga., February 23, 1874; attended the public schools; was graduated from Jasper (Fla.) Normal College in 1895 and from the law department of the University of Georgia at Athens in 1898; was admitted to the bar and commenced practice in Valdosta, Lowndes County, Ga., in 1900; member of the Georgia State house of representatives in 1907 and 1908; elected as a Democrat to the Sixty-third and to the two succeeding Congresses (March 4, 1913-March 3, 1919); unsuccessful candidate for renomination in 1918 to the Sixty-sixth Congress; moved to Eldorado, Ark., and resumed the practice of law; returned to Blackshear, Ga., where he died; interment in the Walker family burying grounds in Pierce County, Ga.

**WALKER, John Williams** (father of Percy Walker and great-great-grandfather of Richard Walker Bolling), a Senator from Alabama; born in Amelia County, Va., August 12, 1783; attended a private school; graduated from The College of New Jersey (now Princeton University) in 1806; studied law; was admitted to the bar in 1810 and commenced practice in Huntsville, Ala.; member, Territorial house of representatives 1817, and served as speaker; president of the State constitutional convention in 1819; upon the admission of Alabama as a State into the Union was elected to the United States Senate and served from December 14, 1819, to December 12, 1822, when he resigned; died in Huntsville, Madison County, Ala., April 23, 1823; interment in Maple Hill Cemetery.

**Bibliography:** Bailey, Hugh C. *John Williams Walker: Life of the Old Southwest.* University, Ala.: University of Alabama Press, 1964; Owsley, Frank L. "John Williams Walker." *Alabama Review* 9 (1956): 100-19.

**WALKER, Joseph Henry,** a Representative from Massachusetts; born in Boston, Mass., December 21, 1829; moved with his parents to Hopkinton in 1830 and to Worcester, Mass., in 1843; attended the public schools; engaged in the manufacture of boots and shoes; established the business of manufacturing leather in Chicago, Ill., in 1868; member of the common council of Worcester 1852-1854; served in the Massachusetts house of representatives in 1879, 1880, and 1887; elected as a Republican to the Fifty-first and to the four succeeding Congresses (March 4, 1889-March 3, 1899); chairman, Committee on Banking and Currency (Fifty-fourth and Fifty-fifth Congresses); unsuccessful candidate for reelection in 1898 to the Fifty-sixth Congress; resumed his former business pursuits; died in Worcester, Mass., April 3, 1907; interment in the Rural Cemetery.

**WALKER, Lewis Leavell,** a Representative from Kentucky; born in Lancaster, Garrard County, Ky., February 15, 1873; attended Lancaster (Ky.) Academy, Garrard College, Lancaster, Ky., and Central University, Richmond, Ky.; studied law; was admitted to the bar in 1894 and commenced practice in Lancaster, Ky.; also engaged in banking; prosecuting attorney of Garrard County in 1901; city attorney of Lancaster 1907-1910; served as trustee of the University of Kentucky, at Lexington, Ky., 1908-1915; judge of the thirteenth judicial district of Kentucky in 1910 and 1911; elected as a Republican to the Seventy-first Congress (March 4, 1929-March 3, 1931); was not a candidate for renomination in 1930; continued the practice of law in Lancaster, Ky., until his death there on June 30, 1944; interment in Lancaster Cemetery.

**WALKER, Percy** (son of John Williams Walker and great-great-uncle of Richard Walker Bolling), a Representative from Alabama; born in Huntsville, Madison County, Ala., in December 1812; completed preparatory studies; was graduated from the medical department of the University of Pennsylvania at Philadelphia in 1835; commenced the practice of medicine in Mobile, Ala.; served in the campaign against the Creek Indians; studied law; was admitted to the bar and practiced in Mobile; State's attorney for the sixth judicial district; member of the State house of representatives in 1839, 1847, and 1853; elected as a candidate of the American Party to the Thirty-fourth Congress (March 4, 1855-March 3, 1857); declined to be a candidate for renomination in 1856; died in Mobile, Ala., December 31, 1880; interment in Magnolia Cemetery.

**WALKER, Prentiss Lafayette,** a Representative from Mississippi; born near Taylorsville, Smith County, Miss., August 23, 1917; attended the public schools of Las Cruces, N.Mex., and Taylorsville and Mize, Miss., and Mississippi College at Clinton, Miss., in 1936; entered United States Army in 1944 and served in Pacific Theater; president of Walker Egg Farms, Inc., Mize, Miss., 1955 to present; owner, Walker's Supermarket, 1937-1963; member of the executive committee of the State Game and Fish Commission, 1960; delegate to the Republican National Conventions of 1964 and 1968; elected as a Republican to the Eighty-ninth Congress (January 3, 1965-January 3, 1967); was not a candidate in 1966 for reelection to the House of Representatives, but was an independent candidate for the United States Senate; unsuccessful candidate for nomination to the United States Senate in 1972; engaged in farming and home building; is a resident of Mize, Miss.

**WALKER, Robert Jarvis Cochran,** a Representative from Pennsylvania; born near West Chester, Chester County, Pa., October 20, 1838; attended school at East Hampton and Cambridge, Mass.; was graduated from the law department of Harvard University in 1858; was admitted to the bar in 1859 and commenced practice in Philadelphia; director of the first school district of Pennsylvania; twice elected to the council of Philadelphia; purchased the Saturday Evening Post in 1874 and was its editor for a short time; engaged in the production of oil; moved to Williamsport, Lycoming County, Pa., in 1875 and engaged in land, lumber, and coal developments; elected as a Republican to the Forty-seventh Congress (March 4, 1881-March 3, 1883); declined to be a candidate for renomination in 1882 to the Forty-eighth Congress, but his name was presented by his friends; returned to Philadelphia in 1890 and became a manufacturing chemist; died in Philadelphia, Pa., December 19, 1903; interment in Laurel Hill Cemetery.

**WALKER, Robert John,** a Senator from Mississippi; born in Northumberland, Pa., July 19, 1801; graduated from the University of Pennsylvania at Philadelphia in 1819; studied law; was admitted to the bar in 1821 and commenced practice in Pittsburgh, Pa., the following year; moved to Natchez, Miss., in 1826 and continued the practice of law; elected as a Democrat to the United States Senate; reelected, and served from March 4, 1835, to March 5, 1845, when he resigned; chairman, Committee on Public Lands (Twenty-fourth through Twenty-sixth Congresses); Secretary of the Treasury in the Cabinet of President James K. Polk from March 8, 1845 to March 5, 1849; declined the mission to China tendered by President Franklin Pierce in 1853; resumed the practice of law; appointed Governor of Kansas Territory by President James Buchanan on March 30, 1857, but resigned on December 17, 1857; United States financial agent to Europe, 1863-1864; again engaged in the practice of law at Washington, D.C., and died there November 11, 1869; interment in Oak Hill Cemetery.

**Bibliography:** *DAB*; Dodd, William E. *Robert J. Walker, Imperialist.* Gloucester, Mass.: P. Smith, 1967; Shenton, James P. *Robert John Walker: Politician From Jackson to Lincoln.* New York: Columbia University Press, 1961.

**WALKER, Robert Smith,** a Representative from Pennsylvania; born in Bradford, McKean County, Pa., December 23, 1942; educated in the public schools of Millersville, Pa., and graduated from Penn Manor High School in 1960; attended the College of William and Mary, Williamsburg, Va., 1960-1961; B.S., Millersville University, 1964; M.A., University of Delaware, Newark, 1968; taught in the public schools of Millersville, 1964-1967; served in Pennsylvania National Guard, 1967-1973; legislative assistant, 1967-1974, and administrative assistant, 1974-1976, to Representative Edwin D. Eshleman of Pennsylvania; elected as a Republican to the Ninety-fifth and to the nine succeeding Congresses (January 3, 1977-January 3, 1997); chairman, Committee on Science (One Hundred Fourth Congress); was not a candidate for reelection in 1996 to the One Hundred Fifth Congress; is a resident of East Petersburg, Pa.

**WALKER, Walter,** a Senator from Colorado; born in Marion, Crittenden County, Ky., April 3, 1883; attended the public schools; moved to Grand Junction, Colo., in 1903 and engaged in the daily newspaper business, later becoming editor, manager, and chief owner of the Grand Junction Daily Sentinel; appointed as a Democrat to the United States Senate to fill the vacancy caused by the death of Charles W. Waterman and served from September 26, 1932, until December 6, 1932, when a duly elected successor qualified; unsuccessful candidate for election in 1932 to fill this vacancy; resumed newspaper activities until his death; presidential elector on the Democratic ticket in 1936; died in Grand Junction, Colo., October 8, 1956; interment in Orchard Mesa Cemetery.

**WALKER, William Adams,** a Representative from New York; born in New Hampshire June 5, 1805; attended the common schools and Northampton Law School; was admitted to the bar but never engaged in the practice of law; moved to New York City in 1832; appointed principal of a public school in New York City; county superintendent of common schools 1843-1847; member of the board of aldermen in 1846; defeated for reelection in 1847; served as commissioner of jurors until elected to Congress; elected as a Democrat to the Thirty-third Congress (March 4, 1853-March 3, 1855); declined to be a candidate for renomination in 1854 to the Thirty-fourth Congress; defeated for election to the board of aldermen in 1857; died in Irvington, West Chester County, N.Y., December 18, 1861; interment in Sleepy Hollow Cemetery, Tarrytown, N.Y.

**WALL, Garret Dorset** (father of James Walter Wall), a Senator from New Jersey; born in Middletown, N.J., March 10, 1783; completed preparatory studies; studied law; was licensed as an attorney in 1804 and as a counselor in 1807 and commenced practice in Burlington, N.J.; served in the War of 1812 and commanded a volunteer regiment from Trenton; clerk of the New Jersey State supreme court, 1812-1817; quartermaster general of New Jersey, 1815-1837; member of the State general assembly in 1827; United States district attorney for New Jersey in 1829; elected Governor of New Jersey in 1829, but declined to serve; elected as a Jacksonian to the United States Senate, and served from March 4, 1835 to March 3, 1841; unsuccessful candidate for reelection; chairman, Committee on the Militia (Twenty-fourth and Twenty-fifth Congresses), Committee on the Judiciary (Twenty-fifth and Twenty-sixth Congresses), Committee on Military Affairs (Twenty-fifth Congress); judge of the Court of Errors and Appeals of New Jersey from 1848 until his death in Burlington, N.J., November 22, 1850; interment in the churchyard of St. Mary's Church.

**WALL, James Walter** (son of Garret Dorset Wall), a Senator from New Jersey; born in Trenton, N.J., May 26, 1820; was tutored privately in Flushing, N.Y., and graduated from the College of New Jersey (now Princeton University) in 1838; studied law; was admitted to the bar in 1841 and commenced practice in Trenton; served as commissioner in bankruptcy; moved to Burlington, N.J., in 1847; served as mayor of Burlington in 1850; was tendered the Democratic nomination for Congress in 1850, but declined; unsuccessful candidate for election in 1854 to the Thirty-fourth Congress; elected as a Democrat to the United States Senate to fill the vacancy caused by the death of John R. Thompson, and served from January 14 to March 3, 1863; unsuccessful candidate for reelection; resumed the practice of law in Burlington; also engaged in literary pursuits; moved to Elizabeth, N.J., in 1869, and died there on June 9, 1872; interment in the churchyard of St. Mary's Episcopal Church, Burlington, N.J.

**WALL, William,** a Representative from New York; born in Philadelphia, Pa., March 20, 1800; received a limited schooling; learned the trade of ropemaking and worked as a journeyman; became a manufacturer of rope; moved to Kings County, Long Island, N.Y., in 1822; trustee, commissioner of highways, supervisor, member of the board of finance, and commissioner of waterworks of Williamsburg (now a part of New York City); mayor of Williamsburg in 1853; was one of the incorporators and for a number of years president of the Williamsburg Savings Bank; also one of the founders of the Williamsburg City Bank (later the First National Bank) and of the Williamsburg Dispensary; elected as a Republican to the Thirty-seventh Congress (March 4, 1861-March 3, 1863); declined to be a candidate for renomination in 1862 to the Thirty-eighth Congress; delegate to the Loyalist Convention at Philadelphia in 1866; died in Brooklyn, N.Y., April 20, 1872; interment in Greenwood Cemetery.

**WALLACE, Alexander Stuart,** a Representative from South Carolina; born near York, S.C., December 30, 1810; received a limited schooling; engaged in planting in his native county; member of the State house of representatives, 1852-1855, 1858-1859 and 1865-1866; successfully contested as a Republican the election of William D. Simpson to the Forty-first Congress; reelected to the Forty-second, Forty-third, and Forty-fourth Congresses and served from May 27, 1870, to March 3, 1877; chairman, Committee on Revolutionary Claims (Forty-second Congress); unsuccessful candidate for reelection in 1876 to the Forty-fifth Congress; engaged in agricultural pursuits until his death near York, S.C., June 27, 1893; interment in Rose Hill Cemetery, York, S.C.

**WALLACE, Daniel,** a Representative from South Carolina; born near Laurens, S.C., May 9, 1801; received a limited schooling; moved to Union County in 1833; major general of State militia;

studied law; was admitted to the bar and practiced in Union and Jonesville, Union County, S.C.; also engaged in agricultural pursuits; member of the State house of representatives 1846-1847; elected as a Democrat to the Thirtieth Congress to fill the vacancy caused by the death of James A. Black; reelected to the Thirty-first and Thirty-second Congresses and served from June 12, 1848, to March 3, 1853; resumed agricultural pursuits; died in Jonesville, S.C., May 13, 1859; interment in Old Presbyterian Cemetery, Union, S.C.

**WALLACE, David,** a Representative from Indiana; born near Lewistown, Mifflin County, Pa., April 24, 1799; moved with his parents to Brookville, Ind., in 1817; was graduated from the United States Military Academy at West Point, N.Y., in 1821, and was appointed assistant professor of mathematics in that institution, resigning in 1822; returned to Brookville, Ind.; studied law; was admitted to the bar in 1824 and practiced; member of the Indiana State house of representatives, 1828-1830; moved to Covington, Ind., in 1830 and continued the practice of law; Lieutenant Governor of Indiana 1831-1837; elected Governor of Indiana in 1837, and served from December 6, 1837 to December 9, 1840; settled in Indianapolis and continued the practice of law; elected as a Whig to the Twenty-seventh Congress (March 4, 1841-March 3, 1843); unsuccessful candidate for reelection in 1842 to the Twenty-eighth Congress; resumed the practice of law in Indianapolis; delegate to the State constitutional convention in 1850; judge of the court of common pleas of Marion County from 1856 until his death in Indianapolis, Ind., September 4, 1859; interment in Crown Hill Cemetery.

Bibliography: *DAB.*

**WALLACE, Henry Agard,** a Vice President of the United States; born on a farm near Orient, Adair County, Iowa, October 7, 1888; attended the public schools; graduated from Iowa State College at Ames in 1910; served on the editorial staff of Wallace's Farmer, Des Moines, Iowa, 1910-1924, and was editor, 1924-1929; experimented with breeding high-yielding strains of corn, 1913-1933; in 1915 devised the first corn-hog ratio charts indicating the probable course of markets; author of many publications on agriculture; appointed Secretary of Agriculture in the Cabinet of President Franklin D. Roosevelt in 1933 and served until September 5, 1940, when he resigned, having been nominated for Vice President; elected on November 5, 1940 as Vice President of the United States on the Democratic ticket with President Franklin D. Roosevelt and was inaugurated January 20, 1941, for the term ending January 20, 1945; unsuccessful candidate for renomination in 1944; appointed Secretary of Commerce, and served from March 2, 1945 until his resignation on September 20, 1946; unsuccessful Progressive candidate for election as President of the United States in 1948; resumed his farming interests; was a resident of South Salem, N.Y.; died in Danbury, Conn., November 18, 1965; remains were cremated at Grace Cemetery in Bridgeport, Conn., and the ashes interred in Glendale Cemetery, Des Moines, Iowa.

Bibliography: *DAB*; Markowitz, Norman D. *The Rise and Fall of the People's Century: Henry A. Wallace and American Liberalism, 1941-1948.* New York: Free Press, 1973; Wallace, Henry A. *The Price of Vision: The Diary of Henry A. Wallace, 1942-1946.* John Morton Blum, ed., Boston: Houghton Mifflin, 1973; White, Graham J., and John Maze. *Henry A. Wallace: His Search for a New World Order.* Chapel Hill: University of North Carolina Press, 1995.

**WALLACE, James M.,** a Representative from Pennsylvania; born in Hanover Township, Lancaster (now Dauphin) County, Pa., in 1750; pursued preparatory studies in Philadelphia; participated in the Revolution as a member of Capt. James Roger's, Col. Timothy Green's, and Capt. William Brown's companies, and at the close of the war was major of a battalion of Associators; commanded a company of rangers in defense of the frontier in 1779; became major

of the Dauphin County Militia in 1796; one of the commissioners of the county 1799-1801; member of the Pennsylvania house of representatives 1806-1810; elected as a Republican to the Fourteenth Congress to fill the vacancy caused by the declination of Amos Ellmaker to serve; reelected to the Fifteenth and Sixteenth Congresses and served from October 10, 1815, to March 3, 1821; declined to be a candidate for renomination and retired to his farm; died near Hummelstown, West Hanover Township, Dauphin County, Pa., December 17, 1823; interment in the Old Derry Church Graveyard, Derry (now Hershey), Pa.

**WALLACE, John Winfield,** a Representative from Pennsylvania; born near Beaver Falls, Beaver County, Pa., December 20, 1818; attended Darlington (Pa.) Academy, where he afterward taught; was graduated from Jefferson Medical College at Philadelphia in 1846 and commenced the practice of medicine in Darlington; moved to New Castle, Pa., in 1850; held several local offices; elected as a Republican to the Thirty-seventh Congress (March 4, 1861-March 3, 1863); unsuccessful candidate for reelection in 1862 to the Thirty-eighth Congress; during the Civil War served as paymaster in the Union Army; elected as a Republican to the Forty-fourth Congress (March 4, 1875-March 3, 1877); was not a candidate for renomination in 1876; resumed the practice of medicine in New Castle, Lawrence County, Pa., where he died June 24, 1889; interment in Grandview Cemetery, near Beaver Falls, Beaver County, Pa.

**WALLACE, Jonathan Hasson,** a Representative from Ohio; born in St. Clair Township, Columbiana County, Ohio, October 31, 1824; attended the common schools, and was graduated from Washington College (now Washington and Jefferson University), Washington, Pa., in 1844; studied law; was admitted to the bar and commenced the practice of law in New Lisbon, Ohio; prosecuting attorney of Columbiana County in 1851 and 1853; successfully contested as a Democrat the election of William McKinley, Jr., to the Forty-eighth Congress and served from May 27, 1884, to March 3, 1885; unsuccessful candidate for reelection in 1884 to the Forty-ninth Congress; appointed judge of the court of common pleas by Governor George Hoadley on March 5, 1885, to fill a vacancy and served one year; continued the practice of law until his death in Lisbon, Ohio, October 28, 1892; interment in Lisbon Cemetery.

**WALLACE, Nathaniel Dick,** a Representative from Louisiana; born in Columbia, Maury County, Tenn., October 27, 1845; attended the common schools, and was graduated from Trinity College, Dublin, Ireland, in 1865; returned to the United States in 1867 and engaged in the commission business at New Orleans, La., in 1878; twice elected president of the New Orleans Produce Exchange; active in manufacturing enterprises; elected as a Democrat to the Forty-ninth Congress to fill the vacancy caused by the death of Michael Hahn and served from December 9, 1886, to March 3, 1887; was not a candidate for renomination in 1886 to the Fiftieth Congress; president of Consumers Ice Co., New Orleans, from 1886 until his death July 16, 1894, in Kenilworth, near Asheville, N.C.; interment in Metairie Cemetery, New Orleans, La.

**WALLACE, Robert Minor,** a Representative from Arkansas; born in New London, Union County, Ark., August 6, 1856; attended the common schools, and was graduated from Arizona Seminary, Arizona, La., in 1876; studied law; was admitted to the bar at Little Rock, Ark., in 1879 and commenced the practice of law in El Dorado, Ark.; member of the State house of representatives in 1881 and 1882; United States post office inspector 1887-1891; prosecuting attorney for the thirteenth judicial circuit of Arkansas in 1891 and 1892; assistant United States attorney in 1894; elected as a Democrat to the Fifty-eighth and to the three succeeding Congresses (March 4, 1903-March 3, 1911); unsuccessful candidate for renomination in 1910 to the Sixty-second Congress; resumed the practice of his profession at Hot Springs and Little Rock and also engaged in lecturing for the Chautauqua and for the Anti-Saloon League; moved to Magnolia, Ark., where he died on November 9, 1942; interment in Magnolia Cemetery.

**WALLACE, Rodney,** a Representative from Massachusetts; born in New Ipswich, Hillsborough County, N.H., December 21, 1823; attended the common schools; engaged in the manufacture of paper; was a member of the select council of Fitchburg, Mass., in 1864, 1865, and 1867; served in the Massachusetts house of representatives in 1873; member of the Governor's council 1880-1882; elected as a Republican to the Fifty-first Congress (March 4, 1889-March 3, 1891); was not a candidate for renomination in 1890 to the Fifty-second Congress; again engaged in the manufacture of paper; died in Fitchburg, Worcester County, Mass., on February 27, 1903; interment in Laurel Hill Cemetery.

**WALLACE, William Andrew,** a Senator from Pennsylvania; born in Huntingdon, Pa., November 28, 1827; moved with his parents to Clearfield, Pa., in 1836; attended the local schools; studied law; admitted to the bar and commenced practice in Clearfield; also taught school in Clearfield; member, Pennsylvania senate 1863-1875, and served as speaker 1871; member of the commission to suggest amendments to the constitution of Pennsylvania in 1874; elected as a Democrat to the United States Senate and served from March 4, 1875, to March 3, 1881; unsuccessful candidate for reelection in 1880; chairman, Committee on the Revision of the Laws of the United States (Forty-sixth Congress); resumed the practice of law in Clearfield; member, Pennsylvania senate 1882-1887; became interested in the development of the bituminous coal fields of the Clearfield region; also served as president of the Beech Creek Railroad; died in New York City, May 22, 1896; interment in Hillcrest Cemetery, Clearfield, Pa.

**WALLACE, William Copeland,** a Representative from New York; born in Brooklyn, N.Y., May 21, 1856; was graduated from Adelphi Academy, Brooklyn, N.Y., in 1873, from Wesleyan University, Middletown, Conn., in 1876, and from the law department of Columbia College (now Columbia University), New York City, in 1878; commenced the practice of law in New York City; assistant United States attorney for the southern district of New York 1880-1883; appointed judge advocate general on the staff of Governor Levi P. Morton; elected as a Republican to the Fifty-first Congress (March 4, 1889-March 3, 1891); unsuccessful candidate for reelection in 1890 to the Fifty-second Congress; resumed the practice of his profession in Brooklyn, N.Y.; also engaged extensively in banking; died at his summer home in Warwick, Orange County, N.Y., September 4, 1901; interment in Greenwood Cemetery, Brooklyn, N.Y.

**WALLACE, William Henson,** a Delegate from the Territories of Washington and Idaho; born in Troy, Miami County, Ohio, July 19, 1811; attended the common schools of Indiana; studied law; was admitted to the bar and practiced; moved to Iowa in 1837; appointed colonel of State troops; appointed receiver of public money at Fairfield, Iowa; moved to the Territory of Washington in 1853; member of the Territorial council in 1855 and 1856 and served as president of the council; appointed Governor of the Territory of Washington by President Abraham Lincoln on April 9, 1861, but did not qualify, having been elected as a Republican a Delegate from the Territory of Washington to the Thirty-seventh Congress (March 4, 1861-March 3, 1863); was appointed as the first Governor of the Territory of Idaho by President Abraham Lincoln on March 10, 1863, and served until August 1864; elected as a Republican a Delegate from the Territory of Idaho to the Thirty-eighth Congress, and served from February 1, 1864 to March 3, 1865; died in Steilacoom, Pierce County, Wash., on February 7, 1879; interment in Fort Steilacoom Cemetery.

**Bibliography:** Bird, Annie Laurie. "William Henson Wallace, Pioneer Politician." *Pacific Northwest Quarterly* 49 (April 1958): 61-76.

**WALLEY, Samuel Hurd,** a Representative from Massachusetts; born in Boston, Mass., August 31, 1805; attended the common schools and Phillips Academy, Andover, Mass.; attended Yale College in 1822; graduated from Harvard University in 1826; studied law; admitted to the Suffolk bar in 1831 and practiced in Boston and Roxbury; engaged in banking; treasurer of the Vermont Central Railroad; promoter and first treasurer of the Wisconsin Central Railroad; member of the Massachusetts house of representatives in 1836 and 1840-1846, serving as speaker 1844-1846; corporate member of the American Board of Commissioners of Foreign Missions 1848-1867; elected as a Whig to the Thirty-third Congress (March 4, 1853-March 3, 1855); unsuccessful candidate for reelection in 1854 to the Thirty-fourth Congress; unsuccessful Whig candidate for Governor of Massachusetts in 1855; president of the Revere National Bank; died at Nantasket Beach, Plymouth County, Mass., on August 27, 1877; interment in Mount Auburn Cemetery, Cambridge, Mass.

**WALLGREN, Monrad Charles,** a Representative and a Senator from Washington; born in Des Moines, Iowa, April 17, 1891; moved with his parents to Galveston, Tex., in 1894 and to Everett, Wash., in 1901; attended the public schools and business college of Everett, Wash.; graduated from Washington State School of Optometry at Spokane in 1914; engaged in the retail jewelry and optical business, 1915-1932; during the First World War served in the Coast Artillery Corps of the Washington National Guard, 1917-1919; adjutant of the Third Battalion of the Washington National Guard, 1921-1922; elected as a Democrat to the Seventy-third and to the three succeeding Congresses, and served from March 4, 1933 until his resignation, effective December 19, 1940; elected November 5, 1940, as a Democrat to the United States Senate for the term commencing January 3, 1941; subsequently appointed to the United States Senate to fill the vacancy caused by the resignation of Lewis B. Schwellenbach in the term ending January 3, 1941, and served from December 19, 1940 to January 9, 1945, when he resigned; elected Governor of Washington in 1944, and served from January 8, 1945 to January 10, 1949; unsuccessful candidate for reelection in 1948; nominated by President Harry S Truman as chairman of National Security Resources Board on February 3, 1949; nomination withdrawn May 17, 1949; member of the Federal Power Commission, 1950-1951; engaged in citrus growing in the Coachella Valley, Calif., and the development of uranium claims at Twenty-nine Palms, Calif.; died in Olympia, Wash., September 18, 1961, due to injuries suffered in an automobile accident; interment in Evergreen Cemetery, Everett, Wash.

**Bibliography:** *DAB*.

**WALLHAUSER, George Marvin,** a Representative from New Jersey; born in Newark, Essex County, N.J., February 10, 1900; attended the grade schools and graduated from Barringer High School, Newark, N.J., in 1918; during the First World War served as a hospital corpsman in the United States Naval Reserve, 1918-1922; graduated from the University of Pennsylvania in 1922; associated with United States Realty & Investment Co., Newark, N.J., in 1928, serving on board of directors and as treasurer and vice president in 1940; enrolled in Columbia University in 1941 and completed courses in real-estate appraising in 1942; chairman, Maplewood (N.J.) Planning Board, 1946-1954; member, Maplewood Township Committee, 1954-1957; elected as a Republican to the Eighty-sixth and to the two succeeding Congresses (January 3, 1959-January 3, 1965); was not a candidate for renomination in 1964 to the Eighty-ninth Congress; senior vice president, United States Realty and Investment Company; commissioner, New Jersey Highway

Authority, 1970-1972, and chairman, 1972-1975; was a resident of Maplewood, N.J.; died August 4, 1993.

**WALLIN, Samuel,** a Representative from New York; born in Easton, Northampton County, Pa., July 31, 1856; moved with his parents to Amsterdam, Montgomery County, N.Y., in 1864; attended the public schools and Amsterdam Academy; engaged in the manufacture of carpets and rugs; served as alderman 1889-1892; mayor of Amsterdam in 1901 and 1902; elected as a Republican to the Sixty-third Congress (March 4, 1913-March 3, 1915); was not a candidate for renomination in 1914; resumed his business activities in Amsterdam, N.Y., where he died December 1, 1917; interment in Green Hill Cemetery.

**WALLING, Ansel Tracy,** a Representative from Ohio; born in Otsego County, N.Y., January 10, 1824; moved to Erie County, Pa., where he attended a local academy; studied medicine and practiced a short time; learned the art of printing; moved to Ohio in 1843 and engaged in newspaper work; clerk of the State legislature in 1851 and 1852; studied law; was admitted to the bar in 1852 and practiced; moved to Keokuk, Iowa, and was editor of the Daily Times 1855-1858; delegate to the Democratic National Convention in 1856; returned to Ohio in 1861 and settled in Circleville, Pickaway County, where he resumed the practice of law; member of the State senate in 1865; served in the State house of representatives in 1867 and was elected speaker pro tempore; elected as a Democrat to the Forty-fourth Congress (March 4, 1875-March 3, 1877); unsuccessful candidate for renomination; again engaged in the practice of law; died in Circleville, Ohio, June 22, 1896; interment in Forest Cemetery.

**WALLOP, Malcolm,** a Senator from Wyoming; born in New York City, February 27, 1933; attended the public schools of Big Horn, Wyo., and the Cate School, Carpenteria, Calif.; B.A., Yale University, 1954; entered the United States Army as a second lieutenant in 1955, released as a first lieutenant in 1957 following service with the Two Hundred Sixty-ninth Field Artillery and Fortieth Field Artillery Group, Fifth Army; businessman and cattle rancher; member, Wyoming State house of representatives, 1969-1972; member, Wyoming State senate, 1973-1976; unsuccessful candidate in 1974 for nomination for Governor of Wyoming; elected as a Republican to the United States Senate in 1976; reelected in 1982 and 1988, and served from January 3, 1977 to January 3, 1995; was not a candidate for reelection in 1994; chairman, Frontiers of Freedom Institute; chairman of the advisory committee, Conservative Television Network; is a resident of Big Horn, Wyo.

**WALLS, Josiah Thomas,** a Representative from Florida; born, probably in slavery, in or near Winchester, Frederick County, Va., December 30, 1842; moved as a child to Darkesville, Va. (now in Jefferson County, W.Va.); attended the county normal school in Harrisburg, Pa.; impressed into the Confederate Army and captured by Union forces during the siege of Yorktown, Va., May 1862; entered the Third Infantry Regiment, United States Colored Troops, Philadelphia, Pa., in July 1863; commissioned corporal in October 1863; moved with his regiment to Florida in February 1864 and was discharged in October 1865; worked at a sawmill on the Suwannee River and taught school at Archer in Alachua County; Alachua County delegate to the State constitutional convention in 1868; served in the Florida State assembly, 1868-1871; presented credentials as a Member-elect to the Forty-second Congress, and served from March 4, 1871 to January 29, 1873, when he was succeeded by Silas L. Niblack, who contested his election; elected as a Republican to the Forty-third Congress (March 4, 1873-March 3, 1875); presented credentials as a Member-elect to the Forty-fourth Congress, and served from March 4, 1875 to April 19, 1876, when he was succeeded by Jesse J. Finley, who contested his election; unsuccessful candidate for renomination in 1876 to the Forty-fifth Congress; served in the Florida State senate, 1876-1879; owned and operated a tomato and lettuce farm, sawmill, and orange groves; unsuccessful Republican candidate for nomination, and unsuccessful Independent candidate for election in 1884 to the Forty-ninth Congress; unsuccessful candidate for the State senate in 1890; supervisor of the farm at Florida Normal College (now Florida A&M University); died in Tallahassee, Fla., May 15, 1905; interment in the Negro Cemetery.

**Bibliography:** Klingman, Peter D. *Josiah Walls, Florida's Black Congressman of Reconstruction.* Gainesville: University Presses of Florida, 1976.

**WALN, Robert,** a Representative from Pennsylvania; born in Philadelphia, Pa., February 22, 1765; received a limited schooling; engaged in mercantile pursuits and in East India and China trade; member of the Pennsylvania legislature for several years; member of the city council of Philadelphia and served as president of the select council; elected as a Federalist to the Fifth Congress to fill the vacancy caused by the death of John Swanwick; reelected to the Sixth Congress and served from December 3, 1798, to March 3, 1801; became interested in the operation of ironworks and during the War of 1812 erected a cotton factory in Trenton; served as president of the Philadelphia Insurance Co. and as a trustee of the University of Pennsylvania; died in Philadelphia, January 24, 1836; interment in Friends' Arch Street Burial Ground.

**Bibliography:** *DAB.*

**WALSH, Allan Bartholomew,** a Representative from New Jersey; born in Trenton, N.J., August 29, 1874; attended Immaculate Conception Parochial School and the public schools of Trenton; employed with an electrical concern in Trenton 1900-1911; member of the State house of assembly in 1910 and 1911; secretary of the Mercer County Board of Taxation in 1912 and 1913; elected as a Democrat to the Sixty-third Congress (March 4, 1913-March 3, 1915); unsuccessful candidate for reelection in 1914 to the Sixty-fourth Congress; engaged in the real estate brokerage business; served as an internal-revenue agent in New Jersey and Wisconsin from 1915 to 1920, when he resigned to engage in private practice as a consultant and adviser in the field of federal laws; again appointed as an internal-revenue agent and served from 1933 until 1940, when he retired due to physical disability and resided in Palm Beach, Fla.; died in New York City, August 5, 1953; interment in Our Lady of Lourdes Cemetery, Trenton, N.J.

**WALSH, Arthur,** a Senator from New Jersey; born in Newark, Essex County, N.J., February 26, 1896; educated in the public schools, by private tutor, and at the New York University School of Commerce at New York City; began his career as a recording violinist for Thomas A. Edison in 1915 and later held executive positions with the Edison Enterprises; during the First World War served as a sergeant in the United States Marine Corps 1917-1919; lieutenant in the United States Naval Reserve 1929-1932; colonel in the New Jersey National Guard 1941-1943; member of the New Jersey Workmen's Compensation Investigating Commission 1932-1933; New Jersey director of the Federal Housing Administration 1934-1935, and as deputy and later as assistant administrator at Washington, D.C., 1935-1938; presidential elector in 1940 on the Democratic ticket; member of the New Jersey State Board of Regents in 1941 and 1942; member of the board of directors of the American-Russian Chamber of Commerce in 1943; commissioner of the Port of New York Authority in 1943; appointed as a Democrat to the United States Senate to fill the vacancy caused by the death of W. Warren Barbour and served from November 26, 1943, to December 7, 1944, when a duly elected successor qualified; was not a candidate for election to the vacancy in 1944; chairman, Committee on Naval Affairs (Seventy-eighth Congress); resumed his former business pursuits; died in New York City, N.Y., December 13, 1947; interment in Gate of Heaven Cemetery, East Hanover, N.J.

**WALSH, David Ignatius,** a Senator from Massachusetts; born in Leominster, Worcester County, Mass., November 11, 1872; attended the public schools; graduated from Holy Cross College, Worcester, Mass., in 1893 and from Boston University Law School in 1897; was admitted to the bar and commenced practice at Fitchburg, Mass., in 1897, later practicing in Boston; member, Massachusetts house of representatives, 1900-1901; lieutenant governor of Massachusetts, 1913; elected Governor of Massachusetts in 1913, reelected in 1914 and served from January 8, 1914 to January 6, 1916; unsuccessful candidate for reelection in 1915; delegate at large to the Massachusetts constitutional convention in 1917 and 1918; elected as a Democrat to the United States Senate and served from March 4, 1919, to March 3, 1925; unsuccessful candidate for reelection in 1924; resumed the practice of law in Boston; elected to the United States Senate in 1926 to fill the vacancy caused by the death of Henry Cabot Lodge and took his seat December 6, 1926; reelected in 1928, 1934, and again in 1940 for the term ending January 3, 1947; unsuccessful candidate for reelection in 1946; chairman, Committee on Education and Labor (Seventy-third and Seventy-fourth Congresses), Committee on Naval Affairs (Seventy-fourth through Seventy-seventh and Seventy-ninth Congresses); retired from political activities and resided in Clinton, Mass., until his death; died in Boston, Mass., June 11, 1947; interment in St. John's Cemetery, Clinton, Mass.

Bibliography: *DAB*; Grattan, William J. "David I. Walsh and His Associates: A Study in Political Theory." Ph.D. dissertation, Harvard University, 1958; Wayman, Dorothy G. *David Walsh: Citizen Patriot.* Milwaukee: Bruce Publishing Company, 1952.

**WALSH, James Joseph,** a Representative from New York; born in New York City May 22, 1858; attended the public schools and St. James' Parochial School; was graduated from Manhattan College in 1877 and from the law department of Columbia University, both in New York City, in 1879; was admitted to the bar in 1880 and commenced practice in New York City; inspector of common schools 1889-1894; presented credentials as a Democratic Member-elect to the Fifty-fourth Congress and served from March 4, 1895, to June 2, 1896, when he was succeeded by John M. Mitchell, who had contested his election; resumed the practice of law in New York City; appointed city magistrate in 1905, which office he held until his death in New York City on May 8, 1909; interment in Calvary Cemetery, Long Island City, N.Y.

**WALSH, James Thomas,** (son of William Francis Walsh), a Representative from New York; born in Syracuse, Onondaga County, N.Y., June 19, 1947; graduated, Christian Brothers Academy, Syracuse, 1966; B.A., St. Bonaventure University, 1970; businessman; member, Syracuse common council, 1978-1988, president, 1986-1988; elected as a Republican to the One Hundred First and to the three succeeding Congresses (January 3, 1989-January 3, 1997); is a resident of Syracuse, N.Y.

**WALSH, John Richard,** a Representative from Indiana; born in Martinsville, Morgan County, Ind., May 22, 1913; attended the public schools; was graduated from Indiana University Law School in 1934; was admitted to the bar July 27, 1934, and engaged in the practice of law in Martinsville, Ind., until 1941; Morgan County attorney in 1935 and 1936; deputy attorney general of Indiana in 1941; served in the United States Army with the Thirty-fifth Infantry Division from May 18, 1942, until discharged as a technical sergeant June 15, 1943; in 1943 continued the practice of law in Anderson, Ind.; chief deputy prosecuting attorney of Madison County, Ind., in 1945 and 1946; probate commissioner for Madison County Circuit Court in 1948; elected as a Democrat to the Eighty-first Congress (January 3, 1949-January 3, 1951); unsuccessful candidate for reelection in 1950 and for election in 1954 to the Eighty-fourth Congress; resumed the practice of law in Anderson and continued in practice until his death; member of board of

directors and secretary-treasurer, State Security Life Insurance Co., Anderson, Ind., 1953-1958; secretary of state of Indiana from December 1, 1958, to November 30, 1960; delegate, Democratic National Convention, 1960; county attorney of Madison County, 1964-1965; was a resident of Anderson, Ind., until his death there on January 23, 1975; interment in Greenlawn Cemetery, Martinsville, Ind.

**WALSH, Joseph,** a Representative from Massachusetts; born in Boston (Brighton), Mass., December 16, 1875; attended public schools in Falmouth, Mass., and Boston University Law School; admitted to the bar in 1906 and practiced in New Bedford; served as a fish culturist and clerk in the United States Bureau of Fisheries at Woods Hole, Mass., 1900-1905; also engaged in newspaper reporting in Boston and New Bedford, Mass.; member of the Massachusetts house of representatives in 1905; elected as a Republican to the Sixty-fourth and to the three succeeding Congresses and served from March 4, 1915, to August 2, 1922, when he resigned to accept a judicial position; appointed August 2, 1922, as a justice of the superior court of Massachusetts, in which capacity he served until his death in New Bedford, Mass., January 13, 1946; interment in St. Mary's Cemetery.

**WALSH, Michael,** a Representative from New York; born in Youghal, near Cork, Ireland, May 4, 1810; completed preparatory studies; was graduated from Trinity College, Dublin, Ireland; immigrated to the United States and settled in Baltimore, Md.; learned the trade of lithographic printer; moved to New York City; member of the New York State assembly in 1839; in 1843 established the Subterranean; suspended publication of the Subterranean after two years when convicted for the publication of a libel; elected as a member of the State assembly in 1846 and again in 1848; elected as a Democrat to the Thirty-third Congress (March 4, 1853-March 3, 1855); unsuccessful candidate for reelection in 1854 to the Thirty-fourth Congress; after his term in Congress was employed as a newspaper reporter; died in New York City on March 17, 1859; interment in Greenwood Cemetery, Brooklyn, N.Y.

Bibliography: *DAB*; Ernst, Robert. "The One and Only Mike Walsh." *New York Historical Society Quarterly* 36 (January 1952): 43-65.

**WALSH, Patrick,** a Senator from Georgia; born in Ballingarry, County Limerick, Ireland, January 1, 1840; immigrated to the United States in 1852 with his parents, who settled in Charleston, S.C.; became a journeyman printer in 1857; attended night schools, high school, and Georgetown University, Washington, D.C., 1859-1861; returned to Charleston and entered the State military service; moved to Augusta, Ga., in 1862 and for thirty-two years was connected with the press of that city, most of the time as manager and editor of the Augusta Chronicle; treasurer and general manager of the Southern Associated Press; member of the Augusta city council in 1870; member, Georgia State house of representatives, 1872, 1874, 1876; member of the Democratic National Executive Committee for four years; member of the World's Columbian Exposition Commission at Chicago in 1893; appointed as a Democrat to the United States Senate to fill the vacancy caused by the death of Alfred H. Colquitt; subsequently elected, and served from April 2, 1894 to March 3, 1895; unsuccessful candidate for renomination in 1894; resumed his newspaper interests; mayor of Augusta, 1897-1899; died in Augusta, Ga., March 19, 1899; interment in the City Cemetery.

**WALSH, Thomas James,** a Senator from Montana; born at Two Rivers, Manitowoc County, Wis., June 12, 1859; attended the public schools; taught school; graduated from the law department of the University of Wisconsin at Madison in 1884; was admitted to the bar in 1884 and commenced practice at Redfield, Dakota Territory; moved to Helena, Mont., in 1890 and continued the practice of law; unsuccessful candidate for election in 1906 to the Sixtieth Congress, and in 1910 for the United States Senate; elected as a Democrat to the United States Senate in 1912; reelected in 1918, 1924, and 1930, and served from March 4, 1913 until his death on March 2, 1933, on a train near Wilson, N.C., while en route to Washington, D.C., to accept the appointment as Attorney General in President Franklin D. Roosevelt's Cabinet; chairman, Committee on Mines and Mining (Sixty-third through Sixty-fifth Congresses), Committee on Pensions (Sixty-fifth Congress), Committee on the Disposition of Useless Executive Papers (Sixty-sixth Congress); as a member of the Committee on Public Lands and Surveys, he was an influential figure in the Senate's investigation of the Harding administration's handling of naval reserve oil leases, popularly known as the "Teapot Dome" scandal; funeral services were held in the Chamber of the United States Senate; interment in Resurrection Cemetery, Helena, Mont.

**Bibliography:** *DAB*; Bates, James Leonard. "Senator Walsh of Montana, 1918-1924: A Liberal Under Pressure." Ph.D. dissertation, University of North Carolina, 1952; Duddington, Miles. "Senator Thomas J. Walsh, Independent Democrat in the Wilson Years." Ph.D. dissertation, University of Chicago, 1940.

**WALSH, Thomas Yates,** a Representative from Maryland; born in Baltimore, Md., in 1809; completed preparatory studies and attended St. Mary's College at Baltimore, 1821-1824; studied law; was admitted to the bar on July 30, 1832, and commenced practice in Baltimore; member of the Baltimore city council in 1847 and 1848; elected as a Whig to the Thirty-second Congress (March 4, 1851-March 3, 1853); unsuccessful candidate for reelection in 1852 to the Thirty-third Congress; resumed the practice of law; died in Baltimore, Md., January 20, 1865; interment in St. Paul's Protestant Episcopal Cemetery.

**WALSH, William,** a Representative from Maryland; born near Tullamore, County Kings, Ireland, May 11, 1828; attended a local school; immigrated to the United States in 1842 and settled in Virginia; was graduated from Mount St. Mary's College, Emmitsburg, Md.; studied law; was admitted to the bar in Virginia in 1850 and commenced practice in Cumberland, Md., in 1852; member of the State constitutional convention in 1867; elected as a Democrat to the Forty-fourth and Forty-fifth Congresses (March 4, 1875-March 3, 1879); chairman, Committee on Revision of the Laws (Forty-fifth Congress); declined to be a candidate for renomination in 1878; resumed the practice of law; died in Cumberland, Md., May 17, 1892; interment in St. Patrick's Cemetery.

**WALSH, William Francis** (father of James T. Walsh), a Representative from New York; born in Syracuse, Onondaga County, N.Y., July 11, 1912; graduated from Most Holy Rosary High School, Syracuse, N.Y., 1930; A.B., St. Bonaventure College, 1934; attended Catholic University School of Social Work, 1939-1940; M.A., social work, University of Buffalo, 1949; atttended Syracuse University, Maxwell School, 1950; LL.D., St. Bonaventure University, 1970; enlisted as a private in the United States Army, One Hundred and First Antitank Battalion, 1941; served in Pacific Theater; honorably discharged, 1946, with rank of captain, United States Air Force; elected Welfare Commissioner of Onondaga County, 1959; elected mayor of Syracuse in 1961, reelected in 1965, and served until 1969; member, New York State Public Service Commission, 1970; delegate, New York State Republican conventions, 1966-1970; delegate to the Republican National Convention of 1968; elected as a Republican-Conservative to the Ninety-third and to the two succeeding Congresses (January 3, 1973-January 3, 1979); was not a candidate for reelection in 1978 to the Ninety-sixth Congress; is a resident of Syracuse, N.Y.

**WALTER, Francis Eugene,** a Representative from Pennsylvania; born in Easton, Northampton County, Pa., May 26, 1894; attended the public schools, preparatory school at Princeton, N.J., Lehigh University, Bethlehem, Pa., and George Washington Univer-

sity and Georgetown University, Washington, D.C.; during both World Wars served in the air service of the United States Navy; was admitted to the bar in 1919 and commenced practice in Easton, Pa.; director of the Broad Street Trust Co., Philadelphia, Pa., and of the Easton National Bank, Easton, Pa.; solicitor of Northampton County, Pa., 1928-1933; delegate to the Democratic National Convention in 1928; elected as a Democrat to the Seventy-third and to the fifteen succeeding Congresses, and served from March 4, 1933 until his death in Washington, D.C., May 31, 1963; chairman, Committee on Un-American Activities (Eighty-fourth through Eighty-eighth Congresses); co-sponsor of the McCarran-Walter Act of 1952, (Immigration and Nationality Act) codifying the immigration and nationality laws, tightening the requirements for citizenship, and retaining the immigration quota system under which Great Britain, Germany and Ireland were allotted over two-thirds of the total quota; interment in Arlington National Cemetery, Va.

**Bibliography:** Dimmitt, Marius Albert, Sr. "The Enactment of the McCarran-Walter Act of 1952." Ph.D. dissertation, University of Kansas, 1970.

**WALTERS, Anderson Howell,** a Representative from Pennsylvania; born in Johnstown, Cambria County, Pa., May 18, 1862; attended the public schools and was graduated from Johnstown High School in 1878; employed as a telegrapher and clerk with the Pennsylvania Railroad Co. 1878-1880; entered the service of the Johnstown Water Co. and the Johnstown Gas Co., in 1881 and was assistant superintendent of these companies in 1889 and general manager and secretary 1895-1902; delegate to the Pennsylvania Republican conventions in 1890, 1892, 1898, and 1904; delegate to the Republican National Convention in 1896; chairman of the Republican city committee 1896-1899; member of the Pennsylvania Republican committee 1898-1902; member of the Johnstown City Council 1900-1904; editor and proprietor of the Johnstown Tribune from 1902 until his death; elected as a member of the board of trustees of the Johnstown Savings Bank in 1907; elected as a Republican to the Sixty-third Congress (March 4, 1913-March 3, 1915); was not a candidate for renomination; elected to the Sixty-sixth and Sixty-seventh Congresses (March 4, 1919-March 3, 1923); chairman, Committee on Expenditures in the Department of Labor (Sixty-sixth and Sixty-seventh Congresses); was not a candidate for renomination; elected to the Sixty-ninth Congress (March 4, 1925-March 3, 1927); was not a candidate for renomination; died in Johnstown, Pa., December 7, 1927; interment in Grandview Cemetery.

**WALTERS, Herbert Sanford,** a Senator from Tennessee; born in Leadvale, Jefferson County, Tenn., November 17, 1891; attended the public schools of Jefferson County, the Baker-Himmell School in Knoxville, the Castle Heights Military Academy in Lebanon, the Carson-Newman College in Jefferson City, and the University of Tennessee in Knoxville; chairman of the board of Walters & Prater, Inc., and a prominent banker; member, State house of representatives 1933-1935; commissioner of the State Highway Department 1934-1935; appointed as a Democrat, August 20, 1963, to the United States Senate to fill the vacancy caused by the death of the Estes Kefauver and served from August 20, 1963, to November 3, 1964; was not a candidate for election in 1964 to the unexpired term; trustee, University of Tennessee, Knoxville, Tenn., 1961-1973; president, Walters & Prater, Inc.; died in Knoxville, Tenn., August 17, 1973; interment in Jarnagin Cemetery, Morristown, Tenn.

**Bibliography:** Hill, Howard. *The Herbert Walters Story.* Kingsport, Tenn.: Kingsport Press, 1963.

**WALTHALL, Edward Cary,** a Senator from Mississippi; born in Richmond, Va., April 4, 1831; moved to Mississippi as a child; attended St. Thomas Hall, Holly Springs, Miss.; studied law; was admitted to the bar in 1852 and commenced practice in Coffeeville, Miss.; elected district attorney for the tenth judicial district of

Mississippi in 1856 and reelected in 1859; during the Civil War entered the Confederate Army as a lieutenant; promoted to lieutenant colonel, colonel, brigadier general, and major general; resumed the practice of law in Coffeeville; moved to Grenada, Miss., in 1871 and continued the practice of law until 1885; appointed as a Democrat to the United States Senate to fill the vacancy caused by the resignation of Lucius Q.C. Lamar; was subsequently elected to fill the vacancy; reelected in 1889 and served from March 9, 1885, to January 24, 1894, when he resigned due to ill health; was again elected for the term beginning March 4, 1895, and served from that date until his death in Washington, D.C., April 21, 1898; chairman, Committee on Military Affairs (Fifty-third Congress), Committee on Revolutionary Claims (Fifty-fifth Congress); funeral services were held in the Chamber of the United States Senate; interment in Holly Springs Cemetery, Holly Springs, Miss.

**Bibliography:** *DAB*; Helmes, James. "Edward Carey Walthall: Soldier and Statesman." Ph.D. dissertation, Peabody College, 1928.

**WALTON, Charles Wesley,** a Representative from Maine; born in Mexico, Oxford County, Maine, December 9, 1819; attended the common schools and was instructed at home and by private tutors; studied law; was admitted to the bar in Oxford, Maine, in 1841 and commenced practice in Mexico, Maine, in 1843; also practiced law in Dixfield, Maine; attorney for Oxford County 1847-1851; moved to Auburn, Maine, in 1855 and continued the practice of law; attorney for Androscoggin County 1857-1860; elected as a Republican to the Thirty-seventh Congress and served from March 4, 1861, to May 26, 1862, when he resigned to accept a judicial appointment; associate justice of the State supreme court 1862-1897; was not a candidate for reappointment; resided in Portland, Cumberland County, Maine, until his death on January 24, 1900; interment in Evergreen Cemetery.

**WALTON, Eliakim Persons,** a Representative from Vermont; born in Montpelier, Vt., February 17, 1812; attended the common schools; apprenticed to a printer; studied law, but did not practice; engaged in journalism and compiling; editor of "Walton's Vermont Register"; organizer and first president of the Editors and Publishers' Association, holding the office of president for more than twenty years; after the retirement of his father in 1853 was sole proprietor of the Watchman until 1868; served in the State house of representatives in 1853; elected as a Republican to the Thirty-fifth, Thirty-sixth, and Thirty-seventh Congresses (March 4, 1857-March 3, 1863); declined to be a candidate for reelection and returned to his editorial and literary labors; delegate to the Republican National Convention in 1864; member of the State constitutional convention in 1870; served in the State senate in 1875 and 1877; trustee of the University of Vermont and of the State agricultural college 1875-1887; president of the Vermont Historical Society 1876-1890; died in Montpelier, Washington County, Vt., December 19, 1890; interment in Green Mount Cemetery.

**WALTON, George** (brother of John Walton and cousin of Matthew Walton), a Delegate and a Senator from Georgia; born in Cumberland County, Va., in either 1749 or 1750; apprenticed as a carpenter; attended the common schools; moved to Savannah, Ga., in 1769; studied law; was admitted to the bar in 1774 and commenced practice in Savannah, Ga.; secretary of the Provincial Congress in 1775, and a member of the committee of intelligence; Member of the council of safety in 1775 and later president of that body; member, Georgia State house of representatives; member of the Continental Congress in 1776, 1777, 1780, and 1781; a signer of the Declaration of Independence; served in the Revolutionary War and was captured at Savannah; colonel in the First Georgia Battalion; Governor of Georgia in 1779; commissioner to treat with the Indians and to negotiate a treaty with the Cherokees in Tennessee in 1783; chief justice of Georgia, 1783-1789; member of the Augusta Board of Commissioners, 1784-1785; represented

Georgia in the settlement of the boundary line between South Carolina and Georgia in 1786; elected as a delegate to the convention to frame the Federal Constitution in 1787, but declined; Governor of Georgia from January 7 to November 9, 1789; was appointed first judge of the superior courts of the eastern judicial circuit in 1790; appointed to the United States Senate to fill the vacancy caused by the resignation of James Jackson, and served from November 16, 1795 to February 20, 1796, when a successor was elected; trustee of Richmond Academy and of the University of Georgia; moved to Augusta; again appointed judge of the superior circuit of Georgia and served from 1799 until his death at his home, "College Hill," near Augusta, Richmond County, Ga., February 2, 1804; interment in Rosney Cemetery; reinterment in 1848 beneath the monument in front of the courthouse on Greene Street, Augusta, Ga.

**Bibliography:** *DAB*; Bridges, Edwin. "George Walton: A Political Biography." Ph.D. dissertation, University of Chicago, 1981.

**WALTON, John** (brother of George Walton and cousin of Matthew Walton), a Delegate from Georgia; born in Virginia in 1738; became a planter near Augusta, Ga.; delegate from St. Paul Parish to the Provincial Congress at Savannah, Ga., in 1775; elected to the Continental Congress February 26, 1778; signed the Articles of Confederation on behalf of Georgia on July 24, 1778; held office of surveyor of Richmond County for several years; died at New Savannah, Ga., in 1783.

**WALTON, Matthew** (cousin of George Walton and John Walton), a Representative from Kentucky; received a limited schooling; member of the conventions held in Danville in 1785 and 1787; member of the first Kentucky constitutional convention in 1792; member of the Kentucky house of representatives in 1792, 1795, and 1808; elected as a Republican to the Eighth and Ninth Congresses (March 4, 1803-March 3, 1807); died in Springfield, Ky., January 18, 1819; interment in Springfield Cemetery.

**WALTON, William Bell,** a Representative from New Mexico; born in Altoona, Blair County, Pa., January 23, 1871; attended the public schools and South Jersey Institute, Bridgeton, N.J.; moved to New Mexico in 1891; studied law; was admitted to the bar in 1893 and commenced practice at Deming, N.Mex.; member of the State house of representatives in 1901 and 1902; clerk of Grant County 1903-1906; delegate to the Democratic National Convention in 1908; chairman of the New Mexico Democratic central committee in 1910; member of the New Mexico constitutional convention in 1911; served in the State senate 1912-1916; elected as a Democrat to the Sixty-fifth Congress (March 4, 1917-March 3, 1919); did not seek renomination, but was an unsuccessful candidate for election to the United States Senate in 1918; resumed the practice of law in Silver City, N.Mex.; elected district attorney of the sixth judicial district November 2, 1926; reelected in 1928 and served until 1932; continued the practice of law until 1934, when he retired from active pursuits; died in Silver City, N.Mex., April 14, 1939; interment in the Masonic Cemetery.

**WALWORTH, Reuben Hyde,** a Representative from New York; born in Bozrah, Conn., October 26, 1788; moved to New York with his parents, who settled on a farm near Hoosick in 1796; attended the common schools; taught school; studied law; was admitted to the bar in 1809 and commenced practice in Plattsburgh in 1810; master in chancery and circuit judge in 1811; served in the War of 1812; aide-de-camp to General Benjamin Mooers and division judge advocate with rank of colonel; elected to the Seventeenth Congress (March 4, 1821-March 3, 1823); was not a candidate for renomination in 1822 to the Eighteenth Congress; judge of the fourth judicial district of New York, 1823-1828; moved to Saratoga Springs, N.Y., in October 1828; chancellor of the State of New York from 1828 to 1848, when the office of chancellor was abolished; unsuccessful candidate for election as Governor in 1848; appointed as an Associate Justice of the United States Supreme Court by President John Tyler on March 13, 1844, but the nomination was withdrawn; died in Saratoga Springs, N.Y., November 27, 1867; interment in Greenridge Cemetery.

Bibliography: *DAB*.

**WAMP, Zachary Paul (Zach),** a Representative from Tennessee; born in Fort Benning, Ga., October 28, 1957, and moved with his family to Chattanooga, Tenn., at an early age; graduated, McCallie School, 1976; attended the University of North Carolina, Chapel Hill, and the University of Tennessee; commercial and industrial real estate broker; president, Hamilton County Young Republicans, 1987; regional director, Tennessee State Republican Party, 1989; unsuccessful candidate in 1992 for election to the One Hundred Third Congress; elected as a Republican to the One Hundred Fourth Congress (January 3, 1995-January 3, 1997); is a resident of Chattanooga, Tenn.

**WAMPLER, Fred,** a Representative from Indiana; born in Carriers Mills, Saline County, Ill., October 15, 1909; moved with his parents to Terre Haute, Ind., in 1911 and attended the public schools; graduated from Indiana State Teachers College in 1931, and M.S., 1940; high school athletic director in Bluffton, Ohio, 1931-1933, and football coach in Terre Haute, Ind., 1937-1958; athletic director, Washington Court House, Ohio, in 1936 and 1937; served from January 1944 as a gunnery officer in the United States Navy, with service in the Pacific Theater until discharged as a lieutenant in 1946; served as commanding officer, Naval Reserve activating training center, Terre Haute, Ind., 1946-1949; sports director for a radio station in Terre Haute, Ind., 1947-1949; during the Korean conflict was recalled to active duty as executive officer aboard a troop transport, and served from January 1950 to March 1954; promoted to commander, United States Naval Reserve, May 11, 1960; elected as a Democrat to the Eighty-sixth Congress (January 3, 1959-January 3, 1961); unsuccessful candidate for reelection in 1960 to the Eighty-seventh Congress; appointed to the Indiana-Illinois Wabash Valley Interstate Commission on March 13, 1961, and served until his resignation May 26, 1962; unsuccessful candidate for election in 1962 to the Eighty-eighth Congress; Regional Coordinator, Department of the Interior, 1963-1970; funding coordinator for state-federal programs, Ohio department of natural resources and transportation, 1971-1976; is a resident of Terrace Park, Ohio.

**WAMPLER, William Creed,** a Representative from Virginia; born in Pennington Gap, Lee County, Va., April 21, 1926; attended the public schools of Bristol, Va.; enlisted on May 21, 1943, in the United States Navy as a seaman, and served for twenty-seven months until discharged on September 29, 1945; member of the Naval Reserve, V-6; resumed his education and was graduated from Virginia Polytechnic Institute, Blacksburg, Va., in 1948 and studied law at the University of Virginia, 1948-1950; reporter for a newspaper in Bristol, Va., 1950-1951; reporter and editorial writer, Big Stone Gap (Va.) Post, 1951; reporter and copy editor, Bristol Herald Courier, 1951-1952; member of board of visitors of Emory and Henry College, Emory, Va.; Republican assistant campaign manager for Ninth Congressional District elections in 1948; president of the Young Republican Federation of Virginia in 1950, and served as keynote speaker and permanent chairman of the Ninth District Republican Convention the same year; elected as a Republican to the Eighty-third Congress (January 3, 1953-January 3, 1955); was an unsuccessful candidate for reelection in 1954 to the Eighty-fourth Congress; served with the Atomic Energy Commission, January 1955 to March 1956; unsuccessful candidate for election in 1956 to the Eighty-fifth Congress; vice president and general manager of Wampler Brothers Furniture Co., Bristol, Va., 1957-1960; vice president and general manager, Wampler Carpet Co., 1961-1966; elected to the Ninetieth and to the seven succeeding Congresses (January 3, 1967-January 3, 1983); unsuccessful candidate for reelection in 1982 to the Ninety-eighth Congress; is a resident of Bristol, Va.

**WANGER, Irving Price,** a Representative from Pennsylvania; born in North Coventry, Chester County, Pa., March 5, 1852; attended the public schools of North Coventry and Pottstown, and Hill School in Pottstown; deputy prothonotary of Chester County in 1871; commenced the study of law at Norristown in 1872; deputy prothonotary of Montgomery County 1873-1875; was admitted to the bar December 18, 1875, and commenced the practice of law in Norristown, Pa.; elected burgess of Norristown in 1878; delegate to the Republican National Convention in 1880; elected district attorney of Montgomery County in 1880 and again in 1886; served as chairman of the Montgomery County Republican committee in 1889; unsuccessful candidate for election in 1890 to the Fifty-second Congress; elected as a Republican to the Fifty-third and to the eight succeeding Congresses (March 4, 1893-March 3, 1911); chairman, Committee on Expenditures in the Post Office Department (Fifty-fifth through Sixty-first Congresses); unsuccessful candidate for reelection in 1910 to the Sixty-second Congress; lived for a short time in Wilmington, Del.; resumed the practice of his profession in Media and Norristown, Pa., in 1920; died in Norristown, Pa., January 14, 1940; interment in Mount Zion Cemetery, Pottstown, Pa.

**WARBURTON, Herbert Birchby,** a Representative from Delaware; born in Wilmington, New Castle County, Del., September 21, 1916; attended the public schools of Wilmington, Del., and Reading, Pa.; graduated from University of Delaware, Newark, Del., in June 1938, and from Dickinson School of Law, Carlisle, Pa., in June 1941; took reserve officers training course at University of Delaware and commissioned a second lieutenant; began active Army duty as first lieutenant of the One Hundred and Twenty-second Antiaircraft Battalion in September 1941; graduated from Command and General Staff School, Fort Leavenworth, Kans., in September 1945 and became battalion commander in October 1945; was relieved from active duty as a major in December 1945; was admitted to the Delaware bar in absentia in April 1942 and began the practice of law in Wilmington, Del., in January 1946; city solicitor, 1949-1952; elected as a Republican to the Eighty-third Congress (January 3, 1953-January 3, 1955); was not a candidate for renomination in 1954 but was an unsuccessful candidate for election to the United States Senate; appointed special assistant to Secretary of Labor James P. Mitchell on March 2, 1955, and served until November 7, 1957; general counsel, Post Office Department, from November 7, 1957, to January 20, 1961; minority counsel to the House Government Operations subcommittee, serving from March 1961 to September 1964; executive director, American Orthotics and Prosthetics Association and the American Board for Certification in Orthotics and Prosthetics; was a resident of Frankford, Del., until his death in Lewes, Del., July 30, 1983; cremated and family retained ashes.

**WARBURTON, Stanton,** a Representative from Washington; was born in Sullivan County, Pa., April 13, 1865; moved to Iowa with his parents, who settled in Cherokee in 1868; attended the public schools; was graduated from Cherokee (Iowa) High School in 1884 and from Coe College, Cedar Rapids, Iowa, in 1888; moved to Tacoma, Wash., in 1888; studied law; was admitted to the bar in 1889 and commenced practice in Tacoma; member of the State senate 1896-1904; elected as a Republican to the Sixty-second Congress (March 4, 1911-March 3, 1913); unsuccessful candidate for reelection in 1912 to the Sixty-third Congress; resumed the practice of law in Tacoma, Wash.; died in Boston, Mass., December 24, 1926; interment in Mountain View Burial Park, Tacoma, Wash.

**WARD, Aaron** (uncle of Elijah Ward), a Representative from New York; was born in Sing Sing (now Ossining), N.Y., on July 5, 1790; completed preparatory studies in Mount Pleasant Academy; served in the War of 1812 as lieutenant and captain in the Twenty-ninth Infantry; studied law; was admitted to the bar and commenced practice at Sing Sing; district attorney for Westchester County; served in the State militia as colonel, brigadier general, and major general; elected to the Nineteenth and Twentieth Congresses (March 4, 1825-March 3, 1829); was not a candidate for reelection; elected as a Jacksonian to the Twenty-second, Twenty-third, and Twenty-fourth Congresses (March 4, 1831-March 3, 1837); was not a candidate for reelection to the Twenty-fifth Congress; elected as a Democrat to the Twenty-seventh Congress (March 4, 1841-March 3, 1843); unsuccessful candidate for reelection to the Twenty-eighth Congress; delegate to the State constitutional convention in 1846; unsuccessful Democratic candidate for secretary of state in 1855; trustee of Mount Pleasant Academy; died at the home of his son-in-law in Georgetown, D.C., March 2, 1867; interment in Dale Cemetery, Ossining, N.Y.

**WARD, Andrew Harrison,** a Representative from Kentucky; was born near Cynthiana, Harrison County, Ky., on January 3, 1815; attended the county schools and Transylvania University, Lexington, Ky.; clerk on a steamboat on the Tombigbee River for several years; studied law; admitted to the bar in 1844 and commenced practice in Cynthiana, Ky.; city attorney of Cynthiana in 1860; unsuccessful candidate for election to the Kentucky house of representatives in 1861; member of the Kentucky house of representatives 1863-1865; unsuccessful candidate for election in 1864 to the Thirty-ninth Congress; elected as a Democrat to the Thirty-ninth Congress to fill the vacancy caused by the resignation of Green Clay Smith and served from December 3, 1866, to March 3, 1867; was not a candidate for renomination in 1866; resumed the practice of law and subsequently became president of the National Bank of Cynthiana; died in Cynthiana, Ky., April 16, 1904; interment in Battle Grove Cemetery.

**WARD, Artemas** (father of Artemas Ward, Jr.), a Delegate and a Representative from Massachusetts; born in Shrewsbury, Mass., November 26, 1727; attended the common schools and was prepared for college by a private tutor; graduated from Harvard College in 1748; justice of the peace in 1752; a representative in the Massachusettsgeneral assembly many terms and served in the executive council; lieutenant colonel in the provincial army during the French and Indian War; appointed brigadier general by the provincial congress of Massachusetts on October 27, 1774, and was made commander in chief of the Massachusetts forces on May 19, 1775; appointed by the Continental Congress as major general on June 17, 1775; chief justice of the court of common pleas of Worcester County in 1776 and 1777; president of the Massachusetts Executive Council, 1777-1779; member of the Massachusetts house of representatives, 1779-1785, serving as speaker in 1785; Member of the Continental Congress, 1780-1781; elected to the Second and Third Congresses (March 4, 1791-March 3, 1795); died in Shrewsbury, Mass., October 28, 1800; interment in Mountain View Cemetery.

Bibliography: *DAB*; Martyn, Charles. *The Life of Artemas Ward, The First Commander-in-Chief of the American Revolution.* 1921. Reprint. Port Washington, N.Y.: Kennikat, 1970; Smith, James Ferrell. "The Rise of Artemas Ward, 1727-1777: Authority, Politics, and Military Life in Eighteenth Century Massachusetts." Ph.D. dissertation, University of Colorado, 1990.

**WARD, Artemas, Jr.** (son of Artemas Ward), a Representative from Massachusetts; born in Shrewsbury, Mass., January 9, 1762; graduated from Harvard University in 1783; studied law; admitted to the bar in 1783 and commenced the practice of law in Weston; member of the Massachusetts house of representatives, 1796-1800,

and again in 1811; moved to Charlestown in 1800; member of the board of overseers of Harvard University, 1810-1844; elected as a Federalist to the Thirteenth and Fourteenth Congresses (March 4, 1813-March 3, 1817); served in the Massachusetts senate in 1818 and 1819; member of the Massachusetts constitutional convention in 1820; chief justice of the court of common pleas from 1820 to 1839; died in Boston, Mass., October 7, 1847.

**WARD, Charles Bonnell,** a Representative from New York; born in Newark, N.J., April 27, 1879; attended the public schools and was graduated from Pennsylvania Military College at Chester in 1899; moved to New York and settled in Debruce, Sullivan County, in 1903; engaged in agricultural pursuits; editor and owner of the Liberty Register at Liberty, N.Y., 1910-1928; elected as a Republican to the Sixty-fourth and to the four succeeding Congresses (March 4, 1915-March 3, 1925); declined to be a candidate for reelection in 1924 to the Sixty-ninth Congress; resumed agricultural pursuits; owner and operator of the Debruce Inn Club until his death; died at Liberty, N.Y., May 27, 1946; interment in Mount Pleasant Cemetery, Newark, N.J.

**WARD, David Jenkins,** a Representative from Maryland; born in Salisbury, Wicomico County, Md., September 17, 1871; attended the public schools; engaged in agricultural pursuits, lumbering, and the mercantile business at Salisbury, Md.; member of the State house of delegates 1915-1917; chairman of the Democratic State central committee of Wicomico County 1918-1926; member of the State senate 1926-1934 and from 1938 until his resignation in 1939; elected as a Democrat to the Seventy-sixth Congress to fill the vacancy caused by the resignation of T. Alan Goldsborough; reelected to the Seventy-seventh and Seventy-eighth Congresses and served from June 6, 1939, to January 3, 1945; was an unsuccessful candidate for renomination in 1944; resumed the mercantile, lumber, and real estate businesses; died in Salisbury, Md., February 18, 1961; interment in Parsons Cemetery.

**WARD, Elijah** (nephew of Aaron Ward), a Representative from New York; born in Sing Sing (now Ossining), N.Y., September 16, 1816; pursued classical studies; engaged in commercial pursuits in New York City and at the same time attended the law department of New York University; was admitted to the bar in 1843 and commenced practice in New York City; judge advocate general of the State 1853-1855; delegate to the Democratic National Convention in 1856; elected as a Democrat to the Thirty-fifth Congress (March 4, 1857-March 3, 1859); unsuccessful candidate for reelection in 1858 to the Thirty-sixth Congress; elected to the Thirty-seventh and Thirty-eighth Congresses (March 4, 1861-March 3, 1865); unsuccessful candidate for reelection in 1864 to the Thirty-ninth Congress; resumed the practice of law in New York City; elected to the Forty-fourth Congress (March 4, 1875-March 3, 1877); chairman, Committee on Commerce (Forty-fourth Congress); unsuccessful candidate for reelection in 1876 to the Forty-fifth Congress; died in Roslyn, Nassau County, N.Y., February 7, 1882; interment in Woodlawn Cemetery, New York City.

**WARD, Hallett Sydney,** a Representative from North Carolina; born near Gatesville, Gates County, N.C., August 31, 1870; attended the public schools; was graduated from the law department of the University of North Carolina at Chapel Hill in 1893; was admitted to the bar the same year and commenced practice in Winton, N.C.; member of the State senate in 1899 and 1901; mayor of Plymouth, N.C., in 1902 and 1903; solicitor of the first judicial district of North Carolina 1904-1910; moved to Washington, N.C., in November 1904 and engaged in the practice of law; elected as a Democrat to the Sixty-seventh and Sixty-eighth Congresses (March 4, 1921-March 3, 1925); declined to be a candidate for renomination in 1924; resumed the practice of law; served in the State senate in 1931; died in Washington, N.C., March 31, 1956; interment in Oakdale Cemetery.

**WARD, Hamilton,** a Representative from New York; born in Salisbury, Herkimer County, N.Y., July 3, 1829; attended the common schools and was privately tutored; studied law; was admitted to the bar and commenced practice in Phillipsville (now Belmont), N.Y., in 1851; district attorney of Allegany County 1856-1859 and 1862-1865; appointed in 1862 by the Governor as commissioner to raise and equip troops for the Civil War; elected as a Republican to the Thirty-ninth, Fortieth, and Forty-first Congresses (March 4, 1865-March 3, 1871); chairman, Committee on Revolutionary Claims (Fortieth Congress); was not a candidate for renomination in 1870; delegate to nearly all State conventions from 1858 to 1890; attorney general of New York in 1880 and 1881; member of the State constitutional commission in 1890; appointed and subsequently elected justice of the State supreme court and served from 1891 until his death in Belmont, Allegany County, N.Y., December 28, 1898; interment in Forest Hill Cemetery.

**WARD, James Hugh,** a Representative from Illinois; born in Chicago, Ill., November 30, 1853; attended the public schools of Chicago and was graduated from the University of Notre Dame, Indiana, in 1873; attended the Union College of Law in Chicago, and was graduated in 1876; was admitted to the bar in July 1876, and practiced; was elected supervisor of the town of West Chicago in 1879; elected as a Democrat to the Forty-ninth Congress (March 4, 1885-March 3, 1887); did not seek renomination in 1886; resumed the practice of his profession in Chicago, Cook County, Ill. where he died on August 15, 1916; interment in Calvary Cemetery.

**WARD, Jasper Delos,** a Representative from Illinois; born in Java, Wyoming County, N.Y., February 1, 1829; attended Allegheny College, Meadville, Pa., in 1849 and 1850; studied law; was admitted to the bar in 1852 and commenced practice in Chicago, Ill.; member of the board of aldermen of Chicago in 1855, 1856, 1859, and 1860; during the Civil War enlisted in the Western Engineers Regiment in 1861 and served for about eight months; member of the Illinois State senate, 1862-1870; elected as a Republican to the Forty-third Congress (March 4, 1873-March 3, 1875); unsuccessful candidate for reelection in 1874 to the Forty-fourth Congress; United States attorney for the northern district of Illinois, 1875-1877; moved to Colorado in 1877 and settled in Leadville; appointed by Governor Frederick W. Pitkin as judge of the fifth judicial district of Colorado, and served from March 5, 1881, to January 3, 1882, declining to be a candidate for election to the same office; moved to Denver, Colo., and resumed the practice of law; died in Denver, Colo., August 6, 1902; interment in Fairmount Cemetery.

**WARD, Jonathan,** a Representative from New York; born in the town of Eastchester, N.Y., September 21, 1768; received a limited schooling; assessor of Eastchester in 1791; sheriff of Westchester County 1802-1806; served in the State senate in 1807; member of the council of appointment in 1809; elected as a Republican to the Fourteenth Congress (March 4, 1815-March 3, 1817); member of the State constitutional convention in 1821; surrogate of Westchester County 1828-1840; died in the town of Eastchester, N.Y., September 28, 1842.

**WARD, Marcus Lawrence,** a Representative from New Jersey; born in Newark, N.J., November 9, 1812; received a limited schooling; engaged in candle manufacturing; delegate to the Republican National Conventions of 1860 and 1864; unsuccessful Union candidate for Governor in 1862; elected Governor of New Jersey in 1865, and served from January 16, 1866 to January 19, 1869; was chairman of the Republican National Committee in 1866; elected as a Republican to the Forty-third Congress (March 4, 1873-March 3, 1875); unsuccessful candidate for reelection in 1874 to the Forty-fourth Congress; died in Newark, N.J., April 25, 1884; interment in Mount Pleasant Cemetery.

**Bibliography:** *DAB*.

**WARD, Matthias,** a Senator from Texas; born in Elbert County, Ga., October 13, 1805; was raised in Madison County, Ala.; received a college education in Huntsville, Ala.; taught school for two years; studied law; moved to the Republic of Texas in 1836 and settled in Bowie, Montague County, and subsequently in Clarksville, Red River County, in 1845; engaged in trading; served a number of years in the Congress of the Republic of Texas; moved to Jefferson, Marion County, Tex.; served in the Texas State senate; appointed as a Democrat to the United States Senate to fill the vacancy caused by the death of J. Pinckney Henderson, and served from September 27, 1858 to December 5, 1859, when a successor was elected; died at Warm Springs, near Raleigh, N.C., October 5, 1861; interment in the Old City Cemetery, Nashville, Tenn.

**WARD, Michael D.,** a Representative from Kentucky; born in White Plains, Westchester County, N.Y., January 7, 1951, and moved with his family to Louisville, Ky., in 1956; graduated, Atherton High School, Louisville, 1969; B.S., University of Louisville School of Business, 1974; served as a Peace Corps volunteer in The Gambia, West Africa; owner of an advertising company, 1983-1985; special assistant to the Jefferson County judge-executive, 1985-1989; member, Kentucky house of representatives, 1989-1993; elected as a Democrat to the One Hundred Fourth Congress (January 3, 1995-January 3, 1997); is a resident of Louisville, Ky.

**WARD, Samuel,** a Delegate from Rhode Island; born in Newport, R.I., May 27, 1725; educated privately; settled in Westerly, R.I., in 1745; engaged in agricultural pursuits; member of the general assembly 1756-1759; one of the founders of Rhode Island College (now Brown University), Providence, R.I., in 1756; chief justice of Rhode Island in 1761 and 1762; Governor under the royal charter in 1762, 1763, and 1765-1767; trustee of Brown University 1764-1776; Member of the Continental Congress 1774-1776; died in Philadelphia, Pa., March 26, 1776; interment in the churchyard of the First Baptist Church, Philadelphia, Pa.; reinterment in the Old Cemetery, Newport, R.I., in 1860.

**Bibliography:** *DAB*.

**WARD, Thomas,** a Representative from New Jersey; born in Newark, N.J., about 1759; completed preparatory studies; studied law; was admitted to the bar and commenced practice in Newark, N.J.; served as captain and major during the Whiskey Rebellion of 1794; sheriff of Essex County, N.J., in 1797; elected one of the judges of the Essex County Court in 1804, and was reelected in 1809; member of the legislative council in 1808 and 1809; elected as a Republican to the Thirteenth and Fourteenth Congresses (March 4, 1813-March 3, 1817); was senior officer of the New Jersey Cavalry at the time of his death in Newark, N.J., March 4, 1842; interment in the churchyard of the First Presbyterian Church.

**WARD, Thomas Bayless,** a Representative from Indiana; born in Marysville, Union County, Ohio, April 27, 1835; moved with his parents to La Fayette, Ind., in May 1836; attended Wabash College, Crawfordsville, Ind., and was graduated from Miami University, Oxford, Ohio, in June 1855; clerk of the city of La Fayette in 1855 and 1856; studied law; was admitted to the bar in 1857 and commenced the practice of his profession in La Fayette, Ind.; city attorney in 1859 and 1860; mayor of La Fayette 1861-1865; judge of the superior court of Tippecanoe County, Ind., 1875-1880; elected as a Democrat to the Forty-eighth and Forty-ninth Congresses (March 4, 1883-March 3, 1887); was not a candidate for renomination in 1886 to the Fiftieth Congress; resumed the practice of his profession in La Fayette, Tippecanoe County, Ind., where he died January 1, 1892; interment in Springvale Cemetery.

**WARD, William,** a Representative from Pennsylvania; born in Philadelphia, Pa., January 1, 1837; attended Girard College, Philadelphia, Pa.; learned the art of printing in the office of the Delaware County Republican, Chester, Pa.; studied law; was admitted to the bar in August 1859 and commenced practice in Chester; also engaged in the land business and banking; member of the city council of Chester and city solicitor; elected as a Republican to the Forty-fifth, Forty-sixth, and Forty-seventh Congresses (March 4, 1877-March 3, 1883); was not a candidate for renomination in 1882; resumed the practice of his profession and his former business pursuits in Chester, Pa., where he died February 27, 1895; interment in the Rural Cemetery.

**WARD, William Lukens,** a Representative from New York; born in Pemberwick, town of Greenwich, Fairfield County, Conn., September 2, 1856; moved to Port Chester, N.Y., with his parents in 1863; attended Friends Seminary, New York City, and the school of mines of Columbia College, New York City (class of 1878); engaged in the manufacture of bolts, nuts, and rivets in Port Chester, N.Y.; chairman of the Republican State committee for several years; elected as a Republican to the Fifty-fifth Congress (March 4, 1897-March 3, 1899); resumed his former manufacturing pursuits in Port Chester, Westchester County, N.Y.; member of the Republican National Committee 1904-1912; died in New York City, July 16, 1933; interment in the family mausoleum in Kensico Cemetery, Valhalla, N.Y.

**WARD, William Thomas,** a Representative from Kentucky; born in Amelia County, Va., August 9, 1808; attended the common schools and St. Mary's College, near Lebanon, Ky.; studied law; admitted to the bar and commenced practice in Greensburg, Ky.; served in the Mexican War as major of the Fourth Kentucky Volunteers in 1847 and 1848; member of the Kentucky house of representatives in 1850; elected as a Whig to the Thirty-second Congress (March 4, 1851-March 3, 1853); was not a candidate for renomination in 1852; commissioned brigadier general in the Union Army and served throughout the Civil War; resumed the practice of law in Louisville, Ky., where he died October 12, 1878; interment in Cave Hill Cemetery.

**WARDWELL, Daniel,** a Representative from New York; born in Bristol, R.I., May 28, 1791; was graduated from Brown University, Providence, R.I., in 1811; studied law; was admitted to the bar and commenced practice in Rome, N.Y.; moved to Mannsville, N.Y., in 1814; judge of the court of common pleas for Jefferson County, N.Y.; elected to the State assembly 1825-1828; elected as a Jacksonian to the Twenty-second, Twenty-third, and Twenty-fourth Congresses (March 4, 1831-March 3, 1837); chairman, Committee on Revolutionary Pensions (Twenty-third and Twenty-fourth Congresses); was not a candidate for renomination in 1836; returned to Rome, N.Y., and resumed the practice of law; died in Rome, Oneida County, N.Y., March 27, 1878; interment in Maplewood Cemetery, Mannsville, Jefferson County, N.Y.

**WARE, John Haines, III,** a Representative from Pennsylvania; born in Vineland, Cumberland County, N.J., August 29, 1908; attended the public schools in Oxford, Pa., and Miami, Fla.; B.S., University of Pennsylvania, 1930; public utility executive; burgess, borough of Oxford, 1956-1960; member, Pennsylvania senate, 1961-1970; chairman, Pennsylvania Republican finance committee; trustee of Lincoln University, Pa., and of the University of Pennsylvania; elected as a Republican to the Ninety-first Congress, November 3, 1970, by special election to fill the vacancy caused by the death of G. Robert Watkins, and at the same time elected to the Ninety-second Congress; reelected to the Ninety-third Congress, and served from November 3, 1970 to January 3, 1975; was not a candidate for reelection in 1974 to the Ninety-fourth Congress; is a resident of Oxford, Pa.

**WARE, Nicholas,** a Senator from Georgia; born in Caroline County, Va., in 1769; moved with his parents to Edgefield, S.C., and a few years later to Augusta, Ga.; received a thorough English education; studied medicine; studied law in Augusta and at Litchfield (Conn.) Law School; was admitted to the bar and commenced practice in Augusta; member, State house of representatives 1808-1811, 1814-1815; mayor of Augusta 1819-1821; elected as a Republican to the United States Senate to fill the vacancy caused by the resignation of Freeman Walker and served from November 10, 1821, until his death in New York City September 7, 1824; interment under the annex of Grace Church.

**WARE, Orie Solomon,** a Representative from Kentucky; born in Peach Grove, Pendleton County, Ky., May 11, 1882; attended the public schools of Covington, Ky.; graduated from the private academy of Prof. George W. Dunlap, at Independence, Ky., in 1899, and from the law department of the University of Cincinnati at Cincinnati, Ohio, LL.B., 1903; admitted to the bar in 1903 and commenced practice in Covington, Ky.; also engaged in banking, serving as a director of the First National Bank and Trust Co.; delegate to all Kentucky Democratic conventions 1910-1939; served as postmaster of Covington from September 1, 1914, to July 1, 1921; Commonwealth attorney of the sixteenth judicial circuit, serving from January 1, 1922, to February 1, 1927, when he resigned; elected as a Democrat to the Seventieth Congress (March 4, 1927-March 3, 1929); was not a candidate for renomination in 1928 to the Seventy-first Congress; served as circuit judge, 1957-1958; resumed the practice of law in Covington; resided in Fort Mitchell, Ky., where he died December 16, 1974; interment in Highland Cemetery.

**WARFIELD, Henry Ridgely,** a Representative from Maryland; born in Anne Arundel County, Md., September 14, 1774; completed preparatory studies; held several local offices; settled in Frederick, Md.; elected to the Sixteenth, Seventeenth, and Eighteenth Congresses (March 4, 1819-March 3, 1825); died in Frederick, Md., March 18, 1839.

**WARNER, Adoniram Judson,** a Representative from Ohio; born in Wales, near Buffalo, N.Y., January 13, 1834; moved with his parents to Wisconsin at the age of eleven; attended school in Beloit, Wis., and New York Central College, McGrawville, N.Y.; principal of Lewistown (Pa.) Academy, superintendent of the public schools of Mifflin County, and principal of Mercer Union School, Pennsylvania, 1856-1861; was commissioned captain in the Tenth Pennsylvania Reserves July 21, 1861, lieutenant colonel May 14, 1862, colonel April 25, 1863, and colonel of the Veteran Reserve Corps November 15, 1863; brevetted brigadier general March 13, 1865; studied law; was admitted to the bar in Indianapolis, Ind., in 1865 but never practiced; at the conclusion of the war returned to Pennsylvania, and in 1866 moved to Marietta, Ohio; engaged in the oil, coal, and railroad businesses; elected as a Democrat to the Forty-sixth Congress (March 4, 1879-March 3, 1881); unsuccessful candidate for reelection in 1880 to the Forty-seventh Congress; elected to the Forty-eighth and Forty-ninth Congresses (March 4, 1883-March 3, 1887); was not a candidate for reelection in 1886; delegate to the Democratic National Convention in 1896; engaged in street railway construction in the District of Columbia and in railroad construction in Ohio; from about 1898 until six months before his death engaged in transportation and power development in Georgia; died in Marietta, Washington County, Ohio, August 12, 1910; interment in Oak Grove Cemetery.

**WARNER, Hiram,** a Representative from Georgia; born in Williamsburg, Hampshire County, Mass., on October 29, 1802; received a good common-school training and acquired some knowledge of the classics; in 1819 moved to Georgia and taught school for three years; studied law; was admitted to the bar and commenced practice in Knoxville, Crawford County, Ga., in 1825;

served in the Georgia State general assembly, 1828-1831; declined to be a candidate for reelection; moved to Talbotton in 1830 and continued the practice of his profession; moved to Greenville; elected judge of the Georgia State superior court and served from 1833 to 1840; judge of the Georgia State supreme court from 1846 to 1853, when he resigned; elected as a Democrat to the Thirty-fourth Congress (March 4, 1855-March 3, 1857); declined to be a candidate for reelection in 1856 to the Thirty-fifth Congress; appointed by Governor Charles J. Jenkins as judge of the Coweta Circuit Court and served from 1865 to 1867, when he was appointed chief justice of the Georgia State supreme court; was subsequently elected and served until 1880, when he resigned; died in Atlanta, Ga., June 30, 1881; interment in Town Cemetery, Greenville, Meriwether County, Ga.

**Bibliography:** *DAB.*

**WARNER, John De Witt,** a Representative from New York; born on a farm in the town of Reading, Schuyler County, N.Y., October 30, 1851; moved with his parents to Big Stream (later Glenora), N.Y., and in 1860 settled in Rock Stream, Yates County, N.Y.; completed preparatory studies; attended the district schools and Starkey Seminary, Eddytown, N.Y.; was graduated from Cornell University in 1872; edited the Ithaca Daily Leader for a few months; professor in the Ithaca and Albany Academies for four years; was graduated from Albany Law School in 1876; was admitted to the bar the same year and commenced practice in New York City in 1877; elected as a Democrat to the Fifty-second and Fifty-third Congresses (March 4, 1891-March 3, 1895); declined to be a candidate for renomination in 1894; resumed the practice of law in New York City; president of the Art Commission of New York City 1902-1905; was president of the American Free Trade League 1905-1909; special counsel for the dock department to advise on terminal work in 1911 and 1912; served on the commission to revise the New York banking laws in 1913; also engaged in literary pursuits; engaged in the practice of law until his death in New York City May 27, 1925; interment in Rock Stream Cemetery, Rock Stream, Yates County, N.Y.

**WARNER, John William,** a Senator from Virginia; born in Washington, D.C., February 18, 1927; attended schools in Washington, D.C. and Virginia; served in the United States Navy, 1944-1946; B.S., Washington and Lee University, Lexington, Va., 1949; served in the United States Marine Corps during the Korean conflict 1951-1952; United States Marine Corps Reserve 1952-1964; LL.B., University of Virginia Law School, 1953; cattle farmer; admitted to the Washington, D.C. bar in 1953 and commenced practice the same year; law clerk, United States Court of Appeals for District of Columbia Circuit, 1953-1954; assistant United States attorney, 1956-1960; Under Secretary, United States Navy, 1969-1972; Secretary, United States Navy, 1972-1974; administrator, American Revolution Bicentennial Administration, 1974-1976; elected as a Republican to the United States Senate, November 7, 1978, for the six-year term commencing January 3, 1979; subsequently appointed by the Governor, January 2, 1979, to fill the vacancy caused by the resignation of William Scott for the term ending January 3, 1979; reelected in 1984 and again in 1990 for the term ending January 3, 1997; chairman, Committee on Rules and Administration (One Hundred Fourth Congress); is a resident of Alexandria, Va.

**WARNER, Levi** (brother of Samuel Larkin Warner), a Representative from Connecticut; born in Wethersfield, Hartford County, Conn., October 10, 1831; completed preparatory studies; attended the law department of Yale College and Dane Law School, Cambridge, Mass.; was admitted to the bar in 1859 and commenced practice in Fairfield County, Conn.; moved to Norwalk, Conn., in 1858 and continued the practice of law; elected as a Democrat to the Forty-fourth Congress to fill the vacancy caused by the resignation of William H. Barnum; reelected to the Forty-fifth Congress and

served from December 4, 1876, to March 3, 1879; was not a candidate for renomination in 1878; resumed the practice of law; died in Norwalk, Conn., April 12, 1911; interment in Riverside Cemetery.

**WARNER, Richard,** a Representative from Tennessee; born near Chapel Hill, Marshall County, Tenn., September 19, 1835; attended the public schools and was graduated from the law department of Cumberland University, Lebanon, Tenn., in 1858; was admitted to the bar the same year and commenced practice in Lewisburg, Tenn.; served in the Confederate Army 1861-1865; returned to Lewisburg, Tenn., and resumed the practice of law; delegate to the convention that framed the new constitution of Tennessee in 1870; member of the State house of representatives, 1879-1881; elected as a Democrat to the Forty-seventh and Forty-eighth Congresses (March 4, 1881-March 3, 1885); chairman, Committee on Mines and Mining (Forty-eighth Congress); unsuccessful candidate for renomination in 1884; resumed the practice of law in Lewisburg, Tenn.; died in Nashville, Tenn., March 4, 1915; interment in Warner Cemetery, near Chapel Hill, Tenn.

**WARNER, Samuel Larkin** (brother of Levi Warner), a Representative from Connecticut; born in Wethersfield, Hartford County, Conn., June 14, 1828; attended Wilbraham Academy, Wilbraham, Mass., and the law department of Yale College; was graduated from the law department of Harvard University in 1854; was admitted to the bar in Boston, Mass., in 1854; commenced the practice of law in Portland, Middlesex County, Conn., in 1855; member of the State house of representatives in 1858; moved to Middletown in 1860; mayor 1862-1866; delegate to the Republican National Convention in 1864, 1888, and 1892; elected as a Republican to the Thirty-ninth Congress (March 4, 1865-March 3, 1867); was not a candidate for renomination; resumed the practice of law; died in Middletown, Conn., on February 6, 1893; interment in Indian Hill Cemetery.

**WARNER, Vespasian,** a Representative from Illinois; born in Mount Pleasant (now Farmer City), De Witt County, Ill., April 23, 1842; moved with his parents to Clinton, Ill., in 1843; attended the common and select schools in Clinton and Lombard University, Galesburg, Ill.; studied law in Clinton; enlisted as a private in Company E, Twentieth Regiment, Illinois Volunteer Infantry, June 13, 1861; promoted to sergeant June 23, 1861, second lieutenant February 4, 1862, captain and commissary of subsistence February 10, 1865, brevetted major March 13, 1865, and was mustered out July 13, 1866; was graduated from the law department of Harvard University in 1868; was admitted to the bar the same year and commenced the practice of law in Clinton, Ill.; elected as a Republican to the Fifty-fourth and to the four succeeding Congresses (March 4, 1895-March 3, 1905); chairman, Committee on Revision of the Laws (Fifty-fifth through Fifty-eighth Congresses); served as Commissioner of Pensions from March 4, 1905, to November 25, 1909; engaged in business in Clinton, Ill., as a banker and realty owner and agent; died in Clinton, De Witt County, Ill., on March 31, 1925; interment in Woodlawn Cemetery.

**WARNER, Willard,** a Senator from Alabama; born in Granville, Licking County, Ohio, on September 4, 1826; attended a country school near Roseville, Muskingum County, Ohio; graduated from Marietta College, Ohio, in 1845; engaged in mercantile pursuits at Cincinnati in 1852 and later became manager of the Newark (Ohio) Machine Works; served in the Union Army during the Civil War; brevetted brigadier general and major general in 1865; served two years in the Ohio senate; moved to Prattville, Autauga County, Ala., in 1867 and engaged in cotton planting; member of the Alabama State house of representatives in 1868; held several local offices; upon the readmission of the State of Alabama to representation was elected as a Republican to the United States Senate, and served from July 13, 1868 to March 3, 1871; unsuccessful candidate for reelection; collector of customs of the port of Mobile, Ala., 1871-1872; declined the appointment as Governor of New Mexico Territory in 1872, and also that of Minister to Argentina; moved to Tecumseh, Ala., in 1873 and organized the Tecumseh Iron Co., of which he served as general manager; in 1890 moved to Chattanooga, Tenn., where he engaged in banking and was a director in several corporations; member, Tennessee State house of representatives, 1897-1898; died in Chattanooga, Tenn., November 23, 1906; interment in Cedar Hill Cemetery, Newark, Ohio.

**WARNER, William,** a Representative and a Senator from Missouri; born in Shullsburg, Lafayette County, Wis., June 11, 1840; worked in lead mines as a child and sporadically attended school; taught school and studied law at Lawrence University and the University of Michigan at Ann Arbor; was admitted to the bar in 1861 and commenced practice in Kansas City, Mo.; enlisted in 1862 in the Thirty-third Regiment, Wisconsin Volunteer Infantry; was mustered out at the close of the Civil War with the rank of major; returned to Kansas City, Mo., in 1865 and resumed the practice of law; served as city attorney in 1867, and as circuit attorney in 1868; mayor of Kansas City in 1871; elected as a Republican to the Forty-ninth and Fiftieth Congresses (March 4, 1885-March 3, 1889); was not a candidate for renomination in 1888 to the Fifty-first Congress; elected commander in chief of the Grand Army of the Republic in 1888; unsuccessful Republican candidate for Governor in 1892; United States district attorney for the western district of Missouri, 1882-1884, 1898, 1902-1905; unsuccessful Republican candidate for governor of Missouri in 1892; elected as a Republican to the United States Senate in 1905, and served from March 18, 1905 to March 3, 1911; was not a candidate for reelection; chairman, Committee on the Mississippi and Its Tributaries (Sixtieth and Sixty-first Congresses); resumed the practice of law; appointed as civilian member of the Board of Ordnance and Fortifications; member of the Board of Managers of the National Home for Disabled Volunteer Soldiers; died in Kansas City, Mo., October 4, 1916; interment in Elmwood Cemetery.

Bibliography: *DAB.*

**WARNOCK, William Robert,** a Representative from Ohio; born in Urbana, Ohio, August 29, 1838; attended the public schools; taught school in Urbana 1856-1868; was graduated from Ohio Wesleyan University, Delaware, Ohio, in 1861; commenced the study of law in 1861; entered the Union Army July 21, 1862, as captain of Company G, Ninety-fifth Regiment, Ohio Volunteer Infantry; promoted to major July 28, 1863, and brevetted lieutenant colonel March 15, 1865; chief of staff for the eastern district of Mississippi from April to August 1865; mustered out August 14, 1865; resumed the study of law; was admitted to the bar in 1866 and commenced practice in Urbana; prosecuting attorney 1868-1872; member of the board of school examiners of Champaign County 1870-1876; served as trustee of Ohio Wesleyan University for twenty-five years; member of the State senate in 1876 and 1877; judge of the court of common pleas in the second district of Ohio 1879-1889; president of the National Bank of Urbana; elected as a Republican to the Fifty-seventh and Fifty-eighth Congresses (March 4, 1901-March 3, 1905); chairman, Committee on Expenditures in the Department of War (Fifty-eighth Congress); was not a candidate for renomination; resumed the practice of law; United States pension agent at Columbus, Ohio, 1906-1910; commander of the department of Ohio, Grand Army of the Republic, in 1913 and 1914; died in Urbana, Ohio, July 30, 1918; interment in Oakdale Cemetery.

**WARREN, Cornelius,** a Representative from New York; born in Phillipstown, Putnam County, N.Y., March 15, 1790; completed preparatory studies; studied law; was admitted to the bar and commenced the practice of law; appointed judge of the court of common pleas in 1841; elected as a Whig to the Thirtieth Congress

(March 4, 1847-March 3, 1849); died at Cold Spring, Putnam County, N.Y., July 28, 1849; interment in the Old Cemetery.

**WARREN, Edward Allen,** a Representative from Arkansas; born near Eutaw, Green County, Ala., May 2, 1818; completed preparatory studies; studied law; was admitted to the bar in 1843 and commenced the practice of law in Clinton, Miss.; member of the State house of representatives in 1845 and 1846; moved to Arkansas in 1847 and settled in Camden, where he continued the practice of his profession; member of the State house of representatives in 1848 and 1849, serving as speaker in 1849; judge of the circuit court of the sixth district of Arkansas; elected as a Democrat to the Thirty-third Congress (March 4, 1853-March 3, 1855); elected to the Thirty-fifth Congress (March 4, 1857-March 3, 1859); resumed the practice of law; died in Prescott, Nevada County, Ark., July 2, 1875; interment in Moscow Cemetery, near Prescott, Ark.

**WARREN, Francis Emroy,** a Senator from Wyoming; born in Hinsdale, Berkshire County, Mass., June 20, 1844; attended the common schools and Hinsdale Academy; during the Civil War enlisted in the Forty-ninth Regiment, Massachusetts Volunteer Infantry, and served as a private and noncommissioned officer until he was mustered out of the service; received the Congressional Medal of Honor September 30, 1893 for gallantry on the battlefield at the siege of Port Hudson, La., May 27 to July 9, 1863; later served as captain in the Massachusetts militia; engaged in farming and stock raising in Massachusetts; moved to Wyoming (then a part of the Territory of Dakota) in 1868; became interested in the real estate, mercantile, livestock, and lighting businesses in Cheyenne; member, Territorial senate, 1873-1874, and served as president; member of the city council, 1873-1874; treasurer of Wyoming, 1876, 1879, 1882, 1884; member, Territorial senate, 1884-1885; mayor of Cheyenne, 1885; appointed Governor of the Territory of Wyoming by President Chester A. Arthur in February 1885, but was removed by President Grover Cleveland in November 1886; again appointed Governor by President Benjamin Harrison in March 1889 and served until elected to the position in 1890; elected as the first Governor of the State in September 1890, but resigned on November 24, 1890, having been elected Senator; elected as a Republican to the United States Senate November 18, 1890, and served until March 4, 1893; resumed agricultural pursuits and stock raising; again elected to the United States Senate in 1895; reelected in 1901, 1907, 1913, 1918, and again in 1924, and served from March 4, 1895, until his death in Washington, D.C., November 24, 1929; chairman, Committee on Irrigation and Reclamation of Arid Lands (Fifty-second, Fifty-fourth and Fifty-fifth Congresses), Committee on Claims (Fifty-sixth through Fifty-ninth Congresses), Committee on Irrigation (Fifty-ninth Congress), Committee on Military Affairs (Fifty-ninth through Sixty-first Congresses), Committee on Public Buildings and Grounds (Fifty-ninth Congress), Committee on Agriculture and Forestry (Sixty-first Congress), Committee on Appropriations (Sixty-second and Sixty-sixth through Seventy-first Congresses), Committee on Engrossed Bills (Sixty-third through Sixty-fifth Congresses); funeral services were held in the Chamber of the United States Senate; interment in Lakeview Cemetery, Cheyenne, Wyo.

Bibliography: *DAB*; Gould, Lewis. "Francis E. Warren and the Johnson County War." *Arizona and the West* 9 (Summer 1967): 131-42; Schulp, Leonard. "A Taft Republican: Sen. Francis E. Warren and National Politics." *Annals of Wyoming* 54 (Fall 1982): 62-67.

**WARREN, Joseph Mabbett,** a Representative from New York; born in Troy, N.Y., January 28, 1813; attended the local schools, and in 1827 entered Rensselaer Polytechnic Institute at Troy; was graduated from the Washington (now Trinity) College, Hartford, Conn., in 1834; worked as a clerk in New York for a year and returned to Troy, N.Y., where he engaged in the wholesale grocery business for several years; entered the wholesale hardware business in 1840; one of the directors of the Bank of Troy and of the United National Bank of Troy, and president of the Bank of Troy 1853-1865; trustee of Rensselaer Polytechnic Institute; mayor of Troy in 1852; appointed as a commissioner of the Troy Water Works Company in 1855 and served until 1867, when he resigned; elected as a Democrat to the Forty-second Congress (March 4, 1871-March 3, 1873); was not a candidate for renomination in 1872; resumed his former business activities in Troy, N.Y., where he died September 9, 1896; interment in the Warren Chapel, Oakwood Cemetery.

**WARREN, Lindsay Carter,** a Representative from North Carolina; born in Washington, Beaufort County, N.C., December 16, 1889; pursued preparatory studies at Bingham School, Asheville, N.C., 1903-1906; attended the University of North Carolina at Chapel Hill, 1906-1908, and studied law there in 1911 and 1912; was admitted to the bar in 1912 and commenced practice in Washington, N.C.; attorney of Beaufort County, 1912-1925; chairman of the Democratic executive committee of Beaufort County, 1912-1925; member of the North Carolina State senate in 1917, 1919, 1959, and 1961, serving as president pro tempore in 1919; member of the State code commission for compiling the consolidated statutes in 1919; chairman of the special legislative committee in 1920 on workmen's compensation acts; member of the State house of representatives in 1923; delegate to the Democratic National Conventions of 1932 and 1940; chairman of the Democratic State conventions in 1930, 1934, and temporary chairman and keynoter in 1938; elected as a Democrat to the Sixty-ninth and to the seven succeeding Congresses, and served from March 4, 1925 until his resignation on October 31, 1940; had been renominated to the Seventy-seventh Congress, but later withdrew; chairman, Committee on Accounts (Seventy-second through Seventy-sixth Congresses); appointed Comptroller General of the United States for a fifteen-year term, serving from November 1, 1940 until his retirement on May 1, 1954; died in Washington, N.C., December 28, 1976; interment in Oakdale Cemetery.

**Bibliography:** *DAB*; Porter, David. "Representative Lindsay Warren, The Water Bloc, and the Transportation Act of 1940." *North Carolina Historical Review* 50 (July 1973): 273-88.

**WARREN, Lott,** a Representative from Georgia; born in Burke County, near Augusta, Richmond County, Ga., October 30, 1797; attended the common schools; moved to Dublin, Laurens County, Ga., in 1816; served as a second lieutenant of Volunteers in the expedition against the Seminoles in 1818; studied law; was admitted to the bar in 1821 and commenced practice in Dublin, Laurens County, Ga.; was also a regularly ordained Baptist minister, but never filled a definite charge; moved to Marion in 1825; elected major of the State militia in 1823; member of the State house of representatives in 1824 and 1831; served in the State senate in 1830; solicitor general and judge of the southern circuit of Georgia 1831-1834; moved to Americus, Sumter County, in 1836; elected as a Whig to the Twenty-sixth and Twenty-seventh Congresses (March 4, 1839-March 3, 1843); was not a candidate for renomination in 1842; moved to Albany in 1842; was judge of the superior court of Georgia 1843-1852; resumed the practice of his profession; died in Albany, Dougherty County, Ga., June 17, 1861; interment in Riverside Cemetery.

**WARREN, William Wirt,** a Representative from Massachusetts; born in Brighton (now a part of Boston), Mass., February 27, 1834; pursued classical studies; graduated from Harvard University in 1856; studied law; admitted to the bar and commenced practice in 1857; assessor of internal revenue in the seventh Massachusetts district in 1865; delegate to the Democratic National Convention in 1868; member of the Massachusetts senate in 1870; elected as a Democrat to the Forty-fourth Congress (March 4, 1875-March 3, 1877); unsuccessful candidate for reelection in 1876 to the

Forty-fifth Congress; engaged in the practice of law until his death in Boston, Mass., May 2, 1880; interment in Evergreen Cemetery.

**WARWICK, John George,** a Representative from Ohio; born in County Tyrone, Province of Ulster, Ireland, December 23, 1830; attended the common schools of his native land; immigrated with his brother to the United States about 1850 and resided in Philadelphia, Pa., for a short time; moved to Navarre, Stark County, Ohio, and became a bookkeeper in a dry goods establishment; moved to Massillon, Stark County, Ohio, and clerked in a dry goods store, subsequently becoming interested in flour milling, coal mining, and agricultural pursuits; also was a promoter of railroad construction; elected as Lieutenant Governor of Ohio, and served from 1884 to 1886; unsuccessful candidate for reelection in 1886; elected as a Democrat to the Fifty-second Congress, and served from March 4, 1891 until his death in Washington, D.C., August 14, 1892; interment in Protestant Cemetery, Massillon, Ohio.

**WASHBURN, Cadwallader Colden** (brother of Israel Washburn, Jr., Elihu Benjamin Washburne, and William Drew Washburn), a Representative from Wisconsin; born in Livermore, Androscoggin County, Maine, April 22, 1818; completed preparatory studies and taught school in Wiscasset, Maine, 1838-1839; moved to Davenport, Iowa, in 1839 and was employed in the geological survey of that State; moved to Rock Island, Ill., and studied law; elected surveyor of Rock Island County, Ill., in 1840; moved to Wisconsin and settled in Mineral Point, Iowa County, in 1842; was admitted to the bar the same year and commenced practice at Mineral Point; founder of the Mineral Point Bank in 1852; elected as a Republican to the Thirty-fourth and to the two succeeding Congresses (March 4, 1855-March 3, 1861); chairman, Committee on Private Land Claims (Thirty-sixth Congress); declined to be a candidate for renomination in 1860 to the Thirty-seventh Congress; moved to La Crosse, Wis., in 1861; delegate to the peace convention held in Washington, D.C., in 1861 in an effort to devise means to prevent the impending war; served in the Union Army during the Civil War; commissioned colonel of the Second Regiment, Wisconsin Volunteer Cavalry, on February 6, 1862; appointed brigadier general of Volunteers, July 16, 1862, and major general on November 29, 1862; resigned his commission on May 25, 1865 and returned to La Crosse; elected to the Fortieth and Forty-first Congresses (March 4, 1867-March 3, 1871); chairman, Committee on Expenditures on Public Buildings (Fortieth Congress); was not a candidate for renomination in 1870 to the Forty-second Congress; elected Governor of Wisconsin in 1871, and served from January 1, 1872 to January 5, 1874; unsuccessful candidate for reelection in 1873; engaged in the manufacture of lumber; owned and operated large flour mills in Minneapolis, Minn.; died at Eureka Springs, Carroll County, Ark., on May 15, 1882, while on a visit at the springs for his health; interment in Oak Grove Cemetery, La Crosse, Wis.

**Bibliography:** *DAB*; Bicha, Karel D. *C.C. Washburn and the Upper Mississippi Valley.* New York: Garland Publishers, 1995; Hunt, Gaillard, comp. *Israel, Elihu, and Cadwallader Washburn: A Chapter in American Biography.* New York: Macmillan, 1925; Marquette, Clare L. "The Business Activities of C.C. Washburn." Ph.D. dissertation, University of Wisconsin, 1940.

**WASHBURN, Charles Grenfill,** a Representative from Massachusetts; born in Worcester, Mass., January 28, 1857; was graduated from Worcester Polytechnic Institute in 1875 and from Harvard University in 1880; studied law; was admitted to the Suffolk bar in 1887; connected with various manufacturing enterprises in Worcester; member of the Massachusetts house of representatives in 1897 and 1898; served in the Massachusetts senate in 1899 and 1900; member of the committee to revise the corporation laws of Massachusetts in 1902; delegate to the Republican National Conventions in 1904 and 1916; was elected as a Republican to the Fifty-ninth Congress to fill the vacancy caused by the death of Rockwood Hoar; reelected to the Sixtieth and Sixty-first Congresses and served from December 18, 1906, to March 3, 1911; unsuccessful candidate for reelection in 1910 to the Sixty-second Congress; director of the Federal Reserve Bank of Boston; president of the Washburn Co. of Worcester, Mass., until his death at Lenox, Berkshire County, Mass., May 25, 1928; interment in Rural Cemetery, Worcester, Mass.

**Bibliography:** *DAB.*

**WASHBURN, Henry Dana,** a Representative from Indiana; born in Windsor, Vt., March 28, 1832; attended the common schools; became a tanner and a currier; taught school for several years; moved to Vermillion County, Ind., in 1850; was graduated from the New York State and National Law Schools; was admitted to the bar in 1853 and commenced the practice of law in Newport, Vermillion County, Ind.; county auditor 1854-1861; enlisted on August 16, 1861, and served in the Union Army as lieutenant colonel of the Eighteenth Regiment, Indiana Volunteer Infantry; promoted to colonel July 15, 1862; brevetted brigadier general of Volunteers December 15, 1864, and major general July 26, 1865; mustered out August 26, 1865; successfully contested as a Republican the election of Daniel W. Voorhees to the Thirty-ninth Congress; reelected to the Fortieth Congress and served from February 23, 1866, to March 3, 1869; was not a candidate for renomination in 1868 to the Forty-first Congress; appointed surveyor general of Montana in 1869 and served until his death; in 1870 headed an expedition to find the headwaters of the Yellowstone River and discovered what is now known as Yellowstone Park; Mount Washburn, Mont., is named for him; returned to Clinton, Vermillion County, Ind., where he died on January 26, 1871; interment in Riverside Cemetery.

**WASHBURN, Israel, Jr.** (brother of Elihu Benjamin Washburne, Cadwallader Colden Washburn, and William Drew Washburn), a Representative from Maine; born in Livermore, Androscoggin County, Maine, June 6, 1813; attended the common schools and was educated by private tutors; studied law; was admitted to the bar in 1834 and commenced practice in Orono, Penobscot County, Maine; member of the Maine State house of representatives, 1842-1843; unsuccessful candidate for the Thirty-first Congress in 1848; elected as a Whig to the Thirty-second and Thirty-third Congresses, as a Republican to the Thirty-fourth, Thirty-fifth, and Thirty-sixth Congresses, and served from March 4, 1851 to January 1, 1861, when he resigned, having been elected Governor; chairman, Committee on Elections (Thirty-fourth Congress); elected Governor of Maine in 1860, reelected in 1861, and served from January 2, 1861 to January 7, 1863; declined to be a candidate for renomination; appointed by President Abraham Lincoln as collector of customs at Portland, Maine, and served from October 31, 1863 until March 16, 1877, when he resigned; served as president of the board of trustees of Tufts College, Medford, Mass.; engaged in literary pursuits; died in Philadelphia, Pa., on May 12, 1883; interment in Mount Hope Cemetery, Bangor, Maine.

**Bibliography:** *DAB*; Hunt, Gaillard, comp. *Israel, Elihu, and Cadwallader Washburn: A Chapter in American Biography.* New York: Macmillan, 1925.

**WASHBURN, William Barrett,** a Representative and a Senator from Massachusetts; born in Winchendon, Worcester County, Mass., January 31, 1820; attended Westminster and Hancock Academies and graduated from Yale College in 1844; employed as a store clerk, 1844-1847; engaged in manufacturing pursuits in Erving, Franklin County, Mass., 1847-1857; member of the Massachusetts senate in 1850; member, Massachusetts house of representatives, 1853-1855; moved to Greenfield, Franklin County, in 1858 and engaged in banking; elected as a Republican to the Thirty-eighth and to the four succeeding Congresses, and served from March 4, 1863 to December 5, 1871, when he resigned, having been elected Governor; chairman, Committee on Claims (Forty-first

Congress); elected Governor of Massachusetts in 1871, reelected in 1872 and 1873, and served from January 4, 1872 until April 29, 1874, when he resigned, having been elected a Senator; elected as a Republican to the United States Senate to fill the vacancy caused by the death of Charles Sumner, and served from April 17, 1874 to March 3, 1875; was not a candidate for reelection; president of the Greenfield National Bank; member of the board of trustees of several colleges; director of the Connecticut River Railroad; died in Springfield, Hampden County, Mass., October 5, 1887; interment in Green River Cemetery, Greenfield, Mass.

**WASHBURN, William Drew** (brother of Israel Washburn, Jr., Elihu Benjamin Washburne, and Cadwallader Colden Washburn), a Representative and a Senator from Minnesota; born in Livermore, Androscoggin County, Maine, on January 14, 1831; attended the common schools and graduated from Bowdoin College, Brunswick, Maine, in 1854; studied law in Bangor, Maine; was admitted to the bar in 1857 and commenced practice in Minneapolis, Minn., where he had settled early in 1857; appointed as United States surveyor general of Minnesota by President Abraham Lincoln 1861-1865, residing in St. Paul while holding that office; unsuccessful candidate for the United States House of Representatives in 1864; returned to Minneapolis and engaged in the newspaper, railway, milling, and waterpower businesses; several times a member of the State house of representatives; elected as a Republican to the Forty-sixth, Forty-seventh, and Forty-eighth Congresses (March 4, 1879-March 3, 1885); elected as a Republican to the United States Senate and served from March 4, 1889, to March 3, 1895; unsuccessful candidate for reelection; chairman, Committee on the Improvement of the Mississippi River and Its Tributaries (Fifty-first and Fifty-second Congresses); resumed manufacturing pursuits and also engaged in railroad building; died in Minneapolis, Minn., July 29, 1912; interment in Lakewood Cemetery.

**Bibliography:** *DAB.*

**WASHBURNE, Elihu Benjamin** (brother of Israel Washburn, Jr., Cadwallader Colden Washburn, and William Drew Washburn), a Representative from Illinois; born in Livermore, Androscoggin County, Maine, September 23, 1816; attended the common schools; printer's apprentice; assistant editor of the Kennebec Journal, Augusta; studied law at Kents' Hill Seminary in 1836 and at Harvard Law School in 1839; was admitted to the bar in 1840; moved to Galena, Jo Daviess County, Ill., in 1840 and commenced the practice of law; delegate to the Whig National Conventions of 1844 and 1852; unsuccessful candidate for election in 1848 to the Thirty-first Congress; elected as a Whig to the Thirty-third Congress and reelected as a Republican to the eight succeeding Congresses and served from March 4, 1853, to March 6, 1869, when he resigned; chairman, Committee on Commerce (Thirty-fourth and Thirty-sixth through Fortieth Congresses), Committee on Appropriations (Fortieth Congress); appointed as Secretary of State in the Cabinet of President Ulysses S. Grant on March 5, 1869, but resigned March 16, 1869 to accept appointment as Envoy Extraordinary and Minister Plenipotentiary to France; upon the declaration of the Franco-Prussian War in July 1870 he protected with the American flag the Paris legations of the various German states; remained in Paris during the siege of 1871 and was the only foreign minister who continued at his post during the days of the Commune, March 18 to May 28, 1871; protected not only Germans but all the foreigners left by their ministers; served as Minister until September 1877, when he returned and settled in Chicago, Ill.; engaged in literary pursuits; died in Chicago, Ill., October 23, 1887; interment in Greenwood Cemetery, Galena, Ill.

**Bibliography:** *DAB*; Hunt, Gaillard, comp. *Israel, Elihu, and Cadwallader Washburn: A Chapter in American Biography.* New York: Macmillan, 1925; Nelson, Russell K. "The Early Life and Congressional Career of Elihu B. Washburne." Ph.D. dissertation, University of North Dakota, 1954.

**WASHINGTON, Craig Anthony,** a Representative from Texas; born in Longview, Gregg County, Tex., October 12, 1941; graduated, Fidelity Manor High School, Galena Park, Tex., 1958; B.S., Prairie View (Tex.) A&M University, 1966; J.D., Texas Southern University Law School, 1969; attorney; member, Texas State house of representatives, 1973-1983; member, Texas State senate, 1983-1989; elected as a Democrat to the One Hundred First Congress, December 9, 1989, by special election to fill the vacancy caused by the death of George Thomas (Mickey) Leland; reelected to the One Hundred Second and One Hundred Third Congresses, and served from December 9, 1989 to January 3, 1995; unsuccessful candidate for renomination in 1994 to the One Hundred Fourth Congress; resumed the practice of law; is a resident of Bastrop, Tex.

**WASHINGTON, George** (granduncle of George Corbin Washington), a Delegate from Virginia and 1st President of the United States; born at "Wakefield," near Popes Creek, Westmoreland County, Va., February 22, 1732; raised in Westmoreland County, Fairfax County and King George County; attended local schools and engaged in land surveying; appointed adjutant general of a military district in Virginia with the rank of major in 1752; in November 1753 was sent by Lieutenant Governor Robert Dinwiddie, of Virginia, to conduct business with the French Army in the Ohio Valley; in 1754 was promoted to the rank of lieutenant colonel and served in the French and Indian War, becoming aide-de-camp to General Edward Braddock in 1755; appointed as commander in chief of Virginia forces in 1755; resigned his commission in December 1758 and returned to the management of his estate at Mount Vernon in 1759; served as a justice of the peace, 1760-1774, and as a member of the Virginia house of burgesses, 1758-1774; delegate to the Williamsburg convention of August 1774; Member of the First and Second Continental Congresses in 1774 and 1775; unanimously chosen on June 15, 1775, as commander in chief of all the forces raised or to be raised; commanded the Continental armies throughout the war for independence; resigned his commission on December 23, 1783, and returned to private life at Mount Vernon; was delegate to, and president of, the Federal Convention in Philadelphia in 1787; unanimously elected as the first President of the United States, being inaugurated April 30, 1789, in New York City; unanimously reelected in 1792 and served until March 3, 1797, after declining a renomination; again appointed as lieutenant general and commander of the United States Army on July 3, 1798, and served until his death in Mount Vernon, Va., December 14, 1799; interment in the vault at Mount Vernon.

**Bibliography:** *DAB*; Freeman, Douglas Southall. *George Washington, A Biography.* 7 vols. New York: Charles Scribner's Sons, 1948-1957; Washington, George. *The Papers of George Washington.* Edited by W.W. Abbot. 35 vols. to date. Charlottesville, Va.: The University Press of Virginia, 1983-.

**WASHINGTON, George Corbin** (grandnephew of George Washington), a Representative from Maryland; born on "Haywood Farms," near Oak Grove, Westmoreland County, Va., August 20, 1789; attended Harvard University; studied law, but devoted himself to agricultural pursuits on his plantation in Maryland; resided for the most part at Dumbarton Heights, in Georgetown, D.C.; elected to the Twentieth and to the two succeeding Congresses (March 4, 1827-March 3, 1833); chairman, Committee on District of Columbia (Twenty-second Congress); was not a candidate for renomination in 1832 to the Twenty-third Congress; elected as an Anti-Jacksonian to the Twenty-fourth Congress (March 4, 1835-March 3, 1837); was not a candidate for renomination in 1836 to the Twenty-fifth Congress; president of the Chesapeake & Ohio Canal Co.; was appointed by President John Tyler in 1844 as a commissioner to adjust and settle the claims arising under the treaty of 1835 with the Cherokee Indians; died in Georgetown, D.C., July 17, 1854; interment in Oak Hill Cemetery.

**WASHINGTON, Harold,** a Representative from Illinois; born in Chicago, Ill., April 15, 1922; attended the public schools; B.A., Roosevelt University, Chicago, 1949; J.D., Northwestern University School of Law, Evanston, Ill., 1952; admitted to the Illinois bar in 1953 and commenced practice in Chicago; served in the United States Air Force Engineers, 1942-1946; assistant city prosecutor, Chicago, 1954-1958; arbitrator, Illinois industrial Commission, 1960-1964; member, Illinois State house of representatives, 1965-1976; member, State senate, 1977-1980; elected as a Democrat to the Ninety-seventh and Ninety-eighth Congresses, and served from January 3, 1981 until his resignation on April 30, 1983; elected mayor of Chicago on April 12, 1983; reelected in 1987, and served from April 29, 1983 until his death in Chicago on November 25, 1987; interment in Oakwood Cemetery.

**Bibliography:** Rivlin, Gary. *Fire on the Prairie: Chicago's Harold Washington and the Politics of Race.* New York: Henry Holt and Co., 1992; Travis, Dempsey. *"Harold," The People's Mayor: An Authorized Biography of Mayor Harold Washington.* Chicago: Urban Research Press, 1989.

**WASHINGTON, Joseph Edwin,** a Representative from Tennessee; was born on the family homestead, "Wessyngton," near Cedar Hill, Robertson County, Tenn., November 10, 1851; received his early instruction at home; was graduated from Georgetown College, Washington, D.C., June 26, 1873; studied law with the first law class organized at Vanderbilt University, Nashville, Tenn., in 1874, and was admitted to the bar, but never practiced; engaged in agricultural pursuits; member of the State house of representatives, 1877-1879; elected as a Democrat to the Fiftieth and to the four succeeding Congresses (March 4, 1887-March 3, 1897); chairman, Committee on Territories (Fifty-second Congress); was not a candidate for renomination in 1896; appointed road commissioner and had charge of the road construction work of Robertson County; member of the board of trustees of Vanderbilt University; director of the Nashville, Chattanooga & St. Louis and Nashville & Decatur Railroads; resumed agricultural pursuits upon the family homestead, "Wessyngton," in Robertson County, Tenn., where he died August 28, 1915; interment in the family burying ground on his estate.

**WASHINGTON, William Henry,** a Representative from North Carolina; born near Goldsboro, Wayne County, N.C., February 7, 1813; studied law; was admitted to the bar in 1835 and commenced practice in New Bern, Craven County, N.C.; was elected as a Whig to the Twenty-seventh Congress (March 4, 1841-March 3, 1843); declined to be a candidate for renomination in 1842; served in the State house of commons in 1843 and 1846; member of the State senate in 1848, 1850, and 1852; resumed the practice of law; died in New Bern, N.C., August 12, 1860; interment in Cedar Grove Cemetery.

**WASIELEWSKI, Thaddeus Francis Boleslaw,** a Representative from Wisconsin; born in Milwaukee, Wis., December 2, 1904; attended the parochial schools and South Division High School of his native city; B.A., University of Michigan at Ann Arbor, 1927, and from the law department of Marquette University, Milwaukee, Wis., J.D., 1931; was admitted to the bar in 1931 and commenced practice in Milwaukee, Wis.; served as census supervisor in 1940; elected as a Democrat to the Seventy-seventh and to the two succeeding Congresses (January 3, 1941-January 3, 1947); unsuccessful Democratic candidate for renomination in 1946 and an unsuccessful Independent candidate for election in 1946 to the Eightieth Congress; delegate, Democratic National Convention, 1948; member, Wisconsin State Central Committee, 1942-1948; resumed the practice of law; resided in Milwaukee, Wis., where he died April 25, 1976; interment in St. Adalbert's Cemetery.

**WASKEY, Frank Hinman,** a Delegate from the Territory of Alaska; born in Lake City, Wabasha County, Minn., April 20, 1875; attended the public schools of Minneapolis; moved to Alaska in February 1898, located in Nome, and engaged in mining; president of a mining company; director of a bank and also of a publishing company, both in Nome; elected as a Democrat to the Fifty-ninth Congress as the first Delegate from Alaska and served from August 14, 1906, to March 3, 1907; was not a candidate for renomination in 1906 to the Sixtieth Congress; prospected for minerals in Alaska, fur buyer, and curio dealer, 1911-1955; United States commissioner at Fortuna Ledge, Alaska, 1915-1918; moved to Oakville, Wash., in 1956, where he died January 18, 1964; interment in Shelton Cemetery, Shelton, Wash.

**WASON, Edward Hills,** a Representative from New Hampshire; born in New Boston, Hillsborough County, N.H., September 2, 1865; attended public and private schools and Francestown (N.H.) Academy; was graduated from New Hampshire College of Agriculture and Mechanic Arts at Hanover in 1886 and from Boston (Mass.) University Law School in 1890; was admitted to the bar in 1890 and commenced practice in Nashua, N.H.; sergeant at arms, assistant clerk, and later clerk of the State senate; member of the Nashua Board of Education 1891-1895, serving as its president in 1895; city solicitor of Nashua in 1894 and 1895; president of the common council in 1897 and 1898; served in the State house of representatives in 1899, 1909, and 1913; member of the State constitutional conventions in 1902 and 1912; solicitor of Hillsborough County 1903-1907; president of the Citizens' Guaranty Savings Bank of Nashua 1904-1941; also engaged in agricultural pursuits in Merrimack, N.H., 1906-1941; alderman of Nashua 1906-1908; elected as a Republican to the Sixty-fourth and to the eight succeeding Congresses (March 4, 1915-March 3, 1933); was not a candidate for renomination in 1932; retired from public life in 1933 and resided on his estate near New Boston, N.H., where he died February 6, 1941; interment in New Boston Cemetery.

**WATERMAN, Charles Winfield,** a Senator from Colorado; born in Waitsfield, Washington County, Vt., November 2, 1861; attended the rural schools and St. Johnsbury Academy; graduated from the University of Vermont at Burlington in 1885; taught school in Connecticut and also at Fort Dodge, Iowa, 1885-1888; graduated from the law school of the University of Michigan at Ann Arbor in 1889; was admitted to the bar the same year and commenced practice in Denver, Colo.; elected as a Republican to the United States Senate in 1926 and served from March 4, 1927, until his death in Washington, D.C., August 27, 1932; chairman, Committee on Patents (Seventy-first Congress), Committee on Enrolled Bills (Seventy-second Congress); remains were cremated and the ashes deposited in Cedar Hill Cemetery.

**WATERS, Maxine,** a Representative from California; born in St. Louis, Mo., August 31, 1938; A.B., California State University, Los Angeles, 1970; Democratic National Convention rules committee, 1984; member, California State assembly, 1977-1990; elected as a Democrat to the One Hundred Second and to the two succeeding Congresses (January 3, 1991-January 3, 1997); is a resident of Los Angeles, Calif.

**WATERS, Russell Judson,** a Representative from California; born in Halifax, Windham County, Vt., June 6, 1843; moved with his parents to Franklin County, Mass., in 1846; attended the district schools; learned the machinist's trade in Shelburne Falls, Mass.; taught school at Charlemont Center, Mass.; was graduated from Franklin Institute (later Arms Academy), Shelburne Falls, Mass., where he later was professor of Latin and mathematics; moved to Chicago, Ill., in 1867; studied law; was admitted to the bar in 1868 and practiced in Chicago until 1886; moved to California and settled in Redlands in 1886; city attorney of Redlands in 1888; moved to Los Angeles in 1894; president of the Pasadena Consolidated Gas Co.;

treasurer of the Los Angeles Chamber of Commerce, vice president of the Citizens' Bank, and connected with many public institutions; elected as a Republican to the Fifty-sixth Congress (March 4, 1899-March 3, 1901); was not a candidate for renomination in 1900; resumed banking as president of the Citizens' National Bank, Los Angeles; president of the California Cattle Company, San Jacinto, Calif., 1903-1911; president of the San Jacinto Water Company, 1910-1911; died in Los Angeles, Calif., September 25, 1911; interment in Hollywood Cemetery.

**WATKINS, Albert Galiton,** a Representative from Tennessee; born near Jefferson City, Jefferson County, Tenn., May 5, 1818; was graduated from Holston College, Tennessee; studied law; was admitted to the bar and began practice at Panther Springs, Tenn., in 1839; member of the Tennessee State house of representatives in 1845; elected as a Whig to the Thirty-first and Thirty-second Congresses (March 4, 1849-March 3, 1853); unsuccessful candidate for reelection in 1852 to the Thirty-third Congress; elected as a Democrat to the Thirty-fourth and Thirty-fifth Congresses (March 4, 1855-March 3, 1859); was not a candidate for renomination in 1858 to the Thirty-sixth Congress; engaged in the ministry; died in Mooresburg, Hawkins County, Tenn., November 9, 1895; interment in Westview Cemetery, Jefferson City, Tenn.

**WATKINS, Arthur Vivian,** a Senator from Utah; born in Midway, Wasatch County, Utah, December 18, 1886; attended the public schools, Brigham Young University, Provo, Utah, 1903-1906, and New York University, New York City, 1909-1910; graduated from Columbia University Law School, New York City, in 1912; was admitted to the bar the same year and commenced practice in Vernal, Utah; engaged in newspaper work in 1914; assistant county attorney of Salt Lake County, 1914-1915; engaged in agricultural pursuits from 1919 until 1925; district judge of the fourth judicial district of Utah, 1928-1933; unsuccessful candidate in 1936 for the Republican nomination to the Seventy-fifth Congress; elected as a Republican to the United States Senate in 1946; reelected in 1952, and served from January 3, 1947 to January 3, 1959; unsuccessful candidate for reelection in 1958; chairman, Select Committee on the Censure of Joseph McCarthy (Eighty-third Congress), co-chairman, Joint Committee on Navaho-Hopi Indian Administration (Eighty-third Congress), Joint Committee on Immigration and Naturalization Policy (Eighty-third Congress); member of the Indian Claims Commission, Washington, D.C., from August 1959, until his retirement in September 1967; author; was a resident of Salt Lake City until he moved to Orem, Utah, in 1973, where he died on September 1, 1973; interment in Eastlawn Memorial Hills.

**Bibliography:** Watkins, Arthur. *Enough Rope: The Inside Story of the Censure of Senator Joe McCarthy.* Englewood Cliffs, N.J.: Prentice-Hall, 1969.

**WATKINS, Elton,** a Representative from Oregon; born in Newton, Newton County, Miss., July 6, 1881; attended the common schools of Mississippi, and Webb School of Bell Buckle, Tenn.; was graduated from Washington and Lee University, Lexington, Va., Georgetown University Law School, and George Washington Law School, Washington, D.C.; employed by the Federal Bureau of Investigation, until 1912, when he moved to Oregon; was admitted to the Oregon bar the same year and commenced the practice of law in Portland; prosecutor, Oregon Bar Association, 1914-1918; assistant United States district attorney in 1919; during the First World War was again employed by the Federal Bureau of Investigation; elected as a Democrat to the Sixty-eighth Congress (March 4, 1923-March 3, 1925); unsuccessful candidate for reelection in 1924 to the Sixty-ninth Congress; unsuccessful Democratic candidate for election to the United States Senate in 1930, and for nomination to the United States Senate in 1932; unsuccessful candidate for mayor of Portland in 1932 and in 1940; resumed the practice of law in

Portland, Oreg., until his death there on June 24, 1956; interment in Greenwood Hills Cemetery.

**WATKINS, George Robert,** a Representative from Pennsylvania; born in Hampton, Va., May 21, 1902; attended the public schools of Hampton; learned the trade of shipfitter; went to Chester, Pa., in 1920 and organized the Chester Stevedoring Co., which was sold in 1931; in 1932 organized with a partner the Blue Line Transfer Co., operating a fleet of trucks to all points in the East; sheriff of Delaware County, Pa., 1945-1948; member of the Pennsylvania senate, 1949-1960; Delaware County commissioner, 1960-1964; operated a farm in Delaware County and was a breeder of thoroughbred horses; elected as a Republican to the Eighty-ninth and to the two succeeding Congresses, and served from January 3, 1965, until his death in West Chester, Pa., on August 7, 1970; interment in Birmingham-Lafayette Cemetery, Birmingham Township, Pa.

**WATKINS, John Thomas,** a Representative from Louisiana; born in Minden, Webster Parish, La., January 15, 1854; attended the common schools and spent three years in Cumberland University, Lebanon, Tenn.; studied law; was admitted to the bar in 1878 and commenced the practice of law in Minden; judge of the district court, 1892-1904; resumed the practice of law; elected as a Democrat to the Fifty-ninth and to the seven succeeding Congresses (March 4, 1905-March 3, 1921); chairman, Committee on Revision of the Laws (Sixty-second through Sixty-fifth Congresses); unsuccessful candidate for renomination in 1920 to the Sixty-seventh Congress; engaged in the practice of law in Washington, D.C., until his death on April 25, 1925; interment in Murrell Cemetery, Minden, La.

**WATKINS, Wesley Wade,** a Representative from Oklahoma; born in DeQueen, Sevier County, Ark., December 15, 1938; moved to Bennington, Okla. in 1945 and attended the public schools there; B.S., Oklahoma State University, Stillwater, 1960, and M.S., 1961; also pursued graduate studies toward a doctoral degree; employed by United States Department of Agriculture, Washington, D.C., 1961-1963; returned to Oklahoma State University in 1963 and served as assistant director of admissions for three years; moved to Wilburton, Okla., and served as executive director, Kiamichi Economic Development District of Oklahoma, 1966-1968; engaged in the residential construction business in Ada, Okla., 1968-1976; served in the Oklahoma State senate, 1975-1976; delegate, Oklahoma State Democratic convention, 1972; delegate to the Democratic National Convention of 1972; elected as a Democrat to the Ninety-fifth and to the six succeeding Congresses (January 3, 1977-January 3, 1991); was not a candidate for reelection in 1990 to the One Hundred Second Congress, but was an unsuccessful candidate for nomination for Governor of Oklahoma; announced his affiliation with the Republican Party on January 5, 1996; candidate for election in 1996 to the One Hundred Fifth Congress; is a resident of Ada, Okla.

**WATMOUGH, John Goddard,** a Representative from Pennsylvania; born in Wilmington, Del., December 6, 1793; pursued classical studies and was graduated from Princeton College; was also engaged in postgraduate work at the University of Pennsylvania, Philadelphia; served in the War of 1812 as corporal in the Fourth Company, Fourth Detachment, Pennsylvania Militia, from May 13 to July 31, 1813; appointed second lieutenant in the Regular Army September 2, 1813; brevetted first lieutenant August 15, 1814, for gallant conduct in the defense of Fort Erie, Canada, and resigned on October 1, 1816; elected as an Anti-Jacksonian to the Twenty-second and Twenty-third Congresses (March 4, 1831-March 3, 1835); unsuccessful Whig candidate for reelection in 1834 to the Twenty-fourth Congress; high sheriff of Philadelphia in 1835 and 1836; surveyor of the port of Philadelphia 1841-1845; discontinued active pursuits in 1854 and lived in retirement until his death in

Philadelphia, Pa., November 27, 1861; interment in Christ Church Cemetery.

**WATRES, Laurence Hawley,** a Representative from Pennsylvania; born in Scranton, Lackawanna County, Pa., July 18, 1882; attended the public schools and Hill School, Pottstown, Pa.; was graduated from Princeton (N.J.) University in 1904 and from the law school of Harvard University in 1907; was admitted to the bar in 1907 and commenced practice in Scranton, Pa.; during the First World War served from September 26, 1916, as captain in the One Hundred and Eighth Machine Gun Battalion of the Twenty-eighth Division; promoted to major and discharged May 28, 1919; awarded the Distinguished Service Cross and the Purple Heart Medal; after the war assisted in reorganizing the One Hundred and Ninth Infantry Regiment of the Pennsylvania National Guard and served as lieutenant colonel; elected as a Republican to the Sixty-eighth and to the three succeeding Congresses (March 4, 1923-March 3, 1931); was not a candidate for renomination in 1930; resumed the practice of law in Scranton, Pa., until 1951; moved to East Orange, N.J.; died while vacationing in Puerto Rico, February 6, 1964; interred in Glenwood Mausoleum, South Abington Township, Pa.

**WATSON, Albert William,** a Representative from South Carolina; born in Sumter, S.C., August 30, 1922; attended the public schools of Columbia and North Greenville Junior College; graduated from the University of South Carolina School of Law at Columbia in 1950; commenced practice in Columbia, S.C., in 1951; during the Second World War served in the United States Army Air Corps as a weather specialist (sergeant) in the Mediterranean Theater of Operations, 1942-1946; served in the South Carolina State general assembly, 1955-1958, and 1961-1962; national chairman, Voice of Democracy Program, United States Junior Chamber of Commerce, in 1957; elected as a Democrat to the Eighty-eighth and Eighty-ninth Congresses, and served from January 3, 1963 until he resigned from the Eighty-ninth Congress, February 1, 1965, after being divested of seniority by the House Democratic Caucus because of his support of the Republican presidential nominee; announced his affiliation with the Republican Party on January 12, 1965; reelected as a Republican to the Eighty-ninth Congress, June 15, 1965, by special election to fill the vacancy caused by his own resignation; reelected to the Ninetieth and Ninety-first Congresses, and served from June 15, 1965 to January 3, 1971; was not a candidate for reelection in 1970 to the Ninety-second Congress, but was an unsuccessful candidate for election for Governor of South Carolina; nominated in May 1971 by President Richard M. Nixon to the United States Military Court of Appeals, but the nomination was later withdrawn; appointed an administrative law judge, Social Security Administration, 1973; was a resident of Columbia, S.C., until his death there on September 25, 1994; interment in Crescent Hill Memorial Gardens.

**Bibliography:** Hathorn, Billy B. "The Changing Politics of Race: Congressman Albert William Watson and the S.C. Republican Party, 1965-1970." *South Carolina Historical Magazine* 89 (October 1988): 227-241.

**WATSON, Clarence Wayland,** a Senator from West Virginia; born in Fairmont, Marion County, W.Va., May 8, 1864; attended the public schools of Marion County; employed in the coal-mining industry and later organized a number of coal companies, serving as president of the Consolidation Coal Co., 1903-1911; elected as a Democrat to the United States Senate to fill the vacancy caused by the death of Stephen B. Elkins and served from February 1, 1911, to March 3, 1913; unsuccessful candidate for reelection; commissioned lieutenant colonel in the Ordnance Department of the Army in March 1918 and served with the American Expeditionary Forces in France until January 1919; in 1918, while overseas, was nominated for United States Senator, but was unsuccessful in the election; again president of the Consolidation Coal Co., until 1928; also owned a stock farm and training stables; chairman of the board of directors of the Elk Horn Coal Corporation, later moving to Cincinnati, Ohio; died in Cincinnati, Ohio, May 24, 1940; interment in Woodlawn Cemetery, Fairmont, W.Va.

**WATSON, Cooper Kinderdine,** a Representative from Ohio; born in Jefferson County, Ky., June 18, 1810; pursued preparatory studies; studied law; was admitted to the bar and commenced practice in Delaware, Ohio; moved to Marion, Ohio; unsuccessful candidate for prosecuting attorney of Marion County in 1839; moved to Tiffin, Ohio, and practiced law for twenty years or more; elected as a Republican to the Thirty-fourth Congress (March 4, 1855-March 3, 1857); unsuccessful candidate for reelection in 1856 to the Thirty-fifth Congress; resumed the practice of law; moved to Sandusky, Ohio; member of the State constitutional convention in 1871; appointed judge of the court of common pleas in 1876 and served until his death in Sandusky, Erie County, Ohio, May 20, 1880; interment in Greenlawn Cemetery, Tiffin, Seneca County, Ohio.

**WATSON, David Kemper,** a Representative from Ohio; born near London, Madison County, Ohio, on June 18, 1849; was graduated from Dickinson College, Carlisle, Pa., in 1871 and from the law department of Boston University in 1873; was admitted to the bar and commenced practice; assistant United States district attorney for the southern district of Ohio during the administration of President Chester A. Arthur; elected attorney general of Ohio in 1887 and reelected in 1889; special counsel for the United States in the suits brought by the Government against the Pacific railroads in 1892; elected as a Republican to the Fifty-fourth Congress (March 4, 1895-March 3, 1897); unsuccessful candidate for reelection in 1896 to the Fifty-fifth Congress; appointed by President William McKinley as a member of the commission to revise and codify the laws of the United States; resumed the practice of law; died in Columbus, Ohio, September 28, 1918; interment in Greenlawn Cemetery.

**WATSON, Henry Winfield,** a Representative from Pennsylvania; born in Bucks County, Pa., June 24, 1856; educated in private schools; studied law; was admitted to the bar in 1881 and commenced the practice of his profession in Philadelphia; president of the Washington, Potomac & Chesapeake Railway Co.; director of several banks and of the Langhorne Water Co.; elected as a Republican to the Sixty-fourth and to the nine succeeding Congresses and served from March 4, 1915, until his death in Langhorne, Pa., on August 27, 1933; interment in the Brandywine Cemetery, Wilmington, Del.

**WATSON, James,** a Senator from New York; born in Woodbury, Conn., April 6, 1750; completed preparatory studies; graduated from Yale College in 1776; commissioned lieutenant in a Connecticut regiment in 1776 and resigned as a captain in 1777; studied law; was admitted to the bar and practiced; appointed in 1780 by the assembly as a purchasing commissary for the Connecticut Line; moved to New York City in 1786; engaged in mercantile pursuits; member, State assembly 1791, 1794-1796, serving as speaker 1794; regent of New York University 1795-1806; member, State senate 1796-1798; elected as a Federalist to the United States Senate to fill the vacancy caused by the resignation of John Sloss Hobart and served from August 17, 1798, to March 19, 1800, when he resigned to accept an appointment by President John Adams as United States naval officer at New York City; unsuccessful candidate for lieutenant governor in 1801; member of the Society of the Cincinnati; organizer and first president of the New England Society in New York City, from 1805 until his death there May 15, 1806.

**WATSON, James Eli,** a Representative and a Senator from Indiana; born in Winchester, Randolph County, Ind., November 2, 1864; graduated from De Pauw University, Greencastle, Ind., in 1886; studied law; was admitted to the bar in 1886 and commenced practice in Winchester; moved to Rushville, Ind., in 1893 and resumed the practice of law; elected as a Republican to the Fifty-fourth Congress (March 4, 1895-March 3, 1897); unsuccessful candidate for reelection in 1896 to the Fifty-fifth Congress; elected to the Fifty-sixth and to the four succeeding Congresses (March 4, 1899-March 3, 1909); was not a candidate for renomination in 1908 to the Sixty-first Congress; unsuccessful Republican candidate for Governor of Indiana in 1908; resumed the practice of law in Rushville, Ind.; elected as a Republican to the United States Senate in 1916 to fill the vacancy caused by the death of Benjamin F. Shively; reelected in 1920 and 1926, and served from November 8, 1916 to March 3, 1933; unsuccessful candidate for reelection in 1932; majority leader (Seventy-first and Seventy-second Congresses); chairman, Committee on Woman Suffrage (Sixty-sixth Congress), Committee on Revision of the Laws (Sixty-sixth Congress), Committee on Enrolled Bills (Sixty-eighth Congress), Committee on Interstate Commerce (Sixty-ninth and Seventieth Congresses), Republican Conference (Seventy-first and Seventy-second Congresses); continued the practice of law in Washington, D.C., until his death there on July 29, 1948; interment in Cedar Hill Cemetery.

**Bibliography:** *DAB*; Watson, James Eli. *As I Knew Them: Memoirs of James R. Watson, Former United States Senator from Indiana.* Indianapolis: The Bobbs-Merrill Co., 1936.

**WATSON, Lewis Findlay,** a Representative from Pennsylvania; born in Crawford County, Pa., April 14, 1819; attended the common schools; engaged in mercantile pursuits at Titusville in 1832; moved to Warren, Pa., in 1835 and continued his former pursuits until 1837; clerk in the office of the recorder in 1838; studied law at Warren Academy 1839-1840; resumed his former mercantile pursuits until 1860; engaged as an operator in lumber and in the production of petroleum 1860-1875; organized and was the first president of the Conewango Valley Railroad Co. in 1861; elected president of the Warren Savings Bank at its organization in 1870; elected as a Republican to the Forty-fifth Congress (March 4, 1877-March 3, 1879); elected to the Forty-seventh Congress (March 4, 1881-March 3, 1883); elected to the Fifty-first Congress and served from March 4, 1889, until his death in Washington, D.C., August 25, 1890; interment in Oakland Cemetery, Warren, Pa.

**WATSON, Thomas Edward,** a Representative and a Senator from Georgia; born in Columbia County, near Thomson, Ga., September 5, 1856; attended the common schools and Mercer University, Macon, Ga.; taught school; studied law; was admitted to the bar in 1875 and commenced practice in Thomson, McDuffie County, Ga., in 1876; also engaged in agricultural pursuits; member, State house of representatives 1882-1883; presidential elector on the Democratic ticket in 1888; elected as a Populist to the Fifty-second Congress (March 4, 1891-March 3, 1893); unsuccessful candidate for reelection in 1892 to the Fifty-third Congress and in 1894 for election to the Fifty-fourth Congress; resumed the practice of law in Thomson, Ga.; nominated for Vice President by the Populist National Convention in 1896 and for President by the People's Party in 1904; published a magazine for many years and later engaged in the newspaper business; author; unsuccessful candidate for the United States House of Representatives in 1918; elected as a Democrat to the United States Senate and served from March 4, 1921, until his death in Washington, D.C., September 26, 1922; interment in Thomson Cemetery, Thomson, Ga.

**Bibliography:** *DAB*; Crowe, Charles. "Tom Watson, Populists, and Blacks Reconsidered." *Journal of Negro History* 55 (April 1970): 99-116; Woodward, C. Vann. *Tom Watson: Agrarian Rebel.* New York: The Macmillan Co., 1938.

**WATSON, Walter Allen,** a Representative from Virginia; born in Nottoway County, Va., November 25, 1867; attended "old field" school; graduated from Hampden-Sidney College, Virginia, in 1887; studied law in the University of Virginia at Charlottesville in 1888 and 1889; admitted to the bar in 1893 and commenced practice in Nottoway and adjoining counties of Virginia; member of the Virginia senate 1891-1895; Commonwealth attorney 1895-1904; member of the Virginia Democratic committee in 1901 and 1902; circuit judge of the fourth judicial circuit of Virginia 1904-1912; elected as a Democrat to the Sixty-third and to the three succeeding Congresses and served from March 4, 1913, until his death in Washington, D.C., December 24, 1919; chairman, Committee on Elections No. 3 (Sixty-fifth Congress); interment in the family cemetery on his estate, "Woodland," Nottoway County, Va.

**WATT, Melvin L.,** a Representative from North Carolina; born in Steele Creek, Mecklenberg County, N.C., August 26, 1945; graduated, York Road High School, Charlotte, N.C., 1963; B.S., University of North Carolina at Chapel Hill, 1967; J.D., Yale University School of Law, 1970; attorney, 1971 to present; part owner, East Towne Manor, elderly and handicapped care facility, 1989 to present; appointed to North Carolina State senate, 1985-1986; campaign manager, Harvey Gantt for city council, mayor of Charlotte and United States Senate campaign; elected as a Democrat to the One Hundred Third and One Hundred Fourth Congresses (January 3, 1993-January 3, 1997); is a resident of Charlotte, N.C.

**WATTERSON, Harvey Magee** (father of Henry Watterson), a Representative from Tennessee; born at "Beechgrove," the family homestead, in Bedford County, Tenn., November 23, 1811; pursued classical studies; studied law; admitted to the bar and commenced practice in Shelbyville, Bedford County, Tenn.; established and edited a paper in Shelbyville, Tenn., in 1831; member of the Tennessee State house of representatives in 1835; elected as a Democrat to the Twenty-sixth and Twenty-seventh Congresses (March 4, 1839-March 3, 1843); declined to be a candidate for reelection in 1842 to the Twenty-eighth Congress; sent by President John Tyler on a diplomatic mission to Buenos Aires, where he remained for a year; member of the Tennessee State senate, 1845-1847, and served as speaker; editor and proprietor of the Nashville Union, 1847-1851, and editor of the Washington Union in 1851; delegate to the Democratic National Convention at Baltimore in 1860, and was a presidential elector on the Stephen A. Douglas ticket the same year; appointed by President Andrew Johnson as one of a commission to investigate conditions in the States "lately in rebellion"; practiced law in Washington, D.C., for fourteen years; moved to Louisville, Ky.; member of the editorial staff of the Louisville Courier-Journal; died in Louisville, Ky., October 1, 1891; interment in Cave Hill Cemetery.

**Bibliography:** *DAB.*

**WATTERSON, Henry** (son of Harvey Magee Watterson and nephew of Stanley Matthews), a Representative from Kentucky; born in Washington, D.C., February 16, 1840; completed preparatory studies under private tutors; attended the Academy of the Diocese of Pennsylvania in Philadelphia, Pa.; engaged in newspaper work as correspondent and editorial writer; his first newspaper employment was on the Washington States, a Democratic paper, 1858-1861; became editor of the Republican Banner in Nashville, Tenn., in 1861; during the Civil War entered the Confederate service; aide to General Nathan Bedford Forrest; was on the staff of General Leonidas Polk; chief of scouts in General Joseph E. Johnston's army; edited the Chattanooga Rebel in 1862 and 1863; resumed newspaper pursuits in Nashville after the war; moved to Louisville, Ky., in 1867 and purchased the Louisville Journal, consolidated it with the Courier, and served as editor of the Louisville Courier-Journal for fifty years; temporary chairman of

the Democratic National Convention of 1876; elected as a Democrat to the Forty-fourth Congress to fill the vacancy caused by the death of Edward Y. Parsons and served from August 12, 1876, to March 3, 1877; declined to be a candidate for renomination in 1876 to the Forty-fifth Congress; delegate to the Democratic National Conventions of 1880, 1884, 1888 and 1892; died in Jacksonville, Fla., December 22, 1921; interment in Cave Hill Cemetery, Louisville, Ky.

**Bibliography:** *DAB*; Wall, Joseph Frazier. *Henry Watterson, Reconstructed Rebel.* New York: Oxford University Press, 1956; Watterson, Henry. *"Marse Henry": An Autobiography.* 2 vols. New York: George H. Doran, 1919.

**WATTS, John,** a Representative from New York; born in New York City, August 27, 1749; completed preparatory studies; studied law; last recorder of New York under the Crown; member of the State assembly 1791-1793, serving as speaker of that body in 1792 and 1793; member of the commission to build Newgate Prison, New York City, 1796-1799; elected to the Third Congress (March 4, 1793-March 3, 1795); judge of Westchester County from 1802 to 1807; founded and endowed the Leake and Watts Orphan House; died in New York City September 3, 1836; interment in a vault in Trinity Churchyard.

**WATTS, John Clarence,** a Representative from Kentucky; born in Nicholasville, Jessamine County, Ky., July 9, 1902; attended the public schools; graduated from the University of Kentucky in 1925 and from its law school in 1927; admitted to the bar in 1927 and commenced the practice of law in Nicholasville, Ky.; also operated a farm; police judge of Nicholasville, Ky., 1929-1933; county attorney of Jessamine County, Ky., 1933-1945; member of the State house of representatives in 1947 and 1948, serving as floor leader; commissioner of motor transportation for Commonwealth of Kentucky 1948-1951; elected as a Democrat to the Eighty-second Congress, by special election, April 14, 1951, to fill the vacancy caused by the resignation of Thomas R. Underwood; reelected to the ten succeeding Congresses and served from April 14, 1951, until his death in Lexington, Ky., September 24, 1971; interment in Maple Grove Cemetery, Nicholasville, Ky.

**WATTS, John Sebrie,** a Delegate from the Territory of New Mexico; born in Boone County, Ky., January 19, 1816; moved to Indiana, where he completed preparatory studies; was graduated from Indiana University at Bloomington; studied law; was admitted to the bar and practiced; member of the Indiana State house of representatives in 1846 and 1847; associate justice of the United States court in the Territory of New Mexico from 1851 to 1854, when he resigned; resumed the practice of law; elected as a Republican to the Thirty-seventh Congress (March 4, 1861-March 3, 1863); delegate to the Republican National Convention of 1864; took an active part in equipping troops for the Union Army during the Civil War; appointed chief justice of the supreme court of New Mexico on July 11, 1868, by President Andrew Johnson, and served in that capacity one year; resumed the practice of law in Santa Fe; returned to Bloomington, Monroe County, Ind., where he died June 11, 1876; interment in Rose Hill Cemetery.

**WATTS, Julius Caesar, Jr.,** a Representative from Oklahoma; born in Eufala, McIntosh County, Okla., November 18, 1957; graduated, Eufala High School, 1976; B.A., University of Oklahoma, 1981; professional football player, 1981-1986; member, Oklahoma State Corporation Commission, 1990-1995, Commission chairman, 1993-1995; elected as a Republican to the One Hundred Fourth Congress (January 3, 1995-January 3, 1997); is a resident of Norman, Okla.

**WAUGH, Daniel Webster,** a Representative from Indiana; born near Bluffton, Wells County, Ind., March 7, 1842; attended the country schools and the high school in Bluffton; enlisted in the Union Army in 1861 in Company A, Thirty-fourth Regiment,

Indiana Volunteer Infantry, and served until honorably discharged in September 1864; taught school; engaged in agricultural pursuits; studied law; was admitted to the bar in 1866; settled in Tipton, Ind., in 1867 and practiced; judge of the thirty-sixth judicial circuit 1884-1890; elected as a Republican to the Fifty-second and Fifty-third Congresses (March 4, 1891-March 3, 1895); declined to be a candidate for renomination in 1894; resumed the practice of law; died in Tipton, Ind., March 14, 1921; interment in the mausoleum adjoining Green Lawn Cemetery.

**WAXMAN, Henry Arnold,** a Representative from California; born in Los Angeles, Calif., September 12, 1939; attended Los Angeles public schools; B.A., University of California, Los Angeles, 1961; J.D., University of California, Los Angeles, School of Law, 1964; admitted to the California bar in 1965 and commenced practice in Los Angeles; president, California Federation of Young Democrats, 1965-1967; member, California State assembly, 1969-1974; elected as a Democrat to the Ninety-fourth and to the ten succeeding Congresses (January 3, 1975-January 3, 1997); is a resident of Los Angeles, Calif.

**WAYNE, Anthony** (father of Isaac Wayne), a Representative from Georgia; born in East Town, Chester County, Pa., January 1, 1745; attended Philadelphia Academy; became a land surveyor and was employed for a time in Nova Scotia; returned to Chester County, Pa.; member of the provincial house of representatives, 1774-1775; served in the Revolutionary Army as colonel of the Fourth Regiment of Pennsylvania troops; commissioned as brigadier general on February 21, 1777; brevetted major general on October 10, 1783; elected to the Pennsylvania Assembly in 1784; moved to Georgia and settled upon a tract of land granted him by that State for his military service; delegate to the State convention which ratified the Constitution of the United States in 1788; presented credentials as a Member-elect to the Second Congress, and served from March 4, 1791 to March 21, 1792, when the seat was declared vacant; declined to be a candidate for reelection in 1792 to the Third Congress; again entered the service of the United States Army, as major general and General in Chief of the Army; concluded a treaty on August 3, 1795, with the Indians northwest of the Ohio River; died in Presque Isle (now Erie), Pa., December 15, 1796; remains were moved in 1809 and interred in St. David's Episcopal Church Cemetery, Radnor, Pa.

**Bibliography:** *DAB*; Nelson, Paul David. "Anthony Wayne: Soldier as Politician." *Pennsylvania Magazine of History and Biography* 106 (October 1982): 463-482; Wildes, Harry E. *Anthony Wayne, Trouble Shooter of the American Revolution.* New York: Harcourt, Brace, 1941.

**WAYNE, Isaac** (son of Anthony Wayne), a Representative from Pennsylvania; born near Paoli, Chester County, Pa., in 1772; attended the common schools; graduated from Dickinson College, Carlisle, Pa.; studied law; admitted to the Chester County bar in 1795; member of the Pennsylvania house of representatives 1799-1801 and in 1806; served in the Pennsylvania senate in 1810; during the War of 1812 was captain of a troop of Pennsylvania Horse Cavalry, raised and equipped by himself, and was subsequently colonel of the Second Regiment, Pennsylvania Volunteer Infantry; unsuccessful Federalist candidate for Governor in 1814; elected to the Eighteenth Congress (March 4, 1823-March 3, 1825); engaged in agricultural pursuits; died in Chester County, Pa., October 25, 1852; interment in St. David's Episcopal Church Cemetery, Radnor, Pa.

**WAYNE, James Moore,** a Representative from Georgia; born in Savannah, Ga., in 1790; completed preparatory studies and was graduated from Princeton College in 1808; studied law in New Haven, Conn.; was admitted to the bar in 1810 and commenced practice in Savannah, Ga.; entered the military service during the War of 1812, and served as an officer in the Georgia Hussars; member of the Georgia State house of representatives in 1815 and 1816; mayor of Savannah, 1817-1819; judge of the court of common pleas and oyer and terminer of Savannah, 1820-1822; judge of the superior court of Savannah from 1822 to 1828; elected as a Jacksonian to the Twenty-first and to the two succeeding Congresses and served from March 4, 1829, to January 13, 1835, when he resigned to accept a judicial position; chairman, Committee on Foreign Affairs (Twenty-third Congress); had been reelected to the Twenty-fourth Congress; nominated on January 7, 1835 by President Andrew Jackson as an Associate Justice of the United States Supreme Court; was confirmed by the Senate on January 9, 1835, and served from January 14, 1835, until his death in Washington, D.C., on July 5, 1867; interment in Laurel Grove Cemetery, Savannah, Chatham County, Ga.

**Bibliography:** *DAB*; Lawrence, Alexander A. *James Moore Wayne, Southern Unionist.* Chapel Hill: University of North Carolina Press, 1943.

**WEADOCK, Thomas Addis Emmet,** a Representative from Michigan; born in Ballygarrett, County Wexford, Ireland, on January 1, 1850; immigrated to the United States in infancy with his parents, who settled on a farm near St. Marys, Auglaize County, Ohio; educated in the common schools and the Union School at St. Marys; taught school in the counties of Auglaize, Shelby, and Miami for five years; was graduated from the law department of the University of Michigan at Ann Arbor in March 1873; was admitted to the bar the same year and commenced practice in Bay City, Mich.; served in the State militia 1874-1877; prosecuting attorney of Bay County in 1877 and 1878; chairman of the Democratic State conventions in 1883 and 1894; mayor of Bay City 1883-1885; member of the board of education of Bay City in 1884; elected as a Democrat to the Fifty-second and Fifty-third Congresses (March 4, 1891-March 3, 1895); chairman, Committee on Mines and Mining (Fifty-third Congress); declined to be a candidate for reelection in 1894; delegate at large to the Democratic National Convention in 1896; resumed the practice of law in Bay City, and later moved to Detroit, and continued to practice; unsuccessful Democratic candidate for judge of the supreme court of Michigan in 1904; appointed a professor of law in the University of Detroit in 1912; appointed an associate justice of the State supreme court in 1933; died in Detroit, Mich., November 18, 1938; interment in St. Patrick's Cemetery, Bay City, Mich.

**WEAKLEY, Robert,** a Representative from Tennessee; born in Halifax County, Va., July 20, 1764; attended Princeton (N.J.) schools; joined the Revolutionary Army at the age of sixteen and served until the close of the Revolutionary War; moved in 1785 to that part of North Carolina which later became Tennessee and engaged in agricultural pursuits; member of the North Carolina convention that ratified the Constitution of the United States in 1789; member of the first State house of representatives in 1796; elected as a Republican to the Eleventh Congress (March 4, 1809-March 3, 1811); appointed United States commissioner to treat with the Chickasaw Indians in 1819; member of the State senate in 1823 and 1824, serving as president in 1823; member of the State constitutional convention in 1834; died near Nashville, Tenn., February 4, 1845; interment in the family vault at "Lockland," on his estate in the suburbs of Nashville.

**WEARIN, Otha Donner,** a Representative from Iowa; born on a farm near Hastings, Mills County, Iowa, January 10, 1903; attended the country schools; was graduated from Tabor (Iowa) Academy in 1920 and from Grinnell (Iowa) College in 1924; served as treasurer of the Wearin, Iowa, rural school district, 1926-1928; engaged in agricultural pursuits and also as an author and editor; member, Iowa State house of representatives, 1928-1932; delegate to the Iowa State Democratic Judicial convention in 1930 and served as chairman; delegate to the Democratic National Conventions of 1936 and 1940; elected as a Democrat to the Seventy-third and to the two succeeding Congresses (March 4, 1933-January 3, 1939); was not a candidate in 1938 for renomination to the House of Representatives, but was an unsuccessful candidate for nomination to the United States Senate; resumed agricultural pursuits; member of the Alien Enemy Hearing Board for the southern district of Iowa, 1941-1944; member, Democratic State Central Committee, 1948-1952; member of Mills County Board of Education; unsuccessful candidate in 1950 for nomination to the United States Senate, and in 1952 for Governor of Iowa; staff adviser to Governor Herschel C. Loveless of Iowa, 1959-1961; member, Iowa State Commission on Aging, 1965-1969; author; was a resident of Hastings, Iowa.; died April 3, 1990.

**Bibliography:** Wearin, Otha D. *Country Roads to Washington.* Des Moines, Iowa: Wallace Homestead Company, 1976.

**WEATHERFORD, Zadoc Lorenzo,** a Representative from Alabama; born on a farm in Marion County, Ala., near Vina, Franklin County, February 4, 1888; attended the public schools; was graduated from the medical department of the University of Tennessee at Memphis, M.D., 1914; served as an intern in St. Joseph Hospital, Memphis, Tenn., 1914-1916; moved to Red Bay, Ala., in 1916 and commenced general medical practice; during the First World War served from August 26, 1917, as battalion surgeon in the Three Hundred and Twenty-sixth Infantry and was discharged on October 6, 1920; awarded the Purple Heart Medal; was subdistrict medical officer, United States Veterans' Bureau, Montgomery, Ala., 1922-1924; resumed medical practice in Red Bay, Ala.; also interested in banking and agricultural pursuits, with farming interests in both Alabama and Mississippi; served in the State senate from 1939 until elected to Congress; elected as a Democrat to the Seventy-sixth Congress to fill the vacancy caused by the death of William B. Bankhead and served from November 5, 1940, to January 3, 1941; was not a candidate for the full term; resumed his medical profession, retiring from active practice January 1, 1958; mayor of Red Bay, Ala., 1945-1948; vice chairman Franklin County Democratic Committee, 1933-1937; president of the Bank of Red Bay, 1938-1970; was a resident of Red Bay, Ala., until his death on May 21, 1983.

**WEAVER, Archibald Jerard** (grandfather of Phillip H. Weaver), a Representative from Nebraska; born in Dundaff, Susquehanna County, Pa., April 15, 1843; attended the common schools; was graduated from Wyoming Seminary, Kingston, Pa., and a member of the faculty 1864-1867; was graduated from the law department of Harvard University in 1869; was admitted to the bar in Boston, Mass., in 1869; moved to Falls City, Nebr., in 1869 and commenced the practice of law; member of the State constitutional conventions in 1871 and 1875; district attorney for the first district of Nebraska in 1872; elected judge of the first judicial district of Nebraska in 1875; reelected in 1879 and resigned in 1883; was elected as a Republican to the Forty-eighth and Forty-ninth Congresses (March 4, 1883-March 3, 1887); did not seek renomination in 1886, but was an unsuccessful candidate for election to the United States Senate in 1887; resumed the practice of law; died in Falls City, Richardson County, Nebr., April 18, 1887; interment in Steele Cemetery.

**Bibliography:** Snoddy, Donald D. "The Congressional Career of Archibald Jerard Weaver, 1882-1887." *Nebraska History* 57 (Spring 1976): 83-98.

**WEAVER, Claude,** a Representative from Oklahoma; born in Gainesville, Cooke County, Tex., March 19, 1867; attended the public schools; was graduated from the law department of the University of Texas at Austin in 1887; was admitted to the bar the same year and practiced in Gainesville, Tex., 1887-1895; assistant prosecuting attorney of Cooke County, Tex., in 1892; moved to Pauls Valley, Indian Territory, in 1895 and engaged in the practice of law; moved to Oklahoma City, Okla., in 1902; member of Oklahoma City

Board of Freeholders in 1910; elected as a Democrat to the Sixty-third Congress (March 4, 1913-March 3, 1915); unsuccessful candidate for renomination in 1914 and for election to fill a vacancy in the Sixty-sixth Congress in 1919; postmaster of Oklahoma City, Okla., 1915-1923; acting county attorney of Oklahoma County in 1926; legal adviser and secretary to the Governor, William H. Murray, 1931-1934; district judge of thirteenth Oklahoma district in 1934 and 1935; returned to the practice of law; died in Oklahoma City, Okla., May 19, 1954; interment in Fairlawn Cemetery.

**WEAVER, James Baird,** a Representative from Iowa; born in Dayton, Ohio, June 12, 1833; moved with his parents to Michigan in 1835, and subsequently moved to Iowa and settled on a farm near Bloomfield; attended the common schools; studied law at Bloomfield, 1853-1856; was graduated from the Cincinnati Law School in April 1856; was admitted to the bar in 1856 and commenced practice in Bloomfield; enlisted as a private in the Second Regiment, Iowa Volunteer Infantry, in April 1861; commissioned first lieutenant of Company G on May 27, 1861; major on July 25, 1862; colonel on November 10, 1862; brevetted brigadier general of Volunteers on March 13, 1864; mustered out on May 27, 1864; elected district attorney for the second judicial district of Iowa in 1866 and served four years; appointed assessor of internal revenue for the first district of Iowa by President Andrew Johnson on March 25, 1867, and served until May 20, 1873; elected as a Greenbacker to the Forty-sixth Congress (March 4, 1879-March 3, 1881); was not a candidate for renomination to the Forty-seventh Congress, but was nominated at Chicago on June 9, 1880 by the National Greenback Party as their candidate for President of the United States; unsuccessful candidate for election in 1882 to the Forty-eighth Congress; elected to the Forty-ninth and Fiftieth Congresses (March 4, 1885-March 3, 1889); chairman, Committee on Expenditures in the Department of the Interior (Forty-ninth Congress), Committee on Patents (Fiftieth Congress); unsuccessful candidate for reelection in 1888 to the Fifty-first Congress; nominated in July 1892 by the People's (Populist) Party as their candidate for President of the United States; mayor of Colfax, Iowa, 1901-1903; died in Des Moines, Iowa, February 6, 1912; interment in Woodland Cemetery.

**Bibliography:** *DAB*; Colbert, Thomas Burnell. "Political Fusion in Iowa: The Election of James B. Weaver to Congress in 1878." *Arizona and the West* 20 (Spring 1978): 25-40; Haynes, Fred Emory. *James Baird Weaver.* Iowa City: State Historical Society of Iowa, 1916.

**WEAVER, James Dorman,** a Representative from Pennsylvania; born in Erie, Pa., September 27, 1920; attended the public schools, the Erie Conservatory of Music, and Syracuse (N.Y.) University, 1938-1941; graduated from the Medical School of the University of Pennsylvania at Philadelphia in 1944; while a student, worked on farms in Erie County, and also as a musician with orchestras; entered the United States Army Medical Corps in 1946 and served as a captain and as commanding officer and chief of surgery, Three Hundred and Eighty-second Station Hospital, Ascom City, Korea, 1947-1948; engaged in the practice of medicine in Erie, Pa., 1948-1962; Pennsylvania delegate to White House Conference on Aging in 1961; medical administrator, Pennsylvania Bureau of Vocational Rehabilitation, 1960-1962; elected as a Republican to the Eighty-eighth Congress (January 3, 1963-January 3, 1965); unsuccessful candidate for reelection in 1964 to the Eighty-ninth Congress; was on active duty with the United States Air Force from 1965 until 1983; associate professor of community medicine, Georgetown University, Washington, D.C., 1966-1968; command surgeon, Air National Guard, 1968-1983; consultant, Assistant Secretary of Defense for Reserve Affairs, 1983-1984; medical adviser, National Guard Association, 1984-1995; is a resident of Fairfax, Va.

**WEAVER, James Howard,** a Representative from Oregon; born in Brookings, S.Dak., August 8, 1927; attended public schools in Des Moines, Iowa; moved to Eugene, Oreg., 1947; B.S., University of Oregon, Eugene, 1952; served in the United States Navy, 1945-1946; worked as publisher's representative, 1954-1958; was staff director for the Oregon Legislative Interim Committee on Agriculture, 1959-1960; became a builder and developer of office and apartment building complexes in Oregon, 1960; delegate to the Democratic National Conventions of 1960 and 1964; elected as a Democrat to the Ninety-fourth and to the five succeeding Congresses (January 3, 1975-January 3, 1987); was not a candidate in 1986 for reelection to the House of Representatives, but was the Democratic nominee for the United States Senate until he withdrew his candidacy on August 13, 1986; author; is a resident of Eugene, Oreg.

**WEAVER, Phillip Hart** (grandson of Archibald Jerard Weaver), a Representative from Nebraska; born in Falls City, Richardson County, Nebr., April 9, 1919; attended the public schools of Falls City and Lincoln, Nebr.; student at St. Benedicts College, Atchison, Kans., in 1938 and 1939; A.B., University of Nebraska, Lincoln, 1942; staff announcer for radio stations, 1938-1940; entered the Armed Services on June 1, 1942, and assigned to command, staff, and liaison duties with the Seventeenth Airborne Division, First Allied Ariborne Army, and Headquarters, Berlin District; was discharged as a captain in March 1946; awarded Combat Infantryman's Badge, Glider Wings, and Bronze Star with oak leaf cluster; retired as lieutenant colonel in United States Army Reserves; engaged in the insurance and finance business in Falls City, 1946-1949; director, Falls City Wholesale & Supply, Inc., beginning in 1946; civilian administrative assistant to the G-1, Fifth Army, Chicago, Ill., in 1949 and 1950; established an automobile agency in Falls City in 1950; elected as a Republican to the Eighty-fourth and to the three succeeding Congresses (January 3, 1955-January 3, 1963); unsuccessful for renomination in 1962 to the Eighty-eighth Congress; special consultant, Department of Agriculture, Washington, D.C., 1963-1965; deputy director, Field Cooperations Division, Rural Community Development Service, 1966; regional development coordinator for Department of Agriculture, 1967-1968; acting administrator, Rural Community Development Service, 1969; deputy assistant to the Secretary of Agriculture, 1969-1973; resumed his business interests in Falls City in 1974; was a resident of Falls City, Nebr.; died April 16, 1989.

**WEAVER, Walter Lowrie,** a Representative from Ohio; born in Montgomery County, Ohio, April 1, 1851; attended the public schools and Monroe Academy, and was graduated from Wittenberg College, Springfield, Ohio, in 1870; studied law; was admitted to the bar in 1872 and commenced practice in Springfield, Ohio; elected prosecuting attorney of Clark County in 1874, 1880, 1882, and 1885; elected as a Republican to the Fifty-fifth and Fifty-sixth Congresses (March 4, 1897-March 3, 1901); chairman, Committee on Elections No. 2 (Fifty-sixth Congress); unsuccessful candidate for renomination in 1900; appointed associate justice Choctaw-Chickasaw citizens' court at McAlester, Okla., in 1902; returned to Springfield, Ohio, in 1904 and resumed the practice of law; died in Springfield, Clark County, Ohio, May 26, 1909; interment in Ferncliff Cemetery.

**WEAVER, Zebulon,** a Representative from North Carolina; born in Weaverville, Buncombe County, N.C., May 12, 1872; attended the public schools and was graduated from Weaver College at Weaverville in 1889; studied law at the University of North Carolina at Chapel Hill; was admitted to the bar in 1894 and commenced practice in Asheville, N.C.; member of the State house of representatives 1907-1909; served in the State senate 1913-1915; presented credentials as a Democratic Member-elect to the Sixty-fifth Congress and served from March 4, 1917, to March 1, 1919, when he was succeeded by James J. Britt, who contested his election; elected to the Sixty-sixth and to the four succeeding Congresses (March 4, 1919-March 3, 1929); unsuccessful candidate for reelection in 1928 to the Seventy-first Congress; elected to the Seventy-second and to the seven succeeding Congresses (March 4, 1931-January 3, 1947); unsuccessful candidate for renomination in 1946; resumed the practice of law in Asheville, N.C., until his death there October 29, 1948; interment in Riverside Cemetery.

**WEBB, Edwin Yates,** a Representative from North Carolina; born in Shelby, Cleveland County, N.C., May 23, 1872; attended the Shelby Military Institute, and was graduated from Wake Forest (N.C.) College in June 1893; studied law at the University of North Carolina at Chapel Hill in 1893 and 1894; was admitted to the bar in 1894 and commenced practice in Shelby; entered the University of Virginia Law School at Charlottesville in 1896 and completed a postgraduate course; member of the North Carolina State senate in 1901; appointed a trustee of Wake Forest College in 1898; appointed trustee of the Agricultural and Mechanical College of Raleigh by the legislature in 1899 and served two years; chairman of the Democratic senatorial district in 1896; chairman of the Democratic county executive committee, 1898-1902; temporary chairman of the Democratic State convention in 1900; elected as a Democrat to the Fifty-eighth and to the eight succeeding Congresses, and served from March 4, 1903 to November 10, 1919, when he resigned to accept a judicial position; chairman, Committee on the Judiciary (Sixty-third through Sixty-fifth Congresses); co-sponsor of the Webb-Kenyon Act of 1913, banning the transport of liquor into any state that prohibited its sale; one of the managers appointed by the House of Representatives in 1912 to conduct impeachment proceedings against Robert W. Archbald, judge of the United States Commerce Court; appointed United States district judge for the western district of North Carolina, November 5, 1919, and served until his retirement on March 1, 1948; died in Wilmington, N.C., February 7, 1955, while on a visit; interment in Sunset Cemetery, Shelby, N.C.

**WEBB, William Robert** (grandson of Richard Stanford), a Senator from Tennessee; born near Mount Tirzah, Person County, N.C., November 11, 1842; attended private schools and was a student in Bingham School, Oaks, N.C., 1856-1860; entered the University of North Carolina in 1860, but left to enlist in the Confederate Army; returned to North Carolina in 1865; graduated from the University of North Carolina at Chapel Hill in 1868; taught at Horner's School, Oxford, N.C., 1868-1870; founded the Webb School, a preparatory school, at Culleoka, Tenn., in 1870; moved the school to Bell Buckle, Tenn., in 1886; elected as a Democrat to the United States Senate to fill the vacancy caused by the death of Robert L. Taylor, and served from January 24, 1913 to March 3, 1913; was not a candidate for reelection in 1913; continued teaching until his death in Bell Buckle, Tenn., December 19, 1926; interment in Hazelwood Cemetery.

Bibliography: *DAB*; McMillin, Laurence. *The Schoolmaker: Sawney Webb and the Bell Buckle Story.* Chapel Hill: University of North Carolina Press, 1971; Parks, E.W. "Sawney Webb: Tennessee's Schoolmaster." *North Carolina Historical Review* 12 (July 1935): 233-51.

**WEBBER, Amos Richard,** a Representative from Ohio; born in Hinckley, Medina County, Ohio, January 21, 1852; attended the public schools of Hinckley and was graduated from Baldwin University, Berea, Ohio, in 1876; studied law; was admitted to the bar in 1876 and commenced practice in Elyria, Ohio; prosecuting attorney of Lorain County 1884-1890; judge of the court of common pleas of Lorain County 1900-1903; elected as a Republican to the Fifty-eighth Congress to fill the vacancy caused by the death of William W. Skiles; reelected to the Fifty-ninth Congress and served from November 8, 1904, to March 3, 1907; unsuccessful candidate for renomination in 1906; resumed the practice of law in Elyria, Ohio; engaged in literary pursuits; again elected in 1922 judge of the court of common pleas, serving until his retirement in 1935; died in Elyria, Ohio, February 25, 1948; interment in Ridgelawn Cemetery.

**WEBBER, George Washington,** a Representative from Michigan; born in Newbury, Orange County, Vt., November 25, 1825; attended the common schools and the academy at Alfred, Allegany County, N.Y.; moved to Michigan in 1852 and settled in Manistee County, where he engaged in farming, lumbering, manufacturing, and mercantile pursuits; moved to Ionia, Ionia County, in 1858 and continued the lumber and mercantile business; engaged in the banking business at Ionia in 1870; elected president of the Second National Bank of Ionia in 1872, a position which he held until the time of his death; mayor of Ionia in 1874 and 1875; elected as a Republican to the Forty-seventh Congress (March 4, 1881-March 3, 1883); was not a candidate for renomination in 1882; resumed his former business activities; died in Ionia, Mich., January 15, 1900; interment in Highland Park Cemetery.

**WEBER, Edward Ford,** a Representative from Ohio; born in Toledo, Lucas County, Ohio, July 26, 1931; attended the public schools; A.B., Denison University, Granville, Ohio, 1953; LL.B., Harvard University Law School, 1956; served in the United States Army, 1956-1958; admitted to the Ohio bar in 1956 and commenced practice in Toledo, 1958; instructor, University of Toledo College of Law, 1966-1979; elected as a Republican to the Ninety-seventh Congress (January 3, 1981-January 3, 1983); unsuccessful candidate for reelection in 1982 to the Ninety-eighth Congress; resumed the practice of law; is a resident of Toledo, Ohio.

**WEBER, John Baptiste,** a Representative from New York; born in Buffalo, N.Y., September 21, 1842; attended public and private schools and the Central School of Buffalo; enlisted in the Civil War as a private in the Forty-fourth Regiment, New York Volunteer Infantry, August 7, 1861, and was rapidly promoted, attaining the rank of colonel of the Eighty-ninth United States Colored Infantry; engaged in the wholesale grocery business; assistant postmaster of Buffalo, 1871-1873; sheriff of Erie County, 1874-1876; elected as a Republican to the Forty-ninth and Fiftieth Congresses (March 4, 1885-March 3, 1889); unsuccessful candidate for reelection in 1888 to the Fifty-first Congress; delegate to the Republican National Convention of 1888; grade-crossing commissioner of the city of Buffalo from 1888 until 1908; commissioner of immigration at the port of New York, 1890-1893; commissioner general of the Pan American Exposition at Buffalo in 1901; died in Lackawanna, N.Y., on December 18, 1926; interment in Forest Lawn Cemetery, Buffalo, N.Y.

**WEBER, John Vincent (Vin),** a Representative from Minnesota; born in Slayton, Murray County, Minn., July 24, 1952; attended the public schools; attended the University of Minnesota, Minneapolis, 1970-1974; copublisher, Murray County newspaper; president, Weber Publishing Co.; press secretary to Representative Tom Hagedorn, 1974-1975; senior aide to Senator Rudy Boschwitz, 1977-1980; delegate, Minnesota State Republican conventions, 1972, 1978; elected as a Republican to the Ninety-seventh and to the five succeeding Congresses (January 3, 1981-January 3, 1993); was not a candidate for renomination in 1992 to the One Hundred Third Congress; vice-chairman, Empower America; partner, Clark and Weinstock, Inc.

**WEBSTER, Daniel,** a Representative from New Hampshire and a Representative and a Senator from Massachusetts; born in Salisbury, N.H., January 18, 1782; attended district schools and Phillips Exeter Academy, Exeter, N.H.; graduated from Dartmouth College, Hanover, N.H., in 1801; principal of an academy at Fryeburg, Maine, in 1802; studied law; admitted to the bar in 1805 and commenced practice in Boscawen, near Salisbury, N.H.; moved to Portsmouth, N.H., in 1807 and continued the practice of law; elected as a Federalist from New Hampshire to the Thirteenth and Fourteenth Congresses (March 4, 1813-March 3, 1817); was not a candidate for reelection in 1816 to the Fifteenth Congress; moved to Boston, Mass., in 1816; achieved national fame as counsel representing Dartmouth College before the United States Supreme Court in *Dartmouth College v. Woodward*, 1818-1819; delegate to the Massachusetts constitutional convention in 1820; elected from Massachusetts to the Eighteenth and to the two succeeding Congresses, and served from March 4, 1823 to May 30, 1827; chairman, Committee on the Judiciary (Eighteenth and Nineteenth Congresses); elected June 8, 1827 to the United States Senate for the term beginning March 4, 1827; reelected as a Whig in 1833 and 1839, and served until his resignation, effective February 22, 1841; chairman, Committee on Finance (Twenty-third and Twenty-fourth Congresses); Webster's reply to Senator Robert Y. Hayne of South Carolina, January 26 and 27, 1830 in opposition to the principles of Nullification won him nationwide renown, as did his widely circulated "Seventh of March" speech in 1850, in support of compromise measures to avert possible civil war; unsuccessful Whig candidate for President of the United States in 1836; appointed Secretary of State by President William Henry Harrison and again by President John Tyler, and served from March 5, 1841 to May 8, 1843; again elected as a Whig to the United States Senate, and served from March 4, 1845 to July 22, 1850, when he resigned; appointed Secretary of State by President Millard Fillmore, and served from July 22, 1850 until his death in Marshfield, Mass., October 24, 1852; interment in the Winslow Cemetery.

**Bibliography:** *DAB*; Baxter, Maurice. *One and Inseparable: Daniel Webster and the Union*. Cambridge, Mass.: Belknap Press of Harvard University, 1984; Webster, Daniel. *The Papers of Daniel Webster*. Edited by Charles M. Wiltse, Harold D. Moser, et al. 15 vols. Hanover, N.H.: University Press of New England, 1974-1989.

**WEBSTER, Edwin Hanson,** a Representative from Maryland; born near Churchville, Harford County, Md., March 31, 1829; received a classical training; attended the Churchville (Md.) Academy and the New London Academy, Chester County, Pa., and was graduated from Dickinson College, Carlisle, Pa., in 1847; taught school; studied law; was admitted to the bar in 1851 and commenced practice in Bel Air, Harford County, Md.; member of the Maryland State senate, 1855-1859; during the Civil War was colonel of the Seventh Regiment, Maryland Volunteer Infantry, and served in 1862 and 1863; elected as a candidate of the American Party to the Thirty-sixth Congress, as a Unionist to the Thirty-seventh Congress and as an Unconditional Unionist to the Thirty-eighth and Thirty-ninth Congresses and served from March 4, 1859, until his resignation in July 1865, when he was appointed collector of customs at the port of Baltimore, and served from July 27, 1865, to April 15, 1869; resumed the practice of his profession in Bel Air; was again appointed by President Chester A. Arthur, on February 17, 1882, and served until February 23, 1886; in 1882 he engaged in banking, which he followed until his death; died in Bel Air, Md., April 24, 1893; interment in Calvary Cemetery, near Churchville, Md.

**WEBSTER, John Stanley,** a Representative from Washington; born in Cynthiana, Harrison County, Ky., February 22, 1877; attended the public schools and Smith's Classical School for Boys; studied law at the University of Michigan at Ann Arbor 1897-1899; was admitted to the bar in 1899 and commenced practice in Cynthiana, Ky.; prosecuting attorney of Harrison County, Ky., 1902-1906; moved to Spokane, Wash., in May 1906; chief assistant prosecuting attorney for Spokane County 1907-1909; judge of the superior court of Spokane County 1909-1916; lecturer on criminal and elementary law in Gonzaga University, Spokane, Wash.; associate justice of the State supreme court 1916-1918; elected as a Republican to the Sixty-sixth, Sixty-seventh, and Sixty-eighth Congresses and served from March 4, 1919, to May 8, 1923, when he resigned to become United States district judge for the eastern district of Washington, in which capacity he served until August 31, 1939, when he retired due to ill health; was a resident of Spokane, Wash., until his death there on December 24, 1962; remains were cremated and the ashes interred in the Oakesdale Cemetery, Oakesdale, Wash.

**WEBSTER, Taylor,** a Representative from Ohio; born in Pennsylvania October 1, 1800; moved with his parents to Ohio in 1806, where he received a limited schooling; attended Miami University, Oxford, Ohio, for a short time; editor and publisher of the Western Telegraph, Hamilton, Ohio, 1828-1836; clerk of the State house of representatives in 1829; member of the State house of representatives in 1830 and served as speaker; elected as a Jacksonian to the Twenty-third and Twenty-fourth Congresses and as a Democrat to the Twenty-fifth Congress (March 4, 1833-March 3, 1839); clerk of court of Butler County, Ohio, 1842-1846; resumed his former business pursuits; moved to New Orleans, La., in 1863 and was employed in a clerical position; died in New Orleans, La., April 27, 1876; interment in Lafayette Cemetery No. 1.

**WEDEMEYER, William Walter,** a Representative from Michigan; born near Lima Township, Washtenaw County, Mich., March 22, 1873; attended the district schools and Ann Arbor High School; was graduated from the law department of the University of Michigan at Ann Arbor in 1895; member of the board of school examiners in 1894 and 1895; was admitted to the bar in 1895; county commissioner of schools 1895-1897; deputy commissioner of railroads for Michigan 1897-1899; commenced the practice of law at Ann Arbor in 1899; chairman of the Republican State convention in 1903; American consul at Georgetown, British Guiana, during the summer of 1905; member of the Republican State central committee 1906-1910; elected as a Republican to the Sixty-second Congress and served from March 4, 1911, until his death; was an unsuccessful candidate for reelection in 1912 to the Sixty-third Congress; while on an official visit to Colon, Panama, was accidentally drowned in the harbor of that port on January 2, 1913; remains were never recovered.

**WEEKS, Edgar** (cousin of John Wingate Weeks [1820-1926]), a Representative from Michigan; born at Mount Clemens, Macomb County, Mich., August 3, 1839; attended the public schools; learned the trade of printer; studied law, and was admitted to the bar in January 1861; during the Civil War served in Company B, Fifth Regiment, Michigan Volunteer Infantry, and was first sergeant of the company; first lieutenant and adjutant of the Twenty-second Michigan Infantry in 1862; captain in 1863; appointed assistant inspector general of the Third Brigade, Second Division, Reserve Corps, Army of the Cumberland, in 1863; was mustered out in December 1863; proprietor and editor of a Republican newspaper in Mount Clemens, Mich.; commenced the practice of law in Mount Clemens in 1866; prosecuting attorney 1867-1870; appointed judge of probate of Macomb County 1870-1876; unsuccessful candidate for election in 1884 to the Forty-ninth Congress; elected as a Republican to the Fifty-sixth and Fifty-seventh Congresses (March 4, 1899-March 3, 1903); chairman, Committee on Elections No. 3 (Fifty-seventh Congress); unsuccessful candidate for renomination in 1902; resumed the practice of law; died in Mount Clemens, Mich., December 17, 1904; interment in Clinton Grove Cemetery.

**WEEKS, John Eliakim,** a Representative from Vermont; born in Salisbury, Addison County, Vt., June 14, 1853; attended the county schools and Middlebury High School; engaged in the banking business in 1882; assistant judge of Addison County, 1884-1886; served in the Vermont State house of representatives in 1888; moved to Middlebury, Vt., in 1896; member of the State senate in 1896; elected trustee of the State industrial school (later the Weeks School) in 1898; associate judge, 1902-1904; again served in the State house of representatives in 1912 and 1915, serving as speaker in 1915; director of State institutions, 1917-1923; commissioner of

public welfare, 1923-1926; elected Governor of Vermont in 1926, reelected in 1928, and served from January 6, 1927 to January 8, 1931; elected as a Republican to the Seventy-second Congress (March 4, 1931-March 3, 1933); was not a candidate for renomination in 1932 to the Seventy-third Congress; resumed his banking interests; died in Middlebury, Vt., on September 10, 1949; interment in Salisbury Cemetery, Salisbury, Vt.

**WEEKS, John Wingate** (father of Sinclair Weeks and cousin of Edgar Weeks), a Representative and a Senator from Massachusetts; born near Lancaster, N.H., April 11, 1860; attended the common schools; taught school; graduated from the United States Naval Academy, Annapolis, Md., in 1881; served in the United States Navy as a midshipman, 1881-1883; resigned from the Navy in 1883 and took up the profession of civil engineering; became engaged in the banking and brokerage business in Boston, Mass., 1888-1914; served in the Massachusetts Naval Brigade from 1890 until 1900, acting as commander the last six years; moved to Newton, Mass., in 1893; member of the Board of Visitors to the United States Naval Academy in 1896; served in the Spanish-American War as a lieutenant in the Volunteer Navy, 1898; member of the board of aldermen of Newton, Mass., 1899-1902; mayor of Newton, 1902-1903; elected as a Republican to the Fifty-ninth and to the four succeeding Congresses and served from March 4, 1905, until his resignation effective March 4, 1913, to become United States Senator; chairman, Committee on Expenditures in the Department of State (Fifty-ninth and Sixtieth Congresses), Committee on Post Office and Post Roads (Sixty-first Congress); elected as a Republican to the United States Senate, and served from March 4, 1913 to March 3, 1919; unsuccessful candidate for reelection in 1918; chairman, Committee on the Disposition of Useless Executive Papers (Sixty-fifth Congress); appointed Secretary of War by President Warren G. Harding, and again by President Calvin Coolidge, and served from March 5, 1921 until October 13, 1925, when he resigned due to ill health; died in Lancaster, N.H., July 12, 1926; remains were cremated and the ashes interred in Arlington National Cemetery.

**Bibliography:** *DAB*; Spence, Benjamin. "The National Career of John Wingate Weeks (1904-1925)." Ph.D. dissertation, University of Wisconsin, 1971; Washburn, Charles. *Life of John W. Weeks.* Boston: Houghton Mifflin, Co., 1928.

**WEEKS, John Wingate** (great uncle of John Wingate Weeks), a Representative from New Hampshire; born in Greenland, Rockingham County, N.H., March 31, 1781; attended the common schools; learned the carpenter's trade; during the War of 1812 recruited a company for the Eleventh Regiment of United States Infantry and served as its captain; promoted to the rank of major; after the war resided in Coos County, N.H., where he held several local offices; elected as a Jacksonian to the Twenty-first and Twenty-second Congresses (March 4, 1829-March 3, 1833); died in Lancaster, Coos County, N.H., April 3, 1853; interment in the Old Cemetery.

**Bibliography:** *DAB*.

**WEEKS, Joseph** (grandfather of Joseph Weeks Babcock), a Representative from New Hampshire; born in Warwick, Mass., February 13, 1773; attended the common schools; moved to Richmond, N.H.; engaged in agricultural pursuits; town clerk of Richmond, N.H., 1802-1822; member of the State house of representatives 1807-1809, 1812, 1813, 1821-1826, 1830, and 1832-1834; associate judge of the court of common pleas 1823 and 1827; elected as a Jacksonian to the Twenty-fourth Congress and reelected as a Democrat to the Twenty-fifth Congress (March 4, 1835-March 3, 1839); died in Winchester, Cheshire County, N.H., August 4, 1845.

**WEEKS, Sinclair** (son of John Wingate Weeks), a Senator from Massachusetts; born in West Newton, Middlesex County, Mass., June 15, 1893; attended the public schools; graduated from Harvard University, Cambridge, Mass., in 1914; engaged in the banking business at Boston, Mass., 1914-1923; served on the Mexican border with the Massachusetts National Guard in 1916; during the First World War served from 1917, as a lieutenant and later as a captain of the One Hundred and First Field Artillery in the Twenty-sixth Division, and was discharged in 1919; engaged in the manufacture of metal products, 1923-1953; alderman of Newton, 1923-1930; mayor of Newton, 1930-1935; member of the Republican National Committee, 1941-1953, serving as treasurer from 1940 until 1944; appointed as a Republican to the United States Senate on February 8, 1944, to fill the vacancy caused by the resignation of Henry Cabot Lodge, Jr., and served from February 8, 1944, to December 19, 1944, a successor having been elected; was not a candidate for election to the vacancy; overseer of Harvard University, 1948-1954; Secretary of Commerce in the Cabinet of President Dwight D. Eisenhower from January 21, 1953 until his resignation on November 12, 1958; chairman, partner, and director of several manufacturing, investment and insurance firms; retired in 1970 and resided in Lancaster, N.H.; died in Concord, Mass., February 7, 1972; interment in Summer Street Cemetery, Lancaster, N.H.

**WEEMS, Capell Lane,** a Representative from Ohio; born in Whigville, Noble County, Ohio, July 7, 1860; attended the common schools and normal academy, Caldwell, Ohio; studied law; was admitted to the bar in 1883 and commenced practice in Caldwell; elected prosecuting attorney of Noble County in 1884; member of the State house of representatives in 1888 and 1889; moved to St. Clairsville in 1890; prosecuting attorney of Belmont County 1890-1896; elected as a Republican to the Fifty-eighth Congress to fill the vacancy caused by the resignation of Joseph J. Gill; reelected to the Fifty-ninth and Sixtieth Congresses and served from November 3, 1903, to March 3, 1909; resumed the practice of law and was solicitor for the Pennsylvania Railroad; died in Steubenville, Ohio, January 5, 1913; interment in Union Cemetery, St. Clairsville, Ohio.

**WEEMS, John Crompton,** a Representative from Maryland; born in Waterloo, Calvert County, Md., in 1778; attended St. John's College, Annapolis, Md.; engaged in planting; elected to the Nineteenth Congress to fill the vacancy caused by the resignation of Joseph Kent; reelected to the Twentieth Congress and served from February 1, 1826, to March 3, 1829; resumed agricultural pursuits; died on his plantation, "Loch Eden," in Anne Arundel County, Md., January 20, 1862; interment in a private cemetery on his estate.

**WEFALD, Knud,** a Representative from Minnesota; born in Kragero, Norway, November 3, 1869; attended the local schools and high school of his native land; immigrated to the United States in 1887 and in 1896 settled in Hawley, Clay County, Minn., engaged in agricultural pursuits; also manager and part owner of a lumber business; member of the village council of Hawley, serving as president in 1907-1912, 1917, and 1918; member of the State house of representatives 1913-1915; elected on the Farmer-Labor ticket to the Sixty-eighth and Sixty-ninth Congresses (March 4, 1923-March 3, 1927); unsuccessful candidate for reelection in 1926 to the Seventieth Congress; resumed his former business pursuits; editor of a Norwegian newspaper at Fargo, N.Dak., 1929-1931; executive secretary of the commission of administration and finance of Minnesota in 1931 and 1932; served as railroad and warehouse commissioner of Minnesota from January 1933 until his death; died in St. Paul, Minn., October 25, 1936; interment in Hawley Cemetery, Hawley, Minn.

**Bibliography:** Wefald, Jon M. "Congressman Knud Wefald: A Minnesota Voice for Farm Parity." *Minnesota History* 38 (December 1962): 177-85.

**WEICHEL, Alvin F.,** a Representative from Ohio; born in Sandusky, Ohio, September 11, 1891; attended the public schools of Sandusky, Ohio; during the First World War enlisted on December 14, 1917, and assigned to Company P, Ordnance Training Camp, and later to Headquarters Supply Company at Camp Hancock, Ga., and was discharged a sergeant January 31, 1919; appointed second lieutenant, Ordnance Section, Officers' Reserve Corps, December 10, 1918, and commission terminated December 8, 1928; was graduated from Ferris Institute, Big Rapids, Mich., from the University of Michigan at Ann Arbor, and from the Michigan College of Law in 1924; was admitted to the bar in 1924; served as commissioner of insolvents for the State of Ohio; prosecuting attorney of Erie County, Ohio, 1931-1937; served as special counsel for the attorney general of Ohio; lecturer, School Police Administration, Ohio State University, Columbus, Ohio; elected as a Republican to the Seventy-eighth and to the five succeeding Congresses (January 3, 1943-January 3, 1955); chairman, Committee on Merchant Marine and Fisheries (Eightieth and Eighty-third Congresses); was not a candidate for renomination in 1954; resumed the practice of law; died in Sandusky, Ohio, November 27, 1956; interment in Calvary Cemetery.

**WEICKER, Lowell Palmer, Jr.,** a Representative and a Senator from Connecticut; born in Paris, France, May 16, 1931; graduated, Lawrenceville Academy, 1949; B.A., Yale University, 1953; LL.B., University of Virginia School of Law, 1958; served in the United States Army during the Korean conflict as a first lieutenant, artillery, 1953-1955; captain, United States Army Reserve, 1959-1964; admitted to the Connecticut bar in 1960; member, Connecticut State house of representatives, 1963-1969; First Selectman, town of Greenwich, 1964-1968; elected as a Republican to the Ninety-first Congress (January 3, 1969-January 3, 1971); was not a candidate in 1970 for reelection to the House of Representatives, but was elected to the United States Senate; reelected in 1976 and 1982, and served from January 3, 1971, to January 3, 1989; unsuccessful candidate for reelection in 1988; chairman, Committee on Small Business (Ninety-seventh through Ninety-ninth Congresses); elected Governor of Connecticut as an Independent in 1990, and served from January 9, 1991 to January 4, 1995; declined to be a candidate for reelection in 1994; chairman, DLW Health; visiting professor, George Washington University School of Government; is a resident of Greenwich, Conn.

**Bibliography:** Weicker, Lowell P., Jr., and Barry Sussman. *Maverick: A Life in Politics.* Boston: Little, Brown and Co., 1995.

**WEIDEMAN, Carl May,** a Representative from Michigan; born in Detroit, Wayne County, Mich., March 5, 1898; attended the public schools and the University of Michigan at Ann Arbor from 1914 until the outbreak of the First World War; attended the Naval Officers Training School at Ann Arbor, Mich.; enlisted in the United States Navy as an apprentice seaman; member of the United States Naval Reserve 1918-1922; Detroit (Mich.) College of Law, LL.B., in 1921 but was previously admitted to the bar in 1920; commenced practice in Detroit, Mich.; delegate to the Democratic State conventions 1932-1944 and to the Democratic National Convention in 1940; elected as a Democrat to the Seventy-third Congress (March 4, 1933-January 3, 1935); unsuccessful candidate for renomination in 1934 to the Seventy-fourth Congress; resumed the practice of law in Detroit, Mich.; elected circuit court commissioner of Wayne County, Mich., in 1936, 1942, and 1948, and served from January 1, 1937, to April 30, 1950; circuit judge for the third judicial circuit of the State of Michigan May 1, 1950-September 15, 1968; resided in Grosse Pointe Park, Mich., where he died March 5, 1972; interment in Woodlawn Cemetery, Detroit, Mich.

**WEIGHTMAN, Richard Hanson,** a Delegate from the Territory of New Mexico; born in Washington, D.C., December 28, 1816; attended private schools in Washington, D.C., and Alexandria, Va.;

was graduated from the University of Virginia at Charlottesville in 1834; attended the United States Military Academy at West Point 1835-1837; studied law; was admitted to the bar in 1841 in the District of Columbia, but did not practice; moved to St. Louis, Mo., and on May 28, 1846, was elected captain of Clark's Battalion, Missouri Volunteer Light Artillery, in the Mexican War; he served as Additional Paymaster, Volunteers, in the Army in 1848 and 1849; moved to New Mexico in 1851 and edited a newspaper in Santa Fe; appointed agent for Indians in New Mexico in July 1851; elected as a Democrat and the Territory's first Delegate to the Thirty-second Congress (March 4, 1851-March 3, 1853); was not a candidate for reelection in 1852; resumed newspaper work; moved to Kickapo and Atcheson, Kans., in 1858, and went to Independence, Mo., in 1861; elected colonel, First Regiment Cavalry, Eighth Division, Missouri State Guard, Confederate States Army, June 11, 1861; promoted to command of First Brigade, Eighth Division, June 20, 1861; killed while commanding the First Brigade at Wilson Creek, Mo., August 10, 1861; interment on the battlefield near Springfield, Mo.

**WEIS, Jessica McCullough,** a Representative from New York; born in Chicago, Ill., July 8, 1901; moved to Rochester, N.Y., in 1921; attended the Franklin School, Buffalo, N.Y.; graduate of Miss Wright's School, Bryn Mawr, Pa., and Madam Rieffel's School, New York City; appointed to Inter-American Commission of Women; vice chairman, Monroe County Republican committee, 1937-1952; president, National Federation of Republican Women, in 1940 and 1941; member of the Republican National Committee 1944-1963; delegate at large to the Republican National Conventions in 1940, 1944, 1948, 1952, and 1956; appointed by President Dwight D. Eisenhower in 1953 as a member of the National Civil Defense Advisory Council, reappointed in 1956, and 1960; elected as a Republican to the Eighty-sixth and Eighty-seventh Congresses (January 3, 1959-January 3, 1963); was not a candidate for reelection in 1962 to the Eighty-eighth Congress; died in Rochester, N.Y., May 1, 1963; interment in Mount Hope Cemetery.

**WEISS, Samuel Arthur,** a Representative from Pennsylvania; born in Krotowocz, Poland, April 15, 1902; immigrated to the United States in 1903 with his parents, who settled in Glassport, Pa.; attended the public schools; B.S., Duquesne University, Pittsburgh, Pa., 1925 and from the law department of the same university, LL.B., 1927 and J.D., 1929; admitted to the bar in 1927 and commenced practice in Pittsburgh, Pa.; director of the Roselia Maternity Hospital, Pittsburgh, Pa.; served in the Pennsylvania house of representatives 1935-1939; elected as a Democratic to the Seventy-seventh Congress; reelected to the two succeeding Congresses and served from January 3, 1941, until his resignation on January 7, 1946; elected in November 1945 a judge of Common Pleas Court of Allegheny County, Pa., for the term commencing in January 1946; reelected in 1955 for the term ending January 1966, and again in 1965 for the term ending January 1976; retired in 1967; president, Pennsylvania State Judicial Administration, 1968; died in Pittsburgh, Pa., February 1, 1977; interment in B'nai Israel Cemetery.

**WEISS, Theodore S.,** a Representative from New York; born in Gava, Hungary, September 17, 1927; attended the primary schools of Hungary until 1938 when he emmigrated to the United States and settled in South Amboy, N.J.; continued his education in the public schools of South Amboy; graduated from Hoffman High School, 1946; B.A., Syracuse (N.Y.) University, 1951; LL.B., Syracuse University School of Law, 1952; admitted to the New York bar in 1953 and commenced practice in New York City; served in the United States Army, 1946-1947; naturalized citizen of the United States, 1953; served as New York County assistant district attorney, 1955-1959; engaged in the private practice of law in New York City, 1959-1976; member, Council of the city of New York, 1962-1977; delegate, New York State Democratic convention, 1962; delegate to the Democratic National Convention of 1972; elected as a Democrat to the Ninety-fifth and to the seven succeeding Congresses, and served from January 3, 1977 until his death on September 14, 1992.

**WEISSE, Charles Herman,** a Representative from Wisconsin; born near Sheboygan Falls, Sheboygan County, Wis., October 24, 1866; attended the public schools and St. Paul Lutheran School; in 1880 started to work in a tannery and became a partner in 1888; president of the city council of Sheboygan Falls, Wis., 1893-1896; treasurer of the school board 1897-1900; delegate to the Democratic National Conventions in 1904 and 1908; unsuccessful Democratic candidate for election in 1900 to the Fifty-seventh Congress; elected as a Democrat to the Fifty-eighth and to the three succeeding Congresses (March 4, 1903-March 3, 1911); was not a candidate for renomination in 1910 to the Sixty-second Congress; engaged in the manufacture of leather and in various other business enterprises in his native city; accidentally killed in Sheboygan Falls, Wis., October 8, 1919; interment in Falls Cemetery.

**WELBORN, John** a Representative from Missouri; born near Aullville, Lafayette County, Mo., on November 20, 1857; attended the public schools; studied law at Warrensburg (Mo.) State Normal School; was admitted to the bar in 1880 and practiced in Lexington, Lafayette County, Mo.; city recorder in 1890 and 1891; mayor of Lexington 1896-1920; delegate to the Republican National Convention in 1900; elected as a Republican to the Fifty-ninth Congress (March 4, 1905-March 3, 1907); unsuccessful candidate for reelection in 1906 to the Sixtieth Congress; resumed the practice of law; died in Lexington, Mo., October 27, 1907; interment in Machpelah Cemetery.

**WELCH, Adonijah Strong,** a Senator from Florida; born in East Hampton, Conn., April 12, 1821; attended the public schools; moved to Michigan in 1839 and settled in Jonesville; graduated from the University of Michigan at Ann Arbor in 1846; studied law and was admitted to the bar in 1847; high school principal 1847-1849; principal of the Michigan State Normal School, Ypsilanti, Mich., 1851-1865; trustee of the Michigan Agricultural College at East Lansing; moved to Pensacola, Fla., in 1865 and later to Jacksonville, where he established a lumber mill and also engaged in orange growing; upon the readmission of the State of Florida to representation was elected as a Republican to the United States Senate and served from June 25, 1868, to March 3, 1869; declined renomination to accept the presidency of the Iowa State Agricultural College at Ames, Iowa, and served from 1869 to 1883, when he resigned; commissioner to inspect foreign colleges of agriculture 1882-1883; professor of psychology and history in the Iowa State Agricultural College 1885-1889; was an author and engaged in educational work; died in Pasadena, Los Angeles County, Calif., March 14, 1889; interment in the Iowa State College Cemetery, Ames, Iowa.

**Bibliography:** *DAB.*

**WELCH, Frank,** a Representative from Nebraska; born at Bunker Hill, Charlestown, Mass., February 10, 1835, moved with his parents to Boston in early childhood; was graduated from the Boston High School; adopted the profession of civil engineering; moved to the Territory of Nebraska in 1857 and engaged in mercantile pursuits at Decatur, Burt County; served as postmaster of Decatur; served in the Territorial council in 1864; member of the Territorial house of representatives in 1865 and 1866, serving as presiding officer in 1865; register of the land office at West Point, Nebr., 1871-1876; elected as a Republican to the Forty-fifth Congress and served from March 4, 1877, until his death in Neligh, Nebr., September 4, 1878; interment in Forest Hills Cemetery, Jamaica Plain, Mass.

**WELCH, John,** a Representative from Ohio; born near New Athens, Harrison County, Ohio, October 28, 1805; received a liberal schooling and was graduated from Franklin College; moved to Athens County in 1828 and settled in Rome Township; engaged in the milling business; studied law; was admitted to the bar and commenced practice in Athens, Ohio, in 1833; prosecuting attorney of Athens County 1841-1843; member of the State senate 1845-1847; elected as a Whig to the Thirty-second Congress (March 4, 1851-March 3, 1853); declined to be a candidate for renomination in 1852; delegate to the Whig National Convention in 1852; resumed the practice of law; judge of the court of common pleas 1862-1865; associate justice of the supreme court of Ohio 1865-1878 and was chief justice in 1877 and 1878; died in Athens, Ohio, August 5, 1891; interment in West Union Street Cemetery.

**WELCH, Philip James,** a Representative from Missouri; born in St. Joseph, Buchanan County, Mo., April 4, 1895; educated in the public schools; engaged in the furniture business 1916-1931; treasurer of city of St. Joseph 1932-1936 and mayor 1936-1946; delegate to Democratic National Convention in 1940; assistant director of Reconstruction Finance Corporation, Kansas City, Mo., in 1946 and 1947; elected as a Democrat to the Eighty-first and Eighty-second Congresses (January 3, 1949-January 3, 1953); was not a candidate for renomination in 1952 to the Eighty-third Congress but was unsuccessful for the Democratic gubernatorial nomination; served with the State civil defense and later with the State industrial inspection division; was a resident of St. Joseph, Mo., until his death in Methodist Hospital April 26, 1963; interment in Memorial Park Cemetery.

**WELCH, Richard Joseph,** a Representative from California; born in Monroe County, N.Y., February 13, 1869; educated in the public schools; moved to California in early boyhood and settled in San Francisco; served in the State senate 1901-1913; harbor master for the port of San Francisco 1903-1907; supervisor of the city and county of San Francisco from 1916 until September 30, 1926, when he resigned, having been elected to Congress; elected as a Republican to the Sixty-ninth Congress to fill the vacancy caused by the death of Lawrence J. Flaherty; reelected to the Seventieth and to the eleven succeeding Congresses and served from August 31, 1926, until his death in a hospital in Needles, Calif., September 10, 1949; chairman, Committee on Labor (Seventy-first Congress), Committee on Public Lands (Eightieth Congress); interment in Holy Cross Cemetery, San Francisco, Calif.

**WELCH, William Wickham,** a Representative from Connecticut; born in Norfolk, Litchfield County, Conn., December 10, 1818; studied medicine; was graduated from the medical department of Yale College in 1839 and commenced practice in Norfolk; member of the State house of representatives 1848-1850; served in the State senate in 1851 and 1852; elected as a candidate of the American Party to the Thirty-fourth Congress (March 4, 1855-March 3, 1857); resumed the practice of his profession; again a member of the State house of representatives in 1869 and 1881; died in Norfolk, Conn., July 30, 1892; interment in Center Cemetery.

**Bibliography:** *DAB.*

**WELDON, David Joseph,** a Representative from Florida; born in Amityville, Suffolk County, N.Y., August 31, 1953; graduated, Farmingdale (N.Y.) High School, 1971; B.S., State University of New York, Stony Brook, 1978; M.D., State University of New York, Buffalo, 1981; served in the United States Army as major, medical corps, 1981-1987, and in the United States Army Reserve, 1987-1992; co-founder, Space Coast Family Forum; private practice, internal medicine; elected as a Republican to the One Hundred Fourth Congress (January 3, 1995-January 3, 1997); is a resident of Palm Bay, Fla.

**WELDON, Wayne Curtis,** a Representative from Pennsylvania; born in Marcus Hook, Delaware County, Pa., July 22, 1947; attended public schools and graduated from Media (Pa.) High School in 1965; B.A., West Chester (Pa.) State College, 1969; engaged in graduate work at Cabrini College, Wayne, Pa., Temple University, and St. Joseph's University, Philadelphia; school teacher and administrator, 1969-1976; director, manpower training and development, Cigna Corporation, 1976-1981; mayor of Marcus Hook, 1977-1982; member, Delaware County council, 1981-1986, chairman, 1984-1986; unsuccessful candidate for election in 1984 to the Ninety-ninth Congress; elected as a Republican to the One Hundredth and to the four succeeding Congresses (January 3, 1987-January 3, 1997); is a resident of Aston, Pa.

**WELKER, Herman,** a Senator from Idaho; born in Cambridge, Washington County, Idaho, December 11, 1906; attended public school and the University of Idaho at Moscow; graduated from the law school of the University of Idaho at Moscow in 1929; was admitted to the bar in 1929; prosecuting attorney of Washington County, Idaho; moved to Los Angeles, Calif., in 1936 and practiced law until 1943; during the Second World War served in the United States Air Corps, 1943-1944; returned to Payette, Idaho, and practiced law from 1944 until 1950; also interested in farming and livestock raising in Idaho; member, Idaho State senate, 1948-1950; elected as a Republican to the United States Senate in 1950, and served from January 3, 1951 to January 3, 1957; unsuccessful candidate for reelection in 1956; engaged in the practice of law and farming; died in Bethesda, Md., October 30, 1957; interment in Arlington National Cemetery, Va.

**Bibliography:** *DAB.*

**WELKER, Martin,** a Representative from Ohio; born in Knox County, Ohio, April 25, 1819; attended the common schools; studied law; was admitted to the bar in 1840 and commenced practice at Millersburg, Ohio; clerk of the court of common pleas for Holmes County, 1846-1851; unsuccessful candidate for election in 1852 to the Thirty-third Congress; judge of the sixth judicial district of Ohio, 1852-1857; moved to Wooster, Ohio, in 1857; Lieutenant Governor of Ohio in 1857 and 1858 on the ticket with Salmon P. Chase; declined to be a candidate for renomination in 1858; was appointed aide-de-camp, with rank of colonel, to Governor William Dennison, Jr. of Ohio on August 10, 1861; judge advocate general of the State of Ohio in 1861; appointed superintendent of drafting with the rank of colonel under Governor David Tod on August 15, 1862; assistant adjutant general in 1862; enlisted in the Union Army as a private in Company I, One Hundred and Eighty-eighth Regiment, Ohio Volunteer Infantry, February 16, 1865; mustered out on September 21, 1865; unsuccessful candidate for election in 1862 to the Thirty-eighth Congress; elected as a Republican to the Thirty-ninth and to the two succeeding Congresses (March 4, 1865-March 3, 1871); was not a candidate for renomination in 1870 to the Forty-second Congress; appointed United States judge for the northern district of Ohio by President Ulysses S. Grant in 1873 and served until 1889, when he retired; professor of political science and international law at Wooster University from 1873 to 1890; died in Wooster, Ohio, March 15, 1902; interment in Wooster Cemetery.

**WELLBORN, Marshall Johnson,** a Representative from Georgia; born near Eatonton, Putnam County, Ga., May 29, 1808; attended the University of Georgia at Athens; studied law; was admitted to the bar in 1826 and practiced in Columbus, Ga.; held several local offices; member of the State house of representatives in 1833 and 1834; judge of the superior court of Georgia 1838-1842; elected as a Democrat to the Thirty-first Congress (March 4, 1849-March 3, 1851); studied theology and was ordained as a Baptist minister in 1864 and continued in the ministry until his death in Columbus, Ga., October 16, 1874; interment in Oakland Cemetery, Atlanta, Ga.

**WELLBORN, Olin,** a Representative from Texas; born in Cumming, Forsyth County, Ga., June 18, 1843; attended the common schools, Emory College, Oxford, Ga., and the University of North Carolina at Chapel Hill; enlisted in the Confederate Army in 1861 and served throughout the Civil War, attaining the rank of captain in Company B, Fourth Georgia Cavalry; at the close of the war settled in Atlanta, Ga.; studied law; was admitted to the bar in 1866 and commenced the practice of law in Atlanta; moved to Dallas, Tex., in 1871 and continued the practice of his profession; elected as a Democrat to the Forty-sixth and to the three succeeding Congresses (March 4, 1879-March 3, 1887); chairman, Committee on Indian Affairs (Forty-eighth and Forty-ninth Congresses); unsuccessful candidate for renomination in 1886 to the Fiftieth Congress; moved to San Diego, Calif., in 1887 and continued the practice of his profession for six years; moved to Los Angeles, Calif., in 1893; appointed by President Grover Cleveland as United States judge for the southern district of California in 1895, which office he held until January 20, 1915, when he retired; died in Los Angeles, Calif., December 6, 1921; interment in Rosedale Cemetery.

**WELLER, Gerald C. (Jerry),** a Representative from Illinois; born in Streator, La Salle County, Ill., July 7, 1957; graduated, Dwight (Ill.) High School, 1975; attended Joliet (Ill.) Junior College, 1976; B.S., University of Illinois, 1979; staff assistant to Representative Thomas J. Corcoran of Illinois; assistant to the director, Illinois State department of agriculture; special representative of United States Secretary of Agriculture John R. Block; member, Illinois State house of representatives, 1988-1994; founder and past president, Grundy County Young Republicans; elected as a Republican to the One Hundred Fourth Congress (January 4, 1995-January 4, 1997); is a resident of Morris, Ill.

**WELLER, John B.,** a Representative from Ohio and a Senator from California; born in Hamilton County, Ohio, February 22, 1812; attended the public schools and Miami University, Oxford, Ohio; studied law; was admitted to the bar and practiced in Butler County, Ohio; prosecuting attorney of Butler County, 1833-1836; elected as a Democrat from Ohio to the Twenty-sixth and to the two succeeding Congresses (March 4, 1839-March 3, 1845); was not a candidate for renomination in 1844 to the Twenty-ninth Congress; served in the Mexican War, 1846-1847; unsuccessful Democratic candidate for governor of Ohio in 1848; member of the commission to establish the boundary line between California and Mexico in 1849 and 1850; moved to California and engaged in the practice of law; elected as a Democrat from California to the United States Senate for the term commencing March 4, 1851, and served from January 30, 1852, to March 3, 1857; unsuccessful candidate for reelection; chairman, Committee on Military Affairs (Thirty-fourth Congress); elected Governor of California in 1857, and served from January 8, 1858 to January 9, 1860; appointed Minister to Mexico on November 17, 1860 and was recalled in May 1861; moved to New Orleans, La., in 1867 and continued the practice of law; died in New Orleans, La., August 17, 1875; interment in Girod Street Cemetery; cemetery destroyed in 1959 and unclaimed remains commingled with 15,000 others and deposited beneath Hope Mausoleum, St. John's Cemetery, New Orleans, La.

Bibliography: *DAB.*

**WELLER, Luman Hamlin,** a Representative from Iowa; born in Bridgewater, Litchfield County, Conn., on August 24, 1833; received a common-school and an academic training; attended the State normal school at New Britain, and the Suffield (Conn.) Literary Institute; moved to Chickasaw County, Iowa, in 1859 and engaged in agricultural pursuits; justice of the peace in 1865; unsuccessful independent candidate for the Iowa State house of representatives in 1867; studied law; was admitted to the bar in 1869 and commenced practice in Bradford, Iowa; elected as a Greenbacker to the Forty-eighth Congress (March 4, 1883-March 3, 1885); unsuccessful candidate for reelection in 1884 to the Forty-ninth Congress; resumed the practice of law and also engaged in agricultural pursuits near Nashua, Iowa; for twenty years was proprietor and editor of the Farmers' Advocate, a weekly paper, published at Independence, Iowa; upon the organization of the People's Party in 1890 was appointed as a member of its national committee, and served until his death; served as president of the Chosen Farmers of America; twice unsuccessful candidate for judge of the supreme court of Iowa; was an unsuccessful candidate of the People's Party for Governor of Iowa in 1901; died in a sanitarium at Minneapolis, Minn., March 2, 1914; interment in Greenwood Cemetery, near Nashua, Chickasaw County, Iowa.

**WELLER, Ovington Eugene,** a Senator from Maryland; born in Reisterstown, Baltimore County, Md., on January 23, 1862; attended the public schools; entered the United States Naval Academy, Annapolis, Md., in 1877 and graduated in 1881; after two years of service in the Navy, was honorably discharged in 1883; employed as a clerk in the Post Office Department, Washington, D.C., 1883-1887; graduated from the National Law School, Washington, D.C., in 1887; was admitted to the bar in 1888 and practiced law for three years; engaged in banking and in manufacturing, and was a member of a stock brokerage firm; retired in 1901 and traveled extensively; chairman of the State Roads Commission of Maryland, 1912-1916; unsuccessful candidate in 1915 for election for governor of Maryland; treasurer of the Republican National Senatorial Committee, 1918-1920; elected as a Republican to the United States Senate in 1920, and served from March 4, 1921 to March 3, 1927; unsuccessful candidate for reelection in 1926; chairman, Committee on Manufactures (Sixty-ninth Congress); resumed the practice of law in Baltimore, Md., until his death there on January 5, 1947; interment in Arlington National Cemetery, Va.

**WELLER, Royal Hurlburt,** a Representative from New York; born in New York City, July 2, 1881; attended the public schools and the College of the City of New York; was graduated from the New York Law School in 1901; was admitted to the bar in 1902 and commenced practice in New York City; assistant district attorney of New York County from 1911 to 1917, when he resigned to reenter the practice of law; counsel for the Alien Property Custodian in 1918 and 1919; elected as a Democrat to the Sixty-eighth and to the two succeeding Congresses, and served from March 4, 1923 until his death; had been reelected to the Seventy-first Congress; died in New York City, March 1, 1929; interment in Woodlawn Cemetery.

**WELLING, Milton Holmes,** a Representative from Utah; born in Farmington, Davis County, Utah, January 25, 1876; attended the common schools, the Latter-day Saints' University, and the University of Utah at Salt Lake City; engaged in agricultural and mercantile pursuits and also in banking; was elected a member of the board of trustees of Brigham Young College, Logan, Utah, in 1906; served in the State house of representatives 1911-1915; elected as a Democrat to the Sixty-fifth and Sixty-sixth Congresses (March 4, 1917-March 3, 1921); did not seek renomination, but was an unsuccessful Democratic candidate for the United States Senate in 1920; director of registration for the State of Utah 1925-1928; elected secretary of state of Utah in 1928; reelected in 1932 and served until January 1, 1937; trustee of Utah State Agricultural College 1926-1936; regent of University of Utah 1928-1936; appointed by Secretary of Interior Harold L. Ickes to make a survey of public grazing lands in 1937 and 1938; resumed agricultural and mining operations; in January 1943 accepted war service appointment as auditor with Army Air Forces and also served with the War Assets Administration at Salt Lake City, Utah, until his death May 28, 1947; interment in Fielding Cemetery, Fielding, Utah.

**WELLINGTON, George Louis,** a Representative and a Senator from Maryland; born in Cumberland, Allegany County, Md., January 28, 1852; attended a German school and received private instruction; clerk in the Second National Bank of Cumberland in 1870 and later was teller; treasurer of Allegany County 1882-1888, 1890; unsuccessful candidate for election as comptroller of Maryland in 1889; assistant treasurer of the United States at Baltimore 1890-1893; unsuccessful candidate for election to the Fifty-third Congress; elected as a Republican to the Fifty-fourth Congress (March 4, 1895-March 3, 1897); elected to the United States Senate and served from March 4, 1897, to March 3, 1903; was not a candidate for reelection; chairman, Committee to Establish the University of the United States (Fifty-fifth and Fifty-sixth Congresses); unsuccessful candidate on the Progressive ticket for election to the United States Senate in 1913; engaged in civic activities; president of two banks and interested in the electric railways and lighting companies of Cumberland, Md.; died in that city March 20, 1927; interment in Rose Hill Cemetery.

**WELLS, Alfred,** a Representative from New York; born in Dagsboro, Sussex County, Del., May 27, 1814; pursued classical studies; studied law; was admitted to the bar in 1837 and commenced practice in Ithaca, Tompkins County, N.Y.; one of the owners of the Ithaca Journal and Advertiser 1839-1853; district attorney of Tompkins County, N.Y., 1845-1847; judge of Tompkins County Court from 1847 to 1851; attended the Anti-Nebraska Conventions at Saratoga and Auburn in 1854; elected as a Republican to the Thirty-sixth Congress (March 4, 1859-March 3, 1861); unsuccessful candidate for renomination in 1860; appointed United States assessor of internal revenue at Ithaca in 1862 and served until his death in Ithaca, N.Y., July 18, 1867; interment in the City Cemetery.

**WELLS, Daniel, Jr.,** a Representative from Wisconsin; born in West Waterville, Maine, July 16, 1808; attended the public schools; taught school; engaged in the mercantile business at Palmyra, Maine; moved to Milwaukee, Wis., in 1838 and engaged in banking and lumbering pursuits; appointed probate judge of Milwaukee in 1838; member of the Territorial council 1838-1840; elected as a Democrat to the Thirty-third and Thirty-fourth Congresses (March 4, 1853-March 3, 1857); chairman, Committee on Expenditures in the Department of State (Thirty-third Congress); was not a candidate for renomination in 1856; engaged in the development of railroads; a director of the Chicago, Milwaukee & St. Paul Railroad in 1865 and 1866; president of the La Crosse & Milwaukee Railroad, the Southern Minnesota Railroad, and the St. Paul & Minnesota Valley Railroad; died in Milwaukee, Wis., March 18, 1902; interment in Forest Home Cemetery.

**WELLS, Erastus,** a Representative from Missouri; born in Sackets Harbor, Jefferson County, N.Y., December 2, 1823; attended the public schools; moved to St. Louis, Mo., in 1842; established the first omnibus line in that city and subsequently inaugurated the first street railroad company; member of the board of aldermen of St. Louis 1853-1867; president of the Missouri Railroad Co. 1859-1883; elected as a Democrat to the Forty-first and to the three succeeding Congresses (March 4, 1869-March 3, 1877); unsuccessful candidate for reelection in 1876 to the Forty-fifth Congress; elected to the Forty-sixth Congress (March 4, 1879-March 3, 1881); was not a candidate for renomination in 1880; president of the Laclede Gas Light Co. 1880-1883; died in St. Louis, Mo., October 2, 1893; interment in Bellefontaine Cemetery.

Bibliography: *DAB*.

**WELLS, Guilford Wiley,** a Representative from Mississippi; born in Conesus Center, Livingston County, N.Y., February 14, 1840; attended the Genesee Wesleyan Seminary and College, Lima, N.Y.; enlisted in the Union Army as a private in the Twenty-seventh New York Infantry May 21, 1861; promoted to second lieutenant in the One Hundred and Thirtieth New York Infantry in 1862 and subsequently to first lieutenant and captain in the Nineteenth New York Cavalry; mustered out February 10, 1865, as a lieutenant colonel; was graduated from the law department of Columbian College (later George Washington University); Washington, D.C., in 1867; was admitted to the bar in 1867 and commenced practice in Holly Springs, Miss.; United States attorney for the northern district of Mississippi 1870-1875; elected as an Independent Republican to the Forty-fourth Congress (March 4, 1875-March 3, 1877); declined to be a candidate for renomination in 1876; consul general at Shanghai, China, from June 23, 1877, to May 26, 1879; settled in Los Angeles, Calif., in 1879 and resumed the practice of law; died in Santa Monica, Calif., March 21, 1909; interment in Evergreen Cemetery, Los Angeles, Calif.

**WELLS, John,** a Representative from New York; born in Johnstown, Fulton County, N.Y., July 1, 1817; attended Johnstown Academy, and was graduated from Union College, Schenectady, N.Y., in 1835; studied law; was admitted to the bar in 1839 and commenced practice in Palmyra, N.Y.; returned to Johnstown, N.Y., and continued the practice of law; elected judge of Fulton County and served from June 1847 until his resignation in December 1851, having been elected to Congress; elected as a Whig to the Thirty-second Congress (March 4, 1851-March 3, 1853); declined to be a candidate for reelection in 1852 to the Thirty-third Congress; resumed the practice of law and also engaged in literary pursuits; died in Johnstown, N.Y., May 30, 1877; interment in Johnstown Cemetery.

**WELLS, John Sullivan,** a Senator from New Hampshire; born in Durham, Strafford County, N.H., October 18, 1803; attended Pembroke (N.H.) Academy; studied law; was admitted to the bar in 1828 and practiced in Guildhall, Vt., 1828-1835; moved to Lancaster, N.H., in 1836 and continued the practice of law until 1846; solicitor of Coos County 1838-1847; moved to Exeter, Rockingham County, N.H., and resumed the practice of law; member, State house of representatives 1839-1841, serving as speaker in 1841; attorney general of New Hampshire 1847; member and president of the State senate 1851-1852; appointed to the United States Senate to fill the vacancy caused by the death of Moses Norris and served from January 16 to March 3, 1855; died in Exeter, N.H., August 1, 1860.

**WELLS, Owen Augustine,** a Representative from Wisconsin; born in Catskill, Greene County, N.Y., February 4, 1844; moved with his parents to a farm near Empire, Fond du Lac County, Wis., in 1850; attended public and private schools; studied law; was admitted to the bar in 1870 and commenced practice in Fond du Lac; also engaged in agricultural pursuits and stock raising; appointed by President Grover Cleveland as collector of internal revenue for the third Wisconsin district in 1885, serving until 1887, when that district was consolidated with the Milwaukee district; delegate to the Democratic National Convention of 1888, and to the Gold Democratic National Convention in 1896, also to numerous State conventions of his party; elected as a Democrat to the Fifty-third Congress (March 4, 1893-March 3, 1895); unsuccessful candidate for reelection in 1894 to the Fifty-fourth Congress; declined to accept any public office and resumed the practice of law in Fond du Lac; retired in 1901 and resided in Fond du Lac, Wis., until his death there on January 29, 1935; interment in Rienzi Cemetery.

**WELLS, William Hill,** a Senator from Delaware; born in Burlington, N.J., January 7, 1769; received a liberal schooling; engaged in mercantile pursuits at Dagsboro and Millsboro, Del.; studied law; was admitted to the bar and practiced at Georgetown, Del.; moved to Dover, Del.; member, Delaware general assembly 1794-1798; elected as a Federalist to the United States Senate to fill the vacancy caused by the death of Joshua Clayton and served from January 17, 1799, to November 6, 1804, when he resigned; again elected as a Federalist to the United States Senate to fill the vacancy caused by the resignation of James A. Bayard and served from May 28, 1813, to March 3, 1817; was not a candidate for reelection in 1816; resumed the practice of law and was interested in the oil business in Pennsylvania, where the town of Wellsboro was named in his honor; died near Dagsboro, Sussex County, Del., on March 11, 1829; interment in Prince George's Churchyard, near Dagsboro.

**WELLSTONE, Paul David,** a Senator from Minnesota; born in Washington, D.C., July 21, 1944; attended Charles A. Stuart Grammar School and Wakefield and Yorktown High Schools, Arlington, Va.; B.A., University of North Carolina, 1965, and Ph.D., political science, 1969; teacher, Carleton College, Northfield, Minn.; director, Minnesota Community Energy Program; elected as a Democrat to the United States Senate in 1990 for the term commencing January 3, 1991; is a resident of Minneapolis, Minn.

**WELSH, George Austin,** a Representative from Pennsylvania; born near Bay View, Cecil County, Md., August 9, 1878; attended the country schools and the public schools of Philadelphia, Pa.; took business and academic courses at Temple University, Philadelphia, Pa.; engaged as a legislative stenographer and reporter from 1895 to 1901; graduated from the law department of Temple University in 1905; was admitted to the bar the same year and commenced practice in Philadelphia; secretary to the mayor of Philadelphia in 1905 and 1906; assistant solicitor for Philadelphia in 1906 and 1907; assistant district attorney for Philadelphia County 1907-1922; secretary of Temple University 1914-1938, and served as first vice president from 1938 until his death; president of the Republican district executive committee 1914-1932; attended officers' training camp at Fort Niagara, N.Y., 1917; member of the Board of Education of Philadelphia County 1921-1932; elected as a Republican to the Sixty-eighth and to the four succeeding Congresses and served from March 4, 1923, until his resignation May 31, 1932, having been appointed judge of the United States district court for the eastern district of Pennsylvania, in which capacity he served until 1957, when he retired as judge to become senior judge; chairman, Committee on Industrial Arts and Expositions (Sixty-ninth Congress); resided in Lima, Pa., where he died October 22, 1970; cremated; ashes scattered privately by his family.

**WELTNER, Charles Longstreet,** a Representative from Georgia; born in Atlanta, Fulton County Ga., December 17, 1927; attended the public schools of Fulton County, Ga.; graduated from Oglethorpe University at Atlanta, Ga., in 1948 and from Columbia University School of Law at New York City, in 1950; M.A., Columbia Theological Seminary, Decatur, Ga., 1983; LL.M., University of Virginia Law School, 1983; commenced practice in Atlanta, Ga., in 1950; served as a first lieutenant in the United States Army, 1955-1957; elected as a Democrat to the Eighty-eighth and Eighty-ninth Congresses (January 3, 1963-January 3, 1967); was not a candidate for reelection in 1966 to the Ninetieth Congress; unsuccessful candidate for election in 1968 to the Ninety-first Congress; deputy chairman, Democratic National Committee, and director of young Americans division, 1967; resumed the practice of law; unsuccessful candidate in 1973 for nomination for mayor of Atlanta; judge, Superior Court, Atlanta Judicial Circuit, 1976-1981; chairman, Judicial Council of Georgia, 1980-1981; justice, Supreme Court of Georgia, 1981-1992, chief justice from June 1992 until his death; was a resident of Atlanta, Ga., until his death there on August 31, 1992; interment in Arlington Memorial Park.

Bibliography: Dimon, Joseph H., IV. "Charles L. Weltner and Civil Rights." *Atlanta Historical Journal* 24 (Fall 1980): 7-20; Weltner, Charles L. *Southerner*. Philadelphia: J.B. Lippincott, 1966.

**WELTY, Benjamin Franklin,** a Representative from Ohio; born near Bluffton, Allen County, Ohio, August 9, 1870; attended the common schools and the Tri-State Normal College of Indiana; was graduated from the Ohio Northern University at Ada in 1894 and

from the University of Michigan at Ann Arbor in 1896; studied law; was admitted to the bar in 1896 and commenced practice in Lima, Allen County, Ohio; city solicitor of Bluffton 1897-1909; served as a private during the Spanish-American War; prosecuting attorney of Allen County 1905-1910; lieutenant colonel in the Ohio National Guard 1908-1913; special counsel to the State attorney general 1911-1913; special assistant in the United States Department of Justice 1913-1915; elected as a Democrat to the Sixty-fifth and Sixty-sixth Congresses (March 4, 1917-March 3, 1921); unsuccessful candidate for reelection in 1920 to the Sixty-seventh Congress; employed with Inland Waterways Association 1921-1924; resumed the practice of law until 1951, when he retired; died in Dayton, Ohio, October 23, 1962; interment in Woodlawn Cemetery, Shawnee Township, Allen County, Ohio.

**WEMPLE, Edward,** a Representative from New York; born in Fultonville, Montgomery County, N.Y., October 23, 1843; attended the common schools in Fultonville and Ashland Academy in Green County, and was graduated from Union College, Schenectady, N.Y., in 1866; studied law for a time and then engaged in the foundry business; served as president of the village of Fultonville in 1873; supervisor of the town of Glen 1874-1876; member of the State assembly in 1877 and 1878; elected as a Democrat to the Forty-eighth Congress (March 4, 1883-March 3, 1885); unsuccessful candidate for reelection in 1884; continued his former business pursuits; served in the State senate in 1885; elected comptroller of the State of New York in 1887, and served two terms; unsuccessful candidate for reelection; died in Fultonville, N.Y., December 18, 1920; interment in Maple Avenue Cemetery.

**WENDOVER, Peter Hercules,** a Representative from New York; born in New York City August 1, 1768; received a liberal schooling; held several local offices; member of the volunteer fire department of New York City in 1796; delegate to the State constitutional conventions in 1801 and 1821; member of the State assembly in 1804; elected as a Republican to the Fourteenth, Fifteenth, and Sixteenth Congresses (March 4, 1815-March 3, 1821); sheriff of New York County 1822-1825; died in New York City September 24, 1834; interment in the Dutch Reformed Church Cemetery.

**WENE, Elmer H.,** a Representative from New Jersey; born on a farm near Pittstown, Hunterdon County, N.J., May 1, 1892; attended the public schools and Rutgers University, New Brunswick, N.J.; in 1918 engaged in agricultural pursuits near Vineland, N.J.; served on the New Jersey State board of agriculture, 1925-1934; elected as a Democrat to the Seventy-fifth Congress (January 3, 1937-January 3, 1939); unsuccessful candidate for reelection in 1938 to the Seventy-sixth Congress; member of the Board of Chosen Freeholders of Cumberland County, N.J., 1939-1941; elected to the Seventy-seventh and Seventy-eighth Congresses (January 3, 1941-January 3, 1945); was not a candidate in 1944 for renomination to the House of Representatives, but was an unsuccessful candidate for election to the United States Senate; resumed agricultural pursuits and poultry raising; also president and owner of two radio stations in New Jersey; in 1945 was an adviser to the Secretary of Agriculture; elected to the New Jersey State senate in 1946; delegate to the State constitutional convention in 1947; on June 26, 1948, was given a recess appointment by President Harry S Truman as Under Secretary of Agriculture; unsuccessful candidate for election for Governor of New Jersey in 1949; unsuccessful candidate for election in 1950 to the Eighty-second Congress; unsuccessful candidate for nomination for Governor in 1953; died in Philadelphia, Pa., January 25, 1957; interment in Locust Grove Cemetery, Quakertown, Pa.

**WENTWORTH, John** (grandson of John Wentworth, Jr.), a Representative from Illinois; born in Sandwich, Carroll County, N.H., March 5, 1815; educated in the common schools and academies at Gilmanton, Wolfeboro, and New Hampton, N.H., and South Berwick, Maine; taught school for several years, and contributed political articles to newspapers; was graduated from Dartmouth College, Hanover, N.H., in 1836; moved to Chicago, Ill., in 1836, where he engaged as a clerk in a law office, and also studied law; editor and manager of the Chicago Democrat; appointed aide-de-camp to Governor Carlin in 1838; attended the law department of Harvard University in 1841; was admitted to the bar in 1841 and commenced practice in Chicago, Ill.; elected as a Democrat to the Twenty-eighth and to the three succeeding Congresses (March 4, 1843-March 3, 1851); elected to the Thirty-third Congress (March 4, 1853-March 3, 1855); Republican mayor of Chicago 1857-1863; delegate to the State constitutional convention in 1861; elected as a Republican to the Thirty-ninth Congress (March 4, 1865-March 3, 1867); resumed the practice of law; died in Chicago, Ill., October 16, 1888; interment in Rosehill Cemetery.

**Bibliography:** *DAB*; Fehrenbacher, Don Edward. *Chicago Giant: A Biography of Long John Wentworth*. Madison, Wis.: American History Research Center, 1957; Wentworth, John. *Congressional Reminiscences*. Chicago: Fergus Printing Co., 1882.

**WENTWORTH, John, Jr.** (grandfather of John Wentworth), a Delegate from New Hampshire; born at Salmon Falls, Strafford County, N.H., July 17, 1745; prepared for college by private tutors; was graduated from Harvard College in 1768; studied law; was admitted to the bar and commenced practice in Dover, N.H., in 1771; register of probate of Strafford County 1773-1787; appointed on January 10, 1774, a member of the committee of correspondence; member of the State house of representatives 1776-1780; appointed in June 1777 a member of the State committee of safety; served as moderator 1777-1786; Member of the Continental Congress in 1778; one of the signers of the Articles of Confederation; member of the State council 1780-1784; served in the State senate 1784-1786; died in Dover, N.H., on January 10, 1787; interment in Pine Hill Cemetery.

**WENTWORTH, Tappan,** a Representative from Massachusetts; born in Dover, N.H., February 24, 1802; received a liberal schooling; studied law; admitted to the bar in 1826 and commenced practice in York County, Maine; moved to Lowell, Mass., in 1833 and continued the practice of law; member of the common council 1836-1841; served in the Massachusetts house of representatives in 1851, 1859, 1860, 1863, and 1864; member of the Massachusetts senate in 1848, 1849, 1865, and 1866; elected as a Whig to the Thirty-third Congress (March 4, 1853-March 3, 1855); unsuccessful candidate for reelection in 1854 to the Thirty-fourth Congress; engaged in the practice of his profession until his death in Lowell, Mass., June 12, 1875; interment in Lowell Cemetery.

**WERDEL, Thomas Harold,** a Representative from California; born in Emery, Hanson County, S.Dak., September 13, 1905; moved with his parents to Kern County, Calif., in 1915; attended the public schools and Kern County Union High School; was graduated from the University of California at Berkeley in 1930, and from the University of California Law School in 1936; was admitted to the bar in 1936 and commenced the practice of law in Bakersfield, Calif.; member of the California State assembly from the thirty-ninth district in the legislative sessions of 1943 and 1945; elected as a Republican to the Eighty-first and Eighty-second Congresses (January 3, 1949-January 3, 1953); was an unsuccessful candidate for reelection in 1952 to the Eighty-third Congress; resumed the practice of law; candidate for Vice President of the United States in 1956 on the States' Rights ticket headed by T. Coleman Andrews; died in Bakersfield, Calif., September 30, 1966; interment in Greenlawn Memorial Park.

**WERNER, Theodore B.,** a Representative from South Dakota; born in Ossian, Winneshiek County, Iowa, June 2, 1892; attended the public and parochial schools; moved to Rapid City, S.Dak., in 1909; engaged in the newspaper publishing and commercial printing business; editor and publisher of the Gate City Guide; served as postmaster of Rapid City, 1915-1923; commissioner of Rapid City, 1927-1930; served as mayor in 1929 and 1930; unsuccessful candidate for election in 1930 to the Seventy-second Congress; elected as a Democrat to the Seventy-third and Seventy-fourth Congresses (March 4, 1933-January 3, 1937); unsuccessful candidate for reelection in 1936 to the Seventy-fifth Congress; resumed the newspaper publishing business until 1965; was a resident of Rapid City, S.Dak.; died January 24, 1989.

**WERTZ, George M.,** a Representative from Pennsylvania; born near Johnstown, Cambria County, Pa., July 19, 1856; attended the public schools, Ebensburg (Pa.) Academy, and the National Normal School, Lebanon, Ohio; taught school 1876-1884; school director 1886-1894; county commissioner 1893-1896; sheriff of Cambria County 1897-1901; member of the Pennsylvania senate 1908-1912, serving as president pro tempore in 1911 and 1912; organized and directed the Johnstown (Pa.) Daily Leader 1911-1917; comptroller of Cambria County 1914-1916; elected as a Republican to the Sixty-eighth Congress (March 4, 1923-March 3, 1925); unsuccessful candidate for renomination in 1924; engaged in the real estate business until his death in Johnstown, Pa., November 19, 1928; interment in Grand View Cemetery.

**WEST, Charles Franklin,** a Representative from Ohio; born in Mount Vernon, Knox County, Ohio, January 12, 1895; attended the public schools; was graduated from Ohio Wesleyan University, Delaware, Ohio, in 1918; attended Harvard University in 1920 and 1922-1924; served as American vice consul at Naples, Italy, in 1918 and 1919; instructor of government at the College of Wooster, Wooster, Ohio, 1920-1922 and at Harvard University, 1922-1924; professor of political science at Denison University, Granville, Ohio, 1924-1930; elected as a Democrat to the Seventy-second and Seventy-third Congresses (March 4, 1931-January 3, 1935); was not a candidate in 1934 for renomination to the House of Representatives, but was an unsuccessful candidate for nomination to the United States Senate; served as special assistant to the governor of the Farm Credit Administration from February 25, 1935, to August 4, 1935; appointed Under Secretary of the Interior on August 5, 1935, and served until May 10, 1938; delegate to the Democratic National Convention of 1936; member of United States Processing Tax Board of Review until October 1940; engaged in private business from 1940 until 1947; became professor of political science at Akron (Ohio) University in 1947; received the Democratic nomination in 1954 to the Eighty-fourth Congress, but withdrew before the November election; died in Bradenton, Fla., December 27, 1955; interment in Mound View Cemetery, Mount Vernon, Ohio.

**WEST, George,** a Representative from New York; born in Bradninch, Devonshire County, England, February 17, 1823; attended the common schools; immigrated to the United States in February 1849 and settled at Ballston Spa, Saratoga County, N.Y.; engaged in paper manufacturing; member of the State assembly 1872-1876; delegate to the Republican National Convention in 1880; president of the First National Bank of Ballston Spa; elected as a Republican to the Forty-seventh Congress (March 4, 1881-March 3, 1883); unsuccessful candidate for reelection in 1882 to the Forty-eighth Congress; elected to the Forty-ninth and Fiftieth Congresses (March 4, 1885-March 3, 1889); was not a candidate for renomination in 1888; resumed his former business activities; died in Ballston Spa, N.Y., September 20, 1901; interment in Ballston Spa Cemetery.

**Bibliography:** *DAB*.

**WEST, Joseph Rodman,** a Senator from Louisiana; born in New Orleans, La., September 19, 1822; moved with his parents to Philadelphia in 1824; educated in private schools; attended the University of Pennsylvania, 1836-1837; moved to New Orleans in 1841; captain attached to Maryland and District of Columbia Volunteers in the Mexican War, 1847-1848; moved to California in 1849 and engaged in newspaper work in San Francisco; proprietor of the San Francisco Price Current; during the Civil War entered the Union Army as lieutenant of the First Regiment, California Volunteer Infantry, in 1861; promoted to the rank of colonel and brigadier general, and was brevetted major general in 1866; returned to New Orleans, La.; deputy United States marshal; auditor for customs, 1867-1871; elected as a Republican to the United States Senate and served from March 4, 1871, to March 3, 1877; was not a candidate for reelection; chairman, Committee on Railroads (Forty-fourth Congress); member of the Board of Commissioners of the District of Columbia, 1882-1885; retired from public life in 1885; died in Washington, D.C., October 31, 1898; interment in Arlington National Cemetery, Va.

**WEST, Milton Horace,** a Representative from Texas; born on a farm near Gonzales, Gonzales County, Tex., June 30, 1888; attended the public schools and the West Texas Military Academy at San Antonio; served with Company C, Texas Rangers, 1911-1912; studied law; was admitted to the bar in 1915 and began practice in Floresville, Tex.; moved to Brownsville, Tex., in 1917 and continued the practice of law; district attorney for the twenty-eighth judicial district of Texas, 1922-1925, and assistant district attorney, 1927-1930; member of the Texas State house of representatives, 1930-1933; elected as a Democrat to the Seventy-third Congress to fill the vacancy caused by the resignation of John Nance Garner; reelected to the Seventy-fourth and to the six succeeding Congresses, and served from April 22, 1933 until his death in Washington, D.C., October 28, 1948; chairman, Committee on Elections No. 1 (Seventy-fifth Congress); was not a candidate for renomination in 1948 to the Eighty-first Congress; interment in Buena Vista Cemetery, Brownsville, Tex.

**WEST, William Stanley,** a Senator from Georgia; was born near Buena Vista, Marion County, Ga., on August 23, 1849; moved with his parents to Lowndes (now Brooks) County, Ga.; attended the country schools and preparatory schools at Lookout Mountain, Tenn., and Penfield, Ga.; taught school about four years; graduated from the law department of Mercer University, Macon, Ga., in 1876 and from the literary department in 1880; was admitted to the bar in 1876 and commenced practice in Statenville, Ga.; moved to Valdosta, Lowndes County, Ga.; engaged as a planter and millman; also interested in other enterprises; member, Georgia State house of representatives, 1892-1901; member, State senate, 1901-1906, serving as president, 1905-1906; chairman of the board of trustees of South Georgia State Normal College at Valdosta and ex officio member of the board of trustees of the University of Georgia at Athens; appointed to the United States Senate to fill the vacancy caused by the death of Augustus O. Bacon, and served from March 2 to November 3, 1914, when a successor was elected and qualified; chairman, Committee on Expenditures in the Post Office Department (Sixty-third Congress); resumed his occupation as a planter and lumberman; died in Valdosta, Ga., on December 22, 1914; interment in Sunset Hill Cemetery.

**WESTBROOK, John,** a Representative from Pennsylvania; born in Sussex County, N.J., January 9, 1789; moved with his parents to Pike County, Pa., in 1792 and settled near Dingmans Ferry; attended private schools; engaged in lumbering and agricultural pursuits; colonel in the Pennsylvania militia in 1812; sheriff of Pike County in 1817; member of the Pennsylvania house of representatives in 1833; elected as a Democrat to the Twenty-seventh Congress (March 4, 1841-March 3, 1843); declined to be a candidate for reelection in 1842 to the Twenty-eighth Congress; resumed agricultural pursuits; died near Dingmans Ferry, Pike County, Pa., October 8, 1852; interment in Laurel Hill Cemetery, Milford, Pa.

**WESTBROOK, Theodoric Romeyn,** a Representative from New York; born in Fishkill, Dutchess County, N.Y., November 20, 1821; attended the common schools and was graduated from Rutgers College, New Brunswick, N.J., in 1838; studied law; was admitted to the bar in 1843 and commenced practice in Kingston, Ulster County, N.Y.; elected as a Democrat to the Thirty-third Congress (March 4, 1853-March 3, 1855); declined to be a candidate for renomination in 1854; resumed the practice of his profession at Kingston, N.Y.; elected a justice of the supreme court in 1873; died while holding court in Troy, Rensselaer County, N.Y., on October 6, 1885; interment in Wiltwyck Cemetery, Kingston, N.Y.

**WESTCOTT, James Diament, Jr.,** a Senator from Florida; born in Alexandria, Va., May 10, 1802; moved to New Jersey, where he received a liberal schooling; studied law; was admitted to the bar in 1824 and commenced practice; clerk in the Consular Bureau, Washington, D.C.; secretary of Florida Territory 1830-1834; United States attorney for the middle district of Florida 1834-1836; member, Territorial house of representatives 1832; delegate to the State constitutional conventions in 1838 and 1839; upon the admission of Florida as a State into the Union was elected as a Democrat to the United States Senate and served from July 1, 1845, to March 3, 1849; was not a candidate for reelection in 1848; chairman, Committee on Territories (Twenty-ninth Congress), Committee on Patents and the Patent Office (Thirtieth Congress); settled in New York City in 1850 and practiced law; moved to Canada in 1862; died in Montreal, Canada, January 19, 1880; interment in City Cemetery, Tallahassee, Fla.

**WESTERLO, Rensselaer,** a Representative from New York; born in Albany, N.Y., April 29, 1776; was graduated from Columbia College, New York City, in 1795; studied law; was admitted to the bar and practiced; elected as a Federalist to the Fifteenth Congress (March 4, 1817-March 3, 1819); was not a candidate for reelection; resumed the practice of law; died in Albany, N.Y., April 18, 1851; interment in the Albany Rural Cemetery.

**WESTLAND, Alfred John (Jack),** a Representative from Washington; born in Everett, Snohomish County, Wash., December 14, 1904; attended the local schools and was graduated from the University of Washington Law School, at Seattle in 1926; engaged in the cotton goods business in New York City and Chicago, Ill., 1926-1930; in the investment brokerage business in Chicago, Ill., 1930-1936, and in Seattle, Wash., 1936-1941; enlisted in the United States Navy in the summer of 1940 and was commissioned a lieutenant (junior grade) in November 1940; was called to active duty on May 1, 1941; served in the Pacific until separated from the service as a commander in February 1946; returned to Everett, Wash., and operated an insurance agency until 1954; National Amateur Golf Champion in 1953, and the winner of such titles as French Amateur, Western Amateur, Pacific Northwest Champion, and was twice selected for the Walker Cup team; elected as a Republican to the Eighty-third and to the five succeeding Congresses (January 3, 1953-January 3, 1965); was an unsuccessful candidate for reelection in 1964 to the Eighty-ninth Congress; automobile dealer in Monterey, Calif.; was a resident of Pebble Beach, Calif, until his death there on November 3, 1982; interment in Arlington National Cemetery, Va.

**WETHERED, John,** a Representative from Maryland; born near Wetheredville, Baltimore County, Md., on May 8, 1809; completed preparatory studies; held several local offices; engaged in the manufacture of woolen goods at Wetheredville, Md.; elected as a Whig to the Twenty-eighth Congress (March 4, 1843-March 3, 1845);

resumed the manufacture of woolen goods; delegate from Baltimore County to the State convention which framed the constitution of Maryland in 1867; retired from active pursuits in 1868 and lived on his estate, "Ashland," near Catonsville, Md., where he died February 15, 1888; interment in Greenmount Cemetery, Baltimore, Md.

**WETMORE, George Peabody,** a Senator from Rhode Island; born during a visit of his parents abroad, in London, England, August 2, 1846; received his early education at a private school; graduated from Yale College in 1867 and from the law department of Columbia College, New York City, in 1869; was admitted to the bar of Rhode Island and of New York in 1869, but never practiced; trustee of several institutions; presidential elector on the Republican ticket in 1880 and 1884; elected Governor of Rhode Island in 1885, reelected in 1886 and served from May 26, 1885 to May 31, 1887; unsuccessful candidate for reelection in 1887; unsuccessful candidate for election to the United States Senate in 1889; elected as a Republican to the United States Senate in 1894; reelected in 1900 and served from March 4, 1895, to March 3, 1907; elected January 22, 1908, to fill the vacancy caused by the failure of the legislature to elect in the term commencing March 4, 1907, and served until March 3, 1913; declined to be a candidate for reelection in 1912; chairman, Committee on Manufactures (Fifty-fourth Congress), Committee on the Library (Fifty-fifth through Sixty-second Congresses); died in Boston, Mass., on September 11, 1921; interment in Island Cemetery, Newport, R.I.

**WEVER, John Madison,** a Representative from New York; born in Ganges, Allegan County, Mich., February 24, 1847; attended the common schools and Albion (Mich.) College; during the Civil War entered the Union Army at the age of sixteen and served in the Army of the Cumberland and the Army of the Ohio; at the close of the war settled in Plattsburgh, Clinton County, N.Y., and engaged in banking; elected county treasurer of Clinton County in 1884 and reelected in 1887; elected as a Republican to the Fifty-second and Fifty-third Congresses (March 4, 1891-March 3, 1895); was not a candidate for renomination in 1894 to the Fifty-fourth Congress; cashier and later president of the Merchants' National Bank of Plattsburgh, N.Y.; died in Plattsburgh, N.Y., September 27, 1914; interment in Riverside Cemetery.

**WEYMOUTH, George Warren,** a Representative from Massachusetts; born in West Amesbury (now Merrimac), Mass., August 25, 1850; attended the public schools and the Merrimac High School; moved to Fitchburg, Mass., in 1882 and engaged in the carriage business; later became manager of the Simonds Rolling Machine Co.; trustee of the Fitchburg Savings Bank 1891-1901 and director of the Fitchburg National Bank 1892-1901; director in other corporations; member of the common council of Fitchburg in 1886; served in the Massachusetts house of representatives in 1896; delegate to the Republican National Convention in 1896; elected as a Republican to the Fifty-fifth and Fifty-sixth Congresses (March 4, 1897-March 3, 1901); was not a candidate for renomination in 1900; moved to Fairhaven; president of the Atlas Tack Corp. of Fairhaven, Mass., 1897-1910; killed in an automobile accident near Bingham, Maine, September 7, 1910; interment in Riverside Cemetery, Fairhaven, Bristol County, Mass.

**WHALEN, Charles William, Jr.,** a Representative from Ohio; born in Dayton, Montgomery County, Ohio, July 31, 1920; graduated from Oakwood High School; B.S., University of Dayton, 1942; M.B.A., Harvard University Graduate School of Business, 1946; enlisted in the United States Army during the Second World War; discharged as a first lieutenant in 1946; vice president of the Dayton Dress Company, 1946-1952; professor of economics and chairman of the department, University of Dayton, 1962-1966; Ohio State representative, 1955-1960; Ohio State senator, 1961-1966; elected as a Republican to the Ninetieth and to the five succeeding Congresses (January 3, 1967-January 3, 1979); was not a candidate for reelection in 1978 to the Ninety-sixth Congress; is a resident of Bethesda, Md.

**Bibliography:** Lynch, Patricia Louise. "An Analysis of the Rhetorical Dialogue of Charles W. Whalen, Jr., in Ohio's Third Congressional District." Ph.D. dissertation, Ohio State University, 1976.

**WHALEY, Kellian Van Rensalear,** a Representative from Virginia and from West Virginia; born in Onondaga County, near Utica, N.Y., May 6, 1821; moved to Ohio and attended the public schools; moved to Virginia in 1842, settled in Ceredo, and engaged in the lumbering business; elected as a Unionist from Virginia to the Thirty-seventh Congress (March 4, 1861-March 3, 1863); during the Civil War recruited several regiments for the Union Army; upon the admission of West Virginia as a State into the Union was elected as an Unconditional Unionist to the Thirty-eighth and Thirty-ninth Congresses, and served from December 7, 1863 to March 3, 1867; chairman, Committee on Invalid Pensions (Thirty-eighth Congress), Committee on Revolutionary Claims (Thirty-ninth Congress); was not a candidate for renomination in 1866 to the Fortieth Congress; delegate to the Republican (National Union) Convention of 1864; collector of customs at Brazos de Santiago, Tex., in 1868; returned to West Virginia and settled in Point Pleasant, Mason County, where he died on May 20, 1876; interment in Lone Oak Cemetery.

**WHALEY, Richard Smith,** a Representative from South Carolina; born in Charleston, S.C., July 15, 1874; attended the Episcopal High School, Alexandria, Va., and was graduated from the law department of the University of Virginia at Charlottesville in 1897; was admitted to the bar in 1897 and commenced practice in Charleston, S.C.; member of the State house of representatives 1901-1910, 1913; served as speaker 1907-1910 and as speaker pro tempore in 1913; presiding officer of the Democratic State convention in 1910 and of the Democratic city convention in 1911; delegate to the Democratic National Conventions in 1912 and 1920; elected as a Democrat to the Sixty-third Congress to fill the vacancy caused by the death of George S. Legaré; reelected to the Sixty-fourth, Sixty-fifth, and Sixty-sixth Congresses and served from April 29, 1913, to March 3, 1921; was not a candidate for renomination in 1920; resumed the practice of law; appointed commissioner of the United States Court of Claims in 1925; appointed judge of the Court of Claims by President Herbert Hoover in 1930, and was designated chief justice in 1939; retired as chief justice in 1947; died in Charleston, S.C., November 8, 1951; interment in Magnolia Cemetery.

**WHALLEY, John Irving,** a Representative from Pennsylvania; born in Barnesboro, Cambria County, Pa., September 14, 1902; attended the public schools and Cambria Rowe Business College; engaged in the automobile, banking and coal businesses; member of advisory board of Johnstown College, University of Pittsburgh; chairman of Somerset County Redevelopment Authority and Windber Planning Commission; member of Windber School Board 1935-1947; member of the Pennsylvania house of representatives 1951-1955 and served in the Pennsylvania senate 1955-1960; appointed by President Richard M. Nixon to serve as delegate to United Nations for the 1969 session; elected as a Republican to the Eighty-sixth Congress, by special election, November 8, 1960, to fill the vacancy caused by the death of Douglas H. Elliott, and at the same time elected to the Eighty-seventh Congress; reelected to the five succeeding Congresses and served from November 8, 1960, to January 3, 1973; was not a candidate for reelection in 1972 to the Ninety-third Congress; died March 8, 1980, at Pompano Beach, Fla.; interment in Grandview Cemetery, Johnstown, Pa.

**WHALLON, Reuben,** a Representative from New York; born in Bedminster, Somerset County, N.J., December 7, 1776; attended the common schools; moved to Argyle, Washington County, N.Y.; appointed justice of the peace for the township of Argyle March 13,

1806, and served until 1811; moved to Essex, Essex County, N.Y., in 1814; was a large landowner, farmer, merchant, mill owner, and ironmaster; served as captain and major in the New York State Militia 1803-1814; member of the State assembly in 1808, 1809, and 1811; supervisor of the town of Essex in 1818, 1819, 1827, and 1828; first judge of Essex County Court of Common Pleas 1831-1838; elected as a Jacksonian to the Twenty-third Congress (March 4, 1833-March 3, 1835); chairman, Committee on Expenditures on Public Buildings (Twenty-third Congress); again engaged in his former business pursuits; died on his estate at Whallons Bay, town of Essex, N.Y., on April 15, 1843; interment in Whallons Bay Cemetery.

**WHARTON, Charles Stuart,** a Representative from Illinois; born in Aledo, Mercer County, Ill., April 22, 1875; moved to Chicago with his parents in 1878; attended the public schools; was graduated from the law department of the University of Michigan at Ann Arbor in 1896; was admitted to the bar in 1896 and commenced practice in Chicago, Ill.; prosecuting attorney for the town of Lake in 1899; appointed assistant city attorney of Chicago in 1903; elected as a Republican to the Fifty-ninth Congress (March 4, 1905-March 3, 1907); unsuccessful candidate for reelection in 1906 to the Sixtieth Congress; resumed the practice of law in Chicago, Ill.; member of the board of exemption and Government appeal agent at Chicago during the First World War; served as an assistant corporation counsel in 1919; appointed assistant State's attorney in 1920 and served in this capacity until December 1923, when he resigned; resumed the practice of law in Chicago, Ill., until 1929; operated a restaurant; author of several books; died in Chicago, Ill., September 4, 1939; interment in Mount Hope Cemetery.

**WHARTON, James Ernest,** a Representative from New York; born in Binghamton, Broome County, N.Y., October 4, 1899; attended the public schools of Richmondville, N.Y.; was graduated from Union University and from Albany Law School; during the First World War served with the United States Army; was admitted to the bar in 1923; employed with the Travelers Insurance Co., 1920-1929; commenced the private practice of law in 1929 at Richmondville, N.Y.; owned and operated a farm; district attorney of Schoharie County, N.Y., 1932-1941; elected surrogate, county judge, and judge of children's court of Schoharie County, 1941-1951; elected as a Republican to the Eighty-second and to the six succeeding Congresses (January 3, 1951-January 3, 1965); was an unsuccessful candidate for reelection in 1964 to the Eighty-ninth Congress; engaged in real estate development; was a resident of Richmondville, N.Y.; died January 19, 1990.

**WHARTON, Jesse** (grandfather of Wharton Jackson Green), a Representative and a Senator from Tennessee; born in Covesville, Albemarle County, Va., July 29, 1782; completed preparatory studies; studied law; was admitted to the bar and commenced practice in Albemarle County; moved to Tennessee; elected as a Republican to the Tenth Congress (March 4, 1807-March 3, 1809); appointed to the United States Senate to fill the vacancy caused by the resignation of George W. Campbell and served from March 17, 1814, to October 10, 1815, when a successor was elected; resumed the practice of his profession; member of the board of visitors to the United States Military Academy, West Point, N.Y., in 1832; died in Nashville, Tenn., July 22, 1833; interment in Mount Olivet Cemetery.

**WHARTON, Samuel,** a Delegate from Delaware; born in Philadelphia, Pa., May 3, 1732; received a liberal schooling; engaged in mercantile pursuits; speculated in western lands and promoted the Vandalia Company; signed the nonimportation resolutions of 1765; Member of the Continental Congress from Delaware in 1782 and 1783; justice of the peace for the district of Southwark 1784-1786; judge of the court of common pleas 1790-1791 and resigned in the latter year; died at his country home near Philadelphia, Pa., in March 1800.

Bibliography: *DAB*.

**WHEAT, Alan Dupree,** a Representative from Missouri; born in San Antonio, Bexar County, Tex., October 16, 1951; attended elmentary schools in Wichita, Kans., and in Seville, Spain; graduated from Airline High School, Bossier City, La., 1968; B.A., Grinnell College, Grinnell, Iowa, 1972; economist; legislative aide to county executive, Jackson County, Mo.; elected, Missouri general assembly, 1977-1982; delegate, Missouri State Democratic convention, 1978; elected as a Democrat to the Ninety-eighth and to the five succeeding Congresses (January 3, 1983-January 3, 1995); was not a candidate in 1994 for renomination to the House of Representatives, but was an unsuccessful candidate for election to the United States Senate; is a resident of Kansas City, Mo.

**WHEAT, William Howard,** a Representative from Illinois; born in Kahoka, Clark County, Mo., February 19, 1879; attended the public schools of Brookfield and Chillicothe, Mo., and Chaddock College and Gem City Business College, Quincy, Ill.; clerk in clothing stores in Quincy and Bloomington, Ill.; moved to Thomasboro, Ill., in 1900, becoming engaged as bookkeeper and later cashier of a bank; in 1909 moved to Rantoul, Ill., and served as vice president and president of banking institutions; also interested in agriculture; school treasurer of Rantoul, Ill., for a number of years; unsuccessful candidate for election in 1936 to the Seventy-fifth Congress; elected as a Republican to the Seventy-sixth and to the two succeeding Congresses and served from January 3, 1939, until his death in Washington, D.C., January 16, 1944; interment in Maplewood Cemetery, Rantoul, Ill.

**WHEATON, Horace,** a Representative from New York; born in New Milford, Litchfield County, Conn., February 24, 1803; moved with his parents to Pompey, Onondaga County, N.Y., in 1810; received a limited schooling; was graduated from Pompey (N.Y.) Academy; engaged in mercantile pursuits; member of the State assembly in 1834; one of the commissioners to build a railroad between Syracuse and Utica; postmaster of Pompey, N.Y., 1840-1842; supervisor of Pompey; city treasurer; elected as a Democrat to the Twenty-eighth and Twenty-ninth Congresses (March 4, 1843-March 3, 1847); was not a candidate for renomination in 1846; moved to Syracuse, N.Y., in 1846; mayor of Syracuse 1851-1853; city treasurer of Syracuse in 1857 and 1858; engaged in hardware, saddlery, and mercantile pursuits; died in Syracuse, N.Y., June 23, 1882; interment in Oakwood Cemetery.

**WHEATON, Laban,** a Representative from Massachusetts; born in Mansfield, Bristol County, Mass., on March 13, 1754; attended Wrentham (Mass.) Academy; graduated from Harvard College in 1774; studied theology under private instructor at Woodstock, Conn.; also studied law; admitted to the bar in 1788 and commenced practice in Milton, Mass.; judge of the Bristol County Court; member of the Massachusetts house of representatives 1803-1808 and again in 1825; elected as a Federalist to the Eleventh and to the three succeeding Congresses (March 4, 1809-March 3, 1817); appointed chief justice of the court of common pleas of Bristol County May 18, 1810, which position he held until appointed chief justice of the court of sessions on May 25, 1819, for life; died in Norton, Bristol County, Mass., March 23, 1846; interment in Norton Cemetery.

**WHEELER, Burton Kendall,** a Senator from Montana; born in Hudson, Middlesex County, Mass., February 27, 1882; attended the common schools; worked as a stenographer in Boston, Mass.; graduated from the law department of the University of Michigan at Ann Arbor in 1905; was admitted to the bar the same year and commenced practice in Butte, Silver Bow County, Mont.; member, Montana State house of representatives, 1910-1912; United States district attorney for Montana, 1913-1918; resumed the practice of law in Butte; unsuccessful Democratic candidate for governor of Montana in 1920; elected as a Democrat to the United States Senate in 1922 for the term ending March 3, 1929; unsuccessful candidate for Vice President of the United States in 1924 on the Progressive Party ticket headed by Robert M. LaFollette; reelected to the United States Senate in 1928, 1934, and 1940, and served from March 4, 1923 to January 3, 1947; unsuccessful candidate for renomination in 1946; chairman, Committee on Indian Affairs (Seventy-third Congress), Committee on Interstate Commerce (Seventy-fourth through Seventy-ninth Congresses); resumed the practice of law; died in Washington, D.C., January 6, 1975; interment in Rock Creek Cemetery.

**Bibliography:** Anderson, John Thomas. "Senator Burton K. Wheeler and United States Foreign Relations." Ph.D. dissertation, University of Virginia, 1982; Wheeler, Burton Kendall. *Yankee From the West: The Candid, Turbulent Life Story of the Yankee-Born U.S. Senator from Montana.* 1962. Reprint. New York: Octagon Books, 1977.

**WHEELER, Charles Kennedy,** a Representative from Kentucky; born near Hopkinsville, Christian County, Ky., April 18, 1863; received his early education from a private tutor; graduated from Southwestern University, Clarksville, Tenn., in 1879 and from the Lebanon Law School, Lebanon, Tenn., in 1880; admitted to the bar the same year through the enactment of a special grant by the Kentucky legislature, and commenced practice in Paducah, Mc-Cracken County, Ky.; city solicitor of Paducah 1894-1896; elected as a Democrat to the Fifty-fifth, Fifty-sixth, and Fifty-seventh Congresses (March 4, 1897-March 3, 1903); did not seek renomination in 1902; practiced law in Paducah, Ky., until his death in that city June 15, 1933; interment in Oak Grove Cemetery.

**WHEELER, Ezra,** a Representative from Wisconsin; born in Chenango County, N.Y., December 23, 1820; received a liberal preparatory schooling and was graduated from Union College, Schenectady, N.Y., in 1842; moved to Berlin, Green Lake County, Wis., in 1849; studied law; was admitted to the bar and commenced practice in Berlin, Wis.; member of the State assembly in 1853; judge of Green Lake County 1854-1862; elected as a Democrat to the Thirty-eighth Congress (March 4, 1863-March 3, 1865); resumed the practice of law in Berlin, Wis.; on account of ill health, moved to Pueblo, Colo., in 1870; appointed register of the land office at Pueblo on June 27, 1871, and served until his death in that city on September 19, 1871; interment in Oakwood Cemetery, Berlin, Wis.

**WHEELER, Frank Willis,** a Representative from Michigan; born in Chaumont, Jefferson County, N.Y., March 2, 1853; attended the common schools; moved to Michigan in 1864 with his parents, who settled in East Saginaw; attended the Saginaw High School and the Ypsilanti State Normal School; engaged in boatbuilding; moved to West Bay City, Mich., in 1876; became master of the Saginaw River Tug Association; engaged in shipbuilding at the Bay Cities for many years; elected as a Republican to the Fifty-first Congress (March 4, 1889-March 3, 1891); was not a candidate for renomination in 1890; engaged in his former pursuits until 1899, when he moved to Detroit; returned to Saginaw in 1917 and organized the Saginaw Shipbuilding Co., and was engaged in building boats for the United States Government; died in Saginaw, Mich., August 9, 1921; interment in Elm Lawn Cemetery, Bay City, Mich.

**WHEELER, Grattan Henry,** a Representative from New York; born near Providence, R.I., August 25, 1783; attended public and preparatory schools; moved to New York with his parents, who settled in Steuben County about 1800; agriculturist and lumberman near Wheeler, N.Y.; member of the State assembly in 1822, 1824, and 1826; served in the State senate 1826-1830; elected as an Anti-Masonic candidate to the Twenty-second Congress (March 4, 1831-March 3, 1833); unsuccessful candidate for reelection to the Twenty-third Congress; resumed former pursuits; presidential elector on the Whig ticket in 1840; died in Wheeler, Steuben County, N.Y., March 11, 1852; interment in a private cemetery on the Wheeler homestead.

**WHEELER, Hamilton Kinkaid,** a Representative from Illinois; born in Ballston Township, Saratoga County, N.Y., August 5, 1848; moved to Illinois in 1852 with his parents, who settled near Grant Park, Kankakee County; attended public and private schools in Kankakee County; studied law; was admitted to the bar in 1871 and commenced practice in the city of Kankakee; member of the State senate in 1884; elected as a Republican to the Fifty-third Congress (March 4, 1893-March 3, 1895); was not a candidate for renomination in 1894 to the Fifty-fourth Congress; resumed the practice of law in Kankakee, Ill.; delegate to the Republican National Conventions in 1896 and 1900; died in Kankakee, Ill., July 19, 1918; interment in Mound Grove Cemetery.

**WHEELER, Harrison H.,** a Representative from Michigan; born at Farmers Creek, Lapeer County, Mich., March 22, 1839; attended the common schools; taught school until 1861; during the Civil War enlisted in the Union Army November 1, 1861, as a private in Company C, Tenth Regiment, Michigan Volunteer Infantry; promoted to second lieutenant in June 1862; first lieutenant of Company E, same regiment, in April 1863; captain of Company F, same regiment, in April 1865; settled in Bay City, Mich., at the close of the war; elected clerk of Bay County in 1866; studied law; was admitted to the bar in 1868 and commenced practice in Bay City; member of the State senate in 1870 and 1872; moved to Ludington, Mason County, Mich., in 1873; appointed circuit judge in 1874 and later elected to the office; resigned in June 1878; appointed postmaster April 16, 1878, and served until his successor was appointed, April 26, 1882; resumed the practice of law in Ludington; elected as a Democrat to the Fifty-second Congress (March 4, 1891-March 3, 1893); unsuccessful candidate for reelection in 1892 to the Fifty-third Congress; appointed United States pension agent at Detroit February 8, 1894, and served until his death; died at Farmers Creek, near Lapeer, Mich., July 28, 1896; interment in Lakeview Cemetery, Ludington, Mich.

**WHEELER, John,** a Representative from New York; born in Humphreysville (now Seymour), New Haven County, Conn., February 11, 1823; attended the common schools at Cheshire, Conn.; moved to New York City in 1843 and was engaged in the hotel business with his father; became a dry-goods clerk; elected as a Democrat to the Thirty-third and Thirty-fourth Congresses (March 4, 1853-March 3, 1857); declined to be a candidate for renomination in 1856 to the Thirty-fifth Congress; commissioner and president of the Department of Taxes and Assessments of New York City 1872-1880; member of the Board of Estimates and Apportionments and commissioner of accounts of New York City; was a lawyer, but did not practice; died in New York City April 1, 1906; interment in Woodlawn Cemetery.

**WHEELER, Joseph,** a Representative from Alabama; born in Augusta, Ga., September 10, 1836; attended local schools and the Episcopal Academy, Cheshire, Conn.; was graduated from the United States Military Academy at West Point, 1859; attended the Cavalry School at Carlisle, Pa., 1859-1860; transferred to the Mounted Rifles on June 26, 1860; commissioned a second lieutenant on September 1, 1860, and served in New Mexico; resigned from the United States Army on February 27, 1861; appointed lieutenant of Artillery in the Confederate Army on April 3, 1861; successively promoted to the grade of colonel, brigadier general (October 30, 1862), and major general (January 20, 1863), and was commissioned lieutenant general in February 1865; in 1862 was assigned to the command of the Army Corps of Cavalry of the Western Army, continuing in that position until the war closed; commissioned senior Cavalry general of the Confederate Armies on May 11, 1864;

studied law; was admitted to the bar and engaged in practice at Wheeler, Ala., and also became a planter; presented credentials as a Democratic Member-elect to the Forty-seventh Congress, and served from March 4, 1881 to June 3, 1882, when he was succeeded by William M. Lowe, who contested his election; subsequently elected to the same Congress to fill the vacancy caused by the death of William M. Lowe, and served from January 15 to March 3, 1883; elected as a Democrat to the Forty-ninth and to the seven succeeding Congresses, and served from March 4, 1885 to April 20, 1900, when he resigned; chairman, Committee on Expenditures in the Department of the Treasury (Fiftieth Congress), Committee on Territories (Fifty-third Congress); served in the Spanish-American War; commissioned major general of Volunteers on May 4, 1898, and assigned to command of a Cavalry division, United States Army; senior member of the commission which negotiated the surrender of Santiago and the Spanish Army in Cuba; during the Philippine Insurrection commanded the First Brigade, Second Division, Eighth Army Corps, in the Tarlac campaign, and in several other operations in central Luzon from July 8, 1899, to January 24, 1900; commissioned brigadier general in the United States Regular Army on June 16, 1900; retired on September 10, 1900; died in Brooklyn, N.Y., January 25, 1906; interment in Arlington National Cemetery, Va.

**Bibliography:** *DAB*; Dyer, John Percy. *"Fightin' Joe" Wheeler.* University, La.: Louisiana State University Press, 1941.

**WHEELER, Loren Edgar,** a Representative from Illinois; born in Havana, Mason County, Ill., October 7, 1862; attended the public schools and Graylock Institute, South Williamstown, Mass.; moved to Springfield, Ill., in 1880 and engaged in the ice and coal business until 1910 when he became identified with the advertising business; member of the board of aldermen 1895-1897; mayor of Springfield 1897-1901; delegate to the Republican National Convention in 1900; postmaster of Springfield 1901-1913; elected as a Republican to the Sixty-fourth and to the three succeeding Congresses (March 4, 1915-March 3, 1923); chairman, Committee on Railways and Canals (Sixty-sixth and Sixty-seventh Congresses); unsuccessful candidate for reelection in 1922 to the Sixty-eighth Congress; again elected to the Sixty-ninth Congress (March 4, 1925-March 3, 1927); unsuccessful candidate for reelection in 1926 to the Seventieth Congress; continued his former business activities in Springfield, Ill., until his death there on January 8, 1932; interment in Oak Ridge Cemetery.

**WHEELER, Nelson Platt,** a Representative from Pennsylvania; born in Portville, Cattaraugus County, N.Y., November 4, 1841; attended the public schools and academies in Olean and Deposit, N.Y.; became a surveyor and civil engineer; moved to Endeavor, Forest County, Pa.; engaged in the lumber business and also interested in agricultural pursuits and banking; elected county commissioner in 1866; held various township offices; member of the Pennsylvania house of representatives in 1878 and 1879; declined to be a candidate for renomination; elected as a Republican to the Sixtieth and Sixty-first Congresses (March 4, 1907-March 3, 1911); unsuccessful candidate for renomination in 1910, but the primary election being contested, his opponent subsequently withdrew and he was tendered the congressional nomination, but declined; resumed his former business pursuits in Endeavor, Pa.; owing to ill health, moved to Pasadena, Los Angeles County, Calif., in 1915, and died there on March 3, 1920; interment in Mountain View Cemetery.

**WHEELER, William Almon,** a Representative from New York and a Vice President of the United States; born in Malone, Franklin County, N.Y., June 30, 1819; completed preparatory studies; attended the Franklin Academy at Malone and the University of Vermont at Burlington; studied law; was admitted to the bar in 1845 and practiced in Malone, N.Y.; district attorney for Franklin County, N.Y., 1846-1849; member, New York State assembly, 1850-1851; member, New York State senate, 1858-1860; elected as a Republican to the Thirty-seventh Congress (March 4, 1861-March 3, 1863); delegate to the State constitutional conventions in 1867 and 1868; elected to the Forty-first and to the three succeeding Congresses (March 4, 1869-March 3, 1877); was not a candidate for reelection in 1876 to the Forty-fifth Congress, having been nominated for Vice President of the United States on the Republican ticket headed by Rutherford B. Hayes; elected Vice President of the United States, November 7, 1876; inaugurated on March 5, 1877 and served until March 4, 1881; retired from public life and active business pursuits because of ill health; died in Malone, N.Y., June 4, 1887; interment in Morningside Cemetery.

**Bibliography:** *DAB*; Otten, James T. "Grand Old Party Man: William A. Wheeler and the Republican Party, 1850-1880." Ph.D. dissertation, University of South Carolina, 1976.

**WHEELER, William McDonald,** a Representative from Georgia; born near Alma, Bacon County, Ga., July 11, 1915; attended the public schools and South Georgia College at Douglas, Middle Georgia College at Cochran, Georgia Teachers College at Statesboro, and Atlanta Law School, LL.B., 1966; engaged in agricultural pursuits; taught school and also served as principal of the junior high schools in Bacon and Appling Counties 1936-1941; enlisted as a private in the Army Air Force on May 30, 1942; was promoted through the ranks to captain and discharged on June 4, 1946; delegate, Democratic National Convention, 1952; elected as a Democrat to the Eightieth and to the three succeeding Congresses (January 3, 1947-January 3, 1955); unsuccessful candidate for renomination in 1954; employed with the Georgia Motor Vehicle Division in the Internal Revenue Department, Atlanta, Ga., in 1955 and 1956; engaged in sales and public relations; tax examiner, State of Georgia; coordinator, Federal programs, Bacon County, Ga., Board of Education; assistant director, Governor's Highway Safety Program, State of Mississippi; is a resident of Alma, Ga.

**WHELCHEL, Benjamin Frank,** a Representative from Georgia; born in Lumpkin County, near Gainesville, Ga., December 16, 1895; attended the public schools; studied law privately in Gainesville, Ga.; was admitted to the bar in 1925 and commenced the practice of law in Gainesville, Ga.; judge of the city court of Hall County 1932-1934; elected as a Democrat to the Seventy-fourth and to the four succeeding Congresses (January 3, 1935-January 3, 1945); was not a candidate for renomination in 1944; resumed the practice of law; died in Gainesville, Ga., May 11, 1954; interment in West View Abbey, Atlanta, Ga.

**WHERRY, Kenneth Spicer,** a Senator from Nebraska; born in Liberty, Gage County, Nebr., February 28, 1892; attended the public schools; B.A., University of Nebraska, Lincoln, 1914; attended Harvard University, 1915-1916; during the First World War served as a cadet in the United States Navy Flying Corps, 1917-1918; engaged in the sale of automobiles, farm implements, furniture, and real estate; studied law; was admitted to the bar and commenced practice in Pawnee City, Nebr.; president, Pawnee County Agricultural Society, 1927-1944; member of the Pawnee City council in 1927 and 1929; mayor of Pawnee City, 1929-1931, and 1938-1943; member, Nebraska State senate, 1929-1932; unsuccessful candidate for nomination for Governor in 1932; unsuccessful candidate for nomination for United States Senator in 1934; western director for the Republican National Committee, 1941-1942; elected as a Republican to the United States Senate in 1942; reelected in 1948, and served from January 3, 1943 until his death in Washington, D.C., November 29, 1951; Republican whip 1944-1949; minority leader (Eighty-first and Eighty-second Congresses); chairman, Special Committee on Problems of Small Business (Eightieth Congress); interment in Pawnee City Cemetery, Pawnee City, Nebr.

**Bibliography:** *DAB*; Dalstrom, Harl A. "Kenneth S. Wherry." Ph.D. dissertation, University of Nebraska, 1965; Stromer, Marvin. *The Making of a Political Leader, Kenneth S. Wherry.* Lincoln: University of Nebraska Press, 1969.

**WHIPPLE, Thomas, Jr.,** a Representative from New Hampshire; born in Lebanon, Grafton County, N.H., in 1787; completed preparatory studies; moved to Warren, N.H., in 1811; studied medicine in Haverhill and Hanover, N.H., and was graduated from Dartmouth College, Hanover, N.H., in 1814; commenced practice in Wentworth, N.H.; member of the State house of representatives 1818-1820; elected to the Seventeenth and to the three succeeding Congresses (March 4, 1821-March 3, 1829); resumed the practice of medicine; died in Wentworth, Grafton County, N.H., January 23, 1835; interment in Wentworth Village Cemetery.

**WHIPPLE, William,** a Delegate from New Hampshire; born in Kittery, York County, Maine, January 14, 1730; became a sailor and engaged in the slave trade; freed his slaves and engaged in mercantile pursuits in Portsmouth, N.H.; delegate to the Provincial Congress at Exeter in 1775; Member of the Continental Congress 1776-1779; declined to be a candidate for renomination; one of the signers of the Declaration of Independence; commissioned a brigadier general in 1777; member of the State assembly 1780-1784; participated in several battles in the Revolutionary War; appointed judge of the State supreme court in 1782; financial receiver for New Hampshire 1782-1784; died in Portsmouth, N.H., November 28, 1785; interment in the Old North Burial Ground.

Bibliography: *DAB.*

**WHITACRE, John Jefferson,** a Representative from Ohio; born in Decatur, Burt County, Nebr., December 28, 1860; attended the public schools, Hiram (Ohio) College, and the University of Michigan at Ann Arbor; engaged as a manufacturer of hollow building tile; delegate to the Democratic National Convention in 1912; unsuccessful candidate in 1908 to the Sixty-first Congress; elected as a Democrat to the Sixty-second and Sixty-third Congresses (March 4, 1911-March 3, 1915); resumed his former manufacturing pursuits; president of the Whitacre Engineering Co. and the Whitacre-Greer Fireproofing Co.; died in Miami, Fla., December 2, 1938; interment in Magnolia Cemetery, Magnolia, Ohio.

**WHITAKER, John Albert** (grandson of Addison Davis James), a Representative from Kentucky; born in Russellville, Logan County, Ky., October 31, 1901; attended the public schools, Bethel College, and the University of Kentucky; studied law; was admitted to the bar in 1926 and commenced practice in Russellville, Ky.; county attorney of Logan County, Ky., 1928-1948; delegate to all Kentucky conventions 1924-1950; elected as a Democrat to the Eightieth Congress to fill the vacancy caused by the resignation of Earle C. Clements; reelected to the Eighty-first and Eighty-second Congresses and served from April 17, 1948, until his death in Russellville, Ky., December 15, 1951; interment in Maple Grove Cemetery.

**WHITCOMB, James,** a Senator from Indiana; born in Windsor County, Vt., December 1, 1795; attended Transylvania University, Lexington, Ky.; studied law; was admitted to the bar and commenced practice in Bloomington, Ind., in 1824; prosecuting attorney for Monroe County, 1826-1829; member, Indiana State senate, 1830-1831, 1832-1836; appointed by President Andrew Jackson as Commissioner of the General Land Office, 1836-1841; resumed the practice of law in Terre Haute, Ind.; elected Governor of Indiana in 1843, reelected in 1846, and served from December 6, 1843 until his resignation on December 27, 1848; elected as a Democrat to the United States Senate, and served from March 4, 1849 until his death in New York City, October 4, 1852; chairman, Committee on Claims (Thirty-first and Thirty-second Congresses), Committee on Public Buildings (Thirty-second Congress); interment in Crown Hill Cemetery, Indianapolis, Ind.

Bibliography: *DAB.*

**WHITE, Addison** (cousin of John White), a Representative from Kentucky; born in Abingdon, Washington County, Va., May 1, 1824; received an academic education; was graduated from Princeton College in 1844; engaged in agricultural pursuits and cotton raising; elected as a Whig to the Thirty-second Congress (March 4, 1851-March 3, 1853); during the Civil War served in the Confederate Army; moved to Huntsville, Ala., and resumed agricultural pursuits; died in Huntsville, Ala., February 4, 1909; interment in Maple Hill Cemetery.

**WHITE, Albert Smith,** a Representative and a Senator from Indiana; born in Orange County, N.Y., October 24, 1803; graduated from Union College, Schenectady, N.Y., in 1822; studied law; was admitted to the bar in 1825 and practiced; moved to Lafayette, Ind.; assistant clerk of the State house of representatives 1830-1831, and clerk 1832-1835; unsuccessful candidate for election in 1832 to the Twenty-third Congress; presidential elector on the Whig ticket in 1836; elected as a Whig to the Twenty-fifth Congress (March 4, 1837-March 3, 1839); was not a candidate for renomination in 1838; elected as a Whig to the United States Senate and served from March 4, 1839, to March 3, 1845; declined to be a candidate for reelection; chairman, Committee to Audit and Control the Contingent Expense (Twenty-seventh Congress), Committee on Indian Affairs (Twenty-seventh and Twenty-eighth Congress); president of several railroads; moved to Stockwell, Ind., and resumed the practice of law; elected as a Republican to the Thirty-seventh Congress (March 4, 1861-March 3, 1863); was not a candidate for renomination in 1862; appointed by President Abraham Lincoln one of three commissioners to adjust the claims of citizens of Minnesota and Dakota against the government for Indian depredations; appointed judge of the United States Court for the District of Indiana in 1864 and served until his death in Stockwell, Ind., September 4, 1864; interment in Greenbush Cemetery, Lafayette, Ind.

Bibliography: *DAB.*

**WHITE, Alexander,** a Representative from Alabama; born in Franklin, Williamson County, Tenn., October 16, 1816; moved with his parents to Courtland, Ala., in 1821; pursued an academic course and attended the University of Tennessee at Knoxville; served in the Seminole War in 1836; moved to Talladega, Ala., in 1837; studied law; was admitted to the bar in 1838 and commenced practice in Talladega; elected as a Whig to the Thirty-second Congress (March 4, 1851-March 3, 1853); moved to Selma, Ala., in 1856 and continued the practice of law; delegate to the State constitutional convention in 1865; member of the State house of representatives in 1872; elected as a Republican to the Forty-third Congress (March 4, 1873-March 3, 1875); unsuccessful candidate for reelection in 1874 to the Forty-fourth Congress; appointed an associate justice of the United States Court for the Territory of Utah in 1875, serving only a few months; moved to Dallas, Tex., in 1876 and resumed the practice of law; died in Dallas December 13, 1893; interment in Greenwood Cemetery.

**WHITE, Alexander,** a Representative from Virginia; born in Frederick County, Va., in 1738; studied law at the Inner Temple, London, in 1762 and attended Gray's Inn in 1763; member, Virginia House of Burgesses, 1772-1773; member of the Virginia house of delegates 1782-1786 and in 1788; delegate to the Virginia convention in 1788; elected to the First and Second Congresses (March 4, 1789-March 3, 1793); again a member of the Virginia house of delegates 1799-1801; appointed by President George Washington May 18, 1795, one of the three commissioners to lay out the city of Washington, D.C., and erect the public buildings, and served until May 1, 1802, when the board was abolished; died on his estate, "Woodville," in Frederick County, Va., October 9, 1804.

Bibliography: *DAB.*

**WHITE, Alexander Colwell,** a Representative from Pennsylvania; was born near Kittanning, Armstrong County, Pa., December 12, 1833; attended the public schools; taught school; attended the Jacksonville Institute and the Dayton Union Academy; moved to Jefferson County, Pa., in 1860 where he studied law; was admitted to the bar in 1862, and commenced practice in Punxsutawney, Pa.; enlisted in the Union Army as a private in Company I, Eighth Regiment, Pennsylvania Volunteer Infantry; moved to Brookville, Jefferson County, Pa., and continued the practice of his profession; elected district attorney in 1867 and 1870; elected as a Republican to the Forty-ninth Congress (March 4, 1885-March 3, 1887); was not a candidate for reelection in 1886 to the Fiftieth Congress; resumed the practice of his profession; justice of the peace for Rose Township; died near Brookville, Pa., June 11, 1906; interment in Brookville Cemetery.

**WHITE, Allison,** a Representative from Pennsylvania; born in Pine Township, near Jersey Shore, Pa., December 21, 1816; attended the public schools and was graduated from Allegheny College, Meadville, Crawford County, Pa.; studied law; was admitted to the bar and commenced practice in Lock Haven, Pa.; was elected as a Democrat to the Thirty-fifth Congress (March 4, 1857-March 3, 1859); chairman, Committee on Expenditures on Public Buildings (Thirty-fifth Congress); unsuccessful candidate for reelection in 1858 to the Thirty-sixth Congress; engaged in the lumber and coal business at Philadelphia; died in Philadelphia, Pa., on April 5, 1886; interment in Highland Cemetery, Lock Haven, Clinton County, Pa.

**WHITE, Bartow,** a Representative from New York; born in Yorktown, Westchester County, N.Y., November 7, 1776; attended the common schools and completed preparatory studies; studied medicine with his father, Dr. Ebenezer White, and commenced practice in Fishkill, N.Y., in 1800; elected to the Nineteenth Congress (March 4, 1825-March 3, 1827); resumed the practice of medicine; presidential elector on the Whig ticket in 1840; died in Fishkill, Dutchess County, N.Y., December 12, 1862; interment in the Dutch Reformed Church Cemetery.

**WHITE, Benjamin,** a Representative from Maine; born in Goshen (now Vienna), Maine, May 13, 1790; attended the common schools; moved to Winthrop, Maine, in 1802 and was employed on a farm until 1808 when he entered Farmington Academy; taught school for several years; during the War of 1812 was in Augusta, Maine, and assisted in raising troops, later serving as a noncommissioned officer with troops stationed at Castine and Eastport, Maine; again engaged in teaching in Montville, Maine, until 1821, when he also engaged in the sawmill business and agricultural pursuits; served as town selectman; member of the State house of representatives in 1829, 1841, and 1842; elected as a Democrat to the Twenty-eighth Congress (March 4, 1843-March 3, 1845); resumed his former pursuits; died in Montville, Maine, on June 7, 1860; interment in Halldale Cemetery, North Montville, Maine.

**WHITE, Campbell Patrick,** a Representative from New York; born in Ireland November 30, 1787; received a limited education; immigrated to the United States in 1816 and engaged in mercantile pursuits in New York City; elected as a Jacksonian to the Twenty-first and to the three succeeding Congresses and served from March 4, 1829, until his resignation in 1835, which occurred before the convening of the Twenty-fourth Congress; chairman, Committee on Naval Affairs (Twenty-third Congress); resumed mercantile pursuits; appointed quartermaster general of the State militia on January 24, 1831; delegate to the New York State constitutional convention in 1845; resided in New York City, where he died February 12, 1859; interment in St. Paul's Cemetery.

**WHITE, Cecil Fielding,** a Representative from California; born in Temple, Bell County, Tex., December 12, 1900; attended the public schools of Fort Smith, Ark.; at sixteen years of age joined the United States Army and served on the Mexican border; went to France as a sergeant in the One Hundred and Forty-second Field Artillery, Thirty-ninth Division, 1916-1919; worked in the Los Angeles office of a cotton broker; associated with cotton mills in California, Arkansas and Tennessee; owner and operator of the Cecil F. White Ranches, Inc., Devils Den, Calif.; elected as a Democrat to the Eighty-first Congress (January 3, 1949-January 3, 1951); unsuccessful candidate for reelection in 1950 to the Eighty-second Congress; unsuccessful candidate for election in 1966 to the Ninetieth Congress; died March 29, 1992.

**WHITE, Chilton Allen,** a Representative from Ohio; born in Georgetown, Brown County, Ohio, February 6, 1826; attended the public schools; taught school; served in the Mexican War with Company G, First Regiment, Ohio Volunteers; studied law; was admitted to the bar in 1848 and commenced the practice of law in Georgetown, Ohio; prosecuting attorney of Brown County from 1852 to 1854; member of the State senate in 1859 and 1860; elected as a Democrat to the Thirty-seventh and Thirty-eighth Congresses (March 4, 1861-March 3, 1865); unsuccessful for reelection in 1864 to the Thirty-ninth Congress; resumed the practice of law in Georgetown; delegate to the State constitutional convention in 1873; unsuccessful candidate for secretary of state in 1896; died in Georgetown, Ohio, December 7, 1900; interment in Confidence Cemetery.

**WHITE, Compton Ignatius** (father of Compton Ignatius White, Jr.), a Representative from Idaho; born in Baton Rouge, La., July 31, 1877; at an early age moved with his parents to Rankin County, Miss., and to Clark Fork, Bonner County, Idaho, in 1890; attended the public schools, Metropolitan Business College, Chicago, Ill., and Gonzaga University, Spokane, Wash.; railway telegraph operator, 1897-1903, trainman, 1903-1906, and conductor, 1906-1910; engaged in agricultural, lumbering, and mining work in Clark Fork; also engaged in stock raising; member of the board of trustees of Clark Fork; delegate to the Democratic National Conventions of 1928, 1932, and 1936; unsuccessful candidate for election in 1930 to the Seventy-second Congress; elected as a Democrat to the Seventy-third and to the six succeeding Congresses (March 4, 1933-January 3, 1947); chairman, Committee on Irrigation (Seventy-fourth through Seventy-eighth Congresses), Committee on Coinage, Weights, and Measures (Seventy-ninth Congress); unsuccessful candidate for reelection in 1946 to the Eightieth Congress; elected to the Eighty-first Congress (January 3, 1949-January 3, 1951); was not a candidate in 1950 for renomination to the House of Representatives, but was an unsuccessful candidate for nomination to the United States Senate; unsuccessful candidate for nomination in 1952 to the Eighty-third Congress; resumed stock raising and the maintenance of his mining interests at Clark Fork, Idaho; died in Spokane, Wash., March 31, 1956; interment in the family cemetery, east of Clark Fork, Idaho.

**WHITE, Compton Ignatius, Jr.** (son of Compton Ignatius White), a Representative from Idaho; born in Spokane, Wash., December 19, 1920; attended the public schools of Clark Fork, Idaho, and Washington, D.C.; attended George Washington University, Washington, D.C., 1938-1939 and the University of Idaho at Moscow, 1939-1942; engaged as breeder of livestock, and also in mining and logging; during the Second World War was an analysis and experimental flight test engineer for Boeing Aircraft, Co., Seattle, Wash.; member of school board and Clark Fork Board of Trustees, serving as chairman, 1947-1950; unsuccessful candidate in 1960 for nomination to the United States Senate; mayor of Clark Fork, 1958-1962; elected as a Democrat to the Eighty-eighth and Eighty-ninth Congresses (January 3, 1963-January 3, 1967);

unsuccessful candidate for reelection in 1966 to the Ninetieth Congress; consultant, Department of the Treasury, 1967; resumed ranching pursuits; member, Clark Fork City Council; is a resident of Clark Fork, Idaho.

**WHITE, David,** a Representative from Kentucky; born in 1785; completed preparatory studies; studied law; admitted to the bar and commenced practice in New Castle, Ky.; member of the Kentucky house of representatives in 1826; elected to the Eighteenth Congress (March 4, 1823-March 3, 1825); died in Franklin County, Ky., October 19, 1834.

**WHITE, Dudley Allen,** a Representative from Ohio; born in New London, Huron County, Ohio, January 3, 1901; attended the public schools and was graduated from the New London High School in 1918; during the First World War served as an enlisted man in the United States Navy; employed with a rubber company in Akron, Ohio, in 1919 and 1920, and also engaged in the insurance business; moved to Uhrichsville, Ohio, and engaged in the dry-goods business in 1920 and 1921; returned to New London, Ohio, and became associated with a company manufacturing regalia and uniforms 1921-1925; entered the newspaper business at Norwalk, Ohio, in 1925, later becoming editor and general manager; delegate to the Republican National Conventions in 1928 and 1948; State commander of the American Legion in Ohio in 1929 and 1930; elected as a Republican to the Seventy-fifth and Seventy-sixth Congresses (January 3, 1937-January 3, 1941); did not seek renomination in 1940, but was unsuccessful for the Republican nomination for United States Senator; called to active duty in the United States Navy in 1942 as a lieutenant commander; promoted to captain and served as director of recruiting and induction until 1946; director of the Citizens National Bank and president of a broadcasting company in Norwalk, Ohio; served as executive director of President Dwight D. Eisenhower's Commission on Intergovernmental Relations in 1954 and 1955; president and publisher of the Norwalk Reflector-Herald and the Sandusky Register at time of death; died in Delaware, Ohio, October 14, 1957; interment in Woodlawn Cemetery, Norwalk, Ohio.

**WHITE, Edward Douglass** (son of James White and father of Edward Douglass White [1845-1921]), a Representative from Louisiana; born in Nashville, Tenn., in March 1795; moved with his father to what is now St. Martin Parish, La., in 1799; attended the common schools, and was graduated from the University of Nashville, Tennessee, in 1815; studied law; was admitted to the bar and commenced practice in Donaldsonville, La.; was appointed judge of the city court of New Orleans and moved there in 1825; elected to the Twenty-first and to the two succeeding Congresses and served from March 4, 1829, to November 15, 1834, when he resigned; elected Governor of Louisiana by the Legislature, and served from February 4, 1835 to February 4, 1839; moved to Thibodaux; elected as a Whig to the Twenty-sixth and Twenty-seventh Congresses (March 4, 1839-March 3, 1843); resumed the practice of his profession; also engaged as a planter; died in New Orleans, La., April 18, 1847; interment in St. Joseph's Catholic Cemetery, Thibodaux, La.

**Bibliography:** *DAB.*

**WHITE, Edward Douglass** (son of Edward Douglass White [1795-1847], and grandson of James White), a Senator from Louisiana; born near Thibodaux, Lafourche Parish, La., November 3, 1845; attended Mount St. Mary's College, near Emmitsburg, Md., the Jesuit College in New Orleans, La., and Georgetown College, Washington, D.C.; served in the Confederate Army during the Civil War; studied law; was admitted to the bar and commenced practice in New Orleans, La., in 1868; member, Louisiana State senate, 1874; associate justice of the supreme court of Louisiana, 1879-1880; resumed the practice of law; elected as a Democrat to the United States Senate and served from March 4, 1891, until his resignation,

effective March 12, 1894; chairman, Committee to Audit and Control the Contingent Expense (Fifty-third Congress); nominated on February 19, 1894 by President Grover Cleveland as an Associate Justice of the United States Supreme Court; was confirmed by the Senate the same day; nominated on December 12, 1910 by President William Howard Taft as Chief Justice of the United States; was confirmed by the Senate the same day, and served until his death in Washington, D.C., May 19, 1921; interment in Oak Hill Cemetery.

**Bibliography:** *DAB*; Highsaw, Robert. *Edward Douglass White, Defender of the Conservative Faith.* Baton Rouge: Louisiana State University Press, 1981; Klinkhammer, Marie. *Edward Douglass White, Chief Justice of the United States.* Washington, D.C.: Catholic University of America Press, 1943.

**WHITE, Francis,** a Representative from Virginia; born near Winchester, Frederick County, Va.; attended the common schools at Winchester; engaged in agricultural pursuits; elected a member of the Virginia house of delegates in 1794, 1809-1813, and 1818; elected as a Federalist to the Thirteenth Congress (March 4, 1813-March 3, 1815); served in the Virginia senate in 1823 and 1824; appointed sheriff of Hampshire County, Va. (now West Virginia), on December 9, 1823, by the Governor; died in Hampshire County, on the Capon River, in November 1826.

**WHITE, Francis Shelley (Frank),** a Senator from Alabama; born in Prairie, Noxubee County, Miss., March 13, 1847; attended the common schools and was tutored at home; during the Civil War served in the Confederate Army as a private; after the close of the war engaged in agricultural pursuits until 1868; studied law; was admitted to the bar in 1869 and commenced practice in West Point, Miss.; member, State house of representatives 1875, 1882-1883; moved to Birmingham, Jefferson County, Ala., in 1886 and continued the practice of law; elected as a Democrat to the United States Senate to fill the vacancy caused by the death of Joseph F. Johnston and served from May 11, 1914, to March 3, 1915; was not a candidate for renomination; chairman, Committee on Revolutionary Claims (Fifty-third Congress); resumed the practice of his profession until his death in Birmingham, Ala., August 1, 1922; interment in Elmwood Cemetery.

**WHITE, Frederick Edward,** a Representative from Iowa; born in Prussia, Germany, January 19, 1844; immigrated to the United States in 1857 with his mother, who settled on a farm in Keokuk County, Iowa; joined the Eighth Regiment, Iowa Volunteer Infantry, in 1861 but was rejected on account of age; enlisted in February 1862 in the Thirteenth Regiment, Iowa Volunteer Infantry, and was mustered out in August 1865; returned to Keokuk County and engaged in agricultural pursuits and stock raising; elected as a Democrat to the Fifty-second Congress (March 4, 1891-March 3, 1893); unsuccessful candidate for reelection in 1892 to the Fifty-third Congress; retired from public life and resumed agricultural pursuits; died in Sigourney, Keokuk County, Iowa, January 14, 1920; interment in Sigourney Cemetery.

**WHITE, George,** a Representative from Ohio; born in Elmira, Chemung County, N.Y., August 21, 1872; moved with his parents to Titusville, Crawford County, Pa., in 1874; attended the common schools; was graduated from the local high school in 1891 and from Princeton College in 1895; taught school for several years; mined in the Klondike region, 1898-1901; moved to Washington County, Ohio, in 1902 and settled in Marietta; engaged in the production of oil; member of the Ohio State house of representatives, 1905-1908; unsuccessful candidate for election in 1908 to the Sixty-first Congress; elected as a Democrat to the Sixty-second and Sixty-third Congresses (March 4, 1911-March 3, 1915); unsuccessful candidate for reelection in 1914 to the Sixty-fourth Congress; elected to the Sixty-fifth Congress (March 4, 1917-March 3, 1919); was an unsuccessful candidate for reelection in 1918 to the Sixty-sixth

Congress; served as chairman of the Democratic National Committee from July 1920 to November 1921; resumed his former activities in the oil business; elected Governor of Ohio in 1930, reelected in 1932 and served from January 12, 1931 to January 14, 1935; chairman of the Northwest Territory (Federal) Commission in 1938; vice chairman of the Marietta College Board of Trustees; vice president and a director of People's Banking & Trust Co. of Marietta, Ohio; died in West Palm Beach, Fla., December 15, 1953; interment in Oak Grove Cemetery, Marietta, Ohio.

**Bibliography:** Queenan, Thomas J. "The Public Career of George White, 1905-1941." Ph.D. dissertation, Kent State University, 1976.

**WHITE, George Elon,** a Representative from Illinois; born in Millbury, Worcester County, Mass., March 7, 1848; attended the public schools; during the Civil War enlisted as a private in the Fifty-seventh Regiment, Massachusetts Veteran Volunteers; after the close of the war entered a commercial college in Worcester, Mass.; moved to Chicago, Ill., in 1867 and engaged in the lumber business and also became interested in banking; member of the board of aldermen of Chicago; member of the State senate 1878-1886; elected as a Republican to the Fifty-fourth and Fifty-fifth Congresses (March 4, 1895-March 3, 1899); unsuccessful candidate for reelection in 1898 to the Fifty-sixth Congress; resumed his former business pursuits in Chicago, Ill., and served as president of the White Lumber Co.; died in Chicago, Ill., on May 17, 1935; interment in the mausoleum in Rosehill Cemetery.

**WHITE, George Henry,** a Representative from North Carolina; born in Rosindale, Bladen County, N.C., December 18, 1852; attended the public schools, and was graduated from Howard University, Washington, D.C., in 1877; studied law; was admitted to the bar in 1879 and commenced practice in New Bern, N.C.; principal of the State Normal School of North Carolina; member of the State house of representatives in 1881; served in the State senate in 1885; solicitor and prosecuting attorney for the second judicial district of North Carolina 1886-1894; delegate to the Republican National Conventions in 1896 and 1900; elected as a Republican to the Fifty-fifth and Fifty-sixth Congresses (March 4, 1897-March 3, 1901); was not a candidate for renomination in 1900 to the Fifty-seventh Congress; resumed the practice of law and also engaged in banking; died in Philadelphia, Pa., December 28, 1918; interment in Eden Cemetery.

**Bibliography:** Reid, George W. "A Biography of George H. White, 1852-1918." Ph.D. dissertation, Howard University, 1974.

**WHITE, Harry,** a Representative from Pennsylvania; born in Indiana, Indiana County, Pa., January 12, 1834; attended Indiana (Pa.) Academy; graduated from Princeton College in 1854; studied law; admitted to the bar in June 1855 and commenced practice in Indiana, Pa.; entered the Union Army as major of the Sixty-seventh Regiment, Pennsylvania Volunteer Infantry, on December 13, 1861; mustered out February 22, 1865; member of the Pennsylvania senate during his military service and attended its sessions in the winter of 1862-1863; reelected to the Pennsylvania senate and served from 1865 to 1874, being speaker at the close of the last term; delegate to the Pennsylvania constitutional convention in 1872; unsuccessful candidate for Governor of Pennsylvania in 1872; elected as a Republican to the Forty-fifth and Forty-sixth Congresses (March 4, 1877-March 3, 1881); was not a candidate for renomination in 1880; elected a judge of Indiana County, Pa., in 1884; reelected in 1894 and served until 1904; resumed the practice of law and engaged in banking; died in Indiana, Pa., June 23, 1920; interment in Oakland Cemetery.

**Bibliography:** Shankman, Arnold. "John P. Penney, Harry White and the 1864 Pennsylvania Senate Deadlock." *Western Pennsylvania Historical Magazine* 55 (January 1972): 77-86.

**WHITE, Hays Baxter,** a Representative from Kansas; born near Fairfield, Jefferson County, Iowa, on September 21, 1855; attended the rural schools of his native county; engaged in agricultural pursuits; moved to Jewell County, Kans., in 1875 and engaged in agricultural pursuits near Mankato; taught school at Mankato in 1876; member of the State house of representatives 1888-1890; member of the State senate 1900-1904; mayor of Mankato in 1914 and 1915; member of the State tax commission in 1915-1918; elected as a Republican to the Sixty-sixth and to the four succeeding Congresses (March 4, 1919-March 3, 1929); chairman, Committee on Election of President, Vice President, and Representatives (Sixty-eighth through Seventieth Congresses); election unsuccessfully contested by W.H. Clark; was not a candidate for renomination in 1928; died in Mankato, Kans., September 29, 1930; interment in Mount Hope Cemetery.

**WHITE, Hugh,** a Representative from New York; born in Whitestown, Oneida County, N.Y., on December 25, 1798; attended the common schools; was graduated from Hamilton College, Clinton, N.Y., in 1823; studied law but did not practice; entered business at Chittenango in 1825 and afterwards at Rondout; active in the building of the Michigan Southern & Northern Indiana Railroad; moved to Cohoes, N.Y., in 1830; was greatly interested in the development of water power from the Mohawk River; organized the Rosendale Cement Works; elected as a Whig to the Twenty-ninth, Thirtieth, and Thirty-first Congresses (March 4, 1845-March 3, 1851); chairman, Committee on Agriculture (Thirtieth Congress); resumed his business activities; died in Waterford, N.Y., October 6, 1870; interment in Albany Rural Cemetery.

**WHITE, Hugh Lawson,** a Senator from Tennessee; born in Iredell County, N.C., October 30, 1773; moved with his parents in 1785 to that part of North Carolina which now is Knox County, Tenn.; participated in an expedition against the Cherokees around 1793; pursued classical studies in Philadelphia, Pa., and studied law in Lancaster, Pa.; was admitted to the bar in 1796 and commenced practice in Knoxville, Tenn.; judge of the State superior court 1801-1807; member, State senate 1807-1809; appointed United States district attorney in 1808; judge of the State supreme court 1809-1815; president of the State bank; member, State senate 1817-1825; elected to the United States Senate to fill the vacancy caused by the resignation of Andrew Jackson; reelected in 1829 and 1835, as a Jacksonian, and served from October 28, 1825, to January 13, 1840, when he resigned because he could not conscientiously obey the instructions of his constituents; served as President pro tempore of the Senate during the Twenty-second and Twenty-third Congresses; chairman, Committee on Indian Affairs (Twentieth through Twenty-sixth Congresses); died in Knoxville, Tenn., April 10, 1840; interment in First Presbyterian Church Cemetery.

**Bibliography:** *DAB*; Gresham, Lunia. "The Public Career of Hugh Lawson White." Ph.D. dissertation, Vanderbilt University, 1943; Scott, Nancy, ed. *A Memoir of Hugh Lawson White.* Philadelphia: J. B. Lippincott and Co., 1856.

**WHITE, James** (father of Edward Douglass White [1795-1847] and grandfather of Edward Douglass White [1845-1921]), a Delegate from North Carolina and from the Territory South of the River Ohio (now the State of Tennessee); born in Philadelphia, Pa., June 16, 1749; attended a Jesuit College in St. Omer, France; returned to the United States and studied medicine in the University of Pennsylvania at Philadelphia; also studied law; moved to North Carolina and settled in Davidson County; member of the North Carolina General Assembly in 1785; Member of the Continental Congress from North Carolina 1786-1788; superintendent of Indian affairs for the southern district in 1786; after the creation of the Territory South of the River Ohio (later the State of Tennessee) in 1790, served in the house of representatives of the first Territorial legislature from Davidson County in 1794; elected as a Delegate to the Third and

Fourth Congresses from the Territory South of the River Ohio and served from September 3, 1794, to June 1, 1796, when the Territory was admitted into the Union as the State of Tennessee; moved to Louisiana in 1799; appointed judge of Attakapas district in 1804 and later of St. Martin Parish; died in Attakapas, La., in October 1809.

**WHITE, James Bain,** a Representative from Indiana; born in Stirlingshire, Scotland, June 26, 1835; attended the common schools; immigrated to the United States in 1854 and settled in Fort Wayne, Ind.; a calico printer and a tailor until the outbreak of the Civil War; enlisted as a private in Company I, Thirteenth Regiment, Indiana Volunteers; elected captain of the company and served until December 1862, when he resigned; was wounded in the Battle of Shiloh, Tenn., April 7, 1862; elected a member of the common council of Fort Wayne, Ind., in 1874; operated a department store; engaged in the manufacture of wheels and was also interested in banking; elected as a Republican to the Fiftieth Congress (March 4, 1887-March 3, 1889); unsuccessful candidate for reelection in 1888 to the Fifty-first Congress; delegate to the Republican National Convention of 1892; commissioner to the World's Columbian Exposition at Chicago in 1893; died in Fort Wayne, Ind., October 9, 1897; interment in Linwood Cemetery.

**WHITE, James Bamford,** a Representative from Kentucky; born near Winchester, Clark County, Ky., on June 6, 1842; attended the common schools and the Mount Zion Academy, Macon County, Ill.; entered the Confederate Army in the fall of 1863 and served in the commands of Generals John C. Breckinridge and John Hunt Morgan until the close of the Civil War, when he was honorably discharged; engaged in teaching at Irvine, Estill County, Ky.; studied law while teaching; was admitted to the bar in 1867 and commenced the practice of law in Irvine; prosecuting attorney of Estill County 1872-1880; elected as a Democrat to the Fifty-seventh Congress (March 4, 1901-March 3, 1903); continued the practice of his profession in Irvine, Ky., until his retirement in 1919; died in Irvine, Ky., March 25, 1931; interment in Oakdale Cemetery.

**WHITE, John** (cousin of Addison White and uncle of John Daugherty White), a Representative from Kentucky; born near Cumberland Gap (now Middlesboro), Ky., February 14, 1802; received a limited schooling; studied law; was admitted to the bar and commenced practice in Richmond, Madison County, Ky.; member of the Kentucky house of representatives in 1832; elected as a Whig to the Twenty-fourth and to the four succeeding Congresses (March 4, 1835-March 3, 1845); Speaker of the House of Representatives (Twenty-seventh Congress); appointed judge of the nineteenth judicial district of Kentucky, and served from February 8, 1845 until his death in Richmond, Ky., September 22, 1845; interment in the State Cemetery, Frankfort, Franklin County, Ky.

**WHITE, John Daugherty** (nephew of John White), a Representative from Kentucky; born near Manchester, Clay County, Ky., January 16, 1849; attended a private school until 1865 and Eminence (Ky.) College and the University of Kentucky at Lexington until 1870; graduated from the law department of the University of Michigan at Ann Arbor in 1872; also attended the medical department of the same institution; admitted to the bar by the Kentucky Court of Appeals in 1875 and practiced; elected as a Republican to the Forty-fourth Congress (March 4, 1375-March 3, 1877); declined to be a candidate for renomination; chairman of the Kentucky Republican convention at Louisville in 1879; member of the Kentucky house of representatives in 1879 and 1880; resigned in 1880; endorsed and reelected without opposition during the sitting of the legislature; delegate to the Republican National Convention in 1880; unsuccessful Republican candidate for the United States Senate in 1881; elected as a Republican to the Forty-seventh and Forty-eighth Congresses (March 4, 1881-March 3, 1885); declined to be a candidate for renomination in 1884 and resumed the practice of law in Louisville, Ky.; unsuccessful candidate of the Kentucky

Prohibition Party for Governor of Kentucky in 1903; unsuccessful candidate of the Progressive Party for judge of the Kentucky Court of Appeals in 1912; died near Manchester, Ky., January 5, 1920; interment in the family burying ground near Manchester, Clay County, Ky.

**WHITE, Joseph Livingston,** a Representative from Indiana; born in Cherry Valley, Otsego County, N.Y.; completed preparatory studies; studied law in Utica, N.Y.; was admitted to the bar, and commenced practice in Madison, Ind.; elected as a Whig to the Twenty-seventh Congress (March 4, 1841-March 3, 1843); moved to New York City and resumed the practice of law; while on a business trip to Nicaragua, Central America, he was shot by a Mr. Gavett as he was leaving the ship at Corinto (Punta Ycacos), Nicaragua, January 5, 1861, dying at Corinto on January 12; interment in the cemetery at Corinto, Nicaragua.

**WHITE, Joseph M.,** a Delegate from Florida Territory; born in Franklin County, Ky., May 10, 1781; completed preparatory studies; studied law; was admitted to the bar and practiced; moved to Pensacola, Fla., in 1821; one of the commissioners under the act of Congress of May 8, 1822, "for ascertaining claims and titles to lands within the Territory of Florida"; elected to the Nineteenth and to the five succeeding Congresses (March 4, 1825-March 3, 1837); unsuccessful candidate for reelection to the Twenty-fifth Congress; author of a "New Collection of Laws, Charters, etc., of Great Britain, France, and Spain Relating to Cessions of Lands, with the Laws of Mexico," in two volumes published in 1839; died in St. Louis, Mo., October 19, 1839.

**WHITE, Joseph Worthington,** a Representative from Ohio; born in Cambridge, Guernsey County, Ohio, October 2, 1822; attended the common schools and Cambridge Academy; engaged in mercantile pursuits; studied law; was admitted to the bar in 1844, and commenced practice in Cambridge; prosecuting attorney of Guernsey County 1845-1847; mayor of Cambridge; delegate to the Democratic National Convention in 1860; elected as a Democrat to the Thirty-eighth Congress (March 4, 1863-March 3, 1865); unsuccessful for reelection in 1864 to the Thirty-ninth Congress; resumed the practice of law; died in Cambridge, Ohio, August 6, 1892; interment in the South Cemetery.

**WHITE, Leonard,** a Representative from Massachusetts; born in Haverhill, Essex County, Mass., May 3, 1767; graduated from Harvard University in 1787; member of the Massachusetts house of representatives in 1809; held many local offices; elected as a Federalist to the Twelfth Congress (March 4, 1811-March 3, 1813); town clerk of Haverhill; cashier of the Merrimack Bank of Haverhill 1814-1836; died in Haverhill, Mass., October 10, 1849; interment in Pentucket Cemetery.

**WHITE, Michael Doherty,** a Representative from Indiana; born in Clark County, Ohio, September 8, 1827; moved with his parents to Tippecanoe County, Ind., in 1829; pursued classical studies; moved to Crawfordsville, Crawfordsville County, Ind., in 1848; attended the county seminary and Wabash College, Crawfordsville; clerked in a store for one year; studied law; was admitted to the bar in 1854 and commenced the practice of his profession in Crawfordsville; law partner of General Lew Wallace; prosecuting attorney of Montgomery and Boone Counties 1854-1856; member of the State senate 1860-1864; elected as a Republican to the Forty-fifth Congress (March 4, 1877-March 3, 1879); was not a candidate for renomination in 1878; continued the practice of law in Crawfordsville, Ind., until 1911, and died there on February 6, 1917; interment in the Masonic Cemetery.

**WHITE, Milo,** a Representative from Minnesota; born in Fletcher, Franklin County, Vt., August 17, 1830; attended the common schools and Bakersfield Academy; moved to Chatfield, Fillmore County, Minn., in 1855 and engaged in mercantile pursuits; chairman of the board of supervisors of Chatfield upon its organization in 1858; served in the State senate 1872-1876, 1881, and 1882; elected as a Republican to the Forty-eighth and Forty-ninth Congresses (March 4, 1883-March 3, 1887); unsuccessful candidate for election in 1898 to the Fifty-sixth Congress; resumed mercantile pursuits; mayor of Chatfield for several terms; member of the school board until his death in Chatfield, Minn., May 18, 1913; interment in Chatfield Cemetery.

**WHITE, Phillips,** a Delegate from New Hampshire; born in Haverhill, Mass., on October 28, 1729; completed preparatory studies and attended Harvard College; during the French and Indian War was an officer in the colonial army at Lake George in 1755; moved to New Hampshire; member of the State house of representatives 1775-1782, and served as speaker in 1775 and 1782; probate judge of Rockingham County, N.H., 1776-1790; Member of the Continental Congress in 1782 and 1783; councilor 1792-1794; retired to his farm near South Hampton, N.H.; died in South Hampton on June 24, 1811; interment in the Old Cemetery.

**WHITE, Phineas,** a Representative from Vermont; born in South Hadley, Hampshire County, Mass., October 30, 1770; was graduated from Dartmouth College, Hanover, N.H., in 1797; studied law; was admitted to the bar in 1800 and commenced practice in Pomfret, Vt.; register of probate for Windsor County 1800-1809; county attorney in 1813; judge of Windham County in 1814, 1815, 1817, and 1820; also judge of probate of the district of Westminster in 1814 and 1815; member of the constitutional convention in 1814; served in the State house of representatives 1815-1820; elected to the Seventeenth Congress (March 4, 1821-March 3, 1823); member of the State constitutional convention in 1836; served in the State senate in 1836 and 1837; trustee of Middlebury College; died in Putney, Windham County, Vt., on July 6, 1847; interment in Maple Grove Cemetery.

**WHITE, Richard Alan (Rick),** a Representative from Washington; born in Bloomington, Monroe County, Ind., November 6, 1953; B.A., Dartmouth College, 1975; pursued academic studies at the University of Paris, Pantheon-Sorbonne; J.D., Georgetown University School of Law, 1980; clerk to United States Judge Charles Clark of the Fifth Circuit Court of Appeals; founder and director of a literacy program for children; member, Queen Anne (Wash.) Community Council, 1986-1988; practiced law in Seattle, Wash., 1983-present; elected as a Republican to the One Hundred Fourth Congress (January 3, 1995-January 3, 1997); is a resident of Bainbridge Island, Wash.

**WHITE, Richard Crawford,** a Representative from Texas; born in El Paso, Tex., April 29, 1923; graduated from Dudley Primary School, and the El Paso High School, and the Citizen's Military Training Camp at San Antonio, Tex.; attended Texas Western College, 1940-1942; graduated from the University of Texas in 1946 and from the law school of the same university in 1949; was admitted to the bar in 1949 and began the practice of law in El Paso; served in the United States Marine Corps as a rifleman and Japanese interpreter in the Pacific Theater, 1942-1945; was awarded the Purple Heart; served in the Texas State house of representatives, 1955-1958; served as El Paso county chairman, 1963-1965; elected as a Democrat to the Eighty-ninth and to the eight succeeding Congresses (January 3, 1965-January 3, 1983); was not a candidate for reelection in 1982 to the Ninety-eighth Congress; returned to the practice of law; is a resident of El Paso, Tex.

**WHITE, Samuel,** a Senator from Delaware; born near Dover, Mispillion Hundred, Kent County, Del., in December 1770; attended Cokesbury College, Maryland; studied law; was admitted to the bar in 1793 and commenced practice in Dover, Del.; served two years as a captain in the United States Army; adjutant general of Delaware in 1803; appointed in 1801 and subsequently elected as a Federalist to the United States Senate to fill the vacancy caused by the resignation of Henry Latimer; reelected in 1803 and 1809 and served from February 28, 1801, until his death in Wilmington, Del., November 4, 1809; interment in the Old Swede Churchyard.

**Bibliography:** *DAB*.

**WHITE, Sebastian Harrison,** a Representative from Colorado; born on a farm near Maries County, Mo., December 24, 1864; attended the rural schools in Dallas County and the Marionville (Mo.) Collegiate Institute (later the Ozark Wesleyan College at Carthage, Mo.); taught school for several years; elected president of the Hickory County Teachers Institute in 1886; elected superintendent of schools of Hickory County in 1887; while a teacher studied law; was admitted to the bar in 1889 and commenced practice in Pueblo, Colo.; delegate to the Democratic State convention in 1892; chairman of the Pueblo County Democratic central committee in 1892; served as city attorney of Pueblo 1897-1899; public trustee of Pueblo County 1900-1903 and 1905-1909; district attorney of the tenth judicial district 1904-1908; elected justice of the State supreme court in 1908 for a term of ten years 1909-1919, and served as chief justice from 1917 until 1918, when he retired; engaged in the practice of law in Denver, Colo., in 1919; elected as a Democrat to the Seventieth Congress to fill the vacancy caused by the death of William N. Vaile and served from November 15, 1927, to March 3, 1929; unsuccessful candidate for reelection in 1928 to the Seventy-first Congress; resumed the practice of law in Denver, Colo.; died in a hospital in Colorado Springs, Colo., December 21, 1945; remains were cremated in Fairmount Cemetery, Denver, Colo., and the ashes scattered over the cemetery.

**WHITE, Stephen Mallory,** a Senator from California; born in San Francisco, Calif., January 19, 1853; moved with his parents to Santa Cruz County, Calif.; attended private and common schools and St. Ignatius College in San Francisco; graduated from Santa Clara College, Santa Clara, Calif., in 1871; studied law; was admitted to the bar in 1874 and commenced practice in Los Angeles, Calif.; district attorney of Los Angeles County 1883-1884; member, State senate 1887-1891, serving as president pro tempore both sessions; was an unsuccessful candidate for election to the United States Senate in 1890; elected as a Democrat to the United States Senate and served from March 4, 1893, to March 3, 1899; did not seek reelection; chairman, Committee on Irrigation and Reclamation of Arid Lands (Fifty-third through Fifty-fifth Congresses); died in Los Angeles, Calif., February 21, 1901; interment in Calvary Cemetery.

**Bibliography:** *DAB*; Dobie, Edith. *The Political Career of Stephen Mallory White: A Study of Party Politics Under the Convention System.* 1927. Reprint. New York: AMS Press, 1971; Grassman, Curtis. "Prologue to Progressivism: Senator Stephen M. White and the California Reform Impulse, 1875-1905." Ph.D. dissertation, University of California, Los Angeles, 1970.

**WHITE, Stephen Van Culen,** a Representative from New York; born in Chatham County, N.C., August 1, 1831; moved to Illinois with his parents, who settled near Otterville, Jersey County, Ill.; attended the free school founded by Dr. Silas Hamilton in Otterville, Ill., and was graduated from Knox College, Galesburg, Ill., in 1854; entered a mercantile house in St. Louis, Mo.; studied law and was admitted to the bar November 4, 1856; moved to Des Moines, Iowa, in 1856, and practiced law until January 1, 1865; acting United States district attorney for Iowa in 1864; moved to New York City in 1865 and engaged in banking; member of the New York Stock

Exchange; was an astronomer and upon the organization of the American Astronomical Society in 1883 was elected its first president; elected as a Republican to the Fiftieth Congress (March 4, 1887-March 3, 1889); was not a candidate for renomination in 1888 to the Fifty-first Congress; resumed the practice of law; died in Brooklyn, N.Y., January 18, 1913; interment in Greenwood Cemetery.

Bibliography: *DAB.*

**WHITE, Wallace Humphrey, Jr.** (grandson of William Pierce Frye), a Representative and a Senator from Maine; born in Lewiston, Androscoggin County, Maine, August 6, 1877; attended the public schools of Lewiston; graduated from Bowdoin College, Brunswick, Maine, in 1899; assistant clerk to the Committee on Commerce, United States Senate, and secretary to his grandfather, the President pro tempore, 1899-1903; studied law; was admitted to the bar and commenced practice in Lewiston, Maine; elected as a Republican to the Sixty-fifth and to the six succeeding Congresses (March 4, 1917-March 3, 1931); chairman, Committee on Expenditures in the Department of Justice (Sixty-sixth Congress), Committee on Woman Suffrage (Sixty-seventh through Sixty-ninth Congresses), Committee on Merchant Marine and Fisheries (Seventieth and Seventy-first Congresses); served as a presidential appointee on a variety of commissions; was not a candidate in 1930 for reelection to the House of Representatives, but was elected to the United States Senate; reelected in 1936 and again in 1942, and served from March 4, 1931 to January 3, 1949; was not a candidate for renomination in 1948; minority leader (Seventy-eighth and Seventy-ninth Congresses); majority leader (Eightieth Congress); chairman, Committee on Interstate and Foreign Commerce (Eightieth Congress); retired from political and business activities; died in Auburn, Maine, March 31, 1952; interment in Mount Auburn Cemetery.

**WHITE, Wilbur McKee,** a Representative from Ohio; born near Hillsboro, Highland County, Ohio, February 22, 1890; educated in the rural schools and the Hillsboro High School; Marietta (Ohio) College, M.A., 1914; engaged in teaching at Marietta, Ohio, in 1914 and 1915; correspondent for a Dayton, Ohio, newspaper in 1916; served in the United States Army on the Mexican border as a private and first sergeant in Company H, Third Ohio Infantry, in 1916; during the First World War served from August 15, 1917, as a first lieutenant and later as a captain in the Three Hundred and Thirty-second Regiment, United States Infantry, in Italy and France; associated with the Toledo Times in 1919 and served as managing editor 1925-1930 and associate editor in 1930 and 1931; elected as a Republican to the Seventy-second Congress (March 4, 1931-March 3, 1933); unsuccessful candidate for reelection in 1932 and for election in 1940 to the Seventy-seventh Congress; employed in a glass manufacturing concern in 1933; served as secretary and as executive director of the Safety Glass Association 1934-1958; engaged in independent highway safety work 1958-1961; died in Chillicothe, Ohio, December 31, 1973; interment in Hillsboro Cemetery, Hillsboro, Ohio.

**WHITE, William John,** a Representative from Ohio; born at Rice Lake, Ontario, Canada, October 7, 1850; moved to the United States in 1857 with his parents, who settled in Cleveland, Ohio; attended the district schools; entered business as a candy maker in 1869, and later began the manufacture of chewing gum; mayor of West Cleveland in 1889; elected as a Republican to the Fifty-third Congress (March 4, 1893-March 3, 1895); declined to be a candidate for renomination in 1894; was first president of the American Chicle Co. and later president of the W.J. White Chicle Co.; died in Cleveland, Ohio, on February 16, 1923; interment in Lake View Cemetery.

**WHITEAKER, John,** a Representative from Oregon; born in Dearborn County, near Fort Wayne, Ind., May 4, 1820; was self-educated and engaged in agricultural pursuits and stock raising; moved to the Pacific coast in 1849, and settled in Lane County, Oreg., in 1852; elected judge of probate for Lane County in 1855; member of the Territorial legislature in 1857; elected Governor of Oregon in 1858, and served from March 3, 1859 to September 10, 1862; member of the State house of representatives in 1866 and 1868, and served as speaker; again elected to the State house of representatives in 1870; member of the State board of equalization in 1872, and served as chairman; member of the commission to examine, report upon, and receive the locks and canal at the falls of the Willamette River; member of the State senate, 1876-1880, and served as president of the sessions of 1876 and 1878; elected as a Democrat to the Forty-sixth Congress (March 4, 1879-March 3, 1881); chairman, Committee on Revolutionary Pensions (Forty-sixth Congress); was an unsuccessful candidate for reelection in 1880 to the Forty-seventh Congress; appointed internal revenue collector for the district of Oregon, and served from June 20, 1885 to February 27, 1890; moved to Eugene, Lane County, Oreg., in 1889, and died there on October 2, 1902; interment in the Masonic Cemetery.

**WHITEHEAD, Joseph,** a Representative from Virginia; born near Mount Airy, Pittsylvania County, Va., October 31, 1867; attended the public schools of his native city; graduated from the academic department of Richmond College (now the University of Richmond), Richmond, Va., in 1889, and from the law department of the University of Virginia at Charlottesville in 1892; admitted to the bar the same year and commenced the practice of law in Chatham, Pittsylvania County, Va.; served in the Virginia senate 1899-1904; elected as a Democrat to the Sixty-ninth, Seventieth, and Seventy-first Congresses (March 4, 1925-March 3, 1931); unsuccessful candidate for renomination in 1930; resumed the practice of his chosen profession until his death at Chatham, Va., on July 8, 1938; interment in Chatham Cemetery.

**WHITEHEAD, Thomas,** a Representative from Virginia; born in Lovingston, Nelson County, Va., December 27, 1825; received a limited schooling; engaged in mercantile pursuits; studied law; admitted to the bar in 1849 and commenced practice in Amherst, Va.; during the Civil War served in the Confederate Army as captain of Company E, Second Virginia Cavalry, 1861-1865; elected to the Virginia senate in 1865, but did not qualify; elected prosecuting attorney for Amherst County in 1866 and again in 1869, resigning in November 1873, having been elected to Congress; elected as a Democrat to the Forty-third Congress (March 4, 1873-March 3, 1875); was not a candidate for renomination in 1874; editor of the Lynchburg News in 1876 and the Lynchburg Advance in 1880; resumed the practice of law; elected commissioner of agriculture for the Commonwealth of Virginia in 1888 and served in this capacity until his death; died near Lynchburg, Campbell County, Va., July 1, 1901; interment in Spring Hill Cemetery, Lynchburg, Va.

**WHITEHILL, James** (son of John Whitehill and nephew of Robert Whitehill), a Representative from Pennsylvania; born in Strasburg, Lancaster County, Pa., on January 31, 1762; studied law; was admitted to the bar and commenced practice in Strasburg; associate judge of the Lancaster County Court from January 3, 1811, to February 1, 1813, when he resigned, having been elected to Congress; served in the War of 1812 as major general of Pennsylvania Militia; elected as a Republican to the Thirteenth Congress and served from March 4, 1813, to September 1, 1814, when he resigned; engaged in mercantile pursuits in Strasburg; burgess of Strasburg in 1816; again associate judge of the county court from October 17, 1820, until his death in Strasburg, Pa., on February 26, 1822; interment in the Presbyterian Church Cemetery, Leacock, Lancaster County, Pa.

**WHITEHILL, John** (father of James Whitehill and brother of Robert Whitehill), a Representative from Pennsylvania; born in Salisbury Township, Lancaster County, Pa., December 11, 1729;

completed preparatory studies; studied law; was admitted to the bar and commenced practice in Lancaster County; was appointed justice of the peace and justice of the orphans' court of Lancaster County, March 31, 1777; member of the Pennsylvania house of representatives 1780-1782 and 1793; member of the council of censors in 1783; was delegate to the supreme executive council in 1784; member of the Pennsylvania ratification convention in 1787; associate judge of Lancaster County in 1791; elected as a Republican to the Eighth and Ninth Congresses (March 4, 1803-March 3, 1807); died in Salisbury Township, Lancaster County, Pa., September 16, 1815; interment in Pequea Presbyterian Church Cemetery.

**WHITEHILL, Robert** (brother of John Whitehill and uncle of James Whitehill), a Representative from Pennsylvania; born in Pequea, Lancaster County, Pa., July 21, 1738; attended the common schools; settled in Cumberland County; member of the Pennsylvania constitutional convention in July 1776 that approved the Declaration of Independence; member of the council of safety in 1777; delegate to the Pennsylvania constitutional convention in 1790; member of the Pennsylvania house of representatives 1797-1800; served in the Pennsylvania senate 1801-1804, and was speaker of the senate in 1804 during the impeachment trials of the supreme court judges of Pennsylvania; elected as a Republican to the Ninth Congress to fill the vacancy caused by the death of John A. Hanna; reelected to the Tenth and to the three succeeding Congresses and served from November 7, 1805, until his death at Lauther Manor, Cumberland County, Pa., April 8, 1813; interment in the Silver Spring Presbyterian Church Cemetery, Hampden Township, near Camp Hill, Pa.

**Bibliography:** *DAB*; Crist, Robert Grant. *Robert Whitehill and the Struggle for Civil Rights*. Lemoyne, Pa.: Lemoyne Trust Co., 1958.

**WHITEHOUSE, John Osborne,** a Representative from New York; born in Rochester, Strafford County, N.H., July 19, 1817; received a common-school education; moved to New York City in 1835 and was engaged as a clerk until 1839, when he moved to Brooklyn, N.Y., and engaged as a merchant and manufacturer of shoes; moved to Poughkeepsie, Dutchess County, N.Y., in 1860 and continued the shoe manufacturing business; elected as a Democrat to the Forty-third and Forty-fourth Congresses (March 4, 1873-March 3, 1877); chairman, Committee on Reform in the Civil Service (Forty-fourth Congress); was not a candidate for reelection in 1876 to the Forty-fifth Congress; resumed the shoe manufacturing business; also interested in banking and railroading; owner of the Daily News 1872-1880; died in Poughkeepsie, N.Y., August 24, 1881; interment in Greenwood Cemetery, Brooklyn, N.Y.

**WHITEHURST, George William,** a Representative from Virginia; born in Norfolk, Va., March 12, 1925; educated in Norfolk public schools; B.A., Washington and Lee University, Lexington, Va., 1950; M.A., University of Virginia, 1951; Ph.D., history, West Virginia University, 1962; served in the United States Navy as an aviation radioman in the Pacific Theater, 1943-1946; member, Department of History, Old Dominion College, Norfolk, Va., 1950-1968; member, public affairs and news department, television station WTAR, Norfolk, Va.; elected as a Republican to the Ninety-first and to the eight succeeding Congresses (January 3, 1969-January 3, 1987); was not a candidate for reelection in 1986 to the One Hundredth Congress; university lecturer in public affairs, Old Dominion University, Norfolk, Va.; television news analyst, station WVEC; is a resident of Norfolk, Va.

**Bibliography:** Whitehurst, G. William. *Diary of a Congressman*. Norfolk, Va.: The Donning Company, 1983; Whitehurst, G. William. *Diary of a Congressman, Vol. 2: ABSCAM and Beyond*. Norfolk, Va.: The Donning Company, 1985.

**WHITELAW, Robert Henry,** a Representative from Missouri; born on a farm near Lloyds, Essex County, Va., January 30, 1854; moved with his father to Cape Girardeau County, Mo., in 1856; returned to Essex County, Va., in 1866; attended private schools in Tappahannock and Staunton, Va., and the law department of the University of Michigan at Ann Arbor; was admitted to the bar in 1873 and commenced practice in Cape Girardeau, Mo.; city attorney in 1873; prosecuting attorney of Cape Girardeau County 1874-1878; member of the State house of representatives in 1883 and 1887; elected as a Democrat to the Fifty-first Congress to fill the vacancy caused by the death of James Peter Walker and served from November 4, 1890, to March 3, 1891; was not a candidate for election in 1890 to the Fifty-second Congress; resumed the practice of law in Cape Girardeau, Mo.; retired from active law practice in 1927 and moved to Blodgett, Mo., and in 1934 to Blytheville, Ark., where he died on July 27, 1937; interment in Lorimier Cemetery, Cape Girardeau, Mo.

**WHITELEY, Richard Henry,** a Representative from Georgia; born in County Kildare, Ireland, December 22, 1830; immigrated to the United States in 1836 with his parents, who settled in Georgia; received private instruction in elementary education; engaged in manufacturing; studied law; was admitted to the bar in 1860 and commenced practice in Bainbridge, Ga.; opposed secession, but after the adoption of the ordinance entered the Confederate Army and served throughout the Civil War, attaining the rank of major; member of the State constitutional convention in 1867; unsuccessful candidate for election in 1866 to the Fortieth Congress; presented credentials as a Senator-elect to the United States Senate on July 15, 1870, to fill the vacancy in the term beginning March 4, 1865, but as the election took place prior to the readmission of Georgia into the Union was not admitted to a seat; elected as a Republican to the Forty-first Congress to fill the vacancy caused by the House declaring Nelson Tift not entitled to the seat; reelected to the Forty-second and Forty-third Congresses and served from December 22, 1870, to March 3, 1875; unsuccessful candidate for reelection to the Forty-fourth Congress and for election to the Forty-fifth Congress; moved to Boulder, Colo., in 1877 and resumed the practice of his profession; died in Boulder, Colo., September 26, 1890; interment in the Masonic Cemetery.

**WHITELEY, William Gustavus,** a Representative from Delaware; born near Newark, Del., August 7, 1819; attended Bullock's School at Wilmington, Del., and was graduated from Princeton College in 1838; studied law; was admitted to the bar in 1841 and began practice in Wilmington, Del.; prothonotary of New Castle County 1852-1856; elected as a Democrat to the Thirty-fifth and Thirty-sixth Congresses (March 4, 1857-March 3, 1861); chairman, Committee on Agriculture (Thirty-fifth Congress); was not a candidate for renomination in 1860; again prothonotary of New Castle County 1862-1867; mayor of Wilmington, Del., 1875-1878; member of commission to settle fishery disputes between New Jersey and Delaware in 1877; census enumerator for Delaware in 1880; associate judge of the superior court of Delaware from March 31, 1884, until his death in Wilmington, Del., April 23, 1886; interment in Bridgeton Cemetery, Bridgeton, N.J.

**WHITENER, Basil Lee,** a Representative from North Carolina; born in York County, S.C., May 14, 1915; educated in public schools of Gaston County; graduated from Lowell High School in 1931 and from Rutherford College in 1933; attended the University of South Carolina, 1933-1935; graduated from Duke University Law School in 1937; admitted to the North Carolina bar the same year and commenced the practice of law in Gastonia, N.C.; member of the State house of representatives in 1941 and renominated in 1942 but resigned to enter the United States Navy; served as gunnery officer and was separated from the service in November 1945 with rank of lieutenant; appointed solicitor, fourteenth solicitorial district, in

January 1946 and elected in November 1946, reelected in 1950 and 1954, and served until December 31, 1956; delegate to the Democratic National Convention of 1948; elected as a Democrat to the Eighty-fifth and to the five succeeding Congresses (January 3, 1957-January 3, 1969); unsuccessful candidate for reelection in 1968 to the Ninety-first Congress; unsuccessful candidate for election in 1970 to the Ninety-second Congress; resumed the practice of law; was a resident of Gastonia, N.C.; died March 20, 1989.

**WHITESIDE, Jenkin,** a Senator from Tennessee; born in Lancaster, Pa., in 1772; pursued preparatory studies; studied law and was admitted to the bar; moved to Tennessee and commenced practice in Knoxville; one of the commissioners of Knoxville in 1801 and 1802; elected as a Republican to the United States Senate in 1809 to fill the vacancy caused by the resignation of Daniel Smith; reelected the same year and served from April 11, 1809, to October 8, 1811, when he resigned; resumed the practice of law; died in Nashville, Tenn., September 25, 1822; interment was probably in the Old Cemetery west of the Nashville sulphur spring.

**WHITESIDE, John,** a Representative from Pennsylvania; born near Lancaster, Pa., in 1773; attended the common schools and Chestnut Level Academy; employed on his father's farm; later engaged in the hotel business and operated a distillery; justice of the peace; member of the Pennsylvania house of representatives in 1810 and 1811; elected as a Republican to the Fourteenth and Fifteenth Congresses (March 4, 1815-March 3, 1819); resumed the hotel business in Lancaster, Pa.; register of wills; again a member of the Pennsylvania house of representatives in 1825; died in Lancaster, Pa., July 28, 1830; interment in Lancaster Cemetery.

**WHITFIELD, John Wilkins,** a Delegate from the Territory of Kansas; born in Franklin, Williamson County, Tenn., March 11, 1818; attended the local schools; served in the Mexican War in 1846; moved to Independence, Mo., in 1853 to serve as Indian agent to the Pottawatomies at Westport, Mo., and to the Arkansas Indians in 1855 and 1856; upon the admission of the Territory of Kansas to representation was elected as a Democrat to the Thirty-third Congress and served from December 20, 1854, to March 3, 1855; presented credentials as a Delegate-elect to the Thirty-fourth Congress and served from March 4, 1855, to August 1, 1856, when the seat was declared vacant; again elected to the Thirty-fourth Congress to fill the vacancy caused by the action of the House of Representatives in declaring the seat vacant and served from December 9, 1856, to March 3, 1857; register of the land office at Doniphan, Kans., 1857-1861; began his military career as captain of the Twenty-seventh Texas Cavalry in 1861; promoted to the rank of major in 1862; commissioned brigadier general May 9, 1863; at the close of the war in 1865 went to Texas and settled in Lavaca County and engaged in agricultural pursuits and stock raising; member of the State house of representatives; died near Hallettsville, Lavaca County, Tex., October 27, 1879; interment in Hallettsville Cemetery.

**WHITFIELD, Wayne Edward,** a Representative from Kentucky; born in Hopkinsville, Christian County, Ky., May 25, 1943; graduated, Madisonville (Ky.) High School; B.S., University of Kentucky, 1965; attended Wesley Theological Seminary and American University, Washington, D.C.; J.D., University of Kentucky School of Law, 1969; served in the United States Army Reserve as a first lieutenant, 1967-1970; practicing attorney; member, Kentucky house of representatives, 1973-1975; owner and operator of an oil distributorship in western Kentucky; counsel to the president, Seaboard System Railroad, 1979-1983; vice president of state relations, 1983-1988, and vice president for railroad affairs, 1988-1991, CSX Corp.; attorney adviser to Chairman Edward J. Philbin of the Interstate Commerce Commission, 1991-1993; elected as a Republican to the One Hundred Fourth Congress (January 3, 1995-January 3, 1997); is a resident of Hopkinsville, Ky.

**WHITING, Justin Rice,** a Representative from Michigan; born in Bath, Steuben County, N.Y., February 18, 1847; moved to Michigan in 1849 with his parents, who settled in St. Clair; attended the public schools and the University of Michigan at Ann Arbor 1863-1865; engaged as a merchant and manufacturer; mayor of St. Clair in 1879; member of the State senate in 1882; elected as a Democrat to the Fiftieth Congress and reelected to the Fifty-first, Fifty-second, and Fifty-third Congresses (March 4, 1887-March 3, 1895); resumed his former business pursuits in St. Clair; unsuccessful Democratic candidate for Governor in 1898 and also for election in 1900 to the Fifty-seventh Congress; chairman of the Democratic State central committee; died in St. Clair, Mich., January 31, 1903; interment in Hillside Cemetery.

**WHITING, Richard Henry** (uncle of Ira Clifton Copley), a Representative from Illinois; born in West Hartford, Conn., January 17, 1826; attended the common schools; moved to Altona, Ill., in 1850, thence to Galesburg, Ill., in 1860, where he built a gas works; during the Civil War served in the Union Army as paymaster of Volunteers 1862-1866; appointed assessor of internal revenue for the fifth district of Illinois in February 1870, serving until May 20, 1873, when the office was abolished; appointed collector of internal revenue for the same district May 20, 1873, with office at Peoria, Ill., and served until his resignation on March 4, 1875, having been elected to Congress; elected as a Republican to the Forty-fourth Congress (March 4, 1875-March 3, 1877); was not a candidate for renomination in 1876; delegate to the Republican National Convention in 1884; died in New York City, May 24, 1888; interment in Springdale Cemetery, Peoria, Ill.

**WHITING, William,** a Representative from Massachusetts; born in Concord, Mass., on March 3, 1813; attended Concord Academy and was graduated from Harvard University in 1833; taught school in Plymouth and Concord, Mass.; was graduated from the law department of Harvard University in 1838; was admitted to the bar the same year and commenced practice in Boston; solicitor of the War Department 1862-1865; elected as a Republican to the Forty-third Congress and served from March 4, 1873, until death in Boston, Mass., June 29, 1873; interment in Sleepy Hollow Cemetery, Concord, Mass.

**Bibliography:** *DAB.*

**WHITING, William,** a Representative from Massachusetts; born in Dudley, Worcester County, Mass., May 24, 1841; attended the public schools; graduated from Amherst College, Amherst, Mass.; engaged in the manufacture of paper in Holyoke, Mass., in 1865; member of the Massachusetts senate in 1873; city treasurer of Holyoke in 1876 and 1877; mayor of Holyoke in 1878 and 1879; delegate to the Republican National Convention in 1876 and 1896; elected as a Republican to the Forty-eighth, Forty-ninth, and Fiftieth Congresses (March 4, 1883-March 3, 1889); was not a candidate for renomination in 1888; commissioner to the World's Exposition in Paris, France, in 1900; resumed his former manufacturing pursuits; died in Holyoke, Hampden County, Mass., January 9, 1911; interment in Forestdale Cemetery.

**WHITLEY, Charles Orville,** a Representative from North Carolina; born in Siler City, Chatham County, N.C., January 3, 1927; attended the public schools of Siler City; B.A., Wake Forest University, 1949, and LL.B., 1950; M.A., George Washington University, Washington, D.C., 1974; admitted to the North Carolina bar in 1950 and commenced practice in Mount Olive; served in the United States Army, 1944-1946; practiced law in Mount Olive, 1950-1960; served as Mount Olive city attorney from 1961 until 1967; administrative assistant to Representative David Henderson of North Carolina, 1961-1976; elected as a Democrat to the Ninety-fifth and to the four succeeding Congresses, and served from January 3, 1977 until his resignation on December 31, 1986; was not a candidate for reelection in 1986 to the One Hundredth Congress; is a resident of Mount Olive, N.C.

**WHITLEY, James Lucius,** a Representative from New York; born in Rochester, N.Y., May 24, 1872; attended the public schools; was graduated from the Rochester Free Academy and from the law department of Union University, Albany, N.Y., in 1898; during the Spanish-American War served as a sergeant in the Seventh Battery, United States Volunteers; was admitted to the bar in 1899 and commenced practice in Rochester, N.Y.; served as assistant corporation counsel, city of Rochester, in 1900 and 1901; chief examiner of the Civil Service Commission 1902-1904; member of the State assembly 1905-1910; served in the State senate 1918-1928; delegate to the Republican State conventions for twenty years; elected as a Republican to the Seventy-first, Seventy-second, and Seventy-third Congresses (March 4, 1929-January 3, 1935); unsuccessful candidate for reelection in 1934 to the Seventy-fourth Congress; returned to the practice of law; died in Rochester, N.Y., May 17, 1959; interment in Mount Hope Cemetery.

**WHITMAN, Ezekiel,** a Representative from Massachusetts and from Maine; born in East Bridgewater, Mass., March 9, 1776; graduated from Brown University, Providence, R.I., in 1795; studied law; admitted to the bar and practiced in New Gloucester, Maine (until 1820 a district of Massachusetts), 1799-1807 and in Portland, Maine, 1807-1852; unsuccessful candidate for election in 1806 to the Tenth Congress; elected as a Federalist from Massachusetts to the Eleventh Congress (March 4, 1809-March 3, 1811); member of the executive council in 1815 and 1816; elected to the Fifteenth and Sixteenth Congresses (March 4, 1817-March 3, 1821); delegate to the convention in 1819 that framed the first State constitution of Maine; elected to the Seventeenth Congress from Maine and served from March 4, 1821, to June 1, 1822, when he resigned; judge of the court of common pleas of Maine 1822-1841; unsuccessful candidate for election in 1838 to the Twenty-sixth Congress; served as chief justice of the Massachusetts Supreme Court 1841-1848; retired in 1852 and returned to East Bridgewater, Mass., where he died on August 1, 1866.

**Bibliography:** *DAB.*

**WHITMAN, Lemuel,** a Representative from Connecticut; born in Farmington, Conn., June 8, 1780; completed preparatory studies; was graduated from Yale College in 1800; taught in a seminary in Bermuda in 1801; studied law and was graduated from the Litchfield Law School; was admitted to the bar and commenced practice in Farmington; appointed judge of the superior court in 1818; associate judge of the Hartford County Court 1819-1821, and chief judge 1821-1823; one of a committee of three to prepare a revision of the statutes of the State in 1821; member of the State senate in 1822; elected to the Eighteenth Congress (March 4, 1823-March 3, 1825); resumed the practice of law; again a member of the State house of representatives in 1831 and 1832; died in Farmington, Conn., on November 13, 1841.

**WHITMORE, Elias,** a Representative from New York; born in Pembroke, N.H., March 2, 1772; completed preparatory studies; moved to New York and settled in Windsor; engaged in mercantile pursuits; elected to the Nineteenth Congress (March 4, 1825-March 3, 1827); resumed his former business pursuits in Windsor, N.Y., until his death in that city December 26, 1853; interment in the Village Cemetery.

**WHITMORE, George Washington,** a Representative from Texas; born in McMinn County, Tenn., on August 26, 1824; attended the public schools; moved to Texas in 1848; studied law; was admitted to the bar and practiced in Tyler, Smith County, Tex.; member of the State house of representatives in 1852, 1853, and 1858; district attorney for the ninth judicial district in 1866; appointed register in bankruptcy in 1867; upon the readmission of

Texas to representation was elected as a Republican to the Forty-first Congress and served from March 30, 1870, to March 3, 1871; unsuccessful candidate for reelection in 1870 to the Forty-second Congress; resumed the practice of law; died in Tyler, Tex., October 14, 1876; interment in Oakwood Cemetery.

**WHITNEY, Thomas Richard,** a Representative from New York; born in New York City May 2, 1807; pursued classical studies and engaged in newspaper work; member of the State assembly in 1854 and 1855; elected as the candidate of the American Party to the Thirty-fourth Congress (March 4, 1855-March 3, 1857); died in New York City April 12, 1858; interment in Greenwood Cemetery, Brooklyn, N.Y.

**WHITTAKER, Robert Russell,** a Representative from Kansas; born in Eureka, Greenwood County, Kans., September 18, 1939; attended the Greenwood County public schools; attended Kansas University, 1957-1959; attended Emporia (Kans.) State College (now Emporia State University) during the summer of 1959; O.D., Illinois College of Optometry, 1962; optometrist; clinic director, Kansas Low Vision Clinic, 1973; project director, Eyeglasses for the Poor, Montemoroles, Mexico; member, Kansas State house of representatives, 1974-1977; precinct committeeman and member of the Augusta, Kans., city planning commission, 1970-1974; elected as a Republican to the Ninety-sixth and to the five succeeding Congresses (January 3, 1979-January 3, 1991); was not a candidate for reelection in 1990 to the One Hundred Second Congress; is a resident of Augusta, Kans.

**WHITTEMORE, Benjamin Franklin,** a Representative from South Carolina; born in Malden, Middlesex County, Mass., May 18, 1824; attended the public schools of Worcester, and received an academic education at Amherst; engaged in mercantile pursuits until 1859; studied theology and became a minister in the Methodist Episcopal Church of the New England Conference in 1859; during the Civil War served as chaplain of the Fifty-third Regiment, Massachusetts Volunteers, and later with the Thirtieth Regiment, Veteran Volunteers; after the war settled in Darlington, S.C.; delegate to the State constitutional convention in 1867; elected president of the Republican State executive board in 1867; founded the New Era in Darlington; member of the State senate in 1868; delegate to the Republican National Convention in 1868; upon the readmission of South Carolina to representation was elected as a Republican to the Fortieth and Forty-first Congresses and served from July 18, 1868, to February 24, 1870, when he resigned, pending the investigation of his conduct in connection with certain appointments to the United States Military and Naval Academies; censured by the House of Representatives on February 24, 1870, following his resignation; presented credentials of a second election to the same Congress on June 18, 1870, but the House declined to allow him to take his seat; again a member of the State senate in 1877; resigned from the State senate and returned to Massachusetts, settling in Woburn; became a publisher; died in Montvale, Mass., on January 25, 1894; interment in the Salem Street Cemetery, Woburn, Mass.

**WHITTEN, Jamie Lloyd,** a Representative from Mississippi; born in Cascilla, Tallahatchie County, Miss., April 18, 1910; attended the public schools and the literary and law departments of the University of Mississippi at Oxford; was admitted to the bar in 1932 and commenced the practice of law in Charleston, Miss.; principal of the Cowart School in Tallahatchie County, Miss., in 1930 and 1931; member of the Mississippi State house of representatives in 1931 and 1932; elected district attorney of the seventeenth district of Mississippi, 1933-1941; elected as a Democrat to the Seventy-seventh Congress, November 4, 1941, by special election to fill the vacancy caused by the resignation of Wall Doxey; reelected to the twenty-six succeeding Congresses and served from November 4, 1941, to January 3, 1995; co-chairman, Joint Committee on Budget

Control (Ninety-second and Ninety-third Congresses); chairman, Committee on Appropriations (Ninety-sixth through One Hundred Second Congresses); was not a candidate for reelection in 1994 to the One Hundred Fourth Congress; retired from active pursuits; was a resident of Charleston, Miss., until his death in Oxford, Miss., on September 9, 1995.

**WHITTHORNE, Washington Curran,** a Representative and a Senator from Tennessee; born near Farmington, Marshall County, Tenn., April 19, 1825; attended the common schools, an academy in Arrington, Williamson County, and Campbell Academy, Lebanon, Tenn.; graduated from the University of Tennessee at Knoxville in 1843; studied law and was admitted to the bar in 1845 at Columbia, Maury County, Tenn.; served as auditor's clerk and in other local government positions until 1848, when he commenced the practice of law in Columbia, Tenn.; member, State senate 1855-1858; member, State house of representatives, and speaker in 1859; presidential elector on the John C. Breckinridge and Lane ticket in 1860; during the Civil War served as assistant adjutant general in the provisional army of Tennessee in 1861 and in the Confederate service as adjutant general of the State 1861-1865; his political disabilities were removed by act of Congress in 1870; elected as a Democrat to the Forty-second and to the five succeeding Congresses (March 4, 1871-March 3, 1883); chairman, Committee on Naval Affairs (Forty-fourth through Forty-sixth Congresses); appointed and subsequently elected as a Democrat to the United States Senate to fill the vacancy caused by the resignation of Howell E. Jackson and served from April 16, 1886, to March 3, 1887; elected to the Fiftieth and Fifty-first Congresses (March 4, 1887-March 3, 1891); died in Columbia, Tenn., September 21, 1891; interment in Rose Hill Cemetery.

**WHITTINGTON, William Madison,** a Representative from Mississippi; born in Little Springs, Franklin County, Miss., May 4, 1878; attended the public schools of Franklin County; was graduated from Mississippi College at Clinton in 1898 and from the law department of the University of Mississippi at Oxford in 1899; was admitted to the bar in 1899 and commenced practice in Roxie, Franklin County, Miss., January 1, 1901; in January 1904 moved to Greenwood, Miss., where he continued the practice of law and also engaged in agricultural pursuits; member of the city council, Greenwood, Miss., from January 1, 1907, to January 1, 1911; member of the State senate from January 1, 1916, to January 1, 1920; reelected in 1923 for a four-year term and served from January 1 to August 16, 1924, when he resigned to accept the Democratic nomination for Representative in Congress; delegate to the Democratic National Conventions in 1920, 1928, 1936, 1940, and 1948; elected as a Democrat to the Sixty-ninth and to the twelve succeeding Congresses (March 4, 1925-January 3, 1951); chairman, Committee on Flood Control (Seventy-fifth through Seventy-ninth Congresses), Committee on Public Works (Eighty-first Congress); was not a candidate for renomination in 1950; resumed the practice of law; was a resident of Greenwood, Miss., until his death August 20, 1962; interment in Odd Fellows Cemetery.

**WHITTLESEY, Elisha** (uncle of William Augustus Whittlesey and cousin of Frederick Whittlesey and Thomas Tucker Whittlesey), a Representative from Ohio; born in Washington, Conn., October 19, 1783; in early youth moved with his parents to Salisbury, Conn.; attended the common schools at Danbury, Conn.; studied law in Danbury; was admitted to the bar of Fairfield County and practiced in Danbury and Fairfield County; also practiced in New Milford, Conn., in 1805; moved to Canfield, Mahoning County, Ohio, in 1806; practiced law and taught school; prosecuting attorney of Mahoning County; served as military and private secretary to General William Henry Harrison, and as brigade major in the Army of the Northwest in the War of 1812; member of the Ohio State house of representatives in 1820 and 1821; elected to the Eighteenth through

Twenty-second Congresses, elected as an Anti-Masonic candidate to the Twenty-third Congress, and elected as a Whig to the Twenty-fourth and Twenty-fifth Congresses and served from March 4, 1823, to July 9, 1838, when he resigned; chairman, Committee on Claims (Twenty-first through Twenty-fifth Congresses); Sixth Auditor of the Treasury from March 18, 1841, until December 18, 1843, when he resigned and resumed the practice of law in Canfield; appointed general agent of the Washington Monument Association in 1847; appointed by President Zachary Taylor as First Comptroller of the Treasury and served from May 31, 1849, to March 26, 1857, when he was removed by President James Buchanan; was reappointed by President Lincoln on April 10, 1861, and served until his death in Washington, D.C., January 7, 1863; interment in the Canfield Village Cemetery, Canfield, Mahoning County, Ohio.

**Bibliography:** Davison, Kenneth E. "Forgotten Ohioan: Elisha Whittlesey, 1783-1863." Ph.D. dissertation, Western Reserve University, 1953.

**WHITTLESEY, Frederick** (cousin of Elisha Whittlesey and Thomas Tucker Whittlesey), a Representative from New York; born in New Preston, Conn., June 12, 1799; pursued academic studies; was graduated from Yale College in 1818; studied law; was admitted to the bar in Utica, N.Y., in 1821 and commenced practice in Cooperstown, N.Y., early in 1822; later in the year moved to Rochester, N.Y.; treasurer of Monroe County in 1829 and 1830; elected as an Anti-Masonic candidate to the Twenty-second and Twenty-third Congresses (March 4, 1831-March 3, 1835); chairman, Committee on Expenditures in the Department of War (Twenty-third Congress); resumed the practice of law; city attorney of Rochester in 1838; vice chancellor of the eighth judicial district of New York 1839-1847; justice of the State supreme court in 1847 and 1848; professor of law at Genesee College in 1850 and 1851; died in Rochester, N.Y., September 19, 1851; interment in Mount Hope Cemetery.

**WHITTLESEY, Thomas Tucker** (cousin of Elisha Whittlesey and Frederick Whittlesey), a Representative from Connecticut; born in Danbury, Conn., December 8, 1798; attended the public schools and was graduated from Yale College in 1817; attended Litchfield Law School; was admitted to the bar in 1818 and commenced practice in Danbury, Conn.; served as probate judge; elected as a Jacksonian to the Twenty-fourth Congress to fill the vacancy caused by the death of Zalmon Wildman; reelected as a Democrat to the Twenty-fifth Congress and served from April 29, 1836, to March 3, 1839; unsuccessful candidate for reelection in 1838 to the Twenty-sixth Congress; moved to Pheasant Branch, near Madison, Wis., in 1846; resumed the practice of law and also engaged in agricultural pursuits; member of the State senate in 1853 and 1854; died at Pheasant Branch, Dane County, Wis., August 20, 1868; interment in Forest Hill Cemetery, Madison, Wis.

**WHITTLESEY, William Augustus** (nephew of Elisha Whittlesey), a Representative from Ohio; born in Danbury, Conn., July 14, 1796; attended the common schools and was graduated from Yale College in 1816; taught school; moved to Canfield, Ohio, in 1818; studied law; was admitted to the bar in 1821 and commenced practice in Canfield; moved to Marietta, Ohio, in 1821; auditor of Washington County 1825-1837; member of the State house of representatives in 1839 and 1840; elected as a Democrat to the Thirty-first Congress (March 4, 1849-March 3, 1851); did not seek renomination in 1850; resumed the practice of law; mayor of Marietta in 1856, 1860, and 1862; died in Brooklyn, N.Y., where he had gone for medical treatment, on November 6, 1866; interment in Mound Cemetery, Marietta, Ohio.

**WHYTE, William Pinkney,** a Senator from Maryland; born in Baltimore, Md., August 9, 1824; was instructed by a private teacher and attended Baltimore College; engaged in banking in Baltimore, 1842-1844; studied law in Baltimore and attended the law school of

Harvard University, 1844-1845; was admitted to the bar in 1846 and practiced in Baltimore; member, Maryland State house of delegates, 1847-1848; unsuccessful candidate for election in 1850 to the Thirty-second Congress; comptroller of the treasury of Maryland, 1853-1855; appointed as a Democrat to the United States Senate to fill the vacancy caused by the resignation of Reverdy Johnson, and served from July 13, 1868 to March 3, 1869; was not a candidate for renomination in 1868; elected Governor of Maryland in 1871, and served from January 10, 1872 until March 4, 1874, when he resigned, having been elected Senator; counsel for Maryland before the arbitration board in the boundary dispute between Virginia and Maryland in 1874; elected as a Democrat to the United States Senate, and served from March 4, 1875 to March 3, 1881; unsuccessful candidate for reelection in 1880; chairman, Committee on Printing (Forty-sixth Congress); mayor of Baltimore, 1881-1882; attorney general of Maryland, 1887-1891; Baltimore city solicitor, 1900-1903; appointed and subsequently elected to the United States Senate to fill the vacancy caused by the death of Arthur Pue Gorman, and served from June 8, 1906 until his death in Baltimore, Md., March 17, 1908; interment in Greenmount Cemetery.

**WICK, William Watson,** a Representative from Indiana; born in Canonsburg, Washington County, Pa., February 23, 1796; moved with his parents to Western Reserve in 1800; completed preparatory studies; moved to Cincinnati, Ohio, in 1816; taught school; studied medicine until 1818 and then law; was admitted to the bar in Franklin, Johnson County, Ind., in 1819 and commenced practice in Connersville, Fayette County, Ind., in 1820; clerk of the State house of representatives 1820; assistant clerk of the State senate 1821; president judge of the fifth judicial State circuit 1822-1825; secretary of state 1825-1829; prosecuting attorney of the fifth judicial circuit 1829-1831; again president judge 1834-1837; elected as a Democrat to the Twenty-sixth Congress (March 4, 1839-March 3, 1841); unsuccessful candidate for reelection in 1840 to the Twenty-seventh Congress; resumed the practice of law in Indianapolis; elected to the Twenty-ninth and Thirtieth Congresses (March 4, 1845-March 3, 1849); was not a candidate for renomination; president judge for a third time, serving from 1850 to 1853; postmaster of Indianapolis, Ind., from April 9, 1853, to April 6, 1857; adjutant general in the State militia; moved to Franklin, Ind., in 1857, where he continued the practice of law, and died there May 19, 1868; interment in Greenlawn Cemetery.

**WICKER, Roger F.,** a Representative from Mississippi; born in Pontotoc, Miss., July 5, 1951; graduated, Pontotoc High School; B.A., University of Mississippi, 1973; J.D., University of Mississippi School of Law, 1975; served in the United States Air Force as judge advocate, 1976-1980, and in the United States Air Force Reserve from 1980 to present; House Committee on Rules staff counsel to Representative Trent Lott, 1980-1982; practiced law in Tupelo, Miss., 1980-1995; Tupelo City judge pro tem; Lee County public defender; member, Mississippi State senate, 1988-1994; elected as a Republican to the One Hundred Fourth Congress (January 3, 1995-January 3, 1997); is a resident of Tupelo, Miss.

**WICKERSHAM, James,** a Delegate from the Territory of Alaska; born in Patoka, Marion County, Ill., August 24, 1857; attended the common schools; studied law; was admitted to the bar in 1880 and commenced practice in Springfield, Sangamon County, Ill.; served in the Governor's guards, Springfield Militia; moved to Washington Territory in 1883; probate judge of Pierce County, Wash., 1884-1888; city attorney of Tacoma, Wash., in 1894; member of the Washington State house of representatives in 1898; moved to Eagle, Alaska, when he was appointed United States district judge for the Territory of Alaska in 1900; moved to Nome in 1901, to Valdez in 1902, and to Fairbanks in 1903; served as district judge until January 1908, when he resigned to run for Congress; elected as a Republican to the Sixty-first and to the three succeeding

Congresses (March 4, 1909-March 3, 1917); successfully contested the election of Charles A. Sulzer to the Sixty-fifth Congress, and served from January 7 to March 3, 1919; successfully contested the election of Charles A. Sulzer to the Sixty-sixth Congress, and served from March 1 to March 3, 1921, succeeding George B. Grigsby, who had qualified on credentials of a special election held to fill the vacancy caused by the death of Mr. Sulzer, which occurred on April 28, 1919, while the contest was pending; was not a candidate for renomination in 1920 to the Sixty-seventh Congress; moved to Juneau, Alaska, in 1921 and resumed the practice of law; elected to the Seventy-second Congress (March 4, 1931-March 3, 1933); unsuccessful candidate for reelection in 1932 to the Seventy-third Congress; continued the practice of law in Juneau, Alaska; writer on ethnological and historical subjects; editor of Alaska Territory Law Reports, and of Old Yukon and Alaskan literature; died in Juneau, Alaska, October 24, 1939; remains were cremated and the ashes deposited in Old Tacoma Cemetery, Tacoma, Wash.

**Bibliography:** Atwood, Evangeline. *Frontier Politics: Alaska's James Wickersham*. Portland, Ore.: Binford and Mort, 1979.

**WICKERSHAM, Victor Eugene,** a Representative from Oklahoma; born on a farm near Lone Rock, Baxter County, Ark., February 9, 1906; moved to Mangum, Greer County, Okla., with his parents in 1915; educated in the public schools of Oklahoma; employed in the office of the county clerk of Greer County, Okla., 1924-1926; Greer County clerk, 1926-1935; chief clerk, Oklahoma State board of affairs, 1935-1936; engaged as a building contractor in Oklahoma City, 1937-1938, and in the life insurance business, 1938-1941; elected as a Democrat to the Seventy-seventh Congress to fill the vacancy caused by the death of Sam C. Massingale; reelected to the Seventy-eight and Seventy-ninth Congresses, and served from April 1, 1941 to January 3, 1947; unsuccessful candidate for renomination in 1946 to the Eightieth Congress; elected to the Eighty-first and to the three succeeding Congresses (January 3, 1949-January 3, 1957); unsuccessful candidate for renomination in 1956 to the Eighty-fifth Congress, and for nomination in 1958 to the Eighty-sixth Congress; elected to the Eighty-seventh and to the Eighty-eighth Congresses (January 3, 1961-January 3, 1965); unsuccessful candidate for renomination in 1964 to the Eighty-ninth Congress; real estate, insurance, and investment broker; member, Oklahoma State legislature, January 3, 1971 to January 3, 1979, and again from February 9, 1988 until his death in Oklahoma City, Okla., on March 15, 1988.

**WICKES, Eliphalet,** a Representative from New York; born in Huntington, Long Island, N.Y., April 1, 1769; during the Revolution was employed as an express rider; studied law; was admitted to the bar and commenced practice in Jamaica, Long Island, N.Y.; elected as a Republican to the Ninth Congress (March 4, 1805-March 3, 1807); appointed July 1, 1797, the first postmaster of Jamaica, Long Island, N.Y., and served until April 1, 1806; reappointed January 1, 1807, and served until April 27, 1835; district attorney of Queens County 1818-1821; master in chancery; died in Troy, N.Y., on June 7, 1850; interment in Oakwood Cemetery.

**WICKHAM, Charles Preston,** a Representative from Ohio; born in Norwalk, Huron County, Ohio, September 15, 1836; attended the public schools and the Norwalk Academy; learned the printer's trade; was graduated from the Cincinnati Law School; admitted to the bar in 1858 and practiced in Norwalk, Ohio; enlisted as a private in Company D, Fifty-fifth Regiment, Ohio Volunteers, in September 1861 and was mustered out of the service July 11, 1865; was commissioned lieutenant colonel by brevet; resumed the practice of law in Norwalk in 1865; prosecuting attorney 1866-1870; elected judge of the court of common pleas of the fourth judicial district in 1880 and 1885; resigned in 1886; elected as a Republican to the Fiftieth and Fifty-first Congresses (March 4, 1887-March 3, 1891); chairman, Committee on Coinage, Weights, and Measures

(Fifty-first Congress); unsuccessful candidate for renomination; resumed the practice of law; died in Norwalk, Ohio, March 18, 1925; interment in Woodlawn Cemetery.

**WICKLIFFE, Charles Anderson** (grandfather of Robert Charles Wickliffe and John Crepps Wickliffe Beckham), a Representative from Kentucky; born near Springfield, Washington County, Ky., June 8, 1788; completed preparatory studies; studied law; admitted to the bar in 1809 and commenced practice in Bardstown; served in the War of 1812; was aide to General Winlock; member of the Kentucky house of representatives in 1812 and 1813; again entered the Army as aide to General Caldwell; again a member of the Kentucky house of representatives in 1822, 1823, and 1833-1835, and served as speaker in 1834; elected to the Eighteenth Congress; reelected to the Nineteenth Congress and reelected as a Jacksonian to the Twentieth through Twenty-second Congresses (March 4, 1823-March 3, 1833); chairman, Committee on Public Lands (Twenty-first and Twenty-second Congresses); was not a candidate for renomination in 1832 to the Twenty-third Congress; one of the managers appointed by the House of Representatives in 1830 to conduct the impeachment proceedings against James H. Peck, United States judge for the district of Missouri; Lieutenant Governor in 1836; became Governor of Kentucky upon the death of Governor James Clark and served from October 5, 1839 to June 1, 1840; Postmaster General in the Cabinet of President John Tyler from October 13, 1841 to March 6, 1845; sent on a secret mission by President James K. Polk to the Republic of Texas in 1845; member of the Kentucky constitutional convention in 1849; member of the peace conference held at Washington, D.C., in 1861 in an effort to devise means to prevent the impending war; elected as a Unionist to the Thirty-seventh Congress (March 4, 1861-March 3, 1863); was not a candidate for renomination in 1862 to the Thirty-eighth Congress; unsuccessful candidate for Governor in 1863; delegate to the Democratic National Convention of 1864; died near Ilchester, Md., October 31, 1869; interment in Bardstown Cemetery, Bardstown, Ky.

**Bibliography:** *DAB.*

**WICKLIFFE, Robert Charles** (grandson of Charles Anderson Wickliffe and cousin of John Crepps Wickliffe Beckham), a Representative from Louisiana; born in Bardstown, Ky., May 1, 1874, while his parents were on a visit to relatives in that State; attended the public schools of St. Francisville, La.; was graduated from Centre College, Danville, Ky., in 1895 and from the law department of Tulane University, New Orleans, La., in 1897; was admitted to the bar in 1898 and commenced practice in St. Francisville, La.; member of the State constitutional convention in 1898; enlisted as a private in Company E, First Regiment, Louisiana Volunteer Infantry, during the Spanish-American War; was mustered out of the service in October 1898; returned to West Feliciana Parish; district attorney of the twenty-fourth judicial district of Louisiana 1902-1906; elected as a Democrat to the Sixty-first and Sixty-second Congresses and served from March 4, 1909, until June 11, 1912, when he was killed while crossing a railroad bridge in Washington, D.C.; interment in Cave Hill Cemetery, Louisville, Ky.

**WIDGERY, William,** a Representative from Massachusetts; probably born in Devonshire, England, about 1753; immigrated to America with his parents, who settled in Philadelphia; attended the common schools; engaged in shipbuilding; served in the Revolutionary War as a lieutenant on a privateer; studied law; admitted to the bar and commenced practice in Portland, Maine (until 1820 a district of Massachusetts), about 1790; member of the Massachusetts house of representatives 1787-1793 and 1795-1797; delegate to the Massachusetts constitutional convention in 1788; served in the Massachusetts senate in 1794; member of the executive council in 1806 and 1807; elected as a Republican to the Twelfth Congress (March 4, 1811-March 3, 1813); unsuccessful for reelection in 1812

to the Thirteenth Congress; judge of the court of common pleas 1813-1821; died in Portland, Maine, July 31, 1822; interment in the Eastern Cemetery.

**WIDNALL, William Beck,** a Representative from New Jersey; born in Hackensack, Bergen County, N.J., March 17, 1906; attended the public schools; Brown University, Providence, R.I., Ph.B., 1926 and from the New Jersey Law School (now part of Rutgers University), LL.B., 1931; was admitted to the bar in 1932 and commenced the practice of law in Hackensack, N.J.; member of the State house of assembly 1946-1950; delegate, Republican National Convention, 1968; elected as a Republican to the Eighty-first Congress, by special election, February 6, 1950, to fill the vacancy caused by the resignation of J. Parnell Thomas; reelected to the twelve succeeding Congresses and served from February 6, 1950, until his resignation December 31, 1974; unsuccessful candidate for reelection in 1974 to the Ninety-fourth Congress; chairperson of the National Commission on Electronic Fund Transfers from November 1975 to 1981; was a resident of Ridgewood, N.J., until his death there December 28, 1983; interment in Gate of Heaven Cemetery, Hawthorne, N.Y.

**WIER, Roy William,** a Representative from Minnesota; born in Redfield, Spink County, S.Dak., February 25, 1888; moved with his parents in 1896 to Minneapolis, Hennepin County, Minn.; attended the public schools and North High School; learned the telephone and electrical trade, later going into theatrical stage-lighting work; during the First World War served in the United States Army for eighteen months, with overseas service; in 1920 became active in the trade-union movement in Minneapolis and had been officially a representative of the Trades and Labor Assembly of Minneapolis; member of the State house of representatives 1933-1939; member of the Minneapolis Board of Education 1939-1948 and the board of directors of Hennepin County Red Cross; elected as a Democrat to the Eighty-first and to the five succeeding Congresses (January 3, 1949-January 3, 1961); unsuccessful candidate for reelection in 1960 to the Eighty-seventh Congress; was a resident of Minneapolis, Minn., until May 1962, when he moved to Edmonds, Wash.; died in Seattle, Wash., June 27, 1963; remains were cremated and the ashes deposited in the columbarium of Evergreen Washelli Cemetery.

**WIGFALL, Louis Trezevant,** a Senator from Texas; was born near Edgefield, Edgefield District, S.C., April 21, 1816; pursued classical studies; attended the University of Virginia and graduated from South Carolina College (now the University of South Carolina) at Columbia in 1837; served as a lieutenant of Volunteers in the Seminole War in Florida in 1835; attended the law department of the University of Virginia at Charlottesville; was admitted to the bar in 1839 and commenced practice in Edgefield, S.C.; moved to Marshall, Tex., in 1848; member, Texas State house of representatives, 1849-1850; member, State senate, 1857-1860; elected as a Democrat to the United States Senate to fill the vacancy caused by the death of J. Pinckney Henderson, and served from December 5, 1859 until March 23, 1861, when he withdrew; expelled from the Senate by a resolution of July 11, 1861 for support of the Confederacy; commissioned a brigadier general in the Confederate Army on October 21, 1861, and served until his resignation February 20, 1862, having been elected to the Confederate Congress; after the war moved to London, England; returned to the United States in 1873 and settled in Baltimore, Md.; died in Galveston, Tex., February 18, 1874; interment in the Episcopal Cemetery.

**Bibliography:** *DAB*; King, Alvy. *Louis T. Wigfall: Southern Fire-Eater.* Baton Rouge: Louisiana State University Press, 1970; Ledbetter, Billy. "The Election of Louis T. Wigfall to the United States Senate, 1859: A Reevaluation." *Southwestern Historical Quarterly* 77 (October 1973): 241-54.

**WIGGINS, Charles Edward,** a Representative from California; born in El Monte, Los Angeles County, Calif., December 3, 1927; attended the public schools in El Monte, Calif.; served in the United States Army, Infantry, 1945-1948, and 1950-1952, with thirty-two months overseas during the Second World War and Korea; B.S., University of Southern California, 1953; LL.B., University of Southern California School of Law, 1956; admitted to the bar and commenced practice in El Monte, Calif., in 1957; member and chairman of the El Monte Planning Commission, 1954-1960; councilman and mayor of El Monte, Calif., 1960-1966; member of the California State Republican Central committee, and elected to the Los Angeles County Republican Central committee; elected as a Republican to the Ninetieth and to the five succeeding Congesses (January 3, 1967-January 3, 1979); was not a candidate for reelection in 1978 to the Ninety-sixth Congress; appointed judge, United States Court of Appeals, Ninth Circuit, October 11, 1984; is a resident of Reno, Nev.

**WIGGINTON, Peter Dinwiddie,** a Representative from California; born in Springfield, Sangamon County, Ill., September 6, 1839; moved to Wisconsin with his parents in 1843; completed preparatory studies and attended the University of Wisconsin at Madison; studied law; was admitted to the bar in 1859 and practiced; editor of the Dodgeville (Wis.) Advocate; moved to Snelling, Merced County, Calif., in 1862, and continued the practice of law; district attorney of Merced County 1864-1868; elected as a Democrat to the Forty-fourth Congress (March 4, 1875-March 3, 1877); successfully contested the election of Romualdo Pacheco to the Forty-ninth Congress and served from February 7, 1878, to March 3, 1879; settled in San Francisco in 1880 and resumed the practice of law; nominated by the American Party as candidate for Vice President in 1888 in place of James R. Geer; died in Oakland, Calif., July 7, 1890; interment in Mountain View Cemetery.

**WIGGLESWORTH, Richard Bowditch,** a Representative from Massachusetts; born in Boston, Mass., April 25, 1891; was graduated from Milton Academy, Milton, Mass., in 1908, from Harvard University in 1912, and from the law department of the same university in 1916; assistant private secretary to the Governor General of the Philippine Islands in 1913; admitted to the bar in 1916 and commenced practice in Boston, Mass.; during the First World War served overseas as captain, Battery E, and as commanding officer, First Battalion, Three Hundred and Third Field Artillery, Seventy-sixth Division, 1917-1919; legal adviser to the Assistant Secretary of the Treasury in charge of foreign loans and railway payments, and secretary of the World War Debt Commission, 1922-1924; assistant to the agent general for reparation payments, Berlin, Germany, 1924-1927; general counsel and Paris representative for organizations created under the Dawes plan in 1927 and 1928; elected as a Republican to the Seventieth Congress to fill the vacancy caused by the death of Louis A. Frothingham; reelected to the Seventy-first and to the fourteen succeeding Congresses and served from November 6, 1928, until his resignation November 13, 1958; was not a candidate for renomination in 1958 to the Eighty-sixth Congress; appointed by President Dwight D. Eisenhower as Ambassador to Canada on October 29, 1958, and served until his death in Boston, Mass., October 22, 1960; interment in Arlington National Cemetery, Va.

**Bibliography:** Weeks, Sinclair. *Richard Bowditch Wigglesworth: Way-Stations of a Fruitful Life.* N.p.: The author, 1964.

**WIKE, Scott,** a Representative from Illinois; born in Meadville, Pa., April 6, 1834; moved with his parents to Quincy, Ill., in 1838 and to Pike County in 1844; was graduated from Lombard University, in Galesburg, in 1857; studied law; admitted to the bar in 1858; was graduated from Harvard Law School in 1859 and commenced practice the same year in Pittsfield, Pike County, Ill.; member of the Illinois State house of representatives, 1863-1867;

elected as a Democrat to the Forty-fourth Congress (March 4, 1875-March 3, 1877); unsuccessful candidate for renomination in 1876 to the Forty-fifth Congress; elected to the Fifty-first and Fifty-second Congresses (March 4, 1889-March 3, 1893); unsuccessful candidate for renomination in 1892 to the Fifty-third Congress; appointed an Assistant Secretary of the Treasury during the second administration of President Grover Cleveland, and served from July 1, 1893 to May 4, 1897; resumed the practice of law in Pittsfield, Ill.; died near Barry, Pike County, Ill., January 15, 1901.

**WILBER, David** (father of David Forrest Wilber), a Representative from New York; born near Quaker Street, Schenectady County, N.Y., October 5, 1820; moved with his parents to Milford, Otsego County, N.Y.; attended the common schools; engaged in the lumbering trade, hop business, and agricultural pursuits; member of the board of supervisors of Otsego County in 1858, 1859, 1862, 1865, and 1866; director of the Albany & Susquehanna Railroad; director of the Second National Bank of Cooperstown, N.Y.; president of the Wilber National Bank of Oneonta 1874-1890; elected as a Republican to the Forty-third Congress (March 4, 1873-March 3, 1875); was not a candidate for renomination in 1874; elected to the Forty-sixth Congress (March 4, 1879-March 3, 1881); was not a candidate for renomination in 1880; delegate to the Republican National Conventions in 1880 and 1888; moved to Oneonta, N.Y., in 1886; again elected as a Republican to the Fiftieth Congress; reelected to the Fifty-first Congress, but owing to ill health took the oath of office at his home and never attended a session; served from March 4, 1887, until his death in Oneonta, Otsego County, N.Y., April 1, 1890; interment in Glenwood Cemetery.

**WILBER, David Forrest** (son of David Wilber), a Representative from New York; born in Milford, Otsego County, N.Y., December 7, 1859; attended the public schools; was graduated from Cazenovia (N.Y.) Seminary in 1879; engaged in the hop business at Milford in 1879 and at Oneonta, N.Y., in 1880; also interested in the real estate business, agricultural pursuits, and stock breeding; twice represented Oneonta on the board of supervisors; vice president and director on the Wilber National Bank of Oneonta 1883-1896; trustee of the Cazenovia Seminary; elected as a Republican to the Fifty-fourth and Fifty-fifth Congresses (March 4, 1895-March 3, 1899); was not a candidate for renomination in 1898; served as United States consul to Barbados 1903-1905; served as consul general to Singapore 1905-1907, Halifax 1907-1909, Kobe 1909-1910, Vancouver 1910-1913, Zurich 1913-1915, Genoa 1915-1921, and Auckland and Wellington 1922-1923; retired in June 1923 and returned to Oneonta, N.Y., to care for his business interests; member of the Republican State committee 1924-1927; died at his summer camp at Upper Dam, Oxford County, Maine, August 14, 1928; interment in Glenwood Cemetery, Oneonta, N.Y.

**WILBOUR, Isaac,** a Representative from Rhode Island; born in Little Compton, R.I., April 25, 1763; completed preparatory studies; studied law; was admitted to the bar in 1793 and practiced; also engaged in agricultural pursuits; held various local offices from 1793 to 1800; member of the Rhode Island State house of representatives in 1805 and 1806 and served as speaker the last year; Lieutenant Governor in 1806 and 1807 and Acting Governor in 1806; elected as a Republican to the Tenth Congress (March 4, 1807-March 3, 1809); unsuccessful candidate for reelection in 1808 to the Eleventh Congress and for election in 1812 to the Thirteenth Congress; in 1807 received a commission from Governor James Fenner, appointing him as his successor to the United States Senate for the remainder of the term ending March 3, 1811, which he declined; again Lieutenant Governor in 1810 and 1811; associate justice of the supreme court of Rhode Island in 1818 and chief justice from 1819 to 1827, when he resigned; died in Little Compton, R.I., on October 4, 1837; interment in the Seaconnet Cemetery.

**WILCOX, James Mark,** a Representative from Florida; born in Willacoochee, Atkinson County, Ga., May 21, 1890; attended the public schools and Emory College, Atlanta, Ga.; was graduated from the law department of Mercer University, Macon, Ga., in 1910; was admitted to the bar the same year and commenced practice in Hazelhurst, Ga.; solicitor of Jeff Davis County, Ga., 1911-1918; moved to Brunswick, Ga., in 1919 and to West Palm Beach, Fla., in 1925, continuing the practice of law; city attorney of West Palm Beach 1928-1933; a member of the taxation committee of President Hoover's Conference on Home Ownership in 1931; elected as a Democrat to the Seventy-third, Seventy-fourth, and Seventy-fifth Congresses (March 4, 1933-January 3, 1939); was not a candidate for renomination in 1938, but was an unsuccessful candidate for the Democratic nomination for United States Senator; resumed the practice of law in Miami, Fla.; attorney general for the Dade County Port Authority from 1945 until his death at his farm near White Springs, Fla., February 3, 1956; interment in Woodlawn Park Cemetery, Miami, Fla.

**WILCOX, Jeduthun** (father of Leonard Wilcox), a Representative from New Hampshire; born in Middletown, Conn., November 18, 1768; studied law; was admitted to the bar in 1802 and commenced practice in Orford, N.H.; member of the State house of representatives 1809-1811; elected as a Federalist to the Thirteenth and Fourteenth Congresses (March 4, 1813-March 3, 1817); died in Orford, Grafton County, N.H., July 18, 1838; interment in Orford Cemetery.

**WILCOX, John A.,** a Representative from Mississippi; born in Greene County, N.C., April 18, 1819; moved to Tennessee; attended the common schools; moved to Mississippi and settled in Aberdeen; secretary of the State senate; served in the Mexican War as lieutenant, adjutant, and lieutenant colonel; elected as a Unionist to the Thirty-second Congress (March 4, 1851-March 3, 1853); unsuccessful candidate for reelection in 1852 to the Thirty-third Congress; moved to Texas in 1853; member of the Confederate Congress; died in Richmond, Va., February 7, 1864; interment in Hollywood Cemetery.

**WILCOX, Leonard** (son of Jeduthun Wilcox), a Senator from New Hampshire; born in Hanover, N.H., January 29, 1799; graduated from Dartmouth College, Hanover, N.H., in 1817; studied law; was admitted to the bar in 1820 and commenced practice in Orford, Grafton County, N.H.; member, State house of representatives 1828-1834; judge of the superior court 1838-1840; bank commissioner 1838-1842; appointed as a Democrat to the United States Senate to fill the vacancy caused by the resignation of Franklin Pierce; subsequently elected and served from March 1, 1842, to March 3, 1843; resumed the practice of law; judge of the court of common pleas of New Hampshire 1847-1848; again appointed judge of the superior court in 1848, and served until his death in Orford, N.H., June 18, 1850; interment in the West Congregational Churchyard.

**WILCOX, Robert William,** a Delegate from the Territory of Hawaii; born in Kahalu, Honuaula, island of Maui, Hawaiian Islands, February 15, 1855; attended the Haleakala Boarding School, Makawao, island of Maui; taught school at Honuaula for several years; elected to the legislature as a representative from Wailukua, island of Maui, in 1880; later pursued an academic course in the Royal Military Academy, Turin, Italy, 1881-1885 and became a sublieutenant of artillery; entered the Royal Application School for Engineer and Artillery Officers in Turin in 1885; recalled by the Hawaiian Government in 1887; moved to San Francisco, Calif., in 1887 and engaged in the surveying business; returned to Hawaii in 1889 and became leader of the revolution of 1889; tried for treason but acquitted by a Hawaiian jury; elected to the legislature as a representative from Honolulu in 1890 and from Koolauloa, island of Oahu, in 1892; again a revolutionary leader in 1895 in an effort to restore Liliuokalani to the throne; was court-martialed and sentenced to death, but the sentence was commuted to thirty-five years; pardoned by President Sanford B. Dole of Hawaii in 1898; elected the first Delegate from Hawaii to the Fifty-sixth Congress; reelected to the Fifty-seventh Congress and served from November 6, 1900, to March 3, 1903; unsuccessful candidate for reelection in 1902 to the Fifty-eighth Congress; died in Honolulu, Hawaii, October 23, 1903; interment in the Catholic Cemetery.

**WILDE, Richard Henry,** a Representative from Georgia; born in Dublin, Ireland, September 24, 1789; immigrated to the United States in 1797 with his parents, who settled in Baltimore, Md.; received a limited schooling; moved to Augusta, Ga., in 1802; engaged in mercantile pursuits; studied law; was admitted to the bar in 1809 and commenced practice in Augusta; solicitor general of the superior court of Richmond County and by virtue of this office attorney general of Georgia 1811-1813; elected as a Republican to the Fourteenth Congress (March 4, 1815-March 3, 1817); unsuccessful candidate for reelection in 1816 to the Fifteenth Congress; elected to the Eighteenth Congress to fill the vacancy caused by the resignation of Thomas W. Cobb and served from February 7 to March 3, 1825; unsuccessful candidate for reelection in 1824 to the Nineteenth Congress and for election in 1826 to the Twentieth Congress; subsequently elected to the Twentieth Congress to fill the vacancy caused by the resignation of John Forsyth; reelected to the Twenty-first, Twenty-second, and Twenty-third Congresses and served from November 17, 1827, to March 3, 1835; unsuccessful candidate for reelection in 1834 to the Twenty-fourth Congress; engaged in literary pursuits while traveling in Europe 1835-1840; moved to New Orleans in 1843 and continued the practice of law; professor of constitutional law in the University of Louisiana at New Orleans; died in New Orleans, La., September 10, 1847; interment in a vault in a cemetery in New Orleans; reinterred at Sand Hill family burying ground near Augusta, Ga., in 1854 and again in 1886 in the City Cemetery, Augusta, Ga.

**Bibliography:** *DAB*; Tucker, E.L. *Richard Henry Wilde; His Life and Selected Poems.* Athens: University of Georgia Press, 1966.

**WILDER, Abel Carter,** a Representative from Kansas; born in Mendon, Worcester County, Mass., March 18, 1828; completed preparatory studies; engaged in mercantile pursuits; moved to Rochester, N.Y., and continued mercantile pursuits; moved to Leavenworth, Kans., in 1857 and again engaged in mercantile pursuits; delegate to the Osawatomie convention in 1859; delegate to the Republican National Convention in 1860 and elected its chairman; served as a captain in the Kansas brigade for one year in the Civil War; elected as a Republican to the Thirty-eighth Congress (March 4, 1863-March 3, 1865); delegate to the Republican National Conventions in 1864, 1868, and 1872; returned to Rochester, N.Y., in 1865 and published the Morning and Evening Express until 1868, when he retired from active business pursuits; elected mayor of Rochester in 1872, but resigned in 1873; died in San Francisco, Calif., December 22, 1875, while there for his health; interment in Mount Hope Cemetery, Rochester, N.Y.

**WILDER, William Henry,** a Representative from Massachusetts; born in Belfast, Waldo County, Maine, May 14, 1855; moved with his parents to Massachusetts in 1866; attended the common schools; engaged in the mercantile and manufacturing business at Gardner, Mass.; president of the Wilder Industries (Inc.); studied law; admitted to the bar in 1900; was admitted to practice before the United States Supreme Court in 1909; studied the monetary systems in Europe in 1909 and wrote many articles and pamphlets on monetary questions; elected as a Republican to the Sixty-second and Sixty-third Congresses and served from March 4, 1911, until his death in Washington, D.C., September 11, 1913; interment in Crystal Lake Cemetery, Gardner, Worcester County, Mass.

**WILDMAN, Zalmon,** a Representative from Connecticut; born in Danbury, Fairfield County, Conn., February 16, 1775; completed preparatory studies; manufacturer of hats; established the first hat stores in Charleston, S.C., and Savannah, Ga., in 1802; first president of Danbury National Bank 1824-1826; member of the State house of representatives in 1818 and 1819; appointed postmaster of Danbury, Conn., and served from April 9, 1805, to May 26, 1835; elected as a Jacksonian to the Twenty-fourth Congress and served from March 4, 1835, until his death in Washington, D.C., December 10, 1835; interment in Wooster Cemetery, Danbury, Conn.

**WILDRICK, Isaac,** a Representative from New Jersey; born in Marksboro, Warren County, N.J., March 3, 1803; attended the common schools; engaged in agricultural pursuits near Blairstown, Warren County, N.J.; constable from 1827 to 1832; coroner 1829-1831; justice of the peace 1834-1839; judge in 1839; sheriff 1839-1841; director of the county poorhouse 1842-1848; member freeholder 1845-1848; elected as a Democrat to the Thirty-first and Thirty-second Congresses (March 4, 1849-March 3, 1853); was not a candidate for renomination in 1852; resumed agricultural pursuits; again a freeholder 1856-1859; member of the State assembly 1882-1885; died in Blairstown, N.J., March 22, 1892; interment in the Presbyterian Cemetery, Marksboro, N.J.

**WILEY, Alexander,** a Senator from Wisconsin; born in Chippewa Falls, Chippewa County, Wis., May 26, 1884; attended the public schools, Augsburg College, Minneapolis, Minn., and the University of Michigan at Ann Arbor; graduated from the law department of the University of Wisconsin at Madison in 1907; was admitted to the bar the same year and commenced practice in Chippewa Falls, Wis.; district attorney of Chippewa County 1909-1915; unsuccessful Republican candidate for governor in 1936; engaged in agricultural pursuits and banking; elected as a Republican to the United States Senate in 1938; reelected in 1944, 1950, and again in 1956, and served from January 3, 1939, to January 3, 1963; unsuccessful candidate for reelection in 1962; chairman, Committee on the Judiciary (Eightieth Congress), Committee on Foreign Relations (Eighty-third Congress), resided in Washington, D.C., until a few days before his death, May 26, 1967, at High Oaks Christian Science Church Sanitarium in Germantown, Pa.; interment in Forest Hill Cemetery, Chippewa Falls, Wis.

Bibliography: Wiley, Alexander. *Laughing With Congress.* New York: Crown Publishers, 1947.

**WILEY, Ariosto Appling** (brother of Oliver Cicero Wiley), a Representative from Alabama; born in Clayton, Barbour County, Ala., November 6, 1848; moved with his parents to Troy, Pike County, Ala.; attended the common schools and was graduated from Emory and Henry College, Emory, Va., in 1870; studied law; was admitted to the bar in 1871 and commenced practice in Clayton, Ala.; moved to Montgomery, Ala., the same year and continued the practice of law; was captain of a Cavalry troop of the Alabama National Guard and later a lieutenant colonel commanding the Second Regiment of Infantry of the Alabama National Guard; member of the Alabama State house of representatives in 1884, 1885, 1888, 1889, 1896, and 1897; served in the Alabama State senate, 1890-1893, 1898, and 1899; appointed by President William McKinley on June 9, 1898, lieutenant colonel of the Fifth Regiment, United States Volunteer Infantry, and served during the Spanish-American War; legal adviser and chief of staff to General Henry W. Lawton in Santiago, Cuba, and assisted General Leonard Wood in the establishment of civil government in the eastern Province; delegate to the Democratic National Convention of 1888; elected as a Democrat to the Fifty-seventh and to the three succeeding Congresses and served from March 4, 1901, until his death at Hot Springs, Bath County, Va., June 17, 1908; interment in Oakwood Cemetery, Montgomery, Ala.

**WILEY, James Sullivan,** a Representative from Maine; born in Mercer, Somerset County, Maine, January 22, 1808; moved to Bethel, Oxford County, Maine, in 1826; attended Gould's Academy and was graduated from Colby College, Waterville, Maine, in 1836; moved to Dover, Maine, and was an instructor in Foxcroft Academy; studied law; was admitted to the Piscataquis County bar in 1839 and commenced practice in Dover; elected as a Democrat to the Thirtieth Congress (March 4, 1847-March 3, 1849); resumed the practice of law in Dover; moved to Fryeburg, Maine, in 1889 and continued the practice of law until his death in that city on December 21, 1891; interment in Smart Hill Cemetery.

**WILEY, John McClure,** a Representative from New York; born in Londonderry, Ireland, August 11, 1846; immigrated to the United States in 1850 with his parents, who settled in Erie County, N.Y.; attended the common schools; engaged in mercantile pursuits and the real estate business in Colden, N.Y.; member of the New York State assembly in 1871 and 1872; delegate to the Democratic National Conventions of 1884, 1888, and 1892; elected as a Democrat to the Fifty-first Congress (March 4, 1889-March 3, 1891); declined to be a candidate for renomination in 1890 to the Fifty-second Congress; appointed consul at Bordeaux, France, by President Grover Cleveland on April 24, 1893, and served until July 31, 1897; resided in Jacksonville, Fla., during the winter and in Colden, N.Y., during the summer months; died in St. Catharines, Ontario, Canada, August 13, 1912; interment in Crown Hill Cemetery, Indianapolis, Ind.

**WILEY, Oliver Cicero** (brother of Ariosto Appling Wiley), a Representative from Alabama; born in Troy, Pike County, Ala., January 30, 1851; attended the common schools; member of the town council for five years; chairman of the Democratic executive committee of Pike County 1884-1886; member of the Democratic State executive committee in 1888; was president of the Alabama Midland Railway during its construction, from 1887 to 1892; president of the board of directors of the State normal college at Troy, Ala.; director of the Farmers & Merchants' National Bank at Troy; vice president and general manager of the Standard Chemical & Oil Co. at Troy; elected as a Democrat to the Sixtieth Congress to fill the vacancy caused by the death of his brother, Ariosto Appling Wiley, and served from November 3, 1908, to March 3, 1909; died in Troy; Ala., October 18, 1917; interment in Oakwood Cemetery.

**WILEY, William Halsted,** a Representative from New Jersey; born in New York City July 10, 1842; attended private schools; was graduated from the College of the City of New York in 1861; entered the Union Army in 1860 as a member of the Seventh New York Volunteers; was promoted to first lieutenant of Volunteers in 1862, and mustered out with the rank of brevet major in 1864 by the consolidation of his regiment; was graduated from the Rensselaer Polytechnic Institute, Troy, N.Y., in 1866; attended the Columbia College School of Mines in 1868; engaged in civil engineering and also as a superintendent of a mine for several years; member of the township committee of East Orange, N.J., 1886-1888, and served as president for one year; in 1897 was president of one of the juries at the International Exposition in Brussels and a member of the superior jury; appointed by Governor Franklin Murphy of New Jersey as a member of the commission for the Louisiana Purchase Exposition at St. Louis, Mo., in 1904; elected as a Republican to the Fifty-eighth and Fifty-ninth Congresses (March 4, 1903-March 3, 1907); was an unsuccessful candidate for renomination in 1906 to the Sixtieth Congress; elected to the Sixty-first Congress (March 4, 1909-March 3, 1911); unsuccessful candidate for reelection in 1910 to the Sixty-second Congress; a publisher in New York City, with residence in East Orange, N.J.; during the First World War served as the representative of the American Society of Mechanical Engineers on the National Preparedness Committee and became its chairman; died in East Orange, N.J., May 2, 1925; interment in Rosedale Cemetery.

**WILFLEY, Xenophon Pierce,** a Senator from Missouri; born near Mexico, Audrain County, Mo., March 18, 1871; attended the country schools; graduated from Clarksburg College in 1891 and from Central College, at Fayette, in 1894; taught in Central College one year and in Sedalia High School for three years; graduated from the Washington University Law School at St. Louis, Mo., in 1899 and commenced practice in that city; chairman of the board of election commissioners of St. Louis 1917-1918; appointed as a Democrat to the United States Senate to fill the vacancy caused by the death of William J. Stone and served from April 30, to November 5, 1918, when a successor was elected; unsuccessful candidate for the nomination to fill the vacancy in 1918; chairman, Committee on Industrial Expositions (Sixty-fifth Congress); resumed the practice of his profession; president of the Missouri Bar Association in 1925; died in St. Louis, Mo., May 4, 1931; interment in Oak Grove Cemetery.

**WILKIN, James Whitney** (father of Samuel Jones Wilkin) a Representative from New York; born in Wallkill, Orange (now Ulster) County, N.Y., in 1762; served in the Revolutionary War; was graduated from Princeton College in 1785; studied law; was admitted to the bar in 1788 and began practice in Goshen, N.Y.; member of the State assembly in 1800; entered the State militia and rose through successive grades to the rank of major general; served in the State senate 1801-1804 and 1811-1814; member of the State assembly in 1808 and 1809, and served as speaker in the latter year; member of the council of appointment in 1802, 1811, and 1813; elected as a Republican to the Fourteenth Congress to fill the vacancy caused by the resignation of Jonathan Fisk; reelected to the Fifteenth Congress and served from June 7, 1815, to March 3, 1819; unsuccessful candidate for United States Senator in 1815; county clerk of Orange County 1819-1821; county treasurer for several years; died in Goshen, N.Y., February 23, 1845; interment in Slate Hill Cemetery.

**WILKIN, Samuel Jones** (son of James Whitney Wilkin), a Representative from New York; born in Goshen, Orange County, N.Y., December 17, 1793; was graduated from Princeton College in 1812; studied law; was admitted to the bar in 1815 and began practice in Goshen; member of the State assembly in 1824 and 1825; elected as an Anti-Jacksonian to the Twenty-second Congress (March 4, 1831-March 3, 1833); unsuccessful Whig candidate for election in 1844 as Lieutenant Governor of New York; member of the State senate in 1848 and 1849; canal appraiser in 1850; died in Goshen, N.Y., March 11, 1866; interment in Slate Hill Cemetery.

**WILKINS, Beriah,** a Representative from Ohio; born near Richwood, Union County, Ohio, July 10, 1846; attended the common schools of Marysville, Ohio; enlisted as a private in Company H, One Hundred and Thirty-sixth Regiment, Ohio Volunteer Infantry, May 2, 1864, and served until honorably discharged on August 31, 1864; engaged in banking in Uhrichsville, Tuscarawas County, Ohio; member of the Ohio State senate 1880 and 1881; member of the Democratic State central committee in 1882; elected as a Democrat to the Forty-eighth and to the two succeeding Congresses (March 4, 1883-March 3, 1889); chairman, Committee on Banking and Currency (Fiftieth Congress); settled in Washington, D.C.; became majority owner and publisher of the Washington Post in 1889, and in 1894 acquired the entire stock ownership of the newspaper, serving as editor until his death in Washington, D.C., June 7, 1905; interment in Rock Creek Cemetery.

**WILKINS, William,** a Senator and a Representative from Pennsylvania; born in Carlisle, Pa., December 20, 1779; attended Dickinson College, Carlisle, Pa.; studied law; was admitted to the bar in 1801 and commenced practice in Pittsburgh, Pa.; assisted in organizing the Pittsburgh Manufacturing Co. in 1810; first president of the Bank of Pittsburgh; president of the common council, 1816-1819; member of the Pennsylvania house of representatives in 1820; judge of the fifth judicial district of Pennsylvania, 1821-1824; judge of the United States District Court for western Pennsylvania, 1824-1831; unsuccessful candidate for election in 1826 to the Twentieth Congress; elected as a Democrat to the Twenty-first Congress, but resigned before qualifying; elected as a Jacksonian to the United States Senate and served from March 4, 1831, to June 30, 1834, when he resigned; chairman, Committee on the Judiciary (Twenty-second Congress), Committee on Foreign Relations (Twenty-third Congress); appointed United States Minister to Russia on June 30, 1834 and served until December 1835; unsuccessful candidate for election in 1840 to the Twenty-seventh Congress; elected as a Democrat to the Twenty-eighth Congress, and served from March 4, 1843 to February 14, 1844, when he resigned; chairman, Committee on the Judiciary (Twenty-eighth Congress); appointed Secretary of War by President John Tyler and served from February 15, 1844 to March 4, 1845; member, Pennsylvania senate, 1855-1857; major general of the Pennsylvania Home Guards in 1862; died in "Homewood," near Pittsburgh, Allegheny County, Pa., June 23, 1865; interment in Homewood Cemetery, Wilkinsburg, Pa., a town named for him.

**Bibliography:** *DAB*; Slick, S.E. "The Life of William Wilkins." Ph.D. dissertation, University of Pittsburgh, 1931.

**WILKINSON, Morton Smith,** a Senator and a Representative from Minnesota; born in Skaneateles, Onondaga County, N.Y., January 22, 1819; attended the common schools; moved to Illinois in 1837 and was employed in railroad work two years; returned to Skaneateles in 1840; studied law; was admitted to the bar in 1842 and commenced practice in Eaton Rapids, Mich., in 1843; moved to Stillwater, Washington County, Minn., in 1847; elected to the first legislature of Minnesota Territory in 1849; register of deeds of Ramsey County 1851-1853; moved to Mankato in 1858; member of the board of commissioners to prepare a code of laws for the Territory of Minnesota in 1858; elected as a Republican to the United States Senate and served from March 4, 1859, to March 3, 1865; unsuccessful candidate for reelection; chairman, Committee on Revolutionary Claims (Thirty-eighth Congress); elected as a Republican to the Forty-first Congress (March 4, 1869-March 3, 1871); unsuccessful candidate for renomination in 1870; moved to Wells, Faribault County; member of the State senate 1874-1877; prosecuting attorney of Faribault County 1880-1884; resumed the practice of his profession; died in Wells, Minn., February 4, 1894; interment in Glenwood Cemetery, Mankato, Blue Earth County, Minn.

**WILKINSON, Theodore Stark,** a Representative from Louisiana; born on Point Celeste plantation in Plaquemines Parish, near New Orleans, La., December 18, 1847; educated by private tutors and attended the common schools; was graduated from Washington and Lee University, Lexington, Va., in 1870; engaged in sugar planting in 1870; member of the school board of Plaquemines Parish; member and president of the board of levee commissioners for the third levee district; elected as a Democrat to the Fiftieth and Fifty-first Congresses (March 4, 1887-March 3, 1891); declined to be a candidate for renomination in 1890; chairman of the Louisiana antilottery convention in 1892; collector of the port of New Orleans 1893-1898; unsuccessful candidate for Governor in 1898; again engaged in sugar planting; delegate to the Democratic National Convention in 1912; died in New Orleans, La., on February 1, 1921; interment in Metairie Cemetery.

**WILLARD, Charles Wesley,** a Representative from Vermont; born in Lyndon, Caledonia County, Vt., June 18, 1827; was graduated from Dartmouth College, Hanover, N.H., in 1851; studied law; was admitted to the bar and commenced practice in Montpelier in 1853; secretary of state of Vermont 1855 and 1856; declined a reelection; member of the State senate 1860 and 1861; became editor and publisher of the Montpelier Freeman in 1861; elected as a Republican to the Forty-first, Forty-second, and Forty-third Congresses (March 4, 1869-March 3, 1875); chairman, Committee on Revolutionary Pensions (Forty-first and Forty-second Congresses); unsuccessful candidate for reelection in 1874 to the Forty-third Congress; resumed the practice of law in Montpelier; member of the commission to revise the laws of Vermont in 1879 and 1880; died in Montpelier, Vt., on June 8, 1880; interment in Green Mount Cemetery.

**WILLARD, George,** a Representative from Michigan; born in Bolton, Vt., March 20, 1824; attended school and received instruction from his father; moved with his parents to Battle Creek, Mich., in 1836; was graduated from Kalamazoo (Mich.) College in 1844; taught school and also studied theology, and was ordained a minister of the Episcopal Church in 1848; rector of churches in Coldwater, Battle Creek, and Kalamazoo, Mich., until 1863; professor of Latin in Kalamazoo (Mich.) College in 1863 and 1864; engaged in newspaper work in Battle Creek, Calhoun County, Mich.; member of the Michigan State Board of Education 1857-1863; regent of the University of Michigan at Ann Arbor 1863-1872; member of the State house of representatives in 1866 and 1867; member of the State constitutional convention in 1867; delegate to the Republican National Convention in 1872; elected as a Republican to the Forty-third and Forty-fourth Congresses (March 4, 1873-March 3, 1877); was not a candidate for renomination in 1876; resumed newspaper work in Battle Creek, Mich.; editor and owner of the Battle Creek Journal until his death in Battle Creek, Mich., March 26, 1901; interment in Oak Hill Cemetery.

**WILLCOX, Washington Frederick,** a Representative from Connecticut; born in Killingworth, Middlesex County, Conn., August 22, 1834; prepared for college at a private school, Madison Academy, and Hopkins Grammar School, New Haven; was graduated from Yale Law School in 1862; was admitted to the bar the same year and commenced practice in Deep River, Middlesex County, Conn.; member of the State house of representatives in 1862 and 1863; served in the State senate in 1875 and 1876; State's attorney 1875-1883; elected as a Democrat to the Fifty-first and Fifty-second Congresses (March 4, 1889-March 3, 1893); was not a candidate for renomination in 1892; resumed the practice of law in Deep River, Conn., and also engaged in banking; State railroad commissioner 1897-1905; died at his home in Chester, Conn., March 8, 1909; interment in Fountain Hill Cemetery, Deep River, Conn.

**WILLETT, William Forte, Jr.,** a Representative from New York; born in Brooklyn, N.Y., November 27, 1869; attended the public schools of his native city and was graduated from the law department of New York University, New York City, in 1895; was admitted to the bar the following year and commenced the practice of his profession in New York City; elected as a Democrat to the Sixtieth and Sixty-first Congresses (March 4, 1907-March 3, 1911); was not a candidate for renomination in 1910; engaged in the real estate business; died in New York City, February 12, 1938; interment in Evergreen Cemetery, Brooklyn, N.Y.

**WILLEY, Calvin,** a Senator from Connecticut; born in East Haddam, Conn., September 15, 1776; attended the common schools; studied law; was admitted to the bar in 1798 and commenced practice in Chatham, Conn.; moved to Stafford, Conn., in 1800; member, Connecticut State house of representatives, 1805-1806; postmaster of Stafford Springs, Conn., 1806-1808; moved to Tolland, Conn., in 1808; member of the State house of representatives in 1810, 1812, 1820-1821; postmaster of Tolland, 1812-1816; probate judge of Stafford district, 1818-1825; member, State senate, 1823-1824; presidential elector in 1824; elected to the United States Senate for the term commencing March 4, 1825, and served from

May 4, 1825 to March 3, 1831; chairman, Committee on Agriculture (Nineteenth Congress); resumed the practice of law in Tolland, Conn.; died in Stafford, Conn., August 23, 1858; interment in Skungamaug Cemetery, Tolland, Conn.

**WILLEY, Earle Dukes,** a Representative from Delaware; born in Greenwood, Sussex County, Del., July 21, 1889; attended the public schools and George Washington University Law School, Washington, D.C.; was graduated from Dickinson College, Carlisle, Pa., in 1911; principal of Greenwood High School, 1911-1915; secretary to Representative Thomas W. Miller of Delaware, Washington, D.C., 1915-1917; was admitted to the bar in 1920 and commenced practice in Dover, Del.; Delaware State librarian, 1917-1921; deputy attorney general and prosecuting attorney for Kent County, Del., 1921-1931; judge of the court of common pleas of Kent County, 1931-1939; judge of the juvenile court of Kent and Sussex Counties, 1933-1939; unsuccessful candidate for Lieutenant Governor in 1940; Delaware secretary of state, 1941-1943; trustee of the University of Delaware, of the Elizabeth W. Murphey School for Orphan Children, and of the State College for Colored Students; elected as a Republican to the Seventy-eighth Congress (January 3, 1943-January 3, 1945); unsuccessful candidate for reelection in 1944 to the Seventy-ninth Congress; resumed the practice of law in Dover, Del., until his death on March 17, 1950; interment in St. Johnstown Cemetery, near Greenwood, Del.

**WILLEY, Waitman Thomas,** a Senator from Virginia and from West Virginia; born in Monongalia County, Va., in what is now a part of Marion County, W.Va., October 18, 1811; graduated from Madison (Pa.) College in 1831; studied law; was admitted to the bar in 1833 and commenced practice in Morgantown, Va. (now West Virginia); appointed clerk of the county court of Monongalia County in 1841, and later clerk of the circuit superior court, and held both positions until 1852; delegate to the Virginia constitutional convention in 1850 and 1851; elected as a Unionist to the United States Senate from Virginia to fill the vacancy caused by the retirement of James M. Mason, and served from July 9, 1861 to March 3, 1863; chairman, Committee on Enrolled Bills (Thirty-seventh Congress); delegate to the State constitutional convention of West Virginia; upon the admission of West Virginia as a State into the Union was elected as a Unionist to the United States Senate; reelected in 1865 as a Republican, and served from August 4, 1863 to March 3, 1871; chairman, Committee on Engrossed Bills (Thirty-ninth Congress), Committee on Patents and the Patent Office (Thirty-ninth and Fortieth Congresses); again served as clerk of the county court of Monongalia County, 1882-1896; retired from public life; died in Morgantown, W.Va., May 2, 1900; interment in Oak Grove Cemetery.

Bibliography: *DAB*; Ambler, Charles. *Waitman Thomas Willey: Orator, Churchman, Humanitarian.* Huntington, W.Va.: Standard Print and Publishing Co., 1954; Bayless, R.W. "Peter Van Winkle and Waitman T. Willey in the Impeachment Trial of Andrew Johnson." *West Virginia History* 13 (January 1952): 75-89.

**WILLFORD, Albert Clinton,** a Representative from Iowa; born in Vinton, Benton County, Iowa, September 21, 1877; attended the country and town schools and Tilford's Academy, Vinton, Iowa; employed as chief engineer of the electric light, power, and water company at Vinton 1900-1907; moved to Waterloo, Black Hawk County, Iowa, in 1907 and engaged in the manufacture of ice until 1910, when he engaged in the seed, feed, and coal business; trustee of the Waterloo Public Library 1918-1930; served on the Black Hawk County Jury Commission 1922-1924; president of the Iowa Stationary Engineers Association for one year; president of the Izaak Walton League of America for Iowa 1927-1929 and served as a National and State director; president of the Waterloo Baseball Club 1923-1927; elected as a Democrat to the Seventy-third Congress (March 4, 1933-January 3, 1935); unsuccessful candidate for reelection in 1934 to the Seventy-fourth Congress and for election in 1936 to the Seventy-fifth Congress; resumed his former pursuits in Waterloo, Iowa, until his death there on March 10, 1937; interment in Memorial Park Cemetery.

**WILLIAMS, Abram Pease,** a Senator from California; born in New Portland, Somerset County, Maine, February 3, 1832; attended the common schools and completed an academic course at North Anson (Maine) Academy 1846-1848; attended normal school at Farmington, Maine, 1848-1853; taught school at North Anson; moved to Fairfield, Somerset County, Maine, in 1853 and engaged in mercantile pursuits; moved to California in 1858 and engaged in mining in Tuolumne County; resumed mercantile pursuits in 1859; moved to San Francisco in 1861 and became an importer, stock raiser, and farmer; one of the founders of the San Francisco Board of Trade, serving as its first president; member of the San Francisco chamber of commerce; elected as a Republican to the United States Senate to fill the vacancy caused by the death of John F. Miller and served from August 4, 1886, to March 3, 1887; was not a candidate for renomination in 1887; resumed the wholesale mercantile business in San Francisco, Calif., where he died October 17, 1911; interment in Maplewood Cemetery, Fairfield, Maine.

**WILLIAMS, Alpheus Starkey,** a Representative from Michigan; born in Saybrook, Middlesex County, Conn., September 20, 1810; was graduated from Yale College in 1831; studied law; was admitted to the bar in 1837 and commenced practice in Detroit, Mich.; judge of probate, 1840-1844; editor of the Detroit Daily Advertiser, 1843-1847; served in the war with Mexico; commissioned lieutenant colonel of the First Michigan Infantry on December 8, 1847, and was mustered out July 29, 1848; postmaster of Detroit, 1849-1853; commissioned brigadier general of Michigan Volunteers on April 24, 1861, and of United States Volunteers on May 17, 1861; brevetted major general of Volunteers on January 12, 1865, and was mustered out January 15, 1866; unsuccessful candidate in 1866 for election for Governor of Michigan; appointed Minister Resident to El Salvador on August 16, 1866, and served until October 1869; elected as a Democrat to the Forty-fourth and Forty-fifth Congresses, and served from March 4, 1875 until his death in Washington, D.C., December 21, 1878; chairman, Committee on District of Columbia (Forty-fifth Congress); interment in Elmwood Cemetery, Detroit, Mich.

Bibliography: *DAB*; Charnley, Jeffrey Gordon. "'Neglected Honor': The Life of General A.S. Williams of Michigan, 1810-1878." Ph.D. dissertation, Michigan State University, 1983; Williams, Alpheus S. *From the Cannon's Mouth: The Civil War Letters of General Alpheus S. Williams.* Edited with an introduction by Milo M. Quaife. 1959. Reprint. Lincoln: University of Nebraska Press, 1995.

**WILLIAMS, Andrew,** a Representative from New York; born in Ormstown, Province of Quebec, Canada, August 27, 1828; received a limited schooling; engaged in mercantile pursuits; immigrated to the United States in 1852 and settled in Plattsburgh, N.Y.; engaged in the manufacture of nails, 1863-1865, and subsequently in the mining of iron ore, in the lumber trade, and in the manufacture of horseshoe nails and wagons; one of the organizers of the Iron National Bank at Plattsburgh in 1881, and served as its president until 1888; elected as a Republican to the Forty-fourth and Forty-fifth Congresses (March 4, 1875-March 3, 1879); was not a candidate for renomination in 1878 to the Forty-sixth Congress; member of the board of supervisors of Dannemora for two years, and for a number of years represented Plattsburgh in a like capacity; superintendent of the Plattsburgh waterworks, 1889-1902; elected Clinton county treasurer in 1890; reelected in 1893, 1896, 1899, 1902, and 1905; member of the board of education; died in Plattsburgh, N.Y., October 6, 1907; interment in Riverside Cemetery.

**WILLIAMS, Archibald Hunter Arrington** (nephew of Archibald Hunter Arrington), a Representative from North Carolina; born near Louisburg, Franklin County, N.C., October 22, 1842; attended the common schools and Emory and Henry College, Emory, Va.; enlisted as a private in the Confederate Army during the Civil War; served four years in the Army of Northern Virginia, and at the surrender at Appomattox was captain of his company; after the war engaged in agricultural pursuits and in retail trade in Oxford, Granville County, N.C.; developer and president of the Oxford & Henderson Railroad; member of the State house of representatives 1883-1885; elected as a Democrat to the Fifty-second Congress (March 4, 1891-March 3, 1893); unsuccessful candidate for reelection in 1892 to the Fifty-third Congress; died in Chase City, Mecklenburg County, Va., September 5, 1895; interment in Elmwood Cemetery, Oxford, N.C.

**WILLIAMS, Arthur Bruce,** a Representative from Michigan; born in Ashland, Ashland County, Ohio, January 27, 1872; attended the common schools of Eaton County, and was graduated from Olivet College, in that county, in 1892; was admitted to the bar in 1894 and commenced practice at Battle Creek, Mich.; interested in agricultural pursuits at his summer home, Gull Lake, Mich.; director of the Old National Bank, Battle Creek; vice president and general counsel of the Postum Cereal Co.; president of the Michigan Manufacturers' Association; elected as a Republican to the Sixty-eighth Congress to fill the vacancy caused by the death of John M.C. Smith; reelected to the Sixty-ninth Congress and served from June 19, 1923, until his death in Baltimore, Md., May 1, 1925; interment in Maple Hill Cemetery, Charlotte, Eaton County, Mich.

**WILLIAMS, Benjamin,** a Representative from North Carolina; born near Smithfield, Johnston County, N.C., January 1, 1751; attended the country schools; engaged in agricultural pursuits; member of the provincial congress in 1774 and 1775; served in the Revolutionary Army as second lieutenant; promoted to captain in the Second Regiment on July 19, 1776; promoted to colonel for gallantry at Guilford, N.C., July 12, 1781; member of the North Carolina State house of commons in 1779, 1785, and 1789; member of the North Carolina State senate in 1780, 1781, April 1784, October 1784, and 1786, and again in 1807 and 1809; elected to the Third Congress (March 4, 1793-March 3, 1795); was not a candidate for renomination in 1794 to the Fourth Congress; Governor of North Carolina from 1799 until 1802, and from December 1, 1807 until December 12, 1808; died in Moore County, N.C., July 20, 1814; interment in the family cemetery in Moore County, near Carbonton, N.C.; reinterment in 1970 at his last residence in Moore County, now known as "The House in the Horseshoe," a mile and a half from his original grave on Governor's Creek.

**WILLIAMS, Charles Grandison,** a Representative from Wisconsin; born in Royalton, Niagara County, N.Y., October 18, 1829; pursued an academic course and studied law in Rochester, N.Y.; moved to Wisconsin in 1856 and settled in Janesville; was admitted to the bar and commenced practice in Janesville; served in the State senate 1869-1872; twice chosen president pro tempore of that body; elected as a Republican to the Forty-third and to the four succeeding Congresses (March 4, 1873-March 3, 1883); chairman, Committee on Foreign Affairs (Forty-seventh Congress); unsuccessful candidate for reelection in 1882 to the Forty-eighth Congress; resumed the practice of law; died in Watertown, Codington County, S.Dak., March 30, 1892; interment in Oak Hill Cemetery, Janesville, Rock County, Wis.

**WILLIAMS, Christopher Harris** (grandfather of John Sharp Williams), a Representative from Tennessee; born near Hillsboro, Orange County, N.C., December 18, 1798; pursued an academic course and attended the University of North Carolina at Chapel Hill; studied law; was admitted to the bar about 1820 and practiced;

elected as a Whig to the Twenty-fifth, Twenty-sixth, and Twenty-seventh Congresses (March 4, 1837-March 3, 1843); unsuccessful candidate for reelection in 1842 to the Twenty-eighth Congress; elected to the Thirty-first and Thirty-second Congresses (March 4, 1849-March 3, 1853); was not a candidate for renomination in 1852; resumed the practice of law in Lexington, Henderson County, Tenn., and died there November 27, 1857; interment in Lexington Cemetery.

**WILLIAMS, Clyde,** a Representative from Missouri; born on a farm near Grubville, Jefferson County, Mo., October 13, 1873; attended the county schools, De Soto High School, and the State normal school at Cape Girardeau; was graduated from the law department of the University of Missouri at Columbia in 1901; was admitted to the bar the same year and commenced practice in De Soto, Mo.; prosecuting attorney of Jefferson County 1902-1908; elected as a Democrat to the Seventieth Congress (March 4, 1927-March 3, 1929); unsuccessful candidate for reelection in 1928 to the Seventy-first Congress; resumed the practice of law; elected to the Seventy-second and to the five succeeding Congresses (March 4, 1931-January 3, 1943); unsuccessful candidate for reelection in 1942 to the Seventy-eighth Congress; engaged in legal work for the Reconstruction Finance Corporation in Washington, D.C., 1943-1945; served as president of the Jefferson Trust Co. in Hillsboro and president of the Bank of Hillsboro; died in St. Louis, Mo., November 12, 1954; interment in Hillsboro Cemetery, Hillsboro, Mo.

**WILLIAMS, David Rogerson,** a Representative from South Carolina; born in Robbins Neck, S.C., March 8, 1776; attended school at Wrentham, Mass., and Rhode Island College (now Brown University), Providence, R.I.; studied law; was admitted to the bar in 1797 and practiced for three years in Providence, R.I.; editor and proprietor of the City Gazette and Weekly Carolina Gazette of Charleston, S.C., 1801-1803; engaged in cotton planting and manufacturing in Darlington County, S.C., from 1803 until his death; built the first cottonseed oil mill in South Carolina; elected as a Republican to the Ninth and Tenth Congresses (March 4, 1805-March 3, 1809); elected to the Twelfth Congress (March 4, 1811-March 3, 1813); commissioned a brigadier general in the United States Army on July 9, 1813, and served until April 6, 1814, when he resigned; elected Governor of South Carolina by the Legislature, and served from December 1814 to December 1816; member of the State senate from 1824 until he was accidentally killed November 17, 1830, while superintending the construction of a bridge over Lynchs Creek, Witherspoons Ferry, on the road to Georgetown, S.C.; interment on his plantation near Society Hill, Darlington County, S.C.

**Bibliography:** *DAB*; Cook, Harvey Tolliver. *The Life and Legacy of David Rogerson Williams.* New York, 1916.

**WILLIAMS, Elihu Stephen,** a Representative from Ohio; born in New Carlisle, Clark County, Ohio, January 24, 1835; educated in the common schools and attended Antioch College, Yellow Springs, Ohio, two years; studied law in Dayton, Ohio, and was admitted to the bar in 1861; during the Civil War enlisted as a private in the Seventy-first Regiment, Ohio Volunteer Infantry, in October 1861; commissioned first lieutenant February 14, 1862; promoted to captain February 10, 1863; detailed to the command of the military post at Carthage, Smith County, Tenn., in September 1863 and remained there until the close of the war; attorney general of the sixth judicial district of Tennessee from April 1865 to 1867; member of the Tennessee house of representatives 1867-1869; moved to Troy, Miami County, Ohio, in January 1875; elected as a Republican to the Fiftieth and Fifty-first Congresses (March 4, 1887-March 3, 1891); editor of the Buckeye; died in Troy, Ohio, December 1, 1903; interment in Riverside Cemetery.

**WILLIAMS, George Fred,** a Representative from Massachusetts; born in Dedham, Norfolk County, Mass., July 10, 1852; attended private schools, and was graduated from the Dedham High School in 1868 and from Dartmouth College, Hanover, N.H., in 1872; studied at the Universities of Heidelberg and Berlin; taught school in West Brewster, Mass., in 1872 and 1873; became a reporter on the Boston Globe; member of the Dedham school committee; studied law at Boston University, Boston, Mass.; was admitted to the bar in 1875 and practiced in Boston; edited Williams' Citations of Massachusetts Cases in 1878 and volumes 10 to 17 of the Annual Digest of the United States, 1880-1887; member of the Massachusetts house of representatives in 1890; elected as a Democrat to the Fifty-second Congress (March 4, 1891-March 3, 1893); unsuccessful candidate for reelection in 1892 to the Fifty-third Congress; was an unsuccessful Democratic candidate for election for Governor in 1895, 1896, and 1897; resumed the practice of law in Boston, Mass.; delegate to several Massachusetts conventions; delegate to the Democratic National Conventions of 1896, 1900, 1904 and 1908; appointed Minister to Greece and Montenegro on December 22, 1913 and served until September 1914; resumed the practice of law until his retirement in 1930; died in Brookline, Mass., July 11, 1932; interment in the Old Village Cemetery, Dedham, Mass.

**WILLIAMS, George Henry,** a Senator from Oregon; born in New Lebanon, Columbia County, N.Y., March 26, 1823; completed preparatory studies; studied law; was admitted to the bar in 1844 and commenced practice at Fort Madison, Iowa Territory; judge of the first judicial district of Iowa, 1847-1852; presidential elector on the Democratic ticket in 1852; chief justice of the Territory of Oregon, 1853-1857; reappointed by President James Buchanan but declined; member of the Oregon constitutional convention of 1858; elected as a Republican to the United States Senate and served from March 4, 1865, to March 3, 1871; unsuccessful candidate for reelection; Attorney General in the Cabinet of President Ulysses S. Grant from January 10, 1872 to May 15, 1875; nominated by President Grant as Chief Justice of the Supreme Court of the United States on December 1, 1873, but his name was withdrawn at his own request; mayor of Portland, Oreg., 1902-1905; died in Portland, Oreg., April 4, 1910; interment in Riverview Cemetery.

**Bibliography:** *DAB*; Teiser, Sidney. "Almost Chief-Justice: George H. Williams." *Oregon Historical Quarterly* 47 (September 1946): 256-80, 47 (December 1946): 417-40.

**WILLIAMS, George Howard,** a Senator from Missouri; born in California, Moniteau County, Mo., on December 1, 1871; attended the public schools; graduated from the preparatory department of Drury College, Springfield, Mo., in 1890, from Princeton University in 1894, and from the Washington University Law School, St. Louis, Mo., in 1897; was admitted to the bar in 1897 and commenced practice in St. Louis; judge of the circuit court of the city of St. Louis, 1906-1912; delegate at large to the Missouri constitutional convention in 1922 and 1923; appointed as a Republican to the United States Senate to fill the vacancy caused by the death of Selden P. Spencer, and served from May 25, 1925 to December 5, 1926, when a duly elected successor qualified; was an unsuccessful candidate for election to fill the vacancy in 1926; chairman, Committee to Audit and Control the Contingent Expense (Thirty-ninth Congress), Committee on Private Land Claims (Fortieth and Forty-first Congresses); resumed the practice of law in St. Louis until 1943, when he retired and moved to Sarasota, Fla., where he died on November 25, 1963; interment in Masonic Cemetery, California, Mo.

**WILLIAMS, George Short,** a Representative from Delaware; born in Ocean View, Sussex County, Del., October 21, 1877; attended the public schools and Wilmington Conference Academy, Dover, Del.; was graduated from Dickinson College, Carlisle, Pa., in 1900; instructor in Ironwood (Mich.) High School, 1902-1904; engaged in the lumber business in Delaware and North Carolina, 1905-1923;

also interested in banking; mayor of Millsboro, Del., 1921-1927; treasurer of the State of Delaware, 1929-1933; president of the State board of education, 1927-1934; deputy motor vehicle commissioner, 1935-1937; delegate to the Republican National Convention of 1940; elected as a Republican to the Seventy-sixth Congress (January 3, 1939-January 3, 1941); unsuccessful candidate for reelection in 1940 to the Seventy-seventh Congress; motor vehicle commissioner, 1941-1946; administrative assistant to Senator John J. Williams from January 1947 to January 1959; died in Millsboro, Del., November 22, 1961; interment in Union Cemetery, Georgetown, Del.

**WILLIAMS, Guinn,** a Representative from Texas; born near Beuela, Calhoun County, Miss., April 22, 1871; moved with his parents to Texas and settled in Decatur, Wise County, in 1876; attended the public schools; was graduated from the commercial branch of Transylvania College, Lexington, Ky., in 1890; engaged in the livestock business, agricultural pursuits, and banking; county clerk of Wise County, Tex., 1898-1902; member of the State senate from 1920 to May 1922, when he resigned, having been elected to Congress; elected as a Democrat to the Sixty-seventh Congress to fill the vacancy caused by the death of Lucian W. Parrish; reelected to the Sixty-eighth and to the four succeeding Congresses and served from May 13, 1922, to March 3, 1933; chairman, Committee on Territories (Seventy-second Congress); was not a candidate for renomination in 1932 to the Seventy-third Congress; manager of the Regional Agricultural Credit Corporation in San Angelo, Tex., in 1933; also engaged in the livestock business and ranching; died in San Angelo, Tex., on January 9, 1948; interment in Decatur Cemetery, Decatur, Tex.

**WILLIAMS, Harrison Arlington, Jr. (Pete),** a Representative and a Senator from New Jersey; born in Plainfield, Union County, N.J., December 10, 1919; attended the public schools; A.B., Oberlin (Ohio) College, 1941; engaged in newspaper work in Washington, D.C., and studied at Georgetown University Foreign Service School until called to active duty as a seaman in the United States Naval Reserve in 1941; became a naval aviator and was discharged as a lieutenant (junior grade) in 1945; employed in the steel industry for a short time; LL.B., Columbia University Law School, 1948; admitted to the bar in 1948 and commenced practice in New Hampshire; returned to Plainfield, N.J., in 1949 and continued to practice law; was an unsuccessful candidate for the New Jersey State house of assembly in 1951, and for city councilman in 1952; elected as a Democrat to the Eighty-third Congress to fill the vacancy caused by the resignation of Clifford Case; reelected to the Eighty-fourth Congress and served from November 3, 1953, to January 3, 1957; unsuccessful candidate for reelection in 1956 to the Eighty-fifth Congress; elected to the United States Senate in 1958; reelected in 1964, 1970, and again in 1976, and served from January 3, 1959 until his resignation; chairman, Special Committee on Aging (Ninetieth and Ninety-first Congresses), Committee on Labor and Public Welfare (Ninety-second through Ninety-fifth Congresses), Committee on Human Resources (Ninety-fifth Congress), Committee on Labor and Human Resources (Ninety-sixth Congress); resigned on March 11, 1982, eight days after the Senate began debate on a resolution of expulsion following Williams' conviction and sentencing on charges related to the Federal Bureau of Investigation's ABSCAM operation; is a resident of Bedminster, N.J.

**WILLIAMS, Henry,** a Representative from Massachusetts; born in Taunton, Bristol County, Mass., November 30, 1805; completed preparatory studies; studied law; admitted to the bar in 1829 and commenced practice in Taunton, Mass.; member of the Massachusetts house of representatives in 1834; served in the Massachusetts senate in 1836 and 1837; elected as a Democrat to the Twenty-sixth Congress (March 4, 1839-March 3, 1841); unsuccessful candidate for reelection in 1840 to the Twenty-seventh Congress; was elected to the Twenty-eighth Congress (March 4, 1843-March 3, 1845);

resumed the practice of law; died in Taunton, Mass., on May 8, 1887; interment in Mount Pleasant Cemetery.

**WILLIAMS, Hezekiah,** a Representative from Maine; born near Woodstock, Vt., July 28, 1798; was graduated from Dartmouth College, Hanover, N.H., in 1820; studied law; was admitted to the bar and commenced practice in Castine, Hancock County, Maine, in 1825; register of probate for Hancock County 1824-1838; selectman of Castine 1833-1835; trustee of the school fund in 1834; member of school committee in 1840; served in the State senate 1839-1841; again a selectman of Castine in 1843 and 1844; elected as a Democrat to the Twenty-ninth and Thirtieth Congresses (March 4, 1845-March 3, 1849); resumed the practice of law; died in Castine, Maine, October 23, 1856; interment in Castine Cemetery.

**WILLIAMS, Isaac, Jr.,** a Representative from New York; born in Goshen, Conn., April 5, 1777; received a limited schooling; moved with his father to Otsego County, N.Y., in 1793; was appointed undersheriff of Otsego County in 1810; afterward appointed sheriff by the council of appointment in 1811 and served until 1813; successfully contested as a Republican the election of John M. Bowers to the Thirteenth Congress to fill the vacancy caused by the death of William Dowse and served from December 20, 1813, to March 3, 1815; elected to the Fifteenth Congress (March 4, 1817-March 3, 1819); elected to the Eighteenth Congress (March 4, 1823-March 3, 1825); unsuccessful candidate for sheriff in 1828; died in Cooperstown, Otsego County, N.Y., November 9, 1860; interment in Warren Cemetery, Otsego, N.Y.

**WILLIAMS, James,** a Representative from Delaware; born in Philadelphia, Pa., August 4, 1825; completed preparatory studies; moved to Kenton, Kent County, Del., in 1844 and engaged in agricultural pursuits; member of the State house of representatives in 1856 and 1862; served in the State senate in 1866 and 1871; delegate to the Democratic National Convention in 1872; elected as a Democrat to the Forty-fourth and Forty-fifth Congresses (March 4, 1875-March 3, 1879); was not a candidate for renomination in 1878; resumed agricultural pursuits; moved to Smyrna, Del., in 1891 and continued farming until his death on April 12, 1899; interment in St. Peter's Cemetery.

**WILLIAMS, James Douglas,** a Representative from Indiana; born in Pickaway County, Ohio, January 16, 1808; moved with his parents to Indiana and settled in Knox County in 1818; received a limited education; engaged in agricultural pursuits; justice of the peace of Vincennes, Ind., 1839-1843; from 1855 was identified with the Indiana State board of agriculture for sixteen years, serving four years as its president; member of the State house of representatives in 1843, 1847, 1851, 1856, and 1868; served in the State senate in 1858, 1862, and 1870; delegate to the Democratic National Convention of 1872; was the caucus nominee of his party, which was in the minority, for United States Senator in 1872; was elected as a Democrat to the Forty-fourth Congress, and served from March 4, 1875 to December 1, 1876, when he resigned, having been elected Governor; chairman, Committee on Accounts (Forty-fourth Congress); elected Governor of Indiana in 1876, and served from January 8, 1877 until his death in Indianapolis, Ind., November 20, 1880; interment in Walnut Grove Cemetery, near Monroe City, Knox County, Ind.

**Bibliography:** *DAB.*

**WILLIAMS, James Robert,** a Representative from Illinois; born in Carmi, White County, Ill., December 27, 1850; attended the common schools; was graduated from Indiana State University at Bloomington in 1875 and from Union College of Law, Chicago, Ill., in 1876; was admitted to the bar in 1876 and commenced practice in Carmi, Ill.; master in chancery 1880-1882; county judge of White County 1882-1886; elected as a Democrat to the Fifty-first Congress to fill the vacancy caused by the death of Richard W. Townsend;

reelected to the Fifty-second and Fifty-third Congresses and served from December 2, 1889, to March 3, 1895; elected to the Fifty-sixth, Fifty-seventh, and Fifty-eighth Congresses (March 4, 1899-March 3, 1905); resumed the practice of his profession; died in Loma Linda, San Bernardino County, Calif., November 8, 1923; interment in Maple Ridge Cemetery, Carmi, Ill.

**WILLIAMS, James Wray,** a Representative from Maryland; born in that State October 8, 1792; completed preparatory studies; member of the State house of delegates; was speaker in 1830; elected as a Democrat to the Twenty-seventh Congress and served from March 4, 1841, until his death on Prieshford farm, Deer Creek, Harford County, Md., December 2, 1842; interment in the family cemetery on Prieshford farm.

**WILLIAMS, Jared,** a Representative from Virginia; born in Montgomery County, Md., March 4, 1766; pursued classical studies; engaged in agricultural pursuits; member of the Virginia house of delegates from 1812 to 1817; elected to the Sixteenth, Seventeenth, and Eighteenth Congresses (March 4, 1819-March 3, 1825); died near Newton, Va., January 2, 1831.

**WILLIAMS, Jared Warner,** a Representative and a Senator from New Hampshire; born in West Woodstock, Conn., December 22, 1796; graduated from Brown University, Providence, R.I., in 1818; studied law in the Litchfield (Conn.) Law School; was admitted to the bar in 1822 and commenced practice in Lancaster, Coos County, N.H.; member, New Hampshire State house of representatives, 1830-1831, and 1835-1836; member, State senate, 1832-1834; elected as a Democrat to the Twenty-fifth and Twenty-sixth Congresses (March 4, 1837-March 3, 1841); elected Governor of New Hampshire in 1847, reelected in 1848, and served from June 3, 1847 to June 7, 1849; appointed as a Democrat to the United States Senate to fill the vacancy caused by the death of Charles G. Atherton, and served from November 29, 1853 to July 15, 1854; died in Lancaster, N.H., September 29, 1864; interment in Summer Street Cemetery.

**WILLIAMS, Jeremiah Norman,** a Representative from Alabama; born near Louisville, Barbour County, Ala., May 29, 1829; attended the preparatory schools of Barbour County and was graduated from the University of South Carolina at Columbia in 1852; studied law in Montgomery and Tuskegee; was admitted to the bar in 1855 and commenced practice in Clayton, Barbour County, Ala.; volunteered for service in the Confederate Army during the Civil War and was made captain of the Clayton Guards, later becoming major of the First Regiment, Alabama Infantry; elected a member of the State house of representatives in 1872, but was not allowed to take his seat; elected as a Democrat to the Forty-fourth and Forty-fifth Congresses (March 4, 1875-March 3, 1879); chairman, Committee on Expenditures in the Post Office Department (Forty-fifth Congress); chancellor of the third division 1893-1899; resumed the practice of law in Clayton, Ala.; member of the State constitutional convention in 1901; died in Clayton, Ala., May 8, 1915; interment in the City Cemetery.

**WILLIAMS, John,** a Representative from New York; born in Barnstable, England, in September 1752; received a liberal education; studied medicine and surgery in St. Thomas Hospital, London; served for one year as surgeon's mate on an English man-of-war; immigrated to America in 1773 and settled in New Perth, Charlotte County (now Salem, Washington County), N.Y.; engaged in an extensive medical practice; member of the State Provincial Congress in 1775, to which body he was reelected and served until its dissolution in 1777; appointed surgeon of the State forces in 1775; colonel of the Charlotte County Regiment in 1776 and retained command throughout the Revolutionary War; served in the State senate in 1777 and 1778; member of the State assembly in 1781 and 1782; again a member of the State senate 1782-1785;

appointed a member of the first board of regents of New York University in 1784; brigadier general of militia in 1786; delegate to the State ratification convention in 1788; member of the council of appointment in 1789; elected as a Federalist to the Fourth and Fifth Congresses (March 4, 1795-March 3, 1799); was a large landholder; a promoter and director of a company organized to build the Erie Canal as a private enterprise, the project later being taken over and completed by the State; judge of the county court; died in Salem, N.Y., July 22, 1806; interment in Salem Cemetery.

**WILLIAMS, John,** a Representative from New York; born in Utica, N.Y., January 7, 1807; spent his youth and completed preparatory studies in Sackets Harbor, N.Y.; moved to Rochester, N.Y., in 1824 and engaged in mercantile pursuits and the manufacture of flour; member of the board of aldermen in 1844; mayor of Rochester in 1853; elected as a Democrat to the Thirty-fourth Congress (March 4, 1855-March 3, 1857); again engaged in the milling business 1858-1870; was major general of the Seventh Division of the National Guard at the time of his death; excise commissioner and manager of the house of refuge in 1870; city treasurer from 1871 until his death; died in Rochester, N.Y., March 26, 1875; interment in Mount Hope Cemetery.

**WILLIAMS, John,** a Delegate from North Carolina; born in Hanover County, Va., March 14, 1731; moved to North Carolina in 1745 with his parents, who settled in Granville County; donated the land and laid out the town of Williamsboro, N.C.; studied law; was admitted to the bar and commenced practice in Williamsboro; one of the founders of the University of North Carolina at Chapel Hill; deputy attorney general in 1768; delegate to the Provincial Congress of 1775; member of the State house of commons in 1777 and 1778 and served as speaker; Member of the Continental Congress in 1778 and 1779; judge of the supreme court of North Carolina from 1779 until his death in Montpelier, near Williamsboro, N.C., October 10, 1799; interment in the family cemetery, Montpelier, N.C.

**WILLIAMS, John** (brother of Lewis Williams and Robert Williams, father of Joseph Lanier Williams, and cousin of Marmaduke Williams), a Senator from Tennessee; born in Surry County, N.C., January 29, 1778; completed preparatory studies; captain in the Sixth Regiment, United States Infantry 1799-1800; studied law in Salisbury, N.C.; was admitted to the bar of Knox County, Tenn., in 1803 and commenced practice in Knoxville, Tenn.; captain of regular troops in the War of 1812 and was colonel of a regiment of East Tennessee Mounted Volunteers in the expedition against the Seminoles in Florida in 1812 and 1813; colonel of the Thirty-ninth Regiment, United States Infantry, in 1813, and subsequently served under General Andrew Jackson in the expedition against the Creek Indians in Alabama; elected in 1815 as a Republican to the United States Senate to fill the vacancy caused by the resignation of George W. Campbell; was subsequently appointed to fill the vacancy in the regular term caused by a recess of the legislature; was then elected in 1817 and served from October 10, 1815, to March 3, 1823; unsuccessful candidate for reelection; chairman, Committee on Military Affairs (Fourteenth through Seventeenth Congresses); appointed by President John Quincy Adams as Chargé d'Affaires to the Central American Federation 1825-1826; member, State senate 1827-1828; died near Knoxville, Tenn., August 10, 1837; interment in the First Presbyterian Church Cemetery.

**Bibliography:** *DAB.*

**WILLIAMS, John Bell,** a Representative from Mississippi; born in Raymond, Hinds County, Miss., December 4, 1918; attended the public schools; was graduated from Hinds Junior College, Raymond, Miss., in 1936, from the University of Mississippi at Oxford in 1938, and from Jackson (Miss.) School of Law in 1940; was admitted to the bar in 1940 and commenced practice in Raymond, Miss.; enlisted as an aviation cadet in the United States Army,

November 5, 1941; was commissioned as a pilot July 3, 1942; retired from active service because of injuries received in the line of duty on April 29, 1944; prosecuting attorney of Hinds County, Miss., from May 20, 1944, to October 1, 1946; elected as a Democrat to the Eightieth and to the ten succeeding Congresses, and served from January 3, 1947, to January 16, 1968, when he resigned; elected Governor of Mississippi in 1967 and served from January 16, 1968 to January 18, 1972; practiced law in Jackson, Miss., until he retired on January 1, 1981; resided in Brandon, Miss., until his death there on March 25, 1983; interment in Raymond Cemetery, Raymond, Miss.

**Bibliography:** Vance, Sandra Stringer. "The Congressional Career of John Bell Williams, 1947-1967." Ph.D. dissertation, Mississippi State University, 1976.

**WILLIAMS, John James,** a Senator from Delaware; born on a farm near Frankford, Sussex County, Del., May 17, 1904; attended the public schools at Frankford; moved to Millsboro, Del., in 1922 and engaged in the grain business; elected as a Republican to the United States Senate in 1946; reelected in 1952, 1958, and again in 1964 and served from January 3, 1947, until his resignation December 31, 1970; was not a candidate for reelection in 1970; died on January 11, 1988, in Lewes, Del.; interment in Millsboro Cemetery, Millsboro, Del.

**WILLIAMS, John McKeown Snow,** a Representative from Massachusetts; born in Richmond, Henrico County, Va., August 13, 1818; moved to Boston, Mass.; attended the public schools; engaged in mercantile pursuits and was also a shipowner; member of the Massachusetts house of representatives in 1856; served in the Massachusetts senate in 1858; elected as a Republican to the Forty-third Congress (March 4, 1873-March 3, 1875); unsuccessful candidate for reelection in 1874 to the Forty-fourth Congress; resumed his former business pursuits; died in Cambridge, Middlesex County, Mass., March 19, 1886; interment in Mount Auburn Cemetery.

**WILLIAMS, John Patrick (Pat),** a Representative from Montana; born in Helena, Lewis and Clark County, Mont., October 30, 1937; attended the public schools and graduated from Butte High School in 1956; attended the University of Montana, Missoula, 1956-1957; B.A., University of Denver, Colo., 1961; served in the Colorado and Montana National Guard, 1961-1969; teacher in Butte, Mont., 1963-1969; served in the Montana State house of representatives, 1967-1969; executive director of the Montana presidential campaign of Hubert H. Humphrey in 1968, and co-chair of the Montana presidential campaign of Jimmy Carter in 1976; executive assistant to Representative John Melcher of Montana, 1969-1971; unsuccessful candidate for nomination in 1974 to the Ninety-fourth Congress; coordinator, Montana Family Education Program, 1971-1978; member, Governor's Employment and Training Council, 1972-1978; member, Montana Reapportionment Commission, 1972-1973; elected as a Democrat to the Ninety-sixth and to the eight succeeding Congresses (January 3, 1979-January 3, 1997); was not a candidate for reelection in 1996 to the One Hundred Fifth Congress; is a resident of Helena, Mont.

**WILLIAMS, John Sharp** (grandson of Christopher Harris Williams), a Representative and a Senator from Mississippi; born in Memphis, Tenn., July 30, 1854; after the death of his parents moved to Yazoo County, Miss.; attended private schools, the Kentucky Military Institute near Frankfort, the University of the South, Sewanee, Tenn., the University of Virginia at Charlottesville, and the University of Heidelberg, at Baden, Germany; subsequently studied law at the University of Virginia and in Memphis, Tenn.; was admitted to the bar in 1877; moved to Yazoo City, Miss., in 1878; engaged in the practice of law and also interested in cotton planting; elected as a Democrat to the Fifty-third and to the seven succeeding Congresses (March 4, 1893-March 3, 1909); was not a candidate for

renomination in 1908; minority leader in the Fifty-eighth, Fifty-ninth, and Sixtieth Congresses; chairman, Committee on Party Leaders (Fifty-eighth through Sixtieth Congresses); elected as a Democrat to the United States Senate in 1910; reelected in 1916 and served from March 4, 1911, to March 3, 1923; declined to be a candidate for renomination in 1922; chairman, Committee to Audit and Control the Contingent Expense (Sixty-third Congress), Committee on the Library (Sixty-fourth and Sixty-fifth Congresses), Committee on the University of the United States (Sixty-sixth Congress); retired from public life and lived on his plantation, "Cedar Grove," near Yazoo City, Miss., until his death there September 27, 1932; interment in the family cemetery on his plantation.

**Bibliography:** *DAB*; Dickson, Harris. *An Old-Fashioned Senator: A Biography of John Sharp Williams.* New York: Frederick Stokes Company, 1925; Osborn, George C. *John Sharp Williams: Planter-Statesman of the Deep South.* Gloucester, Mass.: P. Smith, 1964.

**WILLIAMS, John Stuart,** a Senator from Kentucky; born near Mount Sterling, Montgomery County, Ky., July 10, 1818; attended the common schools; graduated from Miami University, Oxford, Ohio, in 1839; studied law; admitted to the bar in 1840 and commenced practice in Paris, Bourbon County, Ky.; served in the Mexican War, first as a captain of an independent company attached to the Sixth Regiment, United States Infantry, and afterward as a colonel of the Fourth Regiment, Kentucky Volunteers; member, Kentucky house of representatives 1851, 1853; during the Civil War served in the Confederate Army as a colonel in 1861; promoted to brigadier general in 1862 and surrendered in 1865; engaged in agricultural pursuits, with residence in Winchester, Ky.; member, Kentucky house of representatives 1873 and 1875; was an unsuccessful candidate for governor in 1875; presidential elector on the Democratic ticket in 1876; elected as a Democrat to the United States Senate and served from March 4, 1879, to March 3, 1885; was an unsuccessful candidate for reelection; engaged in agricultural pursuits; died in Mount Sterling, Ky., on July 17, 1898; interment in Winchester Cemetery, Winchester, Ky.

**WILLIAMS, Jonathan,** a Representative from Pennsylvania; born in Boston, Mass., May 20, 1750; completed preparatory studies and worked in a bank in Boston; went to France as secretary to Benjamin Franklin in 1770 and served until 1775, part of this time as commercial agent for the United States; studied military science; returned to the United States in 1785 and settled in Philadelphia; was judge of the court of common pleas; entered the United States Army as major of the Second Regiment of Artillerists and Engineers February 16, 1801; commanded the post at West Point, N.Y., and was the first Superintendent of the United States Military Academy in 1802; promoted through the ranks to colonel; planned and built the inner forts for the defense of New York Harbor; resigned July 31, 1812; returned to Philadelphia, Pa., and engaged in literary and scientific pursuits; was the author of several military and philosophical papers; elected to the Fourteenth Congress and served from March 4, 1815, until his death, before the assembling of the Congress, in Philadelphia, Pa., May 16, 1815.

**Bibliography:** *DAB*.

**WILLIAMS, Joseph Lanier** (son of John Williams, of Tennessee), a Representative from Tennessee; born near Knoxville, Knox County, Tenn., October 23, 1810; completed preparatory studies; attended the University of East Tennessee and the United States Military Academy at West Point; studied law; was admitted to the bar and commenced practice in Knoxville, Tenn.; elected as a Whig to the Twenty-fifth, Twenty-sixth, and Twenty-seventh Congresses (March 4, 1837-March 3, 1843); unsuccessful candidate for renomination in 1842; engaged in the practice of law in Washington, D.C.; appointed judge of the United States District Court of Dakota

Territory by President Lincoln; died in Knoxville, Tenn., December 14, 1865; interment in Old Gray Cemetery.

**WILLIAMS, Lawrence Gordon,** a Representative from Pennsylvania; born in Pittsburgh, Pa., September 15, 1913; moved to Philadelphia in June of 1922; graduated from Frankfort High School, and attended Drexel Institute of Technology; was a commissioner, 1952-1966, and president of the board, 1960-1966, township of Springfield, Pa.; employed by the Curtis Publishing Co., 1936-1966, and retired as assistant to the senior vice president in charge of manufacturing; served in the Army Air Corps during the Second World War; Delaware County's representative on the policy committee on the Penn-Jersey Transportation Study, 1959-1966, Delaware Valley Regional Planning Commission, and the Southeastern Pennsylvania Transportation Authority; past president of the Pennsylvania State Association of Township Commissioners; elected as a Republican to the Ninetieth and to the three succeeding Congresses (January 3, 1967-January 3, 1975); unsuccessful candidate for renomination in 1974 to the Ninety-fourth Congress; appointed by President Gerald R. Ford as special assistant to the Cochairman of the Ozarks Regional Commission and served in that capacity from January 20, 1975, until his death; resided in Springfield, Pa.; died in Philadelphia, Pa., July 13, 1975; interment in Edgewood Memorial Park, Concordville, Pa.

**WILLIAMS, Lemuel,** a Representative from Massachusetts; born in Taunton, Mass., June 18, 1747; was graduated from Harvard College in 1765; studied law; was admitted to the bar and practiced in Bristol and Worcester Counties, Mass.; town clerk of New Bedford, Mass., 1792-1800; elected as a Federalist to the Sixth, Seventh, and Eighth Congresses (March 4, 1799-March 3, 1805); member of the Massachusetts house of representatives in 1806; resumed the practice of law; died in Acushnet, Mass., November 8, 1828; interment in Acushnet Cemetery.

**WILLIAMS, Lewis** (brother of John Williams, of Tennessee, and Robert Williams and cousin of Marmaduke Williams), a Representative from North Carolina; born in Surry County, N.C., February 1, 1782; was graduated from the University of North Carolina at Chapel Hill in 1808; member of the State house of commons in 1813 and 1814; elected as a Republican to the Fourteenth Congress; reelected to the Fifteenth through Twenty-third Congresses and reelected as a Whig to the Twenty-fourth through Twenty-seventh Congresses and served from March 4, 1815, until his death; chairman, Committee on Claims (Fifteenth through Twenty-first Congresses), Committee on Territories (Twenty-third Congress); died in Washington, D.C., February 23, 1842; interment in Panther Creek Cemetery, Surry County, N.C.

**WILLIAMS, Lyle,** a Representative from Ohio; born in Philippi, Barbour County, W.Va., August 23, 1942; attended the public schools of North Bloomfield, Ohio; graduated from North Bloomfield High School, 1960; served in the United States Army Reserve, 1960-1968; barber; member, Bloomfield local school board, 1970-1972; Trumbull County Commissioner, 1972-1976; elected as a Republican to the Ninety-sixth and to the two succeeding Congresses (January 3, 1979-January 3, 1985); unsuccessful candidate for reelection in 1984 to the Ninety-ninth Congress; member of the external affairs staff, Office of Surface Mining, Department of the Interior, 1987; is a resident of Warren, Ohio.

**WILLIAMS, Marmaduke** (cousin of John Williams, of Tennessee, Lewis Williams, and Robert Williams), a Representative from North Carolina; born in Caswell County, N.C., April 6, 1774; completed preparatory studies; studied law; was admitted to the bar and practiced; member of the North Carolina State senate in 1802; elected as a Republican to the Eighth and to the two succeeding Congresses (March 4, 1803-March 3, 1809); was not a candidate for renomination in 1808 to the Eleventh Congress; moved to

Mississippi Territory in 1810, and later to Huntsville, Madison County, Ala.; in 1818 settled in Tuscaloosa, Ala.; delegate to the State constitutional convention in 1819, and the same year was an unsuccessful candidate for Governor of Alabama; member of the Alabama State house of representatives, 1821-1839; judge of the Tuscaloosa County Court, 1832-1842; died in Tuscaloosa, Ala., October 29, 1850; interment in Greenwood Cemetery.

**WILLIAMS, Morgan B.,** a Representative from Pennsylvania; born in Rhandir-Mwyn, parish of Llanfair-ar-y-Bryn, Carmarthenshire, Wales, September 17, 1831; attended the public schools; went to Australia in 1856; returned to Wales in August 1861; immigrated to the United States in March 1862 and settled in Scranton, Pa., where he worked in the coal mines; moved to Wilkes-Barre, Pa., in September 1865; appointed superintendent for the Lehigh & Wilkes-Barre Coal Co., which position he held for fourteen years; member of the school board and of the city council for twelve years; served in the Pennsylvania senate in 1884; member of the Chicago World's Fair Commission; elected as a Republican to the Fifty-fifth Congress (March 4, 1897-March 3, 1899); unsuccessful candidate for reelection in 1898 to the Fifty-sixth Congress; engaged in coal mining, and was vice president and general manager of the Red Ash Coal Co.; died in Wilkes-Barre, Pa., October 13, 1903; interment in Hollenback Cemetery.

**WILLIAMS, Nathan,** a Representative from New York; was born in Williamstown, Mass., December 19, 1773; attended the common schools in Bennington, Vt.; moved with his parents to Troy, N.Y., in 1786; studied law; was admitted to the bar in 1795 and commenced practice in Utica, N.Y.; assisted in the establishment of Utica Public Library, of which he was librarian for a number of years; president of the village corporation; president of the Manhattan Bank; district attorney for the sixth district 1801-1813; elected as a Republican to the Ninth Congress (March 4, 1805-March 3, 1807); served in the War of 1812; member of the State assembly 1816-1818 and in 1819; regent of the University of the State of New York from January 28, 1817, to February 13, 1824; district attorney of Oneida County 1818-1821; delegate to the State constitutional convention in 1821; judge of the circuit court 1823-1833; appointed clerk of the State supreme court in 1834 and moved to Geneva, Ontario County, N.Y., where he died September 25, 1835; interment in the "Burying Ground," Utica, Oneida County, N.Y.; reinterment in Forest Hill Cemetery.

**WILLIAMS, Reuel,** a Senator from Maine; born in Hallowell, Maine, June 2, 1783; attended Hallowell Academy; studied law; was admitted to the bar in 1804 and commenced practice in Augusta, Maine; member, State legislature 1812-1829, 1832, 1848; commissioner of public buildings in 1831; presidential elector on the Democratic ticket in 1836; elected February 22, 1837, as a Democrat to the United States Senate to fill the vacancy caused by the resignation of Ether Shepley and served from March 4, 1837, to February 15, 1843, when he resigned; chairman, Committee on Naval Affairs (Twenty-sixth Congress); manager of a railroad for twelve years; died in Augusta, Maine, on July 25, 1862; interment in the family cemetery on the banks of the Kennebec River, Augusta, Maine.

**Bibliography:** *DAB.*

**WILLIAMS, Richard,** a Representative from Oregon; born in Findlay, Hancock County, Ohio, November 15, 1836; attended the common schools; moved to Monroe County, Oreg., in 1851; was educated at the Willamette University, Salem, Oreg.; studied law; was admitted to the bar in 1857 and commenced practice in Kirbyville, Josephine County, Oreg.; moved to Portland, Oreg., in 1865 and practiced law; unsuccessful Republican candidate for election in 1874 to the Forty-fourth Congress; elected as a Republican to the Forty-fifth Congress (March 4, 1877-March 3, 1879); was not a candidate for renomination in 1878; resumed the practice of law in Portland, Oreg.; elected a member of the Portland School Board in 1890 and served for twenty years; died in Portland, Oreg., June 19, 1914; interment in Riverview Cemetery.

**WILLIAMS, Robert** (brother of John Williams, of Tennessee, and Lewis Williams and cousin of Marmaduke Williams), a Representative from North Carolina; born in Prince Edward County, Va., July 12, 1773; moved with his parents to Surry County, N.C.; received a liberal education; studied law; was admitted to the bar and commenced practice in what is now Rockingham County; member of the State senate 1792-1795; elected as a Republican to the Fifth, Sixth, and Seventh Congresses (March 4, 1797-March 3, 1803); appointed by President Jefferson in 1803 a member of a commission to ascertain the rights of persons claiming lands west of the Pearl River in Mississippi Territory and served in this capacity until 1807; Governor of Mississippi Territory from May 10, 1805, to March 3, 1809, when he resigned; subsequently resided in Mississippi and North Carolina, where he practiced law and engaged in planting; adjutant general of North Carolina; moved to Ouachita, Union Parish, La., where he died January 25, 1836; interment on his plantation near Monroe, Ouachita Parish, La.

**WILLIAMS, Seward Henry,** a Representative from Ohio; born in Amsterdam, Montgomery County, N.Y., November 7, 1870; attended the common schools, the Amsterdam Academy, Williams College, Williamstown, Mass., and Princeton College; was graduated in law from Washington and Lee University, Lexington, Va., in 1895; was admitted to the bar in 1895 and commenced practice the same year; city solicitor of Lorain, Ohio, 1901-1904; member of the State house of representatives 1910-1913; elected as a Republican to the Sixty-fourth Congress (March 4, 1915-March 3, 1917); unsuccessful candidate for reelection in 1916 to the Sixty-fifth Congress; resumed the practice of law; died in Lorain, Ohio, September 2, 1922; interment in Elmwood Cemetery.

**WILLIAMS, Sherrod,** a Representative from Kentucky; born in Pulaski County, Ky., in 1804; moved with his parents to Wayne County; received a limited education; learned the trade of brickmaker in Monticello when about fifteen years of age; studied law; was admitted to the bar and practiced; member of the Kentucky house of representatives 1829-1834 and in 1846; elected as a Whig to the Twenty-fourth, Twenty-fifth, and Twenty-sixth Congresses (March 4, 1835-March 3, 1841); chairman, Committee on Invalid Pensions (Twenty-sixth Congress); was not a candidate for reelection; moved to one of the Southern States, where he died.

**WILLIAMS, Thomas,** a Representative from Alabama; born near Richmond, Greensville County, Va., on August 11, 1825; attended preparatory schools and was graduated from the University of East Tennessee, Knoxville, Tenn.; studied law; was admitted to the bar in 1852 and commenced practice in Wetumpka, Elmore County, Ala.; justice of the peace; register in chancery; appointed prison inspector in 1872; member of the State house of representatives in 1878; elected as a Democrat to the Forty-sixth, Forty-seventh, and Forty-eighth Congresses (March 4, 1879-March 3, 1885); engaged in agricultural pursuits and resided in Wetumpka, Ala., until his death April 13, 1903; interment in the City Cemetery.

**WILLIAMS, Thomas,** a Representative from Pennsylvania; born in Greensburg, Westmoreland County, Pa., August 28, 1806; attended the common schools, and was graduated from Dickinson College, Carlisle, Pa., in 1825; studied law; was admitted to the bar in 1828 and commenced practice in Greensburg, Pa.; moved to Pittsburgh, Pa., in 1832 and continued the practice of law; served in the State senate 1838-1841; elected as a Republican to the Thirty-eighth, Thirty-ninth, and Fortieth Congresses (March 4, 1863-March 3, 1869); one of the managers appointed by the House of Representatives in 1868 to conduct the impeachment proceedings against President Andrew Johnson; was not a candidate for

renomination in 1868 to the Forty-first Congress, and lived in retirement until his death in Allegheny City, Pa., on June 16, 1872; interment in Allegheny Cemetery, Pittsburgh, Pa.

**WILLIAMS, Thomas Hickman,** a Senator from Mississippi; born in Williamson County, Tenn., January 20, 1801; attended the common schools; moved to Mississippi and settled in Pontotoc County; engaged in planting; appointed and subsequently elected as a Democrat to the United States Senate to fill the vacancy caused by the resignation of James F. Trotter and served from November 12, 1838, to March 3, 1839; secretary and treasurer of the University of Mississippi at Oxford 1845-1851; known as "Father of the State University," being the first to propose it and also aiding to secure it; died on his plantation south of Pontotoc, Pontotoc County, Miss., May 3, 1851; interment in the private cemetery on the family estate.

**WILLIAMS, Thomas Hill,** a Senator from Mississippi; born in North Carolina in 1780; completed preparatory studies; studied law; was admitted to the bar and practiced; register of the land office for the Territory of Mississippi in 1805; secretary of the Territory, 1805; Acting Governor in 1806; reappointed secretary, 1807; Acting Governor from March 4 to June 30, 1809, filling the vacancy caused by the resignation of Governor Robert Williams; collector of customs at New Orleans, 1810; delegate to the State constitutional convention; upon the admission of Mississippi as a State into the Union in 1817 was elected as a Republican to the United States Senate; reelected in 1823 and served from December 10, 1817, to March 3, 1829; chairman, Committee on Public Lands (Sixteenth Congress); moved to Tennessee, where he died, in Robertson County, in 1840.

**WILLIAMS, Thomas Scott,** a Representative from Connecticut; born in Wethersfield, Conn., June 26, 1777; completed preparatory studies; was graduated from Yale College in 1794; studied law; was admitted to the bar in 1799 and commenced practice in Mansfield, Conn.; moved to Hartford, Conn., in 1803; appointed attorney of the board of managers of the school fund of Hartford 1809-1810; served in the State house of representatives in 1813, 1815, and 1816; clerk of the house in 1815 and 1816; elected as a Federalist to the Fifteenth Congress (March 4, 1817-March 3, 1819); again a member of the State house of representatives in 1819, 1825, and 1827-1829; appointed in 1829 an associate judge of the supreme court of errors and of the superior court, and in May 1834 appointed chief justice, holding the position until his resignation in May 1847; mayor of Hartford 1831-1835; resigned from public office; president of the American Tract Society of New York from May 1848 until his death; died in Hartford, Conn., December 15, 1861; interment in Old North Cemetery.

**Bibliography:** *DAB.*

**WILLIAMS, Thomas Sutler,** a Representative from Illinois; born in Louisville, Clay County, Ill., February 14, 1872; attended Willis district school, Louisville High School, and Austin College, Effingham, Ill.; studied law; was admitted to the bar in 1897 and commenced practice in Louisville; city attorney 1897-1899; member of the State house of representatives 1899-1901; mayor of Louisville 1907-1909; prosecuting attorney of Clay County 1908-1915; became the owner and publisher of the Clay County Republican at Louisville in 1920; moved to Harrisburg, Salina County, Ill., in 1926; elected as a Republican to the Sixty-fourth and to the seven succeeding Congresses and served from March 4, 1915, until his resignation November 11, 1929, having been appointed a judge for the Court of Claims of the United States and served until his death in Washington, D.C., April 5, 1940; chairman, Committee on Expenditures in the Department of Commerce (Sixty-sixth Congress); interment in Cedar Hill Cemetery.

**WILLIAMS, Thomas Wheeler,** a Representative from Connecticut; born in Stonington, Conn., September 28, 1789; attended the public schools; at the age of fifteen was employed as a clerk in New York City, and before he was twenty-one was employed on a business mission to Norway, Sweden, and Russia; for about eight years was engaged in the shipping business; moved to New London, Conn., in 1818 and became a prominent figure in the whaling business; elected as a Whig to the Twenty-sixth and Twenty-seventh Congresses (March 4, 1839-March 3, 1843); chairman, Committee on Mileage (Twenty-sixth and Twenty-seventh Congresses); member of the State house of representatives in 1846 and 1847; president of the New London, Willamantic and Palmer Railroad (later the New London Northern Railroad) in 1847 and for many years thereafter; died in New London, Conn., December 31, 1874; interment in Cedar Grove Cemetery.

**WILLIAMS, William,** a Delegate from Connecticut; born in Lebanon, Conn., March 29, 1731; completed preparatory studies; was graduated from Harvard College in 1751; studied theology for a year; engaged in mercantile pursuits; town clerk of Lebanon 1753-1796; member of a military expedition to Lake George in 1755; member of the State house of representatives 1757-1762, 1763-1776, and 1780-1784, serving as speaker in 1775 and 1781-1783; Member of the Continental Congress in 1776 and 1777; a signer of the Declaration of Independence; member of the council of safety during the Revolution; judge of the county court of Windham 1776-1804; judge of probate for the Windham district 1776-1808; became an assistant councilor in 1780 and served as assistant and as councilor for twenty-four years; member of the Connecticut ratification convention in 1787; died in Lebanon, Conn., August 2, 1811; interment in the Trumbull Tomb, East Cemetery.

Bibliography: *DAB*; Stark, Bruce P. *Connecticut Signer: William Williams.* Chester, Conn.: Pequot Press, 1975.

**WILLIAMS, William,** a Representative from Indiana; born near Carlisle, Cumberland County, Pa., May 11, 1821; attended the common schools and received a very limited education; studied law; was admitted to the bar in 1845 and commenced practice in Warsaw, Kosciusko County, Ind.; treasurer of Kosciusko County in 1852; resigned the office of treasurer in order to become a candidate for Lieutenant Governor; unsuccessful candidate for Lieutenant Governor in 1853; managed the Bank of Warsaw for several years; director of the Fort Wayne and Chicago Railway, 1854-1856; director of the Michigan City prison, 1859-1862; served in the Union Army as commandant of Camp Allen, Fort Wayne, Ind., in 1862 and as paymaster of Volunteers, with headquarters at Louisville, Ky., until the close of the war; elected as a Republican to the Fortieth and to the three succeeding Congresses (March 4, 1867-March 3, 1875); chairman, Committee on Expenditures in the Department of War (Fortieth through Forty-third Congresses); was not a candidate for renomination in 1874 to the Forty-fourth Congress; resumed the practice of law in Warsaw, Ind.; appointed by President Chester A. Arthur as Chargé d'Affaires to Paraguay and Uruguay on April 12, 1882, and served until February 14, 1885, when he resigned; returned to Warsaw in 1885 and retired from active business pursuits; died in Warsaw, Ind., April 22, 1896; interment in Oakwood Cemetery.

**WILLIAMS, William,** a Representative from New York; born in Bolton, Conn., September 6, 1815; received a common-school education; clerk in a bank in Windham, Conn.; moved to Sandusky, Ohio, in 1838, and to Buffalo, N.Y., in 1839, where he engaged in banking; also served as a railroad manager and president; member of the State assembly in 1866 and 1867; elected as a Democrat to the Forty-second Congress (March 4, 1871-March 3, 1873); unsuccessful candidate for reelection in 1872 to the Forty-third Congress; withdrew from public life and active business pursuits, and lived in retirement until his death in Buffalo, N.Y., September 10, 1876; interment in Forest Lawn Cemetery.

**WILLIAMS, William Brewster,** a Representative from Michigan; born in Pittsford, Monroe County, N.Y., July 28, 1826; attended the common schools and received an academic education; was graduated from the State and National Law School, Ballston Spa, N.Y., in 1851; was admitted to the bar the same year and commenced practice in Rochester, N.Y.; moved to Allegan, Mich., in 1855; judge of probate, 1857-1865; member of the Michigan State senate, 1866-1870, serving as president pro tempore in 1869; member of the State constitutional convention in 1867; appointed by Governor Henry P. Baldwin in 1871 as a member of the State board for the supervisory control of the charitable, penal, and beneficiary institutions, which position he resigned upon his election to Congress; elected as a Republican to the Forty-third Congress to fill the vacancy caused by the death of Wilder D. Foster; reelected to the Forty-fourth Congress, and served from December 1, 1873 to March 3, 1877; was not a candidate for renomination in 1876 to the Forty-fifth Congress; railroad commissioner of Michigan, 1877-1883; resumed the practice of law; died in Allegan, Mich., March 4, 1905; interment in Oakwood Cemetery.

**WILLIAMS, William Elza,** a Representative from Illinois; born near Detroit, Pike County, Ill., May 5, 1857; attended the public schools and Illinois College, Jacksonville, Ill.; studied law; was admitted to the bar in 1880 and practiced in Detroit and Pittsfield, Ill.; State's attorney of Pike County 1886-1892; member of the board of aldermen of Pittsfield; member of the board of education; became trial lawyer for the City Railway Co. of Chicago in 1903; elected as a Democrat to the Fifty-sixth Congress (March 4, 1899-March 3, 1901); resumed the practice of law in Pittsfield, Ill.; elected to the Sixty-third and Sixty-fourth Congresses (March 4, 1913-March 3, 1917); unsuccessful candidate for reelection in 1916 and for election in 1918 to the Sixty-sixth Congress; continued the practice of law until his death in Pittsfield, Ill., September 13, 1921; interment in Pittsfield West Cemetery.

**WILLIAMS, William Robert,** a Representative from New York; born in Brookfield, Madison County, N.Y., August 11, 1884; moved to Cassville, Oneida County, N.Y., with his parents in 1891; attended the public schools of Bridgewater, N.Y.; salesman with Standard Oil Co., of New York, 1907-1910; engaged in farming at Cassville, N.Y.; member of the State assembly 1935-1943; sheriff of Oneida County 1943-1951; elected as a Republican to the Eighty-second and to the three succeeding Congresses (January 3, 1951-January 3, 1959); was not a candidate for renomination in 1958 to the Eighty-sixth Congress; chairman, Oneida County Republican Committee, 1959-1961; resumed and continued his interests in farming at Cassville, N.Y., where he died May 9, 1972; interment in Sauquoit Valley Cemetery, Sauquoit, N.Y.

**WILLIAMSON, Ben Mitchell,** a Senator from Kentucky; born in White Post, Pike County, Ky., October 16, 1864; attended the rural schools of Kentucky and Bethany (W.Va.) College; engaged in the wholesale hardware business at Catlettsburg, Ky., from 1886 until 1924, and at Ashland, Ky., in 1924; also engaged in banking and in the mining of coal; one of the founders of the Kentucky Crippled Children's Commission, serving as president from 1924 to 1941; member of the board of charities and correction for the Commonwealth of Kentucky, 1929-1930; director of the International Society for Crippled Children; elected as a Democrat to the United States Senate on November 4, 1930, to fill the vacancy caused by the resignation of Frederic M. Sackett and served from December 1, 1930, to March 3, 1931; was not a candidate for election to the full term; resumed the wholesale hardware business at Ashland, Ky., with residence in Catlettsburg, Ky.; also interested financially in various other business enterprises; died in Cincinnati,

Ohio, June 23, 1941; interment in Ashland Cemetery Mausoleum, Ashland, Ky.

**WILLIAMSON, Hugh,** a Delegate and a Representative from North Carolina; born on Oterara Creek, in West Nottingham Township, Pa., December 5, 1735; attended the common schools; prepared for college at Newark, Del., and was graduated from the University of Pennsylvania at Philadelphia in 1757; studied theology, and was licensed to preach in 1758; resigned, owing to ill health, in 1760; professor of mathematics in the College of Philadelphia; studied medicine in Edinburgh, Scotland, and Utrecht, The Netherlands; returned to Philadelphia and practiced; engaged in business; member of the American Philosophical Society, and was a member of the commission to observe the transits of Venus and Mercury in 1773; at the time of the "Boston Tea Party" he was examined in England by the privy council regarding it; returned to America in 1776 and settled in Edenton, N.C.; engaged in mercantile pursuits; during the Revolutionary War was surgeon general of the North Carolina troops 1779-1782; Member of the State house of commons in 1782 and 1785; member of the Continental Congress 1782-1785, and 1788; delegate to the Federal Convention in 1787; member of the State ratification convention in 1789; elected as a Federalist to the First and Second Congresses and served from March 19, 1790, until March 3, 1793; moved to New York City in 1793; engaged extensively in literary pursuits until his death in New York City, May 22, 1819; interment in the Apthrop tomb in Trinity Churchyard.

**Bibliography:** *DAB*; Potts, Louis W. "Hugh Williamson: The Poor Man's Franklin and the National Domain." *North Carolina Historical Review* 64 (October 1987): 371-93.

**WILLIAMSON, John Newton,** a Representative from Oregon; born near Junction City, Lane County, Oreg., November 8, 1855; attended the country schools; attended Willamette University, Salem, Oreg.; moved to Prineville, Oreg., and engaged in livestock raising; sheriff of Cook County, 1886-1888; member of the Oregon State house of representatives from 1888 until 1898; served in the State senate, 1900-1902; elected as a Republican to the Fifty-eighth and Fifty-ninth Congresses (March 4, 1903-March 3, 1907); declined to be a candidate for renomination in 1906 to the Sixtieth Congress; engaged in stock raising and agricultural pursuits; appointed postmaster at Prineville, Cook County, Oreg., March 21, 1922; reappointed on May 18, 1926, and served until June 30, 1934, when he retired to his farm in Central Oregon; died in Prineville, Oreg., August 29, 1943; interment in the Masonic Cemetery.

**WILLIAMSON, William,** a Representative from South Dakota; born near New Sharon, Mahaska County, Iowa, October 7, 1875; moved with his parents to Plankinton, Aurora County, S.Dak., in 1882; attended the public schools and the Wayne (Nebr.) Normal School; engaged in agricultural pursuits and also taught school for several years; was graduated from the University of South Dakota at Vermilion in 1903 and from the law department of that university in 1905; was admitted to the bar in 1905 and commenced practice in Oacoma, Lyman County, S.Dak.; founder, with his brother, of the Murdo Coyote and the Prairie Sun; prosecuting attorney of Lyman County from 1905 until 1911; circuit judge of the eleventh judicial district from 1911 to 1921; delegate to the Republican National Convention of 1912; elected as a Republican to the Sixty-seventh and to the five succeeding Congresses (March 4, 1921-March 3, 1933); chairman, Committee on Expenditures in the Department of the Interior (Sixty-eighth and Sixty-ninth Congresses), Committee on Expenditures in Executive Departments (Seventieth and Seventy-first Congresses); unsuccessful candidate for reelection in 1932 to the Seventy-third Congress; resumed the practice of law in Rapid City, S.Dak.; special assistant attorney general of South Dakota and assigned as general counsel for the Public Utilities Commission, 1939-1951, and also the Department of Insurance of

South Dakota the last five years; officer with an insurance company from 1950 until 1972; member of the Mount Rushmore National Memorial Commission from 1928 to 1972; died in Custer, S.Dak., July 15, 1972; interment in Pine Lawn Cemetery, Rapid City, S.Dak.

**Bibliography:** Williamson, William. *William Williamson; Student, Homesteader, Teacher, Lawyer, Judge, Congressman and Trusted Friend; An Autobiography.* Rapid City, S.Dak.: The Author, 1964.

**WILLIAMSON, William Durkee,** a Representative from Maine; born in Canterbury, Conn., July 31, 1779; moved in boyhood with his father to Amherst, Mass.; attended the common schools and Williams College, Williamstown, Mass.; was graduated from Brown University, Providence, R.I., in 1804; studied law; was admitted to the bar and commenced practice in Bangor, Maine (then a district of Massachusetts), in 1807; State's attorney for Hancock County from 1808 until 1815; postmaster of Bangor, Maine, from 1810 to 1821; member of the Massachusetts senate from 1816 until the separation of Maine from Massachusetts in 1820; served in the Maine State senate in 1820 and 1821 and was elected its president both years; as president of the State senate he became Governor upon the resignation of Governor William King in 1821; elected to the Seventeenth Congress (March 4, 1821-March 3, 1823); was not a candidate for renomination in 1822 to the Eighteenth Congress; judge of probate for Penobscot County from 1824 until 1840; bank commissioner, 1838-1841; died in Bangor, Maine, May 27, 1846; interment in Mount Hope Cemetery.

**Bibliography:** *DAB*.

**WILLIE, Asa Hoxie,** a Representative from Texas; born in Washington, Wilkes County, Ga., October 11, 1829; attended private schools and pursued an academic course; moved to Washington County, Tex., in 1846 and settled in Brenham; studied law; was admitted to the bar in 1848 and commenced practice in Brenham; district attorney of the third judicial district of Texas, 1852-1854; during the Civil War served in the Confederate Army under General John Gregg with the rank of major; moved to Galveston, Tex., in 1866; elected associate justice of the Texas State supreme court the same year but was removed in 1867 by the military commander; elected as a Democrat to the Forty-third Congress (March 4, 1873-March 3, 1875); declined to be a candidate for renomination in 1874 to the Forty-fourth Congress; resumed the practice of law in Galveston; elected chief justice of the Texas State supreme court in November 1882 and served until his resignation on March 3, 1888; resumed the practice of law; died in Galveston, Tex., March 16, 1899; interment in Episcopal Cemetery.

**Bibliography:** *DAB*.

**WILLING, Thomas,** a Delegate from Pennsylvania; born in Philadelphia, Pa., December 19, 1731; completed preparatory studies in Bath, England; studied law in London at the Inner Temple; returned to Philadelphia and engaged in mercantile pursuits until 1793; member of the common council in 1755; alderman in 1759; associate justice of the city court October 2, 1759; justice of the court of common pleas February 28, 1761; mayor of Philadelphia in 1763; associate justice of the supreme court of Pennsylvania 1767-1777; member of the committee of correspondence in 1774 and of the committee of safety in 1775; served in the colonial house of representatives; Member of the Continental Congress in 1775 and 1776; president of the Bank of North America; first president of the Bank of the United States 1791-1811; resumed mercantile pursuits; died in Philadelphia, Pa., January 19, 1821; interment in Christ Churchyard.

**Bibliography:** *DAB*; Slaski, Eugene R. "Thomas Willing: Moderation during the American Revolution." Ph.D. dissertation, Florida State University, 1971.

**WILLIS, Albert Shelby,** a Representative from Kentucky; born in Shelbyville, Shelby County, Ky., January 22, 1843; attended the common schools, and was graduated from the Louisville (Ky.) Male High School in 1860; taught school four years; was graduated from the Louisville Law School in 1866; was admitted to the bar and commenced the practice of law in Louisville; prosecuting attorney for Jefferson County, 1874-1877; elected as a Democrat to the Forty-fifth and to the four succeeding Congresses (March 4, 1877-March 3, 1887); chairman, Committee on Rivers and Harbors (Forty-eighth and Forty-ninth Congresses); unsuccessful candidate for renomination in 1886 to the Fiftieth Congress; resumed the practice of law; appointed Minister to Hawaii by President Grover Cleveland on September 13, 1893, and served until his death in Honolulu, Hawaii, January 6, 1897; interment in Cave Hill Cemetery, Louisville, Ky.

**Bibliography:** *DAB.*

**WILLIS, Benjamin Albertson,** a Representative from New York; born in Roslyn, Queens County, N.Y., March 24, 1840; was graduated from Union College in 1861; studied law; was admitted to the bar in 1862 and commenced practice in New York City; during the Civil War enlisted in the Union Army in 1862; captain in the One Hundred and Nineteenth New York Volunteers, and subsequently colonel of the Twelfth Regiment, New York State Volunteers; honorably discharged in 1864; resumed the practice of law; member of the State assembly 1872-1878; elected as a Democrat to the Forty-fourth and Forty-fifth Congresses (March 4, 1875-March 3, 1879); chairman, Committee on Expenditures in the Department of the Navy (Forty-fifth Congress); unsuccessful candidate for reelection in 1878 to the Forty-sixth Congress; engaged in the practice of law and also in the real estate business; died in New York City on October 14, 1886; interment in Friends Cemetery, Westbury, Long Island; reinterment in Woodlawn Cemetery.

**WILLIS, Edwin Edward,** a Representative from Louisiana; born in Arnaudville, St. Martin Parish, La., October 2, 1904; graduated from St. Martin Parish public schools and from the law school of Loyola University, New Orleans, La., in 1926; was admitted to the bar in 1926 and commenced the practice of law in New Orleans, La., and in St. Martinville, La., beginning in 1936; law lecturer in evening classes, 1926-1936; owner and operator of a plantation in St. Martin Parish; elected to the Louisiana State senate in January 1948, and served until elected to Congress; delegate to the Democratic National Convention of 1956; elected as a Democrat to the Eighty-first and to the nine succeeding Congresses (January 3, 1949-January 3, 1969); chairman, Committee on Un-American Activities (Eighty-eighth through Ninetieth Congresses); unsuccessful candidate for renomination in 1968 to the Ninetieth Congress; legislative consultant and author; operated a 1,000-acre farm near Arnaudville, La.; died in St. Martinville, La., October 24, 1972; interment in St. Martin of Tours Catholic Cemetery.

**WILLIS, Francis,** a Representative from Georgia; born in Frederick County, Va., January 5, 1745; received a liberal education; served as captain and colonel in the Revolutionary War in 1777 and 1778; moved to Wilkes County, Ga., in 1784; elected to the Second Congress (March 4, 1791-March 3, 1793); moved to Maury County, Tenn.; died January 25, 1829.

**WILLIS, Frank Bartlett,** a Representative and a Senator from Ohio; born in Lewis Center, Delaware County, Ohio, December 28, 1871; attended the common schools; graduated from the Ohio Northern University at Ada in 1894; studied law; was admitted to the bar in 1906; professor of history and economics at Ohio Northern University from 1894 until 1906; professor of economics and law, 1906-1910; member, Ohio State house of representatives, 1900-1904; was elected as a Republican to the Sixty-second and Sixty-third Congresses, and served from March 4, 1911 to January 9, 1915, when he resigned, having been elected Governor; elected Governor of Ohio in 1914, and served from January 11, 1915 to January 8, 1917; unsuccessful candidate for reelection in 1916, and for election as Governor in 1918; elected as a Republican to the United States Senate in 1920 for the term commencing March 4, 1921, and subsequently appointed in January 1921 to fill the vacancy in the term ending March 3, 1921, caused by the resignation of Warren G. Harding; reelected in 1926, and served from January 14, 1921 until his death in Delaware, Ohio, March 30, 1928, while campaigning for the Republican presidential nomination; chairman, Committee on Territories and Insular Possessions (Sixty-eighth through Seventieth Congresses); interment in Oak Grove Cemetery.

**Bibliography:** Ridinger, Gerald. "The Political Career of Frank B. Willis." Ph.D. dissertation, Ohio State University, 1957.

**WILLIS, Jonathan Spencer,** a Representative from Delaware; born in Oxford, Talbot County, Md., April 5, 1830; attended the district schools and studied under private tutors; taught school seven years and then entered the ministry of the Methodist Episcopal Church; served charges in Maryland, Delaware, Philadelphia, Pa., New York City, and Stamford, Conn.; retired from the ministry in 1884; settled on a farm near Milford, Del., and engaged in fruit growing; unsuccessful Republican candidate for election in 1892 to the Fifty-third Congress; elected as a Republican to the Fifty-fourth Congress (March 4, 1895-March 3, 1897); unsuccessful candidate for reelection in 1896 to the Fifty-fifth Congress; engaged in agricultural pursuits; died in Milford, Sussex County, Del., November 24, 1903; interment in Barrett's Chapel Cemetery, near Frederica, Kent County, Del.

**WILLIS, Raymond Eugene,** a Senator from Indiana; born in Waterloo, De Kalb County, Ind., August 11, 1875; attended the public schools and graduated from Wabash College, Crawfordsville, Ind., in 1896; learned the printer's trade in Waterloo, Ind.; moved to Angola, Ind., and engaged in the newspaper publishing business in 1898; postmaster of Angola 1910-1914; during the First World War served as chairman of Steuben County Council of Defense 1917-1918; member, State house of representatives 1919-1921; unsuccessful candidate for election to the United States Senate in 1938; elected as a Republican to the United States Senate in 1940, and served from January 3, 1941, to January 3, 1947; was not a candidate for renomination in 1946; resumed the publishing business as president of the Steuben Printing Co.; trustee of Tri-State College at Angola; died in Angola, Ind., March 21, 1956; interment in Circle Hill Cemetery.

**WILLITS, Edwin,** a Representative from Michigan; born at Otto, Cattaraugus County, N.Y., April 24, 1830; moved to Michigan with his parents in September 1836; was graduated from the University of Michigan at Ann Arbor in June 1855; settled in Monroe, Mich., in April 1856; editor of the Monroe Commercial, 1856-1861; studied law; was admitted to the bar in December 1857 and commenced practice in Monroe; prosecuting attorney of Monroe County, 1860-1862; member of the State board of education 1860-1872; appointed postmaster of Monroe on January 1, 1863, by President Abraham Lincoln, and removed by President Andrew Johnson on October 15, 1866; member of the commission to revise the constitution of the State in 1873; elected as a Republican to the Forty-fifth and to the two succeeding Congresses (March 4, 1877-March 3, 1883); chairman, Committee on Expenditures in the Department of Justice (Forty-seventh Congress); was not a candidate for renomination in 1882 to the Forty-eighth Congress; principal of the Michigan State normal school at Ypsilanti, 1883-1885; president of the Michigan Agricultural College, 1885-1889; First Assistant Secretary of Agriculture from March 23, 1889, to December 31, 1893; continued the practice of law in Washington, D.C., until his death there October 22, 1896; interment in Woodlawn Cemetery, Monroe, Mich.

**Bibliography:** Bald, F. Clever. "Edwin Willits." In *Michigan and the Cleveland Era*. Edited by Earl D. Babst and Lewis G. Vander Velde. Ann Arbor: University of Michigan Press, 1948.

**WILLOUGHBY, Westel, Jr.,** a Representative from New York; born in Goshen, Conn., November 20, 1769; moved to Newport, N.Y.; studied medicine and engaged in practice; appointed judge of the court of common pleas of Herkimer County in 1805 and served until 1821; president of the Herkimer County Medical Society 1806-1816 and 1818-1836; served in the State assembly in 1808 and 1809; president of the College of Physicians and Surgeons for the Western District of New York 1812-1844; member of the medical staff of the militia and served in the War of 1812; successfully contested as a Republican the election of William S. Smith to the Fourteenth Congress and served from December 13, 1815, to March 3, 1817; founded the town of Willoughby, Ohio, and also Willoughby College (now a part of Syracuse University); died in Newport, Herkimer County, N.Y., October 3, 1844; interment in the First Baptist Church Cemetery.

**WILMOT, David,** a Representative and a Senator from Pennsylvania; born in Bethany, Pa., January 20, 1814; completed preparatory studies in the academy at Aurora, N.Y.; studied law; was admitted to the bar of Bradford County, Pa., in 1834 and commenced practice in Towanda, Bradford County, Pa.; elected as a Democrat to the Twenty-ninth and to the two succeeding Congresses (March 4, 1845-March 3, 1851); was not a candidate for renomination in 1850 to the Thirty-second Congress; sponsor of the "Wilmot Proviso" of 1846, which stated that slavery would not be permitted to exist in any part of new territory acquired from Mexico, and was proposed as an amendment to a Mexican War appropriations bill; took a leading part in the founding of the Republican Party in 1854; presiding judge of the thirteenth judicial district from 1851 until 1861; unsuccessful Republican candidate for governor of Pennsylvania in 1857; elected as a Republican to the United States Senate to fill the vacancy caused by the resignation of Simon Cameron, and served from March 14, 1861 to March 3, 1863; was not a candidate for reelection in 1862; member of the peace convention of 1861, held in Washington, D.C., in an effort to devise means to prevent the impending war; appointed by President Abraham Lincoln a judge of the United States Court of Claims in 1863 and served until his death in Towanda, Pa., March 16, 1868; interment in Riverside Cemetery.

**Bibliography:** *DAB*; Going, Charles. *David Wilmot: Free-Soiler, A Biography of the Great Advocate of the Wilmot Proviso*. 1924. Reprint. Gloucester, Mass.: P. Smith, 1966.

**WILSHIRE, William Wallace,** a Representative from Arkansas; born in Shawneetown, Gallatin County, Ill., on September 8, 1830; educated in the country schools; spent three years in California in gold mining, from 1852 to 1855, when he returned to his home in Port Byron and engaged in the coal mining and mercantile business; studied law, and was admitted to the bar in 1859; entered the Union Army as major in the One Hundred and Twenty-sixth Regiment, Illinois Volunteer Infantry, and served from July 16, 1862, to July 16, 1864, when he resigned his commission on account of ill health; after the war located in Little Rock, Ark., and commenced the practice of law; appointed solicitor general of the State in 1867; chief justice of the State supreme court from 1868 to 1871, when he resigned and resumed the practice of law; presented credentials as a Republican Member-elect to the Forty-third Congress and served from March 4, 1873, to June 16, 1874, when he was succeeded by Thomas M. Gunter, who contested his election; elected as a Democrat to the Forty-fourth Congress (March 4, 1875-March 3, 1877); was not a candidate for renomination in 1876; engaged in the practice of law in Washington, D.C., where he died August 19, 1888; interment in Mount Holly Cemetery, Little Rock, Ark.

**WILSON, Alexander,** a Representative from Virginia; born in that State; completed preparatory studies; member of the Virginia house of delegates in 1803 and in 1804; elected as a Republican to the Eighth Congress to fill the vacancy caused by the resignation of Andrew Moore; reelected to the Ninth and Tenth Congresses, and served from December 4, 1804 to March 3, 1809.

**WILSON, Benjamin,** a Representative from West Virginia; born in Wilsonburg, Harrison County, Va. (now West Virginia), April 30, 1825; attended the Northwestern Virginia Academy at Clarksburg and the law school in Staunton, Va.; was admitted to the bar in 1848 and commenced practice in Clarksburg, Harrison County, Va. (now West Virginia); Commonwealth attorney for Harrison County 1852-1860; member of the State constitutional convention in 1861; member of the State constitutional convention of West Virginia in 1871; delegate to the Democratic National Convention in 1872; unsuccessful candidate for election in 1872 to the Forty-third Congress; elected as a Democrat to the Forty-fourth and to the three succeeding Congresses (March 4, 1875-March 3, 1883); Assistant Attorney General of the United States 1885-1893; died in Clarksburg, W.Va., April 26, 1901; interment in the Odd Fellows Cemetery.

**WILSON, Charles,** a Representative from Texas; born in Trinity, Tex., June 1, 1933; attended the public schools and graduated from Trinity High School in 1951; while a student at Sam Houston State University at Huntsville, Tex., was appointed to the United States Naval Academy and received a B.S. from the Academy in 1956; served in the United States Navy, with rank of lieutenant, 1956-1960; engaged in the lumber business; elected to the Texas State house of representatives, 1960-1966; elected to the Texas State senate, 1966-1972; elected as a Democrat to the Ninety-third and to the eleven succeeding Congresses (January 3, 1973-January 3, 1997); was not a candidate for reelection in 1996 to the One Hundred Fifth Congress; is a resident of Lufkin, Tex.

**WILSON, Charles Herbert,** a Representative from California; born in Magna, Salt Lake County, Utah, February 15, 1917; with his parents, moved to Los Angeles, Calif., in 1922 and attended the public schools there and in Inglewood; employee of a bank, 1935-1942; served as a staff sergeant in the United States Army from June 1942 to December 1945, with overseas service in the European Theater of Operations; in 1945, established an insurance agency in Los Angeles, Calif.; served in the State legislature, 1954-1962, as assemblyman from the Sixty-sixth Assembly District; elected as a Democrat to the Eighty-eighth and to the eight succeeding Congresses (January 3, 1963-January 3, 1981); censured by the House of Representatives on June 10, 1980, for financial misconduct; unsuccessful candidate for renomination in 1980 to the Ninety-seventh Congress; was a resident of Tantallon, Md., until his death in Clinton, Md., on July 21, 1984; interment in Inglewood Park Cemetery, Inglewood, Calif.

**WILSON, Earl,** a Representative from Indiana; born on a farm near Huron, Lawrence County, Ind., on April 18, 1906; attended the public schools and Purdue University, Lafayette, Ind.; was graduated from the Coyne Electrical School, Chicago, Ill., in 1928 and from Indiana University at Bloomington in 1931; taught high school in Dubois, White, and Decatur Counties, Ind., 1931-1938; high school principal in Jackson County, Ind., in 1939 and 1940; elected as a Republican to the Seventy-seventh and to the eight succeeding Congresses (January 3, 1941-January 3, 1959); unsuccessful candidate for reelection in 1958 to the Eighty-sixth Congress; elected to the Eighty-seventh and to the Eighty-eighth Congresses (January 3, 1961-January 3, 1965); unsuccessful candidate for reelection in 1964 to the Eighty-ninth Congress; elected to the Indiana State senate, ninety-sixth and ninety-seventh sessions; was a resident of Bedford, Ind.; died April 27, 1990.

**WILSON, Edgar,** a Representative from Idaho; born in Armstrong County, Pa., near the city of Pittsburgh, February 25, 1861; attended the public schools; was graduated from the law department of the University of Michigan at Ann Arbor in 1884 and admitted to the bar; moved to Idaho in 1884, settled in Boise City and commenced the practice of law; elected city attorney of Boise City in 1887 and district attorney in 1888; member of the constitutional convention that framed the State constitution in 1890; elected as a Republican to the Fifty-fourth Congress (March 4, 1895-March 3, 1897); was not a candidate for reelection, having been nominated as a candidate for the bench; unsuccessful candidate for justice of the State supreme court in 1896; elected as a Silver Republican to the Fifty-sixth Congress (March 4, 1899-March 3, 1901); resumed the practice of law in Boise, Idaho, where he died January 3, 1915; interment in Morris Hill Cemetery.

**WILSON, Edgar Campbell** (son of Thomas Wilson of Virginia and father of Eugene McLanahan Wilson), a Representative from Virginia; born in Morgantown, Monongalia County, Va. (now West Virginia), October 18, 1800; completed preparatory studies; studied law; was admitted to the bar June 24, 1832, and commenced practice in Morgantown; elected as an Anti-Jacksonian to the Twenty-third Congress (March 4, 1833-March 3, 1835); was an unsuccessful candidate for reelection in 1834 to the Twenty-fourth Congress; resumed the practice of law in Morgantown; appointed prosecuting attorney in the circuit court of Marion County in 1842; died in Morgantown, Va. (now West Virginia), April 24, 1860; interment in Oak Grove Cemetery.

**WILSON, Emmett** (grandson of Augustus Emmett Maxwell), a Representative from Florida; born during the temporary residence of his parents at Belize, British Honduras, Central America, September 17, 1882; moved with his parents to Chipley, Fla.; attended the public schools and Florida State College at Tallahassee; employed as a railroad telegrapher and later as a stenographer; was graduated from the law department of the John B. Stetson University at De Land in 1904; was admitted to the bar the same year and commenced practice in Marianna, Fla.; moved to Pensacola in 1906 and continued the practice of law; appointed assistant United States attorney for the northern district of Florida February 1, 1907, and United States attorney for the same district October 7, 1907, holding the position until March 1909; State's attorney for the first judicial circuit of Florida 1911-1913; elected as a Democrat to the Sixty-third and Sixty-fourth Congresses (March 4, 1913-March 3, 1917); unsuccessful candidate for renomination in 1916; resumed the practice of law in Pensacola, Fla., and died there on May 29, 1918; interment in St. John's Cemetery.

**WILSON, Ephraim King** (father of Ephraim King Wilson [1821-1891]), a Representative from Maryland; born near Snow Hill, Somerset (now Worcester) County, Md., September 15, 1771; received instruction in private schools and was graduated from Princeton College in 1790; studied law; was admitted to the bar in 1792 and commenced practice in Snow Hill, Md.; elected to the Twentieth Congress and reelected as a Jacksonian to the Twenty-first Congress (March 4, 1827-March 3, 1831); was not a candidate for renomination in 1830 to the Twenty-second Congress; resumed the practice of law until his death in Snow Hill, Md., on January 2, 1834; interment in the Makemie Presbyterian Churchyard.

**WILSON, Ephraim King** (son of Ephraim King Wilson [1771-1834]), a Representative and a Senator from Maryland; born in Snow Hill, Worcester County, Md., December 22, 1821; attended Union Academy at Snow Hill and Washington Academy, Princess Anne, Md.; graduated from Jefferson College, Canonsburg, Pa., in 1840; taught school for six years; studied law; was admitted to the bar in 1848 and commenced practice in Snow Hill, Md.; member, State house of delegates 1847; presidential elector on the Democratic ticket in 1852; because of impaired health abandoned the practice of law in 1867 and retired to his farm; examiner and treasurer of the school board of Worcester County in 1868; elected as a Democrat to the Forty-third Congress (March 4, 1873-March 3, 1875); declined to be a candidate for renomination in 1874; judge of the first judicial circuit of Maryland 1878-1884; elected as a Democrat in 1884 to the United States Senate and served from March 4, 1885, until his death; had been reelected in 1890 for the term beginning March 4, 1891; died in Washington, D.C., February 24, 1891; interment in Makemie Presbyterian Churchyard, Snow Hill, Md.

**WILSON, Eugene McLanahan** (son of Edgar Campbell Wilson, grandson of Thomas Wilson of Virginia, and great-grandson of Isaac Griffin), a Representative from Minnesota; born in Morgantown, Monongalia County, Va. (now West Virginia), December 25, 1833; attended the common schools and Morgantown Academy; was graduated from Jefferson College, Canonsburg, Pa., in 1852; studied law; was admitted to the bar in 1855 and commenced practice in Winona, Minn.; United States attorney for the district of Minnesota with residence in Minneapolis 1857-1861; continued the practice of law in Minneapolis; served in the Union Army during the Civil War as captain of Company A, First Minnesota Mounted Rangers; elected as a Democrat to the Forty-first Congress (March 4, 1869-March 3, 1871); was not a candidate for renomination in 1870; resumed the practice of law; elected mayor of Minneapolis in 1872 and 1874; unsuccessful candidate for election in 1874 to the Forty-fourth Congress; delegate to the Democratic National Convention in 1876; member of the State senate in 1878 and 1879; unsuccessful candidate for Governor in 1888; died while on a visit to regain his health in Nassau, New Providence Island, British West Indies, April 10, 1890; interment in Lakewood Cemetery, Minneapolis, Minn.

**WILSON, Francis Henry,** a Representative from New York; born in Clinton, Oneida County, N.Y., February 11, 1844; lived in Utica, N.Y., until ten years of age, when he moved with his parents to the Westmoreland farm; attended the district school, Dwight's Preparatory School, Clinton, N.Y., and was graduated from Yale College in 1867; taught in a preparatory school four years; was graduated from the Columbia College Law School, New York City, in 1875; was admitted to the bar in 1882 and commenced practice in New York City; one of the founders of the Union League Club and its president in 1888 and 1889; elected as a Republican to the Fifty-fourth and Fifty-fifth Congresses and served from March 4, 1895, to September 30, 1897, when he resigned to become postmaster; appointed postmaster of Brooklyn, N.Y., and served from October 1897 until December 1901; resumed the practice of law; died in Brooklyn, N.Y., September 25, 1910; interment in Greenwood Cemetery.

**WILSON, Frank Eugene,** a Representative from New York; born in Roxbury, Delaware County, N.Y., December 22, 1857; attended the public schools and the Poughkeepsie Military Academy; was graduated from the Jefferson Medical College, Philadelphia, Pa., in 1882; practiced medicine in Pleasant Valley, Dutchess County, N.Y., until April 1888; moved to Brooklyn, N.Y., in 1888 and continued the practice of medicine; senior physician, a director, and member of the board of governors of the Bushwick Hospital and visiting physician to the Swedish Hospital, both of Brooklyn, N.Y.; elected as a Democrat to the Fifty-sixth, Fifty-seventh, and Fifty-eighth Congresses (March 4, 1899-March 3, 1905); unsuccessful candidate for reelection in 1904 to the Fifty-ninth Congress; delegate to the Democratic National Convention in 1900; elected to the Sixty-second and Sixty-third Congresses (March 4, 1911-March 3, 1915); was not a candidate for renomination in 1914; resumed the practice of medicine in Brooklyn, N.Y., until his death there July 12, 1935; remains were cremated and the ashes deposited in Roxbury Cemetery, Roxbury, N.Y.

**WILSON, George Allison,** a Senator from Iowa; born on a farm near Menlo, Adair County, Iowa, April 1, 1884; attended the rural schools; later attended Grinnell (Iowa) College and graduated from the law school of the State University of Iowa at Iowa City in 1907; was admitted to the bar the same year and commenced practice in Des Moines, Iowa; assistant county attorney of Polk County, Iowa, 1912-1914 and county attorney, 1915-1916; district judge, 1917-1921; member, Iowa State senate, 1925-1935; unsuccessful candidate in 1936 for Governor; elected Governor of Iowa in 1938, reelected in 1940, and served from January 12, 1939 to January 14, 1943; elected as a Republican to the United States Senate for the term beginning January 3, 1943, but was not sworn in until January 14, 1943, continuing as Governor during the interim, and served from January 14, 1943 to January 3, 1949; unsuccessful candidate for reelection in 1948; resumed the practice of law; died in Des Moines, Iowa, September 8, 1953; interment in Glendale Cemetery.

**WILSON, George Howard,** a Representative from Oklahoma; born in Mattoon, Coles County, Ill., August 21, 1905; moved with his parents to Oklahoma and attended the public schools of Enid; graduated from Phillips University, Enid, Okla., in 1926; student at the University of Michigan Law School in 1926 and 1927, and graduated from the law school of the University of Oklahoma in 1929; was admitted to the bar in 1928 and commenced the practice of law in 1929 in Enid, Okla.; deputy district court clerk of Garfield County, Okla., in 1928; special agent, Federal Bureau of Investigation, 1934-1938; city attorney of Enid, Okla., 1939-1942; served as a colonel in Judge Advocate General's Department, United States Army, with overseas duty in the South Atlantic Theater of Operations 1942-1946; elected as a Democrat to the Eighty-first Congress (January 3, 1949-January 3, 1951); unsuccessful for reelection in 1950 to the Eighty-second Congress; director of Oklahoma State Crime Bureau in 1951; State judge, Superior Court, Garfield County, Okla., 1952-1968; chief judge, State Administrative Zone No. 1, 1967; president, Oklahoma Judicial Conference, 1968; district judge, 1969 to date; chief judge, Division No. 1, Judicial District No. 4; was a resident of Enid, Okla., until his death there July 16, 1985; interment in Memorial Park Cemetery.

**WILSON, George Washington,** a Representative from Ohio; born in Brighton, Clark County, Ohio, February 22, 1840; attended the common schools and Antioch College, Yellow Springs, Ohio; enlisted in the Ninety-fourth Regiment, Ohio Volunteer Infantry, August 8, 1862; commissioned second lieutenant and later first lieutenant; first lieutenant in the First Regiment, United States Veteran Volunteer Engineers, July 2, 1864, and afterward captain; mustered out October 1, 1865; studied law; was admitted to the bar August 7, 1866, and practiced in London, Ohio; prosecuting attorney of Madison County 1866-1870; member of the State house of representatives 1871-1874; served in the State senate 1877-1881; elected as a Republican to the Fifty-third and Fifty-fourth Congresses (March 4, 1893-March 3, 1897); resumed the practice of law in London, Ohio; delegate to the Republican National Convention in 1896; mayor of New London; prosecuting attorney of Madison County; died in London, Ohio, November 27, 1909; interment in Kirkwood Cemetery.

**WILSON, Henry,** a Senator from Massachusetts and a Vice President of the United States; born Jeremiah Jones Colbath in Farmington, N.H., February 16, 1812; worked on a farm; attended the common schools; had his name legally changed by the legislature to Henry Wilson in 1833; moved to Natick, Mass., in 1833 and learned the shoemaker's trade; attended the Strafford, Wolfsboro, and Concord Academies for short periods; taught school in Natick, Mass., where he later engaged in the manufacture of shoes; member of the Massachusetts legislature between 1841 and 1852; owner and editor of the Boston Republican, 1848-1851; unsuccessful candidate for election in 1852 to the Thirty-third

Congress; delegate to the Massachusetts constitutional convention in 1853; unsuccessful candidate for Governor of Massachusetts in 1853; elected in 1855 to the United States Senate by a coalition of Free-Soilers, Americans, and Democrats to fill the vacancy caused by the resignation of Edward Everett; reelected as a Republican in 1859, 1865, and 1871, and served from January 31, 1855 to March 3, 1873, when he resigned to become Vice President; chairman, Committee on Military Affairs and the Militia (Thirty-seventh through Fortieth Congresses), Committee on Military Affairs (Forty-first and Forty-second Congresses); in 1861 he raised and commanded the Twenty-second Regiment, Massachusetts Volunteer Infantry; elected Vice President of the United States in 1872 on the Republican ticket with President Ulysses S. Grant, and served from March 4, 1873 until his death in the Capitol Building at Washington, D.C., on November 22, 1875; interment in Old Dell Park Cemetery, Natick, Mass.

**Bibliography:** *DAB*; Abbott, Richard. *Cobbler in Congress: The Life of Henry Wilson, 1812-1875*. Lexington: University Press of Kentucky, 1972; McKay, Ernest. *Henry Wilson: Practical Radical, A Portrait of a Politician*. Port Washington, N.Y.: Kennikat Press, 1971.

**WILSON, Henry,** a Representative from Pennsylvania; born in Dauphin, Dauphin County, Pa., in 1778; completed preparatory studies; studied law in Harrisburg, Pa.; was admitted to the bar December 21, 1812, and commenced practice in Allentown, Pa.; prothonotary and clerk of Lehigh County Courts, 1815-1821; elected to the Eighteenth and Nineteenth Congresses and served from March 4, 1823, until his death in Allentown, Pa., August 14, 1826; interment in Union Cemetery.

**WILSON, Isaac,** a Representative from New York; born in Middlebury, Vt., June 25, 1780; served in the War of 1812 as captain of Cavalry; moved to Genesee County, N.Y.; member of the State assembly in 1816 and 1817; served in the State senate 1818-1821; judge of the Genesee County Court from May 9, 1821, to February 10, 1823; presented credentials as a Member-elect to the Eighteenth Congress and served from March 4, 1823, to January 7, 1824, when he was succeeded by Parmenio Adams, who contested his election; again judge of the Genesee County Court from February 2, 1830, to January 23, 1836; moved to Batavia, Kane County, Ill.; appointed postmaster of Batavia on February 6, 1841, and served until July 21, 1846, when his successor was appointed; died in Batavia, Ill., on October 25, 1848; interment in East Batavia Cemetery.

**WILSON, James** (father of John Lockwood Wilson), a Representative from Indiana; born in Crawfordsville, Montgomery County, Ind., April 9, 1825; was graduated from Wabash College, Crawfordsville, Ind., in 1842; studied law; was admitted to the bar in 1848 and commenced practice in Crawfordsville, Ind.; served in the Mexican War from June 17, 1846, to June 16, 1847; during the Civil War was appointed captain of Volunteers, November 26, 1862, and honorably discharged on December 6, 1865, as brevet lieutenant colonel; elected as a Republican to the Thirty-fifth and Thirty-sixth Congresses (March 4, 1857-March 3, 1861); appointed Minister to Venezuela on May 31, 1866, and served until his death in Caracas, Venezuela, August 8, 1867; interment in Oak Hill Cemetery, Crawfordsville, Ind.

**WILSON, James,** a Representative from Iowa; born on a farm in Ayrshire, Scotland, August 16, 1835; immigrated to the United States in 1852 with his parents, who settled in Norwich, Conn.; moved to Iowa in 1855 and located in Traer, Tama County; attended the public schools and Grinnell (Iowa) College; engaged in agricultural pursuits; taught school; member of the Iowa State house of representatives, 1867-1871, serving as speaker in 1870 and 1871; regent of the State university, 1870-1874; elected as a Republican to the Forty-third and Forty-fourth Congresses (March 4, 1873-March 3, 1877); member of the Iowa Railway Commission,

1878-1883; presented credentials as a Member-elect to the Forty-eighth Congress, and served from March 4, 1883 until the closing day, March 3, 1885, when he was succeeded by Benjamin T. Frederick, who contested his election; director of the agricultural experiment station and professor of agriculture in the Iowa Agricultural College at Ames, 1891-1897; was Secretary of Agriculture in the Cabinets of Presidents William McKinley, Theodore Roosevelt, and William Howard Taft, and served from March 5, 1897 to March 3, 1913; editor of the Agricultural Digest; died in Traer, Iowa, August 26, 1920; interment in Buckingham Cemetery.

**Bibliography:** *DAB*; Wilcox, Earley Vernon. *Tama Jim*. Boston: The Stratford Co., 1930.

**WILSON, James** (father of James Wilson [1797-1881]), a Representative from New Hampshire; born in Peterboro, N.H., August 16, 1766; attended Phillips Academy, Andover, Mass., and was graduated from Harvard University in 1789; studied law; was admitted to the bar in 1792 and commenced practice in Peterboro, N.H.; member of the State house of representatives 1803-1808 and 1812-1814; elected as a Federalist to the Eleventh Congress (March 4, 1809-March 3, 1811); was not a candidate for renomination in 1810; resumed the practice of law; moved to Keene, Cheshire County, N.H., in 1815 and continued the practice of law; died in Keene, N.H., January 4, 1839; interment in Woodland Cemetery.

**WILSON, James** (son of James Wilson [1766-1839]), a Representative from New Hampshire; born in Peterboro, N.H., March 18, 1797; attended the academies at New Ipswich, Atkinson, and Exeter; moved with his parents to Keene, N.H., in 1815; was graduated from Middlebury College in 1820; member of the State militia 1820-1840 and successively promoted from captain to major general; studied law; was admitted to the bar in 1823 and commenced practice in Keene, Cheshire County, N.H.; member of the State house of representatives 1825-1837, 1840, and 1846, and served as speaker in 1828; unsuccessful candidate for Governor in 1835 and 1838; delegate to the Whig National Convention in 1840; surveyor general of public lands in the Territories of Wisconsin and Iowa 1841-1845; elected as a Whig to the Thirtieth and Thirty-first Congresses and served from March 4, 1847, to September 9, 1850, when he resigned; chairman, Committee on Expenditures in the Post Office Department (Thirtieth Congress); appointed one of the commissioners to settle private land claims in California in 1851 and served in this capacity until 1853; settled in San Francisco and remained there until 1867, when he returned to Keene, N.H.; again a member of the State house of representatives in 1871 and 1872; died in Keene, N.H., May 29, 1881; interment in Woodland Cemetery.

**WILSON, James,** a Delegate from Pennsylvania; born in Carskerdo, near St. Andrews, Scotland, September 14, 1742; attended the Universities of St. Andrews, Glasgow, and Edinburgh; immigrated to the United States in 1765; resided in New York City until 1766, when he moved to Philadelphia, Pa.; tutor in the College of Philadelphia (now the University of Pennsylvania); studied law; admitted to the bar in 1767; practiced in Reading and Carlisle, Pa., and for a short time, during Sir William Howe's occupation of Philadelphia, in Annapolis, Md.; also engaged in literary pursuits; member of the Provincial Convention of Pennsylvania in 1774; Member of the Continental Congress, 1775-1777, 1783, and 1785-1786; chosen colonel of the Fourth Battalion of Associators in 1775; advocate general for France in America and guided that country's legal relations to the Confederation; member of the board of war; brigadier general of the Pennsylvania militia; a signer of the Declaration of Independence; a delegate from Pennsylvania to the Federal Convention in 1787, and a delegate to the Pennsylvania ratification convention; settled in Philadelphia in 1778 and resumed the practice of law; first professor of law in the College of Philadelphia in 1790 and in the University of Pennsylvania when

they were united in 1791; nominated on September 24, 1789 by President George Washington as an Associate Justice of the United States Supreme Court; was confirmed by the Senate on September 26, 1789, and served until his death in Edenton, N.C., August 21, 1798; interment in the Johnston burial ground on the Hayes plantation near Edenton, N.C.; reinterment in Christ Churchyard, Philadelphia, Pa., in 1906.

**Bibliography:** *DAB*; Smith, Charles Page. *James Wilson, Founding Father, 1742-1798*. Chapel Hill: University of North Carolina Press, 1956; Wilson, James. *Selected Political Essays of James Wilson*. Edited with an introductory essay by Randolph G. Adams. New York: Knopf, 1930.

**WILSON, James,** a Representative from Pennsylvania; born in Millerstown (now Fairfield), Pa., April 28, 1779; attended the common schools; learned the trade of cabinetmaker; engaged in mercantile pursuits and also interested in the real estate business; justice of the peace, 1811-1822; elected to the Eighteenth and to the two succeeding Congresses (March 4, 1823-March 3, 1829); again a justice of the peace from 1830 until 1859; engaged in the real estate business; died in Gettysburg, Adams County, Pa., July 19, 1868; interment in Evergreen Cemetery.

**WILSON, James Clifton,** a Representative from Texas; born in Palo Pinto, Palo Pinto County, Tex., June 21, 1874; attended the public schools and Weatherford (Tex.) College; was graduated from the law department of the University of Texas at Austin in 1896; was admitted to the bar the same year and commenced practice in Weatherford, Tex.; assistant prosecuting attorney of Parker County 1898-1900 and prosecuting attorney 1902-1908; chairman of the Democratic county executive committee 1908-1912; moved to Fort Worth in November 1912 and served as assistant district attorney of Tarrant County until July 1913; United States attorney for the northern district of Texas from July 1913 to March 1917; elected as a Democrat to the Sixty-fifth and Sixty-sixth Congresses and served from March 4, 1917, to March 3, 1919, when he resigned; appointed by President Woodrow Wilson as United States district judge for the northern district of Texas, serving from March 13, 1919, until his retirement in 1947; died in Fort Worth, Tex., August 3, 1951; interment in Rose Hill Cemetery.

**WILSON, James Falconer,** a Representative and a Senator from Iowa; born in Newark, Licking County, Ohio, October 19, 1828; pursued an academic course; apprenticed to the harnessmaker's trade; studied law; was admitted to the bar in 1851 and practiced in Newark, Ohio, 1851-1853; moved to Fairfield, Jefferson County, Iowa, in 1853 and resumed the practice of law; member of the Iowa constitutional convention in 1857; member of the Iowa State house of representatives in 1857 and 1859; member, Iowa State senate, 1859-1861, and was its president in 1861; elected as a Republican to the Thirty-seventh Congress to fill the vacancy caused by the resignation of Samuel R. Curtis; reelected to the three succeeding Congresses, and served from October 8, 1861 to March 3, 1869; was not a candidate for renomination in 1868 to the Forty-first Congress; chairman, Committee on the Judiciary (Thirty-eighth through Fortieth Congresses); one of the managers appointed by the House of Representatives in 1868 to conduct the impeachment proceedings against President Andrew Johnson; was tendered the position of Secretary of State in the Cabinet of President Ulysses S. Grant, but declined; subsequently appointed by President Grant as government director of the Union Pacific Railroad and served eight years; unsuccessful candidate for the Republican nomination for United States Senator in 1872; elected as a Republican to the United States Senate in 1882; reelected in 1888, and served from March 4, 1883 to March 3, 1895; was not a candidate for reelection in 1894; chairman, Committee on Mines and Mining (Forty-eighth Congress), Committee on Expenditures of Public Money (Forty-eighth Congress), Committee on Revision of the Laws of the United States

(Forty-ninth through Fifty-second Congresses), Committee on Education and Labor (Fifty-second Congress); died in Fairfield, Iowa, April 22, 1895; interment in Fairfield-Evergreen Cemetery.

**Bibliography:** *DAB*; Schlup, Leonard. "Republican Loyalist: James F. Wilson and Party Politics, 1855-1895." *Annals of Iowa* 52 (Spring 1993): 123-149.

**WILSON, James Jefferson,** a Senator from New Jersey; born in Essex County, N.J., in 1775; attended the common schools; editor and publisher of the True American of Trenton 1801-1824; clerk in the State general assembly in 1804; judge advocate and captain, Hunterdon Brigade, New Jersey Militia, in 1806; surrogate of Hunterdon County in 1808; member, State general assembly 1809-1811; brigadier general and adjutant general of New Jersey 1810-1812; reappointed brigadier general and adjutant general of New Jersey in 1814; captain in the Third Regiment, Hunterdon Brigade, 1814; captain in the New Jersey Militia 1814; brigadier general and quartermaster general of New Jersey 1821-1824; elected as a Republican to the United States Senate and served from March 4, 1815, to January 8, 1821, when he resigned; was an unsuccessful candidate for reelection; chairman, Committee on Post Office and Post Roads (Fourteenth and Fifteenth Congresses), Committee on Claims (Sixteenth Congress); appointed postmaster of Trenton, N.J., in 1821 and served until his death in that city July 28, 1824; interment in the First Baptist Church Cemetery.

**WILSON, Jeremiah Morrow,** a Representative from Indiana; born near Lebanon, Warren County, Ohio, November 25, 1828; completed preparatory studies; studied law; was admitted to the bar and practiced; moved to Indiana and settled in Connersville and continued the practice of law; judge of the court of common pleas 1860-1865; elected judge of the circuit court in October 1865 and served until his election to Congress; elected as a Republican to the Forty-second and Forty-third Congresses (March 4, 1871-March 3, 1875); was not a candidate for reelection in 1874; resumed the practice of his profession in Washington, D.C., where he died September 24, 1901; interment in Rock Creek Cemetery.

**WILSON, John,** a Representative from Massachusetts; born in Peterboro, N.H., January 10, 1777; graduated from Harvard University in 1799; studied law; admitted to the bar in 1802 at Peterboro, N.H., and commenced practice in Belfast, Maine (then a district of Massachusetts); served as a captain in the Massachusetts militia; elected as a Federalist to the Thirteenth Congress (March 4, 1813-March 3, 1815); unsuccessful candidate for reelection in 1814 to the Fourteenth Congress; resumed the practice of his profession in Belfast; was elected to the Fifteenth Congress (March 4, 1817-March 3, 1819); unsuccessful candidate for renomination in 1818; engaged in the practice of law until his death in Belfast, Maine, August 9, 1848; interment in Grove Cemetery.

**WILSON, John,** a Representative from South Carolina; born at Wilson's Ferry (now Pelzer), Anderson County, S.C., August 11, 1773; attended the common schools; engaged in agricultural pursuits in Anderson County, near Golden Grove, S.C.; also operated a public ferry across the Saluda River at what is now known as Pelzer; member, State house of representatives, 1812-1817; elected to the Seventeenth, Eighteenth, and Nineteenth Congresses (March 4, 1821-March 3, 1827); unsuccessful candidate for reelection in 1826 to the Twentieth Congress; died at his home near Golden Grove, in Anderson County, S.C., August 13, 1828; interment in the family cemetery on his plantation, which is now a part of the industrial city of Pelzer, S.C.

**WILSON, John Frank,** a Delegate from the Territory of Arizona; born near Pulaski, Giles County, Tenn., May 7, 1846; moved with his parents to Alabama; attended the common schools and Rhuhama (Ala.) College; served in the Confederate Army as a member of Company B, First Battalion, Volunteer Infantry, and later on staff duty under General Thomas C. Hindman until 1863, after which he served as lieutenant colonel of a regiment; studied law; was admitted to the bar in 1866 and commenced practice in Fayetteville, Ark.; member of the Arkansas State house of representatives in 1877 and 1878; prosecuting attorney for the fourth judicial district in 1885 and 1886; moved to the Territory of Arizona; settled in Prescott in 1887 and continued the practice of law; member of the constitutional convention in 1891; probate judge of Yavapai County, 1893-1895; delegate to the Democratic National Convention of 1896; appointed attorney general of the Territory of Arizona by Governor Benjamin J. Franklin and served during 1896 and 1897; elected as a Democrat to the Fifty-sixth Congress (March 4, 1899-March 3, 1901); was not a candidate for renomination in 1900 to the Fifty-seventh Congress; elected to the Fifty-eighth Congress (March 4, 1903-March 3, 1905); was not a candidate for renomination in 1904 to the Fifty-ninth Congress; resumed the practice of his profession; died in Prescott, Ariz., April 7, 1911; interment in Mountain View Cemetery.

**WILSON, John Haden,** a Representative from Pennsylvania; born in Nashville, Tenn., August 20, 1867; moved with his parents to Harmony, Butler County, Pa., the same year; attended the public schools; was graduated from Harmony (Pa.) Collegiate Institute, Zelienople (Pa.) Academy, and from Grove City (Pa.) College; studied law and was admitted to the bar in Butler, Pa., in 1893; taught school; commenced the practice of law in Butler in 1896; member of the Pennsylvania National Guard for three years and served during the Homestead riots; was solicitor for the city of Butler 1906-1934, except while a Member of Congress; delegate to the Democratic National Conventions in 1916, 1932, 1936, and 1940; elected as a Democrat to the Sixty-sixth Congress to fill the vacancy caused by the death of Representative-elect Edward E. Robbins and served from March 4, 1919, to March 3, 1921; unsuccessful candidate for reelection in 1920 to the Sixty-seventh Congress; resumed the practice of law; served as judge of the several courts of Butler County, Pa., 1933-1943; died in Butler, Pa., on January 28, 1946; interment in North Cemetery.

**WILSON, John Henry,** a Representative from Kentucky; born in Crab Orchard, Lincoln County, Ky., January 30, 1846; pursued preparatory studies; graduated from Tusculum College, Greeneville, Tenn., in June 1870; studied law; admitted to the bar in September 1871 and commenced practice in Barbourville, Knox County, Ky.; was also greatly interested in agricultural pursuits and the construction of the Dixie Highway; member of the Kentucky senate 1883-1887; elected as a Republican to the Fifty-first and Fifty-second Congresses (March 4, 1889-March 3, 1893); unsuccessful candidate for reelection in 1892 to the Fifty-third Congress; resumed the practice of his profession in Barbourville, Ky.; died in Louisville, Ky., January 14, 1923; interment in Barbourville Cemetery.

**WILSON, John Lockwood** (son of James Wilson of Indiana [1825-1867]), a Representative and a Senator from Washington; born in Crawfordsville, Montgomery County, Ind., August 7, 1850; attended the common schools; messenger during the Civil War; graduated from Wabash College, Crawfordsville, Ind., in 1874; studied law; was admitted to the bar in 1878 and commenced practice in Crawfordsville; member, State house of representatives 1880; appointed by President Chester A. Arthur as receiver of public moneys at Spokane Falls and Colfax, Washington Territory 1882-1887; upon the admission of Washington as a State into the Union was elected as a Republican to the Fifty-first Congress; reelected to the Fifty-second and Fifty-third Congresses and served from November 20, 1889, to February 18, 1895, when he resigned to become Senator; elected as a Republican to the United States Senate on February 1, 1895, to fill the vacancy in the term commencing March 4, 1893, but did not assume his senatorial duties until February 19, 1895; served until March 3, 1899; was an unsuccessful candidate for reelection in 1898; chairman, Committee on Indian Depredations (Fifty-fourth and Fifty-fifth Congresses); published the Seattle Post-Intelligencer, Seattle, Wash.; died in Washington, D.C., on November 6, 1912; interment in Oak Hill Cemetery, Crawfordsville, Ind.

Bibliography: *DAB*.

**WILSON, John Thomas,** a Representative from Ohio; born in Bell, Highland County, Ohio, April 16, 1811; received a limited schooling; engaged in mercantile and agricultural pursuits; during the Civil War was appointed first lieutenant of Company E, Seventieth Regiment, Ohio Volunteer Infantry, November 2, 1861, and was discharged as captain November 27, 1862; member of the State senate 1863-1866; elected as a Republican to the Fortieth, Forty-first, and Forty-second Congresses (March 4, 1867-March 3, 1873); chairman, Committee on Agriculture (Forty-first and Forty-second Congresses); unsuccessful candidate for reelection in 1872 to the Forty-third Congress; engaged in the handling of loans and mortgages; died in Tranquillity (near what is now known as Seaman), Adams County, Ohio, on October 6, 1891; interment in Tranquillity Cemetery.

**WILSON, Joseph Franklin,** a Representative from Texas; born in Corsicana, Navarro County, Tex., March 18, 1901; attended the elementary school at Corsicana; at the age of twelve moved to Memphis, Tex. (in the Panhandle), and attended the public schools until 1916; during the First World War enrolled at Peacock Military College, San Antonio, Tex., from September 1917 to June 1918 and at Tennessee Military Institute at Sweetwater from September 1918 to June 1919, advancing through the grades to first sergeant; graduated from Baylor University Law School, Waco, Tex., in 1923; was admitted to the bar the same year and commenced practice in Dallas, Tex.; delegate to the Democratic National Convention in 1936; chairman of the Dallas County Democratic Executive Committee 1942-1945; district judge of the criminal district court of Texas in 1943 and 1944; elected as a Democrat to the Eightieth and to the three succeeding Congresses (January 3, 1947-January 3, 1955); was not a candidate for renomination in 1954; appointed judge of Criminal District Court No. 1, Dallas, Tex., in 1955, in which capacity he served until September 1968, when he retired due to illness; died in Dallas, Tex., October 13, 1968; interment in Hillcrest Memorial Park.

**WILSON, Joseph Gardner** (cousin of James Willis Nesmith), a Representative from Oregon; born in Acworth, Sullivan County, N.H., December 13, 1826; moved with his parents to Cincinnati, Ohio, in 1828 and later to a farm near Reading, Hamilton County; attended the district schools until 1840 and Cary's Academy from 1840 to 1842; was graduated from Marietta (Ohio) College in 1846; professor in Farmer's College, near Cincinnati, in 1849; was graduated from the Cincinnati Law School in 1852 and was admitted to the bar; moved to Oregon Territory in 1852 and commenced the practice of law in Salem, Oreg.; clerk of the Territorial legislature in 1853; first secretary of the Willamette Woolen Co. when it was established in 1854; prosecuting attorney of Marion County 1860-1862; associate judge of the State supreme court 1864-1866 and 1868-1870; unsuccessful candidate for election in 1870 to the Forty-second Congress; resumed the practice of his profession; elected as a Republican to the Forty-third Congress and served from March 4, 1873, until his death in Marietta, Ohio, July 2, 1873; interment in Pioneer Cemetery, The Dalles, Oreg.

**WILSON, Nathan,** a Representative from New York; born in Bolton, Worcester County, Mass., December 23, 1758; moved with his family to Greenwich, Hampshire County, Mass., where he attended school; served two enlistments in Massachusetts regiments during the Revolutionary War in 1777 and 1780; moved to New Perth (now Salem), Washington County, N.Y.; enlisted as a private in the Sixteenth Regiment, Albany County Militia; appointed by Governor George Clinton in 1791 as adjutant in the Washington County Militia Regiment; town collector in 1801 and 1802; sheriff of Washington County, 1802-1806; elected as a Republican to the Tenth Congress to fill the vacancy caused by the resignation of David Thomas and served from June 3, 1808, to March 3, 1809; justice of the peace, 1808-1816; engaged in agricultural pursuits; died near Salem, Washington County, N.Y., July 25, 1834; interment in Evergreen Cemetery, Salem, N.Y.

**WILSON, Peter Barton (Pete),** a Senator from California; born in Lake Forest, Lake County, Ill., August 23, 1933; attended private school in St. Louis, Mo.; B.A., Yale University, 1955; J.D., University of California School of Law, Berkeley, 1962; served in the United States Marine Corps, 1955-1958; admitted to the California bar in 1963 and commenced practice in San Diego; member, California State legislature, 1966-1971; mayor of San Diego, Calif., 1971-1983; elected as a Republican to the United States Senate in 1982; reelected in 1988, and served from January 3, 1983 to January 7, 1991, when he resigned, having been elected Governor of California in 1990 for the four-year term beginning January 7, 1991; reelected Governor in 1994 for the four-year term beginning January 9, 1995; is a resident of San Diego, Calif.

**WILSON, Riley Joseph,** a Representative from Louisiana; born near Goldonna, Winn Parish, La., November 12, 1871; attended the public schools and Beeson College, Arcadia, La.; was graduated from Iuka (Miss.) Normal Institute in 1894; principal of Harrisonburg High School, 1895-1897; studied law; was admitted to the bar in 1898 and commenced practice in Harrisonburg, La.; member of the Louisiana State constitutional convention in 1898; edited the Catahoula News, 1898-1904; member of the Louisiana State house of representatives, 1900-1904; district attorney of the eighth judicial district from December 1, 1904, until his resignation on May 1, 1910, to accept a judicial appointment; judge of the eighth judicial district from May 1, 1910, until his resignation on December 1, 1914, having been elected to Congress; delegate to the Democratic National Convention of 1920; elected as a Democrat to the Sixty-fourth and to the ten succeeding Congresses (March 4, 1915-January 3, 1937); chairman, Committee on Elections No. 1 (Sixty-fifth Congress), Committee on Flood Control (Seventy-second through Seventy-fourth Congresses); unsuccessful candidate for renomination in 1936 to the Seventy-fifth Congress; unsuccessful candidate in 1928 for Governor of Louisiana; retired from public and political activities; died in Ruston, La., February 23, 1946; interment in Greenwood Cemetery.

**WILSON, Robert,** a Senator from Missouri; born near Staunton, Va., in November 1803; moved to Howard County, Mo., in 1820; taught school; probate judge of Howard County in 1825; clerk of the circuit and county courts from 1829 until 1840; appointed brigadier general of the State forces in 1837 and served during the so-called "Mormon war"; studied law; was admitted to the bar and commenced practice in 1840; moved to Huntsville, Mo.; member of the Missouri State house of representatives in 1844; moved to Andrew County, Mo., in 1852; member of the State senate in 1854; Union delegate to the State convention called to determine the attitude on secession in 1861 and elected vice president of the convention, later acting as president; appointed as a Unionist to the United States Senate to fill the vacancy caused by the expulsion of Waldo P. Johnson, and served from January 17, 1862 to November 13, 1863, when a successor was elected; engaged in agricultural pursuits; died in Marshall, Saline County, Mo., on May 10, 1870; interment in Mount Mora Cemetery, St. Joseph, Mo.

**WILSON, Robert Carlton,** a Representative from California; born in Calexico, Imperial County, Calif., April 5, 1916; attended California public schools; attended San Diego State College, 1933-1935, and Otis Art Institute; during the Second World War operated Conship Commissary and served as a private in the United

States Army; lieutenant colonel, United States Marine Corps Reserve; partner in two advertising agencies in San Diego; president of the San Diego Junior Chamber of Commerce in 1951; chairman, Republican Congressional Campaign Committee, 1962-1966; elected as a Republican to the Eighty-third and to the thirteen succeeding Congresses (January 3, 1953-January 3, 1981); was not a candidate for reelection in 1980 to the Ninety-seventh Congress; chairman, Washington Industrial Team and Air-Space America; is a resident of San Diego, Calif.

**WILSON, Robert Patterson Clark,** a Representative from Missouri; born in Boonville, Cooper County, Mo., August 8, 1834; moved with his parents to Platte County; attended William Jewell College, Liberty, Mo., and was graduated from Centre College, Danville, Ky., in 1853; studied law; was admitted to the bar in 1854 and commenced practice in Seguin, Tex., in 1855; returned to Missouri in 1858; moved to Leavenworth, Kans., in 1860; was a member of the first State house of representatives of Kansas from March to June 4, 1861; returned to Missouri in 1861; member of the State house of representatives of Missouri in 1871 and 1872 and served as speaker both years; member of the State senate in 1879 and 1880; delegate to the Democratic National Convention in 1888; president of the school board of Platte City, Mo.; elected as a Democrat to the Fifty-first Congress to fill the vacancy caused by the death of James N. Burnes; reelected to the Fifty-second Congress and served from December 2, 1889, to March 3, 1893; chairman, Committee on Pensions (Fifty-second Congress); resumed the practice of his profession in Platte City, Platte County, Mo.; died in Kansas City, Mo., December 21, 1916; interment in Marshall Cemetery, Platte City, Mo.

**WILSON, Stanyarne,** a Representative from South Carolina; born in Yorkville (now York), S.C., January 10, 1860; attended Kings Mountain Military School and Washington and Lee University, Lexington, Va.; studied law; was admitted to the bar by an act of the legislature in 1880, then being a minor; settled in Spartanburg, Spartanburg County, S.C., in 1881; practiced law and was also interested in cotton manufactures, gold mining, iron works, and agriculture; member of the State house of representatives 1884-1886 and 1890-1892; served in the State senate 1892-1895; member of the State constitutional convention in 1895; elected as a Democrat to the Fifty-fourth, Fifty-fifth, and Fifty-sixth Congresses (March 4, 1895-March 3, 1901); continued the practice of law in Spartanburg, S.C., and later in Richmond, Va., where he moved in 1913; returned to Spartanburg, S.C., in January 1928, and died there February 14, 1928; interment in Church of the Advent Cemetery.

**WILSON, Stephen Fowler,** a Representative from Pennsylvania; born in Columbia, Pa., September 4, 1821; received an academic education; studied law; admitted to the bar and practiced; held several local offices; member of the Pennsylvania senate 1863-1865 and served in one session after he had been elected a Representative to Congress; delegate to the Republican National Convention in 1864; elected as a Republican to the Thirty-ninth and Fortieth Congresses (March 4, 1865-March 3, 1869); appointed additional judge of the fourth judicial district of Pennsylvania in 1871 to fill a vacancy; elected additional judge and served ten years; appointed associate justice of the supreme court of the Territory of New Mexico by President Chester A. Arthur on October 16, 1884; president judge of the fourth judicial district of Pennsylvania from 1887 to 1889; resumed the practice of his profession in Wellsboro, Tioga County, Pa., where he died March 30, 1897; interment in Wellsboro Cemetery.

**WILSON, Thomas,** a Representative from Minnesota; born in Dungannon, County Tyrone, Ireland, May 16, 1827; attended the common schools; immigrated to the United States in 1839 with his parents, who settled in Venango County, Pa.; was graduated from Allegheny College, Meadville, Pa., in 1852; studied law; was

admitted to the bar in February 1855 and commenced practice in Winona, Minn.; member of the Minnesota constitutional convention in 1857; judge of the third judicial district court 1857-1864; associate justice of the supreme court of Minnesota in 1864; chief justice from 1864 to July 1869, when he resigned; resumed the practice of law; member of the State house of representatives 1880-1882; served in the State senate 1882-1885; elected as a Democrat to the Fiftieth Congress (March 4, 1887-March 3, 1889); unsuccessful candidate for reelection; unsuccessful candidate for Governor in 1890; delegate to the Democratic National Convention in 1892; general counsel for the Chicago, St. Paul, Minneapolis & Omaha Railroad until his death in St. Paul, Minn., April 3, 1910; interment in Woodlawn Cemetery, Winona, Minn.

**WILSON, Thomas,** a Representative from Pennsylvania; born near Sunbury, Northumberland County, Pa., in 1772; attended the common schools; had the contract for supplying the western forts of the United States from Niagara to New Orleans; engaged in shipbuilding in Erie, Pa., in 1805; built vessels for commerce on the Great Lakes; burgess of Erie in 1807; town clerk in 1808; treasurer of Erie County 1809-1812; county commissioner in 1811; justice of the peace; elected as a Republican to the Thirteenth Congress to fill the vacancy caused by the resignation of Abner Lacock; reelected to the Fourteenth Congress and served from May 4, 1813, to March 3, 1817; member of the Pennsylvania house of representatives 1817-1820; prothonotary and clerk of court of Erie County 1819-1824; died in Erie, Pa., October 4, 1824.

**WILSON, Thomas** (father of Edgar Campbell Wilson and grandfather of Eugene McLanahan Wilson), a Representative from Virginia; born in Staunton, Va., September 11, 1765; studied law in Staunton, Va.; admitted to the bar September 21, 1789, and commenced practice in Morgantown, Va. (now West Virginia); member of the Virginia senate 1792-1795; served in the Virginia house of delegates in 1799 and 1800; again a member of the Virginia senate 1800-1804; elected as a Federalist to the Twelfth Congress (March 4, 1811-March 3, 1813); again a member of the Virginia house of delegates in 1816 and 1817; resumed the practice of law; died in Morgantown, Va., January 24, 1826; interment in Oak Grove Cemetery.

**WILSON, Thomas Webber,** a Representative from Mississippi; born in Coldwater, Tate County, Miss., January 24, 1893; attended the public schools of his native city; was graduated from the law department of the University of Mississippi at Oxford in 1913; was admitted to the bar the same year and commenced the practice of law in Laurel, Miss.; prosecuting attorney of Jones County 1915-1919; district attorney for the twelfth judicial district of Mississippi 1919-1923; elected as a Democrat to the Sixty-eighth, Sixty-ninth, and Seventieth Congresses (March 4, 1923-March 3, 1929); was not a candidate for renomination in 1928 but was an unsuccessful candidate for the nomination for United States Senator; engaged in the private practice of law 1928-1933; appointed a Federal judge for the Virgin Islands and served from 1933 until 1935; member of the Parole Board in the Justice Department, Washington, D.C., 1935-1947; died in Coldwater, Miss., January 31, 1948; interment in Magnolia Cemetery.

**WILSON, William,** a Representative from Ohio; born in New Boston, Hillsboro County, N.H., March 19, 1773; attended the public schools and was graduated from Dartmouth College, Hanover, N.H., in 1797; studied law in Johnstown, N.Y., and was admitted to the bar; moved to Ohio and settled in Chillicothe about 1805; engaged in the practice of law; moved to Newark, Ohio, in 1808, having been appointed chief judge of the court of common pleas, and served until 1823; elected to the Eighteenth, Nineteenth, and Twentieth Congresses and served from March 4, 1823, until his death in Newark, Licking County, Ohio, June 6, 1827; chairman, Committee on Expenditures in the Post Office Department (Nineteenth

Congress); interment in the Old Cemetery; reinterment on March 23, 1853, in Cedar Hill Cemetery.

**WILSON, William,** a Representative from Pennsylvania; elected as a Republican to the Fourteenth and Fifteenth Congresses (March 4, 1815-March 3, 1819).

**WILSON, William Bauchop,** a Representative from Pennsylvania; born in Blantyre, Scotland, April 2, 1862; immigrated to this country with his parents, who settled in Arnot, Tioga County, Pa., in 1870; attended the common schools; engaged in coal mining from 1871 until 1898; international secretary-treasurer of the United Mine Workers of America, 1900-1908; elected as a Democrat to the Sixtieth and to the two succeeding Congresses (March 4, 1907-March 3, 1913); chairman, Committee on Labor (Sixty-second Congress); unsuccessful candidate for reelection in 1912 to the Sixty-third Congress, and for election in 1914 to the Sixty-fourth Congress; appointed Secretary of Labor in the Cabinet of President Woodrow Wilson, and served from March 5, 1913 to March 5, 1921; during the First World War was a member of the Council of National Defense; member of the Federal Board for Vocational Education, 1914-1921 and also chairman of the board in 1920 and 1921; appointed on March 4, 1921, a member of the International Joint Commission, created to prevent disputes regarding the use of the boundary waters between the United States and Canada, and served until March 21, 1921, when he resigned; unsuccessful candidate for election to the United States Senate in 1926; engaged in mining and agricultural pursuits near Blossburg, Tioga County, Pa.; died on a train near Savannah, Ga., May 25, 1934; interment in Arbon Cemetery, Blossburg, Pa.

**Bibliography:** *DAB*; Gengarelly, W. Anthony. "Secretary of Labor William B. Wilson and the Red Scare, 1919-1920." *Pennsylvania History* 47 (October 1980): 311-30; Wilhelm, Clarke L. "William B. Wilson: The First Secretary of Labor." Ph.D. dissertation, Johns Hopkins University, 1967.

**WILSON, William Edward,** a Representative from Indiana; born in Mount Vernon, Posey County, Ind., March 9, 1870; attended the public schools and the Evansville Commercial College, with which he was associated as teacher, principal, and owner from 1888 to 1904; retired from school work and engaged in the insurance business at Evansville, Ind.; deputy auditor of Vanderburg County, Ind., 1910-1912; clerk of the circuit court of Vanderburg County 1912-1920; unsuccessful candidate for election in 1920 to the Sixty-seventh Congress; elected as a Democrat to the Sixty-eighth Congress (March 4, 1923-March 3, 1925); unsuccessful candidate for reelection in 1924 to the Sixty-ninth Congress; engaged in banking and was later employed by the Chrysler Corp.; died in Evansville, Ind., September 29, 1948; interment in Oak Hill Cemetery.

**WILSON, William Henry,** a Representative from Pennsylvania; born in Philadelphia, Pa., December 6, 1877; attended the public and high schools; graduated from the law department of the University of Pennsylvania at Philadelphia in 1898; admitted to the bar in 1899 and commenced the practice of law in Philadelphia, Pa.; served as assistant city solicitor 1900-1909; member of the Pennsylvania house of representatives 1913-1915; served as director of public safety, Philadelphia, 1916-1920; elected as a Republican to the Seventy-fourth Congress (January 3, 1935-January 3, 1937); unsuccessful candidate for reelection in 1936 to the Seventy-fifth Congress; died in Santa Barbara, Calif., August 11, 1937; remains were cremated and placed in Forest Lawn Memorial Park, Glendale, Calif.

**WILSON, William Lyne,** a Representative from West Virginia; born near Charles Town, Jefferson County, Va. (now West Virginia), May 3, 1843; attended Charles Town Academy; was graduated from Columbian College (now George Washington University), Washington, D.C., in 1860 and subsequently studied in the University of Virginia at Charlottesville; during the Civil War served in the Confederate Army as a private in the Twelfth Virginia Cavalry; taught for several years in Columbian College, during which time he was graduated from its law school; was admitted to the bar in 1869 and commenced practice in Charles Town, W.Va.; delegate to the Democratic National Convention of 1880; chosen president of the West Virginia University at Morgantown and entered upon the office on September 4, 1882; elected as a Democrat to the Forty-eighth and to the five succeeding Congresses (March 4, 1883-March 3, 1895); chairman, Committee on Ways and Means (Fifty-third Congress); appointed Postmaster General in the Cabinet of President Grover Cleveland, and served from April 4, 1895 to March 5, 1897; president of the Washington and Lee University, Lexington, Va.; died in Lexington, Rockbridge, County, Va., October 17, 1900; interment in Edgehill Cemetery, Charles Town, W.Va.

**Bibliography:** *DAB*; Summers, Festus P. *William L. Wilson and Tariff Reform*. New Brunswick, N.J.: Rutgers University Press, 1953; Tull, Thomas R. "The Shift to Republicanism: William L. Wilson and the Election of 1894." *West Virginia History* 37 (October 1975): 17-33; Wilson, William Lyne. *A Borderland Confederate*. Edited by Festus P. Summers. Pittsburgh: University of Pittsburgh Press, 1962.

**WILSON, William Warfield,** a Representative from Illinois; born in Ohio, Bureau County, Ill., March 2, 1868; attended the public schools of Ohio, Ill., and the University of Michigan at Ann Arbor; was graduated from the Chicago-Kent College of Law in 1893; was admitted to the bar the same year and commenced practice in Chicago, Ill.; elected as a Republican to the Fifty-eighth and to the four succeeding Congresses (March 4, 1903-March 3, 1913); unsuccessful candidate for election in 1912 to the Sixty-third Congress; elected to the Sixty-fourth, Sixty-fifth, and Sixty-sixth Congresses (March 4, 1915-March 3, 1921); was not a candidate for renomination in 1920; appointed general counsel of the Alien Property Custodian of the United States in 1922, serving until 1927; resumed the practice of law; died in Chicago, Ill., July 22, 1942; interment in Union Cemetery, Ohio, Ill.

**WINANS, Edwin Baruch,** a Representative from Michigan; born in Avon, Livingston County, N.Y., May 16, 1826; moved with his parents to Michigan in 1834; attended Albion College, Michigan; went to California and engaged in mining on the North Yuba River, near Placerville, in 1850; worked in different parts of the State until 1857; returned to Michigan in 1858 and settled in Hamburg, Livingston County, where he engaged in agricultural pursuits; member of the Michigan State house of representatives, 1861-1865; delegate to the State constitutional convention of May 15, 1867; probate judge of Livingston County, 1877-1881; elected as a Democrat to the Forty-eighth and Forty-ninth Congresses (March 4, 1883-March 3, 1887); resumed agricultural pursuits in Livingston County, Mich.; elected Governor of Michigan in 1890, and served from January 1, 1891 to January 1, 1893; died in Hamburg, Mich., July 4, 1894; interment in Hamburg Cemetery.

**WINANS, James January,** a Representative from Ohio; born in Maysville, Ky., June 7, 1818; moved with his parents to Greene County, Ohio; attended the common schools and the University of Lexington, Kentucky; studied law; was admitted to the bar in Lexington, Ky., in 1841 and commenced practice in Indiana; moved to Xenia, Greene County, Ohio, in 1843 and continued the practice of law; clerk of the Greene County Courts 1845-1851; served in the State senate in 1857; member of the State house of representatives in 1863; judge of the court of common pleas 1864-1871; elected as a Republican to the Forty-first Congress (March 4, 1869-March 3, 1871); unsuccessful candidate for reelection in 1870 to the Forty-second Congress; resumed the practice of law; died in Xenia, Ohio, April 28, 1879; interment in Woodlawn Cemetery.

**WINANS, John,** a Representative from Wisconsin; born in Vernon, Sussex County, N.J., September 27, 1831; studied law and was admitted to the bar in 1855; moved to Janesville, Rock County, Wis., in 1857 and practiced his profession; member of the board of aldermen of Janesville in 1861; city attorney, 1865-1875; member of the Wisconsin State assembly in 1874, 1882, 1887, and 1891; delegate to the Democratic National Convention of 1864; served as colonel on the staff of Governor William R. Taylor in 1874 and 1875; mayor of Janesville, 1885-1887; elected as a Democrat to the Forty-eighth Congress (March 4, 1883-March 3, 1885); was not a candidate for renomination in 1884 to the Forty-ninth Congress; engaged in the practice of law in Janesville, Wis., until his death January 17, 1907; interment in Oak Hill Cemetery.

**WINCHESTER, Boyd,** a Representative from Kentucky; born in Ascension Parish, La., September 23, 1836; pursued preparatory studies; attended Centre College, Danville, Ky., and the University of Virginia at Charlottesville; was graduated from the law department of the University of Louisville, Kentucky, in 1857 and commenced practice in Louisville; member of the Kentucky senate in 1867 and 1868; resigned in 1868; elected as a Democrat to the Forty-first and Forty-second Congresses (March 4, 1869-March 3, 1873); was not a candidate for renomination in 1872 to the Forty-third Congress; resumed the practice of law in Louisville, Ky.; president of an insurance company, 1875-1877; president of the Democratic State convention in 1884; appointed Minister Resident and consul general to Switzerland on May 7, 1885, and served until May 1889; died in Louisville, Ky., May 18, 1923; interment in Cave Hill Cemetery.

**WINDOM, William,** a Representative and a Senator from Minnesota; born in Belmont County, Ohio, on May 10, 1827; pursued an academic course at Martinsburg, Ohio; studied law; was admitted to the bar in 1850 and commenced practice in Mount Vernon, Ohio; prosecuting attorney of Knox County in 1852; moved to Winona, Winona County, Minnesota Territory, in 1855; elected as a Republican to the Thirty-sixth and to the four succeeding Congresses (March 4, 1859-March 3, 1869); chairman, Committee on Indian Affairs (Thirty-eighth through Fortieth Congresses); appointed as a Republican to the United States Senate to fill the vacancy in the term ending March 3, 1871, caused by the death of Daniel S. Norton, and served from July 15, 1870 to January 22, 1871, when a successor was elected to complete the term; elected to the United States Senate in 1871; reelected in 1877, and served from March 4, 1871 to March 7, 1881, when he resigned to accept a Cabinet portfolio; appointed Secretary of the Treasury by President James A. Garfield, and served from March 8, 1881 until his resignation on November 14, 1881, having been elected Senator; elected to the United States Senate on October 26, 1881, to fill the vacancy caused by his own resignation, and served from November 15, 1881 to March 3, 1883; unsuccessful candidate for reelection in 1883; chairman, Committee on Enrolled Bills (Forty-second Congress), Committee on Appropriations (Forty-fourth and Forty-fifth Congresses), Committee on Foreign Relations (Forty-seventh Congress); moved to New York City in 1883 and practiced law; appointed Secretary of the Treasury in the Cabinet of President Benjamin Harrison, and served from March 7, 1889 until his death in New York City on January 29, 1891; interment in Rock Creek Cemetery, Washington, D.C.

**Bibliography:** *DAB*; Salisbury, Robert Seward. *William Windom: Apostle of Positive Government.* Lanham, Md.: University Press of America, 1993.

**WINFIELD, Charles Henry,** a Representative from New York; born in Crawford, N.Y., April 22, 1822; completed preparatory studies; studied law; was admitted to the bar in 1846 and commenced practice in Goshen, N.Y.; district attorney for Orange County 1850-1856; elected as a Democrat to the Thirty-eighth and Thirty-ninth Congresses (March 4, 1863-March 3, 1867); was not a candidate for renomination in 1866; resumed the practice of his profession; died in Walden, N.Y., June 10, 1888; interment in Wallkill Valley Cemetery.

**WING, Austin Eli,** a Delegate from Michigan; born in Conway, Hampshire County, Mass., February 3, 1792; in early youth moved with his parents to Marietta, Ohio; attended the common schools, the academy at Chillicothe, Ohio, and Athens College, Ohio; was graduated from Williams College, Williamstown, Mass., in 1814; moved to Detroit, Mich.; elected to the Nineteenth and Twentieth Congresses (March 4, 1825-March 3, 1829); moved to Monroe, Mich.; elected to the Twenty-second Congress (March 4, 1831-March 3, 1833); affiliated with the Whig Party after its formation; member of the State house of representatives in 1842; served as a member of the board of regents of the University of Michigan from 1845 until 1850; appointed United States marshal for the district of Michigan on February 24, 1846, and served until 1849; died in Cleveland, Ohio, on August 27, 1849; interment in Woodlawn Cemetery, Monroe, Mich.

**WINGATE, Joseph Ferdinand,** a Representative from Maine; born in Haverhill, Essex County, Maine (until 1820 a district of Massachusetts), June 29, 1786; received a limited schooling; engaged in the mercantile business in Bath, Maine; member of the Massachusetts house of representatives in 1818 and 1819; collector of customs at the port of Bath 1820-1824; elected to the Twentieth and Twenty-first Congresses (March 4, 1827-March 3, 1831); moved to Windsor, Maine; died in South Windsor, Kennebec County, Maine; interment in Rest Haven Cemetery.

**WINGATE, Paine,** a Delegate, a Senator, and a Representative from New Hampshire; born in Amesbury, Mass., May 14, 1739; graduated from Harvard College in 1759; studied theology and was ordained a minister of the Congregational Church in 1763, holding a pastorate in Hampton Falls, N.H., until 1776; moved to Stratham, N.H., in 1776 and engaged in agricultural pursuits; member of the State constitutional convention in 1781; member, State house of representatives 1783; Member of the Continental Congress in 1788; elected to the United States Senate and served from March 4, 1789, to March 3, 1793; elected to the Third Congress (March 4, 1793-March 3, 1795); member, State house of representatives 1795; judge of the superior court of New Hampshire 1798-1809; withdrew from political life and resumed agricultural pursuits; died in Stratham, N.H., on March 7, 1838; interment in Stratham Cemetery.

**Bibliography:** *DAB*; Wingate, Charles. *The Life and Letters of Paine Wingate.* 2 vols., Medford, Mass.: Mercury Printing Co., 1930.

**WINGO, Effiegene Locke** (wife of Otis Theodore Wingo and great-great-great-grandaughter of Matthew Locke), a Representative from Arkansas; born in Lockesburg, Sevier County, Ark., April 13, 1883; attended public and private schools and Union Female College, Oxford, Miss.; was graduated from Maddox Seminary, Little Rock, Ark., in 1901; moved to Texarkana, Ark., in 1895 and to De Queen, Ark., in 1897; elected as a Democrat on November 4, 1930, to the Seventy-first Congress to fill the vacancy caused by the death of her husband, Otis Theodore Wingo, and on the same day was elected to the Seventy-second Congress and served from November 4, 1930, to March 3, 1933; was not a candidate for renomination in 1932; co-founder in 1934 of National Institute of Public Affairs, Washington, D.C.; engaged in educational and research work; was a resident of De Queen, Sevier County, Ark.; died September 19, 1962, in Burlington, Ontario, Canada, while visiting her son; interment in Rock Creek Cemetery, Washington, D.C.

**WINGO, Otis Theodore** (husband of Effigene Wingo), a Representative from Arkansas; born in Weakley County, Tenn., June 18, 1877; attended the public schools, Bethel College at McKenzie, Tenn., McFerrin College at Martin, Tenn., and Valparaiso (Ind.) University; taught school; studied law; was admitted to the bar in 1900 and commenced practice in De Queen, Sevier County, Ark.; member of the State senate 1907-1909; resumed the practice of his profession in De Queen, Ark.; elected as a Democrat to the Sixty-third and to the eight succeeding Congresses and served from March 4, 1913, until his death in Baltimore, Md., October 21, 1930; interment in Rock Creek Cemetery, Washington, D.C.

**WINN, Edward Lawrence, Jr. (Larry),** a Representative from Kansas; born in Kansas City, Jackson County, Mo., August 22, 1919; attended public schools in Kansas City, Mo.; B.A., University of Kansas, 1941; two years with a radio station in Kansas City, Mo.; two years with North American Aviation; two years as a private builder; vice president, Winn-Rau Corp., 1950 to 1966; national director, National Association of Home Builders, fourteen years; past president, Home Builders Association of Kansas; elected as a Republican to the Ninetieth and to the eight succeeding Congresses (January 3, 1967-January 3, 1985); was not a candidate for reelection in 1984 to the Ninety-ninth Congress; is a resident of Prairie Village, Kans.

**WINN, Richard,** a Representative from South Carolina; born in Fauquier County, Va., in 1750; attended the common schools; moved to Georgia and then to Fairfield County in South Carolina in 1768; served as a clerk in a countinghouse; engaged in cotton buying and other mercantile pursuits, and was a land surveyor; entered the Revolutionary Army as a lieutenant and attained the rank of colonel of State militia; after the war was promoted to the rank of major general of militia; member, South Carolina State assembly, 1779-1786; appointed superintendent of Indian affairs for the Creek Nation in 1788; elected to the Third Congress, and reelected as a Republican to the Fourth Congress (March 4, 1793-March 3, 1797); elected to the Seventh Congress to fill the vacancy caused by the resignation of Thomas Sumter; reelected to the Eighth and to the four succeeding Congresses, and served from January 24, 1803 to March 3, 1813; moved to Tennessee in 1813; became a planter, and continued in the mercantile business until his death on his plantation at Duck River, Maury County, Tenn., December 19, 1818; interment at Winnsboro, Fairfield County, S.C.

**WINN, Thomas Elisha,** a Representative from Georgia; born near Athens, Clarke County, Ga., May 21, 1839; attended Carrollton (Ga.) Masonic Institute, and was graduated from Emory and Henry College, Emory, Va., in 1860; studied law; was admitted to the bar in 1861 and commenced practice in Alpharetta, Milton County, Ga.; solicitor of the county court of Milton County; entered the Confederate Army as a first lieutenant in 1861; promoted to captain, afterward, a major, and finally a lieutenant colonel, Twenty-fourth Regiment, Georgia Infantry, and served with General Robert E. Lee's army until the close of the Civil War; engaged in agricultural pursuits in 1868; county school commissioner of Gwinnett County from 1876 to 1890, when he resigned; elected as a Democrat to the Fifty-second Congress (March 4, 1891-March 3, 1893); did not seek renomination in 1892 to the Fifty-third Congress; resumed agricultural pursuits in Greene County, Ga.; died in Atlanta, Ga., on June 5, 1925; interment in Ridge Grove Cemetery, near Greensboro, Greene County, Ga.

**WINSLOW, Samuel Ellsworth,** a Representative from Massachusetts; born in Worcester, Mass., April 11, 1862; attended the public schools; graduated from Worcester Classical High School in 1880, from Williston Seminary, Easthampton, Mass., in 1881, and from Harvard University in 1885; engaged in the manufacture of skates; appointed as a colonel on the staff of Governor John Q.A. Brackett in 1890; chairman of the Republican city committee of Worcester, 1890-1892; chairman of the Massachusetts Republican committee in 1893 and 1894; delegate to the Republican National Convention of 1908; elected as a Republican to the Sixty-third and to the five succeeding Congresses (March 4, 1913-March 3, 1925); chairman, Committee on Interstate and Foreign Commerce (Sixty-seventh and Sixty-eighth Congresses); was not a candidate for renomination in 1924 to the Sixty-ninth Congress; appointed by President Calvin Coolidge in 1926 as a member of the United States Board of Mediation, for the disposition of disputes between carriers and their employees, and was subsequently chosen chairman, serving until 1934; moved in 1935 to Worcester, Mass., where he died July 11, 1940; remains were cremated and the ashes interred in Hope Cemetery.

**WINSLOW, Warren,** a Representative from North Carolina; born in Fayetteville, Cumberland County, N.C., January 1, 1810; was graduated from the University of North Carolina at Chapel Hill in 1827; studied law; was admitted to the bar and commenced practice in Fayetteville; member of the North Carolina State senate, and served as speaker; became Acting Governor of North Carolina following the resignation of Governor David S. Reid, and served from December 6, 1854 to January 1, 1855; elected as a Democrat to the Thirty-fourth and to the two succeeding Congresses (March 4, 1855-March 3, 1861); died in Fayetteville, N.C., August 16, 1862; interment in Cross Creek Cemetery.

**WINSTEAD, William Arthur,** a Representative from Mississippi; born near Philadelphia, Neshoba County, Miss., January 6, 1904; attended the public schools, Clarke Memorial College, Newton, Miss., and the University of Alabama at Tuscaloosa; was graduated from Mississippi Southern College at Hattiesburg in 1931; engaged in agricultural pursuits; superintendent of education of Neshoba County, Miss., 1935-1942; elected as a Democrat to the Seventy-eighth and to the ten succeeding Congresses (January 3, 1943-January 3, 1965); unsuccessful candidate for reelection in 1964 to the Eighty-ninth Congress; resumed agricultural pursuits; automobile dealer; commissioner, Mississippi department of Public Welfare, 1968-1971; was a resident of Philadelphia, Miss., until his death in Jackson, Miss., on March 14, 1995.

**WINSTON, Joseph,** a Representative from North Carolina; born in Louisa County, Va., June 17, 1746; moved in 1766 to that part of Rowan County which later became Stokes County, N.C.; participated in expeditions against the hostile frontier Indians; member of the Hillsboro convention in 1775; member of the commission that concluded a treaty with the Cherokees in 1777; appointed entry taker for Surry County in 1778; chief ranger of Surry County; served as major in the Revolutionary Army; member of the North Carolina State senate in 1790, 1791, 1802, 1807, and 1812; elected to the Third Congress (March 4, 1793-March 3, 1795); elected as a Republican to the Eighth and Ninth Congresses (March 4, 1803-March 3, 1807); died near Germanton, Stokes County, N.C., April 21, 1815; interment in the family burial ground near Germanton; reinterment on Guilford Battle Grounds, N.C.

**Bibliography:** *DAB*; Hendricks, J. Edwin. "Joseph Winston: North Carolina Jeffersonian." *North Carolina Historical Review* 45 (July 1968): 284-297.

**WINTER, Charles Edwin,** a Representative from Wyoming; born in Muscatine, Iowa, September 13, 1870; attended the public schools and Iowa Wesleyan University at Mount Pleasant; was graduated from the Nebraska Wesleyan University at Lincoln in 1892; studied law; was admitted to the bar in 1895 and commenced practice in Omaha, Nebr.; moved to Encampment, Carbon County, Wyo., in 1902 and to Casper, Natrona County, Wyo., in 1903; delegate to the Republican National Convention in 1908; judge of the sixth judicial district of Wyoming 1913-1919; resigned from the bench and resumed the practice of law at Casper, Wyo.; elected as a

Republican to the Sixty-eighth, Sixty-ninth, and Seventieth Congresses (March 4, 1923-March 3, 1929); was not a candidate for renomination in 1928, but was an unsuccessful candidate for election to the United States Senate; attorney general of Puerto Rico in 1932 and 1933, and served as Acting Governor; resumed the practice of law; died in Casper, Wyo., April 22, 1948; interment in Highland Cemetery.

**WINTER, Elisha I.,** a Representative from New York; born in New York City, July 15, 1781; moved about 1806 to that portion of the township of Peru, Clinton County, which was later included in the township of Ausable, and engaged in mining ore; was elected as a Federalist to the Thirteenth Congress (March 4, 1813-March 3, 1815); unsuccessful candidate for reelection in 1814 to the Fourteenth Congress; moved to a farm near Lexington, Ky., and engaged as a planter; was also instrumental in building the first railroad in that locality, and subsequently became president of the Lexington & Ohio Railroad; died in Lexington, Fayette County, Ky., June 30, 1849; interment in Lexington Cemetery.

**WINTER, Thomas Daniel,** a Representative from Kansas; born in Columbus, Cherokee County, Kans., July 7, 1896; attended the public and high schools; during the First World War served as a private in the United States Air Corps in 1918 and 1919; court reporter of the district court of Crawford County, Kans., 1921-1927; studied law; was admitted to the bar in 1926 and commenced practice in Girard, Kans.; assistant county attorney of Crawford County, Kans., in 1927 and 1928 and county attorney in 1929 and 1930; commissioner of public utilities of Girard 1933-1935; commissioner of finance of Girard 1936-1938; elected as a Republican to the Seventy-sixth and to the three succeeding Congresses (January 3, 1939-January 3, 1947); unsuccessful candidate for renomination in 1946; returned to Girard, Kans., and continued to practice law; died in Pittsburg, Kans., November 7, 1951; interment in Park Cemetery, Columbus, Kans.

**WINTHROP, Robert Charles,** a Representative and a Senator from Massachusetts; born in Boston, Mass., May 12, 1809; graduated from Harvard University in 1828; studied law with Daniel Webster; was admitted to the bar in 1831 and practiced in Boston; member, Massachusetts house of representatives, 1835-1840, and served as speaker, 1838-1840; elected as a Whig to the Twenty-sixth Congress to fill the vacancy caused by the resignation of Abbott Lawrence; reelected to the Twenty-seventh Congress, and served from November 9, 1840 to May 25, 1842, when he resigned; subsequently elected to the Twenty-seventh Congress to fill the vacancy caused by the resignation of his successor, Nathan Appleton; reelected to the Twenty-eighth and to the three succeeding Congresses, and served from November 29, 1842 to July 30, 1850, when he again resigned to become Senator; Speaker of the House of Representatives during the Thirtieth Congress; appointed as a Whig to the United States Senate, July 27, 1850, to fill the vacancy caused by the resignation of Daniel Webster, and served from July 30, 1850 to February 1, 1851, when a successor was elected; unsuccessful candidate for election to the vacancy in 1851; was an unsuccessful Whig candidate for Governor of Massachusetts the same year; presidential elector on the Whig ticket in 1852; engaged in literary, historical, and philanthropic pursuits; died in Boston, Mass., November 16, 1894; interment in Mount Auburn Cemetery, Cambridge, Mass.

Bibliography: *DAB*; Winthrop, Robert, Jr. *Memoir of Robert Charles Winthrop*. Boston: Little, Brown and Co., 1897.

**WIRTH, Timothy Endicott,** a Representative and a Senator from Colorado; born in Santa Fe, N.Mex., September 22, 1939; A.B., Harvard University, 1961; M.Ed., Harvard Graduate School of Education, 1964; Ph.D., education, Stanford University, 1973; United States Army Reserve, 1961-1967; White House fellow, Department of Health, Education and Welfare, 1967-1968; Deputy Assistant Secretary of Health, Education and Welfare, 1970-1971; vice president, Great Western United Corp., 1970-1971; manager, Rocky Mountain office, Arthur D. Little, Inc., 1971-1974; elected as a Democrat to the Ninety-fourth and to the five succeeding Congresses and served from January 3, 1975, to January 3, 1987; was not a candidate for reelection in 1986 to the House of Representatives, but was elected to the United States Senate and served from January 3, 1987 to January 3, 1993; was not a candidate for reelection in 1992; appointed a member of the President's Committee on the Arts and the Humanities, September 19, 1994; nominated as Counselor of the Department of State, March 9, 1993, and confirmed by the Senate on April 21, 1993; is a resident of Washington, D.C.

**WISE, George Douglas** (cousin of John Sergeant Wise and Richard Alsop Wise and nephew of Henry Alexander Wise), a Representative from Virginia; born at "Deep Creek," the Wise estate in Accomack County, near Onancock, Va., June 4, 1831; was graduated from Indiana University at Bloomington; studied law in the College of William and Mary, Williamsburg, Va.; was admitted to the bar and commenced practice in Richmond, Henrico County, Va.; captain in the Confederate Army during the Civil War; Commonwealth attorney of the city of Richmond from 1870 to 1889, when he resigned; elected as a Democrat to the Forty-seventh and to the three succeeding Congresses (March 4, 1881-March 3, 1889); chairman, Committee on Manufactures (Forty-ninth Congress); presented credentials as a Member-elect to the Fifty-first Congress and served from March 4, 1889, to April 10, 1890, when he was succeeded by Edmund Waddill, Jr., who contested his election; elected to the Fifty-second and Fifty-third Congresses (March 4, 1891-March 3, 1895); chairman, Committee on Interstate and Foreign Commerce (Fifty-second and Fifty-third Congresses); died in Richmond, Va., February 4, 1898; interment in Hollywood Cemetery.

**WISE, Henry Alexander** (father of John Sergeant Wise and Richard Alsop Wise and uncle of George Douglas Wise), a Representative from Virginia; born in Drummondtown, Accomack County, Va., December 3, 1806; was privately tutored until his twelfth year and then entered Margaret Academy, near Pungoteague, Accomack County; was graduated from Washington College, Pennsylvania, in 1825; studied law in Winchester, Va.; was admitted to the bar in 1828 and commenced practice in Nashville, Davidson County, Tenn.; returned to Virginia in 1830; held several local offices; elected as a Jacksonian to the Twenty-third and Twenty-fourth Congresses, as a Whig to the Twenty-fifth through Twenty-seventh Congresses, and as a Democrat to the Twenty-eighth Congress and served from March 4, 1833, until his resignation on February 12, 1844; chairman, Committee on Naval Affairs (Twenty-seventh and Twenty-eighth Congresses); was appointed Minister to France in 1843, but was not confirmed; appointed Minister to Brazil on February 8, 1844 and served until August 1847; delegate to the Virginia constitutional convention in 1850; elected Governor of Virginia in 1855 and served from January 1, 1856 to December 31, 1859; delegate to the Virginia Convention, 1861; appointed a brigadier general in the Confederate Army on June 5, 1861, and served throughout the Civil War; resumed the practice of law in Richmond, Henrico County, Va.; served on the commission to fix the boundary line between Virginia and Maryland; died in Richmond, Va., September 12, 1876; interment in Hollywood Cemetery.

Bibliography: *DAB*; Simpson, Craig M. *A Good Southerner: The Life of Henry A. Wise of Virginia*. Chapel Hill: University of North Carolina Press, 1985; Wise, Henry Alexander. *Seven Decades of the Union*. Philadelphia: J.B. Lippincott, 1872.

**WISE, James Walter,** a Representative from Georgia; born near McDonough, Henry County, Ga., March 3, 1868; attended the common schools; studied law at Emory College, Oxford, Ga.; was admitted to the bar in 1892 and commenced practice in Fayetteville, Fayette County, Ga., in January 1893; member of the State house of representatives 1902-1908; was mayor of Fayetteville 1904-1906; solicitor general of the Flint judicial circuit 1908-1912; elected as a Democrat to the Sixty-fourth and to the four succeeding Congresses (March 4, 1915-March 3, 1925); declined to be a candidate for renomination in 1924; owing to prolonged illness was unable to qualify for or attend the Sixty-eighth Congress; died in Atlanta, Ga., on September 8, 1925; interment in McDonough Cemetery, McDonough, Ga.

**WISE, John Sergeant** (son of Henry Alexander Wise, grandson of John Sergeant, brother of Richard Alsop Wise, and cousin of George Douglas Wise), a Representative from Virginia; born in Rio de Janeiro, Brazil, December 27, 1846, while his father was United States Minister to that country; attended preparatory schools in Goochland and Princess Anne Counties, Va., and the Virginia Military Institute at Lexington in 1862; participated with the institute cadets in the Battle of New Market, Va., May 15, 1864; subsequently became a lieutenant in the Confederate Army; was graduated from the law department of the University of Virginia at Charlottesville in 1867; was admitted to the bar the same year and commenced practice in Richmond, Henrico County, Va.; unsuccessful candidate for election in 1880 to the Forty-seventh Congress; United States attorney for the eastern district of Virginia from May 1882 to March 1883, when he resigned, having been elected to Congress; elected as a Readjuster to the Forty-eighth Congress (March 4, 1883-March 3, 1885); was not a candidate for renomination in 1884 to the Forty-ninth Congress; unsuccessful Republican candidate in 1885 for election for Governor of Virginia; moved to New York City and engaged in the practice of his profession; died near Princess Anne, Somerset County, Md., May 12, 1913; interment in Hollywood Cemetery, Richmond, Va.

Bibliography: *DAB*; Campbell, Otho Carlino. "John Sergeant Wise: A Case Study in Conservative-Readjuster Politics in Virginia, 1869-1889." Ph.D. dissertation, University of Virginia, 1979; Davis, Curtis C. "Very Well-Rounded Republican: The Several Lives of John S. Wise." *Virginia Magazine of History and Biography* 71 (October 1963): 461-87.

**WISE, Morgan Ringland,** a Representative from Pennsylvania; born in West Bethlehem, Washington County, Pa., June 7, 1825; attended the public schools; taught school; emigrated west and engaged in gold mining in California in 1850; while there volunteered, under Major Stammins, to defend the miners against the depredations of the Indians; returned to Pennsylvania, and was graduated from Waynesburg (Pa.) College in 1856; engaged in agricultural pursuits; member of the Pennsylvania house of representatives from 1874 to 1878; elected as a Democrat to the Forty-sixth and Forty-seventh Congresses (March 4, 1879-March 3, 1883); chairman, Committee on Manufactures (Forty-sixth Congress); was not a candidate for renomination in 1882 to the Forty-eighth Congress; moved to Arizona and engaged in cattle raising; consular agent at Nogales, Mexico, from February 20, 1888 to May 31, 1900; died in Coraopolis, Allegheny County, Pa., April 13, 1903; interment in Greenmount Cemetery, Waynesburg, Pa.

**WISE, Richard Alsop** (son of Henry Alexander Wise, grandson of John Sergeant, brother of John Sergeant Wise, and cousin of George Douglas Wise), a Representative from Virginia; born in Philadelphia, Pa., September 2, 1843; attended private schools in Richmond, Va., Harrison's Academy, Albemarle County, Va., and the College of William and Mary, Williamsburg, Va., for two years; during the Civil War served in the Confederate Army as a private in General J.E.B. Stuart's cavalry and as assistant inspector general of Wise's brigade, Army of Northern Virginia; graduated in medicine from the Medical College of Virginia in 1867 and practiced; professor at the College of William and Mary 1869-1881; delegate to all Virginia Republican conventions from 1879 to 1900; superintendent of the Eastern Lunatic Asylum of Virginia 1882-1885; member of the Virginia house of delegates 1885-1887; clerk of the circuit and county courts of the city of Williamsburg and county of James City 1888-1894; delegate to the Republican National Conventions in 1892, 1896, and 1900; successfully contested as a Republican the election of William A. Young to the Fifty-fifth Congress and served from April 26, 1898, to March 3, 1899; was again successful in contesting the election of William A. Young to the Fifty-sixth Congress and served from March 12, 1900, until his death in Williamsburg, Va., December 21, 1900; interment in Hollywood Cemetery, Richmond, Va.

**WISE, Robert Ellsworth, Jr.,** a Representative from West Virginia; born in Washington, D.C., January 6, 1948; attended public schools in Charleston, W.Va., and graduated from George Washington High School in 1966; B.A., Duke University, Durham, N.C., 1970; J.D., Tulane University School of Law, New Orleans, La., 1975; admitted to the West Virginia bar in 1975 and commenced practice in Charleston; legislative counsel to the West Virginia State house of delegates judiciary committee, 1977-1978; director, West Virginians for Fair and Equitable Assessment of Taxes, Inc., 1977-1980; West Virginia State senator, 1980-1982; elected as a Democrat to the Ninety-eighth and to the six succeeding Congresses (January 3, 1983-January 3, 1997); is a resident of Clendenin, W.Va.

**WISNER, Henry,** a Delegate from New York; born near Florida, Orange County, N.Y., in 1720; completed academic studies; invested in real estate and built a gristmill near Goshen, N.Y.; assistant justice of the court of common pleas; member of the colonial assembly 1759-1769; delegate to the New York provincial convention in 1775; Member of the Continental Congress 1775-1776; voted for the Declaration of Independence, but was absent at the time it was signed, attending the Provincial Congress in New York, to which he had just been elected; member of the Provincial Congress in 1776 and 1777; erected three powder mills in the vicinity of Goshen, Orange County, N.Y., and supplied powder to the Continental Army during the Revolution; one of the committee that framed the first constitution of New York in 1777; member of the commission to provide for fortifying the Hudson River in 1777 and 1778; served in the State senate 1777-1782; established an academy at Goshen in 1784; member of the first board of regents of the University of the State of New York 1784-1787; served as a member of the State ratification convention in 1788; died in Goshen, N.Y., on March 4, 1790; interment in the Old Wallkill Cemetery, Phillipsburg, N.Y.

Bibliography: *DAB*.

**WITCHER, John Seashoal,** a Representative from West Virginia; born in Cabell County, Va. (now West Virginia), July 15, 1839; attended the public schools; elected clerk of the circuit court of Cabell County in 1861; enrolled in the Union Army as a first lieutenant, Third Regiment, West Virginia Volunteer Cavalry, December 13, 1862; promoted to captain September 8, 1863, major May 23, 1864, lieutenant colonel May 6, 1865; honorably mustered out June 30, 1865; member of the State house of delegates in 1865; secretary of state of West Virginia 1866-1869; elected as a Republican to the Forty-first Congress (March 4, 1869-March 3, 1871); unsuccessful candidate for reelection in 1870 to the Forty-second Congress; appointed by President Ulysses S. Grant as collector of internal revenue for the third district of West Virginia and served from April 1, 1871, to October 1, 1876; served as United States pension agent at Washington, D.C., from July 7, 1878, to October 3, 1880; major and paymaster, United States Army, from October 5, 1880, until he retired September 8, 1899; moved to Salt

Lake City, Utah, in 1891, and died there July 8, 1906; interment in Mount Olivet Cemetery.

**WITHERELL, James,** a Representative from Vermont; born in Mansfield, Mass., June 16, 1759; completed preparatory studies; served in the Revolutionary Army as a member of the Eleventh Massachusetts Regiment 1775-1783; studied medicine and was licensed to practice in 1788; moved to Hampton, Vt., in 1788 and to Fair Haven, Vt., in 1789 and continued the practice of his profession; member of the State house of representatives 1798-1802; associate county judge 1801-1803; judge of Rutland County 1803-1806; executive councilor 1802-1806; elected as a Republican to the Tenth Congress and served from March 4, 1807, to May 1, 1808, when he resigned; appointed United States judge for the Territory of Michigan in 1808 and served until 1828, when he resigned to become secretary of the Territory; during the War of 1812 was in command of the troops at Detroit in the absence of General Hull, and was taken prisoner when the latter surrendered; lived in Fair Haven, Vt., while on parole; was exchanged and returned to his duties in Detroit; secretary of Michigan Territory by appointment of President John Quincy Adams 1828-1830; died in Detroit, Mich., January 9, 1838, interment in the Russell Street Cemetery; reinterment in Elmwood Cemetery.

**WITHERS, Garrett Lee,** a Senator and a Representative from Kentucky; born on a farm in Webster County, near Clay, Ky., June 21, 1884; student of Providence M. and F. Academy and Southern Normal School, Bowling Green, Ky.; was admitted to the bar in 1908; practicing attorney in Webster County, Ky., 1911-1953; clerk of Webster County Circuit Court 1910-1912, and master commissioner 1913-1917; member, Kentucky Highway Commission 1932-1936; referee in bankruptcy 1941-1945; appointed commissioner, Kentucky Department of Highways 1947-1949; appointed as a Democrat to the United States Senate to fill the vacancy caused by the resignation of Alben W. Barkley, and served from January 20, 1949, to November 26, 1950; was not a candidate for election to the vacancy; member, Kentucky house of representatives 1951; elected as a Democrat to the Eighty-second Congress to fill the vacancy caused by the death of John A. Whitaker; reelected to the Eighty-third Congress and served from August 2, 1952, until his death in the naval hospital at Bethesda, Md., April 30, 1953; interment in the I.O.O.F. Cemetery, Clay, Ky.

**WITHERS, Robert Enoch** (cousin of Thomas Withers Chinn), a Senator from Virginia; born near Lynchburg, Campbell County, Va., September 18, 1821; attended private schools; graduated from the medical department of the University of Virginia at Charlottesville in 1841 and commenced practice in Campbell County; moved to Danville, Pittsylvania County, Va., in 1858; during the Civil War entered the Confederate Army as major of Infantry in 1861 and was promoted to colonel of the Eighteenth Virginia Infantry, which he commanded until retired in consequence of numerous disabling wounds; appointed to command the post at Danville, Va., which position he held until the close of the war; moved to Lynchburg, Va., in 1866 and established the Lynchburg News, a daily paper devoted to the interests of the Conservative Party; nominated for governor by that party, but withdrew; presidential elector on the Democratic ticket in 1872; elected lieutenant governor in 1873; elected as a Democrat to the United States Senate and served from March 4, 1875, to March 3, 1881; unsuccessful candidate for reelection in 1881; chairman, Committee on Pensions (Forty-sixth Congress); appointed by President Grover Cleveland as United States consul at Hong Kong, China, 1885-1889, when he resigned; returned to Wytheville, Wythe County, Va.; died at "Ingleside," Wytheville, Va., September 21, 1907; interment in the East End Cemetery.

**Bibliography:** Withers, Robert E. *Autobiography of an Octogenarian.* Roanoke: The Stone Printing Co., 1907.

**WITHERSPOON, John,** a Delegate from New Jersey; born in Gifford, Haddingtonshire, Scotland, February 5, 1723; completed preparatory studies; was graduated from Edinburgh University in 1739; studied theology at Edinburgh; was licensed in 1743 and ordained minister of the parish of Beith in 1745; was the author of various religious pamphlets; installed pastor at Paisley on June 16, 1757; moderator of the synod of Glasgow and Ayr in 1758; became president of the College of New Jersey (now Princeton University) in 1768; appointed a member of the committee on correspondence from Somerset County on July 28, 1775; member of the Provincial Congress of New Jersey from June 10 to June 22, 1776; Member of the Continental Congress from 1776 to 1782; a signer of the Declaration of Independence; member of the secret committee of the Congress on the conduct of the war and member of the board of war in 1778; member of the State council in 1780; drafted the instructions of June 1781 to the American peace commissioners; served in the New Jersey State general assembly in 1783 and 1789; member of the State ratification convention in 1787; after the war returned to Princeton, where he continued his duties as president; died on his farm near Princeton, N.J., November 15, 1794; interment in the Princeton Cemetery.

**Bibliography:** *DAB*; Collins, Varnum Lansing. *President Witherspoon.* 2 vols. Reprint. 1925. New York: Arno Press, 1969; Stohlman, Martha Lou Lemmon. *John Witherspoon: Parson, Politician, Patriot.* 1976. Reprint. Louisville, Ky.: Westminster/John Knox Press, 1989; Witherspoon, John. *The Selected Writings of John Witherspoon.* Edited by Thomas Miller. Carbondale: Southern Illinois University Press, 1990.

**WITHERSPOON, Robert** (great-great-grandfather of Robert Witherspoon Hemphill), a Representative from South Carolina; born near Kingstree, Williamsburg County, S.C., January 29, 1767; attended local schools; elected State treasurer in 1800 and served one term; was a member of the State house of representatives, 1792-1794, 1802-1804, 1806-1808, 1816-1817; elected as a Republican to the Eleventh Congress (March 4, 1809-March 3, 1811); declined to be a candidate for reelection; had large planting interests in Sumter County, S.C.; opposed the nullification act in 1832; died near Mayesville, Sumter County, S.C., October 11, 1837; interment in the Salem Brick Church Cemetery.

**WITHERSPOON, Samuel Andrew,** a Representative from Mississippi; born near Columbus, Lowndes County, Miss., May 4, 1855; attended the public schools; in 1872 moved with his mother to Oxford, Miss.; was graduated from the University of Mississippi at Oxford in 1876; professor in the University of Mississippi 1876-1879; studied law; was admitted to the bar in 1879 and commenced practice in Meridian, Lauderdale County, Miss., the same year; elected as a Democrat to the Sixty-second, Sixty-third, and Sixty-fourth Congresses and served from March 4, 1911, until his death in Meridian, Miss., November 24, 1915; interment in Rose Hill Cemetery.

**WITHROW, Gardner Robert,** a Representative from Wisconsin; born in La Crosse, Wis., October 5, 1892; attended the grade and high schools; after two years of legal training entered the train service of the Chicago, Burlington and Quincy Railroad Company; was engaged in railroading as a fireman and conductor from 1912 until 1931; member of the Wisconsin State assembly in 1926 and 1927; served as State representative for the railroad brotherhoods, 1928-1931; elected as a Republican to the Seventy-second and Seventy-third Congresses and as a Progressive to the Seventy-fourth and Seventy-fifth Congresses (March 4, 1931-January 3, 1939); unsuccessful candidate for reelection in 1938 to the Seventy-sixth Congress; unsuccessful candidate for election in 1940 to the Seventy-seventh Congress, and for election in 1942 to the Seventy-eighth Congress; resumed activities as State representative for the Brotherhood of Railroad Trainmen; elected as a Republican to the Eighty-first and to the five succeeding Congresses (January 3, 1949-January 3, 1961); was not a candidate for renomination in 1960 to the Eighty-seventh Congress; was a resident of La Crosse, Wis., until his death on September 23, 1964; interment in Oak Grove Cemetery.

**WITTE, William Henry,** a Representative from Pennsylvania; born in Columbia, Morris County, N.J., October 4, 1817; moved to Springtown, Bucks County, Pa., and attended the common schools; moved to Philadelphia in 1840; engaged in mercantile pursuits and the real estate business; elected as a Democrat to the Thirty-third Congress (March 4, 1853-March 3, 1855); engaged in newspaper work and resumed real estate interests; died in Philadelphia, Pa., November 24, 1876; interment in Durham Cemetery, Durham, Bucks County, Pa.

**WOFFORD, Harris Llewellyn,** a Senator from Pennsylvania; born in New York City, April 9, 1926; B.A., University of Chicago, 1948; LL.B., Yale University Law School, 1954; J.D., Howard University Law School, Washington, D.C., 1954; United States Army Air Force service, 1944-1945; attorney; former staff member, United States Commission on Civil Rights; adviser to Senator John F. Kennedy, 1960 presidential campaign; special assistant to the President and chairman, Sub-Cabinet Group on Civil Rights, 1960-1962; aided in launching Peace Corps and served as its special representative to Africa then as its associate director; president, State University of New York College at Old Westbury, 1966-1970; president, Bryn Mawr (Pa.) College, 1970-1978; assistant professor of law, Notre Dame University; chairman, Pennsylvania Democratic State Committee, 1986; Secretary of Labor and Industry to Governor Robert P. Casey, Pennsylvania; appointed as a Democrat to the United States Senate to fill the vacancy caused by the death of Henry John Heinz III, elected for the remainder of the term expiring January 3, 1995, and served from May 9, 1991 to January 3, 1995; unsuccessful candidate in 1994 for election to a full term; appointed by President William J. Clinton as chief executive officer of the Corporation for National and Community Service, and served from September 29, 1995 to present; is a resident of Bryn Mawr, Pa.

**Bibliography:** Wofford, Harris. *Of Kennedys and Kings: Making Sense of the Sixties.* 1980. Reprint. Pittsburgh: University of Pittsburgh Press, 1992.

**WOFFORD, Thomas Albert,** a Senator from South Carolina; born in Madden Station, Laurens County, S.C., September 27, 1908; attended the public schools; graduated from the University of South Carolina at Columbia 1928, and from Harvard University Law School in 1931; was admitted to the bar in 1931 and commenced the practice of law in Greenville, S.C.; assistant solicitor of thirteenth judicial circuit, 1935-1936; assistant United States district attorney, 1937-1944; member, board of trustees, Winthrop College, Rock Hill, S.C., 1944-1956; appointed as a Democrat, April 5, 1956, to the United States Senate to fill the vacancy caused by the resignation of Strom Thurmond, and served from April 5, 1956 to November 6, 1956; was not a candidate for election to fill the vacancy; engaged in the practice of law; member, South Carolina State senate, 1966-1972; changed party affiliation to Republican; resided in Greenville, S.C., where he died on February 25, 1978; interment in Woodlawn Memorial Park.

**WOLCOTT, Edward Oliver,** a Senator from Colorado; born in Long Meadow, Hampden County, Mass., March 26, 1848; attended the common schools; served in the One Hundred and Fiftieth Regiment, Ohio Volunteer Infantry, during the Civil War; attended Yale College; graduated from the law department of Harvard University in 1875; moved to Colorado; taught school and practiced law; elected district attorney in 1876; moved to Denver in 1879; member, State senate 1879-1882; elected in 1889 as a Republican to the United States Senate; reelected in 1895 and served from March 4, 1889, to March 3, 1901; unsuccessful candidate for reelection in

1901 and again in 1902 and 1903; chairman, Committee on Civil Service and Retrenchment (Fifty-first and Fifty-second Congresses), Committee on Post Office and Post Roads (Fifty-fourth through Fifty-sixth Congresses); resumed the practice of law in Denver, Colo.; died in Monte Carlo, Principality of Monaco, March 1, 1905; remains were cremated in Paris, France, and the ashes interred in Woodlawn Cemetery, New York City.

**Bibliography:** *DAB*; Dawson, Thomas. *Life and Character of Edward Oliver Wolcott.* 2 vols., New York: The Knickerbocker Press, 1911.

**WOLCOTT, Jesse Paine,** a Representative from Michigan; born in Gardner, Worcester County, Mass., March 3, 1893; attended the common and high schools at Gardner, Mass., and the Detroit (Mich.) Technical Institute; was graduated from the Detroit College of Law, Detroit, Mich., in 1915; was admitted to the bar the same year and commenced practice in Detroit, Mich.; during the First World War served overseas as a second lieutenant in a machine gun company of the Twenty-sixth Infantry, First Division, 1917-1919; after the war settled in Port Huron, Mich., and resumed the practice of law; assistant police judge of Port Huron in 1921; assistant prosecuting attorney of St. Clair County, Mich., 1922-1926; prosecuting attorney 1927-1930; elected as a Republican to the Seventy-second and to the twelve succeeding Congresses (March 4, 1931-January 3, 1957); chairman, Committee on Banking and Currency (Eightieth and Eighty-third Congresses), Joint Committee on Economic Report (Eighty-third Congress); was not a candidate for renomination in 1956; appointed a director of the Federal Deposit Insurance Corporation by President Dwight D. Eisenhower in 1958, and served as chairman until January 1964; resided in Chevy Chase, Md., until his death on January 28, 1969; interment in Arlington National Cemetery, Va.

**WOLCOTT, Josiah Oliver,** a Senator from Delaware; born in Dover, Del., October 31, 1877; attended the public schools and Wilmington Conference Academy, Dover, Del., and graduated from Wesleyan University, Middletown, Conn., in 1901; studied law; was admitted to the bar in 1904 and commenced practice in Wilmington, Del.; deputy attorney general of Delaware 1909-1913; attorney general of Delaware 1913-1917; elected as a Democrat to the United States Senate and served from March 4, 1917, to July 2, 1921, when he resigned to accept a judicial position; chairman, Committee on Expenditures in the Department of Commerce (Sixty-fifth Congress); appointed chancellor of Delaware in 1921 and served until his death in Dover, Del., November 11, 1938; interment in Lake Side Methodist Episcopal Cemetery.

**WOLCOTT, Oliver,** a Delegate from Connecticut; born in Windsor, Conn., November 20, 1726; graduated from Yale College in 1747; commissioned a captain by the Governor of New York in 1747; raised a company of Volunteers and served on the northwestern frontier until the peace of Aix-la-Chapelle in 1748; returned to Connecticut and settled in Litchfield; studied medicine, but did not practice; elected sheriff of the newly organized county of Litchfield, Conn., in 1751; member of the State council from 1774 to 1786, and at the same time judge of the county court of common pleas; judge of probate for the Litchfield district many years; major general of militia; appointed by the Continental Congress in 1775 as one of the commissioners of Indian affairs for the northern department, intrusted with the task of inducing the Iroquois Indians to remain neutral; Member of the Continental Congress, 1776-1778, and 1780-1783; a signer of the Declaration of Independence; commander of the fourteen Connecticut regiments sent for the defense of New York in 1776, and divided his time between Army service and service in Congress; commanded a brigade of militia which took part in the defeat of General John Burgoyne in 1777; Lieutenant Governor of Connecticut, 1786-1796; elected Governor of Connecticut in 1796, reelected in 1797, and served from January 5, 1796 until his death in Litchfield, Conn., December 1, 1797; interment in the East Cemetery.

**Bibliography:** *DAB*; Bland, James E. "The Oliver Wolcotts of Connecticut: The National Experience, 1775-1800." Ph.D. dissertation, Harvard University, 1970.

**WOLD, John Schiller,** a Representative from Wyoming; born in East Orange, Essex County, N.J., August 31, 1916; attended St. Andrews University, Scotland; A.B., Union College, Schenectady, N.Y., 1938; M.S., Cornell University, 1939; consulting physicist, Bureau of Ordnance, Department of the Navy, 1941-1942; gunnery and executive officer, destroyer escort duty, Atlantic and Pacific Theaters, during the Second World War; member, Wyoming State house of representatives, 1957-1959; Wyoming Republican State chairman, 1960-1964; chairman, Western States Republican State Chairmen's Association; member, Republican National Committee, 1960-1964; executive committee, Republican National Committee, 1962-1964; unsuccessful Republican candidate in 1964 for election to the United States Senate; geologist, specializing in oil, gas, coal, and uranium exploration, 1939-1968; elected as a Republican to the Ninety-first Congress (January 3, 1969-January 3, 1971); was not a candidate in 1970 for reelection to the House of Representatives, but was an unsuccessful candidate for election to the United States Senate; president of an oil and gas company, 1969 to present; is a resident of Casper, Wyo.

**WOLF, Frank Rudolph,** a Representative from Virginia; born in Philadelphia, Pa., January 30, 1939; attended the public schools; attended the University of Mississippi, 1957-1958; B.A., Pennsylvania State University, University Park, 1961; LL.B., Georgetown University Law School, Washington, D.C., 1965; served in the United States Army 1962-1963; United States Army Signal Corps Reserve, 1963-1967; admitted to the Virginia bar in 1966; executive, trade association, Washington, D.C., 1963-1968; legislative assistant to Representative Edward G. Biester, Jr. of Pennsylvania, 1968-1971; assistant to Secretary of Interior Rogers C.B. Morton, 1971-1974; Deputy Assistant Secretary for Congressional and Legislative Affairs, Department of the Interior, 1974-1975; practiced law, 1975-1980; elected as a Republican to the Ninety-seventh and to the seven succeeding Congresses (January 3, 1981-January 3, 1997); is a resident of Vienna, Va.

**WOLF, George,** a Representative from Pennsylvania; born in Allen Township, Northampton County, Pa., August 12, 1777; pursued preparatory studies; studied law; was admitted to the bar in 1799 and commenced practice in Easton, Pa.; postmaster of Easton in 1802 and 1803; clerk of the orphans' court of Northampton County, 1803-1809; member of the Pennsylvania house of representatives in 1814; elected to the Eighteenth Congress to fill the vacancy caused by the resignation of Thomas J. Rogers; reelected to the three succeeding Congresses, and served from December 9, 1824 until his resignation in 1829 before the convening of the Twenty-first Congress; chairman, Committee on Revolutionary Claims (Twentieth Congress); elected Governor of Pennsylvania in 1829, reelected in 1832, and served from December 15, 1829 to December 15, 1835; was an unsuccessful candidate for reelection in 1835; first Comptroller of the Treasury of the United States from June 18, 1836 to February 23, 1838; appointed collector of customs of the port of Philadelphia in 1838, and served until his death in Philadelphia, Pa., on March 11, 1840; interment in Harrisburg Cemetery, Harrisburg, Pa.

**Bibliography:** *DAB*.

**WOLF, Harry Benjamin,** a Representative from Maryland; born in Baltimore, Md., June 16, 1880; attended the public schools of Baltimore and was graduated from the law department of the University of Maryland at Baltimore in 1901; was admitted to the bar the same year and commenced the practice of law in Baltimore;

also engaged in the real estate business and hotel property investments; member of the State house of delegates 1906-1908; elected as a Democrat to the Sixtieth Congress (March 4, 1907-March 3, 1909); unsuccessful candidate for reelection in 1908 to the Sixty-first Congress; resumed the practice of his profession and other business interests in Baltimore, Md.; died in Baltimore, Md., February 17, 1944; interment in Hebrew Friendship Cemetery.

**WOLF, Leonard George,** a Representative from Iowa; born on a farm in Dane County, near Mazomanie, Wis., October 29, 1925; attended the public schools of Mazomanie, Wis.; served in the United States Navy 1944-1946, with service in the Pacific Theater; graduated from the University of Wisconsin in agricultural economics in 1949 and moved to Elkader, Iowa, the same year; retail feed dealer in Elkader, Iowa, 1952-1958; also public speaker and lecturer; unsuccessful candidate for election in 1956 to the Eighty-fifth Congress; elected as a Democrat to the Eighty-sixth Congress (January 3, 1959-January 3, 1961); unsuccessful candidate for reelection in 1960 to the Eighty-seventh Congress; in 1961 was appointed special assistant to the director, International Cooperation Administration Mission in Brazil and served until 1965; in 1966, coordinator for the child feeding program for Latin America; in 1967, coordinated famine relief activities in India following drought; in 1968, appointed executive director of the American Freedom From Hunger Foundation; died in Washington, D.C., March 28, 1970; interment in St. Barnabas Cemetery, Mazomanie, Wis.

**WOLF, William Penn,** a Representative from Iowa; born in Harrisburg, Stark County, Ohio, December 1, 1833; attended the public schools and Holbrook Seminary; moved to Cedar County, Iowa, in 1856; studied law; was admitted to the bar in 1859 and commenced practice in Tipton, Cedar County, Iowa; superintendent of public schools; member of the State house of representatives in 1863 and 1864; served in the Union Army as captain of Company I, Forty-sixth Regiment, Iowa Volunteer Infantry; appointed assistant assessor of internal revenue in 1865; member of the State senate 1867-1869; elected as a Republican to the Forty-first Congress to fill the vacancy caused by the death of William Smyth and served from December 6, 1870, to March 3, 1871; resumed the practice of law in Tipton, Iowa; again a member of the State house of representatives 1881-1885, and was chosen speaker in 1884; elected judge of the eighteenth judicial district in the fall of 1894 and continued in this capacity until his death in Tipton, Iowa, on September 19, 1896; interment in the Masonic Cemetery.

**WOLFE, Simeon Kalfius,** a Representative from Indiana; born near Georgetown, Floyd County, Ind., February 14, 1824; attended Floyd County schools, and was graduated from the law department of the University of Indiana at Bloomington in 1850; was admitted to the bar in 1851 and commenced practice in Corydon, Harrison County, Ind.; edited and published the Corydon Democrat from 1857 to 1865; member of the State senate 1860-1864; delegate to the Democratic National Conventions at Charleston and Baltimore in 1860; moved to New Albany in 1870 and continued the practice of law; elected as a Democrat to the Forty-third Congress (March 4, 1873-March 3, 1875); was not a candidate for renomination in 1874; resumed the practice of law; judge of the Floyd and Clark circuit court 1880-1884; died in New Albany, Floyd County, Ind., November 18, 1888; interment in Fairview Cemetery.

**WOLFENDEN, James,** a Representative from Pennsylvania; born in Cardington, Delaware County, Pa., on July 25, 1889; attended the public schools, the Friends' Central School, and Penn Charter Academy, Philadelphia, Pa.; engaged in the manufacture of cotton and woolen goods, Cardington, Pa.; elected as a Republican to the Seventieth Congress to fill the vacancy caused by the death of Thomas S. Butler; reelected to the Seventy-first and to the eight succeeding Congresses and served from November 6, 1928, to January 3, 1947; was not a candidate for renomination in 1946; died in Philadelphia, Pa., April 8, 1949; interment in Friends Cemetery, Upper Darby, Pa.

**WOLFF, Joseph Scott,** a Representative from Missouri; born on a farm in Westmoreland County near Greensburg, Pa., June 14, 1878; attended the public schools; served with the Fourth United States Cavalry in the Philippine Islands during the Spanish-American War 1899-1901; moved to St. Louis, Mo., in 1901; was graduated from the dental department of Washington University, St. Louis, Mo., in 1905 and practiced his profession in St. Louis and Festus, Mo.; mayor of Festus, Jefferson County, Mo., 1907-1911, and 1915-1917; member of the Missouri State house of representatives, 1913-1915; was graduated from the St. Louis College of Law and Finance in 1923; was admitted to the bar the same year and commenced practice in Festus, Mo.; elected as a Democrat to the Sixty-eighth Congress (March 4, 1923-March 3, 1925); unsuccessful candidate for reelection in 1924 to the Sixty-ninth Congress; moved to Kansas City in 1924 and continued the practice of dentistry and law until his retirement in 1957; died in Kansas City, Mo., February 27, 1958; interment in Gambel Cemetery, Festus, Mo.

**WOLFF, Lester Lionel,** a Representative from New York; born in New York City, January 4, 1919; attended the public schools of New York City; student at New York University, 1935-1939; lecturer at New York University, 1939-1941; during the Second World War served in the United States Army Air Corps, 1941-1945; head of marketing department of Collegiate Institute, 1945-1949; major, public relations officer, and squadron commander in the Civil Air Patrol, United States Air Force Auxilliary, 1945-1950; colonel, commanding Congressional Squadron, Civil Air Patrol, United States Air Force Auxiliary, 1968-1980; chairman of the board, Coordinated Marketing Agency, 1950-1964; member of the board of Noramco (Dugan's), 1963-1964, and of the Madison Life Insurance Co., 1963-1968; engaged in television as a moderator and producer, 1948-1960; member of the United States Trade Mission to the Philippines in 1962 and to Malaysia and Hong Kong in 1963; chairman of the Advisory Committee of the Subcommittee on Consumers Study by the House of Representatives in 1957; elected as a Democrat to the Eighty-ninth and to the seven succeeding Congresses (January 3, 1965-January 3, 1981); chairman, Select Committee on Narcotics Abuse and Control (Ninety-fourth through Ninety-sixth Congresses); unsuccessful candidate for reelection in 1980 to the Ninety-seventh Congress; chairman, Pacific Community Institute, 1984 to present; television commentator, Public Broadcasting System; member of the board, Critton Corp.; chairman, International Trade and Development Agency, Inc., and International Information Agency, Inc.; is a resident of Great Neck, N.Y.

**WOLFORD, Frank Lane,** a Representative from Kentucky; born near Columbia, Adair County, Ky., September 2, 1817; attended the common schools; studied law; admitted to the bar and commenced practice in Liberty, Casey County, Ky.; member of the Kentucky house of representatives in 1847, 1848, 1865, and 1866; during the Civil War served as colonel of the First Kentucky Volunteer Cavalry 1861-1864; adjutant general of the Commonwealth of Kentucky in 1867 and 1868; elected as a Democrat to the Forty-eighth and Forty-ninth Congresses (March 4, 1883-March 3, 1887); unsuccessful candidate for reelection in 1886 to the Fiftieth Congress; continued the practice of law in Columbia, Ky., until his death there August 2, 1895; interment in Columbia Cemetery.

**WOLPE, Howard Eliot, III,** a Representative from Michigan; born in Los Angeles, Calif., November 2, 1939; attended the public schools of Los Angeles; graduated from University High School, Los Angeles, 1956; B.A., Reed College, Portland, Oreg., 1960; Ph.D., political science, Massachusetts Institute of Technology, Cambridge, 1967; guest lecturer in political science, Boston University, 1965-1966; consultant to the Foreign Service Institute and the Department of State, 1962-1972, and to the Peace Corps, 1966-1967;

associate professor, Western Michigan University, Kalamazoo, 1967-1972; regional representative to Senator Donald W. Riegle, Jr. of Michigan, 1976-1978; member, Michigan State legislature, 1972-1976; Kalamazoo City Commissioner, 1969-1972; delegate, Michigan State Democratic conventions, 1972-1978; elected as a Democrat to the Ninety-sixth and to the six succeeding Congresses (January 3, 1979-January 3, 1993); was not a candidate for reelection in 1992 to the One Hundred Third Congress; unsuccessful candidate in 1994 for election for Governor of Michigan; distinguished visiting professor, University of Michigan and Western Michigan University, 1993-1994; visiting fellow, Brookings Institution; appointed Special Envoy of the President and Secretary of State for Burundi Peace Negotiations, June 17, 1996; is a resident of Reston, Va.

**WOLVERTON, Charles Anderson,** a Representative from New Jersey; born in Camden, N.J., October 24, 1880; attended the public schools and was graduated from the law department of the University of Pennsylvania at Philadelphia in 1900; was admitted to the bar in 1901 and began practice in Camden, N.J.; assistant prosecutor of Camden County, N.J., 1906-1913; special assistant attorney general of New Jersey in 1913 and 1914; member of the New Jersey State house of assembly, 1915-1918, serving as speaker in 1918; Federal food administrator for Camden County, 1917-1919; prosecutor of pleas of Camden County, 1918-1923; elected as a Republican to the Seventieth and to the fifteen succeeding Congresses (March 4, 1927-January 3, 1959); chairman, Committee on Interstate and Foreign Commerce (Eightieth and Eighty-third Congresses); was not a candidate for renomination in 1958 to the Eighty-sixth Congress; resumed the practice of law in Camden, where he died on May 16, 1969; interment in Harleigh Cemetery.

**WOLVERTON, John Marshall,** a Representative from West Virginia; born in Big Bend, Calhoun County, W.Va., January 31, 1872; attended country schools and Glenville and Fairmont State Normal Schools; was graduated from the law department of the West Virginia University at Morgantown in 1901; was admitted to the bar the same year and commenced practice in Grantsville, Calhoun County, W.Va.; moved to Richwood in 1904; mayor of Richwood in 1918 and 1919; prosecuting attorney of Nicholas County, 1913-1917, and 1921-1925; elected as a Republican to the Sixty-ninth Congress (March 4, 1925-March 3, 1927); unsuccessful candidate for reelection in 1926 to the Seventieth Congress; elected to the Seventy-first Congress (March 4, 1929-March 3, 1931); unsuccessful candidate for reelection in 1930 to the Seventy-second Congress; unsuccessful candidate for election in 1932 to the Seventy-third Congress, and in 1936 to the Seventy-fifth Congress; resumed the practice of law in Richwood, W.Va., where he died on August 19, 1944; interment in the Odd Fellows Cemetery.

**WOLVERTON, Simon Peter,** a Representative from Pennsylvania; born in Rush Township, Northumberland County, Pa., January 28, 1837; attended the common schools and Danville (Pa.) Academy, and was graduated from Lewisburg University (now Bucknell University), Lewisburg, Pa., in 1860; principal of Sunbury (Pa.) Academy, 1860-1862; studied law; was admitted to the bar in 1862 and commenced practice in Sunbury; during the Civil War raised a company of emergency men, of which he was made captain in 1862, and served in the Eighteenth Regiment, Pennsylvania Volunteers; chosen captain of Company F, Thirty-sixth Regiment, Pennsylvania Volunteers, in June 1863; member of the Pennsylvania senate in 1878, 1880, and 1884; Democratic nominee for the United States Senate in the joint convention of 1884; elected as a Democrat to the Fifty-second and Fifty-third Congresses (March 4, 1891-March 3, 1895); was not a candidate for renomination in 1894 to the Fifty-fourth Congress; continued the practice of law; died in Sunbury, Northumberland County, Pa., October 25, 1910; interment in Pomfret-Manor Cemetery.

**WON PAT, Antonio Borja,** the first Delegate from the Territory of Guam, born in Sumay, Guam, December 10, 1908; educated in Guam public schools; became school teacher in 1926; principal in the school systems of Piti, Inarajan, and Sumay, 1934-1939; taught school at George Washington High School, Agana, Guam, from 1940 until the end of the Second World War; first elected to the Advisory Guam Congress in 1936; reelected in 1948 as speaker of the Guam Assembly; speaker of the first, second, fourth, fifth, sixth, and seventh Guam Legislatures; elected in 1965 as Guam's first representative to Washington, D.C.; reelected to the same position in 1968; delegate to the Democratic National Convention of 1972; elected as a Democrat a Delegate to the Ninety-third and to the five succeeding Congresses (January 3, 1973-January 3, 1985); unsuccessful candidate for reelection in 1984 to the Ninety-ninth Congress; was a resident of Sinajana, Guam until his death in Silver Spring, Md., on May 1, 1987; interment in Veterans Cemetery, Piti, Guam.

**WOOD, Abiel,** a Representative from Massachusetts; born in Wiscasset, Maine (then a district of Massachusetts), July 22, 1772; attended the common schools; engaged in mercantile pursuits; member of the Massachusetts house of representatives 1807-1811, and again in 1816; elected as a Republican to the Thirteenth Congress (March 4, 1813-March 3, 1815); unsuccessful candidate for reelection in 1814 to the Fourteenth Congress; delegate to the constitutional convention of Maine in 1819; State councilor of Maine in 1820 and 1821; resumed mercantile pursuits and also engaged in shipping; bank commissioner for Maine until his death in Belfast, Waldo County, Maine, October 26, 1834; interment in Woodlawn Cemetery, Wiscasset, Lincoln County, Maine.

**WOOD, Alan, Jr.** (nephew of John Wood), a Representative from Pennsylvania; born in Philadelphia, Pa., July 6, 1834; attended private schools; employed in his father's mill at Delaware Iron Works, near Wilmington, Del.; moved to Conshohocken, Montgomery County, Pa., in 1857; engaged in iron manufacturing and banking; elected as a Republican to the Forty-fourth Congress (March 4, 1875-March 3, 1877); was not a candidate for renomination in 1876; resumed his former business activities and also engaged in agricultural pursuits; president of the Alan Wood Iron & Steel Co.; died in Philadelphia, Pa., October 31, 1902; interment in Woodland Cemetery.

**WOOD, Amos Eastman,** a Representative from Ohio; born in Ellisburg, N.Y., January 2, 1810; attended the common schools; moved to Sandusky County, Ohio, in 1833 and engaged in agricultural pursuits; member of the State house of representatives 1840-1842; served in the State senate in 1845; elected as a Democrat to the Thirty-first Congress to fill the vacancy caused by the death of Rudolphus Dickinson and served from December 3, 1849, until his death in Fort Wayne, Ind., November 19, 1850; interment in Woodville Cemetery, Woodville, Sandusky County, Ohio.

**WOOD, Benjamin** (brother of Fernando Wood), a Representative from New York; born in Shelbyville, Shelby County, Ky., October 13, 1820; moved to New York City with his parents; attended the public schools; entered the shipping business; purchased the Daily News in 1860 and was its editor and publisher until his death; chairman of Democratic Editors in 1860; elected as a Democrat to the Thirty-seventh and Thirty-eighth Congresses (March 4, 1861-March 3, 1865); member of the State senate in 1866 and 1867; elected to the Forty-seventh Congress (March 4, 1881-March 3, 1883); died in New York City February 21, 1900; interment in Calvary Cemetery, Long Island City, N.Y.

Bibliography: Mushkat, Jerome. "Ben Wood's 'Fort Lafayette': A Source for Studying the Peace Democrats." *Civil War History* 21 (June 1975): 160-71.

**WOOD, Benson,** a Representative from Illinois; born near Bridgewater, Susquehanna County, Pa., on March 31, 1839; attended the common schools, Montrose (Pa.) Academy, and Wyoming (Pa.) Seminary; moved to Illinois in 1859 and for two years was principal of a village school in Lee County; enlisted as first lieutenant of Company C, Thirty-fourth Regiment, Illinois Volunteer Infantry, September 7, 1861; promoted to captain May 1, 1862; honorably discharged January 29, 1863; was graduated from the law department of the University of Chicago in 1864; was admitted to the bar in 1864 and engaged in the practice of law in Effingham, Effingham County, Ill.; member of the State house of representatives in 1872; delegate to the Republican National Convention in 1876 and 1888; mayor of Effingham 1881-1883; elected as a Republican to the Fifty-fourth Congress (March 4, 1895-March 3, 1897); was an unsuccessful candidate for reelection in 1896 to the Fifty-fifth Congress; resumed the practice of law in Effingham, Ill.; president of the Effingham State Bank 1903-1912, and chairman of the board of directors 1912-1915; died in Effingham, Ill., on August 27, 1915; interment in Oakridge Cemetery.

**WOOD, Bradford Ripley,** a Representative from New York; born in Westport, Conn., September 3, 1800; attended the common schools and was graduated from Union College at Schenectady, N.Y., in 1824; was engaged in teaching and lecturing; studied law at the Litchfield (Conn.) Law School; was admitted to the bar in 1827 and commenced practice in Albany, N.Y.; on May 29, 1827, was made solicitor in the court of chancery of New York State, and on June 6, 1830, rose to the position of chancellor of the same court; became counselor in the New York Supreme Court in 1835, and in the United States Supreme Court in 1845; member of the Albany County board of supervisors in 1844; was elected as a Democrat to the Twenty-ninth Congress (March 4, 1845-March 3, 1847); unsuccessful candidate for reelection in 1846 to the Thirtieth Congress; president of the Young Men's Temperance Society in 1851; trustee of Union College, Williams College, and the Albany Law School; vice president of the Albany Medical College; one of the founders of the Republican Party in New York State in 1856; vice president of the American Home Missionary Society; founder of the First Congregational Church in Albany; appointed Minister to Denmark on March 22, 1861 and served until November 1865; died in Albany, N.Y., September 26, 1889; interment in Albany Rural Cemetery, Albany County, N.Y.

**WOOD, Ernest Edward,** a Representative from Missouri; born in Chico, Butte County, Calif., August 24, 1875; attended the public schools and was graduated from the Stockton (Calif.) High School in 1892; appointed as a cadet to the United States Military Academy at West Point in 1893 and remained two years; studied law; was admitted to the bar in 1898 and commenced practice in St. Louis, Mo.; presented credentials as a Democratic Member-elect to the Fifty-ninth Congress and served from March 4, 1905, to June 23, 1906, when he was succeeded by Harry M. Coudrey, who contested his election; moved to Los Angeles, Calif., in 1907 and resumed the practice of law; died in Los Angeles, Calif., January 10, 1952; interment in Hollywood Cemetery, Hollywood, Calif.

**WOOD, Fernando** (brother of Benjamin Wood), a Representative from New York; born in Philadelphia, Pa., June 14, 1812; attended the public schools; moved with his father to New York City in 1820; was engaged in business as a shipping merchant in 1831; elected as a Democrat to the Twenty-seventh Congress (March 4, 1841-March 3, 1843); unsuccessful candidate for reelection in 1842 to the Twenty-eighth Congress; appointed by Secretary of State John C. Calhoun dispatch agent for the State Department at the port of New York; reappointed to the position by Secretary of State James Buchanan and served from 1844 to 1847; unsuccessful candidate for mayor of New York in 1850 and in 1867; retired as a shipping merchant in 1850; mayor of New York City in 1855-1858,

1861, and 1862; elected as a Democrat to the Thirty-eighth Congress (March 4, 1863-March 3, 1865); unsuccessful candidate for reelection in 1864 to the Thirty-ninth Congress; elected to the Fortieth and to the seven succeeding Congresses and served from March 4, 1867, until his death at Hot Springs, Ark., February 14, 1881, before the beginning of the Forty-seventh Congress, to which he had been reelected; chairman, Committee on Ways and Means (Forty-fifth and Forty-sixth Congresses); censured by the Fortieth Congress on January 15, 1868, for use of unparliamentary language; interment in Trinity Cemetery, New York City.

Bibliography: *DAB*; Anbinder, Tyler G. "Fernando Wood and New York City's Secession from the Union: A Political Reappraisal." *New York History* 68 (January 1987): 67-92; Mushkat, Jerome. *Fernando Wood: A Political Biography*. Kent, Ohio: Kent State University Press, 1990; Pleasants, Samuel A. *Fernando Wood of New York*. New York: Columbia University Press, 1948.

**WOOD, Ira Wells,** a Representative from New Jersey; born in Wilkes-Barre, Pa., on June 19, 1856; was graduated from Princeton College in 1877; studied law; was admitted to the bar in 1880 and commenced practice in Trenton, N.J.; was a member of the city board of education 1894-1896; served in the city council 1896-1900; president of the Board of Trade of Trenton 1896-1900; member of the State assembly in 1899 and 1900; commissioner for New Jersey to the Louisiana Purchase Exposition held in St. Louis, Mo., in 1904; delegate to the Interparliamentary Peace Union at Brussels, Belgium, in 1905; elected as a Republican to the Fifty-eighth Congress to fill the vacancy caused by the resignation of William M. Lanning; reelected to the Fifty-ninth and to the three succeeding Congresses and served from November 8, 1904, to March 3, 1913; declined to be a candidate for reelection to the Sixty-third Congress; resided in Trenton, N.J., until his death there on October 5, 1931; interment in Mercer Cemetery.

**WOOD, John** (uncle of Alan Wood, Jr.), a Representative from Pennsylvania; born in Philadelphia, Pa., September 6, 1816; attended the Friends Society schools of Philadelphia; employed by his father in the manufacture of tools and agricultural machinery 1832-1840; engaged in the manufacture of iron and steel near Wilmington, Del., 1841-1844; moved to Conshohocken, Montgomery County, Pa., in 1844 and engaged in the milling of iron and steel; first burgess of Conshohocken, Pa.; elected as a Republican to the Thirty-sixth Congress (March 4, 1859-March 3, 1861); was not a candidate for renomination in 1860; resumed his former manufacturing pursuits; died in Conshohocken, Pa., May 28, 1898; interment in Montgomery Cemetery, Norristown, Montgomery County, Pa.

**WOOD, John Jacob,** a Representative from New York; born in Clarkstown (now New City), Rockland County, N.Y., February 16, 1784; town clerk of Clarkstown 1809-1812; inspector of schools in 1815, 1823, 1829-1831, 1835-1836; elected to the Twentieth Congress (March 4, 1827-March 3, 1829); again inspector of schools 1829-1831, 1835-1837; surrogate of Rockland County in 1837; delegate to the State constitutional convention in 1846; died at New City, Rockland County, N.Y., May 20, 1874; interment in Old Wood Burying Ground.

**WOOD, John M.,** a Representative from Maine; born in Minisink, Orange County, N.Y., November 17, 1813; attended the common schools; engaged in railroad construction in New Jersey; moved to Portland, Maine, in 1846; was one of the contractors in the construction of the Atlantic and St. Lawrence Railroad; also engaged in banking; member, Rhode Island State house of representatives, 1852-1853; owner and publisher of the Portland Daily Advertiser, 1853-1857; elected as a Republican to the Thirty-fourth and Thirty-fifth Congresses (March 4, 1855-March 3, 1859); contractor for building the Air Line Railroad between Woonsocket, R.I. and New Haven, Conn.; died while on a visit in Boston, Mass., December 24, 1864; interment in Greenwood Cemetery, Brooklyn, N.Y.

**WOOD, John Stephens,** a Representative from Georgia; born on a farm near Ball Ground, Cherokee County, Ga., February 8, 1885; attended the public schools and the North Georgia Agricultural College at Dahlonega; was graduated from the law department of Mercer University, Macon, Ga., in 1910; was admitted to the bar the same year and commenced practice in Jasper, Ga.; member of the State house of representatives in 1917; served as solicitor general of the Blue Ridge judicial circuit of Georgia 1921-1925, and as judge of superior courts of the Blue Ridge judicial circuit 1925-1931; elected as a Democrat to the Seventy-second and Seventy-third Congresses (March 4, 1931-January 3, 1935); unsuccessful candidate for renomination in 1934; resumed the practice of law; elected to the Seventy-ninth and to the three succeeding Congresses (January 3, 1945-January 3, 1953); chairman, Committee on Un-American Activities (Seventy-ninth, Eighty-first, and Eighty-second Congresses); was not a candidate for renomination in 1952; resumed law practice in Canton, Ga., until failing health forced his retirement; died in Marietta, Ga., September 12, 1968; interment in Arlington Cemetery, Sandy Springs, Atlanta, Ga.

**WOOD, John Travers,** a Representative from Idaho; born in Wakefield, England, November 25, 1878; immigrated to the United States with his parents in 1889 and settled in Woodridge, N.Dak.; naturalized in 1901; attended the public schools; taught school for six years; graduated from Detroit College of Medicine in 1904 and practiced medicine in Hannah, N.Dak., for one year; moved to Coeur d'Alene, Idaho, in 1905 and licensed to practice medicine in 1906; surgeon for Chicago, Milwaukee & St. Paul Railroad 1910-1950; mayor of Coeur d'Alene in 1911 and 1912; founder and first president of Coeur d'Alene Hospital in 1908; during the First World War served as a lieutenant in the Medical Corps; elected as a Republican to the Eighty-second Congress (January 3, 1951-January 3, 1953); was an unsuccessful candidate for reelection in 1952 to the Eighty-third Congress; resumed the practice of medicine; died in Coeur d'Alene, Idaho, November 2, 1954; interment in Forest Cemetery.

**WOOD, Joseph,** a Delegate from Georgia; born in Pennsylvania in 1712; moved to Sunbury, St. John's Parish (afterward Liberty County), Ga., about 1774; served in the Revolutionary War as major, lieutenant colonel, and colonel of the Second Pennsylvania Battalion, which later became the Third Pennsylvania Regiment, and was on duty in Canada in 1776; returned to Georgia and engaged in planting; member of the State council of safety; Member of the Continental Congress 1777-1778; died on his plantation near Sunbury, Ga., in September 1791.

**WOOD, Reuben Terrell,** a Representative from Missouri; born on a farm near Springfield, Greene County, Mo., August 7, 1884; attended the public schools and received private instructions; apprenticed as a cigar maker in Springfield, Mo., in 1898; employed as a labor organization officer 1902-1912; served as president of the Missouri State Federation of Labor 1912-1932; elected as a Democrat to the Seventy-third and to the three succeeding Congresses and served from March 4, 1933, to January 3, 1941; chairman, Committee on War Claims (Seventy-sixth Congress); was an unsuccessful candidate for election in 1940 to the Seventy-seventh Congress; resumed office as president of the Missouri State Federation of Labor until his retirement in May 1953; member of the Missouri Constitutional convention in 1944; died in Springfield, Mo., July 16, 1955; interment in Greenlawn Cemetery.

**WOOD, Silas,** a Representative from New York; born in West Hills, near Huntington, Suffolk County, N.Y., September 14, 1769; pursued classical studies; was graduated from Princeton College in 1789 and during the five succeeding years was a teacher at that institution; studied law; was admitted to the bar and commenced practice in Huntington, N.Y.; was appointed district attorney of Suffolk County in 1818 and 1821; elected to the Sixteenth and to the four succeeding Congresses (March 4, 1819-March 3, 1829); chairman, Committee on Expenditures in the Department of State (Seventeenth and Eighteenth Congresses); unsuccessful candidate for reelection in 1828 to the Twenty-first Congress; died in Huntington, N.Y., March 2, 1847; interment in the Old Public Cemetery on Main Street.

**WOOD, Thomas Jefferson,** a Representative from Indiana; born in Athens County, Ohio, September 30, 1844; moved with his parents to Vigo County, Ind., in 1853; attended the common schools; taught school two years; studied law in Terre Haute, Ind., and was graduated from the law department of the University of Michigan at Ann Arbor in 1867; moved to Crown Point, Lake County, Ind., in November 1867 and practiced law; corporation treasurer 1870-1872; prosecuting attorney of Lake County 1872-1876; member of the State senate 1878-1882; elected as a Democrat to the Forty-eighth Congress (March 4, 1883-March 3, 1885); unsuccessful candidate for reelection; resumed the practice of law; died in Crown Point, Ind., October 13, 1908; interment in Maplewood Cemetery.

**WOOD, Walter Abbott,** a Representative from New York; born in Mason, N.H., October 23, 1815; moved to New York in 1816 with his parents, who settled in Rensselaerville; attended the common schools; moved to Hoosick Falls in 1835; became an inventor and manufacturer of reapers, mowers, and binders; elected as a Republican to the Forty-sixth and Forty-seventh Congresses (March 4, 1879-March 3, 1883); was not a candidate for renomination; returned to Hoosick Falls, N.Y., and resumed his former pursuits; died in Hoosick Falls, N.Y., January 15, 1892; interment in Maple Grove Cemetery.

**Bibliography:** *DAB.*

**WOOD, William Robert,** a Representative from Indiana; born in Oxford, Benton County, Ind., on January 5, 1861; attended the public schools of Oxford and was graduated from the law department of the University of Michigan at Ann Arbor in 1882; was admitted to the bar the same year and commenced practice in LaFayette, Tippecanoe County; prosecuting attorney of Tippecanoe County 1890-1894; member of the State senate 1896-1914, and served as president pro tempore 1899-1907; Republican floor leader of the State senate for four sessions; delegate to the Republican National Conventions in 1912, 1916, 1920, and 1924; chairman of the Republican National congressional committee 1920-1933; elected as a Republican to the Sixty-fourth and to the eight succeeding Congresses (March 4, 1915-March 3, 1933); chairman, Committee on Appropriations (Seventy-first Congress); unsuccessful candidate for reelection in 1932 to the Seventy-third Congress; died while on a visit in New York City March 7, 1933; interment in Spring Vale Cemetery, LaFayette, Ind.

**Bibliography:** *DAB.*

**WOODARD, Frederick Augustus,** a Representative from North Carolina; born near Wilson, Wilson County, N.C., February 12, 1854; attended private schools in Wilson County; studied law at the law school of Chief Justice Richmond Mumford Pearson; was admitted to the bar in 1873 and commenced practice in Wilson, N.C.; vice president of the First National Bank of Wilson; elected as a Democrat to the Fifty-third and Fifty-fourth Congresses (March 4, 1893-March 3, 1897); unsuccessful candidate for reelection to the Fifty-fifth Congress; resumed the practice of law in Wilson, N.C., and died there May 8, 1915; interment in Maplewood Cemetery.

**WOODBRIDGE, Frederick Enoch,** a Representative from Vermont; born in Vergennes, Addison County, Vt., August 29, 1818; was graduated from the University of Vermont at Burlington in 1840; studied law; was admitted to the bar in 1843 and commenced practice in Vergennes; member of the State house of representatives in 1849, 1857, and 1858; mayor of Vergennes for five years; State auditor 1850-1852; prosecuting attorney 1854-1858; engaged in the construction of railroads; member of the State senate in 1860 and 1861 and served as president pro tempore in the latter year; elected as a Republican to the Thirty-eighth, Thirty-ninth, and Fortieth Congresses (March 4, 1863-March 3, 1869); resumed the practice of his profession; died in Vergennes, Vt., April 25, 1888; interment in Prospect Cemetery.

**WOODBRIDGE, William,** a Delegate and a Senator from Michigan; born in Norwich, Conn., August 20, 1780; studied law; moved to Ohio in 1799; was admitted to the Ohio bar in 1806 and commenced the practice of law in Marietta; member, Ohio State house of representatives, 1807; prosecuting attorney for New London (now Washington) County, Ohio, 1808-1814; member, Ohio State senate, 1808-1814; moved to Detroit, Mich.; collector of customs, Michigan Territory, 1814-1829; appointed secretary of Michigan Territory in 1814, and served until appointed judge of the Territory in 1828; elected as a Delegate to the Sixteenth Congress and served from March 4, 1819, to August 9, 1820, when he resigned; judge of the supreme court of Michigan Territory, 1828-1832; delegate to the State constitutional convention in 1835; member, Michigan State senate, 1838-1839; elected Governor of Michigan in 1839 and served from January 7, 1840 until his resignation February 23, 1841; elected as a Whig to the United States Senate and served from March 4, 1841, to March 3, 1847; was not a candidate for reelection; chairman, Committee on Public Lands (Twenty-eighth Congress), Committee on Patents and the Patent Office (Twenty-ninth Congress); retired from public life and devoted his time to horticulture; died in Detroit, Mich., October 20, 1861; interment in Elmwood Cemetery.

**Bibliography:** *DAB*; Lanman, Charles. *The Life of William Woodbridge.* Washington, D.C.: Blanchard and Mahun, 1867.

**WOODBURN, William,** a Representative from Nevada; born in County Wicklow, Ireland, April 14, 1838; immigrated with his parents to the United States in 1849; attended St. Charles College, Maryland; studied law; was admitted to the bar in 1866 and commenced the practice of law in Virginia City, Nev.; district attorney of Storey County, Nev., in 1871 and 1872; elected as a Republican to the Forty-fourth Congress (March 4, 1875-March 3, 1877); elected to the Forty-ninth and Fiftieth Congresses (March 4, 1885-March 3, 1889); resumed the practice of his profession in Virginia City, Storey County, Nev.; unsuccessful candidate for election in 1892 to the Fifty-third Congress; died in Carson City, Nev., January 15, 1915; interment in St. Theresa Cemetery.

**WOODBURY, Levi,** a Senator from New Hampshire; born in Francestown, N.H., December 22, 1789; graduated from Dartmouth College, Hanover, N.H., in 1809; studied law in Litchfield, Conn., Boston, Mass., and Exeter, N.H.; was admitted to the bar in 1812 and practiced in Francestown, N.H., 1813-1816; judge of the superior court of New Hampshire, 1816-1823; moved to Portsmouth, N.H., in 1819; elected Governor of New Hampshire in 1823, and served from June 5, 1823 to June 2, 1824; unsuccessful candidate for reelection in 1824; member, New Hampshire State house of representatives, 1825, and served as speaker; elected to the United States Senate for the term beginning March 4, 1825, and served from March 16, 1825, to March 3, 1831; chairman, Committee on Commerce (Twentieth and Twenty-first Congresses); nominated for the New Hampshire State senate in 1831, but declined; appointed Secretary of the Navy in the Cabinet of President Andrew Jackson, and served from May 23, 1831 to June 30, 1834; appointed Secretary of the Treasury, and served in the Cabinets of President Jackson and President Martin Van Buren from June 30, 1834 until March 3, 1841; appointed chief justice of the superior court of New Hampshire but declined to serve; elected to the United States Senate as a Democrat, and served from March 4, 1841 to November 20, 1845, when he resigned; chairman, Committee on Finance (Twenty-ninth Congress); declined appointment as Minister to Great Britain;

unsuccessful candidate for the Democratic presidential nomination in 1848; nominated on December 23, 1845 by President James K. Polk as an Associate Justice of the United States Supreme Court; was confirmed by the Senate on January 3, 1846, and served until his death in Portsmouth, N.H., September 4, 1851; interment in Harmony Grove Cemetery.

**Bibliography:** *DAB*; Capowski, Vincent. "The Making of a Jacksonian Democrat: Levi Woodbury, 1789-1851." Ph.D. dissertation, Fordham University, 1966; Woodbury, Levi. *Writings of Levi Woodbury*. 3 vols. Boston: Little, Brown and Co., 1852.

**WOODCOCK, David,** a Representative from New York; was born in Williamstown, Berkshire County, Mass., in 1785; attended the public schools; studied law; was admitted to the bar and practiced; moved to Ithaca, Seneca (now Tompkins) County, N.Y.; commissioned postmaster of Ithaca November 19, 1808; appointed master of the court of chancery in 1808; member of the State assembly in 1814 and 1815; appointed district attorney of Tompkins County in April 1817; surrogate and assistant attorney general of the State in 1817; president of the Cayuga Steamboat Co. in 1819; elected to the Seventeenth Congress (March 4, 1821-March 3, 1823); president and trustee of the village of Ithaca in 1823, 1824, and 1826; resumed the practice of law; again a member of the State assembly in 1826; took a prominent part in the Anti-Masonic Crusade and State Convention at Utica, N.Y., in 1827; elected to the Twentieth Congress (March 4, 1827-March 3, 1829); unsuccessful candidate for reelection in 1828 to the Twenty-first Congress; resumed the practice of his profession; died in Ithaca, N.Y., September 18, 1835; interment in the City Cemetery.

**WOODFORD, Stewart Lyndon,** a Representative from New York; born in New York City, September 3, 1835; was graduated from Columbia College (now Columbia University), New York City, in 1854; studied law; was admitted to the bar in 1857 and commenced practice in New York City; delegate to the Republican National Conventions of 1860 and 1872; assistant attorney for the United States in New York City, 1861-1862; during the Civil War served in the Union Army; commissioned lieutenant colonel of the One Hundred and Twenty-seventh New York Volunteers, September 8, 1862; colonel of the One Hundred and Third United States Colored Infantry, March 3, 1865; brevetted brigadier general of Volunteers, May 12, 1865; resigned on August 23, 1865; was the first Union military commander of Charleston, S.C., and of Savannah, Ga.; Lieutenant Governor of New York, 1867-1869; unsuccessful candidate in 1870 for election for Governor; elected as a Republican to the Forty-third Congress, and served from March 4, 1873 to July 1, 1874, when he resigned; United States attorney for the southern district of New York, 1877-1883; appointed United States Envoy Extraordinary and Minister Plenipotentiary to Spain on June 19, 1897, and served until he left his post on April 21, 1898, the United States being about to declare war on Spain; resumed the practice of law in New York City, and died there on February 14, 1913; interment in Woodland Cemetery, Stamford, Conn.

**Bibliography:** *DAB*.

**WOODHOUSE, Chase Going,** a Representative from Connecticut; born in Victoria, British Columbia, Canada, March 3, 1890; attended the public schools in San Francisco, Calif., Aberdeen, S.Dak., and Science Hill School, Shelbyville, Ky.; graduated from McGill University of Montreal, Canada, in 1912; engaged in graduate work at the University of Berlin and the University of Chicago; taught economics at Smith College in Northampton, Mass., 1918-1925, and at summer sessions at Teachers College of Columbia University in New York City, University of Texas at Austin, and the University of Iowa at Iowa City; professor of economics at Connecticut College in New London, Conn., 1934-1946; managing director, Institute of Women's Professional Relations at Connecticut College, 1929-1946; personnel director, Woman's College, University

of North Carolina at Greensboro, 1929-1934; senior economist, Bureau of Home Economics, United States Department of Agriculture, 1926-1928; consultant, National Roster of Scientific and Specialized Personnel, War Manpower Commission, 1942-1944; chairman of New London Democratic Town Committee, 1942-1943; secretary of state of Connecticut, 1941-1942; president of the Connecticut Federation of Democratic Women's Clubs, 1943-1948; elected as a Democrat to the Seventy-ninth Congress (January 3, 1945-January 3, 1947); unsuccessful candidate for reelection in 1946 to the Eightieth Congress; executive director, women's division, Democratic National Committee, Washington, D.C., from February 1947 to April 1948; visiting expert on the staff of General Lucius D. Clay, Allied Military Governor of Germany, in 1948; elected to the Eighty-first Congress (January 3, 1949-January 3, 1951); unsuccessful candidate for reelection in 1950 to the Eighty-second Congress; special assistant to the Director of Price Stabilization, 1951-1953; member, Connecticut State Constitutional Convention, 1965; was a resident of Sprague, Conn., until her death at New Canaan, Conn., on December 12, 1984.

**WOODMAN, Charles Walhart,** a Representative from Illinois; born in Aalborg, Denmark, March 11, 1844; was educated in the schools of his native country; followed the sea 1860-1863; arrived in Philadelphia, Pa., in 1863 and immediately enlisted in the Gulf Squadron of the United States Navy; moved to Chicago, Ill., in 1865; graduated from the law department of Chicago University in 1871; was admitted to the Illinois bar the same year and commenced practice in Chicago; appointed prosecuting attorney of the lower courts in 1877; appointed justice of the peace by the judges of Cook County in 1881; elected as a Republican to the Fifty-fourth Congress (March 4, 1895-March 3, 1897); unsuccessful candidate for reelection in 1896 to the Fifty-fifth Congress; engaged in the practice of his profession until his death; died in Elgin, Ill., March 18, 1898; interment in Rose Hill Cemetery, Chicago, Ill.

**WOODRUFF, George Catlin,** a Representative from Connecticut; born in Litchfield, Conn., on December 1, 1805; was graduated from Yale College in 1825; studied law; was admitted to the bar in 1827 and began practice in Litchfield; postmaster of Litchfield from January 4, 1832, to January 27, 1842, and from September 2, 1842, to September 28, 1846; member of the State house of representatives in 1851, 1866, and 1874; elected as a Democrat to the Thirty-seventh Congress (March 4, 1861-March 3, 1863); unsuccessful candidate for reelection in 1862 to the Thirty-eighth Congress; continued the practice of law until his death in Litchfield, Conn., November 21, 1885; interment in East Cemetery.

**WOODRUFF, John,** a Representative from Connecticut; born in West Hartford, Hartford County, Conn., February 12, 1826; received a limited schooling; moved to Catskill, Greene County, N.Y., in 1835; returned to Connecticut in 1841 and settled in Bristol, where he worked in a clock factory until 1845; moved to New Haven in 1845; elected a member of the common council in 1848 and served several terms; member of the general assembly in 1852; elected as a candidate of the American Party to the Thirty-fourth Congress (March 4, 1855-March 3, 1857); unsuccessful candidate for reelection in 1856 to the Thirty-fifth Congress; elected as a Republican to the Thirty-sixth Congress (March 4, 1859-March 3, 1861); upon establishment of the office in 1862 was appointed collector of internal revenue for the second district of Connecticut and served until his death in New Haven, Conn., May 20, 1868; interment in Evergreen Cemetery.

**WOODRUFF, Roy Orchard,** a Representative from Michigan; born at Eaton Rapids, Eaton County, Mich., March 14, 1876; attended the common schools and the high school of Eaton Rapids; apprenticed to the printing business from 1891 until 1899; enlisted as a corporal in Company G, Thirty-third Regiment, Michigan Volunteer Infantry, during the Spanish-American War; saw active service and was mustered out; was graduated from the dental department of the College of Medicine, Detroit, Mich., in 1902 and practiced dentistry in Bay City, Mich., 1902-1911; mayor of Bay City, 1911-1913; elected as a Progressive to the Sixty-third Congress (March 4, 1913-March 3, 1915); was not a candidate for renomination in 1914 to the Sixty-fourth Congress; served for two years in the First World War as an Infantry officer, acquiring the rank of major during his service in France; elected as a Republican to the Sixty-seventh and to the fifteen succeeding Congresses (March 4, 1921-January 3, 1953); was not a candidate for renomination in 1952 to the Eighty-third Congress; died in Washington, D.C., February 12, 1953; interment in Elm Lawn Cemetery, Bay City, Mich.

**WOODRUFF, Thomas M.,** a Representative from New York; born in New Jersey, May 3, 1804; elected as a candidate of the American Party to the Twenty-ninth Congress (March 4, 1845-March 3, 1847); employed as a cabinetmaker and later engaged in the furniture business in New York City; died in New York City, March 28, 1855; interment in the First Presbyterian Church Cemetery, Newark, N.J.

**WOODRUM, Clifton Alexander,** a Representative from Virginia; born in Roanoke, Roanoke County, Va., April 27, 1887; attended the public schools of his native city and the University College of Medicine (now combined with the Medical College of Virginia), Richmond, Va.; became a registered pharmacist and engaged in his profession in Roanoke; studied law at Washington and Lee University, Lexington, Va.; was admitted to the bar in 1908 and commenced practice in Roanoke, Va.; Commonwealth attorney of Roanoke 1917-1919; judge of the Hustings Court of Roanoke 1919-1922; elected as a Democrat to the Sixty-eighth and to the eleven succeeding Congresses and served from March 4, 1923, until his resignation on December 31, 1945, to become president of the American Plant Food Council, Inc.; died in Washington, D.C., October 6, 1950; interment in Fairview Cemetery, Roanoke, Va.

**Bibliography:** Sargeant, James E. "Clifton A. Woodrum of Virginia: A Southern Progressive in Congress, 1923-1945." *Virginia Magazine of History and Biography* 89 (July 1981): 341-64.

**WOODS, Frank Plowman,** a Representative from Iowa; born near Sharon, Walworth County, Wis., December 11, 1868; attended the public schools and the Northern Indiana Normal School, Valparaiso, Ind.; moved to Estherville, Emmett County, Iowa, in 1887 and worked in a newspaper office for two years; engaged in the mortgage-loan business and private banking; chairman of the Republican State central committee in 1906 and 1907; elected as a Republican to the Sixty-first and to the four succeeding Congresses (March 4, 1909-March 3, 1919); unsuccessful candidate for renomination in 1918; chairman of the Republican National Congressional Committee 1913-1918; resided in Altadena, Calif., until his death there April 25, 1944; interment in Mountain View Cemetery.

**WOODS, Henry** (brother of John Woods [1761-1816]), a Representative from Pennsylvania; born in Bedford, Bedford County, Pa., in 1764; received a limited schooling; attended the subscription schools of Bedford County, Pa.; studied law; was admitted to the bar in 1792 and commenced practice in Bedford, Pa.; elected as a Federalist to the Sixth and Seventh Congresses (March 4, 1799-March 3, 1803); engaged as a land speculator; died in Bedford, Pa., in 1826.

**WOODS, James Pleasant,** a Representative from Virginia; born near Roanoke, Roanoke County, Va., February 4, 1868; attended the common schools; was graduated from Roanoke College in 1892; studied law at the University of Virginia at Charlottesville in 1892 and 1893; was admitted to the bar in the latter year and commenced practice in Roanoke, Va.; mayor of Roanoke 1898-1900; elected as a Democrat to the Sixty-fifth and Sixty-sixth Congresses

to fill the vacancies caused by the resignation of Carter Glass; was reelected to the Sixty-seventh Congress and served from February 25, 1919, to March 3, 1923; unsuccessful candidate for renomination in 1922; delegate to the Democratic National Convention in 1920; president of the board of trustees of Roanoke College; member of the board of trustees of the Randolph-Macon system of colleges; rector of the board of visitors of the Virginia Polytechnic Institute; resumed the practice of law; died in Roanoke, Va., July 7, 1948; interment in Evergreen Burial Park.

**WOODS, John,** a Representative from Ohio; born in Johnstown, Dauphin County, Pa., October 18, 1794; moved with his parents to Ohio, where he attended the common schools; served in the War of 1812; after the war operated a school near Springborough for two years; studied law; was admitted to the bar in 1819 and commenced the practice of his profession in Hamilton, Butler County, Ohio; prosecuting attorney of Butler County 1820-1825; elected to the Nineteenth and Twentieth Congresses (March 4, 1825-March 3, 1829); unsuccessful candidate for reelection in 1828 to the Twenty-first Congress; became editor and publisher of the Hamilton Intelligencer in 1829; State auditor of Ohio from 1845 to 1851; president of the Cincinnati, Hamilton & Indianapolis Railroad; died in Hamilton, Ohio, July 30, 1855; interment in Greenwood Cemetery.

**WOODS, John** (brother of Henry Woods), a Representative from Pennsylvania; born in Bedford, Bedford County, Pa., in 1761; studied law; admitted to the bar in Washington County, Pa., in December 1783, in Westmoreland County and Fayette County in 1784, in Allegheny County on December 16, 1788, and in Bedford County in 1791; practiced extensively in those counties; assisted in laying out the city of Pittsburgh in 1784; member of the Pennsylvania senate in 1797; elected as a Federalist to the Fourteenth Congress (March 4, 1815-March 3, 1817); owing to illness never attended or qualified; died in Brunswick County, Va., December 16, 1816, while on a journey to the South to regain his health.

**WOODS, Samuel Davis,** a Representative from California; born in Mount Pleasant, Maury County, Tenn., September 19, 1845; moved with his parents to Stockton, Calif., in February 1850; attended the public schools; studied law; was admitted to the California bar in April 1875 and engaged in practice in Stockton and in the city and county of San Francisco; elected as a Republican to the Fifty-sixth Congress to fill the vacancy caused by the resignation of Marion De Vries; reelected to the Fifty-seventh Congress and served from December 3, 1900, to March 3, 1903; was not a candidate for reelection in 1902 to the Fifty-eighth Congress; resumed the practice of law in San Francisco, Calif., and died there December 24, 1915; interment in Mount Olivet Cemetery, San Mateo County, Calif.

**WOODS, William,** a Representative from New York; born in Washington County, N.Y., in 1790; received a limited schooling; moved to Bath, Steuben County, N.Y., in 1813; studied law; was admitted to the bar and practiced in Bath, N.Y.; member of the State assembly 1823-1825; elected to the Eighteenth Congress to fill the vacancy caused by the resignation of William B. Rochester and served from November 3, 1823, to March 3, 1825; resumed the practice of his profession; surrogate of Steuben County 1827-1835; died in Bath, N.Y., August 7, 1837; interment in Grove Cemetery.

**WOODSON, Samuel Hughes** (father of Samuel Hughes Woodson [1815-1881]), a Representative from Kentucky; born near Charlottesville, Albemarle County, Va., September 15, 1777; completed preparatory studies; studied law; admitted to the bar in 1802 and commenced practice in Nicholasville, Jessamine County, Ky.; clerk of Jessamine County Circuit Court 1803-1819; elected to the Seventeenth Congress (March 4, 1821-March 3, 1823); unsuccessful candidate for reelection in 1822 to the Eighteenth Congress; resumed the practice of his profession in Nicholasville; member of the Kentucky house of representatives in 1825 and 1826; died at "Chaumiere," Jessamine County, Ky., July 28, 1827; interment in the Crocket Burying Ground.

**WOODSON, Samuel Hughes** (son of Samuel Hughes Woodson [1777-1827]), a Representative from Missouri; born near Nicholasville, Jessamine County, Ky., October 24, 1815; attended the public schools; was graduated from Centre College, Danville, Ky., and the law department of Transylvania University, Lexington, Ky.; was admitted to the bar in 1838 and commenced the practice of law in Independence, Jackson County, Mo., in 1840; member of the State house of representatives in 1853 and 1854; delegate to the State constitutional convention in 1855; elected on the American Party ticket to the Thirty-fifth and Thirty-sixth Congresses (March 4, 1857-March 3, 1861); was not a candidate for renomination in 1860; resumed the practice of his profession in Independence; became affiliated with the Democratic Party; was judge of the twenty-fourth judicial circuit of Missouri from March 1875 until his death in Independence, Mo., June 23, 1881; interment in Woodlawn Cemetery.

**WOODWARD, George Washington,** a Representative from Pennsylvania; born in Bethany, Wayne County, Pa., March 26, 1809; attended Geneva Seminary (now Hobart College), Geneva, N.Y., and Wilkes-Barre (Pa.) Academy; studied law; was admitted to the bar in 1830 and commenced practice in Wilkes-Barre, Pa.; delegate to the Pennsylvania constitutional convention in 1837; president judge of the fourth judicial district, 1841-1851; unsuccessful candidate for United States Senator in 1845; nominated on December 23, 1845 by President James K. Polk as an Associate Justice of the Supreme Court of the United States, but the Senate, on January 22, 1846, refused to confirm the nomination; associate judge of the supreme court of Pennsylvania, 1852-1863 and chief justice, 1863-1867; unsuccessful Democratic candidate for Governor in 1863; elected as a Democrat to the Fortieth Congress to fill the vacancy caused by the death of Charles Denison; reelected to the Forty-first Congress and served from November 21, 1867, to March 3 1871; was not a candidate for renomination in 1870 to the Forty-second Congress; delegate to the Democratic National Convention of 1868; unsuccessful candidate for president judge of the eleventh judicial district in 1870; moved to Philadelphia in 1871 and continued the practice of his profession; was a delegate to the Pennsylvania constitutional convention in 1873; traveled abroad in 1874 and died in Rome, Italy, on May 10, 1875; interment in Hollenback Cemetery, Wilkes-Barre, Pa.

**WOODWARD, Gilbert Motier,** a Representative from Wisconsin; born in Washington, D.C., December 25, 1835; educated in the common schools; studied law; was admitted to the bar in 1861 and commenced practice in La Crosse, Wis., in February 1860; served more than three years in the Union Army during the Civil War as a private, first sergeant, second lieutenant, first lieutenant, and adjutant in the Second Regiment, Wisconsin Volunteer Infantry; district attorney of La Crosse County 1866-1873; mayor of the city of La Crosse in 1874 and 1875; city attorney 1876-1882; elected as a Democrat to the Forty-eighth Congress (March 4, 1883-March 3, 1885); unsuccessful for reelection in 1884 to the Forty-ninth Congress; resumed the practice of law in La Crosse, Wis.; unsuccessful Democratic candidate for Governor of Wisconsin in 1886; delegate to the Democratic National Convention in 1888; died in La Crosse, Wis., March 13, 1913; interment in Oak Grove Cemetery.

**WOODWARD, Joseph Addison** (son of William Woodward), a Representative from South Carolina; born in Winnsboro, Fairfield County, S.C., on April 11, 1806; received an academic training and was graduated from the University of South Carolina at Columbia; studied law; was admitted to the bar and practiced; member of the State house of representatives, 1834-1835, 1840-1841; elected as a Democrat to the Twenty-eighth and to the four succeeding Congresses (March 4, 1843-March 3, 1853); declined to be a candidate for reelection in 1852 to the Thirty-third Congress; moved to Alabama and resumed the practice of his profession; died in Talladega, Talladega County, Ala., on August 3, 1885; interment in Oak Hill Cemetery.

**WOODWARD, William** (father of Joseph Addison Woodward), a Representative from South Carolina; member, State house of representatives, 1818-1823; elected as a Republican to the Fourteenth Congress (March 4, 1815-March 3, 1817).

**WOODWORTH, James Hutchinson,** a Representative from Illinois; born in Greenwich, N.Y., December 4, 1804; received a limited schooling; moved to Fabius, Onondaga County, N.Y., and taught school; engaged in mercantile pursuits in 1823; inspector of the common schools in 1826; moved to Erie, Pa., in 1827; justice of the peace, 1829-1832; moved to Chicago, Ill., in 1833 and engaged in the dry-goods business; served in the Illinois State senate, 1839-1842; member of the Illinois State house of representatives, 1842-1847; owner and manager of the Chicago Hydraulic Flouring Mills for ten years; member of the Chicago City Council, 1845-1848; mayor of Chicago, 1848-1850; elected as a Republican to the Thirty-fourth Congress (March 4, 1855-March 3, 1857); retired to private life until appointed by Governor Richard Yates to serve on the board of auditors on war claims; served as president of the Merchants & Mechanics' Bank of Chicago, and was president of the Treasury Bank of Chicago at the time of his death; one of the founders of Chicago University; died in Highland Park, Ill., March 26, 1869; interment in Oakland Cemetery, Chicago, Ill.

**WOODWORTH, Laurin Dewey,** a Representative from Ohio; born in Windham, Portage County, Ohio, September 10, 1837; attended the common schools, Windham (Ohio) Academy, Hiram (Ohio) College, and the Ohio State University at Columbus; studied law at Union Law College, Cleveland, Ohio; was admitted to the bar in 1859 and commenced practice in Ravenna, Ohio; member of the Portage County Board of School Examiners; served in the Union Army as major of the One Hundred and Fourth Ohio Volunteer Infantry from July 1862 to December 1862; moved to Youngstown, Mahoning County, Ohio, in 1864 and resumed the practice of law; elected to the State senate in 1867; reelected in 1869 and served as president pro tempore; elected as a Republican to the Forty-third and Forty-fourth Congresses (March 4, 1873-March 3, 1877); was an unsuccessful candidate for renomination in 1876 to the Forty-fifth Congress; continued the practice of law in Youngstown, Ohio, until his death there on March 13, 1897; interment in Windham Cemetery, Windham, Portage County, Ohio.

**WOODWORTH, William W.,** a Representative from New York; born in New London, Conn., March 16, 1807; moved to Hyde Park, Dutchess County, N.Y., in 1834; received a limited schooling; supervisor of Hyde Park in 1838, 1841, and 1843; appointed judge of Dutchess County in 1838 and reappointed in 1843; unsuccessful candidate for election in 1842 to the Twenty-eighth Congress; elected as a Democrat to the Twenty-ninth Congress (March 4, 1845-March 3, 1847); unsuccessful candidate for renomination in 1846; held interests in Cuba and formed a stock company of the Hudson River State Co. at Clinton, N.Y.; contractor for building a section of the Hudson River Railroad; moved to Yonkers, N.Y., December 1, 1849, and engaged in the real estate business and banking; elected president of Yonkers in 1857 and 1858; elected receiver of taxes in 1870; died in Yonkers, N.Y., February 13, 1873; interment in Oakland Cemetery.

**WOODYARD, Harry Chapman,** a Representative from West Virginia; born in Spencer, Roane County, W.Va., November 13, 1867; attended the common schools; engaged in the wholesale grocery and lumber business; member of the State senate in 1898; elected as a Republican to the Fifty-eighth and to the three succeeding Congresses (March 4, 1903-March 3, 1911); unsuccessful candidate for reelection in 1910 to the Sixty-second Congress; elected to the Sixty-fourth Congress to fill the vacancy caused by the death of Hunter H. Moss, Jr.; reelected to the Sixty-fifth, Sixty-sixth, and Sixty-seventh Congresses and served from November 7, 1916, to March 3, 1923; unsuccessful candidate for reelection in 1922 to the Sixty-eighth Congress; elected to the Sixty-ninth Congress (March 4, 1925-March 3, 1927); was not a candidate for reelection to the Seventieth Congress; resumed his former business pursuits; died in Spencer, W.Va., on June 21, 1929; interment in Spencer Mausoleum.

**WOOLSEY, Lynn C.,** a Representative from California; born in Seattle, Wash., November 3, 1937; graduated from Lincoln High School, Seattle; B.S., University of San Francisco, 1981; human resources manager, Harris Digital Systems, Novato, Calif., 1969-1980; owner, Woolsey Personnel Service, 1980 to present; teacher, Marin Community College, Indian Valley, Calif.; instructor, Dominican College of San Rafael, Calif.; member, Petaluma (Calif.) city council, 1985-1992, vice mayor, 1991-1992; elected as a Democrat to the One Hundred Third and One Hundred Fourth Congresses (January 3, 1993-January 3, 1997); is a resident of Petaluma, Calif.

**WOOMER, Ephraim Milton,** a Representative from Pennsylvania; born in Jonestown, Lebanon County, Pa., January 14, 1844; attended the common schools; during the Civil War enlisted in Company A, Ninety-third Regiment, Pennsylvania Volunteer Infantry, in September 1861; promoted to sergeant; taught school until 1869; engaged in mercantile pursuits; clerk of the orphans' court of Lebanon County 1869-1872; cashier of the People's Bank of Lebanon; member of the council of the borough of Lebanon 1884-1886; president of the select council of the city of Lebanon 1886-1890; delegate to the Republican National Convention in 1888; elected as a Republican to the Fifty-third and Fifty-fourth Congresses (March 4, 1893-March 3, 1897); unsuccessful candidate for renomination in 1896; again engaged in banking; died in Lebanon, Pa., November 29, 1897; interment in Mount Lebanon Cemetery.

**WOOTEN, Dudley Goodall,** a Representative from Texas; born near Springfield, Greene County, Mo., June 19, 1860; moved in infancy with his parents to Texas during the Civil War; attended private schools in Paris, Tex., and was graduated from Princeton College in 1875; attended Johns Hopkins University, Baltimore, Md., and was graduated from the law department of the University of Virginia at Charlottesville; was admitted to the bar in 1880 and practiced in Austin, Tex.; prosecuting attorney of Austin 1884-1886; moved to Dallas, Tex., in 1888; judge of the Dallas County district court 1890-1892; member of the State house of representatives in 1898 and 1899; delegate to the National Antitrust Conference at Chicago in 1899; member of the executive council of the National Civic Federation in 1900; delegate to the National Tax Conference at Buffalo in 1901; elected as a Democrat to the Fifty-seventh Congress to fill the vacancy caused by the death of Robert E. Burke and served from July 13, 1901, to March 3, 1903; unsuccessful candidate for renomination in 1902; continued the practice of law in Seattle, Wash.; served as special judge of the superior court at various times; delegate to the National Rivers and Harbors Congress in 1912; delegate to the National Conservation Congress in 1913; appointed a member of the State board of higher curricula by the Governor in 1919; professor of law at the University of Notre Dame, Notre Dame, Ind., 1924-1928; died, while on a visit, in Austin, Tex., on February 7, 1929; interment in Calvary Cemetery, Seattle, Wash.

**WORCESTER, Samuel Thomas,** a Representative from Ohio; born in Hollis, Hillsborough County, N.H., August 30, 1804; attended the common schools and was graduated from Harvard University in 1830; studied law; was admitted to the bar in 1835 and began practice in Norwalk, Huron County, Ohio; member of the State senate in 1849 and 1850; served as judge of the court of common pleas in 1859 and 1860; elected as a Republican to the Thirty-seventh Congress to fill the vacancy caused by the resignation of John Sherman and served from July 4, 1861, to March 3, 1863; resumed the practice of law and engaged in literary pursuits; died in Nashua, N.H., on December 6, 1882; interment in the South Cemetery, Hollis, N.H.

**WORD, Thomas Jefferson,** a Representative from Mississippi; born in Surry County, N.C.; member of the State house of commons in 1832; moved to Mississippi and settled in Pontotoc, Pontotoc County; contested the election of Samuel J. Gholson to the Twenty-fifth Congress, and the election was set aside by the House; subsequently elected as a Whig to fill the vacancy caused by this action, and served from May 30, 1838, to March 3, 1839.

**WORKS, John Downey,** a Senator from California; born near Rising Sun, Ohio County, Ind., March 29, 1847; attended private schools; during the Civil War served in the Tenth Regiment, Indiana Volunteer Cavalry, of the Union Army; studied law; was admitted to the bar in 1868 and commenced practice in Vevay, Ind.; member, State house of representatives 1878-1880; moved to San Diego, Calif., in 1883 and continued the practice of law; judge of the superior court of San Diego County 1886-1887; associate justice of the supreme court of California 1888-1891; moved to Los Angeles in 1896; president of the city council of Los Angeles 1910; elected as a Republican to the United States Senate and served from March 4, 1911, to March 3, 1917; was not a candidate for renomination; chairman, Committee on Expenditures in the War Department (Sixty-second Congress), Committee on Fisheries (Sixty-second Congress); resumed the practice of law for a short time; died in Los Angeles, Calif., June 6, 1928; remains were cremated and the ashes deposited in Inglewood Cemetery.

**Bibliography:** Works, John D. *Man's Duty to Man: A Study of Social Conditions and How They May Be Improved.* New York: Neale Publishing Co., 1919; Works, John D. *What's Wrong With the World?* Boston: The Stratford Co., 1922.

**WORLEY, Francis Eugene,** a Representative from Texas; born to Lone Wolf, Kiowa County, Okla., October 10, 1908; moved to Shamrock, Tex., in 1922; attended the public schools, the Texas Agricultural and Mechanical College at College Station in 1927 and 1928, and the law school of the University of Texas at Austin 1930-1935; was admitted to the bar in 1935 and commenced practice in Shamrock, Tex.; member of the State house of representatives from 1935 to 1940, when he resigned, having been elected to Congress; served as a lieutenant commander in the United States Navy from December 1941 to August 1942, while a Member of Congress; elected as a Democrat to the Seventy-seventh Congress; reelected to the four succeeding Congresses and served from January 3, 1941, until his resignation April 3, 1950; chairman, Committee on Election of President, Vice President, and Representatives (Seventy-eighth Congress); appointed an associate judge of the United States Court of Customs and Patent Appeals, Washington, D.C., and served from April 4, 1950, to May 4, 1959; appointed chief judge May 4, 1959; resided in Arlington, Va., until his death in Naples, Fla., December 17, 1974; cremated; ashes interred at Columbia Gardens, Arlington, Va.

**WORMAN, Ludwig,** a Representative from Pennsylvania; born in Tinicum Township, Bucks County, Pa., in 1761; received a limited schooling; learned the tanning business; moved to Earl Township, Berks County, Pa., in 1784 and established a tannery; elected as a Federalist to the Seventeenth Congress and served from March 4,

1821, until his death; unsuccessful candidate for reelection in 1822 to the Eighteenth Congress; died in Earl Township, Berks County, Pa., October 17, 1822; interment in Earl Township Cemetery.

**WORTENDYKE, Jacob Reynier,** a Representative from New Jersey; born in Chestnut Ridge, near Hackensack, Bergen County, N.J., November 27, 1818; completed preparatory studies under a private tutor; was graduated from Rutgers College, New Brunswick, N.J., 1839; taught school for ten years; studied law; was admitted to the bar in 1853 and commenced practice in Jersey City, N.J.; elected as a Democrat to the Thirty-fifth Congress (March 4, 1857-March 3, 1859); unsuccessful candidate for reelection in 1858 to the Thirty-sixth Congress; resumed the practice of law; trustee of Rutgers College 1862-1868; president of the water board, Jersey City, 1860-1868; president of the Riparian Commission of New Jersey 1865-1868; delegate to the Democratic National Convention in 1868; died in Jersey City, N.J., November 7, 1868; interment in the Dutch Reformed Church Cemetery, Park Ridge, Bergen County, N.J.

**WORTHINGTON, Henry Gaither,** a Representative from Nevada; born in Cumberland, Md., February 9, 1828; completed preparatory studies; studied law; was admitted to the bar and commenced practice in Tuolumne County, Calif.; traveled in Central America and Mexico and upon his return settled in San Francisco, Calif.; member of the California State house of representatives in 1861; moved to Nevada in 1862 and settled in Austin; upon the admission of Nevada as a State into the Union was elected as a Republican to the Thirty-eighth Congress, and served from October 31, 1864 to March 3, 1865; appointed Minister to Argentina and Uruguay on June 5, 1868 by President Andrew Johnson, and served until July 1869; major general of militia; moved to South Carolina in 1872; collector of the port of Charleston, S.C.; left South Carolina in 1877; defeated by two votes for election to the United States Senate from Nebraska; served as a pallbearer at the funeral of President Abraham Lincoln; died in Washington, D.C., July 29, 1909; interment in Congressional Cemetery.

**WORTHINGTON, John Tolley Hood,** a Representative from Maryland; born at "Shewan," near Baltimore, Baltimore County, Md., November 1, 1788; received a limited schooling; engaged in agricultural pursuits; elected as a Jacksonian to the Twenty-second Congress (March 4, 1831-March 3, 1833); unsuccessful candidate for reelection in 1832 to the Twenty-third Congress and for election in 1834 to the Twenty-fourth Congress; elected as a Democrat to the Twenty-fifth and Twenty-sixth Congresses (March 4, 1837-March 3, 1841); resumed agricultural pursuits; died at "Shewan," Baltimore County, Md., April 27, 1849; interment in a private cemetery on his farm; reinterment in St. John's Episcopal Churchyard, Worthington Valley, Baltimore County, Md.

**WORTHINGTON, Nicholas Ellsworth,** a Representative from Illinois; born in Brooke County, Va. (now West Virginia), March 30, 1836; was graduated from Allegheny College, Meadville, Pa.; studied law; was admitted to the bar in 1860 and commenced practice in Peoria, Ill.; superintendent of schools of Peoria County, 1865-1872; member of the Illinois State board of education, 1869-1872; elected as a Democrat to the Forty-eighth and Forty-ninth Congresses (March 4, 1883-March 3, 1887); unsuccessful candidate for reelection in 1886 to the Fiftieth Congress, and for election in 1888 to the Fifty-first Congress; resumed the practice of law; elected circuit judge of the tenth judicial district of Illinois in 1891; reelected in 1897, and served until his retirement on June 15, 1915; appointed by President Grover Cleveland a member of the commission to investigate labor strikes in 1894; died in Peoria, Ill., March 4, 1916; interment in Springdale Cemetery.

**WORTHINGTON, Thomas,** a Senator from Ohio; born in Jefferson County, Va. (now West Virginia), on July 16, 1773; completed preparatory studies; went to sea; studied surveying; moved to Ross County, Ohio, in 1796; member of the first and second Territorial legislatures, 1799-1803; delegate to the State constitutional convention in 1803; elected as a Republican to the United States Senate, and served from April 1, 1803 to March 3, 1807; member of the Ohio State house of representatives in 1807; unsuccessful candidate for Governor in 1808 and again in 1810; again elected to the United States Senate to fill the vacancy caused by the resignation of Return J. Meigs, Jr., and served from December 15, 1810 until December 1, 1814, when he resigned, having been elected Governor; elected Governor of Ohio in 1814, reelected in 1816, and served from December 8, 1814 to December 14, 1818; member, State house of representatives, 1821-1822; canal commissioner from 1818 until his death in New York City on June 20, 1827; interment in Grandview Cemetery, Chillicothe, Ohio.

**Bibliography:** *DAB*; Sears, Alfred. *Thomas Worthington: Father of Ohio Statehood.* Columbus: Ohio State University Press, 1958.

**WORTHINGTON, Thomas Contee** (nephew of Benjamin Contee), a Representative from Maryland; born near Annapolis, Anne Arundel County, Md., November 25, 1782; received a limited schooling; served as a captain in the War of 1812; brigadier general of the Ninth Brigade, Maryland Militia, 1818-1847; studied law; was admitted to the bar in 1817 and commenced practice in Annapolis, Md.; member of the executive council in 1830 under the first State constitution; moved to Frederick, Frederick County, Md., in 1818 and continued the practice of law; member of the State house of representatives in 1818; elected to the Nineteenth Congress (March 4, 1825-March 3, 1827); resumed the practice of law in Frederick, Md., and died there on April 12, 1847; interment in Mount Olivet Cemetery.

**WORTLEY, George Cornelius,** a Representative from New York; born in Syracuse, N.Y., December 8, 1926; attended St. Lucy's Academy, Syracuse, and graduated from Tully (N.Y.) Central School; B.S., Syracuse University, 1948; attended Kings Point Academy, 1945-1946; cadet midshipman, MMR-United States Naval Reserve, 1945-1946; president of a publishing company; publisher-editor, Eagle Bulletin; director, Bank of New York (central region); director, Wortley Drug Store, Inc.; president, National Editorial Foundation, 1968-1973; president, New York Press Association, 1966; National Commission on Historical Publications and Records, 1977-1980; director, Greater Syracuse Chamber of Commerce, 1979-1982; elected as a Republican to the Ninety-seventh and to the three succeeding Congresses (January 3, 1981-January 3, 1989); was not a candidate for reelection in 1988 to the One Hundred First Congress; member of Dierman, Wortley, Zola and Associates, public policy consultants; is a resident of Washington, D.C., and Fort Lauderdale, Fla.

**WREN, Thomas,** a Representative from Nevada; born in McArthurstown, Ohio, January 2, 1826; received a common-school education; moved with his parents to Illinois; crossed the Plains to California in 1850; engaged in mining for three years; deputy clerk of Eldorado County, Calif., 1855-1857; studied law; was admitted to the bar and commenced practice in Downeyville, Calif.; moved to Nevada in 1863, where he resided successively in Austin, Hamilton, Pioche, Eureka, and Reno, being engaged in the practice of law at each place; city attorney of Austin, 1874-1876; president and attorney for the Richmond Mining Co. in Eureka; member of the State house of representatives in 1875; elected as a Republican to the Forty-fifth Congress (March 4, 1877-March 3, 1879); resumed the practice of law; died in Reno, Nev., February 5, 1904; interment in the Masonic Cemetery.

**WRIGHT, Ashley Bascom,** a Representative from Massachusetts; born in Hinsdale, Berkshire County, Mass., May 25, 1841; attended the public schools and Lincoln Academy at Hinsdale; moved to North Adams, Mass., in 1861; appointed chief deputy collector of internal revenue for the tenth district of Massachusetts in 1861; resigned in 1865 and engaged in mercantile pursuits; elected selectman; commissioner for the county of Berkshire 1884-1887 and chairman for one year; member of the Massachusetts executive council in 1890 and 1891; elected as a Republican to the Fifty-third, Fifty-fourth, and Fifty-fifth Congresses and served from March 4, 1893, until his death in North Adams, Berkshire County, Mass., August 14, 1897; chairman, Committee on Mileage (Fifty-fourth and Fifty-fifth Congresses); interment in Hinsdale Cemetery.

**WRIGHT, Augustus Romaldus,** a Representative from Georgia; born in Wrightsboro, Ga., June 16, 1813; attended the public schools at Appling, Ga., the grammar school, Franklin College, and the University of Georgia at Athens; studied law at Litchfield (Conn.) Law School; was admitted to the bar in 1835 and commenced practice in Crawfordville, Ga., moving the following year to Cassville; served as judge of the superior courts of the Cherokee circuit from 1842 until he resigned in 1849 to resume the practice of law; moved to Rome, Ga., in 1855 and continued the practice of law; elected as a Democrat to the Thirty-fifth Congress (March 4, 1857-March 3, 1859); delegate to Georgia Secession Convention (opposing secession) and to the Confederate Secession Convention; offered provisional governorship of Georgia by President Lincoln, but declined; served as a member of the Confederate Congress; during the Civil War organized Wright's Legion, which was mustered in with the Thirty-eighth Georgia Infantry; after the Civil War resumed the practice of law at Rome, Ga.; member of the Georgia Constitutional Convention of 1877; died March 31, 1891, at his home "Glenwood," later a part of the Berry School, near Rome, Ga.; interment in Myrtle Hill Cemetery.

**WRIGHT, Charles Frederick** (brother of Myron Benjamin Wright), a Representative from Pennsylvania; born in Forest Lake Township, Susquehanna County, Pa., on May 3, 1856; attended the public schools and was graduated from the Montrose (Pa.) Academy in 1874; teller of the First National Bank of Montrose, Pa., 1875-1881; was assistant cashier, cashier, and president of the First National Bank of Susquehanna Depot 1882-1899; delegate to the Republican National Conventions in 1896, 1904, and 1908; elected as a Republican to the Fifty-sixth, Fifty-seventh, and Fifty-eighth Congresses (March 4, 1899-March 3, 1905); chairman, Committee on Expenditures in the Department of Agriculture (Fifty-eighth Congress); was not a candidate for renomination in 1904; State treasurer 1911-1913; commissioner of public service in 1915 and 1916; resumed banking pursuits; died in Susquehanna, Pa., November 10, 1925; interment in Evergreen Cemetery.

**WRIGHT, Daniel Boone,** a Representative from Mississippi; born near Mount Pleasant, Giles County, Tenn., February 17, 1812; attended the common schools and was graduated from Cumberland University, Lebanon, Tenn., in 1837; studied law; was admitted to the bar in 1840 and commenced practice in Ashland, Benton County, Miss.; moved to Salem (later Hudsonville), Benton County, Miss., in 1850 and continued the practice of law and also engaged in agricultural pursuits; elected as a Democrat to the Thirty-third and Thirty-fourth Congresses (March 4, 1853-March 3, 1857); was not a candidate for renomination in 1856 to the Thirty-fifth Congress; resumed the practice of law at Ashland, Miss.; during the Civil War was appointed, on April 16, 1862, lieutenant colonel of the Thirty-fourth Regiment of Mississippi Infantry in the Confederate Army; appointed colonel of Cavalry to take effect June 6, 1864, and served as a judge of military courts in General Nathan Bedford Forrest's Cavalry Division; resumed the practice of his profession in Ashland, Miss., and was also interested in agricultural pursuits in

Benton County; died in Ashland, Miss., December 27, 1887; interment in the McDonald (private) Cemetery, near Ashland, Miss.

**WRIGHT, Edwin Ruthvin Vincent,** a Representative from New Jersey; born in Hoboken, N.J., January 2, 1812; completed preparatory studies; engaged in newspaper work in 1835; editor of the Jersey Blue in 1836, a newspaper published in Hoboken, N.J.; studied law; was admitted to the bar in 1839 and commenced practice in Jersey City; subsequently settled in Hudson City and continued the practice of law; member of the State council in 1843; district attorney for Hudson County, 1851-1855; mayor of Hudson, N.J., in 1855; elected as a Democrat to the Thirty-ninth Congress (March 4, 1865-March 3, 1867); owing to ill health, was not a candidate for renomination in 1866 to the Fortieth Congress; died in Jersey City, N.J., January 21, 1871; interment in Hoboken Cemetery, New Durham, Hudson County, N.J.

**WRIGHT, George Grover** (brother of Joseph Albert Wright), a Senator from Iowa; born in Bloomington, Monroe County, Ind., March 24, 1820; attended private schools and graduated from Indiana University at Bloomington in 1839; studied law in Rockville, Ind.; was admitted to the bar in 1840 and commenced practice in Keosauqua, Iowa Territory; prosecuting attorney of Van Buren County, Iowa, 1847-1848; member, State senate 1849-1851; justice of the State supreme court 1854-1870; served as president of the Iowa Agricultural Society 1860-1865; moved to Des Moines, Iowa, in 1865; one of the founders of the College of Law, University of Iowa; professor in the law department of the State university 1865-1871; elected as a Republican to the United States Senate and served from March 4, 1871, to March 3, 1877; was not a candidate for reelection; chairman, Committee on the Judiciary (Forty-second Congress), Committee on Civil Service and Retrenchment (Forty-third Congress), Committee on Claims (Forty-fourth Congress); resumed the practice of his profession in Des Moines and also engaged in banking; president of the American Bar Association 1887-1888; died in Des Moines, Iowa, on January 11, 1896; interment in Woodland Cemetery.

**Bibliography:** *DAB.*

**WRIGHT, George Washington,** a Representative from California; was born in Concord, Mass., on June 4, 1816; attended the public schools; employed in the business department of the Boston Courier in 1835 and later engaged in mercantile pursuits in Boston; moved to California and settled in San Francisco in 1849; again engaged in mercantile pursuits and also became interested in banking and mining; one of the founders of the banking house of Palmer, Cook & Co. in San Francisco; upon the admission of California as a State into the Union was elected as an Independent to the Thirty-first Congress and served from September 11, 1850, to March 3, 1851; declined to be a candidate for renomination; affiliated with the Republican Party; moved to Washington, D.C., and served as attorney of the Choctaw Indians; engaged in private scientific work; moved to Dorchester, Mass., in 1880 and retired from active pursuits; died in Dorchester, Mass., April 7, 1885; interment in Sleepy Hollow Cemetery, Concord, Middlesex County, Mass.

**WRIGHT, Hendrick Bradley,** a Representative from Pennsylvania; born in Plymouth, Luzerne County, Pa., April 24, 1808; attended the Wilkes-Barre Grammar School; graduated from Dickinson College, Carlisle, Pa., in 1829; studied law; admitted to the bar November 8, 1831, and commenced practice in Wilkes-Barre, Luzerne County; appointed district attorney for Luzerne County in 1834; member of the Pennsylvania house of representatives 1841-1843 and served the last year as speaker; delegate to the Democratic National Conventions in 1844, 1848, 1852, 1856, 1860, 1868, and 1876; unsuccessful candidate for election to the Thirty-second Congress in 1850; elected as a Democrat to the Thirty-third Congress (March 4, 1853-March 3, 1855); unsuccessful candidate for reelection in 1854 to the Thirty-fourth Congress; elected to the Thirty-seventh Congress to fill the vacancy caused by the death of George W. Scranton and served from July 4, 1861, to March 3, 1863; resumed the practice of his profession; elected as a Democrat to the Forty-fifth Congress and reelected as a Greenbacker to the Forty-sixth Congress (March 4, 1877-March 3, 1881); chairman, Committee on Manufactures (Forty-fifth Congress); unsuccessful candidate for reelection in 1880; died in Wilkes-Barre, Pa., September 2, 1881; interment in Hollenback Cemetery.

**Bibliography:** *DAB*; Curran, Daniel J. "Hendrick B. Wright: A Study in Leadership." Ph.D. dissertation, Fordham University, 1962.

**WRIGHT, James Assion,** a Representative from Pennsylvania; born in Carnegie, Allegheny County, Pa., on August 11, 1902; attended the public schools; was graduated from Holy Cross College, Worcester, Mass., in 1923 and from the law department of the University of Pittsburgh, Pittsburgh, Pa., in 1927; was admitted to the bar in 1927 and commenced practice in Carnegie, Pa.; served as assistant county solicitor of Allegheny County, Pa., 1935-1941; elected as a Democrat to the Seventy-seventh and Seventy-eighth Congresses (January 3, 1941-January 3, 1945); unsuccessful candidate for reelection in 1944 to the Seventy-ninth Congress; resumed the practice of law; died in Scott Township, Pa., November 7, 1963; interment in Holy Souls Cemetery, Carnegie, Pa.

**WRIGHT, James Claude, Jr.,** a Representative from Texas; born in Fort Worth, Tarrant County, Tex., December 22, 1922; attended the public schools of Fort Worth and Dallas, Tex.; student at Weatherford (Tex.) College, 1939-1940, and the University of Texas, 1940-1941; enlisted in the United States Army Air Force in December 1941; commissioned in 1942 and flew combat missions in the South Pacific; was awarded the Distinguished Flying Cross; partner in a national trade extension and advertising firm; member of the Texas State house of representatives, 1947-1949; mayor of Weatherford, Tex., 1950-1954; served as president of the League of Texas Municipalities in 1953; delegate to the Democratic National Conventions of 1956, 1960, 1964, and 1968, and Convention chairman in 1988; elected as a Democrat to the Eighty-fourth and to the seventeen succeeding Congresses, and served from January 3, 1955 until his resignation on June 30, 1989; majority leader (Ninety-fifth through Ninety-ninth Congresses), Speaker of the House of Representatives (One Hundredth and One Hundred First Congresses); is a resident of Fort Worth, Tex.

**Bibliography:** Wright, Jim. *Balance of Power: Presidents and Congress from the Era of McCarthy to the Age of Gingrich*. Atlanta: Turner Publishing, 1996; Wright, Jim. *Reflections of a Public Man*. Fort Worth: Madison Publishing Company, 1984; Wright, Jim. *Worth It All: My War for Peace*. Washington: Brassey's, 1993.

**WRIGHT, John Crafts,** a Representative from Ohio; born in Wethersfield, Conn., August 17, 1783; completed preparatory studies; learned the trade of printer; moved to Troy, N.Y., and edited the Troy Gazette for several years; studied law in Litchfield, Conn.; was admitted to the bar and commenced practice in Steubenville, Ohio, in 1809; United States district attorney in 1817; elected to the Seventeenth Congress, but resigned on March 3, 1821, before the beginning of the congressional term; reelected to the three succeeding Congresses (March 4, 1823-March 3, 1829); unsuccessful candidate for reelection in 1828 to the Twenty-first Congress; elected to the Ohio Supreme Court in 1831 and served until February 2, 1835, when he resigned; moved to Cincinnati in 1835 and engaged in newspaper work, and for thirteen years published the Cincinnati Gazette; director of the Cincinnati, Hamilton & Dayton Railway Co.; delegate to and honorary president of the peace congress held in Washington, D.C., in 1861 in an effort to devise means to prevent the impending war, and died while serving in that capacity at Washington, D.C., February 13, 1861; interment in Spring Grove Cemetery, Cincinnati, Ohio.

**Bibliography:** Gunderson, Robert Gray. "John C. Wright and 'The Old Gentlemen's Convention.'" *Bulletin of the Historical and Philosophical Society of Ohio* 12 (April 1954): 109-118.

**WRIGHT, John Vines,** a Representative from Tennessee; born in Purdy, McNairy County, Tenn., June 28, 1828; completed preparatory studies; attended the University of Tennessee at Knoxville, where he pursued courses in medicine and law, graduating from the law department; was admitted to the bar and commenced practice in Purdy, Tenn.; elected as a Democrat to the Thirty-fourth and to the two succeeding Congresses (March 4, 1855-March 3, 1861); during the Civil War served in the Confederate Army as colonel of the Thirteenth Regiment, Tennessee Infantry, in 1861; elected to the First and Second Confederate Congresses; judge of the circuit court of Tennessee; chancellor and judge of the State supreme court; practiced law in Nashville, Tenn., from 1865 to 1886; unsuccessful candidate as an Anti-Repudiation Democrat for Governor of Tennessee in 1880; was chairman of the Northwest Indian Commission in 1886 and member of the commission to treat with the Great Sioux Nation in Dakota; appointed to the law division of the General Land Office in 1887, and served until his death in Washington, D.C., June 11, 1908; interment in Rock Creek Cemetery.

**WRIGHT, Joseph Albert** (brother of George Grover Wright), a Representative and a Senator from Indiana; born in Washington, Pa., April 17, 1810; moved to Indiana about 1820 with his parents, who settled in Bloomington, Monroe County; attended the common schools; graduated from Indiana University at Bloomington in 1825; studied law; was admitted to the bar in 1829 and commenced practice in Rockville, Parke County, Ind.; member, Indiana State house of representatives, 1833, 1836; member of the State senate in 1840; elected as a Democrat to the Twenty-eighth Congress (March 4, 1843-March 3, 1845); unsuccessful candidate for reelection in 1844 to the Twenty-ninth Congress; elected Governor of Indiana in 1849, reelected in 1852, and served from December 5, 1849 to January 12, 1857; appointed by President James Buchanan as Envoy Extraordinary and Minister Plenipotentiary to Prussia on June 1, 1857, and served until July 1861; appointed as a Unionist to the United States Senate to fill the vacancy caused by the expulsion of Jesse D. Bright, and served from February 24, 1862 to January 14, 1863; was not a candidate for the succeeding term; appointed United States commissioner to the Hamburg Exhibition in 1863; again appointed Envoy Extraordinary and Minister Plenipotentiary to Prussia on June 30, 1865, and served until his death in Berlin, Germany, May 11, 1867; interment in New York City.

**Bibliography:** *DAB*; Crane, Philip M. "Governor Jo Wright: Hoosier Conservative." Ph.D. dissertation, Indiana University, 1963; Joachim, Martin D. "Governor Joseph A. Wright, Librarian." *Indiana Magazine of History* 78 (September 1982): 242-248.

**WRIGHT, Myron Benjamin** (brother of Charles Frederick Wright), a Representative from Pennsylvania; born at Forest Lake, Susquehanna County, Pa., June 12, 1847; attended the common schools and pursued an academic course; taught school; clerk in the First National Bank of Susquehanna in 1865 and 1866; elected assistant cashier of the bank in 1867 and cashier in 1869; interested in several financial, business, and manufacturing enterprises; elected as a Republican to the Fifty-first, Fifty-second, and Fifty-third Congresses and served from March 4, 1889, until his death before the close of the Fifty-third Congress; had been reelected to the Fifty-fourth Congress; died while on a trip for the benefit of his health in Trenton, Canada, November 13, 1894; interment in the Grand Street Cemetery, Susquehanna, Pa.

**WRIGHT, Robert** (cousin of Turbutt Wright), a Senator and a Representative from Maryland; born at "Narborough," near Chestertown, Queen Annes County, Md., November 20, 1752; attended the common schools and Washington College, Chestertown, Md.; studied law; was admitted to the bar in 1773 and commenced practice in Chestertown; served in the Revolutionary War as private, lieutenant, and later as captain; member, Maryland State house of delegates, 1784-1786; member of the State senate in 1801; elected as a Republican to the United States Senate on November 19, 1801, for the term commencing March 4, 1801, and served until his resignation on November 12, 1806, having been elected Governor; delegate to the Farmers' National Convention in 1803; elected Governor of Maryland by the General Assembly, and served from November 12, 1806 until his resignation on May 6, 1809; served as clerk of Queen Annes County in 1810; elected to the Eleventh and Twelfth Congresses to fill the vacancy caused by the resignation of John Brown; reelected to the Thirteenth and Fourteenth Congresses, and served from November 29, 1810 to March 3, 1817; unsuccessful candidate for reelection in 1816 to the Fifteenth Congress; elected to the Seventeenth Congress (March 4, 1821-March 3, 1823); was not a candidate for renomination in 1822 to the Eighteenth Congress; district judge of the lower Eastern Shore district of Maryland from 1823 until his death at "Blakeford," Queen Annes County, Md., September 7, 1826; interment in the private burying ground of the DeCourcy family at "Cheston-on-Wye," Queen Annes County, Md.

**Bibliography:** *DAB.*

**WRIGHT, Samuel Gardiner,** a Representative from New Jersey; born in Wrightstown, N.J., November 18, 1781; was mainly self-educated; engaged in mercantile pursuits in Philadelphia, Pa., with a country place near Imlaystown, N.J.; owned several iron furnaces in New Jersey and Delaware; was elected as a Whig to the Twenty-ninth Congress and served from March 4, 1845, until his death near Imlaystown, Monmouth County, N.J., July 30, 1845, before the assembling of Congress; interment in the East Branch Cemetery, near Imlaystown, N.J.

**WRIGHT, Silas, Jr.,** a Representative and a Senator from New York; born in Amherst, Mass., May 24, 1795; moved with his father to Wyebridge, Vt., in 1796; graduated from Middlebury (Vt.) College in 1815; moved to Sandy Hill, Washington County, N.Y., in 1816; studied law; was admitted to the bar in 1819 and commenced practice in Canton, St. Lawrence County, N.Y.; surrogate of St. Lawrence County, 1821-1824; member, New York State senate, 1824-1827; appointed brigadier general of State militia in 1827; elected to the Twentieth Congress, and served from March 4, 1827 to February 16, 1829, when he resigned; successfully contested the election of George Fisher to the Twenty-first Congress, but declined to qualify; comptroller of the State of New York, 1829-1833; elected to the United States Senate in 1833 as a Jacksonian to fill the vacancy caused by the resignation of William L. Marcy; reelected in 1837, and served from January 4, 1833 to November 26, 1844, when he resigned, having been elected Governor; chairman, Committee on Finance (Twenty-fourth through Twenty-sixth Congresses); declined the Democratic nomination for Vice President of the United States in 1844; elected Governor of New York in 1844, and served from January 1, 1845 to January 1, 1847; unsuccessful candidate for reelection in 1846; died in Canton, N.Y., August 27, 1847; interment in Old Canton Cemetery.

**Bibliography:** *DAB*; Chanceloor, William *A Life of Silas Wright, 1795-1847.* New York: W.C. O'Donnell, Jr., 1913; Garraty, John A. *Silas Wright.* 1949. Reprint. New York: AMS Press, 1970; Mallam, William D. *Silas Wright: The Farmer Statesman.* Canton, N.Y.: St. Lawrence County Historical Association at the Silas Wright Museum, 1994.

**WRIGHT, Turbutt** (cousin of Robert Wright), a Delegate from Maryland; born at "White Marsh," near Chester Mills (now Centerville), Queen Annes County, Md., on February 5, 1741; engaged in agricultural pursuits; member of the General Assembly of Maryland in 1773 and 1774; one of the signers of the Association of Freemen of Maryland July 26, 1775; member of the Maryland constitutional convention in 1776; appointed February 3, 1777, by the council of Maryland as a member of the council of safety to fill the place of James Lloyd Chamberlaine, resigned, and served until the dissolution of the council on March 21, 1777; commissioned a justice of Queen Annes County in 1779; register of wills of Queen Annes County in 1779 and 1780; Member of the Continental Congress in 1782; again served in the State general assembly in 1781 and 1782; died on his estate, "White Marsh," near Centerville, Md., in 1783; interment in the family burial plot on the homestead.

**WRIGHT, William,** a Representative and a Senator from New Jersey; born in Clarksville, Rockland County, N.Y., November 13, 1794; attended the public schools and Poughkeepsie Academy; was a volunteer for the defense of Stonington, Conn., in the War of 1812; learned the saddler's trade and engaged in business in Bridgeport, Conn.; moved to Newark, N.J., in 1821 and ran a saddlery and leather business; mayor of Newark, 1840-1843; elected as a Whig to the Twenty-eighth and Twenty-ninth Congresses (March 4, 1843-March 3, 1847); unsuccessful Whig candidate for election for Governor of New Jersey in 1847; affiliated with the Democratic Party in 1850; elected as a Democrat to the United States Senate, and served from March 4, 1853 to March 3, 1859; unsuccessful candidate for reelection in 1858; chairman, Committee on Manufactures (Thirty-third and Thirty-fourth Congresses), Committee to Audit and Control the Contingent Expense (Thirty-fifth Congress), Committee on Engrossed Bills (Thirty-fifth Congress); again elected as a Democrat to the United States Senate, and served from March 4, 1863 until his death in Newark, N.J., November 1, 1866; interment in Mount Pleasant Cemetery.

**Bibliography:** *DAB.*

**WRIGHT, William Carter,** a Representative from Georgia; born on a farm in Carroll County, Ga., January 6, 1866; moved with his parents to Newnan, Coweta County, Ga., in 1869; attended the common and high schools of Newnan; studied law; was admitted to the bar in 1886 and commenced practice in Newnan, Ga.; also interested in banking and agricultural pursuits; city attorney for Newnan 1892-1895; solicitor of the city court of Newnan 1894-1903; member of the board of education 1910-1918; chairman of the Democratic State executive committees in 1910 and 1911; elected as a Democrat to the Sixty-fifth Congress to fill the vacancy caused by the resignation of William C. Adamson; reelected to the Sixty-sixth and to the six succeeding Congresses and served from January 24, 1918, to March 3, 1933; did not seek renomination in 1932; died in Newnan, Ga., June 11, 1933; interment in Oak Hill Cemetery.

**WURTS, John,** a Representative from Pennsylvania; born in Flanders, Morris County, N.J., August 13, 1792; after his father's death in 1793 the family resided in Montville, Morris County, and subsequently moved to Philadelphia, Pa.; graduated from Princeton College in 1813; studied law; admitted to the bar in 1816 and commenced practice in Philadelphia, Pa.; member of the Pennsylvania house of representatives in 1817; served in the Pennsylvania senate in 1820; elected to the Nineteenth Congress (March 4, 1825-March 3, 1827); was not a candidate for renomination; United States district attorney 1827-1831; member of the city council of Philadelphia; president of the Delaware & Hudson Canal Co. 1831-1858; went abroad for his health in 1859; died in Rome, Italy, on April 23, 1861; interment in the family cemetery at Pleasant Mills, near Batsto, Atlantic County, N.J.

**WURZBACH, Harry McLeary** (uncle of Robert Christian Eckhardt), a Representative from Texas; born in San Antonio, Tex., May 19, 1874; attended the public schools, and was graduated from the law department of Washington and Lee University, Lexington, Va., in 1896; was admitted to the bar the same year and commenced practice in San Antonio, Tex.; during the Spanish-American War volunteered as a private in Company F, First Regiment, Texas

Volunteer Infantry; after the war moved to Seguin, Tex., in 1900 and continued the practice of law; prosecuting attorney of Guadalupe County 1900-1902; judge of Guadalupe County 1904-1910; elected as a Republican to the Sixty-seventh and to the three succeeding Congresses (March 4, 1921-March 3, 1929); successfully contested the election of Augustus McCloskey to the Seventy-first Congress; reelected to the Seventy-second Congress and served from February 10, 1930, until his death; delegate to the Republican National Convention in 1924; died in San Antonio, Tex., November 6, 1931; interment in Military Cemetery.

**WYANT, Adam Martin,** a Representative from Pennsylvania; born near Kittanning, Armstrong County, Pa., September 15, 1869; attended the public schools, Mount Pleasant Institute, and Bucknell University, Lewisburg, Pa.; was graduated from the University of Chicago in 1895; moved to Greensburg, Westmoreland County, Pa., in 1896; studied law; was admitted to the Westmoreland County Bar in 1902 and commenced the practice of law in Greensburg; interested in coal mining and other business enterprises; elected as a Republican to the Sixty-seventh and to the five succeeding Congresses (March 4, 1921-March 3, 1933); was an unsuccessful candidate for reelection in 1932 to the Seventy-third Congress; resumed his former business pursuits; died in Greensburg, Pa., on January 5, 1935; interment in St. Clair Cemetery.

**WYATT, Joseph Peyton, Jr.,** a Representative from Texas; born in Victoria, Tex., October 12, 1941; attended the Bloomington, Texas (Victoria County) public schools; attended Victoria College, 1964; B.A., University of Texas, 1968; engaged in graduate work at the University of Houston Law School, 1970; served in the United States Marine Corps Reserve, 1966-1970; served on the staffs of Texas State Senator William N. Patman, United States Representative Clark W. Thompson, and Vice President Lyndon B. Johnson; auditor, Texas Alcoholic Beverage Commission, Austin, Tex.; director of community affairs, private firm, Victoria, Tex.; member, Texas State house of representatives, 1971-1979; served on the Southern Legislative Conference and the National Conference of State Legislatures; delegate, Texas State Democratic conventions, 1968-1978; delegate to the Democratic National Convention of 1964; elected as a Democrat to the Ninety-sixth Congress (January 3, 1979-January 3, 1981); was not a candidate for reelection in 1980 to the Ninety-seventh Congress; special projects consultant; is a resident of Victoria, Tex.

**WYATT, Wendell,** a Representative from Oregon; born in Eugene, Lane County, Oreg., June 15, 1917; attended the public schools; graduated from the Jefferson High School in Portland, Oreg., in 1935; LL.B., University of Oregon, Eugene, 1941; was admitted to the bar in 1941 and commenced the practice of law in Portland, Oreg.; special agent, Federal Bureau of Investigation, 1941-1942; served in the Marine Air Corps, 1942-1946; chairman of the Oregon State Republican Central committee, 1955-1957; elected as a Republican to the Eighty-eighth Congress, November 3, 1964, by special election to fill the vacancy caused by the death of Walter Norblad, and at the same time elected to the Eighty-ninth Congress; reelected to the four succeeding Congresses, and served from November 3, 1964 to January 3, 1975; was not a candidate for reelection in 1974 to the Ninety-fourth Congress; is a resident of Lake Oswego, Oreg.

**WYDEN, Ronald Lee,** a Representative and a Senator from Oregon; born in Wichita, Sedgwick County, Kans., May 3, 1949; attended the public schools of Palo Alto, Calif., and graduated from Palo Alto High School in 1967; attended the University of California, Santa Barbara, 1967-1969; A.B., Stanford University, Palo Alto, 1971; J.D., University of Oregon Law School, Eugene, 1974; admitted to the bar in 1975; instructor at the Wallace School of Community Service and Public Affairs, University of Oregon, 1975-1976, and at Portland (Oreg.) State University, 1979-1980;

staff, crime prevention division, city of Portland, Oreg., 1976-1977; co-founder and director, Oregon Gray Panthers, 1974-1980; director, Oregon Legal Services for the Elderly, 1977-1979; public member, Oregon State Board of Examiners of Nursing Home Administrators, 1978-1979; elected as a Democrat to the Ninety-seventh and to the seven succeeding Congresses, and served from January 3, 1981 until his resignation on February 5, 1996, having been elected Senator; elected to the United States Senate, January 30, 1996, by special election to fill the vacancy in the term ending January 3, 1999, caused by the resignation of Robert W. Packwood, and served from February 6, 1996 to January 3, 1999; is a resident of Portland, Oreg.

**WYDLER, John Waldemar,** a Representative from New York; born in Brooklyn, N.Y., June 9, 1924; attended West School of Long Beach, Long Beach High School, and Brown University, Providence, R.I.; enlisted as a private in the United States Army Air Corps November 16, 1942, was promoted to staff sergeant in a chemical weapons company and assigned to the China-Burma-India Theater, and was discharged in November 1945; served as a lieutenant in the judge advocate's office, and in Air Force Reserve, 1945-1955; resumed studies at Brown University until 1947; LL.B., Harvard University Law School, 1950; was admitted to the bar in October 1950; served in the United States attorney's office, Eastern District of New York, 1953-1959; entered the private practice of law in Mineola, N.Y., in 1959; delegate, Republican National Convention, 1968; elected as a Republican to the Eighty-eighth and to the eight succeeding Congresses (January 3, 1963-January 3, 1981); was not a candidate for reelection in 1980 to the Ninety-seventh Congress; chairman, Long Island Development Agency; was a resident of Garden City, N.Y., until his death in Washington, D.C., on August 4, 1987; interment in Holy Rood Cemetery, Garden City, N.Y.

**WYLIE, Chalmers Pangburn,** a Representative from Ohio; born in Norwich, Muskingum County, Ohio, November 23, 1920; attended the public schools of Pataskala, Ohio, Otterbein College, Westerville, Ohio, and Ohio State University; J.D., Harvard University Law School, 1948; enlisted in United States Army as a private, attained rank of first lieutenant and served with Thirtieth Infantry Division in Europe during the Second World War; colonel in the Army Reserves (retired); assistant attorney general of Ohio, 1951-1954; assistant city attorney of Columbus, Ohio, 1949-1950; elected city attorney of Columbus, Ohio, 1954-1956; administrator of Bureau of Workman's Compensation for the State of Ohio in 1957; appointed first assistant to Governor C. William O'Neill of Ohio in 1957; elected president of the Ohio Municipal League in 1957; practicing attorney, 1959-1967; served three terms in the Ohio State Legislature, 1961-1967; elected as a Republican to the Ninetieth and to the twelve succeeding Congresses (January 3, 1967-January 3, 1993); was not a candidate for renomination in 1992 to the One Hundred Third Congress; is a resident of Columbus, Ohio.

**WYMAN, Louis Crosby,** a Representative and a Senator from New Hampshire; born in Manchester, Hillsborough County, N.H., March 16, 1917; B.S., University of New Hampshire, Durham, 1938; J.D., Harvard University Law School, 1941; was admitted to the bar of Massachusetts and New Hampshire in 1941, and of Florida in 1957, and commenced the practice of law with Ropes Gray in Boston, Mass.; during the Second World War served in the Alaskan Theater as lieutenant in the United States Naval Reserve, 1942-1946; general counsel to a United States Senate committee in 1946; secretary to Senator Styles Bridges of New Hampshire in 1947; counsel, Joint Congressional Committee on Foreign Economic Cooperation, 1948-1949; attorney general of New Hampshire from 1953 until 1961; president, National Association of Attorneys General, 1957; legislative counsel to Governor Wesley Powell of New Hampshire in 1961; member and chairman of several State legal and judicial commissions; elected as a Republican to the Eighty-eighth Congress (January 3, 1963-January 3, 1965); unsuccessful candidate for reelection in 1964 to the Eighty-ninth Congress; elected to the Ninetieth and to the three succeeding Congresses and served from January 3, 1967, until his resignation December 31, 1974; was not a candidate in 1974 for reelection to the House of Representatives, but was a candidate for the United States Senate for the six-year term commencing January 3, 1975; certified elected by the State of New Hampshire by a two vote margin; subsequently appointed December 31, 1974, to fill the vacancy caused by the resignation of Norris Cotton, for the term ending January 3, 1975, and served until that date; due to the contested election of November 5, 1974, the United States Senate declared the seat, for the six-year term commencing January 3, 1975, vacant as of August 8, 1975; unsuccessful candidate in a special election held September 16, 1975, to fill the vacancy; associate justice, New Hampshire Superior Court, 1978-1987; is a resident of Manchester, N.H.

**Bibliography:** Tibbetts, Donn. *The Closest United States Senate Race in History.* Manchester, N.H.: J.W. Cummings Enterprises, 1976.

**WYNKOOP, Henry,** a Delegate and a Representative from Pennsylvania; born in Northampton Township, Bucks County, Pa., March 2, 1737; completed English and classical studies; member of the Pennsylvania Assembly in 1760 and 1761; associate justice of Bucks County Courts 1764-1777 and president judge 1777-1789; member of the committee of observation in 1774; delegate to the provincial conferences of July 15, 1774, and June 18, 1775; major of Bucks County Associated Battalions; member of the general committee of safety in 1776 and 1777; Member of the Continental Congress from 1779 to 1782; justice of the high court of errors and appeals from 1783 to 1789; elected to the First Congress (March 4, 1789-March 3, 1791); appointed associate justice of Bucks County, Pa., and served until his death in that county on March 25, 1816; interment in the graveyard of the Low Dutch Reformed Church, Richboro, Pa.

**Bibliography:** Beatty, Joseph M., Jr. "The Letters of Judge Henry Wynkoop, Representative From Pennsylvania to the First Congress of the United States." *Pennsylvania Magazine of History and Biography* 38 (January 1914): 39-64, 183-205.

**WYNN, Albert Russell,** a Representative from Maryland; born in Philadelphia, Pa., September 10, 1951; graduated, DuVal High School, Lanham, Md., 1969; B.A., University of Pittsburgh, 1973; Howard University, Washington, D.C., graduate study; J.D., Georgetown University School of Law, 1977; executive director, Prince Georges County, Md., Consumer Protection Commission; chair, Metropolitan Washington Council of Consumer Agencies; attorney, 1981 to present; member, Maryland State house of delegates, 1982-1986; member, Maryland State senate, 1986-1993, deputy majority whip; delegate, Democratic National Convention; elected as a Democrat to the One Hundred Third and One Hundred Fourth Congresses (January 3, 1993-January 3, 1997); is a resident of Largo, Md.

**WYNN, William Joseph,** a Representative from California, born in San Francisco, Calif., June 12, 1860; attended the public schools of San Francisco; apprenticed to the machinist's trade, and subsequently worked in the principal manufacturing establishments of San Francisco; member of the board of supervisors of the city and county of San Francisco from January 8, 1902 to March 4, 1903; elected as a Democrat to the Fifty-eighth Congress (March 4, 1903-March 3, 1905); unsuccessful candidate for reelection in 1904 to the Fifty-ninth Congress; engaged in the insurance business in San Francisco, Calif., until his death in that city on January 4, 1935; interment in Holy Cross Cemetery, Colma, Calif.

**WYNNS, Thomas,** a Representative from North Carolina; born near Barfields, Hertford County, N.C., in 1764; received his education in England; captured at sea on a vessel called the *Fair American* in 1780, and with several other colonists was carried to London; returned to North Carolina and settled as a planter in Hertford County; one of the first trustees of the University of North Carolina at Chapel Hill; member of the North Carolina House of Commons in 1787; delegate to the State conventions for the ratification of the Federal Constitution in 1788 and 1789; served in the North Carolina State senate 1790-1802 and 1807-1817; elected as a Republican to the Seventh Congress to fill the vacancy caused by the death of Charles Johnston; reelected to the Eighth and Ninth Congresses and served from December 7, 1802, to March 3, 1807; resumed planting in Hertford County; member of the North Carolina Executive Council 1818-1824; brigadier general of militia; died near Winton, Hertford County, N.C., on June 3, 1825; interment in Maneys Cemetery, near Maneys Ferry, N.C.

**WYTHE, George,** a Delegate from Virginia; born near Back River, Elizabeth City County, Va., in 1726; privately instructed by his mother and attended the College of William and Mary, Williamsburg, Va.; studied law; admitted to the bar in 1746 and commenced practice in Elizabeth City County in 1755; moved to Williamsburg about 1755; member of the Virginia house of burgesses 1758-1768; appointed a member of the committee of correspondence in 1759; moved to his estate in Elizabeth City County in 1763 and returned to Williamsburg in 1768; clerk of the Virginia house of burgesses 1768-1775; Member of the Continental Congress 1775-1776; a signer of the Declaration of Independence; speaker of the house of delegates in 1777; judge of the Virginia Chancery Court in 1777; appointed sole chancellor of Virginia in 1778; professor of law at the College of William and Mary from 1779 to 1791, when he resigned and moved to Richmond, Va.; conducted a private school in Richmond and continued teaching until his death; delegate to the Federal Convention at Philadelphia, Pa., in 1787; a member of the Virginia ratification convention in 1788; died in Richmond, Va., June 8, 1806; interment in St. John's Churchyard.

**Bibliography:** *DAB*; Boyd, Julian P. "The Murder of George Wythe." *William and Mary Quarterly* 3rd Ser., 12 (October 1955): 513-42; Kirtland, Robert B. "George Wythe: Lawyer, Revolutionary, Judge." Ph.D. dissertation, University of Michigan, 1983.

# Y

**YANCEY, Bartlett** (cousin of John Kerr), a Representative from North Carolina; born near Yanceyville, Caswell County, N.C., February 19, 1785; attended a private school and Hyco Academy in Caswell County; student at the University of North Carolina at Chapel Hill 1804-1806; studied law; was admitted to the bar in 1807 and practiced; elected as a Republican to the Thirteenth and Fourteenth Congresses (March 4, 1813-March 3, 1817); chairman, Committee on Claims (Thirteenth and Fourteenth Congresses); declined to be a candidate for renomination in 1816; member of the State senate and served as its presiding officer 1817-1827; died near Yanceyville, N.C., August 30, 1828; interment in the family cemetery upon the homestead.

**YANCEY, Joel,** a Representative from Kentucky; born in Albemarle County, Va., October 21, 1773; member of the Kentucky house of representatives 1809-1811; served in the Kentucky senate 1816-1820 and 1824-1827; elected as a Jacksonian to the Twentieth and Twenty-first Congresses (March 4, 1827-March 3, 1831); chairman, Committee on Expenditures in the Post Office Department (Twenty-first Congress); unsuccessful candidate for reelection in 1830 to the Twenty-second Congress; died in Barren County, Ky., in April 1838; interment in that county.

**YANCEY, William Lowndes** (uncle of Joseph Haynsworth Earle), a Representative from Alabama; born at the Falls of the Ogeechee, Warren County, Ga., August 10, 1814; attended preparatory school and Williams College, Williamstown, Mass.; studied law in Sparta, Ga., was admitted to the bar in 1834 and commenced practice in Greenville, S.C.; moved to Cahawba, Ala., in 1836; temporarily abandoned the practice of law and became a cotton planter; editor of the Cahawba Democrat and the Cahawba Gazette; moved to Wetumpka, Ala., in 1839 and resumed the practice of law; member of the State house of representatives in 1841; served in the State senate in 1843; elected as a Democrat to the Twenty-eighth Congress to fill the vacancy caused by the resignation of Dixon H. Lewis; reelected to the Twenty-ninth Congress and served from December 2, 1844, to September 1, 1846, when he resigned; moved to Montgomery, Ala., in 1846; delegate to the Democratic National Convention in 1848, 1856, and 1860; member of the State constitutional convention which convened in Montgomery January 7, 1861; appointed chairman of the commission sent to Europe in 1861 to present the Confederate cause to the Governments of England and France; elected to the first Confederate States Senate February 21, 1862; died at his plantation home, near Montgomery, Ala., July 26, 1863; interment in Oakwood Cemetery.

**Bibliography:** *DAB*; Draughon, Ralph Brown, Jr. "William Lowndes Yancey: From Unionist to Secessionist 1814-1852." Ph.D. dissertation, University of North Carolina at Chapel Hill, 1968; Mitchell, Rexford S. "William Lowndes Yancey: Orator of Southern Constitutional Rights." Ph.D. dissertation, University of Wisconsin, 1937.

**YANGCO, Teodoro Rafael,** a Resident Commissioner from the Philippine Islands; born in San Antonio, Province of Zambales, Philippine Islands, on November 9, 1861; attended the Ateneo de Manila (Jesuit College), and was graduated from the University of St. Thomas in 1881; pursued a commercial course in London, England, 1882-1886; engaged in the construction and repair of vessels, in the operation of a line of ferries, and also in mercantile pursuits; director of a life insurance company and interested in various commercial and charitable organizations in Manila; elected as a Nationalist a Resident Commissioner to the United States, and served from March 4, 1917, to March 3, 1920; was not a candidate for renomination in 1920; resumed his former business activities in Manila, Philippine Islands, until his death on April 20, 1939; interment in the Cementerio del Norte.

**YAPLE, George Lewis,** a Representative from Michigan; born in Leonidas, St. Joseph County, Mich., on February 20, 1851; moved with his parents to Mendon, Mich., in 1857; attended the common schools and Albion (Mich.) College; was graduated from the Northwestern University, Evanston, Ill., in 1871 and completed a postgraduate course in 1874; studied law; was admitted to the bar in 1872, but was engaged in agricultural pursuits until 1877, when he commenced the practice of law at Mendon, Mich.; unsuccessful Greenback candidate for election in 1880 to the Forty-seventh Congress; elected as a Democrat to the Forty-eighth Congress (March 4, 1883-March 3, 1885); unsuccessful candidate for reelection in 1884 to the Forty-ninth Congress; unsuccessful candidate for election as Governor in 1886; delegate to the Democratic National Convention in 1888; resumed the practice of law in Mendon, Mich.; circuit judge of the fifteenth circuit of Michigan 1894-1911; became a member of the Republican Party in 1916; retired from active pursuits and resided in Mendon, Mich., until his death December 16, 1939; interment in Mendon Cemetery.

**YARBOROUGH, Ralph Webster,** a Senator from Texas; born in Chandler, Henderson County, Tex., June 8, 1903; attended the public schools of Chandler and Tyler, Tex., and graduated from Tyler High School in 1919; attended the United States Military Academy, West Point, N.Y., in 1919 and 1920, and the Sam Houston State Teachers College, Huntsville, Tex., in 1921; taught school for three years in Delta and Martin Springs, Henderson County, Tex.; spent one year working and studying foreign trade and international relations in Europe, mostly in Germany as assistant secretary for the American Chamber of Commerce in Berlin; served in the Thirty-sixth Division, Texas National Guard, from private to staff sergeant, 1923-1926; LL.B., University of Texas Law School, 1927; was admitted to the bar and commenced practice in El Paso, Tex.; assistant attorney general of Texas, 1931-1934; member of the board of directors of the Lower Colorado River Authority in 1935; unsuccessful candidate for State attorney general in 1938; lectured on land law at University of Texas Law School in 1935; elected and served as district judge of the Fifty-third Judicial district, Austin, Tex., 1936-1941, and for three years was presiding judge for the third administrative judicial district; during the Second World War served in Army ground forces in Europe and Japan from 1943 until discharged as a lieutenant colonel in June 1946; author; member of the Texas Board of Law Examiners, 1947-1951; unsuccessful candidate in 1952, 1954 and 1956 for nomination for Governor of Texas; elected as a Democrat to the United States Senate, April 2, 1957, by special election to fill the vacancy caused by the resignation of Price Daniel for the term ending January 3, 1959; reelected in 1958, and again in 1964, and served from April 29, 1957 to January 3, 1971; unsuccessful candidate for renomination in 1970, and for nomination in 1972; chairman, Committee on Labor and Public Welfare (Ninety-first Congress); member, Interparliamentary Union Group, 1961-1970; member, board of directors, Gallaudet College, 1969-1971; member, constitutional revision commission of Texas, 1973-1974; member, Texas State library and archives commission, 1983-1989; practiced law in Austin from 1971 to 1995; was a resident of Austin, Tex., until his death there on January 27, 1996; interment in Texas State Cemetery.

**Bibliography:** Adams, Mark, and Creekmore Fath. *Yarborough, Portrait of a People's Senator: A Political Profile.* Austin, Tex.: Chaparral Press, 1957; Phillips, William G. *Yarborough of Texas.* Washington, D.C.: Acropolis Books, 1969.

**YARDLEY, Robert Morris,** a Representative from Pennsylvania; born in Yardley, Bucks County, Pa., October 9, 1850; attended public and private schools in Yardley and Doylestown; studied law; was admitted to the bar in 1872 and commenced practice in Doylestown, Pa.; district attorney of Bucks County 1880-1884; delegate to the Republican National Convention in 1884; elected as a Republican to the Fiftieth and Fifty-first Congresses (March 4, 1887-March 3, 1891); chairman, Committee on Expenditures in the Department of War (Fifty-first Congress); declined to be a candidate for renomination in 1890; resumed the practice of law in Bucks County; member of the Doylestown School Board; director of several financial and public service corporations; died in Doylestown, Pa., December 8, 1902; interment in Doylestown Cemetery.

**YATES, Abraham** (uncle of Peter Waldron Yates), a Delegate from New York; born in Albany, N.Y., August 23, 1724; completed preparatory studies; sheriff of Albany County 1755-1759; deputy to the Provincial Convention in 1775; delegate to the Provincial Congress 1775-1777, and served as president pro tempore of that body November 2, 1775, August 10, 1776, and as president August 28, 1776; member of the council of appointment in 1777; member of the first and second councils of safety May 3, 1777, to January 7, 1778; served in the State senate 1778-1790; receiver of Albany in 1778 and 1779; first postmaster of Albany in 1783; Member of the Continental Congress in 1787 and 1788; mayor of Albany 1790-1796; died in Albany, N.Y., June 30, 1796; interment in Albany Rural Cemetery.

**Bibliography:** *DAB.*

**YATES, John Barentse,** a Representative from New York; born in Schenectady, N.Y., February 1, 1784; completed preparatory studies and was graduated from Union College at Schenectady in 1802; studied law; was admitted to the bar in 1805 and commenced practice in Schenectady; served in the War of 1812 under General Wade Hampton on the northern frontier and was subsequently appointed aide-de-camp to Governor Daniel D. Tompkins; elected as a Republican to the Fourteenth Congress (March 4, 1815-March 3, 1817); chairman, Committee on Expenditures in the Department of State (Fourteenth Congress); did not seek renomination in 1816 to the Fifteenth Congress; aided in the construction of the Welland Canal between Lakes Erie and Ontario; founded the Yates Polytechnic Institute in 1825; moved to Chittenango, Madison County, N.Y., in 1816; judge of Madison County in 1835 and 1836; elected a member of the New York State assembly in 1836 and served until his death in Chittenango, N.Y., July 10, 1836; interment in Walnut Grove Cemetery, near Chittenango, N.Y.

**Bibliography:** Aitken, Hugh G.J. "J. Yates and McIntyre's Lottery Managers." *Journal of Economic History* 13 (Winter 1953): 36-57.

**YATES, Peter Waldron** (nephew of Abraham Yates), a Delegate from New York; born in Albany, N.Y., August 23, 1747; studied law; was admitted to the bar and commenced practice in Albany; member of the committee on correspondence in 1775; resigned and was reelected, but declined to serve; regent of the University of the State of New York in 1784; served in the State assembly in 1784 and 1785; Member of the Continental Congress in 1786; resumed the practice of law; died in Caughnawaga, N.Y., March 9, 1826.

**YATES, Richard** (father of Richard Yates [1860-1936]), a Representative and a Senator from Illinois; born in Warsaw, Gallatin County, Ky., January 18, 1815; attended the common schools; moved to Illinois in 1831; graduated from Illinois College, Jacksonville, Ill, in 1835; studied law at Transylvania University, Lexington, Ky.; was admitted to the bar in 1837 and commenced practice in Jacksonville, Ill.; member, Illinois State house of representatives, 1842-1845, 1848-1849; elected as a Whig to the Thirty-second and Thirty-third Congresses (March 4, 1851-March 3, 1855); unsuccessful candidate for reelection in 1854 to the Thirty-fourth Congress; elected Governor of Illinois in 1860, and served from January 14, 1861 to January 16, 1865; unsuccessful candidate for election to the United States Senate in 1863; elected as a Republican to the United States Senate and served from March 4, 1865, to March 3, 1871; was not a candidate for reelection; chairman, Committee on Revolutionary Claims (Thirty-ninth and Forty-first Congresses), Committee on Territories (Fortieth Congress); appointed by President Ulysses S. Grant as a United States commissioner to inspect a land subsidy railroad; died suddenly in St. Louis, Mo., on November 27, 1873; interment in Diamond Grove Cemetery, Jacksonville, Ill.

**Bibliography:** *DAB*; Reavis, Logan. *The Life and Public Services of Richard Yates.* St. Louis: J.A. Chambers and Co., 1881.

**YATES, Richard** (son of Richard Yates [1815-1873]), a Representative from Illinois; born in Jacksonville, Morgan County, Ill., December 12, 1860; attended public schools and Illinois Woman's College, Jacksonville, Ill., 1870-1874; city editor of the Daily Courier in 1878 and 1879, and of the Daily Journal, 1881-1883; was graduated from the Illinois College, Jacksonville, Ill., in 1880 and from the law department of the University of Michigan at Ann Arbor in 1884; commenced practice in Jacksonville, Ill.; city attorney of Jacksonville, 1885-1890; private in Company I, Fifth Infantry, Illinois National Guard, 1885-1890; county judge of Morgan County, 1894-1897; United States collector of internal revenue for the eighth internal revenue district, 1897-1900; elected Governor of Illinois in 1900 and served from January 14, 1901 to January 9, 1905; member of the Illinois State public utilities commission, 1914-1917; assistant attorney general of the State of Illinois in 1917 and 1918; elected as a Republican to the Sixty-sixth and to the six succeeding Congresses (March 4, 1919-March 3, 1933); unsuccessful candidate for renomination in 1928 to the Seventy-first Congress, but on July 27, 1928 was appointed nominee by the Republican State central committee in place of Henry R. Rathbone, who had died twelve days before; unsuccessful candidate for reelection in 1932 to the Seventy-third

Congress; resided in Harbor Springs, Mich., and Springfield, Ill., while engaged in writing his memoirs; died in Springfield, Ill., April 11, 1936; interment in Diamond Grove Cemetery, Jacksonville, Ill.

**Bibliography:** Yates, Richard. *Serving the Republic . . . An Autobiography.* Edited by John H. Krenkel. Danville, Ill.: Interstate Printers and Pubs., 1968.

**YATES, Sidney Richard,** a Representative from Illinois; born in Chicago, Ill., August 27, 1909; attended the elementary and high schools of Chicago; B.Ph., University of Chicago, 1931; J.D., University of Chicago School of Law, 1933; was admitted to the bar in 1933 and commenced the practice of law in Chicago, Ill.; assistant attorney for Illinois State bank receiver, 1935-1937; assistant attorney general attached to Illinois Commerce Commission as traction attorney, 1937-1940; served as a lieutenant in the United States Navy, 1944-1946; editor of "Bulletin of Decalogue Society of Lawyers," in 1947; elected as a Democrat to the Eighty-first and to the six succeeding Congresses (January 3, 1949-January 3, 1963); was not a candidate for renomination in 1962 to the House of Representatives, but was an unsuccessful candidate for election to the United States Senate; United States Representative to the Trusteeship Council of the United Nations with rank of Ambassador, 1963-1964; elected to the Eighty-ninth and to the fifteen succeeding Congresses (January 3, 1965-January 3, 1997); is a resident of Chicago, Ill.

**YATRON, Gus,** a Representative from Pennsylvania; born in Reading, Berks County, Pa., October 16, 1927; graduated from Reading High School, 1946; graduated from Kutztown State Teachers College, 1950; served on the Reading School Board, 1955-1960; member, Pennsylvania house of representatives, 1956-1960; member, Pennsylvania senate, 1960-1968; engaged in the manufacture of ice cream with other members of his family in Reading, Pa., 1950-1968; elected as a Democrat to the Ninety-first and to the eleven succeeding Congresses (January 3, 1969-January 3, 1993); was not a candidate for renomination in 1992 to the One Hundred Third Congress; is a resident of Reading, Pa.

**YEAMAN, George Helm,** a Representative from Kentucky; born in Hardin County, Ky., November 1, 1829; completed preparatory studies; studied law; was admitted to the bar in 1852 and commenced practice in Owensboro, Ky.; judge of Davis County in 1854; member of the Kentucky house of representatives in 1861; elected as a Unionist to the Thirty-seventh Congress to fill the vacancy caused by the death of James S. Jackson; reelected to the Thirty-eighth Congress, and served from December 1, 1862 to March 3, 1865; unsuccessful candidate for reelection in 1864 to the Thirty-ninth Congress; appointed Minister to Denmark on August 25, 1865 and served until November 1870; settled in New York City; lecturer on constitutional law at Columbia College; president of the Medico-Legal Society of New York; died in Jersey City, N.J., February 23, 1908; interment in Webb Memorial Chapel, Madison, N.J.

**YEATES, Jesse Johnson,** a Representative from North Carolina; born near Murfreesboro, Hertford County, N.C., May 29, 1829; attended private schools and Emory and Henry College, Emory, Va.; studied law; was admitted to the bar in 1855 and commenced practice in Murfreesboro; prosecuting attorney of Hertford County, 1855-1860; member of the North Carolina State house of commons, 1860-1862; solicitor of the first judicial district, 1860-1866; served in the Confederate Army as captain and major of the Thirty-first North Carolina Infantry during the Civil War; member of the Governor's council during Governor Jonathan Worth's administration; declined appointment by Governor William W. Holden as judge of the first judicial district in 1868; delegate to the Democratic State convention in 1871; member of the North Carolina State constitutional convention in 1871; elected as a Democrat to the Forty-fourth and Forty-fifth Congresses (March 4,

1875-March 3, 1879); successfully contested the election of Joseph J. Martin to the Forty-sixth Congress and served from January 29 to March 3, 1881; declined to be a candidate for renomination in 1880 to the Forty-seventh Congress; resumed the practice of his profession in Washington, D.C., and died there on September 5, 1892; interment in Glenwood Cemetery.

**YELL, Archibald,** a Representative from Arkansas; born in North Carolina in 1797; moved to Tennessee in his youth and settled in Bedford County; took part in the Creek campaign; participated in the War of 1812 and served under General Jackson at the Battle of New Orleans; studied law; was admitted to the bar of Tennessee and commenced practice in Fayetteville, Lincoln County, Tenn., and continued until 1832; declined the governorship of the Territory of Florida; appointed judge of the Territory of Arkansas by President Jackson in 1832, with residence at Fayetteville, Ark., and served until 1835; upon the admission of Arkansas as a State into the Union was elected as a Jacksonian to the Twenty-fourth Congress; reelected as a Democrat to the Twenty-fifth Congress, and served from August 1, 1836 to March 3, 1839; elected Governor of Arkansas in 1840, and served from November 4, 1840 until his resignation on April 29, 1844; elected to the Twenty-ninth Congress, and served from March 4, 1845 to July 1, 1846, when he resigned to take part in the Mexican War; served as colonel of the First Regiment, Arkansas Volunteer Cavalry, and was killed in the Battle of Buena Vista, near Monterrey, Mexico, February 22, 1847; interment in Fayetteville Cemetery, Fayetteville, Ark.

**Bibliography:** *DAB*; Hughes, William W. *Archibald Yell.* Foreword by John S.D. Eisenhower. Fayetteville: University of Arkansas Press, 1988.

**YOAKUM, Charles Henderson,** a Representative from Texas; born near Tehuacana, Lincoln (now Limestone) County, Tex., July 10, 1849; attended Larissa College in Cherokee County and Cumberland College; studied law; was admitted to the bar in 1874 and commenced practice in Emory, Rains County, Tex.; served as prosecuting attorney for Rains County in 1876; moved to Hunt County in 1883 and continued the practice of law in Greenville; district attorney for the eighth judicial district 1886-1890; member of the State senate 1892-1896; elected as a Democrat to the Fifty-fourth Congress (March 4, 1895-March 3, 1897); continued the practice of law in Greenville, Tex., until 1900, when he moved to Los Angeles, Calif.; returned to Texas in 1904; died in Fort Worth, Tex., January 1, 1909; interment in Myrtle Cemetery, Ennis, Tex.

**YOCUM, Seth Hartman,** a Representative from Pennsylvania; born in Catawissa, Columbia County, Pa., August 2, 1834; attended the rural schools; went to Philadelphia in 1850 and learned the printer's trade; taught school for several years; was graduated from Dickinson College, Carlisle, Pa., in 1860; during the Civil War entered the Union Army as a private and was promoted to first lieutenant of the Fifth Pennsylvania Cavalry; studied law; was admitted to the Schuylkill County bar in 1865 and commenced practice in Ashland, Pa.; moved to Bellefonte, Center County, in 1873 and continued the practice of law; district attorney of Center County 1875-1879; elected as a Greenbacker to the Forty-sixth Congress (March 4, 1879-March 3, 1881); was not a candidate for renomination in 1880; moved to Johnson City, Tenn., and engaged in the tanning business; mayor of Johnson City, Tenn., in 1885; moved to Pasadena, Calif., and became engaged in the orange-growing business; died in Santa Monica, Calif., April 19, 1895; interment in Mountain View Cemetery, Pasadena, Calif.

**YODER, Samuel S.,** a Representative from Ohio; born in Berlin, Holmes County, Ohio, August 16, 1841; attended the common schools and Wooster (Ohio) University, and was graduated from the University of Michigan at Ann Arbor; enlisted in the Union Army in the One Hundred and Twenty-eighth Regiment, Ohio Volunteer Infantry, April 19, 1862; rose to the rank of lieutenant and served until the end of the war; studied medicine and practiced in Bluffton, Ohio; mayor of Bluffton, 1868-1878; moved to Lima, Ohio, in 1878; studied law; was admitted to the bar in 1880 and commenced practice in Lima; member of the Democratic State executive committee, 1883-1885; judge of the probate court of Allen County from February 1882 to October 1886, when he resigned, having been elected to Congress; elected as a Democrat to the Fiftieth and Fifty-first Congresses (March 4, 1887-March 3, 1891); was not a candidate for renomination in 1890 to the Fifty-second Congress; Sergeant at Arms of the House of Representatives from December 8, 1891 to August 7, 1893; continued the practice of law and also engaged in the real estate business in Washington, D.C., until his death on May 11, 1921; interment in Arlington National Cemetery, Va.

**YON, Thomas Alva,** a Representative from Florida; born near Blountstown, Calhoun County, Fla., March 14, 1882; at the age of five years moved with his parents to a farm in Jackson County, Fla.; attended rural schools, and was graduated from Lanier Southern Business College, Macon, Ga., in 1903; returned to Blountstown, Fla., the same year and engaged in mercantile pursuits until 1906; engaged as a traveling salesman at Tallahassee, Fla., 1906-1927; delegate to the Democratic National Convention in 1920; elected as a Democrat to the Seventieth, Seventy-first, and Seventy-second Congresses (March 4, 1927-March 3, 1933); unsuccessful candidate for renomination in 1932; special and commercial agent in the Bureau of Foreign and Domestic Commerce, United States Department of Commerce, Washington, D.C., 1933-1940; assistant investigator, Division of Investigation, General Accounting Office, from 1941 until his retirement in January 1946; engaged in development and sale of his Florida real estate holdings after retirement; died in Tallahassee, Fla., February 16, 1971; interment in Oakland Cemetery.

**YORK, Tyre,** a Representative from North Carolina; born in Rockford, Surry County, N.C., May 4, 1836; attended the common schools; studied medicine at the Charleston (S.C.) Medical College and commenced practice in Traphill, Wilkes County, N.C., in 1859; also engaged in agricultural pursuits; served during the latter part of the Civil War as surgeon of the Wilkes County Home Guards; was a member of the State house of representatives in 1865, 1866, 1879, and 1887; served in the State senate in 1876 and 1881; elected as an Independent Democrat to the Forty-eighth Congress (March 4, 1883-March 3, 1885); did not seek renomination in 1884 to the Forty-ninth Congress, but was an unsuccessful candidate for Governor of North Carolina in 1884; resumed agricultural pursuits; died in Traphill, N.C., January 28, 1916; interment in Traphill Cemetery.

**YORKE, Thomas Jones,** a Representative from New Jersey; born at Hancocks Bridge, Salem County, N.J., March 25, 1801; attended the common schools and the Salem Academy; during the War of 1812 served as a scout for the United States forces; studied law, but did not practice; engaged in mercantile pursuits at Salem; county collector of Salem County in 1830; judge of the Salem County court of common pleas in 1833, 1834, and 1845-1854 and for a portion of the latter term was presiding judge; member of the State general assembly in 1835; elected as a Whig to the Twenty-fifth Congress (March 4, 1837-March 3, 1839); presented credentials as a Member-elect to the Twenty-sixth Congress, but the House declined to seat him; elected to the Twenty-seventh Congress (March 4, 1841-March 3, 1843); chairman, Committee on Expenditures in the Department of the Navy (Twenty-seventh Congress); director of the West Jersey Railroad Co., serving as secretary and treasurer in 1853 and as president 1866-1875; also president of the Cape May & Millville Railroad Co.; served as director at various times of the Swedesborough Railroad Co., Salem Railroad Co., Camden & Philadelphia Ferry Co., and West Jersey Marl & Transportation Co.;

died in Salem, N.J., April 4, 1882; interment in St. John's Episcopal Cemetery.

**YORTY, Samuel William,** a Representative from California; born in Lincoln, Lancaster County, Nebr., October 1, 1909; attended the public schools of Lincoln, Nebr.; moved to Los Angeles, Calif., in 1927; completed prelegal work and studied law at Southwestern University and La Salle University; also studied at University of Southern California, 1946-1950, and extension courses at University of California in 1948; was admitted to the bar in 1939 and commenced the practice of law in Los Angeles; member of the California State assembly from 1936 until 1940; served as a captain, Combat Intelligence, United States Air Corps, with service in New Guinea and the Philippine Islands, 1942-1945; again a member of the State assembly in 1949 and 1950; elected as a Democrat to the Eighty-second and Eighty-third Congresses (January 3, 1951-January 3, 1955); was not a candidate in 1954 for renomination to the House of Representatives, but was an unsuccessful candidate for election to the United States Senate; unsuccessful candidate for the Democratic nomination for United States Senator in 1956; resumed the practice of law; elected mayor of Los Angeles in May 1961 for a four-year term; reelected in 1965 and again in 1969; unsuccessful candidate for reelection in 1973; returned to the practice of law in Los Angeles; host of a radio and television show; unsuccessful candidate for the Republican nomination to the United States Senate in 1980; unsuccessful candidate for mayor of Los Angeles in 1981; is a resident of Studio City, Calif.

Bibliography: Bollens, John C., and Grant B. Geyer. *Yorty: Politics of a Constant Candidate.* Pacific Palisades, Calif.: Palisades Publishers, 1973.

**YOST, Jacob,** a Representative from Virginia; born in Staunton, Augusta County, Va., April 1, 1853; attended the public schools and Mossy Creek Academy; learned the printing trade and was associated in publishing the Valley Virginian; engaged in civil engineering; unsuccessful Republican candidate for election in 1884 to the Forty-ninth Congress; elected mayor of Staunton in May 1886 and served until January 1887, when he resigned, having been elected to Congress; elected as a Republican to the Fiftieth Congress (March 4, 1887-March 3, 1889); unsuccessful candidate for reelection in 1888 to the Fifty-first Congress; elected to the Fifty-fifth Congress (March 4, 1897-March 3, 1899); declined to be a candidate for renomination in 1898; engaged in the management and development of iron ore and coal lands; moved to Palo Alto, Calif., in 1925 and lived there in retirement until his death on January 25, 1933; interment in Thornrose Cemetery Staunton, Va.

**YOST, Jacob Senewell,** a Representative from Pennsylvania; born in Pottsgrove Township, near Pottstown, Montgomery County, Pa., July 29, 1801; attended the common schools and Fourth Street Academy, Philadelphia, Pa.; engaged in agricultural pursuits; publisher and editor of the La Fayette (Pa.) Aurora; member of the Pennsylvania house of representatives 1836-1839; elected as a Democrat to the Twenty-eighth and Twenty-ninth Congresses (March 4, 1843-March 3, 1847); chairman, Committee on Engraving (Twenty-ninth Congress); resumed agricultural pursuits near Pottstown, Pa.; United States marshal for the eastern district of Pennsylvania at Philadelphia, Pa., by appointment of President James Buchanan and served from 1857 until his resignation in 1860; resumed agricultural pursuits; died in Pottstown, Pa., on March 7, 1872; interment in Edgewood Cemetery.

**YOUMANS, Henry Melville,** a Representative from Michigan; born in Otego, Otsego County, N.Y., May 15, 1832; attended the common schools; was in the employ of the York & Erie Railroad Co., on the Susquehanna division, for ten years; moved to East Saginaw, Mich., in 1862; engaged in the manufacture of lumber and salt 1863-1878; moved to St. Clair County, Mich., in 1878 and engaged in farming and lumbering until 1884 when he returned to East Saginaw; mayor of East Saginaw in 1886 and 1887; served four terms as alderman; elected as a Democrat to the Fifty-second Congress (March 4, 1891-March 3, 1893); chairman, Committee on Expenditures on Public Buildings (Fifty-second Congress); unsuccessful candidate for reelection in 1892 to the Fifty-third Congress; member of the State senate in 1896 and 1897; engaged in agricultural pursuits at Bridgeport, Mich., until his death in Saginaw, Mich., July 8, 1920; interment in Brady Hill Cemetery.

**YOUNG, Andrew Jackson, Jr.,** a Representative from Georgia; born in New Orleans, Orleans Parish, La., March 12, 1932; educated in public schools of New Orleans, Gilbert Academy, and Dillard University; B.S., Howard University, 1951; B.D., Hartford Theological Seminary, 1955; ordained by the United Church of Christ; served as pastor in Marion, Ala., and in Thomasville and Beachton, Ga.; associate director, Department of Youth Work, National Council of Churches, 1957-1961; executive director, Southern Christian Leadership Conference, 1964; executive vice president, Southern Christian Leadership Conference, 1967; chairman, Atlanta Community Relations Commission, 1970-1972; elected as a Democrat to the Ninety-third and to the two succeeding Congresses, and served from January 3, 1973 until his resignation January 29, 1977, to become United States representative to the United Nations with the rank of Ambassador, and served in that capacity until his resignation September 23, 1979; elected mayor of Atlanta, Ga., October 27, 1981; reelected in 1985, and served from 1982 to 1990; co-chairman, Atlanta Committee for the Olympic Games; is a resident of Atlanta, Ga.

Bibliography: Young, Andrew. *A Way Out of No Way: The Spiritual Memoirs of Andrew Young.* Nashville: Thomas Nelson Publishers, 1994; Young, Andrew. *An Easy Burden: The Civil Rights Movement and the Transformation of America.* New York: Harper Collins Publishers, 1996.

**YOUNG, Augustus,** a Representative from Vermont; born in Arlington, Bennington County, Vt., March 20, 1784; completed preparatory studies; studied law; was admitted to the bar in 1810 and commenced practice in Stowe, Vt.; moved to Craftsbury, Vt., in 1812; member of the State house of representatives 1821-1824, 1826, 1828-1830, and 1832; State's attorney for Orleans County 1824-1828; judge of probate in 1830 and 1831; served in the State senate 1836-1838; elected as a Whig to the Twenty-seventh Congress (March 4, 1841-March 3, 1843); declined to be a candidate for renomination in 1842; resumed the practice of law and engaged in literary pursuits; moved to St. Albans in 1847; assistant judge of the Franklin County Court 1851-1854; died in St. Albans, Vt., June 17, 1857; interment in Greenwood Cemetery.

**YOUNG, Bryan Rust** (brother of William Singleton Young and uncle of John Young Brown), a Representative from Kentucky; born near Bardstown, Nelson County, Ky., January 14, 1800; attended the common schools; graduated from the University of Louisville, Louisville, Ky.; studied medicine and practiced his profession in Nelson County, Ky.; member of Kentucky house of representatives in 1858-1859, 1861-1862, and 1863-1864; elected as a Whig to the Twenty-ninth Congress (March 4, 1845-March 3, 1847); resumed the practice of medicine; died in Elizabethtown, Ky., May 14, 1882; interment in Elizabethtown Cemetery.

**YOUNG, Charles William (Bill),** a Representative from Florida; born in Harmarville, Allegheny County, Pa., December 16, 1930; attended the public schools of Pennsylvania and Florida; served in the Army National Guard, 1948-1957, with honorable discharge as master sergeant; elected to the Florida State senate, 1960; reelected in 1964, 1966, 1967 (special election), and 1968 and served as minority leader in 1966; national committeeman, Florida Young Republicans, 1957-1959; State chairman, Florida Young Republicans, 1959-1961; member, Florida Constitution Revision Commission, 1965-1967; Pinellas County Republican Executive

Committee, 1958-1966; chairman, Southern Highway Policy Committee, 1966-1968; delegate to the Republican National Conventions of 1968, 1972, 1976 and 1984; elected as a Republican to the Ninety-second and to the twelve succeeding Congresses (January 3, 1971-January 3, 1997); is a resident of Indian Rocks Beach, Fla.

**YOUNG, Clarence Clifton,** a Representative from Nevada; born in Lovelock, Pershing County, Nev., November 7, 1922; attended the public schools of his native city; B.A., University of Nevada, Reno, 1943; during the Second World War served in the United States Army ground forces from May 1943 to October 1946, with twenty months' overseas duty in the European Theater with the One Hundred and Third Infantry Division, and was discharged as a major; LL.B., Harvard University Law School, 1949; was admitted to the Nevada bar in 1949 and commenced practice in Reno, Nev.; public administrator of Washoe County, 1950-1952; president of the Young Republicans of Nevada in 1952; delegate to the Republican National Convention of 1952; elected as a Republican to the Eighty-third and Eighty-fourth Congresses (January 3, 1953-January 3, 1957); was not a candidate in 1956 for renomination to the House of Representatives, but was an unsuccessful candidate for election to the United States Senate; engaged in the practice of law in Reno; member, Nevada State senate, 1966-1980; president, National Wildlife Federation, 1981-1983; elected associate justice of the Nevada Supreme Court in 1984, reelected in 1990 for the six-year term ending in January 1997, chief justice, 1989-1990; is a resident of Reno, Nev.

**YOUNG, Donald Edwin,** a Representative from Alaska; born in Meridian, Sutter County, Calif., June 9, 1933; attended the public schools; B.A., Chico (Calif.) State College, 1958; teacher; mayor of Fort Yukon, Alaska, 1960-1968; river boat captain, 1968-1972; member, city council, Fort Yukon, 1960-1968; member, Alaska State house of representatives, 1966-1970; member, Alaska State senate, 1970-1973; delegate, Alaska State Republican conventions, 1964, 1966, 1968, and 1972; elected as a Republican to the Ninety-third Congress, March 6, 1973, by special election to fill the vacancy caused by the death of Nick Begich; reelected to the eleven succeeding Congresses and served from March 6, 1973, to January 3, 1997; chairman, Committee on Resources (One Hundred Fourth Congress); is a resident of Fort Yukon, Alaska.

**YOUNG, Ebenezer,** a Representative from Connecticut; born in Killingly, Windham County, Conn., on December 25, 1783; was graduated from Yale College in 1806; studied law; was admitted to the bar and commenced practice in Westfield (now Danielson), Conn.; engaged in the manufacture of cloth at East Killingly, Conn.; elected as a Federalist a member of the State house of representatives in 1810, 1811, 1816, and 1817; served in the State senate 1823-1825; again a member of the State house of representatives 1826-1828, serving as speaker in 1827 and 1828; elected to the Twenty-first, Twenty-second, and Twenty-third Congresses (March 4, 1829-March 3, 1835); chairman, Committee on Expenditures on Public Buildings (Twenty-second Congress); died in West Killingly, Conn., August 18, 1851; interment in Westfield Cemetery, Danielson, Conn.

**YOUNG, Edward Lunn,** a Representative from South Carolina; born in Florence, Florence County, S.C., September 7, 1920; attended the public schools; B.S., Clemson (S.C.) College, 1941; served in the United States Army Air Corps as a fighter pilot in Southwest Pacific, 1942-1946; awarded the Distinguished Flying Cross and the Air Medal with nine oak leaf clusters; discharged as major in the Reserve; engaged in farming and real estate; member, South Carolina State house of representatives, 1958-1960; delegate, South Carolina State Republican conventions, 1968, 1970; delegate to the Republican National Convention of 1968; elected as a Republican to the Ninety-third Congress (January 3, 1973-January 3, 1975); unsuccessful candidate for reelection in 1974 to the

Ninety-fourth Congress, and for election in 1976 to the Ninety-fifth Congress; unsuccessful candidate in 1978 for election for Governor of South Carolina; unsuccessful candidate for nomination in 1980 to the Ninety-seventh Congress; farmer and businessman; is a resident of Florence, S.C.

**YOUNG, George Morley,** a Representative from North Dakota; born in Lakelet, Huron County, Ontario, Canada, December 11, 1870; when a boy moved to the United States and settled in St. Charles, Mich.; attended the public schools; was graduated from the law department of the University of Minnesota at Minneapolis in 1894; was admitted to the bar the same year and commenced practice in Valley City, N.Dak.; member of the board of aldermen in 1898 and 1899; member of the State house of representatives 1900-1902; served in the State senate 1904-1908 and was president pro tempore during the entire term; elected as a Republican to the Sixty-third and to the five succeeding Congresses and served from March 4, 1913, to September 2, 1924, when he resigned to accept a judicial position; appointed as a member of the United States Customs Court at New York City in 1924; served as associate judge until 1932 and as presiding judge until his death in New York City, May 27, 1932; interment in Woodbine Cemetery, Valley City, N.Dak.

**YOUNG, Hiram Casey,** a Representative from Tennessee; born in Tuscaloosa, Tuscaloosa County, Ala., December 14, 1828; moved with his parents to a farm near Byhalia, Marshall County, Miss., in 1838; attended the local schools and was tutored by his father and also attended Marshall Institute in Marshall County, Miss.; studied law; was admitted to the bar in 1859 and commenced practice in Memphis, Tenn.; served in the Civil War 1861-1865 as lieutenant colonel of Cavalry and on the brigade staff; Assistant Inspector General, First Division of Cavalry, in 1864; elected as a Democrat to the Forty-fourth, Forty-fifth, and Forty-sixth Congresses (March 4, 1875-March 3, 1881); unsuccessful candidate for reelection in 1880; elected to the Forty-eighth Congress (March 4, 1883-March 3, 1885); chairman, Committee on Expenditures in the Department of the Interior (Forty-eighth Congress); was not a candidate for renomination; resumed the practice of law; died in Memphis, Tenn., August 17, 1899; interment in Elmwood Cemetery.

**YOUNG, Horace Olin,** a Representative from Michigan; born in New Albion, Cattaraugus County, N.Y., August 4, 1850; attended the common schools and high school of Albion, N.Y., and Randolph (N.Y.) Institute; moved to Ishpeming, Mich.; engaged in accounting; studied law; was admitted to the bar in 1879 and commenced practice in Ishpeming, Mich.; member of the State house of representatives in 1879; prosecuting attorney of Marquette County 1886-1896; elected as a Republican to the Fifty-eighth and to the four succeeding Congresses (March 4, 1903-March 3, 1913); presented credentials as a Member-elect to the Sixty-third Congress and served from March 4, 1913, until his resignation, effective May 16, 1913, while a contest for the seat was pending; president of the Miners' National Bank in Ishpeming; died in Ishpeming, Mich., August 5, 1917; interment in the City Cemetery.

**YOUNG, Isaac Daniel,** a Representative from Kansas; born near Pleasantville, Marion County, Iowa, on March 29, 1849; attended high school and Oskaloosa College in Iowa; began teaching at the age of fifteen and continued in that profession for ten years; moved to Mitchell County, Kans., in 1874 and settled on a homestead in Turkey Creek Township; engaged in agricultural pursuits for eleven years; superintendent of public instruction of Mitchell County, Kans., 1876-1880; member of the State senate 1884-1888; moved to Beloit, Kans., in 1885; studied law; was admitted to the bar in 1889 and commenced practice in Beloit, Kans.; again a member of the State senate 1904-1908; elected as a Republican to the Sixty-second Congress (March 4, 1911-March 3, 1913); unsuccessful for reelection in 1912; resumed the practice of law in Beloit, Kans., until his death December 10, 1927; interment in Elmwood Cemetery.

**YOUNG, James,** a Representative from Texas; born in Henderson, Rusk County, Tex., July 18, 1866; attended the public schools; was graduated from the law department of the University of Texas at Austin in July 1891; was admitted to the bar the same year and commenced practice in Kaufman, Tex.; elected as a Democrat to the Sixty-second and to the four succeeding Congresses (March 4, 1911-March 3, 1921); declined to be a candidate for renomination in 1920; again engaged in the practice of law in Kaufman, Tex.; unsuccessful candidate for the Democratic gubernatorial nomination in 1930; moved to Henderson, Tex., in 1931, and continued the practice of law until 1937, when he moved to Dallas, Tex., where he died April 29, 1942; interment in the Kaufman Cemetery, Kaufman, Tex.

**YOUNG, James Rankin,** a Representative from Pennsylvania; born in Philadelphia, Pa., March 10, 1847; attended the common schools and Philadelphia High School; enlisted in the Union Army in June 1863 in the Thirty-second Regiment, Pennsylvania Volunteer Infantry; one of the founders of the Philadelphia Evening Star in 1866; attended all Republican National Conventions 1864-1908; served as chief of the Washington bureau of the New York Tribune from June 1866 to December 1870; chief executive clerk of the United States Senate from December 1873 to March 1879; chief clerk of the Department of Justice from September 1882 to December 1883; again chief executive clerk of the United States Senate from December 1883 to April 1892; elected as a Republican to the Fifty-fifth, Fifty-sixth, and Fifty-seventh Congresses (March 4, 1897-March 3, 1903); chairman, Committee on Expenditures in the Department of War (Fifty-seventh Congress); superintendent of the Dead Letter Office of the Post Office Department 1905-1913; superintendent of the postal savings depository in Philadelphia until 1915; was a resident of Washington, D.C., until his death December 18, 1924; interment in Glenwood Cemetery.

**YOUNG, John,** a Representative from New York; born in Chelsea, Orange County, Vt., June 12, 1802; moved to New York State in 1806 with his parents, who settled in Conesus, Livingston County, where he attended the public schools; studied law; was admitted to the bar in 1829 and commenced practice in Geneseo, N.Y.; member of the New York State assembly in 1833, 1844, and 1845; elected as a Whig to the Twenty-fourth Congress to fill the vacancy caused by the resignation of Philo C. Fuller, and served from November 9, 1836 to March 3, 1837; declined to be a candidate for reelection in 1836 to the Twenty-fifth Congress; elected to the Twenty-seventh Congress (March 4, 1841-March 3, 1843); was not a candidate for reelection in 1842 to the Twenty-eighth Congress; elected Governor of New York in 1846, and served from January 1, 1847 to January 1, 1849; delegate to the Whig National Convention in 1848; appointed assistant treasurer of the United States at New York on June 28, 1849, and served until his death in New York City, April 23, 1852; interment in Temple Hill Cemetery, Geneseo, N.Y.

Bibliography: *DAB.*

**YOUNG, John Andrew,** a Representative from Texas; born in Corpus Christi, Nueces County, Tex., November 10, 1916; attended the Incarnate Word Academy and Corpus Christi College-Academy; B.A., St. Edwards University, Austin, Tex., 1937; LL.B., University of Texas School of Law, 1940; was admitted to the bar in 1940 and commenced the practice of law; volunteered for service in the United States Navy in 1941, before Pearl Harbor, served in all theaters of war, and was separated from the service in 1945 as a lieutenant commander for physical disability incurred in line of duty; awarded the Presidential Unit Citation for service beyond the call of duty; assistant county attorney of Nueces County in 1946; assistant district attorney of Nueces County, 1947-1950; county attorney in 1951 and 1952; county judge of Nueces County, 1953-1956; elected as a Democrat to the Eighty-fifth and to the ten succeeding Congresses (January 3, 1957-January 3, 1979); unsuccessful candidate for renomination in 1978 to the Ninety-sixth Congress; resumed the practice of law in Washington, D.C.; consultant; is a resident of McLean, Va.

**YOUNG, John Duncan,** a Representative from Kentucky; born in Owingsville, Bath County, Ky., September 22, 1823; attended the common schools; studied law; was admitted to the bar in 1854 and practiced in Owingsville, Ky., and later engaged in agricultural pursuits; acting marshal of Kentucky during the administration of President Franklin Pierce; elected judge of the quarterly court of Bath County in 1858 and served four years; again elected in 1866 and served until 1867 when he resigned, having been elected to Congress; presented credentials as a Member-elect to the Fortieth Congress in 1867, but was not permitted to qualify; elected as a Democrat to the Forty-third Congress (March 4, 1873-March 3, 1875); was not a candidate for renomination in 1874 to the Forty-fourth Congress; resumed agricultural pursuits; Kentucky railroad commissioner, 1884-1889; again served as judge of the quarterly court of Bath County, 1890-1895; died in Mount Sterling, Ky., December 26, 1910; interment in Machpelah Cemetery.

**YOUNG, John Smith,** a Representative from Louisiana; born near Raleigh, Wake County, N.C., November 4, 1834; moved with his father to Fayette County, Tenn., in 1836, and to Columbia County, Ark., in 1848; was graduated from Centenary College, Jackson, La., in 1855; moved to Homer, Claiborne Parish, La., in September 1855; studied law; was admitted to the bar in 1860 and practiced in Homer; enlisted in the Confederate Army as a private on May 3, 1861, and was successively promoted until he attained the rank of lieutenant colonel; returned to Homer at the close of the war and resumed the practice of law; judge of Claiborne Parish Court, 1870-1872; member of the Louisiana State house of representatives, 1872-1876; judge of the eleventh judicial district of Louisiana, 1876-1878; elected as a Democrat to the Forty-fifth Congress to fill the vacancy caused by the death of John E. Leonard, and served from November 5, 1878 to March 3, 1879; was not a candidate for renomination in 1878 to the Forty-sixth Congress; resumed the practice of law in Homer, La.; moved to Monroe, La., and later to Shreveport in 1880, where he continued the practice of his profession; sheriff of Caddo Parish from 1892 until 1900; died in Shreveport, La., October 11, 1916; interment in Oakland Cemetery.

**YOUNG, Lafayette,** a Senator from Iowa; born near Eddyville, Monroe County, Iowa, May 10, 1848; attended country schools and night school in St. Louis, where he learned the printing trade; founded and published the Atlantic (Iowa) Telegraph 1871-1890; member, State senate 1874-1880, 1886-1888; established the Des Moines Capital in 1890 and was editor until his death; during the Spanish-American War was in Cuba as a war correspondent in 1898; presidential elector on the Republican ticket in 1908; appointed as a Republican to the United States Senate to fill the vacancy caused by the death of Jonathan P. Dolliver and served from November 12, 1910, to April 11, 1911, when a successor was elected; unsuccessful candidate for election to fill this vacancy; war correspondent for four months in Europe in 1915; Chautauqua lecturer in 1915; chairman of the State council for defense for Iowa during the First World War; was made a knight of the Order of Leopold II of Belgium in recognition of his work in raising funds in Iowa for the children of Belgium; died in Des Moines, Iowa, November 15, 1926; interment in Woodlawn Cemetery.

Bibliography: *DAB.*

**YOUNG, Milton Ruben,** a Senator from North Dakota; born in Berlin, La Moure County, N.Dak., on December 6, 1897; attended the public schools of La Moure County; attended the North Dakota State Agricultural College at Fargo, and Graceland College in Lamoni, Iowa; engaged in agricultural pursuits near Berlin, N.Dak.;

elected to the North Dakota State house of representatives in 1932; member, North Dakota State senate, 1934-1945; appointed to the United States Senate on March 12, 1945, to fill the vacancy caused by the death of John Moses; subsequently elected as a Republican to the United States Senate, by special election, on June 25, 1946, to complete the six-year term ending January 3, 1951; reelected in 1950, 1956, 1962, 1968, and again in 1974, and served from March 12, 1945 to January 3, 1981; was not a candidate for renomination in 1980; served as President pro tempore of the Senate during the Ninety-sixth Congress; resided in Sun City, Ariz., until his death on May 31, 1983; interment at Berlin Cemetery, Berlin, N.Dak.

**Bibliography:** Sylvester, Stephen G. "Water on Both Shoulders: The Political Ascendancy of Milton R. Young." *North Dakota Quarterly* 56 (Fall 1988): 222-244.

**YOUNG, Pierce Manning Butler,** a Representative from Georgia; born in Spartanburg, Spartanburg County, S.C., on November 15, 1836; moved with his parents to Georgia in 1839; studied under private tutors and was graduated from Georgia Military Institute at Marietta in 1856; studied law; entered the United States Military Academy, West Point, N.Y., in 1857 and resigned two months before graduation to enter the Confederate Army as a second lieutenant; served throughout the Civil War, attaining the rank of major general on September 28, 1863; settled in Cartersville, Ga., after the war and engaged in agricultural pursuits; upon the readmission of the State of Georgia to representation was elected as a Democrat to the Fortieth Congress, and served from July 25, 1868 to March 3, 1869; presented credentials as a Member-elect to the Forty-first Congress, but the House decided he was not entitled to the seat; subsequently elected to fill the vacancy thus caused; reelected to the Forty-second and Forty-third Congresses, and served from December 22, 1870 to March 3, 1875; unsuccessful candidate for renomination in 1874 to the Forty-fourth Congress; delegate to the Democratic National Conventions of 1872, 1876, and 1880; resumed agricultural pursuits; appointed United States commissioner to the Paris Exposition in 1878; consul general at St. Petersburg, Russia, 1885-1887; Envoy Extraordinary and Minister Plenipotentiary to Guatemala and Honduras by appointment of President Grover Cleveland, and served from April 14, 1893 until May 1896; died in New York City, July 6, 1896; interment in Oak Hill Cemetery, Cartersville, Ga.

**Bibliography:** *DAB*; Holland, Lynwood Mathis. *Pierce M.B. Young: The Warwick of the South.* Athens: University of Georgia Press, 1964.

**YOUNG, Richard,** a Representative from New York; born in Londonderry, Ireland, August 6, 1846; immigrated to the United States in 1851 with his parents, who settled in Philadelphia, Pa.; attended the public schools and was graduated from Crittenden's Commercial College in Philadelphia; moved to Flatbush, N.Y., in 1866 and engaged in an extensive leather trade in New York City; member of the board of school commissioners of Brooklyn 1895-1902; park commissioner for the Boroughs of Brooklyn and Queens in 1902 and 1903; engaged in banking and also interested in numerous corporations and business enterprises; elected as a Republican to the Sixty-first Congress (March 4, 1909-March 3, 1911); declined to be a candidate for reelection in 1910; resumed his interest in the leather industry; also engaged in banking and various business enterprises in Brooklyn and resided in Flatbush, Brooklyn, N.Y., until his death there June 9, 1935; interment in Greenwood Cemetery.

**YOUNG, Richard Montgomery,** a Senator from Illinois; born in Fayette County, Ky., February 20, 1798; attended the country schools and Forest Hill Academy, Jessamine County, Ky.; studied law and was admitted to the bar in Kentucky in 1816; member of the Kentucky Militia; moved to Illinois in 1817 and commenced the practice of law in Jonesboro; appointed captain in the Illinois

Militia; member, State house of representatives 1820-1822; circuit judge of the fifth circuit 1825-1837, when he resigned, having been elected to the United States Senate; elected as a Democrat to the United States Senate and served from March 4, 1837, to March 3, 1843; chairman, Committee on Roads and Canals (Twenty-fifth and Twenty-sixth Congresses); member of the mission to England to negotiate a loan for the State of Illinois in 1839; associate justice of the State supreme court 1843-1847, when he resigned; appointed by President James Polk as Commissioner of the General Land Office 1847-1849; Clerk of the United States House of Representatives 1850-1851; resumed the practice of law in Washington, D.C., where he died November 28, 1861; interment in the Congressional Cemetery.

**YOUNG, Robert Anton, III,** a Representative from Missouri; born in St. Louis, Mo., November 22, 1923; attended the primary schools of Vinita Park, Mo.; graduated from Normandy High School, St. Louis, 1941; pipefitter; served in the United States Army, 1943-1945: Three Hundred First Military Police Escort in Guard Company, First Amphibious Engineers Battalion, First Army, on Utah Beach, France, June 1944; Eighty-seventh Infantry Division, Three Hundred Forty-sixth Infantry Regiment, H Company, Third Army; awarded Bronze Star, European-African Theater Campaign Medal with five battle stars, Combat Infantryman's Badge, Army Commendation Ribbon, Croix de Guerre with palm, Presidential Distinguished Unit Citation; member, Missouri State house of representatives, 1957-1963; Missouri State senator, 1963-1976; delegate, Missouri State Democratic conventions, 1952-1976; delegate to the Democratic National Conventions of 1960, 1964, 1968, 1972, 1976, 1980, 1984 and 1988; elected as a Democrat to the Ninety-fifth and to the four succeeding Congresses (January 3, 1977-January 3, 1987); unsuccessful candidate for reelection in 1986 to the One Hundredth Congress; is a resident of Maryland Heights, Mo.

**YOUNG, Samuel Hollingsworth,** a Representative from Illinois; born in Casey, Clark County, Ill., December 26, 1922; graduated from Urbana (Ill.) High School, 1940; LL.B., University of Illinois, 1947; J.D., University of Illinois Law School, 1948; served in the United States Army Paratroops, 1943-1946, attained the rank of captain; admitted to the Illinois bar in 1948, to the Florida bar in 1978, and to the District of Columbia bar in 1985; commenced practice in Chicago in 1948 with the Securities and Exchange Commission; engaged in the private practice of law, 1949 to present; instructor in economics, University of Illinois, 1947-1948, and business finance, Northwestern University, 1949-1950; securities commissioner of Illinois, 1953-1955; assistant secretary of State, 1955-1957; financial vice president, secretary, and treasurer, hospital supply company, 1964-1966; delegate, Illinois State Republican conventions, 1951-1973; elected as a Republican to the Ninety-third Congress (January 3, 1973-January 3, 1975); unsuccessful candidate for reelection in 1974 to the Ninety-fourth Congress, and for election in 1976 to the Ninety-fifth Congress; is a resident of Glenview, Ill., and Marco Island, Fla.

**YOUNG, Stephen Marvin,** a Representative and a Senator from Ohio; born on a farm near Norwalk, Huron County, Ohio, May 4, 1889; attended the public schools and Kenyon and Adelbert Colleges; LL.B., Western Reserve University, Cleveland, Ohio, 1911; was admitted to the bar the same year and commenced practice in Norwalk, Ohio; member, Ohio State house of representatives, 1913-1917; assistant prosecuting attorney of Cuyahoga County, 1917-1918; served as a private in Company F, Third Ohio Infantry, on the Mexican border in 1916, and during the First World War served in the Field Artillery; chief assistant prosecuting attorney of Cuyahoga County, 1919-1920; unsuccessful candidate for attorney general in 1922; unsuccessful Democratic candidate for the gubernatorial nomination in 1930; member of the Ohio Commission on Unemployment Insurance, 1931-1932; elected as a Democrat to the Seventy-third and Seventy-fourth Congresses (March 4, 1933-January 3, 1937); was not a candidate in 1936 for renomination to the House of Representatives, but was an unsuccessful candidate for the gubernatorial nomination; special counsel to the attorney general of Ohio, 1937-1939; elected to the Seventy-seventh Congress (January 3, 1941-January 3, 1943); unsuccessful candidate for reelection in 1942 to the Seventy-eighth Congress; during the Second World War was commissioned a major in the United States Army in 1943, served in North Africa and Italy, and was discharged as a lieutenant colonel in 1946; resumed the practice of law in Cleveland, Ohio, and Washington, D.C.; elected to the Eighty-first Congress (January 3, 1949-January 3, 1951); unsuccessful candidate for reelection in 1950 to the Eighty-second Congress; unsuccessful candidate in 1956 for attorney general of Ohio; elected as a Democrat to the United States Senate in 1958; reelected in 1964, and served from January 3, 1959, to January 3, 1971; was not a candidate for reelection in 1970; was a resident of Washington, D.C., until his death there on December 1, 1984; interment in Norwalk Cemetery, Norwalk, Ohio.

**Bibliography:** Young, Stephen M. *Tales Out of Congress.* Philadelphia: J.B. Lippincott, 1964.

**YOUNG, Thomas Lowry,** a Representative from Ohio; born in Killyleagh, County Down, Ireland, December 14, 1832; immigrated to the United States with his parents in 1847; enlisted in the United States Army as a musician and advanced through the ranks to first sergeant of Company A, Third Artillery, and served from March 25, 1848 to January 28, 1858; settled in Cincinnati and was instructor in the State reform school; during the Civil War was commissioned captain of the Benton Cadets, Missouri Volunteers, on September 6, 1861; resigned on December 10, 1861; commissioned major of the One Hundred and Eighteenth Regiment, Ohio Volunteer Infantry, September 17, 1862; appointed lieutenant colonel, April 17, 1863, and colonel on April 11, 1864; resigned his commission on September 14, 1864; was graduated from the Cincinnati Law School; was admitted to the bar in 1865 and commenced practice in Cincinnati, Ohio; assistant city auditor of Cincinnati in 1865; member of the Ohio State house of representatives, 1866-1868; elected recorder of Hamilton County in 1867; appointed supervisor of internal revenue in 1868; delegate to the Republican National Convention of 1868; member of the State senate, 1871-1873; Lieutenant Governor in 1875; became Governor of Ohio after Governor Rutherford B. Hayes resigned to assume office as President of the United States, and served from March 2, 1877 to January 14, 1878; elected as a Republican to the Forty-sixth and Forty-seventh Congresses (March 4, 1879-March 3, 1883); chairman, Committee on Patents (Forty-seventh Congress); unsuccessful candidate for renomination in 1882 to the Forty-eighth Congress; resumed the practice of law; member of the board of public affairs of Cincinnati, 1886-1888; died in Cincinnati, Ohio, July 20, 1888; interment in Spring Grove Cemetery.

**YOUNG, Timothy Roberts,** a Representative from Illinois; born in Dover, N.H., November 19, 1811; completed preparatory studies; attended Phillips Exeter (N.H.) Academy and was graduated from Bowdoin College, Brunswick, Maine, in 1835; studied law in Dover, N.H., and was admitted to the bar; moved to Marshall, Ill., in the spring of 1838 and practiced law for ten years; elected as a Democrat to the Thirty-first Congress (March 4, 1849-March 3, 1851); moved to Mattoon, Ill., and became interested in the manufacture of plug tobacco, in which he continued for ten years; engaged in agricultural pursuits near Casey, Clark County, Ill.; died at Oilfield, near Casey, Ill., May 12, 1898; interment in Marshall Cemetery, Marshall, Ill.

**YOUNG, William Albin,** a Representative from Virginia; born in Norfolk, Va., May 17, 1860; attended the public schools and St. Mary's Academy at Norfolk; studied law, but abandoned it before obtaining a license and devoted himself to mercantile pursuits; clerk of the circuit and corporation courts of the city of Norfolk for six years; delegate to the Democratic National Convention in 1892; presented credentials as a Member-elect to the Fifty-fifth Congress and served from March 4, 1897, to April 26, 1898, when he was succeeded by Richard A. Wise, who contested his election; presented credentials as a Member-elect to the Fifty-sixth Congress and served from March 4, 1899, to March 12, 1900, when he was again succeeded by Richard A. Wise, who contested his election; engaged in the real estate business at Norfolk, Va., where he died March 12, 1928; interment in St. Mary's Cemetery.

**YOUNG, William Singleton** (brother of Bryan Rust Young and uncle of John Young Brown), a Representative from Kentucky; born near Bardstown, Nelson County, Ky., April 10, 1790; studied medicine with Dr. Bemiss, of Bloomfield, and was graduated from the University of Louisville, Louisville, Ky.; commenced practice in Bloomfield, Nelson County, Ky.; moved to Elizabethtown, Hardin County, Ky., in 1814 and continued the practice of law; elected to the Nineteenth Congress; reelected to the Twentieth Congress and served from March 4, 1825, until his death in Elizabethtown, September 20, 1827, before the assembling of the Twentieth Congress; interment in Elizabethtown Cemetery.

**YOUNGBLOOD, Harold Francis,** a Representative from Michigan; born in Detroit, Wayne County, Mich., August 7, 1907; attended the public schools; was graduated from St. Joseph's Commercial College in 1927; employed in Detroit office of the secretary of State of Michigan in 1927 and 1928; member of staff of Wayne County Board of Auditors 1928-1935; engaged as a plumbing and heating contractor in 1940; elected as a Republican to the Eightieth Congress (January 3, 1947-January 3, 1949); unsuccessful candidate for reelection in 1948 to the Eighty-first Congress; special assistant to the Director of Foreign Operations Administration in Berlin area in 1954 and 1955; engaged in construction contracting; was a resident of Tucson, Ariz., until his death there on May 10, 1983; interment in East Lawn Cemetery.

**YOUNGDAHL, Oscar Ferdinand,** a Representative from Minnesota; born in Minneapolis, Minn., October 13, 1893; attended the public schools and Hamline University, St. Paul, Minn.; was graduated from Gustavus Adolphus College, St. Peter, Minn., in 1916; principal of Ortonville (Minn.) High School and instructor of dramatics and public speaking 1916-1918; during the First World War served as a seaman second class in the United States Navy in 1918 and 1919; engaged in the sale of bonds and securities 1919-1925; was graduated from the Minnesota College of Law at Minneapolis in 1925; was admitted to the bar the same year and commenced practice in Minneapolis, Minn.; unsuccessful candidate for attorney general in 1936; elected as a Republican to the Seventy-sixth and Seventy-seventh Congresses (January 3, 1939-January 3, 1943); unsuccessful candidate for renomination in 1942; resumed the practice of law until his death in Minneapolis, Minn., February 3, 1946; interment in Lakewood Cemetery.

**YOUNGER, Jesse Arthur,** a Representative from California; born in Albany, Linn County, Oreg., April 11, 1893; moved to Kirkland, Wash., in 1904; attended the public schools; graduated from the University of Washington at Seattle in 1915 and served as graduate manager of athletics until 1917; during the First World War was called into Federal service in August 1917 with the Washington National Guard; served overseas for ten months with the Forty-eighth Coast Artillery Corps, and discharged as a captain in June 1919; officer and president of loan companies in Seattle, 1920-1934; appraiser with the Home Owners Loan Corporation, the Home Loan Bank Board, and Chief of the Savings and Loan Division of the Federal Home Loan Bank Board 1934-1937; moved to San Mateo, Calif., in 1937; executive vice president of Citizens Federal Savings & Loan Association in San Francisco 1937-1952; elected as a Republican to the Eighty-third and to the seven succeeding Congresses and served from January 3, 1953, until his death in Washington, D.C., on June 20, 1967; interment in Cypress Lawn Memorial Park, Colma, Calif.

**YULEE, David Levy,** a Delegate and a Senator from Florida; born David Levy in St. Thomas, West Indies, June 12, 1810; at the age of nine was sent to the United States to Norfolk, Va. to attend a private school; studied law in St. Augustine, Fla.; was admitted to the bar in 1836 and practiced in St. Augustine, Fla.; delegate to the State constitutional convention in 1838; clerk to the Territorial legislature in 1841; elected as a Whig-Democrat, a Territorial delegate to the Twenty-seventh and Twenty-eighth Congresses (March 4, 1841-March 3, 1845); did not seek renomination, having become a candidate for the Senate; upon the admission of Florida as a State into the Union was elected as a Democrat to the United States Senate and served from July 1, 1845, to March 3, 1851; unsuccessful candidate for reelection; chairman, Committee on Private Land Claims (Twenty-ninth and Thirtieth Congresses), Committee on Naval Affairs (Thirty-first Congress); by an act of the Florida Legislature and at his request his name was changed to David Levy Yulee in 1846; again elected to the United States Senate in January 1855 and served from March 4, 1855, until his withdrawal January 21, 1861; chairman, Committee on Post Office and Post Roads (Thirty-fifth and Thirty-sixth Congresses); president of the Atlantic & Gulf Railroad; served in the Confederate Congress throughout the Civil War; was a prisoner at Fort Pulaski in 1865; moved to Washington, D.C., in 1880; died in New York City, October 10, 1886; interment in Oak Hill Cemetery, Washington, D.C.

**Bibliography:** *DAB*; Adler, Joseph. "The Public Career of Senator David Levy Yulee." Ph.D. dissertation, Case Western Reserve, 1973; Thompson, Arthur. "David Yulee: A Study of 19th Century American Thought and Enterprise." Ph.D. dissertation, Columbia University, 1954.

# Z

**ZABLOCKI, Clement John,** a Representative from Wisconsin; born in Milwaukee, Wis., November 18, 1912; attended parochial school and Marquette University High School; Ph.B., Marquette University, 1936; taught high school in Milwaukee in 1938 and 1939; organist and choir director, 1932-1948; member of the Wisconsin State senate, 1942-1948; chairman of the Democratic State convention in 1948; delegate to the Democratic National Conventions of 1952, 1956, 1960, 1964, and 1968; was an unsuccessful candidate for the office of city controller of Milwaukee in 1948; United States delegate to the fourteenth session of the United States General Assembly in 1959; lieutenant colonel in the United States Air Force Reserve; unsuccessful candidate in 1957 for nomination to the United States Senate in a special primary; elected as a Democrat to the Eighty-first and to the sixteen succeeding Congresses, and served from January 3, 1949 until his death in Washington, D.C., on December 3, 1983; chairman, Committee on International Relations (Ninety-fifth Congress), Committee on Foreign Affairs (Ninety-sixth through Ninety-eighth Congresses); interment in St. Adalbert's Cemetery, Milwaukee, Wis.

**Bibliography:** Leahy, Stephen Michael. "Polonia's Child: The Public Life of Clement J. Zablocki." Ph.D. dissertation, Marquette University, 1994.

**ZEFERETTI, Leo C.,** a Representative from New York; born in Brooklyn, N.Y., July 15, 1927; attended public schools in Brooklyn; attended New York University, 1963, and the Bernard M. Baruch School of the City University of New York, 1964-1966; served in the United States Navy, 1944-1946; corrections officer with the Department of Correction, New York City, 1957-1974; president,

Correction Officers Benevolent Association, 1968-1974; member, New York State Crime Control Planning Board, 1972-1974; representative to the President's Conference on Correction, 1971; elected as a Democrat to the Ninety-fourth and to the three succeeding Congresses (January 3, 1975-January 3, 1983); chairman, Select Committee on Narcotics Abuse and Control (Ninety-seventh Congress); unsuccessful candidate for reelection in 1982 to the Ninety-eighth Congress; is a resident of Washington, D.C., and Miami, Fla.

**ZELENKO, Herbert,** a Representative from New York; born in New York City, March 16, 1906; attended public schools; graduated from Columbia University in 1926 and from Columbia Law School in 1928; was admitted to the bar in 1929 and commenced the practice of law in New York City; lecturer, Practicing Law Institute and Law Science Institute; former assistant United States attorney for the southern district of New York; elected as a Democrat to the Eighty-fourth and to the three succeeding Congresses (January 3, 1955-January 3, 1963); unsuccessful candidate for renomination in 1962 to the Eighty-eighth Congress; resumed the practice of law; died in New York City, February 23, 1979; interment at Sharon Gardens, Valhalla, N.Y.

**ZELIFF, William,** a Representative from New Hampshire; born in East Orange, Essex County, N.J., June 12, 1936; graduated from Milford (Conn.) High School, 1954; B.S., University of Connecticut at Storrs, 1959; United States Army National Guard service; innkeeper, Christmas Farm Inn, Yesterdays Restaurant in Jackson, N.H.; E.I. DuPont de Nemours and Co., 1961-1976; sales and marketing manager, Consumer Products Division, Milford Manufacturing Co.; unsuccessful candidate in 1984 for nomination to the New Hampshire State senate; elected as a Republican to the One Hundred Second and to the two succeeding Congresses (January 3, 1991-January 3, 1997); was not a candidate for reelection in 1996 to the One Hundred Fifth Congress, but was an unsuccessful candidate for nomination for Governor of New Hampshire; is a resident of Jackson, N.H.

**ZENOR, William Taylor,** a Representative from Indiana; born near Corydon, Harrison County, Ind., April 30, 1846; attended the common schools and the seminary of James G. May; studied law in New Albany, Ind.; was admitted to the bar in 1870 and commenced practice in Corydon; moved to Leavenworth, Crawford County, Ind., in 1871 and continued the practice of law; prosecuting attorney of Crawford and Harrison Counties 1879-1885; judge of the third judicial circuit 1885-1897; elected as a Democrat to the Fifty-fifth and to the four succeeding Congresses (March 4, 1897-March 3, 1907); resumed the practice of law in Corydon, Ind.; moved to New Albany, Ind., in 1910 and continued the practice of law until his death there June 2, 1916; interment in Cedar Hill Cemetery, Corydon, Ind.

**ZIEGLER, Edward Danner,** a Representative from Pennsylvania; born in Bedford, Bedford County, Pa., March 3, 1844; attended the common schools, and was graduated from Pennsylvania College at Gettysburg in 1865; engaged in teaching in the York County Academy; studied law; was admitted to the bar on November 4, 1868, and commenced practice in York, Pa.; commissioner's clerk in 1871 and 1872; counsel to the board of commissioners; district attorney of York County 1881-1883; delegate to the Democratic National Convention in 1884; elected as a Democrat to the Fifty-sixth Congress (March 4, 1899-March 3, 1901); unsuccessful candidate for renomination in 1900; resumed the practice of law; appointed by the judge of the court of common pleas of York County; auditor of the offices of prothonotary, register of wills, clerk of the court, treasurer, and recorder of York County and served from 1923 to 1925; resumed the practice of law in York, Pa., until his death there on December 21, 1931; interment in Prospect Hill Cemetery.

**ZIHLMAN, Frederick Nicholas,** a Representative from Maryland; born in Carnegie, Allegheny County, Pa., October 2, 1879; moved to Maryland with his parents, who settled in Cumberland in 1882; attended the public schools; entered a glass factory in 1890 and apprenticed as a glass blower; president of the local flint-glass workers' union 1904-1909 and was a member of the national executive board in 1905 and 1906; president of the Allegany Trades Council 1904-1909; president of the Maryland State Federation of Labor in 1906 and 1907; member of the Maryland State senate 1909-1917, serving as Republican floor leader in 1914 and 1916; engaged in the real estate and insurance business in Cumberland, Md., in 1912; was an unsuccessful candidate for election in 1914 to the Sixty-fourth Congress; elected as a Republican to the Sixty-fifth and to the six succeeding Congresses (March 4, 1917-March 3, 1931); chairman, Committee on Expenditures in the Post Office Department (Sixty-sixth and Sixty-seventh Congresses), Committee on District of Columbia (Sixty-seventh Congress and Sixty-ninth through Seventy-first Congresses), Committee on Labor (Sixty-seventh and Sixty-eighth Congresses); was an unsuccessful candidate for reelection in 1930 and for election in 1934 to the Seventy-fourth Congress; resumed his former business pursuits in Cumberland, Md., where he died on April 22, 1935; interment in St. John's Cemetery, Forest Glen, Md.

**ZIMMER, Richard Alan,** a Representative from New Jersey; born in Newark, N.J., August 16, 1944; graduated from Glen Ridge (N.J.) High School, 1962; B.A., Yale University, 1966; LL.B., Yale University School of Law, 1968; admitted to the New Jersey bar in 1969; practicing attorney, New York City, 1969-1975; attorney, Johnson and Johnson, 1975-1990; counsel to the gubernatorial campaigns of Thomas H. Kean, 1981, 1985; member, New Jersey State assembly, 1982-1990; elected as a Republican to the One Hundred Second and to the two succeeding Congresses (January 3, 1991-January 3, 1997); was not a candidate for reelection in 1996 to the House of Representatives, but was a candidate for election to the United States Senate; is a resident of Flemington, N.J.

**ZIMMERMAN, Orville,** a Representative from Missouri; born on a farm near Glenallen, Bollinger County, Mo., December 31, 1880; attended the public schools and Mayfield-Smith Academy, Marble Hill, Mo.; was graduated from the Southeast Missouri State College at Cape Girardeau in 1904 and from the law department of the University of Missouri at Columbia in 1911; principal of Dexter (Mo.) High School 1904-1908; was admitted to the bar in 1911 and commenced practice in Kennett, Mo.; during the First World War served as a private in the United States Army in 1918; member of the board of education of Kennett, Mo., 1928-1936; member of the board of regents of Southeast Missouri State College 1933-1948; elected as a Democrat to the Seventy-fourth and to the six succeeding Congresses and served from January 3, 1935, until his death in Washington, D.C., April 7, 1948; interment in Oak Ridge Cemetery, Kennett, Mo.

**ZION, Roger Herschel,** a Representative from Indiana; born in Escanaba, Delta County, Mich., September 17, 1921; attended public schools in Evansville, Ind., and Milwaukee, Wis.; B.A., University of Wisconsin, Madison, 1943; attended Harvard Graduate School of Business Administration, 1944-1945; served in the United States Navy, 1943-1946, in the Asiatic-Pacific area and was discharged a lieutenant; became associated with Mead, Johnson and Co., eventually becoming director of training and professional relations, 1946-1965; elected as a Republican to the Ninetieth and to the three succeeding Congresses (January 3, 1967-January 3, 1975); unsuccessful candidate for reelection in 1974 to the Ninety-fourth Congress; president, Resources Development Inc., Washington, D.C.; is a resident of Washington, D.C.

**Bibliography:** Zion, Roger H. *The Hallowed Howls of Congress.* Indianapolis: Guild Press of Indiana, 1994.

**ZIONCHECK, Marion Anthony,** a Representative from Washington; born in Kety, Galicia, Poland, December 5, 1901; immigrated to the United States in 1905 with his parents who settled in Seattle, Wash.; attended the public schools; attended the University of Washington at Seattle from 1919 until graduated from the law department in 1929; was admitted to the bar the same year and commenced practice in Seattle, Wash.; delegate to the Democratic State conventions in 1932 and 1934; elected as a Democrat to the Seventy-third and Seventy-fourth Congresses, and served from March 4, 1933 until his death by suicide, August 7, 1936, in Seattle, Wash.; interment in Evergreen Cemetery.

**ZOLLICOFFER, Felix Kirk,** a Representative from Tennessee; born in Bigbyville, Maury County, Tenn., May 19, 1812; attended the "old field" schools and Jackson College, Columbia, Tenn.; became a printer; engaged in newspaper work in Paris, Tenn., 1828-1830, Knoxville, Tenn., in 1831 and 1832, and Huntsville, Ala., 1835-1843; elected State printer of Tennessee in 1835; served as a lieutenant in the war against the Seminoles in Florida in 1836; owner and editor of the Columbia Observer and the Southern Agriculturist in 1837; editor of the Republican Banner, the State organ of the Whig Party, in 1843; comptroller of the State treasury, 1845-1849; served in the Tennessee State senate, 1849-1852; delegate to the Whig National Convention in 1852; elected as a Whig to the Thirty-third Congress and reelected as a candidate of the American Party to the Thirty-fourth and Thirty-fifth Congresses (March 4, 1853-March 3, 1859); declined to be a candidate for renomination in 1858 to the Thirty-sixth Congress; member of the peace convention of 1861 held in Washington, D.C., in an effort to devise means to prevent the impending war; during the Civil War was commissioned a brigadier general in the Confederate Army, July 9, 1861; died from wounds received at the Battle of Logan Cross Roads, Ky., January 19, 1862; interment in the Old City Cemetery, Nashville, Tenn.

**Bibliography:** *DAB*; Parks, Edd. Winfield. "Zollicoffer: Southern Whig." *Tennessee Historical Quarterly* 11 (December 1952): 346-55; Stamper, James C. "Felix K. Zollicoffer: Tennessee Editor and Politician." *Tennessee Historical Quarterly* 28 (Winter 1969): 356-76.

**ZORINSKY, Edward,** a Senator from Nebraska; born in Omaha, Douglas County, Nebr., November 11, 1928; attended the public schools; attended the University of Minnesota, 1945-1946, and Creighton (Nebr.) University, 1946-1948; B.S., University of Nebraska, 1949; engaged in graduate work at Harvard University in 1966; engaged in the wholesale tobacco and candy business from 1950 until 1973; served in the United States Army Reserve, 1949-1962; mayor of Omaha, Nebr., 1973-1977; member, Nebraska Judicial Qualifications Commission, 1968-1971; member, board of directors, Omaha Public Power District, 1969-1973; elected as a Democrat to the United States Senate on November 2, 1976, for the six-year term commencing January 3, 1977; subsequently appointed, December 28, 1976, to fill the vacancy caused by the resignation of Roman L. Hruska for the term ending January 3, 1977; reelected in 1982, and served from December 28, 1976 until his death in Omaha, Nebr., March 6, 1987; interment in Beth El Cemetery, Omaha.

**ZSCHAU, Edwin Van Wyck,** a Representative from California; born in Omaha, Douglas County, Nebr., January 6, 1940; attended public schools in Omaha; A.B., Princeton University, 1961; M.B.A., Stanford University, Palo Alto, Calif., 1963, M.S., 1964, and Ph.D., 1967; professor, Graduate School of Business, Stanford University, 1965-1969; visiting professor, Harvard University Business School, 1967-1968; founder and president of Systems Industries, Inc., a computer equipment manufacturer; elected as a Republican to the Ninety-eighth and to the Ninety-ninth Congresses (January 3, 1983-January 3, 1987); was not a candidate in 1986 for reelection to the House of Representatives, but was an unsuccessful candidate for election to the United States Senate; became a partner of Brentwood Associates in 1987; general manager, IBM Storage Systems

Division, until 1996; senior lecturer of business administration, Harvard University; is a resident of Los Altos, Calif.

**ZUBLY, John Joachim,** a Delegate from Georgia; born in St. Gall, Switzerland, August 27, 1724; immigrated to America and settled in South Carolina; was engaged as a clerk in Wando Neck; ordained to the ministry in 1744; was the first pastor of the Presbyterian Church in Savannah (later the Independent Presbyterian Church) in 1760; served in the Provincial Congress of Georgia in 1775; Member of the Continental Congress from July 4, 1775, to November 1775, when he resigned; was accused of having furnished information to Sir James Wright, the royal governor, and narrowly escaped severe punishment; was banished from the State and one-half of his property was confiscated; resided in South Carolina 1777-1779; returned to Georgia and resumed pastoral duties in Savannah, where he died July 23, 1781; interment in what was later known as Colonial Park.

**Bibliography:** *DAB*; Martin, Roger A. "John Joachim Zubly: Preacher, Planter and Politician." Ph.D. dissertation, University of Georgia, 1976.

**ZWACH, John Matthew,** a Representative from Minnesota; born in Gales Township, Redwood County, Minn., February 8, 1907; attended the public schools and graduated from Milroy High School in 1926; received a teaching certificate from Mankato State College in 1927; B.S., University of Minnesota, 1933; served in the Minnesota State house of representatives, 1934-1946; Minnesota State senator, 1946-1966, majority leader, 1959-1966; member of the Interim Agriculture Commission, 1955-1957; school teacher and superintendent for fourteen years; farmer; elected as a Republican to the Ninetieth and to the three succeeding Congresses (January 3, 1967-January 3, 1975); was not a candidate for reelection in 1974 to the Ninety-fourth Congress; was a resident of Lucan, Minn.; died November 11, 1990.